INTERNATIONAL HANDBOOK OF UNIVERSITIES

2017

twenty-eighth edition

Volume 1

palgrave
macmillan

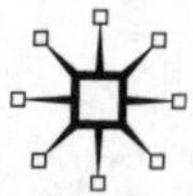

IAU ISBN 978-92-9002-203-9 (hardback)
ISBN 978-1-137-50851-5

Edited by the IAU/UNESCO Information Centre on Higher Education,
International Association of Universities
Director of Publication: Isabelle Turmaine
Manager, Reference Publications: Carine Sébast

Printed on acid-free paper.

The Palgrave imprint is published by Springer Nature.
The registered company is Macmillan Publishers Ltd. London.

Printed in China

CONTENTS

PREFACE

The International Association of Universities (IAU) and its IAU/UNESCO Information Centre on Higher Education are pleased to present the Twenty-eighth edition of the *International Handbook of Universities*, which offers updated, comprehensive information on universities and university-level institutions worldwide.

The *Handbook* was first published by the International Association of Universities in 1959 in response to the growing demand for authoritative information about higher education institutions worldwide. It has grown considerably over the years in both the quantity and the quality of its entries. Today, it includes over 18,000 institutions extracted from the lists provided by the competent authorities or academic bodies in over 180 countries and territories, their websites or official documents. The *Handbook* also comprises basic information on the education system of all countries and two indexes (institutions and fields of study). Only higher education institutions offering at least a postgraduate degree or a professional diploma in four years or more are included in the *Handbook*.

The compilation of the *Handbook* involves working on documents in many languages, covering a wide range of continuously evolving systems of higher education. The information concerning all the countries registered in the WHED are assembled with the greatest care. However, IAU cannot be held responsible for the consequences of errors or incomplete information in the country data. The IAU/UNESCO Information Centre on Higher Education is indebted to those many higher education institutions, governmental agencies and academic bodies which have provided material for this edition in order to make it a unique and authoritative source of information. Where information was not available in time for inclusion, entries have remained the same as in the previous edition. The date of the latest update is indicated at the bottom of each entry.

The full wealth of data held by the IAU/UNESCO Information Centre - including the information in the *Handbook*, as well as more comprehensive data on higher education systems and credentials offered in over 180 countries - is available at www.whed.net, the World Higher Education Database (WHED) Portal. Free single-user access to advanced features of the WHED Portal is available to all purchasers of the *Handbook* for 12 months following the publication date, and offers users the opportunity to search, browse, and print the information with ease and convenience.

The production of the *Handbook* and of the WHED Portal is part of the drive by the International Association of Universities (IAU) to provide access to information on higher education institutions, systems, and credentials worldwide. The IAU quarterly scholarly *Journal Higher Education Policy*[1] provides a deeper and more analytical understanding of higher education policy worldwide.

[1]Higher Education Policy, Palgrave Macmillan (see p. xviii).

GUIDE TO THE ENTRIES

This edition of the *International Handbook of Universities* comprises entries for over 18,000 universities and university-level institutions in over 180 countries and territories.

COUNTRY CHAPTERS

A short presentation of the education system based upon the information provided by the appropriate higher education authorities in the countries concerned or found on their official website or documentation is provided for each country. It comprises a short description of the overall structure of the higher education system; the different stages of study; the admission requirements (including for foreign students); the quality assurance/recognition system; and information on national bodies responsible for higher education. The designations employed for countries and territories are those in use in the United Nations system and do not imply any expression of opinion with regard to their status or the delimitations of their frontiers.

INSTITUTIONAL ENTRIES

Entries are selected on the basis of the information contained in the listings provided by the appropriate higher education authorities in the countries concerned or found on their official websites. Questionnaires are then sent to those degree-granting institutions which offer at least a post-graduate degree and/or a professional diploma in four years or more to obtain more detailed information. The inclusion or omission of an institution, therefore, does not imply any judgement on the part of the IAU/UNESCO Information Centre on Higher Education as to the status or quality of that institution.

Membership of a higher education institution in the International Association of Universities is indicated by IAU preceding its name. Higher education institutions wishing to become members should contact: iau@iau-aiu.net.

The institutional entries within each country are generally listed within Public and Private Sections (when the information is available we do not include for-profit institutions), where relevant, with their postal address, email and website information. The name of each institution is given first in English, followed by the name in the national language(s), where appropriate. Where available, the names and full contact details of the Academic Head, the Chief Administrative Officer, and the Director of International Relations are given.

The lists of faculties, colleges, departments, schools, institutes, etc., are intended primarily as a general guide to the academic structure of the institution of which they form a part. They normally include the various fields of study offered (standardized list). This information is followed by a brief description of the history and structure of the institution.

Admission requirements are usually listed for courses leading to a first degree or similar qualification. Special requirements for admission to studies leading to higher degrees and specialized diplomas are indicated where appropriate.

The names of degrees, diplomas and professional qualifications are generally given in the language of the country concerned. Tuition fees and student services and facilities available in each university are also indicated if provided.

Overall academic staff (including staff with doctorates) and student enrolment statistics complete the entry and include a breakdown of number of foreign students and part-time, distance education students and students with disabilities, if available. A breakdown by men and women for both academic staff and students is also given where available.

LIST OF FIELDS OF STUDY

The complete list of fields of study used in the *Handbook* is provided to help users in their search of the field of study index.

INDEXES

An index to higher education institutions which comprises the name of each institution in English, in the national language (when available) and the alternative name (when appropriate) is provided at the end of the *Handbook*.

An index to fields of study is also provided to allow for searches of institutions providing courses in a specific specialty.

LIST OF REGIONAL/INTERNATIONAL ORGANIZATIONS

A list of regional/international organizations by country is provided at the end of the preface.

IAU - THE INTERNATIONAL ASSOCIATION OF UNIVERSITIES

The International Association of Universities (IAU), founded in 1950, is a worldwide organization with Member Institutions and Organizations in some 120 countries. It cooperates with a vast network of international, regional and national bodies. Its permanent Secretariat, the International Universities Bureau, is located at UNESCO headquarters, Paris, France, and provides a wide variety of services to Member Institutions and Organizations and to the international higher education community at large. Institutions/organizations interested in becoming members should contact iau@iau-aiu.net.

MEETINGS

The IAU provides a forum for higher education leaders to discuss major current trends and issues in higher education and higher education policy. Heads of all Member Institutions and Organizations or their representatives are invited to the IAU quadrennial General Conference as well as to annual international events. These events are organized by the Association, either alone or in cooperation with other academic bodies, and provide unique opportunities for the exchange of experience and ideas on issues of international interest and importance. The 14th General Conference was held in San Juan, Puerto Rico in November 2012, and discussed the theme "Higher Education and the Global Agenda: Alternative Paths to the Future".

PUBLICATIONS

Services offered to Member Institutions and Organizations include the right to receive the Association's publications either on a complimentary basis or at considerably reduced rates. As from 2014, these include the *International Handbook of Universities* and advanced access to the World Higher Education Database (WHED) Portal, the quarterly journal *Higher Education Policy*, a quarterly Newsletter *IAU Horizons*, the monthly *IAU e-Bulletin* and the *IAU Highlights from the Press*. The WHED Portal provides detailed information on thousands of higher education institutions worldwide as well as comprehensive data on higher education systems and credentials, and many search facilities. The *Guide to Higher Education in Africa* is published once every three years. The academic publication *Higher Education Policy* focuses on policy issues and the role of higher education in society today, offering a platform for the exchange and sharing of information and debate within the world community of higher education.

INFORMATION SERVICES

Also available to Member Institutions and Organizations is the vast body of information housed in the specialized IAU/UNESCO Information Centre on Higher Education. The Centre, managed by the IAU, contains over 50,000 volumes on higher education worldwide and operates two major databases (WHED, mentioned above, and HEDBIB, the Higher Education Bibliographical Database) from which the two directories (*International Handbook of Universities* and *Guide to Higher Education in Africa*) and the WHED Portal are produced. Different types of information services (topical bibliographies, institutional data, and address labels) are also provided. The IAU website (http://www.iau-aiu.net) is another important source of information and links.

COOPERATION

The IAU, through its unique networking capacity, provides an important clearing house function to Members for academic exchange and cooperation, implying active involvement and participation of Member universities in the important mission of bringing a real international perspective to the life of universities. Among the major areas retained for cooperation are Sustainable Development; Internationalization; Doctoral Programmes in Africa; and Information and Communication Technologies (ICTs).

HEADQUARTERS

International Association of Universities
1, rue Miollis
75732 Paris Cedex 15, France
Telephone: + 33 1-45-68-48-00
Fax: + 33 1-47-34-76-05
E-Mail: iau@iau-aiu.net
Website: http://www.iau-aiu.net

PRESIDENT

Dzulkifli Abdul Razak, Former Vice-Chancellor, University Sains Malaysia and Former Vice-Chancellor, Albukhary International University, Malaysia

SECRETARY-GENERAL

Eva Egron-Polak, Executive Director International Association of Universities

OFFICERS OF THE INTERNATIONAL ASSOCIATION OF UNIVERSITIES

Administrative Board 2012–2016

President

Dzulkifli ABDUL RAZAK	Former Vice-Chancellor, University Sains Malaysia and Former Vice-Chancellor, Albukhary International University, Malaysia

Vice-Presidents

Pam FREDMAN	Rector, University of Gothenburg, Sweden
Manuel J. FERNÓS	President, Interamerican University of Puerto Rico, Puerto Rico
Pornchai MONGKHONVANIT	President, Siam University, Thailand
Olive MUGENDA	Vice-Chancellor, Kenyatta University, Kenya

Immediate Past President

Juan Ramón de la FUENTE	Former Rector, National Autonomous University of Mexico, Mexico

Members

AFRICA

Ernest ARYEETEY	Vice-Chancellor, University of Ghana, Ghana
Hope C. SADZA	Vice-Chancellor, Women's University in Africa, Zimbabwe

AMERICAS

Stephen FREEDMAN	Provost, Fordham University, USA
Eon Nigel HARRIS	Vice-Chancellor, The University of the West Indies, Jamaica
Juan TOBIAS	Rector, University of Salvador, Argentina

ASIA & PACIFIC

Anna CICCARELLI	Deputy Vice-Chancellor and Former Vice-President, The University of Queensland, Australia
Walid MOUSSA	President, Notre Dame University-Louaize, Lebanon
Khalid OMARI	President, Jerash University, Jordan
Yutaka TSUJINAKA	Executive Advisor to the President, University of Tsukuba, Japan
Jianhua LIN	President, Zhejiang University, China

EUROPE

Howard NEWBY	Vice-Chancellor, University of Liverpool, UK
Patricia POL	Policy Advisor for European and International Affairs, Université Paris-Est Créteil Val de Marne, France
Angelo RICCABONI	Rector, University of Siena, Italy
Daniel Hernández RUIPEREZ	Rector, University of Salamanca, Spain

IAU – INTERNATIONAL ASSOCIATION OF UNIVERSITIES LIST OF PUBLICATIONS

For a worldwide Association, sharing information, expertise and experience amongst leaders and decision-makers on the central issues facing higher education, is key. The IAU has made - and continues to make - a very substantial input to informed debate on public policy. It maintains databases and produces reference works on higher education systems, institutions and credentials and brings out state of the art research on vital issues that concern higher education. By doing so, it serves the academic community and its leadership, stimulating discussion and advancing action.

Major publications resulting from this commitment are:

REFERENCE WORKS

- *International Handbook of Universities.*
- *Guide to Higher Education in Africa.*

PUBLISHED BY: Palgrave Macmillan, Houndmills, Basingstoke, Hampshire RG21 6XS and 175 Fifth Avenue, New York, N.Y. 10010. www.palgrave.com

HIGHER EDUCATION POLICY

IAU Quarterly Journal

Editor: Professor Jeroen Huisman, Ghent University, Belgium

SUBSCRIPTIONS AT: Palgrave Macmillan, Houndmills, Basingstoke, Hampshire, RG21 6XS and 175, Fifth Avenue, suite 203, New York, N.Y. 10010. www.palgrave-journals.com/hep/subscribe.html

OTHER PUBLICATIONS

- *Internationalization of Higher Education: Growing expectations, fundamental values.* Paris, IAU, 2014
- *IAU Horizons/AIU Horizons* - A quarterly magazine.

AVAILABLE FROM: International Association of Universities, UNESCO House, 1, rue Miollis, 75732 Paris Cedex 15, France. Tel: +33-1-45 68 48-00 - Fax: +33-1-47-34 76 05 iau@iau-aiu.net and on IAU website.

- *IAU E-Bulletin/Bulletin électronique de l'AIU* – A monthly electronic publication.

FREE SUBSCRIPTION AT: http://www.iau-aiu.net/iau_e_bulletin.html

- *IAU Highlights from the Press*

AVAILABLE AT: http://www.iau-aiu.net/content/electronic-publications

- IAU Website/Site Web de l'AIU: http://www.iau-aiu.net

LIST OF REGIONAL/INTERNATIONAL ORGANIZATIONS

Academic Cooperation Association - ACA
President: Sijbolt Noorda
Director: Bernd Waechter
Egmontstraat 15
Brussel 1000
BELGIUM
Tel: +32(2) 513-2241
Fax: +32(2) 513-1776
EMail: info@aca-secretariat.be
WWW: http://www.aca-secretariat.be

African Academy of Sciences - AAS
President: Aderemi Kuku
PO Box 24916
Nairobi 00502
KENYA
Tel: +254(20) 8060674
Fax: +254(20) 8060675
EMail: aas@aasciences.org; communication@aasciences.org
WWW: http://www.aasciences.org
The overall goals are to strengthen science and technology capacity, to mobilize science and technology resources in the continent and among the African diaspora, to stimulate problem-solving research and development in pivotal areas of the continent's development, and to market the Academy's activities widely for greater impact on African social development and economic growth.

African Council for Distance Education - ACDE
President: Primrose Kurasha
Secretary-General: James K. Tuitoek
PO Box 8023
Nairobi 00100
KENYA
Tel: +254(20) 26274818
EMail: director@acde-africa.org
WWW: http://www.acdeafrica.org
The African Council for Distance Education (ACDE) is a continental educational organization comprising African universities and other higher education institutions, which are committed to expanding access to quality education and training through open and distance learning.

African Network for the Internationalisation of Education - ANIE
Chair: Chika Trevor Sehoole
Secretary/Executive Director: James Otieno Jowi
c/o Margaret Thatcher Library, Moi University
PO Box 3900
Eldoret 30100
KENYA
Tel: +254 721 917 461
Fax: +254(53) 43047
EMail: sec@anienetwork.org
WWW: http://www.anienetwork.org
ANIE is an independent, non-profit, non-governmental membership organisation whose aim is to develop research capacity and constitute an expert network in advancing the understanding of internationalisation of higher education to meet the professional needs of individuals, institutions and organisations.

African Network of Scientific and Technological Institutions - ANSTI
Chair: George Albert Magoha
PO Box 30592
Nairobi 00100
KENYA
Tel: +254(20) 7622619
Fax: +254(20) 7622538
EMail: info@ansti.org
WWW: http://www.ansti.org
The aim of ANSTI is to develop active collaboration among African scientific institutions so as to promote research and development in areas of relevance to the development of the region.

African Quality Assurance Network - AfriQAN
Accra
GHANA
EMail: jcmba@aau.org
WWW: http://afriqan.aau.org
To provide assistance to institutions concerned with quality assurance in higher education in Africa.

Agence universitaire de la Francophonie - AUF
Secrétaire-général: Abdellatif Miraoui
Rector: Jean-Paul de Gaudemar
Case postale du Musée, C.P. 49714
Montréal
Québec H3T 2A5
CANADA
Tel: +1(514) 343-6630
Fax: +1(514) 343-2107
EMail: rectorat@auf.org
WWW: http://www.auf.org

All-Africa Students Union - AASU
President: Mohammed Sallah
Secretary-General: Fred Awaah
PO Box M 274
Accra
GHANA
Tel: +233(30) 225-8484
EMail: info@aasuonline.org; secgen@aasuonline.org
WWW: http://www.aasuonline.org

ASEAN University Network - AUN
Executive Director: Nantana Gajaseni
17th Floor, Chamchuri 10 Building
Chulalongkorn University, Phayathai Road
Bangkok 10330
THAILAND
Tel: +66(2) 215-3640
Fax: +66(2) 216-8808
EMail: nantana@aunsec.org

Asia-Pacific Association for International Association - APAIE
President: Susan Elliott
Executive Director: Grace Kim
Room 312 Lyceum, Korea University,
Anam-Dong, Seongbuk-Gu
Seoul 136-701
KOREA (REPUBLIC OF)
Tel: +82(2) 3290-2935
Fax: +82(2) 921-0684
EMail: apaie@apaie.org; serena@apaie.org
WWW: http://www.apaie.org
Non-profit organization whose aims are to achieve greater cooperation among those responsible for international education and internationalization in Asia-Pacific higher education institutions and promote the quality of international programmes, activities, and exchanges.

Asian Association of Open Universities - AAOU
President: Wong Yuk Shan
Secretary-General: Li Kam Cheong
c/o The Open University of Hong Kong,
Homantin
Kowloon
CHINA - HONG KONG SAR
Tel: +852 3120 2785
Fax: +852 2769 7533
EMail: aaou@ouhk.edu.hk
WWW: http://www.aaou.org
Non-profit organization of higher learning institutions that are primarily concerned with education at a distance. AAOU was founded in 1987.

Asociación de Universidades de América Latina y el Caribe para la Integración - AUALCPI
President: German Anzola Montero
Executive Assistant: Laura Phillips Sanchez
Calle 222 # 55 - 30
Bogotá
COLOMBIA
Tel: +57 (1) 668 4700 Ext. 220
EMail: info@aualcpi.net
WWW: http://www.aualcpi.net/

Asociación de Universidades Grupo Montevideo
President: Carlos Alexandre Netto
Executive Secretary: Alvaro Maglia
Guayabos 1729 Ap. 502
Montevideo 11200
URUGUAY
Tel: +598 2400 5411
Fax: +598 2400 5401
EMail: secretariaejecutiva@grupomontevideo.org
WWW: http://www.grupomontevideo.edu.uy

Asociación de Universidades Privadas de Centro América - AUPRICA (Association of Private Universities of Central America)
President: Manuel Sandí Murillo
Calle Florida
San José 11303
COSTA RICA
EMail: erodriguez@unibe.ac.cr
WWW: http://www.auprica.com

Asociación Iberoamericana de Educación Superior a Distancia - AIESAD (Ibero-American Association for Open University Education)
President: Carlos Eduardo Bielschowsky
Permanent Secretary: Rosario Domingo Navas
Secretaria-Permanente, Calle Bravo Murillo, 38-6 planta
Madrid 28015
SPAIN
Tel: +34(91) 398-7430
Fax: +34(91) 398-7497
EMail: vrector-relint@adm.uned.es
WWW: http://aiesad.cederj.edu.br/
The association works to promote distance higher education, especially among the 13 nations that make up the association. The Association seeks to contribute to the academic life of managers, teachers and students of its member universities, through its various projects and quality assurance in distance education.

Associação das Universidades de Língua Portuguesa - AULP (Association of Portuguese Language Universities - APLU)
President: Rui Martins
Avenida Santos Dumont, 67, 2°
Lisboa 1050-203
PORTUGAL
Tel: +351(217) 816 360
Fax: +351(217) 816 369
EMail: aulp@aulp.org
WWW: http://aulp.org
The aim of this international association is the development of cooperation between universities and higher research institutions by means of promoting the interchange of researchers and students and the development of joint projects of scientific and technological research as well as the exchange of information.

Associação de Universidades Amazonicas - UNAMAZ (Association of Amazonian Universities)
A. Tancredo Neves 2501 Barrio Montese Campos da UFRA
Belém Pará 66077-530
BRAZIL
Tel: +55(91) 3210-5230
EMail: unamaz@ufpa.br
WWW: http://www.unamaz.org
Network of higher education institutions from Bolivia, Brazil, Colombia, Ecuador, Guyana, Peru, Suriname, and Venezuela created in 1993 to promote higher education cooperation for the sustainable development of the Amazonian region.

IAU Association des Universités africaines - AUA (Association of African Universities)
President: Olusola Oyewole
Secretary-General: Etienne E. Ehile
PO Box 5744
Accra
GHANA
Tel: +233(21) 774 495
Fax: +233(21) 774 821
EMail: info@aau.org
WWW: http://www.aau.org
International non-governmental organization founded in Rabat, Morocco in November 1967 having its headquarters in Accra, Ghana.

Association des Universités de l'Atlantique (Association of Atlantic Universities - AAU)
President: Eddy Campbell
Suite 403, 5657 Spring Garden Road
Halifax
Nova Scotia B3J 3R4
CANADA
Tel: +1(902) 425-4230
Fax: +1(902) 425-4233
EMail: info@atlanticuniversities.ca
WWW: http://atlanticuniversities.ca
A voluntary association of the 16 universities in the Atlantic region and in the West Indies which offer programmes leading to a degree or have degree-granting status.

Association for Tertiary Education Management - ATEM
President: Carl Rallings
Executive Director: Paul Abela
Building M, University of Sydney
Cumberland College
75 East Street
(PO Box 170)
Lidcombe
NSW 2141
AUSTRALIA
Tel: +61(2) 9351-9456
Fax: +61(2) 6125-5262
EMail: info@atem.org.au
WWW: http://www.atem.org.au
A professional body for tertiary education administrators and managers in Australasia.

IAU Association internationale des Universités - AIU (International Association of Universities - IAU)
President: Dzulkifli Abdul Razak
Secretary-General: Eva Egron-Polak
UNESCO House
1, Rue Miollis
Cedex 15
Paris 75732
FRANCE
Tel: +33(0)1 4568 4800
Fax: +33(0)1 4734 7605
EMail: iau@iau-aiu.net
WWW: http://www.iau-aiu.net

IAU Association of Arab Universities - AArU
Secretary-General: Sultan Abu Orabi
PO Box 401
Jubeyha
Amman

JORDAN
Tel: +962(6) 506-2048
Fax: +962(6) 506-2051
EMail: secgen@aaru.edu.jo
WWW: http://www.aaru.edu.jo

Association of Christian Universities and Colleges in Asia - ACUCA
President: Mangadar Situmorang
General Secretary: Hadrianus Tedjoworo, OSC
c/o Parahyangan Catholic University,
Jalan Ciumbuleuit 94
Bandung 40141
INDONESIA
Tel: +62(22) 203-1110
EMail: acuca@unpar.ac.id
WWW: http://www.acuca.net
The Association of Christian Universities and Colleges in Asia (ACUCA) was formally established at a founding conference held on December 6-9, 1976 in Manila.

IAU Association of Commonwealth Universities - ACU
Chairperson: Olive Mugenda
Secretary-General: John Wood
Woburn House
20-24 Tavistock Square
London
WC1H 9HF
UNITED KINGDOM
Tel: +44 20 7380 6700
Fax: +44 20 7387 2655
EMail: info@acu.ac.uk
WWW: http://www.acu.ac.uk

IAU Association of Pacific Rim Universities - APRU
Chair: C.L. Max Nikias
Secretary-General: Christopher Tremewan
Shaw Foundation Alumni House
2F, 11 Kent Ridge Drive
Singapore 119244
SINGAPORE
Tel: +65 6516-3140
Fax: +65 6778-2285
EMail: apru@apru.org
WWW: http://apru.org/
Established in 1997 with universities across the Americas, Asia and Australasia, to contribute to the development of an increasingly integrated Pacific Rim community, and now consists of some 45 member universities.

Association of Southeast Asian Institutions of Higher Learning - ASAIHL
President: Mohd Fauzi Ramlan
Secretary-General: Ninnat Olanvoravuth
Bangkok
THAILAND
WWW: http://www.seameo.org/asaihl/
Assisting member institutions in their development through cooperation.

Association of the Carpathian Region Universities - ACRU
President: Paul-Serban Agachi
Secretary-General: Jana Mojžišová
University of Veterinary Medicine and Pharmacy in Košice, Komenského 73
Košice 041 81
SLOVAK REPUBLIC
EMail: mojzisova@uvlf.sk
WWW: http://acru.uvlf.sk/
The Association has 24 higher education member institutions from Slovakia, Poland, Ukraine, Romania, Hungary and Serbia.

Association of Universities of Asia and the Pacific - AUAP
President: Shawn Chen
Secretary-General: Ricardo Pama
Suranaree University of Technology
111 University Avenue, Suranaree Sub-district
Muang
Nakhon Ratchasima 30000
THAILAND
Tel: +66 85 768 7474
EMail: auapheadquarter@gmail.com
WWW: http://www.e-auap.org

Association of West African Universities - AWAU
Chair: D.D. Kupoole
Acting Secretary-General: Is-haq Oloyede
245 Samuel Ademulegun Way, Central Business District, Opp Arewa Suites
Abuja
NIGERIA
EMail: info@awau.org
WWW: http://www.awau.org
Provides coordination and networking for universities in West Africa.

IAU Bibliotheca Alexandrina
Director: Ismael Serageldin
Director, Centre for Special Studies and Programmes: Mohammed El-Faham
PO Box 138 - Chatby

Alexandria 21526
EGYPT
Tel: +20(3) 483 99 99
EMail: Secretariat@bibalex.org
WWW: http://www.bibalex.org
The Bibliotheca Alexandrina aims to be a center of excellence in the production and dissemination of knowledge and to be a place of dialogue, learning and understanding between cultures and peoples.

Caribbean Area Network for Quality Assurance in Tertiary Education – CANQATE
President: Ruby S. Alleyne
The University of Trinidad and Tobago (UTT),
O'Meara Estate
Arima
TRINIDAD AND TOBAGO
Tel: +868 642-8888
Fax: +868 643-0268
EMail: canqateinfo@gmail.com
WWW: http://www.canqate.org/

Centro Interuniversitario de Desarrollo - CINDA (Inter-University Development Centre)
President: José Tadeu Jorge
Executive Director: María José Lemaitre del Campo
Santa Magdalena 75, Piso 11, Providencia
Santiago
CHILE
Tel: +56 2 2234 1128
Fax: +56 2 2234 1117
EMail: cinda@cinda.cl
WWW: http://www.cinda.cl/

Commonwealth of Learning - COL
President and Chief Executive Officer: Asha S. Kanwar
4710 Kingsway, Suite 2500
Burnaby
British Columbia V5H 4M2
CANADA
Tel: +1(604) 775-8200
Fax: +1(604) 775-8210
EMail: info@col.org
WWW: http://www.col.org
The Commonwealth of Learning (COL) is an intergovernmental organisation created by Commonwealth Heads of Government to encourage the development and sharing of open learning/distance education knowledge, resources and technologies.

Conseil africain et malgache pour l'Enseignement supérieur - CAMES (African and Malagasy Council for Higher Education)
Secretary-General: Bertrand Mbatchi
01 BP 134
Ouagadougou
BURKINA FASO
Tel: +226 5036-8146
Fax: +226 5036-8573
EMail: cames@lecames.org;cames@bf.refer.org
WWW: http://www.lecames.org
Regional body aiming at research dissemination in Africa and in the long-term at accreditation provision within the region.

Consejo Centroamericano de Acreditación de la Educación Superior - CCA (Central American Higher Education Accreditation Council)
President: Lea Azucena Cruz Cruz
Executive Director: Esteban Arias Monge
100 m. norte y 75 m. este de Office Depot, Avenida Central, San Pedro, Montes de Oca
San José
COSTA RICA
Tel: +506 2511 1453
Fax: +506 2224 6903
EMail: cca@ucr.ac.cr
WWW: http://www.cca.ucr.ac.cr/
The Council was created with the purpose of establishing regional mechanisms to harmonize, and give validity to international quality accreditation of higher education in the region.

Consejo Superior Universitario Centroamericano - CSUCA (Central-American University Higher Council)
Secretary-General: Alfonso Fuentes Soria
Avenida las Américas, 1-03 Zona 14, Interior Club Los Arcos
Guatemala 01014
GUATEMALA
Tel: +502 2502-7500
Fax: +502 2502-7501
EMail: macomuy@csuca.org
WWW: http://www.csuca.org/
Regional organization that promotes the integration and strengthening of higher education in Central America.

Consortium for North American Higher Education Collaboration - CONAHEC
President of the Board: David Longanecker
Executive Director: Sean Manley-Casimir
University of Arizona
PO Box 210300
Tucson Arizona 85721-0300
UNITED STATES OF AMERICA
Tel: +1(520) 621-7761
Fax: +1(520) 626-2675
EMail: mariannv@email.arizona.edu
WWW: http://www.conahec.org/
To foster academic collaboration among higher education institutions, organizations and agencies in North America and with their peers around the world. Principal activities include: encouraging student exchange within their member institutions; convening the higher education community; providing online information and networking; conducting comparative research on educational policy issues affecting North America; providing professional development opportunities; preparing future leaders by involving students in regional dialogue; honouring social responsibilities.

Donaurektorenkonferenz (Danube Rectors' Conference)
President: Doru Pamfil
Manager of the DRC Secretariat: Sebastian Schäffer
DRC Secretariat
Hahngasse 6/24
Wien 1090
AUSTRIA
Tel: +43(1) 319 72 58 - 32
EMail: info@drc-danube.org
WWW: http://www.drc-danube.org
A network of almost 70 universities in the Danube Region aiming to improve higher education in teaching and research in theregion, and in particular the advancement of our member universities, by establishing and facilitating bilateral and multilateral contacts between the universities.

European Access Network - EAN
President: Mary Tupan-Wenno
Executive Director: Fran Ferrier
Lawrence Building,
University of Roehampton,
Roehampton Lane
London SW15 5PJ
UNITED KINGDOM
Tel: +44 20 8392 3857
Fax: +44 20 8392 3148
EMail: info@ean-edu.org
WWW: http://www.ean-edu.org/
The European Access Network encourages wider access to higher education for those who are currently under-represented, whether for reasons of gender, ethnic origin, nationality, age, disability, family background, vocational training, geographic location, or earlier educational disadvantage. The EAN is the only European-wide, non-governmental organisation for widening participation in higher education. It is organised for educational purposes and operates under English Law.

European Alliance for Subject-Specific and Professional Accreditation an Quality Assurance - EASPA
President: Iring Wasser
c/o ASIIN
PO Box 101139
Düsseldorf 40002
GERMANY
Tel: +49(211) 900977-0
Fax: +49(211) 900977-99
WWW: http://www.easpa.eu

European Association for International Education - EAIE
President: Laura Howard
Director: Leonard Engel
PO Box 11189
Amsterdam 1001 GD
NETHERLANDS
Tel: +31(20) 344 5100
Fax: +31(20) 344 5119
EMail: eaie@eaie.nl;info@eaie.org
WWW: http://www.eaie.org

European Association for Quality Assurance in Higher Education - ENQA
President: Padraig Walsh
Director: Maria Kelo
Avenue de Tervuren, 38 - bte 4
Brussels 1040
BELGIUM
Tel: +32(2) 735-5659
Fax: +32(2) 736-9850
EMail: secretariat@enqa.eu
WWW: http://www.enqa.eu

European Association for University Lifelong Learning - EUCEN
Executive Secretary: Carme Royo
Balmes, 132-134
Barcelona 08008
SPAIN
Tel: +34(93) 542-1825
Fax: +34(93) 542-2975
EMail: office@eucen.eu
WWW: http://www.eucen.eu
The aim of the association is too contribute to the economic and cultural life of Europe through the promotion and advancement of lifelong learning within higher education institutions in Europe and elsewhere, and to foster universities' influence in the development of lifelong learning knowledge and policies throughout Europe.

European Association of Distance Teaching Universities - EADTU
President: Anja Oskamp
Managing Director: George Ubachs
PO Box 2960
Heerlen 6401
NETHERLANDS
Tel: +31(45) 576 2214
Fax: +31(45) 574 1473
EMail: secretariat@eadtu.eu
WWW: http://www.eadtu.eu

European Association of Institutions in Higher Education - EURASHE
President: Stéphane Lauwick
Secretary General: Johan Cloet
Ravensteingalerij 27/3
Brussels 1000
BELGIUM
Tel: +32(2) 211-4197
Fax: +32(2) 211-4199
EMail: eurashe@eurashe.eu
WWW: http://www.eurashe.eu
EURASHE is the association of European Higher Education Institutions – Polytechnics, Colleges, University Colleges, etc. – devoted to Professional Higher Education and related research within the Bachelor-Masters structure.

European Consortium of Innovative Universities - ECIU
President: Lluís Tort
Secretary-General: Katrin Dircksen
c/o Katrin Dircksen, University of Twente
PO Box 217
Enschede 7500 AE
NETHERLANDS
Tel: +31(53) 489 2684
EMail: k.dircksen@utwente.nl
WWW: http://www.eciu.org
Network of universities with its base in Europe, but building on the experience and insights of institutions in other parts of the world.

European Council of Doctoral Candidates and Junior Researchers - EURODOC
President: Margaux Kersschot
Secretary: Miia Ijäs
Rue d'Egmont 11
Brussels 1000
BELGIUM
EMail: board@eurodoc.net
WWW: http://www.eurodoc.net
International federation of 34 national organizations of PhD candidates, and more generally of young researchers from 33 countries of the European Union and the Council of Europe.

European University Association - EUA
President: Rolf Tarrach
Secretary-General: Lesley Wilson
Avenue de l'Yser, 24
Brussels 1040
BELGIUM
Tel: +32(2) 230-5544
Fax: +32(2) 230-5751
EMail: info@eua.be
WWW: http://www.eua.be

Fédération internationale des Universités catholiques - FIUC (International Federation of Catholic Universities - IFCU)
President: Fr Pedro Rubens Ferreira Oliveira
Secretary-General: Mgr Guy-Réal Thivierge
Head, Communication: Loïc Roche
21 rue d'Assas
Paris 75270
FRANCE
Tel: +33(0)1 4439 5226
Fax: +33(0)1 4439 5228
EMail: sgfiuc@bureau.fiuc.org
WWW: http://fiuc.org/en
Created by a Decree of the Holy See in 1948, it was recognized by Pope Pius XII in 1949 and became the International Federation of Catholic Universities (IFCU) in 1965.

Federation of the Universities of the Islamic World - FIUW
Secretary-General: Abdulaziz Bin Othman Altwaijri
ISESCO, Avenue de F.A.R., Hay Ryad
BP 2275
Rabat 10104
MOROCCO
Tel: +212 5 3756 6012
Fax: +212 5 3756 6053
EMail: fumi@isesco.org.ma
WWW: http://www.isesco.org.ma/fuiw.org/en

Global University Network for Innovation - GUNI
President: Sergi Bonet
C. Sant Antoni Maria Claret 167, Pav. Sant Leopold S1, Recinte Històric de Sant Pau
Barcelona 08025
SPAIN
Tel: +34(93) 401-7009
EMail: info@guninetwork.org
WWW: http://www.guninetwork.org

Groupement International des Secrétaires Généraux des Universités Francophones - GISGUF (International Group of Secretary-Generals of Francophone Universities)
President: Stéphane Berthet
Secretary: Luc Maurice
Maison des Universités
103 Boulevard Saint Michel
Paris 75006
FRANCE
WWW: http://www.gisguf.org/

Grupo Compostela de Universidades (Compostela Group of Universities)
President: Marek Kreglewski
Executive Secretary: Isabel Lirola Delgado
Casa da Cuncha - rúa da Conga, no. 1
Santiago de Compostela 15782
SPAIN
Tel: +34(981) 812-931
Fax: +34(981) 812-932
EMail: lucia.castro@usc.es
WWW: http://www.gcompostela.org
The Compostela Group of Universities is a non-profit association aimed at fostering cooperation and promoting dialogue in all fields related to higher education.

International Association of University Presidents - IAUP
Secretary-General: Alvaro Romo
President: Toyoshi Satow
809 United Nations Plaza
New York
NY 10017-3580
UNITED STATES OF AMERICA
WWW: http://www.iaup.org
An NGO and association of university chief executives from higher education institutions around the world. Membership is limited to those individuals who serve as Presidents, Rectors or Vice-Chancellors at regionally accredited colleges or universities. Its mission is: to increase the exchange of experiences, levels of collaboration and networking between university leaders; to provide a well informed forum for university leaders throughout the world; to contribute to a worldwide vision of higher education; to strengthen the international mission of institutions throughout the world; to make every effort for the voice of educational leaders to be heard; to support sustainable development in a context of global competency; to promote peace and international understanding through education.

International Council for Open and Distance Education - ICDE
President: Mandla Makhanya
Secretary-General: Gard Titlestad
Lilleakerveien 23
Oslo 0283
NORWAY
Tel: +47 2206 2630
Fax: +47 2206 2631
EMail: icde@icde.org
WWW: http://www.icde.org
Global membership organization for open, distance, flexible and online education, including e-learning, that draws its membership from institutions, educational authorities, commercial actors, and individuals. ICDE was founded in 1938 in Canada as the International Council for Correspondence Education.

International Education Association - ISANA
President: Mary Ann Seow
228 Liverpool Street
Hobart TAS7000
AUSTRALIA

Tel: +61(3) 6231-0253
Fax: +61(3) 6231-1522
EMail: isana@isana.org.au
WWW: http://www.isana.org.au
ISANA, a body for international education professionals in Australia and New Zealand, works in student services, advocacy, teaching, and policy development in Australia and New Zealand.

International Federation of University Women - IFUW
President: Catherine Bell
Executive Director: Danièle Castle
10 rue du Lac
Geneva 1207
SWITZERLAND
Tel: +41(22) 731 2380
Fax: +41(22) 738 0440
EMail: info@ifuw.org
WWW: http://www.ifuw.org/
IFUW advocates for women's rights, equality and empowerment through access to quality secondary and tertiary education, and training up to the highest levels.

International Network for Quality Assurance Agencies in Higher Education - INQAAHE
President: Jagannath Patil
The Catalan University Quality Assurance Agency, AQU Catalunya
C. dels Vergós, 36-42
Barcelona 08017
SPAIN
Tel: +34(93) 268-8950
EMail: secretariat@inqaahe.org
WWW: http://www.inqaahe.org
The International Network for Quality Assurance Agencies in Higher Education (INQAAHE) is a world-wide association of over 200 organisations active in the theory and practice of quality assurance in higher education.

IAU International Student Identity Card Association - ISIC
Secretary-General: Todd Almeida
Keizersgracht 174
Amsterdam 1016 DW
NETHERLANDS
Tel: +31(20) 520 08 40
EMail: admin@isic.org;academic@isicnederland.nl
WWW: http://www.isicnederland.nl

Inter-University Council for East Africa - IUCEA
Executive Secretary: Alexandre Lyambabje
Plot 4 Nile Avenue
3rd Floor, EADB Building
PO Box 7110
Kampala
UGANDA
Tel: +256(41) 425-6251
Fax: +256(41) 434-2007
EMail: info@iucea.org
WWW: http://www.iucea.org
The mission of the IUCEA is to encourage and develop mutually beneficial collaboration between its member Universities, and between them and Governments and other organisations, both public and private. Its aim is to help its members to contribute to meeting national and regional development needs, to the resolution of problems in every appropriate sector of activity in the region, and to the development of human resource capacity particularly in the disciplines of Science, Technology and Business Studies.

Islamic Educational, Scientific and Cultural Organization - ISESCO
Director General: Abdulaziz Bin Othman Altwaijri
Avenue des F.A.R., Hay Ryad
PO Box 2275
Rabat 10104
MOROCCO
Tel: +212(537) 56 60 52
Fax: +212(537) 56 60012
EMail: press@isesco.org.ma
WWW: http://www.isesco.org.ma

IAU Magna Charta Observatory
President: Sijbolt Noorda
Secretary-General: David Lock
Via Zamboni 25
Bologna 40126
ITALY
Tel: +39.051 2098709
Fax: +39.051 2098710
EMail: magnacharta@unibo.it
WWW: http://www.magna-charta.org/
The Magna Charta Observatory aims to gather information, express opinions and prepare documents relating to the respect for, and protection of, the fundamental university values and rights laid down in the Magna Charta Universitatum signed in Bologna in 1988 by 388 Rectors of worldwide main universities.

Network of Universities from the Capitals of Europe - UNICA
President: Luciano Saso
Secretary-General: Kris Dejonckheere
C/o University Foundation
rue d'Egmont n°11
Brussels 1000
BELGIUM
Tel: +32(2) 514-7800
Fax: +32(2) 514-7900
EMail: office@unica-network.eu
WWW: http://www.unica-network.eu
UNICA is a network of 40 universities from the capital cities of Europe. Its role is to promote academic excellence, integration and co-operation between member universities throughout Europe.

IAU Observatory on Borderless Higher Education - OBHE
Chairperson: Drummond Bone
Director: Richard Garrett
Redhill Chambers, 2d High Street
Redhill Surrey RH1 1RJ
UNITED KINGDOM
Tel: +44 20 7222 7890
Fax: +44 20 7182 7152
EMail: info@obhe.ac.uk
WWW: http://www.obhe.ac.uk/
A higher education think tank with institutional members across 30 countries. They offer analysis on trends, business models and policy frameworks, with the aim of providing strategic intelligence for education leaders and policymakers attempting to navigate the opportunities and threats of borderless higher education.

IAU Organisation universitaire interaméricaine - OUI (Inter-American Organisation for Higher Education - IOHE)
President: Allan Cahoon
Executive Director: David Julien
Université de Montréal, 3744, Jean-Brillant, bureau 592
Montreal
Québec H3T 1P1
CANADA
Tel: +1(514) 343-6980
EMail: info@oui-iohe.org
WWW: http://www.oui-iohe.org

Red de Macrouniversidades de América Latina y del Caribe (Network of of Macrouniversities of Latin America and the Caribbean)
President: Alberto Barbieri
Secretary-General: Raúl Perdomo
Regional Coordinator: Rosamaría Villarello Reza México
MEXICO
EMail: secprivada@rec.uba.ar
WWW: http://www.redmacro.unam.mx/

IAU Réseau africain francophone de la Formation supérieure et de l'Enseignement technique - RAFSET (Francophone African Network for Higher Training and Technical Education)
President: Bassabi Kagbara
Route de Kpalimé, à côté de la Poste
BP 8619
Lomé
TOGO
Tel: +228 22 51 65 81
Fax: +228 22 51 44 21
EMail: rafset_togo@yahoo.fr
Contributes to the creation of an African area for the promotion of education by training, institutional capacity building and improving management quality in administrations and enterprises.

Santander Group - European Universities' Network
President: Albert Corhay
Executive Secretary: Wioletta Wegorowska
Rue de Stassart 119
Brussels 1050
BELGIUM
Tel: +32(2) 511-6620
Fax: +32(2) 502-9611
EMail: sgroup@sgroup.be
WWW: http://www.sgroup.be
The SGroup European Universities' Network aims to strengthen the institutional capacities of its member universities to reinforce their international visibility, to expand their collaboration opportunities in education and research and to improve the quality of their governance, teaching, research and administrative practices. It seeks to achieve this through the transfer of knowledge, the development of strategic alliances and the improvement of intercultural understanding.

SEAMEO Regional Centre for Higher Education and Development - RIHED
Director: Chantavit Sujatanond
5th Floor, Commission on Higher Education Building,
328 Sri Ayuthaya Road,
Rajthewee
Bangkok 10400
THAILAND
Tel: +66(2) 644-9856
Fax: +66(2) 644-5421
EMail: rihed@rihed.seameo.org
WWW: http://www.rihed.seameo.org

IAU Southern African Regional Universities Association - SARUA
CEO: Piyushi Kotecha
PO Box 662
Wits 2050
SOUTH AFRICA
Tel: +27(11) 717 3952
Fax: +27(11) 717 3950
EMail: info@sarua.org
WWW: http://www.sarua.org
SARUA is an association for the public universities in the SADC region. SARUA aims to promote, strengthen and increase higher education, training and research through expanded inter-institutional collaboration and capacity building initiatives across the region and promotes universities as major contributors towards national and regional socio-economic development.

UNESCO - Instituto Internacional para la Educación Superior en América Latina y el Caribe - IESALC (UNESCO Institute for Higher Education in Latin America and the Caribbean)
Director: Pedro Henríquez Guajardo
Head, University Networks: Débora Ramos
Edificio Asovincar
1052-A Av, Los Chorros c/c Calle Acueducto,
Altos de Sebucán
Apartado Postal 68.39
Caracas
VENEZUELA
Tel: +58 (212) 286 0555
Fax: +58 (212) 286 0527
EMail: iesalc@unesco.org.ve
WWW: http://www.iesalc.unesco.org.ve/

IAU Unión de Universidades de América Latina - UDUAL (Association of Universities of Latin America and the Caribbean)
President: José Tadeu Jorge
Secretary-General: Roberto Escalante Semerena
Apartado postal 70232
Cuidad Universitaria
México D.F.04510
MEXICO
Tel: +52(55) 5616-2383
Fax: +52(55) 5622-0092
EMail: contacto@udual.org
WWW: http://www.udual.org/

Universitas 21
Chairperson: David Eastwood
Secretary-General: Jane Usherwood
Strathcona 109
c/o University of Birmingham
Edgbaston
Birmingham B15 2TT
UNITED KINGDOM
Tel: +44 121 415 8870
Fax: +44 121 415 8873
EMail: u21@universitas21.com
WWW: http://www.universitas21.com
A global network of research-intensive universities, working together to foster global citizenship and institutional innovation through research-inspired teaching and learning, student mobility, connecting our students and staff, and wider advocacy for internationalisation.

University Network of the European Capitals of Culture - UNeECC
President: Flora Carrijn
Lucian Blaga University of Sibiu
10 Victoriei Bvd
Sibiu 550024
ROMANIA
EMail: uneecc@ulbsibiu.ro
WWW: http://www.uneecc.org/
The aim of UNeECC is to to ensure the recognition of the role and contribution of universities to the success of the cities conferred the title "European Capital of Culture"; to provide the member universities with the possibility of continuous and full participation in the European Capitals of Culture movement enhanced by "Universities of the Year"; and to foster inter-university cooperation to develop and reshape the universities' regional position to create new activities for city and university collaboration.

Vives University Network (Xarxa Vives d'Universitats)
President: Francisco José Mora Mas
1st Vice President: Francesc Xavier Grau i Vidal
Edifici Àgora Universitat Jaume I,
Campus del Riu Sec

Castelló de la Plana 12006
SPAIN
Tel: +34(964) 72 89 93
EMail: xarxa@vives.org
WWW: http://www.vives.org
A non-profit institution that represents and coordinates joint action in higher education, research and culture of a number of universities from 4 different European countries. Since 1994 it has offered a platform leader in services for universities, public and private organizations and society. Its main objective is contributing to the construction process of this cross-border interuniversity region in Mediterranean Europe and its social and economic development.

WC2 University Network
International Development
City University London
Northampton Square
London EC1V 0HB
UNITED KINGDOM
Tel: +44 20 7040 0113
EMail: internationalpartnerships@city.ac.uk
WWW: http://www.wc2network.org/
The WC2 University Network has been developed with the goal of bringing together top universities located in the heart of major world cities in order to address cultural, environmental and political issues of common interest to world cities and their universities.

INTERNATIONAL HANDBOOK OF UNIVERSITIES

2017

twenty-eighth edition

Volume 1

Afghanistan

STRUCTURE OF HIGHER EDUCATION SYSTEM

Description:

The higher education system is centralized and under the responsibility of the Ministry of Higher Education. Higher education institutions reopened in 2002.

Stages of studies:

University level first stage: *Bachelor's Degree*

The first stage of higher education leads in Arts, Education, Social Science, Engineering, Veterinary Medicine, Science and Agriculture, to the award of the Bachelor's degree after four years of study. Studies in Medicine last for seven years (including one year pre-medical and one year internship).

University level second stage:

The second stage of higher education leads in Literature, Dari, Pashto, Public Administration and Islamic Studies, to the award of the Master's degree after two years of study.

ADMISSION TO HIGHER EDUCATION

Admission to university-level studies:

Name of secondary school credential required: Baccaluria

Admission requirements: According to Article 21 of the Law on Universities, admission to University is carried out by competitive examinations, with the exceptions provided for in Article 56.

RECOGNITION OF STUDIES

Quality assurance system:

A quality assurance and accreditation system is currently being developed by the Ministry of Higher Education.

Bodies dealing with recognition:

Ministry of Education

Froshgah, Deh Afghanan Main Road
Kabul
WWW: http://moe.gov.af

NATIONAL BODIES

Ministry of Higher Education

Minister: Farida Mohmand
Karte 4
Kabul
WWW: http://www.mohe.gov.af

Ministry of Education

Minister: Asadullah Balkhi Hanif
Froshgah, Deh Afghanan Main Road
Kabul
WWW: http://moe.gov.af

Data for academic year: 2012-2013

Source: IAU from the UNESCO Office Kabul, from the Ministry of Higher Education in Kabul, 2012. Bodies 2016.

INSTITUTIONS

PUBLIC INSTITUTIONS

ALBERONI UNIVERSITY

Kapisa Main Road, Gulbahar, Kapisa
Website: http://www.au.edu.af/

Chancellor: Abdul Rashid Aziz

Vice-Chancellor: Moh. Naeem Shareef (2005-) Tel: +799 181-883

International Relations: Abdul Malik Hamwar Tel: +799 302-429

Faculty
Agriculture (Agriculture; Botany; Zoology); **Engineering** (Civil Engineering; Engineering); **Languages and Literature** (English; Journalism; Literature; Modern Languages; Native Language); **Law and Political Science** (Administrative Law; International Law; International Relations; Law; Political Sciences); **Medical and Health Sciences** (Health Sciences; Medicine); **Shari'a** (Islamic Law; Islamic Studies)

History: Founded 1999. Acquired present status 2005.

Academic Year: March to December

Fees: None

Main Language(s) of Instruction: Dari

Accrediting Agency: Ministry of Higher Education

Degrees and Diplomas: *Bachelor's Degree*: **Agriculture; Education; Engineering; Law; Literature; Medicine; Political Sciences.**

Student Services: Academic Counselling, Canteen, Cultural Activities, Health Services, Language Laboratory, Nursery Care, Social Counselling, Sports Facilities

Academic Staff *2010-2011*	MEN	WOMEN	**TOTAL**
FULL-TIME	68	6	**74**
Student Numbers *2010-2011*			
All (Foreign included)	2,220	194	**2,414**

Last Updated: 08/11/12

BADAKHSHAN INSTITUTE OF HIGHER EDUCATION

Faizabad main road, Faizabad, Badakhshan
Website: http://www.badakhshan-in.edu.af

Chancellor: Abdul Qadir Mehan

Faculty
Agriculture (Agriculture); **Education** (Biology; Chemistry; Islamic Studies; Mathematics; Physics); **Literature and Social Sciences** (Literature; Social Sciences)

History: Founded 1961 as a Teacher Training Centre. Successively renamed Institution of Teacher Training 1987 and Nasir Khusraw Pedagogical College 1988. Acquired present status 2003.

Accrediting Agency: Ministry of Higher Education

Degrees and Diplomas: *Bachelor's Degree*: **Agriculture; Economics; Education; Literature.**

Academic Staff *2010-2011*	MEN	WOMEN	**TOTAL**
FULL-TIME	29	3	**32**
Student Numbers *2010-2011*			
All (Foreign included)	234	614	**848**

Last Updated: 08/11/12

BAGHLAN UNIVERSITY

Puli Khumri, Baghlan

Chancellor: Aman Zeyayee

Faculty
Agriculture (Agriculture); **Education** (Education)

History: Founded 2004.

Accrediting Agency: Ministry of Higher Education

Degrees and Diplomas: *Bachelor's Degree*: **Agriculture; Education; Engineering.**

Academic Staff *2010-2011*	MEN	WOMEN	**TOTAL**
FULL-TIME	53	6	**59**
Student Numbers *2010-2011*			
All (Foreign included)	1,315	176	**1,491**

Last Updated: 09/11/12

BALKH UNIVERSITY

Rawze Sakhi Street, Mazar-e Sharif, Balkh
Tel: +93 50-3487 +93 50-3554
EMail: balkh_university@yahoo.com
Website: http://www.ba.edu.af/

Chancellor: Mukammal Alokozai

Faculty
Agriculture (Agriculture; Animal Husbandry; Botany; Forest Products); **Economics** (Economics; Finance); **Education** (Education; Foreign Languages Education; Mathematics Education; Native Language Education; Science Education); **Engineering** (Chemical Engineering; Electrical Engineering; Geology; Industrial Engineering; Mathematics; Mining Engineering; Physics); **Law and Political Sciences** (Criminal Law; International Law; Political Sciences; Public Law); **Literature and Human Science** (English; History; Journalism; Oriental Languages); **Medicine** (Anaesthesiology; Anatomy; Biochemistry; Biology; Chemistry; Dermatology; Epidemiology; Gynaecology and Obstetrics; Mathematics; Medicine; Neurology; Ophthalmology; Otorhinolaryngology; Paediatrics; Pathology; Pharmacology; Physics; Physiology; Social and Preventive Medicine; Surgery); **Shari'a (Islamic Law)** (Islamic Law; Islamic Theology)

History: Founded 1988.

Admission Requirements: Secondary school certificate (baccalaureate) or equivalent

Main Language(s) of Instruction: Dari, Pashtu, English

Accrediting Agency: Ministry of Higher Education

Degrees and Diplomas: *Bachelor's Degree*: **Agriculture; Business Administration; Computer Science; Engineering; Journalism; Law; Literature; Medicine; Political Sciences.**

Student Services: Academic Counselling, Canteen, Careers Guidance, Cultural Activities, Health Services, Language Laboratory, Nursery Care, Social Counselling, Sports Facilities

Academic Staff *2010-2011*	MEN	WOMEN	**TOTAL**
FULL-TIME	193	61	**254**
Student Numbers *2010-2011*			
All (Foreign included)	4,442	1,401	**5,843**

Last Updated: 08/11/12

BAMYAAN UNIVERSITY (BU)

Bamyaan city, Bamyaan 32
Website: http://bu.afghanistan.af/fa

Chancellor: Sakhidad Salim

Faculty
Agriculture (Agriculture); **Education** (Education)

History: Founded 1997. Closed during the Taliban Regime. Re-inaugurated 2004.

Accrediting Agency: Ministry of Higher Education

Degrees and Diplomas: *Bachelor's Degree*: **Agriculture; Economics; Geology; Higher Education.**

Academic Staff *2010-2011*	MEN	WOMEN	**TOTAL**
FULL-TIME	63	6	**69**
Student Numbers *2010-2011*			
All (Foreign included)	1,041	167	**1,208**

Last Updated: 08/11/12

FARYAB UNIVERSITY (FU)

Faryab, Faryab Province

Chancellor: Ahmad Zai Habibi

Faculty

Agriculture (Agriculture); **Pedagogy** (Pedagogy)

History: Founded 1977. Formerly Faryab Pedagogical College and Faryab Higher Education Institute. Acquired present status and title 2013.

Accrediting Agency: Ministry of Higher Education

Degrees and Diplomas: *Bachelor's Degree*: **Agriculture; Economics; Higher Education; Social Sciences.**

Academic Staff *2010-2011*	MEN	WOMEN	TOTAL
FULL-TIME	41	13	**54**
Student Numbers *2010-2011*			
All (Foreign included)	970	326	**1,296**

Last Updated: 26/03/14

GHAZNI UNIVERSITY

Central Ghazni Street, Ghazni
Website: http://www.ghi.edu.af

Chancellor: Ahmad Shah Rafiqi

Faculty

Agriculture (Agriculture); **Teacher Training** (Teacher Training)

History: Founded 2009.

Accrediting Agency: Ministry of Higher Education

Degrees and Diplomas: *Bachelor's Degree*: **Agriculture; Education.**

Academic Staff *2010-2011*	MEN	WOMEN	TOTAL
FULL-TIME	25	–	**25**
Student Numbers *2010-2011*			
All (Foreign included)	438	76	**514**

Last Updated: 08/11/12

HERAT UNIVERSITY

Herat, Herat Province
Tel: +93 40 226-770 +93 40 223-570
EMail: nazir@heratuniversity.org
Website: http://www.hu.edu.af/

Chancellor: Mir Ghulam Osman Bariz Hossanini
Tel: +93 79554-0570 EMail: barizhossaini@yahoo.com

Faculty

Agriculture (Agriculture; Agronomy; Animal Husbandry); **Computer Science** (Computer Networks; Computer Science); **Economics** (Economics; Management); **Engineering** (Civil Engineering; Engineering); **Fine Art** (Fine Arts; Painting and Drawing; Writing); **Islamic Studies** (Islamic Law; Islamic Theology; Theology); **Language and Literature** (Arabic; Asian Studies; English; German; International Relations; Journalism; Literature; Modern Languages); **Law and Political Sciences** (Law; Political Sciences); **Science**; **Social Science** (Social Sciences); **Veterinary Medicine** (Veterinary Science)

History: Founded 1988.

Admission Requirements: Secondary school certificate (baccalaureate) or equivalent

Accrediting Agency: Ministry of Higher Education

Degrees and Diplomas: *Bachelor's Degree*

Academic Staff *2010-2011*	MEN	WOMEN	TOTAL
FULL-TIME	221	55	**276**
Student Numbers *2010-2011*			
All (Foreign included)	4,545	2,061	**6,606**

Last Updated: 08/11/12

JAWZJAN UNIVERSITY (JU)

Sheberghan balahesar, Jawzjan
Website: http://ju.afghanistan.af/fa

Chancellor: Gul Ahmad Fazli

Faculty

Agriculture (Agriculture); **Engineering** (Civil Engineering); **Science** (Teacher Training); **Social Sciences** (Social Sciences; Teacher Training)

History: Founded 2002.

Accrediting Agency: Ministry of Higher Education

Degrees and Diplomas: *Bachelor's Degree*: **Agriculture; Civil Engineering; Economics; Geology; Higher Education.**

Academic Staff *2010-2011*	MEN	WOMEN	TOTAL
FULL-TIME	46	29	**75**
Student Numbers *2010-2011*			
All (Foreign included)	1,870	435	**2,305**

Last Updated: 09/11/12

KABUL EDUCATION UNIVERSITY (KEU)

Near to the Kabul police Academy, Afshar-Silo, Kabul
Tel: +93 75 201-4369
EMail: yasserhoseini2008@yahoo.com
Website: http://www.keu.edu.af/

Chancellor: Amanullah Hamidzai

Faculty

Language and Literature (Arabic; English; Literature; Modern Languages; Native Language; Russian); **Natural Sciences** (Biology; Chemistry; Computer Science; Mathematics; Natural Sciences; Physics); **Physical Education** (Physical Education; Sports); **Social Sciences** (Geography; History; Islamic Studies; Social Sciences; Sociology); **Special Education** (Education of the Handicapped; Special Education); **Vocational Education** (Education; Psychology; Vocational Education)

History: Founded 1913 as Teachers Training Centre. Changed name to Darul Malimeen (DM). Became a Teacher Training Academy (TTA) 1946. Transformed into Kabul Institute of Pedagogy (KIP) 1984. Acquired present status and title 2003.

Admission Requirements: High school leaving certificate; entrance examination

Fees: None

Main Language(s) of Instruction: Pashtu and Dari, English (for candidates of scholarship or upon organisational request)

Accrediting Agency: Ministry of Higher Education

Degrees and Diplomas: *Bachelor's Degree*: **Literature; Natural Sciences.** *Master's Degree*: **Education.**

Student Services: Language Laboratory, Sports Facilities

Publications: Payam-e-Maarifat

Academic Staff *2010-2011*	MEN	WOMEN	TOTAL
FULL-TIME	129	50	**179**
Student Numbers *2010-2011*			
All (Foreign included)	2,553	2,071	**4,624**

Last Updated: 08/11/12

KABUL MEDICAL UNIVERSITY (KMU)

Karte Sakhi, Kabul
Tel: +93 20 250-0327
Fax: +93 20 250-0326
EMail: info@kmu.edu.af
Website: http://www.kmu.edu.af

Chancellor: Shirin Aqa Zarif

Faculty

Curative Medicine (Medicine); **Nursing** (Nursing); **Paediatrics** (Paediatrics); **Stomatology** (Stomatology)

History: Founded 1932 as Kabul Medical Faculty (KMF). Initially maintained by collaboration with the Turkish and French governments, it acquired a status of single self-autonomous University in 2005.

Admission Requirements: Secondary school certificate (baccalaureate) or equivalent

Main Language(s) of Instruction: Dari

Accrediting Agency: Ministry of Higher Education

Degrees and Diplomas: *Bachelor's Degree*: **Health Sciences; Medicine; Nursing; Public Health; Stomatology.**

Academic Staff 2010-2011	MEN	WOMEN	TOTAL
FULL-TIME	207	39	**246**
Student Numbers 2010-2011			
All (Foreign included)	1,066	666	**1,732**

Last Updated: 08/11/12

KABUL POLYTECHNIC UNIVERSITY (KPU)

Kabul
Tel: +93 20 220-1114
Website: http://www.polytechnic-kabul.org

Chancellor: Ezatullah Amed
Tel: +93(0) 75200-1933 EMail: chancellor@kpu.edu.af

Vice-Chancellor, Administrative Affairs: Akbar Jan Arzomand
EMail: arzomand@polytechnic-kabul.org

Vice-Chancellor, Student's Affairs: Abdul Ahad Khaleqi
EMail: rahmani@polytechnic-kabul.org

Faculty

Construction and Civil Engineering (Architecture; Civil Engineering; Construction Engineering; Environmental Engineering; Hydraulic Engineering; Islamic Studies; Road Engineering); **Electromechanics** (Automotive Engineering; Mathematics; Mechanics; Modern Languages; Physics; Power Engineering); **Geology and Mining** (Chemical Engineering; Chemistry; Geological Engineering; Geology; Mining Engineering; Petroleum and Gas Engineering; Sports)

Course

Computer Science (Computer Engineering; Computer Science; Information Technology)

History: Founded 1963. Acquired present status 1979.

Academic Year: March to December (March-July; September-December)

Admission Requirements: Secondary school certificate (baccalaureate) or equivalent

Fees: None

Main Language(s) of Instruction: Dari, Pashtu

Accrediting Agency: Ministry of Higher Education

Degrees and Diplomas: *Bachelor's Degree*: **Chemical Engineering; Computer Science; Electrical Engineering; Geology; Mechanical Engineering; Mining Engineering; Surveying and Mapping.** *Master's Degree*: **Agricultural Equipment; Architecture; Chemical Engineering; Civil Engineering; Geological Engineering; Hydraulic Engineering; Industrial Engineering; Mining Engineering; Petroleum and Gas Engineering; Surveying and Mapping.**

Student Services: Academic Counselling, Canteen, Cultural Activities, Foreign Studies Centre, Health Services, Language Laboratory, Nursery Care, Social Counselling, Sports Facilities

Publications: Kabul Polytechnic Institute Academic Journal; Science and Technology

Academic Staff 2010-2011	MEN	WOMEN	TOTAL
FULL-TIME	159	26	**185**
Student Numbers 2010-2011			
All (Foreign included)	2,721	139	**2,860**

Last Updated: 08/11/12

KABUL UNIVERSITY

Pohantoon Kabul
Karte Sakhi, Kabul
Tel: +93 20 250-0326 +93 70 276-174 (mobile)
Fax: +93 20 250-0326
EMail: info@ku.edu.af
Website: http://www.ku.edu.af/

Chancellor: Habibullah Habib (2012-)

Vice Chancellor for Administrative Affairs: Mohammad Hadi Hedayati Tel: +93 785504620 EMail: hhedayati@ku.edu.af

Vice Chancellor for Academic Affairs: Mohammad Salim Rahimi
Tel: +93 202500238 EMail: srahimi55@yahoo.com

Faculty

Agriculture (Agriculture; Animal Husbandry; Forestry); **Computer Science** (Computer Science); **Economics** (Economics); **Engineering** (Architecture; Engineering); **Fine Arts** (Fine Arts); **Geosciences** (Geology); **Journalism** (Journalism); **Language and Literatures** (Literature; Modern Languages); **Law** (Law); **Pharmacy** (Pharmacy); **Psychology and Educational Sciences** (Educational Sciences; Psychology); **Science** (Mathematics and Computer Science; Natural Sciences); **Social Sciences** (Social Sciences); **Veterinary Science** (Veterinary Science)

History: Founded 1932 as a Faculty of Medicine. Became University by State Decree 1945. Co-educational since 1958. Faculty of Medicine detached 1979. A State institution under the jurisdiction of the Ministry of Higher Education.

Academic Year: March to January (March-July; September-January)

Admission Requirements: Secondary school certificate (baccalaureate) or equivalent

Fees: None

Main Language(s) of Instruction: Dari (Persian), Pashtu, English

Accrediting Agency: Ministry of Higher Education

Degrees and Diplomas: *Bachelor's Degree*; *Master's Degree*

Student Services: Canteen, Cultural Activities, Health Services, Language Laboratory, Nursery Care, Sports Facilities

Publications: Journal of Da Kabul Pohantoon

Academic Staff 2010-2011	MEN	WOMEN	TOTAL
FULL-TIME	565	128	**693**
Student Numbers 2010-2011			
All (Foreign included)	10,206	3,503	**13,709**

Last Updated: 07/11/12

KANDAHAR UNIVERSITY (KU)

loya wiyala new Eid gah Kandahar Afghanistan - District 9, Kandahar 25000
Tel: +93 79 930-5478
Website: http://kan.edu.af/

Chancellor: Hazrat Mir Totakhil
Tel: +93 707259635 EMail: chancellor@kandahar-university.af

Vice-Chancellor: Abdul Tawab Balakarzai
Tel: +93 700318932 EMail: tawab@kandahar-university.af

Faculty

Agriculture (Agriculture); **Economics** (Economics); **Education** (Education); **Engineering** (Engineering); **Journalism** (Journalism); **Medicine** (Medicine); **Theology (Sharia)** (Islamic Law; Theology)

Further Information: Branch in Helmand (Faculties of Agriculture and Education)

History: Founded 1990.

Admission Requirements: Secondary school certificate (baccalaureate) or equivalent

Accrediting Agency: Ministry of Higher Education

Degrees and Diplomas: *Bachelor's Degree*: **Agriculture; Economics; Education; Engineering; Journalism; Medicine.**

Academic Staff 2010-2011	MEN	WOMEN	TOTAL
FULL-TIME	103	–	**103**
Student Numbers 2010-2011			
All (Foreign included)	2,626	114	**2,740**

Last Updated: 08/11/12

KUNDUZ UNIVERSITY

Kunduz main road, Kunduz

Chancellor: Abdul Qudus Zarifi

Vice Chancellor: Sayeed Kamal Manawee

Faculty

Agriculture (Agriculture); **Economics** (Economics); **Education** (Education); **Law** (Law)

History: Founded as a training centre 1967. Became Higher Education Institute 1994. Acquired present status and title 2011.

Accrediting Agency: Ministry of Higher Education

Degrees and Diplomas: *Bachelor's Degree*: **Agriculture; Economics; Higher Education; Law; Political Sciences.**

Academic Staff *2010-2011*	MEN	WOMEN	TOTAL
FULL-TIME	32	7	**39**
Student Numbers *2010-2011*			
All (Foreign included)	1,031	205	**1,236**

Last Updated: 08/11/12

NANGARHAR UNIVERSITY (NU)

Jalalabad main road, Jalalabad, Nangarhr
Tel: +93(0) 2076-5423
EMail: info@nu.edu.af
Website: http://www.nu.edu.af/

Chancellor: Mohammad Saber
EMail: chancellor@nu.edu.af; mohammadsaber@hotmail.de

Faculty

Agriculture (Agricultural Economics; Agriculture; Agronomy; Animal Husbandry; Horticulture; Plant and Crop Protection); **Computer Science** (Computer Networks; Computer Science; Software Engineering); **Economics** (Business Administration; Economics); **Education** (Education); **Engineering** (Agricultural Engineering; Electrical Engineering; Engineering); **Languages and Literature** (Arabic; English; Hindi; Literature; Native Language); **Law and Political Sciences** (Law; Political Sciences); **Medicine** (Medicine); **Science** (Natural Sciences); **Shariah** (Islamic Law; Theology); **Veterinary Science** (Veterinary Science)

History: Founded 1962 from Medical Faculty of Kabul University. Reorganized in 1978.

Academic Year: September to June

Main Language(s) of Instruction: Pashtu

Accrediting Agency: Ministry of Higher Education

Degrees and Diplomas: *Bachelor's Degree*: **Agriculture; Civil Engineering; Computer Science; Economics; Education; Islamic Law; Law; Literature; Medicine; Modern Languages; Political Sciences; Veterinary Science.**

Student Services: Academic Counselling, Careers Guidance, Language Laboratory

Academic Staff *2010-2011*	MEN	WOMEN	TOTAL
FULL-TIME	313	11	**324**
Student Numbers *2010-2011*			
All (Foreign included)	6,081	236	**6,317**

Last Updated: 05/08/13

PAKTIA UNIVERSITY (PU)

Paktia province main road, Gardez, Paktia
Tel: +93 20 220-0239
Website: http://www.pu.edu.af/

Chancellor: Abdul Rahim Fahari

Faculty

Agriculture (Agriculture); **Economics** (Economics); **Education** (Education); **Engineering** (Engineering); **Law & Political Science** (Law; Political Sciences); **Literature** (Literature); **Medicine** (Medicine)

History: Founded 2004. Incorporated Aryana University (Faculties of Medicine, Engineering and Law and Political Science) 2010.

Accrediting Agency: Ministry of Higher Education

Degrees and Diplomas: *Bachelor's Degree*

Academic Staff *2010-2011*	MEN	WOMEN	TOTAL
FULL-TIME	45	–	**45**
Student Numbers *2010-2011*			
All (Foreign included)	1,058	–	**1,058**

Last Updated: 08/11/12

PARWAN HIGHER EDUCATION INSTITUTION

Charikar main road, Charikar, Parwan
Website: http://www.parwan-in.edu.af

Chancellor: Atta Mohammad Poya

Faculty

Agriculture (Agriculture; Animal Husbandry; Horticulture; Plant and Crop Protection); **Economics** (Administration; Banking; Economics; Management); **Education** (Arts and Humanities; Biology; Chemistry; Computer Science; Education; English; Geography; Islamic Studies; Mathematics; Vocational Education)

History: Founded 1961 as Primary Teacher training centre in the addition to Numan High School in this province. Upgraded into a Teacher Training Centre 1967. Acquired present status 1999.

Accrediting Agency: Ministry of Higher Education

Degrees and Diplomas: *Bachelor's Degree*: **Agriculture; Economics; Higher Education.**

Academic Staff *2010-2011*	MEN	WOMEN	TOTAL
FULL-TIME	8	39	**47**
Student Numbers *2010-2011*			
All (Foreign included)	1,250	121	**1,371**

Last Updated: 08/11/12

SAMANGAN PEDAGOGICAL COLLEGE

Aibuck Main Road, Aibuck, Samangan

Chancellor: M. Adebi

Faculty

Agriculture (Agriculture); **Education** (Education)

History: Founded 2008.

Accrediting Agency: Ministry of Higher Education

Degrees and Diplomas: *Bachelor's Degree*: **Agriculture; Education.**

Academic Staff *2010-2011*	MEN	WOMEN	TOTAL
FULL-TIME	7	–	**7**
Student Numbers *2010-2011*			
All (Foreign included)	210	60	**270**

Last Updated: 08/11/12

SHAIKH ZAYED UNIVERSITY (KHOST)

Kabul-Khust, Khost
Tel: +93 88-216 +93 52 001-649
EMail: info@szu.edu.af
Website: http://szu.edu.af/en

Chancellor: Mohammad Rasool Barawy (2012-)
EMail: chancellor@szu.edu.af; barawy1@hotmail.com

Faculty

Agriculture (Agriculture); **Computer Science** (Computer Science); **Economics** (Economics); **Education** (Education); **Engineering** (Engineering); **Journalism** (Journalism); **Law and Political Sciences** (Law; Political Sciences); **Medicine** (Medicine); **Sharia** (Islamic Law; Theology)

History: Founded 2005. Previously located in Peshawar, Pakistan, under the name "Afghan University Peshawar".

Accrediting Agency: Ministry of Higher Education

Degrees and Diplomas: *Bachelor's Degree*: **Agriculture; Business Administration; Computer Science; Education; Engineering; Journalism; Law; Literature; Medicine.**

Publications: Sheikh Zayed University Academic Magazine

Academic Staff *2010-2011*	MEN	WOMEN	TOTAL
FULL-TIME	127	–	**127**
Student Numbers *2010-2011*			
All (Foreign included)	2,691	15	**2,706**

Last Updated: 08/11/12

TAKHAR UNIVERSITY (TU)

Taloqan, Takhar
Tel: +93 70-071-2462
Website: http://tu.edu.af/en

President: Kashifi Barmaki

Faculty

Agriculture (Agriculture); **Education** (Education); **Engineering** (Engineering); **Languages and Literature** (Literature; Modern Languages); **Medicine** (Medicine); **Theology** (Theology)

History: Founded as Abdullah Bin Masoud University and registered with the MoHE 1995.

Accrediting Agency: Ministry of Higher Education

Degrees and Diplomas: *Bachelor's Degree*: **Agriculture; Education; Engineering; Law; Literature.**

Academic Staff *2010-2011*	MEN	WOMEN	**TOTAL**
FULL-TIME	54	6	**60**
Student Numbers *2010-2011*			
All (Foreign included)	1,780	265	**2,045**

Last Updated: 08/11/12

PRIVATE INSTITUTIONS

AMERICAN UNIVERSITY OF AFGHANISTAN

P.O. Box 458, Central Post Office, Darul-Aman Road, Kabul
Tel: +93 797 200 400
EMail: communications@auaf.edu.af
Website: http://www.auaf.edu.af

President: Michael Smith

Registrar: Paul Revere EMail: prevere@auaf.edu.af

Department

Business (Business Administration); **English** (Communication Studies; English; Literature); **Information Technology** (Computer Science; Information Technology); **Mathematics and Science** (Mathematics; Natural Sciences); **Political Science and Public Administration** (Political Sciences; Public Administration)

History: Founded 2006.

Main Language(s) of Instruction: English

Accrediting Agency: Ministry of Higher Education

Degrees and Diplomas: *Bachelor's Degree*: **Business Administration; Communication Arts; Computer Science; Information Technology; Public Administration.** *Master's Degree*: **Business Administration.**

Academic Staff *2010-2011*	MEN	WOMEN	**TOTAL**
FULL-TIME	20	7	**27**
Student Numbers *2010-2011*			
All (Foreign included)	287	61	**348**

Last Updated: 07/11/12

ARIA INSTITUTE OF HIGHER EDUCATION

Ettefaq Village Street, Mazar-e Sharif, Balkh
Tel: +93 750902583; +93 786137373
EMail: info@aria.edu.af
Website: http://www.aria.edu.af/en/

Chancellor: Nasratyar

History: Founded 2009.

Accrediting Agency: Ministry of Higher Education

Degrees and Diplomas: *Bachelor's Degree*: **Computer Science; Economics; Engineering; Law; Medicine.**

Academic Staff *2010-2011*	MEN	WOMEN	**TOTAL**
FULL-TIME	56	–	**56**
Student Numbers *2010-2011*			
All (Foreign included)	1,116	363	**1,479**

Last Updated: 07/11/12

ARIANA INSTITUTE OF HIGHER EDUCATION

Main Campus, Chaknoori Watt, Jalalabad, Nangarhr
Tel: +93 798929691
EMail: ariana.university2@gmail.com
Website: http://www.ariana.edu.af

Chancellor: Daneshmal

Faculty

Economics (Economics); **Engineering** (Civil Engineering; Electrical Engineering; Mechanical Engineering); **Law and Political Science** (International Relations; Law); **Medical Sciences** (Medical Technology; Medicine; Midwifery; Pharmacy)

History: Founded 2009.

Accrediting Agency: Ministry of Higher Education

Degrees and Diplomas: *Bachelor's Degree*: **Banking; Business Administration; Civil Engineering; Economics; Finance; International Relations; Law; Medicine; Political Sciences.** *Master's Degree*: **Medicine.**

Last Updated: 07/11/12

BAKHTAR UNIVERSITY

Karte Char, Kabul 1004
Tel: +93 7863-53535
EMail: info@bakhtar.edu.af; hayat_economist@hotmail.com
Website: http://www.website.bakhtar.edu.af/

Chancellor: Abdul Latif Roshan (2007-)
EMail: abdul.latif@bakhtar.edu.af

Vice-Chancellor: Waheed Rokham
Tel: +93 786-7773 EMail: waheed.rokahn@bakhtar.edu.af

International Relations: Umar Hayat, Academic Director
Tel: +92 3339-212540 EMail: hayat_economist@hotmail.com

Faculty

Computer Science (Computer Science); **Management Sciences** (Business and Commerce; Management)

History: Founded 2005 as Bakhtar Institute of Higher Education. Acquired current title and status 2012.

Admission Requirements: High school certificate

Fees: 3,000 per semester (Afghani)

Main Language(s) of Instruction: Dari, English, Pushto

Accrediting Agency: Ministry of Higher Education

Degrees and Diplomas: *Bachelor's Degree*: **Computer Science; Finance; Human Resources; Marketing; Political Sciences.** *Master's Degree*: **Business Administration.**

Academic Staff *2013-2014*	**TOTAL**
FULL-TIME	**180**
PART-TIME	**120**
STAFF WITH DOCTORATE	
FULL-TIME	**60**
Student Numbers *2013-2014*	
All (Foreign included)	**3,012**

Last Updated: 13/09/14

DAWAT UNIVERSITY

PO Box 11086, 5th district, Khoshal Mina, Kabul, 1046
Tel: +93 7749 33600
EMail: dawat.university@gmail.com
Website: http://www.dawat.edu.af/

President: Abdul Rab Rasoul Sayyaf (2009-)
Tel: +93 7890 75407 EMail: sayaf.forpresidency@gmail.com

Vice-chancellor for Administrative and Finance: Alhaj Mohammad Bashir Sarwari
Tel: +93 7929 96090 EMail: dawat.university@gmail.com

International Relations: Abdul Rahman Mansour, Head of International Relations
Tel: +93 7032 72727 EMail: abdurahman.m33@gmail.com

Faculty

Economics (Administration; Banking; Finance; Management; Statistics); **Engineering** (Civil Engineering; Electrical Engineering); **Journalism** (Cultural Studies; Information Technology; Journalism;

Radio and Television Broadcasting); **Law and Political Sciences** (Law; Political Sciences); **Medicine for Ladies** (Gynaecology and Obstetrics; Medicine; Paediatrics); **Pharmacy** (Pharmacy); **Sharia** (Islamic Law)

History: Created 2009.

Academic Year: April to September; September to January

Admission Requirements: High School Certifiacte; entrance exam

Fees: 12,000 - 25,00 per semester, undergraduate; 35,000 per semester, postgraduate (Afghani)

Main Language(s) of Instruction: Pushto, Arabic, English, Dari

Accrediting Agency: Ministry of Higher Education

Degrees and Diplomas: *Bachelor's Degree*: **Administration; Banking; Civil Engineering; Electrical Engineering; Finance; Information Technology; International Relations; International Studies; Islamic Law; Law; Management; Radio and Television Broadcasting; Religious Education.** *Master's Degree*: **Islamic Law.**

Academic Staff *2014-2015*	MEN	WOMEN	**TOTAL**
FULL-TIME	–	–	**140**
PART-TIME	–	–	**290**
STAFF WITH DOCTORATE			
FULL-TIME	–	–	**34**
Student Numbers *2014-2015*			
All (Foreign included)	7,705	1,049	**8,754**

Last Updated: 08/09/14

GHALIB INSTITUTE OF HIGHER EDUCATION

Gharbe Parke Taraqi, Hirat 1009
Tel: +93 7996-97795
EMail: qadira032@gmail.com
Website: http://ghalib.edu.af/

Vice-Chancellor: Abdul Qadir (2010-)
EMail: qadira032@gmail.com

General Director: Sabaoon Muhammad
Tel: +93 7841-41525 EMail: Muhammad.sabaoon@hotmail.com

International Relations: Assad Ullah, Internationl Relation Coordinator Tel: +92 34697-99178 EMail: asaddkhan@outlook.com

Faculty
Economics (Economics); **Law and Political Science** (Law; Political Sciences); **Medicine** (Medicine)

History: Created 2010.

Admission Requirements: High school certificate

Fees: 50,000 per annum (Afghani)

Main Language(s) of Instruction: Dari, English, Pushto

Accrediting Agency: Ministry of Higher Education

Degrees and Diplomas: *Bachelor's Degree*: **Economics; Law; Medicine; Political Sciences.** BSc in Medicine in 5 years; all others - 4 years.

Academic Staff *2013-2014*	**TOTAL**
FULL-TIME	**350**
PART-TIME	**130**
STAFF WITH DOCTORATE	
FULL-TIME	**260**
Student Numbers *2013-2014*	
All (Foreign included)	**3,812**

Last Updated: 13/09/14

KARDAN INSTITUTE OF HIGHER EDUCATION (KIHE)

Charahi Parwan II, Kabul
Tel: +93 799528393; +93 777528383
EMail: info@kardan.edu.af
Website: http://www.kardan.edu.af/

Chancellor: Royeen Rahmani

Vice Chancellor: Syed Umar Farooq

Department
Business Administration (Business Administration); **Civil Engineering** (Civil Engineering); **Computer Science** (Computer Science); **Economics** (Economics); **Law** (Law)

History: Founded 2006.

Accrediting Agency: Ministry of Higher Education

Degrees and Diplomas: *Bachelor's Degree*: **Computer Science; Economics; Engineering.**

Academic Staff *2010-2011*	MEN	WOMEN	**TOTAL**
FULL-TIME	46	–	**46**
Student Numbers *2010-2011*			
All (Foreign included)	2,233	239	**2,472**

Last Updated: 07/11/12

KATEB INSTITUTE OF HIGHER EDUCATION

Pole Sorkh, Kabul
Website: http://kateb.ac.af/english/

Chancellor: Mohd Arefi

History: Founded 2007.

Accrediting Agency: Ministry of Higher Education

Degrees and Diplomas: *Bachelor's Degree*: **Computer Science; Economics; Law; Medicine; Political Sciences.**

Academic Staff *2010-2011*	MEN	WOMEN	**TOTAL**
FULL-TIME	55	8	**63**
Student Numbers *2010-2011*			
All (Foreign included)	901	244	**1,145**

Last Updated: 07/11/12

KHATAM-U-NABIEEN INSTITUTE OF HIGHER EDUCATION

Karte 4, Tamaddun Road, Kabul 25000

Chancellor: Wahid Benish

History: Founded 2007.

Accrediting Agency: Ministry of Higher Education

Degrees and Diplomas: *Bachelor's Degree*: **Economics; Engineering; Medicine.**

Academic Staff *2010-2011*	MEN	WOMEN	**TOTAL**
FULL-TIME	22	3	**25**
Student Numbers *2010-2011*			
All (Foreign included)	524	164	**688**

Last Updated: 07/11/12

KHURASAN UNIVERSITY

Phase-3 Joe Haft, Jalalabad 26000
Tel: +93(77) 2529525
EMail: info@khurasan.edu.af
Website: http://www.khurasan.edu.af/

Rector: Ahmad Tariq Kamal EMail: atkamal@khurasan.edu.af

Director of Academic Affairs: Haddad Hafizullah
EMail: haddad_hafizulah@yahoo.com

International Relations: Mohmand Fazalullah, Coordinator of International Affairs EMail: kihe.oia@gmail.com

Faculty
Computer Science (Computer Science); **Engineering** (Engineering); **Journalism and Mass Communications** (Journalism; Mass Communication); **Linguistics** (English; Linguistics; Native Language); **Management Sciences** (Business Administration)

History: Founded 2006. Previously known as Khurasan Institute of Higher Education, acquired current title and status 2014.

Academic Year: April to June

Admission Requirements: Shahdatnama (12th Grade Diploma)

Main Language(s) of Instruction: Pashto, English

Accrediting Agency: Ministry of Higher Education

Degrees and Diplomas: *Bachelor's Degree*: **Arabic; Business Administration; Civil Engineering; Computer Science; Economics; English; Journalism; Linguistics.** *Master's Degree*: **Business Administration.**

Academic Staff *2014-2015*	MEN	WOMEN	TOTAL
FULL-TIME	–	–	**46**
PART-TIME	–	–	**7**
STAFF WITH DOCTORATE			
FULL-TIME	–	3	**3**
Student Numbers *2014-2015*			
All (Foreign included)	–	–	**2,284**

Last Updated: 23/02/15

MAIWAND INSTITUTE OF HIGHER EDUCATION (MIHE)

Taimany Project, 4th Street, Kabul
Tel: +93 788481599

Chancellor: Abdul Ghani Zarmati

History: Founded 1987.

Accrediting Agency: Ministry of Higher Education

Degrees and Diplomas: *Bachelor's Degree*: **Computer Science; Economics.**

Academic Staff *2010-2011*	MEN	WOMEN	TOTAL
FULL-TIME	29	–	**29**
Student Numbers *2010-2011*			
All (Foreign included)	1,002	97	**1,099**

Last Updated: 07/11/12

MARYAM INSTITUTE OF HIGHER EDUCATION

Taimany Project, 3th Street, Chahari Sedarat, Kabul
Tel: +93 700 034 903
EMail: info@mu.edu.af
Website: http://www.mu.edu.af/Mission.htm

Chancellor: Shahla Rashid EMail: Dr.shahla@mu.edu.af

History: Founded 2007.

Accrediting Agency: Ministry of Higher Education

Degrees and Diplomas: *Bachelor's Degree*: **Computer Science; Economics.**

Academic Staff *2010-2011*	MEN	WOMEN	TOTAL
FULL-TIME	18	–	**18**
Student Numbers *2010-2011*			
All (Foreign included)	610	66	**676**

Last Updated: 07/11/12

MAWLANA JALAL-U-DIN PRIVATE HIGHER EDUCATION

Keyan Building, Dushte Shor Street, Mazar-e Sharif

Chancellor: Mohd Zarif Anwari

History: Founded 2007.

Accrediting Agency: Ministry of Higher Education

Degrees and Diplomas: *Bachelor's Degree*: **Economics; Education; Journalism; Law.**

Academic Staff *2010-2011*	MEN	WOMEN	TOTAL
FULL-TIME	–	34	**34**
Student Numbers *2010-2011*			
All (Foreign included)	812	120	**932**

Last Updated: 07/11/12

SALAM UNIVERSITY

Kolola Poshta, Traffic Intersection, 40-Meter Road, Kabul 1001
Tel: +93(20) 2230 6640
EMail: salamuk@salam.edu.af
Website: http://www.salam.edu.af/

President: Mohammad Ismail Labib Balkhi (2012-)

Vice-President Administration: Atta Rafiullah

International Relations: Paiman Obaidullah, Quality Assurance and External Relations Manager
EMail: obaid_paiman@yahoo.com

Faculty

Computer Science (Computer Science); **Economics** (Business Administration; Economics); **Engineering** (Civil Engineering; Electrical Engineering; Engineering); **Law and Political Science** (Law; Political Sciences); **Shari and Law** (Islamic Law; Islamic Theology; Law)

History: Created in 2009 as an Institute of Higher Education. Acquired current status and title 2013.

Academic Year: Spring semester starts in March; Autumn semester starts in September.

Admission Requirements: Grade 12 Certificate

Fees: Law and Political Science, 24,000; Economics and Business Administration, 27,000; Computer Science 27,000; Shari and Law, 15,000; Civil Engineering, Electric Engineering, 33,000. Fees per semester (Afghani)

Main Language(s) of Instruction: Pashto/Pushto, English

Accrediting Agency: Ministry of Higher Education

Degrees and Diplomas: *Bachelor's Degree*: **Business Administration; Computer Science; Economics; Engineering; Information Technology; Islamic Law; Law; Political Sciences.** *Master's Degree*: **Islamic Law; Law.**

Academic Staff *2013-2014*	TOTAL
FULL-TIME	**128**
PART-TIME	**160**
STAFF WITH DOCTORATE	
FULL-TIME	**12**
Student Numbers *2013-2014*	
All (Foreign included)	**4,000**

Last Updated: 20/05/14

Albania

STRUCTURE OF HIGHER EDUCATION SYSTEM

Description:

Higher education is offered by public and private institutions. All higher education (HE) institutions are governed by the Law on Higher Education (2007). Universities offer up to third cycle study programmes; higher schools and professional colleges offer mainly first cycle and sometimes second cycle programmes. Research is carried out mainly in universities, but higher education schools and professional colleges may carry out research in Arts, Sports, etc., depending on their statutes. Study programmes are offered full-time and part-time, distance learning is also available.

Admission. The National Exam Agency, under the Ministry of Education and Science, governs admission procedures. Admission to all public and private HE institutions requires successful completion of secondary education and the 4 State Matura Exams. In certain study programmes requiring specific skills like Arts, Sports, Architecture, and some foreign languages, there is an admission/ entrance examination at the HE institution level. The number of admissions to public HE institutions is determined each year by the Government in a special Act, based on proposals made by the HE institutions.

Study Programmes. Pre-Bologna Programmes: The first cycle usually consisted of 4 years' study (for primary teachers and a few others, 3 years'), followed by the Postgraduate School (1-2 years) and the PhD, consisting of a doctoral thesis only. Within the 2007 HE Law, these 4-year programmes were recognized at the level of Integrated Second Cycle (Bologna's 3+2). The Postgraduate School has been recognized at Post Master's level (and can also cover the 60 ECTS of the first doctoral year). Post Bologna Programmes: There are non-university HE study programmes of 120 ECTS, basically in applied fields. The first cycle programmes are no less than 180 ECTS with 60 ECTS per year. The completion of the first cycle leads to the second cycle of (i) 120 ECTS, of 2 years' length for the Master of Science or the Master of Fine Arts or (ii) 60-90 ECTS, of 1,5 years for Professional Masters. In field such as Medicine, Stomatology, Pharmacy, Veterinary Science and Architecture, HE institutions offer integrated second cycle programmes with a minimum of 300 ECTS and of 5 years' length. To receive their second cycle diploma, students are required to provide evidence of an internationally recognized English language test in accordance with the Common European Framework of Reference for Languages. Only the completion of the second cycle programme, leading to a Master of Science or Master of Fine Arts, gives access to the third cycle. The third cycle includes: a) Long term specialization studies, basically in Medicine, Stomatology, Pharmacy, Veterinary Science, Engineering and Law, lasting for 2 years as stipulated by the law on regulated professions; and b) Doctoral programmes, lasting for at least 3 academic years with 60 ECTS for taught subjects leading to the award of the Doctor diploma. Doctoral students have to prepare and defend a thesis and submit evidence of English language command in accordance with the Common European Framework of Reference for Languages. The holders of the former Master of the Second Level or the Post University School, may have such credits transferred and have the 60 ECTS completed, passing directly to the doctoral thesis. After 2007, research is mainly carried out at universities. The former Research Institutes have been integrated into universities and academies. Some units at the department or faculty levels are mainly focused on research but can also teach. The other departments focus on teaching, but may carry out a little research. The Inter-University Center of Albanological Studies mostly focuses on research.

Accreditation. Accreditation falls under the responsibility of the National Accreditation Council. There is accreditation at the institution and study programme levels for all three cycles. A new HE institution has to be recognized by a Government Act, based on a proposal from the Ministry of Education and Science. Prior to the Act, the National Agency of Accreditation carries out a pre-accreditation. Following recognition, the new HE institution will have to undergo accreditation, and only after that, it will be allowed to award degrees. Accreditation usually takes place once every 6 years

Stages of studies:

University level first stage: *Bachelor - First Cycle Degree*
Studies last for a minimum of 3 years. Undergraduate study programmes include at least 180 credits and are offered at universities and professional colleges. If the profession is not regulated, the degree can give access to the labour market. Academically, it can give access to the second cycle of higher education or to the Master of Science or to the Professional Master. A thesis is not a standard requirement. The study programme must be accredited.

University level second stage: *Master of Science, Master of Fine Arts, Professional Master - Second Cycle Degree*
The second cycle degree of Master of Science or Master of Fine Arts confers 120 ECTS and studies last for 2 years. Students must prepare a thesis. It is the required standard for a number of professions. In certain fields like Medicine, Pharmacy, Dentistry, Veterinary Medicine, Architecture, universities offer only integrated first and second cycle study programmes of a length of no less than 5 years of study. The study programme must be accredited. It provides for entry to the third cycle study programme – a) long term specialization; and/or b) PhD study programmes. The Professional Master is open to those with at least a first cycle degree. It is mainly professional. Teachers, in particular, need this Master in their field. It comprises no less than 60 ECTS. It includes taught subjects and training. It does not give access to the third cycle. It cannot lead directly to third cycle programmes, but holders may have access to a Master of Science or Master of Fine Arts programme, with credits being transferred.

University level third stage: *Long term specialization studies; Doktor i Shkencave (Doctor of Sciences)*
With studies lasting for at least 2 years and comprising a minimum of 120 ECTS, the long-term specialization studies advance theoretical and professional knowledge and skills in Medicine, Pharmacy, Stomatology, Veterinary science, Engineering, Law, etc. These studies comprise both taught subjects and research. Holders of this diploma may enter a doctoral programme and may not have to take the 60 ECTS of taught subjects which are normally compulsory for doctoral programmes. Students have to take the English Language Test in accordance with the Common European Framework of Refence for Languages. The Doktor i Shkencave (Doctor of Sciences) studies last at least for 3 years. They comprise 60 ECTS of taught subjects and a doctoral thesis after individual study and research (while working). The title of Doktor i Shkencave is conferred. The candidate, under the supervision of a scientific researcher, must prepare and defend a thesis. He/she needs to fulfill the requirement of the English language test and other criteria set out by HEIs.

ADMISSION TO HIGHER EDUCATION

Admission to university-level studies:

Name of secondary school credential required: Diplomë e Maturës Shtetërore

Minimum score/requirement: Minimum score of 25 out of 100

For entry to: all HE programmes.

Alternatives to credentials: “A” level equivalents such as the International Baccalaureate (IB) or a pass in year 1 or an undergraduate programme from a recognized university abroad. IB points of certain points.

Admission requirements: Certain undergraduate programmes require candidates to pass an interview, a written test conducted by the university.

Foreign students admission:

Quotas: Set by special decree of the Council of Ministers.

Admission requirements: The same as for Albanian nationals.

Language proficiency: Albanian language test at scores set by HEIs.

RECOGNITION OF STUDIES

Quality assurance system:

The first part of QA is the licensing procedure. Within the framework of the Government's Act for the opening of a new higher education institution or a new study programme, the Accreditation Council checks the fulfillment of standards and requirements. Only a positive evaluation from the Accreditation Council can lead to the Government's license. Until the award of the first diplomas, the new HE institution will have to undergo institutional and study programme accreditation. The new HE Law provides for internal QA which is under the responsibility of each HE institution. The external QA leads then to the final procedures for accreditation. The National Agency of Accreditation is responsible for the implementation of these procedures. The Accreditation Council may decide to approve, reject or grant conditional accreditation based on internal and external evaluation reports. Relying on recommendations from the Accreditation Council, the Minister of Education and Science, or the Minister in charge in case of specific HE institutions, then issues the accreditation decree.

Bodies dealing with recognition:

Agjencia Publike e Akreditimit të Arsimit të Lartë - APAAL (National Agency for the Accreditation of Higher Education)

Director:Dhurata Bozo
Bulevardi "Zhan D'Ark", Pallatet e Lanës, Nr 2
Tiranë
Tel: +355(4) 224-3423
WWW: http://www.aaal.edu.al

Special provisions for recognition:

Recognition for university level studies: According to the Law on Higher Education, HE institutions are responsible for recognition when the purpose of recognition is enrolment in higher levels of education. (Article 38 of Law No. 9741 on HE). Recognition of post secondary qualifications is done by the Ministry of Education and Science, through its Diploma Recognition Unit (Article 37 of the same Law). Albania has ratified the Lisbon Convention on Recognition.Further provisions on recognition requirements and procedures, should be found in the HE institutions' charters. For details on the recognition procedures and requirements by the Ministry of Education and Science, see www.mash.gov.al (Arsimi i Lartë (Higher Education), Njohja e Diplomave (Diploma Recognition).

The Division for Diploma Recognition (serving also as the Albanian ENIC-NARIC) is responsible for assuring the authenticity and comparability of foreign higher education qualifications with the levels of higher education.

For access to advanced studies and research: In accordance with Law no. 9741, dated 21.05.2007, with amendments, Article 38, academic recognition is vested with the universities. Therefore, in the case of advanced studies and research, universities have the power to recognize qualifications from foreign HE institutions.

For exercising a profession: The Law no. 10171, dated 22.10.2009 "On regulated professions in the Republic of Albania" with amendments, provides for the exercise of several regulated professions such as: Medicine, Pharmacy, Stomatology, Nursing, Midwifery, Physiotherapy, Veterinary Medicine, Law, Urban Planning, Architecture, Construction, Teaching etc. In the case of unregulated professions, recognition is at the discretion of employers.

Continuous efforts are being made to introduce standards such as those under the 2005/36 EU Directive.

NATIONAL BODIES

Ministria e Arsimit dhe Sportit (Ministry of Education and Sport)

Minister: Lindita Nikolla
Rruga e Durrësit Nr. 23
Tiranë 1001
Tel: +355(4) 223-0289
EMail: info@arsimi.gov.al
WWW: http://www.arsimi.gov.al

Role of national body: Organizes the system of higher education and research and is responsible for expenditure on institutions and specialized institutions.

Albanian Rectors' Conference

c/o Ministry of Education and Science
Rruga e Durrësit, 23
Tirana

Data for academic year: 2011-2012
Source: IAU from the Albanian ENIC-NARIC, 2011. Bodies 2016.

INSTITUTIONS

PUBLIC INSTITUTIONS

AGRICULTURAL UNIVERSITY OF TIRANA

Universiteti Bujqësor i Tiranës (AUT/UBT)
Kodër Kamëz, Tiranë
Tel: +355(47) 200893
Fax: +355(47) 353893
EMail: iroaut@yahoo.com
Website: http://www.ubt.edu.al

Rector: Fatos Harizaj

Faculty

Agriculture and Environment (Agricultural Business; Agricultural Economics; Agronomy; Animal Husbandry; Aquaculture; Food Technology; Horticulture; Plant and Crop Protection); **Biotechnology and Food Technology** (Biotechnology; Food Technology); **Economy and Agribusiness** (Agricultural Business; Agricultural Economics; Economics); **Forestry** (Forestry; Harvest Technology; Wood Technology); **Veterinary Science** (Veterinary Science)

History: Founded 1951 as the Higher Agricultural Institute. Acquired present status 1991.

Academic Year: October to July

Admission Requirements: High school certificate and entrance examination

Main Language(s) of Instruction: Albanian

Accrediting Agency: Ministria e Arsimit dhe Shkences (MASH) (Ministry of Education and Science)

Degrees and Diplomas: *Bachelor – Diplomë e Ciklit të Parë*: **Agriculture; Environmental Studies.** *Master Profesional*: **Agricultural Business; Agricultural Economics; Agricultural Management; Environmental Management; Horticulture; Plant and Crop Protection.** *Master i Shkencave/Master i Arteve të Bukura*: **Agricultural Business; Agricultural Economics; Agricultural Engineering; Agricultural Equipment; Agricultural Management; Agronomy; Animal Husbandry; Aquaculture; Forestry; Horticulture; Oenology; Plant and Crop Protection; Veterinary Science; Viticulture; Wood Technology.** *Doktor*: **Agricultural Business; Agricultural Economics; Agricultural Management; Agronomy; Animal Husbandry; Biotechnology; Environmental Studies; Food Science; Forestry; Horticulture; Plant and Crop Protection; Veterinary Science; Wood Technology.**

Student Services: Canteen, Cultural Activities, Health Services, Sports Facilities

Last Updated: 29/06/15

ALEKSANDËR MOISIU UNIVERSITY OF DURRES

Universiteti Aleksandër Moisiu i Durrësit
Lagja 1, Rr. Currilave, Durrës
Tel: +355(5) 239161
Fax: +355(5) 239162
EMail: contacts@uamd.edu.al
Website: http://www.uamd.edu.al

Rector: Mit'hat Mema

Faculty

Business (Administration; Banking; Economics; Finance; Management; Public Administration); **Education** (Computer Education; Education; Foreign Languages Education; Mathematics Education; Primary Education; Science Education; Teacher Training); **Information Technology** (Information Technology); **Political Science and Law** (Administration; Law; Political Sciences)

History: Founded 2006.

Main Language(s) of Instruction: Albanian

Degrees and Diplomas: *Bachelor – Diplomë e Ciklit të Parë*: **Business Administration; Education.** *Master Profesional*: **Business Administration; Education; Finance; Public Administration; Tourism.** *Master i Shkencave/Master i Arteve të Bukura*: **Business Administration; Computer Science; Education; Finance; Public Administration.**

Last Updated: 29/06/15

ALEKSANDËR XHUVANI UNIVERSITY OF ELBASAN

Universiteti i Elbasanit Aleksandër Xhuvani
Rr. Rinia, Elbasan
Tel: +355(54) 52593
Fax: +355(54) 52593
EMail: info@uniel.edu.al
Website: http://www.uniel.edu.al

Rector: Liman Varoshi

Faculty

Economics (Accountancy; Business Administration; Economics; Finance); **Education** (Education; Teacher Training); **Humanities** (Albanian; Geography; History; Journalism; Literature; Modern Languages); **Medical Sciences** (Health Administration; Medical Auxiliaries; Medical Technology; Midwifery; Nursing; Rehabilitation and Therapy); **Natural Sciences** (Biology; Chemistry; Mathematics; Nursing; Physics)

History: Founded 1909, acquired present status 1991.

Academic Year: October to July (October-February; March-July)

Admission Requirements: Secondary school certificate and entrance examination

Main Language(s) of Instruction: Albanian

Accrediting Agency: Ministria e Arsimit dhe Shkences (MASH) (Ministry of Education and Science)

Degrees and Diplomas: *Bachelor – Diplomë e Ciklit të Parë*: **Arts and Humanities; Business Administration; Education; Information Technology; Natural Sciences.** *Master Profesional*: **Business Administration; Cultural Studies; Educational Administration; Foreign Languages Education; Geography; History; Humanities and Social Science Education; Linguistics; Marketing; Mathematics Education; Modern Languages; Science Education; Secondary Education; Social Work.** *Master i Shkencave/Master i Arteve të Bukura*: **Applied Mathematics; Education; Educational Psychology; Environmental Studies; Linguistics; Social Work.** *Doktor*: **History; Linguistics.**

Student Services: Academic Counselling, Canteen, Careers Guidance, Cultural Activities, Facilities for disabled people, Foreign Studies Centre, Health Services, Language Laboratory, Nursery Care, Social Counselling, Sports Facilities

Last Updated: 29/06/15

IAU EQREM ÇABEJ UNIVERSITY OF GJIROKSTRA

Universiteti 'Eqrem Çabej' Gjirokastër (UGJ)
Lagja "18 Shtatori", Gjirokstër
Tel: +355(842) 63408
Fax: +355(842) 63776
EMail: rektori@uogj.edu.al
Website: http://www.uogj.edu.al

Rector: Gëzim Sala (2008-)
Tel: +355(842) 66146
EMail: gezimsala@yahoo.com; rektori@uogj.edu.al; rectorsecretary@uogj.edu.al

Chancellor: Sotira Goçi
Tel: +355(842) 67571 EMail: sotiragoci@yahoo.com

International Relations: Liljana Reçka, Vice-Rector, Science and International Relations
Tel: +355(842) 68024 EMail: liljanarecka@yahoo.com

Faculty

Education and Social Sciences (Albanian; Economics; Education; Educational Sciences; Geography; Greek; Greek (Classical); History; Modern Languages; Social Sciences; Teacher Training);

Natural Sciences (Biology; Chemistry; Information Technology; Mathematics; Mathematics and Computer Science; Nursing)

History: Founded 1971. Acquired current status in 1991.

Academic Year: October to September

Admission Requirements: Secondary school certificate.

Main Language(s) of Instruction: Albanian, Greek, English, Italian

Accrediting Agency: Ministria e Arsimit dhe Shkences (MASH) (Ministry of Education and Science)

Degrees and Diplomas: *Bachelor – Diplomë e Ciklit të Parë*: **Accountancy; Albanian; Biology; Chemistry; Computer Science; English; Finance; Geography; Greek; History; Italian; Literature; Management; Mathematics; Modern Languages; Nursing; Physics; Public Administration.** *Master Profesional*: **Accountancy; Education; Finance; Foreign Languages Education; Greek; Information Technology; Literature; Native Language Education; Nursing; Primary Education; Public Administration; Science Education; Secondary Education; Tourism.** *Master i Shkencave/Master i Arteve të Bukura*: **Archaeology; Art Management; Linguistics; Literature; Science Education.**

Student Services: Academic Counselling, Canteen, Careers Guidance, Cultural Activities, Foreign Studies Centre, Health Services, Language Laboratory, Nursery Care, Social Counselling, Sports Facilities

Publications: Journal of Mathematics and Natural Sciences; Journal of Social, Economics and Educational Sciences

Last Updated: 24/04/15

FAN S. NOLI UNIVERSITY KORCE

Universiteti 'Fan S. Noli' Korçë

Rr. Gjergj Kastrioti, Korçë

Tel: +355(824) 2580

Fax: +355(824) 2230

EMail: iro@unkorce.edu.al

Website: http://www.unkorce.edu.al

Rector: Gjergji Mero EMail: rektorati@unkorce.edu.al

Faculty

Agriculture (Agriculture; Farm Management; Food Science; Horticulture); **Economics** (Economics; Finance; Management; Marketing; Tourism); **Education and Philology** (Education; History; Modern Languages); **Natural and Human Sciences** (Information Technology; Mathematics; Mathematics and Computer Science; Midwifery; Natural Sciences; Nursing; Philosophy; Sociology)

History: Founded 1971 as Higher Agricultural Institute. Acquired present status and title 1992.

Academic Year: October to July

Admission Requirements: Secondary school certificate and entrance examination

Main Language(s) of Instruction: Albanian

Accrediting Agency: Ministria e Arsimit dhe Shkences (MASH) (Ministry of Education and Science)

Degrees and Diplomas: *Bachelor – Diplomë e Ciklit të Parë*: **Agriculture; Arts and Humanities; Business Administration; Economics; Education; Natural Sciences; Nursing.** *Master Profesional*: **Accountancy; Agriculture; Business Administration; Education; Foreign Languages Education; Marketing; Mathematics Education; Natural Sciences; Science Education; Secondary Education; Tourism.** *Master i Shkencave/Master i Arteve të Bukura*: **Business Administration; Finance; Primary Education; Social Sciences; Tourism.** *Doktor*: **Horticulture.**

Student Services: Canteen, Cultural Activities, Health Services, Nursery Care, Social Counselling, Sports Facilities

Last Updated: 29/06/15

LUIGJ GURAKUQI UNIVERSITY OF SHKODRA

Universiteti i Shkodrës 'Luigj Gurakuqi' (USH)

Sheshi 2 Prilli, Shkodër

Tel: +355(22) 800651

EMail: info@unishk.edu.al

Website: http://www.unishk.edu.al

Rector: Artan Haxhi
EMail: rektori@unishk.tirana.al; ahaxhi@unishk.edu.al

Faculty

Economics (Accountancy; Business Administration; Finance; Tourism); **Education Sciences** (Art Education; Humanities and Social Science Education; Pedagogy; Physical Education; Preschool Education; Primary Education; Psychology; Science Education; Secondary Education; Social Work; Teacher Training); **Foreign Languages** (English; French; German; Italian; Modern Languages); **Law** (Law); **Natural Sciences** (Biology; Chemistry; Mathematics; Nursing; Physics); **Social Sciences** (Geography; History; Linguistics; Literature)

History: Founded 1957 as Higher Pedagogical Institute. Acquired present status and title 1991.

Academic Year: October to July (October-January; February-July)

Admission Requirements: Secondary school certificate and entrance examination

Main Language(s) of Instruction: Albanian

Accrediting Agency: Ministria e Arsimit dhe Shkences (MASH) (Ministry of Education and Science)

Degrees and Diplomas: *Bachelor – Diplomë e Ciklit të Parë*: **Arts and Humanities; Business Administration; Education; Law; Modern Languages; Natural Sciences; Social Work; Tourism.** *Master Profesional*: **Albanian; Foreign Languages Education; Humanities and Social Science Education; Linguistics; Mathematics Education; Native Language Education; Physical Education; Science Education; Secondary Education; Translation and Interpretation.** *Master i Shkencave/Master i Arteve të Bukura*: **Accountancy; Biology; Business Administration; Clinical Psychology; Finance; Industrial and Organizational Psychology; Law; Native Language Education; Psychology; Science Education; Tourism.** *Doktor*: **Albanian.**

Student Services: Academic Counselling, Canteen, Cultural Activities, Health Services, Nursery Care, Sports Facilities

Last Updated: 29/06/15

MEDICAL UNIVERSITY, TIRANA

Universiteti i Mjekësisë, Tiranë

Rruga e "Dibës" Nr. 371, Tiranë 1005

Tel: +355(4) 236443

Fax: +355(4) 236443

EMail: info@umed.edu.al

Website: http://www.umed.edu.al

Rector: Arben Gjata

Faculty

Dentistry (Dentistry); **Medicine** (Medicine); **Pharmacy** (Pharmacy); **Public Health** (Public Health); **Technical Medical Sciences** (Medical Auxiliaries; Medical Technology)

History: Founded 2013.

Main Language(s) of Instruction: Albanian

Degrees and Diplomas: *Bachelor – Diplomë e Ciklit të Parë*: **Health Sciences; Midwifery; Nursing; Public Health; Rehabilitation and Therapy.** *Master Profesional*: **Health Administration; Medical Auxiliaries; Medical Technology; Nursing; Physical Therapy; Public Health; Radiology.** *Master i Shkencave/Master i Arteve të Bukura*: **Dentistry; Medical Auxiliaries; Medical Technology; Medicine; Midwifery; Nursing; Pharmacy; Physical Therapy.** *Doktor*: **Anatomy; Cardiology; Epidemiology; Forensic Medicine and Dentistry; Gynaecology and Obstetrics; Medical Technology; Neurology; Neurosciences; Ophthalmology; Otorhinolaryngology; Paediatrics; Pharmacology; Pharmacy; Public Health; Surgery.**

Last Updated: 30/06/15

POLYTECHNIC UNIVERSITY OF TIRANA

Universiteti Politeknik i Tiranës

Sheshi "Nene Tereza", Nr.4, Tiranë

Tel: +355(42) 27914

Fax: +355(42) 27914

Website: http://www.upt.al

Rector: Jorgaq Kacani EMail: jorgaqkacani@yahoo.com

Faculty

Architecture and Urbanism (Architecture; Town Planning); **Civil Engineering** (Civil Engineering; Construction Engineering; Environmental Engineering; Geological Engineering; Structural Architecture; Town Planning; Urban Studies); **Electrical Engineering** (Electrical Engineering); **Geology and Mining** (Earth Sciences; Geology; Mining Engineering); **Information Technology** (Electronic Engineering; Information Technology; Telecommunications Engineering); **Mathematical Engineering and Physical Engineering** (Chemistry; Mathematics; Physical Engineering; Physics); **Mechanical Engineering** (Energy Engineering; Mechanical Engineering; Production Engineering; Textile Technology)

Institute

Geo-sciences and Energy, Water and Environment (Energy Engineering; Geological Engineering; Seismology; Surveying and Mapping; Water Management)

History: Founded 1957 incorporating former institutes of Engineering, Medicine, Economics, Law and Sciences. Acquired present status 1991.

Academic Year: October to July (October-January; February-July)

Admission Requirements: Secondary school certificate and entrance examination

Main Language(s) of Instruction: Albanian

Accrediting Agency: Ministria e Arsimit dhe Shkences (MASH) (Ministry of Education and Science)

Degrees and Diplomas: *Bachelor – Diplomë e Ciklit të Parë*: **Engineering; Information Technology.** *Master Profesional*: **Engineering.** *Master i Shkencave/Master i Arteve të Bukura*: **Civil Engineering; Computer Engineering; Electrical Engineering; Electronic Engineering; Environmental Engineering; Geological Engineering; Hydraulic Engineering; Materials Engineering; Mechanical Engineering; Physical Engineering; Telecommunications Engineering; Textile Technology.** *Doktor*: **Architecture; Computer Engineering; Construction Engineering; Electrical Engineering; Environmental Engineering; Geological Engineering; Mechanical Engineering; Physical Engineering; Telecommunications Engineering.**

Student Services: Academic Counselling, Cultural Activities, Health Services, Sports Facilities

Last Updated: 30/06/15

TIRANA UNIVERSITY OF SPORT

Universiteti i Sporteve të Tiranës
Rr. Muhamet Gjollesha, Tiranë
Tel: +355(4) 226652
Fax: +355(4) 226652
EMail: contact@ust.edu.al
Website: http://www.ust.edu.al

Rector: Juel JARANI Jarani

Department

Individual Sports (Sports); **Professional Education and Sciences** (Arts and Humanities; Natural Sciences); **Sports Medicine** (Sports Medicine); **Team Sports** (Sports)

History: Founded 1948. Previously known as Akademia e Edukimit Fizik dhe Sporteve Vojo Kushi (Vojo Kushi Academy of Physical Education). Acquired present title 2010.

Main Language(s) of Instruction: English, Italian, French, German

Accrediting Agency: Ministria e Arsimit dhe Shkences (MASH) (Ministry of Education and Science)

Degrees and Diplomas: *Bachelor – Diplomë e Ciklit të Parë*: **Sports.** *Master Profesional*: **Sports.** *Master i Shkencave/Master i Arteve të Bukura*: **Sports.** *Doktor*: **Sports.**

Last Updated: 29/06/15

UNIVERSITY OF ARTS

Universiteti i Arteve
Bulevardi "Dëshmoret e Kombit", Sheshi "Nënë Tereza", Tiranë
Tel: +355(42) 25488
Fax: +355(42) 25488
Website: http://www.artacademy.al

Rector: Petrit Malaj EMail: rektori@uart.edu.al

Faculty

Fine Arts (Fine Arts; Multimedia; Painting and Drawing; Sculpture); **Music** (Conducting; Music; Music Theory and Composition; Musicology); **Performing Arts** (Acting; Dance; Theatre)

History: Founded 1966 as High Institute of Arts, incorporating the Conservatory, the High School of Figurative Arts and the High School of Actors. Became Akademia e Arteve (Academy of Fine Arts) 1991, and acquired current title and status 2011.

Admission Requirements: Secondary school certificate

Main Language(s) of Instruction: Albanian

Accrediting Agency: Ministria e Arsimit dhe Shkences (MASH) (Ministry of Education and Science)

Degrees and Diplomas: *Bachelor – Diplomë e Ciklit të Parë*: **Conducting; Music Theory and Composition; Musicology.** *Master Profesional*: **Music; Music Education.** *Master i Shkencave/Master i Arteve të Bukura*: **Dance; Fine Arts; Music; Theatre.**

Student Services: Academic Counselling

Last Updated: 30/06/15

UNIVERSITY OF TIRANA

Universiteti i Tiranës
Sheshi "Nënë Tereza", Kutia Postare Nr 183, Tiranë
Tel: +355(4) 222840
Fax: +355(4) 2223981
EMail: info@unitir.edu.al
Website: http://www.unitir.edu.al

Rector: Dhori Kule EMail: dhorikule@unitir.edu.al

Faculty

Economics (Accountancy; Business Administration; Economics; Finance; Management; Marketing; Tourism); **Foreign Languages** (English; French; German; Italian; Modern Languages); **History and Philology** (Albanian; Geography; History; Journalism; Linguistics; Literature; Philology); **Law** (Civil Law; Criminal Law; Law; Public Law); **Natural Sciences** (Biology; Biotechnology; Chemistry; Computer Science; Industrial Chemistry; Mathematics; Natural Sciences; Pharmacy; Physics); **Social Sciences** (Pedagogy; Philosophy; Political Sciences; Psychology; Social Work; Sociology)

Further Information: Branches in: Bérat, Durrës, Elbasan, Korça, Shkodër, Vlorë

History: Founded 1957 incorporating former institutes of Engineering, Medicine, Economics, Law and Science.

Academic Year: October to July (October-December; January-July).

Admission Requirements: Secondary school certificate and admission exam

Main Language(s) of Instruction: Albanian

Accrediting Agency: Ministria e Arsimit dhe Shkences (MASH) (Ministry of Education and Science)

Degrees and Diplomas: *Bachelor – Diplomë e Ciklit të Parë*: **Economics; Geography; History; Journalism; Law; Modern Languages; Natural Sciences; Social Sciences.** *Master Profesional*: **Archiving; Biology; Biotechnology; Computer Science; Documentation Techniques; Educational Administration; Government; Law; Mathematics; Modern Languages; Philosophy; Physics; Social Policy; Social Work; Teacher Training.** *Master i Shkencave/Master i Arteve të Bukura*: **Archaeology; Biology; Business Administration; Chemical Engineering; Chemistry; Computer Science; Development Studies; Economics; Educational Psychology; Finance; Food Science; Food Technology; Geography; History; Industrial and Organizational Psychology; Journalism; Law; Library Science; Linguistics; Literature; Mathematics; Physics; Plant Pathology; Political Sciences; Public Relations; Social Work; Sociology; Tourism; Translation and Interpretation.** *Doktor*: **Accountancy; Biotechnology; Chemistry; Criminology; Economics; Finance; Law; Linguistics; Literature; Management; Marketing; Mass Communication; Molecular Biology; Pedagogy; Philosophy; Physics; Political Sciences; Psychology; Social Work; Sociology; Statistics.**

Student Services: Canteen, Cultural Activities, Health Services, Sports Facilities

Publications: Buletini i shkencave mjeksore; Buletini i shkencave te Natyres; Bulletini i shkencave Ekonomike

Last Updated: 29/06/15

UNIVERSITY OF VLORA 'ISMAIL QEMALI'

Universiteti i Vlorës 'Ismail Qemali' (UV)
L. Pavarësia, Vlorë 9400
Tel: +355(33) 222288
Fax: +355(33) 224952
EMail: info@univlora.edu.al
Website: http://univlora.edu.al

Rector: Albert Qarri (2012-)
EMail: berti.qarri@univlora.edu.al; rektorati@univlora.edu.al

Faculty

Economics (Accountancy; Administration; Finance; Hotel and Restaurant; Management; Marketing; Public Administration; Real Estate; Tourism); **Humanities** (Albanian; Educational Sciences; English; Italian; Law; Preschool Education; Special Education; Teacher Training); **Public Health** (Midwifery; Nursing; Public Health); **Technical Sciences** (Actuarial Science; Biology; Chemistry; Computer Education; Computer Science; Electrical Engineering; Fishery; Information Technology; Marine Engineering; Marine Science and Oceanography; Mathematics; Mathematics Education; Mechanical Engineering; Physics)

History: Founded 1994 as a Technological University.

Academic Year: October-January; February-May; July-September

Admission Requirements: Secondary school certificate and entrance examination

Main Language(s) of Instruction: Albanian

Accrediting Agency: Ministria e Arsimit dhe Shkences (MASH) (Ministry of Education and Science)

Degrees and Diplomas: *Bachelor – Diplomë e Ciklit të Parë*: **Business Administration; Education; Engineering; Information Sciences; Mathematics and Computer Science; Natural Sciences; Public Health.** *Master Profesional*: **Computer Science; English; Information Technology; Italian; Marine Engineering; Mathematics; Mechanical Engineering; Nautical Science; Physics; Public Administration; Tourism.** *Master i Shkencave/Master i Arteve të Bukura*: **Computer Science; Finance; Physics.** *Doktor*: **Mathematics.**

Student Services: Academic Counselling, Canteen, Careers Guidance, Facilities for disabled people, Foreign Studies Centre, Health Services, Language Laboratory, Sports Facilities

Publications: Albanian Journal of Mathematics; Bulletini Shkencor

Last Updated: 29/06/15

PRIVATE INSTITUTIONS

ALBANIAN UNIVERSITY

Rruga e Durrësit, Tiranë
Tel: +355(4) 2223562
EMail: informacioni@albanianuniversity.edu.al
Website: http://www.albanianuniversity.edu.al

Rector: Vera Ostreni EMail: v.ostreni@albanianuniversity.edu.al

Faculty

Architecture and Engineering (Architecture; Engineering); **Economics** (Business Administration; Economics); **Medical Sciences** (Dentistry; Nursing; Pharmacy); **Social Sciences** (Communication Studies; Law; Political Sciences; Psychology)

History: Founded 2004 as UFO University. Acquired current title 2010.

Accrediting Agency: Ministria e Arsimit dhe Shkences (MASH) (Ministry of Education and Science)

Degrees and Diplomas: *Bachelor – Diplomë e Ciklit të Parë*: **Architecture; Business Administration; Economics; Engineering; Health Sciences; Information Technology; Political Sciences.** *Master Profesional*: **Administration; Business and Commerce; Clinical Psychology; Criminology; Education; Educational Psychology; Finance; Health Administration; International Relations; Law; Nursing.** *Master i Shkencave/Master i Arteve të Bukura*: **Advertising and Publicity; Architecture; Banking; Business Administration; Clinical Psychology; Computer Engineering; Dentistry; Developmental Psychology; Educational Psychology; Electronic Engineering; Information Technology; International Relations; Journalism; Law; Mechanical Engineering; Pharmacy; Primary Education; Psychology; Public Administration; Public Relations.** *Doktor*: **Administration; Architecture; Clinical Psychology; Finance; International Relations; Law; Pharmacy.** *Certifikate Specializimi*: **Dentistry.**

Last Updated: 24/04/15

ALDENT UNIVERSITY

Universiteti Aldent
Rruga e Dibrës, nr.235, Tiranë
Tel: +355(4) 2231835
EMail: info@ual.edu.al
Website: http://www.ual.edu.al

President: Adem Alushi

Programme

Dental Technician (Dental Technology); **Nursing** (Nursing); **Pharmacy** (Pharmacy); **Physical Therapy** (Physical Therapy); **Stomatology** (Stomatology)

History: Created 2009.

Degrees and Diplomas: *Bachelor – Diplomë e Ciklit të Parë*: **Dental Technology; Nursing; Physical Therapy.** *Master Profesional*: **Nursing.** *Master i Shkencave/Master i Arteve të Bukura*: **Dentistry; Medicine; Orthodontics; Physical Therapy; Stomatology.**

Last Updated: 02/07/15

CANADIAN INSTITUTE OF TECHNOLOGY

Institucioni Kanadez i Teknologjisë
Qendra Zayed, Rruga Andon Zako Çajupi, Tiranë
Tel: +355(4) 2229778
EMail: info@cit.edu.al
Website: http://www.cit.edu.al/

School

Business (Business Administration; Information Technology); **Engineering** (Industrial Engineering; Software Engineering)

History: Created 2011 and acquired current status 2013.

Main Language(s) of Instruction: English

Degrees and Diplomas: *Bachelor – Diplomë e Ciklit të Parë*: **Business Administration; Engineering.** *Master Profesional*: **Business Administration; Industrial Engineering; Software Engineering.** *Master i Shkencave/Master i Arteve të Bukura*: **Business Administration; Industrial Engineering; Software Engineering.**

Last Updated: 30/06/15

EPOKA UNIVERSITY

Universiteti Epoka
Rr. Tiranë-Rinas, Km 12, Tiranë 1039
Tel: +355(4) 223-2086
Fax: +355(4) 222-2117
EMail: info@epoka.edu.al; communications@epoka.edu.al
Website: http://www.epoka.edu.al

Rector: Remzi Altin (2012-) EMail: raltin@epoka.edu.al

International Relations: Alba Gërdeci, Head, International Relations EMail: iro@epoka.edu.al; agerdeci@epoka.edu.al

Faculty

Economics and Administrative Sciences (Banking; Business Administration; Economics; Finance; International Relations; Political Sciences); **Engineering and Architecture** (Architecture; Civil Engineering; Computer Engineering)

Research Centre

Continuous Education; **European Studies**; **Research and Design in Architecture**

History: Created 1992. Accredited from 2008. Power to award doctoral degrees from 2012/2013.

Admission Requirements: Secondary school certificate and entrance exam.

Accrediting Agency: Agjencia Publike e Akreditimit të Arsimit të Lartë (Public Agency for the Accreditation of Higher Education of the Republic of Albania)

Degrees and Diplomas: *Bachelor – Diplomë e Ciklit të Parë*: **Architecture; Banking; Business Administration; Business Computing; Civil Engineering; Computer Engineering; Economics; Finance; International Relations; Marketing; Political Sciences; Telecommunications Engineering; Transport Management.** *Master Profesional*: **Architecture; Banking; Business Administration; Civil Engineering; Computer Engineering; Educational Administration; European Studies; Finance; International Relations; Political Sciences.** *Master i Shkencave/Master i Arteve të Bukura*: **Architecture; Banking; Business Administration; Civil Engineering; Communication Arts; Computer Engineering; Construction Engineering; Economics; Electronic Engineering; European Studies; Finance; International Relations; Political Sciences; Telecommunications Engineering.** *Doktor*: **Architecture; Business Administration; Civil Engineering; Computer Engineering; Economics; Political Sciences.**

Last Updated: 29/06/15

EUROPEAN UNIVERSITY IN TIRANA

Universiteti Europian i Tiranës

Bulevardi "Gjergj Fishta", Nr.2, Tiranë 10423
Tel: +355(4) 2421806
EMail: info@uet.edu.al
Website: http://www.uet.edu.al

Rector: Tonin Gjuraj EMail: tonin.gjuraj@uet.edu.al

Faculty

Economics and Information Technology (Economics; Finance; Information Technology; Management; Mathematics; Statistics); **Law** (Commercial Law; Constitutional Law; European Union Law; International Law; Law; Public Law); **Social Sciences and Education** (Communication Studies; Education; Public Relations; Social Sciences)

School

Doctoral Studies (Business Administration; Law; Social Sciences)

History: Created 2006.

Degrees and Diplomas: *Bachelor – Diplomë e Ciklit të Parë*: **Business Administration; Education; Law; Social Sciences.** *Master Profesional*: **Educational Psychology; Finance; Information Management; International Relations; Law; Management; Marketing; Political Sciences; Public Relations; Teacher Training.** *Master i Shkencave/Master i Arteve të Bukura*: **Banking; Business Administration; Business Computing; Commercial Law; Communication Studies; Criminal Law; Educational Sciences; Finance; International Law; International Relations; Political Sciences; Private Law; Psychology; Public Law; Sociology.** *Doktor*: **Civil Law; Commercial Law; Communication Studies; Economics; Educational Psychology; Finance; Information Management; International Law; International Relations; Management; Political Sciences; Public Law; Sociology.**

Last Updated: 30/06/15

HËNA E PLOTË (BEDËR) UNIVERSITY

Shkolla e Lartë 'Hëna e Plotë (Bedër)'

Rr. Jordan Misja, Tiranë 1001
Tel: +355(4) 241-9200
Fax: +355(4) 241-9333
EMail: info@beder.edu.al
Website: http://beder.edu.al/

Rector: Ferdinand Gjana (2011-) EMail: fgjana@beder.edu.al

Chancellor: Bledar Uku EMail: buku@beder.edu.al

International Relations: Klodian Shehi, Head of International Relations Office EMail: kshehi@beder.edu.al

Department

Communication Sciences (Communication Studies); **Education Sciences** (Education; Educational Sciences); **English Language and Literature** (English; Literature); **Islamic Sciences** (Islamic Studies); **Law** (Law); **Turkish Language and Literature** (Literature; Turkish)

History: Created 2011.

Academic Year: Oct to Feb; Mar to Jun. Also summer school in July and August.

Admission Requirements: Undergraduate: Cumulative GPA above 8, high school diploma, admission test for border-line cases; Postgraduate: Bachelor degree (or equivalent).

Fees: 1,100.00 - 2,000.00 per annum (Euro)

Main Language(s) of Instruction: Albanian, English, Turkish

Accrediting Agency: Public Accreditation Agency for Higher Education

Degrees and Diplomas: *Bachelor – Diplomë e Ciklit të Parë*: **Communication Studies; Educational and Student Counselling; English; Islamic Studies; Law; Preschool Education; Primary Education; Turkish.** *Master Profesional*: **Educational and Student Counselling; Foreign Languages Education.** *Master i Shkencave/Master i Arteve të Bukura*: **Criminal Law; Educational Administration; Educational and Student Counselling; English; International Law; Islamic Studies; Journalism; Public Relations; Turkish.**

Academic Staff *2014-2015*	**TOTAL**
FULL-TIME	**57**
PART-TIME	**38**
STAFF WITH DOCTORATE	
FULL-TIME	**42**
Student Numbers *2014-2015*	
All (Foreign included)	**845**
FOREIGN ONLY	**287**

Last Updated: 12/03/15

LUARASI UNIVERSITY

Universiteti Luarasi

Rr. "Dritan Hoxha", Nr. 127/1, Tiranë
Tel: +355(4) 267200
Fax: +355(4) 267200
EMail: info@luarasi-univ.edu.al
Website: http://www.luarasi-univ.edu.al

Rector: Irakli Koçollari EMail: rector@luarasi-univ.edu.al

Faculty

Economics (Business Administration; Economics; Law); **Law** (Civil Law; Criminal Law; Law; Private Law; Public Law)

History: Founded 2003.

Main Language(s) of Instruction: Albanian

Accrediting Agency: Ministria e Arsimit dhe Shkences (MASH) (Ministry of Education and Science)

Degrees and Diplomas: *Bachelor – Diplomë e Ciklit të Parë*: **Business Administration; Law.** *Master Profesional*: **Accountancy; Administrative Law; Commercial Law; Finance; Fiscal Law; Law; Marketing.** *Master i Shkencave/Master i Arteve të Bukura*: **Banking; Civil Law; Commercial Law; Criminal Law; Management; Public Law.**

Last Updated: 30/06/15

MARIN BARLETI UNIVERSITY

Universiteti 'Marin Barleti'

Rr. "Sami Frashëri", nr. 41, Tiranë
Tel: +355(4) 2430333
EMail: info@umb.edu.al
Website: http://www.umb.edu.al

Faculty

Applied Sciences and Economics (Architecture; Business Administration; Economics; Finance; Information Technology); **Law and Political and Social Sciences** (Law; Modern Languages; Political Sciences; Psychology; Sociology)

History: Created 2005.

Main Language(s) of Instruction: Albanian

Degrees and Diplomas: *Bachelor – Diplomë e Ciklit të Parë*: **Architecture; Business Administration; Economics; Information Technology; Law; Modern Languages; Political Sciences; Social Sciences.** *Master Profesional*: **Architecture; Business Administration; Education; Educational Administration;**

Political Sciences; Psychology; Sociology. *Master i Shkencave/ Master i Arteve të Bukura*: **Business Administration; Political Sciences; Social Sciences.**
Last Updated: 30/06/15

OUR LADY OF GOOD COUNSEL CATHOLIC UNIVERSITY

Universiteti Katolik "Zoja e Këshillit të Mirë"
Rruga r Durresit, Kompleksi Spitalor, Tiranë
Tel: +355(4) 2273290
EMail: info@unizkm.edu.al
Website: http://www.unizkm.edu.al

Rector: Paolo Ruatti

Vice-Rector: Tritan Shehu

Faculty
Applied Sciences (Natural Sciences); **Economics and Political Science** (Economics; Political Sciences); **Medicine** (Dentistry; Medicine; Nursing; Physical Therapy; Stomatology; Surgery); **Pharmacy** (Pharmacy)

History: Founded 2004.

Main Language(s) of Instruction: Albanian

Accrediting Agency: Ministria e Arsimit dhe Shkences (MASH) (Ministry of Education and Science)

Degrees and Diplomas: *Bachelor – Diplomë e Ciklit të Parë*: **Business Administration; Health Sciences; International Relations; Political Sciences.** *Master Profesional*: **Finance; Management.** *Master i Shkencave/Master i Arteve të Bukura*: **Dentistry; Economics; European Studies; Health Administration; International Relations; Management; Medicine; Orthodontics; Pharmacy.**
Last Updated: 30/06/15

POLIS UNIVERSITY

Universiteti POLIS (U-POLIS)
Rr. Bylis 12, Autostrada Tiranë-Durrës, Km 5, Kashar, Tiranë 2995
Tel: +355(4) 2407420
Fax: +355(4) 2407422
EMail: contact@universitetipolis.edu.al
Website: http://www.universitetipolis.edu.al

Rector: Besnik Aliaj EMail: besnik_aliaj@universitetipolis.edu.al

Faculty
Architecture and Design (Architectural and Environmental Design; Architecture; Design); **Planning, Environment, and Urban Management** (Environmental Management; Town Planning)

History: Created 2006. Also known as Universiteti POLIS - Shkolla nderkombetare e Arkitektures dhe politikave te zhvillimit urban (POLIS University International School of Architecture and Urban Development Policies).

Admission Requirements: Diploma e shkolles se mesme (High school Diploma); Entrance exam; English proficiency

Main Language(s) of Instruction: Albanian

Accrediting Agency: Agjensia e akreditimit per arsimin e larte (AAAL) (Higher Education Accreditation Agency); Ministria e Arsimit dhe Shkences (MASH) (Ministry of Education and Science)

Degrees and Diplomas: *Bachelor – Diplomë e Ciklit të Parë*: **Architecture; Construction Engineering; Environmental Studies; Town Planning.** *Master Profesional*: **Business Administration; Design; Town Planning.** *Master i Shkencave/Master i Arteve të Bukura*: **Architecture; Civil Engineering; Design; Environmental Management; Town Planning.**

Student Services: Academic Counselling, Canteen, Facilities for disabled people, Language Laboratory, Social Counselling
Last Updated: 30/06/15

UNIVERSITY OF NEW YORK AT TIRANA

Universiteti i New York-ut në Tiranë
Kodra e Diellit, Tiranë 1046
Tel: +355(4) 4512345
Fax: +355(4) 2441329
EMail: admissions@unyt.edu.al; info@unyt.edu.al
Website: http://www.unyt.edu.al

President: Elias Foutsis

Department
Computer Science (Computer Networks; Computer Science; Information Management); **Economics, Business and Administrative Sciences** (Business Administration; Economics; Finance; Management; Marketing); **English Language and Literature** (English; Literature); **Humanities and Social Sciences** (Communication Studies; English; International Relations; Journalism; Law; Political Sciences; Psychology); **Mathematics and Natural Sciences** (Mathematics; Natural Sciences)

History: Founded 2002. Acquired present status 2004.

Accrediting Agency: Ministria e Arsimit dhe Shkences (MASH) (Ministry of Education and Science)

Degrees and Diplomas: *Bachelor – Diplomë e Ciklit të Parë*: **Business Administration; Law; Mathematics and Computer Science; Natural Sciences; Political Sciences; Psychology.** *Master i Shkencave/Master i Arteve të Bukura*: **Accountancy; Business Administration; Commercial Law; Computer Science; Finance; International Law; International Relations.** *Doktor*: **Business Administration; Computer Science; Law; Political Sciences.** MBA (in collaboration with the Institut Universitaire Kurt Bösch in Sion, Switzerland and the University of Sunderland)
Last Updated: 30/06/15

Algeria

STRUCTURE OF HIGHER EDUCATION SYSTEM

Description:

Higher education falls under the responsibility of the Ministry of Higher Education and Scientific Research. The introduction of the three-tier system (LMD) has started as from the 2004/2005 academic year but until now the two systems (traditionnal and LMD) are co-existing.

Stages of studies:

University level first stage:
At undergraduate level, higher education is divided into a short (three-year) cycle, leading to a Diplôme d'Etudes universitaires appliquées (DEUA), and a long (four- to seven-year) cycle, leading to the Licence, the Diplôme d'Etudes supérieures, the Diplôme d'Ingénieur or the Diplôme de Docteur. Courses for the Diplôme in Engineering, Dental Surgery, Pharmacy, Architecture and Veterinary Medicine last for five years while the title of Doctor in Medicine is awarded after seven years' study. In 2004/2005 a new undergraduate level consisting of a Licence awarded three years after the Baccalauréat was introduced as part of the three-tier system reform which is in the process of being implemented.

University level second stage:
The Master is awarded after two years' study following upon an undergraduate degree.

University level third stage:
The last stage leads to the Doctorat. Lasting three years after the Master, studies involve individual research work and the submission of a thesis.

ADMISSION TO HIGHER EDUCATION

Admission to university-level studies:

Name of secondary school credential required: Baccalauréat général
Name of secondary school credential required: Baccalauréat technique

Foreign students admission:

Admission requirements: Students must hold the Baccalauréat or an equivalent qualification.

Entry regulations: Foreign students must hold a visa or copy of agreement between their country and Algeria (e.g. proof of an equivalence agreement).

Language proficiency: Students must have good knowledge of Arabic. Arabic language courses are compulsory for specialized studies.

RECOGNITION OF STUDIES

Bodies dealing with recognition:

Ministère de l'Enseignement supérieur et de la Recherche scientifique (Ministry of Higher Education and Scientific Research)

11 Chemin Doudou Mokhtar
Ben Aknoun
Alger
Tel: +213(21) 91-23-23
Fax: +213(21) 91-17-17
EMail: info@mesrs.dz
WWW: http://www.mesrs.dz

NATIONAL BODIES

Ministère de l'Enseignement supérieur et de la Recherche scientifique (Ministry of Higher Education and Scientific Research)

Minister: Tahar Hadjar
11 Chemin Doudou Mokhtar
Ben Aknoun
Alger
Tel: +213(21) 91-23-23
Fax: +213(21) 91-17-17
EMail: info@mesrs.dz
WWW: http://www.mesrs.dz
Role of national body: Coordinates higher education.

Data for academic year: 2012-2013
Source: IAU from the website of the Ministry of Higher Education and IBE, 2012. Bodies 2016.

INSTITUTIONS

8 MAY 1945 UNIVERSITY OF GUELMA

Université 8 mai 1945 de Guelma
BP 401, Avenue du 19 mai 1956, 24000 Guelma
Tel: +213(37) 20-62-95
Fax: +213(37) 20-87-58
EMail: recteur@univ-guelma.dz
Website: http://www.univ-guelma.dz

Recteur: Mohamed Nemamcha
Tel: +213(37) 20-62-95 EMail: nemamcha@yahoo.fr

Faculty
Economics, Commerce and Management *(Souidani Boudjemaa campus)* (Accountancy; Business and Commerce; Economics; Management); **Humanities and Social Sciences** *(Souidani Boudjemaa campus)* (Archaeology; Arts and Humanities; Communication Studies; Information Sciences; Psychology; Social Sciences; Sociology); **Languages and Letters** *(New campus)* (Arabic; English; French; Literature); **Law and Political Science** *(Héliopolis campus)* (Law; Political Sciences); **Matter Sciences, Mathematics, and Computing Science** (Computer Science; Materials Engineering; Mathematics; Physics); **Natural and Life Sciences and Earth and Universe Sciences** (Biology; Earth Sciences; Ecology; Environmental Engineering; Natural Sciences); **Science and Technology** (Automation and Control Engineering; Chemical Engineering; Civil Engineering; Electrical and Electronic Engineering; Mechanical Engineering; Telecommunications Engineering)

History: Founded 1992 as Centre universitaire de Guelma. Acquired present status 2001, modified 2004 and 2010.

Accrediting Agency: Ministère de l'Enseignement supérieur et de la Recherche scientifique

Degrees and Diplomas: *Licence (LMD)*; *Master*, *Doctorat*
Last Updated: 07/06/12

20 AUGUST 1955 UNIVERSITY OF SKIKDA

Université 20 août 1955 de Skikda
BP 26, 26 Route El Hadaiek, 21000 Skikda
Tel: +213(38) 70-10-24
EMail: rectorat@univ-skikda.dz
Website: http://www.univ-skikda.dz

Recteur: Ali Kouadria Tel: +213(38) 70-10-00

Vice-Recteur: Mouloud Belachia EMail: belachia@yahoo.fr

International Relations: Amara Otmani
EMail: amara_otmani@yahoo.fr

Faculty
Engineering (Civil Engineering; Computer Engineering; Electrical Engineering; Mechanical Engineering); **Law** (Administration; Law); **Management and Economics** (Economics; Management); **Science** (Agriculture; Biological and Life Sciences; Biology; Mathematics and Computer Science; Natural Sciences; Physics); **Social Sciences and Human Sciences** (Arabic; English; French; Literature; Psychology; Social Sciences; Sociology)

History: Founded 1986. Acquired present status 2001.

Academic Year: September to June

Fees: (Algerian Dinars): 200 per annum

Main Language(s) of Instruction: Arabic and French

Accrediting Agency: Ministère de l'Enseignement supérieur et de la Recherche scientifique

Degrees and Diplomas: *Diplôme d'Etudes universitaires appliquées*; *Licence (LMD)*; *Diplôme d'Etudes supérieures*; *Diplôme d'Ingénieur*

ABBÈS LAGHROUR UNIVERSITY OF KHENCHELA

Université Abbès Laghrour de Khenchela
BP 1252, Route de Constantine, El Houria, 4004 Khenchela
Tel: +213(32) 33-19-66
Fax: +213(32) 33-19-63
EMail: cuniv_khenchela@cuniv-khenchela.edu.dz
Website: http://www.univ-khenchela.dz

Directeur: Azzeddine Haftari

Institute
Economics, Commerce and Management (Business and Commerce; Economics; Management); **Law and Administration** (Administration; Law); **Literature and Languages** (Arabic; English; French; Literature; Modern Languages); **Natural and Life Sciences** (Biochemistry; Biology; Ecology; Genetics; Microbiology; Molecular Biology); **Science and Technology** (Computer Science; Technology)

History: Founded 2001. Acquired present status and title 2012.

Degrees and Diplomas: *Licence (LMD)*; *Diplôme d'Ingénieur*, *Master*, *Doctorat*
Last Updated: 06/12/12

ABDELHAMID IBN BADIS UNIVERSITY OF MOSTAGANEM

Université Abdelhamid Ibn Badis de Mostaganem (UNIV MOSTA)
BP 227, 27000 Mostaganem
Tel: +213(45) 26-54-55 +213(45) 30-10-18/19
Fax: +213(45) 26-54-52 +213(45) 30-10-16
EMail: recteur@univ-mosta.dz
Website: http://www.univ-mosta.dz

Recteur: Mohammed Salah Eddine Seddiki

Secrétaire Generale: Abid Charef Ounassa
Tel: +213(45) 30-10-20

International Relations: Ahmed Chaalal
EMail: achaalal@univ-mosta.dz

Faculty
Arts and Humanities (Arts and Humanities); **Economics, Commerce and Management** (Business and Commerce; Economics; Management); **Exact, Natural and Life Sciences** (Agronomy; Biology; Biotechnology; Fishery; Mathematics; Natural Sciences; Physics); **Law and Political Science** (Law; Political Sciences); **Science and Technology** (Architecture; Civil Engineering; Computer Science; Electronic Engineering; Engineering; Industrial Chemistry; Mathematics; Measurement and Precision Engineering; Mechanical Engineering); **Social Sciences** (Philosophy; Psychology; Social Sciences; Sociology)

Institute
Physical Training and Sports (Physical Education; Sports)

History: Founded 1978 as Centre universitaire de Mostaganem. Acquired present status and title 1998, modified in 2004.

Academic Year: September-June

Admission Requirements: Baccalaureat

Fees: (Algerian Dinars): 200

Main Language(s) of Instruction: Arabic, French, English

Accrediting Agency: Ministère de l'Enseignement supérieur et de la Recherche scientifique

Degrees and Diplomas: *Diplôme d'Etudes universitaires appliquées*; *Licence (LMD)*: **Arabic; Arts and Humanities; Civil Engineering; Computer Science; Electrical Engineering; English; Fine Arts; French; Law; Mathematics; Mechanical Engineering; Social Sciences; Spanish; Sports.** *Diplôme d'Ingénieur*: **Architecture; Civil Engineering; Computer Science; Electrical Engineering; Electronic Engineering; Mechanical Engineering.** *Licence*: **Arabic; Civil Engineering; Communication Studies; Computer Science; Electrical Engineering; English; Fine Arts; French; Mathematics; Mechanical Engineering; Psychology; Sociology; Spanish; Sports.** *Master*: **Civil Engineering; Communication Studies; Education; Fine Arts; Law; Mechanical Engineering; Psychology; Social Sciences.** *Doctorat*: **Arabic; Chemistry; English; French; Mathematics; Physics; Sports.** Also Magistère (6 yrs): Mathematics; Engineering; Arts and Humanities; Social Sciences; Physical Training and Sports; Arabic; English; Law; Business and Commerce; Psychology; Sociology; Agronomy; Biology; Physics; Natural Sciences; Architecture

Student Services: Academic Counselling, Canteen, Careers Guidance, Cultural Activities, Facilities for disabled people, Health Services, Nursery Care, Social Counselling, Sports Facilities

Publications: Revue des Sciences de l'Ingénieur

ABDELLAH ARBAOUI NATIONAL SCHOOL OF HYDRAULIC ENGINEERING OF BLIDA

Ecole nationale supérieure d'Hydraulique Abdellah Arbaoui de Blida (ENSH)
BP 31, 29 route de Soumaa, 09000 Blida
Tel: +213(25) 39-74-47
Fax: +213(25) 39-74-46
EMail: contact@ensh.dz
Website: http://www.ensh.dz

Directeur: M.S. Benhafid EMail: mbenhafid@ensh.dz

Programme
Hydraulic Engineering and Environment (Environmental Engineering; Hydraulic Engineering); **Irrigation and Draining** (Irrigation); **Non-conventional Water Re-use** (Water Management; Water Science); **Urban Hydraulics** (Hydraulic Engineering); **Urban Techniques** (Urban Studies)

History: Founded 1972. Acquired present status 1998.

Admission Requirements: Competitive examination following two years of a preparatory course

Accrediting Agency: Ministère de l'Enseignement supérieur et de la Recherche

Degrees and Diplomas: *Diplôme d'Ingénieur*, *Master*, *Doctorat*
Last Updated: 31/05/12

ABDERAHMANE MIRA UNIVERSITY OF BÉJAÏA

Université Abderrahmane Mira de Béjaïa
Rue Terga Ouzemour, 06000 Béjaïa
Tel: +213(34) 21-43-33
Fax: +213(34) 21-43-32
EMail: rectorat@univ-bejaia.dz
Website: http://www.univ-bejaia.dz

Recteur: Djoudi Merabet EMail: dmerabet@univ-bejaia.dz
Secrétaire général: Brahim Mira

Faculty
Economics, Commerce and Management (Business and Commerce; Economics; Management); **Exact Sciences** (Chemistry; Computer Science; Mathematics; Operations Research; Physics); **Humanities** (Arabic; Arts and Humanities; English; French; Literature; Modern Languages; Oriental Languages); **Law** (Business and Commerce; Economics; Law; Management); **Letters and Languages** (Arabic; English; Literature); **Medicine** (Medicine); **Natural and Life Sciences** (Biochemistry; Biological and Life Sciences; Chemistry; Food Science); **Technology** (Civil Engineering; Earth Sciences; Electronic Engineering; Hydraulic Engineering; Mechanical Engineering)

History: Founded 1983 as Centre universitaire de Béjaia. Acquired present status 1998, modified in 2004.

Degrees and Diplomas: *Diplôme d'Etudes universitaires appliquées*; *Licence (LMD)*; *Diplôme d'Etudes supérieures*; *Diplôme d'Ingénieur*, *Doctorat*

ADVANCED SCHOOL OF COMMERCE

Ecole supérieure de Commerce (ESC)
1 Rampe Salah Gharbi, Alger
Tel: +213(21) 42-32-31
Fax: +213(21) 42-37-32
EMail: contact@esc-alger.com
Website: http://www.esc-alger.com

Recteur: Abdelaziz Sebboua

Department
Accountancy (Accountancy); **Finance** (Finance); **Management** (Management); **Marketing** (Marketing)

History: Founded 1900 under French administration. Linked to the Université d'Alger 1966. Became an independent institution in 1985.

Degrees and Diplomas: *Licence (LMD)*; *Master*, *Doctorat*
Last Updated: 31/05/12

AHMED DRAYA UNIVERSITY - ADRAR

Université Ahmed Draïa d'Adrar
Rue 11 décembre, 1960 Adrar
Tel: +213(49) 96-85-32
Fax: +213(49) 96-75-71
EMail: recteur@univ-adrar.dz
Website: http://www.univadrar.org/francais/Francais.html

Recteur: A. Abassi

Faculty
Arts and Humanities (Arabic; English; French; Law; Literature); **Science and Engineering** (Agricultural Engineering; Computer Science); **Social Sciences and Islamic Studies** (Islamic Studies; Social Sciences)

History: Founded 2001. Acquired present status 2004.

Accrediting Agency: Ministère de l'Enseignement supérieur et de la Recherche scientifique

Degrees and Diplomas: *Licence (LMD)*; *Master*
Publications: El-Hakika
Last Updated: 01/06/12

AKLI MOHAND OULHAD UNIVERSITY OF BOUIRA

Université Akli Mohand Oulhadj de Bouira
Bouira
EMail: info@cu-bouira.dz
Website: http://www.univ-bouira.dz

Recteur: Abadli Mohand-Tahar

Faculty
Economics, Commerce and Management (Business and Commerce; Economics; Management); **Languages and Languages** (Arabic; Literature; Modern Languages); **Law and Political Science** (Law; Political Sciences); **Natural, Life and Earth Sciences** (Biological and Life Sciences; Earth Sciences; Natural Sciences); **Social Sciences and Humanities** (Arts and Humanities; History; Philosophy; Social Sciences)

Institute
Physical Education (Physical Education)

History: Founded 2005. Acquired present status 2012.

Main Language(s) of Instruction: Arabic

Degrees and Diplomas: *Licence (LMD)*; *Master*, *Doctorat*
Last Updated: 12/12/12

ALGERIAN BUSINESS SCHOOL

Ecole supérieure algérienne des Affaires
BP 63F, Les Pins Maritimes, Mohammadia, 16130 Alger
Tel: +213(21) 21 90 09
Fax: +213(21) 21 00 89
EMail: contact@esaa.dz
Website: http://www.esaa.dz

Directeur: Lilian Cadet

Programme
Business Administration (Business Administration); **Management** (Management)

History: Founded 2005.

Main Language(s) of Instruction: French

Degrees and Diplomas: *Master*. Also MBA
Last Updated: 31/05/12

ALGERIAN PETROLEUM INSTITUTE

Institut algérien du Pétrole
Avenue 1er Novembre, 35000 Boumerdès
Tel: +213(24) 81 90 56
EMail: iap@iap.dz
Website: http://www.iap.dz

Président: Salah Khebri

Unit
Drilling, Production and Reservoir Engineering (Petroleum and Gas Engineering); **Gas Engineering and Refining** (Petroleum and Gas Engineering); **Geosciences and Mines** (Geological Engineering; Geology; Geophysics; Mining Engineering); **Industrial Maintenance** (Industrial Maintenance); **Instrumentation and Electrical Engineering** (Electrical Engineering); **Languages and Communication** (Communication Studies; English); **Polymers, Petrochemicals and Plastics** (Petrology; Polymer and Plastics Technology)

Department
Petroleum Economics and Management (Economics; Management)

Further Information: Also branches in Oran and Skikda

History: Founded 1965.

Admission Requirements: Competitve entrance examination

Accrediting Agency: Ministère de l'Industrie et de l'Energie

Degrees and Diplomas: *Master*. Also Diplôme d'Ingénieur spécialisé

ALGIERS MANAGEMENT SCHOOL

Ecole nationale supérieure de Management
37 rue Larbi Ben M'hedi, Alger
EMail: contact@ensm.dz
Website: http://www.ensm.dz

Directeur: Cherif Belmihoub

Programme
Management (Business Administration; Economics; Management)

History: Founded 2008.

Admission Requirements: Higher education degree

Accrediting Agency: Ministère de l'Enseignement supérieur et de la Recherche scientifique

Degrees and Diplomas: *Master*
Last Updated: 06/12/12

AMAR TELIDJI UNIVERSITY OF LAGHOUAT

Université Amar Telidji de Laghouat (UATL)
BP 37 G, route de Ghardaia, 03000 Laghouat
Tel: +213(29) 93-17-91
Fax: +213(29) 93-26- 98
EMail: dep.inf@mail.lagh-univ.dz
Website: http://web.lagh-univ.dz/web/fr/index.php

Recteur: Azib Makhlouf Tel: +213(29) 93-10-24

Faculty
Economics, Commerce and Management (Business and Commerce; Economics; Management); **Engineering** (Architecture; Biology; Civil Engineering; Computer Engineering; Electrical Engineering; Engineering; Hydraulic Engineering; Industrial Chemistry; Mechanical Engineering; Technology); **Law and Political Science** (Law; Political Sciences); **Letters and Languages** (Literature; Modern Languages); **Technology** (Architecture; Civil Engineering; Electronic Engineering; Mechanical Engineering; Technology)

History: Founded 1986 as a high school for technical teaching. Became university centre 1997. Acquired present status 2001, modified in 2004.

Admission Requirements: Secondary school certificate (baccalauréat)

Fees: None

Main Language(s) of Instruction: Arabic and French

Accrediting Agency: Ministère de l'Enseignement supérieur et de la Recherche scientifique

Degrees and Diplomas: *Diplôme d'Etudes universitaires appliquées*; *Licence (LMD)*; *Diplôme d'Ingénieur*: **Engineering.** *Master*

Student Services: Health Services, Sports Facilities
Last Updated: 11/12/12

AMINE ELOKKAL EL HADJ MOUSSA EGAKHAMOUK UNIVERSITY CENTRE OF TAMANRASSET

Centre Universitaire Amine Elokkal El Hadj Moussa Egakhamouk de Tamanrasset
PO Box 10034, 11000 Tamanrasset
Tel: +213(29) 44 77 34
Fax: +213(29) 34 91 86
Website: http://www.cu-tamanrasset.dz

Directeur: Daddah Moïse Boulkheir

Institute
Arts and Languages (Arabic; French; Literature); **Economics, Commerce and Management** (Banking; Business and Commerce; Economics; Finance; Management); **Humanities and Social Sciences** (Clinical Psychology; Demography and Population; Psychology; Social Sciences); **Law and Political Science** (Criminal Law; Law; Political Sciences); **Science and Technology** (Analytical Chemistry; Earth Sciences; Geology; Mathematics; Microbiology; Physics)

History: Founded 2005.

Main Language(s) of Instruction: Arabic

Degrees and Diplomas: *Master*: **Banking; Criminal Law; Human Resources.** Also Bachelors of Academic Specialization.

BADJI MOKHTAR UNIVERSITY OF ANNABA

Université Badji Mokhtar Annaba (UBMA)
BP 12 Sidi Ammar, 23000 Annaba
Tel: +213(38) 87-24-10
Fax: +213(38) 87-24-36
EMail: vr.graduation@univ-annaba.dz
Website: http://www.univ-annaba.org

Recteur: Abdelkrim Kadi
Tel: +213(38) 87-15-19 EMail: abdelkrim.kadi@univ-annaba.org

Secrétaire général: Ahmad Hamdaou
Tel: +213(38) 87-15-19 EMail: sg@univ-annaba.org

International Relations: Hannoune Abdelmadjid
EMail: vr.reccm@univ-annaba.org

Faculty
Arts and Humanities and Social Sciences (Arabic; Arts and Humanities; Modern Languages; Psychology; Sociology; Translation and Interpretation); **Earth Sciences** *(Sidi-Amar)* (Architecture; Earth Sciences; Geology; Mining Engineering; Regional Planning); **Economics and Management** *(Sidi-Achour)* (Communication Studies; Economics; Finance; Management); **Engineering** *(Sidi Amar)* (Civil Engineering; Computer Science; Electronic Engineering; Hydraulic Engineering; Materials Engineering; Mechanical Engineering; Production Engineering); **Law** *(Annaba)* (Law; Political Sciences; Private Law; Public Law); **Medicine** *(Annaba)* (Medicine; Pharmacy; Stomatology); **Science** (Biochemistry; Biology; Chemistry; Marine Science and Oceanography; Mathematics; Physics)

Research Centre
Entrepreneurial Training (Management); **Environment** (Environmental Studies; Sanitary Engineering); **Industrial Health** (Occupational Health); **Materials Science** (Materials Engineering)

History: Founded 1975 as Institute of Mining and Metallurgy, acquired present status 1999.

Academic Year: September to July (September-February; March-July)

Admission Requirements: Secondary school certificate (baccalauréat) or foreign equivalent

Main Language(s) of Instruction: Arabic, French

Accrediting Agency: Ministry of Higher Education and Scientific Research

Degrees and Diplomas: *Licence (LMD); Diplôme d'Etudes supérieures; Diplôme d'Ingénieur; Master; Doctorat*

Student Services: Canteen, Cultural Activities, Facilities for disabled people, Health Services, Sports Facilities

Publications: El-Tawassol; Synthèse

BENYOUCEF BENKHEDDA UNIVERSITY OF ALGIERS

Université d'Alger Benyoucef Benkhedda
2, rue Didouche Mourad, 16000 Alger
Tel: +213(21) 64-69-70
Fax: +213(21) 63-53-03
EMail: Contact@admin.univ-alger.dz
Website: http://www.univ-alger.dz

Faculty
Islamic Studies (Arabic; Islamic Law; Islamic Studies; Law; Middle Eastern Studies; Religious Studies); **Law** (Law; Private Law; Public Law); **Medicine** (Dentistry; Medicine; Pharmacy; Stomatology)

History: Founded 1859 as a School of Medicine and Pharmacy, followed in 1879 by schools of Law, Science, and Letters. Formally established as University 1909. Acquired present status 1984, modified in 2004. Acquired present title 2010.

Academic Year: October to June (October-December; January-April; April-June)

Admission Requirements: Secondary school certificate (baccalauréat) or recognized equivalent or entrance examination

Main Language(s) of Instruction: Arabic, French

Accrediting Agency: Ministry of Higher Education and Scientific Research

Degrees and Diplomas: *Licence (LMD); Diplôme de Docteur.* **Dentistry; Medicine; Pharmacy.** *Master; Doctorat*
Last Updated: 01/06/12

BÉCHAR UNIVERSITY

Université de Béchar
BP 417 Route Kenadsa-Béchar, 08000 Béchar
Tel: +213(7) 81-55-81
Fax: +213(7) 81-52-44
EMail: a.slimani@mesrs.dz
Website: http://www.univ-bechar.dz/

Recteur: Slimani Abd Al-Kader

Faculty
Economics, Management and Commerce (Business and Commerce; Economics; Management); **Law and Political Science** (Administration; Law; Political Sciences); **Letters, Languages, and Human and Social Sciences** (Arabic; Arts and Humanities; English; French; History; Literature; Social Sciences; Translation and Interpretation); **Science and Technology** (Architecture; Biology; Computer Science; Materials Engineering; Technology)

Institute
Electrical Engineering (Electrical Engineering)

History: Founded 1986 as Institut National d'Étude Supérieure. Became Centre Universitaire de Bechar 1992. Acquired present status 2009.

Degrees and Diplomas: *Licence (LMD); Master; Doctorat*
Last Updated: 01/06/12

CONSTANTINE 2 UNIVERSITY

Université Constantine 2
Nouvelle Ville Ali Mendjeli - BP: 67A, Constantine
EMail: rectorat@univ-constantine2.dz
Website: http://www.univ-constantine2.dz

Recteur: Mohamed -El Hadi Latrèche

Faculty
Economics, Commerce and Management (Business and Commerce; Economics; Management); **Humanities and Social Sciences** (Archaeology; History; Philosophy; Psychology); **Information and Communication Technology** (Communication Studies; Information Technology); **Psychology and Educational Sciences** (Clinical Psychology; Educational Sciences; Psychology)

Institute
Library Science (Library Science); **Physical Education and Sports** (Physical Education; Sports)

History: Founded 2011.

Degrees and Diplomas: *Licence; Master; Doctorat*
Last Updated: 09/08/13

DJILLALI LIABES UNIVERSITY OF SIDI BEL ABBÈS

Université Djillali Liabes de Sidi Bel Abbès
BP 89, 22000 Sidi-Bel-Abbès
Tel: +213(48) 54-30-18
Fax: +213(48) 54-11-52
EMail: rectorat@univ-sba.dz
Website: http://www.univ-sba.dz

Recteur: Abdel Nacer Tou

Faculty
Arts and Humanities (Arabic; Arts and Humanities; History; Literature; Modern Languages; Philosophy; Political Sciences; Psychology; Sociology; Translation and Interpretation); **Commerce** (Business and Commerce); **Engineering** (Civil Engineering; Computer Science; Electrical Engineering; Hydraulic Engineering; Mathematics; Mechanical Engineering; Technology; Telecommunications Engineering); **Law**; **Medicine** *(M.S. Taleb)* (Dentistry; Medicine; Pharmacy; Stomatology); **Science** (Biology; Chemistry; Mathematics; Natural Sciences; Physics)

History: Founded 1978. Acquired university status 1989, present status 1995, present title 1996.

Degrees and Diplomas: *Licence (LMD); Diplôme d'Ingénieur; Master; Doctorat*
Last Updated: 01/06/12

DR TAHAR MOULAY UNIVERSITY OF SAÏDA

Université Dr Tahar Moulay de Saïda
BP 138, Cité ENNASR, Saïda
Tel: +213(48) 47-11-24
Fax: +213(48) 47-76-85
EMail: derkaoui@univ-saida.dz
Website: http://www.univ-saida.dz/

Recteur: Berrezoug Belgoumène

Faculty
Economics, Commerce and Management (Business and Commerce; Economics; Management); **Law and Political Science** (Administration; Law; Political Sciences); **Letters, Languages, Humanities and Social Sciences** (Arts and Humanities; Literature; Modern Languages; Social Sciences); **Science and Technology** (Biology; Chemistry; Civil Engineering; Computer Science; Electronic Engineering; Hydraulic Engineering; Mathematics; Natural Sciences; Physics; Technology)

History: Founded 1986. Acquired present title and status 2009.

Degrees and Diplomas: *Licence (LMD)*: **Arabic; Chemistry; Law; Literature; Mathematics; Physics.** *Diplôme d'Etudes supérieures*; *Diplôme d'Ingénieur*: **Electrical Engineering; Electronic Engineering; Hydraulic Engineering.** *Master*, *Doctorat*
Last Updated: 31/05/12

DR YAHIA FARÈS UNIVERSITY OF MEDEA

Université Dr Yahia Farès de Médéa
Quartier Ain D'heb, 26000 Médéa
Tel: +213(25) 58-16-87
Fax: +213(25) 58-28-09
EMail: sg@univ-medea.dz
Website: http://www.univ-medea.dz/fr

Recteur: Ahmed Zaghdar EMail: rectorat@univ-medea.dz

Faculty
Economics, Commerce and Management (Business and Commerce; Economics; Management); **Law** (Law); **Letters, Languages, Social Sciences and Humanities** (Arabic; Communication Studies; Heritage Preservation; Literature; Modern Languages; Psychology; Sociology); **Science and Technology** (Civil Engineering; Computer Engineering; Electrical and Electronic Engineering; Materials Engineering; Mechanical Engineering)

History: Founded 2000. Acquired present status 2004.

Academic Year: September to June (September-December; January-March; April-June)

Admission Requirements: Baccalaureat (A-Level)

Fees: (Algerian Dinars): 200 per annum

Main Language(s) of Instruction: Arabic, French

Accrediting Agency: Ministry of Higher Education and Scientific Research

Degrees and Diplomas: *Diplôme d'Etudes universitaires appliquées*; *Licence (LMD)*: **Arabic; Business and Commerce; Communication Studies; Economics; Finance; French; Law; Literature; Management.** *Diplôme d'Ingénieur*: **Civil Engineering; Electrical and Electronic Engineering; Industrial Chemistry; Mechanical Engineering.** *Master*: **Arabic; Business and Commerce; Civil Engineering; Economics; Electrical and Electronic Engineering; Finance; French; Industrial Chemistry; Literature; Management.** *Doctorat*

Student Services: Canteen, Cultural Activities, Health Services, Nursery Care, Sports Facilities
Last Updated: 01/06/12

EMIR ABDELKADER UNIVERSITY OF ISLAMIC SCIENCES, CONSTANTINE

Université des Sciences Islamiques Emir Abdelkader
BP 137, 25000 Constantine
Tel: +213(31) 93-92-92
Fax: +213(31) 93-80-73
EMail: usieak1@ist.cerist.dz
Website: http://www.univ-emir.dz

Recteur: Abdullah Boukhelkhal

Faculty
Humanities (Administration; Arabic; Arts and Humanities; Economics; Koran; Literature); **Oussoul Eddine, Shariah and Islamic Civilization** (Islamic Law; Islamic Studies; Islamic Theology)

History: Founded 1984. Acquired present status 2004.

Academic Year: September to June (September-February; February-June)

Admission Requirements: Secondary school certificate (baccalauréat)

Fees: None

Main Language(s) of Instruction: Arabic

Degrees and Diplomas: *Licence (LMD)*; *Master*, *Doctorat*

Publications: Revue de l'Université

Publishing House: Emir Abdelkader University Press
Last Updated: 01/06/12

FERHAT ABBAS UNIVERSITY OF SÉTIF 1

Université Ferhat Abbas de Sétif 1
Cité Mabouda, 19000 Sétif
Tel: +213(36) 90-00-80
Fax: +213(36) 90-38-79
EMail: relationexterieure@yahoo.fr
Website: http://www.univ-setif.dz

Recteur: Abdelmadjid Djenane (2014-)
Tel: +213(36) 92-51-20 EMail: recteur_ufas@univ-setif.dz

Faculty
Arts and Languages (Arabic; Arts and Humanities; Modern Languages; Psychology; Social Sciences; Sociology); **Economics, Commerce and Management** (Business and Commerce; Economics; Management); **Humanities and Social Sciences** (Arts and Humanities; Social Sciences); **Law and Political Science** (Law; Political Sciences; Private Law; Public Law); **Medicine** (Medicine; Pharmacy; Stomatology); **Natural and Life Sciences** (Agronomy; Biochemistry; Biology; Ecology; Microbiology; Physiology); **Science** (Chemistry; Computer Science; Mathematics; Physics); **Technology** (Civil Engineering; Computer Science; Electronic Engineering; Engineering; Industrial Chemistry; Measurement and Precision Engineering)

Institute
Architecture and Earth Sciences (Architecture; Earth Sciences); **Optics and Precision Mechanics** (Measurement and Precision Engineering; Optics)

History: Founded 1978 as Centre universitaire, acquired present status and title 1989, modified 2004.

Academic Year: September to June (September-January; March-June)

Admission Requirements: Secondary school certificate (baccalauréat)

Main Language(s) of Instruction: Arabic, French

Accrediting Agency: Ministry of Higher Education and Scientific Research

Degrees and Diplomas: *Licence (LMD)*; *Diplôme d'Ingénieur*, *Master*, *Doctorat*
Last Updated: 27/11/14

HADJ LAKHDAR UNIVERSITY OF BATNA

Université Hadj Lakhdar de Batna
1, avenue Chahid Boukhlouf, 05000 Batna
Tel: +213(33) 86.06.02
EMail: recteur@univ-batna.dz
Website: http://www.univ-batna.dz

Recteur: Tahar Benabid
Tel: +213(33) 81-24-80 EMail: tbenabid06@yahoo.fr

Faculty
Economics and Management (Business and Commerce; Economics; Management); **Humanities, Social Sciences, Islamic Sciences** (Arts and Humanities; Islamic Studies; Sociology); **Law and Political Science** (Law; Political Sciences); **Letters and Languages** (Arabic; Arts and Humanities; English; French); **Medicine** (Health Sciences; Medicine; Pharmacy); **Science** (Agronomy;

Biology; Chemistry; Earth Sciences; Mathematics; Natural Sciences; Physics; Veterinary Science); **Technology** (Electronic Engineering; Engineering; Industrial Engineering; Mechanical Engineering)

Institute

Civil and Hydraulic Engineering and Architecture (Architecture; Civil Engineering; Hydraulic Engineering); **Hygiene and Industrial Security** (Hygiene; Industrial Maintenance); **Veterinary Science and Agronomy** (Agronomy; Food Technology; Veterinary Science)

History: Founded 1977 as Centre universitaire. Acquired present status 2001, modified 2004.

Accrediting Agency: Ministère de l'Enseignement supérieur et de la Recherche scientifique

Degrees and Diplomas: *Licence (LMD)*; *Diplôme d'Ingénieur*; *Diplôme de Docteur*: **Animal Husbandry; Medicine; Veterinary Science.** *Master*

Publishing house: University of Batna Press

Last Updated: 06/12/12

HASSIBA BEN BOUALI UNIVERSITY OF CHLEF

Université Hassiba Ben Bouali de Chlef

Hay Salem, route nationale N° 19, 02000 Chlef

Tel: +213(27) 72-10-67

Fax: +213(27) 72-17-88

EMail: rectorat@univ-chlef.dz

Website: http://www.univ-chlef.dz/

Recteur: Mostefa Bessedik EMail: m.bessedik@univ-chlef.dz

Faculty

Civil Engineering and Architecture (Architecture; Civil Engineering; Hydraulic Engineering); **Economics, Commerce and Management** (Business and Commerce; Economics; Management); **Humanities and Social Sciences** (Arts and Humanities; Social Sciences); **Law and Political Science** (Law; Political Sciences); **Letters and Languages** (Arabic; English; French; Literature); **Science** (Biology; Chemistry; Computer Science; Mathematics; Physics); **Technology** (Electronic Engineering; Mechanical Engineering; Technology)

Institute

Agronomy (Agronomy; Hydraulic Engineering); **Physical Education and Sports** (Physical Education; Sports)

History: Founded 1983. Acquired present status 2001.

Accrediting Agency: Ministère de l'Enseignement supérieur et de la Recherche scientifique

Degrees and Diplomas: *Licence (LMD)*; *Master*, *Doctorat*

Last Updated: 06/12/12

HOUARI BOUMEDIÈNE UNIVERSITY OF SCIENCE AND TECHNOLOGY

Université des Sciences et de la Technologie Houari Boumediène (USTHB)

BP 32, El Alia, Bab-Ezzouar, 16123 Alger

Tel: +213(21) 24-79-50

Fax: +213(21) 24-79-92

EMail: recteur@usthb.dz

Website: http://www.usthb.dz

Recteur: Benali Benzaghou

Faculty

Biological Sciences (Biological and Life Sciences; Cell Biology; Ecology; Molecular Biology; Physiology); **Chemistry** (Applied Chemistry; Chemistry; Organic Chemistry; Physical Chemistry); **Civil Engineering** (Civil Engineering; Hydraulic Engineering; Materials Engineering); **Earth Sciences, Geography and Regional Planning** (Earth Sciences; Geography; Geology; Geophysics; Regional Planning); **Electronic and Computer Science** (Automation and Control Engineering; Computer Science; Electronic Engineering; Telecommunications Engineering); **Mathematics** (Mathematics); **Mechanical and Process Engineering** (Energy Engineering; Mechanical Engineering; Production Engineering; Systems Analysis); **Physics** (Physics)

History: Founded 1974 as Université des Sciences et de la Technologie d'Alger. Became Université des Sciences et de la Technologie Houari Boumediène 1980. Reorganized 2001.

Academic Year: September to June (September-December; January-April; April-June)

Admission Requirements: Secondary school certificate (baccalauréat)

Main Language(s) of Instruction: Arabic, French

Accrediting Agency: Ministry of Higher Education and Scientific Research

Degrees and Diplomas: *Licence (LMD)*; *Diplôme d'Ingénieur*; *Master*, *Doctorat*

Student Services: Academic Counselling, Canteen, Careers Guidance, Cultural Activities, Health Services, Social Counselling, Sports Facilities

Last Updated: 01/06/12

IBN KHALDOUN UNIVERSITY OF TIARET

Université Ibn Khaldoun de Tiaret (UIKT)

BP 78, Zaaroura, 14000 Tiaret

Tel: +213(46) 42-42-13

Fax: +213(46) 42-47-10

EMail: vicerectorat1_uikt@mail.univ-tiaret.dz

Website: http://www.univ-tiaret.dz

Recteur: Mustapha Rahmoun

Tel: +213(46) 45-22-14 EMail: rectorat@mail.univ-tiaret.dz

Faculty

Economics, Commerce and Management (Business and Commerce; Economics; Management); **Humanities and Social Sciences** (Accountancy; Arabic; Business Administration; Business and Commerce; Fiscal Law; French; Law; Literature; Management); **Law and Political Science** (Law; Political Sciences); **Letters and Languages** (Literature; Modern Languages); **Natural and Life Sciences** (Biological and Life Sciences; Natural Sciences); **Technology and Matter Engineering** (Chemistry; Mathematics; Organic Chemistry; Physics)

Institute

Veterinary Science (Veterinary Science)

History: Founded 1980 as Centre Universitaire de Tiaret. Restructured 2010.

Admission Requirements: Baccalauréat

Main Language(s) of Instruction: Arabic, French

Accrediting Agency: Agence nationale du Développement de la Recherche universitaire (ANDRU), Agence nationale du Développement de la Recherche en Santé (ANDRS)

Degrees and Diplomas: *Diplôme d'Etudes universitaires appliquées*: **Accountancy; Biology; Computer Science; Electrical Engineering; Fiscal Law; Hydraulic Engineering; Mechanics; Veterinary Science.** *Licence (LMD)*: **Administrative Law; Arabic; Business and Commerce; Literature; Management.** *Diplôme d'Etudes supérieures*: **Biology; Chemistry; Physics.** *Diplôme d'Ingénieur*: **Agronomy; Electrical Engineering; Mechanics; Nutrition.** *Diplôme de Docteur*: **Animal Husbandry; Veterinary Science.** *Master*: **Arabic; Business and Commerce; Chemistry; Environmental Studies; Literature; Management; Mechanics; Physical Engineering.**

Student Services: Academic Counselling, Canteen, Cultural Activities, Foreign Studies Centre, Health Services, Nursery Care, Social Counselling, Sports Facilities

Publications: Revue d'Ecologie et d'Environnement

Last Updated: 06/12/12

KASDI MERBAH UNIVERSITY OF OUARGLA

Université Kasdi Merbah Ouargla

Route Ghardaia, Ouargla

Tel: +213(29) 71-24-68

Fax: +213(29) 71-51-61

EMail: info@ouargla-univ.dz

Website: http://www.univ-ouargla.dz

Recteur: Ahmed Boutarfaia EMail: aboutarfaia@yahoo.fr

International Relations: Foudil Dahou
EMail: dahoufoudil@gmail.com

Faculty

Economics, Management and Commerce (Business and Commerce; Economics; Management); **Humanities and Social Sciences** (Educational Sciences; Psychology; Sociology; Sports); **Law and Political Science** (Economics; Law; Management; Political Sciences); **Letters and Languages** (Arabic; English; French; Literature; Translation and Interpretation); **Natural and Life Sciences and Earth and Universe Sciences** (Agronomy; Biological and Life Sciences; Earth Sciences; Ecology; Geology; Natural Sciences); **Science and Technology and Science of Matter** (Chemical Engineering; Civil Engineering; Engineering; Hydraulic Engineering; Materials Engineering; Mathematics and Computer Science; Mechanical Engineering; Natural Sciences)

History: Founded 1987 as Ecole Nationale Supérieure. Became University Centre 1997. Acquired present status 2001, modified 2004.

Academic Year: September to June

Admission Requirements: Baccalauréat

Fees: (Algerian Dinars): 200 per annum

Main Language(s) of Instruction: Arabic and French

Degrees and Diplomas: *Licence (LMD)*; *Diplôme d'Ingénieur*, *Master*, *Doctorat*

Student Services: Canteen, Cultural Activities, Health Services, Social Counselling, Sports Facilities

Publications: El-Athar; El-Bahith

LARBI BEN M'HIDI UNIVERSITY OUM-EL BOUAGHI

Université Larbi Ben M'hidi de Oum-El Bouaghi
BP 358, Route de Constantine, 04000 Oum-El Bouaghi
Tel: +213(32) 42-10-36
Fax: +213(32) 42-10-36
EMail: sec-general@univ-oeb.dz
Website: http://www.univ-oeb.dz

Recteur: Ahmed Bouras (2005-)
Tel: +213(32) 42-73-17 EMail: a.bouras@univ-oeb.dz

Secrétaire général: Boudjamaâ Belefreikh

International Relations: Haddoun Abd el Hakim
EMail: a.hadoune@univ-oeb.dz

Faculty

Economics, Commerce and Management (Business and Commerce; Economics; Management); **Law and Political Sciences** (Law; Political Sciences); **Letters and Languages** (Arabic; Arts and Humanities; Communication Studies; English; French; Psychology; Sociology); **Natural Sciences** (Biological and Life Sciences; Materials Engineering; Mathematics and Computer Science; Natural Sciences); **Science and Technology** (Computer Engineering; Electronic Engineering; Hydraulic Engineering; Mechanical Engineering; Technology)

Institute

Urban Technical Management (Urban Studies)

History: Founded 1983. Acquired present status 1997.

Admission Requirements: Baccalaureat

Fees: (Algerian Dinars): 200

Main Language(s) of Instruction: Arabic, French

Degrees and Diplomas: *Licence (LMD)*; *Master*, *Doctorat*

Student Services: Academic Counselling, Canteen, Cultural Activities, Facilities for disabled people, Health Services, Language Laboratory, Nursery Care, Social Counselling, Sports Facilities

LARBI TEBESSI UNIVERSITY OF TEBESSA

Université Larbi Tebessi de Tebessa
Route de Constantine, 12002 Tebessa
Tel: +213(37) 49-02-48
Fax: +231(37) 49-03-02
EMail: sg@univ-tebessa.dz
Website: http://www.univ-tebessa.dz

Recteur: Said Fekra

Faculty

Economics, Commerce and Business Administration (Business Administration; Business and Commerce; Economics; International Business; Management); **Exact Sciences and Natural and Life Sciences** (Biological and Life Sciences; Biology; Chemistry; Earth Sciences; Geography; Geology; Mathematics; Natural Sciences; Physics; Regional Planning); **Law and Political Science** (Law; Political Sciences; Private Law); **Literature, Humanities and Social Sciences** (Anthropology; Arabic; Arts and Humanities; Communication Studies; History; Literature; Modern Languages; Social Sciences; Sociology); **Science and Technology**

History: Founded 1992. Acquired present status 2009.

Academic Year: September to June

Admission Requirements: Baccalauréat

Fees: None

Main Language(s) of Instruction: French and Arabic

Degrees and Diplomas: *Licence (LMD)*; *Diplôme d'Etudes supérieures*; *Diplôme d'Ingénieur*, *Master*, *Doctorat*

Student Services: Academic Counselling, Canteen, Cultural Activities, Facilities for disabled people, Foreign Studies Centre, Health Services, Language Laboratory, Nursery Care, Social Counselling, Sports Facilities

MESSAADIA MOHAMED CHÉRIF UNIVERSITY OF SOUK-AHRAS

Université Messaadia Mohamed Chérif de Souk-Ahras
B.P. 1553, Route de Aannaba, 41000 Souk-Ahras
Tel: +213(37) 75-30-15
Fax: +213(37) 35-12-68
Website: http://www.univ-soukahras.dz/

Recteur: Youcef Berrich

Faculty

Arab Literature and Foreign Languages (Arabic; Arts and Humanities; French; Literature); **Economics, Commerce and Management** (Business and Commerce; Economics; Management); **Law and Administration** (Administration; Law); **Natural and Life Sciences** (Biological and Life Sciences; Natural Sciences; Physical Education; Sports); **Science and Technology** (Civil Engineering; Computer Science; Electrical Engineering; Engineering; Materials Engineering; Mathematics; Mechanical Engineering; Production Engineering)

Institute

Agronomy and Veterinary Science (Agronomy; Veterinary Science); **Physical Education and Sport** (Physical Education; Sports)

History: Founded 2001. Acquired present status and title 2012.

Degrees and Diplomas: *Licence (LMD)*; *Master*

Last Updated: 11/12/12

M'HAMED BOUGARA UNIVERSITY OF BOUMERDÈS

Université M'Hamed Bougara de Boumerdès
Avenue de l'Indépendance, 35000 Boumerdès
Tel: +213(24) 81-64-20
Fax: +213(24) 81-63-73
EMail: rectorat@umbb.dz
Website: http://www.umbb.dz

Recteur: Ouiza Cherifi

Secrétaire général: Ahmed Boufellah
Tel: +213(24) 81-69-29 EMail: secr-gener@umbb.dz

International Relations: Abdelaziz Tairi, Vice-Recteur
Tel: +213(24) 81-99-87 EMail: vrpgr@umbb.dz

Faculty

Economics, Management and Commerce (Business and Commerce; Economics; Management); **Engineering** (Energy Engineering; Engineering; Environmental Engineering; Industrial Engineering; Materials Engineering; Mechanical Engineering); **Hydrocarburates and Chemistry** (Automation and Control Engineering; Chemical Engineering; Engineering Management; Industrial Management; Marketing; Mining Engineering; Petroleum and Gas Engineering); **Law** (Law; Private Law; Public Law); **Science**

Institute

Electrical and Electronic Engineering (Electrical and Electronic Engineering)

History: Founded 1998 following merger of six former national institutes, modified 2004.

Admission Requirements: Baccalauréat

Fees: (Algerian Dinars): 200

Main Language(s) of Instruction: Arabic, French, English

Accrediting Agency: Ministry of Higher Education and Scientific Research

Degrees and Diplomas: *Diplôme d'Etudes universitaires appliquées*: **Biology; Business Computing; Chemistry; Civil Engineering; Computer Science; Electrical Engineering; Food Technology; Industrial Engineering; International Business; Materials Engineering; Mechanical Engineering.** *Licence (LMD)*: **Administration; Business and Commerce; Law; Management; Social Sciences.** *Diplôme d'Ingénieur*: **Biology; Chemistry; Civil Engineering; Computer Science; Electrical Engineering; Food Technology; Industrial Engineering; Materials Engineering; Mechanical Engineering; Statistics; Water Science.** *Master*: **Computer Science; Electrical Engineering.** *Doctorat*

Student Services: Canteen, Cultural Activities, Health Services, Language Laboratory, Nursery Care, Social Counselling, Sports Facilities

Publications: Lettre de la Faculté des Sciences

Last Updated: 06/12/12

MOHAMED BOUDIAF UNIVERSITY OF SCIENCE AND TECHNOLOGY OF ORAN

Université des Sciences et de la Technologie d'Oran Mohamed Boudiaf (USTOMB)

BP 1505, M'Naouer, 31000 Oran
Tel: +213(41) 56-03-33
Fax: +213(41) 56-03-22
EMail: mekdam@univ-usto.dz
Website: http://www.univ-usto.dz

Recteur: A. Derdour

Faculty

Architecture and Civil Engineering (Architecture; Civil Engineering; Hydraulic Engineering); **Electrical Engineering** (Automation and Control Engineering; Electrical Engineering; Electronic Engineering); **Mechanical Engineering** (Marine Engineering; Mechanical Engineering; Metallurgical Engineering; Mining Engineering); **Science** (Biotechnology; Chemistry; Computer Science; Mathematics; Natural Sciences; Physics)

Institute

Physical Education (Physical Education)

History: Founded 1975. Acquired present status 1984, modified 2004.

Academic Year: September to June

Admission Requirements: Secondary school certificate (baccalauréat) or equivalent

Main Language(s) of Instruction: French

Accrediting Agency: Ministry of Higher Education and Scientific Research

Degrees and Diplomas: *Licence (LMD)*; *Diplôme d'Ingénieur*; *Master*; *Doctorat*

Last Updated: 01/06/12

MOHAMED EL BACHIR EL IBRAHIMI UNIVERSITY OF BORDJ BOU ARRERIDJ

Université Mohamed El Bachir El Ibrahimi de Bordj Bou Arréridj

Bordj Bou Arreridj
Tel: +213(35) 66-63-01
EMail: direction@univ-bba.dz
Website: http://www.univ-bba.dz

Faculty

Economics, Commerce and Management (Business and Commerce; Economics; Management); **Law and Political Science** (Law; Political Sciences); **Letters and Languages** (Arabic; Arts and Humanities; Literature; Modern Languages); **Mathematics and Computer Science** (Computer Science; Mathematics); **Natural, Life, Earth and Universe Sciences** (Astronomy and Space Science; Biological and Life Sciences; Earth Sciences; Natural Sciences); **Science and Technology** (Biological and Life Sciences; Civil Engineering; Electronic Engineering; Environmental Engineering; Mechanical Engineering; Natural Sciences; Technology); **Social Sciences and Humanities** (Arts and Humanities; Social Sciences)

History: Founded 2001. Acquired present status and title 2012.

Accrediting Agency: Ministère de l'Enseignement supérieur et de la Recherche scientifique

Degrees and Diplomas: *Licence (LMD)*; *Diplôme d'Ingénieur*; *Master*; *Doctorat*

Last Updated: 11/12/12

MOHAMED KHIDER UNIVERSITY OF BISKRA

Université Mohamed Khider de Biskra

BP 145, 07000 Biskra
Tel: +213(33) 73-32-06
Fax: +213(33) 73-32-07
EMail: info@umkbiskra.net
Website: http://www.umkbiskra.net

Recteur: Belkacem Selatnia EMail: recteur@univ-biskra.dz

Secrétaire général: Nacer Ghamri
Tel: +213(33) 74-61-63 EMail: sg@univ-biskra.dz

Faculty

Economics, Commerce and Management (Business and Commerce; Economics; Management); **Exact, Natural and Life Sciences** (Agronomy; Biological and Life Sciences; Chemistry; Computer Science; Mathematics; Physics); **Humanities and Sociology** (Arabic; Arts and Humanities; Demography and Population; English; Literature; Social Sciences; Sociology); **Law and Political Science** (Law; Political Sciences); **Literature and Languages** (Literature; Modern Languages); **Science and Technology** (Architecture; Automation and Control Engineering; Civil Engineering; Electronic Engineering; Hydraulic Engineering; Industrial Chemistry; Mechanical Engineering; Metallurgical Engineering)

History: Founded 1998, acquired present status 2004.

Degrees and Diplomas: *Licence (LMD)*; *Master*

MOHAMED SEDDIK BEN YAHIA UNIVERSITY OF JIJEL

Université Mohamed Seddik Ben Yahia de Jijel

BP 98, Ouled Aissa, 18000 Jijel
Tel: +213(34) 49-80-16
Fax: +213(34) 49-55-78
EMail: rectorat@univ-jijel.dz
Website: http://www.univ-jijel.dz

Recteur: Kaddour Lamara

Faculty

Economics, Commerce and Management (Business and Commerce; Economics; Management); **Exact, Natural and Life Sciences** (Biological and Life Sciences; Cell Biology; Chemistry; Earth Sciences; Geology; Mathematics; Molecular Biology; Physics); **Law and Political Sciences** (Law; Political Sciences); **Letters, Languages and Social Sciences** (Arabic; English; French; Sociology); **Science and Technology** (Architecture; Automation and Control Engineering; Civil Engineering; Computer Science; Ecology; Electronic Engineering; Mechanical Engineering)

History: Founded 2003.

Accrediting Agency: Ministère de l'Enseignement supérieur et de la Recherche scientifique

Degrees and Diplomas: *Licence (LMD)*: **Chemistry; Law; Management; Mathematics; Physics.** *Diplôme d'Ingénieur*: **Agronomy; Automation and Control Engineering; Biology; Chemical Engineering; Civil Engineering; Computer Science; Electrical and Electronic Engineering; Geology; Regional Planning.** *Master*; *Doctorat*

MOULOUD MAMMERI UNIVERSITY OF TIZI-OUZOU

Université Mouloud Mammeri de Tizi-Ouzou (UMMTO)

BP 17, 15000 Tizi-Ouzou
Tel: +213(26) 21-53-14
Fax: +213(26) 21-29-68
EMail: univ_tizi@mail.ummto.dz
Website: http://www.ummto.dz/

Recteur: Naceur Eddine Hannachi
Tel: +213(26) 21-89-95 EMail: univ_tizi@mail.ummto.dz

Faculty
Biology and Agronomy (Agronomy; Biology); **Construction Engineering** (Construction Engineering; Engineering); **Economics, Commerce and Management** (Business and Commerce; Economics; Management); **Electrical and Computer Engineering** (Computer Engineering; Electrical Engineering); **Humanities and Social Sciences** (Arts and Humanities; Psychology; Social Sciences); **Law and Political Science** (Law; Political Sciences); **Letters and Languages** (Arabic; Educational Sciences; English; French; Psychology; Social Sciences; Translation and Interpretation); **Medicine** (Medicine); **Science** (Mathematics; Natural Sciences)

History: Founded 1977 as University Centre of Tizi-Ouzou. Became university 1989, modified 2004.

Academic Year: September to June (September-January; February-June)

Admission Requirements: Secondary school certificate (baccalauréat) and entrance examination

Main Language(s) of Instruction: Arabic, French

Accrediting Agency: Ministry of Higher Education and Scientific Research

Degrees and Diplomas: *Licence (LMD)*; *Diplôme d'Etudes supérieures*; *Diplôme d'Ingénieur*; *Doctorat*: **Medicine.**

NATIONAL GRADUATE SCHOOL OF POLITICAL SCIENCE

Ecole nationale supérieure de Sciences politiques

Chemin Doudou Mokhtar, n° 64, Ben Aknoun, Alger
Website: http://www.enssp.net

Directeur: Med Bouacha

Department
Military and Strategic Studies (Military Science); **Political Sociology and International Relations** (International Relations; Sociology); **Public Policy** (Political Sciences)

History: Founded 2009.

Degrees and Diplomas: *Master*

Last Updated: 13/12/12

NATIONAL INSTITUTE OF PLANNING AND STATISTICS

Institut national de la Planification et de la Statistique (INPS)

11 chemin Doudou Mokhtar, Ben Aknoun, Alger
Tel: +213(21) 91-21-33
Fax: +213(21) 91-21-39
EMail: inps-dz@wissal.dz
Website: http://www.inps-alger.dz/

Directeur général: Ahmed Zakane
Tel: +213(21) 91-21-33 EMail: zakane-dg@inps-alger.dz

Department
Planning and Statistics (Statistics)

History: Founded 1970 as institut des techniques de planification. Acquired present title 1983.

Degrees and Diplomas: *Diplôme d'Ingénieur*, *Doctorat*

NATIONAL INSTITUTE OF POST, INFORMATION AND COMMUNICATION TECHNOLOGIES

Institut national de la Poste et des Technologies de l'Information et de la Communication

BP 156 Route de l'arbaa, Eucalyptus, 16220 Alger
Tel: + 213(21) 50- 01-51
Fax: + 213(21) 50-00-98
EMail: inptic@inptic.edu.dz
Website: http://www.inptic.edu.dz

Directeur: Rachid Outemzabet

Programme
Communication (Information Technology); **Telecommunications and Computer Networks** (Computer Networks; Telecommunications Engineering)

Accrediting Agency: Ministère de la Poste et des Technologies de l'Information et de la Communication (MPTIC) et du Ministère de l'Enseignement Supérieur et de la Recherche Scientifique (MESRS)

Degrees and Diplomas: *Licence (LMD)*; *Master*

NATIONAL INSTITUTE OF TELECOMMUNICATIONS AND INFORMATION AND COMMUNICATION TECHNOLOGIES

Institut National des Télécommunications et des Technologies de l'Information et de la Communication

BP 1518, Route de Senia, 31000 Oran
Tel: +213(41) 29-93-21
Fax: +213(41) 29-93-08
Website: http://www.ito.dz

Directeur: Abdelmajid Boutaleb

Programme
Information and Communications Technology (Information Technology); **Telecommunications Engineering** (Telecommunications Engineering)

History: Founded 1964 as École Nationale des Télécommunications in Algiers. Became Institut des Télécommunications à Oran 1971. Acquired present title 2008.

Accrediting Agency: Ministère de la Poste et des Technologies de l'Information et de la Communication (MPTIC) et du Ministère de l'Enseignement Supérieur et de la Recherche Scientifique (MESRS)

Degrees and Diplomas: *Diplôme d'Etudes universitaires appliquées*; *Diplôme d'Ingénieur*, *Master*, *Doctorat*

Last Updated: 06/12/12

NATIONAL MARINE SCIENCE AND COASTAL MANAGEMENT SCHOOL

Ecole nationale supérieure des Sciences de la Mer et de l'Aménagement du Littoral (ISMAL)

BP 19, Campus universitaire de Delly Brahim, Alger
Tel: +213(21) 91-77-87
Fax: +213(21) 91-77-87
EMail: dg_enssmal@enssmal.dz
Website: http://www.enssmal.dz

Directeur: Djamel-Eddine Zouakh Tel: +213(21) 91-77-91

Programme
Aquaculture (Aquaculture); **Coast Planning** (Coastal Studies); **Fishery** (Aquaculture; Fishery); **Marine Environment** (Biochemistry; Ecology; Environmental Studies; Marine Biology)

History: Founded 1964 as Institut d'Océanographie d'Alger. Became Institut national des Sciences de la Mer et de l'Aménagement du Littoral 1983. Acquired present title 2008.

Admission Requirements: Baccalauréat

Accrediting Agency: Ministère de l'Enseignement supérieur et de la Recherche scientifique

Degrees and Diplomas: *Diplôme d'Ingénieur*, *Master*

Last Updated: 31/05/12

NATIONAL POLYTECHNIC OF ORAN

Ecole nationale polytechnique d'Oran
BP 1523, El-M'naouer, 31000 Oran
Tel: +213(41) 41-98-05
Fax: +213(41) 41-98-06
Website: http://www.enset-oran.dz

Directeur: Abdelbaki Benziane EMail: benziane_baki@yahoo.fr

Department

Civil Engineering (Civil Engineering); **Electrical Engineering** (Electrical Engineering); **Languages** (Arabic; French); **Management** (Industrial Management; Management; Transport Management); **Mathematics and Computer Science** (Computer Science; Mathematics); **Mechanical Engineering** (Mechanical Engineering); **Physics and Chemistry** (Chemistry; Physics)

History: Founded 1970 as Ecole Normale Supérieure d'Enseignement polytechnique, became Ecole normale supérieure d'Enseignement technique 1984. Acquired present status and title 2012.

Degrees and Diplomas: *Master*. Diplôme de Professeur de l'Enseignement Secondaire Technique; Postgraduation

NATIONAL SCHOOL OF ADMINISTRATION

Ecole nationale d'Administration (ENA)
13 Chemin Abdelkader Gadouche, Hydra, Alger
Tel: +213(21) 60-13-50
Fax: +213(21) 60-49-41
EMail: ena@wissal.dz
Website: http://www.ena.dz/

Directeur: Hocine Cherhabil

Programme

Economics and Finance (Economics; Finance); **International Institutions** (International Relations); **Law** (Private Law; Public Law); **Public Administration** (Public Administration)

History: Founded 1964. Acquired present status 2006.

Admission Requirements: Licence de l'enseignement supérieur, diplôme d'ingénieur d'État or equivalent and competitive examination

Publications: IDARA

NATIONAL SCHOOL OF AGRONOMY

Ecole nationale supérieure Agronomique (ENSA)
10, avenue Hassen Badi, El-Harrach, Alger
Tel: +213(21) 52-50-84
Fax: +213(21) 82-27-29
EMail: ina@ina.dz
Website: http://www.ina.dz

Directrice: Rosa Issolah

Department

Agricultural Engineering (Agricultural Engineering; Agricultural Equipment); **Animal Production** (Animal Husbandry; Cattle Breeding; Zoology); **Botany** (Botany; Plant Pathology); **Food Technology** (Food Technology); **Forestry** (Forestry); **Plant Production** (Plant and Crop Protection); **Rural Economics** (Agricultural Economics; Management); **Soil Science** (Soil Science); **Zoology**

History: Founded 1905 as Ecole d'Agriculture d'Alger. Acquired present title 2009.

Accrediting Agency: Ministère de l'Enseignement supérieur et de la Recherche

Degrees and Diplomas: *Diplôme d'Ingénieur*; *Master*; *Doctorat*
Last Updated: 06/06/12

NATIONAL SCHOOL OF CIVIL ENGINEERING

Ecole nationale supérieure des Travaux publics (ENSTP)
BP 32, Rue Sidi Garidi, 16051 Alger
Tel: +213(21) 28-68-38
Fax: +213(21) 28-87-61
EMail: entp@entp.edu.dz
Website: http://www.entp.edu.dz

Programme

Civil Engineering (Civil Engineering); **Computer Science** (Computer Science); **Hydraulics** (Hydraulic Engineering); **Transport** (Transport and Communications)

History: Founded 1966. Acquired present status 1998.

Accrediting Agency: Ministère de l'Enseignement supérieur et de la Recherche scientifique; Ministère des Travaux publics

Degrees and Diplomas: *Diplôme d'Ingénieur*, *Master*, *Doctorat*. Post-graduation Spécialisée

Publications: Algérie Équipement
Last Updated: 31/05/12

NATIONAL SCHOOL OF COMPUTER SCIENCE

Ecole nationale supérieure d'Informatique (ESI)
BP 68 M Oued Smar, El Harrach, 16270 Alger
Tel: +213(21) 51-60-77
Fax: +213(21) 51-61-56
EMail: de@esi.dz
Website: http://www.esi.dz/

Directeur général: Mouloud Koudil EMail: m_koudil@esi.dz

Programme

Computer Science (Computer Science)

History: Founded 1969 as Institut national de Formation en Informatique.

Degrees and Diplomas: *Diplôme d'Ingénieur*, *Master*, *Doctorat*

NATIONAL SCHOOL OF SPORTS SCIENCE

Ecole nationale supérieure en Sciences et Technologie du Sport de Dely Ibrahim
BP 71, El Biar, Alger
Tel: +213(21) 92-23-44
Website: http://www.ists.dz

Programme

Sports (Physical Education; Sports; Sports Management)

History: Created 1975 as Institut National de Formation Supérieure en Sciences et Technologie du Sport. Acquired status 2011.

Admission Requirements: Baccalauréat général or Licence (which determines the length of the course).

Accrediting Agency: Ministère de la Jeunesse et des Sports; Ministère de l'Enseignement supérieur et de la Recherche scientifique.

Degrees and Diplomas: *Diplôme d'Etudes supérieures*; *Master*
Last Updated: 07/09/12

NATIONAL SCHOOL OF TECHNOLOGY

Ecole nationale supérieure de Technologie
Alger
EMail: enst@wissal.dz
Website: http://www.enst.dz

Directeur: Mohamed Tellache

Department

Electrical Engineering and Industrial Computing (Computer Science; Electrical Engineering; Industrial Engineering; Telecommunications Engineering); **Industrial Engineering and Maintenance** (Industrial Engineering; Industrial Maintenance); **Mechanical and Production Engineering** (Mechanical Engineering; Production Engineering)

History: Founded 2009.

Accrediting Agency: Ministère de l'Enseignement supérieur et de la Recherche scientifique

Degrees and Diplomas: *Licence*; *Master*, *Doctorat*
Last Updated: 06/12/12

NATIONAL SCHOOL OF VETERINARY SCIENCE

Ecole nationale supérieure vétérinaire d'Alger (ENSV)
10 Avenue Hassen Badi, El Harrach, 16000 Alger
Tel: +213(21) 52-51-32
Fax: +213(21) 82-44-81
EMail: de@env.dz
Website: http://www.ensv.dz

Directeur: Youcef Hamdi-Pacha

Programme

Veterinary Science (Health Sciences; Veterinary Science)

History: Founded 1970.

Academic Year: September to December (September-December; January-March; April-June)

Admission Requirements: Baccalaureate in Mathematics, Experimental Science, Natural and Life Sciences, Exact Sciences

Main Language(s) of Instruction: French

Accrediting Agency: Ministère de l'Enseignement supérieur et de la Recherche scientifique

Degrees and Diplomas: *Diplôme de Docteur*: **Veterinary Science.** *Master*; *Doctorat*: **Veterinary Science.** Also Postgraduation spécialisée (PGS) 1 yr

Student Services: Academic Counselling, Health Services, Language Laboratory

Publications: Revue des Sciences Vétérinaires

Last Updated: 06/06/12

SAAD DAHLAB UNIVERSITY OF BLIDA

Université Saad Dahlab de Blida (USDB)

BP 270, Route de Soumma, 09000 Blida
Tel: +213(25) 43-36-25
Fax: +213(25) 43-38-64
EMail: contact@univ-blida.dz
Website: http://www.univ-blida.dz

Recteur: Abdellatif Baba Ahmed
Tel: +213(25) 43-81-38 EMail: rectorat@mail.univ-blida.dz

Secrétaire Générale: Rafika Soussi

International Relations: Oukid-Khouas Saliha, Vice-Rector
Tel: +213(25) 43-04-66 EMail: osalyha@yahoo.com

Faculty

Agro-Veterinary and Biological Science (Agronomy; Biology; Biotechnology; Cell Biology; Embryology and Reproduction Biology; Genetics; Molecular Biology; Nutrition; Parasitology; Pharmacology; Veterinary Science); **Arts and Social Sciences** (Arabic; Demography and Population; Italian; Modern Languages; Psychology; Social Sciences; Sociology; Special Education; Speech Therapy and Audiology); **Economics and Management** (Accountancy; Banking; Economics; Finance; Management; Marketing); **Engineering** (Aeronautical and Aerospace Engineering; Architecture; Civil Engineering; Electronic Engineering; Engineering; Industrial Chemistry; Mechanical Engineering); **Law** (Criminology; International Law; Law); **Medicine** (Dentistry; Medicine; Pharmacy); **Science** (Chemistry; Computer Science; Mathematics; Physics)

History: Founded 1981. Acquired present status 1989, modified 2004.

Academic Year: (Algerian Dinars): 200 per annum

Admission Requirements: Baccalaureat

Main Language(s) of Instruction: Arabic, French

Accrediting Agency: Ministry of Higher Education and Scientific Research

Degrees and Diplomas: ; *Licence (LMD)*: **Arts and Humanities; Biological and Life Sciences; Economics; Law; Management; Modern Languages; Natural Sciences.** *Diplôme d'Etudes supérieures; Diplôme d'Ingénieur*: **Agronomy; Biology.** *Master*: **Biological and Life Sciences; Natural Sciences.** *Doctorat*: **Dentistry; Medicine; Pharmacy; Veterinary Science.**

Student Services: Canteen, Health Services, Nursery Care, Sports Facilities

Last Updated: 05/06/12

SCHOOL OF ARCHITECTURE AND TOWN PLANNING

Ecole polytechnique d'Architecture et d'Urbanisme (EPAU)

BP 177, route de beaulieu, El Harrache, 16200 Alger
Tel: +213(21) 52-47-26/27
Fax: +213(21) 82-17-57
EMail: zerouala54@yahoo.com
Website: http://www.epau-alger.edu.dz

Directeur: Mohamed Salah Zerouala

Programme

Architecture and Town Planning (Architecture; Town Planning)

History: Founded 1970.

Degrees and Diplomas: *Diplôme d'Ingénieur*: **Architecture.** *Master*; *Doctorat*

Last Updated: 31/05/12

SCHOOL OF BANKING

Ecole supérieure de Banque (ESB)

BP 156, Route de Baïnem Bouzaréah, 16340 Alger
Tel: +213(21) 90-29-29
Fax: +213(21) 90-43-16
Website: http://www.esb.edu.dz

Directeur général: Mahmoud Hemidet Tel: +213(21) 90-38-15

Programme

Banking I (Accountancy; Banking; Economics; Finance; Law); **Banking II** *(Formation qualifiante)* (Accountancy; Banking; Economics; Finance; Law); **Computer Science and Audiovisual Studies** (Cinema and Television; Computer Science)

History: Founded 1995.

Admission Requirements: Secondary School certificate (baccalauréat), Licence

Fees: (Algerian Dinars): 300 per annum (including accommodation)

Main Language(s) of Instruction: French

Degrees and Diplomas: *Master*. Brevet Supérieur de la Banque (BSB, 30 months), Diplôme Supérieur des Études Bancaires; Postgraduate diplomas (Master in collaboration with the Ecole supérieure de Commerce d'Amiens, France)

Student Services: Canteen, Careers Guidance, Cultural Activities, Health Services, Nursery Care, Social Counselling, Sports Facilities

Last Updated: 31/05/12

SCHOOL OF COMMERCE

Ecole des Hautes Etudes Commerciales (EHEC ALGER)

11, Chemin Doudou Mokhtar, Ben Aknoun, Alger
Tel: +213(21) 91-11-76
Fax: +213(21) 91-54-51
EMail: contact@hec.dz
Website: http://www.hec.dz

Directeur: Abdesselam Saadi EMail: directeur@hec.dz

Programme

Accounting and Audit (Accountancy); **Business Management** (Business Administration; Management); **Enterprise Management** (Management); **Human Resources and Communication** (Communication Studies; Human Resources); **International Business** (International Business); **Management** (Management); **Marketing** (Marketing)

History: Founded in 1970 as Institut de Technologie du Commerce. Became Institut National de Commerce in 1983. Acquired present status and title 2009.

Admission Requirements: Baccalauréat; Preparatory school

Main Language(s) of Instruction: French

Degrees and Diplomas: *Licence (LMD)*; *Master*, *Doctorat*

Last Updated: 01/06/12

SCHOOL OF ENGINEERING OF ALGIERS

Ecole nationale polytechnique d'Alger (ENP)

BP 162, 10, Avenue Hassen Badi, El Harrach, 16200 Alger
Tel: +213(21) 52-10-27
EMail: enp@enp.edu.dz
Website: http://www.enp.edu.dz

Directrice: Ghania Nezzal

Department

Automation (Automation and Control Engineering); **Chemical Engineering** (Chemical Engineering); **Civil Engineering** (Civil Engineering); **Electrical Engineering** (Electrical Engineering); **Electronics** (Electronic Engineering; Information Management; Microwaves; Telecommunications Engineering); **Environmental Engineering** (Environmental Engineering); **Industrial Engineering** (Industrial Engineering); **Languages** (English; Modern Languages);

Mechanical Engineering (Mechanical Engineering); **Metallurgical Engineering** (Metallurgical Engineering); **Mining Engineering** (Mining Engineering)

History: Founded 1925 as Institut Industriel d'Algérie. Acquired present status 1966.

Degrees and Diplomas: *Diplôme d'Ingénieur, Master, Doctorat*

SCHOOL OF HEALTH MANAGEMENT AND ADMINISTRATION

Ecole nationale de Management et de l'Administration de la Santé

Alger

Tel: +213(21) 86-10-75

EMail: enmas@sante.dz

Website: http://www.sante.dz/ensp/lasante.htm

Programme

Health Administration (Health Administration)

History: Founded 1989. Acquired present title and status 2009.

SCHOOL OF MAGISTRACY

Ecole supérieure de la Magistrature (ESM)

Boulevard du 11 décembre 1960, El Biar, Alger

Tel: +213(21) 91-51-92

Fax: +213(21) 91-52-01

EMail: webmaster@esm.dz

Website: http://www.esm.dz

Directeur: Hocine Cherhabil Tel: +213(21) 91-51-99

Programme

Law (Administrative Law; Commercial Law; Criminal Law; Law; Maritime Law)

History: Founded 1964.

Admission Requirements: Licence en droit (eight semesters) or equivalent and competitive entrance examination

Last Updated: 07/12/12

TEACHER TRAINING SCHOOL OF CONSTANTINE

Ecole normale supérieure de Constantine (ENSC)

Plateau du Mansourah, Constantine

Tel: +213(31) 61-21-53

Fax: +213(31) 63-00-75

EMail: directeur@ens-constantine.dz

Website: http://www.ens-constantine.dz/

Directeur: Mohamed Reghioua

Secrétaire général: Cherif Touami

International Relations: Azzouz Dilmi Tel: +213(31) 62-48-60

Department

Arabic Language and Literature (Arabic; Literature); **English** (English); **French** (French); **Mathematics and Computer Science** (Computer Science; Mathematics); **Philosophy, History and Geography** (Geography; History; Philosophy)

History: Founded 1984. Acquired present status 2008.

Fees: None

Main Language(s) of Instruction: Arabic, French, English

Accrediting Agency: Ministère de l'Enseignement supérieur et de la Recherche scientifique

Degrees and Diplomas: *Licence; Master, Doctorat*

Student Services: Academic Counselling

Publications: Forum de l'Enseignement

Last Updated: 31/05/12

TEACHER TRAINING SCHOOL OF KOUBA

Ecole normale supérieure de Kouba (ENS-KOUBA)

BP 92, 16050 Kouba, Alger

Tel: +213(21) 29-75-11

Fax: +213(21) 28-20-67

EMail: info@ens-kouba.dz

Website: http://www.ens-kouba.dz

Directeur: Abdelhamid Meraghni (2000-)
EMail: meraghni@ens-kouba.dz

Sous-Directeur: Omar Guenane

International Relations: Abdelmalek Bouzari, Chef de Service des Relations extérieures
EMail: malek_bouzari@yahoo.fr; bouzari@ens-kouba.dz

Department

Chemistry (Chemistry); **Computer Science** (Computer Science); **Distance Education** (Distance Education); **Educational Sciences** (Educational Sciences); **Mathematics** (Mathematics); **Music** (Music); **Natural Sciences** (Natural Sciences); **Physics** (Physics); **Postgraduate Studies and Scientific Research**

History: Founded 1964.

Academic Year: September to June

Admission Requirements: Baccalaureat; Licence for Post Graduate Studies

Main Language(s) of Instruction: Arabic, French, English

Degrees and Diplomas: *Licence (LMD); Master, Doctorat*

Student Services: Cultural Activities, Health Services, Language Laboratory, Nursery Care, Social Counselling, Sports Facilities

Publications: Cahier d'Ibn al-Haytham; Revue Maghrébine de Mathématiques

Last Updated: 31/05/12

UNIVERSITY CENTRE OF AIN TÉMOUCHENT

Centre Universitaire d'Ain Témouchent

Route de Sidi Bellabes - BP 284, 46000 Aïn Témouchent

Tel: +213(43) 60 34 31

EMail: cuaintemouchent@yahoo.fr

Website: http://www.cuniv-aintemouchent.dz/planification.html

Directeur: Abdelmalek Bekkouche

Institute

Economics, Commerce and Management (Business and Commerce; Economics; Management); **Literature and Languages** (Literature; Modern Languages); **Science and Technology** (Natural Sciences; Technology)

History: Founded 2005.

Main Language(s) of Instruction: Arabic

Degrees and Diplomas: *Licence*

Last Updated: 07/12/12

UNIVERSITY CENTRE OF MILA

Centre Universitaire de Mila

Mila

EMail: directeur@centre-univ-mila.dz

Website: http://www.centre-univ-mila.dz/

Directeur: Ali Boukaroura

Institute

Economics, Commerce and Management (Business and Commerce; Economics; Management); **Literature and Languages** (Literature; Modern Languages); **Science and Technology** (Natural Sciences; Technology)

History: Founded 2008.

Main Language(s) of Instruction: Arabic

Degrees and Diplomas: *Licence*

UNIVERSITY CENTRE OF RÉLIZANE

Centre Universitaire de Rélizane

BP:48000, Bormadia

EMail: cur48@cu-relizane.dz

Website: http://www.cu-relizane.dz

Directeur: Benaissa Bekouche

Institute

Economics, Commerce and Management (Business and Commerce; Economics; Management); **Law and Administration** (Administration; Commercial Law; Law; Public Administration); **Literature and Languages** (Arabic; French; Literature); **Science and Technology** (Biological and Life Sciences; Computer Science;

Mathematics; Natural Sciences; Technology); **Social Sciences** (Arts and Humanities; Social Sciences)

History: Founded 2008.

Main Language(s) of Instruction: Arabic

Degrees and Diplomas: *Licence*

UNIVERSITY CENTRE OF TISSEMSILT

Centre Universitaire de Tissemsilt
Tissemsilt
Tel: +213(46) 47-94-36
EMail: cutissemsilt@yahoo.fr

Directeur: Bendjemaa Tayeb

Institute
Economics, Commerce and Management (Business and Commerce; Economics; Management); **Law and Administration** (Administration; Law); **Literature and Languages** (Literature; Modern Languages); **Science and Technology** (Technology)

History: Founded 2005.

Degrees and Diplomas: *Licence*

UNIVERSITY CONSTANTINE 1

Université Constantine 1
BP 325, Route de Aïn-El-Bey, 25017 Constantine
Tel: +213(31) 61-43-48
Fax: +213(31) 61-43-49
EMail: Universite-mentouri@umc.edu.dz
Website: http://www.umc.edu.dz

Recteur: Abdelhamid Djekoun
Tel: +231(31) 81-88-92 EMail: rectorat@umc.edu.dz

Secrétaire général: Foudil Belaouira
Tel: +213(31) 92-57-79 EMail: secretariat-g@umc.edu.dz

International Relations: Farida Hobar, Vice-Recteur des Relations extérieures
Tel: +213(31) 81-86-83 EMail: vicerect-relex@umc.edu.dz

Faculty
Earth Sciences, Geography and Regional Planning (Architecture; Earth Sciences; Regional Planning; Town Planning); **Economics and Management** (Economics; Management); **Engineering** (Civil Engineering; Computer Engineering; Electronic Engineering; Industrial Chemistry; Mechanical Engineering; Meteorology); **Exact Sciences** (Chemistry; Mathematics; Physics); **Humanities and Social Sciences** (Arts and Humanities; History; Library Science; Philosophy; Psychology; Social Sciences; Sociology); **Languages and Literature** (Arabic; French; Literature; Modern Languages; Translation and Interpretation); **Law** (Law; Political Sciences; Private Law; Public Law); **Medicine** (Medicine; Pharmacy; Stomatology); **Natural and Life Sciences** (Biochemistry; Biological and Life Sciences; Biology; Ecology; Microbiology; Veterinary Science)

Institute
Nutrition and Food Technology (Food Technology; Nutrition)

Further Information: Also Audiovisual Centre

History: Founded 1969 as University Centre, acquired present status 1984, modified 2006.

Academic Year: September to June (September-January; February-June)

Admission Requirements: Secondary school certificate (baccalauréat)

Main Language(s) of Instruction: Arabic, French, English

Accrediting Agency: Ministry of Higher Education and Scientific Research

Degrees and Diplomas: *Diplôme d'Etudes universitaires appliquées*; *Licence (LMD)*; *Diplôme d'Etudes supérieures*; *Diplôme d'Ingénieur*. **Architecture.** *Diplôme de Docteur*. **Animal Husbandry; Veterinary Science.** *Master*, *Doctorat*

UNIVERSITY SETIF 2

Université Sétif 2
Pôle d'El Hidhaba, Sétif
Website: http://www.univ-setif2.dz/

Recteur: Khier Guechi (2012-)
Tel: +212 36-66-11-25 EMail: rectorat@univ-setif2.dz

Faculty
Humanities and Social Sciences (Archaeology; Arts and Humanities; Educational Sciences; History; Information Sciences; Philosophy; Social Sciences; Sociology; Speech Therapy and Audiology); **Law and Political Science** (Law; Political Sciences); **Letters and Languages** (Arabic; French; Literature; Modern Languages; Translation and Interpretation)

History: Founded 2011.

Degrees and Diplomas: *Licence*; *Master*. **Arabic; Arts and Humanities; Law; Literature; Social Sciences.** *Doctorat*: **Arabic; Literature.**

Last Updated: 05/06/12

UNIVERSITY OF ALGIERS 2

Université d'Alger 2
Boulevard Djamel Eddine, El Afghani Bouzareah, Alger
Tel: +213(21) 90-95-78
Fax: +213(21) 90-89-92
EMail: contact@univ-alger2.dz
Website: http://www.univ-alger2.dz

Recteur: Abdelkader Henni

Faculty
Human and Social Sciences (History; Library Science; Philosophy; Psychology; Sociology); **Letters and Languages** (Arabic; English; French; Literature)

Institute
Archaeology (Archaeology)

History: Founded 1984 as Ecole normale supérieure des Lettres et Sciences humaines de Bouzareah. Acquired present status and title 2010.

Admission Requirements: Baccalauréat

Degrees and Diplomas: *Licence (LMD)*; *Master*

Last Updated: 01/06/12

UNIVERSITY OF ALGIERS 3

Université d'Alger 3
02, Rue Ahmed Oukade, Dely-Ibrahim, 16320 Alger
Website: http://www.univ-alger3.dz

Recteur: Rabah Cheriet

Faculty
Economics, Commerce and Management (Business and Commerce; Economics; Management); **Political Science and Information** (Information Sciences; Political Sciences)

Institute
Physical Education and Sports (Physical Education; Sports)

History: Founded 2009 as Université de Dély Ibrahim. Acquired present title 2010.

Degrees and Diplomas: *Licence*; *Master*, *Doctorat*

Last Updated: 05/06/12

UNIVERSITY OF EL OUED

Université d'El Oued
BP 789, El Oued
Tel: +213(32) 24-41-81
Fax: +213(32) 24-47-67
EMail: admin@mail.univ-eloued.dz
Website: http://www.univ-eloued.dz

Directeur: Azzedine Haftari (2007-)

Faculty
Economics, Commerce, and Management (Business and Commerce; Economics; Management); **Law and Political Science** (Law; Political Sciences); **Literature and Languages** (Literature; Modern Languages); **Natural and Life Sciences** (Biological and Life Sciences; Natural Sciences); **Science and Technology** (Natural Sciences; Technology); **Social Sciences and Humanities** (Arts and Humanities; Social Sciences)

History: Founded 2001. Acquired present status and title 2012.
Degrees and Diplomas: *Licence*; *Master*, *Doctorat*
Last Updated: 01/06/12

UNIVERSITY OF EL TARF

Université d'El Tarf
BP 73, Route de Matroha, 36000 El Tarf
Tel: +213(38) 60-15-33
Fax: +213(38) 60-14-17
EMail: directeur@cuniv-eltaref.edu.dz
Website: http://www.cuniv-eltaref.edu.dz

Directeur: Rachid Siab
Tel: +213(38) 60-18-93 EMail: r.siab@mesrs.dz

Faculty

Economics, Commerce and Management (Business and Commerce; Economics; Management); **Languages and Literature** (Arabic; English; French; Literature; Sociology); **Law and Political Science** (Law; Political Sciences); **Natural and Life Sciences** (Biological and Life Sciences; Biology; Biotechnology; Natural Sciences; Plant and Crop Protection); **Science and Technology** (Natural Sciences; Technology); **Social Sciences and Humanities** (Arts and Humanities; Social Sciences)

History: Founded as Agro-veterinary Institute of Annaba University 1992. Acquired present status 2012.

Academic Year: September to June

Admission Requirements: Secondary school certificate (baccalauréat)

Fees: None

Main Language(s) of Instruction: Arabic, French

Degrees and Diplomas: *Licence (LMD)*; *Diplôme d'Etudes supérieures*; *Diplôme d'Ingénieur*, *Diplôme de Docteur*: **Veterinary Science.** *Master*, *Doctorat*

Student Services: Academic Counselling, Canteen, Health Services, Sports Facilities

Last Updated: 11/12/12

UNIVERSITY OF GHARDAIA

Université de Ghardaia
Ghardaia
Website: http://www.cu-ghardaia.edu.dz

Directeur: Mohamed Rajraj

Faculty

Economics, Commerce and Management (Business and Commerce; Economics; Management); **Law and Political Science** (Law; Political Sciences); **Letters and Languages** (Literature; Modern Languages); **Natural, Life and Earth Sciences** (Biological and Life Sciences; Earth Sciences; Natural Sciences); **Science and Technology** (Natural Sciences; Technology); **Social Sciences and Humanities** (Arts and Humanities; Social Sciences)

History: Founded 2005.

Degrees and Diplomas: *Licence*; *Master*

Last Updated: 11/12/12

UNIVERSITY OF KHEMIS MILIANA

Université de Khemis Miliana
Route de theniet el-had, 44225 Khemis Miliana
Tel: +213(27) 66-42-32
Fax: +213(27) 66-48-63
EMail: cukm@cukm.org
Website: http://www.cu-km.dz

Directeur: Mohamed Bezzina

Faculty

Economics, Commerce and Management (Business and Commerce; Economics; Management); **Law and Political Science** (Law; Political Sciences); **Letters and Languages** (Arabic; French; Literature; Modern Languages); **Natural, Life and Earth Sciences** (Agronomy; Animal Husbandry; Biological and Life Sciences; Biology; Earth Sciences; Environmental Studies; Geology; Natural Sciences; Water Science); **Social Sciences and Humanities** (Arts and Humanities; Communication Studies; Geography; History; Library Science; Media Studies; Philosophy; Social Sciences; Sociology)

Institute

Physical and Sports Activities (Physical Education; Sports); **Science and Technology** (Automation and Control Engineering; Civil Engineering; Computer Science; Electrical Engineering; Energy Engineering; Mathematics; Mechanical Engineering; Physical Chemistry; Thermal Engineering)

History: Founded 2001. Acquired present status and title 2012.

Degrees and Diplomas: *Licence (LMD)*; *Diplôme d'Ingénieur*, *Licence*; *Master*, *Doctorat*

Publications: Economics

Last Updated: 07/12/12

UNIVERSITY OF MASCARA

Université de Mascara
BP 305, Route de Mamounia, 29000 Mascara
Tel: +231(45) 80-41-69
Fax: +231(45) 80-41-69
EMail: rectorat@univ-mascara.dz
Website: http://www.univ-mascara.dz/

Recteur: Khaloufi Benabdeli

Faculty

Economics, Commerce and Management (Business and Commerce; Economics; Management); **Law and Administration** (Administration; Law; Political Sciences); **Letters, Languages, Humanities and Social Sciences** (Arts and Humanities; Literature; Modern Languages; Social Sciences); **Natural and Life Sciences** (Biological and Life Sciences; Natural Sciences); **Science and Technology** (Natural Sciences; Technology)

History: Founded 1986. Acquired present status 1992.

Degrees and Diplomas: *Licence (LMD)*: **Economics; Law; Management.** *Diplôme d'Ingénieur*: **Agronomy; Biology; Computer Science; Hydraulic Engineering; Mechanical Engineering.** *Master*

Last Updated: 05/06/12

UNIVERSITY OF M'SILA

Université de M'sila
BP 166, Ichbilia, 28000 M'sila
Tel: +231(35) 55-09-06
Fax: +231(35) 55-04-04
EMail: sdpunivmsila@yahoo.fr
Website: http://www.univ-msila.dz

Recteur: Slimane Barhoumi

Secrétaire général: Djamel Khaldoune Tel: +213(35) 55-64-68

International Relations: Lahcène Mezrag
EMail: lmezrag@yahoo.fryes

Faculty

Arts and Social Sciences (Arabic; Arts and Humanities; French; History; Literature; Psychology; Sociology); **Economics, Management and Commerce** (Business and Commerce; Economics; Management); **Law** (Administration; Communication Studies; Law; Political Sciences); **Mathematics and Computer Science** (Computer Science; Information Technology; Mathematics); **Science** (Agronomy; Biological and Life Sciences; Chemistry; Natural Sciences; Physics); **Technology** (Civil Engineering; Electrical Engineering; Electronic Engineering; Hydraulic Engineering; Mechanical Engineering)

Institute

Physical Education and Sports (Physical Education; Sports); **Town Planning** (Town Planning)

History: Founded 1985 as Institute of Mechanical Engineering. Became university centre 1992. Acquired present status 2001.

Academic Year: September to July

Admission Requirements: Baccalauréat

Fees: (Algerian Dinars): 200 per annum

Main Language(s) of Instruction: Arabic, French, English

Accrediting Agency: Ministère de l'Enseignement supérieur et de la Recherche scientifique

Degrees and Diplomas: *Licence (LMD)*; *Master*, *Doctorat*

Student Services: Academic Counselling, Canteen, Cultural Activities, Facilities for disabled people, Health Services, Language Laboratory, Social Counselling, Sports Facilities

Last Updated: 01/06/12

UNIVERSITY OF ORAN

Université d'Oran

BP 1524, El-M'Naouer, 31000 Oran

Tel: +213(41) 58-19-47

EMail: vrre-oran@univ-oran.dz

Website: http://www.univ-oran.dz

Recteur: Larbi Chahed

Faculty

Earth Sciences, Geography and Regional Planning (Earth Sciences; Geography; Regional Planning); **Economics, Management and Commerce** (Business and Commerce; Economics; Management); **Humanities and Islamic Civilization** (Arts and Humanities; History; Islamic Studies; Library Science); **Law and Political Science** (Law; Political Sciences; Private Law; Public Law); **Letters, Languages and Arts** (Arabic; English; French; German; Literature; Russian; Spanish; Theatre; Translation and Interpretation); **Medicine** (Medicine; Pharmacy; Stomatology); **Science** (Biology; Biotechnology; Chemistry; Computer Science; Mathematics; Physics); **Social Sciences** (Demography and Population; Philosophy; Psychology; Social Sciences; Sociology)

Institute

Industrial Maintenance (Industrial Maintenance)

History: Founded 1961 as Centre universitaire d'Oran attached to the University of Algiers. Became University 1966.

Academic Year: October to July (October-February; March-July)

Admission Requirements: Secondary school certificate (baccalauréat)

Main Language(s) of Instruction: Arabic, French

Degrees and Diplomas: *Licence (LMD)*; *Diplôme d'Ingénieur*, *Diplôme de Docteur*. **Medicine; Pharmacy.** *Master*, *Doctorat*

Publications: Applied Biology and Biotechnology (ABB); Résolang

Last Updated: 01/06/12

UNIVERSITY OF TLEMCEN

Université Abou Bekr Belkaid de Tlemcen

BP 119, 22 rue Abi Ayed Abdelkrim, Faubourg Pasteur, 13000 Tlemcen

Tel: +213(43) 20-23-36

Fax: +213(43) 20-41-89

EMail: vrcms@univ-bejaia.dz

Website: http://www.univ-tlemcen.dz

Recteur: Noureddine Ghouali

Faculty

Economics, Commerce and Management (Accountancy; Business and Commerce; Economics; Management); **Humanities and Social Sciences** (Archaeology; Arts and Humanities; History; Literature; Sociology); **Law and Political Science** (Law; Political Sciences); **Letters and Languages** (Arabic; English; French; Literature); **Medicine** (Medicine; Pharmacy; Stomatology); **Natural and Life Sciences and Earth and Universe Sciences** (Agronomy; Biological and Life Sciences; Earth Sciences; Ecology; Environmental Studies; Forestry; Geology); **Science** (Chemistry; Computer Science; Mathematics; Physics); **Technology** (Architecture; Civil Engineering; Electronic Engineering; Engineering; Hydraulic Engineering; Mechanical Engineering; Technology)

History: Founded as Centre universitaire de Tlemcen 1974, acquired present status and title 1998, modified in 2004.

Academic Year: September to July (September-December; January-March; April-July)

Admission Requirements: Secondary school certificate (baccalauréat) or equivalent

Main Language(s) of Instruction: Arabic, French

Accrediting Agency: Ministry of Higher Education and Scientific Research

Degrees and Diplomas: *Licence (LMD)*; *Diplôme d'Etudes supérieures*; *Diplôme d'Ingénieur*, *Diplôme de Docteur*. **Medicine.** *Master*, *Doctorat*

Student Services: Canteen, Health Services, Sports Facilities

Publications: Arabic Literature Magazine; Popular Culture Magazine

Last Updated: 07/06/12

ZIANE ACHOUR UNIVERSITY OF DJELFA

Université Ziane Achour de Djelfa

Route Moudjbara - BP 3117, 17000 Djelfa

Tel: +213(27) 90-02-03

Fax: +213(27) 90-02-01

EMail: webmaster@univ-djelfa.dz

Website: http://web.univ-djelfa.dz

Recteur: Ali Choukri EMail: recteur@univ-djelfa.dz

Secrétaire Général: Mohamed Teta EMail: sg@univ-djelfa.dz

Faculty

Economics, Commerce and Management (Business and Commerce; Economics; Management); **Law and Political Science** (Law; Political Sciences); **Literature and Languages and Social Sciences and Humanities** (Arts and Humanities; Literature; Modern Languages; Social Sciences); **Natural and Life Sciences** (Biological and Life Sciences; Natural Sciences); **Science and Technology** (Natural Sciences; Technology)

History: Founded 2000.

Main Language(s) of Instruction: Arabic

Degrees and Diplomas: *Diplôme d'Etudes universitaires appliquées*: **Computer Science; Electronic Engineering.** *Licence (LMD)*; *Diplôme d'Ingénieur*. **Electronic Engineering.**

Last Updated: 07/12/12

Andorra

STRUCTURE OF HIGHER EDUCATION SYSTEM

Description:

Higher education is provided by one public institution (Universitat d'Andorra) offering courses in Nursing, Computer Science, Business and Administration, Educational Studies, in on-campus and distance modes; and two private institutions, one specialized in the field of Dentistry, the other in online Business and Computing studies. For other higher education degrees, students enter the French or the Spanish higher education systems.

Stages of studies:

University level first stage: *Estudis universitaris*

Bàtxelor - 180 ECTS

University level second stage: *Estudis universitaris*

Bàtxelor d'especialització - 120 ECTS; Màster - 300 ECTS

University level third stage: *Estudis universitaris*

Doctorat (3 years)

ADMISSION TO HIGHER EDUCATION

Admission to university-level studies:

Name of secondary school credential required: Títol de Batxiller

For entry to: 1st year university studies.

Alternatives to credentials: - Títol de Batxiller Professional.

- Diplomas enabling access to higher education issued by Member Countries of the EHEA are accepted as Títol de Batxiller.

Admission requirements: When too many people wish to study a specific field of study, the University organises an entrance exam.

Foreign students admission:

Definition of foreign student: All those non Andorran or not living in Andorra.

Admission requirements: Diplomas enabling access to higher education issued by Member countries of the EHEA are accepted as Títol de Batxiller.

Entry regulations: Foreign students must fulfill the immigration requirements.

Language proficiency: The main teaching language is Catalan.

RECOGNITION OF STUDIES

Quality assurance system:

Department of Higher Education and Research of the Ministry of Education and Youth is in charge of academic recognition of diplomas. The Department of Labour within the Ministry of the Interior is in charge of professional recognition. The Ministry of Education and Youth evaluates credentials for professional recognition upon request of the Ministry of the Interior.

Bodies dealing with recognition:

Departament d'Ensenyament Superior i Recerca (Department of Higher Education and Research)

Ministeri d'Educació i Joventut
Av. Rocafort, 21-23, Ed. El Molí, 5a planta
Sant Julià de Lòria AD600
Tel: +376 743-300
Fax: +376 743-310
EMail: esuperior.gov@andorra.ad
WWW: http://www.ensenyamentsuperior.ad

Special provisions for recognition:

Recognition for university level studies: Department of Higher Education and Research of the Ministry of Education and Youth evaluates by Law all foreign credentials for access to a Bachelor's degree.

For access to advanced studies and research: Department of Higher Education and Research of the Ministry of Education and Youth evaluates credentials for access to this level of education upon request of the HEI.

For exercising a profession: The Department of Labour within the Ministry of the Interior is in charge of professional recognition. The Ministry of Education and Youth evaluates credentials for professional recognition upon request of the Ministry of the Interior.

NATIONAL BODIES

Ministeri d'Educació i Ensenyament Superior (Ministry of Education and Higher Education)

Minister: Eric Jover Comas
Edifici El Molí
Av. Rocafort, 21-23
Sant Julià de Lòria AD600
Tel: +376 743-300
Fax: +376 743-313
EMail: educacio@govern.ad
WWW: http://www.educacio.ad

Departament d'Ensenyament Superior i Recerca (Department of Higher Education and Research)

Ministeri d'Educació i Joventut
Av. Rocafort, 21-23, Ed. El Molí, 5a planta
Sant Julià de Lòria AD600
Tel: +376 743-300
Fax: +376 743-310
EMail: esuperior.gov@andorra.ad
WWW: http://www.ensenyamentsuperior.ad

Agència de Qualitat de l'Ensenyament Superior d'Andorra - AQUA (Andorran Agency for Quality Assurance)

Ed. El Molí
Av. Rocafort, 21-23
Sant Julià de Lòria AD600
EMail: info@aqua.ad
WWW: http://www.ensenyamentsuperior.ad/suport-a-l-ensenyament-superior/aqua

Data for academic year: 2014-2015

Source: Department of Higher Education and Research, Ministry of Education and Youth, Government of Andorra, 2014. Bodies 2016.

INSTITUTIONS

PUBLIC INSTITUTION

UNIVERSITY OF ANDORRA

Universitat d'Andorra
Plaça de la Germandat 7, AD 600 Sant Julià de Lòria
Tel: +376 743-000
Fax: +376 743-043
EMail: uda@uda.ad
Website: http://www.uda.ad

Rector: Miquel Nicolau i Vila (2015-)
Tel: +376 743-000 EMail: mnicolau@uda.ad.

Manager: Joan Obiols

School

Computer Science and Administration (Accountancy; Business Administration; Computer Science; Finance; Information Technology; Management; Marketing); **Nursing** (Anatomy; Child Care and Development; Community Health; Demography and Population; Dietetics; Environmental Studies; Epidemiology; Ethics; Family

Studies; Gerontology; Health Administration; Health Education; Microbiology; Nursing; Nutrition; Parasitology; Pharmacology; Physiology; Psychiatry and Mental Health; Psychology; Public Health; Statistics)

Centre
Virtual Studies and Continuing Education

History: Higher education in Andorra started in 1988 with two faculties: the School of Nursing and the School of Computer Systems. The University of Andorra was formally created by law in July 1997. Now, the University of Andorra is constituted by public centres devoted to higher education.

Admission Requirements: Established by the government depending on the degree

Fees: 600 per semester (Euro)

Main Language(s) of Instruction: Catalan, English, French, Spanish

Accrediting Agency: Comissio per a la qualitat del sistema universitari d'Andorra

Degrees and Diplomas: *Diploma Professional Avançat*; *Bàtxelor*: **Business Administration; Computer Science; Education; Gynaecology and Obstetrics; Midwifery; Nursing.** *Doctorat*: **Catalan.** Agreement with the Open University of Catalonia (UOC) to jointly offer double Bachelor's degree in: Business Administration, Law, Arts in Humanities, Computer Science, Media Studies, Mass Communication, Catalan, Literature

Last Updated: 19/12/14

PRIVATE INSTITUTIONS

OPEN UNIVERSITY OF LA SALLE

Universitat Oberta La Salle (UOLS)
Av. del Través 31, Local A-2, La Massana, AD400
Tel: +376 815388
EMail: info@uols.org
Website: http://www.uols.org

Rector: Lluís Vicent Safont EMail: vicent@uols.org

Manager: Ramon Ollé Ribalta EMail: r.olle@uols.org

Programme
Business and Management (Business Administration; Computer Science; E- Business/Commerce; Finance; Management)

Research Institute
Higher Research Institute (Education; Educational Technology)

History: Created 2010.

Degrees and Diplomas: *Bàtxelor*: **Computer Science.** *Bàtxelor d'Especialització*: **Business Administration; Finance; Management.** *Màster*: **Business Administration; E- Business/Commerce.** *Doctorat*: **Education; Educational Technology.** Professional Development non-degree programme in E-Business, Computer Science, Environmental Management, Educational Technology.

Last Updated: 23/01/15

UNIVERSITY OF THE VALLEYS

Universitat de les Valls (UDV)
Av. Meritxell, 28, 500 Andorra la Vella
Tel: +376 813-781
Fax: +376 813-981
EMail: info@udv.ad
Website: http://www.udv.ad

Vice-Chancellor: Philip Garcia Ricart
Tel: +376 81-37-81 EMail: rector@udv.ad

School
Dentistry (Biochemistry; Cell Biology; Chemistry; Dental Hygiene; Dental Technology; Dentistry; Gerontology; Medicine; Molecular Biology; Nursing; Nutrition; Orthodontics; Pharmacology; Radiology)

History: Created 2011.

Main Language(s) of Instruction: Spanish, English

Degrees and Diplomas: *Màster*: **Dentistry.**

Student Services: Residential Facilities

Last Updated: 23/01/15

Angola

STRUCTURE OF HIGHER EDUCATION SYSTEM

Description:

Since 2010, higher education falls under the supervision of the Ministry of Higher Education, Science and Technology. It is structured around two types of higher education institutions: university level institutions (composed of universidades and academias) and polytecnics (composed of escolas superiores and institutos superiores). The higher education system offers undergraduate (Bacharelato and Licenciatura) and post-graduate courses (Mestrado and Doutoramento). There are both academic and professional post-graduate courses. Universidades and academias are placed under the supervision of a Rector, escolas superiores and institutos superiores under the supervision of a Director-General. The higher education sector is composed of public, public-private, and private institutions.

Stages of studies:

University level first stage: *Graduação*
The Bacharelato is obtained after three years' study. The Licenciadura is obtained after four to six years' study.

University level second stage: *Pos-Graduação*
There are two types of post-graduate degrees in Angola. The first is the pós-graduação academico which leads to the Mestrado in two to three years and to the Doutoramento after four to five years following the Licenciatura. The second, the pós-graduação profissional, offers Especialização of various durations. All post-graduate degrees are the Licenciatura or the Licenciatura or the Mestrado for the Doutoramento.

ADMISSION TO HIGHER EDUCATION

Admission to university-level studies:

Name of secondary school credential required: Secondary School-Leaving Certificate
Admission requirements: Entrance examination

Foreign students admission:

Admission requirements: Secondary-school-leaving certificate or equivalent and success in the entrance examination.
Language proficiency: Good knowledge of Portuguese

RECOGNITION OF STUDIES

Quality assurance system:

The process of establishing private higher education institutions comprises 3 phases: 1. credibility assessment; 2. evaluation of the facilities; 3. authorization.

NATIONAL BODIES

Ministério de Ciência e Tecnologia - MESCT (Ministry of Science and Technology)

Minister: Maria Candida Teixeira
Luanda
WWW: http://www.minct.gov.ao
Role of national body: The Ministry proposes and implements the higher education policy.

Data for academic year: 2012-2013
Source: IAU from the website of the Ministry of Higher Education, 2012. Bodies 2016.

INSTITUTIONS

PUBLIC INSTITUTIONS

AGOSTINHO NETO UNIVERSITY

Universidade Agostinho Neto
Caixa postal 815, Avenida 4 de Fevereiro 7, 2° andar, Luanda
EMail: info@uan-angola.org
Website: http://www.agostinhoneto.co.ao/

Reitor: Orlando da Mata
EMail: orlandomata@hotmail com; orlandomata@yahoo com

Faculty
Agrarian Sciences *(Huambo)* (Agricultural Engineering; Agriculture; Agronomy; Veterinary Science); **Economics** *(Luanda)* (Economics); **Engineering** *(Luanda)* (Engineering); **Law** *(Luanda)* (Law); **Letters** (History; Modern Languages; Political Sciences; Psychology; Public Administration; Social Sciences; Sociology); **Medicine** *(Luanda)* (Medicine; Surgery); **Science** (Biology; Chemistry; Engineering; Geophysics; Mathematics; Physics)

Higher Institute
Educational Sciences *(Lubango)* (Education); **Educational Sciences** *(Luanda)* (Education); **Educational Sciences** *(Benguela)* (Education); **Nursing** (Nursing)

History: Founded 1962 as Estudos Gerais Universitários, became University of Luanda 1968, University of Angola 1976 and acquired present title 1985. An autonomous State institution.

Academic Year: October to June (October-February; March-June)

Admission Requirements: Secondary school certificate and entrance examination

Fees: None

Main Language(s) of Instruction: Portuguese

Degrees and Diplomas: *Bachalerato*; *Licenciatura*: **Medicine.** *Mestrado*; *Doutoramento*: **Environmental Management; Natural Resources; Waste Management.**

Student Services: Canteen, Cultural Activities, Social Counselling, Sports Facilities
Last Updated: 07/12/12

NATIONAL INSTITUTE OF PUBLIC ADMINISTRATION

Institut national d'Administration publique (INAP)
BP 6852, Estrago do Futungo, Luanda
Tel: +244(222) 351-160
Fax: +244(222) 354-555

Direitor: José Joào Lourenço

Programme
Economics (Economics); **Law** (Law); **Political Science** (Political Sciences); **Public Administration** (Public Administration); **Social Sciences** (Social Sciences)

PRIVATE INSTITUTIONS

AGRARIAN SCHOOL OF KUANZA-SUL

Escola Superior Agrária do Kwanza Sul (ESAKS)
Sumbe, Kwanza-Sul
Tel: +244 923-379-361

Director-General: Octavio Isaac Manuel Spinola

Programme
Accountancy (Accountancy); **Agronomy** (Agronomy); **Management** (Management)

History: Founded 2007. Acquired present status 2009.

Main Language(s) of Instruction: Portuguese

Degrees and Diplomas: *Licenciatura*
Last Updated: 07/12/12

BELAS UNIVERSITY

Universidade de Belas (UNIBELAS)
Bairro Benfica, Município da Samba, Luanda
Tel: +244(222) 401 679
EMail: unibelas@hotmail.com
Website: http://www.unibelas.org/unibelas_site/default.aspx

Rector: Agatângelo Estêvão Zua

Faculty
Economics and Social Sciences (Accountancy; Business Administration; Management; Marketing; Psychology); **Engineering** (Computer Engineering; Petroleum and Gas Engineering); **Health Sciences** (Dentistry; Health Administration; Nursing; Nutrition; Pharmacy); **Law** (Law)
History: Founded 2007.

Main Language(s) of Instruction: Portuguese

Degrees and Diplomas: *Licenciatura*
Last Updated: 07/12/12

CATHOLIC UNIVERSITY OF ANGOLA

Universidade Católica de Angola (UCAN)
Caixa postal 2064, Rua Nossa Sennhora da Muxima 29, Luanda
Tel: +244(222) 331-973
Fax: +244(222) 398-759
EMail: info@ucan.edu
Website: http://www.ucan.edu

Reitor: Damião António Franklin
EMail: damiaofranklin@ucan.edu; damiaof@ucan.edu

Vice-Reitor: Jerónimo Cahinga

Faculty
Economics and Management (Economics; Management); **Engineering** (Engineering); **Humanities** (English; Portuguese; Psychology; Social Sciences; Translation and Interpretation); **Law** (Law); **Theology** (Theology)

History: Founded 1997.
Degrees and Diplomas: *Licenciatura*
Last Updated: 07/12/12

GREGÓRIO SEMEDO UNIVERSITY

Universidade Gregório Semedo (UGS)
Rua Kwamme N'Krumah, 16-18, Ingombotas, Luanda
Tel: +244(222) 239-4668
Fax: +244 923 690-274
EMail: ugs@snet.co.ao
Website: http://www.ugs.ed.ao/

Reitor: José António Lopes Semedo

Faculty
Economics and Business Studies (Business Administration; Economics); **Engineering and New Technologies** (Computer Engineering; Technology); **Law and Political Science**; **Social Sciences and Human Development** (Human Resources; Social Sciences)

History: Founded 2003.

Main Language(s) of Instruction: Portuguese

Degrees and Diplomas: *Licenciatura*: **Business Administration; Business Computing; Computer Engineering; Human Resources; Law; Marketing.**
Last Updated: 07/12/12

HIGHER INSTITUTE OF SOCIAL SCIENCES AND INTERNATIONAL RELATIONS

Instituto superior de Ciencias Sociais e Relações Internacionais (ISCRI)
Talatona, Luanda
Tel: +244(222) 406-886
EMail: geral@cis-edu.org
Website: http://www.cis-edu.org/

Director Geral: Emmanuel Moeira Carneiro

Programme
Economics (Economics); **International Relations** (International Relations); **Political Science** (Political Sciences); **Public Administration** (Public Administration); **Sociology** (Sociology)

History: Founded 2007.

Degrees and Diplomas: *Licenciatura*
Last Updated: 30/05/12

HIGHER TECHNICAL INSTITUTE OF ANGOLA

Instituto Superior Técnico de Angola (ISTA)
Bairro do Grafanil, Rua da Cor, Luanda
Tel: +244 222 401 193
EMail: secretaria.geral@ista-angola.com
Website: http://www.ista-angola.com/

Director académico: Joaquim Pascoal Silva

Programme
Accounting and Administration (Accountancy; Administration); **Engineering** (Computer Engineering; Electronic Engineering; Telecommunications Engineering); **Law** (Law); **Psychology** (Psychology)

History: Founded 2007.

Degrees and Diplomas: *Licenciatura*
Last Updated: 07/12/12

INDEPENDENT UNIVERSITY OF ANGOLA

Universidade Independente de Angola (UNIA)
Rua da Missão, Barrio Morro Bento II Corimba, Luanda
Tel: +224(222) 33-89-70
Fax: +244(222) 33-89-68
EMail: unia@unia.ao
Website: http://www.unia.ao

Reitor: Carlos Alberto Burity da Silva
EMail: reitor@unia.ao

Vice-Rector: Filipe Silvino de Pina Zau

Department
Civil Engineering (Civil Engineering; Construction Engineering); **Communication Sciences** (Journalism; Radio and Television Broadcasting); **Computer Engineering** (Computer Engineering); **Electronic Engineering and Telecommunications** (Electronic Engineering; Telecommunications Engineering); **Law** (Law); **Management and Marketing** (Management; Marketing); **Natural Resources and Environmental Engineering** (Environmental Engineering; Natural Resources); **Social Sciences** (Social Sciences)

History: Founded 2004.

Degrees and Diplomas: *Licenciatura*
Last Updated: 18/06/12

JEAN PIAGET UNIVERSITY OF ANGOLA

Universidade Jean Piaget de Angola (UNIPIAGET DE ANGOLA)
Caixa postal 81, Bairro Capalanca, Viana, Luanda
Tel: +244(222) 29-04-48
Fax: +244(222) 29-02-59
EMail: info@angola.ipiaget.org

Reitor: Pedro Domingos Peterson

Vice-Rector: José Eduardo do Carmo Nelumba

Course
Clinical Psychology (Clinical Psychology); **Computer Engineering** (Computer Engineering); **Construction Engineering and Territorial Planning** (Construction Engineering); **Dentistry** (Dentistry); **Economics and Management**; **Electrical and Mechanical Engineering** (Electrical Engineering; Mechanical Engineering); **Human Motricity and Rehabilitation**; **Law** (Criminal Law; Law); **Medicine**; **Nursing** (Nursing); **Petroleum Engineering** (Petroleum and Gas Engineering); **Pharmacy** (Pharmacy); **Physiotherapy** (Physical Therapy); **Portuguese** (Native Language; Portuguese); **Sociology** (Sociology)

History: Founded 2000.

Main Language(s) of Instruction: Portuguese

Degrees and Diplomas: *Licenciatura*

METHODIST UNIVERSITY OF ANGOLA

Universidade Metodista de Angola (UMA)
Rua Nossa Senhora da Muxima, 10, Kinaxixi, Luanda
Tel: +224(222) 338-984
Fax: +224(222) 330-572
EMail: geral@uma.co.ao
Website: http://www.uma.co.ao/UMA

Reitora: Teresa José Adelina da Silva Neto
EMail: tjasn@uma.co.ao

Vice-Presidente do Conselho de Administração: Pedro Sebastião EMail: ps@uma.co.ao

Faculty
Architecture (Architecture; Art History; Design; Town Planning); **Economics and Business Administration** (Accountancy; Banking; Business Administration; Finance; Management); **Engineering and Environmental Studies** (Civil Engineering; Computer Engineering; Electrical and Electronic Engineering; Environmental Studies; Industrial Engineering; Mechanical Engineering; Rural Planning); **Health Sciences** (Public Health); **Humanities and Social Sciences** (Portuguese; Theology); **Law** (Administrative Law; Constitutional Law; International Law; Law)

History: Founded 2007.

Main Language(s) of Instruction: Portuguese

Degrees and Diplomas: *Licenciatura*; *Mestrado*
Last Updated: 18/06/12

OSCAR RIBAS UNIVERSITY

Universidade Óscar Ribas (UOR)
Rua Direita do Centro de Convenções s/n, Luanda
Tel: +244 3750 10 87
Fax: +244 23 70 22 12
EMail: reitoria@uor.ed.ao
Website: http://www.uor.ed.ao

Rector: Alberto Chocolate
Tel: +244 923-608-652

Secretary-General: Madaleno De Andrade
Tel: +244 923-307-902; +244 912-688-514

International Relations: Maria Fatima, Vice Rector
Tel: +244 925-482-765 EMail: geral.vraa@uor.ed.ao

Department
Civil Engineering; **Engineering** (Computer Science; Electrical Engineering; Engineering; Mechanical Engineering; Telecommunications Engineering); **International Relations** (International Relations); **Law** (Law); **Management** (Management); **Psychology**

History: Founded 2007.

Admission Requirements: Certificate of Secondary Studies

Fees: (US Dollars): 250 per month for Social Science course; 280 per month for Engineering course

Main Language(s) of Instruction: Portuguese

Degrees and Diplomas: *Licenciatura*

Student Services: Academic Counselling, Canteen, Language Laboratory, Nursery Care
Last Updated: 18/06/12

PRIVATE UNIVERSITY OF ANGOLA

Universidade Privada de Angola (UPRA)
Estrada de Catete- Edificio da Filda, Luanda
Tel: +244(222) 265-645
EMail: upra@upra.lubango.org
Website: http://www.upralubango.org/apresentacao

Reitor: Carlos Alberto Pinto de Sousa

International Relations: Helena Coelho
Tel: +244(925) 184-047 EMail: helena@upra.ao

Department

Accountancy and Business Administration (Accountancy; Business Administration); **Architecture** (Architecture); **Civil Engineering** (Civil Engineering); **Computer Science** (Computer Science); **Dentistry** (Dentistry); **International Relations** (International Relations); **Nursing** (Nursing); **Pharmacy** (Pharmacy); **Physiotherapy** (Physical Therapy); **Psychology** (Psychology); **Social Communication** (Communication Studies); **Tourism and Hotel Management** (Hotel Management; Tourism)

History: Founded 2000 as Instituto Superior Privado de Angola. Acquired present status and title 2007.

Main Language(s) of Instruction: Portuguese

Degrees and Diplomas: *Licenciatura*; *Mestrado*: **Health Administration.**

Last Updated: 07/12/12

TECHNICAL UNIVERSITY OF ANGOLA

Universidade Técnica de Angola (UTANGA)
Bairro Capolo II, Rua A4 N°. 14, Kilamba Kiaxi, Luanda
Tel: +244(222) 262 064
Fax: +244(222) 263 642
EMail: info@utanga.co.ao
Website: http://www.utanga.co.ao

Reitor: Paulo Victorino dos Reis Afonso

Secretario-General: Filipe Zeferino

Faculty

Economics and Management; **Engineering** (Computer Engineering; Electronic Engineering; Environmental Engineering; Mining Engineering; Telecommunications Engineering)

Course

Architecture and Town Planning (Architecture; Town Planning); **Computer Engineering** (Business Computing; Computer Engineering); **English Language and Literature** (English; Literature); **Geology and Mining Engineering** (Geology; Mining Engineering); **Law** (Law); **Modern Languages** (English); **Political Sciences and International Relations** (International Relations; Political Sciences); **Psychology** (Psychology)

History: Founded 2007.

Degrees and Diplomas: *Licenciatura*

Argentina

STRUCTURE OF HIGHER EDUCATION SYSTEM

Description:

Higher education is provided by public and private universities and institutes. The Consejo Interuniversitario Nacional (CIN) coordinates policies of the State-run universities and their relationship with public and private, national and foreign bodies; draws up proposals for the national recognition of complete and partial studies and related degrees and diplomas, and for the national validation of foreign qualifications. Private universities are autonomous but must be recognized by the State, and their statutes, courses and programmes must be approved by it. They are grouped under the Consejo de Rectores de Universidades Privadas (CRUP). Through their Steering Committees, CIN and CRUP form part of the University (Consejo de Universidades) and Higher Education Regional Planning Councils (CPRES), to which the Ministry turns to in order to address some affairs regarding university policies. The Consejo Nacional de Evaluación y Acreditación Universitaria (CONEAU) oversees the external evaluations of all universities and provides authorization for the establishment of new universities. It also accredits graduate programmes and some undergraduate programmes where the public interest needs to be protected (e.g. Medicine and Engineering). State-run higher education institutions do not generally charge any fees but private universities do.

Stages of studies:

University level first stage: *Grado*

The first stage of university level education lasts between four and six years. It leads to the award of the Licenciatura or a professional qualification. The first stage corresponds to the study of basic subjects and practical experience in a given subject. In fields such as Architecture, Law and Medicine, first professional degrees are awarded after 5-6 years of study.

University level second stage: *Posgrado*

The Especialización consists in further training in a profession. It leads to the title of Especialista in a given field after a minimum of one year or 360 hours. The Maestría offers further training in a discipline or in an interdisciplinary field and is conferred after two years of further study or 540 hours. Training includes carrying out a research project or defending a thesis under the guidance of a supervisor which is evaluated by a jury which comprises at least one member that is external to the University. It leads to a Título Académico de Magister and the specification of the field of study. The Doctorado is the highest degree. Candidates must submit a thesis. Since it is not a prerequisite for the practice of a profession, no time limit is imposed.

ADMISSION TO HIGHER EDUCATION

Admission to university-level studies:

Name of secondary school credential required: Bachillerato

Admission requirements: There is an entrance examination or a year of preparatory course in some cases.

RECOGNITION OF STUDIES

Quality assurance system:

Higher education institutions and courses are assessed and accredited by the National Commission for University Evaluation and Accreditation (Comisión Nacional de Evaluación y Acreditación Universitaria - CONEAU).

NATIONAL BODIES

Ministerio de Educación (Ministry of Education)

Minister: Alberto Estanislao Sileoni

Secretary, University Policies: Aldo Luis Caballero

Pizzurno 935

Buenos Aires 1020
Tel: +54(11) 4129-1000
WWW: http://portal.educacion.gov.ar
Role of national body: Body in charge of the development of national education policies and strategies as per the national education law.

Comisión Nacional de Evaluación y Acreditación Universitaria - CONEAU (National Commission for University Evaluation and Accreditation)
Director, Development, Planning and International Relations: Martín Pablo Strah
Av. Santa Fe 1385, Piso 4
Buenos Aires C1059ABH
Tel: +54(11) 4819 9050
Fax: +54(11) 4815 0744
EMail: consulta@coneau.edu.ar
WWW: http://www.coneau.edu.ar
Role of national body: Its main functions are: evaluation of institutional projects of new private and state institutions; external evaluation of institutions; accreditation of undergraduate careers regulated by the state; and accreditation of graduate careers.

Consejo de Rectores de Universidades Privadas - CRUP (Council of Rectors of Private Universities)
President: Juan Carlos Mena
Montevideo 1910 PB
Buenos Aires C1021AAH
Tel: +54(11) 4811 6435
Fax: +54(11) 4811 0947
WWW: http://www.crup.org.ar
Role of national body: Coordinates the activities of private universities.

Consejo Interuniversitario Nacional - CIN (National Interuniversity Council)
President: Jorge Calzoni
Director-General: Oscar Spada
Pacheco de Melo 2084
Buenos Aires C1126AAF
Tel: +54(11) 4806 2269
EMail: info@cin.edu.ar
WWW: http://www.cin.edu.ar
Role of national body: Coordinates university activities, recommends the creation of academic units, participates in university policy planning and makes recommendations to the Ministry.

Data for academic year: 2015-2016
Source: IAU from the website of the Ministry of Education, Argentina, Estudiar en Argentina (http://estudiarenargentina.siu.edu.ar/), and NUFFIC's Education System Argentina (https://www.nuffic.nl/en/library/education-system-argentina.pdf), 2015.

INSTITUTIONS

PUBLIC INSTITUTIONS

ARTURO JAURETCHE NATIONAL UNIVERSITY

Universidad Nacional Arturo Jauretche (UNAJ)
Av. San Martín y Granaderos, Florencia Valera, Buenos Aires
EMail: info@unaj.edu.ar
Website: http://www.unaj.edu.ar

Rector: Ernesto Fernando Villanueva
EMail: rectorado@unaj.edu.ar

International Relations: Mariano F. Ameghino
EMail: internacionales@unaj.edu.ar

Institute
Engineering and Agronomy (Agriculture; Bioengineering; Computer Engineering; Electronic Engineering; Industrial Engineering; Mechanical Engineering; Petroleum and Gas Engineering; Vegetable Production); **Health Sciences** (Biochemistry; Cardiology; Health Sciences; Medicine; Nursing); **Social Sciences and Administration** (Administration; Economics; Environmental Management; Labour and Industrial Relations; Social Work)

History: Founded 2009.

Degrees and Diplomas: *Licenciatura*: **Agriculture; Business Administration; Computer Engineering; Economics; Electronic Engineering; Environmental Management; Health Sciences; Industrial Engineering; Labour and Industrial Relations; Mechanical Engineering; Nursing; Petroleum and Gas Engineering; Social Sciences.** *Especialización*: **Cardiology.** *Maestría*: **Health Sciences.**

Last Updated: 28/08/15

AUTONOMOUS UNIVERSITY OF ENTRE RÍOS

Universidad Autónoma de Entre Ríos (UADER)

Avenida F. Ramirez 1143, 3100 Paraná, Entre Ríos

Tel: +54(343) 420-7880

EMail: administrativa@uader.edu.ar

Website: http://www.uader.edu.ar

Rector: Anibal Javier Sattler EMail: rectorado@uader.edu.ar

Secretario Académico: Patricia Lucero
EMail: academica@uader.edu.ar

Faculty

Humanities, Arts and Social Sciences (Arts and Humanities; Education; English; Fine Arts; French; Geography; Gerontology; History; Italian; Literature; Modern Languages; Music; Philosophy; Portuguese; Psychology; Social Sciences; Special Education; Visual Arts); **Life and Health Sciences** (Biological and Life Sciences; Health Sciences; Nursing; Physical Education); **Management** (Archiving; Business Administration; Economics; Hotel Management; International Business; Management; Marketing; Public Administration; Tourism); **Science and Technology** (Biology; Computer Networks; Computer Science; Criminal Law; Earth Sciences; Environmental Management; Technology)

History: Founded 2000.

Degrees and Diplomas: *Licenciatura*: **Archiving; Biology; Business Administration; Computer Networks; Computer Science; Criminal Law; Economics; Educational Sciences; Environmental Studies; Geography; History; Hotel Management; International Business; Management; Marketing; Philosophy; Psychology; Public Administration; Social Sciences; Technology; Tourism; Visual Arts.** *Maestría*: **Earth Sciences.**

Last Updated: 26/08/15

GENERAL SARMIENTO NATIONAL UNIVERSITY

Universidad Nacional de General Sarmiento (UNGS)

Juan M. Gutiérrez 1150, 1613 Los Polvorines, Buenos Aires

Tel: +54(11) 4469-7500

EMail: info@ungs.edu.ar

Website: http://www.ungs.edu.ar

Rectora: Gabriela Leticia Diker EMail: gdiker@ungs.edu.ar

Vicerrector: Pablo Daniel Bonaldi EMail: pbonaldi@ungs.edu.ar

Secretario Académico: Oscar Graizer
EMail: ograizer@ungs.edu.ar

Institute

Human Development *(IDH)* (Communication Studies; Cultural Studies; Economics; Education; History; Mathematics; Philosophy; Physics; Political Sciences); **Industry** *(IDEL)* (Business Administration; Industrial and Production Economics; Industrial Engineering; Industrial Management; Social Sciences); **Science** *(ICI)* (Arts and Humanities; Mathematics and Computer Science; Natural Sciences; Social Sciences); **Urban Studies** *(Conurbano, ICO)* (Ecology; Public Administration; Social Policy; Urban Studies)

History: Founded 1993.

Academic Year: March to December

Admission Requirements: Secondary school certificate or equivalent

Main Language(s) of Instruction: Spanish

Degrees and Diplomas: *Licenciatura*; *Especialización*; *Maestría*: **Economics; Engineering Management; Industrial and Production Economics; Small Business; Social Studies; Technology.** *Doctorado*: **Natural Sciences; Social Sciences; Technology; Urban Studies.**

Student Services: Academic Counselling, Canteen, Facilities for disabled people, Library

Last Updated: 01/09/15

LATIN AMERICAN FACULTY OF SOCIAL SCIENCES

Facultad Latinoamericana de Ciencias Sociales (FLACSO)

Ayacucho 555 (C1026AAC), Buenos Aires

Tel: + 54(11) 5238-9300

Website: http://www.flacso.org.ar

Director: Luis Alberto Quevedo EMail: vroselli@flacso.org.ar

Secretaria Académica: Myriam Southwell
EMail: msouthwell@flacso.org.ar

Area

Communication and Culture (Communication Studies; Cultural Studies); **Development, Innovation and State-Society Relations** (Development Studies; Sociology); **Economics and Technology** (Economics; Technology); **Education** (Education); **Ethics, Law and Global Public Goods** (Ethics; Law); **Gender, Society and Politics** (Gender Studies; Political Sciences; Sociology); **International Relations** (International Relations); **Latin American Studies** (Latin American Studies); **Social Anthropology and Political Science** (Anthropology; Political Sciences); **The State and Public Policy** (Political Sciences)

History: Founded 1974.

Main Language(s) of Instruction: Spanish

Degrees and Diplomas: *Especialización*: **Education; Ethics; Public Law.** *Maestría*: **Agriculture; Anthropology; Education; Ethics; Labour and Industrial Relations; Law; Political Sciences; Social Sciences.** *Doctorado*: **Social Sciences.**

Last Updated: 25/08/15

NATIONAL TECHNICAL UNIVERSITY

Universidad Tecnológica Nacional (UTN)

Sarmiento 440, Piso 3, 5, 6, 7, 8, 1347 Buenos Aires, Capital Federal

Tel: +54(11) 5371-5600

Fax: +54(11) 5371-5697

EMail: sec-admin@utn.edu.ar

Website: http://www.utn.edu.ar

Rector: Héctor Carlos Brotto
Tel: +54(11) 5371-5700 EMail: privada@utn.edu.ar

Vicerrector: Pablo Andrés Rosso
Tel: +54(11) 5371-5702 EMail: v-rector@utn.edu.ar

International Relations: Ruben Soro
EMail: internacionales@rec.utn.edu.ar

Faculty

Avellaneda Regional Faculty *(Avellaneda, Buenos Aires.)* (Business Administration; Chemical Engineering; Civil Engineering; Computer Engineering; Electrical Engineering; Electronic Engineering; Environmental Engineering; Food Technology; Higher Education Teacher Training; Industrial Engineering; Mechanical Engineering; Medicine; Sound Engineering (Acoustics)); **Bahía Blanca Regional Faculty** *(Bahía Blanca, Buenos Aires.)* (Business Administration; Civil Engineering; Electrical and Electronic Engineering; Environmental Engineering; Mechanical Engineering); **Buenos Aires Regional Faculty** *(Buenos Aires)* (Business Administration; Chemical Engineering; Computer Engineering; Educational Sciences; Electrical and Electronic Engineering; Environmental Engineering; Food Technology; Higher Education Teacher Training; Industrial Engineering; Information Sciences; Information Technology; Marine Engineering; Mechanical Engineering; Nuclear Engineering; Textile Technology); **Chubut Regional Faculty** *(Puerto Madryn, Chubut)* (Fishery; Industrial Management); **Concepción del Uruguay Regional University** *(Concepción del Uruguay, Between Rivers.)* (Business Administration; Civil Engineering; Computer Engineering; Environmental Engineering; Industrial Management; Sound Engineering (Acoustics)); **Concordia Regional Faculty** *(Concordia, Entre Rios)* (Civil Engineering; Electrical Engineering; Environmental Engineering); **Córdoba Regional Faculty** *(Córdoba, Cordova)* (Business Administration; Chemical Engineering; Civil Engineering; Electrical and Electronic Engineering; Engineering; Higher Education Teacher Training; Industrial Engineering; Information Sciences; Mechanical Engineering; Metallurgical Engineering; Transport and Communications); **Del Neuquén Regional Faculty** *(Plaza Huincul, Neuquén)* (Business Administration; Chemical Engineering; Electronic Engineering); **Delta Regional Faculty** *(Campana, Buenos Aires)* (Business Administration; Chemical Engineering; Electrical and Electronic Engineering; Electrical Engineering; Engineering; Information Sciences); **General Pacheco Regional Faculty** *(General Pacheco, Buenos Aires)* (Automotive Engineering; Business Administration; Civil Engineering; Computer Engineering; Electrical Engineering; Higher Education Teacher Training; Mechanical Engineering); **Haedo Regional Faculty** *(Haedo, Buenos Aires.)* (Aeronautical and Aerospace Engineering; Business Administration; Computer Science; Engineering; Environmental Engineering; Higher Education Teacher Training; Sound Engineering (Acoustics)); **La Plata Regional Faculty** *(La Plata, Buenos Aires)* (Chemical Engineering; Civil Engineering; Electrical Engineering; Engineering; Higher Education Teacher Training; Industrial Engineering; Information Sciences; Marine Engineering; Mechanical Engineering); **La Rioja Regional Faculty** *(La Rioja Capital, The Rioja)* (Business Administration; Civil Engineering; Electrical Engineering; Electronic Engineering; Higher Education Teacher Training); **Mendoza Regional Faculty** *(Mendoza, Mendoza)* (Civil Engineering; Computer Engineering; Electrical Engineering; Engineering; Health Sciences; Higher Education Teacher Training; Information Sciences; Mechanical Engineering; Sound Engineering (Acoustics)); **Paraná Regional Faculty** *(Paraná, Entre Rios)* (Business Administration; Civil Engineering; Electrical Engineering; Electronic Engineering; Mechanical Engineering); **Rafaela Regional Faculty** *(Rafaela, Santa Fe)* (Business Administration; Civil Engineering; Industrial Engineering; Mechanical Engineering); **Reconquista Regional Faculty** *(Reconquista, Santa Fe)* (Agricultural Management; Electronic Engineering; Mechanical Engineering); **Resistencia Regional Faculty** *(Resistance, Chaco)* (Business Administration; Electronic Engineering; Engineering; Higher Education Teacher Training; Information Sciences; Mechanical Engineering); **Río Grande Regional Faculty** *(Río Grande, Tierra del Fuego)* (Business Administration; Chemical Engineering; Electronic Engineering; Fishery; Industrial Engineering); **Rosario Regional Faculty** *(Rosario, Santa Fe)* (Chemical Engineering; Civil Engineering; Computer Engineering; Electrical Engineering; Environmental Engineering; Food Technology; Higher Education Teacher Training; Information Sciences; Mechanical Engineering); **San Francisco Regional Faculty** *(San Francisco, Cordova)* (Business Administration; Chemical Engineering; Electrical and Electronic Engineering; Engineering; Higher Education Teacher Training; Information Sciences); **San Nicolás Regional Faculty** *(San Nicolás, Buenos Aires)* (Agricultural Management; Business Administration; Electrical Engineering; Health Sciences; Higher Education Teacher Training; Industrial Engineering; Industrial Management; Mechanical Engineering; Metallurgical Engineering); **San Rafael Regional Faculty** *(San Rafael, Mendoza)* (Civil Engineering; Computer Engineering; Electrical Engineering; Fishery; Industrial Engineering; Marine Engineering; Mechanical Engineering); **Santa Cruz Regional Faculty** *(Río Gallegos, Santa Cruz)* (Electronic Engineering; Industrial Engineering); **Santa Fe Regional Faculty** *(Santa Fe, Santa Fe)* (Civil Engineering; Electrical Engineering; Engineering; Environmental Engineering; Industrial Engineering; Information Sciences; Mechanical Engineering; Transport and Communications); **Trenque Lauquen Regional Faculty** *(Lauquen Dam, Buenos Aires)* (Agricultural Management; Industrial Engineering); **Tucumán Regional Faculty** *(San Miguel de Tucuman, Tucuman)* (Business Administration; Civil Engineering; Electrical Engineering; Electronic Engineering; Higher Education Teacher Training; Information Sciences; Mechanical Engineering); **Venardo Tuerto Regional Faculty** *(Venardo Tuerto, Santa Fe)* (Business Administration; Civil Engineering; Electrical Engineering; Mechanical Engineering); **Villa María Regional Faculty** *(Villa María, Córdoba)* (Business Administration; Chemical Engineering; Electronic Engineering; Environmental Engineering; Food Technology; Information Sciences; Mechanical Engineering)

Unit

Mar del Plata Academic Unit *(Buenos Aires)* (Environmental Engineering; Fishery; Marine Engineering)

History: Founded 1948 as Universidad Obrera Nacional. Acquired present status and title 1959.

Academic Year: February to November (February-July; August-November)

Admission Requirements: Secondary school certificate (bachillerato)

Main Language(s) of Instruction: Spanish

Degrees and Diplomas: *Licenciatura*: **Agricultural Management; Industrial Management.** *Especialización*: **Aeronautical and Aerospace Engineering; Civil Engineering; Computer Science; Electrical and Electronic Engineering; Industrial Engineering; Information Sciences; Mechanical Engineering; Metallurgical Engineering; Physical Engineering; Railway Transport.** *Maestría*: **Business Administration; Computer Engineering; Environmental Engineering; Food Science; Higher Education Teacher Training; Medicine; Sound Engineering (Acoustics).** *Doctorado*: **Engineering; Materials Engineering.**

Student Services: Academic Counselling, Canteen, Careers Guidance, Cultural Activities, Facilities for disabled people, Health Services, Nursery Care, Social Counselling, Sports Facilities

Publications: Revista de la Universidad Tecnológica Nacional

Last Updated: 30/12/15

NATIONAL UNIVERSITY INSTITUTE OF ARTS

Universidad Nacional de las Artes (IUNA)

Azcuénaga 1129, C1115AAG Buenos Aires, Capital Federal

Tel: +54(11) 5777-1300

EMail: secretariaprivada@iuna.edu.ar

Website: http://www.iuna.edu.ar

Rectora: Sandra Daniela Torlucci EMail: rectora@iuna.edu.ar

Vicerrector: Julio César García Cánepa
EMail: vicerrector@iuna.edu.ar

Secretaria de Asuntos Académicos: Yamila Volnovich
EMail: rectorado.academica@iuna.edu.ar

Area

Art Criticism; **Folklore** (Dance; Folklore); **Multimedia** (Multimedia); **Teacher Training** (Teacher Training)

Department

Audiovisual Arts (Cinema and Television); **Dance** *(María Ruanova)* (Dance; Folklore); **Drama** *(Antonio Cunill Cabanellas)* (Theatre); **Music and Sound** *(Carlos López Buchardo)* (Music; Music Education; Music Theory and Composition; Musical Instruments; Singing); **Visual Arts** *(Prilidiano Pueyrredón)* (Ceramic Art; Design; Painting and Drawing; Sculpture; Visual Arts)

History: Founded 1996.

Admission Requirements: Secondary school certificate and other minimum requirements

Main Language(s) of Instruction: Spanish

Accrediting Agency: Ministerio de Educación, Ciencia y Tecnología; Comisión Nacional de Evaluación y Acreditación Universitaria

Degrees and Diplomas: *Licenciatura*: **Dance; Folklore; Multimedia; Music; Theatre; Visual Arts.** *Especialización*: **Art Management; Art Therapy; Dance; Multimedia; Theatre; Visual Arts.** *Maestría*: **Dance; Theatre; Visual Arts.** *Doctorado*: **Fine Arts.**

Student Services: Canteen

Last Updated: 26/08/15

NATIONAL UNIVERSITY OF AVELLANEDA

Universidad Nacional de Avellaneda (UNDAV)

España 350 esq. Colón, Buenos Aires

Tel: +54(11) 4229-2400

EMail: info@undav.edu.ar

Website: http://www.undav.edu.ar

Rector: Jorge Fabián Calzoni EMail: rectorado@undav.edu.ar

Secretaria Académica: Julia Denazis
EMail: secacad@undav.edu.ar

Department

Communication and Information Technology *(Transversal)* (Computer Engineering; Journalism); **Culture and Art** (Art Management; History; Museum Studies; Visual Arts); **Environmental Sciences and Tourism** (Architecture; Environmental Studies; Tourism); **Health and Community Development** *(Transversal)*

(Law; Nursing); **Physical Education, Sport and Recreation** (Physical Education; Sports); **Production and Work** (Business Administration; Industrial Design; Materials Engineering)

History: Founded 2009.

Degrees and Diplomas: *Licenciatura*: **Art Management; Business Administration; Environmental Management; History; Journalism; Museum Studies; Physical Education; Sports; Tourism; Visual Arts.** *Maestría*: **Architecture; Computer Engineering; Materials Engineering; Physical Education.**

Student Services: Library

Last Updated: 28/08/15

NATIONAL UNIVERSITY OF CATAMARCA

Universidad Nacional de Catamarca (UNCA)

Esquiú 612, 4700 San Fernando del Valle de Catamarca, Catamarca

Tel: +54(3833) 424-099

EMail: protocolo@unca.edu.ar

Website: http://www.unca.edu.ar

Rector: Flavio Sergio Fama

Secretaria Académica y de Posgrado: Raúl Edgardo Caro
EMail: rcaro@unca.edu.ar

Faculty

Agriculture (Agricultural Engineering; Agriculture; Landscape Architecture); **Economics and Administration** (Accountancy; Administration; Economics); **Exact and Natural Sciences** (Biology; Chemistry; Environmental Studies; Mathematics; Natural Sciences; Physics; Technology); **Health Sciences** (Health Sciences; Nursing; Nutrition; Physical Education; Public Health); **Humanities** (Arts and Humanities; Educational Sciences; English; French; Geography; History; Literature; Philosophy; Social Work; Teacher Training); **Law** (Law); **Technology and Applied Sciences** (Electrical Engineering; Geology; Mining Engineering; Natural Sciences; Technology)

School

Archaeology (Archaeology)

History: Founded 1972. An autonomous State institution.

Academic Year: March to November

Admission Requirements: Secondary school certificate (bachillerato) or equivalent

Main Language(s) of Instruction: Spanish

Degrees and Diplomas: *Diploma de Técnico Superior*: **Administration; Haematology; Nursing.** *Licenciatura*: **Arts and Humanities; Biology; Chemistry; Education; English; French; Geography; Geology; History; Mathematics; Nursing; Philosophy; Physics.** *Especialización*: **Education; Engineering; Environmental Management; Finance; Social Sciences; Telecommunications Engineering.** *Maestría*: **Agriculture; Environmental Management; Public Health.** *Doctorado*: **Biology; Chemistry; Computer Science; Cultural Studies; Education; Environmental Studies; Literature; Mathematics; Modern Languages; Physics; Social Studies.**

Student Services: Library

Last Updated: 01/09/15

NATIONAL UNIVERSITY OF CHACO AUSTRAL

Universidad Nacional del Chaco Austral (UNCAUS)

Cmte. Fernández 755, Sáenz Peña, Chaco

Tel: +54(364) 442-0137

Website: www.uncaus.edu.ar

Rector: Walter Gustavo Lopez EMail: rector@uncaus.edu.ar

Secretario Académico: Daniel Leguiza
EMail: academica@uncaus.edu.ar

Department

Basic and Appled Sciences (Biotechnology; Chemical Engineering; Chemistry; Computer Engineering; Food Technology; Industrial Engineering; Mathematics; Nutrition; Optometry; Pharmacy); **Social and Human Sciences** (Accountancy; Administration; Chemistry; Environmental Studies; Mathematics Education; Physics)

Degrees and Diplomas: *Licenciatura*; *Especialización*; *Maestría*; *Doctorado*: **Food Technology; Pharmacy.**

Last Updated: 03/09/15

NATIONAL UNIVERSITY OF CHILECITO

Universidad Nacional de Chilecito (UNDEC)

9 de Julio 22, 5333 Chilecito, La Rioja

Tel: +54(3825) 42-2631

EMail: infoinstitucional@undec.edu.ar

Website: http://www.undec.edu.ar

Rector: Norberto Raúl Caminoa EMail: ncaminoa@undec.edu.ar

Secretario Gestion Académica: Jorge Arias
EMail: jarias@undec.edu.ar

Department

Exact, Physical and Natural Sciences (Agricultural Engineering; Agronomy; Biology; Systems Analysis); **Social, Legal and Economic Sciences** (Economics; Law; Social Sciences)

History: Founded 2003.

Main Language(s) of Instruction: Spanish

Degrees and Diplomas: *Licenciatura*. Also posgrado in social communication

Last Updated: 01/09/15

NATIONAL UNIVERSITY OF COMAHUE

Universidad Nacional del Comahue (UNCOMA)

Buenos Aires 1400, 8300 Neuquén, Neuquén

Tel: +54(299) 449-0300

EMail: secretaria.academica@central.uncoma.edu.ar

Website: http://www.uncoma.edu.ar

Rector: Gustavo Crisafuli (2014-)
EMail: rectorado@central.uncoma.edu.ar

Secretaria Académica: María Alejandra Minelli
Tel: +54(299) 449-0356
EMail: secretaria.academica@central.uncoma.edu.ar

Faculty

Agriculture *(Cinco Saltos)* (Agricultural Engineering; Agriculture; Animal Husbandry; Biotechnology; Water Science); **Computer Science** (Computer Science); **Economics and Administration** (Administration; Economics); **Educational Sciences** *(Cipoletti)* (Education; Pedagogy; Psychology); **Engineering** (Chemical Engineering; Chemistry; Civil Engineering; Electrical and Electronic Engineering; Engineering; Mechanical Engineering; Mining Engineering; Petroleum and Gas Engineering; Physics); **Environmental and Health Sciences** (Environmental Studies; Health Sciences); **Humanities** (Arts and Humanities; Geography; History; Literature; Philosophy); **Languages** *(General Roca)* (English; Modern Languages; Translation and Interpretation); **Law and Social Sciences** *(General Roca)* (Law; Social and Community Services; Social Sciences; Sociology); **Medicine** *(Cipolletti)* (Medical Technology; Medicine); **Tourism** (Leisure Studies; Tourism)

Institute

Marine Biology and Fisheries *(San Antonio Oeste)* (Fishery; Marine Biology)

History: Founded 1965 as Universidad del Neuquén, acquired present status 1972.

Academic Year: March to December (March-July; August-December)

Admission Requirements: Secondary school certificate (bachillerato)

Fees: None for undergraduate studies

Main Language(s) of Instruction: Spanish

Accrediting Agency: CONEAU

Degrees and Diplomas: *Licenciatura*; *Especialización*; *Maestría*

Student Services: Academic Counselling, Canteen, Careers Guidance, Cultural Activities, Facilities for disabled people, Health Services, Language Laboratory, Social Counselling, Sports Facilities

Last Updated: 15/12/15

ATLANTIC ZONE REGIONAL CENTRE

CENTRO UNIVERSITARIO REGIONAL 'ZONA ATLÁNTICA' (CURZA)

Monseñor Esandi y Ayacucho, 8500 Viedma, Río Negro
Tel: +54(2920) 42-2921
Fax: +54(2920) 42-3198
EMail: curza@uncoma.edu.ar
Website: http://curza.net

Directora administrativa: Irma Guerra

Secretaria Académica: Constanza Ginestet

Programme

Nursing (Nursing)

Department

Agricultural Management (Agricultural Management; Business Administration); **Agricultural Production Technology** (Agricultural Engineering); **Language, Literature and Communication** (Communication Studies; Literature; Modern Languages); **Political Science** (Political Sciences); **Psychopedagogy** (Educational Psychology); **Public Administration** (Public Administration); **Science and Technology** (Computer Science; Software Engineering)

Degrees and Diplomas: *Licenciatura*; *Especialización*

Student Services: Library

BARILOCHE REGIONAL UNIVERSITY CENTRE

CENTRO REGIONAL UNIVERSITARIO 'BARILOCHE' (CRUB)

Quintral s/n 1250, Barrio Jardín Botánico, 8400 San Carlos de Bariloche, Río Negro
Tel: +54(2944) 42-3374
Fax: +54(2944) 42-2111
Website: http://crubweb.uncoma.edu.ar

Decano: Víctor Humberto Báez

Secretaria Académica: María Inés Sánchez
EMail: academica@crub.uncoma.edu.ar

Programme

Biological Sciences (Biology); **Engineering** (Chemical Engineering; Civil Engineering; Electrical and Electronic Engineering; Mechanical Engineering; Petroleum and Gas Engineering); **History** (History); **Mathematics** (Mathematics); **Nursing** (Nursing)

Main Language(s) of Instruction: Spanish

Degrees and Diplomas: *Licenciatura*; *Especialización*; *Maestría*; *Doctorado*: **Biology.**

Student Services: Library

SAN MARTÍN DE LOS ANDES BRANCH

ASENTAMIENTO UNIVERSITARIO 'SAN MARTÍN DE LOS ANDES' (AUSMA)

Pasaje de la Paz 235, 8370 San Martín de Los Andes, Neuquén
Tel: +54(2972) 42-7618
Fax: +54(2972) 42-7164
EMail: ausma@smandes.com.ar
Website: http://ausmaweb.uncoma.edu.ar

Presidente: Virginia Fontana

Programme

Forestry Engineering (Forestry); **Tourism** (Tourism)

History: Founded 1975 as Centro Universitario Regional de San Martín de los Andes. Acquired present status and title 1985.

Main Language(s) of Instruction: Spanish

Degrees and Diplomas: *Diploma de Técnico Superior*

ZAPALA BRANCH

ASENTAMIENTO UNIVERSITARIO 'ZAPALA' (AUZA)

Avenida 12 de Julio y Rahue, 8340 Zapala, Neuquén
Tel: +54(2942) 42-1574
Fax: +54(2942) 42-1847
EMail: secretaria.academica@auza.uncoma.edu.ar
Website: http://auzaweb.uncoma.edu.ar

Directora: Mónica Luciana Rueda

Programme

Mining Engineering (Mining Engineering); **Plant Science** (Plant Pathology)

History: Founded 1975.

Main Language(s) of Instruction: Spanish

Degrees and Diplomas: *Licenciatura*

NATIONAL UNIVERSITY OF CÓRDOBA

Universidad Nacional de Córdoba (UNC)

Haya de la Torre s/n, Ciudad Unversitaria, Pabellón Argentina, 5000 Córdoba, Córdoba
Tel: +54(351) 535-3751
EMail: internacionales@pri.unc.edu.ar
Website: www.unc.edu.ar

Rector: Francisco Antonio Tamarit EMail: rector@unc.edu.ar

Vicerrector: Silvia Noemi Barei
EMail: sbarei@vicerrectorado.unc.edu.ar

Secretaria de Asuntos Académicos: Ana María Alderete
EMail: secretarioacad@saa.unc.edu.ar

International Relations: Guillermo Badenes, Head of ORI (2)
Tel: +543515353751 EMail: guillermobadenes@pri.unc.edu.ar

Faculty

Agriculture (Agriculture); **Architecture, Town Planning, and Design** (Architecture; Design; Town Planning); **Arts** (Fine Arts; Performing Arts); **Chemistry** (Chemistry); **Dentistry** (Dentistry); **Economics** (Accountancy; Economics; Management); **Exact, Physical and Natural Sciences** (Natural Sciences; Physics); **Languages** (Modern Languages); **Law and Social Sciences** (Information Sciences; Law; Social Welfare); **Mathematics, Astronomy, and Physics** (Astronomy and Space Science; Mathematics; Physics); **Medical Sciences** (Ergotherapy; Medical Technology; Medicine; Nursing; Nutrition; Physical Therapy; Speech Therapy and Audiology); **Philosophy and Humanities** (Archiving; Education; History; Library Science; Philosophy); **Psychology** (Psychology)

School

Archives (Archiving); **Arts** (Fine Arts); **Audiology** (Speech Therapy and Audiology); **Educational Sciences** (Educational Sciences); **History** (History); **Information Sciences** (Information Sciences); **Kinesiology and Physical Therapy** (Physical Therapy); **Letters** (Arts and Humanities); **Library Science** (Library Science); **Medical Technology** (Medical Technology); **Nursing** (Nursing); **Nutrition** (Nutrition); **Philosophy** (Philosophy); **Public Health** (Public Health); **Social Work** (Social Work)

Centre

Microscope Electronics (Microelectronics)

History: Founded 1613.

Academic Year: February to December (February-July; August-December)

Main Language(s) of Instruction: Spanish

Accrediting Agency: CONEAU Ministerio de Educación de la Nación

Degrees and Diplomas: *Bachillerato*: **Accountancy; Aeronautical and Aerospace Engineering; Agricultural Engineering; Architecture and Planning; Educational Administration; Industrial Design.** *Diploma de Técnico Superior*: **Electrical Engineering; Floriculture; Landscape Architecture; Mechanical Engineering.** *Licenciatura*: **Administration; Business Education; Cinema and Television; Conducting; Finance; Home Economics Education; Music Theory and Composition; Musical Instruments; Painting and Drawing; Sculpture; Secondary Education; Teacher Trainers Education; Theatre; Visual Arts.**

Student Services: Academic Counselling, Canteen, Careers Guidance, Cultural Activities, Facilities for disabled people, Foreign Studies Centre, Health Services, IT Centre, Language Laboratory, Library, Nursery Care, Sports Facilities, eLibrary

Publications: Actualidad Económica; Agriscientia; Anuario de Investigaciones de la Facultad de Psicología; Anuario de la Escuela de Historia Virtual; Anuarios Estadísticos de la UNC; Apertura; Astrolabio; Bitácora Digital; Boletín de la Sociedad Argentina de

Botánica; Cardinalis; Cuadernos de Educación; Cuadernos de Historia. Serie Economía y Sociedad; E+E: Estudios de Extensión en Humanidades; El Cactus, revista de Comunicación; Estudios; Estudios de Derecho Empresario; Ética&Cine Journal; ExT: Revista de Extensión de la UNC; Huellas: revista de vinculación con la comunidad de la Facultad de Odontología; Integración y Conocimiento; Intersticios de la política y la cultura. Intervenciones latinoamericanas; Miscelánea. Academia Nacional de Ciencias; Nombres: Revista de Filosofía; Prácticas y Residencias en Formación Docente: memorias, experiencias y horizontes; Pymes, Innovación y Desarrollo; RECIAL Revista del CIFFyH Área Letras; RECORDIP; Revista Académica PROCOAS-AUGM; Revista Argentina de Ciencias del Comportamiento; Revista de Economía y Estadística; Revista de Educación Matemática; Revista de Enseñanza de la Física; Revista de la Facultad de Ciencias Exactas, Físicas y Naturales; Revista de la Facultad de Ciencias Médicas; Revista de la Facultad de Derecho; Revista de la Red Intercátedras de Historia de América Latina Contemporánea Segunda Época; Revista de la Universidad Nacional de Córdoba; Revista de Salud Pública; Revista de Vivienda y Ciudad; Revista del Museo de Antropología; REVISTA Deodoro; Revista Digital de Políticas Lingüísticas (RDPL); Revista Evaluar; REVISTA TESIS Facultad de Psicología; TOMA UNO; V Jornadas de la RedVITEC: 10 años de experiencias de cooperación: Universidad – Entorno Socioproductivo – Estado; Virtualidad, Educación y Ciencia

Academic Staff *2014*	MEN	WOMEN	**TOTAL**
FULL-TIME	616	745	**1,361**
PART-TIME	4,216	3,923	**8,139**
STAFF WITH DOCTORATE			
FULL-TIME	943	899	**1,842**
Student Numbers *2014*			
All (Foreign included)	45,615	75,173	**120,788**
FOREIGN ONLY	959	1,215	**2,174**

Part-time students, –

Last Updated: 18/08/15

NATIONAL UNIVERSITY OF CUYO

Universidad Nacional de Cuyo (UNCUYO)

Centro Universitario, M5500JMA Mendoza, Mendoza

Tel: +54(261) 413-5000

EMail: cicun@uncu.edu.ar

Website: http://www.uncu.edu.ar

Rector: Daniel Ricardo Pizzi EMail: rectorpizzi@uncu.edu.ar

Secretaria Académica: Adiana Aída García EMail: adrianagarcia@uncu.edu.ar

Vicerrector: Jorge Horacio Barón EMail: vicerrector@uncu.edu.ar

Faculty

Agriculture *(Chacras de Coria)* (Agricultural Engineering; Agriculture; Oenology); **Art and Design** (Ceramic Art; Design; Fine Arts; Music; Theatre; Visual Arts); **Dentistry** (Dentistry); **Economics** (Accountancy; Administration; Economics; Statistics); **Elementary and Special Education** (Curriculum; Educational Administration; Physical Education; Primary Education; Special Education; Speech Therapy and Audiology); **Engineering** *(Mendoza)* (Civil Engineering; Engineering; Industrial Engineering; Petroleum and Gas Engineering); **Law** (Law); **Medical Sciences** (Cardiology; Community Health; Medical Auxiliaries; Medicine; Nursing; Pneumology; Psychiatry and Mental Health; Public Health); **Philosophy and Literature** (English; French; Geography; History; Philosophy; Science Education); **Political and Social Sciences** (Political Sciences; Public Administration; Social Sciences; Social Work; Sociology); **Science Applied to Industry** *(San Rafael)* (Analytical Chemistry; Chemical Engineering; Food Technology; Industrial Chemistry; Industrial Engineering)

Institute

Public Safety (Civil Security)

Further Information: Also Nuclear Medicine School Foundation

History: Founded 1939 as a State institution to serve the three provinces of Cuyo.

Academic Year: April to November (April-July; August-November)

Admission Requirements: Secondary school certificate (bachillerato) and entrance examination

Main Language(s) of Instruction: Spanish

Degrees and Diplomas: *Licenciatura*: **Administration; Arts and Humanities; Chemistry; Economics; Education; English; French; Geography; History; Literature; Mathematics; Music; Painting and Drawing; Philosophy; Physics; Psychology; Public Administration; Sculpture; Social Sciences; Sociology.** *Especialización*; *Maestría*: **Biological and Life Sciences; International Business; Water Science.** *Doctorado*: **Agronomy; Biology; Dentistry; Economics; Educational Sciences; Engineering; Geography; History; Industrial Engineering; Law; Literature; Medicine; Nuclear Engineering; Philosophy; Physics; Social Sciences.**

Student Services: Library

Publications: Acta Cuyana de Ingeniería; Anales; Anales de Arqueología y Etnología; Anales del Instituto de Investigaciones Psicopedagógicas; Anales del Instituto de Lingüística; Artes Plásticas; Boletín de Estudios Geográficos: Serie I, Fuentes Documentales; Serie III Ensayos (History); Boletín de Estudios Germánicos; Boletín de Estudios Políticos y Sociales; Cuadernos de Filosofía; Cuadernos de Historia del Arte; Cuadernos de la Escuela de Pedagogía; Cuadernos de Psiquiatría; Cuadernos del Instituto de Investigaciones Políticas y Sociales; Filosofía; Noticias de Ingeniería de Petróleos; Nuestro Mundo; Revista de Estudios Clásicos; Revista de Historia Americana y Argentina; Revista de la Facultad de Ciencias Agrarias; Revista de la Facultad de Ciencias Económicas; Revista de Literaturas Modernas; Serie de Cuadernos

Last Updated: 01/09/15

NATIONAL UNIVERSITY OF ENTRE RÍOS

Universidad Nacional de Entre Ríos (UNER)

Eva Perón 24, 3260 Concepción del Uruguay, Entre Ríos

Tel: +54(3442) 42-1500

Fax: +54(3442) 42-1563

EMail: sprivada@rect.uner.edu.ar

Website: http://www.uner.edu.ar

Rector: Jorge Amado Gerard EMail: rector@uner.edu.ar

Vicerrectora: Cristina Benintende EMail: vicerrectora@uner.edu.ar

Secretaria Académica: Roxana Gabriela Puig EMail: sacademica@uner.edu.ar

Faculty

Administration *(Concordia)* (Accountancy; Administration; Tourism); **Agriculture** *(Oro Verde)* (Agricultural Engineering; Agriculture); **Bromatology** *(Gualeguaychú)* (Chemistry; Food Science); **Economics** *(Paraná)* (Accountancy; Economics); **Educational Sciences** *(Paraná)* (Education); **Engineering** *(Oro Verde)* (Bioengineering; Biomedical Engineering); **Food Science** *(Concordia)* (Food Technology); **Health Sciences** (Health Sciences; Nursing; Physical Therapy); **Social Work** *(Paraná)* (Social Work)

Further Information: Also branches in Paraná, Concordia and Gualeguaychú

History: Founded 1973. An autonomous State institution.

Academic Year: April to November (April-July; August-November)

Admission Requirements: Secondary school certificate (bachillerato) or equivalent

Main Language(s) of Instruction: Spanish

Degrees and Diplomas: *Licenciatura*: **Accountancy; Administration; Education; Food Science; Information Sciences.** *Especialización*; *Maestría*; *Doctorado*: **Education; Engineering; Social Sciences.**

Student Services: Health Services, Library, Sports Facilities

Last Updated: 01/09/15

NATIONAL UNIVERSITY OF FORMOSA

Universidad Nacional de Formosa (UNAF)

Don Bosco 1082, 3600 Formosa, Formosa

Tel: +54(3717) 43-0485

Fax: +54(3717) 43-0485

EMail: rectorado@unf.edu.ar

Website: http://www.unf.edu.ar

Rector: Martín René Romano EMail: rectorado@unf.edu.ar

Vicerrector: Roque Fabian Silguero Tel: +54(3717) 42-3930 EMail: rsilguero@arnet.com.ar

Secretaria General Académica: Ofelia Inés Fantin
EMail: secadem@unf.edu.ar

Faculty

Business, Administration and Economics (Business Administration; Business and Commerce; Economics); **Health Sciences** (Health Sciences; Laboratory Techniques; Nursing; Nutrition; Radiology); **Humanities** (Arts and Humanities; Educational Psychology; Geography; Literature); **Natural Resources** (Agricultural Business; Civil Engineering; Forestry; Natural Resources; Zoology); **Production and Environment** (Environmental Studies; Tourism)

History: An autonomous State institution since 1988.

Academic Year: February to December

Admission Requirements: Secondary school certificate (Bachillerato)

Fees: None

Main Language(s) of Instruction: Spanish

Degrees and Diplomas: *Licenciatura*: **Food Science; Gynaecology and Obstetrics; International Business; Natural Sciences; Nursing; Nutrition.** *Especialización*: **Curriculum; Pedagogy.** *Maestría*: **Forestry; Medicine.**

Student Services: Academic Counselling, Canteen, Health Services, Social Counselling, Sports Facilities

Publications: Revista de Ciencia y Tecnología de la Universidad Nacional De Formosa; Revista de Geografía; Revista de la Facultad de Ciencias de la Salud; Revista de la Facultad de Recursos Naturales - Serie Forestal

Last Updated: 01/09/15

NATIONAL UNIVERSITY OF GENERAL SAN MARTÍN

Universidad Nacional de General San Martín (UNSAM)

Campus Miguelete, Edificio de Gobierno: 25 de Mayo y Francia, 1650 San Martín, Buenos Aires
Tel: +54(11) 4006-1500
Fax: +54(11) 4006-1511
EMail: investigacion@unsam.edu.ar
Website: http://www.unsam.edu.ar

Rector: Carlos Rafael Ruta (2006-)
EMail: rectorado@unsam.edu.ar

Vicerrector: Daniel Di Gregorio
EMail: vicerrectorado@unsam.edu.ar

School

Economics and Business *(San Martín)* (Business and Commerce; Economics); **Humanities** *(San Martín)* (Arts and Humanities; Education; Museum Studies; Performing Arts; Social Sciences); **Political Science and Government** *(Buenos Aires)* (Government; Political Sciences); **Science and Technology** *(Villa Ballester)* (Biomedical Engineering; Computer Networks; Computer Science; Natural Sciences; Radiology; Technology)

Institute

Arts *(Mauricio Kagel)* (Dance; Film; Music; Painting and Drawing; Performing Arts; Photography); **Biotechnological Research** *(Migueletes)* (Biotechnology); **Higher Social Studies** *(Buenos Aires)* (Social Sciences); **Industrial Quality** *(INCALIN)* (Safety Engineering); **Law** (Law); **Nuclear Technology** *(Dan Beninson)* (Nuclear Engineering); **Rehabilitation and Movement Sciences** *(Belgrano, Buenos Aires)* (Rehabilitation and Therapy); **Technology** *(Sabato)* (Materials Engineering)

History: Founded 1992, acquired present status 1994. Previously known as National University General de San Martín (Universidad Nacional de General San Martín)

Academic Year: March to December

Admission Requirements: Secondary school certificate (bachillerato)

Main Language(s) of Instruction: Spanish

Accrediting Agency: Consejo Nacional de Evaluación y Acreditación Universitaria (CONEAU)

Degrees and Diplomas: *Licenciatura*; *Especialización*: **Education; Environmental Studies; Family Studies; International Relations; Latin American Studies.** *Maestría*: **Biotechnology; Education; Environmental Studies; Family Studies; International Relations; Latin American Studies; Technology.** *Doctorado*: **Anthropology; Biotechnology; Chemistry; Education; Engineering; History; Microbiology; Molecular Biology; Philosophy; Political Sciences; Sociology; Technology.**

Student Services: Academic Counselling, Careers Guidance, Cultural Activities, Language Laboratory, Library, Social Counselling, Sports Facilities

Publications: Nómada

Last Updated: 01/09/15

NATIONAL UNIVERSITY OF JOSÉ CLEMENTE PAZ

Universidad Nacional de José Clemente Paz (UNPAZ)

Avenida Leandro N. Alem 4731, José C. Paz, Buenos Aires
EMail: rectorado@unpaz.edu.ar
Website: www.unpaz.edu.ar

Rector: Héctor Hugo Trinchero

Secretario Académico: Gonzalo Kodelia
EMail: secretariaacademica@unpaz.edu.ar

Programme

Administration (Administration); **History** (History); **Law** (Law); **Nursing** (Nursing); **Physical Education** (Physical Education); **Social Work** (Social Work); **Surgical Instruments** (Medical Technology)

History: Founded 2009.

Main Language(s) of Instruction: Spanish

Degrees and Diplomas: *Licenciatura*

Last Updated: 01/09/15

NATIONAL UNIVERSITY OF JUJUY

Universidad Nacional de Jujuy (UNJU)

Avenida Bolivia N° 1239, 4600 San Salvador de Jujuy, Jujuy
Tel: +54(388) 422-1502
Fax: +54(388) 422-1507
EMail: seu@unju.edu.ar
Website: http://www.unju.edu.ar

Rector: Rodolfo Alejandro Tecchi EMail: rtecchi@unju.edu.ar

Vicerrector: Jorge Eugenio Griot
Tel: +54(388) 4221-501 EMail: vicerrector@unju.edu.ar

Faculty

Agriculture (Agricultural Engineering; Agronomy; Biology); **Economics** (Accountancy; Administration; Economics); **Engineering** (Chemical Engineering; Computer Engineering; Engineering; Food Technology; Geology; Industrial Engineering; Mining Engineering); **Humanities and Social Sciences** (Anthropology; Arts and Humanities; Communication Studies; Education; Health Education; History; Social Sciences; Social Work)

History: Founded 1972 as provincial University, acquired present status and title 1974. An autonomous State institution.

Academic Year: February to December (February-June; August-December)

Admission Requirements: Secondary school certificate (bachillerato) or equivalent

Main Language(s) of Instruction: Spanish

Degrees and Diplomas: *Diploma de Técnico Superior*; *Licenciatura*: **Anthropology; Arts and Humanities; Chemistry; Educational Sciences.** *Especialización*; *Maestría*; *Doctorado*: **Food Technology; Social Sciences.**

Student Services: Library

Publications: Didactic Notes of the School of Agriculture; Geological Sciences Review; Revista XUXUY

Publishing House: Secretaría de Extensión Universitaria - Editorial UNJU

Last Updated: 01/09/15

NATIONAL UNIVERSITY OF LA MATANZA

Universidad Nacional de La Matanza (UNLAM)
Florencio Varela 1903, B 1754 JEC San Justo, Buenos Aires
Tel: +54(11) 4651-8339
Fax: +54(11) 4480-8962
EMail: rectorado@unlam.edu.ar
Website: http://www.unlam.edu.ar

Rector: Daniel Eduardo Martínez (1999-)
EMail: rectorado@unlam.edu.ar

Vicerrector: Victor René Nicoletti EMail: nicoletti@unlam.edu.ar

Secretario Académico: Gustavo H Duek
EMail: gduek@unlam.edu.ar

School

Continuing Education (Applied Mathematics; Educational Administration; Environmental Management; History; Insurance; International Business; Literature; Marketing; Modern Languages; Nursing; Physical Education); **Postgraduate Studies** (Banking; Communication Studies; Economics; Environmental Management; Finance; Higher Education; Information Technology; International Economics; International Relations; Justice Administration; Law; Psychiatry and Mental Health; Social Sciences)

Department

Economics (Accountancy; Administration; Economics; International Business); **Engineering and Technological Research** (Computer Engineering; Electronic Engineering; Engineering; Industrial Engineering; Technology); **Health Sciences** (Medicine; Nursing; Nutrition; Physical Therapy); **Humanities and Social Sciences** (Arts and Humanities; Labour and Industrial Relations; Physical Education; Social Sciences; Social Work); **Law and Political Science** (Law; Political Sciences; Private Law; Public Law)

History: An autonomous State institution since 1989.

Academic Year: February to December

Admission Requirements: Secondary school certificate (bachillerato) or equivalent and admission examination

Fees: None

Main Language(s) of Instruction: Spanish

Degrees and Diplomas: *Especialización*: **Agriculture; Banking; Business Administration; Health Sciences; Higher Education Teacher Training; Law; Service Trades.** *Maestría*: **Computer Science; Economics; Education; Engineering Drawing and Design; Environmental Engineering; Health Sciences; International Economics; Law; Social Sciences.** *Doctorado*: **Economics; Law.**

Student Services: Academic Counselling, Canteen, Careers Guidance, Cultural Activities, Facilities for disabled people, Health Services, Language Laboratory, Social Counselling, Sports Facilities

Academic Staff *2012-2013*	**TOTAL**
FULL-TIME	**710**
PART-TIME	**1,627**
STAFF WITH DOCTORATE	
FULL-TIME	**57**
Student Numbers *2012-2013*	
All (Foreign included)	**36,126**

Last Updated: 30/12/15

NATIONAL UNIVERSITY OF LA PAMPA

Universidad Nacional de La Pampa (UNLPAM)
Coronel Gil 353 3°, 6300 Santa Rosa, La Pampa
Tel: +54(2954) 451600
Fax: +54(2954) 433408
EMail: info@unlpam.edu.ar
Website: http://www.unlpam.edu.ar

Rector: Sergio Aldo Baudino EMail: rector1@unlpam.edu.ar

Secretaria Académica: Maria Esther Folco
EMail: secacademica@unlpam.edu.ar

Faculty

Agronomy (Agricultural Engineering; Agricultural Management; Agriculture; Agronomy; Dairy); **Economics and Law** (Accountancy; Law); **Engineering** (Computer Engineering; Electronic Engineering; Industrial Engineering; Mechanical Engineering); **Exact and Natural Sciences** (Biological and Life Sciences; Chemistry; Computer Science; Geology; Mathematics; Natural Resources; Physics); **Human Sciences** (Education; English; Geography; History; Humanities and Social Science Education; Physical Education; Social Work); **Veterinary Science** *(General Pico)* (Veterinary Science)

Institute

Labour Studies (Labour and Industrial Relations; Labour Law)

Further Information: Branch in General Pico

History: Founded 1958 as a provincial University, became National University 1973.

Academic Year: March to November (March-July; August-November)

Admission Requirements: Secondary school certificate (bachillerato) or equivalent

Main Language(s) of Instruction: Spanish

Degrees and Diplomas: *Licenciatura*: **Educational Sciences; English; Geography; History; Literature; Modern Languages.** *Especialización*; *Maestría*: **Business Administration; Criminal Law; Water Science.**

Student Services: Academic Counselling, Canteen, Health Services, Language Laboratory, Sports Facilities

Publications: Contexto Universitario

Last Updated: 01/09/15

NATIONAL UNIVERSITY OF LA PLATA

Universidad Nacional de La Plata (UNLP)
Calle 7 N° 776, 1900 La Plata, Buenos Aires
Tel: +54(221) 423-6804
Fax: +54(221) 425-6967
EMail: privada@presi.unlp.edu.ar
Website: http://www.unlp.edu.ar

Presidente: Raúl Anibal Perdomo
EMail: secretaria.privada@presi.unlp.edu.ar

Secretario General: Leonardo González
EMail: secretaria.general@presi.unlp.edu.ar

Faculty

Agriculture and Forestry (Agricultural Engineering; Agriculture; Forestry); **Architecture and Town Planning** (Architecture; Town Planning); **Astronomy and Geophysics** (Astronomy and Space Science; Geophysics); **Computer Science** (Computer Networks; Computer Science; Software Engineering); **Dentistry** (Dentistry); **Economics** (Accountancy; Administration; Economics; Tourism); **Engineering** (Aeronautical and Aerospace Engineering; Chemical Engineering; Civil Engineering; Electrical and Electronic Engineering; Hydraulic Engineering; Metallurgical Engineering; Telecommunications Engineering); **Exact Sciences** (Biotechnology; Chemistry; Mathematics; Molecular Biology; Optics; Optometry; Physics); **Fine Arts** (Conducting; Fine Arts; Industrial Design; Music Theory and Composition; Musical Instruments; Theatre; Visual Arts); **Humanities and Education** (Arts and Humanities; Biology; Education; Educational Sciences; English; Geography; History; Library Science; Literature; Philosophy; Physical Education; Psychology; Sociology); **Journalism and Social Communication** (Communication Studies; Journalism); **Law and Social Sciences** (Law; Social Sciences); **Medical Sciences** (Gynaecology and Obstetrics; Medicine; Nursing; Speech Therapy and Audiology); **Natural Sciences** (Anthropology; Biology; Ecology; Geology; Natural Sciences; Paleontology); **Social Work** (Social Work); **Veterinary Science** (Veterinary Science)

Further Information: Also 43 research laboratories, institutes and regional university centres of Junín, San Carlos de Bariloche, Viedma and Río Gallegos

History: Founded 1897 by law as a provincial University with faculties of Law, Chemistry, Medicine, and Physical and Mathematical Sciences. Reorganized 1906 and became a National University.

Academic Year: March to November (March-June; June-September; September-November)

Admission Requirements: Secondary school certificate (bachillerato) or equivalent. Foreign qualifications are recognized if covered by formal international agreements

Main Language(s) of Instruction: Spanish

Degrees and Diplomas: *Licenciatura*: **Administration; Arts and Humanities; Astronomy and Space Science; Biochemistry; Biology; Chemistry; Economics; Education; Geography; Geology; Geophysics; History; Library Science; Mathematics; Music; Painting and Drawing; Pharmacy; Philosophy; Physics; Sculpture; Zoology.** *Especialización*; *Maestría*; *Doctorado*: **Architecture; Arts and Humanities; Astronomy and Space Science; Biochemistry; Chemistry; Dentistry; Economics; Education; Geology; Geophysics; History; Law; Mathematics; Medicine; Natural Sciences; Pharmacy; Philosophy; Physics; Social Sciences; Town Planning; Veterinary Science.**

Student Services: Canteen, Careers Guidance, Cultural Activities, Health Services, Library, Nursery Care, Sports Facilities

Publications: Revista de la Universidad

Publishing House: Imprenta de la Universidad

Last Updated: 02/09/15

NATIONAL UNIVERSITY OF LA RIOJA

Universidad Nacional de La Rioja (UNLAR)
Av. Dr. René Favaloro S/N, 5300 La Rioja, La Rioja
Tel: +54(3822) 457-000
Fax: +54(3822) 457-000
EMail: unlar@unlar.edu.ar
Website: http://www.unlar.edu.ar

Rector: Fabián Alejandro Calderón EMail: rector@unlar.edu.ar

Vicerrector: José Gaspanello EMail: vice@unlar.edu.ar

Department

Applied Sciences (Agricultural Engineering; Applied Chemistry; Applied Physics; Engineering; Mining Engineering; Natural Sciences); **Exact, Physical and Natural Sciences** (Mathematics; Natural Sciences); **Health and Educational Sciences** (Educational Sciences; Medicine); **Humanities** (Educational and Student Counselling; Psychology); **Social Sciences, Law and Economics** (Economics; Social Sciences)

Further Information: Branches in Chamical, Chepes, Aimogasta, Villa Unión and Catuna

History: Founded 1993 from the Universidad Provincial de La Rioja, founded 1973.

Academic Year: March to November (March-July; August-November)

Admission Requirements: Secondary school certificate (bachillerato) and entrance examination

Fees: None

Main Language(s) of Instruction: Spanish, French, English

Accrediting Agency: Organización Universitaria Interamericana (OUI); International Association of University Presidents (IAUP)

Degrees and Diplomas: *Licenciatura*: **Administration; Law; Medicine; Nursing; Teacher Training.** *Especialización*; *Doctorado*: **Agronomy; Geology; Health Sciences; Industrial Engineering.**

Student Services: Academic Counselling, Canteen, Cultural Activities, Health Services, Language Laboratory, Library, Nursery Care, Sports Facilities

Publications: UNLaR Ciencia

Last Updated: 02/09/15

NATIONAL UNIVERSITY OF LANÚS

Universidad Nacional de Lanús (UNLA)
29 de Septiembre 3901, Remedios de Escalada, 1826 Lanús, Buenos Aires
Tel: +54(11) 5533-5600
Fax: +54(11) 5533-5600
EMail: info@unla.edu.ar
Website: http://www.unla.edu.ar

Rectora: Ana María Jaramillo EMail: mfund@unla.edu.ar

Vicerrector: Nerio Neirotti EMail: nneirotti@unla.edu.ar

Department

Arts and Humanities (Arts and Humanities; Design; Industrial Design; Museum Studies; Music; Philosophy; Translation and Interpretation); **Community Health** (Community Health; Epidemiology; Nursing; Physical Education; Psychiatry and Mental Health); **Planning and Public Policy** (Government; Public Administration; Social Work; Town Planning); **Production and Technology** (Business Administration; Environmental Management; Food Technology; Labour and Industrial Relations; Leather Techniques; Tourism)

History: Founded 1995.

Academic Year: April to November (April-July; August-November)

Admission Requirements: Secondary school certificate (bachillerato) and entrance examination

Main Language(s) of Instruction: Spanish

Degrees and Diplomas: *Licenciatura*: **Business and Commerce; Civil Security; Communication Arts; Economics; Educational Administration; Educational Technology; Fine Arts; Food Science; Government; Industrial Design; Music; Nursing; Painting and Drawing; Physical Education; Radio and Television Broadcasting; Social Work; Technology; Tourism; Town Planning; Visual Arts.** *Especialización*: **Educational Research; Health Administration; Tourism.** *Maestría*: **Business Administration; Energy Engineering; Epidemiology; Ethics; Food Technology; Health Sciences.** *Doctorado*: **Community Health; Education; Human Rights; Philosophy; Psychiatry and Mental Health.**

Last Updated: 02/09/15

NATIONAL UNIVERSITY OF LOMAS DE ZAMORA

Universidad Nacional de Lomas de Zamora (UNLZ)
Camino de Cintura y Juan XXIII, 1836 Lomas de Zamora, 1836 Buenos Aires, Capital Federal
Tel: +54(11) 4282-8045
EMail: sacademica@unlz.edu.ar
Website: http://www.unlz.edu.ar

Rector: Diego Molea EMail: rector@unlz.edu.ar

Secretario Académico: Hugo Galderisi

Faculty

Agriculture (Agricultural Engineering; Agriculture; Zoology); **Economics** *(Lomas de Zamora)* (Accountancy; Administration; Economics); **Engineering** *(Lomas de Zamora)* (Industrial Engineering; Mechanical Engineering); **Law** *(Lomas de Zamora)* (Law); **Social Sciences** *(Lomas de Zamora)* (Advertising and Publicity; Education; Educational Sciences; Journalism; Labour and Industrial Relations; Literature; Public Relations; Social Sciences; Social Work)

History: Founded 1972. An autonomous State institution.

Academic Year: March to December (March-July; August-December)

Admission Requirements: Secondary school certificate (bachillerato) or equivalent

Main Language(s) of Instruction: Spanish

Degrees and Diplomas: *Licenciatura*: **Administration; Education; International Studies; Journalism; Labour and Industrial Relations; Public Relations.** *Especialización*; *Maestría*; *Doctorado*: **Industrial Engineering; Law; Mechanical Engineering.**

Student Services: Library

Last Updated: 02/09/15

NATIONAL UNIVERSITY OF LUJÁN

Universidad Nacional de Luján (UNLU)
Int. Ruta 5 y Avenida Constitución, 6700 Luján, Buenos Aires
Tel: +54(2323) 423-979
Fax: +54(2323) 42-5795
EMail: informes@unlu.edu.ar
Website: http://www.unlu.edu.ar

Rector: Osvaldo Pedro Arizio EMail: rector@mail.unlu.edu.ar

Vicerrectora: María Cristina Serafini EMail: privada@unlu.edu.ar

Department

Basic Sciences (Biology; Chemistry; Mathematics and Computer Science; Natural Sciences; Physics; Statistics); **Education** (Adult Education; Distance Education; Education; Modern Languages; Pedagogy; Psychology); **Social Sciences** (Administration; Business Administration; Economics; Geography; History; Law; Social Studies; Sociology); **Technology** (Agronomy; Food Technology; Natural Sciences; Technology)

Further Information: Regional Centres in Campana, Chivilcoy, General Sarmiento

History: Founded 1972. Acquired present status 1984. An autonomous State institution.

Academic Year: March to November

Admission Requirements: Secondary school certificate (bachillerato) or equivalent

Fees: None

Main Language(s) of Instruction: Spanish

Degrees and Diplomas: *Diploma de Técnico Superior*, *Licenciatura*: **Administration; Biology; Computer Engineering; Educational Sciences; Geography; History; Information Management; International Business.** *Especialización*; *Maestría*: **Educational Administration; Social Sciences.** *Doctorado*: **Arts and Humanities; Natural Sciences; Social Sciences.**

Student Services: Academic Counselling, Canteen, Careers Guidance, Health Services, Library, Sports Facilities

Publications: UNlu Ciencia

Last Updated: 02/09/15

NATIONAL UNIVERSITY OF MAR DEL PLATA

Universidad Nacional de Mar del Plata (UNMDP)

Diagonal Juan Bautista Alberdi 2659, B 7600 GYI Mar del Plata, Buenos Aires
Tel: +54(223) 492-1705
Fax: +54(223) 492-1711
Website: http://www.mdp.edu.ar

Rector: Francisco Antonio Morea EMail: rector@mdp.edu.ar

Vicerrector: Raúl Horacio Conde EMail: vicerect@mdp.edu.ar

Secretaria Académica: Paula A. Meschini
EMail: academica@mdp.edu.ar

Faculty

Agriculture *(Balcarce)* (Agricultural Economics; Agricultural Engineering; Agriculture; Animal Husbandry; Food Technology; Plant and Crop Protection; Soil Science; Vegetable Production); **Architecture, Town Planning and Design** (Architecture; Industrial Design; Town Planning); **Economics and Social Sciences** (Accountancy; Administration; Economics; Social Sciences; Tourism); **Engineering** (Chemical Engineering; Electrical Engineering; Electronic Engineering; Engineering; Materials Engineering; Mechanical Engineering); **Exact and Natural Sciences** (Biology; Chemistry; Mathematics; Natural Sciences; Physics); **Health Sciences and Social Work** (Health Sciences; Nursing; Occupational Therapy; Social and Community Services; Social Work); **Humanities** (Arts and Humanities; English; Geography; History; Library Science; Literature; Pedagogy; Philosophy); **Law** (Civil Law; Criminal Law; Law; Public Law); **Psychology** (Psychoanalysis; Psychology)

Further Information: Also 26 Regional Distance and Lifelong Centres

History: Founded 1961 as provincial University, acquired present status and title 1975. An autonomous State institution.

Academic Year: April to March

Admission Requirements: Secondary school certificate (bachillerato) or equivalent

Fees: For postgraduate studies

Main Language(s) of Instruction: Spanish

Degrees and Diplomas: *Diploma de Técnico Superior*: **Cultural Studies; Library Science.** *Licenciatura*: **Arts and Humanities; Biology; Economics; Geography; Mathematics; Psychology; Tourism.** *Especialización*: **Administrative Law; Animal Husbandry; Business Administration; Ethics; Fishery; Health Sciences; Higher Education; Occupational Health; Social Studies.** *Maestría*: **Agriculture; Arts and Humanities; Economics; Engineering; Political Sciences; Town Planning.** *Doctorado*: **Agriculture; Biology; Chemistry; History; Law; Literature; Mathematics; Physics; Psychology.**

Student Services: Academic Counselling, Careers Guidance, Health Services, Language Laboratory, Library, Nursery Care, Social Counselling, Sports Facilities

Publications: Revista 'Nexos'

Last Updated: 02/09/15

NATIONAL UNIVERSITY OF MISIONES

Universidad Nacional de Misiones (UNAM)

Campus Universitario, Ruta Nacional 12, Km. 7 1/2, Miguel Lanús, 3304 Posadas, Misiones
Tel: +54(3752) 48-0916
Fax: +54(3752) 48-0500
EMail: info@unam.edu.ar
Website: http://www.unam.edu.ar

Rector: Javier Gortari EMail: rector@unam.edu.ar

Secretaria General Académica: Susana Caceres
EMail: scaceres@campus.unam.edu.ar

Vicerrector: Fernando Luis Kramer
EMail: vicerrector@unam.edu.ar

Faculty

Arts and Design *(Oberá)* (Ceramic Art; Fine Arts; Graphic Design; Industrial Design; Painting and Drawing; Photography); **Economics** (Accountancy; Administration; Business Administration; Economics; Finance); **Engineering** *(Oberá)* (Civil Engineering; Electronic Engineering; Engineering; Hygiene; Industrial Engineering; Mechanical Engineering); **Exact, Natural and Chemical Sciences** *(Posadas)* (Biochemistry; Biology; Chemical Engineering; Chemistry; Food Science; Food Technology; Genetics; Mathematics; Microbiology; Natural Sciences; Nursing; Pharmacy; Physics); **Forestry** *(Eldorado)* (Agronomy; Biology; Forestry; Wood Technology); **Humanities and Social Sciences** *(Posadas)* (Anthropology; Arts and Humanities; Literature; Portuguese; Social Sciences; Social Work; Special Education; Tourism)

School

Eldorado Agro-technical (Agriculture; Technology); **Nursing** *(Posadas)* (Nursing)

History: Founded 1973. An autonomous State institution.

Academic Year: February to December (February-July; August-December)

Admission Requirements: Secondary school certificate (bachillerato) or equivalent

Main Language(s) of Instruction: Spanish

Degrees and Diplomas: *Diploma de Técnico Superior*: **Library Science; Nursing; Secretarial Studies; Tourism.** *Licenciatura*: **Business Administration; Genetics; History; Literature; Social Work; Tourism.** *Especialización*; *Maestría*; *Doctorado*: **Administration; Anthropology; Arts and Humanities; Industrial Engineering; Natural Sciences; Social Sciences.**

Student Services: Library

Last Updated: 02/09/15

NATIONAL UNIVERSITY OF MORENO

Universidad Nacional de Moreno

Av. Bartolomé Mitre 1891, Gran Buenos Aires, B1744OHC Buenos Aires
Tel: +54(237) 466-4365
EMail: unm@unm.edu.ar
Website: http://www.unm.edu.ar

Rector: Hugo Omar Andrade (2013-) EMail: rectorado@unm.edu.ar

Secretaria Académica: Adriana Sánchez
EMail: sec.academica@unm.edu.ar

Department

Applied Science and Technology (Electronic Engineering; Environmental Management; Environmental Studies); **Architecture, Design and Town Planning** (Architecture; Town Planning); **Economics and Administration** (Accountancy; Administration; Economics; Labour and Industrial Relations); **Humanities and Social**

Sciences (Multimedia; Primary Education; Secondary Education; Social Work)

History: Founded 2009.

Main Language(s) of Instruction: Spanish

Degrees and Diplomas: *Licenciatura*

Last Updated: 02/09/15

NATIONAL UNIVERSITY OF PATAGONIA SAN JUAN BOSCO

Universidad Nacional de la Patagonia San Juan Bosco (UNPSJB)

Ciudad Universitaria Km 4, 9005 Comodoro Rivadavia, Chubut
Tel: +54(297) 455-7856
Fax: +54(297) 455-7453
Website: http://www.unp.edu.ar

Rector: Alberto César Ayape EMail: rector@unp.edu.ar

Vicerrectora: Antonia Lidia Blanco EMail: virectorado@unp.edu.ar

Secretaria Académica: Alicia Liliana Balocchi
EMail: secacademica@unp.edu.ar

Faculty

Economics *(Ushuaia)* (Accountancy; Economics; Tourism); **Engineering** (Chemical Engineering; Civil Engineering; Computer Science; Electronic Engineering; Engineering; Forest Management; Industrial Engineering; Mathematics; Mechanical Engineering; Petroleum and Gas Engineering); **Humanities and Social Sciences** (Communication Studies; Educational Sciences; Environmental Management; Geography; History; Literature; Political Sciences; Social Work; Tourism); **Law** (Law); **Natural Sciences** (Biochemistry; Biology; Forestry; Geology; Marine Biology; Microbiology; Nursing; Pharmacy)

Further Information: Also branches in Trelew; Esquel and Puerto Madryn

History: Founded 1980, following merger of Universidad de la Patagonia, founded 1963, and Universidad Nacional de la Patagonia founded in 1974. An autonomous State institution.

Academic Year: March to November

Admission Requirements: Secondary school certificate (bachillerato) or equivalent

Main Language(s) of Instruction: Spanish

Degrees and Diplomas: *Licenciatura*; *Especialización*; *Maestría*: **Biochemistry; Biology; Geology; Pharmacy.** *Doctorado*: **Biochemistry; Biology; Chemistry; Geology; Pharmacy.**

Student Services: Library

Publications: Naturalia Patagónica

Publishing House: Editorial Universitaria de la Patagonia

Last Updated: 02/09/15

NATIONAL UNIVERSITY OF QUILMES

Universidad Nacional de Quilmes (UNQ)

Roque Sáenz Peña 352, B1876BXD Bernal, Buenos Aires
Tel: +54(11) 4365-7100
Fax: +54(11) 4365-7101
EMail: info@unq.edu.ar
Website: http://www.unq.edu.ar

Rector: Mario Enrique Lozano EMail: mario.lozano@unq.edu.ar

Secretaria Académica: Sara Pérez EMail: sperez@unq.edu.ar

Vicerrector: Alejandro Villar EMail: avillar@unq.edu.ar

Department

Science and Technology (Automation and Control Engineering; Bioengineering; Food Technology; Naval Architecture; Technology); **Social Sciences** (Communication Studies; Education; Hotel Management; International Business; Music; Music Theory and Composition; Occupational Therapy; Social Sciences)

Centre

Studies and Research

History: Founded 1989. An autonomous State institution.

Admission Requirements: Secondary school certificate (bachillerato) or equivalent and approval of the admission course

Fees: No tuition fees for graduate students

Main Language(s) of Instruction: Spanish

Accrediting Agency: Comisión Nacional de Evaluación y Acreditación Universitaria (CONEAU)

Degrees and Diplomas: *Licenciatura*; *Especialización*; *Maestría*; *Doctorado*: **Arts and Humanities; Economics; Natural Sciences; Social Sciences; Technology.**

Last Updated: 18/08/15

NATIONAL UNIVERSITY OF RÍO CUARTO

Universidad Nacional de Río Cuarto (UNRC)

Ruta Nacional 36 Km. 601, 5800 Río Cuarto, Córdoba
Tel: +54(358) 467-6200
Fax: +54(358) 468-0280
Website: http://www.unrc.edu.ar

Rector: Roberto Rovere EMail: secpriv@rec.unrc.edu.ar

Secretaria Académica: Ana Vogliotti

Vicerrector: Jorge González

Faculty

Agronomy and Veterinary Science (Agricultural Engineering; Agronomy; Veterinary Science); **Economics** (Accountancy; Administration; Economics; Finance; Marketing); **Engineering** (Chemical Engineering; Electrical Engineering; Engineering; Mechanical Engineering; Telecommunications Engineering); **Exact, Natural and Physical Chemistry Sciences** (Biology; Chemistry; Computer Networks; Geology; Mathematics; Microbiology; Natural Sciences; Physical Chemistry; Physics); **Human Sciences** (Arts and Humanities; Communication Studies; English; French; Geography; History; Law; Linguistics; Literature; Nursing; Pedagogy; Philosophy; Physical Education; Political Sciences; Social Sciences)

History: Founded 1971. An autonomous State institution.

Academic Year: March to November (March-July; August-November)

Admission Requirements: Secondary school certificate (bachillerato) or equivalent

Main Language(s) of Instruction: Spanish

Accrediting Agency: CONEAU

Degrees and Diplomas: *Diploma de Técnico Superior*: **Nursing.** *Licenciatura*: **Biology; Business Administration; Chemistry; Communication Arts; Computer Science; Economics; Education; Educational Psychology; Mathematics; Physical Education; Political Sciences; Teacher Training.** *Especialización*: **Animal Husbandry; Education; Environmental Studies; Geology; Health Sciences; Human Resources; Statistics.** *Maestría*: **Agriculture; Animal Husbandry; Applied Mathematics; Biotechnology; Chemical Engineering; Electrical Engineering; Industrial Chemistry; Mathematics Education; Mechanical Engineering; Veterinary Science.** *Doctorado*: **Animal Husbandry; Biology; Chemistry; Communication Studies; Economics; Educational Sciences; Engineering; Geology; Physics; Social Sciences.**

Student Services: Cultural Activities, Health Services, Library, Nursery Care, Social Counselling, Sports Facilities

Publications: Revista

Publishing House: Departamento de Imprenta y Publicaciones

Last Updated: 02/09/15

NATIONAL UNIVERSITY OF RÍO NEGRO

Universidad Nacional de Río Negro (UNRN)

Belgrano 526, 8500 Viedma, Río Negro
Tel: 54 02920 428 601
Fax: 54 02920 428 601
Website: http://www.unrn.edu.ar

Rector: Juan Carlos Del Bello
EMail: jcdelbello@unrn.edu.ar; rector@unrn.edu.ar

Vicerrector: Roberto Kozulj EMail: rkozulj@unrn.edu.ar

Area

Applied Science (Agronomy; Anthropology; Computer Science; Criminal Law; Design; Environmental Studies; Furniture Design;

Geology; Interior Design; Paleontology); **Economics** (Accountancy; Administration; Business Administration; Economics; International Business; Marketing; Tourism); **Engineering** (Agricultural Engineering; Biotechnology; Electronic Engineering; Environmental Engineering; Food Technology; Telecommunications Engineering); **Health Sciences** (Dentistry; Physical Therapy; Veterinary Science); **Humanities** (Administration; Education; Literature; Physical Education; Primary Education; Teacher Training; Theatre; Visual Arts); **Social Sciences** (Communication Studies)

Further Information: Also Sede Andina, Sede Alto Valle y Valle Medio and Sede Atlántica

History: Founded 2007.

Academic Year: March to December

Main Language(s) of Instruction: Spanish

Degrees and Diplomas: *Licenciatura*; *Especialización*; *Maestría*

Last Updated: 24/09/15

NATIONAL UNIVERSITY OF ROSARIO

Universidad Nacional de Rosario (UNR)

Rectorado, Cordoba 1814, S2000AXD Rosario, Santa Fé
Tel: +54(341) 480-2621
Fax: +54(341) 480-2621
EMail: academica@unr.edu.ar
Website: http://www.unr.edu.ar

Rector: Héctor Floriani EMail: rector@unr.edu.ar

Vicerrector: Fabián Biccíré EMail: svicerrectorado@unr.edu.ar

International Relations: Mariano Gárate, Secretary of International Relations EMail: rrii@unr.edu.ar

Faculty

Agriculture *(Zavalla)* (Agricultural Engineering; Agriculture; Harvest Technology; Natural Resources; Plant and Crop Protection); **Architecture, Planning and Design** (Architectural and Environmental Design; Architecture; Architecture and Planning; Design); **Biochemistry and Pharmacy** (Analytical Chemistry; Biochemistry; Microbiology; Organic Chemistry; Pharmacy; Physical Chemistry; Physiology); **Dentistry** (Dentistry); **Economics and Statistics** (Accountancy; Business Administration; Economics; Statistics); **Exact Sciences, Engineering and Land Surveying** (Civil Engineering; Electrical Engineering; Industrial Engineering; Mathematics; Mechanical Engineering; Physics; Rural Planning; Surveying and Mapping); **Humanities and Arts** (Anthropology; Arts and Humanities; Educational Sciences; Fine Arts; History; Literature; Music; Philosophy); **Law** (Law); **Medical Sciences** (Health Sciences; Medicine; Nursing; Speech Therapy and Audiology); **Political Science and International Relations** (Communication Studies; International Relations; Political Sciences; Social Work); **Psychology** (Psychology); **Veterinary Science** *(Casilda)* (Veterinary Science)

School

Agricultural Technology *(Libertador San Martín)* (Agricultural Equipment); **Business** *(Libertador General San Martín)* (Accountancy; Business and Commerce; Communication Arts; Economics; English; French; Law; Mathematics; Music; Physical Education; Social Sciences; Theatre)

Higher Institute

Polytechnic *(General San Martín)* (Chemistry; Computer Science; Electrical Engineering; Food Technology; Industrial Management; Mathematics; Mechanical Engineering; Optics; Physical Education; Physics; Polymer and Plastics Technology; Technology)

Centre

Interdisciplinary Studies (International Studies; Public Health)

History: Founded 1968. A State Institution.

Academic Year: March to November (March-June; August-November)

Admission Requirements: Secondary school certificate (bachillerato)

Main Language(s) of Instruction: Spanish

Degrees and Diplomas: *Licenciatura*: **Architecture; Arts and Humanities; Economics; History; International Relations; Journalism; Law; Mathematics; Medicine; Midwifery; Nursing; Pharmacy; Philosophy; Physics; Political Sciences; Visual Arts.** *Especialización*; *Maestría*; *Doctorado*: **Accountancy; Administration; Agriculture; Anthropology; Architecture; Biology; Biomedicine; Chemistry; Computer Science; Economics; Education; Engineering; Fine Arts; History; International Relations; Law; Linguistics; Literature; Mathematics; Medicine; Music; Nursing; Philosophy; Physics; Political Sciences; Psychology; Social Work; Speech Therapy and Audiology; Veterinary Science.**

Student Services: Academic Counselling, Cultural Activities, Health Services, Library, Social Counselling, Sports Facilities

Publications: Revista de la Universidad

Last Updated: 02/09/15

NATIONAL UNIVERSITY OF SALTA

Universidad Nacional de Salta (UNSA)

Av. Bolivia 5150, 4400 Salta, Salta
Tel: +54(387) 425-5307
EMail: info@unsa.edu.ar
Website: http://www.unsa.edu.ar

Rector: Victor Hugo Claros
Tel: +54(387) 425-5427 EMail: rector@unsa.edu.ar

Secretaria Académica: Marta Elena Torino
Tel: +54(387) 425-5574 EMail: secadem@unsa.edu.ar

International Relations: Viviana Murgia
Tel: +54(387) 425-5533 EMail: coreinte@unsa.edu.ar

Faculty

Economics, Law and Social Sciences (Accountancy; Administration; Business Administration; Economics; Law; Social Sciences); **Engineering** (Chemical Engineering; Civil Engineering; Electronic Engineering; Engineering; Food Technology; Industrial Engineering; Mechanical Engineering); **Exact Sciences** (Chemistry; Computer Science; Electronic Engineering; Mathematics; Natural Sciences; Physics; Systems Analysis); **Health Sciences** (Health Sciences; Nursing; Nutrition; Public Health); **Humanities** (Anthropology; Arts and Humanities; Communication Studies; Educational Sciences; History; Philosophy); **Natural Sciences** (Agricultural Engineering; Biology; Environmental Studies; Geology; Natural Sciences)

Institute

Accountancy (Accountancy); **Administration** (Administration); **Chemical Research** *(INIQUI)* (Chemistry); **Distance Education**; **Ecology and Human Environment** (Ecology; Environmental Studies); **Economic Research** (Economics); **Folklore and Regional Literature** *(Augusto Raúl Cortazár)* (Folklore; Literature); **Food Research** *(IIASA)* (Food Science); **Geology** *(GEONORTE)* (Geology); **Human Nutrition Evaluation** *(IIEMPO)* (Food Science); **Industrial Chemistry Research** *(INIQUI)* (Industrial Chemistry); **Mathematics** (Mathematics); **Natural Resources and Ecological Development** *(IRNED)* (Ecology); **Non-conventional Energy Research** *(INENCO)* (Ecology); **Rural Development** (Development Studies); **Social Studies** (Social Studies)

Centre

History and Anthropology Research *(CEPIHA)* (Anthropology; History); **Interdisciplinary Research** *(CICIO, Oran)*; **Public Health** *(CESAP)* (Public Health); **Tropical Cultivation** *(CE.CU.TRO)* (Tropical Agriculture)

Group

Demography Studies (Demography and Population)

Laboratory

Experimental Pathology (Pathology)

Further Information: Also Regional Centres in Orán, Rosario de la Frontera, Tartagal

History: Founded 1973, incorporating the Faculty of Natural Sciences, Department of Economics, and Institute of Endocrinology of the National University of Tucumán. An autonomous State institution.

Academic Year: March to November (March-June; August-November)

Admission Requirements: Secondary school certificate (bachillerato) or equivalent

Main Language(s) of Instruction: Spanish

Degrees and Diplomas: *Licenciatura*: **Agriculture; Engineering; Social Work.** *Especialización*: **Accountancy; Business Administration; Civics; Economics; Ethics; Law; Natural Resources; Public Administration; Public Health; Social Welfare.** *Maestría*; *Doctorado*: **Arts and Humanities; Biology; Chemistry; Civil Engineering; Educational Research; Industrial Engineering; Natural Resources.**

Student Services: Canteen, Cultural Activities, Health Services, Sports Facilities

Publications: Andes; Castañares; Literatura de Salta

Publishing House: Dirección de Publicaciones e Impresiones

Last Updated: 02/09/15

NATIONAL UNIVERSITY OF SAN JUAN

Universidad Nacional de San Juan (UNSJ)
Mitre 396 (E), J5402CWH San Juan, San Juan
Tel: +54(264) 429-5000
Website: http://www.unsj.edu.ar

Rector: Oscar Herminio Nasisi EMail: rector@unsj.edu.ar

Vicerrectora: Mónica Coca EMail: vicerec@unsj.edu.ar

Faculty

Architecture, Town Planning and Design *(Rivadavia)* (Architecture; Graphic Design; Industrial Design; Town Planning); **Engineering** (Bioengineering; Chemical Engineering; Civil Engineering; Electrical and Electronic Engineering; Food Technology; Mechanical Engineering; Mining Engineering; Surveying and Mapping); **Exact, Physical and Natural Sciences** *(Rivadavia)* (Astronomy and Space Science; Biology; Geology; Geophysics; Information Sciences); **Philosophy, Humanities and Arts** (Arts and Humanities; Chemistry; Education; English; Fine Arts; History; Literature; Mathematics; Music; Pedagogy; Philosophy; Physics; Technology; Tourism; Visual Arts); **Social Sciences** *(Rivadavia)* (Business Administration; Economics; Journalism; Law; Political Sciences; Public Administration; Social Sciences; Social Work; Sociology)

Further Information: Also 26 institutes

History: Founded 1973, incorporating faculties and schools of the National University of Cuyo. An autonomous State institution.

Academic Year: April to November (April-July; August-November)

Admission Requirements: Secondary school certificate (bachilerato) or equivalent

Main Language(s) of Instruction: Spanish

Degrees and Diplomas: *Licenciatura*: **Business Administration; Communication Arts; Educational Administration; Geology; Geophysics; Political Sciences; Social Work; Sociology.** *Especialización*; *Maestría*; *Doctorado*: **Architecture; Astronomy and Space Science; Biology; Chemical Engineering; Civil Engineering; Electrical Engineering; Geology; Geophysics; Urban Studies.**

Student Services: Library

Last Updated: 02/09/15

NATIONAL UNIVERSITY OF SAN LUIS

Universidad Nacional de San Luis (UNSL)
Avenida Ejército de los Andes 950, D5700HHW San Luis, San Luis
Tel: +54(2652) 452-0300
Website: http://www.unsl.edu.ar

Rector: Félix Daniel Nieto Quintas EMail: rector@unsl.edu.ar

Secretaria Académica: Edilma Olinda Gagliardi EMail: sacade@unsl.edu.ar; oli@unsl.edu.ar

Faculty

Chemistry, Biochemistry, and Pharmacy (Biochemistry; Chemistry; Pharmacy); **Engineering and Socio-Economics** *(Villa Mercedes)* (Chemical Engineering; Electrical and Electronic Engineering; Food Science; Industrial Engineering); **Health Sciences** (Nursing; Nutrition; Physical Therapy; Speech Therapy and Audiology); **Human Sciences** (Education; Journalism; Literature; Radio and Television Broadcasting); **Physics, Mathematics, and Natural Sciences** (Geology; Information Sciences; Mathematics; Mining Engineering; Physics); **Psychology** (Psychology); **Tourism and Urban Studies** (Tourism; Urban Studies)

School

Teacher Training *(Juan Pascal Pringles)* (Teacher Training)

History: Founded 1973. An autonomous State institution.

Academic Year: March to November

Admission Requirements: Secondary school certificate (bachilerato) or equivalent

Main Language(s) of Instruction: Spanish

Degrees and Diplomas: *Diploma de Técnico Superior*: **Speech Therapy and Audiology; Statistics.** *Licenciatura*: **Administration; Biochemistry; Chemistry; Education; Geology; Mathematics; Physics; Psychology.** *Especialización*; *Maestría*; *Doctorado*: **Biochemistry; Biology; Chemistry; Computer Engineering; Computer Science; Education; Geology; Mathematics; Pharmacy; Physics; Speech Therapy and Audiology.**

Student Services: Library

Last Updated: 02/09/15

NATIONAL UNIVERSITY OF SANTIAGO DEL ESTERO

Universidad Nacional de Santiago del Estero (UNSE)
Avenida Belgrano Sur 1912, 4200 Santiago del Estero, Santiago del Estero
Tel: +54(385) 450-9500
Fax: +54(385) 450-9544
EMail: info@unse.edu.ar
Website: http://www.unse.edu.ar

Rector: Natividad Nassif EMail: rectora@unse.edu.ar

Secretario Académico: Víctor Hugo Ledesma EMail: academia@unse.edu.ar

International Relations: Graciela Cazaux de Castiglione, Dirección de Relaciones Internacionales EMail: mgcastig@unse.edu.ar

Faculty

Agronomy and Food Industry (Agronomy; Chemistry; Food Science; Food Technology); **Exact Sciences and Technology** (Civil Engineering; Electrical Engineering; Electronic Engineering; Hydraulic Engineering; Mathematics; Natural Sciences; Technology); **Forestry** (Ecology; Forestry; Wood Technology); **Humanities, Social Sciences and Health** (Accountancy; Administration; Arts and Humanities; Communication Studies; Education; English; Gynaecology and Obstetrics; Health Sciences; History; Law; Literature; Modern Languages; Nursing; Philosophy; Psychology; Social Sciences; Social Work; Sociology)

School

Educational Innovation (Education)

Centre

Rural Education *(Secondary level)* (Rural Studies; Secondary Education)

History: Founded 1973. An autonomous State institution.

Academic Year: February to December (March-July; August-December)

Admission Requirements: Secondary school certificate (bachilerato) or equivalent

Main Language(s) of Instruction: Spanish

Degrees and Diplomas: *Licenciatura*; *Especialización*; *Maestría*; *Doctorado*: **Food Technology.**

Student Services: Library

Publications: Quebracho; Revista de Ciencia y Técnica

Last Updated: 02/09/15

NATIONAL UNIVERSITY OF SOUTHERN PATAGONIA

Universidad Nacional de la Patagonia Austral (UNPA)
Lisandro de la Torre 860, 9400 Río Gallegos, Santa Cruz
Tel: +54(2966) 44-2376
Fax: +54(2966) 44-2376
EMail: info@unpa.edu.ar
Website: http://www.unpa.edu.ar

Rector: Eugenia Márquez (2007-) EMail: emarquez@unpa.edu.ar

Vicerrector: Hugo Santos Rojas EMail: hrojas@unpa.edu.ar

Secretaria General Académica: María José Leno
EMail: mjleno@unpa.edu.ar

School

Administration and Economics (Administration; Economics; Management); **Basic and Exact Sciences** (Mathematics); **Communication** (Communication Studies); **Computer Science** (Computer Engineering; Computer Science; Software Engineering); **Education** (Educational Sciences; Primary Education); **Engineering and Risk Prevention** (Chemical Engineering; Electronic Engineering; Mechanical Engineering; Mining Engineering); **Geography, Territorial Administration and Geoinformatics** (Geography); **History** (History); **Letters** (Literature); **Natural Resources** (Fruit Production; Horticulture); **Nursing** (Nursing); **Psychopedagogy** (Educational Psychology); **Social Work** (Social Work); **Tourism** (Tourism)

Further Information: Also branches in Caleta Olivia, San Julián and Río Turbio

History: Founded 1962, acquired present status and title 1994.

Main Language(s) of Instruction: Spanish

Degrees and Diplomas: *Diploma de Técnico Superior*, *Licenciatura*; *Especialización*; *Maestría*

Student Services: Library

Last Updated: 02/09/15

NATIONAL UNIVERSITY OF THE CENTRE OF THE PROVINCE OF BUENOS AIRES

Universidad Nacional del Centro de la Provincia de Buenos Aires (UNCPBA)

General Pinto 399, B7000GHG Tandil
Buenos Aires
Tel: +54(2293) 42-2000
Fax: +54(2293) 42-1608
EMail: sprivada@rec.unicen.edu.ar
Website: http://www.unicen.edu.ar

Rector: Roberto Tassara EMail: rector@rec.unicen.edu.ar

Secretaria Académica: Mabel Pacheco
Tel: +54(2293) 42-1876 EMail: academica@rec.unicen.edu.ar

International Relations: Ana Taborga, Secretaria de Relaciones Institucionales EMail: ataborga@rec.unicen.edu.ar

Faculty

Agronomy *(Azul)* (Agricultural Business; Agricultural Management; Agronomy; Biology; Water Science); **Art** (Theatre); **Economics** (Accountancy; Administration); **Engineering** *(Olavarría)* (Chemical Engineering; Civil Engineering; Computer Engineering; Electronic Engineering; Food Technology; Industrial Engineering; Mechanical Engineering; Medical Technology; Technology); **Exact Sciences** (Computer Engineering; Computer Science; Mathematics; Mathematics Education; Physics); **Human Sciences** (Arts and Humanities; Education; Educational Sciences; Environmental Management; Geography; History; International Relations; Primary Education; Social Studies; Social Work; Surveying and Mapping); **Social Sciences** *(Olavarría)* (Anthropology; Archaeology; Communication Studies; Cultural Studies; Media Studies; Social Policy; Social Sciences; Social Studies); **Veterinary Science** (Animal Husbandry; Apiculture; Biology; Dairy; Epidemiology; Veterinary Science; Zoology)

Higher School

Health Sciences (Nursing)

Further Information: Branches in Azul and Olavarría

History: Founded 1964 as University of Tandil, a private institution. Acquired present status and title 1974, incorporating previously existing institutions in Olavarría and Azul. An autonomous State institution.

Academic Year: March to December (March-July; August-December)

Admission Requirements: Secondary school certificate (bachillerato) or equivalent

Fees: None

Main Language(s) of Instruction: Spanish

Degrees and Diplomas: *Licenciatura*; *Especialización*; *Maestría*; *Doctorado*: **Administration; Animal Husbandry; Archaeology; Computer Science; Engineering; Physics.**

Student Services: Academic Counselling, Canteen, Careers Guidance, Cultural Activities, Health Services, Language Laboratory, Library, Nursery Care, Social Counselling, Sports Facilities

Publications: Espacios en Blanco; Estudios Socioterritoriales; Intersecciones en Antropología; Intersecciones en Comunicación; Revista Alternativas; Revista de la Escuela de Perfeccionamiento en Investigación Operativa; Revista El Peldaño-Cuaderno de Teatrología; Revista La Escalera

Publishing House: Departamento de Impresiones

Last Updated: 03/09/15

NATIONAL UNIVERSITY OF THE COAST

Universidad Nacional del Litoral (UNL)

Bulevar Pellegrini 2750, S3000ADQ Santa Fé, Santa Fé
Tel: +54(342) 457-1110
Fax: +54(342) 457-1110
EMail: informes@unl.edu.ar
Website: http://www.unl.edu.ar

Rector: Miguel Irigoyen (2015-) EMail: rector@unl.edu.ar

Secretario Académico: Miguel Irigoyen
EMail: academica@unl.edu.ar

Faculty

Agronomy (Agricultural Engineering; Apiculture; Dairy); **Architecture, Design and Town Planning** (Architecture; Industrial Design; Town Planning); **Biochemistry and Biological Sciences** (Biochemistry; Biotechnology; Nutrition); **Chemical Engineering** (Chemical Engineering; Chemistry; Food Technology; Industrial Engineering; Mathematics); **Economics** (Accountancy; Administration; Economics); **Humanities and Sciences** (Biology; Geography; History; Literature; Philosophy; Political Sciences; Sociology); **Hydraulic Resources Sciences** (Computer Engineering; Environmental Engineering; Hydraulic Engineering; Measurement and Precision Engineering; Surveying and Mapping); **Law and Social Sciences** (Law; Library Science; Social Sciences; Social Studies); **Veterinary Science**

School

Agriculture and Farming

Higher School

Food Analysis (Food Technology); **Food Studies** (Food Science; Food Technology); **Health Services** *(Ramon Carrillo)* (Environmental Studies; Public Health); **Industrial Engineering**; **Medicine** *(School)*

Higher Institute

Music (Music)

History: Founded 1889 as provincial University, became National University by law in 1919. An autonomous State institution.

Academic Year: March to November

Admission Requirements: Secondary school certificate (bachillerato)

Main Language(s) of Instruction: Spanish

Degrees and Diplomas: *Licenciatura*: **Education; Food Science; Health Sciences; Music; Theatre.** *Especialización*: **Agriculture; Education; Health Sciences; Social Sciences.** *Maestría*: **Agriculture; Architecture; Business Administration; Chemical Engineering; Computer Science; Health Sciences; Higher Education Teacher Training; Law; Mathematics; Physics; Social Sciences.** *Doctorado*: **Agriculture; Architecture; Arts and Humanities; Biological and Life Sciences; Chemical Engineering; Chemistry; Engineering; Food Science; Law; Mathematics; Public Administration.**

Student Services: Academic Counselling, Canteen, Careers Guidance, Cultural Activities, Facilities for disabled people, Foreign Studies Centre, Health Services, Language Laboratory, Nursery Care, Social Counselling, Sports Facilities

Publications: Conciencia

Last Updated: 04/09/15

NATIONAL UNIVERSITY OF THE NORTH-EAST

Universidad Nacional del Nordeste (UNNE)
Calle 25 de Mayo 868, 3400 Corrientes, Corrientes
Tel: +54(3783) 42-5064
Fax: +54(3783) 42-4678
Website: http://www.unne.edu.ar

Rectora: María Delfina Veiravé EMail: rector@unne.edu.ar

Secretaria Académica: Viviana Godoy Guglielmone
EMail: secacad@unne.edu.ar

Faculty

Agricultural Sciences (Agricultural Engineering; Agriculture); **Agroindustry** *(Saenz Peña)* (Agricultural Engineering; Chemical Engineering; Food Technology; Forestry; Pharmacy); **Architecture and Town Planning** *(Resistencia)* (Architecture; Town Planning); **Art, Design and Cultural Studies** (Cultural Studies; Design; Fine Arts); **Dentistry** (Dentistry); **Economics** *(Resistencia)* (Accountancy; Economics; Public Administration); **Engineering** *(Resistencia)* (Civil Engineering; Computer Engineering; Electrical Engineering; Engineering; Hydraulic Engineering; Mechanical Engineering; Thermal Engineering); **Exact Natural Sciences and Surveying** (Biology; Chemistry; Computer Science; Educational Psychology; Engineering; Mathematics; Natural Sciences; Physics; Surveying and Mapping); **Humanities** *(Resistencia)* (Arts and Humanities; Educational Sciences; Geography; History; Literature; Modern Languages; Philosophy); **Law, Social Sciences and Political Science** (Law; Political Sciences; Social Sciences); **Medicine** (Medicine; Nursing; Physical Therapy); **Veterinary Science** (Veterinary Science)

Institute

Criminology and Criminal Science (Criminal Law); **Regional Medicine** (Health Sciences; Medicine)

History: Founded 1956, incorporating various schools attached to the National University of the Coast. The institution, which enjoys academic and administrative autonomy, is responsible to the Ministry of Education and Culture.

Academic Year: March to November (March-July; July-November)

Admission Requirements: Secondary school certificate (bachillerato) or equivalent

Main Language(s) of Instruction: Spanish

Degrees and Diplomas: *Licenciatura*: **Botany; Chemistry; Economics; Education; Geography; History; Literature; Mathematics; Philosophy; Physics; Zoology.** *Maestría*; *Doctorado*: **Administration; Biology; Chemistry; Economics; Education; Geography; History; Law; Literature; Philosophy; Physics; Veterinary Science.**

Student Services: Library

Publications: Anales del Instituto de Patología Regional; Bomplandia; Nordeste; Revista de la Facultad de Derecho; Revista Veterinaria

Last Updated: 03/09/15

NATIONAL UNIVERSITY OF THE NORTH-WEST OF THE PROVINCE OF BUENOS AIRES

Universidad Nacional del Noroeste de la Provincia de Buenos Aires (UNNOBA)
Libertad 555, B6000FJJ Junín, Buenos Aires
Tel: +54(2362) 444-4213
EMail: secretariaprivada@unnoba.edu.ar
Website: http://www.unnoba.edu.ar

Rector: Guillermo Ricardo Tamarit (2007-)
EMail: secretariaprivada@unnoba.edu.ar

Secretaria Académica: María Florencia Castro
EMail: academica@unnoba.edu.ar

International Relations: Gabriela Messing
Tel: +54(2477) 42-9614 +54(2477) 42-9569
EMail: rrii@unnoba.edu.ar

School

Agrarian, Natural and Environmental Sciences (Agronomy; Biological and Life Sciences; Food Science; Genetics; Natural Sciences); **Economics and Law** (Accountancy; Administration; Economics; Law; Public Administration); **Technology** (Computer Science; Design; Industrial Engineering; Industrial Maintenance; Mechanical Engineering)

Further Information: Also branches in Pergamino and Junín

History: Founded 2002.

Admission Requirements: High School Certificate

Fees: None

Main Language(s) of Instruction: Spanish

Degrees and Diplomas: *Diploma de Técnico Superior*: **Agronomy; Animal Husbandry; Computer Science; Food Science; Industrial Maintenance; Mechanics; Nursing; Public Administration.** *Licenciatura*: **Administration; Agronomy; Computer Science; Fashion Design; Food Science; Genetics; Graphic Design; Journalism; Nursing; Textile Design.** *Especialización*; *Maestría*

Student Services: Language Laboratory, Sports Facilities

Last Updated: 03/09/15

NATIONAL UNIVERSITY OF THE SOUTH

Universidad Nacional del Sur (UNS)
Avenida Colón 80, B8000FTN Bahía Blanca, Buenos Aires
Tel: +54(291) 459-5015
Fax: +54(291) 459-5016
Website: http://www.uns.edu.ar

Rector: Mario Ricardo Sabbatini EMail: rector@uns.edu.ar

Secretaria General Académica: Graciela Petra Brizuela
EMail: secac@uns.edu.ar

International Relations: Gastón Milanesi, Secretario General
EMail: institucionales@uns.edu.ar

Department

Administration (Accountancy; Administration; Business Administration); **Agronomy** (Agriculture; Agronomy; Animal Husbandry; Apiculture; Horticulture; Soil Science); **Biology, Biochemistry and Pharmacy** (Biochemistry; Biological and Life Sciences; Biology; Pharmacy); **Chemical Engineering** (Chemical Engineering; Food Science); **Chemistry** (Chemistry); **Computer Science and Engineering** (Computer Engineering; Computer Science); **Economics** (Economics); **Electrical Engineering** (Electrical Engineering; Electronic Engineering); **Engineering** (Civil Engineering; Engineering; Industrial Engineering; Mechanical Engineering); **Geography and Tourism** (Geography; Tourism); **Geology** (Geology); **Health Sciences** (Health Sciences); **Humanities** (Arts and Humanities; History; Literature; Modern Languages; Philosophy); **Law** *(Bahia Bianca)* (Law); **Mathematics** (Mathematics); **Physics** (Physics)

Institute

Applied Mechanics *(IMA)* (Mechanical Engineering); **Electrical Engineering** *(Alfredo Desages)*; **Mathematics** *(Bahía Bianca)* (Mathematics); **Oceanography** *(Argentina (IADO))* (Marine Science and Oceanography); **Pilot Chemical Engineering Plant** *(PLAPIQUI)* (Food Technology; Polymer and Plastics Technology; Production Engineering)

Centre

Renewable Resources in the Semi-Arid Region *(CERZOS)* (Arid Land Studies; Natural Resources)

Research Institute

Biochemical *(Bahía Blanca (INIBIBB))* (Biochemistry; Biophysics; Biotechnology)

History: Founded 1946 as Instituto Tecnológico del Sur, became National University 1956. An autonomous State institution.

Academic Year: February to December

Admission Requirements: Secondary school certificate (bachillerato) or equivalent and entrance examination

Main Language(s) of Instruction: Spanish

Accrediting Agency: National Commission of University Accreditation (CONEAU) - Ministerio de Educación, Ciencia y Tecnología

Degrees and Diplomas: *Licenciatura*: **Administration; Arts and Humanities; Biology; Chemistry; Computer Science; Economics; Geography; Geology; History; Mathematics; Philosophy; Physics; Tourism.** *Especialización*: **Accountancy; Agriculture; Biology; Economics; Electrical and Electronic Engineering.**

Maestría; *Doctorado*: **Administration; Agronomy; Arts and Humanities; Biochemistry; Biology; Chemical Engineering; Chemistry; Computer Science; Economics; Engineering; Food Technology; Geography; Geology; History; Literature; Mathematics; Philosophy.**

Student Services: Academic Counselling, Cultural Activities, Health Services, Language Laboratory, Library, Social Counselling, Sports Facilities

Publications: Cuadernos del Sur; Escritos Contables (Ciencias de la Administración); Latin American Applied Research (PLAPIQUI); Revista Estudios Económicos; Revista Universitaria de Geografía

Last Updated: 24/09/15

NATIONAL UNIVERSITY OF THE THIRD OF FEBRUARY

Universidad Nacional de Tres de Febrero (UNTREF)

Mosconi 2736, B1674AHF Sáenz Peña, Buenos Aires

Tel: +54(11) 4519–6010

Website: http://www.untref.edu.ar

Rector: Aníbal Yazbeck Jozami
EMail: ajozami@untref.edu.ar; rectorado@untref.edu.ar

Vicerrector: Martín Kaufmann EMail: mkaufmann@untref.edu.ar

International Relations: Agustín Colombo Sierra
EMail: relacionesinstitucionales@untref.edu.ar

Department

Administration and Economics (Administration; Economics); **Art and Culture** (Arts and Humanities; Cultural Studies); **Engineering** (Engineering); **Health and Social Security** (Health Sciences; Social and Preventive Medicine; Social Welfare); **Methodology, Statistics and Mathematics** (Mathematics; Statistics); **Social Sciences** (Social Sciences)

Further Information: Also Caseros, Aromos, Centro Cultural Borges, Villa Lynch units

History: Founded 1995.

Academic Year: March to December

Admission Requirements: Secondary school certificate and admission course

Fees: (US Dollars): 200-250 per month

Main Language(s) of Instruction: Spanish

Accrediting Agency: CONEAU

Degrees and Diplomas: *Licenciatura*; *Especialización*; *Maestría*; *Doctorado*: **Education.**

Student Services: Academic Counselling, Canteen, Careers Guidance, Cultural Activities, Facilities for disabled people, Language Laboratory, Social Counselling

Publications: Cibertronic

Last Updated: 02/09/15

NATIONAL UNIVERSITY OF THE WEST

Universidad Nacional del Oeste

Belgrano 369, 1718 San Antonio de Padua, Buenos Aires

Tel: +54(220) 483-4150

EMail: info@uno.edu.ar

Website: http://www.uno.edu.ar

Rector: Martín Alfredo Othacehé EMail: rectorado@uno.edu.ar

Secretario Académico: Hernán Piotti López
EMail: academica@uno.edu.ar

School

Administration (Administration; Public Administration); **Computer Science** (Computer Science); **Engineering** (Chemical Engineering); **Health Sciences** (Nursing); **Humanities** (Educational Administration; Physical Education)

History: Founded 2009.

Degrees and Diplomas: *Licenciatura*

Student Services: Library

Last Updated: 03/09/15

NATIONAL UNIVERSITY OF TIERRA DEL FUEGO, ANTARTICA AND SOUTH ATLANTIC ISLANDS

Universidad Nacional de Tierra del Fuego, Antártida e Islas del Atlàntico Sur

Darwin s/n, 9410 Ushuaia, Tierra del Fuego

Tel: +54(2901) 43-4163

EMail: info@untdf.edu.ar

Website: http://www.untdf.edu.ar

Rector: Roberto Domecq EMail: rdomecq@untdf.edu.ar

Secretaria Académica: Claudia Bogosian
EMail: cbogosian@untdf.edu.ar

Institute

Culture, Society and State (Communication Studies; Political Sciences; Sociology); **Economic Development and Innovation** (Accountancy; Business Administration; Computer Science; Economics; Industrial Engineering; Tourism); **Education and Knowledge** (Biology; Literature; Mathematics Education; Modern Languages; Teacher Training); **Polar Sciences, Environment and Natural Resources** (Biology; Environmental Studies; Geology)

History: Founded 2009.

Main Language(s) of Instruction: Spanish

Degrees and Diplomas: *Licenciatura*: **Business Administration; Industrial Engineering.** *Especialización*: **Teacher Training.**

Student Services: Library

Last Updated: 03/09/15

NATIONAL UNIVERSITY OF TUCUMÁN

Universidad Nacional de Tucumán (UNT)

Ayacucho 491, 4000 San Miguel de Tucumán, Tucumán

Tel: +54(381) 424-7752

Fax: +54(381) 424-8025

EMail: academica@rectorado.unt.edu.ar

Website: http://www.unt.edu.ar

Rectora: Alicia Bardón EMail: direint@rectorado.unt.edu.ar

Vicerrector: José García

Faculty

Agronomy and Animal Husbandry (Agronomy; Animal Husbandry; Veterinary Science); **Architecture and Town Planning** (Architecture; Town Planning); **Arts** (Arts and Humanities; Dance; Interior Design; Painting and Drawing; Theatre); **Biochemistry, Chemistry and Pharmacy** (Biochemistry; Biological and Life Sciences; Chemistry; Pharmacy); **Dentistry** (Dentistry); **Economics** (Accountancy; Business Administration; Economics); **Exact Sciences and Technology** (Chemical Engineering; Chemistry; Civil Engineering; Computer Engineering; Computer Science; Electrical and Electronic Engineering; Industrial Engineering; Mechanical Engineering; Natural Sciences; Physics; Technology); **Law and Social Sciences** (Law; Social Sciences); **Medicine** (Medicine); **Natural Sciences** *(Instituto 'Miguel Lillo')* (Archaeology; Biology; Geology; Natural Sciences); **Philosophy and Letters** (Arts and Humanities; Chemistry; Educational Sciences; Geography; History; Literature; Mathematics; Philosophy; Physics); **Physical Education** (Physical Education); **Psychology** (Psychology)

School

Cinema, Video and Television (Cinema and Television; Video); **Nursing** *(Agüilares)* (Nursing)

History: Founded 1912, and inaugurated 1914 as a provincial University. Became a National University 1921.

Academic Year: February to December

Admission Requirements: Secondary school certificate (bachillerato). Foreign qualifications are recognized if covered by formal international agreements

Main Language(s) of Instruction: Spanish

Degrees and Diplomas: *Licenciatura*: **Arts and Humanities; Biology; Chemistry; Economics; Education; English; French; Geography; History; Mathematics; Music; Nursing; Painting and Drawing; Philosophy; Physics; Psychology; Sculpture.** *Especialización*; *Maestría*; *Doctorado*: **Arts and Humanities; Biochemistry; Chemistry; Dentistry; Educational Sciences; Engineering; Food Technology; Geology; Industrial Engineering;**

Law; Literature; Medicine; Nursing; Philosophy; Psychology; Social Sciences; Statistics.

Student Services: Language Laboratory, Library

Publications: Acta Zoológica Lilloana; Archivos de Bioquímica; Boletín de Jurisprudencia; Eventos del Paleozoico Inferior América Latina; Geología de América del Sur; Humanitas; Lilloa; Química y Farmacia; Revista Agronómica del Nordeste Argentino; Revista de Medicina; Revista Desarollo Rural; Revista Entomológica Argentina; Revista Jurídica; Revista Matemáticas y Física Teórica

Last Updated: 03/09/15

NATIONAL UNIVERSITY OF VILLA MARÍA

Universidad Nacional de Villa María (UNVM)

Av. Arturo Jauretche 1555, 5900 Villa María, Córdoba

Tel: +54(353) 453-9100/5

Fax: +54(353) 453-9117

EMail: informes@unvm.edu.ar

Website: http://www.unvm.edu.ar

Rector: Martín Rodrigo Gill
EMail: martingill@unvm.edu.ar; rectorado@unvm.edu.ar

Secretaria Académica: Luisa Margarita Schweitzer
EMail: secacad@rec.unvm.edu.ar

International Relations: Marta Susana Ancarani
EMail: internacionales@unvm.edu.ar

Institute

Basic and Applied Sciences (Agricultural Engineering; Computer Science; Food Technology; Industrial Design; Ophthalmology; Veterinary Science); **Human Sciences** (Arts and Humanities; Computer Graphics; Design; Education; Educational Administration; Educational Psychology; Educational Sciences; English; Literature; Mathematics; Modern Languages; Music; Nursing; Occupational Therapy; Pedagogy; Physical Education); **Social Sciences** (Accountancy; Administration; Business Administration; Communication Studies; Development Studies; Economics; Political Sciences; Social Sciences; Social Work; Sociology)

Centre

Antonio Sobral; Mediterranean Studies

History: Founded 1995.

Academic Year: March to November (March-June; August-November)

Admission Requirements: Secondary school certificate. Adults over 25 years of age not holding a secondary school certificate may register after complying with specific requirements

Main Language(s) of Instruction: Spanish

Degrees and Diplomas: *Licenciatura*: **Business Administration; Communication Studies; Computer Science; Design; Development Studies; Economic and Finance Policy; Educational Administration; Educational Psychology; Educational Sciences; Film; Music; Nursing; Occupational Therapy; Ophthalmology; Optometry; Physical Education; Political Sciences; Protective Services; Social Work; Sociology.** *Especialización*; *Maestría*: **Arts and Humanities; Development Studies.**

Student Services: Academic Counselling, Canteen, Careers Guidance, Health Services, Language Laboratory, Library, Social Counselling, Sports Facilities

Last Updated: 03/09/15

NATIONAL UNIVERSITY OF VILLA MERCEDES

Universidad Nacional de Villa Mercedes (UNVIME)

Las Heras N° 383, Villa Mercedes, San Luis

Tel: +54(2657) 422-154

EMail: info@unvime.edu.ar

Website: http://www.unvime.edu.ar

Rectora: Gladys María Ciuffo EMail: rectora@unvime.edu.ar

Secretario Académico: César Almeida
EMail: academica@unvime.edu.ar

School

Business Administration and Economics (Business Administration; Economics); **Engineering** (Bioengineering; Computer Science); **Environment and Biotechnology** (Environmental Management; Food Technology); **Health Sciences** (Gynaecology and Obstetrics; Nursing; Physical Therapy)

History: Founded 2009.

Main Language(s) of Instruction: Spanish

Degrees and Diplomas: *Licenciatura*

Last Updated: 03/09/15

PEDAGOGICAL UNIVERSITY OF THE PROVINCE OF BUENOS AIRES

Universidad Pedagógica de la Provincia de Buenos Aires (UNIPE)

Camino Centenario 2565, Gonnet, B1897AVA Buenos Aires

Tel: +54(221) 484-2697

Website: http://unipe.edu.ar

Rector: Adrián Canelotto EMail: rectorado@unipe.edu.ar

Secretaria Académica: Graciela Misirlis
EMail: secretaria.academica@unipe.edu.ar

Department

Teacher Training (Teacher Training)

Degrees and Diplomas: *Licenciatura*; *Especialización*; *Maestría*

Student Services: Library

Last Updated: 04/09/15

UNIVERSITY INSTITUTE OF AERONAUTICS

Instituto Universitario Aeronáutico (IUA)

Avenida Fuerza Aérea 6500, X5010JMX Guarnición Aérea, Córdoba

Tel: +54(351) 568-8800

Fax: +54(351) 568-8800

EMail: informes@iua.edu.ar

Website: http://www.iua.edu.ar

Rector: Edgar Mario Karpowicz (2013-)
EMail: rector@iua.edu.ar; ayudantia@iua.edu.ar

Secretario Académico: Héctor Carlos Riso
EMail: sacademica@iua.edu.ar

International Relations: José María Zarate, Head, Institutional Relations Tel: +54(351) 568-8837 EMail: rrii@iua.edu.ar

Faculty

Administration (Accountancy; Administration; Business Administration; Human Resources; Management; Transport Management); **Engineering** (Aeronautical and Aerospace Engineering; Computer Engineering; Electronic Engineering; Telecommunications Engineering)

Centre

Applied Research (Aeronautical and Aerospace Engineering)

Further Information: Distance Learning Programmes offered.

History: Founded 1947 as School of Aeronautical Engineering (Escuela Superior de Aeronáutica), acquired present status and title 1971.

Academic Year: February to December (February-June; July-December)

Admission Requirements: Certificate of Completion of secondary education. Admission exam required for some study tracks.

Fees: (Pesos): Administration programme, 270 per month; Engineering programme, 380 per month

Main Language(s) of Instruction: Spanish

Accrediting Agency: Ministerio de Educación, Ciencia y Tecnología; CONEAU

Degrees and Diplomas: *Licenciatura*: **Administration; Human Resources.** *Especialización*: **Engineering.** *Maestría*: **Aeronautical and Aerospace Engineering; International Studies; Law.**

Student Services: Academic Counselling, Canteen, Careers Guidance, Cultural Activities, Facilities for disabled people, Health Services, Language Laboratory, Nursery Care, Sports Facilities

Publications: Noticias de Nuestra Universidad

Last Updated: 25/08/15

UNIVERSITY OF BOLOGNA ARGENTINA

Università di Bologna Argentina
Marcelo T. de Alvear 1149, 4° piso, C1058AAQ Buenos Aires
Tel: +54(11) 4570-3000
EMail: administracion@unibo.edu.ar
Website: http://www.ba.unibo.it

Director: Angelo Manaresi EMail: amanaresi@unibo.edu.ar

Directora Administrativa: María Elena Turchi
EMail: mturchi@unibo.edu.ar

Programme

International Relations (International Relations)

Degrees and Diplomas: *Maestría*

Last Updated: 04/09/15

UNIVERSITY OF BUENOS AIRES

Universidad de Buenos Aires (UBA)
Calle Viamonte 430/444, C1053ABH Buenos Aires, Capital Federal
Tel: +54(11) 4511-8120
Fax: +54(11) 4511-8155
EMail: academico@rec.uba.ar
Website: http://www.uba.ar

Rector: Alberto Eduardo Barbieri EMail: rector@rec.uba.ar

Secretaria de Asuntos Académicos: María Catalina Nosiglia
EMail: privadasaa@rec.uba.ar

Faculty

Agronomy (Agricultural Business; Agricultural Economics; Agronomy; Environmental Studies; Floriculture; Food Science; Food Technology; Horticulture; Landscape Architecture); **Architecture, Design and Town Planning** (Architecture; Design; Graphic Design; Industrial Design; Landscape Architecture; Town Planning); **Dentistry** (Dentistry); **Economics** (Accountancy; Actuarial Science; Administration; Economics; Information Management); **Engineering** (Agricultural Engineering; Chemical Engineering; Civil Engineering; Computer Engineering; Electrical Engineering; Engineering; Food Technology; Industrial Engineering; Mechanical Engineering; Systems Analysis); **Exact and Natural Sciences** (Biology; Chemistry; Computer Science; Food Technology; Geology; Marine Science and Oceanography; Mathematics; Meteorology; Natural Sciences; Paleontology; Physics; Science Education); **Law** (Law; Translation and Interpretation); **Medicine** (Gynaecology and Obstetrics; Medicine; Nursing; Nutrition; Physical Therapy; Radiology; Speech Therapy and Audiology; Surgery); **Pharmacy and Biochemistry** (Biochemistry; Food Science; Food Technology; Pharmacy); **Philosophy and Literature** (Anthropology; Archaeology; Art History; Arts and Humanities; Communication Studies; Economics; Educational Sciences; Fine Arts; History; Information Sciences; Library Science; Linguistics; Literature; Music; Painting and Drawing; Philosophy; Sculpture; Sociology); **Psychology** (Occupational Therapy; Psychology; Rehabilitation and Therapy); **Social Sciences** (Communication Studies; Labour and Industrial Relations; Political Sciences; Social Sciences; Social Work; Sociology); **Veterinary Science** (Veterinary Science)

Further Information: Also 75 Research institutes, and regional university centres. SISBI, integrating 19 university libraries, 10 museums, 6 university health centres and hospitals

History: Founded 1821. Acquired present status 1881. An autonomous State institution.

Academic Year: March to December (March-July; August-December)

Admission Requirements: Secondary school certificate (bachillerato) and entrance examination

Fees: None

Main Language(s) of Instruction: Spanish

Accrediting Agency: No accrediting agency for undergraduate programmes; National Commission for University Evaluation and Accreditation (CONEAU) for Graduate programmes

Degrees and Diplomas: *Licenciatura*; *Especialización*; *Maestría*; *Doctorado*: **Agronomy; Anthropology; Archaeology; Architecture; Art History; Biochemistry; Biology; Chemistry; Classical Languages; Computer Science; Dentistry; Design; Economics; Educational Sciences; Engineering; Geology; History; Law; Library Science; Linguistics; Literature; Marine Science and Oceanography; Mathematics; Medicine; Pharmacy; Philosophy; Physics; Psychology; Social Sciences; Town Planning; Veterinary Science.**

Student Services: Academic Counselling, Canteen, Careers Guidance, Cultural Activities, Health Services, Language Laboratory, Library, Nursery Care, Social Counselling, Sports Facilities

Publications: Cien por Cien, Ciencia y Técnica

Publishing House: Editorial Universitaria De Buenos Aires-EUDEBA

Last Updated: 27/08/15

PRIVATE INSTITUTIONS

ARGENTINE BUSINESS UNIVERSITY

Universidad Argentina de la Empresa (UADE)
Lima 775 Edificio Lima 3, P.B., C1073AAO Buenos Aires, Capital Federal
Tel: +54(11) 4000-7600
EMail: contactouade@uade.edu.ar
Website: http://www.uade.edu.ar

Rector: Ricardo Orosco

Secretario Académico: Eduardo J. Fasulino
EMail: secretariaacademica@uade.edu.ar

International Relations: Eduardo Andrés Ossoinak
EMail: relinter@uade.edu.ar

Faculty

Communication and Design (Advertising and Publicity; Communication Arts; Communication Studies; Design; Public Relations; Tourism); **Economics** (Accountancy; Business Administration; Economics; Finance; Human Resources; Labour and Industrial Relations; Marketing); **Engineering and Applied Sciences** (Computer Engineering; Food Technology; Industrial Engineering; Information Technology; Mathematics and Computer Science; Production Engineering); **Law and Social Sciences** (English; Government; International Relations; Law; Modern Languages; Psychology; Social Sciences; Translation and Interpretation)

School

Business (Business Administration)

History: Founded 1957 as a private Foundation, and officially recognized by the government 1963 as a private University. Acquired present status 1982.

Academic Year: March to December (March-July; August-December)

Admission Requirements: Secondary school certificate (bachillerato) or recognized equivalent

Fees: (Pesos): Tuition, 700 per annum

Main Language(s) of Instruction: Spanish

Degrees and Diplomas: *Licenciatura*: **Agricultural Management; Biotechnology; Business Administration; Business and Commerce; Communication Arts; Communication Studies; Computer Science; Economics; Electronic Engineering; English; Finance; Food Technology; Government; Graphic Design; Hotel and Restaurant; Hotel Management; Human Resources; International Business; International Relations; Marketing; Mechanical Engineering; Production Engineering; Psychology; Textile Design; Tourism.** *Especialización*; *Maestría*: **Business Administration; Business and Commerce; Communication Studies; Finance; Human Resources; Information Sciences.** *Doctorado*: **Economics.**

Student Services: Academic Counselling, Canteen, Careers Guidance, Cultural Activities, Health Services, Sports Facilities

Publications: Base de datos del Sector Construcción; Construcción y Mercado Inmobiliario; Indice de Producción Industrial; Información de AFJP; Panorama Industrial; Principales Indicadores de la Economía Argentina

Last Updated: 26/08/15

ATLÁNTIDA ARGENTINA UNIVERSITY

Universidad Atlántida Argentina
Diagonal Rivadavia 515, 7109 Mar de Ajó, Buenos Aires
Tel: +54(2257) 42-0388
EMail: atlantida@atlantida.edu.ar
Website: http://www.atlantida.edu.ar

Rector: Amado Zogbi EMail: rectorado@atlantida.edu.ar

Secretaria Académica: María Florencia Dorigoni
EMail: academica@atlantida.edu.ar

Faculty

Economics (Accountancy; Administration; Economics); **Engineering** (Engineering; Systems Analysis); **Humanities** (Arts and Humanities; Tourism); **Law and Social Sciences** (Law; Social Sciences); **Psychology** (Psychology)

Further Information: Also Branches in Mar del Plata and Dolores

History: Founded 1994.

Main Language(s) of Instruction: Spanish

Degrees and Diplomas: *Licenciatura*

Last Updated: 26/08/15

BLAS PASCAL UNIVERSITY

Universidad Blas Pascal (UBP)
Av. Donato Álvarez 380, 5147 Argüello, Córdoba
Tel: +54(351) 414-4444
Fax: +54(351) 414-4400
EMail: informes@ubp.edu.ar
Website: http://www.ubp.edu.ar

Rector: José Alejandro Consigli EMail: secrectorado@ubp.edu.ar

Vicerrector de Asuntos Académicos: Roberto Raúl Rossi
EMail: rrossi@ubp.edu.ar

School

Córdoba Management School *(Córdoba, Córdoba)* (Business Administration)

Department

Architecture and Design (Architecture; Graphic Design); **Business Management** (Banking; Human Resources; Management; Marketing); **Communication** (Advertising and Publicity; Mass Communication; Public Relations); **Education** (Educational Sciences; Physical Education); **Environment and Tourism** (Tourism); **Legal** (Law; Notary Studies); **Technology** (Computer Engineering)

History: The origin of Pascal University Foundation goes back to the existence of a tertiary level setting incorporated to formal education, under the name of "Instituto Superior Pascal' (ISP). The Institute has began his activities in 1980, driven by a group of teachers from Córdoba with an educational proposal based on an innovative curriculum. The first educational offerings belonged to the area of ã computer science, mathematics and administration. When Blaise Pascal University began working in 1990, the higher authorities decided to stop the activities of the Institute in order to concentrate all academic and financial resources within the University. The Blas Pascal University has launched his distance education in 2000.

Academic Year: from March to December

Fees: National: 30000 per year (Argentine Peso), International: 6300 (US Dollar)

Main Language(s) of Instruction: Spanish, English

Accrediting Agency: CONEAU (Comisión Nacional de Evaluación y Acreditación Universitaria)

Degrees and Diplomas: *Diploma de Técnico Superior*: **Agricultural Management; Banking; Small Business.** *Licenciatura*: **Accountancy; Architecture; Business Administration; Communication Arts; Computer Engineering; Educational Administration; Environmental Management; Graphic Design; Human Resources; Journalism; Law; Marketing; Multimedia; Notary Studies; Physical Education; Public Relations; Telecommunications Engineering; Tourism.** *Especialización*: **Civil Law; Commercial Law; Constitutional Law; Criminal Law; Management Systems.**

Student Services: Academic Counselling, Canteen, Careers Guidance, Cultural Activities, Facilities for disabled people, Foreign Studies Centre, Health Services, IT Centre, Language Laboratory, Library, Residential Facilities, Social Counselling, Sports Facilities, eLibrary

Publications: "Revista de Estudios de Derecho Notarial y Registral" belongs to the Advocatus Magazine publisher and is intended for the attorney community, legal and their students.; "Revista Tendencias" is published twice a year and each issue is devoted to a science or specific problems addressed through a holistic view, often interdisciplinary.; The digital publication "ENFOCO" aims to show the wealth of activities being conducted by the educational institution.; The scientific publication "Revista de Derecho Privado" is intended for the legal community, teachers and students.

Academic Staff *2013-2014*	MEN	WOMEN	**TOTAL**
FULL-TIME	–	–	**500**
Student Numbers *2013-2014*			
All (Foreign included)	–	–	c. **10,000**
FOREIGN ONLY	23	59	**82**

Last Updated: 30/12/15

BUENOS AIRES TECHNOLOGY INSTITUTE

Instituto Tecnológico de Buenos Aires (ITBA)
Avenida Eduardo Madero 399, C1106ACD Buenos Aires, Capital Federal
Tel: +54(11) 2150-4800
EMail: informes@itba.edu.ar
Website: http://www.itba.edu.ar

Rector: José Luis Roces EMail: jlroces@itba.edu.ar

Secretario Académico: Jorge Oscar Ratto
EMail: secacad@itba.edu.ar

School

Engineering and Management (Administration; Computer Science; Economics; Finance; Industrial Engineering; Law); **Engineering and Technology** (Bioengineering; Chemical Engineering; Electrical and Electronic Engineering; Engineering; Mathematics; Mechanical Engineering; Petroleum and Gas Engineering; Physics)

History: Founded 1960 as a private institution, recognized by the federal government and operating under its supervision. Financed from private sources.

Academic Year: March to November (March-July; August-November)

Admission Requirements: Secondary school certificate and entrance examination

Main Language(s) of Instruction: Spanish

Accrediting Agency: CONEAU

Degrees and Diplomas: *Licenciatura*; *Especialización*: **Data Processing; Environmental Management; Petroleum and Gas Engineering.** *Maestría*; *Doctorado*: **Computer Science; Engineering.**

Publications: Revista

Last Updated: 25/08/15

BUSINESS UNIVERSITY OF THE TWENTY-FIRST CENTURY

Universidad Empresarial Siglo 21 (UE21)
Ituzaingó 484, 5000 Nueva Córdoba, Córdoba
Tel: +54(351) 420-4003
EMail: informes@uesiglo21.edu.ar
Website: http://www.uesiglo21.edu.ar

Rectora: María Belén Mendé

Vicerrector Académico: Manuel Ignacio Velasco

Area

Business Studies (Administration; Agricultural Management; Business Administration; Environmental Management; Hotel Management; Human Resources; Hygiene; Labour and Industrial Relations; Marketing; Tourism); **Communication and Design** (Advertising and Publicity; Communication Studies; Graphic Design; Industrial Design; Public Relations; Textile Design); **Computer Science** (Computer Science; Software Engineering); **Economics** (Accountancy; Administration; Agricultural Business; Business Administration; Business and Commerce; Hotel Management; International Business); **Law and Political Science** (International

Relations; Law; Political Sciences); **Psychology and Social Sciences** (Education; Psychology; Sociology)

History: Founded 1995.

Academic Year: March to November (March-July; August-November)

Admission Requirements: Secondary school certificate (bachillerato)

Main Language(s) of Instruction: Spanish, English, Portuguese

Degrees and Diplomas: *Diploma de Técnico Superior*: **Agricultural Management; Graphic Design; Human Resources; International Business; Technology.** *Licenciatura*: **Advertising and Publicity; Agricultural Management; Business Administration; Clinical Psychology; Computer Science; Graphic Design; Human Resources; Industrial and Organizational Psychology; International Business; Marketing; Sociology.** *Especialización*; *Maestría*. Also Diplomaturas

Student Services: Academic Counselling, Canteen, Careers Guidance, Cultural Activities, Facilities for disabled people, Health Services, Library, Social Counselling, Sports Facilities

Last Updated: 28/08/15

CAECE UNIVERSITY

Universidad CAECE (CAECE)

Tte. Gral. J.D.Perón 2933, 1198 Buenos Aires, Capital Federal
Tel: +54(11) 5217-7888
Fax: +54(11) 4878-7898
EMail: info@caece.edu.ar
Website: http://www.caece.edu.ar

Rector: Francisco F. von Wuthenau
EMail: rectorado@caece.edu.ar

Vicerrector Académico: Leonardo Gargiulo

Department

Administration (Accountancy; Administration; Business Administration; Human Resources; Marketing); **Biological Sciences** (Biological and Life Sciences; Environmental Management); **Humanities and Social Sciences** (Advertising and Publicity; Arts and Humanities; Biology; Chemistry; Communication Studies; Graphic Design; Hotel Management; Journalism; Music Education; Physical Education; Physics; Tourism); **Mathematics** (Mathematics; Mathematics and Computer Science); **Psychology and Pedagogical Sciences** (Education; Pedagogy; Psychology); **Systems** (Computer Networks; Systems Analysis)

Centre

Biomedical Sciences (Biomedicine)

History: Founded 1967.

Academic Year: April to November (April-June; August-November)

Admission Requirements: Secondary school certificate (bachillerato)

Degrees and Diplomas: *Licenciatura*; *Maestria*

Publications: Mathematical Elements (Scientific publication)

Publishing House: Editorial CAECE

Last Updated: 26/08/15

CATHOLIC UNIVERSITY OF ARGENTINA

Pontificia Universidad Católica Argentina Santa María de los Buenos Aires (UCA)

Edificio Santa María de los Buenos Aires, Avenida Alicia Moreau de Justo 1300 2° Piso, C1107AAZ Buenos Aires, Capital Federal
Tel: +54(11) 4349-0200
Fax: +54(11) 4349-0271
EMail: info@uca.edu.ar
Website: http://www.uca.edu.ar

Rector: Víctor Manuel Fernández (2009-)
Tel: +54(11) 4349-0251 EMail: rector@uca.edu.ar

Vicerrector: Gabriel Fernando Limodio
EMail: gabriel_limodio@uca.edu.ar

International Relations: Soledad Zapiola, Coordinator, International Relations
Tel: +54(11) 4338-0606 EMail: uca_internacional@uca.edu.ar

Faculty

Agriculture *(Buenos Aires Campus)* (Agriculture; Animal Husbandry; Food Technology); **Arts and Music** *(Buenos Aires Campus)* (Conducting; Music; Music Theory and Composition; Musicology); **Canon Law** *(Graduate School; Buenos Aires Campus)* (Canon Law); **Chemistry and Engineering** *(Fray R. Bacon, Rosario Campus)* (Chemistry; Engineering); **Economics (Mendoza Campus)** *(Mendoza Campus)* (Accountancy; Business Administration; Safety Engineering; Systems Analysis); **Economics (Rosario Campus)** (Accountancy; Business Administration; Economics); **Humanities** *(Teresa de Ávila, Paraná Campus)* (Arts and Humanities; History; Library Science; Philosophy; Psychology); **Humanities and Education** *(Mendoza Campus)* (Arts and Humanities; Education); **Law** *(Buenos Aires and Paraná Campus)* (Law); **Law and Social Sciences** *(Rosario Campus)* (Arts and Humanities; Education; History; Law; Social Sciences); **Medical Sciences** *(Buenos Aires Campus)* (Health Sciences; Medicine); **Philosophy and Letters** (English; History; Literature; Philosophy; Translation and Interpretation); **Physics, Mathematical Sciences and Engineering** *(Buenos Aires Campus)* (Civil Engineering; Computer Engineering; Electronic Engineering; Engineering; Environmental Engineering; Environmental Studies; Industrial Engineering); **Psychology and Educational Sciences** (Education; Educational Psychology; Psychology); **Social Sciences and Economics** *(Buenos Aires Campus)* (Accountancy; Business Administration; Economics; Social Sciences; Sociology); **Theology** *(Buenos Aires Campus)* (Theology)

Institute

Bioethics *(Graduate; Buenos Aires Campus)* (Biology; Ethics); **Marriage and Family Studies** (Family Studies); **Political Science and International Relations** *(Buenos Aires and Paraná Campus)* (International Relations; Political Sciences); **Social Communication, Journalism and Advertising** (Advertising and Publicity; Communication Arts; Journalism); **Social Communication, Journalism and Publicity** *(Buenos Aires Campus)* (Advertising and Publicity; Communication Studies; Journalism); **Spirituality and Pastoral Activities** (Pastoral Studies)

Further Information: Branches in Rosario, Paraná and Mendoza

History: Founded 1958 as a private University based on former Institute of Catholic Culture created in 1922. Accorded status of Pontifical University by the Holy See 1960. The University and the degrees it awards are formally recognized by the National Government. Financed by student fees and gifts. The Archbishop of Buenos Aires is Grand Chancellor.

Academic Year: March to December

Admission Requirements: Secondary school certificate (bachillerato) or equivalent and competitive entrance examination

Main Language(s) of Instruction: Spanish

Accrediting Agency: CONEAU, AMBA

Degrees and Diplomas: *Licenciatura*: **Agriculture; Animal Husbandry; Arts and Humanities; Business Administration; Canon Law; Conducting; Education; Educational Administration; English; Environmental Studies; History; Hygiene; Industrial Chemistry; International Studies; Journalism; Music; Music Theory and Composition; Musicology; Pedagogy; Philosophy; Political Sciences; Psychology; Public Administration; Public Relations; Systems Analysis.** *Especialización*: **Administrative Law; Cardiology; Constitutional Law; Criminal Law; Environmental Studies; Labour Law; Nephrology; Oncology; Ophthalmology; Orthodontics; Otorhinolaryngology; Paediatrics; Periodontics; Psychiatry and Mental Health; Respiratory Therapy; Software Engineering; Sports Medicine; Stomatology; Surgery.** *Maestría*: **Biomedicine; Business Administration; Civil Law; Communication Studies; Economics; Environmental Engineering; Labour Law; Sociology.** *Doctorado*: **Biomedicine; Business Administration; Canon Law; Economics; Educational Psychology; History; Law; Literature; Music; Philosophy; Political Sciences; Psychology; Sociology; Theology.**

Student Services: Academic Counselling, Canteen, Careers Guidance, Cultural Activities, Facilities for disabled people, Library, Sports Facilities

Publications: Antiguo Oriente; Anuario Argentino de Derecho Canónico; Colección; Consonancias; Creciendo en Familia; Cultura Económica; El Derecho; Estudios de Historia de Espana; Lecturas Sociales y Económicas; Prudentia Juris; Res Gesta; Revista de

Psicologia; Revista Teología; Sapientia; Stylos; Temas de Historia Argentina y Americana; Universitas; Vida e Ética

Publishing House: EDUCA - Editorial de la Universidad Católica Argentina

Student Numbers *2014*	MEN	WOMEN	TOTAL
All (Foreign included)	8,958	10,147	c. **19,105**

Last Updated: 16/12/15

CATHOLIC UNIVERSITY OF CÓRDOBA

Universidad Católica de Córdoba (UCC)
Obispo Trejo 323, X5000IG Córdoba, Córdoba
Tel: +54(351) 493-8000
Fax: +54(351) 493-8002
EMail: secrec@uccor.edu.ar
Website: http://www.ucc.edu.ar

Rector: Alfonso José Gomez EMail: rector@uccor.edu.ar

Vicerrector Académico: Diego Osvaldo Fonti EMail: vra@uccor.edu.ar

International Relations: Milton Ernesto Escobar, Secretario de Asuntos Internacionales EMail: dirderex@uccor.edu.ar

Faculty

Agriculture (Agriculture; Animal Husbandry; Food Technology; Vegetable Production; Veterinary Science); **Architecture** (Architecture; Landscape Architecture; Structural Architecture); **Chemistry** (Biochemistry; Food Technology; Pharmacy); **Economics and Administration** (Accountancy; Administration); **Education** (Educational Psychology; Educational Sciences; Higher Education Teacher Training; Special Education); **Engineering** (Civil Engineering; Computer Engineering; Electrical and Electronic Engineering; Electronic Engineering; Engineering; Industrial Engineering; Mechanical Engineering; Systems Analysis); **Law and Social Sciences** (Law; Notary Studies); **Medicine** (Dentistry; Medicine; Nursing; Nutrition; Occupational Therapy); **Philosophy and Humanities** (Arts and Humanities; History; Philosophy; Psychology; Religious Studies); **Political Science and International Relations** (Government; International Relations; Political Sciences; Public Administration)

School

Administration (Administration; Finance; Health Administration; Human Resources; Management; Public Administration)

History: Founded 1956 as Institute, became University and received government recognition 1959, authorized to award degrees and professional qualifications. A private institution under the direction of the Society of Jesus within the Archbishopric of Córdoba.

Academic Year: February to December (February-July; July-December)

Admission Requirements: High school Diploma (bachillerato) or recognized equivalent and entrance examination

Fees: (Pesos): Registration, 425; tuition, 420, 535 or 585 per month depending on the faculty

Main Language(s) of Instruction: Spanish

Degrees and Diplomas: *Diploma de Técnico Superior*: **Management; Social Sciences.** *Licenciatura*: **Accountancy; Animal Husbandry; Biochemistry; Business Administration; Educational Sciences; Engineering; Food Technology; History; International Relations; Law; Literature; Pharmacy; Philosophy; Religious Studies; Veterinary Science.** *Especialización*: **Cattle Breeding; Management.** *Maestría*: **Architectural and Environmental Design; Business Administration; Food Technology; Health Administration; Management.** *Doctorado*: **Agronomy; Biochemistry; Medicine.**

Student Services: Canteen, Facilities for disabled people, Foreign Studies Centre, Health Services, Language Laboratory, Library, Sports Facilities

Publications: Dialogos Pedagógicos; Studia Politicae

Last Updated: 26/08/15

CATHOLIC UNIVERSITY OF CUYO

Universidad Católica de Cuyo (UCCUYO)
Avenida Jose Ignacio la Roza 1516 Oeste, 5400 Rivadavia, San Juan
Tel: +54(264) 429-2300
Fax: +54(264) 429-2310
Website: http://www.uccuyo.edu.ar

Rector: Claudio Marcelo Larrea Arnau EMail: rectorado@uccuyo.edu.ar

Secretaria Académica: Maria Laura Simonassi EMail: s.academica@uccuyo.edu.ar

International Relations: Beatriz Farah de Aracena, Secretaria de Extensión y Relaciones Institucionales EMail: extension@uccuyo.edu.ar

Faculty

Economics and Business Science *(San Luis)* (Accountancy; Business Administration; Economics; Hotel Management; International Business; Marketing; Tourism); **Education** (Education; Educational Administration; Educational Psychology; Physical Education; Special Education); **Food Science, Biochemistry and Pharmacy** (Biochemistry; Food Science; Food Technology; Oenology; Pharmacy); **Law and Social Sciences** *(Cervantes Institute-Rio Cuarto Córdoba)* (Law; Social Sciences); **Medicine** *(Immaculate Conception Institute- Mendoza- Cervantes Institute-Río Cuarto- Córdoba)* (Medicine; Nursing; Nutrition; Physical Therapy); **Philosophy and Humanities** *(Immaculate Conception Institute- Mendoza- Cervantes Institute- Río Cuarto- Córdoba)* (Arts and Humanities; Human Resources; Philosophy)

School

Religious and Pastoral Studies (Pastoral Studies; Religious Studies)

Institute

Santa Maria (Religious Studies)

History: Founded 1959.

Academic Year: March to November

Admission Requirements: Secondary school certificate (bachillerato); Egresado del Nivel Polimodal

Fees: (US Dollars): c. 600 per trimester

Main Language(s) of Instruction: Spanish

Accrediting Agency: CONEAU; DGU; Ministry of Education, Science and Technology

Degrees and Diplomas: *Licenciatura*: **Economics; Education; Food Technology; Law; Medicine; Nursing.** *Especialización*; *Maestría*; *Doctorado*: **Education.**

Student Services: Academic Counselling, Canteen, Cultural Activities, Language Laboratory, Library, Nursery Care, Sports Facilities

Last Updated: 26/08/15

CATHOLIC UNIVERSITY OF LA PLATA

Universidad Católica de La Plata (UCALP)
Calle 13 N° 1227, 1900 La Plata, Buenos Aires
Tel: +54(221) 439-3100
EMail: info@ucalp.edu.ar
Website: http://www.ucalp.edu.ar

Rector: Hernán Mathieu EMail: rectorado@ucalp.edu.ar

Vicerrector Académico: Eduardo Ventura EMail: eduardo.ventura@ucalp.edu.ar

Faculty

Architecture and Design (Architecture; Graphic Design; Interior Design); **Dentistry** (Dentistry); **Economics and Social Sciences** (Accountancy; Business Administration; Economics; Human Resources; Tourism); **Exact Sciences and Engineering** (Computer Engineering; Environmental Engineering; Hygiene; Information Sciences); **Health Sciences** (Gynaecology and Obstetrics; Nutrition; Occupational Therapy; Rehabilitation and Therapy; Speech Therapy and Audiology); **Humanities** (Educational Psychology; Educational Sciences; History; Literature; Philosophy; Physical Education); **Law and Social Sciences** (Criminal Law; International Relations; Law; Notary Studies; Political Sciences)

Institute
Bioethics (Ethics; Family Studies)

Further Information: Also Branch in Bernal

History: Founded 1964 as a private institution. Recognized by the government and authorized to award degrees.

Academic Year: March to November

Main Language(s) of Instruction: Spanish

Degrees and Diplomas: *Licenciatura*: **Accountancy; Administration; Applied Mathematics; Architecture; Economics; Education; Law; Sociology; Statistics; Systems Analysis; Teacher Training.** *Especialización*; *Maestría*

Student Services: Library

Publications: Revista

Last Updated: 26/08/15

CATHOLIC UNIVERSITY OF LAS MISIONES

Universidad Católica de las Misiones (UCAMI)
Avenida Jauretche 1036, Esquina Av. Urquiza., Misiones
Tel: +54(376) 446-3718
EMail: info@ucami.edu.ar
Website: http://www.ucami.edu.ar

Rectora: Claudia Adriana Aguilera EMail: rectorado@ucami.edu.ar

Vicerrectora Académica: Ana María Teresita Foth
EMail: vicerr_acad@ucami.edu.ar

Faculty
Health Sciences (Gynaecology and Obstetrics; Medicine; Psychology); **Humanities** (English; Literature)

History: Founded 2012.

Main Language(s) of Instruction: Spanish

Degrees and Diplomas: *Licenciatura*

Last Updated: 26/08/15

CATHOLIC UNIVERSITY OF SALTA

Universidad Católica de Salta (UCS)
Casilla 18, Ciudad Universitaria, 4400 Campo Castañares, Salta
Tel: +54(387) 426-8924
EMail: informes@ucasal.ar
Website: http://www.ucasal.ar

Rector: Jorge Antonio Manzaraz EMail: rectorado@ucasal.net

Vicerrectora Académica: María Isabel Virgili de Rodriguez
EMail: vicerrectorado@ucasal.net

Faculty
Agriculture and Veterinary Science (Animal Husbandry; Forestry; Veterinary Science); **Architecture and Town Planning** (Architecture; Interior Design; Town Planning); **Arts and Science** (Arts and Humanities; Communication Studies; English; Graphic Design; History; Natural Sciences; Philosophy; Psychology; Radio and Television Broadcasting; Translation and Interpretation); **Economics and Administration** (Accountancy; Administration; Agricultural Management; Business Administration; Economics; Human Resources; Public Relations; Secretarial Studies); **Engineering** (Building Technologies; Civil Engineering; Computer Science; Engineering; Industrial Engineering; Telecommunications Engineering); **Law** (Criminal Law; International Relations; Law)

Programme
Distance Education (Accountancy; Business Administration; International Relations; Law)

School
Commerce (Business and Commerce); **Health Sciences** (Dentistry; Medicine; Nursing; Speech Therapy and Audiology); **Music** (Music); **Physical Education** (Physical Education); **Social Work** (Social Welfare; Social Work); **Tourism** (Tourism)

Further Information: Also Academic Centres in Metan and Buenos Aires

History: Founded 1963 and began regular courses 1967. Recognized by the government 1968 and authorized to award degrees and professional qualifications. A private institution operated with the co-operation of the Society of Jesus.

Academic Year: March to December (March-July; August-December)

Admission Requirements: Secondary school certificate (bachillerato) and entrance examination

Main Language(s) of Instruction: Spanish

Degrees and Diplomas: *Licenciatura*: **Agricultural Business; Business Administration; Business and Commerce; Criminal Law; Economics; History; Human Resources; International Relations; Literature; Modern Languages; Music; Philosophy; Physical Education; Psychology; Public Relations; Safety Engineering; Social Work; Tourism.** *Especialización*; *Maestría*

Student Services: Library

Last Updated: 26/08/15

CATHOLIC UNIVERSITY OF SANTA FE

Universidad Católica de Santa Fe (UCSF)
Echagüe 7151, 3000 Santa Fé, Santa Fé
Tel: +54(342) 460-3030
Fax: +54(342) 460-3030
EMail: ucsf@ucsf.edu.ar
Website: http://www.ucsf.edu.ar

Rector: Ricardo Mario Rocchetti EMail: rector@ucsf.edu.ar

Vicerrector Académico: Eugenio Martín De Palma

Faculty
Architecture (Architecture); **Economics** (Accountancy; Administration; Economics); **Humanities** (Arts and Humanities; Education; Educational Administration; Educational Psychology; Fine Arts; Multimedia; Social Sciences); **Law and Political Science** (Law; Political Sciences); **Philosophy** (Literature; Philosophy); **Psychology** (Psychology)

Department
Philosophy and Theology (Philosophy; Theology)

Further Information: Also Branch in Posadas

History: Founded 1957, became University 1960.

Academic Year: March to December

Admission Requirements: Secondary school certificate (bachillerato) or equivalent

Main Language(s) of Instruction: Spanish

Degrees and Diplomas: *Licenciatura*: **Accountancy; Administration; Architecture; Communication Arts; Communication Studies; Display and Stage Design; Economics; Education; Educational Psychology; Environmental Studies; Law; Philosophy; Soil Science; Teacher Training.** *Especialización*: **International Relations.** *Maestría*: **Environmental Management.** *Doctorado*: **Education; Law; Philosophy.**

Student Services: Library

Publishing house: Editorial Universidad Católica de Santa Fé

Last Updated: 26/08/15

CATHOLIC UNIVERSITY OF SANTIAGO DEL ESTERO

Universidad Católica de Santiago del Estero (UCSE)
Campus Universitario, Avenida Alsina y Dalmacio Vélez Sársfield, 4200 Santiago del Estero, Santiago del Estero
Tel: +54(385) 421-1777
Fax: +54(385) 421-1777
EMail: ucserec@ucse.edu.ar
Website: http://www.ucse.edu.ar

Rector: Luis Eugenio Lucena EMail: luis.lucena@ucse.edu.ar

Vicerrectora: Silvia Corina Carreras
EMail: silvia.carreras@ucse.edu.ar

Faculty
Applied Mathematics (Applied Mathematics; Computer Engineering; Computer Science; Electronic Engineering); **Economics** (Accountancy; Business Administration; Economics; International Business; Tourism); **Education** (Communication Studies; Education; Educational Administration; Geography; Psychology; Special Education); **Law and Political and Social Sciences** (Criminology; Human Rights; International Law; Labour Law; Law; Political Sciences; Social Sciences)

History: Founded 1960 as University institute attached to the Universidad Católica de Santa Fé. Recognized by the national government as an independent autonomous University 1969.

Academic Year: April to November (April-June; August-November)

Admission Requirements: Secondary school certificate (bachillerato) or foreign equivalent and entrance examination

Fees: (US Dollars): Registration, 150; tuition, 150 per month

Main Language(s) of Instruction: Spanish

Degrees and Diplomas: *Licenciatura*: **Accountancy; Business Administration; Business and Commerce; Design; Educational Administration; Educational Psychology; Educational Sciences; Engineering; Geography; International Relations; Journalism; Law; Mathematics Education; Psychology; Radio and Television Broadcasting; Sociology; Special Education; Theology; Tourism.** *Especialización*: **Human Resources.** *Maestría*: **Business Administration.** Also Diplomaturas Universitarias

Student Services: Academic Counselling, Canteen, Careers Guidance, Facilities for disabled people, Health Services, Sports Facilities

Publications: Revista 'Nuevas Propuestas'; Revista de la Secretaria de Ciencia y Técnica; Señales

Last Updated: 27/08/15

OLIVOS UNIT

SEDE OLIVOS

Avenida Corrientes 180, 1636 Olivos, Buenos Aires
Tel: +54(11) 4790-4110/8327
Fax: +54(11) 4790-4110
EMail: info.daba@ucse.edu.ar
Website: http://newsite.ucse.edu.ar/index.php/ucse-sedes/olivos

Directora: Liliana Bruzzo

Programme

Administration (Administration); **Education** (Educational Sciences); **Educational Institutions Administration** (Educational Administration; Public Administration); **Geography** (Geography); **Law** (Law); **Marketing** (Marketing); **Public Administration** (Public Administration)

History: Founded 1994.

Main Language(s) of Instruction: Spanish

Degrees and Diplomas: *Licenciatura*: **Accountancy; Administration; Business and Commerce; Educational Administration; Law.**

RAFAELA UNIT

SEDE RAFAELA

Boulevard Hipólito Irigoyen 1502, 2300 Rafaela, Santa Fé
Tel: +54(3492) 433-408
EMail: secextension.dar@ucse.edu.ar
Website: http://newsite.ucse.edu.ar/index.php/ucse-sedes/rafaela

Director: Edgardo Agustín Allochis

Secretario Administrativo: Jorge Alberto

Programme

Accountancy (Accountancy); **Administration** (Administration); **Computer Engineering** (Computer Engineering); **Education** (Educational Psychology); **Finance** (Finance); **Law** (Law); **Psychology** (Psychology); **Public Administration** (Public Administration); **Tourism** (Tourism)

History: Founded 2003.

Main Language(s) of Instruction: Spanish

Degrees and Diplomas: *Licenciatura*: **Accountancy; Administration; Educational Administration; Law.** *Especialización*

SAN SALVADOR DE JUJUY UNIT

SEDE SAN SALVADOR DE JUJUY

Lavalle 333, 4600 San Salvador de Jujuy, Jujuy
Tel: +54(388) 423-6881
EMail: infodass@.ucse.edu.ar
Website: http://newsite.ucse.edu.ar/index.php/ucse-sedes/jujuy

Directora: Delly Brunelli de Antoraz
EMail: dantoraz@dass.ucse.edu.ar

Programme

Business Administration (Business Administration); **Computer Engineering**; **Computer Science** (Computer Science); **International Relations** (International Relations); **Journalism** (Journalism); **Law** (Law); **Notary Studies** (Notary Studies); **Nutrition** (Nutrition); **Political Science** (Political Sciences); **Psychology** (Psychology); **Psychopedagogy** (Educational Psychology); **Tourism** (Tourism)

History: Founded 1993.

Main Language(s) of Instruction: Spanish

Degrees and Diplomas: *Licenciatura*

CEMA UNIVERSITY

Universidad del CEMA (UCEMA)

Avenida Córdoba 374, C1054AAP Buenos Aires, Capital Federal
Tel: +54(11) 6314-3000
Fax: +54(11) 4314-1654
EMail: info@ucema.edu.ar
Website: http://www.ucema.edu.ar

Rector: Carlos Alfredo Rodriguez EMail: rectorado@cema.edu.ar

Secretario Académico: Guillermo Marcos Gallacher
EMail: gmg@ucema.edu.ar

International Relations: Eugenia Napolitano, Director, Department for Professional Development EMail: men03@ucema.edu.ar

Department

Accountancy (Accountancy); **Business Administration** (Business Administration); **Economics** (Economics); **Engineering** (Computer Science; Engineering); **Finance** (Finance); **Mathematics** (Mathematics); **Political Science** (Political Sciences)

History: Founded 1978 as Centro de Estudios Macroeconómicos de Argentina (CEMA), acquired present status and title 1995.

Academic Year: March to December

Admission Requirements: Secondary school certificate (bachillerato) or recognized equivalent and entrance examination

Main Language(s) of Instruction: Spanish

Accrediting Agency: Association of MBAs (AMBA); Association to Advanced Collegiate Schools of Business (AACSB); National Commission for University Evaluation and Accreditation (CONEAU); Ministerio de Educación, Ciencia y Tecnología

Degrees and Diplomas: *Licenciatura*: **Accountancy; Business Administration; Computer Engineering; Economics; International Relations; Marketing; Political Sciences.** *Especialización*; *Maestría*: **Agricultural Business; Banking; Business Administration; Economics; Finance.** *Doctorado*: **Business Administration; Economics; Finance.**

Student Services: Academic Counselling, Canteen, Careers Guidance, Cultural Activities, Facilities for disabled people, Foreign Studies Centre, Library, Sports Facilities

Publications: Journal of Applied Economics; Revista Temas de Management; Revista UCEMA

Publishing House: Departamento Editorial de la Universidad del CEMA

Last Updated: 28/08/15

CEMIC UNIVERSITY INSTITUTE

Instituto Universitario CEMIC (IUC)

Valdenegro 4337, 1431 Buenos Aires, Capital Federal
Tel: +54(11) 5299-0914
EMail: institutouniversitario@iuc.edu.ar
Website: http://www.cemic.edu.ar

Director General: Hugo Magonza

School

Medicine (Medicine; Nursing; Nutrition; Physical Therapy)

Further Information: Also 2 Teaching Hospitals and 6 ambulatory care centres

History: Founded 1958 as Centro de Educación Médica e Investigaciones Clínicas (CEMIC) 'Norberto Quirno'. CEMIC University Institute was founded by CEMIC 1997.

Academic Year: March to December (undergraduate); June to May (postgraduate)

Main Language(s) of Instruction: Spanish

Accrediting Agency: Comisión Nacional de Evaluación y Acreditación Universitaria (CONEAU)

Degrees and Diplomas: *Licenciatura*; *Especialización*: **Dermatology; Epidemiology; Genetics; Nephrology; Urology.** *Maestría*: **Medicine.** Also Diploma in Cytotechnology (2 yrs)

Student Services: Academic Counselling, Canteen, Facilities for disabled people, Health Services, Library

Publications: Revista

Publishing House: Main University Press

Last Updated: 22/09/15

CHAMPAGNAT UNIVERSITY

Universidad Champagnat
Belgrano 721, 5501 Godoy Cruz
Tel: +54(261) 424-8443
EMail: informes@uch.edu.ar
Website: http://www.uch.edu.ar

Rector: Raúl Mercau EMail: raulmercau@uch.edu.ar

Vicerrectora Académica: María Eugenia de la Rosa EMail: medelarosa@uch.edu.ar

Faculty

Business Administration and Public Management (Accountancy; Business Administration; Economics; International Business; Tourism); **Computer Science and Design** (Computer Science; Design); **Law** (Law)

Further Information: Also San Rafael and Valle de Uco campuses

History: Founded 1991. Acquired present status 1994.

Main Language(s) of Instruction: Spanish

Degrees and Diplomas: *Licenciatura*

Last Updated: 27/08/15

DEL PLATA ADVENTIST UNIVERSITY

Universidad Adventista del Plata (UAP)
25 de Mayo 99, 3103 Libertador San Martín, Entre Ríos
Tel: +54(343) 491-8000
Fax: +54(343) 491-0300
EMail: informes@uap.edu.ar
Website: http://www.uapar.edu

Rector: Oscar Anibal Ramos EMail: rectorado@uapar.edu

International Relations: Juan Francisco Darrichón, Vicerrector EMail: direlins@uapar.edu

Faculty

Economics and Administration (Accountancy; Administration; Business Administration; Computer Science; Secretarial Studies); **Health Sciences** (Health Sciences; Medicine; Nursing); **Humanities** (Arts and Humanities; Communication Studies; Education; Educational Psychology; English; Modern Languages; Physical Education; Preschool Education; Primary Education; Psychology; Social Sciences; Translation and Interpretation); **Theology** (Pastoral Studies; Religion; Religious Education; Theology)

History: Founded as College 1898, acquired present status and title 1990.

Academic Year: March to November (March-June; August-November)

Admission Requirements: Secondary school certificate (bachillerato); admission approval by the University; entrance examination

Fees: (US Dollars): 2,400-3,900 per annum

Main Language(s) of Instruction: Spanish

Accrediting Agency: National Board of University Accreditation and Assesment; Accrediting Association of Seventh-Day Adventist Schools, Colleges and Universities

Degrees and Diplomas: *Diploma de Técnico Superior*, *Licenciatura*: **Administration; Computer Science; Educational Psychology; Nursing; Nutrition; Physical Therapy; Psychology; Theology.** *Maestría*: **Missionary Studies; Theology.** *Doctorado*: **Theology.**

Student Services: Academic Counselling, Cultural Activities, Foreign Studies Centre, Health Services, Language Laboratory, Nursery Care, Social Counselling, Sports Facilities

Publications: Davarlogos; Enfoques; Sumando

Last Updated: 26/08/15

DR PLACIDO MARIN UNIVERSITY OF SAN ISIDRO

Universidad de San Isidro Dr Placido Marín (USI)
Av. del Libertador 17115, B1643CRD Buenos Aires
EMail: info@usi.edu.ar
Website: http://www.usi.edu.ar

Rector: Gustavo Carlos Mangisch EMail: manisch@usi.edu.ar

Vicerrectora Académica: María Irma Marabotto EMail: marabotto@usi.edu.ar

Faculty

Education and Communication (Advertising and Publicity; Communication Studies; Education); **Law and Administration** (Business Administration; Commercial Law; Criminal Law; Law; Private Law; Public Law)

Main Language(s) of Instruction: Spanish

Degrees and Diplomas: *Licenciatura*

Last Updated: 28/08/15

FAVALORO UNIVERSITY

Universidad Favaloro
Solís 453, C1078AAI Buenos Aires, Ciudad Autónoma de Buenos Aires
Tel: +54 (11) 4378-1169
Fax: +54 (11) 4378-1161
EMail: info@favaloro.edu.ar
Website: http://www.favaloro.edu.ar

Rector: Facundo Francisco Manes EMail: rectorado@favaloro.edu.ar

Secretaria General: Claudia Gabriela Saracino EMail: csaracino@favaloro.edu.ar; secretariageneral@favaloro.edu.ar

International Relations: Diego Sebastián Sica, National and International Cooperation Secretary EMail: dsica@favaloro.edu.ar

Faculty

Engineering and Exact and Natural Sciences (Biology; Biomedical Engineering; Physical Engineering); **Human and Behavioural Sciences** (Psychology); **Medical Sciences** (Dietetics; Medicine; Nursing; Rehabilitation and Therapy)

Unit

Rectorship (Dentistry; Orthodontics)

Research Centre

Science and Technology (Biology; Biomedical Engineering; Biomedicine; Biotechnology; Cardiology; Cell Biology; Electronic Engineering; Embryology and Reproduction Biology; Gastroenterology; Mechanics; Medicine; Molecular Biology; Neurosciences; Nuclear Physics; Physics; Physiology; Surgery)

History: Founded 1992. Acquired present status 1998. A private Institution named after René Gerónimo Favaloro.

Academic Year: March to February.

Admission Requirements: High school certificate for undergraduate degree, and undergraduate degree for graduate certification.

Main Language(s) of Instruction: Spanish

Accrediting Agency: The National Commission of University Evaluation and Accreditation (Comisión Nacional de Evaluación y Acreditación Universitaria - CONEAU)

Degrees and Diplomas: *Licenciatura*: **Biological and Life Sciences; Dietetics; Nursing; Psychology; Rehabilitation and Therapy.** *Especialización*: **Cardiology; Dentistry; Endocrinology; Nursing; Orthodontics; Rehabilitation and Therapy;**

Respiratory Therapy. *Maestría*: Biomedical Engineering; Health Administration; Molecular Biology; Psychiatry and Mental Health. *Doctorado*: Biomedical Engineering; Medicine. Also intermediate degrees.

Student Services: Academic Counselling, Library, Social Counselling, Sports Facilities, eLibrary

Last Updated: 21/08/15

GASTÓN DACHARY UNIVERSITY

Universidad Gastón Dachary (IUGD)

Salta y Colón Piso 2, 3300 Posadas, Misiones
Tel: +54(3752) 43-8677
Fax: +54(3752) 43-8677
EMail: secretaria_rectorado@dachary.edu.ar
Website: http://www.dachary.edu.ar

Rector: Luis Enrique Lichowski
EMail: lichowski@dachary.edu.ar; secretaria_rectorado@dachary.edu.ar

Secretario Académico: Luciano J. Duarte
EMail: academica@dachary.edu.ar

Department

Design and Communication (Communication Studies; Industrial Design); **Economics and Business Studies** (Accountancy; Administration; Business and Commerce; Hotel Management; Marketing; Tourism); **Engineering and Production Sciences** (Agronomy; Animal Husbandry; Computer Engineering; Computer Science); **Health Sciences** (Nutrition; Physical Education; Physical Therapy); **Social Sciences and Law** (Educational Psychology; Law)

History: Founded 1990 as Instituto Privado de Estudios Superiores de Misiones (IPESMI), acquired present status and title 2009.

Main Language(s) of Instruction: Spanish

Accrediting Agency: Comisión Nacional de Evaluación y Acreditación Universitaria

Degrees and Diplomas: *Licenciatura*; *Especialización*; *Maestría*

Student Services: Library

Last Updated: 28/08/15

INTERAMERICAN OPEN UNIVERSITY

Universidad Abierta Interamericana (UAI)

Chacabuco 90, 1° Piso, 1069 Buenos Aires, Capital Federal
Tel: +54(11) 4342-7788
Fax: +54(11) 4342-7654
EMail: contacto@uai.edu.ar
Website: http://www.uai.edu.ar

Rector: Rodolfo N De Vincenzi

Administrative Vice President: Alfredo Fernandez

Faculty

Architecture (Architecture); **Business Administration** (Accountancy; Administration; Business Administration; Business and Commerce; Management; Marketing); **Communication Sciences** (Advertising and Publicity; Cinema and Television; Communication Studies; Graphic Design; Journalism; Mass Communication; Performing Arts); **Computer Technology** (Computer Engineering; Computer Science; Mathematics; Software Engineering; Systems Analysis); **Educational Development and Research** (Educational Sciences; Pedagogy; Preschool Education; Teacher Trainers Education; Teacher Training); **Human Development and Sport** (Education of the Handicapped; Physical Therapy; Sports); **Law and Political Sciences** (International Relations; Law; Political Sciences); **Medicine and Health Sciences** (Dentistry; Health Administration; Medicine; Nursing; Nutrition; Rehabilitation and Therapy); **Psychology and Human Relations** (Occupational Therapy; Psychology); **Tourism and Hotel Management** (Hotel Management; Tourism)

History: Founded 1995.

Academic Year: February to December

Admission Requirements: Secondary school certificate (bachillerato)

Fees: (Pesos): 148-937 per month

Main Language(s) of Instruction: Spanish

Accrediting Agency: Ministerio de Educación, Ciencia y Tecnología. Comisión de Evaluación y Acreditación Universitaria (CONEAU)

Degrees and Diplomas: *Diploma de Técnico Superior*: Business Administration; Dentistry; Management; Nursing; Tourism. *Licenciatura*: Advertising and Publicity; Art Therapy; Business Administration; Business and Commerce; Education; Educational Administration; Educational Psychology; Educational Sciences; Engineering; Fine Arts; Graphic Design; Health Administration; Hotel Management; Information Sciences; International Business; International Relations; Journalism; Marketing; Mass Communication; Music; Nursing; Nutrition; Occupational Therapy; Physical Education; Physical Therapy; Preschool Education; Psychology; Radio and Television Broadcasting; Radiology; Sports; Sports Management; Technology; Tourism. *Especialización*; *Maestría*: Business Administration; Computer Engineering; Educational Technology; Industrial and Organizational Psychology; International Business; Pharmacology. *Doctorado*: Medicine.

Student Services: Academic Counselling, Canteen, Careers Guidance, Cultural Activities, Health Services, Language Laboratory, Nursery Care, Social Counselling, Sports Facilities

Publications: Conexión Abierta

Last Updated: 16/12/15

ISALUD UNIVERSITY

Universidad ISALUD

Venezuela 925/31, C1095AAS Buenos Aires, Capital Federal
Tel: +54(11) 5239-4000
Fax: +54(11) 5239-4003
EMail: informes@isalud.edu.ar
Website: http://www.isalud.org

Rector: Rubén Torres EMail: rector@isalud.edu.ar

Secretaria Académica: Silvia Zambonini
EMail: academica@isalud.org

International Relations: Claudio Mate Rothgerber
EMail: mate@isalud.com

Programme

Environmental Management (Environmental Management); **Health Administration** (Health Administration); **Nursing** (Nursing); **Nutrition** (Nutrition); **Physiotherapy** (Physical Therapy)

History: Founded 1991.

Main Language(s) of Instruction: Spanish

Accrediting Agency: Comisión Nacional de Evaluación y Acreditación Universitaria (CONEAU)

Degrees and Diplomas: *Licenciatura*; *Especialización*; *Maestría*

Student Services: Library

Last Updated: 24/09/15

ITALIAN UNIVERSITY INSTITUTE OF ROSARIO

Instituto Universitario Italiano de Rosario (IUNIR)

Virasoso 1249, S2001ODA Rosario, Santa Fé
Tel: +54(341) 485-8893
Fax: +54(341) 482-5065
EMail: iunir@iunir.edu.ar
Website: http://www.iunir.edu.ar

Rector: Mario A. Secchi EMail: rectoria@iunir.edu.ar

Secretario Académico: Walter A. Bordino
EMail: secretariaacademica@iunir.edu.ar

School

Dentistry (Dentistry); **Medicine** (Cardiology; Child Care and Development; Gynaecology and Obstetrics; Haematology; Immunology; Surgery; Urology); **Nursing** (Biology; Computer Science; Nursing; Social Sciences); **Psychology**

Further Information: Also Teaching Hospital

History: Founded 1999.

Main Language(s) of Instruction: Spanish

Accrediting Agency: Comisión Nacional de Evaluación y Acreditación Universitaria (CONEAU)

Degrees and Diplomas: *Licenciatura*; *Especialización*: **Medicine; Surgery.** *Maestría*: **Medicine.** *Doctorado*: **Biomedicine.**
Last Updated: 22/09/15

JOHN F. KENNEDY ARGENTINE UNIVERSITY

Universidad Argentina John F. Kennedy (UK)
Calle Bartolomé Mitre 1411, 1° Piso, 1037 Buenos Aires, Capital Federal
Tel: +54(11) 4116-1000
Fax: +54(11) 4116-1000
EMail: info@kennedy.edu.ar
Website: http://www.kennedy.edu.ar

Rector: Oscar Antonio Cámpoli EMail: rectorado@kennedy.edu.ar

Department

Anthropology (Anthropology); **Architecture** (Architecture; Building Technologies); **Art** (Art Management; Fine Arts; Graphic Design; Painting and Drawing; Photography; Theatre); **Chemistry** (Chemistry; Inorganic Chemistry; Organic Chemistry); **Communications and Design** (Communication Studies; Design); **Computer Science** (Computer Science); **Economics and Administration** (Business Administration; Economics); **Health Sciences** (Biology; Dentistry); **Law** (Law; Private Law; Public Law); **Literature** (Literature); **Mathematics and Physics** (Mathematics; Physics); **Modern Languages** (English; Portuguese); **Psychology** (Clinical Psychology; Psychology); **Social Sciences** (Anthropology; Art History; Arts and Humanities; Educational Sciences; History; Pedagogy; Philosophy; Political Sciences; Social and Community Services; Sociology); **Tourism** (Demography and Population; Tourism)

History: Founded 1964 as college, became University 1981. A private institution authorized by governmental decree and responsible to the Ministry of Education and Justice.

Academic Year: March to November; December to March

Admission Requirements: Secondary school certificate (bachillerato)

Main Language(s) of Instruction: Spanish

Degrees and Diplomas: *Diploma de Técnico Superior*: **Teacher Training.** *Licenciatura*; *Especialización*; *Maestría*; *Doctorado*: **Law; Psychology.**
Last Updated: 23/09/15

JUAN AGUSTÍN MAZA UNIVERSITY

Universidad Juan Agustín Maza (UMAZA)
Avenida de Acceso Este Lateral Sur N° 2245, 5519 Guaymallén, Mendoza
Tel: +54(261) 405-6200
EMail: informes@umaza.edu.ar
Website: http://www.umaza.edu.ar

Rector: Daniel Roberto Miranda EMail: rector@umaza.edu.ar
Vicerrectora Académica: Viviana Catalano
EMail: vcatalano@umaza.edu.ar

International Relations: Eduardo José Salvarini, Vicerrector de Extensión Universitaria EMail: esalvarini@umaza.edu.ar

Faculty

Business Administration and Law (Accountancy; Business Administration; Human Resources); **Education** (Dance; Education; Physical Education; Teacher Training); **Engineering** (Engineering); **Environmental and Veterinary Sciences** (Environmental Studies; Veterinary Science); **Journalism** (Advertising and Publicity; Journalism); **Kinesiology and Physiotherapy** (Physical Therapy); **Nutrition** (Nutrition); **Oenology and Agricultural Industries** (Fruit Production; Horticulture; Oenology); **Pharmacy and Biochemistry** (Biochemistry; Pharmacy)

History: Founded 1960. Acquired present status 1980.

Academic Year: April to March

Admission Requirements: Completed intermediary, secondary or polymodal studies

Main Language(s) of Instruction: Spanish

Degrees and Diplomas: *Licenciatura*: **Accountancy; Advertising and Publicity; Computer Science; Human Resources; Nutrition; Oenology; Pharmacy; Physical Education; Physical Therapy.** *Especialización*: **Accountancy; Higher Education; Management; Physical Therapy; Surveying and Mapping; Veterinary Science.** *Maestría*: **Communication Arts; Management; Viticulture.**

Student Services: Academic Counselling, Canteen, Facilities for disabled people, Language Laboratory, Library, Sports Facilities

Publications: UJAM News
Last Updated: 28/08/15

MAIMÓNIDES UNIVERSITY

Universidad Maimónides (UM)
Hidalgo 775, 1013 Buenos Aires, Capital Federal
Tel: +54(11) 4905-1101
Fax: +54(11) 4982-8181
Website: http://www.maimonides.edu.ar

Chairman of Board of Governors: Ernesto Goberman
EMail: rectorado@maimonides.edu

Secretario Académico: Alejandra Marinaro
EMail: marinaro.alejandra@maimonides.edu

Faculty

Health Sciences (Biochemistry; Biology; Dentistry; Dermatology; Medicine; Nursing; Nutrition; Physical Therapy); **Humanities, Social and Managerial Sciences** (Administration; Arts and Humanities; Business and Commerce; Education; Educational Sciences; Gerontology; Human Resources; Law; Music; Psychology; Social Sciences; Tourism)

School

Multimedia (Information Technology; Multimedia)

Further Information: Distance learning courses in Contemporary Strategy; Geopolitics; International Relations; Political Science; Strategy

History: Founded 1990.

Academic Year: March to December (March-June; August-December)

Admission Requirements: Secondary school certificate (bachillerato) or equivalent

Fees: (US Dollars): 1,200-9,000 per annum

Main Language(s) of Instruction: Spanish

Accrediting Agency: CONEAU

Degrees and Diplomas: *Licenciatura*: **Family Studies; Health Administration; Medicine; Peace and Disarmament; Social Problems.** *Especialización*: **Dentistry; Forensic Medicine and Dentistry; Medical Technology; Medicine; Paediatrics; Paramedical Sciences; Psychotherapy; Radiology.** *Maestría*: **Administration; Child Care and Development; Dentistry; Ecology; International Relations.** *Doctorado*: **Medicine; Psychology.**

Student Services: Academic Counselling, Cultural Activities, Facilities for disabled people, Language Laboratory, Library, Sports Facilities
Last Updated: 28/08/15

METROPOLITAN UNIVERSITY FOR EDUCATION AND LABOUR

Universidad Metropolitana para la Educación y el Trabajo (UMET)
Sarmiento 2037, C1044AAE Buenos Aires, Buenos Aires
Tel: +54(11) 53 54 66 69
EMail: info@umet.edu.ar
Website: http://umet.edu.ar

Rector: Nicolás Trotta EMail: trotta.n@umet.edu.ar

Vicerrectora: Alejandra García Martínez
EMail: agarciamartinez.a@umet.edu.ar

International Relations: Pablo Javier Zardini, Head of International Relations EMail: zardini.p@umet.edu.ar

Faculty

School of Applied Technology (Building Technologies; Crafts and Trades; Electrical and Electronic Equipment and Maintenance; Industrial Maintenance; Mechanical Equipment and Maintenance; Technology); **School of Organization Development and Management** (Management; Real Estate; Social Policy; Social Problems; Social Studies; Welfare and Protective Services); **School of**

Private Policies and Environmental Management (Environmental Management; Government; Leadership; Social Policy; Social Problems; Social Studies; Social Welfare; Urban Studies); **School of Tourism, Physical Education and Sports** (Physical Education; Sports; Tourism)

History: Founded 2012.

Academic Year: From March to December

Admission Requirements: High school certificate (or original transcript legalized) with its photocopy, original passport with its photocopy and 2 color photos 4 x 4 updated (photocopies not accepted). In the case of not having the secondary title, registration is conditional until the first call to examination tables, when should submit: original certificate of title pending. Foreign Students: in addition to the documentation requested by the institution, to finish the official enrollment form, the applicant must validate the mid-level title spread by the origin country to the program office Equivalence and Recognition of Qualifications. For applicants from countries with which Argentina has Convention: Montevideo 950 Capital Federal. Tel: 41 29 13 17. For applicants from countries with which Argentina has not Convention: 55. Emerald Capital Federal. During the period until the title is properly presented and approved, the student may not take exams that prove the continuity of the course. More information on Department of Students.

Main Language(s) of Instruction: Spanish

Degrees and Diplomas: *Licenciatura*: **Building Technologies; Business Administration; Computer Science; Ecology; Education; Environmental Management; Environmental Studies; Industrial Maintenance; Maintenance Technology; Mathematics; Physical Education; Real Estate; Social Policy; Social Problems; Social Studies; Sports; Systems Analysis; Teacher Trainers Education; Teacher Training; Tourism; Urban Studies.** Also bachelor's degrees in: Social and Organizations Management, Operational Management of Intelligent Buildings, Real State Management, Tourism, Public Policies and Government, Environmental Management and Sustainable Development and Teacher Training College in Physical Education and Sports.

Student Services: Academic Counselling, Canteen, Careers Guidance, Cultural Activities, Facilities for disabled people, IT Centre, Language Laboratory, Library, Sports Facilities, eLibrary

Publications: Editorial Octubre; Editorial UMET

Academic Staff *2013-2014*	**TOTAL**
FULL-TIME	60
PART-TIME	78
STAFF WITH DOCTORATE	
FULL-TIME	12
Student Numbers *2013-2014*	
All (Foreign included)	1,050

Last Updated: 18/08/15

SAINT THOMAS AQUINUS UNIVERSITY OF THE NORTH

Universidad del Norte Santo Tomás de Aquino (UNSTA)

9 de Julio 165, 4000 San Miguel de Tucumán, Tucumán
Tel: +54(381) 422-8805
EMail: info@unsta.edu.ar
Website: http://www.unsta.edu.ar

Rector: Luis Raúl Alcaide EMail: lralcaide@unsta.edu.ar

Secretaria Académica: Liliana Oterino
EMail: loterino@unsta.edu.ar

Faculty

Economics and Administration (Accountancy; Administration; Business Administration; Economics; Tourism); **Engineering** (Computer Engineering; Environmental Management; Graphic Design; Hygiene; Industrial Engineering; Multimedia; Transport Management); **Health Sciences** (Health Sciences; Nutrition; Occupational Therapy; Psychology; Radiology); **Humanities** (Modern Languages; Philosophy); **Law and Political Science** (Law; Notary Studies; Political Sciences)

Centre

Institutional Studies (Public Administration)

Further Information: Also University Centre in Concepción

History: Founded 1956 as institute, acquired present status and title 1965.

Academic Year: March to November

Admission Requirements: Secondary school certificate (bachillerato)

Main Language(s) of Instruction: Spanish

Degrees and Diplomas: *Licenciatura*: **Business Administration; Educational Administration; Graphic Design; Law; Nutrition; Philosophy; Psychology; Tourism.** *Especialización*; *Maestría*

Student Services: Academic Counselling, Health Services, Language Laboratory, Library, Sports Facilities

Publications: Propuestas; Sto. Tomás Moro; STUDIUM Filosofía y Teología

Last Updated: 28/08/15

SAN ANDRÉS UNIVERSITY

Universidad de San Andrés (UDESA)

Vito Dumas 284, B1644BID Victoria, Buenos Aires
Tel: +54(11) 4725-7000
EMail: rectorado@udesa.edu.ar
Website: http://www.udesa.edu.ar

Rector: Fernando Rosenkrantz EMail: rosenkrantz@udesa.edu.ar

Vicerrector: Roberto Bouzas EMail: rbouzas@udesa.edu.ar

School

Administration and Business (Accountancy; Administration; Business Administration; Human Resources; Management; Marketing); **Education** (Education)

Department

Economics (Economics); **Humanities** (Arts and Humanities; History; Literature; Philosophy); **Law** (Law); **Mathematics and Science** (Mathematics; Statistics); **Social Sciences** (Communication Studies; International Relations; Political Sciences)

Chair

Entrepreneurship *(Karl Steur)* (Business Administration; Finance; Management)

History: Founded 1838 as Escuela Escocesa San Andrés by members of 'St. Andrew's Scots' School, an educational institution established by the Presbiterian Church. Acquired present status and title 1988.

Academic Year: March to December (March-July; August-December)

Admission Requirements: Secondary school certificate (bachillerato) and entrance examination

Main Language(s) of Instruction: Spanish, English

Degrees and Diplomas: *Licenciatura*; *Especialización*; *Maestría*; *Doctorado*: **Economics; Education; History.**

Student Services: Academic Counselling, Canteen, Careers Guidance, Cultural Activities, Facilities for disabled people, Foreign Studies Centre, Language Laboratory, Sports Facilities

Publications: Investigaciones; Trabajos Docentes

Last Updated: 28/08/15

SOUTHERN UNIVERSITY

Universidad Austral

Cerrito 1250, C1010AAZ Buenos Aires, Capital Federal
Tel: +54(11) 5239-8000
EMail: admisiones@austral.edu.ar
Website: http://www.austral.edu.ar

Rector: Fernando Fraguiero EMail: rectorado@austral.edu.ar

Vicerrector Académico: Juan Cianciardo

Faculty

Biomedical Sciences *(Derqui, Pilar)* (Biomedicine); **Business Studies** (Accountancy; Business Administration); **Communication** (Communication Studies; Journalism); **Engineering** (Automation and Control Engineering; Computer Engineering; Engineering; Systems Analysis); **Law** (Law)

School

Business *(IAE, Derqui, Pilar)* (Business Administration; Business and Commerce; Management); **Education** (Education; Educational Administration; Higher Education)

Institute
Family Studies (Family Studies); **Philosophy** (Philosophy)

Further Information: Also University Hospital

History: Founded as Graduate School of Business (IAE), acquired present status and title 1991. A private institution promoted by the Asociación Civil de Estudios Superiores.

Academic Year: March to November (March-July; August-November)

Admission Requirements: Secondary school certificate (bachillerato) or equivalent and competitive entrance examination

Fees: (US Dollars): 3,000 per annum; graduate, 5,000-17,000

Main Language(s) of Instruction: Spanish

Degrees and Diplomas: *Licenciatura*; *Especialización*; *Maestría*; *Doctorado*: **Business Administration; Communication Studies; Law; Medicine.**

Student Services: Canteen, Careers Guidance, Facilities for disabled people, Language Laboratory, Library, Sports Facilities

Last Updated: 26/08/15

UNIVERSITY INSTITUTE - ARGENTINA BUSINESS SCHOOL

Instituto Universitario Escuela Argentina de Negocios (IUEAN)

Av. Córdoba 1690, C1055AAT Buenos Aires, Capital Federal
Tel: +54(11) 5032-3900
EMail: informes@iuean.edu.ar
Website: http://www.iuean.edu.ar

Rectora: Ariana De Vincenzi
EMail: ariana.devincenzi@iuean.edu.ar

Vicerrectora Académica: Beatríz Checchia
EMail: beatriz.checchia@iuean.edu.ar

Programme
Business Administration (Business Administration); **Computer Engineering** (Computer Engineering); **Hotel Management** (Hotel Management); **Human Resources** (Human Resources); **International Business** (International Business); **Marketing** (Marketing)

Area
E-Learning and Distance Education (Distance Education)

Further Information: Also another site in Martinez

History: Founded 1993. Acquired present status 2004.

Academic Year: March to December

Admission Requirements: Secondary school certificate; Basic knowledge of spanish

Fees: (Pesos): 5,820 per annum

Main Language(s) of Instruction: Spanish

Accrediting Agency: Comisión Nacional de Evaluation y Acreditacion Universitaria (CONEAU)

Degrees and Diplomas: *Licenciatura*: **Computer Engineering; Hotel Management; Human Resources; International Business; Marketing.** Also Diplomado (6-9 months), Analista Universitario 3 yrs

Student Services: Academic Counselling, Careers Guidance, Language Laboratory

Publications: Carrera & Negocios; Innova

Last Updated: 22/09/15

UNIVERSITY INSTITUTE - GRADUATE SCHOOL OF ECONOMICS AND BUSINESS ADMINISTRATION

Instituto Universitario Escuela Superior de Economía y Administración de Empresas (ESEADE)

Uriarte 2472, 1425 Buenos Aires, Capital Federal
Tel: +54(11) 4773-5825 +54(11) 4773-3735
Fax: +54(11) 4773-3735
EMail: info@eseade.edu.ar
Website: http://www.eseade.edu.ar

Rector: Luis Del Prado

Vicerrector - Secretario Académico (A/c): Adrián Pin
EMail: pin@eseade.edu.ar

Director del Departamento de Administración y Formación Empresaria: Alfredo Blousson EMail: blousson@eseade.edu.ar

International Relations: Pablo Lannello, Coordinador de Relaciones Internacionales EMail: lanello@eseade.edu.ar

Department
Administration and Business Studies (Administration; Business Administration); **Art and Design** (Design; Fine Arts); **Economics and Social Sciences** (Economics; Social Sciences); **Humanities and Communication** (Arts and Humanities; Communication Studies)

History: Founded 1978. Acquired present status 1999. A private Graduate School.

Main Language(s) of Instruction: Spanish

Degrees and Diplomas: *Licenciatura*; *Especialización*; *Maestría*: **Business Administration.** *Doctorado*: **Business Administration.**

Student Services: Academic Counselling

Publications: Libertas

Last Updated: 25/08/15

UNIVERSITY INSTITUTE OF BIOMEDICAL SCIENCES OF CORDOBA

Instituto Universitario de Ciencias Biomedicas de Córdoba (IUCBC)

Córdoba
EMail: info@iucbc.edu.ar
Website: http://www.iucbc.edu.ar

Rector: Luis María Amuchastegui EMail: rectorado@iucbc.edu.ar

Secretaria Académica: Cecilia Cravero
EMail: cecravero@yahoo.es

Area
Humanities (Anthropology; Ethics; Literature; Philosophy; Sociology); **Medicine** (Gynaecology and Obstetrics; Medicine; Paediatrics; Surgery)

UNIVERSITY INSTITUTE OF HEALTH SCIENCES - HÉCTOR A. BARCELÓ FOUNDATION

Instituto Universitario de Ciencias de la Salud Fundación Héctor A. Barceló (IUCS)

Avenida Las Heras 2191, 1127 Capital Federal, Buenos Aires
Tel: +54(11) 4800-0200
Fax: +54(11) 4800-0239
EMail: rectorado@barcelo.edu.ar
Website: http://www.barcelo.edu.ar

Rector: Héctor Alejandro Barceló (2006-)
EMail: rectorado@barcelo.edu.ar

Vicerrector: Alfredo Cáceres EMail: vicerectorado@barcelo.edu.ar

Secretario Académico: Ricardo Znaidak
EMail: secretariaacademica@barcelo.edu.ar

Faculty
Medicine (Health Sciences; Medical Technology; Medicine; Neurology; Nursing; Pharmacology; Physical Therapy; Psychology; Surgery)

Department
Health Sciences *(La Rioja)* (Dietetics; Health Administration; Health Sciences; Medical Technology; Medicine; Physical Therapy)

Further Information: Branches in La Rioja and Santo Tomé. Also 3 Teaching Hospitals

History: Founded 1968 as Biological Foundation and Research Institute. Acquired present status and title 1992.

Academic Year: February to December

Admission Requirements: Secondary school certificate (bachillerato) Introduction Course

Fees: (US Dollars): c.4,200 per annum; Medicine, c.6,600; Postgraduate, c.2,400

Main Language(s) of Instruction: Spanish

Accrediting Agency: Ministerial Resolution No. 1247 of 26/06/1992. Comisión Nacional de Evaluación y Acreditación Universitaria (CONEAU).

Degrees and Diplomas: *Licenciatura*; *Especialización*; *Maestría*; *Doctorado*: **Health Sciences.**

Student Services: Academic Counselling, Canteen, Careers Guidance, Cultural Activities, Facilities for disabled people, Foreign Studies Centre, Health Services, Language Laboratory, Library, Nursery Care, Residential Facilities, Social Counselling, Sports Facilities, eLibrary

Academic Staff *2013-2014*	MEN	WOMEN	TOTAL
FULL-TIME	–	–	**400**
PART-TIME	–	–	**400**
STAFF WITH DOCTORATE			
FULL-TIME	60	10	c. **70**
Student Numbers *2013-2014*			
All (Foreign included)	3,000	4,000	c. **7,000**
FOREIGN ONLY	300	300	**600**

Last Updated: 19/08/15

UNIVERSITY INSTITUTE OF MENTAL HEALTH OF THE BUENOS AIRES PSYCHOANALYTICAL ASSOCIATION (APDEBA)

Instituto Universitario de Salud Mental de la Asociación Psicoanalítica de Buenos Aires (APdeBA) (IUSAM)

Maure 1850, C1426CUH Buenos Aires, Capital Federal
Tel: +54(11) 4775-7867/7985
Fax: +54(11) 4775-7867/7985, Ext.16
EMail: info@iusam.edu.ar
Website: http://www.iusam.edu.ar

Rector: Rodolfo Moguillansky EMail: moguilla@gmail.com

Vicerrectora Académica: Sara Zac de Filc

Area

Culture (Cultural Studies); **Psychoanalysis** (Psychoanalysis); **Psychopathology** (Family Studies; Psychiatry and Mental Health)

Department

Research on Psychoanalysis and Mental Health

History: Founded 2005. Part of the International Psychoanalytical Association (IPA)

Academic Year: March to December

Admission Requirements: A Degree in Medicine or Psychology; University Degree or equivalent for Masters

Fees: 1,640-4,990 per annum depending on subjects (Argentine Peso)

Main Language(s) of Instruction: Spanish

Accrediting Agency: Provisional authorization Decree No. 352 of 2005. Comisión Nacional de Evaluación y Acreditación Universitaria (CONEAU)

Degrees and Diplomas: *Especialización*: **Psychoanalysis.** *Maestría*: **Art Therapy; Family Studies.**

Student Services: Academic Counselling, Facilities for disabled people

Publications: Revista Psicoanálisis

Last Updated: 16/12/15

UNIVERSITY INSTITUTE SCHOOL OF MEDICINE OF THE ITALIAN HOSPITAL

Instituto Universitario Escuela de Medicina del Hospital Italiano (IUHI)

Potosí 4240, 1119 Buenos Aires, Capital Federal
Tel: +54(11) 4959-0200 (Int. 4161)
Fax: +54(11) 4983-2624
EMail: escuelademedicina@hospitalitaliano.org.ar
Website: http://www.hospitalitaliano.org.ar/educacion/iuhi

Rector: Marcelo Fernando Figari
EMail: marcelo.figar@hospitalitaliano.org.ar

Secretaria Académica: Elsa Mercedes Nucifora
EMail: enucifora@hitalba.edu.ar

Secretaria: Matilde Acosta
EMail: matilde.acosta@hospitalitaliano.org.ar

Department

Applied Biochemistry (Biochemistry); **Cell and Molecular Biology** (Cell Biology; Molecular Biology); **Diagnostics and Medical Treatment** (Health Sciences; Medicine); **Health Professions and Research** (Health Sciences); **Immunology**; **Medical Computer Science** (Computer Science); **Medicine** (Medicine); **Nursing** (Nursing); **Paediatrics** (Paediatrics); **Pathology** (Pathology); **Pharmacology and Toxicology** (Pharmacology; Pharmacy; Toxicology); **Physiology** (Physiology); **Public Health** (Public Health); **Surgery** (Surgery)

History: Founded 2000.

Fees: (US Dollars): Tuition, 300

Main Language(s) of Instruction: Spanish

Accrediting Agency: Comisión Nacional de Evaluación y Acreditación Universitaria (CONEAU)

Degrees and Diplomas: *Licenciatura*: **Medicine; Nursing.** *Especialización*; *Maestría*

Last Updated: 25/08/15

UNIVERSITY OF ARGENTINIAN SOCIAL STUDIES

Universidad del Museo Social Argentino (UMSA)

Avenida Corrientes 1723, 1042 Buenos Aires, Capital Federal
Tel: +54(11) 4375-4601
Fax: +54(11) 4375-4600
EMail: informes@umsa.edu.ar
Website: http://www.umsa.edu.ar

Rector: Alejandra Garbarini Islas EMail: rectorado@umsa.edu.ar

Secretario General: Aníbal Luzuriaga

Faculty

Arts (Art History; Heritage Preservation; Interior Design; Landscape Architecture; Museum Management; Museum Studies; Restoration of Works of Art; Visual Arts); **Economics** (Accountancy; Business Administration; Business and Commerce; Economics; International Business); **Human Sciences** (Psychology; Social and Community Services; Speech Therapy and Audiology); **Law and Social Sciences** (Human Resources; Journalism; Law; Social Studies); **Modern Languages** (English; Translation and Interpretation)

History: Founded 1956, acquired present status 2001.

Academic Year: March to November (March-June; July-November)

Admission Requirements: Secondary school certificate, and other minimum requirements

Main Language(s) of Instruction: Spanish

Accrediting Agency: Comisión Nacional de Evaluación y Acreditación Universitaria (CONEAU) and National Evaluation and Acreditation Commission

Degrees and Diplomas: *Licenciatura*: **Art History; Arts and Humanities; Business Administration; Business and Commerce; Communication Studies; Education; Heritage Preservation; International Business; Journalism; Labour and Industrial Relations; Library Science; Museum Studies; Pedagogy; Psychology; Speech Therapy and Audiology; Visual Arts.** *Especialización*; *Maestría*: **Information Sciences.** *Doctorado*: **Speech Therapy and Audiology.**

Student Services: Academic Counselling, Canteen, Careers Guidance, Cultural Activities, Language Laboratory, Library, Sports Facilities

Publications: Conceptos; Foro Politico/Foro Economico

Last Updated: 16/12/15

UNIVERSITY OF BELGRANO

Universidad de Belgrano (UB)

Zabala 1837/51 2° Piso, 1426 Buenos Aires, Capital Federal
Tel: +54(11) 4788-5400
Fax: +54(11) 4788-5400, Ext. 2557
EMail: ingresos@ub.edu.ar
Website: http://www.ub.edu.ar

Presidente: Avelino Jose Porto (1964-)
Tel: +54(11) 4576-3928 EMail: avelino.porto@ub.edu.ar

Vicepresidente de Gestión Técnica y Administrativa: Eustaquio Castro EMail: eustaquio.castro@ub.edu.ar

Faculty

Agriculture (Agricultural Business; Agriculture); **Architecture and Town Planning** (Advertising and Publicity; Architecture; Graphic Design; Interior Design; Town Planning); **Distance Learning Education** *(2-yr programmes)* (Farm Management; International Business; Sales Techniques; Small Business; Tourism); **Economics** (Accountancy; Business Administration; Economics; Hotel Management; Human Resources; International Business; Marketing; Sales Techniques); **Engineering and Computer Technology** (Civil Engineering; Computer Science; Electrical and Electronic Engineering; Engineering; Industrial Engineering; Mechanical Engineering; Telecommunications Engineering); **Exact and Natural Sciences** (Biological and Life Sciences; Biology; Chemistry; Food Science; Food Technology; Natural Sciences; Pharmacy); **Graduate Studies** (International Economics; International Relations; Political Sciences; Sociology); **Health Sciences** (Health Sciences; Nutrition); **Humanities** *(Undergraduate)* (Cinema and Television; Clinical Psychology; Industrial and Organizational Psychology; Psychology; Public Relations; Radio and Television Broadcasting; Tourism); **Law and Social Sciences** *(Undergraduate)* (International Relations; Journalism; Law; Political Sciences)

School

Economics and International Business *(Graduate)* (Agricultural Business; Banking; Business Administration; Economics; Finance; Human Resources; International Business; Management; Marketing); **Languages and Foreign Studies** (English; Modern Languages; Translation and Interpretation)

Department

Postgraduate Studies and Continuing Education (Business Administration; Communication Studies; Economics; Finance; Human Resources; Management; Marketing)

Further Information: Also Study Abroad programmes. Courses for foreign students

History: Founded 1964. A private institution under the jurisdiction of the Federal Government.

Academic Year: March to December (March-July; August-December)

Admission Requirements: Secondary school certificate (bachillerato) or equivalent

Main Language(s) of Instruction: Spanish

Degrees and Diplomas: *Licenciatura*; *Especialización*; *Maestría*; *Doctorado*: **Political Sciences.** Also Diplomado Internacional en Management Estratégico

Student Services: Academic Counselling, Canteen, Careers Guidance, Cultural Activities, Health Services, Language Laboratory, Social Counselling, Sports Facilities

Publishing house: Editorial de Belgrano

Last Updated: 27/08/15

UNIVERSITY OF BUSINESS AND SOCIAL SCIENCES

Universidad de Ciencias Empresariales y Sociales (UCES)

Paraguay 1401, C1057AAV Buenos Aires, Capital Federal
Tel: +54(11) 4815-3290
Fax: +54(11) 4813-5635
EMail: informes@uces.edu.ar
Website: http://www.uces.edu.ar

Rector: Gastón Alejandro ÓDonnell EMail: rectorado@uces.edu.ar

Secretaria Académica: Viviana Dopchiz
EMail: vdopchiz@uces.edu.ar

Faculty

Business Administration (Business Administration; International Business; Marketing; Tourism); **Communication** (Advertising and Publicity; Communication Studies; Graphic Design; Journalism); **Economics** (Accountancy; Business Administration; Economics; Finance; Human Resources); **Health Sciences** (Health Administration; Health Sciences; Medicine; Nursing; Nutrition; Physical Therapy); **Law and Political Sciences** (Law; Political Sciences); **Psychology and Social Sciences** (Educational Sciences; Philosophy; Psychology; Social Sciences; Sociology)

Further Information: Also Regional Centre

History: Founded 1988.

Main Language(s) of Instruction: Spanish

Degrees and Diplomas: *Licenciatura*; *Especialización*; *Maestría*; *Doctorado*: **Law; Psychology; Public Health.**

Student Services: Library

Last Updated: 27/08/15

UNIVERSITY OF CINEMA STUDIES

Universidad del Cine (UCINE)

Pasaje J. M. Giuffra 330, San Telmo, C1064ADD Buenos Aires, Capital Federal
Tel: +54(11) 4300-1413
Fax: +54(11) 4300-0674
EMail: ucine@ucine.edu.ar
Website: http://www.ucine.edu.ar

Rector: Manuel Antín (1991-) EMail: m-antin@ucine.edu.ar

Secretaria Académica: Graciela B. Fernández Toledo
EMail: gfernandeztoledo@ucine.edu.ar

International Relations: María Marta Antín
EMail: mmantin@ucine.edu.ar

Faculty

Cinema (Cinema and Television; Display and Stage Design; Film); **Communication Sciences** (Communication Studies; Distance Education; Graphic Design; Visual Arts)

History: Founded 1991, acquired present status and title 1993.

Academic Year: March to December

Admission Requirements: Secondary school certificate (bachillerato)

Fees: (US Dollars): 3,850-5,500 per annum

Main Language(s) of Instruction: Spanish

Degrees and Diplomas: *Licenciatura*: **Cinema and Television; Design; Educational Sciences; Publishing and Book Trade; Theatre.** *Maestría*

Student Services: Academic Counselling, Canteen, Careers Guidance, Cultural Activities, Language Laboratory, Social Counselling

Last Updated: 18/08/15

UNIVERSITY OF CONCEPCIÓN DEL URUGUAY

Universidad de Concepción del Uruguay (UCU)

8 de Junio 522, 3260 Concepción del Uruguay, Entre Ríos
Tel: +54(3442) 42-5606
Fax: +54(3422) 42-7721
EMail: info@ucu.edu.ar
Website: http://www.ucu.edu.ar

Rector: Héctor César Sauret
EMail: rectorado@ucu.universia.com.ar

Secretaria Académica: Mauricio Lopéz
EMail: academica@ucu.edu.ar

Faculty

Agricultural Sciences (Agricultural Engineering); **Architecture and Town Planning** (Architecture; Interior Design; Town Planning); **Communication and Education** (Educational Administration; English; Journalism; Physical Education); **Economics** (Accountancy; Administration; Business and Commerce; Economics; International Business; Marketing); **Law and Social Sciences** (Law; Sociology); **Medicine** (Haematology; Immunology; Medicine; Nutrition)

Further Information: Also Regional Centres in Gualeguaychú, Paraná, and Rosario

History: Founded 1971.

Academic Year: February to December

Main Language(s) of Instruction: Spanish

Degrees and Diplomas: *Licenciatura*; *Especialización*; *Maestría*

Last Updated: 27/08/15

UNIVERSITY OF CONGRESS

Universidad de Congreso

Avenida Colón 90, M5500GEN Mendoza, Mendoza
Tel: +54(261) 423-0630
EMail: info@ucongreso.edu.ar
Website: http://www.ucongreso.edu.ar

Rector: Francisco Piñón EMail: pinonf@ucongreso.edu.ar

Vicerrector de Gestión Académica: Víctor Eugenio Duplancic EMail: duplancicv@ucongreso.edu.ar

International Relations: María Landa EMail: landama@ucongreso.edu.ar

Department

Architecture (Architecture); **Business** (Accountancy; Administration; Business Administration; Business and Commerce; Human Resources; International Business); **Communication Studies** (Communication Studies); **Computer Science** (Computer Science); **Environmental Sciences** (Environmental Studies); **Law** (Law)

Further Information: Also branch in Cordoba

History: Founded 1994.

Academic Year: March to February

Admission Requirements: Secondary school certificate (bachillerato) and competitive entrance examination

Fees: (Pesos): 250 per annum

Main Language(s) of Instruction: Spanish, English and Portuguese

Degrees and Diplomas: *Licenciatura*: **Accountancy; Business Administration; Communication Arts; Information Technology; International Relations; Law; Marketing.** *Especialización*; *Maestría*

Student Services: Academic Counselling, Canteen, Cultural Activities, Language Laboratory, Sports Facilities

Publications: Magazine of Trasandinian Studies

Last Updated: 27/08/15

UNIVERSITY OF FLORES

Universidad de Flores (UFLO)

Av. Nazca 274, 1406 Buenos Aires, Capital Federal
Tel: +54(11) 4611-4800
Fax: +54(11) 4613-3636
EMail: informes@uflo.edu.ar
Website: http://www.uflo.edu.ar

Rector: Néstor Blanco EMail: secretariarectorado@uflo.edu.ar

Vicerrectora Académica: Ruth Fische EMail: Sacademica@uflo.edu.ar

Faculty

Administration (Accountancy; Administration); **Engineering** (Environmental Engineering; Safety Engineering); **Law** (Law); **Physical Education and Sports** (Physical Education; Sports); **Psychology and Social Sciences** (Communication Studies; Psychology); **Socio-environmental Design** (Architectural and Environmental Design; Architecture and Planning; Graphic Design; Town Planning)

Further Information: Also Teaching Hospitals. Branch in Comahue

History: Founded 1995.

Academic Year: March to December (March-July; August-December)

Admission Requirements: Secondary school certificate (bachillerato); entrance examination for students over 25 without secondary title

Main Language(s) of Instruction: Spanish

Degrees and Diplomas: *Licenciatura*: **Administration; Architecture; Environmental Engineering; Graphic Design; Law; Psychology; Sports; Toxicology.** *Maestría*; *Doctorado*: **Psychology.**

Student Services: Academic Counselling, Canteen, Cultural Activities, Facilities for disabled people, Health Services, Social Counselling, Sports Facilities

Publishing house: Editorial UFLO. Editorial IPPEM

Last Updated: 27/08/15

UNIVERSITY OF MENDOZA

Universidad de Mendoza (UM)

Boulogne sur Mer 683, 5500 Mendoza, Mendoza
Tel: +54(261) 420-2017
Fax: +54(261) 420-1100
EMail: rectorado@um.edu.ar
Website: http://www.um.edu.ar

Rector: Emilio Vázquez Viera (1993-) EMail: rectorado@um.edu.ar

Secretaria Académica: María José Reina EMail: maria.reina@um.edu.ar

Faculty

Architecture, Town Planning and Design (Architecture; Design; Interior Design; Textile Design; Town Planning); **Economics** (Accountancy; Business Administration); **Engineering** (Bioengineering; Computer Engineering; Electrical and Electronic Engineering; Industrial Engineering; Systems Analysis; Telecommunications Engineering); **Health Sciences** (Dentistry; Medicine; Physical Therapy; Psychology); **Law and Social Sciences** (Law; Social Sciences)

Further Information: Also branch in San Rafael

History: Founded 1959. A private institution officially recognized by the government.

Academic Year: March to November (March-June; August-November)

Admission Requirements: Secondary school certificate (bachillerato) and entrance examination

Main Language(s) of Instruction: Spanish

Degrees and Diplomas: *Licenciatura*: **Systems Analysis.** *Especialización*; *Maestría*; *Doctorado*: **Architecture; Engineering; Law; Social Sciences.** Also Diplomados

Publications: Revista Idearium (Law and Social Sciences)

Publishing House: Editorial 'Idearium'

Last Updated: 27/08/15

UNIVERSITY OF MORÓN

Universidad de Morón (UM)

Cabildo 134, B1708JPD Morón, Buenos Aires
Tel: +54(11) 5627-2000
EMail: coopint@unimoron.edu.ar
Website: http://www.unimoron.edu.ar

Rector: Hector Norberto Porto Lemma (2005-) EMail: sec-rectorado@unimoron.edu.ar; hporto@unimoron.edu.ar

Secretario General: Walter Oscar Fernández

International Relations: Alejandro Gavric, Director de la Oficina de Comunicaciones y Relaciones Institucionales

Faculty

Agronomy and Food Science (Agricultural Economics; Agriculture; Agronomy; Farm Management; Food Science); **Architecture, Design, Art and Town Planning** (Architecture; Design; Interior Design; Theatre; Town Planning; Visual Arts); **Computer Science and Communication** (Communication Studies; Computer Science; Technology; Translation and Interpretation); **Economics and Business** (Business Administration; Business and Commerce; Economics; Human Resources; International Business; Public Relations); **Education and Humanities** (Arts and Humanities; Education; History; Latin American Studies; Literature; Philosophy; Teacher Training); **Engineering** (Civil Engineering; Electrical and Electronic Engineering; Engineering; Industrial Engineering; Surveying and Mapping; Telecommunications Engineering); **Exact and Natural Sciences and Chemistry** (Biochemistry; Biology; Biotechnology; Chemistry; Cosmetology; Ecology; Genetics; Natural Sciences; Optics; Pharmacy); **Health Sciences** (Medicine; Nursing; Nutrition; Physical Therapy; Surgery); **Law, Political and Social Sciences** (International Relations; Law; Notary Studies; Political Sciences; Social Sciences); **Sciences Applied to Tourism and Population Studies** (Anthropology; Demography and Population; Food Science; Geography; Hotel Management; Leisure Studies; Physical Education; Sociology; Tourism)

School

Social Services (Social and Community Services)

History: Founded 1960.

Academic Year: April to November (April-July; August-November)

Admission Requirements: Secondary school certificate (bachillerato)

Main Language(s) of Instruction: Spanish

Degrees and Diplomas: *Diploma de Técnico Superior*: **Hotel Management; Tourism.** *Licenciatura*: **Advertising and Publicity; Arts and Humanities; Business Administration; Chemistry; Computer Science; Economics; Education; History; Human Resources; Marketing; Occupational Health; Pharmacy; Philosophy; Psychology; Public Relations; Taxation; Tourism.** *Especialización*; *Maestría*; *Doctorado*: **Law; Medicine; Philosophy.**

Student Services: Careers Guidance, Cultural Activities, Language Laboratory, Library, Sports Facilities

Publications: UM - Labor; UM - Saber

Last Updated: 28/08/15

UNIVERSITY OF NOTARIAL STUDIES

Universidad Notarial Argentina (UNA)

Avenida 51, N° 435, B1900AVI La Plata, Buenos Aires
Tel: +54(221) 421-9283
Fax: +54(221) 421-0552
EMail: uninotlp@universidadnotarial.edu.ar
Website: http://www.universidadnotarial.edu.ar

Rector: Cristina Noemi Armella
EMail: cristinaarmella@universidadnotarial.edu.ar

Vicerrectora: Adriana N. Abella
EMail: adrianaabella@universidadnotarial.edu.ar

Institute

Administrative Law (Administrative Law); **Civil Law** (Civil Law); **Commercial Law** (Commercial Law); **Comparative and Integrative Law** (Comparative Law); **Constitutional Law** (Constitutional Law); **Consumer Law** (Consumer Studies); **Copyright** (Law); **Customary Law** (Taxation); **Environmental Law** (Environmental Studies); **International Private Law** (International Law; Private Law); **Justice Studies** (Law); **Law** (Law); **Law and Mass Communication** (Law; Mass Communication); **Minorities Rights** (Demography and Population; Law); **Notarial Computer Systems** (Notary Studies; Software Engineering); **Notarial Further Training** (Notary Studies); **Notarial History** (Notary Studies); **Notarial Law** (Law; Notary Studies); **Notarial Management** (Notary Studies); **Notarial Studies** (Notary Studies); **Public, Provincial, Municipal Law and Town Planning** (Public Law; Regional Planning; Town Planning)

Further Information: Branches in Morón; Corrientes; Paraná; Rosario and Santa Fé

History: Founded 1962 and recognized by the federal government as a private postgraduate institution 1968.

Academic Year: March to December (March-July; August-December)

Admission Requirements: A University degree (in Law and Social Sciences, Philosophy, Economics)

Main Language(s) of Instruction: Spanish

Degrees and Diplomas: *Especialización*; *Maestría*

Publications: Cuadernos Notariales

Last Updated: 15/12/15

UNIVERSITY OF PALERMO

Universidad de Palermo (UP)

Av. Córdoba 3501, esq. Mario Bravo, 1175ABT Buenos Aires, Capital Federal
Tel: +54(11) 4964-4610
Fax: +54(11) 4963-1560
EMail: informes@palermo.edu
Website: http://www.palermo.edu

Rector: Ricardo H. Popovsky (1990-)
EMail: rectorado@palermo.edu

Secretario Administrativo Académico: Federico Kamegawa
EMail: fkameg@palermo.edu

International Relations: Matías Popovsky, Head, International Relations EMail: mpopov@palermo.edu

Faculty

Architecture (Architecture; Town Planning); **Business and Economics** (Accountancy; Administration; Business Administration; Finance; Human Resources; International Business; Management; Marketing); **Design and Communication** (Advertising and Publicity; Cinema and Television; Design; Film; Fine Arts; Public Relations); **Engineering** (Computer Engineering; Computer Networks; Computer Science; Electronic Engineering; Engineering; Industrial Engineering; Information Technology; Telecommunications Engineering); **Law** (Administrative Law; Civil Law; Commercial Law; Constitutional Law; Criminal Law; Labour Law; Law); **Psychology** (Psychology); **Social Sciences** (Arts and Humanities; Education; Fine Arts; Health Sciences; Social Sciences)

Graduate School

Business (Business Administration; Business and Commerce)

Further Information: Branch in Catalinas

History: Founded 1986 as Community College, acquired present status and title 1990.

Academic Year: March to June; August to December

Admission Requirements: Secondary school certificate (bachillerato)

Fees: (US Dollars): 4,900 per annum, undergraduate; 5,000-9,000 per annum, postgraduate

Main Language(s) of Instruction: Spanish

Accrediting Agency: CONEAU (Comisión Nacional de Evaluación y Acreditación Universitaria); RIBA (Royal Institute of British Architects).

Degrees and Diplomas: *Licenciatura*; *Especialización*; *Maestría*; *Doctorado*: **Design; Higher Education; Law; Psychology.**

Student Services: Academic Counselling, Canteen, Careers Guidance, Cultural Activities, Facilities for disabled people, Foreign Studies Centre, Language Laboratory, Social Counselling, Sports Facilities

Publications: Creación y Producción en Diseño y Comunicación; Cuadermos del Centro de Estudios; Palermo Business Review; Revista de Ciencia y Tecnología; Revista Escritos en la Facultad - Diseño y Comunicación; Revista Jurídica Revista Juridica

Publishing House: Editorial Universidad de Palermo

Last Updated: 28/08/15

UNIVERSITY OF SALVADOR

Universidad del Salvador (USAL)

Viamonte 1856, C1056ABB Buenos Aires, Capital Federal
Tel: +54(11) 4813-9630
Fax: +54(11) 4812-4625
EMail: uds-rect@salvador.edu.ar
Website: http://www.salvador.edu.ar

Rector: Juan Alejandro Tobias (1985-)
EMail: uds-rect@salvador.edu.ar

Vice-Rectora Académica: Zulma Barada (2015-)
EMail: uds-rect@salvador.edu.ar

Vice-Rectora de Investigación y Desarrollo: Luciana Tondello (2015-) EMail: uds-rect@usal.edu.ar

Faculty

Administration (Administration; Business and Commerce; Human Resources); **Economics** (Accountancy; Actuarial Science; Banking; Economics; Finance; International Business; Management; Taxation); **Education and Social Communication** (Advertising and Publicity; Communication Studies; Education; Journalism); **Engineering** (Industrial Engineering; Information Technology); **History, Geography and Tourism** (Arts and Humanities; Environmental Studies; Geography; History; Tourism); **Law** (Law); **Medicine** (Art Therapy; Dentistry; Medicine; Nursing; Occupational Therapy; Physical Therapy; Radiology; Rehabilitation and Therapy; Speech Therapy and Audiology; Sports Medicine); **Philosophy and Literature** (Literature; Philosophy); **Psychology and Psychopedagogy** (Educational Psychology; Performing Arts; Psychology); **Social Sciences** (International Relations; Political Sciences; Social Sciences; Social Work; Sociology)

School

Agronomy *(Graduate)* (Agronomy; Food Technology); **Arts and Architecture** (Architecture; Theatre); **Graphic Design** (Graphic Design); **Modern Languages** (English; Portuguese; Translation and Interpretation); **Oriental Studies** (Asian Studies; Middle Eastern Studies); **Veterinary Science** *(Graduate)* (Veterinary Science)

Institute

Continuous Training (Continuing Education); **International Complex Thought** (Philosophy)

Centre

Technological Applications (Technology)

Research Institute

Administration (Administration); **Applied Geomatics** (Surveying and Mapping); **Drug Dependency** (Toxicology); **East/West Comparative Studies** (Comparative Politics); **Economics** (Economics); **Education and Social Communication** (Education; Social Studies); **Environment and Ecology** (Ecology; Environmental Studies); **Geopolitics, Defence and Security** (International Relations); **History and Geography** (Geography; History); **Law** (Law); **Linguistics** (Linguistics); **Medicine** (Medicine); **Philosophy** (Philosophy); **Psychology** (Psychology); **Psychopedagogic Counselling** (Educational Psychology); **Remote Sensors** (Surveying and Mapping); **Social Sciences** (Social Sciences); **Tourism** (Tourism)

Further Information: Campuses in Pilar, Gobernador Virasoro, Corrientes

History: Founded 1944 as Instituto Superior de Filosofía, reorganized as faculty 1954 and officially recognized as University 1956. Since 1975, it is administered by a Civil Association.

Academic Year: January to December

Admission Requirements: Secondary school certificate (bachillerato) or equivalent

Fees: 42000 per annum (Argentine Peso)

Main Language(s) of Instruction: Spanish

Accrediting Agency: Comisión Nacional de Evaluación y Acreditación Universitaria (CONEAU)

Degrees and Diplomas: *Diploma de Técnico Superior*: **Teacher Training.** *Licenciatura*: **Administration; Advertising and Publicity; Art Therapy; Arts and Humanities; Business and Commerce; Economics; English; Environmental Studies; Geography; History; Human Resources; Information Technology; International Business; International Relations; Journalism; Music; Nutrition; Oriental Studies; Pedagogy; Physical Education; Physical Therapy; Political Sciences; Social and Community Services; Sociology; Speech Therapy and Audiology; Theatre; Tourism.** *Especialización*: **Bilingual and Bicultural Education; Business Computing; Cardiology; Distance Education; E- Business/Commerce; Economic and Finance Policy; Finance; Forensic Medicine and Dentistry; Gastroenterology; Health Administration; Human Resources; Institutional Administration; Insurance; Marketing; Oncology; Ophthalmology; Philology; Private Law; Psychiatry and Mental Health; Psychometrics; Public Law; Radiology; Surgery; Taxation.** *Maestría*: **Accountancy; Administration; Advertising and Publicity; Commercial Law; Comparative Law; Diabetology; E-Business/Commerce; Education; Finance; Gastroenterology; Hepatology; Human Resources; Information Management; International Business; International Relations; Journalism; Leadership; Management; Marketing; Nursing; Orthodontics; Pedagogy; Psychoanalysis; Public Administration; Public Relations; Social and Preventive Medicine; Social Welfare.** *Doctorado*: **Criminal Law; Geography (Human); History; International Relations; Law; Literature; Philosophy; Political Sciences; Psychology.**

Student Services: Academic Counselling, Canteen, Careers Guidance, Cultural Activities, Facilities for disabled people, Foreign Studies Centre, Health Services, Language Laboratory, Library, Social Counselling, Sports Facilities, eLibrary

Publications: Aequitas; Aequitas Virtual; Anuario de Investigación USAL; El Equilibrista; Épocas; Gramma; Huellas en papel; Institutas: Revista de Derecho Procesal; Iushistoria investigaciones; Miriada: Investigación en Ciencias Sociales; Psicología y Psicopedagogía; Ser y estar; SIGNOS EAD (Revista de educación a distancia); SIGNOS ELE (Revista de español como lengua extranjera); Signos Universitarios

Academic Staff *2015*	MEN	WOMEN	TOTAL
FULL-TIME	30	27	**57**
PART-TIME	–	–	**2,167**
STAFF WITH DOCTORATE			
FULL-TIME	56	61	c. **117**
Student Numbers *2015*			
All (Foreign included)	8,619	15,973	c. **24,592**
FOREIGN ONLY	1,055	480	**1,535**

Last Updated: 16/12/15

UNIVERSITY OF SAN PABLO-TUCUMÁN

Universidad de San Pablo-Tucumán (UPST)
24 de Septiembre 476, San Pablo, Tucumán
Tel: +54(381) 4530-630
EMail: informes@uspt.edu.ar
Website: http://www.uspt.edu.ar

Rector: Juan Pablo Lichtmajer
EMail: juanpablo.plichtmajer@gmail.com

Vicerrector: Ramiro Albarracin EMail: ralbarracin@uspt.edu.ar

Institute

Development and Technical Innovation for Competitivity (Agricultural Business; Food Technology; Industrial Design; Textile Design); **Health Sciences and Quality of Life** (Medicine); **Social, Political and Cultural Studies** (Cultural Studies; Finance; International Relations; Law; Political Sciences; Social Sciences)

History: Founded 2007.

Degrees and Diplomas: *Licenciatura*; *Especialización*

Last Updated: 28/08/15

UNIVERSITY OF THE ACONCAGUA

Universidad del Aconcagua (UDA)
Catamarca 147, 5500 Mendoza, Mendoza
Tel: +54(261) 520-1637
Website: http://www.uda.edu.ar

Rector: Osvaldo S. Caballero EMail: rectorado@uda.edu.ar

Secretaria Académica: María Ester Gibbs
EMail: megibbs@uda.edu.ar

Faculty

Economics and Law (Accountancy; Business and Commerce; Economics; Law; Marketing); **Medical Sciences** (Gynaecology and Obstetrics; Hygiene; Medicine; Speech Therapy and Audiology); **Psychology** (Criminology; Psychoanalysis; Psychology); **Social Sciences and Administration** (Administration; Advertising and Publicity; Computer Science; International Business; Software Engineering; Telecommunications Engineering)

School

Foreign Languages (English; Modern Languages; Translation and Interpretation)

History: Founded 1966 as Instituto de Enseñanza Superior del Aconcagua. Acquired present status and title 1973.

Main Language(s) of Instruction: Spanish

Degrees and Diplomas: *Licenciatura*: **Accountancy; Business Administration; Business and Commerce; Psychology.** *Especialización*; *Maestría*; *Doctorado*: **Psychology.**

Student Services: Library

Last Updated: 28/08/15

UNIVERSITY OF THE EAST

Universidad del Este (UDE)
Palacio Gibert, Diag. 80 N° 723, Buenos Aires
Tel: +54(221) 422-4636
EMail: info@ude.edu.ar
Website: http://www.ude.edu.ar

Rectora: María de las Mercedes Reitano
EMail: mreitano@ude.edu.ar

Secretaria Académica: Isabel Noemi Pozurama
EMail: ipozurama@ude.edu.ar

Faculty
Design and Communication (Advertising and Publicity; Design; Graphic Design; Interior Design; Textile Design); **Economics** (Accountancy; Administration; Business and Commerce); **Humanities** (Educational Administration); **Law and Social Sciences** (Law; Social Sciences)

History: Founded 2008.

Main Language(s) of Instruction: Spanish

Degrees and Diplomas: *Licenciatura*

Student Services: Library

Last Updated: 28/08/15

UNIVERSITY OF THE LATIN AMERICAN EDUCATIONAL CENTRE

Universidad del Centro Educativo Latinoamericano (UCEL)

Avenida Pellegrini 1332, S2000BUN Rosario, Santa Fé

Tel: +54(341) 449-9292

Fax: +54(341) 449-1241

Website: http://www.ucel.edu.ar

Rectora: Stella Maris Requena
EMail: rectorado@ucel.edu.ar

Secretaria Académica: Noemi Lagreca
EMail: Secacademica@ucel.edu.ar

International Relations: Fanny Sloer de Godfrid
EMail: relacionesinternacionales@ucel.edu.ar

Faculty
Chemistry (Chemistry; Computer Science; Environmental Management; Food Technology; Nutrition); **Economics and Business Administration** (Business Administration; Business and Commerce; Economics; Hotel Management; Labour and Industrial Relations; Marketing); **Social Sciences and Law** (Law; Social Sciences; Translation and Interpretation)

History: Founded 1993. Acquired present status 2007.

Academic Year: March to November

Main Language(s) of Instruction: Spanish

Degrees and Diplomas: *Licenciatura*: **Accountancy; Business Administration; Business and Commerce; Economics; English; Food Technology; Labour and Industrial Relations; Literature.** *Especialización*; *Maestría*

Last Updated: 28/08/15

UNIVERSITY OF THE MERCHANT NAVY

Universidad de la Marina Mercante (UDEMM)

Avenida Rivadavia 2258, 1034 Buenos Aires, Capital Federal

Tel: +54(11) 4953-9000

Fax: +54(11) 4953-9000

EMail: info@udemm.edu.ar

Website: http://www.udemm.edu.ar

Rector: Norberto Fraga
EMail: nfraga@udemm.edu.ar

Secretario General: Mirko E. Mayer
EMail: secgeneral@udemm.edu.ar

Faculty
Administration and Economics (Accountancy; Administration; Human Resources; International Business; Marine Transport; Marketing; Tourism; Transport and Communications); **Engineering** (Computer Science; Electrical and Electronic Engineering; Engineering; Hygiene; Mechanical Engineering; Naval Architecture; Systems Analysis); **Humanities** (Educational Psychology; Psychology); **Law, Social Sciences and Communication** (Communication Studies; Human Resources; Law; Management; Public Relations; Tourism)

History: Founded 1968 as private University.

Main Language(s) of Instruction: Spanish

Degrees and Diplomas: *Licenciatura*; *Maestría*

Last Updated: 27/08/15

UNIVERSITY OF THE SANTO TOMÁS DE AQUINO FRATERNITY

Universidad de las Fraternidades de Agrupaciones Santo Tomás de Aquino (FASTA)

Gascón 3145, 7600 Mar del Plata, Buenos Aires

Tel: +54(223) 499-0400

Fax: +54(223) 499-0417

EMail: informes@ufasta.edu.ar

Website: http://www.ufasta.edu.ar

Rector: Juan Carlos Mena (11) EMail: jcmena@ufasta.edu.ar

Vicerrector Académico: Alejandro Gabriel Campos
EMail: vicerrectoradoacademico@ufasta.edu.ar

International Relations: Fernando Mumare, Secretario de Relaciones Institucionales EMail: dai@ufasta.edu.ar

Faculty
Economics (Accountancy; Administration; Business and Commerce; Human Resources; Marketing); **Educational Sciences** (Educational Sciences; Pedagogy; Teacher Training); **Engineering** (Computer Science; Engineering; Environmental Engineering; Hygiene; Safety Engineering); **Law and Social Sciences** (Civil Security; Criminology; Law; Real Estate); **Medical Sciences** (Health Sciences; Medicine; Nutrition; Physical Therapy; Speech Therapy and Audiology)

School
Communication (Communication Studies); **Humanities** (Religious Education)

Further Information: Also Branch in Bariloche

History: Founded on the initiative of the Fraternity of St. Thomas Aquinas Groups (FASTA) which was founded in 1962 as a youth movement in the Catholic Church. Recognized 1971 as a lay institution of the Dominican Order.

Academic Year: March to July

Main Language(s) of Instruction: Spanish

Accrediting Agency: CONEAU

Degrees and Diplomas: *Licenciatura*; *Especialización*

Student Services: Academic Counselling, Canteen, Careers Guidance, Cultural Activities, Facilities for disabled people, Foreign Studies Centre, Health Services, IT Centre, Language Laboratory, Library, Sports Facilities, eLibrary

Publications: In Itinere - Magazine humanities University

Last Updated: 18/08/15

UNIVERSITY OF THE VALLEY OF THE PLATA

Universidad de la Cuenca del Plata (UCP)

Lavalle 50, 3400 Corrientes, Corrientes

Tel: +54(3783) 43-6236

EMail: informaciones@ucp.edu.ar

Website: http://www.ucp.edu.ar

Rector: Ángel Enrique Rodriguez (1994-) EMail: rector@ucp.edu.ar

Vicerrectora Académica: Ana María Petrone de Maló
EMail: viceacademica@ucp.edu.ar

International Relations: Norma Benitez Boulock
EMail: cooperacion@ucp.edu.ar

Faculty
Art, Design and Communication (Advertising and Publicity; Graphic Design; Multimedia; Photography; Textile Design); **Business Studies** (Accountancy; Administration; Hotel Management; International Business; Secretarial Studies; Tourism); **Engineering and Technology** (Engineering; Food Technology; Nutrition); **Law and Political Science** (Law; Public Administration; Taxation); **Psychology, Education and Human Relations** (Educational Psychology; Psychology)

Further Information: Also branches in Goya, Formosa, Posadas and Paso de los Libres

History: Founded 1993.

Academic Year: February to December

Fees: (Pesos): Tuition, 3,420 per annum

Main Language(s) of Instruction: Spanish

Degrees and Diplomas: *Licenciatura*: **Administration; Advertising and Publicity; Educational Sciences; International Business; Journalism; Psychology.** *Especialización*

Student Services: Academic Counselling, Canteen, Language Laboratory, Library, Social Counselling, Sports Facilities

Last Updated: 27/08/15

UNIVERSITY OF TORCUATO DI TELLA

Universidad Torcuato di Tella (UTDT)

Miñones 2177, C1428ATG Buenos Aires, Capital Federal

Tel: +54(11) 5169-7000

Website: http://www.utdt.edu

Rector: Ernesto Schargrodsky
EMail: eschargr@utdt.edu; rectorado@utdt.edu

Secretaria Académica: Andrea Rotnitzky
EMail: Sacademica@utdt.edu

School

Architecture and Urban Studies (Architecture; Urban Studies); **Business** (Banking; Business Administration; Business and Commerce; Economics; Finance; Management; Marketing); **Government** (Economics; Education; Social Policy); **Law** (Law)

Department

Arts (Cinema and Television; Fine Arts); **Economics** (Economics); **History** (Arts and Humanities; Contemporary History; History; Journalism; Modern History); **Mathematics and Statistics** (Mathematics; Statistics); **Political Science and International Relations** (International Relations; Political Sciences)

Further Information: Also another site in Saenz Valiente

History: Founded jointly by the Foundation and the Instituto Torcuato Di Tella 1991.

Academic Year: March to December

Admission Requirements: Secondary school certificate and entrance examination

Fees: (Pesos): 14,400 per annum for Economics; Business; History; Political Science; International Studies. 11,520 per annum for Law and Architecture

Main Language(s) of Instruction: Spanish

Accrediting Agency: CONEAU (Ministerio de Educación, Ciencia y Tecnología)

Degrees and Diplomas: *Licenciatura*; *Especialización*; *Maestría*: **Architecture; Business Administration; Cultural Studies; Economics; Educational Administration; Finance; History; International Studies; Journalism; Law; Management; Public Administration; Town Planning; Urban Studies.** *Doctorado*: **Economics; History; Political Sciences.**

Student Services: Academic Counselling, Canteen, Careers Guidance, Facilities for disabled people, Health Services, Library, Sports Facilities

Publications: Block - Revista de Arquitectura; Revista Argentina de Teoría Jurídica; Working Papers CIF

Publishing House: Press Department

Last Updated: 04/09/15

Armenia

STRUCTURE OF HIGHER EDUCATION SYSTEM

Description:

The aim of higher professional education is to provide high quality education and training that meets the needs of the economy. There are state and private HEIs. The two-level (Bachelor-Master) educational system was introduced in 2007. The third level (Aspirantura) is in the process of being reformed.

Stages of studies:

University level first stage: *Bachelor's degree; Medical Doctor*

The Bachelor's degree is awarded to those having completed secondary education and four years of higher education. For medical studies, the Bachelor's degree (Medical Doctor) is awarded after a minimum of 5 years, depending on the specialization.

University level second stage: *Master's degree*

The Master's degree is conferred on those who hold a Bachelor's degree and have completed two further years of higher education. Clinical Ordinate and Pharmaceutics degrees are granted to those having studied Medicine and completed at least one year of postgraduate study. The Specialist diploma is conferred on those having completed secondary education and five years of higher education. The academic year 2010/2011 saw the award of the last Specialist diplomas.

University level third stage: *Postgraduate education*

A Researcher's or Candidate of Science (PhD) degree is granted to those who hold a Master's or Specialist diploma degree upon completion of three years of postgraduate studies. For the Candidate of Science degree, it is necessary to defend a thesis.

ADMISSION TO HIGHER EDUCATION

Admission to university-level studies:

Name of secondary school credential required: Mijnakarg Yndhanur Krtoutian Attestat

For entry to: Higher education institutions

Alternatives to credentials: Diploma of Vocational Education (Mijin masnagitakan diplom)

Admission requirements: Entrance examination

Foreign students admission:

Quotas: According to international agreements.

Admission requirements: Foreign students must hold a secondary school leaving certificate and sit for an entrance examination.

Entry regulations: All foreign candidates must have a residence visa and be recommended by a competent body in their country.

Health requirements: Medical certificate

RECOGNITION OF STUDIES

Bodies dealing with recognition:

National Center for Professional Education Quality Assurance Foundation - ANQA

22 Orbeli Street
Yerevan 0028
Tel: +374(10) 229-146
Fax: +376(10) 229-148
EMail: info@anqa.am
WWW: http://www.anqa.am

National Information Centre of Academic Recognition and Mobility - ARMENIC
Executive Director: Gayane Harutyunyan
27 Amiryan Street
Yerevan 0010
Tel: +374(10) 530 904
Fax: +374(10) 530 904
EMail: armENIC@cornet.am
WWW: http://www.armenic.am/

Special provisions for recognition:

Recognition for university level studies: The National Information Centre for Academic Recognition and Mobility is responsible for academic and professional recognition. For further information please visit: http://www.armenic.am.

For access to advanced studies and research: The National Information Centre for Academic Recognition and Mobility is responsible for academic and professional recognition. For further information please visit: http://www.armenic.am.

NATIONAL BODIES

Ministry of Education and Science
Minister: Armen Ashotyan
Government Building 3, Republic Square
Yerevan 375010
Tel: +374(10) 526-602
Fax: +374(10) 527-343
EMail: info@edu.am
WWW: http://www.edu.am
Role of national body: Elaborates and implements the policies of the Republic of Armenia Government in the education and science sectors.

Council of Rectors of State Higher Educational Institutions
Alex Manoogian Street 1
Yerevan 0025
Tel: +374(10) 554 629
Fax: +374(10) 554 641

Council of Rectors of Private Higher Educational Institutions
Yerevan

Data for academic year: 2011-2012
Source: IAU from National Information Center for Academic Recognition and Mobility, Armenia, 2011. Bodies 2016.

INSTITUTIONS

PUBLIC INSTITUTIONS

ARMENIAN STATE AGRARIAN UNIVERSITY

Hayastani Petakan Agrarayin Hamalsaran (ASAU)
Teryan Street 74, 0009 Yerevan
Tel: +374(10) 524-541 +374(10) 581-912
Fax: +374(10) 522-361 +374(10) 581-597
EMail: info@anau.am
Website: http://www.anau.am/

Rector: Arshaluys Tarverdyan (1998-) Tel: +374(10) 524-541

Vice-rector on Educational Affairs: Yuri Marmaryan Tel: +374(1) 521-565 EMail: marmaryan@armenia.com

International Relations: Hovik Sayadyan, Head, Department of International Relations
Tel: +374(10) 567-411
EMail: hovik_s@yahoo.com; inter@anau.am; sayadyan@anau.am

Faculty

Agribusiness and Marketing (Agricultural Business; Law; Management; Marketing; Political Sciences; Statistics); **Agriculture Mechanization and Automobile Transportation** (Agricultural Engineering; Agricultural Equipment; Automotive Engineering; Electrical Engineering; Machine Building; Mathematics); **Agronomy** (Agriculture; Armenian; Biology; Ecology; Forestry; Horticulture; Modern Languages; Plant and Crop Protection; Russian; Vegetable Production); **Economics** (Accountancy; Agricultural Business;

Agricultural Economics; Banking; Computer Science; Economics; Finance; Mathematics); **Foodstuff Technologies** (Animal Husbandry; Chemistry; Food Technology; Horticulture; Leather Techniques; Packaging Technology; Physical Education; Physics; Thermal Physics); **Hydro Melioration, Land Management and Land Cadastre** (Construction Engineering; History; Materials Engineering; Philosophy; Real Estate; Soil Conservation; Water Management); **Veterinary Medicine and Sanety Expertize** (Anatomy; Animal Husbandry; Biochemistry; Epidemiology; Gynaecology and Obstetrics; Hygiene; Microbiology; Parasitology; Pathology; Pharmacology; Physiology; Rehabilitation and Therapy; Veterinary Science; Virology; Zoology)

Further Information: Also a branch in Vanadzor and Sisian.

History: Founded 1930 as Armenian Agricultural Academy. Acquired present status 1994 and title 2005.

Fees: 1,000-1,200 per annum (US Dollar)

Main Language(s) of Instruction: Armenian

Accrediting Agency: Ministry of Education and Science of Armenia

Degrees and Diplomas: *Bakalavri Vorakavorum*; *Magistrosi Vorakavorum*: **Accountancy; Agricultural Business; Agricultural Economics; Agricultural Equipment; Agricultural Management; Agronomy; Animal Husbandry; Automation and Control Engineering; Biotechnology; Dairy; Ecology; Electrical Engineering; Finance; Fishery; Food Science; Food Technology; Forestry; Genetics; Information Technology; Insurance; Landscape Architecture; Leather Techniques; Management; Marketing; Meat and Poultry; Packaging Technology; Plant and Crop Protection; Real Estate; Regional Planning; Soil Management; Transport Management; Veterinary Science; Viticulture; Water Science.** *Candidate/Doctor of Science*: **Accountancy; Agricultural Equipment; Animal Husbandry; Applied Chemistry; Banking; Biochemistry; Botany; Cell Biology; Construction Engineering; Ecology; Economics; Finance; Food Technology; Forestry; Fruit Production; Genetics; Geophysics; Gynaecology and Obstetrics; Horticulture; Machine Building; Management; Mechanical Engineering; Mineralogy; Molecular Biology; Oncology; Pathology; Pharmacology; Plant and Crop Protection; Real Estate; Soil Science; Statistics; Surgery; Surveying and Mapping; Veterinary Science; Viticulture; Water Science.**

Student Services: Academic Counselling, Canteen, Careers Guidance, IT Centre, Language Laboratory, Library, Nursery Care, Sports Facilities

Last Updated: 04/05/15

ARMENIAN STATE INSTITUTE OF PHYSICAL CULTURE

Phizikakan Culturayi Haykakan Petakan Institut (ASIPC)

11 Alek Manukyan Street, 375070 Yerevan

Tel: +374(10) 55-62-81

Fax: +374(10) 55-41-04

EMail: info@asipc.am

Website: http://www.asipc.am

Rector: Vahram Arakelyan (1998-)
Tel: +374(10) 556-281 EMail: rector@asipc.am

Head, Educational Unit: Yuri Kupalyan

Vice-Rector for Administrative Affairs: Edward Kantarchyan

International Relations: Haroutun Babayan
Tel: +374(10) 554-406

Faculty

Sports and Health Recovery (Anatomy; Dance; Journalism; Physical Therapy; Physiology; Sports; Sports Medicine); **Training Pedagogy** (Modern Languages; Pedagogy; Physical Education; Psychology; Social Sciences; Sports)

Course

Correspondence Studies (Dance; Journalism; Physical Education; Sports)

History: Founded 1945.

Main Language(s) of Instruction: Armenian

Accrediting Agency: Ministry of Education and Science of Armenia

Degrees and Diplomas: *Bakalavri Vorakavorum*; *Magistrosi Vorakavorum*: **Journalism; Pedagogy; Physical Education.** Postgraduate studies, 3 yrs

Student Services: Academic Counselling, Canteen, Health Services, Library, Sports Facilities

Student Numbers *2014-2015*: Total 2,765

Last Updated: 26/05/15

ARMENIAN STATE PEDAGOGICAL UNIVERSITY AFTER KHACHATUR ABOVYAN

Kh. Abovyani Anvan Petakan Manakavarzhakan Hamalsaran (ASPU)

Tigran Mets 17, 010 Yerevan

Tel: +374(1) 597-049

Fax: +374(1) 597-008

EMail: info@aspu.am

Website: http://www.armspu.am

Rector: Rouben Mirzakhanyan
Tel: +374(10) 597-001 EMail: rector@armspu.am

Vice-Rector for General Affairs: Armen Liparit Tamazyan
Tel: +374(10) 59-70-02 EMail: vicerector-gen@armspu.am

International Relations: Ara Vladimir Yeremyan, Vice Chancellor of Personnel and International Cooperation
Tel: +374(10) 597-004 EMail: vicerector-intercop@armspu.am

Faculty

Art Education (Art History; Conducting; Cultural Studies; Design; Fine Arts; Handicrafts; Music; Music Education; Musical Instruments; Singing); **Biology, Chemistry and Geography** (Biology; Chemistry; Geography; Physiology; Science Education; Zoology); **Culture** (Architectural Restoration; Cinema and Television; Cultural Studies; Dance; Journalism; Museum Studies; Music; Photography; Radio and Television Broadcasting); **Educaional Psychology and Sociology** (Developmental Psychology; Educational Psychology; Psychology; Social Work; Sociology); **Education Management** (Educational Administration); **Foreign Languages** (English; Foreign Languages Education; German; Modern Languages; Romance Languages; Russian); **History and Jurisprudence** (History; History of Law; Humanities and Social Science Education; Law; Political Sciences); **Mathematics, Physics and Informatics** (Computer Science; Materials Engineering; Mathematics; Mathematics Education; Mechanical Engineering; Physics; Science Education); **Philology** (Ancient Languages; Armenian; Humanities and Social Science Education; Literature; Philology); **Preschool Education** (Mathematics Education; Native Language Education; Preschool Education; Primary Education); **Special Education** (Psychology; Special Education; Speech Therapy and Audiology)

College

Basic Studies *(ASPU Yerevan Basic College SNGO)* (Biology; Mathematics; Physics)

Centre

Democracy and Human Rights Education (Human Rights)

Research Centre

Pedagogy (Pedagogy)

History: Founded 1922, acquired present status 2008.

Academic Year: September to July

Admission Requirements: Secondary school certificate

Fees: 260,000-585,000 per annum (Armenian Dram)

Main Language(s) of Instruction: Armenian

Accrediting Agency: Ministry of Education and Science of Armenia

Degrees and Diplomas: *Bakalavri Vorakavorum*; *Magistrosi Vorakavorum*: **Armenian; Art History; Biology; Chemistry; Cinema and Television; Computer Science; Cultural Studies; Dance; Ecology; Educational Administration; English; Environmental Management; Fine Arts; Geography; German; History; Information Sciences; Journalism; Library Science; Literature; Management; Mathematics; Museum Studies; Music Education; Natural Sciences; Painting and Drawing; Pedagogy; Photography; Physics; Preschool Education; Primary Education; Psychology; Radio and Television Broadcasting; Russian; Social Work; Sociology; Spanish; Special Education; Technology.** *Candidate/Doctor of Science*: **Biology; Chemistry; Cultural Studies; Engineering; Geography; History; Mathematics; Pedagogy; Philology; Physics; Psychology; Sociology.**

Student Services: Academic Counselling, Canteen, Careers Guidance, Cultural Activities, Facilities for disabled people, Foreign Studies Centre, Health Services, IT Centre, Language Laboratory, Library, Social Counselling, Sports Facilities

Publications: Apaga Mankavarzh (Future Pedagogue); Armenian Studies Review; Pedagogical University official newspaper; Scientific Bulletin; Scientific Periodical of Interuniversity Consortium; The Basic Problems in Pedagogy and Psychology

Publishing House: Mankavarzh

Last Updated: 06/05/15

ARMENIAN STATE UNIVERSITY OF ECONOMICS

Hayastani Petakan Tntesagitakan Hamalsaran (ASUE)
128 Nalbandyan str., 0025 Yerevan
Tel: +374(10) 521-720
Fax: +374(10) 528-864
EMail: asue@asue.am; int@asue.am
Website: http://www.asue.am

Rector: Koryun Atoyan (2011-)
Tel: +374(10) 521-720
EMail: k.atoyan@asue.am; rector@asue.am

Vice Rector on Education-Methodological Affairs: Paruyr Kalantaryan Tel: +374(10) 593-428 EMail: p.kalantaryan@asue.am

International Relations: Gagik Vardanyan, Vice-Rector of Science and International Relations
Tel: +374(10) 593-427 EMail: g.vardanyan@asue.am

Department

Accounting and Auditing (Accountancy; Finance; Management); **Computer Science and Statistics** (Applied Mathematics; Computer Science; Information Technology; Statistics); **Finance** (Banking; Finance; Insurance); **Management** (Economics; Educational Administration; Industrial and Production Economics; Management; Tourism); **Marketing and Business Administration** (Business Administration; Business and Commerce; E- Business/Commerce; Marketing); **Regulation of Economy and International Economic Relations** (Economics; International Economics)

Chair

Armenian and Russian Languages (Armenian; Russian); **Foreign Languages** (Modern Languages); **Higher Mathematics** (Mathematics); **Philosophy and Armenian History** (History; Philosophy); **Physical Training, Emergency Situations and Civil Defense** (Physical Education; Protective Services); **Political Science and Law** (Law; Political Sciences)

History: Founded 1975 as Yerevani Petakan Tntesagitakan Institut (Yerevan State Institute of Economics). Acquired present status and title 2006.

Academic Year: September to July

Fees: 400,000-450,000 per annum (Armenian Dram)

Main Language(s) of Instruction: Armenian

Accrediting Agency: Ministry of Education and Science of Armenia

Degrees and Diplomas: *Bakalavri Vorakavorum*; *Magistrosi Vorakavorum*: **Accountancy; Applied Mathematics; Business and Commerce; Business Computing; E- Business/Commerce; Economic and Finance Policy; Economics; Finance; Fiscal Law; Information Technology; Insurance; International Economics; Journalism; Labour Law; Management; Marketing; Real Estate; Statistics; Taxation.** *Candidate/Doctor of Science*: **Accountancy; Applied Mathematics; Economics; Finance; International Economics; Management.**

Student Services: Academic Counselling, Canteen, Health Services, Language Laboratory, Social Counselling, Sports Facilities

Publications: "Tntesaget" Magazine (Economist)

Last Updated: 05/05/15

GYUMRI BRANCH
GYUMRII MASNACHUOH
32 Leningradyan Street, 377526 Gyumri
Tel: +374(312) 370-08
Website: http://www.asue.am/en/about-asue/branches/gyumri-branch-249

Rector: Samson Davoyan

Programme

Accounting (Accountancy); **Commerce** (Business and Commerce); **Finance** (Finance); **International Economic Relations** (International Economics); **Management** (Management)

Main Language(s) of Instruction: Armenian

Degrees and Diplomas: *Bakalavri Vorakavorum*; *Magistrosi Vorakavorum*: **Accountancy; Business Administration; Business and Commerce; Finance.**

Student Numbers *2014-2015*: Total: c. 500

YEGHEGNADZOR BRANCH
YEGHEGNADZOR MASNACHUOH
4 Vayk str., Yeghegnadzor, Vayots Dzor
Tel: +374(281) 254-10
EMail: sos.khachikyan@gmail.com
Website: http://www.asue.am/en/about-asue/branches/yeghegnadzor-branch-248

Director: Sos Khachikyan

Programme

Finance (Finance); **International Economic Relations** (International Economics); **Management and Tourism Management** (Management; Tourism)

Main Language(s) of Instruction: Armenian

Degrees and Diplomas: *Bakalavri Vorakavorum*; *Magistrosi Vorakavorum*: **Finance; Management.**

CRISIS MANAGEMENT STATE ACADEMY OF THE EMERGENCY SITUATIONS OF THE REPUBLIC OF ARMENIA

1 Acharyan Str., 0040 Yerevan
Tel: +374(10) 61-19-24 +374(10) 61-19-21 +374(10) 61-47-60
EMail: cmsa_ema@yahoo.com

Rector: Hamlet Matevosyan

Programme

Civil protection (Civil Security); **Crisis Management** (Protective Services); **Crisis management (Graduate)** (Protective Services); **Exploitation and Equipment of Special Transport and Fire Rescue Equipment** (Fire Science; Transport and Communications); **Fire protection** (Fire Science); **Management** (Management); **Protection in Emergency Situations** (Protective Services); **Rescue Work** (Protective Services); **Rescue Work (Graduate)** (Protective Services)

History: Founded 1992.

Main Language(s) of Instruction: Armenian

Degrees and Diplomas: *Bakalavri Vorakavorum*; *Magistrosi Vorakavorum*: **Protective Services.**

Academic Staff *2014-2015*: Total 46

Last Updated: 31/05/15

EUROPEAN REGIONAL EDUCATIONAL ACADEMY

Evropakan Krtakan Taratsashrjanain Akademia (EREA)
10 Davit Anhaght, Zeitun district, 0037 Yerevan
Tel: +374(10) 246-371
Fax: +374(10) 241-891
EMail: info@era.am
Website: http://www.eriicta.am

Rector: Arman Avagyan Tel: +374(10) 242-746

Vice-Rector for Teaching-Methodological Affairs: Husik Z. Gevorgyan EMail: husikgz@yahoo.com

Department
Economics and Management (Economics; International Business; International Economics; Management); **Informational Technologies** (Applied Mathematics; Computer Science; Information Technology); **Law and International Relations** (International Relations; Law); **Linguistics and Tourism** (Linguistics; Tourism); **Pedagogy and Psychology** (Pedagogy; Psychology)

History: Created 2001. Offers both academic and vocational training using both traditional Armenian and European curricula.

Academic Year: September to May

Admission Requirements: Mijnakarg Yndhanur Krtoutian Attestat or equivalent secondary school certificate.

Fees: National: Master, 450,000-690,000 per annum; Doctor, 288,000-360,000 per annum (Armenian Dram), International: Master, 900,000-960,000 per annum; Doctor, 864,000-1,080,000 per annum (Armenian Dram)

Main Language(s) of Instruction: Armenian, English

Accrediting Agency: Ministry of Education and Science of Armenia; Armenian National Academy of Science

Degrees and Diplomas: *Bakalavri Vorakavorum*: **Business Administration; Electronic Engineering; Information Management; Information Technology; International Economics; International Relations; Law; Linguistics; Management; Pedagogy; Psychology; Software Engineering; Tourism.** *Magistrosi Vorakavorum*: **Business Administration; Electronic Engineering; Information Management; Information Technology; International Business; International Economics; International Relations; Law; Linguistics; Management; Pedagogy; Psychology; Software Engineering; Tourism.** *Candidate/Doctor of Science*: **Automation and Control Engineering; Economics; International Economics; Law; Linguistics; Management; Tourism.**

Student Services: Academic Counselling, Canteen, Careers Guidance, Cultural Activities, Foreign Studies Centre, Health Services, Language Laboratory, Social Counselling, Sports Facilities

Last Updated: 05/05/15

FRENCH UNIVERSITY OF ARMENIA

Hayastani Fransiakan Hamalsaran (UFAR)
David Anhaght Street 10, 0037 Yerevan
Tel: +374(10) 249-661
Fax: +374(10) 249-645
EMail: info@ufar.am
Website: http://www.ufar.am

Rector: Joëlle Le Morzellec
Tel: +374(10) 249-644 EMail: recteur@ufar.am

Faculty
Finance (Finance; Insurance); **Law** (Law); **Management** (Accountancy; Finance; Management); **Marketing** (International Business; Marketing)

History: Founded 2000.

Fees: Undergraduate, 580,000-640,000 per annum; Graduate, 650,000-690-000 per annum (Armenian Dram)

Main Language(s) of Instruction: Armenian, French

Accrediting Agency: Ministry of Education and Science of Armenia

Degrees and Diplomas: *Bakalavri Vorakavorum*: **European Union Law; Finance; Insurance; Management; Marketing; Political Sciences.** *Magistrosi Vorakavorum*: **Accountancy; Commercial Law; European Union Law; Finance; Insurance; International Business; International Law; Management; Marketing.** Also Master's degree in Communication Studies, Art Management and Tourism offered in partnership with Université Toulouse 1 Capitole (France)

Student Services: IT Centre, Library, Sports Facilities

Student Numbers *2014-2015*: Total: c. 900

Last Updated: 04/05/15

GAVAR STATE UNIVERSITY

Gavari Petakan Hamalsaran (GSU)
1 Hrant Hakobyan st., 378630 Gavar, Gegharkunik Region
Tel: +374(264) 257-75 +374(60) 46-12-99 +374(60) 46-02-01
Fax: +374(60) 46-02-01
EMail: info@gsu.am
Website: http://gsu.am/

Rector: Ruzanna Hakobyan (2006-)
Tel: +374(10) 60-46-02-01 +374(264) 2-57-75
EMail: Rusakob@yahoo.com; rector@gsu.am

Vice-Rector: Nelly Albert Kutuzyan

Faculty
Economics (Accountancy; Finance; Management); **Humanities** (History; Law; Social Sciences); **Natural Sciences** (Biology; Computer Engineering; Computer Science; Ecology; Geography; Physics); **Philology** (Armenian; Literature; Modern Languages; Russian)

Course
Correspondense (Accountancy; Armenian; Biology; Chemistry; Computer Engineering; Computer Science; Ecology; Geography (Human); History; Law; Literature; Natural Resources; Pedagogy; Primary Education; Russian; Surveying and Mapping; Tourism)

History: Founded 1993.

Academic Year: September to June

Admission Requirements: Secondary school certificate and state entrance examination

Main Language(s) of Instruction: Armenian

Accrediting Agency: Ministry of Education and Science

Degrees and Diplomas: *Bakalavri Vorakavorum*; *Magistrosi Vorakavorum*: **Accountancy; Armenian; Biology; Chemistry; Computer Engineering; Computer Science; Ecology; English; Environmental Management; Finance; Geography; History; Law; Literature; Management; Pedagogy; Primary Education.**

Student Services: Academic Counselling, Canteen, Health Services, Library, Sports Facilities, eLibrary

Publications: Collection of Scientific Papers

Last Updated: 30/04/15

GORIS STATE UNIVERSITY

Gorisi Petakan Hamalsaran
Avangard Street, House 4, 3204 Goris, Syunik Region
Tel: +374(284) 22-767
Fax: +374(284) 23-603
EMail: seua_goris@mail.ru; karapetyandiana@rambler.ru
Website: http://www.gorsu.am

Rector: Yuri Safaryan

Faculty
Economics (Economics; Management; Modern Languages); **Engineering** (Electronic Engineering; Energy Engineering; Engineering; Marine Engineering; Physics); **Humanities** (Armenian; History; Law; Literature; Pedagogy; Physical Education; Primary Education; Psychology; Teacher Training); **Natural Sciences** (Biology; Chemistry; Mathematics)

History: Founded 1967 acquired present status 1984.

Main Language(s) of Instruction: Armenian

Degrees and Diplomas: *Bakalavri Vorakavorum*; *Magistrosi Vorakavorum*: **Armenian; Biological and Life Sciences; Chemistry; Economics; Law; Literature; Mathematics; Primary Education.**

Student Services: Library

Last Updated: 04/05/15

GYUMRI STATE PEDAGOGICAL INSTITUTE NAMED AFTER M. NALBANDIAN

Gyumrii M. Nalbandiani Anvan Petakan Mankavaržhakan Institut (GSPI)
Paruir Sevak Street 4, 3126 Gyumri, Shirak Region
Tel: +374(312) 694-94
Fax: +374(312) 32-199
EMail: info@gspi.am; pedinst@gspi.am
Website: http://www.gspi.am

Rector: Vardevan Grigoryan Tel: +374(312) 32-199

First Vice-Rector: Razmik Matevosian EMail: gspi@gspi.am

International Relations: Lilit Margaryan, Head of the Office of International Relations EMail: gspi.intpro@gmail.com

Faculty

Biology and Geography (Biology; Chemistry; Ecology; Geography; Natural Sciences; Pharmacology; Science Education); **Foreign Languages** (English; Foreign Languages Education; French; German; Literature; Modern Languages; Russian); **History and Philology** (Armenian; History; Humanities and Social Science Education; Journalism; Law; Literature; Native Language Education; Philology); **Pedagogy** (Art Education; Music; Music Education; Painting and Drawing; Pedagogy; Preschool Education; Primary Education; Psychology; Social Work); **Physical Education and Primary Military Training** (Military Science; Physical Education); **Physics, Mathematics and Economics** (Computer Education; Computer Science; Economics; Mathematics; Physics)

Chair

All-Institute (Philosophy; Social Sciences)

History: Founded 1934.

Main Language(s) of Instruction: Armenian

Accrediting Agency: Ministry of Education and Science of Armenia

Degrees and Diplomas: *Bakalavri Vorakavorum*; *Magistrosi Vorakavorum*: **Armenian; Biology; Chemistry; Computer Science; English; Geography; History; Law; Literature; Management; Mathematics; Pedagogy; Physics; Psychology; Russian; Teacher Training.**

Student Services: Library

Last Updated: 30/04/15

INTERNATIONAL SCIENTIFIC-EDUCATIONAL CENTER OF THE NATIONAL ACADEMY OF SCIENCES OF REPUBLIC OF ARMENIA

M. Baghramyan 24d, 0019 Yerevan
Tel: +374(10) 56-80-32
EMail: info@isec.am; isec@sci.am; fordep@isec.am
Website: http://www.isec.am

Rector: Albert Sargsyan (2002-)

Division

Armenology and Social Sciences (Archaeology; Central European Studies; Economics; Ethnology; Fine Arts; History; Law; Literature; Modern Languages; Oriental Studies; Philosophy); **Chemistry and Earth Sciences** (Applied Chemistry; Geology; Geophysics; Inorganic Chemistry; Organic Chemistry; Seismology); **Mathematical and Technical Sciences** (Automation and Control Engineering; Computer Science; Mathematics; Mechanics); **Natural Sciences** (Biochemistry; Biotechnology; Botany; Ecology; Microbiology; Molecular Biology; Natural Sciences; Physiology; Zoology); **Physics and Astrophysics** (Applied Physics; Astrophysics; Electronic Engineering; Physics; Radiophysics)

History: Founded 1997.

Fees: Master, 250,000-550,000 per annum in full-time mode and 200,000-500,000 per annum in part-time mode; Ph.D, 450,000-500,000 per annum for programmes in Law and Economics and 350,000-450,000 for other specializations

Main Language(s) of Instruction: Armenian

Degrees and Diplomas: *Magistrosi Vorakavorum*: **Applied Chemistry; Applied Mathematics; Armenian; Biotechnology; Business Administration; Cell Biology; Computer Engineering; Computer Science; Economics; Environmental Management; Finance; Geology; History; International Relations; Journalism; Law; Literature; Management; Marketing; Molecular Biology; Neurosciences; Oriental Studies; Pedagogy; Political Sciences; Psychology; Sociology; Telecommunications Engineering.** *Candidate/Doctor of Science*: **Anthropology; Applied Mathematics; Archaeology; Architecture; Art History; Astrophysics; Automation and Control Engineering; Biochemistry; Biotechnology; Botany; Building Technologies; Cell Biology; Computer Engineering; Computer Networks; Criminal Law; Criminology; Design; Ethnology; Fine Arts; Genetics; Handicrafts; History; History of Law; Inorganic Chemistry; Law; Literature; Logic; Mathematics; Mechanics; Molecular Biology; Music; Optics; Organic Chemistry; Philosophy; Physical Chemistry; Physics; Physiology; Radiophysics; Sociology; Software Engineering; Solid State Physics; Sound Engineering (Acoustics).** Also Part-time Master's Degree Prgrammes in: Political Science, Management, Finance, Law, Journalism, Psychology, Pedagogy, Sociology, Library Science and Information Sciences, Business Administration, Tourism.

Student Services: Library

Last Updated: 31/05/15

NATIONAL POLYTECHNIC UNIVERSITY OF ARMENIA

Hayastani Petakan Tchartaragitakan Hamalsaran (NPUA)

105, Teryan Str., 0009 Yerevan
Tel: +374(10) 524-629 +374(10) 567-968
Fax: +374(10) 545-843
EMail: info@seua.am; papash@mail.ru; seuavan@yahoo.com; seua@synik.am
Website: http://polytech.am

Rector: Hovhannes V. Tokmajyan EMail: rector@seua.am

Academic Secretary: Henry Balabanyan Tel: +374(1) 525-997 EMail: hbalabanyan@seua.am

International Relations: Maria Mangasarova, Head of International Office Tel: +374(1) 567-968 EMail: intof@seua.am

Faculty

Applied Mathematics (Applied Mathematics); **Chemical Technology and Environmental Engineering** (Biotechnology; Chemical Engineering; Chemistry; Environmental Management); **Computer Systems and Informatics** (Automation and Control Engineering; Computer Engineering; Computer Networks; Computer Science; Information Management; Information Technology; Software Engineering); **Correspondence Education**; **Cybernetics** (Automation and Control Engineering; Biomedical Engineering; Electronic Engineering; Measurement and Precision Engineering); **Electrical Engineering** (Electrical Engineering); **Foreign Students** (Applied Mathematics; Biomedical Engineering; Chemical Engineering; Computer Science; Electrical Engineering; Electronic Engineering; Engineering; Information Technology; Microelectronics; Telecommunications Engineering); **Machine Building** (Automation and Control Engineering; Economics; Machine Building); **Mechanics and Machine Study** (Machine Building; Mechanics); **Mining and Metallurgy** (Economics; Environmental Engineering; Management; Materials Engineering; Metallurgical Engineering; Mining Engineering); **Power Engineering** (Economics; Electrical Engineering; Environmental Engineering; Power Engineering); **Radio Engineering and Communication Systems** (Economics; Management; Telecommunications Engineering); **Transportation Systems** (Air Transport; Transport and Communications; Transport Management)

Campus

Gyumri (Applied Mathematics; Computer Graphics; Computer Science; Engineering; Microelectronics); **Kapan** (Engineering); **Vanadzor** (Engineering; Industrial and Production Economics; Information Technology; Natural Sciences)

History: Founded 1933 as Yerevan Polytechnic. Acquired present status and renamed State Engineering University of Armenia 1991, and State Engineering University of Armenia - Polytechnic 2005. Acquired present title 2014.

Academic Year: September to June (September-January; February-June)

Admission Requirements: Secondary school certificate and entrance examination

Fees: National: Undergraduate, 800-1,050 per annum; Graduate (Master) 1,050-1,200 per annum; Postgraduate 700 per annum (US Dollar), International: Preparatory programme 1,500 per annum; Undergraduate 2,500 per annum; Master, 3,500 per annum; Doctorate, 4,000 per annum (US Dollar)

Main Language(s) of Instruction: Armenian

Accrediting Agency: Ministry of Education and Science of Armenia

Degrees and Diplomas: *Bakalavri Vorakavorum*: **Applied Mathematics; Automation and Control Engineering; Biological and Life Sciences; Biomedicine; Economics; Engineering**

Management; Environmental Studies; Information Technology; Materials Engineering; Metallurgical Engineering; Mining Engineering; Transport and Communications. *Magistrosi Vorakavorum*: **Applied Mathematics; Automation and Control Engineering; Biological and Life Sciences; Biomedicine; Economics; Electrical Engineering; Electronic Engineering; Engineering Management; Environmental Studies; Information Technology; Mechanical Engineering; Metallurgical Engineering; Mining Engineering; Power Engineering; Sociology; Transport and Communications.** *Candidate/Doctor of Science*: **Automation and Control Engineering; Biotechnology; Chemical Engineering; Economics; Electrical Engineering; Electronic Engineering; Engineering Management; Environmental Studies; Information Technology; Mathematics; Mechanics; Metallurgical Engineering; Mining Engineering; Power Engineering; Transport and Communications.** Also Junior Engineer Degree, 3 yrs; Programmes in Russian and English for Foreign students

Student Services: Academic Counselling, Canteen, Cultural Activities, Foreign Studies Centre, Health Services, Library, Nursery Care, Sports Facilities

Publications: Bulletin of State Engineering University of Armenia; Bulletin of the National Academy of Sciences and the State Engineering University of Armenia; Mathematics in Higher School; Modeling, Optimization and Control

Student Numbers *2014-2015*: Total: c. 10,000
Last Updated: 26/05/15

PUBLIC ADMINISTRATION ACADEMY OF REPUBLIC OF ARMENIA (PAARA)

Kievyan 8, Yerevan
Tel: +374(10) 26-92-59
Fax: +374(10) 22-89-42
EMail: info@paara.am; aspa.paara@gmail.com
Website: http://paara.am

Rector: Arsen Lokyan (2011-)

Vice-Rector for Educational Affairs: Khachatur Bezirjyan

International Relations: Tereza Khechoyan, Vice-Rector for External Relations

Chair

Languages and Information Technology (Finance; Management); **Law** (Law); **Political Governance and Political Analysis** (Political Sciences); **Psychology of Management** (Industrial and Organizational Psychology); **Public Administration** (Public Administration)

History: Founded 1994.

Main Language(s) of Instruction: Armenian

Degrees and Diplomas: *Magistrosi Vorakavorum*: **English; Finance; Information Technology; Law; Political Sciences; Psychology; Public Administration.** *Candidate/Doctor of Science*: **Economics; Finance; Law; Political Sciences; Psychology; Public Administration.**

Student Services: Library

Publications: "Public Administration" scientific journal; "Public Service" weekly newspaper

Last Updated: 31/05/15

RUSSIAN-ARMENIAN (SLAVONIC) UNIVERSITY

Rus-Haikakan (Slavonakan) Hamalsaran (RAU)

123 Hovsep Emin str., 0051 Yerevan
Tel: +374(10) 27-70-52
Fax: +374(10) 22-14-63
EMail: rector@rau.am
Website: http://www.rau.am

Rector: Armen Darbinyan (2001-)
Tel: +374(10) 229-254 +374(10) 289-700
EMail: laghajanyan@rambler.ru

Vice-Rector: Gagik Sargsyan
Tel: +374(10) 269-701 EMail: gzsarg@rau.am

International Relations: Emma Yeghiazaryan
Tel: +374(10) 270-523

Institute

Economics and Business (Business Administration; Economics; Finance; Management; Tourism); **Humanities** (Arts and Humanities; Communication Studies; Journalism; Literature; Modern Languages; Psychology; Russian); **Law and Politics** (Civil Law; Constitutional Law; Criminal Law; European Union Law; History of Law; International Law; International Relations; Law; Political Sciences; Public Law); **Mathematics and High Technology** (Automation and Control Engineering; Bioengineering; Biological and Life Sciences; Chemistry; Electronic Engineering; Information Technology; Materials Engineering; Mathematics; Physics); **Media, Advertising and Film Art** (Advertising and Publicity; Cinema and Television; Journalism; Media Studies; Public Relations)

History: Founded 1998 following the agreement between the Governments of Russian Federation and Armenia. Acquired present status 2000.

Academic Year: September to June

Admission Requirements: Secondary school certificate

Fees: 900-2,500 per annum (US Dollar)

Main Language(s) of Instruction: Russian

Accrediting Agency: Ministry of Education and Science of the Republic of Armenia and the Russian Federation

Degrees and Diplomas: *Bakalavri Vorakavorum*: **Advertising and Publicity; Applied Mathematics; Biochemistry; Bioengineering; Cinema and Television; Computer Science; Construction Engineering; Economics; Electronic Engineering; Film; International Relations; Journalism; Law; Linguistics; Management; Nanotechnology; Pharmacy; Philology; Philosophy; Political Sciences; Psychology; Public Relations; Regional Studies; Tourism.** *Magistrosi Vorakavorum*: **Accountancy; Administration; Administrative Law; Automation and Control Engineering; Biochemistry; Bioengineering; Business Computing; Chinese; Cinema and Television; Civil Law; Commercial Law; Computer Engineering; Constitutional Law; Criminal Law; Criminology; Data Processing; Economics; Educational Administration; Electronic Engineering; European Union Law; Finance; Foreign Languages Education; History of Law; International Economics; International Law; International Relations; Journalism; Law; Literature; Management; Mathematics; Nanotechnology; Pharmacology; Political Sciences; Protective Services; Psychology; Public Law; Russian; Software Engineering; Statistics; Telecommunications Engineering; Tourism; Translation and Interpretation.** *Candidate/Doctor of Science*: **Accountancy; Automation and Control Engineering; Biochemistry; Biophysics; Cell Biology; Computer Networks; Computer Science; Criminal Law; Criminology; Economics; Finance; Germanic Languages; History; History of Law; International Economics; International Law; Journalism; Law; Mathematics; Molecular Biology; Organic Chemistry; Physics; Political Sciences; Private Law; Psychology; Public Law; Science Education; Slavic Languages; Software Engineering; Statistics; Telecommunications Engineering; Zoology.** Also SBS Swiss Business School MBA programmes; Also Candidate/Doctoral recognised by the Ministry of Education of the Republic of Russia in: Physics, Organic Chemistry, Biochemistry, Mathematics, Software Engineering, Computer Engineering, Computer Networks, Computer Science, Information Technology, Information Management, Economics, Finance, Banking, International Economics, Literature, Journalism, Constitutional Law, Administrative Law, Civil Law, Commercial Law, Private Law, International Law, Criminal Law, Criminology, European Union Law, Political Science, History, International Relations, Development Studies.

Student Services: Canteen, Careers Guidance, Cultural Activities, Health Services, Language Laboratory, Library, Sports Facilities

Publications: Vestnik

Last Updated: 27/05/15

VANADZOR STATE UNIVERSITY NAMED AFTER HOVHANNES TOUMANYAN

Vanadzori Hovhannes Tumanyani Anvan Petakan Hamalsaran (VSU)

Tigran Mets Street 36, 377200 Vanadzor, Lori Region
Tel: +374(322) 46-387
Fax: +374(322) 41-856
EMail: rector@vspi.am
Website: http://www.vspi.am

Rector: Gurgen Khachatryan (2006-)
EMail: gxchatryan@yahoo.com

Vice-Rector: Susanna Toumanyan
Tel: +374(322) 43-114 EMail: stoumanyan@vspi.am

International Relations: Sirapi Arustamyan, Department Manager
Tel: +374(322) 41-853 EMail: foreign@vspi.am

Faculty

Chemistry and Biology (Biology; Chemistry; Ecology; Natural Sciences; Pharmacology; Physical Education; Sports); **History and Geography** (Cultural Studies; Geography; Government; History; Law; Management; Social Work); **Pedagogy** (Educational Administration; Educational Psychology; Music Education; Painting and Drawing; Pedagogy; Preschool Education; Primary Education; Sociology); **Philology** (Armenian; English; Foreign Languages Education; Journalism; Literature; Russian; Translation and Interpretation); **Physics and Mathematics** (Applied Mathematics; Information Technology; Management; Mathematics; Physics; Small Business; Technology)

History: Founded 1969. Acquired present title 2014. Formerly known as Vanadzori Hovhannes Toumanyani anvan Petakan Mankavaržakan Institut (Vanadzor State Pedagogical Institute named after Hovhannes Toumanyan).

Admission Requirements: Secondary school certificate and entrance examination

Fees: 500-900 per annum (US Dollar)

Main Language(s) of Instruction: Armenian

Accrediting Agency: Ministry of Education and Science of Armenia

Degrees and Diplomas: *Bakalavri Vorakavorum*; *Magistrosi Vorakavorum*: **Applied Mathematics; Armenian; Biology; Chemistry; Educational Administration; Educational Psychology; English; Foreign Languages Education; History; Humanities and Social Science Education; Information Technology; Literature; Mathematics; Native Language Education; Pedagogy; Physics; Public Administration; Russian; Science Education.** *Doctor of Science*: **Computer Engineering; Inorganic Chemistry; Literature; Mathematics; Pedagogy; Physical Chemistry; Slavic Languages.**

Student Services: Canteen, IT Centre, Language Laboratory, Library, Nursery Care, Sports Facilities

Publications: Apaga Mankavarjh

Publishing House: Yes

Last Updated: 26/05/15

YEREVAN STATE ACADEMY OF FINE ARTS

Yerevani Gegharvesti Petakan Academia (YSAFA)
Isahakyan 36, 0009 Yerevan
Tel: +374(10) 56-07-26
Fax: +374(10) 54-27-06
EMail: yafa@yafa.am; info@yafa.am
Website: http://www.yafa.am

Rector: Aram Issabekyan (1994-)
Tel: +374(10) 56-07-26 EMail: aram.isabekyan@yafa.am

Vice-Rector for Education and Sciences: Susanna Karakhanyan
Tel: +374(10) 56-06-15 EMail: vicerector@yafa.am

International Relations: Marine Patvakanyan, Head, International Relations Department
Tel: +374(1) 54-27-06 EMail: m.patvakanyan@yafa.am

Faculty

Design and Decorative Applied Arts (Computer Graphics; Design; Fashion Design; Fine Arts; Graphic Arts; Handicrafts; Sculpture); **Fine Arts** (Art History; Fine Arts; Graphic Arts; Painting and Drawing; Sculpture)

History: Founded 1945 as Yerevan State Institute of Fine Arts, acquired present status and title 1999.

Main Language(s) of Instruction: Armenian

Accrediting Agency: Ministry of Education and Science of Armenia

Degrees and Diplomas: *Bakalavri Vorakavorum*; *Magistrosi Vorakavorum*: **Art History; Computer Graphics; Design; Fashion Design; Fine Arts; Graphic Design; Painting and Drawing; Sculpture.** *Candidate/Doctor of Science*: **Design; Fine Arts; Handicrafts.**

Last Updated: 28/05/15

DILIJAN BRANCH
DILIJAN MASNACHUOH
Getapnya aj, Dilijan
Tel: 374(268) 26-184
EMail: ghazar.ghazaryan@yafa.am

Dean: Ghazar Ghazaryan

Division

Applied Arts and Handicrafts (Fine Arts; Handicrafts)

History: Founded 1999.

Degrees and Diplomas: *Bakalavri Vorakavorum*; *Magistrosi Vorakavorum*: **Fine Arts; Handicrafts.**

GYUMRI BRANCH
GYUMRII MASNACHUOH
Ankakhutyan Street 1, Gyumri
Tel: +374(312) 22-355
EMail: gcca@shirak.am
Website: http://www.yafa.am/en/?page_id=1603

Director: Hambardzum Ghukassian (1997-) Tel: +374(322) 22-355

Department

Graphic Arts (Graphic Arts); **History and Theory of Fine Arts** (Art History; Fine Arts); **Painting** (Painting and Drawing); **Sculpture** (Sculpture)

Section

Decorative Applied Arts/Potter's Art (Handicrafts); **Folk Crafts** (Fashion Design; Textile Design)

History: Founded 1997.

Main Language(s) of Instruction: Armenian

Degrees and Diplomas: *Bakalavri Vorakavorum*; *Magistrosi Vorakavorum*: **Design; Fine Arts; Visual Arts.**

Student Services: IT Centre

YEREVAN STATE CONSERVATORY AFTER KOMITAS

Yerevani Komitasi Anvan Petakan Conservatoria (YSC)
1A, Sajat-Nova Street, 0001 Yerevan
Tel: +374(10) 58-11-64
Fax: +374(10) 56-35-40
EMail: yksc@conservatory.am
Website: http://www.conservatory.am/

Rector: Sh. Shahinian

Acting Vice-Rector, Administrative Affairs: A. Hakobyan

International Relations: Arkadi Avanesov, Vice-Rector, International Affairs

Faculty

Orchestra (Musical Instruments); **Piano** (Musical Instruments); **Vocal Theory** (Conducting; Music Theory and Composition; Singing)

History: Founded 1921.

Academic Year: September to June

Admission Requirements: Secondary school certificate

Fees: National: c. 600,000 per annum (Armenian Dram), International: 900,000 per annum (Armenian Dram)

Main Language(s) of Instruction: Armenian

Accrediting Agency: Ministry of Education and Science of Armenia

Degrees and Diplomas: *Bakalavri Vorakavorum*; *Magistrosi Vorakavorum*: **Conducting; Music Theory and Composition; Musical Instruments; Musicology; Singing.** *Candidate/Doctor of Science*: **Music.** Also Certificate of Postgraduate Studies in Musicology, a further 3 yrs

Student Services: Academic Counselling, Canteen, Foreign Studies Centre, Language Laboratory, Library, Social Counselling, Sports Facilities

Publications: Yeražshtakan Hayastan

Student Numbers *2014-2015*: Total: c. 1,000

Last Updated: 29/05/15

GYUMRI BRANCH

GYUMRII MASNACHUOH (YSCGC)

Ankakhutyan Square 1, 377526 Gyumri
Tel: +374(312) 36-937

Rector: Karine Avdalyan

History: Founded 1997.

Main Language(s) of Instruction: Armenian

YEREVAN STATE INSTITUTE OF THEATRE AND CINEMA

Yerevani Tatroni ev Kinoi Petakan Institut (YSITC)
Abovyan St. 26, 0002 Yerevan
Tel: +374(10) 53-62-21
Fax: +374(10) 536-233
EMail: bccp@arminco.com
Website: http://www.ysitc.am

Rector: David E. Muradian Tel: +374(10) 536-221

International Relations: Artur Ghukasyan

Department

Art History, Theory and Management (Art History; Art Management); **Film, TV and Animation** (Cinema and Television; Clothing and Sewing; Display and Stage Design; Film; Sound Engineering (Acoustics); Visual Arts); **Part-Time Studies** (Acting; Art History; Art Management; Arts and Humanities; Cinema and Television; Dance; Singing; Theatre); **Theatre** (Acting; Theatre)

Campus

Gyumri (Acting; Cinema and Television)

Further Information: Also branches in Goris and Vanadzor

History: Founded 1944, acquired present status and title 1997.

Academic Year: September to June

Admission Requirements: Secondary school certificate; College graduation or diploma of other institution

Fees: National: 500-750 per annum (US Dollar), International: 1,000-1,400 per annum (US Dollar)

Main Language(s) of Instruction: Armenian

Accrediting Agency: Ministry of Education and Science of Armenia

Degrees and Diplomas: *Bakalavri Vorakavorum*: **Art Criticism; Art Management; Cinema and Television; Performing Arts; Theatre.** *Magistrosi Vorakavorum*: **Acting; Art Management; Cinema and Television; Cultural Studies; Dance; Painting and Drawing; Theatre; Writing.** *Candidate/Doctor of Science*: **Cinema and Television; Theatre.**

Student Services: Academic Counselling, Canteen, Cultural Activities, Facilities for disabled people, Foreign Studies Centre, Health Services, Language Laboratory, Library, Nursery Care, Social Counselling, Sports Facilities

Publications: Arvest; Handes

Last Updated: 29/05/15

YEREVAN STATE LINGUISTIC UNIVERSITY NAMED AFTER V. BRUSOV

Yerevani V. Brusovi Anvan Petakan Lezerabanakan Hamalsaran (YSLU)
42 Toumanyan Street, 375002 Yerevan
Tel: +374(10) 53-05-52
Fax: +374(10) 53-05-52
EMail: info@brusov.am; yslu@brusov.am
Website: http://www.brusov.am/index.php

Rector: Gayane Gasparyan
Tel: +374(10) 530-552 EMail: ggasparyan@brusov.am

Vice-Rector for Legal, Administrative and Economic Affairs: Gabriel Kimi Balayan
Tel: +374(10) 534-172 EMail: gabrbal@brusov.am

International Relations: L. Fljyan, Vice Rector for Science and International Relations
Tel: +374(10) 533-331 EMail: vicerector_si@brusov.am

Faculty

Foreign Languages (Armenian; English; European Languages; Foreign Languages Education; French; German; Korean; Linguistics; Oriental Languages; Pedagogy; Physical Education; Romance Languages); **Russian Language, Literature and Foreign Languages** (Literature; Russian; Slavic Languages); **Translation and Intercultural Communication** (Communication Studies; English; French; German; Journalism; Linguistics; Political Sciences; Psychology; Regional Studies; Tourism; Translation and Interpretation; Turkish)

History: Founded 1935. Acquired present status and title 2000.

Academic Year: September to June

Admission Requirements: Secondary school certificate

Fees: c. 350,000 per annum (Armenian Dram)

Main Language(s) of Instruction: Armenian, Russian

Accrediting Agency: Ministry of Education and Science of Armenia

Degrees and Diplomas: *Bakalavri Vorakavorum*; *Magistrosi Vorakavorum*: **Communication Studies; European Languages; International Relations; Journalism; Linguistics; Literature; Modern Languages; Political Sciences; Public Administration; Russian; Service Trades.** *Candidate/Doctor of Science*: **English; French; German; Linguistics.**

Student Services: Academic Counselling, Canteen, Careers Guidance, Cultural Activities, Health Services, IT Centre, Language Laboratory, Library, Social Counselling, Sports Facilities

Publications: "Polyglot" Student Journal; Newspapers; Research Papers

Last Updated: 31/05/15

YEREVAN STATE MEDICAL UNIVERSITY NAMED AFTER M. HERATSI

Yerevani Mkhitar Heratsu Anvan Petakan Bjshkakan Hamalsaran (YSMU)
2 Koryun str., 0025 Yerevan
Tel: +374(10) 58-25-32
Fax: +374(10) 58-25-32
EMail: info@ysmu.am
Website: http://www.ysmu.am

Rector: Michael Z. Narimanyan (2012-)
Tel: +374(10) 58-18-02 EMail: rector@ysmu.am

Vice-Rector for Academic Affairs: Samvel A. Avetisyan
Tel: +374(10) 58-11-52 EMail: vice-edu@ysmu.am

International Relations: Yervand S. Sahakyan, Vice-Rector for External Affairs and International Partnerships
Tel: +374(10) 560-594 EMail: international@ysmu.am

Faculty

General Medicine (Anaesthesiology; Anatomy; Endocrinology; Gynaecology and Obstetrics; Haematology; Laboratory Techniques; Medicine; Neurology; Oncology; Orthopaedics; Paediatrics; Pharmacology; Radiology; Surgery; Urology); **Military Medicine** (Medicine; Military Science; Rehabilitation and Therapy; Surgery); **Pharmacy** (Anatomy; Armenian; History; Management; Microbiology; Modern Languages; Organic Chemistry; Pathology; Pharmacology; Pharmacy; Philosophy; Physical Education; Physiology; Surgery); **Postgraduate and Continuing Education** (Alternative Medicine; Anaesthesiology; Cardiology; Cosmetology; Dentistry; Dermatology; Endocrinology; Gynaecology and Obstetrics; Health Administration; Medicine; Neurology; Nursing; Oncology; Ophthalmology; Orthodontics; Orthopaedics; Paediatrics; Pharmacology; Plastic Surgery; Radiology; Rehabilitation and Therapy; Stomatology; Surgery; Venereology); **Public Health** (Dermatology; Ecology; Epidemiology; Gender Studies; Health Administration; Health Sciences; Hygiene; Law; Physical Therapy; Pneumology; Psychiatry and Mental Health; Psychology; Public Health; Rehabilitation and Therapy; Venereology); **Stomatology** (Biochemistry; Biology; Chemistry; Dental Technology; Forensic Medicine and Dentistry; Histology; Orthodontics; Paediatrics; Physics; Physiology; Rehabilitation and Therapy; Stomatology; Surgery)

History: Founded 1920, acquired present status and title 1995.

Academic Year: September to June (September-January; February-June)

Admission Requirements: Secondary school certificate

Fees: Undergraduate, 580,000-800,000 per annum; Graduate, 650,000-900,000 per annum (Armenian Dram)

Main Language(s) of Instruction: Armenian, Russian, English

Accrediting Agency: Ministry of Education and Science of Armenia

Degrees and Diplomas: *Bakalavri Vorakavorum*: **Dentistry; Medicine; Pharmacy.** *Magistrosi Vorakavorum*: **Dentistry; Health Education; Medicine; Pharmacology; Public Health; Stomatology.** *Candidate/Doctor of Science*: **Cardiology; Dental Technology; Dentistry; Gynaecology and Obstetrics; Medicine; Pharmacy; Rehabilitation and Therapy; Surgery.** Also Post-Doctoral degrees of 'Professor'

Student Services: Academic Counselling, Canteen, Cultural Activities, Health Services, Language Laboratory, Library, Nursery Care, Social Counselling, Sports Facilities

Publications: Apaga Bjisk-Future Doctor; Hajastani Bjshkagitutjun-Medical Science of Armenia; Medicus; The New Armenian Medical Journal

Student Numbers *2014-2015*: Total: c. 3,000

Last Updated: 29/04/15

YEREVAN STATE UNIVERSITY

Yerevani Petakan Hamalsaran (YSU)

Alex Manoogian Street 1, 0025 Yerevan

Tel: +374(10) 55-52-40 +374(10) 55-46-29

Fax: +374(10) 554-641

EMail: info@ysu.am; pr-int@ysu.am; international@ysu.am

Website: http://www.ysu.am

Rector: Aram Simonyan (2006-)
Tel: +374(10) 55-43-12 +374(60) 71-01-00 EMail: rector@ysu.am

Vice-Rector on Educational Affairs: Alexander Grigoryan
Tel: +374(10) 55-46-01 +374(60) 71-01-07
EMail: agrigoryan@ysu.am

International Relations: Gegham G. Gevorgyan, Vice-Rector for Scientific Policy and Int Cooperation (2008-)
Tel: +374(10) 554-702 EMail: ggg@ysu.am

Faculty

Armenian Philology (Armenian; Art Criticism; Linguistics; Literature; Pedagogy); **Biology** (Biochemistry; Biology; Biophysics; Biotechnology; Botany; Cell Biology; Ecology; Environmental Management; Genetics; Microbiology; Physiology; Plant and Crop Protection; Zoology); **Economics and Management** (Accountancy; Business Administration; Economics; Finance; International Economics; Management; Mathematics); **Geography and Geology** (Geochemistry; Geography; Geography (Human); Geological Engineering; Geology; Geophysics; Mineralogy; Petrology; Surveying and Mapping); **History** (Archaeology; Art History; Cultural Studies; Demography and Population; Ethnology; History); **Informatics and Applied Mathematics** (Applied Mathematics; Computer Science; Information Technology; Software Engineering; Systems Analysis); **International Relations** (Communication Studies; History; International Relations; Political Sciences; Public Administration); **Journalism** (Journalism; Radio and Television Broadcasting); **Law** (Civil Law; Constitutional Law; Criminal Law; Criminology; European Union Law; International Law; Law; Public Law); **Mathematics and Mechanics** (Actuarial Science; Finance; Insurance; Mathematics; Mechanics; Statistics); **Oriental Studies** (Arabic; Oriental Studies; Persian; Turkish); **Pharmacology and Chemistry** (Analytical Chemistry; Chemistry; Ecology; Inorganic Chemistry; Organic Chemistry; Pharmacology; Physical Chemistry); **Philosophy and Psychology** (Ethics; Logic; Philosophy; Psychology; Social Psychology); **Physics** (Astrophysics; Nuclear Physics; Optics; Physics; Solid State Physics); **Radiophysics** (Mathematics; Microelectronics; Microwaves; Physics; Radiophysics; Telecommunications Engineering); **Romance and Germanic Philology** (English; French; German; Literature; Philology; Romance Languages; Translation and Interpretation); **Russian Philology** (Linguistics; Literature; Russian); **Sociology** (Social Work; Sociology); **Theology** (History of Religion; Theology)

History: Founded 1919.

Academic Year: September to June (September-January; February-June)

Admission Requirements: Competitive entrance examination following general or special secondary school certificate

Fees: None for 70% of students; for others: c. 600 per annum (US Dollar)

Main Language(s) of Instruction: Armenian

Accrediting Agency: Ministry of Education and Science of Armenia

Degrees and Diplomas: *Bakalavri Vorakavorum*; *Magistrosi Vorakavorum*: **Accountancy; Actuarial Science; Applied Chemistry; Applied Mathematics; Arabic; Archaeology; Armenian; Art Criticism; Art History; Astrophysics; Atomic and Molecular Physics; Banking; Biochemistry; Biological and Life Sciences; Biology; Biophysics; Biotechnology; Botany; Business Administration; Business Computing; Cell Biology; Civil Law; Clinical Psychology; Commercial Law; Communication Studies; Computer Engineering; Computer Networks; Computer Science; Constitutional Law; Criminal Law; Criminology; Cultural Studies; Demography and Population; Developmental Psychology; Ecology; Economic and Finance Policy; Educational Administration; English; Environmental Management; Ethics; Ethnology; European Studies; European Union Law; Finance; French; Genetics; Geochemistry; Geography (Human); Geological Engineering; Geology; Geophysics; German; Higher Education; History; History of Religion; Industrial and Organizational Psychology; Inorganic Chemistry; Insurance; International Economics; International Law; International Relations; Islamic Studies; Italian; Journalism; Linguistics; Literature; Management; Mass Communication; Mathematics; Mathematics and Computer Science; Mechanics; Media Studies; Meteorology; Microelectronics; Microwaves; Mineralogy; Nuclear Physics; Optics; Organic Chemistry; Oriental Studies; Peace and Disarmament; Persian; Petrology; Pharmacology; Philosophy; Physical Chemistry; Physics; Physiology; Political Sciences; Psychology; Psychotherapy; Public Administration; Public Law; Public Relations; Radiophysics; Religion; Russian; Service Trades; Social Policy; Social Psychology; Social Studies; Social Work; Sociology; Spanish; Statistics; Surveying and Mapping; Telecommunications Engineering; Theology; Tourism; Translation and Interpretation; Turkish; Zoology.** *Candidate/Doctor of Science*: **Applied Mathematics; Biology; Computer Science; Economics; Geography; Geology; History; Journalism; Law; Philology; Radiophysics; Sociology; Theology.**

Student Services: Health Services, Library, Sports Facilities

Publications: Transactions

Academic Staff *2014-2015*: Total: c. 3,000

Student Numbers *2014-2015*: Total: c. 18,000

Last Updated: 29/05/15

IJEVAN BRANCH

IJEVAN MASNACHUOGH

Usanoghakan Street 3, 377260 Ijevan

Tel: +374(263) 32-202 +374(263) 36-597

EMail: ijevan@ysu.am

Director: Samvel Arakelyan (2000-)

Department

Applied Decoration Art (Handicrafts); **Applied Mathematics** (Applied Mathematics); **Armenian Language and Literature** (Natural Sciences); **History** (History); **National Trade** (Business and Commerce); **Pedagogy** (Pedagogy); **Physics** (Physics); **Psychology** (Psychology)

History: Founded 1994.

Academic Year: September to June (September-January; February-June)

Main Language(s) of Instruction: Armenian

Degrees and Diplomas: *Bakalavri Vorakavorum*

Student Numbers *2014-2015*: Total: c. 900

YEREVAN STATE UNIVERSITY OF ARCHITECTURE AND CONSTRUCTION

Yerevani Tchartarapetutyan ev Shinararutyan Institut (YSUAC)

Teryan Street 105, 3750009 Yerevan
Tel: +374(10) 54-74-25
Fax: +374(10) 58-72-84
EMail: info@ysuac.am; manager@ysuac.am
Website: http://www.ysuac.am

Rector: Gagik Galstyan

Vice Rector Academic Affairs: Arkadi Barkhudaryan

International Relations: Vardges Edoyan, Vice-rector on International Affairs

Faculty

Architecture (Architectural and Environmental Design; Architectural Restoration; Architecture; Art History; Environmental Studies; Fine Arts); **Design** (Computer Graphics; Design; Heating and Refrigeration; Hydraulic Engineering; Painting and Drawing; Water Management); **Management and Technology** (Accountancy; Economics; Management; Technology)

Department

Construction (Building Technologies; Construction Engineering; Geology; Surveying and Mapping)

History: Founded 1921, acquired present status and title 1989.

Academic Year: September to August

Admission Requirements: Secondary school certificate or university diploma and entrance examination

Fees: Preparatory Group, 600 per annum; Faculty of Architecture, 900 per annum; other faculties, 800 per annum; Postgraduate Course, 1,000 per annum (US Dollar)

Main Language(s) of Instruction: Armenian, Russian, French

Accrediting Agency: Ministry of Education and Science of Armenia

Degrees and Diplomas: *Bakalavri Vorakavorum*; *Magistrosi Vorakavorum*: **Accountancy; Architecture; Automotive Engineering; Building Technologies; Computer Graphics; Computer Science; Construction Engineering; Design; Economics; Environmental Management; Environmental Studies; Fine Arts; Industrial Engineering; Information Technology; Maintenance Technology; Management; Natural Resources; Real Estate; Road Transport; Safety Engineering; Service Trades; Surveying and Mapping; Translation and Interpretation; Transport Management; Urban Studies; Water Management.** *Candidate/Doctor of Science*: **Architecture; Building Technologies; Civil Engineering; Construction Engineering; Economics; Hydraulic Engineering; Industrial Maintenance; Management; Surveying and Mapping; Transport Engineering; Water Management.**

Student Services: Canteen, Cultural Activities, Health Services, Language Laboratory, Social Counselling, Sports Facilities

Publications: Proceedings of the Institute Scientific Workers and Professor Staff; Proceedings of the Institute Young Scientific Workers and Post-graduates

Last Updated: 29/05/15

PRIVATE INSTITUTIONS

AMERICAN UNIVERSITY OF ARMENIA

Hayastani Amerikyan Hamalsaran (AUA)

40 Marshal Baghramyan Avenue, 0019 Yerevan
Tel: +374(10) 324-040 +374(60) 694-040
Fax: +374(60) 612-512
EMail: info@aua.am; admissions@aua.am
Website: http://www.aua.am

President: Armen Der Kiureghian (2014-)
Tel: +374(60) 612-526 EMail: president@aua.am

Interim Provost: Donald Fuller
Tel: +374(60) 612-526 EMail: dfuller@aua.am

International Relations: Chaghig Arzrouni-Chahinian, Registrar
Tel: +374(60) 612-790 EMail: carzroun@aua.am

College

Business and Economics (Business Administration; Economics); **Humanities and Social Sciences** (Arts and Humanities; Economics; Foreign Languages Education; International Relations; Law; Philosophy; Political Sciences; Psychology; Social Sciences); **Science and Engineering** (Computer Science; Engineering; Information Sciences; Natural Sciences)

School

Public Health (Public Health)

Centre

Business Research and Development (Business Administration; Management); **Engineering Research** (Engineering); **Environment** *(Acopian)* (Environmental Studies); **Health Services Research and Development** (Health Sciences); **Legal Resource** (Law); **Policy Analysis** *(Turpanjian)* (Political Sciences); **Research in Applied Linguistics** (Applied Linguistics; English); **Rural Development** *(Turpanjian)* (Rural Planning)

Further Information: Branch in Oakland, California (USA)

History: Founded 1991. An Institution of Graduate Studies.

Academic Year: February to November (February-May; June-August; September-November)

Admission Requirements: Undergraduate degree. English language proficiency (TOEFL = 550), GRE or GMAT

Fees: National: Undergraduate, 1,500,000-1,080,000 per annum; Graduate, 960,000-1,280,000 per annum; Certificates and professional studies, 45,000-90,000 per credit (Armenian Dram), International: Undergraduate, 2,160,000-3,000,000 per annum; Graduate, 2,880,000-3,840,000 per annum; Certificates and professional studies, 125,000-275,000 per credit (Armenian Dram)

Main Language(s) of Instruction: English

Accrediting Agency: Ministry of Education and Science; Western Association of Schools and Colleges Senior College and University Commission (WSCUC)

Degrees and Diplomas: *Bakalavri Vorakavorum*: **Business Administration; Communication Studies; English.** *Magistrosi Vorakavorum*: **Business Administration; Computer Science; Economics; Engineering; Foreign Languages Education; Industrial Engineering; Information Sciences; International Relations; Law; Management Systems; Political Sciences; Public Health.** Also Certificates in: Teaching English as a Foreign Language, 1 yr; Translation, 1 yr

Student Services: Academic Counselling, Canteen, Careers Guidance, Facilities for disabled people, Health Services, IT Centre, Language Laboratory, Library

Academic Staff *2011*	**TOTAL**
FULL-TIME	**30**
PART-TIME	**60**
STAFF WITH DOCTORATE	
FULL-TIME	c. **20**

Student Numbers *2011*	
All (Foreign included)	c. **260**
FOREIGN ONLY	**30**

Last Updated: 06/05/15

ARMENIAN MEDICAL INSTITUTE

Haikakan Bžhshkakan Hamalsaran (AMI)

Titogradyan 14, 0087 Yerevan
Tel: +374(10) 451-923; +374(10) 470-844
Fax: +374(10) 451-923
EMail: info@armedin.com; ami@web.am
Website: http://www.armedin.com/

Rector: Mushegh Astabatsyan EMail: rector@armedin.com

Faculty

Dentistry (Dentistry; Stomatology); **Medicine** (Medicine)

Further Information: Cooperation agreements with 26 clinics of Yerevan that serve as training facilities

History: Founded 1990. Acquired present status 2001.

Fees: 800 per annum (US Dollar)

Main Language(s) of Instruction: Armenian, Russian

Accrediting Agency: Ministry of Education and Science of Armenia

Degrees and Diplomas: Graduates are awarded a State Diploma equivalent to a Bachelor and Master's Degree in Medicine (6 yrs) and Stomatology (5 yrs)

Student Services: Academic Counselling, Canteen, Careers Guidance, Sports Facilities

Academic Staff *2014-2015*: Total: c. 130

Last Updated: 04/05/15

ARMENIAN-RUSSIAN INTERNATIONAL UNIVERSITY MKHITAR GOSH

Vanadzori Mkhitar Gosh hay-rusakan Midjazgayn Hamalsaran

Tigran Mec 30a, Vanadzor, Lori Region
Tel: +374(322) 4-03-11
Fax: +374(322) 4-04-11
EMail: mguniv@rambler.ru; mguniv@mail.ru
Website: http://www.mkhitargosh.com

Rector: Vachik Brutyan

Faculty

Armenian Philology (Armenian); **Computer Science and Automation** (Automation and Control Engineering; Computer Science); **Economics** (Accountancy; Business and Commerce; Finance; International Economics; Management); **International Relations** (International Relations); **Journalism** (Journalism); **Law** (Law); **Medicine** (Medicine; Pharmacy; Stomatology); **Romance-Germanic Philology** (English; French; German; Modern Languages)

History: Founded 1996. Acquired present status 2002.

Accrediting Agency: Ministry of Education and Science of Armenia

Degrees and Diplomas: *Bakalavri Vorakavorum*: **Automation and Control Engineering; Computer Engineering; Computer Science; English; French; German; Law; Management; Modern Languages; Primary Education.** *Magistrosi Vorakavorum*: **Automation and Control Engineering; Computer Engineering; Computer Science; French; German; Law; Management; Modern Languages; Primary Education.**

Student Services: Sports Facilities

Student Numbers *2014-2015*: Total: c. 1,000

Last Updated: 27/05/15

AZPAT-VETERAN INSTITUTE OF FORENSIC SCIENCE AND PSYCHOLOGY

Azpat-Veteran Datakan Porcagitutyan ev Hogebanutyan Institut

Hanrapetutyan 19, 0010 Yerevan
Tel: +374(10) 522-781
Fax: +374(10) 522-644
EMail: tadevosyan-group@mail.ru; tadevosyangroup@mail.ru

Head: Azat Tadevosyan

Executive Director: Jevon Tadevosyan

Programme

Law (Law)

History: Acquired present status 2002.

Main Language(s) of Instruction: Armenian

Accrediting Agency: Ministry of Education and Science of Armenia

Degrees and Diplomas: *Bakalavri Vorakavorum*: **Law.**

Student Services: Academic Counselling, Canteen, Careers Guidance, Health Services, Language Laboratory, Nursery Care, Sports Facilities

Last Updated: 29/04/15

EURASIA INTERNATIONAL UNIVERSITY

Yevrasia Mijazgain Hamalsaran (EIU)

Azatutyan 24/2, next to administrative building of "ArmenTel", 0014 Yerevan
Tel: +374(10) 299-088 +374(10) 249-438 +374(10) 299-077
Fax: +374(10) 249-438
EMail: info@eiu.am
Website: http://www.eiu.am/

Rector: Souren Hekim Ohanyan (1996-)
Tel: +374(10) 249-438 EMail: president@eiu.am

Vice Rector for Academic Affairs: A. Aghabekyan
EMail: vp@eiu.am

Faculty

Foreign Languages (English; French; German; Modern Languages; Spanish); **Law** (Law); **Management and Economics** (Economics; Finance; Management)

History: Founded 1996 as Mkhitar Gosh Migazgain Hamalsaran - Yerevan. Acquired present status 2001 and title 2004.

Academic Year: September to May (September-December; February-May)

Admission Requirements: Secondary school certificate and entrance examination

Fees: National: 250,000 per annum; Doctor, 380,000 per annum (Armenian Dram), International: Doctor 570 000 per annum (Armenian Dram)

Main Language(s) of Instruction: Armenian, English

Accrediting Agency: Ministry of Education and Science of Armenia

Degrees and Diplomas: *Bakalavri Vorakavorum*; *Magistrosi Vorakavorum*: **Finance; Law; Management; Modern Languages.** *Candidate/Doctor of Science*: **Economics; German; Management.** Dual Degree Master Programmes in Electronic Business Administration (e-Business) offered in collaboration with Lithuanian Mykolas Romeris University, with the support of Microsoft Armenia and the Union of Information Technology Enterprises (UITE).

Student Services: Academic Counselling, Canteen, Health Services, Library, Residential Facilities, Sports Facilities

Publications: Periodical of Conference Articles

Last Updated: 05/05/15

FINANCIAL ACADEMY

Finansakan Akademia

Pushkin Street 25, 375010 Yerevan
Tel: +374(10) 53-86-07 +374(10) 53-43-96
Fax: +374(10) 53-91-48
EMail: adm@npc.am; mfbfinakad@mail.ru
Website: http://www.finacademy.am

Rector: Eduard Gasparyan
Tel: +374(10) 539-148 EMail: rector@finacademy.am

Director: Karen E. Gasparyan

Institute

Banking and Economics (Accountancy; Finance; Information Technology)

History: Founded 1999 as Banking Economical Institute. Acquired present title and state status 2001.

Admission Requirements: Atestat

Main Language(s) of Instruction: Armenian, Russian

Accrediting Agency: Ministry of Education and Science of Armenia

Degrees and Diplomas: *Bakalavri Vorakavorum*: **Accountancy; Banking; Finance; Information Technology; Management; Real Estate; Taxation.** *Magistrosi Vorakavorum*: **Accountancy; Banking; Finance; Information Technology.**

Student Services: Cultural Activities, Health Services, Language Laboratory, Sports Facilities

Publications: Finansist Magazine

Last Updated: 29/04/15

GYUMRI PROGRESS UNIVERSITY

Gyumrii Progres Hamalsaran

Tigran Mets Street 1, 3101 Gyumri, Shirak Region
Tel: +374(312) 5-77-35 +374(312) 5-51-80
Fax: +374(312) 5-86-03
EMail: progress_am@rambler.ru
Website: http://progress-hamalsaran.am

Rector: Rafik Z. Khachatryan

Vice-Rector: Karen Tonoyan

Faculty
Humanities (Journalism; Linguistics; Modern Languages; Pedagogy; Psychology; Teacher Training)

College
Medical (Dentistry; Midwifery; Nursing; Pharmacy)

School
Economics (Business Administration; Economics; Finance); **Law** (Law)

History: Founded 1990. Acquired present status 2001.

Admission Requirements: Armenian Secondary school certificate

Fees: 150,000-225,000 per annum (Armenian Dram)

Main Language(s) of Instruction: Armenian

Accrediting Agency: Ministry of Education and Science of Armenia

Degrees and Diplomas: *Bakalavri Vorakavorum*: **Armenian; Biochemistry; Dentistry; Design; Finance; Journalism; Law; Literature; Modern Languages; Pedagogy; Psychology; Teacher Training.** *Magistrosi Vorakavorum*: **Biochemistry; Economics; Law; Psychology.**

Student Services: Academic Counselling, Canteen, Cultural Activities, Health Services, Language Laboratory, Library, Nursery Care, Residential Facilities, Social Counselling, Sports Facilities

Academic Staff *2014-2015*: Total: c. 40

Student Numbers *2014-2015*: Total: c. 850

Last Updated: 04/05/15

HRAZDAN INSTITUTE OF HUMANITIES

Hrazdani Humanitar Institut (HIH)
Hrazdan Centre, Kotayk Region, 2301 Hrazdan
Tel: +374(223) 214-97
Fax: +374(223) 255-18
EMail: hrhumanitar@mail.ru
Website: http://www.hinstitute.am

Rector: Liparit Arakelyan (1996-)
Tel: +374(223) 2-55-18 EMail: liparitar@mail.ru

Vice-Rector, Educational Affairs: Rafael Yeghyan

International Relations: Christine Ghazaryan
EMail: kristarm@mail.ru

Faculty
Economics (Accountancy; Banking; Business Administration; Economic and Finance Policy; Economics; Finance; Geography (Human); History; Industrial and Production Economics; Marketing; Taxation); **Law** (Administrative Law; Banking; Civil Law; Constitutional Law; Criminal Law; Finance; History of Law; Labour Law; Law; Private Law; Public Administration; Real Estate)

Programme
Pedagogy (Education; Pedagogy; Primary Education)

History: Founded 1996. Acquired present status 2002.

Academic Year: September to June

Admission Requirements: Secondary school certificate and entrance examination

Main Language(s) of Instruction: Armenian

Accrediting Agency: Ministry of Education and Science of Armenia

Degrees and Diplomas: *Bakalavri Vorakavorum*; *Magistrosi Vorakavorum*

Student Services: Academic Counselling, Canteen, Cultural Activities, IT Centre, Language Laboratory, Library, Social Counselling, Sports Facilities

Publications: Newspaper

Last Updated: 04/05/15

HUMANITY UNIVERSITY OF YEREVAN

Amiryan 26, Yerevan
Tel: +374(10) 530-973
Fax: +374(10) 530-973

Rector: Michael Amirxanyan

Programme
Translation Studies (Translation and Interpretation)

Main Language(s) of Instruction: Armenian

Degrees and Diplomas: *Bakalavri Vorakavorum*: **Translation and Interpretation.**

Last Updated: 04/05/15

IMASTASER ANANIA SHIRAKATSI UNIVERSITY OF GYUMRI

Gyumrii Imastaser Anania Shirakatsi Hamalsaran (IASU)
Sayat-Nova Street 1, 377500 Gyumri, Shirak Region
Tel: +374(312) 39-394
Fax: +374(312) 33-015
EMail: roman@gyumri.am

Rector: Robert Manvelyan EMail: roman@gyumri.am

Pro-Rector: Levon Manandyan

International Relations: Gayane Grigoryan, Lecturer
Tel: +374(312) 4-06-75 EMail: gayaneg73@yahoo.com

Faculty
Economics and Law (Economics; Information Technology; Law; Management); **Philology** (Armenian; English; French; Literature; Modern Languages; Philology)

History: Founded 1991. Acquired present status 2001.

Main Language(s) of Instruction: Armenian

Accrediting Agency: Ministry of Education and Science of Armenia

Degrees and Diplomas: *Bakalavri Vorakavorum*: **Armenian; Economics; English; French; Law; Literature; Management.**

Student Services: Academic Counselling, Canteen, Cultural Activities, Language Laboratory, Nursery Care

Publications: Anania Shirakatsi

Last Updated: 30/04/15

INTERLINGUA LINGUISTIC UNIVERSITY OF YEREVAN

Yerevani Interlingva Lezvagitakan Hamalsaran
Pushkin Street, 21, 0010 Yerevan
Tel: +374(10) 52-63-07
Fax: +374(10) 58-60-72
EMail: inlingua@arminco.com

Rector: Iveta Arakelyan
Tel: +374(10) 54-36-85 +374(10) 58-60-72

Programme
Foreign Language (English; Modern Languages; Philology); **Translation** (English; French; Spanish; Translation and Interpretation)

History: Founded 1996. Acquired present status 2002.

Main Language(s) of Instruction: Armenian

Accrediting Agency: Ministry of Education and Science of Armenia

Degrees and Diplomas: *Bakalavri Vorakavorum*: **English; Translation and Interpretation.** *Magistrosi Vorakavorum*: **English.**

Last Updated: 28/05/15

INTERNATIONAL ACCOUNTANCY TRAINING CENTER (IATC)

1 Charents St., 9th floor, 0025 Yerevan
Tel: +374(10) 575-940 +374(10) 575-238
Fax: +374(10) 574-579
EMail: info@iatc.am
Website: http://www.iatc.am/

Executive Director: Hasmik Sahakyan EMail: iatc@iatc.am

Deputy Director Administration: Knarik Mkrtchyan
EMail: admin@iatc.am

Programme
Accountancy and Audit (Accountancy; Finance)

Course
English (English)

History: Founded 1998.

Main Language(s) of Instruction: Armenian
Degrees and Diplomas: *Magistrosi Vorakavorum*: **Accountancy.**
Student Services: Library
Last Updated: 04/05/15

NATIONAL ACADEMY OF FINE ARTS

Gegecik Arvestneri Azgain Academia (NAFA)
Hakob Hakobyan St., 3, 033 Yerevan
Tel: +374(10) 23-00-89 +374(10) 27-76-69
EMail: geghecik_arvestner@yahoo.com
Website: http://www.education.am/english/education/NAFA.htm

Rector: Eduard A. Sedrakyan (1996-)

Programme
Decorative Design (Design); **Fashion Design** (Fashion Design); **Graphic Design** (Graphic Design); **Interior and Exterior Design** (Design; Interior Design)

History: Founded 1996. Acquired present status 2002.

Fees: 130,000 (College)-230,000 (Academy) per semester (Armenian Dram)

Main Language(s) of Instruction: Armenian, Italian, Russian

Accrediting Agency: Ministry of Education and Science of Armenia

Degrees and Diplomas: *Bakalavri Vorakavorum*: **Design; Fine Arts.** *Magistrosi Vorakavorum*: **Design; Fine Arts.**

Student Services: Academic Counselling, Cultural Activities
Last Updated: 29/04/15

NORTHERN UNIVERSITY

Hyusisain Hamalsaran
Alek Manougyan Street 15/9, 0070 Yerevan
Tel: +374(10) 573-317
EMail: hyusisayin@gmail.com
Website: http://www.northern.am/en/

Rector: Boris Makichyan
Tel: +373(10) 55-40-52 EMail: hyusisayin@gmail.com

Department
Economics, Management and Informatics (Computer Engineering; Computer Science; Economics; Management); **Law and Journalism** (Journalism; Law; Social Sciences); **Pedagogy, Psychology and Language** (Armenian; Literature; Modern Languages; Pedagogy; Psychology)

History: Founded 1996. Acquired present status 2002.

Main Language(s) of Instruction: Armenian

Accrediting Agency: Ministry of Education and Science of Armenia

Degrees and Diplomas: *Bakalavri Vorakavorum*; *Magistrosi Vorakavorum*: **Armenian; Computer Engineering; Economics; Journalism; Law; Modern Languages; Philology; Teacher Training.**

Student Services: Library
Last Updated: 04/05/15

PEDAGOGICAL INSTITUTE OF VARDENIS NAMED AFTER V. HAMBARDZUMYAN

7 Azgaldyan Str., Vardenis
Tel: +374(269) 249-05

Programme
Armenian Language and Literature (Armenian; Literature); **History** (History); **Teacher's Training** (Pedagogy; Primary Education; Teacher Training)
Main Language(s) of Instruction: Armenian
Degrees and Diplomas: *Bakalavri Vorakavorum*
Last Updated: 26/05/15

SYUNIQ INSTITUTE OF GORIS

Goris Syuniq Institute
Mashtots 2, Goris
Tel: +374(284) 22-997
Fax: +374(94) 429-544

Rector: Gravik Babayan

Programme
Finance (Banking; Finance); **Law** (Law)
Main Language(s) of Instruction: Armenian
Degrees and Diplomas: *Bakalavri Vorakavorum*
Last Updated: 30/04/15

UNIVERSITY OF ECONOMY AND LAW NAMED AFTER AVETIK MKRTCHYAN

Avetik Mkrtchyan Tntesairavagitakan Hamalsaran
Shahumyan 32/1, 0015 Yerevan
Tel: +374(10) 569-161 +374(10) 569-163
Fax: +374(10) 569-162
EMail: info-mtih@mail.ru; l.mkrtchyan@edu.mtih.am
Website: http://www.mtih.am

President: Laura Mkrtchyan EMail: laura.mkrtchyan@mtih.am

Department
Finance and Credit (Banking; Finance); **Foreign Languages/English** (English; Modern Languages); **International Affairs** (International Relations); **Law** (Law); **Pedagogy and Education Methodology** (Education; Pedagogy; Primary Education; Teacher Training); **Psychology** (Psychology)

History: Founded 1990 as Yerevani Tntesairavagitakan Hamalsaran (Yerevan University of Economics and Law). Acquired present status 2001. Acquired present title 2008.

Main Language(s) of Instruction: Armenian

Accrediting Agency: Ministry of Education and Science of Armenia

Degrees and Diplomas: *Bakalavri Vorakavorum*; *Magistrosi Vorakavorum*: **Banking; English; Finance; International Relations; Law; Modern Languages; Psychology.**

Student Services: Library
Last Updated: 29/04/15

UNIVERSITY OF PRACTICAL PSYCHOLOGY AND SOCIOLOGY URARTU

Yerevani Gorcnakan Hogebanutyan ev Sociologiai Urartu Hamalsaran
Koryuni 19a str., 7th floor, Yerevan
Tel: +374(10) 528-242
Fax: +374(10) 566-463
EMail: urartuuniversity@yahoo.com; urartu1@mail.ru
Website: http://www.urartuuniversity.com

Rector: Sedrak Sedrakyan (1991-)
Tel: +374(10) 586-961 EMail: sedraks@urartuuniversity.com

Vice-Rector for Educational Matters: Ruzan Kostanyan

International Relations: Anahit Sedrakyan, Vice-Rector for International Affairs

Faculty
Psychology (Clinical Psychology; Educational Psychology; Industrial and Organizational Psychology; Physical Therapy; Psychology; Psychotherapy); **Social Work** (Arts and Humanities; Modern Languages; Natural Sciences; Pedagogy; Social Work; Sociology)

History: Founded 1991. Acquired present status 2002.

Academic Year: September to June

Admission Requirements: High school diploma

Fees: (Drams): 250,000 per annum

Main Language(s) of Instruction: Armenian, English

Accrediting Agency: Ministry of Education and Science of Armenia

Degrees and Diplomas: *Bakalavri Vorakavorum*: **Psychology; Social Work.** *Magistrosi Vorakavorum*: **Clinical Psychology; Educational Psychology; Industrial and Organizational Psychology; Pedagogy; Psychology; Psychotherapy; Social Work.** *Candidate/Doctor of Science*: **Psychology; Social Sciences.** Doctoral Programmes are taught in 3 different languages: Armenian, Russian and English.

Student Services: Academic Counselling, Canteen, Careers Guidance, Cultural Activities, Facilities for disabled people, Foreign Studies Centre, Health Services, Language Laboratory, Library, Social Counselling, Sports Facilities

Publications: University Newspaper

Publishing House: 'Zangak-97' publishing house
Last Updated: 28/05/15

UNIVERSITY OF TRADITIONAL MEDICINE

Avandakan Bžhshkutyan Hamalsaran
Babajanyan 38a, Avan., 375040 Yerevan
Tel: +374(10) 616-290 +374(10) 616-470
EMail: tradmeduni@mail.ru
Website: http://www.tradmed-uni.am/

Rector: Norik Kh. Saribekyan
Tel: +374(10) 616-290 EMail: saribekyan@tradmed-uni.am

Vice-Chacellor for Training: Vahagn P. Kirakosyan

Vice-Chancellor for Scientific activity: Inna G. Persoyan
EMail: inna_persyan@list.ru

Department
Complementary and Alternative Medicine *(CAM)* (Alternative Medicine); **General and Private Surgery** (Oncology; Orthopaedics; Surgery; Urology); **General and Private Therapeutic Studies** (Endocrinology; Nursing; Pharmacology); **Humanities** (Armenian; Arts and Humanities; Economics; English; History; Latin; Law; Modern Languages; Philosophy; Social Studies; Terminology); **Medical and Biological Sciences** (Anatomy; Biological and Life Sciences; Biology; Embryology and Reproduction Biology; Epidemiology; Histology; Hygiene; Immunology; Medicine; Pharmacology; Physics; Physiology; Social and Preventive Medicine; Virology); **Natural and Science** (Biochemistry; Chemistry; Mathematics; Medicine; Natural Sciences; Pharmacology); **Prophylactics** (Social and Preventive Medicine); **Special Professional and Clinical Studies** (Dermatology; Epidemiology; Forensic Medicine and Dentistry; Gynaecology and Obstetrics; Medicine; Ophthalmology; Otorhinolaryngology; Paediatrics; Psychiatry and Mental Health; Psychology; Rehabilitation and Therapy; Stomatology; Surgery); **Stomatology N1** (Orthodontics; Stomatology); **Stomatology N2** (Orthopaedics; Stomatology); **Traditional Medicine** (Acupuncture; Homeopathy; Physical Therapy; Traditional Eastern Medicine)

History: Founded 1991. Acquired present status 2001.

Academic Year: From September to June (Sep-Jan; Apr-June)

Main Language(s) of Instruction: Armenian

Accrediting Agency: Ministry of Education and Science of Armenia

Degrees and Diplomas: *Bakalavri Vorakavorum*: **Medicine; Stomatology.** *Magistrosi Vorakavorum*: **Medicine; Stomatology.**

Student Services: Academic Counselling, Canteen, Language Laboratory, Library, Nursery Care

Last Updated: 28/04/15

USEL UNIVERSITY

Usel Hamalsaran (USEL)
12/1 Yervand Kochar St., 0009 Yerevan
Tel: +374(77) 000-187 +374(91) 721-937
EMail: info@usel.am; useluniversity@gmail.com
Website: http://www.usel.am

Rector: Dayana Moskovyan

Faculty
Economic Theory (Economics); **Foreign Languages and Literature** (Linguistics; Modern Languages; Pedagogy; Translation and Interpretation); **Journalism** (Journalism); **Law** (Law)

History: Founded 1991 as Grigor Zohrab University. Acquired present status and title 2006.

Main Language(s) of Instruction: Armenian

Degrees and Diplomas: *Bakalavri Vorakavorum*: **Economics; English; Foreign Languages Education; Journalism; Law; Literature; Modern Languages.** *Magistrosi Vorakavorum*: **Economics; English; Foreign Languages Education; Journalism; Law; Literature; Modern Languages.**

Student Services: Careers Guidance, Library

Last Updated: 26/05/15

YEREVAN AGRICULTURAL UNIVERSITY

Yerevani Gyughatntesakan Hamalsaran (YAU)
Futchiki 27/5, 0048 Yerevan
Tel: +374(10) 34-13-00
Fax: +374(93) 67-72-70
Website: http://www.yau.am

Rector: Liana Azizbekyan

Vice-Rector: Zhanna Azizbekyan

Faculty
Design (Design); **Economics** (Economics); **Law** (Law); **Technology** (Technology); **Veterinary Medicine** (Veterinary Science)

History: Founded 1992.

Main Language(s) of Instruction: Armenian

Degrees and Diplomas: *Bakalavri Vorakavorum*; *Magistrosi Vorakavorum*: **Design; Finance; Law; Technology; Veterinary Science.**

Student Services: Careers Guidance, Library

Last Updated: 28/05/15

YEREVAN ANANIA SHIRAKATSI UNIVERSITY OF INTERNATIONAL RELATIONS

Yerevani Anania Shirakatsi Mijazgain Haraberutyunneri Hamalsaran (SUIR)
Tigran Mets Street 65A, 0005 Yerevan
Tel: +374(10) 571-177
Fax: +374(10) 573-806
EMail: info@shirakatsi.com; suir@netsys.am

Rector: Seyran Afyan

Programme
Foreign Languages (English; German; Modern Languages); **International Economics** (International Relations); **Journalism** (Journalism); **Law** (Law)

History: Founded 1990. Acquired present status 2002.

Main Language(s) of Instruction: Armenian

Accrediting Agency: Ministry of Education and Science of Armenia

Degrees and Diplomas: *Bakalavri Vorakavorum*: **English; German; International Economics; Journalism; Law.**

Last Updated: 27/05/15

YEREVAN ARMENIAN OPEN UNIVERSITY NAMED AFTER LORIS KHALASHYAN

Abelyan 6, Yerevan
Tel: +374(10) 39-06-98 +374(10) 39-61-61
EMail: info@academedu.org; openuni@academedu.org
Website: http://www.academedu.org

Rector: Vladimir Mkrtchyan

Programme
Fine Arts projects of Textile and Light Industry Production (Fine Arts; Textile Design); **Law** (Law); **Management** (Management); **Teacher Training and Psychology** (Psychology; Teacher Training)

Main Language(s) of Instruction: Armenian

Degrees and Diplomas: *Bakalavri Vorakavorum*

Student Services: Library, Sports Facilities

Last Updated: 31/05/15

YEREVAN FINANCIAL BANKING AND STOCK EXCHANGE UNIVERSITY

Yerevani Finansabankayin ev Borsayakan Hamalsaran
Byuzandi 1/3, 6th floor, Yerevan
Tel: +374(10) 522-720

Rector: Yura Alaverdyan Tel: +374(91) 417-138

Programme
Finance and Credit (Banking; Finance); **Law** (Law)

History: Founded 1996.

Main Language(s) of Instruction: Armenian

Degrees and Diplomas: Diploma Specialist: Law; Finance and Banking

Last Updated: 27/05/15

YEREVAN GALIK UNIVERSITY

Yerevani Galik Hamalsaran
Teryan Street 105a, 0009 Yerevan
Tel: +374(10) 58-96-98 +374(10) 56-60-67 +374(10) 56-65-17
Fax: +374(10) 52-56-51
EMail: unigalick@gmail.com; galick@hi-tech.am
Website: http://galick.do.am/

Rector: Frunze Kharatyan

Department

Foreign Languages (English; Foreign Languages Education; French; German; Modern Languages; Philology; Translation and Interpretation); **Journalism** (Journalism; Publishing and Book Trade; Radio and Television Broadcasting); **Law** (Civil Law; Constitutional Law; Criminal Law; International Law; International Relations; Law; Notary Studies); **Management and Administration** (Accountancy; Administration; Automation and Control Engineering; Banking; Economics; Finance; International Economics; International Relations; Management; Marketing)

History: Founded 1989.

Main Language(s) of Instruction: Armenian

Accrediting Agency: Ministry of Education and Science of Armenia

Degrees and Diplomas: *Bakalavri Vorakavorum*; *Magistrosi Vorakavorum*: **Foreign Languages Education; Journalism; Law; Management; Translation and Interpretation.**

Last Updated: 27/05/15

YEREVAN GLADZOR UNIVERSITY

Gladzor Karavarman Hamalsaran
G. Lousavorchi Street 7/1, 375015 Yerevan
Tel: +374(10) 545-987
Fax: +374(10) 545982
EMail: gladzor_um@xter.net
Website: http://www.gladzor.am

Rector: Zhora Jhangiryan

Faculty

Armenian Language and Literature (Armenian; Literature); **Economics** (Economics); **Foreign Language** (English; French; German; Spanish); **Information Technologies and Systems** (Information Technology; Mathematics and Computer Science); **International Relations** (International Relations); **Journalism** (Journalism); **Law** (Law)

History: Founded 1990. Acquired present status 2001.

Fees: 250,000-300,000 per annum (Armenian Dram)

Main Language(s) of Instruction: Armenian

Accrediting Agency: Ministry of Education and Science of Armenia

Degrees and Diplomas: *Bakalavri Vorakavorum*; *Magistrosi Vorakavorum*: **Banking; Civil Law; Criminal Law; Cultural Studies; English; Finance; Foreign Languages Education; Information Technology; International Law; International Relations; Journalism; Linguistics; Literature; Public Law; Radio and Television Broadcasting; Taxation; Translation and Interpretation.** *Candidate/Doctor of Science*: **Administrative Law; Banking; Civil Law; Commercial Law; Computer Science; Constitutional Law; Economics; European Union Law; Finance; Fiscal Law; German; History; International Law; Labour Law; Law; Literature; Management; Mass Communication; Private Law; Public Law; Romance Languages.**

Student Services: IT Centre, Library, Sports Facilities

Last Updated: 30/04/15

YEREVAN HAYBUSAK UNIVERSITY

Yerevani Haybusak Hamalsaran (YHU)
Abelyan 6, 375038 Yerevan
Tel: +374(10) 390-698
Fax: +374(10) 399-015
EMail: info@haybusak.org; aybusak@academedu.org
Website: http://www.haybusak.org

Rector: Anahit L. Harutyunyan

Vice-Rector for Academic Affairs: Bogdan G. Gasparyan

Faculty

Economics (Business Administration; Computer Science; Economics; Finance; Information Technology; Management; Public Health; Tourism); **Humanities** (Armenian; Journalism; Literature; Modern Languages; Pedagogy; Psychology; Teacher Training); **Law and International Relations after Lazarian** (Arabic; International Relations; Oriental Studies; Persian; Political Sciences; Tourism); **Medicine** (Dentistry; Medicine; Pharmacy)

Institute

Design *(Roslin)* (Design; Fashion Design; Graphic Arts)

History: Founded 1990. Acquired present status 2001. Joined with Armenian Open University after L. Kalashyan, International Relations Institute after H. Lazaryan, and Yerevan Haybusak University base College into a structure called International Academy of Education (IAE) 2006.

Fees: 600,000-850,000 per annum (Armenian Dram)

Main Language(s) of Instruction: Armenian, English, Russian

Accrediting Agency: Ministry of Education and Science of the Republic of Armenia

Degrees and Diplomas: *Bakalavri Vorakavorum*; *Magistrosi Vorakavorum*: **Dentistry; Design; International Relations; Law; Linguistics; Literature; Management; Medicine; Oriental Studies; Pedagogy; Pharmacy; Psychology.** *Doctor of Science*: **Arts and Humanities.** Also Post-graduate Degree programmes in Medicine, Pharmacy, Stomatology

Student Services: Canteen, Careers Guidance, IT Centre, Sports Facilities

Last Updated: 28/05/15

YEREVAN HRACHYA ACHARYAN UNIVERSITY

Yerevani Hrachya Acharyan Hamalsaran
Moskovyan 3, 0001 Yerevan
Tel: +374(10) 52-67-11
Fax: +374(10) 56-15-51
EMail: hau@info.am; hau@dolphin.am

Rector: Avag Khachatryan (2010-) Tel: +374(10) 52-58-69

Programme

Armenian Language and Literature (Armenian; Literature); **Foreign Languages/English** (English; Modern Languages); **History** (History); **International Affairs** (International Relations); **Journalism** (Journalism); **Law** (Law); **Management** (Management); **Oriental Studies** (Oriental Studies); **Speech Therapy** (Speech Therapy and Audiology); **Teachers' Training and Methodics for Elementary Education** (Primary Education; Teacher Training); **World Economy** (International Economics)

History: Founded 1991. Acquired present status 2001. Rector reportedly wrote to the Ministry of Education to ask for supsension of academic activities in 2012.

Main Language(s) of Instruction: Armenian

Accrediting Agency: Ministry of Education and Science of Armenia

Degrees and Diplomas: *Bakalavri Vorakavorum*. Also Diploma Specialist

Last Updated: 29/05/15

YEREVAN MARTIG UNIVERSITY OF INTERNATIONAL ECONOMIC RELATIONS

Yerevani Martig Artakin Tntesakan Kaperi Hamalsaran (MARTIG UIER)
Miasnikyan 5, 0025 Yerevan
Tel: +374(10) 589-198 +374(10) 561-646
EMail: martig@arminco.com
Website: http://uier-edu.am

Rector: Marianna Voskanyan

School

Accountancy (Accountancy; Behavioural Sciences; Economics; Finance; Marketing; Statistics; Taxation); **Computer Sciences** (Computer Engineering; Computer Graphics; Computer Networks; Computer Science; Data Processing; Software Engineering; Statistics); **Economics** (Agricultural Economics; Banking; Econometrics; Economics; Environmental Studies; Finance; International Business; International Economics; Mathematics; Statistics);

Finance (Business Administration; Commercial Law; Economics; Finance; Government; International Business; Management; Real Estate); **Law** (Civil Law; Constitutional Law; Criminal Law; Environmental Studies; Ethics; European Union Law; History of Law; Insurance; International Law; Labour Law; Law; Taxation); **Management** (Accountancy; Business Computing; Commercial Law; Communication Studies; Management; Marketing)

History: Founded 1991. Acquired present status 2002.

Main Language(s) of Instruction: Armenian

Accrediting Agency: Ministry of Education and Science of Armenia

Degrees and Diplomas: *Bakalavri Vorakavorum*; *Magistrosi Vorakavorum*: **Accountancy; Computer Science; Finance; Law.**

Student Services: IT Centre, Library
Last Updated: 28/05/15

YEREVAN UNIVERSITY NAMED AFTER MESROP MASHTOTS

Yerevani Mesrop Mashtoci Anvan Mankavargakan Hamalsaran
Heratsu 2/1, 025 Yerevan
Tel: +374(10) 57-50-12

Rector: Zaven V. Sargsyan

Programme
Accounting and Audit (Accountancy; Business Administration; Economics); **Armenian Language and Literature** (Armenian; Literature); **Design** (Design; Fashion Design; Industrial Design); **Foreign Languages** (French; Modern Languages); **Law** (Civil Law; International Law; Law); **Socio-cultural Services and Tourism** (Social and Community Services; Tourism); **Teacher Training and Methodics for Elementary Education** (Primary Education; Teacher Training); **Teacher Training and Psychology** (Psychology; Teacher Training)

History: Founded 1990. Acquired present status 2002.

Main Language(s) of Instruction: Armenian

Accrediting Agency: Ministry of Education and Science of Armenia

Degrees and Diplomas: *Bakalavri Vorakavorum*
Last Updated: 29/05/15

YEREVAN UNIVERSITY NAMED AFTER MOVSES KHORENATSI

Yerevani Movses Khorenatsu Anvan Hamalsaran
Teryan 105, 1st Building, 4th Floor, 0009 Yerevan
Tel: +374(10) 52-05-41
Fax: +374(10) 52-05-41
Website: http://www.mkhu.am

Rector: Arthur Aghababyan Tel: +374(91) 41-15-30

Faculty
Economics (Accountancy; Banking; Economic and Finance Policy; Economics; Finance; International Economics; Management; Marketing); **Informatics and Applied Mathematics** (Applied Mathematics; Automation and Control Engineering; Computer Engineering; Computer Graphics; Computer Science; Foreign Languages Education; Mathematics Education); **Law** (International Law; Law; Notary Studies); **Philology** (Armenian; Humanities and Social Science Education; Linguistics; Literature; Native Language Education; Philology); **Romance-Germanic Languages** (English; French; German; Linguistics; Translation and Interpretation); **School Education** (Education; Educational Psychology; Hygiene; Pedagogy; Primary Education; Teacher Training)

History: Founded 1996. Acquired present status 2002.

Fees: 135,000-200,000 per annum (Armenian Dram)

Main Language(s) of Instruction: Armenian

Accrediting Agency: Ministry of Education and Science of Armenia

Degrees and Diplomas: *Bakalavri Vorakavorum*; *Magistrosi Vorakavorum*: **Accountancy; Armenian; Banking; Criminology; English; Finance; French; German; Humanities and Social Science Education; International Economics; International Law; Law; Linguistics; Literature; Management; Marketing; Native Language Education; Notary Studies.**

Student Services: Careers Guidance

Academic Staff *2014-2015*: Total 64

Student Numbers *2014-2015*: Total: c. 130
Last Updated: 29/05/15

YEREVAN UNIVERSITY OF MANAGEMENT AND INFORMATION TECHNOLOGY

Yerevani Karavarman ev Informacion Tecnologianeri Hamalsaran (YUMIT)
Kievyan 16, 375028 Yerevan
Tel: +374(10) 266-780
EMail: info@yumit.am

Rector: Vitaly Aleksandryan Tel: +374(10) 266-882

Pro-Rector: Edward Gharslyan

Programme
Information Sciences (Information Management; Information Sciences; Information Technology)

History: Founded 1991. Acquired present status 2002.

Main Language(s) of Instruction: Armenian

Accrediting Agency: Ministry of Education and Science of Armenia

Degrees and Diplomas: *Bakalavri Vorakavorum*: **Information Sciences.**
Last Updated: 28/05/15

Aruba

STRUCTURE OF HIGHER EDUCATION SYSTEM

Description:

Higher education in Aruba is offered at two public higher education institutions and several private institutions.

Stages of studies:

University level first stage: *Bachelor's degree*
Studies last three years and students are awarded a Bachelor's degree which gives access to Master's level programmes.
University level second stage: *Master's degree*
The Master's degree is awarded after one year of study and graduates may proceed to PhD-level studies.

ADMISSION TO HIGHER EDUCATION

Admission to university-level studies:

Name of secondary school credential required: Advanced High School (VWO) Certificate

Name of secondary school credential required: HAVO Diploma

RECOGNITION OF STUDIES

Quality assurance system:

Quality assurance of higher education in Aruba is carried out in cooperation with higher education institutions in Curaçao, the Netherlands, the United States and locally. For example, Aruban education institutes can apply for accreditation to the Accreditation Organisation of the Netherlands and Flanders (NVAO) - www.nvao.net.

NATIONAL BODIES

Ministerio di Enseñansa y Famia (Ministry of Education and Family)

Minister: Michelle Janice Hooyboer-Winklaar
L.G. Smith Boulevard 76
Oranjestad
Tel: +297 528-4971
Fax: +297 582-7531

Data for academic year: 2014-2015
Source: IAU from NUFFIC's Country Module for Aruba, 2014. Bodies 2016.

INSTITUTIONS

ARUBA PEDAGOGICAL INSTITUTE

Instituto Pedagogico Arubano
Isaac Wagemakerstraat 11, San Nicolas
Tel: +297 524-3100
Fax: +297 584-3943
EMail: info@ipa.aw
Website: http://www.ipaaruba.com

Programme
Teacher Training (Physical Education; Primary Education; Secondary Education; Special Education; Teacher Training)
History: Created 1990.
Accrediting Agency: Department of Education Aruba
Degrees and Diplomas: *Bachelor*: **Physical Education; Primary Education; Secondary Education.** *Master*: **Special Education.**
Last Updated: 18/08/15

UNIVERSITY OF ARUBA

J. Irausquinplein 4, Oranjestad
Tel: +297 526-2200
Fax: +297 583-1770
EMail: info@ua.aw
Website: http://www.ua.aw

Faculty

Accounting, Finance and Marketing (Accountancy; Finance; Marketing); **Arts and Science** (Management; Social Work); **Hospitality and Tourism Management** (Hotel and Restaurant; Tourism); **Law** (Law)

History: Created 1988.

Accrediting Agency: Department of Education Aruba

Degrees and Diplomas: *Bachelor*: **Accountancy; Finance; Hotel and Restaurant; Law; Management; Tourism.** *Master*: **International Business; Law; Social Work; Tourism.**

Last Updated: 18/08/15

Australia

STRUCTURE OF HIGHER EDUCATION SYSTEM

Description:

Higher education in Australia refers to university and non university higher education institutions which award degree or sub degree qualifications based on the Australian Qualifications Framework. Australia has self accrediting public and private universities, self accrediting higher education institutions, and accredited higher education institutions. Universities and other self accrediting higher education institutions are established or recognised under state and territory or Commonwealth legislation. Non self accrediting higher education institutions and their programmes are accredited by state and territory government authorities. The Australian Qualifications Framework register lists self accrediting institutions and links to lists of non self accrediting institutions in each state and territory (http://www.aqf.edu.au/register/aqf-register/). Universities are autonomous multidisciplinary institutions that are responsible for their own management structure, budgets, resource allocation, staff, student enrolments, accreditation of qualifications, quality assurance and curriculum. Australia also has around 170 higher education institutions accredited by state and territory authorities to offer higher education courses. Non university higher education institutions tend to offer programmes in only one or two fields of study. The Australian Government is responsible for higher education policy and finance through the Department of Education. State and territory governments have legislative responsibility. Consultation between the Australian Government and the states and territories occurs at Ministerial level through the Ministerial Council for Tertiary Education and Employment (MCTEE), and at an official level through the Joint Committee on Higher Education (JCHE), which advises the MCTEE on higher education matters. Higher education students in Australia are subject to a range of fees. There are several financial support options available to students. Australian students can undertake higher education studies at an approved Australian higher education provider as a Commonwealth supported student. Students pay a subsidised student contribution for their education, but the Government pays for the majority of costs.

Stages of studies:

University level first stage: *Undergraduate studies*

Undergraduate studies include several qualifications, both sub degree and degree level. The Diploma and Advanced Diploma on the Australian Qualifications Framework are dual sector qualifications. The other sub degree qualification is the Associate degree, which is at the same AQF level as the Advanced Diploma. Associate degrees and Advanced Diplomas can provide advanced standing into a Bachelor degree programme in a similar field. This is usually 1 1/2 years for an Advanced Diploma or 2 years for an Associate degree. The other qualification offered at the undergraduate level is the Bachelor degree. Australian Bachelor degrees are diverse and range from 3 to 6 years of study. There are several types of Bachelor degrees including 3 year degrees, 4 year degrees, professional degrees, combined degrees and Bachelor Honours degrees.

University level second stage: *Postgraduate studies*

Postgraduate qualifications on the AQF include the Graduate Certificate, Graduate Diploma and Master degree. Length of study varies between one semester and four years. Admission is normally based on a Bachelor degree. Graduate Certificate and Graduate Diploma programmes are specialised and can be professionally oriented. There are three types of Master degree programmes: coursework, research and extended.

University level third stage: *Doctoral studies*

The final stage of higher education is Doctoral degree studies. There are three types of Doctoral degree research, professional and higher. A typical Doctoral degree programme requires 3 to 4 years of full time study and research. Students are expected to make a substantial original contribution to knowledge in the form of new knowledge or significant and original adaptation, application and interpretation of existing knowledge. Admission is based on a Master degree, or a Bachelor Honours degree.

ADMISSION TO HIGHER EDUCATION

Admission to university-level studies:

Name of secondary school credential required: Senior Secondary Certificate of Education

Minimum score/requirement: Varies according to course and institution, student's age, whether student has disabilities or special needs

For entry to: For Diploma and Advanced Diploma, Associate degree and Bachelor degree courses

Alternatives to credentials: Entry may be based on prior experience or other learning.

Numerus clausus: Entry to a higher education course is normally determined by the student's tertiary entrance score, rank or index. This is calculated on the basis of results in the Senior Secondary Certificate of Education. Tertiary Admissions Centres in New South Wales, Queensland, South Australia, Victoria and Western Australia coordinate admissions.

Other requirements: A portfolio, interview, audition or exam may also be taken into account in conjunction with the tertiary entrance score for certain courses. There are also alternative schemes for mature age students, students with disabilities and students with special needs.

Foreign students admission:

Definition of foreign student: A student who is not an Australian citizen, but is enrolled in (or will enrol in) a course of study with an Australian education provider.

Admission requirements: Individual institutions determine the acceptability of overseas qualifications for the purposes of admission or credit transfer.

Entry regulations: Students require confirmation of enrolment, a student visa and sufficient funds to support themselves.

Health requirements: Students must undergo a medical examination as part of their visa application and must have Overseas Students Health Cover for the period covered by their visa.

Language proficiency: Students should have a good command of the English language and may be required to pass an English test.

RECOGNITION OF STUDIES

Quality assurance system:

Quality assurance in Australia's higher education system is based on a strong partnership between the Australian Government, state and territory governments and the higher education sector. In 2011, the Australian Government established a new national regulatory and quality agency for higher education, the Tertiary Education Quality and Standards Agency (TEQSA). TEQSA is an independent regulatory body which monitors quality and establishes standards for university and non-university higher education providers. TEQSA registers providers, evaluates standards and performance, quality assures international education and consolidate current regulatory arrangements. TEQSA works with state and territory regulatory bodies and assumes quality assurance responsibilities previously undertaken by the Australian Universities Quality Agency (AUQA).

Bodies dealing with recognition:

AEI-NOOSR

Manager:Liz Campbell-Dorning
GPO Box 9880
Canberra 2601
EMail: qualsrecognition@education.gov.au
WWW: https://internationaleducation.gov.au/services-and-resources/pages/qualifications-recognition.aspx

Special provisions for recognition:

Recognition for university level studies: Individual institutions determine the acceptability of qualifications and studies for admission purposes.

For access to advanced studies and research: Individual institutions determine the acceptability of qualifications and studies for admission purposes.

For exercising a profession: Professional recognition is undertaken by the relevant professional body. The Australian Skills Recognition Information website, http://www.immi.gov.au/asri, lists assessing authorities, registration/licensing authorities and industry bodies for professional occupations within Australia and provides full contact details.

NATIONAL BODIES

Department of Education and Training

Minister: Simon Birmingham
GPO Box 9880
Canberra, ACT 2601
WWW: http://education.gov.au

Role of national body: Responsible for national policies and programmes that help Australians access quality early childhood education, school education, higher education, vocational education and training, international education and research.

Australian Qualifications Framework Council - AQFC

Governance, Quality s education system. Expert consultative bodies are convened as required to advise Ministers on any AQF policy matters which arise.

Tertiary Education Quality and Standards Agency -TEQSA

CEO: Anthony McClaran
Chief Commissioner: Nick Saunders
GPO Box 1672
Melbourne, Victoria 3001
EMail: enquiries@teqsa.gov.au
WWW: http://www.teqsa.gov.au

Role of national body: Independent body with powers to regulate university and non university higher education providers, monitor quality and set standards. Incorporated Australian Universities Quality Agency (AUQA) in 2014.

Council of Private Higher Education - COPHE

Chief Executive Officer: Adrian McComb
Suite 59, Level 5, Tower Building
47 Neridah Street
Chatswood, NSW 2067
Tel: +61(2) 8021-0841
WWW: http://cophe.edu.au

Role of national body: COPHE provides a voice for private higher education institutions calling for equitable higher education policy for all students. Our members cater for students studying from diploma to doctorate level at more than 60 campuses around Australia.

International Education Association of Australia - IEAA

President: Christopher Ziguras
PO Box 12917
Melbourne, VIC 8006
Tel: +61(3) 9925-4579
Fax: +61(3) 9925-2023
EMail: admin@ieaa.org.au
WWW: http://www.ieaa.org.au

Role of national body: The International Education Association of Australia is an association of international education professionals. The Association has been established to serve the needs and interests of the large number of individuals working in international education across all education sectors, to encourage informed and ethical professional practice among members, and to promote international education to governments, education organisations and within the community.

Universities Australia

Chief Executive: Belinda Robinson
GPO Box 1142
Canberra, ACT 2601
Tel: +61(2) 6285-8100
Fax: +61(2) 6285-8101
EMail: contact@universitiesaustralia.edu.au
WWW: http://www.universitiesaustralia.edu.au
Role of national body: Represents higher education institutions nationally and internationally and advances higher education through voluntary, cooperative and coordinated action.

IDP Education Pty Ltd - IDP

Chief Executive Officer, Managing Director: Andrew Barkla
Level 8, 535 Bourke Street
Melbourne, VIC 3000
Tel: +61(3) 9612-4400
EMail: info.melbourne@idp.com
WWW: http://www.idp.com
Role of national body: IDP Education Pty Ltd (IDP) is a company offering student placement and English language testing services. It places students into all sectors of the Australian education system, including higher education, vocational education and training (VET), English language intensive courses for overseas students (ELICOS) and schools.

Data for academic year: 2012-2013
Source: IAU from Educational and Professional Recognition Unit (AEI-NOOSR), Australian Government Department of Industry, Innovation, Science, Research and Tertiary Education, 2013. Bodies 2015.

INSTITUTIONS

PUBLIC INSTITUTIONS

AUSTRALIAN CATHOLIC UNIVERSITY (ACU)

PO Box 968, North Sydney, New South Wales 2059
Tel: +61(2) 9739 2368
EMail: futurestudents@acu.edu.au; study.international@acu.edu.au
Website: http://www.acu.edu.au

Vice-Chancellor: Greg Craven (2008-) EMail: vc@acu.edu.au
International Relations: Chris Riley, Executive Director
EMail: chris.riley@acu.edu.au

Faculty
Arts and Sciences (Arts and Humanities; Chemistry; History; Information Technology; Literature; Modern Languages; Music; Physics; Psychology; Social Sciences; Social Work; Theology; Visual Arts); **Business** (Accountancy; Business Administration; Commercial Law; Finance; Management; Marketing); **Education** (Adult Education; Continuing Education; Education; Primary Education; Religious Education; Secondary Education; Special Education); **Health Sciences** (Health Sciences; Midwifery; Nursing; Physical Therapy); **Theology and Philosophy** (Philosophy; Theology)

Campus
Adelaide; **Ballarat**; **Brisbane**; **Canberra**; **Melbourne**; **North Sydney**; **Strathfield**

History: Founded 1991 by amalgamation of institutions of higher education in Australian Capital Territory, New South Wales, Queensland, and Victoria.

Academic Year: February to November (February-June; July-November)

Admission Requirements: Secondary school certificate with matriculation or Australian Year 12 Equivalent.

Main Language(s) of Instruction: English

Degrees and Diplomas: *Diploma*; *Bachelor Degree*: **Arts and Humanities; Business Administration; Business and Commerce; Communication Studies; Education; Health Sciences; Media Studies; Physical Therapy; Religion; Social Sciences; Visual Arts; Welfare and Protective Services.** *Bachelor Honours Degree*: **Arts and Humanities; Business Administration; Communication Studies; Education; Health Sciences; Information Sciences; Media Studies; Social Sciences; Theology; Visual Arts; Welfare and Protective Services.** *Graduate Certificate/Diploma*: **Arts and Humanities; Business Administration; Education; Health Sciences; Information Sciences; Religion; Social Sciences; Visual Arts; Welfare and Protective Services.** *Master Degree*: **Accountancy; Arts and Humanities; Business Administration; Education; Health Sciences; Social Sciences; Theology; Welfare and Protective Services.** *Doctoral Degree*: **Arts and Humanities; Business and Commerce; Education; Health Sciences; Social Sciences; Theology.**

Student Services: Academic Counselling, Canteen, Careers Guidance, Facilities for disabled people, Social Counselling, Sports Facilities

Last Updated: 21/03/14

BATCHELOR INSTITUTE OF INDIGENOUS TERTIARY EDUCATION

Post Office Batchelor, Batchelor, Northern Territory 0845
Tel: +61(8) 8939-7111
Fax: +61(8) 8939-7100
EMail: enquiries@batchelor.edu.au
Website: http://www.batchelor.edu.au/

Director: Adrian Mitchell

Programme

Education (Natives Education; Preschool Education; Primary Education); **Health** (Community Health; Health Administration; Health Education; Health Sciences; Nursing); **Indigenous Knowledges and Policy** (Indigenous Studies; Natives Education)

History: Founded 1965, acquired present status and title 1999.

Degrees and Diplomas: *Diploma*; *Bachelor Degree*; *Bachelor Honours Degree*; *Graduate Certificate/Diploma*; *Master Degree*; *Doctoral Degree*

Last Updated: 24/03/14

CENTRAL QUEENSLAND UNIVERSITY (CQU)

Building 5 Bruce Highway, Rockhampton, Queensland 4702
Tel: +61(7) 4930-9000
Fax: +61(7) 4923-2100
EMail: international-enquiries@cqu.edu.au
Website: http://www.cqu.edu.au

Vice-Chancellor and President: Scott Bowman
EMail: vc-cquniversity@cqu.edu.au

School

Business and Law (Accountancy; Business Administration; Finance; Hotel Management; Human Resources; International Business; Management; Marketing); **Education and the Arts** (Arts and Humanities; Education; Multimedia; Music; Preschool Education; Primary Education; Secondary Education; Theatre); **Engineering and Technology** (Engineering; Information Technology; Surveying and Mapping; Telecommunications Engineering); **Human, Health and Social Sciences** (Clinical Psychology; Environmental Studies; Occupational Therapy; Physical Therapy; Podiatry; Psychology; Speech Therapy and Audiology); **Medical and Applied Sciences** (Agricultural Business; Chiropractic; Environmental Management; Food Science; Medical Auxiliaries; Medical Technology; Nursing; Public Health); **Nursing and Midwifery** (Midwifery; Nursing)

Further Information: Campuses in Bundaberg, Gladstone, Mackay, Noosa, Rockhampton, Brisbane, Melbourne and Sydney.

History: Founded 1967 as Queensland Institute of Technology (Capricornia), acquired university status 1992 and title 1994.

Academic Year: Queensland Regional and Head Campus in Rockhampton, three terms year from March to November (March-June; July-November; November-February)

Admission Requirements: Secondary school certificate with matriculation or recognized foreign equivalent. English Language proficiency: IELTS of 6.0 or TOEFL score of 550 or equivalent for undergraduate and postgraduate programmes; IETLS of 6.5 or equivalent for research programmes

Fees: 1,350-2,298 per course (Australian Dollar)

Main Language(s) of Instruction: English

Degrees and Diplomas: *Bachelor Degree*; *Bachelor Honours Degree*; *Graduate Certificate/Diploma*; *Master Degree*; *Doctoral Degree*. Also undergraduate Diplomas

Last Updated: 24/03/14

CHARLES DARWIN UNIVERSITY (CDU)

Casuarina Campus, Ellengowan Drive,
Darwin, Northern Territory 0810
Tel: +61(8) 8946-6666
Fax: +61(8) 8946-6642
EMail: international@cdu.edu.au
Website: http://www.cdu.edu.au

Vice-Chancellor: Simon Maddocks EMail: vc@cdu.edu.au

International Relations: Monica Turvey, Director International Strategy and Development
EMail: monica.turvey@cdu.edu.au; samantha.ambridge@cdu.edu.au

Faculty

Engineering, Health, Science and the Environment (Computer Engineering; Computer Networks; Engineering; Environmental Management; Environmental Studies; Health Sciences; Information Technology; Medical Technology; Midwifery; Nursing; Pharmacy; Psychology; Social Work; Software Engineering; Sports); **Law, Education, Business and Arts** (Accountancy; Architecture; Arts and Humanities; Business Administration; Business and Commerce; Design; Education; Indigenous Studies; Law; Music; Native Language; Preschool Education; Primary Education; Secondary Education; Tourism; Visual Arts); **Vocational Education and Training** *(Offers pre-bachelor certificates and diplomas.)*

Further Information: Campuses at Casuarina, Palmerson and Alice Springs, Jabiru, Katherine, Nhulunbuy and Tennant Creek.

History: Founded 1989 as Northern Territory University, amalgamating the University College of the Northern Territory and Darwin Institute of Technology. Acquired present title 2003 after merger with Centralian College in Alice Springs.

Academic Year: February to October (February-June; July-October); Vocational Education and Training (VET) courses, February to December (February-June; July-December)

Admission Requirements: Secondary school certificate or recognized foreign equivalent, or previous tertiary study. Direct entrance to second year on successful completion of studies in another tertiary institution

Fees: VET courses, c. 4250-17,000; Undergraduate Courses, c. 5,900-74,500; Postgraduate, c. 6,650-69,200 (Australian Dollar)

Main Language(s) of Instruction: English

Degrees and Diplomas: *Bachelor Degree*; *Bachelor Honours Degree*; *Graduate Certificate/Diploma*; *Master Degree*; *Doctoral Degree*

Last Updated: 24/03/14

CHARLES STURT UNIVERSITY (CSU)

Bathurst, New South Wales 2795
Tel: +61(2) 6338-6077
EMail: inquiry@csu.edu.au
Website: http://www.csu.edu.au

Vice-Chancellor and President: Andrew Vann
EMail: vc@csu.edu.au

Faculty

Arts (Acting; Advertising and Publicity; Business Administration; Criminology; Design; Fine Arts; Graphic Design; Islamic Theology; Journalism; Leisure Studies; Photography; Police Studies; Protective Services; Psychology; Public Relations; Radio and Television Broadcasting; Social Sciences; Social Work; Theology); **Business** (Accountancy; Business Administration; Computer Science; Finance; Management; Marketing; Mathematics)

Institute

Land, Water and Society (Social Studies; Soil Management; Soil Science; Water Management; Water Science)

Research Centre

Management of Dryland Salinity (Bioengineering; Farm Management; Plant and Crop Protection; Soil Science; Water Management); **National Wine and Grape Industry** (Oenology; Viticulture); **Public and Contextual Theology** (Theology); **Rural Social Research** (Gender Studies; Rural Studies; Social Policy)

Research Institute

Professional Practice, Learning and Education *(RIPPLE)* (Educational Research)

Campus Abroad

Canada *(Located in Burlington,Ontario)* (Education; Preschool Education; Primary Education)

History: Founded 1989. A federated network Institution incorporating the former Mitchell College of Advanced Education at Bathurst and Riverina-Murray Institute of Higher Education at Wagga Wagga and Albury-Wodonga. Campuses are located in Bathurst, Wagga Wagga, Albury-Wodonga and Dubbo.

Academic Year: February to November (February-June; July-November)

Admission Requirements: New South Wales higher school certificate, or equivalent. Also previous tertiary or postsecondary studies

Main Language(s) of Instruction: English

Degrees and Diplomas: *Bachelor Degree*; *Bachelor Honours Degree*; *Graduate Certificate/Diploma*; *Master Degree*; *Doctoral Degree*

Student Services: Academic Counselling, Canteen, Careers Guidance, Facilities for disabled people, Health Services, Language Laboratory, Nursery Care, Social Counselling, Sports Facilities
Last Updated: 24/03/14

CURTIN UNIVERSITY

GPO Box U1987, Perth, Western Australia 6845
Tel: +61(8) 9266-9266
Fax: +61(8) 9266-3131
Website: http://www.curtin.edu.au

Vice-Chancellor: Deborah Terry
EMail: deborah.terry@curtin.edu.au

Division

Health Sciences (Biomedicine; Dental Hygiene; Health Sciences; Midwifery; Nursing; Occupational Therapy; Pharmacy; Physical Therapy; Psychology; Public Health; Speech Therapy and Audiology); **Humanities** (Anthropology; Architecture; Arts and Humanities; Cultural Studies; Design; Education; Fine Arts; History; Indigenous Studies; Information Sciences; Leisure Studies; Library Science; Modern Languages; Performing Arts; Publishing and Book Trade; Social Sciences; Social Work; Technology; Town Planning; Welfare and Protective Services; Writing); **Science and Engineering** (Applied Physics; Biology; Chemical Engineering; Chemistry; Civil Engineering; Computer Engineering; Electrical and Electronic Engineering; Mathematics; Mechanical Engineering; Petroleum and Gas Engineering; Physics; Sound Engineering (Acoustics); Statistics)

School

Business (Accountancy; Business Computing; Economics; Finance; Law; Management; Marketing)

Centre

Aboriginal Studies (Community Health; Indigenous Studies; Natives Education)

Further Information: Campuses in Bentley, Geraldton, Kalgoorlie, Margaret River, Northam, Shenton Park, Sydney. Overseas Campus: Miri, Sarawak, Malaysia

History: Founded 1967 as Western Australian Institute of Technology, became Curtin University of Technology in 1987, and acquired current name 2010.

Academic Year: 2 semesters, commencing February and July (12 weeks each)

Admission Requirements: Secondary graduation and demonstrated competence in English, plus attainment of a sufficiently high Tertiary Entrance Rank (TER) or recognized international equivalent. Some courses require specific subjects to have been satisfactorily completed prior to entry

Main Language(s) of Instruction: English

Degrees and Diplomas: *Bachelor Degree*; *Bachelor Honours Degree*; *Graduate Certificate/Diploma*; *Master Degree*; *Doctoral Degree*

Student Services: Academic Counselling, Canteen, Careers Guidance, Cultural Activities, Facilities for disabled people, Foreign Studies Centre, Health Services, Language Laboratory, Nursery Care, Social Counselling, Sports Facilities
Last Updated: 14/11/14

DEAKIN UNIVERSITY

Locked Bag 20000, Geelong, Victoria 3220
Tel: +61(3) 5227-1100
Fax: +61(3) 5227-2001
EMail: deakin-international@deakin.edu.au
Website: http://www.deakin.edu.au

Vice-Chancellor: Jane den Hollander
EMail: vcoffice@deakin.edu.au

Faculty

Arts and Education (Asian Studies; Communication Arts; Education; Fine Arts; Heritage Preservation; History; International Studies; Pacific Area Studies; Political Sciences; Social Sciences); **Business and Law** (Accountancy; Business Administration; Economics; Finance; Information Technology; Law; Management; Marketing; Social Sciences); **Health** (Health Sciences; Medicine; Midwifery; Nursing; Nutrition; Physical Education; Psychology; Social and Preventive Medicine); **Science and Technology** (Architecture and Planning; Biological and Life Sciences; Engineering; Environmental Engineering; Environmental Studies; Information Sciences; Information Technology; Mathematics and Computer Science; Natural Sciences; Technology)

Institute

Research *(Alfred Deakin)*; **Koorie Education**; **Teaching and Learning**; **Technology Research and Innovation**

Further Information: Also Melbourne campus at Burwood; Geelong Waterfront campus; Geelong campus at Waurn Ponds; Warrnambool campus

History: Founded 1974. It was Victoria's only regionally based University. Following the mergers with Warrnambool Institute of Advanced Education, 1990 and Victoria College 1991, Deakin is a multi-campus institution. A second Geelong campus was established at the Geelong Waterfront in 1996.

Academic Year: March to November (March-June; July-October; November-February)

Admission Requirements: Victorian Certificate of Education (VCE) or equivalent qualification, or tertiary or TAFE study.

Fees: 17,500-52,290 (undergraduate); 18,500-26,580 (postgraduate) per annum (Australian Dollar)

Main Language(s) of Instruction: English

Degrees and Diplomas: *Bachelor Degree*; *Bachelor Honours Degree*; *Graduate Certificate/Diploma*; *Master Degree*; *Doctoral Degree*

Student Services: Academic Counselling, Canteen, Careers Guidance, Cultural Activities, Facilities for disabled people, Health Services, Nursery Care, Social Counselling, Sports Facilities

Student Numbers *2012-2013*: Total 43,316
Last Updated: 28/03/14

EDITH COWAN UNIVERSITY (ECU)

270 Joondalup Drive, Joondalup, Western Australia 6027
Tel: +61(8) 6304-0000
EMail: enquiries@ecu.edu.au
Website: http://www.ecu.edu.au

Vice-Chancellor: Steve Chapman (2015-) EMail: vc@ecu.edu.au

Faculty

Business and Law (Accountancy; Business Administration; Commercial Law; Finance; Hotel Management; Human Resources; International Business; Law; Management; Tourism); **Education and Arts** (Acting; Cinema and Television; Communication Arts; Cultural Studies; Dance; Design; Display and Stage Design; Education; Journalism; Media Studies; Music; Performing Arts; Photography; Public Relations; Theatre); **Health, Engineering and Science** (Aeronautical and Aerospace Engineering; Biological and Life Sciences; Biology; Chemical Engineering; Chemistry; Civil Engineering; Computer Science; Electronic Engineering; Engineering; Information Sciences; Marine Engineering; Mechanical Engineering; Midwifery; Nursing; Nutrition; Occupational Therapy; Physical Therapy; Psychology; Social Sciences; Sports; Telecommunications Engineering)

Further Information: Also Mount Lawley and South West (Bunbury) campuses.

History: Founded 1991 with four campuses: Bunbury, Churchlands, Joondalup, and Mount Lawley. Formerly the Western Australia College of Advanced Education. Roots extend back to 1902 when first tertiary institution was established in Western Australia.

Academic Year: February to November (February-June; July-November). Summer Session: December-January.

Admission Requirements: Secondary school certificate with matriculation or recognized foreign equivalent

Main Language(s) of Instruction: English

Degrees and Diplomas: *Bachelor Degree*; *Bachelor Honours Degree*: **Business Administration; Computer Science; Health Sciences; Law; Natural Sciences; Performing Arts; Sports; Teacher Training; Tourism.** *Graduate Certificate/Diploma*; *Master Degree*: **Biological and Life Sciences; Business Administration; Chemistry; Computer Science; Mathematics; Midwifery;**

Nursing; Performing Arts; Public Health; Social Sciences; Sports. *Doctoral Degree*: **Health Administration; Information Technology.**

Student Services: Academic Counselling, Canteen, Careers Guidance, Cultural Activities, Facilities for disabled people, Foreign Studies Centre, Health Services, Language Laboratory, Nursery Care, Social Counselling, Sports Facilities
Last Updated: 24/03/14

IAU FEDERATION UNIVERSITY AUSTRALIA

P.O. Box 663, Ballarat, Victoria 3353
Tel: +61(3) 5327-8510
Fax: +61(3) 5327-8001
EMail: international@federation.edu.au
Website: http://federation.edu.au/

Vice-Chancellor and President: David Battersby
Tel: +61(3) 5327-9000 EMail: vc@federation.edu.au

Public Relations Manager: Le-Anne O'Brien
Tel: +61(3) 5327-9637 EMail: l.obrien@federation.edu.au

International Relations: Rowena Coutts, Senior Deputy Vice-Chancellor
Tel: +61(3) 5327-9506 EMail: r.coutts@federation.edu.au

Faculty

Business (Accountancy; Business Administration; Business and Commerce; Economics; Information Technology; Leadership; Public Administration); **Education and Arts** (Art Education; Arts and Humanities; Ceramic Art; Curriculum; Education; Educational Administration; Fine Arts; Graphic Design; Music; Painting and Drawing; Pedagogy; Performing Arts; Preschool Education; Primary Education; Secondary Education; Social Sciences; Theatre); **Health** (Biomedicine; Food Science; Health Sciences; Midwifery; Nursing; Nutrition; Occupational Health; Psychology; Sports); **Science** (Engineering; Information Technology; Mathematics; Natural Sciences)

Further Information: Six campuses in Ararat, Camp Street, Horsham, Stawell, Mt Helen, and Gippsland.

History: Founded 1870 as School of Mines and Industries Ballarat. Became University of Ballarat in 1994. Merged with the Horsham-based Wimmera Institute of TAFE 1998, to become a dual sector university incorporating both higher education and technical and further education. Acquired current title 2014.

Academic Year: February to November (February-June; July-November)

Admission Requirements: Successful completion of an approved year 12 course of study

Main Language(s) of Instruction: English

Degrees and Diplomas: *Advanced Diploma*; *Diploma*; *Bachelor Degree*; *Graduate Certificate/Diploma*; *Master Degree*; *Doctoral Degree*

Student Numbers *2011-2012*: Total: c. 25,810
Last Updated: 21/03/14

FLINDERS UNIVERSITY

GPO Box 2100, Adelaide, South Australia 5001
Tel: +61(8) 8201-3911
Website: http://www.flinders.edu.au

Vice-Chancellor and President: Michael N. Barber
EMail: kay.anderson@flinders.edu.au

Faculty

Education, Humanities and Law (Archaeology; Education; English; Fine Arts; French; Greek; Italian; Literature; Philosophy; Spanish; Theatre; Theology; Tourism; Writing); **Medicine, Nursing and Health Sciences** (Community Health; Dietetics; Medicine; Midwifery; Nursing; Optometry; Physical Therapy; Public Health; Speech Therapy and Audiology); **Science and Engineering** (Biological and Life Sciences; Biology; Biomedical Engineering; Chemistry; Civil Engineering; Computer Science; Electrical and Electronic Engineering; Engineering; Environmental Studies; Information Technology; Mathematics; Mechanical Engineering; Physics; Statistics); **Social and Behavioural Sciences** (American Studies; Asian Studies; Business Administration; Development Studies; History; International Relations; International Studies; Psychology; Social Work; Sociology)

History: Flinders University of South Australia founded 1966 by proclamation of Act of South Australian Parliament. The Sturt Campus of the South Australian College of Advanced Education was amalgamated with the University 1991.

Academic Year: March to November (March-June; July-November)

Admission Requirements: South Australian Certificate of Education or recognized equivalent. Credit for work done at other recognized institutions may be counted towards a Flinders award. Applicants from countries where English is not the first language are required to demonstrate a minimum standard of English language competence (TOEFL score of 550, IELTS score of 6, or 213 in the computer-based TOEFL)

Main Language(s) of Instruction: English

Degrees and Diplomas: *Bachelor Degree*; *Bachelor Honours Degree*; *Graduate Certificate/Diploma*; *Master Degree*; *Doctoral Degree*

Student Services: Academic Counselling, Canteen, Careers Guidance, Facilities for disabled people, Health Services, Language Laboratory, Nursery Care, Social Counselling, Sports Facilities
Last Updated: 24/03/14

IAU GRIFFITH UNIVERSITY

The Chancellery, Parklands Drive, Southport, Queensland 4222
Tel: +61(7) 3735-7111
EMail: international@griffith.edu.au
Website: http://www.griffith.edu.au

Vice-Chancellor and President: Ian O'Connor
EMail: vc@griffith.edu.au; i.oconnor@griffith.edu.au

Director, External Relations: Meredith Jackson
EMail: meredith.jackson@griffith.edu.au

International Relations: Christopher Madden, Pro-Vice Chancellor (International) EMail: c.madden@griffith.edu.au

School

Applied Psychology (Psychology); **Arts, Education and Law** (Arts and Humanities; Education; Law); **Biomolecular and Physical Sciences** (Biomedical Engineering; Molecular Biology); **Business** (Asian Studies; International Business); **Criminology and Criminal Justice** (Criminal Law; Criminology); **Dentistry and Oral Health** (Dentistry; Oral Pathology); **Education and Professional Studies** (Art Education; Curriculum; Education; Foreign Languages Education; Pedagogy; Special Education; Technology; Technology Education; Vocational Education); **Engineering** (Electronic Engineering; Engineering; Environmental Engineering; Microelectronics); **Environment** (Environmental Management; Environmental Studies); **Human Services and Social Work** (Social and Community Services; Social Welfare); **Humanities** (Arts and Humanities); **Information and Communication Technology** (Computer Engineering; Computer Science; Information Technology; Telecommunications Engineering); **Languages and Linguistics** (Linguistics; Modern Languages); **Law** (Law); **Management** (Management); **Medical Science** (Biomedical Engineering; Biomedicine; Molecular Biology; Natural Sciences); **Medicine** (Medicine); **Nursing and Midwifery** (Midwifery; Nursing); **Pharmacy** (Pharmacy); **Physiotherapy and Exercise Science** (Physical Therapy; Physiology; Rehabilitation and Therapy); **Public Health** (Anatomy; Dentistry; Health Sciences; Medicine; Nursing; Oral Pathology; Pharmacy; Physical Therapy; Psychology; Public Health); **Science, Environment, Engineering and Technology** (Computer Engineering; Engineering; Environmental Engineering; Information Technology; Microelectronics); **Vocational, Technology and Arts Education** (Art Education; Technology Education)

Department

Accountancy, Finance and Economics (Accountancy; Economics; Finance); **Employment Relations and Human Resources** (Human Resources; Industrial Management); **International Business and Asian Studies** (Accountancy; Asian Studies; Business and Commerce; Finance; Hotel Management; Human Resources; International Business; Leisure Studies; Management; Marketing; Political Sciences; Sports Management; Tourism); **Marketing** (Marketing); **Politics and Public Policy** (Political Sciences; Public Administration); **Tourism, Leisure, Hotel and Sport Management**

(Hotel Management; Leisure Studies; Sports Management; Tourism)

Conservatory

Conservatorium *(Queensland)* (Music)

Further Information: Also Campuses at Nathan, Mount Gravatt, Gold Coast, Logan and South Bank. the Gold Coast in south-east Queensland. Over 30 Reseach centres. Several independent academic centres, institutes and colleges

History: Founded 1971 and officially opened 1975. The University has adopted a 'School' Structure as its academic unit.

Academic Year: January to December (February-June; July-November; November-February)

Admission Requirements: Secondary school certificate or recognized foreign equivalent, or previous tertiary study. Candidates who have completed relevant studies from another institution may apply for exemption from some studies

Fees: 14,720-61,520 per annum (Australian Dollar)

Main Language(s) of Instruction: English

Degrees and Diplomas: *Bachelor Degree*; *Bachelor Honours Degree*; *Graduate Certificate/Diploma*; *Master Degree*; *Doctoral Degree*

Student Services: Academic Counselling, Canteen, Careers Guidance, Cultural Activities, Facilities for disabled people, Foreign Studies Centre, Health Services, Language Laboratory, Nursery Care, Social Counselling, Sports Facilities

Last Updated: 24/03/14

JAMES COOK UNIVERSITY (JCU)

1 James Cook Drive, Townsville, Queensland 4811
Tel: +61(7) 4781-4111
Fax: +61(7) 4779-6371
EMail: registrar@jcu.edu.au
Website: http://www.jcu.edu.au

Vice-Chancellor: Sandra Harding
EMail: vc@jcu.edu.au; sandra.harding@jcu.edu.au

Senior Deputy Vice-Chancellor: Chris Cocklin
EMail: chris.cocklin@jcu.edu.au

Faculty

Arts, Education and Social Sciences (Arts and Humanities; Education; Social Sciences); **Law, Business and Creative Arts** (Arts and Humanities; Business and Commerce; Economics; Fine Arts; Law); **Medicine, Health and Molecular Sciences** (Health Sciences; Medicine; Molecular Biology); **Science and Engineering** (Engineering; Natural Sciences)

Institute

Gas Research *(Coalseam)*; **Interdisciplinary Studies**; **Northern Australia Social Research**; **Sports and Exercise Science**; **Tropical Medical Laboratory Science**

Centre

Advanced Analytical; **Astronomy** *(Co-operative Research)*; **Australian Tropical Freshwater Research**; **Biotechnology Applications Research**; **Coastal Zone Estuary and Waterway Management**; **Comparative Genomics**; **Coral Reef Biodiversity**; **Disaster Studies**; **English Language**; **Great Barrier Reef World Heritage Area** *(Co-operative Research)*; **Interactive Multimedia**; **Melanesian Studies**; **North Queensland Magnetic Resonance**; **Remote Sensing**; **Rural Education Research and Development**; **Study of Teaching and Teacher Development**; **Sustainable Development of Tropical Savannas**; **Sustainable Sugar Production**; **Sustainable Tourism**; **Tropical Freshwater Research**; **Tropical Health and Medicine** *(Anton Breinl)*; **Tropical Marine Studies** *(Sir George)*; **Tropical Rainforest Ecology and Management** *(Co-operative Research)*; **Tropical Urban and Regional Planning**; **Women's Studies**

Further Information: Also campuses at Mackay, Cairns, Mount Isa, Brisbane, Singapore and Thursday Island.

History: Founded 1961 as University College of Townsville, acquired present status and title 1970. Townsville College of Advanced Education amalgamated with the University 1982.

Academic Year: February to November (February-June; July-November)

Admission Requirements: Secondary school certificate or recognized foreign equivalent, or previous tertiary study. Credit may be granted for studies in another tertiary institution. Students whose language is not English must show proficiency in English (6.0 IELTS, with non-component lower than 5.5 or 550 TOEFL minimum, with a test of written English-minimum score of 19) (iscadmissions@jcu.edu.au)

Main Language(s) of Instruction: English

Degrees and Diplomas: *Bachelor Degree*; *Bachelor Honours Degree*; *Graduate Certificate/Diploma*; *Master Degree*; *Doctoral Degree*

Last Updated: 24/03/14

LA TROBE UNIVERSITY

Melbourne, Victoria 3086
Tel: +61(3) 9627-4805
EMail: international@latrobe.edu.au
Website: http://www.latrobe.edu.au

Vice-Chancellor: John Dewar EMail: vc@latrobe.edu.au

Faculty

Education (Education); **Health Sciences** (Health Sciences); **Humanities and Social Sciences** (Communication Disorders; European Studies; Social Sciences; Visual Arts); **Law and Management**; **Science, Technology and Engineering** (Engineering; Natural Sciences; Technology)

School

Accounting (Accountancy); **Business** *(Regional)* (Business Administration); **Communication, Arts and Critical Enquiry** (Cinema and Television; English; Gender Studies; Linguistics; Logic; Media Studies; Philosophy; Religious Studies; Theatre; Visual Arts); **Dentistry and Oral Health** (Dentistry; Oral Pathology); **Economics and Finance** (Economics; Finance); **Education** (Art Education; Cultural Studies; Education; English; Foreign Languages Education; Health Education; Natural Resources; Physical Education; Preschool Education; Primary Education; Secondary Education; Special Education; Tourism); **Engineering and Mathematical Sciences** (Civil Engineering; Computer Engineering; Computer Science; Electronic Engineering; Mathematics; Physics; Statistics); **Historical and European Studies** (American Studies; Archaeology; Art History; Catalan; Cultural Studies; European Studies; French; German; Greek; History; Italian; Latin American Studies; Portuguese; Religion; Religious Studies; Spanish); **Human Biosciences** (Biological and Life Sciences); **Human Communication Sciences** (Speech Therapy and Audiology); **Law** (Commercial Law; Law; Public Law); **Life Sciences** (Agriculture; Botany; Ecology; Environmental Management; Environmental Studies; Microbiology; Zoology); **Management** (Human Resources; Information Sciences; Management; Marketing; Sports Management; Tourism); **Molecular Sciences** (Biochemistry; Chemistry; Genetics; Pharmacy); **Nursing and Midwifery** (Midwifery; Nursing); **Occupational Therapy** (Occupational Therapy); **Physiotherapy** (Physical Therapy); **Podiatry** (Podiatry); **Psychology** (Psychology); **Public Health** (Public Health); **Social Sciences** (Anthropology; Asian Studies; Development Studies; Indigenous Studies; International Relations; Law; Pacific Area Studies; Peace and Disarmament; Political Sciences; Social Sciences; Sociology); **Social Work and Social Policy** (Social Policy; Social Work); **Sport, Tourism and Hospitality Management** (Hotel Management; Leisure Studies; Sports; Tourism); **Visual Arts and Design** (Design; Visual Arts)

Institute

Australian Institute for Primary Care; **Australian Institute of Archaeology**; **Human Security**; **Institute of Latin American Studies**; **Italian Australian Institute**; **La Trobe Institute of Indian and South Asian Studies**; **Michael J Osborne Institute for Advanced Study** *(Research activity in any discipline by distinguished visiting scholars)*; **Molecular Sciences**; **National Institute for Deaf Studies and Sign Language Research**; **Social and Environmental Sustainability**; **Social Participation**

Centre

Advanced Materials Manufacturing *(Victorian)*; **Australian Centre for Evidence Based Aged Care**; **Centre for China Studies**; **Centre for Dialogue**; **Centre for Ergonomics and Human Factors**; **Centre for Professional Development**; **Centre for Public Health Law**; **Centre for Sustainable Regional Communities**;

Centre for the Study of Professions; Philippines Australian Study Centre; Prosthetics and Orthodontics *(National)*; **The Bouverie Centre; Thesis Eleven Centre for Critical Theory**

Graduate School
Management

Research Centre
A D Trendall Research Centre; Agribioscience (Agrobiology); **Australian Research Centre in Sex, Health and Society; Centre for Excellence for Mathematics and Statistics of Complex Systems** *(ARC)*; **Computer, Communication and Social Innovation; Conflict Resolution; Excellence for Coherent X-Ray Science** *(Australian Research Council (ARC))*; **Greek Studies; Innovative Universities European Research Centre; Linguistic Typology; Materials and Surface Science; Mother and Child Health; Murray Darling Frenswater Reasearch Centre; Musculoskeletal; Olga Tennison Austim; Public Sector Governance and Accountability Research Centre; Technology Infusion**

Research Unit
Refugee Health Research Unit

Further Information: Campuses in Melbourne, Albury-Wodonga, Bendigo, Franklin Street, Mildura, Shepparton, and Sydney.

History: Founded 1964, admitted first students 1967.

Academic Year: March to October (March-June; July-October)

Admission Requirements: Secondary school certificate or recognized international equivalent, or previous tertiary study

Main Language(s) of Instruction: English

Degrees and Diplomas: *Bachelor Degree*; *Bachelor Honours Degree*; *Graduate Certificate/Diploma*; *Master Degree*; *Doctoral Degree*

Student Services: Academic Counselling, Canteen, Facilities for disabled people, Foreign Studies Centre, Language Laboratory, Sports Facilities

Last Updated: 24/03/14

MACQUARIE UNIVERSITY

Balaclava Road, North Ryde, Sydney, New South Wales 2109
Tel: +61(2) 9850-7111
Website: http://www.mq.edu.au

Vice-Chancellor: S Bruce Dowton EMail: vc@mq.edu.au

Faculty
Arts (Ancient Civilizations; Anthropology; Cultural Studies; English; History; Indigenous Studies; International Studies; Law; Media Studies; Music; Philosophy; Police Studies; Sociology); **Business and Economics** (Accountancy; Actuarial Science; Business Administration; Economics; Finance; Management; Marketing); **Human Sciences** (Cognitive Sciences; Education; Linguistics; Medicine; Psychology); **Science** (Astronomy and Space Science; Biological and Life Sciences; Biology; Chemistry; Chiropractic; Computer Science; Earth Sciences; Engineering; Geography; Physics; Statistics)

History: Founded 1964 by an Act of the N.S.W. State Parliament. First postgraduate students accepted 1966 and undergraduate teaching began 1967. Institute of Early Childhood at Waverley became a school of the University 1990. In order to break down divisions between Humanities, Sciences and Social Sciences and to allow students as much freedom as possible in choice of studies, the University is organized as a single integrated body composed of 9 Divisions, with Departments and Academic Units, and 3 Academic Colleges.

Academic Year: March to December (March-July; July-December)

Admission Requirements: Secondary New South Wales higher school certificate or interstate recognized foreign equivalent, or previous tertiary study. Advanced standing for studies in recognized tertiary institution

Main Language(s) of Instruction: English

Degrees and Diplomas: *Bachelor Degree*; *Bachelor Honours Degree*; *Graduate Certificate/Diploma*; *Master Degree*; *Doctoral Degree*

Student Services: Academic Counselling, Canteen, Careers Guidance, Facilities for disabled people, Foreign Studies Centre, Health Services, Language Laboratory, Nursery Care, Social Counselling, Sports Facilities

Last Updated: 24/03/14

MONASH UNIVERSITY

Melbourne, Victoria 3800
Tel: +61(3) 9902-6011
EMail: study@monash.edu.au
Website: http://www.monash.edu.au

Vice-Chancellor and President: Edward Byrne
EMail: kerrie.edwards@monash.edu

Faculty
Art and Design (Architecture; Design; Fine Arts; Multimedia); **Arts** (Ancient Civilizations; Anthropology; Arts and Humanities; Communication Studies; Comparative Literature; Cultural Studies; Eastern European Studies; English; Environmental Studies; Geography; Germanic Studies; Greek; History; Indigenous Studies; International Studies; Japanese; Journalism; Linguistics; Music; Oriental Languages; Oriental Studies; Philosophy; Political Sciences; Religion; Romance Languages; Social Sciences; Social Work; Theology; Visual Arts); **Business and Economics** (Accountancy; Banking; Business and Commerce; Economics; Finance; Management; Marketing; Taxation); **Education** (Education; Preschool Education; Primary Education; Secondary Education; Sports); **Engineering** (Aeronautical and Aerospace Engineering; Bioengineering; Chemical Engineering; Civil Engineering; Computer Engineering; Electrical Engineering; Engineering; Materials Engineering; Mechanical Engineering); **Information Technology** (Archiving; Computer Engineering; Computer Science; Information Management; Information Technology; Library Science; Software Engineering); **Law** (Law); **Medicine, Nursing and Health Sciences** (Anatomy; Biochemistry; Biomedicine; Clinical Psychology; Community Health; Epidemiology; Gynaecology and Obstetrics; Haematology; Immunology; Medicine; Midwifery; Molecular Biology; Nursing; Nutrition; Occupational Therapy; Paediatrics; Pharmacology; Physiology; Psychiatry and Mental Health; Psychology; Surgery); **Science** (Biological and Life Sciences; Chemistry; Earth Sciences; Ecology; Genetics; Mathematics; Natural Sciences; Physics; Psychology)

College
Pharmacy *(Victorian)* (Pharmacy)

Further Information: Campuses outside Australia in Italy (Prato Centres), in Malaysia (Monash University Sunway Campus), and South Africa (Monash University South Africa), as well as domestic campuses (Berwick, Caulfield, Clayton, Peninsula, Parkville).

History: Founded 1958.

Academic Year: February to November (February-June; July-November)

Admission Requirements: Victorian Certificate of Education or national or international equivalent

Main Language(s) of Instruction: English

Degrees and Diplomas: *Bachelor Degree*; *Bachelor Honours Degree*; *Graduate Certificate/Diploma*; *Master Degree*; *Doctoral Degree*

Student Services: Academic Counselling, Canteen, Careers Guidance, Cultural Activities, Facilities for disabled people, Health Services, Nursery Care, Social Counselling, Sports Facilities

Last Updated: 24/03/14

MURDOCH UNIVERSITY

90 South Street, Murdoch, Western Australia 6150
Tel: +61(8) 9360-6000
EMail: international@murdoch.edu.au
Website: http://www.murdoch.edu.au

Vice-Chancellor: Richard Higgott
EMail: r.higgott@murdoch.edu.au

School
Arts (Asian Studies; Communication Studies; Computer Graphics; English; History; Indigenous Studies; Indonesian; Japanese; Journalism; Media Studies; Philosophy; Photography; Public Relations; Religion; Theatre; Theology; Writing); **Education** (Adult Education; Education; Education of the Gifted; Mathematics Education;

Preschool Education; Primary Education; Secondary Education); **Engineering and Information Technology** (Automation and Control Engineering; Chemical Engineering; Chemistry; Computer Science; Energy Engineering; Engineering; Information Management; Information Technology; Mathematics; Measurement and Precision Engineering; Metallurgical Engineering; Nanotechnology; Physics; Power Engineering; Software Engineering; Statistics); **Health Professions** (Chiropractic; Health Administration; Nursing); **Law** (Commercial Law; Criminology; Law); **Management and Governance** (Accountancy; Banking; Business Administration; Economics; Finance; Hotel Management; Human Resources; International Business; International Studies; Management; Marketing; Political Sciences; Tourism); **Psychology and Exercise Science** (Clinical Psychology; Cognitive Sciences; Industrial and Organizational Psychology; Neurosciences; Psychology; Sports); **Public Policy and International Affairs** *(Sir Walter Murdoch)* (Development Studies; International Studies; Management; Public Administration); **Veterinary and Life Sciences** (Animal Husbandry; Biological and Life Sciences; Biomedicine; Biotechnology; Environmental Management; Forensic Medicine and Dentistry; Marine Science and Oceanography; Molecular Biology; Plant and Crop Protection; Toxicology; Veterinary Science)

Further Information: Also Co-operative Multimedia Centre; Office of Continuing Veterinary Education

History: First admitted students to the Murdoch campus in 1975 and in 1996 opened a regional campus at Rockingham. Peel campus at Mandurah opened 2005.

Academic Year: February to November (Semesters: February-July; July-November. Trimesters: January-April; May-August; August-November)

Admission Requirements: Demonstrated merit and evidence of suitability for a university education. Western Australian school leavers must demonstrate competence in English or English literature and obtain a sufficiently high Tertiary Entrance Rank (TER) score.

Main Language(s) of Instruction: English

Degrees and Diplomas: *Bachelor Degree*; *Bachelor Honours Degree*; *Graduate Certificate/Diploma*; *Master Degree*; *Doctoral Degree*

Last Updated: 25/03/14

QUEENSLAND UNIVERSITY OF TECHNOLOGY (QUT)

GPO Box 2434, George Street, Brisbane, Queensland 4001
Tel: +61(7) 3183-2111
EMail: qut.international@qut.edu.au
Website: http://www.qut.edu.au

Vice-Chancellor: Peter Coaldrake (2003-)
EMail: p.coaldrake@qut.edu.au

International Relations: Scott Sheppard, Deputy Vice-Chancellor (International and Development) EMail: scott.sheppard@qut.edu.au

Faculty

Built Environment and Engineering (Aeronautical and Aerospace Engineering; Architecture; Civil Engineering; Computer Engineering; Construction Engineering; Electrical and Electronic Engineering; Industrial Design; Interior Design; Landscape Architecture; Mechanical Engineering; Medical Technology; Production Engineering; Real Estate; Regional Planning; Software Engineering; Surveying and Mapping; Town Planning; Urban Studies); **Business** (Accountancy; Advertising and Publicity; Banking; Business and Commerce; E- Business/Commerce; Economics; Finance; Human Resources; International Business; Management; Marketing; Public Relations); **Creative Industries** (Acting; Cinema and Television; Communication Studies; Dance; Fashion Design; Film; Information Sciences; Journalism; Leisure Studies; Literature; Mass Communication; Media Studies; Music; Sound Engineering (Acoustics); Theatre; Visual Arts; Writing); **Education** (Cultural Studies; Mathematics Education; Modern Languages; Preschool Education; Science Education; Technology); **Health** (Human Rights; Midwifery; Nursing; Optometry; Psychology; Public Health; Social and Community Services; Social Welfare); **Law and Justice** (Justice Administration; Law); **Science and Technology** (Biochemistry; Biomedical Engineering; Chemistry; Computer Science; Forensic Medicine and Dentistry; Information Sciences; Mathematics; Molecular Biology; Natural Sciences; Pharmacy; Radiology)

Institute

Creative Industries and Innovation; **Health and Biomedical Innovation**; **Information Security**; **Sustainable Resources**

History: Founded 1965 as Queensland Institute of Technology, acquired present status and title 1989. Brisbane College of Advanced Education incorporated 1990.

Academic Year: February to December (February-June; July-November). Summer programme, November to February

Admission Requirements: Secondary school certificate or recognized foreign equivalent, or previous tertiary study

Main Language(s) of Instruction: English

Degrees and Diplomas: *Bachelor Degree*; *Bachelor Honours Degree*; *Graduate Certificate/Diploma*; *Master Degree*; *Doctoral Degree*

Student Services: Academic Counselling, Canteen, Careers Guidance, Cultural Activities, Facilities for disabled people, Foreign Studies Centre, Health Services, Nursery Care, Social Counselling, Sports Facilities

Student Numbers *2012-2013*: Total 4,400
Last Updated: 28/03/14

ROYAL MELBOURNE INSTITUTE OF TECHNOLOGY (RMIT UNIVERSITY)

PO Box 2476, Melbourne, Victoria 3001
Tel: +61(3) 9925-2000
Fax: +61(3) 9663-2764
EMail: admissions@rmit.edu.au
Website: http://www.rmit.edu.au

Vice-Chancellor and President: Martin Bean (2015-)
EMail: vc@rmit.edu.au

International Relations: Saskia Loer Hansen, Director International Relations EMail: saskia.hansen@rmit.edu.au

School

Business (Accountancy; Business Administration; Business Computing; Economics; Finance; Law; Management; Marketing); **Design and Social Context** (Architecture; Communication Studies; Design; Education; Fashion Design; Fine Arts; International Studies; Media Studies; Social Studies; Textile Design; Urban Studies); **Science, Engineering and Health** (Aeronautical and Aerospace Engineering; Biomedicine; Biotechnology; Chemical Engineering; Chiropractic; Civil Engineering; Computer Engineering; Computer Science; Electrical Engineering; Environmental Engineering; Information Technology; Mechanical Engineering; Midwifery; Nursing; Occupational Therapy; Pharmacy; Physical Education; Production Engineering; Psychology; Traditional Eastern Medicine)

Research Centre

Advanced Composite Structures; **Aerospace Studies** *(Sir Lawrence Wackett)*; **Bushfires**; **Construction Innovation**; **Globalism**; **Governance, Work and Technologies**; **Intelligent Manufacturing Systems and Technologies**; **Interaction Design**; **Management Quality Research**; **Polymers**; **Satellite Positioning for Atmosphère, Climate and Environmment Studies** *((SPACE))*; **SMART Internet Technology**; **Water Quality and Treatment**

Research Institute

Australian Housing and Urban Studies; **Design** *(RMIT)*; **Global Cities** *(RMIT)*; **Health Innovations** *(RMIT)*; **Platform Technologies** *(RMIT)*

Campus Abroad

RMIT Vietnam *(Ho Chi Minh City and Hanoi (http://www.rmit.edu.vn/))* (Business Administration; Design; Engineering; Information Technology)

Further Information: Campuses in Brunswick and Bundoora.

History: Founded 1887 as Melbourne Working Men's College, renamed Melbourne Technical College 1934, and acquired present title of Royal Melbourne Institute of Technology (RMIT) 1960. Established as University of Technology by Act of State Parliament of Victoria 1992, amalgamating with Phillip Institute of Technology.

RMIT is one of Australia's largest multi-level universities offering a fully-integrated programme of courses at Diploma, Degree and Postgraduate levels. The University emphasizes education for employment and for research which uses technology to solve real world problems.

Academic Year: March to November (March-July; July-November)

Admission Requirements: For Bachelor degree programme, satisfactory completion of interstate secondary schooling or Victorian Certificate of Education (VCE), or recognized foreign equivalent

Fees: National: 4,355-9,080 per annum (Australian Dollar), International: 15,000 -18,750 per annum (Australian Dollar)

Main Language(s) of Instruction: English

Degrees and Diplomas: *Bachelor Degree*; *Bachelor Honours Degree*; *Graduate Certificate/Diploma*; *Master Degree*; *Doctoral Degree*

Student Services: Academic Counselling, Canteen, Careers Guidance, Cultural Activities, Facilities for disabled people, Health Services, Nursery Care, Social Counselling, Sports Facilities

Last Updated: 17/03/15

SOUTHERN CROSS UNIVERSITY

PO Box 157, Lismore, New South Wales 2480
Tel: +61(2) 6620-3000
Fax: +61(2) 6622-3700
EMail: enquiry@scu.edu.au
Website: http://www.scu.edu.au

Vice-Chancellor: Peter Lee EMail: vc@scu.edu.au

College

Indigenous Australian Peoples (Indigenous Studies)

School

Arts and Social Sciences (Arts and Humanities; Education; Music; Secondary Education; Social Sciences; Social Work; Visual Arts); **Business** (Accountancy; Business Administration; Computer Science; Human Resources; Information Technology); **Education** (Education; Preschool Education; Primary Education; Secondary Education); **Environment, Science and Engineering** (Biology; Environmental Studies; Forestry; Marine Science and Oceanography); **Health and Human Sciences** (Midwifery; Nursing; Nutrition; Occupational Therapy; Osteopathy; Podiatry; Psychology; Speech Therapy and Audiology; Sports); **Law and Justice** (Law); **Tourism and Hospitality Management** (Hotel Management; Tourism)

Further Information: Campuses in Coffs Harbour and Tweed Gold Coast.

History: Founded 1971. Began operations under current title 1994.

Academic Year: February to November (February-June; June-October; November-February)

Admission Requirements: Qualifications deemed equivalent to completion of secondary school in Australia. Specific information available on request. Recognition of prior learning (RPL) applies to specific awards

Fees: 15,000-20,000 per annum; graduate,16,000-22,500 per annum (Australian Dollar)

Degrees and Diplomas: *Bachelor Degree*; *Bachelor Honours Degree*; *Graduate Certificate/Diploma*; *Master Degree*; *Doctoral Degree*

Student Services: Academic Counselling, Canteen, Careers Guidance, Cultural Activities, Facilities for disabled people, Foreign Studies Centre, Health Services, Language Laboratory, Nursery Care, Social Counselling, Sports Facilities

Last Updated: 25/03/14

SWINBURNE UNIVERSITY OF TECHNOLOGY (SUT)

PO Box 218, Hawthorn, Victoria 3122
Tel: +61(3) 9214-8000
EMail: international@swinburne.edu.au
Website: http://www.swinburne.edu.au/

Vice-Chancellor: Linda Kristjanson
EMail: vc@swin.edu.au; mstephens@swin.edu.au

Faculty

Business and Enterprise (Accountancy; Advertising and Publicity; Business Administration; Human Resources; Management; Public Relations; Sports Management; Transport Management); **Health, Arts and Design** (Communication Arts; Design; Education; Film; Health Sciences; Industrial Design; Interior Design; Media Studies; Psychology; Social Sciences); **Science, Engineering and Technology** (Aeronautical and Aerospace Engineering; Astronomy and Space Science; Biotechnology; Chemistry; Civil Engineering; Construction Engineering; Electrical Engineering; Marine Engineering; Mathematics; Mechanical Engineering; Physics; Production Engineering; Robotics; Software Engineering; Telecommunications Engineering)

Division

Technical and Further Education *(TAFE; Hawthorn, Lilydale, Prahran, Healesville, Wantirna, Croydon)* (Applied Chemistry; Business Administration; Child Care and Development; Computer Science; Design; Engineering; Environmental Studies; Fine Arts; Fire Science; Horticulture; Industrial Management; Information Technology; Occupational Health; Performing Arts; Social and Community Services; Social Sciences; Social Welfare; Technology; Tourism; Visual Arts; Writing)

Centre

Advanced Internet Architectures (Architecture); **Astrophysics and Superconducting** (Astrophysics); **Atom Optics and Ultrafast Laser Spectroscopy**; **Business and Management Research** *(CBMR)* (Business Administration; Business and Commerce; Management); **e-Business and Communication** *(Lilydale)* (Business Computing; Information Technology; Telecommunications Engineering); **Emerging Technologies and Society** *(Australian Centre)* (Social Studies; Technology); **Environment and Biotechnology** (Applied Chemistry; Biochemistry; Biomedicine; Biotechnology; Environmental Studies; Microbiology; Molecular Biology; Nanotechnology; Packaging Technology; Paper Technology); **Gender and Cultural Diversity** *(National Centre)* (Cultural Studies; Gender Studies); **Imaging and Applied Optics** (Applied Physics; Laser Engineering; Optical Technology; Optics); **Intelligent Systems and Complex Processes** *(CISCP)* (Artificial Intelligence; Computer Science); **International Agents and Multi Agent Systems** (Software Engineering); **Internet Computing and e-Business** (Computer Networks; E-Business/Commerce); **Mathematical Modelling** (Mathematics and Computer Science); **Microphotonics** (Optical Technology); **Molecular Stimulation**; **Neuropsychology** (Industrial and Organizational Psychology; Psychology); **Psychological Services** (Psychology); **Software Engineering** (Software Engineering)

Campus Abroad

Sarawak *(Malaysia (http://www.swinburne.edu.my/))* (Design; Engineering; Information Sciences; Information Technology; Natural Sciences)

History: Founded 1908. Affiliated with Victorian Institute of Colleges 1965. Acquired university status 1992 by Act of Parliament. It has two divisions - Higher Education and Technical and Further Education (TAFE). It comprises six campuses at Hawthorn, Prahan, Lilydale, Wantima, Croydon and Healesville. Responsible to Commonwealth and State Ministries of Education and Training.

Academic Year: Higher Education Division: February to November (February-May; July-November). Summer School: December-February. Technical and Further Education Division: February to December (February-April; April-June; July-September; October-December)

Admission Requirements: Victorian Certificate of Education (VCE) or recognized foreign equivalent

Fees: 8,500-15,000 per annum; 29,400 for MBA (Australian Dollar)

Main Language(s) of Instruction: English

Degrees and Diplomas: *Bachelor Degree*; *Bachelor Honours Degree*; *Graduate Certificate/Diploma*; *Master Degree*; *Doctoral Degree*

Student Services: Academic Counselling, Canteen, Careers Guidance, Facilities for disabled people, Foreign Studies Centre, Health Services, Language Laboratory, Nursery Care, Social Counselling, Sports Facilities

Last Updated: 25/03/14

THE AUSTRALIAN NATIONAL UNIVERSITY (ANU)

Canberra, ACT 0200
Tel: +61(2) 6125-5111
EMail: international.enquiry@anu.edu.au
Website: http://www.anu.edu.au

Vice-Chancellor: Ian Young EMail: vc@anu.edu.au

International Relations: Erik Lithander, Pro Vice-Chancellor (International and Outreach) EMail: pvc.io@anu.edu.au

School

Archaeology and Anthropology (Anthropology; Archaeology; Development Studies; Indigenous Studies); **Art** (Art History; Ceramic Art; Fine Arts; Furniture Design; Glass Art; Painting and Drawing; Photography; Sculpture; Textile Design); **History** (History); **Literature, Languages and Linguistics** (Ancient Civilizations; Applied Linguistics; Classical Languages; Cultural Studies; English; Film; History; Linguistics; Modern Languages; Theatre); **Music** (Music); **Philosophy** (Philosophy); **Politics and International Relations** (International Relations; Political Sciences); **Sociology** (Sociology)

Institute

Demographic and Social Research (Demography and Population)

Centre

Aboriginal Economic Policy Research (Economic and Finance Policy; Economics; Indigenous Studies); **Arab and Islamic Studies** (Arabic; Islamic Studies; Middle Eastern Studies); **Archaeological Research** (Archaeology); **Arts and Technology** (Fine Arts; Technology); **Contemporary Pacific** (Pacific Area Studies); **Continuing Education** (Education); **Cross-Cultural Research** (Anthropology; Cultural Studies); **Democratic Institutions** (Institutional Administration; Political Sciences); **Educational Development and Academic Methods**; **Epidemiology and Population Health** (Community Health; Epidemiology); **Financial Mathematics** (Finance; Mathematics); **Humanities Research** (Arts and Humanities); **Immigration and Multicultural Studies** (Cultural Studies; Demography and Population); **International and Public Law** (International Law; Public Law); **Mathematics and its Applications** (Applied Mathematics); **Mental Health Research** (Health Sciences); **Mind** (Psychology); **Public Awareness of Science** (Administration; Natural Sciences); **Resource and Environmental Studies** (Environmental Studies; Leisure Studies; Welfare and Protective Services); **Science and Engineering Materials** (Materials Engineering; Natural Sciences); **Study of the Chinese Southern Diaspora** (Demography and Population); **Sustainable Energy Systems** (Energy Engineering); **Theoretical Physics** (Physics); **Visual Sciences** (Natural Sciences); **Women's Studies** (Women's Studies)

History: Founded 1946 by Act of Parliament of the Commonwealth of Australia. The original function of the University, research and research training, now carried out by the Institute of Advanced Studies. The Faculties provide teaching and undertake research training at all levels. Merged with Canberra University College 1960 and with the Institute of the Arts in 1992.

Academic Year: March to November

Admission Requirements: Secondary school certificate with matriculation or recognized foreign equivalent. Direct entrance to second year on completion of studies in another tertiary institution

Main Language(s) of Instruction: English

Degrees and Diplomas: *Bachelor Degree*; *Bachelor Honours Degree*; *Graduate Certificate/Diploma*; *Master Degree*; *Doctoral Degree*

Last Updated: 25/03/14

THE UNIVERSITY OF ADELAIDE

Adelaide, South Australia 5005
Tel: +61(8) 8313-4455
Fax: +61(8) 8313-4401
EMail: student.centre@adelaide.edu.au
Website: http://www.adelaide.edu.au

Vice-Chancellor: Warren Bebbington
EMail: vice-chancellor@adelaide.edu.au

Faculty

Engineering, Computer and Mathematical Sciences (Chemical Engineering; Civil Engineering; Computer Science; Electrical and Electronic Engineering; Mathematics; Mechanical Engineering; Mining Engineering; Petroleum and Gas Engineering); **Health Sciences** (Community Health; Dentistry; Medicine; Nursing; Paediatrics; Psychology); **Humanities and Social Sciences** (Anthropology; Asian Studies; Demography and Population; Development Studies; English; French; Gender Studies; German; Hispanic American Studies; History; Linguistics; Music; Philosophy; Political Sciences; Spanish; Writing); **Science** (Agriculture; Animal Husbandry; Chemistry; Earth Sciences; Environmental Studies; Molecular Biology; Oenology; Physics; Veterinary Science); **The Professions** (Architecture; Business Administration; Economics; Education; Law)

Further Information: Also North Terrace, Roseworthy, Waite, and Thebarton campuses.

History: Founded 1874 by Act of provincial legislature. Became autonomous under Act of Parliament. Member of the Group of Eight (Australia's leading research universities).

Academic Year: March to November (1st semester: March-April; April-June; 2nd semester: July-September; October-November). Summer Semester (January-February); Winter Semester (June-July).

Admission Requirements: South Australian Certificate of Education (SACE), International Baccalaureate or recognized foreign equivalent. Special Entry Schemes for mature students, Aboriginal and Torres Strait Islander students, and non-award students in the Faculty of Humanities and Social Sciences

Main Language(s) of Instruction: English

Degrees and Diplomas: *Bachelor Degree*; *Bachelor Honours Degree*; *Graduate Certificate/Diploma*; *Master Degree*; *Doctoral Degree*

Student Services: Academic Counselling, Canteen, Careers Guidance, Cultural Activities, Facilities for disabled people, Health Services, Language Laboratory, Nursery Care, Social Counselling, Sports Facilities

Last Updated: 25/03/14

THE UNIVERSITY OF NEWCASTLE

University Drive, Callaghan, New South Wales 2308
Tel: +61(2) 4921-5000
Fax: +61(2) 4921-4200
EMail: international@newcastle.edu.au
Website: http://www.newcastle.edu.au

Vice-Chancellor and President: Caroline McMillen
EMail: Caroline.McMillen@newcastle.edu.au

International Relations: Winnie Eley, Pro Vice-Chancellor International and Advancement EMail: Winnie.Eley@newcastle.edu.au

Faculty

Business and Law (Accountancy; Business Administration; Business and Commerce; Economics; Finance; Human Resources; International Business; Law; Marketing); **Education and Arts** (Ancient Civilizations; Anthropology; Art Education; Chinese; Classical Languages; Cultural Studies; Dance; Education; English; Film; Fine Arts; French; German; History; Japanese; Linguistics; Media Studies; Music; Music Education; Performing Arts; Philosophy; Preschool Education; Primary Education; Religion; Secondary Education; Social Work; Sociology; Speech Therapy and Audiology; Theatre; Theology; Writing); **Engineering and Built Environment** (Architecture; Chemical Engineering; Civil Engineering; Computer Science; Electrical and Electronic Engineering; Engineering Management; Environmental Engineering; Mechanical Engineering; Surveying and Mapping); **Health and Medicine** (Biomedicine; Dentistry; Dietetics; Health Administration; Medicine; Midwifery; Nursing; Nutrition; Occupational Health; Occupational Therapy; Pharmacy; Physical Therapy; Podiatry; Public Health; Radiology); **Science and Information Technology** (Biological and Life Sciences; Biotechnology; Chemistry; Clinical Psychology; Communication Arts; Development Studies; Earth Sciences; Environmental Management; Environmental Studies; Food Science; Geography; Information Technology; Marine Science and Oceanography; Mathematics; Physics; Psychology; Sports; Statistics)

Campus Abroad

Singapore (Business Administration; Electrical Engineering; Information Technology; Mass Communication; Mechanical Engineering; Occupational Health)

Further Information: Also Newcastle Callaghan, Newcastle City, Central Coast, Port Macquarie, and Sydney campuses.

History: Founded 1951 as College of New South Wales University of Technology. Became an autonomous Institution 1965 and amalgamated with the Hunter Institute of Higher Education 1989.

Academic Year: March to November (March-June; July-November)

Admission Requirements: Higher School Certificate (HSC) or recognized foreign equivalent, or previous tertiary study. Admission to some undergraduate courses requires additional testing, audition or portfolio. Prior tertiary studies may be recognized for course credit

Main Language(s) of Instruction: English

Degrees and Diplomas: *Bachelor Degree*; *Bachelor Honours Degree*; *Graduate Certificate/Diploma*; *Master Degree*; *Doctoral Degree*

Last Updated: 25/03/14

THE UNIVERSITY OF QUEENSLAND (UQ)

St Lucia, Brisbane, Queensland 4072
Tel: +61(7) 3365-1111
Fax: +61(7) 3365-1266
EMail: study@uq.edu.au
Website: http://www.uq.edu.au

Vice-Chancellor and President: Peter Høj (2012-)
EMail: vc@uq.edu.au

AO Executive Director (Operations) and University Secretary: Maurie Mcnarn EMail: m.mcnarn@uq.edu.au

International Relations: Andrew Everett, Acting Vice-President (International)
EMail: j.saunders2@uq.edu.au; lyndall.grant@uq.edu.au.

Faculty

Arts (Art History; Classical Languages; Cultural Studies; English; History; Media Studies; Modern Languages; Music; Philosophy; Religion); **Business Economics and Law** (Business Administration; Economics; Law; Leisure Studies; Tourism); **Engineering, Architecture and Information Technology** (Architecture and Planning; Chemical Engineering; Civil Engineering; Electrical Engineering; Engineering; Information Technology; Mechanical Engineering; Mining Engineering; Water Management); **Health Sciences** (Community Health; Dentistry; Health Sciences; Medicine; Midwifery; Nursing; Pharmacy; Public Health; Rehabilitation and Therapy; Toxicology; Tropical Medicine); **Science** (Agriculture; Animal Husbandry; Biological and Life Sciences; Biomedical Engineering; Biomedicine; Earth Sciences; Ecology; Environmental Engineering; Environmental Management; Environmental Studies; Food Science; Food Technology; Geography; Marine Science and Oceanography; Mathematics; Microbiology; Molecular Biology; Nanotechnology; Nutrition; Physics; Regional Planning; Toxicology; Veterinary Science; Zoology); **Social and Behavioural Sciences** (Archaeology; Communication Studies; Education; International Studies; Journalism; Political Sciences; Psychology; Social Sciences; Social Work)

Further Information: Also Teaching Hospitals, University Mine, Veterinary Science facilities and Agricultural Farms, Marine Research Stations and Study Abroad, Study Exchange and Twinning Programmes, Institute for Continuing and TESOL Education (ICTE), and 8 research institutes

History: Established by Act of the Queensland Parliament 1909. Officially founded 1910, it began teaching in 1911. In 1990, it merged with the Queensland Agricultural College (now UQ Gatton) as part of a unified national system abolishing the binary system of universities and colleges of advanced education. In 1999, opened UQ Ipswich.

Academic Year: February to December (February-July; July-December). Summer session (November-February) for some courses

Admission Requirements: Senior secondary school certificate or recognized foreign equivalent with appropriate grades and prerequisites. English language proficiency is required either via IELTS-test, overall band score of at least 6.5, with a writing band score of at least 6; or TOEFL test score of 550, with a writing band of 5. Higher English language proficiency is required for some programs of study

Fees: 8,800 - 27,500 per semester (Australian Dollar)

Main Language(s) of Instruction: English

Degrees and Diplomas: *Bachelor Degree*; *Bachelor Honours Degree*; *Graduate Certificate/Diploma*; *Master Degree*; *Doctoral Degree*

Student Services: Academic Counselling, Canteen, Careers Guidance, Facilities for disabled people, Health Services, Language Laboratory, Nursery Care, Social Counselling, Sports Facilities

Last Updated: 25/03/14

THE UNIVERSITY OF SYDNEY (USYD)

Building A14, Sydney, New South Wales 2006
Tel: +61(2) 9351-2222
Fax: +61(2) 9351-4596
EMail: info.centre@sydney.edu.au
Website: http://www.usyd.edu.au

Vice-Chancellor: Michael Spence
EMail: vice.chancellor@sydney.edu.au

Provost and Deputy Vice-Chancellor: Stephen Garton
EMail: dvc.provost@sydney.edu.au

Faculty

Agriculture, Food and Natural Resources (Agricultural Economics; Agricultural Engineering; Agriculture; Agrobiology; Agronomy; Animal Husbandry; Crop Production; Food Science; Plant and Crop Protection; Soil Science; Water Science); **Architecture** (Architectural Restoration; Architecture; Landscape Architecture; Regional Planning; Structural Architecture; Town Planning); **Arts** (Ancient Civilizations; Anthropology; Applied Linguistics; Archaeology; Art History; Arts and Humanities; Asian Studies; Celtic Languages and Studies; Chinese; Classical Languages; Contemporary History; English; Fine Arts; French; German; Grammar; Greek; Hebrew; History; Indic Languages; Italian; Japanese; Korean; Latin; Linguistics; Literature; Mathematics; Medieval Studies; Modern History; Modern Languages; Music; Philology; Philosophy; Phonetics; Prehistory; Russian; South and Southeast Asian Languages; Spanish; Speech Studies; Statistics; Terminology; Thai Languages; Translation and Interpretation; Writing); **Dentistry** (Dental Hygiene; Dental Technology; Dentistry; Oral Pathology; Orthodontics; Periodontics; Radiology); **Economics and Business** (Accountancy; Administration; Banking; Business Administration; Business and Commerce; Econometrics; Economic History; Economics; Finance; Human Resources; Industrial Management; Institutional Administration; International Business; Labour and Industrial Relations; Law; Management; Management Systems; Marketing; Public Administration; Transport Economics); **Education and Social Work** (Curriculum; Education; Educational Psychology; Educational Sciences; Higher Education Teacher Training; Literacy Education; Primary Education; Secondary Education; Social Policy; Special Education); **Engineering** (Aeronautical and Aerospace Engineering; Chemical Engineering; Civil Engineering; Electrical Engineering; Engineering; Environmental Engineering; Information Technology; Mechanical Engineering); **Health Sciences** (Community Health; Dietetics; Health Sciences; Hygiene; Occupational Health; Public Health; Social and Preventive Medicine; Sports Medicine); **Law** (Administrative Law; Civil Law; Commercial Law; Comparative Law; Constitutional Law; Criminal Law; Human Rights; International Law; Labour Law; Law; Public Law); **Medicine** (Anaesthesiology; Cardiology; Community Health; Dermatology; Endocrinology; Epidemiology; Gastroenterology; Gerontology; Gynaecology and Obstetrics; Haematology; Medicine; Nephrology; Neurology; Oncology; Ophthalmology; Paediatrics; Parasitology; Pathology; Psychiatry and Mental Health; Radiology; Urology; Venereology; Virology); **Nursing** (Anatomy; Chemistry; Community Health; Dietetics; Hygiene; Microbiology; Nursing; Pharmacology; Physics; Physiology; Psychology; Public Health; Sociology); **Pharmacy** *(Orange Campus)* (Pharmacology; Pharmacy); **Rural Management** *(Orange College)* (Agricultural Business; Agricultural Economics; Agriculture; Farm Management; Horticulture; Management; Rural Planning); **Science** (Applied Physics; Astronomy and Space Science; Astrophysics; Biochemistry; Biological and Life Sciences; Biophysics; Chemistry; Computer Science; Entomology; Geography; Geology; Geophysics; Immunology; Marine Science and Oceanography; Mathematics; Microbiology; Natural Sciences; Neurosciences; Nuclear Physics; Nutrition; Optics; Pharmacy; Physics; Psychology; Soil Science; Solid State Physics; Statistics; Thermal Physics; Zoology); **Sydney College of Arts**; **Sydney Conservatorium of Music** (Conducting; Music; Music Education; Music Theory and Composition; Musical Instruments; Musicology; Performing Arts; Singing); **Veterinary Science** (Animal Husbandry; Cell Biology; Chemistry; Genetics; Veterinary Science)

Unit
Electron Microscope (Atomic and Molecular Physics; Optical Technology); **Spatial Science Innovation Unit**

College
Health Sciences (Dentistry; Health Administration; Health Sciences; Medicine; Nursing; Pharmacy; Public Health; Rehabilitation and Therapy; Surgery; Treatment Techniques); **Humanities and Social Sciences** (Arts and Humanities; Business Administration; Economics; Education; Fine Arts; Information Sciences; Law; Music; Social Sciences; Social Work; Vocational Counselling); **Sciences and Technology** (Agriculture; Architecture; Engineering; Natural Sciences; Rural Planning; Science Education; Technology; Veterinary Science)

Institute
Astronomy (Astronomy and Space Science); **Marine Science** (Marine Science and Oceanography); **Medical Physics**; **Plant Breeding** (Plant and Crop Protection); **Teaching and Learning**; **Transport Studies** (Transport and Communications; Transport Management); **Wildlife Research** (Wildlife)

Centre
Advanced Materials Technology (Polymer and Plastics Technology); **Advanced Structural Engineering** (Civil Engineering); **Advanced Technologies in Animal Genetics** *(Reprogen)*; **Animal Immunology Research** (Immunology; Zoology); **Australian Mekong Resource Centre** *(AMRC)*; **Australian National Genomic Information Service** (Biology; Genetics); **Biological Information and Technology** *(SUBIT)* (Biotechnology); **Celtic Studies** (Celtic Languages and Studies); **Classical Civilizations** (Ancient Civilizations; Classical Languages); **Clinical Trials** *(National Health and Medical Council Centre of)* (Clinical Psychology); **Design Computing and Cognition** *(Key Centre)* (Computer Graphics; Design); **English Teaching** (English); **Environmental Law** *(Australian Centre)*; **European Studies**; **Finite Element Analysis** (Aeronautical and Aerospace Engineering); **Geotechnical Research** (Civil Engineering); **Health Economics Research and Evaluation** *(CHERE)*; **Health Promotion** *(Australian Centre)* (Health Education); **Heavy Metals Research** (Chemistry); **Human Aspects of Science and Technology**; **Industrial Relations Research and Teaching** *(ACIRRT)* (Industrial Management; Labour and Industrial Relations); **Innovation and International Competitiveness** (International Business; Marketing); **Mathematics Learning** (Mathematics); **Medieval Studies**; **Molonglo Observatory** (Astronomy and Space Science); **Nitrogen Fixation** *(SUNfix; Syndey University Nitrogen Fixation Centre)*; **Optical Fibre Technology** (Information Technology; Optical Technology); **Organic Synthesis** (Organic Chemistry); **Peace and Conflict Studies** (Peace and Disarmament); **Polymer Colloids** *(Key Centre)* (Polymer and Plastics Technology); **Precision Agriculture** *(Australian Centre)* (Agricultural Management; Agriculture; Crop Production); **Risk, Envrionment, Systems Technology and Analysis** (Chemical Engineering); **Rural Sustainability**; **Salinity Assessment and Management** (Soil Science; Water Science); **Visualisation Lab** *(VISLAB)* (Computer Graphics; Computer Networks; Data Processing)

Graduate School
Government; **Government** *(Run jointly with the University of New South Wales)* (Administration; Government)

Research Centre
Accountancy Foundation (Accountancy; Business and Commerce); **Advanced Composite Structures** *(Australian Cooperative)* (Materials Engineering); **Asian Agribusiness** (Agricultural Business); **Australian Marine Mammal** (Marine Biology); **Autonomous** *(Australian Research Council Centre of Excellence)*; **Biological Control of Pest Animals** *(Australian Cooperative Research Centre)* (Pest Management); **Biosecurity, Emerging Infectious Diseases** *(Australian Cooperative Research Centre)* (Immunology); **Ecological Impacts of Coastal Cities** (Coastal Studies; Ecology; Environmental Studies); **Field Robotics** *(Australian Key Research Centre(ACFR))*; **Fruit Fly** (Fruit Production; Pest Management); **Herbal Medicines** *(Research and Education Centre)* (Alternative Medicine); **IA Watson Grains** (Crop Production; Food Science); **Ian Buchan Fell Housing**; **Innovation Dairy Products** *(Australian Cooperative Research Centre)* (Crop Production; Food Science); **Innovative Grain Food Products** *(Australian Cooperative Research Centre)* (Crop Production; Food Science); **Mining** *(Australian Cooperative Research Centre)* (Mining Engineering); **Nursing** *(Sydney Nursing Research Centre)* (Midwifery; Nursing); **One Tree Island** (Biology; Marine Biology); **Photonics** *(Australian Cooperative Research Center)* (Optical Technology); **Polymers** *(Australian Cooperative Research Centre)* (Polymer and Plastics Technology); **Quaternary Dating** (Archaeology; Prehistory); **Rehabilitation** (Rehabilitation and Therapy); **Structural Biology and Structural Chemistry** (Biology; Chemistry); **Stuttering Research** (Speech Therapy and Audiology); **Sustainable Cotton Production** *(Australian Cooperative Research Centre)* (Crop Production); **Sustainable Resource Processing** *(Australian Cooperative Research Centre)* (Chemical Engineering); **Sustainable Rice Production** *(Australian Cooperative Research Centre)* (Crop Production; Food Science); **Technology Enabled Capital Markets** *(Australian Cooperative Research Centre)* (Electrical and Electronic Engineering); **Theoretical Astrophysics** (Astrophysics); **Ultra-high-Bandwidth Devices for Optical Systems** *(Australian Cooperative Research Centre(CUDOS))* (Optical Technology); **Value-added Wheat Cooperative** (Crop Production; Food Science); **Wave Physics**

Research Institute
Asia and Pacific (Asian Studies; Pacific Area Studies); **Asian and Pacific Law** (Comparative Law; Law); **Criminology** (Criminology); **Humanities and Social Sciences** *(RIHSS)*; **Rural Management** (Agricultural Management)

Foundation
Chemical Engineering (Chemical Engineering); **Chemistry** *(Cornforth)* (Chemistry); **Civil Engineering**; **Dairy Research**; **Earth Resources** (Natural Resources); **Electrical Engineering**; **Information Technology** *(Research Foundation)* (Information Technology); **Inorganic Chemistry**; **Nutrition Research**; **Physics** *(Science Foundation)* (Physics); **Planning Research** (Public Administration; Urban Studies); **Poultry Research** (Food Science; Meat and Poultry); **Save Sight Institute** (Ophthalmology); **Veterinary Science** (Veterinary Science); **Veterinary Science** *(Postgraduate)* (Veterinary Science); **Warren Centre of Advanced Engineering** (Engineering)

Further Information: Also Teaching Hospitals and Study Abroad Programme

History: Founded 1850. The oldest University in Australia. Cumberland College of Health Sciences, Sydney College of the Arts, N.S.W. State Conservatorium of Music and two parts of Sydney College of Advanced Education, Institute of Nursing Studies, and Sydney Institute of Education (formerly Sydney Teachers' College) amalgamated with the University 1990.

Academic Year: February to December (February-June; July-December)

Admission Requirements: Secondary higher school certificate or recognized foreign equivalent, or previous tertiary study. Direct entrance to second year on completion of studies in another tertiary institution. Overseas students must show proficiency in English (6.5 IELTS or 577 TOEFL minimum with a test of written English minimum of 4.5)

Main Language(s) of Instruction: English

Degrees and Diplomas: *Bachelor Degree*; *Bachelor Honours Degree*; *Graduate Certificate/Diploma*; *Master Degree*; *Doctoral Degree*. Also postgraduate certificates and undergraduate and postgraduate diplomas

Student Services: Academic Counselling, Canteen, Careers Guidance, Facilities for disabled people, Foreign Studies Centre, Health Services, Language Laboratory, Nursery Care, Social Counselling, Sports Facilities

Last Updated: 27/03/14

THE UNIVERSITY OF WESTERN AUSTRALIA

35 Stirling Highway, Crawley, Western Australia 6009
Tel: +61(8) 6488-6000
Fax: +61(8) 6488-1380
EMail: general.enquiries@uwa.edu.au
Website: http://www.uwa.edu.au

Vice-Chancellor: Paul Johnson
EMail: vc@uwa.edu.au; paul.johnson@uwa.edu.au

Registrar and Executive Director Corporate Services: Peter Curtis EMail: peter.curtis@uwa.edu.au

Faculty
Architecture, Landscape and Visual Arts (Architecture; Art History; Landscape Architecture; Visual Arts); **Arts** (Arts and Humanities; Cultural Studies; History; Modern Languages; Music); **Education** (Education; Preschool Education; Primary Education; Secondary Education); **Engineering, Computing and Mathematics** (Chemical Engineering; Civil Engineering; Computer Engineering; Computer Science; Electrical and Electronic Engineering; Engineering; Environmental Engineering; Mathematics; Mechanical Engineering; Mining Engineering; Software Engineering; Statistics); **Medicine, Dentistry and Health Sciences** (Community Health; Dentistry; Medicine; Neurosciences; Paediatrics; Pathology; Pharmacology; Psychiatry and Mental Health; Surgery); **Science** (Agricultural Economics; Anatomy; Biochemistry; Biology; Chemistry; Earth Sciences; Physics; Physiology; Plant Pathology; Psychology; Sports; Zoology)

School
Business (Accountancy; Business Administration; Economics; Human Resources; Management; Marketing); **Indigenous Studies** (Indigenous Studies); **Law** (Law)

Institute
Advanced Studies; **Agriculture** (Agriculture); **Confucius** (Chinese); **Energy and Minerals** (Energy Engineering; Mineralogy); **Oceans** (Marine Science and Oceanography); **Regional Development** (Regional Studies)

Centre
Aboriginal Medical and Dental Health; **Advanced Consumer Research**; **Atomic, Molecular and Surface Physics**; **Callaway**; **Child and Adolescent Related Disorders** (Behavioural Sciences); **Child Study** (Child Care and Development); **Crime Research**; **Ear Sciences** (Otorhinolaryngology); **Ecohydrology**; **Electro-Optic Propagation and Sensing** (Optical Technology); **Energy Systems** (Energy Engineering); **Engineering Design and Consultancy** (Engineering Drawing and Design); **Evolutionary Biology**; **Excellence in Natural Resource Management**; **Forensic Science** (Forensic Medicine and Dentistry); **Geomechanics** *(Australian)* (Geological Engineering; Mechanical Engineering); **Health Services Research** (Health Administration); **Indigenous History and the Arts**; **Industrial Solid Mechanics**; **Infectious Diseases Research** *(Marshall)*; **Integrated Human Sciences**; **Intelligent Information Processing Systems**; **Labour Market Research** (Social Studies); **Land Rehabilitation**; **Legumes in Mediterranean Agriculture** (Agriculture; Vegetable Production); **Microscopy, Characterisation and Analysis**; **Mining, Energy and Natural Resources Law**; **Mobile Health Care Solutions** *(e-Med)*; **Musculoskeletal Studies** (Anatomy); **Music** (Music); **Muslim States and Societies**; **Neuromuscular and Neurological Disorders**; **Offshore Foundation Systems**; **Ophthalmology and Visual Science**; **Organisational Research** (Management; Psychology); **Plant Energy Biology**; **Plant Metabolomics** (Plant and Crop Protection); **Remote and Rural Oral Health** (Oral Pathology); **Rural Health** *(Combined Universities)* (Health Sciences); **Software Practice** (Software Engineering); **Strategic Nano-Fabrication** (Nanotechnology); **Sustainable Mine Lakes**; **Timber Technology** (Wood Technology); **Western Australian History** (History)

Research Centre
Advanced Mineral and Materials Processing; **Anthropological**; **Applied Cancer Studies**; **Applied Dynamics and Optimization**; **Archaeological** *(Eureka)* (Archaeology); **Asthma, Allergy and Respiratory**; **Clinical Research in Neuropsychiatry** (Neurology; Psychiatry and Mental Health); **Consumer** *(Advanced)*; **Crystallography**; **Energy Systems**; **Future Farm Industries** *(Cooperative)*; **Global Studies** *(Australian)*; **Gravitational** *(Australian International)*; **Medical Engineering** *(Australian)*; **Molecular Immunology and Instrumentation**; **Oil and Gas Engineering**; **Urban Research**; **Water Research**

Further Information: Also 30 Teaching Hospitals

History: Founded 1911, endowed by an Act of the State legislature with Royal Assent.

Academic Year: February to November (February-June; July-November)

Admission Requirements: Western Australia Tertiary Entrance Examination following secondary school certificate or recognized foreign equivalent, or previous tertiary study. Direct entrance to second year on satisfactory completion of studies in another recognized tertiary institution

Fees: 22,000 - 46,000 per annum (Australian Dollar)

Main Language(s) of Instruction: English

Degrees and Diplomas: *Bachelor Degree*; *Bachelor Honours Degree*; *Graduate Certificate/Diploma*; *Master Degree*; *Doctoral Degree*

Last Updated: 25/03/14

UNIVERSITY OF CANBERRA (UC)

Canberra, ACT 2601
Tel: +61(2) 6201-5111
Fax: +61(2) 6201-5999
EMail: international@canberra.edu.au
Website: http://www.canberra.edu.au

Vice-Chancellor: Stephen Parker (2007-)
EMail: ovc@canberra.edu.au

Faculty
Arts and Design (Advertising and Publicity; Architecture; Communication Studies; Foreign Languages Education; Graphic Design; Industrial Design; Interior Design; International Studies; Journalism; Landscape Architecture; Marketing; Media Studies; Modern Languages; Writing); **Business, Government and Law** (Administration; Banking; Economics; Finance; Government; Management; Marketing; Regional Planning; Tourism; Urban Studies); **Education, Science, Technology and Maths** (Biological and Life Sciences; Education; Engineering; Environmental Studies; Information Technology; Mathematics; Pharmacy; Statistics); **Health** (Nursing; Pharmacy; Physical Therapy; Psychology; Sports)

Further Information: Also research centres

History: Founded as Canberra College of Advanced Education. Acquired present title and status 1989.

Academic Year: February to November (February-June; July-November)

Admission Requirements: Higher school certificate (HSC) or national or international equivalent. Advanced standing may be granted on satisfactory completion of studies in another recognized higher education institution

Fees: 15,000 per annum (Australian Dollar)

Main Language(s) of Instruction: English

Degrees and Diplomas: *Bachelor Degree*; *Bachelor Honours Degree*; *Graduate Certificate/Diploma*; *Master Degree*; *Doctoral Degree*

Last Updated: 26/03/14

UNIVERSITY OF MELBOURNE

Melbourne, Victoria 3010
Tel: +61(3) 8344-4000
Website: http://www.unimelb.edu.au

Vice-Chancellor: Glyn Conrad Davis, AC
EMail: vc@unimelb.edu.au

Senior Vice-Principal: R. Ian Marshman
EMail: i.marshman@unimelb.edu.au

International Relations: Sue Elliott, Deputy Vice-Chancellor (Engagement) EMail: s.elliott@unimelb.edu.au

Faculty
Architecture, Building and Planning (Architecture; Civil Engineering; Environmental Management; Landscape Architecture; Rural Planning; Town Planning); **Arts** (Ancient Civilizations; Anthropology; Applied Linguistics; Arabic; Art History; Arts and

Humanities; Asian Studies; Chinese; Criminology; Development Studies; Economics; English; Environmental Studies; European Studies; French; Gender Studies; Geography; German; Hebrew; Indigenous Studies; Indonesian; International Studies; Islamic Studies; Italian; Japanese; Jewish Studies; Latin American Studies; Law; Linguistics; Media Studies; Philosophy; Political Sciences; Psychology; Russian; Sociology; Spanish; Theatre; Writing); **Business and Economics** (Accountancy; Business Administration; Economics; Finance; Management; Marketing); **Medicine, Dentistry and Health Sciences** (Biomedicine; Community Health; Dental Hygiene; Dental Technology; Dentistry; Epidemiology; Medicine; Nursing; Physical Therapy; Public Health; Social Work); **Science** (Biochemistry; Chemistry; Earth Sciences; Environmental Studies; Mathematics; Natural Sciences; Physics; Statistics); **Veterinary Science** (Veterinary Science)

College

Arts (Cinema and Television; Dance; Fine Arts; Performing Arts; Theatre)

School

Engineering (Biomedical Engineering; Chemical Engineering; Computer Engineering; Electrical and Electronic Engineering; Information Technology; Mechanical Engineering); **Land and Environment** (Agriculture; Animal Husbandry; Environmental Management; Food Science; Forestry; Horticulture); **Law** (Law)

Conservatory

Music (Music; Music Theory and Composition; Musicology)

Graduate School

Education (Education; Educational Administration; Educational Testing and Evaluation; Preschool Education; Primary Education; Secondary Education)

Further Information: Also Burnley, Creswick, Dookie, Parkville, Shepparton, Southbank, and Werribee Campuses.

History: Founded 1853 by an Act of the Victorian State Parliament, Melbourne was Victoria's first University and Australia's second. Funding is through the Australian Government and non-governmental sources. The University amalgamated with the Melbourne College of Advanced Education in 1989, with the Hawthorn Institute of Education in 1996 and with the Victorian College of Agriculture and Horticulture in 1997. Victorian College of the Arts became a full faculty in 2007.

Academic Year: March to December (March-June; July-December)

Admission Requirements: Satisfactory completion of an approved final year of high school equivalent to the Victorian Certificate of Education (VCE) or, in countries without a recognised high school qualification, completion of a foundation programme in Australia or first year standing from a recognised overseas tertiary institution, and satisfactory completion of any special course requirements; admission quotas apply and completion of entrance qualifications does not guarantee right of entry.

Fees: Up to 64,000 per annum (Australian Dollar)

Main Language(s) of Instruction: English

Degrees and Diplomas: *Bachelor Degree*; *Bachelor Honours Degree*; *Graduate Certificate/Diploma*; *Master Degree*; *Doctoral Degree*

Student Services: Academic Counselling, Canteen, Careers Guidance, Cultural Activities, Facilities for disabled people, Health Services, Nursery Care, Social Counselling, Sports Facilities

Last Updated: 27/03/14

UNIVERSITY OF NEW ENGLAND (UNE)

Armidale, New South Wales 2351
Tel: +61(2) 6773-3333
Website: http://www.une.edu.au

Vice-Chancellor: Annabelle Duncan EMail: vc@une.edu.au

School

Arts (Chinese; English; French; German; Indonesian; Italian; Japanese; Media Studies; Music; Spanish; Theatre; Writing); **Behavioural, Cognitive and Social Sciences** (Criminology; Geography; Linguistics; Psychology; Regional Planning; Sociology; Town Planning); **Business** (Accountancy; Agricultural Business; Agricultural Economics; Business Administration; Econometrics; Economics; Finance; Human Resources; Management); **Education** (Art Education; Education; Educational Psychology; Humanities and Social Science Education; Mathematics Education; Physical Education; Preschool Education; Primary Education; Science Education; Special Education; Technology Education); **Environmental and Rural Science** (Agriculture; Agronomy; Botany; Earth Sciences; Ecology; Environmental Engineering; Farm Management; Meat and Poultry; Paleontology; Plant Pathology; Veterinary Science); **Health** (Health Administration; Nursing; Social Work); **Humanities** (Ancient Civilizations; Archaeology; Asian Studies; Classical Languages; History; Indigenous Studies; International Studies; Islamic Studies; Peace and Disarmament; Political Sciences; Religious Studies); **Law** (Law); **Rural Medicine** (Medicine); **Science and Technology** (Biomedicine; Cell Biology; Chemistry; Computer Science; Mathematics; Molecular Biology; Pharmacy; Sports; Statistics)

Further Information: Also Clinical Schools, International Office, and Off-shore Programmes

History: Founded 1938 as New England University College, acquired present status and title 1954.

Academic Year: February to November (February-June; July-November).

Admission Requirements: Secondary school certificate or recognized foreign equivalent, or previous tertiary study. Overseas applicants must provide evidence of proficiency in English

Fees: 14,175 (Undergraduate) - 24,100 (PhD) per annum (Australian Dollar)

Degrees and Diplomas: *Bachelor Degree*; *Bachelor Honours Degree*; *Graduate Certificate/Diploma*; *Master Degree*; *Doctoral Degree*

Student Services: Academic Counselling, Canteen, Careers Guidance, Facilities for disabled people, Foreign Studies Centre, Health Services, Language Laboratory, Nursery Care, Social Counselling, Sports Facilities

Last Updated: 27/03/14

UNIVERSITY OF NEW SOUTH WALES (UNSW)

High St, Kensington, New South Wales 2052
Tel: +61(2) 9385-1000
EMail: internationaloffice@unsw.edu.au
Website: http://www.unsw.edu.au

Vice-Chancellor and President: Ian Jacobs (2015-)
EMail: vice-chancellor@unsw.edu.au

Faculty

Arts and Social Sciences (Anthropology; Asian Studies; Chinese; Criminology; Dance; Development Studies; Education; English; European Studies; Film; French; Gender Studies; German; History; Indigenous Studies; Philosophy; Political Sciences; Sociology; Spanish; Theatre; Women's Studies; Writing); **Built Environment** (Architecture; Industrial Design; Interior Design; Landscape Architecture; Rural Planning; Town Planning); **Engineering** (Biomedical Engineering; Chemical Engineering; Civil Engineering; Computer Engineering; Computer Science; Electrical Engineering; Energy Engineering; Engineering; Environmental Engineering; Mechanical Engineering; Mining Engineering; Petroleum and Gas Engineering; Production Engineering; Telecommunications Engineering); **Law** (Law); **Medicine** (Community Health; Gynaecology and Obstetrics; Medicine; Paediatrics; Psychiatry and Mental Health; Public Health); **Science** (Anatomy; Archaeology; Biological and Life Sciences; Biology; Biotechnology; Cell Biology; Chemistry; Coastal Studies; Earth Sciences; Ecology; Environmental Management; Food Science; Genetics; Geochemistry; Geography; Marine Science and Oceanography; Materials Engineering; Mathematics; Microbiology; Molecular Biology; Neurosciences; Pharmacology; Physics; Physiology; Psychology; Statistics)

College

Fine Arts (Art Education; Design; Fine Arts)

School

Business (Accountancy; Actuarial Science; Banking; Business Administration; Commercial Law; Economics; Finance; Management; Marketing; Taxation)

History: Founded 1949 as the New South Wales University of Technology, acquired present status and title 1958.

Academic Year: February to November (March-June; July-November)

Admission Requirements: Higher School Certificate or recognized national or foreign equivalent, or previous post-secondary study.

Fees: Undergraduate, 54,000-200,000 for full programme (Bachelor); Postgraduate coursework, 16,300-33,600 (Australian Dollar)

Main Language(s) of Instruction: English

Degrees and Diplomas: *Bachelor Degree*; *Bachelor Honours Degree*; *Graduate Certificate/Diploma*; *Master Degree*; *Doctoral Degree*

Student Services: Academic Counselling, Canteen, Careers Guidance, Cultural Activities, Facilities for disabled people, Health Services, Nursery Care, Social Counselling, Sports Facilities
Last Updated: 27/03/14

UNIVERSITY OF SOUTH AUSTRALIA (UNISA)

PO Box 2471, Adelaide, South Australia 5001
Tel: +61(8) 8302-6611
Fax: +61(8) 8302-2466
EMail: international.office@unisa.edu.au
Website: http://www.unisa.edu.au

Vice-Chancellor and President: David Lloyd
EMail: david.lloyd@unisa.edu.au

International Relations: Nigel Relph, Deputy Vice Chancellor International and Advancement, EMail: nigel.relph@unisa.edu.au

Division
Business (Accountancy; Administration; Banking; Business Administration; Business and Commerce; Criminal Law; Economics; Finance; Hotel Management; Human Resources; Labour and Industrial Relations; Labour Law; Law; Leadership; Leisure Studies; Marketing; Private Law; Public Law; Real Estate; Sports Management; Taxation; Tourism); **Education, Arts and Social Sciences** (Architecture; Art History; Art Management; Behavioural Sciences; Cinema and Television; Cognitive Sciences; Communication Studies; Cultural Studies; Dance; Design; Education; Educational Sciences; Fine Arts; Gender Studies; Handicrafts; Indigenous Studies; Industrial Design; Interior Design; International Studies; Journalism; Linguistics; Mass Communication; Media Studies; Modern Languages; Multimedia; Performing Arts; Political Sciences; Psychology; Radio and Television Broadcasting; Social and Community Services; Social Policy; Social Welfare; Social Work; Sociology; Special Education; Teacher Training; Theatre; Visual Arts); **Health Sciences** (Health Sciences); **Information Technology, Engineering and the Environment** (Civil Engineering; Computer Engineering; Electrical and Electronic Engineering; Energy Engineering; Environmental Studies; Industrial Engineering; Information Management; Information Technology; Materials Engineering; Mathematics; Mechanical Engineering; Parks and Recreation; Production Engineering; Statistics; Surveying and Mapping; Water Science)

Centre
Centre for Regional Engagement (Business Administration; Management; Midwifery; Nursing; Social Policy; Social Work)

Research Centre
Accounting, Governance and Sustainability; **Advanced Computing**; **Applied Psychological Research**; **Comparative Water Policies and Law** (Law; Water Management); **Defence and Systems Institute**; **Environmental Risk Assessment and Remediation**; **Human Resource Management** (Human Resources); **Industrial and Applied Mathematics** (Applied Mathematics; Mathematics and Computer Science); **Languages and Culture**; **Nutritional Physiology Research**; **Regulation and Market Analysis**; **Rural Health and Community Development**; **Sleep Research**; **Sustainable Design and Behaviour** *(Zero Waste SA)*; **Water Management and Reuse** (Water Management); **Work and Life**

Research Group
Tourism and Leisure Management (Leisure Studies; Tourism)

Research Institute
Bartbara Handy; **Ian Wark** (Polymer and Plastics Technology); **Marketing Science** *(Ehrenberg-Bass)*; **Mawson Institute**; **Sansom Institute** (Medicine; Pharmacy); **Sustainable Societies** *(Hawke)*; **Sustainable Systems and Technologies**; **Telecommunications Research** (Telecommunications Engineering)

History: Founded 1991 through the amalgamation of the South Australian Institute of Technology and several campuses of the South Australian College of Advanced Education.

Academic Year: February to November (February - June; July - November); Summer programme, December - February

Admission Requirements: Undergraduate entrants require senior secondary school (year 12) certificate or recognised foreign equivalent with appropriate grades and prerequisites. Postgraduate entrants shall normally hold a recognised University undergraduate degree or equivalent professional experience. The minimum English language entry requirements for international students who speak English as a foreign language are: International English Language Testing System (IELTS) Academic - overall 6.0 obtained within the last two years or corresponding results from an equivalent test. Note that many programs have a higher IELTS (Academic) requirement, some of which include specific subscore requirements.

Main Language(s) of Instruction: English, Chinese

Degrees and Diplomas: *Bachelor Degree*; *Bachelor Honours Degree*; *Graduate Certificate/Diploma*; *Doctoral Degree*

Student Services: Academic Counselling, Canteen, Careers Guidance, Cultural Activities, Facilities for disabled people, Foreign Studies Centre, Health Services, Language Laboratory, Nursery Care, Social Counselling, Sports Facilities
Last Updated: 28/03/14

UNIVERSITY OF SOUTHERN QUEENSLAND (USQ)

West Street, Toowoomba, Queensland 4350
Tel: +61(7) 4631-2100
Fax: +61(7) 4631-2893
EMail: international@usq.edu.au; study@usq.edu.au
Website: http://www.usq.edu.au

Vice-Chancellor: Jan Thomas EMail: vc@usq.edu.au

Faculty
Arts (Arts and Humanities; International Studies; Mass Communication; Multimedia; Music; Social Sciences; Theatre; Visual Arts); **Business and Law** (Business and Commerce; Economics; Human Resources; Information Technology; International Business; Labour and Industrial Relations; Law; Marketing; Transport Management); **Education** (Child Care and Development; Distance Education; Education; Educational Administration; Primary Education; Secondary Education; Special Education); **Engineering and Surveying** (Agricultural Engineering; Civil Engineering; Electrical and Electronic Engineering; Engineering; Mechanical Engineering; Surveying and Mapping); **Science** (Astronomy and Space Science; Biology; Biomedicine; Information Technology; Mathematics and Computer Science; Midwifery; Natural Sciences; Nursing; Oenology; Psychology)

Section
Distance and E-Education; **Kumbari/Ngurpai Lage Higher Education** *(academic and personal support for Aboriginal and Torres Strait Islander students)* (Higher Education); **Learning and Teaching Support Unit**; **Preparatory and Academy Support**

Research Centre
Computational Engineering and Science (Computer Engineering; Computer Science); **Public Memory**; **Rural and Remote Area Health** (Health Sciences); **Sustainable Catchments** *(Australian)*; **Systems Biology** (Biology); **Transformative Pedagogies**

Further Information: Campuses at Fraser Coast and Springfield.

History: Founded 1992 by Act of the Queensland Parliament; previously University College of Southern Queensland (1990), Institute of Technology, Darling Downs (1967).

Academic Year: February to November (February-July; July-November). (Summer Term, November to February)

Admission Requirements: Completion of 12 years of schooling or equivalent with passes at required levels

Main Language(s) of Instruction: English

Degrees and Diplomas: *Diploma*; *Graduate Certificate/Diploma*; *Master Degree*; *Doctoral Degree*

Student Services: Academic Counselling, Canteen, Careers Guidance, Cultural Activities, Facilities for disabled people, Foreign Studies Centre, Health Services, Language Laboratory, Nursery Care, Social Counselling, Sports Facilities
Last Updated: 21/03/14

UNIVERSITY OF TASMANIA (UTAS)

Private Bag 51, Hobart, Tasmania 7001
Tel: +61(3) 6226-2999
Fax: +61(3) 6226-2018
EMail: admissions@utas.edu.au
Website: http://www.utas.edu.au

Vice-Chancellor: Peter Rathjen
EMail: Vice.Chancellor@utas.edu.au

Faculty
Arts (Classical Languages; European Studies; Furniture Design; Gender Studies; Geography; Latin; Medieval Studies; Political Sciences; Sculpture); **Business and Economics** (Business Administration; Economics; Hotel Management; Tourism); **Education** (Education; Health Education; Physical Education; Preschool Education; Primary Education; Science Education; Secondary Education); **Health** (Biomedicine; Health Administration; Medicine; Midwifery; Nursing; Pharmacy; Psychology; Public Health; Radiology); **Law** (Law); **Science, Engineering and Technology** (Agriculture; Architecture; Biochemistry; Chemistry; Computer Science; Engineering; Environmental Studies; Furniture Design; Geography; Geology; Interior Design; Landscape Architecture; Marine Science and Oceanography; Mathematics; Physics; Plant Pathology; Psychology; Science Education; Surveying and Mapping; Zoology)

College
Australian Maritime College (Aquaculture; Marine Engineering; Marine Science and Oceanography; Marine Transport; Nautical Science; Naval Architecture; Transport Management)

Institute
Marine and Antarctic Studies (Marine Biology; Marine Science and Oceanography)

Further Information: Campuses in Sandy Bay (Hobart), Newnham (Launceston) and Cradle Coast (Burnie).

History: Founded 1890 as University of Tasmania in Hobart, amalgamated with Tasmanian State Institute of Technology in Launceston to form new University 1991.

Academic Year: February to November (February-June; July-November)

Admission Requirements: Secondary school certificate or recognized foreign equivalent, or previous tertiary studies in another tertiary institution

Main Language(s) of Instruction: English

Degrees and Diplomas: *Bachelor Degree*; *Bachelor Honours Degree*; *Graduate Certificate/Diploma*; *Master Degree*; *Doctoral Degree*

Last Updated: 25/03/14

UNIVERSITY OF TECHNOLOGY, SYDNEY (UTS)

15 Broadway, Ultimo, New South Wales 2007
Tel: +61(2) 9514-2000
EMail: international@uts.edu.au
Website: http://www.uts.edu.au

Vice-Chancellor and President: Attila Brungs
EMail: attila.brungs@uts.edu.au; vc@uts.edu.au

International Relations: William Purcell, Deputy Vice-Chancellor and Vice-President (International and Development)
EMail: sarah.idziak@uts.edu.au

Faculty
Arts and Social Sciences (Communication Studies; Education; International Studies); **Business** (Accountancy; Administration; Art Management; Business Administration; Business and Commerce; Economics; Finance; Management; Marketing; Sports Management; Tourism); **Design, Architecture and Building** (Architecture; Building Technologies; Communication Studies; Construction Engineering; Design; Fashion Design; Industrial Design; Interior Design; Management; Photography; Town Planning; Visual Arts); **Engineering and Information Technology** (Civil Engineering; Computer Engineering; Construction Engineering; Electrical Engineering; Engineering; Environmental Engineering; Information Technology; Mechanical Engineering; Software Engineering; Telecommunications Engineering); **Law** (Law); **Nursing, Midwifery and Health** (Health Administration; Health Sciences; Midwifery; Nursing); **Science** (Applied Physics; Biological and Life Sciences; Biomedicine; Biotechnology; Cell Biology; Chemistry; Clinical Psychology; Earth Sciences; Environmental Studies; Forensic Medicine and Dentistry; Horticulture; Mathematics; Mathematics and Computer Science; Medicine; Molecular Biology; Natural Sciences; Technology)

School
Accountancy (Accountancy); **Business** *(Graduate)* (Business and Commerce); **Economics** (Economics); **Finance** (Finance); **Leisure, Sports and Tourism** (Leisure Studies; Sports; Tourism); **Management** (Management); **Marketing** (Marketing)

Department
Communication (Communication Studies; Cultural Studies; History of Societies; Humanities and Social Science Education; Information Sciences; Journalism; Media Studies; Music; Social Sciences; Social Studies; Sound Engineering (Acoustics); Writing); **Education** (Adult Education; Applied Linguistics; Education; English; Indigenous Studies; Literacy Education; Primary Education; Secondary Education; Special Education; Staff Development; Teacher Training; Vocational Education); **International Studies** (Cultural Studies; Modern Languages)

Institute
Interactive Multimedia and Learning (Media Studies; Multimedia); **International Studies** (International Studies); **Sustainable Futures** (Development Studies)

Centre
Anti-Slavery Australia; **Australasian Legal Information**; **Cardiovascular and Chronic Care**; **Child and Youth Culture and Wellbeing**; **China Research**; **Communitcation Law Centre**; **Community Organizations and Management**; **Cooperative Research and Development**; **E-Business and Knowledge Management**; **Ecotoxicology**; **Electrical Machines and Power Electronics**; **Event Management**; **Forensic Science**; **Health Services Management**; **Independent Journalism**; **Information and Knowledge Management**; **Local Government**; **Media Arts Innovation**; **Midwifery, Child and Family Health**; **New Writing**; **Nursing, Midwifery and Health Development** *(WHO Collaborating)* (Health Sciences; Midwifery; Nursing); **Object Technology Applications and Research**; **Popular Education**; **Public Communication**; **Public History**; **Research and Education in the Arts**; **Training and Development Services**; **Vocational Education and Training**

Research Centre
Built Infrastructure; **Corporate Governance**; **Cosmopolitan Civil Societies**; **Creative Practices and Cultural Economy**; **Entreprise Distributed Systems Technology** *(Cooperative)*; **Health Communication** (Health Sciences); **Health Economics Research and Evaluation**; **Health Technologies**; **Human Centred Technology Design**; **Innovation in IT Services and Applications**; **Intelligent Mechatronic Systems**; **Learning and Change**; **Organizational Researchers on Collaborations and Alliances**; **Quantitative Finance Research**; **Quantum Computation and Intelligent Systems**; **Real-time Information Networks**; **Renewable Energy** *(Cooperative)*; **Satellite Systems** *(Cooperative)*; **Sustainable Aquaculture of Finfish** *(Cooperative)*; **Technology Enabled Capital Markets** *(Cooperative)*; **Technology in Water and Waste Water** *(Cooperative)*; **Transforming Cultures**

Research Institute
Infection, Immunity and Innovation (Immunology; Medicine; Parasitology; Virology); **Nanoscale Technology**; **Plant Functional Biology and Climate Change Cluster (C3)** (Earth Sciences; Environmental Studies)

Further Information: Also campuses in Kuring-Gai. Study Abroad Programme. Most of the University's extensive range of undergraduate and postgraduate courses are available to international students. Detailed course information may be obtained at the following Web site: http://www.uts.edu.au/international

History: Founded 1965 as New South Wales Institute of Technology, acquired present status and title 1988. Kuring-gai College of Advanced Education and the Institute of Technology and Adult Teacher Education of Sydney College of Advanced Education amalgamated with the University 1990.

Academic Year: March to November (March-June; August-November). Summer session November-February

Admission Requirements: New South Wales higher school Certificate (NSW HSC) with matriculation, or recognized equivalent

Fees: National: None for local undergraduate students; Local postgraduates 5,000-18,000 per annum (Australian Dollar), International: Undergraduates, 19,000-22,000; postgraduates, 20,000-24,000 (Australian Dollar)

Degrees and Diplomas: *Bachelor Degree*; *Bachelor Honours Degree*; *Graduate Certificate/Diploma*; *Master Degree*; *Doctoral Degree*

Student Services: Academic Counselling, Canteen, Careers Guidance, Facilities for disabled people, Health Services, Language Laboratory, Nursery Care, Social Counselling, Sports Facilities

Last Updated: 27/03/14

UNIVERSITY OF THE SUNSHINE COAST (USC)

Maroochydore DC, Queensland 4558
Tel: +61(7) 5430-1234
Fax: +61(7) 5430-1111
EMail: information@usc.edu.au
Website: http://www.usc.edu.au

Vice-Chancellor and President: Greg Hill
EMail: ghill@usc.edu.au; vcoffice@usc.edu.au

Deputy Vice-Chancellor: Birgit Lohmann
EMail: BLohmann@usc.edu.au

International Relations: Robert Elliot, Pro Vice-Chancellor (International and Quality) EMail: elliot@usc.edu.au

Faculty

Arts and Business (Accountancy; Business Administration; Communication Arts; Development Studies; Geography; History; Hotel Management; Human Resources; Indigenous Studies; International Business; Law; Management; Marketing; Political Sciences; Psychology; Regional Planning; Rural Planning; Social Sciences; Social Work; Sociology; Tourism); **Science, Health, Education and Engineering** (Civil Engineering; Community Health; Education; Engineering; Mechanical Engineering; Midwifery; Nursing; Occupational Therapy; Preschool Education; Primary Education; Psychology; Public Health; Secondary Education)

History: Founded as Sunshine Coast University College 1994. Acquired present status and title 1998.

Academic Year: Undergraduate and postgraduate: February to November (February-June; July-November). Postgraduate Business: Business Administration and International Business coursework programs run on a session basis.

Admission Requirements: Senior secondary school certificate comparable to Australian Year 12. Entry is competitive and admission dependent on standard of results

Fees: (Aus Dollars): Undergraduate, 17,200-23,000 per annum; Postgraduate, 17,200-23,000 per annum (fees are suject to annual review)

Main Language(s) of Instruction: English

Degrees and Diplomas: *Bachelor Degree*; *Bachelor Honours Degree*; *Graduate Certificate/Diploma*; *Master Degree*; *Doctoral Degree*. Also Combined Degree, 4 yrs

Student Services: Academic Counselling, Canteen, Careers Guidance, Facilities for disabled people, Foreign Studies Centre, Language Laboratory, Social Counselling, Sports Facilities

Last Updated: 27/03/14

UNIVERSITY OF WESTERN SYDNEY (UWS)

Locked Bag 1797, Penrith, New South Wales 2751
Tel: +61(2) 9852-5222
Website: http://www.uws.edu.au

Vice-Chancellor: Barney Glover (2014-)
EMail: vc@uws.edu.au; B.Glover@uws.edu.au

School

Business (Accountancy; Business and Commerce; Business Computing; Economics; Finance; Hotel Management; Human Resources; International Business; International Economics; International Relations; Management; Marketing; Real Estate; Sports Management); **Computing, Engineering and Mathematics** (Applied Mathematics; Computer Science; Design; Engineering; Fire Science; Health Administration; Industrial Design; Industrial Management; Information Technology; Mathematical Physics; Safety Engineering); **Education** (Education; Preschool Education; Primary Education; Secondary Education; Special Education; Teacher Training); **Humanities and Communication Arts** (Advertising and Publicity; Arabic; Chinese; Design; Fine Arts; International Studies; Japanese; Journalism; Law; Music; Primary Education; Public Relations; Spanish; Translation and Interpretation); **Law** (Commercial Law; Law); **Medicine** (Anatomy; Cell Biology; Gynaecology and Obstetrics; Health Education; Medicine; Microbiology; Oncology; Paediatrics; Pathology; Pharmacology; Psychiatry and Mental Health; Surgery); **Nursing and Midwifery** (Community Health; Health Administration; Midwifery; Nursing; Psychiatry and Mental Health); **Science and Health** (Acupuncture; Alternative Medicine; Biology; Chemistry; Environmental Management; Environmental Studies; Food Technology; Forensic Medicine and Dentistry; Health Sciences; Mathematics; Natural Sciences; Nutrition; Occupational Therapy; Parks and Recreation; Physical Therapy; Podiatry; Public Health; Rehabilitation and Therapy; Sports; Zoology); **Social Sciences and Psychology** (Art Therapy; Clinical Psychology; Criminology; Geography; Peace and Disarmament; Police Studies; Psychology; Rural Planning; Social Welfare; Social Work; Sociology; Tourism; Town Planning; Urban Studies)

Further Information: Also Bankstown, Blacktown, Campbelltown, Hawkesbury, Parramatta campuses and Nirimba Education Precinct and Westmead Precinct.

History: Founded 1989 as a federated network of three members (UWS Hawkesbury, UWS Macarthur, and UWS Nepean) under the banner of the University of Western Sydney. In 2000 the federated network became a unified entity with six campuses.

Academic Year: Autumn (March to June); Spring (July to November)

Admission Requirements: Secondary School diploma or equivalent.

Degrees and Diplomas: *Bachelor Degree*; *Bachelor Honours Degree*; *Graduate Certificate/Diploma*; *Master Degree*; *Doctoral Degree*

Student Services: Academic Counselling, Canteen, Careers Guidance, Cultural Activities, Facilities for disabled people, Foreign Studies Centre, Health Services, Language Laboratory, Nursery Care, Social Counselling, Sports Facilities

Last Updated: 27/03/14

UNIVERSITY OF WOLLONGONG (UOW)

Administrative Building, Northfields Avenue,
Wollongong, New South Wales 2522
Tel: +61(2) 4221-3555
Fax: +61(2) 4221-3233
EMail: uniadvice@uow.edu.au
Website: http://www.uow.edu.au

Vice-Chancellor and Principal: Paul Wellings
EMail: paul_wellings@uow.edu.au

International Relations: Joe Chicharo, Deputy Vice-Chancellor (International) and Managing Director (ITC)
EMail: chicharo@uow.edu.au

Faculty

Arts (Arts and Humanities; Social Sciences); **Commerce** (Business and Commerce; Economics; Finance; Management; Marketing); **Creative Arts** (Fine Arts; Music; Theatre); **Educational Sciences** (Educational Sciences; Physical Education; Special Education; Teacher Trainers Education); **Engineering** (Civil Engineering; Computer Engineering; Electrical Engineering; Engineering; Environmental Engineering; Management; Materials Engineering; Mechanical Engineering; Physics; Telecommunications

Engineering); **Health and Behavioural Sciences** (Behavioural Sciences; Biomedical Engineering; Dietetics; Health Sciences; Midwifery; Nursing; Psychology; Public Health); **Informatics** (Information Management; Information Technology; Mass Communication; Mathematics and Computer Science); **Law** (Administrative Law; Civil Law; Commercial Law; Comparative Law; Constitutional Law; Criminal Law; Human Rights; International Law; Labour Law; Law; Maritime Law); **Science** (Biological and Life Sciences; Chemistry; Earth Sciences; Marine Science and Oceanography; Natural Sciences; Physics)

Institute
Biomolecular Science (Molecular Biology); **Conservation Biology and Law** (Biological and Life Sciences; Ethics; Law); **Social Change and Critical Enquiry** (Social Sciences; Social Studies)

Centre
Asia-Pacific Social Transformation (Asian Studies; Pacific Area Studies; Social Studies); **Canadian-Australian Studies** (Canadian Studies; Pacific Area Studies); **Equity Research in Education** (Education; Ethics); **Health Services Development** (Health Administration; Health Sciences); **Landscape Change** (Environmental Management; Landscape Architecture); **Medical Radiation Physics** (Radiology); **Smart Foods** *(Key Centre)* (Food Science)

Research Centre
Advanced Materials Processing (Materials Engineering); **Bulk Solids and Particulate Technologies** *(Key Centre)* (Solid State Physics); **Digital Media Initiative** (Electronic Engineering); **Engineering Mechanics** (Mechanical Engineering); **Image, Performance and Text** (Film; Graphic Arts; Performing Arts; Photography; Writing); **Industrial Automation** (Automation and Control Engineering); **Intelligent Manufacturing Systems** *(CRC)* (Production Engineering); **Legal Intersection** (Ethics; Law); **Metabolic Research** (Biological and Life Sciences); **Ocean and Coastal Research** (Coastal Studies; Marine Science and Oceanography); **Railway Engineering and Technologies** *(CRC)* (Railway Engineering); **Smart Internet Technology** *(CRC)* (Computer Networks); **Sustainable Earth Research** (Earth Sciences); **Welded Structures** *(CRC)* (Metal Techniques)

Research Group
Atmospheric Chemistry (Chemistry; Meteorology)

Research Institute
Brain and Behaviour (Behavioural Sciences; Neurosciences; Psychology); **Intelligent Polymer** (Polymer and Plastics Technology); **Mathematical Modelling and Computational Systems** (Mathematics and Computer Science); **Steel Processing and Products** *(BHP)* (Metal Techniques; Metallurgical Engineering); **Superconducting and Electronic Materials** (Conducting; Electronic Engineering; Materials Engineering); **Telecommunications and Information Technology** (Information Technology; Telecommunications Engineering)

Further Information: Also Shoalhaven campus.

History: Founded 1951 as Division of New South Wales University of Technology. Became later College of University of New South Wales. In 1975 University of Wollongong was established as an autonomous institution.

Academic Year: February to December (February-July; July-December). Also optional Summer Session (December-January)

Admission Requirements: Candidates must achieve the required mark in an Australian Yr 12, Senior secondary school certificate or recognized foreign equivalent. Any tertiary studies completed prior to enrolment may lead to advanced standing or credit

Main Language(s) of Instruction: English

Degrees and Diplomas: *Bachelor Degree*; *Bachelor Honours Degree*; *Graduate Certificate/Diploma*; *Master Degree*; *Doctoral Degree*

Student Services: Academic Counselling, Canteen, Careers Guidance, Cultural Activities, Facilities for disabled people, Foreign Studies Centre, Health Services, Language Laboratory, Nursery Care, Social Counselling, Sports Facilities

Student Numbers *2012-2013*: Total 17,405
Last Updated: 28/03/14

VICTORIA UNIVERSITY (VU)

PO Box 14428, Melbourne, Victoria 8001
Tel: +61(3) 9688-4000
Fax: +61(3) 9688-4069
EMail: vice-chancellor@vu.edu.au
Website: http://www.vu.edu.au

Vice-Chancellor and President: Peter Dawkins

College
Arts (Asian Studies; Communication Studies; Gender Studies; History; Media Studies; Performing Arts; Political Sciences; Psychology; Sociology; Vietnamese; Visual Arts); **Business** (Accountancy; Business Administration; Finance; Management; Marketing; Transport Management); **Education** (Education; Educational Administration; Physical Education; Preschool Education; Primary Education; Secondary Education); **Engineering and Science** (Architecture; Civil Engineering; Computer Science; Information Technology; Mechanical Engineering; Sports); **Health and Biomedicine** (Anatomy; Biology; Cell Biology; Dietetics; Midwifery; Nursing; Nutrition; Osteopathy; Psychiatry and Mental Health); **Law and Justice** (Law); **Sport and Exercise Science** (Leisure Studies; Sports; Sports Management)

Further Information: Also City Flinders, City Flinders Lane, City King, City Queen, Footscray Nicholson, Footscray Park, Melton, St Albans, Sunshine, VU Sydney, and Werribee campuses.

History: Founded 1916 as Footscray Technical College. Established as Victoria University of Technology in 1990. Acquired present status and title 2005. Federally funded.

Academic Year: February to November

Admission Requirements: Victorian Certificate of Education or equivalent

Degrees and Diplomas: *Bachelor Degree*; *Bachelor Honours Degree*; *Graduate Certificate/Diploma*; *Master Degree*; *Doctoral Degree*

Student Services: Academic Counselling, Canteen, Careers Guidance, Facilities for disabled people, Health Services, Nursery Care, Social Counselling, Sports Facilities
Last Updated: 28/03/14

PRIVATE INSTITUTIONS

ADELAIDE CENTRAL SCHOOL OF ART

PO Box 225, Fullarton, South Australia 5063
Tel: +61(8) 8299-7300
Fax: +61(8) 8172-0504
EMail: info@acsa.sa.edu.au
Website: http://www.acsa.sa.edu.au/

Chaire, Board of Governors: Alan Young

Programme
Visual Arts (Painting and Drawing; Photography; Sculpture; Visual Arts)

History: Created 1982, bachelor degrees awarded from 1998 and in 2010 restructured its degree system to offer 4 year honours degrees.

Degrees and Diplomas: *Bachelor Degree*: **Visual Arts.** *Bachelor Honours Degree*: **Visual Arts.**
Last Updated: 28/03/14

ALPHACRUCIS COLLEGE

PO Box 337, Parramatta, New South Wales 2124
Tel: +61(2) 8893-9099
EMail: info@ac.edu.au
Website: http://ac.edu.au/

Principal: Stephen Fogarty

School
Christian Studies (Christian Religious Studies; Missionary Studies; Theology); **Professional Studies** (Business Administration; Primary Education)

History: Created 1948

Degrees and Diplomas: *Bachelor Degree*: **Business Administration; Missionary Studies; Theology.** *Graduate Certificate/Diploma*; *Master Degree*: **Christian Religious Studies; Primary Education; Theology.**
Last Updated: 28/03/14

ASIA PACIFIC INTERNATIONAL COLLEGE

55 Regent Street, Chippendale, New South Wales 2008
Tel: +61(2) 9698-5206
EMail: programs@apicollege.edu.au
Website: http://www.apicollege.edu.au/

Programme

Business Administration (Business Administration; Management)

Degrees and Diplomas: *Graduate Certificate/Diploma*: **Business Administration.** *Master Degree*: **Business Administration.**
Last Updated: 28/03/14

AUSTRALIAN COLLEGE OF APPLIED PSYCHOLOGY (ACAP)

Level 5 Wynyard Green, 11 York Street,
Sydney, New South Wales 2000
EMail: info.acap@navitas.com
Website: http://www.acap.edu.au/

Principal and Executive General Manager: Andrew Little

Programme

Applied Psychology (Clinical Psychology; Psychoanalysis; Psychology; Psychotherapy); **Criminal Justice** (Criminology); **Elite Athlete Mentoring** (Sports; Sports Management)

History: Created 1983.

Degrees and Diplomas: *Bachelor Degree*: **Psychology; Sports; Sports Management.** *Bachelor Honours Degree*: **Psychology.** *Graduate Certificate/Diploma*: **Psychology; Sports; Sports Management.** *Master Degree*: **Clinical Psychology; Psychology; Psychotherapy.**
Last Updated: 08/04/14

AUSTRALIAN COLLEGE OF NURSING

14 Railway Parade, Burwood, New South Wales 2134
Tel: +61(2) 9745-7500
EMail: ssc@acn.edu.au
Website: http://www.acn.edu.au/

President: Carmen Morgan

Programme

Nursing (Health Administration; Nursing)

Degrees and Diplomas: *Graduate Certificate/Diploma*: **Health Administration; Nursing.**
Last Updated: 28/03/14

AUSTRALIAN FILM, TELEVISION, AND RADIO SCHOOL

Building 130, The Entertainment Quarter, Moore Park,
Sydney, New South Wales 2021
Tel: +61(2) 9805-6611
Website: http://www.aftrs.edu.au/

Chief Executive Officer: Sandra Levy
EMail: executiveassistant@aftrs.edu.au

Programme

Film (Art Management; Cinema and Television; Film; Radio and Television Broadcasting)

History: Created 1972. A self-accrediting higher education provider.

Degrees and Diplomas: *Bachelor Degree*: **Cinema and Television.** *Graduate Certificate/Diploma*: **Art Management; Cinema and Television; Film; Radio and Television Broadcasting.** *Master Degree*: **Art Management; Cinema and Television.**
Last Updated: 28/03/14

AUSTRALIAN INSTITUTE FOR RELATIONSHIP STUDIES

Unit 2 Macquarie Link, 277 Lane Cove Road,
Macquarie Park, New South Wales 2113
Tel: +61(02) 8874 8090
EMail: airs@ransw.org.au
Website: http://www.nsw.relationships.com.au/

Chief Executive Officer: Frank Francis

Programme

Couple and Family Therapy (Psychology; Social Welfare)

Degrees and Diplomas: *Graduate Certificate/Diploma*: **Social Welfare.**
Last Updated: 08/04/14

AUSTRALIAN INSTITUTE OF BUSINESS (AIB)

27 Currie Street, Adelaide, South Australia 5000
Tel: +61(8) 8212-8111
Fax: +61(8) 8212-0032
EMail: enquiries@aib.edu.au
Website: http://www.aib.edu.au

Chief Executive: Param Abraham (2006-)
EMail: param.abraham@aib.edu.au

Director Operations and Corporate Affairs: Sanjay Abraham
EMail: sanjay.abraham@aib.edu.au

International Relations: Olga Carroll, International Marketing Manager EMail: olga.carroll@aib.edu.au

Department

Business Administration (Business Administration)

History: Created 1984. Acquired status 1994. AIB was formerly known as Gibaran Graduate School of Business. The other members of the Gibaran Learning Group (Australian Institute of Business Administration, Entrepreneurship Institute Australia and Tourism Institute Australia) were merged with AIB as part of a corporate restructuring exercise.

Academic Year: Student intake in March, June and November.

Admission Requirements: Undergraduate: a qualification deemed equivalent to year 12 under the Australian Qualifications Framework; Postgraduate: relevant undergraduate degree, and/or work experience in some cases; Doctorates: relevant Master's degree and relevant work experience. All candidates whose native language is not English must show proof of English proficiency (undergraduate applicants: TOEFL 550, or 6.0 IELTS, or a credit or better in English in the GCE 'O' or 'A' levels or equivalent; postgraduate and doctoral applicants: TOEFL 575, or 6.5 IELTS). More detailed information available from the institution.

Fees: (Aus Dollars): 17,000 – 48,000. Total fees per course and vary according to whether domestic or overseas students, and distance learning students. Contact institution for more details

Main Language(s) of Instruction: English

Accrediting Agency: Department of Further Education, Employment, Science and Technology, South Australia

Degrees and Diplomas: *Bachelor Honours Degree*: **Business Administration.** *Graduate Certificate/Diploma*: **Business Administration.** *Master Degree*: **Business Administration.** *Doctoral Degree*: **Business and Commerce; Management.** Also Advanced MBA. All degrees offered full time as well as intensive mode.

Student Services: Academic Counselling, Facilities for disabled people, Foreign Studies Centre, Social Counselling

Publications: Gibaran Journal of Applied Management
Last Updated: 21/03/14

AUSTRALIAN INSTITUTE OF MANAGEMENT

Cnr Boundary and Rosa Streets, Spring Hill, Queensland 4000
Tel: +61(7) 3227 4888
Fax: +61(7) 3832 2497
EMail: enquiry@aim.com.au
Website: http://www.aim.com.au

President: Brian Nye

Programme
Management *(Melbourne)* (Management); **Management** (Management); **Management** *(Hindmarsh)* (Business Administration; Management)

History: Created 1949.

Degrees and Diplomas: *Graduate Certificate/Diploma*: **Management.** *Master Degree*: **Business Administration.**

Last Updated: 07/04/14

AUSTRALIAN INSTITUTE OF POLICE MANAGEMENT

PO Box 168, Manley, New South Wales 1655
Tel: +61(2) 9934 4800
Fax: +61(2) 9934 4780
EMail: reception@aipm.gov.au
Website: http://www.aipm.gov.au/

Chair: Tony Negus

Programme
Policing and Emergency Services (Civil Security; Police Studies)

History: Created 1995.

Degrees and Diplomas: *Graduate Certificate/Diploma*: **Civil Security; Police Studies.**

Last Updated: 07/04/14

AUSTRALIAN INTERNATIONAL CONSERVATORIUM OF MUSIC

114 Victoria Road, Rozelle, Sydney, New South Wales 2039
Tel: +61(2) 9555 1666
Fax: +61(2) 8076 7685
EMail: admin@aicm.edu.au
Website: http://www.aicm.edu.au

Programme
Music (Music)

Degrees and Diplomas: *Bachelor Degree*: **Music.** *Graduate Certificate/Diploma*: **Music.** *Master Degree*: **Music.**

Last Updated: 07/04/14

AVONDALE COLLEGE OF HIGHER EDUCATION

PO Box 19, Cooranbong, New South Wales 2265
Tel: +61(2) 4980-2222
EMail: reception@avondale.edu.au
Website: http://www.avondale.edu.au

President: Ray Roennfeldt
EMail: ray.roennfeldt@avondale.edu.au

School
Business (Accountancy; Business Administration; Business and Commerce; Human Resources; Information Technology; Management; Marketing); **Education** (Education; Humanities and Social Science Education; Mathematics Education; Preschool Education; Primary Education; Science Education; Secondary Education); **Humanities and Creative Arts** (Arts and Humanities; Communication Arts; Fine Arts; Theology); **Ministry** (Bible; Religious Studies; Theology); **Nursing** (Midwifery; Nursing); **Science and Mathematics** (Biological and Life Sciences; Chemistry; Food Science; Geography; Information Technology; Mathematics; Nutrition; Physics)

Campus
Sydney

History: Founded 1897 by the Seventh-Day Adventist Church. A self-accrediting authority

Degrees and Diplomas: *Diploma*; *Bachelor Degree*; *Bachelor Honours Degree*; *Graduate Certificate/Diploma*; *Master Degree*; *Doctoral Degree*

Last Updated: 24/03/14

BLUE MOUNTAINS INTERNATIONAL HOTEL MANAGEMENT SCHOOL

540 George Street, Sydney, New South Wales 2780
Tel: +61(2) 9307 4600
EMail: nquiry@bluemountains.edu.au
Website: http://www.bluemountains.edu.au/

Programme
Hotel Management (Business Administration; Hotel Management)

History: Created 1991.

Degrees and Diplomas: *Bachelor Degree*: **Business Administration; Hotel Management.** *Graduate Certificate/Diploma*: **Business Administration; Hotel Management.** *Master Degree*: **Business Administration; Hotel Management.**

Last Updated: 07/04/14

BOND UNIVERSITY

14 University Drive (Off Cottesloe Drive), Robina, Queensland 4226
Tel: +61(7) 5595 1111
EMail: international@bond.edu.au
Website: http://www.bond.edu.au

Vice-Chancellor: Tim Brailsford EMail: vc@bond.edu.au

Faculty
Business (Business Administration; Finance; Multimedia); **Health Sciences and Medicine** (Biomedical Engineering; Forensic Medicine and Dentistry; Health Sciences; Medicine; Physical Therapy; Sports; Sports Management; Surgery); **Humanities and Social Sciences** (Advertising and Publicity; Applied Linguistics; Arts and Humanities; Austronesian and Oceanic Languages; Behavioural Sciences; Communication Studies; Computer Science; Criminology; Film; International Relations; Journalism; Media Studies; Modern Languages; Multimedia; Philosophy; Psychology; Public Relations; Radio and Television Broadcasting; Social Sciences); **Law** (Commercial Law; Criminal Law; E- Business/Commerce; International Law; Law; Public Law)

College
Bond; **Bond University English Language School** *(BUELI)* (English)

Institute
Sustainable Development and Architecture (Architecture; Building Technologies; Constitutional Law; Environmental Management; Environmental Studies; Management; Real Estate; Surveying and Mapping; Town Planning; Urban Studies)

Centre
Applied Research in Learning, Engagement, Andragogy and Pedagogy *(LEAP)* (Educational Sciences; Pedagogy); **Autism Spectrum Disorder** *(CASD)*; **Commercial Law**; **Dispute Resolution** (Family Studies; Peace and Disarmament); **Family Business** (Business and Commerce; Family Studies); **Film, Television and Screen-Based Media**; **Global Trade and Finance**; **Health Informatics** (Computer Science; Health Sciences); **Health, Exercise and Sports Sciences** (Health Sciences; Sports); **Law, Gouvernance and Public Policy**; **Leadership Studies** (Leadership); **Owen Dixon Society**; **Population Health and Neuroimmunology** *(PHANU)* (Media Studies); **Primary Health Care Research, Evaluation and Development (PHCRED) Collaboration**; **Psychology Clinic**; **Technology Innovation** (Technology)

Research Centre
Health, Exercises and Sports Science *(BURCHESS)* (Health Sciences; Sports); **Research in Evidence Based Practice** *(CREBP)*; **Software Assurance** (Software Engineering); **Sustainable Healthy Communities**

History: Founded 1987 by Act of the Queensland Parliament. The first non-profit, privately funded and independent university to be established in Australia. Classes started May 1989.

Academic Year: January to December (January-April; May-August; September-December)

Admission Requirements: Selection on the basis of a combination of academic merit, work experience and references, as well as other factors considered important indicators for success at Bond University. In some cases an interview may be required.

Main Language(s) of Instruction: English

Degrees and Diplomas: *Bachelor Degree*; *Graduate Certificate/ Diploma*; *Master Degree*; *Doctoral Degree*

Student Services: Canteen, Careers Guidance, Facilities for disabled people, Health Services, Social Counselling, Sports Facilities

Last Updated: 21/03/14

BOX HILL INSTITUTE (BHI)

Private Bag 2014, Box Hill, Victoria 3128
Tel: +61(3) 9286-9222
EMail: ceooffice@boxhill.edu.au
Website: http://www.bhtafe.edu.au/

Chief Executive Office: Norman Gray AM
EMail: ceooffice@boxhill.edu.au; norman.gray@boxhill.edu.au

Manager, Higher Education and Learning Partnerships: Christine Hepperle EMail: c.hepperle@boxhill.edu.au

International Relations: Carole Ross, Centre Manager, International Student Services EMail: c.ross@boxhill.edu.au

Centre

Biotechnology and Animal Sciences (Animal Husbandry; Biotechnology; Veterinary Science); **Building and Furniture Studies** (Building Technologies); **Business Programmes** (Business and Commerce); **Creative Industries** (Fashion Design; Music); **Health and Community Services** (Child Care and Development; Preschool Education); **Hospitality and Tourism** (Hotel Management; Tourism); **Information and Communications Technology** (Computer Science; Information Technology)

History: Created 1984 as Box Hill College of Technical and Further Education.

Academic Year: Feb to June; July to Nov

Admission Requirements: Please consult website.

Fees: 13,248 - 16,000 per annum (Australian Dollar)

Main Language(s) of Instruction: English

Accrediting Agency: Tertiary Education Quality Standards Agency; Australian Skills Quality Authority

Degrees and Diplomas: *Bachelor Degree*: **Biotechnology; Business Administration; Business and Commerce; Computer Science; Environmental Studies; Fashion Design; Hotel Management; Information Management; Library Science; Music; Preschool Education.** *Graduate Certificate/Diploma*: **Computer Networks; Literacy Education; Management; Preschool Education.** *Master Degree*: **Business and Commerce; Computer Networks.**

Academic Staff *2013*	**TOTAL**
FULL-TIME	**48**
PART-TIME	**23**
STAFF WITH DOCTORATE	
FULL-TIME	**15**
Student Numbers *2013*	
All (Foreign included)	**4,843**
FOREIGN ONLY	**2144**

Distance students, 186.

Last Updated: 21/03/14

CARNEGIE MELLON UNIVERSITY AUSTRALIA

Torrens Building, 220 Victoria Square,
Adelaide, South Australia 5000
Tel: +61(8) 8110 9900
EMail: info@cmu.edu.au
Website: http://www.australia.cmu.edu/

Programme

Information Technology (Information Technology)

Degrees and Diplomas: *Master Degree*: **Information Technology.**

Last Updated: 07/04/14

CHRISTIAN HERITAGE COLLEGE

PO Box 2246, Mansfield BC, Queensland 4122
Tel: +61(7) 3347 7900
Fax: +61(7) 3347 7911
EMail: enquiries@chc.edu.au
Website: http://www.chc.edu.au/

Acting Chief Executive Officer: Johan Roux
EMail: jroux@chc.edu.au

School

Business (Business Administration; Management); **Education and Humanities** (Education; Preschool Education; Primary Education; Secondary Education); **Ministries** (Christian Religious Studies; Pastoral Studies); **Social Sciences** (Behavioural Sciences; Educational and Student Counselling; Social Sciences)

History: Created 1986

Degrees and Diplomas: *Bachelor Degree*: **Business Administration; Christian Religious Studies; Education; Pastoral Studies.** *Graduate Certificate/Diploma*: **Christian Religious Studies; Education; Management; Pastoral Studies; Social Sciences.** *Master Degree*: **Education; Pastoral Studies; Social Sciences.**

Last Updated: 07/04/14

HOLMES INSTITUTE

185 Spring Street, Melbourne, Victoria 3000
Tel: +61(3) 9662 2055
Fax: +61(3) 9662 2083
EMail: melbourne@holmes.edu.au
Website: http://www.holmes.edu.au/

Programme

Business (Accountancy; Business Administration; Management)

History: Created 1963. Acquired current status 2001.

Degrees and Diplomas: *Bachelor Degree*: **Business Administration.** *Graduate Certificate/Diploma*: **Business Administration.** *Master Degree*: **Accountancy; Business Administration.**

Last Updated: 07/04/14

HOLMESGLEN INSTITUTE

PO Box 42, Holmesglen, Victoria 3148
Tel: +61(3) 9564 1555
EMail: info@holmesglen.edu.au
Website: http://www.holmesglen.edu.au/

Chief Executive Officer: Mary Faraone
EMail: mary.faraone@holmesglen.edu.au

Division

Art and Design (Fashion Design; Graphic Design); **Building and Construction** (Building Technologies; Engineering Management; Surveying and Mapping); **Business and Finance** (Administration; Business Administration; Finance; Management; Marketing); **Community and Health Sciences** (Community Health; Nursing); **Education and Languages** (Preschool Education); **Fitness and Wellbeing** (Leisure Studies; Sports); **Horticulture and Environment** (Landscape Architecture); **Hospitality and Tourism** (Hotel Management; Tourism); **Information Technology** (Information Technology)

History: Created 1982.

Degrees and Diplomas: *Bachelor Degree*: **Business Administration; Engineering Management; Fashion Design; Hotel Management; Nursing; Preschool Education.** *Graduate Certificate/Diploma*: **Business Administration; Engineering Management.**

Last Updated: 07/04/14

INSTITUTE OF CHARTERED ACCOUNTANTS IN AUSTRALIA

33 Erskine Street, Sydney, New South Wales 2000
Tel: +61(2) 9290 1344
Fax: +61(2) 9262 1512
EMail: service@charteredaccountants.com.au
Website: http://www.charteredaccountants.com.au/

Chief Executive Officer: Lee White

Programme

Accountancy (Accountancy)

History: Created 1928.

Degrees and Diplomas: *Graduate Certificate/Diploma*: **Accountancy.**

Last Updated: 08/04/14

INTERNATIONAL COLLEGE OF MANAGEMENT SYDNEY

151 Darley Road, Manley, Sydney, New South Wales 2095
Tel: +61(2) 9977 0555
Fax: +61(2) 9977 0333
EMail: info@icms.edu.au
Website: http://www.icms.edu.au

Managing Director: Frank Prestipino

Programme

Business (Business Administration; Hotel Management; Management; Sports Management; Tourism)

History: Created 1996.

Degrees and Diplomas: *Bachelor Degree*: **Business Administration; Hotel Management; Management; Sports Management.** *Graduate Certificate/Diploma*: **Business Administration.** *Master Degree*: **Hotel Management; International Business; Management; Sports Management.**

Last Updated: 07/04/14

JOHN PAUL II INSTITUTE FOR MARRIAGE AND FAMILY (JPII INST)

278 Victoria Parade, East Melbourne, Victoria 3002
Tel: +61(3) 9417-4349
EMail: info@jp2institute.org
Website: http://www.jp2institute.org/

Director: Peter Elliott

Registrar: Toby Hunter EMail: thunter@jp2institute.org

Programme

Ethics (Ethics); **Philosophy** (Philosophy); **Religion** (Catholic Theology)

History: Created 2001 under the auspices of the Melbourne Archdiocese.

Academic Year: February to November

Admission Requirements: Bachelor's degree

Fees: 875 per subject unit (Australian Dollar)

Main Language(s) of Instruction: English

Accrediting Agency: Victorian Registration and Qualifications Authority

Degrees and Diplomas: *Graduate Certificate/Diploma*: **Ethics; Health Sciences; Theology.** *Master Degree*: **Ethics; Health Sciences; Theology.** *Doctoral Degree*: **Ethics; Health Sciences; Theology.**

Student Services: Social Counselling

Last Updated: 24/03/14

KAPLAN BUSINESS SCHOOL

Level 8, 540 George Street, Sydney, New South Wales 2000
Tel: +61(2) 8248 6758
Fax: +61(2) 8248 6770
EMail: kbs.enquiries@kbs.edu.au
Website: http://www.kbs.edu.au/

Programme

Business Administration (Accountancy; Business Administration)

Degrees and Diplomas: *Bachelor Degree*: **Business Administration.** *Graduate Certificate/Diploma*: **Accountancy; Business Administration.** *Master Degree*: **Accountancy; Business Administration.**

Last Updated: 07/04/14

KING'S OWN INSTITUTE (KOI)

Level 1, 545 Kent Street, Sydney, New South Wales 2000
Tel: +61(2) 9283 3583
Fax: +61(2) 9283 3683
EMail: ask@koi.edu.au
Website: http://koi.edu.au

Chief Executive Officer and Dean: Doug Hinchliffe

Programme

Business Administration (Accountancy; Business Administration; Finance; Management)

Degrees and Diplomas: *Bachelor Degree*: **Accountancy; Business Administration; Finance.** *Graduate Certificate/Diploma*: **Business Administration.** *Master Degree*: **Accountancy.**

Last Updated: 07/04/14

LE CORDON BLEU AUSTRALIA

Days Road, Regency Park, South Australia 5010
Tel: +61(8) 8348 3000
Fax: +61(8) 8346 3755
EMail: australia@cordonbleu.edu
Website: http://www.lecordonbleu.com.au/

President: André J. Cointreau

Programme

Hotel Management (Cooking and Catering; Hotel and Restaurant; Hotel Management; Tourism)

Degrees and Diplomas: *Bachelor Degree*: **Hotel and Restaurant; Hotel Management.** *Master Degree*: **Hotel and Restaurant; Hotel Management.**

Last Updated: 08/04/14

LEO CUSSEN CENTRE FOR LAW

360 Little Bourke Street, Melbourne, Victoria 3000
Tel: +61(3) 9602 3111
Fax: +61(3) 9670 3242
Website: http://www.leocussen.vic.edu.au/

Executive Director: Elizabeth Loftus
EMail: eloftus@leocussen.vic.edu.au

Programme

Law (Law)

History: Created 1972.

Degrees and Diplomas: *Graduate Certificate/Diploma*: **Law.**

Last Updated: 08/04/14

MARCUS OLDHAM COLLEGE

Private Bag 116, Mail Centre, Geelong, Victoria 3221
Tel: +61(3) 5243-3533
Fax: +61(3) 5244-1263
Website: http://www.marcusoldham.vic.edu.au

Principal: Simon Livingstone
EMail: livingstone@marcusoldham.vic.edu.au

Programme

Agribusiness (Agricultural Business; Agricultural Management); **Horse Business Management** (Agricultural Business; Agricultural Management; Animal Husbandry)

History: Founded 1961.

Degrees and Diplomas: *Advanced Diploma*; *Associate Degree*; *Diploma*; *Bachelor Degree*: **Agricultural Business; Farm Management.** *Graduate Certificate/Diploma*: **Agricultural Business.**

Last Updated: 15/11/13

MAYFIELD EDUCATION

2-10 Camberwell Road, Hawthorn, East Victoria 3123
Tel: +61(3) 9882 7644
Fax: +61(3) 9882 7518
Website: http://www.mayfield.edu.au/

Chief Executive Officer: Mavis E. Smith
EMail: msmith@mayfield.edu.au

Programme
Diabetes Education and Health Care (Dietetics; Nutrition; Public Health)
Degrees and Diplomas: *Graduate Certificate/Diploma*: **Dietetics; Nutrition; Public Health.**
Last Updated: 07/04/14

MELBOURNE INSTITUTE OF TECHNOLOGY

388-392 Lonsdale Street, Melbourne, Victoria 3000
Tel: +61(3) 8600 6700
Fax: +61(3) 8600 6761
EMail: enquiries@mit.edu.au
Website: http://www.mit.edu.au/

Chief Executive Officer: Shesh Ghale

School
Business (Accountancy; Business and Commerce); **Information Technology and Engineering** (Computer Networks; Telecommunications Engineering)
Further Information: Campus also in Sydney.
History: Created 1996.
Degrees and Diplomas: *Bachelor Degree*: **Business and Commerce; Computer Networks; Telecommunications Engineering.** *Graduate Certificate/Diploma*: **Accountancy; Computer Networks; Telecommunications Engineering.** *Master Degree*: **Accountancy; Computer Networks; Telecommunications Engineering.**
Last Updated: 08/04/14

MIECAT - MELBOURNE INSTITUTE FOR EXPERIENTIAL AND CREATIVE ARTS THERAPY

15-17 Victoria Street, Fitzroy, Victoria 3065
Tel: +61(3) 9486 9081
Website: http://www.miecat.org.au/

Director: Jan Allen

Programme
Experiential and Creative Arts Practice (Art Therapy; Fine Arts)
History: Created 1997.
Degrees and Diplomas: *Graduate Certificate/Diploma*: **Art Therapy; Fine Arts.** *Master Degree*: **Art Therapy; Fine Arts.** *Doctoral Degree*: **Art Therapy; Fine Arts.** Professional Doctorate
Last Updated: 07/04/14

MONTESSORI WORLD EDUCATIONAL INSTITUTE, AUSTRALIA

Unit 3/20 Comserv Loop, Ellenbrook, Western Australia 6069
Tel: +61(8) 6296 7900
Fax: +61(8) 6296 7911
EMail: info@mwei.edu.au
Website: http://www.mwei.edu.au/

National Director: Rachael Stevens

Programme
Education (Education; Preschool Education; Primary Education)
Degrees and Diplomas: *Graduate Certificate/Diploma*: **Education; Preschool Education; Primary Education.**
Last Updated: 08/04/14

NAN TIEN INSTITUTE

180 Berkeley Road, Berkeley, New South Wales 2506
Tel: +61(2) 4272 0648
Fax: +61(2) 4271 7862
EMail: info@nantien.edu.au
Website: http://www.nantien.edu.au/

President: Grier Lin EMail: grier.lin@nantien.edu.au

Programme
Applied Buddhist Studies (Esoteric Practices; Philosophy); **Health and Social Wellbeing** (Community Health; Social Welfare)
History: Created 2009. Graduated first cohort in 2012. A secular tertiary Institute, providing a range of courses designed to educate non-Buddhists, and the world's growing Buddhist community. It caters for those interested in subjects that are connected to Buddhist values and culture, and whose careers link them with Buddhist philosophy, culture, practices and international relations.
Degrees and Diplomas: *Graduate Certificate/Diploma*: **Esoteric Practices.** *Master Degree*: **Esoteric Practices.**
Last Updated: 08/04/14

NATIONAL ART SCHOOL

Forbes Street, Darlinghurst, New South Wales 2010
Tel: +61(2) 9339 8744
Fax: +61(2) 9339 8740
EMail: enquiries@nas.edu.au
Website: http://www.nas.edu.au/

Chair: Nicholas Johnson

Programme
Fine Art (Art History; Ceramic Art; Fine Arts; Painting and Drawing; Photography; Printing and Printmaking; Sculpture)
History: Created 1926. First bachelor's degrees accredited 1998, and honours and master's degrees in 2001.
Degrees and Diplomas: *Bachelor Degree*: **Fine Arts.** *Bachelor Honours Degree*: **Fine Arts.** *Master Degree*: **Fine Arts.**
Last Updated: 08/04/14

NATIONAL INSTITUTE OF DRAMATIC ART (NIDA)

215 Anzac Parade, Kensington, New South Wales 2033
Tel: +61(2) 9697 7600
Fax: +61(2) 9662 7415
EMail: info@nida.edu.au
Website: http://www.nida.edu.au/

Director, Chief Executive Officer: Lynne Williams

Programme
Dramatic Art (Acting; Display and Stage Design; Theatre)
History: Created 1959.
Degrees and Diplomas: *Bachelor Degree*: **Acting; Display and Stage Design; Theatre.** *Master Degree*: **Acting; Theatre.**
Last Updated: 08/04/14

NEW SOUTH WALES INSTITUTE OF PSYCHIATRY

Locked Bag 7118, Parramatta BC, New South Wales 2124
Tel: +61(2) 9840 3833
Fax: +61(2) 9840 3838
EMail: institute@nswiop.nsw.edu.au
Website: http://www.nswiop.nsw.edu.au/

Programme
Psychiatry (Psychiatry and Mental Health; Psychology; Psychotherapy)
Degrees and Diplomas: *Graduate Certificate/Diploma*: **Psychiatry and Mental Health.** *Master Degree*: **Psychiatry and Mental Health.**
Last Updated: 08/04/14

OASES GRADUATE SCHOOL

2 Minona Street, Hawthorn, Victoria 3122
Tel: +61(3) 9819 3502
EMail: info@oases.edu.au
Website: http://www.oases.edu.au/

Chair of Academic Council: Chris Lloyd
EMail: chris.lloyd@oases.edu.au

Programme
Sustainability and Social Change (Ecology; Environmental Studies)
Degrees and Diplomas: *Graduate Certificate/Diploma*: **Ecology; Environmental Studies.** *Master Degree*: **Ecology; Environmental Studies.**
Last Updated: 08/04/14

RAFFLES COLLEGE OF DESIGN AND COMMERCE

Level 18, 99 Mount Street, Syndey, New South Wales 2060
Tel: +61(2) 9922-4278
Fax: +61(2) 9922-7862
EMail: contact@raffles.edu.au
Website: http://www.raffles.edu.au/

CEO: Isaac Ng

Programme
Accountancy (Accountancy); **Arts** (Art Management; Computer Graphics; Multimedia; Photography; Visual Arts); **Commerce** (Finance; Management; Marketing); **Design** (Design; Fashion Design; Graphic Design; Interior Design)
History: Created 2005.
Degrees and Diplomas: *Associate Degree*; *Bachelor Degree*; *Graduate Certificate/Diploma*; *Master Degree*
Last Updated: 21/03/14

S P JAIN SCHOOL OF GLOBAL MANAGEMENT

5 FigTree Drive, Sydney Olympic Park,
Sydney, New South Wales 2127
Tel: +61(2) 8970 6800
Fax: +61(2) 8970 6820
EMail: gmbasydney@spjain.org
Website: http://www.spjain.org/

President and Director: Nitish Jain

Programme
Business Administration (Business Administration)
Further Information: Campuses also in Singapore, Dubai, and Mumbai (India)
History: Createdd 2012.
Degrees and Diplomas: *Bachelor Degree*: **Business Administration.** *Master Degree*: **Business Administration.**
Last Updated: 08/04/14

SYDNEY COLLEGE OF DIVINITY

Unit 6B, 5 Talavera Rd, North Ryde, New South Wales 2113
Tel: +61(2) 9889 1969
Fax: +61(2) 9889 2281
Website: http://scd.edu.au/

Dean, Chief Executive Officer: Diane Speed
EMail: dianes@scd.edu.au

Programme
Theology (Bible; Christian Religious Studies; Religious Studies; Theology)
History: Created 1983.
Degrees and Diplomas: *Bachelor Degree*: **Theology.** *Bachelor Honours Degree*: **Theology.** *Graduate Certificate/Diploma*: **Theology.** *Master Degree*: **Theology.** *Doctoral Degree*: **Theology.**
Last Updated: 08/04/14

TAFE NSW HIGHER EDUCATION

Level 2, 35 Bridge Street, Sydney, New South Wales 2001
Tel: +61(2) 9217 3797
EMail: si.internationalstudents@tafensw.edu.au
Website: http://www.highered.tafensw.edu.au/

Chair, Governing Council: Mark Wainwright

Programme
Postgraduate (Leadership); **Undergraduate** (Child Care and Development; Computer Graphics; Computer Networks; Finance; Interior Design; Preschool Education)
Degrees and Diplomas: *Bachelor Degree*: **Child Care and Development; Computer Graphics; Computer Networks; Interior Design; Preschool Education.** *Graduate Certificate/Diploma*: **Leadership.**
Last Updated: 08/04/14

THE AUSTRALIAN COLLEGE OF PHYSICAL EDUCATION

1 Figtree Drive, Sydney Olympic Park, New South Wales 2127
Tel: +61(2) 8263-1888
Fax: +61(2) 9267-0531
Website: http://www.acpe.edu.au/

Dean and Head of College: Brian Nook

Programme
Postgraduate (Leisure Studies; Physical Education; Sports; Sports Management); **Undergraduate** (Leisure Studies; Physical Education; Sports; Sports Management)
Degrees and Diplomas: *Bachelor Degree*: **Physical Education; Sports; Sports Management.** *Graduate Certificate/Diploma*: **Physical Education; Sports; Sports Management.**
Last Updated: 28/03/14

THE AUSTRALIAN INSTITUTE OF MUSIC

1-55 Foveaux Street, Surry Hills, New South Wales 2010
Tel: +61(2) 9219 5444
EMail: enquiries@aim.edu.au
Website: http://www.aim.edu.au/

Executive Dean: Ian Bofinger

Programme
Music (Art Management; Music)
Further Information: Campus also in Melbourne.
History: Created 1968.
Degrees and Diplomas: *Bachelor Degree*: **Music.** *Graduate Certificate/Diploma*: **Music.** *Master Degree*: **Music.**
Last Updated: 08/04/14

THE CAIRNMILLAR INSTITUTE SCHOOL OF PSYCHOLOGY COUNSELLING AND PSYCHOTHERAPY

993 Burke Road, Camberwell, Victoria 3124
Tel: +61(03) 9813 3400
Fax: +61(03) 9882 9764
Website: http://www.cairnmillar.edu.au/

Executive Director: Francis Macnab

Programme
Psychology and Psychotherapy (Clinical Psychology; Psychology; Psychotherapy)
History: Created 1961.
Degrees and Diplomas: *Graduate Certificate/Diploma*: **Psychology; Psychotherapy.** *Master Degree*: **Psychology; Psychotherapy.**
Last Updated: 08/04/14

THE COLLEGE OF LAW

2 Chandos Street, St Leonards, New South Wales 2065
Tel: +61(2) 9965 7000
Fax: +61(2) 9436 1265
Website: http://www.collaw.edu.au/

Chair, Board of Governors: Joseph Catanzariti

Programme
Law
History: Created 1973.
Degrees and Diplomas: *Graduate Certificate/Diploma*: **Law.** *Master Degree*: **Law.**
Last Updated: 08/04/14

THE INSTITUTE OF INTERNAL AUDITORS IN AUSTRALIA

Level 7, 133 Castlereagh Street, Sydney, New South Wales 2000
Tel: +61(2) 9267 9155
Fax: +61(2) 9264 9240
EMail: enquiry@iia.org.au
Website: http://www.iia.org.au/

President: Stephen Horne

Programme
Internal Auditing (Accountancy)

History: Created 1952. Became a national institute in 1986.

Degrees and Diplomas: *Graduate Certificate/Diploma*: **Accountancy.**
Last Updated: 08/04/14

THE UNIVERSITY OF NOTRE DAME AUSTRALIA

19 Mouat Street, Fremantle, Western Australia 6959
Tel: +61(8) 9433-0555
Fax: +61(8) 9433-0544
EMail: international@nd.edu.au; fremantle.reception@nd.edu.au
Website: http://www.nd.edu.au

Vice-Chancellor: Celia Hammond EMail: VC@nd.edu.au

School
Arts and Sciences (Advertising and Publicity; Archaeology; Behavioural Sciences; Biology; Business Administration; Communication Arts; English; Environmental Studies; Geography; Greek; History; Human Resources; International Relations; Italian; Journalism; Marketing; Mathematics; Media Studies; Modern Languages; Political Sciences; Public Relations; Theatre); **Business** (Accountancy; Business Administration; Human Resources; Management; Marketing); **Education** (Education; Higher Education Teacher Training; Preschool Education; Primary Education; Secondary Education); **Health Sciences** (Health Education; Physical Education; Sports); **Law** (Law); **Medicine** (Medicine); **Nursing** (Midwifery; Nursing); **Philosophy and Theology** (Pastoral Studies; Philosophy; Religious Education; Theology); **Physiotherapy** (Physical Therapy)

Further Information: Campuses also in Sydney and Broome.

History: Founded 1990. A private institution established under its own Act of Parliament. In the process of development, as a Catholic university.

Academic Year: February to November

Admission Requirements: Secondary school certificate with matriculation or recognized foreign equivalent. Direct entrance to second year on completion of studies in another tertiary institution

Fees: 18,000 per annum (Australian Dollar)

Main Language(s) of Instruction: English

Degrees and Diplomas: *Bachelor Degree*; *Bachelor Honours Degree*; *Graduate Certificate/Diploma*; *Master Degree*; *Doctoral Degree*

Student Services: Academic Counselling, Canteen, Careers Guidance, Cultural Activities, Facilities for disabled people, Foreign Studies Centre, Health Services, Language Laboratory, Social Counselling, Sports Facilities
Last Updated: 27/03/14

THINK: COLLEGES

Level 3, 80 Pacific Highway, North Sydney, New South Wales 2060
Tel: +61(2) 9955 1122
Fax: +61(2) 9957 1811
EMail: enquiries@think.edu.au
Website: http://www.think.edu.au/

Chief Executive Officer: Linda Brown

Programme
Business (Human Resources; Marketing; Retailing and Wholesaling; Tourism); **Counselling** (Psychotherapy); **Design** (Communication Arts; Design; Graphic Design; Multimedia); **Health Sciences** (Alternative Medicine; Traditional Eastern Medicine)

Degrees and Diplomas: *Bachelor Degree*: **Business and Commerce; Design; Health Sciences; Psychotherapy.** *Graduate Certificate/Diploma*: **Psychotherapy.** *Master Degree*: **Psychotherapy.**
Last Updated: 08/04/14

TOP EDUCATION INSTITUTE

Administration Office, 1 Central Avenue, Australian Technology Park, Eveleigh, New South Wales 2015
Tel: +61(2) 9209 488
Fax: +61(2) 9209 4887
EMail: info@top.edu.au
Website: http://www.top.edu.au/

Principal: Minshen Zhu

Programme
Business Administration (Accountancy; Business Administration; International Business; Marketing; Public Relations); **Law** (Law)

History: Created 2012.

Degrees and Diplomas: *Bachelor Degree*: **International Business; Law.** *Graduate Certificate/Diploma*: **Accountancy; Management; Marketing; Public Relations.** *Master Degree*: **Accountancy; International Business; Marketing; Public Relations.**
Last Updated: 08/04/14

TORRENS UNIVERSITY AUSTRALIA

GPO Box 2025, Adelaide, South Australia 5001
Tel: +61(8) 8113 7888
Website: http://www.tua.edu.au/

Vice-Chancellor and President: Fred McDougall

Programme
Business Administration (Business Administration; Business and Commerce); **Education** (Education; Literacy Education; Preschool Education); **Global Project Management** (Management); **Public Health** (Public Health)

History: Created 2012.

Degrees and Diplomas: *Bachelor Degree*: **Business and Commerce.** *Graduate Certificate/Diploma*: **Business Administration; Management; Public Health.** *Master Degree*: **Business Administration; Literacy Education; Management; Preschool Education; Public Health.**
Last Updated: 08/04/14

UNIVERSAL BUSINESS SCHOOL

Tower 2, 1 Lawson Square, Redfern, Sydney, NSW 2016
Tel: +61(2) 1300 422 422
Fax: +61(2) 9310-1548
Website: http://www.ubss.edu.au

Dean: Angus Hook

Programme
Business (Accountancy; Business Administration)

Degrees and Diplomas: *Bachelor Degree*: **Business Administration.** *Graduate Certificate/Diploma*: **Business Administration.** *Master Degree*: **Business Administration.**
Last Updated: 15/02/16

UNIVERSITY OF DIVINITY

21 Highbury Grove, Kew, Victoria 3101
Tel: +61(3) 9853 3177
Fax: +61(3) 9853 6695
EMail: enquiries@divinity.edu.au
Website: http://www.divinity.edu.au/

Vice-Chancellor: Peter Sherlock EMail: vc@divinity.edu.au

Programme
Religion (Christian Religious Studies; Pastoral Studies; Religion; Religious Studies); **Religious Education** (Religious Education); **Theology** (Theology)

History: Created 1910 as Melbourne College of Divinity. Acquired current status and title 2012.

Degrees and Diplomas: *Bachelor Degree*: **Pastoral Studies; Theology.** *Graduate Certificate/Diploma*: **Religious Education.** *Master Degree*: **Religious Education; Theology.** *Doctoral Degree*: **Philosophy; Theology.**
Last Updated: 07/04/14

WESLEY INSTITUTE

PO Box 534, Drummoyne, New South Wales 1470
Tel: +61(2) 9819 8888
Website: http://www.wi.edu.au/

Chair: Phillip Cave

Programme

Counselling (Educational and Student Counselling; Psychology); **Education** (Education; Primary Education; Religious Education; Secondary Education); **Graphic Design** (Graphic Design); **Performing Arts** (Acting; Dance; Music; Theatre)

Degrees and Diplomas: *Bachelor Degree*: **Design; Performing Arts; Theology.** *Graduate Certificate/Diploma*: **Education; Religious Education; Secondary Education.** *Master Degree*: **Education; Educational and Student Counselling; Music; Primary Education; Religious Education; Theology.**

Last Updated: 08/04/14

WHITEHOUSE INSTITUTE OF DESIGN

2 Short Street, Surry Hills, New South Wales 2010
Tel: +61(2) 9267 8799
Fax: +61(2) 9267 6947
EMail: enquiry@whitehouse-design.edu.au
Website: http://whitehouse-design.edu.au/

Chief Executive Officer: Ian Tudor

Programme

Design (Design; Fashion Design; Interior Design)

History: Created 1988.

Degrees and Diplomas: *Bachelor Degree*: **Design; Fashion Design.** *Graduate Certificate/Diploma*: **Design.** *Master Degree*: **Design.**

Last Updated: 08/04/14

Austria

STRUCTURE OF HIGHER EDUCATION SYSTEM

Description:

Higher education: Various educational paths are open to students after completion of their secondary education, that is, after passing the Reifeprüfung (upper secondary school leaving examination); or after passing the Studienberechtigungsprüfung (the university entrance examination); or the Berufsreifeprüfung (external upper secondary school leaving examination). Higher education is provided by public universities, universities of applied sciences (Fachhochschulen, introduced in 1994), private universities (introduced in 2000), university colleges of education (Pädagogische Hochschulen), and Schools of Theology under the auspices of the Catholic Church. There are also Academies (e.g. Medical-Technical Colleges). Study programmes lead to the following degrees: Degree programmes: - Diploma (after 8-12 semesters), or, respectively Diploma (FH) (after 8-10 semesters); - Bachelor (6-8 semesters); - Master (2-4 semesters after the bachelor); - Doctor (6 semesters after the master or diploma degree), only at public and private universities.

Further education programmes: Certificate ("Akademische/r ..."); Master.

The 2002 University Reform redefined the relationship between universities and the State. Universities remain State institutions, and the State continues to finance them. Universities are, however, fully autonomous in terms of their statutes, internal affairs and curricula. The law provides for the establishment of a university board (Universitätsrat) at each institution which comprises leading figures from public life and the private sector. It is also responsible for providing the Federal Minister of Science and Research with expert opinion on issues of the given university and launching evaluation measures. The University Assembly elects the rector. The Ministry assumes a supervisory function only in legal affairs and continues to be responsible for strategic planning and research. The law establishes which groups of degree programmes may be introduced at universities and lays down general rules concerning admissions and the award of academic degrees. In 1999, the University Accreditation Act was enacted which allows private institutions to obtain accreditation as a private university by the Accreditation Council which works under the supervision of the Ministry. At private universities, study programmes can be offered either in accordance with state programmes and degrees, or without reference to them.

Stages of studies:

University level first stage: *Bachelor*

Bachelor programmes are offered by public universities, universities of applied sciences, private universities and university colleges of education. Access to Bachelor programmes is normally based on the Reifeprüfung Certificate. Bachelor programmes last for 3-4 years and end with a Bachelor examination (Bachelorprüfung). They lead to the academic degree of Bachelor. The former diploma programmes, however, can be continued instead of Bachelor and Master programmes.

University level second stage: *Master*

Master programmes are offered by public universities, universities of applied sciences and private universities. Access to Master programmes is based on completion of a relevant Bachelor programme. Master programmes last for 1-2 years and require a master thesis and end with a Master examination (Masterprüfung). They lead to the academic degree of Master, in Engineering to the Diplom Ingenieur/Diplom Ingenieurin.

University level third stage: *Doktorat*

Doctoral studies, which are offered only by universities, generally require a minimum of 6 semesters. Access is based on completion of a relevant Master programme at a university, university of applied sciences or private university. Doctoral programmes demand greater independence of students in their scientific work. Doctoral candidates are required to present a thesis approved by at least two professors and an examining Commission, and pass the final oral examination (Rigorosum). They can be Doctor or PhD programmes; the latter are subdivided into a more study-oriented and a purely scientific stages.

University level fourth stage: *Habilitation*
The Habilitation is acquired within the university system and is based on special research achievements after the Doctorate and production of a research monograph. It is awarded with the title Universitätsdozent/in or Privatsdozent/in, respectively. This is not an academic degree, but a special university qualification. It is often, but not necessarily, a prerequisite to be appointed professor at a university.

ADMISSION TO HIGHER EDUCATION

Admission to university-level studies:
Name of secondary school credential required: Reifeprüfung/Reife- und Diplomprüfung

Minimum score/requirement: 4

For entry to: All higher education institutions (public universities, universities of applied sciences, private universities, university colleges of teacher education).

Alternatives to credentials: Studienberechtigungsprüfung: examination giving access to higher education to Austrian nationals who are over 22 years of age and do not possess a Reifezeugnis, but who have a professional or non-professional experience. It is valid only for those fields of study for which it has been taken. Relevant professional qualification in combination with certain additional examinations in subjects of general education.

Numerus clausus: At universities in some fields of study (e.g. Medicine, artistic programmes); at universities of applied sciences, most private universities and all university colleges of education.

Other requirements: Besondere Universitätsreife (special university entrance qualification) additional qualifications specific to the requirements of a given study programme in addition to Reifeprüfung in the country of its origin (this does not apply to EU citizens)

Foreign students admission:
Definition of foreign student: A person who does not have Austrian citizenship. Foreign nationals who enjoy equal status with Austrian nationals are: EU citizens, children of diplomats, refugees and some other groups.

Quotas: The prerequisite is that there are sufficient places available for foreign students. EU and EEA citizens are admitted regardless of the number of places available.

Admission requirements: Foreign students are admitted to study courses at university if their qualifications are equivalent to the "Matura" (Reifezeugnis) and qualify them for entry to a university in their own country. They also must give evidence that a higher education institution in the awarding country would accept them immediately for university studies in the respective field. This does not apply to EC citizens.

Language proficiency: Good knowledge of German is essential. In case of doubt, students must pass the compulsory German language examination (both written and oral) at the university before registering as full-time students. German language study facilities are available in all university towns and at a number of language schools. For students from the Near East, special courses are also conducted by the Hammer-Purgstall Society.

RECOGNITION OF STUDIES

Quality assurance system:
Since March 2012, a single agency is responsible for external quality assurance in the HE sector (Public Universities, Universities of Applied Sciences, Private Universities). It replaced the Österreichischer Akkreditierungsrat, Fachhochschulrat, and Österreichische Qualitätssicherungsagentur.

Bodies dealing with recognition:

ENIC NARIC AUSTRIA
Head: Heinz Kasparovsky
Deputy: Ingrid Wadsack-Köchl

Abteilung III/7
Teinfaltstrasse 8
Wien 1014
Tel: +43(1) 53120 5921
Fax: +43(1) 53120 7890
EMail: naric@bmwf.gv.at
WWW: http://wissenschaft.bmwfw.gv.at/bmwfw/studium/academic-mobility/enic-naric-austria

Special provisions for recognition:

Recognition for university level studies: Higher education entrance qualifications are declared equivalent according to international agreements, such as the Lisbon Recognition Convention or bilateral agreements with certain European countries.

For access to advanced studies and research: This is decided by the receiving higher education institution; in some cases multilateral or bilateral agreements will apply.

For exercising a profession: Regulated professions: either professional recognition on the basis of the Directive on the recognition of professional qualifications, 2005/36/EC, or, if this is not applicable, nostrification by a higher education institution.
Non-regulated professions: no formal recognition; decision lies with the employer. In any case, the Federal Ministry for Science and Research (ENIC NARIC AUSTRIA) provides advice to employers or public authorities as well as assessments of diplomas in single cases.

NATIONAL BODIES

Bundesministerium für Wissenschaft, Forschung und Wirtschaft – BMWFW (Federal Ministry of Science, Research and Economy)

Minister: Reinhold Mitterlehner
Minoritenplatz 5
Vienna 1014
Tel: +43(1) 531200
EMail: ministerium@bmwf.gv.at; infoservice@bmwf.gv.at
WWW: http://www.bmwf.gv.at
Role of national body: Central authority which is politically responsible for higher education and research.

Bundesministerium für Bildung und Frauen (Federal Ministry for Education and Women)

Minister: Gabriele Heinisch-Hosek
Minoritenplatz 5
Wien 1014
Tel: +43(1) 53 120-0
Fax: +43(1) 53 120-3099
EMail: ministerium@bmukk.gv.at; redaktion@bmukk.gv.at
WWW: http://www.bmukk.gv.at
Role of national body: Central authority which is politically responsible for school education.

Agentur für Qualitätssicherung und Akkreditierung Austria - AQ (Agency for Quality Assurance and Accreditation Austria)

President: Anke Hanft
Managing Director: Achim Hopbach
Renngasse 5
Wien 1010
Tel: +43(1) 532 0220-0
EMail: office@aq.ac.at
WWW: http://www.aq.ac.at
Role of national body: A single agency created in 2012 responsible for external quality assurance in the HE sector (Public Universities, Universities of Applied Sciences, Private Universities). It replaced the Österreichischer Akkreditierungsrat, Fachhochschulrat, and Österreichische Qualitätssicherungsagentur

Österreichische Austauschdienst GmbH – OeAD GmbH (Austrian Agency for International Cooperation in Education and Research)

Chair: Elmar Pichl
Ebendorferstraße 7
Wien 1010
Tel: +43(1) 53408-0
Fax: +43(1) 53408-999
EMail: info@oead.at
WWW: http://www.oead.ac.at
Role of national body: Limited Society for all kinds of foreign exchange of students and scholars, acting on the operational level unter the authority of the relevant Ministries.

Österreichische Fachhochschul-Konferenz - FHK (Association of Universities of Applied Sciences)

President: Helmut Holzinger
Secretary-General: Kurt Koleznik
Bösendorferstraße 4/11
Vienna 1010
Tel: +43(1) 890 6345 10
EMail: office@fhk.ac.at
WWW: http://www.fhk.ac.at
Role of national body: Umbrella organization for universities of applied sciences at national level

Österreichische Privatuniversitäten Konferenz – ÖPUK (Austrian Private University Conference)

President: Karl Wöber
WWW: http://www.privatuniversitaeten.at
Role of national body: Umbrella organization for private universities at national level.

Österreichische Universitätenkonferenz - UNIKO (Universities Austria)

President: Sonja Hammerschmid
Secretary-General: Elisabeth Fiorioli
Floragasse 7/7
Wien 1040
Tel: +43(1) 310 5656-0
Fax: +43(1) 310 5656-22
EMail: office@uniko.ac.at
WWW: http://www.uniko.ac.at
Role of national body: Umbrella organization for public universities at national level.

Data for academic year: 2014-2015
Source: IAU from ENIC NARIC AUSTRIA, BMWFW, 2015. Bodies 2016.

INSTITUTIONS

PUBLIC INSTITUTIONS

ACADEMY OF FINE ARTS VIENNA

Akademie der bildenden Künste Wien (BIKU)

Schillerplatz 3, 1010 Wien, Vienna
Tel: +43(1) 588-160
Fax: +43(1) 588-16-1898
EMail: info@akbild.ac.at
Website: http://www.akbild.ac.at

Rector: Eva Blimlinger (2011-)
Tel: +43(1) 58816-1000 EMail: rektorin@akbild.ac.at

International Relations: Gabriele Reinharter-Schrammel
Tel: +43(1) 588-16-2100 EMail: international@akbild.ac.at

Institute
Art and Architecture (Architecture; Arts and Humanities); **Art Theory and Cultural Studies** (Arts and Humanities; Cultural Studies); **Conservation and Restoration** (Restoration of Works of Art); **Education in the Arts** (Art Education); **Fine Arts** (Fine Arts); **Natural Sciences and Technologies in Art** (Natural Sciences; Technology)

History: Founded 1696, acquired present status 2004.

Academic Year: October to June (October-February; March-June)

Admission Requirements: Entrance examination

Fees: 363,36 per semester for students from Austria or other EU or EEA member states; students from other countries, 726,72 per semester (Euro)

Main Language(s) of Instruction: German

Degrees and Diplomas: *Bachelor's Degree*: **Architecture; Fine Arts.** *Master's Degree*: **Architecture; Fine Arts.** *Doctor of Philosophy*: **Cultural Studies; Fine Arts; Natural Sciences; Technology.** Also Diploma in Scenography

Student Services: Canteen, Nursery Care

Last Updated: 17/04/15

DANUBE UNIVERSITY KREMS

Donau-Universität Krems (DUK)

Dr.-Karl-Dorrek-Strasse 30, 3500 Krems, Lower Austria

Tel: +43(2732) 893-6000

Fax: +43(2732) 893-4000

EMail: info@donau-uni.ac.at

Website: http://www.donau-uni.ac.at

Rector: Friedrich Faulhammer (2013)
Tel: +43(2732) 893-2210
EMail: friedrich.faulhammer@donau-uni.ac.at

Study Director: Vera Ehgartner (2012-)
Tel: +43(2732) 893-2280 EMail: vera.ehgartner@donau-uni.ac.at

International Relations: Sabina Ertl
Tel: +43(2732) 893-2216 EMail: sabina.ertl@donau-uni.ac.at

Faculty

Business and Globalization (Banking; Commercial Law; Communication Studies; Economics; European Union Law; Finance; Information Sciences; Information Technology; Journalism; Law; Management; Media Studies; Political Sciences; Public Administration); **Education, Arts and Architecture** (Architecture; Cultural Studies; Education; Educational Administration; Educational Technology; Engineering; Film; Media Studies; Multimedia; Music; Real Estate; Safety Engineering); **Health and Medicine** (Biomedicine; Biotechnology; Clinical Psychology; Dentistry; Epidemiology; Health Sciences; Medicine; Neurosciences; Psychotherapy; Social and Preventive Medicine)

History: Founded 1994. The first University in Austria offering only postgraduate and continuing education programmes. A special cost-splitting model reinforces the autonomous character of the University. The Austrian Federal Government assumes the basic costs of personnel, investments and running operations. Province of Lower Austria has planned facilities at its disposal and is responsible for maintaining them. The University is run along the guidelines of a private enterprise.

Academic Year: October to July (October-February; February-July)

Admission Requirements: University degree and professional experience, and/or equivalent professional experience

Main Language(s) of Instruction: German, English

Accrediting Agency: Foundation for International Business Administration Accreditation

Degrees and Diplomas: *Master's Degree*: **Banking; Business Administration; European Studies; Finance; Fine Arts; Law; Natural Sciences; Public Administration.**

Student Services: Academic Counselling, Canteen, Cultural Activities, Facilities for disabled people, Nursery Care, Social Counselling, Sports Facilities

Academic Staff *2013*	MEN	WOMEN	**TOTAL**
FULL-TIME	203	383	**586**
Student Numbers *2014-2015*			
All (Foreign included)	–	–	**8,641**

Last Updated: 16/04/15

FERDINAND PORSCHE FERNFH

Lothringerstrasse 4-8, 1040 Wien, Wien

Tel: +43(1) 505-77-78

Fax: +43(1) 505-32-28

EMail: office@fernfh.ac.at

Website: http://www.fernfh.ac.at/

Managing Director: Axel Jungwirth
Tel: +43(1) 505-77-78-48 EMail: axel.jungwirth@fernfh.ac.at

Area

Aging serving Management (Management); **Business computer science** (Business and Commerce; Computer Science); **Industrial and Organizational Psychology** (Industrial and Organizational Psychology; Psychology)

History: Founded 2006.

Admission Requirements: Secondary school certificate (Reifezeugnis) and cover letter

Fees: 363,36 per semester (Euro)

Main Language(s) of Instruction: German

Degrees and Diplomas: *Bachelor's Degree*: **Business and Commerce; Computer Science; Industrial and Organizational Psychology; Management.** *Master's Degree*: **Business and Commerce; Computer Science; Industrial and Organizational Psychology.** For Master and Bachelor programmes, a semester consists of three attendance phases (on Friday and Saturday) and two distance learning phases.

Last Updated: 21/04/15

GRAZ UNIVERSITY OF TECHNOLOGY

Technische Universität Graz (TU GRAZ)

Rechbauerstrasse 12, 8010 Graz, Styria

Tel: +43(316) 873-0

Fax: +43(316) 873-6562

EMail: info@TUGraz.at

Website: http://www.tugraz.at/

Rektor: Harald Kainz (2011-2015)
Tel: +43(316) 873-6000 EMail: rektor@tugraz.at

Head of Rectorate's Office: Ursula Tomantschger-Stessl
Tel: +43(664) 60-873-6061
EMail: ursula.tomantschger-stessl@tugraz.at

International Relations: Sabine Prem, Director of the International Office Tel: +43(316) 873-6417 EMail: sabine.prem@tugraz.at

Faculty

Architecture (Architecture); **Civil Engineering** (Civil Engineering; Economics; Geophysics); **Computer Science and Biomedical Engineering** (Biomedical Engineering; Computer Graphics; Computer Science); **Electrical Engineering and Information Technology** (Electrical Engineering; Information Technology); **Mathematics, Physics and Geodesy** (Geophysics; Mathematics; Physical Engineering); **Mechanical Engineering and Economic sciences** (Chemical Engineering; Economics; Mechanical Engineering); **Technical Chemistry, Chemical and Process Engineering and Biotechnology** (Biotechnology; Chemical Engineering; Chemistry; Engineering Management)

Laboratory

Structural Engineering (Engineering)

Further Information: Also 104 Institutes; Interuniversity Centre; Women Studies Co-ordination Centre

History: Founded 1811, acquired University rank and new status 1865/66 and right to award doctorate 1901. Reorganized 1955 with limited autonomy. Latest University Organization Act passed 2002.

Academic Year: October to June (October-February; March-June)

Admission Requirements: Secondary school certificate (Reifezeugnis) or recognized equivalent

Fees: 363,36 per semester; 726,72 for non-Eu students (Euro)

Main Language(s) of Instruction: German, English

Degrees and Diplomas: *Bachelor's Degree*: **Architecture; Biomedical Engineering; Chemical Engineering; Chemistry; Civil Engineering; Computer Engineering; Computer Science; Earth Sciences; Electrical Engineering; Environmental Studies; Geophysics; Information Sciences; Mathematics; Mechanical Engineering; Molecular Biology; Natural Sciences; Physics; Software Engineering; Technology.** *Diplom-Ingenieur*: **Engineering.** *Master's Degree*: **Architecture; Astronomy and Space Science; Biochemistry; Biomedical Engineering; Biotechnology; Botany; Chemical Engineering; Chemistry; Civil Engineering; Computer Science; Electrical Engineering; Engineering; Environmental Studies; Geophysics; Hydraulic Engineering; Management; Materials Engineering; Mechanical Engineering; Microbiology; Natural Sciences; Physics;**

Software Engineering; Technology. *Doctor of Philosophy*: **Engineering; Natural Sciences.**

Student Services: Academic Counselling, Canteen, Facilities for disabled people, Foreign Studies Centre, Language Laboratory, Social Counselling, Sports Facilities

Publications: Research Journal

Academic Staff *2012-2013*: Total 1,392
Student Numbers *2012-2013*: Total 12,323
Last Updated: 14/04/15

JOHANNES KEPLER UNIVERSITY LINZ

Johannes Kepler Universität Linz
Altenberger Strasse 69, 4040 Linz, Upper Austria
Tel: +43(732) 2468-0
Fax: +43(732) 2468-8822
EMail: bdr@jku.at
Website: http://www.jku.at

Rector: Richard Hagelauer
Tel: +43(732) 2468-3360 EMail: rektor@jku.at

Vice-Rector of Academic Affairs: Herbert Kalb
Tel: +43(732) 2468-3204 EMail: herbert.kalb@jku.at

International Relations: Christine Hinterleitner
Tel: +43(732) 2468-3290
EMail: christine.hinterleitner@jku.at; auslandsbuero@jku.at

Faculty

Law (Law); **Medicine** (Health Sciences; Medicine); **Social Sciences, Economics and Business** *(SoWi)* (Business Administration; Business Education; Economics; Social Sciences; Sociology; Statistics); **Technology and Natural Sciences** (Chemistry; Computer Science; Electronic Engineering; Engineering; Mathematics; Mechanical Engineering; Physics; Polymer and Plastics Technology)

Further Information: Also 58 institutes

History: Founded 1966 as Hochschule für Sozial-und Wirtschaftswissenschaften. Acquired present status and title 1975. A State institution under the jurisdiction of the Federal Ministry of Education, Science and Culture.

Academic Year: October to July (October-February; March-July)

Admission Requirements: Completed secondary or commercial education or foreign equivalent

Fees: 363.36 per semester for students from EU or EEA countries; non EU students, 726,72 (Euro)

Main Language(s) of Instruction: German

Degrees and Diplomas: *Bachelor's Degree*: **Arts and Humanities; Business Administration; Economics; Engineering; Law; Mathematics; Mathematics and Computer Science; Medicine; Natural Sciences; Sociology; Statistics.** *Diplom-Ingenieur*: **Chemistry; Computer Science; Economics; Electronic Engineering; Mathematics; Mechanical Engineering; Physics.** *Master's Degree*: **Business and Commerce; Business Computing; Business Education; Chemistry; Computer Science; Economics; Law; Mathematics Education; Medicine; Physics; Social Sciences; Sociology; Statistics; Teacher Training.** *Doctor of Philosophy*: **Arts and Humanities; Economics; Engineering; Law; Natural Sciences; Social Sciences.**

Student Services: Academic Counselling, Canteen, Careers Guidance, Cultural Activities, Facilities for disabled people, Health Services, Language Laboratory, Nursery Care, Social Counselling, Sports Facilities

Publishing house: Stabsstelle für Public Relations
Last Updated: 15/04/15

KLAGENFURT UNIVERSITY

Alpen-Adria-Universität Klagenfurt
Universitätsstrasse 65-67, 9020 Klagenfurt, Carinthia
Tel: +43(463) 2700-9200
Fax: +43(463) 2700-9299
EMail: rektorat@aau.at
Website: http://www.uni-klu.ac.at

Rector: Oliver Vitouch (2012-)
Tel: +43(463) 2700-9201 EMail: rektorat@aau.at

Vice-Rector, Head of Administration: Martin Hitz
Tel: +43(463) 2700-9240 EMail: vr-pers@aau.at

International Relations: Cristina Beretta, Vice Rector for Education and International
Tel: +43(463) 2700-9212 EMail: vr-lehre@aau.at

Faculty

Arts and Humanities (American Studies; Communication Studies; Cultural Studies; Education; Educational Sciences; English Studies; Germanic Studies; History; Literature; Mass Communication; Media Studies; Musicology; Philosophy; Psychology; Romance Languages; Slavic Languages; Speech Therapy and Audiology; Teacher Training); **Economics** (Economics; Environmental Management; Finance; Geography; Health Administration; International Economics; Law; Management; Public Administration; Regional Planning; Sociology; Sports Management; Tourism); **Interdisciplinary Studies** (Communication Studies; Ecology; Ethics; Health Sciences; Management; Peace and Disarmament; Teacher Training; Technology); **Technical Sciences** (Computer Education; Computer Networks; Information Technology; Mathematics and Computer Science; Mathematics Education; Statistics; Technology)

History: Founded 1970 as college, acquired present status and title 1975. A State institution under the jurisdiction of the Federal Ministry of Education, Science and Culture.

Academic Year: October to June (October-January; March-June)

Admission Requirements: Secondary school certificate (Reifezeugnis)

Main Language(s) of Instruction: German, English

Degrees and Diplomas: *Bachelor's Degree*: **Business Administration; Communication Studies; Computer Science; Cultural Studies; Economics; Educational Sciences; Geography; German; History; Industrial Engineering; Information Management; Information Technology; International Business; Law; Mathematics; Media Studies; Philosophy; Psychology; Romance Languages; Slavic Languages.** *Master's Degree*: **American Studies; Business Administration; Business and Commerce; Communication Studies; Computer Science; Cultural Studies; Ecology; Education; English Studies; Geography; German; Germanic Studies; History; Information Management; Information Technology; International Business; Law; Mathematics; Media Studies; Philosophy; Psychology; Regional Studies; Romance Languages; Slavic Languages.** *Doctor of Philosophy*: **Cognitive Sciences; Economics; Engineering; Natural Sciences; Philosophy; Social Sciences.**

Student Services: Academic Counselling, Canteen, Careers Guidance, Cultural Activities, Facilities for disabled people, Nursery Care, Social Counselling, Sports Facilities

Publications: UNISONO
Last Updated: 15/04/15

MEDICAL UNIVERSITY OF GRAZ

Medizinische Universität Graz
Auenbruggerplatz 2, A-8036 Graz
Tel: +43(316) 385-0
EMail: rektor@medunigraz.at
Website: http://www.meduni-graz.at

Rector: Josef Smolle
Tel: +43(316) 385-72011 EMail: rektor@medunigraz.at

Programme

Dental Medicine (Dentistry); **Human Medicine** (Anaesthesiology; Dermatology; Gynaecology and Obstetrics; Health Sciences; Medicine; Neurology; Oncology; Ophthalmology; Orthopaedics; Plastic Surgery; Psychiatry and Mental Health; Psychology; Radiology; Surgery; Urology; Venereology); **Nursing** (Nursing)

History: Founded 2004 from the Medical Faculty of the University of Graz.

Academic Year: October to September (October - February; February - September)

Fees: 363,36 per semester (Euro)

Main Language(s) of Instruction: German

Degrees and Diplomas: *Bachelor's Degree*: **Nursing.** *Doktor der gesamten Heilkunde (Doktor der Zahnheilkunde)*: **Dentistry; Medicine; Natural Sciences.** *Master's Degree*: **Health Sciences; Nursing.** *Doctor of Philosophy*: **Microbiology.**
Last Updated: 14/04/15

MEDICAL UNIVERSITY OF INNSBRUCK

Medizinische Universität Innsbruck
Christoph-Probst-Platz 1, Innrain 52, 6020 Innsbruck, Tyrol
Tel: +43(512) 9003-0
EMail: rektorat@i-med.ac.at
Website: http://www.i-med.ac.at

Rector: Helga Fritsch (2013-)
Tel: +43(512) 9003-70001 EMail: rektorat@i-med.ac.at
International Relations: Christine Bandtlow, Vice-Rector for Research and International Affairs
Tel: +43(512) 9003-70064
EMail: international-relations@i-med.ac.at

Department
Theoretical Studies

Institute
Neurosciences (Neurosciences)

Centre
Medical Studies (Anaesthesiology; Dentistry; Dermatology; Gynaecology and Obstetrics; Medical Technology; Medicine; Neurology; Ophthalmology; Oral Pathology; Orthopaedics; Otorhinolaryngology; Paediatrics; Plastic Surgery; Psychiatry and Mental Health; Psychology; Psychotherapy; Radiology; Surgery; Toxicology; Urology; Venereology)

Laboratory
Animal Facilities (Veterinary Science)

History: Founded 2004 from the Medical Faculty of the University of Innsbruck.
Academic Year: October to June
Fees: 363,36 - 726,72 (Euro)
Main Language(s) of Instruction: German
Degrees and Diplomas: *Doktor der gesamten Heilkunde (Doktor der Zahnheilkunde)*: **Dentistry; Medicine.** *Doctor of Philosophy*: **Health Sciences.**
Last Updated: 14/04/15

MEDICAL UNIVERSITY OF VIENNA

Medizinische Universität Wien
Spitalgasse 23, 1090 Wien, Vienna
Tel: +43(1) 40160-0
Fax: +43(1) 40160-910000
EMail: infopoint-meduni@meduniwien.ac.at
Website: http://www.meduniwien.ac.at/

Rector: Wolfgang Schütz
Tel: +43(1) 40160-10001
EMail: buero-universitaetsleitung@meduniwien.ac.at

Programme
Applied Medical Science (Health Sciences); **Dentistry** (Dentistry); **Human Medicine** (Health Sciences); **Medical Informatics** (Biomedical Engineering; Computer Science; Health Sciences); **Medical Science** (Medicine)

History: Founded 2004.
Academic Year: October to June
Fees: 382,06 - 745,42 (Euro)
Main Language(s) of Instruction: German
Degrees and Diplomas: *Doktor der gesamten Heilkunde (Doktor der Zahnheilkunde)*; *Doctor of Philosophy*: **Dentistry; Health Sciences; Medicine.** Also a Maters' programme in Medical Informatics

Student Numbers *2013*: Total 7,584
Last Updated: 14/04/15

UNIVERSITY MOZARTEUM SALZBURG

Universität Mozarteum Salzburg
Mirabell Platz 1, 5020 Salzburg, Salzburg
Tel: +43(662) 6198-0
Fax: +43(662) 6198-3033
EMail: presse@moz.ac.at
Website: http://www.moz.ac.at

Rector: Siegfried Mauser (2006-)
Tel: +43(662) 6198-2000 EMail: Rektor@moz.ac.at
Vice-Rector for Academics Affairs: Matthias Seidel
Tel: +43(662) 6198-2001 EMail: Vizerektor.SEIDEL@moz.ac.at
International Relations: Elisabeth Skärbäck
Tel: +43(662) 6198-2230 EMail: elisabeth.skaerbaeck@moz.ac.at

Programme
Music (Conducting; Music; Music Education; Music Theory and Composition; Musical Instruments; Musicology; Performing Arts; Singing); **Theatre** (Performing Arts; Theatre); **Visual Arts** (Art Education; Fine Arts; Visual Arts)

Institute
Chamber Music *(Sándor Végh Institute for chamber music)* (Music); **Drama** *(Thomas Bernhard Institute)* (Acting; Theatre); **Early Music** (Music); **Game research** (Music; Music Theory and Composition); **History of musical reception and interpretation** (Music); **Mozart-Operas interpretation** (Opera; Singing); **Music and Dance Education** *(Carl Orff)* (Dance; Music; Performing Arts); **New Music** (Music; Music Theory and Composition)

Further Information: Also Abteilung Musikerziehung in Innsbruck
History: Founded 1841, transferred to the Mozarteum Foundation 1881, became Conservatory 1914, a State institution 1921 and Akademie 1953 and University institution with title of Hochschule 1970. Acquired present title 1998.
Academic Year: October to September (October-February; March-September)
Admission Requirements: Entrance examination
Main Language(s) of Instruction: German
Degrees and Diplomas: *Bachelor's Degree*; *Master's Degree*; *Doctor of Philosophy*: **Music Education; Musicology.**
Student Services: Academic Counselling, Canteen, Social Counselling
Last Updated: 15/04/15

UNIVERSITY OF APPLIED ARTS VIENNA

Universität für angewandte Kunst Wien
Oskar Kokoschka Platz 2, 1010 Wien, Vienna
Tel: +43(1) 71133-0
EMail: info@uni-ak.ac.at
Website: http://www.dieangewandte.at/

Rector: Gerald Bast (2003-)
Tel: +43(1) 71133-2000
EMail: gerald.bast@uni-ak.ac.at; pr@uni-ak.ac.at
Vice-Rector: Josef Kaiser EMail: josef.kaiser@uni-ak.ac.at
International Relations: Jürgen Gschiel
Tel: +43(1) 71133-2003 EMail: juergen.gschiel@uni-ak.ac.at

Institute
Architecture (Architecture; Structural Architecture); **Art and Society** (Design; Fine Arts); **Art and Technology** (Ceramic Art; Chemistry; Heritage Preservation; Metal Techniques; Textile Technology; Visual Arts; Wood Technology); **Art Sciences and Art Education** (Art Education; Art History; Cultural Studies; Design; Philosophy; Textile Technology); **Artistic Sciences, Art Education and Communication** (Art Education; Art History; Cultural Studies; Philosophy; Textile Design); **Design** (Design; Fashion Design; Graphic Design; Industrial Design; Landscape Architecture); **Fine and Media Arts** (Ceramic Art; Fine Arts; Graphic Arts; Painting and Drawing; Photography); **Language Arts** (Literature; Writing); **Restoration and Conservation** (Heritage Preservation; Restoration of Works of Art)

History: Founded 1867 as School, reorganized 1940 and 1945, and became Academy 1948 and University institution with title of Hochschule 1970. Acquired present status 1998. A State institution.

Academic Year: October to September (October-March; March-September)

Admission Requirements: Secondary school certificate (Reifezeugnis) or equivalent and entrance examination

Fees: EU citizens, 382,06 per semester; non EU citizens, 745,42 per semester (Euro)

Main Language(s) of Instruction: German

Degrees and Diplomas: *Bachelor's Degree*: **Art Education; Writing.** *Master's Degree*: **Architecture; Communication Studies; Cultural Studies; Economics; Fine Arts; Management.** *Doctor of Philosophy*

Student Services: Academic Counselling, Canteen
Last Updated: 15/04/15

UNIVERSITY OF APPLIED SCIENCES FOR HEALTH - TYROL

Fachhochschule gesundheit (FHG)

Zentrum für Gesundheitsberufe Tirol GmbH, Innrain 98, 6020 Innsbruck, Tirol
Tel: +43(512) 5322-0
Fax: +43(512) 5322-75200
Website: https://www.fhg-tirol.ac.at

Director: Walter Draxl (2006-)
Tel: +43(512) 5322-76701 EMail: walter.draxl@fhg-tirol.ac.at
Director of Studies: Max Laimböck
Tel: +43(512) 5322-76777 EMail: max.laimboeck@fhg-tirol.ac.at
International Relations: Bettina Kaufmann
Tel: +43(512) 5322-76718 EMail: bettina.kaufmann@fhg-tirol.ac.at

Programme
Health sciences (Biomedicine; Dietetics; Health Administration; Health Education; Midwifery; Nursing; Nutrition; Occupational Therapy; Osteopathy; Physical Therapy; Public Health; Speech Therapy and Audiology; Treatment Techniques)

History: Founded in 2006 as Center for Health Sciences Tyrol.

Admission Requirements: Entrance examination. Secondary school certificate (Reifepruefungszeugnis) or foreign equivalent

Fees: 363,36 per semester (Euro)

Main Language(s) of Instruction: German

Degrees and Diplomas: *Bachelor's Degree*: **Biomedicine; Dietetics; Midwifery; Occupational Therapy; Physical Therapy; Speech Therapy and Audiology; Treatment Techniques.** *Master's Degree*: **Health Administration.**
Last Updated: 22/04/15

UNIVERSITY OF APPLIED SCIENCES FOR HEALTH PROFESSIONS - UPPER AUSTRIA

Fachhochschulen Gesundheitsberufe

Semmelweisstrasse 34/D3, 4020 Linz, Oberösterreich
Tel: +43(50) 344-20000
EMail: office@fhgooe.ac.at
Website: http://www.fh-gesundheitsberufe.at/index.php?id=home&L=2

Managing Director: Bettina Schneebauer
Tel: +43(50) 344-20000 EMail: Bettina.Schneebauer@fhgooe.ac.at
International Relations: Barbara Peinhaupt
Tel: +43(50) 344-20060 EMail: barbara.peinhaupt@fhgooe.ac.at

Programme
Health Sciences (Biomedicine; Dietetics; Health Administration; Health Education; Midwifery; Occupational Therapy; Physical Therapy; Radiology; Speech Therapy and Audiology; Treatment Techniques)

Further Information: Also campus in Steyr
History: Founded 2010
Academic Year: September to September (September- February; February-September)

Admission Requirements: Entrance examination. General university eligibility, adequate specific secondary school vocational certificate, certificate of access to higher education, relevant professional qualifications

Fees: Bachelor and Master programmes: No fees; "University Didactics for Health Professional Education" Master course: 2,500 per semester (Euro)

Main Language(s) of Instruction: German

Degrees and Diplomas: *Bachelor's Degree*: **Biomedicine; Dietetics; Midwifery; Occupational Therapy; Physical Therapy; Radiology; Speech Therapy and Audiology.** *Master's Degree*: **Health Administration; Health Education.**
Last Updated: 21/04/15

UNIVERSITY OF ART AND INDUSTRIAL DESIGN LINZ

Universität für künstlerische und industrielle Gestaltung Linz

Hauptplatz 8, 4010 Linz, Upper Austria
Tel: +43(732) 7898
Fax: +43(732) 783-508
EMail: international.office@ufg.ac.at; ufg.presse@lists.ufg.ac.at
Website: http://www.ufg.ac.at

Rector: Reinhard Kannonier
Tel: +43(732) 7898-222
EMail: reinhard.kannonier@ufg.ac.at; heidemarie.gehmair@ufg.at
International Relations: Regina Dicketmüller-Pointinger
Tel: +43(732) 7898-269 EMail: international.office@ufg.at

Institute
Architecture and Design (Architecture; Industrial Design); **Art and Design** (Ceramic Art; Design; Fashion Design; Fine Arts; Textile Design); **Fine Arts and Cultural Studies** (Cultural Studies; Fine Arts); **Media Studies** (Communication Arts)

History: Founded as School of Art 1947, acquired present status 1998. A State institution under the jurisdiction of the Federal Ministry of Education, Science and Culture. Financed by the Federal Government, the Land Oberösterreich and the City of Linz.

Academic Year: October to June (October-January; March-June)

Admission Requirements: Secondary school certificate (Reifezeugnis) for secondary Art teacher's education and/or entrance examination for Art study programmes

Fees: 363.36 - 726.72 per semester (Euro)

Main Language(s) of Instruction: German

Degrees and Diplomas: *Bachelor's Degree*; *Master's Degree*: **Architecture; Design; Media Studies; Photography; Textile Design; Visual Arts.** *Doctor of Philosophy*: **Architecture; Design; Multimedia; Urban Studies; Visual Arts.**

Student Services: Canteen, Cultural Activities, Social Counselling, Sports Facilities
Last Updated: 16/04/15

UNIVERSITY OF GRAZ

Karl-Franzens-Universität Graz

Universitätsplatz 3, 8010 Graz, Styria
Tel: +43(316) 380-0
Fax: +43(316) 380-9030
EMail: info@uni-graz.at
Website: http://www.uni-graz.at

Rector: Christa Neuper (2011-)
Tel: +43(316) 380-2201 EMail: rektorin@uni-graz.at
Vice-Rector for Financial Affairs, Resources and Location Development: Peter Riedler
Tel: +43(316) 380-1740 EMail: vizerektor.finanzen@uni-graz.at
International Relations: Sabine Pendl
Tel: +43(316) 380-2211
EMail: sabine.pendl@uni-graz.at; international@uni-graz.at

Faculty
Arts and Humanties (American Studies; Archaeology; Art History; Classical Languages; English Studies; Ethnology; German; History; Linguistics; Modern Languages; Musicology; Philosophy; Romance Languages; Slavic Languages; Teacher Training; Translation and Interpretation); **Business, Economics and Social Sciences** (Business Administration; Business Education; Economics; Gender Studies; Sociology); **Catholic Theology** (Catholic Theology; Comparative Religion; Religious Education); **Environmental, Regional**

and Educational Sciences (Educational Sciences; Environmental Management; Regional Studies; Special Education; Sports Management); **Law** (Law); **Natural Sciences** (Biological and Life Sciences; Chemistry; Earth Sciences; Mathematics; Molecular Biology; Pharmacy; Physics; Psychology)

History: Founded 1585 with faculties of philosophy and theology in a Jesuit College. Became lyceum 1782. Re-established as Karl-Franzens Universität 1827. Moved to present campus 1870. Karl-Franzens Universität is an autonomous university under the jurisdiction of the Federal Ministry of Education, Science and Culture.

Academic Year: October to June (October-January; March-June)

Admission Requirements: Secondary school certificate (Reifezeugnis) or recognized equivalent

Fees: National: 363 per semester (Euro), International: 363 per semester (EU); 727 per semester (other nationalities) (Euro)

Main Language(s) of Instruction: German, English

Degrees and Diplomas: *Bachelor's Degree*; *Master's Degree*: **Adult Education; American Studies; Ancient Civilizations; Archaeology; Astronomy and Space Science; Behavioural Sciences; Biological and Life Sciences; Biotechnology; Botany; Business Administration; Chemistry; Classical Languages; Earth Sciences; Ecology; Economics; Education; English Studies; Environmental Studies; Ethics; Ethnology; Gender Studies; Geography; History; Linguistics; Literature; Mathematics and Computer Science; Meteorology; Modern Languages; Musicology; Pedagogy; Philosophy; Physics; Psychology; Regional Planning; Religion; Romance Languages; Sociology; Sports; Surveying and Mapping; Translation and Interpretation; Urban Studies; Women's Studies.** *Doctor of Philosophy*: **Catholic Theology; Economics; Education; Environmental Studies; Law; Natural Sciences; Philosophy; Regional Planning; Religion.** Also: Diploma programme of Law; Teacher training programmes; joint Master programme

Student Services: Academic Counselling, Canteen, Careers Guidance, Cultural Activities, Facilities for disabled people, Foreign Studies Centre, IT Centre, Language Laboratory, Library, Nursery Care, Social Counselling, Sports Facilities, eLibrary

Publications: UNIZEIT

Academic Staff *2014*: Total 4,129

Student Numbers *2014-2015*: Total 31,909

Last Updated: 14/04/15

UNIVERSITY OF INNSBRUCK

Leopold-Franzens Universität Innsbruck

Innrain 52, 6020 Innsbruck, Tyrol
Tel: +43(512) 507-0
EMail: international-relations@uibk.ac.at
Website: http://www.uibk.ac.at

Rector (Acting): Tilmann Märk
Tel: +43(512) 507-2000 EMail: rektor@uibk.ac.at

Public Relations: Uwe Steger
Tel: +43(512) 507-32000 EMail: uwe.steger@uibk.ac.at

International Relations: Mathias Schennach, Head of International Relations Office
Tel: +43(512) 507-32401 EMail: international-relations@uibk.ac.at

Faculty

Architecture (Architecture); **Biology** (Biology); **Catholic Theology** (Bible; Christian Religious Studies; Religious Practice; Theology); **Chemistry and Pharmacy** (Chemistry; Pharmacy); **Economics and Statistics** (Economic History; Economics; Finance; Political Sciences; Statistics); **Education** (Education; Educational Research; Teacher Training); **Engineering Science** *(Former Faculty of Civil engineering)* (Applied Mathematics; Civil Engineering; Construction Engineering; Environmental Engineering; Hydraulic Engineering; Materials Engineering; Mechanics; Structural Architecture; Surveying and Mapping; Transport Engineering); **Geo- and Atmospheric Sciences** (Geography; Geology; Geophysics; Meteorology; Mineralogy; Paleontology; Petrology); **Humanities I (Philosophy and History)** (Arts and Humanities; History; Philosophy); **Humanities II ((Language and Literature)** (Literature; Modern Languages); **Law** (Civil Law; Commercial Law; Criminal Law; European Union Law; International Law; Labour Law; Law; Private Law; Public Law); **Mathematics, Computer Science and Physics** (Computer Science; Mathematics; Physics); **Psychology and Sport Science** (Psychology; Sports)

School

Catholic Theology (Catholic Theology; Religion); **Education** (Education); **Management** *(Innsbruck University School of Management)* (Accountancy; Banking; Finance; Information Technology; Management; Marketing; Modern Languages; Taxation; Tourism; Transport Management); **Political Science and Sociology** (Political Sciences; Sociology)

Further Information: Also 73 Institutes of the Faculties

History: Founded 1669, acquired present status 1862. A State institution under the jurisdiction of the Federal Ministry of Education, Science and Culture.

Academic Year: October to July (October-February; March-July)

Admission Requirements: Secondary school certificate (Reifezeugnis) or foreign equivalent

Fees: 363,36-726,72 per semester (Euro)

Main Language(s) of Instruction: German

Degrees and Diplomas: *Bachelor's Degree*; *Master's Degree*: **Architecture and Planning; Arts and Humanities; Business Administration; Civil Engineering; Ecology; Economics; Education; Engineering; Environmental Engineering; Environmental Management; Environmental Studies; Ethnology; Mathematics and Computer Science; Modern Languages; Music; Musicology; Nanotechnology; Natural Sciences; Performing Arts; Political Sciences; Religion; Social Sciences; Sports; Translation and Interpretation; Zoology.** *Doctor of Philosophy*: **Arts and Humanities; Economics; Education; Engineering; Law; Management; Mathematics and Computer Science; Natural Sciences; Philosophy; Political Sciences; Sociology; Sports; Theology.**

Student Services: Language Laboratory, Sports Facilities

Last Updated: 14/04/15

UNIVERSITY OF LEOBEN

Montanuniversität Leoben (MUL)

Franz-Josef-Strasse 18, 8700 Leoben, Styria
Tel: +43(3842) 402-0
Fax: +43(3842) 402-7702
EMail: international@unileoben.ac.at
Website: http://www.unileoben.ac.at

Rector: Wilfried Eichlseder (2011-2015)
Tel: +43(3842) 402-7001
EMail: rektor@unileoben.ac.at; ursula.papst-morina@unileoben.ac.at

International Relations: Cornelia Praschag
Tel: +43(3842) 402-7201
EMail: cornelia.praschag@unileoben.ac.at

Department

Applied Geological Sciences and Geophysics (Environmental Engineering; Geology; Geophysics; Mineralogy; Petroleum and Gas Engineering; Soil Science; Systems Analysis); **Economics and Business Management** (Business Administration; Economics; Industrial Management); **Environmental and Energy Process Engineering** (Chemical Engineering; Energy Engineering; Environmental Engineering; Environmental Studies; Technology; Thermal Engineering; Waste Management); **General, Analytical and Physical Chemistry** (Analytical Chemistry; Chemistry; Physical Chemistry); **Materials Physics** (Atomic and Molecular Physics; Physics); **Mathematics and Information Technology** (Information Technology; Mathematics); **Metallurgy** (Heating and Refrigeration; Metallurgical Engineering); **Mineral Ressources Engineering** (Engineering; Geological Engineering; Mineralogy; Mining Engineering; Technology); **Petroleum Engineering** (Petroleum and Gas Engineering; Production Engineering); **Physical Metallurgy and Materials Testing** (Metal Techniques; Metallurgical Engineering; Physical Engineering); **Physics** (Physics); **Polymer Technology** (Chemistry; Materials Engineering; Polymer and Plastics Technology); **Product Engineering** (Automation and Control Engineering; Mechanical Engineering; Polymer and Plastics Technology; Production Engineering; Technology); **Structural and**

Functional Ceramics (Ceramics and Glass Technology; Engineering)

Institute

Electrical Engineering (Electrical Engineering); **Mechanics** (Mechanics); **Metal forming** (Metal Techniques); **Polymer Processing** (Polymer and Plastics Technology)

History: Founded 1840 as a Mining Institute, acquired University status 1904, and present title by law 1975. A State institution under the jurisdiction of the Federal Ministry of Education, Science and Culture.

Academic Year: October to June (October-February; February-June)

Admission Requirements: Secondary school certificate (Reifezeugnis) or recognized foreign equivalent (Matura/Abitur)

Fees: EU residents, 363,36 per semester; international students, 726,72 per semester (Euro)

Main Language(s) of Instruction: German, English

Degrees and Diplomas: *Diplom-Ingenieur*: **Engineering.** *Master's Degree*: **Business Administration; Chemical Engineering; Construction Engineering; Earth Sciences; Engineering; Environmental Engineering; Geological Engineering; Industrial Engineering; Industrial Management; Management; Materials Engineering; Metallurgical Engineering; Mineralogy; Mining Engineering; Natural Resources; Petroleum and Gas Engineering; Polymer and Plastics Technology; Technology; Waste Management.** *Doctor of Philosophy*: **Engineering.**

Student Services: Academic Counselling, Canteen, Careers Guidance, Cultural Activities, Social Counselling, Sports Facilities

Publishing house: Springer-Verlag, Wien

Last Updated: 15/04/15

UNIVERSITY OF MUSIC AND PERFORMING ARTS GRAZ

Universität für Musik und darstellende Kunst Graz (KUG)

Leonhardstrasse 15, Palais Meran, 8010 Graz, Styria
Tel: +43(316) 389-0
EMail: info@kug.ac.at
Website: http://www.kug.ac.at

Rector: Elisabeth Freismuth (2015-)
Tel: +43(316) 389-1106 EMail: rektorin@kug.ac.at

University Director: Astrid Wedenig
Tel: +43(316) 389-1162 EMail: astrid.wedenig@kug.ac.at

International Relations: Irene Hofmann-Wellenhof, International Coordinator
Tel: +43(316) 389-1162
EMail: irene.hofmann-wellenhof@kug.ac.at

Institute

Aesthetics of Music (Aesthetics; Art Criticism); **Composition, Music Theory, Music History and Conducting** (Conducting; Music Theory and Composition; Musicology); **Dramatic Arts** (Acting; Literature; Speech Studies; Theatre); **Early Music and Performance Practice**; **Electronic Music and Acoustics** (Music; Music Theory and Composition); **Ethnomusicology** (Musicology); **Jazz**; **Jazz Research** (Jazz and Popular Music); **Music Education** (Music Education); **Musical Instruments and Singing** *(Institut Oberschützen)* (Musical Instruments); **Opera** (Music; Theatre); **Piano** (Musical Instruments); **Stage Design** (Display and Stage Design); **String Instruments** (Musical Instruments); **Voice, Lied and Oratorio** (Singing); **Wind and Percussion Instruments** (Musical Instruments)

History: Founded as provincial School of Music 1816, became Conservatory 1920, Akademie 1963, and University Institution with title of Hochschule 1970. Acquired title of University of Music and Dramatic Arts Graz in 1998, became University of Music and Performing Arts Graz in 2009. A State institution.

Academic Year: October to June (October-January; March-June)

Admission Requirements: Secondary school certificate (Reifezeugnis) and entrance examination

Fees: 363,36 per semester; 726,72 for certain non-EU nationals (Euro)

Main Language(s) of Instruction: German

Accrediting Agency: Federal Ministry of Science and Research

Degrees and Diplomas: *Bachelor's Degree*; *Master's Degree*; *Doctor of Philosophy*: **Music; Performing Arts; Theatre.**

Student Services: Canteen, Careers Guidance, Cultural Activities, Social Counselling, Sports Facilities

Publications: Research publications

Student Numbers *2012-2013*: Total 2,300

Last Updated: 15/04/15

UNIVERSITY OF MUSIC AND PERFORMING ARTS VIENNA

Universität für Musik und darstellende Kunst Wien

Anton-von-Webern-Platz 1, 1030 Wien, Vienna
Tel: +43(1) 71155-0
Fax: +43(1) 71155-6099
EMail: rektorsbuero@mdw.ac.at
Website: http://www.mdw.ac.at

Rector: Werner Hasitschka (2010-)
Tel: +43(1) 71155-6001 EMail: rektorsbuero@mdw.ac.at

International Relations: Andrea Kleibel Kleibel, Vice-Rector for International and Public Relations (2011-)
EMail: internationaloffice@mdw.ac.at

Institute

Acting, Production and Directing *(Max-Reinhart-Seminar)* (Acting; Theatre); **Analysis, Theory and History of Music** (Musicology); **Chamber Music** *(Joseph Haydn)*; **Composition and Electroacoustics** (Music Theory and Composition); **Conducting and Accompaniment** (Conducting; Music Theory and Composition; Musical Instruments); **Cultural Management and Culture Studies** *(IKM)* (Cultural Studies; Management); **Film and Television** *(Film Academy Vienna)* (Cinema and Television; Film; Photography); **Folk Music and Ethno-musicology** (Folklore; Music; Musicology); **Keyboard Instruments** (Musical Instruments); **Keyboard Instruments in Music Education** *(Ludwig van Beethoven)* (Music Education; Musical Instruments; Teacher Training); **Music Acoustics** *(Viennese Style)* (Music; Sound Engineering (Acoustics)); **Music Education** (Music Education); **Music Education, Rhythmic and Musical Therapy** (Music Education); **Music Sociology**; **Music Theory, Aural Training, Ensemble Conducting** *(Anton Bruckner)* (Conducting; Music; Music Theory and Composition); **Musical Style Research** (Music; Musicology); **Organ, Organ Research and Church Music** (Musical Instruments; Religious Music); **Popular Music** (Jazz and Popular Music; Music); **Singing in Music Education** *(Antonio Salieri)* (Music Education; Opera); **String Instruments** (Musical Instruments); **String Instruments in Music Education** *(Hellmesberger)* (Music Education; Musical Instruments; Teacher Training); **Voice and Music Theatre** (Music; Theatre); **Wind and Percussion Instruments** *(Leonard Bernstein)* (Musical Instruments); **Wind and Percussion Instruments in Music Education** *(Franz Schubert)* (Music Education; Musical Instruments; Teacher Training)

History: Founded 1817 as Konservatorium der Gesellschaft der Musikfreunde in Wien, became Academy and State Institution 1909 and University 1998.

Academic Year: October to June (October-February; March-June)

Admission Requirements: Secondary school certificate (Reifezeugnis) and entrance examination (depends on branch of study)

Fees: 363,36 - 726,72 per semester (Euro)

Main Language(s) of Instruction: German

Degrees and Diplomas: *Bachelor's Degree*: **Film; Music; Music Education; Performing Arts; Video.** *Master's Degree*: **Art Therapy; Film; Fine Arts; Music; Music Education; Performing Arts; Video.** *Doctor of Philosophy*: **Performing Arts.** Also Diploma in Acting and Drama Directing

Student Services: Academic Counselling, Canteen, Careers Guidance, Language Laboratory, Social Counselling

Last Updated: 15/04/15

UNIVERSITY OF NATURAL RESOURCES AND APPLIED LIFE SCIENCES, VIENNA

Universität für Bodenkultur Wien (BOKU)
Gregor-Mendel-Strasse 33, 1180 Wien, Vienna
Tel: +43(1) 47-654-0
Fax: +43(1) 47-654-1055
EMail: bdr@boku.ac.at
Website: http://www.boku.ac.at

Rector: Martin Gerzabek
Tel: +43(1) 47-654-1001 EMail: rektorat@boku.ac.at

Vice-Rector for Teaching and International Affairs: Barbara Hinterstoisser
Tel: +43(1) 47-654-1004 EMail: barbara.hinterstoisser@boku.ac.at

International Relations: Sabina Moshammer
Tel: +43(1) 47654-2600
EMail: sabina.moshammer@boku.ac.at; international@boku.ac.at

Department

Agrobiotechnology (IFA-Tulln) (Agriculture; Biotechnology); **Applied Genetics and Cell Biology** (Cell Biology; Genetics); **Applied Plant Sciences and Plant Biotechnology** (Biotechnology; Horticulture; Plant and Crop Protection); **Biotechnology** *(DBT)* (Biotechnology); **Chemistry** *(DCH)* (Analytical Chemistry; Biochemistry; Chemistry; Natural Resources; Organic Chemistry); **Civil Engineering and Natural Hazards** (Civil Engineering); **Crop sciences** *(DNW)* (Agriculture; Agronomy; Plant and Crop Protection; Vegetable Production; Viticulture); **Economics and Social Sciences** *(WiSo)* (Economics; Social Sciences); **Food Science and Technology** *(DLWT)* (Biotechnology; Food Science; Food Technology); **Forest and Soil Sciences** (Forest Products; Forestry; Natural Resources; Water Management; Wildlife; Wood Technology); **Integrative Biology and Biodiversity Research** *(DIB)* (Botany; Mathematics; Wildlife; Zoology); **Landscape, Spatial and Infrastructure Science** (Bioengineering; Design; Landscape Architecture; Regional Planning); **Material Sciences and Process Engineering** *(MAP)* (Materials Engineering); **Nanobiotechnology** *(DNBT)* (Biotechnology; Nanotechnology); **Sustainable Agricultural Systems** (Agriculture; Botany; Plant and Crop Protection; Soil Science; Zoology); **Water, Atmosphere and Environment** *(WAU)* (Civil Engineering; Transport Management; Waste Management; Water Management)

Centre

Agricultural Sciences (Agriculture); **Bio-ressources and Technology** (Natural Resources; Technology); **BOKU Network for Bioconversion of Renewables** (Natural Resources); **Development Research** (Development Studies); **Global Change and Sustainability** *(ZGWN)* (Environmental Studies); **Scientific Initiatives**; **Vienna Institute of BioTechnology** *(VIBT Muthgasse)* (Biotechnology)

History: Founded 1872 as Hochschule. Acquired present title 1975. A State institution.

Academic Year: October to June (October-February; February-June)

Admission Requirements: Secondary school certificate (Reifezeugnis)

Fees: 363,36 per semester; 726,72 per semester for non-EU/non-EEA citizens (Euro)

Main Language(s) of Instruction: German, English

Degrees and Diplomas: *Bachelor's Degree*: **Agriculture; Biotechnology; Environmental Engineering; Environmental Management; Environmental Studies; Food Science; Forestry; Landscape Architecture; Natural Resources; Wood Technology.** *Master's Degree*: **Agricultural Economics; Agriculture; Alternative Medicine; Biotechnology; Botany; Environmental Engineering; Environmental Management; Food Science; Forest Biology; Forestry; Landscape Architecture; Limnology; Mountain Studies; Natural Resources; Technology; Water Management; Wildlife; Wood Technology.** *Doctor of Philosophy*: **Biological and Life Sciences; Economics; Nanotechnology; Natural Resources; Social Sciences; Technology.**

Student Services: Academic Counselling, Canteen, Careers Guidance, Language Laboratory

Publications: Blick Ins Land; BOKU INSIGHT; Die Bodenkultur; Ökoenergie

Last Updated: 15/04/15

UNIVERSITY OF SALZBURG

Universität Salzburg
Kapitelgasse 4-6, 5020 Salzburg, Salzburg
Tel: +43(662) 8044-0
Fax: +43(662) 8044-145
EMail: international@sbg.ac.at
Website: http://www.uni-salzburg.at

Rector: Heinrich Schmidinger (2001-)
Tel: +43(662) 8044-2000 EMail: heinrich.schmidinger@sbg.ac.at

Vice-Rector for International Relations and Communication: Sylvia Hahn
Tel: +43(662) 8044-2440 EMail: sylvia.hahn@sbg.ac.at

International Relations: Markus Bayer, Head of the International Office Tel: +43(662) 8044-2040 EMail: markus.bayer@sbg.ac.at

Faculty

Arts and Humanities (Communication Studies; Cultural Studies; Dance; English; Fine Arts; German; History; Linguistics; Music; Philosophy; Political Sciences; Romance Languages; Slavic Languages; Social Sciences; Sociology); **Catholic Theology** (Bible; Catholic Theology; History of Religion; Philosophy; Theology); **Law** (European Union Law; Labour Law; Law; Private Law; Public Law); **Natural Sciences** (Cell Biology; Computer Science; Geography; Geology; Mathematics; Molecular Biology; Natural Sciences; Physics; Psychology)

Centre

GeoInformatics (Computer Science); **Interdisciplinary Research on Medieval Studies** (History; Medieval Studies); **Interdisciplinary Research on Metamorphic Changes in the Arts** (Aesthetics; Cultural Studies; Social Studies); **Jewish Culture History** (Jewish Studies); **Neurocognitive Linguistics** (Linguistics); **Poverty Research**

Research Centre

BioScience and Health (Biological and Life Sciences; Health Sciences); **Education and Art** (Education; Fine Arts); **Information and Communication Technologies and Society** *(ICT&S)* (Communication Studies; Information Technology); **Law, Economics and Employment** (Economics; Law)

Further Information: Also 51 Institutes

History: Founded 1617 as School by Archbishop Paris Lodron, became University 1622, dissolved 1810. Re-established 1962. A State institution financed by the Federal Ministry of Education, Science and Culture.

Academic Year: October to June (October-January; March-June)

Admission Requirements: Secondary school certificate (Reifezeugnis), or recognized foreign equivalent

Fees: EU citizens, 363,36 per semester; non EU citizens, 726,72 (Euro)

Main Language(s) of Instruction: German

Degrees and Diplomas: *Bachelor's Degree*; *Diplom-Ingenieur*: **Engineering.** *Master's Degree*: **Arts and Humanities; Law; Mathematics; Natural Sciences; Performing Arts; Philosophy; Social Sciences; Sports; Theology.** *Doctor of Philosophy*: **Catholic Theology; Economics; Education; Law; Natural Sciences; Philosophy.** Also teacher training courses

Student Services: Academic Counselling, Canteen, Facilities for disabled people, Nursery Care, Social Counselling, Sports Facilities

Publishing house: Universitätsdirektion

Last Updated: 14/04/15

UNIVERSITY OF VETERINARY MEDICINE, VIENNA

Veterinärmedizinische Universität Wien (VMU)
Veterinärplatz 1, A1210 Wien, Vienna
Tel: +43(1) 250-77-0
Fax: +43(1) 250-77-1090
EMail: ursula.schober@vetmeduni.ac.at
Website: http://www.vetmeduni.ac.at

Rector: Sonja Hammerschmid
Tel: +43(1) 250-77-1004
EMail: gerda.obermueller@vetmeduni.ac.at

International Relations: Ursula Schober
Tel: +43(1) 250-77-1107 EMail: ursula.schober@vetmeduni.ac.at

Department

Biomedical Sciences (Animal Husbandry; Biochemistry; Biotechnology; Genetics; Histology; Pharmacology; Physics; Physiology; Toxicology); **Companion Animals and Horses** *(Clinical)* (Anaesthesiology; Animal Husbandry; Epidemiology; Gynaecology and Obstetrics; Ophthalmology; Surgery); **Farm Animals and Veterinary Public Health** (Animal Husbandry; Botany; Epidemiology; Food Science; Hygiene; Nutrition; Pharmacology; Public Health); **Integrative Biology and Evolution** (Biology; Environmental Studies; Wildlife); **Pathobiology** (Anatomy; Embryology and Reproduction Biology; Forensic Medicine and Dentistry; Histology; Hygiene; Parasitology; Pathology; Virology; Zoology)

Further Information: Also Veterinary Teaching Hospital

History: Founded 1765 as a school, achieved University status 1908 and was granted the same rights and privileges as other Austrian Universities 1920. Acquired present title 1975.

Academic Year: October to June (October-January; March-June)

Admission Requirements: Secondary school leaving certificate (Reifezeugnis) or equivalent

Fees: EU citizens, 363,36 per semester; non EU citizens, 726,72 per semester (Euro)

Main Language(s) of Instruction: German

Degrees and Diplomas: *Bachelor's Degree*: **Animal Husbandry; Biomedical Engineering; Biotechnology.** *Master's Degree*: **Biomedical Engineering; Biotechnology.** *Doctor of Philosophy*: **Veterinary Science.** Also Doktor: Veterinary Medicine

Student Services: Academic Counselling, Canteen, Cultural Activities, Facilities for disabled people, Foreign Studies Centre, Nursery Care, Sports Facilities

Publications: VetmedMagazin; Wiener Tierärztliche Monatsschrift

Academic Staff *2014*: Total 1,335

Student Numbers *2015*: Total 2,344

Last Updated: 15/04/15

UNIVERSITY OF VIENNA

Universität Wien

Universitätsring 1, 1010 Wien, Vienna
Tel: +43(1) 4277-0
Fax: +43(1) 4277-9100
EMail: buero.rektorat@univie.ac.at
Website: http://www.univie.ac.at

Rector: Heinz W. Engl (2011-)
Tel: +43(1) 4277-10010
EMail: heinz.engl@univie.ac.at; rektor@univie.ac.at

Vice Rector for Human Resources Development and International Relations: Heinz Fassmann
Tel: +43(1) 4277-100-30
EMail: personal.rektorat@univie.ac.at; internationales.rektorat@univie.ac.at

International Relations: Lottelis Moser, Director of International Relations
Tel: +43(1) 4277-18216 EMail: lottelis.moser@univie.ac.at

Faculty

Business, Economics and Statistics (Business Administration; Business and Commerce; Commercial Law; Economics; Finance; Modern Languages; Statistics); **Catholic Theology** (Catholic Theology; Theology); **Chemistry** (Chemistry); **Computer Science** (Computer Science); **Earth Sciences, Geography and Astronomy** (Astronomy and Space Science; Earth Sciences; Geography); **Historical-Cultural Sciences** (Ancient Civilizations; Cultural Studies; Ethnology; History); **Law** (Law); **Life Sciences** (Biological and Life Sciences; Biology; Molecular Biology; Pharmacy); **Mathematics** (Mathematics; Mathematics Education); **Philological-Cultural Sciences** (Cultural Studies; Philology); **Philosophy and Educational Sciences** (Educational Sciences; Pedagogy; Philosophy); **Physics** (Physics); **Protestant Theology** (Protestant Theology; Religion; Religious Education; Theology); **Psychology** (Psychology); **Social Sciences** (Political Sciences; Social Sciences; Sociology)

Centre

Molecular Biology (Molecular Biology); **Sports Sciences and University Sports** (Sports); **Teacher Education** *(ZLB)* (Education; Teacher Training); **Translation studies** (Communication Studies; Translation and Interpretation)

History: Founded 1365. Reorganized 1377, 1384 and 1850 and 2004. A State institution under the jurisdiction of the Federal Ministry of Education, Science and Culture.

Academic Year: October to June (October-January; March-June)

Admission Requirements: Secondary school certificate (Reifezeugnis) or recognized foreign equivalent

Fees: c. 363.36 per semester; 726.72 for certain non-EU nationals; tuition waivers for some countries (Euro)

Main Language(s) of Instruction: German

Degrees and Diplomas: *Bachelor's Degree*; *Master's Degree*: **Anthropology; Archaeology; Arts and Humanities; Astronomy and Space Science; Behavioural Sciences; Biological and Life Sciences; Botany; Business Administration; Chemistry; Classical Languages; Cultural Studies; Earth Sciences; Ecology; Economics; Education; Environmental Studies; Gender Studies; Geography; Information Sciences; Mass Communication; Mathematics and Computer Science; Meteorology; Modern Languages; Musicology; Natural Sciences; Nursing; Nutrition; Performing Arts; Political Sciences; Psychology; Regional Planning; Religion; Social Sciences; Sociology; Sports; Surveying and Mapping; Technology; Theology; Translation and Interpretation; Urban Studies; Zoology.** *Doctor of Philosophy*: **Arts and Humanities; Biological and Life Sciences; Business Administration; Economics; Education; Engineering; Law; Natural Sciences; Philosophy; Social Sciences; Statistics; Theology.** The University of Vienna also offers continuing education courses

Student Services: Academic Counselling, Canteen, Careers Guidance, Language Laboratory, Social Counselling, Sports Facilities

Academic Staff *2013-2014*	MEN	WOMEN	**TOTAL**
FULL-TIME	–	–	**9,703**

Student Numbers *2013-2014*			
All (Foreign included)	24,356	41,956	c. **66,312**
FOREIGN ONLY	9,807	15,779	**25,586**

Last Updated: 14/04/15

VIENNA UNIVERSITY OF ECONOMICS AND BUSINESS

Wirtschaftsuniversität Wien (WU)

Welthandelsplatz 1, 1020 Wien, Vienna
Tel: +43(1) 313-36-0
EMail: rektorat@wu.ac.at
Website: http://www.wu.ac.at

Rector: Edeltraud Hanappi-Egger (2015-)
EMail: edeltraud.hanappi-egger@wu.ac.at

International Relations: Stefan Pichler, Vice-Rector, Research, International Affairs and External Relations
EMail: clemens.rogi@wu.ac.at

Department

Business, Employment and Social Security Law (Business Administration; Civil Law; European Union Law; Labour Law); **Economics** (Economics; Finance; International Economics; Social Policy); **Finance, Accounting and Statistics** (Accountancy; Banking; Finance; Insurance; Mathematics; Statistics; Taxation); **Foreign Language Business Communication** (English; Romance Languages; Slavic Languages); **Global Business and Trade** (Business Administration; International Business; Small Business; Transport Management); **Information Systems and Operations** (Industrial and Production Economics; Information Management; Information Technology; Media Studies; Production Engineering); **Management** (Management); **Marketing** (Advertising and Publicity; International Business; Leisure Studies; Marketing; Retailing and Wholesaling; Tourism); **Public Law and Tax Law** (Criminal Law; European Union Law; International Law; Public Law); **Socio-economics** (Economic History; Economics; Environmental Management; Geography; Geography (Human); Regional Studies; Social Policy; Social Sciences; Sociology; Technology); **Strategic**

Management and Innovation (Industrial Management; Management; Public Administration)

Research Institute

Capital Markets (Business Administration); **Co-Operation and Co-Operatives**; **Computational Methods** (Computer Science); **Economics of Ageing**; **European Affairs** (European Studies; Management; Marketing); **Family Businesses**; **Gender and Diversity in Organizations** (Gender Studies); **Health Care Management and Economics** (Health Administration); **Human Capital and Development**; **Independent Professions**; **International Taxation** (International Business; Taxation); **Legal Studies** (Law); **Managing Sustainability** (Management); **Regulatory Economics** (Economics); **Spatial and Real Estate Economics** (Real Estate); **Supply Chain Management** (Management); **Urban Management and Governance** (Government; Urban Studies)

Further Information: International Studies Centre; Career Planning and Placement Centre

History: Founded 1898 as Imperial Export Academy, soon took on the characteristics of a university, received the right to confer doctorates in 1930. Became Vienna University of Economics and Business Administration 1975. It gained full institutional autonomy 2004 through the University Act of 2002. Renamed WU (Vienna University of Economics and Business) in 2009.

Academic Year: October to June (October-January; March-June)

Admission Requirements: Secondary school certificate (Reifepruefungszeugnis) or foreign equivalent at Bachelor level. Bachelor degree or equivalent requirements at Master level (language skills, program-specific knowledge, GPA, GMAT etc.) Master degree or equivalent at Doctoral and PhD level.

Fees: 363,36 per semester. Tuition fees are waived for EU-citizens, EEA-citizens and refugees under the provisions of the Geneva Convention for the length of the standard duration of their degree program, plus two extra semesters (Euro)

Main Language(s) of Instruction: German, English

Degrees and Diplomas: *Bachelor's Degree*: **Business and Commerce; Commercial Law; Economics; Social Studies.** *Master's Degree*: **Accountancy; Business Education; Commercial Law; Economics; Finance; Information Technology; International Business; Management; Taxation.** *Doctor of Philosophy*: **Commercial Law; Economics; Finance; International Business; Social Sciences.**

Student Services: Academic Counselling, Canteen, Careers Guidance, Foreign Studies Centre, Language Laboratory, Nursery Care, Social Counselling

Publications: Journal für Betriebswirtschaft

Academic Staff *2013-2014*	TOTAL
FULL-TIME	1,043
Student Numbers *2013-2014*	
All (Foreign included)	22,781
FOREIGN ONLY	6241

Last Updated: 15/04/15

VIENNA UNIVERSITY OF TECHNOLOGY

Technische Universität Wien (TU WIEN)

Karlsplatz 13, 1040 Wien, Vienna
Tel: +43(1) 58801-0
Fax: +43(1) 58801-41088
EMail: webmaster@tuwien.ac.at
Website: http://www.tuwien.ac.at

Rector: Sabine Seidler
Tel: +43(1) 58801-406 000 EMail: sabine.seidler@tuwien.ac.at

Vice Rector for Academic Affairs: Adalbert Prechtl
Tel: +43(1) 58801-40139 EMail: adalbert.prechtl@tuwien.ac.at

International Relations: Andreas Zemann, Head of the International Office
Tel: +43(1) 58801-41552 EMail: andreas.zemann@tuwien.ac.at

Faculty

Architecture and Planning (Architecture and Planning; Regional Planning); **Civil Engineering** (Civil Engineering); **Computer Science** (Computer Science); **Electrical Engineering and Information Technology** (Electrical Engineering; Electronic Engineering; Information Technology); **Mathematics and Geoinformation** (Computer Science; Geophysics; Mathematics; Statistics); **Mechanical and Industrial Engineering** (Engineering Management; Industrial Engineering; Mechanical Engineering); **Physics** (Physics); **Technical Chemistry** (Chemistry)

History: Founded 1815 as institute of technology, acquired University status 1872 and right to award doctorates 1901. Reorganized 1955, acquired present status and title 1975. A State institution.

Academic Year: October to June (October-January; March-June)

Admission Requirements: Secondary school certificate (Reifezeugnis) or recognized foreign equivalent

Fees: 363,36 per semester for EU residents; 726,72 for non EU residents (Euro)

Main Language(s) of Instruction: German, English

Degrees and Diplomas: *Bachelor's Degree*; *Master's Degree*: **Architecture; Biomedical Engineering; Chemical Engineering; Civil Engineering; Computer Science; Electrical Engineering; Materials Engineering; Mathematics; Mechanical Engineering; Physics; Regional Planning; Surveying and Mapping; Urban Studies.** *Doctor of Philosophy*: **Economics; Natural Sciences; Social Sciences.** Also Doctoral programme in Technical sciences

Student Services: Academic Counselling, Canteen, Cultural Activities, Facilities for disabled people, Foreign Studies Centre, Language Laboratory, Social Counselling, Sports Facilities

Academic Staff *2013-2014*: Total 4,528
Student Numbers *2013-2014*: Total 27,923
Last Updated: 14/04/15

PRIVATE INSTITUTIONS

ANTON BRUCKNER UNIVERSITY

Anton Bruckner Privatuniversität

Wildergstrasse 18, 4040 Linz, Upper Austria
Tel: +43(732) 701000-0
Fax: +43(732) 701000-30
EMail: information@bruckneruni.at
Website: http://www.bruckneruni.at

Rector: Ursula Brandstätter
Tel: +43(732) 701000-70 EMail: u.brandstaetter@bruckneruni.at

Vice-Rector: Josef Eidenberger
Tel: +43(732) 701000-79 EMail: j.Eidenberger@bruckneruni.at

International Relations: Johanna Breuer
Tel: +43(732) 70-1000 EMail: j.breuer@bruckneruni.at

Programme

Classical Music (Music); **Dance** (Dance; Performing Arts); **Elementary Music Education** (Music Education); **Jazz and Improvization** (Jazz and Popular Music); **Theatre** (Theatre)

History: Founded in 1799.

Academic Year: October to June (October-February; March-June)

Admission Requirements: Entrance examination

Fees: Bachelor and Masters degrees: 300 per semester (Euro)

Main Language(s) of Instruction: German

Degrees and Diplomas: *Bachelor's Degree*: **Dance; Music; Music Education; Performing Arts; Theatre.** *Master's Degree*: **Dance; Music; Music Education; Performing Arts.**

Last Updated: 17/04/15

CAMPUS 02 UNIVERSITY OF APPLIED SCIENCES

Campus 02 Fachhochschule der Wirtschaft GmbH

Körblergasse 126, 8010 Graz, Styria
Tel: +43(316) 6002-177
EMail: info@campus02.at
Website: http://www.campus02.at

Rector: Franz Schrank
Tel: +43(316) 6002-322 EMail: franz.schrank@campus02.at

Managing Director: Erich Brugger
Tel: +43(316) 6002-311 EMail: erich.brugger@campus02.at

International Relations: Barbara Schantl
Tel: +43(316) 6002-786
EMail: international@campus02.at; barbara.schantl@campus02.at

Programme

Accountancy and Auditing (Accountancy; Management); **Automation Technology** (Automation and Control Engineering; Engineering; Technology); **Information Technology and Business Informatics** (Business and Commerce; Information Sciences; Information Technology); **Innovation Management** (Leadership; Management); **International Marketing and Sales Management** (Business and Commerce; International Business; Management; Marketing)

History: Founded 1996.

Academic Year: October to June

Admission Requirements: Graduation from high school (Matura) and entrance examination

Fees: 363,36 per semester (Euro)

Main Language(s) of Instruction: German

Degrees and Diplomas: *Bachelor's Degree*: **Automation and Control Engineering; Business and Commerce; Information Technology; Management; Marketing.** *Diplom-Ingenieur*: **Automation and Control Engineering; Information Technology.** *Master's Degree*: **Accountancy; Engineering; International Business; Management; Marketing.**

Student Services: Canteen, Facilities for disabled people, Language Laboratory

Last Updated: 17/04/15

CATHOLIC THEOLOGICAL PRIVATE UNIVERSITY LINZ

Katholisch-Theologische Privat Universität Linz
Bethlehemstrasse 20, 4020 Linz, Upper Austria
Tel: +43(732) 7842-93
Fax: +43(732) 7842-934-155
EMail: rektorat@ktu-linz.ac.at
Website: http://www.ktu-linz.ac.at

Rector: Franz Gruber (2014-)
Tel: +43(732) 78-42-93 EMail: f.gruber@ktu-linz.ac.at

Vice Rector: Ewald Volgger
Tel: +43(732) 78-42-93 EMail: e.volgger@ktu-linz.ac.at

Faculty

Arts and Humanities (Arts and Humanities; Fine Arts); **Philosophy** (Philosophy); **Theology** (Bible; Canon Law; History of Religion; Pastoral Studies; Philosophy; Religion; Religious Education; Theology)

Further Information: Also 12 Institutes

History: Founded 1672. Acquired present status 2001.

Main Language(s) of Instruction: German

Degrees and Diplomas: *Bachelor's Degree*: **Fine Arts; Philosophy; Religion.** *Lizentiat*: **Catholic Theology.** *Master's Degree*: **Catholic Theology; Fine Arts; Philosophy; Religious Education.** *Doctor of Philosophy*: **Catholic Theology; Fine Arts; Philosophy.** Also teacher training programme

Last Updated: 17/04/15

DANUBE PRIVATE UNIVERSITY (DPU)

Steiner Landstraße 124, 3500 Krems-Stein
Tel: +43(676) 842-419-305
Fax: +43(2732) 70478-7060
EMail: info@DP-Uni.ac.at
Website: http://www.danube-private-university.at/

President: Marga B. Wagner Pischel
Tel: +43(676) 842 -419-302
EMail: M.B.Wagner-Pischel@DP-Uni.ac.at

Director of Marketing and Management: Stefanie Arco-Zinneberg
Tel: +43(676) 842-419-304 EMail: Stefanie.Arco@DP-Uni.ac.at

Programme

Dentistry (Dentistry); **Medical Journalism and Public Relations** (Journalism; Public Relations)

Admission Requirements: Secondary school certificate (Reifezeugnis), written entrance examination and interview.

Fees: 4,000 - 13,000 per semester (Euro)

Main Language(s) of Instruction: German, English

Accrediting Agency: AQ Austria (Agentur für Qualitätssicherung und Akkreditierung Austria);

Degrees and Diplomas: *Bachelor's Degree*: **Dental Hygiene; Journalism; Public Relations.** *Master's Degree*: **Dentistry; Journalism; Public Relations.**

Student Services: Sports Facilities

Last Updated: 22/04/15

FHWIEN UNIVERSITY OF APPLIED SCIENCES

FHWien-Studiengänge der Wirtschaftskammer Wien
Währinger Gürtel 97, 1180 Wien, Vienna
Tel: +43(1) 47677-5744
Fax: +43(1) 47677-5745
EMail: studienzentrum@fh-wien.ac.at
Website: http://www.fh-wien.ac.at

Managing Director: Michael Heritsch
Tel: +43(1) 47677-5705 EMail: michael.heritsch@fh-wien.ac.at

International Relations: Elena Domaschkina
Tel: +43(1) 47677-5751 EMail: elena.domaschkina@fh-wien.ac.at

Programme

Business Management (Business Administration); **Communications Management** (Communication Studies); **Coorporate Communication** (Communication Studies); **Corporate Communication** (Communication Studies); **Entrepreneurship - Executive Management** (Business Administration; Management); **Finance, Accounting and Taxation** (Accountancy; Finance); **Financial Management** (Finance); **Financial Management and Controlling** (Finance); **Hospitality and Tourism Management** (Tourism); **Human Resources Management** (Human Resources); **Journalism and Media Management** (Journalism; Media Studies); **Management and Entrepreneurship** (Management); **Marketing and Sales** (Marketing; Sales Techniques); **Real Estate Management** (Real Estate); **Tourism Management** (Tourism)

History: Founded 1996.

Academic Year: September to June

Admission Requirements: Secondary school certificate (Reifezeugnis) or foreign equivalent

Main Language(s) of Instruction: German

Accrediting Agency: Fachhochschule Council

Degrees and Diplomas: *Bachelor's Degree*: **Accountancy; Business and Commerce; Communication Studies; Finance; Human Resources; Journalism; Management; Marketing; Media Studies; Real Estate; Taxation; Tourism.** *Master's Degree*: **Communication Studies; Finance; Human Resources; Journalism; Leadership; Management; Marketing; Media Studies; Real Estate; Tourism.**

Student Services: Canteen, Library

Student Numbers *2013*: Total 2,518

Last Updated: 22/04/15

IMC UNIVERSITY OF APPLIED SCIENCES OF KREMS

IMC Fachhochschule Krems (IMC)
Piaristengasse 1, 3500 Krems, Lower Austria
Tel: +43(2732) 802
Fax: +43(2732) 802-4
EMail: office@fh-krems.ac.at
Website: http://www.fh-krems.ac.at/

Rector: Eva Werner
Tel: +43(2732) 802-250 EMail: eva.werner@fh-krems.ac.at

CEO: Ulrike Prommer
Tel: +43 2732 802-562 EMail: ulrike.prommer@fh-krems.ac.at

International Relations: Maxililian Schachner, Head of International Department
Tel: +43(2732) 802-150 EMail: max.schachner@fh-krems.ac.at

School

Business (Business Administration; Health Administration; International Business; Management; Marketing; Tourism); **Health** (Art Therapy; Health Sciences; Midwifery; Nursing; Physical Therapy); **Life Sciences** (Biological and Life Sciences; Biotechnology; Pharmacology)

History: Founded 1994.

Academic Year: September to June

Admission Requirements: Secondary school leaving certificate or equivalent and entrance examination

Fees: National: EU citizens: 363,36 per semester (Euro), International: Non EU citizens: 3900 per semester (Euro)

Main Language(s) of Instruction: German, English

Accrediting Agency: Fachhochschule Council

Degrees and Diplomas: *Bachelor's Degree*: **Art Therapy; Biotechnology; Business Administration; Business and Commerce; Health Administration; Health Sciences; Management; Midwifery; Nursing; Occupational Therapy.** *Master's Degree*: **Art Therapy; Biotechnology; Environmental Management; Health Administration; International Business; Leisure Studies; Management; Marketing; Tourism.**

Student Services: Academic Counselling, Canteen

Last Updated: 16/04/15

KARL LANDSTEINER PRIVATE UNIVERSITY OF HEALTH SCIENCES

Karl Landsteiner Privatuniversität für Gesundheitswissenschaften (KL)

Dr. Karl-Dorrek Strasse 30, 3500 Krems
Tel: +43(2732) 720-90-0
Fax: +43(2732) 720-90-500
EMail: office@kl.ac.at
Website: http://www.kl.ac.at/

Rector and CEO: Rudolf Mallinger
Tel: +43(2732) 72090 - 200 EMail: rektorat@kl.ac.at

Prorector and CEO: Sabine Siegl EMail: rektorat@kl.ac.at

Programme

Health Sciences (Health Sciences); **Human Medicine** (Medicine); **Neurorehabilitation Sciences** (Rehabilitation and Therapy); **Psychotherapy and Counselling Sciences** (Psychotherapy)

Admission Requirements: Secondary school certificate (Reifezeugnis), vocational matriculation examination or general university entrance examination for medical degree programmes, or recognized foreign equivalent; written test and interview

Fees: 4,000 - 7,000 per semester (Euro)

Main Language(s) of Instruction: German, English

Accrediting Agency: Agency for Quality Assurance and Accreditation Austria (AQ Austria)

Degrees and Diplomas: *Bachelor's Degree*: **Health Sciences; Psychotherapy.** *Master's Degree*: **Medicine; Rehabilitation and Therapy.**

Student Services: Canteen

Last Updated: 22/04/15

LAUDER BUSINESS SCHOOL, UNIVERSITY OF APPLIED SCIENCES (LBS-VIC)

Hofzeile 18-20, 1190 Wien, Vienna
Tel: +43(1) 3691818
Fax: +43(1) 3691817
EMail: office@lbs.ac.at
Website: http://www.lbs.ac.at

President: Ronald S. Lauder

Executive Manager: Alexander Zirkler
Tel: +43(1) 369-1818-710 EMail: katja.seebohm@lbs.ac.at

International Relations: Elisabeth Kuebler
EMail: elisabeth.kuebler@lbs.ac.at

Programme

Banking, Finance and Compliance (Banking; Finance; Management); **International Business Administration** (Business Administration); **International Management and Leadership** (International Business; Leadership; Management)

Further Information: LBS is an EU-accredited institution of higher learning offering a four-year Master's degree programme in International Marketing and Management in English as the language of instruction. Foreign languages, German as a second language, and Jewish Studies are also offered, as well as electives in various fields (Philosophy, Psychology, Social and Political Sciences, International Relations, Legal Studies, Information Technology). Students take courses in core subjects of Accountancy, Finance, Management and Marketing in the first 4 semesters, and select specialized courses according to interests in the fifth and sixth semester. A semester of practical training (internship) takes place during the 7th semester, and the writing of a Master's thesis in the 8th and final semester.

History: Founded 2003 by former US ambassador to Austria Ronald S. Lauder with the support of the city of Vienna, the Ronald S. Lauder Foundation and other private donors.

Academic Year: October to June

Admission Requirements: High school diploma with university entrance; TOEFL test, placement test and interview, ability to contribute to and benefit from programme (Bachelor's degree not required although advanced standing of up to 2 years may be granted).

Main Language(s) of Instruction: English

Accrediting Agency: Ministry of Education, Science and Culture; Fachhochschulrat

Degrees and Diplomas: *Bachelor's Degree*: **International Business.** *Master's Degree*: **Finance; International Business; Management.**

Student Services: Academic Counselling, Canteen, Careers Guidance, Language Laboratory, Social Counselling

Last Updated: 17/04/15

MANAGEMENT CENTER INNSBRUCK (MCI)

Universitätsstrasse 15, 6020 Innsbruck, Tyrol
Tel: +43(512) 2070-0
Fax: +43(512) 2070-1099
EMail: office@mci.edu
Website: http://www.mci.edu

Rector and Executive Director: Andreas Altmann (2011-)
Tel: +43(512) 2070-1050 EMail: andreas.altmann@mci.edu

Director of Infrastructure and Organisation: Tommy Mayr
EMail: tommy.mayr@mci.edu

International Relations: Susanne Lichtmannegger, Head of International Relations
Tel: +43(512) 2070-1610
EMail: international@mci.edu; susanne.lichtmannegger@mci.edu

Programme

Biotechnology (Biotechnology); **Business and Management** (Business Administration; Economics; Management); **Engineering and Environmental Management** (Chemical Engineering; Chemistry; Electrical and Electronic Engineering; Engineering; Engineering Management; Environmental Management; Mathematics; Physics); **Engineering and Environmental Management** (Electronic Engineering; Mechanical Engineering); **General Management Executive MBA** (Business Administration; Business and Commerce; Economics; Finance; Human Resources; International Studies; Management; Marketing); **Management and Applied Informatics** (Artificial Intelligence; Business Administration; Computer Science; Information Sciences; Management); **Management and Law** (Business Administration; European Union Law; International Business; International Law; Labour Law; Law; Management; Private Law; Public Law); **Non Profit, Social and Health Care Management** (Business Administration; Economics; Health Administration; Law; Political Sciences; Social Studies); **Social Work** (Social Work); **Tourism and Leisure** (Business Administration; Hotel and Restaurant; Leadership; Leisure Studies; Management; Tourism)

Further Information: Also Summer Schools and non degree programmes

History: Founded 1996 by the Business Faculty of the University of Innsbruck and other partners, acquired present status 1997.

Academic Year: September to July

Admission Requirements: High school certificate or equivalent and/or relevant professional qualification; Selection process (written exam, interview)

Fees: 363 per semester (Euro)

Main Language(s) of Instruction: German, English

Accrediting Agency: Austrian Ministry of Education, Science and Culture; Austrian Accrediting Board for University of Applied Sciences

Degrees and Diplomas: *Bachelor's Degree*: **Business and Commerce; Engineering; Social Sciences.** *Master's Degree*: **Business and Commerce; Social Sciences.**

Student Services: Academic Counselling, Canteen, Foreign Studies Centre, Language Laboratory, Social Counselling, Sports Facilities

Student Numbers *2014-2015*: Total 2,939

Last Updated: 17/04/15

MODUL UNIVERSITY

Am Kahlenberg 1, Josefsdorf 2, 1190 Wien, Vienna
Tel: +43(1) 3203555-101; +43(1) 47670-257
Fax: +43(1) 3203555-901; +43(1) 47670-258
EMail: office@modul.ac.at
Website: http://www.modul.ac.at/

President: Karl Wöber
Tel: +43(1) 3203555-300 EMail: karl.woeber@modul.ac.at

Head of Marketing and Communications: Andreas Eder
Tel: +43(1) 3203555-104 EMail: andreas.eder@modul.ac.at

Managing Director: Christian Hoffmann
Tel: +43(1) 3203555-100 EMail: christian.hoffmann@modul.ac.at

Department

Applied Statistics and Economics (Economics; Statistics); **International Management** (International Business; Management); **New Media Technology** (Mass Communication; Media Studies); **Public Governance and Sustainable Development** (Development Studies; Government; Management; Public Administration; Regional Planning; Tourism); **Tourism and Service Management** (Management; Tourism)

History: Founded 2007.

Academic Year: September to July

Admission Requirements: High school certificate for Bachelor, university degree for Master

Fees: 5,166 - 6,250 per semester (Euro)

Main Language(s) of Instruction: German, English

Degrees and Diplomas: *Bachelor's Degree*: **Hotel and Restaurant; Hotel Management; Tourism.** *Master's Degree*: **Development Studies; Management; Public Administration; Tourism.** Also Doctorate in Business and Socioeconomic Sciences

Student Services: Canteen, Library

Last Updated: 20/04/15

NEW DESIGN UNIVERSITY

Privatuniversität der Kreativwirtschaft (NDU)
Mariazeller Strasse 97, 3100 St. Pölten, Lower Austria
Tel: +43(2742) 890-2411
Fax: +43(2742) 890-2413
EMail: office@ndu.ac.at
Website: http://www.ndu.ac.at

Rector: Stephan Schmidt-Wulffen EMail: rektor@ndu.ac.at

Vice Rector: Johannes Zederbauer
EMail: johannes.zederbauer@ndu.ac.at

International Relations: Monika Weiß-Svoboda
Tel: +43(2742) 890-2424 EMail: international@ndu.ac.at

Programme

Design (Business and Commerce; Design; Graphic Design; Interior Design); **Events Engineering**; **Graphic Arts** (Graphic Arts); **Information science and big data analytics** (Information Sciences)

History: Founded 2004

Admission Requirements: Entrance examination

Main Language(s) of Instruction: German

Degrees and Diplomas: *Bachelor's Degree*: **Business and Commerce; Design.** *Master's Degree*: **Business and Commerce; Design; Information Sciences; Natural Resources.**

Last Updated: 20/04/15

PARACELSUS PRIVATE MEDICAL UNIVERSITY

Paracelsus Medizinische Privatuniversität
Strubergasse 21, 5020 Salzburg, Salzburg
Tel: +43(662) 2420-0
Fax: +43(662) 2420-80009
EMail: pmu@pmu.ac.at
Website: http://www.pmu.ac.at

Rector: Herbert Resch EMail: herbert.resch@pmu.ac.at

Vice Rector: Wolfgang Soellner
Tel: +49(911) 398-2839 EMail: wolfgang.soellner@pmu.ac.at

Programme

Medicine (Medicine); **Nursing** (Nursing)

Institute

Anatomy (Anatomy; Health Sciences); **General Practice, Family Medicine and Preventive Medicine** (Medicine); **Nursing Sciences** (Nursing); **Pharmacology and Toxicology** (Pharmacology; Toxicology); **Physiology and Pathophysiology** (Health Sciences; Physiology)

History: Founded 2002. Formerly known as Private Medizinische Universität Salzburg.

Academic Year: October to June

Main Language(s) of Instruction: German

Degrees and Diplomas: *Bachelor's Degree*: **Nursing.** *Master's Degree*: **Nursing.** *Doctor of Philosophy*: **Medicine; Microbiology.**

Last Updated: 20/04/15

PRIVATE UNIVERSITY FOR HEALTH SCIENCES, MEDICAL INFORMATICS AND TECHNIQUES

Private Universität für Gesundheitswissenschaften, Medizinische Informatik und Technik (UMIT)
Eduard Wallnöfer-Zentrum I, 6060 Hall, Tyrol
Tel: +43(50) 8648-3000
Fax: +43(50) 8648-673001
EMail: rektorat@umit.at
Website: http://www.umit.at

Rector: Sabine Schindler
Tel: +43(50) 8648-3890 EMail: rektorat@umit.at

Vice Rector and CEO: Philipp Unterholzne
Tel: +43(50) 8648-3920 EMail: vizerektorat@umit.at

Department

Biomedical computer science and mechatronics (Automation and Control Engineering; Biomedical Engineering; Computer Science; Electrical Engineering; Technology); **Nursing and Gerontology** (Gerontology; Nursing); **Psychology, Medical Sciences and Health Systems Management** (Health Administration; Health Sciences; Psychology); **Public Health and Health Technology Assessment** *(Department of Public Health and HTA)* (Behavioural Sciences; Health Administration; Medical Technology; Public Health)

Institute

Automation and Control Engineering (Automation and Control Engineering); **Behavioural Medicine and Prevention** (Medicine; Social and Preventive Medicine); **Bioinformatics and**

Translational Research (Computer Science; Technology); **Electrical and Biomedical Engineering** (Biomedical Engineering; Electrical Engineering); **Gerontology and Demographic Development** (Demography and Population; Gerontology); **Nursing** (Nursing); **Public Health, Medical Decision Making and HTA** (Medical Technology; Medicine; Public Health); **Quality and Ethics in Health Care** (Ethics; Public Health)

History: Founded 2001. Formerly known as Private Universität für Medizinische Informatik und Technik Tirol.

Academic Year: October to June

Fees: 2,600 - 3,600 per semester (Euro)

Main Language(s) of Instruction: German

Degrees and Diplomas: *Bachelor's Degree*: **Economics; Electronic Engineering; Health Administration; Nursing; Physical Therapy; Psychology; Sports.** *Master's Degree*: **Electronic Engineering; Health Sciences; Nursing; Psychology.** *Doctor of Philosophy*: **Biomedical Engineering; Computer Science; Health Administration; Leisure Studies; Medical Technology; Nursing; Psychology; Public Health; Sports.**

Last Updated: 20/04/15

PRIVATE UNIVERSITY SCHLOSS SEEBURG

Privatuniversität Schloss Seeburg

Seeburgstrasse 8, 5201 Seekirchen am Wallersee, Salzburg
Tel: +43(6212) 2626-0
Fax: +43(6212) 2626-39
EMail: Info@uni-seeburg.at
Website: http://www.uni-seeburg.at/

Rector: Achim Hecker (2013-)
Tel: +43(6212) 2626-10 EMail: achim.hecker@uni-seeburg.at

Managing Director: Christian Werner
Tel: +43(6212) 2626 EMail: christian.werner@uni-seeburg.at

International Relations: Eva-Maria Leitner
Tel: +43(6212) 2626-13 EMail: eva-maria.leitner@uni-seeburg.at

Programme

Business Administration (Business Administration; Management; Sports Management); **Business Psychology** (Industrial and Organizational Psychology); **Educational Management** (Educational Administration)

History: Founded in 2008

Admission Requirements: General university entrance (Matura) or equivalent

Fees: Bachelor: 390 per semester; Master: 450 per semester; MBA: 14,900 per annum (Euro)

Main Language(s) of Instruction: German

Accrediting Agency: Agentur für Qualitätssicherung und Akkreditierung Austria (Austria AQ)

Degrees and Diplomas: *Bachelor's Degree*: **Business Administration; Industrial and Organizational Psychology; Management; Sports Management.** *Master's Degree*: **Business Administration; Educational Administration; Industrial and Organizational Psychology; Management; Sports Management.** Semi-virtual study: attendance phases (three times per semester for a week) and distance learning phases. Also MBA

Student Services: Careers Guidance

Student Numbers *2012-2013*: Total 259
Last Updated: 22/04/15

SIGMUND FREUD PRIVATE UNIVERSITY OF VIENNA

Sigmund Freud Privatuniversität Wien

Freudplatz 1, 1020 Wien, Vienna
Tel: +43(1) 798-4098
Fax: +43(1) 798-4098/900
EMail: office@sfu.ac.at
Website: http://sfu.ac.at/

Rector: Alfred Pritz EMail: alfred.pritz@sfu.ac.at

Vice Rector: Jutta Fiegl EMail: jutta.fiegl@sfu.ac.at

International Relations: Elisabeth Vykoukal, Head of International Programmes
Tel: +43(1) 798-40-98-455 EMail: elisabeth.vykoukal@sfu.ac.at

Department

Child and Adolescent Psychotherapy (Psychotherapy); **Neuroscientific Principles of Psychotherapy** (Neurosciences; Psychotherapy); **Psychotherapy in the Health Care System** (Health Sciences; Psychotherapy); **Schools of Psychotherapy** (Psychotherapy); **Transcultural and Historical Research in Psychotherapy** (Psychotherapy)

Institute

Wealthibility and Wealth Psychology (Psychology)

Further Information: Also University Outpatient Clinic

History: Acquired present status 2005.

Academic Year: September to July (September-January; March-July)

Admission Requirements: secondary school certificate (Matura), vocational certificate (Berufsreifeprüfung), or foreign equivalent. Two admission interviews.

Fees: Bachelor's Degree Program: 6,300 per semester; Master's Degree Programme: 6,830 per semester (Euro)

Main Language(s) of Instruction: German

Degrees and Diplomas: *Bachelor's Degree*: **Psychotherapy.** *Master's Degree*: **Psychotherapy.** Also Doctoral programme in Psychotherapy

Last Updated: 20/04/15

UNIVERSITY OF APPLIED SCIENCES OF BFI VIENNA

Fachhochschule des bfi Wien GmbH

Wohlmutstrasse 22, 1020 Wien, Vienna
Tel: +43(1) 7201286
Fax: +43(1) 7201286-19
EMail: info@fh-vie.ac.at
Website: http://www.fh-vie.ac.at

Managing Director: Helmut Holzinger (1998-)
Tel: +43(1) 7201286-10 EMail: helmut.holzinger@fh-vie.ac.at

International Relations: Elisabeth Brunner-Sobanski, Head of the International Office
Tel: +43(1) 7201286-956 EMail: elisabeth.brunner@fh-vie.ac.at

Programme

Banking and Finance Studies *(Full time and career-parallel studies)* (Banking; Finance); **European Economy and Business Management Studies** *(career-parallel studies)* (Business Administration; Economics; European Studies; Management); **Film, TV and Media Production** (Film; Media Studies); **Logistics and Transport Management** *(Full time studies)* (Transport Management); **Project Management and Information Technology** *(Full-time and parallel studies)* (Information Technology; Management)

Graduate School

Risk Management (Management)

History: Founded 1996, acquired present status 2002.

Academic Year: October to July (October-February; March-July)

Admission Requirements: Secondary school leaving certificate (Reifezeugnis) or foreign equivalent, or university entrance qualification

Fees: 363,36 per semester (Euro)

Main Language(s) of Instruction: German, English

Accrediting Agency: Fachhochschule Council Vienna (Fachhochschulrat Wien)

Degrees and Diplomas: *Bachelor's Degree*: **Banking; Business and Commerce; Economics; European Studies; Finance; Management; Mass Communication; Transport Management.** *Master's Degree*: **Banking; Economics; European Studies; Finance; Insurance; International Business; Management; Transport Management.** Also MBA and MSc

Student Services: Academic Counselling, Canteen, Facilities for disabled people, Language Laboratory, Social Counselling

Publications: Research Magazine

Last Updated: 16/04/15

UNIVERSITY OF APPLIED SCIENCES OF BURGENLAND

Fachhochschule Burgenland GmbH

Campus 1, 7000 Eisenstadt, Burgenland
Tel: +43(5) 9010609-0
Fax: +43(5) 9010609-15
EMail: office@fh-burgenland.at
Website: http://www.fh-burgenland.at

Rector: Gernot Hanreich
Tel: +43(3357) 45370-1133
EMail: gernot.hanreich@fh-burgenland.at

Administrative Officer: Georg Pehm
Tel: +43(5) 9010-603-12 EMail: georg.pehm@fh-burgenland.at

International Relations: Petra Hauptfeld-Göllner, Head of international
Tel: +43(5) 9010-601-22 EMail: petra.hauptfeld@fh-burgenland.at

Department

Building Technology and Management *(Pinkafeld)* (Building Technologies; Engineering; Management); **Economics** (Economics; European Studies; Human Resources; International Business; Management; Marketing); **Energy and Environment Management** *(Pinkafeld)* (Energy Engineering; Engineering; Environmental Management); **Health** (Health Administration; Information Management; Information Technology; Nursing; Physical Therapy); **Information Technology and Information Management** (Communication Studies; Computer Engineering; Engineering; Information Sciences; Information Technology; Management; Media Studies); **Social Work** (Social Work)

History: Founded 1994.

Academic Year: September to August (September-February; February-August)

Admission Requirements: Secondary school leaving certificate (Matura) and entrance examination

Fees: None

Main Language(s) of Instruction: German, English

Degrees and Diplomas: *Bachelor's Degree*: **Environmental Management; Health Administration; International Business; Media Studies; Physical Therapy; Social Work.** *Diplom-Ingenieur*: **Building Technologies; Energy Engineering; Environmental Management; Management.** *Master's Degree*: **Building Technologies; Computer Engineering; Energy Engineering; Environmental Management; Health Administration; Human Resources; Information Management; International Business; Management.**

Student Services: Academic Counselling, Canteen, Careers Guidance, Cultural Activities, Facilities for disabled people, Foreign Studies Centre, Language Laboratory, Social Counselling, Sports Facilities

Last Updated: 17/04/15

UNIVERSITY OF APPLIED SCIENCES OF CAMPUS VIENNA

Fachhochschule Campus Wien

Favoritenstraße 226, 1100 Wien, Vienna
Tel: +43(1) 606-6877-6600
EMail: office@fh-campuswien.ac.at
Website: http://www.fh-campuswien.ac.at

Rector: Arthur Mettinger
Tel: +43(1) 606-6877-1501
EMail: arthur.mettinger@fh-campuswien.ac.at

Chief Executive Officer: Wilhelm Behensky
Tel: +43(1) 606-6877-1000 EMail: office@fh-campuswien.ac.at

International Relations: Wolfgang Sünder
Tel: +43(1) 6066-877-6151
EMail: wolfgang.suender@fh-campuswien.ac.at

Department

Applied ILife science (Bioengineering; Biotechnology; Computer Science; Management; Technology); **Building and Design** (Building Technologies; Civil Engineering; Construction Engineering; Management); **Engineering** (Biomedical Engineering; Computer Engineering; Electronic Engineering; Engineering; Information Technology; Management; Safety Engineering; Technology; Telecommunications Engineering); **Health Science** (Biomedical Engineering; Biomedicine; Dietetics; Health Sciences; Midwifery; Nursing; Occupational Health; Physical Therapy; Radiology; Speech Therapy and Audiology); **Public sector** (Insurance; Leadership; Management; Public Administration; Taxation); **Social Work** (Economics; Management; Social Work)

History: Founded 1999.

Academic Year: October to June

Admission Requirements: Secondary school certificate (Reifezeugnis) or recognized foreign equivalent, Higher education entrance qualification; written selection test and Interview

Fees: 363,36 per semester (Euro)

Main Language(s) of Instruction: German

Accrediting Agency: Fachhochschule Council

Degrees and Diplomas: *Bachelor's Degree*: **Bioengineering; Biomedical Engineering; Biotechnology; Building Technologies; Civil Engineering; Construction Engineering; Dietetics; Electrical Engineering; Information Technology; Midwifery; Nursing; Occupational Therapy; Public Administration; Radiology; Social Work; Speech Therapy and Audiology; Taxation; Technology; Telecommunications Engineering.** *Master's Degree*: **Biomedical Engineering; Biotechnology; Building Technologies; Civil Engineering; Computer Engineering; Computer Science; Construction Engineering; Engineering; Insurance; Leadership; Management; Public Administration; Social Work; Taxation; Technology.**

Last Updated: 16/04/15

UNIVERSITY OF APPLIED SCIENCES OF CARINTHIA

Fachhochschule Kärnten

Villacher Strasse 1, 9800 Spittal an der Drau, Carinthia
Tel: +43(5) 90500-0
Fax: +43(5) 90500-1110
EMail: international@fh-kaernten.at
Website: http://www.fh-kaernten.at/

Rector: Dietmar Brodel
Tel: +43(5) 90500-1200 EMail: d.brodel@fh-kaernten.at

Executive Director: Siegried Spanz
Tel: +43(5) 90500-9900 EMail: siegfried.spanz@fh-kaernten.at

International Relations: Aleksandra Jama, Head of the International Office Tel: +43(5) 90500-9902 EMail: a.jama@fh-kaernten.at

School

Civil Engineering and Architecture *(Spittal)* (Architecture; Civil Engineering); **Geoinformation** *(Villach)* (Geography; Geophysics; Surveying and Mapping); **Health and Care** *(Feldkirchen)* (Health Administration); **Management** *(Villach)* (International Business; Management; Public Administration); **Medical Information Technology** *(Klagenfurt)* (Health Administration; Information Technology; Medical Technology); **Social Work** *(Feldkirchen)*; **Systems Engineering** (Electronic Engineering; Engineering Management; Mechanical Engineering); **Telematics and Network Engineering** (Computer Networks; Telecommunications Engineering)

Further Information: Campuses in Spittal, Villach, Klagenfurt and Feldkirchen.

History: Founded 1995. Previously known as Fachhochschule Technikum Kärnten.

Academic Year: October to September.

Admission Requirements: an Austrian certificate of the university entrance examination or foreigne equivalent

Main Language(s) of Instruction: German, English

Accrediting Agency: Fachhochschule Council

Degrees and Diplomas: *Bachelor's Degree*: **Architecture; Civil Engineering; Computer Engineering; Engineering; Health Administration; Information Technology; Management; Mechanical Engineering; Medicine; Social Work; Surveying and Mapping.** *Diplom-Ingenieur*, *Master's Degree*: **Architecture; Civil Engineering; Communication Arts; Design; Health Administration; Health Sciences; International Business; Management; Social Work; Systems Analysis.**

Student Services: Academic Counselling, Canteen, Facilities for disabled people, Language Laboratory, Sports Facilities

Last Updated: 16/04/15

UNIVERSITY OF APPLIED SCIENCES OF JOANNEUM

Fachhochschule Joanneum
Alte Poststraße 147 - 154, Eggenberger Allee 9 - 13, 8020 Graz, Styria
Tel: +43(316) 5453-0
Fax: +43(316) 5453-8801
EMail: international@fh-joanneum.at
Website: http://www.fh-joanneum.at

Rector and Managing Director: Karl Peter Pfeiffer
Tel: +43(316) 5453-8860 EMail: karl-peter.pfeiffer@fh-joanneum.at

Commercial Director: Günter Riegler
Tel: +43(316) 5453-8870 EMail: guenter.riegler@fh-joanneum.at

International Relations: Birgit Hernády, Head of International Relations
Tel: +43(316) 5453-8827
EMail: birgit.hernady @fh-joanneum.at; international@fh-joanneum.at

Department

Applied Computer Sciences (Computer Engineering; Information Management; Information Technology); **Building, Energy and Society** (Architecture; Building Technologies; Construction Engineering; Design; Energy Engineering; Environmental Engineering; Environmental Management; Social Work; Transport Management); **Engineering** (Aeronautical and Aerospace Engineering; Automotive Engineering; Electronic Engineering; Mechanical Engineering; Production Engineering); **Health Sciences** *(Bad Gleichenberg)* (Biomedical Engineering; Business and Commerce; Dietetics; English; Health Administration; Midwifery; Nutrition; Occupational Health; Physical Therapy; Radiology); **Management** (Banking; Health Administration; Industrial Management; Insurance; International Business; Tourism); **Media and Design** (Communication Studies; Design; Furniture Design; Journalism; Mass Communication; Public Relations)

History: Founded 1995. Formerly known as Fachhochschul-Studiengänge Technikum Joanneum.

Academic Year: September to July

Admission Requirements: Secondary school certificate (Reifezeugnis) or foreign equivalent and entrance examination

Fees: Non-EU/EEA students: 727 per semester (Euro)

Main Language(s) of Instruction: German

Degrees and Diplomas: *Bachelor's Degree*: **Aeronautical and Aerospace Engineering; Automotive Engineering; Banking; Biomedicine; Computer Engineering; Computer Science; Design; Dietetics; Electronic Engineering; Energy Engineering; Environmental Management; Health Administration; Industrial Design; Industrial Management; Information Management; Information Technology; Insurance; Journalism; Management; Midwifery; Nutrition; Occupational Therapy; Production Engineering; Public Relations; Radiology; Social Work; Software Engineering; Speech Therapy and Audiology; Tourism; Transport Management.** *Master's Degree*: **Aeronautical and Aerospace Engineering; Architecture; Automotive Engineering; Business and Commerce; Communication Studies; Computer Science; Construction Engineering; Design; Electronic Engineering; Energy Engineering; Health Sciences; Industrial Design; Industrial Management; Information Management; Management; Media Studies; Production Engineering; Social Work; Tourism; Transport Management.**

Student Services: Academic Counselling, Canteen, Facilities for disabled people, Language Laboratory

Last Updated: 17/04/15

UNIVERSITY OF APPLIED SCIENCES OF KUFSTEIN TIROL

Fachhochschule Kufstein Tirol
Andreas Hofer Strasse 7, 6330 Kufstein, Tyrol
Tel: +43(5372) 71819
Fax: +43(5372) 71819-104
EMail: info@fh-kufstein.ac.at
Website: http://www.fh-kufstein.ac.at

Rector: Johannes Lüthi
Tel: +43(5372) 71819-172
EMail: Johannes.Luethi@fh-kufstein.ac.at; rektorat@fh-kufstein.ac.at

CEO Managing Director: Thomas Madritsch
Tel: +43(5372) 71819-301
EMail: Thomas.Madritsch@fh-kufstein.ac.at

International Relations: Noureddine Rafili (Head of International Relations Office)
Tel: +43(5372) 71819-113
EMail: Noureddine.Rafili@fh-kufstein.ac.at

Programme

Business Engineer Sciences (Business Administration); **Business Management** (Business Administration); **Corporate Restructuring** (Business Administration); **ERP-Systems and Business Process Management** (Management); **European Energy Business** (Business Administration); **Facility and Real Estate Management** (Real Estate); **International Business Studies** (International Business; Management); **Marketing and Communication Management** (Communication Studies; Management; Marketing); **Real Estate and Facility Management** (Architecture; Building Technologies; Business Administration; Real Estate); **Sports, Culture and Event Management** (Cultural Studies; Sports Management); **Web-Business and Technology** (Computer Networks; E-Business/Commerce)

History: Founded 1997.

Academic Year: September to July (September-February; March-July)

Admission Requirements: Secondary school certificate (Reifeprüfung) or foreign equivalent

Fees: 363,36 per semester (Euro)

Main Language(s) of Instruction: German, English

Degrees and Diplomas: *Bachelor's Degree*: **Business Administration; Business and Commerce; Computer Networks; E-Business/Commerce; Industrial Engineering; International Business; Management; Marketing; Real Estate; Sports Management; Technology.** *Master's Degree*: **Business Administration; Computer Networks; E-Business/Commerce; Management; Marketing; Real Estate; Sports Management.**

Student Services: Academic Counselling, Careers Guidance, Language Laboratory, Library, Social Counselling, Sports Facilities

Last Updated: 17/04/15

UNIVERSITY OF APPLIED SCIENCES OF SALZBURG

Fachhochschule Salzburg
Urstein Süd 1, 5012 Puch, Salzburg
Tel: +43(50) 2211-0
EMail: office@fh-sbg.ac.at
Website: http://www.fh-salzburg.ac.at

Rector: Kerstin Fink (2011-)
Tel: +43(50) 2211-1010 EMail: kerstin.fink@fh-salzburg.ac.at

Managing Director: Raimund Ribitsch
Tel: +43-(50) 2211-100 EMail: raimund.ribitsch@fh-salzburg.ac.at

International Relations: Claudia Prätor, Head of International Office
Tel: +43-(50) 2211-1031 EMail: claudia.praetor@fh-salzburg.ac.at

Programme

Business and Information Management (Business Administration; Information Management); **Business Development in Tourism** (Management; Tourism); **Construction and Design with Wood** (Construction Engineering; Design; Wood Technology); **Design and Product Management** (Industrial Design; Industrial Management); **Digital Television** (Radio and Television Broadcasting; Telecommunications Engineering); **Forest Products Technology and Management** (Wood Technology); **Health sciences** (Biomedicine; Midwifery; Nursing; Rehabilitation and Therapy; Treatment Techniques); **Information Technology and Systems Management** (Information Management; Information Technology); **Multimedia Art-Creation and Production** (Multimedia); **Social Work** (Social Work)

History: Founded 1996. Incorporated Holztechnikum Kuchl as a branch 2003.

Academic Year: September to July

Admission Requirements: Secondary school certificate (Reifezeugnis) or recognized foreign equivalent

Fees: 363 per semester (Euro)

Main Language(s) of Instruction: German

Degrees and Diplomas: *Bachelor's Degree*: **Biomedicine; Building Technologies; Forest Products; Forestry; Health Sciences; Management; Midwifery; Multimedia; Nursing; Occupational Therapy; Social Work; Technology; Treatment Techniques.** *Master's Degree*: **Computer Engineering; Computer Graphics; Forest Products; Forestry; Information Technology; Management; Multimedia; Technology; Tourism.**

Student Services: Academic Counselling, Canteen, Careers Guidance, Foreign Studies Centre, Health Services, Language Laboratory, Social Counselling, Sports Facilities

Last Updated: 16/04/15

UNIVERSITY OF APPLIED SCIENCES OF ST. PÖLTEN

Fachhochschule St. Pölten

Matthias Corvinus-Strasse 15, 3100 St. Pölten, Lower Austria
Tel: +43(2742) 313-228-200
Fax: +43(2742) 313-228-339
EMail: international@fhstp.ac.at
Website: https://www.fhstp.ac.at/en

Rector: Barbara Schmid

Executive Director: Gernot Kohl
Tel: +43(2742) 313-228-202 EMail: gernot.kohl@fhstp.ac.at

Executive Director: Gabriela Fernandes
Tel: +43(2742) 313-228-205
EMail: gabriela.fernandes@fhstp.ac.at

International Relations: Barbara Zimmer, Head of the International Office
Tel: +43(2742) 313-228-261 EMail: barbara.zimmer@fhstp.ac.at

Programme

Business (Management; Media Studies); **Health and Social Sciences** (Dietetics; Physical Therapy; Social Work); **Technology** (Media Studies; Railway Engineering; Telecommunications Engineering)

History: Founded 1996.

Academic Year: September to June (September-February; February-June)

Admission Requirements: Secondary school certificate (Matura or Studienberechtigungsprüfung)

Fees: 363,36 per semester; Higher tuition fees may apply to non EU students (Euro)

Main Language(s) of Instruction: German

Degrees and Diplomas: *Bachelor's Degree*: **Computer Science; Dietetics; Health Sciences; Media Studies; Railway Engineering; Social Work; Technology.** *Master's Degree*: **Computer Science; Media Studies; Multimedia; Railway Engineering; Social Work; Technology.**

Student Services: Academic Counselling, Facilities for disabled people, Language Laboratory

Student Numbers *2011*: Total 1,776

Last Updated: 16/04/15

UNIVERSITY OF APPLIED SCIENCES OF TECHNIKUM VIENNA

Fachhochschule Technikum Wien

Höchstädtplatz 6, 1200 Wien, Vienna
Tel: +43(1) 333 4077-0
EMail: info@technikum-wien.at
Website: http://www.technikum-wien.at

Rector: Fritz Schmöllebeck
Tel: +43(1) 333-4077-261
EMail: nicole.sagmeister@technikum-wien.at

Vice-Rector: Christian Kollmitzer

International Relations: Sandra Allmayer
Tel: +43(1) 333-4077-323
EMail: sandra.allmayer@technikum-wien.at

Department

Advanced Engineering Technologies (Automation and Control Engineering; Electronic Engineering; Materials Engineering; Mechanical Engineering; Robotics; Technology); **Applied Mathematics and Science** (Applied Mathematics; Natural Sciences); **Biochemical Engineering** (Biochemistry; Engineering); **Biomedical Engineering** (Biomedical Engineering); **Computer Science** (Computer Science); **Electronic Engineering** (Electronic Engineering); **Embedded Systems** (Computer Engineering); **Humanities** (Arts and Humanities; Cultural Studies; Modern Languages); **Information Engineering and Security** (Information Technology); **Information Systems Management** (Information Technology); **Management, Business and Law** (Business Administration; Law; Management); **Renewable Energy** (Energy Engineering); **Social Competence and Management Methods** (Management); **Sports Engineering and Biomechanics** (Sports; Technology); **Telecommunication and Internet Technologies** (Computer Engineering; Computer Science; Information Technology; Technology; Telecommunications Engineering)

History: Founded 1994.

Admission Requirements: Secondary school certificate (Allgemeine Hochschulreife)

Fees: 363,36 per semester (Euro)

Main Language(s) of Instruction: German, English

Accrediting Agency: Fachhochschule Council

Degrees and Diplomas: *Bachelor's Degree*: **Biomedical Engineering; Business and Commerce; Computer Science; Electronic Engineering; Engineering; Environmental Studies; Information Sciences; International Business; Mechanical Engineering; Natural Resources; Robotics; Sports; Technology.** *Master's Degree*: **Biomedical Engineering; Computer Engineering; Computer Science; Electronic Engineering; Engineering; Environmental Management; Information Management; Information Sciences; International Business; Leisure Studies; Management; Medical Technology; Natural Resources; Robotics; Software Engineering; Sports; Technology; Telecommunications Engineering; Transport Engineering.**

Student Services: Academic Counselling, Careers Guidance, Facilities for disabled people, Foreign Studies Centre, Language Laboratory, Social Counselling

Last Updated: 16/04/15

UNIVERSITY OF APPLIED SCIENCES OF VORARLBERG

Fachhochschule Vorarlberg

Hochschulstrasse 1, 6850 Dornbirn, Vorarlberg
Tel: +43(5572) 792-0
Fax: +43(5572) 792-9500
EMail: info@fhv.at
Website: http://www.fhv.at

Rector: Rudi Feurstein (2005-)
Tel: +43(5572) 792-1000 EMail: rektorat@fhv.at

Managing Director: Stefan Fitz-Rankl
Tel: +43(5572) 792-2001 EMail: stefan.fitz-rankl@fhv.at

International Relations: Karin Wüstner-Dobler, Head of International Office
Tel: +43(5572) 792-1201
EMail: karin.wuestner-dobler@fhv.at; international@fhv.at

Programme

Social Sciences and Organization Studies (Social Sciences; Social Work)

Department

Computer Science (Computer Science; Information Technology; Mathematics); **Design and Mediabased Communication** (Communication Studies; Design; Graphic Design; Media Studies; Visual Arts); **Engineering** (Automation and Control Engineering; Electronic Engineering; Mechanical Engineering; Robotics); **Management and Business Administration** (Business Administration; Management)

History: Founded 1994.

Academic Year: October to June

Admission Requirements: Secondary school certificate and entrance examination

Main Language(s) of Instruction: German, English

Accrediting Agency: Fachhochschulrat, Vienna

Degrees and Diplomas: *Bachelor's Degree*: **Computer Engineering; Electrical Engineering; Engineering Management; International Business; Mechanical Engineering; Multimedia; Social Work.** *Master's Degree*: **Accountancy; Business Administration; Computer Science; Energy Engineering; Finance; International Business; Marketing; Mechanical Engineering; Multimedia; Social Work; Technology.** Also degrees in Professional Training courses

Student Services: Academic Counselling, Canteen, Careers Guidance, Facilities for disabled people, Sports Facilities

Last Updated: 16/04/15

UNIVERSITY OF APPLIED SCIENCES WIENER NEUSTADT

Fachhochschule Wiener Neustadt

Johannes-Gutenberg-Strasse 3, 2700 Wiener Neustadt, Lower Austria

Tel: +43(2622) 89084-0

Fax: +43(2622) 89084-99

EMail: international@fhwn.ac.at

Website: http://www.fhwn.ac.at

Rector: Ferry Stocker
Tel: +43(2622) 89-084-300 EMail: stocker@fhwn.ac.at

CEO: Susanne Scharnhorst
Tel: +43 (2622)/ 89-084-100
EMail: susanne.scharnhorst@fhwn.ac.at

International Relations: Bettina Lichtenwörther
Tel: +43 (2622) 89-084-451
EMail: bettina.lichtenwoerther@fhwn.ac.at

Faculty

Business (Business Administration; Business and Commerce; International Business; Leadership; Management; Marketing); **Engineering** (Aeronautical and Aerospace Engineering; Biotechnology; Business and Commerce; Computer Engineering; Electronic Engineering; Engineering; Information Technology; Microelectronics; Natural Resources); **Health Studies** (Biomedicine; Health Sciences; Nursing; Occupational Therapy; Radiology; Speech Therapy and Audiology); **Security** (Police Studies; Protective Services); **Sports** (Sports)

History: Founded 1994.

Academic Year: September to June (September-January; February- June)

Admission Requirements: Secondary school certificate (Matura)

Fees: 363,36 per semester (Euro)

Main Language(s) of Instruction: German, English

Degrees and Diplomas: *Bachelor's Degree*: **Biomedicine; Biotechnology; Business Administration; Business and Commerce; Computer Science; Health Sciences; International Business; Management; Marketing; Mechanical Engineering; Nursing; Occupational Therapy; Police Studies; Radiology; Speech Therapy and Audiology; Sports.** *Master's Degree*: **Aeronautical and Aerospace Engineering; Biotechnology; Business Administration; Business and Commerce; Computer Science; International Business; Leadership; Management; Marketing; Mechanical Engineering; Natural Resources; Protective Services; Sports.**

Student Services: Academic Counselling, Canteen, Careers Guidance, Facilities for disabled people, Foreign Studies Centre, Language Laboratory, Social Counselling

Last Updated: 16/04/15

UPPER AUSTRIA UNIVERSITY OF APPLIED SCIENCES

Fachhochschul-Studiengänge Oberösterreich

Franz-Fritsch Strasse 11, 4600 Wels, Upper Austria

Tel: +4(5) 0804-10

Fax: +43(5) 0804-11900

EMail: info@fh-ooe.at

Website: http://www.fh-ooe.at

University President: Gerald Reisinger
Tel: +43 50804-11110 EMail: gerald.reisinger@fh-ooe.at

Executive Vice-President: Regina Aichinger
Tel: +43 50804-12110 EMail: regina.aichinger@fh-ooe.at

International Relations: Vanessa Prüller, Head of International Office Tel: +43 50804-43140 EMail: international@fh-wels.at

Programme

Automation Engineering *(Wels Campus)* (Automation and Control Engineering); **Bio- and Environmental Technology** *(Wels Campus)* (Biotechnology; Environmental Engineering); **Bioinformatics** *(Undergraduate, Hagenberg Campus)* (Biology; Computer Science); **Communication and Knowledge Media** *(Undergraduate, Hagenberg Campus)* (Communication Studies; Computer Science; Engineering; Media Studies); **Computer and Media Security** *(Undergraduate, Hagenberg Campus)* (Computer Science; Media Studies); **Digital Media** *(Graduate, Hagenberg Campus)* (Computer Science; Design; Media Studies); **e-Business** *(Steyr Campus)*; **Eco-Energy Engineering** *(Wels Campus)* (Energy Engineering; Environmental Studies); **Hardware/Software Co-Engineering** *(Undergraduate, Hagenberg Campus)*; **Human Services for Individuals with Special Needs** *(Linz Campus)* (Social and Community Services); **Human Services Management** *(Linz Campus)*; **Information Engineering and Management** *(Graduate, part-time; Hagenberg Campus)* (Computer Science; Software Engineering); **Innovation and Product Management** *(Wels Campus)* (Engineering; Industrial and Production Economics; Management); **Materials and Process Engineering** *(Wels Campus)* (Materials Engineering; Metallurgical Engineering; Polymer and Plastics Technology); **Mechanical Engineering** *(Wels Campus)* (Mechanical Engineering); **Mechatronics and Management** *(Wels Campus)* (Electronic Engineering; Management); **Media Technology and Design** *(Undergraduate, Hagenberg Campus)* (Computer Science; Design; Media Studies); **Medical Device Technology** *(Linz Campus)*; **Mobile Computing** *(Graduate, Hagenberg Campus)*; **Mobile Computing** *(Undergraduate, Hagenberg Campus)* (Computer Science); **Public Administration** *(Linz Campus)* (Public Administration); **Secure Information Systems** *(Graduate, Hagenberg Campus)*; **Social Work** *(Linz Campus)* (Criminal Law; Social Welfare; Social Work; Welfare and Protective Services); **Software Engineering** *(Undergraduate, Hagenberg Campus)* (Software Engineering); **Software Engineering** *(Graduate, Hagenberg Campus)*

Further Information: Also campuses in Hagenberg, Steyr and Lynz

History: Founded 1994.

Academic Year: October to June (October-January; March-June)

Admission Requirements: High school diploma or equivalent

Main Language(s) of Instruction: German, English

Degrees and Diplomas: *Bachelor's Degree*: **Accountancy; Automation and Control Engineering; Biomedical Engineering; Biotechnology; Business Administration; Business and Commerce; Civil Engineering; Communication Studies; Computer Engineering; Electrical Engineering; Energy Engineering; Environmental Studies; Food Technology; Management; Marketing; Materials Engineering; Mechanical Engineering; Media Studies; Public Administration; Social Work; Software Engineering.** *Master's Degree*: **Accountancy; Automation and Control Engineering; Biomedical Engineering; Biotechnology; Business Administration; Computer Engineering; Computer Science; Energy Engineering; Environmental Engineering; Health Administration; Information Management; Landscape Architecture; Management; Marketing; Materials Engineering; Mechanical Engineering; Multimedia; Public Administration.**

Student Numbers *2014-2015*: Total 5,362

Last Updated: 17/04/15

VIENNA CONSERVATOIRE PRIVATE UNIVERSITY

Konservatorium Wien Privatuniversität

Johannesgasse 4a, 1010 Wien, Vienna

Tel: +43(1) 5127747-89332

Fax: +43(1) 5127747-99

EMail: studieninfo@konswien.at

Website: http://www.konservatorium-wien.ac.at/

Rector: Franz Patay
Tel: +43(1) 51277-47-89306 EMail: a.schmid@konswien.at

Vice-Rector: Susana Zapke
Tel: +43(1) 51277-47-89307 EMail: s.zapke@konswien.at

Programme

Music (Conducting; Jazz and Popular Music; Music; Music Education; Musical Instruments); **Performing Arts** (Dance; Opera; Performing Arts; Singing; Theatre)

History: Founded 1945

Admission Requirements: Entrance examination

Fees: 300 per semester (Euro)

Main Language(s) of Instruction: German

Degrees and Diplomas: *Bachelor's Degree*: **Conducting; Dance; Music; Music Theory and Composition; Performing Arts; Theatre.** *Master's Degree*: **Art Education; Conducting; Music; Music Theory and Composition; Performing Arts.**

Last Updated: 17/04/15

WEBSTER UNIVERSITY VIENNA

Webster University Wien

Palais Wenkheim, Praterstrasse 23, 1020 Wien, Vienna
Tel: +43(1) 269-9293-0
EMail: info@webster.ac.at
Website: http://www.webster.ac.at

Director: Arthur Hirsh (2001-) EMail: hirsh@webster.edu

Director of Finance and Administration: Olivier Schindler
EMail: schindle@webster.edu

International Relations: Debbie Pierce, Director of the Center for International Education
Tel: +43(314) 246-7432 EMail: deborahpierce40@webster.edu

Department

Business and Management (Business Administration; Management); **International Relations** (International Relations); **Media Communications** (Communication Studies; Media Studies); **Psychology** (Psychology)

History: Founded 1981.

Main Language(s) of Instruction: English

Accrediting Agency: Higher Learning Commission (HLC); Commission on Institutions of Higher Education (USA); Austrian Federal Ministry for Education, Science and Culture; FIBAA (Foundation for International Business Administration Accreditation)

Degrees and Diplomas: *Bachelor's Degree*: **Business Administration; Economics; International Relations; Management; Media Studies; Psychology; Video.** *Master's Degree*: **Business Administration; Finance; International Business; International Relations; Marketing; Psychology.**

Student Services: Academic Counselling, Canteen, Careers Guidance, Cultural Activities, Language Laboratory, Social Counselling

Last Updated: 21/04/15

Azerbaijan

STRUCTURE OF HIGHER EDUCATION SYSTEM

Description:

Higher education is governed by the Cabinet of Ministers and the Ministry of Education. The higher education system consists of state and private institutions. Azerbaijan joined the Bologna process in 2005, and it defined contours of the reforms carried out in the higher education field.

Stages of studies:

University level first stage: *Bakalavr (Bachelor)*

This stage lasts for three to four years and leads to the Bachelor's degree (Bakalavr).

University level second stage: *Magistr (Master)*

During the second stage, which lasts between one-and-a-half and two years and leads to the Master's degree (Magistr), students acquire in-depth knowledge and professional training.

University level third stage: *Doctor*

The best graduates of the Master stage are admitted to the doctoral stage. After successful completion of their studies (two or three years), they obtain the Doctoral degree (Ph.D).

ADMISSION TO HIGHER EDUCATION

Admission to university-level studies:

Name of secondary school credential required: Certificate of General Education

For entry to: All higher education institutions

Admission requirements: Students must sit for a National Entrance examination.

Foreign students admission:

Admission requirements: For admission to higher education institutions, foreign students must submit a document proving they have completed secondary education.

Entry regulations: Visas are not required for students from Turkey and CIS (the Commonwealth of Independent States) countries.

Health requirements: Foreign students must submit a health certificate.

Language proficiency: One-year preparatory language courses are organized for those students who have no knowledge one of the three languages of instruction (Azerbaijani, Russian or English)

NATIONAL BODIES

Ministry of Education

Minister: Mikayil Jabbarov
49 Khatai Avenue
Baku 1008
Tel: +994(12) 599-1155
Fax: +994(12) 496-3483
WWW: http://www.edu.gov.az

Data for academic year: 2011-2012
Source: IAU from the website of the Ministry of Education, 2011. Bodies 2016.

INSTITUTIONS

PUBLIC INSTITUTIONS

ADA UNIVERSITY UNDER THE MINISTRY OF FOREIGN AFFAIRS OF THE REPUBLIC OF AZERBAIJAN

ul. Ahmadbeja Agogly, 11, Baku 1008
Tel: +994(12) 437-32-35
Fax: +994(12) 437-32-36
EMail: admissions@ada.edu.az; info@ada.edu.az
Website: http://www.ada.edu.az

Rector: Hafiz Pashayev EMail: Rector@ada.edu.az

Registrar: Elchin Rizayev EMail: erizayev@ada.edu.az

School
Business (Business Administration; Economics); **Education** *(Operates as a general education facility.)* (Arts and Humanities); **Information Technologies and Engineering** (Computer Science; Information Technology); **Public and International Affairs** (International Relations; International Studies; Public Administration)

History: Created 2006 by the Ministry of Foreign Affairs of Azerbaijan as the Azerbaijan Diplomatic Academy with the main objective of training specialists for a diplomatic career in Azerbaijani foreign affairs. Programmes were expanded and the name changed to ADA University in 2014.

Accrediting Agency: Ministry of Education

Degrees and Diplomas: *Bakalavr*: **Business Administration; Computer Science; Economics; Information Technology; International Relations; International Studies.** *Magistr*: **Business Administration; International Relations; Public Administration.**
Last Updated: 07/08/15

AZERBAIJAN ACADEMY OF FINE ARTS

prosp. Geidara Aliyeva, 58, Baku 1029
Tel: +994(12) 566-98-34
Fax: +994(12) 566-56-37
EMail: rector@art-academy.net; adra@azeurotel.com
Website: http://adra.edu.az/

Programme
Fine Arts

History: Created 2002.

Accrediting Agency: Ministry of Education

Degrees and Diplomas: *Bakalavr*: **Fine Arts.** *Magistr*: **Fine Arts.**
Last Updated: 07/08/15

AZERBAIJAN INSTITUTE OF TOURISM

Korgoly Ragimov, 822/23, Baku 1000
Tel: +994(12) 564-42-33
Fax: +994(12) 564-42-34
EMail: ATI@tourism.edu.az
Website: http://tourism.edu.az

Rector: Sefer Memmed Seferov

Programme
Hotel Management (Hotel Management); **Tourism** (Tourism)

History: Created 2006.

Degrees and Diplomas: *Bakalavr*: **Hotel Management; Tourism.** *Magistr*: **Hotel Management; Tourism.**
Last Updated: 08/09/15

AZERBAIJAN MEDICAL UNIVERSITY (ATU)

ul. Bakihanov 23, Baku AZ 1022
Tel: +994(12) 495-35-66
Fax: +994(12) 495-38-70
EMail: admin@amu.edu.az; vtm@amu.edu.az
Website: http://www.amu.edu.az

Rector: Ahliman Amiraslanov (1992-) EMail: rektor@amu.edu.az

Faculty
Dentistry (Dental Hygiene; Dentistry); **General Medicine** (Medicine); **General Medicine II** (Medicine); **Military Medicine** (Medicine); **Paediatrics** (Medicine; Paediatrics); **Pharmacy** (Pharmacology; Pharmacy); **Prophylactic Medicine and Biology** (Biology; Hygiene; Social and Preventive Medicine)

History: Founded 1919 as Medical Faculty of Azerbaijan State University. Reorganized 1930 as Azerbaijan Medical Institute, an independent institution. Named after Nariman Narimanov 1957, and acquired present status and title 1991.

Academic Year: September to May (September-January; February-May)

Admission Requirements: General or special secondary school certificate (Attestat) and Competitive entrance examination

Main Language(s) of Instruction: Azeri, Russian

Accrediting Agency: Ministry of Education

Degrees and Diplomas: *Bakalavr*: **Pharmacy.** *Magistr*: **Dentistry; Medicine; Paediatrics.**

Student Services: Academic Counselling, Canteen, Careers Guidance, Cultural Activities, Facilities for disabled people, Foreign Studies Centre, Health Services, Language Laboratory, Social Counselling, Sports Facilities
Last Updated: 24/07/15

AZERBAIJAN NATIONAL CONSERVATORY

ul. Mirzy Ibrahimova, 8, Baku
Tel: +994(12) 539-70-47
Fax: +994(12) 539-70-48
EMail: national@conservatory.az
Website: http://conservatory.az

Rector: Siyavuş Kerimi

Faculty
History and Theory of Music (Music); **Performance** (Music)
History: Created 2001.
Accrediting Agency: Ministry of Education
Degrees and Diplomas: *Bakalavr*: **Music.** *Magistr*: **Music.** *Doktor*: **Music.**
Last Updated: 07/08/15

AZERBAIJAN STATE ACADEMY FOR PHYSICAL TRAINING AND SPORTS

prosp. Fatali Khan Khoyski 98, Baku 1072
Tel: +994(12) 564-2610
Fax: +994(12) 564-4731

Programme
Physical Education and Sports (Physical Education; Sports)

History: Founded 1930 as Azerbaijan State Institute of Physical Culture, acquired present status and title 2000.

Main Language(s) of Instruction: Russian, Azerbaijani

Accrediting Agency: Ministry of Education

Degrees and Diplomas: *Bakalavr*: **Physical Education; Sports.** *Magistr*
Last Updated: 24/07/15

AZERBAIJAN STATE AGRICULTURAL UNIVERSITY (ASAU)

prosp. Ataturka, 262, Gandja 2000
Tel: +994(22) 256-5733
Fax: +994(22) 256-2408
EMail: info@adau.edu.az
Website: http://adau.edu.az

Rector: Ibrahim Jafarov

Faculty
Agricultural Economics (Agricultural Economics; Agriculture); **Agricultural Technology** (Agrobiology; Food Technology; Landscape Architecture; Plant and Crop Protection; Soil Science); **Agronomy** (Agronomy); **Electrical Engineering and Information Technology** (Electrical Engineering; Information Technology); **Engineering** (Automation and Control Engineering; Electrical Engineering); **Veterinary Medicine and Pharmacology** (Pharmacy; Veterinary Science)

History: Founded 1929 as Azerbaijan Agricultural Academy. Acquired present status and title 2009.

Main Language(s) of Instruction: Azerbaijani, Russian

Accrediting Agency: Ministry of Education

Degrees and Diplomas: *Bakalavr*: **Agriculture; Engineering; Veterinary Science.** *Magistr*: **Agricultural Business; Agricultural Economics; Agricultural Engineering; Agricultural Management; Agriculture; Agronomy; Architecture; Environmental Studies; Forestry; Landscape Architecture; Mechanical Equipment and Maintenance; Plant and Crop Protection; Soil Science; Transport Management; Veterinary Science; Viticulture.** *Doktor*

Last Updated: 24/07/15

AZERBAIJAN STATE MARINE ACADEMY

ul. Zarifa Aliyeva 18, Baku 1000
Tel: +994(12) 493-7521
Fax: +994(12) 493-7521
EMail: akademiya@adda.edu.az
Website: http://adda.edu.az

Rector: Rasim Javad oglu Bashirov
EMail: Rasim-agmail@rambler.ru

Faculty
Marine Engineering and Shipping (Marine Engineering; Marine Science and Oceanography; Nautical Science)

History: Founded 1881 as a Centre for training seamen, acquired present status and title 1996.

Admission Requirements: Secondary school certificate

Main Language(s) of Instruction: Azerbaijani, Russian

Accrediting Agency: Ministry of Education

Degrees and Diplomas: *Bakalavr*: **Marine Engineering; Marine Transport.** *Magistr*: **Electrical Engineering; Electronic Engineering; Marine Engineering; Marine Transport; Naval Architecture; Transport Management.**

Student Services: Academic Counselling, Canteen, Careers Guidance, Cultural Activities, Health Services, Language Laboratory, Nursery Care, Social Counselling, Sports Facilities

Last Updated: 24/07/15

AZERBAIJAN STATE OIL ACADEMY

pros. Azadlyg 20, Baku 1010
Tel: +994(12) 493-28-46
EMail: info@asoa.edu.az
Website: http://www.asoa.edu.az

Rector: Siyavush Garayev (1997-) EMail: sgaraev@mail.az

Faculty
Chemical Engineering (Chemical Engineering; Ecology; Environmental Engineering; Polymer and Plastics Technology; Safety Engineering); **Economics, International Economics and Management** (Applied Mathematics; Economics; Engineering Management; International Economics; Management); **Geology and Prospecting** (Earth Sciences; Geological Engineering; Geology; Petroleum and Gas Engineering); **Mechanical Engineering** (Machine Building; Materials Engineering; Mechanical Engineering; Production Engineering); **Petroleum Production** (Mining Engineering; Petroleum and Gas Engineering); **Power Engineering** (Electrical Engineering; Energy Engineering; Hydraulic Engineering; Power Engineering); **Production Processing Automation** (Automation and Control Engineering; Business Administration; Computer Engineering; Computer Science; Electrical and Electronic Engineering; Electronic Engineering; Information Management; Information Technology; Measurement and Precision Engineering; Software Engineering)

History: Founded 1920, acquired present status 1992.

Academic Year: September to July

Admission Requirements: Competitive entrance examination following general or special secondary school certificate (Attestat)

Main Language(s) of Instruction: Azeri, Russian

Accrediting Agency: Ministry of Education

Degrees and Diplomas: *Bakalavr*: **Computer Science; Engineering.** *Magistr*: **Computer Science; Engineering; Industrial Management.** *Doktor*: **Chemical Engineering; Chemistry; Environmental Engineering; Materials Engineering; Mechanical Engineering; Petroleum and Gas Engineering.**

Student Services: Canteen, Foreign Studies Centre, Health Services, Language Laboratory, Nursery Care, Sports Facilities

Last Updated: 02/07/15

AZERBAIJAN STATE PEDAGOGICAL UNIVERSITY

ul. Uzeir Hajibejov 34, Baku 1000
Tel: +994(12) 493-0032
Fax: +994(12) 498-8933
EMail: adpu@azeri.com

Rector: Yusif Mamedov

Faculty
Biology (Biology; Hygiene); **Chemistry** (Biology; Chemistry); **Drawing and Imitation Arts** (Painting and Drawing; Performing Arts); **Elementary Military Education and Physical Training and Geography** (Geography; Physical Education); **History** (History); **Mathematics and Computer Science** (Computer Science; Mathematics); **Pedagogy** (Music; Primary Education); **Pedagogy and Psychology (Preschool)** (Child Care and Development; Pedagogy; Preschool Education; Primary Education; Psychology); **Philology** (English; French; Literature; Native Language; Philology); **Physics** (Physics)

History: Founded 1921.

Admission Requirements: Secondary school certificate (Attestat)

Main Language(s) of Instruction: Russian, Azerbaijani

Accrediting Agency: Ministry of Education

Degrees and Diplomas: *Bakalavr*: **Education.** *Magistr*: **Education.**

Student Services: Academic Counselling, Canteen, Careers Guidance, Cultural Activities, Foreign Studies Centre, Health Services, Language Laboratory, Social Counselling, Sports Facilities

Last Updated: 24/07/15

AZERBAIJAN STATE UNIVERSITY OF CULTURE AND FINE ARTS

pros. Insaatchilar, 39, Baku 1065
Tel: +994(12) 438-4310
Fax: +994(12) 438-9348
EMail: info@admiu.edu.az
Website: http://www.admiu.edu.az

Rector: Farah Shirmammad Aliyeva (2014-)
EMail: rector@admiu.edu.az

Faculty
Cultural Studies (Cultural Studies); **Fine Arts** (Art Criticism; Art Management; Fine Arts; Industrial Arts Education); **Management** (Management); **Music** (Music); **Painting** (Painting and Drawing); **Theatre and Cinema** (Cinema and Television; Theatre)

History: Founded 1945.

Academic Year: September to July

Admission Requirements: Competitive entrance examination following general or special secondary school certificate (Attestat)

Main Language(s) of Instruction: Azerbaijani

Accrediting Agency: Ministry of Education

Degrees and Diplomas: *Magistr*: **Cultural Studies; Fine Arts.**

Student Services: Canteen, Careers Guidance, Cultural Activities, Health Services, Language Laboratory, Social Counselling, Sports Facilities

Last Updated: 24/07/15

AZERBAIJAN STATE UNIVERSITY OF ECONOMICS (ASEU)

ul. Istiglaliyat, 6, Baku 1001
Tel: +994(12) 437-1086
Fax: +994(12) 492-5940
EMail: aseu@aseu.az
Website: http://www.aseu.az

Rector: Adalat Muradov (2014-)

Faculty

Accountancy (Accountancy; Statistics); **Business Administration** (Business Administration; Human Resources; International Business; Management); **Commerce** (Business and Commerce; International Business; Marketing); **Economics** (Economics; Tourism); **Finance** (Accountancy; Finance; Insurance; Taxation); **Industry and Services Production** (Industrial and Production Economics); **Information Science and Management** (Business Administration; Business Computing; Computer Science; Management); **International Economic Relations** (Economics; International Business; International Economics; International Relations; Marketing; Taxation); **Merchandising** (Advertising and Publicity; Business and Commerce; Marketing); **Technology and Design** (Dairy; Food Science; Food Technology; Industrial Design; Meat and Poultry; Oenology; Technology); **Turkish World** (International Economics; International Relations)

Further Information: Branch in Derbent, Daghestan Republic

History: Founded 1930. Acquired present status and title 2008.

Academic Year: September to June

Admission Requirements: Secondary school certificate (Attestat); SSAC (State Student Admission Commission) test results

Main Language(s) of Instruction: Russian, English, Turkish, Azerbaijani

Accrediting Agency: Ministry of Education

Degrees and Diplomas: *Bakalavr*: **Business Administration; Ecology; Economics; Food Technology; Hotel and Restaurant; Information Technology; International Relations; Tourism.** *Magistr*: **Accountancy; Business and Commerce; Ecology; Economics; Finance; Food Technology; Hotel Management; Information Technology; International Economics; International Relations; Management; Marketing; Statistics; Tourism.** *Doktor*: **Accountancy; Econometrics; Economic and Finance Policy; Finance; Food Technology; International Economics.**

Student Services: Academic Counselling, Canteen, Careers Guidance, Cultural Activities, Foreign Studies Centre, Health Services, Language Laboratory, Social Counselling, Sports Facilities

Last Updated: 24/07/15

AZERBAIJAN STATE UNIVERSITY OF LANGUAGES

ul. Rashid Bahbudov 60, Baku 1010
Tel: +994(12) 440-3505
Fax: +994(12) 441-5863
EMail: info@adu.edu.az
Website: http://www.adu.edu.az

Rector: Samad Seyidov (2000-)

Faculty

English, Romance and German Philology (Dutch; English; French; German; Germanic Languages; Modern Languages; Romance Languages); **German, French, English and Regional Studies** (English Studies; French Studies; Germanic Studies; Regional Studies); **Pedagogy** (Foreign Languages Education; Literacy Education; Native Language Education; Primary Education; Secondary Education); **Translation and Interpretation** (English; French; German; Italian; Korean; Spanish; Translation and Interpretation)

History: Founded 1937 as Azerbaijan State Institute of Foreign Languages, acquired present status and title 2000.

Admission Requirements: School certificate and entrance examination

Main Language(s) of Instruction: Azerbaijani, Russian

Accrediting Agency: Ministry of Education

Degrees and Diplomas: *Bakalavr*: **Education; Journalism; Modern Languages; Translation and Interpretation.** *Magistr*: **Foreign Languages Education; Linguistics; Literature; Modern Languages; Native Language; Native Language Education; Translation and Interpretation.** *Doktor*

Last Updated: 24/07/15

AZERBAIJAN TEACHERS INSTITUTE (AMI)

ul. K. Rahimova, 104, Baku
Tel: +99(12) 564-8047
Fax: +99(12) 564-8047
EMail: ami-az@hotmail.com
Website: http://www.ami.az

Rector: Agiya Nakhchivanli

Faculty

Pedagogy (Computer Science; Education; Foreign Languages Education; Humanities and Social Science Education; Mathematics; Mathematics Education; Native Language Education; Pedagogy; Preschool Education; Primary Education; Science Education); **Phillology** (Literature; Modern Languages; Philology)

Further Information: Branches in Sumgait, Agjabedi, Sheki, Jalilabad, Guba, Zagatala, Gazakh, Mingachevir, Ganja, Salyan, and Shamakhi.

History: Founded 1929.

Main Language(s) of Instruction: Azerbaijani

Degrees and Diplomas: *Bakalavr*: **Education; Teacher Training.** *Magistr*: **Educational Psychology; Preschool Education; Primary Education.** *Doktor*: **Education; Literature; Pedagogy.**

Last Updated: 31/08/15

AZERBAIJAN TECHNICAL UNIVERSITY

H. Cavid prospekti 25, Baku 1073
Tel: +994(12) 538-3383
Fax: +994(12) 538-3280
EMail: aztu@aztu.edu.az
Website: http://www.aztu.az

Rector: Havar Mamedov (2000-) EMail: rector@aztu.org

Faculty

Automation and Computer Engineernig (Automation and Control Engineering; Measurement and Precision Engineering); **Electrical and Power Engineering** (Electrical Engineering; Power Engineering); **Engineering Business and Management** (Economics; Management); **Machine Building** (Machine Building; Mechanical Engineering); **Metallurgy** (Metallurgical Engineering); **Radio Engineering and Communication** (Electronic Engineering; Telecommunications Engineering); **Technological and Light Industry Machines** (Electrical Engineering; Mechanical Equipment and Maintenance; Technology); **Transport** (Automotive Engineering; Transport Management)

History: Founded 1920 as Baku Polytechnical University. Reorganized 1950 as Azerbaijan Polytechnical Institute. Acquired present status and title 1991.

Academic Year: September to June (September-January; February-June)

Admission Requirements: Secondary school certificate (Attestat)

Main Language(s) of Instruction: Russian, Azerbaijani

Accrediting Agency: Ministry of Education

Degrees and Diplomas: *Bakalavr*: **Business Administration; Engineering; Mathematics and Computer Science; Transport and Communications.** *Magistr*: **Automation and Control Engineering; Business Administration; Computer Engineering; Economics; Energy Engineering; Engineering Management; Mechanical Engineering; Metallurgical Engineering; Railway Transport; Telecommunications Engineering; Telecommunications Services; Transport Economics; Transport Engineering; Transport Management.** *Doktor*: **Chemistry; Computer Science; Economics; Energy Engineering; Mathematics; Mechanical Engineering; Mechanics; Organic Chemistry; Physics; Thermal Engineering; Transport Engineering; Transport Management.**

Last Updated: 24/07/15

AZERBAIJAN UNIVERSITY OF ARCHITECTURE AND CONSTRUCTION

ul. A. Sultanova 5, Baku 1073
Tel: +994(12) 434-1597
Fax: +994(12) 434-1597
EMail: interreldep@azmiu.edu.az
Website: http://www.azmiu.edu.az

Rector: Gulchohra Mammadova (1976-)
Tel: +994(12) 438-3001 EMail: rector@azmiu.edu.az

Vice-Rector: Farhad Jafarov
Tel: +994(12) 439-07-45
EMail: prorector-ti@azmiu.edu.az; prorektorti@edu.az

International Relations: Farid Aliyev, Head, Department for International Relations
Tel: +994(12) 434-1597 EMail: interreldep@azmiu.edu.az

Faculty
Architecture (Architecture); **Building Technology** (Building Technologies; Construction Engineering); **Construction** (Construction Engineering); **Construction Economics** (Economics; Engineering Management); **Mechanization and Automation** (Automation and Control Engineering; Power Engineering); **Transport Engineering** (Bridge Engineering; Road Engineering; Surveying and Mapping; Transport Engineering; Transport Management); **Water Supply and Engineering Systems** (Ecology; Engineering; Hydraulic Engineering; Water Management)

College
Construction (Building Technologies; Construction Engineering)

History: Azerbaijan University of Architecture and Construction (AUAC) was founded as construction faculty incorporated with the Polytechnic Institute in 1920; from 1930 to 1934 it functioned as an autonomous Construction Institute and since 1934 it functioned as a civil engineering department within Azerbaijan Industrial Institute. In 1975, Azerbaijan Civil Engineering Institute began life as an autonomous institution of higher education. In 2000, Azerbaijan Civil Engineering Institute was named Azerbaijan University of Architecture and Construction.

Academic Year: September - June

Admission Requirements: School leaving certificate

Fees: National: 650-1000,00 per annum (Azerbaijanian Manat), International: 1000,00 - 3000,00 per annum (US Dollar)

Main Language(s) of Instruction: Russian, English, Azerbaijani

Accrediting Agency: Ministry of Education

Degrees and Diplomas: *Bakalavr*: **Architecture and Planning; Engineering.** *Magistr*: **Architecture; Bridge Engineering; Construction Engineering; Engineering Management; Environmental Engineering; Road Engineering; Surveying and Mapping; Transport Engineering.** *Doktor*: **Agriculture; Architecture and Planning; Engineering; Industrial and Production Economics; Mathematics; Mechanics; Physics; Soil Science.**

Student Services: Academic Counselling, Canteen, Careers Guidance, Cultural Activities, Facilities for disabled people, Foreign Studies Centre, Health Services, Language Laboratory, Nursery Care, Social Counselling, Sports Facilities

Publications: Ecology and water economy; Scientific works; Theoretical and applied mechanics; Urbanizm

Publishing House: Inshaatci Kadrlar

Last Updated: 02/07/15

AZERBAIJAN UNIVERSITY OF TECHNOLOGY

prosp. Hatai, 103, Gandja 2011
Tel: +994(22) 57-56-29
EMail: rektorat@aztun.edu.az
Website: https://www.aztun.edu.az

Rector: Akif Shamil oglu Suleimanov

Faculty
Consumer Products Technology and Expertise (Consumer Studies; Telecommunications Engineering); **Economics and Management** (Economics; Marketing); **Food Production and Tourism** (Food Science; Tourism); **Standardization and Technological Machinery** (Automation and Control Engineering; Food Technology; Industrial Engineering; Measurement and Precision Engineering; Technology)

History: Founded 1970. Acquired present status 2000.

Admission Requirements: Secondary school certificate

Main Language(s) of Instruction: Azerbaijani, Russian

Degrees and Diplomas: *Bakalavr*: **Business Administration; Service Trades; Technology.** *Magistr*: **Business Administration; Service Trades; Technology.**

Student Services: Academic Counselling, Canteen, Cultural Activities, Facilities for disabled people, Health Services, Language Laboratory, Nursery Care, Social Counselling, Sports Facilities

Last Updated: 31/08/15

BAKU BRANCH OF MOSCOW STATE UNIVERSITY NAMED AFTER M.V. LOMONOSOV

prosp. G. Džavida, 133, Baku 1143
Tel: +994(12) 510-96-08
Fax: +994(12) 510-97-07
EMail: info@msu.az
Website: http://www.msu.az

Rector: Nargiz Arif Pashaeva EMail: rector@msu.az

Faculty
Chemistry (Chemistry); **Economics** (Economics); **Mathematics and Computer Science** (Applied Mathematics; Computer Science; Mathematics); **Philology** (Literature; Modern Languages; Philology); **Psychology** (Psychology)

History: Created 2007

Accrediting Agency: Ministry of Education

Degrees and Diplomas: *Bakalavr*: **Chemistry; Computer Science; Economics; Mathematics; Modern Languages; Philology; Psychology.** *Magistr*: **Applied Mathematics; Chemistry; Philology; Psychology.**

Last Updated: 07/08/15

BAKU MUSIC ACADEMY 'UZER HAJIBEJOV'

ul. Šamsi Badelbeyli 98, Baku 1014
Tel: +994(12) 493-22-48
Fax: +994(12) 493-19-28
EMail: info@musigi-dunya.az
Website: http://musakademiya.musigi-dunya.az

Rector: Farhad Badalbeyli

Programme
Music (Music; Music Theory and Composition; Musical Instruments; Musicology)

History: Founded 1922.

Main Language(s) of Instruction: Russian, Azerbaijani

Accrediting Agency: Ministry of Education

Degrees and Diplomas: *Bakalavr*: **Music.** *Magistr*: **Music.** *Doktor*: **Music.**

Last Updated: 07/08/15

BAKU SLAVIC UNIVERSITY

ul. Suleiman Rustam 25, Baku 1014
Tel: +994(12) 441-50-68
Fax: +994(12) 440-27-70
EMail: bakslavuniver@hotmail.com
Website: http://bsu-edu.org

Rector: Asif A. Hajiev (2014-)

Faculty
International Relations and Regional studies (European Studies; Foreign Languages Education; International Relations; Political Sciences; Russian); **Pedagogy** (Educational Psychology; Information Technology; Mathematical Physics; Pedagogy; Primary Education; Russian); **Philology** (English; Foreign Languages Education; French; German; Journalism; Native Language; Russian; Translation and Interpretation); **Translation** (Literature; Translation and Interpretation)

History: Founded 1946 as Azerbaijan Pedagogical Institute of Russian Language and Literature 'Mirza Fatali Akhundov'. Acquired present status and title 2000.

Main Language(s) of Instruction: Russian, Azerbaijani

Accrediting Agency: Ministry of Education

Degrees and Diplomas: *Bakalavr.* **Education; International Relations; Linguistics; Modern Languages; Translation and Interpretation.** *Magistr.* **Education; International Relations; Journalism; Linguistics; Philology; Regional Studies.** *Doktor.* **Foreign Languages Education; International Relations; Linguistics; Literature; Native Language; Native Language Education; Pedagogy; Psychology; Slavic Languages; Turkish.**

Last Updated: 07/08/15

BAKU STATE UNIVERSITY (BSU)

ul. Zahad Halilov 23, Baku 1148
Tel: +994(12) 539-0535
Fax: +994(12) 598-3376
EMail: info@bsu.az
Website: http://www.bsu.az

Rector: Abel Mammadali Maharramov (1999-)
EMail: rector@bsu.az

Faculty

Applied Mathematics and Cybernetics (Applied Mathematics; Computer Science; Mathematics); **Biology** (Biology); **Chemistry** (Chemistry); **Ecology and Soil Science** (Ecology; Soil Science); **Geography** (Geography; Geology); **Geology** (Geology); **History** (History); **International Relations and Economics** (International Law; International Relations); **Journalism** (Journalism); **Law** (Law); **Library Science and Information Sciences** (Information Sciences; Library Science); **Mechanics and Mathematics** (Mathematics; Mechanics); **Oriental Studies** (Oriental Studies); **Philology** (Philology); **Physics** (Physics); **Social Science and Psychology** (Psychology; Social Sciences; Social Work; Sociology); **Theology** (Islamic Law; Islamic Theology)

History: Founded 1919 on former Baku Transcaucasus University (founded 1918).

Academic Year: September to July

Admission Requirements: Competitive entrance examination following general or special secondary school certificate (Attestat)

Main Language(s) of Instruction: Russian, English, Azerbaijani

Accrediting Agency: Ministry of Education

Degrees and Diplomas: *Bakalavr.* **Applied Mathematics; Biochemistry; Biology; Chemistry; Computer Science; Ecology; Foreign Languages Education; Geography; Geology; Marine Science and Oceanography; Mathematics; Mathematics Education; Meteorology; Modern Languages; Philology; Physics; Rural Planning; Science Education; Soil Science; Tourism; Town Planning.** *Magistr.* **Applied Mathematics; Atomic and Molecular Physics; Biochemistry; Biophysics; Botany; Chemistry; Computer Science; Ecology; Entomology; Fishery; Geography; Geology; Literature; Marine Science and Oceanography; Mathematics; Mechanics; Meteorology; Microbiology; Modern Languages; Molecular Biology; Physics; Regional Planning; Rural Planning; Soil Science; Tourism; Town Planning.** *Doktor.* **Chemistry; Computer Science; Mathematical Physics; Mathematics; Mechanics; Physics; Solid State Physics.**

Last Updated: 06/08/15

GANDJA STATE UNIVERSITY (GDU)

prosp. Khatai 187, Gandja 2000
Tel: +994(22) 567-310
Fax: +994(22) 56-19-63
EMail: info@gsu.az
Website: http://www.gsu.az

Rector: Yusif Oglu Amirali Yousibov (2015-)

Faculty

Chemistry and Biology (Biology; Chemistry); **Educational Psychology** (Educational Psychology; Teacher Training); **Engineering Education** (Engineering; Technology Education); **Foreign Languages** (English; French; German); **History** (History); **Mathematics and Computer Science** (Computer Science; Mathematics); **Philology** (Oriental Languages; Philology); **Physics** (Physics)

History: Founded 1938 as Gandja State Pedagogical Institute, named after H. Zardabi 2000, acquired present title 2002.

Admission Requirements: General or secondary school certificate (Attestat)

Main Language(s) of Instruction: Russian, Azerbaijani

Accrediting Agency: Ministry of Education

Degrees and Diplomas: *Bakalavr*; *Magistr*; *Doktor*

Student Services: Canteen, Careers Guidance, Cultural Activities, Foreign Studies Centre, Health Services, Language Laboratory, Nursery Care

Publications: Handbook of Science Labour

Last Updated: 06/08/15

LANKARAN STATE UNIVERSITY (LSU)

ul. General H. Aslanov 50, Lankaran 4200
Tel: +994(25) 255-0340
Fax: +994(25) 255-2786
EMail: office@lsu.edu.az
Website: http://www.lsu.edu.az

Rector: Asaf Iskanderov EMail: rector@lsu.edu.az

Faculty

Economics and Management (Agricultural Economics; Agricultural Management; Economics; Management); **Humanities** (History; Literature; Modern Languages; Philosophy); **Natural Sciences** (Biology; Computer Engineering; Geography; Mathematics and Computer Science); **Pedagogy** (English; French; Music; Pedagogy; Physical Education; Primary Education; Psychology)

History: Founded 1991 as branch of Baku State University, acquired present independent status and title 1992.

Academic Year: September to June (September-January; February-June)

Admission Requirements: Secondary school certificate (orta tehsil haqqinda attestat) and competitive entrance examination or diploma

Main Language(s) of Instruction: Russian, Azerbaijani

Accrediting Agency: Ministry of Education

Degrees and Diplomas: *Bakalavr.* **Agriculture; Business Administration; Education; Natural Sciences.** *Magistr.* **Biology; Geography; History; Industrial and Production Economics; Linguistics; Management; Mathematics; Philology.** *Doktor.* **English; Geography; Literature; Mathematics; Pedagogy.**

Student Services: Academic Counselling, Canteen, Careers Guidance, Cultural Activities, Facilities for disabled people, Language Laboratory, Social Counselling, Sports Facilities

Last Updated: 06/08/15

NAKHCHIVAN STATE UNIVERSITY (NSU)

University Campus, Nakhchivan Az7000
Tel: +994(136) 45-72-88
Fax: +994(136) 45-72-88
EMail: ndu@ndu.edu.az
Website: http://www.ndu.edu.az

Rector: Saleh Heydar Oglu Maharramov EMail: rector@ndu.edu.az

Faculty

Architecture and Engineering (Architecture; Energy Engineering; Environmental Engineering; Road Engineering; Transport Engineering); **Art** (Acting; Art Education; Music; Music Education); **Economics** (Accountancy; Economics; International Economics; Management); **History and Philology** (Heritage Preservation; Journalism; Library Science; Literature; Museum Studies; Native Language); **International Relations and Foreign Languages** (Foreign Languages Education; International Relations; Russian; Translation and Interpretation); **Mathematics and Physics** (Mathematics Education; Science Education); **Medicine** (Dentistry; Medicine; Pharmacy); **Natural History and Agriculture** (Ecology; Science Education; Veterinary Science); **Pedagogy** (Educational Technology; Pedagogy; Physical Education; Primary Education;

Sports); **Social Management and Law** (Hotel Management; Law; Public Administration; Social Work; Tourism)

History: Founded 1967, acquired present status and title 1990.

Academic Year: September to July (September-January; February-July)

Admission Requirements: Secondary school certificate

Main Language(s) of Instruction: Azeri

Accrediting Agency: Ministry of Education

Degrees and Diplomas: *Bakalavr*: **Architecture; Arts and Humanities; Dentistry; Education; Engineering; Law; Mathematics and Computer Science; Medicine; Music; Natural Sciences; Pharmacy; Teacher Training; Tourism.** *Magistr*: **Accountancy; Administrative Law; Arabic; Archaeology; Art History; Astrophysics; Botany; Civil Law; Computer Science; Economics; Energy Engineering; English; Ethnology; French; Geography; German; History; Information Technology; Inorganic Chemistry; Journalism; Library Science; Management; Mathematics; Music; Musical Instruments; Native Language; Native Language Education; Pedagogy; Persian; Physical Chemistry; Physiology; Primary Education; Public Administration; Restoration of Works of Art; Russian; Taxation; Tourism; Transport Management; Veterinary Science; Zoology.** *Doktor*: **Agriculture; Archaeology; Architecture; Botany; Chemistry; Ecology; Economics; Ethnology; Geography; Germanic Languages; History; Inorganic Chemistry; Linguistics; Literature; Mathematics; Music; Native Language; Pedagogy; Physical Chemistry; Physics; Romance Languages; Zoology.**

Student Services: Academic Counselling, Canteen, Careers Guidance, Cultural Activities, Facilities for disabled people, Foreign Studies Centre, Health Services, Language Laboratory, Nursery Care, Social Counselling, Sports Facilities

Last Updated: 06/08/15

NAKHCHIVAN TEACHERS INSTITUTE

pros. Geidara Aliyeva, 1, Nakhchivan
Tel: +994(36) 45-32-02
Fax: +994(36) 45-46-76
Website: http://www.naxmi.com

Rector: Oruc Qafar Hesenli EMail: oruc-hesenli@mail.ru

International Relations: Jahangir Hesenli, Head of International Relations EMail: h.eyvazli@gmail.com

Faculty

Pedagogy (Educational Psychology; Mathematics and Computer Science; Pedagogy; Preschool Education; Primary Education)

History: Founded 2000, in the base of the Nakhchivan Polytechnic technical school. It was the branch of the Teachers Institute of Azerbaijan in Nakhchivan from 2000-2003. Acquired present title and status 2003.

Main Language(s) of Instruction: Azerbaijani

Accrediting Agency: Ministry of Education

Degrees and Diplomas: *Bakalavr*: **Education; Teacher Training.** *Magistr*: **Educational Psychology; Preschool Education; Primary Education.**

Last Updated: 07/08/15

NATIONAL AVIATION ACADEMY

Bina Settlement, Airport, Baku 370009
Tel: +994(12) 97-28-29
Fax: +994(12) 97-28-29
EMail: meil@naa.edu.az
Website: http://naa.edu.az

Rector: Arif Mir Jalal oglu Pachayev

Department

Aviation (Air Transport)

Main Language(s) of Instruction: Russian, Azerbaijani

Accrediting Agency: Ministry of Education

Degrees and Diplomas: *Bakalavr*: **Aeronautical and Aerospace Engineering; Air Transport.** *Magistr*: **Aeronautical and Aerospace Engineering; Air Transport; Economics; Law; Transport Economics; Transport Management.**

Last Updated: 02/07/15

SUMGAIT STATE UNIVERSITY

Sumgait
EMail: sdu@sdu.edu.az
Website: http://www.sdu.edu.az

Rector: Elkhan Bahadur oglu Husseynov

Faculty

Chemistry and Biology (Biology; Botany; Chemistry; Zoology); **Economics and Management** (Accountancy; Business Administration; Economics; Management); **Engineering** (Automation and Control Engineering; Computer Engineering; Computer Science; Energy Engineering; Information Technology); **History and Geography** (Geography; History; Humanities and Social Science Education; Political Sciences; Sociology); **Mathematics** (Computer Science; Mathematics; Mathematics Education); **Philology** (Linguistics; Literature; Modern Languages; Native Language Education; Philology; Primary Education); **Physics and Electronic Engineering** (Electrical and Electronic Engineering; Physics; Science Education)

History: Created 1961 as Azerbaijan Industrial Institute. Acquired current status 2000.

Accrediting Agency: Ministry of Education

Degrees and Diplomas: *Bakalavr*: **Biology; Business Administration; Chemistry; Computer Education; Ecology; Economics; Engineering; Geography; History; Humanities and Social Science Education; Mathematics Education; Native Language; Native Language Education; Philology; Physics; Preschool Education; Science Education.** *Magistr*: **Automation and Control Engineering; Biology; Botany; Chemistry; Computer Engineering; Computer Science; Continuing Education; Energy Engineering; History; Humanities and Social Science Education; Information Technology; Literature; Mathematics; Mathematics Education; Native Language; Native Language Education.** *Doktor*: **Chemistry; Computer Engineering; Linguistics; Literature; Philology.**

Last Updated: 07/08/15

THE ACADEMY OF PUBLIC ADMINISTRATION UNDER THE PRESIDENT OF THE REPUBLIC OF AZERBAIJAN

ul. Lermontova 74, Baku 1001
Tel: +994(12) 492-6529
Fax: +994(12) 492-6515
EMail: dia@azeurotel.com
Website: http://www.dia.edu.az/

Rector: Urkhan Kazim oglu Alekperov EMail: rector@dia.org.az

Faculty

Political Administration (International Relations; International Studies; Modern Languages; Philosophy; Political Sciences; Public Administration; Social Psychology); **State Administration** (Administration; Government; Information Technology; Management; Public Administration; Public Law)

History: Created in 1999 to train quality civil servants and to offer further professional training to current civil servants. Previously known as Academy of Management under the President of the Republic of Azerbaijan.

Accrediting Agency: Ministry of Education

Degrees and Diplomas: *Bakalavr*: **Administration; International Relations.** *Magistr*: **Administration; International Relations.**

Student Services: Canteen

Last Updated: 06/08/15

PRIVATE INSTITUTIONS

AZERBAIJAN COOPERATION UNIVERSITY

prosp. Nariman Narimanov 8b, Baku 370106
Tel: +994(12) 462-85-17
Fax: +994(12) 462-83-46
EMail: info@aku.gen.az
Website: http://aku.edu.az

Rector: Eldar Allahyar Quliyev

Faculty
Economics (Economics); **Finance** (Accountancy; Finance); **International Economics** (International Business; International Economics); **Marketing and Management** (Management; Marketing)

History: Created 1964.

Main Language(s) of Instruction: Azeri, Russian

Accrediting Agency: Ministry of Education

Degrees and Diplomas: *Bakalavr*; *Magistr*. **Accountancy; Finance; International Economics; Management; Marketing; Mathematics; Tourism.**
Last Updated: 02/07/15

AZERBAIJAN UNIVERSITY (AZUN)

Nasimi district R. Safarov-17, Baku 1102
Tel: +994(12) 430-51-79
Fax: +994(12) 430-49-29
EMail: rector@au.edu.az
Website: http://www.au.edu.az

Rector: Farid Akhmadov (2015-)

Faculty
Business Administration (Business Administration; International Relations); **Economics and Management** (Accountancy; Economics; Finance; Management; Marketing; Public Administration); **Humanities** (History; Philology; Social Work; Translation and Interpretation)

School
Graduate Studies

History: Founded 1991, acquired present status 1995.

Academic Year: September to June (September-December; February-June)

Admission Requirements: Competitive entrance examination following general or secondary school certificate (Attestat)

Main Language(s) of Instruction: Azerbaijani, English

Accrediting Agency: Ministry of Education

Degrees and Diplomas: *Bakalavr*, *Magistr*, *Doktor*

Student Services: Canteen, Cultural Activities, Foreign Studies Centre, Health Services, Language Laboratory, Sports Facilities

Publications: Felsefe ve social-siyasi elmler (Philosophy and Social-Political Sciences); Ipek Yolu (Silk Road); Newspaper

Publishing House: Azerbaijan University Press
Last Updated: 06/08/15

BAKU ASIA UNIVERSITY

A.Salamzade St. 28, Baku 370102
Tel: +994(12) 430-52-40
Fax: +994(12) 431-36-99
Website: http://www.asia.baku.az

Rector: Jalil Nagiyev

Faculty
Economics (Economics); **Law and International Relations** (Law); **Philology** (Arabic; English; Japanese; Journalism; Native Language; Philology)

History: Founded 1993 as a private University. Registered 1995 by the decision of the Cabinet of Ministries of the Azerbaijan Republic.

Academic Year: September to June (September-January; February-June)

Main Language(s) of Instruction: Azeri, Russian

Accrediting Agency: Ministry of Education

Degrees and Diplomas: *Bakalavr*, *Magistr*
Last Updated: 02/07/15

BAKU BUSINESS UNIVERSITY (BBU)

ul. H. Zardabi 88a Str, Baku 1011
Tel: +994(12) 431-79-51
Fax: +994(12) 430-07-80
EMail: info@bbu.edu.az; relation@bbu.edu.az
Website: http://www.bbu.edu.az

President: Ibad Abbasov (1993-)

International Relations: Eshgin Ali Oglu Bayramov, Vice-Rector, International Relations EMail: relation@bbu.edu.az

Faculty
Business and Management (Business Administration; Business and Commerce; Economics; Industrial Management; Management; Marketing; Taxation); **Economics and Management** (Accountancy; English; Finance; International Economics; Translation and Interpretation)

History: Founded 1993. Acquired present status 1997.

Academic Year: September to June

Admission Requirements: Secondary school certificate

Main Language(s) of Instruction: Russian, English, Azerbaijani

Accrediting Agency: Ministry of Education

Degrees and Diplomas: *Bakalavr*. **Business Administration; Economics.** *Magistr*. **Accountancy; Administration; Banking; Economics; Law; Management.**

Student Services: Canteen, Careers Guidance, Cultural Activities, Foreign Studies Centre, Health Services, Language Laboratory, Social Counselling, Sports Facilities
Last Updated: 06/08/15

BAKU EURASIA UNIVERSITY

ul. akad. G. Aliyeva, 135A, Baku 1073
Tel: +994(12) 564-63-67
Fax: +994(12) 564-42-72
EMail: info@baau.edu.az
Website: http://baau.edu.az

Rector: Nazim Hüseynli

International Relations: Sayavush Gasimov, Vice-Rector EMail: info@baau.edu.az

Faculty
Philology (Modern Languages; Philology; Translation and Interpretation); **Regional Economics** (Economics; Regional Studies)

History: Created 1992 as a college of diplomacy and international relations. Acquired current title and status 2006.

Degrees and Diplomas: *Bakalavr*. **Economics; Foreign Languages Education; Modern Languages; Philology; Translation and Interpretation.** *Magistr*. **Economics; Modern Languages; Philology; Translation and Interpretation.** *Doktor*. **Economics; Philology.**
Last Updated: 24/11/15

BAKU ISLAMIC UNIVERSITY

ul. Mirza Fatali 7, Baku
Tel: +994(12) 492-82-23

Programme
Islamic Studies (Islamic Law; Islamic Studies; Islamic Theology; Koran)

Main Language(s) of Instruction: Azeri, Russian

Accrediting Agency: Ministry of Education

Degrees and Diplomas: *Bakalavr*. **Religious Studies.** *Magistr*. **History of Religion; Islamic Theology; Religious Studies.**
Last Updated: 02/07/15

BAKU WOMEN'S UNIVERSITY

ul. Movsuma Sanani, 14, Baku 1078
Tel: +994(12) 595-30-02
Fax: +994(12) 594-69-86
EMail: info@bqu.edu.az
Website: http://www.bqu.edu.az

Rector: Agarehim Ragimov

Faculty
Foreign Languages (Modern Languages); **History** (History); **Language and Literature** (Literature; Modern Languages); **Natural Sciences** (Natural Sciences); **Pedagogy** (Pedagogy; Teacher Training); **Psychology** (Educational Psychology)

History: Created 1992 to train female teachers. Acquired current title and status 2005.

Degrees and Diplomas: *Bakalavr*: **Computer Education; Foreign Languages Education; Humanities and Social Science Education; Mathematics Education; Native Language Education; Primary Education; Psychology; Teacher Training.** *Magistr*: **History; Pedagogy; Philology; Primary Education.**

Last Updated: 08/09/15

KHAZAR UNIVERSITY

ul.Mehseti 11, Baku 1096
Tel: +994(12) 421-79-27
Fax: +994(12) 498-93-79
EMail: contact@khazar.org
Website: http://www.khazar.org

Acting Rector: Mahammad Nuriyev EMail: mnouriev@khazar.org

School

Economics and Management (Accountancy; Business Administration; Economics; Finance; Information Technology; International Business; International Economics; Management; Marketing); **Education** (Biology; Chemistry; Education; Geography; History; Primary Education); **Engineering and Applied Science** (Civil Engineering; Computer Engineering; Engineering; Environmental Engineering; Management; Mathematics; Mathematics and Computer Science; Petroleum and Gas Engineering); **Humanities and Social Sciences** (Arts and Humanities; Design; English; International Relations; Journalism; Linguistics; Literature; Persian; Political Sciences; Psychology; Regional Studies; Translation and Interpretation)

Further Information: Also Teaching Hospitals: Sabuncu Hospital; National Centre of Oncology; Institute of Obstetrics and Gynaecology

History: Founded 1991.

Academic Year: September to August (September-January; February-June; June-August)

Admission Requirements: Secondary school certificate (Attestat)

Main Language(s) of Instruction: English, Azerbaijani

Accrediting Agency: Ministry of Education

Degrees and Diplomas: *Bakalavr*: **Biomedical Engineering; Business Administration; Chemical Engineering; Civil Engineering; Computer Education; Computer Engineering; Computer Science; Economics; English; Humanities and Social Science Education; International Relations; Journalism; Literature; Mathematics Education; Native Language Education; Petroleum and Gas Engineering; Political Sciences; Primary Education; Psychology; Science Education; Telecommunications Engineering; Translation and Interpretation.** *Magistr*: **Business Administration; Clinical Psychology; Computer Engineering; Computer Science; Educational Administration; Educational Sciences; English; Foreign Languages Education; International Relations; Linguistics; Literature; Mathematics; Native Language; Petroleum and Gas Engineering; Political Sciences; Psychology; Telecommunications Engineering; Translation and Interpretation.** *Doktor*: **Biochemistry; Computer Science; Economics; Educational Administration; Finance; Germanic Languages; History; International Economics; International Relations; Management; Mathematics; Molecular Biology; Native Language; Pedagogy; Petroleum and Gas Engineering; Philosophy; Political Sciences.**

Student Services: Academic Counselling, Canteen, Careers Guidance, Cultural Activities, Health Services, Language Laboratory, Social Counselling, Sports Facilities

Publications: Journal of Azerbaijan Archaeology; Khazar Journal of Humanities and Social Sciences; Khazar Journal of Mathematics; Khazar Journal of Science and Technology; Khazar View

Publishing House: Khazar University Press

Last Updated: 05/08/15

NAKHCHIVAN PRIVATE UNIVERSITY

Babeskij raijon, 1, Nakhchivan
Tel: +994(36) 545-07-45
Fax: +994(36) 545-07-45
Website: http://nu.edu.az

Rector: Ismayil Aliyev EMail: rector@nu.edu.az

Faculty

Economics (Accountancy; Economics; Finance); **Management** (Management); **Pedagogy** (Foreign Languages Education; Humanities and Social Science Education; Mathematics Education; Primary Education; Science Education; Teacher Training)

History: Created 1999.

Accrediting Agency: Ministry of Education

Degrees and Diplomas: *Bakalavr*: **Business Administration; Economics; Education; Modern Languages.** *Magistr*: **Economics; English; Literature; Native Language; Pedagogy.**

Last Updated: 11/08/15

ODLAR YURDU UNIVERSITY

Odlar Yurdu Universiteti

ul. Koroglu Rahimov 835, Baku 1072
Tel: +994(12) 465-82-00
Fax: +994(12) 465-67-05
EMail: info@oyu.edu.az
Website: http://www.oyu.edu.az

Rector: Ahmad Valiyev (1995-) EMail: rektor@oyu.edu.az

Faculty

Economics and Business (Business Administration; Economics; Finance; International Economics); **Law and International Relations** (International Relations; Law); **Mathematics and Information Technology** (Computer Education; Computer Engineering; Computer Science; Information Technology; Mathematics Education; Pedagogy; Petroleum and Gas Engineering); **Medicine and Biology** (Biological and Life Sciences; Dentistry; Medicine; Surgery); **Translation and Pedagogy** (English; Modern Languages; Translation and Interpretation)

History: Founded 1995. Acquired present status 1996.

Academic Year: September to June

Main Language(s) of Instruction: Russian, English, Azerbaijani

Degrees and Diplomas: *Bakalavr*, *Magistr*, *Doktor*

Last Updated: 18/09/15

QAFQAZ UNIVERSITY (QU)

Baku-Sumgayit Highway 16th km, Khirdalan, Baku 0101
Tel: +994(12) 448-2862
EMail: info@qu.edu.az
Website: http://www.qu.edu.az

Rector: Ahmet Sanic (2005-)
Tel: +994(12) 44-82-862 EMail: rector@qu.edu.az

Faculty

Economic and Administrative Sciences (Administration; Banking; Business Administration; International Economics; Political Sciences; Public Administration); **Education** (Arabic; Chemistry; Computer Education; English; Literature; Mathematics Education; Physical Education; Primary Education; Translation and Interpretation; Turkish); **Engineering** (Chemical Engineering; Computer Engineering; Engineering; Industrial Engineering; Information Technology; Mechanical Engineering); **Law** (European Studies; International Law; International Relations; Journalism)

History: Founded 1993. Acquired present status 1995.

Academic Year: September to June (September-December; February-June)

Admission Requirements: Written statement, secondary school certificate (mekteb attestat)

Fees: 2,000-4,000 per annum (Azerbaijanian Manat)

Main Language(s) of Instruction: English, Azerbaijani

Accrediting Agency: Ministry of Education

Degrees and Diplomas: *Bakalavr*: **Business Administration; Education; Engineering; International Law; Literature; Modern Languages.** *Magistr*: **Arabic; Asian Studies; Banking; Business Administration; Computer Engineering; English; Industrial Engineering; International Economics; International Law; International Relations; Literature; Management; Public Administration; Turkish.** *Doktor*: **Atomic and Molecular**

Physics; Computer Science; Economics; Mathematics; Mechanical Engineering; Pedagogy; Philology.

Student Services: Academic Counselling, Canteen, Careers Guidance, Cultural Activities, Facilities for disabled people, Foreign Studies Centre, Health Services, Language Laboratory, Nursery Care, Social Counselling, Sports Facilities

Publications: Journal of Qafqaz

Publishing House: Qafqaz University Press

Last Updated: 06/08/15

TAFACCUR UNIVERSITY

ul. Tabriz 19, Baku 1008
Tel: +994(12) 441-45-35 +994(12) 496-38-26
Fax: +994(12) 441-55-82
EMail: tafaccur@ab.az
Website: http://universitet-tefekkur.com

President: Musfig Atakishiyev (2002-)
EMail: mushfig_atakishiyev@yahoo.com

Faculty

Economics and Engineering (Business Administration; Economics; Management; Mechanical Engineering; Transport Engineering; Transport Management); **Philology and Biology** (Education; English; Foreign Languages Education; Journalism; Native Language; Philology; Primary Education)

History: Founded 1992, recognized by the State 1995.

Academic Year: September to July

Admission Requirements: Competitive entrance examination following general or special secondary school certificate (Attestat)

Main Language(s) of Instruction: Azerbaijani

Accrediting Agency: Ministry of Education

Degrees and Diplomas: *Bakalavr*; *Magistr*

Student Services: Academic Counselling, Canteen, Careers Guidance, Cultural Activities, Health Services, Social Counselling, Sports Facilities

Last Updated: 24/08/15

WESTERN UNIVERSITY (WU)

ul. Istiglalliyyat 27, Baku 1001
Tel: +994(12) 492-74-18
Fax: +994(12) 492-67-01
EMail: administration@wu.edu.az; iro@wu.edu.az
Website: http://www.wu.edu.az/

Rector: Zenfira Mammadova

School

Business Administration (Banking; Business and Commerce; Hotel Management; International Business; Marketing; Tourism); **Computer Sciences** (Computer Science; Information Technology); **Design** (Design; Fine Arts); **Political Science and International Relationsin** (International Relations; Journalism; Political Sciences); **Western Languages** (English; French; German; Native Language; Russian; Spanish; Translation and Interpretation)

History: Founded 1991, acquired present title 1993.

Academic Year: September to June (September-January; February-June)

Admission Requirements: Competitive entrance examination following general or special secondary school certificate (Attestat)

Main Language(s) of Instruction: English, Russian, Azerbaijani

Accrediting Agency: Ministry of Education

Degrees and Diplomas: *Bakalavr*: **Business Administration; Computer Engineering; Ecology; Economics; English; Finance; Fine Arts; Graphic Design; Hotel Management; Information Technology; Interior Design; International Economics; International Relations; Landscape Architecture; Law; Literature; Political Sciences; Psychology; Regional Studies; Tourism; Translation and Interpretation.** *Magistr*: **Business Administration; Design; Economics; English; Information Technology; International Relations; Journalism; Leisure Studies; Political Sciences; Public Administration; Regional Studies.**

Student Services: Academic Counselling, Careers Guidance, Cultural Activities, Foreign Studies Centre, Language Laboratory

Last Updated: 07/08/15

Bahamas

STRUCTURE OF HIGHER EDUCATION SYSTEM

Description:

In the Bahamas, higher education is provided principally by the College of the Bahamas which offers Associate and Bachelor's degrees in various fields and several Master's degrees independently or in conjunction with overseas universities. The Bahamas is also affiliated with the University of the West Indies (UWI) which is a regional institution with campuses in Jamaica, Trinidad and Barbados. The UWI maintains an administrative office and a full-time representative in Nassau, through whom Bahamian students may seek admission to any campus. Furthermore, the UWI Centre for Hotel and Tourism Management is located in Nassau. In addition, some American universities offer degree programmes in the Bahamas. Higher education is under the jurisdiction of the Ministry of Education which is considering the conversion of the College of the Bahamas into a full university. Higher education is also provided by institutions that are privately managed, including religious and overseas-based institutions.

Stages of studies:

University level first stage:
The Bachelor's degree is awarded after three or five years' study.

University level second stage:
Some Master's degrees are awarded independently and others in collaboration with foreign universities after one or two years' study.

ADMISSION TO HIGHER EDUCATION

Admission to university-level studies:

Name of secondary school credential required: Bahamas General Certificate of Secondary Education

Admission requirements: An admission test is required in most institutions.

RECOGNITION OF STUDIES

Quality assurance system:

All higher education institutions wanting to operate in the Bahamas have to seek registration with the Accreditation Council. If the evaluation is positive, the registration will then be submitted to the Minister for approval.

Bodies dealing with recognition:

Ministry of Education, Science and Technology
P.O. Box N-3913
Thompson Boulevard
Nassau
Tel: +1(242) 502-2700
Fax: +1(242) 322-8491
EMail: info@bahamaseducation.com
WWW: http://bahamaseducation.com/

NATIONAL BODIES

Ministry of Education, Science and Technology
Minister: Jerome Fitzgerald
P.O. Box N-3913
Thompson Boulevard
Nassau

Tel: +1(242) 502-2700
Fax: +1(242) 322-8491
EMail: info@bahamaseducation.com
WWW: http://bahamaseducation.com/
Role of national body: Responsible for the education policy and its implementation in the country.

National Accreditation and Equivalency Council of the Bahamas - NAECOB
Nassau

Data for academic year: 2016-2017
Source: IAU from the website of the Ministry of Education and documentation, 2016

INSTITUTION

PUBLIC INSTITUTION

THE COLLEGE OF THE BAHAMAS (COB)

Oakes Field Campus, Poinciana Drive and Thompson Boulevard, PO Box N4912, Nassau, N.P.
Tel: +1(242) 302-4300
Fax: +1(242) 302-4539
EMail: cob@cob.edu.bs
Website: http://www.cob.edu.bs

President: Rodney D. Smith

International Relations: Valdez Russell, Vice-President, Research, Graduate Programmes and International Relations
Tel: +1(242) 302-4379 EMail: vkrussell@cob.edu.bs

School
School of Business - SBUS (Business Administration); **School of Chemistry, Environmental and Life Sciences - SCELS** (Agriculture; Biology; Chemistry); **School of Communication and Creative Arts - SCCA** (Communication Studies; Fine Arts; Journalism; Modern Languages; Music); **School of Education - SEDUC** (Education); **School of English Studies - SES** (English Studies); **School of Mathematics, Physics and Technology - SMPT** (Architecture; Engineering; Mathematics; Physics); **School of Nursing and Allied Health Professions - SNAHP** (Nursing); **School of Social Sciences - SOSC** (Criminal Law; History; Law; Psychology; Public Administration; Religious Studies; Social Sciences; Social Work; Sociology; Theology)

Institute
Culinary and Hospitality Management Institute - CHMI (Hotel and Restaurant); **International Languages and Cultures Institute - ILCI** (Modern Languages)

Centre
Continuing Education and Extension Services (CEES)

Further Information: 3 Campuses: Oakes Field, Grosvenor Close, and Northern Bahamas Campus.

History: Founded 1974.

Degrees and Diplomas: *Associate Degree*; *Bachelor's Degree*. Various Master's Degrees programmes offered in collaboration with overseas institutions.

Last Updated: 08/04/16

Bahrain

STRUCTURE OF HIGHER EDUCATION SYSTEM

Description:

Higher education is provided by universities, colleges and institutes.

Stages of studies:

University level first stage: *Bachelor's degree*

Four-year courses lead to the Bachelor's degree in Arabic, Biology, Chemistry, Education, English, Mathematics, Physics, Accounting, Business and Management, Computing, Engineering and Office Management. A Bachelor's degree in general nursing takes four years to complete. A BSc in Medical Studies is conferred following a two-year pre-medical course followed by a two-year pre-clinical internship.

University level second stage: *Master's degree, Postgraduate diploma*

The second stage leads, after two to four years' study, to the Master's degree in Education, Biology, Chemistry, Physical Education and Business Administration. An MD is conferred after a three-year clinical internship following upon the BSc in Medical Studies. A three-year part-time MBA is also available. Postgraduate diplomas are conferred after one year's study.

University level third stage: *Doctoral studies*

A doctoral degree is awarded after three to five years of study and research following the master's degree.

ADMISSION TO HIGHER EDUCATION

Admission to university-level studies:

Name of secondary school credential required: Tawjihiya

Admission requirements: Students must sit an entrance exam.

Foreign students admission:

Quotas: 5% reservation for non-Bahraini students to the College of Arts, Science and Education and College of Health Sciences.

Admission requirements: Foreign students should have qualifications equivalent to the Bahrain Secondary School Leaving Certificate.

Entry regulations: Only Gulf State nationals do not require visas.

Language proficiency: Students should have a good knowledge of Arabic and English.

RECOGNITION OF STUDIES

Quality assurance system:

The Ministry has established a Committee for the evaluation of academic qualifications made up of representatives of specialized bodies or who are related to academic fields. The Ministerial decree no 6/186-1/85, 1986 indicates the basic conditions to evaluate qualifications and the Committee's role, procedure and techniques.

NATIONAL BODIES

Ministry of Education

Minister: Majid bin Ali Al-Naimi
PO Box 43
Manama

Tel: +973 1727-8999
Fax: +973 1727-3656
EMail: moe@moe.gov.bh; minister@moe.gov.bh
WWW: http://www.education.gov.bh

Data for academic year: 2007-2008
Source: IAU from Ministry of Education, Manama, 2007. Bodies 2015.

INSTITUTIONS

PUBLIC INSTITUTIONS

ARABIAN GULF UNIVERSITY (AGU)

P.O. Box 26671, Manama
Tel: +973 1723-9999
Fax: +973 1727-2555
EMail: info@agu.edu.bh
Website: http://www.agu.edu.bh/

President: Khalid Abdul Rahman Al Ohaly (2009-)
Tel: +973 239-801 EMail: layla@agu.edu.bh; info@agu.edu.bh

International Relations: Khaled Tabbara, Vice-President
Tel: +973 239-701 EMail: farzanahj@agu.edu.bh

College
Graduate Studies (Arid Land Studies; Biotechnology; Distance Education; Education; Education of the Gifted; Environmental Management; Special Education; Technology; Water Management); **Medicine and Medical Sciences** (Anaesthesiology; Anatomy; Biochemistry; Community Health; Demography and Population; Gynaecology and Obstetrics; Health Sciences; Immunology; Laboratory Techniques; Medicine; Microbiology; Paediatrics; Pathology; Pharmacology; Physiology; Surgery)

School
Management and Finance *(French Arabian)* (Business Administration; Finance; Health Administration)

History: Founded 1979 by the seven Gulf States. A regional autonomous scientific institution with public status, sponsored by the six GCC countries. Jointly managed by the member countries on the basis of equal representation in the General Conference and on the Board of Trustees.

Academic Year: September to June

Admission Requirements: Must be a national of one of the GCC member states that founded the University. Secondary school certificate with cumulative average of 90%.

Main Language(s) of Instruction: English, Arabic

Degrees and Diplomas: *Bachelor's Degree*; *Medical Doctor Degree*: **Medicine.** *Postgraduate Diploma in Education*; *Master's Degree*: **Arid Land Studies; Biotechnology; Environmental Management; Water Management.** *Doctor's Degree*

Student Numbers *2013*: Total 1,340
Last Updated: 12/02/13

COLLEGE OF HEALTH SCIENCES

PO Box 12, Manama
Tel: +973 1728-5910
Fax: +973 1728-5920
EMail: CHS@health.gov.bh
Website: http://www.chs.edu.bh

Dean: Aneesa Al Sindi

Division
Allied Health (Dental Hygiene; Laboratory Techniques; Pharmacy; Public Health; Radiology); **Integrated Sciences** (Behavioural Sciences; Biomedicine; Social Sciences); **Nursing** (Nursing)

History: Founded 1976.
Degrees and Diplomas: *Bachelor's Degree*
Last Updated: 21/11/11

GULF COLLEGE OF HOSPITALITY AND TOURISM

PO Box 22088, Muharraq
Tel: +973 320-191
Fax: +973 332-547

Principal: Abdul Raheem Abdulla Al-Khaja (1983-)

Administrator: Haider Hasan Al-Jamea

Programme
Hospitality (Hotel and Restaurant; Hotel Management); **Tourism** (Tourism)

History: Founded 1975.

Degrees and Diplomas: *Bachelor's Degree*; *Master's Degree*

GULF UNIVERSITY
Al-Jame'a Al-Khaleejia

P.O. Box 26489, Adliya 26489
Tel: +973 1762-0092
Fax: +973 1762-2230
EMail: info@gulfuniversity.net
Website: http://www.gulfuniversity.edu.bh

President: Mona R. Al-Zayani
Tel: +973 3964-5749 EMail: president@gulfuniversity.net

Vice-President for Academic Affairs: Yehya T. Mohammed Al-Rawi
Tel: +973 3921-3146 EMail: prof.yehya.alrawi@gulfuniversity.net

International Relations: Mohammed Al-Azzawi
Tel: +973 3676-3762
EMail: dr.mohammed.alazzawi@gulfuniversity.net

College
Administrative and Financial Sciences (Accountancy; Finance); **Computer Engineering and Science** (Computer Engineering); **Education** (Curriculum; Education; Educational Administration; Educational and Student Counselling; Educational Psychology; Educational Technology; Pedagogy); **Engineering** (Architectural and Environmental Design; Civil Engineering; Electrical Engineering; Electronic Engineering; Mechanical Engineering); **Law** (Administrative Law; Commercial Law; Constitutional Law; Criminal Law)

Centre
English Language Development (English); **Professional Certification and Consultation**

History: Founded 2001.

Academic Year: September to July

Admission Requirements: Bahrain Secondary School Certificate or equivalent

Fees: (Bahraini Dinars) 1500 per semester

Main Language(s) of Instruction: Arabic and English

Accrediting Agency: Ministry of Education

Degrees and Diplomas: *Bachelor's Degree*; *Master's Degree*; *Doctor's Degree*
Last Updated: 21/11/11

UNIVERSITY COLLEGE OF BAHRAIN

P.O. Box 55040, Manama
Tel: +973(17) 790-828
EMail: president@ku.edu.bh
Website: http://www.ucb.edu.bh

President: Khalid Bin Mohammed Al-Khalifa
EMail: President@ucb.edu.bh

Registrar: Isam Ahmed Al-Saraf EMail: al-saraf@ucb.edu.bh

Programme

Business Administration (Accountancy; Business Administration; Finance; Management; Marketing); **Communication and Media** (Graphic Design; Journalism; Media Studies; Public Relations; Radio and Television Broadcasting); **Information Technology** (Computer Science; Information Technology; Software Engineering)

Academic Year: September to June

Admission Requirements: Bahraini Secondary School Completion Certificate or equivalent

Degrees and Diplomas: *Bachelor's Degree*; *Master's Degree*
Last Updated: 21/11/11

UNIVERSITY OF BAHRAIN (UOB)

PO Box 32038, Manama, Sakhir, Southern Directorate
Tel: +973(17) 438-888
Fax: +973(17) 449-900
EMail: uobpresident@admin.uob.bh
Website: http://www.uob.edu.bh

President: Ebrahim Mohammed Janahi
Tel: +973(17) 438-200 EMail: uobpresident@admin.uob.bh

Vice-President (Academic Programmes and Research): Khalid Ahmed Abdulla Bugahoos Tel: +973(17) 438-090

International Relations: Hussain Al Ruffai, Director of Information and Public Relations
Tel: +973(17) 438-555 EMail: pri@admin.uob.bh

College

Applied Studies (Business Administration; Chemical Engineering; Civil Engineering; Electrical Engineering; Electronic Engineering; Information Technology; Instrument Making; Mechanical Engineering); **Arts** *(Sukhair)* (Arabic; Arts and Humanities; Communication Studies; English; Fine Arts; Islamic Studies; Literature; Social Sciences; Tourism); **Bahrain Teachers College** *(BTC)* (Curriculum; Education; Educational Technology; Psychology); **Business Administration** *(Sukhair)* (Accountancy; Administration; Business Administration; Economics; Marketing); **Engineering** *(Isa Town)* (Architecture; Chemical Engineering; Civil Engineering; Electrical Engineering; Engineering; Mechanical Engineering); **Law** *(Sukhair)* (Law; Private Law; Public Law); **Physical Education and Physiotherapy** (Physical Education; Physical Therapy); **Science** *(Sukhair)* (Biology; Chemistry; Mathematics; Natural Sciences; Physics)

Centre

American Studies (American Studies); **E-Learning** (Distance Education); **English Language** (English); **French Studies** (French; French Studies); **German Studies** (Germanic Studies); **Japanese Studies** (Japanese); **Measurement and Evaluation; Road and Transport Studies** (Road Transport; Transport and Communications)

History: Founded 1986, incorporating the University College of Arts, Science and Education, founded 1978 and the Gulf Polytechnic, College of Business and Administration and Engineering, founded 1981.

Academic Year: September to September (September-January; February-June; June-September)

Admission Requirements: Secondary school certificate (Twajihia) or equivalent

Fees: (Bahraini Dinars): 120 per semester

Main Language(s) of Instruction: Arabic, English

Degrees and Diplomas: *Bachelor's Degree*; *Postgraduate Diploma in Education*; *Master's Degree*: **Business and Commerce; Education; Engineering; Fine Arts; Information Technology.** *Doctor's Degree*: **Education; Engineering; Physical Education.**

Student Services: Academic Counselling, Canteen, Careers Guidance, Cultural Activities, Facilities for disabled people, Health Services, Language Laboratory, Social Counselling, Sports Facilities

Publications: Journal of Education and Psychological Sciences; Journal of Human Sciences; Journal of Thaqafat; The Arabian Journal of Accounting
Last Updated: 20/03/12

PRIVATE INSTITUTIONS

AHLIA UNIVERSITY (AU)

PO Box 10878, GOSI Complex, Manama
Tel: +973 1729-8999
Fax: +973 1729-0083
EMail: info@ahliauniversity.edu.bh
Website: http://www.ahliauniversity.edu.bh/

President: Abdulla Y. Al-Hawaj
EMail: aalhawaj@ahliauniversity.edu.bh

College

Arts, Science and Education (Arabic; Graphic Design; Interior Design; Mass Communication; Mathematics; Modern Languages; Public Relations); **Banking and Finance** (Accountancy; Business Administration; Economics; Finance; Information Management; Management; Marketing); **Engineering** (Computer Engineering; Telecommunications Engineering); **Information Technology** (Information Technology; Multimedia); **Medical and Health Sciences** (Physical Therapy)

History: Founded 2001.

Main Language(s) of Instruction: English and Arabic

Degrees and Diplomas: *Associate Diploma*; *Bachelor's Degree*; *Master's Degree*
Last Updated: 21/11/11

AMA INTERNATIONAL UNIVERSITY - BAHRAIN

P.O. Box 18041, Salmabad
Website: http://www.amaiu.edu.bh

President: Amable R. Aguiluz V

College

Administrative and Financial Sciences (Business Administration; Business Computing; International Studies); **Computer Studies** (Computer Science); **Engineering** (Computer Engineering; Electronic Engineering; Mechanical Engineering); **Medicine** (Medicine)

History: Founded 2002. Part of the AMA Education System (AMAES) based in the Philippines.

Accrediting Agency: Ministry of Education

Degrees and Diplomas: *Bachelor's Degree*; *Master's Degree*
Last Updated: 08/12/11

APPLIED SCIENCE UNIVERSITY

PO Box 5055, Manama
Tel: +973 1772-8777
Fax: +973 1772-8915
EMail: info@asu.edu.bh
Website: http://www.asu.edu.bh/

President: Ghassan F. Aouad (2014-)
EMail: president@asu.edu.bh; prof.ghassan@asu.edu.bh

International Relations: Fahad A. Abdulkarim, International Relations Officer EMail: fahad@asu.edu.bh; fahad_free@yahoo.co.uk

College

Administrative Sciences (Accountancy; Business Administration; Finance; Marketing; Political Sciences); **Arts and Sciences** (Computer Science; Graphic Design; Interior Design); **Law** (Commercial Law; Law; Private Law; Public Law)

History: Founded 2004.

Main Language(s) of Instruction: English and Arabic

Degrees and Diplomas: *Bachelor's Degree*: **Accountancy; Business Administration; Computer Science; Finance; Graphic Design; Information Sciences; Interior Design; Law; Marketing.** *Master's Degree*: **Accountancy; Business Administration; Commercial Law; Computer Science; Finance; Human Resources; Law.**
Last Updated: 21/11/11

ARAB OPEN UNIVERSITY - BAHRAIN BRANCH

P.O Box: 18211, AL-Haram Plaza, Sahla Street, Manama
Tel: + 973 1740-7077
Fax: + 973 1740-0916
EMail: info@aou.org.bh
Website: http://www.aou.org.bh

Branch director: Samir Qasim Fakhro

Department

Business (Business Administration; Business and Commerce); **English** (English); **Information Technology** (Information Technology)

History: Founded 2002.

Degrees and Diplomas: *Bachelor's Degree*
Last Updated: 21/11/11

DELMON UNIVERSITY FOR SCIENCE AND TECHNOLOGY

P.O. Box 2469, Exhibition Avenue, Manama
Tel: +973 1729-4400 +973 1729-5500
Fax: +973 1729-2010 +973 1729-3300
EMail: Info@delmon.bh
Website: http://www.delmon.edu.bh

President: Hasan Al-Qadhi EMail: hassan@delmon.bh

Vice President for Academic Affairs: Saad Darwish EMail: saad@delmon.bh

Faculty

Administrative and Financial Sciences (Business Administration; Economics; Finance; Marketing); **Arts** (Arabic; English; Journalism; Mass Communication; Sociology; Translation and Interpretation); **Education** (Curriculum; Education; Educational Administration; Educational Psychology; Pedagogy); **Fine Arts** (Graphic Design; Interior Design); **Information Technology and Computer Science** (Computer Science; Information Technology); **Law** (Public Law)

History: Founded in 1992. Acquired current title and status 2004.

Academic Year: September to January; February to May

Admission Requirements: Tawjihiya or equivalent secondary school certificate

Main Language(s) of Instruction: Arabic and English

Accrediting Agency: Ministry of Education

Degrees and Diplomas: *Bachelor's Degree*; *Master's Degree*
Last Updated: 21/11/11

ROYAL COLLEGE OF SURGEONS IN IRELAND - MEDICAL UNIVERSITY OF BAHRAIN

P.O. Box 15503, Adliya, Busaiteen, Manama 228
Tel: +973 1735-1450
Fax: +973 1733-0906
EMail: info@rcsi-mub.com
Website: http://www.rcsibahrain.edu.bh/

President: Thomas Collins (2011-) EMail: president@rcsi-mub.com

Vice President for Administration and Finance: Mary Alexander EMail: malexander@rcsi-mub.com

International Relations: Fadi Ghosn, Regulatory Affairs Administrator EMail: fghosen@rcsi-mub.com

School

Medicine (Health Administration; Medicine); **Midwifery** (Midwifery; Nursing); **Postgraduate Studies and Research** (Health Administration; Nursing)

History: Created 2004.

Academic Year: September to June

Admission Requirements: Recognized secondary school certificate for undergraduate degrees. For Master's courses, a recognized Bachelor's degree is required. Full information available from the institution.

Fees: (US Dollars): Undergraduate, Medicine, 38,250; Nursing, 11,630; Master's degree, Nursing, 14,550, Ethics and Law, 18,630, all per annum

Main Language(s) of Instruction: English

Accrediting Agency: Gulf Cooperation Council Medical School Dean's Committee; Bahrain Quality Assurance Authority for Education and Training (QAAET)

Degrees and Diplomas: *Bachelor's Degree*: **Nursing.** *Medical Doctor Degree*: **Gynaecology and Obstetrics; Medicine; Surgery.** *Master's Degree*: **Ethics; Health Administration; Law; Nursing; Public Health.** Also Bridging courses in Nursing, 1 1/2 yrs

Student Services: Academic Counselling, Canteen, Facilities for disabled people, Health Services, Language Laboratory, Social Counselling, Sports Facilities

Publications: RCSIsmj: Royal College of Surgeons in Ireland Student Medical Journal; Surgeon: journal of the Royal Colleges of Surgeons of Edinburgh and Ireland

Academic Staff *2011-2012*	MEN	WOMEN	**TOTAL**
FULL-TIME	48	53	**101**
PART-TIME	56	36	**92**
STAFF WITH DOCTORATE			
FULL-TIME	19	9	**28**
Student Numbers *2011-2012*			
All (Foreign included)	342	672	**1,014**
FOREIGN ONLY	203	193	**396**

Last Updated: 20/02/12

ROYAL UNIVERSITY FOR WOMEN (RUW)

PO Box 37400, West Riffa
Tel: +973 1776-4444
Fax: +973 1776-4445
EMail: info@ruw.edu.bh
Website: http://www.ruw.edu.bh/

President: Mazin Mohammed Ali Tel: +973 1776-4429

Vice-President for Academic Affairs: L. Sykes EMail: rmokha@ruw.edu.bh

Faculty

Art and Design (Fashion Design; Graphic Design; Interior Design); **Business and Financial Sciences** (Banking; Finance; Human Resources; International Business; Management; Marketing); **Education** (Education; English; Preschool Education; Primary Education; Special Education)

Centre

General Studies

History: Founded 2004.

Academic Year: September to January; February to June

Fees: (Bahraini dinars): 160-180 per credit

Accrediting Agency: Ministry of Education

Degrees and Diplomas: *Diploma*: **Graphic Design.** *Bachelor's Degree*: **Business Administration; Computer Science; Design; Education; Fine Arts; Information Technology.**
Last Updated: 21/11/11

THE KINGDOM UNIVERSITY

PO Box 40434, Manama
Tel: +973(17) 238-899
Fax: +973(17) 271-001
EMail: info@ku.edu.bh
Website: http://www.ku.edu.bh

President: Yousef Abdul Ghaffar Abdulla (2003-2015)

International Relations: Amanulla Mohammed Salih, International Relations Officer EMail: a.salih@ku.edu.bh

College
Arts (Media Studies; Public Relations); **Business Administration** (Banking; Business Administration; Finance; Insurance; International Business; Marketing); **Computing and Information Technology** (Computer Science; Information Technology); **Engineering** (Architecture; Interior Design); **Law** (Law; Private Law)

History: Founded 2002.

Academic Year: September to July

Admission Requirements: High school certificate or equivalent (Tawjeheya)

Fees: (Bahraini Dinars): Bachelor's Degree: 195 per subject

Main Language(s) of Instruction: Arabic, with some courses in English

Degrees and Diplomas: *Bachelor's Degree*; *Master's Degree*

Last Updated: 21/11/11

Bangladesh

STRUCTURE OF HIGHER EDUCATION SYSTEM

Description:

The management of the higher education system falls under the Ministry of Education, its Directorate of Secondary and Higher Education (DSHE), and the University Grants Commission (UGC). Higher education is offered in general, technical, engineering, agriculture, business, and medical streams. The minimum requirement for admission to higher education is the higher secondary certificate (HSC). There are both public and private universities. There is also tertiary level of Madrasah education. Madrasah education comprises Islamic religious education along with general education. This level is comprised of 4 (2+2) years of formal education. The minimum requirement for admission to higher level of Madrasah education is the Alim (equivalent to HSC) certificate. Alim pass students are qualified to enroll in 2-year Fazil education. After successful completion of the Fazil degree, one can enroll in 2-year Kamil education.

Stages of studies:

University level first stage: *Bachelor's degree*

Pass degrees are obtained after three years' study and Honours degrees after four years.

University level second stage: *Master's degree*

Most postgraduate courses leading to a Master's degree in general universities are of two years' duration for Pass graduates and one year for Honours graduates.

University level third stage: *Master of Philosophy (MPhil), Doctor's degree (PhD)*

The MPhil course is of one year's duration after MA or MSc. The Doctor of Philosophy (PhD) is the highest university qualification, usually awarded following two to three years' study beyond the Master's degree. It is only offered in specific fields of study (Engineering, Medicine, Education). Candidates must submit a thesis following research.

ADMISSION TO HIGHER EDUCATION

Admission to university-level studies:

Name of secondary school credential required: Higher Secondary Certificate

Admission requirements: There are admission tests.

Foreign students admission:

Entry regulations: Foreign students must hold a visa.

Language proficiency: Students should be proficient in English.

RECOGNITION OF STUDIES

Quality assurance system:

It is mandatory for all institutions to be recognised by the appropriate national level statutory bodies established by the Government. All universities come under the jurisdiction of the University Grants Commission (UGC).

NATIONAL BODIES

Ministry of Education - MOEDU

Minister: Nurul Islam Nahid
Building 6, Floor 17th and 18th, Bangladesh Secretariat
Dhaka 1000
Tel: +88(2) 9540-395
Fax: +88(2) 9514-114
EMail: info@moedu.gov.bd
WWW: http://www.moedu.gov.bd

Role of national body: To formulate policies and programmes for the development of post-primary to higher education including Madrasah, technical, and vocational education. To formulate laws, rules, and regulations for the management and administration of post-primary education.

Directorate of Secondary and Higher Education - DSHE

Director: Fahima Khatun
Ministry of Education, Building 6, Floor 17th and 18th, Bangladesh Secretariat
Dhaka 1000
EMail: info@dshe.gov.bd
WWW: http://www.dshe.gov.bd/index.html
Role of national body: To implement the education policy of the Government in respect to secondary and higher education (Bachelors and Masters).

University Grants Commission of Bangladesh - UGC

Chair: Abdul Mannan
Agargaon
Dhaka 1207
Tel: +88(2) 8113-242
Fax: +88(2) 8122-948
EMail: chairmanugc@yahoo.com; publicrelations.ugc@gmail.com
WWW: http://www.ugc.gov.bd
Role of national body: To supervise, maintain, promote and coordinate university education; to maintain standards and quality in all public and private universities in Bangladesh; to assess the needs of public universities in terms of funding; to advise the Government in various issues related to higher education in Bangladesh.

Bangladesh Bureau of Educational Information and Statistics - BANBEIS

Director: Mohammed Fashiullah
1 Sonargaon Road
Dhaka 1205
Tel: +88(2) 9665-457
EMail: banbeis@banbeis.gov.bd; info@banbeis.gov.bd
WWW: http://www.banbeis.gov.bd
Role of national body: To keep educational information at all levels.

IAU Association of Universities of Bangladesh - AUB

Executive Secretary: S.M. Saifuddin
University Grants Commission Office Building
Agargaon, Shar-e-Bangla Nagar
Dhaka 1207
EMail: duregstr@bangla.net

Association of Private Universities of Bangladesh - APUB

Dhaka

Data for academic year: 2013-2014
Source: IAU from "National Education Policy 2010" and Ministry of Education and UGC websites, 2013. Bodies 2016.

INSTITUTIONS

PUBLIC INSTITUTIONS

BANGABANDHU SHEIKH MUJIBUR MEDICAL UNIVERSITY

PO Box 3048, Shahbag, Dhaka 1000
Tel: +880(2) 966-1065
Fax: +880(2) 956-7899
EMail: vc@bsmmu.edu.bd
Website: http://www.bsmmu.edu.bd

Vice-Chancellor: Pran Gopal Datta
Registrar: Muhammad A. Gafur Tel: +880(2) 966-1064

Faculty

Alternative Medicine (Alternative Medicine); **Basic Science and Para Clinical Science** (Biochemistry; Microbiology; Pathology; Pharmacy; Physiology; Virology); **Dentistry** (Dentistry; Orthodontics; Surgery); **Medical Technology** (Medical Technology); **Medicine** (Anatomy; Cardiology; Dermatology; Gastroenterology; Haematology; Hepatology; Medicine; Nephrology; Oncology; Ophthalmology; Orthopaedics; Paediatrics; Pathology; Pharmacology;

Physical Therapy; Physiology; Psychiatry and Mental Health; Radiology; Rehabilitation and Therapy); **Nursing** (Nursing); **Preventive and Social Medicine** (Ophthalmology; Public Health); **Surgery** (Anaesthesiology; Cardiology; Gynaecology and Obstetrics; Midwifery; Ophthalmology; Surgery; Urology)

History: Founded 1965 as Institute of Postgraduate Medicine and Research, acquired present status and title 1998.

Degrees and Diplomas: *Master's Degree*

Student Services: Library

Last Updated: 07/07/14

BANGABANDHU SHEIKH MUJIBUR RAHMAN AGRICULTURAL UNIVERSITY (BSMRAU)

Salna 1706
Tel: +880(2) 893-1515
Fax: +880(2) 920-5338 +880(2) 920-5333
EMail: info@bsmrau.edu.bd
Website: http://www.bsmrau.edu.bd

Vice-Chancellor: Md. Mahbubar Rahman

Faculty

Agricultural Economics and Rural Development (Agricultural Business; Agricultural Economics; Statistics); **Agriculture** (Agricultural Economics; Agricultural Engineering; Agriculture; Agronomy; Biochemistry; Biotechnology; Botany; Crop Production; Entomology; Environmental Studies; Farm Management; Genetics; Horticulture; Plant Pathology; Soil Science); **Agroforestry & Environment** (Agriculture; Environmental Engineering; Forestry); **Fisheries** (Aquaculture; Fishery); **Veterinary Science and Animal Science** (Animal Husbandry; Dairy; Meat and Poultry; Public Health; Radiology; Surgery; Veterinary Science)

History: Founded 1980 as Bangladesh College of Agricultural Sciences. Acquired present title 1998.

Admission Requirements: SSC (Science Group) and HSC (Science Group) examinations or equivalent examinations from a recognized Board or Institution with at least GPA 3 in each of the examinations. Total GPA of both the examinations should be at least 7. (b) must have at least B grade in Physics, Chemistry, Biology, Mathematics and English in HSC or equivalent examinations.

Fees: (Taka): Bachelor, c. 9,000 per annum; Master, c. 8,000; PhD, c. 10,000

Main Language(s) of Instruction: English

Accrediting Agency: University Grants Commission (UGC)

Degrees and Diplomas: *Bachelor of Science*: **Agriculture.** *Master's Degree*: **Agriculture.** *Ph. D.*: **Agriculture; Horticulture; Plant Pathology; Soil Science.**

Student Services: Academic Counselling, Canteen, Cultural Activities, Health Services, Library, Social Counselling, Sports Facilities

Publications: Annals of Bangladesh Agriculture; Research Abstract

Last Updated: 07/07/14

BANGLADESH AGRICULTURAL UNIVERSITY

BAU Main Road, Mymensingh 2202
Tel: +880(91) 556-95
Fax: +880(91) 527-80 +880(91) 558-10
EMail: vcbau@bd.drik.net
Website: http://bau.edu.bd

Vice-Chancellor: Md. Rafiqul Hoque

Faculty

Agricultural Economics and Rural Sociology (Agricultural Economics; Finance; Rural Studies; Sociology; Statistics); **Agricultural Engineering and Technology** (Agricultural Engineering; Farm Management; Food Technology; Irrigation; Water Management); **Agriculture** (Agriculture; Agronomy; Biochemistry; Crop Production; Entomology; Forestry; Genetics; Horticulture; Plant Pathology; Soil Science); **Animal Husbandry** (Animal Husbandry; Dairy; Meat and Poultry; Nutrition); **Fishery** (Aquaculture; Fishery); **Veterinary Science** (Anatomy; Histology; Hygiene; Medicine; Microbiology; Parasitology; Pathology; Pharmacology; Physiology; Surgery; Veterinary Science)

Institute

Advanced Studies and Research; **Graduate Training**; **Research System**

Centre

Extension

History: Founded 1961 as East Pakistan Agricultural University, acquired present status and title 1972. A teaching, examining and affiliating body, its main purpose is to provide facilities for higher education and research in agriculture and allied fields.

Academic Year: July to June

Admission Requirements: Higher secondary certificate (HSC) or foreign equivalent and entrance examination

Fees: (Taka): 150-600

Main Language(s) of Instruction: Bengali, English

Degrees and Diplomas: *Bachelor's Degree (Pass)*; *Bachelor's Degree (Hons)*; *Master's Degree*; *Ph. D.*: **Agricultural Economics; Agricultural Engineering; Agriculture; Animal Husbandry; Fishery.**

Publications: Agricultural Economics (professional scientific journal); Agricultural Science (professional scientific journal); Animal Sciences (professional scientific journal); Aquaculture (professional scientific journal); Crop Science (professional scientific journal); Extension Education (professional scientific journal); Fisheries (professional scientific journal); Horticulture (professional scientific journal); Plant Pathology (professional scientific journal); Progressive Agriculture (professional scientific journal); Training and Development (professional scientific journal); Veterinarian, Agricultural Engineering (professional scientific journal); Veterinary Science (professional scientific journal)

Last Updated: 07/07/14

BANGLADESH OPEN UNIVERSITY

Board Bazar, Gazipur 1704
Tel: +880(2) 980-0801
Fax: +880(2) 929-1130
EMail: arahman@bou.edu.bd
Website: http://www.bou.edu.bd

Vice-Chancellor: M.A. Manna (2013-) EMail: vc@bou.bangla.net

School

Agriculture and Rural Development (Agriculture; Crop Production; Fishery; Forestry; Horticulture; Meat and Poultry; Plant and Crop Protection); **Business** (Accountancy; Banking; Business and Commerce; Economics; Management; Marketing); **Education** (Education); **Open** (Mathematics; Natural Sciences); **Science and Technology** (Computer Science; Demography and Population; Health Sciences; Nursing; Nutrition); **Social Sciences, Humanities and Language** (Arabic; Arts and Humanities; English; Social Sciences)

History: Founded 1992.

Academic Year: July to June

Fees: (US Dollars): c. 700

Main Language(s) of Instruction: Bengali, English

Degrees and Diplomas: *Diploma*; *Bachelor's Degree (Pass)*; *Master's Degree*; *Master of Philosophy*

Last Updated: 07/07/14

BANGLADESH UNIVERSITY OF ENGINEERING AND TECHNOLOGY (BUET)

Dhaka 1000
Tel: +880(2) 966-5650
Fax: +880(2) 861-3046
EMail: daers@buet.edu
Website: http://www.buet.ac.bd

Vice-Chancellor: S. M. Nazrul Islam

Registrar: A.K.M. Masud EMail: regt@regtr.buet.ac.bd

Faculty

Architecture and Planning (Architecture and Planning; Regional Planning; Town Planning); **Civil Engineering** (Civil Engineering; Environmental Engineering; Structural Architecture; Transport Engineering; Water Science); **Electrical and Electronic Engineering** (Computer Engineering; Electrical and Electronic Engineering; Industrial Engineering); **Engineering** (Chemical

Engineering; Chemistry; Engineering; Materials Engineering; Mathematics; Metallurgical Engineering; Mineralogy; Petroleum and Gas Engineering; Physics); **Mechanical Engineering** (Industrial Engineering; Marine Engineering; Mechanical Engineering; Naval Architecture; Production Engineering)

Institute
Accident Research; **Appropriate Technology** (Technology); **Information and Communication Technology** (Computer Science; Information Technology); **Water and Flood Management** (Safety Engineering; Water Management; Water Science)

Centre
Biomedical Engineering Research (Biomedical Engineering); **Energy Studies** (Energy Engineering); **Environmental Resources Management** (Environmental Engineering)

History: Founded 1846 as Dhaka Survey School. Became Ahsanullah Engineering College as a Faculty of Engineering under the University of Dhaka1947. Became East Pakistan Engineering University 1962 and acquired present title and status 1971. A State Institution.

Academic Year: January to December

Admission Requirements: Secondary school certificate (SSC) and higher secondary certificate (HSC) or foreign equivalent. Major with Mathematics, Physics, Chemistry and admission test

Fees: (Taka): 1,000 per term

Main Language(s) of Instruction: English

Degrees and Diplomas: *Bachelor of Science*; *Master's Degree*: **Agricultural Engineering; Architecture; Chemical Engineering; Civil Engineering; Computer Science; Electrical and Electronic Engineering; Industrial Engineering; Marine Engineering; Mechanical Engineering; Mining Engineering; Naval Architecture; Petroleum and Gas Engineering; Production Engineering; Rural Planning; Town Planning; Water Management; Water Science.** *Master of Philosophy*: **Chemistry; Mathematics; Physics.** *Ph. D.*: **Agricultural Engineering; Architecture; Chemical Engineering; Civil Engineering; Computer Science; Electrical and Electronic Engineering; Industrial Engineering; Marine Engineering; Mechanical Engineering; Mining Engineering; Naval Architecture; Petroleum and Gas Engineering; Production Engineering; Rural Planning; Town Planning; Water Management; Water Science.** Also offers post-graduate diplomas in one year in Water Resources Development; Information and Communication Technology.

Student Services: Academic Counselling, Canteen, Cultural Activities, Health Services, Library, Sports Facilities

Publications: BUET Studies; Research Abstracts; Technical Journal

Last Updated: 08/07/14

BANGLADESH UNIVERSITY OF PROFESSIONALS

Mirpur Cantonment, Dhaka 1216
Tel: +880(2) 800-0368
Fax: +880(2) 800-0443
EMail: info@bup.edu.bd
Website: http://www.bup.edu.bd

Vice-Chancellor: Mamun Khaled

Faculty
Business Studies (Business Computing; Finance; Human Resources; Management Systems; Marketing)

History: Created 2008 out of the Military Institute of Science and Technology (MIST).

Main Language(s) of Instruction: English

Degrees and Diplomas: *Bachelor's Degree (Pass)*: **Business Administration.** *Master's Degree*: **Business Administration.** *Master of Philosophy*. Also Executive Masters.

BANGLADESH UNIVERSITY OF TEXTILES

92 Shaheed Tajuddin Ahmed Avenue, Tejgaon, Dhaka 1208
Tel: +880(2) 911-4260
Fax: +880(2) 912-4255
EMail: vc@butex.edu.bd
Website: http://www.butex.edu.bd

Vice-Chancellor: Nitai Chandra Sutradhar

Faculty
Textile Chemical Processing Engineering & Applied Science (Chemical Engineering; Chemistry; Mathematics; Physics); **Textile Clothing, Fashion Design & Business Studies** (Business Administration; Clothing and Sewing; Fashion Design); **Textile Manufacturing Engineering** (Production Engineering; Textile Technology)

History: Founded 1921 as East Bengal Textile Institute. Became East Pakistan Textile Institute in 1950. Acquired present status and title 2010.

Degrees and Diplomas: *Bachelor's Degree (Pass)*; *Master's Degree*

Student Services: Library

Last Updated: 09/07/14

BEGUM ROKEYA UNIVERSITY

Rangpur 5400
Tel: +880(521) 66731
Website: http://www.brur.ac.bd

Vice-Chancellor: A.K.M. Nurun Nabi

Faculty
Arts (Archaeology; Arts and Humanities; English; History; Native Language Education); **Business** (Accountancy; Banking; Business Administration; Finance; Management; Marketing); **Engineering & Technology** (Computer Engineering; Computer Science; Electrical Engineering; Telecommunications Engineering); **Life & Earth Sciences** (Environmental Engineering; Geography (Human)); **Science** (Chemistry; Mathematics; Natural Sciences; Physics; Statistics); **Social Sciences** (Economics; Gender Studies; Journalism; Mass Communication; Political Sciences; Public Administration; Sociology; Women's Studies)

History: Founded 2008.

Degrees and Diplomas: *Bachelor's Degree (Pass)*; *Master's Degree*

Student Services: Library

Last Updated: 08/07/14

CHITTAGONG UNIVERSITY OF ENGINEERING AND TECHNOLOGY (CUET)

Chittagong 4349
Tel: +880(31) 71-4951
EMail: admin@cuet.ac.bd
Website: http://www.cuet.ac.bd

Vice-Chancellor: Md. Jahangir Alam EMail: vc@cuet.ac.bd

Registrar: Faruque-Uz-Zaman Chowdhury
EMail: registrar@cuet.ac.bd

Faculty
Architecture and Planning (Architecture; Town Planning); **Civil Engineering** (Civil Engineering; Environmental Engineering); **Electrical and Computer Engineering** (Computer Engineering; Electrical Engineering; Telecommunications Engineering); **Engineering and Technology** (Chemistry; Mathematics; Physics); **Mechanical Engineering** (Mechanical Engineering; Petroleum and Gas Engineering)

Institute
Earthquake Engineering (Seismology); **Energy Technology** (Energy Engineering); **Information and Communication Technology** (Information Technology)

History: Founded as an Engineering College 1968. Became an Institute of Technology 1986. Acquired present status 2003.

Academic Year: July to June

Admission Requirements: Higher Secondary Certificate

Main Language(s) of Instruction: English

Degrees and Diplomas: *Bachelor's Degree (Pass)*; *Master's Degree*; *Master of Philosophy*; *Ph. D.*

Student Services: Academic Counselling, Canteen, Health Services, Library, Sports Facilities

Last Updated: 08/07/14

CHITTAGONG VETERINARY AND ANIMAL SCIENCES UNIVERSITY

Zakir Hossain Road, Khulshi, Chittagong 4202
Tel: +880(31) 659-093 +880(31) 659-492
Fax: +880(31) 659-620
EMail: vccvasu@gmail.com
Website: http://www.cvasu.ac.bd

Vice-Chancellor: A. S. Mahfuzul Bari
EMail: bari.bau.bd@gmail.com

Faculty

Fisheries (Aquaculture; Fishery; Harvest Technology; Marine Science and Oceanography); **Food Science and Technology** (Applied Chemistry; Food Science; Food Technology; Mathematics; Physics); **Veterinary Medicine** (Agricultural Economics; Anatomy; Animal Husbandry; Biochemistry; Dairy; Histology; Meat and Poultry; Medicine; Microbiology; Parasitology; Pathology; Physiology; Social Sciences; Surgery; Veterinary Science)

Research Centre

Poultry (Meat and Poultry)

History: Created 1996 as Chittagong Government Veterinary College (then part of the University of Chittagong). Acquired current title and status 2006.

Degrees and Diplomas: *Bachelor's Degree (Hons)*; *Master's Degree*; *Ph. D.*. Also Doctor of Veterinary Medicine (DVM) in 5 yrs

Last Updated: 08/07/14

COMILLA UNIVERSITY

Kotbari, Comilla
Tel: +880 81-6681
EMail: registrarcou@gmail.com
Website: http://www.cou.ac.bd

Vice-Chancellor: Md. Ali Ashraf

Registrar: Muzibur Rahman Mozumdar

School

Arts and Humanities (Archaeology; English; Native Language Education); **Business** (Accountancy; Banking; Finance; Management; Marketing); **Science** (Chemistry; Mathematics; Pharmacy; Physics; Statistics); **Social Sciences** (Anthropology; Economics; Public Administration; Sociology)

History: Founded 2000.

Degrees and Diplomas: *Bachelor's Degree (Pass)*; *Bachelor's Degree (Hons)*; *Master's Degree*

Last Updated: 09/07/14

DHAKA UNIVERSITY OF ENGINEERING AND TECHNOLOGY (DUET GAZIPUR)

Gazipur 1700
Tel: +880(2) 920-4703
Fax: +880(2) 920-4701
EMail: mala403@yahoo.co.uk
Website: http://www.duet.ac.bd

Vice-Chancellor: Mohammed Alauddin

Registrar: Md. Asaduzzaman Chowdhury
EMail: reg_duet@duet.ac.bd

Faculty

Civil Engineering (Architecture; Chemistry; Civil Engineering; Mathematics; Physics); **Electrical and Electronic Engineering** (Computer Engineering; Computer Science; Electrical and Electronic Engineering); **Mechanical Engineering** (Arts and Humanities; Mechanical Engineering; Textile Technology)

History: Founded 1980 as Dakha Engineering College, became Bangladesh Institute of Technology, 1986. Acquired present name and status 2003.

Admission Requirements: Secondary School Certificate, 3-year Diploma in Engineering from Polytechnic Institute of Bangladesh

Main Language(s) of Instruction: English

Degrees and Diplomas: *Bachelor's Degree (Pass)*; *Master's Degree*; *Master of Philosophy*; *Ph. D.*

Student Services: Academic Counselling, Canteen, Careers Guidance, Cultural Activities, Health Services, Language Laboratory, Nursery Care, Social Counselling, Sports Facilities

Last Updated: 09/07/14

HAJEE MOHAMMAD DANESH UNIVERSITY OF SCIENCE AND TECHNOLOGY (HMDSTU)

Dinajpur 5200
Tel: +880(531) 65-429
Fax: +880(531) 61-344
EMail: registrar@hstu.ac.bd
Website: http://www.hstu.ac.bd

Vice-Chancellor: M. Afzal Hossain

Registrar: R.I. Mahmood Tel: +880(531) 61-355

Faculty

Agriculture (Agricultural Economics; Agriculture; Agronomy; Animal Husbandry; Biochemistry; Botany; Chemistry; Entomology; Forestry; Genetics; Horticulture; Plant Pathology; Soil Science; Statistics); **Agro-Industrial and Food Processing Engineering**; **Business Studies**; **Computer Science and Engineering** (Computer Engineering; Computer Science; Electrical and Electronic Engineering; Electronic Engineering; Information Technology; Mathematics; Physics; Social Sciences; Telecommunications Engineering); **Fisheries**; **Postgraduate Studies** (Agriculture; Agronomy; Biochemistry; Entomology; Horticulture; Plant Pathology; Soil Science)

History: Founded 1976 as Bangladesh Agricultural Research Institute. Acquired present status 2002.

Academic Year: January to December

Fees: (Taka): 2,000 per semester

Main Language(s) of Instruction: English

Degrees and Diplomas: *Bachelor's Degree (Pass)*: **Agriculture.** *Master's Degree*: **Agriculture.** *Ph. D.*

Student Services: Academic Counselling, Canteen, Careers Guidance, Cultural Activities, Health Services, Language Laboratory, Nursery Care, Social Counselling, Sports Facilities

Publications: Journal of Science and Technology

Last Updated: 10/07/14

ISLAMIC UNIVERSITY

Shantidanga-Dulalpur, Kushtia 7000
Tel: +880(71) 530-29 +880(71) 546-00
Fax: +880(71) 544-00
Website: http://www.iubd.net

Vice-Chancellor: M. Allaudin (2009-) Tel: +880(71) 546-00

International Relations: M.G. Saklayen
Tel: +880(71) 530-29, Ext. 241

Faculty

Applied Sciences and Technology (Applied Chemistry; Applied Physics; Biotechnology; Computer Science; Food Science; Information Sciences; Natural Sciences; Technology); **Business Administration** (Accountancy; Business Administration; Management); **Humanities and Social Sciences** (Arabic; Arts and Humanities; Economics; English; Indic Languages; Political Sciences; Public Administration; Social Sciences); **Law and Sh'ariah** (Islamic Law); **Theology and Islamic Studies** (Islamic Studies; Islamic Theology)

History: Founded 1979 as a unitary teaching and residential University. Acquired present status and title 2000.

Academic Year: July to June

Admission Requirements: Higher school certificate or equivalent

Main Language(s) of Instruction: English, Bengali, Arabic

Accrediting Agency: Government of Bangladesh

Degrees and Diplomas: *Bachelor's Degree (Pass)*; *Bachelor's Degree (Hons)*; *Master's Degree*; *Master of Philosophy*; *Ph. D.*

Student Services: Academic Counselling, Sports Facilities

Publishing house: Islamic University Press

JAGANNATH UNIVERSITY

9-10 Chittaranjan Avenue, Dhaka 1100
Tel: +880(2) 711-9731
Fax: +880(2) 711-3752
EMail: admission@jagannathuniversity.org
Website: http://www.jnuni.net/index1.html

Vice-Chancellor: Mijanur Rahman

Registrar: Md. Ohiduzzaman

Faculty

Arts (English; History; Islamic Studies; Native Language; Philosophy); **Business Studies** (Accountancy; Finance; Management; Marketing); **Law** (Law); **Life and Earth Sciences** (Biotechnology; Botany; Environmental Engineering; Geography; Microbiology; Pharmacy; Psychology; Zoology); **Science** (Chemistry; Computer Engineering; Computer Science; Mathematics; Physics; Statistics); **Social Science** (Anthropology; Ecology; Economics; Journalism; Mass Communication; Political Sciences; Public Administration; Social Work; Sociology)

History: Created in 1858 as Dhaka Brahma School. Offered degree courses from 1949 as Jagannath Intermediate College. Began honours and masters programmes in 1975. Obtained current status and title 2005.

Degrees and Diplomas: *Bachelor's Degree (Hons)*; *Master's Degree*; *Master of Philosophy*; *Ph. D.*: **English; Physics; Social Sciences.**

Publications: Jagannath University Journal of Social Sciences; Jagannath University Journal of Arts; Jagannath University Journal of Business Studies; Jagannath University Journal of Science

Last Updated: 11/07/14

JAHANGIRNAGAR UNIVERSITY

Savar, Dhaka 1342
Tel: +880(2) 770-8478
Fax: +880(2) 770-8069
EMail: registr@juniv.edu
Website: http://www.juniv.edu

Vice-Chancellor: Farzana Islam
EMail: prof.farzanaislam@gmail.com

Registrar: Abu Bakr Siddique

Faculty

Arts and Humanities (Archaeology; Arts and Humanities; English; History; Journalism; Media Studies; Philosophy; Theatre); **Biological Sciences** (Biochemistry; Botany; Microbiology; Molecular Biology; Pharmacy; Zoology); **Business Studies** (Accountancy; Banking; Finance; Management; Marketing); **Mathematical and Physical Sciences** (Chemistry; Computer Science; Electronic Engineering; Environmental Studies; Geology; Mathematics; Physics; Statistics); **Social Sciences** (Anthropology; Economics; Environmental Studies; Geography; Government; International Relations; Public Administration; Regional Planning; Social Sciences; Town Planning)

Institute

Business Administration (Business Administration); **Information Technology** (Information Technology)

History: Founded 1970, as a unitary teaching and residential University by the Jahangirnagar Muslim University Ordinance promulgated by the then government of E. Pakistan, now Bangladesh. Acquired present title 1972.

Academic Year: July to June

Admission Requirements: Secondary school certificate (SSC) and higher secondary certificate (HSC) or foreign equivalent and admission test

Main Language(s) of Instruction: English, Bengali

Degrees and Diplomas: *Bachelor's Degree (Pass)*; *Master's Degree*; *Master of Philosophy*; *Ph. D.*

Student Services: Library

Publications: Anthropology Journal; Asian Studies (Department of Government and Policy); Bangla Shahitya Patra (Department of Bengali); Bhugol Patrika (Department of Geography); Clio (Department of History); Copula (Department of Philosophy); Harvest (Department of English); Jahangirnagar Economics Review; Jahangirnagar Physical Studies; Jahangirnagar Review; Journal of Life Sciences; Journal of Mathematical and Mathematics Sciences; Journal of Statistical Studies; Rasayan Samikha (Department of Chemistry)

Last Updated: 11/07/14

JATIYA KABI KAZI NAZRUL ISLAM UNIVERSITY

House # 76, Road # 19, Sector # 14, Uttara Model Town, Dhaka
EMail: contact@jkkniu.edu.bd
Website: http://www.jkkniu.edu.bd

Vice-Chancellor: Mohit Ul Alam EMail: syed_ahmed@yahoo.com

Registrar: Md. Humayun Kabi

Faculty

Arts (English; Fine Arts; Literature; Music; Native Language; Performing Arts; Theatre); **Business Studies** (Accountancy; Banking; Business Administration; Finance; Human Resources; Management); **Science and Engineering** (Computer Engineering; Computer Science; Electrical and Electronic Engineering); **Social Science** (Economics; Public Administration)

History: Founded 2005.

Degrees and Diplomas: *Bachelor's Degree (Pass)*; *Master's Degree*

Student Services: Library, Residential Facilities

Last Updated: 16/07/14

JESSORE SCIENCE AND TECHNOLOGY UNIVERSITY

Shadhinota Shorok (Independence Road), Jessore 7408
EMail: registrar@just.edu.bd
Website: http://www.just.edu.bd

Vice-Chancellor: Abdus Sattar

Faculty

Applied Science and Technology (Applied Chemistry; Chemical Engineering; Environmental Management; Environmental Studies; Food Technology; Nutrition); **Biological Science and Technology** (Aquaculture; Biotechnology; Fishery; Genetics; Microbiology); **Engineering and Technology** (Computer Engineering; Computer Science; Industrial Engineering; Mining Engineering; Petroleum and Gas Engineering); **Physical Education, Language and Ethical Studies** (English; Physical Education); **Science** (Chemistry; Mathematics; Physics; Statistics)

History: Founded 2008.

Degrees and Diplomas: *Bachelor of Science*; *Bachelor's Degree (Hons)*; *Master's Degree*

Student Services: Library

Last Updated: 15/07/14

KHULNA UNIVERSITY

Gollamara, Khulna 9208
Tel: +880(41) 721-791 +880(41) 720-171
Fax: +880(41) 731-244
EMail: ku@bdonline.com
Website: http://www.ku.ac.bd

Vice-Chancellor: Mohammad Fayek Uzzaman

Registrar: Molla Amir Hossen

School

Arts and Humanities (English; Literature; Native Language); **Life Sciences** (Agricultural Engineering; Biological and Life Sciences; Biotechnology; Environmental Studies; Fishery; Forest Management; Natural Resources; Pharmacy; Soil Science; Wood Technology); **Management and Business Administration** (Accountancy; Business Administration; Communication Studies; Computer Science; Economics; English; Finance; Management); **Science, Engineering and Technology** (Architecture; Arts and Humanities; Computer Engineering; Computer Science; Construction Engineering; Electronic Engineering; Engineering;

Environmental Studies; Mathematics; Natural Sciences; Physics; Rural Planning; Social Sciences; Software Engineering; Technology; Telecommunications Engineering; Town Planning); **Social Sciences** (Development Studies; Economics; Sociology)

Institute

Fine Arts (Fine Arts)

History: Founded 1987, classes formally inaugurated 1991.

Academic Year: July to June (July-December; January-June)

Admission Requirements: Higher secondary certificate examination, or Pass in Aleem from any Madrasha in Bangladesh

Fees: (Taka): Registration, 2,500; foreign students, (US Dollars): 1,000

Main Language(s) of Instruction: English, Bengali

Degrees and Diplomas: *Bachelor's Degree (Pass)*; *Bachelor's Degree (Hons)*; *Master's Degree*: **Agronomy.**

Student Services: Academic Counselling, Canteen, Careers Guidance, Cultural Activities, Health Services, Language Laboratory, Library, Residential Facilities, Sports Facilities

Publications: Khulna University Studies

Last Updated: 15/07/14

KHULNA UNIVERSITY OF ENGINEERING AND TECHNOLOGY

Khulna 9203
Tel: +880(41) 774-584
EMail: info@kuet.ac.bd
Website: http://www.kuet.ac.bd

Vice-Chancellor: Muhammed Alamgir
EMail: alamgir63dr@yahoo.com

Faculty

Civil Engineering (Arts and Humanities; Chemistry; Civil Engineering; Mathematics; Physics; Regional Planning; Town Planning); **Electrical and Electronic Engineering** (Biomedical Engineering; Computer Engineering; Electrical and Electronic Engineering; Energy Engineering); **Mechanical Engineering** (Industrial Engineering; Leather Techniques; Mechanical Engineering; Textile Technology)

History: Founded 1967 as Khulna Engineering College. Became Bangladesh Institute of Technology (BIT), Khulna 1986. Acquired present status 2003.

Main Language(s) of Instruction: English

Degrees and Diplomas: *Bachelor's Degree (Pass)*; *Master's Degree*; *Master of Philosophy*; *Ph. D.*: **Engineering.**

Student Services: Library, Residential Facilities

Last Updated: 15/07/14

MAWLANA BHASHANI SCIENCE AND TECHNOLOGY UNIVERSITY

Santosh, Tangail, Dhaka 1902
Tel: +880(921) 51-899
Fax: +880(921) 55-400
EMail: registrar@mbstu.ac.bd
Website: http://mbstu.ac.bd

Vice-Chancellor: Md. Alauddin

Faculty

Business Studies (Business Administration); **Engineering** (Computer Engineering; Computer Science; Information Technology; Telecommunications Engineering; Textile Technology); **Life Science** (Biotechnology; Criminology; Environmental Studies; Food Technology; Genetics; Natural Resources; Nutrition; Police Studies); **Science** (Chemistry; Mathematics; Physics; Statistics); **Social Sciences** (Economics)

History: Founded 2002.

Degrees and Diplomas: *Bachelor's Degree (Pass)*; *Bachelor's Degree (Hons)*; *Master's Degree*

Student Services: Library

Last Updated: 16/07/14

NATIONAL UNIVERSITY

Board Bazar, Gazipur 1704
Tel: +880(2) 980-0655 +880(2) 980-0657
Fax: +880(2) 811-0261
EMail: vc@nu.edu.bd
Website: http://www.nu.edu.bd

Vice-Chancellor: Harun-or- Rashid EMail: harun@du.ac.bd

Pro-Vice-Chancellor (Academic): Mohammed Ashlam Bhuiyan

School

Undergraduate Studies (Administration; Business Administration; Education; Home Economics; Law)

Institute

Postgraduate Studies

Centre

Curriculum Development and Evaluation (Curriculum); **Postgraduate Education, Training and Research** (Education)

History: Founded 1992 by act of Bangladesh Government. Composed of numerous affiliated colleges.

Academic Year: July to June

Main Language(s) of Instruction: English, Bengali

Degrees and Diplomas: *Bachelor's Degree (Pass)*; *Bachelor's Degree (Hons)*; *Master's Degree*

Student Services: Academic Counselling, Social Counselling

Last Updated: 16/07/14

PABNA UNIVERSITY OF SCIENCE AND TECHNOLOGY

Rajapur, Pabna
Tel: +880(731) 66742
EMail: pabna@quantummethod.org.bd
Website: http://www.pust.ac.bd

Vice-Chancellor: Al-Nakib Chowdhury
EMail: nakib@chem.buet.ac.bd

Faculty

Business Studies (Business Administration); **Engineering and Technology** (Architecture; Civil Engineering; Computer Engineering; Computer Science; Electrical and Electronic Engineering; Information Technology; Telecommunications Engineering); **Humanities and Social Science** (Economics; Native Language); **Life and Earth Science** (Environmental Engineering; Geography; Town Planning); **Science** (Mathematics; Pharmacy; Physics)

History: Founded 2008.

Degrees and Diplomas: *Bachelor of Science*; *Bachelor's Degree (Hons)*; *Master's Degree*; *Master of Philosophy*; *Ph. D.*: **Engineering.**

Student Services: Library, Residential Facilities

Last Updated: 17/07/14

PATUAKHALI SCIENCE AND TECHNOLOGY UNIVERSITY (PSTU)

Dumki, Patuakali 8602
Tel: +880(442) 756011
Fax: +880(442) 756009
EMail: vc@pstu.ac.bd
Website: http://pstu.ac.bd

Vice-Chancellor: Md. Shams-Ud-Din

Faculty

Agriculture (Agriculture; Horticulture; Meat and Poultry; Plant Pathology; Soil Science); **Animal Science and Veterinary Medicine** (Biochemistry; Dairy; Meat and Poultry; Medicine; Microbiology; Nutrition; Pathology; Pharmacy; Physiology; Surgery; Veterinary Science); **Business Administration** (Business Administration; Management); **Computer Science and Engineering** (Computer Engineering; Computer Science); **Disaster Management** (Management); **Fishery** (Fishery); **Nutrition and Food Science** (Food Science; Nutrition)

History: Founded 2002 in the campus of former Patuakhali Agricultural College.

Degrees and Diplomas: *Bachelor's Degree (Pass)*; *Bachelor of Science*; *Bachelor's Degree (Hons)*; *Master's Degree*; *Ph. D.*: **Agriculture; Food Science; Horticulture.**

Student Services: Library

Last Updated: 17/07/14

RAJSHAHI UNIVERSITY

Motihar, Rajshahi 6205
Tel: +880(721) 750-041
Fax: +880(721) 750-064
EMail: registrar@ru.ac.bd
Website: http://www.ru.ac.bd

Vice-Chancellor: M. Abdus Sobhan
Tel: +880(721) 750-783 +880(721) 750-320

Registrar: M.A. Salam Tel: +880(721) 750-244

International Relations: Md. Mahbubar Rahman
Tel: +880(721) 750-025

Faculty

Agriculture (Agronomy; Animal Husbandry; Biotechnology; Crop Production; Fishery; Genetics; Veterinary Science); **Arts** (Arabic; Arts and Humanities; Cultural Studies; English; History; Indic Languages; Islamic Studies; Modern Languages; Philosophy); **Business Studies** (Accountancy; Banking; Finance; Management; Marketing); **Law** (Law); **Life and Earth Sciences** (Botany; Earth Sciences; Geography; Geology; Mining Engineering; Psychology; Zoology); **Medicine**; **Science** (Applied Chemistry; Applied Mathematics; Applied Physics; Biochemistry; Chemistry; Computer Engineering; Computer Science; Demography and Population; Electronic Engineering; Information Technology; Materials Engineering; Mathematics; Molecular Biology; Pharmacy; Physics; Statistics); **Social Sciences** (Economics; Information Sciences; Library Science; Mass Communication; Political Sciences; Public Administration; Social Sciences; Social Work; Sociology)

Institute

Bangladesh Studies; **Biological Sciences** (Biological and Life Sciences)

History: Founded 1953.

Academic Year: July to June

Admission Requirements: Secondary school certificate (SSC) and/or higher secondary certificate (HSC) or foreign equivalent. The University has its own admission test

Main Language(s) of Instruction: English, Bengali

Degrees and Diplomas: *Bachelor's Degree (Hons)*; *Master's Degree*; *Master of Philosophy*; *Ph. D.*

Publications: Rajshahi University Studies

Publishing House: Rajshahi University Press

Last Updated: 09/03/11

RAJSHAHI UNIVERSITY OF ENGINEERING AND TECHNOLOGY (RUET)

Dhaka-Natore Road, Kazla, Rajshahi 6204
Tel: +880 721- 750742
EMail: registrar@ru.ac.bd
Website: http://www.ruet.ac.bd

Vice-Chancellor: Mohd. Rafiqul Alam Beg

Faculty

Civil Engineering (Architecture; Chemistry; Civil Engineering; Mathematics; Physics; Regional Planning; Town Planning); **Electrical and Computer Engineering** (Computer Engineering; Computer Science; Electrical and Electronic Engineering; Telecommunications Engineering); **Mechanical Engineering** (Arts and Humanities; Ceramics and Glass Technology; Industrial Engineering; Mechanical Engineering; Production Engineering)

History: Founded 2003.

Degrees and Diplomas: *Bachelor's Degree (Pass)*; *Bachelor of Science*; *Master's Degree*; *Ph. D.*: **Chemistry; Engineering; Mathematics; Physics.**

Student Services: Library

Last Updated: 17/07/14

SHAHJALAL UNIVERSITY OF SCIENCE AND TECHNOLOGY

Kumargaon, Sylhet 3114
Tel: +880(821) 714-479
Fax: +880(821) 715-257
EMail: registrar@sust.edu
Website: http://www.sust.edu

Vice-Chancellor: Md. Aminul Haque Bhuyan EMail: vc@sust.edu

Registrar: Mohd Ishfaqul Hussain

School

Agriculture and Mineral Sciences (Environmental Studies; Forestry); **Applied Sciences and Technology** (Architecture; Chemical Engineering; Civil Engineering; Computer Science; Electronic Engineering; Environmental Engineering; Petroleum and Gas Engineering; Polymer and Plastics Technology; Technology); **Life Sciences** (Biological and Life Sciences; Biotechnology; Genetics; Molecular Biology); **Management and Business Administration** (Business Administration; Management); **Medical Sciences** (Medicine); **Physical Sciences** (Chemistry; Geography; Mathematics; Physics; Statistics); **Social Sciences** (Anthropology; Economics; Political Sciences; Social Welfare; Sociology)

History: Founded 1987 by Act of Parliament. Teaching started 1990.

Academic Year: July to June

Admission Requirements: Secondary school certificate (SSC) and higher secondary certificate (HSC); both second division or Ordinary ('O') level in 5 subjects and Advanced ('A') level in 3 subjects

Main Language(s) of Instruction: English, Bengali

Degrees and Diplomas: *Bachelor's Degree (Hons)*; *Master's Degree*

Last Updated: 21/07/14

SHER-E-BANGLA AGRICULTURAL UNIVERSITY

Sher-e-Banglanagar, Dhaka 1207
Tel: +880(2) 911-0351
Fax: +880(2) 911-2649
EMail: vcsau@dhaka.net
Website: http://www.sau.edu.bd

Vice-Chancellor: Md. Shadat Ulla

Faculty

Agribusiness Management (Agricultural Economics; Banking; Business Administration; Finance; Marketing; Rural Studies); **Agriculture** (Agricultural Engineering; Agriculture; Agronomy; Animal Husbandry; Entomology; Fishery; Forestry; Harvest Technology; Horticulture; Plant Pathology; Soil Science); **Animal Science and Veterinary Medicine** (Animal Husbandry; Biochemistry; Cattle Breeding; Chemistry; Dairy; Meat and Poultry; Molecular Biology; Pathology; Physiology; Public Health; Veterinary Science)

History: Founded 1938 as Bangladesh Agricultural Institute. Acquired present status and title 2001.

Main Language(s) of Instruction: English

Accrediting Agency: University Grants Commission (UGC)

Degrees and Diplomas: *Bachelor's Degree (Pass)*: **Agricultural Business.** *Bachelor of Science*: **Animal Husbandry; Veterinary Science.** *Bachelor's Degree (Hons)*: **Agriculture.** *Master's Degree*: **Agriculture; Agronomy; Biochemistry; Biotechnology; Botany; Chemistry; Entomology; Forestry; Horticulture; Plant Pathology; Soil Science.** *Ph. D.*: **Agronomy; Botany; Chemistry; Horticulture; Plant Pathology; Soil Science.**

Last Updated: 21/07/14

SYLHET AGRICULTURAL UNIVERSITY

SIU, Shamimabad, Bagbari Sylhet
Tel: +880(821) 761-980
EMail: siu_syl@yahoo.com
Website: http://www.sylhetagrivarsity.edu.bd

Vice-Chancellor: Md. Shahid Ullah Talukder

Faculty

Agricultural Business and Economics (Agricultural Business; Rural Planning); **Agriculture** (Agricultural Equipment; Agronomy; Biotechnology; Botany; Chemistry; Crop Production; Entomology; Environmental Studies; Forestry; Horticulture; Plant Pathology; Soil Science); **Fisheries** (Aquaculture; Fishery); **Veterinary and Animal Science** (Anatomy; Animal Husbandry; Biochemistry; Cattle Breeding; Chemistry; Dairy; Epidemiology; Genetics; Histology; Immunology; Meat and Poultry; Medicine; Microbiology; Parasitology; Pathology; Pharmacology; Physiology; Surgery; Toxicology)

History: Founded 2006.

Degrees and Diplomas: *Bachelor's Degree (Pass)*. Also Doctor of Veterinary Medicine

UNIVERSITY OF BARISAL

4/A Lake Circus, Kalabagan, Dhaka
EMail: info.barisaluniv@gmail.com
Website: http://www.barisaluniv.edu.bd

Vice-Chancellor: Harunor Rashid Khan

Faculty

Arts and Humanities (English; Native Language); **Bio-Sciences and Agriculture** (Botany; Crop Production; Soil Science); **Business Studies** (Accountancy; Banking; Finance; Management; Marketing); **Law** (Law); **Science and Engineering** (Chemistry; Computer Engineering; Mathematics); **Social Sciences** (Economics; Political Sciences; Public Administration; Sociology)

History: Founded 2011.

Degrees and Diplomas: *Bachelor's Degree (Pass)*; *Bachelor's Degree (Hons)*

Last Updated: 23/07/14

UNIVERSITY OF CHITTAGONG (CU)

Hathazari, Chittagong 4331
Tel: +880(31) 716-552 +880(31) 716-558
Fax: +880(31) 726-311 +880(31) 726-314
EMail: vc_cu66@yahoo.com
Website: http://www.cu.ac.bd

Vice-Chancellor: Md. Anwarul Azim Arif

Registrar: Mohammed Shafiul Alam

Faculty

Arts and Humanities (Arabic; Arts and Humanities; Education; English; Fine Arts; History; Islamic Studies; Journalism; Oriental Languages; Persian; Philosophy; Theatre); **Biological Science** (Biochemistry; Biology; Biotechnology; Geography; Molecular Biology; Pharmacy; Psychology; Soil Science; Zoology); **Business Administration** (Accountancy; Business and Commerce; Finance; Management; Marketing); **Engineering** (Applied Physics; Computer Engineering; Computer Science; Electronic Engineering); **Law** (Law); **Science** (Biochemistry; Botany; Chemistry; Computer Science; Electronic Engineering; Geography; Mathematics; Microbiology; Natural Sciences; Physics; Soil Science; Statistics; Zoology); **Social Sciences** (Anthropology; Economics; Political Sciences; Public Administration; Social Sciences; Sociology)

Institute

Forestry and Environmental Science (Environmental Studies; Forestry)

Research Centre

Mathematical and Physical Science

History: Founded 1964. Acquired present status 1966. A State Institution.

Academic Year: July to June

Admission Requirements: Secondary school certificate (SSC) and higher secondary certificate (HSC) or foreign equivalent and admission test

Fees: (Taka): 1,412-1,558

Main Language(s) of Instruction: English (Examination: Bengali or English)

Degrees and Diplomas: *Bachelor's Degree (Hons)*; *Master's Degree*. Also Postgraduate Diploma

Student Services: Academic Counselling, Canteen, Careers Guidance, Facilities for disabled people, Health Services, Language Laboratory, Library, Sports Facilities

Publications: Bangla Sahitya Samity (Department of Bengali); Eco (Department of Economics); Hisab Bijyan (Department of Accountancy); Itihas Patrica (Journal in Bengali, Department of History); Managire (Department of Management)

Last Updated: 23/07/14

UNIVERSITY OF DHAKA

Ramna, Dhaka 1000
Tel: +880(2) 966-1900
Fax: +880(2) 861-5583
EMail: registrar@du.ac.bd
Website: http://www.univdhaka.edu

Vice-Chancellor: A. M. S. Arefin Siddique (2009-)
Tel: +800(2) 861-8383

Faculty

Arts (Arabic; Arts and Humanities; Asian Religious Studies; Comparative Religion; English; History; Indic Languages; Information Sciences; Islamic Studies; Journalism; Library Science; Linguistics; Mass Communication; Music; Persian; Philosophy; Sanskrit; Theatre; Urdu); **Biological Sciences** (Aquaculture; Biochemistry; Biological and Life Sciences; Biotechnology; Botany; Clinical Psychology; Educational and Student Counselling; Educational Psychology; Fishery; Molecular Biology; Psychology; Soil Science; Water Science; Zoology); **Business Studies** (Accountancy; Banking; Business and Commerce; Finance; Hotel and Restaurant; Insurance; Management; Marketing; Tourism); **Earth and Environmental Sciences** (Earth Sciences; Environmental Studies; Geography; Geology; Marine Science and Oceanography); **Education** (Education); **Engineering and Technology** (Applied Chemistry; Applied Physics; Computer Engineering; Computer Science; Electronic Engineering; Nuclear Engineering); **Fine Arts** (Art History; Ceramic Art; Fine Arts; Graphic Design; Handicrafts; Painting and Drawing; Printing and Printmaking; Sculpture); **Law** (Law); **Medicine** (Medical Technology; Medicine; Nursing; Occupational Therapy; Physical Therapy; Public Health; Speech Therapy and Audiology; Surgery); **Pharmacy** (Pharmacy); **Science** (Applied Chemistry; Applied Physics; Chemistry; Electronic Engineering; Geography; Geology; Mathematics; Natural Sciences; Physics; Statistics); **Social Sciences** (Anthropology; Cinema and Television; Criminal Law; Demography and Population; Economics; Film; International Relations; Journalism; Mass Communication; Peace and Disarmament; Political Sciences; Public Administration; Social Sciences; Sociology; Women's Studies)

Institute

Business Administration (Business Administration); **Education and Research** (Education; Educational Research); **Energy** (Energy Engineering); **Health Economics** (Health Administration); **Information Technology** (Information Technology); **Leather Engineering and Technology** (Leather Techniques); **Modern Languages** (Arabic; Chinese; French; German; Indic Languages; Korean; Modern Languages; Persian; Russian; Spanish; Turkish); **Nutrition and Food Science** (Food Science; Nutrition); **Social Welfare and Research** (Social Welfare; Welfare and Protective Services); **Statistical Research and Training** (Statistics)

Further Information: Also Research Centres

History: Founded 1921 by Act of Parliament. A State Institution.

Academic Year: July to June (July-December; January-June)

Admission Requirements: Secondary school certificate (SSC) and higher secondary certificate (HSC) or foreign equivalent and admission test

Fees: (Taka): Undergraduate c. 3,365 per session (Arts, Business Studies, Law, Social Sciences); c. 3,450 per session (Biological Sciences, Pharmacy, Science); Postgraduate (MPhil), c. 3,230 per session (Arts, Business Studies, Law, Social Sciences), c. 4580 (Biological Sciences, Pharmacy, Science; c. 3,000-4,400. (US Dollars): Foreign students, 1,200 per annum (SAARC Countries, 500)

Main Language(s) of Instruction: Bengali, English

Degrees and Diplomas: *Bachelor's Degree (Pass)*; *Bachelor's Degree (Hons)*; *Master's Degree*; *Master of Philosophy*: **Biological and Life Sciences; Business and Commerce; Education; Fine Arts; Law; Pharmacy; Social Sciences.** *Ph. D.*: **Biological and**

Life Sciences; Business and Commerce; Education; Fine Arts; Law; Pharmacy; Social Sciences.

Student Services: Library

Publications: Bangladesh Journal of Nutrition; Dakha University Journal of Psychology; Dhaka Bishwabidyala Patrika; Dhaka University Studies (Part A); Dhaka University Studies (Part B); Dhaka University Studies (Part C); Dhaka University Studies (Part D); Dhaka University Studies (Part E); Dhaka University Studies (Part F); IML Patrika; Journal of Arabic; Journal of Management; Journal of Statistical Research

Publishing House: Dhaka University Grantha Sangstha

Last Updated: 24/07/14

PRIVATE INSTITUTIONS

AHSANULLAH UNIVERSITY OF SCIENCE AND TECHNOLOGY (AUST)

141-142 Love Road, Tejgaon Industrial Area, Dhaka 1208
Tel: +880(2) 887-0422
Fax: +880(2) 887-0417-18
EMail: regr@aust.edu; info@aust.edu
Website: http://www.aust.edu

Vice-Chancellor: A.M.M. Safiullah (2011-)
Tel: +880(2) 887-0414 EMail: vc@aust.edu

Registrar: Muhammad Abdul Gafur
Tel: +880(2) 887-0416 EMail: regr@aust.edu

Faculty

Architecture and Planning (Architecture and Planning); **Business and Social Sciences** (Business Administration); **Education** (Education); **Engineering** (Civil Engineering; Computer Engineering; Computer Science; Electrical and Electronic Engineering; Engineering; Industrial Engineering; Mathematics; Textile Technology)

Institute

Technical and Vocational Education and Training (Architecture; Chemical Engineering; Civil Engineering; Computer Engineering; Electrical Engineering; Electronic Engineering)

History: Founded 1995 under the Private University Act of 1992. Sponsored by Dhaka Ahsania Mission, the largest Bangladeshi Non-Governmental Organization involved in extensive programmes of Education, Health and Socio-Economic sectors in the country. Also known as Ahsanullah Biggyan O Projucti Bishwabiddalaya.

Academic Year: April to March

Admission Requirements: Higher secondary certificate (HSC), or 'A' level or equivalent. Only students with high performance in HSC/'A' level or equivalent can apply for admission

Main Language(s) of Instruction: English

Degrees and Diplomas: *Diploma*; *Bachelor's Degree (Pass)*: **Architecture; Business Administration; Engineering.** *Master's Degree*: **Business Administration; Education; Mathematics.**

Student Services: Health Services, Library, Sports Facilities

Publications: AUST Journal of Science and Technology

Student Numbers *2012-2013*: Total 6,500

Last Updated: 07/07/14

AMERICAN INTERNATIONAL UNIVERSITY-BANGLADESH (AIUB)

83/B, Rd 4, Banani, Kemal Ataturk, Dhaka 1213
Tel: +880(2) 881-1749 +880(2) 988-5907
Fax: +880(2) 881-3233
EMail: info@aiub.edu
Website: http://www.aiub.edu

Vice-Chancellor: Carmen Z. Lamagna (1999-)
Tel: +880(2) 989-0415 EMail: clamagna@aiub.edu

Vice President, Treasury, HR and Administration: Hasanul Hasan EMail: habedin@aiub.edu

International Relations: Ishtiaque Abedin, Vice-President, Director, International Affairs
Tel: +880(2) 988-5907 EMail: iabedin@aiub.edu

Faculty

Arts and Social Sciences (Economics; English; Mass Communication; Media Studies; Public Health); **Business Administration** (Accountancy; Agricultural Business; Business Computing; Economics; Finance; Hotel Management; Human Resources; International Business; Management; Marketing; Tourism); **Engineering** (Computer Engineering; Electrical and Electronic Engineering; Engineering; Telecommunications Engineering)

Department

Architecture (Architecture)

History: Founded 1994.

Academic Year: September to August

Admission Requirements: Secondary school certificate (SSC) and higher secondary certificate (HSC), or 5 'O' Levels and 2 'A' levels, or any US high school certificate or equivalent and admission test

Fees: 110,000 per annum (Taka)

Main Language(s) of Instruction: English

Accrediting Agency: University Grants Commission (UGC)

Degrees and Diplomas: *Bachelor's Degree (Pass)*: **Accountancy; Banking; Business Administration; Commercial Law; Communication Arts; Computer Engineering; Computer Science; Economics; Electrical and Electronic Engineering; Finance; Human Resources; International Economics; Labour and Industrial Relations; Management; Marketing; Statistics; Taxation.** *Master's Degree*: **Accountancy; Agricultural Business; Business Administration; Economics; Finance; Human Resources; Marketing.** Also Executive MBA

Student Services: Academic Counselling, Canteen, Careers Guidance, Cultural Activities, Facilities for disabled people, Foreign Studies Centre, Health Services, Language Laboratory, Social Counselling, Sports Facilities

Publications: AIUB Journal of Business and Economics; AIUB Journal of Science and Technology

Student Numbers *2012-2013*: Total 4,275

Last Updated: 14/03/13

ASA UNIVERSITY

ASA Tower, 23/3, Bir Uttam A.N.M Nuruzzaman Sarak, (Formerly Known as Khilji Road), Shyamoli, Mohammadpur, Dhaka 1207
Tel: +880(2) 812-2555
EMail: info@asaub.edu.bd
Website: http://www.asaub.edu.bd

Vice-Chancellor: Dalem Ch. Barman

Faculty

Arts and Social Sciences (English; Linguistics; Literature; Sociology); **Business** (Business Administration); **Law** (Law); **Science and Engineering** (Pharmacy; Public Health)

History: Founded 2006.

Degrees and Diplomas: *Bachelor's Degree (Pass)*; *Master's Degree*

Student Services: Library

Last Updated: 07/07/14

ASIAN UNIVERSITY FOR WOMEN

20/A M.M. Ali Road, Chittagong 4000
Tel: +880(31) 2854980
Fax: +880(31) 2854988
EMail: info@auw.edu.bd
Website: http://www.auw.edu.bd/

Chief Academic Officer: John Schroeder (2015-)
EMail: john.schroeder@auw.edu.bd

International Relations: Herman Salton, Co-Director, Center for International Programs EMail: herman.salton@auw.edu.bd

International Relations: Sarah Shehabuddin, Co-Director, Center for International Programs EMail: sarah.shehabuddin@auw.edu.bd

History: Created 2008

Academic Year: August - June

Degrees and Diplomas: *Bachelor of Science*: **Biological and Life Sciences; Computer Science; Environmental Studies; Information Technology; Public Health.** *Bachelor's Degree (Hons)*: **Asian Studies; Economics; Philosophy; Political Sciences.**

Academic Staff *2014-2015*	TOTAL
FULL-TIME	22
PART-TIME	14
STAFF WITH DOCTORATE	
FULL-TIME	23
Student Numbers *2014-2015*	
All (Foreign included)	473

Last Updated: 20/08/15

ASIAN UNIVERSITY OF BANGLADESH (AUB)

House 25, Road 5, Sector 7, Uttara Model Town, Dhaka 1230
Tel: +880(2) 891-6116
Fax: +880(2) 891-6521
EMail: info@aub-bd.org
Website: http://www.aub.edu.bd

Vice-Chancellor: Abulhasan M. Sadeq

Registrar: A.K.M. Salahuddin

School

Arts (Arts and Humanities; English; Islamic Studies; Native Language Education; Oriental Languages); **Business** (Accountancy; Business Administration; Finance; Human Resources; International Business; Management Systems; Marketing); **Education and Training** (Education); **Science and Engineering** (Computer Engineering; Computer Science); **Social Sciences** (Anthropology; Economics; Government; Information Management; Library Science; Political Sciences; Social Sciences; Sociology)

Further Information: Also Viz and Dhanmondi campuses

History: Founded 1996.

Admission Requirements: Higher secondary certificate, Advanced ('A') level

Fees: (Taka): 3,600-26,950 per semester

Main Language(s) of Instruction: English

Accrediting Agency: University Grants Commission (UGC); Ministry of Education; Academy for the Promotion of International Culture and Scientific Exchange (APICS), Switzerland

Degrees and Diplomas: *Bachelor's Degree (Pass)*; *Bachelor's Degree (Hons)*: **Asian Studies; Islamic Studies; Literature.** *Master's Degree*: **Accountancy; Asian Studies; Business Administration; Education; Finance; Government; Human Resources; Islamic Studies; Literature; Management Systems; Marketing; Social Sciences.**

Student Services: Academic Counselling, Canteen, Careers Guidance, Cultural Activities, Language Laboratory, Library, Social Counselling, Sports Facilities

Last Updated: 07/07/14

ATISH DIPANKAR UNIVERSITY OF SCIENCE AND TECHNOLOGY

House:-83, Road:- 4, Block:- B, Banani, Dhaka 1212
Tel: +880(2)881-6762
EMail: info@atishdipankaruniversity.edu.bd
Website: http://www.atishdipankaruniversity.edu.bd

Vice-Chancellor: Abul Hossain Sikder (Acting)

Faculty

Agriculture, Biological Science and Biotechnology; **Arts and Social Sciences** (Education; English; Law; Public Health); **Business** (Agricultural Business; Business Administration); **Science and Technology** (Computer Engineering; Computer Science; Electronic Engineering; Pharmacy; Textile Technology)

History: Founded 2004.

Degrees and Diplomas: *Bachelor's Degree (Pass)*; *Master's Degree*

Last Updated: 07/07/14

BANGLADESH ISLAMI UNIVERSITY

Gazaria Tower, 89/12, R. K. Mission Road (Maniknagar Bishwa Road), Dhaka 1203
Tel: +880(2)7552-495
EMail: biudhaka@yahoo.com
Website: http://www.biu.ac.bd

Vice-Chancellor: Anwarullah Chowdhury

Department

Business Studies (Accountancy; Banking; Business Administration; Finance; Management; Marketing); **GED** (Anthropology; Political Sciences; Sociology); **Islamic Studies** (Islamic Studies); **Law** (Law)

History: Founded 2005.

Admission Requirements: At least second division both in SSC & HSC Examination with minimum GPA 2.50 or equivalent or at least 'O' level in 3 subjects & 'A' level in 2 subjects passed.

Degrees and Diplomas: *Bachelor's Degree (Pass)*; *Master's Degree*

Last Updated: 07/07/14

BANGLADESH UNIVERSITY

15/1, Iqbal Road, Mohammadpur, Dhaka
Tel: +880(2) 913-6061
EMail: info@bu.edu.bd
Website: http://bu.edu.bd/

Faculty

Arts, Social Sciences and Law (Economics; Education; English; Law; Public Administration; Sociology); **Business and Economics** (Accountancy; Business Administration; Economics; English; Marketing); **Science, Engineering and Technology** (Architecture; Computer Engineering; Computer Science; Electrical and Electronic Engineering; Mathematics; Pharmacy)

Degrees and Diplomas: *Bachelor's Degree (Pass)*; *Master's Degree*

Last Updated: 07/07/14

BANGLADESH UNIVERSITY OF BUSINESS AND TECHNOLOGY (BUBT)

Dhaka Commerce College Road, Mirpur-2, Dhaka 1216
Tel: +880(2) 8057-581 +880(2) 8057-582
Fax: +880(2) 8057-583
EMail: info@bubt.edu.bd
Website: http://www.bubt.edu.bd/

Vice-Chancellor: Md. Abu Saleh (2007-)

Registrar: Enayet Hossain Mia

Faculty

Arts and Humanities (English); **Business** (Accountancy; Banking; Business Administration; Finance; Management; Marketing); **Engineering and Applied Sciences** (Computer Engineering; Computer Science; Electrical and Electronic Engineering; Textile Technology); **Law** (Law); **Mathematical and Physical Science** (Mathematics); **Social Sciences** (Economics)

History: Founded 2003 by Dhaka Commerce College

Academic Year: Autumn: October-January; Summer: June-September; Spring: February-May

Admission Requirements: Secondary School Certificate (or equivalent) for undergraduate programmes; Relevant undergraduate degree for postgraduate programmes.

Main Language(s) of Instruction: English

Degrees and Diplomas: *Bachelor's Degree (Pass)*; *Bachelor of Science*; *Bachelor's Degree (Hons)*; *Master's Degree*

Student Services: Academic Counselling, Canteen, Careers Guidance, Cultural Activities, Facilities for disabled people, Foreign Studies Centre, Health Services, Language Laboratory, Library, Social Counselling, Sports Facilities

Last Updated: 08/07/14

BGC TRUST UNIVERSITY BANGLADESH

BGC Viddyanagar, Chandanaish, Chittagong
Tel: +880(31) 636-548 +880(31) 627-040
EMail: info@bgctub-edu.com
Website: http://www.bgctub-edu.com

Vice-Chancellor: Saroj Kanti Singh Hazari

Registrar: Farid Ahmed Tel: +1713 120863 (mob.)

Faculty

Business Administration (Business Administration); **Computer Science and Engineering** (Computer Engineering; Computer Science; Engineering); **English** (English); **Law** (Law); **Pharmacy** (Pharmacy)

History: Founded 2001.

Academic Year: Higher secondary certificate

Main Language(s) of Instruction: English

Accrediting Agency: UGC and Ministry of Education, Bangladesh

Degrees and Diplomas: *Bachelor's Degree (Pass)*; *Bachelor's Degree (Hons)*; *Master's Degree*

Student Services: Academic Counselling, Canteen, Cultural Activities, Health Services, Language Laboratory, Social Counselling, Sports Facilities

Last Updated: 08/07/14

BRAC UNIVERSITY (BU)

66 Mohakhali, Dhaka 1212
Tel: +880(2) 988-1265
Fax: +880(2) 881-0383
EMail: info@bracuniversity.ac.bd
Website: http://www.bracuniversity.ac.bd

Vice-Chancellor: Ainun Nishat EMail: vc@bracuniversity.ac.bd

Registrar: Muhammad Sahool Afzal
EMail: registrar@bracuniversity.ac.bd

School

Business *(BRAC)* (Banking; Business Administration; Business and Commerce); **Engineering and Computer Science** (Computer Engineering; Computer Science; Electrical and Electronic Engineering); **Law** (Law); **Public Health** *(James P. Grant)* (Public Health)

Department

Architecture (Architecture); **Economics and Social Sciences** (Anthropology; Development Studies; Economics; Gender Studies; Social Sciences); **English and Humanities** (Arts and Humanities; English; Linguistics; Literature; Modern Languages); **Mathematics and Natural Sciences** (Applied Physics; Biotechnology; Mathematics; Natural Sciences; Physics); **Pharmacy** (Pharmacy)

Institute

Development (Development Studies); **Educational Development** (Education); **Global Health** *(James P. Grant)* (Midwifery; Public Health); **Governance Studies** (Government); **Languages** (Arabic; Chinese; English; French; Korean; Native Language; Spanish)

History: Founded 2001.

Academic Year: September to August

Admission Requirements: Higher Secondary Certificate: 'A' Level and Admission test

Fees: (Taka): 3,000-4,000 per credit

Main Language(s) of Instruction: English

Accrediting Agency: University Grants Commission (UGC), Ministry of Education

Degrees and Diplomas: *Bachelor's Degree (Pass)*; *Bachelor of Science*; *Bachelor's Degree (Hons)*; *Master's Degree*. Also six months' certificate courses and one-year post-graduate diplomas.

Student Services: Academic Counselling, Canteen, Careers Guidance, Cultural Activities, Facilities for disabled people, Health Services, Language Laboratory, Library, Residential Facilities, Social Counselling, Sports Facilities

Publications: BRAC University Journal

Last Updated: 08/07/14

BRITANNIA UNIVERSITY

Paduar Bazar, Bishwa Road, Comilla
EMail: info@britannia.ac
Website: http://www.britannia.ac

School

Business Administration (Business Administration); **Law** (Law)

Department

Computer Science and Engineering (Computer Engineering; Computer Science); **Economics** (Economics); **English** (English)

History: Founded 2012.

Degrees and Diplomas: *Bachelor's Degree (Pass)*; *Bachelor's Degree (Hons)*; *Master's Degree*

Last Updated: 09/07/14

CENTRAL WOMEN'S UNIVERSITY

1 RK Mission Road, Ittefaq bhaban, Dhaka 1203
Tel: +880(2) 959-1551
EMail: info@cwu-bd.net
Website: http://cwu-bd.net

Vice-Chancellor: Perween Hasan Tel: +880(2) 955-9452

Registrar: Firdaus Ali

Faculty

Arts and Humanities (English; Gender Studies; Geography (Human); Journalism; Law; Media Studies; Political Sciences; Sociology); **Science and Information** (Computer Engineering; Computer Science)

School

Business (Business Administration)

History: Founded 1993.

Admission Requirements: Secondary school certificate (SSC) and Higher secondary school certificate (HSC)

Fees: (US Dollars): 500

Main Language(s) of Instruction: English

Degrees and Diplomas: *Bachelor's Degree (Hons)*; *Master's Degree*

Student Services: Academic Counselling, Cultural Activities, Language Laboratory, Library

Last Updated: 08/07/14

CHITTAGONG INDEPENDENT UNIVERSITY

Minhaj Complex, 12,Jamal Khan Road, Chittagong
Tel: +880(3) 162-2946
EMail: info@ciu.edu.bd
Website: http://www.ciu.edu.bd

Vice-Chancellor: Irshad Kamal

School

Business (Accountancy; Finance; Human Resources; Management; Marketing); **Engineering and Computer Science** (Computer Engineering; Computer Science; Electrical and Electronic Engineering; Telecommunications Engineering); **Liberal Arts and Social Sciences** (English; Literature)

History: Founded in 1999 as the Chittagong Campus of Independent University, Bangladesh (IUB). Due to legislative changes in the beginning of 2010, the Chittagong Campus of IUB applied to function as an autonomous University. Acquired present status and title 2013.

Admission Requirements: HSC and SSC pass certificates with minimum CGPA of 3.00 in both; O'Level in minimum 5 subjects with a GPA 2.50 and A'Level in 2 subjects with a minimum GPA 2.00; International Baccalaureate; High School Diploma; GED with SSC/O-Levels at 410 each Subjects; 12 years equivalent degree

Degrees and Diplomas: *Bachelor's Degree (Pass)*; *Master's Degree*

Student Services: Library

Last Updated: 28/08/14

CITY UNIVERSITY (CU)

40, Kemal Ataturk Avenue, Banani, Dhaka 1213
Tel: +880(2) 989-3983
Fax: +880(2) 956-4020
EMail: frs1101@yahoo.com
Website: http://www.cityuniversity.edu.bd

Vice-Chancellor: N.R.M. Borhan Uddin

Registrar: R.A.M.Obaidul Muktadir Chowdhury

Faculty

Business Administration (Business Administration); **Computer Science and Engineering** (Computer Engineering; Computer Science); **English** (Arts and Humanities; English); **Law** (Law); **Social Sciences** (Social Sciences); **Textile Engineering** (Textile Technology)

History: Founded 2002.

Academic Year: September to August

Admission Requirements: Higher secondary school certificate (HSC)/ A-Level/ GED and admission test

Fees: (Taka): Undergraduate, 2,000 per credit; Graduate Programmes, 2,500

Main Language(s) of Instruction: English

Accrediting Agency: University Grants Commission; Ministry of Education

Degrees and Diplomas: *Bachelor's Degree (Pass)*: **Accountancy; Business Administration; Computer Science; Economics; Engineering; English; Finance; Management; Marketing.** *Master's Degree*: **Accountancy; Banking; Business Administration; Economic and Finance Policy; Finance; Management; Marketing.**

Student Services: Academic Counselling, Canteen, Careers Guidance, Cultural Activities, Foreign Studies Centre, Language Laboratory, Social Counselling, Sports Facilities

Last Updated: 09/03/11

COX'S BAZAR INTERNATIONAL UNIVERSITY

Dynamic Cox Kingdom, Kolatoli Circle, Cox's Bazar 4700
Tel: +880(3) 415-2510
Fax: +880(3) 415-2511
EMail: cbiu.bd@gmail.com
Website: http://www.cbiu.ac.bd

Vice-Chancellor: Quazi Mustain Billah

Department

Business Administration (Business Administration); **Computer Science and Engineering** (Computer Engineering; Computer Science); **Electrical and Electronic Engineering** (Electrical and Electronic Engineering); **English** (English); **Hospitality & Tourism Management** (Hotel and Restaurant; Tourism); **Law** (Law)

History: Founded 2013.

Admission Requirements: Minimum GPA 2.50 in both SSC & HSC/ equivalent exams or, GPA 6.00 in SSC & HSC/ equivalent exams. combined, but not less than GPA 2.00 in SSC or HSC/ equivalent exam.

Degrees and Diplomas: *Bachelor's Degree (Pass)*; *Master's Degree*

Last Updated: 10/07/14

DAFFODIL INTERNATIONAL UNIVERSITY (DIU)

102, Shukrabad, Mirpur Road, Dhaka 1207
Tel: +880(2) 913-8234
Fax: +880(2) 913-1947
EMail: info@daffodilvarsity.edu.bd; international@daffodilvarsity.edu.bd
Website: http://www.daffodilvarsity.edu.bd

Vice-Chancellor: M. Lutfar Rahman
EMail: vcoffice@daffodilvarsity.edu.bd

Faculty

Allied Health (Biotechnology; Dietetics; Food Science; Food Technology; Genetics; Medical Technology; Nutrition; Pharmacy; Public Health); **Business and Economics** (Accountancy; Business Administration; Business and Commerce; Economics; Finance; Human Resources; Management; Marketing; Real Estate); **Humanities and Social Sciences** (English; Journalism; Law; Mass Communication); **Science and Information Technology** (Computer Engineering; Computer Science; Electronic Engineering; Environmental Studies; Food Technology; Information Management; Information Technology; Software Engineering; Telecommunications Engineering; Textile Technology)

Further Information: Also Uttara Campus

History: Founded 2002.

Academic Year: Jan-Apr; May-Aug; Sep-Dec

Admission Requirements: Higher Secondary Certificate

Main Language(s) of Instruction: English

Degrees and Diplomas: *Bachelor's Degree (Pass)*: **Business Administration; Real Estate.** *Bachelor of Science*: **Computer Engineering; Computer Science; Electrical and Electronic Engineering; Electronic Engineering; Environmental Studies; Fine Arts; Food Technology; Multimedia; Nutrition; Safety Engineering; Software Engineering; Technology; Telecommunications Engineering.** *Bachelor's Degree (Hons)*: **Business and Commerce; English; Journalism; Law; Mass Communication; Pharmacy.** *Master's Degree*: **Business Administration; Computer Science; Electronic Engineering; English; Journalism; Law; Mass Communication; Telecommunications Engineering.** Also Postgraduate Diploma

Student Services: Academic Counselling, Canteen, Careers Guidance, Cultural Activities, Facilities for disabled people, Foreign Studies Centre, Health Services, Language Laboratory, Library, Social Counselling, Sports Facilities

Publications: Daffodil International University Journal of Business and Economics; Daffodil International University Journal of Science and Technology

Academic Staff *2011-2012*	MEN	WOMEN	TOTAL
FULL-TIME	136	61	**197**
PART-TIME	59	4	**63**
STAFF WITH DOCTORATE			
FULL-TIME	26	1	**27**
Student Numbers *2011-2012*			
All (Foreign included)	6,195	1,487	**7,682**
FOREIGN ONLY	6	8	**14**

Last Updated: 09/07/14

DARUL IHSAN UNIVERSITY, DHAKA (DIU)

House 21, Road 9/A, Dhanmondi R/A, Dhaka
Tel: +880(2) 912-5190
Fax: +880(2) 811-4746
EMail: info@diu.dc.bd
Website: http://www.diu.ac.bd

Vice-Chancellor: Anwar Islam EMail: vc@diu.edu

Faculty

Human Sciences (Education; English; Law; Literature); **Natural Sciences** (Computer Engineering; Computer Science; Information Technology; Telecommunications Engineering); **Religious Sciences** (Arabic; Islamic Studies; Islamic Theology; Religious Studies)

Institute

Business Studies (Business Administration)

History: Founded 1989.

Academic Year: January to December (January-June; July-December)

Admission Requirements: Higher secondary certificate (HSC) or equivalent and entrance examination

Main Language(s) of Instruction: Bengali, English, Arabic.

Accrediting Agency: University Grants Commission (UGC); Ministry of Education

Degrees and Diplomas: *Bachelor's Degree (Pass)*: **Business Administration; Communication Arts; Computer Science; Information Technology.** *Bachelor's Degree (Hons)*: **English; Islamic Studies.** *Master's Degree*: **Business Administration; English; Islamic Studies.**

Student Services: Academic Counselling, Canteen, Careers Guidance, Cultural Activities, Health Services, Language Laboratory, Social Counselling, Sports Facilities

Publications: Journal of the Institute of Business Studies

Last Updated: 09/07/14

DHAKA INTERNATIONAL UNIVERSITY (DIU)

House # 4, Road # 1, Block - F, Banani, Dhaka 1213
Tel: +880(2) 985-8734
Fax: +880(2) 987-1556
EMail: info@diu.net.bd
Website: http://www.diu.net.bd

Vice-Chancellor: K. M. Mohsin

Faculty

Arts and Social Sciences (Arts and Humanities; Education; English; Political Sciences; Sociology); **Business Studies** (Business Administration; Business and Commerce); **Law** (Law); **Pharmacy** (Pharmacy); **Science and Engineering** (Computer Engineering; Computer Science; Electrical and Electronic Engineering; Telecommunications Engineering)

History: Founded 1995. Acquired present status 2000.

Academic Year: July to June

Admission Requirements: Secondary school certificate

Main Language(s) of Instruction: Bengali and English

Degrees and Diplomas: *Bachelor's Degree (Pass)*; *Bachelor's Degree (Hons)*: **Business Administration; Computer Science; English; Law; Sociology.** *Master's Degree*: **Business Administration; English; Law; Sociology.**

Student Services: Academic Counselling, Canteen, Careers Guidance, Cultural Activities, Facilities for disabled people, Health Services, Language Laboratory, Library, Sports Facilities

Last Updated: 09/07/14

EAST DELTA UNIVERSITY

1267/A Goshaildanga, Agrabad, Chittagong
Tel: +880(31) 251-4441
EMail: enquiry@eastdelta.edu.bd
Website: http://www.eastdelta.edu.bd

Vice-Chancellor: Muhammad Sekandar Khan

School

Business Administration (Business Administration); **Liberal Arts and Social Sciences** (Economics; English); **Science, Engineering and Technology** (Computer Engineering; Computer Science; Electrical and Electronic Engineering; Telecommunications Engineering)

History: Founded 2006.

Academic Year: Spring semester (January – April) Summer semester (May – August) Fall semester (September – December)

Admission Requirements: Minimum GPA 2.5 in both SSC and HSC separately. Minimum GPA 2.0 in either SSC or HSC. But the combined GPA is not less than 6.0. 5 subjects in 'O' Level and 2 Subjects in 'A' Level.

Main Language(s) of Instruction: English

Degrees and Diplomas: *Bachelor's Degree (Pass)*; *Bachelor's Degree (Hons)*; *Master's Degree*

Student Services: Library

Last Updated: 09/07/14

EAST WEST UNIVERSITY (EWU)

A/2, Jahurul Islam Avenue, Jahurul Islam City, Aftabnagar, Dhaka 1212
Tel: +880(2) 985-8261
EMail: info@ewubd.edu
Website: http://www.ewubd.edu

Vice-Chancellor: Ahmed Shafee EMail: vc@ewubd.edu

Faculty

Business and Economics (Business Administration; Economics); **Liberal Arts and Social Sciences** (English; Social Sciences; Sociology); **Science and Engineering** (Biotechnology; Computer Engineering; Computer Science; Electrical and Electronic Engineering; Pharmacy; Statistics; Telecommunications Engineering)

History: Founded 1996.

Academic Year: January to December (January-May; June-July; August-December)

Admission Requirements: Second division in secondary school certificate (SSC) and Higher secondary school certificate (HSC). GCE with passes in 5 subjects at ordinary ('O') level

Main Language(s) of Instruction: English

Accrediting Agency: University Grants Commission (UGC)

Degrees and Diplomas: *Bachelor's Degree (Pass)*; *Master's Degree*

Student Services: Academic Counselling, Canteen, Careers Guidance, Cultural Activities, Health Services, Language Laboratory, Library, Sports Facilities

Publications: East West Journal of Humanities

Last Updated: 09/07/14

EASTERN UNIVERSITY

House 26, Road 5, Dhanmondi, Dhaka 1205
Tel: +880(2) 967-6031
Fax: +880(2) 967-5981
EMail: info@easternuni.edu.bd
Website: http://www.easternuni.edu.bd/

Vice-Chancellor: Abdur Rab EMail: vc@easternuni.edu.bd

Faculty

Arts (English); **Business Administration** (Business Administration); **Engineering and Technology** (Computer Engineering; Computer Science; Electrical and Electronic Engineering; Information Technology); **Law** (Law)

History: Founded 2003.

Degrees and Diplomas: *Bachelor's Degree (Pass)*; *Bachelor's Degree (Hons)*; *Master's Degree*

Last Updated: 10/07/14

EUROPEAN UNIVERSITY OF BANGLADESH

Rupayan Shelford, Plot, 23/6, Block- B, Mirpur Road, Shyamoli, Dhaka 1207
Tel: +880(2) 911-0847
Website: http://www.eub.edu.bd

Vice-Chancellor: Abdul Manaan

Faculty

Arts and Social Sciences (English; Law); **Business and Industrial Management** (Business Administration; Hotel and Restaurant; Management; Tourism); **Science and Engineering** (Civil Engineering; Electrical and Electronic Engineering; Textile Technology)

History: Founded 2012.

Degrees and Diplomas: *Bachelor's Degree (Pass)*; *Bachelor's Degree (Hons)*; *Master's Degree*

Student Services: Library

Last Updated: 10/07/14

FAR EAST INTERNATIONAL UNIVERSITY

R.S.R Tower, House # 50, Road # 11, Block - C, Banani, Dhaka 1213
Tel: +880(2) 989-1453
Fax: +880(2) 989-1845
EMail: info@fiu.edu.bd
Website: http://www.fiu.edu.bd/

Vice-Chancellor: M Mozzammel Hoque

Faculty

Engineering (Architecture; Civil Engineering; Computer Engineering; Computer Science; Electrical and Electronic Engineering; Environmental Engineering; Fashion Design; Textile Design; Textile Technology); **Liberal Arts and Social Sciences** (Economics; English; Islamic Studies; Journalism; Law; Mass Communication; Native Language; Social Sciences); **Science** (Chemistry; Mathematics; Pharmacy; Physics; Public Health)

School

Business (Business Administration)

History: Founded 2013.

Admission Requirements: SSC + HSC or equivalent.

Degrees and Diplomas: *Bachelor's Degree (Pass)*; *Bachelor's Degree (Hons)*; *Master's Degree*

Last Updated: 11/07/14

FENI UNIVERSITY

Trunk Road, Feni 3900
EMail: registrar@feniuniversity.edu.bd
Website: http://www.feniuniversity.edu.bd

Vice-Chancellor: Md Fashiul Alam
EMail: vc@feniuniversity.edu.bd

Faculty
Arts, Social Science and Law (Economics; English; Journalism; Law); **Business Administration** (Business Administration); **Science and Engineering** (Computer Engineering; Computer Science; Electrical and Electronic Engineering; Textile Technology)

History: Founded 2010.

Degrees and Diplomas: *Bachelor's Degree (Pass)*; *Bachelor's Degree (Hons)*; *Master's Degree*
Last Updated: 11/07/14

FIRST CAPITAL UNIVERSITY OF BANGLADESH

Shahnaz Mansion, Alamdanga Road (Pouro College Para), Chuadanga 7200
EMail: first_capital_bd@yahoo.com
Website: http://fcubd.net

Vice-Chancellor: Obaidul Islam Joarder

Faculty
Agriculture (Agricultural Economics; Agricultural Equipment; Agronomy; Crop Production; Entomology; Forestry; Horticulture; Plant Pathology; Soil Science; Vegetable Production); **Law** (Law)

Department
Business Administration (Banking; Business Administration; Commercial Law; Human Resources; Management; Marketing); **Computer Science and Engineering** (Computer Engineering; Computer Science; Information Technology); **Electrical and Electronic Engineering** (Electrical and Electronic Engineering); **English** (English; Linguistics; Literature); **Public Health** (Child Care and Development; Community Health; Health Administration; Nutrition; Public Health); **Sociology** (Sociology)

History: Founded 2012.

Admission Requirements: Minimum GPA 2.5 in both SSC & HSC

Degrees and Diplomas: *Bachelor's Degree (Pass)*; *Bachelor's Degree (Hons)*; *Master's Degree*
Student Services: Library
Last Updated: 16/07/14

GONO UNIVERSITY

Gonoshasthaya Kendra Complex Nayarhat, Savar, Dhaka 1344
Tel: 880(2) 770-8004
Fax: 880(2) 770-8336
EMail: admin@gonouniversity.edu.bd
Website: http://www.gonouniversity.edu.bd

Vice-Chancellor: Mesbah Uddin Ahmad
EMail: mesbahuahmad@gmail.com

Registrar: Delower Hossain
EMail: register@gonouniversity.edu.bd; mddelhossain@gmail.com

Faculty
Arts and Social Sciences (Business Administration; English; Law; Literature; Native Language; Political Sciences; Social Work; Sociology); **Health and Medical Sciences** (Medicine; Microbiology; Pharmacy; Physical Therapy); **Physical and Mathematical Sciences** (Applied Mathematics; Biochemistry; Biomedical Engineering; Computer Engineering; Computer Science; Molecular Biology; Physics); **Postgraduate Studies** (Biochemistry; English; Microbiology; Molecular Biology; Pharmacy; Physical Therapy; Political Sciences; Social Work; Sociology)

History: Founded 1998.

Admission Requirements: Higher Secondary Certificate/A level and entrance examination

Main Language(s) of Instruction: Bengali, English

Accrediting Agency: University Grants Commission (UGC)

Degrees and Diplomas: *Bachelor's Degree (Pass)*; *Bachelor's Degree (Hons)*; *Master's Degree*
Last Updated: 10/07/14

GREEN UNIVERSITY OF BANGLADESH

Malek Tower, 31, Tejkunipara, Farm Gate, Dhaka 1215
Tel: +880(2) 913-9614
Fax: +880(2) 812-4611
EMail: infogub@yahoo.com
Website: http://green.edu.bd

Vice-Chancellor: Md. Golam Samdani Fakir
EMail: samdani@green.edu.bd

Faculty
Arts and Social Sciences (Anthropology; English; Media Studies; Sociology); **Law** (Law); **Science and Engineering** (Computer Engineering; Computer Science; Electrical and Electronic Engineering; Textile Technology)

Department
Business Administration (Business Administration)

Degrees and Diplomas: *Bachelor's Degree (Pass)*; *Bachelor's Degree (Hons)*; *Master's Degree*

Student Services: Library
Last Updated: 10/07/14

INDEPENDENT UNIVERSITY, BANGLADESH (IUB)

Plot 16, Block B, Aftabuddin Ahmed Road Bashundhara R/A, Dhaka 1219
Tel: +880(2) 986-2386-90 +880(2) 988-4498
Fax: +880(2) 882-3959 +880(2) 885-0226
EMail: info@iub.edu.bd
Website: http://www.iub.edu.bd

Vice-Chancellor: M. Omar Rahman (2010-)
EMail: orahman@iub.edu.bd

Registrar: Tanvir A. Khan

School
Business (Accountancy; Banking; Business Administration; Economics; Finance; Human Resources; Management; Marketing); **Engineering and Computer Science** (Computer Engineering; Computer Networks; Computer Science; Electrical and Electronic Engineering; Telecommunications Engineering); **Environmental Science and Management** (Ecology; Environmental Studies; Soil Science; Water Science); **Liberal Arts and Science** (Arts and Humanities; Communication Studies; Computer Science; Cultural Studies; Heritage Preservation; Media Studies; Modern Languages; Social Sciences); **Life Sciences** (Biochemistry; Biology; Microbiology); **Public Health** (Epidemiology; Public Health)

History: Founded 1993.

Academic Year: August to July

Admission Requirements: Higher Secondary Education Certificate or equivalent

Fees: (Taka): Admission: 15,000 per annum; 3,300 per credit per semester

Main Language(s) of Instruction: English

Accrediting Agency: University Grants Commission (UGC)

Degrees and Diplomas: *Bachelor's Degree (Pass)*: **Accountancy; Economics; Finance; Management; Marketing.** *Bachelor of Science*: **Computer Engineering; Computer Science; Demography and Population; Electrical and Electronic Engineering; Electronic Engineering; Environmental Management; Environmental Studies; Information Sciences; Landscape Architecture; Telecommunications Engineering; Water Management.** *Bachelor's Degree (Hons)*: **Communication Studies; Media Studies.** *Master's Degree*: **Computer Science; Development Studies; Public Health; Social Sciences; Telecommunications Engineering.**

Student Services: Academic Counselling, Canteen, Careers Guidance, Foreign Studies Centre, Sports Facilities
Last Updated: 10/07/14

INTERNATIONAL BUSINESS ADMINISTRATION AND INFORMATION SYSTEM (IBAIS) UNIVERSITY

House – 16, Road – 5, Sector – 4, Uttara, Dhaka 1230
Tel: +880(2) 892-3899
Fax: +880(2) 891-5999
EMail: registrar@ibais.edu.bd
Website: http://www.ibais.edu.bd

Vice-Chancellor: Zakaria Lincoln

Faculty

Arts (Arts and Humanities; English; Hotel Management; Linguistics; Literature; Tourism); **Business and Economics** (Accountancy; Banking; Business Administration; E- Business/Commerce; Finance; Human Resources; Management; Marketing); **Science and Engineering** (Computer Engineering; Computer Science; Electrical and Electronic Engineering)

History: Founded 1997. Acquired present status 2002.

Admission Requirements: Higher Secondary Certificate or equivalent

Fees: (Taka): 15,000

Main Language(s) of Instruction: English

Accrediting Agency: University Grants Commission (UGC)

Degrees and Diplomas: *Bachelor's Degree (Pass)*: **Business Administration; Business and Commerce; Computer Engineering; Computer Science; Economics; Electrical and Electronic Engineering; Electrical Engineering; English; Hotel Management; Pharmacy; Tourism.** *Master's Degree*: **Business Administration; Business and Commerce; Computer Engineering; Computer Science; Economics; Electrical and Electronic Engineering; Electrical Engineering; English; Health Sciences; Hotel Management; Pharmacy; Tourism.**

Student Services: Academic Counselling, Canteen, Careers Guidance, Cultural Activities, Language Laboratory, Social Counselling, Sports Facilities

Publications: IBAISU Quarterly

Last Updated: 10/07/14

INTERNATIONAL ISLAMIC UNIVERSITY CHITTAGONG (IIUC)

154/A, College Road, Chittagong 4203
Tel: +880(2) 610-085
Fax: +880(2) 610-307
EMail: info@iiuc.ac.bd
Website: http://www.iiuc.ac.bd

Vice-Chancellor: A.K.M. Azharul Islam EMail: vc@iiuc.ac.bd

Registrar: Muhammad Nurul Islam

International Relations: Murtaza Ahmed
EMail: acad_iiuc@fnfbd.net

Faculty

Arts and Humanities (Arabic; Arts and Humanities; English; Literature); **Business Studies** (Banking; Business Administration; Economics); **Law** (Law); **Science and Engineering** (Computer Engineering; Computer Science; Electrical and Electronic Engineering; Pharmacy); **Shariah and Islamic Studies** (Islamic Law; Islamic Studies; Koran)

History: Founded 1995 by the Islamic University Chittagong Trust.

Admission Requirements: A level Certificate with minimum 2nd division/2.5 GPA (average)

Fees: (Taka): 27,000-289,000

Main Language(s) of Instruction: English, Arabic

Accrediting Agency: University Grants Commission (UGC)

Degrees and Diplomas: *Bachelor's Degree (Pass)*; *Bachelor's Degree (Hons)*; *Master's Degree*

Student Services: Academic Counselling, Canteen, Careers Guidance, Cultural Activities, Foreign Studies Centre, Health Services, Language Laboratory, Library, Sports Facilities

Publications: Shar'iah Faculty Journal

Last Updated: 10/07/14

INTERNATIONAL UNIVERSITY OF BUSINESS, AGRICULTURE AND TECHNOLOGY (IUBAT)

4 Embankment Drive Road, Sector 10, Uttara Model Town, Dhaka 1230
Tel: +880(2) 892-3469
Fax: +880(2) 892-2625
EMail: info@iubat.edu
Website: http://www.iubat.edu

Vice-Chancellor: M. Alimullah Miyan (1993-)
EMail: miyan@iubat.edu

Registrar: M A Hannan

College

Agricultural Sciences (Agricultural Economics; Agriculture; Agronomy; Animal Husbandry; Dairy; Farm Management; Fishery; Floriculture; Horticulture; Meat and Poultry; Plant Pathology; Veterinary Science); **Arts and Science** (Arts and Humanities; Biological and Life Sciences; Demography and Population; Econometrics; Economics; English; Physics; Social Sciences; Social Welfare; Social Work); **Business Administration** (Accountancy; Banking; Business Administration; Business Computing; Finance; Human Resources; Management); **Engineering and Technology** (Business Computing; Civil Engineering; Computer Engineering; Computer Networks; Computer Science; Electrical and Electronic Engineering; Environmental Engineering; Hydraulic Engineering; Marine Engineering; Measurement and Precision Engineering; Mechanical Engineering; Software Engineering; Surveying and Mapping; Transport Engineering); **Health Sciences and Medical Education** (Community Health; Dentistry; Health Sciences; Medicine; Midwifery; Occupational Health; Social and Preventive Medicine; Surgery); **Nursing** (Midwifery; Nursing); **Tourism and Hospitality Management** (Hotel Management; Tourism)

History: Founded 1991, acquired present status 1993.

Academic Year: January to December (January-April; May-August; September-December)

Admission Requirements: Higher secondary certificate (HSC)

Fees: 650 - 1,040 per semester (US Dollar)

Main Language(s) of Instruction: English

Accrediting Agency: University Grants Commission (UGC)

Degrees and Diplomas: *Bachelor's Degree (Pass)*: **Agriculture; Business Administration; Civil Engineering; Computer Science; Economics; Electrical and Electronic Engineering; Hotel and Restaurant; Mechanical Engineering; Nursing; Tourism.** *Master's Degree*: **Business Administration.**

Student Services: Academic Counselling, Canteen, Careers Guidance, Cultural Activities, Health Services, Language Laboratory, Social Counselling, Sports Facilities

Academic Staff *2013-2014*	**TOTAL**
FULL-TIME	**215**
PART-TIME	**35**
STAFF WITH DOCTORATE FULL-TIME	**57**
Student Numbers *2013-2014*	
All (Foreign included)	**9,043**

Last Updated: 11/07/14

ISHAKHA INTERNATIONAL UNIVERSITY

461, Nilganj Road, Sholakia, Kishorganj 2300
EMail: ishakhauniversity@gmail.com
Website: http://www.ishakha.edu.bd/site

Vice-Chancellor: Durgadas Bhattacharjee

Faculty

Agriculture (Agriculture); **Arts & Social Science** (English; Literature); **Business Administration** (Banking; Business Administration); **Law** (Law)

History: Founded 2012.

Academic Year: January to April; May to August; September to December

Degrees and Diplomas: *Bachelor's Degree (Pass)*; *Bachelor's Degree (Hons)*; *Master's Degree*

Last Updated: 15/07/14

ISLAMIC UNIVERSITY OF TECHNOLOGY (IUT)

Board Bazar, Gazipur 1704
Tel: +880(2) 929-1250 +880(2) 929-1252
Fax: +880(2) 929-1260
EMail: vc@iut-dhaka.edu
Website: http://www.iutoic-dhaka.edu

Vice-Chancellor: M. Imtiaz Hossain (2008-)
EMail: vc@iut-dhaka.edu

Registrar: Muhammad Ahsan Habib EMail: regstrar@iut-dhaka.edu

Department
Civil and Environmental Engineering *(CEE)* (Civil Engineering; Environmental Engineering); **Computer Science and Information Technology** *(CIT)* (Computer Science; Information Technology); **Electrical and Electronic Engineering** (Electrical and Electronic Engineering); **Instructor Training and General Studies** *(ITS)* (Engineering; Teacher Training; Technology); **Mechanical and Chemical Engineering** *(MCE)* (Chemical Engineering; Mechanical Engineering)

History: Founded by OIC 1981, acquired present status 2001.

Academic Year: December to October

Admission Requirements: Higher/upper secondary school certificate or equivalent in Science with good grades in Mathematics, Physics, Chemistry and English for undergraduate programmes in Engineering and Technology

Fees: (US Dollars): Bachelor's Degree, 5,000 (for 4 yrs); Postgraduate studies, 5,000 per annum. Higher diploma free

Main Language(s) of Instruction: English

Accrediting Agency: Accrediting agencies of OIC Member States

Degrees and Diplomas: *Bachelor's Degree (Pass)*; *Master's Degree*; *Ph. D.*: **Technology.** Also postgraduate diploma 1 yr following upon Bachelor's Degree

Student Services: Academic Counselling, Canteen, Careers Guidance, Cultural Activities, Foreign Studies Centre, Health Services, Language Laboratory, Social Counselling, Sports Facilities

Publications: Journal of Engineering and Technology

Last Updated: 11/07/14

KHWAJA YUNUS ALI UNIVERSITY

Enaetpur, Chowhali, Sirajgonj
EMail: info@kyau.edu.bd
Website: http://www.kyau.edu.bd

Vice-Chancellor: Abdul Quadir Bhuiyan EMail: vc@kyau.edu.bd

School
Bio-medical Science (Biochemistry; Biotechnology; Microbiology; Pharmacy); **Business** (Business Administration; Computer Science; Management); **Human Science** (English; Islamic Studies; Library Science); **Law** (Law); **Science and Engineering** (Physics; Textile Technology)

History: Founded 2012.

Admission Requirements: At least 2nd division or a minimum GPA of 2.5 or an equivalent grade separately in SSC and HSC or equivalent public examinations

Degrees and Diplomas: *Bachelor's Degree (Pass)*; *Master's Degree*

Student Services: Library

Last Updated: 15/07/14

LEADING UNIVERSITY

Modhubon, Sylhet 31000
Tel: +880(821) 720303
EMail: info@lus.ac.bd
Website: http://www.lus.ac.bd

Vice-Chancellor (Acting): Kabir Hossain

Faculty
Arts and Language (English; Law); **Business** (Business Administration); **Modern Science** (Architecture; Civil Engineering; Computer Engineering; Computer Science; Electrical and Electronic Engineering)

History: Founded 2001.

Degrees and Diplomas: *Bachelor's Degree (Pass)*; *Master's Degree*

MANARAT INTERNATIONAL UNIVERSITY (MIU)

Plot Number 16, Road Number 106, Gulshan, Dhaka 1212
Tel: +880(2) 881-7525
EMail: info@manarat.ac.bd
Website: http://www.manarat.ac.bd

Vice-Chancellor: Choudhury Mahmood Hasan

Registrar: Abul Basher Khan

School
Arts and Humanities (English; Law); **Business and Economics** (Business Administration); **Science and Technology** (Computer Engineering; Computer Science; Electronic Engineering; Pharmacy; Telecommunications Engineering)

History: Founded 2001.

Admission Requirements: At least GPA 2.5 or Second Division both SSC & HSC and "A" Level in two subjects with minimum average grade "C" of US High School Diploma or equivalent.(CSE & ECE applicants must have physics & maths, and Pharmacy applicants must have chemistry at HSC or equivalent levels)

Accrediting Agency: University Grants Commission (UGC)

Degrees and Diplomas: *Bachelor's Degree (Pass)*; *Bachelor's Degree (Hons)*; *Master's Degree*

Student Services: Library

Last Updated: 16/07/14

METROPOLITAN UNIVERSITY

Al-Hamra, Zindabazar, Sylhet
Tel: +880(821) 713-077
EMail: info@metrouni.edu.bd
Website: http://www.metrouni.edu.bd

Vice-Chancellor: Md. Saleh Uddin (2009-)

School
Business (Business Administration); **Humanities and Social Sciences** (English); **Law** (Law); **Science** (Computer Engineering; Computer Science; Electrical and Electronic Engineering)

History: Founded 2003.

Degrees and Diplomas: *Bachelor's Degree (Pass)*; *Bachelor's Degree (Hons)*; *Master's Degree*

Last Updated: 16/07/14

NORTH BENGAL INTERNATIONAL UNIVERSITY

42, Khanika, Binodpur Bazar, Motihar, Rajshahi
Tel: +880(72) 177-3561
EMail: nbiu.edu@gmail.com
Website: http://www.nbiu.edu.bd

Vice-Chancellor: Abdul Khaleque

Faculty
Arts (English; History; Islamic Studies; Literature; Native Language); **Business Studies** (Business Administration); **Social Science & Law** (Communication Arts; Folklore; Journalism; Law; Political Sciences; Sociology)

History: Founded 2013.

Admission Requirements: Total GPA 5.50 with minimum 2.50 in S.S.C and H.S.C for the students of Arts and Commerce group; Total GPA 5.50 with minimum 2.50 in S.S.C and H.S.C/Diploma for the students of Science group; Minimum GP 2.5 in three Subjects at O-Level and minimum GP 2.5 in two subjects at A-Level.

Degrees and Diplomas: *Bachelor's Degree (Pass)*; *Bachelor's Degree (Hons)*; *Master's Degree*

Student Services: Library

Last Updated: 16/07/14

NORTH EAST UNIVERSITY BANGLADESH

Telihaor, Shekhghat, Sylhet 3100
EMail: info@neub.edu.bd
Website: http://www.neub.edu.bd

Vice-Chancellor: Khalilur Rahman

Faculty

Natural Sciences and Engineering (Computer Engineering; Computer Science; Environmental Engineering; Mathematics); **Social Sciences and Humanities** (English; Law; Public Health)

School

Business (Accountancy; Business Administration; Finance; Human Resources; Insurance; Management; Marketing)

History: Founded 2010.

Degrees and Diplomas: *Bachelor's Degree (Pass)*; *Bachelor's Degree (Hons)*; *Master's Degree*

Student Services: Library, Residential Facilities
Last Updated: 16/07/14

NORTH SOUTH UNIVERSITY

Plot 15, Block B, Bashundhara, Dhaka 1229
Tel: +880(2) 885-2000
Fax: +880(2) 885-2016
EMail: registrar@northsouth.edu
Website: http://www.northsouth.edu

Vice-Chancellor: Amin U. Sarkar
EMail: aminsarkar@northsouth.edu

Registrar: Md Shahjahan EMail: mali@northsouth.edu

School

Business (Accountancy; Business Administration; Finance; Human Resources; International Business; Marketing); **Engineering and Physical Sciences** (Architecture; Computer Engineering; Computer Science; Environmental Management; Environmental Studies; Mathematics; Physics); **Health & Life Sciences** (Biology; Chemistry; Environmental Engineering; Pharmacy; Public Health); **Humanities and Social Sciences** (English; History; Law; Modern Languages; Philosophy; Political Sciences; Sociology)

Institute

Modern Languages (Modern Languages)

History: Founded 1992. The first private university in Bangladesh. Established by NSU Foundation.

Accrediting Agency: Universities Grants Commission

Degrees and Diplomas: *Bachelor's Degree (Pass)*: **Business Administration; Computer Science; Economics; English; Environmental Studies.** *Master's Degree*: **Business Administration; Development Studies; Economics.**

Student Services: Library
Last Updated: 16/07/14

NORTH WESTERN UNIVERSITY

236, M.A Bari Road, Sonadanga, Khulna
Tel: +880(41)722-744
EMail: info@nwu.edu.bd
Website: http://nwu.edu.bd

Vice-Chancellor: Khondoker Bazlul Hoque

Faculty

Business Studies (Business Administration); **Liberal Arts & Human Science** (English; Law; Literature); **Science & Technology** (Architecture; Civil Engineering; Computer Engineering; Computer Science; Electrical and Electronic Engineering; Marine Engineering; Pharmacy; Textile Technology); **Social Sciences** (Economics; Social Sciences; Sociology)

History: Founded 2013.

Degrees and Diplomas: *Bachelor's Degree (Hons)*; *Master's Degree*

Student Services: Library
Last Updated: 16/07/14

NORTHERN UNIVERSITY BANGLADESH (NUB)

93, Kazi Nazrul Islam Avenue, Kawran Bazar, Dhaka 1215
Tel: +880(2) 815-3437-39
Fax: +880(2) 913-5562
EMail: info@nub.ac.bd
Website: http://www.nub.ac.bd

Vice-Chancellor: Shamsul Haque EMail: vc@nub.ac.bd

Treasurer: Abu Bakar Siddique EMail: treasurer@nub.ac.bd

International Relations: Md. Lutfor Rahman, Director, Human Resource Development EMail: director@nub.ac.bd

Faculty

Arts and Humanities (English; Literature); **Business** (Accountancy; Banking; Business Administration; Economics; Finance; Management; Marketing); **Health Sciences** (Health Sciences; Pharmacy; Public Health); **Law** (Law); **Science and Engineering** (Civil Engineering; Computer Engineering; Computer Science; Electrical and Electronic Engineering; Engineering; Textile Technology)

History: Founded 2002. A private university approved by Government.

Academic Year: January to December

Main Language(s) of Instruction: English

Degrees and Diplomas: *Bachelor's Degree (Pass)*; *Bachelor's Degree (Hons)*; *Master's Degree*

Student Services: Academic Counselling, Canteen, Careers Guidance, Health Services, Language Laboratory, Residential Facilities, Social Counselling, Sports Facilities
Last Updated: 17/07/14

PORT CITY INTERNATIONAL UNIVERSITY

7 - 14, Nikunja Housing Society, South Khulshi, Chittagong
Tel: +88(31) 286-9877
EMail: portcityuniversity@gmail.com
Website: http://www.portcity.edu.bd

Vice-Chancellor: Md. Nural Anwar EMail: vc@portcity.edu.bd

Faculty

Business Studies (Business Administration); **Humanities & Social Sciences** (Economics; English; Journalism; Media Studies); **Law** (Law); **Science & Engineering** (Civil Engineering; Computer Engineering; Computer Science; Electrical and Electronic Engineering; Fashion Design; Textile Technology)

History: Founded 2012.

Admission Requirements: Arts, Law, Social Science and Business Related Programmes: Minimum GPA 2.50 in both S.S.C and H.S.C or equivalent; Minimum 5 subjects in O-Level and 2 subjects in A-Level with minimum grade of B in 4 subjects and C in 3 subjects Science and Engineering Related Programmes: Minimum GPA 2.50 in both S.S.C and H.S.C with science background or equivalent; Minimum 5 subjects in O-Level and 2 subjects in A-Level with minimum grade of B in 4 subjects and C in 3 subjects from science group

Degrees and Diplomas: *Bachelor of Science*; *Bachelor's Degree (Hons)*; *Master's Degree*
Last Updated: 17/07/14

PREMIER UNIVERSITY (PUC)

1/A, O.R. Nizam Road, Panchlaish, Chittagong
Tel: +880(31) 656-917
Fax: +880(31) 687-892
EMail: info@puc.ac.bd
Website: http://www.puc.ac.bd

Vice-Chancellor: Anupam Sen (2006-)
EMail: profdrsen@yahoo.com

Registrar: Mohammed Ibrahim

Faculty

Arts and Social Sciences (Economics; English; Literature); **Business Studies** (Business Administration); **Engineering** (Computer Engineering; Computer Science; Electrical and Electronic Engineering); **Law** (Law)

History: Founded 2001.

Degrees and Diplomas: *Bachelor's Degree (Pass)*; *Bachelor's Degree (Hons)*; *Master's Degree*
Last Updated: 17/07/14

PRESIDENCY UNIVERSITY

Tower Building 11a, Road No: 92, Gulshan - 2, Dhaka
EMail: info@presidency.edu.bd
Website: http://www.presidency.edu.bd

Vice-Chancellor (Acting): Tapan Kumar Chakraborty
EMail: vc@presidency.edu.bd

School

Business *(Moazzam Hossain)* (Business Administration); **Engineering** *(Azimur Rahman)* (Civil Engineering; Electrical Engineering; Electronic Engineering; Telecommunications Engineering); **Liberal Arts and Social Sciences** *(Shamsul Alamin)* (Economics; English; Social Sciences)

History: Founded 2003.

Degrees and Diplomas: *Bachelor's Degree (Pass)*; *Master's Degree*

Student Services: Library
Last Updated: 17/07/14

PRIME UNIVERSITY (PU)

2A/1 North East of Darus Salam Road, Section-1 Mirpur, Dhaka 1216
Tel: +880(2) 805-5646
Fax: +880(2) 805-5647
EMail: info@primeuniversity.edu.bd
Website: http://primeuniversity.edu.bd

Vice-Chancellor: C. Profulla EMail: vc@primeuniversity.edu.bd

Faculty

Arts and Social Sciences (Arts and Humanities; Education; English; Literature); **Business Studies** (Business Administration); **Engineering** (Computer Engineering; Computer Science; Electrical Engineering; Electronic Engineering; Telecommunications Engineering); **Information Technology** (Applied Mathematics; Computer Science; Information Technology)

History: Founded 2002.

Admission Requirements: Minimum 2.5 in S.S.C or equivalent and 2.5 in H.S.C or equivalent examination

Degrees and Diplomas: *Bachelor's Degree (Pass)*; *Master's Degree*

Student Services: Library
Last Updated: 17/07/14

PRIMEASIA UNIVERSITY

12 Kemal Ataturk Avenue, Banani, Dhaka 1213
Tel: +880(2) 982-2133
EMail: info@primeasia.edu.bd
Website: http://www.primeasia.edu.bd

Vice-Chancellor: Gias uddin Ahmad EMail: vc@primeasia.edu.bd

School

Business (Business Administration); **Engineering** (Architecture; Computer Engineering; Computer Science; Electrical and Electronic Engineering; Mechanical Engineering; Textile Technology); **Law** (Law); **Science** (Biochemistry; Microbiology; Nutrition; Pharmacy; Public Health)

History: Founded 2003.
Degrees and Diplomas: *Bachelor's Degree (Pass)*; *Bachelor of Science*; *Master's Degree*

Student Services: Library
Last Updated: 17/07/14

QUEENS UNIVERSITY

House 43/E, Road 17/A, Banani, Dhaka
EMail: info@queensuniversity.edu.bd
Website: http://www.queensuniversity.edu.bd/

Vice-Chancellor: Abdul Khaleque

School

Arts (English); **Business Administration** (Business Administration); **Law** (Law); **Science** (Computer Science; Engineering)

History: Founded 1996, acquired present status 1997.

Academic Year: March to February (March to August; September to February)

Admission Requirements: At least Second Division in both the S.S.C. & H.S.C. Examination or equivalent.

Fees: (Taka): 30,000 per semester; 60,000 per annum

Main Language(s) of Instruction: English

Degrees and Diplomas: *Bachelor's Degree (Pass)*: **Computer Science; Engineering.** *Bachelor's Degree (Hons)*; *Master's Degree*: **Business Administration.**

Student Services: Cultural Activities, Sports Facilities
Last Updated: 17/07/14

RAJSHAHI SCIENCE AND TECHNOLOGY UNIVERSITY

VIP Tower, Holding # 112, Dhaka Road, Bara Harishpur, Natore Sadar, Natore
EMail: rstuniversity@yahoo.com
Website: http://www.rstu.edu.bd

School

Business (Business Administration); **Liberal Arts and Social Sciences** (Economics; English; Journalism; Law; Media Studies; Sociology); **Science and Engineering** (Civil Engineering; Computer Engineering; Computer Science; Electrical and Electronic Engineering; Pharmacy; Textile Technology)

History: Founded 2013.

Degrees and Diplomas: *Bachelor's Degree (Pass)*; *Bachelor of Science*; *Bachelor's Degree (Hons)*; *Master's Degree*
Last Updated: 17/07/14

RANODA PRASHAD SHAHA UNIVERSITY

25, Sultan Giasuddin Road, Naryanganj 1400
EMail: info@rpsu.edu.bd
Website: http://rpsu.edu.bd/rpsu

Faculty

Arts and Social Science (Economics; English; Human Rights; Law); **Business** (Business Administration); **Engineering** (Computer Engineering; Computer Science; Electrical and Electronic Engineering); **Life Science and Health** (Pharmacy)

History: Founded 2013.

Admission Requirements: For Business Administration/Science • Minimum GPA 2.75 in SSC and HSC separately. Total GPA 6.00. Mathematics must be included in HSC level for Science students. • Minimum GPA 2.5 in O-Levels in five subjects and A-Levels in two subjects. Total GPA 6.00 (Scale A = 5, B = 4, C = 3, D = 2 and E = 1). Mathematics must be included at A- Level for Science students. For Engineering • Minimum GPA 3.00 in SSC and HSC separately. Total GPA 6.00. Mathematics must be included in HSC level. • Minimum GPA 3.00 in O-Levels in five subjects and A-Levels in two subjects. Total GPA 6.00 (Scale A = 5, B = 4, C = 3, D = 2 and E = 1). Mathematics must be included at A- Level. For Arts and Social Science • Minimum GPA 2.75 in SSC and HSC separately. Total GPA 5.50. • Minimum GPA 2.5 in O-Levels in five subjects and A-Levels in two subjects. Total GPA 5.00 (Scale A = 5, B = 4, C = 3, D = 2 and E = 1). Mathematics must be included at A- Level.

Degrees and Diplomas: *Bachelor's Degree (Pass)*; *Bachelor of Science*; *Bachelor's Degree (Hons)*
Last Updated: 21/07/14

ROYAL UNIVERSITY OF DHAKA

House No# 2, Road No#10, Block # E, Banani, Dhaka 1213
Tel: +880(2) 988-6150
Fax: +880(2) 882-6971
EMail: registrar@royal.edu.bd
Website: http://www.royal.edu.bd

Vice-Chancellor: Hasan Imtiaz Chowdhury

Faculty

Arts and Social Sciences (Education; English; Hotel and Restaurant; Library Science; Tourism); **Business** (Banking; Business Administration); **Science** (Computer Science; Rural Planning; Technology; Town Planning)

History: Founded 2004

Degrees and Diplomas: *Bachelor's Degree (Pass)*; *Master's Degree*

Last Updated: 21/07/14

SHANTO MARIAM UNIVERSITY OF CREATIVE TECHNOLOGY

House No. 01, Road No. 14, sector No. 13, Uttara, Dhaka 1230
Tel: +880(2) 892-3167
Fax: +880(2) 891-5308,
EMail: smuctbd@yahoo.com
Website: http://www.smuct.edu.bd

Vice-Chancellor: Shamsul Haq

Faculty

Design and Technology (Architecture; Ceramic Art; Clothing and Sewing; Computer Science; Fashion Design; Graphic Design; Handicrafts; Interior Design; Jewellery Art; Textile Design; Weaving); **Fine and Performing Arts** (Dance; Fine Arts; Music; Painting and Drawing; Printing and Printmaking); **Management & General Studies** (Accountancy; Anthropology; Banking; Business Administration; Education; English; Finance; Human Resources; Islamic Studies; Law; Management; Marketing; Native Language; Political Sciences; Sociology)

History: Founded 2003.

Degrees and Diplomas: *Bachelor's Degree (Pass)*; *Bachelor's Degree (Hons)*; *Master's Degree*

Student Services: Library, Residential Facilities

Last Updated: 21/07/14

SONARGAON UNIVERSITY

Kawran Bazar, Dhaka 1215
EMail: su.edu.bd@gmail.com
Website: http://www.su.edu.bd

Vice-Chancellor: M.A. Razzaque

Faculty

Business & Economics (Accountancy; Business Administration; Finance; Human Resources; Management; Marketing); **Humanities & Social Science** (Criminal Law; Development Studies; Economics; English; History; Islamic Studies; Journalism; Media Studies; Political Sciences; Safety Engineering); **Law & Justice** (Law); **Science & Engineering** (Architecture; Civil Engineering; Computer Engineering; Electrical and Electronic Engineering; Fashion Design; Marine Engineering; Mechanical Engineering; Naval Architecture; Textile Technology)

History: Founded 2012.

Degrees and Diplomas: *Bachelor's Degree (Pass)*; *Bachelor of Science*; *Bachelor's Degree (Hons)*; *Master's Degree*

Last Updated: 22/07/14

SOUTHEAST UNIVERSITY (SEU)

House -64/B, Road-18, Banani, Dhaka 1213
Tel: +880(2) 988-2914
Fax: +880(2) 989-2914
EMail: info@seu.ac.bd
Website: http://www.seu.ac.bd

Vice-Chancellor: Anwar Hossain

Registrar: Md. Anwarul Islam

School

Arts and Social Sciences (Development Studies; Economics; Education; English; Islamic Studies; Law; Native Language); **Business Studies** (Business Administration); **Science and Engineering** (Architecture; Computer Engineering; Computer Science; Electrical and Electronic Engineering; Pharmacy; Telecommunications Engineering; Textile Technology)

History: Founded 2002.

Academic Year: January to December (January - April; May - August; September - December)

Admission Requirements: Higher Secondary School Certificate (HSC)

Fees: (Taka): 40,000-325,000 per programme; distance students, 40,000-70,000

Main Language(s) of Instruction: English

Degrees and Diplomas: *Bachelor's Degree (Pass)*; *Bachelor's Degree (Hons)*; *Master's Degree*

Student Services: Academic Counselling, Canteen, Careers Guidance, Health Services, Library, Residential Facilities, Sports Facilities

Last Updated: 22/07/14

SOUTHERN UNIVERSITY BANGLADESH (SOUTHERN)

739/ A Mehdibag Road, Chittagong 4000
Tel: +880(31) 285-1336-9 +880(31) 626-744
Fax: +880(31) 285-1340
EMail: info@southern.edu.bd
Website: http://www.southern.edu.bd

Vice-Chancellor: Mohammad Ali

International Relations: Sarwar Jahan, Vice-President (OP)
EMail: southern.edu@gmail.com

Faculty

Business Administration (Accountancy; Administration; Banking; Business Administration; Business and Commerce; E- Business/ Commerce; Finance; Human Resources; International Business; Management; Marketing); **Science and Engineering** (Civil Engineering; Computer Science; Electrical and Electronic Engineering; Information Technology; Pharmacy; Public Health; Telecommunications Engineering)

Academy

Arts, Law and Social Sciences (English; Islamic Studies; Law)

History: Southern University is located at the port city of Chittagong on the South-eastern part of Bangladesh. Present campus only at Mehedibag Road, Chittagong, Bangladesh. The University began its life as an Institute in 1998 which was an affiliated Bangladesh Campus of USA and UK universities. In 2002, the university received approval from the Ministry of Education, Government of Bangladesh as non-government private university under the Universities act of 1992 and 1998.

Academic Year: January to December

Admission Requirements: Minimum 12 (Twelve) years of schooling prior to undergraduate programme or equivalents. (2.5/ 5.0 GPA) in the examinations.

Fees: National: Undergraduate: 1,50,000 to 2,76,000 per program for four years; Post Graduate: 40,000 to 1,25,000 per program for one to two years (Taka), International: Same as for national students

Main Language(s) of Instruction: English, Bengali

Accrediting Agency: UGC

Degrees and Diplomas: *Bachelor's Degree (Pass)*: **Business Administration; Computer Science; English; Law.** *Bachelor of Science*; *Master's Degree*: **Business Administration; Computer Science; English; Information Technology; Islamic Studies; Law.**

Student Services: Academic Counselling, Careers Guidance, Cultural Activities, Language Laboratory, Sports Facilities

Publications: Journal of Business and Society; The Journal of Engineering and Science; The Journal of General Education

Last Updated: 24/08/15

STAMFORD UNIVERSITY BANGLADESH

744, Satmosjid Road, Dhanmondi R/A, Dhaka 1209
Tel: +880(2) 815-3168
Fax: +880(2) 811-9956
EMail: admission@stamforduniversity.edu.bd
Website: http://www.stamforduniversity.edu.bd

Vice-Chancellor: M. Feroze Ahmed

Registrar: S. M. Ikramul Haque

Department

Architecture (Architecture); **Business Administration** (Business Administration; Human Resources); **Civil Engineering** (Civil Engineering); **Computer Science** (Computer Engineering; Computer Science; Information Technology); **Economics** (Economics); **Electrical and Electronic Engineering** (Electrical and Electronic Engineering); **English** (English); **Environmental Science** (Environmental Studies); **Film and Media** (Film; Media Studies); **Journalism and Media Studies** (Journalism; Media Studies); **Law** (Law); **Microbiology** (Microbiology); **Pharmacy** (Pharmacy)

History: Founded 1994 as Stamford College Group. Acquired present status 2001.

Accrediting Agency: Government

Degrees and Diplomas: *Bachelor's Degree (Pass)*; *Master's Degree*

Student Services: Library

Last Updated: 23/07/14

STATE UNIVERSITY OF BANGLADESH

77 Satmasjid Road, Dhanmondi, Dhaka 1205
Tel: +880(2) 815-1781
Fax: +880(2) 812-3296
EMail: info@subd.net
Website: http://www.subd.net

Vice-Chancellor: Iftekhar Ghani Chowdhury

Registrar: A.Y.M. Ekram-ud Daulah
EMail: registrar@subd.net

International Relations: Dil Afroze
Tel: +880(2) 812-6272 EMail: afroze@subd.net

School

Business and Social Studies (Business Administration; English; Law); **Health Sciences** (Food Science; Food Technology; Nutrition; Optometry; Pharmacy; Public Health); **Science and Technology** (Architecture; Computer Engineering; Computer Science; Environmental Studies)

History: Founded 2002.

Admission Requirements: Secondary school certificate

Main Language(s) of Instruction: English

Degrees and Diplomas: *Bachelor's Degree (Pass)*; *Master's Degree*

Student Services: Academic Counselling, Canteen, Careers Guidance, Facilities for disabled people, Foreign Studies Centre, Health Services, Language Laboratory, Social Counselling, Sports Facilities

Last Updated: 23/07/14

SYLHET INTERNATIONAL UNIVERSITY (SIU)

Shamimabad, Bagbari, Sylhet
Tel: +880(821) 717-193 +880(821) 720-771
Fax: +880(821) 725-644
EMail: info@siu.edu.bd
Website: http://siu.edu.bd

Vice-Chancellor: Susanta Kumar Das (2010-)
EMail: skdas@siu.edu.bd; skdas.phy@gmail.com

Faculty

Business Administration (Business Administration); **Computer Science and Engineering** (Electrical and Electronic Engineering; Engineering); **Humanities and Social Sciences** (English; Islamic Studies); **Law** (Law)

History: Created 2001.

Accrediting Agency: University Grants Commission (UGC)

Degrees and Diplomas: *Bachelor's Degree (Pass)*; *Bachelor's Degree (Hons)*; *Master's Degree*: **Business Administration.**

Last Updated: 23/07/14

THE MILLENNIUM UNIVERSITY

Momenbagh, Rajarbagh, Dhaka 1217
Tel: +880(2) 936-0836
EMail: khanfoundation@hotmail.com
Website: http://www.themilleniumuniversity.edu.bd

Vice-Chancellor: Abu Ayub Md. Baquer

Faculty

Business Studies (Business Administration); **Computer Science and Technology** (Computer Engineering; Computer Science; Information Technology); **Humanities** (English); **Law** (Law)

Degrees and Diplomas: *Bachelor's Degree (Pass)*; *Bachelor's Degree (Hons)*; *Master's Degree*

Last Updated: 23/07/14

THE PEOPLE'S UNIVERSITY OF BANGLADESH

3/2, Block-A Asad Avenue, Mohammadpur, Dhaka-1207, Dhaka 1207
Tel: +880(2) 812-8676 +880(2) 913-0726
Fax: +880(2) 912-8009
EMail: info@pub.ac.bd
Website: http://www.pub.ac.bd

Vice-Chancellor: Md. Abdul Mannan Chowdhury
EMail: vc@pub.ac.bd

Registrar: Mohammed Mufakker EMail: registrar@pub.ac.bd

International Relations: Ummay Kulsum

School

Applied Science and Engineering (Computer Engineering; Computer Science; Electronic Engineering; Telecommunications Engineering); **Arts** (English; Islamic Studies); **Business Administration** (Business Administration; Business Computing; Hotel Management; Tourism); **Health Science** (Physical Therapy); **Social Sciences** (Law; Social Sciences; Social Work; Sociology); **Textile Engineering** (Textile Technology)

History: Founded 1992. Opened 1996.

Academic Year: January-December (January-July; August-December)

Admission Requirements: In science subjects, students passing SSC and SSC examination or equivalent with Physics, Chemistry and Mathematics/Biology obtaining at least 2nd Division in both SSC and HSC examinations or their equivalent may apply for admission to BS Hons programmes.

Fees: (US Dollars): undergraduate, c. 3,000-5,000; postgraduate, c. 1,200

Main Language(s) of Instruction: English

Accrediting Agency: University Grants Commission (UGC)

Degrees and Diplomas: *Bachelor's Degree (Pass)*; *Bachelor's Degree (Hons)*; *Master's Degree*. Admission to postgraduate courses leading to MPhil and PhD degrees in related subjects is available.

Student Services: Academic Counselling, Canteen, Cultural Activities, Health Services, Language Laboratory, Library, Sports Facilities

Publications: The Journal of the People's University of Bangladesh

Publishing House: Centre for Multi-disciplinary Studies

Last Updated: 23/07/14

THE UNIVERSITY OF ASIA PACIFIC

House 73, Road 5A, Dhanmondi R/A, Dhaka 1209
Tel: +880(2) 966-1193
Fax: +880(2) 966-4950
EMail: registrar@uap-bd.edu
Website: http://www.uap-bd.edu

Vice-Chancellor: Jamilur Reza Choudory EMail: vc@uap-bd.edu

School

Business (Business Administration); **Engineering** (Civil Engineering; Computer Engineering; Computer Science; Electrical and Electronic Engineering); **Environmental Sciences and Design** (Architecture); **Law** (Human Rights; Law); **Medicine** (Pharmacy); **Science** (Mathematics)

History: Founded 1996.

Admission Requirements: At least higher second division in the Secondary School Certificate (SSC) and Higher Secondary Certificate (HSC) examinations

Fees: (Taka): c. 40,000 per semester

Accrediting Agency: University Grants Commission (UGC)

Degrees and Diplomas: *Bachelor's Degree (Hons)*; *Master's Degree*: **Business Administration.**

Last Updated: 23/07/14

UNITED INTERNATIONAL UNIVERSITY (UIU)

House 80, Road 8/A, Satmasjid Road, Dhanmondi, Dhaka 1209
Tel: +880(2) 912-5912
Fax: +880(2) 912-5916
EMail: info@uiu.ac.bd
Website: http://uiu.ac.bd

Vice-Chancellor: Mohammad Rezwan Khan

Registrar: A. S. M. Salahuddin EMail: su@uiu.ac.bd

School

Business and Economics (Accountancy; Banking; Business Administration; Economics; Finance; Management; Marketing); **Science and Engineering** (Civil Engineering; Computer Engineering; Computer Science; Electrical and Electronic Engineering; Electronic Engineering)

Institute

English Language (English); **Natural Sciences** (Applied Chemistry; Applied Mathematics; Applied Physics; Physics)

History: Founded 2003.

Admission Requirements: Higher Secondary Certificate or 5 O level subjects and 2 A level subjects with minimum GPA of 2.0 or American High School Diploma or equivalent

Fees: (Taka): Undergraduate, 1,800 per credit; Graduate, 2,500 per credit

Main Language(s) of Instruction: English

Accrediting Agency: Government; University Grants Commission (UGC)

Degrees and Diplomas: *Bachelor's Degree (Pass)*; *Bachelor of Science*; *Master's Degree*

Student Services: Library

Last Updated: 23/07/14

UNIVERSITY OF DEVELOPMENT ALTERNATIVE (UODA)

80 Satmasjid Road, Dhanmondi Residential Area, Dhaka 1209
Tel: +880(2) 914-5741
Fax: +880(2) 815-7339
EMail: registrar@uoda.edu.bd
Website: http://www.uoda.edu.bd

Vice-Chancellor: Emajuddin Ahamed
Tel: +880(2) 914-5741 EMail: president@uoda.org

Registrar: Iffat Chowdhury EMail: iffat@uoda.org

International Relations: Md. Haider Faruque
EMail: haider_faruque@yahoo.com

Faculty

Arts and Social Sciences (Development Studies; Human Rights; Law; Media Studies; Music; Native Language Education; Political Sciences); **Business Administration** (Business Administration); **Fine Arts** (Art History; Fine Arts; Painting and Drawing); **Life Sciences** (Biological and Life Sciences; Biotechnology; Genetics; Molecular Biology; Pharmacy); **Science and Technology** (Computer Engineering; Computer Science; Mathematics; Telecommunications Engineering)

History: Founded 2002.

Academic Year: January to December (January-April; May-August; September-December)

Admission Requirements: Secondary school certificate (SSC) and higher secondary certificate (HSC)

Fees: (Taka): 14,000 per semester

Main Language(s) of Instruction: English

Accrediting Agency: University Grants Commission (UGC)

Degrees and Diplomas: *Bachelor's Degree (Hons)*; *Master's Degree*

Student Services: Academic Counselling, Canteen, Careers Guidance, Cultural Activities, Health Services, Nursery Care, Social Counselling, Sports Facilities

Publications: UODA Studies: A Scientific Journal

Last Updated: 23/07/14

UNIVERSITY OF INFORMATION TECHNOLOGY AND SCIENCES (UITS)

GA - 37/1, Jamalpur Twin Tower (Tower 2), Pragati Sharani, Baridhara View, Gulshan-2, Dhaka 1212
Tel: +880(2) 889-9751
Fax: +880(2) 889-9753
EMail: info@uits.edu.org
Website: http://www.uits.edu.bd

Vice-Chancellor: Muhammad Samad EMail: vc@uits.edu.bd

Registrar: Abdullah Al Mamun Choudhury
EMail: amamunchy@yahoo.com

School

Business (Accountancy; Banking; Finance; Insurance; Management; Marketing); **Liberal Arts and Social Sciences** (English; Law); **Science and Engineering** (Civil Engineering; Computer Engineering; Computer Science; Electrical and Electronic Engineering; Information Technology; Natural Sciences; Pharmacy; Social Problems)

History: Founded 2003.

Academic Year: September to June

Admission Requirements: Secondary school certificate (SSC) and higher secondary certificate (HEC) or foreign equivalent.

Fees: (Taka): 7,500-9,000 per month

Main Language(s) of Instruction: English

Accrediting Agency: University Grants Commission (UGC)

Degrees and Diplomas: *Bachelor's Degree (Pass)*; *Bachelor's Degree (Hons)*; *Master's Degree*: **Business Administration; Computer Engineering; Computer Science; English; Law; Telecommunications Engineering.**

Student Services: Academic Counselling, Canteen, Language Laboratory, Library, Sports Facilities

Last Updated: 23/07/14

UNIVERSITY OF LIBERAL ARTS BANGLADESH

House 56, Rd 4/A @ Satmasjid Road, Dhanmond, Dhaka 1209
Tel: +880(2) 966-1255
EMail: info@ulabd.edu.bd
Website: http://www.ulab.edu.bd

Vice-Chancellor: Imran Rahman

School

Arts and Humanities (Arts and Humanities; English); **Business** (Business Administration); **Science and Technology** (Computer Engineering; Computer Science; Electronic Engineering; Telecommunications Engineering); **Social Sciences** (Journalism; Media Studies)

History: Founded 2004.

Degrees and Diplomas: *Bachelor's Degree (Pass)*; *Bachelor of Science*; *Master's Degree*

Student Services: Library

Last Updated: 24/07/14

UNIVERSITY OF SCIENCE AND TECHNOLOGY, CHITTAGONG

Main Campus, Foy's Lake, Khulshi, Pahartali, Chittagong 4202
Tel: +880(31) 659-070
Fax: +880(31) 659-545
EMail: ustc-cst@spnetctg.com; ustc-ctag@gmail.com
Website: http://www.ustc.ac.bd

Vice-Chancellor: Nurul Islam
Tel: 880(2) 861-4959 EMail: ustcbd@bangla.net

Registrar: Farid Uddin Ahmed

Faculty
Basic Medical and Pharmaceutical Sciences (Biochemistry; Biotechnology; Pharmacy); **Business Administration** (Banking; Business Administration); **Medicine** (Gynaecology and Obstetrics; Medicine; Paediatrics; Surgery); **Science, Engineering and Technology** (Computer Engineering; Computer Science; Electrical and Electronic Engineering; Engineering; Technology; Telecommunications Engineering); **Social Sciences and Humanities** (English)
History: Founded 1992.

Degrees and Diplomas: *Bachelor's Degree (Pass)*: **Business Administration; Computer Science; Engineering; Medicine; Pharmacy.** *Master's Degree*: **Business Administration; Engineering.**

UNIVERSITY OF SOUTH ASIA

House 76 & 78, Road 14, Block B, Banani, Dhaka,
Tel: +880(2) 985-7074
EMail: mail@southasia-uni.org
Website: http://www.southasia-uni.org

Vice-Chancellor: A. H. Syedur Rahman

School
Business *(South Asia)* (Business Administration); **Engineering and Technology** *(South Asia)* (Computer Engineering; Computer Science; Information Technology; Textile Technology); **Humanities** (English); **Public Health and Life Sciences** *(South Asia)* (Environmental Engineering; Food Science; Nutrition; Optometry; Public Health)

History: Founded 2003.

Admission Requirements: A higher secondary certificate or its equivalent in Science, Arts, Commerce or other fields of study. Minimum qualifying points to be eligible to apply is 5.

Degrees and Diplomas: *Bachelor's Degree (Pass)*; *Master's Degree*
Last Updated: 28/07/14

UTTARA UNIVERSITY

House-5, Road-15, Sector-6, Uttara, Dhaka
Tel: +880(2) 891-9794
EMail: info@uttarauniversity.edu.bd
Website: http://www.uttarauniversity.edu.bd/

Vice-Chancellor: Azizur Rahman
EMail: dma_rahman@yahoo.com

School
Arts and Social Sciences (Education; English; Islamic Studies; Native Language); **Business** (Business Administration); **Civil, Environmental and Industrial Engineering** (Civil Engineering; Computer Engineering; Computer Science; Environmental Engineering; Fashion Design); **Education and Physical Education** (Education; Physical Education)

History: Founded 2003.

Degrees and Diplomas: *Bachelor's Degree (Pass)*; *Master's Degree*

VARENDRA UNIVERSITY

Kazla, Motihar, Rajshahi
Tel: +880(721) 750-570
EMail: info@vu.edu.bd
Website: http://www.vu.edu.bd

Vice-Chancellor: Osman Goni Talukder

Department
Business Administration (Business Administration); **Computer Science & Engineering** (Computer Engineering; Computer Science); **Economics** (Economics); **Electrical and Electronic Engineering** (Electrical and Electronic Engineering; Telecommunications Engineering); **English** (English; Literature); **Journalism, Communication and Media Studies (JCMS)** (Communication Arts; Journalism; Mass Communication; Media Studies); **Law** (Law); **Pharmacy** (Pharmacy); **Sociology** (Sociology)

History: Founded 2012.

Degrees and Diplomas: *Bachelor's Degree (Pass)*; *Bachelor's Degree (Hons)*; *Master's Degree*
Last Updated: 29/07/14

VICTORIA UNIVERSITY OF BANGLADESH

69 K, Panthapath, Dhaka 1205
Tel: +880(2) 862-2634
Fax: +880(2) 862-2635
EMail: info@vub.edu.bd
Website: http://www.vub.edu.bd

Vice-Chancellor: M. R. Khan

School
Arts and Humanities (English); **Business and Management** (Accountancy; Banking; Business Administration; Finance; Hotel and Restaurant; Insurance; Management; Marketing; Tourism); **Education and Training** (Education); **Science** (Computer Engineering; Computer Science; Information Technology)

History: Founded 2003.

Admission Requirements: Higher Secondary Certificate or equivalent Certificate. In order to be eligible for admission a student must secure a minimum of GPA 2.5 at all levels

Degrees and Diplomas: *Bachelor's Degree (Pass)*; *Bachelor's Degree (Hons)*; *Master's Degree*
Last Updated: 29/07/14

IAU WORLD UNIVERSITY OF BANGLADESH (WUB)

Administrative Building, Building 3/A, Road No 4, Dhaka 1205
Tel: +880(2) 961-1410
Fax: +880(2) 967-7474
EMail: info@wub.edu
Website: http://www.wub.edu

Vice-Chancellor: Mabdul Mannan Choudury
EMail: amchoudhury@wub.edu.bd

International Relations: Ushan Ara Badal, International Relations Officer EMail: int.affairs@wub.edu.bd

International Relations: Abdul Jalil Masud, Assistant Registrar, International Office EMail: int.affairs@wub.edu.bd

Faculty
Arts and Humanities (Education; English; Law); **Business Studies** (Business and Commerce; Hotel Management; Management; Tourism); **Science and Engineering** (Architecture; Civil Engineering; Computer Engineering; Computer Science; Electrical and Electronic Engineering; Mechanical Engineering; Pharmacy; Textile Technology)

History: Founded 2001. Acquired present status 2003.

Academic Year: January to December

Admission Requirements: Higher Secondary Certificate or foreign equivalent

Fees: 4,400-28,000 per annum (Taka)

Main Language(s) of Instruction: English

Accrediting Agency: University Grants Commission - UGC

Degrees and Diplomas: *Bachelor's Degree (Pass)*; *Bachelor of Science*: **Civil Engineering; Computer Science; Mechanical Engineering; Textile Technology.** *Bachelor's Degree (Hons)*: **English.** *Master's Degree*: **Business Administration; Business Education; Education; English; Law.**

Student Services: Academic Counselling, Canteen, Careers Guidance, Cultural Activities, Facilities for disabled people, Foreign Studies Centre, Health Services, Language Laboratory, Social Counselling, Sports Facilities

Academic Staff *2014-2015*	**TOTAL**
FULL-TIME	**247**
PART-TIME	**3**
STAFF WITH DOCTORATE	
FULL-TIME	**20**
Student Numbers *2014-2015*	
All (Foreign included)	**1,631**

Last Updated: 20/08/15

Z.H. ZIKDER UNIVERSITY OF SCIENCE AND TECHNOLOGY

Madhupur, Kartikpur, Bhedorgonj, Shariatpur, Dhaka
Tel: +880(2) 811-5965
EMail: zhsust2012@gmail.com
Website: http://zhsust.edu.bd/sust

Vice-Chancellor: Muhammed Abdul Malek

Faculty

Business Studies (Accountancy; Banking; Business Administration; Finance; Human Resources; Management; Marketing); **Engineering and Technology** (Chemical Engineering; Civil Engineering; Computer Engineering; Computer Science; Electrical and Electronic Engineering; Environmental Engineering); **Humanities and Social Science** (Economics; English; Law)

History: Founded 2012.

Admission Requirements: For Engineering/Science/Architecture: A total GPA of 6.5 in SSC & HSC with Science background at HSC. Math must be included at HSC level. Minimum GPA 3.0 (in both 0 and A Levels separately) with no grade lower than 'C' among best 5 subjects in O' level and best 2 subjects in A' level. Math must be included at A' level. (Scale: A = 5, B = 4, C = 3, D = 2 & E= 1). High School Diploma/International Baccalaureate with minimum grade B in Math. For Business Administration: A total GPA of 6.0 in SSC C among best 5 subjects in O' level and best 2 subjects in A1 level. (Scale: A = 5, B = 4,C = 3,D = 2&E= 1).High School Diploma/International Baccalaureate with minimum grade B. For Humanities and Social Science: A total GPA of 5.5 in SSC D'among best 5 subjects in O' level and best 2 subjects in A' level. (Scale: A = 5,B = 4, C = 3,D = 2 & E= 1). High School Diploma/ International Baccalaureate with minimum grade C. Also entrance test

Degrees and Diplomas: *Bachelor's Degree (Pass)*; *Bachelor's Degree (Hons)*; *Master's Degree*

Last Updated: 30/07/14

Barbados

STRUCTURE OF HIGHER EDUCATION SYSTEM

Description:

Higher education is provided at academic, vocational and technical colleges as well as at the University of the West Indies, Cave Hill Campus.

Stages of studies:

University level first stage: *Bachelor's degree*

Bachelor's degree courses last for three to four years.

University level second stage: *Master's degree*

Master's degrees usually take one year following upon a first degree. They are offered at the University of the West Indies.

University level third stage: *Doctorate*

Doctorates take a further three years, following upon the Master's degree. They are offered at the University of the West Indies.

ADMISSION TO HIGHER EDUCATION

Admission to university-level studies:

Name of secondary school credential required: Caribbean Advanced Proficiency Certificate

Foreign students admission:

Language proficiency: Knowledge of English is essential.

RECOGNITION OF STUDIES

Quality assurance system:

In November 2004, the Barbados Accreditation Council was established by an Act of Parliament to register institutions offering post-secondary/tertiary education and programmes of study, accredit programmes and institutions in Barbados, and deal with recognition and equivalency of local and foreign-based qualifications.

Bodies dealing with recognition:

Barbados Accreditation Council

Plaza Centrale, Roebuck St.
St.Michael
Tel: +1(246) 622-1090
Fax: +1(246) 622-1089
EMail: info@bac.gov.bb
WWW: https://bac.gov.bb/

NATIONAL BODIES

Ministry of Education, Science, Technology and Innovation

Minister: Ronald D. Jones
Senior Education Officer, Tertiary Section: Gertrude Welch
Elsie Payne Complex
Constitution Road
St. Michael
Tel: +1(246) 430-2700
Fax: +1(246) 436-2411

EMail: info@mes.gov.bb
WWW: http://www.mes.gov.bb

Barbados Accreditation Council

Executive Director: Valda Alleyne
Plaza Centrale, Roebuck St.
St.Michael
Tel: + 1(246) 622-1090
Fax: + 1(246) 622-1089
EMail: info@bac.gov.bb
WWW: https://bac.gov.bb/
Role of national body: Government agency with responsibility for assuring the quality and integrity of post-secondary or tertiary education and training in Barbados.

National Council for Science and Technology - NCST

Reef Road, Fontabelle
St.Michael
Tel: + 1(246) 427-5270
Fax: + 1(246) 427-5765
EMail: lennox.chandler@commerce.gov.bb
WWW: http://www.ncst.gov.bb/
Role of national body: NCST was set up in 1977 under the aegis of the Ministry of Finance and Planning to coordinate local activities in science and technology.

Data for academic year: 2016-2017
Source: IAU from the websites of the Ministry of Education and the Barbados Accreditation Council, 2016.

INSTITUTION

PUBLIC INSTITUTION

UNIVERSITY OF THE WEST INDIES - CAVE HILL CAMPUS

Bridgetown
Tel: + 1(246) 417-4000
Fax: + 1(246) 425-1327
EMail: officeoftheprincipal@cavehill.uwi.edu
Website: http://www.cavehill.uwi.edu/

Principal and Pro-Vice-Chancellor: Hilary Beckles
Tel: + 1(246) 417-4030
EMail: hilary.beckles@cavehill.uwi.edu

Campus Registrar: Jacqueline Wade
Tel: + 1(246) 417-4052
EMail: cregoffice@cavehill.uwi.edu

International Relations: Anthony Fisher
Tel: + 1 (246) 417- 4542
EMail: internationaloffice@cavehill.uwi.edu

Faculty
Humanities and Education (Education; History; Linguistics; Literature; Modern Languages; Philosophy); **Law** (Administrative Law; Commercial Law; Criminal Law; International Law; Law; Private Law; Public Law); **Medical Sciences** (Anaesthesiology; Epidemiology; Medicine; Ophthalmology; Paediatrics; Psychiatry and Mental Health; Surgery); **Pure and Applied Sciences** (Biological and Life Sciences; Chemistry; Electronic Engineering; Mathematics; Mathematics and Computer Science; Natural Sciences; Physics); **Social Sciences** (Economics; Government; Management; Social Work; Sociology; Tourism)

School
Business (Business Administration)

Centre
Caribbean Law *(CLIC)* (Law); **Resource Management and Environmental Studies** *(CERMES)*; **Shridath Ramphal** (International Business); **Social and Economic Studies** *(Sir Arthur Lewis Institute)* (Economics; Social Studies)

Research Centre
Chronic Disease (Medicine)

Research Unit
Gender and Development Studies (Development Studies; Gender Studies)

Further Information: St. Augustine Campus (Trinidad and Tobago), Mona Campus (Jamaica).

History: Founded 1962 when the University of the West Indies (UWI) was granted its charter.

Academic Year: August to July

Admission Requirements: General Certificate of Education, CXC's, Associate degree or equivalent

Main Language(s) of Instruction: English

Degrees and Diplomas: *Bachelor's Degree*: **Education; Fine Arts; Law; Natural Sciences.** *Doctor of Medecine*; *Master's Degree*: **Banking; Biology; Caribbean Studies; Chemistry; Computer Science; Cultural Studies; Education; Environmental Studies; Finance; Fine Arts; History; Law; Linguistics; Management; Marketing; Mathematics; Physics; Public Health; Sociology; Sports.** *Ph.D.*

Student Services: Academic Counselling, Canteen, Facilities for disabled people, Health Services, Language Laboratory, Social Counselling, Sports Facilities

Publications: Pelican

Last Updated: 08/04/16

Belarus

STRUCTURE OF HIGHER EDUCATION SYSTEM

Description:

The Belarusian system of higher education includes educational, research and governing institutions that use unified official standards and rules in the processes of teaching, management, assessment and research. Higher education is provided by public (State) and private (non State) accredited higher education institutions (HEIs). Education in public HEIs is free of charge for students who pass the entrance competition. In private HEIs, all students pay tuition fees. Higher education is under the supervision of the Ministry of Education, which is responsible for applying the State Educational Standards. The current higher education system includes 2 stages; after completion of the first stage (4-6 years) a diploma of higher education is issued, after completion of the second stage (1 to 2 years following the first degree) the diploma of Master is issued.

Stages of studies:

University level first stage:
The first stage of higher education provides specialists with both research and professional proficiency and gives direct access to work. The Diploma of Higher Education (Diplom o Vyshem Obrazovanii) is awarded in all fields (except Medicine) after defending a Diploma project and sitting for a final state exam. The nominal length of study is 4 to 6 years (in Medicine and Architecture). The Diploma of Higher Education gives access to Master studies (Magistratura).

University level second stage: *Magistratura*
The second stage of higher education leads to the Diploma of Magistr (Master's degree) following the first stage. Access to these programmes is competitive. The Magistr is awarded after one to two years of study and the presentation and defense of a thesis. The Magistr gives access to postgraduate studies (Aspirantura).

University level third stage: *Aspirantura and Doktorantura*
This stage corresponds to the training of scientific and pedagogical staff. Studies follow a two-step route: 1) the Candidate of Sciences requires at least 3-4 years of study in postgraduate courses, special examinations and the public defense of a thesis. Following this, students are awarded the degree of Kandidat Nauk (Candidate of Sciences); 2) Holders of the Kandidat Nauk can prepare a Doctorate. After following the required research programme and public defense of a doctoral thesis, candidates are awarded the highest scientific degree of Doktor Nauk (Doctor of Sciences). The Dissertation Councils are supervised by the Supreme Attestation Committee (Vishaya Attestatsionnaya Komissiya, VAK) of the Republic of Belarus. It is possible to do doctorate research and sit for a scientific degree without following postgraduate courses. Higher education and research institutions support this type of students and provide them with a supervisor.

ADMISSION TO HIGHER EDUCATION

Admission to university-level studies:

Name of secondary school credential required: Attestat ob Obschem Srednem Obrazovanii

Alternatives to credentials: Diploma of Professional Technical Education, Diploma of Specialized Secondary Education

Admission requirements: Centralized test program (three subjects)

Other requirements: There can be an interview in one subject instead of several exams. The applicant can enter a preparatory department and study for one year before trying to enter the higher education institution.

Foreign students admission:

Definition of foreign student: A foreign citizen who trains at a Belarusian higher education institution and does not have Belarusian citizenship

Admission requirements: Students must hold a secondary school-leaving certificate or an equivalent qualification to that of general secondary school in Belarus.

Entry regulations: Students must hold a visa and have financial guarantees.

Health requirements: A medical certificate is required.

Language proficiency: Foreign students who have no command of the language of instruction can follow a one-year course at a preparatory department of the institution where they study the language of instruction and specialization subjects that are relevant for the chosen course. At the end of the year, they must sit for an examination. Successful students obtain a graduation certificate and are admitted to the basic course of study in the chosen speciality. Those who fail are dismissed from the institution and asked to leave the country.

RECOGNITION OF STUDIES

Quality assurance system:

Recognition of academic and scientific degrees and titles lies within the competence of the Higher Attestation Commission of the Republic of Belarus.The procedure for the assessment of foreign educational qualifications is a function of the National Institute for Higher Education (NIHE).

Qualifications assessment for academic purposes is done by educational institutions or NIHE. Qualifications assessment for professional purposes id done by NIHE.

Bodies dealing with recognition:

Otdel Expertiz i Priznanii Dokumentov (Foreign Credentials Assessment Department, Belarusian ENIC)

Head of Department:Ina Mitskevich
Moskovskaja Str. 15 room 219
Minsk 220007
Tel: +375(17) 228-13-13
Fax: +375(17) 222-83-15
EMail: mitskevich@nihe.by; enicbelarus@gmail.com
WWW: http://www.nihe.bsu.by

Vishaya attestacionnaya komissiya - VAK (Supreme Attestation Committee)

Chair: Gennadij Pal'chik
Prospekt Nezavisimosti, 66
Minsk 220072
Tel: +375(17) 284-06-90
EMail: mail@vak.org.by
WWW: http://www.vak.org.by

Special provisions for recognition:

Recognition for university level studies: Applicants must submit complete official academic documents together with their application form to the institution.

For access to advanced studies and research: Applicants must submit complete official academic documents to the National Institute for Higher Education.

For exercising a profession: Applicants must submit complete official academic documents to the National Institute for Higher Education.

NATIONAL BODIES

Ministerstvo obrazovaniya Respubliki Belarus (Ministry of Education of the Republic of Belarus)

Minister: Mikhail Zhuravkov
Ul. Sovetskaja 9
Minsk 220010
EMail: root@minedu.unibel.by
WWW: http://edu.gov.by

Role of national body: Provides State education policy, controls the quality of education, finances educational institutions in the limits of budget allocations, licenses new institutions, grants accreditation.

Academy for Postgraduate Education
Rector: Andrei Petrovich Monastyrnyj
Ul. Nekrasova 20
Minsk 220040
Tel: +375(17) 285-78-68
Fax: +375(17) 285-78-68
EMail: info@academy.edu.by
WWW: http://www.academy.edu.by

National Institute for Higher Education
Rector: Viktor Gaisenok
Ul. Moskovskaja 15
Minsk 220007
EMail: rector@nihe.by; enicbelarus@gmail.com
WWW: http://www.nihe.bsu.by
Role of national body: Responsible for educational research and information on higher education, the Institute also provides training courses to new rectors, deans and department heads and acts as Belarusian ENIC.

Respublikanskij sovet rektorov vysshykh učebnykh zavedenij (Rectors' Council of Higher Educational Institutes of Belarus)
President: Vladimir Shimov
WWW: http://srrb.niks.by

Data for academic year: 2014-2015
Source: IAU from National Institute for Higher Education, Minsk, November 2014. Bodies 2015.

INSTITUTIONS

PUBLIC INSTITUTIONS

ACADEMY OF PUBLIC ADMINISTRATION UNDER THE AEGIS OF THE PRESIDENT OF THE REPUBLIC OF BELARUS

Akademija Kiravanja pry Prezidence Respubliki Belarus
17 Moskovskaya St, 220007 Minsk
Tel: +375(17) 229-51-11
Fax: +375(17) 222-82-64
EMail: post@pac.by
Website: http://www.pac.by/en

Rector: Marat Zhylinski Tel: +375(17) 229-51-11

Vice-Rector for Academic Affairs: Ihar Hancharonak
Tel: +375(17) 222-83-62 EMail: gancher@pac.by

International Relations: Tatsiana Samasiuk, Director, Centre for International Cooperation and Educational Programmes
Tel: +375(17) 229-53-55 EMail: interbiz@pac.by

Department
Academic and Methodological

Institute
Civil Service (Agricultural Business; Agricultural Management; Business Administration; Economics; Industrial and Organizational Psychology; Industrial Management; International Relations; Law; Management; Modern Languages; Philosophy; Public Administration; Social Studies; Sociology); **Managerial Education** (Administration; Administrative Law; Applied Mathematics; Arabic; Business Administration; Civil Law; Commercial Law; Constitutional Law; Econometrics; Economics; English; French; German; History of Law; Information Management; Latin; Law; Management; Physical Education; Public Administration; Spanish; Turkish)

Research Institute
Theory and Practice of Public Administration

History: Founded 1991, acquired present status and title 1995.

Admission Requirements: Secondary school certificate (Attestat o srednjem obrazovanii), entrance examination and interview

Main Language(s) of Instruction: Russian, Belarusian

Accrediting Agency: Ministry of Education

Degrees and Diplomas: *Diplom o Vyshem Obrazovanii*; *Diplom Magistra*: **Banking; Econometrics; Economics; Finance; International Economics; Law; Management; Political Sciences.** *Kandidat Nauk*: **Economics; Political Sciences.** Also Specialist Diploma; Certificate in improvement of professional skills and Diploma in retraining at the level of higher education

Student Services: IT Centre, Library, Sports Facilities

Student Numbers *2014-2015*: Total: c. 9,000
Last Updated: 03/02/15

ACADEMY OF THE MINISTRY OF INTERNAL AFFAIRS OF THE REPUBLIC OF BELARUS

Akademija Ministerstva Unutrannyh Sprau Respubliki Belarus (AMIA)
6 Masherov Avenue, 220005 Minsk
Tel: +375(17) 284-89-39
Fax: +375(17) 284-89-39
EMail: info@amia.unibel.by
Website: http://www.academy.mia.by

Head of the Academy: Vladimir Bachila
Tel: +375(17) 289-23-30 EMail: pressa@amia.unibel.by

International Relations: Alexander Podupeyko, Deputy Head for International Cooperation and Training of Foreign Specialists

Faculty

Advanced Studies and Retraining (Police Studies); **Criminal and Executive Activities** (Military Science; Sports); **Extra-mural Studies** (Police Studies); **Investigation and Legal Expertise** (Criminal Law; Criminology; Law; Protective Services); **Law** (Law); **Police Training** (Administration; Commercial Law; Criminology; Law; Protective Services); **Scientific and Pedagogical Studies** (Administrative Law; Civil Law; Constitutional Law; Criminal Law; Criminology; Fiscal Law; History; Law; Private Law; Protective Services; Psychology)

History: Founded 1958, acquired present status and title 1995. Trains specialists in the area of law enforcement.

Academic Year: September to July

Admission Requirements: Secondary school certificate (Attestat o srednjem obrazovanii) and entrance examination

Fees: None

Main Language(s) of Instruction: Russian, Belarusian

Accrediting Agency: Ministry of Education

Degrees and Diplomas: *Diplom o Vyshem Obrazovanii*: **Commercial Law; Criminology; Law.** *Diplom Magistra*: **Law.** *Kandidat Nauk*: **Law.**

Student Services: Canteen, Health Services, IT Centre, Library, Residential Facilities, Sports Facilities

Publications: Vestnik of the Academy

Publishing House: Publishing Department

Student Numbers *2014-2015*: Total: c. 300
Last Updated: 03/02/15

BARANOVICHI STATE UNIVERSITY

Baranavickij Dzjaržauny Universitet (BARSU)
vul. Voikava, 21, 225404 Baranoviči
Tel: +375(163) 45-78-60
Fax: +375(163) 45-78-31
EMail: BarSU@brest.by
Website: http://www.barsu.by

Rector: Vassily Ivanovich Kochurko Tel: +375(163) 45-71-09

Vice-rector for Acadmic Affairs: Pavel Popko
Tel: +375(163) 45-75-45

Faculty

Distance Education; **Economics and Law** (Accountancy; Business Administration; Economics; Law; Marketing); **Education and Psychology** (Art Criticism; Education; History; Mathematics Education; Music Education; Pedagogy; Philology; Philosophy; Physical Education; Preschool Education; Psychology; Science Education; Technology Education); **Engineering** (Agricultural Engineering; Agronomy; Animal Husbandry; Automation and Control Engineering; Engineering; Information Technology; Machine Building; Mechanical Engineering; Production Engineering); **Pre-University Training** (Economics; English; Linguistics; Technology); **Slavic and Germanic Languages** (English; German; Literature; Modern Languages; Native Language; Slavic Languages)

Institute

Refresher Training and Re-Training (Accountancy; Economics; Industrial Management; Law; Marketing)

Centre

Turkish Language and Culture (Tourism; Turkish)

History: Founded 2004.

Main Language(s) of Instruction: Russian, Belarusian

Accrediting Agency: Ministry of Education

Degrees and Diplomas: *Diplom o Vyshem Obrazovanii*; *Diplom Magistra*: **Educational Sciences; Engineering; Machine Building; Pedagogy.** *Kandidat Nauk*: **Mechanical Engineering.**

Student Services: IT Centre, Library, Residential Facilities, Sports Facilities

Academic Staff *2014-2015*: Total 390
Student Numbers *2014-2015*: Total: c. 10,000
Last Updated: 03/02/15

BELARUS STATE AGRARIAN AND TECHNICAL UNIVERSITY

Belaruskij Dzjaržauny Agrarny Tehničny Universitet (BSATU)
99 Nezavisimosti Avenue, 220023 Minsk
Tel: +375(17) 267-47-71
Fax: +375(17) 267-41-16
EMail: rektorat@batu.edu.by
Website: http://www.batu.edu.by

Rector: Ivan Shyla
Tel: +375(17) 264-61-91 EMail: rektor@batu.edu.by

First Vice-Rector: Mikalai Ramaniuk Tel: +375(17) 264-47-90

International Relations: Mikhail Hurnovich, Head, Department of International Relations Tel: +375(17) 267-07-84

Faculty

Agro-Mechanical Engineering (Agricultural Engineering; Agricultural Equipment; Mechanical Engineering); **Agro-Power Engineering** (Agricultural Engineering; Automation and Control Engineering; Electrical and Electronic Engineering; Power Engineering); **Business Administration and Management** (Business Administration; Management); **Electrification (Extramural Education)** (Energy Engineering); **Engineering and Technology** (Agricultural Engineering; Food Technology; Safety Engineering); **Farm Machinery** (Agricultural Engineering; Agricultural Equipment; Maintenance Technology); **Mechanization (Extramural Education)** (Agricultural Engineering; Agricultural Equipment; Agriculture; Maintenance Technology; Safety Engineering; Transport Management)

Institute

Professional Development and Retraining of Agribusiness Specialists (Agricultural Business)

History: Founded 1954 as Belarusian Institute of Mechanization and Electrification of Agriculture. Became Belarusian Agrarian Technical University 1992. Acquired present status and title 2000.

Academic Year: September to July

Admission Requirements: General or special secondary school certificate (Attestat o srednjem/specialnom/obrazovanii)

Fees: None

Main Language(s) of Instruction: Russian, Belarusian

Accrediting Agency: Ministry of Agriculture and Food; Ministry of Education

Degrees and Diplomas: *Diplom o Vyshem Obrazovanii*; *Diplom Magistra*: **Agricultural Engineering; Agriculture; Economics; Food Technology; Maintenance Technology.**

Student Services: Academic Counselling, Canteen, Careers Guidance, Cultural Activities, Facilities for disabled people, Health Services, Language Laboratory, Library, Social Counselling, Sports Facilities

Publications: Agropanorama; Proceedings of Conferences

Student Numbers *2014-2015*: Total: c. 15,000
Last Updated: 05/02/15

BELARUS STATE ECONOMICS UNIVERSITY

Belaruskij Dzjaržauny Ekanamičny Universitet (BSEU)
26, Partizanski Ave, 220070 Minsk
Tel: +375(17) 209-88-88 +375(17) 209-88-32
Fax: +375(17) 368-01-60 +375(17) 296-23-66
EMail: umoms@bseu.by
Website: http://www.bseu.by/

Rector: Vladimir Nikolaievich Shimov (2002-)

First Deputy Rector: Viktor Sadovs

International Relations: Natalia Skriba, Head of International Office
Tel: +375(17) 209-79-71 +375(17) 209-79-70
EMail: dinu@bseu.by

Faculty

Commerce, Economics and Management (Business and Commerce; Economics; Management)

School

Accounting and Economics (Accountancy; Banking; Statistics); **Finance and Banking** (Banking; Finance; Information Technology; Taxation); **International Business Communication** (Communication Studies; International Business); **International Economic Relations** (Economic History; International Business; International Economics); **Law** (Civil Law; Commercial Law; Law; Public Law); **Management** (Applied Mathematics; Economics; Management); **Marketing and Logistics** (Marketing; Transport Management)

Higher School

Business and Management (Banking; Business Administration; Economics; Finance; Management); **Tourism** (Management; Tourism)

Campus

Bobruisk (English; German; Mathematics and Computer Science; Romance Languages)

History: Founded 1933. Acquired present status and title 1992.

Fees: Undergraduate studies, 2,800-3,000 per annum; Graduate studies, 3,200-3,600 per annum (US Dollar)

Main Language(s) of Instruction: Russian, Belarusian

Accrediting Agency: Ministry of Education

Degrees and Diplomas: *Diplom o Vyshem Obrazovanii*; *Diplom Magistra*: **Accountancy; Banking; Business Administration; Business and Commerce; Economics; Finance; International Economics; Management; Marketing.** *Kandidat Nauk*: **Accountancy; Civil Law; Commercial Law; Econometrics; Economic and Finance Policy; Economics; Finance; International Economics; International Law; Mathematics; Private Law; Statistics.** *Doktor Nauk*: **Accountancy; Banking; Econometrics; Economic and Finance Policy; Economics; Finance; Mathematics; Statistics.** Some programmes offered in English

Student Services: IT Centre, Library, Residential Facilities, Sports Facilities

Publications: "Belorusskiy ekonomicheskiye" Journal; "The BSEU Herald" Magazine; "Uchet, finansy i audit" Journal

Last Updated: 05/02/15

BELARUSIAN NATIONAL TECHNICAL UNIVERSITY

Belaruski Nacyjanal'ny Tehnichny Universitet (BNTU)

Nezavisimosty Ave., 65, 220013 Minsk

Tel: +375(17) 331-01-15 +375 (29) 753-43-07

Fax: +375(17) 292-91-37

EMail: bntu@bntu.by; press@bntu.by

Website: http://www.bntu.by

Rector: Boris Mikhailavich Khroustalev (2000-)
Tel: +375(17) 292-40-55 EMail: rector@bntu.by

First Vice-Rector: Fiodar I. Pantsialeyenka
Tel: +375(17) 292-76-64 EMail: firstprorektor@bntu.by

International Relations: Julian J. Jarmak, Dean of International Cooperation Faculty Tel: +375(17) 292-74-26 EMail: icd@bntu.by

Faculty

Architecture (Architecture); **Automotive and Tractor** (Automotive Engineering; Design; Petroleum and Gas Engineering; Road Transport; Transport and Communications; Transport Engineering; Transport Management); **Civil Engineering** (Civil Engineering; Construction Engineering; Industrial Engineering); **Engineering and Pedagogy** (Engineering; Pedagogy); **Information Technologies and Robotics** (Artificial Intelligence; Automation and Control Engineering; Information Technology; Robotics; Software Engineering); **Instrument Making** (Engineering; Instrument Making; Laser Engineering; Measurement and Precision Engineering; Safety Engineering; Sports); **International Relations** (International Relations; Slavic Languages); **Management Technology and Humanities** (Administration; Business and Commerce; Energy Engineering; Engineering Management; Management; Packaging Technology; Power Engineering; Taxation; Technology); **Marketing, Management and Entrepreneurship** (Business Administration; Economics; International Economics; Management; Marketing); **Mechanical and Technological Engineering** (Engineering; Materials Engineering; Mechanical Engineering; Metal Techniques; Metallurgical Engineering; Technology); **Mechanical Engineering** (Automation and Control Engineering; Building Technologies; Machine Building; Materials Engineering; Mechanical Engineering; Metal Techniques; Metallurgical Engineering); **Military Engineering** (Automotive Engineering; Building Technologies; Machine Building; Road Engineering); **Mining Engineering and Engineering Ecology** (Environmental Engineering; Mining Engineering); **Power Engineering** (Electrical Engineering; Heating and Refrigeration; Industrial Engineering; Power Engineering); **Power Plant Construction and Engineering Services** (Construction Engineering; Heating and Refrigeration; Hydraulic Engineering; Marine Engineering; Marine Transport; Naval Architecture; Nuclear Engineering; Petroleum and Gas Engineering; Power Engineering); **Soligorsk** (Economics; Industrial Engineering; Mineralogy; Mining Engineering); **Sports** (Physical Education; Sports); **Transport Communication** (Road Engineering; Transport and Communications)

Institute

Distance Education (*International Institute*) (Computer Science; Economics; Information Technology; Management); **Improvement of Professional Skills and Staff Retraining on New Directions of Engineering** (Engineering; Technology Education); **Innovative Technologies** (*Republican Institute*) (Technology); **Staff Training and Retraining on Management and Personnel Development** (*Inter-sectoral Institute of Higher Qualification and Re-Training*) (Human Resources; Management)

Further Information: Also UNESCO Chair "Energy Conservation and Renewable Energies" with Prof. Victor Bashtovoi.

History: Founded 1920 as Belarusian State Polytechnical Institute. In 1991 renamed Belarusian State Polytechnic Academy. Acquired present status and title 2002.

Academic Year: September to June (September-January; February-June)

Admission Requirements: General or special secondary school certificate (Attestat o srednjem/specialnom/obrazovanii) and entrance examination

Fees: National: 1,300-1,600 per annum; Graduate, 4,200 per annum (Euro), International: 1,300-1,600 per annum (Euro)

Main Language(s) of Instruction: Belarusian, French, German, Russian

Accrediting Agency: Ministry of Education

Degrees and Diplomas: *Diplom o Vyshem Obrazovanii*: **Architecture; Automotive Engineering; Civil Engineering; Electronic Engineering; Engineering Management; Environmental Engineering; Information Technology; Laser Engineering; Management; Marketing; Measurement and Precision Engineering; Mechanical Engineering; Metallurgical Engineering; Mining Engineering; Power Engineering; Robotics; Sports; Technology Education; Transport Engineering.** *Diplom Magistra*: **Automation and Control Engineering; Computer Engineering; International Economics; Production Engineering.** *Kandidat Nauk*: **Architecture; Automation and Control Engineering; Automotive Engineering; Biology; Bridge Engineering; Building Technologies; Civil Engineering; Computer Engineering; Computer Graphics; Construction Engineering; Earth Sciences; Ecology; Economics; Electrical Engineering; Electronic Engineering; Engineering; Geological Engineering; Heating and Refrigeration; Hydraulic Engineering; Information Management; Laser Engineering; Machine Building; Materials Engineering; Mathematics; Measurement and Precision Engineering; Mechanics; Medical Technology; Metallurgical Engineering; Mining Engineering; Optical Technology; Optics; Pedagogy; Petroleum and Gas Engineering; Physics; Power Engineering; Road Engineering; Robotics; Rural Planning; Social Sciences; Taxation; Thermal Engineering; Thermal Physics; Town Planning; Transport Engineering; Water Science.** *Doktor Nauk*: **Architecture; Automotive Engineering; Biology; Bridge Engineering; Building Technologies; Civil Engineering; Computer Engineering; Construction Engineering; Earth Sciences; Ecology; Economics; Electrical Engineering; Engineering; Heating and Refrigeration; Hydraulic Engineering; Information Management; Laser Engineering; Machine Building; Management; Materials Engineering; Mathematics; Measurement and Precision Engineering; Mechanical Engineering; Mechanics; Metallurgical Engineering; Optics; Pedagogy; Petroleum and Gas Engineering; Physics; Power Engineering; Road Engineering; Rural Planning;**

Taxation; Thermal Engineering; Town Planning; Transport Engineering; Water Science. Also some courses in English; Russian as a Foreign Language Programme.

Student Services: Academic Counselling, Canteen, Careers Guidance, Cultural Activities, Foreign Studies Centre, Health Services, Language Laboratory, Library, Residential Facilities, Social Counselling, Sports Facilities

Publications: Energetika/Power Engineering; VESTNIK BNTU

Publishing House: Yes

Student Numbers *2014-2015 14538*: Total: c. 35,000
Last Updated: 04/02/15

BELARUSIAN STATE ACADEMY OF ARTS

Belaruskaja Dzjaržaunaja Akademija Mastastvau (BSAA)
Prospect Nezavisimosti 81, 220012 Minsk
Tel: +375(17) 292-15-42 292
Fax: +375(17) 292-20-41
EMail: info@bdam.by
Website: http://bdam.by/

Rector: Mikhail Barazna (2010-)

Vice President for Academic Affairs: Bohan Elena

International Relations: Ekaterina Kenigsberg, Head of the International Relations Department
Tel: +375(17) 202-11-21 EMail: international@bdam.by

Faculty

Design and Decorative Arts and Applied Arts (Art History; Design; Graphic Arts; Graphic Design; Handicrafts; Industrial Design; Interior Design; Painting and Drawing; Sculpture; Textile Design); **Film-Making** (Art History; Art Management; Cinema and Television; Film; Sound Engineering (Acoustics)); **Fine Arts** (Fine Arts; Graphic Arts; Painting and Drawing; Sculpture; Visual Arts); **Further Training and Retraining** (Design; Fine Arts); **Theatre** (Acting; Singing; Speech Studies; Theatre)

Department

General Disciplines Studies *(Interfaculty)* (Art History; Arts and Humanities; Fine Arts; Physical Education)

History: Founded 1945, reorganized 1991 as Belarus Academy of Arts, and acquired present status and title 2001.

Fees: 3,000-5,300 per annum (US Dollar)

Main Language(s) of Instruction: Russian, Belarusian

Accrediting Agency: Ministry of Education

Degrees and Diplomas: *Diplom o Vyshem Obrazovanii*: **Acting; Art Criticism; Art History; Cinema and Television; Design; Film; Fine Arts; Graphic Design; Handicrafts; Painting and Drawing; Sculpture; Theatre.** *Diplom Magistra*: **Art History; Design; Film; Theatre.** *Kandidat Nauk*: **Aesthetics; Architecture; Design; Film; Fine Arts; Handicrafts; Theatre.** *Doktor Nauk*: **Architecture; Film; Fine Arts; Handicrafts; Theatre.**

Student Services: Library, Residential Facilities

Student Numbers *2014-2015*: Total: c. 1,300
Last Updated: 04/02/15

BELARUSIAN STATE ACADEMY OF MUSIC

Belaruskaja Dzjaržaunaja Akademija Muzyki (BGAM)
vul. Internaciyanalnaja, 30, 220030 Minsk
Tel: +375(17) 327-49-42
Fax: +375(17) 206-55-01
EMail: uo-gam@kultura.by; international@tut.by
Website: http://www.bgam.edu.by

Rector: Ekaterina Nikolaevna Dulova
Tel: +375(17) 327-49-42 EMail: rector@bgam.edu.by

Prorector for Academic Affairs: Pyotr F. Dudarenko

International Relations: Aleksandra Vitalievna Makarova, Head, International Relations
Tel: +375(17) 328-55-02 EMail: international@tut.by

Division

Interdepartmental Studies (Art History; Arts and Humanities; Conducting; Modern Languages; Music Education; Musical Instruments; Performing Arts; Physical Education; Social Sciences)

Department

Folk Instruments (Conducting; Music Education; Musical Instruments; Pedagogy); **Mogilyov Branch** (Conducting; Music Education; Musical Instruments); **Orchestra** (Musical Instruments); **Piano, Musicology and Composition** (Computer Science; Music; Music Education; Music Theory and Composition; Musical Instruments; Musicology; Pedagogy; Philosophy); **Preparatory Education; Vocal and Choir** (Conducting; Opera; Singing); **Vocational Training and Retraining**

Further Information: Branch in Mogiliev

History: Founded 1932, acquired present status and title 1992.

Academic Year: September to June (September-January; February-June)

Admission Requirements: General or special secondary school certificate (Attestat o srednjem/specialnom/obrazovanii). Interview for foreign students. Knowledge of Russian language required, except for performance Diploma programmes

Fees: National: None, International: Undergraduate, 2,500 per annum; Graduate and postgraduate, 4,000 (US Dollar)

Main Language(s) of Instruction: Russian, Belarusian

Accrediting Agency: Ministry of Education

Degrees and Diplomas: *Diplom o Vyshem Obrazovanii*: **Conducting; Music; Music Education; Music Theory and Composition; Musical Instruments; Musicology; Singing.** *Diplom Magistra*: **Music; Music Education.** *Kandidat Nauk*: **Musicology.** *Doktor Nauk*: **Musicology.**

Student Services: Academic Counselling, Canteen, Careers Guidance, Cultural Activities, Facilities for disabled people, Foreign Studies Centre, Health Services, IT Centre, Language Laboratory, Library, Social Counselling, Sports Facilities

Publications: Scientific Papers; Vesti Belaruskaja Akademii Musyki (Belarus Academy of Music News)

Publishing House: Belarussian State Academy of Music Press

Student Numbers *2014-2015*: Total: c. 1,200
Last Updated: 04/02/15

BELARUSIAN STATE AGRICULTURAL ACADEMY

Belaruskaja Dzjaržaunaja Sel'skagaspadarčaja Akademija (BSAA)
vul. Michurina, 5, 213407 Gorki
Tel: +375(29) 79641
Fax: +375(29) 79641
EMail: kancel@baa.by
Website: http://www.baa.by/

Rector: Pavel A. Saskevich
Tel: +375(2233) 5-95-45 EMail: rector@baa.by

Vice Rector for Academic Affairs and Information: Sergei Gudkov Tel: +375(2233) 5-99-84

International Relations: Svetlana Naskova, Head of International Office Tel: +375(2233) 79664

Faculty

Accountancy (Accountancy; Finance); **Agro-Ecology** (Agriculture; Applied Chemistry; Ecology; Fruit Production; Soil Science; Vegetable Production); **Agronomy** (Agronomy; Crop Production); **Business and Law** (Business and Commerce; Economics; Law; Marketing; Social Sciences); **Economics** (Agricultural Business; Agricultural Economics; Agricultural Management; Econometrics; Economic and Finance Policy; Economics; International Economics; International Relations; Law; Marketing); **Farm Mechanization** (Agricultural Engineering; Agricultural Equipment; Mechanical Equipment and Maintenance; Water Science); **Land Reclamation** (Agricultural Engineering; Agricultural Management; Rural Planning; Water Management); **Land Use and Planning** (Rural Planning; Soil Conservation; Surveying and Mapping); **Zoo Engineering** (Animal Husbandry; Biotechnology; Fishery; Meat and Poultry)

Higher School
Agribusiness (Accountancy; Agricultural Business; Business Administration; Economics; Finance; Management; Marketing)

Further Information: Also Preparatory Department; Branches in Pinsk and Polessky

History: Founded 1840 as Gory-Gorecky Agricultural School. Reorganized 1928 as Belarusian Agricultural Academy incorporating Belarusian Institute of Agriculture (founded 1922). Acquired present status and title 1997.

Academic Year: September to June (September-January; February-June)

Admission Requirements: Secondary school certificate (Attestat o srednjem obrazovanii) and entrance examination

Fees: National: None, International: 1,850 (except for Doctoral programmes, 2,200 per annum) (US Dollar)

Main Language(s) of Instruction: Russian, Belarusian

Accrediting Agency: Ministry of Education

Degrees and Diplomas: *Diploma of Professional Technical Education*; *Diplom o Vyshem Obrazovanii*: **Accountancy; Agricultural Business; Agricultural Engineering; Agricultural Equipment; Agriculture; Agronomy; Animal Husbandry; Applied Chemistry; Business Administration; Business and Commerce; Business Computing; Crop Production; Ecology; Economics; Finance; Fishery; Food Science; Fruit Production; Horticulture; International Economics; Landscape Architecture; Law; Management; Marketing; Plant and Crop Protection; Rural Planning; Social Sciences; Soil Science; Vegetable Production; Water Management.** *Diplom Magistra*: **Accountancy; Agricultural Engineering; Agricultural Equipment; Agronomy; Animal Husbandry; Ecology; Economics; Food Science; Management; Plant and Crop Protection; Rural Planning; Soil Management; Soil Science; Statistics.** *Kandidat Nauk*: **Animal Husbandry; Soil Management; Soil Science.** *Doktor Nauk*: **Agriculture.**

Student Services: Canteen, Careers Guidance, Cultural Activities, Health Services, Language Laboratory, Library, Nursery Care, Residential Facilities, Social Counselling, Sports Facilities

Publishing house: Gorki Printing House

Academic Staff *2014-2015*	**TOTAL**
FULL-TIME	**600**
Student Numbers *2014-2015*	
All (Foreign included)	c. **6,500**
FOREIGN ONLY	**500**

Last Updated: 04/02/15

BELARUSIAN STATE MEDICAL UNIVERSITY

Belaruskij Dzjaržauny Medycynski Universitet (BSMU)

83, Dzerzinski Ave, 220116 Minsk
Tel: +375(17) 272-61-96
Fax: +375(17) 272-61-97
EMail: bsmu@bsmu.by
Website: http://www.bsmu.by/

Rector: Anatol Sikorski
Tel: +375(17) 272-61-96 EMail: rektor@bsmu.by

First Vice-Rector: Siarhei Zhavaranak
Tel: +375(17) 272-64-98 EMail: primprorektor@bsmu.by

International Relations: Boyko Varvara Vadimovna, Head, Department of International Relations
Tel: +375(17) 277-16-72 EMail: intdept@bsmu.by

Faculty
Career Guidance and pre-University Training (Biological and Life Sciences; Medicine); **Dentistry** (Child Care and Development; Dental Hygiene; Dentistry; Oral Pathology; Periodontics; Plastic Surgery); **General Medicine** (Anaesthesiology; Cardiology; Endocrinology; Gynaecology and Obstetrics; Haematology; Hepatology; Medicine; Nephrology; Orthopaedics; Physical Therapy; Surgery; Venereology); **Medical Studiesl for International Students** (Anatomy; Biochemistry; Biology; Cell Biology; Embryology and Reproduction Biology; Genetics; Histology; Hygiene; Medicine; Microbiology; Ophthalmology; Organic Chemistry; Otorhinolaryngology; Paediatrics; Pathology; Pharmacology; Physiology; Psychiatry and Mental Health; Surgery; Tropical Medicine); **Military Medicine** (Medicine); **Paediatrics** (Paediatrics); **Pharmacy** (Pharmacy); **Preventive Medicine** (Epidemiology; Medicine; Social and Preventive Medicine; Virology)

Further Information: Also courses for foreign students. Preparatory department for postgraduate Medical Training. Postgraduate research courses

History: Founded 1921 as part of Department of Medicine of Belarus State University, reorganized as Minsk State Medical Institute 1930, and acquired present status and title 2002.

Academic Year: September to June (September-January; February-June)

Admission Requirements: General or special secondary school certificate (Attestat o srednjem/specialnom/obrazovanii)

Fees: 2,500-4,800 per annum (US Dollar)

Main Language(s) of Instruction: Russian

Accrediting Agency: Ministry of Health; Ministry of Education

Degrees and Diplomas: *Diplom o Vyshem Obrazovanii*: **Dentistry; Medicine; Paediatrics; Pharmacy; Social and Preventive Medicine.** *Diplom Magistra*: **Anaesthesiology; Anatomy; Biochemistry; Cell Biology; Dentistry; Epidemiology; Forensic Medicine and Dentistry; Gynaecology and Obstetrics; Histology; Hygiene; Immunology; Microbiology; Nephrology; Oncology; Ophthalmology; Orthopaedics; Otorhinolaryngology; Paediatrics; Pathology; Pharmacology; Pharmacy; Physiology; Pneumology; Psychiatry and Mental Health; Radiology; Surgery; Urology; Venereology; Virology.** *Kandidat Nauk*: **Anaesthesiology; Anatomy; Biochemistry; Biological and Life Sciences; Cardiology; Cell Biology; Dentistry; Ecology; Embryology and Reproduction Biology; Endocrinology; Epidemiology; Forensic Medicine and Dentistry; Gynaecology and Obstetrics; Health Sciences; Histology; Hygiene; Immunology; Microbiology; Nephrology; Neurology; Oncology; Ophthalmology; Orthopaedics; Otorhinolaryngology; Paediatrics; Parasitology; Pathology; Pharmacology; Physical Therapy; Physiology; Psychiatry and Mental Health; Public Health; Radiology; Rehabilitation and Therapy; Rheumatology; Sports Medicine; Surgery; Urology; Venereology.** *Doktor Nauk*: **Medicine.** Also Clinical Residency.

Student Services: Academic Counselling, Canteen, Cultural Activities, Foreign Studies Centre, Health Services, IT Centre, Language Laboratory, Library, Nursery Care, Residential Facilities, Social Counselling, Sports Facilities

Publications: Belarusian Medical Journal; Proceedings of Minsk State Medical University

Student Numbers *2014-2015*: Total: c. 7,050
Last Updated: 05/02/15

BELARUSIAN STATE PEDAGOGICAL UNIVERSITY NAMED AFTER MAXIM TANK

Belaruskij Dzjaržauny Pedagogiskij Universitet imja Maksima Tanka (BSPU)

Sovetskaya str, 18, 220050 Minsk
Tel: +375(17)123-45-67
Fax: +375(17)123-45-67
EMail: bspu@bspu.unibel.by; webmaster@bspu.unibel.by
Website: http://www.bspu.unibel.by

Rector: Alexander Zhuk (2014-) Tel: +375(17) 226-40-20

First Vice-Rector: Alexander Andaraĭ Tel: +375(17) 226-56-23

Faculty
Aesthetic and Communications (Art Education; Communication Studies; Computer Graphics; Fine Arts; Music Education; Performing Arts); **Belarus and Russian Philology** (Cultural Studies; Literature; Philology; Russian; Slavic Languages); **History** (History); **Mathematics** (Mathematics; Mathematics and Computer Science); **Natural Sciences** (Biology; Chemistry; Geography; Natural Sciences); **Physical Education** (Leisure Studies; Physical Education; Tourism); **Physics** (Computer Science; Physics); **Pre-University Training** (Higher Education; Pedagogy); **Preschool Education and Communications** (Communication Studies; Preschool Education); **Primary Education and Communications** (Communication Studies; Primary Education); **Psychology** (Educational Psychology; Psychology; Social Psychology); **Socio-pedagogical**

Technologies (Humanities and Social Science Education; Pedagogy; Social Work); **Special Education** (Rehabilitation and Therapy; Special Education; Speech Therapy and Audiology; Sports)

History: Founded 1914, acquired present status and title 1994. Formerly known as the Minsk State Pedagogical Institute named after Maxim Gorky Moscow State Pedagogical Institut.

Academic Year: September to June

Admission Requirements: General or special secondary school certificate (Attestat o srednjem/specialnom/obrazovanii) and entrance examination

Main Language(s) of Instruction: Russian, Belarusian

Accrediting Agency: Ministry of Education

Degrees and Diplomas: *Diplom o Vyshem Obrazovanii*; *Diplom Magistra*: **Art Criticism; Art Education; Biology; Chemistry; Communication Studies; Computer Education; Educational Administration; History; Humanities and Social Science Education; Linguistics; Mathematics; Mathematics Education; Music Education; Native Language Education; Pedagogy; Physical Education; Physics; Preschool Education; Primary Education; Psychology; Psychotherapy; Science Education; Special Education; Teacher Training.** *Kandidat Nauk*: **Aesthetics; Archaeology; Biochemistry; Biological and Life Sciences; Botany; Cultural Studies; Developmental Psychology; Economics; Educational Psychology; Entomology; Environmental Studies; Folklore; Genetics; Geography; Geography (Human); History; Inorganic Chemistry; Linguistics; Literature; Mathematics; Modern Languages; Organic Chemistry; Pedagogy; Philosophy; Physical Education; Physics; Plant and Crop Protection; Political Sciences; Psychology; Radiophysics; Russian; Social Psychology; Soil Science; Zoology.** *Doktor Nauk*: **Cultural Studies; Developmental Psychology; Educational Psychology; Geography; History; Literature; Pedagogy; Physical Education; Physics; Psychology; Russian; Social Psychology.**

Student Services: Academic Counselling, Canteen, Careers Guidance, Cultural Activities, Health Services, IT Centre, Library, Social Counselling, Sports Facilities, eLibrary

Publications: Nastaunik

Publishing House: Press service BSPU

Last Updated: 05/02/15

BELARUSIAN STATE TECHNOLOGICAL UNIVERSITY

Belaruskij Dzjaržauny Tehnalagičny Universitet (BSTU)

Sverdlov st., 13a, 220006 Minsk
Tel: +375(17) 327-62-17 +375(17) 327-30-21
Fax: +375(17) 227-62-17 +375(17) 327-30-21
EMail: root@belstu.by
Website: http://www.bstu.unibel.by

Rector: Ivan Zharski (1987-)

Faculty

Chemical Technology and Engineering (Chemical Engineering; Chemistry; Technology); **Economic Engineering** (Accountancy; Economics; Management; Marketing); **Forestry** (Forestry; Landscape Architecture); **Forestry Engineering and Wood Technology** (Forestry; Machine Building; Power Engineering; Wood Technology); **Information Technology** (Computer Graphics; Computer Science; History; Information Technology; Political Sciences); **Organic Substances Technology** (Biotechnology; Ecology; Organic Chemistry); **Printing and Publishing** (Printing and Printmaking; Publishing and Book Trade)

History: Founded 1930 as Forestry Institute, became Forestry Technical Institute, 1932, Belarusian Institute of Technology, 1961. Acquired present status and title 1993.

Academic Year: September to June

Admission Requirements: General or special secondary school certificate (Attestat o srednjem/specialnom/obrazovanii)

Fees: 1,600 (US Dollar)

Main Language(s) of Instruction: Russian, Belarusian

Accrediting Agency: Ministry of Education

Degrees and Diplomas: *Diplom o Vyshem Obrazovanii*; *Diplom Magistra*: **Automation and Control Engineering; Biotechnology; Chemical Engineering; Computer Engineering; Computer Science; Cosmetology; Earth Sciences; Ecology; Electronic Engineering; Forest Management; Forest Products; Forestry; Information Management; Inorganic Chemistry; Journalism; Machine Building; Materials Engineering; Organic Chemistry; Plant and Crop Protection; Polymer and Plastics Technology; Printing and Printmaking; Wood Technology.** *Kandidat Nauk*: **Applied Chemistry; Automation and Control Engineering; Biotechnology; Chemical Engineering; Computer Engineering; Computer Science; Ecology; Forest Management; Forest Products; Forestry; Information Management; Information Technology; Inorganic Chemistry; Machine Building; Materials Engineering; Microbiology; Nanotechnology; Organic Chemistry; Physical Chemistry; Physics; Plant and Crop Protection; Polymer and Plastics Technology; Printing and Printmaking; Solid State Physics; Thermal Engineering; Wood Technology.** *Doktor Nauk*: **Agriculture; Arts and Humanities; Biological and Life Sciences; Geography; Geology; History; Mathematics; Physics.** Also Graduate Engineer in Science, 5 yrs

Student Services: Canteen, Careers Guidance, Cultural Activities, Health Services, Nursery Care, Residential Facilities, Social Counselling, Sports Facilities

Publications: Chemistry and Inorganic Substances Technology; Chemistry and Organic Substances Technology; Economics and Management; Forestry; Physico-Mathematical and Computer Sciences; Political Science, Philosophy, History and Linguistics; Printing and Publishing; Teaching and Teaching Methods; Timber and Wood-Working Industry

Academic Staff *2014-2015*: Total: c. 650

Student Numbers *2014-2015*: Total 13,000

Last Updated: 06/02/15

BELARUSIAN STATE UNIVERSITY

Belaruskij Dzjaržauny Universitet (BSU)

4 Nezavisimosti avenue, 220030 Minsk
Tel: +375(17) 209-50-85
Fax: +375(17) 226-59-40
EMail: bsu@bsu.by
Website: http://www.bsu.by

Rector: Sergey V. Ablameyko (2003-)
Tel: +375(17) 209-5203
EMail: rector@bsu.by; Ablameyko@bsu.by

Vice-rector for Administrative and Maintenance Work: Vladimir V. Rogovitsky Tel: +375(17) 209-52-31

Faculty

Applied Mathematics and Computer Science (Applied Mathematics; Computer Science); **Biology** (Biochemistry; Biology; Botany; Ecology; Genetics; Microbiology; Molecular Biology; Physiology; Zoology); **Chemistry** (Analytical Chemistry; Chemistry; Inorganic Chemistry; Organic Chemistry); **Economics** (Economics); **Geography** (Earth Sciences; Ecology; Geography; Geology; Soil Science); **History** (Archaeology; Contemporary History; Ethnology; History; Modern History); **International Relations** (European Union Law; International Law; International Relations; Private Law); **Law** (Law); **Liberal Education** (Clinical Psychology; Cultural Studies; Design; Ecology; Health Administration; Information Technology; Translation and Interpretation); **Mathematics and Mechanics** (Mathematics; Mechanics); **Military Faculty** (Military Science); **Philology** (Applied Linguistics; English; German; Linguistics; Literature; Philology; Romance Languages; Russian; Slavic Languages); **Philosophy and Social Studies** (Philosophy; Psychology; Social Sciences; Sociology); **Physics** (Physics); **Pre-University Education** (Chemistry; Economics; Literature; Mathematics; Physics; Regional Studies; Russian); **Radiophysics and Computer Technology** (Computer Science; Electronic Engineering; Radiophysics)

School

Business and Management of Technology

Institute

Journalism (Journalism); **Management and Social Technologies** (Business Administration; Economics; Finance; Law; Management; Real Estate; Rehabilitation and Therapy; Social Work); **Theology named after Sts. Cyril and Methodius** (Theology)

History: Founded 1921.

Academic Year: September to June

Admission Requirements: Secondary school certificate (Attestat o srednjem/specialnom/obrazovanii)

Fees: 1,500-3,000 per annum (US Dollar)

Main Language(s) of Instruction: Belarusian, Russian

Accrediting Agency: Ministry of Education

Degrees and Diplomas: *Diplom o Vyshem Obrazovanii*; *Diplom Magistra*: **Actuarial Science; Anthropology; Applied Mathematics; Archaeology; Archiving; Art Criticism; Banking; Biochemistry; Biology; Business Administration; Chemistry; Chinese; Computer Science; Cultural Studies; Design; Ecology; Economics; Educational Sciences; Electronic Engineering; English; Ethnology; Finance; French; Geography; Geography (Human); Geology; German; Heritage Preservation; History; Human Resources; Information Management; Information Sciences; International Business; International Economics; International Law; International Relations; Italian; Journalism; Law; Linguistics; Literature; Management; Mathematics; Mathematics and Computer Science; Mechanics; Microbiology; Mineralogy; Museum Studies; Oriental Languages; Oriental Studies; Pedagogy; Pharmacology; Philology; Philosophy; Physics; Political Sciences; Psychology; Radiophysics; Restoration of Works of Art; Romance Languages; Russian; Science Education; Slavic Languages; Social Work; Sociology; Software Engineering; Surveying and Mapping; Tourism; Translation and Interpretation; Transport Management.** *Kandidat Nauk*: **Economics; International Economics; International Law; International Relations; Oriental Languages; Oriental Studies; Tourism.** *Doktor Nauk*: **Actuarial Science; Administrative Law; Aesthetics; Analytical Chemistry; Anthropology; Applied Mathematics; Archaeology; Biochemistry; Biology; Biotechnology; Bulgarian; Chemistry; Chinese; Civil Law; Commercial Law; Communication Studies; Computer Science; Constitutional Law; Criminal Law; Criminology; Cultural Studies; Czech; Demography and Population; Design; Ecology; Econometrics; Economics; Educational Psychology; Educational Sciences; Electronic Engineering; English; Ethics; Ethnology; European Union Law; Fiscal Law; Folklore; French; Geochemistry; Geography; Geology; German; History; History of Law; Industrial and Production Economics; Information Management; Information Sciences; Inorganic Chemistry; International Economics; International Law; International Relations; Italian; Journalism; Labour Law; Laser Engineering; Law; Literature; Logic; Management; Mathematical Physics; Mathematics; Mathematics and Computer Science; Mechanics; Microbiology; Mineralogy; Museum Studies; Nuclear Physics; Optics; Organic Chemistry; Oriental Languages; Oriental Studies; Peace and Disarmament; Pedagogy; Pharmacology; Philology; Philosophy; Physical Chemistry; Physical Education; Physics; Political Sciences; Private Law; Psychology; Radiophysics; Restoration of Works of Art; Russian; Science Education; Slavic Languages; Social Psychology; Social Studies; Social Work; Sociology; Software Engineering; Soil Science; Sports; Statistics; Surveying and Mapping; Thermal Engineering; Tourism; Translation and Interpretation; Transport Management.**

Student Services: Academic Counselling, Canteen, Careers Guidance, Cultural Activities, Facilities for disabled people, Foreign Studies Centre, Health Services, Language Laboratory, Nursery Care, Social Counselling, Sports Facilities

Publications: Belarusian Historical Magazine; International Relations; Sociology

Publishing House: Publishing Centre

Last Updated: 06/02/15

BELARUSIAN STATE UNIVERSITY OF CULTURE AND ARTS

Belaruskij Dzjaržauny Universitet Kul'tury I Mastatstvau (BUK)

Rabkorovskaya Street, 17, 220007 Minsk
Tel: +375(17) 222-83-71 +375(17) 222-24-10
Fax: +375(17) 222-24-09 +375(17) 222-24-09
EMail: buk@buk.by; bukinterdep@yahoo.com
Website: http://www.buk.by/

Rector: Yuri P. Cooper (2013-)
Tel: +375(17) 222-83-71 EMail: rector@buk.by

Vice-Rector for General Affairs: Nasenov Vladimir Selivestrovich
Tel: +375(17) 256-08-74
EMail: total@buk.by; bguki-teh@yandex.ru

International Relations: Vadim V. Kryshtanosav, Head of International Relations Tel: +375(17) 222-83-50

Faculty

Culturology and Socio-Cultural Activity (Art Criticism; Cultural Studies; Information Technology; International Relations; Management; Philosophy); **Further Education**; **Information and Documentary Communications** (Heritage Preservation; Information Sciences; Information Technology; Library Science; Museum Studies); **Musical Art** (Conducting; Music; Music Education; Musical Instruments; Singing); **Part-time Training (FPT)** (Arts and Humanities; Cultural Studies; Fine Arts; Information Sciences; Performing Arts; Social Sciences); **Traditional Belarusian Culture and Contemporary Art** (Arts and Humanities; Dance; Ethnology; Folklore; Performing Arts; Theatre)

History: Founded 1975 as as Minsk Institute of Culture, acquired present status and title 2004.

Academic Year: September to June

Fees: National: 300 per annum (US Dollar), International: 3,600-4350 per annum for full-time mode; 2,250-3300 per annum for distance mode (US Dollar)

Main Language(s) of Instruction: Russian, Belarusian

Accrediting Agency: Ministry of Education

Degrees and Diplomas: *Diplom o Vyshem Obrazovanii*: **Art Criticism; Cultural Studies; Dance; Fine Arts; Folklore; Heritage Preservation; Library Science; Museum Studies; Musical Instruments; Singing; Social Sciences.** *Diplom Magistra*: **Art Criticism; Art Management; Cultural Studies; Heritage Preservation; Library Science; Museum Studies; Welfare and Protective Services.** *Kandidat Nauk*: **Art History; Cultural Studies; Heritage Preservation; Library Science; Museum Studies; Welfare and Protective Services.** *Doktor Nauk*: **Art History; Cultural Studies; Heritage Preservation; Library Science; Museum Studies; Welfare and Protective Services.**

Student Services: Academic Counselling, Canteen, Careers Guidance, Language Laboratory, Library, Nursery Care, Residential Facilities, Social Counselling, Sports Facilities

Publications: Vestnik Belaruskaga Dzarzaunaga Universiteta Kultury i Mastatstvau

Academic Staff *2014-2015*: Total: c. 300

Student Numbers *2014-2015*: Total: c. 5,000

Last Updated: 09/02/15

BELARUSIAN STATE UNIVERSITY OF INFORMATICS AND RADIOELECTRONICS

Belaruskij Dzjaržauny Universitet Informatyki i Radyjoelektroniki (BSUIR)

P. Browka Str., 6, 220013 Minsk
Tel: +375(17) 293-23-33
Fax: +375(17) 293-23-33
EMail: remina@bsuir.by; shuam@bsuir.by; edu@bsuir.by
Website: http://www.bsuir.by

Rector: Mikhail Paylavich Batura (2000-)
Tel: +375(17) 292-32-35 EMail: rector@bsuir.by

First Vice-Rector: Anatoly Osipov
Tel: +375(17) 292-42-51 EMail: osipov@bsuir.by

International Relations: Anna Titovich, Head of Department
Tel: +375(17) 293-85-72
EMail: titovich@bsuir.by; international@bsuir.by

Faculty

Computer Systems and Networks (Computer Engineering; Computer Networks; Computer Science; Information Technology; Software Engineering); **Computer-Aided Design** (Computer Engineering; Computer Graphics; Electronic Engineering; Information Technology; Medical Technology; Optical Technology; Safety Engineering); **Continuous and Distance Training** (Artificial Intelligence; Automation and Control Engineering; Computer Science;

Data Processing; Engineering; Information Technology; Marketing; Software Engineering); **Engineering and Economics** (Business Computing; E- Business/Commerce; Economics; Information Technology; Marketing; Transport Management); **Extra-mural Training** (Automation and Control Engineering; Computer Engineering; Computer Graphics; Computer Networks; Economics; Electronic Engineering; Industrial Management; Information Sciences; Information Technology; Microelectronics; Nanotechnology; Radio and Television Broadcasting; Safety Engineering; Telecommunications Engineering); **Information Technology and Control** (Artificial Intelligence; Automation and Control Engineering; Electronic Engineering; Industrial Engineering; Information Technology); **Military** (Engineering; Information Technology; Telecommunications Engineering); **Pre-University Preparation** (Computer Science; Mathematics; Physics; Russian); **Radioengineering and Electronics** (Automation and Control Engineering; Electronic Engineering; Materials Engineering; Microelectronics; Nanotechnology); **Telecommunication** (Computer Networks; Information Technology; Measurement and Precision Engineering; Multimedia; Radio and Television Broadcasting; Telecommunications Engineering)

Further Information: Also courses for foreign students. Distance and part time learning also available.

History: Founded 1964 as Minsk Radioengineering Institute, acquired present status and title 1993.

Academic Year: September to June (September-January; February-June)

Admission Requirements: General or special secondary school certificate (Attestat o srednjem/specialnom/obrazovanii) and entrance examination

Fees: Russian-taught programmes, 2,000-3,300 per annum; English-taught programmes, 4,000-5,000 (US Dollar)

Main Language(s) of Instruction: Russian, Belarusian

Accrediting Agency: Ministry of Education

Degrees and Diplomas: *Diplom o Vyshem Obrazovanii*; *Diplom Magistra*: **Applied Mathematics; Artificial Intelligence; Automation and Control Engineering; Business Administration; Computer Engineering; Computer Networks; Computer Science; Ecology; Econometrics; Economics; Electronic Engineering; Engineering; Industrial and Organizational Psychology; Information Management; Information Technology; Instrument Making; Materials Engineering; Mathematics; Measurement and Precision Engineering; Medical Technology; Microelectronics; Microwaves; Nanotechnology; Occupational Health; Optical Technology; Radiophysics; Safety Engineering; Software Engineering; Sound Engineering (Acoustics); Telecommunications Engineering.** *Kandidat Nauk*: **Automation and Control Engineering; Computer Engineering; Computer Graphics; Computer Networks; Computer Science; Econometrics; Economics; Electrical Engineering; Electronic Engineering; Information Management; Information Technology; Materials Engineering; Mathematics; Measurement and Precision Engineering; Medical Technology; Microelectronics; Microwaves; Nanotechnology; Optics; Radio and Television Broadcasting; Radiophysics; Safety Engineering; Software Engineering; Solid State Physics; Telecommunications Engineering.** *Doktor Nauk*: **Automation and Control Engineering; Computer Engineering; Computer Graphics; Computer Networks; Computer Science; Econometrics; Economics; Electrical Engineering; Electronic Engineering; Information Management; Information Technology; Materials Engineering; Medical Technology; Microelectronics; Microwaves; Nanotechnology; Optics; Radio and Television Broadcasting; Radiophysics; Safety Engineering; Software Engineering; Solid State Physics; Telecommunications Engineering.** Some English-taught programmes: 1st Degree in Information Technology, Telecommunications Engineering, Information Technology, Automation and Control Engineering, Data Processing. Master's Degree in Nanotechnology, Electronic Engineering, Telecommunication Engineering, Computer Networks, Information Management, Information Technology.

Student Services: Academic Counselling, Canteen, Careers Guidance, Cultural Activities, Facilities for disabled people, Foreign Studies Centre, Health Services, IT Centre, Language Laboratory, Library, Residential Facilities, Sports Facilities

Publications: Doklady Belorusskogo gosudartvennogo universiteta informatiki i radioelektroniki

Publishing House: Publishing Department of University

Academic Staff *2014-2015*	**TOTAL**
FULL-TIME	c. **2,200**
Student Numbers *2014-2015*	
All (Foreign included)	c. **16,000**
FOREIGN ONLY	**450**

Last Updated: 09/02/15

BELARUSIAN STATE UNIVERSITY OF PHYSICAL EDUCATION

Belaruskij Dzjaržauny Universitet Fizičnaj Kul'tury (BSUPC)

Pobediteley Ave., 105, 220020 Minsk
Tel: +375(17) 250-80-08 +375(17) 250-30-84
Fax: +375(17) 250-80-08
EMail: mobgufk@mail.ru
Website: http://www.sportedu.by

Rector: Gregory P. Kosyachenko
Tel: +375(17) 250-68-78 EMail: rektor@sportedu.by

Vice-Rector for Academic Affairs: Elena Filgina

Faculty

Physical Education and Tourism (Anatomy; Biochemistry; Physical Education; Physical Therapy; Physiology; Rehabilitation and Therapy; Russian; Slavic Languages; Sports; Tourism); **Pre-Master; Sport and Education - Mass Sports** (Pedagogy; Psychology; Sports; Sports Medicine); **Sport and Education - Sports and Martial Arts** (History; Philosophy; Physical Education; Sports); **Training and Retraining** (Communication Studies; Tourism)

Institute

Tourism (Tourism)

History: Founded 1937, acquired present status and title 2003.

Academic Year: September to June (September-January and February-June)

Admission Requirements: Secondary school certificate (Attestat o srednjem obrazovanii) and entrance examination.

Fees: 1,500 per annum; postal tuition, 800; preparatory faculty, 900 magistracy, c. 1,500; postgraduate courses, c. 1,700 (US Dollar)

Main Language(s) of Instruction: Russian, Belarusian

Accrediting Agency: Ministry of Sport and Tourism

Degrees and Diplomas: *Diplom o Vyshem Obrazovanii*; *Diplom Magistra*: **Physical Education; Sports; Tourism.** *Kandidat Nauk*: **Physical Education; Physiology; Sports.** *Doktor Nauk*: **Physical Education; Sports.**

Student Services: Academic Counselling, Canteen, Cultural Activities, Facilities for disabled people, Foreign Studies Centre, Health Services, Language Laboratory, Library, Social Counselling, Sports Facilities

Last Updated: 08/02/15

BELARUSIAN STATE UNIVERSITY OF TRANSPORT

Belaruskij Dzjaržauny Universitet Transpartu (BELGUT)

st. Kirova. 34, 246653 Gomel
Tel: +375(232) 77-72-15
Fax: +375(232) 77-44-83
EMail: belsut@belsut.gomel.by
Website: http://www.belsut.gomel.by

Rector: Benjamin I. Senko
Tel: +375(232) 95-39-41
EMail: rector@belsut.gomel.by

First Vice-Rector: Viktor Negrej
Tel: +375(232) 95-39-81

International Relations: Nikolai Volkov
Tel: +7(23) 255-11-68 EMail: npvolkov@belsut.gomel.by

Faculty
Construction (Construction Engineering; Road Engineering); **Electrical Engineering** (Automation and Control Engineering; Electrical and Electronic Engineering; Electrical Engineering; Telecommunications Engineering); **Extramural Education** (Transport and Communications); **Foreign Students** (Transport and Communications); **Humanities and Economics** (Accountancy; Economics; Humanities and Social Science Education; Management); **Industrial and Civil Engineering** (Architecture; Building Technologies; Civil Engineering; Industrial Engineering; Road Engineering); **Master Training and Guidance** (Biology; Chemistry; Engineering Drawing and Design; Mathematics; Physics; Russian; Slavic Languages; Transport and Communications); **Mechanical Engineering** (Mechanical Engineering); **Military Transport** (Transport and Communications); **Transport Management** (Transport and Communications; Transport Management)

Department
Design (Design)

Laboratory
Structural and Tribological Materials (NFI KTM) (Materials Engineering)

Research Centre
Complex Transport Problems (NC QFT) (Railway Engineering); **Environmental Security and Energy Efficiency in Transport (SIC EiET)** (Ecology; Railway Transport)

Research Institute
Railway Transport *(NIIZHT)* (Railway Transport)

Research Laboratory
Brakes Rolling Stock (O'Neill TSPS) (Transport and Communications); **Electric Power Supply of Transport (NFI SET)** (Electrical Engineering; Transport and Communications); **Estimation of Rolling Stock Units** (Railway Transport); **Safety and Electromagnetical Compatibility of Technical Means** (Safety Engineering; Technology); **Soil, Base and Foundation Mechanics** (Mechanics); **Surface and Thin Films Physics** (Materials Engineering); **Track Studies** (Materials Engineering); **Traffic Control (NFI SCP)** (Transport Management); **Transport Communications (SRL TC)** (Transport and Communications)

Further Information: Also Russian language preparatory course for foreign students

History: Founded 1953 as Belarusian Institute of Railway Engineering, acquired present status and title 1993.

Academic Year: September to July (September-January; February-July)

Admission Requirements: General or special secondary school certificate (Attestat o srednjem/specialnom/obrazovanii) and competitive entrance examination

Fees: Foreign students, 1,000-1,500 per annum (US Dollar)

Main Language(s) of Instruction: Russian, Belarusian

Accrediting Agency: Ministry of Education

Degrees and Diplomas: *Diplom o Vyshem Obrazovanii*; *Diplom Magistra*: **Accountancy; Architecture; Automation and Control Engineering; Automotive Engineering; Business Administration; Business and Commerce; Civil Engineering; Construction Engineering; Ecology; Economics; Electrical and Electronic Engineering; Energy Engineering; Industrial Engineering; Information Management; Information Technology; Maintenance Technology; Materials Engineering; Mechanical Engineering; Mechanics; Physics; Railway Engineering; Road Engineering; Transport and Communications; Transport Economics; Transport Management; Water Management.** *Kandidat Nauk*: **Architecture; Civil Engineering; Economics; Materials Engineering; Mathematics; Mechanical Engineering; Mechanics; Railway Engineering; Regional Planning; Rural Planning; Software Engineering; Town Planning; Transport Management.** *Doktor Nauk*: **Mechanical Engineering; Railway Engineering; Transport Management.**

Student Services: Canteen, Careers Guidance, Cultural Activities, Health Services, Language Laboratory, Library, Social Counselling, Sports Facilities, eLibrary

Publications: Science and Transport

Last Updated: 09/02/15

BELARUSIAN-RUSSIAN UNIVERSITY

Belaruska-Rasijskij Universitet (BRU)

Prospect Mira, 43, 212000 Mogilev

Tel: +375(222) 26-61-00

Fax: +375(222) 22-58-21

EMail: bru@bru.by

Website: http://www.bru.by/

Rector: Igor Sergeevich Sazonov (1998-)
Tel: +375(222) 26-61-00 EMail: rektor@bru.by

Vice-Rector for Administration: Komar Viktor Leonidovich
Tel: +375(222) 25-13-23 EMail: pr_ahr@bru.by

International Relations: Alexander Korotkevich
Tel: +375(222) 25-28-30 EMail: interstudy@bru.mogilev.by

Faculty
Automotive Engineering (Automotive Engineering; Mechanical Engineering; Russian; Slavic Languages); **Construction Engineering** (Civil Engineering; Construction Engineering; Industrial Engineering; Road Engineering; Safety Engineering); **Economics** (Accountancy; Business Administration; Business and Commerce; Business Computing; Economics; Finance; Management; Marketing; Mathematics; Transport Management); **Electrical Engineering** (Automation and Control Engineering; Electrical Engineering; Electronic Engineering; Information Technology; Software Engineering); **Engineering** (Machine Building; Materials Engineering; Mechanical Engineering; Mechanics; Metal Techniques; Metallurgical Engineering); **Engineering and Economics** (Biotechnology; Computer Engineering; Computer Science; Electrical Engineering; Power Engineering; Software Engineering; Transport Engineering)

College
Architecture and Civil Engineering (Architecture; Civil Engineering)

Department
Humanities (Arts and Humanities); **Physical Education and Sports** (Physical Education; Sports)

Institute
Advanced Studies and Retraining

History: Founded 1961 as Mogilev Mechanical Engineering Institute. Became Mogilev State Technical University (MSTU). Acquired present status and title 2003.

Academic Year: September to June (September-January; February-June)

Admission Requirements: General or special secondary school certificate (Attestat o srednjem specialnom obrazovanii) and entrance examination

Fees: c. 13-15 m. per annum (Russian Ruble)

Main Language(s) of Instruction: Russian

Accrediting Agency: Ministry of Education; Federal Agency on Education of Ministry of Education and Science of the Russian Federation

Degrees and Diplomas: *Diplom o Vyshem Obrazovanii*: **Automation and Control Engineering; Automotive Engineering; Business Administration; Civil Engineering; Computer Engineering; Computer Science; Economics; Electrical Engineering; Transport Management.** *Diplom Magistra*: **Automation and Control Engineering; Computer Engineering; Economics; Energy Engineering; Machine Building; Management; Materials Engineering; Mechanical Engineering; Mining Engineering; Transport Engineering.** *Kandidat Nauk*: **Automation and Control Engineering; Building Technologies; Civil Engineering; Computer Engineering; Electrical Engineering; Machine Building; Mechanical Engineering; Metallurgical Engineering; Road Engineering; Social Sciences.** *Doktor Nauk*: **Automotive Engineering; Machine Building; Social Sciences.**

Student Services: Academic Counselling, Canteen, Cultural Activities, Foreign Studies Centre, Health Services, Language Laboratory, Library, Nursery Care, Social Counselling, Sports Facilities

Publications: Conference Works

Student Numbers *2014-2015*: Total: c. 7,500

Last Updated: 04/02/15

BREST STATE TECHNICAL UNIVERSITY

Brestskij Gosudarstvennyj Tehnicheskij Universitet (BSTU)

267 Moskovskaya str, 224017 Brest
Tel: +375(162) 42-05-48
Fax: +375(162) 42-21-27
EMail: canc@bstu.by
Website: http://www.bstu.by

Rector: Piotr S. Poyta (2002-) Tel: +375(162) 42-74-57

Vice-Rector: Vecheslav I. Dragan
Tel: +375(162) 42-03-61 EMail: 1strector@bstu.by

International Relations: Liana I. Kholodar
Tel: +375(162) 40-83-74
EMail: liholodar@bstu.by; ttc@bstu.by; ttc.bstu@gmail.com

Faculty

Civil Engineering (Civil Engineering; Construction Engineering; Real Estate; Road Engineering; Structural Architecture); **Economics** (Accountancy; Banking; Business and Commerce; Economic and Finance Policy; Economics; Finance; International Economics; Management; Marketing); **Electronics Information Systems** (Artificial Intelligence; Computer Engineering; Computer Networks; Computer Science; Data Processing; Electronic Engineering; Industrial Engineering); **Engineering Systems and Ecology Faculty** (Chemistry; Ecology; Engineering Drawing and Design; Environmental Engineering; Heating and Refrigeration; Soil Conservation; Water Management; Water Science); **Extra-Mural Studies** (Accountancy; Banking; Business and Commerce; Civil Engineering; Data Processing; Economics; Finance; Industrial Management; Machine Building; Maintenance Technology; Management; Marketing; Road Engineering; Water Management); **Innovation, Management and Finance** (Banking; Civil Engineering; Economics; Electronic Engineering; Finance; Industrial Engineering; Machine Building; Maintenance Technology; Management; Soil Management; Water Management); **Mechanical Engineering** (Automation and Control Engineering; Automotive Engineering; Building Technologies; Maintenance Technology; Mechanical Engineering); **Pre-University Training** (Russian; Slavic Languages)

Further Information: Also Language Courses for foreign students; Study Abroad programmes in Poland and Germany

History: Founded 1966 as Civil Engineering Institute, reorganized as Polytechnical Institute, and acquired present status and title 2000.

Academic Year: September to July (September-January; February-July)

Admission Requirements: General or special secondary school certificate (Attestat o srednjem/specialnom/obrazovanii)

Fees: National: 1,766,600 per annum (Belarussian Ruble), International: 2,000-4,200 per annum (US Dollar)

Main Language(s) of Instruction: Russian, Belarusian

Accrediting Agency: Ministry of Education

Degrees and Diplomas: *Diplom o Vyshem Obrazovanii*; *Diplom Magistra*: **Accountancy; Architecture; Automation and Control Engineering; Building Technologies; Civil Engineering; Construction Engineering; Economics; International Economics; Mathematics; Mechanical Engineering; Real Estate; Road Engineering; Rural Planning; Soil Conservation; Soil Management; Structural Architecture.** *Kandidat Nauk*: **Building Technologies; Computer Engineering; Construction Engineering; Ecology; Economics; Geology; Heating and Refrigeration; Industrial Engineering; Machine Building; Mechanical Engineering; Mechanics; Power Engineering; Structural Architecture; Thermal Physics; Water Management.** Some programmes are conducted in English at undergraduate level (in Information Technology, Civil Engineering, Water Management, Soil Conservation, Economics), Graduate level (in Information Technology, Architecture) and Doctorate level (in Information Technology).

Student Services: Canteen, Health Services, IT Centre, Language Laboratory, Social Counselling, Sports Facilities

Publications: Collected Papers

Last Updated: 09/02/15

BREST STATE UNIVERSITY NAMED AFTER A.S. PUSHKIN

Brestskij Dzjaržauny Universitet imja A.S. Puškina (BRSU)

21 Kosmonavtov Boulevard, 224016 Brest
Tel: +375(162) 23-33-40
Fax: +375(162) 23-09-96
EMail: box@brsu.brest.by
Website: http://www.brsu.by/

Rector: Mechyslau Edvardavich Chasnouski (2002-)
Tel: +375(162) 23-01-41

Vice-Rector: Stanislav Grigor'evich Rachevky
Tel: +375(162) 23-33-42

International Relations: Vladimir Stanislavovich Sekerzickij, Vice-Rector Tel: +375(162) 23-33-44

Faculty

Biology (Biology; Botany; Chemistry; Ecology; Genetics; Zoology); **Foreign Languages** (English; German; Modern Languages); **Geography** (Geography; Tourism); **History** (History); **Law** (Law); **Philology** (Literature; Native Language; Philology; Russian); **Physical Education and Sports** (Physical Education; Rehabilitation and Therapy; Sports); **Physics and Mathematics** (Mathematics; Physics); **Pre-University Education** (Education); **Psychology and Pedagogy** (Educational Psychology; Foreign Languages Education; Native Language Education; Pedagogy; Primary Education; Psychology; Science Education); **Sociology and Pedagogy** (Pedagogy; Sociology)

Laboratory

Fizpraktikum (Physics)

Further Information: Also Branch in Pinsk

History: Founded 1945 as teachers' institute. Transformed into Brest State Pedagogical institute 1950. Acquired present status and renamed into Brest State University 1995. Acquired present title 1999.

Main Language(s) of Instruction: Russian, Belarusian

Accrediting Agency: Ministry of Education

Degrees and Diplomas: *Diplom o Vyshem Obrazovanii*; *Diplom Magistra*: **Art Education; Biology; Chemistry; Economics; Educational Sciences; Geography; History; Law; Linguistics; Literature; Mathematics; Mathematics Education; Music Education; Pedagogy; Physical Education; Physics; Preschool Education; Psychology.** *Kandidat Nauk*: **Archaeology; Arts and Humanities; Biochemistry; Biological and Life Sciences; Biology; Botany; Developmental Psychology; Earth Sciences; Economics; Educational Psychology; Educational Sciences; Geochemistry; Geography; Geography (Human); History; Linguistics; Literature; Mathematics; Mathematics Education; Pedagogy; Philology; Physics; Psychology; Slavic Languages; Social Sciences; Vocational Education.**

Student Services: Health Services, Library, Residential Facilities, Sports Facilities

Academic Staff *2014-2015*: Total: c. 600
Student Numbers *2014-2015*: Total: c. 10,000
Last Updated: 09/02/15

COMMAND AND ENGINEERING INSTITUTE OF THE MINISTRY OF EMERGENCY SITUATIONS

Kamandna-Inžynerny Instytut MNS Respubliki Belarus'

Mashinostroiteley str., 25, 220118 Minsk
Tel: +375(17) 340-35-57
Fax: +375(17) 340-35-57
EMail: mail@kii.gov.by; oic@kii.gov.by
Website: http://kii.gov.by/

Rector: Ivan Polevoda Tel: +375(17) 240-35-58

First Vice-Rector: Dmitry Petrovich Lukyanchikov

Faculty

Commanding (Safety Engineering); **Distance Learning** (Safety Engineering); **Engineering** (Safety Engineering); **Retraining and Professional Development** (Industrial Engineering; Safety Engineering)

Programme
Fire and Industrial Safety *(Ph.D.)* (Fire Science; Industrial Engineering; Safety Engineering); **Graduate Studies** (Safety Engineering)
History: Founded 1933, acquired present status and title 1992.
Academic Year: September to July (September-January; February-July)
Admission Requirements: General or special secondary school certificate (Attestat o srednjem/specialnom/obrazovanii)
Fees: c.15m (Belarussian Ruble)
Main Language(s) of Instruction: Russian, Belarusian
Accrediting Agency: Ministry of Education; Ministry of Emergencies of Republic of Belarus
Degrees and Diplomas: *Diplom o Vyshem Obrazovanii*; *Diplom Magistra*: **Safety Engineering.** *Kandidat Nauk*: **Fire Science; Safety Engineering.**
Student Services: Canteen, Careers Guidance, Cultural Activities, Health Services, IT Centre, Library, Residential Facilities, Social Counselling, Sports Facilities
Publications: Scientific Journal "Bulletin" (Vestnik)
Publishing House: Publishing Centre of the Belarusian State University
Last Updated: 10/02/15

FRANCISK SKORINA GOMEL STATE UNIVERSITY

Gomel'skij Dzjaržauny Universitet imja Franciska Skarany (GSU)
Sovetskaya str., 104, 246019 Gomel
Tel: +375(232) 60-73-71 +375(232) 60-31-13
Fax: +375(232) 57-81-11
EMail: mail@gsu.by
Website: http://www.gsu.by

Rector: A.V. Rogachev (2004-)
Tel: +375(232) 60-31-13 EMail: rector@gsu.unibel.by
First Vice-Rector: Yuri Kulazhenko
Tel: +375(232) 57-34-40
EMail: vice-rector@gsu.unibel.by
International Relations: Ludmila Protchenko
Tel: +375(232) 60-31-78
EMail: interaffairs@gsu.unibel.by

Faculty
Biology (Analytical Chemistry; Anatomy; Biochemistry; Biology; Botany; Cell Biology; Chemistry; Forestry; Genetics; Microbiology; Molecular Biology; Organic Chemistry; Physiology; Zoology); **Economics** (Accountancy; Business Administration; Business and Commerce; Economics; Industrial and Production Economics; Industrial Management; International Business; Management; Marketing; Taxation); **Foreign Languages** (English; French; German; Grammar; Italian; Modern Languages; Phonetics; Translation and Interpretation; Writing); **Geology and Geography** (Crystallography; Ecology; Geography; Geology; Geophysics; Mineralogy); **History** (Ancient Civilizations; Contemporary History; History; Medieval Studies; Modern History; Prehistory); **Law** (Administrative Law; Civil Law; Constitutional Law; Criminal Law; History of Law; International Law; Labour Law; Law); **Mathematics** (Mathematics; Mathematics and Computer Science; Statistics; Systems Analysis); **Philology** (Grammar; Latin; Linguistics; Native Language; Philology; Phonetics; Russian; Speech Studies); **Physical Education** (Physical Education; Sports; Sports Medicine); **Physics** (Applied Physics; Atomic and Molecular Physics; Electronic Engineering; Nuclear Physics; Optics; Physics; Radiophysics); **Preparatory Education for Teaching and Learning of Foreign Students**; **Psychology** (Psychology; Social Psychology)

Department
Distance Education (Administration; English; Forestry; German; Information Technology; Psychology; Software Engineering)

Institute
Management *(Institut Franco-Biélorusse de Gestion)* (Management); **Professional Skills Development** (Accountancy; Computer Education; Computer Science; Education; Higher Education; Psychology; Secretarial Studies; Vocational Education)

Centre
Marketing (MRC) *(Regional)* (Marketing)
History: Founded 1930, acquired present status and title 1969.
Academic Year: September to July (September-February; February-July)
Admission Requirements: General or special secondary school certificate (Attestat o srednjem/specialnom/obrazovanii) and competitive entrance examination
Fees: 950-11,295 per annum (US Dollar)
Main Language(s) of Instruction: Russian
Accrediting Agency: Ministry of Education
Degrees and Diplomas: *Diplom o Vyshem Obrazovanii*; *Diplom Magistra*: **Analytical Chemistry; Arts and Humanities; Botany; Civil Law; Criminal Law; Criminology; Ecology; Economics; English; Folklore; Genetics; Geology; History of Law; Law; Literature; Mathematics; Pedagogy; Philology; Physiology; Psychology; Public Law; Slavic Languages; Zoology.** *Kandidat Nauk*: **Accountancy; Administrative Law; Ecology; Economics; Finance; Fiscal Law; Geography; Geology; Geophysics; Law; Literature; Mathematics; Mineralogy; Nuclear Physics; Pedagogy; Petroleum and Gas Engineering; Philology; Psychology; Russian; Science Education; Slavic Languages; Soil Science; Statistics; Water Science.** *Doktor Nauk*: **Computer Engineering; Computer Networks; Ecology; Geography; Geology; Mathematics; Optics; Russian; Science Education; Slavic Languages.**
Student Services: Academic Counselling, Canteen, Cultural Activities, Health Services, Language Laboratory, Social Counselling, Sports Facilities
Last Updated: 10/02/15

GOMEL ENGINEERING INSTITUTE OF THE MINISTRY OF EMERGENCY SITUATIONS

Gomel'skij Inžynerny Instytut MNS Respubliki Belarus'
35Å, Retchitski av., 246023 Gomel
Tel: +375(232) 46-13-13
Fax: +375(232) 46-00-13
EMail: gii@mail.gomel.by
Website: http://gii.by/

Rector: Andrei V. Borodako Tel: +375(232) 46-00-00
First Vice-Rector: Igor I. Sutorma Tel: +375(232) 46-00-04

Department
Automatic Fire Safety Systems (Fire Science; Safety Engineering); **Emergency Protection Management** (Protective Services); **Emergency Response** (Protective Services); **Fire and Industrial Safety** (Fire Science; Safety Engineering); **Fire and Rescue Equipment** (Fire Science); **Fire Rescue and Physical Training** (Fire Science; Physical Education); **Humanities** (Cultural Studies; Economics; Educational Psychology; Ethics; History; Modern Languages; Native Language; Philosophy; Political Sciences; Sociology); **Modern Languages** (English; German; Modern Languages); **Natural Sciences** (Information Sciences; Information Technology; Mathematics; Mechanics; Physics)
History: Creating in 2000 as an institution for fire-fighting and fire-prevention. Acquired present status and title 2003.
Main Language(s) of Instruction: Russian
Accrediting Agency: Ministry of Education
Degrees and Diplomas: *Diplom o Vyshem Obrazovanii*; *Diplom Magistra*: **Data Processing; English; Fire Science; German; Information Technology; Management; Natural Sciences; Philosophy; Physics; Psychology; Safety Engineering; Secondary Education.**
Publications: Emergencies: Education and Science
Last Updated: 10/02/15

GOMEL STATE MEDICAL UNIVERSITY

Gomel'skij Dzjaržauny Medycynski Universitet
st. Lange, 5, 246000 Gomel
Tel: +375(232) 74-41-21
Fax: +375(232) 74-98-31
EMail: gsmu@gsmu.by
Website: http://www.gsmu.by/

Rector: Anatoliy N. Lizikov (1990-) Tel: +375(232) 74-41-21

Vice-Rector for Academic Affairs: Alexander Kozlovsky Tel: +375(232) 53-06-23

International Relations: Vladimir V. Aničkin

Department

Medical and Diagnostic Studies (Biological and Life Sciences; Hygiene; Laboratory Techniques; Medicine; Microbiology); **Pre-university Training and Vocational Guidance** (Biology; Physics; Russian); **Specialists Training for Foreign Countries** (Medicine); **Therapy** (Medicine; Public Health)

History: Founded 1990 as Institute, acquired present status and title 2000.

Fees: 16,8m. per annum (Belarussian Ruble)

Main Language(s) of Instruction: Russian, Belarusian

Accrediting Agency: Ministry of Education

Degrees and Diplomas: *Diplom o Vyshem Obrazovanii*: **Medicine.** *Diplom Magistra*: **Medicine.** *Kandidat Nauk*: **Anaesthesiology; Anatomy; Biochemistry; Biological and Life Sciences; Biomedicine; Cardiology; Dermatology; Endocrinology; Epidemiology; Gastroenterology; Gynaecology and Obstetrics; Health Sciences; Hygiene; Immunology; Laboratory Techniques; Medicine; Nephrology; Oncology; Ophthalmology; Otorhinolaryngology; Paediatrics; Parasitology; Pathology; Pharmacology; Physical Therapy; Physiology; Public Health; Rehabilitation and Therapy; Rheumatology; Social and Preventive Medicine; Sports Medicine; Surgery; Venereology.** *Doktor Nauk*: **Medicine; Physiology; Surgery.**

Student Services: Library

Publications: "36 and 6" Newspaper

Last Updated: 06/02/15

GRODNO STATE AGRARIAN UNIVERSITY

Grodnenskij Dzjarzhauny Agrarny Universitet (GRSAU)

Tereshkova street, 28, 230008 Grodno
Tel: +375(152) 72-13-65
Fax: +375(152) 72-13-65
EMail: ggau@ggau.by
Website: http://www.ggau.by

Rector: Vitold Kazimirovitch Pestis Tel: +375(152) 47-01-68 EMail: obr@ggau.by

First Vice-Rector: Alexander Duduk Tel: +375(152) 72-00-25

Faculty

Accounting (Accountancy; Banking; Finance); **Agronomy** (Agricultural Equipment; Agronomy; Botany; Fruit Production; Physical Education; Plant and Crop Protection; Sports; Vegetable Production); **Biotechnology** (Animal Husbandry; Biotechnology; Genetics; Veterinary Science; Zoology); **Economics** (Agricultural Economics; Economics); **Engineering and Technology** (Agricultural Engineering; Agricultural Equipment; Chemistry; Machine Building; Plant and Crop Protection); **Plant Protection** (Agriculture; Entomology; Meteorology; Physics; Plant and Crop Protection; Plant Pathology; Soil Science); **Preparatory Education for International Students** (Arts and Humanities; Biology; Chemistry; Computer Science; Economics; Mathematics; Physics; Russian; Social Sciences); **Veterinary Medicine** (Animal Husbandry; Veterinary Science)

Higher School

Management (Economics; Management)

Further Information: Also preparatory Department

History: Founded 1951 as Grodno Agricultural Institute, acquired present status and title 2000.

Academic Year: September to June (September-November; February-June)

Admission Requirements: General or special secondary school education (Attestat o srednjem/specialnom/obrazovanii) and competitive entrance examination

Fees: First level and Master's degree, 2,000 per annum; PhD, 3,000 per annum (US Dollar)

Main Language(s) of Instruction: Belarusian, Russian

Accrediting Agency: Ministry of Agriculture; Ministry of Education

Degrees and Diplomas: *Diplom o Vyshem Obrazovanii*: **Accountancy; Agriculture; Biotechnology; Economics; Engineering; Technology; Veterinary Science.** *Diplom Magistra*: **Agriculture; Agronomy; Animal Husbandry; Chemistry; Economics; Food Science; Food Technology; Veterinary Science.** *Kandidat Nauk*: **Agriculture; Animal Husbandry; Chemistry; Crop Production; Economics; Food Science; Food Technology; Plant and Crop Protection.** *Doktor Nauk*: **Animal Husbandry.**

Student Services: Academic Counselling, Canteen, Careers Guidance, Cultural Activities, Health Services, Library, Residential Facilities, Sports Facilities

Academic Staff *2014-2015*	**TOTAL**
FULL-TIME	c. 340
Student Numbers *2014-2015*	
All (Foreign included)	**7,896**
FOREIGN ONLY	**188**

Last Updated: 11/02/15

GRODNO STATE MEDICAL UNIVERSITY

Grodnenskij Dzjaržauny Medycynski Universitet (GRMSU)

80 Gorkogo St., 230009 Grodno
Tel: +375(152) 43-26-61 +375(152) 43-54-51
Fax: +375(152) 43-53-41 +375(152) 43-53-41
EMail: mailbox@grsmu.by; ief@grsmu.by; grsmuinternational@mail.ru
Website: http://www.grsmu.by/

Rector: Viktor A. Snerzhitskiy Tel: +375(152) 33-03-65

International Relations: Zhanna Motylevich Tel: +375(152) 33-55-61 EMail: grsmuinternational@mail.ru

Faculty

General Medicine (Medicine); **Medical Diagnostics** (Medicine); **Medical Studies for International Students** (Medicine); **Mental Health Medicine** (Psychiatry and Mental Health); **Paediatrics** (Paediatrics)

Laboratory

Central Research (Medicine); **Narcotics** (Toxicology)

Research School

Hepatology (Hepatology)

Further Information: Also 21 Clinics. Courses for foreign students

History: Founded 1958, acquired present status and title 2000.

Academic Year: September to June (September-January; February-June)

Admission Requirements: General or special secondary school certificate (Attestat o srednjem/specialnom/obrazovanii)

Fees: National: c. 1,500 per annum (US Dollar), International: 3,500 per annum for courses in Russian; 4,100 per annum for courses in English (US Dollar)

Main Language(s) of Instruction: Russian, English

Accrediting Agency: Ministry of Education

Degrees and Diplomas: *Diplom o Vyshem Obrazovanii*: **Medicine; Nursing.** *Diplom Magistra*: **Medicine.** *Kandidat Nauk*: **Medicine.** Practical and theoretical courses offered in the Medical Studies for International Students available in English

Student Services: Canteen, Cultural Activities, Health Services, Library, Residential Facilities, Sports Facilities

Last Updated: 10/02/15

HIGHER STATE COLLEGE OF COMMUNICATIONS

Vyšejšy Dzjaržauny Kaledž Suvjazi (UO VGKS/HSCC)

B.2, House 8, F. Scorina Str., 220114 Minsk
Tel: +375(17) 267-44-14 +375(17) 217-56-06
Fax: +375(17) 264-44-14
EMail: vks@vks.belpak.by
Website: http://vks.belpak.by/

Rector: Andrey O. Zenevih Tel: +375(17) 267-44-14

Faculty

Engineering and Technology Communication (Arts and Humanities; Economics; Information Technology; Management; Postal Services; Telecommunications Engineering); **Telecommunication** (Mathematics; Physical Education; Physics; Software Engineering; Sports; Telecommunications Engineering; Telecommunications Services)

History: Founded 1993, acquired present status and title 2000.

Main Language(s) of Instruction: Russian, Belarusian

Accrediting Agency: Ministry of Education

Degrees and Diplomas: *Diplom o Vyshem Obrazovanii*: **Economics; Engineering; Management; Marketing; Postal Services; Radio and Television Broadcasting; Software Engineering; Telecommunications Engineering; Telecommunications Services.**

Student Services: Language Laboratory, Library, Residential Facilities, Sports Facilities

Last Updated: 08/02/15

INTERNATIONAL SAKHAROV ENVIRONMENTAL UNIVERSITY

Mižnarodny Dzjaržauny Ekalagičny Universitet imja A.D. Saharova (ISEU)

23 Dolgobrodskaya St, 220070 Minsk

Tel: +375(17) 230-69-98

Fax: +375(17) 230-68-97

EMail: info@iseu.by

Website: http://www.iseu.by

Acting Rector, Vice-rector for Research: Sergey L. Kabak Tel: +375(29) 230-73-32 EMail: kabak@bsmu.by; rector@iseu.by

Vice-rector for Educational and Ideological Work: Vladimir I. Krasouski Tel: +375(17) 230-73-81 EMail: vikras@iseu.by

Vice-rector for Administration and Maintenance: Nikolay N. Vayzekhovitch Tel: +375(17) 230-28-96

International Relations: Helen Alexeichik, International Officer Tel: +375(17) 230-6888 EMail: id@iseu.by

Faculty

Advanced Training and Staff Re-training (Environmental Management; Nuclear Engineering; Physics; Power Engineering); **Correspondent Education**; **Environmental Medicine** (Biochemistry; Biology; Biophysics; Ecology; Environmental Studies; Epidemiology; Genetics; Hygiene; Immunology; Medicine; Modern Languages; Molecular Biology; Physical Education; Radiology; Science Education); **Environmental Monitoring and Management** (Data Processing; Economics; Energy Engineering; Environmental Engineering; Environmental Management; Environmental Studies; Information Technology; Mathematics; Nuclear Engineering; Philosophy; Physics; Safety Engineering; Sociology); **Pre-university Training** (Biology; Chemistry; Computer Science; Mathematics; Physics; Russian)

Further Information: Also Field Station in Hoiniky (Gomel Region) and Pilot Station in Volma (Minsk Region)

History: Founded 1992 as International 'Saharov' College by Decree of Council of the Ministers following a resolution passed at the First International Saharov Memorial Congress and with support of the UN. Reorganized 1994 as International Saharov Institute of Radioecology, and acquired present status and title 1999.

Academic Year: September to July (September-December; January-April; May-July)

Admission Requirements: General or special secondary school certificate (Attestat o srednjem/specialnom/obrazovanii), and entrance examination

Fees: 850 per annum (US Dollar)

Main Language(s) of Instruction: Russian, English

Accrediting Agency: Ministry of Education

Degrees and Diplomas: *Diplom o Vyshem Obrazovanii*; *Diplom Magistra*: **Biochemistry; Biology; Ecology; Energy Engineering; Environmental Engineering; Mathematics; Measurement and Precision Engineering; Preschool Education; Primary Education.** *Kandidat Nauk*: **Biochemistry; Biology; Biophysics; Ecology; Measurement and Precision Engineering; Preschool Education; Radiophysics; Secondary Education.**

Student Services: Academic Counselling, Careers Guidance, Cultural Activities, Health Services, IT Centre, Language Laboratory, Library, Sports Facilities

Publications: Sakharov Readings

Last Updated: 04/02/15

MINSK STATE HIGHER AVIATION COLLEGE

Minski Dzjaržauny Vyšejšy Avijacyjny Kaledž (MSHAC)

77 Uborevich St., 220096 Minsk

Tel: +375(17) 341-66-32 +375(17) 345-32-81

Fax: +375(17) 341-66-32

EMail: college@avia.mtk.by; aviacollege@ivcavia.com

Website: http://mgvak.by/

Rector: Alexander A. Laptsevich

Faculty

Civil Aviation (Aeronautical and Aerospace Engineering; Air Transport; Electrical and Electronic Engineering; Electrical and Electronic Equipment and Maintenance; Engineering; Maintenance Technology; Natural Sciences; Physical Education; Sports); **Military Aviation** (Aeronautical and Aerospace Engineering; Air Transport; Electrical and Electronic Engineering; Electrical and Electronic Equipment and Maintenance; Engineering; Maintenance Technology); **Training and Retraining** (Air Transport; Arts and Humanities; English; Social Sciences)

Department

Distance Learning (Air Transport; Computer Engineering; Maintenance Technology); **Secondary Special Education** (Air Transport; Maintenance Technology)

History: Founded 1974, acquired present status and title 2001.

Fees: c.11m (Belarussian Ruble)

Main Language(s) of Instruction: Russian, Belarusian

Accrediting Agency: Ministry of Education

Degrees and Diplomas: *Diplom o Vyshem Obrazovanii*: **Aeronautical and Aerospace Engineering; Air Transport; Maintenance Technology.**

Last Updated: 08/02/15

MINSK STATE HIGHER RADIO-ENGINEERING COLLEGE

Minski Dzjaržauny Vyšejšy Radiotehničny Kaledž

62 Nezavisimosty Ave, 220005 Minsk

Tel: +375(17) 292-62-85

Fax: +375(17) 331-89-45

EMail: office@mgvrk.by

Website: http://www.mgvrk.by

Rector: Sergey N. Ankuda (2010-) EMail: rector@mgvrk.by

Department

Computer Programming (Computer Engineering); **Distance Education**; **Electronics** (Electrical and Electronic Engineering; Microelectronics); **Radio Engineering** (Engineering); **Vocational Education**

History: Founded 1960.

Main Language(s) of Instruction: Russian, Belarusian

Accrediting Agency: Ministry of Education

Degrees and Diplomas: *Diplom o Vyshem Obrazovanii*: **Computer Engineering; Electrical and Electronic Engineering.**

Student Services: IT Centre, Library, Residential Facilities, Sports Facilities

Academic Staff *2014-2015*: Total 192

Student Numbers *2014-2015*: Total 2,500

Last Updated: 08/02/15

MINSK STATE LINGUISTICS UNIVERSITY

Minski Dzjaržauny Lingvistyčny Universitet (MSLU)

21 Zakharov St, 220034 Minsk
Tel: +375(17) 294-76-63
Fax: +375(17) 294-75-04
EMail: info@mslu.by
Website: http://www.mslu.by

Rector: Natalia Petrovna Baranova (1995-)
Tel: +375(17) 288-15-44 EMail: mslu@mslu.by

Vice-Rector for Research: Anatoly M. Gorlatov
Tel: +375(17) 284-80-33

School

English (English; Grammar; Literature; Phonetics); **French** (French; Grammar; Phonetics); **German** (German; Grammar; Phonetics); **Intercultural Communication** (Communication Studies; Modern Languages; Speech Studies; Translation and Interpretation); **Retraining and Teacher Development** (Teacher Training); **Russian as a Foreign Language** *(for foreign students)* (Russian); **Spanish** (Grammar; Phonetics; Spanish); **Translation and Interpreting** (Translation and Interpretation)

Further Information: Also classes in Russian/Belarusian languages and cultures for non-Russian speaking students. Branches in Sloynik and Padručnik

History: Founded 1948 as Pedagogical Institute, acquired present status and title 1993.

Academic Year: September to June (September-January; February-June)

Admission Requirements: General or special secondary school certificate (Attestat o srednjem/specialnom/obrazovanii), and competitive entrance examination

Fees: c. 1,100 per annum (US Dollar)

Main Language(s) of Instruction: Russian, Belarusian

Accrediting Agency: Ministry of Education

Degrees and Diplomas: *Diplom o Vyshem Obrazovanii*; *Diplom Magistra*: **Applied Linguistics; Communication Studies; Cultural Studies; English; Fine Arts; Foreign Languages Education; French; German; Information Technology; Linguistics; Literature; Pedagogy; Philology; Psychology; Spanish; Translation and Interpretation.** *Kandidat Nauk*: **Educational Psychology; Foreign Languages Education; Linguistics; Modern Languages; Pedagogy.** *Doktor Nauk*: **Educational Psychology; Foreign Languages Education; Linguistics; Modern Languages; Pedagogy.**

Student Services: Academic Counselling, Canteen, Cultural Activities, Health Services, IT Centre, Language Laboratory, Library, Residential Facilities, Social Counselling, Sports Facilities

Publications: Lingua (Pedagogics); Vestnik (Philology)

Publishing House: Publishing House of Minsk State Linguistic University

Academic Staff *2014-2015*	**TOTAL**
FULL-TIME	**781**
FOREIGN ONLY	**680**

Last Updated: 11/02/15

MOGILEV STATE UNIVERSITY NAMED AFTER A.A.KULESHOV

Magiljouski Dzjaržauny Universitet imja A.A. Kuljašova (MSU)

1 Kosmonavtov Ave., 212022 Mogilev
Tel: +375(222) 28-41-11
Fax: +375(222) 28-36-26
EMail: msu@msu.mogilev.by
Website: http://msu.mogilev.by/

Rector: Konstantin Bondarenko EMail: rector@msu.mogilev.by

First Vice-Rector: Dmitry Lavrinovich

International Relations: Sergej Machekin, Head of the International Relations Department
Tel: +375(222) 283-949 EMail: ird-msu@mail.ru

Faculty

Economics and Law (Economics; Law; Management; Political Sciences; Sociology); **Elementary Education** (Music; Music Education; Musical Instruments; Native Language; Pedagogy; Primary Education; Russian); **Foreign Languages** (English; French; German; Modern Languages; Philology; Romance Languages); **History** (Archaeology; History; Philosophy); **Natural Sciences** (Biology; Chemistry; Geography); **Pedagogy and Childhood Psychology** (Child Care and Development; Family Studies; Pedagogy; Psychology); **Physical Education** (Physical Education; Sports); **Physics and Mathematics** (Mathematics; Physics); **Slavonic Philology** (Journalism; Literature; Native Language; Philology; Russian)

Further Information: Also Regional Lyceums in Krichev and Mogilev

History: Founded 1913 as Teacher Training Institute, reorganized 1918 as Pedagogical Institute, and acquired present status and title 1997.

Academic Year: September to June (September-January; February-June)

Admission Requirements: General or special secondary school certificate (Attestat o srednjem/specialnom/obrazovanii)

Fees: 1,8502,200 per annum (US Dollar)

Main Language(s) of Instruction: Russian, Belarusian

Accrediting Agency: Ministry of Education

Degrees and Diplomas: *Diplom o Vyshem Obrazovanii*; *Diplom Magistra*: **Educational Sciences; History; Pedagogy; Psychology.**

Student Services: Academic Counselling, Canteen, Careers Guidance, Cultural Activities, Health Services, Language Laboratory, Library, Residential Facilities, Social Counselling, Sports Facilities

Publications: Young University Scientists Works

Publishing House: Mogilev University Publishing House

Academic Staff *2014-2015*: Total 450
Student Numbers *2014-2015*: Total: c. 4,600
Last Updated: 11/02/15

MOGILEV STATE UNIVERSITY OF FOOD TECHNOLOGY

Magiljouski Dzjaržauny Universitet Harčavannja (MSFU)

3 Smidta Ave., 212027 Mogilev
Tel: +375(222) 44-32-27
Fax: +375(222) 48-00-11
EMail: mgup@mogilev.by
Website: http://www.mgup.mogilev.by/

Rector: Vyacheslav A. Sharshunov (2003-)
Tel: +375(222) 48-03-63 EMail: rector@mogilev.by

First Vice-Rector: Nosikov Alexander Stepanovich
Tel: +375(222) 48-32-29

International Relations: Igor Davidovich, Vice-Rector for Academic Affairs
Tel: +375(222) 41-05-12 EMail: igor_davidovich@tut.by

Faculty

Chemical Engineering (Chemical Engineering; Dairy; Ecology; Food Technology; Meat and Poultry; Technology); **Correspondence** (Business Administration; Economics; Engineering; Mechanical Engineering); **Economics** (Accountancy; Business Administration; Economics; Industrial Management); **Mechanical Engineering** (Automation and Control Engineering; Food Science; Heating and Refrigeration; Mechanical Engineering; Production Engineering); **Preparatory Education** (Chemistry; English; French; German; Mathematics; Physics; Russian; Slavic Languages); **Technology** (Crop Production; Food Technology; Technology)

Institute

Advanced Studies and Retraining (Accountancy; Computer Graphics; Finance; Food Technology; Information Technology)

History: Founded 1973 as Mogilev Technological Institute, acquired present status and title 2002.

Academic Year: September to June (September-January; February-June)

Admission Requirements: General or special secondary school certificate (Attestat o srednjem/specialnom/obrazovanii)

Fees: National: Full-time, 14,6m. per annum; Part-time, c. 5,2m. per annum (Belarussian Ruble), International: 1,000 per annum (US Dollar)

Main Language(s) of Instruction: Russian, Belarusian

Accrediting Agency: Ministry of Education

Degrees and Diplomas: *Diplom o Vyshem Obrazovanii*; *Diplom Magistra*: **Automation and Control Engineering; Biotechnology; Chemical Engineering; Chemistry; Dairy; Economics; Energy Engineering; Fishery; Food Technology; Fruit Production; Industrial Management; Machine Building; Meat and Poultry; Polymer and Plastics Technology; Production Engineering; Vegetable Production; Viticulture.** *Kandidat Nauk*: **Accountancy; Animal Husbandry; Automation and Control Engineering; Chemical Engineering; Chemistry; Energy Engineering; Environmental Studies; Food Science; Food Technology; Heating and Refrigeration; Industrial Management; Information Technology; Mechanical Engineering; Production Engineering.**

Student Services: Canteen, IT Centre, Library, Residential Facilities, Sports Facilities

Publications: Bulletin of the Mogilev State University of Food; Mogilev Technological Institute Works

Last Updated: 10/02/15

MOZYR STATE PEDAGOGICAL UNIVERSITY NAMED AFTER I.P. SHAMYAKIN

Mozyrskij Dzjaržauny Pedagogičny Universitet imja I. P. Shamyakin (MDPI)

28, Studencheskaya Str., 247760 Mozyr
Tel: +375(236) 32-43-17
Fax: +375(236) 32-54-26
EMail: mgpu@mail.gomel.by; sajtmzr@mail.ru
Website: http://www.mspu.by/

Rector: Valentin V. Valetoff (1997-)
Tel: +375(236) 32-43-16

First Pro-Rector: Valery S. Bolbas
Tel: +375(236) 32-50-61

International Relations: Tatsiana N. Chechko, Head, International Affairs Department Tel: +375(236) 32-98-29

Faculty

Biology (Biology; Chemistry); **Engineering and Pedagogy** (Agricultural Engineering; Construction Engineering; Economics; Management; Mechanical Engineering; Power Engineering); **Philology** (Cultural Studies; English; German; History; Humanities and Social Science Education; Literature; Modern Languages; Political Sciences; Russian; Slavic Languages; Social Sciences); **Physical Education** (Health Sciences; Parks and Recreation; Physical Education; Sports; Sports Management; Tourism); **Physics and Mathematics** (Applied Mathematics; Computer Science; English; Mathematics; Pedagogy; Physics); **Pre-school and Primary Education** (Physical Education; Preschool Education; Primary Education; Psychology; Speech Therapy and Audiology); **Pre-university Tuition and Professional Guidance** (Accountancy; Information Technology; Psychology; Software Engineering; Speech Therapy and Audiology); **Professional Development and Retraining** (Accountancy; Child Care and Development; Educational Psychology; Preschool Education; Psychology; Software Engineering; Speech Therapy and Audiology); **Technology** (Fine Arts; Handicrafts; Painting and Drawing; Pedagogy; Physics; Technology; Technology Education)

History: Founded 1944 as Mozyr Teachers' Institute, acquired present status and title 2006.

Academic Year: September to June (September-January; February-June)

Admission Requirements: General or special secondary school certificate (Attestat o srednjem/specialnom/obrazovanii)

Fees: 900,000 per annum (Belarussian Ruble)

Main Language(s) of Instruction: Russian, Belarusian

Accrediting Agency: Ministry of Education

Degrees and Diplomas: *Diplom o Vyshem Obrazovanii*; *Diplom Magistra*: **Art Criticism; Biology; Educational Sciences; Linguistics; Literature; Pedagogy; Physical Education; Physics; Sports.** *Kandidat Nauk*: **Educational Sciences; Mathematics Education; Optics; Pedagogy; Physical Education; Primary Education; Russian; Slavic Languages; Solid State Physics.**

Student Services: Canteen, Cultural Activities, Health Services, IT Centre, Language Laboratory, Library, Residential Facilities, Social Counselling, Sports Facilities

Publications: Vesnik Mazyrskaga Dzaržaunaga Pedagogičnaga Universiteta

Publishing House: Mozyr pedinstitut

Student Numbers *2014-2015*: Total: c. 6,000
Last Updated: 11/02/15

PAVEL SUKHOI STATE TECHNICAL UNIVERSITY OF GOMEL

Gomel'skij Dzjaržauny Tehničny Universitet imja P.O. Suhogo (GSTU)

Pr. Octiabria, No 48, 246746 Gomel
Tel: +375(232) 40-20-36
Fax: +375(232) 47-91-65
EMail: rector@gstu.gomel.by; interdep@gstu.by
Website: https://www.gstu.by/

Rector: Sergei Timoshin (2001-)
Tel: +375(232) 48-16-00 EMail: rector@gstu.by

First Vice-Rector: Oleg D. Asenchik
Tel: +375(232) 48-00-20 EMail: prorector@gstu.by

Faculty

Automation and Information Systems (Automation and Control Engineering; Electronic Engineering; Information Technology; Mathematics); **Correspondence** (Economics; Machine Building; Management; Metal Techniques; Power Engineering; Production Engineering); **Economics and Humanities** (Commercial Law; Economics; History; Management; Marketing; Philosophy; Political Sciences; Sociology); **Mechanical Engineering** (Automation and Control Engineering; Engineering Drawing and Design; Machine Building; Petroleum and Gas Engineering; Technology); **Power Engineering** (Electrical Engineering; Physics; Power Engineering; Thermal Engineering); **Pre-University Studies** (Arts and Humanities); **Technology** (Agricultural Equipment; Mechanical Equipment and Maintenance; Mechanics; Metal Techniques; Technology)

Department

Physical Training and Sports (Physical Education; Sports)

Institute

Upgrading and Retraining (Accountancy; Advertising and Publicity; Business Administration; Computer Graphics; Energy Engineering; English; Finance; French; German; Industrial Management; Management; Marketing; Mechanical Engineering; Mining Engineering; Safety Engineering; Small Business; Software Engineering; Tourism; Transport Management)

History: Founded 1981, acquired present status and title 1998.

Academic Year: September to June

Admission Requirements: General or special secondary school certificate, (Attestat o srednjem/specialnom/obrazovanii) and certificate of centralised testing.

Main Language(s) of Instruction: Belarusian, Russian

Accrediting Agency: Ministry of Education

Degrees and Diplomas: *Diplom o Vyshem Obrazovanii*; *Diplom Magistra*: **Automation and Control Engineering; Economics; Electronic Engineering; Engineering; Materials Engineering; Mathematics; Mechanical Engineering; Metallurgical Engineering; Power Engineering; Production Engineering.** *Kandidat Nauk*: **Computer Engineering; Economics; Electronic Engineering; Engineering; Hydraulic Engineering; Industrial Engineering; Machine Building; Materials Engineering; Mechanical Engineering; Metallurgical Engineering; Petroleum and Gas Engineering; Power Engineering.** *Doktor Nauk*: **Power Engineering.**

Student Services: Canteen, Careers Guidance, Cultural Activities, Health Services, Library, Social Counselling, Sports Facilities

Publications: Vestnik GSTU

Academic Staff *2014-2015*: Total: c. 400
Student Numbers *2014-2015*: Total: c. 10,000
Last Updated: 10/02/15

POLESSKY STATE UNIVERSITY

Palesskij Dzjaržauny Universitet
Dneprovskoy Flotilii, 23, 225710 Pinsk
Tel: +375(165) 31-21-60 +375(165) 31-08-81
Fax: +375(165) 31-21-95
EMail: polessu@nbrb.by; polessky.edu@gmail.com
Website: http://www.psunbrb.by

Rector: Konstantin K. Shebeko Tel: +375(165) 31-21-60

Vice-Rector for Academic Affairs: Lidiya S. Tsvirko
Tel: +375(165) 31-08-40

Faculty

Banking (Accountancy; Banking; Finance; Information Technology); **Biotechnology** (Aquaculture; Biology; Biotechnology; Landscape Architecture); **Economics** (Agricultural Economics; Agricultural Management; Business Administration; Economics; Hotel and Restaurant; Management; Marketing; Tourism); **Healthy Lifestyle** (Health Sciences; Occupational Therapy; Physical Education; Physical Therapy; Rehabilitation and Therapy); **Preparatory Studies** (Biology; Chemistry; English; German; History; Mathematics; Physics; Russian; Slavic Languages); **Retraining and Qualification Upgrading** (Banking; Business Administration; Management; Sports Management)

History: Created 1944 as Pinskij Višejšy Bankauski Kaledž (Pinsk Higher Banking College). Acquired current title and status 2006.

Fees: National: Undergraduate, 2,000 per annum (US Dollar), International: Undergraduate, 2,500 per annum (US Dollar)

Main Language(s) of Instruction: Belarusian, Russian

Accrediting Agency: Ministry of Education

Degrees and Diplomas: *Diplom o Vyshem Obrazovanii*; *Diplom Magistra*: **Banking; Business Administration; Economics; Finance; Vocational Education.** *Kandidat Nauk*: **Banking; Economics; Finance; Physical Education; Sports Management.**

Student Services: Library, Residential Facilities, Sports Facilities

Publications: Economy and Banks; Health for Everyone; Nature Bulletin of Palesky State University Series in Natural Sciences; Series Iin Social Sciences And Humanities; Society Bulletin of Palesky State University

Academic Staff *2014-2015*: Total 243
STAFF WITH DOCTORATE: Total 19
Student Numbers *2014-2015*: Total: c. 4,080
Distance students, 1389.
Last Updated: 10/02/15

POLOTSK STATE UNIVERSITY

Polatskij Dzjaržauny Universitet (PSU)
29 Blokhin Street, 211440 Novopolotsk
Tel: +375(214) 53-21-61 +375(214) 51-13-93
Fax: +375(214) 53-42-63
EMail: post@psu.by
Website: http://www.psu.by/

Rector: Dmitry M. Lazovsky (2003-)
Tel: +375(214) 53-20-12 EMail: d.lazovski@psu.by

First Pro-rector: Vasily Boulakh
Tel: +375(214) 53-28-98 EMail: v.boulakh@psu.by

International Relations: Sergey Peshkun, Head of the International Office
Tel: +375(214) 53-63-40
EMail: inter.office@yahoo.co.uk; int.office@psu.by

Faculty

Civil Engineering (Architecture; Civil Engineering; Construction Engineering; Industrial Engineering); **Engineering Technology** (Chemical Engineering; Chemistry; Heating and Refrigeration; Hydraulic Engineering; Petroleum and Gas Engineering; Safety Engineering; Water Management); **Finance and Economics** (Accountancy; Economics; Finance; Human Resources; Management); **Geodesy** (Geography; Surveying and Mapping); **History and Philology** (English; French; German; History; Modern Languages; Philology); **Information Technology** (Computer Networks; Computer Science; Information Technology; Software Engineering); **Law** (Law); **Machine Building** (Building Technologies; Machine Building; Mechanical Engineering); **Physical Education** (Physical Education; Sports; Teacher Trainers Education); **Pre-university Training**; **Radio Engineering** (Electrical and Electronic Engineering; Telecommunications Engineering)

Further Information: Also Russian courses for foreign specialists (3-6 months). Continuing education programmes in Economics and Chemical Engineering

History: Founded 1968 as Novopolock Polytechnical Institute, acquired present status and title 1993.

Academic Year: September to June (September-February; February-June)

Admission Requirements: General or special secondary school certificate (Attestat o srednjem/specialnom/obrazovanii)

Fees: c. 1,300 per annum (US Dollar)

Main Language(s) of Instruction: Russian, Belarusian

Accrediting Agency: Ministry of Education

Degrees and Diplomas: *Diplom o Vyshem Obrazovanii*; *Diplom Magistra*: **Chemical Engineering; Computer Graphics; Computer Networks; Construction Engineering; Economics; Energy Engineering; Engineering Drawing and Design; Foreign Languages Education; Geology; Geophysics; History; Law; Literature; Machine Building; Maintenance Technology; Materials Engineering; Mathematics; Petroleum and Gas Engineering; Physical Education; Safety Engineering; Sports; Surveying and Mapping; Telecommunications Engineering.** *Kandidat Nauk*: **Automation and Control Engineering; Chemical Engineering; Civil Engineering; Construction Engineering; Economics; Electrical Engineering; Electronic Engineering; Geology; Heating and Refrigeration; Literature; Machine Building; Maintenance Technology; Materials Engineering; Mathematics; Mechanical Engineering.**

Student Services: Academic Counselling, Canteen, Cultural Activities, Health Services, IT Centre, Language Laboratory, Library, Social Counselling, Sports Facilities

Publications: Bulletin of Polock State University (Humanities and Applied Sciences)

Last Updated: 11/02/15

VITEBSK STATE ACADEMY OF VETERINARY MEDICINE

Vitebskaja Dzjaržaunaja Akademija Veterynarnaj Medycyny (VSAVM)
1st Dovatora str. 7/11, 210602 Vitebsk
Tel: +375(212) 37-07-37 +375(212) 37-20-37
+375(212) 37-23-22
Fax: +375(212) 37-02-84
EMail: vet.by@mail.ru
Website: http://www.vsavm.com/

Rector: Anton Ivanovič Yatusevich (1997-)

First Vice-Rector for Academic Affairs: Rostislav G. Kuzmich

Faculty

Animal Science (Animal Husbandry; Arts and Humanities; Chemistry; Farm Management; Fishery; Meat and Poultry; Physics; Physiology; Veterinary Science; Zoology); **Environmental Engineering** (Agricultural Economics; Agricultural Engineering; Environmental Engineering; Geological Engineering; Geology; Irrigation; Law; Management; Marketing; Real Estate; Soil Management; Soil Science; Water Management); **Veterinary Medicine** (Veterinary Science)

Department

Accounting and Finance (Accountancy; Finance)

Centre

Humanitarian Affairs and Communications (Arts and Humanities; Economics; History; Modern Languages; Pedagogy; Philosophy; Physical Education; Psychology; Sports); **Professional**

Retraining (Higher Education Teacher Training; Secondary Education)

Research Institute

Engineering and Agroengineering (Agricultural Engineering; Chemistry; Engineering; Machine Building; Maintenance Technology; Metal Techniques; Physics)

History: Founded 1924 as Higher Agricultural Technical School, acquired present status and title 1994.

Academic Year: September to July (September-January; February-July)

Admission Requirements: General or special secondary school certificate (Attestat o srednjem/specialnom/obrazovanii) and entrance examination

Fees: 750-800 per annum (US Dollar)

Main Language(s) of Instruction: Russian, Belarusian

Accrediting Agency: Ministry of Agriculture and Food; Ministry of Education

Degrees and Diplomas: *Diplom o Vyshem Obrazovanii*: **Veterinary Science.** *Diplom Magistra*: **Veterinary Science.** *Kandidat Nauk*: **Agricultural Engineering; Animal Husbandry; Veterinary Science.** *Doktor Nauk*: **Agricultural Engineering.**

Student Services: Academic Counselling, Canteen, Cultural Activities, Health Services, Library, Social Counselling, Sports Facilities

Publications: Jurnal Veterinarnaja Medicina Belarusi

Student Numbers *2014-2015*: Total: c. 5,600

Last Updated: 12/02/15

VITEBSK STATE MEDICAL UNIVERSITY

Vitebskij Dzjaržauny Medycynski Universitet (VSMU)

27 Frunze Ave, 210023 Vitebsk

Tel: +375(212) 24-04-33 +375 (212) 60-14-49

Fax: +375(212) 37-09-37 +375(212) 37-21-07

EMail: admin@vsmu.by; admin@vgmu.vitebsk.by; interdep.vitmed@gmail.com

Website: http://www.vsmu.by/

Rector: Valery P. Deykalo (2005-)
Tel: +375(212) 60-13-97 EMail: admin@vgmu.vitebsk.by

Vice-rector of Educational Work and International Affairs: Natalia Yurievna Konevalova Tel: +375(212) 60-13-91

Faculty

Advanced Training and Personnel Development (Anaesthesiology; Gynaecology and Obstetrics; Immunology; Laboratory Techniques; Oncology; Paediatrics; Pharmacology; Pharmacy; Rehabilitation and Therapy; Surgery); **Advanced Training in Pedagogics and Psychology** (Developmental Psychology; Educational Technology; Information Technology; Pedagogy; Psychology; Social Psychology; Vocational Education); **Medicine** (Anaesthesiology; Anatomy; Biochemistry; Biology; Cell Biology; Chemistry; Dermatology; Ecology; Embryology and Reproduction Biology; Epidemiology; Genetics; Gynaecology and Obstetrics; Health Sciences; Histology; Hygiene; Information Technology; Medicine; Microbiology; Neurology; Oncology; Ophthalmology; Organic Chemistry; Orthopaedics; Otorhinolaryngology; Paediatrics; Pathology; Pharmacology; Physics; Physiology; Pneumology; Psychiatry and Mental Health; Psychology; Public Health; Surgery; Toxicology); **Overseas Students Training** (Anatomy; Biochemistry; Biological and Life Sciences; Botany; Epidemiology; Gynaecology and Obstetrics; Medical Technology; Medicine; Neurology; Otorhinolaryngology; Pedagogy; Pharmacology; Pharmacy; Physiology; Psychiatry and Mental Health; Psychology; Rehabilitation and Therapy; Russian; Stomatology; Surgery; Toxicology; Urology); **Pharmacy** (Analytical Chemistry; Biochemistry; Botany; Chemistry; Laboratory Techniques; Microbiology; Organic Chemistry; Pharmacology; Pharmacy; Toxicology); **Professional Orientation and Preparatory Training (FOPT)** (Biology; Chemistry; Native Language; Russian); **Stomatology** (Stomatology)

Further Information: University Clinic; Teaching Hospitals; Teaching Educative-Industrial Drugstore "Vitunipharm"; University Dental Clinic; Control-Analytic Laboratory; Republican Centre "Infection in Surgery"; Lipid Centre; Etc.

History: Founded 1934 as Vitebsk State Medical Institute. Acquired present status and title 1998.

Academic Year: September to June (September-January; February-June)

Admission Requirements: Secondary school certificate (Attestat o srednjem obrazovanii) with good estimations (not less than 50%) on Biology, Chemistry, Physics and Mathematics.

Fees: National: 2,300-2,500 per annum (US Dollar), International: Undergraduate, 4,200-4,300 per annum for English language programmes and 1,700-4,100 per annum for English language programmes; Postgraduate, 2,030-3,600 annum (depending on the speciality and medium of training) (US Dollar)

Main Language(s) of Instruction: Russian, English

Accrediting Agency: Ministry of Health of the Republic of Belarus; Ministry of Education

Degrees and Diplomas: *Diplom o Vyshem Obrazovanii*: **Medicine; Pharmacy; Stomatology.** *Diplom Magistra*: **Anaesthesiology; Anatomy; Gynaecology and Obstetrics; Immunology; Medical Technology; Medicine; Oncology; Pathology; Pharmacology; Pharmacy; Physiology; Psychiatry and Mental Health; Public Health; Social and Preventive Medicine; Stomatology; Surgery; Toxicology.** *Kandidat Nauk*: **Anaesthesiology; Anatomy; Biochemistry; Botany; Cardiology; Cell Biology; Dermatology; Endocrinology; Epidemiology; Forensic Medicine and Dentistry; Gastroenterology; Gynaecology and Obstetrics; Histology; Hygiene; Immunology; Laboratory Techniques; Microbiology; Nephrology; Oncology; Ophthalmology; Orthopaedics; Otorhinolaryngology; Paediatrics; Parasitology; Pathology; Pharmacology; Pharmacy; Physical Therapy; Physiology; Pneumology; Psychiatry and Mental Health; Public Health; Radiology; Rehabilitation and Therapy; Social and Preventive Medicine; Sports Medicine; Surgery; Urology; Venereology.**

Student Services: Academic Counselling, Canteen, Careers Guidance, Cultural Activities, Foreign Studies Centre, Health Services, Library, Social Counselling, Sports Facilities

Publications: Bulletin of Pharmacy; Bulletin of VSMU; Immunology, Allergology, Infectology; Maternity and Childhood Protection; Medvuzovets; News of Surgery

Academic Staff *2014-2015*: Total: c. 280

Student Numbers *2014-2015*: Total: c. 7,000

Last Updated: 11/02/15

VITEBSK STATE TECHNOLOGICAL UNIVERSITY

Vitebskij Dzjaržauny Tehnalagičny Universitet (VSTU)

72, Moskovski Ave, 210035 Vitebsk

Tel: +375(212) 25-50-26

Fax: +375(212) 25-74-01

EMail: vstu@vitebsk.by

Website: http://vstu.by/

Rector: Valeriy S. Bashmetov (1993-) Tel: +375(212) 27-50-26

Vice-Rector: Sergeij Ivanovich Malashenkov

Faculty

Artistic Design and Technology (Applied Mathematics; Design; Textile Design; Textile Technology; Weaving); **Correspondence** (Business Administration; Economics; Engineering; Marketing); **Design and Technology** (Chemistry; Clothing and Sewing; Design; Ecology; Occupational Health; Physical Education; Technology; Textile Design; Weaving); **Economics** (Accountancy; Banking; Business Administration; Business and Commerce; Economics; Finance; Industrial Management; Management; Marketing); **Mechanics and Technology** (Automation and Control Engineering; Engineering Drawing and Design; Graphic Design; Machine Building; Mechanical Equipment and Maintenance; Mechanics; Physics; Technology); **Pre-university Training and Vocational Guidance** (Arts and Humanities; Economics; Engineering; English; Fine Arts; German; History; Mathematics; Painting and Drawing; Physics; Russian); **Qualifications Improvement and Staff Retraining** (Automation and Control Engineering; Communication Studies; Computer Science; Economics; Fine Arts; Handicrafts; Industrial Management; Management; Metallurgical Engineering; Safety

Engineering; Vocational Education; Welfare and Protective Services)

History: Founded 1965. Acquired present status 1999.

Fees: Full-time, 2,200 per annum; Part-time, 900 per annum; Preparatory faculty, 1,000 per annum (US Dollar)

Main Language(s) of Instruction: Russian, Belarusian

Accrediting Agency: Ministry of Education

Degrees and Diplomas: *Diplom o Vyshem Obrazovanii*; *Diplom Magistra*: **Automation and Control Engineering; Business Administration; Economics; Industrial Engineering; Machine Building; Management; Mechanical Engineering; Production Engineering; Textile Technology.** *Kandidat Nauk*: **Automation and Control Engineering; Ecology; Industrial Engineering; Industrial Management; Machine Building; Mechanical Engineering; Production Engineering; Textile Technology.** *Doktor Nauk*: **Textile Technology.**

Student Services: Health Services, IT Centre, Library, Residential Facilities, Sports Facilities

Last Updated: 10/02/15

VITEBSK STATE UNIVERSITY NAMED AFTER P.M. MASHEROV

Vitebskij Dzjaržauny Universitet imja P.M. Mašerova (VSU)

33 Moskovskiy Ave, 210038 Vitebsk
Tel: +375(212) 23-82-81
Fax: +375(212) 21-49-59
EMail: vsu@vsu.by
Website: http://www.vsu.by

Rector: Alexandr P. Solodkov (2014-)
Tel: +375(212) 21-58-66 EMail: rector@vsu.by

International Relations: Oksana Anatolieva Tulinova
Tel: +375(212) 21-99-16 EMail: szs@vsu.by

Faculty

Art and Graphics (Art Education; Education; Fine Arts; Handicrafts; Painting and Drawing; Technology; Visual Arts); **Belarusian Philology and Culture** (Cultural Studies; Educational Psychology; History; Journalism; Native Language; Philology); **Biology** (Biology; Chemistry; Ecology; Geography; Natural Sciences); **History** (History); **Law** (Law); **Mathematics** (Applied Mathematics; Information Technology; Mathematics; Mechanics); **Pedagogy** (Pedagogy); **Philology** (English; German; Literature; Philology; Russian; Slavic Languages); **Physical Education and Sports** (Physical Education; Sports; Sports Medicine); **Physics** (Astronomy and Space Science; Physical Engineering; Physics); **Preliminary Training; Social Pedagogy and Psychology** (Arts and Humanities; Preschool Education; Psychology; Social Psychology; Social Sciences)

Institute

Staff Upgrading and Retraining (Accountancy; Communication Studies; Computer Science; Economics; Educational Administration; Health Sciences; Industrial Management; Law; Occupational Health; Pedagogy; Physical Education; Preschool Education; Protective Services; Psychology; Speech Therapy and Audiology; Tourism; Vocational Education)

History: Founded 1910 as Teacher Training Institute, acquired present status and title 1995.

Academic Year: September to June (September-January; February-June)

Admission Requirements: General or special secondary school certificate (Attestat o srednjem/specialnom/obrazovanii) and entrance examination

Main Language(s) of Instruction: Belarusian, Russian

Accrediting Agency: Ministry of Education

Degrees and Diplomas: *Diplom o Vyshem Obrazovanii*; *Diplom Magistra*: **Art Criticism; Art Education; Biology; Educational Sciences; English; Foreign Languages Education; French; German; History; Humanities and Social Science Education; Mathematics; Music Education; Native Language Education; Pedagogy; Physical Education; Physics; Science Education; Sports; Teacher Training.** *Kandidat Nauk*: **Art Education; Biochemistry; Computer Education; Ecology; Educational Psychology; Educational Sciences; Entomology; History; Literature; Mathematics; Mathematics Education; Mechanics; Pedagogy; Philosophy; Physics; Russian; Slavic Languages; Vocational Education; Zoology.**

Student Services: Canteen, Careers Guidance, Cultural Activities, Health Services, Library, Sports Facilities

Publications: Vestnik Vitebskogo Gosudarstvennogo Universiteta (Bulletin of the Vitebsk State University)

Publishing House: Vitebsk State University Publishing House (Izdatelstvo Vitebskogo Gosudarstvennogo Universiteta)

Last Updated: 11/02/15

YANKA KUPALA STATE UNIVERSITY OF GRODNO

Grodnenskij Dzjaržauny Universitet imja Janki Kupaly (YKSUG)

22 Ozheshko str., 230023 Grodno
Tel: +375(152) 73-19-00
Fax: +375(152) 73-19-10
EMail: mail@grsu.by
Website: http://www.grsu.by

Rector: Andrei Karol Tel: +375(152) 73-19-01

Senior Vice-Rector: Sviatlana Ahiyavets
EMail: +375(152) 73-19-02

International Relations: Olga Minova, Head of International Cooperation Office
Tel: +375(152) 72-24-68 EMail: ominova@grsu.by

Faculty

Arts and Design (Conducting; Fashion Design; Fine Arts; Music; Musical Instruments; Singing); **Biology and Ecology** (Biochemistry; Biology; Botany; Chemical Engineering; Chemistry; Ecology; Environmental Studies; Physiology; Zoology); **Economics and Management** (Accountancy; Business Administration; Economics; Finance; Management); **Engineering and Construction** (Building Technologies; Materials Engineering); **History, Communications and Tourism** (Archaeology; Ethnology; History; Journalism; Sociology; Translation and Interpretation); **Innovative Mechanic Engineering** (Materials Engineering; Mechanical Engineering); **Law** (Commercial Law; Criminal Law; Criminology; International Law; Labour Law; Law; Private Law); **Mathematics and Informatics** (Applied Mathematics; Artificial Intelligence; Computer Science; Economics; Information Technology; Mathematics Education; Software Engineering); **Military Science** (Military Science); **Pedagogy** (Education of the Handicapped; English; Fine Arts; Music; Musical Instruments; Pedagogy; Preschool Education; Primary Education); **Philology** (English; Foreign Languages Education; German; Linguistics; Philology; Slavic Languages; Translation and Interpretation); **Physical Education** (Physical Education; Sports; Sports Medicine); **Physico-technical Studies** (Electrical and Electronic Engineering; Industrial Engineering; Materials Engineering; Measurement and Precision Engineering; Physics); **Pre-University Training** (Russian; Technology); **Psychology** (Psychology)

Department

Socio-Humanitarian (Cultural Studies; Economics; Philosophy; Political Sciences)

Further Information: Also Russian language foundation programme; Intensive Russian/Belarusian languages courses; Vocational schools

History: Founded 1940 as State Teacher Training Institute. Placed under the authority of the Ministry of Education of the Republic of Belarus. Financed by the State. Acquired present status and title 1978.

Academic Year: September to June (September-January; February-June). Winter and Summer Sessions

Admission Requirements: General or special secondary school certificate (Attestat o srednjem/specialnom/obrazovanii) and competitive entrance examination; For Doctoral programmes, Master's degree is required

Fees: Russian/Belarusian Language Courses, c. 100 per week; the Russian/Belarusian Foundation Programme, 1,100 per annum; First Degree, 1,000-1,900 per annum; Doctoral Programmes, 1,500 per annum (US Dollar)

Main Language(s) of Instruction: Russian, Belarusian, English

Accrediting Agency: Ministry of Education

Degrees and Diplomas: *Diplom o Vyshem Obrazovanii*; *Diplom Magistra*: **Applied Linguistics; Applied Mathematics; Biology; Civil Engineering; Commercial Law; Computer Science; Ecology; Educational Administration; Foreign Languages Education; German; International Economics; International Law; Journalism; Latin; Law; Linguistics; Literature; Machine Building; Management; Mathematics; Military Science; Music; Pedagogy; Physical Education; Physics; Political Sciences; Preschool Education; Primary Education; Psychology; Public Law; Radiophysics; Social Psychology; Sociology; Transport Engineering.** *Kandidat Nauk*: **Art Criticism; Biochemistry; Biotechnology; Civil Law; Commercial Law; Constitutional Law; Criminology; Cultural Studies; Developmental Psychology; Econometrics; Economics; Educational Psychology; Educational Sciences; History; History of Law; Humanities and Social Science Education; International Law; Laser Engineering; Linguistics; Literature; Mathematics; Mechanical Engineering; Mechanical Equipment and Maintenance; Microbiology; Optics; Pedagogy; Philosophy; Physical Education; Physics; Physiology; Polymer and Plastics Technology; Private Law; Production Engineering; Radiophysics; Russian; Science Education; Slavic Languages; Solid State Physics; Sports.** *Doktor Nauk*: **Mathematics; Optics; Physics.**

Student Services: Academic Counselling, Canteen, Cultural Activities, Foreign Studies Centre, Health Services, IT Centre, Language Laboratory, Library, Social Counselling, Sports Facilities

Publications: Vestnik GRGU

Publishing House: Editorial and Publishing Department

Academic Staff *2014-2015*: Total 831

Student Numbers *2014-2015*: Total 15,527

Last Updated: 11/02/15

PRIVATE INSTITUTIONS

BELARUSIAN INSTITUTE OF LAW

BIP-Instytut Pravaznaustva (BIP)

3 Korolya Street, 220004 Minsk

Tel: +375(17) 211-01-58

Fax: +375(17) 211-01-58

EMail: bnip@user.unibel.by

Website: http://www.bip-ip.info/

Rector: V. Golovanov Tel: +375(17) 211-01-45

First Vice-Rector: Stepan Sokol Tel: +375(17) 200-92-93

International Relations: Vasiliy Bonko, Vice-Rector for Research Tel: +375(17) 202-40-59

Faculty

Economics and Law (Accountancy; Economics; Information Technology; Mathematics); **International Law and Legal Psychology** (International Law; Philosophy; Political Sciences; Psychology)

School

Law (Civil Law; Criminal Law; Fiscal Law; History of Law; Law)

Department

Foreign Languages (English; French; German); **Physical Education** (Physical Education)

Campus

Grodno (Civil Law; Criminal Law; Criminology; History of Law; International Law; Law; Philosophy; Political Sciences; Psychology); **Mogilev** (Arts and Humanities; Economics; Law)

History: Founded 1990, acquired present status and title 2005.

Academic Year: September to June

Admission Requirements: School Certificate

Main Language(s) of Instruction: Russian, Belarusian

Accrediting Agency: Ministry of Education

Degrees and Diplomas: *Diplom o Vyshem Obrazovanii*: **Accountancy; Business Administration; Commercial Law; Economics; Fiscal Law; International Law; Law; Political Sciences; Psychology.** *Diplom Magistra*: **Economics; Law; Management.** *Kandidat Nauk*: **Civil Law; Commercial Law; History of Law; International Law; Private Law.**

Student Services: Academic Counselling, Canteen, Careers Guidance, Foreign Studies Centre, Health Services, IT Centre, Library, Social Counselling, Sports Facilities

Publications: Law and Life; Social, Economic and Law Researches

Publishing House: "BIP-S Plus" Publishing House

Last Updated: 05/02/15

BELARUSIAN TRADE AND ECONOMICS UNIVERSITY OF CONSUMER COOPERATIVES

Belaruskij Gandljova-Ekanamičny Universitet Spažyveckaj Kaaperacyi (BTEU)

pr. Oktyabrya 50, 246029 Gomel

Tel: +375(232) 48-17-07 +375(232) 48-09-83

Fax: +375(232) 47-80-68 +375(232) 48-10-62

EMail: gki@mail.gomel.by; bteu@bks.by; Ppriem@bteu.by; interbteu@mail.ru

Website: http://www.i-bteu.by/

Rector: Svetlana Lebedeva Tel: +375(232) 48-17-07

Vice-Rector: Ludmila V. Misnikova
Tel: +375(232) 48-05-58 EMail: lmis@bteu.by

Faculty

Accountancy and Finance (Accountancy; Banking; Finance; Modern Languages); **Commerce** (Business and Commerce; Marketing; Physical Education; Sports; Transport Management); **Economics and Management** (Agricultural Business; Economics; Information Technology; International Economics; Law; Management; Statistics); **Training and Retraining** (Economics; Law)

History: Founded 1964 as Gomel Cooperative Institute, acquired present title 2001.

Academic Year: September to June (September-February; March-June)

Admission Requirements: General or special secondary school certificate (Attestat o srednjem/specialnom/obrazovanii)

Fees: 14,6m. per annum (Belarussian Ruble)

Main Language(s) of Instruction: Russian, Belarusian

Accrediting Agency: Belarus Republican Union of Consumer Societies; Ministry of Education

Degrees and Diplomas: *Diplom o Vyshem Obrazovanii*; *Diplom Magistra*: **Accountancy; Banking; Business Administration; Business Computing; Economics; Finance; Food Technology; International Economics; Management; Marketing; Statistics; Tourism; Transport Management.** *Kandidat Nauk*: **Accountancy; Banking; Economics; Finance; Food Technology; Statistics.**

Student Services: Academic Counselling, Canteen, Careers Guidance, Cultural Activities, Health Services, IT Centre, Library, Nursery Care, Residential Facilities, Social Counselling, Sports Facilities

Publications: Potrebitelskaya cooperatsiya

Publishing House: Polygraphy

Academic Staff *2014-2015*	**TOTAL**
FULL-TIME	**258**
Student Numbers *2014-2015*	
All (Foreign included)	c. **7,000**
FOREIGN ONLY	**130**

Last Updated: 09/02/15

INSTITUTE OF ENTREPRENEURIAL ACTIVITY

Instytut Pradprymal'nickaj Dzejnasci

Seraphimovich St, 11, 220033 Minsk

Tel: +375(17) 247-08-77 +375(17) 247-06-22

Fax: +375(17) 298-38-10

EMail: uoipd@tut.by

Website: http://www.uoipd.org/

Rector: Viktor L. Tsybovsky

First Vice-Rector: Vladimir V. Sheverdov

Faculty
Economics and Business (Business Administration; Economics; Management; Mathematics and Computer Science); **Foreign Economic Activity and Entrepreneurship** (Arts and Humanities; Management; Marketing; Physical Education; Tourism; Translation and Interpretation)

History: Founded 1992.

Main Language(s) of Instruction: Russian, Belarusian

Accrediting Agency: Ministry of Education

Degrees and Diplomas: *Diplom o Vyshem Obrazovanii*; *Diplom Magistra*: **Administration; Management.**

Student Services: Library

Academic Staff *2014-2015*: Total 142
Student Numbers *2014-2015*: Total: c. 2,750
Last Updated: 11/02/15

INSTITUTE OF MANAGEMENT AND BUSINESS

Častnij Instytut Kiravannja i Pradprymal'nictva
ul.Slavinskogo, 1, Bldg. 3, 220086 Minsk
Tel: +375(17) 263-79-83
Fax: +375(17) 263-56-33
EMail: imb@imb.by
Website: http://www.imb.by

Rector: Alexander Semeshko
Tel: +375(17) 263-00-49 EMail: Rectorat@imb.by

Provost for Academic and Scientific Affairs: Michael I. Ovseets
Tel: +375(17) 263-38-26

Faculty
Economics (Accountancy; Banking; Economics; Finance; Human Resources; Information Technology; International Economics; International Relations; Management; Mathematics); **Law** (Arts and Humanities; Civil Law; Criminal Law; Law; Modern Languages; Physical Education; Public Law); **Personnel Retraining** (Accountancy; Economics; Finance; Human Resources; Physical Education; Small Business)

History: Founded 1993. Acquired present status 2001.

Main Language(s) of Instruction: Russian, Belarusian

Accrediting Agency: Ministry of Education

Degrees and Diplomas: *Diplom o Vyshem Obrazovanii*; *Diplom Magistra*: **Economics.**

Student Services: IT Centre, Library, Sports Facilities
Last Updated: 10/02/15

INSTITUTE OF MODERN KNOWLEDGE

Instytut Sučasnyh Vedau
ul. Filimonov, 69, 220114 Minsk
Tel: +375(17) 263-77-42
Fax: +375(17) 285-70-83
EMail: zao@isz.minsk.by
Website: http://www.isz.minsk.by

Rector: A.L. Kapilov Tel: +375(17) 285-70-83

Vice-Rector for Academic Affairs: Valentina Rostovtcev
EMail: +375 (17) 263-00-43

Faculty
Art (Computer Graphics; Design; Fine Arts; Interior Design; Music; Musical Instruments; Singing; Textile Design); **Humanities** (Art Management; Arts and Humanities; Cultural Studies; English; Finance; German; Italian; Management; Translation and Interpretation)

History: Created in 1990. Acquired status 2001.

Main Language(s) of Instruction: Russian, Belarusian

Accrediting Agency: Ministry of Education

Degrees and Diplomas: *Diplom o Vyshem Obrazovanii*: **Communication Studies; Cultural Studies; Design; Fine Arts.**

Student Services: Library
Last Updated: 06/02/15

INSTITUTE OF PARLIAMENTARISM AND ENTREPRENEURSHIP

Instytut Parlamentaryzma i Pradprymal'nictva (IPE)
65A Timiryazev Street, 220035 Minsk
Tel: +375(17) 209-06-67
Fax: +375(17) 209-06-83
EMail: ipp@ipp.by
Website: http://www.ipp.by

Rector: Alexander Gorelik Tel: +375(17) 290-82-01

First Vice-Rector: Markov Andrei Viktorovich
Tel: +375(17) 209-06-89

Department
Economics and Management (Accountancy; Banking; Business Administration; Economics; Finance; Management; Small Business); **Journalism** (Journalism); **Political Science** (Information Management; Information Sciences; Political Sciences)

History: Founded 1993, acquired present status and title 2004.

Main Language(s) of Instruction: Russian, Belarusian

Accrediting Agency: Ministry of Education

Degrees and Diplomas: *Diplom o Vyshem Obrazovanii*; *Diplom Magistra*: **Leadership; Management; Political Sciences.**

Student Services: Library
Last Updated: 06/02/15

INTERNATIONAL HUMANITARIAN AND ECONOMICS INSTITUTE

Mižnarodny Gumanitarna-Ekanamičny Instytut (IHEI)
129A, Mayakovskogo St., 220028 Minsk
Tel: +375(17) 392-69-13 +375(017) 328-23-30
Fax: +375(17) 210-58-75
EMail: mgei2006@tut.by
Website: http://www.mgei.org

Rector: Alexander N. Alpeev

Chancellor: Tamara M. Alpeev

Faculty
Accounting and Audit (Accountancy); **Economics and Management** (Accountancy; Business Administration; Economics; Finance; Management); **Finances and Credit** (Banking; Finance); **International Economics** (International Economics); **International Law** (International Law; Modern Languages); **International Relations** (International Relations); **Law** (Law); **Political Science** (Political Sciences); **Psychology** (Psychology); **Sociology** (Sociology)

History: Founded 1994.

Main Language(s) of Instruction: Russian, Belarusian

Accrediting Agency: Ministry of Education

Degrees and Diplomas: *Diplom o Vyshem Obrazovanii*

Student Services: Library
Last Updated: 11/02/15

INTERNATIONAL UNIVERSITY MITSO

Mižnarodny Universitet "MITSO"
1/3 Kazintsa St., 220099 Minsk
Tel: +375(17) 207-04-04
Fax: +375(17) 207-04-04
EMail: mitso@mitso.by
Website: http://mitso.by/

Rector: Stanislav Knyazev (2011-)
Tel: +375(17) 207-04-04 EMail: knyazev@mitso.by

First Vice-Rector: Gennady Podgorny Tel: +375(17) 279-98-98

International Relations: Elena A. Kulago, International Relations Officer Tel: +375(17) 278-60-29 EMail: international@mitso.by

Faculty
International Economic Relations and Management (Economics; Finance; Management; Marketing; Transport Management); **Law** (Chinese; Commercial Law; English; French; German; International Law; Italian; Labour Law; Law; Spanish); **Pre-University Training** (Business Administration; Civil Law; Commercial Law;

Economics; English; German; Labour Law; Mathematics; Russian; Social Sciences)

Further Information: Branches in Gomel and Vitebsk

History: Founded 1992 as Mižnarodny Instytut Pracounyh i Sacyjal'nyh Adnosin (International Institute of Labour and Social Relations). Acquired present status and title 2011.

Main Language(s) of Instruction: Russian, Belarusian

Accrediting Agency: Ministry of Education

Degrees and Diplomas: *Diplom o Vyshem Obrazovanii*; *Diplom Magistra*: **Economics; Law.** *Kandidat Nauk*: **Economics; Law.** *Doktor Nauk*: **Economics; Law.**

Student Services: Canteen, Library, Residential Facilities, Sports Facilities

Publications: Labor Trade Union Society

Last Updated: 11/02/15

MINSK INSTITUTE OF MANAGEMENT

Minskij Instytut Kiravannja (MIM)

12 Lazo Street, 220102 Minsk

Tel: +375(17) 291-26-27

Fax: +375(17) 243-67-61

EMail: miu@miu.by

Website: http://www.miu.by/

Rector: Nikolay Vasilyevich Susha (1994-)
Tel: +375(17) 291-26-27 EMail: nsusha@tut.by; miu@miu.by

Vice-Rector for Academic Affairs: Branislau A. Hedranovich
Tel: +375(17) 273-76-22

International Relations: Valiantsina V. Hedranovich
Tel: +375(17) 243-54-72

Faculty

Advanced Training and Retraining *("Higher School of Management")* (Accountancy; Banking; Economics; Finance; Graphic Design; Industrial Management; Information Technology; Management; Marketing; Psychology; Software Engineering); **Economics** (Accountancy; Banking; Business Administration; Economics; Finance; Industrial Management; Information Technology; Transport Management); **Engineering and Information** (Computer Engineering; Computer Science; Engineering; Information Management; Information Technology; Management; Marketing; Mathematics; Software Engineering); **Law** (Architectural and Environmental Design; Commercial Law; Design; English; German; Law; Modern Languages; Psychology; Translation and Interpretation)

History: Founded 1991, acquired present status and title 2001.

Main Language(s) of Instruction: Russian, Belarusian

Accrediting Agency: Ministry of Education

Degrees and Diplomas: *Diplom o Vyshem Obrazovanii*; *Diplom Magistra*: **Accountancy; Architectural and Environmental Design; Banking; Business Administration; Computer Engineering; Computer Science; Economics; Finance; Germanic Languages; Information Management; International Economics; Law; Management; Marketing; Psychology; Social Psychology; Software Engineering; Statistics.** *Kandidat Nauk*: **Civil Law; Commercial Law; Economics; International Law; Private Law.** *Doktor Nauk*: **Economics.**

Student Services: IT Centre, Language Laboratory, Library, Sports Facilities

Publications: Actual Problems of Science of the XXI Century; Economics and Management

Last Updated: 11/02/15

Belgium - Flemish Community

STRUCTURE OF HIGHER EDUCATION SYSTEM

Description:

Within the Bologna Process, participating countries have committed to elaborating national qualifications frameworks by 2010 and to launch this work by 2007. The aim was to establish a European Higher Education Area by 2010. Countries have been invited to carry out self-certification exercises to verify the compatibility with the overarching framework of qualifications of the European Higher Education Area (EHEA) http://www.ehea.info/. As these self-certification exercises are completed, the self-certification reports will be published at http://www.enic-naric.net/index.aspx?s=n&r=ena&d=qf.

Thanks to the Bologna Process, all higher education programmes in Flanders (Belgium) were transformed into the Three-Tier structure, "Bachelor-Master-Doctor"-structure, by the Law on Higher Education Reform of 4 April 2003. The National Framework of Qualifications in Higher Education in Flanders is compatible with the overarching Framework for Qualifications of the European Higher Education Area. This is stated by NVAO following the conclusion of an independent and international external verification committee. The self-certification report of Flanders is published at http://www.nvao.net/nqf-fl as well as at http://www.enic-naric.net/index.aspx?s=n&r=ena&d=qf.

The learning outcomes of all programmes in Flanders (Belgium) are legally outlined in cycle descriptors. The higher education in Flanders has a binary structure at Bachelor level. Professional Bachelor's programmes have the objective to bring students to a level of general and specific knowledge and competences required to perform a particular profession or group of professions independently. A professional Bachelor's programme can therefore lead directly to a place on the labour market.

The main objective of the academic Bachelor's programmes is that students will go on to a Master's programme. Thus, they are geared towards bringing the students to a certain level of scientific or artistic knowledge and competences, required for scientific or artistic work in general, and towards a specific field of sciences or arts in particular. Preparing students for the labour market is only a secondary objective. Some Bachelor's programmes are a follow-up to another (professional) Bachelor's programme. This follow-up programme is geared towards the broadening of or specializing in competences acquired during the initial Bachelor's programme.

Master's programmes have the objective to bring students to an advanced level of scientific or artistic knowledge and competences required for scientific or artistic work in general, and to a specific domain of sciences and arts in particular, which is required for autonomous scientific or artistic work or to apply this scientific or artistic knowledge independently in one or a group of professions. Some Master's programmes are considered as advanced or further studies.

The qualification of Doctor is granted by a panel of researchers after a public presentation of the Doctor's thesis in which the writer/researcher/student has demonstrated to be able to conceive new scientific knowledge based on independent research. The doctoral thesis should have the potential to lead to publications in scientific journals.

Only people who have been conferred the title of Bachelor, Master or Doctor, pursuant to the Law of 2003, may carry the corresponding title of Bachelor, Master or Doctor and the legally protected abbreviations "Dr" and "PhD".

The European Qualifications Framework for Lifelong Learning (EQF for LLL) was approved by the European Parliament and the European Council in 2008. http://ec.europa.eu/education/lifelong-learning-policy/eqf_en.htm. The EQF for LLL is a translation tool to make qualifications expressed in competences intelligible and comparable at European level. Subsequent to this European development, Flanders introduced by law in 2009 - totally comparable with the European Qualifications Framework for Lifelong learning (EQF for LLL) - the National Qualification Framework (NQF) of Flanders also with eight levels. The level descriptors of Bachelor, Master and Doctor are legally declared equal to the level descriptors of level 6, level 7 and level 8 of the NQF Flanders and EQF for LLL. Since a secondary school leaving certificate of Flanders is at level 4, Flanders introduced at level 5 "Hoger Beroepsonderwijs" leading to the new qualification in higher education, namely "Diploma van gegradueerde", officially translated as "Associate degree".

Stages of studies:

University level first stage: *Bachelor - NQF Flanders level 6*

Bachelor programmes have a study load of 180 credits. There are Bachelor's programmes with a professional orientation and Bachelor's programmes with an academic orientation. Professional Bachelor's programmes have the objective to bring students to a level of general and specific knowledge and competences required to perform a particular profession or group of professions independently. A professional Bachelor's programme can therefore lead directly to a place on the labour market. Only the university colleges offer professional Bachelor's programmes. The main objective of the academic Bachelor's programmes is that students will go on to a Master's programme. Thus, they are geared towards bringing the students to a certain level of scientific or artistic knowledge and competences, required for scientific or artistic work in general, and towards a specific field of sciences or arts in particular. Preparing students for the labour market is only a secondary objective. University colleges and universities may offer academic Bachelor's programmes. Some Bachelor's programmes are a follow-up to another (professional) Bachelor's programme. This follow-up programme is geared towards the broadening of or specializing in competences acquired during the initial Bachelor's programme. Only the university colleges may offer such advanced Bachelor's programmes. The study load of these programmes is at least 60 credits.

University level second stage: *Master - NQF Flanders level 7*

All Master programmes have a study load of minimum 60 credits. Master's programmes have the objective to bring students to an advanced level of scientific or artistic knowledge and competences required for scientific or artistic work in general, and to a specific domain of sciences and arts in particular, which is required for autonomous scientific or artistic work or to apply this scientific or artistic knowledge independently in one or a group of professions. Some Master's programmes are advanced or further studies aiming at deepening the knowledge and/or competences in a certain field of study. University colleges and universities may offer Master's programmes. Postgraduate Certificate programmes have the goal to increase the professional knowledge and skills by broadening and/or enlarging the competences obtained by graduation after a Bachelor's programme or Master's programme. University colleges and universities may offer such programmes. The study load of Postgraduate Certificate programmes is at least 20 credits.

University level third stage: *Doctor - NQF Flanders level 8*

The qualification of Doctor is granted by a panel of researchers after a public presentation of the Doctor's thesis in which the writer/researcher/student has demonstrated to be able to conceive new scientific knowledge based on independent research. The doctoral thesis should have the potential to lead to publications in scientific journals. The organisation of doctoral studies is the autonomous decision of the universities. It can include courses or not and there are different approaches to interdisciplinary training. The common practice is as follows: 1) no credits are used for doctoral studies, but a few universities do use credits but only for the course part of the programme; 2) the normal duration is 4 years of full-time study and this is the standard for the doctoral grant system to doctoral students; 3) each university has a set of rules and procedures on the supervision structure. Doctoral students present a study and research plan to their respective Faculty or Department for approval. The student will be guided by a supervisor and an accompanying committee of professors to which the student has to report at regular intervals, usually every 2 years. The committee can impose a course programme to the student, but this is not obligatory. Most universities have doctoral schools with the mission: 1) to advertise and recruit internationally, 2) to optimize the guidance of doctoral students, 3) to help expand and develop the skills of young researchers. In the doctoral schools they offer doctoral education programmes which have to be completed before admission to the doctoral defence. The aim is to train the doctoral student by enlarging the scientific knowledge (truncus communis) and by acquiring diverse competences. The truncus communis is compulsory and has the following elements: publications, doctoral seminars linked with the own research topic and more general relevant topics, presentations on international conferences, attending doctoral seminars and courses and submitting reports regarding the doctoral progress. The qualification of Doctor is only awarded by universities.

ADMISSION TO HIGHER EDUCATION

Admission to university-level studies:

Name of secondary school credential required: Diploma van Secundair Onderwijs

For entry to: Bachelor's degrees

Alternatives to credentials: The board of the institution may, pursuant to the regulations, facilitate the access to a particular programme on the basis of deviatory admission requirements, solely based on humanitarian grounds; medical, psychological or social grounds; the overall level of the candidate, which is assessed by the board of the institution. A student who has already obtained a Bachelor's degree can enter another Bachelor's programme without having to take up all the credits of that programme.

Admission requirements: Entrance examinations must be sat for in Civil Engineering, Civil Engineering-Architect, Dental Sciences and Medical Sciences.

Other requirements: Entrance examinations must be sat for Dental and Medical Sciences.

Foreign students admission:

Definition of foreign student: Holders of a foreign qualification. Nationality is not at all an issue regarding this matter, namely access to higher education.

Admission requirements: Foreign students who can justify having obtained a secondary school leaving certificate giving access to higher education in their country may start higher education in Flanders. Foreign students also have to pass the entrance examinations for Nautical sciences, Fine Arts, Dental and Medical sciences. Foreign students holding a higher education diploma may obtain a reduction of the total study load of a programme.

Language proficiency: Students must be proficient in Dutch for undergraduate studies. Candidates may be required to sit for a language test. The universities organize language courses during the summer.

RECOGNITION OF STUDIES

Quality assurance system:

The concept of accreditation has been incorporated into the Higher Education Act 2003. The accreditation system is organised in close cooperation with the Netherlands by an independent Dutch Flemish Accreditation Body (Nederlands Vlaams Accreditatie Orgaan NVAO) which was set up in September 2003. In Flanders, accreditation is a formal decision by the NVAO that a programme meets the predefined quality criteria. These criteria are laid down in NVAO's (initial) accreditation frameworks. Accreditation is however only one part of the whole quality assurance system of higher education in Flanders. This quality assurance system consists of three parts: an internal part, an external part and the part where the formal decision is taken.

(1) Internal Quality Assurance: the self-evaluation. The self-evaluation of the programme is organized by the higher education institution itself and results in the self-evaluation report.

(2) External Quality Assurance: external quality assessment. The self-evaluation report is the starting point of the external quality assessment. The result of the external quality assessment is the assessment report. The external quality assessment is organised by the VLHORA and VLIR.

The VLHORA, the Council of Flemish University Colleges, was established in 1996 and was awarded the statute of public utility institution by law in 1998. The VLHORA gives advice to the Flemish authorities on all policy aspects regarding university college education, applied research, social services and the practice of the arts. Moreover the VLHORA organises and stimulates consultation between the institutions on all issues related to the university colleges. Cf. http://www.vlhora.be/.

In 1976, the Flemish Interuniversity Council (VLIR) was set up as an autonomous public body with its own institutional status. The council consists of members who represent the Flemish universities. It defends the interests of the universities and gives advice to the Flemish government on university matters (consultation, advice and recommendations). In addition, the council organises consultation between the universities. Cf. http://www.vlir.be/. VLHORA and VLIR organise and coordinate external quality assurance through the external reviews of programmes. In 2010 they merged to VLUHR, "Vlaamse Universiteiten en Hogescholen Raad". VLUHR organizes these assessments by setting up an independent assessment panel of experts responsible for assessing all the programmes in a certain field of study. The assessment panel consists of experts in the field of study, experts in quality assurance, educational/pedagogical experts and experts in the international development of the field of study. Students are always involved and represented in the assessment panel.

(3) The formal decision: accreditation. The Netherlands and Flanders have set up an independent accreditation organization by international treaty, the Nederlands-Vlaamse Accreditatieorganisatie (NVAO). Cf. http://www.nvao.net. Higher education programmes that have successfully gone through the external quality assessment send their assessment report to the NVAO. The NVAO then evaluates the thoroughness of the external assessment and accepts or rejects its findings. If the accreditation decision is positive, the programme is accredited. This means that the programme is included in the Higher Education Register. This registration

means that the degree awarded by the programme is recognised by the national authority, Flanders. Additionally, accredited programmes can receive public funding and the students enrolled in these programmes can receive student support (e.g. grants). However, public funding and student support are normally not available for programmes offered by private institutions. A positive accreditation decision by the NVAO is kept or listed in the Higher Education Register for 8 years. If the accreditation decision is negative, the programme loses accreditation. This means the programme is deleted from the Higher Education Register and can no longer be offered. However there is a possibility of temporary recognition during a recovery period. After the negative accreditation decision, the institution has the opportunity to submit an application to the Flemish government for a temporary recognition. This has to be done within one month after the notification of the negative decision. A detailed plan for improvement has to be put forward together with the application. Following advice from the Recognition Commission, the Flemish government takes a decision within three months of the application. Temporary recognition may have a validity of one to three years. In the NVAO's accreditation system, learning outcomes are made use of at the three levels. A programme is expected to explicitly define its intended learning outcomes. These are the competences a graduate should acquire during his studies. An assessment panel first judges whether a programme's intended learning outcomes are in line with the required level and the subject of the programme. The level is evaluated by matching the intended learning outcomes to the Framework for Qualifications of the European Higher Education Area. Additionally, the assessment panel assesses whether these intended learning outcomes are in line with what is (inter)nationally expected of a programme in that subject. NVAO secondly judges the potential learning outcomes. These are the competences a student can achieve in the programme as it is offered. This is mainly done by checking the content of the curriculum with the intended learning outcomes. Thirdly, NVAO assesses the achieved learning outcomes. These are the competences a graduate has actually acquired during his or her studies. An assessment panel needs to read students' work such as essays, end of term papers and theses to be able to judge the achieved learning outcomes and then match those with the required learning outcomes. The required learning outcomes are of course the level-specific and intended subject-specific learning outcomes as defined by the programme and (positively) assessed by the panel Accreditation is a prerequisite for awarding Bachelor's or Master's degrees education funding and study financing for students.

Bodies dealing with recognition:

NARIC-Vlaanderen - NARIC-Flanders

Hendrik Consciencegebouw Toren C2
Koning Albert II-laan 15
Brussels 1210
Tel: +32(2) 553-8958
Fax: +32(2) 553-9845
EMail: naric@vlaanderen.be
WWW: http://www.ond.vlaanderen.be/naric

Nederlands-Vlaams Accreditatie Orgaan - NVAO

Postbus 85498
Den Haag 2508
Tel: +31(70) 312-2300
Fax: +31(70) 312-2301
EMail: info@nvao.net
WWW: http://www.nvao.net

NATIONAL BODIES

Ministerie van Onderwijs en Vorming (Ministry of Education and Training)

Minister: Hilde Crevits
Hendrik Consciencegebouw
Koning Albert II-laan 15
Brussels, Vlaams-Brabant 1210
Tel: +32(2) 553-5070
WWW: http://www.ond.vlaanderen.be

Role of national body: The Higher Education Policy Unit belongs to the Department of Education and Training of the Flemish Ministry of Education and Training. It is responsible for policy development and evaluation of higher education. In cooperation with the higher education institutions and other organisations the Higher Education Policy Unit improves, develops and stimulates pro-active initiatives regarding higher education and research.

Vlaamse Onderwijsraad - VLOR (Flemish Educational Council)

Administrator General: Mia Douterlungne
Kunstlaan 6 bus 6
Brussels 1210
Tel: +32(2) 219-4299
Fax: +32(2) 219-8118
EMail: info@vlor.be
WWW: http://www.vlor.be

Role of national body: The VLOR is the Strategic Advisory Council for the education and training policy of Flanders. It plays a role in the policy-making process. The council operates independent of the Department of Education and Training and of the competent Minister. Representatives of all the different stakeholders in education and training meet in the VLOR. Together they look for ways to further improve education and training in Flanders.

Vlaamse Interuniversitaire Raad - VLIR (Flemish Interuniversity Council)

Secretary-General: Rosette S'Jegers
Ravensteingalerij 27, Bus 3
Brussels 1000
Tel: +32(2) 792-5500
Fax: +32(2) 211-4199
EMail: administratie@vlir.be
WWW: http://www.vlir.be

Role of national body: In 1976, the Flemish Interuniversity Council (VLIR) was set up as an autonomous public body with its own institutional status. The council consists of members who represent the Flemish universities. It defends the interests of the universities and gives advice to the Flemish government on university matters (consultation, advice and recommendations). In addition, the council organises consultation between the universities. VLHORA and VLIR organise and coordinate external quality assurance through the external reviews of programmes. In 2010, the VLHORA and VLIR merged to VLUHR, "Vlaamse Universiteiten en Hogescholen Raad".

Vlaamse Hogescholenraad - VLHORA (Flemish Council of University Colleges)

Secretary-General: Marc Vandewalle
Ravensteingalerij 27 bus 3 - 1e verd
Brussels 1000
Tel: +32(2) 211-4190
Fax: +32(2) 211-4199
EMail: info@vlhora.be
WWW: http://www.vlhora.be

Role of national body: The VLHORA, the Council of Flemish University Colleges, was established in 1996 and was awarded the statute of public utility institution by law in 1998. The VLHORA gives advice to the Flemish authorities on all policy aspects regarding university college education, applied research, social services and the practice of the arts. Moreover the VLHORA organises and stimulates consultation between the institutions on all issues related to the university colleges.

VLHORA and VLIR organise and coordinate external quality assurance through the external reviews of programmes. In 2010, they merged to VLUHR, "Vlaamse Universiteiten en Hogescholen Raad".

NARIC-Vlaanderen - NARIC-Flanders

Coordinator: Daniël De Schrijver
Hendrik Consciencegebouw Toren C2
Koning Albert II-laan 15
Brussels 1210
Tel: +32(2) 553-8958
Fax: +32(2) 553-9845

EMail: naric@vlaanderen.be
WWW: http://www.ond.vlaanderen.be/naric
Role of national body: NARIC-Flanders, is the recognition and information centre of Flanders (Belgium) within the ENIC and NARIC Networks of the European Commission, the Council of Europe and UNESCO. It is in charge of the academic recognition of foreign (higher education) qualifications and the professional recognition of teachers based upon the applicable European Directive 2005/36/EC. It belongs to the Agency for Quality Assurance in Education and Training. That Agency belongs to the Ministry of Education and Training (of Flanders).

Data for academic year: 2011-2012
Source: IAU from the Higher Education Policy Unit, Department of Education and Training, Flemish Ministry of Education and Training, Belgium, 2012. Bodies 2015.

INSTITUTIONS

ANTWERP MARITIME ACADEMY

Hogere Zeevaartschool Antwerpen (HZS)
Noordkasteel Oost 6, 2030 Antwerpen
Tel: +32(3) 205-64-30
Fax: +32(3) 225-06-39
EMail: info@hzs.be
Website: http://www.hzs.be

Algemeen Directeur: Patrick Blondé EMail: patrick.blonde@hzs.be

Administratief Directeur: Anne Courbois
EMail: anne.courbois@hzs.be

International Relations: Willem Bruyndonx
EMail: willem.bruyndonx@hzs.be

Faculty
Marine Engineering (Marine Engineering); **Nautical Sciences** (Nautical Science)

History: Founded 1800. Acquired present status 1834.

Academic Year: October to July

Admission Requirements: Secondary school certificate

Fees: EU students, c. 460 per annum; foreign students, 3,815 (Euro)

Main Language(s) of Instruction: Dutch, French. English on request for special courses

Degrees and Diplomas: *Bachelor*: **Marine Engineering; Nautical Science.** *Master*: **Nautical Science.**

Student Services: Academic Counselling, Canteen, Careers Guidance, Health Services, Language Laboratory, Social Counselling, Sports Facilities
Last Updated: 25/02/15

ARTESIS PLANTIJN UNIVERSITY COLLEGE

Artesis Plantijn Hogeschool Antwerpen (HA)
Lange Nieuwstraat 101, 2000 Antwerpen, Antwerpen
Tel: +32(3) 220-54-00
EMail: info@ap.be
Website: https://www.ap.be/english

Algemeen Directeur: Pascale De Groote
Tel: +32(3) 213-93-04 EMail: liliane.huyben@artesis.be

Department
Education and Training (Secondary Education; Teacher Training); **Health and Social Care** *(Antwerp and Mechelen)* (Gynaecology and Obstetrics; Midwifery; Nursing; Occupational Therapy; Physical Therapy; Social Work); **Management and Communication** *(Antwerp and Lier)* (Business Administration; Business and Commerce; Hotel Management; Journalism; Law; Management; Marketing); **Science and Technology** *(Antwerp, Mechelen and Turnhout)* (Building Technologies; Chemistry; Construction Engineering; Electrical Engineering; Electronic Engineering; Industrial Engineering; Mechanical Engineering; Medical Technology; Surveying and Mapping; Technology)

Academy
Fine Arts *(Antwerp)* (Fashion Design; Graphic Design; Jewellery Art; Painting and Drawing; Photography; Printing and Printmaking; Sculpture)

Conservatory
Conservatoire *(Royal, Antwerp)* (Dance; Music)

History: Founded from merger Artesis University College and Plantijn University College.

Academic Year: September to July

Admission Requirements: Secondary school certificate, or equivalent

Main Language(s) of Instruction: Dutch

Degrees and Diplomas: *Bachelor*, *Master*

Student Services: Canteen, Careers Guidance, Cultural Activities, Facilities for disabled people, Health Services, Language Laboratory, Social Counselling, Sports Facilities
Last Updated: 27/02/15

CATHOLIC UNIVERSITY COLLEGE OF BRUGES–OSTEND

Katholieke Hogeschool Brugge-Oostende (KHBO)
Xaverianenstraat 10, 8200 Brugge, West-Flanders
Tel: +32(50) 30-51-00
Fax: +32(50) 30-51-01
EMail: info@khbo.be
Website: http://www.khbo.be/3837

Algemeen Directeur: Joris Hindryckx

Faculty
Education and Teacher Training *(Bruges)* (Education; Preschool Education; Primary Education; Secondary Education; Teacher Training); **Engineering Technology** *(Ostende)* (Aeronautical and Aerospace Engineering; Chemical Engineering; Construction Engineering; Electrical Engineering; Energy Engineering; Materials Engineering; Mechanical Engineering); **Health Care** *(Bruges)* (Laboratory Techniques; Midwifery; Nursing; Nutrition; Public Health; Rehabilitation and Therapy; Speech Therapy and Audiology); **Management and Business Studies** *(Bruges)* (Accountancy; Finance; Hotel Management; Insurance; Marketing; Secretarial Studies; Tourism; Translation and Interpretation)

History: Founded 1995.

Academic Year: October to July (October-February; February-July)

Admission Requirements: Secondary school certificate

Main Language(s) of Instruction: Dutch

Degrees and Diplomas: *Bachelor*, *Master*

Student Services: Academic Counselling, Canteen, Careers Guidance, Cultural Activities, Facilities for disabled people, Health Services, Social Counselling, Sports Facilities
Last Updated: 26/02/15

CATHOLIC UNIVERSITY OF LEUVEN

Katholieke Universiteit Leuven (KULEUVEN)

Naamssestraat 22, 3000 Leuven
Tel: +32(16) 32-40-27
Fax: +32(16) 32-40-22
EMail: secr@dir.kuleuven.ac.be
Website: http://www.kuleuven.ac.be

Rector: Rik Torfs

General Administrator: Koenraad De Backere
EMail: Koenraad.Debackere@abh.kuleuven.be

International Relations: Bart De Moor, Vice-Rector, International Policy

Faculty

Arts (American Studies; Archaeology; Arts and Humanities; European Studies; Fine Arts; Latin American Studies; Linguistics; Literature; Medieval Studies; Modern Languages; Musicology); **Bioengineering Sciences** (Bioengineering; Food Technology; Management; Molecular Biology; Nanotechnology; Natural Resources; Water Science); **Business and Economics** (Business Administration; Economics); **Canon Law** (Canon Law); **Engineering** (Architecture; Chemical Engineering; Civil Engineering; Computer Engineering; Electronic Engineering; Engineering); **Kinesiology and Rehabilitation Science** (Physical Education; Physical Therapy; Rehabilitation and Therapy); **Law** (Law); **Medicine** (Medicine); **Pharmaceutical Sciences** (Pharmacy); **Psychology and Educational Sciences** (Education; Psychology); **Science** (Astronomy and Space Science; Biology; Chemistry; Earth Sciences; Environmental Studies; Mathematics; Natural Sciences; Physics); **Social Sciences** (Anthropology; Communication Studies; Cultural Studies; Political Sciences; Social Sciences; Sociology); **Theology** (Ethics; Religious Studies; Theology)

Institute

Energy (Energy Engineering); **Language** *(Leuven)* (Modern Languages); **Philosophy** (Philosophy)

Higher Institute

Labour Studies (Labour and Industrial Relations)

Centre

Agrarian Bio and Environment Ethics (Agriculture; Environmental Studies; Ethics); **Biomedical Ethics and Law** *(Interfaculty)* (Biomedicine; Ethics; Law); **Ethics** *(European)* (Ethics); **Risk and Insurance Studies** (Insurance)

History: Founded 1425 by Bull of Pope Martin V on the initiative of Duke John of Brabant. Collegium Trilingue established by Erasmus 1517. Suppressed 1797 under French occupation and closed during the reigns of Napoleon and William I of Holland. Re-established 1834 as Catholic University by Belgian episcopate. Reorganized 1969 with two divisions, the Katholieke Universiteit te Leuven and the Université catholique de Louvain which became separate legal entities in 1970. The titular head of the University is the Cardinal Archbishop of Malines; it is independent of direct State control but receives a full State subvention.

Academic Year: September to June (September-January; February-June)

Admission Requirements: Secondary school leaving certificate or foreign equivalent if formally recognized under agreements concluded with the Belgian Government. Other foreign qualifications subject to the approval of the faculty concerned

Fees: (Euros): 505 per annum

Main Language(s) of Instruction: Dutch, English

Degrees and Diplomas: *Bachelor*: **Archaeology; Bioengineering; Canon Law; Criminology; Economics; Education; Engineering; History; Law; Medicine; Modern Languages; Notary Studies; Pharmacy; Philosophy; Physical Education; Psychology; Social Sciences; Theology.** *Master*: **Archaeology; Criminology; Education; History; Law; Modern Languages; Natural Sciences; Notary Studies; Philosophy; Physical Education; Social Sciences; Theology.** *Doctor*

Student Services: Academic Counselling, Canteen, Careers Guidance, Cultural Activities, Facilities for disabled people, Health Services, Nursery Care, Social Counselling, Sports Facilities

Publications: Reviews of faculties and institutes

Publishing House: University Press

Last Updated: 26/02/15

CAMPUS KULAK KORTRIJK

AFDELING KULAK KORTRIJK

Etienne Sabbelaan 53, 8500 Kortrijk
Tel: +32(56) 24-61-11
Fax: +32(56) 24-69-95
EMail: info@kulak.be
Website: http://www.kuleuven-kulak.be

Campus Rector: Marc Depaepe

Faculty

Arts (Arts and Humanities; History; Modern Languages); **Business and Economics** (Business Administration; Economics); **Law** (Law); **Medicine** (Medical Technology); **Psychology and Educational Sciences** (Educational Sciences; Pedagogy; Psychology); **Science and Technology** (Biochemistry; Biology; Biotechnology; Chemistry; Computer Science; Natural Sciences; Physics)

COLLEGE OF EUROPE

Europacollege

Dijver 11, 8000 Brugge
Tel: +32(50) 47-71-11
Fax: +32(50) 47-71-10
EMail: info@coleurope.eu
Website: http://www.coleurope.eu

Rector: Paul Demaret

Programme

EU International Relations and Diplomacy Studies (International Relations); **European Economic Studies** (Economics; European Studies); **European General Studies** (Economics; European Studies; Government; Political Sciences); **European Law** (European Union Law); **European Political and Administrative Studies** (Administration; European Studies; Political Sciences)

Further Information: Campus also in Natolin (Warsaw), Poland.

History: Created 1948. Natolin Campus, Warsaw, Poland opened 1993.

Fees: Tuition fees: 15,000 (Euro)

Degrees and Diplomas: *Master*

Last Updated: 25/02/15

ERASMUS UNIVERSITY COLLEGE, BRUSSELS

Erasmushogeschool Brussel (EHB)

Nijverheidskaai 170, 1070 Brussel
Tel: +32(2) 559-15-15
Fax: +32(2) 523-37-57
EMail: info@ehb.be
Website: http://www.ehb.be

Algemeen Directeur: Luc Van de Velde
EMail: luc.van.de.velde@ehb.be

Administratief Directeur: Ann Langenakens
EMail: ann.langenakens@ehb.be

International Relations: Annelore Schittecatte
EMail: annelore.schittecatte@ehb.be

Department

Applied Languages (Danish; Dutch; English; French; German; Greek; Italian; Portuguese; Russian; Spanish; Swedish; Translation and Interpretation; Turkish); **Architecture** (Landscape Architecture); **Audiovisual Arts and Techniques** (Film; Radio and Television Broadcasting; Theatre); **Communications** (Business and Commerce; Communication Studies; Journalism; Public Relations; Translation and Interpretation); **Health Care** (Dietetics; Midwifery; Nursing; Nutrition; Pharmacy); **Hotel and Tourism** (Hotel Management; Tourism); **Industrial and Technical Sciences**

(Computer Science; Industrial Engineering); **Social Sciences** (Human Resources; Social Sciences; Social Work); **Teacher Training** (Teacher Training)

Conservatory

Music *(Royal)* (Music)

History: Founded 1995 as a merger of several university colleges. A university-level institution, financed by the State and tuition fees, which is responsible to the Ministry of Education.

Academic Year: End of September to July (October-February; February-July)

Admission Requirements: Secondary school certificate

Fees: c. 600 per annum (Euro)

Main Language(s) of Instruction: Dutch

Degrees and Diplomas: *Bachelor*; *Master*

Publications: Medium

Last Updated: 25/02/15

FLANDERS OPERASTUDIO

Operastudio Vlaanderen

Bijlokekaai 6, 9160 Gent, Oost-Vlaanderen
Tel: +32(9) 233-24-30
Fax: +32(9) 233-37-65
EMail: info@ioacademy.be
Website: http://www.operastudio.be

Director: Ronny Lauwers (2004-)
EMail: ronny.lauwers@operastudio.be

Financial Assistant: Dirk Cornelius
EMail: dirk.cornelis@operastudio.be

International Relations: Kristien Heirman, Communication and Student Administration EMail: kristien.heirman@operastudio.be

Department

Piano (Musical Instruments; Musicology); **Singing** (Music; Opera; Singing)

History: Created in 1998.

Admission Requirements: Admission by audition.

Fees: 1,000 per annum (Euro)

Main Language(s) of Instruction: English

Degrees and Diplomas: Two-year postgraduate diploma in Singing and Pianist-Repetitor.

Student Services: Canteen

Last Updated: 26/02/15

FREE UNIVERSITY OF BRUSSELS

Vrije Universiteit Brussel (VUB)

Pleinlaan 2, 1050 Brussel
Tel: +32(2) 629-21-11
Fax: +32(2) 629-22-82
EMail: info@vub.ac.be
Website: http://www.vub.ac.be

Rector: Paul De Knop EMail: rector@vub.ac.be

Algemeen Operationeel Directeur: Jim Van Leemput
Tel: +32(2) 629-21-42 EMail: algemeen.directeur@vub.ac.be

International Relations: Jacqueline Couder
EMail: international.relations@vub.ac.be

Faculty

Arts and Philosophy *(Etterbeek)* (Archaeology; Classical Languages; Communication Studies; Ethics; Germanic Languages; History; Library Science; Linguistics; Literature; Modern Languages; Philosophy; Romance Languages); **Economic and Social Sciences and Solvay Business School** *(with Solvay Business School)* (Business and Commerce; Business Computing; Economics; Management; Political Sciences); **Engineering** *(Etterbeek)* (Architecture; Chemical Engineering; Civil Engineering; Computer Science; Electronic Engineering; Engineering; Materials Engineering; Natural Resources); **Law and Criminology** *(Etterbeek)* (Criminology; Law; Notary Studies); **Medicine and Pharmacy** *(Medical Campus Jette)* (Biomedicine; Medical Technology; Medicine; Nursing; Pharmacy); **Physical Education and Physiotherapy** *(Etterbeek)* (Physical Education; Physical Therapy; Rehabilitation and Therapy); **Psychology and Educational Sciences** *(Etterbeek)* (Educational Sciences; Psychology; Teacher Training); **Science and Bio-Engineering Science** *(Etterbeek)* (Artificial Intelligence; Astrophysics; Biology; Chemistry; Computer Science; Geography; Geology; Mathematics; Physics; Software Engineering)

College

Vesalius (Business Education; Communication Studies; International Studies)

Institute

Contemporary Chinese Studies *(Brussels)* (Chinese); **European Studies** (European Studies; European Union Law; International Law)

Further Information: Also University Hospital

History: Founded 1970 when the former Vrije Universiteit Brussels, founded 1834, was replaced by separate Dutch and French-speaking Universities. A private autonomous institution receiving substantial financial support from the State.

Academic Year: September to July

Admission Requirements: Secondary school certificate or recognized foreign equivalent and entrance examination for Bachelor degree in Medicine

Fees: 564-7000 per annum (Euro)

Main Language(s) of Instruction: Dutch, English

Degrees and Diplomas: *Bachelor*: **Archaeology; Architecture; Bioengineering; Biology; Biomedical Engineering; Business and Commerce; Chemistry; Communication Arts; Computer Science; Criminology; Economics; Engineering; Ethics; Geography; History; Law; Linguistics; Literature; Mathematics; Medicine; Pharmacy; Philosophy; Physical Education; Physics; Political Sciences; Psychology; Sociology; Sports.** *Master*: **American Studies; Business and Commerce; Criminology; Ecology; Economics; Education; Engineering; European Studies; European Union Law; Fine Arts; International Law; Law; Linguistics; Management; Medicine; Nuclear Engineering; Pharmacy; Philosophy; Physical Education; Physical Therapy; Psychology; Urban Studies.** *Doctor*: **Arts and Humanities; Biological and Life Sciences; Education; Engineering; Medicine; Natural Sciences; Psychology.**

Student Services: Academic Counselling, Canteen, Careers Guidance, Cultural Activities, Facilities for disabled people, Foreign Studies Centre, Health Services, Language Laboratory, Nursery Care, Social Counselling, Sports Facilities

Publications: Akademos

Publishing House: VUB University Press

Academic Staff *2010-2011*	MEN	WOMEN	**TOTAL**
FULL-TIME	1,176	707	**1,883**
Student Numbers *2010-2011*			
All (Foreign included)	4,385	5,813	**10,198**
FOREIGN ONLY		-	**1,406**

Last Updated: 09/04/15

GHENT UNIVERSITY

Universiteit Gent (UGENT)

Sint-Pietersnieuwstraat 25, 9000 Gent
Tel: +32(9) 264-31-11 +32(9) 264-70-03
Fax: +32(9) 264-31-31
EMail: GUIDe@Ugent.be; secretariaatAIB@ugent.be
Website: http://www.ugent.be

Rector: Anne De Paepe (2013-)
EMail: rector@Ugent.be; anne.depaepe@ugent.be

International Relations: Luc François, Chief International Officer
Tel: +32(9) 264-70-66 EMail: luc.francois@UGent.be

Faculty

Arts and Philosophy (African Languages; African Studies; Archaeology; Cultural Studies; Dutch; Eastern European Studies; English; Fine Arts; French; German; Greek; History; Latin; Medieval Studies; Modern History; Musicology; Nordic Studies; North African Studies; Oriental Studies; Philosophy; Romance Languages; Slavic Languages; Southeast Asian Studies; Theatre); **Bioscience Engineering** (Agricultural Economics; Agricultural Engineering;

Agriculture; Animal Husbandry; Applied Chemistry; Applied Mathematics; Biochemistry; Crop Production; Ecology; Environmental Studies; Food Technology; Forest Management; Nutrition; Organic Chemistry; Plant and Crop Protection; Soil Management; Water Management); **Economics and Business Administration** (Accountancy; Business Administration; Business Computing; Economics; Finance; Management; Management Systems; Marketing); **Engineering** (Applied Physics; Architecture; Automation and Control Engineering; Chemical Engineering; Civil Engineering; Electrical and Electronic Engineering; Industrial Management; Information Technology; Mathematics; Mechanics; Telecommunications Engineering; Textile Technology; Thermal Engineering; Town Planning); **Law**; **Medicine and Health Sciences** (Anaesthesiology; Biochemistry; Chemistry; Dentistry; Dermatology; Forensic Medicine and Dentistry; Genetics; Gynaecology and Obstetrics; Immunology; Medical Technology; Medicine; Microbiology; Ophthalmology; Orthopaedics; Otorhinolaryngology; Paediatrics; Pathology; Pharmacology; Physical Therapy; Psychiatry and Mental Health; Psychology; Public Health; Radiology; Rehabilitation and Therapy; Sports Medicine; Surgery; Urology); **Pharmaceutical Sciences** (Pharmacy); **Political and Social Sciences** (Communication Studies; Development Studies; Political Sciences; Sociology); **Psychology and Educational Sciences** (Education; Educational Sciences; Educational Technology; Experimental Psychology; Industrial and Organizational Psychology; Pedagogy; Psychoanalysis; Psychology; Special Education); **Sciences**; **Veterinary Medicine** (Animal Husbandry; Veterinary Science)

Further Information: Also University Hospital; courses for foreign students; interuniversity courses

History: Founded 1817 by King William I of the Netherlands. The official language of the University was originally Latin; this changed to French 1830 and to Dutch 1930. Ghent University is today one of the most important academic institutions of Belgium and has an important international educational and scientific role. Acquired present status and title 1991.

Academic Year: October to September

Admission Requirements: Secondary school certificate or recognized foreign equivalent and entrance examination for engineering and medicine

Main Language(s) of Instruction: Dutch

Degrees and Diplomas: *Bachelor*; *Master*; *Doctor*

Student Services: Academic Counselling, Canteen, Careers Guidance, Cultural Activities, Facilities for disabled people, Health Services, Language Laboratory, Nursery Care, Social Counselling, Sports Facilities

Student Numbers *2012-2013*: Total: c. 38,000

Last Updated: 09/04/15

GROUP T-INTERNATIONAL UNIVERSITY COLLEGE LEUVEN

Groep T - Internationale Hogeschool Leuven'

Campus Versalius, Vesaliusstraat 13, 3000 Leuven, Vlaams-Brabant
Tel: +32(16) 30-10-30
Fax: +32(16) 30-10-40
EMail: group-t@group-t.be
Website: http://www.group-t.be

President: Johan De Graeve
EMail: johan.de.graeve@group-t.academy

Administrator General: Ingrid Ilsbroux

International Relations: Wim Polet Tel: +32(16) 30-10-04

College

Anticipative Continuing Education (Modern Languages); **Education** (Preschool Education; Primary Education; Secondary Education; Teacher Training); **Engineering** (Biochemistry; Chemical Engineering; Electrical and Electronic Engineering; Engineering; Hydraulic Engineering; Information Technology; Management; Mass Communication; Mechanical Engineering; Media Studies)

History: Founded 1960 as Technical Institute. Granted legal status as a university-level institution 1977. Merged with the Teacher College of the Flemish-Brabant province and acquired present title 2008.

Academic Year: October to July (October-January; February-July)

Admission Requirements: Secondary school certificate or recognized foreign equivalent

Fees: EU students, 523 per annum; non-EU students, 5,600 (Euro)

Main Language(s) of Instruction: Dutch, English

Degrees and Diplomas: *Bachelor*: **Bioengineering; Chemical Engineering; Electrical Engineering; Electronic Engineering; Mechanical Engineering.** *Master*: **Biochemistry; Chemical Engineering; Electrical Engineering; Electronic Engineering; Mechanical Engineering; Multimedia.** Postgraduate Programme in Enterprising; Professional Bachelor in Education 3 years.

Student Services: Academic Counselling, Canteen, Careers Guidance, Facilities for disabled people, Foreign Studies Centre, Health Services, Language Laboratory, Social Counselling, Sports Facilities

Last Updated: 03/03/15

HASSELT UNIVERSITY

Universiteit Hasselt (UHASSELT)

Agoralaan gebouw D, BE 3590 Diepenbeek
Tel: +32(11) 26-81-11
Fax: +32(11) 26-81-99
EMail: info@uhasselt.be
Website: http://www.uhasselt.be

Rector: Luc De Schepper (2004-) EMail: luc.deschepper@luc.ac.be

Faculty

Applied Economics (Business Administration; Computer Science; Economics; Marketing); **Architecture and Art** (Architecture; Interior Design); **Industrial Engineering** (Industrial Engineering); **Law** (Law); **Medicine** (Dentistry; Health Sciences); **Science** (Biology; Chemistry; Computer Science; Mathematics; Natural Sciences; Physics)

Institute

Transport Sciences (Transport and Communications)

Further Information: Also campus at Diepenbeek

History: Founded 1971 as 'Limburgs Universitair Centrum' (LUC). Acquired present status 2005.

Academic Year: October to September

Admission Requirements: Secondary school certificate or recognized equivalent

Main Language(s) of Instruction: Dutch, English

Degrees and Diplomas: *Bachelor*: **Biology; Biomedical Engineering; Business Administration; Chemistry; Computer Science; Data Processing; Mathematics; Medicine; Physics; Transport and Communications.** *Master*: **Biological and Life Sciences; Biomedical Engineering; Business Administration; Computer Science; Data Processing; Economics; Information Technology; International Business; Management; Statistics; Transport and Communications.**

Student Services: Academic Counselling, Canteen, Careers Guidance, Facilities for disabled people, Foreign Studies Centre, Health Services, Language Laboratory, Social Counselling, Sports Facilities

Last Updated: 27/02/15

INSTITUTE OF TROPICAL MEDICINE ANTWERP

Prins Leopold Instituut voor Tropische Geneeskunde (ITG - ANTWERPEN)

Nationalestraat 155, 2000 Antwerpen
Tel: +32(3) 247-66-66
Fax: +32(3) 216-14-31
EMail: info@itg.be
Website: http://www.itg.be

Director: Bruno Gryseels EMail: bgryseels@itg.be

Department

Biomedical Sciences (Medical Parasitology; Microbiology); **Clinical Sciences** (Medicine); **Public Health** (Epidemiology; Public Health)

History: Founded 1906.

Main Language(s) of Instruction: Dutch, English, French

Degrees and Diplomas: *Master*: **Tropical Medicine; Veterinary Science.** *Doctor*: **Health Sciences; Natural Sciences.** Also Postgraduate Certificates in Tropical Medicine and International Health

Last Updated: 26/02/15

KAREL DE GROTE UNIVERITY COLLEGE, ANTWERP

Karel de Grote-Hogeschool Antwerpen (KDG)

Brusselstraat 45, 2018 Antwerpen
Tel: +32(3) 613-13-13
EMail: info@kdg.be
Website: http://www.kdg.be

Algemeen Directeur: Dirk Broos

Department

Applied Social Studies *(SAW)* (Social Work; Special Education); **Arts and Design** *(ABK)* (Fine Arts; Graphic Design; Jewellery Art); **Commercial Sciences and Business Administration** (Business Administration; Business and Commerce; Business Computing; Management); **Health Care** *(GEZ)* (Midwifery; Nursing); **Industrial Sciences and Technology** *(IWT)* (Automotive Engineering; Chemistry; Electronic Engineering; Engineering; Mechanical Engineering; Mechanics; Medical Technology; Photography); **Teacher Training** *(DLO)* (Preschool Education; Primary Education; Secondary Education; Teacher Training)

History: Founded 1994 incorporating 13 Catholic institutions of higher education.

Academic Year: September to July (September-February; February-July)

Admission Requirements: Secondary school certificate (Diploma secundair onderwijs) and entrance examination for Department of Arts

Fees: 100-578 per annum; postgraduate courses, 495-1,000 (Euro)

Main Language(s) of Instruction: Dutch (with some study programmes in English)

Degrees and Diplomas: *Bachelor*, *Master*

Student Services: Academic Counselling, Canteen, Careers Guidance, Cultural Activities, Facilities for disabled people, Health Services, Language Laboratory, Nursery Care, Social Counselling, Sports Facilities

Academic Staff *2010-2011*	**TOTAL**
FULL-TIME	630
PART-TIME	320
STAFF WITH DOCTORATE	
FULL-TIME	c. 20
Student Numbers *2010-2011*	
All (Foreign included)	c. 8,000
FOREIGN ONLY	310

Last Updated: 26/02/15

LEUVEN UNIVERSITY COLLEGE

Katholieke Hogeschool Leuven (KH LEUVEN)

Abdij van Park 9, 3001 Heverlee
Tel: +32(16) 375-700
Fax: +32(16) 375-799
EMail: administratie@khleuven.be
Website: http://www.khleuven.be

Algemeen Directeur: Toon Martens
EMail: toon.martens@khleuven.be

Department

Business Studies (Accountancy; Business Administration; Business and Commerce; Finance; Insurance; Management; Marketing; Secretarial Studies; Taxation); **Health Care and Technology** *(Rega)* (Biochemistry; Biology; Chemistry; Dietetics; Environmental Studies; Food Technology; Information Technology; Laboratory Techniques; Midwifery; Nursing; Nutrition; Pharmacy; Secretarial Studies; Technology); **Social Work** (Social Studies; Social Work; Welfare and Protective Services); **Teacher Training** *(Leuven and Diest)* (Education; Preschool Education; Primary Education; Secondary Education)

History: Founded 1995, incorporating six existing Colleges of higher education.

Admission Requirements: Secondary school certificate (Flemish Certificate) or equivalent

Degrees and Diplomas: *Bachelor*, *Master*. Also Advanced Bachelor Degrees and Postgraduaat

Last Updated: 26/02/15

LIMBURG CATHOLIC UNIVERSITY COLLEGE

Katholieke Hogeschool Limburg (KHLIM)

Agoralaan Gebouw B, Bus 1, 3590 Diepenbeek, Limburg
Tel: +32(11) 23-07-70
Fax: +32(11) 23-07-89
EMail: informatie@ad.khlim.be
Website: http://www.khlim.be

Algemeen Directeur: Theo Creemers

Faculty

Media, Arts and Design *(MDa, Genk)* (Advertising and Publicity; Fine Arts; Graphic Design; Media Studies; Photography; Video)

Department

Commercial Sciences and Business Administration *(HB, Diepenbeek)* (Accountancy; Business Administration; Business and Commerce; Marketing; Secretarial Studies; Taxation); **Health Care** *(GEZ, Hasselt)* (Health Sciences; Midwifery; Nursing); **Industrial Sciences and Technology** *(IWT, Diepenbeek)* (Automation and Control Engineering; Biochemistry; Chemical Engineering; Chemistry; Electrical Engineering; Energy Engineering; Industrial Engineering; Laboratory Techniques; Mechanical Engineering); **Social Work** *(SAW, Hasselt)* (Social Work; Special Education); **Teacher Training** *(LER, Hasselt)* (Teacher Training)

History: Founded 1995, incorporating other existing institutes of higher education. A private university-level institution recognized by and receiving financial support from the State.

Academic Year: September to July (September-February; February-July)

Admission Requirements: Secondary school certificate

Fees: 523 per annum (Euro)

Main Language(s) of Instruction: Dutch

Accrediting Agency: Nederlands Vlaamse Accreditering Organisatie (NVAO)

Degrees and Diplomas: *Bachelor*, *Master*

Student Services: Academic Counselling, Canteen, Careers Guidance, Social Counselling, Sports Facilities

Last Updated: 26/02/15

LUCA SCHOOL OF ARTS

Paleizenstraat 70, 1030 Brussel
Tel: +32(2) 250-11-00
Fax: +32(2) 250-11-11
EMail: info@sintlukas.be
Website: http://www.sintlukas.be

Directeur-generaal: Maria De Smet

Programme

Audiovisual Arts *(C Mine campus, Genk campus Sint-Lukas, Brussels)* (Film; Video); **Construction** *(Sint-Lukas campus, Brussels)* (Building Technologies; Construction Engineering); **Drama** *(Lemmens campus, Leuven)* (Theatre); **Fine Arts** *(campus Sint-Lucas, Ghent, campus Sint-Lukas, Brussels)* (Fine Arts; Graphic Arts; Painting and Drawing; Sculpture); **Graphic Design** *(campus Sint-Lucas, Ghent; campus Sint-Lukas, Brussels)* (Design; Graphic Arts; Graphic Design); **Interior Design** *(campus Sint-Lucas, Ghent and campus Sint-Lukas, Brussels)* (Architecture; Interior Design); **Music** *(Lemmens campus, Leuven)* (Music); **Photography** (Photography)

History: Founded 1884 on the basis of a Roman Catholic neo-Gothic Art Philosophy. A private university-level institution. Acquired present status 1991.

Admission Requirements: Entrance examination

Fees: 513 per annum (Euro)

Main Language(s) of Instruction: Dutch

Degrees and Diplomas: *Bachelor*, *Master*. Also Advanced Master's Degree

Student Services: Canteen, Facilities for disabled people, Foreign Studies Centre, Social Counselling

Last Updated: 03/03/15

ODISEE (HUB)

Warmoesberg 26, 1000 Brussel
Tel: +32(2) 210-12-11
EMail: info@odisee.be
Website: http://www.odisee.be

Algemeen Directeur: Dirk De Ceulaer (2002-)
EMail: dirk.deceulaer@hubrussel.be

International Relations: Martine Vanheulenbrouck
EMail: martine.vanheulenbrouck@hubrussel.be

Area

Applied Social Studies *(Brussels)* (Family Studies; Social Sciences; Social Work); **Biotechnology** *(Sint Niklaas)* (Biotechnology); **Business Studies** *(Aalst; Brussels, Ghent)* (Business Administration; Computer Science; Economics; International Business; Management); **Education** *(Aalst, Brussels, Sint Niklaas)* (Preschool Education; Primary Education; Secondary Education); **Health Care** *((Aalst - Brussels - Ghent - Sint-Niklaas)* (Food Science; Medical Technology; Midwifery; Nursing; Occupational Therapy; Optics; Optometry; Radiology); **Technology** *(Aalst, Ghent)* (Building Technologies; Chemistry; Design; Electrical Engineering; Electronic Engineering; Energy Engineering; Information Technology; Mechanical Engineering; Production Engineering; Real Estate)

Further Information: Also campuses in Ghent, Aalst and Sint-Niklaas.

History: Founded 1925. Officially recognized 1937. Acquired present status 2014 following the merger of Hogeschoolã Universiteit Brussel (HUB) and Katholieke Hogeschool Sintã Lieven (KAHO)

Academic Year: September to June

Admission Requirements: Secondary school certificate or recognized equivalent

Fees: 578 per annum (Euro)

Main Language(s) of Instruction: Dutch, some courses in English

Degrees and Diplomas: *Bachelor*, *Master*

Student Services: Academic Counselling, Canteen, Careers Guidance, Cultural Activities, Facilities for disabled people, Language Laboratory, Social Counselling, Sports Facilities

Last Updated: 26/02/15

PXL UNIVERSITY COLLEGE

Hogeschool PXL (PHL)
Elfde-Liniestraat 24, 3500 Hasselt
Tel: +32(11) 77-55-55
Fax: +32(11) 77-55-59
EMail: pxl@pxl.be
Website: http://www.pxl.be/

Algemeen Directeur: Ben Lambrechts
Tel: +32(11) 23-86-12 EMail: Ben.Lambrechts@phl.be

Department

Business (Accountancy; Business and Commerce; Commercial Law; Computer Science; Environmental Management; Finance; Insurance; Law; Marketing; Secretarial Studies; Taxation; Translation and Interpretation); **Education** (Preschool Education; Primary Education; Secondary Education; Teacher Training); **Health Care** (Midwifery; Nursing; Occupational Therapy; Physical Therapy); **Information Technology** (Computer Science; Information Technology); **Media and Tourism** (Communication Studies; Journalism; Leisure Studies; Tourism); **Music** (Jazz and Popular Music); **Plastic Arts** (Advertising and Publicity; Ceramics and Glass Technology; Design; Fine Arts; Glass Art; Graphic Arts; Jewellery Art; Multimedia; Painting and Drawing; Sculpture; Visual Arts); **Social Work** (Social Work)

Further Information: Also campus at Diepenbeek

History: Founded 1994.

Main Language(s) of Instruction: Dutch, English

Degrees and Diplomas: *Bachelor*, *Master*

Last Updated: 03/03/15

THOMAS MORE UNIVERSITY COLLEGE

Thomas More Hoogeschool (KHK)
Kleinhoefstraat 4, 2440 Geel
Tel: +32(14) 56-23-10
EMail: info.geel@thomasmore.be
Website: http://www.thomasmore.be

Algemeen Directeur: Machteld Verbruggen

Faculty

Biomedical, Behavioural & Social Studies *(Antwerp, Lier, Mechelen, Turnhout)* (Medical Technology; Midwifery; Nursing; Nutrition; Occupational Therapy; Orthopaedics; Psychology; Social Work; Speech Therapy and Audiology); **Management & Education** *(Mechelen, Turnhout, Vorselaar)* (Business Administration; Journalism; Management; Preschool Education; Primary Education; Secondary Education; Tourism); **Technology & Design** (Agrobiology; Automation and Control Engineering; Biotechnology; Computer Science; Construction Engineering; Electrical Engineering; Electronic Engineering; Energy Engineering; Information Technology; Interior Design; Mechanical Engineering; Production Engineering)

History: Founded 2014 through the merger of Katholieke Hogeschool Kempen, Lessius Antwerp and Lessius Mechelen

Academic Year: September to July (September-January; February-July)

Admission Requirements: Secondary school certificate

Main Language(s) of Instruction: Dutch

Degrees and Diplomas: *Bachelor*: **Agriculture; Biotechnology; Business and Commerce; Chemistry; Computer Science; Dietetics; Electrical Engineering; Electronic Engineering; Health Education; Information Technology; Laboratory Techniques; Management; Mechanical Engineering; Midwifery; Nursing; Nutrition; Occupational Therapy; Orthopaedics; Primary Education; Secondary Education; Social Work; Transport Management.** *Master*

Student Services: Academic Counselling, Canteen, Careers Guidance, Health Services, Social Counselling

Publications: Agora

Last Updated: 26/02/15

UNIVERSITY COLLEGE GHENT

Hogeschool Gent (HOGENT)
Geraard de Duivelstraat 5, 9000 Gent
Tel: +32(9) 243-33-02
Fax: +32(9) 243-33-53
EMail: info@hogent.be
Website: http://www.hogent.be

Principal: Robert Hoogewijs (2004-)
EMail: bert.hoogewijs@hogent.be

International Relations: Kathleen Poma, Director, Central Education Office EMail: kathleen.poma@hogent.be

Faculty

Business and Information Management (Business Administration; Computer Science; Information Management; Retailing and Wholesaling); **Education, Health and Social Work** (Biomedicine; Laboratory Techniques; Nursing; Occupational Therapy; Preschool Education; Primary Education; Secondary Education; Social Work; Speech Therapy and Audiology); **Science and Technology** (Agrobiology; Biotechnology; Chemistry; Electronic Engineering; Fashion Design; Mechanics; Real Estate; Technology; Textile Technology; Wood Technology)

School

Fine Arts *(Royal Academy)* (Design; Film; Interior Design; Landscape Architecture; Music; Theatre; Visual Arts)

History: Founded 1995, incorporating 13 Hogescholen. A university-level institution. Merged with the university college of the Province of East-Flanders. in 2001.

Academic Year: October to July (October-January; February-July)

Admission Requirements: Secondary school certificate (Diploma secundar onderwijs) or equivalent

Fees: 540 per annum (Euro)

Main Language(s) of Instruction: Dutch

Accrediting Agency: Nederlands Vlaamse Accreditatie Organisatie (NVAO)

Degrees and Diplomas: *Bachelor*: **Agriculture; Biotechnology; Business Administration; Business and Commerce; Chemistry; Computer Science; Dietetics; Electrical Engineering; Electronic Engineering; Fashion Design; Information Sciences; Information Technology; Interior Design; Laboratory Techniques; Landscape Architecture; Linguistics; Management; Mechanical Engineering; Music; Nursing; Nutrition; Occupational Therapy; Preschool Education; Primary Education; Public Administration; Radio and Television Broadcasting; Real Estate; Secondary Education; Speech Therapy and Audiology; Textile Technology; Theatre; Visual Arts; Wood Technology.** *Master*: **Agriculture; Biochemistry; Business Administration; Chemistry; Communication Studies; Computer Science; Electrical Engineering; Electronic Engineering; Fine Arts; Food Technology; Horticulture; Information Technology; Mechanical Engineering; Midwifery; Modern Languages; Music; Nursing; Public Administration; Radio and Television Broadcasting; Social Work; Textile Technology; Theatre; Translation and Interpretation.** Also Advanced Masters

Student Services: Academic Counselling, Canteen, Careers Guidance, Facilities for disabled people, Health Services, Social Counselling, Sports Facilities

Student Numbers *2011-2012*: Total 18,000
Last Updated: 08/04/15

UNIVERSITY COLLEGE OF WEST FLANDERS

Hogeschool West-Vlaanderen (HOWEST)

Marksesteenweg 58, 8500 Kortrijk
Tel: +32(56) 24-12-90
Fax: +32(56) 24-12-92
EMail: info@howest.be
Website: http://www.howest.be

Algemeen Directeur: Lode De Geyter
EMail: lode.de.geyter@howest.be

International Relations: Isabelle Pertry, Head
EMail: international.office@howest.be

Department

Architecture; **Business Studies and Management** *(HIEPSO)* (Business Administration; Communication Arts; Computer Science; Journalism; Leisure Studies; Management; Management Systems; Telecommunications Services; Tourism); **Education** *(HPI, Brugge)* (Preschool Education; Primary Education; Secondary Education; Teacher Training); **Engineering and Technology** (Biochemistry; Chemistry; Communication Studies; Electronic Engineering; Environmental Studies; Industrial Design; Mechanical Engineering; Multimedia; Technology); **Medical Sciences** *(Simon Stevin, Sint-Michels)* (Biomedical Engineering; Nursing; Occupational Therapy); **Social Sciences** *(Vesalius-Hiss De Haan, Oostende)* (Psychology; Social Work)

Further Information: Intensive Dutch course for foreigners. International Semester in English: Digital Business Management (30 ECTS-Fall sem.); Multimedia Communication (30 ECTS -Spring sem). Also 5 Branches: Hiespo and PIH in Kortrijk; Simon Stevin and Leranopleiding in Brugge; Vesalius in Oostende.

History: Founded 1879 as technical institute, acquired present status and title 1977. A university-level provincial institution receiving financial support from the State. Merged and acquired present status 1995.

Academic Year: September to September

Admission Requirements: Secondary school certificate

Fees: 490 per annum (Euro)

Main Language(s) of Instruction: Dutch (with some modules in English)

Accrediting Agency: Ministry of Education and Training

Degrees and Diplomas: *Bachelor*: **Architecture; Biochemistry; Biomedical Engineering; Business and Commerce; Chemistry; Communication Arts; Computer Science; Economics; Electrical Engineering; Electronic Engineering; Environmental Studies; Industrial Design; Information Technology; Journalism; Laboratory Techniques; Leisure Studies; Management; Mechanical Engineering; Multimedia; Nursing; Occupational Therapy; Psychology; Social Work; Telecommunications Engineering; Tourism.** *Master*: **Architecture; Biochemistry; Biomedical Engineering; Business and Commerce; Chemistry; Communication Arts; Computer Science; Economics; Electrical Engineering; Electronic Engineering; Environmental Studies; Industrial Design; Information Technology; Journalism; Laboratory Techniques; Leisure Studies; Management; Mechanical Engineering; Multimedia; Nursing; Occupational Therapy; Psychology; Social Work; Telecommunications Engineering; Tourism.** Two international semesters are offered, taught in English.

Student Services: Academic Counselling, Canteen, Careers Guidance, Facilities for disabled people, Language Laboratory, Social Counselling
Last Updated: 27/02/15

UNIVERSITY OF ANTWERP

Universiteit Antwerpen (UA)

Prinsstraat, 13, BE-2000 Antwerpen
Tel: +32(3) 265-41-11
Fax: +32(3) 265-44-20
EMail: internationaloffice@uantwerp.be
Website: https://www.uantwerpen.be/nl/

Rector: Alain Verschoren EMail: alain.verschoren@uantwerpen.be

International Relations: Piet Van Hove
Tel: +32(3) 220-46-27 EMail: piet.vanhove@uantwerpen.be

Faculty

Applied Economics (Business Administration; Business and Commerce; Economic and Finance Policy; Economics; Information Sciences; Management Systems); **Applied Engineering** (Construction Engineering; Electrical Engineering; Information Technology; Mechanical Engineering); **Arts** (History; Linguistics; Literature; Philosophy); **Design Science** (Architecture; Heritage Preservation; Interior Design); **Law** (Commercial Law; European Union Law; International Law; Law); **Medicine and Health Sciences** (Medicine; Midwifery; Nursing; Physical Therapy; Psychiatry and Mental Health; Surgery); **Pharmaceutical, Biomedical and Veterinary Sciences** (Biomedicine; Pharmacy; Veterinary Science); **Political and Social Sciences** (Communication Studies; Political Sciences; Sociology; Women's Studies); **Science** (Biochemistry; Biological and Life Sciences; Biology; Biotechnology; Chemistry; Computer Science; Mathematics; Physics)

Institute

Development Policy and Management *(IDPM)* (Development Studies); **Education and Information Sciences** (Education; Information Sciences)

History: Founded 2003, incorporating Universitaire Instelling Antwerpen (UIA), Universitaire Faculteiten St. Ignatius te Antwerpen (UFSIA) and Universitair Centrum Antwerpen (RUCA).

Academic Year: September/October to June/July

Admission Requirements: Secondary school certificate or recognized equivalent

Fees: 525 per annum (Euro)

Main Language(s) of Instruction: Dutch, English

Degrees and Diplomas: *Bachelor*, *Master*, *Doctor*

Student Services: Academic Counselling, Canteen, Careers Guidance, Facilities for disabled people, Foreign Studies Centre, Health Services, Language Laboratory, Social Counselling, Sports Facilities
Last Updated: 26/02/15

VLERICK BUSINESS SCHOOL (VLGMS)

Reep 1, 9000 Gent
Tel: +32(9) 210-97-11
Fax: +32(9) 210-97-00
EMail: info@vlerick.com
Website: http://www.vlerick.com

Dean: Philippe Haspeslagh (2008-)
EMail: philippe.haspeslagh@vlerick.be

Division
Accounting and Finance (Accountancy; Finance); **Governance and Ethics** (Ethics; Government); **Human Resource Management** (Human Resources; Management); **Innovation and Entrepreneurship** (Management); **Marketing and Sales** (E-Business/ Commerce; Marketing; Sales Techniques); **Organisational Behaviour** (Leadership; Management); **Specific Industries** (Industrial Arts Education); **Strategy** (Management)

Further Information: Also campuses in Leuven, Brussels and St Petersburg (Russia)

History: Founded 1953. Acquired title 2012. The management school of the Katholieke Universiteit Leuven and Ghent University.

Academic Year: September to July

Admission Requirements: University degree; GMAT; TOEFL

Fees: Full-time MBA, 24,500 per annum; Masters, 7,500-8,750 per annum (Euro)

Main Language(s) of Instruction: English

Accrediting Agency: EQUIS, AACSB, AMBA, Flemish Government

Degrees and Diplomas: *Master*: **Business Administration; Finance; Management.** Also Executive Masters, and long- and short-education executive training programmes.

Student Services: Academic Counselling, Canteen, Careers Guidance, Facilities for disabled people, Foreign Studies Centre, Social Counselling

Last Updated: 27/02/15

Belgium - French Community

STRUCTURE OF HIGHER EDUCATION SYSTEM

Description:

Higher education is established on a binary scheme which refers to the co-existence of "short-type" or professionalising education and "long-type" or academic education. "Short-type" or professionalising higher education, which closely relates theory and practice in terms of pedagogy, is organised by the university colleges (Hautes Ecoles), the arts colleges (Ecoles supérieures des Arts) and the institutions of social promotion education (établissements d'enseignement de promotion sociale). "Long-type" higher education, which is based on fundamental concepts, experimentations and illustrations, is organised by the universities, the Hautes Ecoles, the Ecoles supérieures des Arts and the Etablissements d'enseignement de promotion sociale.

Stages of studies:

University level first stage: *Bachelier ("long-type" higher education)*
The first stage of university level studies is offered at Universities, Hautes Ecoles, Ecoles supérieures des Arts and Etablissements de promotion sociale. It leads to the title of Bachelier after three years' study and 180 ECTS credits.

University level second stage: *Master; Médecin; Médecin vétérinaire*
The second stage of university-level studies is offered at Universities, Hautes Ecoles, Ecoles supérieures des Arts and Etablissements d'enseignement de promotion sociale. It leads to the title of Master after one or two years' study and 60 or 120 ECTS credits; of Médecin (Medicine) after three years' study and 180 ECTS credits; and of Médecin vétérinaire (Veterinary Medicine) after three years' study and 180 ECTS credits.

University level third stage: *Doctorat*
The third stage of university-level studies is offered at universities. Doctoral training lasts generally 3 years corresponding to 180 ECTS.

ADMISSION TO HIGHER EDUCATION

Admission to university-level studies:

Name of secondary school credential required: Certificat d' Enseignement secondaire supérieur

For entry to: All institutions.

Alternatives to credentials: Attestation of success in one of the admissions examinations organised by the higher education institutions or a jury of the French Community - Academic title conferred by a higher education or university institution and in some cases by social promotion institutions.

Admission requirements: Students seeking admission to first cycle programme in Medical sciences must participate in a compulsory orientation test (non-binding results), which is identical and simultaneous across all universities. Special entrance examination for access to Civil Engineering studies.

Foreign students admission:

Definition of foreign student: A foreign student is a person enrolled at a higher education institution in Belgium (French-speaking Community) who is not a permanent resident.

Admission requirements: Students must obtain the equivalence of their secondary school leaving certificate with the Certificat d'enseignement secondaire supérieur (CESS).

Entry regulations: Students must register with the communal administration of their town of residence, present proof of their enrolment, as well as financial guarantees.

Language proficiency: Admission to the first cycle of studies requires sufficient level of knowledge in French. Language proficiency tests are organised by the Académie de Recherche et d'Enseignement supérieur (ARES).

RECOGNITION OF STUDIES

Quality assurance system:

Competences over the academic recognition of foreign higher education degrees in the Federation Wallonia-Brussels are shared between the Ministry (DGENORS) and the higher education institutions. The Ministry is competent for the recognition of foreign higher education degrees when requested for professional purposes. The higher education institutions are competent for the recognition of foreign first and second cycle degrees, when requested for study purposes, as well as foreign doctorate degrees.

Bodies dealing with recognition:

Centre ENIC-NARIC de la Fédération Wallonie-Bruxelles

Attaché: Kevin Guillaume
Rue Lavallée, 1
Bruxelles 1080
Tel: +32(2) 690-8747
Fax: +32(2) 690-8760
EMail: enic-naric@cfwb.be
WWW: http://www.enseignement.be/enic-naric

Direction générale de l'Enseignement non obligatoire et de la Recherche scientifique (Directorate General Non-Compulsory Education and Scientific Research)

Ministère de la Fédération Wallonie-Bruxelles
Administration générale de l'Enseignement et de la Recherche scientifique
Direction générale de l'Enseignement non obligatoire et de la Recherche scientifique
Rue Adolphe Lavallée, 1
Bruxelles 1080
EMail: info@enseignement.be
WWW: http://www.enseignement.be

NATIONAL BODIES

Direction générale de l'Enseignement non obligatoire et de la Recherche scientifique (Directorate General Non-Compulsory Education and Scientific Research)

Minister of Higher Education, Research and Media: Jean-Claude Marcourt
Ministère de la Fédération Wallonie-Bruxelles
Administration générale de l'Enseignement et de la Recherche scientifique
Direction générale de l'Enseignement non obligatoire et de la Recherche scientifique
Rue Adolphe Lavallée, 1
Bruxelles 1080
EMail: info@enseignement.be
WWW: http://www.enseignement.be
Role of national body: Governing and decision-making role for higher education

Académie de Recherche et d'Enseignement supérieur - ARES

Administrateur: Julien Nicaise
Rue d'Egmont, 5
Bruxelles 1000
EMail: info@ares-ac.be
WWW: http://www.ares-ac.be

Agence pour l'Evaluation de la Qualité de l'Enseignement Supérieur

President: Philippe Lepoivre
Head of the Executive Unit: Caty Duykaerts
Boulevard Léopold II, 44
2e étage
Brussels 1080
EMail: info@aeqes.be
WWW: http://www.aeqes.be

Role of national body: Created in 2002, the AEQES is an independent public service agency, a full member of the European Network for Quality Assurance (ENQA) and included on the European Quality Assurance Register (EQAR) which develops a formative approach to quality assurance.

Conseil des Recteurs des Universités francophones de Belgique - CREF

President: Didier Viviers
Rue d'Egmont, 5
Bruxelles 1000
Fax: +32(2) 504-9343
EMail: elisabeth.kokkelkoren@cref.be
WWW: http://www.cref.be

Data for academic year: 2014-2015
Source: Directorate General for Education and Scientific Research, ENIC-NARIC centre of the Federation Wallonia-Brussels, 2014. Bodies 2015.

INSTITUTIONS

ACADÉMIE ROYALE DES BEAUX-ARTS DE LA VILLE DE BRUXELLES - ÉCOLE SUPÉRIEURE DES ARTS (ARBA-ESA)

144 Rue du Midi, 1000 Bruxelles
Tel: + 32(2) 506-10-10
Fax: +32(2) 506-10-28
EMail: info@arba-esa.be
Website: http://www.arba-esa.be

Directeur: Marc Partouche
Tel: +32(2) 511-04-91 EMail: direction@arba-esa.be

Programme
Plastic Arts, Visual Arts and Graphic Arts (Architectural and Environmental Design; Communication Arts; Engraving; Fine Arts; Graphic Arts; Interior Design; Painting and Drawing; Photography; Sculpture; Textile Design; Visual Arts; Weaving)

Institute
Arts and Choreography (Dance; Fine Arts)

History: Founded 1711, acquired present status 1980.

Academic Year: September to June

Admission Requirements: Secondary school certificate or foreign equivalent and entrance examination

Main Language(s) of Instruction: French

Degrees and Diplomas: Bachelor 3 yrs; Master 1 yr and Master à finalité (3 options: Master approfondi (préparation au doctorat), Master didactique, Master spécialisé

Student Services: Canteen, Social Counselling

Publications: La Part de l'Oeil
Last Updated: 05/02/15

ARTS - ÉCOLE SUPÉRIEURE DES ARTS (ESAPV)

rue de Nimy 7, 7000 Mons, Hainaut
Tel: +32(65) 34-73-77
EMail: direction@artsaucarre.be
Website: http://www.esapv.be

Directeur: Michel Stockhem

Division
Music *(Conservatoire royal)* (Music; Music Theory and Composition; Musical Instruments); **Theatre** *(Conservatoire royal)* (Theatre); **Visual Arts** *(long cycle)* (Engraving; Fine Arts; Furniture Design; Interior Design; Multimedia; Painting and Drawing; Sculpture; Visual Arts)

History: Founded following the merger of the Conservatoire royal de Mons and the Ecole supérieure des arts plastiques et visuels (ESAPV).

Admission Requirements: Secondary school certificate and artistic examination

Fees: 310-400 (Euro)

Main Language(s) of Instruction: French

Accrediting Agency: Communauté française de Belgique

Degrees and Diplomas: *Bachelier (enseignement universitaire et enseignement supérieur de type long)*; *Master*. Doctorate in collaboration with the University

Student Services: Canteen, Nursery Care, Social Counselling
Last Updated: 04/02/15

CATHOLIC UNIVERSITY OF LOUVAIN

Université catholique de Louvain (UCL)
Place de l'Université, 1, 1348 Louvain-la-Neuve
Tel: +32(10) 47-21-11
Fax: +32(10) 47-29-99
EMail: info-cio@uclouvain.be
Website: http://www.uclouvain.be

Recteur: Vincent Blondel (2014-) EMail: rectorat@uclouvain.be

Administrateur général: Dominique Opfergelt
EMail: Dominique.Opfergelt@uclouvain.be

International Relations: Vincent Wertz, Prorecteur
EMail: vincent.wertz@uclouvain.be

Faculty
Architecture, Architectural Engineering and Urban Planning (Architecture; Regional Planning; Structural Architecture; Town Planning); **Biological, Agricultural and Environmental Engineering** (Agronomy; Biological and Life Sciences; Environmental Engineering); **Economic, Social and Political Sciences and Communication** (Business Administration; Communication Studies; Demography and Population; Development Studies; Economics; Political Sciences; Social Sciences); **Law and Criminology** (Criminal Law; Criminology; Law); **Medicine and Dentistry** *(Brussels)* (Biomedicine; Dentistry; Medicine; Pharmacy; Public Health); **Motor Science** (Physical Education; Physical Therapy; Rehabilitation and Therapy); **Pharmacy and Biomedical Sciences** (Biomedicine; Pharmacy); **Philosophy, Arts and Letters** (Ancient Civilizations; Archaeology; Art History; Arts and Humanities; Chinese; Classical Languages; Communication Studies; Cultural Studies; Dutch; English; French; German; Greek; History; Information Technology; Italian; Latin; Linguistics; Literature; Medieval Studies; Modern Languages; Musicology; Oriental Languages; Performing

Arts; Philosophy; Romance Languages); **Psychology and Educational Sciences** (Education; Educational Psychology; Family Studies; Psychology); **Public Health** (Public Health); **Science** (Biology; Chemistry; Geography; Mathematics; Natural Sciences; Physics); **Theology** (Canon Law; Theology)

School

Engineering (Architecture; Civil Engineering; Computer Engineering; Electrical Engineering; Environmental Engineering; Materials Engineering; Mechanical Engineering; Town Planning); **Management** *(Louvain)* (Management)

Further Information: Also Research Centres and Institutes (http://www.uclouvain.be/secteurs.html)

History: Founded 1425, UCL is one of the oldest universities in the world. Erasmus, Jansenius, Vesalius, Mercator, Georges Lemaître worked or taught at the UCL. In 1970, separation into two distinct universities, the Flemish-speaking one remained on the original site in Leuven. The French-speaking University moved to Wallonia (Louvain-la-Neuve). The faculty of Medicine moved to Brussels.

Academic Year: September to July (September-February; February-July)

Admission Requirements: Secondary school certificate and entrance examination, or foreign qualifications if recognized under agreement concluded with the Belgian Government. Other foreign qualifications subject to the approval of the faculty concerned

Main Language(s) of Instruction: French

Degrees and Diplomas: *Bachelier (enseignement supérieur de type court)*; *Master*: **Actuarial Science; Agricultural Engineering; Ancient Languages; Anthropology; Applied Mathematics; Archaeology; Architecture; Biochemistry; Bioengineering; Biological and Life Sciences; Biology; Biomedical Engineering; Biomedicine; Business and Commerce; Chemical Engineering; Chemistry; Christian Religious Studies; Communication Studies; Computer Engineering; Computer Science; Construction Engineering; Criminology; Demography and Population; Dentistry; Development Studies; Economics; Education; Electrical Engineering; Engineering; Environmental Management; Environmental Studies; Ethics; European Studies; Family Studies; French; Gender Studies; Geography; History; Human Resources; Information Technology; Law; Linguistics; Literature; Management; Materials Engineering; Mathematics; Mechanical Engineering; Medicine; Modern Languages; Performing Arts; Pharmacy; Philosophy; Physical Education; Physical Engineering; Physical Therapy; Physics; Political Sciences; Psychology; Public Administration; Public Health; Religious Studies; Sociology; Statistics; Theology.** *Doctorat*: **Archaeology; Architecture; Art History; Civil Engineering; Communication Studies; Computer Science; Economics; Education; History; Management; Natural Sciences; Philosophy; Physical Therapy; Political Sciences; Psychology; Social Sciences; Translation and Interpretation; Veterinary Science.**

Student Services: Academic Counselling, Careers Guidance

Publications: La Lucarne; Louvain medical; Revue Louvain

Publishing House: Presses universitaires de Louvain

Student Numbers *2012-2013*: Total 28,632

Last Updated: 10/04/15

CATHOLIC UNIVERSITY OF MONS

Université catholique de Mons (UCM)

151 Chaussée de Binche, 7000 Mons

Tel: +32(65) 32-32-11

Fax: +32(65) 31-56-91

EMail: secretariat.etudes@fucam.ac.be

Website: http://www.fucam.ac.be

Recteur: Vincent Blondel EMail: rectorat@fucam.ac.be

Administrateur général: Dominique Opfergelt EMail: dominique.opfergelt@uclouvain.be

Faculty

Economics, Social Sciences,Poltical Science and Communication (Communication Studies; Economics; Political Sciences; Social Sciences)

School

Management *(Louvain)* (Management)

History: Founded as Facultés Universitaires Catholiques de Mons (FUCaM). Acquired present title 2011.

Academic Year: September to June (September-December; January-May)

Admission Requirements: Secondary school certificate in relevant fields or recognized equivalent and compulsory French as a foreign language test for non-French-speaking students

Main Language(s) of Instruction: French

Degrees and Diplomas: *Bachelier (enseignement supérieur de type court)*; *Master*: **Business and Commerce; Engineering; International Relations; Management; Public Administration.** *Doctorat*: **Economics; Information Technology; Management; Political Sciences; Social Sciences.**

Student Services: Canteen, Careers Guidance, Facilities for disabled people, Social Counselling

Last Updated: 10/04/15

CONSERVATOIRE ROYAL DE BRUXELLES

Rue de la Régence, 30, 1000 Bruxelles

Tel: +32(2) 511-04-27

Fax: +32(2) 512-69-79

EMail: info@conservatoire.be

Website: http://www.conservatoire.be

Directeur: Frédéric de Roos EMail: direction@conservatoire.be

Programme

Music (Conducting; Music; Music Theory and Composition; Musical Instruments; Singing; Theatre); **Theatre** (Speech Studies; Theatre)

History: Founded 1832 as Conservatoire royal de Musique de Bruxelles.

Main Language(s) of Instruction: French

Degrees and Diplomas: *Bachelier (enseignement supérieur de type court)*; *Master*

Last Updated: 04/02/15

CONSERVATOIRE ROYAL DE LIÈGE

Boulevard Piercot, 29, 4000 Liège

Tel: +32(4) 222-03-06

Fax: +32(4) 222-03-84

EMail: info@crlg.be

Website: http://www.crlg.be

Directeur: Nathanaël Harcq EMail: direction@crlg.be

Programme

Music (Conducting; Music; Music Theory and Composition; Musical Instruments; Singing; Theatre); **Theatre** (Speech Studies; Theatre)

History: Founded 1826 as Conservatoire royal de Musique de Liège.

Main Language(s) of Instruction: French

Degrees and Diplomas: *Bachelier (enseignement supérieur de type court)*; *Master*. Specialised Master

Last Updated: 04/02/15

ÉCOLE NATIONALE SUPÉRIEURE DES ARTS VISUELS DE LA CAMBRE

Abbaye de La Cambre, 21, 1000 Bruxelles

Tel: +32(2) 626-17-80

Fax: +32(2) 640-96-93

EMail: lacambre@lacambre.be

Website: http://www.lacambre.be

Directrice: Caroline Mierop EMail: direction@lacambre.be

Division

Fine Arts *(long cycle)* (Ceramic Art; Display and Stage Design; Engraving; Fashion Design; Film; Furniture Design; Graphic Arts; Graphic Design; Industrial Design; Painting and Drawing; Photography; Printing and Printmaking; Publishing and Book Trade; Restoration of Works of Art; Sculpture; Video; Visual Arts)

History: Founded 1927.

Degrees and Diplomas: *Bachelier (enseignement supérieur de type court); Master*
Last Updated: 04/02/15

ÉCOLE SUPÉRIEURE DES ARTS DE LA VILLE DE LIÈGE

Rue des Anglais, 21, 4000 Liège
Tel: +32(4) 221-70-70
Fax: +32(4) 221-38-20
EMail: arba.liege@sup.cfwb.be
Website: http://www.acasupliege.be

Directeur: Daniel Sluse

Programme

Graphic and Visual Arts *(long cycle)* (Advertising and Publicity; Engraving; Graphic Arts; Painting and Drawing; Sculpture; Video; Visual Arts)

History: Founded 1775 as Académie royale des Beaux-Arts de Liège.

Admission Requirements: Secondary school certificate (Baccalauréat)

Main Language(s) of Instruction: French

Degrees and Diplomas: *Bachelier (enseignement supérieur de type court); Master*

Student Services: Academic Counselling, Canteen, Social Counselling

Last Updated: 05/02/15

ÉCOLE SUPÉRIEURE DES ARTS - ÉCOLE DE RECHERCHE GRAPHIQUE (ERG)

87 rue du Page, 1050 Bruxelles
Tel: +32(2) 538-98-29
Fax: +32(2) 539-33-93
EMail: secretariat@erg.be
Website: http://www.erg.be

Directrice: Corinne Diserens EMail: direction@erg.be

Division

Graphic and Visual Arts *(long cycle)* (Film; Graphic Arts; Painting and Drawing; Performing Arts; Photography; Sculpture; Video; Visual Arts)

History: Founded 1972 as Institut supérieur libre des Arts plastiques - Ecole de Recherche graphique. ERG is associated to Instituts Saint-Luc.

Main Language(s) of Instruction: French

Degrees and Diplomas: *Bachelier (enseignement supérieur de type court); Master.* Also Master a finalité 60 credits (5yrs)

Last Updated: 04/02/15

ÉCOLE SUPÉRIEURE DES ARTS SAINT-LUC DE BRUXELLES (ESA)

Rue d'Irlande, 57, 1060 Bruxelles
Tel: +32(2) 537-08-70
Fax: +32(2) 537-00-63
EMail: info@stluc-bruxelles-esa.be
Website: http://www.stluc-bruxelles-esa.be/

Directrice: Françoise Klein EMail: f.klein@brutele.be

Directeur Adjoint: Marc Streker EMail: m.streker@brutele.be

Course

Advertising and Publicity (Advertising and Publicity); **Architectural and Planning** (Architecture; Architecture and Planning); **Architecture** (Architecture); **Comics** (Painting and Drawing); **Computer Graphics** (Computer Graphics); **Interior Architecture**; **Interior Design** (Interior Design)

History: Founded 1863 as Institut Saint-Luc.

Main Language(s) of Instruction: French

Degrees and Diplomas: *Bachelier (enseignement supérieur de type court); Master*

Last Updated: 04/02/15

ÉCOLE SUPÉRIEURE DES ARTS SAINT-LUC DE LIÈGE

Boulevard de la Constitution, 41, 4020 Liège
Tel: +32(4) 341-80-00
Fax: +32(4) 341-80-80
EMail: beaux-arts@stluc.com
Website: http://www.saintluc-liege.be

Directrice: Anne-Marie Wynants

Programme

Plastic Arts (Advertising and Publicity; Fine Arts; Graphic Arts; Industrial Design; Interior Design; Painting and Drawing; Photography; Restoration of Works of Art; Sculpture)

History: Founded as Institut supérieur des Beaux-Arts 'Saint-Luc'.

Main Language(s) of Instruction: French

Degrees and Diplomas: *Bachelier (enseignement supérieur de type court); Master*

Last Updated: 04/02/15

FINE-ARTS ACADEMY OF TOURNAI

Académie des Beaux-Arts de Tournai (AC'T)
Rue de l'Hôpital Notre-Dame, 14, 7500 Tournai
Tel: +32(69) 84-12-63
Fax: +32(69) 84-32-53
EMail: info@actournai.be
Website: http://www.actournai.be

Directeur: Bernard Bay

International Relations: Patrick Winberg

Programme

Fine Arts *(long cycle)* (Advertising and Publicity; Graphic Arts; Interior Design; Painting and Drawing; Textile Design; Visual Arts)

History: Founded 1757 as Académie royale des Beaux-Arts et des Arts décoratifs de Tournai.

Admission Requirements: Baccalauréat and entrance examination

Main Language(s) of Instruction: French

Degrees and Diplomas: *Bachelier (enseignement supérieur de type court); Master*

Student Services: Cultural Activities, Social Counselling

Last Updated: 04/02/15

HAUTE ECOLE CHARLEMAGNE

Rue des Rivageois, 6, B4000 Liège
Tel: +32(4) 254-76-11
Fax: +32(4) 253-39-15
EMail: secr.presidence@hech.be
Website: http://www.hech.be

Directrice-Présidente: Corine Matillard
EMail: corine.matillard@hecharlemagne.be

Department

Agronomy *(Huy - Gembloux)* (Agricultural Engineering; Agronomy; Horticulture; Landscape Architecture); **Economics** *(Huy)* (Economics; Hotel Management; Real Estate; Tourism; Transport Management); **Paramedical Sciences** *(Liège-Sart Tilman)* (Biomedicine; Chemistry); **Pedagogy** *(Verviers, Liège)* (Biology; Chemistry; Economics; Ethics; French; Geography; Germanic Languages; History; Physical Education; Physics; Social Sciences; Teacher Training); **Technology** *(Gembloux; Sart Tilman)* (Biology; Chemistry; Electronic Engineering; Engineering; Industrial Engineering; Materials Engineering; Mathematics; Packaging Technology; Statistics)

History: Founded 1878. Acquired present status and title 1996.

Academic Year: September to July

Admission Requirements: Secondary school certificate or recognized equivalent for foreigners

Fees: 475 per annum (Euro)

Main Language(s) of Instruction: French

Degrees and Diplomas: *Bachelier (enseignement supérieur de type court):* **Agronomy; Business and Commerce; Education; Paramedical Sciences; Preschool Education; Primary**

Education. *Master*: **Agronomy; Industrial Engineering; Landscape Architecture.**

Student Services: Academic Counselling, Canteen, Careers Guidance, Language Laboratory, Social Counselling, Sports Facilities

Publications: Bulletin International Charlemagne

Last Updated: 04/02/15

HAUTE ECOLE DE BRUXELLES (HEB)

Chaussée de Waterloo, 749, 1180 Bruxelles
Tel: +32(2) 340-12-95
Fax: +32(2) 347-52-64
EMail: heb@heb.be
Website: http://www.heb.be

Directrice-Présidente: Marianne Coessens
EMail: mcoessens@heb.be

International Relations: Jean Gomez, Head, International Office
EMail: jgomez@heb.be

School

Computer Science *(Ecole supérieure d'Informatique)* (Business Computing; Computer Networks; Computer Science; Telecommunications Engineering)

Institute

Pedagogy *(Institut pédagogique Defré)* (Pedagogy); **Translation and Interpretation** *(Institut supérieur de Traducteurs et Interprètes)* (Translation and Interpretation)

History: Founded 1996, incorporating existing institutions.

Admission Requirements: Secondary school certificate

Fees: 322 per annum (Euro)

Main Language(s) of Instruction: French

Degrees and Diplomas: *Bachelier (enseignement supérieur de type court)*; *Master*; *Doctorat*: **Translation and Interpretation.**

Student Services: Language Laboratory, Social Counselling

Publications: Equivalences

Last Updated: 05/02/15

HAUTE ECOLE DE LA PROVINCE DE LIÈGE

Avenue Montesquieu, 6, 4101 Jemeppe-sur-Meuse
Tel: +32(4) 237-96-01
Fax: +32(4) 237-95-51
EMail: epl@provincedeliege.be
Website: http://haute-ecole.provincedeliege.be/

Directeur-Président: Toni Bastianelli
EMail: Toni.Bastianelli@provincedeliege.be

Department

Agronomy *(La Reid)* (Agricultural Management; Agronomy; Biotechnology; Environmental Studies; Forestry); **Chemistry, Biochemistry, Biotechnology** *(Liège)* (Biochemistry; Biotechnology; Chemistry); **Communication** *(Jemeppe)* (Communication Studies; Documentation Techniques; Library Science; Multimedia); **Computer Graphics** *(Seraing)* (Computer Graphics); **Computer Science** *(Seraing)* (Computer Networks; Computer Science; Industrial Engineering; Systems Analysis; Telecommunications Engineering); **Construction** *(Verviers)* (Construction Engineering; Industrial Engineering); **Economics** *(Jemeppe)* (Accountancy; E- Business/Commerce; Economics; International Business; Management; Marketing; Transport Management); **Education** *(Jemeppe)* (Education; Educational Psychology; Physical Education); **Electrical and Mechanical Engineering** *(Seraing)* (Electrical Engineering; Industrial Engineering; Mechanical Engineering; Production Engineering); **Law** *(Jemeppe)* (Law); **Paramedical** *(Liège)* (Biotechnology; Community Health; Dietetics; Ergotherapy; Gerontology; Laboratory Techniques; Midwifery; Nursing; Oncology; Paediatrics; Physical Therapy; Psychiatry and Mental Health; Rehabilitation and Therapy); **Social Studies** *(Jemeppe)* (Human Resources; Social Studies; Social Work)

History: Founded 1995, following the merger of three Hautes Ecoles provinciales: Rennequin Sualem, Léon-Eli Troclet and André Vésale.

Academic Year: September to June

Admission Requirements: Secondary school certificate or foreign equivalent

Fees: (Euros): Registration, 175 per annum (Euro)

Main Language(s) of Instruction: French

Degrees and Diplomas: *Bachelier (enseignement supérieur de type court)*; *Master*

Student Services: Academic Counselling, Canteen, Careers Guidance, Facilities for disabled people, Social Counselling

Last Updated: 05/02/15

HAUTE ÉCOLE DE LA VILLE DE LIÈGE

Rue Hazinelle, 2, 4000 Liège
Tel: +32(4) 223-28-08
Fax: +32(4) 221-08-42
EMail: info@hel.be
Website: http://www.hel.be/

Directeur-Président: Patrick Delcour Nossent
EMail: patrick.delcour@hel.be

School

Economics *(ECSSAC)* (Economics; Hotel Management; Public Administration; Public Relations; Secretarial Studies); **Pedagogy** *(Ecole Normale Jonfosse)* (Germanic Languages; Mathematics; Natural Sciences; Preschool Education; Primary Education; Secondary Education; Teacher Training); **Physical Therapy** *(Ecole supérieure de Logopédie)* (Speech Therapy and Audiology); **Translation and Interpretation** (Translation and Interpretation)

Institute

Technical Studies *(Institut Supérieur d'Enseignement Technologique)* (Automotive Engineering; Chemistry; Computer Science; Electronic Engineering; Publishing and Book Trade)

History: Founded 1995.

Main Language(s) of Instruction: French

Degrees and Diplomas: *Bachelier (enseignement supérieur de type court)*; *Master*

Last Updated: 10/04/15

HAUTE ÉCOLE DE NAMUR-LIÈGE-LUXEMBOURG (HENAM)

Rue Saint-Donat, 130, 5002 Namur
Tel: +32(81) 46-85-00
EMail: info@henallux.be
Website: http://www.henallux.be

Directeur-Président: Daniel Chavée
EMail: daniel.chavee@henallux.be

Department

Economics, Technology and Pedagogy *(Namur)* (Accountancy; Automation and Control Engineering; Business Computing; Computer Science; Law; Marketing; Teacher Training); **Economics, Technology and Social Studies** *(Arlon)* (Accountancy; Electronic Engineering; Mechanical Engineering; Secretarial Studies; Social Work); **Paramedical** *(Sainte Elisabeth, Namur)* (Midwifery; Nursing); **Pedagogy** *(Bastogne, Champion, Malonne)* (Teacher Training); **Pedagogy and Social Studies** *(Malonne)* (Documentation Techniques; Library Science); **Social Work** *(Namur)* (Human Resources; Management; Social Work); **Technical** *(Marche-en-Famenne, Seraing, Virton)* (Computer Science; Electronic Engineering; Industrial Engineering; Mechanical Engineering)

History: Founded 2011 following merger of the Haute École de Namur and the Haute École Blaise Pascal.

Admission Requirements: Secondary school certificate

Main Language(s) of Instruction: French

Degrees and Diplomas: *Bachelier (enseignement supérieur de type court)*; *Master*

Last Updated: 05/02/15

HAUTE ECOLE EN HAINAUT

Rue Pierre-Joseph Duménil, 4, 7000 Mons
Tel: +32(65) 34-79-83
Fax: +32(65) 39-45-25
EMail: directeur-president@hecfh.be
Website: http://www.hecfh.be

Directeur-Président: Denis Dufrane

Campus

Economics *(Institut supérieur économique de Tournai)* (Economics; Law; Secretarial Studies; Tourism); **Pedagogy** *(Institut supérieur d'Enseignement pédagogique)* (Arts and Humanities; Economics; Education; Educational Technology; Fine Arts; French; Germanic Languages; Mathematics; Natural Sciences; Pedagogy; Preschool Education; Primary Education; Special Education; Teacher Training); **Social** (Social Studies); **Technical** *(Mons)* (Biotechnology; Chemical Engineering; Computer Engineering; Computer Graphics; Construction Engineering; Electronic Engineering; Industrial Engineering)

Degrees and Diplomas: *Bachelier (enseignement supérieur de type court); Master*

Student Services: Academic Counselling, Social Counselling

Last Updated: 05/02/15

HAUTE ECOLE FRANCISCO FERRER (HEFF)

Rue de la Fontaine, 4, 1000 Bruxelles, Brabant
Tel: +32(2) 279-58-10
Fax: +32(2) 279-58-29
EMail: heff.europe@he-ferrer.eu
Website: http://www.he-ferrer.eu/

Directeur-Président: Pierre Lambert Tel: +32(2) 279-58-12

Unit

Applied Mathematics (Applied Mathematics); **Physical Education** (Physical Education)

Department

Applied Arts (Advertising and Publicity; Fashion Design; Textile Design); **Economics** *(Cooremans)* (Accountancy; Administration; Business Administration; Insurance; Public Administration; Secretarial Studies; Transport Management); **Paramedical Studies** (Medical Technology; Midwifery; Nursing); **Pedagogy** (Economics; French; Germanic Languages; Mathematics; Natural Sciences; Physical Education; Preschool Education; Primary Education; Secondary Education); **Technical** (Electronic Engineering; Graphic Design); **Translation and Interpretation** (Translation and Interpretation)

History: Founded 1996.

Main Language(s) of Instruction: French

Degrees and Diplomas: *Bachelier (enseignement supérieur de type court); Master*

Last Updated: 05/02/15

HAUTE ECOLE GALILÉE (HEG)

Rue des Grands Carmes, 23, 1000 Bruxelles, Brabant
Tel: +32(2) 289-63-30
Fax: +32(2) 289-63-39
EMail: heg@galilee.be
Website: http://www.galilee.be

Directeur-Président: John Van Tiggelen
EMail: directeur.president@galilee.be

Department

Economics (Hotel Management; Secretarial Studies; Tourism)

Institute

Nursing *(Institut supérieur Soins infirmiers Galilée Bruxelles)* (Nursing); **Pedagogy** *(Institut supérieur pédagogique Galilée)* (Biology; Chemistry; Dutch; Economics; English; Fine Arts; French; Geography; History; Mathematics; Pedagogy; Physics; Religion; Social Sciences; Teacher Training); **Social Communication** *(Institut des Hautes Etudes des Communications sociales)* (Advertising and Publicity; Communication Studies; Journalism; Media Studies; Modern Languages; Public Relations)

History: Founded 1996, incorporating 5 existing institutes.

Academic Year: September to June

Admission Requirements: Secondary school certificate and entrance examination in french

Fees: EU Students, 396-793 per annum. Non-EU Students, 1,388-1,784 (Euro)

Main Language(s) of Instruction: French

Degrees and Diplomas: *Bachelier (enseignement supérieur de type court); Master*

Last Updated: 10/04/15

HAUTE ECOLE GROUPE ICHEC - ISC SAINT LOUIS - ISFSC

Boulevard Brand Whitlock, 6, 1150 Bruxelles
Tel: +32(2) 739-37-00
Fax: +32(2) 739-38-03
EMail: info@ichec.be
Website: http://www.he-ichec-isfsc.be

Recteur: Brigitte Chanoine

School

Management *(Brussels (ICHEC))* (Business Administration; Cultural Studies; E-Business/Commerce; Fiscal Law; Management; Taxation)

Institute

Social Work and Communication (Communication Studies; Multimedia; Social and Community Services; Social Welfare; Social Work)

History: Founded 1996, incoporating existing institutions.

Academic Year: September to June

Admission Requirements: Secondary school certificate or equivalent. TOEFL exam for foreign students

Fees: 780-805 per annum; Foreign Students 2,279-2,775 per annum (Euro)

Main Language(s) of Instruction: French

Degrees and Diplomas: *Bachelier (enseignement supérieur de type court); Master*

Student Services: Academic Counselling, Canteen, Careers Guidance, Foreign Studies Centre, Language Laboratory, Social Counselling

Last Updated: 05/02/15

HAUTE ECOLE LÉONARD DE VINCI (HELDV)

Place de l'Alma, 2, 1200 Bruxelles
Tel: +32(2) 761-06-80
Fax: +32(2) 761-06-89
EMail: info@vinci.be
Website: http://www.vinci.be

Directeur-Président: Damien Huvelle

School

Pedagogy *(Ecole Normale Catholique du Brabant wallon)* (Pedagogy; Teacher Training)

Institute

Industrial Engineering *(ECAM, Institut supérieur industriel)* (Automation and Control Engineering; Computer Engineering; Construction Engineering; Electronic Engineering; Industrial Engineering; Mechanical Engineering; Surveying and Mapping); **Libre Marie Haps** (Clinical Psychology; Educational Psychology; Speech Therapy and Audiology; Translation and Interpretation); **Nursing** *(Institut Supérieur d'Enseignement Infirmier)* (Anaesthesiology; Community Health; Gerontology; Midwifery; Nursing; Oncology; Paediatrics; Psychiatry and Mental Health); **Parnasse Deux Alices** (Ergotherapy; Nursing; Physical Education; Physical Therapy; Podiatry); **Paul Lambin** (Biomedicine; Business Computing; Chemistry; Dietetics; Laboratory Techniques; Medical Technology)

History: Founded 1994 incorporating existing institutes. A university-level institution financially supported by the State.

Main Language(s) of Instruction: French

Degrees and Diplomas: *Bachelier (enseignement supérieur de type court); Master.* Also Agrégé(e) de l'enseignement secondaire inférieur.

Last Updated: 05/02/15

HAUTE ECOLE LIBRE DE BRUXELLES ILYA PRIGOGINE (HELB-IP)

Avenue Besme 97, 1090 Bruxelles
Tel: +32(2) 349-68-11
Fax: +32(2) 349-68-31
EMail: direction.presidence@helb-prigogine.be
Website: http://www.helb-prigogine.be

Directrice-Présidente: Nicole Bardaxoglou

Institute

Applied Humanities *(Ecole Ouvrière Supérieure)* (Social Welfare; Social Work); **Economics and Paramedical Sciences** *(Institut Libre d'Enseignement Supérieur Economique et Paramédical de Bruxelles)* (Business Computing; Physical Therapy; Public Relations); **Paramedical Studies** *(ISCAM)* (Community Health; Ergotherapy; Gerontology; Midwifery; Nursing; Oncology; Paediatrics; Physical Therapy; Podiatry); **Radioelectricity and Cinema** *(Institut National de Radioélectricité et de Cinématographie)* (Cinema and Television; Electrical Engineering; Electronic Engineering; Photography)

History: Founded 1995

Main Language(s) of Instruction: French

Degrees and Diplomas: *Bachelier (enseignement supérieur de type court); Master*

Last Updated: 10/04/15

HAUTE ECOLE LIBRE MOSANE (HELMO)

Mont Saint-Martin 41, 4000 Liège
Tel: +32(4) 222-22-00
EMail: info@helmo.be
Website: http://www.helmo.be/

Directeur-Président: Alexandre Lodez

International Relations: Julie Guiot
Tel: +32(4) 229-86-69

Institute

HELMo ESAS (Social Welfare; Social Work); **HELMo Huy** (Primary Education; Teacher Training); **HELMo Lancin** (Physical Education); **HELMo Mode** (Fashion Design); **HELMo Saint Laurent** (Automation and Control Engineering; Biomedicine; Business and Commerce; Computer Science); **HELMo Saint Roch** (Primary Education; Teacher Training); **HELMo Saint-Martin** (Business Administration; Law); **HELMo Sainte Julienne** (Midwifery; Nursing); **HELMo Sainte-Croix** (Preschool Education; Primary Education; Secondary Education; Teacher Training); **HELMo Sainte-Marie** (Accountancy; Insurance; International Business; Marketing); **HELMo Verviers** (Modern Languages; Secretarial Studies); **HELMo-Gramm** (Industrial Engineering)

Centre

HELMo-CFEL *(Centre de Formation Éducationnelle Liégeois (CFEL))* (Teacher Training)

History: Founded 1996. Acquired present title 2008 following merger with ISELL.

Academic Year: September to June (September-January; February-June)

Admission Requirements: Secondary school certificate

Main Language(s) of Instruction: French

Degrees and Diplomas: *Bachelier (enseignement supérieur de type court); Master*

Student Services: Academic Counselling, Careers Guidance, Social Counselling

Last Updated: 05/02/15

HAUTE ECOLE LOUVAIN EN HAINAUT

159 Chaussée de Binche, 7000 Mons, Hainaut
Tel: +32(65) 40-41-42
Fax: +32(65) 34-04-52
EMail: isabelle.graulich@helha.be
Website: http://www.helha.be

Directeur-Président: Jean-Luc Vreux (1998-)

Division

Agronomy *(Fleurus)* (Agricultural Business; Biotechnology); **Applied Arts** *(Mons)* (Advertising and Publicity); **Economics** *(Mons, La Louvière, Charleroi, Fleurus, Montignies-sur-Sambre, Mouscron)* (Accountancy; Business Administration; Business Computing; Hotel Management; Marketing; Public Relations; Secretarial Studies; Tourism); **Paramedical Studies** *(Fleurus, Montignies-sur-Sambre, Gilly, La Louvière, Mouscron, Tournai)* (Biomedicine; Ergotherapy; Medical Technology; Midwifery; Nursing; Physical Therapy); **Pedagogy** *(Gosselles, Braine le Comte, Leuze-en-Hainaut, Mons, Loverval)* (Teacher Training); **Social Work** *(Montignies-sur-Sambre, Louvain la Neuve, Mons, Tournai)* (Communication Studies; Social Work); **Technology** *(Mons, Charleroi, Tournai)* (Automotive Engineering; Chemistry; Computer Science; Construction Engineering; Electronic Engineering; Industrial Engineering)

History: Founded 2009 following merger of the Haute École Charleroi Europe, the Haute École Libre du Hainaut Occidental and the Haute École Roi Baudouin

Academic Year: September to July

Admission Requirements: Secondary school certificate

Fees: c. 245-570 per annum (Euro)

Main Language(s) of Instruction: French

Degrees and Diplomas: *Bachelier (enseignement supérieur de type court); Master*

Student Services: Academic Counselling, Canteen, Language Laboratory, Social Counselling

Last Updated: 05/02/15

HAUTE ECOLE LUCIA DE BROUCKÈRE (HELDB)

Avenue Emile Gryzon, 1, 1070 Bruxelles
Tel: +32(2) 526-73-00
Fax: +32(2) 524-30-82
EMail: info@heldb.be
Website: http://www.heldb.be

Directrice-Présidente: Anne-Marie Duquesne

Department

Site Ferry (Accountancy; Medical Technology; Primary Education; Teacher Training)

Institute

Economics *(Site d'Ixelles)* (Law; Marketing); **Haulot** (Dietetics; Hotel Management; Landscape Architecture; Public Relations; Tourism; Urban Studies); **Meurice** (Biochemistry; Chemistry; Industrial Engineering); **Pedagogy and Economics** *(Jodoigne)* (Secretarial Studies; Special Education; Teacher Training)

History: Founded 1891 as Institut Meurice. Acquired present title 1995.

Fees: c. 200 per annum (Euro)

Main Language(s) of Instruction: French

Degrees and Diplomas: *Bachelier (enseignement supérieur de type court); Master*

Student Services: Academic Counselling, Canteen, Careers Guidance, Facilities for disabled people, Social Counselling, Sports Facilities

Last Updated: 05/02/15

HAUTE ECOLE PAUL-HENRI SPAAK

Haute Ecole de la Communauté française Paul-Henri Spaak (HEPHS)

Rue Royale, 150, 1000 Bruxelles
Tel: +32(2) 227-35-01
Fax: +32(2) 227-35-22
EMail: contact@he-spaak.be
Website: http://www.he-spaak.be

Directeur-Président: François Debast EMail: debast@isib.be

Institute

Economics *(Institut supérieur d'Etudes économiques)* (Economics; Law; Secretarial Studies); **Ergotherapy and Physical Therapy** *(Institut d'Enseignement supérieur d'Ergothérapie et de Kinésithérapie)* (Occupational Therapy; Physical Therapy); **Industry** *(Institut Supérieur Industriel de Bruxelles)* (Aeronautical and Aerospace Engineering; Chemistry; Computer Science; Electrical Engineering; Electronic Engineering; Industrial Engineering; Mechanical Engineering; Nuclear Engineering; Physical Engineering); **Pedagogy** *(Institut d'Enseignement supérieur pédagogique)* (Biology; Chemistry; Economics; Geography; History; Literature; Mathematics; Modern Languages; Physical Education; Physics; Social Sciences; Teacher Training); **Social Work, Library and Documentation Sciences** *(Institut d'Enseignement supérieur social des Sciences* *de l'Information et de la Documentation)* (Documentation Techniques; Library Science; Social Work)

History: Founded 1996.

Academic Year: September to July (September-February, February-July)

Admission Requirements: Secondary school certificate (Certificat d'Enseignement secondaire supérieur)

Main Language(s) of Instruction: French

Degrees and Diplomas: *Bachelier (enseignement supérieur de type court); Master.* Also Spécialisation 1 yr

Student Services: Academic Counselling, Careers Guidance, Language Laboratory, Social Counselling

Last Updated: 05/02/15

HAUTE ECOLE ROBERT SCHUMAN (HERS)

Chemin de Weyler 2, B-6700 Arlon
Tel: +32(63) 41-00-00
Fax: +32(63) 41-00-13
EMail: cel.adm@hers.be
Website: http://www.hers.be

Directeur-Président: Marc Fourny EMail: dp@hers.be

Department

Economics *(Libramont)* (Accountancy; Business Computing; Computer Science; Secretarial Studies; Tourism); **Paramedical** (Nursing; Physical Therapy; Speech Therapy and Audiology); **Pedagogy** *(Virton)* (Arts and Humanities; Economics; Ethics; French; Germanic Languages; Mathematics; Natural Sciences; Physical Education; Preschool Education; Primary Education); **Social Work** (Social Work); **Technical** *(Arlon)* (Building Technologies; Chemistry; Construction Engineering; Electronic Engineering; Industrial Engineering; Mechanical Engineering; Wood Technology)

Admission Requirements: Secondary school certificate

Main Language(s) of Instruction: French

Degrees and Diplomas: *Bachelier (enseignement supérieur de type court); Master.* Also Agrégé de l'enseignement secondaire inférieur

Last Updated: 05/02/15

HAUTE ECOLE PROVINCIALE DE HAINAUT CONDORCET (HEPCUT)

17, Chemin du Champ de Mars, 7000 Mons
Tel: +32(65) 40 12 20
Website: http://www.condorcet.be

Directeur-Président: Pascal Lambert

Department

Agronomy *(Ath)* (Agricultural Business; Agricultural Engineering; Agronomy; Forestry; Horticulture; Rural Planning); **Economics** *(Mons,Charleroi, Mouscron, Tournai, Saint-Ghislain)* (Accountancy; Business Computing; E- Business/Commerce; Economics; Hotel Management; Insurance; International Business; Law; Marketing; Real Estate; Retailing and Wholesaling; Secretarial Studies; Tourism); **Fine Arts** *(Saint-Ghislain)* (Graphic Arts); **Paramedical Sciences** *(Charleroi, Tournai, Saint-Ghislain, Mons)* (Dietetics; Ergotherapy; Medical Technology; Midwifery; Nursing; Physical Therapy); **Pedagogy** *(Charleroi, Mons, Morlanwelz)* (Arts and Humanities; French; Germanic Languages; Mathematics; Physical Education; Special Education; Teacher Training); **Social Work** *(Charleroi)* (Communication Studies; Multimedia; Social Work); **Technical Studies** *(Ath, Charleroi, Tournai)* (Aeronautical and Aerospace Engineering; Automation and Control Engineering; Biochemistry; Biotechnology; Chemistry; Electrical Engineering; Industrial Engineering; Mechanical Engineering)

History: Founded 2009 following merger of the Haute École Provinciale Mons-Borinage-Centre (HEPMBC), the Haute École Provinciale du Hainaut Occidental (HEPHO) and the Haute École Provinciale Charleroi-Université du travail (HEPCUT).

Admission Requirements: Secondary school certificate

Main Language(s) of Instruction: French

Degrees and Diplomas: *Bachelier (enseignement supérieur de type court); Master*

Student Services: Academic Counselling, Canteen, Careers Guidance, Facilities for disabled people, Health Services, Language Laboratory, Social Counselling, Sports Facilities

Last Updated: 05/02/15

IEPSCF

Institut d'enseignement de promotion sociale de la Communauté française (IEPSCF) d'Uccle

95 rue Gatti de Gamond, Uccle (Brussels)
Website: http://www.iepscf-uccle.be/

Department

Computer Science (Computer Science; Software Engineering); **Economics** (Accountancy; International Business; Tourism); **Languages** (Arabic; Chinese; Dutch; English; French; German; Italian; Spanish); **Technology** (Construction Engineering; Electronic Engineering; Industrial Engineering; Mechanical Engineering)

Degrees and Diplomas: *Bachelier (enseignement supérieur de type court); Master*

Last Updated: 05/02/15

INSTITUT D'URBANISME ET DE RÉNOVATION URBAINE

Rue d'Irlande 57, 1060 Bruxelles
EMail: isuru@skynet.be
Website: http://www.isuru.be

Area

Regional and Town Planning (Regional Planning; Town Planning)

History: Founded 1947. Master offered as from 2012

Degrees and Diplomas: *Master*

Last Updated: 05/02/15

INSTITUT NATIONAL SUPÉRIEUR DES ARTS DU SPECTACLE ET DES TECHNIQUES DE DIFFUSION (INSAS)

Rue Thérésienne, 8, 1000 Bruxelles
Tel: +32(2) 511-92-86
Fax: +32(2) 511-02-79
EMail: info@insas.be
Website: http://www.insas.be

Directeur: Laurent Gross

Division

Audio-visual Arts (Cinema and Television; Radio and Television Broadcasting; Writing); **Theatre** (Acting; Theatre)

History: Founded 1962.

Main Language(s) of Instruction: French

Degrees and Diplomas: *Bachelier (enseignement supérieur de type court); Master*

Last Updated: 05/02/15

INSTITUT SUPÉRIEUR DE MUSIQUE ET DE PÉDAGOGIE (IMEP)

28 Rue Juppin, 5000 Namur
Tel: +32(81) 73-64-37
Fax: +32(81) 73-95-14
EMail: info@imep.be
Website: http://www.imep.be/

Directeur: Guido Jardon EMail: direction@imep.be

Secrétaire générale: Brigitte Darasse

Programme

Music (Music; Singing); **Musical Instruments** (Musical Instruments); **Musical Pedagogy** (Music Education)

Institute

Fugue and Composition (Music; Music Theory and Composition)

History: Founded 1970, acquired present title and status 1975.

Admission Requirements: Secondary school certificate and entrance examination in solfeggio and instrument playing

Fees: c. 800 per annum (Euro)

Main Language(s) of Instruction: French

Degrees and Diplomas: *Bachelier (enseignement supérieur de type court)*: **Music Education.** *Master*; *Master de spécialisation*

Student Services: Canteen

Publications: Les échos de l'IMEP

Last Updated: 05/02/15

INSTITUTE OF MEDIA ARTS

Institut des Arts de Diffusion (IAD)

Rue des Wallons, 77, B-1348 Louvain-la-Neuve
Tel: +32(10) 47-80-20
Fax: +32(10) 45-11-74
EMail: iad@iad-arts.be
Website: http://www.iad-arts.be

Directeur: Serge Flamé EMail: flame@iad-arts.be

Directeur adjoint: Michel Wouters EMail: wouteks@iad-arts.be

International Relations: Nathalie Degimbe
EMail: degimbe@iad-arts.be

Division

Arts (Cinema and Television; Computer Graphics; Multimedia; Radio and Television Broadcasting; Sound Engineering (Acoustics); Theatre)

History: Founded 1959, acquired present status 1962.

Academic Year: September to June

Admission Requirements: Secondary school certificate and entrance examination

Fees: 1,017-1,192 per annum (Euro)

Main Language(s) of Instruction: French

Degrees and Diplomas: *Bachelier (enseignement supérieur de type court)*; *Master*

Student Services: Academic Counselling, Careers Guidance, Social Counselling

Last Updated: 05/02/15

SAINT-LAURENT INSTITUTE

Institut Saint-Laurent - enseignement de promotion sociale

Rue Saint-Laurent, 33, 4000 Liège
Website: http://www.isl.be

Directeur: Claude Tilkin

Last Updated: 06/02/15

UNIVERSITÉ LIBRE DE BRUXELLES (ULB)

50 avenue Roosevelt, 1050 Bruxelles
Tel: +32(2) 650-21-11
Fax: +32(2) 650-35-95
EMail: epi@ulb.ac.be
Website: http://www.ulbruxelles.be/

Recteur: Didier Viviers (2010-) EMail: recteur@admin.ulb.ac.be

Responsible des R.P: Isabelle Pollet
EMail: isabelle.pollet@ulb.ac.be

International Relations: Pierre Quertenmont, Responsable des Relations internationales EMail: dri@dri.ulb.ac.be

Faculty

Applied Sciences (Biomedical Engineering; Chemical Engineering; Civil Engineering; Computer Engineering; Construction Engineering; Electrical Engineering; Electronic Engineering; Mechanical Engineering; Structural Architecture); **Architecture** *(La Cambre-Horta)* (Architecture; Art History; Construction Engineering; Fine Arts); **Law and Criminology** (Civil Law; Commercial Law; Criminology; Law; Notary Studies; Private Law; Public Law); **Medicine** (Biomedicine; Dentistry; Health Sciences; Medicine); **Pharmacy** (Pharmacy); **Philosophy and Letters** (Archaeology; Arts and Humanities; Communication Studies; History; Linguistics; Literature; Modern Languages; Philosophy); **Psychology and Education** (Educational Sciences; Psychology; Speech Studies); **Public Health** (Public Health); **Science** (Actuarial Science; Agronomy; Biochemistry; Bioengineering; Biology; Cell Biology; Chemistry; Computer Science; Ecology; Environmental Management; Geography; Geology; Mathematics; Molecular Biology; Physics; Tourism); **Social and Political Sciences** (Anthropology; Business Administration; Economics; Political Sciences; Social Sciences; Sociology)

School

Economics and Management *(Solvay)* (Economics; Management)

Institute

Motor Sciences (Osteopathy; Physical Education; Physical Therapy; Rehabilitation and Therapy; Sports Medicine)

Further Information: Campuses at: Solbosch, Plaine, Erasme, Nivelles (province of Brabant), Treignes, Charleroi; also an academic hospital "Erasme".

History: The Université libre de Bruxelles has 13 faculties, schools and specialized institutes that cover all the disciplines, closely combining academic input and research. It offers almost 40 undergraduate programmes and 235 graduate programmes. It also partners 20 Doctoral schools, with almost 1,600 PhD in progress.

Academic Year: September to July

Admission Requirements: Secondary school certificate or recognized foreign equivalent, or entrance examination. Entrance examination obligatory for the Faculty of Applied Sciences

Fees: 835 (for EU students). More details on http://www.ulb.ac.be/enseignements/inscriptions-english/index.html (Euro)

Main Language(s) of Instruction: French

Degrees and Diplomas: *Bachelier (enseignement supérieur de type court)*; *Master*, *Doctorat*: **Actuarial Science; Archaeology; Architecture; Astrophysics; Biology; Computer Science; Criminal Law; Economics; Fine Arts; History; Mathematics; Mechanical Engineering; Medicine; Modern Languages; Multimedia; Pharmacology; Philosophy; Physics; Physiology; Public Health; Social Sciences; Statistics; Theology; Town Planning.**

Student Services: Canteen, Careers Guidance, Health Services, Language Laboratory, Nursery Care, Social Counselling, Sports Facilities

Publications: Esprit Libre

Publishing House: Les Editions de l'Université de Bruxelles

Student Numbers *2013-2014*: Total 24,000

Last Updated: 06/02/15

UNIVERSITY OF LIÈGE

Université de Liège (ULG)

Place du 20 Août, 9, 4000 Liège
Tel: +32(4) 366-21-11
Fax: +32(4) 366-57-00
EMail: info.etudes@ulg.ac.be
Website: http://www.ulg.ac.be

Recteur: Albert Corhay (2014-) EMail: Recteur@ulg.ac.be

International Relations: Annick Comblain
EMail: A.Comblain@ulg.ac.be

Faculty

Agro-Bio Tech *(Gembloux)* (Agronomy; Bioengineering; Landscape Architecture); **Applied Sciences** (Architecture; Chemical Engineering; Computer Engineering; Construction Engineering; Geological Engineering; Mechanical Engineering; Mining Engineering; Physical Engineering); **Architecture** (Architecture); **Law, Political Science and Criminology** (Criminology; Law; Political Sciences); **Medicine** (Biomedicine; Dentistry; Medicine; Pharmacy; Physical Education; Physical Therapy; Public Health); **Philosophy and Letters** (Art History; Classical Languages; Germanic Languages; History; Information Sciences; Modern Languages; Oriental Languages; Philosophy; Romance Languages); **Psychology and Education** (Educational Sciences; Psychology; Speech Therapy and Audiology); **Science** (Biochemistry; Biological and Life Sciences; Chemistry; Environmental Management; Geography; Geology; Mathematics; Physics); **Veterinary Science** (Veterinary Science)

School

Management (Economics; Engineering Management; Management; Social Sciences)

Institute

Human and Social Science (Anthropology; Arts and Humanities; Demography and Population; Labour and Industrial Relations; Social Sciences; Sociology)

Further Information: Also French language courses for foreign students. Inter-University study programmes. Teaching hospital. Teaching veterinary hospital

History: Founded 1817 under King William I of the Netherlands. Following the independence of Belgium designated in 1835 as a State University. In 1959 provision was made for the transfer of the University to a new campus. The University enjoys limited autonomy and receives the major share of its income from the Communauté française de Belgique.

Academic Year: September to July (September-January; January-July)

Admission Requirements: Secondary school certificate or recognized foreign equivalent and entrance examination in French for non-native speakers. Entrance examination for engineers

Fees: 835 per annum (Euro)

Main Language(s) of Instruction: French

Degrees and Diplomas: *Bachelier (enseignement supérieur de type court)*; *Master*, *Doctorat*: **Aeronautical and Aerospace Engineering; Applied Chemistry; Archaeology; Architecture; Art History; Civil Engineering; Communication Studies; Computer Science; Electrical and Electronic Engineering; History; Information Sciences; Literature; Management; Mechanical Engineering; Modern Languages; Philosophy; Town Planning; Translation and Interpretation; Veterinary Science.**

Student Services: Academic Counselling, Canteen, Careers Guidance, Cultural Activities, Facilities for disabled people, Health Services, Nursery Care, Social Counselling, Sports Facilities

Last Updated: 05/02/15

UNIVERSITY OF MONS

Université de Mons

Place du Parc 20, 7000 Mons
Tel: +32(65) 37-30-14
EMail: info.mons@umons.ac.be
Website: http://www.umons.ac.be

Recteur: Calogero Conti (2009-)
EMail: recteur@umons.ac.be

Faculty

Architecture and Urban Planning *(Formerly Institut supérieur d'Architecture Intercommunal - Site de Mons)* (Architecture; Town Planning); **Engineering** (Architecture; Chemical Engineering; Civil Engineering; Electrical Engineering; Engineering; Mechanical Engineering; Mining Engineering); **Medicine and Pharmacy** (Medicine; Pharmacy); **Psychology and Education** (Education; Educational Sciences; Psychology); **Science** (Biology; Chemistry; Computer Science; Mathematics; Physics); **Translation and Interpretation** *(School of International Interpreters)* (American Studies; Danish; Dutch; English; German; Italian; Linguistics; Russian; Spanish; Translation and Interpretation)

School

Business and Economics *(Warocqué)* (Business Administration; Economics; Management)

Institute

Humanities and Social Sciences (Communication Studies; Educational Sciences; Management; Political Sciences; Psychology; Social Sciences); **Language Sciences** (Communication Studies; Linguistics); **Legal Studies** (Criminology; Law)

History: Created 2009 from the merger of Faculté polytechnique de Mons (Faculty of Engineering, Mons, created 1837) and Université de Mons-Hainaut (University of Mons-Hainaut, created 1899).

Academic Year: September to September (September-December; January-May; June-September

Admission Requirements: Secondary school certificate or recognized equivalent and entrance examination

Fees: c.835 per annum (Euro)

Main Language(s) of Instruction: French

Degrees and Diplomas: *Bachelier (enseignement supérieur de type court)*; *Master*, *Doctorat*: **Biology; Biomedicine; Chemistry; Computer Science; Educational Sciences; Engineering; Mathematics; Medicine; Pharmacy; Political Sciences; Psychology; Town Planning.**

Student Services: Academic Counselling, Canteen, Careers Guidance, Cultural Activities, Facilities for disabled people, Health Services, Social Counselling

Last Updated: 05/02/15

UNIVERSITY OF NAMUR

Université de Namur

Rue de Bruxelles, 61, 5000 Namur
Tel: +32(81) 72-41-11
Fax: +32(81) 23-03-91
EMail: vice.recteur@unamur.be
Website: http://www.unamur.be

Recteur: Yves Poullet EMail: yves.poullet@fundp.ac.be
Vice-recteur: Robert Sporken

Faculty

Computer Science (Computer Science); **Economics, Social Sciences and Management** (Communication Studies; Economics; Management; Political Sciences; Social Sciences); **Law** (Law); **Medicine** (Biomedicine; Medicine; Pharmacy); **Philosophy and Letters** (Archaeology; Art History; Arts and Humanities; Classical Languages; Germanic Studies; History; Literature; Philology; Philosophy; Romance Languages); **Science** (Biology; Chemistry; Geography; Geology; Mathematics; Natural Sciences; Physics; Veterinary Science)

Further Information: Campus in Charleroi

History: Founded 1831 as college by the Society of Jesus and reconstituted under present title 1833. Independent but recognized and financially supported by the State. First authorized to award degrees 1929, granted full University status 1971. Previously known as Facultés universitaires Notre-Dame de la Paix. Acquired current title 2012.

Academic Year: September to August (September-January; January-August)

Admission Requirements: Secondary school certificate or recognized foreign equivalent

Fees: 835 euros per annum (Euro)

Main Language(s) of Instruction: French

Degrees and Diplomas: *Bachelier (enseignement supérieur de type court)*: **Archaeology; Biology; Biomedicine; Chemistry; Communication Studies; Computer Science; Economics; Geography; Geology; History; Law; Management; Mathematics; Medicine; Modern Languages; Pharmacy; Philosophy; Physics; Veterinary Science.** *Master*: **Computer Science; Economics; Management.** *Doctorat*: **Archaeology; Biomedicine; Communication Studies; Economics; History; Law; Management; Medicine; Modern Languages; Pharmacy; Philosophy; Veterinary Science.**

Student Services: Academic Counselling, Canteen, Careers Guidance, Cultural Activities, Health Services, Nursery Care, Social Counselling, Sports Facilities

Publications: Annales de la Société scientifique de Bruxelles; Cahier de Recherche de la Faculté de Sciences économiques et sociales; Cahiers de Formation continue de la Faculté des Sciences économiques et sociales; Documents et Points de Vue de la Faculté des Sciences économiques et sociales; Journal de Réflexion sur l'Informatique; Les Etudes classiques; Revue des Questions scientifiques; Revue régionale de Droit

Publishing House: Presses Universitaires de Namur

Last Updated: 05/02/15

UNIVERSITY SAINT-LOUIS, BRUSSELS

Université Saint-Louis - Bruxelles (USL-B)

Boulevard du Jardin Botanique, 43, 1000 Bruxelles
Tel: +32(2) 211-78-11
Fax: +32(2) 211-79-97
EMail: info@usaintlouis.be
Website: http://www.usaintlouis.be/

Recteur: Pierre Jadoul (2013-) EMail: pierre.jadoul@usaintlouis.be

International Relations: Bertrand Hamaide, Conseiller du Recteur pour les relations internationales
Tel: +32(2) 792-35-16 EMail: hamaide@fusl.ac.be

Faculty

Economics, Political Science, Social Sciences (Anthropology; Communication Studies; Economics; Management; Political Sciences; Sociology); **Law** (Law); **Philosophy, Letters and Humanities** (Germanic Studies; History; Literature; Modern Languages; Philosophy; Romance Languages)

School

Philosophical and Religious Studies (Philosophy; Religious Studies)

Institute

European Studies (European Studies)

Research Centre

Economics (Economics); **Environmental Law** (Law); **History of Law and Institutions** (History of Law); **Juridical Studies** (Law); **Linguistics** (Linguistics); **Literature** (Literature); **Political Philosophy** (Philosophy); **Political Science** (Political Sciences); **Regional Studies** (Regional Studies); **Religious History** (Religion); **Sociology** (Sociology)

Further Information: Also Research Networks on Interdisciplinary Approach of Society and on Urban and Regional Issues

History: Founded 1858 as Section de Philosophie. First authorized to award degrees 1890; reorganized 1969 with separate Dutch and French sections which became legally distinct institutions in 1974. A private, state supported institution with full university status. Previously known as Facultés universitaires Saint-Louis, Bruxelles. Acquired current title 2012.

Academic Year: September to September

Admission Requirements: Secondary school certificate or foreign recognized equivalent

Main Language(s) of Instruction: French

Degrees and Diplomas: *Bachelier (enseignement supérieur de type court)*: **Economics; German; History; Information Technology; Law; Literature; Management; Philosophy; Sociology.** *Master*, *Doctorat*: **Archaeology; Art History; Communication Studies; History; Law; Literature; Management; Modern Languages; Philosophy; Political Sciences; Social Sciences; Translation and Interpretation.**

Student Services: Academic Counselling, Canteen, Cultural Activities, Social Counselling, Sports Facilities

Publications: Cahiers du CRHIDI; Revue Anthropologique; Revue interdisciplinaire d'Etudes juridiques

Publishing House: Publications des Facultés universitaires Saint-Louis

Student Numbers *2012-2013*: Total 2,800

Last Updated: 06/02/15

Belize

STRUCTURE OF HIGHER EDUCATION SYSTEM

Description:

The Ministry of Education is responsible for all levels of education. Higher education includes post-secondary institutions, such as sixth-form establishments-junior colleges, professional training institutions and the University of Belize. Degree courses are mostly offered by the University of Belize, founded in 2000 by the merger of the University College of Belize (originally created in 1986), Belize School of Nursing, and Belize Teachers College. The University is directly financed by the Ministry of Education and offers its own Bachelor's degree courses under the authority of the Government of Belize. Through an extra-mural Department, Belize is also affiliated to the University of the West Indies, which is a regional institution with campuses in Jamaica, Barbados and Trinidad.

Stages of studies:

University level first stage: *Associate degree; Bachelor's degree*
Associate degrees are awarded after two years of study and Bachelor's degrees after two years following upon the Associate degree.

University level second stage: *Master degree*
A Master degree is offered in partnership with the University of West Indies.

ADMISSION TO HIGHER EDUCATION

Admission to university-level studies:

Name of secondary school credential required: Caribbean Advanced Proficiency Examination
Name of secondary school credential required: General Certificate of Education Advanced Level

Foreign students admission:

Admission requirements: Foreign students should have a general certificate of education or equivalent.
Language proficiency: A good knowledge of English is requested.

RECOGNITION OF STUDIES

Quality assurance system:

The Ministry of Education is in charge of ensuring relevant quality education through the development and monitoring of the implementation of national standards.

Bodies dealing with recognition:

Ministry of Education, Youth, Sports and Culture
West Block Building - 3rd Floor
Belmopan
Tel: +011 501 822-3163
Fax: +011 501 822-0102
EMail: moeducation@moes.gov.bz
WWW: http://moe.gov.bz/

NATIONAL BODIES

Ministry of Education, Youth, Sports and Culture
Minister: Patrick Jason Faber
Deputy Director, Tertiary and Post-Secondary Services: Deryck Satchwell
West Block Building - 3rd Floor
Belmopan, Cayo District

Tel: +011 501 822-3163
Fax: +011 501 822-0102
EMail: moeducation@moes.gov.bz
WWW: http://moe.gov.bz/

Data for academic year: 2016-2017
Source: IAU from the website of the Ministry of Education, Belize, 2016

INSTITUTIONS

PUBLIC INSTITUTION

UNIVERSITY OF BELIZE (UB)

PO Box 340, University Drive, Belmopan
Cayo District
Tel: +501(822) 3680
Fax: +501(822) 1107
Website: http://www.ub.edu.bz

President: Alan Slusher

Faculty

Education and Arts (Anthropology; Education; English; History); **Management and Social Sciences** (Accountancy; Business Administration; Business and Commerce; Hotel and Restaurant; Law; Marketing; Public Administration; Tourism); **Nursing, Allied Health and Social Work** (Health Sciences; Laboratory Techniques; Pharmacy; Social Work); **Science and Technology** (Agriculture; Architecture; Biology; Chemistry; Engineering; Information Technology; Marine Science and Oceanography; Mathematics; Natural Resources; Physics)

Department

Adult and Continuing Education

Further Information: Also Belize City Campus; Central Farm in the Cayo District; Punta Gorda in the the Toledo District; and two marine sites at Hunting Caye and Calabash Caye.

History: Founded August 2000 by the merger of the University College of Belize, Belize School of Nursing, Belize Teacher Training College.

Main Language(s) of Instruction: Spanish

Degrees and Diplomas: *Associate Degree*; *Bachelor's Degree*

Last Updated: 07/04/16

PRIVATE INSTITUTION

GALEN UNIVERSITY

62.5 Western Highway, Cayo District, Cayo
Tel: +501 (824) 3226
Fax: +501 (824) 3723
EMail: admissions@galen.edu.bz
Website: http://www.galen.edu.bz

President: Nancy Adamson (2010-) Tel: +501(824) 3226, Ext.106 EMail: nadamson@galen.edu.bz; vicepresident@galen.edu.bz

International Relations: Marion Cayetano, Vice-President, Planning EMail: planning@galen.edu.bz

Faculty

Arts and Sciences (Anthropology; Archaeology; Criminal Law); **Business and Entrepreneurship** (Accountancy; Banking; Economics; Finance; International Business; Management; Marketing); **Education** (Primary Education); **Science and Technology** (Computer Science; Environmental Studies)

History: Founded in 2003.

Academic Year: September to December; January to April; May to August. Students may enrol in any semester

Admission Requirements: (Undergraduate): Original essay; $60.00 Application Fee (non-refundable); One (1) official High School transcript; One (1) copy of transcript One (1) copy of diploma; One (1) copy of any of the following test scores: ATLIB, CXC, ACT, SAT

Fees: (Belize dollars): local students, undergraduate, Full-time, 1 semester (15 credits) $6,750

Main Language(s) of Instruction: English

Degrees and Diplomas: *Bachelor's Degree*

Student Services: Academic Counselling, Canteen, Careers Guidance, Facilities for disabled people, Health Services, Social Counselling

Last Updated: 07/04/16

Benin

STRUCTURE OF HIGHER EDUCATION SYSTEM

Description:

The higher education sector falls under the responsibility of the Ministry of Higher Education and Scientific Research. It is provided by State and private institutions. The three-tier system based on the Bologna system and called LMD (for Licence - Master - Doctorat) was introduced in 2011/2012.

ADMISSION TO HIGHER EDUCATION

Admission to university-level studies:

Name of secondary school credential required: Baccalauréat

Admission requirements: Competitive examination in some cases.

Other requirements: In professional schools, portfolio.

Foreign students admission:

Admission requirements: Students should hold a Secondary School Leaving Certificate (Baccalauréat) or its equivalent. For vocational education, the students' files are studied. They may have to sit for an examination.

Language proficiency: Good knowledge of French is indispensable.

NATIONAL BODIES

Ministère de l'Enseignement supérieur et de la Recherche Scientifique (Ministry of Higher Education and Scientific Research)

Minister: François Adebayo Abiola
PO Box 348
Cotonou
Tel: +229(21) 300681
Fax: +229(21) 305795
EMail: sgm@recherche.gouv.bj
WWW: http://www.recherche.gouv.bj

Data for academic year: 2012-2013

Source: IAU from IBE, National Education website, and docuemntation, 2012. Bodies 2016.

INSTITUTIONS

PUBLIC INSTITUTIONS

ABOMEY-CALAVI UNIVERSITY

Université d'Abomey-Calavi (UAC)
01 BP 526, Calavi, Cotonou, Littoral
Tel: +229 36-00-74
Fax: +229 36-00-28
EMail: vrcireip.uac@uac.bj
Website: http://www.uac.bj

Recteur: Brice Sinsin Tel: +229 36-00-28

Vice-Président des Affaires académiques: Maxime Da Cruz

Faculty

Agronomy *(Abomey-Calavi Campus)* (Agronomy; Animal Husbandry; Environmental Management; Food Technology; Nutrition; Rural Studies; Vegetable Production); **Arts and Humanities** (Anthropology; Archaeology; Arts and Humanities; Communication Studies; English; Geography; History; Literature; Modern Languages; Philosophy; Regional Planning; Sociology); **Economics and Management** (Economics; Management); **Health Sciences** (Medicine; Pharmacy; Social Work); **Law and Political Science** *(Abomey-Calavi Campus)* (Law; Political Sciences); **Science and Technology** (Biochemistry; Biology; Chemistry; Ecology; Geology; Mathematics; Natural Sciences; Physics; Technology)

School

Applied Economics and Management *(National)* (Economics; Management); **Polytechnic** *(Abomey-Calavi Campus)* (Animal Husbandry; Biology; Computer Science; Electronic Engineering; Energy Engineering; Environmental Engineering; Mechanical Engineering; Radiology; Telecommunications Engineering); **Teacher Training** *(ENS, Campus of Porto Novo)* (Teacher Training);

Technical Teacher Training *(ENS, Lokossa Campus)* (Teacher Training)

Institute

Arabic Language and Islamic Culture *(Abomey-Calavi Campus)* (Arabic; Islamic Studies); **Mathematics and Physics** *(Dangbo Campus)* (Mathematics; Physics); **Sports and Physical Education** *(Campus of Porto-Novo)* (Physical Education; Sports); **Technology** *(Campus of Lokossa)* (Civil Engineering; Computer Science; Electronic Engineering; Mechanics)

History: Founded 1970 as Université du Dahomey and incorporating departments of former Institut d'Enseignement supérieur du Bénin, established 1962. Acquired present status 1976 and present title 2000. A State Institution responsible to the Ministry of Higher Education and Scientific Research.

Academic Year: October to July (October-January; January-March; April-July)

Admission Requirements: Secondary school certificate (baccalauréat) or equivalent

Fees: (CFA Francs): 6,200

Main Language(s) of Instruction: French

Accrediting Agency: African and Malagasy Council for Higher Education (CAMES)

Degrees and Diplomas: *Licence*: **Arts and Humanities; Economics; Law; Natural Sciences; Technology.** *Doctorat en Médecine*: **Health Sciences.** *Master*: **Arts and Humanities; Economics; Law; Natural Sciences; Technology.** *Doctorat*

Student Services: Academic Counselling, Canteen, Health Services, Sports Facilities

Publications: Annales de la Faculté des Lettres, Arts et Sciences Humaines; Annales de la Faculté des Sciences Agronomiques; Bénin Médical; Cahiers d'Etudes linguistiques; Revue générale des Sciences juridiques, économiques et politiques

Publishing House: Services des Publications Universitaires

Last Updated: 05/07/12

PARAKOU UNIVERSITY

Université de Parakou (UP)
BP 123, Parakou, Borgou
Tel: +229 23-61-07-12
Fax: +229 23-61-07-12
EMail: univ_parakou@borgou.net
Website: http://www.up.bj/

Rector: Simon Akpona (2006-)
Tel: +229 23-61-15-41 EMail: akponasimon@yahoo.fr

Secretary-General: Marc-Abel Ayedoun
Tel: +229 231-12-06 EMail: mayedoun@hotmail.com

International Relations: Nestor Sokpon
Tel: +229 97-16-49-91 EMail: nsokpon@yahoo.fr

Faculty

Agronomy *(Parakou Campus)* (Agronomy); **Law and Political Science** (Law; Political Sciences; Private Law; Public Law); **Law, Economics and Management** (Economics; Law; Management); **Medicine** (Medicine)

School

Teacher Training *(Natitingou Campus)* (Teacher Training)

Institute

Technology *(IUT)* (Banking; Business Administration; Business Computing; Management; Technology)

History: Founded 2001 by Ministerial decree. Created from the breaking down of the National University of Benin into two national Universities: Abomey Calavi University and Parakou University in line with the Government's desire to accommodate the influx of upper six formers (holders of Baccalaureate) wishing to gain admission into higher institutions under adequate conditions.

Admission Requirements: Baccalaureat

Fees: (CFA Francs): 15,000 (Classical Faculties); 260,000 to 418,000 (for Schools)

Main Language(s) of Instruction: French

Degrees and Diplomas: *Licence*; *Master*

Student Services: Academic Counselling, Canteen, Health Services, Language Laboratory, Nursery Care, Social Counselling, Sports Facilities

Last Updated: 05/07/12

PRIVATE INSTITUTIONS

ADONAÏ INSTITUTE OF MANAGEMENT STUDIES

Institut supérieur de Management Adonaï
Saint Jean, derrière la Gazette du Golfe, Cotonou
Tel: +229(21) 32 85 97
EMail: ismadonai@yahoo.fr
Website: http://www.ismadonai.net

Programme

Accountancy (Accountancy); **Audit and Management** (Management); **Banking, Finance and Insurance** (Banking; Finance; Insurance); **Business Administration** (Business Administration); **Human Resource Management** (Human Resources; Management); **Marketing and Communication** (Communication Studies; Marketing); **Project Management** (Management)

Further Information: Campuses in Calavi, Parakou and Lomé

Accrediting Agency: CAMES

Degrees and Diplomas: *Licence*; *Master*

Last Updated: 05/07/12

ADVANCED SCHOOL OF ECONOMICS AND MANAGEMENT

Ecole supérieure d'Economie et de Gestion (ESEG)
02 BP 1092, Boulevard du Renouveau démocratique, Agontinkon, Immeuble Ecobank Etoile 3ème Etage, Cotonou, Atlantique-littoral
Tel: +229 21-30-68-55
Fax: +229 95-96-43-91
EMail: eseg_africa@yahoo.com

Directeur: Ambroise Akpatcha

Programme

Banking Administration (Administration; Banking); **Banking and Finance** (Banking; Finance); **Business Administration** (Business Administration); **Economic Policy** (Economic and Finance Policy); **International Business** (International Business); **Management of Decentralised Economies** (Economics; Management); **Management of Microfinance Institutions** (Business Administration; Finance)

History: Founded 2001.

Degrees and Diplomas: *Licence*; *Master*. Also Diploma in Business Administration; Certificate in Economic and Professional English; Certificate in Advanced academic English

Last Updated: 21/03/12

AFRICAN UNIVERSITY OF TECHNOLOGY AND MANAGEMENT

Université Africaine de Technologie et de Management (UATM/GASA-FORMATION)
04 BP 1361, Qtier Gbegamey, Cadjehoun, Cotonou, Atlantique
Tel: +229 21-30-86-87
Fax: +229 21-30-89-85
EMail: info@uatm-gasaformation.com
Website: http://www.uatm-gasaformation.com

Président: Théophane Ayi

Programme

Administration and Business Management (Accountancy; Banking; Communication Studies; Finance; Human Resources; Insurance; International Business; International Relations; Management; Marketing); **Agronomy** (Agronomy); **Biotechnology** (Biotechnology; Food Technology; Industrial Engineering);

Economic Science (Economics); **Electrical Engineering** (Computer Networks; Electrical Engineering; Software Engineering; Telecommunications Engineering); **Juridical and Political Sciences** (Law; Political Sciences); **Science and Technology** (Computer Networks; Computer Science; Industrial Engineering; Telecommunications Engineering)

Further Information: Also campuses in Agla, Akpakpa, Pahou and Porto-Novo.

Fees: (CFA Francs): BTS, 210,000-325,000 per annum; Licence, 170,000 per annum; Professional Licence, 365-000-430,000 per annum

Degrees and Diplomas: *Licence*; *Master*; *Doctorat*
Last Updated: 25/06/12

BENIN UNIVERSITY OF SCIENCE AND TECHNOLOGY

Université des Sciences et Technologies du Bénin (USTB)

03 BP 2332, Lot 413 bis Domaine Universitaire de Kpondéhou, Cotonou, Atlantique
Tel: +229(21) 33-60-11
Fax: +229(21) 33-60-13
EMail: info@ustbenin.org
Website: http://ustbweb.org

Président: Claudide Dohou Tel: +229(21) 33-88-93

Secrétaire Général: Dieudonné Agbannekpo
Tel: +229(21) 33-26-11 EMail: agbovincent@yahoo.fr

International Relations: Nina Attignon, Directrice de l'Administration et des Relations Internationales
Tel: +229(21) 33-60-10 EMail: ninattignon@yahoo.fr

Faculty

Agronomy *(FASA)* (Agronomy); **Economics** *(FASE)* (Economics); **Fundamental and Applied Sciences** *(FAFSA)* (Biological and Life Sciences; Biotechnology; Chemistry; Earth Sciences; Mathematics; Physics; Technology); **Humanities, Arts and Social Sciences** *(FLASS)* (Arts and Humanities; Chinese; English; Geography (Human); German; History; Philosophy; Social Sciences; Sociology; Spanish); **Law** *(FAD)* (Administration; International Relations; Law; Political Sciences); **Management** *(FASG)* (Management)

Higher School

Applied Informatics *(ESIA)* (Business Computing; Computer Engineering; Computer Science); **Civil Engineering, Mining and Geology** *(ESTPMG)* (Civil Engineering; Construction Engineering; Mechanical Engineering; Production Engineering; Surveying and Mapping); **Communication Studies** *(ESCOM)* (Communication Studies; Multimedia); **Industrial Technology** *(ESTI)* (Automation and Control Engineering; Chemistry; Computer Engineering; Computer Networks; Electrical Engineering; Electronic Engineering; Energy Engineering; Industrial Engineering; Maintenance Technology; Thermal Engineering); **Management and Business Administration** *(ESMAE)* (Accountancy; Administration; Banking; Business Administration; Business and Commerce; Finance; Human Resources; International Business; Management; Marketing; Safety Engineering; Secretarial Studies)

History: Founded 1996. Acquired present status 2002.

Academic Year: October to June

Admission Requirements: Secondary school certificate (baccalauréat) or foreign equivalent

Main Language(s) of Instruction: French, English, German, Spanish, Chinese

Accrediting Agency: African and Malagasy Council for Higher Education (CAMES)

Degrees and Diplomas: *Licence*; *Master*; *Doctorat*

Student Services: Academic Counselling, Canteen, Careers Guidance, Facilities for disabled people, Foreign Studies Centre, Health Services, Nursery Care, Social Counselling, Sports Facilities

Publications: Le Manager; Message

Publishing House: USTB-Info

Last Updated: 05/07/12

CATHOLIC UNIVERSITY OF WESTERN AFRICA

Université Catholique de l'Afrique de l'Ouest

Unité Universitaire de Cotonou, 04 BP 928, Cotonou
Tel: +(229) 21-30-51-18
Fax: +(229) 2130- 51-17
EMail: ucao@ucaobenin.com
Website: http://www.ucaobenin.com

Président: Père Pierre Able Dago

Faculty

Agronomy and Environment (Agricultural Business; Agricultural Management; Agronomy; Animal Husbandry; Environmental Management; Environmental Studies)

School

Electrical and Computer Engineering (Automation and Control Engineering; Computer Networks; Electrical Engineering; Telecommunications Engineering); **Management and Applied Economics** (Accountancy; Banking; Business Computing; Finance; Human Resources; Management; Marketing)

History: Founded 2001.

Fees: (CFA Francs): 350,000 per annum

Degrees and Diplomas: *Licence*; *Master*
Last Updated: 25/06/12

COLLEGE OF SURVEYING AND MAPPING

Ecole supérieure des Ingénieurs Géomètres Topographes (ESIGT)

03 BP 1941, Jéricho, Cotonou
Tel: +229 21-32-08-64 +229 954-212-70
Fax: +229 21-32-08-64

Directeur: Constantin Bah EMail: bah_constantin@yahoo.fr

Administrative Officer: Armand Folly

International Relations: Constantin Bah, Managing Director

Programme

Surveying and Mapping (Surveying and Mapping)

History: Founded 2001.

Admission Requirements: Engineers: BTS, Licence, Master in Science

Fees: (CFA Francs): 600,000 per annum (Social fee), 2m. (Tuition)

Main Language(s) of Instruction: French

Accrediting Agency: Ministry of Higher Education and Scientific Research (MESRS)

Degrees and Diplomas: *Master*

Student Services: Academic Counselling, Careers Guidance, Health Services, Language Laboratory, Nursery Care, Sports Facilities

Publications: L'arpenteur

HIGHER INSTITUTE OF VOCATIONAL EDUCATION

Institut supérieur de Formation professionnelle (ISFOP)

01 BP, Cotonou, Littoral 1206
Tel: +229 21-30-36-18
EMail: contact@isfop-benin.com
Website: http://isfop-benin.com

Directeur: Marius Dakpogan EMail: mariusdakpogan@yahoo.fr

Programme

Accountancy and Management (Accountancy; Management); **Agricultural Production** (Agriculture); **Bank Management** (Banking); **Banking and Corporate Finance** (Banking; Finance); **Business Administration** (Business Administration); **Business Computing** (Business Computing); **Marketing and Commercial Action** (Marketing; Sales Techniques); **Regional Planning** (Regional Planning)

History: Founded 1993.

Degrees and Diplomas: *Licence*; *Master*
Last Updated: 07/12/12

HOUDEGBE NORTH AMERICAN UNIVERSITY BENIN (HNAUB)

06 BP 2080, Cotonou 229
Tel: +229 21-33-21-27 +229 90-90-27-77
Fax: +229 21-33-35-88
EMail: info@houdegbeuniversity.com

Chancellor and President: Octave Cossi Houdegbe (2001-)
Tel: +229 95-15-10-49 EMail: hnaub-cotonou@hotmail.com

Administrator: Apollinaire Hacheme
Tel: +229 95-01-05-03 EMail: hachemepo@yahoo.fr

International Relations: Victorin Degbo, Special Assistant of Chancellor Tel: +229 97-68-46-34 EMail: degbovic@yahoo.fr

School

Business Administration and Economics *(Léon Sullivan School)* (Accountancy; Banking; Business Administration; Economics; Finance; Management; Marketing; Sociology); **International Affairs, Political Science and Public Administration** *(Dr. Kwame Nkrumah School)* (Education; International Relations; Law; Political Sciences; Public Administration); **Law** *(Kessington Adebukunola Adebutu)* (Commercial Law; International Law; Law; Maritime Law; Private Law; Public Law); **Medicine and Pharmacy** *(Dr. Maryam Babanguida School)* (Anatomy; Biochemistry; Community Health; Medicine; Nursing; Pharmacy; Physiology); **Science and Information Technology** (Computer Engineering; Computer Science; Information Sciences; Information Technology; Technology)

Institute

Languages and Translation *(Andre Kollingba)* (English; French; German; Modern Languages; Secretarial Studies; Spanish; Translation and Interpretation)

History: Founded 1992 as College Preparatoire International HOUDEGBE. Acquired present status 2001.

Admission Requirements: GCE ('O') Level, West African School Certificate or Baccalaureate (BAC)

Fees: (CFA Francs): 1m-1.5m per annum, including room and board (where applicable)

Main Language(s) of Instruction: English, French

Accrediting Agency: Ministry of Higher Education and Scientific Research (MESRS); National Universities Commission (NUC)

Degrees and Diplomas: *Licence*: **Business Administration; International Relations; Law; Modern Languages; Translation and Interpretation.** *Master*: **Economics; International Relations; Law; Translation and Interpretation.**

Student Services: Academic Counselling, Canteen, Cultural Activities, Health Services, Social Counselling, Sports Facilities

Last Updated: 25/06/12

INTERNATIONAL POLYTECHNIC UNIVERSITY OF BENIN

Université Polytechnique Internationale du Bénin (UPIB)

Étoile Rouge, 02 BP 8133, Cotonou, Atlantique-Littoral
Tel: +229 21-32-83-95
Website: http://www.cepib-formation.com

Président: Valère K. Glele

School

Law *(International)* (Criminal Law; Law; Private Law; Public Law); **Management** *(University)* (Banking; Finance; Human Resources; Insurance; Management; Marketing; Transport Management)

Institute

Audit *(African)* (Accountancy; Actuarial Science; Finance); **Business Administration** *(International)* (Banking; Business Administration; Finance; Human Resources; Insurance; Marketing; Sales Techniques)

Centre

Computer Science (Business Computing; Computer Networks; Computer Science; Electronic Engineering; Telecommunications Engineering)

Further Information: Also campuses at Porto Novo and Parakou

History: Founded 1992.

Fees: (CFA Francs): 560,000 to 1430, 000 per annum

Degrees and Diplomas: *Licence*; *Master*

Last Updated: 05/07/12

LE CITOYEN POLYTECHNIC INSTITUTE

Institut Polytechnique Le Citoyen (IPC)

01 BP 3524, C 156 lot O, rue du Commissariat de Cadjehoun, Domaine le Citoyen, Cotonou, Littoral
Tel: +229 21-30-51-06 +229 90-90-39-70
Fax: +229 21-30-23-73

Head: Abraham Voglozin

Programme

Accountancy/Management (Accountancy; Management); **Corporate Banking and Finance** (Banking; Finance); **Development Communication** (Communication Studies); **Education/Pedagogy** (Education; Pedagogy); **Financial Resources Management** (Finance; Management); **Human Resources Management** (Human Resources; Management); **Secretarial Studies** (Secretarial Studies)

History: Founded 1998.

Degrees and Diplomas: *Licence*; *Master*

PANAFRICAN SCHOOL OF APPLIED MANAGEMENT

Ecole supérieure panafricaine de Management appliqué (ESPAM-FORMATION)

06 BP1378, Cite Vie Nouvelle d' Akpakpa, Cotonou
Tel: +229 21 33 42 96 +229 21 33 47 27
EMail: info@espam-formationuc.org
Website: http://www.espam-formationuc.org/

Président: Martial Lipeb
Tel: +229 95 75 88 91 EMail: mrfranklin@espam-formationuc.org

International Relations: Franklin Nwankwo, Registrar
Tel: +229 66 26 09 30 EMail: mrfranklin@espam-formationuc.org

International Relations: Victor Ogar, International Relations Officer
Tel: +229 94 65 82 26 EMail: victor93@yahoo,com

Faculty

Applied Science (Nursing; Pharmacy); **Management Science** (Accountancy; Business Administration; Economics); **Social Science** (International Relations; Mass Communication)

History: Created 2007. Acquired status 2009.

Degrees and Diplomas: *Licence*; *Master*

Academic Staff *2011-2012*	TOTAL
FULL-TIME	15
PART-TIME	20
STAFF WITH DOCTORATE	
FULL-TIME	18
Student Numbers *2011-2012*	
All (Foreign included)	123

Last Updated: 24/09/12

PIGIER BENIN

Pigier Bénin

01 BP 2411 RP, Carré 10 - rue 503, Antikanmey Cotonou, Cotonou, Littoral
Tel: +229 21-31-16-44
Fax: +229 21-31-30-47
EMail: pigiercotonou@yahoo.fr
Website: http://www.cie-formation.com

Directeur général: Henri Tafou

Directeur pédagogique: Gérard Akindes

Programme

Accountancy and Management (Accountancy; Management); **Accountancy Audit and Management Control** (Accountancy; Management); **Bilingual Executive Assistant** (Secretarial Studies); **Commercial Action**; **Corporate Banking and Finance** (Banking; Finance); **Finance and Expertise** (Finance); **Journalism and Communication** (Communication Studies; Journalism);

Negociation and Multimedia Communication (Communication Studies; Multimedia); **Secretarial Studies** (Secretarial Studies)

History: Founded 1993.

Admission Requirements: Baccalauréat or Licence

Fees: (CFA Francs): 800,000 per annum

Main Language(s) of Instruction: French and English

Degrees and Diplomas: *Licence*; *Master*

Student Services: Health Services, Nursery Care

Last Updated: 05/07/12

PROTESTANT UNIVERSITY OF WESTERN AFRICA

Université Protestante d'Afrique de l'Ouest (UPAO)

01 BP 176, 1er Arrondissement Ahouanticomè, Porto-Novo, Ouémé
Tel: +229 20-21-29-30
Fax: +229 20-21-29-62
EMail: upaoben@intnet.bj

Rector: Marcellin S. Dossou (2002-)

Director of Academic Services: Timothée A. Gandonou

International Relations: Gaéton-Pierre Avademe, Director, Finance and Administration

Institute

Accountancy and Finance Management (Accountancy; Finance; Management); **Education Sciences** (Educational Sciences; Pedagogy); **Human Resources Management** (Human Resources; Management); **Theology** (Theology)

History: UPAO belongs to four churches in three countries and was founded as a Theological college in 1924 before acquiring university status in 2003.

Academic Year: September to June

Admission Requirements: Secondary school certificate (Baccalauréat)

Fees: (CFA Francs): Registration, 300,000-500,000 per annum; students sent by member churches, 75%

Main Language(s) of Instruction: French, English

Accrediting Agency: ASTHEOL; University of Benin and Private Universities Association

Degrees and Diplomas: *Licence*: **Accountancy; Finance; Human Resources; Theology.** *Master*: **Accountancy; Finance; Human Resources; Theology.**

Student Services: Academic Counselling, Health Services, Nursery Care, Social Counselling, Sports Facilities

Publishing house: C.L.E. Yaoundé

Last Updated: 07/12/12

SCHOOL OF COMMERCE AND MANAGEMENT

Haute Ecole de Commerce et de Management (HECM)

01 BP 3842, Lot 485 Bar Tito, Cotonou Oueme-Plateau
Tel: +229 21-32-57-28
EMail: contact@hecm-afrique.net
Website: http://www.hecm-benin.net

Directeur: Natondé Ake

Programme

Accountancy and Management (Accountancy; Management); **Administration and Human Resources Management** (Administration; Human Resources; Management); **Banking and Finance** (Banking; Finance); **Business Computing** (Business Computing); **Communication and Commercial Negociation** (Business and Commerce); **Corporate Communication** (Communication Studies); **Electronics** (Electronic Engineering); **Finance and Management Control** (Finance; Management); **Food Chemistry and Quality Control** (Chemistry; Food Science); **Human Resources Management** (Human Resources; Management); **Industrial Informatics and Maintenance** (Business Computing; Industrial Maintenance); **Journalism** (Journalism); **Management Informatics and NICT** (Business Computing; Information Technology; Management); **Marketing and Commercial Action** (Business and Commerce; Marketing); **Tourism and Leisure** (Leisure Studies; Tourism)

History: Founded 1999.

Admission Requirements: Secondary school leaving certificate (Baccalauréat); Bachelor for graduate programmes.

Fees: (CFA Francs): BTS, 395,000 per annum; Licence, 650,000 per annum

Degrees and Diplomas: *Licence*; *Master*

Last Updated: 25/06/12

SCHOOL OF MANAGEMENT, COMPUTER SCIENCE AND SCIENCE

Ecole supérieure de Gestion, d'Informatique et des Sciences

Bd de l'Ouémé Jérico, Cotonou
Tel: +229 32 47 73
EMail: esgis.benin@gmail.com

Programme

Accountancy (Accountancy); **Computer Science** (Computer Engineering; Computer Networks; Computer Science; Telecommunications Engineering); **Finance** (Finance); **International Management** (Management)

Degrees and Diplomas: *Licence*; *Master*. Also Mastère spécialisé

Last Updated: 10/07/12

UNIVERSITY INSTITUTE OF BENIN

Institut universitaire du Bénin (IUB)

06 BP 3116, Aïdjèdo, rue du Centre d'Accueil Mgr Parisot, Cotonou, Littoral 06
Tel: +229 21-32-81-97 +229 97-10-37-89
Fax: +229 21-32-78-32
EMail: secretariat@iubformations.org

Président: Albert Gandonou
Tel: +229 97-47-72-90 EMail: gandalert@yahoo.fr

Department

Communication Studies (Communication Studies); **Computer Engineering** (Computer Engineering); **French Language** (French; Literature; Translation and Interpretation); **Sociology** (Sociology)

History: Founded 2002.

Academic Year: October to December (October-December; January-March; April-June)

Admission Requirements: Baccalauréat

Main Language(s) of Instruction: French

Degrees and Diplomas: *Master*: **Banking; Communication Studies; Computer Science; Development Studies; Finance; Human Resources; Insurance.**

Student Services: Language Laboratory, Nursery Care, Sports Facilities

Last Updated: 07/12/12

UNIVERSITY OF APPLIED SCIENCES AND MANAGEMENT

Université des Sciences appliquées et du Management (USAM)

221/224 rue et n°144 Accron-Gogankomey, Porto-Novo, Oueme 01 BP 3582
Tel: +229 20-21-54 +229 90-90-05-32
Fax: +229 22-54-05-31
EMail: info@univ-usam.net

Institute

Advanced Business Studies *(IHEC)* (Business Administration); **Alternative and Continuous Training** (Continuing Education); **Applied Sciences and Technology** (Natural Sciences; Technology); **Political and Social Sciences Rights** *(IDSPS)* (Political Sciences; Social Sciences)

History: Founded 2003. Acquired present status 2004.

Main Language(s) of Instruction: French, English

Degrees and Diplomas: *Licence*; *Master*

VERECHAGUINE A.K. SCHOOL OF CIVIL ENGINEERING

Ecole supérieure de Génie Civil Verechaguine (ESGC VAK)

02 BP 244, C/753 Gbegamey, Cotonou, Atlantique
Tel: +229 90-92-33-31 +229 97-97-00-96
Fax: +229 21-30-69-08
EMail: secretariat_general_vak@yahoo.fr
Website: http://www.verechaguine.com

Directeur: Gérard Léopold Gbaguidi Aisse
Tel: +229 21-30-69-17 EMail: dg_vak@yahoo.fr

Chef de Service Administratif et Financier: Svetlana Gbaguidi
Tel: +229 21-30-69-17

International Relations: Jeanne-Marie Menou, Chef de Service
Tel: +229 21-30-69-17

Programme
Civil Engineering (Civil Engineering)

History: Founded 1998.

Admission Requirements: Secondary school certificate (baccalauréat); DT(BTP,DPB)

Main Language(s) of Instruction: French

Accrediting Agency: Ministry of Higher Education and Scientific Research; Direction des Etablissements Privés d'Enseignement Supérieur

Degrees and Diplomas: *Licence*: **Civil Engineering; Surveying and Mapping.** *Master*. Also Diplôme de Technicien (3 yrs)

Student Services: Health Services, Language Laboratory, Social Counselling, Sports Facilities

Last Updated: 25/06/12

Bhutan

STRUCTURE OF HIGHER EDUCATION SYSTEM

Description:

Tertiary education in Bhutan is education offered after Class XII. It encompasses both degree and diploma programmes and consists of both professional and general programmes that can be offered at undergraduate, post-graduate and doctoral levels.
The Department of Adult and Higher Education within the Ministry of Education is in charge of the sector.

Stages of studies:

University level first stage: *Bachelor's degree*
Bachelor's degrees are conferred in various subjects after three to four years to students who have passed the Class XII examinations.

University level second stage: *Postgraduate diploma/certificate; Master's degree*

ADMISSION TO HIGHER EDUCATION

Admission to university-level studies:

Name of secondary school credential required: Bhutan Higher Secondary Education Certificate

RECOGNITION OF STUDIES

Quality assurance system:

Universities in Bhutan are required to create and maintain an effective quality assurance system that covers all programmes. The Bhutan Accreditation Council has established the Bhutan Qualifications Framework (2012). Private institutions must obtain the Gold leaf from the Ministry of Education and be incorporated under the Companies Act of the Kingdom of Bhutan 2000. Not-for-profit institutions are governed by the Civil Society Organizations Act of the Kingdom of Bhutan 2007.

NATIONAL BODIES

Ministry of Education

Minister: Mingbo Dukpa
PO Box 112
Thimphu
Tel: +975(2) 322223
Fax: +975(2) 323154
WWW: http://www.education.gov.bt

Royal Education Council - REC

Director: Sonam Nima
PO Box 1468
Motithang
Thimphu
Tel: +975(2) 336136
Fax: +975(2) 336253
EMail: snima@rec.org.bt
WWW: http://www.rec.org.bt
Role of national body: The Royal Education Council was established through a Royal Command in August 2007 to initiate and implement education reforms across the entire spectrum covering school, technical and tertiary education.

Quality Assurance and Accreditation Division - QAAD
Department of Adult and Higher Education, Ministry of Education, PO Box 112
Thimphu
Tel: +975(2) 332068
Fax: +975(2) 334101
EMail: qaad2012dahe@gmail.com
WWW: http://www.education.gov.bt

Data for academic year: 2013-2014
Source: IAU from the Royal Government of Bhutan website; "Tertiary Education Policy of the Kingdom of Bhutan, 2010", Ministry of Education; "National Education Framework, 2012", Royal Education Council; and "Bhutan Qualifications Framework, 2012", Bhutan Accreditation Council, 2013. Bodies 2016.

INSTITUTION

ROYAL UNIVERSITY OF BHUTAN (RUB)

PO Box 708, Lower Motithang, Semtokha, Thimphu
Tel: +975(2) 336-454 +975(2) 336-523 +975(2) 336-524
Fax: +975(2) 336-453 +975(2) 336-456
EMail: tandindorji@hotmail.com
Website: http://www.rub.edu.bt

Vice-Chancellor: Pema Thinley
Tel: +975(2) 336-451 EMail: pavc.ovc@rub.edu.bt

Registrar: Gajel Lhendup
Tel: +975(2) 336-459 EMail: gajel_lhundup.ovc@rub.edu.bt

International Relations: Dorji Thinley, Director, Research and External Relations
Tel: +975(2) 336-455 EMail: dthinley.ovc@rub.edu.bt

College

Business Studies *(Gedu, Chukha)* (Business Administration; Business and Commerce); **Education** *(Samtse)* (Education; Teacher Training); **Natural Resources** *(Lobesa, Thimphu)* (Agriculture; Animal Husbandry; Forestry); **Science and Technology** *(Phuentsholing, Chukha)* (Civil Engineering; Electrical Engineering; Electronic Engineering; Telecommunications Engineering); **Sherubtse** *(Kanglung, Trashigang)* (Arts and Humanities; Biological and Life Sciences; History; Information Technology; Mathematics; Natural Sciences; Political Sciences; Social Sciences)

Institute

Health Sciences *(Thimphu, Changzamto)* (Health Sciences; Medical Technology; Midwifery; Nursing); **Language and Cultural Studies** *(Semtokha, Thimphu)* (Cultural Studies; Native Language); **Polytechnic** *(Dewathang, Samdrup, Jongkhar)* (Civil Engineering; Electrical Engineering; Mechanical Engineering); **Traditional Medicine** *(Thimphu, Kawajangsa)* (Traditional Eastern Medicine)

History: Founded 2003 by Royal Decree. A federated organization of ten member colleges and institutes.

Academic Year: July to June or February to December, depending on each college or institute.

Admission Requirements: Secondary School Certificate

Main Language(s) of Instruction: English

Degrees and Diplomas: *Bachelor's Degree*: **Agriculture; Biological and Life Sciences; Biology; Business Administration; Chemistry; Civil Engineering; Computer Science; Demography and Population; Economics; Electrical Engineering; English; Environmental Engineering; Environmental Studies; Forestry; Geography; Information Technology; Literature; Mathematics; Media Studies; Modern Languages; Natural Resources; Physics; Tibetan; Traditional Eastern Medicine.** *Postgraduate Diploma/Certificate*: **Education; Educational Administration; Educational and Student Counselling; English Studies; Mathematics.**

Student Services: Academic Counselling, Canteen, Careers Guidance, Cultural Activities, Facilities for disabled people, Foreign Studies Centre, Health Services, Language Laboratory, Nursery Care, Social Counselling, Sports Facilities

Publications: Bhutan Journal of Research and Development; Building Our Institutional Futures; Men-jong So-rig; Rabsel; Rig-Gter; Sherub Doenme: Academic Journal of Sherubtse College; The Personal Helicon; Yonten

Academic Staff *2012-2013*	MEN	WOMEN	**TOTAL**
FULL-TIME	389	101	**490**
Student Numbers *2012-2013*			
All (Foreign included)	–	–	**7,432**

Last Updated: 28/02/14

Bolivia (Plurinational State of)

STRUCTURE OF HIGHER EDUCATION SYSTEM

Description:

Higher education is offered in universities and higher technical institutes. There are different kinds of universities (public, foreign, indigenous, military, and private). The Executive Committee of the Bolivian University (CEUB) is responsible for public and autonomous universities, the only ones entitled to public national funds. It also coordinates and implements the decisions of the supreme governing body. Private universities, most of which were created after 1985, are organized in an association, the Asociacion Nacional de Universidades Privadas (ANUP), founded in 1992, but are supervised by the Ministry of Education.

Stages of studies:

University level first stage: *Pre Grado*

Undergraduate studies comprise diplomas de Técnico Superior (from 1 1/2 to 3 years' studies) and degrees of Licenciaturas (4 to 5 or more years in specific fields).

University level second stage: *Post Grado*

Post-graduate courses comprise diplomas de Diplomado and Especialidad and degrees of Maestria, Doctorado, and Post Doctorado.

ADMISSION TO HIGHER EDUCATION

Admission to university-level studies:

Name of secondary school credential required: Bachillerato

Foreign students admission:

Admission requirements: Foreign students must hold a Secondary School Leaving Certificate equivalent to the Diploma de Bachiller. Some universities require an entrance examination (Pre-Grado).

Entry regulations: Students should hold a visa

Language proficiency: Students should be proficient in Spanish.

NATIONAL BODIES

Ministerio de Educación (Ministry of Education)

Minister: Roberto Aguilar Gómez
Vice-Minister, Higher Education: Jiovanny Edward Samanamud Ávila
Avenida Arce no. 2147
Casilla de correo 3116
La Paz
Tel: +591(2) 244 2144
WWW: http://www.minedu.gob.bo/

Asociacíon Nacional de Universidades Privadas - ANUP (National Association of Private Universities)

La Paz

Comisión Nacional de Acreditación de Carreras Universitarias – CNACU (National Accreditation Council)

MINEDU
La Paz
Role of national body: CNACU assesses and accredits public and private university education.

Comité Ejecutivo de la Universidad Boliviana - CEUB (Executive Committee of the Bolivian University)

National Executive Secretary: Gustavo Rojas Ugarte
C.H. Manchego No 2559
Casilla 4722
La Paz

Tel: +591(2) 243 5217
Fax: +591(2) 243 5276
EMail: secejen@ceub.edu.bo
WWW: http://www.ceub.edu.bo
Role of national body: CEUB coordinates and represents the Bolivian university system.

Data for academic year: 2015-2016
Source: IAU from the websites of the Ministry of Education and Culture and CEUB, 2015.

INSTITUTIONS

PUBLIC INSTITUTIONS

AUTONOMOUS UNIVERSITY OF BENI

Universidad Autónoma del Beni José Ballivián (UABJB)
Casilla Postal 38, Avenida 6 de Agostos N° 5715, Calle Sucre, Trinidad, Beni
Tel: +591(3) 462-1590 +591(3) 462-0744
Fax: +591(3) 462-0236
EMail: secretariogeneral@uabjb.edu.bo
Website: http://www.uabjb.edu.bo

Rector: Luis Carlos Zambrano Aguirre (2010-)
EMail: rector@uabjb.edu.bo; secretariarectorado@uabjb.edu.bo

Vicerrector: Freddy Machado Flores
Tel: +591(3) 462-4101 EMail: pregrado@uabjb.edu.bo

Faculty
Agriculture (Agricultural Engineering; Agriculture; Animal Husbandry); **Animal Husbandry** (Animal Husbandry; Cattle Breeding; Veterinary Science); **Economics** (Accountancy; Business Administration; Economics); **Engineering and Technology** (Civil Engineering; Computer Engineering); **Forestry** (Forestry); **Health Sciences** (Biochemistry; Health Sciences; Medicine; Nursing; Pharmacy); **Humanities and Education Sciences** (Education; Pedagogy; Tourism); **Law and Political and Social Science** (Communication Studies; Law; Political Sciences)

Institute
Arts (Fine Arts)

History: Founded 1967 as Universidad Técnica del Beni 'Mariscal José Ballivián', acquired present title and status 2005.

Main Language(s) of Instruction: Spanish

Degrees and Diplomas: *Técnico Universitario Medio*; *Licenciatura*; *Especialización*; *Maestría*; *Doctorado*: **Educational Administration; International Business.**

Publications: Revista Científica AGROCIENCIAS AMAZONIA

Last Updated: 25/09/15

BOLIVIAN APIAGUAIKI TUPA INDIGENOUS UNIVERSITY

Universidad Indígena Boliviana Guarani Apiagûaiki Tûpa (UNIBOL GUARANI)
Casilla 88-Ecobol-Camiri-Santa Cruz, Territorio Guaraní - Ivo, Chuquisaca
EMail: guaraniunibol@gmail.com
Website: http://unibolguarani.edu.bo

Rector: Roberto Gualuo

Vicerrector: Gonzalo Medina

Faculty
Fishery (Fishery); **Forestry** (Forestry); **Petroleum and Gas Engineering** (Petroleum and Gas Engineering); **Veterinary Science** (Veterinary Science)

History: Founded 2008.

Main Language(s) of Instruction: Guarani

Degrees and Diplomas: *Licenciatura*: **Fishery; Forestry; Petroleum and Gas Engineering; Veterinary Science.**

Last Updated: 25/09/15

BOLIVIAN AYMARATUPAK KATARI INDIGENOUS UNIVERSITY

Universidad Indígena Boliviana Aymara Tupak Katari (UNIBOL-A-TK)
Plaza Elizardo Pérez s/n - Canton Warisata, Achacachi
Tel: +561(2) 222-3576
EMail: info@utupakkatari.edu.bo
Website: http://www.utupakkatari.edu.bo

Rector: Lucio Choquehuanca Yujra

Faculty
Agronomy of the Altiplano (Agronomy); **Food Technology** (Food Technology); **Textile Technology** (Textile Technology); **Veterinary Science** (Veterinary Science)

History: Founded 2008.

Main Language(s) of Instruction: Aymara

Degrees and Diplomas: *Licenciatura*: **Agronomy; Food Technology; Textile Technology; Veterinary Science.** *Diplomado*; *Maestría*; *Doctorado*

Last Updated: 25/09/15

CASIMIRO HUANCA QUECHUA INDIGENOUS UNIVERSITY

Universidad Indígena Quechua Casimiro Huanca (UNIBOL QUECHUA)
Santa Cruz Km. 191 Chimore zona "La Jota", Cochabamba
Tel: +591(4) 413-6832
EMail: unibolquechua@hotmail.com
Website: http://www.unibolquechua.edu.bo

Rector: José Cáceres Guzmán

Programme
Agricultural Engineering (Agricultural Engineering); **Fishery** (Fishery); **Food Technology** (Food Technology); **Forestry** (Forestry)

History: Founded 2008.

Main Language(s) of Instruction: Quechua

Degrees and Diplomas: *Licenciatura*: **Fishery; Food Technology; Forestry; Tropical Agriculture.**

Last Updated: 29/09/15

EL ALTO PUBLIC UNIVERSITY

Universidad Pública de El Alto (UPEA)
Av. Sucre s/n Zona Villa Esperanza, El Alto, La Paz
Tel: +59 (12) 284-4177
EMail: upeamilenium@gmail.com
Website: http://www.upea.edu.bo

Rector: Romualdo Ricardo Nogales

Vicerrector: Luz Soraya Vega Zenteno

Area
Education (Educational Sciences; Preschool Education); **Health Sciences** (Dentistry; Dietetics; Medicine; Nursing; Nutrition; Veterinary Science); **Social Sciences** (Accountancy; Architecture; Business Administration; Communication Studies; Development Studies; Economics; Fine Arts; History; International Business; Law; Linguistics; Modern Languages; Political Sciences; Psychology; Social Work; Sociology; Tourism); **Technology** (Agricultural Engineering; Automation and Control Engineering; Civil Engineering; Computer Engineering; Electrical and Electronic Engineering; Environmental Engineering; Production Engineering; Textile Technology)

History: Founded 2000.

Main Language(s) of Instruction: Spanish

Degrees and Diplomas: *Licenciatura*: **Accountancy; Agricultural Engineering; Architecture; Business Administration; Business and Commerce; Business Computing; Civil Engineering; Dentistry; Development Studies; Economics; Education; Electronic Engineering; Engineering; Law; Linguistics; Medicine; Nursing; Petroleum and Gas Engineering; Social Work; Sociology; Veterinary Science.**

Last Updated: 30/09/15

GABRIEL RENÉ MORENO AUTONOMOUS UNIVERSITY

Universidad Autónoma Gabriel René Moreno (UAGRM)

Avenidas Centenario, Venezuela y Av. 26 de Febrero, Santa Cruz de la Sierra, Santa Cruz
Tel: +591(3) 336-5533
Fax: +591(3) 334-2160
EMail: uagrm@uagrm.edu.bo
Website: http://www.uagrm.edu.bo

Rector: Saúl Rosas Ferrufino
EMail: rectorado@uagrm.edu.bo

Faculty
Accountancy (Accountancy); **Agriculture** (Agricultural Engineering; Agriculture; Agronomy; Biology; Forestry); **Economics and Finance** (Business Administration; Business and Commerce; Economics; Finance); **Exact Sciences and Technology** (Chemical Engineering; Civil Engineering; Computer Engineering; Electrical Engineering; Environmental Engineering; Food Science; Industrial Engineering; Mechanical Engineering; Petroleum and Gas Engineering; Physics; Technology); **Habitat, Arts and Design** (Design; Fine Arts; Interior Design); **Health Sciences** (Biochemistry; Health Sciences; Medicine; Nursing; Pharmacy); **Humanities** (Arts and Humanities; Communication Studies; Educational Sciences; Modern Languages; Philology; Psychology; Sociology); **Integral Del Chaco** (Accountancy; Agricultural Engineering; Computer Engineering; Nursing; Petroleum and Gas Engineering); **Integral Del Norte** (Accountancy; Computer Engineering; Finance; Industrial Engineering; Law; Medicine; Nursing; Petroleum and Gas Engineering; Veterinary Science); **Law, Political and Social Sciences** (International Relations; Law; Political Sciences; Social Sciences; Social Work); **Polytechnic** (Construction Engineering; Electrical Engineering; Electronic Engineering; Engineering; Mechanical Engineering; Surveying and Mapping; Technology); **Technology** *(Universitario Vallegrande)* (Agriculture); **Veterinary Science** (Veterinary Science; Zoology)

History: Founded 1880 as Universidad de Santo Tomás de Aquino, became autonomous in 1911.

Academic Year: February to December (February-June; July-December)

Admission Requirements: Secondary school certificate (bachillerato) and entrance examination

Main Language(s) of Instruction: Spanish

Degrees and Diplomas: *Licenciatura*: **Accountancy; Agriculture; Economics; Engineering; Law.** *Especialización*: **Engineering; Town Planning.**

Last Updated: 02/11/15

JUAN MISAEL SARACHO AUTONOMOUS UNIVERSITY

Universidad Autónoma Juan Misael Saracho (UAJMS)

Casilla Postal 51, Avenida Victor Paz E. No 149, Tarija, Cercado
Tel: +591(4) 66431-10
Fax: +591(4) 61123-22
EMail: rector@uajms.edu.bo
Website: http://www.uajms.edu.bo

Rector: Marcelo Hoyos Montecinos
EMail: rector@mail.uajms.edu.bo

Secretario General: Gustavo Succi EMail: secun@uajms.edu.bo

International Relations: Eduardo Trigo
EMail: ppaunesco@mail.uajms.edu.bo

Faculty
Agriculture and Forestry (Agriculture; Agronomy; Forestry); **Dentistry** (Dentistry); **Economics and Finance** (Accountancy; Business Administration; Economics; Finance; Statistics); **Health Sciences** (Biochemistry; Health Sciences; Nursing); **Humanities** (Arts and Humanities; Modern Languages; Psychology); **Law and Political Sciences** (Law; Political Sciences); **Science and Technology** (Architecture; Chemical Engineering; Civil Engineering; Computer Engineering; Food Science; Mathematics and Computer Science; Technology)

Programme
Journalism (Journalism)

Further Information: Also campuses in Yacuiba, Caraparí, El Palmar, Villa Montes and Bermejo

History: Founded 1946. A State institution.

Academic Year: March to December (March-July; August-December)

Admission Requirements: Secondary school certificate (bachillerato) and entrance examination

Fees: (US Dollars): Registration, c. 1,600; foreign students, c. 3,300 per annum

Main Language(s) of Instruction: Spanish

Degrees and Diplomas: *Técnico Universitario Superior*: **Accountancy; Agriculture; Agronomy; Animal Husbandry; Veterinary Science; Zoology.** *Licenciatura*: **Accountancy; Agriculture; Architecture; Biochemistry; Business Administration; Chemical Engineering; Civil Engineering; Computer Engineering; Dentistry; Economics; Food Science; Forestry; Law; Modern Languages; Nursing; Pharmacy; Psychology.**

Student Services: Health Services, Library, Sports Facilities

Publications: Revista Nueva Economía; Tercer Milenio

Publishing House: Imprenta Universitaria

Last Updated: 25/09/15

LA PAZ MILITARY ENGINEERING SCHOOL

Escuela Militar de Ingeniería La Paz (EMI)

Avenida Arce 2642, La Paz
Tel: +591(2) 243-2266
EMail: lapaz@adm.emi.edu.bo
Website: http://www.emi.edu.bo

Rector: Álvaro Ríos Oliver

Vicerrector: Gherson Peñaloza Cordova

Area
Engineering (Civil Engineering; Computer Engineering; Electronic Engineering; Environmental Engineering; Industrial Engineering; Mechanical Engineering; Petroleum and Gas Engineering; Telecommunications Engineering)

Further Information: Also branches in Santa Cruz, Cochabamba and Riberalta

Main Language(s) of Instruction: Spanish

Degrees and Diplomas: *Maestría*; *Doctorado*: **Education.**

Last Updated: 25/09/15

NATIONAL UNIVERSITY OF SIGLO VEINTE

Universidad Nacional de Siglo XX (UNSXX)
C.Campero No 36, Llallagua-Potosi
Tel: +591(2) 582-0222
Fax: +591(2) 582-2591
EMail: unsxx@unsxx.edu.bo
Website: http://www.unsxx.edu.bo

Rector: Jose Guillermo Dalence Salinas

Vicerrector: Edwin Sinforiano Ilacio Nina

Area
Health Sciences (Biochemistry; Dentistry; Laboratory Techniques; Nursing; Pharmacy); **Social Sciences** (Accountancy; Communication Studies; Educational Sciences; Law); **Technology** (Agricultural Engineering; Automotive Engineering; Civil Engineering; Computer Engineering; Electrical Engineering; Mechanical Engineering; Mining Engineering)

History: Founded in 1985.

Main Language(s) of Instruction: Spanish

Degrees and Diplomas: *Técnico Universitario Superior*; *Licenciatura*

Last Updated: 25/09/15

PEDAGOGICAL UNIVERSITY

Universidad Pedagógica
Avenida del Maestro No. 331, Sucre, Chuquisaca
Tel: +591(4) 646-2669
Fax: +591(4) 645-3890
EMail: upedagogica@upedagogica.edu.bo
Website: http://upedagogica.edu.bo

Rector: Luz Jiménez Quispe

Faculty
Educational Sciences (Education; Educational Sciences; Pre-school Education; Primary Education; Secondary Education; Teacher Training)

History: Founded 1999.

Main Language(s) of Instruction: Spanish

Degrees and Diplomas: *Técnico Universitario Superior*: **Arts and Humanities; Education; Natural Sciences.** *Licenciatura*: **Educational Sciences.** *Especialización*: **Education.** *Maestría*: **Educational Sciences; Mathematics Education; Science Education; Teacher Training.** *Doctorado*: **Education.**

Last Updated: 06/11/15

ROYAL, PONTIFICAL UNIVERSITY SAN FRANCISCO XAVIER DE CHUQUISACA

Universidad Mayor, Real y Pontificia de San Francisco Xavier de Chuquisaca (USFX)
Casilla Postal 212, Calle Junín esq. Estudiantes, Sucre, Chuquisaca
Tel: +591(4) 64533-08
Fax: +591(4) 64553-08
EMail: r_internacionales@usfx.edu.bo
Website: http://www.usfx.edu.bo

Rector: Eduardo Rivero Zurita EMail: rector@usfx.edu.bo

Vicerrector: Walter Arizaga Cervantes
Tel: +591(4) 64535-04 EMail: vcerector@usfx.edu.bo

Faculty
Accountancy (Accountancy); **Agronomy** (Agricultural Engineering; Agriculture; Animal Husbandry; Crop Production; Forest Products; Forestry; Fruit Production; Natural Resources; Veterinary Science; Zoology); **Architecture and Habitat** (Architecture); **Biochemistry and Pharmacy** (Biochemistry; Pharmacy); **Dentistry** (Dentistry); **Economics and Administration** (Administration; Economics); **Humanities** (Arts and Humanities; Education; Modern Languages; Pedagogy; Psychology; Tourism); **Law, Political and Social Sciences** (Law; Political Sciences; Social Sciences); **Medical Technology** (Laboratory Techniques; Medical Technology; Nutrition; Physical Therapy); **Medicine** (Biochemistry; Dentistry; Health Sciences; Medicine; Nursing; Pharmacy; Physical Therapy; Radiology); **Nursing** (Nursing); **Technical** (Automation and Control Engineering; Construction Engineering; Electrical and Electronic Engineering; Engineering; Industrial Engineering; Mechanical Engineering; Technology); **Technology** (Architecture; Chemical Engineering; Civil Engineering; Computer Engineering; Electrical Engineering; Food Technology; Industrial Engineering; Mechanical Engineering; Systems Analysis; Technology; Telecommunications Engineering)

History: Founded 1624 by Father Juan de Frías y Herrán of the Society of Jesus and by Papal Bull and Royal Decree. Higher education came under State control 1852 and the University was reorganized and granted autonomous status 1930.

Academic Year: March to December (March-August; September-December)

Admission Requirements: Secondary school certificate (bachillerato) or equivalent and entrance examination

Main Language(s) of Instruction: Spanish

Degrees and Diplomas: *Técnico Universitario Superior*; *Licenciatura*; *Especialización*; *Diplomado*; *Maestría*; *Doctorado*

Publications: Boletín de la Universidad popular; Boletín del Museo Antropológico; Boletín del Museo Colonial 'Charcas'; Ciencias políticas y sociales; Revista de la Facultad de Ciencias económicas; Revista de la Facultad de Ciencias médicas; Revista de la Facultad de Derecho; Revista del Instituto de Sociología Boliviana

Last Updated: 25/09/15

SAN SIMÓN UNIVERSITY

Universidad Mayor de San Simón (UMSS)
Casilla 992, Avenida Oquendo y Sucre, Cochabamba
Tel: +591(4) 422-0717
Fax: +591(4) 452-2114
EMail: rector@umss.edu.bo
Website: http://www.umss.edu.bo

Rector: Juan Ríos del Prado EMail: rector@umss.edu.bo

Vicerrector: J. Walter López Valenzuela
EMail: vice@umss.edu.bo

Faculty
Agriculture, Animal Husbandry and Forestry (Agriculture; Agronomy; Animal Husbandry; Forestry; Rural Planning; Veterinary Science); **Architecture and Habitat** (Architecture; Graphic Design; Interior Design; Tourism); **Biochemistry and Pharmacy** (Biochemistry; Pharmacy); **Dentistry** (Dentistry); **Economics** (Accountancy; Administration; Economics; Statistics); **Humanities and Education** (Arts and Humanities; Bilingual and Bicultural Education; Educational Sciences; Linguistics; Psychology; Social Sciences; Social Work); **Law and Political Science** (Law; Political Sciences); **Medicine** (Medicine; Nutrition; Physical Therapy); **Polytechnic** *(del Valle Alto)* (Agricultural Equipment; Civil Engineering; Construction Engineering; Food Science; Industrial Chemistry; Mechanical Engineering; Nursing; Statistics); **Science and Technology** (Biology; Chemical Engineering; Chemistry; Civil Engineering; Computer Engineering; Computer Science; Electrical and Electronic Engineering; Industrial Engineering; Mathematics; Mechanical Engineering; Natural Sciences; Physics; Technology); **Social Sciences** (Anthropology; Social Sciences; Sociology)

School
Forestry (Forestry)

History: Founded 1832 as School of Science and Arts. Granted autonomous status by law 1930. The University is financed by the State. It is part of the Bolivian Public University System.

Academic Year: February to December (February-June; July-December)

Admission Requirements: Secondary school certificate (bachillerato) and entrance examination

Fees: (Bolivianos): 100-800 (fees vary according to faculty)

Main Language(s) of Instruction: Spanish

Degrees and Diplomas: *Técnico Universitario Superior*, *Licenciatura*; *Diplomado*; *Maestría*; *Doctorado*: **Business Administration.**

Student Services: Canteen, Health Services, Language Laboratory, Sports Facilities

Publishing house: Imprenta Universitaria

Last Updated: 25/09/15

SIMON BOLIVAR ANDEAN UNIVERSITY

Universidad Andina Simón Bolívar (UASB)

Calle R. Audiencia No. 73, Sucre, Chuquisaca

Tel: +591(4) 646-0265

Fax: +591(4) 646-0833

EMail: info@uasb.edu.bo

Website: http://www.uasb.edu.bo

Rector: Jose Luis Gutierrez Sardán
EMail: jlgsardan@uasb.edu.bo

Programme

Economics (Economics; International Business; Management); **Environmental Studies** (Agricultural Management; Environmental Studies); **Health Sciences** (Forensic Medicine and Dentistry; Orthodontics; Physical Therapy); **Information and Communication Technology** (Information Technology; Software Engineering); **Law** (Constitutional Law; Fiscal Law; Law); **Sustainable Development** (Agricultural Management; Ecology; Environmental Management; Food Science); **Tourism and Culture** (Tourism)

Further Information: Branch in La Paz

Degrees and Diplomas: *Especialización*: **Ecology; Environmental Studies.** *Diplomado*: **Cultural Studies; Ecology; Environmental Studies; Justice Administration; Law.** *Maestría*: **Business Administration; Dentistry; Ecology; Environmental Studies; Finance; Information Technology; International Business; Law.** *Doctorado*: **Neurosciences; Public Health.**

Last Updated: 02/11/15

TECHNICAL UNIVERSITY OF ORURO

Universidad Técnica de Oruro (UTO)

Casilla Postal 49, Av. 6 de Octubre 5715 entre Cochabamba y Ayacucho, Oruro

Tel: +591(2) 525-01-00

Fax: +591(2) 524-22-15

EMail: vicerrectorado@uto.edu.bo

Website: http://www.uto.edu.bo

Rector: Carlos Antezana García EMail: rector@uto.edu.bo

Secretario General: Marco Ernesto Jaimes Molina
EMail: striagal@uto.edu.bo

International Relations: José Cortes Gumucio
Tel: +591(252) 757-98 EMail: dpic@uto.edu.bo

Faculty

Agriculture and Veterinary Science *(Oruro, Challapta)* (Agricultural Engineering; Agriculture; Rural Planning; Veterinary Science); **Architecture and Town Planning** (Architecture; Town Planning); **Economics, Finance and Administration** (Accountancy; Administration; Business Administration; Economics; Finance); **Engineering** *(National)* (Chemical Engineering; Civil Engineering; Computer Engineering; Electrical Engineering; Electronic Engineering; Geological Engineering; Industrial Engineering; Mechanical Engineering; Metallurgical Engineering; Mining Engineering; Systems Analysis); **Health Sciences** (Cardiology; Epidemiology; Medicine; Nursing; Public Health; Surgery); **Law, Political and Social Sciences** (Anthropology; Law; Political Sciences; Social Sciences); **Technical Studies** (Automation and Control Engineering; Building Technologies; Industrial Chemistry; Industrial Maintenance; Mechanical Engineering; Technology)

Further Information: Branches in Oruro and Challapta

History: Founded 1892 as provincial University. Became autonomous in 1937. Formerly known as the Universidad Autónoma de San Agustín. Financed by the State.

Academic Year: January to December

Admission Requirements: Secondary school certificate (bachillerato en humanidades) and entrance examination

Fees: (US Dollars): 200 per annum

Main Language(s) of Instruction: Spanish

Degrees and Diplomas: *Técnico Universitario Superior*, *Licenciatura*: **Accountancy; Agriculture; Chemistry; Civil Engineering; Economics; Electrical Engineering; Law; Mechanical Engineering; Metallurgical Engineering; Mining Engineering.** *Diplomado*; *Maestría*; *Doctorado*: **Business Administration; Economics.**

Student Services: Academic Counselling, Cultural Activities, Health Services, Language Laboratory, Social Counselling, Sports Facilities

Publications: Cultura Boliviana; Revista de Agronomía; Revista de Derecho; Revista de Metalurgía

Publishing House: Editora Universitaria

Last Updated: 30/09/15

TOMAS FRIAS AUTONOMOUS UNIVERSITY

Universidad Autónoma Tomás Frías (UATF)

Av. Del Maestro-Av. Cívica s/n, Potosí

Tel: +591(2) 622-7300

Fax: +591(2) 622-6663

Website: http://www.uatf.edu.bo

Rector: Luis Ferrufino Terceros EMail: rectoruatf@cotapnet.com.bo

Vicerrector: Pedro Guido Lopez Cortes Asesores

Faculty

Agriculture and Animal Husbandry (Agricultural Engineering; Agronomy; Animal Husbandry; Veterinary Science); **Arts** (Music; Visual Arts); **Economics, Finance and Administration** (Accountancy; Administration; Economics; Finance); **Engineering** (Civil Engineering; Construction Engineering; Surveying and Mapping); **Geological Engineering** (Environmental Engineering; Geological Engineering); **Health Sciences** (Nursing); **Humanities and Social Sciences** (Linguistics; Social Work; Tourism); **Law** (Law); **Medicine** (Medicine); **Mining Engineering** (Mining Engineering); **Pure Science** (Chemistry; Information Sciences; Mathematics; Physics; Statistics); **Technology** (Automation and Control Engineering; Electrical and Electronic Engineering; Mechanical Engineering)

History: Founded 1892, the University was at first attached to the Universidad Francisco Xavier Sucre but became independent and autonomous. Acquired present title and status 1937.

Academic Year: February to December (January-July; July-December)

Admission Requirements: Secondary school certificate (bachiller) and entrance examination

Main Language(s) of Instruction: Spanish

Accrediting Agency: Comité Ejecutivo de la Universidad Boliviana (CEUB)

Degrees and Diplomas: *Técnico Universitario Superior*: **Accountancy; Chemistry; Construction Engineering; Electrical and Electronic Engineering; Fine Arts; Mathematics; Mechanical Engineering; Music; Physics; Tourism.** *Licenciatura*: **Accountancy; Agricultural Engineering; Animal Husbandry; Business Administration; Chemistry; Civil Engineering; Economics; Electrical and Electronic Engineering; Fine Arts; Information Sciences; Law; Linguistics; Mathematics; Mechanical Engineering; Medicine; Mining Engineering; Music; Nursing; Physics; Social Work; Statistics; Tourism; Veterinary Science.** *Diplomado*: **Education; Geology; Marketing; Metallurgical Engineering; Statistics.** *Maestría*

Student Services: Academic Counselling, Canteen, Cultural Activities, Health Services, Language Laboratory, Nursery Care, Social Counselling, Sports Facilities

Publications: Libros de texto

Publishing House: University Press

Last Updated: 25/09/15

UNIVERSITY OF SAN ANDRES

Universidad Mayor de San Andrés (UMSA)

Casilla Postal 6042, Monoblock, Avenida Villazón 1995, La Paz

Tel: +591(2) 2441-690

EMail: informate@umsa.bo

Website: http://www.umsa.bo

Rector: Waldo Albarracín Sánchez EMail: rector@umsa.bo

Vicerrector: Alberto Quevedo Iriarte

Faculty

Agronomy (Agricultural Engineering; Agriculture; Agronomy); **Architecture, Art, Design and Town Planning** (Architecture; Design; Fine Arts; Town Planning; Urban Studies); **Dentistry** (Dentistry); **Economics and Finance** (Business Administration;

Economics; Finance); **Engineering** (Civil Engineering; Electrical Engineering; Food Technology; Industrial Engineering; Mechanical Engineering; Petroleum and Gas Engineering); **Geology** (Environmental Engineering; Geography; Geology); **Humanities and Education** (Education; History; Library Science; Linguistics; Literature; Philosophy; Psychology; Tourism); **Law and Political Science** (Law; Political Sciences); **Medicine, Nursing, Nutrition and Medical Technology** (Dietetics; Medical Technology; Medicine; Nursing; Nutrition); **Pharmacy and Biochemistry** (Biochemistry; Pharmacy); **Pure and Natural Sciences** (Biology; Chemistry; Computer Science; Ecology; Mathematics; Physics; Statistics); **Social Sciences** (Anthropology; Archaeology; Communication Studies; Social Work; Sociology); **Technology** (Air Transport; Automation and Control Engineering; Electrical Engineering; Electronic Engineering; Industrial Chemistry; Mechanical Equipment and Maintenance; Surveying and Mapping; Telecommunications Engineering)

Institute

Altitude Studies *(Bolivian)* (Mountain Studies); **Genetics** (Genetics); **Hydraulics** (Hydraulic Engineering)

History: Founded 1830, acquired present title 1972. An autonomous institution financially supported by the State and by special taxes.

Academic Year: February to December

Admission Requirements: Secondary school certificate (bachillerato) and entrance examination

Main Language(s) of Instruction: Spanish

Degrees and Diplomas: *Técnico Universitario Superior*; *Licenciatura*; *Diplomado*; *Maestria*: **Agricultural Economics; Development Studies; Higher Education; Public Health.** Also Especializaciones

Student Services: Academic Counselling, Cultural Activities, Health Services, Nursery Care, Social Counselling, Sports Facilities

Publications: Revista, Memoria Universitaria

Last Updated: 25/09/15

PRIVATE INSTITUTIONS

ADVENTIST UNIVERSITY OF BOLIVIA

Universidad Adventista de Bolivia (UAB)

Av. Simón I. Patiño Km 1, Vinto, Cochabamba

Tel: +591 (4) 426-3330

Fax: +591 (4) 426-3336

EMail: info@uab.edu.bo

Website: http://www.uab.edu.bo

Rector: Efraín Choque EMail: rector@uab.edu.bo

Vicerrector: Raúl Tancara EMail: raul.tancara@adventistas.org.bo

Faculty

Economics and Administration (Accountancy; Administration; Business Administration; Economics); **Education and Humanities** (Education; Pedagogy; Physical Education; Psychology); **Engineering** (Computer Engineering; Engineering; Systems Analysis); **Health Sciences** (Health Sciences; Nursing; Nutrition; Physical Therapy); **Theology** (Theology)

History: Founded 1928. Acquired present status 2012.

Main Language(s) of Instruction: Spanish

Degrees and Diplomas: *Técnico Universitario Superior*; *Licenciatura*; *Maestria*: **Administration; Educational Administration.**

Last Updated: 25/09/15

AQUINAS UNIVERSITY BOLIVIA

Universidad De Aquino Bolivia (UDABOL)

Pasaje Isaac Eduardo no 2643, Capitan Ravelo, La Paz

Tel: +591(2) 441-044

Fax: +591(2) 441-873

EMail: info@udabol.edu.bo

Website: http://www.udabol.edu.bo

Rector: Antonio Saavedra EMail: postgrado@scz.udabol.edu.bo

Vicerrectora: Claudia Saavedra

Faculty

Architecture and Tourism (Architecture; Tourism); **Economics and Finance** (Accountancy; Business and Commerce; Economics; Finance; Marketing); **Health Sciences** (Biochemistry; Dentistry; Medicine; Nursing; Pharmacy; Physical Therapy); **Science and Technology** (Petroleum and Gas Engineering; Systems Analysis; Technology; Telecommunications Engineering); **Social and Human Sciences** (Communication Studies; International Relations; Law; Psychology; Social Sciences)

Further Information: Also branches in Cochabamba, Oruro and Santa Cruz

History: Founded 1995. Acquired present status 2001.

Main Language(s) of Instruction: Spanish

Degrees and Diplomas: *Técnico Universitario Superior*, *Licenciatura*; *Diplomado*; *Maestria*

Last Updated: 25/09/15

BOLIVAR UNION UNIVERSITY

Universidad Unión Bolivariana (UB)

Av. 6 de Marzo entre Calles 5 y 6, El Alto, La Paz

Tel: +591(2) 282-3513

Fax: +591(2) 2822-389

EMail: universidad@ub.edu.bo

Website: http://www.ub.edu.bo

Rectora: Ericka Molina Davila EMail: gsarector@ub.edu.bo

Programme

Accountancy (Accountancy); **Business Administration** (Business Administration; Economics; Finance; International Business; International Relations; Marketing; Public Administration); **Education** (Curriculum; Education; Educational Psychology; Educational Sciences; Educational Technology; International and Comparative Education; Pedagogy); **Law** (Law); **Systems Engineering** (Computer Engineering; Computer Networks; Software Engineering)

History: Acquired present status 2004.

Degrees and Diplomas: *Licenciatura*

Last Updated: 01/10/15

BOLIVIAN EVANGELICAL UNIVERSITY

Universidad Evangélica Boliviana (UEB)

Barrio Cruz del Sur, Ave Miguel Servet, Santa Cruz de la Sierra

Tel: +591(3) 3560-990

EMail: uebmail@ueb.edu.bo

Website: http://www.ueb.edu.bo

Rector: Timoteo Sánchez Bejarano

Vicerrectora Académica: Marcela Valenzuela de Camacho

Faculty

Agriculture, Forestry and Veterinary Science (Agriculture; Forestry; Veterinary Science); **Business Studies** (Accountancy; Administration); **Communication and Culture** (Communication Studies; English; Music); **Health Sciences** (Biochemistry; Clinical Psychology; Dietetics; Health Sciences; Nursing; Nutrition; Pharmacy); **Science and Technology** (Electronic Engineering; Technology); **Theology, Education and Social Sciences** (Psychology; Social Work; Theology)

History: Founded 1982. Acquired present status 1985.

Main Language(s) of Instruction: Spanish

Degrees and Diplomas: *Técnico Universitario Superior*, *Licenciatura*; *Diplomado*; *Maestria*

Last Updated: 25/09/15

BOLIVIAN PRIVATE UNIVERSITY, COCHABAMBA

Universidad Privada Boliviana (UPB)

Av. Victor Ustariz Km 6.5, Cochabamba

Tel: +591(4) 426-8287

Fax: +591(4) 426-8288

EMail: upb@upb.edu

Website: http://www.upb.edu

Rector: Manuel Olave Sarmiento EMail: molave@upb.edu

Faculty

Engineering and Architecture (Architecture; Civil Engineering; Computer Science; Engineering; Industrial Engineering; Petroleum and Gas Engineering; Production Engineering; Systems Analysis); **Entrepreneurial Sciences and Law** (Business Administration; Business and Commerce; Communication Studies; Economics; Finance; Graphic Design; Law; Marketing)

College

Graduate Studies (Business Administration; Commercial Law)

Research Centre

Economics Research (Economics); **Energy** (Energy Engineering); **Entrepreneurship** (Business Administration)

Further Information: Also branches in La Paz, Santa Cruz, Oruro and Tarija

History: Founded 1992 by the Federation of Private Entrepreneurs of Cochabamba and the Confederation of Private Entrepreneurs of Bolivia.

Academic Year: February to December

Admission Requirements: Diploma de Bachiller en Humanidades, Prueba de Aptitud Académica of the College Board

Main Language(s) of Instruction: Spanish and English

Accrediting Agency: Bolivian Government; Vice-Ministry of Higher Education

Degrees and Diplomas: *Licenciatura*: **Architecture; Business Administration; Business and Commerce; Economics; Engineering; Finance; Graphic Design; Law.** *Maestría*: **Business Administration; Commercial Law; International Business.** *Doctorado*: **Business Administration; Economics.**

Student Services: Academic Counselling, Canteen, Careers Guidance, Language Laboratory, Library, Social Counselling, Sports Facilities

Last Updated: 29/09/15

BOLIVIAN UNIVERSITY OF COMPUTER SCIENCE

Universidad Boliviana de Informática (UBI)
Rosendo Villa No. 146 al 150, Sucre, Chuquisaca
Tel: +591(4) 644-76-70 +591(4) 644-31-61
Fax: +591(4) 644-76-70
EMail: info@ubi.edu.bo
Website: http://www.ubi.edu.bo

Rector: René Pasquier

Programme

Agroindustry Engineering (Agricultural Engineering); **Agronomy** (Agronomy); **Architecture** (Architecture); **Auditing** (Accountancy); **Civil Engineering** (Civil Engineering); **Commercial Engineering** (Business and Commerce); **Hardware Engineering** (Computer Engineering); **Law** (Law); **Medicine** (Medicine); **Social Work** (Social Work); **Software Engineering** (Software Engineering); **Systems Engineering** (Systems Analysis); **Veterinary Science** (Veterinary Science); **Zootechniques** (Zoology)

Further Information: Also branches in El Alto and La Paz

History: Founded 1994.

Main Language(s) of Instruction: Spanish

Degrees and Diplomas: *Técnico Universitario Superior*; *Técnico Universitario Medio*; *Licenciatura*

Last Updated: 04/01/16

BOLIVIAN UNIVERSITY OF TECHNOLOGY

Universidad Tecnológica Boliviana (UTB)
Calle Colombia N° 154, Zona San Pedro, La Paz
Tel: +591(2) 235-7734
Fax: +591(2) 239-0731
EMail: infolp@utb.edu.bo
Website: http://www.utb.edu.bo

Rector: Víctor Kenny La Fuente Cámara
EMail: napaza@utb.edu.bo

Programme

Accountancy (Accountancy); **Business Administration** (Business Administration); **Civil Engineering** (Civil Engineering); **Commerce** (Business Administration; Business and Commerce); **Ecology and Environmental Engineering** (Ecology; Environmental Engineering); **Electronic Engineering** (Electronic Engineering); **Information Systems** (Information Management); **International Business** (International Business); **Law** (Law); **Systems Engineering** (Computer Engineering)

Further Information: Also branch in El Alto

History: Founded 1993.

Degrees and Diplomas: *Técnico Universitario Superior*; *Técnico Universitario Medio*; *Licenciatura*; *Maestría*

Last Updated: 01/10/15

CENTRAL UNIVERSITY

Universidad Central (UNICEN)
Calle Santivañez No 216, Cochabamba
Tel: +591(4) 4252-987
Fax: +591(4) 4254-613
EMail: info@unicen.edu.bo
Website: http://www.unicen.edu.bo

Rector: Walker Romiro Bustamente García
EMail: rector@unicen.edu.bo

Vicerrector: Fernando Molina Guzmán
EMail: deu.cba@unicen.edu.bo

Programme

Accountancy (Accountancy); **Advertising and Marketing** (Advertising and Publicity; Marketing); **Business Administration** (Business Administration); **Commercial Engineering** (Business and Commerce; Finance); **Educational Sciences** (Educational Sciences); **Journalism** (Journalism); **Law** (Law); **Physiotherapy and Rehabilitation** (Physical Therapy; Rehabilitation and Therapy); **Psychology** (Psychology); **Social Work** (Social Work); **Tourism and Hotel Management** (Hotel Management; Tourism)

Further Information: Branches in the cities of La Paz and Santa Cruz de la Sierra

History: Founded 1990.

Academic Year: It is divided in 2 semesters, one begins in Marchand the other in August.

Main Language(s) of Instruction: Spanish

Degrees and Diplomas: *Técnico Universitario Superior*, *Licenciatura*. Also postgrados

Last Updated: 16/09/15

CHRISTIAN UNIVERSITY OF BOLIVIA

Universidad Cristiana de Bolivia (UCEBOL)
Km 5 Carr.al Norte, Santa Cruz, Santa Cruz de la Sierra
Tel: +591(3) 342-6311
Fax: +591(3) 342-2356
EMail: info@ucebol.edu.bo
Website: http://www.ucebol.edu.bo

Rector: Eun Shil Chung

Vicerrector Académico: Wiston Montero

Programme

Agricultural Engineering (Agricultural Engineering; Agronomy); **Biochemistry and Pharmacy** (Biochemistry; Pharmacy); **Business Administration** (Business Administration); **Commercial Engineering** (Business and Commerce); **Computer Engineering** (Computer Engineering); **Dentistry** (Dentistry); **Educational Sciences and Pedagogy** (Educational Sciences; Pedagogy); **Medicine and Surgery** (Medicine; Surgery); **Physiotherapy** (Physical Therapy); **Theology** (Theology); **Tourism** (Tourism)

History: Founded 1990.

Main Language(s) of Instruction: Spanish

Degrees and Diplomas: *Licenciatura*; *Especialización Médica*; *Diplomado*; *Maestría*

Last Updated: 25/09/15

COSMOS PRIVATE TECHNICAL UNIVERSITY

Universidad Técnica Privada Cosmos (UNITEPC)
Av. Blanco Galindo Km 71/2, Florida Norte, Cochabamba
Tel: +591(4) 4370352
Fax: +591(4) 4370325
EMail: info@unitepc.edu.bo
Website: http://www.unitepc.edu.bo

Rector: Hernán García Arce

Vicerrector Académico: Hugo Fuentes Rojas

Faculty
Exact Sciences and Technology (Computer Engineering; Electronic Engineering; Engineering; Sound Engineering (Acoustics)); **Health Sciences** (Dental Technology; Dentistry; Health Sciences; Medicine; Nursing; Physical Therapy; Veterinary Science); **Law, Social Sciences and Political Sciences** (Law; Political Sciences; Social Sciences)

Further Information: Also branch in El Alto

History: Founded 1993.

Main Language(s) of Instruction: Spanish

Degrees and Diplomas: *Técnico Universitario Superior*, *Licenciatura*; *Diplomado*; *Maestria*
Last Updated: 30/09/15

CUMBRE PRIVATE UNIVERSITY

Universidad Privada Cumbre
Av. Cañoto 580 entre Calle México y Av. Centenario, Santa Cruz, Santa Cruz de la Sierra
Tel: +591(3) 3330-088
Fax: +591(3) 336-1319
EMail: info@cumbre.edu.bo
Website: http://www.cumbre.edu.bo

Rectora: Salome Nasica Azogue EMail: luisbert_hf@hotmail.com

Vicerrector: José Samir Makaren Chávez

Programme
Business Administration (Accountancy; Business Administration; Business and Commerce; International Business); **Law** (Law); **Social Communication** (Communication Studies); **Technology** (Computer Engineering)

History: Founded 2001.

Main Language(s) of Instruction: Spanish

Degrees and Diplomas: *Técnico Universitario Superior*, *Licenciatura*; *Diplomado*
Last Updated: 01/10/15

DOMINGO SAVIO S.A. PRIVATE UNIVERSITY

Universidad Privada Domingo Savio S.A. (UPDS)
Av. Beni Tercer Anillo Externo, Santa Cruz de la Sierra, Santa Cruz de la Sierra
Tel: +591(3) 342-6600
Fax: +591(3) 342-6820
EMail: universidad@upds.edu.bo
Website: http://www.upds.edu.bo

Rector: Carlos Cuéllar Aguilera EMail: ccuellar@upds.edu.bo

International Relations: Isabel Estrada, Secretaria General
Tel: +591(3) 342-6600, Ext: 211 EMail: iestrada@upds.edu.bo

Faculty
Business Administration (Accountancy; Advertising and Publicity; Business Administration; Marketing); **Law** (Law); **Social Sciences** (Communication Studies; International Relations; Political Sciences; Psychology; Public Relations; Tourism); **Technology** (Computer Engineering; Environmental Engineering; Industrial Engineering; Petroleum and Gas Engineering; Technology; Telecommunications Engineering)

Further Information: Also branch in Tarija and Potosi

History: Founded 2000.

Main Language(s) of Instruction: Spanish

Degrees and Diplomas: *Licenciatura*; *Diplomado*; *Maestría*; *Doctorado*
Last Updated: 30/09/15

FRANZ TAMAYO PRIVATE UNIVERSITY

Universidad Privada Franz Tamayo (UNIFRANZ)
Calle Héroes del Acre N°1855, esq. Landaeta, Casilla No 4780, La Paz
Tel: +591(2) 487-700 +591(2) 487-744
Fax: +591(2) 492-395
EMail: unifranz@unifranz.edu.bo
Website: http://www.unifranz.edu.bo

Rectora: Verónica Agreda Nogales de Pazos

Vicerrector Académico: Erick Gustavo Montaño

Faculty
Design and Technology Crossroads (Advertising and Publicity; Architecture; Graphic Design; Marketing); **Economics and Business** (Accountancy; Business Administration; Economics; Hotel and Restaurant); **Engineering** (Finance; Systems Analysis); **Health Sciences** (Biochemistry; Dentistry; Medicine; Nursing; Pharmacy); **Law and Social Sciences** (Civil Law; Criminal Law; Education; Law; Psychology)

Further Information: Branches in El Alto, Santa Cruz and Cochabamba

History: Founded 1993.

Main Language(s) of Instruction: Spanish

Degrees and Diplomas: *Técnico Universitario Superior*, *Licenciatura*; *Diplomado*
Last Updated: 30/09/15

LA SALLE UNIVERSITY

Universidad La Salle (ULS)
Av. Jorge Carrasco esq. Las Palmas N°450 (Bolognia), La Paz
Tel: +591(2) 272-3588 +591(2) 277-3672
Fax: +591(2) 277-3671
EMail: info@ulasalle.edu.bo
Website: http://www.ulasalle.edu.bo

Rector: Enrique A. González Álvarez

Vicerrector Académico: José Gil Iñiguez

Programme
Accountancy (Accountancy); **Commerce and Business Administration** (Business Administration; Business and Commerce); **Education** (Education); **Law** (Law); **Psychology** (Psychology); **Systems Engineering** (Computer Engineering); **Tourism** (Tourism)

Further Information: Also branch in El Alto

History: Founded 2003.

Main Language(s) of Instruction: Spanish

Degrees and Diplomas: *Técnico Universitario Superior*, *Licenciatura*; *Diplomado*

Publications: Fides et Ratio
Last Updated: 29/09/15

LATIN AMERICAN PRIVATE OPEN UNIVERSITY

Universidad Privada Abierta Latinoamericana (UPAL)
Av. América N° 524, Cochabamba
Tel: +591(4) 486-100
Fax: +591(4) 116-857
EMail: upal@upal.edu
Website: http://www.upal.edu

Rectora: Patricia Miranda Chávez

Vicerrectora Académica: Miriam Camacho Zenteno

Programme
Biochemistry and Pharmacy (Biochemistry; Pharmacy); **Dentistry** (Dentistry); **Marketing** (Marketing); **Medicine** (Medicine); **Physiotherapy** *(Oruro)* (Physical Therapy); **Psychology** (Psychology); **Social Communication** (Communication Studies; Journalism)

Further Information: Also branch in Oruro

History: Founded 1990.

Admission Requirements: Bachiller and prueba de aptitud académica or equivalent

Fees: (US Dollars): 440-750

Main Language(s) of Instruction: Spanish

Degrees and Diplomas: *Técnico Universitario Superior*, *Licenciatura*; *Diplomado*; *Maestría*

Student Services: Health Services, Sports Facilities

Publications: Revista Cientifica Voces

Last Updated: 29/09/15

LOYOLA UNIVERSITY

Universidad Loyola (UL)

Av. Busch No. 1191, Edificio El Sauce, La Paz

Tel: +591(2) 224-522

Fax: +591(2) 224-522

EMail: uloyola@loyola.edu.bo

Website: http://www.loyola.edu.bo

Rector: Julio Estrada Vásquez EMail: rector@loyola.edu.bo

Vicerrector Académico: Ramiro Aguilar Calderón
EMail: ramiro.aguilar@loyola.edu.bo

Faculty

Administration, Economics and Finance (Accountancy; Administration; Business Administration; Business and Commerce; Economics; Finance); **Natural Sciences** (Agronomy; Environmental Engineering; Food Technology; Natural Sciences; Veterinary Science; Zoology); **Social Sciences** (Communication Studies; Law; Music; Social Sciences); **Technology** (Building Technologies; Civil Engineering; Electronic Engineering; Industrial Engineering; Mechanical Engineering; Surveying and Mapping; Systems Analysis; Technology)

History: Founded 1995.

Main Language(s) of Instruction: Spanish

Degrees and Diplomas: *Licenciatura*; *Diplomado*; *Maestría*

Last Updated: 29/09/15

NATIONAL UNIVERSITY OF ECOLOGY

Universidad Nacional Ecológica

Km. 5 1/2 Carretera a Cotoca, Santa Cruz, Santa Cruz de la Sierra

Tel: +591(3) 349-9199

EMail: info@uecologica.edu.bo

Website: http://www.uecologica.edu.bo/

Rector: Carlos Hugo Molina Saucedo

Programme

Biochemistry (Biochemistry); **Dentistry** (Dentistry); **Environmental Engineering** (Environmental Engineering); **Food Technology** (Food Technology); **Management** (Management); **Medicine** (Medicine); **Nursing** (Nursing); **Nutrition** (Nutrition); **Physical Therapy** (Physical Therapy)

History: Founded 1999.

Main Language(s) of Instruction: Spanish

Degrees and Diplomas: *Técnico Universitario Superior*, *Licenciatura*; *Diplomado*; *Maestría*

Last Updated: 29/09/15

NATIONAL UNIVERSITY OF THE EAST

Universidad Nacional del Oriente (UNO)

Libertad esq. Andrés Ibañez, Santa Cruz, Santa Cruz de la Sierra

Tel: +591(3) 333-7577

Fax: +591(3) 336-8453

EMail: uno@uno.edu.bo

Website: http://www.uno.edu.bo

Rector: Carlos Hurtado Aburdene EMail: rector@uno.edu.bo

Administrative Officer: Carola Vargas Meneses
EMail: vicerrectorado@uno.edu.bo

Faculty

Economics and Finance; **Health Sciences** (Biochemistry; Dental Technology; Dentistry; Health Sciences; Nursing; Pharmacy; Physical Therapy; Rehabilitation and Therapy); **Technology** (Forestry; Systems Analysis; Technology)

Further Information: Also branch in Montero

History: Founded 1997.

Main Language(s) of Instruction: Spanish

Degrees and Diplomas: *Técnico Universitario Superior*, *Licenciatura*

Last Updated: 29/09/15

NUESTRA SEÑORA DE LA PAZ UNIVERSITY

Universidad Nuestra Señora de La Paz (UNSLP)

Calle Presbítero Medina N° 2412, La Paz

Tel: +591(2) 242-323

Fax: +591(2) 241-0255

EMail: unslp@unslp.edu.bo; contacto@unslp.edu.bo

Website: http://www.unslp.edu.bo

Rector: Jorge Paz Navajas

Faculty

Administration and Economics (Administration; Economics); **Architecture and Design** (Architecture; Design; Interior Design); **Engineering** (Environmental Engineering; Food Technology; Industrial Engineering; Systems Analysis); **Medicine** (Medicine); **Odontology** (Dentistry); **Political and Social Sciences** (International Relations; Law; Political Sciences; Public Administration; Social Sciences)

History: Founded 1992.

Main Language(s) of Instruction: Spanish

Degrees and Diplomas: *Técnico Universitario Superior*, *Licenciatura*; *Diplomado*; *Maestría*

Student Services: Library

Last Updated: 29/09/15

NUR UNIVERSITY

Universidad Nur

Av. Cristo Redentor no 100, Santa Cruz, Santa Cruz de la Sierra

Tel: +591(3) 336-3939

Fax: +591(3) 331-1850

EMail: info@nur.edu

Website: http://www.nur.edu

Rector: Willy Shoaie EMail: rectorado@nur.edu

Vicerrector: Gustavo Ortega

Programme

Accountancy (Accountancy); **Administration** (Administration); **Agricultural Economics** (Agricultural Economics); **Finance** (Finance); **International Relations** (International Relations); **Law** (Law); **Marketing** (Marketing); **Public Relations** (Public Relations); **Social Communication** (Communication Studies); **Systems Engineering** (Systems Analysis); **Tourism for Sustainable Development** (Tourism)

Further Information: Also branches in La Paz, Sucre and Cochabamba

History: Founded 1984.

Main Language(s) of Instruction: Spanish

Degrees and Diplomas: *Técnico Universitario Superior*, *Licenciatura*; *Diplomado*

Last Updated: 29/09/15

POSTGRADUATE UNIVERSITY FOR STRATEGIC RESEARCH IN BOLIVIA

Universidad de Postgrado para la Investigación Estratégica en Bolivia (UPIEB)

Av. Arce 2799 esq. Calle Cordero, Edificio Fortaleza piso 6, Of. 601, La Paz

Tel: +591(2) 243-2582

Fax: +591(2) 243-5235

EMail: upieb@upieb.edu.bo

Website: http://www.upieb.edu.bo

Rector: Godofredo Sandoval Zapata

Administrative Officer: Mario Yapu Condo
EMail: marioyapu@upieb.edu.bo

Programme

Economics (Economics); **Social Sciences** (Peace and Disarmament; Social Sciences)

History: Founded 2002. Acquired present status 2011.

Main Language(s) of Instruction: Spanish

Degrees and Diplomas: *Diplomado*: **Educational Research; Social Sciences; Social Studies.** *Maestría*: **Educational Research; Social Sciences.**

Student Services: Library

Publications: Formación y Desarrollo

Last Updated: 29/09/15

PRIVATE UNIVERSITY OF ORURO

Universidad Privada de Oruro (UNIOR)

C. Junín N° 348 esq. Potosí, Oruro
Tel: +591(2) 527-3780
Fax: +591(2) 528-0745
EMail: informaciones@unior.edu.bo; www.unior.edu.bo
Website: http://www.unior.edu.bo

Rectora: Maria Beatriz Cortez EMail: rectorado@unior.edu.bo

Vicerrectora Administrativa: Asunción Ramirez Aliendre
EMail: viceadmin@unior.edu.bo

Vicerrector Académico: Felipe Alfredo Ayala Dorado
EMail: academico@unior.edu.bo

Programme

Accountancy (Accountancy); **Business Administration** (Business Administration; Management); **Law** (Law); **Medicine** (Medicine); **Nursing** (Nursing); **Odontology** (Dentistry); **Systems Engineering** (Computer Engineering)

History: Founded 1999.

Degrees and Diplomas: *Técnico Universitario Superior*, *Licenciatura*

Last Updated: 30/09/15

PRIVATE UNIVERSITY OF SANTA CRUZ DE LA SIERRA

Universidad Privada de Santa Cruz de la Sierra (UPSA)

Casilla Postal 2944, Av. Paraguá y 4° anillo, Zona Parque Industrial, Santa Cruz de la Sierra, Andrés Ibañez 2944
Tel: +591(3) 346-4000
Fax: +591(3) 346-5757
EMail: informaciones@upsa.edu.bo
Website: http://www.upsa.edu.bo

Rector: Lauren Müller de Pacheco
EMail: laurenmuller@upsa.edu.bo

Secretario General: Roberto Antelo Scott
EMail: robertoantelo@upsa.edu.bo

Faculty

Architecture, Design and Town Planning (Architecture; Building Technologies; Industrial Design; Interior Design; Landscape Architecture); **Business Studies** (Accountancy; Advertising and Publicity; Business Administration; Business and Commerce; Economics; Finance; Human Resources; International Business; Marketing); **Engineering** (Civil Engineering; Computer Engineering; Computer Networks; Electronic Engineering; Engineering; Industrial Engineering; Petroleum and Gas Engineering; Systems Analysis; Telecommunications Engineering); **Humanities and Communication** (Communication Studies; Fashion Design; Graphic Design; Journalism; Psychology); **Law** (Law)

Programme

Higher Education (Higher Education)

History: Founded 1984.

Main Language(s) of Instruction: Spanish

Degrees and Diplomas: *Técnico Universitario Superior*, *Licenciatura*; *Especialización*; *Diplomado*: **Business Administration; Design; Engineering; Finance; Higher Education; Human Resources.** *Maestría*: **Business Administration; Commercial Law; Communication Studies.**

Last Updated: 02/11/15

PRIVATE UNIVERSITY OF THE VALLEY

Universidad Privada del Valle (UNIVALLE)

Av. Ayacucho 256, Cochabamba
Tel: +591(4) 431-8800
Fax: +591(4) 431-5886
EMail: relinternational@univalle.edu
Website: http://www.univalle.edu

Rector: Gonzalo Ruiz Martinez EMail: rectoradocba@univalle.edu

International Relations: Marco Vélez Ocampo V.
EMail: relinternacional@univalle.edu

Faculty

Architecture and Tourism *(Trinidad)* (Architecture; Cooking and Catering; Hotel and Restaurant; Interior Design; Landscape Architecture; Tourism; Town Planning); **Architecture and Tourism** *(Cochabamba)* (Architecture; Cooking and Catering; Hotel Management; Interior Design; Landscape Architecture; Tourism; Town Planning); **Architecture and Tourism** *(Sucre)* (Architecture; Cooking and Catering; Hotel and Restaurant; Interior Design; Landscape Architecture; Tourism; Town Planning); **Computer Science and Electronics** *(La Paz)* (Biomedical Engineering; Computer Engineering; Computer Science; Electronic Engineering; Telecommunications Engineering); **Computer Science and Electronics** *(Cochabamba)* (Biomedical Engineering; Computer Engineering; Computer Science; Electronic Engineering; Telecommunications Engineering); **Computer Science and Electronics** *(Trinidad)* (Biomedical Engineering; Computer Engineering; Computer Science; Electronic Engineering; Telecommunications Engineering); **Health Sciences** *(La Paz)* (Biochemistry; Dentistry; Health Sciences; Medicine; Pharmacy; Physical Therapy); **Health Sciences** *(Cochabamba)* (Biochemistry; Dentistry; Health Sciences; Medicine; Pharmacy; Physical Therapy); **Social Sciences and Administration** *(Cochabamba)* (Accountancy; Business Administration; Business and Commerce; Communication Studies; Economics; Finance; Hotel Management; International Business; Journalism; Law; Marketing; Psychology; Tourism); **Social Sciences and Administration** *(Trinidad)* (Administration; Business Administration; Journalism; Law; Social Sciences); **Social Sciences and Administration** *(Sucre)* (Accountancy; Business Administration; Business and Commerce; Communication Studies; Economics; Finance; Hotel Management; International Business; Journalism; Law; Marketing; Psychology; Tourism); **Social Sciences and Administration** *(La Paz)* (Accountancy; Business Administration; Business and Commerce; Communication Studies; Economics; Finance; Hotel Management; International Business; Journalism; Law; Marketing; Psychology; Tourism); **Technology** *(Cochabamba)* (Automation and Control Engineering; Civil Engineering; Computer Engineering; Food Technology; Industrial Engineering; Mechanical Engineering; Petroleum and Gas Engineering); **Technology and Architecture** *(La Paz)* (Architecture; Automation and Control Engineering; Civil Engineering; Computer Engineering; Food Technology; Industrial Engineering; Mechanical Engineering; Petroleum and Gas Engineering; Town Planning)

Further Information: Branches in La Paz, Sucre and Trinidad

History: Founded 1988.

Main Language(s) of Instruction: Spanish

Degrees and Diplomas: *Licenciatura*; *Diplomado*: **Administration; Computer Networks; Higher Education; Law.** *Maestría*: **Business Administration; Commercial Law; Computer Science; Engineering; Finance; Food Science; Higher Education; Information Technology; Marketing; Pharmacy; Social Psychology.** *Doctorado*: **Administration; Economics; Educational Sciences.**

Last Updated: 30/09/15

ROYAL UNIVERSITY

Universidad Real (UREAL)

Capitan Ravelo 2329, Sopocachi, La Paz
Tel: +591(2) 443-635
EMail: info@ureal.edu.bo
Website: http://www.ureal.edu.bo

Rectora: Esmeralda Capriles EMail: ecapriles@ureal.edu.bo

Vicerrectora: Giovanna Torres Salvador
EMail: vicerrectorado@ureal.edu.bo

Programme

Audiovisual Communication (Communication Studies); **Computer Science** (Computer Science); **Financial Administration** (Administration; Finance); **International Trade** (International Business); **Law** (Law); **Marketing** (Marketing); **Tourism and Management** (Tourism)

History: Founded 1999.

Main Language(s) of Instruction: Spanish

Degrees and Diplomas: *Técnico Universitario Superior*: **English; Hotel Management; Marketing; Tourism.** *Licenciatura*: **Business Computing; Cinema and Television; Finance; Hotel Management; International Business; Law; Marketing; Tourism.**

Last Updated: 30/09/15

SAINT PAUL UNIVERSITY

Universidad Saint Paul (USP)

Calle Yanacocha No. 875, La Paz

Tel: +591(2) 228-0787

Fax: +591(2) 228-0787

EMail: uni_saintpaul@hotmail.com

Website: http://www.usp.edu.bo

Rector: Juan Paz Villarroel Rodriguez

EMail: jpwillarroel@hotmail.com

Faculty

Economics and Finance (Accountancy; Business Administration; Economics; Finance); **Engineering** (Civil Engineering; Electronic Engineering; Food Technology; Industrial Engineering; Systems Analysis); **Health Sciences** (Dentistry; Health Sciences; Medicine; Nursing); **Social Sciences** (Communication Studies; Education; Law; Tourism)

History: Founded 2003.

Main Language(s) of Instruction: Spanish

Degrees and Diplomas: *Técnico Universitario Superior*, *Licenciatura*

Last Updated: 30/09/15

COCHABAMBA CAMPUS

Cochabamba

Tel: +591(4) 425-2165

EMail: jpvvillarroel@hotmail.com

Website: http://www.usp.edu.bo

Faculty

Dentistry; **Law** (Law); **Medicine** (Medicine); **Nursing** (Nursing); **System Analysis** (Computer Engineering; Systems Analysis)

Degrees and Diplomas: *Licenciatura*: **Computer Engineering; Dentistry; Law; Medicine; Nursing.**

SALESIAN UNIVERSITY OF BOLIVIA

Universidad Salesiana de Bolivia

Casilla postal 13102, Avda. Chacaltaya N. 1258 (Esq. Ramos Gavilán, Plaza Don Bosco), La Paz

Tel: +591(2) 230-5210

Fax: +591(2) 230-5111

EMail: usalesiana@usb.edu.bo

Website: http://www.usalesiana.edu.bo

Rector: Thelian Argeo Corona Cortés

Vicerrector Académico: José Manuel Rojas

International Relations: Pablo Aranda Manrique

Tel: +591(2) 230-5844 EMail: aranda@hotmail.com

Programme

Accountancy (Accountancy); **Law** (Law); **Psychomotricity, Education and Sports** (Education; Educational Psychology; Physical Education); **Systems Engineering** (Systems Analysis)

Further Information: Also branch in Camiri

History: Founded 1998.

Main Language(s) of Instruction: Spanish

Degrees and Diplomas: *Técnico Universitario Superior*, *Licenciatura*; *Diplomado*; *Maestria*

Last Updated: 30/09/15

SAN FRANCISCO DE ASIS UNIVERSITY

Universidad San Francisco de Asís (USFA)

Casilla postal 5772, Av. 20 de Octubre esq. Belisario Salinas, La Paz

Tel: +591(2) 440-894

Fax: +591(2) 443-773

EMail: info@usfa.edu.bo

Website: http://www.usfa.edu.bo

Rector: Boris Crespo Toranzo

EMail: bcrespo@usfa.edu.bo; rectorado@usfa.edu.bo

Programme

Business Administration (Business Administration); **Commerce** (Business and Commerce); **Educational Sciences** (Educational Sciences); **Journalism** (Journalism); **Law** (Law); **Preschool and Primary Education** (Preschool Education; Primary Education); **Psychology** (Psychology); **Social Communication** (Communication Studies); **Systems Analysis** (Systems Analysis); **Systems Engineering** (Computer Engineering); **Urban Studies** (Urban Studies)

Further Information: Also branch in Tupiza

History: Founded 1998.

Main Language(s) of Instruction: Spanish

Degrees and Diplomas: *Técnico Universitario Superior*, *Licenciatura*; *Diplomado*: **Marketing; Public Administration.** *Maestría*: **Marketing; Public Administration.**

Last Updated: 02/11/15

SAN PABLO BOLIVIAN CATHOLIC UNIVERSITY

Universidad Católica Boliviana San Pablo (UCB)

Casilla Postal 4805, Av. 14 de Septiembre N° 4807 Obrajes, La Paz

Tel: +591(2) 278-3148

Fax: +591(2) 278-3932

EMail: info@ucb.edu.bo

Website: http://www.ucb.edu.bo

Rector: Marco Antonio Fernández Calderón (2013-)

EMail: rector@ucb.edu.bo

Vicerrector: Jesús Muñoz Diez EMail: jmunoz@ucb.edu.bo.

International Relations: Jimena Sainz EMail: rrppint@ucb.edu.bo

Faculty

Economics and Finance (Accountancy; Business Administration; Economics; Finance); **Engineering** (Biomedical Engineering; Chemical Engineering; Civil Engineering; Computer Engineering; Electronic Engineering; Engineering; Environmental Engineering; Industrial Engineering; Mechanical Engineering; Telecommunications Engineering); **Law and Political Science** (Law; Political Sciences); **Social Sciences and Humanities** (Communication Studies; Education; Educational Psychology; Religious Studies; Theology)

School

Production and Competitivity (Business Administration)

Department

Architecture and Graphic Design (Architecture; Graphic Design)

Institute

Democracy (Political Sciences); **Professional Ethics Studies** (Ethics); **Socio-Economic Research** (Economics; Social Studies)

History: Founded 1966. A public institution under the administration of the Conferencia Episcopal de Bolivia.

Academic Year: January to December (January-June; August-December)

Admission Requirements: Secondary school certificate (bachillerato) and entrance examination

Main Language(s) of Instruction: Spanish

Degrees and Diplomas: *Técnico Universitario Superior*, *Licenciatura*; *Especialización*; *Diplomado*; *Maestría*; *Doctorado*: **Computer Engineering; Psychology.**

Student Services: Canteen, Cultural Activities, Health Services, Language Laboratory, Sports Facilities

Last Updated: 25/09/15

COCHABAMBA CAMPUS

Casilla Postal 4105, Avenida América, Esq. General Galindo, Tupuraya, Cochabamba
Tel: +591(4) 293-100
Fax: +591(4) 291-145
Website: http://www.ucbcba.edu.bo

Rector regional: Luis Alfonso Via Reque
EMail: viareque@ucbcba.edu.bo

Faculty

Nursing *(Elizabeth Seton)* (Nursing)

Department

Administration, Economics and Finance (Accountancy; Business Administration; Economics; Finance); **Exact Sciences and Engineering** (Chemical Engineering; Civil Engineering; Computer Engineering; Electronic Engineering; Engineering; Environmental Engineering; Industrial Engineering; Mechanical Engineering; Telecommunications Engineering); **Social Sciences and Humanities** (Anthropology; Educational Administration; Law; Modern Languages; Pedagogy; Philosophy; Psychology; Social Sciences)

Institute

Bioethics (Biology; Ethics); **Missiology** (Missionary Studies); **Research in Applied Computer Science** (Computer Science); **Theological Studies** (Theology)

Centre

Computer Science and Education (Computer Science); **Radio and Television Training Service for Development** *(SECRAD)* (Radio and Television Broadcasting)

History: Founded 1971.

Main Language(s) of Instruction: Spanish

Degrees and Diplomas: *Licenciatura*; *Maestría*; *Doctorado*: **Communication Studies; Information Sciences.**

Student Services: Canteen, Cultural Activities, Health Services, Language Laboratory, Sports Facilities

SANTA CRUZ CAMPUS

Casilla Postal 3201, Calle España 368, Santa Cruz
Tel: +591(3) 337-815
Fax: +591(3) 332-389
Website: http://www.ucbscz.edu.bo

Rector regional: Jorge Ybarnegaray Urquidi
EMail: rector@ucbscz.edu.bo

Academic Regional Head: María Josefina Ortíz

Department

Administration, Economics and Finance (Accountancy; Administration; Economics; Finance); **Architecture** (Architecture); **Exact Sciences and Engineering** (Engineering; Science Education); **Health Sciences** (Dentistry; Medicine)

Institute

Ethics Studies (Ethnology)

History: Founded 1993.

Main Language(s) of Instruction: Spanish

Degrees and Diplomas: *Licenciatura*; *Diplomado*

Student Services: Canteen, Cultural Activities, Health Services, Language Laboratory, Sports Facilities

TARIJA CAMPUS

Calle Colón no 0734, Tarija
Tel: +591(4) 664-7971
EMail: secre@ucbtja.edu.bo
Website: http://www.ucbtja.edu.bo

Rector regional: Enrique Farfán Torrez
EMail: rector@ucbtja.edu.bo

Academic Regional Head: Jose Santos Loaiza
EMail: diracad@ucbtja.edu.bo

Department

Architecture and Town Planning (Architecture; Town Planning); **Engineering and Exact Sciences** (Civil Engineering; Computer Engineering; Electronic Engineering; Environmental Engineering; Industrial Engineering; Mechanical Engineering; Science Education); **Pastoral Studies** (Pastoral Studies); **Social Sciences, Business Administration and Culture** (Business Administration; Finance)

History: Founded 1999.

Main Language(s) of Instruction: Spanish

Student Services: Canteen, Cultural Activities, Health Services, Sports Facilities

SIMON I. PATINO UNIVERSITY

Universidad Simón I. Patiño (USIP)

Av. Villazón Nro 22 Km. 1 a, Sacaba, Cochabamba
EMail: info@usip.edu.bo
Website: http://usip.edu.bo

Rector: Santiago Sologuren Paz

Director académico: Ciro Miranda Uribe

Faculty

Administration and Finance (Business Administration; Finance); **Engineering** (Computer Engineering; Electrical Engineering; Mechanical Engineering; Software Engineering; Telecommunications Engineering); **Law and Social Sciences** (Law); **Natural Resources and Environment** (Bioengineering; Environmental Engineering); **Science and Arts** (Architecture; Mathematics)

History: Founded 2006.

Main Language(s) of Instruction: Spanish

Degrees and Diplomas: *Licenciatura*; *Diplomado*; *Maestría*

Last Updated: 30/09/15

TECHNOLOGICAL PRIVATE UNIVERSITY OF SANTA CRUZ

Universidad Tecnológica Privada de Santa Cruz (UTEPSA)

Casilla postal 4146, 3er Anillo Interno entre Av. Busch y Av. San Martin, Santa Cruz, Santa Cruz de la Sierra
Tel: +591(3) 341-1919, Ext:1640
Fax: +591(3) 341-1919
EMail: informaciones@utepsa.edu
Website: http://www.utepsa.edu

Rector: Antonio Carvalho Suárez EMail: rectorado@utepsa.edu

Vicerrector, Administración y Finanzas: Hussein Rezvani
EMail: hrezvani@utepsa.edu

International Relations: Claudia Quezada, Vicerrector
EMail: cquezada@utepsa.edu; international@utepsa.edu

Faculty

Economics, Finance and Administration *(FEFA)* (Accountancy; Administration; Advertising and Publicity; Business and Commerce; Economics; Finance; Human Resources; International Business; Marketing; Tourism); **Law and Social Sciences** (International Relations; Law); **Science and Technology** (Computer Engineering; Computer Networks; Computer Science; Electronic Engineering; Industrial Engineering; Management Systems; Petroleum and Gas Engineering; Telecommunications Engineering)

History: Founded 1994, acquired present status 2001.

Academic Year: February to December (February-July; August-December)

Admission Requirements: Secondary school certificate (bachillerato)

Fees: (US Dollars): 416 per semester

Main Language(s) of Instruction: Spanish

Degrees and Diplomas: *Técnico Universitario Superior*; *Licenciatura*; *Diplomado*; *Maestría*

Student Services: Academic Counselling, Canteen, Careers Guidance, Cultural Activities, Facilities for disabled people, Foreign Studies Centre, Health Services, Language Laboratory, Nursery Care, Sports Facilities

Publishing house: Imprenta El Deber

Last Updated: 01/10/15

UNIVERSITY OF THE ANDES

Universidad de Los Andes (UNANDES)

Avenida los Leones No 10, Zona Obrajes, La Paz
Tel: +591(2) 278-7308 +591(2) 278-7135
Fax: +591(2) 278-7308
EMail: info@udelosandes.edu.bo
Website: http://www.udelosandes.edu.bo

Rector: Pedro Saénz Muñoz

Vicerrectora: Maria Ester Burela de Hubner

Faculty

Automotive Engineering (Automotive Engineering); **Business** (Business Administration; Business and Commerce; Business Computing; Management; Marketing; Public Administration); **Gastronomy and Hotel Management** (Cooking and Catering; Hotel and Restaurant; Hotel Management); **Law** (Law)

History: Founded 2002.

Main Language(s) of Instruction: Spanish

Degrees and Diplomas: *Técnico Universitario Superior*, *Licenciatura*; *Diplomado*

Last Updated: 25/09/15

UNIVERSITY OF THE CORDILLERA

Universidad de la Cordillera (UCORDILLERA)

Chaco No 1161, La Paz
Tel: +591(2) 215-2278 +591(2) 241-6973
EMail: info@cordillera.edu.bo
Website: http://www.ucordillera.edu.bo

Rector: Paola Vargas Huamán

Programme

Anthropology (Anthropology); **Business Administration** (Business Administration); **Economics** (Economics); **History and Geography** (Geography; History); **Political Science and Philosophy** (Philosophy; Political Sciences); **Social Communication** (Communication Studies); **Sociology** (Sociology)

History: Founded 1997.

Main Language(s) of Instruction: Spanish

Degrees and Diplomas: *Licenciatura*; *Diplomado*

Last Updated: 25/09/15

Bosnia and Herzegovina

STRUCTURE OF HIGHER EDUCATION SYSTEM

Description:

According to the Framework Law on Higher Education in BiH ("Official Gazette of BiH", No. 59/07), higher education institutions in Bosnia and Herzegovina comprise universities and colleges. The title "university" is limited to the higher education institutions undertaking both teaching and research, offering academic degrees in all three cycles, while the title "college" (visoka skola) is limited to higher education institutions accredited to offer first cycle diplomas and degrees. All higher education activities are subject to national (Republic Srpska) or cantonal (in the Federation of B&H) laws. Access to higher education is granted to all students having completed four years of secondary school.

Stages of studies:

University level first stage: *First cycle*
The first cycle leading to the academic title of completed undergraduate studies (Bachelor's degree) is obtained after three to four years of full time study following a secondary school leaving certificate. It is valued between 180 and 240 ECTS credit points. Studies in Medical Sciences are longer and valued at 360 ECTS credit points.

University level second stage: *Second cycle*
The second cycle leads to the academic title of Master or equivalent. It is obtained after the completion of undergraduate studies and one or two years' study and has a value of 60 to 120 ECTS credit points, in such a way that the total number of credits obtained when adding the ones obtained in the first cycle amounts to 300 ECTS points.

University level third stage: *Third cycle*
The third cycle leads to the academic degree of Doctor or equivalent. The studies last for three years and are valued at 180 ECTS credit points. The public defence of a doctoral thesis is required.

ADMISSION TO HIGHER EDUCATION

Admission to university-level studies:

Name of secondary school credential required: Svjedočanstvo

Foreign students admission:

Definition of foreign student: All those who do not possess Bosnian and Herzegovinan citizenship

RECOGNITION OF STUDIES

Quality assurance system:

In the Republic of Srpska, the recognition bodies are higher education institutions and the Ministry of Education and Culture of the Republic of Srpska. For the purpose of further studies, higher education institutions at which holders of qualifications want to continue their studies are responsible for recognition. For professional purposes, there is the Committee for Information and Recognition of Documents in Higher Education.

In the Federation of Bosnia and Herzegovina, higher education is at the cantonal level. There are ten cantons and every canton is competent for the recognition of qualifications on its own teritory. Furthermore, some cantons have their own laws on recognition of foreign qualifications, some use the old Law on Recognition from 1988 as Bosnia and Herzegovina existed as one of six republics of former Yugoslavia and one canton still doesn't have a law on recognition because there is no higher education institution on its teritory and for professional purposes, recognition is conducted in other cantons or by other entities. Regarding the Brcko District of Bosnia and Herzegovina, there also is no law on recognition, so the holders of qualifications have to have their qualifications recognized by one of two entities: the Republic of Srpska or the Federation of Bosnia and Herzegovina.

Bodies dealing with recognition:

Ministarstvo prosvjete i kulture Republike Srpske (Ministry of Education and Culture of the Republic of Srpska)

Ministarstvo obrazovanja, nauke, kulture i sporta Unsko-sanskog kantona (Ministry of Education, Science, Culture and Sport of the Una-Sana Canton)

Ministarstvo prosvjete, znanosti, kulture i športa Županije Posavske (Ministry of Education, Science, Culture and Sport of the Posavina Canton)

Ministarstvo obrazovanja, nauke, kulture i sporta Tuzlanskog kantona (Ministry of Education, Science, Culture and Sport of the Tuzla Canton)

Ministarstvo za obrazovanje, nauku, kulturu i sport Zeničko-dobojskog kantona (Ministry of Education, Science, Culture and Sport of the Zenica-Doboj Canton)

Ministarstvo za obrazovanje, mlade, nauku, kulturu i sport Bosansko-podrinjskog kantona (Ministry of Education, Youth, Science, Culture and Sport of the Bosnian-Podrinje Canton)

Ministarstvo obrazovanja, nauke, kulture i sporta Srednjobosanskog Kantona (Ministry of Education, Science, Culture and Sport of the Central Bosnia Canton)

Ministarstvo obrazovanja, nauke, kulture i sporta Hercegovačko-neretvanskog kantona/županije (Ministry of Education, Science, Culture and Sport of the Herzegovina-Neretva Canton)

Ministarstvo obrazovanja, znanosti, kulture i športa Županije Zapadnohercegovačke (Ministry of Education, Science, Culture and Sport of the West Herzegovina Canton)

Ministarstvo za obrazovanje, nauku i mlade Kantona Sarajevo (Ministry for Education, Science and Youth of the Sarajevo Canton)

Ministarstvo znanosti, prosvjete, kulture i športa Hercegbosanske županije (Ministry of Education, Science, Culture and Sport of the Hercegbosnian Canton)

Special provisions for recognition:

Recognition for university level studies: stipulated by recognition laws and the internal provisions of higher education institutions (access requirements).

For access to advanced studies and research: stipulated by the recognition laws and the internal provisions of higher education institutions (access requirements).

For exercising a profession: stipulated by the recognition laws.

NATIONAL BODIES

Ministarstvo Civilnih Poslova BiH (Ministry of Civil Affairs of Bosnia and Herzegovina)

Minister: Adil Osmanovic
TRG BiH I
Sarajevo 71000
Tel: +387(33) 221-073
Fax: +387(33) 221-074
EMail: zorica.rulj@mcp.gov.ba
WWW: http://www.mcp.gov.ba

Federalno Ministarstvo Obrazovanja i Nauke (Federal Ministry of Education and Science)

Minister: Elvira Dilberović
Dr. Ante Starčevića bb
Mostar
Tel: +387(36) 355-700
Fax: +387(36) 355-742
EMail: info@fmon.gov.ba; kabinet@fmon.gov.ba
WWW: http://www.fmon.gov.ba

Ministarstvo prosvjete i kulture Republike Srpske (Ministry of Education and Culture of the Republic of Srpska)

Ministarstvo obrazovanja, nauke, kulture i sporta Unsko-sanskog kantona (Ministry of Education, Science, Culture and Sport of the Una-Sana Canton)

Ministarstvo prosvjete, znanosti, kulture i športa Županije Posavske (Ministry of Education, Science, Culture and Sport of the Posavina Canton)

Ministarstvo obrazovanja, nauke, kulture i sporta Tuzlanskog kantona (Ministry of Education, Science, Culture and Sport of the Tuzla Canton)

Ministarstvo za obrazovanje, nauku, kulturu i sport Zeničko-dobojskog kantona (Ministry of Education, Science, Culture and Sport of the Zenica-Doboj Canton)

Ministarstvo za obrazovanje, mlade, nauku, kulturu i sport Bosansko-podrinjskog kantona (Ministry of Education, Youth, Science, Culture and Sport of the Bosnian-Podrinje Canton)

Ministarstvo obrazovanja, nauke, kulture i sporta Srednjobosanskog Kantona (Ministry of Education, Science, Culture and Sport of the Central Bosnia Canton)

Ministarstvo obrazovanja, nauke, kulture i sporta Hercegovačko-neretvanskog kantona/županije (Ministry of Education, Science, Culture and Sport of the Herzegovina-Neretva Canton)

Ministarstvo obrazovanja, znanosti, kulture i športa Županije Zapadnohercegovačke (Ministry of Education, Science, Culture and Sport of the West Herzegovina Canton)

Ministarstvo za obrazovanje, nauku i mlade Kantona Sarajevo (Ministry for Education, Science and Youth of the Sarajevo Canton)

Ministarstvo znanosti, prosvjete, kulture i športa Hercegbosanske županije (Ministry of Education, Science, Culture and Sport of the Hercegbosnian Canton)

Agencija za Razvoj Visokog Obrazovanja i Osiguranje Kvaliteta Bosne i Hercegovine (Agency for the Development of Higher Education and Quality Assurance)

Director: Husein Nanic
Public Relations: Slavica Škoro
Ulica akademika Jovana Surutke 13
Banjaluka 78000
Tel: +387(51) 430-510
Fax: +387(51) 462-302
EMail: info@hea.gov.ba
WWW: http://www.hea.gov.ba

Role of national body: The Agency for the Development of Higher Education and Quality Assurance, as an autonomous administrative organization, shall among other things assist the relevant education authorities in the process of accreditation and licensing of higher education institutions, establish criteria and standards for quality assurance, provide advice and recommendations for removal of drawbacks in the quality of studies and higher education institutions, and the like.

Centar za informisanje/informiranje i priznavanje dokumenata iz oblasti/područja visokog obrazovanja (Centre for Information and Recognition of Qualifications in Higher Education)

Director: Borko Sorajić
Head of Department for Information and Cooperation: Dženan Omanović
Kneza Branimira 12
Mostar 88000
Tel: +387(36) 333-980
Fax: +387(36) 333-991
EMail: dzenan.omanovic@cip.gov.ba
WWW: http://www.cip.gov.ba

Data for academic year: 2014-2015

Source: IAU from Centre for Information and Recognition of Qualifications in Higher Education, Mostar, 2015. Bodies 2015.

INSTITUTIONS

PUBLIC INSTITUTIONS

DŽEMAL BIJEDIĆ UNIVERSITY OF MOSTAR

Univerzitet Džemal Bijedić, Mostar
USRC "Mithad Hudjur Hujka", 88 104 Mostar
Tel: +387(36) 570-727
Fax: +387(36) 570-032
EMail: info@unmo.ba
Website: http://www.unmo.ba

Rektor: Fuad Ćatović (2011-) EMail: Fuad.Catovic@unmo.ba

Secretary General: Zoran Kazazić
EMail: Zoran.Kazazic@unmo.ba

Faculty
Agro-Mediterranean (Agriculture; Mediterranean Studies); **Business Management** (Business Administration); **Civil Engineering** (Civil Engineering); **Humanities** (Arts and Humanities; Communication Studies; English; History; Theatre); **Information Technology** (Information Technology); **Law** (Law); **Mechanical Engineering** (Mechanical Engineering)

Department
Information Technology (Information Technology)

Academy
Teacher Training (Pedagogy)

History: Founded 1977. Previously the Advanced School for Pedagogy.

Admission Requirements: Secondary school certificate

Fees: (Konvertibilna Marka): 100 per annum for full-time; part-time, 800

Main Language(s) of Instruction: Bosanski, Hrvatski, Srpski

Degrees and Diplomas: *Degree of Bachelor*: **Agriculture; Arts and Humanities; Civil Engineering; Economics; Information Technology; Law; Mechanical Engineering; Mediterranean Studies; Teacher Training.** *Master*

Student Services: Canteen, Language Laboratory

Publications: Monografija; Pregledi Predavanja

Last Updated: 10/02/15

UNIVERSITY OF BANJA LUKA

Univerzitet u Banjoj Luci
Bulevar vojvode Petra Bojovića 1A, 78000 Banja Luka
Tel: +387(51) 321-112
Fax: +387(51) 315-694
EMail: info@unibl.rs
Website: http://www.unibl.org

Rektor: Stanko Stanić EMail: mirjanicd@blic.net

Generalni Sekretar: Dušanka Dragić

Faculty
Agriculture (Animal Husbandry; Crop Production; Rural Studies); **Architecture and Civil Engineering** (Architecture; Civil Engineering); **Economics** (Economics); **Electrical Engineering** (Computer Science; Electrical Engineering; Information Technology; Power Engineering; Telecommunications Engineering); **Forestry** (Forestry); **Law** (Law); **Mathematics and Natural Sciences** (Mathematics; Natural Sciences); **Mechanical Engineering** (Mechanical Engineering); **Medicine** (Medicine); **Mining** (Mining Engineering); **Philology** (English; French; German; Italian; Literature; Philology; Serbocroatian); **Philosophy** (History; Pedagogy; Philosophy; Preschool Education; Psychology); **Physical Education and Sports** (Physical Education; Sports); **Political Science** (Journalism; Political Sciences; Social Work; Sociology); **Technology** (Biotechnology; Environmental Engineering; Food Technology; Technology; Textile Technology)

Institute
Genetic Resources (Genetics)

Academy
Arts (Fine Arts; Music; Theatre)

History: Founded 1975, incorporating faculties formerly attached to the University of Sarajevo.

Academic Year: October to September

Admission Requirements: Svjedočanstvo and entrance examination

Fees: (Konvertibilna Marka): 300 per semester

Main Language(s) of Instruction: Serbian

Accrediting Agency: Agencija za razvoj visokog obrazovanja i osiguranje kvaliteta Bosne i Hercegovina

Degrees and Diplomas: *Degree of Bachelor*, *Master*, *Doktor*: **Information Technology.**

Student Services: Cultural Activities, Health Services, Sports Facilities

Last Updated: 10/02/15

UNIVERSITY OF BIHAĆ

Univerzitet u Bihaću
Pape Ivana Pavla II 2/II, 77000 Bihać
Tel: +387(37) 222-022
Fax: +387(37) 222-022
EMail: rektorat@unbi.ba
Website: http://www.unbi.ba

Rektor: Refik Šahinović EMail: refik.sahinovic@unbi.ba

Generalni Sekretar: Asija Cucak EMail: asija.cucak@unbi.ba

International Relations: Ekrem Pehlić
EMail: ekrem.pehlic@unbi.ba

Faculty
Biotechnology (Biotechnology); **Economics** (Economics); **Education** *(Islamic)* (Education); **Law** (Law); **Pedagogy** (Pedagogy); **Technical Engineering** (Engineering; Technology)

College
Nursing (Nursing)

History: Founded 1997.

Admission Requirements: Secondary school certificate (Maturska Svjedodzba)

Main Language(s) of Instruction: Bosnian

Degrees and Diplomas: *Degree of Bachelor*, *Master*, *Doktor*

Student Services: Academic Counselling, Canteen, Cultural Activities, Health Services, Nursery Care, Sports Facilities

Publications: Research Papers

Last Updated: 10/02/15

UNIVERSITY OF EAST SARAJEVO

Univerzitet u Istočnom Sarajevu
Vuka Karadžića 30, Lukavica, 71123 Istočno Sarajevo
Tel: +387(57) 340-464
Fax: +387(57) 340-263
EMail: univerzitet@paleol.net
Website: http://www.ues.rs.ba/en/university/about-university/university-management

Rector: Radoslav Grujić EMail: radslav.grujic@ues.rs.ba

Faculty
Agriculture (Agriculture); **Business and Economics** (Business and Commerce; Economics); **Dental Medicine** *(Foca)* (Dentistry); **Economics** *(Brcko)* (Economics); **Economics** *(Pale)* (Economics); **Education** (Education); **Electrical Engineering** (Electrical Engineering); **Law** *(Pale)* (Law); **Mechanical Engineering** (Mechanical Engineering); **Medicine** *(Foca)* (Medicine); **Orthodox Theology** *(St. Basil of Ostrog (Foca))* (Orthodox Theology); **Philosophy** *(Pale)* (Philosophy); **Physical Education and Sports** *(Pale)* (Physical Education; Sports); **Production and Management** *(Trebinje)* (Management; Production Engineering); **Technology** *(Zvornik)*

(Technology); **Transport and Traffic Engineering** *(Doboj)* (Transport Engineering; Transport Management)

Academy

Fine Arts *(Trebinje)* (Fine Arts); **Music** (Music); **Theology** *(Srbinje)* (Theology)

Accrediting Agency: Agencija za razvoj visokog obrazovanja i osiguranje kvaliteta Bosne i Hercegovina

Degrees and Diplomas: *Degree of Bachelor, Master, Doktor.* **Agriculture; Dentistry; Economics; Medicine; Nursing; Philology.**

Last Updated: 11/02/15

UNIVERSITY OF MOSTAR

Sveučilište u Mostaru
Trg hrvatskih velikana 1, 88000 Mostar
Tel: +387(36) 310-778
Fax: +387(36) 320-885
EMail: mail@sve-mo.ba
Website: http://www.sve-mo.ba

Rektor: Ljerka Ostojić EMail: rektor@sve-mo.ba

Faculty

Agronomy (Agricultural Economics; Agriculture; Animal Husbandry; Food Technology; Plant and Crop Protection); **Civil Engineering** (Civil Engineering; Construction Engineering; Design; Industrial Engineering; Production Engineering); **Computer Engineering and Mechanical Engeenering** (Computer Engineering; Information Technology; Mechanical Engineering); **Economics** (Accountancy; Economics; Finance; Management; Marketing); **Health Science** (Health Sciences; Nursing; Physical Therapy; Radiology); **Law** (Law); **Medicine** (Medicine); **Natural Science and Pedagogy** (Archaeology; Art History; Biology; Chemistry; Computer Science; Education; English; Geography; German; History; Journalism; Latin; Literature; Mathematics; Music; Pedagogy; Physics; Preschool Education; Primary Education; Psychology; Slavic Languages; Teacher Training); **Philosophy** (Philosophy)

Academy

Fine Arts (Art History; Fine Arts; Graphic Design; Painting and Drawing; Sculpture)

History: Founded 1977, acquired present title 1992.

Main Language(s) of Instruction: Croatian

Degrees and Diplomas: *Degree of Bachelor, Master, Doktor.* **Agronomy; Ecology; Economics; Geography; Pedagogy.**

Last Updated: 10/02/15

UNIVERSITY OF SARAJEVO

Univerzitet u Sarajevu
Obala Kulina Bana 7/II, 71000 Sarajevo
Tel: +387(33) 663-392
Fax: +387(33) 663-393
EMail: rektorat@unsa.ba
Website: http://www.unsa.ba

Rector: Muharem Avdispahic EMail: kabinet.rektora@unsa.ba

Faculty

Agriculture (Agriculture); **Architecture and Town Planning** (Architecture; Town Planning); **Civil Engineering** (Civil Engineering); **Criminology** (Criminology); **Dentistry** (Dentistry); **Economics** (Economics); **Electrical Engineering** (Automation and Control Engineering; Computer Science; Electrical Engineering; Electronic Engineering; Information Sciences; Telecommunications Engineering; Telecommunications Services); **Forestry** (Forestry; Horticulture); **Law** (Law); **Mechanical Engineering** (Automotive Engineering; Mechanical Engineering; Production Engineering; Wood Technology); **Medicine** (Medicine); **Natural Sciences and Mathematics** (Biology; Chemistry; Geography; Mathematics; Natural Sciences; Physics); **Pharmacy** (Pharmacy); **Philosophy** (Education; English; Germanic Languages; History; Library Science; Literature; Middle Eastern Studies; Philosophy; Psychology; Romance Languages; Slavic Languages; Sociology); **Physical Education** (Physical Education); **Political Science** (Journalism; Military Science; Political Sciences; Social Work; Sociology); **Transport and Communication** (Transport and Communications; Transport Engineering); **Veterinary Medicine** (Veterinary Science)

School

Nursing (Nursing)

Institute

Crime against Humanity Research and International Law (Criminology; International Law); **Genetic Engineering and Biotechnology** (Biotechnology; Genetics); **History** (History); **Oriental Research** (Oriental Studies)

Academy

Drama (Acting; Theatre); **Fine Arts** (Fine Arts); **Music** (Music); **Pedagogy** (Pedagogy)

History: Founded 1949.

Academic Year: September to June

Admission Requirements: Secondary school certificate (Maturska Svjedodzba) or recognized equivalent and entrance examination

Fees: None

Main Language(s) of Instruction: Bosnian

Accrediting Agency: Agencija za razvoj visokog obrazovanja i osiguranje kvaliteta Bosne i Hercegovina

Degrees and Diplomas: *Degree of Bachelor, Master, Doktor.* **Agriculture; Archaeology; Biology; Business and Commerce; Chemistry; Civil Engineering; Conducting; Economics; Electronic Engineering; Food Science; Geography; History; Law; Management; Mathematics; Music Theory and Composition; Musical Instruments; Musicology; Philosophy; Physics; Postal Services; Psychology; Railway Transport; Road Transport; Sociology; Structural Architecture; Telecommunications Services.**

Student Services: Canteen, Cultural Activities, Health Services

Publications: Bibliography of Doctoral Thesis; Lecture Review

Last Updated: 10/02/15

UNIVERSITY OF TUZLA

Univerzitet u Tuzli
Muharema Fizovića Fiska 6, 75000 Tuzla, Tuzla Canton
Tel: +387(35) 300-500
Fax: +387(35) 300-547
EMail: rektorat@untz.ba
Website: http://www.untz.ba

Rektor: Enver Halilović

General Secretary: Jasmina Berbič

International Relations: Mensura Aščerić, Vice-Rector

Faculty

Economics (Accountancy; Finance; Management; Marketing); **Electrical Engineering** (Computer Engineering; Power Engineering); **Law** (Law); **Mechanical Engineering** (Mechanical Engineering; Power Engineering; Production Engineering); **Medicine** (Medicine); **Mining, Geology and Civil Engineering** (Civil Engineering; Geology; Health Sciences; Hydraulic Engineering; Mining Engineering; Safety Engineering); **Pharmacy** (Pharmacy); **Philosophy** (Computer Science; English; Foreign Languages Education; German; History; Journalism; Literature; Pedagogy; Psychology; Slavic Languages; Social Work; Teacher Training; Technology Education; Turkish); **Science** (Biology; Chemistry; Geography; Mathematics; Physics); **Special Education and Rehabilitation** (Rehabilitation and Therapy; Special Education); **Sport and Physical Education** (Physical Education; Sports); **Technology** (Agronomy; Chemical Engineering; Ecology; Environmental Engineering; Food Technology)

Academy

Performing Arts (Acting; Film)

History: Founded 1976, incorporating former faculties of the University of Sarajevo. Became Faculty of Mining 1960, Faculty of Medicine 1976. Acquired present status and title 2000.

Academic Year: September to June (September-February; February-June)

Admission Requirements: Secondary school diploma (Maturska Svjedodzba)

Fees: (Konvertibilna Marka): 1,200-4,000 per annum

Main Language(s) of Instruction: Bosnian, Serbian, Croatian

Degrees and Diplomas: *Degree of Bachelor*: **Biology; Civil Engineering; Economics; Electrical Engineering; English; Geography; Geology; German; History; Journalism; Law; Mathematics Education; Mechanical Engineering; Mining Engineering; Native Language Education; Pedagogy; Psychology; Science Education; Social Work; Technology; Turkish.** *Master*, *Doktor*: **Medicine.**

Student Services: Canteen, Careers Guidance, Cultural Activities, Facilities for disabled people, Health Services, Sports Facilities
Last Updated: 10/02/15

UNIVERSITY OF ZENICA

Univerzitet u Zenici (UNZE)
Fakultetska 1, 72000 Zenica, Zenica-Doboj Canton
Tel: +387(32) 449-420
Fax: +387(32) 449-425
EMail: rektorat@unze.ba
Website: http://www.unze.ba

Rector: Dževad Zecic EMail: dzevad.zecic@unze.ba
Secretary-General: Medina Arnaut EMail: mediha.arnaut@unze.ba

Faculty

Economics (Accountancy; Business Administration; Economics); **Education** (Arts and Humanities; Computer Science; Education; Educational Sciences; Literature; Mathematics; Mathematics and Computer Science; Modern Languages; Teacher Training); **Health** (Health Administration; Medicine); **Islamic Pedagogy** (Islamic Studies; Religion; Religious Education); **Law** (Law); **Mechanical Engineering** (Maintenance Technology; Mechanical Engineering); **Metallurgy and Materials Science** (Engineering; Materials Engineering; Metal Techniques; Metallurgical Engineering; Mining Engineering; Production Engineering; Technology; Vocational Counselling; Welfare and Protective Services; Wood Technology); **Philosophy** (Philosophy); **Polytechnic** (Civil Engineering)

History: Founded 2000.

Admission Requirements: Secondary school certificate or equivalent

Fees: (Euros): 750-1,000 per semester for postgraduate courses

Main Language(s) of Instruction: Bosnian, Serbian and Croatian

Accrediting Agency: Agencija za razvoj visokog obrazovanja i osiguranje kvaliteta Bosne i Hercegovina

Degrees and Diplomas: *Degree of Bachelor*: **Economic and Finance Policy; Environmental Engineering; Foreign Languages Education; Law; Materials Engineering; Mechanical Engineering; Metallurgical Engineering.** *Master*

Student Services: Academic Counselling, Canteen, Facilities for disabled people, Health Services, Language Laboratory, Nursery Care, Sports Facilities

Publications: Didakticki Putokazi - Didactical Trends; Mechanical Engineering Journal
Last Updated: 11/02/15

PRIVATE INSTITUTIONS

AMERICAN UNIVERSITY IN BOSNIA AND HERZEGOVINA

Americki Univerzitet u Bosni i Hercegovini (AUBIH)
Fra Anđela Zvizdovića 1, 71000 Sarajevo
Tel: + 387(33) 296-415
Fax: + 387(33) 296-416
EMail: contact@aubih.edu.ba
Website: http://www.aubih.edu.ba

President: Esmir Ganić

College

International Law *(Banja Luka)* (International Law)

School

Economics *(American)* (Economics; Finance; International Business; International Economics; Marketing; Sales Techniques); **Government** *(American)* (International Law; International Relations; Political Sciences; Public Administration); **Technology** *(American)* (Industrial Management; Information Technology)

Institute

Research and Development (Comparative Law; Economics; European Studies; Information Technology; Media Studies; Public Administration)

Academy

Modern Art *(American)* (Graphic Arts; Graphic Design; Journalism; Media Studies; Multimedia)

Further Information: Also branches in Banja Luka, Mostar and Tuzla

Academic Year: October-mid January; February-May

Degrees and Diplomas: *Degree of Bachelor*, *Master*, *Doktor*. Some degrees are issued by the State University of New York
Last Updated: 09/02/15

HERZEGOVINA UNIVERSITY

Sveučilište Hercegovina
Blajburških žrtava 100, 88000 Mostar
Tel: +387 (36) 83 33 91
EMail: rektorat@hercegovina.edu.ba
Website: http://hercegovina.edu.ba/hr/

Rector: Milenko Brkić

Faculty

International Relations and Diplomacy (International Relations); **Social Sciences** (Social Sciences)

Degrees and Diplomas: *Degree of Bachelor*, *Master*, *Doktor*: **International Relations; Social Sciences.**
Last Updated: 10/02/15

INDEPENDENT UNIVERSITY OF BANJA LUKA

Nezavisni Univerzitet Banja Luka
Ulica Veljka Mlađenovića 12 E, 78000 Banja Luka
Tel: +387(51) 456-600
Fax: +387(51) 456-602
EMail: info@nubl.org
Website: http://www.nubl.org/
Rector: Žarko Pavić

Faculty

Computer Science (Computer Science; Software Engineering); **Ecology** (Ecology); **Economics** (Accountancy; Banking; Business Administration; Economics; Finance; Insurance; Management); **Political Sciences** (Political Sciences); **Social Sciences** (Social Sciences)

History: Founded 2005.

Accrediting Agency: Agencija za razvoj visokog obrazovanja i osiguranje kvaliteta Bosne i Hercegovina

Degrees and Diplomas: *Degree of Bachelor*, *Master*
Last Updated: 09/02/15

INTERNATIONAL BURCH UNIVERSITY

Internacionalni Burč univerzitet (IBU)
Francuske revolucije bb, Ilidža, 71000 Sarajevo
Tel: +387(33) 782-100
Fax: +387(33) 782-131
EMail: info@ibu.edu.ba
Website: http://www.ibu.edu.ba

Rector: Mehmet Uzunoğlu EMail: rector@ibu.edu.ba

Faculty

Economics and Social Sciences (Banking; Business Administration; Economics; European Studies; Finance; International Business; International Relations; Management); **Education** (Education; English; Literature; Oriental Languages; Philology); **Engineering and Information Technology** (Architecture; Bioengineering; Electrical and Electronic Engineering; Engineering; Genetics; Information Technology)

History: Founded 2008.

Admission Requirements: High School Diploma

Fees: 1,500-3,600 depending on programmes (Euro)

Accrediting Agency: Agencije za razvoj visokog obrazovanja i osiguranje kvaliteta Bosne i Hercegovine

Degrees and Diplomas: *Degree of Bachelor, Master, Doktor*: **Architecture; Bioengineering; Electrical and Electronic Engineering; English; Genetics; Information Technology; Turkish.**

Student Services: Canteen, Sports Facilities

Last Updated: 09/02/15

INTERNATIONAL UNIVERSITY OF GORAZDE

Internacionalni univerzitet u Goraždu
Ibrahima Čelika bb, 73000 Goražde
EMail: info@univerzitetgorazde.com
Website: http://univerzitetgorazde.com

Rector: Mehmed Avdagić

Faculty

Economics (Banking; Economics; Management); **Educational Sciences** (Psychology; Turkish); **Engineering** (Architecture; Building Technologies; Construction Engineering; Electrical Engineering; Surveying and Mapping); **Health Sciences** (Dentistry; Medicine; Pharmacy); **Law** (Law)

Degrees and Diplomas: *Degree of Bachelor, Master, Doktor*

Last Updated: 09/02/15

INTERNATIONAL UNIVERSITY OF SARAJEVO

Internacionalni Univerzitet u Sarajevu (IUS)
Paromlinska 66, 71000 Sarajevo
Tel: +387(33) 720 600
Fax: +387(33) 720 625
EMail: info@ius.edu.ba
Website: http://www.ius.edu.ba/

Rector: Yücel Oğurlu EMail: rector@ius.edu.ba

International Relations: Edina Hadžiahmetović, Manager, Quality Assurance Office EMail: ehadziahmetovic@ius.edu.ba

Faculty

Arts and Social Sciences (Cultural Studies; English; Literature; Political Sciences; Social Sciences; Visual Arts); **Business and Administration** (Economics; International Relations; Leadership; Management); **Engineering and Natural Sciences** (Bioengineering; Biology; Computer Engineering; Computer Science; Industrial Engineering; Materials Engineering; Microelectronics)

School

English Language (English)

History: Founded 2004.

Academic Year: September to June

Accrediting Agency: Agencije za razvoj visokog obrazovanja i osiguranje kvaliteta Bosne i Hercegovine

Degrees and Diplomas: *Degree of Bachelor, Master, Doktor*: **Architecture; Bioengineering; Computer Engineering; Computer Science; Cultural Studies; Economics; Electrical and Electronic Engineering; English; Genetics; International Relations; Leadership; Literature; Management; Mechanical Engineering; Political Sciences; Psychology; Social Sciences; Visual Arts.**

Last Updated: 09/02/15

INTERNATIONAL UNIVERSITY OF TRAVNIK

Internacionalni Univerzitet Travnik
Bunar bb - Dolac, 72 270 Travnik
Tel: +387(30) 540-586
Website: http://www.iu-travnik.com

Rector: Ibrahim Jusufranic

Faculty

Ecology (Ecology); **Economics** (Banking; Economics; Finance; Management; Marketing; Tourism); **Law** (Law); **Media and Communications** (Communication Studies; Media Studies); **Polytechnic Sciences** (Architecture; Automation and Control Engineering; Electronic Engineering; Energy Engineering); **Traffic** (Transport Engineering; Transport Management)

History: Founded 2006. Acquired present status and title 2010.

Degrees and Diplomas: *Degree of Bachelor, Master, Doktor*: **Banking; Communication Studies; Ecology; Economics; Engineering; Finance; History; Management; Marketing; Media Studies.**

Last Updated: 09/02/15

PAN-EUROPEAN UNIVERSITY APEIRON

Panevropski univerzitet Apeiron
Pere Krece 13, 78102 Banja Luka
Tel: +387(51) 430-890
Fax: +387(51) 430-891
EMail: info@apeiron-uni.eu
Website: http://www.apeiron-uni.eu/

Rector: Dragan Danelišen EMail: risto.k@apeiron-uni.eu

Vice-Rector: Esad Jakupovic

College

Business Economics (Banking; Business Administration; Finance; Management; Public Administration); **Computer Science** (Computer Education; Computer Science; Information Technology); **Health Care and Nursing** (Health Administration; Health Sciences; Medical Technology; Nursing; Occupational Therapy; Physical Therapy; Sanitary Engineering); **Law** (Commercial Law; Law); **Philology** (Philology); **Sports** (Sports; Sports Management)

History: Founded 2007.

Degrees and Diplomas: *Degree of Bachelor, Master, Doktor*: **Computer Science; Law; Nursing.**

Last Updated: 09/02/15

SARAJEVO SCHOOL OF SCIENCE AND TECHNOLOGY (SSST)

Bistrik 7, 71000 Sarajevo
Tel: +387(33) 563-030
Fax: +387(33) 563-033
EMail: admissions@ssst.edu.ba
Website: http://ssst.edu.ba/

Rector: Ejup Ganić

Department

Computer Science (Computer Science); **Economics** (Economics); **Engineering** (Electrical and Electronic Engineering; Energy Engineering; Engineering; Environmental Engineering; Mathematics; Mechanical Engineering); **Information Systems** (Information Technology; Systems Analysis); **Modern Languages** (English; German); **Political Sciences and International Relations** (International Relations; Political Sciences)

Institute

Conflict Resolution, Responsibility and Reconciliation *(Balkan)* (Peace and Disarmament)

History: Founded 2004.

Degrees and Diplomas: *Degree of Bachelor, Master, Doktor*: **Economics; Electrical Engineering; International Relations; Political Sciences.** In cooperation with the University of Buckingham, SSST organizes postgraduate study for a Master of Science (MSc) and Doctor's degree

Last Updated: 09/02/15

SLOBOMIR P UNIVERSITY

Slobomir P Univerzitet
PF 70, Pavlovica put bb, 76300 Slobimir
Tel: +387(55) 231-101
Fax: +381(55) 231-176
EMail: info@spu.ba
Website: http://www.spu.ba

Rector: Desanka Trakilovic EMail: desanka.trakilovic@spu.ba

Faculty

Economics and Management (Business Computing; Economics; Management; Marketing); **Information Technology** (Information Technology); **Law** (Law); **Phillology** (English; Philology)

Academy
Arts (Cinema and Television; Design; Graphic Design; Music; Theatre); **Fiscal** (Taxation)

History: Founded 2003.

Degrees and Diplomas: *Degree of Bachelor*, *Master*, *Doktor*. **Economics; Law; Management; Philology.**
Last Updated: 09/02/15

UNIVERSITY FOR BUSINESS ENGINEERING AND MANAGEMENT (PIM)

Univerzitet za poslovni inženjering i menadžment Banja Luka
Banja Luka
Website: http://univerzitetpim.com/

Rector: Zarko Pavic EMail: zarkopavic@yahoo.com

Pro-Rector: Ilija Dzombic EMail: idzombic@yahoo.com

Programme
Economics (Economics); **Finance and Banking** (Banking; Finance); **Graphic Arts and Design** (Design; Graphic Arts; Industrial Design); **Law** (Law); **Management** (Management); **Marketing** (Marketing); **Psychology** (Psychology)

History: Founded 2003. Acquired present status 2007.
Last Updated: 10/04/15

UNIVERSITY ITC INTERLOGOS CENTER IN KISELJAK

ITC-Interlogos centar Sveučilište/Univerzitet Kiseljak
Kiseljak
Tel: +387 (0) 30 877 670
Fax: +387 (0) 30 877 673
EMail: info@itc.edu.ba
Website: http://www.itc.edu.ba/

Degrees and Diplomas: *Degree of Bachelor*
Last Updated: 10/04/15

UNIVERSITY OF BIJELJINA

Univerzitet Bijeljina
Pavlovica put bb, 76300 Bijeljina
Tel: +387(55) 355 222
EMail: sekretar@ubn.rs.ba
Website: http://www.ubn.rs.ba/

Director: Ljiljana Tomic

Faculty
Agriculture (Agricultural Economics; Agriculture); **Health Studies** (Nursing); **Pharmacy** (Pharmacy); **Psychology** (Psychology)

Degrees and Diplomas: *Degree of Bachelor*
Last Updated: 10/02/15

UNIVERSITY OF BUSINESS STUDIES

Univerzitet za poslovne studije Banja Luka
Ul. Jovana Dučića br. 25, 78000 Banja Luka
Tel: +387(51) 222-537
EMail: ups@univerzitetps.com
Website: http://www.univerzitetps.com/

Rector: Radovan Klincov EMail: rektor@univerzitetps.com

Faculty
Applied Economics (Economics); **Business and Financial Studies** (Business Administration; Finance); **Ecology** (Ecology); **Information Technology and Design** (Information Technology); **Journalism and Communication** (Communication Studies; Journalism); **Law** (Law); **Tourism and Hotel Management** (Hotel Management; Tourism)
History: Founded 2005.

Accrediting Agency: Agencija za razvoj visokog obrazovanja i osiguranje kvaliteta Bosne i Hercegovina

Degrees and Diplomas: *Degree of Bachelor*, *Master*
Last Updated: 10/02/15

UNIVERSITY OF MODERN SCIENCES CKM - MOSTAR

Univerzitet modernih znanosti CKM - Mostar
Mostar
Website: http://web.ckm.ba

UNIVERSITY OF TRAVNIK

Univerzitet u Travniku
Alley consul no. 5, Travnik
EMail: info@unt.ba
Website: http://www.unt.ba

Rector: Rasim Dacic

Faculty
Education (Education); **Law** (Law); **Management and Business Economics** (Business and Commerce; Economics; Management); **Pharmacy and Health** (Dentistry; Health Sciences; Pharmacy; Physical Therapy; Radiology); **Technology** (Computer Science; Textile Technology)

History: Founded 2007. Acquired present status 2010.

Degrees and Diplomas: *Degree of Bachelor*, *Master*, *Doktor*. **Biomedicine; Economics; Law; Management.**
Last Updated: 10/02/15

UNIVERSITY SINERGIJA

Univerzitet Sinergija
Raje Baničića, Bijeljina
Tel: +387(55) 213-132
Fax: +387(55) 224-571
EMail: office@sinergija.edu.ba
Website: http://www.sinergija.edu.ba

Rector: Milovan Stanišic EMail: mstanisic@sinergija.edu.ba

Faculty
Business Economics (Accountancy; Business Administration; Marketing); **Computing and Informatics** (Computer Science); **Drama and Film Arts** (Film; Theatre); **Law** (Law); **Philology** (Philology)

Accrediting Agency: Agencija za razvoj visokog obrazovanja i osiguranje kvaliteta Bosne i Hercegovina

Degrees and Diplomas: *Degree of Bachelor*, *Master*. MBA programmes with Lincoln University
Last Updated: 10/02/15

VITEZ UNIVERSITY

Sveučilište/Univerzitet "Vitez"
Ulica školska 23, 72270 Travnik
Tel: +387(30) 509-750
EMail: info@unvi.edu.ba
Website: http://unvi.edu.ba/en/

Rector: Mirko Puljić

Faculty
Business Economics (Accountancy; Agricultural Management; Banking; Business Administration; Economics; Finance; Insurance; Management; Marketing; Public Administration; Tourism); **Business Informatics** (Business Computing; Computer Science; Information Technology); **Health Care** (Gynaecology and Obstetrics; Health Administration; Health Sciences; Nursing; Occupational Therapy; Physical Therapy); **Law** (Law)

Degrees and Diplomas: *Degree of Bachelor*, *Master*, *Doktor*
Last Updated: 10/02/15

Botswana

STRUCTURE OF HIGHER EDUCATION SYSTEM

Description:

Higher education falls under the mandate of the Tertiary Education Council. In 2008, the Council prepared the White Paper on Tertiary Education. Higher education is offered at both public and private institutions.

Stages of studies:

University level first stage: *First Degree*

Bachelor's degrees are offered after four years' study or five years in the case of Law and Engineering.

University level second stage: *Postgraduate Level*

At postgraduate level, there are one-year Postgraduate programmes and one-and-a-half to three-year Master programmes. A PhD (Doctor of Philosophy) may be obtained after the Master's degree and a minimum period of three to four years' research devoted to preparing a thesis.

ADMISSION TO HIGHER EDUCATION

Admission to university-level studies:

Name of secondary school credential required: Botswana General Certificate of Secondary Education

Minimum score/requirement: Grade B

For entry to: BA (Humanities or Social Sciences)/BSc/BEd/BNS, etc

Foreign students admission:

Definition of foreign student: All students who are not Botswana nationals.

Quotas: At University level all foreign students are free to apply.

Entry regulations: Visas are required for some countries.

Language proficiency: Students must be proficient in English.

RECOGNITION OF STUDIES

Quality assurance system:

The Tertiary Education Council (TEC) is responsible for the registration of tertiary institutions and the quality assurance of programmes of learning. All institutions interested in offering tertiary education from Diploma programmes and above are required to register with the Tertiary Education Council. The institutions would go through a process of accreditation after three years of registration or one year of operation.

NATIONAL BODIES

Ministry for Education and Skills Development

Minister: Unity Dow
Building Block 6, Private Bag 005
Government enclave
Gaborone
Tel: +267 365 5440
Fax: +267 365 5458
WWW: http://www.gov.bw/en/Ministries–Authorities/Ministries/Ministry-of-Education-and-Skills-Development/

Tertiary Education Council - TEC

Executive Secretary: Patrick D. Molutsi
Private Bag BR 108
Gaborone

Tel: +267 393-0741
Fax: +267 393-0814
EMail: info@tec.org.bw
WWW: http://www.tec.org.bw
Role of national body: Parastatal body responsible for the coordination of Tertiary Education and for determining and maintening standards of teaching, examination and research in tertiary institutions in Botswana.

Data for academic year: 2012-2013
Source: IAU from the website of the Tertiary Education Council and IBE, 2012. Bodies 2016.

INSTITUTION

PUBLIC INSTITUTION

UNIVERSITY OF BOTSWANA (UB)

Private Bag 0022, Gaborone
Tel: +267(31) 355-0000
Fax: +267(31) 395-6591
EMail: webadmin@mopipi.ub.bw
Website: http://www.ub.bw

Vice-Chancellor: Thabo T. Fako (2011-)
Tel: +267(31) 355-2032
EMail: vc@mopipi.ub.bw

Director, Public Affairs: Mhitshane Reetsang (2009-)
Tel: +267(31) 355-2286
EMail: directorpa@mopipi.ub.bw

Executive Assistant: Gaboikanngwe G. Maphakwane
Tel: +267 (31) 355 4799 +267 (31) 395 2252
EMail: maphakwg@mopipi.ub.bw

Faculty

Business (Accountancy; Business Administration; Business and Commerce; International Business; Management; Marketing; Tourism); **Education** (Adult Education; Education; Educational Administration; Educational Sciences; Family Studies; Home Economics; Physical Education; Primary Education; Science Education; Secondary Education; Special Education); **Engineering and Technology** (Architecture; Civil Engineering; Construction Engineering; Design; Electrical Engineering; Electronic Engineering; Engineering; Geological Engineering; Industrial Design; Industrial Engineering; Mechanical Engineering; Mining Engineering; Real Estate; Regional Planning; Technology; Town Planning); **Health Sciences** (Environmental Studies; Health Sciences; Laboratory Techniques; Medicine; Nursing); **Humanities** (African Languages; Archaeology; Arts and Humanities; Chinese; English; Environmental Studies; French; History; Information Management; Information Sciences; Library Science; Media Studies; Performing Arts; Religious Studies; Sociology; Theology; Visual Arts); **Science** (Biological and Life Sciences; Biology; Chemistry; Computer Science; Environmental Studies; Geology; Information Management; Mathematics; Microbiology; Natural Sciences; Physics; Statistics); **Social Sciences** (Demography and Population; Development Studies; Economics; Law; Political Sciences; Psychology; Public Administration; Social Sciences; Social Work; Sociology; Statistics)

School

Graduate Studies; **Medicine** (Medicine)

Centre

Academic Development; **Continuing Education**

Research Centre

Okavango Research Institute; **Research and Development**

Further Information: Also Legal Clinic and Business Clinic

History: Founded 1964 as University of Basutoland, Bechuanaland and Swaziland. Acquired present status and title 1982.

Academic Year: August to May (August-December; January-May)

Admission Requirements: Botswana General Certificate of Secondary Education (BGCSE); Cambridge Overseas School Certificate (COSC) or General Certificate of Education (GCE) or recognized foreign equivalent. Direct entrance to second year on completion of studies in another tertiary Institution

Fees: National: c.9,350-24,470 per annum (Pula), International: 14,025-48,940 per annum (Pula)

Main Language(s) of Instruction: English

Degrees and Diplomas: *Bachelor's Degree*: **Accountancy; Civil Engineering; Computer Science; Construction Engineering; Education; Educational Administration; Electrical and Electronic Engineering; Environmental Studies; Finance; Fine Arts; Geophysics; Hotel and Restaurant; Information Sciences; Information Technology; Law; Library Science; Management; Marketing; Mechanical Engineering; Medical Technology; Medicine; Meteorology; Mining Engineering; Nursing; Physical Education; Physics; Primary Education; Social Work; Tourism.** *Post-Graduate Diploma*: **Education.** *Master's Degree*: **Biological and Life Sciences; Chemistry; Education; Fine Arts; Law; Mathematics; Medicine; Natural Resources; Nursing; Paediatrics; Pathology; Philosophy; Physics; Public Health; Statistics.** *PhD*. Also Certificates

Student Services: Academic Counselling, Canteen, Careers Guidance, Facilities for disabled people, Foreign Studies Centre, Health Services, Social Counselling, Sports Facilities

Academic Staff *2010-2011*	MEN	WOMEN	**TOTAL**
FULL-TIME	813	–	**813**
Student Numbers *2010-2011*			
All (Foreign included)	6,934	8,797	**15,731**

BOTSWANA COLLEGE OF AGRICULTURE (BCA)

Private Bag 0027, Gaborone
Tel: +267(31) 365-0100
Fax: +267(31) 392-8753
Website: http://www.bca.bw

Principal: Ricks G. Chabo (2009-)

Department

Agricultural Economics, Education and Extension *(AEE)* (Agricultural Economics; Agricultural Education); **Agricultural Engineering and Land Planning** *(AEL)* (Agricultural Education; Agricultural Engineering; Agricultural Equipment; Agriculture; Food Science; Harvest Technology; Power Engineering; Soil Science; Water Management); **Animal Science and Production** (Animal Husbandry; Cattle Breeding; Zoology); **Basic Sciences** (Biology; Botany; Chemistry; Mathematics; Natural Sciences; Physics); **Crop Science and Production** (Agronomy; Crop Production; Forestry; Horticulture; Plant and Crop Protection; Soil Science); **Food Science & Technology** (Food Science; Food Technology)

Centre

In-service and Continuing Education

Further Information: Animal Health Clinic and Ambulatory Services

History: Founded 1967 as Botswana Agricultural College. Acquired present status and title 1991.

Degrees and Diplomas: *Bachelor's Degree*: **Agricultural Business; Agricultural Economics; Agricultural Education; Agricultural Equipment; Agriculture; Crop Production; Veterinary Science.** *Master's Degree*: **Agricultural Education; Agricultural Engineering; Crop Production; Veterinary Science.**

Student Services: Academic Counselling, Canteen, Careers Guidance, Facilities for disabled people, Health Services, Social Counselling, Sports Facilities

Academic Staff *2010-2011*	MEN	WOMEN	**TOTAL**
FULL-TIME	75	28	**103**
Student Numbers *2010-2011*			
All (Foreign included)	625	385	**1,010**

Brazil

STRUCTURE OF HIGHER EDUCATION SYSTEM

Description:

Higher education is under the responsibility of the Ministry of Education (MEC). It is provided in public federal, state, municipal or confessional and private universities and other higher education institutions, foundations, federations and independent establishments. It is organized at two levels: Graduação (undergraduate) programmes which take usually from 4 to 6 years of study and Pós-graduação (graduate) programmes lasting for 1 and 1/2 to 4 years following upon a first degree. Post-secondary professional education (curso superiore de tecnologia) is also available.

Stages of studies:

University level first stage: *Graduação (Bacharel)*

The first stage of higher education leads to the award of a Bacharelado which is usually obtained after four to six years of study, depending on the institution and the field of study (Odontology and Agriculture, four years; Architecture and Law, five years; Medicine, six years).

University level second stage: *Pós-graduação (Certificado de Especialização; Mestrado; Doutorado)*

The second stage leads to the Certificado de Especialização after studies lasting between 360 hours to 2 years. The Mestrado is awarded upon completion of 1 and 1/2 to two years' study following upon the Bacharelado. The Doutorado, the highest degree, is awarded upon completion of four years' study and research and the submission of a thesis following upon the Mestrado.

ADMISSION TO HIGHER EDUCATION

Admission to university-level studies:

Name of secondary school credential required: Certificado de Ensino Médio

Minimum score/requirement: 3 in Portuguese, 3 in another discipline and above 1 in all the others.

For entry to: All courses

Name of secondary school credential required: Técnico de Nivel Medio

Admission requirements: Results of ENEM (Exame Nacional do Ensino Médio), and/or Concurso Vestibular.

Numerus clausus: A Numerus clausus is applied if/when there are more candidates than available places. Overall achievement in secondary school and the Matura or final examination results are taken into account. According to the Regulations on Studies of Foreigners, the number of foreign students must not exceed 5% of all full-time study places available (and 50% of part-time study places).

Other requirements: Good knowledge of Portuguese.

Foreign students admission:

Admission requirements: Foreign students must hold a secondary school-leaving certificate that is recognized by the Ministry of Education and pass an examination (Concurso Vestibular) comprising papers in Portuguese language and Brazilian History and Geography. Students from Latin American and African countries which have signed cultural agreements with Brazil are exempted from this examination and from paying tuition fees.

Language proficiency: Foreign students must have a good command of Portuguese.

RECOGNITION OF STUDIES

Quality assurance system:

The Ministry of Education is responsible for the quality assessment of higher education, with CONAES being in charge of evaluating undergraduate courses and CAPES of graduate courses.

Bodies dealing with recognition:

Ministério da Educação (Ministry of Education)

Esplanada dos Ministérios
Bloco L, 8° Andar - Gabinete
Brasília 70047-900

Tel: +55(61) 2022-7828
EMail: gabinetedoministro@mec.gov.br
WWW: http://portal.mec.gov.br/

Comissão Nacional de Avaliação do Ensino Superior - CONAES (National Commission for the Evaluation of Higher Education)

Edifício Sede do Conselho Nacional de Educação - CNESGAS, Av. L2 Sul, Quadra 607, Lote 50 - Térreo - Sala 16
Brasilia 70200-670
Tel: +55 (61) 2022-7680
Fax: +55 (61) 2022-7796
EMail: conaes@mec.gov.br
WWW: http://portal.mec.gov.br/conaes-comissao-nacional-de-avaliacao-da-educacao-superior

Coordenação de Aperfeiçoamento de Pessoal de Nível Superior - CAPES (Coordination for the Improvement of Higher Education Personnel)

Setor Bancário Norte
Quadra 2, Bloco L, Lote 06, Edifício Capes
Brasilia 70040-020
WWW: http://www.capes.gov.br

Special provisions for recognition:

Recognition for university level studies: Access to university-level studies is based on secondary school certification and the passing of examinations in each institution.

For access to advanced studies and research: Graduate study diploma.

For exercising a profession: Professional diploma.

NATIONAL BODIES

Ministério da Educação (Ministry of Education)

Minister: Aloizio Mercadante
Secretario de Educaçao Superior: Jesualdo Pereira Farias
Esplanada dos Ministérios
Bloco L, 8° Andar - Gabinete
Brasília, DF 70047-900
Tel: +55(61) 2022-7828
EMail: gabinetedoministro@mec.gov.br
WWW: http://portal.mec.gov.br/

Associação Brasileira das Universidades Comunitárias - ABRUC (Brazilian Association of Community Universities)

President: Pedro Rubens Ferreira Oliveira
Executive Secretary: José Carlos Aguilera
Setor de Clubes Sul, Trecho 3, Conjunto 6, Associação Médica do Brasîlia
Brasilia 70200-003
Fax: +55 (61) 3349-3300
EMail: se@abruc.org.br
WWW: http://www.abruc.org.br/
Role of national body: Represents 66 not-for-profit community universities (ICES).

Associação Nacional dos Dirigentes das Instituições Federais de Ensino Superior - ANDIFES (National Association of Heads of Federal Higher Education Institutions)

President: Maria Lucia Cavalli Neder
Executive Secretary: Gustavo Henrique de Sousa Balduino
SCS, Quadra 01, Bloco K, Ed. Denasa, N° 30, 8° andar
Brasilia, DF 70398-900
Tel: +55(61) 3321-6341

EMail: andifes@andifes.org.br
WWW: http://www.andifes.org.br
Role of national body: Created in 1989, it represents 2 CEFETs, 2 IFETS and 63 federal universities.

Conselho de Reitores das Universidades Brasileiras - CRUB (Brazilian University Rectors' Conference)
President: Benedito Guimarães Aguiar Neto
Executive Secretary: Fernanda Figueirêdo Torres Póvoa
Prédio da Associação Médica de Brasília (AMBr), Setor de Clubes Esportivos Sul Trecho 3, Conj. 06, 3° andar
Brasília, DF 70200-003
Tel: +55(61) 3349-9010
Fax: +55(61) 3274-4621
EMail: crub@crub.org.br
WWW: http://www.crub.org.br
Role of national body: Created in 1966, it promotes exchanges and cooperation between Brazilian universities.

Coordenação de Aperfeiçoamento de Pessoal de Nível Superior - CAPES (Coordination for the Improvement of Higher Education Personnel)
President: Carlos A. Nobre
Setor Bancário Norte
Quadra 2, Bloco L, Lote 06, Edifício Capes
Brasilia, DF 70040-020
WWW: http://www.capes.gov.br
Role of national body: In charge of the development and strengthening of post-graduate education (Masters and Doctorates) throughout the country.

Instituto Nacional de Estudos e Pesquisas Educacionais Anísio Teixeira - INEP (National Educational Research Institute)
President: José Francisco Soares
Director, Higher Education Evaluation (DAES): Claudia Maffini Griboski
SIG Quadra 04 lote 327
Zona Industrial
Brasilia, DF 70610-908
WWW: http://portal.inep.gov.br/
Role of national body: Studies and conducts research on the educational system to inform policies.

Data for academic year: 2015-2016
Source: IAU from the website of the Ministry of Education and Education system Brazil (https://www.epnuffic.nl/en/publications/education-system-brazil.pdf), NUFFIC, 2015.

INSTITUTIONS

PUBLIC INSTITUTIONS

ALAGOAS STATE UNIVERSITY OF HEALTH SCIENCES

Universidade Estadual de Ciências da Saúde de Alagoas (UNCISAL)
Campus Governador Lamenha Filho, Rua Doutor Jorge de Lima, 113, Trapiche da Barra, Maceió, Alagoas 57010-300
Tel: +55(82) 3315-6701 +55(82) 3315-6705 +55(82) 3315-6702
Fax: +55(82) 3315-6704
EMail: ecmal@zipmail.com.br
Website: http://www.uncisal.edu.br

Reitor: Paulo José Medeiros de Souza Costa
Tel: +55(82) 3315-6703 EMail: reitoria@uncisal.edu.br

Pró-Reitora de Gestão Administrativa: Lavínia Guimarães
Tel: +55(82) 3315-6708 EMail: progad@uncisal.edu.br

Centre
Distance Education (Education; Health Administration; Health Sciences; Information Technology); **Health Sciences** (Health Sciences; Medicine; Nursing; Occupational Therapy; Physical Therapy; Rehabilitation and Therapy; Speech Therapy and Audiology); **Integrated Sciences** (Anatomy; Biological and Life Sciences; Microbiology); **Technology** (Biological and Life Sciences; Biomedicine; Management; Nursing; Radiology; Systems Analysis)

History: Founded 1970

Main Language(s) of Instruction: Portuguese

Degrees and Diplomas: *Técnico de Nivel Medio*; *Tecnólogo*; *Bacharelado*; *Licenciatura*; *Especialização/Aperfeiçoamento*: **Biological and Life Sciences; Educational Technology; Gerontology; Higher Education Teacher Training; Pharmacology; Statistics.** Also Medical Residencies

Last Updated: 01/04/16

ANTONINO FREIRE INSTITUTE OF EDUCATION

Instituto Superior de Educação Antonino Freire (ISEAF)
Praça Firmina Sobreira, s/n, Matinha, Teresina, PI 64002-190
Tel: +55(86) 3216-3271
EMail: iseaf2004@yahoo.com.br
Website: http://www.iseaf.pi.gov.br

Diretora Geral: Maria Aurilucia Moreira da Silva

Course

Teacher Training (Teacher Training)

History: Founded 1915.

Main Language(s) of Instruction: Portuguese

Degrees and Diplomas: *Licenciatura*

Student Services: eLibrary
Last Updated: 12/04/16

CELSO SUCKOW DA FONSECA FEDERAL CENTRE OF TECHNOLOGICAL EDUCATION

Centro Federal de Educação Tecnológica Celso Suckow da Fonseca (CEFET/RJ)
Avenida Maracanã 229, Maracanã,
Rio de Janeiro, Rio de Janeiro 20271-110
Tel: +55(21) 2568-8890
Fax: +55(21) 2204-0978
EMail: sespi@cefet-rj.br
Website: http://www.cefet-rj.br

Director: Carlos Henrique Figueiredo Alves

Vice-Director: Maurício Saldanha Motta

Unit

Itaguai (Mechanical Engineering); **Maracanã** (Automation and Control Engineering; Civil Engineering; Computer Science; Electrical Engineering; Electronic Engineering; Environmental Management; Industrial Management; Information Technology; Mechanical Engineering; Production Engineering; Telecommunications Engineering); **Nova Friburgo** (Physics; Tourism); **Nova Iguaçu** (Automation and Control Engineering; Production Engineering); **Petrópolis** (Physics; Tourism)

Further Information: Also branches in Maria da Graça and Nova Iguaçu

History: Founded 1909. Acquired present status 1978.

Academic Year: March to December

Admission Requirements: Secondary school certificate

Main Language(s) of Instruction: Portuguese

Accrediting Agency: Ministério de Educação (MEC), Coordenação Nacional de Aperfeiçoamento de Pessoal de Nível Superior (CAPES); Instituto Nacional de Estudos e Pesquisas Educacionais (INEP)

Degrees and Diplomas: *Bacharelado*; *Licenciatura*; *Mestrado*: **Education; Electrical Engineering; Materials Engineering; Mathematics Education; Mechanical Engineering; Optics; Social Sciences; Technology.** *Doutorado*: **Education; Natural Sciences; Optics; Technology.**

Student Services: Academic Counselling, Canteen, Careers Guidance, Facilities for disabled people, Health Services, Language Laboratory, Library, Nursery Care, Sports Facilities

Publications: Tecnologia & Cultura
Last Updated: 18/06/15

DARCY RIBEIRO STATE UNIVERSITY OF THE NORTH OF THE STATE OF RIO DE JANEIRO

Universidade Estadual do Norte Fluminense Darcy Ribeiro (UENF)
Av. Alberto Lamego, 2000, Parque Califórnia,
Campos dos Goytacazes, Rio de Janeiro 28013-602
Tel: +55(24) 2739-7010 +55(24) 2739-7002 +55(24) 2739-7006
Fax: +55(24) 2739-7173
EMail: uenf@uenf.br; prograd@uenf.br
Website: http://www.uenf.br

Reitor: Luis Passoni
Tel: +55(22) 2739-7003 EMail: reitoria@uenf.br

Diretora Geral de Administração: Patrícia Gonçalves Magalhães
Tel: +55(22) 2739-7014 EMail: dgadiretor@uenf.br; dga@uenf.br

Vice-Reitor: Teresa de Jesus Peixoto Faria
Tel: +55(22) 2739-7006 EMail: reitoria@uenf.br

International Relations: Carlos Logullo, Assessor para Relações Internacionais Tel: +55(22) 2748-6004 EMail: assaii@uenf.br

Centre

Agricultural Sciences and Technologies (CCTA) (Agronomy; Animal Husbandry; Veterinary Science); **Biosciences and Biotechnology (CBB)** (Biological and Life Sciences; Biology); **Human Sciences (CCH)** (Pedagogy; Public Administration; Social Sciences); **Science and Technology (CCT)** (Biological and Life Sciences; Chemistry; Civil Engineering; Computer Science; Mathematics; Mathematics Education; Metallurgical Engineering; Petroleum and Gas Engineering; Physics; Production Engineering; Science Education)

History: Founded 1990. A State institution.

Academic Year: Secondary school certificate and entrance examination

Fees: None

Main Language(s) of Instruction: Portuguese

Degrees and Diplomas: *Bacharelado*; *Licenciatura*; *Mestrado*: **Animal Husbandry; Biological and Life Sciences; Biotechnology; Botany; Civil Engineering; Cognitive Sciences; Ecology; Genetics; Horticulture; Materials Engineering; Natural Resources; Natural Sciences; Petroleum and Gas Engineering; Political Sciences; Production Engineering; Social Policy; Sociology.** *Doutorado*: **Animal Husbandry; Biological and Life Sciences; Biotechnology; Botany; Civil Engineering; Ecology; Genetics; Horticulture; Materials Engineering; Natural Resources; Natural Sciences; Petroleum and Gas Engineering; Political Sciences; Sociology.**

Student Services: Cultural Activities, IT Centre, Language Laboratory, Library, Social Counselling, Sports Facilities
Last Updated: 01/03/16

EUCLID FACULTY OF CUNHA

Faculdade Euclides da Cunha (FEUC)
Avenida Dep. Eduardo Vicente Nasser, 1020,
São José do Rio Pardo, SP
Tel: +55(19) 3608-4704
EMail: direcao@feucriopardo.edu.br;
vicediretora@feucriopardo.edu.br; lidia@feucriopardo.edu.br
Website: http://www.feucriopardo.edu.br

Diretora: Isabela Custódio Talora Bozzini
EMail: diretor@feucriopardo.edu.br

Course

Administration (Business Administration); **Art** (Fine Arts); **Biology** (Biology); **Commercial Management** (Business and Commerce); **History** (History); **Letters** (Literature); **Pedagogy** (Pedagogy); **Physical Education** (Physical Education); **Physics** (Physics)

History: Founded 1964 as Faculdade de Filosofia, Ciências e Letras de São José do Rio Pardo. Acquired present title 2005.

Main Language(s) of Instruction: Portuguese

Degrees and Diplomas: *Tecnólogo*; *Bacharelado*; *Licenciatura*. Also Especialização offered through Universidade de São Caetano do Sul (USCS)

Student Services: IT Centre, Library
Last Updated: 01/12/15

FACULTIES OF THE EDUCATIONAL FOUNDATION OF MOCOCA

Faculdades da Fundação de Ensino de Mococa (FAFEM)
Praça Madre Cabrini N°87, Vila Mariana,
Mococa, São Paulo 13730-330
Tel: +55(19) 3656-5516
EMail: direcao@fafem.com.br
Website: http://www.fafem.com.br

Diretor: Jorge dos Santos Gomes Soares

Course
Accountancy (Accountancy); **Administration** (Administration); **Computer Science** (Computer Science); **Literature** (Literature); **Pedagogy** (Pedagogy)

History: Founded 1972 as Instituto de Ensino Superior de Mococa. Acquired present status and title 2002.

Main Language(s) of Instruction: Portuguese

Degrees and Diplomas: *Bacharelado*; *Licenciatura*; *Especialização/Aperfeiçoamento*

Last Updated: 11/06/15

FACULTY OF AGRICULTURE OF ARARIPINA

Faculdade de Ciências Agrárias de Araripina (FACIAGRA)

Avenida Florentino Alves Batista, s/n Campus Universitário Centro, Araripina, PE 56280-000
Tel: +55(81) 3873-1001
Fax: +55(81) 3873-1001
EMail: aeda@htnet.com.br
Website: http://www.portalaeda.com.br

Diretora: Serliete de Carvalho Mendes Schneider
Tel: +55(87) 3873-0440

Course
Agronomy (Agriculture; Agronomy); **Environmental Management** (Environmental Management)

History: Founded 1986.

Main Language(s) of Instruction: Portuguese

Accrediting Agency: Ministry of Education

Degrees and Diplomas: *Bacharelado*

Last Updated: 23/10/15

FACULTY OF ANICUNS

Faculdade de Anicuns (FECHA)

Avenida Bandeirantes, 1140, Setor Roosevelt, Anicuns, Goiás 76170-000
Tel: +55(62) 3564-1499
Fax: +55(62) 3564-2522
EMail: contatos@faculdadeanicuns.edu.br
Website: http://www.faculdadeanicuns.edu.br

Diretora: Ana Mônica Beltrão da Silva

Course
Accountancy (Accountancy); **Business Administration** (Administration; Business Administration); **Law** (Law); **Pedagogy** *(FECHA)* (Education; Pedagogy)

History: Founded 1985.

Main Language(s) of Instruction: Portuguese

Accrediting Agency: Ministry of Education

Degrees and Diplomas: *Bacharelado*; *Licenciatura*; *Especialização/Aperfeiçoamento*: **Civil Law; Criminal Law; Higher Education; Special Education.**

Student Services: Library

Last Updated: 20/10/15

FACULTY OF APPLIED AND SOCIAL SCIENCES OF PETROLINA

Faculdade de Ciências Aplicadas e Sociais de Petrolina (FACAPE)

Campus Universitário, s/n, Vila Eduardo, Petrolina, Pernambuco 56328-903
Tel: +55(81) 3866-3200
Fax: +55(81) 3866-3204 +55(81) 3866-3253
EMail: direcao@facape.br
Website: http://www.facape.br/

President: Rinaldo Remigio Mendes

Diretor Acadêmico: Antonio Henrique Habib Carvalho

Course
Accountancy (Accountancy); **Administration** (Administration); **Computer Science** (Computer Science); **Economics** (Economics); **Foreign Trade** (International Business); **Information Technology** (Information Technology); **International Business** (International Business); **Law** (Law); **Secretarial Studies** (Secretarial Studies); **Social Services** (Social and Community Services); **Tourism** (Tourism)

History: Founded 1976.

Main Language(s) of Instruction: Portuguese

Accrediting Agency: Ministry of Education

Degrees and Diplomas: *Bacharelado*; *Especialização/Aperfeiçoamento*: **Human Resources; Information Technology; Public Administration; Software Engineering.**

Last Updated: 23/10/15

FACULTY OF APPLIED SCIENCES OF LIMOEIRO

Faculdade de Ciências Aplicadas do Limoeiro (FACAL)

Av. Jerônimo Heráclio, 81, Centro, Limoeiro, PE 55700-000
Tel: +55(81) 3628-1397
Fax: +55(81) 3628-1397
EMail: facal@facal.edu.br
Website: http://www.facal.edu.br

Diretora: Marli Maria da Silva

Course
Accountancy (Accountancy); **Administration** (Administration); **Graduate Studies** (Management; Marketing; Public Administration)

History: Founded 1973 as Faculdade de Ciências da Administração do Limoeiro.

Main Language(s) of Instruction: Portuguese

Accrediting Agency: Ministry of Education

Degrees and Diplomas: *Bacharelado*; *Especialização/Aperfeiçoamento*: **Accountancy; Business Administration; Finance; Management.**

Student Services: Library

Last Updated: 23/10/15

FACULTY OF EDUCATION, SCIENCES AND LETTERS OF PARAISO DO TOCANTINS

Faculdade de Educação, Ciências e Letras de Paraiso do Tocantins (FEPAR-FECIPAR)

Rua L 20, Setor Interlagos, Paraíso do Tocantins, TO 77600-000
Tel: +55(63) 3602-6649
EMail: fepar@fecipar.edu.br
Website: http://fecipar.edu.br/v2

Diretora Presidenta: Sonia Maria França

Diretor Adm.-Financeiro: Sebastião Ozair B. de Bastos

Course
Accountancy (Accountancy); **Administration** (Administration; Business Administration); **Letters** (Literature; Portuguese; Spanish); **Pedagogy** (Pedagogy); **Postgraduate Studies** (Educational and Student Counselling; Higher Education Teacher Training; Information Sciences; Peace and Disarmament; Taxation)

History: Founded 1993.

Main Language(s) of Instruction: Portuguese

Degrees and Diplomas: *Bacharelado*; *Licenciatura*; *Especialização/Aperfeiçoamento*: **Educational and Student Counselling; Higher Education Teacher Training; Information Sciences; Peace and Disarmament; Taxation.**

Last Updated: 16/07/15

FACULTY OF HEALTH SCIENCES OF SERRA TALHADA

Faculdade de Ciências da Saúde de Serra Talhada (FACISST)

Avenida Afonso Magalhães, até 446/447, São Cristóvão, Serra Talhada 56912-380
Tel: +55(87) 3831-2311
EMail: facisst@gmail.com
Website: http://facisst.blogspot.fr

Course

Psychology (Clinical Psychology; Developmental Psychology; Educational Psychology; Experimental Psychology; Industrial and Organizational Psychology; Psychology)

History: Founded 2010.

Main Language(s) of Instruction: Portuguese

Degrees and Diplomas: *Bacharelado*

Last Updated: 25/11/15

FACULTY OF HUMAN AND APPLIED SOCIAL SCIENCES OF CABO DE SANTO AGOSTINHO

Faculdade de Ciências Humanas e Sociais Aplicadas do Cabo de Santo Agostinho (FACHUCA)

Rua Sebastião Juventino, s/n, Destilaria, Cabo de Santo Agostinho, PE 54500-000
Tel: +55(81) 3521-0400 +55(81) 3524-0707
Fax: +55(81) 3521-0483
EMail: factuta@uol.com.br
Website: http://www.fachuca.edu.br

Diretora: Tereza de Jesus Sales Lyra e Silva

Secretário Geral: Emerson Tenório Alves

Course

Administration (Administration); **Law** (Law); **Mathematics** (Mathematics); **Pedagogy** (Education)

History: Founded 1992

Main Language(s) of Instruction: Portuguese

Degrees and Diplomas: *Bacharelado*; *Licenciatura*; *Especialização/Aperfeiçoamento*: **Business Education.**

Student Services: Library

Last Updated: 23/06/15

FACULTY OF HUMAN SCIENCES OF SERTÃO CENTRAL

Faculdade de Ciências Humanas do Sertão Central (FACHUSC)

Rua Antonio Filgueira Sampaio, n° 134, Bairro Nossa Senhora das Graças, Salgueiro, PE 56000-000
Tel: +55(87) 3871-0217
Fax: +55(81) 3871-1553
EMail: fachusc2000@yahoo.com.br
Website: http://www.fachusc.com.br

Diretora: Verônica Rejane Lima Teixeira

Course

Biological Sciences (Biological and Life Sciences); **Education** (Education); **Geography** (Geography (Human)); **History** (History); **Law** (Law); **Literature** (Literature); **Mathematics** (Mathematics); **Post-graduate Studies** (History; Mathematics; Portuguese; Psychiatry and Mental Health)

History: Founded 1984.

Main Language(s) of Instruction: Portuguese

Degrees and Diplomas: *Bacharelado*: **Law.** *Licenciatura*: **Biological and Life Sciences; English; Geography (Human); History; Literature; Mathematics; Pedagogy.** *Especialização/Aperfeiçoamento*: **History; Mathematics; Portuguese; Psychiatry and Mental Health.** Postgraduate Degree Porgrammes are offered in partnership with Universidade de Pernambuco (UPE) and Autarquia Educacional de Araripina (AEDA)

Last Updated: 10/06/15

FACULTY OF HUMAN SCIENCES OF THE VALLEY OF PIRANGA

Faculdade de Ciências Humanas do Vale do Piranga (FAVAP)

Rua Cantídio Drumond 92, Centro, Ponte Nova, Minas Gerais 35430-006
Tel: +55(31) 4062-7007
Fax: +55(31) 3817-4503
EMail: direcao@favap.com.br; secretaria@favap.com.br; coordenacao@favap.com.br; fach@pontenet.com.br
Website: http://www.favap.com.br

Diretor: Luiz Raimundo

Course

Geography (Geography); **History** (History); **Literature** (English; Literature; Portuguese); **Post-graduate Studies** (Education)

History: Founded 1974.

Main Language(s) of Instruction: Portuguese

Degrees and Diplomas: *Licenciatura*: **English; Geography (Human); Literature; Portuguese.** *Mestrado*: **Education.**

Last Updated: 11/06/15

FACULTY OF HUMANITIES AND SOCIAL SCIENCES OF ARARIPINA

Faculdade de Ciências Humanas e Sociais de Araripina (FACISA)

Estrada Vicinal, s/n, Lagoa de Dentro, Araripina, PE 56280-000
Tel: +51(8 7) 3873-2603
Fax: +51(8 7) 3873-2603
EMail: facisaaeda@hotmail.com
Website: http://portalaeda.edu.br/facisa

Diretora: Morgana de Moura Costa Silva

Secretária Acadêmica: Widilane Fernandes da Silva

Course

Accounting (Accountancy); **Law** (Law)

History: Founded 2006.

Main Language(s) of Instruction: Portuguese

Degrees and Diplomas: *Bacharelado*

Last Updated: 03/12/15

FACULTY OF HUMANITIES AND SOCIAL SCIENCES OF SERRA TALHADA

Faculdade de Ciencias Humanas e Sociais de Serra Talhada (FACHUSST)

Avenida Afonso Magalhães, s/n, Várzea, Serra Talhada 56912-902
Tel: +55(87) 3831-2311
EMail: fachusst@hotmail.com; magna.mourato@hotmail.com
Website: http://fafopst.webnode.com/aeset/fachusst

Course

Social Services (Social and Community Services)

Main Language(s) of Instruction: Portuguese

Degrees and Diplomas: *Bacharelado*

Last Updated: 07/12/15

FACULTY OF LAW OF CONSELHEIRO LAFAIETE

Faculdade de Direito de Conselheiro Lafaiete (FDCL)

Rua Lopes Franco, 1001 bl., C/D Carijós, Conselheiro Lafaiete Minas Gerais 36400-000
Tel: +55(31) 3769-1919
Fax: +55(31) 3769-1919
EMail: chrysthiane.pi@fdcl.edu.br; fdcl@fdcl.edu.br
Website: http://www.fdcl.edu.br

Diretor: Hamilton Junqueira

Diretora de Controle Acadêmico: Elma Terezinha de Melo

Diretora Administrativa: Geralda Clemente Santana

School
Law (Administrative Law; Civil Law; Commercial Law; Fiscal Law; Labour Law; Law; Police Studies; Private Law; Social Welfare)
History: Founded 1970
Main Language(s) of Instruction: Portuguese
Degrees and Diplomas: *Bacharelado*
Student Services: Library
Last Updated: 29/06/15

FACULTY OF LAW OF FRANCA

Faculdade de Direito de Franca (FDF)
Avenida Major Nicácio, 2377, Bairro São José, Franca, São Paulo 14401-135
Tel: +55(16) 3713-4000
Fax: +55(16) 3713-4000
EMail: secretaria.fdf@direitofranca.br
Website: http://www.direitofranca.br

Diretor: Decio Antonio Piola

Course
Law (Law)
History: Founded 1958
Main Language(s) of Instruction: Portuguese
Degrees and Diplomas: *Bacharelado*; *Especialização/Aperfeiçoamento*: **Civil Law; Commercial Law.**
Last Updated: 29/06/15

FACULTY OF LAW OF SÃO BERNARDO DO CAMPO

Faculdade de Direito de São Bernardo do Campo (FDSBC)
Autarquia Municipal, Rua Java 425 Jardim do Mar, São Bernardo do Campo São Paulo 09750-650
Tel: +55(11) 4123-0222
Fax: +55(11) 4123-0222
EMail: secretariageral@direitosbc.br; diretoria@direitosbc.br
Website: http://www.direitosbc.br

Diretor: Marcelo José Ladeira Mauad
Vice-Diretor: Rui Décio Martins

Department
Basic Disciplines (Economics; Law; Philosophy; Sociology); **Civil Procedure** (Civil Law); **Criminal Law and Forensic Medicine** (Criminal Law; Forensic Medicine and Dentistry); **Labour and Social Welfare** (Labour Law); **Private Law** (Civil Law; Commercial Law); **Public Law** (Administrative Law; Constitutional Law; Fiscal Law; International Law; Political Sciences)
History: Founded 1964
Main Language(s) of Instruction: Portuguese
Degrees and Diplomas: *Bacharelado*; *Especialização/Aperfeiçoamento*: **Civil Law; Fiscal Law; Labour Law; Real Estate; Social Welfare.**
Student Services: Library, Sports Facilities
Last Updated: 29/06/15

FACULTY OF MEDICINE OF JUNDIAI

Faculdade de Medicina de Jundiaí (FMJ)
Rua Francisco Telles 250, Vila Arens, Caixa Postal 1295, Jundiaí, São Paulo 13202-550
Tel: +55(11) 4587-1095
Fax: +55(11) 4587-1095
EMail: fmj@fmj.br
Website: http://www.fmj.br

Diretor: Itibagi Rocha Machado
Gerente de Administração: José Carlos Tresmondi

Course
Graduate Studies (Health Sciences); **Medicine** (Medicine); **Nursing** (Nursing)
History: Founded 1968
Main Language(s) of Instruction: Portuguese
Degrees and Diplomas: *Bacharelado*; *Especialização/Aperfeiçoamento*: **Health Sciences.** *Mestrado*: **Health Sciences.**
Last Updated: 15/07/15

FACULTY OF MEDICINE OF MARILIA

Faculdade de Medicina de Marília (FAMEMA)
Av. Monte Carmelo, 800, Marilia, São Paulo 17519-030
Tel: +55(14) 3402-1744
Fax: +55(14) 3413-2594
EMail: info@famema.br
Website: http://www.famema.br

Diretor Geral: Paulo Roberto Teixeira Michelone
Diretor Administrativo: Gilson Caleman

Course
Medicine (Medicine); **Nursing** (Nursing)
History: Founded 1967
Main Language(s) of Instruction: Portuguese
Degrees and Diplomas: *Bacharelado*; *Especialização/Aperfeiçoamento*: **Psychology; Psychotherapy.** *Mestrado*: **Health Sciences.**
Student Services: IT Centre, Library
Last Updated: 15/07/15

FACULTY OF MEDICINE OF SÃO JOSÉ DO RIO PRETO

Faculdade de Medicina de São José do Rio Preto (FAMERP)
Av. Brigadeiro Faria Lima, 5416, Vila São Pedro, São José do Rio Preto, São Paulo 15090-000
Tel: +55(17) 3201-5700
Fax: +55(17) 3229-1777
EMail: secretariageral@famerp.br
Website: http://www.famerp.br

Diretor Geral: Dulcimar Donizeti de Souza
Diretor Adjunto de Administração: Aldenis Albaneze Borim

Course
Medicine (Medicine); **Nursing** (Nursing)
History: Founded 1974
Main Language(s) of Instruction: Portuguese
Degrees and Diplomas: *Bacharelado*; *Especialização/Aperfeiçoamento*: **Biology; Cosmetology; Dermatology; Educational Psychology; Genetics; Health Education; Health Sciences; Medicine; Molecular Biology; Nursing; Nutrition; Occupational Health; Oncology; Paediatrics; Pharmacy; Physical Education; Physical Therapy; Psychology; Psychotherapy; Public Administration; Public Health; Rehabilitation and Therapy; Safety Engineering; Surgery.** *Mestrado*: **Health Sciences; Medicine; Nursing.** *Doutorado*: **Health Sciences; Medicine.**
Student Services: Library
Last Updated: 15/07/15

FACULTY OF PHILOSOPHY AND HUMANITIES OF GOIATUBA

Faculdade de Filosofia e Ciências Humanas de Goiatuba (FAFICH)
Rod Go 320, s/n, Jardim Santa Paula, Goiatuba, Goiás 75600-000
Tel: +55(64) 3495-1560 +55(64) 3495-8100
Fax: +55(64) 3495-8102
EMail: fafich@fafich.org.br; contato@fafich.org.br; ouvidoria@fafich.org.br
Website: http://www.fafich.org.br

Diretora: Dulcimar Rosa Ferreira EMail: dulce@fafich.org.br

Course
Accountancy (Accountancy); **Administration** (Administration); **Agronomy** (Agronomy); **Civil Engineering** (Civil Engineering); **Environmental Management** (Civil Engineering); **Graduate Studies** (Accountancy; Environmental Management; Human Resources; Law; Literacy Education; Marketing; Physical Education; Teacher Training); **Law** (Law); **Literature** (English; Literature;

Portuguese); **Nursing** (Nursing); **Pedagogy** (Pedagogy); **Physical Education** (Physical Education); **Public Administration** (Public Administration)

History: Founded 1988

Main Language(s) of Instruction: Portuguese

Degrees and Diplomas: *Bacharelado*; *Licenciatura*; *Especialização/Aperfeiçoamento*: **Accountancy; Human Resources; Law; Literacy Education; Marketing; Physical Education; Teacher Training.** Also MBA in Environmental Management

Student Services: Library

Last Updated: 06/07/15

FACULTY OF PHILOSOPHY, SCIENCE AND LETTERS OF ALEGRE

Faculdade de Filosofia, Ciências e Letras de Alegre (FAFIA)

Rua Belo Amorim, n° 100, Centro, Alegre, ES 29500-000
Tel: +55(27) 3552-1412
Fax: +55(27) 3552-1412
EMail: fafia@fafia.edu.br
Website: http://fafia.srvroot.com/site

Diretora: Rosane Maria Souza dos Santos

Course

Biology *(Licenciatura)* (Biology); **Biology** *(Bacharelado)* (Biology); **Graduate Studies** (Educational Administration; Environmental Studies; Literacy Education; Natural Resources; Psychology); **History** (History); **Literature** (Literature); **Mathematics** (Mathematics); **Nursing** (Nursing); **Pedagogy** (Pedagogy); **Pharmacy** (Pharmacy); **Psychology** *(Licenciatura)* (Psychology); **Psychology** (Psychology); **Social Services** (Social and Community Services)

History: Founded 1967

Main Language(s) of Instruction: Portuguese

Degrees and Diplomas: *Bacharelado*; *Licenciatura*; *Especialização/Aperfeiçoamento*: **Educational Administration; Environmental Management; Environmental Studies; History; Literacy Education; Literature; Psychology.** Especializaçao degree courses were launched in 2015.

Last Updated: 07/07/15

FACULTY OF PHILOSOPHY, SCIENCE AND LETTERS OF IBITINGA

Faculdade de Filosofia, Ciências e Letras de Ibitinga (FAIBI)

Rua Roque Raineri, 81, Jd. Centenário, Ibitinga, São Paulo 14940-000
Tel: +55(16) 3342-7303
Fax: +55(16) 3342-7303
EMail: contato@faibi.com.br; faibi@faibi.com.br
Website: http://www.faibi.com.br

Diretora: André Luiz Oliveira

Vice Diretora Geral: Maria Eliza Nakamura

Course

Administration (Administration); **Pedagogy** (Pedagogy); **Tourism** (Tourism)

History: Founded 2001.

Main Language(s) of Instruction: Portuguese

Degrees and Diplomas: *Bacharelado*; *Licenciatura*

Student Services: IT Centre, Library

Last Updated: 06/07/15

FACULTY OF PHILOSOPHY, SCIENCE AND LETTERS OF MANDAGUARI

Faculdade de Filosofia, Ciências e Letras de Mandaguari (FAFIMAN)

Rua Renê Taccola, Mandaguari, PR 86975000
Tel: +55(44) 3233-1356
Fax: +55(44) 3233-2411
EMail: secretaria@fafiman.br
Website: http://www.fafiman.br

Diretor: José Natal de Oliveira EMail: joseno@fafiman.br

Secretária: Terezinha Mosconi de Freitas
EMail: terezinhafafiman@gmail.com

Course

Accountancy (Accountancy); **Administration** (Administration); **Agricultural Business** (Agricultural Business); **Biological Sciences** (Biology); **Computer Science** (Computer Science); **English and Portuguese Literature** (English; Literature; Portuguese); **Graduate Studies** (Accountancy; Biology; Computer Science; Environmental Management; Foreign Languages Education; Humanities and Social Science Education; Industrial Management; Linguistics; Literature; Management; Mathematics Education; Native Language Education; Physical Education; Public Health; Special Education; Transport Management); **History** (History); **Law** (Law); **Mathematics** (Mathematics); **Nursing** (Nursing); **Pedagogy** (Pedagogy); **Physical Education** (Physical Education)

History: Founded 1966.

Main Language(s) of Instruction: Portuguese

Degrees and Diplomas: *Bacharelado*; *Licenciatura*; *Especialização/Aperfeiçoamento*: **Biology; Computer Science; Foreign Languages Education; Humanities and Social Science Education; Mathematics Education; Native Language Education; Physical Education; Public Health; Special Education.** Also MBA in Industrial Management, Transport Management, Management

Student Services: IT Centre, Library

Last Updated: 08/07/15

FACULTY OF SCIENCE AND TECHNOLOGY OF BIRIGUI

Faculdade de Ciências e Tecnológia de Birigui (FATEB)

Rua Antônio Simões, 04, Centro, Birigüi, São Paulo 16200-027
Tel: +55(18) 3649-2200
Fax: +55(18) 3649-2201
EMail: fateb@fateb.br; secretaria@fateb.br
Website: http://www.fateb.br

Interim Director: Renata de Freitas Góis Comparoni

Course

Accountancy (Accountancy); **Administration** (Administration; Business Administration); **Design** (Industrial Design); **Graduate Studies** (Education; Educational Sciences); **Information Systems** (Computer Science); **Literature** *(Extension)* (Literature; Portuguese); **Pedagogy** (Educational Administration; Pedagogy; Teacher Training)

History: Founded 1985.

Main Language(s) of Instruction: Portuguese

Degrees and Diplomas: *Bacharelado*; *Licenciatura*; *Especialização/Aperfeiçoamento*: **Educational Sciences.**

Student Services: IT Centre, Library, eLibrary

Last Updated: 09/06/15

FACULTTY OF SCIENCE AND TECHNOLOGY OF GOIANA

Faculdade de Ciências e Tecnologia de Goiana (FADIMAB)

Rua Poco Rei, s/n, Centro, Goiana, PE 55900-000
Tel: +55(81) 3626-0740
Fax: +55(81) 3626-0617
EMail: fadimab@fadimab.edu.br
Website: http://www.fadimab.edu.br

Diretor: Marcos Sérgio de Souza Leão Ribeiro

Vice-Diretora: Zuleide Elisa Almeida Moreira

Course

Biology (Biology); **Geography** (Geography); **History** (History); **Literature** (Literature); **Mathematics** (Mathematics); **Physical Education** (Physical Education); **Teacher Training** (Teacher Training)

History: Founded as Instituto Superior de Educação de Goiana, 1972.

Main Language(s) of Instruction: Portuguese

Degrees and Diplomas: *Bacharelado*; *Licenciatura*

Last Updated: 13/04/16

FACULTY OF SCIENCE OF THE FOUNDATION TECHNOLOGICAL INSTITUTE OF OSASCO

Faculdade de Ciências da Fundação Instituto Tecnológico de Osasco (FAC-FITO)
Av. das Flores, 711, Jardim Das Flores,
Osasco, São Paulo 06110-100
Tel: +55(11) 3652-3090
Fax: +55(11) 3652-3094
EMail: fac@fito.br
Website: http://www.fito.edu.br/faculdade/

Presidente: Rubens Aniz

Diretoria Geral de Ensino: Marinalva Oliveira

Course

Accountancy (Accountancy); **Administration** (Administration; Business Administration); **Computer Science** (Computer Science); **Economics** (Economics); **Electrical Engineering** (Electrical Engineering); **Music** (Music; Musical Instruments); **Pedagogy** (Education; Pedagogy)

History: Founded 1968.

Main Language(s) of Instruction: Portuguese

Accrediting Agency: Ministry of Education

Degrees and Diplomas: *Bacharelado*; *Licenciatura*

Student Services: Library

Last Updated: 05/11/15

FACULTY OF SOCIAL SCIENCES OF PALMARES

Faculdade de Ciências Sociais dos Palmares
Br 101 K 186 Sul s/n, Engenho São Manoel,
Palmares, PE 55540-000
Tel: +55(81) 3661-1876
Fax: +55(81) 3661-1876
EMail: facip_educ@hotmail.com
Website: http://www.famasul.edu.br

Diretor: Paulo de Assis Mendes da Silva

Course

Administration (Administration)

History: Founded 2003.

Main Language(s) of Instruction: Portuguese

Degrees and Diplomas: *Bacharelado*: **Administration.**

Last Updated: 25/06/15

FACULTY OF TECHNOLOGICAL EDUCATION OF THE STATE OF RIO DE JANEIRO

Faculdade de Educação Tecnológica do Estado do Rio de Janeiro
Rua Clarimundo de Melo, 847, Quintino Bocaiuva,
Rio de Janeiro, RJ 21311-280
Tel: +55(21) 2332-4048
Fax: +55(21) 2332-4048
EMail: ist-rio@faetec.rj.gov.br
Website: http://www.faeterj-rio.edu.br

Reitor: Fernando Mota

Unit

Itabapoana *(FAETERJ BJ Itabapoan)* (Pedagogy); **Itaperuna** *(FAETERJ ITAPERUNA)* (Pedagogy); **Santo Antônio de Pádua** *(FAETERJ S Ant. de Pádua)* (Pedagogy); **Três Rios** *(FAETERJ Três Rios)* (Pedagogy; Transport Management)

Course

Postgraduate Studies (Educational Technology; Information Technology; Software Engineering); **Systems Analysis and Development** (Systems Analysis)

Main Language(s) of Instruction: Portuguese

Degrees and Diplomas: *Tecnólogo*; *Licenciatura*; *Especialização/Aperfeiçoamento*: **Educational Technology; Information Technology.**

Publications: Democratizar; RevISTa

Last Updated: 09/12/15

FACULTY OF TECHNOLOGY OF AMERICANA

Faculdade de Tecnologia de Americana (FATEC)
Rua Emílio de Menezes, s/n°, Vila Amorim,
Americana, São Paulo 13469-101
Tel: +55(19) 3406-3297 +55(19) 3406-5776
Fax: +55(19) 3406-5776
EMail: direcao@fatec.edu.br; academica@fatec.edu.br
Website: http://www.fatec.br

Diretor: Rafael Ferreira Alves EMail: direcao@fatec.edu.br

Diretora de Serviço Área Administrativa: Fabiana Morell EMail: servicos@fatec.edu.br

Course

Business Administration (Business Administration); **Digital Games** (Software Engineering); **Information Security** (Information Management); **Logistics** (Transport Management); **Postgraduate Studies** (Business and Commerce; Information Technology; Textile Technology); **Systems Analysis and Development** (Systems Analysis); **Textile Production** (Textile Technology); **Textiles and Fashion** (Fashion Design; Textile Design)

History: Founded 1986 as Faculdade de Tecnologia Têxtil de Americana. Acquired present title 1986.

Main Language(s) of Instruction: Portuguese

Degrees and Diplomas: *Tecnólogo*; *Bacharelado*; *Licenciatura*; *Especialização/Aperfeiçoamento*: **Business and Commerce; Information Technology; Textile Technology.**

Student Services: Library

Last Updated: 19/08/15

FACULTY OF TECHNOLOGY OF PRAIA GRANDE

Faculdade de Tecnologia de Praia Grande (FATECPG)
Praça 19 de janeiro, 144, Praia Grande, SP 11700-100
Tel: +55 (13) 3591-1303 +55(13) 3591-6968
Website: http://www.fatecpg.com.br

Diretora: Luciana Maria Guimarães

Course

Business Administration; **Chemical Processes** (Chemistry); **Graduate Studies** (Business and Commerce; Management); **International Business** (International Business); **Systems Analysis and Development** (Systems Analysis)

History: Founded 2002.

Main Language(s) of Instruction: Portuguese

Degrees and Diplomas: *Tecnólogo*; *Especialização/Aperfeiçoamento*: **Business and Commerce.**

Last Updated: 20/08/15

FACULTY OF TECHNOLOGY OF SÃO JOSÉ DO RIO PRETO

Faculdade de Tecnologia de São José do Rio Preto (FATECRP)
Rua Fernandópolis, 2510, Eldorado,
São José do Rio Preto, SP 15043-020
Tel: +55(17) 3219-1433
Fax: +55(17) 3219-1433
EMail: faleconosco@fatecriopreto.edu.br; diretoriaservicos@fatecriopreto.edu.br
Website: http://www.fatecriopreto.edu.br

Diretor: Waldir Barros Fernandes Jr. EMail: direcao@fatecriopreto.edu.br

Course

Agribusiness (Agricultural Business); **Business Administration** (Business Administration); **Business Computing** (Business Computing); **Graduate Studies** (Business Administration; Computer Science; Information Technology; Management); **Systems Analysis and Development** (Systems Analysis)

Main Language(s) of Instruction: Portuguese

Degrees and Diplomas: *Tecnólogo*; *Especialização/Aperfeiçoamento*: **Business Administration; Information Technology; Management.**

Last Updated: 20/08/15

FACULTY OF TECHNOLOGY OF SÃO PAULO

Faculdade de Tecnologia de São Paulo (FATEC-SP)
Praça Coronel Fernando Prestes, 30, Bom Retiro,
São Paulo, São Paulo 01124-060
Tel: +55(11) 3322-2200 +55(11) 3322-2249
Fax: +55(11) 3315-0383
EMail: ataa@fatecsp.br
Website: http://www.fatecsp.br

Diretor: Luciana Reyes Pires Kassab EMail: secdir@fatecsp.br

Diretora de Serviços Acadêmicos: Márcia Sumiko Ito

Course

Buildings (Civil Engineering); **Business Administration** (Business Administration); **Environmental Sanitation** (Environmental Management); **Industrial Electronics** (Electronic Engineering); **Materials Engineering** (Materials Engineering); **Materials, Processes and Electronic Components** (Electronic Engineering; Materials Engineering); **Office Automation and Secretarial Studies** (Business Computing; Secretarial Studies); **Paving** (Civil Engineering); **Postgraduate** (Business Administration; Computer Science; Environmental Engineering; Management; Systems Analysis); **Precision Mechanics** (Mechanics); **Production Engineering** (Production Engineering); **Projects** (Mechanics); **Systems Analysis and Development** (Systems Analysis); **Tourism** (Tourism); **Welding** (Metal Techniques)

History: Founded 1973.

Main Language(s) of Instruction: Portuguese

Degrees and Diplomas: *Tecnólogo*; *Especialização/Aperfeiçoamento*: **Business Administration; Computer Science; Environmental Engineering; Management; Systems Analysis.**

Student Services: IT Centre, Library

Publications: Boletim Técnico; CNPq

Last Updated: 20/08/15

FEDERAL CENTRE OF TECHNOLOGICAL EDUCATION OF MINAS GERAIS

Centro Federal de Educação Tecnológica de Minas Gerais (CEFET-MG)
Avenida Amazonas 5253, Nova Suiça,
Belo Horizonte, Minas Gerais 30421-169
Tel: +55(31) 3319-7002
Fax: +55(31) 3319-7009
EMail: gabinete@adm.cefetmg.br
Website: http://www.cefetmg.br

Diretor Geral: Márcio Silva Basílio

Course

Administration (Administration); **Automation and Control Engineering** (Automation and Control Engineering); **Automation and Industrial Engineering** (Automation and Control Engineering; Industrial Engineering); **Chemical Technology** (Chemical Engineering); **Civil Engineering** (Civil Engineering); **Computer Engineering** (Computer Engineering); **Electrical Engineering** (Electrical Engineering); **Environmental Engineering** (Environmental Engineering); **Languages** (Modern Languages); **Materials Engineering** (Materials Engineering); **Mathematics and Computer Science** (Mathematics and Computer Science); **Mechanical Engineering** (Mechanical Engineering); **Mechatronics Engineering** (Electronic Engineering; Mechanical Engineering); **Quality and Normalisation** (Safety Engineering); **Radiology** (Radiology); **Teacher Training** (Teacher Training; Technology Education)

Further Information: Also branches in Leopoldina, Araxá and Divinópolis

History: Founded 1909 as Escola de Aprendizes Artífices de Minas Gerais. Acquired present status 1978.

Main Language(s) of Instruction: Portuguese

Degrees and Diplomas: *Tecnólogo*; *Bacharelado*; *Licenciatura*; *Especialização/Aperfeiçoamento*: **Industrial Engineering; Modern Languages; Technology; Transport Management.** *Mestrado*: **Administration; Civil Engineering; Electrical Engineering; Energy Engineering; Information Technology; Materials Engineering; Mathematics and Computer Science; Modern Languages; Technology Education.** *Doutorado*: **Literature; Mathematics and Computer Science; Modern Languages.** Also MBA

Student Services: Library

Last Updated: 19/06/15

FEDERAL INSTITUTE OF EDUCATION, SCIENCE AND TECHNOLOGY OF ALAGOAS

Instituto Federal de Educação, Ciência e Tecnologia de Alagoas (IFAL)
Rua Odilon Vasconcelos, 103, Maceió, Alagoas 57035-660
Tel: +55(82) 3194-1150
EMail: portal@ifal.edu.br
Website: http://www.ifal.edu.br

Reitor: Sérgio Teixeira Costa
Tel: +55(82) 3194-1194/1195 EMail: secgab@ifal.edu.br

Course

Biology (Biology); **Chemistry** (Chemistry); **Civil Engineering** (Civil Engineering); **Environmental Management** (Environmental Management); **Food Science and Technology** (Food Science; Food Technology); **Hotel Management** (Hotel Management); **Information Systems** (Computer Science; Information Technology); **Interior Design** (Interior Design); **Mathematics** (Mathematics); **Portuguese** (Portuguese); **Tourism** (Tourism); **Town Planning** (Town Planning)

Further Information: Also 11 campuses located in Maceio, Palmeira do Índios, Satuba, Marechal Deodoro, Arapiraca, Piranhas, Penedo, Maragogi, Murici, São Miguel dos Campos and Santana do Ipanema

History: Founded 1999 as Centro Federal de Educação Tecnológica de Alagoas. Acquired present title following merger with Escola Agrotécnica Federal de Satuba 2008.

Main Language(s) of Instruction: Portuguese

Degrees and Diplomas: *Tecnólogo*; *Bacharelado*; *Licenciatura*

Student Services: Library

Last Updated: 05/04/16

FEDERAL INSTITUTE OF EDUCATION, SCIENCE AND TECHNOLOGY OF BAHIA

Instituto Federal de Educação, Ciência e Tecnologia da Bahia (IFBA)
Rua Emídio dos Santos s/n, Barbalho, Salvador, Bahia 40300-010
Tel: +55(71) 2102-9400
EMail: gabinete@ifba.edu.br
Website: http://www.portal.ifba.edu.br

Pró-Reitor: Luiz Gustavo da Cruz Duarte
Tel: +55 (71) 3221-0330 EMail: prpgi@ifba.edu.br

Diretor Executivo: Antonio Carlos Peixoto Bitencourt
Tel: +55(71) 3221-0336

Department

Applied Sciences (Applied Chemistry; Applied Mathematics; Applied Physics; Computer Science; Engineering); **Electrical and Electronic Engineering** (Electrical and Electronic Engineering); **Human Sciences and Languages** (Linguistics; Modern Languages; Philosophy); **Industrial Engineering** (Industrial Engineering); **Mechanical and Materials Engineering** (Materials Engineering; Mechanical Engineering)

History: Founded 1993 as Centro Federal de Educação Tecnológica da Bahia. Acquired present title: Instituto Federal de Educação, Ciência e Tecnologia da Bahia, 2008.

Main Language(s) of Instruction: Portuguese

Degrees and Diplomas: *Tecnólogo*; *Bacharelado*; *Licenciatura*; *Especialização/Aperfeiçoamento*: **Chemical Engineering; Computer Engineering; Educational Administration; Environmental Studies; Health Sciences; Technology Education; Vocational Education.** *Mestrado*: **Computer Science; Linguistics; Modern Languages; Philosophy.** *Doutorado*: **Materials Engineering; Statistics.**

Student Services: Library

Last Updated: 04/04/16

FEDERAL INSTITUTE OF EDUCATION, SCIENCE AND TECHNOLOGY OF BRASILIA

Instituto Federal de Educaçâo, Ciencia e Tecnologia de Brasilia

Via L2 Norte, SGAN 610, Módulo D, E, F e G, Brasília, DF
Tel: +502 (61) 2103-2154
EMail: sic@ifb.edu.br
Website: http://www.ifb.edu.br

Reitor: Wilson Conciani

Further Information: Also campuses in Ceilândia, Estrutural, Gama, Planaltina, Riacho Fundo, Samambaia, São Sebastião, Taguatinga, Taguatinga Centro

History: Founded 2008.

Main Language(s) of Instruction: Portuguese

Degrees and Diplomas: *Bacharelado*; *Licenciatura*

Last Updated: 15/04/16

FEDERAL INSTITUTE OF EDUCATION, SCIENCE AND TECHNOLOGY OF CEARÁ

Instituto Federal de Educação, Ciência e Tecnologia do Ceará (IFCE)

Avenida Rui Barbosa 2847, Joaquim Távora,
Fortaleza, Ceará 60115-222
Tel: +55(85) 3401-2500
Fax: +55(85) 3401-2323
EMail: reitoria@ifce.edu.br
Website: http://www.ifce.edu.br

Reitor: Virgílio Augusto Sales Araripe

Programme

Postgraduate Studies (Education; Environmental Studies; Irrigation; Tourism); **Undergratuate Studies** (Adult Education; Automation and Control Engineering; Chemistry; Civil Engineering; Computer Engineering; Computer Networks; Construction Engineering; Electronic Engineering; Engineering; Environmental Engineering; Environmental Management; Environmental Studies; Fine Arts; Folklore; Food Technology; Hotel and Restaurant; Irrigation; Mathematics; Mathematics Education; Mechanical Engineering; Nutrition; Performing Arts; Physical Education; Physics; Public Health; Sports Management; Telecommunications Engineering; Theatre; Tourism; Visual Arts)

Further Information: Also 22 extensions (Aracati, Baturité, Camocim, Caucaia, Jaguaribe, Morada Nova, Tabuleiro do Norte, Tauá, Tianguá, Ubajara and more)

History: Founded 1999 as Centro Federal de Educação Tecnológica do Ceará. Acquired present status and title 2008.

Main Language(s) of Instruction: Portuguese

Degrees and Diplomas: *Tecnólogo*; *Bacharelado*; *Licenciatura*; *Especialização/Aperfeiçoamento*: **Education; Food Technology; Fruit Production; Physical Education; Social Sciences; Technology; Tourism.**

Student Services: Library

Last Updated: 08/04/16

FEDERAL INSTITUTE OF EDUCATION, SCIENCE AND TECHNOLOGY OF ESPÍRITO SANTO

Instituto Federal de Educação, Ciência e Tecnologia do Espírito Santo (IFES)

Avenida Vitória 1729, Jucutuquara,
Vitória, Espirito Santo 29040-780
Tel: +55(27) 3331-2110
Fax: +55(27) 3331-2222
EMail: gabinete@ifes.edu.br; gps@ifes.edu.br
Website: http://www.ifes.edu.br

Reitor: Denio Rebello Arantes

Course

Postgraduate Studies (Agriculture; Ecology; Education; Metal Techniques; Metallurgical Engineering); **Undergraduate Studies** (Adult Education; Agricultural Engineering; Agriculture; Aquaculture; Automation and Control Engineering; Biology; Chemistry; Computer Engineering; Computer Networks; Computer Science; Ecology; Education; Electrical Engineering; Environmental Studies; Information Sciences; Materials Engineering; Mathematics; Metal Techniques; Metallurgical Engineering; Occupational Health; Production Engineering; Public Administration; Teacher Trainers Education; Tropical Agriculture)

Further Information: Also 22 campuses across the country

History: Founded 1999 as Centro Federal de Educação Tecnológica do Espírito Santo (CEFET/ES). Acquired present status and title 2008 following merger with Escola Agrotécnicas de Alegre, Escola de Colatina and Escola de Santa Teresa.

Main Language(s) of Instruction: Portuguese

Degrees and Diplomas: *Tecnólogo*; *Licenciatura*; *Especialização/Aperfeiçoamento*: **Adult Education; Agriculture; Business Administration; Computer Education; Distance Education; Ecology; Electrical Engineering; Environmental Management; Pedagogy; Primary Education; Public Administration; Secondary Education; Sports; Technology Education; Vocational Education.** *Mestrado*: **Agriculture; Ecology; Materials Engineering; Mathematics Education; Metallurgical Engineering; Portuguese; Science Education; Technology.**

Student Services: Library

Last Updated: 08/04/16

FEDERAL INSTITUTE OF EDUCATION, SCIENCE AND TECHNOLOGY OF FARROUPILHA

Instituto Federal de Educação, Ciência e Tecnologia Farroupilha (IFFARROUPILHA)

Rua Esmeralda, 430, Faixa Nova, Camobi,
Santa Maria, RS 97110-767
Tel: +55(55) 3218-9800
Fax: +55(55) 3218-9800
EMail: gabreitoria@iffarroupilha.edu.br
Website: http://www.iffarroupilha.edu.br

Reitor: Carla Comerlato Jardim
Tel: +55(55) 9980-8111 EMail: carla.jardim@iffarroupilha.edu.br

Course

Agricultural Business (Agricultural Business); **Agricultural Engineering** (Agricultural Engineering); **Agroindustry** (Agricultural Management); **Biological Sciences** (Biological and Life Sciences); **Chemistry** (Chemistry); **Computer Science** (Computer Science); **Crop Production** (Crop Production); **Food Science** (Food Science); **Mathematics** (Mathematics); **Public Administration** (Public Administration); **Systems Analysis and Development** (Systems Analysis); **Systems for the Internet** (Computer Science); **Zootechnics** (Animal Husbandry)

Further Information: Also following Campuses: Alegrete, Júlio de Castilhos, Panambi, São Borja, Santa Rosa, Santo Augusto, São Vicente do Sul

History: Founded 2002 as Centro Federal Tecnológico de São Vicente do Sul - CEFETSVS. Acquired present status and title 2008 following merger with Escola Agrotécnica Federal de Alegrete, Unidade Descentralizada de Júlio de Castilhos and Unidade Descentralizada de Santo Augusto.

Main Language(s) of Instruction: Portuguese

Degrees and Diplomas: *Tecnólogo*; *Licenciatura*; *Especialização/Aperfeiçoamento*: **Animal Husbandry; Computer Education; Education; Environmental Studies; Public Administration; Rural Studies; Technology Education; Vocational Education.**

Student Services: Library

Last Updated: 11/04/16

FEDERAL INSTITUTE OF EDUCATION, SCIENCE AND TECHNOLOGY OF GOIÁNIA

Instituto Federal de Educação, Ciência e Tecnologia de Goiás (IFG)

Avenida Assis Chateaubriand, n° 1.658, Setor Oeste,
Goiânia, Goiás 74130-012
Tel: +55(62) 3612-2233
EMail: gabinete.reitoria@ifg.edu.br
Website: http://www.ifg.edu.br

Reitor: Jerônimo Rodrigues da Silva

Course
Undergraduate (Bachalerado) (Automation and Control Engineering; Civil Engineering; Computer Engineering; Electrical Engineering; Environmental Engineering; Mechanical Engineering); **Undergraduate (Licentiatura)** (Biology; Chemistry; Mathematics; Music; Pedagogy; Physics); **Undergraduate (Tecnólogo)** (Chemistry; Construction Engineering; Hotel Management; Hygiene; Road Transport; Technology; Telecommunications Engineering; Tourism; Transport Management)

Campus
Inhumas; **Itumbiara** (Chemistry); **Jataí** (Mathematics Education; Science Education; Technology); **Uruaçu** (Chemical Engineering; Chemistry; Construction Engineering; Environmental Engineering; Hotel and Restaurant; Industrial Engineering; Information Technology; Mining Engineering; Surveying and Mapping; Telecommunications Engineering; Tourism; Transport and Communications)

History: Founded 1909 as Escolas de Aprendizes Artífices. Became Escola Técnica Federal de Goiás 1965. Became Centro Federal de Educação Tecnológica de Goiás (CEFET-GO) 1999. Acquired present status and title 2008.

Main Language(s) of Instruction: Portuguese

Degrees and Diplomas: *Tecnólogo*; *Bacharelado*; *Licenciatura*; *Especialização/Aperfeiçoamento*: **Mathematics; Mathematics Education; Science Education; Telecommunications Engineering; Vocational Education.** *Mestrado*: **Mathematics Education; Science Education.**

Student Services: Library

Last Updated: 05/04/16

FEDERAL INSTITUTE OF EDUCATION, SCIENCE AND TECHNOLOGY OF GOIANO

Instituto Federal de Educação, Ciência e Tecnologia Goiano (IF GOIANO)

Rua 88, n°310, Setor Sul, Nova Suiça, GO 74085-010
Tel: +55(62) 3605-3601/3602
EMail: reitoria@ifgoiano.edu.br
Website: http://www.ifgoiano.edu.br

Reitor: José Donizete Borges EMail: reitoria@ifgoiano.edu.br

Course
Undergraduate (Agricultural Engineering; Agronomy; Civil Engineering; Computer Engineering; Environmental Engineering; Food Technology; Information Technology; Mathematics; Systems Analysis; Veterinary Science)

Campus
Avançado Catalão; **Avançado Cristalina**; **Avançado Hidrolândia**; **Avançado Ipameri**; **Campos Belos**; **Ceres** (Administration; Agronomy; Biological and Life Sciences; Computer Science); **Iporá** (Agricultural Business; Agronomy; Chemistry; Systems Analysis); **Morrinhos** (Agronomy; Chemistry; Computer Science); **Posse**; **Rio Verde** (Agricultural Business; Agronomy; Animal Husbandry; Biological and Life Sciences; Chemistry; Crop Production; Environmental Engineering; Food Technology); **Trindade**; **Urutaí** (Agricultural Engineering; Agronomy; Biological and Life Sciences; Food Technology; Information Technology; Mathematics; Systems Analysis; Water Management)

History: Founded 2002 as Centro Federal de Educação Tecnológica de Rio Verde. Acquired present status and title 2008.

Degrees and Diplomas: *Tecnólogo*; *Bacharelado*; *Licenciatura*; *Especialização/Aperfeiçoamento*: **Energy Engineering.** *Mestrado*: **Agriculture; Animal Husbandry; Biological and Life Sciences; Crop Production; Irrigation; Natural Resources; Plant and Crop Protection.** *Doutorado*: **Agriculture.**

Student Services: Library

Last Updated: 11/04/16

FEDERAL INSTITUTE OF EDUCATION, SCIENCE AND TECHNOLOGY OF MARANHÃO

Instituto Federal de Educação, Ciência e Tecnologia do Maranhão (IFMA)

Av. Marechal Castelo Branco, n° 789 - São Francisco,
São Luís, Maranhão 65076-091
Tel: +55(98) 3215-1701
EMail: gabinete@ifma.edu.br
Website: http://www.ifma.edu.br

Reitor: Roberto Brandão

Campus
Açailândia; **Alcântara** (Tourism); **Buriticupu** (Biology; Public Administration); **Centro Histórico**; **Codó** (Agriculture; Chemistry; Mathematics); **Imperatriz** (Physics); **Maracanã** (Rural Studies); **Monte Castelo**; **Monte Castelo** (Agriculture; Biology; Chemistry; Civil Engineering; Computer Science; Distance Education; Electrical Engineering; Environmental Engineering; Industrial Engineering; Information Sciences; Materials Engineering; Mathematics; Mechanical Engineering; Physics; Telecommunications Engineering; Water Management); **Santa Inês**; **Zé Doca** (Chemistry; Food Science)

History: Founded 1989 as Centro Federal de Educação Tecnológica do Maranhão (CEFET-MA). Acquired present status and title 2008 following merger with Escola Agrotécnicas Federais de Codó, Escola de São Luís and Escola de São Raimundo das Mangabeiras é Autarquia.

Main Language(s) of Instruction: Portuguese

Degrees and Diplomas: *Bacharelado*; *Licenciatura*; *Especialização/Aperfeiçoamento*: **Agriculture; Cultural Studies; Ecology; Environmental Studies; Rural Studies.** *Mestrado*: **Chemistry; Materials Engineering; Physics.**

Student Services: Library

Last Updated: 08/04/16

FEDERAL INSTITUTE OF EDUCATION, SCIENCE AND TECHNOLOGY OF MATO GROSSO

Instituto Federal de Educação, Ciência e Tecnologia de Mato Grosso (IFMT)

Avenida Sen. Filinto Müller, 953 - Bairro: Duque de Caxias, Ed. Tarcom - Sala 12, Centro, Cuiabá, MT 78043-400
Tel: +55(65) 3616-4100
EMail: gabinete@ifmt.edu.br
Website: http://www.ifmt.edu.br

Reitor: José Bispo Barbosa Tel: +55(65) 3616-4105

Campus
Alta Floresta (Administration; Zoology); **Campo Novo do Parecis** (Agricultural Management; Agronomy; Management Systems; Mathematics); **Confresa** (Agriculture; Agronomy; Chemistry); **Cuiabá** (Automation and Control Engineering; Computer Engineering; Computer Networks; Construction Engineering; Energy Engineering; Forestry; Secretarial Studies; Surveying and Mapping); **Cuiabá - Bela Vista** (Environmental Management; Food Technology); **Juína** (Agricultural Business; Biology); **Pontes e Lacerda** (Computer Networks; International Business; Physics); **Primavera do Leste** (Automation and Control Engineering); **Rondonópolis** (Systems Analysis); **São Vicente** (Agronomy; Food Technology; Natural Sciences; Systems Analysis; Zoology); **Sorriso** (Crop Production; Environmental Management)

Further Information: Also campuses in Barra do Garças, Cuiabá - Bela Vista, Cáceres, Confresa, Cuiabá, Juína, Campo Novo do Parecis, Pontes e Lacerda, Rondonópolis, São Vicente. Also Distance Education programmes.

History: Founded 2008 through merger of Centro Federal de Educação Tecnológica de Mato Grosso, Centro Federal de Educação Tecnológica de Cuiabá, and Escola Agrotécnica Federal de Cáceres.

Main Language(s) of Instruction: Portuguese

Degrees and Diplomas: *Tecnólogo*; *Bacharelado*; *Licenciatura*; *Especialização/Aperfeiçoamento*: **Computer Networks; History.** *Mestrado*: **Food Technology.**

Last Updated: 05/04/16

FEDERAL INSTITUTE OF EDUCATION, SCIENCE AND TECHNOLOGY OF MINAS GERAIS

Instituto Federal de Educação, Ciência e Tecnologia de Minas Gerais (IFMG)

Avenida Professor Mário Werneck, 2590, Buritis,
Belo Horizonte, MG 30575-180
Tel: +55(31) 2513-5222
EMail: gabinete@ifmg.edu.br
Website: http://www.ifmg.edu.br

Reitor: Kléber Gonçalves Glória
Tel: +55(31) 2513-5103 EMail: kleber.gloria@ifmg.edu.br

Campus

Bambui (Administration; Agronomy; Biology; Computer Engineering; Food Technology; Physics; Production Engineering; Systems Analysis; Zoology); **Betim** (Automation and Control Engineering; Mechanical Engineering); **Congonhas** (Mechanical Engineering; Physics; Production Engineering); **Formigas** (Accountancy; Administration; Electrical Engineering; Finance; Mathematics); **Governador Valadares** (Environmental Engineering; Production Engineering); **Itabirito** (Electrical Engineering); **Ouro Branco** (Administration; Computer Science; Metallurgical Engineering); **Ouro Preto** (Cooking and Catering; Geography; Physics; Restoration of Works of Art; Safety Engineering); **Piumhi** (Civil Engineering); **Ribeirao Das Neves** (Management Systems); **Sabara** (Management Systems; Systems Analysis; Transport Management); **Santa Luzia** (Architecture; Civil Engineering; Interior Design; Town Planning); **São João Evangelista** (Agronomy; Forestry; Information Technology; Mathematics)

Further Information: Also 12 campuses: Ambuí, Betim, Congonhas, Formiga, Governador Valadares, Ibirité, Ouro Branco, Ouro Preto, Ribeirão das Neves, Sabará, Santa Luzia and São João Evangelista

History: Founded 2008 from the merging of Escola Agrotécnica Federal de São João Evangelista, and the CEFETs of Ouro Preto and Bambuí and UNEDs of Formiga and Congonhas

Main Language(s) of Instruction: Portuguese

Degrees and Diplomas: *Tecnólogo*; *Bacharelado*; *Licenciatura*; *Especialização/Aperfeiçoamento*: **Environmental Studies; Food Technology; Mathematics Education; Public Administration; Safety Engineering; Special Education.** *Mestrado*: **Environmental Engineering; Mathematics Education.**

Student Services: Library
Last Updated: 06/04/16

FEDERAL INSTITUTE OF EDUCATION, SCIENCE AND TECHNOLOGY OF NORTHERN MINAS GERAIS

Instituto Federal de Educação, Ciência e Tecnologia do Norte de Minas Gerais (ISE ZONA OESTE)

Rua Manoel Caldeira de Alvarenga, 1203,
Quintino-Bocaiúva, Rio de Janeiro 23070-200
Tel: +55(38) 3201-3050
Fax: +55(38) 3201-3075
EMail: ise.uezo@faetec.rj.gov.br
Website: http://www.faetec.rj.gov.br

Reitor: José Ricardo Martins da Silva EMail: reitor@ifnmg.edu.br

Course

Administration (Administration; Business Administration); **Agricultural and Environmental Engineering** (Agricultural Engineering; Environmental Engineering); **Agronomy** (Agronomy); **Biology** (Biology); **Chemistry** (Chemistry); **Irrigation** (Irrigation); **Mathematics** (Mathematics); **Physics** (Physics); **Systems Analysis and Development** (Computer Science; Systems Analysis)

History: Founded 1960 as Escola Agrotécnica de Januária-MG. Renamed Colégio Agrícola de Januária 1964. Transformed into Centro Federal de Educação Tecnológica de Januária - CEFET 2002. Acquired present status and title 2008 following merger with Escola Agrotécnica Federal de Salinas.

Main Language(s) of Instruction: Portuguese

Degrees and Diplomas: *Tecnólogo*; *Bacharelado*; *Licenciatura*
Last Updated: 11/04/16

FEDERAL INSTITUTE OF EDUCATION, SCIENCE AND TECHNOLOGY OF NORTHERN RIO GRANDE

Instituto Federal de Educação, Ciência e Tecnologia do Rio Grande do Norte (IFRN)

Rua Doutor Nilo Bezerra Ramalho, 1692, Tirol,
Natal, Rio Grande do Norte 59015-300
Tel: +55(84) 4005-2600
EMail: proen@ifrn.edu.br
Website: http://www.ifrn.edu.br

Reitor: Belchior de Oliveira Rocha
EMail: gabinete.reitoria@ifrn.edu.br

Pro-Reitor de Ensino: José de Ribamar Silva Oliveira

Course

Postgraduate Studies (Education; Literature; Natural Sciences; Public Administration); **Undergraduate Studies** (Biology; Chemistry; Computer Science; Energy Engineering; Geography; Heating and Refrigeration; Mathematics; Mechanical Engineering; Natural Sciences; Physics; Spanish)

Further Information: Also 20 Campus across the country (Apodi, Canguaretama, Ceará-Mirim, Currais Novos, Ipanguaçu, João Câmara, Lajes, Natal - Central, Nova Cruz, Santa Cruz, São Paulo do Potengi...)

History: Founded 1999 as Centro Federal de Educação Tecnológica do Rio Grande do Norte (CEFET/RN). Acquired present status and title 2008.

Main Language(s) of Instruction: Portuguese

Degrees and Diplomas: *Tecnólogo*; *Licenciatura*; *Especialização/Aperfeiçoamento*: **Distance Education; Education; Environmental Studies; Geography; Literature; Mathematics Education; Portuguese; Primary Education; Public Administration; Rural Studies; Science Education; Technology Education.** *Mestrado*: **Natural Resources; Physics; Vocational Education.**

Student Services: Library
Last Updated: 08/04/16

FEDERAL INSTITUTE OF EDUCATION, SCIENCE AND TECHNOLOGY OF PARÁ

Instituto Federal de Educação, Ciência e Tecnologia do Pará (IFPA)

Av. João Paulo II, 514 - Castanheira, Belém, Pará 66645-240
Tel: +55(91) 3342-0578
Fax: +55(91) 3226-9710
EMail: gabinete.reitoria@ifpa.edu.br
Website: http://www.ifpa.edu.br

Reitor: Claudio Alex Jorge da Rocha
EMail: claudio.alex@ifpa.edu.br

Course

Postgraduate Studies (Education; Management; Public Administration); **Undergraduate** (Agriculture; Aquaculture; Automation and Control Engineering; Biology; Chemistry; Computer Science; Education; Engineering; Environmental Management; Environmental Studies; Geography; Health Administration; Materials Engineering; Mathematics; Pedagogy; Physics; Public Administration; Public Health; Rural Studies; Systems Analysis; Telecommunications Engineering)

History: Founded 1999 as Centro Federal de Educação Tecnológica do Pará (CEFET/PA). Acquired present status and title 2008.

Main Language(s) of Instruction: Portuguese

Degrees and Diplomas: *Tecnólogo*; *Licenciatura*; *Especialização/Aperfeiçoamento*: **Education; Management; Public Administration; Rural Studies.**

Student Services: Library
Last Updated: 08/04/16

FEDERAL INSTITUTE OF EDUCATION, SCIENCE AND TECHNOLOGY OF PARAÍBA

Instituto Federal de Educação, Ciência e Tecnologia da Paraíba (IFPB)

Av. João da Mata, 256, Jaguaribe,
João Pessoa, Paraíba 58015-020
Tel: +55(83) 3612-1200
EMail: gabinete.reitoria@ifpb.edu.br
Website: http://www.ifpb.edu.br

Reitor: Cícero Nicácio do Nascimento Lopes
Tel: +55(83) 3612-9701 EMail: nicacio@ifpb.edu.br

Course

Administration (Administration); **Automation and Industrial Engineering** (Automation and Control Engineering); **Biology** (Biology); **Chemistry** (Chemistry); **Civil Engineering** (Civil Engineering); **Computer Engineering** (Computer Engineering);

Computer Networks (Computer Networks); **Electrical Engineering** (Electrical Engineering); **Graphic Design** (Graphic Design); **Mathematics** (Mathematics); **Physical Education** (Physical Education); **Physics** (Physics); **Real Estate** (Real Estate); **Systems for Internet** (Computer Networks; Computer Science); **Telecommunications Engineering** (Telecommunications Engineering); **Veterinary Science** (Veterinary Science)

Further Information: Also branch in Cajazeiras and Campina Grande.

History: Founded 1909. Became CEFET – Centro Federal de Educação Tecnológica da Paraíba 1999. Acquired present title following merger with Escola Agrotécnica Federal de Souza 2008.

Main Language(s) of Instruction: Portuguese

Degrees and Diplomas: *Tecnólogo*; *Bacharelado*; *Licenciatura*; *Mestrado*: **Electrical Engineering.**

Student Services: Library
Last Updated: 05/04/16

FEDERAL INSTITUTE OF EDUCATION, SCIENCE AND TECHNOLOGY OF PERNAMBUCO

Instituto Federal de Educação, Ciência e Tecnologia de Pernambuco (IFPE)

Avenida Professor Luiz Freire 500, Cidade Universitária,
Recife, Pernambuco 50740-540
Tel: +55(81) 2125-1600
Fax: +55(81) 3271-2338
EMail: gabinete@reitoria.ifpe.edu.br
Website: http://www.ifpe.edu.br

Reitora: Cláudia da Silva Santos Sansil (2011-)
Tel: +55(81) 2125-1608/1607

International Relations: Jussara Pimentel, Assessora de Relações Internacionais EMail: arinter@reitoria.ifpe.edu.br

Campus

Afogados da Ingazeira (Agricultural Business; Computer Science; Hygiene); **Barreiros** (Agriculture; Chemistry; Ecology); **Belo Jardim** (Agricultural Business; Computer Science; Music; Nursing); **Caruaru** (Mechanical Engineering); **Garanhuns** (Computer Science); **Ipojuca** (Automation and Control Engineering; Chemistry; Industrial Engineering; Occupational Health); **Pesqueira** (Construction Engineering; Electronic Engineering; Mathematics; Nursing; Physics); **Recife** (Civil Engineering; Environmental Management; Geography; Graphic Design; Production Engineering; Radiology; Systems Analysis; Tourism); **Vitória de Santo Antão** (Agricultural Business; Agriculture; Animal Husbandry)

History: Founded as Escola de Artifícies do Recife 1910. Became, Centro Federal de Educação Tecnológica de Pernambuco, 1999. Acquired present and status 2008.

Main Language(s) of Instruction: Portuguese

Degrees and Diplomas: *Tecnólogo*; *Bacharelado*; *Licenciatura*; *Especialização/Aperfeiçoamento*: **Mathematics Education; Public Administration.** *Mestrado*: **Environmental Management.**

Student Services: Library
Last Updated: 06/04/16

FEDERAL INSTITUTE OF EDUCATION, SCIENCE AND TECHNOLOGY OF PIAUÍ

Instituto Federal de Educação, Ciência e Tecnologia do Piauí (IFPI)

Av. Presidente Jânio Quadros, 330, Santa Isabel,
Teresina, Piauí 64053-390
Tel: +55(86) 3131-1433
EMail: reitoria@ifpi.edu.br
Website: http://www.ifpi.edu.br

Reitor: Paulo Henrique Gomes de Lima Tel: +55(86) 3131-1443

Course

Undergraduate Studies (Administration; Biological and Life Sciences; Biology; Chemistry; Computer Science; Mathematics; Mechanical Engineering; Physics; Systems Analysis)

Further Information: Also 19 campuses across the country (Campo Maior, Floriano, Paulistana, Piripiri, Teresina Central, Uruçuí...) and Distance Education

History: Founded 1999 as Centro Federal de Educação Tecnológica do Piauí (CEFET/PI). Acquired present status and title 2008.

Main Language(s) of Instruction: Portuguese

Degrees and Diplomas: *Tecnólogo*; *Bacharelado*; *Licenciatura*; *Especialização/Aperfeiçoamento*: **Computer Science; Environmental Management; Environmental Studies; Higher Education Teacher Training; Mathematics Education.** *Mestrado*: **Materials Engineering.**

Student Services: Library
Last Updated: 08/04/16

FEDERAL INSTITUTE OF EDUCATION, SCIENCE AND TECHNOLOGY OF RIO DE JANEIRO

Instituto Federal de Educação, Ciência e Tecnologia do Rio de Janeiro (IFRJ)

Rua Pereira de Almeida, 88, Praça da Bandeira,
Nilópolis, Rio de Janeiro 20260-100
Tel: +55(21) 3293-6000
EMail: dga@ifrj.edu.br
Website: http://www.ifrj.edu.br

Reitor: Paulo Roberto de Assis Passos EMail: gr@ifrj.edu.br

Pró-Reitora de Ensino de Graduação (ProGrad): Elizabeth Augustinho EMail: prograd@ifrj.edu.br

International Relations: Adriana Mesquita Rigueira
Tel: +55(21) 3293-6085 EMail: assint@ifrj.edu.br

Course

Biology (Biology; Biotechnology); **Chemical Processes** (Chemistry; Industrial Chemistry); **Chemistry** (Chemistry); **Cultural Production** (Cultural Studies); **Environmental Management** (Environmental Management); **Industrial Production** (Industrial Engineering; Production Engineering); **Management of Industrial Production** (Industrial Management); **Mathematics** (Mathematics); **Occupational Therapy** (Occupational Therapy); **Pharmacy** (Pharmacy); **Physical Therapy** (Physical Therapy); **Physics** (Physics)

Further Information: Also Unidades Paracambi and Rio de Janeiro

History: Founded 1999 as Centro Federal de Educação Tecnológica de Química de Nilópolis. Acquired present status and title 2008.

Main Language(s) of Instruction: Portuguese

Degrees and Diplomas: *Tecnólogo*; *Bacharelado*; *Licenciatura*; *Especialização/Aperfeiçoamento*: **Adult Education; Art Education; Environmental Management; History; Humanities and Social Science Education; Mathematics Education; Nutrition; Science Education; Teacher Training.** *Mestrado*: **Biochemistry; Biology; Food Technology; Science Education.**

Student Services: Library
Last Updated: 08/04/16

FEDERAL INSTITUTE OF EDUCATION, SCIENCE AND TECHNOLOGY OF RONDONIA

Instituto Federal de Educação, Ciencia e Tecnologia de Rondônia

Av. 7 de Setembro, 2090 - Nossa Senhora das Graças,
Porto Velho, RO 76.804-124
Tel: +502(69) 2182-9600
EMail: reitoria@ifro.edu.br
Website: http://www.ifro.edu.br

Reitor: Uberlando Tiburtino Leite

Course

Physics (Physics)

History: Founded 2008.

Main Language(s) of Instruction: Portuguese

Degrees and Diplomas: *Licenciatura*
Last Updated: 15/04/16

FEDERAL INSTITUTE OF EDUCATION, SCIENCE AND TECHNOLOGY OF RORAIMA

Instituto Federal de Educação, Ciência e Tecnologia de Roraima (IFRR)
Rua Fernão Dias Paes Leme, n° 11 – Calungá,
Boa Vista, Roraima 69303-220
Tel: +55(95) 3624-1224
Fax: +55(95) 3624-1224
EMail: gabinete.reitoria@ifrr.edu.br
Website: http://www.ifrr.edu.br

Reitor: Ademar de Araújo Filho EMail: reitor@ifrr.edu.br

Campus

Amajari (Agriculture; Aquaculture); **Boa Vista Centro** (Biology; Environmental Studies; Health Administration; Literature; Nursing; Physical Education; Public Health; Spanish; Systems Analysis; Tourism); **Boa Vista Zona Oeste** (Business and Commerce; Public Administration); **Bonfim** (Administration; International Business); **Novo Paraíso** (Agriculture)

History: Founded 2002 as Centro Federal de Educação Tecnológica de Roraima (CEFET-RR). Acquired present status and title 2008.

Main Language(s) of Instruction: Portuguese

Degrees and Diplomas: *Tecnólogo*; *Licenciatura*; *Especialização/Aperfeiçoamento*

Last Updated: 06/04/16

FEDERAL INSTITUTE OF EDUCATION, SCIENCE AND TECHNOLOGY OF SANTA CATARINA

Instituto Federal de Educação, Ciencia e Tecnologia Catarinense
Rua das Missões, 100, Blumenau, SC 89051-000
Tel: +502(47) 3331-7800
Website: http://www.ifc.edu.br

Reitora: Sônia Regina de Souza Fernandes

Course

Agriculture (Agriculture); **Agronomy** (Agronomy); **Automation and Control Engineering** (Automation and Control Engineering); **Chemistry** (Chemistry); **Computer Science** (Computer Science); **Food Technology** (Food Technology); **Mathematics** (Mathematics); **Mechanical Engineering** (Mechanical Engineering); **Pedagogy** (Pedagogy); **Physics** (Physics); **Veterinary Science** (Veterinary Science)

Further Information: Also campuses in Belardo Luz, Araquari, Brusque, Camboriú, Concórdia, Fraiburgo, Ibirama, Luzerna, Rio do Sul, Santa Rosa do Sul, São Bento do Sul, São Francisco do Sul, Sombrio e Videira.

History: Founded 1954.

Main Language(s) of Instruction: Portuguese

Degrees and Diplomas: *Bacharelado*; *Licenciatura*; *Especialização/Aperfeiçoamento*

Last Updated: 15/04/16

FEDERAL INSTITUTE OF EDUCATION, SCIENCE AND TECHNOLOGY OF SANTA CATARINA

Instituto Federal de Educação, Ciência e Tecnologia de Santa Catarina (IFSC)
Rua 14 de Julho, 150 - Coqueiros, Centro,
Florianópolis, Santa Catarina 88075-010
Tel: +55(48) 3877-9000
EMail: reitoria@ifsc.edu.br
Website: http://www.ifsc.edu.br/

Reitora: Maria Clara Kaschny Schneider
Tel: +55(48) 3877-9002 EMail: mclara@ifsc.edu.br

Pró-Reitor de Ensino: Luiz Otávio Cabral
EMail: proen@ifsc.edu.br

Campus

Araranguá (Fashion Design; Physics); **Caçador** (Production Engineering); **Cachoeira do Sul/RS** (Public Administration); **Campos Novo** (Public Administration); **Canoinhas** (Food Technology; Systems Analysis); **Chapecó** (Automation and Control Engineering); **Criciúma** (Chemistry; Electrical Engineering; Mechanical Engineering); **Florianópolis** (Civil Engineering; Construction Engineering; Design; Electrical Engineering; Electronic Engineering; Energy Engineering; Information Technology; Mechanical Engineering; Radiology); **Florianópolis Continente** (Cooking and Catering; Hotel Management); **Foz do Iguaçú/PR** (Public Administration); **Gaspar** (Fashion Design; Management; Systems Analysis); **Itajaí** (Electrical Engineering); **Jales/SP** (Public Administration); **Jaraguá do Sul** (Physics); **Jaraguá do Sul GW** (Electrical Engineering; Electronic Engineering; Mechanical Engineering); **Joinville** (Electrical Engineering; Health Administration; Mechanical Engineering); **Lages** (Computer Science; Mechanical Engineering); **Palmitos** (Public Administration); **Prefeitura Municipal de São José** (Public Administration); **São José** (Chemistry; Telecommunications Engineering); **São Miguel do Oeste** (Agronomy; Food Technology); **Urupema** (Food Technology; Oenology); **Xanxerê** (Mechanical Engineering)

Further Information: Also 22 campuses and Distance Education programmes.

History: Founded 1909 as Escola de Aprendizes Artifices de Santa Catarin. Became Liceu Industrial de Florianópolis 1937. Transformed into Escola Industrial de Florianópolis 1942. Name changed to Escola Industrial Federal de Santa Catarina 1965. Became Escola Técnica Federal de Santa Catarina (ETF-SC) 1968. Transformed into Centro Federais de Educação Tecnológica (CEFET-SC) 1994. Acquired present title and status 2008.

Degrees and Diplomas: *Tecnólogo*; *Licenciatura*; *Especialização/Aperfeiçoamento*: **Education; Education of the Handicapped; Electronic Engineering; Health Education; Marine Science and Oceanography; Media Studies; Primary Education; Public Administration; Science Education; Secondary Education; Vocational Education.** *Mestrado*: **Electrical Engineering; Mechanical Engineering.**

Student Services: Library

Last Updated: 06/04/16

FEDERAL INSTITUTE OF EDUCATION, SCIENCE AND TECHNOLOGY OF SÃO PAULO

Instituto Federal de Educação, Ciência e Tecnologia de São Paulo (IFSP)
Rua Pedro Vicente 625, Canindé, São Paulo, São Paulo 01109-010
Tel: +55(11) 3775-4501
EMail: secretariacolegiados@ifsp.edu.br
Website: http://www.ifsp.edu.br

Reitor: Eduardo Antonio Modena EMail: gab@ifsp.edu.br

Course

Architecture and Town Planning (Architecture; Town Planning); **Automation and Control Engineering** (Automation and Control Engineering); **Biological Sciences** (Biological and Life Sciences); **Chemistry** (Chemistry); **Civil Engineering** (Civil Engineering); **Electrical Systems** (Electrical Engineering); **Electronic Systems** (Electronic Engineering); **Geography** (Geography); **Mathematics** (Mathematics); **Mechanical Fabrication** (Mechanical Engineering); **Mechanical Production** (Mechanical Engineering; Production Engineering); **Physics** (Physics); **Systems Analysis and Development** (Systems Analysis); **Tourism** (Tourism)

Further Information: Also following Campuses: São Paulo, Cubatão, Sertãozinho, Guarulhos, Caraguatatuba, São João da Boa Vista, Bragança Paulista, Salto, São Roque, São Carlos, Campos do Jordão.

History: Founded 1999 as Centro Federal de Educação Tecnológica de São Paulo. Acquired present status and title 2008.

Main Language(s) of Instruction: Portuguese

Degrees and Diplomas: *Tecnólogo*; *Bacharelado*: **Administration; Architecture; Automation and Control Engineering; Civil Engineering; Electronic Engineering; Mechanical Engineering; Production Engineering; Town Planning.** *Licenciatura*: **Biology; Chemistry; Geography; Linguistics; Literature; Mathematics; Physics.** *Especialização/Aperfeiçoamento*: **Adult Education; Computer Engineering; Construction Engineering; Education; Information Technology; Primary Education; Software Engineering; Teacher Training; Vocational Education.** *Mestrado*:

Automation and Control Engineering; Mathematics; Mathematics Education; Mechanical Engineering.

Student Services: Library

Last Updated: 06/04/16

FEDERAL INSTITUTE OF EDUCATION, SCIENCE AND TECHNOLOGY OF SERGIPE

Instituto Federal de Educação, Ciência e Tecnologia de Sergipe (IFS)

Avenida Engenheiro Gentil Tavares da Mota, 1166, Bairro Getúlio Vargas, Aracaju, Sergipe 49055-260

Tel: +55(79) 3711-3100

Fax: +55(79) 3711-3155

EMail: direcao@ifs.edu.br

Website: http://www.ifs.edu.br

Reitor: Ailton Ribeiro de Oliveira

Course

Agroecology (Ecology; Plant and Crop Protection); **Automation and Control Engineering** (Automation and Control Engineering); **Chemistry** (Chemistry); **Civil Engineering** (Civil Engineering); **Environmental Studies** (Environmental Studies); **Food Technology** (Food Technology); **Information Systems** (Information Technology); **Logistics** (Transport Management); **Mathematics** (Mathematics); **Physics** (Physics); **Tourism** (Tourism)

Further Information: Also Aracaju, Lagarto, São Cristóvão, Estância, Itabaiana, Nossa Senhora da Glória, Tobias Barreto, and Propriá campuses

History: Founded 2002 as Centro Federal de Educação Tecnológica de Sergipe (CEFETSE). Acquired present status and title 2008.

Main Language(s) of Instruction: Portuguese

Degrees and Diplomas: *Tecnólogo*; *Bacharelado*; *Licenciatura*

Last Updated: 07/04/16

FEDERAL INSTITUTE OF EDUCATION, SCIENCE AND TECHNOLOGY OF SERTÃO PERNAMBUCANO

Instituto Federal de Educação, Ciência e Tecnologia do Sertão Pernambucano

Rua Coronel Amorim, 76, Centro, Petrolina, Pernambuco 56302-320

Tel: +55(87) 2101-2350

EMail: comunicacao@ifsertao-pe.edu.br

Website: http://www.ifsertao-pe.edu.br

Reitor: Adelmo Carvalho Santana (2015-)

EMail: ailson.vanderlei@ifsertao-pe.edu.br

Course

Chemistry (Chemistry); **Computer Science** (Computer Science); **Irrigated Fruit Culture** (Fruit Production); **Music** (Music); **Physics** (Physics); **Semi-Arid Fruit Production** *(Postgraduate)* (Fruit Production); **Viticulture and Oenology** (Oenology; Viticulture)

Further Information: Also Petrolina, Petrolina Zona Rural, Floresta, Salgueiro, Ouricurin, Santa Maria da Boa Vista, Serra Talhada, Campuses.

History: Founded 1999 from Escola Agrotécnica Federal Dom Avelar Vilela. Formerly known as Centro Federal de Educação Tecnológica de Petrolina (CEFET-Petrolina).

Main Language(s) of Instruction: Portuguese

Degrees and Diplomas: *Tecnólogo*; *Bacharelado*: **Agronomy.** *Licenciatura*: **Chemistry; Computer Science; Music; Physics.** *Especialização/Aperfeiçoamento*: **Education; Environmental Engineering; Fruit Production; Horticulture; Primary Education.**

Student Services: Library

Last Updated: 10/04/16

FEDERAL INSTITUTE OF EDUCATION, SCIENCE AND TECHNOLOGY OF SOUTHERN RIO GRANDE - BENTO GONÇALVES CAMPUS

Instituto Federal de Educação, Ciência e Tecnologia do Rio Grande do Sul - Campus Bento Gonçalves (IFRS)

Avenida Osvaldo Aranha, 540, Bairro Juventude da Enologia, Bento Gonçalves, RS 95700-000

Tel: +55(54) 3455-3200

Fax: +55(54) 3455-3246

EMail: gabinete@bento.ifrs.edu.br

Website: http://bento.ifrs.edu.br/site/index.php

Diretora-Geral: Soeni Bellé

Course

Agriculture (Agriculture; Horticulture); **Animal Husbandry** (Animal Husbandry; Cattle Breeding); **Logistics** (Transport Management); **Mathematics** (Mathematics; Physics); **Oenology** (Oenology); **Pedagogy** (Teacher Training); **Physics** (Physics); **Viticulture** (Viticulture)

Further Information: Also Distance Education programmes.

History: Founded 1959 as Colégio de Viticultura e Enologia de Bento Gonçalves. Changed name to Escola Agrotécnica Federal Presidente Juscelino Kubistchek 1985. Became Centro Federal de Educação Tecnológica de Bento Gonçalves (Cefet-BG) 2002. Acquired present status and title 2008.

Main Language(s) of Instruction: Portuguese

Degrees and Diplomas: *Tecnólogo*; *Licenciatura*: **Mathematics; Physics; Teacher Training.** *Especialização/Aperfeiçoamento*: **Adult Education; Education; Viticulture; Vocational Education.**

Student Services: Library

Last Updated: 10/04/16

FEDERAL INSTITUTE OF EDUCATION, SCIENCE AND TECHNOLOGY OF THE AMAZON

Instituto Federal de Educação, Ciência e Tecnologia do Amazonas (IFAM)

Avenida Sete de Setembro 1975 Centro, Manaus, Amazonas 69020-120

Tel: +55(92) 3621-6700

EMail: pcqi@ifam.edu.br

Website: http://www.ifam.edu.br

Reitor: Antonio Venâncio Castelo Branco

Tel: +55(92) 3306-0003 EMail: venancio@ifam.edu.br

Course

Advertising and Publicity (Advertising and Publicity); **Agroecology** (Agriculture; Ecology; Veterinary Science); **Biology** (Biology); **Chemical Processes** (Chemistry); **Chemistry** (Chemistry); **Civil Engineering** (Civil Engineering); **Construction Engineering** (Construction Engineering); **Electronic Systems** (Electronic Engineering); **Food Science** (Food Science); **Mathematics** (Mathematics); **Mechanical Engineering** (Mechanical Engineering); **Software Engineering** (Software Engineering); **System Analyses** (Systems Analysis); **Telecommunications Engineering** (Telecommunications Engineering)

Further Information: Also 15 campuses across the country: Manaus Centro, Manaus Zona Leste, Manaus Distrito Industial, Coari, São Gabriel da Cachoeira, Presidente Figueiredo, Lábrea, Tabatinga, Parintins, and more

History: Founded 2001 as Centro Federal de Educação Tecnológica do Amazonas. Acquired present status and title 2008.

Main Language(s) of Instruction: Portuguese

Degrees and Diplomas: *Tecnólogo*; *Licenciatura*; *Especialização/Aperfeiçoamento*: **Special Education.** *Mestrado*: **Physics; Technology Education.**

Student Services: Library

Last Updated: 07/04/16

FEDERAL INSTITUTE OF EDUCATION, SCIENCE AND TECHNOLOGY OF THE SOUTH OF RIO GRANDE

Instituto Federal de Educação, Ciência e Tecnologia Sul-Rio-Grandense (IFSUL)

Rua Gonçalves Chaves 3798, Bairro Centro,
Pelotas, Rio Grande do Sul 96015-560
Tel: +55(53) 3309-1750
Fax: +55(53) 3309-1766
EMail: reitoria@ifsul.edu.br
Website: http://www.ifsul.edu.br

Reitor: Marcelo Bender Machado

Campus

Bagé; **Camaquã**; **Charqueadas**; **Passo Fundo** (Computer Science); **Pelotas** (Automation and Control Engineering; Chemical Engineering; Computer Science; Design; Education; Electrical Engineering; Environmental Management; Environmental Studies; Industrial Engineering; Modern Languages; Telecommunications Engineering); **Sapucaia do Sul** (Industrial Management; Mechanics); **Venâncio Aires**

History: Founded 1999 as Centro Federal de Educação Tecnológica de Pelotas. Acquired present status and title 2008.

Main Language(s) of Instruction: Portuguese

Degrees and Diplomas: *Tecnólogo*; *Bacharelado*; *Especialização/Aperfeiçoamento*: **Chemistry; Education; Literature; Portuguese; Teacher Training.** *Mestrado*: **Education; Technology.**

Student Services: Library

Last Updated: 11/04/16

FEDERAL INSTITUTE OF EDUCATION, SCIENCE AND TECHNOLOGY OF THE SOUTHEAST OF MINAS GERAIS

Instituto Federal de Educação, Ciência e Tecnologia do Sudeste de Minas Gerais

Avenida Francisco Bernardino, 165, Centro,
Juiz de Fora, Minas Gerais 36013-100
Tel: +55(32) 3216-2366
Fax: +55(32) 3216-2366
EMail: gabinete@ifsudeste.edu.br
Website: http://www.ifsudeste.edu.br

Reitor: Mário Sérgio Costa Vieira
EMail: mario.sergio@ifsudeste.edu.br

Campus

Barbacena; **Juiz de Fora** (Electronic Engineering; Mechanical Engineering; Physics); **Muriaé** (Administration; Fashion Design); **Rio Pomba**

History: Founded 1964 as Ginásio Agrícola de Rio Pomba. Became Colégio Agrícola de Rio Pomba 1968. Became Escola Agrotécnica Federal de Rio Pomba - MG 1979. Transformed into Centro Federal de Educação Tecnológica de Rio Pomba 2002. Acquired present status and title 2008.

Degrees and Diplomas: *Tecnólogo*; *Bacharelado*; *Licenciatura*; *Especialização/Aperfeiçoamento*

Last Updated: 18/04/16

FEDERAL INSTITUTE OF EDUCATION, SCIENCE AND TECHNOLOGY OF TRIÂNGULO MINEIRO

Instituto Federal de Educação, Ciência e Tecnologia do Triângulo Mineiro (IFTM)

Av. Doutor Randolfo Borges Júnior, 2900, Bairro São Benedito,
Uberaba, Minas Gerais 38064-300
Tel: +55(34) 3326-1100
Fax: +55(34)3326-1101
EMail: reitor@iftm.edu.br
Website: http://www.iftm.edu.br

Reitor: Roberto Gil Rodrigues Almeida

Campus

Ituiutaba (Agricultural Business; Computer Science); **Paracatu** (Computer Science; Electronic Engineering); **Patos de Minas** (Electronic Engineering; Transport Management); **Patrocínio** (Business and Commerce; Systems Analysis); **Uberaba** (Agricultural Engineering; Animal Husbandry; Biology; Chemistry; Environmental Management; Food Technology; Social Sciences; Systems Analysis); **Uberlândia** (Agricultural Engineering; Agriculture; Food Technology)

Further Information: Also Avançado Campina Verde, Ituiutaba, Paracatu, Patos de Minas, Patrocínio, Uberaba, Avançado Uberaba Parque Tecnológico, Uberlândia, Uberlândia Centro, campuses and 6 poles.

History: Founded 2002 as Centro Federal de Educação Tecnológica de Uberaba (CEFET Uberaba). Acquired present status and title 2008 following merger with Escola Agrotécnica Federal de Uberlândia.

Main Language(s) of Instruction: Portuguese

Degrees and Diplomas: *Tecnólogo*; *Bacharelado*; *Licenciatura*; *Especialização/Aperfeiçoamento*: **Business Administration; Environmental Studies; Food Technology; Vocational Education.** *Mestrado*: **Food Technology; Technology Education; Vegetable Production.**

Last Updated: 11/04/16

FEDERAL RURAL UNIVERSITY OF PERNAMBUCO

Universidade Federal Rural de Pernambuco (UFRPE)

Rua Dom Manoel de Medeiros s/n Dois Irmãos,
Recife, Pernambuco 52171900
Tel: +55(81) 3320.6011
EMail: reitoria@reitoria.ufrpe.br
Website: http://www.ufrpe.br

Reitor: Valmar Corrêa de Andrade EMail: valmarc@ufrpe.br

Department

Agronomy (Agriculture; Agronomy); **Animal Husbandry** (Animal Husbandry); **Biology** (Biology); **Chemistry** (Chemistry); **Education** (Education); **Fishery and Aquaculture** (Aquaculture; Fishery); **Home Economics** (Home Economics); **Letters and Human Sciences** (Arts and Humanities); **Mathematics** (Mathematics); **Morphology and Animal Physiology** (Zoology); **Physics** (Physics); **Rural Technology** (Agricultural Engineering); **Statistics and Computer Science** (Computer Science; Statistics); **Veterinary Medicine** (Veterinary Science)

History: Founded 1912 as School, became University by State decree 1947, acquired status as Federal Institution 1956. Under the jurisdiction of the Ministry of Education and Sports.

Academic Year: March to December (March-June; August-December)

Admission Requirements: Secondary school certificate and entrance examination

Main Language(s) of Instruction: Portuguese

Degrees and Diplomas: *Bacharelado*: **Agricultural Engineering; Animal Husbandry; Biology; Fishery; Forestry; Social Sciences.** *Licenciatura*: **Home Economics.** *Mestrado*; *Doutorado*. Also teaching qualifications

Publications: Anais; Caderno Omega

Publishing House: Imprensa Universitária

Last Updated: 18/04/16

FEDERAL RURAL UNIVERSITY OF RIO DE JANEIRO

Universidade Federal Rural do Rio de Janeiro (UFRRJ)

BR 465 - Km 7, Seropédica, Rio de Janeiro 23890000
Tel: +55(21) 2682-1210
Fax: +55(21) 2682-1120
EMail: gabinete@ufrrj.br
Website: http://www.ufrrj.br

Reitor: Ricardo Motta Miranda

Vice-Reitora: Ana Maria Dantas Soares

Institute

Agronomy (Agronomy; Geology); **Animal Husbandry** (Animal Husbandry); **Biology** (Biology); **Education** (Agriculture; Education; Physical Education); **Exact Sciences** (Chemistry; Mathematics;

Physics); **Forestry** (Forestry); **Human and Social Sciences** (Administration; Economics; Home Economics; Social Sciences); **Technology** (Chemical Engineering; Food Science; Technology); **Veterinary Medicine** (Veterinary Science)

History: Founded 1910 as Universidade Rural do Brasil, acquired present status and title 1965. A State institution under the jurisdiction of and financially supported by the Ministry of Education and Sports.

Academic Year: March to December (March-July; August-December)

Admission Requirements: Secondary school certificate and entrance examination

Fees: None

Main Language(s) of Instruction: Portuguese

Degrees and Diplomas: *Bacharelado*; *Licenciatura*; *Mestrado*; *Doutorado*. Also combined Licenciatura and Bacharelado, 3 1/2-4 yrs

Student Services: Academic Counselling, Canteen, Health Services, Language Laboratory, Sports Facilities

Publications: Revista Universidade Rural. Série Ciências da Vida; Revista Universidade Rural. Série Ciências Exactas e da Terra; Revista Universidade Rural. Série Ciências Humanas

Last Updated: 18/04/16

FEDERAL RURAL UNIVERSITY OF THE AMAZON

Universidade Federal Rural da Amazônia (UFRA)

Avenida Presidente Tancredo Neves 2501, Terra Firme, Belém, Pará 66077530

Tel: +55(91) 3274-3493 +55(91) 3274-0900

Fax: +55(91) 3274-3814

EMail: reitoria@ufra.edu.br

Website: http://www.ufra.edu.br/

Reitor: Sueo Numazawa

Faculty

Agronomy (Agronomy); **Fishery** (Fishery); **Forestry Engineering**; **Veterinary Science** (Veterinary Science); **Zoology** (Zoology)

History: Founded 1943 as Escola de Agronomia da Amazônia. Became Faculdade de Ciências Agrárias do Pará 1973. Acquired present title and status 2002.

Degrees and Diplomas: *Bacharelado*; *Licenciatura*; *Mestrado*; *Doutorado*

Last Updated: 18/04/16

FEDERAL RURAL UNIVERSITY OF THE SEMI-ARID REGION

Universidade Federal Rural do Semi-Árido (UFERSA)

BR 110 - Km 47 Bairro Pres. Costa e Silva, Mossoró, Rio Grande do Norte 59625900

Tel: +55(84) 312-2100 +55(84) 312-2121

Fax: +55(84) 312-2499

EMail: ufersa@ufersa.edu.br

Website: http://www2.ufersa.edu.br

Reitor: Josivan Barbosa Menezes EMail: reitor@ufersa.edu.br

Department

Agricultural Technology and Social Sciences (Agricultural Engineering; Agronomy; Social Sciences); **Animal Sciences** (Veterinary Science; Zoology); **Botany** (Botany; Horticulture; Plant Pathology); **Environmental Studies**

History: Founded 1967 as Escola Superior de Agricultura de Mossoró. Acquired present status and title 2005.

Main Language(s) of Instruction: Portuguese

Degrees and Diplomas: *Bacharelado*; *Especialização/Aperfeiçoamento*; *Mestrado*; *Doutorado*

Last Updated: 18/04/16

FEDERAL UNIVERSITY OF ABC

Universidade Federal do ABC

Av. dos Estados, 5001, Bairro Bangu, Santo André, São Paulo 09.210-170

Tel: +55(11) 4996-7914/7973

EMail: prograd@ufabc.edu.br

Website: http://www.ufabc.edu.br

Reitor: Klaus Capelle

Tel: +55(11) 3356-7083

EMail: marcos.rubia@ufabc.edu.br; gabinete@ufabc.edu.br

Centre

Engineering, Modelling and Applied Social Sciences (Aeronautical and Aerospace Engineering; Automation and Control Engineering; Biomedical Engineering; Economics; Engineering; Environmental Engineering; Instrument Making; International Relations; Materials Engineering; Power Engineering; Public Administration; Robotics; Social Sciences); **Mathematics, Computer and Cognitive Sciences** (Cognitive Sciences; Computer Engineering; Computer Science; Mathematics; Mathematics Education; Neurosciences); **Natural and Human Sciences** (Architecture and Planning; Arts and Humanities; Biological and Life Sciences; Chemistry; Mathematics; Mathematics Education; Nanotechnology; Natural Sciences; Neurosciences; Philosophy; Physics; Science Education)

Further Information: Also São Bernardo do Campo

History: Founded 2005.

Main Language(s) of Instruction: Portuguese

Degrees and Diplomas: *Bacharelado*; *Licenciatura*; *Mestrado*: **Arts and Humanities; Biological and Life Sciences; Biomedical Engineering; Biotechnology; Chemical Engineering; Chemistry; Cognitive Sciences; Computer Science; Electrical Engineering; Energy Engineering; Engineering; Engineering Management; Environmental Engineering; Environmental Studies; Information Sciences; Materials Engineering; Mathematics; Mathematics Education; Mechanical Engineering; Nanotechnology; Neurosciences; Philosophy; Physics; Public Administration; Regional Planning; Science Education; Social Sciences.** *Doutorado*: **Arts and Humanities; Biological and Life Sciences; Biotechnology; Chemistry; Cognitive Sciences; Computer Science; Energy Engineering; Engineering; Information Sciences; Mathematics; Nanotechnology; Natural Sciences; Neurosciences; Physics; Regional Planning; Social Sciences.** Also Mestrado Profissional in Mathematics Education (PROFMAT) and in Physics Education (MNPEF); Doutorado Acadêmico Industrial

Student Services: Library

Last Updated: 05/02/16

FEDERAL UNIVERSITY OF ACRE

Universidade Federal do Acre (UFAC)

Campus Universitário, BR 364/Km 4, Distrito Industrial, Rio Branco, Acre 69915900

Tel: +55(68) 3901-2500

EMail: reitoria@ufac.br

Website: http://www.ufac.br

Reitora: Olinda Batista Assmar Tel: +55(68) 229-5735/1534

Department

Agronomy; **Economics**; **Education**; **Engineering**; **Geography**; **Health Sciences**; **History**; **Law** (Law); **Literature**; **Mathematics and Statistics**; **Natural Sciences**; **Philosophy and Social Sciences**; **Physical Education and Sports**

History: Founded 1971.

Admission Requirements: Secondary school certificate and entrance examination

Main Language(s) of Instruction: Portuguese

Degrees and Diplomas: *Bacharelado*; *Licenciatura*; *Especialização/Aperfeiçoamento*; *Mestrado*; *Doutorado*

Student Services: Canteen

Last Updated: 18/04/16

FEDERAL UNIVERSITY OF ALAGOAS

Universidade Federal de Alagoas (UFAL)

Km 97, Tabuleiro dos Martins, Maceió, Alagoas 57072900

Tel: +55(82) 3214-1002

Fax: +55(82) 3214-1700

EMail: gr@reitoria.ufal.br

Website: http://www.ufal.edu.br

Reitora: Ana Dayse Rezende Dorea Tel: +55(82) 3214-1006

Centre

Agriculture (Agricultural Economics; Agriculture; Animal Husbandry; Engineering); **Applied Social Sciences** (Accountancy; Economics; Social Sciences; Social Work); **Biological Sciences** (Biological and Life Sciences); **Education** (Education); **Exact and Natural Sciences** (Applied Mathematics; Chemistry; Geography; Geology; Mathematics; Meteorology; Natural Sciences; Physics; Surveying and Mapping); **Exact Sciences and Technology** (Architecture; Building Technologies; Chemical Engineering; Civil Engineering; Energy Engineering; Structural Architecture; Technology; Transport Engineering; Water Management); **Health Sciences** (Dentistry; Health Sciences; Medicine; Nursing; Nutrition; Physical Education; Social and Preventive Medicine; Surgery); **Human Sciences** (Arts and Humanities; Communication Studies; History; Literature; Modern Languages; Music; Pedagogy; Philosophy; Social and Community Services; Social Sciences; Theatre); **Law** (Law)

Further Information: Also University Hospital

History: Founded 1961. Reorganized 1983 and faculties and institutes replaced by academic centres. A State institution financed by the Federal Government.

Academic Year: April to December (April-July; September-December)

Admission Requirements: Secondary school certificate and competitive entrance examination

Main Language(s) of Instruction: Portuguese

Degrees and Diplomas: *Bacharelado*: **Accountancy; Administration; Agricultural Engineering; Animal Husbandry; Architecture; Biology; Chemical Engineering; Chemistry; Civil Engineering; Computer Science; Dentistry; Economics; Geography; Journalism; Law; Mathematics; Medicine; Meteorology; Nursing; Nutrition; Psychology; Public Relations; Social Sciences; Social Work.** *Licenciatura*: **Arts and Humanities; Biology; Education; Geography; History; Mathematics; Music; Performing Arts; Philosophy; Physical Education; Social Sciences.** *Especialização/Aperfeiçoamento*; *Mestrado*: **Administration; Biotechnology; Chemistry; Development Studies; Linguistics; Physics.** *Doutorado*: **Linguistics.**

Student Services: Academic Counselling, Canteen, Cultural Activities, Health Services, Sports Facilities

Publishing house: Edufal/Imprensa e Editora Universitária

Last Updated: 18/04/16

FEDERAL UNIVERSITY OF ALFENAS

Universidade Federal de Alfenas (UNIFAL-MG)

Rua Gabriel Monteiro da Silva 714, Centro, Alfenas, Minas Gerais 37130000

Tel: +55(35) 3299-1061

Fax: +55(35) 3299-1063

EMail: reitoria@unifal-mg.edu.br

Website: http://www.unifal-mg.edu.br

Reitor: Paulo Márcio de Faria e Silva
EMail: paulo.silva@unifal-mg.edu.br

Faculty

Dentistry (Dentistry); **Nutrition**; **Pharmacy** (Pharmacy)

School

Nursing (Nursing)

Institute

Biomedicine; **Exact Sciences** (Mathematics; Physics)

History: Founded 1914 as Escola de Farmácia e Odontologia de Alfenas. Acquired present status and title 2005.

Degrees and Diplomas: *Bacharelado*: **Biological and Life Sciences; Biotechnology; Chemistry; Computer Science; Dentistry; Geography; Mathematics; Nursing; Nutrition; Pedagogy; Pharmacy; Physics.** *Licenciatura*: **Biological and Life Sciences; Chemistry; Geography; Mathematics; Physics.** *Especialização/Aperfeiçoamento*: **Clinical Psychology; Dentistry.** *Mestrado*: **Pharmacy.** *Doutorado*

Last Updated: 18/04/16

FEDERAL UNIVERSITY OF AMAPÁ

Universidade Federal do Amapá (UNIFAP)

Rod. Juscelino Kubitschek, KM-02 - Jardim Marco Zero, Macapá, Amapá 68902280

Tel: +55(96) 3312-1700

EMail: unifap@unifap.br

Website: http://www.unifap.br

Reitor: José Carlos Tavares Carvalho EMail: reitor@unifap.br

Course

Architecture and Town Planning (Architecture; Town Planning); **Arts**; **Arts and Humanities**; **Biological and Life Sciences**; **Education**; **Electrical Engineering** (Electrical Engineering); **Environmental Studies**; **Geography**; **History**; **Law**; **Literature**; **Mathematics**; **Medicine**; **Nursing**; **Pedagogy**; **Pharmacy** (Pharmacy); **Physical Education**; **Physics** (Physics); **Social Sciences**

History: Founded 1990.

Admission Requirements: Secondary school certificate and entrance examination

Main Language(s) of Instruction: Portuguese

Degrees and Diplomas: *Bacharelado*; *Licenciatura*; *Especialização/Aperfeiçoamento*; *Mestrado*

Last Updated: 18/04/16

FEDERAL UNIVERSITY OF AMAZONAS

Universidade Federal do Amazonas (UFAM)

Avenida General Rodrigo Otávio Jordão Ramos 3000, Campus Universitário, Coroado II, Mánaus, Amazonas 69077000

Tel: +55(92) 3647-4314 +55(92) 3647-4415

Fax: +55(92) 3647-4314

EMail: gabinete@ufam.edu.br

Website: http://www.ufam.edu.br

Reitora: Márcia Perales Mendes da Silva Tel: +55(92) 3644-1602

Faculty

Agrarian Sciences (Agricultural Engineering; Agriculture; Fishery; Forestry); **Dentistry** (Dentistry); **Education** (Education); **Law** (Law; Private Law; Public Law); **Medicine**; **Pharmacy**; **Physical Education** (Physical Education); **Social Studies** (Accountancy; Administration; Economics; Social Studies); **Technology** (Civil Engineering; Electrical Engineering; Graphic Design; Industrial Design; Technology)

School

Nursing (Nursing)

Institute

Biological Sciences (Biological and Life Sciences; Biotechnology; Nautical Science; Parasitology); **Exact Sciences** (Chemistry; Data Processing; Geology; Mathematics; Natural Sciences; Physics; Statistics); **Human Sciences and Languages** (Arts and Humanities; Geography; History; Journalism; Library Science; Modern Languages; Philosophy; Social Sciences; Social Work)

Centre

Environmental Sciences (Environmental Studies)

Further Information: Campuses: Centro Universitário de Coari, Centro Universitário de Itacoatiara, Centro Universitário de Humaitá, Centro Universitário de Parintins, Centro Universitário de Benjamin Constant. Also Getúlio Vargas University Hospital

History: Founded 1909 as Escola Universitária Livre de Manáos. Later became Universidade de Manáos. Became Universidade do Amazonas 1962 and Universidade Federal do Amazonas 2002.

Academic Year: March to November (March-June; August-November)

Admission Requirements: Secondary school certificate and entrance examination

Fees: None

Main Language(s) of Instruction: Portuguese

Degrees and Diplomas: *Bacharelado*; *Licenciatura*; *Especialização/Aperfeiçoamento*; *Mestrado*; *Doutorado*

Student Services: Canteen, Facilities for disabled people, Sports Facilities

Publications: Ciências Agrárias; Ciências Humanas; Ciências Tecnológicas; Revista da Universidade; Séries: Ciências da Saúde

Publishing House: Imprensa Universitária

Last Updated: 18/04/16

FEDERAL UNIVERSITY OF BAHIA

Universidade Federal da Bahia (UFBA)
Rua Augusto Viana s/n Palacio da Reitoria, Canela,
Salvador, Bahia 40110060
Tel: +55(71) 263-7000 +55(71) 263-7030
Fax: +55(71) 263-7027
EMail: reitor@ufba.br
Website: http://www.ufba.br

Reitora: Dora Rosa Leal (2010-)

Area

Arts; Biological and Health Sciences (Biological and Life Sciences; Dentistry; Marine Science and Oceanography; Medicine; Natural Sciences; Nursing; Nutrition; Pharmacy; Speech Therapy and Audiology; Veterinary Science); **Literature** (Literature); **Philosophy and Human Sciences** (Accountancy; Administration; Archaeology; Communication Studies; Cultural Studies; Economics; History; Law; Library Science; Museum Studies; Pedagogy; Philosophy; Physical Education; Psychology; Secretarial Studies; Social Sciences); **Physics, Mathematics and Technology** (Architecture; Chemical Engineering; Chemistry; Civil Engineering; Computer Science; Electrical Engineering; Geography; Geology; Geophysics; Industrial Chemistry; Marine Science and Oceanography; Mathematics; Mechanical Engineering; Mining Engineering; Physics; Sanitary Engineering; Statistics; Town Planning)

History: Founded 1575 by the Society of Jesus, became University 1946 incorporating other institutions. Reorganized 1968. A State Institution under the jurisdiction of the Ministry of Education and Sports.

Academic Year: February to December (February-June; August-December)

Admission Requirements: Secondary school certificate and entrance examination

Main Language(s) of Instruction: Portuguese

Degrees and Diplomas: *Bacharelado*: **Accountancy; Animal Husbandry; Architecture; Arts and Humanities; Biology; Chemistry; Conducting; Dance; Engineering; Geography; Geology; History; Mathematics; Medicine; Midwifery; Modern Languages; Museum Studies; Music Theory and Composition; Musical Instruments; Nursing; Nutrition; Pedagogy; Philosophy; Physics; Psychology; Public Administration; Secretarial Studies; Singing; Social Sciences; Theatre; Veterinary Science.** *Licenciatura*: **Arts and Humanities; Biology; Chemistry; Dance; Geography; History; Mathematics; Modern Languages; Music; Philosophy; Physics; Psychology; Social Sciences.** *Mestrado*; *Doutorado*

Publications: Publications of the Faculties and Institutes

Publishing House: Gráfica Universitária

Last Updated: 18/04/16

FEDERAL UNIVERSITY OF CAMPINA GRANDE

Universidade Federal de Campina Grande
Avenida Aprigio Veloso 882, Bodocondo,
Campina Grande, Paraíba 58019-900
Tel: +55(83) 3310-1000
EMail: reitoria@reitoria.ufcg.edu.br
Website: http://www.ufcg.edu.br

Reitor: Thompson Fernandes Mariz

Centre

Biological and Health Sciences (Child Care and Development; Health Sciences; Medicine; Surgery); **Education and Health** *(Cuité Campus)*; **Electrical and Computer Engineering; Food Processing** (Food Science; Food Technology); **Health and Rural Technology** *(Patos Campus)* (Biology; Forest Management; Veterinary Science); **Humanities; Legal and Social Sciences** *(Souza Campus)*; **Science and Technology** (Chemical Engineering; Industrial Design; Materials Engineering; Mathematics; Mechanical Engineering; Physics; Production Engineering); **Teacher Training** *(Cajazeiras - Paraíba Campus)* (Teacher Training); **Technology and Natural Resources** (Natural Resources; Technology)

Further Information: Also branches in Patos, Sousa, Cajazeiras, Cuité

History: Founded 2002.

Main Language(s) of Instruction: Portuguese

Degrees and Diplomas: *Bacharelado*; *Licenciatura*; *Especialização/Aperfeiçoamento*; *Mestrado*; *Doutorado*

Last Updated: 18/04/16

FEDERAL UNIVERSITY OF CEARÁ

Universidade Federal do Ceará (UFC)
Avenida da Universidade 2853, Benfica,
Fortaleza, Ceará 60020181
Tel: +55(85) 4009-7301
Fax: +55(85) 4009-7303
EMail: prplufc@ufc.br
Website: http://www.ufc.br

Reitor: Jesualdo Pereira Farias EMail: reitor@ufc.br

Faculty

Economics (Economics); **Education** (Education); **Law** (Law); **Medicine** *(Porangabuçu)*; **Pharmacy, Dentistry and Nursing** *(Porangabuçu)*

Institute

Culture and Art; Marine Sciences

Centre

Science *(Pici)* (Analytical Chemistry; Biochemistry; Biology; Computer Science; Mathematics; Natural Sciences; Physics); **Agrarian Sciences** *(Pici)* (Agricultural Engineering; Agriculture; Food Science; Soil Science); **Humanities** (Arts and Humanities; Computer Science; History; Literature; Philosophy; Psychology; Social Sciences); **Technology** *(Pici)* (Architecture; Chemical Engineering; Electrical Engineering; Environmental Engineering; Hydraulic Engineering; Mechanical Engineering; Structural Architecture; Technology; Town Planning; Transport Engineering)

Further Information: Also 'Walter Cantídio' University Hospital. 'Assis Chateaubriand' Maternity Hospital. Psychology Clinic. Portuguese Courses for foreign students

History: Founded 1954. A State institution financed by the Federal Government.

Academic Year: March to December (March-July; August-December)

Admission Requirements: Secondary school certificate or equivalent and entrance examination

Fees: None

Main Language(s) of Instruction: Portuguese

Degrees and Diplomas: *Bacharelado*: **Medicine.** *Licenciatura*: **Medicine.** *Mestrado*; *Doutorado*

Student Services: Canteen, Cultural Activities, Health Services, Sports Facilities

Publications: Arquivos de Ciências do Mar; Ciências Agronômicas; Educação em Debate; Engenharia; Geologia; Letras; Odontologia; Olhar Midiático; Psicologia; Revista de Ciências Sociais; Revista de Medicina

Last Updated: 18/04/16

FEDERAL UNIVERSITY OF ESPÍRITO SANTO

Universidade Federal do Espírito Santo (UFES)
Avenida Fernando Ferrari 514 s/n Campus Universitário,
Goiabeiras, Vitória, Espírito Santo 29060900
Tel: +55(27) 4009-2770
Fax: +55(27) 4009-2818
EMail: reitoria@npd.ufes.br
Website: http://www.ufes.br

Reitor: Rubens Rasseli Tel: +55(27) 3335-2222

Centre

Agrarian Sciences (Agriculture; Agronomy; Animal Husbandry; Biology; Chemical Engineering; Computer Science; Floriculture; Food Technology; Geology; Industrial Engineering; Mathematics; Nutrition; Pharmacy; Physics; Veterinary Science; Zoology); **Arts** (Advertising and Publicity; Architecture; Fine Arts; Industrial Design; Journalism; Music; Town Planning; Visual Arts); **Education** (Cultural Studies; Education; Modern Languages; Pedagogy; Political Sciences); **Exact Sciences**; **General Studies** (Biology; Chemistry; Earth Sciences; Literature; Modern Languages; Philosophy; Physics; Psychology; Social Sciences; Statistics); **Human and Natural Sciences** (Biology; Development Studies; Ecology; Geography; History; Literature; Modern Languages; Natural Resources; Philosophy; Psychology; Social Sciences); **Law and Economics** (Business Administration; Communication Studies; Economics; Law; Library Science); **Physical Education and Sport** (Physical Education; Sports); **Technology** (Civil Engineering; Computer Science; Electrical Engineering; Environmental Engineering; Industrial Engineering; Mechanical Engineering; Production Engineering; Technology)

Further Information: Also Teaching Hospital

History: Founded 1954 as a State University incorporating existing colleges. Became a Federal Institution 1961 and reorganized 1966. Financed by the Federal Government.

Academic Year: March to December (March-July; August-December)

Admission Requirements: Secondary school certificate and entrance examination

Fees: None

Main Language(s) of Instruction: Portuguese

Degrees and Diplomas: *Bacharelado*; *Licenciatura*; *Mestrado*; *Doutorado*

Publications: Revista de Cultura

Publishing House: Gráfica Imprensa Universitária

Last Updated: 18/04/16

FEDERAL UNIVERSITY OF GOIÁS

Universidade Federal de Goiás (UFG)

Rodovia Goiânia-Nerópolis km 12, Prédio ICB IV, Campus Samambaia, Goiânia, Goiás 74001970

Tel: +55(62) 3521-1000

Fax: +55(62) 3521-1200

EMail: reitora@reitora.ufg.br

Website: http://www.ufg.br

Reitor: Edward Madureira Brasil

Tel: +55(62) 3521-1146 EMail: reitoria@reitoria.ufg.br

Faculty

Communication and Library Sciences (Advertising and Publicity; Communication Studies; Journalism; Library Science; Public Relations); **Dentistry** (Dentistry); **Education** (Education); **Human Sciences and Letters** (Communication Studies; History; Modern Languages; Philosophy; Social Sciences); **Law** (Law); **Medicine** (Medicine); **Nursing** (Nursing); **Nutrition** (Nutrition); **Pharmacy** (Pharmacy); **Physical Education** (Physical Education)

School

Agriculture (Agriculture); **Engineering** (Building Technologies; Construction Engineering; Electronic Engineering; Engineering; Hydraulic Engineering; Sanitary Engineering; Systems Analysis); **Veterinary Medicine** (Veterinary Science)

Institute

Chemistry (Chemistry)

History: Founded 1960. An autonomous institution under the jurisdiction of the Ministry of Education and Sports.

Academic Year: February to December (February-June; August-December)

Admission Requirements: Secondary school certificate and entrance examination

Main Language(s) of Instruction: Portuguese

Degrees and Diplomas: *Bacharelado*: **Agronomy; Animal Husbandry; Art Education; Biological and Life Sciences; Chemistry; Civil Engineering; Computer Science; Dentistry; Electrical Engineering; Geography; History; Law; Library Science; Mathematics; Medicine; Midwifery; Modern Languages; Music; Musical Instruments; Nursing; Nutrition; Pedagogy; Pharmacy; Philosophy; Physical Education; Physics; Singing; Social Sciences; Veterinary Science; Visual Arts.** *Mestrado*: **Agriculture; Biology; Botany; Education; Genetics; History; Law; Linguistics; Mathematics; Modern Languages; Tropical Medicine.** *Doutorado*

Publications: Anais da Escola de Agronomia e Veterinaria; Boletim do Pessoal; Revista da Faculdade de Direito; Revista de Patologia Tropical; Revista do Instituto de Ciências Humanas e Letras; Revista Goiana de Artes; Revista Goiana de Medicina; Revistas

Publishing House: Centro Editorial e Gráfico da UFG-CEGRAF

Last Updated: 18/04/16

FEDERAL UNIVERSITY OF GRANDE DOURADOS FOUNDATION

Fundaçao Universidade Federal da Grande Dourados (UFGD)

Rua João Rosa Góes, 1761, Vila Progresso, Cx. Postal 322, Dourados, Mato Grosso do Sul 79825-070

Tel: +55(67) 3410-2002 +55(67) 3411-3600 +55(67) 3411-3601

Fax: +55(67) 3411-3637

EMail: reitoria@ufgd.edu.br

Website: http://www.ufgd.edu.br

Rectora: Liane Maria Calarge

Tel: +55(67) 3410-2711 EMail: reitoria@ufgd.edu.br

Pró-reitor de Administração: Lino Sanabria

EMail: prad@ufgd.edu.br

International Relations: Cesar Augusto Silva da Silva, Diretor, Escritório de Assuntos Internacionais

Tel: +55(67) 3410-2745 EMail: esai@ufgd.edu.br

Faculty

Administration, Accountancy and Economics (FACE) (Accountancy; Administration; Economics); **Agrarian Sciences (FCA)** (Agricultural Engineering; Agronomy; Animal Husbandry; Aquaculture); **Biological and Environmental Sciences (FCBA)** (Biological and Life Sciences; Biotechnology; Environmental Studies); **Communication, Arts and Letters (FACALE)** (Arts and Humanities; Linguistics; Literature; Theatre); **Distance Education (EAD)** (Computer Science; Health Administration; Mathematics; Pedagogy; Physics; Public Administration; Software Engineering); **Education (FAED)** (Education; Pedagogy; Physical Education; Teacher Training); **Engineering (FAEN)** (Civil Engineering; Energy Engineering; Food Technology; Mechanical Engineering; Production Engineering); **Exact Sciences and Technology (FACET)** (Biotechnology; Chemistry; Computer Engineering; Environmental Engineering; Environmental Studies; Information Technology; Mathematics; Mathematics Education; Physics; Science Education; Software Engineering); **Health Sciences (FCS)** (Community Health; Health Sciences; Medicine; Nutrition; Public Health); **Human Sciences (FCH)** (Geography (Human); History; Psychology; Social Sciences); **Indigenous Intercultural Studies (FAIND)** (Education; Natives Education); **Law and International Relations (FADIR)** (Civil Security; International Relations; Law)

Further Information: Also Cidade Universitaria Unit

History: Founded 2005.

Main Language(s) of Instruction: Portuguese

Degrees and Diplomas: *Bacharelado*; *Licenciatura*; *Especialização/Aperfeiçoamento*: **Agriculture; Arts and Humanities; Civil Security; Cultural Studies; Educational Sciences; Gender Studies; Law; Linguistics; Mathematics Education; Physical Education; Preschool Education; Public Health; Teacher Training; Theatre.** *Mestrado*: **Agricultural Business; Agricultural Engineering; Agronomy; Animal Husbandry; Anthropology; Arts and Humanities; Biological and Life Sciences; Biology; Chemistry; Education; Entomology; Environmental Engineering; Environmental Studies; Geography (Human); Health Sciences; History; Mathematics; Physics; Public Administration; Science Education; Sociology.** *Doutorado*: **Agronomy; Biology; Biotechnology; Education; Entomology; Environmental Engineering; Environmental Studies; Geography (Human); Health Sciences; History.**

Student Services: Library

Last Updated: 04/02/16

FEDERAL UNIVERSITY OF HEALTH SCIENCES OF PORTO ALEGRE

Universidade Federal de Ciências de Saúde de Porto Alegre (UFCSPA)

Rua Sarmento Leite 245, Centro,
Porto Alegre, Rio Grande do Sul 90050170
Tel: +55(51) 3226-7913
Fax: +55(51) 3224-8822 +55(51) 3224-8178
Website: http://www.ufcspa.edu.br

Reitora: Miriam da Costa Oliveira EMail: reitora@ufcspa.edu.br

Department

Basic Health Sciences (Health Sciences); **Clinical Medicine** (Medicine); **Clinical Surgery**; **Community Health**; **Diagnosis Methods**; **Gynaecology and Obstetrics** (Gynaecology and Obstetrics); **Health Education and Information**; **Nursing**; **Nutrition**; **Paediatrics**; **Pathology and Forensic Medicine** (Forensic Medicine and Dentistry; Pathology); **Physiotherapy** (Physical Therapy); **Psychology** (Psychology); **Speech Therapy**

History: Founded 1961 as Fundação Faculdade Federal de Ciências Médicas de Porto Alegre. Acquired present status and title 2008.

Main Language(s) of Instruction: Portuguese

Degrees and Diplomas: *Bacharelado*; *Especialização/Aperfeiçoamento*; *Mestrado*; *Doutorado*

Last Updated: 18/04/16

FEDERAL UNIVERSITY OF ITAJUBÁ

Universidade Federal de Itajubá (UNIFEI)

Caixa Postal 50, Itajubá, Minas Gerais 37500-903
Tel: +55(35) 3629-1101
Fax: +55(35) 3622-3596
EMail: vestibular@unifei.edu.br
Website: http://www.efei.edu.br/

Reitor: Renato de Aquino Faria Nunes

Institute

Electrical and Energy Engineering; **Exact Sciences** (Chemistry; Mathematics; Mathematics and Computer Science; Physics); **Information Systems**; **Mechanical Engineering**; **Natural Resources** (Environmental Engineering; Natural Resources); **Production Engineering and Management**

History: Founded 1913 as Instituto Eletrotécnico e Mecânico de Itajubá. Became Escola Federal de Engenharia de Itajubá en 1968. Acquired present title and status 2002.

Degrees and Diplomas: *Bacharelado*; *Licenciatura*; *Especialização/Aperfeiçoamento*; *Mestrado*; *Doutorado*

Last Updated: 18/04/16

FEDERAL UNIVERSITY OF JUIZ DE FORA

Universidade Federal de Juiz de Fora (UFJF)

Reitoria, Campus Universitário,
Juiz de Fora, Minas Gerais 36036900
Tel: +55(32) 3229-3902
Fax: +55(32) 3229-3933
Website: http://www.ufjf.br

Reitor: Henrique Duque de Miranda Chaves Filho (2006-)
Tel: +55(32) 3215-6245 EMail: gabinete@ufjf.edu.br

Vice-Reitor: José Luiz Rezende Pereira

Faculty

Administration (Administration; Economics); **Communication** (Communication Studies; Journalism); **Dentistry** (Dentistry); **Economics**; **Education** (Education); **Engineering** (Architecture; Civil Engineering; Construction Engineering; Electrical Engineering; Energy Engineering; Engineering; Environmental Engineering; Mechanical Engineering; Production Engineering; Town Planning; Transport Engineering); **Law** (Law); **Letters**; **Medicine** (Medicine); **Nursing**; **Pharmacy and Biochemistry** (Biochemistry; Pharmacy); **Physical Education** (Physical Education; Sports); **Social Services**

Institute

Arts and Design (Design; Fashion Design; Music; Performing Arts; Visual Arts); **Biological Sciences** (Biology); **Exact Sciences** (Architecture; Chemistry; Mathematics; Mathematics and Computer Science; Physics; Statistics); **Human Sciences** (Arts and Humanities; Geography; History; Philosophy; Psychology; Social Sciences; Tourism); **Literature and Language Studies**

History: Founded 1960 by the Federal Government, incorporating five private institutions.

Academic Year: February to December (February-June; August-December)

Admission Requirements: Secondary school certificate and entrance examination

Fees: None

Main Language(s) of Instruction: Portuguese

Degrees and Diplomas: *Bacharelado*: **Architecture; Civil Engineering; Dentistry; Economics; Electrical Engineering; Journalism; Law; Medicine; Pharmacy; Tourism.** *Licenciatura*: **Biology; Chemistry; Design; Education; Fine Arts; Geography; History; Literature; Mathematics; Philosophy; Physical Education; Physics.** *Especialização/Aperfeiçoamento*; *Mestrado*; *Doutorado*

Publications: Boletim do Centro de Biologia de Reprodução; Educação em Foco; Etica e Filosofia Política; Instrumento; Ipotesi; Libertas; Locus; Lumina; Numen; Revista Brasileira de Zoociências; Revista de Engenharia; Veredas

Last Updated: 18/04/16

FEDERAL UNIVERSITY OF LAVRAS

Universidade Federal de Lavras (UFLA)

Campus Universitário, Lavras, Minas Gerais 37200000
Tel: +55(35) 3829-1502
Fax: +55(35) 3829-1100
EMail: proad@ufla.br
Website: http://www.ufla.br

Reitor: Antônio Nazareno Guimarães Mendes

Department

Administration and Economics; **Agriculture**; **Biology**; **Chemistry**; **Computer Science** (Computer Science); **Education**; **Engineering**; **Entomology**; **Exact Sciences** (Mathematics; Statistics); **Food Sciences**; **Forestry**; **Physical Education**; **Phytopathology**; **Soil Sciences**; **Veterinary Medicine**; **Zoology**

History: Founded 1908 as Instituto Gammon. Became Escola Superior de Agricultura de Lavras, acquired present status and title 1994.

Degrees and Diplomas: *Bacharelado*; *Licenciatura*; *Especialização/Aperfeiçoamento*; *Mestrado*; *Doutorado*

Last Updated: 18/04/16

FEDERAL UNIVERSITY OF MARANHÃO

Universidade Federal do Maranhão (UFMA)

AV. Dos Portugueses, s/n, São Luís, Maranhão 65085-580
Tel: +55(98) 217-8011 +55(98) 217-8094
Fax: +55(98) 217-8026
EMail: procin@ufma.br
Website: http://www.ufma.br

Reitor: Natalino Salgado Filho (2007-)

Centre

Biological and Health Sciences (Biological and Life Sciences; Dentistry; Health Sciences; Medicine; Nursing; Pharmacy; Physical Education); **Exact Sciences and Technology** (Chemistry; Computer Science; Electrical Engineering; Industrial Design; Mathematics; Physics; Technology); **Human Sciences**; **Social Sciences** (Accountancy; Economics; Hotel Management; Law; Library Science; Pedagogy; Social and Community Services; Social Sciences)

History: Founded 1966. An autonomous institution financially supported by the Federal Government. Acquired present status 1969.

Academic Year: March to December (March-June; August-December)

Admission Requirements: Secondary school certificate and entrance examination

Main Language(s) of Instruction: Portuguese

Degrees and Diplomas: *Bacharelado*: **Accountancy; Communication Studies; Dentistry; Economics; Electrical**

Engineering; Industrial Chemistry; Industrial Design; Law; Library Science; Mathematics; Pharmacology; Pharmacy; Social Work. *Licenciatura*: **Arts and Humanities; Chemistry; Design; Education; Fine Arts; History; Mathematics; Physical Education; Physics.** *Especialização/Aperfeiçoamento*; *Mestrado*
Last Updated: 18/04/16

FEDERAL UNIVERSITY OF MATO GROSSO

Universidade Federal de Mato Grosso (UFMT)
Avenida Fernando Corrêa da Costa, s/n Cidade Universitária, Caxipó da Ponte, Cuiabá, Mato Grosso 78060-900
Tel: +55(65) 3615-8203
Fax: +55(65) 3615-8204
EMail: ufmt@cpd.br
Website: http://www.ufmt.br

Reitora: Maria Lúcia Cavalli Neder (2008-)
Tel: +55(65) 3615-8301 EMail: reitor@ufmt.br

Faculty
Administration and Economics (Administration; Economics); **Agriculture and Veterinary Medicine** (Agriculture; Tropical Agriculture; Veterinary Science); **Engineering** (Engineering); **Forestry Engineering** (Forestry); **Law** (Law); **Medical Sciences** (Health Sciences; Medicine); **Nursing and Nutrition** (Nursing; Nutrition); **Physical Education** (Physical Education)

Institute
Biosciences (Biochemistry; Biomedicine; Biophysics); **Education** (Education); **Exact Sciences** (Mathematics and Computer Science; Physics); **Human and Social Sciences** (Anthropology; Arts and Humanities; Geography; History; Social Sciences; Social Work; Sociology); **Languages** (Arts and Humanities; Communication Studies; Modern Languages)

Further Information: Also University Hospital 'Júlio Muller'. Campuses at: Rondonópolis, Médio Araguaia

History: Founded 1970, incorporating the Federal Faculty of Law, founded 1934, the Faculty of Philosophy, Science and Letters of Mato Grosso and the Institute of Science and Letters of Cuiabá. A State institution financed by the Federal Government and responsible to the Ministry of Education and Sports.

Academic Year: March to December (March-July; August-December)

Admission Requirements: Secondary school certificate and entrance examination

Main Language(s) of Instruction: Portuguese, French, Spanish

Degrees and Diplomas: *Bacharelado*; *Licenciatura*; *Mestrado*; *Doutorado*

Student Services: Canteen, Cultural Activities, Sports Facilities

Publishing house: University Press
Last Updated: 18/04/16

FEDERAL UNIVERSITY OF MATO GROSSO DO SUL

Universidade Federal de Mato Grosso do Sul (UFMS)
Campus de Campo Grande, s/n Cidade Universitária, Campo Grande, Mato Grosso do Sul 79070900
Tel: +55(67) 787-3833 +55(67) 787-2491
Fax: +55(67) 787-1081
EMail: reitor@nin.ufms.br
Website: http://www.ufms.br

Reitor: Manoel Peró

Department
Corumbá (Accountancy; Administration; Arts and Humanities; Biology; Education; Geography; History; Mathematics; Psychology); **Dourados** (Accountancy; Agriculture; Arts and Humanities; Education; Geography; History; Mathematics); **Três Lagoas** (Arts and Humanities; Biology; Education; Geography; History; Mathematics)

Centre
Biological and Health Sciences (Biological and Life Sciences; Dentistry; Health Sciences; Medicine; Pharmacy; Veterinary Science); **Exact Sciences and Technology** (Civil Engineering; Computer Science; Electrical Engineering; Mathematics; Natural Sciences; Physics; Technology); **Human and Social Sciences** (Administration; Arts and Humanities; Communication Studies; Education; Physical Education; Social Sciences)

Campus
Aquidauana (Geography; History; Natural Sciences)

History: Founded 1969 as Faculty of Pharmacy and Dentistry, became Institute of Biology 1966, State University 1970, and Federal University 1979.

Academic Year: March to December (March-June; August-December)

Admission Requirements: Secondary school certificate and entrance examination

Main Language(s) of Instruction: Portuguese

Degrees and Diplomas: *Bacharelado*: **Animal Husbandry; Civil Engineering; Dentistry; Electrical Engineering; Journalism; Medicine; Pharmacology; Pharmacy; Veterinary Science.** *Licenciatura*: **Arts and Humanities; Chemistry; Education; Geography; History; Mathematics; Painting and Drawing; Physical Education; Physics; Psychology; Sculpture; Sports.** *Especialização/Aperfeiçoamento*; *Mestrado*; *Doutorado*

Publications: Revista Científica e Cultural
Last Updated: 18/04/16

FEDERAL UNIVERSITY OF MINAS GERAIS

Universidade Federal de Minas Gerais (UFMG)
Avenida Presidente Antônio Carlos 6627, Reitoria Pampulha, Belo Horizonte, Minas Gerais 31270-901
Tel: +55(31) 3499-4124
Fax: +55(31) 3499-4130
EMail: gabinete@reitoria.ufmg.br
Website: http://www.ufmg.br

Reitor: Clélio Campolina Diniz EMail: reitor@ufmg.br

Faculty
Actuarial Sciences; **Agronomy** (Agronomy); **Dentistry** (Dentistry); **Economics** (Accountancy; Business Administration; Demography and Population; Economics); **Education** (Education); **Law** (Law); **Letters** (Literature; Modern Languages); **Medicine** (Medicine); **Pharmacy** (Pharmacy); **Philosophy and Humanities** (Anthropology; Arts and Humanities; History; Philosophy; Political Sciences; Psychology; Sociology); **Physiotherapy** (Physical Therapy)

School
Architecture (Architecture; Town Planning); **Engineering** (Civil Engineering; Electrical Engineering; Hydraulic Engineering; Mechanical Engineering; Production Engineering); **Fine Arts** (Cinema and Television; Fashion Design; Fine Arts; Restoration of Works of Art; Theatre; Visual Arts); **Information Sciences** (Archiving; Information Sciences; Library Science; Museum Studies); **Music** (Music); **Nursing** (Nursing); **Physical Education** (Physical Education); **Veterinary Medicine** (Veterinary Science)

Institute
Agrarian Sciences (Agronomy); **Biology** (Biology); **Exact Sciences** (Mathematics and Computer Science; Natural Sciences); **Geosciences** (Geography; Geology; Tourism)

History: Founded 1927 as a University incorporating Institutions established between 1892 and 1911. Reorganized 1968. A State institution financed by the Federal Government and responsible to the Ministry of Education and Sports.

Academic Year: February to December (February-June; August-December)

Admission Requirements: Secondary school certificate and entrance examination

Fees: 250 per semester

Main Language(s) of Instruction: Portuguese

Degrees and Diplomas: *Bacharelado*: **Accountancy; Actuarial Science; Agronomy; Animal Husbandry; Architecture; Arts and Humanities; Biology; Business Administration; Chemistry; Computer Science; Dentistry; Ecology; Economics; Education; Engineering; Fine Arts; Geology; History; Journalism; Law; Library Science; Mathematics; Medicine; Music; Nursing; Occupational Therapy; Pharmacy; Philosophy; Physical Education; Physical Therapy; Physics; Psychology; Statistics;**

Tourism; Veterinary Science; Zoology. *Especialização/Aperfeiçoamento; Mestrado; Doutorado*

Student Services: Academic Counselling, Canteen, Careers Guidance, Cultural Activities, Health Services, Language Laboratory, Nursery Care, Social Counselling, Sports Facilities

Publications: Diversa; Sistemático

Publishing House: Editora da UFMG

Last Updated: 18/04/16

FEDERAL UNIVERSITY OF OURO PRÊTO

Universidade Federal de Ouro Prêto (UFOP)

Rua Diogo de Vasconcelos 122, Centro,
Ouro Prêto, Minas Gerais 35400000
Tel: +55(31) 3559-1100
Fax: +55(31) 3559-1228
EMail: reitoria@cpd.ufop.br
Website: http://www.ufop.br

Reitor: João Luiz Martins
Tel: +55(31) 3559-1210 EMail: reitoria@cpd.ufop.br

School

Mining Engineering (Civil Engineering; Geological Engineering; Metallurgical Engineering; Mining Engineering; Production Engineering); **Nutrition** (Nutrition); **Pharmacy** (Biochemistry; Pharmacy)

Department

Law (Law); **Museology** (Museum Studies); **Tourism** (Tourism)

Institute

Biological and Exact Sciences (Biological and Life Sciences; Chemistry; Computer Science; Mathematics; Physics); **Philosophy, Arts and Culture** (Arts and Humanities; Cultural Studies; Music; Philosophy; Theatre); **Social and Human Sciences** *(Mariana)* (Arts and Humanities; History; Law; Social Sciences)

Further Information: Campuses at Mariana and Morro do Cruzeiro

History: Founded 1969 incorporating Escola de Minas de Ouro Prêto, founded 1876 as Escola de Farmácia e Bioquímica, 1839. Under the jurisdiction of the Ministry of Education and Sports and financially supported by the Federal Government.

Academic Year: March to November (March-June; August-November)

Admission Requirements: Secondary school certificate and entrance examination

Main Language(s) of Instruction: Portuguese

Degrees and Diplomas: *Bacharelado; Licenciatura; Especialização/Aperfeiçoamento; Mestrado; Doutorado*

Student Services: Academic Counselling, Canteen, Careers Guidance, Cultural Activities, Health Services, Nursery Care, Social Counselling, Sports Facilities

Publications: Revista da Escola de Farmácia; Revista de Escola de Minas

Publishing House: Editora da UFOP

Last Updated: 18/04/16

FEDERAL UNIVERSITY OF PARÁ

Universidade Federal do Pará (UFPA)

Rua Augusto Corréa 01, Prédio da Reitoria - 3° andar,
Belém, Pará 66075110
Tel: +55(91) 3211-1112
Fax: +55(91) 3211-1675
EMail: proplan@ufpa.br
Website: http://www.ufpa.br

Reitor: Carlos Edilson de Almeida Maneschy
Tel: +55(91) 211-1112 EMail: reitor@ufpa.br

Centre

Biological Sciences (Biological and Life Sciences); **Education** (Education; Pedagogy; Physical Education); **Exact and Natural Sciences** (Chemistry; Mathematics and Computer Science; Natural Sciences; Physics; Statistics); **Letters and Arts** (Advertising and Publicity; Art Education; Arts and Humanities; Journalism; Literature); **Philosophy and Human Sciences** (Arts and Humanities; Geography; History; Philosophy; Psychology); **Socio-Economic Studies** (Accountancy; Administration; Economics; Social Studies; Tourism); **Technology** (Engineering; Technology)

History: Founded 1957 and comprising previously existing faculties. Reorganized 1970-71 with a structure comprising centres for professional education. An autonomous institution, financially supported by the State and responsible to the Ministry of Education and Sports.

Academic Year: March to December (March-June; August-December)

Admission Requirements: Secondary school certificate and competitive entrance examination

Fees: None

Main Language(s) of Instruction: Portuguese

Degrees and Diplomas: *Bacharelado*: **Accountancy; Administration; Architecture; Biochemistry; Chemical Engineering; Civil Engineering; Dentistry; Economics; Electrical Engineering; Electronic Engineering; Geology; Industrial Chemistry; Law; Mechanical Engineering; Medicine; Pharmacology; Social Work.** *Licenciatura*: **Arts and Humanities; Education; Geography; History; Library Science; Mathematics; Physics; Social Sciences.** *Mestrado; Doutorado*

Publications: Revista de Ciências Jurídicas, Econômicas e Sociais; Revista de Ciências Médicas; Revista de Letras e Artes

Last Updated: 18/04/16

FEDERAL UNIVERSITY OF PARAÍBA

Universidade Federal da Paraíba (UFPB)

Cidade Universitária, Campus I, Castelo Branco III,
João Pessoa, Paraíba 58059900
Tel: +55(83) 3216-7150
Fax: +55(83) 3225-1901
EMail: gabinete@reitoria.ufpb.br
Website: http://www.ufpb.br

Reitor: Rômulo Soares Polari EMail: reitor@reitoria.ufpb.br

Pró-Reitor Administrativo: Múcio S. Souto
Tel: +55(83) 3216-7410 EMail: mucio@pra.ufpb.br

International Relations: Timothy D. Ireland
Tel: +55(83) 3216-7156 EMail: aai@reitoria.ufpb.br

Centre

Agrarian Sciences *(CCA - Aréia)* (Agriculture; Agronomy; Animal Husbandry); **Applied Social Sciences** *(CCSA)* (Accountancy; Administration; Economics; Library Science; Social Sciences); **Education** *(CE)* (Education; Educational and Student Counselling; Pedagogy); **Exact and Natural Sciences** *(CCEN)* (Biology; Chemistry; Computer Science; Ecology; Geography; Mathematics; Natural Sciences; Physics); **Health and Biological Sciences** *(CCBS, Campina Grande)* (Biology; Child Care and Development; Health Sciences; Social and Preventive Medicine; Surgery); **Health and Rural Technology** *(CSTR, Patos)* (Agricultural Engineering; Forestry; Health Sciences; Mathematics and Computer Science; Natural Sciences; Veterinary Science); **Health Sciences** *(CCS)* (Dentistry; Health Sciences; Medicine; Nursing; Nutrition; Pharmacy; Physical Education); **Human Sciences, Letters and Arts** *(CCHLA)* (Arts and Humanities; Communication Studies; Fine Arts; History; Literature; Modern Languages; Music; Philosophy; Psychology; Social Sciences; Social Work; Tourism); **Humanities** *(CH, Campina Grande)* (Administration; Arts and Humanities; Economics; Education; Fine Arts; Geography; History; Literature; Media Studies; Social Sciences); **Law** *(CCJ)* (Law); **Science and Technology** *(CCT, Campina Grande)* (Agricultural Engineering; Chemical Engineering; Civil Engineering; Computer Engineering; Computer Science; Electrical Engineering; Geology; Industrial Design; Materials Engineering; Mathematics; Mechanical Engineering; Meteorology; Mining Engineering; Natural Sciences; Physics; Statistics; Technology); **Social and Juridical Science** *(CCJS, Souza)*; **Teacher Training** *(CFP, Cajazeiras)* (Geography; History; Literature; Mathematics; Natural Sciences; Pedagogy; Teacher Training); **Technology** (Architecture; Civil Engineering; Food Science; Industrial Chemistry; Materials Engineering; Mechanical Engineering; Production Engineering; Technology); **Technology Training** *(CFT, Bananeiras)* (Technology Education)

Further Information: Also Teaching Hospitals (João Pessoa and Campina Grande)

History: Founded 1955, incorporating Faculties established 1947-52, acquired present status 1960. Reorganized 1974 with a structure comprising Centres for professional education situated in 7 campuses.

Academic Year: March to December (March-June; August-December)

Admission Requirements: Secondary school certificate and entrance examination

Main Language(s) of Instruction: Portuguese

Degrees and Diplomas: *Bacharelado*: **Accountancy; Administration; Agronomy; Animal Husbandry; Architecture; Biology; Chemistry; Computer Science; Dentistry; Economics; Engineering; Fine Arts; Geography; Industrial Chemistry; Industrial Design; Law; Library Science; Mathematics; Media Studies; Medicine; Music; Nursing; Nutrition; Pharmacy; Philosophy; Physics; Psychology; Social Sciences; Tourism.** *Licenciatura*: **Art Education; Arts and Humanities; Chemistry; Education; Geography; History; Mathematics; Philosophy; Physical Education; Physics; Social Sciences; Statistics.** *Mestrado*; *Doutorado*

Student Services: Academic Counselling, Canteen, Careers Guidance, Cultural Activities, Facilities for disabled people, Health Services, Language Laboratory, Nursery Care, Social Counselling, Sports Facilities

Publications: Informação e Sociedade; Revista brasileira de Saúde; Revista brasiliera de Engenharia agrícola e ambiental; Temas em Educação

Publishing House: Editora Universitária UFPB

Last Updated: 18/04/16

FEDERAL UNIVERSITY OF PARANÁ

Universidade Federal do Paraná (UFPR)

Rua XV de Novembro 1299, Reitoria, Centro,
Curitibá, Paraná 80060000
Tel: +55(41) 3360-5000 +55(41) 3360-5121
Fax: +55(41) 3360-5126
EMail: vicerei@ufpr.br
Website: http://www.ufpr.br

Reitor: Zaki Akel Sobrinho
Tel: +55(41) 3360-5001 EMail: gabinetereitor@ufpr.br

School

Technical Studies (Accountancy; Computer Science; Nursing; Periodontics; Technology)

Academy

Agrarian Sciences (Agronomy; Forestry; Veterinary Science); **Applied Social Sciences** (Accountancy; Economics; International Business; Management; Social Sciences); **Biological Sciences** (Anatomy; Biochemistry; Biological and Life Sciences; Botany; Cell Biology; Entomology; Genetics; Physical Education; Physiology; Zoology); **Education** (Education; Pedagogy); **Exact Sciences** (Chemistry; Computer Science; Mathematics; Natural Sciences; Physics; Statistics); **Health Sciences** (Dentistry; Health Sciences; Medicine; Nursing; Nutrition; Pharmacology); **Humanities, Arts and Languages** (Arts and Humanities; Communication Studies; History; Industrial Design; Library Science; Literature; Philosophy; Psychology; Social Sciences; Tourism); **Law** (Law); **Technology** (Architecture; Chemical Engineering; Civil Engineering; Electrical Engineering; Geography; Geology; Mechanical Engineering; Surveying and Mapping; Technology; Town Planning)

Research Centre

Administration (Administration); **Applied Psychology** (Psychology); **Bone Marrow Transplant Studies** (Medicine); **Dermatology and Infectology** *('Souza Araújo')* (Dermatology); **Economics** (Economics); **Education** *(CEPED)* (Education); **Electronic Microscopy** (Electronic Engineering); **Engineering** *(CESEC)* (Engineering); **Environment and Development** (Development Studies; Environmental Engineering); **Food Processing** (Food Technology); **Hydromechanics** *('Parigot de Souza')* (Mechanics); **Marine Biology** (Marine Biology); **Nephrology** (Nephrology); **Veterinary Medicine and Animal Husbandry** (Animal Husbandry; Veterinary Science)

Further Information: Also Clinical Hospital

History: Founded 1911, became Federal University 1950. Reorganized 1974 with a structure comprising sectors for professional education. An autonomous institution, but financially supported by the State, and under the jurisdiction of the Ministry of Education and Sports.

Academic Year: March to December (March-June; August-December)

Admission Requirements: Secondary school certificate and entrance examination, or entrance through international exchange programme

Fees: None

Main Language(s) of Instruction: Portuguese

Degrees and Diplomas: *Bacharelado*; *Licenciatura*; *Mestrado*; *Doutorado*

Student Services: Academic Counselling, Canteen, Cultural Activities, Facilities for disabled people, Health Services, Language Laboratory, Sports Facilities

Publications: Acta Biologica of Paraná; Agrarian Department Journal; Anthropology; DENS; Food Processing and Research Centre; Geosciences of Paraná; Journal of Human Sciences; Nerítica; Pesticides; Pharmaceutic Rostrum; The College of Law Magazine; The Economics Magazine; The Language Magazine

Publishing House: Editora da UFPR

Last Updated: 18/04/16

FEDERAL UNIVERSITY OF PELOTAS

Universidade Federal de Pelotas (UFPEL)

Campus Universitário, Capão do Leão,
Pelotas, Rio Grande do Sul 96010900
Tel: +55(53) 3275-7104
Fax: +55(53) 3275-9023
EMail: reitor@ufpel.edu.br
Website: http://www.ufpel.edu.br/

Reitor: Mauro Augusto Burkert Del Pino
Tel: +55(53) 3275-7104 EMail: reitor@ufpel.edu.br

Vice-Reitor: Carlos Francisco Carlos Rogério Mauch
Tel: +55(53) 3275-7204

International Relations: Gustavo Oliveira Vieira
Tel: +55(53) 3225.3943 EMail: crinter.ufpel@gmail.com

Faculty

Administration and Tourism (Administration; Tourism); **Agronomy** *(Eliseu Maciel)* (Agronomy; Animal Husbandry); **Architecture and Town Planning** (Architecture; Building Technologies; Town Planning); **Education** (Education; Pedagogy); **Home Economics** (Food Science; Home Economics); **Law** (Law); **Medicine** (Medicine); **Meteorology** (Meteorology); **Nursing and Obstetrics** (Gynaecology and Obstetrics; Nursing); **Nutrition** (Nutrition); **Odontology** (Dentistry); **Veterinary Science** (Veterinary Science)

Higher School

Physical Education (Physical Education)

Institute

Arts and Design (Cinema and Television; Dance; Graphic Design; Music; Musical Instruments; Theatre; Visual Arts); **Biology** (Anatomy; Biological and Life Sciences; Botany; Genetics; Microbiology; Parasitology; Pharmacology; Physiology; Zoology); **Chemistry and Geoscience** (Chemistry; Earth Sciences); **Human Sciences** (Anthropology; Arts and Humanities; Economics; Geography; Geography (Human); History; Museum Studies); **Physics and Mathematics** (Computer Engineering; Computer Science; Mathematics; Physics); **Sociology and Political Science** (Philosophy; Political Sciences; Sociology)

Centre

Engineering (Engineering); **Technological Development** (Biotechnology; Geological Engineering; Hydraulic Engineering; Materials Engineering; Mineralogy; Petroleum and Gas Engineering)

Conservatory

Music (Music)

History: Founded 1883 as Escola Imperial de Medicina Veterinária e Agricultura, became Escola de Agronomia Eliseu Maciel 1926, Universidade Rural do Sul 1960, Universidade Federal Rural do Rio

Grande do Sul 1967, and acquired present title and status 1969. Under the jurisdiction of the Ministry of Education and Sports and financially supported by the Federal Government.

Academic Year: March to December (March-July; August-December)

Admission Requirements: Secondary school certificate or equivalent and entrance examination

Fees: None

Main Language(s) of Instruction: Portuguese

Degrees and Diplomas: *Bacharelado*: **Agricultural Engineering; Agronomy; Animal Husbandry; Architecture; Biological and Life Sciences; Chemistry; Computer Science; Dentistry; Economics; Engraving; Food Science; Graphic Design; Gynaecology and Obstetrics; Health Administration; Law; Medicine; Music; Nursing; Nutrition; Painting and Drawing; Physical Education; Social Sciences; Textile Technology; Tourism; Urban Studies; Veterinary Science; Visual Arts.** *Licenciatura*: **Biological and Life Sciences; Chemistry; English; French; Geography; Graphic Design; History; Literature; Mathematics; Music; Pedagogy; Philosophy; Physical Education; Physics; Portuguese; Social Sciences; Spanish; Visual Arts.** *Especialização/Aperfeiçoamento*: **Agricultural Management; Art Therapy; Chemistry; Crop Production; Dentistry; Education; Environmental Studies; Food Science; Heritage Preservation; Latin American Studies; Literature; Mathematics; Music; Nursing; Occupational Health; Oral Pathology; Painting and Drawing; Philosophy; Physical Education; Political Sciences; Public Health; Safety Engineering; Sociology; Sports; Surgery.** *Mestrado*: **Agricultural Engineering; Agriculture; Agronomy; Animal Husbandry; Biotechnology; Botany; Crop Production; Dentistry; Education; Entomology; Epidemiology; Fruit Production; Home Economics; Horticulture; Meteorology; Physiology; Plant Pathology; Soil Science; Technology; Veterinary Science; Zoology.** *Doutorado*: **Agricultural Engineering; Agriculture; Agronomy; Biotechnology; Botany; Crop Production; Entomology; Epidemiology; Plant Pathology; Technology; Zoology.** Also Medical Residency, 2-3 years

Student Services: Academic Counselling, Canteen, Facilities for disabled people, Health Services, Language Laboratory, Nursery Care, Social Counselling, Sports Facilities

Publications: Cadernos de Educação; Dissertatio; História da Educação; RAM - Revista Acadêmica de Medicina; Revista Brasileira de Agrociência; Revista das Ciências Sociais

Last Updated: 18/04/16

FEDERAL UNIVERSITY OF PERNAMBUCO

Universidade Federal de Pernambuco (UFPE)

Avenida Professor Moraes Rego 1235, Campus Universitário, Cidade Universitária, Recife, Pernambuco 5067091

Tel: +55(81) 2126-8000

Fax: +55(81) 2126-8029

EMail: alins@ufpe.br

Website: http://www.ufpe.br

Reitor: Amaro Henrique Pessoa Lins (2003-)
Tel: +55(81) 2126-8001 EMail: reitor@ufpe.br

International Relations: Suzana Monteiro
Tel: +55(81) 2126-8118 EMail: cci@ufpe.br

Centre

Applied Social Sciences (Accountancy; Actuarial Science; Administration; Economics; Secretarial Studies; Social Sciences; Social Work; Tourism); **Arts and Communication** (Architecture; Arts and Humanities; Communication Studies; Design; Fine Arts; Journalism; Music; Town Planning); **Biology** (Anatomy; Biochemistry; Biology; Biophysics; Botany; Embryology and Reproduction Biology; Genetics; Histology; Pharmacology; Physiology; Zoology); **Computer Science**; **Education** (Education; Educational Sciences; Philosophy of Education; Psychology); **Exact and Natural Sciences** (Chemistry; Mathematics; Mathematics and Computer Science; Natural Sciences; Physics; Statistics); **Health Sciences** (Dentistry; Health Sciences; Neurology; Nursing; Nutrition; Pathology; Pharmacy; Physical Therapy; Psychiatry and Mental Health; Social and Preventive Medicine; Tropical Medicine); **Juridical Sciences** (Law); **Philosophy and Human Sciences** (Arts and Humanities; Geography; History; Philosophy; Psychology; Social Sciences); **Technology and Geosciences** (Chemical Engineering; Civil Engineering; Electrical and Electronic Engineering; Geology; Industrial Engineering; Marine Science and Oceanography; Mechanical Engineering; Nuclear Engineering; Surveying and Mapping; Systems Analysis; Technology)

Further Information: Also Clinical Hospital

History: Founded 1946 as Universidade do Recife, incorporating Faculties established 1827-1941. Acquired present title 1965. Under the jurisdiction of the Ministry of Education and Sports and financially supported by the Federal Government.

Academic Year: March to December (March-June; August-December)

Admission Requirements: Secondary school certificate and entrance examination

Main Language(s) of Instruction: Portuguese

Degrees and Diplomas: *Bacharelado*; *Licenciatura*; *Especialização/Aperfeiçoamento*; *Mestrado*; *Doutorado*

Publications: Cadernos de Serviço Social; Clio; Econômia e Desenvolvimento; Estudos de Sociologia; Estudos Filosóficos; Politica Hoje; Revista Administração Escolar; Revista Arte e Comunicação; Revista Biológica Brasílicas; Revista de Geografia; Revista de Oceanografia; Revista Estudos Universitários

Last Updated: 18/04/16

FEDERAL UNIVERSITY OF PIAUÍ

Universidade Federal do Piauí (UFPI)

Campus Universitário, Ministro Petrônio Portela, Bairro Ininga, Teresina, Piauí 64049550

Tel: +55(86) 3215-5625 +55(86) 3215-5621

Fax: +55(86) 3215-5880

EMail: ufpinet@ufpi.br

Website: http://www.ufpi.br

Reitor: Luiz de Sousa Santos Júnior (2004-)
Tel: +55(86) 3237-1362

Centre

Agrarian Sciences (Agricultural Engineering; Agriculture; Soil Science; Veterinary Science; Zoology); **Education** (Education; Music; Visual Arts); **Health Sciences** (Biochemistry; Dentistry; Health Sciences; Medicine; Nursing; Nutrition; Pharmacology; Physiology); **Human Sciences and Letters** (Accountancy; Administration; Arts and Humanities; Economics; Geography; History; Law; Philosophy; Social and Community Services; Social Sciences); **Natural Sciences** (Archaeology; Biology; Chemistry; Computer Science; Mathematics; Natural Sciences; Physics; Statistics); **Technology** (Architecture; Electrical Engineering; Geology; Hydraulic Engineering; Mechanical Engineering; Production Engineering; Technology; Transport and Communications)

History: Founded 1973. Under the jurisdiction of the Ministry of Education and Sports and financially supported by the Federal Government.

Academic Year: March to November (March-June; August-November)

Admission Requirements: Secondary school certificate and entrance examination

Fees: None

Main Language(s) of Instruction: Portuguese

Degrees and Diplomas: *Bacharelado*: **Accountancy; Agricultural Engineering; Animal Husbandry; Business Administration; Cattle Breeding; Civil Engineering; Construction Engineering; Dentistry; Economics; Education; Fine Arts; Law; Medicine; Nursing; Rural Planning; Social Work; Veterinary Science.** *Licenciatura*: **Arts and Humanities; Biology; Business and Commerce; Chemistry; Education; Geography; History; Mathematics; Philosophy; Physical Education; Physics; Social Studies.** *Mestrado*; *Doutorado*

Last Updated: 18/04/16

FEDERAL UNIVERSITY OF RIO DE JANEIRO

Universidade Federal do Rio de Janeiro (UFRJ)

Av. Pedro Calmon, n° 500 - Prédio da Reitoria - 2° andar, Cidade Universitária, Rio de Janeiro, Rio de Janeiro 21941590

Tel: +55(21) 2562-2010

Fax: +55(21) 2560-1805

EMail: reitoria@reitoria.ufrj.br

Website: http://www.ufrj.br

Reitor: Aloisio Teixeira

Unit

Community Health Studies *(NESC)* (Health Sciences); **Health Education** *(NUTES)* (Health Education); **National Museum Studies** (Anthropology; Botany; Entomology; Geology; Paleontology); **Natural Products Research** *(NPPN)* (Ecology)

School

Architecture and Urban Planning *(FAU)* (Architecture; Town Planning); **Business Administration** *(COPPEAD, Graduate)* (Business Administration); **Business Administration and Accountancy** (Accountancy; Business Administration); **Chemistry** *(EQ)* (Chemistry); **Communication** *(ECO)* (Communication Studies); **Dentistry** (Dentistry); **Education** (Education); **Engineering** *(COPPE, Graduate)* (Chemical Engineering; Civil Engineering; Computer Engineering; Electrical Engineering; Engineering; Marine Engineering; Materials Engineering; Mechanical Engineering; Metallurgical Engineering; Nuclear Engineering; Production Engineering; Systems Analysis; Transport Engineering); **Engineering** (Civil Engineering; Electrical Engineering; Electronic Engineering; Engineering; Graphic Arts; Hydraulic Engineering; Industrial Engineering; Marine Engineering; Mechanical Engineering; Metallurgical Engineering; Naval Architecture; Nuclear Engineering; Sanitary Engineering; Structural Architecture); **Fine Arts** *(EBA)* (Fine Arts); **Law** (Law); **Letters** (Arts and Humanities; Classical Languages; English; German; Latin; Linguistics; Literature; Oriental Languages; Philology; Portuguese; Slavic Languages); **Medicine** (Medicine); **Music** (Music); **Nursing** *(EEAN)* (Nursing); **Pharmacy** (Pharmacy); **Physical Education and Sports** *(EEFD)* (Physical Education; Sports); **Social Service** (Social Work)

Institute

Biological and Health Sciences *(ICB)* (Biological and Life Sciences; Health Sciences); **Biology** (Biology); **Biophysics** *(IBCCF)* (Biophysics); **Chemistry** *(IQ)* (Chemistry); **Child Care and Education** *(IPPMG)* (Child Care and Development; Education); **Economics** *(IE)* (Economics); **Geosciences** *(IGEO)* (Earth Sciences); **Gynaecology** (Gynaecology and Obstetrics); **Macromolecules** *(IMA)* (Physics); **Mathematics** (Mathematics; Statistics); **Microbiology** (Microbiology); **Neurology** (Neurology); **Nutrition** (Nutrition); **Philosophy and Social Sciences** *(IFCS)* (Philosophy; Social Sciences); **Physics** (Physics); **Pneumology and Pthisis** (Health Sciences); **Psychiatry** (Psychiatry and Mental Health); **Psychology** (Psychology); **Regional and Urban Planning Research** *(IPPUR)* (Architecture; Regional Planning; Town Planning)

Centre

Arts and Letters *(CLA)* (Architecture; Architecture and Planning; Arts and Humanities; Fine Arts; Music; Town Planning); **Health Sciences** (Health Sciences); **Legal and Economic Sciences** *(CCJE)* (Economics; Law); **Mathematics and Natural Sciences** *(CCMN)* (Mathematics; Natural Sciences); **Philosophy and Humanities** *(CFCH)* (Arts and Humanities; Communication Studies; Education; Philosophy; Psychology; Social Sciences; Social Work); **Technology** *(CT)* (Technology)

Further Information: Also 3 University Hospitals: Clementino Fraga Filho, São Francisco and Maternity

History: Founded 1920, reorganized 1937 as Universidade do Brasil with autonomous status. Acquired present title 1965.

Academic Year: March to December (March-June; August-December)

Admission Requirements: Secondary school certificate and entrance examination

Main Language(s) of Instruction: Portuguese

Degrees and Diplomas: *Bacharelado*: **Civics; Medicine; Musical Instruments; Psychology.** *Licenciatura*; *Mestrado*; *Doutorado*

Student Services: Health Services, Nursery Care, Sports Facilities

Publishing house: University Press

Last Updated: 18/04/16

FEDERAL UNIVERSITY OF RIO GRANDE DO NORTE

Universidade Federal do Rio Grande do Norte (UFRN)

Avenida Senador Salgado Filho 3000, Campus Universitário, Lagoa Nova, Natal, Rio Grande do Norte 59078970

Tel: +55(84) 3215-3119

Fax: +55(84) 3215-3131

EMail: gabinete@reitoria.ufrn.br

Website: http://www.ufrn.br

Reitor: José Ivonildo do Rêgo (2003-)

Vice-Rector: Nilsen Carvalho Filho

International Relations: Djalma Marinho Pereira
Tel: +55(84) 3215-3114 EMail: assint@reitoria.ufrn.br

Centre

Applied Social Sciences *(CCSA)* (Accountancy; Administration; Economics; Law; Library Science; Pedagogy; Social Work; Tourism); **Bioscience** (Biochemistry; Biology; Botany; Cell Biology; Ecology; Genetics; Marine Science and Oceanography; Parasitology; Physiology; Zoology); **Earth and Exact Sciences** *(CCET)* (Computer Engineering; Computer Science; Geology; Materials Engineering; Mathematics; Physics; Statistics); **Health Sciences** *(CCS)* (Dentistry; Gynaecology and Obstetrics; Medicine; Nursing; Nutrition; Pharmacy; Physical Education; Physical Therapy); **Higher Education** *(CERES - Regional)* (Higher Education); **Human Sciences, Letters and Arts** *(CCHLA)* (Arts and Humanities; Communication Studies; Fine Arts; Geography; History; Philosophy; Psychology; Social Sciences); **Natural Sciences** *(CB)* (Aquaculture; Biological and Life Sciences; Biomedicine); **Technology** (Architecture; Chemical Engineering; Civil Engineering; Electrical Engineering; Mechanical Engineering; Production Engineering; Technology; Textile Technology; Town Planning; Zoology)

Further Information: Also 4 University Hospitals

History: Founded 1958 incorporating previously existing Faculties. Became federal institution and acquired present title 1960. Reorganized 1968 - faculties became academic departments

Academic Year: March to December (March-June; August-December)

Admission Requirements: Secondary school certificate and entrance examination

Fees: None

Main Language(s) of Instruction: Portuguese

Degrees and Diplomas: *Bacharelado*: **Accountancy; Administration; Aquaculture; Architecture; Art Education; Biology; Biomedicine; Chemical Engineering; Chemistry; Civil Engineering; Communication Studies; Computer Engineering; Computer Science; Dentistry; Documentation Techniques; Ecology; Economics; Electrical Engineering; Geography; Gynaecology and Obstetrics; Law; Mathematics; Mechanical Engineering; Medicine; Music; Nutrition; Pedagogy; Pharmacy; Philosophy; Physical Education; Physical Therapy; Physics; Production Engineering; Psychology; Radiology; Social Sciences; Social Work; Statistics; Textile Technology; Tourism; Urban Studies; Zoology.** *Mestrado*: **Accountancy; Administration; Architecture; Biochemistry; Chemical Engineering; Chemistry; Computer Engineering; Dentistry; Earth Sciences; Economics; Education; Electrical Engineering; Environmental Studies; Genetics; Geography; Geophysics; Health Sciences; Modern Languages; Molecular Biology; Natural Sciences; Nursing; Oral Pathology; Pharmacy; Philosophy; Physics; Production Engineering; Psychology; Sanitary Engineering; Social Sciences; Social Work; Urban Studies.** *Doutorado*: **Chemical Engineering; Education; Electrical Engineering; Geophysics; Health Sciences; Materials Engineering; Oral Pathology; Physics; Social Sciences.**

Student Services: Academic Counselling, Careers Guidance, Cultural Activities, Health Services, Language Laboratory, Nursery Care, Social Counselling, Sports Facilities

Publications: Educação e Saúde; Educação em Questão; Vivência

Publishing House: Editora Universitária

Last Updated: 18/04/16

FEDERAL UNIVERSITY OF RIO GRANDE DO SUL

Universidade Federal do Rio Grande do Sul (UFRGS)

Avenida Paulo Gama 110, Térreo Faroupilha, Porto Alegre, Rio Grande do Sul 90040060

Tel: +55(51) 3316-7000

EMail: ufrgs@ufrgs.br

Website: http://www.ufrgs.br

Reitor: Carlos Alexandre Netto EMail: reitor@gabinete.ufrgs.br

Faculty

Agronomy (Agriculture; Agronomy; Forestry; Horticulture; Plant and Crop Protection; Soil Science; Zoology); **Architecture**

(Architecture; Design; Town Planning); **Dentistry** (Dentistry; Surgery); **Economics** (Accountancy; Actuarial Science; Economics; International Relations); **Education** (Curriculum; Education); **Law** (Law); **Library Science and Journalism** (Advertising and Publicity; Journalism; Library Science; Museum Studies; Public Relations); **Medicine** (Medicine); **Pharmacy** (Pharmacy); **Veterinary Science** (Veterinary Science)

School

Administration; **Engineering** (Automation and Control Engineering; Civil Engineering; Computer Engineering; Engineering; Environmental Engineering; Physical Engineering); **Nursing** (Nursing); **Physical Education** (Physical Education)

Institute

Arts (Music; Theatre; Visual Arts); **Basic Health Sciences** (Biochemistry; Microbiology; Pharmacology; Physiology); **Bioscience** (Biology; Biotechnology; Botany; Ecology; Genetics; Molecular Biology; Zoology); **Chemistry** (Chemistry); **Food Science and Technology** (Food Science; Food Technology); **GeoSciences** (Earth Sciences; Geography; Geology; Mineralogy; Paleontology; Petroleum and Gas Engineering); **Hydrology Research** (Water Science); **Informatics** (Information Sciences); **Letters** (Arts and Humanities); **Mathematics** (Mathematics); **Philosophy and Humanities** (Arts and Humanities; History; Philosophy; Political Sciences; Social Sciences); **Physics** (Physics); **Psychology**

History: Founded 1934 as Universidade do Pôrto Alegre, incorporating faculties established 1896-1910. Acquired present status and title 1965.

Academic Year: March to November (March-June; August-November)

Admission Requirements: Secondary school certificate and entrance examination

Main Language(s) of Instruction: Portuguese

Degrees and Diplomas: *Bacharelado*: **Accountancy; Actuarial Science; Administration; Agricultural Engineering; Animal Husbandry; Architecture; Arts and Humanities; Biology; Business Administration; Chemistry; Computer Science; Dentistry; Economics; Engineering; Geography; Geology; History; Journalism; Law; Library Science; Mathematics; Medicine; Music; Nursing; Painting and Drawing; Pharmacy; Philosophy; Physics; Psychology; Public Administration; Sculpture; Social Sciences; Statistics; Theatre; Veterinary Science.** *Licenciatura*: **Arts and Humanities; Biology; Chemistry; Education; Geography; History; Mathematics; Philosophy; Physical Education; Physics; Social Sciences.** *Mestrado*; *Doutorado*. Also teaching qualifications

Student Services: Academic Counselling, Canteen, Language Laboratory, Nursery Care, Social Counselling, Sports Facilities

Publications: Aplicação Review

Publishing House: Gráfica e Editora da Universidade

Last Updated: 18/04/16

FEDERAL UNIVERSITY OF RIO GRANDE FOUNDATION

Fundação Universidade Federal do Rio Grande (FURG)

Av. Itália km 8, Bairro Carreiros, Rio Grande, Rio Grande 96201900
Tel: +55(53) 3233-6500 +55(53) 3233-6730
Fax: +55(53) 3230-2248
EMail: reitoria@furg.br
Website: http://www.furg.br

Reitora: Cleuza Maria Sobral Dias

Pró-Reitor, Planejamento e Administração - Proplad: Mozart Tavares Martins Filho

Faculty

Law (FaDir) (Law); **Medicine (FaMed)** (Biomedicine; Demography and Population; Gynaecology and Obstetrics; Medicine; Paediatrics; Surgery)

School

Chemistry and Food Science (EQA) (Chemistry; Food Science; Food Technology); **Computer Sciences (CS)** (Automation and Control Engineering; Computer Engineering; Information Technology); **Engineering (EE)** (Civil Engineering; Computer Graphics; Marine Engineering; Mechanical Engineering); **Nursing (EEnf)** (Nursing)

Institute

Biological Sciences (ICB) (Biological and Life Sciences); **Economics, Administration and Accountancy (ICEAC)** (Accountancy; Administration; Business Administration; Economics); **Education (IE)** (Education); **Human Sciences and Information (ICHI)** (Archaeology; Archiving; Geography (Human); History; Hotel Management; Library Science; Psychology; Public Relations; Sociology; Tourism); **Letters and Arts (ILA)** (Arts and Humanities; Linguistics; Literature; Visual Arts); **Mathematics, Statistics and Physics (IMEF)** (Computer Graphics; Mathematics; Mathematics Education; Physics; Science Education; Statistics); **Oceanography (IO)** (Aquaculture; Environmental Management; Marine Biology; Marine Science and Oceanography)

Centre

Comprehensive Care Centre for Children and Adolescents (CAIC) (Health Sciences; Social and Community Services)

Further Information: Also University Hospital; Cidade, Saúde, Santa Vitória do Palmar, Santo Antônio da Patrulha, São Lourenço do Sul campuses

History: Founded 1969 incorporating previously existing Faculties of Industrial Engineering, Law, Philosophy, Science and Letters, Political and Economic Sciences. A State Institution under the jurisdiction of the Ministry of Education and Sports.

Academic Year: March to November (March-June; August-November)

Admission Requirements: Secondary school certificate and competitive entrance examination

Main Language(s) of Instruction: Portuguese

Degrees and Diplomas: *Tecnólogo*; *Bacharelado*: **Accountancy; Agricultural Engineering; Agriculture; Applied Mathematics; Archaeology; Archiving; Automation and Control Engineering; Bioengineering; Biological and Life Sciences; Business Administration; Chemical Engineering; Civil Engineering; Computer Engineering; Ecology; Economics; Food Technology; Geography; History; Hotel Management; Industrial Engineering; Information Technology; International Business; International Relations; Law; Library Science; Marine Science and Oceanography; Mechanical Engineering; Medicine; Naval Architecture; Physics; Psychology; Special Education; Tourism; Visual Arts.** *Licenciatura*: **Art Education; Chemistry; English; Foreign Languages Education; French; History; Humanities and Social Science Education; Mathematics; Mathematics Education; Native Language Education; Pedagogy; Physical Education; Physics; Portuguese; Science Education; Spanish; Visual Arts.** *Especialização/Aperfeiçoamento*: **Accountancy; Adult Education; Automation and Control Engineering; Botany; Chemistry; Computer Science; Construction Engineering; Cultural Studies; Education; Educational Technology; Electrical Engineering; Environmental Studies; Human Rights; Humanities and Social Science Education; Instrument Making; Linguistics; Mathematics Education; Media Studies; Native Language Education; Naval Architecture; Physical Education; Political Sciences; Production Engineering; Public Administration; Science Education; Social Studies; Sociology; Teacher Training; Technology Education.** *Mestrado*: **Administration; Applied Chemistry; Aquaculture; Business Administration; Chemical Engineering; Computer Engineering; Computer Graphics; Economics; Education; Environmental Studies; Food Science; Food Technology; Geography; Health Sciences; History; Humanities and Social Science Education; Labour Law; Literature; Marine Biology; Marine Engineering; Marine Science and Oceanography; Mathematics; Mechanical Engineering; Nursing; Physics; Physiology; Public Health; Science Education.** *Doutorado*: **Applied Chemistry; Aquaculture; Biological and Life Sciences; Education; Environmental Studies; Food Science; Food Technology; Health Sciences; Literature; Marine Biology; Marine Science and Oceanography; Nursing; Physiology; Science Education.** Also Medical Residency Programmes; the Licenciatura is awarded in the same fields as the Bacharelado

Student Services: Canteen, Library, Nursery Care, Sports Facilities

Publications: Ambiente e Educação; Artexto; Atlântica; Biblos; Juris; Momento; Sinergia; Vitale
Publishing House: Editora e Gráfica da FURG
Last Updated: 08/02/16

FEDERAL UNIVERSITY OF RONDÔNIA FOUNDATION

Fundação Universidade Federal de Rondônia (UNIR)
BR 364, Km 9,5, Porto Velho, Rondônia 76801-059
Tel: +55(69) 2182-2100
EMail: reitoria@unir.br
Website: http://www.unir.br

Reitora: Maria Berenice Alho da Costa Tourinho
Tel: +55(69) 2182-2020 EMail: reitoria@unir.br
Pró-Reitora de Administração: Ivanda Soares da Silva
Tel: +55(69) 2182-2001 +55(69) 8455-7838 EMail: prad@unir.br

Unit
Applied Social Sciences (NUCSA) (Accountancy; Administration; Economics; Law; Library Science); **Exact and Earth Sciences (NCET)** (Biology; Chemistry; Geography; Mathematics; Physics); **Health Sciences (NUSAU)** (Medicine; Nursing; Physical Education; Psychology; Public Health); **Human Sciences (NCH)** (Archaeology; Educational Sciences; English; Fine Arts; History; Literature; Modern Languages; Music; Pedagogy; Philosophy; Portuguese; Social Sciences; Spanish; Theatre; Visual Arts); **Technology (NT)** (Civil Engineering; Computer Science; Electrical Engineering)

Further Information: Also campuses in Ariquemes, Cacoal, Guajará-Mirim, Ji-Paraná, Porto Velho, Rolim de Moura e Vilhena

History: Founded 1982.

Admission Requirements: Secondary school certificate and entrance examination (vestibular)

Main Language(s) of Instruction: Portuguese

Degrees and Diplomas: *Bacharelado*; *Licenciatura*; *Especialização/Aperfeiçoamento*: **Educational Administration; Gynaecology and Obstetrics; Health Administration; Human Rights; Pedagogy; Preschool Education; Protective Services; Public Administration.** *Mestrado*: **Administration; Arts and Humanities; Biology; Cultural Studies; Education; Environmental Studies; Geography (Human); Health Education; History; Literature; Mathematics; Modern Languages; Preschool Education; Psychology; Public Administration; Regional Planning.** *Doutorado*: **Biology; Environmental Studies; Geography (Human); Regional Planning.**

Student Services: Academic Counselling, Canteen, Cultural Activities, Language Laboratory, Library, Social Counselling

Publications: Cadernos de Criação; Presença

Last Updated: 04/02/16

FEDERAL UNIVERSITY OF RORAIMA

Universidade Federal de Roraima (UFRR)
Campus Paricarana, Av. Cap. Enê Garcêz, n° 2413 Bairro Aeroporto, Boa Vista, Roraima 69304-000
Tel: +55(95) 3621-3100 +55(95) 3621-3102
Fax: +55(95) 3621-3101
EMail: reitoria@ufrr.br
Website: http://www.ufrr.br

Reitor: Roberto Ramos Santos
Tel: +55(95) 3621-3102 EMail: robertoramos@ufrr.br

Institute
Geosciences (Geology)

Centre
Administration and Law; **Agriculture**; **Biological and Health Sciences**; **Communication and Letters** (Journalism; Literature; Modern Languages); **Computer Science** (Computer Science); **Education**; **Health Sciences** (Medicine); **Human Sciences**; **Science and Technology**

History: Founded 1985.

Academic Year: March to December (March-June; August-December)

Admission Requirements: Secondary school certificate and entrance examination

Fees: None

Main Language(s) of Instruction: Portuguese

Degrees and Diplomas: *Bacharelado*; *Licenciatura*; *Especialização/Aperfeiçoamento*; *Mestrado*

Student Services: Canteen, Health Services, Language Laboratory, Nursery Care, Sports Facilities

Publications: Texts and Discussions

Publishing House: Federal University of Roraima Press

Last Updated: 18/04/16

FEDERAL UNIVERSITY OF SANTA CATARINA

Universidade Federal de Santa Catarina (UFSC)
Caixa Postal 476, Campus Universitário, Trindade, Florianópolis, Santa Catarina 88040900
Tel: +55(48) 3721-9000
Fax: +55(48) 3234-4069
EMail: gabinete@reitoria.ufsc.br
Website: http://www.ufsc.br

Reitor: Alvaro Toubes Prata (2008-) Tel: +55(48) 3331-9572

Centre
Agrarian Sciences (Agricultural Engineering; Agriculture; Animal Husbandry; Aquaculture; Food Science; Food Technology; Plant and Crop Protection; Rural Planning; Rural Studies); **Biological Sciences** (Anatomy; Biochemistry; Biological and Life Sciences; Pharmacology; Physiology); **Communication and Expression** (Arts and Humanities; Communication Studies; English; French; German; Italian; Journalism; Linguistics; Literature; Portuguese); **Education** (Child Care and Development; Documentation Techniques; Education; Library Science; Pedagogy); **Health Sciences** (Dentistry; Health Sciences; Medicine; Nursing; Nutrition; Pharmacy); **Law** (Law); **Philosophy and Human Sciences** (Anthropology; Arts and Humanities; Cultural Studies; Environmental Studies; Geography; Geography (Human); History; Philosophy; Political Sciences; Psychology; Social Sciences; Sociology); **Physics and Mathematics** (Chemistry; Mathematics; Physics); **Socio-Economic Studies** (Accountancy; Business Administration; Economics; Social Studies; Social Work); **Sports** (Sports); **Technology** (Architecture; Automation and Control Engineering; Chemical Engineering; Civil Engineering; Computer Science; Electrical Engineering; Environmental Engineering; Food Technology; Mechanical Engineering; Production Engineering; Safety Engineering; Sanitary Engineering; Statistics; Technology; Town Planning; Transport and Communications; Transport Engineering)

History: Founded 1960 and comprising previously existing Faculties. Reorganized 1970 with a structure comprising Centres for professional Education and Centres of basic Studies. An autonomous Institution financially supported by the State and responsible to the Ministry of Education and Sports.

Academic Year: March to December (March-June; August-December)

Admission Requirements: Secondary school certificate and entrance examination

Main Language(s) of Instruction: Portuguese

Degrees and Diplomas: *Bacharelado*; *Licenciatura*; *Especialização/Aperfeiçoamento*; *Mestrado*; *Doutorado*

Student Services: Academic Counselling, Canteen, Careers Guidance, Cultural Activities, Health Services, Nursery Care, Social Counselling, Sports Facilities

Publications: Biotemas; Ciências de Saúde; Ciências Humanas; Fragmentos; Geosul; Ilha do Desterro; Katalysis; Perspectiva; Poité; Principia; Seqüência; Travessia

Publishing House: Editora da Universidade

Last Updated: 18/04/16

FEDERAL UNIVERSITY OF SANTA MARIA

Universidade Federal de Santa Maria (UFSM)
Avenida Roraima, n° 1000 Cidade Universitária, Bairro Camobi, Santa Maria, Rio Grande do Sul 97105900
Tel: +55(55) 3220-8000
Fax: +55(55) 3220-8001
EMail: gabinete@adm.ufsm.br
Website: http://www.ufsm.br

Reitor: Felipe Martins Müller

Centre

Arts and Letters (Fine Arts; Industrial Design; Linguistics; Literature; Music; Philology; Visual Arts); **Education** (Educational Administration; Special Education; Teacher Training); **Health Sciences** (Dentistry; Medicine; Nursing; Occupational Therapy; Pharmacy; Physical Therapy; Public Health; Speech Therapy and Audiology); **Natural and Exact Sciences** (Biology; Chemistry; Geography; Mathematics; Meteorology; Physics); **Physical Education and Sports** (Physical Education; Sports); **Rural Sciences** (Agricultural Equipment; Agronomy; Animal Husbandry; Crop Production; Food Science; Forestry; Horticulture; Soil Science; Veterinary Science); **Social and Human Sciences** (Accountancy; Administration; Advertising and Publicity; Archiving; Economics; Information Management; Journalism; Law; Philosophy; Political Sciences; Psychology; Public Relations; Social Sciences; Sociology); **Technology** (Architecture; Chemical Engineering; Civil Engineering; Computer Science; Electrical Engineering; Hydraulic Engineering; Mechanical Engineering; Production Engineering; Technology; Town Planning)

History: Founded 1960, incorporating existing Faculties created since 1931. Reorganized 1970 with a structure comprising Centres for Professional Education. A State institution under the jurisdiction of the Ministry of Education and Sports.

Academic Year: March to December (March-July; August-December)

Admission Requirements: Secondary school certificate and entrance examination

Main Language(s) of Instruction: Portuguese

Degrees and Diplomas: *Bacharelado*: **Accountancy; Agronomy; Animal Husbandry; Arts and Humanities; Biology; Chemistry; Civil Engineering; Communication Arts; Dentistry; Economics; Education; Forestry; Geography; History; Industrial Chemistry; Law; Mathematics; Medicine; Music; Painting and Drawing; Pharmacy; Philosophy; Physical Education; Sculpture; Speech Therapy and Audiology; Veterinary Science.** *Licenciatura*: **Physics.** *Especialização/Aperfeiçoamento*; *Mestrado*: **Agricultural Education; Agricultural Engineering; Agronomy; Animal Husbandry; Education; Electrical Engineering; Mechanical Engineering; Veterinary Science.** *Doutorado*

Student Services: Academic Counselling, Canteen, Health Services, Language Laboratory, Nursery Care, Sports Facilities

Publications: Boletim de Pessoal; Caderno Adulto; Caderno de Educação Especial; Caderno de Ensino; Ensino e Pesquisa; Geografi; Pesquisa e Extensão; Revista Ciência Florestal; Revista Ciência Natura; Revista Ciência Rural; Revista Ciências Biomédicas; Revista do Centro de Tecnologia; Revista do Curso de Farmácia

Last Updated: 18/04/16

FEDERAL UNIVERSITY OF SÃO CARLOS

Universidade Federal de São Carlos (UFSCAR)

Rodovia Washington Luís, Km 235, Monjolinho,
São Carlos, São Paulo 13565905
Tel: +55(16) 3351-8111
Fax: +55(16) 3261-2081
EMail: reitoria@power.ufscar.br
Website: http://www.ufscar.br

Reitor: Targino de Araújo Filho
Tel: +55(16) 3260-8101 EMail: reitor@power.ufscar.br

Pró-Reitor de Administração: Manoel Fernando Martins
Tel: +55(16) 3260-8013 EMail: rss@power.ufscar.br

Centre

Agricultural Sciences (Agricultural Economics; Agricultural Engineering; Agriculture; Biotechnology; Environmental Studies; Natural Resources); **Education and Human Sciences** (Arts and Humanities; Communication Studies; Education; Educational Sciences; Information Sciences; Psychology; Social Sciences); **Exact Sciences and Technology** (Chemical Engineering; Chemistry; Civil Engineering; Computer Science; Materials Engineering; Mathematics; Natural Sciences; Physics; Production Engineering; Statistics; Technology); **Health Sciences and Biology** (Anatomy; Biology; Botany; Ecology; Genetics; Health Sciences; Nursing; Occupational Therapy; Pathology; Physical Education; Physical Therapy; Physiology)

Further Information: Also Campus in Araras

History: Founded 1960 as Universidade Federal de São Paulo, acquired present title 1968. A State institution under the jurisdiction of the Ministry of Education and Sports.

Academic Year: March to December (March-June; August-December)

Admission Requirements: Secondary school certificate and entrance examination

Fees: None

Main Language(s) of Instruction: Portuguese

Degrees and Diplomas: *Bacharelado*: **Agriculture; Education; Engineering; Information Sciences; Mathematics and Computer Science; Natural Sciences; Performing Arts; Social Sciences.** *Licenciatura*; *Especialização/Aperfeiçoamento*; *Mestrado*: **Education; Engineering; Mathematics and Computer Science; Natural Sciences; Philosophy; Social Sciences.** *Doutorado*

Student Services: Academic Counselling, Canteen, Cultural Activities, Facilities for disabled people, Health Services, Language Laboratory, Nursery Care, Social Counselling, Sports Facilities

Publications: Revista Univerciência

Publishing House: Editora da Universidade Federal de São Carlos (EDUFSCar)

Last Updated: 18/04/16

FEDERAL UNIVERSITY OF SÃO JOÃO DEL REI

Universidade Federal de São João del Rei (UFSJ)

Campus Santo Antonio Centro, Praça Frei Orlando 170, Centro,
São João del Rei, Minas Gerais 36307352
Tel: +55(32) 3379-2340 +55(32) 3379-2341
Fax: +55(32) 3379-2525
EMail: reitoria@ufsj.edu.br
Website: http://www.ufsj.edu.br/

Reitor: Helvecio Luiz Reis (2008-)

Department

Biosystems Engineering (Bioengineering); **Computer Science** (Computer Science); **Economics** (Economics); **Educational Sciences** (Educational Sciences); **Electrical Engineering** (Electrical Engineering; Engineering); **Geography** (Geography); **Literature, Arts and Culture** (Cultural Studies; Journalism; Literature; Theatre); **Mathematics and Statistics** (Mathematics; Statistics); **Mechanical Engineering** (Mechanical Engineering); **Music** (Music; Music Education; Musical Instruments; Singing); **Natural Sciences** (Biology; Chemistry; Electrical Engineering; Mathematics; Mechanical Engineering; Physics); **Philosophy and Methods** (Philosophy); **Physical Education and Health** (Health Sciences; Physical Education); **Psychology** (Psychology); **Social Sciences** (Social Sciences); **Thermal and Fluid Sciences** (Thermal Engineering)

History: Founded 1986.

Main Language(s) of Instruction: Portuguese

Degrees and Diplomas: *Bacharelado*; *Especialização/Aperfeiçoamento*; *Mestrado*; *Doutorado*

Last Updated: 18/04/16

FEDERAL UNIVERSITY OF SÃO PAULO

Universidade Federal de São Paulo (UNIFESP)

Rua Botucatú 740, Vila Clementino, São Paulo, São Paulo 4023900
Tel: +55(11) 5549-7699
Fax: +55(11) 5576-4313
EMail: reitoria@unifesp.br
Website: http://www.unifesp.br

Reitor: Walter Manna Albertoni (2009-)
EMail: walter.albertoni@unifesp.br

Secretario Geral: Stephan Geocze
Tel: +55(11) 5549-7890 EMail: geocze@epm.br

International Relations: Benjamin Israel Kopelman, International Relations Coordinator
Tel: +55(11) 5576-4769 EMail: bkopelman@terra.com.br

Department

Biochemistry (Biochemistry; Molecular Biology); **Biophysics** (Biophysics; Physical Chemistry); **Dermatology** (Dermatology; Parasitology); **Diagnostic Medical Imaging** (Medical Technology;

Treatment Techniques); **Gynaecology and Obstetrics** (Gynaecology and Obstetrics); **Health Informatics** (Distance Education; Information Technology); **Immunology, Microbiology, Parasitology** (Cell Biology; Immunology; Microbiology; Parasitology); **Medicine** (Cardiology; Endocrinology; Gastroenterology; Gerontology; Haematology; Medicine; Nephrology; Parasitology; Pneumology; Rheumatology); **Morphology** (Anatomy; Biology; Embryology and Reproduction Biology; Genetics; Histology); **Neurology, Neurosurgery** (Neurology); **Nursing** (Midwifery; Nursing; Public Health); **Ophthalmology** (Ophthalmology); **Orthopaedics and Traumatology** (Orthopaedics; Surgery); **Otorhinolaryngology and Human Communication Disorders** (Communication Disorders; Otorhinolaryngology; Speech Therapy and Audiology); **Paediatrics** (Community Health; Gastroenterology; Immunology; Nutrition; Paediatrics; Rheumatology); **Pathology** (Anatomy; Ethics; Law; Pathology; Surgery); **Pharmacology** (Endocrinology; Pharmacology); **Physiology** (Physiology); **Preventive Medicine** (Epidemiology; Social and Preventive Medicine; Statistics); **Psychiatry** (Psychiatry and Mental Health; Psychology); **Psychobiology** (Biology; Pharmacology); **Surgery** (Anaesthesiology; Plastic Surgery; Surgery; Urology)

Further Information: Also Hospital São Paulo, Hospital Municipal 'Vereador José Stropoli' and Hospital Geral de Pirajussara. Specific courses and programmes for graduate students

History: Founded 1938 as Escola Paulista de Medicina. Acquired present status and title 1994.

Academic Year: February to December (February-June; August-December)

Admission Requirements: Secondary school certificate and entrance examination

Fees: None

Main Language(s) of Instruction: Portuguese

Accrediting Agency: Ministry of Education of Brazil

Degrees and Diplomas: *Bacharelado*: **Biomedical Engineering; Medicine; Nursing; Optical Technology; Speech Therapy and Audiology.** *Mestrado*: **Communication Disorders; Epidemiology; Medicine; Nursing; Nutrition; Rehabilitation and Therapy.** *Doutorado*: **Communication Disorders; Medicine; Nursing; Nutrition; Rehabilitation and Therapy.**

Student Services: Academic Counselling, Canteen, Cultural Activities, Health Services, Nursery Care, Social Counselling, Sports Facilities

Publications: Folia Médica; Revista do Hospital São Paulo

Last Updated: 18/04/16

FEDERAL UNIVERSITY OF SERGIPE

Universidade Federal de Sergipe (UFS)

Cidade Universitária Prof. José, Aloísio de Campos, Av. Marechal Rondon, s/n Jardim Rosa Elze, São Cristovão, Sergipe 49100000

Tel: +55(79) 3212-6600
Fax: +55(79) 3212-6474
EMail: proad@ufs.br
Website: http://www.ufs.br

Reitor: Josué Modesto dos Passos Subrinho
Tel: +55(79) 3212-6404 EMail: reitor@ufs.br

Centre

Applied Social Sciences (Accountancy; Administration; Economics; Law; Social and Community Services; Social Sciences); **Biological and Health Sciences** (Biological and Life Sciences; Dentistry; Health Sciences; Medicine; Nursing; Nutrition; Physical Education); **Education and Humanities** (Arts and Humanities; Education; Geography; History; Philosophy; Psychology; Social Sciences); **Exact Sciences and Technology** (Chemical Engineering; Chemistry; Civil Engineering; Information Sciences; Mathematics; Natural Sciences; Physics; Statistics; Technology)

History: Founded 1967. Reorganized 1978 with a structure comprising centres for professional education. An autonomous institution financially supported by the State and responsible to the Ministry of Education and Sports.

Academic Year: March to December (March-June; August-December)

Admission Requirements: Secondary school certificate and entrance examination

Main Language(s) of Instruction: Portuguese

Degrees and Diplomas: *Bacharelado*: **Accountancy; Administration; Agriculture; Biology; Chemical Engineering; Chemistry; Civil Engineering; Computer Science; Dentistry; Economics; Geography; Industrial Chemistry; Law; Nursing; Physics; Psychology; Social Sciences; Social Work.** *Licenciatura*: **Arts and Humanities; Biology; Chemistry; Education; Geography; History; Mathematics; Physics.** *Especialização/Aperfeiçoamento*; *Mestrado*; *Doutorado*

Publications: Geonordeste

Last Updated: 18/04/16

FEDERAL UNIVERSITY OF THE BAY OF BAHIA

Universidade Federal do Recôncavo da Bahia (UFRB)

Campus Universitario da UFRB, Cruz das Almas, Bahia 44380-000

Tel: +55(75) 3621-2350
Fax: +55(75) 3621-9095
EMail: gabinete@urfb.edu.br
Website: http://www.ufrb.edu.br

Reitor: Paulo Gabriel Nacif

Centre

Agrarian, Environmental and Biological Sciences (Agronomy; Biology; Business Administration; Fishery; Forestry; Veterinary Science; Zoology); **Arts, Humanities and Literature** *(Cachoeira)*; **Exact and Technological Sciences**; **Health Sciences** *(Santo Antônio de Jesus)* (Nursing; Nutrition; Psychology); **Teacher Training** *(Amargosa)*

History: Founded 2005.

Main Language(s) of Instruction: Portuguese

Degrees and Diplomas: *Bacharelado*; *Licenciatura*; *Mestrado*; *Doutorado*

Last Updated: 18/04/16

FEDERAL UNIVERSITY OF THE PAMPAS

Universidade Federal do Pampa (UNIPAMPA)

Rua Melanie Granier, 48, Bagé, Rio Grande do Sul 96400-500

Tel: +55(53) 3247-4549
EMail: reitoria@unipampa.edu.br
Website: http://www.unipampa.edu.br

Rector: Maria Beatriz Luce
Tel: +55(53) 3247-4549 EMail: reitora@unipampa.edu.br

Pro-Rector, Administration: Éverton Bonow
Tel: +55(53) 3241-7483 EMail: everton.bonow@unipampa.edu.br

Campus

Alegrete (Civil Engineering; Computer Science; Electrical Engineering; Mechanical Engineering); **Bagé** (Arts and Humanities; Chemical Engineering; Chemistry; Computer Engineering; Energy Engineering; English; Environmental Engineering; Food Technology; Literature; Mathematics; Physics; Portuguese; Production Engineering; Spanish); **Caçapava do Sul**; **Dom Pedrito** (Agricultural Business; Bioengineering; Zoology); **Itaqui** (Agricultural Engineering; Agronomy); **Jaguarão**; **Santana do Livramento**; **São Borja** (Advertising and Publicity; Journalism; Political Sciences; Social and Community Services; Social Sciences); **São Gabriel** (Agricultural Engineering; Biological and Life Sciences; Biotechnology; Environmental Management; Forest Biology; Forestry); **Uruguaiana**

History: Founded 2008.

Main Language(s) of Instruction: Portuguese

Degrees and Diplomas: *Licenciatura*; *Especialização/Aperfeiçoamento*: **Literature; Modern Languages.** *Mestrado*

Last Updated: 18/04/16

FEDERAL UNIVERSITY OF THE STATE OF RIO DE JANEIRO

Universidade Federal do Estado do Rio de Janeiro (UNIRIO)

Avenida Pasteur 296, Urca,
Rio de Janeiro, Rio de Janeiro 22290240

Tel: +55(21) 2543-5615
Fax: +55(21) 2543-5615
EMail: planejamento@unirio.br
Website: http://www.unirio.br

Reitora: Malvina Tania Tuttman EMail: reitora@unirio.br

Centre

Arts and Letters (Art Education; Arts and Humanities; Modern Languages; Music; Theatre); **Biological and Health Sciences** (Biological and Life Sciences; Health Sciences; Medicine; Nursing; Nutrition); **Humanities** (Archiving; Arts and Humanities; Documentation Techniques; Educational Sciences; Law; Library Science; Museum Studies); **Technological Sciences** (Technology)

History: Founded 1969 as Federação das Escolas Federais Isoladas do Estado Guanabara. Acquired present status and title 1979. Under the jurisdiction and financially supported by the Federal Government.

Academic Year: March to December (March-June; August-December)

Admission Requirements: Secondary school certificate and entrance examination

Main Language(s) of Instruction: Portuguese

Degrees and Diplomas: *Bacharelado*; *Licenciatura*; *Especialização/Aperfeiçoamento*; *Mestrado*; *Doutorado*

Publications: Catálogo da Produção Técnica-Científica e Artística

Publishing House: Printing Office

Last Updated: 18/04/16

FEDERAL UNIVERSITY OF THE TRIÂNGULO MINEIRO

Universidade Federal do Triângulo Mineiro (UFTM)

Rua Frei Paulino 30, Abadia, Uberaba, Minas Gerais 38025180

Tel: +55(34) 3318-5004

Fax: +55(34) 3312-1487

EMail: reitoria@reitoria.uftm.edu.br

Website: http://www.uftm.edu.br

Reitor: Virmondes Rodrigues Júnior (2010-)

Institute

Biological and Natural Sciences; **Education and Arts**; **Exact Sciences and Technology** (Chemical Engineering; Civil Engineering; Electrical Engineering; Environmental Engineering; Mathematics; Mechanical Engineering; Physics; Production Engineering); **Health Sciences** (Biomedicine; Nursing; Nutrition; Occupational Therapy; Physical Therapy); **Human and Social Sciences** (Geography; History; Literature; Psychology; Social and Community Services)

History: Founded 1953 as Faculdade de Medicina do Triângulo Mineiro. Acquired present status and title 2005.

Main Language(s) of Instruction: Portuguese

Degrees and Diplomas: *Bacharelado*; *Especialização/Aperfeiçoamento*; *Mestrado*; *Doutorado*

Last Updated: 18/04/16

FEDERAL UNIVERSITY OF THE VALLEY OF SAN FRANCISCO

Universidade Federal do Vale do Sao Francisco (UNIVASF)

Av. José de Sá Maniçoba, s/n, Campus Universitário - Centro, Petrolina, Pernambuco 56304-917

Tel: +55(87) 2101-6830 +55(87) 2101-6712

Fax: +55(87) 2101-6831

EMail: reitoria@univasf.edu.br; srca@univasf.edu.br; proen@univasf.edu.br; proen.pi@univasf.edu.br

Website: http://www.univasf.edu.br

Reitor: Julianeli Tolentino de Lima
Tel: +55(87) 2101-6705
EMail: reitoria@univasf.edu.br; secretaria.gabinete@univasf.edu.br

Course

Administration (Administration); **Archaeology and Heritage Preservation** (Archaeology; Heritage Preservation); **Biological and Life Sciences** (Biological and Life Sciences); **Ecology and Geography** (Ecology; Geography); **Engineering** (Agricultural Engineering; Civil Engineering; Computer Engineering; Electrical Engineering; Environmental Engineering; Mechanical Engineering; Production Engineering); **Medicine** (Medicine); **Natural Sciences** (Natural Sciences); **Nursing** (Nursing); **Pharmacy** (Pharmacy); **Physical Education** (Physical Education); **Psychology** (Psychology); **Social Sciences** (Humanities and Social Science Education; Social Sciences); **Veterinary Science** (Veterinary Science); **Visual Arts** (Visual Arts); **Zootechnics** (Animal Husbandry)

History: Founded 2002.

Main Language(s) of Instruction: Portuguese

Degrees and Diplomas: *Bacharelado*; *Licenciatura*; *Especialização/Aperfeiçoamento*: **Agronomy; Biological and Life Sciences; Health Sciences; Physical Education.** *Mestrado*: **Agricultural Engineering; Animal Husbandry; Horticulture; Materials Engineering; Mathematics; Natural Resources; Psychology; Science Education; Veterinary Science.**

Student Services: Library

Last Updated: 04/02/16

FEDERAL UNIVERSITY OF THE VALLEYS OF JEQUITINHONHA AND MUCURI

Universidade Federal dos Vales do Jequitinhonha e Mucuri (UFVJM)

Rua da Glória 187 Centro, Diamantino, Mato Grosso 39100000

Tel: +55(38) 3531-1811 +55(38) 3531-1024

Fax: +55(38) 3531-1024 +55(38) 3531-1030

EMail: fafeod@fafeod.br

Website: http://www.fafeod.br

Reitor: Pedro Ângelo Almeida Abreu

Faculty

Agrarian Sciences (Agronomy; Forest Management; Zoology); **Applied and Exact Social Sciences** (Accountancy; Administration; Economics; Mathematics; Social and Community Services); **Biology and Health Sciences** (Biology; Dentistry; Nursing; Nutrition; Pharmacy; Physical Education; Physical Therapy); **Exact Sciences and Technology**; **Human Sciences** (English; Geography; History; Literature; Pedagogy; Spanish; Tourism)

Institute

Humanities (Geography; History; Literature; Pedagogy; Tourism); **Science and Technology** (Technology); **Science and Technology of Mucuri** (Civil Engineering; Hydraulic Engineering; Production Engineering)

History: Founded 1953 as Faculdade Federal de Odontologia de Diamantina. Became Faculdades Federais Integradas de Diamantina 2002. Acquired present status and title 2005.

Main Language(s) of Instruction: Portuguese

Degrees and Diplomas: *Bacharelado*; *Licenciatura*; *Especialização/Aperfeiçoamento*; *Mestrado*

Last Updated: 18/04/16

FEDERAL UNIVERSITY OF TOCANTINS

Universidade Federal do Tocantins (UFT)

Avenida NS 15, 109 Norte, Plano Diretor Norte, Palmas, Tocantins 77001-090

Tel: +55(63) 3232- 8012

Fax: +55(63) 3232-8039

EMail: proad@uft.edu.br; prograd@uft.edu.br; ddrgprograd@uft.edu.br

Website: http://ww1.uft.edu.br

Reitor: Márcio Antônio da Silveira
Tel: +55(63) 3232-8035 EMail: reitor@uft.edu.br

Pró-Reitor de Administração e Finanças: José Pereira Guimarães Neto Tel: +55(63) 3232-8120 EMail: proad@uft.edu.br

International Relations: Márcia Schneider, Diretora de Assuntos Internacionais Tel: +55(63) 3232-8103 EMail: dai@uft.edu.br

Department

Distance Education (EAD) (Agricultural Business; Biology; Chemistry; Physics; Public Administration)

Campus

Araguaína (Agricultural Management; Animal Husbandry; Arts and Humanities; Biology; Chemistry; Geography (Human); History; Mathematics; Physics; Tourism; Transport Management; Tropical Agriculture; Veterinary Science); **Arraias** (Biology; Mathematics; Pedagogy); **Gurupi** (Agricultural Engineering; Agronomy;

Biochemistry; Bioengineering; Biotechnology; Chemistry; Environmental Studies; Forestry; Horticulture); **Miracema** (Pedagogy; Social and Community Services); **Palmas** (Accountancy; Agricultural Business; Architecture; Business Administration; Civil Engineering; Community Health; Computer Science; Development Studies; Economics; Electrical Engineering; Environmental Engineering; Environmental Management; Environmental Studies; Fine Arts; Food Technology; Gerontology; Health Administration; Health Sciences; Law; Mass Communication; Medicine; Natural Resources; Nursing; Nutrition; Pedagogy; Philosophy; Town Planning; Water Science); **Porto Nacional** (Arts and Humanities; Biology; Geography (Human); History; Humanities and Social Science Education; International Relations; Literature; Native Language Education; Portuguese; Science Education; Social Sciences); **Tocantinópolis** (Pedagogy; Social Sciences)

Further Information: Also campuses at Araguaína, Arraias, Gurupi, Miracema, Porto Nacional and Tocantinópolis

History: Founded 2000.

Main Language(s) of Instruction: Portuguese

Degrees and Diplomas: *Tecnólogo*; *Bacharelado*; *Licenciatura*; *Especialização/Aperfeiçoamento*: **Administrative Law; Business Administration; Civil Security; Constitutional Law; Environmental Management; Foreign Languages Education; Gerontology; Humanities and Social Science Education; Journalism; Labour Law; Mass Communication; Preschool Education; Protective Services; Public Administration.** *Mestrado*: **Agricultural Business; Agriculture; Animal Husbandry; Arts and Humanities; Biological and Life Sciences; Biotechnology; Communication Studies; Cultural Studies; Development Studies; Ecology; Education; Energy Engineering; Environmental Engineering; Environmental Management; Environmental Studies; Food Technology; Forestry; Geography (Human); Health Sciences; Horticulture; Human Rights; Humanities and Social Science Education; Law; Mathematics; Native Language Education; Political Sciences; Public Health; Regional Planning; Rural Studies; Science Education; Social Studies; Systems Analysis; Tropical Agriculture.** *Doutorado*: **Animal Husbandry; Education; Environmental Studies; Horticulture; Humanities and Social Science Education; Native Language Education; Tropical Agriculture.** Also MBA

Student Services: Canteen, Library

Last Updated: 01/03/16

FEDERAL UNIVERSITY OF UBERLÂNDIA

Universidade Federal de Uberlândia (UFU)

Avenida Engenheiro Diniz 1178, 3° Andar, Martins,
Uberlândia, Minas Gerais 38401136
Tel: +55(34) 3239-4810
Fax: +55(34) 3235-0099
EMail: celso@reito.ufu.br
Website: http://www.ufu.br

Reitor: Alfredo Júlio Fernandes Neto Tel: +55(34) 3239-4810

Faculty

Accountancy (Accountancy); **Architecture, Town Planning and Design**; **Arts, Philosophy and Social Sciences** (Music; Philosophy; Social Sciences; Theatre; Visual Arts); **Business and Administration** (Public Administration); **Chemical Engineering** (Chemical Engineering); **Civil Engineering** (Civil Engineering); **Computer Science**; **Dentistry**; **Education**; **Electrical Engineering** (Electrical Engineering); **Integrated Sciences** *(Pontal)* (Administration; Biology; Chemistry; Geography; History; Mathematics; Pedagogy; Physics; Production Engineering); **Law** (Law); **Mathematics**; **Medicine** (Medicine; Nursing; Nutrition); **Physical Education**; **Veterinary Science** (Veterinary Science)

Institute

Agrarian Sciences (Agricultural Engineering; Environmental Engineering; Plant and Crop Protection; Plant Pathology; Soil Science); **Biology**; **Biomedicine** (Biomedicine; Immunology; Microbiology; Parasitology; Pharmacology; Physiology); **Chemistry** (Chemistry); **Economics** (Economics; Finance; International Relations); **Genetics and Biochemistry** (Biochemistry; Genetics); **Geography** (Geography); **History**; **Literature and Linguistics** (Linguistics; Literature); **Physics** (Physics); **Psychology**

Further Information: Three campuses. Also University Hospitals

History: Founded 1974, incorporating previously existing faculties. Recognized as a federal institution 1978.

Academic Year: March to December (March-June; August-December)

Admission Requirements: Secondary school certificate or equivalent and entrance examination

Main Language(s) of Instruction: Portuguese

Degrees and Diplomas: *Bacharelado*: **Accountancy; Administration; Animal Husbandry; Architecture; Biological and Life Sciences; Communication Arts; Computer Science; Dentistry; Economics; Education; Engineering; Fine Arts; Interior Design; Law; Medicine; Music; Performing Arts; Philosophy; Psychology; Town Planning; Veterinary Science; Visual Arts.** *Licenciatura*: **Arts and Humanities; Design; Education; Fine Arts; Geography; History; Music; Physical Education; Social Studies.** *Especialização/Aperfeiçoamento*; *Mestrado*; *Doutorado*

Student Services: Canteen, Careers Guidance, Cultural Activities, Sports Facilities

Publications: Centro de Ciências Biomédicas; Economia; Letras e Letras; Psicologia e Trânsito

Publishing House: Editora da Universidade

Last Updated: 18/04/16

FEDERAL UNIVERSITY OF VIÇOSA

Universidade Federal de Viçosa (UFV)

Avenida Peter Henry Rolfs s/n, Reitoria Campus Universitário,
Viçosa, Minas Gerais 36570-000
Tel: +55(31) 3899-2328
EMail: reitoria@ufv.br
Website: http://www.ufv.br

Reitor: Luiz Claudio Costa Tel: +55(31) 3899-2796

Centre

Agriculture (Agricultural Economics; Agricultural Engineering; Agriculture; Forestry; Plant Pathology; Soil Science; Zoology); **Biological and Health Sciences** (Biochemistry; Biological and Life Sciences; Biology; Botany; Health Sciences; Medicine; Microbiology; Molecular Biology; Nursing; Nutrition; Physical Education; Veterinary Science; Zoology); **Exact Sciences and Technology** (Architecture; Chemistry; Civil Engineering; Computer Science; Electrical Engineering; Food Technology; Mathematics; Physics; Production Engineering; Town Planning); **Human Sciences, Letters and Arts** (Accountancy; Administration; Arts and Humanities; Business and Commerce; Economics; Education; Geography; History; Home Economics; Law; Linguistics)

History: Founded 1922 as College of Agriculture, became Universidade Rural do Estado de Minas Gerais 1948 by State decree. Reorganized as a federal University with present title 1969.

Academic Year: February to December (February-July; August-December)

Admission Requirements: Secondary school certificate and entrance examination

Main Language(s) of Instruction: Portuguese

Degrees and Diplomas: *Bacharelado*, *Especialização/Aperfeiçoamento*; *Mestrado*; *Doutorado*

Publications: Revista Ação Ambiental; Revista Arvore; Revista Brasileira de Ciência do Solo; Revista Brasileira de Zootecnia; Revista Ceres; Revista do Direito; Revista Economia Rural; Revista Engenharia na Agricultura; Revista Glaukus; Revista Mineira de Educação Fisica; Revista Oikos; Revista Planta Daninha

Publishing House: Divisão de Grafica Universitária

Last Updated: 18/04/16

FLUMINENSE FEDERAL INSTITUTE OF EDUCATION SCIENCE AND TECHNOLOGY

Instituto Federal de Educação, Ciência e Tecnologia Fluminense (IF FLUMINENSE)

Rua Coronel Walter Kramer, 357, Pq. Santo Antônio,
Campos dos Goytacazes, Rio de Janeiro 28080-565
Tel: +55(22) 2737-5600
Fax: +55(22) 2737-5624
EMail: reitoria@iff.edu.br
Website: http://www.iff.edu.br

Reitor: Luiz Augustos Caldas Pereira

Course

Bacharelado (Architecture; Automation and Control Engineering; Computer Engineering; Electrical Engineering; Food Technology; Systems Analysis; Town Planning); **Graduate Studies** (Adult Education; Computer Science; Cultural Studies; Design; Environmental Engineering; Environmental Studies; Geography; Literature; Marketing; Systems Analysis; Teacher Training); **Licenciatura** (Biology; Chemistry; Geography; Literature; Mathematics; Natural Sciences; Physics; Portuguese); **Technical Studies** (Automation and Control Engineering; Computer Science; Construction Engineering; Electrical Engineering; Electronic Engineering; Graphic Design; Industrial Engineering; Industrial Maintenance; Information Technology; Mechanics; Occupational Health; Road Engineering; Safety Engineering; Systems Analysis; Technology; Telecommunications Engineering); **Young and Adults Education** *(EJA)*

Further Information: Also Centro, Guarus, Cabo Frio, Cambuci, Macaé, Maricà, Bom Jesus do Itabapoana, Quissamã, Rio Paraíba do Sul/Upea, São João da Barra, Santo Antônio de Pádua and Itaperuna campuses.

History: Founded 1909 as Escolas de Aprendizes e Artífices. Became Centro Federal de Educação Tecnológica de Campos 1999. Transformed into Instituto Federal de Educação, Ciência e Tecnologia Fluminense 2008.

Main Language(s) of Instruction: Portuguese

Degrees and Diplomas: *Tecnólogo*; *Bacharelado*; *Licenciatura*; *Especialização/Aperfeiçoamento*: **Cultural Studies; Design; Environmental Studies; Information Technology; Literature; Management; Marketing; Science Education; Teacher Training.** *Mestrado*: **Business Computing; Engineering Management; Environmental Engineering; Physics.**

Student Services: Library

Last Updated: 11/04/16

FLUMINENSE FEDERAL UNIVERSITY

Universidade Federal Fluminense (UFF)
Rua Miguel de Frias 9, 7° Andar, Icaraí,
Niterói, Rio de Janeiro 24220008
Tel: +55(21) 2629-5000
Fax: +55(21) 2629-5207
EMail: gabinete@gar.uff.br
Website: http://www.uff.br

Reitor: Roberto de Souza Salles
Tel: +55(21) 2629-5205 +55(21) 2629-5206 EMail: reitor@uff.br

Vice-Reitor: Emmanuel Paiva de Andrade
Tel: +55(21) 2629-5236 EMail: vicereitor@uff.br

Faculty

Administration, Accountancy and Tourism (Accountancy; Administration; Tourism); **Dentistry** (Dentistry); **Economics** (Economics); **Education** (Education); **Law** (Law); **Medicine** (Medicine); **Nutrition** (Nutrition); **Pharmacy** (Pharmacy); **Veterinary Science** (Veterinary Science)

Unit

Advanced Studies *('José Veríssimo', Oriximiná - Pará)* (Development Studies); **Veterinary Science** *(Iguaba)* (Veterinary Science)

School

Architecture and Town Planning (Architecture; Town Planning); **Engineering** (Chemical Engineering; Engineering; Industrial Engineering; Mechanical Engineering; Metallurgical Engineering; Production Engineering; Telecommunications Engineering); **Nursing** (Nursing); **Social Service** (Social and Community Services)

Higher School

Ildefonso Bastos Borges *(Founded as Bom Jesus do Itabapoana)* (Agriculture); **Nilo Peçanha** (Agriculture)

Institute

Arts and Social Communication (Advertising and Publicity; Archiving; Arts and Humanities; Cinema and Television; Communication Studies; Cultural Studies; Documentation Techniques; Journalism; Library Science; Marketing; Media Studies); **Biology** (Biology; Cell Biology; Immunology; Marine Biology; Molecular Biology; Neurosciences); **Biomedicine** (Biomedicine); **Chemistry** (Chemistry); **Computer Science** (Computer Science); **Earth Sciences** (Earth Sciences; Geography; Geology; Geophysics); **Humanities and Philosophy** (Anthropology; Arts and Humanities; History; Philosophy; Political Sciences; Psychology; Social Sciences; Sociology); **Languages and Literature** (Classical Languages; Literature; Modern Languages); **Mathematics** (Mathematics); **Physics** (Physics)

Centre

Applied Social Studies (Accountancy; Administration; Economics; Education; Law; Social and Community Services; Social Work; Tourism); **General Studies** (Anthropology; Arts and Humanities; Biology; Chemistry; Classical Languages; Communication Studies; Earth Sciences; History; Literature; Mathematics; Modern Languages; Philosophy; Physics; Political Sciences; Psychology; Social Studies); **Medical Science** (Dentistry; Health Sciences; Medicine; Nursing; Nutrition; Pharmacy; Veterinary Science); **Technology** (Architecture and Planning; Chemical Engineering; Civil Engineering; Computer Science; Engineering; Industrial Engineering; Mechanical Engineering; Production Engineering; Town Planning)

Further Information: Four campuses and other unities in Niterói, and in 16 other municipalities of the state of Rio de Janeiro. Also University Hospital and reference centre for AIDS. Portuguese courses for foreign students. Study abroad programmes

History: Founded 1960 as Federal University of the State of Rio de Janeiro, acquired present title 1965. Reorganized 1983. An autonomous institution.

Academic Year: March to December (March-July; August-December)

Admission Requirements: Secondary school certificate and entrance examination

Main Language(s) of Instruction: Portuguese

Accrediting Agency: Ministry of Education and Sports

Degrees and Diplomas: *Bacharelado*; *Especialização/Aperfeiçoamento*; *Mestrado*: **Anthropology; Architecture; Arts and Humanities; Cardiology; Chemistry; Child Care and Development; Civil Engineering; Civil Security; Communication Studies; Computer Science; Dentistry; Earth Sciences; Economic and Finance Policy; Education; Environmental Studies; Fine Arts; Geography; Geophysics; History; Hygiene; Immunology; Information Sciences; International Relations; Law; Literature; Management Systems; Marine Biology; Mathematics; Mechanical Engineering; Medicine; Metallurgical Engineering; Microbiology; Neurology; Nursing; Organic Chemistry; Paediatrics; Pathology; Physics; Political Sciences; Production Engineering; Psychology; Social Policy; Sociology; Surgery; Telecommunications Engineering; Town Planning; Veterinary Science.** *Doutorado*: **Anthropology; Arts and Humanities; Civil Engineering; Communication Studies; Computer Science; Earth Sciences; Economic and Finance Policy; Education; Geochemistry; Geography; Geology; Geophysics; History; Hygiene; Information Sciences; Literature; Marine Science and Oceanography; Surgery; Veterinary Science.** Also Teaching Degrees in all fields, 4-5 years

Student Services: Academic Counselling, Canteen, Cultural Activities, Health Services, Nursery Care, Social Counselling, Sports Facilities

Publications: Antropolitica; Confluências; Contracampo; Econômia; Engevista; Gênero; Gragoatá; Medicina do Esporte; Movimento; Poiesis; Revista de Ciências Médicas; Revista de Ciências Veterinárias; Revista de Psicologia; Tempo

Publishing House: EDUFF - Editora Universitária da UFF - University Publisher; NIU - Núcleo Imprensa Universitária - University Press

Last Updated: 18/04/16

HIGHER EDUCATION CENTRE OF ARCOVERDE

Centro de Ensino Superior de Arcoverde (AESA/CESA)
Rua Gumercindo Cavalcanti, 420, Prédio São Cristovão,
Arcoverde, PE 56500000
Tel: +55(87) 821-0574 +55(87) 821-0530
Fax: +55(87) 3821-1579
EMail: aesa@aesa-cesa.br; presidencia@aesa-cesa.br
Website: http://www.aesa-cesa.br

Diretora: Maria da Penha de Queiroz Moraes (1997-)

Faculty

Nursing *(FENFA)* (Nursing)

Course

Biology (Biology); **Education** (Education; Primary Education; Secondary Education; Teacher Trainers Education); **Geography** (Geography); **History** (History); **Literature** (English; Literature; Portuguese); **Mathematics** (Mathematics); **Physical Education** (Physical Education)

History: Founded 1969.

Degrees and Diplomas: *Licenciatura*

Student Services: Library

Last Updated: 10/06/15

HIGHER EDUCATION CENTRE OF THE SAN FRANCISCO VALLEY

Centro de Ensino Superior do Vale São Francisco (CESVASF)

Campus Alto do Encanto, BR -315, Bairro Nova Olinda, Belém do São Francisco, PE 56440-000

Tel: +55(81) 3876-1248

EMail: cesvasf@cesvasf.com.br

Website: http://www.cesvasf.com.br/

Diretor: Valmir Pires Campos

Vice-Diretor: Ana Gleide De Souza Leal Sa

Course

Biology (Biology); **Geography** (Geography); **Graduate Studies** (English; Environmental Management; History; Portuguese); **History** (History); **Literature** (Literature); **Mathematics** (Mathematics); **Physics** (Physics)

Further Information: Also Campus Petrolândia

History: Founded 1984.

Main Language(s) of Instruction: Portuguese

Degrees and Diplomas: *Licenciatura*; *Especialização/Aperfeiçoamento*: **English; Environmental Management; Mathematics; Portuguese.**

Student Services: Library

Last Updated: 18/06/15

HIGHER EDUCATION UNION OF NOVA MUTUM

União de Ensino Superior de Nova Mutum (UNINOVA)

Av. Das Arapongas 1384N, Centro, Nova Mutum, MT 78450000

Tel: +55(65) 3308-2010

Fax: +55(65) 3308-2224

EMail: uninova@uninova.edu.br

Website: http://uninova.edu.br

Diretora Geral: Telma Pinheiro Saravy

EMail: gestao@uninova.edu.br

Course

Administration (Accountancy; Administration); **Agronomy** (Agronomy); **Pedagogy** (Pedagogy)

History: Founded 1994.

Main Language(s) of Instruction: Portuguese

Degrees and Diplomas: *Bacharelado*; *Licenciatura*

Last Updated: 13/04/16

INSTITUTE OF EDUCATION OF RIO DE JANEIRO

Instituto Superior de Educação do Rio de Janeiro (ISERJ)

Rua Mariz e Barros, 273, Praça da Bandeira, Rio de Janeiro, Rio de Janeiro 20270-003

Tel: +55(21) 2597-9513 +55(21) 2334-1749

Fax: +55(21) 2557-9513 +55(21) 2334-1749

EMail: diretorageral@iserj.net; presidencia@faetec.rj.gov.br

Website: http://www.iserj.edu.br

Diretora Geral: Sandra Regina Pinto dos Santos

Course

Pedagogy (Pedagogy); **Pedagogy (Plano Nacional de Formação dos Professores da Educação Básica - PARFOR)** (Pedagogy); **Postgraduate Studies** (Museum Studies; Science Education); **Teacher Training** (Teacher Training)

History: Founded 1998 through transformation of the Instituto de Educação do Rio de Janeiro (Ierj). Maintained by the Institute of the Fundação de Apoio à Escola Técnica (FAETEC).

Main Language(s) of Instruction: Portuguese

Degrees and Diplomas: *Licenciatura*; *Especialização/Aperfeiçoamento*: **Museum Studies; Science Education.**

Last Updated: 13/04/16

JÚLIO DE MESQUITA FILHO SÃO PAULO STATE UNIVERSITY

Universidade Estadual Paulista Júlio de Mesquita Filho (UNESP)

Rua Quirino de Andrade, 215, São Paulo, São Paulo 01049-010

Tel: +55(11) 5627-0233

Fax: +55(11) 5627-0134

EMail: arex@reitoria.unesp.br

Website: http://www.unesp.br

Acting President: Júlio Cezar Durigan (2010-)

Tel: +55(11) 5627-0519

EMail: reitor@unesp.br; visone@reitoria.unesp.br

Vice-Reitora: Marilza Vieira Cunha Rudge

EMail: beth@reitoria.unesp.br

Pró-Reitoria de Administração: Carlos Antonio Gamero

Tel: +55(11) 5627-0128 EMail: prad@reitoria.unesp.br

International Relations: José Celso Freire Junior, Head of International Relations

Tel: +55(11) 5627-0439

EMail: jcfreire@reitoria.unesp.br; arex@reitoria.unesp.br

Faculty

Agricultural and Veterinary Sciences *(Jaboticabal)* (Agriculture; Veterinary Science); **Agricultural Sciences** *(Botucatu)* (Agriculture); **Architecture, Arts and Communication** *(Bauru)* (Architecture; Fine Arts; Mass Communication); **Chemistry** *(Araraquara)* (Chemistry); **Dentistry** *(Araçatuba)* (Dentistry); **Dentistry** *(Araraquara)* (Dentistry); **Engineering** *(Guaratinguetá)* (Engineering); **Engineering** *(Ilha Solteira)* (Engineering); **Engineering** *(Bauru)* (Engineering); **Humanities and Social Sciences** *(Franca)* (Arts and Humanities; Social Sciences); **Medicine** *(Botucatu)* (Medicine); **Pharmaceutical Sciences** *(Araraquara)* (Pharmacy); **Philosophy and Sciences** *(Marília)* (Natural Sciences; Philosophy); **Science** *(Bauru)* (Natural Sciences); **Science and Letters** *(Assis)* (Arts and Humanities; Natural Sciences); **Science and Letters** (Arts and Humanities; Natural Sciences); **Science and Technology** *(Presidente Prudente)* (Natural Sciences; Technology); **Sciences and Engineering** *(Tupã)* (Engineering; Natural Sciences); **Veterinary Medicine** *(Araçatuba)* (Veterinary Science); **Veterinary Medicine and Animal Science** *(Botucatu)* (Animal Husbandry; Veterinary Science)

Institute

Advanced Marine Studies *(São Vicente)* (Marine Science and Oceanography); **Arts** *(São Paulo)* (Fine Arts); **Biological Sciences** *(Rio Claro)* (Biochemistry; Biomedicine; Biophysics); **Biological Sciences** *(Botucatu)* (Biochemistry; Biomedicine; Biophysics); **Biosciences** *(Botucatu)* (Biological and Life Sciences); **Biosciences** *(Rio Claro)* (Biological and Life Sciences); **Biosciences/ Campus Coastal Paulista** *(São Vicente)* (Biological and Life Sciences); **Biosciences, Letters and Exact Sciences** *(São José do Rio Preto)* (Arts and Humanities; Biochemistry; Biomedicine; Biophysics; Mathematics; Physics); **Biosciences, Letters and Exact Sciences** *(São José do Rio Preto)* (Arts and Humanities; Biological and Life Sciences; Mathematics and Computer Science); **Chemistry** *(Araraquara)* (Chemistry); **Geosciences and Exact Sciences** *(Rio Claro)* (Earth Sciences; Mathematics and Computer Science); **Public Policy and International Relations (IPPRI)** (Comparative Politics; International Relations); **Science and Technology** *(Sorocaba)* (Natural Sciences; Technology); **Science and Technology (Formerly School of Dentistry)** *(São José dos Campos)* (Natural Sciences; Technology); **Theoretical Physics** (Physics)

Centre
Agricultural Sciences and Technologies *(Dracena)* (Agricultural Engineering; Agriculture); **Applied Psychology** *(Bauru)* (Psychology); **Aquaculture** (Aquaculture); **Araraquara Science Centre (CCA)** (Natural Sciences); **Dental Care** *(Araçatuba)* (Dentistry); **Electron Microscopy** *(Botucatu)* (Physics); **Environmental Analysis and Planning** *(Rio Claro)* (Environmental Management; Environmental Studies); **Environmental Studies** *(Rio Claro)* (Environmental Studies); **Oral Oncology** *(Araçatuba)* (Oncology); **Poisons and Venomous Animals Studies (CEVAP)** *(Botucatu)* (Zoology); **Social Insects Study** *(Rio Claro)* (Entomology); **Stable Isotope** *(Botucatu)* (Biological and Life Sciences); **Toxicological Assistance (Ceatox)** *(Botucatu)* (Toxicology); **Tropical Roots and Starches (Cerat)** *(Botucatu)* (Tropical Agriculture)

Research Centre
Dante Moreira Leite Childhood and Adolescents Research Centre (CENPE) *(Araraquara)* (Child Care and Development); **Dra. Betti Katzenstein Applied Psychology** *(Assis)* (Psychology)

Research Institute
Meteorology (IPMet) *(Bauru)* (Meteorology)

Campus
Itapeva Experimental Campus; **Ourinhos Experimental Campus**; **Registro Experimental Campus**; **Rosana Experimental Campus**; **São João da Boa Vista Experimental Campus**

Further Information: Also Teaching Hospital in Botucatu; Luiz de Oliveira Quintilian Veterinary Hospital, Botucatu Veterinary Hospital, Governador Report Natel Veterinary Hospital

History: Founded 1976, incorporating previously existing faculties established 1923-1966. An autonomous institution under the jurisdiction of and financially supported by the State of São Paulo.

Academic Year: February to December (February-June; August-December)

Admission Requirements: Secondary school certificate or equivalent, and entrance examination

Fees: Tuition, none

Main Language(s) of Instruction: Portuguese

Degrees and Diplomas: *Bacharelado*: **Agronomy; Animal Husbandry; Architecture and Planning; Arts and Humanities; Biology; Chemistry; Communication Studies; Computer Science; Dentistry; Ecology; Economics; Engineering; Fine Arts; Geography; History; Industrial Design; Law; Mathematics; Medicine; Music; Nursing; Nutrition; Pharmacy; Physical Education; Physical Therapy; Psychology; Public Administration; Social and Community Services; Social Sciences; Social Work; Speech Therapy and Audiology; Statistics; Veterinary Science.** *Licenciatura*: **Art Education; Arts and Humanities; Biology; Chemistry; Education; Geography; History; Mathematics; Music; Pedagogy; Philosophy; Physical Education; Physics; Psychology; Social Sciences.** *Especialização/Aperfeiçoamento*: **Agriculture; Art Education; Biological and Life Sciences; Business and Commerce; Communication Arts; Cultural Studies; Dental Technology; Dentistry; Ecology; Educational Administration; Engineering; Entomology; Environmental Engineering; Environmental Management; Environmental Studies; Fine Arts; Food Science; Fruit Production; Haematology; Health Administration; Health Sciences; Hydraulic Engineering; Industrial Management; Leadership; Marine Science and Oceanography; Orthodontics; Periodontics; Physical Therapy; Physiology; Preschool Education; Production Engineering; Psychology; Public Health; Rehabilitation and Therapy; Safety Engineering; Special Education; Sports; Stomatology; Technology; Transport Management; Water Management.** *Mestrado*: **Agricultural Engineering; Agriculture; Agronomy; Animal Husbandry; Architecture; Arts and Humanities; Biological and Life Sciences; Biophysics; Biotechnology; Botany; Chemistry; Civil Engineering; Communication Studies; Computer Science; Dentistry; Ecology; Economics; Education; Electrical Engineering; Environmental Studies; Fine Arts; Fishery; Food Science; Food Technology; Forestry; Genetics; Geography; Geology; History; Industrial Design; Information Sciences; Law; Linguistics; Materials Engineering; Mathematics; Mechanical Engineering; Medicine; Microbiology; Nursing; Occupational Therapy; Pharmacology; Pharmacy; Philosophy; Physical Education; Physical Therapy; Physics; Physiology; Political Sciences; Production Engineering; Psychology; Public Health; Social and Community Services; Sociology; Speech Therapy and Audiology; Teacher Training; Town Planning; Veterinary Science; Zoology.** *Doutorado*: **Agricultural Engineering; Agronomy; Animal Husbandry; Arts and Humanities; Biological and Life Sciences; Biophysics; Biotechnology; Botany; Chemistry; Civil Engineering; Dentistry; Ecology; Education; Electrical Engineering; Environmental Studies; Fine Arts; Fishery; Food Science; Food Technology; Forestry; Genetics; Geography; Geology; History; Industrial Design; Information Sciences; Linguistics; Materials Engineering; Mathematics; Mechanical Engineering; Medicine; Microbiology; Nursing; Occupational Therapy; Pharmacology; Pharmacy; Physical Education; Physical Therapy; Physics; Physiology; Political Sciences; Production Engineering; Psychology; Public Health; Social and Community Services; Sociology; Teacher Training; Veterinary Science; Zoology.** Also dual degrees, Bacharelado/Licenciatura (Biology, Geology, Mathematics, Physics, Social Sciences)

Student Services: Academic Counselling, Canteen, Careers Guidance, Cultural Activities, Facilities for disabled people, Foreign Studies Centre, Health Services, IT Centre, Language Laboratory, Library, Nursery Care, Social Counselling, Sports Facilities

Publications: Alfa; Alimentos e Nutrição; Arba; Arte UNESP; Científica; Didática; Eclética Química; Geociêncas; Historia; Naturalia; Perspectivas; Revista de Ciencias Farmacêuticas; Revista de Engenharia e Ciências Aplicadas; Revista de Geografia; Revista de Matematica e Nutrição; Revista de Odontologia da UNESP; Transformação; Veterinária e Zootecnia

Publishing House: Editora da UNESP (UNESP Publishing House)

Last Updated: 08/04/16

MAURÍCIO DE OLIVEIRA FACULTY OF MUSIC OF ESPIRITO SANTO

Faculdade de Música do Espírito Santo Maurício de Oliveira (EMES)

Praça Américo Poli Monjardim, 60, Centro,
Vitória, Espirito Santo 29010-640
Tel: +55(27) 3636-3600
Fax: +55(27) 3636-3608
EMail: aacademica@fames.es.gov.br
Website: http://www.fames.es.gov.br

Diretor Geral: Paulo Henrique Avidos Pelissari
Tel: +55(27) 3636-3607 EMail: direcao@fames.es.gov.br

Assessoria Especial/Administração Geral: Marcel Zuqui Ginelli
Tel: +55(27) 3636-3601
EMail: admgeral@fames.es.gov.br; marcel.zuqui@fames.es.gov.br

Course
Music (Music)

History: Founded 1952.

Main Language(s) of Instruction: Portuguese

Degrees and Diplomas: *Bacharelado*; *Licenciatura*

Student Services: Library

Publications: A Tempo - Revista de Pesquisa em Música; Revista Música Viva

Last Updated: 16/07/15

MAYOR HAMILTON VIEIRA MENDES SCHOOL OF CRUZEIRO

Escola Superior de Cruzeiro Prefeito Hamilton Vieira Mendes (ESC-ESEFIC)

Rua Dr José Rodrigues Alves Sobrinho 191, Vila Suely,
Cruzeiro, SP 12711-690
Tel: +55(12) 3145-1155
Fax: +55(12) 3144-1865
EMail: secretaria@esccultural.com.br
Website: http://www.esccultural.com.br

Diretor Geral: Wagner Streitenberger

Course
Nursing (Nursing); **Pedagogy** (Education; Pedagogy); **Physical Education** (Physical Education); **Physiotherapy** (Physical Therapy)

History: Founded 1973 as Escola Superior de Educação Física de Cruzeiro "Prefeito Hamilton Vieira Mendes". Acquired present title and status 2005.

Main Language(s) of Instruction: Portuguese

Degrees and Diplomas: *Bacharelado*; *Licenciatura*; *Especialização/Aperfeiçoamento*: **Physical Education; Physical Therapy; Sports.**

Student Services: Library

Last Updated: 25/09/15

MILITARY ENGINEERING INSTITUTE

Instituto Militar de Engenharia (IME)
Praça General Tibúrcio 80, Praia Vermelha,
Rio de Janeiro, RJ 22290-270
Tel: +55(21) 2546-7080
EMail: scoms@ime.eb.br
Website: http://www.ime.eb.br/

Comandante: Barroso Magno

Course
Graduate Studies (Chemical Engineering; Computer Engineering; Electrical and Electronic Equipment and Maintenance; Engineering; Materials Engineering; Mechanical Engineering; Nuclear Engineering; Surveying and Mapping; Transport Engineering); **Undergraduate Studies** (Chemical Engineering; Computer Engineering; Construction Engineering; Electrical Engineering; Materials Engineering; Mechanical Engineering; Nuclear Engineering; Surveying and Mapping)

History: Founded 1811 as Academia Real Militar. Succesively changed its name to Imperial Academia Militar (1822), Academia Militar da Corte (1832), Escola Militar (1840) and Escola Central (1858). The school of military engineering started its activities in 1930. Changed name to Escola Técnica do Exército in 1933. Merged with Instituto Militar de Tecnologia and acquired present title 1959. Started admitting civilians in 1964 and women in 1997.

Main Language(s) of Instruction: Portuguese

Degrees and Diplomas: *Bacharelado*; *Especialização/Aperfeiçoamento*; *Mestrado*: **Computer Engineering; Electrical Engineering; Materials Engineering; Mechanical Engineering.** *Doutorado*: **Chemistry; Materials Engineering.**

Student Services: Library

Last Updated: 12/04/16

MINEIROS UNIVERSITY CENTRE

Centro Universitário de Mineiros (UF)
Rua 22 - Setor Aeroporto, Mineiros 75830-000
Tel: +55(64) 3672-5100
Fax: +55(64) 3672-5101
EMail: fimes@fimes.edu.br
Website: http://www.fimes.edu.br

Secretária Acadêmica Geral: Eliane Vilela Melo

Reitora: Ita de Fátima Dias Silva EMail: ita@fimes.edu.br

Unit
Biosciences (Agricultural Engineering; Agronomy; Environmental Engineering; Physical Education; Psychology; Sanitary Engineering; Veterinary Science); **Education** (Humanities and Social Science Education; Native Language Education); **Exact Sciences** (Civil Engineering; Information Technology); **Humanities** (Accountancy; Administration; Law; Pedagogy; Theology)

Programme
Postgraduate Studies (Education; Environmental Studies; Law; Management)

History: Founded as Fundação Integrada Municipal de Ensino Superior 1985. Authorized and accredited as Faculdades Integradas de Mineiros 2004. Acquired current status and title 2011.

Main Language(s) of Instruction: Portuguese

Degrees and Diplomas: *Bacharelado*; *Licenciatura*; *Especialização/Aperfeiçoamento*: **Accountancy; Actuarial Science; Business Administration; Educational Psychology; Environmental Management; Labour Law; Safety Engineering; Social Welfare; Taxation.**

Student Services: Library

Last Updated: 24/11/15

MUNICIPAL FACULTY OF PALHOÇA

Faculdade Municipal de Palhoça (FMP)
Rua Maria Theodora Haeming, 48, Passa Vinte, Palhoça 88133-155
Tel: +55(48) 3341-0616 +55(48) 3342-1833
EMail: fmp@fmpsc.edu.br
Website: http://www.fmpsc.edu.br

Preside: Mariah Terezinha Nascimento Pereira
EMail: mariahnascimento@terra.com.br

Course
Administration (Administration); **Pedagogy** (Pedagogy); **Tourism** (Tourism)

History: Founded 2005.

Main Language(s) of Instruction: Portuguese

Degrees and Diplomas: *Bacharelado*; *Especialização/Aperfeiçoamento*

Student Services: Library

Last Updated: 29/05/15

MUNICIPAL HIGHER EDUCATION INSTITUTE OF ASSIS

Instituto Municipal de Ensino Superior de Assis (IMESA)
Avenida Getúlio Vargas, 1200, Vila Nova Santana,
Assis, SP 19807-30
Tel: +55(18) 3302-1056
Fax: +55(18) 3302-1055
EMail: secretaria.fema@femanet.com.br
Website: http://www.fema.edu.br/

Diretor: Eduardo Augusto Vella Gonçalves

Vice-Diretora: Elizete Mello Da Silva

Course
Administration (Administration); **Advertising** (Advertising and Publicity); **Agricultural Business** (Agricultural Business); **Computer Science** (Computer Science); **Data Processing** (Data Processing); **Industrial Chemistry** (Chemistry; Industrial Chemistry); **Journalism** (Journalism); **Law** (Law); **Mathematics** (Mathematics); **Medicine** (Medicine); **Nursing** (Nursing); **Photography** (Photography); **Systems Analysis** (Systems Analysis)

History: Founded 1988.

Main Language(s) of Instruction: Portuguese

Degrees and Diplomas: *Bacharelado*; *Licenciatura*; *Especialização/Aperfeiçoamento*: **Accountancy; Business Administration; Chemistry; Civil Law; Finance; Human Resources.**

Last Updated: 12/04/16

MUNICIPAL INSTITUTE OF HIGHER EDUCATION OF CATANDUVA

Instituto Municipal de Ensino Superior de Catanduva (IMES)
Avenida Daniel Dalto s/n, Rodovia Washington Luis - SP 310 - Km 382, Catanduva, São Paulo 15800-970
Tel: +55(17) 3531-2200
Fax: +55(17) 3531-2205
EMail: secretaria@fafica.br
Website: http://www.fafica.br

Diretora: Cibelle Rocha Abdo

Course
Accountancy (Accountancy); **Advertising** (Advertising and Publicity); **Biology** (Biology); **Computer Science** (Computer Science); **Dentistry** (Dentistry); **Geography** (Geography); **History** (History); **Journalism** (Journalism); **Law** (Law); **Literature** (English; Literature; Portuguese); **Mathematics** (Mathematics); **Nutrition** (Nutrition); **Pedagogy** (Pedagogy); **Physiotherapy** (Physical Therapy); **Psychology** (Psychology)

History: Founded 1967 as Faculdade de Filosofia, Ciências e Letras de Catanduva. Acquired present status and title 2000.

Main Language(s) of Instruction: Portuguese

Degrees and Diplomas: *Bacharelado*; *Licenciatura*; *Especialização/Aperfeiçoamento*: **Civil Law; Computer Engineering; Computer Networks; Dentistry; Education; Educational Testing and Evaluation; Food Technology; History; Linguistics; Literature; Mathematics Education; Special Education.**

Student Services: Library

Last Updated: 12/04/16

MUNICIPAL INSTITUTE OF HIGHER EDUCATION OF MATAO

Instituto Matonense Municipal de Ensino Superior (IMMES)

Av. Tiradentes, 629 - Centro, Matao, São Paulo
Tel: +55(16) 3383-1353
EMail: immes@immes.br
Website: http://www.immes.edu.br

Diretora General: Valquiria Pereira Tenório

Course

Administration (Administration); **Human Resourses** (Human Resources); **Law** (Law)

History: Founded 1998.

Main Language(s) of Instruction: Portuguese

Degrees and Diplomas: *Bacharelado*; *Especialização/Aperfeiçoamento*: **Labour Law.** Also MBA

Last Updated: 12/04/16

MUNICIPAL INSTITUTE OF HIGHER EDUCATION OF SÃO MANUEL

Instituto Municipal de Ensino Superior de São Manuel (IMESSM)

Rua Quintino Bocaiuva s/n, Distrito Aparecida,
São Manuel, São Paulo 18650-000
Tel: +55(14) 6841-3766
Fax: +55(14) 6841-3766
EMail: secretaria@imessm.edu.br
Website: http://www.imessm.edu.br

Diretora: Clara Benedita Bonome Zeminian

Course

Literature (English; Literature; Portuguese; Spanish); **Pedagogy** (Pedagogy); **Psychology** (Educational Psychology; Psychology)

History: Founded 1972 as Faculdade de Filosofia, Ciências e Letras de São Manuel. Acquired present status and title 1982.

Main Language(s) of Instruction: Portuguese

Degrees and Diplomas: *Licenciatura*; *Especialização/Aperfeiçoamento*: **Educational Psychology.**

Student Services: Library

Last Updated: 12/04/16

MUNICIPAL UNIVERSITY CENTRE OF FRANCA

Centro Universitario Municipal de Franca (UNI-FACEF)

Avenida Major Nicácio, 2433, Bairro São José,
Franca, São Paulo 14401-135
Tel: +55(16) 3713-4688
Fax: +55(16) 3713-4605
EMail: facef@facef.br
Website: http://www.facef.br

Reitor: Alfredo José Machado Neto
Tel: +55(16) 3722-4104 EMail: reitoria@facef.br

Pró-Reitora Acadêmica: Sheila Fernandes Pimenta e Oliveira
EMail: sheila@facef.br

Course

Accountancy (Accountancy); **Administration** (Administration); **Advertising and Publicity** (Advertising and Publicity); **Civil Engineering** (Civil Engineering); **Economics** (Economics); **Information Systems** (Information Sciences); **Literature** (Literature); **Mathematics** (Mathematics); **Production Engineering** (Production Engineering); **Psychology** (Psychology); **Social Communication** (Communication Studies; Social Sciences); **Tourism and Hotel Management** (Hotel Management; Tourism)

Further Information: Also Distance Education

History: Founded 1951 as Faculdade de Ciências Econômicas e Administrativas de Franca

Main Language(s) of Instruction: Portuguese

Accrediting Agency: Ministry of Education.

Degrees and Diplomas: *Bacharelado*; *Licenciatura*; *Especialização/Aperfeiçoamento*: **Business Administration; Development Studies; Modern Languages; Psychology; Regional Studies; Software Engineering.** *Mestrado*: **Development Studies; Regional Studies.** Also MBA.

Student Services: Library

Last Updated: 08/09/15

MUNICIPAL UNIVERSITY CENTRE OF SÃO JOSÉ

Centro Universitário Municipal de São José (USJ)

Rua Silvia Maria Fabro, 97, Kobrasol,
São José, Santa Catarina 88102-310
Tel: +55(48) 3247-6071
EMail: reitoria@usj.edu.br
Website: http://www.usj.edu.br

Reitora: Elisiani Cristina de Souza de Freitas Noronha

Course

Accountancy (Accountancy); **Administration** (Administration); **Pedagogy** (Education; Pedagogy); **Religious Studies** (Religious Studies)

History: Founded 2005.

Main Language(s) of Instruction: Portuguese

Degrees and Diplomas: *Bacharelado*; *Licenciatura*; *Especialização/Aperfeiçoamento*: **Preschool Education; Primary Education.**

Student Services: Library

Last Updated: 01/09/15

MUNICIPAL UNIVERSITY OF SÃO CAETANO DO SUL

Universidade Municipal de São Caetano do Sul (USCS)

Avenida Goiás 3,400, Barcelona,
São Caetano do Sul, São Paulo 09550-051
Tel: +55(11) 4239-3200 +55(11) 4239-3299
Fax: +55(11) 4239-3275
EMail: jovanov@uscs.edu.br; secretaria.academica@uscs.edu.br
Website: http://www.uscs.edu.br

Reitor: Marcos Sidnei Bassi EMail: mbassi@uscs.edu.br

Pró-Reitor Administrativo e Financeiro: Paulo Sérgio Lopes Ruiz
EMail: pruiz@uscs.edu.br

School

Business (Accountancy; Administration; Economics; International Business); **Communication** (Advertising and Publicity; Journalism; Mass Communication; Radio and Television Broadcasting); **Computer Science** (Computer Science; Information Technology); **Education** (Pedagogy); **Engineering** (Production Engineering); **Health Sciences** (Health Sciences; Medicine; Nursing; Nutrition; Pharmacy; Physical Education; Physical Therapy); **Law** (Law); **Psychology** (Psychology); **Technological School of Business** (Business Administration; Business and Commerce; Environmental Management; Fashion Design; Finance; Human Resources; Industrial Management; Marketing; Transport Management)

History: Founded 1967. Acquired present status 2004.

Main Language(s) of Instruction: Portuguese

Degrees and Diplomas: *Tecnólogo*; *Bacharelado*; *Licenciatura*; *Especialização/Aperfeiçoamento*: **Accountancy; Administration; Administrative Law; Architecture; Automation and Control Engineering; Biological and Life Sciences; Biology; Biomedicine; Biotechnology; Cardiology; Civil Engineering; Civil Law; Communication Studies; Computer Engineering; Computer Networks; Cosmetology; Criminal Law; Dance; Dermatology; Economics; Education; Educational Psychology; Engineering; Environmental**

Engineering; Environmental Management; Environmental Studies; Fiscal Law; Food Science; Geography (Human); Gerontology; Gynaecology and Obstetrics; Health Sciences; Higher Education Teacher Training; Human Resources; Information Technology; Labour Law; Law; Leadership; Management; Marketing; Mass Communication; Medicine; Modern Languages; Nursing; Nutrition; Occupational Health; Oncology; Orthopaedics; Pedagogy; Pharmacology; Pharmacy; Philosophy; Physical Education; Physical Therapy; Private Law; Production Engineering; Psychology; Public Health; Rehabilitation and Therapy; Respiratory Therapy; Sanitary Engineering; Social and Community Services; Sociology; Speech Therapy and Audiology; Sports; Sports Management; Systems Analysis; Theology; Toxicology; Transport Engineering. *Mestrado*: **Administration; Education; Mass Communication.** *Doutorado*: **Administration.** Also MBA; Post-doctorate Degree in Administration

Student Services: Library

Last Updated: 06/04/16

MUNICIPALITY OF HIGHER EDUCATION OF GARANHUNS

Autarquia do Ensino Superior de Garanhuns (AESGA)

Avenida Caruaru 508, São José, Garanhuns, PE 55295380

Tel: +55(87) 3761-1596

Fax: +55(87) 3761-1596 +55(81) 3762-6691

EMail: administracao@aesga.edu.br

Website: http://www.aesga.edu.br

Presidente: Giane Maria de Lira Oliveira

EMail: presidencia@aesga.edu.br

Faculty

Administration *(FAGA)* (Administration; Business Administration; Educational Administration; Health Administration; Management; Marketing; Tourism); **Exact Sciences** (Civil Engineering); **Law** *(FDG)* (Law); **Social Sciences and Humanities** *(FAHUG)* (Modern Languages; Secretarial Studies)

History: Founded 1976.

Main Language(s) of Instruction: Portuguese

Degrees and Diplomas: *Bacharelado*; *Especialização/Aperfeiçoamento*: **Business Administration; Civil Law; Criminal Law; Educational Administration; Finance; Health Administration; Human Resources; Law; Management; Public Administration; Transport Management.**

Student Services: Library

Last Updated: 12/06/15

NATIONAL INSTITUTE OF EDUCATION FOR THE DEAF

Instituto Nacional de Educação de Surdos (INES)

Rua das Laranjeiras, 232, Laranjeiras,
Rio de Janeiro, RJ 22240-003

Tel: +55(21) 2285-7546 +55(21) 2285-7949

Fax: +55(21) 2285-7692

EMail: dirge@ines.gov.br

Website: http://www.ines.gov.br/

Diretor Geral: Marcelo Ferreira de Vasconcelos Cavalcanti

EMail: dirge@ines.gov.br

Course

Pedagogy (Pedagogy; Special Education)

History: Founded 2009.

Main Language(s) of Instruction: Portuguese

Degrees and Diplomas: *Licenciatura*: **Pedagogy; Special Education.**

Student Services: Library

Last Updated: 12/04/16

NATIONAL SCHOOL OF STATISTICS

Escola Nacional de Ciências Estatísticas (ENCE)

Rua André Cavalcanti 106, Bairro Santa Teresa,
Rio de Janeiro, Rio de Janeiro 20231-050

Tel: +55(21) 2142-4677

Fax: +55(21) 2142-0501

EMail: ence@ibge.gov.br

Website: http://www.ence.ibge.gov.br

Coordenador Geral: Maysa Sacramento de Magalhães

Course

Environmental and Territorial Management *(Postgraduate Lato Sensu)* (Environmental Management); **Population Studies and Social Research** *(Postgraduate Stricto Sensu)* (Demography and Population); **Statistics** (Statistics)

History: Founded 1953.

Main Language(s) of Instruction: Portuguese

Degrees and Diplomas: *Bacharelado*; *Especialização/Aperfeiçoamento*: **Demography and Population; Environmental Management.** *Mestrado*: **Demography and Population.** *Doutorado*: **Demography and Population.**

Student Services: Library

Last Updated: 23/09/15

PRESIDENT KENNEDY INSTITUTE OF HIGHER EDUCATION - TRAINING CENTRE FOR EDUCATION PROFESSIONALS

Instituto de Educação Superior Presidente Kennedy - Centro de Formação de Profissionais de Educação (IFESP)

Rua Jaguarari 2100, Natal, Rio Grande do Norte 59064-500

Tel: +55(84) 3232- 6231

Fax: +55(84) 3232-6238

EMail: ifesp@ifesp.edu.br

Website: http://www.ifesp.edu.br

Diretora: Marlene F. Ribeiro

Course

Administration (Administration); **Finance** (Finance); **Literature** (Literature); **Mathematics** (Mathematics); **Pedagogy** (Pedagogy); **Teacher Training** (Teacher Training)

Further Information: Also Distance Education

History: Founded 1965 as Instituto de Educação Presidente Kennedy succeeding the Instituto de Educação de Natal. Acquired present name 2001.

Main Language(s) of Instruction: Portuguese

Degrees and Diplomas: *Licenciatura*; *Especialização/Aperfeiçoamento*: **Adult Education; Educational Administration; English; Environmental Studies; Mathematics Education; Preschool Education.**

Student Services: Library

Last Updated: 30/03/16

PROFESSOR DIRSON MACIEL DE BARROS FACULTY OF SCIENCE AND TECHNOLOGY

Faculdade de Ciência e Tecnologia Professor Dirson Maciel de Barros (FADIMAB)

Rua Poço do Rei s/n, Goiânia, Goiás 55900-000

Tel: +55(81) 3626-0740

Fax: +55(81) 3626-0517

EMail: contato@fadimab.edu.br; fadimab@fadimab.edu.br

Website: http://fadimab.edu.br

Diretor: Lourenço Benedito Bezerra

Course

Administration (Administration); **Arts and Humanities** (English; Literature; Portuguese); **Biology** (Biology); **Geography** (Geography); **History** (History); **Mathematics** (Mathematics); **Pedagogy** (Pedagogy); **Physical Education** (Physical Education)

History: Founded 1972

Main Language(s) of Instruction: Portuguese

Degrees and Diplomas: *Bacharelado*; *Licenciatura*

Last Updated: 09/07/15

PROFESSOR FRANCO MONTORO MUNICIPAL FACULTY OF MOGI GUAÇU

Faculdade Municipal Professor Franco Montoro de Mogi Guaçu (FMPFM)
Rua dos Estudantes s/n - Bairro Cachoeira de Cima,
Mogi Guaçu, São Paulo 13840970
Tel: +55(19) 3891-5303
EMail: secretaria.geral@fmpfm.edu.br
Website: http://www.fmpfm.edu.br

Diretor: Estéfano Vizconde Veraszto

Course
Administration (Administration); **Chemical Engineering** (Chemical Engineering); **Computer Science** (Computer Science); **Environmental Engineering** (Environmental Engineering); **Nutrition** (Nutrition); **Psychology** (Psychology)

History: Founded 1999.

Main Language(s) of Instruction: Portuguese

Degrees and Diplomas: *Bacharelado*; *Especialização/Aperfeiçoamento*

Student Services: Library
Last Updated: 29/05/15

PROFESSOR PAULO NEVES DE CARVALHO SCHOOL OF GOVERNMENT

Escola de Governo Professor Paulo Neves de Carvalho (EG)
Alameda dos Oitis, 140, São Luís, Pampulha,
Belo Horizonte, Minas Gerais 31270-810
Tel: +55(31) 3448-9400
Fax: +55(31) 3448-9613
EMail: eg.fjp@fjp.mg.gov.br
Website: http://eg.fjp.mg.gov.br

Diretora: Luciana Raso Sardinha

Course
Public Administration (Public Administration)

Further Information: Also Av. Brasil campus.
History: Founded 1992.
Main Language(s) of Instruction: Portuguese

Degrees and Diplomas: *Bacharelado*; *Especialização/Aperfeiçoamento*: **Public Administration.** *Mestrado*: **Public Administration.**
Student Services: Library
Last Updated: 23/09/15

REGIONAL UNIVERSITY OF BLUMENAU

Universidade Regional de Blumenau (FURB)
Rua Antônio da Veiga, 140, Itoupava Seca,
Blumenau, Santa Catarina 89030-903
Tel: +55(47) 3321-0200
Fax: +55(47) 3322-8818
EMail: proen@furb.br
Website: http://www.furb.br

Reitor: João Natel Pollonio Machado
Tel: +55(47) 3321-0381 EMail: reitoria@furb.br

Vice-Reitor: Udo Schroeder
Tel: +55(47) 3321-0412 EMail: proad@furb.br

International Relations: David Colin Morton Bilsland
Tel: +55(47) 3321-0214 EMail: cri@furb.br

Centre
Applied Social Sciences (CCSA) (Accountancy; Administration; Economics; International Business; Leisure Studies; Marketing; Secretarial Studies; Tourism); **Communication and Human Sciences (CCHC)** (History; Journalism; Mass Communication; Religion; Social and Community Services; Social Sciences); **Education, Arts and Letters (CCEAL)** (English; Fashion Design; German; Literature; Music; Pedagogy; Special Education; Theatre; Visual Arts); **Exact and Natural Sciences (CCEN)** (Biological and Life Sciences; Chemistry; Computer Science; Information Technology; Mathematics; Science Education); **Health Sciences (CCS)** (Dentistry; Health Sciences; Medicine; Nursing; Nutrition; Pharmacy; Physical Education; Physical Therapy; Psychology; Veterinary Science); **Juridical Sciences (CCJ)** (Law); **Technological Sciences (CCT)** (Agricultural Engineering; Architecture; Chemical Engineering; Civil Engineering; Design; Electrical Engineering; Food Technology; Mechanical Engineering; Production Engineering; Telecommunications Engineering; Town Planning)

Research Group
Agricultural Sciences (Agriculture); **Applied Social Sciences** (Social Sciences); **Biological Sciences** (Biological and Life Sciences); **Engineering** (Engineering); **Exact and Earth Sciences** (Mathematics; Natural Sciences); **Health Sciences** (Health Sciences); **Humanities** (Arts and Humanities); **Linguistics, Letters and Arts** (Arts and Humanities; Linguistics; Literature)

Further Information: Also Psychology Clinic; Physiotherapy Ambulatory; University Ambulatory and 4 Cancer Clinics

History: Founded 1964. Under the supervision of the Fundação Universidade Regional de Blumenau.

Academic Year: January to December (January-June; August-December)

Admission Requirements: Secondary school certificate and entrance examination

Main Language(s) of Instruction: Portuguese

Degrees and Diplomas: *Tecnólogo*; *Bacharelado*; *Licenciatura*; *Especialização/Aperfeiçoamento*: **Accountancy; Administration; Architecture; Art Education; Business Administration; Business and Commerce; Business Computing; Computer Science; Education; Electrical Engineering; Environmental Studies; Finance; Fine Arts; Forest Management; Health Administration; Health Sciences; Higher Education Teacher Training; Labour Law; Law; Literacy Education; Management; Marketing; Materials Engineering; Music Education; Orthodontics; Philosophy; Production Engineering; Public Administration; Public Law; Radio and Television Broadcasting; Religious Studies; Safety Engineering; Taxation.** *Mestrado*: **Accountancy; Administration; Agricultural Engineering; Chemical Engineering; Chemistry; Development Studies; Education; Environmental Engineering; Mathematics Education; Public Health; Science Education.** *Doutorado*: **Accountancy; Administration; Development Studies; Environmental Engineering.** Also MBA

Student Services: Academic Counselling, Canteen, Cultural Activities, Health Services, Language Laboratory, Library, Social Counselling, Sports Facilities

Publications: Dynamisis: Revista Tecno-científica; Revista de Divulgação Cultural; Revista de Estudos Ambientais; Revista de Negócios; Revista Jurídica
Last Updated: 07/04/16

REGIONAL UNIVERSITY OF CARIRI

Universidade Regional do Cariri (URCA)
Rua Cel. Antônio Luis, 1161, Pimenta, Crato, Ceará 63100-000
Tel: +55(88) 3102-1212 +55(88) 3102-1204
Fax: +55(88) 3102-1271 +55(88) 3102-1218
EMail: urca@urca.br
Website: http://www.urca.br

Reitor: José Patrício Pereira Melo EMail: gabinete@urca.br

Vice-Reitor: Francisco do Ó de Lima Junior
EMail: vice.reitor@urca.br

International Relations: Fábio José Rodrigues da Costa
EMail: internationalrelations@urca.br

Centre
Applied Social Studies (CESA) (Economics; Geography (Human); History; Social Studies); **Arts (CA)** (Theatre; Visual Arts); **Biological and Health Sciences (CCBS)** (Biological and Life Sciences; Chemistry; Health Sciences; Nursing; Physical Education); **Education (EC)** (Education); **Humanities (CH)** (Arts and Humanities); **Science and Technology (CCT)** (Civil Engineering; Mathematics and Computer Science; Natural Sciences; Physics; Technology)

Laboratory
Herbarium (Botany); **Natural Products Reseach** (Biological and Life Sciences)

History: Founded 1986.

Academic Year: February to December (February-June; August-December)

Admission Requirements: Secondary school certificate and entrance examination

Main Language(s) of Instruction: Portuguese

Degrees and Diplomas: *Bacharelado*; *Licenciatura*; *Especialização/Aperfeiçoamento*: **Civil Engineering; Environmental Engineering.** *Mestrado*: **Biological and Life Sciences; Environmental Management; Humanities and Social Science Education; Molecular Biology; Nursing; Physical Education; Public Health.** Also Interinstitucional Doctorate in History

Last Updated: 07/04/16

SCHOOL OF ENGINEERING OF PIRACICABA

Escola de Engenharia de Piracicaba (EEP-FUMEP)

Avenida Monsenhor Martinho Salgot 560, Vila Areão,
Piracicaba, São Paulo 13414-040
Tel: +55(19) 3412-1100
Fax: +55(19) 3421-3244
EMail: eep@fumep.edu.br
Website: http://www.fumep.edu.br/eep

Diretor: Edson Pigoretti

Diretor Acadêmico: Edson Pigoretti

Centre

Post-Graduation (Engineering; Safety Engineering)

Course

Accountancy (Accountancy); **Administration** (Administration); **Civil Engineering** (Civil Engineering); **Computer Science** (Computer Science); **Environmental Engineering** (Environmental Engineering); **Mechanical Engineering** (Mechanical Engineering); **Mechanical Fabrication** (Mechanical Equipment and Maintenance); **Mechatronic Engineering** (Electronic Engineering; Mechanical Engineering); **Production Engineering** (Production Engineering)

History: Founded 1968.

Main Language(s) of Instruction: Portuguese

Degrees and Diplomas: *Bacharelado*; *Especialização/Aperfeiçoamento*: **Civil Engineering; Safety Engineering; Water Management.**

Student Services: Library

Last Updated: 21/09/15

SCHOOL OF PHYSICAL EDUCATION OF JUNDIAÍ

Escola Superior de Educação Física de Jundiaí (ESEFJ)

Rua Dr. Rodrigo Soares de Oliveira, s/no, Anhangabaú,
Jundiaí, São Paulo 13208-120
Tel: +55(11) 4521-7955
Fax: +55(11) 4521-7955
EMail: educacaofisica@esef.br
Website: http://www.esef.br

Diretor: Pedro Rocha Lemos

Course

Graduate Studies (Dance; Physical Education; Sports; Sports Management); **Physical Education** (Physical Education)

History: Founded 1974.

Main Language(s) of Instruction: Portuguese

Degrees and Diplomas: *Bacharelado*; *Licenciatura*; *Especialização/Aperfeiçoamento*: **Dance; Physical Education; Sports; Sports Management.**

Student Services: Library

Last Updated: 25/09/15

SOUTHWEST BAHIA STATE UNIVERSITY

Universidade Estadual do Sudoeste da Bahia (UESB)

Estrada do Bem Querer, km 4, Caixa Postal 95,
Vitória da Conquista, Bahia 45083-900
Tel: +55(73) 3424-8600
Fax: +55(73) 3423-7038
EMail: uesb@uesb.br
Website: http://www.uesb.br

Reitor: Paulo Roberto Pinto Santos

Pró-reitor de Administração: Adriano Correia

Department

Agricultural Studies and Soil Sicence (DEAS) *(Vitória da Conquista)* (Agriculture; Soil Science); **Basic Studies and Instrumental (DEBIO)** (Mathematics); **Biological Sciences (DCB)** *(Jequié)* (Biological and Life Sciences); **Chemistry and Exact Sciences (DQE)** *(Jequié)* (Chemistry; Natural Sciences); **Geography (DG)** *(Vitória da Conquista)* (Geography); **Health Sciences 1 (DS 1)** *(Jequié)* (Health Sciences); **Health Sciences 2 (DS 2)** *(Jequié)* (Health Sciences); **History (DH)** *(Vitória da Conquista)* (History); **Humanities and Letters (DCHL)** *(Jequié)* (Arts and Humanities); **Language and Literature Studies (DELL)** *(Vitória da Conquista)* (Literature; Modern Languages); **Mathematical Sciences and Technology (DCET)** *(Vitoria da Conquista)* (Mathematics; Technology); **Natural Sciences (DCN)** *(Vitória da Conquista)* (Natural Sciences); **Philosophy and Humanities (DFCH)** *(Vitória da Conquista)* (Arts and Humanities; Philosophy); **Plant and Animal Science (DFZ)** *(Vitória da Conquista)* (Botany; Zoology); **Rural Technology and Animal Husbandry (DTRA)** (Agricultural Engineering; Animal Husbandry); **Social Sciences (DCSA)** *(Vitória da Conquista)* (Social Sciences)

Further Information: Also Jequié and Itapetinga Campuses

History: Founded 1980, incorporating previously existing faculties. Recognized by the Federal Government 1987.

Academic Year: March to December (March-July; September-December)

Admission Requirements: Secondary school certificate and entrance examination

Main Language(s) of Instruction: Portuguese

Degrees and Diplomas: *Bacharelado*; *Licenciatura*; *Especialização/Aperfeiçoamento*: **African Studies; Agriculture; Anthropology; Computer Science; Cultural Studies; Education; Educational Administration; Environmental Studies; Ethnology; Foreign Languages Education; Geography; History; Latin American Studies; Linguistics; Literacy Education; Modern Languages; Native Language Education; Political Sciences; Portuguese; Public Administration; Public Health; Social Studies.** *Mestrado*: **Agronomy; Animal Husbandry; Arts and Humanities; Biological and Life Sciences; Chemistry; Cultural Studies; Education; Environmental Management; Environmental Studies; Ethnology; Floriculture; Food Science; Food Technology; Genetics; Health Sciences; Linguistics; Mathematics; Modern Languages; Nursing; Science Education; Social Sciences; Teacher Training.** *Doutorado*: **Agronomy; Animal Husbandry; Arts and Humanities; Food Science; Food Technology; Health Sciences; Nursing; Social Sciences.**

Student Services: Library

Last Updated: 23/02/16

STATE UNIVERSITY CENTRE OF THE WESTERN ZONE

Centro Universitario Estadual da Zona Oeste (UEZO)

Avenida Manuel Caldeira de Alvarenga, 1203,
Campo Grande, Rio de Janeiro 23070-200
Tel: +55(21) 2332-7530
Fax: +55(21) 2332-7533
EMail: reitoria@uezo.rj.gov.br
Website: http://www.uezo.rj.gov.br

Reitor: Alex da Silva Sirqueira (2013-)

Vice-reitor: João Bosco de Salles

Course

Biology (Biology); **Computer Science** (Computer Science; Systems Analysis); **Metallurgical Engineering** (Metallurgical Engineering); **Pharmacy** (Pharmacy); **Polymer Technology** (Polymer and Plastics Technology); **Production Engineering** (Production Engineering); **Shipbuilding Technology** (Marine Engineering)

History: Founded 2004.

Main Language(s) of Instruction: Portuguese

Degrees and Diplomas: *Bacharelado*; *Mestrado*: **Environmental Engineering; Materials Engineering.**

Student Services: Library

Last Updated: 16/07/15

STATE UNIVERSITY OF ALAGOAS

Universidade Estadual de Alagoas (UNEAL)
Rua Governador Luiz Cavalcante, s/n, Alto Cruzeiro, Arapiraca, Alagoas 57312-270
Tel: +55(82) 3521-3019
Fax: +55(82) 3530-3382
EMail: ascom@uneal.edu.br; gabinete@uneal.edu.br
Website: http://www.uneal.edu.br

Reitor: Jairo José Campos da Costa (2010-)

Vice-Reitor: Clébio Correia de Araújo

Pró-Reitora de Graduação: Maria Helena de Melo Aragão
Tel: +55(82) 3539-6065 EMail: prograd@uneal.edu.br

Campus

Campus I - Arapiraca (Accountancy; Biological and Life Sciences; Business Administration; Chemistry; Geography (Human); History; Law; Literature; Mathematics; Pedagogy); **Campus II - Santana do Ipanema** (Animal Husbandry; Biological and Life Sciences; Pedagogy); **Campus III - Palmeira dos Índios** (Foreign Languages Education; Humanities and Social Science Education; Mathematics Education; Native Language Education; Pedagogy; Science Education); **Campus IV - São Miguel dos Campos** (Accountancy; English; Literature; Portuguese; Spanish); **Campus V - União dos Palmares** (English; Geography (Human); Literature; Portuguese); **Campus VI - Maceió** (Public Administration)

History: Founded 1994. Acquired present status and title 2006.

Main Language(s) of Instruction: Portuguese

Degrees and Diplomas: *Bacharelado*; *Licenciatura*; *Especialização/Aperfeiçoamento*: **Cattle Breeding; Education.** *Mestrado*: **Animal Husbandry; Regional Planning.**

Last Updated: 01/04/16

STATE UNIVERSITY OF CAMPINAS

Universidade Estadual de Campinas (UNICAMP)
Cidade Universitária 'Zeferino Vaz' Barão Geraldo, C.P.6194, Campinas, São Paulo 13083970
Tel: +55(19) 3521-4720
Fax: +55(19) 3788-4789
EMail: cori@reitoria.unicamp.br
Website: http://www.unicamp.br

President: Jose Tadeu Jorge (2013-2017)
Tel: +55(19) 3521-4720 EMail: reitor@reitoria.unicamp.br

Communications director: Clayton Levy
EMail: clayton@reitoria.unicamp.br

Vice Reitor Executivo de Administração: Oswaldo da Rocha Grassiotto EMail: vrea@reitoria.unicamp.br

International Relations: Luis Augusto Barbosa Cortez, Vice Reitor Executivo de Relações Internacionais
Tel: +55(19) 3521-4702
EMail: internationaloffice@reitoria.unicamp.br

Faculty

Agricultural Engineering (Feagri) (Agricultural Engineering); **Applied Sciences (FCA)** (Administration; Nutrition; Production Engineering; Public Administration; Sports); **Chemical Engineering (FEQ)** (Chemical Engineering); **Civil Engineering, Architecture and Town Planning (FEC)** (Architecture; Civil Engineering; Town Planning); **Dentistry (FOP)** *(de Piracicaba)* (Dentistry; Surgery); **Education (FE)** (Education; Pedagogy); **Electrical Engineering and Computer Science (FEEC)** (Computer Engineering; Electrical Engineering); **Food Engineering (FEA)** (Food Technology; Nutrition); **Mechanical Engineering (FEM)** (Mechanical Engineering); **Medical Sciences (FCM)** (Health Sciences; Medicine); **Physical Education (FEF)** (Physical Education); **Technology (FT)** (Civil Engineering; Construction Engineering; Environmental Engineering; Environmental Management; Information Technology; Road Engineering; Sanitary Engineering; Systems Analysis; Telecommunications Engineering)

Institute

Arts (IA) (Dance; Multimedia; Music; Theatre; Visual Arts); **Biology (IB)** (Biology); **Chemistry (IQ)** (Chemistry); **Computer Science (IC)** (Computer Science); **Economics (IE)** (Economics); **Geosciences (IG)** (Earth Sciences; Geography; Geology); **Language Studies (IEL)** (Arts and Humanities; Linguistics; Literature); **Mathematics, Statistics and Computer Science (IMECC)** (Computer Science; Mathematics; Statistics); **Philosophy and Humanities (IFCH)** (Anthropology; Arts and Humanities; History; Philosophy; Political Sciences; Sociology); **Physics (IFGW)** *("Gleb Wataghin")* (Physics)

Centre

Agriculture Teaching and Research (Cepagri) (Agriculture); **Applied Informatics Education (Nied - Interdisciplinary)** (Computer Education); **Biological Research (CEMIB - Multidisciplinary)** (Biological and Life Sciences); **Biomedical Engineering (CEB)** (Biomedical Engineering); **Chemistry, Biology and Agriculture (CPQBA)** (Agriculture; Biological and Life Sciences; Chemistry); **Creativity Development (Nudecri)** (Painting and Drawing; Photography); **Energy Planning (Nipe)** (Energy Engineering); **Food Research (Nepa)** (Food Science); **Gender Studies (Pagu)** (Gender Studies); **Integration and Cultural Dissemination (Ciddic)** (Cultural Studies); **Logic, Epistemology and the History of Science (CLE)** (History; Logic; Philosophy); **Molecular Biology and Genetic Engineering (CBMEG)** (Genetics; Molecular Biology); **Petroleum Studies (Cepetro)** (Petroleum and Gas Engineering); **Population Studies (Nepo - Elza Berquó)** (Demography and Population); **Public Opinion Research (CESOP)** (Social Sciences); **Public Policy Studies (Nepp)** (Economic and Finance Policy); **Semi-Conductor Components (CCS)** (Physics); **Studies and Environmental Research (NEPAM)** (Environmental Studies); **Studies on Sound Communication (Nics - Interdisciplinary)** (Sound Engineering (Acoustics)); **Theatrical Research (Lume - Interdisciplinary)** (Theatre); **Unicamp Memory Centre (CMU)** (Heritage Preservation)

Further Information: Also University Clinical Hospital, Advanced Centre for Technological Education, Technical School of Campinas and Technical School of Limeira

History: Founded 1962 by the State legislature of São Paulo as an autonomous institution.

Academic Year: March to December (March-June; August-December)

Admission Requirements: Secondary school certificate and entrance examination

Main Language(s) of Instruction: Portuguese

Accrediting Agency: Coordination for the Improvement of Higher Education Personnel Foundation, National Council for Scientific and Technological Development, State of São Paulo Research Foundation

Degrees and Diplomas: *Técnico de Nivel Medio*; *Tecnólogo*; *Bacharelado*; *Licenciatura*; *Especialização/Aperfeiçoamento*: **Agricultural Engineering; Industrial and Production Economics; Journalism; Labour and Industrial Relations; Mathematics; Medicine; Neurosciences.** *Mestrado*: **Agricultural Engineering; Anaesthesiology; Analytical Chemistry; Anatomy; Anthropology; Applied Linguistics; Applied Mathematics; Architecture; Art Education; Arts and Humanities; Bioengineering; Biological and Life Sciences; Biology; Biomedicine; Cell Biology; Chemical Engineering; Chemistry; Civil Engineering; Computer Science; Cultural Studies; Dance; Demography and Population; Dental Technology; Dentistry; Development Studies; Ecology; Economic and Finance Policy; Economic History; Economics; Education; Educational Administration; Educational Psychology; Electrical Engineering; Energy Engineering; Environmental Management; Environmental Studies; Food Science; Food Technology; Genetics; Geography; Geology; Gerontology; Gynaecology and Obstetrics; Haematology; Health Administration; Health Education; Health Sciences; History; Humanities and Social Science Education; Information Technology; Inorganic Chemistry; International Relations; Linguistics; Literature; Materials Engineering; Mathematics; Mechanical Engineering; Medicine; Molecular Biology; Multimedia; Music; Natural Resources; Natural Sciences; Neurology; Nursing; Nutrition; Ophthalmology; Oral Pathology; Organic Chemistry; Otorhinolaryngology; Pathology; Performing Arts; Petroleum and Gas Engineering; Pharmacology; Philosophy; Physical Chemistry; Physical Education; Physics; Physiology; Political Sciences; Psychiatry and Mental Health; Public Health; Radiology; Rehabilitation and Therapy; Science Education; Social Policy; Social Sciences; Sociology; Sports; Statistics; Stomatology; Surgery; Technology; Theatre; Town Planning; Visual Arts.** *Doutorado*: **Agricultural Engineering; Analytical Chemistry; Anatomy; Anthropology; Applied**

Linguistics; Applied Mathematics; Architecture; Art Education; Arts and Humanities; Bioengineering; Biological and Life Sciences; Biology; Biomedicine; Cell Biology; Chemical Engineering; Chemistry; Civil Engineering; Computer Science; Cultural Studies; Dance; Demography and Population; Dental Technology; Dentistry; Development Studies; Earth Sciences; Ecology; Economic and Finance Policy; Economic History; Economics; Education; Educational Administration; Educational Psychology; Electrical Engineering; Energy Engineering; Environmental Studies; Food Science; Food Technology; Genetics; Geography; Geology; Gerontology; Gynaecology and Obstetrics; Health Education; Health Sciences; History; Humanities and Social Science Education; Information Technology; Inorganic Chemistry; International Relations; Linguistics; Literature; Materials Engineering; Mathematics Education; Mechanical Engineering; Medicine; Molecular Biology; Multimedia; Music; Natural Resources; Natural Sciences; Neurology; Nursing; Nutrition; Oral Pathology; Organic Chemistry; Otorhinolaryngology; Pathology; Performing Arts; Periodontics; Petroleum and Gas Engineering; Pharmacology; Philosophy; Physical Chemistry; Physical Education; Physics; Physiology; Political Sciences; Psychiatry and Mental Health; Public Health; Radiology; Rehabilitation and Therapy; Science Education; Social Sciences; Social Studies; Sociology; Sports; Stomatology; Surgery; Technology; Theatre; Town Planning; Visual Arts.

Student Services: Academic Counselling, Canteen, Careers Guidance, Facilities for disabled people, Health Services, Language Laboratory, Nursery Care, Social Counselling, Sports Facilities

Publications: Journal de Unicamp

Publishing House: Editora UNICAMP

Last Updated: 08/04/16

STATE UNIVERSITY OF CEARÁ

Universidade Estadual do Ceará (UECE)

Av. Dr. Silas Munguba, 1700, Campus do Itaperi,
Fortaleza, Ceará 60740-000
Tel: +55(85) 3101-9600
Fax: +55(85) 3101-9601
EMail: reitoira@uece.br; uceprograd@gmail.com
Website: http://www.uece.br

Reitor: José Jackson Coelho Sampaio EMail: reitor@uece.br

Vice-Reitor: Hidelbrando dos Santos Soares
EMail: vicereitoria@uece.br

Faculty

Education (FACEDI) *(Itapipoca)* (Education); **Education (FAEC)** *(Crateus, Itapipoca)* (Education); **Education, Sciences and Letters (CECITEC)** *(Inhamuns)* (Biology; Chemistry; Pedagogy); **Education, Sciences and Letters (FECLESC)** *(Sertão Central)* (Arts and Humanities; Biological and Life Sciences; Chemistry; Education; History; Mathematics; Natural Sciences; Pedagogy; Physics); **Education, Sciences and Letters (FECLI)** *(Iguatu)* (Arts and Humanities; Biological and Life Sciences; Education; Mathematics; Pedagogy; Physics); **Philosophy (FAFIDAM)** *(Dom Auréliano Matos)* (Philosophy); **Veterinary Science** (Veterinary Science)

Institute

Biomedicine (Biomedicine)

Centre

Applied Social Studies (CESA) (Social Studies); **Education (CED)** (Education; Pedagogy); **Health Sciences (CCS)** (Biological and Life Sciences; Medicine; Nursing; Nutrition; Physical Education); **Humanities (CH)** (Arts and Humanities; History; Music; Musical Instruments; Philosophy; Psychology; Social Sciences); **Sciences and Technology (CCT)** (Mathematics and Computer Science; Natural Sciences; Technology)

Further Information: Also University Hospital

History: Founded 1975, incorporating previously existing private institutions. A State institution financed by the Federal Government.

Academic Year: March to December (March-July; August-December)

Admission Requirements: Secondary school certificate and entrance examination

Main Language(s) of Instruction: Portuguese

Degrees and Diplomas: *Bacharelado*; *Licenciatura*; *Especialização/Aperfeiçoamento*: **Art Education; Biochemistry; Civil Law; Commercial Law; Community Health; Computer Networks; Constitutional Law; Criminal Law; Educational Administration; Educational Psychology; Environmental Management; Environmental Studies; Finance; Food Science; Foreign Languages Education; Geography; Gerontology; Gynaecology and Obstetrics; Health Administration; Health Sciences; Humanities and Social Science Education; Industrial and Organizational Psychology; Labour Law; Law; Leisure Studies; Linguistics; Literacy Education; Literature; Management; Marketing; Mathematics Education; Molecular Biology; Nursing; Nutrition; Parks and Recreation; Pedagogy; Pharmacology; Physical Education; Physiology; Portuguese; Preschool Education; Private Law; Production Engineering; Psychiatry and Mental Health; Public Health; Science Education; Social and Community Services; Social Policy; Social Work; Software Engineering; Special Education; Sports; Sports Medicine; Teacher Trainers Education; Teacher Training; Tourism; Translation and Interpretation; Water Science.** *Mestrado*: **Applied Linguistics; Arts and Humanities; Biotechnology; Child Care and Development; Community Health; Computer Science; Cultural Studies; Education; Geography; Health Administration; Health Education; Health Sciences; History; Management; Mathematics; Meteorology; Natural Resources; Nursing; Nutrition; Philosophy; Physics; Public Administration; Public Health; Social and Community Services; Social Policy; Social Problems; Teacher Training; Tourism; Veterinary Science.** *Doutorado*: **Applied Linguistics; Education; Geography; Health Sciences; Management; Nursing; Physiology; Public Health; Veterinary Science.** Also joint Doctorate programmes in: Biotechnology (RENORBIO), Public Health with Universidade Federal do Ceará (UFC) and University of Fortaleza (UNIFOR).

Student Services: Canteen, Library

Last Updated: 29/02/16

STATE UNIVERSITY OF FEIRA DE SANTANA

Universidade Estadual de Feira de Santana (UEFS)

Avenida Transnordestina, s/n, Novo Horizonte,
Feira de Santana, Bahia 44036-900
Tel: +55(75) 224-8200 +55(75) 224 8001
Fax: +55(75) 224-2284
EMail: procuradoriaeducacional@uefs.br
Website: http://www.uefs.br

Reitor: Evandro do Nascimento Silva (2015-)
Tel: +55(75) 3161-8002
EMail: reitor@uefs.br; gabinete.reitor@uefs.br

Vice-Reitora: Norma Lúcia Fernandes de Almeida

Pró-Reitor de Administração e Finanças: Carlos Eduardo Cardoso de Oliveira Tel: +5(75) 3161-8034 EMail: proad@uefs.br

International Relations: Eneida Soanne Matos Campos de Oliveira, Assessora Especial de Relações Institucionais
EMail: aeri.soanne@gmail.com

Department

Applied Social Sciences (Accountancy; Administration; Economics; Law); **Biological Sciences** (Agronomy; Biological and Life Sciences; Biotechnology; Botany; Cell Biology; Zoology); **Education** (Education; Foreign Languages Education; Humanities and Social Science Education; Mathematics Education; Native Language Education; Pedagogy; Physical Education; Science Education); **Exact Sciences** (Chemistry; Computer Engineering; Earth Sciences; Environmental Studies; Information Technology; Mathematics; Mathematics and Computer Science; Mathematics Education; Natural Sciences; Science Education); **Health Sciences** (Dentistry; Medicine; Nursing; Pharmacy; Physical Education); **Human Sciences and Philosophy** (Arts and Humanities; Geography; History; Philosophy); **Letters and Arts** (Arts and Humanities; Cultural Studies; Design; English; French; Linguistics; Literature; Music; Native Language Education; Portuguese; Spanish); **Physics** (Physics); **Technology** (Civil Engineering; Computer Engineering; Computer Science; Environmental Engineering; Food Technology; Systems Analysis)

History: Founded 1970 by the State legislature of Bahia, recognized by the Federal Government 1976.

Academic Year: March to December (March-July; August-December)

Admission Requirements: Secondary school certificate and entrance examination

Main Language(s) of Instruction: Portuguese

Degrees and Diplomas: *Bacharelado*: **Accountancy; Administration; Agronomy; Biological and Life Sciences; Civil Engineering; Computer Engineering; Dentistry; Economics; Food Technology; Geography; Law; Medicine; Nursing; Pharmacy; Philosophy; Physics; Psychology.** *Licenciatura*: **Foreign Languages Education; Humanities and Social Science Education; Mathematics Education; Modern Languages; Music Education; Native Language Education; Pedagogy; Physical Education; Science Education.** *Especialização/Aperfeiçoamento*: **Bilingual and Bicultural Education; Cell Biology; Civil Engineering; Computer Science; Design; Education; Environmental Engineering; Health Sciences; Information Technology; Linguistics; Literature; Mathematics; Mathematics Education; Native Language Education; Philosophy; Portuguese; Special Education.** *Mestrado*: **Astronomy and Space Science; Biology; Biotechnology; Botany; Civil Engineering; Computer Science; Cultural Studies; Design; Earth Sciences; Education; Environmental Engineering; Environmental Studies; Genetics; History; Linguistics; Literature; Natural Sciences; Nursing; Pharmacy; Public Health; Regional Planning; Zoology.** *Doutorado*: **Anatomy; Biotechnology; Botany; Genetics; Natural Sciences.** Also Network and Inter-institutional Mestrado and Doutorado

Student Services: Library, Sports Facilities

Last Updated: 01/04/16

STATE UNIVERSITY OF GOIÁS

Universidade Estadual de Goiás (UEG)

Campus BR 153 - Km 98 Caixa Postal 459,
Anápolis, Goiás 75110380
Tel: +55(62) 3328-1178
Fax: +55(62) 3328-1179
EMail: gabinete@ueg.br; brandinafm@hotmail.com
Website: http://www.ueg.br

Reitor: Haroldo Reimer
Tel: +55(62) 3328-1433 EMail: reitor@ueg.br; gabinete@ueg.br

Vice-Reitora: Valcemia Gonçalves de Sousa Novaes
Tel: +55(62) 3328-1102 EMail: vicereitoria@ueg.br

International Relations: Hebert Melo, Coordenador Geral de Relações Internacionais EMail: hebert.melo@ueg.br

Centre

Network Teaching and Learning Centre (CEAR) (Administration; Biological and Life Sciences; Computer Science; History)

Campus

Annapolis Socio-Economic Sciences and Humanities Campus (Accountancy; Administration; English; Geography (Human); History; Literature; Pedagogy; Portuguese; Social Sciences); **Aparecida de Goiânia Campus** (Accountancy; Administration); **Caldas Novas Campus** (Administration; Business and Commerce; Cooking and Catering); **Campos Belos Campus** (English; Literature; Pedagogy; Portuguese); **Ceres Campus** (Nursing); **Crixás Campus** (Computer Networks; Pedagogy); **Edéia Campus** (Agricultural Business; Food Science); **Formosa Campus** (Chemistry; English; Geography (Human); History; Literature; Mathematics; Pedagogy; Portuguese); **Goianésia Campus** (Administration; History; Information Technology; Pedagogy); **Goiânia-Eseffego Campus** (Physical Therapy; Sports Medicine); **Goiânia-Laranjeiras Campus** (Cinema and Television; Cosmetology); **Goiás Campus** (English; Geography (Human); History; Literature; Mathematics; Portuguese; Tourism); **Henrique Santillo Campus of Exact and Technological Sciences Annapolis** (Agricultural Engineering; Architecture; Biological and Life Sciences; Chemistry; Civil Engineering; Industrial Chemistry; Information Technology; Mathematics; Pharmacy; Physics; Town Planning); **Inhumas Campus** (English; Literature; Pedagogy; Portuguese); **Ipameri Campus** (Agricultural Engineering; Agronomy; Forestry); **Iporá Campus** (Biological and Life Sciences; English; Geography (Human); History; Literature; Mathematics; Portuguese); **Itaberaí Campus** (Information Technology; Pedagogy); **Itapuranga Campus** (Biological and Life Sciences; English; Geography (Human); History; Literature; Portuguese); **Itumbiara Campus** (Economics; Nursing; Pharmacy; Physical Education); **Jaraguá Campus** (Accountancy; Fashion Design; Pedagogy); **Jataí Campus** (Food Technology; Transport Management); **Jussara Campus** (English; Literature; Mathematics; Portuguese); **Luziânia Campus** (Administration; Pedagogy); **Minaçu Campus** (Geography (Human); Pedagogy); **Mineiros Campus** (Agriculture; Food Science); **Morrinhos Campus** (Accountancy; Biological and Life Sciences; English; Geography (Human); History; Literature; Mathematics; Portuguese); **Niquelândia Campus** (Mineralogy; Tourism); **Palmeiras de Goiás Campus** (Agronomy; Biological and Life Sciences); **Pirenópolis Campus** (Cooking and Catering; Hotel and Restaurant); **Pires do Rio Campus** (Computer Networks; English; Geography (Human); History; Literature; Pedagogy; Portuguese); **Porangatu Campus** (Biological and Life Sciences; English; Geography (Human); History; Information Technology; Literature; Mathematics; Physical Education; Portuguese); **Posse Campus** (Crop Production; English; Information Technology; Literature; Mathematics; Portuguese); **Quirinópolis Campus** (Biological and Life Sciences; English; Geography (Human); History; Literature; Mathematics; Pedagogy; Physical Education; Portuguese); **Sanclerlândia Campus** (Administration); **Santa Helena Campus** (Administration; Agricultural Engineering; Information Technology; Mathematics); **São Luís de Montes Belos Campus** (Animal Husbandry; Dairy; English; Literature; Pedagogy; Portuguese); **São Miguel do Araguaia Campus** (English; Literature; Pedagogy; Portuguese); **Senador Canedo Campus** (Transport Management); **Silvânia Campus** (Administration); **Trindade Campus** (Computer Networks; Fashion Design); **Uruaçu Campus** (Accountancy; History; Pedagogy)

History: Founded 1961 as Faculdade de Ciências Econômicas de Anápolis, became Universidade Estadual de Anápolis 1990 and acquired present status and title 1999. A State institution.

Admission Requirements: Secondary school certificate and entrance examination

Main Language(s) of Instruction: Portuguese

Degrees and Diplomas: *Tecnólogo*; *Bacharelado*; *Licenciatura*; *Especialização/Aperfeiçoamento*: **Agricultural Business; Agricultural Management; Agriculture; Arts and Humanities; Business and Commerce; Computer Networks; Cosmetology; Cultural Studies; Development Studies; Ecology; Education; Educational Administration; Environmental Management; Environmental Studies; Finance; Fine Arts; Health Administration; Higher Education Teacher Training; Humanities and Social Science Education; Industrial Management; Literacy Education; Literature; Management; Mathematics Education; Media Studies; Modern Languages; Natural Resources; Physical Therapy; Primary Education; Regional Studies; Science Education; Social Sciences; Sports; Teacher Training; Technology; Transport Management; Writing.** *Mestrado*: **Agricultural Engineering; Crop Production; Cultural Studies; Development Studies; Education; Health Sciences; Horticulture; Modern Languages; Molecular Biology; Natural Resources; Regional Studies; Science Education; Technology.** *Doutorado*: **Natural Resources.**

Student Services: Library

Last Updated: 04/04/16

STATE UNIVERSITY OF LONDRINA

Universidade Estadual de Londrina (UEL)

Rodovia Celso Gárcia Cid, PR 445 Km 380, Campus Universitário,
Cx. Postal 10.011, Londrina, Paraná 86057-970
Tel: +55(43) 3371-4000
Fax: +55(43) 3328-4440
EMail: apcdaai@uel.br; proplandaai@uel.br
Website: http://www.uel.br

Reitora: Berenice Quinzani Jordão
Tel: +55(43) 3371-4311 EMail: reitoria@uel.br

Pró-Reitora de Administração: Angela Maria de Sousa Lima

International Relations: Telma Nunes Gimenez, Assessora de Relações Internacionais
Tel: +55(43) 3371-4188 EMail: uelari@uel.br

Centre

Agriculture (Agriculture; Agronomy; Animal Husbandry; Food Science; Food Technology; Veterinary Science); **Applied Social Studies** (Accountancy; Administration; Economics; Private Law; Public Law; Social and Community Services); **Biological Sciences** (Anatomy; Behavioural Sciences; Biological and Life Sciences; Biology; Histology; Microbiology; Pathology; Physiology; Psychoanalysis; Psychology; Social Psychology); **Education, Communication Studies, and Arts** (Archiving; Art Education; Communication Studies; Design; Information Sciences; Library Science; Music; Pedagogy; Performing Arts; Theatre; Visual Arts); **Exact Sciences** (Biochemistry; Biotechnology; Chemistry; Computer Science; Earth Sciences; Mathematics; Physics; Statistics); **Health Sciences** (Dentistry; Gynaecology and Obstetrics; Health Sciences; Medicine; Nursing; Oral Pathology; Paediatrics; Pathology; Pharmacy; Physical Therapy; Public Health; Surgery; Toxicology); **Human Sciences and Letters** (Classical Languages; English; History; Literature; Modern Languages; Native Language; Philosophy; Portuguese; Social Sciences; Spanish); **Physical Education and Sports** (Physical Education; Sports); **Technology and Town Planning** (Architecture; Civil Engineering; Construction Engineering; Electrical Engineering; Structural Architecture; Town Planning)

Further Information: Also University Hospital, Veterinary Hospital, and 3 clinics

History: Founded 1970 incorporating previously existing State faculties. The University is constituted as a State Foundation.

Academic Year: February to December (February-June; August-December)

Admission Requirements: Secondary school certificate or recognized foreign equivalent and entrance examination

Main Language(s) of Instruction: Portuguese

Degrees and Diplomas: *Bacharelado*: **Accountancy; Administration; Agricultural Engineering; Animal Husbandry; Architecture; Arts and Humanities; Biology; Biomedicine; Chemistry; Civil Engineering; Computer Science; Dentistry; Economics; Electronic Engineering; Fashion Design; Geography; Graphic Design; Law; Library Science; Mathematics; Nursing; Pharmacy; Physical Education; Physical Therapy; Physics; Psychology; Social Sciences; Social Work; Sports; Theatre; Veterinary Science.** *Licenciatura*: **Art Education; Arts and Humanities; Chemistry; Geography; History; Mathematics; Music; Pedagogy; Philosophy; Physical Education; Physics; Psychology; Social Sciences.** *Especialização/Aperfeiçoamento*: **Accountancy; Adult Education; Advertising and Publicity; Animal Husbandry; Architecture; Archiving; Art Education; Astronomy and Space Science; Biological and Life Sciences; Biology; Biotechnology; Business and Commerce; Chemistry; Civil Law; Commercial Law; Communication Studies; Computer Graphics; Computer Science; Construction Engineering; Criminal Law; Data Processing; Dentistry; Design; Earth Sciences; Educational Psychology; Educational Technology; Electronic Engineering; English; Environmental Studies; Epidemiology; Fashion Design; Finance; Foreign Languages Education; Genetics; Health Administration; Health Sciences; Higher Education Teacher Training; History; Hotel and Restaurant; Human Resources; Humanities and Social Science Education; Industrial and Organizational Psychology; Industrial and Production Economics; Industrial Management; International Law; Jewellery Art; Law; Library Science; Literature; Management; Marketing; Mathematics Education; Media Studies; Music; Natural Sciences; Nursing; Nutrition; Orthodontics; Pharmacy; Philosophy; Photography; Physical Education; Physical Therapy; Political Sciences; Portuguese; Private Law; Psychiatry and Mental Health; Psychoanalysis; Public Health; Public Law; Rehabilitation and Therapy; Religion; Religious Studies; Safety Engineering; Science Education; Social Psychology; Sociology; Software Engineering; Spanish; Sports; Statistics; Structural Architecture; Taxation; Veterinary Science; Visual Arts.** *Mestrado*: **Administration; Agronomy; Animal Husbandry; Applied Mathematics; Architecture; Arts and Humanities; Behavioural Sciences; Bioengineering; Biological and Life Sciences; Biotechnology; Chemistry; Civil Engineering; Commercial Law; Communication Studies; Computer Science; Dentistry; Economics; Education; Electrical Engineering; Energy Engineering; English; Food Science; Genetics; Geography; Health Sciences; Information Sciences; Literature; Mathematics; Mathematics Education; Microbiology; Modern Languages; Molecular Biology; Nursing; Pathology; Philosophy; Physical Education; Physics; Physiology; Portuguese; Public Health; Rehabilitation and Therapy; Sanitary Engineering; Science Education; Social and Community Services; Social Policy; Social Sciences; Town Planning; Toxicology; Veterinary Science.** *Doutorado*: **Agronomy; Animal Husbandry; Arts and Humanities; Biology; Biotechnology; Chemistry; Education; Food Science; Genetics; Geography; Health Sciences; Mathematics Education; Microbiology; Modern Languages; Molecular Biology; Pathology; Physical Education; Physics; Physiology; Public Health; Rehabilitation and Therapy; Science Education; Social and Community Services; Social Policy.** Also MBA; Medical Residencies

Student Services: Canteen, Facilities for disabled people, Health Services, Library, Nursery Care, Social Counselling, Sports Facilities

Publications: Biosaúde; Boletim do Centro de Letras e Ciências Humanas; Discursos Fotográficos; Entretexto; Geografia: Revista do Departamento de Geociências; Mediações; Olho Mágico; Scientia Iuris; Semina; Semina - Ciências Biológicas e da Saúde; Semina - Ciências Exatas e Tecnológicas; Semina - Ciências Sociais e Humanas; Signun: Estudo da Linguagem

Publishing House: Editora EUEL. (Estudante da Universidade Estadual de Londrina)

Last Updated: 04/04/16

STATE UNIVERSITY OF MARANHÃO

Universidade Estadual do Maranhão (UEMA)

Cidade Universitária Paulo VI, Caixa Postal 09,
São Luís, Maranhão 65055-310
Tel: +55(98) 3245-5461
Fax: +55(98) 3245-5882
EMail: waldirmaranhao@uema.br
Website: http://www.uema.br

Reitor: Gustavo Pereira da Costa EMail: reitoria@uema.br

Pró-Reitor de Administração: Gilson Martins Mendonça
Tel: +55(98) 3245-2833 EMail: gilson.mendonca@uema.br

International Relations: Thales Passos de Andrade, Assessor para Relações Internacionais
Tel: +55(98) 3258-2671 EMail: ARInternacionais@uema.br

Centre

Advanced Studies (Bacabal) (Agriculture; Arts and Humanities; Education; Mathematics; Midwifery; Natural Sciences; Nursing; Philosophy; Social Sciences); **Advanced Studies (Balsas)** (Education; Literature; Mathematics; Nursing); **Advanced Studies (Caxias)** (Biology; Chemistry; Education; Geography; History; Literature; Mathematics; Philosophy; Physics; Social Sciences); **Advanced Studies (Imperatriz)** (Biology; Business Administration; Chemistry; Education; Geography; History; Literature; Mathematics; Philosophy; Physics; Social Sciences); **Advanced Studies (Presidente Dutra)** (Education); **Advanced Studies (Santa Inês)** (Literature; Pedagogy); **Advanced Studies (Timon)** (Arts and Humanities; Business Administration); **Agricultural Sciences** (Agricultural Economics; Agricultural Engineering; Agriculture; Animal Husbandry; Horticulture; Pathology; Veterinary Science); **Applied Social Sciences** (Accountancy; Business Administration; Economics; Law; Social Sciences); **Education, Exact and Natural Sciences** (Biology; Chemistry; Computer Science; Education; Geography; History; Literature; Mathematics; Philosophy; Physical Education); **Technological Sciences** (Architecture; Construction Engineering; Graphic Design; Hydraulic Engineering; Mechanical Engineering; Physics; Production Engineering; Sanitary Engineering; Structural Architecture; Town Planning; Transport and Communications)

History: Founded 1973.

Admission Requirements: Admission Examination

Fees: None

Main Language(s) of Instruction: Portuguese

Degrees and Diplomas: *Tecnólogo*; *Bacharelado*: **Agricultural Engineering; Animal Husbandry; Architecture; Business Administration; Civil Engineering; Computer Engineering; Fishery; Floriculture; Geography; Law; Mechanical Engineering; Medicine; Nursing; Production Engineering; Social**

Sciences; Town Planning; Veterinary Science. *Licenciatura*: **Arts and Humanities; Biological and Life Sciences; Biology; Chemistry; English; Geography; History; Literature; Mathematics; Music; Pedagogy; Physics; Portuguese; Social Sciences.** *Mestrado*: **Agriculture; Animal Husbandry; Arts and Humanities; Biological and Life Sciences; Computer Engineering; Development Studies; Ecology; Education; Environmental Studies; Fishery; Geography; Health Sciences; History; Natural Resources; Political Sciences; Regional Planning; Sanitary Engineering; Surveying and Mapping; Systems Analysis.** Also Network Degree Programmes: Mestrado in Mathematics (PROFMAT); Doutorado in Biotechnology (RENORBIO) and Biological and Life Sciences and Biotechnology (BIONORTE)

Student Services: Canteen, Health Services, IT Centre, Library, Social Counselling, Sports Facilities

Publications: Pesquisa em Foco

Last Updated: 01/03/16

STATE UNIVERSITY OF MARINGÁ

Universidade Estadual de Maringá (UEM)

Avenida Colombo 5790, Escritório de Cooperação Internacional Bloco 101, Sala 09, Maringá, Paraná 87020900

Tel: +55(44) 3261-4441 +55(44) 3261-4238

Fax: +55(44) 3263-4820

EMail: sec-eci@uem.br; sec-pen@uem.br; sec-asp@uem.br; sec-gre@uem.br; dias.mariamadalena@gmail.com; sec-nead@ue

Website: http://www.uem.br

Reitor: Mauro Luciano Baesso
Tel: +55(44) 3011-4200 EMail: sec-gre@uem.br

Pró-Reitora de Administração: Maria Helena Ambrosio Dias
Tel: +55(44) 3261-4220 EMail: mhadias@uem.br

Centre

Agriculture (Agriculture; Animal Husbandry); **Applied Social Sciences** (Accountancy; Administration; Economics; Private Law; Public Law); **Biological Sciences** (Biochemistry; Biological and Life Sciences; Biology; Cell Biology; Genetics; Physiology); **Exact Sciences** (Chemistry; Mathematics; Natural Sciences; Physics; Statistics); **Health Sciences** (Biological and Life Sciences; Dentistry; Health Sciences; Medicine; Nursing; Pharmacology; Pharmacy; Physical Education; Rehabilitation and Therapy); **Humanities, Letters and Arts** (Arts and Humanities; Education; Educational Sciences; Geography (Human); History; Literature; Music; Philosophy; Psychology; Social Sciences); **Technology** (Architecture; Chemical Engineering; Civil Engineering; Computer Science; Mechanical Engineering; Production Engineering; Textile Technology; Town Planning)

History: Founded 1970, incorporating previously existing State faculties. A State foundation.

Academic Year: February to December (February-June; August-December)

Admission Requirements: Secondary school certificate and entrance examination

Main Language(s) of Instruction: Portuguese

Degrees and Diplomas: *Bacharelado*: **Accountancy; Administration; Agricultural Engineering; Agronomy; Architecture; Chemical Engineering; Chemistry; Civil Engineering; Computer Science; Dentistry; Economics; Environmental Engineering; Fashion Design; Food Technology; Law; Mechanical Engineering; Medicine; Midwifery; Modern Languages; Music; Nursing; Pedagogy; Pharmacology; Pharmacy; Philosophy; Production Engineering; Psychology; Secretarial Studies; Textile Technology; Veterinary Science.** *Licenciatura*: **Biology; Geography; History; Mathematics; Modern Languages; Physical Education; Physics; Social Studies.** *Especialização/Aperfeiçoamento*: **Accountancy; Agriculture; Anatomy; Biotechnology; Computer Science; Education; Histology; Pathology; Pharmacology; Physical Education; Physiology; Science Education; Social Policy; Waste Management.** *Mestrado*: **Accountancy; Administration; Agriculture; Agronomy; Animal Husbandry; Architecture; Arts and Humanities; Biological and Life Sciences; Biology; Biotechnology; Chemical Engineering; Chemistry; Civil Engineering; Civil Law; Computer Science; Dentistry; Ecology; Economics; Education; Energy Engineering; Environmental Studies; Food Science; Genetics; Geography; Health Sciences; History; Linguistics; Mathematics; Mathematics Education; Mechanical Engineering; Nursing; Pathology; Pharmacy; Philosophy; Physical Education; Physics; Physiology; Psychology; Science Education; Social Policy; Social Sciences; Statistics; Technology; Town Planning.** *Doutorado*: **Administration; Agronomy; Animal Husbandry; Biological and Life Sciences; Biology; Biotechnology; Chemical Engineering; Economics; Education; Environmental Studies; Food Science; Genetics; Geography; Health Sciences; History; Linguistics; Mathematics; Mathematics Education; Nursing; Pathology; Pharmacy; Physics; Physiology; Science Education.** Also MBA

Student Services: Library

Publishing house: Imprensa Universitária/University Press

Last Updated: 04/04/16

STATE UNIVERSITY OF MATO GROSSO DO SUL

Universidade Estadual de Mato Grosso do Sul (UEMS)

Cidade Universitária, Rodovia Dourados, Itahum Km 12 Cidade Universitaria, Aeroporto, Dourados, Mato Grosso do Sul 79804970

Tel: +55(67) 3411-9000

Fax: +55(67) 3411-9004

EMail: cilene@uems.br; reitoria@uems.br

Website: http://www.uems.br

Reitor: Fábio Edir dos Santos Costa
Tel: +55(67) 3902-2361 EMail: reitoria@uems.br

Pró-Reitor de Administração e Planejamento: Márcio de Araújo Pereira
Tel: +55(67) 3902-2453
EMail: marciopereira@uems.br; proap@uems.br

Vice-Reitor: Laércio Alves de Carvalho
Tel: +55(67) 3902-2362 EMail: vicereitoria@uems.br

Centre

Agricultural, Biological and Health Sciences Centre (NUCABS) (Agricultural Engineering; Agriculture; Agronomy; Animal Husbandry; Biological and Life Sciences; Ecology; Environmental Engineering; Food Science; Food Technology; Forestry; Nursing; Physical Education; Physical Engineering); **Exact Sciences and Technology Centre (NUCET)** (Agricultural Engineering; Chemistry; Computer Education; Computer Science; Forestry; Industrial Chemistry; Information Technology; Mathematics; Physics; Science Education); **Human Sciences Teaching Centre (NUCH)** (English; Geography (Human); History; Humanities and Social Science Education; Literature; Pedagogy; Performing Arts; Portuguese; Social Sciences; Spanish); **Social Sciences Teaching Centre (NUCS)** (Accountancy; Administration; Economics; Law; Public Administration; Tourism)

Further Information: Units in: Água Clara, Amambai, Aquidauana, Bataguassu, Bela Vista, Camapuã, Campo Grande, Cassilândia, Coxim, Dourados, Glória de Dourados, Ivinhema, Jardim, Maracaju, Miranda, Mundo Novo, Naviraí, Nova Andradina, Paranaíba, Ponta Porã, São Gabriel.

History: Founded 1993. Acquired present status 1994.

Admission Requirements: Secondary school certificate and entrance examination

Fees: None

Main Language(s) of Instruction: Portuguese

Degrees and Diplomas: *Tecnólogo*; *Bacharelado*; *Licenciatura*; *Especialização/Aperfeiçoamento*: **Applied Linguistics; Education; Gerontology; Health Administration; History; Human Rights; Law; Linguistics; Literature; Political Sciences; Public Administration; Social Sciences; Special Education; Tourism.** *Mestrado*: **Agronomy; Animal Husbandry; Arts and Humanities; Development Studies; Education; Health Education; Humanities and Social Science Education; Mathematics Education; Natural Resources; Science Education.** *Doutorado*: **Agronomy; Natural Resources.**

Student Services: Academic Counselling, Canteen, Careers Guidance, Cultural Activities, Library, Social Counselling, Sports Facilities

Last Updated: 04/04/16

STATE UNIVERSITY OF MONTES CLAROS

Universidade Estadual de Montes Claros (UNIMONTES)

Campus Universitário Professor Darcy Ribeiro, Vila Mauricéia, Montes Claros, Minas Gerais 39401-089
Tel: +55(38) 3229-8000 +55(38) 3229-8101
Fax: +55(38) 3229-8002 +55(38) 3229-8003
EMail: reitoria@unimontes.br; gabinete.reitor@unimontes.br
Website: http://www.unimontes.br

Reitor: João dos Reis Canela EMail: reitor@unimontes.br

Vice-Reitor: Antonio Alvimar Souza
Tel: +55(38) 3229-8110 EMail: vicereitor@unimontes.br

Centre
Applied Social Sciences (CCSA) (Accountancy; Administration; Economics; Law; Social and Community Services; Social Sciences); **Biology and Health Sciences (CCBS)** (Biological and Life Sciences; Biomedicine; Dentistry; Medicine; Nursing; Physical Education); **Distance Education (CEAD)** (English; Geography (Human); History; Literature; Pedagogy; Physical Education; Portuguese; Public Administration; Religious Studies; Social Sciences; Spanish); **Exact Sciences and Technology (CCET)** (Agronomy; Animal Husbandry; Chemistry; Civil Engineering; Computer Engineering; Information Technology; Mathematics; Physics); **Human Sciences (CCH)** (English; Geography (Human); History; Literature; Music; Performing Arts; Philosophy; Portuguese; Religious Studies; Spanish; Theatre; Visual Arts); **Professional and Technical Education (CEPT)** (Agricultural Business; Public Administration)

History: Founded 1971, acquired present status 1984.

Main Language(s) of Instruction: Portuguese

Degrees and Diplomas: *Tecnólogo*; *Bacharelado*; *Licenciatura*; *Especialização/Aperfeiçoamento*: **Administrative Law; Applied Linguistics; Commercial Law; Community Health; Computer Engineering; Cultural Studies; Development Studies; Education; Environmental Studies; Epidemiology; Gerontology; Health Administration; Health Sciences; History; Justice Administration; Latin American Studies; Philosophy; Private Law; Psychiatry and Mental Health; Public Administration; Social Psychology; Teacher Training.** *Mestrado*: **Animal Husbandry; Arts and Humanities; Biological and Life Sciences; Biotechnology; Development Studies; Health Sciences; History; Horticulture; Literature.** *Doutorado*: **Health Sciences.**

Last Updated: 04/04/16

STATE UNIVERSITY OF PARAÍBA

Universidade Estadual da Paraíba (UEPB)

Rua Baraúnas, 351, Bairro Universitário, Campina Grande, Paraíba 58429-500
Tel: +55(83) 3315-3300 +55(83) 3315-3303
Fax: +55(83) 3315-3300 +55(83) 3315-3421
EMail: reitoria@uepb.edu.br
Website: http://www.uepb.edu.br

Reitor: Antonio Guedes Rangel Junior
Tel: +55(83) 3315-3303 +55(83) 3315-3453
EMail: reitoria@uepb.edu.br

Vice-Reitor: José Etham de Lucena Barbosa

Pró-Reitor de Administração e Finanças: Eli Brandão da Silva
Tel: +55(83) 3315-3350
EMail: prograd@uepb.edu.br; secretariaproeg@uepb.edu.br

Centre
Agrarian and Environmental Sciences (CCAA - Campus II) (Agriculture; Ecology); **Applied Social Sciences (CCSA - Campus I)** (Accountancy; Administration; Mass Communication; Social and Community Services); **Biological and Applied Social Sciences (CCBSA - Campus V)** *(João Pessoa)* (Archiving; Biological and Life Sciences; International Relations); **Biological and Health Sciences (CCBS - Campus I)** (Biological and Life Sciences; Dentistry; Health Sciences; Nursing; Pharmacy; Physical Education; Physical Therapy; Psychology); **Education (CEDUC - Campus I)** (Geography; History; Literature; Pedagogy; Philosophy; Sociology); **Exact and Applied Social Sciences (CCEA - Campus VII)** *(Patos)* (Administration; Computer Science; Mathematics; Physics); **Human and Agrarian Sciences (CCHA - Campus IV)** *(Catolé do Rocha)* (Agriculture; Arts and Humanities; Literature); **Human and Exact Sciences (CCHE - Campus VI)** *(Monteiro)* (Accountancy; Literature; Mathematics); **Humanities (CH - Campus III)** *(Guarabira)* (Arts and Humanities; Geography; History; Law; Literature; Pedagogy); **Juridical Sciences (CCJ - Campus I)** (Private Law; Public Law); **Sciences and Technology (CCT - Campus I)** (Chemistry; Computer Science; Environmental Engineering; Mathematics; Physics; Sanitary Engineering; Statistics); **Sciences, Technology and Health (CCTS - Campus VIII)** *(Araruna)* (Civil Engineering; Dentistry; Natural Sciences)

History: Founded 1966.

Academic Year: August to December

Admission Requirements: Secondary school certificate and entrance examination

Fees: None

Main Language(s) of Instruction: Portuguese

Degrees and Diplomas: *Bacharelado*; *Licenciatura*; *Especialização/Aperfeiçoamento*: **Applied Mathematics; Biological and Life Sciences; Civil Security; Criminology; Educational Sciences; Environmental Management; Ethnology; Mathematics; Natives Education; Peace and Disarmament; Police Studies; Primary Education; Teacher Training.** *Mestrado*: **Agriculture; Arts and Humanities; Biological and Life Sciences; Chemistry; Cultural Studies; Dentistry; Ecology; Environmental Engineering; Environmental Management; Environmental Studies; Health Sciences; International Relations; Literature; Mathematics; Mathematics Education; Natural Resources; Nursing; Pharmacy; Psychology; Public Health; Regional Planning; Science Education; Social and Community Services; Teacher Training.** *Doutorado*: **Biological and Life Sciences; Cultural Studies; Dentistry; Environmental Engineering; Environmental Management; Literature; Nursing.** Also MBA

Student Services: Library

Publishing house: Gráfica Universitária

Last Updated: 01/04/16

STATE UNIVERSITY OF PIAUÍ

Universidade Estadual do Piauí (UESPI)

Rua João Cabral, Pirajá, Teresina, Piauí 64002-150
Tel: +55(86) 213-5195 +55(86) 213-5224
Fax: +55(86) 213-2733
EMail: ascom@uespi.br; censo.uespi.tn@gmail.com
Website: http://www.uespi.br

Reitor: Carlos Alverto Pereira da Silva
Tel: +55(86) 213-5757 EMail: reitoria@uespi.br

Pró-Reitoria de Administração e Recursos Humanos: Benedito Ribeiro da Graça Neto
Tel: +55(86) 3213-1636 EMail: prad@uespi.br

Vice-Reitora: Bárbara Olímpia Ramos de Melo

Centre
Education, Communication and Arts (Mass Communication; Pedagogy); **Health Sciences** (Health Sciences; Medicine; Nursing; Physical Education; Physical Therapy; Psychology); **Human Sciences and Letters** (English; Geography; History; Literature; Portuguese; Spanish); **Natural Sciences** (Biology; Chemistry; Mathematics; Physics); **Social and Applied Sciences** (Accountancy; Administration; Civil Security; Law; Library Science; Tourism); **Technology and Town Planning** (Civil Engineering; Computer Science; Electrical Engineering)

Further Information: Also campuses in Campo Maior, Corrente, Floriano, Parnaiba, Picos, Piripiri, São Raimundo, Nonato (among 25 throughout the State)

History: Founded 1988. Under supervision of the Fundação de Apoio ao Desenvolvimento da Educação do Estado do Piauí (FADEP).

Academic Year: March to December (March-June; August-December)

Admission Requirements: Secondary school certificate and entrance examination

Main Language(s) of Instruction: Portuguese

Degrees and Diplomas: *Bacharelado*; *Licenciatura*; *Especialização/Aperfeiçoamento*; *Mestrado*: **Arts and Humanities; Business Education; Cultural Studies; Education; Educational**

Administration; Educational Psychology; Environmental Management; Higher Education Teacher Training; Humanities and Social Science Education; Linguistics; Literature; Primary Education. *Doutorado*: **Civil Engineering; Geography (Human); Tropical Medicine.**

Student Services: Canteen, Careers Guidance, Health Services, Language Laboratory, Sports Facilities

Last Updated: 05/04/16

STATE UNIVERSITY OF PONTA GROSSA

Universidade Estadual de Ponta Grossa (UEPG)

Avenida Carlos Cavalcanti 4748, Campus de Uvaranas, Reitoria de Uvaranas, Ponta Grossa, Paraná 84030-900

Tel: +55(42) 3220-3000

Fax: +55(42) 3220-3233

EMail: uepg@uepg.br; gabinetedareitoria@uepg.br

Website: http://www.uepg.br

Reitor: Carlos Luciano SantÁna Vargas
Tel: +55(42) 3220-3232 EMail: reitoria@uepg.br

Pró-Reitor de Assuntos Administrativos: Amaury dos Martyres

Vice-Reitora: Gisele Alves de Sá Quimelli

International Relations: Jarem Raul Garcia, Diretor, Escritório de Relações Internacionais
EMail: eai@uepg.br; conv.internacional@uepg.br; mob.internacional@uepg.br

Centre

Agriculture and Technology (Agricultural Engineering; Agriculture; Animal Husbandry; Civil Engineering; Computer Science; Food Technology; Horticulture; Materials Engineering; Soil Science); **Applied Social Sciences** (Accountancy; Administration; Economics; Journalism; Social and Community Services; Tourism); **Biological and Health Sciences** (Biological and Life Sciences; Biology; Dentistry; Genetics; Health Sciences; Medicine; Molecular Biology; Nursing; Pharmacy; Physical Education); **Exact and Natural Sciences** (Chemistry; Earth Sciences; Mathematics; Physics; Statistics); **Humanities, Letters and Arts** (Arts and Humanities; Education; Educational Technology; History; Modern Languages; Pedagogy); **Law** (Civil Law; Labour Law; Law; Public Law)

Further Information: Campuses at: Telêmaco Borba, Palmeira, Castro, São Mateus do Sul, Uvaranas

History: Founded 1970, incorporating Faculties of Philosophy, Science and Languages, Pharmacy, Dentistry, Law, Economics and Business Administration.

Academic Year: March to November (March-June; August-November)

Admission Requirements: Secondary school certificate and entrance examination

Fees: None

Main Language(s) of Instruction: Portuguese

Degrees and Diplomas: *Bacharelado*; *Licenciatura*; *Especialização/Aperfeiçoamento*: **Accountancy; Civil Law; Cultural Studies; Dentistry; Economics; Educational Administration; Finance; Fine Arts; Health Administration; History; International Business; Mathematics Education; Orthodontics; Primary Education; Public Health.** *Mestrado*: **Agronomy; Animal Husbandry; Applied Chemistry; Bioengineering; Biological and Life Sciences; Biomedicine; Computer Science; Dentistry; Education; Energy Engineering; Environmental Engineering; Food Science; Food Technology; Geography (Human); Health Sciences; History; Journalism; Linguistics; Mathematics Education; Modern Languages; Natural Sciences; Pharmacy; Sanitary Engineering; Science Education; Social Sciences.** *Doutorado*: **Agronomy; Chemistry; Dentistry; Education; Food Science; Food Technology; Geography; Natural Sciences; Pharmacy; Social Sciences.**

Student Services: Academic Counselling, Canteen, Careers Guidance, Cultural Activities, Health Services, Library, Nursery Care, Social Counselling, Sports Facilities

Publishing house: University Press

Last Updated: 04/04/16

STATE UNIVERSITY OF RIO GRANDE DO SUL

Universidade Estadual do Rio Grande do Sul (UERGS)

Rua 7 de Setembro, 1156, Centro, Porto Alegre, Rio Grande do Sul 90010-191

Tel: +55(51) 3288-9000

Fax: +55(51) 3288-9000

EMail: proens@uergs.edu.br; rodrigo-sanchotene@uergs.edu.br

Website: http://www.uergs.edu.br

Reitora: Arisa Araujo da Luz
Tel: +55(51) 3288-9010 EMail: reitor@uergs.edu.br

Pró-Reitor de Administração: Ismael Mauri Gewehr Ramadam
Tel: +55(51) 3288-9082
EMail: max-segala@uergs.edu.br; proap@uergs.edu.br

Area

Exact Sciences and Engineering (Automation and Control Engineering; Biotechnology; Computer Engineering; Energy Engineering); **Humanities** (Administration; Agricultural Management; Dance; Health Administration; Industrial Management; Literature; Music; Pedagogy; Portuguese; Public Administration; Rural Planning; Teacher Training; Theatre; Visual Arts); **Life and Environmental Sciences** (Agricultural Business; Agriculture; Agronomy; Biological and Life Sciences; Coastal Studies; Environmental Management; Fishery; Food Science; Food Technology; Fruit Production; Marine Biology)

Further Information: Also Units in Alegrete, Bagé, Bento Gonçalves, Botucaraí - Soledade, Cachoeira do Sul, Caxias do Sul, Cruz Alta, Encantado, Erechim, Frederico Westphalen, Guaíba, Litoral Norte - Osório, Montenegro, Novo Hamburgo, Sananduva, Santa Cruz do Sul, Santana do Livramento, São Borja, São Francisco de Paula, São Luiz Gonzaga, Tapes, Três Passos, Vacaria

History: Founded 2001.

Main Language(s) of Instruction: Portuguese

Degrees and Diplomas: *Tecnólogo*; *Bacharelado*; *Licenciatura*; *Especialização/Aperfeiçoamento*: **Adult Education; Agriculture; Computer Science; Curriculum; Ecology; Educational Administration; Educational Sciences; Environmental Studies; Farm Management; Food Science; Food Technology; Literacy Education; Music Education; Regional Planning; Safety Engineering; Social Studies; Teacher Training.** *Mestrado*: **Environmental Studies.**

Student Services: Library

Last Updated: 29/02/16

STATE UNIVERSITY OF RORAIMA

Universidade Estadual de Roraima (UERR)

Rua 7 de Setembro, 231, Canarinho, Boa Vista, Roraima 69306-530

Tel: +55(95) 2121-0909 +55(95) 2121-0934

Fax: +55(95) 2121-0925

EMail: reitoria@uerr.edu.br; registro@uerr.edu.br

Website: http://www.uerr.edu.br

Reitor: Regys Odlare Lima de Freitas
Tel: +55(95) 2121-0950 EMail: reitoria@uerr.edu.br

Vice-Reitor: Elemar Favreto
Tel: +55(95) 2121-0911 EMail: vice-reitoria@uerr.edu.br

Pró-Reitoria de Planejamento e Administração: Mariano Terço de Melo Tel: +55(95) 2121-0919 EMail: proplad@uerr.edu.br

Course

Accountancy *(Alto Alegre, Caracaraí, São Luiz do Anauá, Rorainópolis)* (Accountancy); **Administration** *(Boa Vista, Iracema, Normandia, São João da Baliza)* (Management); **Agronomy** *(Alto Alegre, Rorainópolis, Normandia)* (Agronomy); **Biological Sciences** *(Mucajaí, Boa Vista)* (Biological and Life Sciences); **Chemistry** *(Rorainópolis, Boa Vista)* (Chemistry); **Computer Science** *(Caracaraí, Pacaraima)* (Computer Science); **Foreign Trade** *(Pacaraima)* (International Business); **Forestry Engineering** *(São João da Baliza)* (Agricultural Engineering; Forestry); **Geography** (Geography); **History** *(Boa Vista, São Luiz do Anauá)* (History); **Law** *(Boa Vista, Caracaraí)* (Law); **Literature** *(Boa Vista, Bonfim, Mucajaí, Rorainópolis, Pacaraima)* (Literature); **Mathematics** *(Boa Vista, Caracaraí, São João da Baliza, Rorainópolis)* (Mathematics); **Natural Sciences** (Natural Sciences); **Nursing** *(Alto Alegre, Boa Vista)* (Nursing); **Pedagogy** *(Boa Vista, Caracaraí, Normandia, Rorainópolis, São Luiz do Anauá)* (Pedagogy); **Philosophy** *(Boa*

Vista, Rorainópolis) (Philosophy); **Physical Education** *(Mucajaí)* (Physical Education); **Physics** (Physics); **Public Safety** (Safety Engineering); **Social Services** *(Mucajaí)* (Social and Community Services); **Sociology** *(Boa Vista, São João da Baliza)* (Sociology); **Tourism** *(Caracaraí, Pacaraima)* (Tourism)

Further Information: Also Campuses in Rorainópolis, Alto Alegre, Caracaraí, São João da Baliza and Pacaraima

History: Founded 2005.

Main Language(s) of Instruction: Portuguese

Degrees and Diplomas: *Bacharelado*; *Licenciatura*; *Especialização/Aperfeiçoamento*: **Education; Educational Administration; Gynaecology and Obstetrics; Higher Education; Nursing.** *Mestrado*: **Agriculture; Biology; Ecology; Education; Fishery; Science Education.** *Doutorado*: **Arts and Humanities; Biology; Fishery; Geography (Human); Literature; Mathematics Education; Science Education.**

Last Updated: 04/04/16

STATE UNIVERSITY OF SANTA CRUZ

Universidade Estadual de Santa Cruz (UESC)

Campus Soane Nazaré de Andrade, Rodovia Jorge Amado, Km 16, Bairro Salobrinho, Ilhéus, Bahia 45662-900
Tel: +55(73) 3680-5002
Fax: +55(73) 3689-1126
EMail: reitoria@uesc.br
Website: http://www.uesc.br

Reitora: Adélia Maria Carvalho de Melo Pinheiro
Tel: +55(73) 3680-5311 EMail: reitoria@uesc.br

Pró-Reitor de Administração e Finanças: Elson Cedro Mira
Tel: +55(73) 3680-5008 EMail: proad@uesc.br

Vice-Reitor: Evandro Sena Freire
Tel: +55(73) 3680-5005 EMail: vice-reitoria@uesc.br

Department

Administration and Accountancy (DCAC) (Accountancy; Administration); **Agricultural and Environmental Sciences (DCAA)** (Agricultural Engineering; Agriculture; Agronomy; Geography; Veterinary Science); **Biological Sciences (DCB)** (Biology; Biomedicine); **Economics (DCEC)** (Economics); **Education (DCIE)** (Education; Educational Sciences); **Exact Sciences and Technology (DCET)** (Chemical Engineering; Chemistry; Civil Engineering; Computer Engineering; Computer Science; Electrical Engineering; Mathematics; Mathematics and Computer Science; Mathematics Education; Mechanical Engineering; Physics; Science Education); **Health Sciences (DCS)** (Health Sciences; Medicine; Nursing; Physical Education); **Law (DCIJUR)** (Law); **Letters and Arts (DLA)** (Arts and Humanities; English; French; International Business; Literature; Mass Communication; Modern Languages; Portuguese; Spanish; Writing); **Philosophy and Human Sciences (DFCH)** (History; Philosophy; Social Sciences)

Centre

Biotechnology and Genetics (CBG) (Biotechnology; Genetics); **Documentation and Regional Memory Studies (CEDOC)** (Archiving; Regional Studies); **Electron Microscopy Centre (CME)** (Physics); **Hélio Simões Portuguese Studies Centre (CEPHAS)** (Portuguese)

Research Centre

Research Centre for Science and Technology Radiation (CPqCTR) (Physics)

History: Founded 1972. A State institution.

Academic Year: March to December

Admission Requirements: Secondary school certificate and entrance examination

Main Language(s) of Instruction: Portuguese

Degrees and Diplomas: *Bacharelado*: **Accountancy; Administration; Agronomy; Biological and Life Sciences; Biomedicine; Chemical Engineering; Chemistry; Civil Engineering; Computer Science; Economics; Electrical Engineering; English; Geography; International Business; Law; Mass Communication; Mathematics; Mechanical Engineering; Medicine; Nursing; Physics; Production Engineering; Veterinary Science.** *Licenciatura*: **Arts and Humanities; Biological and Life Sciences; Chemistry; Geography; History; Humanities and Social Science Education; Mathematics; Mathematics Education; Pedagogy; Philosophy; Physical Education; Physics; Science Education; Social Sciences.** *Especialização/Aperfeiçoamento*: **Accountancy; Agriculture; Art Management; Ecology; Educational Administration; Finance; Foreign Languages Education; History; Humanities and Social Science Education; Industrial and Production Economics; Linguistics; Mathematics Education; Physical Education; Preschool Education; Science Education; Special Education; Sports; Teacher Training; Town Planning.** *Mestrado*: **Arts and Humanities; Botany; Chemistry; Computer Graphics; Computer Science; Development Studies; Economic and Finance Policy; Health Sciences; Humanities and Social Science Education; Literature; Materials Engineering; Mathematics Education; Primary Education; Regional Planning; Science Education; Tropical Agriculture; Zoology.** *Doutorado*: **Biology; Biotechnology; Ecology; Environmental Management; Genetics; Microbiology; Molecular Biology; Vegetable Production; Zoology.** Also Postgraduate Diploma in Development Studies and Environmental Studies (PPGDMA)

Student Services: Academic Counselling, Canteen, Cultural Activities, Language Laboratory, Library, Sports Facilities

Publications: Especiaria; Kàwé

Publishing House: Editus

Last Updated: 04/04/16

STATE UNIVERSITY OF THE CENTRE-WEST

Universidade Estadual do Centro-Oeste (UNICENTRO)

Rua Salvatore Renna - Padre, Salvador, 875 - Santa Cruz, Santa Cruz, Guarapuava, Paraná 85010990
Tel: +55(42) 622-4600 +55(42) 621-1000
Fax: +55(42) 623-8644
EMail: tais@unicentro.br; webmail@unicentro.br
Website: http://www.unicentro.br

Reitor: Aldo Nelson Bona Tel: +55(42) 621-1008

Vice-Reitor: Osmar Ambrósio de Souza

Pró-Reitor de Administração e Finanças: Amarildo Hersen
Tel: +55(42) 3621-1077

Sector

Agrarian and Environmental Sciences (Agricultural Engineering; Agronomy; Biological and Life Sciences; Environmental Engineering; Forestry; Geography; Horticulture; Mathematics; Veterinary Science); **Applied Social Sciences** (Accountancy; Administration; Economics; Secretarial Studies; Social and Community Services; Tourism); **Exact Sciences and Technology** (Applied Chemistry; Chemistry; Computer Science; Engineering; Food Science; Mathematics; Physics); **Health Sciences** (Health Sciences; Nursing; Nutrition; Pharmacy; Physical Education; Physical Therapy; Psychology; Speech Therapy and Audiology); **Human Sciences, Letters and Arts** (Art Education; Arts and Humanities; Education; English; History; Literature; Mass Communication; Pedagogy; Philosophy; Portuguese; Spanish)

Further Information: Campus at Irati, and branches at Laranjeiras do Sul, Pitanga, Prudentópolis and Chopinzinho. Also Polytechnic Centre (CEDETEG)

History: Founded 1990 incorporating existing faculties. Acquired present status 1997. A State institution.

Academic Year: February to November (February-June; August-November)

Admission Requirements: Secondary school certificate and entrance examination

Fees: None

Main Language(s) of Instruction: Portuguese, English, French, Italian, Spanish

Accrediting Agency: Parana State Government

Degrees and Diplomas: *Bacharelado*; *Licenciatura*; *Especialização/Aperfeiçoamento*: **Business Administration; Economics; Educational Administration; Finance; Higher Education Teacher Training; Mass Communication; Media Studies; Orthopaedics; Physical Therapy; Rehabilitation and Therapy; Sports Medicine; Veterinary Science.** *Mestrado*: **Agronomy; Arts and Humanities; Biology; Business Administration; Chemistry; Education; Energy Engineering; Environmental Engineering; Forestry; Geography; History; Mathematics Education;**

Pharmacy; Sanitary Engineering; Science Education; Social and Community Services; Veterinary Science. *Doutorado*: **Agronomy; Chemistry; Horticulture.** Also MBA

Student Services: Academic Counselling, Canteen, Careers Guidance, Cultural Activities, Facilities for disabled people, Health Services, Language Laboratory, Library, Sports Facilities

Publications: Analecta; Revista Guairacá

Publishing House: Editora Universitária

Last Updated: 29/02/16

STATE UNIVERSITY OF THE NORTH OF PARANA

Universidade Estadual do Norte do Paraná (UENP)

Av. Getúlio Vargas, 850, Jacarézinho, Paranà 86400-000

Tel: +55(43) 3525-3589 +55(43) 3542-8098

Fax: +55(43) 3525-3589

EMail: gabinete@uenp.edu.br

Website: http://www.uenp.edu.br

Reitora: Fátima Aparecida da Cruz Padoan (2014-)
Tel: +55(43) 3525-3589 EMail: gabinete@uenp.edu.br

Pró-Reitor de Administração e Finanças: José Paulo Guandelini da Silva EMail: proaf@uenp.edu.br

Campus

Cornélio Procópio (UENP-CCP) (Accountancy; Biological and Life Sciences; Business Administration; Economics; Geography; Literature; Mathematics; Pedagogy); **Jacarezinho (UENP-CJ)** (Arts and Humanities; Biological and Life Sciences; Dentistry; English; History; Law; Literature; Mathematics; Pedagogy; Philosophy; Physical Education; Physical Therapy; Spanish); **Luiz Meneghel de Bandeirantes (UENP-CLM)** (Agronomy; Biological and Life Sciences; Computer Science; Information Technology; Nursing; Veterinary Science)

Further Information: Also Cornélio Procópio and Luiz Meneghel de Bandeirantes Campuses

History: Founded 2006.

Main Language(s) of Instruction: Portuguese

Degrees and Diplomas: *Bacharelado*; *Licenciatura*; *Especialização/Aperfeiçoamento*: **Clinical Psychology; Contemporary History; Cultural Studies; Economics; Educational Administration; Educational Psychology; English; Environmental Studies; Finance; Geography; History; Linguistics; Literature; Mathematics Education; Occupational Therapy; Physical Education; Physical Therapy; Portuguese; Public Health; Science Education; Sociology; Special Education; Sports.** *Mestrado*: **Agronomy; Arts and Humanities; Education; Law.** *Doutorado*: **Law.** Also Residency in Veterinary Science

Student Services: IT Centre, Library

Last Updated: 01/03/16

STATE UNIVERSITY OF THE VALLEY OF THE ACARAU

Universidade Estadual do Vale do Acaraú (UVA)

Av. da Universidade, 850, Campus da Betânia,
Sobral, Ceará 62040-370

Tel: +55(88) 3677-4271 +55(88) 3677-4229 +55(88) 3677-4223

Fax: +55(88) 677-4229 +55(88) 3613-1866

EMail: gabinetereitor@uvanet.br

Website: http://www.uvanet.br

Reitor: Fabianno Cavalcante de Carvalho
Tel: +55(88) 677-4223 EMail: reitoria@uvanet.br

Pró-Reitor de Administração: Raimundo Valmir Leite Filho

Centre

Agrarian and Biological Sciences (CCAB) (Animal Husbandry; Biology; Science Education); **Applied Social Sciences (CCSA)** (Accountancy; Business Administration; Law); **Exact Sciences and Technology (CCET)** (Chemistry; Civil Engineering; Computer Science; Construction Engineering; Mathematics; Physics; Technology); **Health Sciences (CCS)** (Health Sciences; Nursing; Physical Education; Sports); **Human Sciences (CCH)** (Geography; History; Humanities and Social Science Education; Social Sciences); **Philosophy, Letters and Education (CENFLE)** (Arts and Humanities; Pedagogy; Philosophy)

Further Information: Also campuses at: Nova Russas, Camocim, Tianguá, Santa Quitéria, Canindé, Acaraú, Três Lagoas.

History: Founded 1968, acquired present status 1994.

Admission Requirements: Secondary school certificate and entrance examination

Main Language(s) of Instruction: Portuguese

Degrees and Diplomas: *Bacharelado*; *Licenciatura*; *Especialização/Aperfeiçoamento*: **Accountancy; Agricultural Business; Alternative Medicine; Animal Husbandry; Biochemistry; Biological and Life Sciences; Business Administration; Civil Law; Clinical Psychology; Community Health; Computer Science; Constitutional Law; Educational Administration; Educational Psychology; English; Health Administration; Health Sciences; History; Humanities and Social Science Education; Industrial Management; Justice Administration; Labour Law; Linguistics; Literacy Education; Literature; Management; Marketing; Mathematics Education; Molecular Biology; Nursing; Philosophy; Physical Education; Portuguese; Preschool Education; Public Administration; Rehabilitation and Therapy; Safety Engineering; Science Education; Social Studies; Social Welfare; Spanish; Special Education; Sports.** *Mestrado*: **Animal Husbandry; Community Health.**

Student Services: Academic Counselling, Canteen, Careers Guidance, Cultural Activities, Facilities for disabled people, Health Services, Language Laboratory, Library, Nursery Care, Social Counselling, Sports Facilities

Publications: Essentia

Publishing House: Edições UVA

Last Updated: 01/03/16

STATE UNIVERSITY OF WESTERN PARANÁ

Universidade Estadual do Oeste do Paraná (UNIOESTE)

R. Universitária, 1619, Universitário, Cascavel, Paraná 85819-110

Tel: +55(45) 3220-3000

Fax: +55(45) 3324-4590

EMail: gabinete@unioeste.br

Website: http://www.unioeste.br

Reitor: Paulo Sergio Wolff
Tel: +55(45) 3220-3090
EMail: gabinete@unioeste.br; jessica.farias@unioeste.br; marli.santos@unioeste.br

Pró-Reitora de Administração e Finanças: Rosiclei Fátima Luft
Tel: +55(45) 3220-3097

Campus

Cascavel (Accountancy; Agricultural Engineering; Arts and Humanities; Biological and Life Sciences; Business Administration; Civil Engineering; Computer Science; Dentistry; Economics; Health Education; Humanities and Social Science Education; Literature; Mathematics Education; Medicine; Nursing; Pedagogy; Pharmacy; Physical Therapy; Portuguese; Science Education; Spanish); **Foz do Iguaçu** (Accountancy; Business Administration; Computer Science; Electrical Engineering; Health Education; Hotel Management; Humanities and Social Science Education; Law; Literature; Mathematics Education; Mechanical Engineering; Nursing; Pedagogy; Portuguese; Spanish; Tourism); **Francisco Beltrão** (Business Administration; Economics; Environmental Studies; Geography; Geological Engineering; Law; Medicine; Nutrition; Pedagogy; Science Education; Social and Community Services); **Marechal Cândido Rondon** (Accountancy; Agronomy; Animal Husbandry; Arts and Humanities; Business Administration; English; Geography; History; Humanities and Social Science Education; Law; Literature; Physical Education; Portuguese; Science Education; Spanish); **Toledo** (Agricultural Engineering; Chemical Engineering; Chemistry; Economics; Fishery; Humanities and Social Science Education; Philosophy; Science Education; Secretarial Studies; Social and Community Services)

History: Founded 1987 as State Foundation Federation of Higher Education of West Parana, incorporating four Municipal Faculties. Became Foundation State University of West Parana 1988, and acquired present status and title 1994. Now composed of 5 campuses.

Academic Year: February to November

Admission Requirements: Secondary school certificate and entrance examination

Main Language(s) of Instruction: Portuguese

Degrees and Diplomas: *Bacharelado*; *Licenciatura*; *Especialização/Aperfeiçoamento*: **Business Administration; Dental Technology; Education; Mathematics Education.** *Mestrado*: **Accountancy; Agricultural Business; Agricultural Engineering; Agronomy; Animal Husbandry; Arts and Humanities; Biological and Life Sciences; Business Administration; Chemical Engineering; Computer Engineering; Cultural Studies; Dentistry; Development Studies; Economics; Education; Electrical Engineering; Energy Engineering; Environmental Studies; Fishery; Geography; Health Sciences; History; Natural Resources; Pharmacy; Philosophy; Public Health; Regional Planning; Social Sciences; Social Studies; Social Work; Technology.** *Doutorado*: **Agricultural Business; Agricultural Engineering; Agronomy; Animal Husbandry; Arts and Humanities; Chemical Engineering; Cultural Studies; Development Studies; Fishery; History; Philosophy; Regional Planning; Social Studies.** Also Especifico da Profissão; MBA

Student Services: Canteen, Careers Guidance, Cultural Activities, Health Services, Library, Sports Facilities, eLibrary

Publications: Ciências Sociais Aplicadas; Faz Ciência; Línguas e Letras; Plural Space Journal; Science Sociais em Perspectiva; Temas & Matizes; Time of Science; Times Históricos Magazine; Varia Scientia

Last Updated: 01/03/16

TEACHER TRAINING FACULTY OF AFOGADOS DA INGAZEIRA

Faculdade de Formação de Professores de Afogados da Ingazeira (FAFOPAI)

Rua Dr. Osvaldo Gouveia, s/n,
Afogados da Ingazeira, PE 56800-000
Tel: +55(81) 3838-1579 +55(81) 3838-1765
Fax: +55(81) 3838-1579 +55(81) 3838-1765
EMail: aedai@terra.com.br; aedai@zaz.com.br
Website: http://www.aedaifafopai.com

Diretora: Maria do Socorro Dias Marques Pessoa

Diretora-Pedagógica: Maria de Fátima Oliveira

Course
History (History); **Literature** (English; Literature; Portuguese); **Mathematics** (Mathematics); **Pedagogy** (Pedagogy)

History: Founded 1986.

Main Language(s) of Instruction: Portuguese

Degrees and Diplomas: *Licenciatura*

Student Services: Library

Last Updated: 08/07/15

TEACHER TRAINING FACULTY OF ARARIPINA

Faculdade de Formação de Professores de Araripina (FAFOPA)

Avenida Florentino Alves Batista s/n, Araripina,
PE 56280000
Tel: +55(81) 3873-1001
Fax: +55(81) 3873-1001
EMail: fafopa@bol.com.br; diretor_fafopa@portalaeda.edu.br
Website: http://portalaeda.edu.br/fafopa

Diretor: Jamilson Bandeira

Course
Biology (Biology); **Chemistry** (Chemistry); **Geography** (Geography); **History** (History); **Literature** (Literature); **Mathematics** (Mathematics); **Pedagogy** (Pedagogy); **Physics** (Physics)

History: Founded 1979

Main Language(s) of Instruction: Portuguese

Degrees and Diplomas: *Licenciatura*

Last Updated: 08/07/15

TEACHER TRAINING FACULTY OF MATA SUL

Faculdade de Formação de Professores da Mata Sul (FAMASUL)

Br 101 Km 186 Sul, Campus Universitário, Engenho São Manoel,
Palmares, PE 55540-000
Tel: +55(81) 3661-0625
Fax: +55(81) 3661-0625
EMail: aemasul-famasul@bol.com.br; famasul2010@hotmail.com
Website: http://www.famasul.edu.br/2015

Diretor: Vilmar Antônio Carvalho

Coordenador de Administração: Francisco Elpídio Câmara

Course
Biological Sciences (Biological and Life Sciences); **Chemistry** (Chemistry); **Geography** (Geography); **Graduate Studies** (Biology; Chemistry; Education; Literature; Mathematics; Portuguese); **History** (History); **Literature** (Literature; Portuguese); **Mathematics** (Mathematics); **Pedagogy** (Pedagogy)

History: Founded 1970

Main Language(s) of Instruction: Portuguese

Degrees and Diplomas: *Licenciatura*; *Especialização/Aperfeiçoamento*: **Biology; Chemistry; Education; Literature; Mathematics; Portuguese.**

Last Updated: 08/07/15

TEACHER TRAINING FACULTY OF SERRA TALHADA

Faculdade de Formação de Professores de Serra Talhada (FAFOPST)

Avenida Afonso Magalhães, s/n, Prédio, Ns° da Conceição,
Serra Talhada, PE 56900-000
Tel: +55(87) 3831-2311
Fax: +55(81) 3831-2698
EMail: aeset@fafopst.com.br; profeitoza@yahoo.com.br

Diretora: Inaldo Dioniso Neto

Course
Biological Sciences (Biology); **Geography** (Geography); **History** (History); **Literature** (English; Literature); **Mathematics** (Mathematics); **Physical Education** (Physical Education); **Sciences** (Natural Sciences)

History: Founded 1983

Main Language(s) of Instruction: Portuguese

Degrees and Diplomas: *Licenciatura*

Last Updated: 09/07/15

TECHNICAL INSTITUTE OF AERONAUTICAL ENGINEERING

Instituto Tecnólogico de Aeronáutica (ITA)

Praça Marechal Eduardo Gomes 50 Vila das Acácias,
São José dos Campos, São Paulo 12228900
Tel: +55(12) 3947-5732
Fax: +55(12) 3941-3500
EMail: chefeidg@ita.br
Website: http://www.ita.br

Reitor: Anderson Ribeiro Correia EMail: reitor@ita.br

Course
Engineering (Aeronautical and Aerospace Engineering; Civil Engineering; Computer Engineering; Electronic Engineering; Mechanical Engineering)

History: Founded 1950.

Main Language(s) of Instruction: Portuguese

Degrees and Diplomas: *Bacharelado*; *Mestrado*: **Aeronautical and Aerospace Engineering; Astronomy and Space Science; Computer Engineering; Electronic Engineering; Physics.** *Doutorado*: **Aeronautical and Aerospace Engineering; Astronomy and Space Science; Computer Engineering; Electronic Engineering; Physics.**

Last Updated: 13/04/16

TECHNOLOGICAL FEDERAL UNIVERSITY OF PARANÁ

Universidade Tecnológica Federal do Paraná (UTFPR)

Av. Sete de Setembro, 3165, Rebouças,
Curitibá, Paraná 80230-901
Tel: +55(41) 3310-4545
EMail: gadircwb@cefetpr.br; canta@utfpr.edu.br
Website: http://www.utfpr.edu.br

Reitor: Carlos Eduardo Cantarelli (2008-)
Tel: +55(41) 3310-4423
EMail: falecomoreitor@utfpr.edu.br; reitoria@utfpr.edu.br

Vice-Reitor: Luiz Alberto Pilatti
Tel: +55(41) 3310-4423 EMail: cleusaleite@utfpr.edu.br

Pró-Reitor de Planejamento e Administração: Sandroney Fochesatto
Tel: +55(41) 3310-4462 EMail: sandroney@utfpr.edu.br

Campus

Apucarana Campus (Civil Engineering; Computer Science; Electronic Engineering; Environmental Engineering; Food Technology; Science Education); **Campo Mourão Unit** (Civil Engineering; Computer Science; Electronic Engineering; Environmental Engineering; Food Technology; Science Education); **Cornélio Procópio Campus** (Automation and Control Engineering; Computer Engineering; Electrical Engineering; Electronic Engineering; Mathematics Education; Mechanical Engineering; Software Engineering; Systems Analysis); **Curitiba Campus** (Administration; Architecture; Automation and Control Engineering; Chemistry; Civil Engineering; Communication Studies; Computer Engineering; Design; Electrical and Electronic Equipment and Maintenance; Electrical Engineering; Electronic Engineering; English; Environmental Management; Graphic Design; Humanities and Social Science Education; Information Technology; Mathematics Education; Mechanical Engineering; Mechanical Equipment and Maintenance; Physical Education; Portuguese; Radiology; Science Education; Telecommunications Engineering; Town Planning); **Dois Vizinhos Campus** (Agricultural Engineering; Agriculture; Agronomy; Animal Husbandry; Bioengineering; Biological and Life Sciences; Biotechnology; Education; Forestry; Science Education; Software Engineering); **Francisco Beltrão** (Chemical Engineering; Computer Education; Environmental Engineering; Food Technology); **Guarapuava Campus**; **Londrina Campus** (Chemical Engineering; Environmental Engineering; Food Technology; Materials Engineering; Mechanical Engineering; Production Engineering; Science Education); **Medianeira Campus** (Computer Science; Electrical Engineering; Engineering; Environmental Engineering; Environmental Management; Food Technology; Industrial Maintenance; Production Engineering; Science Education); **Pato Branco Campus** (Accountancy; Administration; Agriculture; Agronomy; Chemistry; Civil Engineering; Computer Engineering; Electrical Engineering; Foreign Languages Education; Humanities and Social Science Education; Industrial Maintenance; Mathematics Education; Mechanical Engineering; Native Language Education; Systems Analysis); **Ponta Grossa Campus** (Automation and Control Engineering; Chemical Engineering; Computer Science; Electronic Engineering; Food Technology; Mechanical Engineering; Mechanical Equipment and Maintenance; Production Engineering; Science Education; Systems Analysis); **Santa Helena Campus** (Biological and Life Sciences; Computer Science); **Toledo Campus** (Bioengineering; Biotechnology; Chemistry; Civil Engineering; Computer Engineering; Computer Science; Electronic Engineering; Mathematics Education)

History: Founded 1909. Acquired present name and status 1998.

Main Language(s) of Instruction: Portuguese

Degrees and Diplomas: *Técnico de Nivel Medio*; *Tecnólogo*; *Bacharelado*; *Licenciatura*; *Especialização/Aperfeiçoamento*: **Accountancy; Automation and Control Engineering; Computer Graphics; Computer Networks; Data Processing; Educational Technology; Electrical Engineering; Electronic Engineering; Environmental Management; Finance; Foreign Languages Education; Gerontology; Linguistics; Management; Mathematics; Production Engineering; Safety Engineering; Small Business; Software Engineering.** *Mestrado*: **Administration; Agriculture; Agronomy; Animal Husbandry; Biochemistry; Biological and Life Sciences; Biomedical Engineering; Biotechnology; Business Computing; Chemical Engineering; Chemistry; Civil Engineering; Computer Engineering; Computer Science; Development Studies; Electrical Engineering; Energy Engineering; Environmental Engineering; Environmental Studies; Food Technology; Government; Humanities and Social Science Education; Linguistics; Literature; Materials Engineering; Mathematics; Mathematics Education; Mechanical Engineering; Production Engineering; Public Administration; Regional Studies; Science Education; Technology; Technology Education.** *Doutorado*: **Agronomy; Civil Engineering; Computer Engineering; Electrical Engineering; Materials Engineering; Mechanical Engineering; Production Engineering; Science Education; Technology; Technology Education.** Also MBA

Student Services: Library

Last Updated: 08/04/16

UNIRG UNIVERSITY CENTRE

Centro Universitario UNIRG

Av Guanabara N°1500 Esquina c/Av Engenheiro Bernado Sayão,
Gurupi, TO 77403-080
Tel: +55(63) 3612-7600
EMail: reitoria@unirg.edu.br
Website: http://www.unirg.edu.br

Reitora: Lady Sakay

Course

Accountancy (Accountancy); **Administration** (Administration); **Advertising** (Advertising and Publicity); **Civil Engineering** (Civil Engineering); **Computer Science** (Computer Science); **Dentistry** (Dentistry); **Journalism** (Journalism); **Law** (Law); **Literature** (Literature); **Medicine** (Medicine); **Nursing** (Nursing); **Pedagogy** (Pedagogy); **Pharmacy** (Pharmacy); **Physical Education** (Physical Education); **Physiotherapy** (Physical Therapy); **Psychology** (Psychology)

History: Founded 1985. Acquired present status and title 2008.

Main Language(s) of Instruction: Portuguese

Degrees and Diplomas: *Bacharelado*; *Licenciatura*; *Especialização/Aperfeiçoamento*

Student Services: Library

Last Updated: 03/07/15

UNIVERSITY CENTRE OF UNIÃO DA VITÓRIA

Centro Universitário de União da Vitória (UNIUV)

Avenida Bento Munhoz da Rocha Neto, 3856, São Basílio Magno,
União da Vitória, PR 84600-000
Tel: +55(42) 3522-1837
Fax: +55(42) 3522-1837
EMail: uniuv@uniuv.edu.br
Website: http://www.uniuv.edu.br

Reitor: Alysson Frantz

Vice-Reitor: Lucio Kurten dos Passos

Course

Accountancy (Accountancy); **Administration** (Administration); **Advertising and Publicity** (Advertising and Publicity); **Architecture and Urbanism** (Architecture; Town Planning); **Business Computing** (Business Computing); **Civil Engineering** (Civil Engineering); **Computer Science** (Computer Science; Information Technology); **Economics** (Economics); **Environmental Engineering** (Environmental Engineering); **Executive Secretarial Studies** (Secretarial Studies); **Graduate Studies** (Accountancy; Business Administration; Business and Commerce; Communication Studies; Computer Networks; Dance; Environmental Engineering; Finance; Forestry; Health Administration; Hotel Management; Human Resources; Information Technology; International Business; Marketing; Physical Education; Preschool Education; Primary Education; Production Engineering; Public Administration; Secretarial Studies; Special Education; Sports; Tourism); **Industrial Engineering** *(da Madeira)* (Industrial Engineering); **Journalism** (Journalism); **Ondontology** (Dentistry); **Physical Education** (Physical Education); **Tourism** (Tourism)

Further Information: Also São Mateus do Sul campus.

History: Founded 1974

Main Language(s) of Instruction: Portuguese

Accrediting Agency: Ministry of Education.

Degrees and Diplomas: *Bacharelado*; *Licenciatura*; *Especialização/Aperfeiçoamento*: **Information Management; Production Engineering.** *Mestrado*: **Business Administration; Human Resources; Marketing.** Also MBA.
Student Services: Library
Last Updated: 09/07/15

UNIVERSITY FOR THE DEVELOPMENT OF THE UPPER VALLEY OF THE ITAJAI

Universidade para o Desenvolvimento do Alto Vale do Itajaí (UNIDAVI)
Rua Doutor Guilherme Gemballa 13, Jardim América,
Rio do Sul, Santa Catarina 89160000
Tel: +55(47) 3531-6000
Fax: +55(47) 3531-6001
EMail: unidavi@unidavi.edu.br
Website: http://www.unidavi.edu.br

Reitor: Célio Simão Martignago EMail: reitoria@unidavi.edu.br

Pró-Reitoria de Administração: Alcir Texeira
EMail: proad@unidavi.edu.br

International Relations: Jeancarlo Visentainer
Tel: +55(47) 3531-6048 EMail: ri@unidavi.edu.br

Course

Accounting (Accountancy); **Administration** (Administration); **Advertising and Publicity** (Advertising and Publicity); **Architecture and Urbanism** (Architecture; Town Planning); **Civil Engineering** (Civil Engineering); **Economics** (Economics); **Graphic Design** (Graphic Design); **Industrial Chemistry** (Industrial Chemistry); **Information Systems** (Information Technology); **Institutional Communication** (Communication Studies); **Interior Design** (Interior Design); **International Business** (International Business); **Journalism** (Journalism); **Law** (Law); **Marketing** (Marketing); **Nursing** (Nursing); **Pedagogy** (Pedagogy); **Physical Education** (Physical Education); **Production Engineering** (Production Engineering); **Psychology** (Psychology); **Taió Campus** (Accountancy; Administration; Law)

Campus

Ituporanga Campus (Administration; Law); **Presidente Getúlio Campus** (Administration; Law)

History: Founded 1966.
Main Language(s) of Instruction: Portuguese
Degrees and Diplomas: *Bacharelado*; *Licenciatura*; *Especialização/Aperfeiçoamento*: **Business Administration; Civil Law; Communication Studies; Criminal Law; Environmental Studies; Graphic Design; Human Resources; Information Management; Interior Design; Law; Management; Metallurgical Engineering; Nursing; Occupational Health; Oncology; Physical Education; Psychology; Safety Engineering; Sports; Taxation.** *Mestrado*. Also MBA
Student Services: Library
Last Updated: 01/04/16

UNIVERSITY OF BRASÍLIA

Universidade de Brasília (UNB)
Campus Universitário Darcy Ribeiro s/n, Asa Norte,
Brasília, DF 70910-900
Tel: +55(61) 3307-2022 +55(61) 3307-1750 +55(61) 3307-260
Fax: +55(61) 3272-0003
EMail: unb@unb.br
Website: http://www.unb.br

Reitor: Ivan Marques de Toledo Camargo
Tel: +55(61) 3107-0247 +55(61) 3107-0248 EMail: unb@unb.br

Vice-Reitora: Sonia Báo EMail: agendavrt@unb.br

Decanato de Administração: Luís Afonso Bermúdez
Tel: +55(61) 3107-0362 EMail: daf@unb.br

International Relations: Heitti Satto, Director, Assessoria de Assuntos Internacionais
Tel: +55(61) 3107-0216 EMail: inter@unb.br

Faculty

Agronomy and Veterinary Medicine (FAV) (Agricultural Business; Agronomy; Veterinary Science); **Architecture and Town Planning (FAU)** (Architecture; Town Planning); **Communication (FAC)** (Advertising and Publicity; Communication Studies; Journalism; Mass Communication; Radio and Television Broadcasting); **Economics, Management, Accounting and Public Policy Management (FACE)** (Accountancy; Actuarial Science; Administration; Business and Commerce; Economic and Finance Policy; Economics); **Education (FE)** (Education; Educational Administration; Educational Sciences; Teacher Training); **Health Sciences (FS)** (Dentistry; Health Sciences; Nursing; Nutrition; Pharmacy; Public Health); **Information Science (FCI)** (Archiving; Library Science; Museum Studies); **Law (FD)** (Law); **Medicine (FM)** (Medicine); **Physical Education (FEF)** (Physical Education); **Technology (FT)** (Agricultural Engineering; Civil Engineering; Electrical Engineering; Environmental Engineering; Forestry; Mechanical Engineering); **UnB Ceilândia (FCE)** (Health Administration; Nursing; Occupational Therapy; Pharmacy; Physical Therapy; Speech Therapy and Audiology); **UnB Gama (FGA)** (Aeronautical and Aerospace Engineering; Automotive Engineering; Electronic Engineering; Energy Engineering; Engineering; Software Engineering); **UnB Planaltina (FUP)** (Agricultural Business; Agricultural Management; Education; Environmental Management; Natural Sciences)

Institute

Arts (IdA) (Fine Arts; Industrial Design; Music; Performing Arts; Theatre; Visual Arts); **Biological Sciences (IB)** (Biological and Life Sciences; Botany; Cell Biology; Ecology; Genetics; Physiology; Plant Pathology; Zoology); **Chemistry (IQ)** (Chemistry; Science Education); **Exact Sciences (IE)** (Computer Science; Mathematics; Statistics); **Geosciences (IG)** (Earth Sciences; Geology; Science Education); **Human Sciences (IH)** (Geography; History; Philosophy; Social and Community Services); **International Relations (IREL)** (International Relations); **Letters (IL)** (Classical Languages; English; French; Linguistics; Literature; Native Language; Portuguese; Translation and Interpretation); **Physics (IF)** (Physics; Science Education); **Political Science (IPOL)** (Political Sciences); **Psychology (IP)** (Clinical Psychology; Developmental Psychology; Educational Psychology; Industrial and Organizational Psychology; Psychology; Social Psychology); **Social Sciences (ICS)** (Anthropology; Sociology)

Centre

Advanced Multidisciplinary Studies (CEAM) (African American Studies; Asian Studies; Child Care and Development; Ethics; Gerontology; Higher Education; Human Rights; Modern Languages; Peace and Disarmament; Public Administration; Public Health; Regional Studies; Rural Studies; Social Policy; Statistics; Technology; Urban Studies; Women's Studies); **Applied Cartography and Geographic Information (CIGA)** (Surveying and Mapping); **Athos Bulcão Community**; **Bamboo and Natural Fibers Research and Application (CPAB)** (Textile Technology); **Black Coexistence (CCN)**; **Brazilian Services and Research on Proteins (CBSP)** (Health Sciences); **Cerrado da Chapada dos Veadeiros Studies (UnB Cerrado)**; **Condensed Matter Physics (CIFMC)** *(International)* (Mechanics; Physics); **Continuing Education (Interfoco)**; **Cultural Production and Education (CPCE)** (Cultural Studies; Education); **DF/HUB Oral Cancer (CCB DF)** (Oncology); **Digital Memory (CMD)** (Documentation Techniques; Heritage Preservation); **Distance Education (CEAD)**; **Economics and Finance Research (CIEF)** (Economics; Finance); **Edgar Graeff Documentation Centre (CEDIARTE)** (Architecture); **Events Selection and Promotion (COH)** (Public Relations); **Excellence in Tourism (CET)** (Hotel and Restaurant; Tourism); **Government and Public Administration Advanced Studies (CEAG)** (Government; Public Administration); **Informatics (CPD)** (Computer Science); **Integrated Territorial Planning (Ciord)** (Architectural and Environmental Design; Architecture and Planning; Regional Planning; Town Planning); **Interdisciplinary Transports Studies (CEFTRU)** (Transport and Communications); **Market Regulation Studies (CERME)** (Business Administration); **Medicine for the Elderly (CMI)** (Gerontology); **Nanoscience and Nanotechnology (CNANO)** (Biotechnology; Nanotechnology); **Olympic Centre (CO)** (Physical Education; Sports); **Planning (Ceplan)** (Town Planning); **Primatology** (Zoology); **Psychological Services and Studies (CAEP)** (Psychology); **Reference Centre in Nature Conservation and Recovery of Degraded Areas (CRAD)** (Environmental Management); **Research and Graduate Studies on the Americas (CEPPAC)** (American Studies); **Research in Information Architecture (CPAI)** (Information Sciences); **Research in Management, Innovation and Sustainability (CPGIS)** (Management); **Sports Studies and Leisure Development (CEDES)** (Leisure Studies; Sports); **Sustainable Development (CDS)** (Development Studies; Economics; Environmental Management; Meteorology; Natural

Sciences; Peace and Disarmament; Regional Planning); **Technological Development Support (CDT)** (Technology); **UNB Centre for Public Policy Studies, Research and Evaluation (DataUnB)** (Economic and Finance Policy)

Further Information: Also University Hospital

History: Founded 1962. The University is constituted as a State Foundation.

Academic Year: March to December (March-July; August-December)

Admission Requirements: Secondary school certificate and entrance examination

Main Language(s) of Instruction: Portuguese

Degrees and Diplomas: *Bacharelado*; *Licenciatura*; *Especialização/Aperfeiçoamento*: **Accountancy; Adult Education; Architectural Restoration; Architecture; Artificial Intelligence; Biological and Life Sciences; Christian Religious Studies; Civil Security; Classical Languages; Clinical Psychology; Constitutional Law; Cultural Studies; Dental Technology; Development Studies; Earth Sciences; Economic and Finance Policy; Economics; Education; Educational Administration; Educational Psychology; Engineering; Environmental Studies; Ethics; Finance; Government; Health Administration; Humanities and Social Science Education; Industrial and Organizational Psychology; Information Management; Information Technology; International Relations; Labour Law; Law; Literacy Education; Nursing; Pedagogy; Philosophy; Political Sciences; Protective Services; Psychoanalysis; Psychology; Public Law; Social Policy; Sports; Stomatology; Systems Analysis; Taxation; Town Planning; Tropical Medicine.** *Mestrado*: **Accountancy; Administration; Agricultural Business; Agricultural Engineering; Agriculture; American Studies; Anthropology; Applied Linguistics; Architecture; Behavioural Sciences; Biological and Life Sciences; Botany; Chemistry; Civil Engineering; Clinical Psychology; Computer Science; Cultural Studies; Developmental Psychology; Ecology; Economics; Education; Electrical Engineering; Electronic Engineering; Environmental Engineering; Environmental Studies; Fine Arts; Forestry; Geography (Human); Geological Engineering; Geology; Health Sciences; History; Hydraulic Engineering; Industrial and Organizational Psychology; Information Sciences; International Relations; Law; Linguistics; Literature; Mass Communication; Mathematics; Mechanical Engineering; Medicine; Molecular Biology; Music; Nutrition; Pathology; Philosophy; Physical Education; Physics; Plant Pathology; Political Sciences; Psychology; Social Psychology; Sociology; Town Planning; Transport Engineering; Tropical Medicine.** *Doutorado*: **Agricultural Engineering; American Studies; Anthropology; Architecture; Biological and Life Sciences; Chemistry; Cultural Studies; Ecology; Economics; Education; Electrical Engineering; Environmental Engineering; Environmental Management; Forestry; Geological Engineering; Geology; Health Sciences; History; Hydraulic Engineering; Information Sciences; International Relations; Law; Linguistics; Literature; Mass Communication; Mathematics; Mechanical Engineering; Medicine; Molecular Biology; Pathology; Physics; Plant Pathology; Psychology; Social Policy; Sociology; Town Planning; Transport Engineering; Tropical Medicine.**

Student Services: Academic Counselling, Canteen, Careers Guidance, Cultural Activities, Facilities for disabled people, Foreign Studies Centre, Health Services, Language Laboratory, Library, Nursery Care, Social Counselling, Sports Facilities

Publications: Diogens; Documentação Atualidade Política; Revista Humanidades

Publishing House: Editora Universidade de Brasília

Academic Staff *2015-2016*: Total 2,445

Last Updated: 07/04/16

UNIVERSITY OF PERNAMBUCO

Universidade de Pernambuco (UPE)

Avenida Agamenon Magalhães, s/n, Santo Amaro,
Recife, Pernambuco 50100-010

Tel: +55(81) 3183-3674 +55(81) 3183-3778

Fax: +55(81) 3416-4129 +55(81) 3183-4000

EMail: prograd@upe.br

Website: http://www.upe.br

Reitor: Pedro Henrique de Barros Falcão EMail: reitor@upe.br

Vice-Reitora: Maria do Socorro de Mendonça Cavalcanti EMail: vicereitor@upe.br

Pró-Reitoria de Administração e Finanças: Rivaldo Mendes de Albuquerque
Tel: +55(81) 3183-3651 EMail: rivaldo.mendes@upe.br

International Relations: José Guido Corrêa de Araújo, Assessor de Relações Internacionais
Tel: +55(81) 3183-3662 EMail: internacional@upe.br

Course

Distance Education (Biological and Life Sciences; Literature; Pedagogy; Public Administration)

Campus

Arcoverde Campus (Dentistry; Law); **Benfica Campus** (Administration; Automation and Control Engineering; Civil Engineering; Computer Engineering; Electrical and Electronic Engineering; Electrical Engineering; Industrial Engineering; Mechanical Engineering; Telecommunications Engineering); **Camaragibe Campus** (Dentistry; Law); **Caruaru Campus** (Administration; Information Technology); **Garanhuns Campus** (Biological and Life Sciences; Computer Science; English; Geography (Human); History; Humanities and Social Science Education; Literature; Mathematics Education; Medicine; Pedagogy; Portuguese; Psychology; Science Education); **Mata Norte Campus** (Biological and Life Sciences; English; Geography (Human); History; Humanities and Social Science Education; Literature; Mathematics Education; Pedagogy; Portuguese; Science Education; Transport Management); **Palmares Campus** (Social and Community Services); **Petrolina Campus** (Biological and Life Sciences; English; Geography (Human); History; Humanities and Social Science Education; Literature; Mathematics Education; Nursing; Nutrition; Pedagogy; Physical Therapy; Portuguese; Science Education); **Salgueiro Campus** (Administration); **Santo Amaro Campus** (Biological and Life Sciences; Humanities and Social Science Education; Medicine; Nursing; Physical Education; Public Health); **Serra Talhada Campus** (Medicine)

History: Founded 1960.

Admission Requirements: Secondary school certificate and entrance examination

Main Language(s) of Instruction: Portuguese

Degrees and Diplomas: *Tecnólogo*; *Bacharelado*; *Licenciatura*; *Especialização/Aperfeiçoamento*: **Administration; Anaesthesiology; Applied Linguistics; Business and Commerce; Cardiology; Community Health; Computer Engineering; Construction Engineering; Dental Technology; Dentistry; Dermatology; Educational Administration; Educational Psychology; Energy Engineering; Environmental Management; Environmental Studies; Finance; Gerontology; Gynaecology and Obstetrics; Haematology; Health Administration; Health Sciences; Human Resources; Humanities and Social Science Education; Industrial Engineering; Industrial Maintenance; Literature; Management; Mathematics Education; Medicine; Metallurgical Engineering; Microbiology; Molecular Biology; Native Language Education; Neurology; Nursing; Oncology; Paediatrics; Physical Education; Portuguese; Psychiatry and Mental Health; Public Administration; Public Health; Radiology; Rehabilitation and Therapy; Safety Engineering; Science Education; Software Engineering; Sports; Surgery; Urology.** *Mestrado*: **Arts and Humanities; Cell Biology; Civil Engineering; Computer Engineering; Dentistry; Development Studies; Education; Energy Engineering; Forensic Medicine and Dentistry; Health Sciences; Literature; Molecular Biology; Nursing; Physical Education; Psychiatry and Mental Health.** *Doutorado*: **Cell Biology; Dentistry; Health Sciences; Molecular Biology; Nursing; Physical Education.** Also Postgraduate Interdisciplinary Teacher Training and Practice Degree (PPGFPPI); MBA; Medical Residencies

Student Services: Canteen

Last Updated: 31/03/16

UNIVERSITY OF RIO VERDE

Universidade de Rio Verde (UNIRV)

Fazenda Fontes do Saber, Caixa Postal 104,
Rio Verde, GO 75901-970

Tel: +55(64) 3611-2200 +55(64) 3611-2205

Fax: +55(64) 3611-2201 +55(64) 3611-2204

EMail: secretaria@fesurv.br; helemi@unirv.edu.br

Website: http://www.fesurv.br

Reitor: Sebastião Lázaro Pereira
Tel: +55(64) 3611-2200
EMail: spereira@fesurv.br; reitoria@unirv.edu.br
Vice-Reitora: Maria Flavina das Graças Costa

Pró-Reitor de Administração e Planejamento: Alberto Barella Netto

Campus

Aparecida (Medicine); **Caiapônia Campus** (Administration; Environmental Engineering; Law; Physical Education); **Goianésia** (Medicine); **Rio Verde Campus** (Accountancy; Administration; Agronomy; Biological and Life Sciences; Civil Engineering; Dentistry; Environmental Engineering; Graphic Design; Interior Design; Law; Mechanical Engineering; Medicine; Nursing; Nutrition; Pedagogy; Pharmacy; Physical Education; Physical Therapy; Production Engineering; Psychology; Software Engineering; Veterinary Science)

Further Information: Also Aparecida and Goianésia Campuses

History: Founded 1973.

Main Language(s) of Instruction: Portuguese

Degrees and Diplomas: *Bacharelado*; *Licenciatura*; *Especialização/Aperfeiçoamento*: **Administrative Law; Agricultural Business; Agricultural Management; Civil Law; Communication Studies; Constitutional Law; Criminal Law; Educational Administration; Environmental Studies; Finance; Human Resources; Industrial Management; Labour Law; Management; Marketing; Mathematics; Pharmacology; Preschool Education; Public Health; Public Law; Safety Engineering; Statistics; Teacher Training; Transport Management.** *Mestrado*: **Crop Production.** Also MBA

Student Services: Library
Last Updated: 31/03/16

UNIVERSITY OF SÃO PAULO

Universidade de São Paulo (USP)
Rua da Reitoria 109, Cidade Universitária Butantã,
São Paulo, São Paulo 05508-900
Tel: +55(11) 3091-3500
Fax: +55(11) 3815-5665
EMail: gr@usp.br
Website: http://www.usp.br

Reitor: João Grandino Rodas (2009-) EMail: gr@usp.br
Provost for Culture and Extension: Ruy Alberto Corrêa Altafim
Secretária Geral: Maria Fidela de Lima Navarro
Tel: +55(11) 3091-3414

International Relations: Adnei Melges de Andrade, Vice-Rector, International Relations
Tel: +55(11) 3091-2249 EMail: ccint@usp.br

Faculty

Animal Husbandry and Food Engineering *(Pirassununga)* (Animal Husbandry; Food Science); **Architecture and Urbanism** (Architecture; Design; Town Planning); **Economics, Administration and Accountancy** *(Ribeirão Preto)* (Accountancy; Administration; Economics); **Economics, Administration and Accountancy; Education** (Education; Pedagogy); **Law** (Civil Law; Commercial Law; Criminal Law; Forensic Medicine and Dentistry; International Law; Labour Law; Law); **Law** *(Ribeirão Preto)* (Law); **Medicine** *(Ribeirão Preto)* (Medicine); **Medicine** (Cardiology; Dermatology; Gastroenterology; Medicine; Pneumology; Surgery); **Odontology** *(Bauru)* (Dentistry); **Odontology** (Dentistry); **Odontology** *(Ribeirão Preto)* (Dentistry); **Pharmaceutical Sciences** (Food Science; Nutrition; Pharmacy); **Pharmaceutical Sciences** *(Ribeirão Preto)* (Pharmacy); **Philosophy, Arts, and Human Sciences** (Anthropology; Arts and Humanities; Classical Languages; Comparative Literature; History; Linguistics; Literature; Modern Languages; Oriental Languages; Philosophy; Political Sciences; Psychology; Social Sciences; Sociology); **Philosophy, Science, and Letters** *(Ribeirão Preto)* (Biology; Chemistry; Education; Geology; Mathematics; Natural Sciences; Philosophy; Physics; Psychology); **Public Health** (Epidemiology; Nutrition; Public Health); **Veterinary Medicine and Animal Husbandry** (Animal Husbandry; Pathology; Veterinary Science)

School

Agriculture *(Luiz de Queiroz, Piracicaba)* (Agricultural Business; Agriculture; Biology; Entomology; Floriculture; Nutrition; Plant Pathology; Soil Science); **Arts, Sciences and Humanities; Communications and Arts** (Cinema and Television; Documentation Techniques; Fine Arts; Journalism; Library Science; Music; Painting and Drawing; Performing Arts; Public Relations; Publishing and Book Trade; Radio and Television Broadcasting; Sculpture; Theatre; Tourism); **Engineering** *(São Carlos)* (Architecture and Planning; Electrical Engineering; Engineering; Geological Engineering; Hydraulic Engineering; Materials Engineering; Mechanical Engineering; Sanitary Engineering; Structural Architecture; Transport and Communications); **Engineering** *(Lorena)*; **Nursing** *(Ribeirão Preto)* (Nursing); **Nursing** (Nursing); **Physical Education** *(Ribeirão Preto)* (Physical Education); **Physical Education** (Physical Education); **Polytechnic** (Civil Engineering; Computer Engineering; Engineering; Hydraulic Engineering; Mechanical Engineering; Metallurgical Engineering; Mining Engineering; Naval Architecture; Production Engineering; Sanitary Engineering; Structural Architecture; Technology; Transport and Communications; Transport Engineering)

Institute

Advanced Studies (Environmental Studies; History; International Studies); **Astronomy, Geophysics and Atmospheric Science** (Astronomy and Space Science; Geophysics; Seismology); **Biomedical Sciences** (Biomedicine; Cell Biology; Immunology; Microbiology; Pathology); **Biosciences** (Biochemistry; Biomedicine; Biophysics); **Brazilian Studies** (Latin American Studies); **Chemistry** (Chemistry); **Chemistry** *(São Carlos)* (Chemistry); **Electrotechnical and Power Engineering** (Electrical and Electronic Engineering; Power Engineering); **Geosciences** (Geology; Mineralogy); **International Relations; Mathematical Sciences and Computers** *(São Carlos)* (Computer Science; Mathematics); **Mathematics and Statistics** (Mathematics; Statistics); **Oceanography** (Marine Science and Oceanography); **Physics** *(São Carlos)* (Physics); **Physics** (Physics); **Psychology** (Psychology); **Tropical Medicine** (Tropical Medicine)

Centre

Marine Biology (Marine Biology); **Nuclear Power in Agriculture** (Nuclear Engineering)

Further Information: Also 2 University Hospitals at São Paulo and Bauru

History: Founded 1934. An autonomous institution under the jurisdiction of and financially supported by the State of São Paulo.

Academic Year: March to December (March-June; August-December)

Admission Requirements: Secondary school certificate and entrance examination

Fees: None

Main Language(s) of Instruction: Portuguese

Accrediting Agency: Ministério da Educação

Degrees and Diplomas: *Bacharelado*; *Licenciatura*; *Especialização/Aperfeiçoamento*; *Mestrado*; *Doutorado*

Student Services: Academic Counselling, Canteen, Cultural Activities, Facilities for disabled people, Foreign Studies Centre, Health Services, Language Laboratory, Nursery Care, Social Counselling, Sports Facilities

Publications: Almanack Braziliense; Anais do Museu Paulista: História e Cultura Material; Arquivos de Zoologia; Boletim de Botânica; Brazilian Journal of Oceanography; Brazilian Journal of Veterinary Research and Animal Science; Brazilian Oral Research; Cadernos CERU; Cadernos de Psicologia Social do Trabalho; Clinics; Comunicação e Educação; Educação e Pesquisa; Estilos de Clínica; Estudos Avançados; Estudos Econômicos; Fisioterapia e Pesquisa; Geologia USP - Série Científica; Journal of Applied Oral Science; Journal of Comparative Biology; Paisagem e Ambiente; Papéis Avulsos de Zoologia; Pesquisa em Edução Ambiental; Psicologia USP; Resenhas; Revista Acolhendo a Alfabetização em Países de Língua Portuguesa; Revista Brasileira de Ciências Farmacêuticas; Revista Brasileira de Crescimento e Desenvolvimento Humano; Revista Brasileira de Edução Física e Esporte; Revista da Escola de Enfermagem da USP; Revista da Faculdade de Direito; Revista de Administração da USP; Revista de Antropologia; Revista de História; Revista de Psiquiatria Clínica; Revista de

Saúde Pública; Revista de Terapia Ocupacional; Revista Discurso; Revista do Instituto de Estudos Brasileiros; Revista do Instituto de Medicina Tropical de São Paulo; Revista do Museu de Arqueologia e Etnologia; Revista Latino-Americana de Enfermagem; Revista Literatura e Sociedade; Revista Paidéia; Revista Tempo Social; Revista USP; Saúde e Sociedade; Scientia Agricola

Publishing House: Editora da Universidade de São Paulo (EDUSP)

Student Numbers *2012-2013*: Total 91,019

Last Updated: 18/04/16

UNIVERSITY OF TAUBATÉ

Universidade de Taubaté (UNITAU)

Rua Quatro de Março 432, Centro, Taubaté, São Paulo 12020-270
Tel: +55(12) 3625-4100 +55(12) 3624-4193
Fax: +55(12) 3632-7660 +55(12) 3624-4193
EMail: reitoria@unitau.br; elsa.saldanha@unitau.br
Website: http://www.unitau.br

Reitora: José Rui Camargo
Tel: +55(12) 3625-4121 +55(12) 3624-4193
EMail: reitoria@unitau.br

Pró-reitoria de Administração (Interim): Isnard de Albuquerque Câmara Neto Tel: +55(12) 3632-3500 EMail: pra@unitau.br

Department

Agricultural Sciences (Agriculture; Agronomy); **Architecture** (Architecture); **Biology** (Biological and Life Sciences; Biology); **Civil Engineering** (Civil Engineering); **Computer Science** (Computer Engineering; Computer Science; Information Technology; Systems Analysis); **Dentistry** (Dentistry); **Economics, Accountancy and Administration** (Accountancy; Administration; Economics); **Electrical Engineering** (Electrical Engineering); **Law** (Law); **Mathematics and Physics** (Mathematics; Physics); **Mechanical Engineering** (Mechanical Engineering); **Medicine** (Medicine); **Nursing and Nutrition** (Nursing; Nutrition); **Pedagogy** (Pedagogy); **Physical Education** (Physical Education); **Physical Therapy** (Physical Therapy); **Psychology** (Psychology); **Social Communication** (Journalism; Mass Communication; Public Relations); **Social Sciences and Letters** (Arts and Humanities; Geography; History; Literature; Philosophy; Social Sciences); **Social Service** (Social Work)

Campus

Ubatuba Campus (Agricultural Business; Agriculture; Apiculture; Biological and Life Sciences; Business and Commerce; Chemistry; Ecology; Geography (Human); History; Human Resources; Literature; Management; Mathematics; Pedagogy; Philosophy; Physics; Portuguese; Sociology; Transport Management; Visual Arts)

Further Information: Also University Hospital

History: Founded 1974.

Admission Requirements: Secondary school certificate and entrance examination

Main Language(s) of Instruction: Portuguese

Degrees and Diplomas: *Tecnólogo*; *Bacharelado*; *Licenciatura*; *Especialização/Aperfeiçoamento*: **Advertising and Publicity; Aeronautical and Aerospace Engineering; Agriculture; Arts and Humanities; Automation and Control Engineering; Biological and Life Sciences; Business and Commerce; Civil Law; Communication Studies; Community Health; Dental Technology; Dentistry; Educational Administration; Educational and Student Counselling; Educational Psychology; Electronic Engineering; English; Finance; Health Administration; Health Sciences; Human Resources; Hygiene; Industrial Engineering; Industrial Maintenance; Information Management; Journalism; Labour Law; Literature; Management; Marine Biology; Marketing; Mechanical Equipment and Maintenance; Metallurgical Engineering; Modern Languages; Nursing; Occupational Health; Orthodontics; Portuguese; Psychiatry and Mental Health; Psychotherapy; Public Administration; Public Health; Public Law; Rehabilitation and Therapy; Safety Engineering; Social Policy; Social Work; Stomatology; Surgery; Taxation.** *Mestrado*: **Applied Linguistics; Dentistry; Development Studies; Education; Environmental Studies; Mechanical Engineering; Regional Planning.** *Doutorado*: **Dentistry.** Also MBA; Post-Doctorate Degree in Dentistry

Last Updated: 01/04/16

UNIVERSITY OF THE AMAZON STATE

Universidade do Estado do Amazonas (UEA)

Av. Djalma Batista, 3578 - Flores, Manaus, Amazonas 69050-010
Tel: +55(92) 3214-5770
EMail: faleconosco@uea.edu.br
Website: http://www.uea.edu.br

Reitor: Cleinaldo de Almeida Costa EMail: reitor@uea.edu.br

Pró-Reitoria de Administração: Wlademir Leite Correia Filho
Tel: +55(92) 3214-5771 +55(92) 3878-4493
EMail: proadm@uea.edu.br

School

Teacher Training (Biological and Life Sciences; Curriculum; History; Humanities and Social Science Education; Literature; Mathematics; Mathematics Education; Native Language Education; Pedagogy; Portuguese; Preschool Education; Religious Studies; Science Education)

Higher School

Arts and Tourism (Art Education; Arts and Humanities; Cinema and Television; Conducting; Dance; Literature; Music; Music Education; Musical Instruments; Singing; Theatre; Tourism); **Health Sciences** (Biotechnology; Dentistry; Laboratory Techniques; Medicine; Nursing; Physical Education; Psychology; Public Health; Tropical Medicine); **Social Sciences** (Accountancy; Archaeology; Civil Security; Economics; Government; Human Resources; Human Rights; Humanities and Social Science Education; Law; Management; Military Science; Public Administration); **Technology** (Agricultural Engineering; Automation and Control Engineering; Chemical Engineering; Chemistry; Civil Engineering; Computer Engineering; Computer Science; Educational Technology; Electrical Engineering; Electronic Engineering; Engineering; Environmental Management; Environmental Studies; Information Technology; Marine Engineering; Materials Engineering; Measurement and Precision Engineering; Mechanical Engineering; Meteorology; Petroleum and Gas Engineering; Production Engineering; Safety Engineering; Science Education; Telecommunications Engineering)

Further Information: Also Centres in Tefe, Tabatinga, Itacoatiara, São Gabriel da Cachoeira, Lábrea; 44 other Units: Manacapuru, Presidente Figueiredo, Maués, Coari, Carauari, Boca do Acre, Manicoré, Humaitá, Novo Aripuanã, Eirunepé, Careiro Castanho, Anori, Borba, São Paulo de Olivença, Berubi, Fonte Boa, Itapiranga, Jutaí, Barcelos, Novo Airão, Iranduba, São Sebastião do Uatumã, Tapauá, Japurá, Barreirinha, Juruá, Apuí, Autazes, Maraã, Uarini, Santo Antônio do Içá, Envira, Alvarães, Nova Olinda do Norte, Codajás, Benjamin Constant, Boa Vista do Ramos, Tonantins, Ipixuna, Itamarati, Nhamundá, Atalaia do Norte, Amaturá, Urucará, Anamã, Caapira, Canutama.

History: Founded 2006.

Main Language(s) of Instruction: Portuguese

Degrees and Diplomas: *Tecnólogo*; *Bacharelado*; *Licenciatura*; *Especialização/Aperfeiçoamento*: **Art Education; Business Administration; Civil Security; Community Health; Construction Engineering; Curriculum; Dance; Dental Technology; Dentistry; Earth Sciences; Education; Educational Sciences; Educational Technology; Electronic Engineering; Engineering; Environmental Management; Epidemiology; Gerontology; Government; Gynaecology and Obstetrics; Haematology; Higher Education Teacher Training; Humanities and Social Science Education; Industrial Engineering; Laboratory Techniques; Management; Mathematics Education; Measurement and Precision Engineering; Mechanical Engineering; Native Language Education; Natural Resources; Nursing; Occupational Health; Orthodontics; Paediatrics; Petroleum and Gas Engineering; Physical Education; Preschool Education; Primary Education; Psychiatry and Mental Health; Psychology; Public Administration; Public Health; Rehabilitation and Therapy; Safety Engineering; Science Education; Software Engineering; Stomatology; Telecommunications Engineering; Tourism; Transport Management.** *Mestrado*: **Arts and Humanities; Biochemistry; Biotechnology; Civil Security; Environmental Studies; Haematology; Human Rights; Law; Meteorology; Molecular Biology; Natural Resources; Science Education; Tropical Medicine.** *Doutorado*: **Biochemistry; Biological and Life Sciences; Biotechnology; Environmental Studies; Meteorology; Molecular Biology; Tropical Medicine.** Also

MBA; Residency postgraduate programmes in Dental Surgery and Nursing

Student Services: Library

Last Updated: 05/02/16

UNIVERSITY OF THE EXTREME SOUTH OF SANTA CATARINA

Universidade do Extremo Sul Catarinense (UNESC)

Caixa Postal 3167, Av. Universitária, 1105, Bairro Universitário, Criciúma, Santa Catarina 88806-000

Tel: +55(48) 3431-2500

Fax: +55(48) 3431-2750

EMail: suporteweb@unesc.net; reitoria@unesc.rct-sc.br

Website: http://www.unesc.rct-sc.br

Reitor: Gildo Volpato
Tel: +55(48) 3431-2600 EMail: reitoria@unesc.net

Pró-Reitora de Administração e Finanças: Kátia Aurora Dalla Libera Sorato
Tel: +55(48) 3431-2793 EMail: proadministrativa@unesc.net

Unit

Applied Social Sciences (UnaCSA) (Accountancy; Administration; Business Administration; Child Care and Development; Economics; Finance; Human Resources; International Business; Law; Management; Secretarial Studies; Social Policy; Transport and Communications); **Health Sciences (UNASAU)** (Biomedicine; Dentistry; Health Sciences; Medicine; Nursing; Nutrition; Pharmacology; Pharmacy; Physical Therapy; Psychology; Public Health; Rehabilitation and Therapy); **Humanities, Science and Education (UNAHCE)** (Art History; Biological and Life Sciences; Clinical Psychology; Education; English; Environmental Studies; Geography; History; Literature; Mathematics; Physical Education; Physics; Portuguese; Sociology; Visual Arts); **Science, Engineering and Technology (UnaCET)** (Architecture; Chemical Engineering; Civil Engineering; Computer Science; Design; Environmental Engineering; Fashion Design; Glass Art; Handicrafts; Materials Engineering; Production Engineering; Safety Engineering; Sanitary Engineering; Software Engineering; Surveying and Mapping; Town Planning)

History: Founded 1970, acquired present status 1997.

Admission Requirements: Secondary school certificate and entrance examination

Fees: 400-1800 per month (Brazilian Real)

Main Language(s) of Instruction: Portuguese

Degrees and Diplomas: *Tecnólogo*; *Bacharelado*; *Licenciatura*; *Especialização/Aperfeiçoamento*: **Accountancy; Art History; Biological and Life Sciences; Business and Commerce; Cognitive Sciences; Construction Engineering; Cooking and Catering; Criminal Law; Dental Technology; Ecology; Educational Administration; Educational Psychology; Environmental Studies; Furniture Design; Gynaecology and Obstetrics; Health Administration; Health Sciences; Heritage Preservation; Human Rights; Interior Design; Management; Natural Resources; Nursing; Nutrition; Orthodontics; Orthopaedics; Pharmacology; Physical Education; Physical Therapy; Private Law; Psychiatry and Mental Health; Public Law; Rehabilitation and Therapy; Respiratory Therapy; Safety Engineering; Software Engineering; Stomatology.** *Mestrado*: **Development Studies; Economics; Education; Environmental Studies; Health Sciences; Materials Engineering; Public Health.** *Doutorado*: **Environmental Studies; Health Sciences.** Also MBA

Student Services: Academic Counselling, Canteen, Careers Guidance, Language Laboratory, Library, Social Counselling, Sports Facilities

Last Updated: 08/02/16

UNIVERSITY OF THE STATE OF AMAPÁ

Universidade do Estado do Amapá (UEAP)

Av. Presidente Vargas, n° 650 - Centro, Amapá 68900-070

Tel: +55(96) 2101-0506 +55(96) 2101-0524

EMail: ueap@ueap.edu.br

Website: http://www.ueap.ap.gov.br

Rector: Perseu da Silva Aparício

Pró-Reitor de Planejamento e Administração: Albino Lutiani da Costa Brito
Tel: +55(96) 2101-0511 +55(96) 99124-9670
EMail: albino.brito@ueap.edu.br

Course

Chemical Engineering (Chemical Engineering); **Chemistry** (Chemistry); **Design** (Design); **Environmental Engineering** (Environmental Engineering); **Fishery** (Agricultural Engineering; Fishery); **Forestry** (Agricultural Engineering; Forestry); **Literature** (English; French; Literature; Modern Languages; Spanish); **Music** (Music); **Natural Sciences** (Natural Sciences); **Pedagogy** (Pedagogy); **Philosophy** (Philosophy); **Production Engineering** (Production Engineering)

History: Founded 2006.

Main Language(s) of Instruction: Portuguese

Degrees and Diplomas: *Tecnólogo*: **Design.** *Bacharelado*; *Licenciatura*; *Especialização/Aperfeiçoamento*: **Economics; Environmental Studies; Management.**

Student Services: Library

Publications: Revista de Ciências da Amazônia (RCA)

Last Updated: 05/02/16

UNIVERSITY OF THE STATE OF BAHIA

Universidade do Estado da Bahia (UNEB)

Rua Silveira Martins, 2.555, Cabula, Salvador, Bahia 41150-000

Tel: +55(71) 3117-2200

Fax: +55(71) 3117-2387

EMail: uneb@uneb.br

Website: http://www.uneb.br

Reitora: José Bites de Carvalho
Tel: +55(71) 3117-2353
EMail: jbcarvalho@uneb.br; uneb@listas.uneb.br

Vice Reitora: Carla Liane Nascimento Santos
Tel: +55(71) 3117-2327
EMail: clnsantos@uneb.br; carlavicereitora@uneb.br; vicereitoria@listas.uneb.br

Pró-Reitor de Administração: Jairo Luiz Oliveira de Sá
Tel: +55(71) 3117-2361 +55(71) 3117-2309
EMail: jlsa@uneb.br; proad@listas.uneb.br

International Relations: Jardelina Bispo, Secretaria Especial de Relações Internacionais (Serint)
Tel: +55(71) 3117-2475
EMail: jbnascimento@uneb.br; jardnascimento@hotmail.com

Campus

Campus I - Salvador (Accountancy; Arts and Humanities; Business Administration; Chemistry; Civil Engineering; Design; English; History; Hotel Management; Information Technology; Medicine; Nursing; Nutrition; Pedagogy; Pharmacy; Philosophy; Physical Therapy; Portuguese; Production Engineering; Psychology; Public Relations; Social Sciences; Speech Therapy and Audiology; Tourism; Town Planning); **Campus II - Alagoinhas** (Arts and Humanities; Biological and Life Sciences; English; Environmental Engineering; History; Information Technology; Mathematics; Portuguese; Sanitary Engineering); **Campus III - Juazeiro** (Agricultural Engineering; Law; Pedagogy); **Campus IV - Jacobina** (Arts and Humanities; English; Geography (Human); History; Law; Literature; Physical Education; Portuguese); **Campus IX - Barreiras** (Accountancy; Agricultural Engineering; Arts and Humanities; Biological and Life Sciences; Literature; Mathematics; Pedagogy; Portuguese); **Campus V - Santo Antônio de Jesus** (Administration; Arts and Humanities; English; Geography (Human); History; Literature; Portuguese; Spanish); **Campus VI - Caetité** (Biological and Life Sciences; English; Geography (Human); History; Literature; Mathematics; Portuguese); **Campus VII - Senhor do Bonfim** (Biological and Life Sciences; Mathematics; Pedagogy); **Campus VIII - Paulo Afonso** (Agricultural Engineering; Biological and Life Sciences; Fishery; Mathematics; Pedagogy); **Campus X - Teixeira de Freitas** (Arts and Humanities; Biological and Life Sciences; English; History; Literature; Mathematics; Pedagogy; Physical Education; Portuguese); **Campus XI - Serrinha** (Administration; Pedagogy); **Campus XII - Guanambi** (Administration; Nursing;

Pedagogy; Physical Education); **Campus XIII - Itaberaba** (Arts and Humanities; History; Law; Literature; Pedagogy; Portuguese); **Campus XIV - Conceição do Coité** (Arts and Humanities; English; Literature; Mass Communication; Portuguese; Radio and Television Broadcasting); **Campus XIX- Camaçari** (Accountancy; Law); **Campus XV - Valença** (Pedagogy); **Campus XVI - Irecê** (Administration; Arts and Humanities; Literature; Pedagogy; Portuguese); **Campus XVII - Bom Jesus da Lapa** (Administration; Pedagogy); **Campus XVIII - Eunápolis** (Administration; Arts and Humanities; History; Literature; Portuguese; Tourism); **Campus XX - Brumado** (Arts and Humanities; Literature; Portuguese); **Campus XXI - Ipiaú** (Administration; Arts and Humanities; Literature; Portuguese); **Campus XXII - Euclides da Cunha** (Agricultural Engineering; Arts and Humanities; Literature; Portuguese); **Campus XXIII - Seabra** (Arts and Humanities; English; Linguistics; Pedagogy; Portuguese); **Campus XXIV - Xique-Xique** (Agricultural Engineering; Environmental Engineering; Fishery; Sanitary Engineering)

History: Founded 1983 incorporating various Escolas Superiores. Acquired present status and title 1995.

Academic Year: March to December (March-July; August-December)

Admission Requirements: Secondary school certificate and entrance examination

Fees: None

Main Language(s) of Instruction: Portuguese

Degrees and Diplomas: *Bacharelado*; *Licenciatura*; *Especialização/Aperfeiçoamento*: **Agriculture; Aquaculture; Arid Land Studies; Biology; Business and Commerce; Cultural Studies; Ecology; Educational Administration; Educational Psychology; Environmental Studies; Fiscal Law; Foreign Languages Education; Higher Education Teacher Training; History; Linguistics; Literature; Management; Mass Communication; Mathematics; Mathematics Education; Modern Languages; Nursing; Nutrition; Public Administration; Software Engineering; Teacher Training; Transport Management; Zoology.** *Mestrado*: **Adult Education; Applied Chemistry; Arid Land Studies; Biological and Life Sciences; Cultural Studies; Ecology; Education; Educational Sciences; Educational Technology; English; Environmental Management; Horticulture; Teacher Training.** *Doutorado*: **Education.**

Student Services: Canteen, Cultural Activities, Foreign Studies Centre, Language Laboratory, Library, Social Counselling

Publications: Caderno de Extensão; Caderno de Pesquisa; Revista Canadart; Revista da FAEEBA; Revista de Canudos; Revista de Letras da F.F.P.A.; Revista Logos

Publishing House: Gráfica da UNEB

Last Updated: 09/02/16

UNIVERSITY OF THE STATE OF MATO GROSSO

Universidade do Estado de Mato Grosso (UNEMAT)

Av. Tancredo Neves, 1095 - Cavalhada II,
Cáceres, Mato Grosso 78200-000
Tel: +55(65) 3221-0000
EMail: coordecom@unemat.br
Website: http://www.unemat.br

Reitora: Ana Maria Di Renzo EMail: reitoriaunemat@unemat.br

Pró-reitor de Administração: Valter Gustavo Danzer
EMail: prad@unemat.br

Campus

Alta Foresta (Agricultural Engineering; Agriculture; Biological and Life Sciences); **Alto Araguaia** (Arts and Humanities; Computer Science; Mass Communication); **Barra do Bugres** (Agricultural Engineering; Architecture; Computer Science; Food Technology; Mathematics; Town Planning); **Caceres** (Accountancy; Agronomy; Arts and Humanities; Biological and Life Sciences; Computer Science; Education; Geography (Human); History; Law; Mathematics; Medicine; Nursing; Physical Education); **Colider** (Computer Science; Geography); **Juara campus** (Business Administration; Education); **Nova Xavantina** (Agronomy; Biological and Life Sciences; Tourism); **Pontes e Lacerda** (Literature; Veterinary Science); **Sinop** (Accountancy; Arts and Humanities; Business Administration; Civil Engineering; Economics; Education; Electrical Engineering; Mathematics); **Tangara da Serra** (Accountancy; Agriculture; Arts and Humanities; Biological and Life Sciences; Business Administration; Nursing)

Further Information: Also campuses in Alta Floresta, Alto Araguaia, Barra do Bugres, Cáceres, Colider, Juara, Luciara, Pontes e Lacerda, Nova Xavantina, Sinop, Tangará da Serra.

History: Founded 1978.

Main Language(s) of Instruction: Portuguese

Degrees and Diplomas: *Bacharelado*; *Licenciatura*; *Especialização/Aperfeiçoamento*; *Mestrado*: **Agriculture; Arts and Humanities; Ecology; Education; Environmental Management; Environmental Studies; Genetics; Geography (Human); History; Linguistics; Literature; Mathematics; Mathematics Education; Science Education.** *Doutorado*: **Biotechnology; Ecology; Environmental Management; Linguistics; Literature; Mathematics Education; Science Education.** Also Interinstitutional Doctorates in Sociology, Business Administration, Political Sciences and Law

Student Services: IT Centre, Library

Last Updated: 05/02/16

UNIVERSITY OF THE STATE OF MINAS GERAIS

Universidade do Estado de Minas Gerais (UEMG)

Rodovia Pref. Américo Gianetti, 4143, Ed. Minas - 8° andar,
Belo Horizonte, Minas Gerais 31.630-900
Tel: +55 (31) 3916-0471
Fax: +55(31) 3273-6647
EMail: uemg@uemg.br
Website: http://www.uemg.br

Reitora: Dijon Moraes Júnior EMail: dijon.moraes@uemg.br

Vice-Reitor: José Eustáquio de Brito
EMail: joseeustaquio.brito@uemg.br

Faculty

Education (FaE) (Education; Educational Sciences; Teacher Training); **Tancredo Neves Public Policy (FaPP)** (Art Management; Human Resources; Public Administration)

Unit

Abaeté (Accountancy; Administration; Social and Community Services); **Barbacena** (Pedagogy; Social Sciences); **Campanha** (History; Management; Pedagogy); **Carangola** (Biology; Business Administration; English; Geography; History; Information Technology; Literature; Mathematics; Pedagogy; Portuguese; Social and Community Services; Tourism); **Cláudio** (Accountancy; Business Administration; Pedagogy; Social and Community Services); **Diamantina** (Law); **Divinópolis** (Advertising and Publicity; Arts and Humanities; Biological and Life Sciences; Chemistry; Civil Engineering; Computer Engineering; English; History; Journalism; Mass Communication; Mathematics; Nursing; Pedagogy; Physical Education; Physical Therapy; Portuguese; Production Engineering; Psychology; Science Education; Social and Community Services); **Frutal** (Advertising and Publicity; Agriculture; Business Administration; Food Technology; Geography; Information Technology; Journalism; Law; Mass Communication); **Ibirité** (Arts and Humanities; Biological and Life Sciences; English; Mathematics; Pedagogy; Physical Education; Portuguese); **Ituiutaba** (Agricultural Business; Agronomy; Biological and Life Sciences; Chemistry; Computer Engineering; Electrical Engineering; Environmental Management; Food Science; Information Technology; Law; Pedagogy; Physical Education; Psychology); **João Monlevade** (Civil Engineering; Environmental Engineering; Metallurgical Engineering; Mining Engineering); **Leopoldina** (Pedagogy); **Passos** (Accountancy; Administration; Advertising and Publicity; Agronomy; Arts and Humanities; Biological and Life Sciences; Biomedicine; Business and Commerce; Civil Engineering; Cosmetology; Environmental Engineering; Fashion Design; History; Information Technology; Journalism; Law; Mass Communication; Mathematics; Medicine; Nursing; Nutrition; Pedagogy; Physical Education; Physics; Portuguese; Production Engineering; Social and Community Services); **Poços de Caldas** (Pedagogy); **Santa Vitória** (Pedagogy); **Ubá** (Biological and Life Sciences; Chemistry; Industrial Design)

School
Design (Architectural and Environmental Design; Art Education; Design; Furniture Design; Graphic Design; Industrial Design; Jewellery Art); **Guignard** (Art Management; Visual Arts); **Music (EsMu)** (Music)

Further Information: Associated campuses at Campanha, Carangola, Diamantina, Divinópolis, Ituiutaba, Lavras, Passos, Patos de Minas and Varginha

History: Founded 1994.

Admission Requirements: Secondary school certificate and entrance examination

Main Language(s) of Instruction: Portuguese

Degrees and Diplomas: *Tecnólogo*; *Bacharelado*; *Licenciatura*: **Teacher Training.** *Especialização/Aperfeiçoamento*: **Agriculture; Art Management; Business and Commerce; Civil Law; Communication Studies; Ecology; Education; Educational Administration; Educational Psychology; Environmental Management; Furniture Design; Higher Education Teacher Training; Information Technology; Jewellery Art; Literacy Education; Management; Metallurgical Engineering; Mining Engineering; Music Education; Musical Instruments; Pedagogy; Psychiatry and Mental Health; Psychoanalysis; Public Administration; Safety Engineering; Singing; Visual Arts.** *Mestrado*: **Design; Education; Materials Engineering; Music.** *Doutorado*: **Design; Materials Engineering; Music.**

Student Services: Academic Counselling, Canteen, Cultural Activities, Facilities for disabled people, Library

Publications: Cadernos de Educação; Revista Literária

Last Updated: 05/02/16

UNIVERSITY OF THE STATE OF PARA

Universidade do Estado do Pará (UEPA)
Rua do Una, n° 156, Belém, Pará 66050-540
Tel: +55(91) 3244-5460
Fax: +55(91) 3244-5460
EMail: vicereit@uepa.br; ascom@uepa.br
Website: http://www2.uepa.br/uepa_site

Reitor: Juarez Antonio Simões Quaresma
EMail: reitor@uepa.br; gabinete@uepa.br

Vice-Reitor: Rubens Cardoso da Silva EMail: vicereitor@uepa.br

International Relations: Luzia Jucá, Coordenadora de Relações Internacionais Tel: +55(91) 3299-2281 EMail: luziajuca@uepa.br

Centre
Biological and Health Sciences (CCBS) (Biomedicine; Medicine; Nursing; Occupational Health; Physical Education; Physical Therapy); **Indigenous training** (Natives Education); **Natural Sciences and Technology (CCNT)** (Agricultural Engineering; Design; Environmental Engineering; Food Technology; Production Engineering; Systems Analysis); **Social Sciences and Education (CCSE)** (Arts and Humanities; Biology; Chemistry; English; Geography (Human); History; Mathematics; Music; Natural Sciences; Pedagogy; Philosophy; Physics; Portuguese; Religious Studies; Secretarial Studies; Social Sciences)

Further Information: Also Campuses in Paragominas, Conceição do Araguaia, Marabá, Altamira, Igarapé-Açu, São Miguel do Guamá, Santarém, Tucuruí, Moju, Redenção, Barcarena, Vigia, Cametá, Salvaterra e Castanhal.

History: Founded 1993.

Admission Requirements: Secondary school certificate and entrance examination

Main Language(s) of Instruction: Portuguese

Degrees and Diplomas: *Tecnólogo*; *Bacharelado*; *Licenciatura*; *Especialização/Aperfeiçoamento*: **Air Transport; Linguistics; Literature; Marine Transport; Mathematics Education; Transport Management.** *Mestrado*: **Education; Environmental Studies; Health Administration; Health Sciences; Mathematics Education; Nursing; Parasitology; Religious Studies; Surgery.** *Doutorado*: **Parasitology.**

Student Services: Canteen, Health Services, Library

Last Updated: 05/02/16

UNIVERSITY OF THE STATE OF RIO DE JANEIRO

Universidade do Estado do Rio de Janeiro (UERJ)
Rua São Francisco Xavier 524, Maracanã,
Rio de Janeiro, Rio de Janeiro 20559-900
Tel: +55(21) 2587-7720 +55(21) 2334-0652
Fax: +55(21) 2284-5033 +55(21) 2334-0527
EMail: datauerj@uerj.br
Website: http://www.uerj.br

Reitor: Ricardo Vieiralves de Castro
Tel: +55(21) 2334-2181 EMail: reitoria@uerj.br

Diretoria de Administração Financeira: Maria Thereza Lopes de Azevedo Tel: +55(21) 2334-0885 EMail: daf@uerj.br

Vice-reitor: Paulo Roberto Volpato Dias

International Relations: Cristina Russi Guimarães Furtado, International Relations Director
Tel: +55(21) 2334-2188 EMail: dci@sr2.uerj.br

Faculty
Administration and Finance (FAF) (Accountancy; Administration; Business Administration); **Dentistry (ODO)** (Community Health; Dental Technology; Dentistry; Social and Preventive Medicine); **Economics (FCE)** (Economics); **Education (EDU)** (Adult Education; Continuing Education; Education; Educational Administration; Educational Sciences; Humanities and Social Science Education; Political Sciences; Special Education; Teacher Training); **Education (FEBF - Baixada Fluminense)** *(Campus located at Duque de Caxias City)* (Educational Administration; Educational Sciences; Mathematics Education; Teacher Training); **Engineering (FEN)** (Civil Engineering; Computer Engineering; Electrical Engineering; Electronic Engineering; Energy Engineering; Engineering; Environmental Engineering; Industrial Engineering; Mechanical Engineering; Natural Sciences; Sanitary Engineering; Surveying and Mapping; Telecommunications Engineering; Transport Engineering); **Geology (FGEL)** (Earth Sciences; Geography; Geology; Mineralogy; Paleontology; Surveying and Mapping); **Law (DIR)** (Civil Law; Commercial Law; Criminal Law; Labour Law; Law; Public Law); **Medical Sciences (FCM)** (Education; Gynaecology and Obstetrics; Immunology; Information Technology; Medicine; Microbiology; Paediatrics; Parasitology; Pathology; Public Health; Surgery); **Nursing (ENF)** (Nursing; Public Health); **Oceanography** (Geography; Marine Science and Oceanography; Meteorology); **Social Communication (FCS)** (Journalism; Mass Communication; Public Relations); **Social Services (FSS)** (Social and Community Services; Social Policy); **Teacher Training (FFP)** *(São Gonçalo; campus located at São Gonçalo City)* (Arts and Humanities; Education; Geography (Human); Mathematics; Natural Sciences; Teacher Training); **Technology (FAT)** *(campus located at the city of Resende)* (Chemistry; Computer Science; Engineering; Environmental Studies; Mathematics; Mechanics; Physics; Production Engineering)

School
Industrial Design (ESDI) (Computer Graphics; Industrial Design)

Institute
Application (Fernando Rodrigues da Silveira) (Art Education; Design; Literature; Mathematics; Modern Languages; Natural Sciences; Physical Education; Primary Education; Social Work); **Arts (ART)** (Art Education; Art History; Fine Arts); **Biology (IBRAG)** *(Roberto Alcântara Gomes)* (Anatomy; Biochemistry; Biological and Life Sciences; Biology; Biophysics; Ecology; Embryology and Reproduction Biology; Genetics; Histology; Pharmacology; Physiology; Science Education; Zoology); **Chemistry (QUI)** (Analytical Chemistry; Biochemistry; Chemistry; Industrial Management; Inorganic Chemistry; Organic Chemistry; Physical Chemistry); **Geography (IGEOG)** (Geography; Geography (Human); Tourism); **Letters (ILE/UERJ)** (Arts and Humanities; Classical Languages; English; French; German; Greek (Classical); Italian; Japanese; Latin; Literature; Philology; Portuguese); **Mathematics and Statistics (IME)** (Mathematics; Statistics); **Nutrition (NUT)** (Nutrition); **Philosophy and Human Sciences (IFCH)** (Archaeology; History; International Relations; Philosophy; Social Sciences; Tourism); **Physical Education and Sports (IEFD)** (Physical Education; Sports); **Physics (FIS - Armando Dias Tavares)** (Applied Physics; Electronic Engineering; Energy Engineering; Nuclear Physics; Physics); **Political and Social Science (IESP)** (Political Sciences;

Social Sciences); **Polytechnic (IPRJ)** (Computer Engineering; Computer Graphics; Energy Engineering; Engineering; Materials Engineering; Mechanical Engineering); **Psychology (PSI)** (Clinical Psychology; Psychology; Social Psychology); **Social Medicine (IMS)** (Epidemiology; Health Administration; Health Sciences; Human Rights; Medicine; Public Health; Social Work)

Centre

Biomedical Studies (CBI) (Biomedicine); **Education and Humanities (CEH)** (Documentation Techniques; Information Sciences; Mass Communication; Performing Arts); **Production (CEPUERJ)** (Business Administration; Business and Commerce; Communication Studies; Documentation Techniques; Finance; Management; Marketing); **Social Sciences (CCS)** (African American Studies; African Studies; Caribbean Studies; Communication Studies; Latin American Studies; Religion; Social Sciences); **Technology and Sciences (CTC)** (Natural Sciences; Technology)

Further Information: Also Hospital Universitário Pedro Ernesto (HUPE); Policlínica Piquet Carneiro (PPC); Campus at Ilha Grande

History: Founded 1950.

Academic Year: March to December (March-June; August-December)

Admission Requirements: Secondary school certificate and entrance examination

Fees: None

Main Language(s) of Instruction: Portuguese

Degrees and Diplomas: *Bacharelado*: **Accountancy; Actuarial Science; Archaeology; Biological and Life Sciences; Business Administration; Chemical Engineering; Civil Engineering; Computer Engineering; Computer Science; Dentistry; Economics; Education; Electrical Engineering; Environmental Engineering; Geography; Geology; History; Industrial Design; International Relations; Law; Marine Science and Oceanography; Mass Communication; Mechanical Engineering; Medicine; Modern Languages; Nursing; Nutrition; Philosophy; Physics; Production Engineering; Psychology; Sanitary Engineering; Social and Community Services; Social Sciences; Statistics; Surveying and Mapping; Tourism; Visual Arts.** *Licenciatura*: **Art Education; Art History; Biological and Life Sciences; Chemistry; Education; Geography; History; Mathematics; Modern Languages; Philosophy; Physical Education; Physics; Psychology; Social Sciences; Teacher Training; Visual Arts.** *Especialização/Aperfeiçoamento*: **Accountancy; Business Administration; Business and Commerce; Chemistry; Civil Law; Clinical Psychology; Computer Graphics; Constitutional Law; Curriculum; Dental Hygiene; Dental Technology; Dentistry; Dermatology; Diabetology; Economics; Educational Administration; Educational Psychology; Educational Sciences; Educational Technology; Electronic Engineering; Endocrinology; Engineering; Environmental Engineering; Environmental Studies; Epidemiology; Finance; Gerontology; Gynaecology and Obstetrics; Haematology; Health Administration; Health Sciences; Histology; Information Technology; International Relations; Journalism; Law; Literature; Marketing; Mathematics Education; Medical Parasitology; Multimedia; Neurology; Nursing; Nutrition; Occupational Health; Orthodontics; Periodontics; Petroleum and Gas Engineering; Philosophy; Physical Education; Plastic Surgery; Political Sciences; Polymer and Plastics Technology; Portuguese; Primary Education; Private Law; Psychiatry and Mental Health; Public Administration; Public Health; Public Law; Radiology; Regional Planning; Rehabilitation and Therapy; Sanitary Engineering; Science Education; Service Trades; Social Sciences; Sociology; Stomatology; Surgery; Teacher Training; Transport Management.** *Mestrado*: **Accountancy; Biological and Life Sciences; Biology; Business Administration; Chemical Engineering; Chemistry; Civil Engineering; Civil Law; Computer Engineering; Computer Graphics; Computer Science; Criminal Law; Dental Technology; Dentistry; Design; Ecology; Economics; Education; Electronic Engineering; Environmental Studies; Ethics; Fiscal Law; Forensic Medicine and Dentistry; Geography; Geography (Human); History; Humanities and Social Science Education; International Law; Laboratory Techniques; Law; Linguistics; Marine Science and Oceanography; Mass Communication; Materials Engineering; Mathematics; Mechanical Engineering; Microbiology; Nursing; Nutrition; Orthodontics; Pathology; Periodontics; Philosophy; Physics; Physiology; Political Sciences; Portuguese; Public Health; Public Law; Science Education; Social and Community Services; Social and Preventive Medicine; Social Policy; Social Psychology; Social Sciences; Sociology; Surgery.** *Doutorado*: **Biological and Life Sciences; Biology; Business Administration; Chemical Engineering; Chemistry; Civil Engineering; Civil Law; Comparative Literature; Computer Engineering; Computer Graphics; Criminal Law; Dental Technology; Dentistry; Design; Ecology; Economics; Education; English; Environmental Studies; Ethics; Fiscal Law; Geography; Geography (Human); History; International Law; Law; Linguistics; Literature; Marine Science and Oceanography; Mechanical Engineering; Microbiology; Nursing; Nutrition; Orthodontics; Pathology; Periodontics; Philosophy; Physics; Physiology; Political Sciences; Portuguese; Private Law; Public Health; Public Law; Social and Community Services; Social and Preventive Medicine; Social Policy; Social Psychology; Social Sciences; Sociology; Surgery.**

Student Services: Academic Counselling, Canteen, Careers Guidance, Cultural Activities, Facilities for disabled people, Health Services, Language Laboratory, Nursery Care, Social Counselling, Sports Facilities, eLibrary

Publications: Boletim Aconteceh; Cadernos de Antropologia e Imagem; Cadernos de Graduação; Cadernos do Fórum de Debates; Cadernos do IME; Concinnitas; Geo-UERJ; Interseções: Revista de Estudos Interdisciplinares; Physis-Revista de Saùde Coletiva; Projeto Jornal Philia; Publicação da Jornada de História Antiga; Revista de Enfermagem da UERJ; Revista de Estudos Transdisciplinares; Revista do HUPE; Revista Em Pauta; Revista Estudos e Pequisas em Psicologia; Revista Logos; Revista Open to Discussion; Revista Tamoios; Revista Textos sobre Envelhecimento; Revista Thauma; Revistas Espaço e Cultura; Saùde e Sociedade; Série de Estudos em Saùde Colevita; Teias; UERJ em Questão

Publishing House: ED-UERJ-UERJ's Publishing House
Last Updated: 22/02/16

UNIVERSITY OF THE STATE OF SANTA CATARINA

Universidade do Estado de Santa Catarina (UDESC)

Caixa Postal 6021, Avenida Madre Benvenuta 2007, Itacorubi, Florianópolis, Santa Catarina 88035-901
Tel: +55(48) 3664-8000
Fax: +55(48) 3334-6000
EMail: r4sl@udesc.br
Website: http://www.udesc.br

Reitor: Antonio Heronaldo de Sousa
Tel: +55(48) 3321-8004 EMail: reitor@udesc.br; j2ahs@udesc.br

Pró-Reitor de Administração: Matheus Azevedo Ferreira Fidelis
Tel: +55(48) 3664-8114
EMail: proad@udesc.br; liana.troggian@udesc.br

Vice-Reitor: Marcus Tomasi

International Relations: Cecília Just Milanez Coelho, Secretária de Cooperação Interinstitucional e Internacional
Tel: +55(48) 3664-8080 EMail: cecilia.coelho@udesc.br

Centre

Administration and Management (ESAG) *(Florianópolis)* (Business Administration; Economics; Public Administration); **Agricultural and Veterinary Sciences (CAV)** *(Lages)* (Agricultural Engineering; Agronomy; Environmental Engineering; Forestry; Veterinary Science); **Alto Vale do Itajaí Higher Education Centre (CEAVI)** (Accountancy; Sanitary Engineering; Software Engineering); **Arts (CEART)** *(Florianópolis)* (Art Education; Design; Fashion Design; Fine Arts; Graphic Design; Industrial Design; Music; Music Education; Musical Instruments; Theatre); **Foz do Itajaí Higher Education Centre (CESFI)** (Petroleum and Gas Engineering; Public Administration); **Health Sciences and Sports (CEFID)** *(Florianópolis)* (Physical Education; Physical Therapy; Sports); **Human Sciences and Education (FAED)** *(Florianópolis)* (Geography (Human); History; Humanities and Social Science Education; Information Management; Library Science; Pedagogy); **Planalto Norte Education Centre (CEPLAN)** (Information Technology; Mechanical Engineering; Production Engineering);

Southern Region Higher Education Centre (CERES) (Agricultural Engineering; Architecture; Fishery; Town Planning); **Technological Sciences (CCT)** *(Joinville)* (Chemistry; Civil Engineering; Computer Science; Electrical Engineering; Mathematics; Mechanical Engineering; Physics; Production Engineering; Systems Analysis; Technology); **Western Higher Education Centre (CEO)** (Animal Husbandry; Chemical Engineering; Food Technology; Furniture Design; Nursing; Public Health)

History: Founded 1965.

Academic Year: March to December (March-June; August-December)

Admission Requirements: Secondary school certificate and entrance examination

Fees: None

Main Language(s) of Instruction: Portuguese

Degrees and Diplomas: *Tecnólogo*; *Bacharelado*; *Licenciatura*; *Mestrado*: **Administration; Agricultural Engineering; Animal Husbandry; Computer Science; Design; Development Studies; Education; Electrical Engineering; Environmental Studies; Forestry; History; Horticulture; Information Management; Materials Engineering; Mechanical Engineering; Music; Physical Therapy; Physics; Regional Planning; Soil Science; Sports; Theatre; Visual Arts.** *Doutorado*: **Animal Husbandry; Education; Electrical Engineering; History; Horticulture; Materials Engineering; Soil Science; Sports; Theatre; Visual Arts.**

Student Services: Canteen, Cultural Activities, Health Services, Sports Facilities

Publications: Universidade e Desenvolvimento

Last Updated: 10/02/16

UNIVERSITY OF THE UPPER VALLEY OF PEIXE

Universidade Alto Vale do Rio do Peixe (UNIARP)

Rua Victor Baptista Adami, n° 800, Centro,
Caçador, Santa Catarina 89500-000
Tel: +57(49) 3561-6246
EMail: uniarp@uniarp.edu.br; presidente@uniarp.edu.br; dirca@uniarp.edu.br; ca@uniarp.edu.br
Website: http://www.uniarp.edu.br

Reitor: Adelcio Machado dos Santos EMail: adelcio@uniarp.edu.br

Vice-Reitor de Administração e Planejamento: Paulo Cezar de Campos EMail: administracao@uniarp.edu.br

Secretária Geral: Suzana Franco EMail: suzana@uniarp.edu.br

Course

Accounting (Accountancy); **Administration** (Business Administration); **Aesthetics and Cosmetics** *(Technological)* (Cosmetology); **Agronomy** (Agronomy); **Architecture and Urbanism** (Architecture and Planning); **Automation and Control Engineering** (Automation and Control Engineering); **Biological Sciences** (Biological and Life Sciences); **Biological Sciences Education** (Science Education); **Civil Engineering** (Civil Engineering); **Electrical Engineering** (Electrical Engineering); **Environmental and Sanitary Engineering** (Environmental Engineering; Sanitary Engineering); **Geography Education** (Humanities and Social Science Education); **History Education** (Humanities and Social Science Education); **Information Systems** (Information Technology); **Journalism** (Journalism); **Law** (Law); **Literature - Trilingual Education** (Bilingual and Bicultural Education; Humanities and Social Science Education); **Mathematics Education** (Mathematics Education); **Mechanical Engineering** (Mechanical Engineering); **Nursing** (Nursing); **Pedagogy** (Pedagogy); **Pharmacy** (Pharmacy); **Physical Education** (Physical Education); **Physical Education** (Physical Education); **Physiotherapy** (Physical Therapy); **Postgraduate Studies** (Arts and Humanities; Development Studies; Earth Sciences; Education; Health Sciences; Law; Natural Sciences; Social Sciences; Social Studies); **Psychology** (Psychology); **Social Services** (Social and Community Services); **Visual Arts Education** (Art Education)

Campus

Fraiburgo (Accountancy; Business Administration; Cosmetology; Production Engineering; Psychology)

Further Information: Also Fraiburgo Campus

History: Founded 2009.

Main Language(s) of Instruction: Portuguese

Degrees and Diplomas: *Tecnólogo*; *Bacharelado*; *Licenciatura*; *Especialização/Aperfeiçoamento*: **Clinical Psychology; Educational Psychology; Higher Education Teacher Training; Labour Law; Marketing; Mass Communication; Media Studies; Neurosciences; Orthopaedics; Pharmacy; Physical Therapy; Preschool Education; Psychology; Safety Engineering; Sales Techniques; Software Engineering; Special Education; Sports; Sports Medicine.** *Mestrado*: **Development Studies; Education; Social Studies.** Also MBA

Student Services: Library

Last Updated: 25/11/15

UNIVERSITY OF TOCANTINS

Universidade do Tocantins (UNITINS)

108 Sul Alameda 11 Lote 03, Cx. Postal 173,
Palmas, Tocantins 77020-122
Tel: +55(63) 3218-4936 +55(63) 3218-2902 +55(63) 3218-2974
Fax: +55(63) 3218-2942
EMail: unitins@unitins.br; jucylene.mc@unitins.br
Website: http://www.unitins.br

Reitora: Elizângela Glória Cardoso EMail: reitoria@unitins.br

Pró-Reitor de Administração e Finanças: Senivan Arruda de Almeida

Campus

Araguatins (Arts and Humanities; Pedagogy); **Augustinópolis** (Accountancy; Agricultural Business; Law; Nursing); **Dianópolis** (Accountancy; Business Administration; Law); **Palmas** (Agricultural Engineering; Information Technology; Law; Social and Community Services)

History: Founded 1990. A State institution.

Main Language(s) of Instruction: Portuguese

Degrees and Diplomas: *Tecnólogo*; *Bacharelado*; *Licenciatura*; *Especialização/Aperfeiçoamento*: **Accountancy; Administrative Law; Agricultural Business; Agriculture; Animal Husbandry; Civil Law; Communication Studies; Computer Engineering; Constitutional Law; Criminal Law; Ecology; Educational Administration; Environmental Management; Environmental Studies; Fiscal Law; Fruit Production; Government; Grammar; Health Administration; Higher Education; History; Information Technology; Labour Law; Management; Marketing; Mass Communication; Political Sciences; Private Law; Production Engineering; Public Administration; Public Health; Public Law; Rural Planning; Rural Studies; Taxation; Technology; Tropical Agriculture; Vegetable Production.** Also MBA

Last Updated: 29/02/16

UTRAMIG TECHNICAL EDUCATION CENTRE

Centro de educação técnica da UTRAMIG (UTRAMIG)

Avenida Afonso Peña 3400, Cruzeiro,
Belo Horizonte, Minas Gerais 30130-009
Tel: +55(31) 3263-7500
EMail: vicepresidencia@utramig.mg.gov.br; faleconosco@utramig.mg.gov.br; cet.utramig@yahoo.com.br
Website: http://www.utramig.mg.gov.br

Presidenta: Liza Fernandes Prado
Tel: +55(31) 3263-7536 EMail: presidencia@utramig.mg.gov.br

Diretor, Planejamento, Gestão e Finanças: Francisco José Da Fonseca
Tel: +55(31) 3263-7557
EMail: francisco.fonseca@utramig.mg.gov.br

Course

Postgraduate Studies (Educational Administration; Peace and Disarmament; Special Education); **Teacher Training** (Teacher Training)

Further Information: Also Nova Lima and Uberlandia Units

History: Founded 1965. Acquired present title 1972.

Main Language(s) of Instruction: Portuguese

Degrees and Diplomas: *Técnico de Nivel Medio*; *Licenciatura*; *Especialização/Aperfeiçoamento*: **Educational Administration; Peace and Disarmament; Special Education.**

Student Services: Library

Last Updated: 03/02/16

VALE DO IGUAÇU FACULTY OF DOIS VIZINHOS

Faculdade Vizinhança Vale do Iguaçu (VIZIVALI)

Rua Pedro Alvares Cabral 905, Dois Vizinhos, PR 85660000

Tel: +55(46) 3536-4438

Fax: +55(46) 3536-4438

EMail: secretariavizivali@vizivali.edu.br

Website: http://www.vizivali.edu.br

Director: Paulo Fernando Diel EMail: paulo.diel@cpea.br

Course

Administration (Administration); **Advertising** (Advertising and Publicity); **Computer Technology** (Computer Science; Software Engineering); **Letters** (Literature); **Pedagogy** (Pedagogy); **Visual Arts**

History: Founded 1999.

Main Language(s) of Instruction: Portuguese

Degrees and Diplomas: *Bacharelado*; *Licenciatura*; *Especialização/Aperfeiçoamento*. Also MBA

Student Services: Library

Last Updated: 17/07/15

VIRTUAL UNIVERSITY OF THE STATE OF MARANHÃO

Universidade Virtual do Estado do Maranhão (UNIVIMA)

Rua Portugal, 221, Reviver, São Luís, Maranhão 65010-480

Tel: +55(98) 3266-4602

Fax: +55(98)3266-4666

EMail: gabinete@univima.ma.gov.br

Website: http://www.univima.ma.gov.br

Rector: Othon de Carvalho Bastos

Centre

Technological Capability *(CETECMA)* (Technology); **Vocational Technology** (Technology)

Course

Mathematics (Mathematics)

History: Founded 2003.

Main Language(s) of Instruction: Portuguese

Degrees and Diplomas: *Licenciatura*; *Mestrado*

Last Updated: 18/04/16

VITÓRIO CARDASSI MUNICIPAL INSTITUTE OF HIGHER EDUCATION OF BEBEDOURO

Instituto Municipal de Ensino Superior de Bebedouro Vitório Cardassi (IMESB)

Rua Nelson Domingos Madeira 300, Parque Eldorado, Bebedouro, São Paulo 14706-124

Tel: +55(17) 3345-9366

Fax: +55(17) 3345-9361

EMail: imesb@imesb.br

Website: http://www.imesb.br

Head: Damaris Cunha de Godoy EMail: direcao@imesb.br

Vice-direção: Patrícia Helena de Avila Jacyntho EMail: vicedirecao@imesb.br

Course

Accountancy (Accountancy); **Administration** (Administration); **Agriculture Engineering** (Agricultural Engineering); **Architecture and Town Planning** (Architecture; Town Planning); **Law** (Law); **Social Communication** (Advertising and Publicity; Journalism); **Social Services** (Social and Community Services)

History: Founded 1988.

Main Language(s) of Instruction: Portuguese

Degrees and Diplomas: *Bacharelado*; *Especialização/Aperfeiçoamento*: **Civil Law; Finance; Human Resources; Marketing.**

Student Services: Library

Last Updated: 12/04/16

PRIVATE INSTITUTIONS

ABEU UNIVERSITY CENTRE

Abeu - Centro Universitário (UNIABEU)

Rua Itaiara 301, Bloco A, Centro, Belford Roxo, Rio de Janeiro 26113-400

Tel: +55(21) 2104-0450

Fax: +55(21) 2662-1535

EMail: prmc@abeu.com.br; pesquisador@abeu.edu.br

Website: http://www.uniabeu.edu.br

Rector: Valdir Vilela

Vice-Rector for Academic Affairs: Shirley de Souza Gomes Carreira

Course

Accountancy (Accountancy); **Administration** *(Angra dos Reis)* (Administration); **Arts and Humanities** *(Nilópolis)* (Arts and Humanities; Literature; Portuguese); **Biological and Life Sciences** (Biological and Life Sciences); **Computer Networks** *(Nova Iguaçu)* (Computer Networks); **Graduate Studies** (Anatomy; Bible; Business Administration; Christian Religious Studies; Computer Networks; Cultural Studies; Educational Administration; Educational and Student Counselling; Educational Psychology; Environmental Management; Finance; Higher Education; Human Resources; Literature; Marketing; Mathematics Education; Nursing; Pedagogy; Pharmacy; Physical Education; Physical Therapy; Physiology; Social Policy; Sports; Systems Analysis; Transport Management); **History** *(Nilópolis)* (History); **Law** *(Nilópolis)* (Civil Law; Law); **Mathematics** *(Nilópolis)* (Mathematics); **Nursing** (Nursing); **Pedagogy** *(Nilópolis)* (Pedagogy); **Pharmacy** (Pharmacy); **Physical Education** (Physical Education); **Physical Therapy** (Physical Therapy); **Systems Analysis and Development** (Computer Engineering; Systems Analysis)

Further Information: Also campuses in Nilópolis, Nova Iguacu, Angra dos Reis.

History: Founded 1972. Formerly known as Abeu Faculdades Integradas.

Main Language(s) of Instruction: Portuguese

Degrees and Diplomas: *Bacharelado*; *Licenciatura*; *Especialização/Aperfeiçoamento*: **Business Administration; Civil Law; Clinical Psychology; Computer Networks; Education; English; Health Sciences; Labour Law; Law; Occupational Therapy; Pharmacy; Physical Therapy; Sports; Translation and Interpretation.** *Mestrado*: **Business Administration; Finance; Human Resources; Management; Marketing.** Also MBA

Student Services: Library

Last Updated: 03/06/15

ADVENTIST FACULTY OF HORTOLÂNDIA

Faculdade Adventista de Hortolândia (FAH)

Rua Pastor Hugo Gegembauer, 265, Parque Ortolândia, Hortolândia, SP 13184-010

Tel: +55(19) 2118-8011

Fax: +55(19) 2118-8046

EMail: euler.bahia@unasp.edu.br

Website: http://www.iasp.br/

Diretora: Elna Pereira Nascimento Cres

Tel: +51(19) 2118-8006 EMail: karen.aveiro@unasp.edu.br

Course

Accountancy (Accountancy); **Administration** (Administration); **Information Systems** (Information Technology); **Pedagogy** (Pedagogy); **Physical Education** (Physical Education)

History: Founded 1949.

Main Language(s) of Instruction: Portuguese

Degrees and Diplomas: *Bacharelado*; *Licenciatura*; *Especialização/Aperfeiçoamento*: **Business Administration; Educational Psychology; Higher Education; Physical Education; Special Education.** Also MBA.

Student Services: Library

Last Updated: 29/09/15

ADVENTIST FACULTY OF PARANA

Faculdade Adventista Paranaense (FAP)

Gleba Paiçandu, Lote 80, Zona Rural, Caixa Postal 28, Ivatuba, Paraná 87130-000

Tel: +55(44) 3236-8000

Fax: +55(44) 3236-8051

EMail: adm@iap.org.br; secretariafap@iap.org.br; posgraduacao@iap.org.br; jrconsultoria.educacional@hotmail.com

Website: http://www.iap.org.br

Diretor Geral: Gilberto Damasceno
EMail: gilberto@iap.org.br

School

Arts (Music; Musical Instruments)

Course

Administration (Administration); **Distance Postgraduate Studies** (Business Administration; Educational Administration; Educational and Student Counselling; Educational Psychology; Management; Pedagogy; Preschool Education); **Nursing** (Nursing); **Pedagogy** (Pedagogy); **Theology** (Theology)

History: Founded 2001.

Main Language(s) of Instruction: Portuguese

Degrees and Diplomas: *Bacharelado*; *Licenciatura*; *Especialização/Aperfeiçoamento*: **Educational Administration; Educational and Student Counselling; Educational Psychology; Pedagogy; Preschool Education.** Also MBA

Student Services: Canteen, Library, Residential Facilities, Sports Facilities, eLibrary

Last Updated: 04/02/16

ADVENTIST UNIVERSITY CENTRE OF SÃO PAULO

Centro Universitário Adventista de São Paulo (UNASP)

Estrada de Itapecerica, 5859, São Paulo, São Paulo 05828-001

Tel: +55(11) 2128-6000

EMail: faleconosco-sp@unasp.edu.br

Website: http://www.unasp.br

Reitor: Euler Pereira Bahia (1998-)
Tel: +55(11) 5822-6167
EMail: euler.bahia@sp.unasp.edu.br; reitoria@unasp.edu.br

Pró-Reitor Administrativo: Élnio Álvares de Freitas
EMail: marcia.oliveira@ucb.org.br

Area

Applied Social Science (Accountancy; Administration; Advertising and Publicity; Communication Studies; Journalism; Law; Radio and Television Broadcasting; Social Sciences); **Arts and Humanities** (Arts and Humanities; History; Pedagogy; Psychology; Theology); **Biological Sciences** (Biology); **Engineering** (Architecture; Construction Engineering; Production Engineering; Town Planning); **Health Science** (Nursing; Nutrition; Physical Education; Physical Therapy); **Mathematics and Computer Science** (Computer Networks; Computer Science; Data Processing; Information Technology; Mathematics; Mathematics and Computer Science; Mathematics Education; Systems Analysis); **Modern Language and Arts** (Modern Languages; Music); **Translation and Interpretation** (Translation and Interpretation)

Course

Graduate Studies *(São Paulo)* (Business Administration; Education; Educational Administration; Environmental Management; Gynaecology and Obstetrics; Health Administration; Health Sciences; Mathematics Education; Nursing; Physical Education; Physical Therapy; Physiology; Public Health)

Further Information: Also campuses in Engenheiro Coelho, Hortolândia

History: Founded 1915. Acquired present status 1999.

Academic Year: February to December.

Admission Requirements: Entrance Exam

Fees: 9,300 per semester (Brazilian Real)

Main Language(s) of Instruction: Portuguese

Accrediting Agency: Adventist Accreditation Agency.

Degrees and Diplomas: *Bacharelado*; *Licenciatura*; *Mestrado*: **Business Administration; Health Sciences.** Also MBA.

Student Services: Academic Counselling, Canteen, Careers Guidance, Cultural Activities, Facilities for disabled people, Health Services, Language Laboratory, Nursery Care, Social Counselling, Sports Facilities

Publications: Acta Científica; Escola Adventista

Publishing House: Inmprensa Universitária UNASPRESS

Last Updated: 23/06/15

ALBERT EINSTEIN ISRAELI FACULTY OF HEALTH SCIENCES

Faculdade Israelita de Ciências da Saúde Albert Einstein (FICSAE)

Av. Prof. Francisco Morato, 4.293, Butantã, São Paulo, São Paulo 05521-200

Tel: +55(11) 2151-1001 +55(11) 2151-6808

Fax: +55(11) 2151-1001 +55(11) 3746-1070

EMail: faculdade@einstein.br; facenf@einstein.br

Website: http://www.einstein.br

Diretor Geral: Henrique Sutton de Sousa Neves

Programme

Medicine (Medicine); **Nursing** (Nursing); **Postgraduate Studies** (Biomedicine; Dentistry; Health Administration; Health Education; Health Sciences; Management; Medicine; Nursing; Nutrition; Pharmacy; Physical Therapy; Psychology; Speech Therapy and Audiology; Sports; Surgery; Treatment Techniques)

History: Founded 1989. Recognized 1992.

Main Language(s) of Instruction: Portuguese

Degrees and Diplomas: *Bacharelado*; *Especialização/Aperfeiçoamento*: **Anaesthesiology; Biomedicine; Cardiology; Dentistry; Gastroenterology; Genetics; Gerontology; Gynaecology and Obstetrics; Health Administration; Health Education; Health Sciences; Laboratory Techniques; Medical Technology; Medicine; Nephrology; Neurological Therapy; Neurology; Nursing; Nutrition; Occupational Health; Occupational Therapy; Oncology; Orthopaedics; Paediatrics; Pathology; Pharmacology; Pharmacy; Physical Therapy; Plastic Surgery; Pneumology; Psychiatry and Mental Health; Psychoanalysis; Psychology; Radiology; Rehabilitation and Therapy; Speech Therapy and Audiology; Sports; Surgery; Treatment Techniques; Urology.** *Mestrado*: **Health Sciences; Nursing.** *Doutorado*: **Health Sciences.** Also MBA

Student Services: Library

Last Updated: 26/11/15

ALDETE MARIA ALVES FACULTY

Faculdade Aldete Maria Alves (FAMA)

Avenida Domingos Teixeira, 664, Recanto dos Lagos, Iturama, Minas Gerais 38280-000

Tel: +55(34) 3411-9700

Fax: +55(34) 3411-9705

EMail: secretaria@facfama.edu.br

Website: http://www.facfama.edu.br

Diretor Geral: Randall Freitas Stabile

Course

Accountancy (Accountancy); **Administration** (Administration; Business Administration); **Civil Engineering** (Civil Engineering); **Information System** (Information Technology); **Law** (Labour Law; Law); **Pedagogy** (Education; Educational Administration; Educational Psychology; Higher Education; Pedagogy; Primary Education; Special Education)

History: Founded 1998.

Main Language(s) of Instruction: Portuguese

Degrees and Diplomas: *Bacharelado*; *Licenciatura*; *Especialização/Aperfeiçoamento*: **Business Administration; Criminal Law; Education; Educational Administration; Educational and Student Counselling; Higher Education; Labour Law; Law; Primary Education; Public Administration; Special Education.** Also MBA.

Student Services: Library

Last Updated: 29/09/15

ALFACASTELO FACULTY

Faculdade Alfacastelo (FCGB)

Estr. Dr. Cícero Borges de Moraes, 100, Jardim Regina Alice, Barueri, São Paulo 06407-000

Tel: +55(11) 4198-9822

Fax: +55(11) 4163-2836

EMail: secretaria@alfacastelo.br

Website: http://www.alfacastelo.br

Diretor: Sidney Shirosaki

Course

Accountancy (Accountancy); **Administration** (Administration; Business and Commerce; Business Computing; Commercial Law; Economics; Finance; Human Resources; Information Sciences)

History: Founded 2000. Formerly known as Faculdade de Ciências Gerenciais de Barueri.

Main Language(s) of Instruction: Portuguese

Degrees and Diplomas: *Bacharelado*

Student Services: Library

Last Updated: 29/09/15

ALFREDO NASSER FACULTY

Faculdade Alfredo Nasser (UNIFAN)

Avenida Bela Vista 26, Jardim Esmeraldas, Aparecida de Goiânia, Goiás 74905-020

Tel: +55(62) 3094-9494

Fax: +55(62) 3094-9714

EMail: unifan@unifan.edu.br

Website: http://www.unifan.edu.br

Diretoria Geral: Alcides Ribeiro Filho
EMail: presidencia@unifan.edu.br

Diretoria Acadêmica: Carlos Alberto Vicchiatti
EMail: diretoriaacademica@unifan.edu.br

Course

Accountancy (Accountancy); **Administration** (Administration); **Biomedicine** (Biomedicine); **Economics** (Economics); **Education** (Education); **Geography** (Geography); **Law** (Law); **Mathematics** (Mathematics); **Modern Languages** (English; Portuguese; Spanish); **Nursing** (Nursing); **Pharmacy** (Pharmacy); **Physiotherapy** (Physical Therapy)

History: Founded 2000 as Escola Alfredo Nasser de Ensino Superior. Acquired present title and status 2005.

Main Language(s) of Instruction: Portuguese

Accrediting Agency: Ministry of Education

Degrees and Diplomas: *Bacharelado*; *Licenciatura*; *Especialização/Aperfeiçoamento*: **Business Administration; Civil Law; Distance Education; Educational Psychology; Law; Mathematics Education; Pharmacology.** Also MBA

Student Services: Library

Last Updated: 29/09/15

ANCHIETA FACULTY OF HIGHER EDUCATION OF PARANA

Faculdade Anchieta de Ensino Superior do Paraná

Rua Pedro Gusso, 4150 - Cidade Industrial, Curitiba, Paraná 81315-000

Tel: +55(41) 3069-4040

EMail: faesp@faesppr.edu.br

Website: http://www.faesppr.edu.br

Diretor Geral: Daniel Roberto de Almeida

Directora Acadèmica: Rosane do Carmo Machado

Course

Accountancy (Accountancy); **Administration** (Administration); **Advertising and Publicity** (Advertising and Publicity); **Biomedicine** (Biomedicine); **Environmental Engineering** (Environmental Engineering); **Industrial Management** (Industrial Management); **Information Systems** (Information Technology); **Logistics** (Transport Management); **Pedagogy** (Education; Pedagogy); **Production Engineering** (Production Engineering)

Further Information: Also Campus II – Localizado na Avenida Luiz Xavier n° 75 – Centro - Curitiba

History: Founded 2003.

Main Language(s) of Instruction: Portuguese

Degrees and Diplomas: *Bacharelado*; *Licenciatura*; *Especialização/Aperfeiçoamento*: **Administration; Education; Environmental Studies; Health Sciences; Justice Administration; Literacy Education; Public Administration; Public Health; Special Education.**

Student Services: Library

Last Updated: 29/09/15

ANGEL VIANNA FACULTY

Faculdade Angel Vianna

Rua Jornalista Orlando Dantas, 2, Botafogo, Rio de Janeiro, RJ 22231-010

Tel: +55(21) 2552-0139

Fax: +55(21) 2551-0099

EMail: angel@angelvianna.com.br

Website: http://www.escolaangelvianna.com.br/novo/default.asp

Diretora: Angel Vianna

Vice Diretora: Márcia Feijó de Araújo

Course

Dance (Dance)

Degrees and Diplomas: *Bacharelado*; *Licenciatura*; *Especialização/Aperfeiçoamento*: **Dance.**

Student Services: Library

Last Updated: 29/09/15

ANGLICAN FACULTY OF ERECHIM

Faculdade Anglicana de Erechim (FAE)

Av. Sete de Setembro, 44 - Centro, Erechim, RS 99700-000

Tel: +55(54) 2107-7800

Fax: +55(54) 2107-7800

EMail: contato@faers.com.br

Website: http://www.faers.com.br

Course

Accountancy (Accountancy); **Administration** (Administration); **Design** (Fashion Design); **Industrial Electronics Technology** (Electronic Engineering); **Pedagogy** (Education; Pedagogy); **Systems Analysis** (Systems Analysis)

History: Founded 2002.

Main Language(s) of Instruction: Portuguese

Accrediting Agency: Ministry of Education

Degrees and Diplomas: *Bacharelado*; *Licenciatura*; *Especialização/Aperfeiçoamento*: **Accountancy; Business Administration; Design; Educational Administration; Educational Psychology; Educational Sciences; Human Resources; Industrial Maintenance; Information Technology; Marketing.**
Student Services: Library
Last Updated: 29/09/15

ANGLO-AMERICAN INSTITUTE OF EDUCATION OF FOZ DO IGUACU

Instituto Superior de Educação Anglo-Americano de Foz do Iguaçu (ISEAA)
Avenida Paraná, 5661, Vila A, Foz do Iguaçu, PR 85860-590
Tel: +55(45) 3028-3232
Fax: +55(45) 3028-3698
EMail: angloamericano.ffi@angloamericano.edu.br
Website: http://www.angloamericano.edu.br/

Reitor: Paulo César Martinez y Alonso
EMail: reitorpauloalonso@angloamericano.edu.br

Course
Pedagogy (Pedagogy)
Degrees and Diplomas: *Licenciatura*
Last Updated: 18/04/16

ANGLO-AMERICAN INTEGRATED FACULTIES

Faculdades Integradas Anglo-Americano (FIAA)
Avenida das Américas, 2603 - Barra da Tijuca,
Rio de Janeiro, Rio de Janeiro 22631002
Tel: +55(21) 3388-9133
Fax: +55(21) 3388-9132
EMail: angloamericano.frj@angloamericano.edu.br
Website: http://www.angloamericano.edu.br

Diretor: Paulo César Martinez y Alonso
EMail: reitorpauloalonso@angloamericano.edu.br

Course
Computer Networks (Computer Networks); **Computer Science** (Computer Science); **Environmental Management** (Environmental Management); **International Business** (International Business); **International Relations** (International Relations); **Letters** (Literature); **Marketing** (Marketing); **Pedagogy** (Pedagogy); **Systems Analysis** (Computer Science)
Further Information: Also campuses in Foz do Iguaçu, João Pessoa, Caxias do Sul, Passo Fundo, Campina Grande, Chapeco and Bagé
History: Founded 1973.
Main Language(s) of Instruction: Portuguese
Degrees and Diplomas: *Tecnólogo*; *Bacharelado*
Last Updated: 23/10/15

ANTÔNIO EUFRÁSIO DE TOLEDO UNIVERSITY CENTRE OF PRESIDENTE PRUDENTE

Centro Universitario Antônio Eufrásio de Toledo de Presidente Prudente (FIAETPP)
Praça Raul Furquim 09, Vila Furquim,
Presidente Prudente, São Paulo 19030430
Tel: +55(18) 3901-4000
Fax: +55(18) 3901-4009
EMail: toledo@unitoledo.br
Website: http://www.toledoprudente.edu.br

Reitor: Milton Pennacchi

Course
Accountancy (Accountancy); **Administration** (Administration); **Architecture and Town Planning** (Architecture; Town Planning); **Civil Engineering** (Civil Engineering); **Computer Science** (Computer Science); **Economics** (Economics); **Finance** (Finance); **Law** (Law); **Marketing** (Marketing); **Production Engineering** (Production Engineering); **Social Services** (Social and Community Services)
History: Founded 1961.
Main Language(s) of Instruction: Portuguese
Degrees and Diplomas: *Bacharelado*; *Especialização/Aperfeiçoamento*. Also MBAs
Student Services: Library
Last Updated: 08/07/15

APARÍCIO CARVALHO INTEGRATED FACULTIES

Faculdades Integradas Aparício Carvalho (FIMCA)
Rua das Araras 241, Jardim Eldorado,
Porto Velho, Rondônia 78912640
Tel: +55(69) 3227-8900
EMail: fimca@fimca.com.br
Website: http://www.fimca.com.br

Diretor Geral: Maurício Carvalho
EMail: direcaogeral@fimca.com.br

Course
Accountancy (Accountancy); **Administration** (Administration); **Agronomy** (Agronomy); **Architecture and Town Planning** (Architecture; Town Planning); **Biological and Life Sciences** (Biological and Life Sciences); **Biomedicine** (Biomedicine); **Dentistry** (Dentistry); **Gastronomy** (Cooking and Catering); **Hospital Management** (Health Administration); **Medicine** (Medicine); **Nursing** (Nursing); **Occupational Therapy** (Occupational Therapy); **Pharmacy** (Pharmacy); **Physical Therapy** (Physical Therapy); **Psychology** (Psychology); **Social Services** (Social and Community Services); **Speech Therapy** (Speech Therapy and Audiology); **Tourism** (Tourism); **Veterinary Science** (Veterinary Science); **Zoology** (Zoology)
History: Founded 1998.
Main Language(s) of Instruction: Portuguese
Degrees and Diplomas: *Bacharelado*; *Licenciatura*; *Especialização/Aperfeiçoamento*. Also MBA
Last Updated: 12/06/15

ARCHDIOCESAN FACULTY OF CURVELO

Faculdade Arquidiocesana de Curvelo (FAC)
Rua João Pessoa 88, 2° Andar, Centro,
Curvelo, Minas Gerais 35790-000
Tel: +55(38) 3721-3945
Fax: +55(38) 3721-3945
EMail: fac@fac.br
Website: http://www.fac.br

Diretor: Lindomar Rocha Mota EMail: diretoria@fac.br

Course
Accountancy (Accountancy); **Administration** (Administration; Business and Commerce); **Law** (Law)
History: Founded 1997.
Main Language(s) of Instruction: Portuguese
Accrediting Agency: Ministry of Education
Degrees and Diplomas: *Bacharelado*
Student Services: Library
Last Updated: 22/10/15

ARCHDIOCESE OF MARIANA DOM LUCIANO FACULTY

Faculdade Arquidiocesana de Mariana Dom Luciano (FAM)
Rodovia dos Inconfidentes, Km 108 s/n, Mariana, MG 35420-000
Tel: +55(31) 3558-1439
Fax: +55(31) 3558-1439
EMail: famariana@famariana.edu.br
Website: http://www.famariana.edu.br/

Reitor: Dom Geraldo Lyrio Rocha
Diretor Acadêmico: Edmar José da Silva
EMail: fam.mariana@gmail.com

Course
Philosophy (Philosophy)

History: Founded 1971.

Main Language(s) of Instruction: Portuguese

Degrees and Diplomas: *Bacharelado*

Student Services: Library

Last Updated: 30/09/15

ARMANDO ÁLVARES PENTEADO FOUNDATION

Fundação Armando Alvares Penteado (FAAP)

Rua Alagoas, 903, Higienópolis,
São Paulo 01242-902
Tel: +55(11) 3662-7000
Fax: +55(11) 3662-1662 +55(11) 3662-1173
EMail: posrp.secretaria@faap.br; vestibular@faap.br; possjc.secretaria@faap.br
Website: http://www.faap.br

Diretor-Presidente: Antonio Bias Bueno Guillon

Assessor Administrativo e Financeiro: Tomio Ogassavara

Faculty

Administration *(FAE-FAAP)* (Administration); **Communication and Marketing** *(FACOM-FAAP)* (Advertising and Publicity; Cinema and Television; Journalism; Marketing; Public Relations; Radio and Television Broadcasting; Visual Arts); **Economics** *(FEC-FAAP)* (Economics; International Relations); **Engineering** *(FEFAAP)* (Chemical Engineering; Civil Engineering; Electrical Engineering; Mechanical Engineering; Production Engineering); **Law** *(FAD-FAAP)* (Law); **Visual Arts and Architecture** (Architecture; Cultural Studies; Fashion Design; Graphic Design; Industrial Design; Town Planning; Visual Arts)

Further Information: Also São José dos Campos and Ribeirao Preto Campuses

History: Founded 1947.

Main Language(s) of Instruction: Portuguese

Degrees and Diplomas: *Bacharelado*; *Especialização/Aperfeiçoamento*: **Accountancy; Architecture; Art History; Art Management; Cinema and Television; Civil Engineering; Civil Law; Communication Studies; Construction Engineering; Design; Finance; Graphic Design; Human Resources; Industrial Design; Industrial Management; Interior Design; Jewellery Art; Journalism; Management; Marketing; Mass Communication; Photography; Radio and Television Broadcasting; Visual Arts.** Also MBA in Family Entrepeneurship and Family Business Management, Luxury Management, Executive MBA

Student Services: Library

Last Updated: 08/12/15

ARNALDO JANSSEN FACULTY

Faculdade Arnaldo Janssen (FAJANSSEN)

Praça João Pessoa, 200, Funcionários,
Belo Horizonte, MG 30140-020
Tel: +55(31) 3524-5001
Fax: +55(31) 3524-5005
EMail: contato@faculdadearnaldo.edu.br
Website: http://www.faculdadearnaldo.edu.br

Diretor Executivo: Marcelo Moraes Tavares

Administrative Officer: João Guilherme de Souza Porto
EMail: joaoporto@faculdadearnaldo.edu.br

Course

Administration (Administration; Management); **Law** (Law)

History: Founded 2001.

Main Language(s) of Instruction: Portuguese

Accrediting Agency: Ministry of Education

Degrees and Diplomas: *Bacharelado*; *Especialização/Aperfeiçoamento*: **Law; Management.**

Student Services: Library

Last Updated: 30/09/15

ARTHUR SÁ EARP NETO FACULTY/FACULTY OF MEDICINE OF PETRÓPOLIS

Faculdade Arthur Sá Earp Neto/Faculdade de Medicina de Petrópolis (FMP/FASE)

Av. Barão do Rio Branco, 1003 - Centro,
Petrópolis, Rio de Janeiro 25680-120
Tel: +55(24) 2244-6452/6456
Fax: +55(24) 2244-6496
EMail: fog@fmpfase.edu.br
Website: http://www.fmpfase.edu.br

Supervisora Geral e Diretora da Faculdade Arthur Sá Earp Neto – FASE: Maria Isabel de Sá Earp de Resende Chaves (1998-)

Diretor da Faculdade de Medicina de Petrópolis – FMP: Paulo Cesar Guimarães

Course

Administration (Administration; Health Administration; Information Management; Information Sciences); **Graduate Studies** (Health Administration; Nutrition; Psychology; Public Health; Rehabilitation and Therapy); **Medicine** (Medicine); **Nursing** (Nursing); **Nutrition** (Nutrition)

History: Founded ad Faculdade de Medicina de Petrópolis 1967. Faculdade Arthur Sá Earp Neto founded 1998

Main Language(s) of Instruction: Portuguese

Accrediting Agency: Ministry of Education

Degrees and Diplomas: *Bacharelado*; *Licenciatura*; *Especialização/Aperfeiçoamento*: **Business Administration; Health Administration; Health Sciences; Nutrition; Psychology; Public Health; Rehabilitation and Therapy.**

Student Services: Library

Last Updated: 30/09/15

ASCES FACULTY

Faculdade ASCES

Avenida Portugal 584, Santa Maria, Caruaru, PE 55016400
Tel: +55(81) 2103-2000
EMail: asces@asces.edu.br
Website: http://www.asces.edu.br

Diretor Presidente: Paulo Muniz Lopez

Diretora Acadêmica: Marileide Rosa de Oliveira

Course

Biomedicine (Biomedicine); **Environmental Engineering** (Environmental Engineering); **International Relations** (International Relations); **Journalism** (Journalism); **Law** (Law); **Nursing** (Nursing); **Odontology** (Dentistry); **Pharmacy** (Pharmacy); **Physical Education** (Physical Education); **Physiotherapy** (Physical Therapy); **Production Engineering** (Production Engineering); **Public Administration** (Public Administration); **Public Health** (Public Health); **Social Service** (Social Work; Welfare and Protective Services)

History: Founded 1959. Acquired present status 2005. Maintained by Associação Caruaruense de Ensino Superior e Técnico (Higher Education Association of Caruaru).

Main Language(s) of Instruction: Portuguese

Degrees and Diplomas: *Bacharelado*; *Especialização/Aperfeiçoamento*: **Criminal Law; Criminology; Dentistry; Health Sciences; International Business; International Law; Law; Microbiology; Nursing; Orthodontics; Pharmacy; Physical Education; Physical Therapy; Public Health; Public Law; Safety Engineering; Social and Community Services; Social Welfare; Stomatology.**

Student Services: Library

Last Updated: 30/09/15

ASSESSORITEC FACULTY OF TECHNOLOGY

Faculdade de Tecnologia Assessoritec

Rua Marquês de Pombal, 287, Iririú, Joinville, SC
Tel: +57(47) 3451-0400
EMail: assessoritec@assessoritec.com.br
Website: www.assessoritec.com.br

Diretor Geral: Anelísio Machado

Course

Industrial Maintenance (Industrial Maintenance); **Industrial Management** (Industrial Management); **Mechanical and Manufacturing Engineering** (Mechanical Engineering; Production Engineering); **Postgraduate Studies** (Engineering Management; Finance; Human Resources; Safety Engineering); **Quality Management** (Safety Engineering)

History: Founded 2005. Received accreditation 2007.

Main Language(s) of Instruction: Portuguese

Degrees and Diplomas: *Tecnólogo*; *Especialização/Aperfeiçoamento*: **Engineering Management; Finance; Human Resources; Safety Engineering.**

Student Services: Library

Last Updated: 25/11/15

ASSOCIATED FACULTIES OF SAO PAULO

Faculdades Associadas de São Paulo (FASP)

Avenida Paulista 2000, São Paulo, São Paulo 01310-200

Tel: +55(11) 3016-0233

EMail: secretaria@fasp.br

Website: http://www.fasp.br

Diretor: Nilton Trama

Course

Administration (Administration); **Computer Science** (Computer Science)

History: Founded 1974

Main Language(s) of Instruction: Portuguese

Degrees and Diplomas: *Bacharelado*; *Especialização/Aperfeiçoamento*; *Mestrado*

Last Updated: 18/04/16

ASSOCIATED FACULTIES OF UBERABA

Faculdades Associadas de Uberaba (FAZU)

Avenida do Tutuna 720, Uberaba, Minas Gerais 38061500

Tel: +55(34) 3318-4188

Fax: +55(34) 3318-4188

EMail: fazu@fazu.br

Website: http://www.fazu.br

Diretor Acadêmico: Carlos Henrique Cavallari Machado

Course

Agronomy (Agronomy); **Food Processing** (Food Technology); **Zoology**

History: Founded 1975 as Faculdade de Agronomia e Zootecnia de Uberaba. Acquired present title 2002.

Main Language(s) of Instruction: Portuguese

Degrees and Diplomas: *Bacharelado*; *Especialização/Aperfeiçoamento*

Last Updated: 11/06/15

ASSUNÇÃO UNIVERSITY CENTRE

Centro Universitário Assunção (UNIFAI)

Rua Afonso Celso, 671/711, Vila Mariana, São Paulo 04263100

Tel: +55(11) 5087-0199

EMail: iesp@unifai.edu.br

Website: http://www.unifai.edu.br

Reitor: Edélcio Serafim Ottaviani

Vice-Reitora: Karen Ambra Cordeiro

Course

Accountancy (Accountancy); **Administration** *(Vila Mariana)* (Administration); **Archiving** (Archiving); **Computer Engineering** (Computer Engineering); **Geography** *(Vila Mariana)* (Geography); **History** *(Vila Mariana)* (History); **Information System** (Computer Science; Information Technology); **Language and Literature** *(Vila Mariana)* (Literature; Modern Languages); **Law** *(Vila Mariana)* (Law); **Library Studies** *(Vila Mariana)* (Library Science); **Mathematics** *(Vila Mariana)* (Mathematics); **Pedagogy** *(Vila Mariana)* (Pedagogy; Primary Education); **Philosophy** (Philosophy); **Secretarial Studies** *(Vila Mariana)* (Secretarial Studies); **Social Sciences** *(Vila Mariana)* (Anthropology; Geography; History; Political Sciences; Social Sciences; Sociology); **Tourism** (Hotel and Restaurant; Tourism)

History: Founded 1971. Acquired present title and status 2000.

Main Language(s) of Instruction: Portuguese

Degrees and Diplomas: *Bacharelado*; *Licenciatura*; *Especialização/Aperfeiçoamento*: **Art History; Business Administration; Cultural Studies; Education; Educational Psychology; Higher Education; History; Library Science; Literacy Education; Primary Education; Psychology; Religion.** *Mestrado*

Last Updated: 23/06/15

AUGUSTO MOTTA UNIVERSITY CENTRE

Centro Universitário Augusto Motta (UNISUAM)

Avenida Paris, 72, Bonsucesso, Rio de Janeiro, Rio de Janeiro 21041-020

Tel: +55(21) 3882-9797 +55(21) 3882-9702

Fax: +55(21) 2564-2244

EMail: reitoria@unisuam.edu.br

Website: http://www.unisuam.edu.br

Reitor: Arapuan Medeiros da Motta Netto

Course

Accountancy (Accountancy); **Administration** (Administration); **Advertising and Publicity** (Advertising and Publicity); **Architecture and Urbanism** (Architecture; Town Planning); **Arts and Humanities** (Arts and Humanities; English; Literature; Portuguese); **Biological and Life Sciences** (Biological and Life Sciences); **Chemical Engineering** (Chemical Engineering); **Civil Engineering** (Civil Engineering); **Computer Science** (Computer Science); **Electrical Engineering** (Electrical Engineering); **Esthetics and Cosmetics** (Cosmetology); **Gastronomy** (Cooking and Catering); **Graduate Studies** (Business Administration; Civil Law; Cooking and Catering; Law; Nursing; Nutrition; Occupational Health; Physical Education; Physical Therapy; Portuguese; Social and Community Services; Structural Architecture); **History** (History); **Informatics** (Computer Science); **Journalism** (Journalism); **Law** (Law); **Logistics** (Transport Management); **Marketing** (Marketing); **Mathematics** (Mathematics); **Nursing** (Nursing); **Nutrition** (Nutrition); **Pedagogy** (Pedagogy; Teacher Training); **Petroleum and Gas Engineering** (Petroleum and Gas Engineering); **Pharmacy** (Pharmacy); **Physical Education** (Physical Education); **Physical Therapy** (Physical Therapy); **Production Engineering** (Production Engineering); **Psychology** (Psychology); **Social Service** (Social and Community Services); **Tourism** (Tourism)

History: Founded 1970.

Main Language(s) of Instruction: Portuguese

Accrediting Agency: Ministry of Education.

Degrees and Diplomas: *Tecnólogo*; *Bacharelado*; *Licenciatura*; *Especialização/Aperfeiçoamento*: **Archaeology; Cosmetology; Nutrition; Physical Therapy.** *Mestrado*: **Development Studies; Rehabilitation and Therapy.** *Doutorado*: **Rehabilitation and Therapy.** Also MBA.

Student Services: IT Centre, Library

Last Updated: 24/06/15

AVEC FACULTY OF VILHENA

Faculdade AVEC de Vilhena (FECAV)

Av. Liliana Gonzaga, 1265, Nova Vilhena, Vilhena, RO 76980-000

Tel: +55(69) 3322-2822 +55(69) 3322-3336

Fax: +55(69) 3322-2822

EMail: secretaria@avec.br; reges.denis@gmail.com

Website: http://reges.com.br/vilhena

Presidente: José Gonzaga da Silva Neto

Course

Accountancy (Accountancy); **Administration** *(FCGV)* (Administration); **Graduate Studies**; **Law** (Law); **Pedagogy** (Pedagogy); **Technical Studies** (Computer Networks; Systems Analysis)

History: Founded 1989. Integrated the Rede Gonzaga de Ensino Superior (REGES) Network and acquired current title 2011.

Main Language(s) of Instruction: Portuguese

Degrees and Diplomas: *Tecnólogo*; *Bacharelado*; *Licenciatura*. Also MBA.
Student Services: Library, eLibrary
Last Updated: 30/06/15

BAGOZZI FACULTY

Faculdade Bagozzi

Rua Caetano Marchesini 952, Curitiba, PR 81070-110
Tel: +55(41) 3521-2727
EMail: faculdade@faculdadebagozzi.edu.br
Website: http://www.faculdadebagozzi.edu.br

Diretor: Douglas Oliani

Course
Administration (Administration); **Computer Engineering** (Computer Engineering); **Computer Science** (Computer Science); **Electrical Engineering** (Electrical Engineering); **Environmental Engineering** (Environmental Engineering); **Pedagogy** (Education; Pedagogy); **Philosophy** (Philosophy); **Production Engineering** (Production Engineering); **Social Services** (Social and Community Services)
History: Founded 2002.
Main Language(s) of Instruction: Portuguese
Degrees and Diplomas: *Bacharelado*; *Licenciatura*; *Especialização/Aperfeiçoamento*: **Business Administration; Education; Engineering; Law.** *Mestrado*
Student Services: Library
Last Updated: 30/09/15

BAHIA ADVENTIST UNIVERSITY

Faculdade Adventista da Bahia (FADBA)

BR 101 Km 201, Estrada de Capoeiruçu,
Cachoeira, Bahia 44300000
Tel: +55(75) 3425-8000
EMail: info@adventista.edu.br
Website: http://www.adventista.edu.br

Diretor Geral: Juan Choque Fernández
EMail: diretor.geral@adventista.edu.br

Faculty
Administration; **Pedagogy**; **Physical Therapy** (Physical Therapy); **Psychology and Nursing** (Nursing; Psychology); **Theology** (Theology)

School
Music (Music)
History: Founded 1998. Formerly known as Instituto Adventista de Ensino do Nordeste (Adventist Institute of Education of the North East).
Main Language(s) of Instruction: Portuguese
Degrees and Diplomas: *Bacharelado*; *Especialização/Aperfeiçoamento*. Also MBA
Last Updated: 21/07/15

BAHIA SCHOOL OF MEDICINE AND PUBLIC HEALTH

Escola Bahiana de Medicina e Saúde Pública (EBMSP)

Av. Dom João IV, 274, Brotas, Salvador, Bahia 40290-001
Tel: +55(71) 2101-1900
Fax: +55(71) 3356-1936
EMail: fbdc@bahiana.edu.br
Website: http://www.bahiana.edu.br

Diretora: Maria Luisa Carvalho Soliani

Course
Biomedicine (Biomedicine); **Medicine** (Medicine); **Nursing** (Nursing); **Occupational Therapy** (Occupational Therapy); **Odontology** (Dentistry); **Physical Education** (Physical Education); **Physiotherapy** (Physical Therapy); **Psychology** (Psychology)
Further Information: Also other units in Cabula
History: Founded 1953.
Main Language(s) of Instruction: Portuguese
Degrees and Diplomas: *Bacharelado*; *Especialização/Aperfeiçoamento*: **Art Therapy; Dental Technology; Dentistry; Educational Psychology; Health Sciences; Homeopathy; Medical Technology; Neurosciences; Nursing; Periodontics; Physical Therapy; Psychotherapy; Stomatology; Treatment Techniques.** *Mestrado*: **Dentistry; Medical Technology; Medicine; Public Health.** *Doutorado*: **Medicine; Public Health.**
Student Services: Library
Last Updated: 16/09/15

BAPTIST FACULTY OF MINAS GERAIS

Faculdade Batista de Minas Gerais (FBMG)

Rua Varginha, 630 - Bairro Floresta,
Belo Horizonte, Minas Gerais 31110-130
Tel: +55(31) 3429-7232
EMail: cynthia@sistemabatista.edu.br
Website: http://www.faculdadebatista.com.br/

Diretora: Thaís de Abreu Lacerda

Course
Accountancy (Accountancy); **Administration** (Administration; Educational Administration; Marketing; Public Administration); **Computer Networks** (Computer Networks; Data Processing); **Graduate Studies** (Accountancy; Business and Commerce; Civil Law; Criminal Law; Educational Administration; Finance; Law; Management; Marketing; Philosophy; Theology); **Law** (Law); **Theology** (Bible; Pastoral Studies; Theology)
History: Founded 1999.
Main Language(s) of Instruction: Portuguese
Degrees and Diplomas: *Bacharelado*; *Especialização/Aperfeiçoamento*: **Accountancy; Business Administration; Information Technology; Law; Theology.** Also MBA.
Student Services: Library
Last Updated: 01/10/15

BAPTIST FACULTY OF RIO DE JANEIRO

Faculdade Batista do Rio de Janeiro

Rua José Higino, 416 - Caixa Postal, 24060,
Rio de Janeiro, RJ 20510-412
Tel: +55(21) 2570-1833
EMail: teresaakil@seminariodosul.com.br
Website: http://www.fabat.com.br

Diretor: Luiz Alberto Teixeira Sayão
EMail: diretoria@seminariodosul.com.br
Coordenação Geral Acadêmica: Teresa Akil
EMail: teresaakil@seminariodosul.com.br

Course
Music (Music); **Pedagogy** (Pedagogy); **Theology** (Theology)
History: Founded 2000 as Faculdade de Ciências da Educação. Acquired present title 2004.
Main Language(s) of Instruction: Portuguese
Accrediting Agency: Ministry of Education
Degrees and Diplomas: *Bacharelado*; *Licenciatura*; *Especialização/Aperfeiçoamento*: **Theology.**
Last Updated: 01/10/15

BARÃO DE MAUÁ UNIVERSITY CENTRE

Centro Universitário Barão de Mauá (UFBM)

Rua Ramos de Azevedo, 423, Jardim Paulista,
Ribeirão Preto, São Paulo 14090-180
Tel: +55(16) 3603-6600
Fax: +55(16) 3618-6102
EMail: info@baraodemaua.com.br
Website: http://www.baraodemaua.br

Reitora: Dulce Maria Pamplona Guimarães Guimarães
EMail: reitoria@unisuam.edu.br

Vice-reitor: João Alberto de Andrade Velloso

Centre

Distance Education (Educational Psychology; Higher Education; Special Education)

Course

Administration (Administration); **Architecture and Urbanism** (Architecture; Town Planning); **Arts and Humanities** (Arts and Humanities; English; Portuguese); **Arts Education**; **Biological Sciences** (Biological and Life Sciences); **Biomedicine** (Biomedicine); **Computer Science** (Computer Science; Mathematics and Computer Science); **Environmental Engineering** (Environmental Engineering); **Geography** (Geography); **Graduate Studies** *(MBA)* (Accountancy; Acupuncture; Business Administration; Business and Commerce; Finance; Information Technology; Marketing); **History** (History); **Journalism** (Journalism); **Law** (Law); **Medicine** (Medicine); **Nursing** (Nursing); **Pedagogy** (Pedagogy); **Pharmacy** (Pharmacy); **Physical Therapy** (Physical Therapy); **Production Engineering** (Production Engineering); **Psychology** (Psychology); **Social and Community Services** (Social and Community Services); **Social Communication** (Advertising and Publicity); **Technological Studies** (Agricultural Business; Computer Science; Cooking and Catering; Environmental Management); **Theatre** (Theatre); **Tourism** (Tourism); **Veterinary Science** (Veterinary Science)

Further Information: Also Itatiaia and Camilo Units.

History: Founded 1966. Acquired present title and status 1998.

Main Language(s) of Instruction: Portuguese

Accrediting Agency: Ministry of Education.

Degrees and Diplomas: *Tecnólogo*; *Bacharelado*; *Licenciatura*; *Especialização/Aperfeiçoamento*: **Clinical Psychology; Cultural Studies; Dermatology; Educational Psychology; History; Hotel and Restaurant; Literacy Education; Management; Media Studies; Physical Therapy; Primary Education; Psychology; Special Education.** Also MBA.

Student Services: Academic Counselling, IT Centre, Library

Last Updated: 24/06/15

BARNABITA HIGHER EDUCATION CENTRE

Centro de Educação Superior Barnabita (CESB)

Av. do Contorno n° 6475 - Savassi,
Belo Horizonte, Minas Gerais 30110-039
Tel: +55(31) 3221-0344
Fax: +55(31) 3221-0707
EMail: contato@padremachado.edu.br
Website: http://www.padremachado.edu.br

Direction Padre Machado Institute: Moreira Lima

Diretor: Aldir Remígio de Oliveira Leite

Course

Administration (Administration)

History: Founded 2006. Maintained by Instituto Padre Machado.

Main Language(s) of Instruction: Portuguese

Accrediting Agency: Ministry of Education

Degrees and Diplomas: *Bacharelado*

Last Updated: 09/06/15

BARRIGA VERDE UNIVERSITY CENTRE

Centro Universitario Barriga Verde (UNIBAVE)

Rua Pe. João Leonir DallAlba, Bairro Murialdo,
Orleans, SC 88870-000
Tel: +55(48) 3466-0192
Fax: +55(48) 3466-0192
EMail: secretaria@unibave.net
Website: http://www.unibave.net

Reitor: Elcio Willemann

Course

Accountancy (Accountancy); **Administration** (Administration); **Agricultural Business** (Agricultural Business); **Agronomy** (Agronomy); **Ceramic Engineering** (Ceramics and Glass Technology; Engineering); **Environmental Engineering** (Environmental Engineering); **Graduate Studies** (Accountancy; Alternative Medicine; Business Administration; Education; Educational Administration; Educational Psychology; Educational Sciences; Environmental Management; Environmental Studies; Finance; Health Administration; Human Resources; Law; Linguistics; Literature; Marketing; Mathematics Education; Pedagogy; Public Administration; Safety Engineering; Special Education); **Information Systems** (Information Technology); **Law**; **Mathematics** (Mathematics); **Museology** (Museum Studies); **Nursing** (Nursing); **Pedagogy** (Pedagogy; Teacher Training); **Pharmacy** (Pharmacy); **Physical Education** (Physical Education); **Production Engineering** (Production Engineering); **Psychology** (Psychology); **Veterinary Medicine** (Veterinary Science)

History: Founded 1998.

Main Language(s) of Instruction: Portuguese

Accrediting Agency: Ministry of Education.

Degrees and Diplomas: *Bacharelado*; *Especialização/Aperfeiçoamento*: **Accountancy; Business Administration; Clinical Psychology; Commercial Law; Educational Administration; Educational Psychology; Environmental Management; Finance; Health Administration; Human Resources; Information Technology; Management; Marketing; Pharmacy; Psychology; Safety Engineering.**

Student Services: Library

Last Updated: 24/06/15

BELO HORIZONTE INSTITUTE OF HIGHER EDUCATION

Instituto Belo Horizonte de Ensino Superior (IBHES)

Av. do Contorno, 9384, Barro Preto, Belo Horizonte,
MG 30110-064
Tel: +55(31) 3226-2549
EMail: marcioacbarros@unip.br
Website: http://www.ibhes.edu.br

Diretor Geral: Magno Nascimento Veloso

Course

Accountancy (Accountancy); **Administration** (Administration); **Law** (Law); **Production Engineering** (Production Engineering); **Social Communication** (Advertising and Publicity); **Tourism** (Tourism)

History: Founded 2003.

Main Language(s) of Instruction: Portuguese

Degrees and Diplomas: *Bacharelado*; *Especialização/Aperfeiçoamento*: **Administration.**

Student Services: Library

Last Updated: 29/03/16

BENNETT METHODIST UNIVERSITY CENTRE

Centro Universitario Metodista Bennett

Rua Marques de Abrantes 55 Flamengo,
Rio de Janeiro, Rio de Janeiro 22230-060
Tel: +55(21) 3509-1000
Fax: +55(21) 3509-1055
EMail: proacad@bennett.br, sgeral@metodista.br
Website: http://www.bennett.br

Reitor: Marcio de Moraes

Course

Administration (Administration; Human Resources); **Architecture and Urbanism** (Architecture; Town Planning); **Art Education** (Art Education); **International Relations** (International Relations); **Law** (Law); **Nutrition** (Nutrition); **Pedagogy** (Pedagogy); **Physical Education** (Physical Education); **Theology** (Theology)

History: Founded 1978 as Faculdades Integradas Bennett. Acquired present status and title 2004.

Main Language(s) of Instruction: Portuguese

Degrees and Diplomas: *Bacharelado*; *Licenciatura*

Student Services: Library

Last Updated: 30/07/15

BERTHIER INSTITUTE OF PHILOSOPHY

Instituto Superior de Filosofia Berthier (IFIBE)

Rua Senador Pinheiro, 350, Vila Rodrigues,
Passo Fundo, RS 99070-220
Tel: +55(54) 3045-3277
EMail: ifibe@ifibe.edu.br
Website: http://www.ifibe.edu.br

Diretor Geral: José André da Costa

Diretor Administrativo: Moacir Filipin

Course

Philosophy (Philosophy); **Postgraduate Studies** (Education; Finance)

History: Founded 1981.

Main Language(s) of Instruction: Portuguese

Degrees and Diplomas: *Bacharelado*; *Especialização/Aperfeiçoamento*: **Education; Finance.**

Last Updated: 14/04/16

BÉTHENCOURT DA SILVA FACULTY

Faculdade Béthencourt da Silva (FABES)

Rua Frederico Silva 86, 7° Andar Centro, Praça Onze,
Rio de Janeiro, Rio de Janeiro 20230-210
Tel: +55(21) 2277-7600
Fax: +55(21) 2242-2343
EMail: secretaria@fabes.com.br
Website: http://fabesrj.edu.br/

Diretora: Maysa de Lacerda Freire (1997-)

Course

Accountancy (Accountancy); **Administration** (Administration; Business Administration)

History: Founded 1981.

Main Language(s) of Instruction: Portuguese

Accrediting Agency: Ministry of Education

Degrees and Diplomas: *Bacharelado*; *Licenciatura*; *Especialização/Aperfeiçoamento*: **African Studies; Business Administration; History; International Relations; Public Administration.**

Student Services: Library

Last Updated: 01/10/15

BLAURO CARDOSO DE MATTOS INSTITUTE OF HIGHER EDUCATION

Instituto de Ensino Superior Blauro Cardoso de Mattos

Rua L, Bairro Rosário de Fátima, N° 11, Serra, ES 29161-152
Tel: +55(27) 3318-3079
EMail: faserra@faserra.edu.br
Website: http://www.faserra.edu.br

Diretor: Márcio Rosetti de Castro

Diretora Acadêmica: Andréa Rosetti de Castro

Course

Accountancy (Accountancy)

History: Founded 2000.

Main Language(s) of Instruction: Portuguese

Degrees and Diplomas: *Bacharelado*; *Especialização/Aperfeiçoamento*: **Accountancy; Finance; Public Administration.**

Last Updated: 30/03/16

BLESSED SACRAMENT FACULTY

Faculdade Santíssimo Sacramento (FSSS)

Rua Marechal Deodoro, 118, Alagoinhas, BA 48005-020
Tel: +55(75) 3182-3182
Fax: +55(75) 3182-3181
EMail: fsss@fsssacramento.br
Website: http://www.fsssacramento.br

Diretora Geral: Lúcia Maria Sá Barreto de Freitas

Course

Graduate Studies (Accountancy; Education; Educational Administration; Finance; Higher Education; Information Management; Linguistics; Literature; Management; Marketing; Pedagogy; Petroleum and Gas Engineering; Physical Education; Public Administration; Special Education; Transport Management); **Undergraduate Studies** (Accountancy; Administration; Computer Science; Pedagogy; Production Engineering; Psychology)

History: Founded 2000.

Main Language(s) of Instruction: Portuguese

Degrees and Diplomas: *Bacharelado*; *Licenciatura*; *Especialização/Aperfeiçoamento*. Also MBA.

Last Updated: 10/06/15

BLUE CROSS FACULTY

Faculdade Cruz Azul (FACRAZ/FBCT)

Av. Dr. Luís Carlos, 1000, Bairro da Penha,
São Paulo, SP 03505-000
Tel: +55(11) 2174-2300
EMail: atendimento@fbct.com.br
Website: http://www.fbct.com.br/

Course

Accountancy (Accountancy); **Administration** (Administration)

History: Founded 2008.

Main Language(s) of Instruction: Portuguese

Accrediting Agency: Ministry of Education

Degrees and Diplomas: *Bacharelado*; *Especialização/Aperfeiçoamento*: **Business Administration; Finance; Human Resources; Marketing; Public Administration.**

Student Services: Library

Last Updated: 15/10/15

BOAS NOVAS FACULTY

Faculdade Boas Novas

Avenida General Rodrigo Octávio Jordão Ramos N° 1.655, Centro de convenções Canaã, Japiim, Manaus, AM 69077-000
Tel: +55(92) 3237-2214
EMail: jose.carlos@fbnovas.edu.br
Website: http://www.fbnovas.edu.br/

Diretora Geral: Maria José Costa Lima

Coordinator of Postgraduate Studies: José Carlos Da Silva Lima

Course

Administration (Administration); **Advertising and Publicity** (Advertising and Publicity); **Pedagogy** (Education; Pedagogy); **Social Communication** (Journalism); **Theology** (Theology)

History: Founded 2005.

Main Language(s) of Instruction: Portuguese

Accrediting Agency: Ministry of Education

Degrees and Diplomas: *Bacharelado*; *Licenciatura*; *Especialização/Aperfeiçoamento*: **Business Administration; Communication Studies; Education; Educational Administration; Educational Psychology; Higher Education; History; Primary Education; Religious Studies.**

Student Services: Library

Last Updated: 01/10/15

BRAZIL ASSOCIATED FACULTY

Faculdade Associada Brasil (FAB)

Rua Tiquatira N° 243, Bosque da Saúde, São Paulo, SP 04137-111
Tel: +55(11) 5677-1150
EMail: sec@faculdadebrasil.edu.br
Website: http://www.faculdadebrasil.edu.br/

Reitor: José Feuser

Course

Administration (Administration); **Advertising** (Advertising and Publicity); **Pedagogy** (Education; Pedagogy); **Tourism** (Tourism)

Main Language(s) of Instruction: Portuguese

Degrees and Diplomas: *Bacharelado*; *Especialização/Aperfeiçoamento*: **Art Education; Art Therapy; Business Administration; Education; Educational Administration; Educational Psychology; Health Administration; Health Sciences; Higher Education; Literacy Education; Nursing; Philosophy of Education;**

Primary Education; Public Health; Special Education. Also MBA.
Student Services: Library
Last Updated: 30/09/15

BRAZILIAN BAPTIST FACULTY

Faculdade Batista Brasileira (FBB)

Rua Altino Seberto de Barros, 174, Itaigara, Bahia 41830-492
Tel: +55(71) 3505-3434
EMail: fbb@fbb.br
Website: http://www.fbb.br

Reitor: Bispo Átila Brandão EMail: reitoria@fbb.br

Diretora Geral: Andréa Brandão Kraus
EMail: andrea.kraus@fbb.br

Course
Accountancy (Accountancy); **Administration** (Administration); **Gastronomy** (Cooking and Catering); **Law** (Law); **Pedagogy** (Education; Pedagogy); **Philosophy** (Philosophy); **Production Engineering** (Production Engineering); **Theology** (Theology)

History: Founded 1996.

Main Language(s) of Instruction: Portuguese

Degrees and Diplomas: *Bacharelado*; *Licenciatura*; *Especialização/Aperfeiçoamento*: **Adult Education; Business Administration; Criminology; Dentistry; Education; Health Sciences; Law; Orthodontics; Periodontics; Primary Education; Special Education; Teacher Training; Theology.** Also Postgaduate Diplomas.
Last Updated: 30/09/15

BRAZILIAN INSTITUTE OF HIGHER CONTINUING EDUCATION

Instituto Brasileiro de Educação Superior Continuada

rua Cesar Lemos, 22, 3° piso - Vilar dos Teles,
São João de Meriti, RJ 25576-570
Tel: +55(21) 3757-9906
Fax: +55(21) 3757-9906
EMail: ibec@cimpro.com.br; espindolamichelle@yahoo.com.br; ibrahim@fatmus.com.br
Website: http://www.ibec-rio.com.br

Diretor: Charlie Rangel

Course
Music (Music)

Main Language(s) of Instruction: Portuguese

Degrees and Diplomas: *Licenciatura*

Student Services: Library
Last Updated: 17/04/16

BRAZILIAN MUSIC CONSERVATOIRE - UNIVERSIY CENTRE

Conservatorio Brasileiro de Música - Centro Universitário (CBM/CEU)

Avenida Graça Aranha 57, 12° Andar, Centro,
Rio de Janeiro, Rio de Janeiro 20030-002
Tel: +55(21) 3478-7600
EMail: cbm@cbm-musica.org.br
Website: http://www.cbm-musica.org.br

Diretora Geral: Cecilia Fernandez Conde (1998-)

Course
Art Therapy (Art Therapy); **Conducting** (Conducting); **Music** (Music; Music Education; Music Theory and Composition; Musical Instruments); **Singing** (Singing)

History: Founded 1936.

Main Language(s) of Instruction: Portuguese

Degrees and Diplomas: *Bacharelado*; *Licenciatura*; *Especialização/Aperfeiçoamento*: **Art Education; Art History; Art Therapy; Education; Fine Arts; Latin American Studies; Music; Musical Instruments.**
Last Updated: 15/09/15

BRAZILIAN SCHOOL OF ECONOMICS AND FINANCE

Escola Brasileira de Economia e Finanças (EBEF)

Praia de Botafogo, 190, 11° Andar, Botafogo,
Rio de Janeiro, RJ 22253-900
Tel: +55 (21) 2559-5814
EMail: srarj@fgv.br
Website: http://www.fgv.br/epge

Dean: Rubens Penha Cysne

Course
Economics (Economics)
History: Founded 2002.
Main Language(s) of Instruction: Portuguese
Degrees and Diplomas: *Bacharelado*; *Mestrado*: **Economic and Finance Policy; Economics.** *Doutorado*: **Economics.**
Last Updated: 16/09/15

BRAZILIAN SCHOOL OF PUBLIC AND BUSINESS ADMINISTRATION

Escola Brasileira de Administração Pública e de Empresas (FGV/EBAPE)

Praia de Botafogo, 190, 4° e 5° andares,
Rio de Janeiro, RJ 22253-900
Tel: +55 (21) 3799-5650
EMail: direcao.ebape@fgv.br
Website: http://www.ebape.fgv.br

Diretor: Flávio Carvalho de Vasconcelos
Tel: +55(21) 3799-5711 EMail: flavio.vasconcelos@fgv.br

Vice-Diretor: Alvaro Bruno Cyrino

Course
Business Administration (Administration; Business Administration; Finance; Human Resources; Management; Marketing); **Public Administration** (Public Administration)

History: Founded 1952.

Main Language(s) of Instruction: Portuguese

Degrees and Diplomas: *Bacharelado*; *Mestrado*: **Administration; Business Administration; Public Administration.** *Doutorado*: **Administration.**
Last Updated: 16/09/15

CAMILO CASTELO BRANCO UNIVERSITY

Universidade Camilo Castelo Branco (UNICASTELO)

Rua Carolina Fonseca 584, Itaquera,
São Paulo, São Paulo 8230030
Tel: +55(11) 6170-0023
Fax: +55(11) 205-8226
EMail: unicastelo@unicastelo.br
Website: http://www.unicastelo.br

Reitor: José Carlos Pettorossi Imparato
EMail: reitoria@unicastelo.br

Course
Biology - Descalvado Campus (Animal Husbandry; Nursing; Psychology; Veterinary Science); **Biology - Fernandópolis Campus** (Biomedicine; Dentistry; Medicine; Nutrition; Pharmacy; Psychology; Veterinary Science); **Biology - São Paulo Campus** (Biological and Life Sciences; Dentistry; Nursing; Nutrition; Pharmacy; Physical Education); **Exact Sciences - Descalvado Campus** (Agronomy; Chemistry; Civil Engineering; Production Engineering); **Exact Sciences - Fernandópolis Campus** (Accountancy; Agronomy; Chemical Engineering; Chemistry; Civil Engineering; Electrical Engineering; Environmental Engineering; Mathematics; Sanitary Engineering); **Exact Sciences - São Paulo Campus** (Architecture; Civil Engineering; Computer Engineering; Economics; Electrical Engineering; Environmental Engineering; Finance; Mathematics; Mechanical Engineering; Production Engineering; Radiology; Sanitary Engineering; Systems Analysis; Town Planning); **Humanities - Descalvado Campus** (Administration; Law; Pedagogy); **Humanities - Fernandópolis Campus** (Administration; Architecture; Gerontology; Law; Pedagogy; Social and Community Services; Town Planning); **Humanities - São Paulo Campus** (Administration; Advertising and Publicity; Arts and

Humanities; Geography (Human); History; Human Resources; Law; Marketing; Museum Studies; Music; Pedagogy; Psychology; Public Relations; Safety Engineering; Social and Community Services; Visual Arts)

Further Information: Also Descalvado and Fernandópolis Campuses

History: Founded 1989.

Main Language(s) of Instruction: Portuguese

Degrees and Diplomas: *Bacharelado*; *Licenciatura*; *Especialização/Aperfeiçoamento*: **African Studies; Animal Husbandry; Art Education; Art History; Art Therapy; Construction Engineering; Dental Technology; Dentistry; Educational Psychology; Forensic Medicine and Dentistry; Higher Education; Literacy Education; Mathematics Education; Occupational Health; Orthodontics; Physical Education; Plastic Surgery; Psychoanalysis; Psychology; Social Policy; Social Work.** *Mestrado*: **Animal Husbandry; Bioengineering; Biomedical Engineering; Environmental Studies.** *Doutorado*: **Biomedical Engineering.**

Last Updated: 25/03/16

CAMPO GRANDE FACULTY

Faculdade Campo Grande

Av. Afonso Pena, 275, Amambai, Campo Grande, MS 79005-000
Tel: +55(67) 3384-6949
EMail: diretoriaicg@ig.com.br
Website: http://www.icges.edu.br

Diretor: Ivan Reatte

Coordenadora Pedagógica: Daniela Sopran Gil

Course

Accountancy (Accountancy); **Administration** (Administration); **Computer Science** (Computer Science); **Law** (Law); **Nursing** (Nursing); **Nutrition** (Nutrition); **Pedagogy** (Pedagogy); **Physiotherapy** (Physical Therapy); **Production Engineering** (Production Engineering); **Social Communication** (Advertising and Publicity); **Social Services** (Social and Community Services); **Tourism** (Tourism)

Further Information: Also Campus Mato Grosso

History: Founded 2002 as Instituto Campo Grande de Ensino Superior. Acquired present title 2010.

Main Language(s) of Instruction: Portuguese

Accrediting Agency: Ministry of Education

Degrees and Diplomas: *Bacharelado*

Student Services: IT Centre, Library

Last Updated: 02/10/15

CAMPOS DE ANDRADE UNIVERSITY CENTRE

Centro Universitário Campos de Andrade (UNIANDRADE)

R. João Scuissiato, 1, Santa Quitéria, Curitibá, Paraná 80310-310
Tel: +55(41) 3219-4290
Fax: +55(41) 3223-8919
EMail: ouvidoria@uniandrade.br
Website: http://www.uniandrade.br

Reitor: José Campos de Andrade

Area

Applied Social, Human and Legal Sciences *(Postgraduate)*; **Health Sciences** *(Postgraduate)* (Health Administration; Health Sciences; Nursing; Occupational Health; Public Health)

Centre

Distance Education

Course

Accountancy (Accountancy); **Administration** (Administration); **Architecture and Town Planning** (Architecture; Town Planning); **Biology** (Biology); **Computer Science** (Computer Networks; Computer Science); **Economics** (Economics); **Engineering** (Automation and Control Engineering; Civil Engineering; Computer Engineering; Electrical Engineering; Engineering; Environmental Engineering; Materials Engineering; Mechanical Engineering); **Fashion Design** (Fashion Design); **Geography** (Geography); **History** (History); **Information Systems** (Information Technology); **Law** (Law); **Library Science** (Library Science); **Mathematics** (Mathematics); **Media - Advertising** (Advertising and Publicity; Media Studies); **Media - Journalism** (Journalism; Media Studies); **Media - Public Relations** (Media Studies; Public Relations); **Modern Languages** (Arts and Humanities; English; Portuguese; Spanish); **Nursing** (Nursing); **Nutrition** (Nutrition); **Pedagogy** (Pedagogy); **Pharmacy** (Pharmacy); **Philosophy** (Philosophy); **Physical Education** (Physical Education); **Physical Therapy** (Physical Therapy); **Physics** (Physics); **Psychology** (Psychology); **Secretarial Studies** (Secretarial Studies); **Technological Studies** (Computer Networks; Cosmetology; Environmental Management; Hotel and Restaurant; Human Resources; Interior Design; International Business; Management; Marketing; Occupational Health; Secretarial Studies; Software Engineering; Systems Analysis; Transport Management); **Tourism** (Tourism)

Further Information: Also campuses in Ponta Grossa and Maringá

History: Founded 1999.

Main Language(s) of Instruction: Portuguese

Degrees and Diplomas: *Tecnólogo*; *Bacharelado*; *Licenciatura*; *Especialização/Aperfeiçoamento*: **Civil Law; Cosmetology; Health Administration; Health Sciences; Nursing; Pharmacy; Psychology; Special Education.** *Mestrado*

Student Services: Library

Last Updated: 22/06/15

CAMPOS SALLES INTEGRATED FACULTIES

Faculdades Integradas Campos Salles (FICS)

Rua Nossa Senhora da Lapa 270/284, Lapa, SP 05072000
Tel: +55(11) 3649-7000
Fax: +55(11) 3649-7001
EMail: cs@cs.edu.br
Website: http://www.cs.edu.br

Diretor Geral: Claudinei Senger

Course

Accountancy (Accountancy); **Administration** (Administration); **Computer Science** (Computer Science); **Economics** (Economics); **International Business** (International Business); **Law** (Law); **Pedagogy** (Pedagogy)

History: Founded 1924 as Escola de Comércio Campos Salles. Acquired present status and title 1992.

Main Language(s) of Instruction: Portuguese

Degrees and Diplomas: *Bacharelado*; *Licenciatura*; *Especialização/Aperfeiçoamento*

Last Updated: 01/07/15

CANDIDO MENDES UNIVERSITY

Universidade Candido Mendes (UCAM)

Rua da Assembleia, 10, Centro,
Rio de Janeiro, Rio de Janeiro 20900-010
Tel: +55(21) 3543-6400
EMail: enunes@candidomendes.edu.br
Website: http://www.candidomendes.edu.br

Reitor: Cândido Antônio Mendes de Almeida (1998-)
Tel: +55(21) 531-2310 EMail: cmendes@candidomendes.edu.br

Pró-Reitor Administrativo e Financeiro: Paulo Roberto de Araújo Aguiar

International Relations: Andreya Mendes de Almeida Scherer Navarro, Pró-Reitora de Cooperação e Convênios Internacionais
Tel: +55(21) 531-2496

Faculty

Candido Mendes Law Faculty (FDCM) (Law); **Faculty of Political Sciences and Economics RJ (FCPERJ)** (Economics)

Unit

Araruama Unit (Administration; Civil Law; Educational Administration; Environmental Engineering; Human Resources; Law; Management; Marketing; Pedagogy; Psychology; Safety Engineering; Sanitary Engineering); **Bangu Unit** (Civil Engineering; Electrical Engineering; Production Engineering); **Campos Unit** (Accountancy; Civil Engineering; International Business; International Relations; Law; Management; Mechanical Engineering; Production Engineering); **Friburgo Unit** (Accountancy; Business Administration;

Business Education; Civil Engineering; Civil Law; Cooking and Catering; Education; Human Resources; Journalism; Law; Management; Marketing; Music; Production Engineering; Psychology; Small Business); **Ipanema Unit** (Accountancy; Dance; Fashion Design; Fine Arts; Industrial Design; Interior Design; Law; Management; Psychoanalysis; Social Sciences; Theatre); **Jacarepaguá Unit** (Accountancy; Administration; Engineering; Law; Management); **Méier Unit** (Accountancy; Administration; Law); **Niterói Unit** (Accountancy; Administration; Law; Production Engineering); **Padre Miguel Unit** (Law); **Penha Unit** (Administration; Civil Engineering; Law; Production Engineering); **Santa Cruz Unit** (Accountancy; Civil Engineering; Law; Management; Production Engineering); **Tijuca Unit** (Accountancy; Administration; Civil Engineering; Human Resources; Law; Management; Production Engineering; Safety Engineering); **Vitória Unit** (Accountancy; Administration)

Programme

Campo Grande Unit (Administration; Civil Engineering; Law; Production Engineering)

Institute

Institute of Economics, Business and Management (Accountancy; Business Administration; Management); **Institute of Engineering, Technology and Innovation** (Civil Engineering; Production Engineering; Systems Analysis); **University Institute of Research RJ (IUPERJ)** (Arts and Humanities; Cultural Studies; History; International Relations; Political Sciences; Social Sciences; Translation and Interpretation; Visual Arts)

Further Information: Also 12 centres for study and research

History: Founded 1919, acquired present status 1997. Under the supervision of the Sociedade Brasileira de Instrucção, founded 1902, and recognized by the federal authorities.

Academic Year: February to December (February-June; August-December)

Admission Requirements: Secondary school certificate and entrance examination

Main Language(s) of Instruction: Portuguese

Degrees and Diplomas: *Bacharelado*; *Licenciatura*; *Especialização/Aperfeiçoamento*: **Acupuncture; Administration; Administrative Law; Alternative Medicine; Art Education; Art Therapy; Banking; Business Administration; Business and Commerce; Business Computing; Business Education; Cinema and Television; Civil Law; Civil Security; Clinical Psychology; Cognitive Sciences; Commercial Law; Communication Studies; Community Health; Constitutional Law; Criminal Law; Cultural Studies; Distance Education; Educational Administration; Educational and Student Counselling; Educational Psychology; Educational Sciences; Educational Technology; Environmental Engineering; Environmental Management; Environmental Studies; Finance; Fine Arts; Fiscal Law; Food Technology; Health Administration; Health Education; Health Sciences; Higher Education Teacher Training; History; Human Resources; Human Rights; Industrial Management; Information Technology; International Law; International Relations; Labour Law; Latin American Studies; Law; Literacy Education; Literature; Management; Marketing; Mathematics Education; Museum Management; Neurosciences; Nursing; Nutrition; Oncology; Pedagogy; Philosophy; Photography; Preschool Education; Primary Education; Private Law; Production Engineering; Psychiatry and Mental Health; Psychoanalysis; Psychology; Public Administration; Public Health; Public Law; Real Estate; Rehabilitation and Therapy; Religious Education; Retailing and Wholesaling; Safety Engineering; Sanitary Engineering; Secondary Education; Small Business; Social Problems; Social Sciences; Social Welfare; Sociology; Software Engineering; Special Education; Taxation; Teacher Training; Theatre; Tourism; Transport Management; Visual Arts.** *Mestrado*: **Artificial Intelligence; Economics; Industrial and Production Economics; Law; Management; Operations Research; Political Sciences; Production Engineering; Regional Planning; Sociology; Town Planning.** Also Superior de Tecnologia; MBA

Student Services: Academic Counselling, Canteen, Careers Guidance, Cultural Activities, Health Services, Social Counselling, Sports Facilities

Publications: Arche; Archetypon; Dados

Last Updated: 25/03/16

CANTAREIRA FACULTY

Faculdade Cantareira (FIC)

Rua Marcos Arruda 729, Belém, São Paulo, São Paulo 3020000
Tel: +55(11) 6090-5900
Fax: +55(11) 6090-5900
EMail: fic@cantareira.br; renato@cantareira.br
Website: http://www.cantareira.br

Diretor Geral: Paulo Meinberg Junior

Course

Administration (Administration); **Advertising** (Advertising and Publicity); **Agronomy** (Agronomy); **Graduate Studies** *(Especialização)* (Agricultural Business; Law; Marketing; Music Education); **Law** (Law); **Music** (Music)

History: Founded 1998.

Main Language(s) of Instruction: Portuguese

Accrediting Agency: Ministry of Education

Degrees and Diplomas: *Bacharelado*; *Especialização/Aperfeiçoamento*: **Agricultural Business; Business Administration; Environmental Studies; Finance; Leadership; Marketing; Music Education.** Also MBA.

Student Services: Library

Last Updated: 02/10/15

CARIOCA UNIVERSITY CENTRE

Centro Universitário Carioca (UNICARIOCA)

Avenida Paulo de Frontin 568, Rio Comprido,
Rio de Janeiro, Rio de Janeiro 20261-243
Tel: +55(21) 2563-1919
EMail: dirrc@unicarioca.br
Website: http://www.unicarioca.edu.br

Reitor: Celso Niskier (1996-) EMail: reitoria@unicarioca.edu.br

Course

Accountancy (Accountancy); **Advertising and Publicity** (Advertising and Publicity); **Businesss Administration** (Business Administration; Business Computing; Finance; Human Resources; Management; Marketing); **Computer Engineering** (Computer Engineering); **Computer Science** (Computer Networks; Computer Science; Systems Analysis); **Design** (Design); **Education** (Education; Pedagogy); **Electrical Engineering** (Electrical Engineering); **Environmental Management** (Environmental Management); **Journalism** (Journalism); **Production Engineering** (Production Engineering)

Further Information: Also Méier, Bento Ribeiro and Jacarepaguá Units

History: Founded 1990.

Main Language(s) of Instruction: Portuguese

Accrediting Agency: Ministry of Education.

Degrees and Diplomas: *Tecnólogo*; *Bacharelado*; *Licenciatura*; *Especialização/Aperfeiçoamento*: **Computer Engineering; Computer Science.** *Mestrado*: **Business Administration.** Also Post-graduate Programmes and MBA.

Student Services: Library

Last Updated: 29/06/15

CARLOS DRUMMOND DE ANDRADE FACULTY

Faculdade Carlos Drummond de Andrade

Rua Professor Pedreira de Fraitas 405/415, Tatuapé,
São Paulo, São Paulo 03312-052
Tel: +55(11) 2942-1488
Fax: +55(11) 6941-1488
EMail: relacionamento@drummond.com.br;
drummond@drummond.com.br
Website: http://www.drummond.com.br

Diretor: Osmar Basílio (1998-)

Course

Accountancy (Accountancy); **Administration** (Administration); **Computer Science** (Computer Science); **Electronic Engineering** (Automation and Control Engineering; Electronic Engineering); **Graduate Studies** (Accountancy; Business Administration; Commercial Law; Communication Studies; Educational Administration; Educational Psychology; Finance; Health Administration; Higher

Education Teacher Training; Human Resources; Industrial and Organizational Psychology; Information Technology; Management; Marketing; Private Law; Sports; Transport Management); **Information Systems** (Information Technology); **Law** (Law); **Mathematics** (Mathematics); **Pedagogy** (Pedagogy); **Physical Education** (Physical Education); **Production Engineering** (Production Engineering); **Technology** (Advertising and Publicity; Automation and Control Engineering; Computer Networks; Environmental Management; Fashion Design; Finance; Graphic Design; Health Administration; Human Resources; Information Technology; International Business; Management; Marketing; Public Administration; Real Estate; Safety Engineering; Sports; Sports Management; Systems Analysis; Tourism; Transport Management)
Further Information: Also Penha, Ponte Rasa and Vila Formosa Units.
History: Founded 1998.
Main Language(s) of Instruction: Portuguese
Degrees and Diplomas: *Tecnólogo*; *Bacharelado*; *Licenciatura*; *Especialização/Aperfeiçoamento*: **Accountancy; Business Administration; Communication Studies; Educational Administration; Educational Psychology; Finance; Health Administration; Higher Education Teacher Training; Industrial and Organizational Psychology; Information Technology; Marketing; Sports.** Also MBA in Business Administration (Fashion), Transport Management, Human Resources, Management; Master of Laws (LL.M.) in Commercial Law and Private Law
Last Updated: 08/09/15

CARLOS QUEIROZ FACULTY OF PHILOSOPHY, SCIENCE AND LETTERS

Faculdade de Filosofia, Ciências e Letras Carlos Queiroz

Avenida Coronel Clementino Gonçalves 1561, Vila São Judas Tadeu, Santa Cruz do Rio Pardo, São Paulo 18900-000
Tel: +55(14) 3372-1173
Fax: +55(14) 3372-4073
EMail: fafil.oapec@argon.com.br
Website: http://oapec.com.br/faculdade

Diretora Acadêmica: Adélia de Paula Pimentel (1986-)

Course
Graduate Studies (Business Administration; Finance); **Literature and English** (English; Literature); **Literature and Spanish** (Literature; Spanish); **Pedagogy** (Pedagogy)
History: Founded 1971
Main Language(s) of Instruction: Portuguese
Degrees and Diplomas: *Bacharelado*; *Licenciatura*
Last Updated: 06/07/15

CÁSPER LÍBERO FACULTY

Faculdade Cásper Líbero

Avenida Paulista, 900, 5° Andar, Bela Vista, São Paulo, São Paulo 01310-940
Tel: +55(11) 3170-5883
Fax: +55(11) 3170-5891
EMail: diretoria@casperlibero.edu.br
Website: http://casperlibero.edu.br/

Diretor: Carlos Roberto Da Costa
Tel: +55(11) 3170-5811 EMail: diretoria@casperlibero.edu.br

Course
Advertising and Publicity (Advertising and Publicity); **Journalism** (Journalism); **Public Relations** (Public Relations); **Radio and TV** (Radio and Television Broadcasting)
History: Founded 1947.
Main Language(s) of Instruction: Portuguese
Accrediting Agency: Ministry of Education.
Degrees and Diplomas: *Bacharelado*; *Especialização/Aperfeiçoamento*: **Communication Studies; Journalism; Mass Communication; Public Relations.** *Mestrado*: **Communication Studies.**
Student Services: IT Centre, Library
Last Updated: 05/10/15

CASTELO BRANCO FACULTY

Faculdade Castelo Branco (FCB)

Avenida Brasil 1303 Maria das Graças, Colatina, ES 29705-100
Tel: +55(27)2102-6000
EMail: secretaria@funcab.br
Website: http://www.fcb.edu.br/

Diretor Administrativo: Elodilson Sabadini

Course
Accountancy (Accountancy); **Administration** (Administration); **Economics** (Economics); **Geography** (Geography); **History** (History); **Law** (Law); **Modern Languages** (English; French; Literature; Portuguese); **Pedagogy** (Education; Pedagogy); **Technology and Marketing** (Marketing; Technology)
History: Founded 2001 as Faculdades Integradas Castelo Branco. Acquired present title 2008.
Main Language(s) of Instruction: Portuguese
Accrediting Agency: Ministry of Education
Degrees and Diplomas: *Bacharelado*; *Licenciatura*; *Especialização/Aperfeiçoamento*: **Biotechnology; Business Administration; Civil Law; Education; Educational Administration; Educational and Student Counselling; Educational Psychology; Engineering; Environmental Engineering; Finance; Health Sciences; History; Labour Law; Law; Linguistics; Literacy Education; Literature; Marketing; Mathematics Education; Nursing; Preschool Education; Primary Education; Production Engineering; Public Health; Social and Community Services; Special Education.** Also MBA
Student Services: Library
Last Updated: 05/10/15

CASTELO BRANCO UNIVERSITY - RIO DE JANEIRO

Universidade Castelo Branco (UCB)

Avenida Santa Cruz, 1631, Realengo, Rio de Janeiro, Rio de Janeiro 21710-255
Tel: +55(21) 2406-7700 +55(21) 3216-7700
EMail: reitoria@castelobranco.br
Website: http://www.castelobranco.br

Reitor: Mauricio Magalhães EMail: reitoria@castelobranco.br

School
Applied Social Sciences (Advertising and Publicity; Journalism; Law; Social Work); **Exact Sciences and Technology** (Civil Engineering; Environmental Engineering; Mechanical Engineering; Production Engineering); **Health Sciences and Environmental Studies** (Biological and Life Sciences; Biomedicine; Nursing; Nutrition; Physical Education; Physical Therapy; Veterinary Science); **Management and Technology** (Accountancy; Information Technology; Management); **Teacher Training** (Foreign Languages Education; Humanities and Social Science Education; Mathematics Education; Native Language Education; Pedagogy; Physical Education; Science Education; Teacher Training)
Further Information: Also Guadalupe, Penha, Centro Units
History: Founded 1994 as Faculdade de Educação, Ciências e Letras Marechal Castelo Branco and Faculdade de Educação Física da Guanabara. Became Faculdades Integradas Castelo Branco 1976 and acquired present status and title 1994.
Academic Year: February to December (February-July; August-December)
Admission Requirements: Secondary school certificate
Main Language(s) of Instruction: Portuguese
Degrees and Diplomas: *Bacharelado*; *Licenciatura*; *Especialização/Aperfeiçoamento*: **Anatomy; Art Education; Biological and Life Sciences; Business Education; Cardiology; Chemistry; Civil Law; Clinical Psychology; Commercial Law; Computer Graphics; Criminal Law; Criminology; Educational Administration; Educational and Student Counselling; Educational Psychology; Environmental Engineering; Environmental Management; Forensic Medicine and Dentistry; Gerontology; Health Administration; History; Industrial Management; Laboratory Techniques; Labour Law; Law; Management; Marine Biology; Mathematics Education; Neurology; Neurosciences; Nursing; Paediatrics; Physical Education; Physical Therapy; Physiology; Preschool Education; Protective**

Services; Public Administration; Public Law; Rehabilitation and Therapy; Safety Engineering; Social Policy; Special Education; Visual Arts. Also MBA; Executive MBA

Student Services: Canteen, Careers Guidance, Cultural Activities, Health Services, Library, Sports Facilities

Publications: Boletim da Qualidade; Boletim Desenvolvimento Gerencial

Last Updated: 29/03/16

CATHOLIC FACULTY OF ANAPOLIS

Faculdade Católica de Anápolis

Rua 05 - 580, Cidade Jardim, Anápolis, GO 75080-730
Tel: +55(62) 3328-8900
Fax: +55(62) 3321-1048
EMail: adrianavilela@catolicadeanapolis.edu.br
Website: http://www.catolicadeanapolis.edu.br/

Diretora: Adriana Rocha Vilela Arantes

Vice-Diretora Acadêmica: Maria Inácia Lopes

Course

Administration (Administration); **Pedagogy** (Education; Pedagogy); **Philosophy** (Philosophy); **Theology** (Theology)

History: Founded 1995 as Faculdade de Filosofia São Miguel Arcanjo. Acquired present title 2008.

Main Language(s) of Instruction: Portuguese

Accrediting Agency: Ministry of Education

Degrees and Diplomas: *Bacharelado*; *Licenciatura*; *Especialização/Aperfeiçoamento*: **Business Administration; Clinical Psychology; Education; Educational Administration; Educational Psychology; Health Education; Human Resources; Industrial and Organizational Psychology; Philosophy; Primary Education.**

Student Services: Library

Last Updated: 05/10/15

CATHOLIC FACULTY OF CARIRI

Faculdade Católica do Cariri

Rua Cel. Antônio Luiz, 1068, Pimenta, Crato, Ceará 63105-000
Tel: +55(88) 3521-0880
Website: http://www.catolicadocariri.edu.br

Reitor: Fernando Panico

Course

Philosophy (Philosophy); **Secretarial Studies** (Secretarial Studies)

Main Language(s) of Instruction: Portuguese

Degrees and Diplomas: *Bacharelado*; *Licenciatura*; *Especialização/Aperfeiçoamento*: **Business Administration; Clinical Psychology; Educational Psychology; Health Education; Human Resources; Primary Education; Theology.**

Student Services: Library

Last Updated: 05/10/15

CATHOLIC FACULTY OF POUSO ALEGRE

Faculdade Católica de Pouso Alegre (FACAPA)

Avenida Monsenhor Mauro Tommasini 75,
Pouso Alegre, MG 37550-000
Tel: +55(35) 3421-1820
EMail: secretaria@facapa.edu.br
Website: http://www.facapa.edu.br

Diretor Geral: Daniel Santini Rodrigues

Diretor Acadêmico: Giovanni Marques Santos

Course

Philosophy (Philosophy); **Theology** (Theology)

History: Founded 2003.

Main Language(s) of Instruction: Portuguese

Accrediting Agency: Ministry of Education

Degrees and Diplomas: *Bacharelado*; *Especialização/Aperfeiçoamento*: **Educational Psychology; Philosophy; Psychology.**

Student Services: Library

Last Updated: 05/10/15

CATHOLIC FACULTY OF RONDONIA

Faculdade Católica de Rondônia (FCR)

Rua Gonçalves Dias, 290 - Centro, Porto Velho, RO 78900-030
Tel: +55(69) 3211-4505
EMail: fcrdiradm@gmail.com
Website: http://www.fcr.edu.br

Diretor Geral: Fabio Rychecki Hecktheuer
Tel: +55(69) 3211-4510 EMail: reitor@fcr.edu

Course

Law (Law); **Philosophy** (Philosophy); **Postgraduate** (Administration; Education; Law)

History: Founded 2007.

Main Language(s) of Instruction: Portuguese

Accrediting Agency: Ministry of Education

Degrees and Diplomas: *Bacharelado*; *Especialização/Aperfeiçoamento*: **Accountancy; Business Administration; Civil Law; Criminal Law; Distance Education; Finance; Human Resources; Industrial and Organizational Psychology; Law; Philosophy.** *Mestrado*: **History.** *Doutorado*: **Law; Political Sciences; Psychology.**

Student Services: Library

Last Updated: 05/10/15

CATHOLIC FACULTY OF TOCANTINS

Faculdade Católica do Tocantins (FACTO)

Av. Teotônio Segurado - 1402 Sul Cj. 01, Palmas, TO 77061-002
Tel: +55 (63) 3221-2100
EMail: galileu@catolica-to.edu.br
Website: http://www.catolica-to.edu.br/portal/

Diretor Geral: José Romualdo Degasperi
EMail: romualdo@catolica-to.edu.br

Vice-Diretor Acadêmico: Galileu Marcos Guarenghi

School

Agriculture (Agriculture; Agronomy; Animal Husbandry; Environmental Studies; Veterinary Science); **Engineering** (Civil Engineering; Computer Engineering; Electrical Engineering; Engineering; Environmental Engineering; Production Engineering); **Social and Applied Sciences** (Accountancy; Administration; Law)

History: Founded 2003.

Main Language(s) of Instruction: Portuguese

Accrediting Agency: Ministry of Education

Degrees and Diplomas: *Bacharelado*; *Licenciatura*; *Especialização/Aperfeiçoamento*: **Business Administration; Civil Law; Safety Engineering.** *Doutorado*: **Law.** Also MBA. PhD in cooperation with Sociedade Mineira de Cultura (PUC Minas)

Student Services: Library

Last Updated: 05/10/15

CATHOLIC FACULTY OF UBERLANDIA

Faculdade Católica de Uberlândia (FCU)

Rua Padre Pio, 300, Osvaldo Rezende, MG 38400-386
Tel: +55(34) 3236-0336
Fax: +55(34) 3216-6716
EMail: contato@catolicaonline.com.br
Website: http://catolicaonline.com.br/

Diretora Geral: Marilane Santos
EMail: diretor@catolicaonline.com.br

Course

Administration (Administration); **Environmental Engineering** (Environmental Engineering); **Law** (Law); **Logistics** (Transport Management); **Pedagogy** (Education; Pedagogy; Primary Education); **Philosophy** (Philosophy); **Social Services** (Social and Community Services); **Theology** (Theology)

History: Founded 2002.

Main Language(s) of Instruction: Portuguese

Accrediting Agency: Ministry of Education

Degrees and Diplomas: *Bacharelado*; *Licenciatura*; *Especialização/Aperfeiçoamento*: **Safety Engineering; Social Work.**

Student Services: Library

Last Updated: 05/10/15

CATHOLIC INSITUTE OF ADVANCED STUDIES OF PIAUÍ

Instituto Católico de Estudos Superiores do Piauí (ICESPI)

Rodovia Palmeirais (Pi 130) s/n, Caixa Postal 496, Km8, Teresina, PI 64001-970
Tel: +55(86) 3211-7726 +55(86) 9433-9763
Fax: +55(86) 3211-7726
EMail: contato@icespi.com.br; icespi@hotmail.com
Website: http://www.icespi.com.br

Diretor Geral: Jonilson Torres Resende

Course

Philosophy (Philosophy); **Theology** (Theology)

Main Language(s) of Instruction: Portuguese

Degrees and Diplomas: *Bacharelado*; *Licenciatura*; *Especialização/Aperfeiçoamento*: **Canon Law; Philosophy; Religious Practice.**

Last Updated: 17/04/16

CATHOLIC SALESIAN AUXILIUM UNIVERSITY CENTRE

Centro Universitário Católico Salesiano Auxilium (UNISALESIANO)

Rua Dom Bosco 265, Araçatuba, São Paulo 16400-505
Tel: +55(14) 3533-6200
EMail: academico@unisalesiano.edu.br
Website: http://www.unisalesiano.edu.br

Reitor: Luigi Favero

Director of Academic Affairs: André Luis Ornellas

Course

Accountancy (Accountancy); **Administration** (Administration); **Advertising and Publicity** (Advertising and Publicity); **Architecture** (Architecture); **Arts and Humanities** (Arts and Humanities; English; Literature; Portuguese); **Chemistry** (Chemistry); **Environmental Management** (Administration; Environmental Management); **History** (History); **Internet Systems** (Computer Engineering); **Journalism** (Journalism); **Law** (Law); **Nursing** (Nursing); **Occupational Health** (Occupational Therapy); **Pedagogy** (Pedagogy); **Physical Education** (Physical Education); **Physiotherapy** (Physical Therapy); **Psychology** (Psychology); **Social Work** (Social Work)

Further Information: Also Lins Campus.

History: Founded 1974 as Faculdade de Ciências Contábeis e Atuariais da Alta Noroeste. Acquired present title 2005.

Main Language(s) of Instruction: Portuguese

Accrediting Agency: Ministry of Education.

Degrees and Diplomas: *Tecnólogo*; *Bacharelado*; *Especialização/Aperfeiçoamento*: **Computer Engineering; Computer Graphics; Cosmetology; Education; Educational Psychology; Engineering; Health Sciences; Law; Primary Education; Safety Engineering; Veterinary Science.** Also postgraduate programmes and MBA.

Student Services: Library

Last Updated: 29/06/15

CATHOLIC UNIVERSITY CENTRE OF SANTA CATARINA

Centro Universitário Católica de Santa Catarina

Caixa Postal 251, Rua dos Imigrantes, 500, Vila Rau, Jaraguá do Sul, Santa Catarina 89254-430
Tel: +55(47) 3275-8200
Fax: +55(47) 3275-8200
EMail: reitoria@catolicasc.org.br
Website: http://www.catolicasc.org.br

Reitor: Robert Burnett EMail: reitoria@catolicasc.org.br

Pró-Reitor Administrativo: Paulo Oscar Gielow
EMail: asseadm@catolicasc.org.br

Vice Reitora e Pró-Reitora Acadêmica: Anadir Elenir Pradi Vendruscolo

Campus

Jaraguá do Sul (Accountancy; Architectural Restoration; Architecture and Planning; Automation and Control Engineering; Civil Engineering; Computer Science; Design; Electrical Engineering; Environmental Management; Fashion Design; Human Resources; Law; Mechanical Engineering; Production Engineering); **Joinville** (Accountancy; Administration; Architectural Restoration; Architecture; Business Administration; Civil Engineering; Computer Science; Electrical Engineering; Human Resources; International Business; Law; Marketing; Mechanical Engineering; Nutrition; Production Engineering; Theology; Town Planning)

Further Information: Also a campuses in Joinville and São Bento do Sul.

History: Founded 1976 as Fundação Educacional Regional Jaraguaense (FERJ). Became Centro de Ensino Superior de Jaraguá do Sul, 1985. Became Centro Universitário de Jaraguá do Sul, 2000.

Academic Year: March to December

Admission Requirements: Examination

Main Language(s) of Instruction: Portuguese

Accrediting Agency: Ministry of Education

Degrees and Diplomas: *Tecnólogo*; *Bacharelado*; *Licenciatura*; *Especialização/Aperfeiçoamento*: **Business Administration; Business and Commerce; Civil Law; Higher Education; Human Resources; Labour Law; Marketing; Social and Community Services.**

Student Services: Canteen, Language Laboratory, Library, Sports Facilities

Last Updated: 07/09/15

CATHOLIC UNIVERSITY OF BRASÍLIA

Universidade Católica de Brasília (UCB)

QS 07 Epct Lote 01, Águas Claras, Brasilia, DF 71966-700
Tel: +55(61) 3356-9000
Fax: +55(61) 3356-1800 +55(61) 3356-3010
EMail: leao@ucb.br; reitoria@ucb.br; sybelle@ucb.br; karenk@ucb.br
Website: http://www.ucb.br

Reitor: Gilberto Gonçalves Garcia EMail: reitoria@ucb.br

Pró-Reitor de Administração: Fernando de Oliveira Souza

Pró-Reitor Acadêmico: Daniel Rey de Carvalho

Programme

Accounting (Accountancy); **Administration** (Business Administration); **Architecture and Urbanism** (Architecture; Town Planning); **Biological Sciences** (Biological and Life Sciences); **Biomedicine** (Biomedicine); **Chemistry** (Chemistry); **Civil Engineering** (Civil Engineering); **Computer Science** (Computer Science); **Dentistry** (Dentistry); **Economics** (Economics); **Environmental and Sanitary Engineering** (Environmental Engineering; Sanitary Engineering); **Information Systems** (Information Technology); **International Relations** (International Relations); **Journalism** (Journalism); **Law** (Law); **Letters** (Arts and Humanities); **Mass Communication, Advertising and Publicity** (Advertising and Publicity; Mass Communication); **Mathematics** (Mathematics); **Medicine** (Medicine); **Nursing** (Nursing); **Nutrition** (Nutrition); **Pedagogy** (Pedagogy); **Pharmacy** (Pharmacy); **Philosophy** (Philosophy); **Physical Education** (Physical Education); **Physical Therapy** (Physical Therapy); **Physics** (Physics); **Psychology** (Psychology); **Social Services** (Social and Community Services)

Further Information: Also Avançado Asa Norte and Avançado Asa Sul Campuses

History: Founded 1974 as Faculdade Católica de Ciências Humanas (FCCH). Reorganized 1981 as Faculdades Integradas da Católica de Brasília (FICB), acquired present status and title 1994. A private institution under the supervision of the União Brasiliense de Educação e Cultura.

Academic Year: February to December (February-June; August-December)

Admission Requirements: Secondary school certificate and entrance examination (vestibular)

Main Language(s) of Instruction: Portuguese

Degrees and Diplomas: *Tecnólogo*; *Bacharelado*; *Licenciatura*; *Especialização/Aperfeiçoamento*: **Cinema and Television; Civil Law; Clinical Psychology; Computer Science; Criminal Law; Educational Administration; English; Health Administration; Human Rights; Literacy Education; Literature; Management; Mathematics Education; Peace and Disarmament; Physical Education; Physical Therapy; Physiology; Police Studies; Preschool Education; Psychoanalysis; Psychology; Public Administration; Social and Community Services.** *Mestrado*: **Biotechnology; Communication Studies; Economics; Education; Genetics; Gerontology; Information Technology; Law; Physical Education; Psychology.** *Doutorado*: **Biotechnology; Economics; Education; Genetics; Physical Education; Psychology.**

Student Services: Canteen, Cultural Activities, Health Services, Sports Facilities

Publications: Cadernos da Católica; Revista Universa

Publishing House: Editora Universa

Last Updated: 29/03/16

CATHOLIC UNIVERSITY OF GOIÁS

Universidade Católica de Goiás (UCG)

Av. Universitária n.1069, St. Universitário, Caixa Postal 86, Goiânia, Goiás 74605-160

Tel: +55(62) 3946-1000

EMail: ucg@ucg.br

Website: http://www.ucg.br

Reitor: Wolmir Therezio Amado
Tel: +55(62) 3946-1000 EMail: reitoria@pucgoias.edu.br

Pró-Reitor de Administração: Daniel Rodrigues Barbosa

Vice-Reitora: Olga Izilda Ronchi

Institute

Humid Tropics (Geography); **Prehistory and Anthropology** (Anthropology; Prehistory)

Centre

Economic Research (Economics); **Studies, Research and Psychological Practice** (Biological and Life Sciences)

Course

Accountancy (Accountancy); **Administration** (Business Administration); **Advertising and Publicity** (Advertising and Publicity); **Aeronautics** (Aeronautical and Aerospace Engineering); **Agricultural Business** (Agricultural Business); **Animal Husbandry** (Animal Husbandry); **Archaeology** (Archaeology); **Architecture and Urbanism** (Architecture; Town Planning); **Automation and Control Engineering - Mechatronics** (Automation and Control Engineering; Electronic Engineering); **Biology** (Biology); **Biomedicine** (Biomedicine); **Chemistry** (Chemistry); **Civil Engineering** (Civil Engineering); **Computer Engineering** (Computer Engineering); **Computer Sciences** (Computer Science); **Design** (Design); **Economics** (Economics); **Electrical Engineering** (Electrical Engineering); **Environmental Engineering** (Environmental Engineering); **Environmental Management** (Environmental Management); **Events** (Public Relations); **Food Technology** (Food Technology); **Foreign Languages** (English; French; German; Italian; Spanish); **Gastronomy** (Cooking and Catering); **Geography** (Geography (Human)); **History** (History); **International Relations** (International Relations); **Journalism** (Journalism); **Law** (Law); **Letters** (Arts and Humanities); **Mathematics** (Mathematics); **Medicine** (Medicine); **Nursing** (Nursing); **Nutrition** (Nutrition); **Pedagogy** (Pedagogy); **Pharmacy** (Pharmacy); **Philosophy** (Philosophy); **Physical Education** (Physical Education); **Physical Therapy** (Physical Therapy); **Physics** (Physics); **Production Engineering** (Production Engineering); **Psychology** (Psychology); **Secretarial Studies** (Secretarial Studies); **Social Service** (Social and Community Services); **Speech Pathology** (Speech Therapy and Audiology); **Systems Analysis and Development** (Systems Analysis); **Theology** (Theology)

Research Institute

Central Brazil Historical Studies (History; Latin American Studies)

History: Founded 1959. A non-profit private Institution administered by the Catholic Archdiocese of Goiânia.

Academic Year: March to December (March-July; August-December)

Admission Requirements: Secondary school certificate and entrance examination

Main Language(s) of Instruction: Portuguese

Degrees and Diplomas: *Tecnólogo*; *Bacharelado*; *Licenciatura*; *Especialização/Aperfeiçoamento*: **Administrative Law; Anaesthesiology; Anatomy; Arts and Humanities; Biological and Life Sciences; Cardiology; Cell Biology; Civil Law; Commercial Law; Communication Studies; Constitutional Law; Criminal Law; Dermatology; Education; Educational Psychology; Environmental Studies; Fiscal Law; Forensic Medicine and Dentistry; Genetics; Gynaecology and Obstetrics; Haematology; Health Administration; Health Sciences; Higher Education Teacher Training; History; Labour Law; Law; Management; Mass Communication; Medicine; Microbiology; Multimedia; Neurology; Neurosciences; Nursing; Nutrition; Occupational Health; Oncology; Paediatrics; Pharmacy; Physical Therapy; Physiology; Pneumology; Preschool Education; Production Engineering; Psychiatry and Mental Health; Psychoanalysis; Psychology; Psychotherapy; Public Health; Radiology; Regional Planning; Religious Education; Religious Studies; Social and Community Services; Software Engineering; Special Education; Sports; Sports Medicine.** *Mestrado*: **Arts and Humanities; Ecology; Education; Environmental Studies; Genetics; Health Sciences; History; International Relations; Law; Production Engineering; Psychology; Regional Planning; Religious Studies; Social and Community Services.** *Doutorado*: **Arts and Humanities; Ecology; Environmental Studies; Health Sciences.** Also MBA; Executive MBA

Student Services: Canteen, Cultural Activities, Health Services, Library, Social Counselling, Sports Facilities, eLibrary

Publications: Estudos

Publishing House: Divisão Gráfica e Editorial da UGC

Last Updated: 29/03/16

CATHOLIC UNIVERSITY OF PELOTAS

Universidade Católica de Pelotas (UCPEL)

Rua Felix da Cunha 412, Centro, Pelotas, Rio Grande do Sul 96010-000

Tel: +55(53) 2128-8000

EMail: ucpel@phoenix.ucpel.tche.br

Website: http://www.ucpel.tche.br

Reitor: José Carlos Pereira Bachettini Júnior
Tel: +55(53) 2128-8220 EMail: reitoria@ucpel.edu.br

Pro-Reitor Administrativo: Eduardo Luis Insaurriaga dos Santos

Pró-Reitora Acadêmica: Patrícia Haertel Giusti

International Relations: Fabio Rychecki Hecktheuer, Assessor
Tel: +55(532) 284-8295

Institute

Philosophy (Philosophy); **Religious Studies** (Religious Studies); **Theology** (Theology)

Centre

Education and Communication (Advertising and Publicity; Fashion Design; Journalism; Literature; Mass Communication; Mathematics; Pedagogy; Sound Engineering (Acoustics); Tourism); **Law, Economics and Social Sciences** (Accountancy; Business Administration; Business and Commerce; Civil Security; Economics; Finance; Human Resources; Law; Social and Community Services); **Life and Health Sciences** (Ecology; Medicine; Nursing; Pharmacy; Physical Therapy; Psychology); **Polytechnic** (Architecture; Civil Engineering; Computer Engineering; Electrical Engineering; Electronic Engineering; Town Planning)

Further Information: Also University Hospital

History: Founded 1960. A private Institution under the supervision of the Sociedade Pelotense de Assistência e Cultura, but receives financial support from the Federal Government.

Academic Year: March to November

Admission Requirements: Secondary school certificate or foreign equivalent and entrance examination

Main Language(s) of Instruction: Portuguese

Accrediting Agency: CNPq; FAPERGS; CAPES

Degrees and Diplomas: *Bacharelado*; *Licenciatura*; *Especialização/Aperfeiçoamento*: **Biological and Life Sciences; Civil Engineering; Cosmetology; Design; Educational and Student Counselling; Educational Psychology; Energy Engineering; Environmental Studies; Fashion Design; Fiscal Law; Health Administration; Industrial Design; Laboratory Techniques; Marketing; Nursing; Occupational Health; Preschool Education; Protective Services; Psychotherapy; Rehabilitation and Therapy; Road Transport; Safety Engineering.** *Mestrado*: **Arts and Humanities; Behavioural Sciences; Computer Engineering; Electronic Engineering; Health Sciences; Social Policy.** *Doutorado*: **Arts and Humanities; Behavioural Sciences; Health Sciences; Social Policy.**

Student Services: Academic Counselling, Canteen, Cultural Activities, Facilities for disabled people, Health Services, Language Laboratory, Nursery Care, Social Counselling, Sports Facilities

Publications: ECO Revista; Linguagem & Ensino; Razão e Fé; Revista da Escola de Direito; Revista da Escola de Medicina; Sociedade em Debate

Publishing House: Editora da Universidade Católica de Pelotas - EDUCAT

Last Updated: 29/03/16

CATHOLIC UNIVERSITY OF PERNAMBUCO

Universidade Católica de Pernambuco (UNICAP)

Rua do Principe, 526, Boa Vista, Recife, Pernambuco 50050-900
Tel: +55(81) 2199-4016
Fax: +55(81) 3423-0541
EMail: asseplan@unicap.br
Website: http://www.unicap.br

Reitor: Pedro Rubens Ferreira Oliveira, S.J. (2006-)
Tel: +55(81) 3216-4110 EMail: prubens@unicap.br

Pró-reitor Administrativo: Luciano José Pinheiro Barros
Tel: +55(81) 2119-4142 EMail: ljpb@unicap.br

Pró-reitora Acadêmica: Aline Maria Grego
Tel: +55(82) 2119-4055 EMail: amgrego@unicap.br

International Relations: Paulo Gaspar de Meneses, S.J.
Tel: +55(81) 3216-4110 EMail: pmeneses@unicap.br

Programme

Postgraduate Studies (Civil Engineering; Clinical Psychology; Environmental Management; Law; Modern Languages; Psychology; Religious Studies)

Centre

Biology and Health Sciences (CCBS) (Biological and Life Sciences; Health Administration; Medicine; Nursing; Physical Therapy; Psychology; Speech Therapy and Audiology); **Juridical Sciences (CCJ)** (Law); **Sciences and Technology (CCT)** (Architecture; Chemical Engineering; Chemistry; Civil Engineering; Computer Science; Environmental Engineering; Mathematics; Mathematics Education; Physics; Science Education; Town Planning); **Social Sciences (CCS)** (Accountancy; Administration; Advertising and Publicity; Economics; Journalism; Marine Transport; Photography; Public Relations; Social and Community Services; Software Engineering; Tourism); **Theology and Human Sciences (CTCH)** (Arts and Humanities; History; Pedagogy; Philosophy; Theology)

History: Founded 1951 incorporating Faculty of Economics, established 1942, Faculty of Philosophy, 1943, and School of Engineering, 1912. Reorganized 1973 with a structure comprising centres for professional education. A private institution under the supervision of the Society of Jesus and recognized by the Federal Government.

Academic Year: February to December (February-June; August-December)

Admission Requirements: Secondary school certificate and entrance examination

Fees: 295-729.26 per month according to courses (Brazilian Real)

Main Language(s) of Instruction: Portuguese

Degrees and Diplomas: *Bacharelado*: **Accountancy; Advertising and Publicity; Architecture; Chemical Engineering; Civil Engineering; Computer Science; Economics; Environmental Engineering; Journalism; Law; Nursing; Philosophy; Physical Therapy; Physics; Psychology; Social and Community Services; Software Engineering; Speech Therapy and Audiology; Town Planning.** *Licenciatura*: **Arts and Humanities; Biological and Life Sciences; Chemistry; English; Foreign Languages Education; History; Humanities and Social Science Education; Mathematics; Mathematics Education; Native Language Education; Philosophy; Portuguese; Science Education; Spanish.** *Especialização/Aperfeiçoamento*: **Bible; Cinema and Television; Educational Psychology; Engineering Management; Foreign Languages Education; History; Human Rights; Labour Law; Photography; Physical Therapy; Political Sciences; Portuguese; Psychiatry and Mental Health; Rehabilitation and Therapy; Social Policy.** *Mestrado*: **Civil Engineering; Environmental Studies; Law; Linguistics; Psychology; Religious Studies.** *Doutorado*: **Clinical Psychology; Law; Linguistics; Religious Studies.** Also MBA

Student Services: Academic Counselling, Canteen, Careers Guidance, Cultural Activities, Facilities for disabled people, Health Services, IT Centre, Social Counselling, Sports Facilities

Publications: Ágora Filosófica; Interlocuções; Jus Et Fides; Revista Economia Negócios e Financias; Revista Educacão Teorias e Prácticas; Revista Química e Tecnologia; Revista Symposium; Revista Teologia e Ciencia de Religião

Last Updated: 29/03/16

CATHOLIC UNIVERSITY OF PETRÓPOLIS

Universidade Católica de Petrópolis (UCP)

Campus Benjamin Constant - BC, Rua Benjamin Constant, 213, Centro, Petrópolis, Rio de Janeiro 25610-1300
Tel: +55(24) 2244-4000
Fax: +55(24) 2242-7747
EMail: faleconosco@ucp.br
Website: http://www.ucp.br

Reitor: Pedro Paulo de Carvalho Rosa
EMail: reitoria@ucp.br

Pró-Reitora Acadêmica: Regina Máximo
Tel: +55(24) 2244-4061
EMail: proacad@ucp.br

Pró-Reitor Administrativo: Luis Garcia Mello
EMail: proad@ucp.br

Department

Technological Studies (Construction Engineering; Industrial Maintenance; Safety Engineering; Transport Management)

Centre

Applied Social Sciences (CCSA) (Accountancy; Administration; Advertising and Publicity; Economics; International Relations; Marketing; Mass Communication); **Engineering and Computer Sciences (CEC)** (Architecture; Civil Engineering; Computer Engineering; Electrical Engineering; Electronic Engineering; Mechanical Engineering; Production Engineering; Town Planning); **Health Sciences (CCS)** (Biomedicine; Physical Education; Physical Therapy; Psychology); **Law (CCJ)** (Law); **Theology and Humanities (CTH)** (Arts and Humanities; History; Music; Pedagogy; Philosophy; Theology)

History: Founded as Faculty of Law 1953, became University 1961 with the Diocesan Bishop as Grand Chancellor. Receives some financial support from the Federal Government.

Academic Year: February to December (February-June; August-December)

Admission Requirements: Secondary school certificate and entrance examination

Main Language(s) of Instruction: Portuguese

Degrees and Diplomas: *Tecnólogo*; *Bacharelado*; *Licenciatura*; *Mestrado*: **Education; Engineering; Law; Psychology.** *Doutorado*: **Education.** Especialização and MBA degree programmes to be launched 2016.

Student Services: Library, Sports Facilities

Publications: Revista U.C.P.

Publishing House: Private Press

Last Updated: 29/03/16

CATHOLIC UNIVERSITY OF SALVADOR

Universidade Católica do Salvador (UCSAL)
Largo da Palma, s/n°, Nazaré, Salvador, Bahia 40040-170
Tel: +55(71) 3324-7572
Fax: +55(71) 3328-0162
EMail: reitoria@ucsal.br
Website: http://www.ucsal.br

Reitor: Mauricio Ferreira
EMail: reitoria@ucsal.br

Area

Applied Social Sciences (Accountancy; Advertising and Publicity; Architecture; Business Administration; Cooking and Catering; Geography (Human); Human Resources; Law; Mass Communication; Town Planning); **Education, Culture and Humanities** (Educational Psychology; English; History; Humanities and Social Science Education; Literature; Mathematics; Mathematics Education; Musical Instruments; Pedagogy; Philosophy; Physical Education; Portuguese; Social and Community Services; Theology); **Engineering and Technological Sciences** (Chemical Engineering; Civil Engineering; Computer Networks; Mechanical Engineering; Software Engineering; Systems Analysis); **Natural and Health Sciences** (Biological and Life Sciences; Biomedicine; Nursing; Nutrition; Physical Therapy)

History: Founded 1961.

Academic Year: January to December (January-June; August-December)

Admission Requirements: Secondary school certificate and entrance examination

Main Language(s) of Instruction: Portuguese

Degrees and Diplomas: *Tecnólogo*; *Bacharelado*; *Licenciatura*; *Especialização/Aperfeiçoamento*: **Administrative Law; Business and Commerce; Civil Law; Commercial Law; Cooking and Catering; Criminal Law; Engineering; Environmental Management; Family Studies; Fiscal Law; Gerontology; Haematology; Health Sciences; Higher Education Teacher Training; Labour Law; Law; Mathematics; Nursing; Paediatrics; Pastoral Studies; Physical Therapy; Private Law; Psychiatry and Mental Health; Public Law; Social Policy; Social Work; Sports; Technology.** *Mestrado*: **Development Studies; Environmental Management; Family Studies; Regional Planning; Social Policy.** *Doutorado*: **Development Studies; Environmental Management; Family Studies; Social Policy.** Also MBA

Student Services: Library
Last Updated: 29/03/16

CATHOLIC UNIVERSITY OF SANTOS

Universidade Católica de Santos (UNISANTOS)
Av. Conselheiro Nébias, 300, Santos, Santos, São Paulo 11015-002
Tel: +55(13) (13) 3205-5555 Ext.1307
Fax: +55(13) 3205-5555 +55(13) 3205-5622
EMail: secgeral@unisantos.com.br; lourenco@unisantos.br
Website: http://www.unisantos.com.br

Reitor: Marcos Medina Leite
Tel: +55(13) 3205-5545 EMail: reitor@unisantos.br

Pró-Reitora Administrativa: Mariângela Mendes Lomba Pinho
EMail: administrativa@unisantos.br

International Relations: Cesar Bargo Perez
Tel: +55(13) 3228-1241 EMail: ari@unisantos.br

Faculty

Law (Law)

Centre

Applied Social Sciences and Health (Accountancy; Administration; Cooking and Catering; Economics; International Business; International Relations; Nursing; Nutrition; Pharmacy; Psychology; Social and Community Services; Translation and Interpretation); **Educational Sciences and Communication** (Advertising and Publicity; Foreign Languages Education; History; Journalism; Music; Native Language Education; Pedagogy; Philosophy; Public Relations; Theology); **Exact Sciences, Architecture and Engineering** (Architecture; Chemistry; Civil Engineering; Computer Science; Environmental Engineering; Information Technology; Marine Engineering; Mathematics; Petroleum and Gas Engineering; Production Engineering; Town Planning)

Further Information: Also Boqueirão Campus

History: Founded 1986. A private institution under the jurisdiction of the Sociedade Visconde de São Leopoldo.

Admission Requirements: Secondary school certificate and entrance examination

Main Language(s) of Instruction: Portuguese

Degrees and Diplomas: *Bacharelado*; *Licenciatura*; *Especialização/Aperfeiçoamento*: **Architectural Restoration; Civil Law; Clinical Psychology; Commercial Law; Communication Studies; Criminal Law; Criminology; Educational Psychology; Environmental Management; Human Rights; Information Management; Labour Law; Maritime Law; Music Education; Nutrition; Psychology; Regional Planning; Social Policy; Telecommunications Services; Town Planning; Transport Management.** *Mestrado*: **Education; International Law; Law; Public Health.** *Doutorado*: **Education; Law; Public Health.** Also MBA; Distance Mode Especialização in Maritime Law

Last Updated: 30/03/16

CATUAÍ FACULTY

Faculdade Catuaí
Av. Bento Munhoz da Rocha Neto 210, Cambé, PR 86186-000
Tel: +55(43) 3253-5454
EMail: mvalduga@faculdadecatuai.com.br
Website: http://www.faculdadecatuai.com.br/

Diretor Geral: Oscar Neres Demarchi

Vice-Diretora: Maria Aparecida Tomas Valduga

Course

Administration (Administration); **Law** (Law); **Pedagogy** (Pedagogy)

History: Founded 2002.

Main Language(s) of Instruction: Portuguese

Accrediting Agency: Ministry of Education

Degrees and Diplomas: *Bacharelado*; *Especialização/Aperfeiçoamento*: **Business Administration; Educational Administration; Educational Psychology; Finance; Human Resources; Management; Marketing; Primary Education; Special Education.**

Student Services: Library
Last Updated: 06/10/15

CDL FACULTY

Faculdade CDL
Rua 25 de Março, 882, Centro, Fortaleza, Ceará 60060-120
Tel: +55(85) 3464-5514 +55(85) 3433-3042
Fax: +55(85) 3433-3044
EMail: faleconosco@faculdadecdl.edu.br
Website: http://www.faculdadecdl.edu.br

Diretor Geral: Honório Pinheiro

Course

Accountancy (Accountancy); **Administration** (Administration); **Commercial Management** (Business and Commerce; Management); **Graduate Studies** (Business Administration; International Business; Management; Marketing; Real Estate; Retailing and Wholesaling; Taxation); **Logistics** (Transport Management); **Marketing** (Marketing)

History: Founded 2001.

Main Language(s) of Instruction: Portuguese

Degrees and Diplomas: *Tecnólogo*; *Bacharelado*. Also MBA in Business Administration, International Business, Management, Marketing, Real Estate, Retail and Wholesaling, Taxation

Student Services: IT Centre, Library
Last Updated: 19/08/15

CECAP FACULTY

Faculdade CECAP (CECAP)
Av. Paranoá Quadra 10 Conjunto. 04 Lotes 10 e 11,
Brasília, DF 71515-205
Tel: +55(61) 3408-2111
EMail: cecap@cecap.com.br
Website: http://www.cecap.com.br

Diretora Pedagógica: Katia Carneiro EMail: katia@cecap.com.br

Course
Administration (Administration); **Pedagogy** (Education; Pedagogy); **Secretarial Studies** (Secretarial Studies); **Tourism** (Tourism)

History: Founded 1999.
Main Language(s) of Instruction: Portuguese
Accrediting Agency: Ministry of Education
Degrees and Diplomas: *Bacharelado*; *Licenciatura*; *Especialização/Aperfeiçoamento*: **Educational and Student Counselling; Educational Psychology; Environmental Management; Human Resources; Marketing; Public Administration.**
Last Updated: 06/10/15

CEILÂNDIA PROJECTION FACULTY

Faculdade Projeção de Ceilândia (FACEB)
QNM 30, Módulos H, I e J, Ceilândia, Brasilia, DF 72210-300
Tel: +55(61) 3038-7602
Fax: +55(61) 3038-7602
EMail: catarina@projecao.br
Website: http://www.fapro.edu.br/br/home/

Diretor: Oswaldo Luiz Saenger
Diretor Acadêmico: José Sergio de Jesus

Course
Accountancy (Accountancy); **Administration** (Administration); **Geography** (Geography); **History** (History); **Human Resourses** (Human Resources); **Information Security** (Computer Science); **Information Systems** (Computer Science); **Letters** (Portuguese); **Marketing** (Marketing); **Mathematics** (Mathematics); **Pedagogy** (Pedagogy); **Secretarial Studies** (Secretarial Studies); **Social Services** (Social and Community Services); **Tourism** (Tourism)

Further Information: Also units in Wansbeck, North Taguatinga, Guará, and Sobradinho
History: Founded 2000. Became Faculdade Cenecista de Faculdade Cenecista de Brasilia 2009. In 2014, another unit was incorporated into the Group: the FAJESU (Former Jesus Maria José Faculty).
Main Language(s) of Instruction: Portuguese
Accrediting Agency: Ministry of Education
Degrees and Diplomas: *Bacharelado*; *Especialização/Aperfeiçoamento*: **Advertising and Publicity; Business Administration; Computer Engineering; Criminal Law; Education; Educational Administration; Educational and Student Counselling; Information Technology; Latin American Studies; Law; Social and Community Services; Software Engineering.** Also MBA
Last Updated: 08/10/15

CÉLIA HELENA SCHOOL OF ARTS

Escola Superior de Artes Célia Helena
Avenida São Gabriel, 462, Jardim Paulista,
São Paulo, SP 01435-000
Tel: +55(11) 3050-2280
Fax: +55(11) 3884-8214
EMail: contato@celiahelena.com.br
Website: http://www.celiahelena.com.br/

Diretora: Lígia Cortez

Course
Theatre (Dance; Theatre)

History: Founded 1972.
Degrees and Diplomas: *Bacharelado*; *Especialização/Aperfeiçoamento*: **Dance; Music; Performing Arts.** *Mestrado*: **Theatre.**
Student Services: Library
Last Updated: 24/09/15

CELSO LISBOA UNIVERSITY CENTRE

Centro Universitário Celso Lisboa (UCL)
Rua 24 de Maio, 797, Engenho Novo,
Rio de Janeiro, Rio de Janeiro 20950-092
Tel: +55(21) 3289-4747
Fax: +55(21) 3289-4749
EMail: reitoria@celsolisboa.edu.br
Website: http://www.celsolisboa.com.br

Reitor: Paulo Cesar Teixeira EMail: reitoria@celsolisboa.edu.br

Course
Accountancy (Accountancy); **Administration** (Administration); **Biology** (Biology); **Biomedecine** (Biomedicine); **Environmental Engineering** (Environmental Engineering); **Esthetics and Cosmetology** (Cosmetology); **Human Resource Management** (Human Resources); **Informatics** (Computer Science); **Management** (Management); **Nursing** (Nursing); **Nutrition** (Nutrition); **Pedagogy** (Education; Teacher Training); **Pharmacy** (Pharmacy); **Physical Education** (Physical Education; Sports); **Physiotherapy** (Physical Therapy); **Production Engineering** (Production Engineering); **Psychology** (Psychology)

History: Founded 1971.
Main Language(s) of Instruction: Portuguese
Accrediting Agency: Ministry of Education.
Degrees and Diplomas: *Tecnólogo*; *Licenciatura*; *Especialização/Aperfeiçoamento*: **Higher Education Teacher Training; Nursing; Nutrition; Pharmacology; Pharmacy; Physical Education; Psychology.** Also MBA.
Student Services: Health Services, Library, Sports Facilities
Last Updated: 30/06/15

CENECIST FACULTY OF BENTO GONÇALVES

Faculdade Cenecista de Bento Gonçalves (FACEBG)
Rua Arlindo Franklin Barbosa 460, Bairro São Roque,
Bento Gonçalves, RS 95700-000
Tel: +55(54) 3452-4422
Fax: +55(54) 3452-4422
EMail: administracao@cnecbento.com.br
Website: http://www.cnecbento.com.br/

Diretor: Vercino Franzoloso (1998-)
EMail: vercino@cnecbento.com.br

Course
Accountancy (Accountancy); **Administration** (Administration); **Advertising and Publicity** (Advertising and Publicity); **Biology** (Biology); **Biomedicine** (Biomedicine); **Gastronomy** (Cooking and Catering); **Nursing** (Nursing); **Nutrition** (Nutrition); **Physical Therapy** (Physical Therapy); **Psychology** (Psychology); **Tourism** (Tourism)

History: Founded 1998 as Centro de Ensino Superior de Bento Gonçalves. Acquired present status and title 2004.
Main Language(s) of Instruction: Portuguese
Accrediting Agency: Ministry of Education
Degrees and Diplomas: *Bacharelado*; *Especialização/Aperfeiçoamento*: **Business Administration; Educational Sciences; Finance; Human Resources; Public Health.**
Student Services: Library
Last Updated: 07/10/15

CENECIST FACULTY OF ITABORAÍ

Faculdade Cenecista de Itaboraí (FACNEC)
Rua Presidente Costa e Silva, 212, Centro,
Itaboraí, Rio de Janeiro 24800-055
Tel: +55(21) 2645-3924
Fax: +55(21) 2635-3512
EMail: adm@facnet-ita.br
Website: http://www.facnec-ita.br

Diretor Presidente: Alexandre José Dos Santos

Course
Business Administration (Administration; Business Administration); **Graduate Studies** (Business Administration; Business Education; Educational Administration; Educational Psychology; Higher

Education; Hotel Management; Human Resources; Management; Mathematics; Special Education; Statistics; Tourism; Transport Management); **Literature** (English; Portuguese); **Pedagogy** (Mathematics Education; Pedagogy); **Production Engineering** (Production Engineering)

History: Founded 1998.

Main Language(s) of Instruction: Portuguese

Accrediting Agency: Ministry of Education

Degrees and Diplomas: *Bacharelado*; *Licenciatura*; *Especialização/Aperfeiçoamento*: **Business Administration; Education; Educational Administration; Educational Psychology; Mathematics Education; Portuguese; Primary Education.**

Student Services: Library

Last Updated: 08/10/15

CENECIST FACULTY OF JOINVILLE

Faculdade Cenecista de Joinville (FACE-FJC)

Av. Getúlio Vargas, 1266, Anita Garibaldi,
Joinville, Santa Catarina 89202-002

Tel: +55(47) 3431-0900

Fax: +55 (47) 3431 0950

EMail: fabiane@fcj.com.b

Website: http://www.fcj.com.br

Diretor Geral: Félix José Negherbon

Tel: +55(47) 3431-0900 EMail: felix@fcj.com.br

Course

Business and Commerce (Business Administration; Business and Commerce); **Business and International Commerce** (Business and Commerce; International Business); **Graduate Studies** (Accountancy; Business Administration; Commercial Law; Finance; Management; Marketing; Transport Management); **Law** (Law); **Management** (Management); **Marine Transport** (Marine Transport); **Marketing** (Marketing); **Tourism** (Tourism)

History: Founded 2000.

Main Language(s) of Instruction: Portuguese

Degrees and Diplomas: *Tecnólogo*; *Bacharelado*; *Especialização/Aperfeiçoamento*: **Business Administration; Finance; Human Resources; Transport Management.**

Student Services: IT Centre, Library

Last Updated: 12/10/15

CENECIST FACULTY OF NOVA PETROPÓLIS

Faculdade Cenecista de Nova Petropólis (FACENP)

Rua 28 de Fevereiro, 100, Nova Petrópolis, RS 95150-000

Tel: +55(54) 3281-1067

EMail: faculdadenovapetropolis@cnec.br

Website: http://faculdadenovapetropolis.cnec.br/

Diretor: Jorge Gerson Silva da Silva

Course

Accountancy (Accountancy); **Administration** (Administration)

History: Founded 2004.

Main Language(s) of Instruction: Portuguese

Degrees and Diplomas: *Bacharelado*

Student Services: Library

Last Updated: 12/10/15

CENECIST FACULTY OF OSÓRIO

Faculdade Cenecista de Osório (FACOS)

Rua 24 de Maio, 141, Centro, Osório, RS 95520-000

Tel: +55(51) 2161-0200

EMail: facos@facos.edu.br

Website: http://www.facos.edu.br

Diretor: Júlio César Lindemann EMail: 1905.direcao@cnec.br

Course

Accountancy (Accountancy); **Administration** (Administration); **Arts and Humanities** (Philosophy; Sociology); **Biological Sciences** (Biological and Life Sciences); **Biomedicine** (Biomedicine); **Business and Commerce** (Business and Commerce); **Computer Science** (Computer Science); **Geography** (Geography); **History** (History); **Law** (Law); **Literature** (English; Portuguese); **Mathematics** (Mathematics); **Nursing** (Nursing); **Pedagogy** (Pedagogy; Teacher Training); **Physical Education** (Physical Education); **Physical Therapy** (Physical Therapy); **Psychology** (Psychology)

History: Founded 1987.

Main Language(s) of Instruction: Portuguese

Accrediting Agency: Ministry of Education

Degrees and Diplomas: *Bacharelado*; *Licenciatura*; *Especialização/Aperfeiçoamento*: **Art Education; Business Administration; Education; Educational Administration; Educational and Student Counselling; Educational Psychology; Health Administration; Human Resources; Law; Pedagogy; Physical Education; Psychology; Social and Preventive Medicine.**

Student Services: Library

Last Updated: 12/10/15

CENECIST FACULTY OF RIO BONITO

Faculdade Cenecista de Rio Bonito (FACERB)

Avenida Sete de Maio, 383 - Centro, Rio Bonito, RJ

Tel: +55(21) 2734-2313

EMail: ensinosuperior@cnec.br

Website: http://www.facerb.edu.br

Diretora: Juliana Benício EMail: julianabenicio@cnecrj.com.br

Course

Administration (Administration)

History: Founded 2009.

Main Language(s) of Instruction: Portuguese

Accrediting Agency: Ministry of Education

Degrees and Diplomas: *Bacharelado*

Student Services: Library

Last Updated: 12/10/15

CENECIST FACULTY OF RONDONÓPOLIS

Faculdade Cenecista de Rondonópolis (FACER CNEC)

Av. Sothero Silva, 428, Vila Aurora,
Rondonópolis, Mato Grosso 78740-090

Tel: +55(66) 3422-0120

Fax: +55(66) 3422-3802

EMail: cnec.facer@terra.com.br

Website: http://www.cnecfacer.com.br

Diretor Presidente: Alexander José Dos Santos

Course

Accountancy (Accountancy); **Administration** (Administration); **Journalism** (Journalism); **Social Services** (Social and Community Services)

History: Founded 2004.

Main Language(s) of Instruction: Portuguese

Accrediting Agency: Ministry of Education

Degrees and Diplomas: *Bacharelado*; *Especialização/Aperfeiçoamento*: **Agricultural Business; Business Administration; Social Sciences.**

Student Services: Library

Last Updated: 04/11/15

CENECIST FACULTY OF SENHOR DO BONFIM

Faculdade Cenecista de Senhor do Bonfim (FACESB)

Praça Dr Simões Filho 22, Senhor do Bonfim, BA 48970-000

Tel: +55(74) 3541-4011

Fax: +55(74) 3541-3446

EMail: faculdadecenecistasb@hotmail.com

Website: http://www.facesb.com.br

Diretora: Vera Lúcia Gonçalves

Course

History (History); **Letters** (English; Portuguese)

History: Founded 2007.

Main Language(s) of Instruction: Portuguese

Degrees and Diplomas: *Licenciatura*

Last Updated: 12/10/15

CENECIST FACULTY OF SETE LAGOAS

Faculdade Cenecista de Sete Lagoas (FCSL)
Rua Pedro Gabriel de Lima, 20, Jardim Arizona,
Sete Lagoas, Minas Gerais 35700-377
Tel: +55(31) 3779-2270
Fax: +55(31) 3779-2273
EMail: secretaria@fcsl.edu.br
Website: http://fcsl.cnec.br/

Diretor Geral: Pedro Henrique da Silva EMail: diretoria@fcsl.edu.br

Course

Administration (Administration); **Information Systems** (Information Sciences; Information Technology)

History: Founded 2001.

Main Language(s) of Instruction: Portuguese

Accrediting Agency: Ministry of Education

Degrees and Diplomas: *Bacharelado*; *Especialização/Aperfeiçoamento*: **Business Administration; Education; Educational Administration; Educational Psychology; Environmental Management.**

Student Services: Library
Last Updated: 12/10/15

CENECIST FACULTY OF VARGINHA

Faculdade Cenecista de Varginha (FACECA)
Rua Professor Felipe Tiago Gomes, 173,
Varginha, Minas Gerais 37006-020
Tel: +55(35) 3690-8900
EMail: secretaria@faceca.br
Website: http://www.faceca.br

Diretor: Antônio Carlos Luminatto Tel: +55(35) 3690-8944

Course

Accountancy (Accountancy); **Administration** (Administration; Business Administration; Marketing); **Information Systems** (Information Sciences); **Law** (Law); **Production Engineering** (Production Engineering)

History: Founded 1970 as Faculdade de Ciências Econômicas, Contábeis e Administrativas de Varginha. Acquired present title 2000.

Main Language(s) of Instruction: Portuguese

Accrediting Agency: Ministry of Education

Degrees and Diplomas: *Bacharelado*; *Especialização/Aperfeiçoamento*: **Accountancy; Administration; Business Administration; Civil Law; Information Technology; Labour Law; Law.** *Mestrado*. Also MBA.

Student Services: Library
Last Updated: 12/10/15

CENECIST FACULTY OF VILA VELHA

Faculdade Cenecista de Vila Velha (FACEVV)
Avenida Vitória Régia 2950, Ibes,
Vila Velha, Espírito Santo 29108-660
Tel: +55(27) 3329-9838
Fax: +55(27) 3329-1286
EMail: facevv@facevv.edu.br
Website: http://www.facevv.edu.br

Diretor: Rafael Roldi de Freitas Ribeiro

Course

Administration (Administration; Business Administration); **Pedagogy** (Pedagogy)

History: Founded 2000.

Main Language(s) of Instruction: Portuguese

Accrediting Agency: Ministry of Education

Degrees and Diplomas: *Bacharelado*; *Licenciatura*
Last Updated: 12/10/15

CENECIST INSTITUTE OF HIGHER EDUCATION OF SANTO ÂNGELO

Instituto Cenecista de Ensino Superior de Santo Ângelo (CNEC/IESA)
Rua Doutor João Augusto Rodrigues 471, Centro Sul,
Santo Ângelo, RS 98801015
Tel: +(55) 3313-1922
Fax: +(55) 3313-1745
EMail: iesa@cnecsan.com.br; ensinosuperior@cnec.br
Website: http://cnecsan.cnec.br

Diretor: Gilberto Kierber

Course

Accountancy (Accountancy); **Administration** (Administration); **Biomedicine** (Biomedicine); **Dentistry** (Dentistry); **Law** (Law); **Pedagogy** (Educational Psychology; Pedagogy); **Physical Therapy** (Physical Therapy)

History: Founded 1998 incorporating the Faculties of Law, Administration and Accountancy of Santo Angelo.

Main Language(s) of Instruction: Portuguese

Degrees and Diplomas: *Bacharelado*: **Accountancy; Administration; Biomedicine; Dentistry; Law; Physical Therapy.** *Licenciatura*: **Pedagogy.** *Especialização/Aperfeiçoamento*: **Accountancy; Biomedicine; Civil Law; Educational Psychology; Higher Education; Labour Law; Law; Medical Technology; Pedagogy; Physical Therapy.** Also MBA.

Student Services: Library
Last Updated: 29/03/16

CENECISTA FACULTY OF CAPIVARI

Faculdade Cenecista de Capivari (FACECAP)
Rua Barão do Rio Branco 374, Centro, Capivari, SP 13360-000
Tel: +55(19) 3492-8888
Fax: +55(19) 3492-8880
EMail: cnec@cneccapivari.br; viviani@cneccapivari.br
Website: http://www.fc.edu.br

Diretor: Clever Eduardo Lobo Zuin

Course

Accountancy (Accountancy); **Administration** (Administration); **Information Systems** (Information Management; Information Sciences); **Pedagogy** (Education; Pedagogy)

History: Founded 1946. Acquired present status 2006.

Main Language(s) of Instruction: Portuguese

Degrees and Diplomas: *Bacharelado*; *Especialização/Aperfeiçoamento*: **Business Administration; Educational Psychology; Literacy Education.**

Student Services: Library
Last Updated: 08/10/15

CENTEC FACULTY OF TECHNOLOGY - CARIRI

Faculdade de Tecnologia CENTEC - Cariri (FATEC CARIRI)
Rua Amália Xavier de Oliveira, s/n° - Triângulo,
Juazeiro do Norte, Ceará 63040000
Tel: +55(88) 3566-4048; +55(88) 3566-4053
Fax: +55(88) 3566-4049 +55(88) 3566-4051
EMail: fatec_cariri@centec.org.br
Website: http://www.centec.org.br

Diretor: Cícero Emerson Lacerda de Sousa

Course

Electromechanics (Electronic Engineering; Mechanics); **Environmental Health** (Health Sciences); **Food Science** (Food Science); **Industrial Handling; Irrigation and Drainage** (Irrigation; Water Science)

Degrees and Diplomas: *Tecnólogo*; *Especialização/Aperfeiçoamento*: **Agriculture.**
Last Updated: 01/04/16

CENTEC FACULTY OF TECHNOLOGY - SERTÃO CENTRAL

Faculdade de Tecnologia CENTEC - Sertão Central (FATEC SERTÃO CENTRAL)

Av. Geraldo Bizarria de Carvalho, s/n° - Km 2, Quixeramobim, Ceará 63800-000
Tel: +55(88) 3441-1220
Fax: +55(88) 3441-1220
EMail: fatec_sertaocentral@centec.org.br
Website: http://www.centec.org.br

Diretor: Francisco Jardel Rodrigues da Paixã

Area

Agriculture (Apiculture; Cattle Breeding; Food Science)

Degrees and Diplomas: *Especialização/Aperfeiçoamento*: **Apiculture; Cattle Breeding; Food Science.**
Last Updated: 01/04/16

CESMAC UNIVERSITY CENTRE

Centro Universitário Cesmac (CESMAC)

Rua Cônego Machado 918, Farol, Maceió, Alagoas 57051-160
Tel: +55(82) 3221-5007
Fax: +55(82) 3221-0402
EMail: marketing@cesmac.edu.br
Website: http://www.cesmac.edu.br

Diretor Geral: João Rodrigues Sampaio Filho
EMail: joao.sampaio@cesmac.edu.br
Reitor: Douglas Apratto Tenório

Faculty

Applied Social Sciences *(FCSA)* (Accountancy; Administration; Social Work); **Biological and Health Sciences** *(FCBS)* (Biology; Biomedicine; Dentistry; Medicine; Nursing; Nutrition; Pharmacy; Physical Therapy; Psychology; Veterinary Science); **Education and Communication** *(FECOM)* (Advertising and Publicity; Education; English; History; Journalism; Spanish); **Engineering and Technology** (Architecture; Civil Engineering; Computer Engineering; Electrical Engineering; Engineering; Town Planning); **Law** (Law)

History: Founded 1973 as Centro de Estudos Superiores de Maceió. Acquired present title and status 2012.

Main Language(s) of Instruction: Portuguese

Degrees and Diplomas: *Bacharelado*; *Licenciatura*; *Especialização/Aperfeiçoamento*: **Accountancy; Arts and Humanities; Communication Studies; Computer Engineering; Ecology; Education; Finance; Health Administration; Health Sciences; Higher Education; Homeopathy; Human Resources; Labour Law; Law; Marketing; Mathematics Education; Psychoanalysis; Public Health; Special Education.** *Mestrado*: **Biology.** *Doutorado*: **Law.** Also MBA.
Student Services: Library
Last Updated: 07/09/15

CESUMAR FACULTY

Faculdade CESUMAR

R. Itajubá, 673 - Portão, Curitiba, PR 81070-190
Tel: +55(44) 3027-6360
EMail: fale.conosco@unicesumar.edu.br; lincoln@unicesumar.edu.br
Website: http://www.unicesumar.edu.br/curitiba

President: Wilson de Matos Silva EMail: wilsonf@cesumar.br

Programme

Accountancy (Accountancy); **Administration** (Administration); **Architecture and Town Planning** (Architecture; Town Planning); **Business and Commerce** (Business and Commerce); **Civil Engineering** (Civil Engineering); **Gastronomy** (Cooking and Catering); **Human Resources** (Human Resources); **Interior Design** (Interior Design); **Management** (Management); **Systems Analysis** (Systems Analysis)

History: Founded 1990. Maintained by Centro de Ensino Superior de Maringà - CESUMAR

Main Language(s) of Instruction: Portuguese

Degrees and Diplomas: *Bacharelado*; *Licenciatura*

Student Services: Library
Last Updated: 04/12/15

CESUSC FACULTY

Faculdade CESUSC (CESUSC)

Rod. José Carlos Daux (SC401), 9301 - Km 10, Santo Antônio de Lisboa, Florianópolis, Santa Catarina 88050-001
Tel: +55(48) 3239-2600
EMail: mec@cesusc.com.br
Website: http://www.cesusc.edu.br

Diretora Geral: Betina Ines Backes

Diretor Administrativo Financeiro: Flávio Balbinot

Course

Administration (Administration); **Graduate Studies** (Business Administration; Civil Law; Human Resources; Labour Law; Law; Notary Studies; Real Estate); **Interior Design** (Interior Design); **Law** (Law); **Psychology** (Psychology); **Systems Analysis and Development** (Systems Analysis)

History: Founded 2000 as Faculdade de Ciências Sociais de Florianópolis. Acquired present title 2015.

Main Language(s) of Instruction: Portuguese

Degrees and Diplomas: *Bacharelado*; *Especialização/Aperfeiçoamento*: **Civil Law; Labour Law; Law; Notary Studies; Real Estate.** Also MBA in Human Resources; International Executive MBA

Student Services: Library
Last Updated: 25/06/15

CETEP FACULTY OF TECHNOLOGY

Faculdade de Tecnologia Cetep (CETEP)

Rua Francisco Torres, 768, Curitiba, PR 80060-130
Tel: +55 (41) 3362-1705
Fax: +55 (41) 3362-7924
EMail: diretoria@cetepensino.com.br; atendimento@cetepensino.com.br; cassiano@cetepensino.com.br
Website: http://www.cetepensino.com.br

Diretor Geral: Cassiano Rodycz Vitiuk

Course

Graduate Studies (Automotive Engineering; Electronic Engineering; Industrial Management; Management; Safety Engineering; Technology Education); **Industrial Automation** (Automation and Control Engineering); **Industrial Electronics** (Electronic Engineering); **Quality Management** (Safety Engineering)

History: Founded 1986.

Main Language(s) of Instruction: Portuguese

Degrees and Diplomas: *Tecnólogo*; *Especialização/Aperfeiçoamento*: **Automotive Engineering; Electronic Engineering; Industrial Management; Management; Safety Engineering; Technology Education.**

Student Services: Library
Last Updated: 19/08/15

CEUMA UNIVERSITY

Universidade Do Ceuma (UNICEUMA)

Rua Josué Montello, n°1, Bairro Renascença II, São Luís, Maranhão 65075-120
Tel: +55(98) 3214-4277
Fax: +55(98) 3235-3265
EMail: ceuma@ceuma.br
Website: http://www.ceuma.br

Reitor: Saulo Henrique Brito Matos Martins

Area

Architecture and Engineering (Architecture; Environmental Engineering; Mechanical Engineering; Production Engineering; Town Planning); **Exact Sciences** (Information Sciences; Information Technology); **Health Sciences** (Biology; Dentistry; Medicine; Nursing; Nutrition; Occupational Health; Pharmacy; Physical Education; Physical Therapy; Speech Therapy and Audiology); **Human Sciences** (Accountancy; Administration; Advertising and Publicity; English; Law; Literature; Pedagogy; Portuguese; Psychology; Social and Community Services; Spanish)

Course

Technological Studies (Business Administration; Construction Engineering; Cooking and Catering; Cosmetology; Fashion Design; Interior Design; Marketing; Public Administration; Real Estate; Systems Analysis)

Further Information: Also Cohama, Anil, Bacabal, Imperatriz, Deodoro and Turu Units.

History: Founded 1992.

Main Language(s) of Instruction: Portuguese

Degrees and Diplomas: *Tecnólogo*; *Bacharelado*; *Licenciatura*; *Especialização/Aperfeiçoamento*: **Accountancy; Business Administration; Civil Law; Clinical Psychology; Cosmetology; Criminology; Dentistry; Environmental Engineering; Gynaecology and Obstetrics; Health Education; Human Resources; Interior Design; Labour Law; Law; Management; Marketing; Microbiology; Nutrition; Physical Education; Physical Therapy; Public Health; Safety Engineering; Speech Therapy and Audiology; Stomatology.** *Mestrado*: **Biology; Business Administration; Dentistry.** Also MBA.

Student Services: Library

Last Updated: 05/11/15

CHRISTUS FACULTY OF PIAUÍ

Christus Faculdade do Piauí (CHRISFAPI)

Rua Acelino Resende, 132, Fonte dos Matos, Piripiri, PI 64260-000

Tel: +55(86) 3276-2981

Fax: +55(86) 3276-2981

EMail: chrisfapi@chrisfapi.com.br; chrisfapi@hotmail.com

Website: http://www.chrisfapi.com.br

Diretora Geral: Maria do Carmo Amaral Brito

Diretora de Ensino: Ivonalda Brito de Almeida Morais

Course

Accountancy (Accountancy); **Administration** (Administration; Educational Administration; Health Administration); **Law** (Labour Law; Law); **Nursing** (Nursing); **Pharmacy** (Pharmacy); **Physical Therapy** (Physical Therapy); **Social Welfare** (Social Welfare)

Main Language(s) of Instruction: Portuguese

Degrees and Diplomas: *Bacharelado*; *Especialização/Aperfeiçoamento*: **Higher Education.**

Student Services: Library

Last Updated: 14/09/15

CLARETIAN UNIVERSITY CENTRE

Centro Universitário Claretiano (CEUCLAR)

Rua Dom Bosco 466, Castelo, Batatais, São Paulo 14300-000

Tel: +55(16) 3660-1777

Fax: +55(16) 3761-5030

EMail: secretariat@claretiano.edu.br; proreitoracad@claretiano.edu.br

Website: http://www.claretiano.edu.br

Reitor: Sérgio Ibanor Piva (1997-)

Secretária Geral: Lea Mara Lelis Dal Picolo Biagini
EMail: secretariageral@claretiano.edu.br

Area

Health (Health Sciences); **Management** (Administration; Secretarial Studies); **Teacher Training** (Teacher Training); **Technology** (Human Resources; Information Technology; Marketing; Systems Analysis; Transport Management)

Course

Distance Education; **Postgraduate** (Advertising and Publicity; Art Education; Biological and Life Sciences; Business Administration; Business Education; Communication Studies; Computer Networks; Computer Science; Data Processing; Educational Administration; Educational Psychology; English; Environmental Management; Ethics; Finance; Human Resources; Labour Law; Law; Literature; Marketing; Mathematics Education; Native Language Education; Nursing; Occupational Health; Philosophy; Physical Education; Physical Therapy; Physiology; Primary Education; Science Education; Sociology; Special Education; Sports; Sports Management; Translation and Interpretation; Writing)

Further Information: Also Distance Education programs

History: Founded 1970. Acquired present title 2001.

Main Language(s) of Instruction: Portuguese

Accrediting Agency: Ministry of Education.

Degrees and Diplomas: *Bacharelado*; *Licenciatura*; *Especialização/Aperfeiçoamento*: **Cosmetology; Educational Psychology; Nursing; Nutrition; Occupational Therapy; Physical Education; Physical Therapy; Power Engineering.** Also MBA.

Student Services: Library

Last Updated: 30/06/15

CNA FACULTY OF TECNOLOGY

Faculdade de Tecnologia CNA (FATECNA)

SGAN Quadra 601, Módulo K, Brasília, DF 70830-021

Tel: +55(61) 2109-1643

Fax: +55(61) 2109-1325

EMail: secretaria@faculdadecna.com.br; viviane.moreira@senar.org.br

Website: http://www.faculdadecna.com.br

Diretor Geral: Abdon Soares de Miranda Júnior

Vice-Diretor Administrativo: Francisco Gilson de Almeida Maia

Course

Agricultural Business (Agricultural Business); **Postgraduate Studies** (Agricultural Business; Agricultural Management)

History: Founded 2013.

Main Language(s) of Instruction: Portuguese

Degrees and Diplomas: *Tecnólogo*; *Especialização/Aperfeiçoamento*: **Agricultural Business; Agricultural Management.**

Student Services: Library

Last Updated: 22/03/16

CNEC FACULTY OF CAMPO LARGO

Faculdade CNEC Campo Largo

Rua Rui Barbosa 541, Centro, Campo Largo, Paranà 83601-140

Tel: +55(41) 3116-3300

Fax: +55(41) 3116-3300

EMail: ensinosuperior@cnec.br

Website: http://faculdadecampolargo.cnec.br

Diretor: Vitor Hugo Strozzi

Course

Accountancy; **Administration** (Administration); **Biomedicine** (Biomedicine); **Graduate Studies** (Educational Psychology; Special Education); **Information Systems** (Computer Engineering); **Law** (Law); **Nursing** (Nursing); **Pedagogy** (Pedagogy; Primary Education; Secondary Education; Vocational Education); **Production Engineering** (Production Engineering); **Teachers Training** (Teacher Training)

History: Founded 1999 as Faculdade Cenecista Presidente Kennedy. Became Faculdade Cenecista de Campo Largo. Acquired present title 2015.

Main Language(s) of Instruction: Portuguese

Accrediting Agency: Ministry of Education

Degrees and Diplomas: *Bacharelado*; *Licenciatura*; *Especialização/Aperfeiçoamento*: **Business Administration; Civil Law; Computer Networks; Criminal Law; Education; Educational Administration; Educational Psychology; Finance; Health Administration; Higher Education; Law; Software Engineering; Special Education; Telecommunications Engineering; Transport Management.** Also MBA

Student Services: Library

Last Updated: 07/10/15

CNEC FACULTY OF FARROUPILHA

Faculdade CNEC Farroupilha

Rua 14 de Julho 339, Centro, Farroupilha, RS 95180-000

Tel: +55(54) 3268-2288

Fax: +55(54) 3268-2733

EMail: cneccesf@terra.com.br

Website: http://www.cesfar.edu.br

Diretor: Luiz Fernando Felicetti (1997-)

Course

Administrative Management (Administration; Management); **Business Administration** (Business Administration; Real Estate); **Finance** (Finance); **Graduate Studies** (Education; Educational Psychology; Leisure Studies; Management; Marketing; Tourism); **Information Systems** (Information Management; Management); **Law** (Law); **Management** (Business Administration; Management); **Teacher Training** (Teacher Training); **Tourism** (Tourism); **Transport Management** (Transport Management)

History: Founded 1996 as Centro de Ensino Superior Cenesista de Farroupilha (CESF). Became Campanha Nacional de Escolas da Comunidade (CNEC)

Main Language(s) of Instruction: Portuguese

Accrediting Agency: Ministry of Education.

Degrees and Diplomas: *Bacharelado*; *Licenciatura*; *Especialização/Aperfeiçoamento*: **Business Administration; Commercial Law; Educational Psychology; Human Resources; Labour Law; Law; Management; Marketing.**

Student Services: Library

Academic Staff *2014-2015*: Total 65

Student Numbers *2014-2015*: Total 750

Last Updated: 28/07/15

CNEC FACULTY OF GRAVATAI

Faculdade Cnec Gravatai

Rua Dr. José Loureiro da Silva, 1991, Gravataí, RS 94010-001

Tel: +55(51) 3488-1991

EMail: facensa@facensa.com.br

Website: http://www.facensa.edu.br

Diretora: Eunice Carolina Ohlweiler de Oliveira

Coordenação Geral des Graduações: Maria Maira Picawi EMail: maria@facensa.edu.br

Course

Accountancy (Accountancy); **Administration** (Administration; Business Administration); **Information Systems** (Computer Science); **Law** (Law)

History: Founded 2002 as Faculdade Cenecista Nossa Senhora dos Anjos. Acquired present title 2015.

Main Language(s) of Instruction: Portuguese

Degrees and Diplomas: *Bacharelado*; *Especialização/Aperfeiçoamento*: **Business Administration; Labour Law.** Also MBA

Student Services: Library

Last Updated: 13/10/15

CNEC FACULTY OF ILHA DO GOVERNADOR

Faculdade CNEC Ilha do Governador

Estrada do Galeão, s/n° - Jardim Guanabara, Ilha do Governador, Rio de Janeiro 21941-353

Tel: +55(21) 3975-6804 +55(21) 3975-6807

EMail: marianakarem@cnecrj.com.br

Website: http://faculdadeilhadogovernador.cnec.br

Diretor: André Stein da Silveira EMail: andresilveira@cnecrj.com.br

Course

Accountancy (Accountancy); **Administration** (Administration); **Civil Engineering** (Civil Engineering); **Law** (Law); **Pedagogy** (Education; Pedagogy); **Production Engineering** (Production Engineering)

History: Founded 2002 as Faculdade Cenecista da Ilha do Governador. Maintained by Campanha Nacional de Escolas da Comunidade (CNEC).

Main Language(s) of Instruction: Portuguese

Accrediting Agency: Ministry of Education

Degrees and Diplomas: *Bacharelado*; *Licenciatura*; *Especialização/Aperfeiçoamento*: **Business Administration; Education; Educational Psychology; Environmental Management.**

Student Services: Library

Last Updated: 06/10/15

CNEC UNAI FACULTY

Faculdade CNEC UNAI

Rua Celina Lisboa Frederico 142, Centro, Unaí, Minas Gerais 38610000

Tel: +55(38) 3677-4747

EMail: 2021.secretaria@cnec.br

Website: http://www.inesc.br

Diretor Geral: Romualdo Neiva Gonzaga

Course

Accountancy (Accountancy); **Building Technology** (Building Technologies); **Business Administration** (Administration; Business Administration); **Computer Science** (Computer Science); **Human Resource Management** (Human Resources; Management); **Law** (Law); **Pedagogy** (Pedagogy)

History: Founded 1998 as Instituto de Ensino Superior Cenecista. Acquired present status and title 2015.

Main Language(s) of Instruction: Portuguese

Degrees and Diplomas: *Bacharelado*; *Especialização/Aperfeiçoamento*. Also MBA

Student Services: Library

Last Updated: 08/07/15

COOPERATIVE FACULTY OF TECHNOLOGY - ESCOOP

Faculdade de Tecnologia do Cooperativismo - ESCOOP

Av. Berlim, 409, São Geraldo, Porto Alegre, SP 90240-581

Tel: +55(51) 3222-5500 +55(51) 3323-0000

Fax: +55(51) 3323-0032

EMail: secretaria@escoop.edu.br; derlischmidt@yahoo.com.br

Website: http://escoop.edu.br

Diretor Geral: Derli Schmidt

Course

Cooperative Management (Management); **Postgraduate Studies** (Agricultural Business; Management)

History: Founded 2011.

Fees: Undergraduate, 26.50 per credit (Brazilian Real)

Main Language(s) of Instruction: Portuguese

Degrees and Diplomas: *Tecnólogo*; *Especialização/Aperfeiçoamento*: **Management.** Also MBA

Student Services: IT Centre, Library

Last Updated: 26/11/15

COTIA INSTITUTE OF HIGHER EDUCATION - ASSOCIATED FACULTY OF COTIA

Instituto de Ensino Superior de Cotia - Faculdade Associada de Cotia (IESC/FAAC)

Rua Nelson Raineri 630, Lajeado, Cotia, SP 06700560

Tel: +55(11) 4616-0770

EMail: secretaria@faac.br

Website: http://www.faac.br/

Diretora: Margarida Cecilia Corréa Nogueira Rocha EMail: dir@faac.br

Course

Administration (Administration); **Computer Science** (Computer Networks); **Literature** (Literature); **Marketing** (Marketing); **Nursing** (Nursing); **Pedagogy** (Pedagogy); **Physical Education** (Physical Education); **Tourism**; **Visual Arts**

History: Founded 1999.

Main Language(s) of Instruction: Portuguese

Degrees and Diplomas: *Bacharelado*; *Licenciatura*; *Especialização/Aperfeiçoamento*

Last Updated: 18/04/16

DAMAS FACULTY OF CHRISTIAN INSTRUCTION

Faculdade Damas da Instrução Crista
Av. Rui Barbosa, 1426-B, Graças, Recife, PE
Tel: +55(81) 3426-5026
Fax: +55(81) 3241-7558
EMail: diretoria@faculdadedamas.edu.br
Website: http://www.faculdadedamas.edu.br

Diretora-Presidente: Eulalia Maria Wanderley de Lima

Course

Administration (Administration; Business Administration); **Architecture and Town Planning** (Architecture; Landscape Architecture; Town Planning); **International Relations** (International Relations); **Law** (Law)

History: Founded 2005.

Main Language(s) of Instruction: Portuguese

Accrediting Agency: Ministry of Education

Degrees and Diplomas: *Bacharelado*; *Especialização/Aperfeiçoamento*: **Architecture; Business Administration; Civil Law; Criminal Law; Finance; Law.** *Mestrado*: **Law.**

Student Services: IT Centre, Library

Publications: ARCHITECTON - Revista de Arquitetura e Urbanismo; Caderno de Relações Internacionais; Duc In Altum - Cadernos de Direito

Last Updated: 16/10/15

DEHONIANA FACULTY

Faculdade Dehoniana
Av. Francisco Barreto Leme, N° 550, Vila São Geraldo, Taubaté, SP 12062-000
Tel: +55(12) 3625-8080
Fax: +55(12) 3625-8080
EMail: dehoniana@uol.com.br; tudoaqui@dehoniana.edu.br; dehoniana@uol.com.br
Website: http://www.dehoniana.edu.br

Diretor Geral: Everton dos Santos Carvalho

Vice-Diretor Administrativo: Moacir Francisco Pedrini

Course

Administration (Business Administration); **Philosophy** (Philosophy); **Postgraduate Studies** (Management; Psychology; Theology); **Theology** (Theology)

History: Founded 2001.

Main Language(s) of Instruction: Portuguese

Degrees and Diplomas: *Bacharelado*; *Especialização/Aperfeiçoamento*: **Management; Psychology; Theology.**

Student Services: Library

Publications: Revista Nós; Revista TQ

Last Updated: 26/11/15

DIOCESAN FACULTY OF MOSSORÓ

Faculdade Diocesana de Mossoró (FDM)
Praça Dom João Costa, 511, Santo Antônio, Mossoró, RN 59600-140
Tel: +55(84) 3318-7648
EMail: fdm@fdm.edu.br; fdm@fdm.edu.com.br
Website: http://fdm.edu.br

Diretor: Sátiro Cavalcanti Dantas

Secretária Geral: Iara Maria Linhares

Vice-Diretor: Márcia Eloi Rodrigues

Course

Postgraduate Studies (Accountancy; Special Education; Theology); **Theology** (Theology)

History: Founded 2002.

Main Language(s) of Instruction: Portuguese

Degrees and Diplomas: *Bacharelado*; *Especialização/Aperfeiçoamento*: **Accountancy; Special Education; Theology.**

Student Services: Library

Last Updated: 01/12/15

DIOCESAN FACULTY OF SÃO JOSÉ

Faculdade Diocesana São José (FADISI)
Estrada do Sao Francisco, 1576, Bairro Vitória, Rio Branco, AC 69909-021
Tel: +55(68) 9238-9961
EMail: fadisi.acre@hotmail.com; secretariafadisi@outlook.com
Website: http://fadisi.webs.com

Diretor: Joaquin Pertiñez Fernandez

Course

Philosophical Foundations of Bioethics *(Postgraduate)* (Ethics); **Philosophy** (Philosophy); **Theology** (Theology)

History: Founded 2005.

Main Language(s) of Instruction: Portuguese

Degrees and Diplomas: *Bacharelado*; *Especialização/Aperfeiçoamento*: **Ethics.**

Last Updated: 04/09/15

DOCTUM FACULTY OF LAW OF CARANGOLA

Faculdade de Direito da Doctum de Carangola
Av. Machado de Assis, 172, Triângulo, Carangola, MG 36800-000
Tel: +55(32) 3741-3414
EMail: morgana@doctum.edu.br; heloisa@doctum.edu.br; diretoria@doctum.edu.br
Website: http://www.doctum.edu.br:8080/portal/unidades/carangola

Course

Law (Law)

History: Founded 2007.

Main Language(s) of Instruction: Portuguese

Degrees and Diplomas: *Bacharelado*; *Especialização/Aperfeiçoamento*: **Civil Law.**

Last Updated: 29/06/15

DOCTUM FACULTY OF SERRA

Faculdade Doctum da Serra (DOCTUM)
Rua ID N°80, Civit II, Serra, ES 36700000
Tel: +55(33) 3322-6321
Fax: +55(33) 3321-7559
EMail: diretoria@doctum.edu.br;
Website: http://www.doctum.edu.br

Presidente: Cláudio Cezar Azevedo de Almeida Leitão

Unit

Carangola (Law); **Caratinga** (Accountancy; Administration; Architecture; Civil Engineering; Computer Science; Electrical Engineering; Law; Social and Community Services; Town Planning); **Cataguases** (Information Sciences); **Iúna** (Administration; Pedagogy); **Juiz de Fora** (Law); **Leopoldina** (Administration; Law); **Manhuaçu** (Administration; Law); **Serra** (Administration; Biology; Law; Nursing; Pedagogy; Physical Education; Psychology); **Teófilo Otoni** (Accountancy; Administration; Information Sciences; Law; Nursing; Nutrition; Physical Education; Psychology; Social Work)

Campus

Piauseta (Accountancy)

History: Founded 1936 as Sociedade Colégio Caratinga. Acquired present status 2000.

Main Language(s) of Instruction: Portuguese

Degrees and Diplomas: *Bacharelado*; *Licenciatura*; *Especialização/Aperfeiçoamento*; *Mestrado*

Last Updated: 21/07/15

DOM BOSCO CATHOLIC UNIVERSITY

Universidade Católica Dom Bosco (UCDB)
Av. Tamandaré, 6000, Jardim Seminário, Campo Grande, Mato Grosso do Sul 79117-900
Tel: +55(67) 3312-3300 +55(67) 3312-3800
Fax: +55(67) 3312-3301
EMail: webmaster@ucdb.br; proed@ucdb.br
Website: http://www.ucdb.br

Reitor: Ricardo Carlos EMail: reitoria@ucdb.br

Course
Accountancy (Accountancy); **Administration** (Administration); **Advertising and Publicity** (Advertising and Publicity); **Agronomy** (Agronomy); **Animal Husbandry** (Animal Husbandry); **Architecture and Urbanism** (Architecture; Town Planning); **Automation and Control Engineering** (Automation and Control Engineering); **Biological Sciences** (Biological and Life Sciences); **Biomedicine** (Biomedicine); **Civil Engineering** (Civil Engineering); **Computer Engineering** (Computer Engineering); **Computer Networks** (Computer Networks); **Design** (Design); **Electrical Engineering** (Electrical Engineering); **Geography** (Geography (Human)); **History** (History); **Journalism** (Journalism); **Law** (Law); **Letters** (Arts and Humanities; English; Portuguese); **Mechanical Engineering** (Mechanical Engineering); **Nursing** (Nursing); **Nutrition** (Nutrition); **Pedagogy** (Pedagogy); **Pharmacy** (Pharmacy); **Philosophy** (Philosophy); **Phonoaudiology** (Speech Therapy and Audiology); **Physical Education** (Physical Education); **Physiotherapy** (Physical Therapy); **Psychology** (Psychology); **Radio, TV and Internet** (Multimedia; Radio and Television Broadcasting); **Sanitary and Environmental Engineering** (Environmental Engineering; Sanitary Engineering); **Social Service** (Social and Community Services); **Systems Analysis and Development** (Systems Analysis); **Veterinary Medicine** (Veterinary Science)

History: Founded 1961

Admission Requirements: Secondary school certificate and entrance examination

Main Language(s) of Instruction: Portuguese

Degrees and Diplomas: *Bacharelado*; *Licenciatura*; *Especialização/Aperfeiçoamento*: **Accountancy; Administrative Law; Advertising and Publicity; Behavioural Sciences; Civil Law; Clinical Psychology; Criminal Law; Educational Administration; Educational Psychology; Finance; Graphic Design; Human Resources; Information Technology; Labour Law; Law; Management; Marketing; Occupational Health; Psychology; Rehabilitation and Therapy; Software Engineering.** *Mestrado*: **Agriculture; Biotechnology; Development Studies; Education; Environmental Studies; Psychology.** *Doutorado*: **Agriculture; Biotechnology; Development Studies; Education; Environmental Studies; Psychology.** Also MBA

Student Services: Canteen, Library

Last Updated: 30/03/16

DOM BOSCO FACULTY OF EDUCATION, SCIENCE AND ARTS OF MONTE APRAZIVEL

Faculdade de Educação, Ciências e Artes 'Dom Bosco' de Monte Aprazivel (FAECA DOM BOSCO)

Rua Augusto Chiesa, 679, Monte Aprazível, São Paulo 15150-000
Tel: +55(17) 3275-9660
Fax: +55(17) 3275-9660
EMail: dombosco_faeca@hotmail.com; secfaculdade@faeca.com.br;
Website: http://www.faeca.com.br

Diretor: Vanderlei Pereira (1997-)

Course
Accountancy (Accountancy); **Administration** (Administration); **Graduate Studies** (History; Literacy Education; Psychology; Taxation); **History** (History)

History: Founded 1973.

Main Language(s) of Instruction: Portuguese

Degrees and Diplomas: *Bacharelado*; *Licenciatura*; *Especialização/Aperfeiçoamento*: **History; Literacy Education; Psychology; Taxation.**

Student Services: Library

Last Updated: 02/07/15

DOM BOSCO FACULTY OF GOIOERÊ

Faculdade Dom Bosco de Goioerê (FDBG)

Rua Andirá, 565, Jardim Curitiba, Goioerê, PR 87360-000
Tel: +55(44) 3522-5126
Fax: +55(44) 3222-2211
EMail: fundacaoxingu@outlook.com; brazlima@icloud.com
Website: http://www.faculdadesdombosco.edu.br

Diretora: Julia Ribeiro Costa

Course
Administration (Business Administration); **Pedagogy** (Pedagogy)

History: Founded 2005.

Main Language(s) of Instruction: Portuguese

Degrees and Diplomas: *Bacharelado*; *Licenciatura*

Student Services: Library

Last Updated: 27/11/15

DOM BOSCO FACULTY OF PORTO ALEGRE

Faculdade Dom Bosco de Porto Alegre (FDB)

Rua Marechal José Inácio da Silva, n° 355, Bairro Passo d'Areia, Porto Alegre, RS 90520-280
Tel: +55(51) 3361-6700 +55(51) 3345-3668
Fax: +55(51) 3361-6700 +55(51) 3345-3668
EMail: faculdade@dombosco.net; sandrini@dombosco.net; beta2410@hotmail.com
Website: www.faculdade.dombosco.net

Diretor: Marcos Sandrini

Course
Accounting (Accountancy); **Administration** (Business Administration); **Environmental and Sanitary Engineering** (Environmental Engineering; Sanitary Engineering); **Information Systems** (Information Technology); **Law** (Law); **Potgraduate Studies** (Business Administration; Environmental Management; Marketing; Psychology; Transport and Communications)

History: Founded 2003.

Main Language(s) of Instruction: Portuguese

Degrees and Diplomas: *Bacharelado*; *Especialização/Aperfeiçoamento*: **Environmental Management; Psychology; Transport and Communications.** Also MBA

Student Services: Library

Last Updated: 27/11/15

DOM BOSCO SALESIAN FACULTY

Faculdade Salesiana Dom Bosco (FSDB)

Av. Epaminondas, 57, Centro, Manaus, AM 69010-090
Tel: +55(92) 2125-4690
EMail: meirebotelhodeoliveira@gmail.com
Website: http://www.fsdb.edu.br

Diretor: Francisco Alves de Lima

Course
Graduate Studies (Accountancy; Business Administration; Education; Educational Administration; Educational Psychology; Environmental Management; Environmental Studies; Finance; Gerontology; Higher Education; Management; Marketing; Pedagogy); **Undergraduate Studies** (Accountancy; Administration; Pedagogy; Philosophy; Social and Community Services)

History: Founded 2000.

Degrees and Diplomas: *Bacharelado*; *Licenciatura*; *Especialização/Aperfeiçoamento*. Also Postgraduate diploma.

Student Services: Library

Last Updated: 09/06/15

DOM BOSCO SALESIAN FACULTY OF PIRACICABA

Faculdade Salesiana Dom Bosco de Piracicaba (FSDB)

Rua Boa Morte, 1835, Centro, Piracicaba, SP
Tel: +55(19) 3437-3877
EMail: secr.dbf@domboscopira.com.br
Website: www.domboscopira.com.br

Diretor: Antônio Carlos Galhardo
EMail: galhardo@domboscopira.com.br

Course
Accountancy (Accountancy); **Graduate Studies** (Business Administration; Educational Administration; Finance; Literacy Education; Management; Marketing; Preschool Education; Transport Management); **Undergraduate Studies** (Administration; Information Sciences; Pedagogy)

History: Founded 2004.

Degrees and Diplomas: *Bacharelado*; *Licenciatura*; *Especialização/Aperfeiçoamento*. Also MBA.
Last Updated: 09/06/15

DOM HELDER CÂMARA SCHOOL

Escola Superior Dom Helder Câmara
Rua Álvares Maciel, 628, Sta. Efigênia,
Belo Horizonte, MG 30150-250
Tel: +55(31) 2125-8800
Fax: +55(31) 2125-8818
EMail: contato@domhelder.edu.br
Website: http://www.domhelder.edu.br

Reitor: Paulo Umberto Stumpf SJ

Vice-Reitor: Estêvão D' Ávila Freitas

Course

Graduate Studies *(Stricto Sensu)* (Constitutional Law); **Graduate Studies** *(Lato Sensu)* (Civil Security; Police Studies); **Law** (Administrative Law; Civil Law; Commercial Law; Constitutional Law; Criminal Law; Fiscal Law; International Law; Labour Law; Law)

History: Founded 1998.

Main Language(s) of Instruction: Portuguese

Degrees and Diplomas: *Bacharelado*; *Especialização/Aperfeiçoamento*: **Law.** *Mestrado*: **Constitutional Law; Law.** *Doutorado*: **Law.** PhD in Law offered in partnership with Pontifícia Universidade Católica do Rio de Janeiro (PUC-Rio)

Student Services: Library
Last Updated: 24/09/15

DOM ORIONE CATHOLIC FACULTY

Faculdade Católica Dom Orione (FACDO)
Rua Santa Cruz, 557, Centro, Araguaína, TO 77804-090
Tel: +55(63) 3414-3355
Fax: +55(63) 3414-5441
EMail: diretoriaacademica@catolicaorione.edu.br
Website: http://www.catolicaorione.edu.br/site

Diretor Geral: Josumar dos Santos
Diretor Acadêmico: Eduardo Caliman
EMail: caliman@catolicaorione.edu.br

Course

Administration (Administration); **Finance** (Finance); **Law** (Law)

History: Founded 2005.

Main Language(s) of Instruction: Portuguese

Accrediting Agency: Ministry of Education

Degrees and Diplomas: *Bacharelado*; *Especialização/Aperfeiçoamento*: **Accountancy; Business Administration; Civil Law; Constitutional Law; Criminal Law; Educational Administration; Finance; Higher Education; Law; Management; Marketing; Pedagogy; Public Administration.** Also MBA

Student Services: Library
Last Updated: 06/10/15

DOM PEDRO II INTEGRATED FACULTIES

Faculdades Integradas Dom Pedro II (DOMPEDRO)
Avenida Bady Bassitt N° 3777, Vila Imperial,
São José do Rio Preto, São Paulo 15015700
Tel: +55(17) 2139-1600
Fax: +55(17) 2139-1640
EMail: dompedro@dompedro.com.br
Website: http://www.dompedro.com.br

Diretor: Luiz Alberto Ismael Junior
EMail: ismael@dompedro.edu.br

Course

Accountancy (Accountancy); **Administration** (Administration); **Architecture and Town Planning** (Architecture; Town Planning); **Civil Engineering** (Civil Engineering); **Economics** (Economics)

History: Founded 2003.

Main Language(s) of Instruction: Portuguese

Degrees and Diplomas: *Bacharelado*; *Mestrado*
Last Updated: 23/06/15

DON BOSCO FACULTY OF ECONOMICS, ADMINISTRATION AND COMPUTER SCIENCE

Faculdade de Ciências Econômicas, administrativas e da computação Dom Bosco (FCEACDB)
Av. Cel Prof. Antonio Esteves, n° 01, Campo de Aviação,
Resende, RJ 27523-000
Tel: +55(24) 3383-9000
Fax: +55(24) 3383-9000
EMail: sec@aedb.br; esteves@aedb.br
Website: http://www.aedb.br

Direcor: Anibal Simon Esteves

Faculty

Economics, Administration and Computer Science (Administration; Business Administration; Computer Engineering; Computer Science; Economics; Human Resources; Information Technology; Software Engineering)

History: Founded 1968. Maintained by Don Bosco Educational Association with two other Faculties: Faculdade de Filosofia, Ciências e Letras Dom Bosco and Faculdade de Engenharia de Resende.

Main Language(s) of Instruction: Portuguese

Degrees and Diplomas: *Bacharelado*; *Especialização/Aperfeiçoamento*: **Finance; Human Resources; Management; Transport Management.**

Student Services: Library
Last Updated: 11/06/15

DON BOSCO FACULTY OF PHILOSOPHY, SCIENCE AND LETTERS

Faculdade de Filosofia Ciências e Letras Dom Bosco (FFCLDB)
Av Coronel Professor Antonio Esteves, 01, Campo de Aviação,
Resende, RJ 27523-000
Tel: +55(24) 3383- 9000
Fax: +55(24) 3383- 9000
EMail: sec@aedb.br
Website: http://www.aedb.br

Director: Antonio Carlos Simon Esteves

Faculty

Philosophy, Science and Literature (Biology; Education; Educational Sciences; English; Literature; Portuguese; Spanish; Special Education; Teacher Training)

History: Founded 1974. Maintained by Association Educational Don Bosco with Faculdade de Engenharia de Resende and Faculdade de Ciências Econômicas Dom Bosco.

Main Language(s) of Instruction: Portuguese

Degrees and Diplomas: *Bacharelado*; *Licenciatura*; *Especialização/Aperfeiçoamento*: **Clinical Psychology; Educational Psychology; English; Environmental Management; Literature; Portuguese; Spanish; Water Science.**

Student Services: Library
Last Updated: 11/06/15

DON DOMENICO FACULTY

Faculdade Don Domênico
Rua Dr. Arthur Costa Filho 20, Vila Maia,
Guarujа, São Paulo 11410-080
Tel: +55(13) 3308-3000
Fax: +55(13) 3389-7017
EMail: secretariafaculdade@dondomenico.com.br
Website: http://www.faculdadedondomenico.edu.br

Administrador: Manoel Fernando Passaes

Secretária: Valéria de Freitas

Course

Accountancy (Accountancy); **Administration** (Administration); **Geography** (Geography); **History** (History); **Human Resources Management** (Human Resources); **Letters** (Literature); **Logistics** (Transport Management); **Occupational Safety** (Safety Engineering); **Pedagogy** (Pedagogy); **Postgraduate Studies** (Educational

Psychology; Environmental Management; Human Resources; Social Sciences; Special Education; Transport Management)

Further Information: Also Anna Juliana Campus

History: Founded 1972.

Main Language(s) of Instruction: Portuguese

Degrees and Diplomas: *Bacharelado*; *Licenciatura*; *Especialização/Aperfeiçoamento*: **Educational Psychology; Environmental Management; Human Resources; Social Sciences; Special Education.** Also MBA in Transport Management

Student Services: Canteen, IT Centre, Library

Last Updated: 07/09/15

DR. ARISTIDES DE CARVALHO SCHLOBACH HIGHER EDUCATION INSTITUTE OF TAQUARITINGA

Instituto Taquaritinguense de Ensino Superior Dr Aristides de Carvalho Schlobach (ITES)

159 Praça Dr. Horácio Ramalho, Centro, Taquaritinga, São Paulo 15900000

Tel: +55(16) 3253-3169 +55(16) 3253-3170

Fax: +55(16) 3253-3169 +55(16) 3253-3170

EMail: secretariat@ites.com.br

Website: http://www.ites.com.br/index.php

Diretora: Ligiane Raimundo Gomes

Course

Accountancy (Accountancy); **Administration** (Administration); **Agronomy** (Agronomy); **Civil Engineering** (Civil Engineering); **Pedagogy** (Pedagogy); **Psychology** (Psychology)

History: Founded 1998.

Main Language(s) of Instruction: Portuguese

Degrees and Diplomas: *Bacharelado*

Last Updated: 14/04/16

DR. EDMUNSO ULSON UNIVERSITY CENTRE OF ARARAS

Centro Universitario de Araras Dr Edmunso Ulson (UNAR)

Avenida Ernani Lacerda de Oliveira 100, Parque Santa Cândida, Araras, São Paulo 13603 112

Tel: +55(19) 3541-3047

Fax: +55(19) 3542-7373

EMail: secretaria@unar.edu.br,contato@unar.edu.br

Website: http://www.unar.edu.br

Reitora: Maria Terezinha P.B. Ulson

Vice-Reitor: José Marta Filho

Course

Accountancy (Accountancy); **Administration** (Administration); **Advertising** (Advertising and Publicity); **Agricultural Engineering** (Agricultural Engineering); **Architecture and Town Planning** (Architecture; Town Planning); **Art Education** (Art Education; Visual Arts); **Arts and Humanities** (English; Literature; Spanish); **Civil Engineering** (Civil Engineering); **Geography** (Geography); **History** (History); **Human Resources** (Human Resources); **Information Systems** (Information Sciences); **Journalism** (Journalism); **Law** (Law); **Pedagogy** (Pedagogy; Preschool Education; Primary Education; Secondary Education; Teacher Training); **Philosophy** (Philosophy); **Production Engineering** (Production Engineering); **Sociology** (Sociology); **Theology** (Theology); **Tourism** (Tourism); **Transport Management** (Transport Management)

Further Information: Also Distance Education Programs

History: Founded 1971 as Faculdade de Ciências e Letras de Araras.

Main Language(s) of Instruction: Portuguese

Degrees and Diplomas: *Bacharelado*; *Licenciatura*; *Especialização/Aperfeiçoamento*: **Accountancy; Administration; Art Education; Civil Law; Commercial Law; Communication Studies; Design; Human Resources; Information Management; Landscape Architecture; Latin American Studies; Law; Literacy Education; Special Education; Teacher Training.** *Mestrado*; *Doutorado*

Student Services: Library

Last Updated: 02/07/15

DR. FRANCISCO MAEDA FACULTY

Faculdade Dr. Francisco Maeda (FAFRAM)

Rodovia Jerônimo Nunes Macedo Km 01, Campus Agronomia, Aeroporto, Ituverava, São Paulo 14500-000

Tel: +55(16) 3729-9000

EMail: fafram@feituverav.com.br; marciopereira@feituverava.com.bra

Website: http://www.feituverava.com.br/fafram

Diretor: Márcio Pereira

Course

Agronomy (Agronomy); **Information Systems** (Information Technology); **Law** (Law); **Nursing** (Nursing); **Postgraduate Studies** (Agricultural Business; Agricultural Engineering; Agricultural Management; Computer Engineering; Environmental Studies; Health Administration; Labour Law; Real Estate; Safety Engineering; Transport Management; Veterinary Science); **Veterinary Science** (Veterinary Science)

History: Founded 1987.

Main Language(s) of Instruction: Portuguese

Degrees and Diplomas: *Bacharelado*; *Especialização/Aperfeiçoamento*: **Computer Engineering; Environmental Studies; Labour Law; Real Estate; Safety Engineering; Veterinary Science.** Also MBA in Agricultural Business, Agricultural Management, Health Administration, Transport Management, Agricultural Engineering

Student Services: Canteen, Library

Last Updated: 08/09/15

DR. LEOCÁDIO JOSÉ CORREIA FACULTY

Faculdade Dr. Leocádio José Correia (FALEC)

Rua José Antônio Leprevost 331, Santa Candida, Curitibá, Paraná 82640-070

Tel: +55(41) 3256-5717

Fax: +55(41) 3256-5717 +55(41) 3357-6852

EMail: falec@falec.br; agdamotta@gmail.com; falec.coordenacao@gmail.com

Website: http://www.falec.br

Diretor: Enio José Coimbra de Carvalho

Course

Accountancy (Accountancy); **Administration** (Administration); **Pedagogy** (Pedagogy); **Postgraduate Studies** (Educational Psychology; Environmental Studies; Higher Education Teacher Training; Human Resources; Pedagogy; Religious Studies; Special Education); **Spiritual Theology** (Theology)

History: Founded 2000.

Main Language(s) of Instruction: Portuguese

Degrees and Diplomas: *Bacharelado*; *Especialização/Aperfeiçoamento*: **Educational Psychology; Environmental Studies; Higher Education Teacher Training; Human Resources; Pedagogy; Religious Studies; Special Education.**

Student Services: Library

Last Updated: 08/09/15

DULCINA DE MORAES FACULTY OF ARTS

Faculdade de Artes Dulcina de Moraes (FADM)

SDS Bloco C N°. 30/64, Edifício FBT, Brasília, DF 70392-902

Tel: +55(61) 3224-5369

Fax: +55(61) 3224-5369

EMail: fadmweb@fadm.com.br

Website: http://www.dulcina.art.br

Diretora: Lúcia Andrade EMail: lucia@dulcina.art.br

Secretaria Acadêmica: Maria Celia Alves Gelenske EMail: mmariaccelia@hotmail.com

Course
Acting (Acting); **Fine Arts** (Fine Arts; Visual Arts); **Performing Arts** (Performing Arts; Theatre); **Scenic Arts** (Theatre)
History: Founded 1980.
Main Language(s) of Instruction: Portuguese
Accrediting Agency: Ministry of Education
Degrees and Diplomas: *Bacharelado*; *Licenciatura*; *Especialização/Aperfeiçoamento*: **Art History; Theatre.**
Student Services: Library
Last Updated: 21/10/15

EDUCATIONAL FOUNDATION OF ALÉM PARAÍBA

Fundação Educacional de Além Paraíba (FEAP)

Av. Augusto Perácio, n° 226, São Luiz,
Além Paraíba, MG 36660-000
Tel: +55(32) 3462-7030
EMail: cobranca@feap.edu.br; secretariageral@feap.edu; fundacaoap@ig.com.br
Website: http://www.feap.edu.br

Presidente: José Alves Fortes

Faculty
Alves Fortes Faculty Management - FACE - ALFOR *(Além Paraíba)* (Administration; Civil Engineering; Law); **Archimedes Theodoro Faculty of Health Sciences - FAC - SAUDE ARTHE** *(Além Paraíba)* (Nursing; Nutrition; Physical Education); **Faculty of Management - FCGB** *(Bicas)* (Business Administration); **Professora Nair Fortes Abu-Merhy Faculty of Philosophy, Science and Letters - FAFI - PRONAFOR** *(Além Paraíba)* (Geography; History; Literature; Mathematics; Pedagogy)

Institute
Carlos Chagas Institute of Education - ISECC *(Juiz de Fora)* (Pedagogy); **Institute of Education of Bicas - ISEB** *(Bicas)* (Pedagogy); **Institute of Education of Matias Barbosa - ISEMB** *(Matias Barbosa)* (Pedagogy); **Professora Nair Fortes Abu-Merhy Institute of Education - ISEFOR** *(São José)* (Biology; Environmental Studies; Physical Education; Science Education)
History: Founded 1973.
Main Language(s) of Instruction: Portuguese
Degrees and Diplomas: *Bacharelado*; *Licenciatura*; *Especialização/Aperfeiçoamento*: **Educational Administration; Educational Psychology; Environmental Management; Geography; Higher Education Teacher Training; History; Literature; Mathematics; Pedagogy; Portuguese; Preschool Education.**
Last Updated: 09/12/15

EDUCATIONAL MUNICIPALITY OF BELO JARDIM

Autarquia Educacional do Belo Jardim (AEB)

Rodovia PE-166, Km 5, Belo Jardim,
PE 55150-000
Tel: +55(81) 3726-1800
EMail: csgfabeja@yahoo.com.br
Website: http://www.aeb.edu.br

Diretor: José Wilson Maciel Filho

Diretora da FABEJA: Lindhiane Costa de Farias

Diretora da FAEB: Luciana Uchoa Barbosa

Faculty
Teachers Training (FABEJA) (Accountancy; Administration; Biology; English; Geography; History; Literature; Mathematics; Pedagogy; Portuguese)

School
Nursing (FAEB) (Nursing)
Main Language(s) of Instruction: Portuguese
Degrees and Diplomas: *Bacharelado*: **Administration; Nursing.** *Licenciatura*: **English; Geography; History; Mathematics; Modern Languages; Pedagogy; Portuguese.**
Student Services: Library
Last Updated: 12/06/15

EDUCATIONAL UNION OF BRASILIA

União Educacional de Brasília (UNEB)

SGAS - Avenida W5 Sul Quadra 910 32 Bloco D, Asa Sul,
Brasília, DF 70390100
Tel: +55(61) 3445-3344
Fax: +55(61) 3443-1204
EMail: uneb@uneb.com.br
Website: http://www.uneb.com.br

Diretor: Marcelino Federal Neto

Area
Management (Accountancy; Administration; Business Administration; Economics; Environmental Management; Finance; Health Administration; International Business; Public Administration); **Technology**
History: Founded 1981.
Degrees and Diplomas: *Bacharelado*; *Licenciatura*; *Especialização/Aperfeiçoamento*
Last Updated: 13/04/16

EDUVALE FACULTY OF AVARÉ

Faculdade Eduvale de Avaré

Av. Pref. Misael Euphrásio Leal, 347, Jardim América,
Avaré, SP 18705-050
Tel: +55(14) 3733-8585 +55(14) 3733-8383
EMail: eduvale@eduvaleavare.com.br
Website: http://www.eduvaleavare.com.br

Diretor Acadêmico: Evandro Marcio de Oliveira
EMail: direcao@eduvaleavare.com.br

Diretora Administrativa: Renata C. de Lima
EMail: diretoriaadministrativa@eduvaleavare.com.br

Course
Administration (Administration); **Advertising and Publicity** (Advertising and Publicity); **Agronomy** (Agronomy); **Architecture and Urbanism** (Architecture; Town Planning); **Biology** (Biology); **Law** (Law); **Nutrition** (Nutrition); **Systems Development** (Computer Science); **Zootechnics** (Animal Husbandry)
History: Founded 1999.
Main Language(s) of Instruction: Portuguese
Degrees and Diplomas: *Tecnólogo*; *Bacharelado*
Student Services: IT Centre, Library
Last Updated: 08/09/15

EINSTEIN INTEGRATED FACULTIES OF LIMEIRA

Faculdades Integradas Einstein de Limeira (FIEL)

Rua Jatobá, 200, Vila Queiroz, Limeira,
São Paulo 13480000
Tel: +55(19) 3404-9594
Fax: +55(19) 3444-6612
EMail: diracademica@faculdadeespirita.com.br
Website: http://www.einsteinlimeira.com.br

Diretora Presidente: Rosaly Silvia Affonso Leite

Course
Administration (Administration); **Architecture and Town Planning** (Architecture; Town Planning); **Biomedicine** (Biomedicine); **Civil Engineering** (Civil Engineering); **Computer Science** (Computer Science); **Electrical Engineering** (Electrical Engineering); **Environmental Management** (Environmental Management); **Letters** (Literature); **Mechanical Engineering** (Mechanical Engineering); **Nursing** (Nursing); **Pedagogy** (Pedagogy); **Physical Education**; **Physiotherapy** (Physical Therapy); **Production Engineering** (Production Engineering); **Psychology** (Psychology)
History: Founded 1980.
Main Language(s) of Instruction: Portuguese
Degrees and Diplomas: *Bacharelado*; *Especialização/Aperfeiçoamento*. Also MBAs
Last Updated: 09/07/15

ENTRE RIOS FACULTY OF PIAUÍ

Faculdade Entre Rios do Piauí (FAERPI)

Rua Telegrafista Sebastião Portela, 3,392, São João, PI 64046-480
Tel: +55(86) 3303-8766
Fax: +55(86) 3303-8767
EMail: faleconosco@faculdadeentrerios.com; gildasio@lupa-rj.com.br
Website: http://www.faerpi.com

Diretor: Eylanison Falcão do Vale

Course
Pedagogy (Pedagogy); **Philosophy** (Philosophy); **Theology** (Theology)

History: Founded 2004.

Main Language(s) of Instruction: Portuguese

Degrees and Diplomas: *Bacharelado*; *Licenciatura*; *Especialização/Aperfeiçoamento*: **Administrative Law; Adult Education; Art Education; Bible; Biological and Life Sciences; Business Administration; Civil Law; Clinical Psychology; Commercial Law; Community Health; Criminal Law; Distance Education; Educational Administration; Educational Psychology; Ethics; Finance; Fiscal Law; Gerontology; Health Administration; Health Sciences; Higher Education Teacher Training; Human Resources; Industrial and Organizational Psychology; Labour Law; Law; Literacy Education; Management; Mathematics; Mathematics Education; Music Education; Nursing; Occupational Health; Oncology; Pedagogy; Physiology; Preschool Education; Public Administration; Public Health; Religious Studies; Special Education; Sports; Statistics; Theology; Transport Management.** Also MBA

Last Updated: 27/11/15

EQUIPE FACULTY

Faculdade Equipe (FAE)

Av. Sapucaia, 1376, Centro, Sapucaia do Sul, RS 93210-240
Tel: +55(51) 3474-4515
EMail: contato@faculdadesequipe.com.br
Website: http://www.faculdadesequipe.com.br

Diretor Geral: Joaquim Francisco Müller de Paula
EMail: joaquim@faculdadesequipe.com.br

Diretor Administrativo: Fernando Silva de Paula

Course
Accountancy (Accountancy); **Administration** (Administration); **Logistics** (Transport Management); **Pedagogy** (Pedagogy); **Postgraduate Studies** (Educational Psychology; Human Resources)

History: Founded 1989 as Escola Técnica Equipe. Acquired present status and title 2001.

Main Language(s) of Instruction: Portuguese

Degrees and Diplomas: *Bacharelado*; *Especialização/Aperfeiçoamento*: **Educational Psychology; Human Resources.**

Student Services: IT Centre, Library

Last Updated: 08/09/15

EQUIPE INSTITUTE OF EDUCATION

Instituto Superior de Educaçao Equipe (ISEE)

Av. Sapucaia, 1376, Centro, Sapucaia do Sul, RS 93210-240
Tel: +55(51) 3474-4515
EMail: contato@faculdadesequipe.com.br
Website: http://faculdadesequipe.com.br/portaria-isee

Diretor: Joaquim Francisco Muller de Paula
EMail: joaquim@faculdadesequipe.com.br

Diretor Administrativo: Fernando Silva de Paula
EMail: nandodepaula@gmail.com

Course
Letters (Literature; Native Language Education; Portuguese); **Pedagogy** (Pedagogy)

History: Founded 2002.

Main Language(s) of Instruction: Portuguese

Degrees and Diplomas: *Licenciatura*

Last Updated: 13/04/16

ESIC BUSINESS AND MARKETING SCHOOL

Escola Superior de Gestão Comercial e Marketing (ESIC)

Rua Padre Dehon, 814, Hauer, Curitiba, PR 81630-090
Tel: +55(41) 3376-1417
Fax: +55(41) 3376-1417
EMail: academico@esic.br; diretor@esic.br
Website: http://www.esic.br

Diretor Geral: Ari João Erthal

Course
Administration (Administration; Business Administration; Business and Commerce; Finance; Marketing); **Graduate Studies** (Advertising and Publicity; Business Administration; Communication Studies; Finance; Human Resources; International Relations; Management; Marketing)

History: Founded 2001.

Main Language(s) of Instruction: Portuguese

Degrees and Diplomas: *Bacharelado*; *Mestrado*: **Advertising and Publicity; Business Administration; Finance; Human Resources; International Business; Management; Marketing; Transport Management.** Also MBA.

Student Services: Library

Last Updated: 25/09/15

ESPERANÇA INSTITUTE OF HIGHER EDUCATION

Instituto Esperança de Ensino Superior (IESPES)

Rua Coaracy Nunes 3315, Caranazal, Santarem, PA 68040100
Tel: +55(91) 3529-1760 +55(93) 3529-1765
Fax: +55(91) 3529-1761
EMail: secacademica@iespes.edu.br
Website: http://www.fundacaoesperanca.org/#!iespes/c7iv

Presidente Conselho Diretor: Emmanuel Silva

Course
Accountancy (Accountancy); **Administration** (Administration); **Aesthetics and Cosmetology** (Aesthetics; Cosmetology); **Computer Networks** (Computer Networks); **Environmental Management** (Environmental Management); **Journalism** (Journalism); **Logistics** (Transport Management); **Nursing** (Nursing); **Pedagogy** (Pedagogy; Teacher Training); **Pharmacy** (Pharmacy); **Physiotherapy** (Physical Therapy); **Psychology** (Psychology); **Radiology** (Radiology)

History: Founded 1999.

Main Language(s) of Instruction: Portuguese

Degrees and Diplomas: *Tecnólogo*; *Bacharelado*; *Licenciatura*; *Especialização/Aperfeiçoamento*; *Mestrado*

Student Services: Library

Last Updated: 04/04/16

ESPÍRITA INTEGRATED FACULTIES

Faculdades Integradas Espírita (FIES)

Rua Tobias de Macedo Júnior 333, Santo Inácio, Curitibá, Paraná 82010340
Tel: +55(41) 3111-1717
Fax: +55(41) 3335-3423
EMail: diracademica@faculdadeespirita.com.br
Website: http://www.faculdadeespirita.com.br

Diretor Geral: Ivalino Garcia
EMail: dirgeral@faculdadeespirita.com.br

Course
Acupuncture (Acupuncture); **Biological and Life Sciences** (Biological and Life Sciences; Biology); **Education** (Education; Educational Administration; Educational Psychology; Pedagogy; Physical Education); **Environmental Studies** (Environmental Studies); **Geography** (Geography); **History** (History); **Nutrition** (Nutrition); **Physical Therapy** (Physical Therapy; Psychotherapy; Rehabilitation and Therapy); **Yoga** (Alternative Medicine)

History: Founded 1975. Acquired present status and title 1997.

Main Language(s) of Instruction: Portuguese

Degrees and Diplomas: *Bacharelado*; *Licenciatura*; *Especialização/Aperfeiçoamento*
Student Services: Library
Last Updated: 24/06/15

EST FACULTIES

Faculdades EST
Rua Amadeo Rossi, 467, Morro do Espelho,
São Leopoldo, RS 93030-220
Tel: +55(51) 2111-1400
Fax: +55(51) 2111-1411
EMail: est@est.edu.br
Website: http://www.est.edu.br/

Reitor: Wilhelm Wacholz

Pró-Reior de Ensino e Extensão: Remi Klein

Course
Music (Music); **Musical Therapy** (Art Therapy); **Theology** (Theology)
History: Founded 1946 as Escola de Teologia. Acquired present title 2007.
Main Language(s) of Instruction: Portuguese
Degrees and Diplomas: *Bacharelado*; *Especialização/Aperfeiçoamento*: **Theology.** *Mestrado*: **Theology.** *Doutorado*: **Theology.**
Last Updated: 28/09/15

ESTACIO FACULTY OF FLORIANÓPOLIS

Faculdade Estácio de Florianópolis
Rodovia SC 401, km 01-407, Itacorubi, Florianópolis,
SC 88030-000
Tel: +55(48) 3202-6002 +55(48) 3202-6000
Fax: +55(48) 3202-6002
EMail: cgfassesc@gmail.com; sandro.vaz@estacio.br; pedagogico@assesc.edu.br
Website: http://portal.estacio.br/unidades/faculdade-estacio-de-florianopolis.aspx

Gestor da Unidade: Sandro Roberto Vaz

Course
Accounting (Accountancy); **Administration** (Business Administration); **Distance Education**; **Information Systems** (Systems Analysis); **Information Technology Management** (Information Technology); **Postgraduate Studies** (Arts and Humanities; Health Sciences; Law; Management; Technology); **Social Communication and Electronic Media** (Mass Communication; Multimedia); **Tourism** (Tourism)
Main Language(s) of Instruction: Portuguese
Degrees and Diplomas: *Tecnólogo*; *Bacharelado*; *Especialização/Aperfeiçoamento*: **Cooking and Catering; Management; Marketing; Multimedia.** Also MBA
Student Services: Library
Last Updated: 08/12/15

ESTACIO FACULTY OF MACAPÁ

Faculdade Estácio Macapá (SEAMA)
Avenida Nações Unidas, 1223, Bairro Jesus de Nazaré,
Macapá, Amapá 68908-126
Tel: +55(96) 2101-5151
Fax: +55(96) 2101-5151
EMail: seama@seama.edu.br; cgseama@gmail.com; aylla.silva@estacio.br
Website: http://portal.estacio.br/unidades/faculdade-estacio-de-macapa.aspx

Diretora: Aline Búrigo

Course
Advertising (Advertising and Publicity); **Biomedicine** (Biomedicine); **Computer Networks** (Computer Networks); **Information Systems** (Computer Science); **Journalism** (Journalism); **Law** (Law); **Nursing** (Nursing); **Nutrition** (Nutrition); **Physiotherapy** (Physical Therapy); **Postgraduate Studies** (Business Administration; Engineering; Health Sciences; Law; Management); **Psychology** (Psychology)
History: Founded 2000.
Main Language(s) of Instruction: Portuguese
Degrees and Diplomas: *Tecnólogo*; *Bacharelado*; *Especialização/Aperfeiçoamento*: **Administrative Law; Computer Networks; Constitutional Law; Fiscal Law; Higher Education Teacher Training; Physical Therapy; Public Law.** Also MBA
Last Updated: 08/12/15

ESTACIO FACULTY OF RIO GRANDE DO SUL

Faculdade Estácio do Rio Grande do Sul (FARGS)
R. Mal. Floriano Peixoto, 626, Centro, Porto Alegre, RS 90020-060
Tel: +55(51) 3214-1111
Fax: +55(51) 3214-1111
EMail: secretaria@fargs.br; cgfargs@gmail.com; fernando.romeiro@estacio.br
Website: http://portal.estacio.br/unidades/faculdade-estacio-do-rio-grande-do-sul.aspx

Course
Administration (Business Administration); **Business and Commerce** (Business and Commerce); **Hotel Management** (Hotel Management); **Internet Systems** (Computer Science); **Law** (Law); **Tourism** (Tourism)

Campus
Passo da Areia (Accountancy; Administration; Finance)
History: Founded 1994.
Main Language(s) of Instruction: Portuguese
Degrees and Diplomas: *Tecnólogo*; *Bacharelado*
Student Services: IT Centre, Library
Last Updated: 08/12/15

ESTACIO FACULTY OF THE RIO GRANDE DO SUL

Faculdade Estácio do Rio Grande do Sul (FARGS)
R. Mal. Floriano Peixoto, 626, Centro,
Porto Alegre, Rio Grande do Sul 90020060
Tel: +55(51) 3341-2512 +55(51) 3214-1111
Fax: +55(51) 3341-2512 +55(51) 3214-1111
EMail: fargs@fargs.br; secretaria@fargs.br; cgfargs@gmail.com; fernando.romeiro@estacio.br
Website: http://portal.estacio.br/unidades/faculdade-estacio-do-rio-grande-do-sul.aspx

Diretor: Marcelo Mantelli (1994-)

Course
Administration (Administration); **Commercial Management** (Business and Commerce; Management); **Hotel Management** (Hotel Management); **Internet Systems** (Computer Science); **Law** (Law); **Tourism** (Tourism)

Campus
Passo da Areia (Accountancy; Administration; Finance)
History: Founded 1994.
Main Language(s) of Instruction: Portuguese
Degrees and Diplomas: *Bacharelado*
Student Services: IT Centre, Library

Academic Staff *2015-2016*: Total: c. 120
Last Updated: 02/02/16

ESUDA FACULTY OF HUMAN SCIENCES

Faculdade de Ciências Humanas ESUDA (FCHE)
Rua Bispo Cardoso Ayres, s/n - Santo Amaro,
Recife, Pernambuco 50050480
Tel: +55(81) 3412-4242
Fax: +55(81) 3412-4242
EMail: esuda@esuda.com.br
Website: http://www.esuda.com.br

Presidente: Wilson José Macedo Barreto (1997-)

Vice-Presidente: Maria Lucília De A. Andrade Barretto

Unit

Presencial Postgraduate Studties in Caruaru (Accountancy; Administrative Law; Business and Commerce; Civil Law; Clinical Psychology; Commercial Law; Constitutional Law; Educational Psychology; Environmental Management; Finance; Human Resources; Interior Design; Labour Law; Landscape Architecture; Management; Psychiatry and Mental Health; Psychology; Public Health; Taxation); **Presencial Postgraduate Studties in Palmares** (Accountancy; Administrative Law; Business Administration; Business and Commerce; Civil Law; Clinical Psychology; Commercial Law; Constitutional Law; Criminal Law; Environmental Management; Finance; Industrial and Organizational Psychology; Interior Design; Labour Law; Landscape Architecture; Management; Psychiatry and Mental Health; Psychology; Public Health; Social Psychology; Taxation); **Presencial Postgraduate Studties in Recife** (Accountancy; Administrative Law; Architecture; Business and Commerce; Civil Law; Commercial Law; Constitutional Law; Criminal Law; Educational Administration; Educational Psychology; Engineering Management; Environmental Management; Finance; Higher Education Teacher Training; Industrial and Organizational Psychology; Information Management; Information Technology; Interior Design; International Business; Labour Law; Landscape Architecture; Leadership; Management; Marketing; Production Engineering; Protective Services; Psychoanalysis; Psychology; Psychotherapy; Public Administration; Rehabilitation and Therapy; Safety Engineering; Social Psychology; Special Education; Taxation; Urban Studies)

Department

Distance Postgraduate Studies (Accountancy; Adult Education; African Studies; Agricultural Business; Business Administration; Business Computing; Distance Education; Educational Administration; Educational Psychology; Environmental Management; Finance; Higher Education Teacher Training; Human Resources; Humanities and Social Science Education; Labour Law; Latin American Studies; Leadership; Management; Marketing; Native Language Education; Preschool Education; Primary Education; Public Administration; Public Health; Secondary Education; Small Business; Social Policy; Social Welfare; Special Education; Taxation; Transport Management)

Course

Accountancy (Accountancy); **Administration** (Administration; Finance; Human Resources; Information Technology; Management; Marketing; Transport Management); **Architecture and Urbanism** (Architecture; Town Planning); **Economics** (Economics); **Psychology** (Psychology)

Further Information: Also Distance Education Courses.

History: Founded 1974.

Main Language(s) of Instruction: Portuguese

Degrees and Diplomas: *Bacharelado*; *Especialização/Aperfeiçoamento*: **Accountancy; Administrative Law; Adult Education; African Studies; Agricultural Business; Architecture; Business Administration; Business Computing; Civil Law; Commercial Law; Constitutional Law; Criminal Law; Distance Education; Education of the Handicapped; Educational Administration; Educational Psychology; Engineering Management; Environmental Management; Higher Education Teacher Training; Human Resources; Humanities and Social Science Education; Industrial and Organizational Psychology; Information Technology; Interior Design; Labour Law; Landscape Architecture; Latin American Studies; Management; Native Language Education; Preschool Education; Primary Education; Production Engineering; Protective Services; Psychiatry and Mental Health; Psychology; Psychotherapy; Public Health; Rehabilitation and Therapy; Safety Engineering; Secondary Education; Social Psychology; Special Education; Urban Studies.** Also MBA in Leadership, Marketing, Finance, Taxation, Accountancy, Management, Human Ressources, Information Technology, Transport Management, Business and Commerce, International Business, Public Administration, Information Management

Last Updated: 24/06/15

EUCLIDES DA CUNHA FACULTY OF EDUCATION OF THE STATE OF ACRE - INEC

Faculdade de Educação Acriana Euclides da Cunha - INEC

Rua do Aviário N°204, Bairro Aviário, Rio Branco, AC 69900-000
Tel: +55(68) 3223-5088
EMail: caa.souza@uol.com.br; jessicabatista17@yahoo.com.br; contato@pomini.org
Website: http://www.euclidesdacunha.edu.br

Diretor: Carlos Alberto Alves de Souza

Course

Pedagogy (Pedagogy)

History: Founded 2006.

Main Language(s) of Instruction: Portuguese

Degrees and Diplomas: *Licenciatura*; *Especialização/Aperfeiçoamento*: **Adult Education; Education; Educational Administration; Environmental Studies; Higher Education Teacher Training; History; Preschool Education; Social Policy; Special Education.**

Last Updated: 30/06/15

EUGENE GOMES FACULTY

Faculdade Eugênio Gomes (ISEGO)

Rua Manoel Oliveira e Silva n 127, Campus Universitário ou na Praça Roberto Cintra n° 272, Centro, Ipirá, BA 44600-000
Tel: +55(75) 3254-1685 +55(75) 3254-3389
EMail: contato@faculdadeeugeniogomes.com.br; jc@facebahia.com; ckto@terra.com.br
Website: faculdadeeugeniogomes.com.br

Diretor Geral: Ulysses Rezende Neto
EMail: ulysses@faculdadeeugeniogomes.com.br; ulysses@facebahia.com

Diretora Acadêmica: Ana Lúcia Nogueira Guimarães

Course

Pedagogy (Pedagogy); **Postgraduate Studies** (Education; Health Sciences; Social Sciences); **Theology** (Theology)

History: Founded 2004 as Instituto Superior de Educação Eugênio Gomes (ISEGO).

Main Language(s) of Instruction: Portuguese

Degrees and Diplomas: *Bacharelado*; *Licenciatura*; *Especialização/Aperfeiçoamento*: **Adult Education; Bilingual and Bicultural Education; Curriculum; Educational Administration; Educational Psychology; Higher Education Teacher Training; Pedagogy; Preschool Education; Public Health; Social and Community Services; Social Policy; Teacher Training.**

Student Services: Library

Last Updated: 13/04/16

EURIPIDES UNIVERSITY CENTRE OF MARILIA

Centro Universitario Eurípides de Marília (UNIVEM)

Avenida Hygino Muzy Filho 529, Campus Universitãrio, Marília, São Paulo 17525-901
Tel: +55(14) 2105-0800
Fax: +55(14) 3413-2516
EMail: fundacao@univem.edu.br
Website: http://www.univem.edu.br

Reitor: Luiz Carlos de Macedo Soares
Tel: +55(14) 2105-0845 EMail: reitor@univem.edu.br

Pró-Reitoria Administrativa: Marlene de Fátima Campos Souza
EMail: marlene@univem.edu.br

Course

Accountancy (Accountancy); **Administration** (Administration); **Commercial Management** (Business and Commerce); **Computer Networks** (Computer Engineering; Computer Networks); **Computer Science** (Computer Science); **Graphic Design** (Graphic Design); **Human Resources** (Human Resources); **Information Systems** (Information Sciences); **Information Technology Management** (Information Technology); **Interior Design** (Interior Design); **Law** (Law); **Literature** (English; Literature; Portuguese); **Logistics** (Transport Management); **Managerial Process**

(Management); **Mathematics** (Mathematics); **Production Engineering** (Production Engineering)

History: Founded 1974

Main Language(s) of Instruction: Portuguese

Accrediting Agency: Ministry of Education.

Degrees and Diplomas: *Tecnólogo*; *Bacharelado*; *Licenciatura*; *Especialização/Aperfeiçoamento*: **Labour Law.** *Mestrado*: **Business Administration; Law.** Also MBA

Student Services: Library

Last Updated: 16/07/15

EURO-AMERICAN UNIVERSITY CENTRE

Centro Universitário Euro-Americano (UNIEURO)

Avenida das Nações, Trecho 0, Conjunto 5, Brasília, DF 70200-001

Tel: +55(61) 3445-5888 +55(61) 3445-5700

Fax: +55(61) 3445-5747

EMail: centrouniversitario@unieuro.edu.br

Website: https://www.unieuro.edu.br

Reitor: Myriam Christiano Maia Gonçalves
EMail: myriam@unieuro.edu.br

Pró-Reitora Administrativa: Flávia Marão Fecury
EMail: miguelfecury@unieuro.edu.br

Course

Accountancy (Accountancy); **Administration** (Administration); **Advertising and Publicity** (Advertising and Publicity); **Architecture and Town Planning** (Architecture; Town Planning); **Biomedicine** (Biomedicine); **Civil Engineering** (Civil Engineering); **Gastronomy** (Cooking and Catering); **Human Resources** (Human Resources); **Information Systems** (Information Technology); **Interior Design** (Interior Design); **International Relations** (International Relations); **Journalism** (Journalism); **Law** (Law); **Literature** (English; Literature; Portuguese); **Nursing** (Nursing); **Nutrition** (Nutrition); **Ondontology** (Dentistry); **Pedagogy** (Pedagogy); **Pharmacy** (Pharmacy); **Physical Education** (Physical Education); **Physical Therapy** (Physical Therapy); **Psychology** (Psychology); **Public Administration** (Public Administration); **Social Services** (Social and Community Services); **Technological Studies** (Computer Networks; Construction Engineering; Cooking and Catering; Fashion Design; Finance; Heritage Preservation; Human Resources; Interior Design; Management; Marketing; Public Administration; Real Estate)

Further Information: Also campuses in Asa Norte and Águas Claras

History: Founded 1998.

Main Language(s) of Instruction: Portuguese

Degrees and Diplomas: *Tecnólogo*; *Bacharelado*; *Licenciatura*; *Especialização/Aperfeiçoamento*: **Business Administration; Communication Studies; Cooking and Catering; Dentistry; Educational Psychology; Health Sciences; Industrial and Organizational Psychology; Information Technology; Law; Pharmacology; Pharmacy; Physical Education; Tourism.** Also MBA.

Student Services: Library

Last Updated: 07/09/15

EVANGELICAL FACULTY OF GOIANÉSIA

Faculdade Evangélica de Goianésia

Av. Brasil, n° 1000, Covoa, Goianésia, GO 76380-000

Tel: +55(62) 3389-7350

EMail: evangelica@evangelicagoianesia.com.br

Website: http://www.evangelicagoianesia.edu.br

Diretor: José Mateus dos Santos

Secretária Geral: Maria de Fátima Silva

Course

Administration (Administration); **Agronomy** (Agronomy); **Civil Engineering** (Civil Engineering); **Law** (Law)

History: Founded 2003 as Faculdade Betel de Goianésia. Acquired present titlte 2008.

Main Language(s) of Instruction: Portuguese

Degrees and Diplomas: *Bacharelado*

Student Services: Library

Last Updated: 09/09/15

EVANGELICAL FACULTY OF PARANA

Faculdade Evangélica do Paraná (FEPAR)

Rua Padre Anchieta, 2770, Bigorrilho, Curitibá, Paranà 80730-000

Tel: +55(11) 3240-5500

Fax: +55(11) 3240-5500

EMail: evangelica@fepar.edu.br; fepar@fepar.edu.br; nielcia@fepar.edu.br

Website: http://www.fepar.edu.br

Diretor: Constantino Miguel Neto EMail: dirgeral@fepar.edu.br

Diretora Administrativa e Financeira: Angela Mara da Silva
EMail: angela.silva@fepar.edu.br

Course

Medicine (Medicine); **Nursing** (Nursing); **Nutrition** (Nutrition)

History: Founded 1969.

Main Language(s) of Instruction: Portuguese

Degrees and Diplomas: *Bacharelado*; *Especialização/Aperfeiçoamento*: **Cardiology; Clinical Psychology; Dermatology; Endocrinology; Health Administration; Medicine; Neurology; Nursing; Nutrition; Ophthalmology; Orthopaedics; Paediatrics; Plastic Surgery; Rehabilitation and Therapy; Rheumatology; Surgery.** *Mestrado*: **Anatomy; Medicine; Nutrition; Surgery.** *Doutorado*: **Anatomy; Medicine; Nutrition; Surgery.**

Student Services: Library

Last Updated: 09/09/15

EVANGELICAL FACULTY OF PIAUÍ

Faculdade Evangélica do Piauí (FAEPI)

Rua Treze de Maio, 2660 Bairro Pio XII, Teresina, PI 64018-285

Tel: +55(86) 3218-6059

EMail: faepi@faepi.com.br; prodi@inta.edu.br

Website: http://www.faepi.com.br/novo

Diretor: Hamilton Vale Leitão

Diretor Administrativo: Ricardo Antonio Lima Sousa

Course

Pedagogy (Pedagogy); **Postgraduate Studies** (Community Health; Educational Administration; Health Sciences; Higher Education Teacher Training; Occupational Health; Pedagogy; Psychiatry and Mental Health; Public Administration; Religious Studies; Social Welfare); **Social Services** (Social and Community Services); **Theology** (Theology)

History: Founded 2000.

Main Language(s) of Instruction: Portuguese

Degrees and Diplomas: *Bacharelado*; *Licenciatura*; *Especialização/Aperfeiçoamento*: **Community Health; Educational Administration; Health Sciences; Higher Education Teacher Training; Occupational Health; Pedagogy; Psychiatry and Mental Health; Public Administration; Religious Studies; Social Welfare.**

Student Services: Library, eLibrary

Publications: Pedagogia; Serviço Social; Teologia

Last Updated: 09/09/15

EVANGELICAL FACULTY OF SALVADOR

Faculdade Evangélica de Salvador

Av. Antônio Carlos Magalhães, n.° 3749, 2.° andar, Pituba, Salvador, BA 41850-000

Tel: +55(71) 3333-5446

Fax: +55(71) 3333-5452

EMail: diretoria@facesa.edu.br

Diretor: Ivan Pitzer

Course

Music (Music); **Pedagogy** (Pedagogy)

History: Founded 2001.

Main Language(s) of Instruction: Portuguese

Degrees and Diplomas: *Licenciatura*

Last Updated: 09/09/15

EVANGELICAL FACULTY OF TECHNOLOGY, SCIENCE AND BIOTECHNOLOGY

Faculdade Evangélica de Tecnologia, Ciências e Biotecnologia (FAECAD)
Avenida Vicente de Carvalho, 1083, Vila da Penha,
Rio de Janeiro, 21210-002 RJ
Tel: +55(21) 3015-1000
Fax: +55(21) 2482-7733
EMail: faecad@faecad.com.br; secretaria@faecad.com.br
Website: http://faecad.com.br

Diretor Geral: Germano Soares Silva

Chefe da Secretaria Geral: Fabiana de Almeida Silva

Course
Pedagogy (Pedagogy); **Postgraduate Studies** (History; History of Religion; New Testament; Religious Studies; Theology); **Theology** (Theology)

History: Founded 2005.

Main Language(s) of Instruction: Portuguese

Degrees and Diplomas: *Bacharelado*; *Licenciatura*; *Especialização/Aperfeiçoamento*: **History; History of Religion; New Testament; Religious Studies; Theology.**
Last Updated: 30/11/15

EVANGELICAL FACULTY OF THE MID-NORTH REGION

Faculdade Evangélica do Meio Norte (FAEME)
Rua Nova, N° 429, Coroatá, MA 65415-000
Tel: +55(99) 3641-2812 +55(99) 98217-8477
EMail: faeme.ieb@hotmail.com
Website: http://www.faeme.com.br

Diretor: Osiel Gomes da Silva EMail: drosiel@hotmail.com

Course
Administration (Administration); **Law** (Law)

History: Founded 2002.

Main Language(s) of Instruction: Portuguese

Degrees and Diplomas: *Bacharelado*

Student Services: Library, eLibrary
Last Updated: 09/09/15

FABRA HIGHER EDUCATION CENTRE

Centro de Ensino Superior FABRA
Rua Ipatinga 82, Barcelona, Serra, ES 29166-210
Tel: +55(27) 3241-9093
Fax: +55(27) 3241-9093
EMail: fabra@soufabra.com.br
Website: http://www.soufabra.com.br

Diretora: Patrícia Gonçalves Oliveira

Course
Administration (Accountancy); **Computer Networks** (Computer Engineering; Computer Networks); **English** (English); **Information Systems** (Information Technology); **Pedagogy** (Education; Pedagogy); **Portuguese** (Portuguese); **Theology** (Theology)

History: Founded as Escola de Ensino Superior Alternativo, 2001. Acquired present title and status 2013.

Main Language(s) of Instruction: Portuguese

Degrees and Diplomas: *Bacharelado*; *Licenciatura*; *Especialização/Aperfeiçoamento*: **Biotechnology; Business Administration; Education; Health Sciences; Law; Marketing; Nursing; Nutrition; Pharmacology; Physical Therapy; Protective Services; Public Health; Software Engineering; Technology; Theology.**

Student Services: Library
Last Updated: 22/09/15

FACULTIES OF DRACENA

Faculdades de Dracena (UNIFADRA)
Av Alcides Chacon Couto N° 395, Dracena, São Paulo 17900-000
Tel: +55(18) 3821-9004
EMail: secretaria@fundec.edu.br
Website: http://fundec.edu.br/unifadra

Diretor Geral: Wander Dorival Ramos

Course
Biological and Life Sciences (Biological and Life Sciences); **Computer Science** (Computer Science); **Education** (Art Education; Education; Pedagogy; Physical Education); **Literature** (Literature); **Mathematics** (Mathematics); **Nursing** (Nursing); **Psychology** (Psychology); **Social Services** (Social and Community Services)

History: Founded 1997.

Degrees and Diplomas: *Bacharelado*; *Licenciatura*; *Especialização/Aperfeiçoamento*
Last Updated: 11/06/15

FACULTIES OF PEDRO LEOPOLDO

Faculdades Pedro Leopoldo
Av. Lincoln Diogo Viana, 830, Pedro Leopoldo, MG 33600-000
Tel: +55(31) 3686-1461
Fax: +55(31) 3686-1461
EMail: faleconosco@fpl.edu.br
Website: http://www.unipel.edu.br

Diretora Geral: Carlos Alberto Portela da Silva

Vice-Diretora: Ilza Maria Tavares Gualberto

Diretor de Administração e Finanças: Walter Moreira Rocha

Course
Accountancy (Accountancy); **Administration** (Administration); **Law** *(FADIPEL)* (Law); **Logistics** (Transport Management)

History: Founded 1994.

Main Language(s) of Instruction: Portuguese

Degrees and Diplomas: *Tecnólogo*; *Bacharelado*; *Mestrado*: **Administration.** Also MBA

Student Services: Library
Last Updated: 03/02/16

FACULTIES OF THE PROFESSOR PAULO MARTINS SCHOOL

Faculdades Escola Superior Professor Paulo Martins (ESPAM)
Quadra 04 Área Reservada 01 - Região Administrativa V,
Sobradinho, Brasília, DF 73025-040
Tel: +55(61) 3487-7100
EMail: secretaria@espam.edu.br
Website: http://www.espam.edu.br

Diretor Administrativo: Duilio Reis Canedo

Faculty
Administration (Administration)

Higher School
Accountancy and Mathematics *(Planaltina)* (Accountancy; Mathematics)

Higher Institute
Education *(ISPAM)* (Education)

FACULTIES OF THE VALLEY OF CARANGOLA

Faculdades Vale do Carangola
Praça dos Estudantes, 23 - Santa Emilia,
Carangola, MG 36800-000
Tel: +55(32) 3741-1969
EMail: sac@carangola.br
Website: http://www.carangola.br

Reitor: Dijon Moraes Junior

Course
Administration (Administration); **Biology** (Biology); **Geography** (Geography); **History** (History); **Information Systems** (Computer Science); **Letters** (Literature); **Mathematics** (Mathematics); **Pedagogy** (Pedagogy); **Social Services** (Social and Community Services); **Tourism** (Tourism)

History: Founded 1970 as Faculdade de Filosofia, Clências e Letras de Carangola. Acquired present title 2007.

Main Language(s) of Instruction: Portuguese

Degrees and Diplomas: *Bacharelado*; *Licenciatura*; *Especialização/Aperfeiçoamento*

Last Updated: 18/04/16

FACULTY CENTRE OF MATO GROSSO

Faculdade Centro Mato-Grossense

Rua Rui Barbosa 380, Sorriso, MT 78890-000

Tel: +55(66) 3544-4932

EMail: facem@facem.com.br

Website: http://www.facem.com.br

Diretora Geral: Jaquelini Schardosim Moreira

Diretora Acadêmica: Ariel Diaz Loaces

Course

Aesthetics and Cosmetics (Cosmetology); **Agronomy** (Agronomy); **Human Resources** (Human Resources); **Physical Education** (Physical Education)

History: Founded 2005.

Main Language(s) of Instruction: Portuguese

Degrees and Diplomas: *Bacharelado*; *Especialização/Aperfeiçoamento*: **Cosmetology; Physical Education; Plant and Crop Protection; Teacher Training.**

Student Services: Library

Last Updated: 13/10/15

FACULTY CENTRE OF THE STATE OF SAO PAULO

Faculdade Centro Paulista (FACEP)

Av Prefeito Alberto Alves Casemiro, 1747, Jardim Ternura, Ibitinga, SP 14940-000

Tel: +55(16) 3341-5800

EMail: facep@facep.edu.br

Website: http://www.facep.edu.br

Diretora Interina: Nathalia Longhini dos Santos

Secretária Acadêmica: Paula Oliveira dos Santos

Course

Administration (Administration; Business Administration; Finance; Human Resources; Marketing); **Modern Languages** (English; Literature; Spanish); **Pedagogy** (Education; Pedagogy)

History: Founded as Centro de Ensino Superior de Ibitinga. Part of the Grupo Educational UNIESP since 2012.

Degrees and Diplomas: *Bacharelado*; *Licenciatura*

Student Services: IT Centre, Library

Last Updated: 14/10/15

FACULTY ESPIRITO SANTO

Faculdade do Espírito Santo (FACES)

Av. N. S^{a}. da Penha, 1,800, Barro Vermelho, Vitória, ES 29045-400

Tel: +55(27) 3421-1500

EMail: marcioacbarros@yahoo.com.br

Website: http://www.faces.edu.br

Diretor: Rodrigo Cambará Arantes Garcia de Paiva

Course

Accounting (Accountancy); **Administration** (Business Administration); **Education** (Education); **Law** (Law); **Nursing** (Nursing); **Social Communication, Publicity and Advertisement** (Advertising and Publicity; Mass Communication); **Technological Studies** (Business and Commerce; Hotel and Restaurant; Information Technology; International Business; Marketing; Tourism); **Tourism** (Tourism)

History: Founded 2002.

Main Language(s) of Instruction: Portuguese

Degrees and Diplomas: *Tecnólogo*; *Bacharelado*; *Licenciatura*

Last Updated: 26/11/15

FACULTY FOR THE DEVELOPMENT OF THE SOUTH EAST OF THE STATE OF TOCANTINS

Faculdade para o Desenvolvimento do Sudeste Tocantinense

Praça Aurélio Antonio Araújo n° 2, Centro, Dianópolis, TO 77.300–000

Tel: +55(63) 3692-1949

EMail: fades@fades.com.br

Diretora: Grazziella Povoa Costa Rodrigues

Course

Accountancy (Accountancy); **Administration** (Administration)

History: Founded 2005.

Main Language(s) of Instruction: Portuguese

Degrees and Diplomas: *Bacharelado*; *Especialização/Aperfeiçoamento*

Last Updated: 26/06/15

FACULTY OF ACCOUNTANCY AND ADMINISTRATION OF CACHOEIRO DE ITAPEMIRIM

Faculdade de Ciências Contábeis e Administrativas de Cachoeiro de Itapemirim (FACCACI)

Rod. Cachoeiro X Alegre km 8, ES 482, Morro Grande, Cachoeiro de Itapemirim, ES 29313-220

Tel: +55(28) 2102-6600

Fax: +55(28) 2102-6601

EMail: faccaci@faccaci.edu.br

Website: http://www.faccaci.edu.br

Diretor: Eliseu Crisôstomo de Vargas

Course

Accountancy (Accountancy); **Administration** (Administration; Business Administration; Human Resources); **Graduate Studies** (Business Administration)

History: Founded 1970.

Main Language(s) of Instruction: Portuguese

Accrediting Agency: Ministry of Education

Degrees and Diplomas: *Bacharelado*; *Especialização/Aperfeiçoamento*: **Business Administration.** Also MBA.

Student Services: Library

Last Updated: 26/10/15

FACULTY OF ACCOUNTANCY AND ADMINISTRATION OF THE JURUENA VALLEY

Faculdade de Ciências Contábeis e de Administração do Vale do Juruena (AJES)

Avenida Gabriel Müller, s/n, AJES - Faculdades do Vale do Juruena, Módulo I, Juína, MT 78320-000

Tel: +55(66) 3566-1875

EMail: clodis@ajes.edu.br; secretaria@ajes.edu.br

Website: http://www.ajes.edu.br

Reitor: Clodis Antonio Menegaz.

Course

Accountancy (Accountancy); **Administration** (Administration); **Computer Science** (Computer Science); **Geography** (Geography); **History** (History); **Law** (Law); **Letters** (English; Literature; Portuguese); **Mathematics** (Mathematics); **Nursing** (Nursing); **Pedagogy** (Education; Pedagogy); **Pharmacy** (Pharmacy); **Physical Education** (Physical Education); **Physical Therapy** (Physical Therapy); **Psychology** (Psychology); **Social Communication** (Communication Studies); **Theology** (Theology)

Campus

Guaranta Do Norte (Accountancy; Administration; Nursing; Portuguese; Spanish)

History: Founded 2005.

Main Language(s) of Instruction: Portuguese

Accrediting Agency: Ministry of Education

Degrees and Diplomas: *Bacharelado*; *Especialização/Aperfeiçoamento*: **Business Administration; Educational Psychology; Finance; Human Resources; Management; Marketing; Nursing; Public Health; Safety Engineering.**

Student Services: Library

Last Updated: 26/10/15

FACULTY OF ACCOUNTANCY OF AFONSO CLAÚDIO

Faculdade de Ciências Contábeis de Afonso Claúdio (ISEAC)

Rua Ute Gastin de Padua 49, São Tarcisio,
Afonso Claúdio, ES 29600-000
Tel: +55(27) 3735-2411
Fax: +55(27) 3735-2433
EMail: adm.tudo1@gmail.com

Diretor Presidente: Avacilio Azevedo

Course

Accountancy (Accountancy)

History: Founded 2000. Maintained by Instituto Superior de Eucacacao de Afonso Claudio (ISEAC).

Main Language(s) of Instruction: Portuguese

Accrediting Agency: Ministry of Education

Degrees and Diplomas: *Bacharelado*

Last Updated: 23/10/15

FACULTY OF ACCOUNTANCY OF PONTE NOVA

Faculdade de Ciências Contábeis de Ponte Nova

Rua dos Vereadores 177, Sumaré,
Ponte Nova, Minas Gerais 35430-039
Tel: +55(31) 3817-2010
Fax: +55(31) 3817-2580
EMail: lenydepinho@yahoo.com.br
Website: http://www.facco.edu.br

Diretor Acadêmico: José Geraldo da Silva

Course

Accountancy (Accountancy)

History: Founded 1978

Main Language(s) of Instruction: Portuguese

Accrediting Agency: Ministry of Education

Degrees and Diplomas: *Bacharelado*

Last Updated: 26/10/15

FACULTY OF ACCOUNTANCY OF RECIFE

Faculdade de Ciências Contábeis de Recife (FACCOR)

Avenida Ministro Marcos Freire 2855, Casa Caiada,
Olinda, Pernambuco 53130-540
Tel: +55(81) 3495-0504
EMail: marcioacbarros@yahoo.com.br
Website: http://www.fape-pe.edu.br/FAPEIV/index.asp

Diretor: Newton Roberto Gregório Moraes

Coordinatora: Angela Basante Campos

Course

Accountancy (Accountancy)

History: Founded 1992.

Main Language(s) of Instruction: Portuguese

Accrediting Agency: Ministry of Education

Degrees and Diplomas: *Bacharelado*

Student Services: Library, eLibrary

Last Updated: 26/10/15

FACULTY OF ACCOUNTING AND ADMINISTRATIVE SCIENCES OF CAMAQUA

Faculdade Camaqüense de Ciências Contábeis e Administrativas (FACCCA)

Avenida Cônego Luiz Walter Hanquet 151, Centro,
Camaquã, RS 96180-000
Tel: +55(51) 3671-1855 +55(51) 3671-5905
Fax: +55(51) 3671-1855
EMail: fundasul@fundasul.br; faculdades@fundasul.br
Website: http://www.fundasul.br

Presidente: Rubem Carlos Serafini Machado

Course

Accountancy (Accountancy); **Administration** (Business Administration); **Physical Education** *(Licenciatura)* (Physical Education); **Physical Education** (Physical Education)

History: Founded 1973.

Main Language(s) of Instruction: Portuguese

Degrees and Diplomas: *Técnico de Nivel Medio*; *Bacharelado*; *Licenciatura*

Student Services: Library

Last Updated: 10/12/15

FACULTY OF ADMINISTRATION AND ACCOUNTANCY OF SÃO ROQUE

Faculdade de Administração e Ciências Contábeis de São Roque (FACCSR)

Rua Sotero de Souza, 104, Centro,
São Roque, São Paulo 18130-200
Tel: +55(11) 4719-9300
Fax: +55(11) 4719-9302
EMail: fac@facsaoroque.br
Website: http://www.facsaoroque.br

Diretor: Eduardo Storópoli (1996-)

Course

Accountancy (Accountancy); **Administration** (Administration; Business Administration); **Human Resources** (Human Resources); **Information Technology** (Information Technology); **Law** (Law); **Pedagogy** (Pedagogy)

History: Founded 1995.

Main Language(s) of Instruction: Portuguese

Accrediting Agency: Ministry of Education

Degrees and Diplomas: *Tecnólogo*; *Bacharelado*; *Licenciatura*; *Especialização/Aperfeiçoamento*: **Business Administration; Commercial Law; Educational Psychology; Human Resources.** Also MBA. Postgraduate diplomas offered through Universidad Nove de Julho (UNINOVE).

Student Services: Library

Last Updated: 16/10/15

FACULTY OF ADMINISTRATION AND TECHNOLOGY

Faculdade de Ciências Administrativas e de Tecnologia (FATEC)

Avenida Governador Jorge Teixera, 3500, Setor Industrial,
Porto Velho, Rondônia 76821-064
Tel: +55(69) 3301-3430
EMail: diretoriapedagogica@fatec-ro.br
Website: http://www.fatec-ro.br

Diretor: Marco Antônio de Faria EMail: diretoria@fatec-ro.br

Course

Accountancy (Accountancy); **Administration** (Administration; Business Administration; Health Administration); **Information Systems** (Computer Science; Information Technology); **Pedagogy** (Educational Administration; Educational and Student Counselling; Pedagogy)

History: Founded 1989.

Main Language(s) of Instruction: Portuguese

Degrees and Diplomas: *Tecnólogo*; *Bacharelado*; *Especialização/Aperfeiçoamento*: **Accountancy; Business Administration; Business Education; Educational Administration; Educational and Student Counselling; Educational Psychology; Finance; Higher Education; Human Resources.** Also MBA

Student Services: Library

Last Updated: 23/10/15

FACULTY OF ADMINISTRATION OF ALAGOANA - HIGHER EDUCATION INSTITUTE OF ALAGOANA

Faculdade Alagoana de Administração - Instituto de Ensino Superior de Alagoas (FAA-IESA)

UNIDADE I - Av. Eng. Paulo Brandão Nogueira, 160, Loteamento Stela Maris, Jatiúca, Maceió, Alagoas 57036550
Tel: +55(82) 304-5200
Fax: +55(82) 304-5208
EMail: secretariaacademica@aesa.edu.br
Website: http://www.aesa.edu.br

Diretora: Ana Paula Nunes da Silva

Coordenador Pedagógico: Edson Mario de Alcântara Júnior
EMail: edsonjr.cp@aesa.edu.br

Course
Accountancy (Accountancy); **Administration** (Administration; Business Administration; Hotel Management; Human Resources; International Business; Marketing); **Advertising and Publicity** (Advertising and Publicity); **Computer Science** (Computer Science); **Law** (Law); **Modern Languages** (English; Portuguese); **Physiotherapy** (Physical Therapy); **Social Services** (Social and Community Services); **Tourism** (Tourism)

Further Information: Also UNIDADE II - Av. Humberto Mendes, 140 - Jaraguá - Maceió/AL

History: Founded 1994.

Main Language(s) of Instruction: Portuguese

Degrees and Diplomas: *Tecnólogo*; *Bacharelado*

Student Services: Library

Last Updated: 29/09/15

FACULTY OF ADMINISTRATION OF ALAGOAS - HIGHER EDUCATION INSTITUTE OF ALAGOAS

Faculdade Alagoana de Administração - Instituto de Ensino Superior de Alagoas

Av. Eng° Paulo Brandão Nogueira, 160, Jatiúca - Stella Maris, Maceió, AL
Tel: +502(82) 3304-5200
EMail: gerente@aesa.edu.br
Website: http://www.aesa.edu.br

Course
Accountancy (Accountancy); **Administration** (Administration); **Advertisinng and Publicity** (Advertising and Publicity); **Computer Science** (Computer Science); **Law** (Law); **Literature** (English; Literature; Portuguese); **Physiotherapy** (Physical Therapy); **Social Services** (Social and Community Services); **Tourism** (Tourism)

History: Founded 1995.

Main Language(s) of Instruction: Portuguese

Degrees and Diplomas: *Bacharelado*

Last Updated: 15/04/16

FACULTY OF ADMINISTRATION OF CAMPO BELO

Faculdade de Administração de Campo Belo (FACAMP)

Rua Projetada, s/n°, Arnaldos, Campo Belo, MG 37270-000
Tel: +55(35) 3832-7855
Fax: +55(35) 3832-6376
EMail: cemes@stratus.com.br
Website: http://www.cemes.edu.br

Diretora: Ana Maria Almeida

Course
Accountancy (Accountancy);- **Administration** (Administration; Business Administration); **Pedagogy** (Education; Pedagogy); **Production Engineering** (Production Engineering)

History: Founded 2001.

Main Language(s) of Instruction: Portuguese

Accrediting Agency: Ministry of Education

Degrees and Diplomas: *Bacharelado*; *Especialização/Aperfeiçoamento*: **Business Administration; Educational Psychology; Finance; Human Resources; Sports Management.**

Student Services: Library

Last Updated: 19/10/15

FACULTY OF ADMINISTRATION OF CHAPADÃO DO SUL

Faculdade de Administração Chapadão do Sul

Rua Vinte e Oito, 615, Centro, Chapadão do Sul, MS 79560-000
Tel: +55(67) 3562-2703
EMail: fachasul@fachasul.com.br
Website: http://www.fachasul.com.br/

Diretora: Sandra Mendoca Paulino

Course
Accountancy (Accountancy); **Administration** (Administration)

History: Founded 2002.

Main Language(s) of Instruction: Portuguese

Accrediting Agency: Ministry of Education

Degrees and Diplomas: *Bacharelado*; *Especialização/Aperfeiçoamento*: **Welfare and Protective Services.**

Last Updated: 19/10/15

FACULTY OF ADMINISTRATION OF MARIANA

Faculdade de Administração de Mariana (FAMA)

Rua Dom Silvério, 161, Mariana 35420-000
Tel: +55(31) 3558-2673
EMail: secretaria.faculdade@bol.com.br
Website: http://www.femar.edu.br

Diretor Geral: José Jarbas Ramos Filho.

Course
Administration (Administration; Business Administration); **Environmenal Engineering** (Environmental Engineering); **Production Engineering** (Production Engineering)

History: Founded 2004.

Main Language(s) of Instruction: Portuguese

Accrediting Agency: Ministry of Education

Degrees and Diplomas: *Bacharelado*

Student Services: Library

Last Updated: 19/10/15

FACULTY OF ADMINISTRATION OF SANTA CRUZ DO RIO PARDO

Faculdade de Administração de Santa Cruz do Rio Pardo (FASC)

Avenida Coronel Clementino Gonçalves 1561, São Judas Tadeu, Santa Cruz do Rio Pardo, São Paulo 18900000
Tel: +55(14) 3372-1173
Fax: +55(14) 3372-4073
EMail: fafil.oapec@argon.com.br
Website: http://oapecsuperior.com.br

Diretora: Adelia de Paula Pimentel

Course
Business Administration (Business Administration); **Law** (Law)

History: Founded 2000.

Main Language(s) of Instruction: Portuguese

Accrediting Agency: Ministry of Education

Degrees and Diplomas: *Bacharelado*; *Licenciatura*; *Especialização/Aperfeiçoamento*: **Business Administration.**

Student Services: Library

Last Updated: 19/10/15

FACULTY OF ADMINISTRATION OF THE CITY OF GOVERNADOR VALADARES

Faculdade de Administração de Governador Valadares (FAGV)

Rua José de Tassis 350, Vila Bretas,
Governador Valadares, Minas Gerais 35030-250
Tel: +55(33) 3212-6777
Fax: +55(33) 3212-6768
EMail: faleconosco@fagv.com.br
Website: http://www.fagv.com.br

Diretora Geral: Zenólia Maria de Almeida

Course

Administration (Administration)

History: Founded 1975.

Main Language(s) of Instruction: Portuguese

Accrediting Agency: Ministry of Education

Degrees and Diplomas: *Bacharelado*; *Especialização/Aperfeiçoamento*: **Business Administration; Finance; Management; Marketing; Transport Management.**

Student Services: Library

Last Updated: 19/10/15

FACULTY OF ADMINISTRATION, SCIENCE, EDUCATION AND LETTERS

Faculdade de Administração, Ciêncas, Educação e Letras (FACEL)

Avenida Vicente Machado, 156, Centro, Curitibá,
Paraná 80420010
Tel: +55(41) 3324-1115
Fax: +55(41) 3324-1115
EMail: secretaria@facel.com.br
Website: http://www.facel.com.br

Presidente: José Alves Da Silva

Course

Accountancy (Accountancy); **Administration** (Administration; Business Administration); **Distance Postgraduate Studies** (Accountancy; Administration; Literature; Pedagogy; Philosophy; Psychology; Theology); **English Literature** (English; Literature); **Graduate Studies** (Accountancy; Administration; Literature; Pedagogy; Psychology); **Human Resources** (Human Resources; Marketing; Secretarial Studies; Transport Management); **Modern Languages** (English; Portuguese; Spanish); **Pedagogy** (Pedagogy); **Philosophy** (Philosophy); **Psychology** (Psychology); **Theology** (Theology)

History: Founded 1999.

Main Language(s) of Instruction: Portuguese

Accrediting Agency: Ministry of Education

Degrees and Diplomas: *Tecnólogo*; *Bacharelado*; *Licenciatura*; *Especialização/Aperfeiçoamento*: **Accountancy; Administration; Business Administration; Education; Educational Psychology; English; Pedagogy; Portuguese; Psychology; Spanish; Theology.** Also MBA.

Last Updated: 20/10/15

FACULTY OF AGRICULTURAL AND ENVIRONMENTAL SCIENCES

Faculdade de Ciências Agro-Ambientais (FAGRAM)

Avenida Brasil 9727, Penha,
Rio de Janeiro, Rio de Janeiro 21030-000
Tel: +55(21) 3977-9979
EMail: fagram@fagram.edu.br
Website: http://www.fagram.edu.br

Diretor Geral: Antonio Melo Alvarenga

Course

Zootechnics (Agriculture; Animal Husbandry)

History: Founded 1994.

Main Language(s) of Instruction: Portuguese

Accrediting Agency: Ministry of Education

Degrees and Diplomas: *Bacharelado*

Student Services: Library

Last Updated: 23/10/15

FACULTY OF AGUDOS

Faculdade de Agudos (FAAG)

Av. Marginal Vereador Delfino Tendolo, D1200,
Agudos, SP 17120-000
Tel: +55(14) 3262-9400
Fax: +55(14) 3262-9401
EMail: faag@faag.com.br
Website: http://www.faag.com.br

Diretora: Lúcia Helena Aravechia de Oliveira

Course

Accountancy (Accountancy); **Administration** (Administration; Business Administration); **Graduate Studies** (Business Administration; Education; Educational Administration; Environmental Management; Finance; Industrial Management; Management; Special Education); **Human Resources** (Human Resources); **Pedagogy** (Education; Pedagogy); **Production Engineering** (Production Engineering); **Transport Management** (Transport Management)

History: Founded 2002.

Main Language(s) of Instruction: Portuguese

Accrediting Agency: Ministry of Education

Degrees and Diplomas: *Bacharelado*; *Licenciatura*; *Especialização/Aperfeiçoamento*: **Business Administration; Education; Education of the Handicapped; Educational Administration; Educational Psychology; Environmental Management; Finance; Human Resources; Literacy Education; Management; Marketing; Safety Engineering; Special Education; Translation and Interpretation.** Also MBA.

Student Services: IT Centre, Library

Last Updated: 20/10/15

FACULTY OF AMERICAN INTERACTION

Faculdade Interação Americana

Rua Odeon 150, Vila Alcântara,
São Bernardo do Campo, São Paulo 9720290
Tel: +55(11) 4128-2130
EMail: fainam@fainam.edu.br
Website: http://www.fainam.edu.br

Diretor Geral: Oswaldo Accursi

Faculty

Pedagogy (Pedagogy)

Course

Administration (Administration; Business Administration; Finance; Marketing); **Computer Science** (Computer Science); **Letters** (Literature); **Mathematics** (Mathematics)

History: Founded 1989 as Faculdade Tapajós. Acquired present title 2001.

Main Language(s) of Instruction: Portuguese

Degrees and Diplomas: *Bacharelado*; *Licenciatura*; *Especialização/Aperfeiçoamento*; *Mestrado*

Last Updated: 07/05/15

FACULTY OF AMERICANA

Faculdade de Americana (FAM)

Rua Joaquim Boer, 733, Jardim Luciene,
Americana, São Paulo 13477-360
Tel: +55(19) 3478-2449
Fax: +55(19) 3478-2449
EMail: nicom@fam.br
Website: http://www.fam.br

Diretor Geral: Florindo Corral

Course

Accountancy (Accountancy); **Administration** (Administration); **Automation and Control Engineering** (Automation and Control Engineering); **Biological Sciences** (Biological and Life Sciences); **Computer Science** (Computer Science); **Electrical Engineering** (Electrical Engineering); **Environmental Engineering** (Environmental Engineering); **Law** (Law); **Literature** (English; Literature; Portuguese; Spanish); **Mechanichal Engineering** (Mechanical Engineering); **Nursing** (Nursing); **Nutrition** (Nutrition); **Pedagogy** (Education; Pedagogy); **Pharmacy** (Pharmacy); **Physical Education** (Physical

Education); **Physical Therapy** (Physical Therapy); **Production Engineering** (Production Engineering); **Psychology** (Psychology); **Social Commmunciation - Advertising and Publicity** (Advertising and Publicity; Communication Studies; Marketing; Public Relations); **Transport Management** (Transport Management)

History: Founded 1999.

Main Language(s) of Instruction: Portuguese

Accrediting Agency: Ministry of Education

Degrees and Diplomas: *Bacharelado*; *Licenciatura*; *Especialização/Aperfeiçoamento*: **Business Administration; Commercial Law; Human Resources; Physical Education; Safety Engineering.**

Student Services: Library

Last Updated: 20/10/15

FACULTY OF AMPERE

Faculdade de Ampère (FAMPER)

Rua dos Andradas, 550, Centro, Ampère 85640-000

Tel: +55(46) 3547-3031

Website: http://www.famper.com.br

Area

Business (Business Administration); **Education** (Education); **Social** (Social Welfare)

Degrees and Diplomas: *Especialização/Aperfeiçoamento*: **Business Administration; Education; Social Welfare.** Also MBA

Last Updated: 04/04/16

FACULTY OF APPLIED SOCIAL SCIENCES OF CASCAVEL

Faculdade de Ciências Sociais Aplicadas de Cascavel (UNIVEL)

Avenida Tito Muffato, 2317, Bairro Santa Cruz, Cascavel, Paraná 85806-080

Tel: +55(45) 3036-3636

Fax: +55(45) 3036-3638

EMail: desenvolvimento@univel.br

Website: http://www.univel.br

Diretora Geral: Adriano de Sales Coelho (2015-)

Course

Accountancy (Accountancy); **Administration** (Administration); **Advertising and Publicity** (Advertising and Publicity); **Arts** (Fine Arts); **Graduate Studies** (Accountancy; Business Administration; Business and Commerce; Civil Law; Communication Studies; Human Resources; Labour Law; Law; Management; Marketing; Sales Techniques; Taxation); **Journalism** (Journalism); **Law** (Law); **Pedagogy** (Pedagogy); **Production Engineering** (Production Engineering); **Technological Studies** (Business and Commerce; Cooking and Catering; Environmental Management; Finance; Human Resources; Management; Safety Engineering; Systems Analysis; Transport Management)

History: Founded 1995

Main Language(s) of Instruction: Portuguese

Degrees and Diplomas: *Tecnólogo*; *Bacharelado*; *Licenciatura*; *Especialização/Aperfeiçoamento*: **Business Administration; Civil Law; Labour Law; Law.** Also MBA in Taxation, Management, Business Administration, Finance, Accountancy, Marketing, Communication Studies, Sales Techniques, Human Resources; Executive MBA.

Student Services: Library

Last Updated: 24/06/15

FACULTY OF APPLIED SOCIAL SCIENCES OF EXTREMA

Faculdade de Ciências Sociais Aplicadas de Extrema (FAEX)

Estrada Municipal Pedro Rosa da Silva, 303, Vila Rica, Extrema, Minas Gerais 37640-000

Tel: +55(35) 3435-3988

Fax: +55(35) 3435-4414

EMail: faex@faex.edu.br

Website: http://www.faex.edu.br

Diretora Geral: Terezinha Aparecida Monteiro Onisto
EMail: diretoria@faex.edu.br

Secretária Geral: Eliana Aparecida Del Col Lopes
EMail: secretaria@faex.edu.br

Course

Accounting (Accountancy); **Administration** (Administration); **Automation and Control Engineering** (Automation and Control Engineering); **Civil Engineering** (Electronic Engineering; Industrial Engineering); **Graduate Studies** (Automation and Control Engineering; Business Administration; Business and Commerce; Finance; Human Resources; Leadership); **Human Resources Management** (Human Resources); **Industrial Management** (Industrial Management); **Industrial Mechatronics** (Electronic Engineering; Mechanical Engineering); **Law** (Law); **Logistics** (Transport Management); **Production Engineering** (Production Engineering); **Quality Management** (Safety Engineering); **Systems Analysis and Development** (Systems Analysis)

History: Founded in 1999. Acquired present status 2002.

Admission Requirements: Secondary School Leaving Certificate

Main Language(s) of Instruction: Portuguese

Accrediting Agency: Ministério da Educação

Degrees and Diplomas: *Tecnólogo*; *Bacharelado*; *Licenciatura*; *Especialização/Aperfeiçoamento*: **Automation and Control Engineering.** Also MBA in Finance, Business and Commerce, Human Resources, Leadership

Student Services: Library

Last Updated: 25/06/15

FACULTY OF APPLIED SOCIAL SCIENCES OF THE SOUTH OF MINAS GERAIS

Faculdade de Ciências Sociais Aplicadas do Sul de Minas Gerais (FACESM)

Av. Presidente Tancredo de Almeida Neves, 45, Itajubá, Minas Gerais 37504066

Tel: +55(35) 3629-5700

Fax: +55(35) 3629-5705

EMail: facesm@facesm.br

Website: http://www.facesm.br

Diretor Geral: Hector Gustavo Arango

Course

Accountancy (Accountancy); **Administration** (Administration); **Economics** (Economics); **Graduate Studies** (Accountancy; Business Administration; Business and Commerce; Finance; Health Administration; Human Resources; Industrial Management; International Business; Management; Marketing; Safety Engineering; Taxation; Transport Management)

History: Founded 1966 as Faculdade de Ciências Econômicas do Sul de Minas.

Main Language(s) of Instruction: Portuguese

Degrees and Diplomas: *Bacharelado*; *Especialização/Aperfeiçoamento*: **Management.** Also MBA in Industrial Management, Health Administration, Finance, International Business, Safety Engineering, Business Administration, Transport Management, Marketing, Human Resources, Accountancy, Taxation.

Student Services: Library

Last Updated: 25/06/15

FACULTY OF APPLIED SOCIAL STUDIES OF VIANA

Faculdade de Estudos Sociais Aplicados de Viana (FESAV)

Campus Industrial FESAV, Bairro Industrial, Viana, ES 29135-000

Tel: +55(27) 3344-1533

Fax: +55(27) 3344-1499

EMail: fesav@terra.com.br

Website: http://www.fesav.com.br

Diretor: José Alexandre de Souza Gadioli

Course

Accountancy (Accountancy); **Administration** (Administration); **Pedagogy** (Pedagogy); **Post-graduate Studies** (Accountancy;

Business Administration; Educational Administration; Educational Psychology; Special Education)

History: Founded 1995

Main Language(s) of Instruction: Portuguese

Degrees and Diplomas: *Bacharelado*; *Especialização/Aperfeiçoamento*: **Accountancy; Business Administration; Educational Administration; Educational Psychology; Special Education.**

Student Services: Library

Last Updated: 03/07/15

FACULTY OF APUCARANA

Faculdade de Apucarana (FAP)

Rua Osvaldo de Oliveira, 600, Jardim Flamingos,
Apucarana, Paraná 86811-500
Tel: +55(43) 3033-8900
Fax: +55(43) 3033-8930
EMail: fap@fap.com.br
Website: http://www.cesuap.edu.br

Presidente: Lívia Pinheiro Guimarães Pacheco

Diretora Acadêmica: Rita de Cássia Rosiney Ravelli

Course

Administration (Administration); **Biology** (Biology); **Graduate Studies** (Biological and Life Sciences; Computer Science; Cooking and Catering; Educational Administration; Educational Psychology; Educational Sciences; Law; Marketing; Nursing; Physical Therapy; Special Education); **Information Systems** (Computer Science); **Law** (Law); **Nursing** (Nursing); **Nutrition** (Nutrition); **Pedagogy** (Education; Pedagogy); **Physiotherapy** (Physical Therapy)

History: Founded 1999.

Main Language(s) of Instruction: Portuguese

Accrediting Agency: Ministry of Education

Degrees and Diplomas: *Bacharelado*; *Licenciatura*; *Especialização/Aperfeiçoamento*: **Business Administration; Educational Psychology; Environmental Management; Nutrition; Psychology.**

Last Updated: 20/10/15

FACULTY OF ARACAJU

Faculdade de Aracaju (FACAR)

Rua Oscar Valois Galvão, 355, Grageru, Aracaju, SE 49027-220
Tel: +55(79) 3217-7476
EMail: secretariafacar@infonet.com.br
Website: http://www.unilist.com.br/facar/instituto/destaques.asp

Diretor: Adailton Vilela de Almeida
EMail: diretoriafaser@infonet.com.br

Course

Accountancy (Accountancy); **Administration** (Administration); **Law** (Law); **Nursing** (Nursing); **Pharmacy** (Pharmacy); **Physiotherapy** (Physical Therapy); **Social Communication** (Advertising and Publicity); **Tourism** (Tourism)

History: Founded 2005 as Instituto Aracaju de Ensino e Cultura. Acquired present title 2010.

Main Language(s) of Instruction: Portuguese

Degrees and Diplomas: *Bacharelado*; *Licenciatura*

Student Services: Library

Last Updated: 20/10/15

FACULTY OF ARAÇATUBA

Faculdade de Araçatuba

Rua Sarjob Mendes, 244, Jardim Icaray, Araçatuba, SP 16020-360
Tel: +55(18) 3636-7610
Fax: +55(18) 3636-7610
EMail: fernando@uniesp.edu.br
Website: http://www.faculdadedearacatuba.edu.br

Diretor: Jose Fernando Pinto da Costa

Course

Administration (Administration)

History: Founded 2007.

Main Language(s) of Instruction: Portuguese

Accrediting Agency: Ministry of Education

Degrees and Diplomas: *Bacharelado*

Last Updated: 20/10/15

FACULTY OF ARTS OF SAO PAULO

Faculdade Paulista de Artes (FPA)

Av. Brigadeiro Luiz Antônio, 1224 - Bela Vista,
São Paulo, São Paulo 1321000
Tel: +55(11) 3287-4455
Fax: +55(11) 3287-4455
EMail: secretaria@fpa.art.br
Website: http://www.fpa.art.br

Diretora: Vera Toldedo Piza EMail: verapiza.diretora@fpa.art.br

Course

Advertising (Advertising and Publicity); **Architecture and Town Planning** (Architecture; Town Planning); **Dance** (Dance); **Design** (Design); **Fashion Design** (Fashion Design); **Music** (Music); **Music Therapy** (Art Therapy); **Plastic Arts** (Fine Arts); **Theatre** (Theatre); **Visual Arts** (Visual Arts)

History: Founded 1998.

Main Language(s) of Instruction: Portuguese

Degrees and Diplomas: *Bacharelado*; *Licenciatura*; *Especialização/Aperfeiçoamento*

Last Updated: 03/06/15

FACULTY OF BELFORD ROXO

Faculdade de Belford Roxo (FABEL)

Rua Virgilina Bicchieri, 61, Centro,
Belford Roxo, Rio de Janeiro 26113-510
Tel: +55(21) 2662-0066
EMail: info@fabel.edu.br
Website: http://www.fabel.edu.br

Diretora Geral: Katia Maria Soares (1995-)
EMail: Katia@fabel.edu.br

Course

Administration (Administration); **Computer Science** (Computer Science); **History** (History); **Pedagogy** (Pedagogy)

History: Founded 1995.

Main Language(s) of Instruction: Portuguese

Degrees and Diplomas: *Tecnólogo*; *Bacharelado*; *Licenciatura*; *Especialização/Aperfeiçoamento*: **Educational Administration; Educational and Student Counselling; Human Resources.**

Last Updated: 19/10/15

FACULTY OF BERTIOGA

Faculdade Bertioga

Avenida Manoel da Nóbrega, 966, Jardim Lido, Bertioga 11250-000
Tel: +55(13) 3317-3444
EMail: fabe@faculdadebertioga.com.br
Website: http://www.faculdadebertioga.com.br

Diretor: Fernando Sena Rodrigues

Course

Administration (Administration; Business Administration); **Law** (Law); **Pedagogy** (Education; Pedagogy)

History: Founded 2003.

Main Language(s) of Instruction: Portuguese

Degrees and Diplomas: *Bacharelado*; *Licenciatura*; *Especialização/Aperfeiçoamento*: **Business Administration; Civil Law; Education; Educational Psychology; Special Education.**

Student Services: Library

Last Updated: 01/10/15

FACULTY OF BICO DO PAPAGAIO

Faculdade do Bico do Papagaio (FABIC)

Rua Pedro Ludovico, 535, Setor Boa Vista,
Augustinópolis, TO 77960-000
Tel: +55(63) 3456-1225
Fax: +55(63) 3456-1684
EMail: contato@fabic.edu.br; geunpresidente@gmail.com
Website: http://www.fabic.edu.br

Diretor Geral: Nilton Elias

Course

Accounting (Accountancy); **Agricultural Business Management** (Agricultural Business; Agricultural Management); **Law** (Law); **Nursing** (Nursing)

History: Founded 2006.

Main Language(s) of Instruction: Portuguese

Degrees and Diplomas: *Tecnólogo*; *Bacharelado*

Last Updated: 26/11/15

FACULTY OF BUSINESS ACTIVITIES OF TERESINA

Faculdade das Atividades Empresariais de Teresina (FAETE)

Avenida Dr. Nicanor Barreto, 4381, Vale Quem Tem, Teresina, Piauí 64057-355
Tel: +55(86) 3214-9500
Fax: +55(86) 3214-9500
EMail: info@faete.edu.br
Website: http://www.faete.edu.br

Diretora Geral: Catarina Santos

Course

Administration (Administration); **Information Systems** (Computer Science); **Law** (Law); **Tourism** (Tourism)

History: Founded 2000.

Main Language(s) of Instruction: Portuguese

Degrees and Diplomas: *Bacharelado*; *Especialização/Aperfeiçoamento*: **Accountancy; Civil Law; Economics; Educational Administration; Finance; Higher Education; Human Resources; Law.**

Student Services: Library

Last Updated: 19/10/15

FACULTY OF CAPIM GROSSO

Faculdade Capim Grosso (FCG)

Loteameto das Mangueiras, s/n - Planaltino, Capim Grosso, BA 44695-000
Tel: +55(74) 3651-1543 +55(74) 3651-1586
Fax: +55 (74) 3651-1543
EMail: contato@faculdadecapimgrosso.com.br
Website: http://www.faculdadecapimgrosso.com.br

Diretor: Dario Loureiro Guimarães

Coordenadora Pedagógica: Ana Lúcia N. Guimarães

Course

Accountancy (Accountancy); **Administration** (Administration); **Pedagogy** (Education; Pedagogy)

History: Founded 2003.

Main Language(s) of Instruction: Portuguese

Accrediting Agency: Ministry of Education

Degrees and Diplomas: *Bacharelado*; *Especialização/Aperfeiçoamento*: **Accountancy; Adult Education; Business Administration; Education; Educational Administration; Educational Psychology; Higher Education; Human Resources; Linguistics; Management; Marketing; Mathematics Education; Modern Languages; Primary Education; Social and Community Services; Technology Education.**

Student Services: IT Centre, Library

Last Updated: 05/10/15

FACULTY OF CEARA

Faculdade Cearenses

Av. João Pessoa 3884. Damas, Fortaleza, Ceará 60450680
Tel: +55(85) 3201-7000
EMail: ouvidoria@faculdadescearenses.edu.br
Website: http://www.faculdadescearenses.edu.br

Diretor: José Luiz Torres Mota

Area

Human and Social Sciences (Accountancy; Administration; Advertising and Publicity; Business Administration; Human Resources; Information Sciences; Law; Marketing; Pedagogy; Social and Community Services; Tourism; Transport and Communications)

History: Founded 2002.

Main Language(s) of Instruction: Portuguese

Degrees and Diplomas: *Bacharelado*; *Especialização/Aperfeiçoamento*: **Business Administration; Human Resources; Information Sciences; Law; Marketing; Social and Community Services; Taxation; Transport and Communications.**

Last Updated: 08/07/15

FACULTY OF CENTRO LESTE

Faculdade do Centro Leste (UCL)

Rod. ES 010, km 6, Manguinhos, Serra, ES 29173-087
Tel: +55(27) 3434-0100
Fax: +55(27) 3434-0100
EMail: contato@ucl.br
Website: http://www.ucl.br

Diretora: Maria Ângela Loyola de Oliveira

Secretaria Geral: Liliane Barbosa dos Santos

Course

Administration/Management (Administration; Finance; Human Resources; Marketing; Safety Engineering; Transport Management); **Computer Science** (Computer Science; Information Management; Information Technology; Systems Analysis); **Engineering** (Automation and Control Engineering; Biomedical Engineering; Chemical Engineering; Civil Engineering; Electrical Engineering; Mechanical Engineering; Petroleum and Gas Engineering; Production Engineering); **Postgraduate Studies** (Accountancy; Automation and Control Engineering; Biomedical Engineering; Business Administration; Construction Engineering; Data Processing; Educational Technology; Finance; Industrial Engineering; Industrial Management; Information Management; Information Technology; Maintenance Technology; Management; Petroleum and Gas Engineering; Safety Engineering; Transport Management); **Technology** (Finance; Human Resources; Information Technology; Marketing; Safety Engineering; Systems Analysis; Transport Management)

History: Founded 2000.

Main Language(s) of Instruction: Portuguese

Degrees and Diplomas: *Tecnólogo*; *Bacharelado*; *Especialização/Aperfeiçoamento*: **Automation and Control Engineering; Biomedical Engineering; Business Administration; Data Processing; Educational Technology; Industrial Engineering; Information Management; Petroleum and Gas Engineering; Safety Engineering.** Also MBA in Transport Management, Management, Industrial Management, Maintenance Technology, Safety Engineering, Information Technology, Accountancy, Finance, Construction Engineering

Student Services: Library

Last Updated: 07/09/15

FACULTY OF COLIDER

Faculdade de Colider (FACIDER)

Avenida Senador Julio Campos 995 - Loteamento TREVO, Colider, MT 78500-000
Tel: +55(66) 3541-1081 +55(66) 3541-1080
Fax: +55(66) 3541-1081
EMail: informefacider@gmail.com; faculdadecolider@hotmail.com
Website: http://www.sei-cesucol.edu.br

Diretora Geral: Roze Mirian Saldanha

Course

Administration (Administration); **Law** (Law); **Nursing** (Nursing); **Pharmacy** (Pharmacy); **Physical Education** (Physical Education); **Sequential Studies** (Agricultural Business; Health Administration; Journalism)

History: Founded 2001.

Fees: 406-756 per month (Brazilian Real)

Main Language(s) of Instruction: Portuguese

Degrees and Diplomas: *Bacharelado*
Student Services: Library, eLibrary
Last Updated: 25/06/15

FACULTY OF COMMUNICATION, TECHNOLOGY AND TOURISM OF OLINDA

Faculdade de Comunicação, Tecnologia e Turismo de Olinda
Av. Getulio Vargas, 1360, Bairro Novo, Olinda, PE 53030-010
Tel: +55(81)3429-0772
Fax: +55(81) 3493-2956
EMail: falecom@facottur.org; academico@facottur.org
Website: http://www.facottur.org

Diretor Administrativo e Financeiro: Daniel Lucena

Diretor: Daniel Moraes Rêgo de Lucena

Course

Advertising and Publicity (Advertising and Publicity); **Human Resource Management** (Human Resources); **Logistics** (Transport Management); **Management Processes** (Management); **Marketing** (Marketing); **Nursing** (Nursing); **Physical Education** (Physical Education); **Physiotherapy** (Physical Education); **Postgraduate Studies** (Education; Human Resources; Industrial and Organizational Psychology; Protective Services); **Tourism** (Tourism)

History: Founded 1999.

Main Language(s) of Instruction: Portuguese

Degrees and Diplomas: *Tecnólogo*; *Bacharelado*; *Especialização/Aperfeiçoamento*: **Civil Security; Educational Psychology; Human Resources; Industrial and Organizational Psychology; Police Studies; Protective Services.**
Last Updated: 25/06/15

FACULTY OF COMPUTER SCIENCE OF CUIABÁ

Faculdade de Informática de Cuiabá (FIC)
Rua Alziro Zarur, 1625, Boa Esperança, Cuiabá, MT 78068-780
Tel: +55(65) 3027-2210 +55(65) 3664-3890
Fax: +55(65) 3664-3313
EMail: ficcuiaba@yahoo.com.br
Website: http://www.ficcuiaba.com.br

Diretor: Acomerques Antônio da Silva

Course

Agricultural Business (Agricultural Business); **Information Systems** (Information Technology); **Postgraduate Studies** (Business Administration; Civil Security; Criminology; Educational Administration; Educational Technology; Environmental Management; Higher Education Teacher Training; Special Education); **Secretarial Studies** (Secretarial Studies)

History: Founded 1992.

Main Language(s) of Instruction: Portuguese

Degrees and Diplomas: *Tecnólogo*; *Especialização/Aperfeiçoamento*: **Business Administration; Civil Security; Criminology; Educational Administration; Educational Technology; Environmental Management; Higher Education Teacher Training; Special Education.**
Last Updated: 01/12/15

FACULTY OF DENTISTRY OF MANAUS

Faculdade de Odontologia de Manaus (FOM)
Av. Getúlio Vargas, 1311, Centro, Manaus, Amazonas 69065001
Tel: +55(92) 3087-5659 +55(92) 3622-3989
EMail: f.o.m@uol.com.br
Website: http://www.fom.edu.br

Diretor Geral: Oscar Isamu Shirata

Course

Dental Surgery (Dentistry); **Orthodontics**

History: Founded 2000.

Main Language(s) of Instruction: Portuguese

Degrees and Diplomas: *Bacharelado*

Student Services: Library
Last Updated: 16/07/15

FACULTY OF DENTISTRY OF RECIFE

Faculdade de Odontologia do Recife
Rua Artur Coutinho, 143, Santo Amaro, Recife, PE 50100-280
Tel: +55(81) 3423-7553 +55(81) 3221-3325 +55(81) 3037-3325
EMail: secretaria@for.edu.br
Website: http://www.for.edu.br

Diretor: Homero Luiz Sales Neves

Secretária Geral: Selma Ferreira Drumond

Course

Odontology (Dentistry); **Postgraduate Studies** (Dental Technology; Dentistry; Forensic Medicine and Dentistry; Orthodontics; Periodontics)

History: Founded 2002.

Main Language(s) of Instruction: Portuguese

Degrees and Diplomas: *Bacharelado*; *Especialização/Aperfeiçoamento*: **Dental Technology; Dentistry; Forensic Medicine and Dentistry; Orthodontics; Periodontics.**

Student Services: Library
Last Updated: 16/07/15

FACULTY OF DESIGN OF TATUÍ

Faculdade de Desenho de Tatuí (FDT)
Rua Oracy Gomes, 665, Centro, Tatuí, SP 18270-600
Tel: +55(15) 9979-64675
EMail: contato@fdet.com.br; diretoria@fdet.com.br; vicedirecao@fdet.com.br
Website: http://www.fdet.com.br

Course

Administration (Business Administration); **Industrial Design** (Industrial Design); **Pedagogy, Visual Arts and Administration** (Administration; Pedagogy; Visual Arts)

History: Founded 1985.

Main Language(s) of Instruction: Portuguese

Degrees and Diplomas: *Bacharelado*
Last Updated: 30/11/15

FACULTY OF DISCOVERY

Faculdade do Descobrimento
Rua da Mata s/n, Santa Cruz Cabrália, BA 45807-000
Tel: +55(73) 3672-1641
EMail: diretoria@facdesco.edu.br
Website: http://www.facdesco.edu.br

Diretor: Fernando Moura Neto.

Course

Accountancy (Accountancy); **Administration** (Administration); **Computer Science** (Computer Science); **Tourism** (Tourism)

History: Founded 2002.

Main Language(s) of Instruction: Portuguese

Degrees and Diplomas: *Bacharelado*
Last Updated: 08/07/15

FACULTY OF ECONOMICS OF THE MINING TRIANGLE

Faculdade de Ciências Econômicas do Triângulo Mineiro (FCETM)
Rua Ronan Martins Marques, 487, Bairro Universitário, Uberaba, Minas Gerais 38050-600
Tel: +55(34) 3331-5555
Fax: +55(34) 3331-5555
EMail: fcetm@fcetm.br
Website: http://www.fcetm.br

Director: Giovanna Aléxia Meireles
EMail: dir.geral@fcetm.br

Course

Accountancy (Accountancy); **Accounting and Finance** *(Graduate - MBA)* (Accountancy; Business Administration; Finance);

Accounting, Expertise and Audit *(Graduate - MBA)* (Accountancy; Business Administration); **Administration** (Administration); **Applied Management in Logistics** *(Graduate - MBA)* (Management; Transport Management); **Business Administration Management** *(Graduate MBA)* (Business Administration; Management); **Economics** (Economics); **Unified Social Assistance and Interdisciplinary Specialization** *(Graduate)* (Higher Education; Information Technology; Management; Social Policy; Social Work)

History: Founded 1966.

Main Language(s) of Instruction: Portuguese

Degrees and Diplomas: *Bacharelado*; *Especialização/Aperfeiçoamento*: **Social Work.** Also MBA in Accountancy, Finance, Management, Transport Management

Student Services: IT Centre, Library

Publications: ABCZ; Carta Capital; Conjuntura Econômica; Ensino Superior; Época; Exame; Harvard Business; Revista Convergência; Revista Saberes Acadêmicos

Last Updated: 09/06/15

FACULTY OF EDUCATION AND CULTURE OF CEARA

Faculdade de Ensino e Cultura do Ceará (FAECE)

Rua Caetano Ximenes Aragão, 110, Bairro Eng. Luciano Cavalcante, Fortaleza, Ceará 60813-620

Tel: +55(85) 4009-3400

Fax: +55(85) 4009-3437

EMail: marcioacbarros@yahoo.com.br

Website: http://www.iesc.edu.br

Diretora Geral: Rita Maria Silveira da Silva

Tel: +55(85) 8848-7464 EMail: ritamsilveira@gmail.com

Coordenador de Administração: Carlos Garcia Araújo Neto

Course

Administration (Administration); **Hotel Management** (Hotel Management); **Law** (Law); **Nursing** (Nursing); **Pharmacy** (Pharmacy); **Physical Education** (Physical Education); **Physiotherapy** (Physical Therapy); **Social Communication** (Advertising and Publicity); **Technological Studies** (Communication Studies; Computer Networks; Graphic Design; Health Administration; Management; Multimedia; Sports Management); **Tourism** (Tourism)

History: Founded 2001.

Main Language(s) of Instruction: Portuguese

Degrees and Diplomas: *Tecnólogo*; *Bacharelado*; *Licenciatura*

Student Services: Library

Last Updated: 03/07/15

FACULTY OF EDUCATION AND CULTURE OF PORTO VELHO

Faculdade de Educação e Cultura de Porto Velho (FAEC-PVH)

Av. Rio de Janeiro, 4734, Lagoa, Porto Velho, RO 76812-080

Tel: +55(69) 3225-2171 +55(69) 8424-9497

Fax: +55(69) 3441-7002

EMail: unesc@unescnet.br; rodrigo@unescnet.br

Website: http://www.unescnet.br/pvh/inicio.asp#

Diretor Geral: Ismael Cury

Course

Civil Engineering (Civil Engineering); **Postgraduate Studies** (Business Administration; Computer Engineering; Education; Law; Linguistics; Psychology); **Production Engineering** (Production Engineering)

Main Language(s) of Instruction: Portuguese

Degrees and Diplomas: *Bacharelado*; *Especialização/Aperfeiçoamento*: **Accountancy; Business and Commerce; Civil Law; Computer Networks; Constitutional Law; Educational and Student Counselling; Educational Psychology; Educational Technology; Finance; Grammar; Higher Education Teacher Training; Human Resources; Private Law; Psychology; Public Administration; Taxation; Teacher Training.**

Student Services: IT Centre, Library

Last Updated: 04/12/15

FACULTY OF EDUCATION AND CULTURE VILHENA

Faculdade de Educação e Cultura de Vilhena (FAEV)

Av. 7601, n° 8735, quadra 37, Residencial Orleans, Vilhena, RO 76980-000

Tel: +55(69) 3322-1290 +55(69) 8484-0428

Fax: +55(69) 8484-0428

EMail: unesc@unescnet.br; secretariavilhena@unescnet.br; rodrigo@unescnet.br

Website: http://www.unescnet.br/vilhena/inicio.asp#

Diretor Geral: Ismael Cury

Diretor Administrativo/Financeiro: Fhariz Gibran Cury

Faculty

Environmental Engineering (Environmental Engineering)

Course

Accounting (Accountancy); **Biomedicine** (Biomedicine); **Nursing** (Nursing); **Pharmacy** (Pharmacy); **Physical Education** (Physical Education); **Postgraduate Studies** (Accountancy; Business and Commerce; Civil Law; Computer Networks; Constitutional Law; Criminal Law; Educational Administration; Educational and Student Counselling; Educational Psychology; Educational Technology; Finance; Grammar; Higher Education Teacher Training; Human Resources; Humanities and Social Science Education; Psychology; Public Administration; Public Law)

Main Language(s) of Instruction: Portuguese

Degrees and Diplomas: *Bacharelado*; *Especialização/Aperfeiçoamento*: **Accountancy; Business and Commerce; Civil Law; Computer Networks; Constitutional Law; Criminal Law; Educational Administration; Educational and Student Counselling; Educational Psychology; Educational Technology; Finance; Grammar; Higher Education Teacher Training; Human Resources; Humanities and Social Science Education; Psychology; Public Administration; Public Law.**

Student Services: Canteen, IT Centre, Library

Last Updated: 10/12/15

FACULTY OF EDUCATION AND SOCIAL STUDIES OF GOVERNADOR VALADARES

Faculdade de Educação e Estudos Sociais de Governador Valadares (FUNEES G. VALADARES)

Rua Peçanha, 662, 10° andar, sala 1008, Centro, Governador Valadares, MG 35010-161

Tel: +55(33) 3278-5777

Fax: +55(33) 3271-3099

EMail: proreitoriadeensinobh@gmail.com; kesciacarvalho@yahoo.com.br

Website: http://www.unipacgv.com.br

Course

Environmental Management (Environmental Management); **Normal Superior Education** (Primary Education); **Pedagogy** (Pedagogy)

Main Language(s) of Instruction: Portuguese

Degrees and Diplomas: *Tecnólogo*; *Licenciatura*

Last Updated: 07/12/15

FACULTY OF EDUCATION AND SOCIAL STUDIES OF UBERLÂNDIA

Faculdade de Educação e Estudos Sociais de Uberlândia (FEESU)

Av. Marcos de Freitas Costa, 1510, Bairro Osvaldo Rezende, Uberlândia 38400-328

Tel: +55(34) 3210-8227

Fax: +55(34) 3210-8227

EMail: unipacfeesu@gmail.com; proreitoriadeensinobh@gmail.com; carlafarnesi@unipac.br

Website: http://www.unipacfeesu.com.br

Reitor/Presidente: Bonifácio José Tamm de Andrada

Diretora: Raquel Ribeiro Bouças

EMail: raquel@unipacuberlandia.com.br

Course
Mathematics (Mathematics); **Pedagogy** (Pedagogy); **Postgraduate Studies** (Educational Psychology; Educational Sciences; Educational Technology; Religious Education; Special Education; Teacher Training); **Public Administration** (Public Administration)

History: Founded 2002.

Main Language(s) of Instruction: Portuguese

Degrees and Diplomas: *Tecnólogo*; *Licenciatura*; *Especialização/Aperfeiçoamento*: **Art Education; Business Education; Educational and Student Counselling; Educational Psychology; Educational Technology; Higher Education Teacher Training; Literacy Education; Music Education; Neurosciences; Pedagogy; Physical Education; Preschool Education; Religious Education; Special Education; Teacher Training.**

Student Services: Library, eLibrary
Last Updated: 04/12/15

FACULTY OF EDUCATION - ISECUB

Faculdade de Educação - ISECUB (FDE)
Av. João dos Santos Filho, 223, Ilha de Santa Maria,
Vitória, Espirito Santo 29051-145
Tel: +55(27) 3222-5750
Fax: +55(27) 3222-5750
EMail: direcao@fde.edu.br; adm.tudo1@gmail.com
Website: http://www.fde.edu.br

Diretora: Kelly Santos de Paula

Course
Pedagogy (Education)

History: Founded 2001.

Main Language(s) of Instruction: Portuguese

Degrees and Diplomas: *Licenciatura*

Student Services: IT Centre, Library, eLibrary
Last Updated: 30/06/15

FACULTY OF EDUCATION IN HEALTH SCIENCES

Faculdade de Educação em Ciências da Saúde (FECS)
Rua João Julião, 245 - 1° andar, Paraiso, São Paulo, SP 01323-020
Tel: +55(1) 3549-0654
EMail: contato@fecs.org.br; apjaquel@haoc.com.br
Website: http://www.fecs.org.br

Diretor Geral: Jefferson G. Fernandes

Diretor Administrativo-Financeiro: Francisco da Silva Costa

Programme
MBA (Business Administration; Economics; Health Administration)

Course
Hospital Management (Health Administration); **Postgraduate Studies** (Cardiology; Gastroenterology; Gerontology; Medical Technology; Medicine; Nursing; Nutrition; Physical Therapy; Psychology; Rehabilitation and Therapy; Surgery; Urology)

History: Founded 2014.

Main Language(s) of Instruction: Portuguese

Degrees and Diplomas: *Tecnólogo*; *Especialização/Aperfeiçoamento*: **Cardiology; Gastroenterology; Gerontology; Medical Technology; Medicine; Nursing; Nutrition; Physical Therapy; Psychology; Rehabilitation and Therapy; Surgery; Urology.** Also MBA

Student Services: IT Centre, Library
Last Updated: 01/12/15

FACULTY OF EDUCATION OF BOM DESPACHO

Faculdade de Educação de Bom Despacho (FACEB)
BR 262, Km 480, Caixa Postal 160, Bom Despacho, MG 35600-000
Tel: +55(37) 3521-9550
Fax: +55(37) 3521-9595
EMail: pedagogiafaceb@bdonline.com.br; secretariaacademica@faculdadedebomdespacho.com.br
Website: http://www.unipacbomdespacho.com.br/v2/Faceb

Diretora Geral e Acadêmica: Débora Cristina Brettas Andrade Guerra

Diretoria Administrativa/Financeira: José Letício Ferreira Vilalba

Course
Pedagogy (Pedagogy); **Physical Education** (Physical Education); **Technical Studies** (Accountancy; Administration; Building Technologies; Interior Design; Safety Engineering)

History: Founded 2001.

Main Language(s) of Instruction: Portuguese

Degrees and Diplomas: *Bacharelado*: **Physical Education.** *Licenciatura*: **Pedagogy.**

Student Services: IT Centre, Library
Last Updated: 30/06/15

FACULTY OF EDUCATION OF COLORADO DO OESTE

Faculdade de Educação de Colorado do Oeste (FAEC)
Av. Paulo de Assis Ribeiro, 5681,
Colorado do Oeste, RO 76993-000
Tel: +55(69) 3341-2275
Fax: +55(69) 3341-2327
EMail: faec@avec.br
Website: http://www.faec.br

Presidente: José Gonzaga da Silva Neto

Course
Administration (Administration); **Arts and Humanities** (English; Literature; Portuguese); **Graduate Studies** (Business and Commerce; Educational Psychology; Linguistics; Literature; Marketing); **Pedagogy** (Pedagogy); **Technical Studies** (Nursing)

History: Founded 1998.

Main Language(s) of Instruction: Portuguese

Degrees and Diplomas: *Bacharelado*; *Licenciatura*; *Especialização/Aperfeiçoamento*: **Educational Administration.**

Student Services: Library
Last Updated: 30/06/15

FACULTY OF EDUCATION OF ITABORAÍ

Faculdade de Educação de Itaboraí (FEITA)
Avenida Antônio Gomes, 1250, Prédio Parque Royal,
Itaboraí, Rio de Janeiro 24800-000
Tel: +55(21) 2639-1253
Fax: +55(21) 2639-1234
EMail: semeita@ig.com.br; vf.ss@hotmail.com; magaldri@ig.com.br

Diretor: Marcelo Souza Paula

Course
Pedagogy (Pedagogy)

History: Founded 1974.

Main Language(s) of Instruction: Portuguese

Degrees and Diplomas: *Licenciatura*
Last Updated: 30/06/15

FACULTY OF EDUCATION OF JARU

Faculdade de Educação de Jaru (UNICENTRO)
Avenida Otaviano Pereira Neto, s/n, Setor 02, Jaru, RO 76890-000
Tel: +55(69) 3521-5084
Fax: +55(69) 3521-5606
EMail: unicentro@unicentroro.edu.br
Website: http://www.unicentroro.edu.br

Diretor Geral: Juarez Eduardo de Toledo Prado
EMail: diretoria@unicentroro.edu.br

Diretor Administrativo e Financeiro: Paulo Henrique Correa Meneses EMail: diradm@unicentroro.edu.br

Course
Accountancy (Accountancy); **Administration** (Administration); **Biology** (Biology); **Environmental Management** (Environmental Management); **Graduate Studies** (Accountancy; Educational Administration; Finance; Forest Management; Higher Education

Teacher Training; Special Education); **Pedagogy** (Pedagogy); **Social Services** (Social and Community Services)

History: Founded 2001.

Main Language(s) of Instruction: Portuguese

Degrees and Diplomas: *Bacharelado*; *Licenciatura*; *Especialização/Aperfeiçoamento*: **Accountancy; Educational Administration; Finance; Forest Management; Higher Education Teacher Training; Special Education.**

Student Services: Library

Last Updated: 30/06/15

FACULTY OF EDUCATION OF MINAS GERAIS

Faculdade de Ensino de Minas Gerais (FACEMG)

Av. do Contorno, 9384, Barro Preto, Belo Horizonte, MG 30110-130

Tel: +55(31) 3226-2549

EMail: marcioacbarros@yahoo.com.br

Website: http://www.suafaculdade.com.br/facemg

Diretor Geral: Magno Nascimento Veloso

Course

Accounting (Accountancy); **Administration** (Business Administration); **Civil Engineering** (Civil Engineering); **Law** (Law); **Nursing** (Nursing); **Pharmacy** (Pharmacy); **Physical Education** (Physical Education); **Physical Therapy** (Physical Therapy); **Social Communication, Publicity and Advertising** (Advertising and Publicity; Mass Communication); **Technological Studies** (Business and Commerce; Cosmetology; Health Administration; Human Resources; International Business; Management; Marketing; Tourism); **Tourism** (Tourism)

History: Founded 2009 as Instituto Minas Gerais de Ensino e Cultura (IMGEC). Acquired present title 2010.

Main Language(s) of Instruction: Portuguese

Degrees and Diplomas: *Tecnólogo*; *Bacharelado*. Also Distance Mode Undergraduate and Postgraduate Degree Programmes offered through Universidade Paulista

Student Services: Library

Last Updated: 16/12/15

FACULTY OF EDUCATION OF SERRA

Faculdade de Educação da Serra (FASE)

Av. Carapebus, s/n°, São Geraldo, Serra 29163-103

Tel: +55(27) 3338-3799

EMail: fase@fase.br; secretaria@fase.br

Website: http://www.fase.br

Course

Administration (Business Administration); **Pedagogy** (Pedagogy); **Postgraduate Studies** (Business and Commerce; Education; Health Sciences; Law)

History: Founded 1999.

Main Language(s) of Instruction: Portuguese

Degrees and Diplomas: *Bacharelado*; *Licenciatura*; *Especialização/Aperfeiçoamento*: **Art Education; Art Therapy; Arts and Humanities; Business Administration; Business Education; Civil Law; Educational Administration; Educational and Student Counselling; Educational Psychology; Environmental Management; Environmental Studies; Finance; Fiscal Law; Geography; Health Administration; Higher Education Teacher Training; History; Human Resources; Labour Law; Linguistics; Literacy Education; Marketing; Mathematics Education; Nursing; Occupational Health; Physical Education; Preschool Education; Public Administration; Public Health; Public Law; Rehabilitation and Therapy; Transport Management.**

Last Updated: 30/11/15

FACULTY OF EDUCATION OF VICTORIA

Faculdade de Educação de Vitória (AUFES)

Av. Maruípe, 2535, Santa Martha, Vitória 29045-231

Tel: +1(27) 3324-4343

Fax: +1(27) 3324-4343

EMail: direcaoaufes@gmail.com

Diretor Geral: Max Guilherme Nascimento

Course

Pedagogy (Pedagogy)

Main Language(s) of Instruction: Portuguese

Degrees and Diplomas: *Licenciatura*

Last Updated: 07/12/15

FACULTY OF EDUCATION, ADMINISTRATION AND TECHNOLOGY OF IBAITI

Faculdade de Educação, Administração e Tecnológia de Ibaiti (FEATI)

Av. Tertuliano de Moura Bueno, 1400, Bairro Flamenguinho, Ibaiti, PR 84900-000

Tel: +55(43) 3546-1263

Fax: +55(43) 3546-1263

EMail: feati@feati.com.br

Website: http://www.feati.edu.br/faculdade.asp

Diretora Geral: Edmilsa Bonin Braga

Course

Accountancy (Accountancy); **Administration** (Administration); **Graduate Studies** (Administration; Education; Health Sciences; Information Technology; Law); **Information Systems** (Information Technology); **Law** (Law); **Pedagogy** (Pedagogy)

History: Founded 2000.

Main Language(s) of Instruction: Portuguese

Degrees and Diplomas: *Tecnólogo*; *Bacharelado*; *Licenciatura*; *Especialização/Aperfeiçoamento*: **Civil Law; Criminal Law; Educational Administration; Pedagogy; Primary Education; Public Health; Software Engineering; Special Education.** Also MBA in Public Administration, Administration, Business and Commerce

Student Services: Library

Last Updated: 02/07/15

FACULTY OF EDUCATIONAL SCIENCES AND BUSINESS OF NATAL

Faculdade de Ciências Educacionais e Empresariais de Natal (FACEN)

Campus Natal Avenida Prudente de Morais, 3510, Lagoa Nova, Natal, Rio Grande do Norte 59063-200

Tel: +55(84) 3206-4013 +55(84) 3206-2195

EMail: facencontato@gmail.com; facenm@yahoo.com.br

Website: www.facen.com.br

Diretor: Érico Rodrigues Bacelar

Course

Administration (Administration); **Pedagogy** (Pedagogy); **Postgraduate Studies** (Administration; Business Administration; Computer Science; Education; Health Sciences)

Further Information: Also Liberdade, José de Alencar and Jequitibás campuses.

History: Founded 2000.

Main Language(s) of Instruction: Portuguese

Degrees and Diplomas: *Bacharelado*: **Administration.** *Licenciatura*: **Pedagogy.** The Licenciatura degree is offered through the Instituto Natalense de Educação Superior (INAES)

Last Updated: 09/06/15

FACULTY OF EDUCATIONAL SCIENCES AND INTEGRATED SYSTEMS

Faculdade de Ciências Educacionais e Sistemas Integrados (FACESI)

Rua Ludovico Bruschi, 505, Ibiporã, PR 86200-000

Tel: +55(43) 3258-7991

Fax: +55(43) 3258-7991

EMail: facesi@facesi.edu.br; andrea.bertan@uniesp.edu.br; ckto@terra.com.br; academicosup@uniesp.edu.br

Website: http://www.facesi.edu.br

Director: Andréa Henrique Franco Bertan

Course

Administration (Administration); **Marketing** (Marketing); **Pedagogy** (Pedagogy)

History: Founded 2005.

Main Language(s) of Instruction: Portuguese

Degrees and Diplomas: *Tecnólogo*: **Marketing.** *Bacharelado*: **Administration.** *Licenciatura*: **Pedagogy.**

Student Services: Library

Last Updated: 09/06/15

FACULTY OF ENGINEERING AND SURVEYING OF PIRASSUNUNGA

Faculdade de Engenharia e Agrimensura de Pirassununga (FEAP)

Av. dos Acadêmicos, 1, Posto de Monta,
Pirassununga, São Paulo 13633-490
Tel: +55(19) 3562-5238 +55(19) 3561-3845
Fax: +55(19) 3562-8822
EMail: feap@feap.com.br; contato@feap.com.br
Website: http://www.feap.com.br

Diretor Geral: Antônio Moacir Rodrigues Nogueira (1997-)
EMail: engenheironogueira@gmail.com

Course

Postgraduate Studies (Environmental Studies; Safety Engineering; Surveying and Mapping); **Surveying Engineering** (Construction Engineering; Engineering; Surveying and Mapping); **Technological Studies** (Safety Engineering)

History: Founded 1972.

Main Language(s) of Instruction: Portuguese

Degrees and Diplomas: *Bacharelado*; *Especialização/Aperfeiçoamento*: **Environmental Studies; Safety Engineering; Surveying and Mapping.**

Student Services: Library

Last Updated: 02/07/15

FACULTY OF ENGINEERING OF MINAS GERAIS

Faculdade de Engenharia de Minas Gerais (FEAMIG)

Rua Aquiles Lobo, 524, Bairro Floresta,
Belo Horizonte, Minas Gerais 30150-160
Tel: +55(31) 3274-1974
Fax: +55(31) 3274-5006
EMail: secretaria@feamig.br
Website: http://www.feamig.br

Diretor: Fabiano José dos Santos

Coordenador Administrativo: Milton Nonato de Oliveira

Course

Civil Engineering (Civil Engineering); **Graduate Studies** (Civil Engineering; Environmental Engineering; Safety Engineering; Surveying and Mapping); **MBA** (Safety Engineering); **Production Engineering** (Production Engineering); **Surveying Engineering** (Surveying and Mapping)

Further Information: Also Gameleira Unit.

History: Founded 1962.

Main Language(s) of Instruction: Portuguese

Degrees and Diplomas: *Bacharelado*; *Especialização/Aperfeiçoamento*: **Civil Engineering; Environmental Engineering; Safety Engineering; Surveying and Mapping.** Also MBA in Safety Engineering

Student Services: Library

Last Updated: 03/07/15

FACULTY OF ENGINEERING OF RESENDE

Faculdade de Engenharia de Resende (FER)

Avenida Professor Antonio Esteves, Morada da Colina,
Resende, RJ 27523-000
Tel: +55(24) 3383-9000
Fax: +55(24) 3383-9000
EMail: sec@aedb.br
Website: http://www.aedb.br

Director of FER and FCEACDB: Mario Anibal Simon Esteves
EMail: esteves@aedb.br

Faculty

Engineering (Automotive Engineering; Civil Engineering; Electrical and Electronic Engineering; Engineering; Industrial Engineering; Mechanical Engineering; Metallurgical Engineering; Production Engineering)

History: Founded 1998. This Faculty is part of Dom Bosco Educational Association with two other Faculties (Faculdade de Ciências Econômicas Dom Bosco, and Faculdade de Filosofia, Ciências e Letras Dom Bosco.

Main Language(s) of Instruction: Portuguese

Degrees and Diplomas: *Bacharelado*: **Civil Engineering; Electrical and Electronic Engineering; Mechanical Engineering; Production Engineering; Safety Engineering.** *Especialização/Aperfeiçoamento*: **Automotive Engineering; Industrial Engineering; Safety Engineering.**

Student Services: Library

Last Updated: 11/06/15

FACULTY OF ENGINEERING OF SÃO PAULO

Faculdade de Engenharia São Paulo (FESP)

Av. 9 de Julho, N° 5520, Jardim Europa,
São Paulo, São Paulo 01406-200
Tel: +55(11) 3061-5022
Fax: +55(11) 3061-5022
EMail: fesp@sesp.edu.br
Website: http://www.fesp.br

Diretor Geral: Guilherme Gaspar Silva Dias

Course

Administration (Administration); **Civil Engineering** (Civil Engineering); **Construction aand Metallic Structures** (Metal Techniques); **Electrical Engineering** (Electrical Engineering); **Postgraduate Studies** (Automation and Control Engineering; Business and Commerce; Engineering; Environmental Engineering; Finance; Geological Engineering; Human Resources; Insurance; Marketing; Retailing and Wholesaling; Road Engineering; Sales Techniques; Transport Management)

History: Founded 1975

Main Language(s) of Instruction: Portuguese

Degrees and Diplomas: *Tecnólogo*; *Bacharelado*; *Especialização/Aperfeiçoamento*: **Automation and Control Engineering; Environmental Engineering; Geological Engineering; Road Transport; Transport Management.** Also MBA in Finance, Business Administration, Insurance, Marketing, Human Resources, Retailing and Wholesaling, Sales Techniques

Student Services: Library

Last Updated: 03/07/15

FACULTY OF ENGINEERING OF SOROCABA

Faculdade de Engenharia de Sorocaba (FACENS)

Rodovia Senador José Ermírio de Moraes, 1425, Castelinho km 1,5,
Alto da Boa Vista, Sorocaba, São Paulo 18087-125
Tel: +55(15) 3238-1188
Fax: +55(15) 3238-1188
EMail: facens@facens.br
Website: http://www.facens.br

Diretor: Paulo Roberto Freitas de Carvalho EMail: paulo@facens.br

Course

Chemical Engineering (Chemical Engineering); **Civil Engineering** (Civil Engineering); **Computer Engineering** (Computer Engineering); **Digital Games** (Software Engineering); **Electrical Engineering** (Electrical Engineering); **Graduate Studies** (Business and Commerce; Construction Engineering; Industrial Management; Safety Engineering; Transport Management); **Mechanical Engineering** (Mechanical Engineering); **Mechatronic Engineering** (Electrical Engineering; Mechanical Engineering); **Production Engineering** (Production Engineering)

History: Founded 1976

Main Language(s) of Instruction: Portuguese

Degrees and Diplomas: *Bacharelado*; *Especialização/Aperfeiçoamento*: **Civil Engineering; Industrial Engineering; Safety**

Engineering; Transport Management. Also MBA in Business and Commerce, Industrial Management

Student Services: Canteen, Library, Social Counselling

Last Updated: 03/07/15

FACULTY OF ESPIRITO SANTO - UNICAPE

Faculdade Espirito Santense - UNICAPE (FAESA)

Campus Cariacica, Rua São Jorge, 335, Campo Grande, Cariacica, ES 29150-525
Tel: +55(27) 2122-0700
EMail: adrianapelicioni@faesa.br; siomara@faesa.br
Website: http://unicape.faesa.br

Superintendente: Alexandre Nunes Theodoro
EMail: diretorgeral@faesa.br

Direção Campus Vitória: Juliano Silva Campana
Tel: +55(27) 2122-4130 EMail: direcao@faesa.br

Course

Biomedicine (Biological and Life Sciences; Dentistry; Nursing; Psychology); **Exact Sciences** (Automation and Control Engineering; Chemical Engineering; Chemistry; Civil Engineering; Computer Engineering; Computer Graphics; Computer Networks; Computer Science; Electrical Engineering; Environmental Engineering; Industrial Engineering; Information Technology; Mechanical Engineering; Petroleum and Gas Engineering; Production Engineering; Software Engineering; Systems Analysis); **Human Sciences** (Accountancy; Administration; Advertising and Publicity; Architecture; Fashion Design; Interior Design; Journalism; Law; Pedagogy; Town Planning); **Postgraduate Studies** (Business Administration; Engineering; Environmental Studies; Health Sciences; Information Technology; Mass Communication; Small Business); **Technological Studies** (Computer Networks; Industrial Management; Management; Marketing; Protective Services; Software Engineering; Systems Analysis)

Further Information: Also campuses; Dentistry and Psychology Clinic

History: Founded 2000.

Main Language(s) of Instruction: Portuguese

Degrees and Diplomas: *Bacharelado*; *Especialização/Aperfeiçoamento*: **Computer Networks; Educational Psychology; Environmental Management; Health Administration; Health Sciences; Industrial Design; Information Technology; Mass Communication; Nursing; Occupational Health; Petroleum and Gas Engineering; Production Engineering; Safety Engineering; Small Business; Telecommunications Engineering.** Also MBA in Accountancy, Finance, Management, Business Administration, Marketing, Human Resources, Sales Technique, Maritime Transport

Student Services: Library

Last Updated: 08/09/15

FACULTY OF FORTALEZA

Faculdade de Fortaleza (FAFOR)

Rua Caetano Ximenes Aragão, 110, Água Fria, Fortaleza, Ceará 60813-620
Tel: +55(85) 4009-3400
EMail: marcioacbarros@yahoo.com.br
Website: http://www.fafor.edu.br

Diretor Geral: Rita Maria Silveira da Silva
EMail: ritamsilveira@gmail.com

Coordenadora Geral: Andréa A. Lima

Course

Accounting (Accountancy); **Administration** (Business Administration); **Computer Science** (Computer Science); **Law** (Law); **Pedagogy** (Pedagogy); **Physiotherapy** (Physical Therapy); **Production Engineering** (Production Engineering); **Social Communication, Publicity and Advertising** (Advertising and Publicity; Mass Communication); **Social Services** (Social and Community Services); **Tourism** (Tourism)

History: Founded 2002.

Main Language(s) of Instruction: Portuguese

Degrees and Diplomas: *Tecnólogo*; *Bacharelado*; *Licenciatura*

Student Services: Library

Last Updated: 30/11/15

FACULTY OF GUARARAPES

Faculdade de Guararapes (FAG)

Rua Alfredo Pacheco, 750, Centro, Guararapes, São Paulo 16700-000
Tel: +55(18) 3406-9200
Fax: +55(18) 3406-2800
EMail: mantenedora@uniesp.edu.br; ilma.lorencetti@uniesp.edu.br
Website: http://www.uniesp.edu.br/guararapes

Diretor: Joaquim Santiago Filho

Course

Administration (Administration); **Literature** (English; Literature; Portuguese); **Pedagogy** (Pedagogy)

Main Language(s) of Instruction: Portuguese

Degrees and Diplomas: *Bacharelado*; *Licenciatura*

Last Updated: 09/07/15

FACULTY OF GUARUJA

Faculdade do Guarujá (FAGU)

Avenida Miguel Mussa Gaze 247, Guaruja, São Paulo 11431120
Tel: +55(13) 3383-8273
EMail: diretoria-fagu@uniesp.edu.br
Website: http://www.faculdadedoguaruja.edu.br/index.asp

Diretor Geral: Marat Guedes Barreiros

Secretária Acadêmica: Adriana Fidélis de Souza

Course

Accountancy (Accountancy); **Administration** (Administration); **Information Systems** (Information Technology); **International Business** (International Business); **Law** (Law); **Pedagogy** (Pedagogy)

History: Founded 1999.

Main Language(s) of Instruction: Portuguese

Degrees and Diplomas: *Tecnólogo*; *Bacharelado*; *Licenciatura*

Student Services: Library

Last Updated: 07/09/15

FACULTY OF HEALTH SCIENCES OF UNAÍ

Faculdade de Ciências da Saúde de Unai (FACISA-UNAI)

Av. Governador Valadares, 1441, Centro, Unaí, MG 38610-000
Tel: +55(38) 3677-6030
EMail: contato@facisaunai.com.br; diretoracademico@facisaunai.com.br
Website: http://facisaunai.com.br

Representate da Mantenedora: Pedro Araujo

Course

Nursing (Nursing); **Social Services** (Social and Community Services); **Veterinary Science** (Veterinary Science)

History: Founded 2008.

Main Language(s) of Instruction: Portuguese

Degrees and Diplomas: *Bacharelado*

Last Updated: 04/11/15

FACULTY OF HEALTH TECHNOLOGY - IAHCS

Faculdade de Tecnologia em Saúde - IAHCS (FATESA)

Rua Coronel Corte Real, 75, Porto Alegre, RS
Tel: +55(51) 3331-9555
Fax: +55(51) 3331-0592
EMail: contato@fasaude.com.br; sergio@fasaude.com.br
Website: http://fasaude.com.br

Diretor Geral: Claudio José Allgayer

Course

Hospital Management (Health Administration); **Postgraduate Studies** (Architecture; Health Administration; Medicine; Nursing; Occupational Health; Pharmacy)

History: Founded 2010.
Main Language(s) of Instruction: Portuguese
Degrees and Diplomas: *Tecnólogo*; *Especialização/Aperfeiçoamento*: **Architecture; Health Administration; Medicine; Nursing; Occupational Health; Pharmacy; Safety Engineering.** Also MBA
Student Services: Library
Last Updated: 30/11/15

FACULTY OF HIGHER EDUCATION OF AMAZON

Faculdade de Ensino Superior da Amazônia (FESAM)
Av. José Tupinambá (Antiga Nações Unidas), 1,202, Laguinho, Macapá, AP
Tel: +55(96) 3223-7627 +55(11) 5586-4295
Fax: +55(11) 5586-4295
EMail: marcioacbarros@yahoo.com.br
Website: http://www.suafaculdade.com.br/fesam

Diretor Secretário: Fernando Di Genio Barbosa

Course
Accounting (Accountancy); **Administration** (Business Administration); **Social Communication, Publicity and Advertising** (Advertising and Publicity; Mass Communication); **Tourism** (Tourism)
History: Founded 2006.
Main Language(s) of Instruction: Portuguese
Degrees and Diplomas: *Bacharelado*
Student Services: Library
Last Updated: 16/12/15

FACULTY OF HIGHER EDUCATION OF PARANA

Faculdade de Educação Superior do Paraná (FESP)
Rua Dr. Faivre, 141, Centro, Curitiba, PR
Tel: +55(41) 3028-6500
EMail: secretaria@fesppr.br; fesp@fesppr.br; costa@fesppr.br
Website: http://www.fesppr.br

Presidente: Carlos Eduardo de Athayde Guimarãe
Diretor Administrativo Financeiro: Elcio Orlando Calegari
Diretor Acadêmico: Luiz Fernando Ferreira da Costa

Course
Accountancy (Accountancy); **Administration** (Administration); **Economics** (Economics); **Foreign Trade** (International Business); **Information Systems** (Computer Science); **Law** (Law); **Postgraduate Studies** (Accountancy; Banking; Business Administration; Business and Commerce; Criminal Law; Data Processing; Finance; Information Technology; Justice Administration; Labour Law; Law; Management; Marketing; Public Administration; Taxation)
History: Founded 1974 as Instituto de Ciências Sociais do Paraná. Acquired present title 2010.
Main Language(s) of Instruction: Portuguese
Degrees and Diplomas: *Bacharelado*; *Especialização/Aperfeiçoamento*: **Business Administration; Business and Commerce; Criminal Law; Data Processing; Distance Education; Information Management; Information Technology; Justice Administration; Labour Law; Law; Management; Public Administration; Taxation.** Also MBA in Finance, Banking, Management, Marketing, Finance, Business and Commerce (Oil and Gas Industry)
Student Services: Library
Last Updated: 01/07/15

FACULTY OF HUMAN AND SOCIAL SCIENCES

Faculdade de Ciências Humanas e Sociais (FCHS)
Rua Maris e Barros 612, Tijuca, Rio de Janeiro, Rio de Janeiro 20270-001
Tel: +55(21) 2567-1185 +55(21) 2569-3849
Fax: +55(21) 2567-3849
EMail: secretariaisabel@ig.com.br

Diretora: Eulalia Schiavo

Course
Pedagogy (Pedagogy)
History: Founded 1973
Main Language(s) of Instruction: Portuguese
Degrees and Diplomas: *Licenciatura*
Last Updated: 23/06/15

FACULTY OF HUMAN AND SOCIAL SCIENCES

Faculdade de Ciências Humanas e Sociais (FUCAMP/FACIHUS)
Av. Brasil Oeste, s/n, Jardim Zenith, Monte Carmelo, Minas Gerais 38500-000
Tel: +55(34) 842-5272
Fax: +55(34) 842-2330
EMail: fucamp@fucamp.com.br
Website: http://www.fucamp.com.br

Diretora Geral: Guilherme Marcos Ghelli
Diretor do Setor Administrativo: Juliene de Fátima Alves

Course
Accountancy (Accountancy); **Administration** (Administration); **Agricultural Engineering** (Agricultural Engineering); **Arts and Humanities** (English; Literature; Portuguese); **Biological Sciences** (Biological and Life Sciences); **Civil Engineering** (Civil Engineering); **Graduate Studies** *(MBA)* (Accountancy; Business Administration; Communication Studies; Educational and Student Counselling; Educational Psychology; Environmental Studies; Finance; Higher Education Teacher Training; Information Technology; Management; Plant and Crop Protection; Soil Science); **Law** (Law); **Pedagogy** (Pedagogy); **Systems for Internet** (Information Technology)
History: Founded 2000.
Main Language(s) of Instruction: Portuguese
Degrees and Diplomas: *Bacharelado*; *Licenciatura*; *Especialização/Aperfeiçoamento*: **Accountancy; Business Administration; Communication Studies; Educational Psychology; Environmental Studies; Finance; Higher Education Teacher Training; Information Technology; Plant and Crop Protection; Soil Science.** Also MBA.
Last Updated: 23/06/15

FACULTY OF HUMAN SCIENCES OF CRUREIZO

Faculdade de Ciências Humanas de Cruzeiro (FACIC)
Rua dos Andradas, 1039 - Vila Brasil, Crureizo, SP 12703-030
Tel: +55(12) 3143-3866 +55(12) 3144-0705
EMail: faciccruzeiro@uol.com.br
Website: http://www.faciccruzeiro.com.br

Diretor: Patrícia Baptistella

Course
Accountancy (Accountancy; Computer Science; Finance; Human Resources; Information Technology; Law; Management; Marketing; Taxation); **Administration** (Administration; Finance; Human Resources; Industrial Management; Management); **Engineering** *(Postgraduate)* (Energy Engineering; Safety Engineering); **Law** *(Postgraduate)* (Civil Law; Criminal Law; Labour Law); **Law** (Administrative Law; Civil Law; Commercial Law; Constitutional Law; Criminal Law; Fiscal Law; Human Rights; International Law; Labour Law; Law); **Management** *(Postgraduate)* (Accountancy; Administration; Finance; Human Resources; Management; Marketing); **Pedagogy** *(Postgraduate)* (Educational Administration; Educational Psychology; Special Education); **Pedagogy** (Adult Education; Curriculum; Educational Administration; Educational Psychology; Educational Sciences; Environmental Studies; Literacy Education; Pedagogy; Portuguese; Primary Education); **Production Engineering** (Chemistry; Computer Science; Economics; Electrical and Electronic Engineering; Engineering Drawing and Design; Finance; Industrial Management; Management; Marketing; Materials Engineering; Mathematics; Mechanics; Operations Research; Physics; Production Engineering; Safety Engineering; Statistics)
History: Founded 2006.
Main Language(s) of Instruction: Portuguese
Degrees and Diplomas: *Bacharelado*; *Licenciatura*: **Pedagogy.** *Especialização/Aperfeiçoamento*: **Accountancy; Administration; Civil Law; Criminal Law; Educational Administration;**

Educational Psychology; Finance; Higher Education Teacher Training; Human Resources; Labour Law; Management; Marketing; Safety Engineering; Special Education.
Student Services: eLibrary
Last Updated: 10/06/15

FACULTY OF HUMAN SCIENCES OF CURVELO

Faculdade de Ciências Humanas de Curvelo (FACIC)
Avenida J.K. 1441, Jóquei Clube, Curvelo, Minas Gerais 35790000
Tel: +55(38) 3722-2600
Fax: +55(38) 3722-2600
EMail: facic@facic.br; secretaria@facic.br; michellesoebras@yahoo.com.br; tania.raquel.muniz@hotmail.com; luise
Website: http://www.facic.br

Diretor Geral: Luis Eduardo Carvalho de Souza
EMail: diretoria@facic.br

Course
Graduate Studies (Business Education; Educational Psychology); **History** (History); **Literature** (English; Literature; Portuguese); **Nursing** (Nursing); **Science** (Natural Sciences)
History: Founded 1975.
Main Language(s) of Instruction: Portuguese
Degrees and Diplomas: *Bacharelado*: **Nursing.** *Licenciatura*: **Arts and Humanities; History; Natural Sciences.** *Especialização/ Aperfeiçoamento*: **Business Education; Educational Psychology.**
Student Services: Library
Last Updated: 10/06/15

FACULTY OF HUMAN SCIENCES OF OLINDA

Faculdade de Ciências Humanas de Olinda (FACHO)
Rod PE 015 - Jatobá, Olinda, Pernambuco 53060-775
Tel: +55(81) 3429-4100
Fax: +55(81) 3429-4100
EMail: facho@facho.br
Website: http://www.facho.br

Diretor Geral: José Adailson de Medeiros
Vice-Diretora: Maria de Lourdes Dias de Araújo

Course
Accountancy (Accountancy); **Administration** (Administration); **Arts and Humanities** (English; Literature; Portuguese); **Graduate Studies** (Arts and Humanities; Education; Educational Psychology; Health Sciences; Law; Psychology); **Nursing** (Nursing); **Pedagogy** (Pedagogy); **Psychology** (Psychology)
History: Founded 1973.
Main Language(s) of Instruction: Portuguese
Degrees and Diplomas: *Bacharelado*: **Administration.** *Licenciatura*: **English; Literature; Portuguese; Psychology.** *Especialização/Aperfeiçoamento*: **Arts and Humanities; Clinical Psychology; Educational Administration; Educational Psychology; English; Health Sciences; Law; Literature; Portuguese; Public Health; Teacher Training.**
Student Services: IT Centre, Library
Last Updated: 11/06/15

FACULTY OF HUMANITIES AND SOCIAL SCIENCE OF THE XINGU AND AMAZON

Faculdade de Ciência Humanas e Sociais do Xingu e Amazônia (FACX)
Rua Abel Figueiredo, s/n, Aparecida, Altamira, PA 68371-130
Tel: +55(93) 3515-7778 +55(93) 3515-6813
Fax: +55(93) 3593-0202
EMail: secretaria@facx.com.br; vestibular@facx.com.br; bcrvalle@hotmail.com
Website: http://facx.com.br

Diretor Geral: Odair de Pinho

Course
Accounting (Accountancy); **Administration** (Administration); **Postgraduate Studies** (Accountancy; Agricultural Business; Finance; Health Administration; Management)
History: Founded 2014.
Main Language(s) of Instruction: Portuguese
Degrees and Diplomas: *Bacharelado*; *Especialização/Aperfeiçoamento*: **Accountancy; Agricultural Business; Finance; Health Administration; Management.**
Last Updated: 04/12/15

FACULTY OF HUMANITIES OF ITABIRA

Faculdade de Ciências Humanas de Itabira (FACHI)
Rua Venâncio Augusto Gomes, 50 - Prédio Areão, Bairro Major Lage de Cima, Itabira, MG 35900-842
Tel: +55(31) 3839-3600 +55(31) 3839-3684
Fax: +55(31) 3839-3636
EMail: cln@funcesi.br; yana.magalhaes@funcesi.br; patricia.neves@funcesi.br
Website: www.funcesi.br

Diretora: Yana Torres de Magalhaes

Course
Law (Law); **Postgraduate Studies** (Human Resources; Management)
History: Founded 1968.
Main Language(s) of Instruction: Portuguese
Degrees and Diplomas: *Bacharelado*. Also MBA
Student Services: Library
Last Updated: 02/12/15

FACULTY OF IGARASSU

Faculdade de Igarassú (FACIG)
Rodovia BR 101 Norte Km 25, Cerntro, Igarassu, PE 53600-000
Tel: +55(81) 3543-1205
Fax: +55(81) 3543-1205
EMail: contato@facig-pe.edu.br
Website: http://www.facig-pe.edu.br/site

Diretor: Paulo Roberto de Andrade Gomes
EMail: diretoria@facig-pe.edu.br

Course
Accountancy (Accountancy); **Administration** (Administration); **Human Resources** (Human Resources); **Industrial Management** (Industrial Management); **Law** (Law); **Logistics** (Transport Management); **Mathematics** (Mathematics); **Pedagogy** (Pedagogy); **Postgraduate Studies** (Business Administration; Education)
History: Founded 1998
Fees: Undergraduate, 290-615 per month; Graduate, 250-400 per month (Brazilian Real)
Main Language(s) of Instruction: Portuguese
Degrees and Diplomas: *Bacharelado*; *Licenciatura*; *Especialização/Aperfeiçoamento*: **Educational Administration; Educational Psychology; Environmental Management; Finance; Human Resources; Industrial Management; Mathematics Education; Special Education; Transport Management.**
Last Updated: 09/07/15

FACULTY OF ILHA SOLTEIRA

Faculdade de Ilha Solteira (FAISA)
Alameda Bahia, 490 - C, Centro, Ilha Solteira, São Paulo 15385-000
Tel: +55(18) 3743-3905
Fax: +55(18) 3743-3906
EMail: faisa@projetonet.com.br
Website: http://www.faculdadefaisa.edu.br

Diretora: Karla Handressa Castro de Oliveira

Course
Administration (Administration; Business and Commerce; Human Resources; Marketing); **Pedagogy** (Pedagogy)
History: Founded 2000.
Main Language(s) of Instruction: Portuguese

Degrees and Diplomas: *Bacharelado*; *Licenciatura*
Student Services: Library
Last Updated: 09/07/15

FACULTY OF INDUSTRIAL DESIGN OF MAUA

Faculdade de Desenho Industrial de Mauá (FADIM)
Rua Alonso Vasconcelos Pacheco, 1621, Vila Bocaina, Mauá, São Paulo 9310380
Tel: +55(11) 4547-4688 +55(11) 4516-2850
Fax: +55(11) 4547-4688
EMail: secretaria@fadim.edu.br
Website: http://www.fadim.edu.br

Diretora: Rosane Andréa Tartuce

Course

Environmental Management (Environmental Management); **Human Resources Management** (Human Resources); **Industrial Design** (Industrial Design)

History: Founded 1975

Main Language(s) of Instruction: Portuguese

Degrees and Diplomas: *Bacharelado*

Student Services: IT Centre, Library
Last Updated: 25/06/15

FACULTY OF INTEGRATED THEOLOGY

Faculdade de Teologia Integrada (FATIN)
BR 101 Km 42,5, Igarassu, Recife, PE 53640-900
Tel: +55(81) 3342-2053 +55(81) 3543-3259
Fax: +55(81) 3342-2053
EMail: ouvidoria@fatin.com.br; faculdadefatin@hotmail.com; faculdadefatin@hotmail.com; direcao@fatin.com.br
Website: http://www.fatin.com.br

Diretora: Rosely Pereira Pontes de Oliveira
EMail: direcao@fatin.com.br

Secretária Geral: Juracy Gomes Pereira (+(81) 3543-3259)
EMail: secretariafatinigarassu@hotmail.com; secretaria@fatin.com.br

Course

Business Administration (Business Administration); **Graduate Studies** (Educational Administration; Educational Psychology; Human Resources; Primary Education; Religious Studies; Transport Management); **Theology** (Theology)

History: Founded 2005.

Main Language(s) of Instruction: Portuguese

Degrees and Diplomas: *Bacharelado*; *Especialização/Aperfeiçoamento*: **Educational Administration; Educational Psychology; Human Resources; Primary Education; Religious Studies; Transport Management.** Also Mestrado and Doutorado in Education offered through the Universidade Lusófona de Humanidades e Tecnologias.

Student Services: Library
Last Updated: 03/09/15

FACULTY OF JABOTICABAL

Faculdade de Jaboticabal
Rua Juca Quito 618, Centro, Jaboticabal, SP 14870-260
Tel: +55(16) 3202-3844
Fax: +55(16) 3203-2435
EMail: diretoria@fajab.com.br; secretaria_fajab@hotmail.com
Website: http://www.fajab.com.br

Diretor: Edwin Kenji Takeuti

Course

Administration (Administration)

History: Founded 2001.

Main Language(s) of Instruction: Portuguese

Degrees and Diplomas: *Bacharelado*
Last Updated: 09/07/15

FACULTY OF JANDAIA DO SUL

Faculdade de Jandaia do Sul (FAFIJAN)
Rua Dr. João Maximiano 426, Térreo, Centro, Jandaia do Sul, PR 86900-000
Tel: +55(43) 3432-4141 +55(43) 3432-4646
Fax: +55(43) 3432-4141
EMail: fafijan@fafijan.br
Website: http://www.fafijan.br

Diretor: Maria Gertrudes Gonçalves de Sousa Guimarães

Course

Accountancy (Accountancy); **Biology** (Biology); **Business Administration** (Business Administration); **Geography** (Geography); **Letters - Portuguese and English** (English; Literature; Portuguese); **Letters - Portuguese and Spanish** (Literature; Portuguese; Spanish); **Marketing** (Marketing); **Pedagogy** (Pedagogy); **Postgraduate Studies** (Accountancy; Business Administration; Educational Psychology; Finance; Industrial and Organizational Psychology; Management; Marketing; Portuguese; Psychiatry and Mental Health; Science Education; Special Education); **Psychology** (Psychology)

History: Founded 1966 as Faculdade de Filosofia, Ciências e Letras de Jandaia do Sul.

Main Language(s) of Instruction: Portuguese

Degrees and Diplomas: *Bacharelado*; *Licenciatura*; *Especialização/Aperfeiçoamento*: **Educational Psychology; Environmental Studies; Management; Portuguese; Psychiatry and Mental Health; Science Education; Special Education.** Also MBA in Accountancy, Human Resources, Marketing, Finance, Industrial and Organizational Psychology; Executive MBA in Business Administration.

Student Services: Library
Last Updated: 10/07/15

FACULTY OF JAU

Faculdade Jauense
Rua Edgard Ferraz, 41 - Centro, Jaú, SP 17201-440
Tel: +55(14) 3602-7799
EMail: fajau@fajau.com.br
Website: http://www.faculdadejauense.edu.br

Diretor: Tiago Agostini Massan

Course

Business Administration (Business Administration); **Systems Analysis** (Systems Analysis)

History: Founded 2007.

Main Language(s) of Instruction: Portuguese

Degrees and Diplomas: *Bacharelado*
Last Updated: 26/05/15

FACULTY OF JOSÉ BONIFACIO

Faculdade de José Bonifacio (FJB)
Avenida Joaquim Moreira da Silva, 3200, São José, José Bonifacio, São Paulo 15200-000
Tel: +55(17) 3245-4045
EMail: uibe@fjb.com.br
Website: http://www.fjb.edu.br

Diretora: Débora Marcilene Rossi

Secretária Geral: Adriana Aparecida Bueno Garcia

Course

Accountancy (Accountancy); **Administration** (Administration); **Letters** (English; French; German; Literature; Portuguese); **Pedagogy** (Pedagogy)

History: Founded 1999.

Main Language(s) of Instruction: Portuguese

Degrees and Diplomas: *Bacharelado*; *Licenciatura*; *Especialização/Aperfeiçoamento*: **Educational Psychology.**

Student Services: Library
Last Updated: 10/07/15

FACULTY OF JUNQUEIRÓPOLIS

Faculdade de Junqueirópolis
Rua Piauí, 801, Próximo ao Trevo, Junqueirópolis, SP 17890-000
Tel: +55(18) 3842-1701 +55(18) 3842-1636
EMail: junqueiropolis@reges.com.br; reges.denis@gmail.com
Website: http://junqueiropolis.reges.com.br

Diretora: Gláucia Costa

Course
Pedagogy (Pedagogy); **Special Education** *(Postgraduate)* (Literature)

History: Founded 2001 as Instituto Superior de Educação de Junqueirópolis. Acquired current title 2011.

Main Language(s) of Instruction: Portuguese

Degrees and Diplomas: *Licenciatura*; *Especialização/Aperfeiçoamento*: **Special Education.**

Student Services: Library, eLibrary

Last Updated: 13/04/16

FACULTY OF LAW AND SOCIAL SCIENCES OF LESTE DE MINAS

Faculdade de Direito e Ciências Sociais do Lests de Minas (FADILESTE)
Avenida Marcionilia Breder Sathler, 1, Centro, Reduto, MG 36920-000
Tel: +55(33) 3378-4000
Fax: +55(33) 3378-4000
EMail: adileste.edu@hotmail.com; secretaria@fadileste.edu.br; junior-emilio@bol.com.br
Website: http://www.fadileste.edu.br

Diretora Geral: Maria Clara Gomes

Coordenadora Pedagógica/Secretária Geral: Mariza Salazar

Course
Graduate Studies (Banking; Civil Law; Commercial Law; Criminal Law; Criminology; Labour Law; Notary Studies; Public Administration; Public Law; Real Estate); **Law** (Law)

History: Founded 1990.

Main Language(s) of Instruction: Portuguese

Degrees and Diplomas: *Bacharelado*; *Especialização/Aperfeiçoamento*: **Banking; Civil Law; Consumer Studies; Criminal Law; Criminology; Labour Law; Notary Studies; Public Administration; Public Law; Real Estate.** Also MBA in Commercial Law

Student Services: Library, eLibrary

Last Updated: 29/06/15

FACULTY OF LAW OF CACHOEIRO DO ITAPEMIRIM

Faculdade de Direito de Cachoeiro do Itapemirim (FDCI)
Rod. Engenheiro Fabiano Vivacqua, BR 482 - N° 1759-1877, Morro Grande, Cachoeiro de Itapemirim, ES 29310-015
Tel: +55(27) 2101-0311
Fax: +55(27) 2101-0330
EMail: fdci@fdci.br
Website: http://www.fdci.br

Diretor: Humberto Dias Viana (1996-) EMail: humberto@fdci.br

Vice Diretor: Francisco Ribeiro EMail: francisco@fdci.br

Course
Law (Law)

History: Founded 1965.

Degrees and Diplomas: *Bacharelado*

Student Services: IT Centre, Library

Last Updated: 16/07/15

FACULTY OF LAW OF IPATINGA

Faculdade de Direito de Ipatinga (FADIPA)
R. João Patrício de Araújo, n°195, Veneza I, Ipatinga, MG 35164-226
Tel: +55(31) 3822-8808
Fax: +55(31) 3822-8808
EMail: fadipa@fadipa.br; proreitoriadeensinobh@gmail.com; jesus@fadipa.br
Website: http://www.fadipa.br

Diretor: Jésus Nascimento da Silva

Course
Law (Law); **Postgraduate Studies** (Private Law; Public Law)

History: Founded 1993.

Main Language(s) of Instruction: Portuguese

Degrees and Diplomas: *Bacharelado*: **Law.** *Especialização/Aperfeiçoamento*: **Private Law; Public Law.**

Student Services: Library

Last Updated: 27/11/15

FACULTY OF LAW OF SOROCABA

Faculdade de Direito de Sorocaba (FADI)
Rua Dr[a]. Ursulina Lopes Torres, 123, Vergueiro, Sorocaba, São Paulo 18035380
Tel: +55(15) 2105-1234
Fax: +55(15) 2105-1234
EMail: secretaria@fadi.br
Website: http://www.fadi.br

Diretor e Coordenador Pedagógico: José de Mello Junqueira

Department
Civil Law (Civil Law); **General Theory of Law and Legal Culture** (Economics; Ethics; History of Law; Law; Logic; Philosophy; Political Sciences; Social Studies; Sociology); **Penal and Criminal Procedure** (Criminal Law); **Private Law** (Civil Law; Commercial Law); **Public Law** (Administrative Law; Constitutional Law; Fiscal Law; International Law; Political Sciences; Public Law); **Social and Collective Law** (Human Rights; Labour Law; Social Welfare)

History: Founded 1957

Main Language(s) of Instruction: Portuguese

Degrees and Diplomas: *Bacharelado*; *Especialização/Aperfeiçoamento*: **Civil Law.**

Student Services: Library

Last Updated: 29/06/15

FACULTY OF LAW OF THE SOUTH OF MINAS

Faculdade de Direito do Sul de Minas (FDSM)
Av. Dr. João Beraldo, 1075, Centro, Pouso Alegre, Minas Gerais 37550-000
Tel: +55(35) 3449-8100
Fax: +55(35) 3449-8102
EMail: fdsm@fdsm.edu.br
Website: http://www.fdsm.edu.br

Diretor: Rafael Tadeu Simões
Tel: +(35) 3449-8101 EMail: diretoria@fdsm.edu.br

Course
Graduate Studies *(Lato Sensu)* (Civil Law; Constitutional Law; Criminal Law); **Law** (Law)

History: Founded 1969

Main Language(s) of Instruction: Portuguese

Degrees and Diplomas: *Bacharelado*; *Especialização/Aperfeiçoamento*: **Civil Law; Constitutional Law; Criminal Law; Labour Law.** *Mestrado*: **Law.**

Student Services: IT Centre, Library

Last Updated: 29/06/15

FACULTY OF LAW OF THE VALLEY OF THE DOCE RIVER

Faculdade de Direito do Vale do Rio Doce
R. Dom Pedro II, 244, Centro,
Governador Valadares, MG 35010-090
Tel: +55(33) 3271-2004
EMail: contato@fadivale.com.br; fadivale@fadivale.edu.br; cpd@fadivale.edu.br; bill_gv_brasil@hotmail.com
Website: http://www.fadivale.edu.br

Diretor: Alcyr Nascimento

Course

Civil Procedure *(Postgraduate)* (Civil Law); **Criminal Law Military and Military Criminal Procedure** *(Postgraduate)* (Criminal Law); **Electoral Law and the Electoral Process** *(Postgraduate)* (Public Law); **Law** (Law)

History: Founded 1969.

Main Language(s) of Instruction: Portuguese

Degrees and Diplomas: *Bacharelado*; *Especialização/Aperfeiçoamento*: **Civil Law; Criminal Law; Public Law.**

Student Services: Library

Last Updated: 29/06/15

FACULTY OF LAW OF VARGINHA

Faculdade de Direito de Varginha (FADIVA)
Rua José Gonçalves Pereira, 112, Vila Pinto,
Varginha, Minas Gerais 37010-500
Tel: +55(35) 3221-1900
EMail: secretaria@fadiva.edu.br; diretoria@fadiva.edu.br
Website: http://www.fadiva.edu.br

Diretor: Álvaro Vani Bemfica

Course

Graduate Studies (Civil Law; Law); **Law** (Law)

History: Founded 1966.

Main Language(s) of Instruction: Portuguese

Degrees and Diplomas: *Bacharelado*; *Especialização/Aperfeiçoamento*: **Civil Law; Law.**

Last Updated: 29/06/15

FACULTY OF LEGAL STUDIES AND MANAGEMENT OF OLIVEIRA

Faculdade de Ciências Jurídicas e Gerenciais de Oliveira (FACIJUGO)
Rua Cel. Benjamim Guimarães, 27, Centro, Oliveira, MG 35540-000
Tel: +55(37) 3331-4075 +55(37) 3331-1719
EMail: feol@feol.com.br
Website: http://www.feol.com.br

Presidente: Maria José de Jesus Firmino

Diretor Administrativo: Artur de Melo

Programme

Environmental Management (Environmental Management)

Course

Accounting (Accountancy); **Administration** (Business Administration); **Information Systems** (Information Technology); **Law** (Law); **Pedagogy** (Pedagogy); **Postgraduate Studies** (Accountancy; Business Administration; Literacy Education; Teacher Training); **Systems Analysis and Development** (Systems Analysis)

History: Founded 2004.

Main Language(s) of Instruction: Portuguese

Degrees and Diplomas: *Tecnólogo*; *Bacharelado*; *Especialização/Aperfeiçoamento*: **Accountancy; Business Administration; Literacy Education; Teacher Training.**

Student Services: Library

Last Updated: 01/12/15

FACULTY OF LUCÉLIA

Faculdade de Lucélia
Avenida Internacional, 3000, Centro, Lucélia, São Paulo 17780000
Tel: +55(18) 3551-1849
Fax: +55(18) 3551-2044
EMail: cealpa@terra.com.br
Website: http://lucelia.reges.com.br/

Presidente: José Gonzaga da Silva Neto

Vice-Presidente: Heron Fernando de Sousa Gonzaga

Course

Administration and Accountancy *(CEALPA)* (Accountancy; Administration); **Management** (Management)

History: Founded 1972. Maintained by Centro de Ensino da Alta Paulista - CEALPA.

Main Language(s) of Instruction: Portuguese

Degrees and Diplomas: *Bacharelado*: **Accountancy; Management.**

Student Services: Library

Last Updated: 03/12/15

FACULTY OF LUÍS EDUARDO MAGALHÃES

Faculdade de Luís Eduardo Magalhães (FILEM)
Rua Flamboyant, s/n, QA Lote 20, Jardim Primavera,
Luís Eduardo Magalhães, BA
Tel: +55(77) 3628-4966
Fax: +55(77) 3628-4966
EMail: secretaria@filem.edu.br; ckto@terra.com.br; academicosup@uniesp.edu.br
Website: http://www.filem.edu.br

Diretor: Marcelo de Gois Bernardes
EMail: marcelo.bernardes@uniesp.edu.br

Secretária Acadêmica: Rita Daiane Oliveira Fontana
EMail: rita.fontana@uniesp.edu.br

Course

Agricultural Business (Agricultural Business); **Crop Production** (Crop Production); **Information Systems** (Computer Science); **Law** (Law); **Pedagogy** (Pedagogy)

History: Founded 2005.

Main Language(s) of Instruction: Portuguese

Degrees and Diplomas: *Tecnólogo*; *Bacharelado*; *Licenciatura*

Student Services: Library

Last Updated: 10/07/15

FACULTY OF MANAGEMENT OF SETE LAGOAS

Faculdade Setelagoana de Ciências Gerenciais (FASCIG)
Avenida Marechal Castelo Branco, 3870, Jardim Universitário,
Sete Lagoas, MG 35702-134
Tel: +55(31) 3774-9991
EMail: nayara@faculdadepromove.br

Course

Administration (Administration)

History: Founded 2002.

Main Language(s) of Instruction: Portuguese

Degrees and Diplomas: *Bacharelado*

Last Updated: 25/06/15

FACULTY OF MARINGA

Faculdade Maringá (CESPAR)
Avenida Prudente de Moraes 815 Zona 07,
Maringá, Paraná 87010020
Tel: +55(44) 3027-1100
Fax: +55(44) 3027-1200
EMail: iara@faculdadesmaringa.br
Website: http://www.faculdadesmaringa.br

Diretor Geral: Aparecido Domingos Errerias Lopes
EMail: errerias@faculdadesmaringa.br

Course
Accountancy (Accountancy); **Administration**; **Advertising** (Advertising and Publicity); **Journalism**; **Law**

History: Founded 1996.

Main Language(s) of Instruction: Portuguese

Degrees and Diplomas: *Bacharelado*; *Especialização/Aperfeiçoamento*; *Mestrado*

Student Services: Library

Last Updated: 27/05/15

FACULTY OF MAUÁ

Faculdade de Mauá (FAMA)

Rua Vitorino Dell Antonia, 349 - Vila Noêmia, Mauá, SP 09370-570
Tel: +55(45) 12-6100
EMail: faleconosco@facmaua.edu.br
Website: http://www.facmaua.edu.br

Diretora: Carolina Mouco Viana Sanchez

Secretária Geral: Jane Maria Lima Lopes

Course
Accountancy (Accountancy); **Administration** (Administration); **Finance** (Finance); **Information Systems** (Computer Science); **Management** (Management); **Nursing** (Nursing); **Nutrition** (Nutrition); **Pedagogy** (Pedagogy); **Physical Education** (Physical Education); **Social Services** (Social and Community Services)

History: Founded 2001.

Main Language(s) of Instruction: Portuguese

Degrees and Diplomas: *Bacharelado*; *Licenciatura*; *Especialização/Aperfeiçoamento*: **Curriculum; Educational Psychology; Higher Education Teacher Training; Management; Teacher Training; Translation and Interpretation.**

Student Services: Library

Last Updated: 10/07/15

FACULTY OF MEDICAL AND PARAMEDICAL SCIENCES OF THE STATE OF RIO DE JANEIRO

Faculdade de Ciências Médicas e Paramédicas Fluminense (SEFLU)

Rua Pracinha Wallace Paes Leme, 1338, Centro,
Nilópolis, Rio de Janeiro 26525-045
Tel: +55(21) 2792-0352
Fax: +55(21) 2691-0559
EMail: ouvidoria@seflu.com.br; secretaria@seflu.com.br
Website: http://www.seflu.com.br

Diretora: Lana de Oliveira Goulart EMail: diretoria@seflu.com.br

Vice-Diretor Acadêmico: Carlos Eduardo Martins Costa Medawar

Course
Graduate Studies (Psychology); **Psychology** (Psychology)

History: Founded 1985.

Main Language(s) of Instruction: Portuguese

Degrees and Diplomas: *Bacharelado*; *Especialização/Aperfeiçoamento*: **Psychology.**

Student Services: Library, eLibrary

Last Updated: 24/06/15

FACULTY OF MEDICINE OF ABC

Faculdade de Medicina do ABC (FMABC)

Av. Príncipe de Gales, 821, Príncipe de Gales,
Santo André, São Paulo 09060-650
Tel: +55(11) 4993-5400
EMail: comunicacao@fmabc.br; diretoria@fmabc.br
Website: http://www.fmabc.br

Diretor Geral: Adilson Casemiro Pires

Vice Diretor e Diretor Administrativo e Financeiro: Fernando Fonseca

Course
Environmental Health Management (Health Administration); **Medicine** (Medicine); **Nursing** (Nursing); **Nutrition** (Nutrition); **Occupational Therapy** (Occupational Therapy); **Pharmacy** (Pharmacy); **Physiotherapy** (Physical Therapy)

History: Founded 1969

Main Language(s) of Instruction: Portuguese

Degrees and Diplomas: *Bacharelado*; *Especialização/Aperfeiçoamento*: **Cardiology; Dermatology; Gender Studies; Gerontology; Gynaecology and Obstetrics; Health Administration; Health Sciences; Law; Medical Technology; Neurology; Nursing; Nutrition; Paediatrics; Pathology; Physical Therapy; Physiology; Psychiatry and Mental Health; Psychoanalysis; Psychology; Rehabilitation and Therapy; Respiratory Therapy; Sports Medicine; Stomatology; Teacher Training; Treatment Techniques.** *Mestrado*: **Cell Biology; Health Sciences; Medicine; Molecular Biology; Public Health.** *Doutorado*: **Cell Biology; Health Sciences; Medicine; Molecular Biology; Public Health.** Also MBA in Health Administration, Management; Mestrado Profissional in Health Sciences; Pós-Doutorado in Health Sciences

Student Services: Library

Last Updated: 16/07/15

FACULTY OF MEDICINE OF BARBACENA

Faculdade de Medicina de Barbacena (FAME)

Praça Presidente Antonio Carlos, 08,
Barbacena, Minas Gerais 36202-336
Tel: +55(32) 3339-2950
EMail: fame@funjob.edu.br
Website: http://www.funjob.edu.br

Diretor: Marco Aurélio Bernardes de Carvalho

Course
Medicine (Medicine)

History: Founded 1971

Main Language(s) of Instruction: Portuguese

Degrees and Diplomas: *Bacharelado*

Last Updated: 10/07/15

FACULTY OF MEDICINE OF CAMPOS

Faculdade de Medicina de Campos (FMC)

Avenida Alberto Torres, 217, Centro,
Campos dos Goytacazes, Rio de Janeiro 28035-580
Tel: +55(24) 2101-2929
Fax: +55(24) 2733-2211
EMail: fmc@fmc.br
Website: http://www.fmc.br

Diretor: Nélio Artiles Freitas

Diretor Administrativo: Carlos José Martins Manhães

Course
Medicine (Medicine); **Pharmacy** (Pharmacy); **Postgraduate Studies** (Gynaecology and Obstetrics; Health Sciences; Medicine; Occupational Health; Psychoanalysis; Psychology; Public Health); **Psychology** (Psychology)

History: Founded 1967.

Main Language(s) of Instruction: Portuguese

Degrees and Diplomas: *Bacharelado*; *Especialização/Aperfeiçoamento*: **Gynaecology and Obstetrics; Health Sciences; Medicine; Occupational Health; Pharmacy; Psychoanalysis; Psychology; Public Health.**

Student Services: Library

Publications: Revista Científica da Faculdade de Medicina de Campos

Last Updated: 15/07/15

FACULTY OF MEDICINE OF ITAJUBÁ

Faculdade de Medicina de Itajubá (FMIT)

Av. Renó Júnior, 368, São Vicente,
Itajubá, Minas Gerais 37502-138
Tel: +55(35) 3621-4545 +55(35) 3621-4666
Fax: +55(35) 3621-4555
EMail: secretaria@aisi.edu.br
Website: www.medicinaitajuba.com.br

Diretor: Sérgio Visoni Vargas

Administradora Escolar: Ângela Bacci Fernandes

Course

Medicine (Medicine); **Postgraduate Studies** (Anaesthesiology; Gastroenterology; Gynaecology and Obstetrics; Medicine; Orthopaedics; Otorhinolaryngology; Paediatrics; Pathology; Psychology; Radiology; Surgery)

History: Founded 1968

Main Language(s) of Instruction: Portuguese

Degrees and Diplomas: *Bacharelado*; *Especialização/Aperfeiçoamento*: **Anaesthesiology; Cardiology; Gastroenterology; Gynaecology and Obstetrics; Medicine; Otorhinolaryngology; Paediatrics; Pathology; Psychology; Radiology; Surgery.**

Student Services: Library

Last Updated: 10/07/15

FACULTY OF MEDICINE OF MINAS GERAIS

Faculdade de Ciências Médicas de Minas Gerais (FCMMG)

Alameda Ezequiel Dias, 275,
Belo Horizonte, Minas Gerais 30130-110
Tel: +55(31) 3248-7100
Fax: +55(31) 3248-7132
EMail: fcmmg@fcmmg.br; faleconosco@feluma.org.br
Website: http://www.fcmmg.br

Diretor: Ludércio Rochas de Oliveira

Course

Graduate Studies (Acupuncture; Biotechnology; Business Administration; Cardiology; Dermatology; Gerontology; Health Administration; Health Sciences; Medicine; Nursing; Nutrition; Occupational Health; Osteopathy; Paediatrics; Pathology; Physical Therapy; Physiology; Psychology; Psychotherapy; Public Health; Rehabilitation and Therapy; Speech Therapy and Audiology; Surgery; Urology); **Medicine** (Medicine); **Nursing** (Nursing); **Physiotherapy** (Physical Therapy); **Psychology** (Psychology)

History: Founded 1951.

Main Language(s) of Instruction: Portuguese

Degrees and Diplomas: *Bacharelado*; *Especialização/Aperfeiçoamento*: **Business Administration; Cardiology; Cognitive Sciences; Dermatology; Endocrinology; Health Administration; Human Resources; Marketing; Medicine; Neurology; Nursing; Occupational Health; Orthopaedics; Osteopathy; Physical Therapy; Psychiatry and Mental Health; Psychology; Rehabilitation and Therapy; Respiratory Therapy; Speech Therapy and Audiology; Surgery; Urology.** *Mestrado*: **Health Sciences.**

Last Updated: 24/06/15

FACULTY OF MEDICINE OF SANTA CASA DE SÃO PAULO

Faculdade de Ciências Médicas da Santa Casa de São Paulo (FCMSCSP)

Rua Dr. Cesário Motta Jr., 61, São Paulo, São Paulo 01221-020
Tel: +55(11) 3367-7700
Fax: +55(11) 3367-7833
EMail: faleconosco@fcmsantacasasp.edu.br
Website: http://www.fcmscsp.edu.br

Diretor: Valdir Golin EMail: diretoria@fcmsantacasasp.edu.br

Vice-Diretor: Osmar Monte

Course

Graduate Studies *(Stricto Sensu)* (Communication Studies; Health Sciences; Public Health; Surgery); **Graduate Studies** *(Lato Sensu)* (Engineering; Health Sciences; Medical Technology; Medicine; Neurosciences; Nursing; Occupational Health; Physical Therapy; Psychology; Radiology); **Medicine** (Medicine); **Nursing** (Nursing); **Speech Therapy** (Speech Therapy and Audiology); **Technology in Biomedical Systems** (Biomedical Engineering); **Technology in Radiology** (Radiology)

History: Founded 1963

Main Language(s) of Instruction: Portuguese

Degrees and Diplomas: *Bacharelado*; *Especialização/Aperfeiçoamento*: **Dentistry; Engineering; Health Sciences; Medical Technology; Neurology; Nursing; Occupational Health; Physical Therapy; Psychiatry and Mental Health; Psychology; Radiology.** *Mestrado*: **Communication Studies; Health Sciences; Public Health; Surgery.** *Doutorado*: **Health Sciences; Public Health; Surgery.** Also Postdoctoral Programme in Health Sciences

Student Services: Library

Last Updated: 24/06/15

FACULTY OF NOVA SERRANA

Faculdade de Nova Serrana (FANS)

Rua Lígia Rodrigues, 600, Fausto Pinto da Fonseca,
Nova Serrana, MG 35519-0000
Tel: +55(37) 3226-8200
EMail: comunicacao@fanserrana.com.br
Website: http://www.fans.edu.br

Diretor Geral: Fábio Fonseca Saldanha

Course

Accounting (Accountancy); **Industrial Production Management** (Industrial Management); **Management** (Management); **Pedagogy** (Pedagogy); **Psychology** (Psychology)

History: Founded 2000.

Main Language(s) of Instruction: Portuguese

Degrees and Diplomas: *Tecnólogo*; *Bacharelado*; *Licenciatura*

Student Services: Library

Last Updated: 30/11/15

FACULTY OF NOVO HAMBURGO-IENH FACULTY

Faculdade Novo Hamburgo-Faculdade IENH

Rua Frederico Mentz 526 - Prédio, Novo Hamburgo,
RS 93525-360
Tel: +55(51) 3594-3022
EMail: ienh@ienh.com.br
Website: http://www.ienh.com.br

Diretor Geral: Seno Leonhardt EMail: seno@ienh.com.br

Course

Administration (Administration); **Computer Networks** (Computer Networks); **Psychology** (Psychology); **Systems Analysis** (Computer Science)

History: Founded 2007.

Main Language(s) of Instruction: Portuguese

Degrees and Diplomas: *Bacharelado*; *Licenciatura*; *Especialização/Aperfeiçoamento*

Last Updated: 29/05/15

FACULTY OF OLINDA

Faculdade de Olinda (FOCCA)

Rua do Bonfim, 37, Carmo, Olinda,
Pernambuco 53120-090
Tel: +55(81) 3366-3696
Fax: +55(81) 3429-5965
EMail: focca@focca.com.br
Website: http://www.focca.com.br

Diretora Presidente: Antonieta Alves Chiappetta

Course

Accountancy (Accountancy); **Business Administration** (Administration; Business Administration); **Business and Commerce** (Business and Commerce); **Human Resources Management** (Human Resources); **Law** (Law); **Letters** (English; Literature; Portuguese); **Postgraduate Studies** (Business Administration; Education; Law; Modern Languages); **Transport Management** (Transport Management)

History: Founded 1972.

Fees: 480,00 per month (Brazilian Real)

Main Language(s) of Instruction: Portuguese

Degrees and Diplomas: *Tecnólogo*; *Bacharelado*; *Licenciatura*; *Especialização/Aperfeiçoamento*: **Civil Law; Commercial Law; Educational Sciences; English; Human Rights; Law.** *Mestrado*. Also MBA in Management, Business Administration, Environmental

Management, Marketing, Transport Management, Finance, Accountancy

Student Services: IT Centre, Library

Last Updated: 16/07/15

FACULTY OF OURO PRETO DO OESTE

Faculdade de Ouro Preto do Oeste (UNEOURO)
Rua Alto Alegre, 494, Novo Horizonte,
Ouro Preto do Oeste, RO 76920-00
Tel: +55(69) 3461-4278 +55(69) 3461-3377
EMail: uneouro@uneouro.edu.br; roberto@uneouro.edu.br; adriancury@unescnet.br
Website: http://www.uneouro.edu.br

Diretor: Antonio Carlos da Silva

Course

Accountancy (Accountancy); **Administration** (Administration); **Civil Engineering** (Civil Engineering); **Environmental Engineering** (Environmental Engineering); **Information Systems** (Computer Science); **Letters** (English; Literature; Portuguese); **Nursing** (Nursing); **Pedagogy** (Pedagogy); **Postgraduate Studies** (Accountancy; Educational Administration; Educational and Student Counselling; Educational Psychology; English; Finance; Higher Education Teacher Training; Literature; Management; Portuguese; Psychology; Public Administration; Special Education; Taxation)

History: Founded 2001

Main Language(s) of Instruction: Portuguese

Degrees and Diplomas: *Bacharelado*; *Licenciatura*; *Especialização/Aperfeiçoamento*: **Accountancy; Clinical Psychology; Educational Administration; Educational and Student Counselling; Educational Psychology; English; Higher Education Teacher Training; Literature; Portuguese; Psychology; Public Administration; Special Education; Taxation.** Also MBA

Student Services: Library

Last Updated: 04/12/15

FACULTY OF PARÁ DE MINAS

Faculdade de Pará de Minas (FAPAM)
Rua Ricardo Marinho, 110, São Geraldo,
Pará de Minas, MG 35660-398
Tel: +55(37) 3237-2000
Fax: +55(37) 3236-1308
EMail: fapam@nwm.com.br
Website: http://www.fapam.edu.br

Diretor Geral: Ruperto Benjamin Cabanellas Vega

Vice-Diretor: Flávio Marcus da Silva

Course

Accountancy (Accountancy); **Administration** (Administration); **Agricultural Business** (Agricultural Business); **Environmental Management** (Environmental Management); **Information Technology** (Information Technology); **Law** (Law); **Letters** (Literature; Portuguese); **Mathematics** (Mathematics); **Nursing** (Nursing); **Pedagogy** (Pedagogy); **Postgraduate Studies** (Accountancy; Finance; Law); **Psychology** (Psychology)

History: Founded 1976.

Main Language(s) of Instruction: Portuguese

Degrees and Diplomas: *Bacharelado*; *Licenciatura*; *Especialização/Aperfeiçoamento*: **Law.** Also MBA in Finance, Accountancy

Student Services: Library

Last Updated: 16/07/15

FACULTY OF PARANA

Faculdade Paranaense (FACCAR)
Rua Dom Pedro II 400, Jardim Horácio Cabral,
Rolândia, PR 86600000
Tel: +55(43) 3255-8500
Fax: +55(43) 3255-8503
EMail: pos@faccar.com.br
Website: http://www.faccar.com.br

Diretor: José Roberto Beffa (1997-)

Course

Accountancy (Accountancy); **Administration** (Administration; Business Administration); **Law** (Law); **Letters** (Literature); **Systems Analysis** (Computer Science)

History: Founded 1973 as Faculdade de Ciências Contábeis e Administrativas de Rôlandia. Acquired present status and title 2001.

Main Language(s) of Instruction: Portuguese

Degrees and Diplomas: *Bacharelado*; *Especialização/Aperfeiçoamento*

Student Services: Library

Last Updated: 02/06/15

FACULTY OF PEDAGOGY - ANAEC

Faculdade de Pedagogia - ANAEC
Av. Eurico Soares Andrade 730, Nova Andradina,
MS 79750-000
Tel: +55(67) 3441-1379
EMail: anaec@anaec.com.br; mailsonfigueredo@hotmail.com
Website: http://www.objetivo-anaec.com.br

Diretora: Vera Lucia Martinez Battistetti

Course

Pedagogy (Pedagogy)

History: Founded 1998.

Main Language(s) of Instruction: Portuguese

Degrees and Diplomas: *Licenciatura*

Last Updated: 16/07/15

FACULTY OF PEDAGOGY OF AFONSO CLÁUDIO

Faculdade de Pedagogia de Afonso Claudio (ISEAC)
Rua Ute Amélia Gastim Pádua, 49, São Tarcísio,
Afonso Claúdio, ES 29600-000
Tel: +55(27) 3735-2411
Fax: +55(27) 3735-2433
EMail: robertoadministra@gmail.com; direcao@faac-es.com.br; adm.tudo1@gmail.com
Website: http://www.faac-es.com.br

Diretor: Roberto Alexandre Alcantara

Course

Pedagogy (Pedagogy)

History: Founded 1999.

Main Language(s) of Instruction: Portuguese

Degrees and Diplomas: *Licenciatura*; *Especialização/Aperfeiçoamento*: **Accountancy; Adult Education; Art Education; Arts and Humanities; Banking; Business Administration; Business Education; Civil Law; Education; Educational Administration; Educational Psychology; Educational Technology; Environmental Management; Environmental Studies; Finance; Health Administration; Higher Education Teacher Training; Human Resources; Humanities and Social Science Education; Industrial Management; Law; Literacy Education; Management; Marketing; Mathematics Education; Music Education; Native Language Education; Pedagogy; Physical Education; Political Sciences; Primary Education; Protective Services; Public Administration; Public Health; Religious Education; Science Education; Social Work; Special Education; Teacher Training; Theology; Water Management.**

Last Updated: 16/07/15

FACULTY OF PHILOSOPHY, SCIENCE AND LETTERS OF ALTO SÃO FRANCISCO

Faculdade de Filosofia, Ciências e Letras do Alto São Francisco (FASF)
Avenida Laerton Paulinelli, 153, Bairro Monsenhor Pareiras,
Luz, Minas Gerais 35595-000
Tel: +55(37) 3421-9006 +55(37) 3421-9008
EMail: fasf@catedralnet.com.br
Website: http://www.fasf.edu.br

Diretor: Heloisa Ribeiro dos Santos

Course
Accountancy (Accountancy); **Administration** (Administration); **Biology** (Biology); **Dairy** (Dairy); **Finance** (Finance); **Graduate Studies** (Biology; Environmental Management; Mathematics Education; Native Language Education; Public Law); **Pharmacy** (Pharmacy)

History: Founded 1974 as part of the Catholic University of Minas Gerais. Acquired present status and title 1985.

Main Language(s) of Instruction: Portuguese

Degrees and Diplomas: *Tecnólogo*; *Bacharelado*; *Licenciatura*; *Especialização/Aperfeiçoamento*: **Biology; Environmental Management; Native Language Education; Public Law.** Also MBA in Business and Commerce, Finance, Accountancy, Marketing, Leadership, Business Administration

Student Services: Library
Last Updated: 08/07/15

FACULTY OF PHILOSOPHY, SCIENCE AND LETTERS OF BOA ESPERANÇA

Faculdade de Filosofia, Ciências e Letras de Boa Esperança (FAFIBE)

Av. Aureliano Chaves, 192, Jardin Nova Esperança,
Boa Esperança, Minas Gerais 37170-000
Tel: +55(35) 3851-2211
Fax: +55(35) 3851-1891
EMail: secretaria@fafibemg.edu.com.br
Website: www.fafibe.ieducare.com.br

Diretora: Ilso Stopassola
EMail: ilso@ieducare.com.br

Diretor Acadêmico: Marly Nepomuceno Mendonça Bernardes

Course
Environmental Management (Environmental Management); **Geography** (Geography); **Graduate Studies** (Accountancy; Administration; Agriculture; Education; Health Sciences; Information Technology; Law); **History** (History); **Information Technology** (Information Technology); **Literature** (English; Literature); **Mathematics** (Mathematics); **Pedagogy** (Pedagogy)

History: Founded 1973

Main Language(s) of Instruction: Portuguese

Degrees and Diplomas: *Tecnólogo*; *Bacharelado*; *Licenciatura*; *Especialização/Aperfeiçoamento*: **Accountancy; Agriculture; Community Health; Ecology; Educational Administration; Health Administration; Human Resources; Humanities and Social Science Education; Justice Administration; Law; Literacy Education; Mathematics Education; Medicine; Native Language Education; Primary Education; Psychiatry and Mental Health; Public Administration; Public Health; Science Education; Software Engineering; Special Education.** Also MBA in Agricultural Business

Student Services: IT Centre, Library
Last Updated: 07/07/15

FACULTY OF PHILOSOPHY, SCIENCE AND LETTERS OF CAJAZEIRAS

Faculdade de Filosofia, Ciências e Letras de Cajazeiras (FAFIC)

Rua Pe. Ibiapina, s/n, Centro, Cajazeiras,
Paraiba 58900-000
Tel: +55(83) 3531-3500
Fax: +55(83) 3531-3500
EMail: fafic@fescfafic.edu.br
Website: http://fescfafic.edu.br

Diretor: Agripino Ferreira de Assis

Vice-Diretor Acadêmico: Janilson Rolim Veríssimo
EMail: filosofia@fescfafic.edu.br

Course
Accountancy (Accountancy); **Law** (Law); **Philosophy** (Philosophy); **Postgraduate Studies** (Accountancy; Administrative Law; Criminal Law; Fiscal Law; Philosophy; Public Administration; Special Education; Taxation); **Social Services** (Social and Community Services)

History: Founded 1970

Main Language(s) of Instruction: Portuguese

Degrees and Diplomas: *Bacharelado*; *Licenciatura*; *Especialização/Aperfeiçoamento*: **Accountancy; Administrative Law; Criminal Law; Fiscal Law; Higher Education Teacher Training; Philosophy; Public Administration; Special Education; Taxation.**

Student Services: IT Centre, Library
Last Updated: 07/07/15

FACULTY OF PHILOSOPHY, SCIENCE AND LETTERS OF CARUARU

Faculdade de Filosofia, Ciências e Letras de Caruaru (FAFICA)

Avenida Azevedo Coutinho, s/n, Petrópolis, Caruaru,
PE 55030902
Tel: +55(81) 2103-3900
Fax: +55(81) 2103-3900
EMail: fafica@fafica-pe.edu.br; padrejpaulo@gmail.com
Website: http://www.fafica.com

Diretor Geral: João Paulo de Araújo Gomes

Secretária Geral: Maria das Graças Pereira Galindo

Course
Accountancy (Accountancy); **Administration** (Administration); **Commercial Management** (Business and Commerce); **Computer Networks** (Computer Networks); **Graduate Studies** (Accountancy; Adult Education; Business Administration; Computer Networks; Educational Administration; Educational Psychology; Finance; History; Human Resources; Human Rights; Humanities and Social Science Education; Industrial and Organizational Psychology; Marketing; Native Language Education; Occupational Health; Philosophy; Primary Education; Public Administration; Real Estate; Sales Techniques; Service Trades; Sociology; Software Engineering; Taxation; Technology Education; Transport Management); **History** (History); **Literature and English** (English; Literature); **Literature and Spanish** (Literature; Spanish); **Pedagogy** (Pedagogy); **Philosophy** (Philosophy); **Systems Analysis** (Systems Analysis); **Theology** (Theology)

History: Founded 1960

Main Language(s) of Instruction: Portuguese

Degrees and Diplomas: *Tecnólogo*; *Bacharelado*; *Licenciatura*; *Especialização/Aperfeiçoamento*: **Accountancy; Adult Education; Computer Networks; Educational Administration; Educational Psychology; Higher Education Teacher Training; Human Rights; Humanities and Social Science Education; Native Language Education; Philosophy; Primary Education; Sociology; Software Engineering; Taxation.** Also MBA in Service Trades, Business Administration, Finance, Real Estate, Public Administration, Transport Management, Marketing, Sales Techniques, Industrial and Organisational Psychology, Human Resources, Occupational Health.

Student Services: Library
Last Updated: 07/07/15

FACULTY OF PHILOSOPHY, SCIENCE AND LETTERS OF CONGONHAS

Faculdade de Filosofia Ciências e Letras de Congonhas (FAFIC)

Rua José Danilo Gonçalves Ferreira, s/n°, Praia,
Congonhas, MG 36415-000
Tel: +55(31) 3731- 4165 +55(31) 3731-1541
Fax: +55(31) 3731-4165
EMail: proreitoriadeensinobh@gmail.com;
kesciacarvalho@yahoo.com.br
Website: http://www.fupac.edu.br/unipaccongonhas

Course
Pedagogy (Pedagogy)

Main Language(s) of Instruction: Portuguese

Degrees and Diplomas: *Licenciatura*

Student Services: Library

Last Updated: 04/12/15

FACULTY OF PHILOSOPHY, SCIENCE AND LETTERS OF ITUVERAVA

Faculdade de Filosofia, Ciências e Letras de Ituverava (FFCL)

Rua Flauzino Barbosa Sandoval, 1259, Cidade Universitária, Ituverava, São Paulo 14500-000

Tel: +55(16) 3729-9000

Fax: +55(16) 3729-3199

EMail: ffcl@feituverava.com.br; toca@feituverava.com.br

Website: www.ffcl.com.br

Diretor: Antônio Luis de Oliveira

Course

Accountancy (Accountancy); **Administration** (Administration); **Biology** (Biology); **Civil Engineering** (Civil Engineering); **Geography (Distance Mode)** (Geography (Human)); **Graduate Studies** (Biological and Life Sciences; Education; Educational Psychology; Finance; History; Linguistics; Literacy Education; Literature; Management; Marketing; Mathematics Education; Special Education); **History** (History); **History (Distance Mode)** (History); **Literature** (English; Literature; Portuguese); **Mathematics** (Mathematics); **Mechanical Engineering** (Mechanical Engineering); **Pedagogy** (Pedagogy); **Pedagogy (Distance Mode)** (Pedagogy); **Postgraduate Studies** (Educational Psychology; Environmental Studies; Finance; Human Resources; Literacy Education; Literature; Mathematics Education; Primary Education; Special Education); **Postgraduate Studies (Distance Mode)** (Business Education; Educational Psychology; Literacy Education; Literature; Primary Education; Special Education); **Production Engineering** (Production Engineering)

History: Founded 1971

Main Language(s) of Instruction: Portuguese

Degrees and Diplomas: *Bacharelado*; *Licenciatura*; *Especialização/Aperfeiçoamento*: **Educational Psychology; Environmental Studies; Literacy Education; Literature; Mathematics Education; Primary Education; Special Education.** Also MBA in Human Resources and Finance

Student Services: IT Centre, Library

Last Updated: 07/07/15

FACULTY OF PHILOSOPHY, SCIENCE AND LETTERS OF MACAÉ

Faculdade de Filosofia, Ciências e Letras de Macaé (FAFIMA)

Rua Tenente Rui Lopes Ribeiro 200, Centro, Macaé, Rio de Janeiro 27910-340

Tel: +55(24) 2762-1457

Fax: +55(24) 2762-1457

EMail: fafima@fafima.br

Website: http://www.fafima.br

Diretora Geral: Luiz Guaracy Gasparelli Junior
EMail: luiz.diretoria@fafima.br

Secretária Geral: Denise Moura EMail: denisemoura@fafima.br

Course

Geography (Geography (Human)); **Graduate Studies** (Educational Psychology; English; Portuguese; Primary Education); **History** (History); **Literature** (English; Literature; Portuguese); **Mathematics** (Mathematics); **Pedagogy** (Pedagogy)

History: Founded 1973

Main Language(s) of Instruction: Portuguese

Degrees and Diplomas: *Tecnólogo*; *Licenciatura*; *Especialização/Aperfeiçoamento*: **Educational Psychology; English; Portuguese; Primary Education.**

Student Services: Library

Last Updated: 07/07/15

FACULTY OF PHILOSOPHY, SCIENCE AND LETTERS OF PENÁPOLIS

Faculdade de Filosofia, Ciências e Letras de Penápolis (FAFIPE)

Avenida São José, 400, Vila Martins, Penápolis, SP 16300-000

Tel: +55(18) 3654-7690

Fax: +55(18) 3654-7691

EMail: funepe@funepe.edu.br

Website: http://www.funepe.edu.br

Diretora: Wanderli Aparecido Bastos
EMail: Bastos@funepe.edu.br

Course

Accountancy (Accountancy); **Administration** (Administration); **Agricultural Business** (Agricultural Business); **Agricultural Engineering** (Agricultural Engineering); **Biology** (Biology); **Extension Studies** (Medical Technology; Nursing; Occupational Health); **Graduate Studies** (Accountancy; Business and Commerce; Educational Psychology; Environmental Management; Finance; Marketing; Sales Techniques; Special Education); **Information Systems** (Information Technology); **Mathematics** (Mathematics); **Pedagogy** (Pedagogy); **Physics** (Physics); **Psychology** (Psychology); **Technological Studies** (Agricultural Business; Computer Networks; Dental Hygiene; Nursing; Occupational Health; Transport Management); **Visual Arts** (Visual Arts)

History: Founded 1966.

Main Language(s) of Instruction: Portuguese

Degrees and Diplomas: *Tecnólogo*; *Bacharelado*; *Licenciatura*; *Especialização/Aperfeiçoamento*: **Accountancy; Business and Commerce; Educational Psychology; Environmental Management; Finance; Marketing; Medical Technology; Nursing; Occupational Health; Sales Techniques; Special Education.**

Student Services: IT Centre, Library

Last Updated: 07/07/15

FACULTY OF PHILOSOPHY, SCIENCES AND LETTERS OF DUQUE DE CAXIAS

Faculdade de Filosofia, Ciências e Letras de Duque de Caxias (FFCLDC)

Av. Governador Leonel de Moura Brizola n° 9442ã, São Bento, Duque de Caxias, Rio de Janeiro 25045-002

Tel: +55(21) 2671-0888 +55(21) 2671-4501

Fax: +55(21) 2671-5568

EMail: secretaria@feuduc.edu.br; secfeuduc@gmail.com; vestibular@feuduc.edu.br

Website: http://www.feuduc.edu.br

Diretor Acadêmico: Nielson Bezerra
EMail: diretoria@feuduc.edu.br

Course

Biology (Biology); **English Language/Literature** (English; Literature); **Geography** (Geography); **Graduate Studies** (Biological and Life Sciences; Contemporary History; English; Environmental Studies; Geography; History; Mathematics; Pathology; Portuguese; Religious Studies; Social Sciences; Tourism); **History** (History); **Information Systems** (Information Technology); **Mathematics** (Mathematics); **Portuguese Language/Literature** (English; Literature)

History: Founded 1972. Maintained by Fundação Educacional de Duque de Caxias (FEUDUC).

Main Language(s) of Instruction: Portuguese

Degrees and Diplomas: *Bacharelado*; *Licenciatura*; *Especialização/Aperfeiçoamento*: **Biological and Life Sciences; Contemporary History; English; Environmental Studies; Geography; History; Mathematics; Pathology; Portuguese; Religious Studies; Social Sciences; Tourism.**

Student Services: Library

Last Updated: 03/02/16

FACULTY OF PHYSICAL EDUCATION OF BARRA BONITA

Faculdade de Educação Física de Barra Bonita (FAEFI)

João Gerin, 275, Vila Operária, Barra Bonita, São Paulo 17340-000
Tel: +55(14) 3604-1200
Fax: +55(14) 3604-1200
EMail: prof.nono@funbbe.br; coordenacaofaefi@funbbe.br
Website: http://www.funbbe.br/Default.aspx?alias=www.funbbe.br/faefi

Diretor: Ana Cândida Arroyos
EMail: diretoria.ensinosuperior@funbbe.br

Course
Graduate Studies (Nutrition); **Physical Education** (Physical Education)

History: Founded 1972.

Main Language(s) of Instruction: Portuguese

Degrees and Diplomas: *Licenciatura*; *Especialização/Aperfeiçoamento*: **Nutrition.**

Student Services: Library
Last Updated: 01/07/15

FACULTY OF PHYSICAL EDUCATION OF THE CRISTÁ DE MOÇOS ASSOCIATION OF SOROCABA

Faculdade de Educação Física da Associação Cristá de Moços de Sorocaba (FEFISO)

Rua da Penha, 680, Centro, Sorocaba, São Paulo 18010002
Tel: +55(15) 3234-9115
EMail: fefiso@fefiso.edu.br
Website: http://www.fefiso.edu.br

Diretor: Maurício Massari

Course
Graduate Studies (Physical Education; Physiology; Sports; Sports Management); **Physical Education** (Physical Education)

History: Founded 1971.

Main Language(s) of Instruction: Portuguese

Degrees and Diplomas: *Bacharelado*; *Licenciatura*; *Especialização/Aperfeiçoamento*: **Physical Education; Physiology; Sports; Sports Management.**

Student Services: Library
Last Updated: 01/07/15

FACULTY OF PINDAMONHANGABA

Faculdade de Pindamonhangaba (FAPI)

Rodovia Presidente Eurico Gaspar Dutra s/n - Km 99, Pindamonhangaba, SP 12422-970
Tel: +55(12) 3648-8323
EMail: secretaria@fapi.br
Website: http://www.fapi.br

Diretor: Luís Otávio Palhari EMail: presidencia@funvic.org.br

Vice-Diretor: Juliano Palhari EMail: jpalhari@fapi.br

Area
Biological Sciences (Dentistry; Nursing; Pharmacy; Physical Education; Physical Therapy); **Exact Sciences** (Automation and Control Engineering; Chemical Engineering; Computer Engineering; Environmental Engineering; Industrial Engineering; Information Sciences; Production Engineering); **Human Sciences** (Administration; Human Resources; Pedagogy; Theology; Transport Management)

Course
Postgraduate Studies (Dentistry; Management; Media Studies; Nursing; Physical Education; Physical Therapy)

History: Founded 2002.

Main Language(s) of Instruction: Portuguese

Degrees and Diplomas: *Bacharelado*; *Licenciatura*; *Especialização/Aperfeiçoamento*: **Dental Technology; Dentistry; Management; Media Studies; Nursing; Physical Therapy.**

Student Services: Library, eLibrary
Last Updated: 17/07/15

FACULTY OF PONTA PORÃ

Faculdade de Ponta Porã (FAP)

Rua Antônio João, 1675, Centro, Ponta Porã, Mato Grosso do Sul 79900-000
Tel: +55(67) 3431-7730
Fax: +55(67) 3431-1002
EMail: fap@fap.br; ckto@uniesp.edu.br; academicosup@uniesp.edu.br
Website: http://www.fap.br

Diretora Geral: Marta Sulema Martins Gonzalez Biolchi

Course
Accountancy (Accountancy); **Administration** (Administration); **Geography** (Geography); **History** (History); **Letters** (Literature; Portuguese; Spanish)

History: Founded 1988.

Main Language(s) of Instruction: Portuguese

Degrees and Diplomas: *Bacharelado*; *Licenciatura*

Student Services: Library
Last Updated: 17/07/15

FACULTY OF PRESIDENT EPITÁCIO

Faculdade de Presidente Epitácio

Rua Pernambuco, 17-05, Centro, Presidente Epitácio, São Paulo 19470-000
Tel: +55(18) 3281-9600
EMail: secretaria-fape@uniesp.edu.br
Website: http://www.faculdadefape.edu.br

Diretor Presidente: Maria Antonieta de Carvalho e Silva
EMail: maria.antonieta@uniesp.edu.br

Course
Accountancy (Accountancy); **Administration** (Administration); **Computer Science** (Computer Science); **Law** (Law); **Literature** (English; Literature; Portuguese); **Pedagogy** (Pedagogy); **Tourism** (Tourism); **Visual Arts** (Visual Arts)

History: Founded 1998

Main Language(s) of Instruction: Portuguese

Degrees and Diplomas: *Tecnólogo*; *Bacharelado*; *Licenciatura*
Last Updated: 17/07/15

FACULTY OF PRESIDENT PRUDENTE

Faculdade de Presidente Prudente (FAPEPE)

Avenida Presidente Prudente, 6093, Jardim Aeroporto, Presidente Prudente, São Paulo 19053-210
Tel: +55(18) 3918-4700
Fax: +55(18) 3918-4700
EMail: maria.helena@uniesp.edu.br; ckto@terra.com.br; academicosup@uniesp.edu.br
Website: http://www.faculdadefapepe.edu.br

Diretora: Maria Helena de Carvalho e Silva Bueno

Course
Accountancy (Accountancy); **Administration** (Administration); **Biological Sciences** (Biological and Life Sciences); **Chemistry** (Chemistry); **Civil Engineering** (Civil Engineering); **Evironmental and Health Engineering** (Environmental Engineering; Health Sciences); **Executive Secretarial Studies** (Secretarial Studies); **Fashion Design** (Fashion Design); **Information Systems** (Information Technology); **Law** (Law); **Literature** (English; Literature; Portuguese; Spanish); **Mathematics** (Mathematics); **Nursing** (Nursing); **Pedagogy** (Pedagogy); **Physical Education** (Physical Education); **Physics** (Physics); **Production Engineering** (Production Engineering); **Social Communication - Advertising and Publicity** (Advertising and Publicity; Mass Communication); **Social Communication - Journalism** (Journalism; Mass Communication); **Social Services** (Social and Community Services); **Tourism** (Tourism)

History: Founded 2000

Main Language(s) of Instruction: Portuguese

Degrees and Diplomas: *Bacharelado*; *Licenciatura*
Student Services: Library
Last Updated: 17/07/15

FACULTY OF PRESIDENT VENCESLAU

Faculdade de Presidente Venceslau (FAPREV)

Rua Piracicaba, 47, Jardim Coroados,
Presidente Venceslau, São Paulo 19400-000
Tel: +55(18) 3272-9440
Fax: +55(18) 3271-3100
EMail: fafipreve@fafiprev.edu.br
Website: http://www.faculdadefaprev.edu.br

Diretora: Cinthia Maria Bueno Marturelli Mantovani

Secretario Acadêmico: Igor Antonio Bonifácio de Miranda

Course
Administration (Administration); **Biological Sciences** (Biological and Life Sciences); **Geography** (Geography (Human)); **History** (History); **Literature** (English; Literature; Portuguese); **Mathematics** (Mathematics); **Pedagogy** (Pedagogy); **Physical Education** (Physical Education); **Social Services** (Social and Community Services)

History: Founded 1972. Merged with Faculdade de Filosofia, Ciências e Letras de Presidente Venceslau 2008.

Main Language(s) of Instruction: Portuguese

Degrees and Diplomas: *Bacharelado*; *Licenciatura*
Student Services: Library
Last Updated: 17/07/15

FACULTY OF REALAZA

Faculdade de Realeza (CESREAL)

Rodovia PR 281, km 02, Caixa Postal 11, Realaza,
PR 85770-000
Tel: +55(46) 3543-4444
EMail: cesreal@cesreal.br; secretaria_cesreal@yahoo.com.br
Website: http://www.cesreal.br

Diretor: Denis de Oliveira Junior

Course
Accountancy (Accountancy); **Administration** (Administration); **Postgraduate Studies** (Accountancy; Taxation)

History: Founded 2001.

Main Language(s) of Instruction: Portuguese

Degrees and Diplomas: *Bacharelado*; *Especialização/Aperfeiçoamento*: **Accountancy; Taxation.**
Student Services: Library
Last Updated: 17/07/15

FACULTY OF RECIFE

Faculdade do Recife (FAREC)

Rua Dom Bosco, 1,329, Boa Vista, Recife,
PE 50070-070
Tel: +(81) 3231-1299
Fax: +(81) 3221-5651
EMail: marcioacbarros@yahoo.com.br
Website: http://www.farec.edu.br

Diretora Geral: Ana Paula B. de Melo Oliveira Valença

Course
Accounting (Accountancy); **Administration** (Business Administration); **Civil Engineering** (Civil Engineering); **Computer Science** (Computer Science); **Law** (Law); **Nursing** (Nursing); **Pedagogy** (Pedagogy); **Physiotherapy** (Physical Therapy); **Production Engineering** (Production Engineering); **Social Communication, Publicity and Advertising** (Mass Communication); **Social Services** (Social and Community Services); **Tourism** (Tourism)

History: Founded 2002.

Main Language(s) of Instruction: Portuguese

Degrees and Diplomas: *Tecnólogo*; *Bacharelado*; *Licenciatura*
Student Services: Library
Last Updated: 30/11/15

FACULTY OF REHABILITATION OF THE ASCE

Faculdade de Reabilitação da ASCE (FRASCE)

Rua Uarumã n° 80, Higienópolis,
Rio de Janeiro, Rio de Janeiro 21050-660
Tel: +55(21) 3866-0029 +55(21) 3868-8279
EMail: frasce@uol.com.br; amiltondinascimento@gmail.com; barbara_paulucci@globo.com; amiltondonascimento@gmail
Website: http://www.frasce.edu.br

Diretor: Desembargador Libórni Siqueira

Coordenador do Curso de Administração: Luciano Bispo

Course
Administration (Administration); **Foreign Trade** (International Business); **Information Systems** (Information Technology); **Pedagogy** (Pedagogy); **Physiotherapy** (Physical Therapy); **Postgraduate Studies** (Acupuncture; Dermatology; Gerontology; Health Administration; Orthopaedics; Rehabilitation and Therapy; Respiratory Therapy)

History: Founded 1977.

Fees: Graduate studies, 320 per month (Brazilian Real)

Main Language(s) of Instruction: Portuguese

Degrees and Diplomas: *Bacharelado*; *Licenciatura*; *Especialização/Aperfeiçoamento*: **Acupuncture; Dermatology; Gerontology; Health Administration; Orthopaedics; Physical Therapy; Rehabilitation and Therapy; Respiratory Therapy.**
Student Services: Library
Last Updated: 17/07/15

FACULTY OF RONDÔNIA

Faculdade de Rondônia (FARO)

Br 364 Km 6,5 s/n, Campus FARO,
Porto Velho, Rondônia 78914751
Tel: +55(69) 217-5100
Fax: +55(69) 222-1888
EMail: secretaria@faro.edu.br; subdiretoriaacademica@faro.edu.br
Website: http://www.faro.edu.br

Diretoria Executiva: Sebastião Getúlio de Brito
Tel: +55(69) 3217-5154
EMail: diretoriaexecutiva@faro.edu.br

Subdiretoria Operacional: Francirlene Belo Mendes de Santana
Tel: +55(69) 3217-5176
EMail: subdiretoriaoperacional@faro.edu.br

Course
Accountancy (Accountancy); **Administration** (Administration); **Civil Engineering** (Civil Engineering); **Forestry Engineering** (Forestry); **Law** (Law); **Nursing** (Nursing); **Pedagogy** (Pedagogy); **Postgraduate Studies** (Administrative Law; Civil Law; Communication Studies; Constitutional Law; Educational and Student Counselling; Educational Psychology; Environmental Management; Gerontology; Higher Education Teacher Training; Labour Law; Law; Literature; Marketing; Portuguese; Primary Education; Psychiatry and Mental Health; Psychology; Public Health; Rehabilitation and Therapy; Retailing and Wholesaling; Safety Engineering; Social Psychology; Surveying and Mapping; Transport Management)

History: Founded 1988.

Main Language(s) of Instruction: Portuguese

Degrees and Diplomas: *Bacharelado*; *Licenciatura*; *Especialização/Aperfeiçoamento*: **Administrative Law; Civil Law; Communication Studies; Constitutional Law; Educational and Student Counselling; Educational Psychology; Environmental Studies; Gerontology; Higher Education Teacher Training; Labour Law; Law; Literature; Marketing; Portuguese; Psychiatry and Mental Health; Public Health; Rehabilitation and Therapy; Retailing**

and Wholesaling; Safety Engineering; Surveying and Mapping; Transport Management.

Student Services: Library

Last Updated: 17/07/15

FACULTY OF SABARÁ

Faculdade de Sabará (SOECS)

Rodovia Sabará/BH, Km 14, Bairro Caieira,
Sabará, Minas Gerais 34555000
Tel: +55(31) 3671-2560
Fax: +55(31) 3241-7204
EMail: soecs@faculdadedesabara.edu.br
Website: http://www.faculdadedesabara.edu.br

Reitor: Mário de Lima Guerra

Diretora de Administração e da Secretaria Geral: Maria da Glória Ribeiro

Course

Administration (Administration); **Law** (Law); **Letters** (Literature; Portuguese; Spanish); **Postgraduate Studies** (Applied Linguistics; Business Administration; Educational Psychology; Portuguese; Public Administration)

History: Founded 1998

Main Language(s) of Instruction: Portuguese

Degrees and Diplomas: *Bacharelado*; *Licenciatura*. Registration to postgraduate courses are closed

Student Services: Library

Publications: O Acadêmico

Last Updated: 18/08/15

FACULTY OF SAINT BENEDICT OF RIO DE JANEIRO

Faculdade de São Bento do Rio de Janeiro (FSBRJ)

Rua Dom Gerardo, 68, Centro, Rio de Janeiro,
RJ 20090-030
Tel: +55(21) 2206-8281
EMail: info@faculdadesaobento.org.br
Website: http://www.faculdadesaobento.org.br/

Diretor Geral: Anselmo Chagas de Paiva

Course

Graduate Studies (Ancient Civilizations; Art History; Ethics; Medieval Studies; Philosophy; Portuguese; Religious Studies); **Philosophy** (Philosophy); **Theology** (Theology)

History: Founded 1921 as Escola Teológica da Congregação Beneditina do Brasil. Renamed Instituto de Filosofia e de Teologia São Bento 1999.

Main Language(s) of Instruction: Portuguese

Degrees and Diplomas: *Bacharelado*; *Licenciatura*; *Especialização/Aperfeiçoamento*: **Ancient Civilizations; Art History; Medieval Studies; Philosophy; Portuguese; Religious Studies.**

Student Services: eLibrary

Last Updated: 18/08/15

FACULTY OF SAINT CATHERINE

Faculdade de Santa Catarina (FASC)

Av. Salvador Di Bernardi, 503, Campinas, São José,
SC 88101-201
Tel: +55(48) 3878-2000 +55(48) 3878-5000
EMail: marcioacbarros@yahoo.com.br
Website: http://www.fasc.edu.br/

Diretor Geral: Samir Saliba Murad EMail: diretoria@fasc.edu.br

Coordenação Geral: Adriana de Valgas Ferreira
EMail: adrivalgas.cgc@unip.br

Course

Accountancy (Accountancy); **Administration** (Administration); **Architecture and Urbanism** (Architecture; Town Planning); **Law** (Law); **Mass Communication (Advertising)** (Advertising and Publicity; Mass Communication); **Nursing** (Nursing); **Pedagogy** (Pedagogy); **Tourism** (Tourism)

History: Founded 2002.

Degrees and Diplomas: *Bacharelado*; *Licenciatura*

Student Services: IT Centre, Library

Last Updated: 18/08/15

FACULTY OF SANTOS DUMONT

Faculdade de Santos Dumont (FSD)

Avenida Presidente Getúlio Vargas 547, Centro,
Santos Dumont, MG 36240-000
Tel: +55(32) 3251-3817 +55(32) 3251-3752
Fax: +55(32) 3251-3817
EMail: fsd@fsd.edu.br; fsd@cabangu.com.br
Website: http://www.fsd.edu.br

Presidente: Odílio Fernandes da Fonseca

Faculty

Faculty of Juridical Sciences of Santos Dumont - FCJSD (Law); **Faculty of Managerial Sciences of Santos Dumont - FACIG** (Accountancy; Business Administration; Computer Science)

Institute

Institute of Education of Santos Dumont - ISESD (Arts and Humanities; Pedagogy)

History: Founded 1995.

Main Language(s) of Instruction: Portuguese

Degrees and Diplomas: *Bacharelado*; *Licenciatura*. Also Double Degree (Bacharelado) in Business Administration and Accounting

Student Services: IT Centre, Library

Last Updated: 10/12/15

FACULTY OF SÃO BENTO

Faculdade de São Bento (FSB)

Largo de São Bento, s/no, Centro, São Paulo, SP
Tel: +55(11) 3328-8796
EMail: faculdade@saobento.org.br; filosofiasb@uol.com.br
Website: http://www.saobento.org.br

Diretor: Carlos Eduardo Uchôa

Course

Philosophy (Philosophy); **Postgraduate Studies** (Philosophy); **Theology** (Theology)

History: Founded 1908 as Faculdade de Filosofia, Ciências e Letras. Acquired present status and title 2002.

Main Language(s) of Instruction: Portuguese

Degrees and Diplomas: *Bacharelado*; *Licenciatura*; *Mestrado*: **Philosophy.**

Student Services: Library

Last Updated: 18/08/15

FACULTY OF SÃO BERNARDO DO CAMPO

Faculdade de São Bernardo do Campo (FASB)

Rua Américo Brasiliense, 449 e Rua João Pessoa, 601, Centro,
São Bernardo do Campos, São Paulo 09715020
Tel: +55(11) 4123-1469
Fax: +55(11) 4335-4875
EMail: fasb@facsaobernardo.com.br
Website: http://www.facsaobernardo.com.br

Diretor Executivo: Ariovaldo José Pecora (1994-)

Course

Administration (Administration); **Administration and Commerce (Postgraduate)** (Finance; Management; Transport Management); **Chemical Engineering** (Chemical Engineering); **Chemistry** (Chemistry); **Education (Postgraduate)** (Art Criticism; Educational Psychology; Literature); **Exact Sciences (Postgraduate)** (Cosmetology; Petroleum and Gas Engineering; Safety Engineering); **Letters** (English; Literature; Portuguese; Spanish); **Pedagogy** (Pedagogy); **Production Engineering** (Production Engineering); **Social Studies (History)** (History; Social Sciences)

History: Founded 1971 as Faculdade de Filosofia Ciências e Letras de São Bernardo do Campo. Acquired present status and title 2002.

Main Language(s) of Instruction: Portuguese

Degrees and Diplomas: *Bacharelado*; *Licenciatura*; *Especialização/Aperfeiçoamento*: **Art Criticism; Cosmetology; Educational**

Psychology; Finance; Literature; Management; Petroleum and Gas Engineering; Safety Engineering; Transport Management.
Student Services: IT Centre, Library, eLibrary
Last Updated: 18/08/15

FACULTY OF SÃO LUÍS

Faculdade São Luís
Rua Grande, 1455, Diamante, São Luís, MA 65020-250
Tel: +55(98) 3214-6400
EMail: geraldo@facsaoluis.br

Diretor: Claudio Marcio Piontkewicz

Course
Accountancy (Accountancy); **Administration** (Administration); **Advertising** (Advertising and Publicity); **Philosophy** (Philosophy)
History: Founded 2001.
Main Language(s) of Instruction: Portuguese
Degrees and Diplomas: *Bacharelado*; *Licenciatura*; *Especialização/Aperfeiçoamento*
Last Updated: 11/06/15

FACULTY OF SAO PAULO

Faculdade Paulista
Av. Santo Inácio, 1089, Lupércio, SP 17420-000
Tel: +55(14) 3474-1226
Fax: +55(14) 3474-1551
EMail: contato@faculdadepaulista.edu.br
Website: http://www.faculdadepaulista.edu.br

Course
Agribusiness (Agricultural Business); **Agronomy** (Agronomy); **Pedagogy** (Pedagogy); **Postgraduate Studies** (Business Administration; Education; Health Sciences; Law)
History: Founded 2008.
Main Language(s) of Instruction: Portuguese
Degrees and Diplomas: *Tecnólogo*; *Bacharelado*; *Licenciatura*; *Especialização/Aperfeiçoamento*: **Adult Education; Applied Mathematics; Art Education; Art History; Art Therapy; Business Administration; Chemistry; Clinical Psychology; Constitutional Law; Criminal Law; Criminology; Ecology; Education; Education of the Handicapped; Educational Administration; Educational Psychology; Educational Sciences; Engineering Management; Environmental Management; Environmental Studies; Health Administration; Health Education; Higher Education Teacher Training; Labour Law; Law; Linguistics; Literacy Education; Literature; Management; Mathematics; Neurosciences; Nursing; Pedagogy; Pharmacology; Philosophy; Physical Education; Preschool Education; Primary Education; Psychiatry and Mental Health; Psychology; Public Administration; Rehabilitation and Therapy; Safety Engineering; Secondary Education; Social and Community Services; Social Policy; Sociology; Special Education; Sports Management; Teacher Training; Technology Education; Transport Management; Visual Arts.** Also MBA
Student Services: Library
Last Updated: 27/11/15

FACULTY OF SCIENCE AND LETTERS OF BRAGANÇA PAULISTA

Faculdade de Ciências e Letras de Bragança Paulista (FCLBP)
Avenida Francisco Samuel Lucchesi Filho, 770, Bairro da Penha, Bragança Paulista, São Paulo 12929-600
Tel: +55(11) 4035-7800
Fax: +55(11) 4035-7802
EMail: faculdade@fesb.br
Website: http://www.fesb.br

Director, Academic Affairs: Maria Raquel G. O. C. Negro
EMail: diretoria@fesb.edu.br

Director, Administrative Affairs: Claudemir Baffi Parrão
EMail: claudemir@fesb.edu.br

Course
Agronomy (Agronomy); **Art Education** (Art Education); **Arts and Humanities** (Arts and Humanities; English; Portuguese); **Biology** (Biology); **Chemistry** (Chemistry); **Geography** (Geography); **History** (History); **Mathematics** (Mathematics); **Nutrition** (Nutrition); **Pedagogy** (Pedagogy); **Physical Education** *(Bacharelado)* (Physical Education); **Physical Education** *(Licenciatura)* (Physical Education); **Social Services** (Social Work); **Veterinary Science** (Veterinary Science)
History: Founded 1967.
Main Language(s) of Instruction: Portuguese
Degrees and Diplomas: *Bacharelado*; *Licenciatura*; *Especialização/Aperfeiçoamento*
Student Services: IT Centre, Library
Last Updated: 09/06/15

FACULTY OF SCIENCE AND TECHNOLOGY OF UNAÍ

Faculdade de Ciências e Tecnologia de Unaí (FACTU)
Rua Rio Preto, No 422, Centro, Unaí, Minas Gerais 38610-000
Tel: +55(38) 3676-6222 +55(38) 3676-3490
Fax: +55(38) 3676-6222 +55(38) 3676-3490
EMail: factu@factu.br
Website: http://www.factu.br

Diretor Geral: Adalberto Lucas Capanema

Course
Accountancy (Accountancy); **Administration** (Administration); **Agronomy** (Agronomy); **Law** (Law); **Nursing** (Nursing); **Pedagogy** (Pedagogy); **Physical Education** (Physical Education)
History: Founded 1997.
Main Language(s) of Instruction: Portuguese
Degrees and Diplomas: *Bacharelado*; *Licenciatura*
Student Services: Library
Publications: FACTU Ciência; FACTU Jurídica
Last Updated: 09/06/15

FACULTY OF SCIENCE OF BAHIA

Faculdade de Ciências da Bahia (FACIBA)
Rua Direita da Piedade, 2 Barris, Piedade, Salvador, BA 40070-190
Tel: +55(71) 3321-0251 +55(71) 3011-0251
Fax: +55(71) 3321-0251 +55(71) 3011-0251
EMail: faciba@faciba.com.br; coordenacaoacademica@faciba.com.br
Website: http://www.faciba.com.br/

Diretor Presidente: Afonso Santana de Miranda

Course
Graduate Studies *(Stricto Sensu)* (Administration; Education); **Graduate Studies** *(Lato Sensu)* (Administration; Applied Linguistics; Business Administration; Development Studies; Educational Administration; Educational Psychology; Environmental Management; German; Higher Education; Management; Mathematics Education; Rehabilitation and Therapy; Special Education; Transport Management); **Philosophy**
History: Founded 2005.
Main Language(s) of Instruction: Portuguese
Accrediting Agency: Ministry of Education
Degrees and Diplomas: *Bacharelado*; *Especialização/Aperfeiçoamento*: **Higher Education; Special Education.** *Mestrado*: **Accountancy; Administration; Educational Sciences; Environmental Management; Law; Mathematics; Public Health.** Master and PhD delivered in cooperation with UNIVERSIDAD INTERAMERICANA, de Assunpção/Paraguay.
Last Updated: 26/10/15

FACULTY OF SCIENCE OF TIMBAÚBA

Faculdade de Ciências de Timbaúba (FACET)

Avenida Antonio Xavier de Morais, 05, Sapucaia, Timbaúba, PE 55870-000
Tel: +55(81) 3631-0752 +55(81) 97104-7505
Fax: +55(81) 3631-0752
EMail: facet@bol.com.br; faest@bol.com.br; luciatavaressousa@hotmail.com
Website: http://www.faculdadedetimbauba.edu.br

Director General: Luiz Rodrigues de Souza

Vice Director and Management Course Coordinator: Eric Tavares de Sousa

Course
Accountancy (Accountancy); **Administration** (Administration); **Auditing and Tax Planning** *(Post-graduate)* (Accountancy; Taxation); **Educational Psychology with emphasis in Teaching** *(Post-graduate)* (Educational Psychology); **Guidance and Educational Supervision** *(Post-graduate)* (Educational Administration; Educational and Student Counselling); **Inclusive Education** *(Post-graduate)* (Special Education); **Law** (Law); **MBA in Human Resources Management** *(Post-graduate)* (Human Resources); **Pedagogy** (Pedagogy)

Main Language(s) of Instruction: Portuguese

Degrees and Diplomas: *Bacharelado*: **Accountancy; Administration; Law.** *Licenciatura*: **Pedagogy.** *Especialização/Aperfeiçoamento*: **Accountancy; Educational Administration; Educational and Student Counselling; Educational Psychology; Educational Sciences; Taxation.** Also MBA in Human Resources

Student Services: IT Centre, Library

Last Updated: 08/06/15

FACULTY OF SCIENCE, EDUCATION AND THEOLOGY OF THE NORTH OF BRAZIL

Faculdade de Ciências, Educação e Teologia do Norte do Brasil (FACETEN)

Av. dos Bandeirantes, 900, B. Pricumã, Boa Vista, RR 69309-100
Tel: +55(95) 3625-5477
Fax: +55(95) 3625-5477
EMail: isef.faceten@gmail.com
Website: http://www.faceten.edu.br

Diretora: Rita de Cassia Duarte Sampaio

Course
Management (Management); **Pedagogy** (Pedagogy); **Theology** (Theology)

History: Founded 2000.

Fees: Graduate, 150 per month (Brazilian Real)

Main Language(s) of Instruction: Portuguese

Degrees and Diplomas: *Bacharelado*; *Licenciatura*; *Especialização/Aperfeiçoamento*: **Arts and Humanities; Educational Administration; Educational Psychology; Health Administration; Higher Education Teacher Training; Occupational Health; Special Education.**

Student Services: IT Centre, Library

Last Updated: 26/06/15

FACULTY OF SCIENCES OF TIMBAÚBA

Faculdade de Ciências de Timbaúba

Avenida Antonio Xavier de Morais, 05, Sapucaia, Timbaúba, PE 55870-000
Tel: +55(81) 3631-0752
Fax: +55(81) 3631-0752
EMail: faest@bol.com.br; luciatavaressousa@hotmail.com
Website: http://www.faculdadedetimbauba.edu.br

Diretor Geral: Luiz Rodrigues de Sousa

Vice Diretor e Coordenador do Curso de Administração: Érico Tavares de Sousa

Course
Accountancy (Accountancy); **Administration** (Administration); **Graduate Studies** (Educational and Student Counselling; Educational Psychology; Human Resources; Special Education; Taxation); **Law** (Law); **Pedagogy** (Pedagogy)

History: Founded 1997.

Main Language(s) of Instruction: Portuguese

Degrees and Diplomas: *Bacharelado*; *Licenciatura*; *Especialização/Aperfeiçoamento*: **Educational and Student Counselling; Educational Psychology; Special Education; Taxation.** Also MBA in Human Resources

Student Services: Library

Last Updated: 03/09/15

FACULTY OF SECOND OF JULY

Faculdade Dois de Julho (F2J)

Avenida Leovigildo Filgueiras, n° 81, Garcia, Salvador, Bahia 40100000
Tel: +55(71) 3114-3400
Fax: +55(71) 3114-3406
EMail: faculdade@f2j.edu.br
Website: http://f2j.edu.br

Baruch Portela: Marcos da Silva Mello

Diretora Acadêmica: Lêda Lessa Ribeiro

Course
Administration (Administration); **Advertising and Marketing** (Advertising and Publicity; Marketing); **Journalism** (Journalism); **Law** (Law); **Postgraduate Studies** (Advertising and Publicity; Communication Studies; Human Resources; Law; Management; Marketing; Sports Management; Transport Management)

History: Founded 2000.

Main Language(s) of Instruction: Portuguese

Degrees and Diplomas: *Bacharelado*; *Especialização/Aperfeiçoamento*: **Advertising and Publicity; Communication Studies; Human Resources; Law; Management; Marketing; Sports Management; Transport Management.**

Student Services: IT Centre, Library, eLibrary

Last Updated: 07/09/15

FACULTY OF SELVIRIA

Faculdade de Selviria (FAS)

Avenida Goiás 900, Centro, Selviria, MS 79590-000
Tel: +55(67) 8109-4248
Fax: +55(67) 8109-4248
EMail: fas.escritorio@terra.com.br; vadinei_kadochi@hotmail.com

Diretor Geral: Gentil Fernandes Marques (2006-)
EMail: gentil@fas.edu.br

Course
Administration (Administration); **Postgraduate Studies** (Administration; Adult Education; Aesthetics; Educational Psychology; Educational Sciences; Environmental Studies; Fine Arts; Food Science; Forestry; Geography; Gynaecology and Obstetrics; Higher Education Teacher Training; History; Human Resources; Management; Mathematics; Neurosciences; Orthodontics; Primary Education; Psychoanalysis; Public Administration; Safety Engineering; Secondary Education; Social Work; Special Education; Transport and Communications); **Social Communication** (Mass Communication); **Tourism** (Tourism)

History: Founded 2000.

Main Language(s) of Instruction: Portuguese

Degrees and Diplomas: *Bacharelado*; *Especialização/Aperfeiçoamento*: **Administration; Adult Education; Aesthetics; Educational Psychology; Educational Sciences; Environmental Studies; Fine Arts; Food Science; Forestry; Geography (Human); Gynaecology and Obstetrics; Higher Education Teacher Training; History; Human Resources; Management; Mathematics; Neurosciences; Orthodontics; Primary Education; Psychoanalysis; Public Administration; Safety Engineering; Secondary Education; Social Work; Special Education; Transport and Communications.**

Last Updated: 18/08/15

FACULTY OF SOCIAL SCIENCES OF GUARANTÃ DO NORTE

Faculdade de Ciências Sociais de Guarantã do Norte (FCSGN)

Rua Jequitibá, 40, Aeroporto, Guarantã do Norte, MT 78520-000
Tel: +54(66) 3552-1965
Fax: +54(66) 3552-4327
EMail: fabiana_varanda@hotmail.com; diretoria@faculdadeuniflor.edu.br; fac.guaranta@gmail.com
Website: http://www.faculdadeuniflor.edu.br

Diretora Geral: Fabiana Varanda Jorge

Diretor Administrativo/Financeiro: Cassio Brizzi Trizzi

Course
Accounting (Accountancy); **Administration** (Business Administration); **Agribusiness** *(Technological)* (Agricultural Business); **Architecture and Urbanism** (Architecture and Planning); **Information Systems** (Information Technology); **Letters/Spanish** (Arts and Humanities; Spanish); **Nursing** (Nursing); **Pedagogy** (Pedagogy); **Pharmacy** (Pharmacy); **Postgraduate Studies** (Administration; Arts and Humanities; Business Administration; Education; Educational Sciences; Finance; Management; Natural Sciences; Psychology; Teacher Training; Transport and Communications); **Psychology** (Psychology)
History: Founded 1999.
Main Language(s) of Instruction: Portuguese
Degrees and Diplomas: *Tecnólogo*; *Bacharelado*; *Licenciatura*; *Especialização/Aperfeiçoamento*: **Accountancy; Arts and Humanities; Clinical Psychology; Distance Education; Educational Administration; Educational Psychology; Finance; Higher Education Teacher Training; Human Resources; Industrial Management; Literacy Education; Management; Natural Sciences; Preschool Education; Public Administration; Special Education; Taxation; Transport Management.** Also MBA
Student Services: Library
Last Updated: 27/11/15

FACULTY OF SOCIAL SERVICES OF SÃO CAETANO DO SUL

Faculdade Paulista de Serviço Social de São Caetano do Sul (FAPSS-SCS)

R. João Pessoa, 223 - Centro,
São Caetano do Sul, São Paulo 9571200
Tel: +55(11) 4238-6922
EMail: contato@fapss.net
Website: http://fapss.net

Diretor: Danilo Vieiro

Course
Health Sciences (Health Sciences); **Pedagogy** (Pedagogy); **Social Services** (Social Work)
History: Founded 1966.
Main Language(s) of Instruction: Portuguese
Degrees and Diplomas: *Bacharelado*; *Especialização/Aperfeiçoamento*
Student Services: Library
Last Updated: 03/06/15

FACULTY OF SOCIAL SERVICES OF SAO PAULO

Faculdade Paulista de Serviço Social (FAPSS-SP)

Rua Lopes Chaves 273 275 Barra Funda,
São Paulo, São Paulo 01154010
Tel: +55(11) 3666-0246
Fax: +55(11) 3826-1925
EMail: fapss@fapss.br
Website: http://www.fapss.br

Diretor: Heliton Betetto

Course
Social Services (Social Work)
History: Founded 1940.
Main Language(s) of Instruction: Portuguese
Degrees and Diplomas: *Bacharelado*; *Especialização/Aperfeiçoamento*
Student Services: Library
Last Updated: 03/06/15

FACULTY OF SUSTAINABLE DEVELOPMENT OF CRUZEIRO DO SUL - IEVAL

Faculdade de Desenvolvimento Sustentável de Cruzeiro do Sul - IEVAL

Rodovia BR 307, Km 9 - Bairro Boca da Alemanha - Caixa Postal 66, Cruzeiro do Sul, AC 69980-000
Tel: +55(68) 3311-1500
EMail: ieval@avec.br; veiga.jaime3@gmail.com; secretaria.ieval@gmail.com
Website: http://reges.com.br/ieval

Diretor: João Maria Fagundes Weiber

Course
Accountancy (Accountancy); **Administration** (Administration)
History: Founded 2002.
Main Language(s) of Instruction: Portuguese
Degrees and Diplomas: *Bacharelado*; *Especialização/Aperfeiçoamento*: **Accountancy; Finance.**
Student Services: Library
Last Updated: 26/06/15

FACULTY OF TECHNOLOGY AND SCIENCES OF PERNAMBUCO

Faculdade de Tecnologia e Ciências de Pernambuco (FATEC)

Rua do Progresso 441, Soledade, Recife,
PE 50070-020
Tel: +55(81) 3445-5055
Fax: +55(81) 3445-5688
EMail: fatec@fatecpe.com.br
Website: http://www.fatecpe.com.br

Course
Computer Science (Computer Science); **Graduate Studies** (Educational Administration; Educational Psychology; Environmental Studies; Human Resources; Humanities and Social Science Education; Mathematics Education; Native Language Education; Science Education; Special Education)
History: Founded 2001.
Main Language(s) of Instruction: Portuguese
Degrees and Diplomas: *Bacharelado*; *Especialização/Aperfeiçoamento*: **Educational Administration; Educational Psychology; Environmental Studies; Human Resources; Humanities and Social Science Education; Mathematics Education; Music Education; Science Education; Special Education.**
Last Updated: 09/07/15

FACULTY OF TECHNOLOGY OF ALAGOAS

Faculdade de Tecnologia de Alagoas (FAT)

Av. Presidente Roosevelt, 1200, Serraria, Maceió,
AL 57045-150
Tel: +55(82) 3328-7000 +55(82) 3311-5620
Website: http://www.fat-al.edu.br

Diretora Ensino: Maria de Fátima da Costa Lippo Acioli

Gerente Administrativa: Ângela Barbosa Duarte

Course
Administration (Administration); **Architecture and Urbanism** (Architecture; Town Planning); **Civil Engineering** (Civil Engineering); **Law** (Law); **Nursing** (Nursing); **Odontology** (Dentistry); **Posgraduate Studies** (Advertising and Publicity; Civil Law; Earth Sciences; Engineering Management; Environmental Management; Finance; Food Science; Gerontology; Human Resources; Labour Law; Marketing; Safety Engineering; Systems Analysis; Tourism; Transport Management); **Production Engineering** (Production Engineering); **Psychology** (Psychology); **Social Services** (Social and Community Services)

Further Information: Also Antares Unit

History: Founded 2002 as Centro de Educação Tecnológica de Alagoas – CET/AL. Acquired present status and title 2004.

Main Language(s) of Instruction: Portuguese

Degrees and Diplomas: *Tecnólogo*; *Bacharelado*; *Especialização/Aperfeiçoamento*: **Civil Law; Environmental Engineering; Gerontology; Labour Law; Marketing; Safety Engineering; Transport Management.** Also MBA in Business and Commerce, Management, Transport Management, Finance and Environmental Management

Student Services: Library

Last Updated: 19/08/15

FACULTY OF TECHNOLOGY OF GUARATINGUETÁ

Faculdade de Tecnologia de Guaratinguetá (FATEC)

Av. Prof. João Rodrigues Alckmin, 1501, Jd. Esperança,
Guaratinguetá, SP 12517-475
Tel: +55(12) 3126-2643 +55(12) 3125-6905
Fax: +55(12) 3532-5110 +55(12) 3126-3921
EMail: secretaria@fatecguaratingueta.edu.br; fatecgt@uol.com.br
Website: http://www.fatecguaratingueta.edu.br

Diretor: José Manoel Souza das Neves
EMail: diretoria@fatecguaratingueta.edu.br

Diretora de Serviços Administrativos: Karen Cristina de Carvalho Nunes de Lima EMail: adm@fatecguaratingueta.edu.br

Course

Graduate Studies (Management); **Undergraduate Studies** (Business Administration; Finance; Information Technology; Management; Systems Analysis; Transport Management)

History: Founded 1994.

Main Language(s) of Instruction: Portuguese

Degrees and Diplomas: *Tecnólogo*; *Especialização/Aperfeiçoamento*: **Management.** Also Postgraduate Diploma.

Student Services: Library, eLibrary

Last Updated: 19/08/15

FACULTY OF TECHNOLOGY OF OURINHOS

Faculdade de Tecnologia de Ourinhos (FATEC)

Avenida Vitalina Marcusso 1400, Campus Universitário,
Ourinhos, São Paulo 19900000
Tel: +55(14) 3326-3031
Fax: +55(14) 3326-3031
EMail: dir.fatecourinhos@centropaulasouza.sp.gov.br
Website: http://www.centropaulasouza.sp.gov.br/Fatec/Escolas/Ourinhos.html

Diretor: Lia Cupertino Duarte Albino

Course

Agricultural Business (Agricultural Business); **Data Processing** (Data Processing); **Systems Analysis and Information Technology**

History: Founded 1991. Acquired present status 1997.

Main Language(s) of Instruction: Portuguese

Degrees and Diplomas: *Tecnólogo*

Last Updated: 18/04/16

FACULTY OF THE CITY OF COROMANDEL

Faculdade Cidade de Coromandel (FCC)

Avenida Adolfo Timóteo da Silva 433, Brasil Novo,
Coromandel, Minas Gerais 385500-000
Tel: +55(34) 3841-3405
Fax: +55(34) 3841-3405
EMail: fcc@fcc.edu.br
Website: http://www.fcc.edu.br

Diretor: Paulo César de Souza

Diretor Acadêmica: Estanislan Gonçalves Jovtei

Course

Administration (Administration; Business Administration); **Agricultural Engineering** (Agricultural Engineering); **Modern Languages** (English; Literature; Portuguese); **Nursing** (Nursing); **Pedagogy** (Pedagogy); **Physical Education** (Physical Education); **Systems Analysis** (Systems Analysis); **Veterinary Science** (Veterinary Science)

Further Information: Also Undidade II at Av. Dr. Humberto Machado, 216 Centro - Coromandel-MG

History: Founded 2000.

Main Language(s) of Instruction: Portuguese

Accrediting Agency: Ministry of Education

Degrees and Diplomas: *Bacharelado*; *Licenciatura*; *Especialização/Aperfeiçoamento*: **Agricultural Business; Business Administration; Educational and Student Counselling; Educational Psychology; Finance; Human Resources; Literacy Education; Marketing; Nursing; Physical Education; Primary Education; Public Health; Special Education.**

Student Services: Library

Last Updated: 14/10/15

FACULTY OF THE CITY OF JOÃO PINHEIRO

Faculdade Cidade de João Pinheiro (FCJP)

Av. Zico Dornelas, 380, Santa Cruz II,
João Pinheiro, MG 38770-000
Tel: +55(38) 3561-3900
EMail: direcao.projetos@fcjp.edu.br
Website: http://www.fcjp.edu.br

Diretor: Paulo Cesar de Sousa

Course

Administration (Administration; Business Administration); **Biomedicine** (Biomedicine); **Education** (Biology; Chemistry; Geography; History; Literature; Mathematics; Pedagogy; Physical Education); **Nursing** (Nursing); **Physical Therapy** (Physical Therapy)

History: Founded 2002.

Main Language(s) of Instruction: Portuguese

Accrediting Agency: Ministry of Education

Degrees and Diplomas: *Bacharelado*; *Licenciatura*; *Especialização/Aperfeiçoamento*: **Business Administration; Environmental Studies; Higher Education; Human Resources; Literacy Education; Marketing; Nursing; Physical Education; Public Administration; Public Health.**

Student Services: Library

Last Updated: 14/10/15

FACULTY OF THE CITY OF MACEIÓ

Faculdade da Cidade de Maceió (FACIMA)

Av. Durval de Góes Monteiro, 4,354, Tabuleiro dos Martins,
Maceió, AL
Tel: +55(82) 3214-2800 +55(82) 3223-0033
EMail: marcioacbarros@yahoo.com.br
Website: http://www.facima.edu.br

Diretora Geral: Ana Paula Nunes da Silva

Course

Accounting (Accountancy); **Administration** (Business Administration); **Computer Science** (Computer Science); **Law** (Law); **Nursing** (Nursing); **Pedagogy** (Pedagogy); **Physiotherapy** (Physical Education); **Postgraduate Studies** (Business and Commerce; Education; Health Sciences; Law; Mass Communication); **Production Engineering** (Production Engineering); **Social Communication, Publicity and Advertising** (Advertising and Publicity; Mass Communication); **Technological Studies** (Cosmetology; Transport Management); **Tourism** (Tourism)

History: Founded 2002 as Instituto Maceió de Ensino e Cultura. Acquired current name 2010.

Main Language(s) of Instruction: Portuguese

Degrees and Diplomas: *Tecnólogo*; *Bacharelado*; *Licenciatura*; *Especialização/Aperfeiçoamento*: **Educational Psychology; Health Administration; Law; Public Health.** Also MBA in Human Resources, Management, Finance, Banking, Business Administration, Transport Management; Master in Business Communication (MBC) in Communication Studies and Media Studies.

Student Services: IT Centre, Library, eLibrary

Last Updated: 26/11/15

FACULTY OF THE CITY OF PATOS DE MINAS

Faculdade Cidade de Patos de Minas (FPM)

Rua Major Gote 1408, Centro, Patos de Minas, MG 38700-000

Tel: +55(34) 3818-2300

EMail: direcao.projetos@faculdadepatosdeminas.com

Website: http://faculdadepatosdeminas.edu.br/

Diretor: Paulo de Sousa

EMail: direcao.clinicas@faculdadepatosdeminas.edu.br

Course

Accountancy (Accountancy); **Administration** (Administration); **Biology** (Biology); **Biomedicine** (Biomedicine); **Chemistry** (Chemistry); **Civil Engineering** (Civil Engineering); **Dentistry** (Dentistry); **Electrical Engineering** (Electrical Engineering); **Gastronomy** (Cooking and Catering); **Mathematics** (Mathematics); **Nursing** (Nursing); **Nutrition** (Nutrition); **Ondontology** (Dentistry); **Pedagogy** (Education; Pedagogy); **Pharmacy** (Pharmacy); **Physical Education** (Physical Education); **Physiotherapy** (Physical Therapy); **Producion Engineering** (Production Engineering); **Psychology** (Psychology); **Veterinary Science** (Veterinary Science)

History: Founded 2005.

Main Language(s) of Instruction: Portuguese

Accrediting Agency: Ministry of Education

Degrees and Diplomas: *Bacharelado*; *Licenciatura*; *Especialização/Aperfeiçoamento*: **Business Administration; Dentistry; Educational and Student Counselling; Educational Psychology; Environmental Studies; Finance; Higher Education Teacher Training; Human Resources; Marketing; Orthodontics; Pedagogy; Psychology; Public Health.**

Student Services: Library

Last Updated: 14/10/15

FACULTY OF THE CITY OF SANTA LUZIA

Faculdade da Cidade de Santa Luzia (FACSAL)

Avenida Beira Rio, 2000, Dist. Industrial III, Caixa Postal 3423, Santa Luzia, MG 33040-260

Tel: +55(31) 3079-9000

Fax: +55(31) 3079-9000

EMail: facsal@facsal.br

Website: http://www.facsal.br

Diretor: Raul Carlos de Mello

Course

Accountancy (Accountancy); **Administration** (Administration; Business Administration; Marketing); **Biological Sciences** (Biological and Life Sciences); **Information Systems** (Computer Networks; Computer Science); **Law** (Law); **Literature** (English; Portuguese); **Nursing** (Nursing); **Nutrition** (Nutrition); **Pedagogy** (Pedagogy); **Physical Education** (Physical Education); **Physiotherapy** (Physical Therapy); **Social Communication - Advertising and Publicity** (Advertising and Publicity); **Tourism** (Tourism)

History: Founded 2000.

Main Language(s) of Instruction: Portuguese

Degrees and Diplomas: *Tecnólogo*; *Bacharelado*; *Licenciatura*

Student Services: Library

Last Updated: 15/10/15

FACULTY OF THE CULTURAL UNION OF SÃO PAULO STATE

Faculdade União Cultural do Estado de São Paulo (UCESP)

Rodov. Caran Rezek, Km 1.35, Araçatuba, SP 16078-035

Tel: +55(18) 3622-6654

Fax: +55(18) 3622-6654

EMail: secretaria@ucesp.edu.br

Website: http://www.ucesp.edu.br

Diretor Geral: Valmir Leonardo dos Santos

Course

Administration (Administration); **Pedagogy** (Pedagogy); **Theology** (Theology)

Main Language(s) of Instruction: Portuguese

Degrees and Diplomas: *Bacharelado*; *Licenciatura*

Last Updated: 15/04/16

FACULTY OF THE EDUCATIONAL FOUNDATION OF ARAÇATUBA

Faculdade da Fundação Educacional Araçatuba (FAC-FEA)

Rua Maurício de Nassau, 1191, Santana, Araçatuba, São Paulo 16050-480

Tel: +55(18) 3622-8262

EMail: facfea.mantenedora@terra.com.br

Website: http://www.feata.edu.br/

Diretora Executiva: Carmen Sílvia de Oliveira Santana Casteletto

Tel: +55(18) 3622-8262 EMail: facfea.diretor@terra.com.br

Course

Administration (Administration); **Biological Sciences** (Biological and Life Sciences); **Economics** (Economics); **Graduate Studies** *(Lato sensu)* (Educational Psychology; Psychoanalysis; Public Administration; Special Education); **Mathematics** (Mathematics); **Pedagogy** (Education; Pedagogy); **Psychology** (Psychology)

History: Founded 1989.

Main Language(s) of Instruction: Portuguese

Accrediting Agency: Ministry of Education

Degrees and Diplomas: *Bacharelado*; *Licenciatura*; *Especialização/Aperfeiçoamento*: **Educational Psychology; Psychoanalysis; Psychology; Public Administration; Special Education.**

Student Services: Library

Last Updated: 15/10/15

FACULTY OF THE IMMIGRANTS

Faculdade dos Imigrantes (FAI)

Rua Sinimbu, 1670, Centro, Caxias do Sul, RS 95020-001

Tel: +55(54) 3028-7007

EMail: marco@portalfai.com; regacademico@portalfai.com

Website: http://www.portalfai.com

Diretor Geral: Mauro Trojan

Course

Accounting (Accountancy); **Administration** (Business Administration); **Design** (Design); **Interior Design** (Interior Design)

History: Founded 2002.

Main Language(s) of Instruction: Portuguese

Degrees and Diplomas: *Bacharelado*

Last Updated: 03/12/15

FACULTY OF THE INTEGRATED CENTRES FOR TEACHING, LEARNING AND SOCIAL SERVICES OF UBERLÂNDIA

Faculdade Uberlandense de Núcleos Integrados de Ensino, Serviço Social e Aprendizagem (FAESSA)

Rua Bocaiúva, 82, Morada da Colina, Uberlândia, MG 38411-126
Tel: +55(34) 3254-1213
Fax: +55(34) 3237-9827
EMail: leticia@uniessa.com.br
Website: http://uniessa.com.br

Diretor: José Tadeu Silva

Course
Administration (Administration); **Design** (Design); **Financial Management** (Finance); **Human Resource Management** (Human Resources); **Logistics** (Transport Management); **Marketing** (Marketing)

Main Language(s) of Instruction: Portuguese
Degrees and Diplomas: *Tecnólogo*; *Bacharelado*
Last Updated: 15/04/16

FACULTY OF THE INTERIOR OF THE STATE OF SAO PAULO

Faculdade do Interior Paulista (FIP)

Rua João Gerin, 275, Barra Bonita, São Paulo 17340-000
Tel: +55(14) 3604-1200
Fax: +55(14) 3604-1200
EMail: secretariafunbbe@bol.com.br; coordenacaogeral@funbbe.br
Website: http://www.funbbe.br/v2/fip

Course
Business Administration (Business Administration); **Human Resources** *(Postgraduate)* (Human Resources)

History: Founded 2001.
Main Language(s) of Instruction: Portuguese
Degrees and Diplomas: *Bacharelado*: **Business Administration.** *Especialização/Aperfeiçoamento*: **Human Resources.**
Last Updated: 07/09/15

FACULTY OF THE LAKES REGION

Faculdade da Região dos Lagos (FERLAGOS)

Avenida Júlia Kubitschek, 80, Jardim Flamboyant, Cabo Frio, Rio de Janeiro 28905-000
Tel: +55(24) 2645-6100
Fax: +55(24) 2643-0485
EMail: secretaria@ferlagos.br
Website: http://www.ferlagos.br

Presidente: Andrea Maria Ferreira de Oliveira
EMail: direcao@ferlagos.br

Course
Graduate Studies (Accountancy; Administration; Art Education; Biological and Life Sciences; Business Administration; Cultural Studies; Educational Administration; Educational Psychology; English; Environmental Management; Finance; Geography; History; Human Resources; Literacy Education; Marketing; Mathematics; Mathematics Education; Physical Education; Portuguese; Rehabilitation and Therapy; Translation and Interpretation)

History: Founded 1979.
Main Language(s) of Instruction: Portuguese
Degrees and Diplomas: *Bacharelado*; *Licenciatura*; *Especialização/Aperfeiçoamento*: **Accountancy; Business Administration; Education; Educational and Student Counselling; Educational Psychology; Environmental Studies; Finance; Health Sciences; Human Resources; Marine Biology; Mathematics; Portuguese; Public Administration; Transport Management.**
Student Services: Library
Last Updated: 15/10/15

FACULTY OF THE MUNDIAL FOUNDATION

Faculdade Mundial

Avenida Paulista, 2.200 – 12° andar, São Paulo, SP 01310-300
Tel: (11) 3266-5944
EMail: atendimento@faculdademundial.com.br
Website: http://www.faculdademundial.com.br

Diretor: José Abrão

Course
Administration (Administration; Business Administration); **Advertising** (Advertising and Publicity); **Public Relations** (Public Relations); **Radio, Television and Internet** (Computer Science; Radio and Television Broadcasting)

History: Founded 2009.
Main Language(s) of Instruction: Portuguese
Degrees and Diplomas: *Bacharelado*; *Especialização/Aperfeiçoamento*
Last Updated: 29/05/15

FACULTY OF THE NAUTICAL CLUB OF MOGI DAS CRUZES

Faculdade do Clube Náutico Mogiano (FCNM)

Rua Cabo Diogo Oliver, 758, Mogilar, Mogi das Cruzes, São Paulo 8773000
Tel: +55(11) 4791-7100
EMail: nautico@nautico.edu.br; secretaria@nautico.edu.br
Website: http://www.nautico.edu.br

Diretor: Marcos Paulo Tavares Furlan

Course
Exercice Physiology and Sports Training *(Posgraduate)* (Physiology; Sports); **Physical Education** (Physical Education); **Physical Therapy** (Physical Therapy)

History: Founded 1972.
Main Language(s) of Instruction: Portuguese
Degrees and Diplomas: *Bacharelado*; *Licenciatura*; *Especialização/Aperfeiçoamento*: **Physiology; Sports.**
Student Services: Library
Last Updated: 07/09/15

FACULTY OF THE NORTE NOVO REGION OF APUCARANA

Faculdade do Norte Novo de Apucarana (FACNOPAR)

Av. Zilda Seixas do Amaral, 4350, Pq. Industrial Norte, Apucarana, PR 86806-380
Tel: +55(43) 3420-1700
EMail: facnopar@facnopar.com.br
Website: http://www.facnopar.com.br

Diretor: Danilo Lemos Freire
Secretaria Acadêmica: Josiane Cristina de Sousa
EMail: secretariacademica@facnopar.com.br

Course
Accountancy (Accountancy); **Administration** (Administration); **Agricultural Business** (Agricultural Business); **Human Resources Management** (Human Resources); **Interior Design** (Interior Design); **Law** (Law); **Marketing** (Marketing); **Postgraduate Studies** (Business Administration; Criminology; Labour Law; Management; Occupational Health)

History: Founded 2001.
Main Language(s) of Instruction: Portuguese
Degrees and Diplomas: *Bacharelado*; *Licenciatura*; *Especialização/Aperfeiçoamento*: **Criminology; Labour Law; Occupational Health.** Also MBA in Business Administration, Management
Student Services: Canteen, Library
Last Updated: 07/09/15

FACULTY OF THE PEOPLE

Faculdade do Povo (FAPSP)

Rua Barão de Itapetininga, 163, Edifício Louzã, 1° andar, República, São Paulo, SP 01042-910
Tel: +55(11) 3355-4040
EMail: atendimento@fapsp.com.br
Website: http://www.fapsp.com.br

Diretor: Eber Cocareli
Diretor Acadêmico: Miguel Valione Junior

Course
Advertising and Publicity (Advertising and Publicity); **Journalism** (Journalism); **Organisational Communication** *(Postgraduate)* (Communication Studies); **Radio, TV and Internet** (Information Technology; Radio and Television Broadcasting)
History: Founded 2009.
Main Language(s) of Instruction: Portuguese
Degrees and Diplomas: *Bacharelado*. Also MBA in Communication Studies
Student Services: Library
Last Updated: 07/09/15

FACULTY OF THE SOUTH OF BAHIA

Faculdade do Sul da Bahia (FASB)
Rua Sagrada Família, 120, Bela Vista,
Teixeira de Freitas, BA 45995000
Tel: +55(73) 3011-7000
EMail: ffassis@ffassis.edu.br; sec@ffassis.edu.br
Website: http://www.ffassis.edu.br

Diretora: Lay Alves Ribeiro
Diretora Administrativa: Vera Lúcia Pegoretti Motta

Course
Accountancy (Accountancy); **Administration** (Administration); **Agricultural Business** (Agricultural Business); **Automation and Control Engineering** (Automation and Control Engineering); **Biomedicine** (Biomedicine); **Civil Engineering** (Civil Engineering); **Human Resource Management** (Human Resources); **Journalism** (Journalism); **Law** (Law); **Marketing** (Marketing); **Nursing** (Nursing); **Pedagogy** (Pedagogy); **Petroleum and Gas Engineering** (Petroleum and Gas Engineering); **Postgraduate Studies** (Accountancy; Business Administration; Civil Law; Criminal Law; Educational Administration; Educational Psychology; Energy Engineering; Finance; Gynaecology and Obstetrics; Health Sciences; Higher Education Teacher Training; Human Resources; Labour Law; Literature; Management; Nursing; Occupational Health; Petroleum and Gas Engineering; Primary Education; Public Administration; Safety Engineering; Toxicology; Transport Management); **Production Engineering** (Production Engineering); **Systems Analysis and Development** (Systems Analysis); **Tourism** (Tourism)
History: Founded 2001.
Main Language(s) of Instruction: Portuguese
Degrees and Diplomas: *Tecnólogo*; *Bacharelado*; *Licenciatura*; *Especialização/Aperfeiçoamento*: **Civil Law; Criminal Law; Educational Administration; Educational Psychology; Gynaecology and Obstetrics; Health Sciences; Higher Education Teacher Training; Labour Law; Literature; Nursing; Occupational Health; Primary Education; Safety Engineering; Toxicology.** Also MBA in Management and Energy Engineering, Petroleum and Gas Engineering, Business Administration and Human Resources, Finance, Accountancy, Transport Management, Public Administration.
Student Services: IT Centre, Library
Last Updated: 07/09/15

FACULTY OF THE SOUTHEAST OF MINAS GERAIS

Faculdade do Sudeste Mineiro (FACSUM)
Av. Presidente Itamar Franco, 3,180, São Mateus, Juiz de Fora, MG
Tel: +55(32) 2104-9090 +55(32) 4009-7000
EMail: marcioacbarros@yahoo.com.br
Website: http://www.suafaculdade.com.br/facsum

Diretor: Jussara Barbosa de Rezende Martins
Coordenador Geral: Edina Maria de Oliveira

Course
Accounting (Accountancy); **Administration** (Business Administration); **Architecture and Urbanism** (Architecture; Town Planning); **Law** (Law); **Nursing** (Nursing); **Pedagogy** (Pedagogy); **Pharmacy** (Pharmacy); **Physical Education** (Physical Education); **Postgraduate Studies** (Accountancy; Business Administration; Criminal Law; Educational Psychology; Engineering Management; Finance; Human Resources; International Business; Management; Marketing); **Production Engineering** (Production Engineering); **Social Communication, Publicity and Advertising** (Advertising and Publicity; Mass Communication); **Technological Studies** (Cosmetology; Human Resources; International Business; Marketing; Transport Management); **Tourism** (Tourism)
Main Language(s) of Instruction: Portuguese
Degrees and Diplomas: *Tecnólogo*; *Bacharelado*; *Licenciatura*; *Especialização/Aperfeiçoamento*: **Criminal Law; Educational Psychology.** Also MBA; Distance Mode Undergraduate and Postgraduate Degree Programmes offered through Universidade Paulista (UNIP)
Student Services: Library
Last Updated: 16/12/15

FACULTY OF THE STATE OF MARANHÃO

Faculdade do Estado do Maranhão (FACEM)
Alameda D, 5 - Loteamento Quitandinha, Alto do Calhau,
São Luís, MA 65071-680
Tel: +55(98) 3236-8081 +55(98) 3236-8556
EMail: marcioacbarros@yahoo.com.br
Website: http://www.suafaculdade.com.br/facem

Diretora Geral: Regina Célia Bitencourt Reis Pinho
Coordenação Geral: Lyana Péres Pereira

Course
Accounting (Accountancy); **Administration** (Business Administration); **Law** (Law); **Mathematics** (Mathematics); **Social Communication, Publicity and Advertising** (Advertising and Publicity; Mass Communication); **Technological Studies** (Business and Commerce; Health Administration; Human Resources; International Business; Management; Marketing; Tourism); **Tourism** (Tourism)
History: Founded 2003.
Main Language(s) of Instruction: Portuguese
Degrees and Diplomas: *Tecnólogo*; *Bacharelado*; *Licenciatura*. Also Distance Mode Postgraduate Degree Programmes offered through Universidade Paulista
Student Services: Library, eLibrary
Last Updated: 15/12/15

FACULTY OF THE UNION OF GOYAZES

Faculdade União de Goyazes (FUG)
Rodovia Go-060 Km 19, 3184, Setor Laguna Parque,
Trindade, GO 75380-000
Tel: +55(62) 3506-9300
EMail: secretaria@fug.edu.br
Website: http://www.fug.edu.br

Diretor Geral: Carlos Augusto de Oliveira Botelho

Course
Graduate Studies (Sports); **Undergraduate Studies** (Biological and Life Sciences; Biomedicine; Nursing; Nutrition; Occupational Therapy; Pharmacy; Physical Education; Physical Therapy)
Main Language(s) of Instruction: Portuguese
Degrees and Diplomas: *Bacharelado*; *Licenciatura*; *Especialização/Aperfeiçoamento*
Last Updated: 03/07/15

FACULTY OF TRÊS DE MAIO

Faculdade Três de Maio (SETREM)
Avenida Santa Rosa 2405, Centro, Três de Maio,
RS 98910000
Tel: +55(55) 3535-4600
Fax: +55(55) 3535-4682
EMail: faculdade@setrem.com.br
Website: http://www.setrem.com.br

Diretor Geral: Flavio Magedanz

Course
Administration (Administration; Finance; Marketing); **Agronomy** (Agricultural Engineering; Agronomy); **Computer Networks** (Computer Networks); **Fashion Design** (Fashion Design); **Information**

Systems (Information Management; Information Technology); **Nursing** (Nursing); **Pedagogy** (Education; Educational Administration; Pedagogy); **Production Engineering** (Production Engineering); **Psychology** (Psychology)

History: Founded 1976. Acquired present status 1999.

Main Language(s) of Instruction: Portuguese

Degrees and Diplomas: *Bacharelado*; *Licenciatura*; *Especialização/Aperfeiçoamento*

Last Updated: 02/07/15

FACULTY OF TRÊS PONTAS

Faculdade de Três Pontas (FATEP)

Praça D'Aparecida, 57, Centro, Três Pontas, MG 37190-000

Tel: +55(35) 3266-2020

Fax: +55(35) 3266-2020

EMail: comunicacao@unis.edu.br; p.institucional@unis.edu.br; marcelof@unis.edu.br

Website: http://fateps.unis.edu.br

Diretor: Evandro Santos

Course

Administration (Administration); **Law** (Law); **Pedagogy** (Pedagogy); **Postgraduate Studies** (Banking; Finance; Public Law)

History: Founded 2002.

Main Language(s) of Instruction: Portuguese

Degrees and Diplomas: *Bacharelado*; *Licenciatura*; *Especialização/Aperfeiçoamento*: **Public Law.** Also MBA

Last Updated: 15/04/16

FACULTY OF TUPI PAULISTA

Faculdade de Tupi Paulista

Rua Arcebispo Lemieux, 250, Tupi Paulista, SP 17930-000

Tel: +55(18) 3851-1310 +55(18) 3851-336

EMail: secretaria.cestupi@abcrede.com.br; reges.denis@gmail.com

Website: http://tupipaulista.reges.com.br

Diretor: Antonio Luiz Pioltine

Course

Administration (Administration; Environmental Management); **Graduate Studies** (Clinical Psychology; Educational Psychology); **Pedagogy** (Pedagogy)

History: Founded 2002.

Fees: 220 per month for graduate programme (Brazilian Real)

Main Language(s) of Instruction: Portuguese

Degrees and Diplomas: *Bacharelado*; *Licenciatura*; *Especialização/Aperfeiçoamento*: **Clinical Psychology; Educational Psychology.**

Student Services: Library

Last Updated: 03/09/15

FACULTY OF VITÓRIA

Faculdade de Vitória (UVV VITÓRIA)

Rua Coração de Maria 315, Praia do Canto, Vitória, Espirito Santo 29055-770

Tel: +55(27) 3421-2251

Fax: +55(27) 3421-2251

EMail: uvv@uvv.br

Diretor Geral: Giulianno de Oliveira Bresciani

Course

Administration (Administration)

History: Founded 2001.

Main Language(s) of Instruction: Portuguese

Degrees and Diplomas: *Bacharelado*

Last Updated: 04/09/15

FAE FACULTY OF BLUMENAU

Faculdade FAE Blumenau

Rua Santo Antônio s/n, Centro, Blumenau, SC 89010-110

Tel: +55(47) 2102-3500

Fax: +55(47) 2102-3500

EMail: dlne@fae.edu

Website: http://www.fae.edu/unidades/index/66591082/blumenau.htm

Diretor: Celso Magalhães

Course

Administration (Business Administration); **Postgraduate Studies** (Business Administration; Management)

History: Founded 2004.

Fees: Undergraduate, 776 per month (Brazilian Real)

Main Language(s) of Instruction: Portuguese

Degrees and Diplomas: *Bacharelado*. Also MBA

Student Services: Library

Last Updated: 30/11/15

FAE FACULTY OF SÃO JOSÉ DOS PINHAIS

Faculdade FAE São José dos Pinhais

Rua Paulino Siqueira Cortes, 1450, Centro, São José dos Pinhais, PR 83005-030

Tel: +55(41) 2117-9800

Fax: +55(41) 2117-9824

EMail: dlne@fae.edu

Website: http://www.fae.edu

Diretor: Élcio Douglas Joaquim

Course

Administration (Business Administration); **Law** (Law); **Postgraduate Studies** (Business and Commerce; Commercial Law; Management); **Software Engineering** *(Technological Studies)* (Software Engineering)

History: Founded 2009.

Main Language(s) of Instruction: Portuguese

Degrees and Diplomas: *Tecnólogo*; *Bacharelado*; *Especialização/Aperfeiçoamento*: **Business and Commerce; Commercial Law; Management.**

Student Services: Library

Last Updated: 03/12/15

FAE FACULTY OF SÉVIGNÉ PORTO ALEGRE

Faculdade FAE Sévigné Porto Alegre

Rua Duque de Caxias, 1475, Centro, Porto Alegre, RS 90010-283

Tel: +55(51) 3340-7888

Fax: +55(51) 3340-2568

EMail: marisa@saojudastadeu.com.br

Website: http://www.saojudastadeu.com.br

Course

Administration (Business Administration); **Financial Management** (Finance); **Human Resources Management** (Human Resources); **Pedagogy** (Pedagogy); **Systems Analysis and Development** (Systems Analysis)

Main Language(s) of Instruction: Portuguese

Degrees and Diplomas: *Tecnólogo*; *Bacharelado*; *Licenciatura*

Last Updated: 01/12/15

FAI - HIGHER EDUCATION CENTRE IN MANAGEMENT TECHNOLOGY AND EDUCATION

FAI - Centro de Ensino Superior em Gestão, Tecnologia e Educação (FAI)

Avenida Antônio de Cássia, 472, Jardim Santo Antônio, Santa Rita do Sapucai, Minas Gerais 37540-000

Tel: +55(35) 3473-3000

EMail: fai@fai-mg.br

Website: http://www.fai-mg.br

Presidente: Benedito Ramon Pinto Ferreira

Course
Accountancy (Accountancy); **Administration** (Administration); **Information Systems** (Information Technology); **Pedagogy** (Education; Pedagogy); **Production Engineering** (Production Engineering)

History: Founded 1971 as Faculdade de Administração e Informática.

Main Language(s) of Instruction: Portuguese

Degrees and Diplomas: *Bacharelado*; *Licenciatura*; *Especialização/Aperfeiçoamento*: **Business Administration; Education; Educational Administration; Educational and Student Counselling; Educational Psychology; Finance; Higher Education; Human Resources; Information Technology; Marketing; Special Education.**

Student Services: Library
Last Updated: 19/10/15

FAMA FACULTY OF TECHNOLOGY

Faculdade de Tecnologia FAMA (FAMA)
Rua Benfica, 126, Madalena, Recife, PE 50720-001
Tel: +55(81) 3227-0982 +55(81) 3081-0596
Fax: +55(81) 3227-0982
EMail: secretaria.geral@escolademarketing.com.br; acml1416@gmail.com
Website: http://www.escolademarketing.com.br

President/Diretor Geral: José Lavanère das Chagas Lemos

Diretora Acadêmica: Ana Carla Martins Lemos
EMail: diretoria.academica@escolademarketing.com.br

Course
Administration (Administration); **Commercial Management** (Business and Commerce; Management); **Human Resources** *(Executive MBA)* (Human Resources); **Logistics** (Transport Management)

Main Language(s) of Instruction: Portuguese

Degrees and Diplomas: *Tecnólogo*. Also Executive MBA in Human Resources

Student Services: IT Centre, Library
Last Updated: 31/08/15

FATEC - SENAI FACULTY OF TECHNOLOGY

FATEC - Faculdade Senai de Tecnologia (FATEC)
Avenida Marechal Mascarenhas de Morais, 2235, 29052-121, 29052-121
Tel: +55(27) 3334-5768
Fax: +55(27) 3334-5772
EMail: zteixeira@findes.org.br
Website: http://senai-es.org.br

Diretora Regional: Solange Maria Nunes Siqueira

Course
Automation and Control Engineering (Automation and Control Engineering); **Mechanical Engineering** (Mechanical Engineering)

History: Founded 2012.

Main Language(s) of Instruction: Portuguese

Degrees and Diplomas: *Bacharelado*
Last Updated: 15/04/16

FAYAL CENECIST INSTITUTE OF HIGHER EDUCATION

Instituto Cenecista Fayal de Ensino Superior (CNEC IFES)
Avenida Governador Adolfo Konder 2000, Bairro São Vicente, Itajaí, Santa Catarina 88308000
Tel: +55(47) 3248-2421
Fax: +55(47) 3248-2421
EMail: cnecifes@cnec.br
Website: http://faculdadeitajai.cnec.br

Diretor Geral: José Daniel Tavares

Course
Accountancy (Accountancy); **Administration** (Administration); **Advertising** (Advertising and Publicity); **Civil Engineering** (Civil Engineering); **Graphic Design** (Graphic Design); **Human Resources** (Human Resources); **Pedagogy** (Pedagogy); **Production Engineering** (Production Engineering); **Teacher Training** (Teacher Training); **Tourism** (Tourism)

History: Founded 2000. Became part of the CNEC (Campanha Nacional de Escolas da Comunidade) network since 2012.

Main Language(s) of Instruction: Portuguese

Degrees and Diplomas: *Bacharelado*; *Especialização/Aperfeiçoamento*

Student Services: Library
Last Updated: 29/03/16

FECAP UNIVERSITY CENTRE

Centro Universitário FECAP (FECAP)
Av. Liberdade, 532, Liberdade, São Paulo 01502-001
Tel: +55(11) 3272-2222 +55(11) 3272-2273
Fax: +55(11) 3272-2208
EMail: relacionamento@fecap.br
Website: http://www.fecap.br

Reitor: Edison Simoni EMail: reitoria@fecap.br

Course
Accountancy (Accountancy); **Administration** (Administration); **Advertising and Publicity** (Advertising and Publicity); **Economics** (Economics); **Executive Secretary** (Secretarial Studies); **Graduate Studies** *(Lato Sensu)* (Accountancy; Banking; Business Administration; Educational Administration; Finance; Human Resources; Marketing; Public Administration); **International Relations** (International Relations); **Public Relations** (Public Relations)

Further Information: Also Pinheiros and Largo São Francisco campuses

History: Founded 1902.

Main Language(s) of Instruction: Portuguese

Accrediting Agency: Ministry of Education.

Degrees and Diplomas: *Bacharelado*; *Especialização/Aperfeiçoamento*: **Accountancy; Business Administration; Constitutional Law; Human Resources; Law; Leadership; Management; Marketing.** *Mestrado*: **Accountancy; Administration; Business Administration.** Also MBA

Student Services: Library
Last Updated: 17/07/15

FEEVALE UNIVERSITY CENTRE

Centro Universitário Feevale (FEEVALE)
RS-239, 2755, Novo Hamburgo, Rio Grande do Sul 93525-075
Tel: +55(51) 3586-8800
Fax: +55(51) 3586-8836
EMail: feevale@feevale.br
Website: http://www.feevale.br

Reitora: Inajara Vargas Ramos EMail: reitoria@feevale.br

Pró-reitora de Ensino: Denise Ries Russo

International Relations: Paula Casari Cundari, Head, International Relations EMail: paulacc@feevale.br

Institute
Applied Social Sciences *(ICSA)* (Accountancy; Advertising and Publicity; Business Administration; Finance; Human Resources; Journalism; Law; Management; Protective Services; Public Relations; Social Sciences; Tourism); **Exact Sciences and Technology** *(ICET)* (Architecture; Chemical Engineering; Computer Science; Construction Engineering; Design; Electronic Engineering; Environmental Management; Farm Management; Industrial Engineering; Information Sciences; Mechanical Engineering; Production Engineering; Town Planning); **Health Sciences** *(ICS)* (Biology; Biomedicine; Cosmetology; Health Administration; Health Sciences; Nursing; Nutrition; Pharmacy; Physical Education; Physical Therapy); **Human Sciences, Letters and Arts** *(ICHLA)* (Art Education; Art Therapy; Arts and Humanities; Design; Educational Psychology; Graphic Design; History; Interior Design; Modern Languages; Pedagogy; Photography; Psychology; Teacher Training; Visual Arts)

Course
Graduate Studies *(Lato Sensu)* (Accountancy; Art Therapy; Business Administration; Communication Studies; Cosmetology;

Educational Psychology; Gerontology; Health Administration; Health Sciences; Literature; Marketing; Microbiology; Modern Languages; Music; Occupational Health; Philosophical Schools; Physical Education; Psychology; Safety Engineering; Sports; Toxicology; Visual Arts)

Further Information: Also Campus I at Av. Dr. Maurício Cardoso, 510. Distance Education

History: Founded 1970. Became Centro Universitário Feevale 1999. Acquired present status.

Academic Year: February-July; August-December

Fees: 249,45 per credit (Brazilian Real)

Main Language(s) of Instruction: Portuguese

Degrees and Diplomas: *Tecnólogo*; *Bacharelado*; *Licenciatura*; *Especialização/Aperfeiçoamento*: **Accountancy; Art Education; Biomedicine; Business Administration; Civil Law; Computer Networks; Cosmetology; Design; Electronic Engineering; Gerontology; Health Administration; Health Sciences; Human Resources; Literature; Music; Nursing; Occupational Therapy; Pedagogy; Production Engineering; Safety Engineering; Software Engineering; Toxicology; Visual Arts.** *Mestrado*: **Cultural Studies; Environmental Studies; Materials Engineering; Microbiology; Modern Languages; Social and Community Services.** *Doutorado*: **Cultural Studies; Environmental Studies.**

Student Services: Library

Publications: Jornal da Feevale

Publishing House: Editora Feevale

Last Updated: 07/09/15

FIA FACULTY OF ADMINISTRATION AND BUSINESS

Faculdade FIA de Administração e Negócios (FFIA)

R. José Alves Cunha Lima, 172, Vila Butantã,
São Paulo, SP 05360-050
Tel: +55(11) 3732-3515
Fax: +55(11) 3732-3501
EMail: diretoriafaculdade@fia.com.br
Website: http://www3.fia.com.br/ConhecaFIA/faculdadefia/Paginas/default.aspx

Diretor da Faculdade FIA: James Terence Coulter Wright
Tel: +55(11) 3818-4021 EMail: diretoriafia@fia.com.br

Course

Administration (Business Administration); **Postgraduate Studies** (Business Administration; Communication Studies; Data Processing; Information Technology; Service Trades; Transport Management)

History: Founded 2010.

Main Language(s) of Instruction: Portuguese

Degrees and Diplomas: *Bacharelado*; *Especialização/Aperfeiçoamento*: **Administration; Banking; Business Administration; Business and Commerce; Communication Studies; Data Processing; Engineering; Environmental Management; Finance; Information Technology; Insurance; International Business; Leadership; Management; Marketing; Real Estate; Safety Engineering; Sales Techniques; Service Trades; Small Business; Transport Management.** *Mestrado*: **Business and Commerce.** Also MBA and Post-MBA Programmes

Student Services: Library

Last Updated: 01/12/15

FIAM FAAM UNIVERSITY CENTRE

FIAM FAAM Centro Universitario

Rua Taguá 150 Prédio 1, Liberdade,
São Paulo, São Paulo 01508-010
Tel: +55(11) 3346-6200
EMail: reitoria@fiamfaam.br
Website: http://www.fiamfaam.br/

Reitor: Artur Roquete de Macedo

Pró Reitora FIAM-FAAM: Paula Katakura

Course

Administration (Administration); **Advertising and Publicity** (Advertising and Publicity); **Architecture, Art, Design and Fashion** (Architecture; Design; Fashion Design; Interior Design; Town Planning); **Journalism** (Journalism); **Music** (Music); **Public Relations** (Public Relations); **Radio, TV and Video** (Radio and Television Broadcasting; Video); **Technologial Studies** (Cinema and Television; Interior Design; Photography; Radio and Television Broadcasting; Video)

Further Information: Also Distance Education

History: Founded 1972 as Faculdades Integradas Alcântara Machado. Acquired present status and title 2002.

Main Language(s) of Instruction: Portuguese

Degrees and Diplomas: *Tecnólogo*; *Bacharelado*; *Licenciatura*; *Especialização/Aperfeiçoamento*: **Advertising and Publicity; Business Administration; Journalism; Marketing.** *Mestrado*: **Architecture.**

Student Services: Library

Last Updated: 08/09/15

FIDELIS FACULTY

Faculdade Fidelis

Rua Dr. Danilo Gomes, 834, Boqueirão, Curitiba, PR 81670-250
Tel: +55(41) 3376-4566
Fax: +55(41) 3376-4566
EMail: ouvidoria@fidelis.edu.br; erica@fidelis.edu.br; secretaria@fidelis.edu.br
Website: http://www.fidelis.edu.br

Diretora: Erica Pauls

Course

Pedagogy (Pedagogy); **Postgraduate Studies** (Distance Education; Educational Psychology; Neurosciences; Psychology; Religious Studies; Special Education; Teacher Training; Theology); **Theology** (Theology)

History: Founded 2004.

Fees: 6,300-8,000 per programme (Brazilian Real)

Main Language(s) of Instruction: Portuguese

Degrees and Diplomas: *Bacharelado*; *Licenciatura*; *Especialização/Aperfeiçoamento*: **Distance Education; Educational Psychology; Neurosciences; Psychology; Religious Studies; Special Education; Teacher Training; Theology.**

Student Services: IT Centre, Library, eLibrary

Last Updated: 02/12/15

FIEO UNIVERSITY CENTRE

Centro Universitário FIEO (UNIFEO)

Avenida Franz Voegeli,1743, Jardim Wilson,
Osasco, São Paulo 06020-190
Tel: +55(11) 3654-0816
Fax: +55(11) 3654-0816
EMail: reitoria@unifieo.br
Website: http://www.unifieo.br

Reitor and Pró-Reitor Administrativo: José Cassio Soares Hungria Tel: +55(11) 3651-9933 EMail: reitoria@unifieo.br

Course

Accountancy (Accountancy); **Administration** (Administration); **Advertising and Publicity** (Advertising and Publicity); **Architecture and Town Planning** (Architecture; Town Planning); **Arts and Humanities** (Arts and Humanities; English; Latin; Linguistics; Portuguese); **Automation and Control Engineering** (Automation and Control Engineering); **Biological Sciences** (Biological and Life Sciences); **Chemistry** (Chemistry); **Civil Engineering** (Civil Engineering); **Computer Engineering** (Computer Engineering; Computer Networks); **Computer Science** (Computer Science); **Cosmetology** (Cosmetology); **Digital Design** (Design); **Geography** (Geography); **Human Resources** (Human Resources); **Information Systems** (Information Sciences); **International Trade and Business** (International Business); **Journalism** (Journalism); **Law** (Law); **Management** (Management); **Marketing** (Marketing); **Mathematics** (Mathematics); **Pedagogy** (Education; Educational Sciences; Pedagogy; Teacher Training); **Pharmacy** (Pharmacy); **Physical Education** (Physical Education); **Physical Therapy** (Physical Therapy); **Production Engineering** (Production Engineering); **Psychopedagogy** (Educational Psychology); **Secretarial Studies** (Secretarial Studies); **System Analysis** (Systems

Analysis); **Telecommunications Engineering** (Telecommunications Engineering); **Transport Management** (Transport Management)

Further Information: Also Narciso (law) and Wilson Campuses

History: Founded 1969.

Main Language(s) of Instruction: Portuguese

Accrediting Agency: Ministry of Education.

Degrees and Diplomas: *Tecnólogo*; *Bacharelado*; *Licenciatura*; *Especialização/Aperfeiçoamento*: **Chemical Engineering; Civil Law; Clinical Psychology; Criminal Law; Educational Psychology; Finance; Human Resources; Industrial and Organizational Psychology; Labour Law; Law; Physical Therapy.** *Mestrado*: **Business Administration; Law.** Also MBA.

Student Services: Library

Last Updated: 17/07/15

FILADELFIA UNIVERSITY CENTRE

Centro Universitário Filadélfia (UNIFIL)

Av. Juscelino Kubitscheck, 1626, Caixa Postal 196,
Londrina, Paraná 86020-000
Tel: +55(43) 3375-7400
Fax: +55(43) 3375-7412
EMail: caa@unifil.br
Website: http://www.unifil.br

Reitor: Eleazar Ferreira EMail: reitor@filadelfia.br

Area

Agrarian Sciences (Agronomy; Veterinary Science); **Applied Social Sciences** (Accountancy; Administration; Architecture; Law; Town Planning); **Biological Sciences** (Biological and Life Sciences); **Engineering** (Civil Engineering); **Exact Sciences** (Computer Science; Information Sciences); **Health Sciences** (Biomedicine; Nursing; Nutrition; Pharmacy; Physical Education; Physical Therapy); **Humanities** (Psychology; Theology)

Course

Graduate Studies (Business Administration; Education; Educational Psychology; Health Sciences; Human Resources; Interior Design; Nursing; Nutrition; Psychology; Public Health; Software Engineering; Special Education); **Technological Studies** (Cooking and Catering; Cosmetology; Environmental Management; Transport Management)

History: Founded 1972 as Centro de Estudos Superiores de Londrina (Cesulon). Acquired present status and title 2001.

Main Language(s) of Instruction: Portuguese

Accrediting Agency: Ministry of education.

Degrees and Diplomas: *Tecnólogo*; *Bacharelado*; *Especialização/Aperfeiçoamento*: **Agriculture; Architecture; Clinical Psychology; Educational Psychology; Nursing; Nutrition; Physical Education; Physical Therapy; Psychology; Soil Science.** Also MBA.

Student Services: Library

Last Updated: 20/07/15

FINACI FACULTY OF TECHNOLOGY

Faculdade de Tecnologia FINACI (FINACI)

Praça Pedro Lessa, 41, Centro, São Paulo, SP 01032-030
Tel: +55(11) 3053-4321
EMail: fazio@finaci.com.br
Website: http://www.finaci.com.br

Diretora: Yara Esmeralda Arena

Course

Hospital Management (Health Administration); **Human Resources Management** (Human Resources); **Occupational Safety** (Safety Engineering); **Postgraduate Studies** (Health Administration; Medical Technology; Nutrition; Pathology; Pharmacy; Physiology; Radiology; Safety Engineering); **Radiology** (Radiology)

History: Founded 2007.

Main Language(s) of Instruction: Portuguese

Degrees and Diplomas: *Técnico de Nivel Medio*; *Tecnólogo*; *Especialização/Aperfeiçoamento*: **Health Administration; Medical Technology; Nutrition; Pathology; Pharmacy; Physiology; Radiology; Safety Engineering.** Also MBA

Last Updated: 02/12/15

FLUMINENSE UNIVERSITY CENTRE

Centro Universitario Fluminense (UNIFLU)

Rua Tenente Coronel Cardoso 349,
Campos dos Goytacazes, Rio de Janeiro 28013-460
Tel: +55(22) 2101-3350
Fax: +55(24) 2101-3353
EMail: ouvidoria@uniflu.edu.br
Website: http://www.uniflu.edu.br

Reitor: Inès Cabral Ururahy De Souza

Course

Architecture and Town Planning (Architecture; Town Planning); **Human Resources Management** (Human Resources); **Journalism** (Journalism); **Law** (Civil Law; Criminal Law; Labour Law; Law; Public Law); **Logistics** (Transport Management); **Modern Languages** (English; Portuguese; Spanish); **Odontology** (Dentistry; Orthodontics; Stomatology); **Pedagogy** (Education; Pedagogy; Teacher Training); **Phonoaudiology** (Speech Therapy and Audiology); **Tourism** (Tourism); **Visual Arts** (Visual Arts)

History: Founded 1961

Main Language(s) of Instruction: Portuguese

Accrediting Agency: Ministry of Education

Degrees and Diplomas: *Bacharelado*; *Especialização/Aperfeiçoamento*: **Architecture; Civil Law; Criminal Law; Dentistry; Educational Psychology; Labour Law; Law; Orthodontics; Public Law.**

Student Services: Library

Last Updated: 20/07/15

FOUNDATION FOR HIGHER EDUCATION AND COMMUNICATION OF MACHADO

Fundação Machadense de Ensino Superior e Comunicação (FUMESC)

Rodóvia BR 267 Km 3, s/n Distrito Industrial Parque Industrial,
Machado, Minas Gerais 37750-000
Tel: +55(35) 3295-9800
Fax: +55(35) 3295-9801
EMail: fumesc@fumesc.com.br
Website: http://www.fumesc.com.br

Diretor: Wellington Espanha Moreira

Course

Accountancy (Accountancy); **Administration** (Administration); **Human Resources** (Human Resources); **Law** (Law); **Public Administration** (Public Administration)

History: Founded 1998.

Main Language(s) of Instruction: Portuguese

Degrees and Diplomas: *Bacharelado*: **Law.** *Especialização/Aperfeiçoamento*: **Human Resources; Law.** Also MBA

Student Services: Library

Last Updated: 25/03/16

FOUNDATION SCHOOL OF SOCIOLOGY AND POLITICAL SCIENCE OF SÃO PAULO

Fundação Escola de Sociologia e Política de São Paulo (FESPSP)

Rua General Jardim, 522, Vila Buarque, São Paulo, SP 01223-010
Tel: +55(11) 3868-6901 +55(11) 3123-7800
Fax: +55(11) 3868-6924
EMail: fespsp@fespsp.org.br; edileine@fespsp.org.br
Website: http://www.fespsp.org.br

Diretor Geral: Waltercio Zanvettor (1996-)
Tel: +55(11) 3868-6903 EMail: waltercio@fespsp.org.br

Secretária Geral: Lais da Costa Manso

International Relations: Almiro Vicente Heitor, Financial Director
Tel: +55(11) 3868-6904 EMail: almiro@fespsp.org.br

Faculty
Library Science and Information Sciences (FABCI) (Information Management; Information Sciences; Information Technology; Library Science); **Management of FESPSP (FADFESPSP)** (Business Administration; Management; Public Administration)

School
São Paulo School of Sociology and Politics (ESP) (Anthropology; Archiving; Cultural Studies; International Relations; International Studies; Library Science; Media Studies; Political Sciences; Psychology; Sociology)

History: Founded 1933 as Escola de Sociologia e Politica (ESP). Acquired present status 1946.

Admission Requirements: Secondary school certificate and entrance examination.

Fees: 3986,10 per semester (Brazilian Real)

Main Language(s) of Instruction: Portuguese

Accrediting Agency: Ministry of Education (MEC)

Degrees and Diplomas: *Bacharelado*; *Especialização/Aperfeiçoamento*: **Archiving; Cultural Studies; Information Management; Information Technology; International Relations; International Studies; Latin American Studies; Library Science; Media Studies; Political Sciences; Psychology; Public Administration; Social Psychology; Social Studies; Sociology.** Also MBA

Student Services: Academic Counselling, Canteen, Careers Guidance, Cultural Activities, Facilities for disabled people, Library

Academic Staff *2010-2011*	MEN	WOMEN	TOTAL
FULL-TIME	24	47	**71**
STAFF WITH DOCTORATE			
FULL-TIME	11	14	**25**
Student Numbers *2010-2011*			
All (Foreign included)	388	552	**940**

Last Updated: 03/02/16

FRANCISCAN UNIVERSITY CENTRE

Centro Universitário Franciscano (UNIFRA)

Rua dos Andradas, 1614, Centro,
Santa Maria, Rio Grande do Sul 97010-032
Tel: +55(55) 3220-1200
Fax: +55(55) 3222-6484
EMail: reitoria@unifra.br
Website: http://www.unifra.br

Reitora: Irani Rupolo (1997-) Tel: +55(55) 3220-1200

Pró-Reitor Administrativo: Inacir Pederiva

Course
Administration (Administration); **Advertising and Publicity** (Advertising and Publicity); **Architecture and Town Planning** (Architecture; Town Planning); **Biomedicine** (Biomedicine); **Chemistry** (Chemistry); **Computer Science** (Computer Science); **Design** (Design); **Economics** (Economics); **Environmental Engineering** (Environmental Engineering); **Geography** (Geography); **Graduate Studies** *(Lato Sensu)* (Business Administration; Communication Studies; Educational Psychology; Environmental Management; Health Administration; Marketing; Pharmacy; Public Health; Safety Engineering; Welfare and Protective Services); **Graduate Studies** *(Stricto Sensu)* (Mathematics Education; Science Education); **History** (History); **Information Systems** (Information Sciences); **Journalism** (Journalism); **Law** (Law); **Literature** (Literature); **Literature** (Literature; Portuguese); **Materials Engineering** (Materials Engineering); **Mathematics** (Mathematics); **Nursing** (Nursing); **Nutrition** (Nutrition); **Occupational Therapy** (Occupational Therapy); **Odontology** (Dentistry); **Pedagogy** (Pedagogy); **Pharmacy** (Pharmacy); **Philosophy** (Philosophy); **Physical Therapy** (Physical Therapy); **Physics** (Physics); **Psychology** (Psychology); **Social Service** (Social and Community Services); **Technical Studies** (Nursing); **Tourism** (Tourism)

History: Founded 1955. Acquired present status 1998.

Academic Year: March to December (March-July; August-December)

Admission Requirements: Secondary school leaving certificate and Vestibular

Fees: 9,125,82 per semester (Brazilian Real)

Main Language(s) of Instruction: Portuguese

Accrediting Agency: Ministry of Education.

Degrees and Diplomas: *Bacharelado*; *Licenciatura*; *Especialização/Aperfeiçoamento*: **Accountancy; Acupuncture; Architecture; Business Administration; Cinema and Television; Civil Engineering; Civil Law; Dentistry; Educational Administration; Educational Psychology; Environmental Engineering; Family Studies; Finance; Health Sciences; Human Resources; Industrial and Organizational Psychology; Information Technology; Labour Law; Law; Literacy Education; Literature; Marketing; Modern Languages; Oncology; Orthodontics; Periodontics; Pharmacy; Physical Therapy; Public Health; Safety Engineering; Social Sciences; Town Planning; Traditional Eastern Medicine.** *Mestrado*: **Mathematics Education; Nanotechnology; Public Health; Science Education.** *Doutorado*: **Mathematics Education; Nanotechnology; Science Education.**

Student Services: Academic Counselling, Canteen, Facilities for disabled people, Language Laboratory, Library

Publications: Disciplinarum Scientia; Vidya

Last Updated: 27/07/15

FRASSINETTI FACULTY OF RECIFE

Faculdade Frassinetti do Recife (FAFIRE)

Av. Conde da Boa Vista, 921, Boa Vista,
Recife, Pernambuco 50060-002
Tel: +55(81) 2122-3500
Fax: +55(81) 2122-3580
EMail: comunica@fafire.br; mdasgracas@fafire.br
Website: http://www.fafire.br

Diretora: Maria das Graças Soares da Costa

Vice-Diretora: Maria do Socorro Lopes Souza

Course
Administration (Administration); **Biological Sciences** (Biological and Life Sciences); **Letters** (English; Literature; Portuguese); **Pedagogy** (Pedagogy); **Postgraduate Studies** (Accountancy; Biology; Business Administration; Business and Commerce; Communication Studies; Education; Finance; Human Resources; Information Technology; Law; Management; Marketing; Psychology; Service Trades; Social Work; Telecommunications Services; Tourism; Transport Management); **Psychology** (Psychology); **Technological Studies** (Business and Commerce; Finance; Human Resources; Transport Management); **Tourism** (Tourism)

History: Founded 1941 as Instituto Superior de Pedagogia, Ciências e Letras Paula Frassinetti. Renamed Faculdade de Filosofia do Recife 1941.

Main Language(s) of Instruction: Portuguese

Degrees and Diplomas: *Tecnólogo*; *Bacharelado*; *Licenciatura*; *Especialização/Aperfeiçoamento*: **Business Administration; Business and Commerce; Communication Studies; Finance; Human Resources; Management; Marketing; Service Trades; Social Work; Telecommunications Services; Transport Management.**

Student Services: IT Centre, Library, eLibrary

Publications: Anais; Lumen; Revista FAFIRE

Last Updated: 09/09/15

FUCAPE BUSINESS SCHOOL

Avenida Fernando Ferrari 1358, Boa Vista, Vitória, ES 29075-505
Tel: +55 (27) 4009-4444
Fax: +55(27) 4009-4422
EMail: fucape@fucape.br
Website: http://www.fucape.br

Diretor: Arilton Teixeira

Diretor Acadêmico: Bruno Funchal EMail: secretaria@fucape.br

Course
Accountancy (Accountancy); **Administration** (Administration); **Economics** (Economics)

History: Founded 2004.

Main Language(s) of Instruction: Portuguese

Degrees and Diplomas: *Bacharelado*; *Licenciatura*; *Mestrado*: **Accountancy.** *Doutorado*: **Accountancy; Administration.** Also MBA
Student Services: Library
Last Updated: 25/03/16

FUCAPI FACULTY

Faculdade FUCAPI (FUCAPI-CESF)

Avenida Governador Danilo Areosa 381, Distrito Industrial, Manaus, Amazonas 69075-351
Tel: +55(92) 2127-3034
EMail: direcaocesf@fucapi.br
Website: http://www.fucapi.br

Diretor: Antônio Luiz da Silva Maués

Course
Administration (Administration); **Bioprocess Engineering** (Bioengineering); **Civil Engineering** (Civil Engineering); **Computer Engineering** (Computer Engineering); **Computer Science** (Computer Science); **Design** (Design); **Electrical Engineering** (Electrical Engineering); **Environmental Engineering** (Environmental Engineering); **Information Systems** (Systems Analysis); **Mechanical Engineering** (Mechanical Engineering); **Product Design Technology** (Computer Science; Industrial Design); **Production Engineering** (Production Engineering); **Software Engineering** (Software Engineering); **Telecommunications Engineering** (Telecommunications Engineering)

History: Founded 1998 as Instituto de Ensino Superior FUCAPI – CESF.
Main Language(s) of Instruction: Portuguese
Degrees and Diplomas: *Bacharelado*; *Especialização/Aperfeiçoamento*: **Automation and Control Engineering; Computer Engineering; Design; Electrical Engineering; Production Engineering; Software Engineering.** *Mestrado*: **Design.** Also MBA
Student Services: Library
Last Updated: 01/04/16

FUMEC UNIVERSITY

Universidade FUMEC

Av. Afonso Pena, 3880, Cruzeiro, Belo Horizonte, Minas Gerais 30130-009
Tel: +55(31) 3269-5250 +55(31) 3269-5255
Fax: +55(31) 3269-5206
EMail: fumec@fumec.br
Website: http://www.fumec.br

Reitor: Fernando de Melo Nogueira
Tel: +55(31) 3269-5250 EMail: reitoria@fumec.br
Pró-reitor de Planejamento e Administração: Márcio Dario da Silva
International Relations: Maria Fernanda F. Loureiro
Tel: +55(31) 3269-5220 EMail: relint@fumec.br

Faculty
Business Administration (FACE) (Accountancy; Administration; Computer Science; International Business); **Engineering and Architecture (FEA)** (Aeronautical and Aerospace Engineering; Architecture; Bioengineering; Civil Engineering; Energy Engineering; Environmental Engineering; Fashion Design; Industrial Design; Interior Design; Production Engineering; Telecommunications Engineering; Town Planning); **Human, Social and Health Sciences (FCH)** (Advertising and Publicity; Biomedicine; Journalism; Law; Mass Communication; Pedagogy; Physical Therapy; Psychology)

Sector
FUMEC Virtual Studies (Accountancy; Administration; Business Administration; Educational Psychology; Finance; Higher Education Teacher Training; Human Resources; Information Technology; Management; Pedagogy; Physical Education; Protective Services)

History: Founded 1965. Became Centro Universitário FUMEC 2000 following merger of Faculdade de Ciências Econômicas, Administrativas e Contábeis de Belo Horizonte (FACE), Faculdade de Ciências Humanas (FCH) e Faculdade de Engenharia e Arquitetura (FEA). Acquired present status 2005.
Main Language(s) of Instruction: Portuguese
Degrees and Diplomas: *Tecnólogo*; *Bacharelado*; *Especialização/Aperfeiçoamento*: **Architecture; Biological and Life Sciences; Biomedicine; Child Care and Development; Civil Law; Commercial Law; Computer Engineering; Cultural Studies; Distance Education; Educational Psychology; Engineering; Environmental Studies; Health Sciences; Higher Education; Human Rights; Mathematics Education; Molecular Biology; Neurology; Notary Studies; Photography; Plastic Surgery; Psychology; Psychotherapy; Public Law; Rehabilitation and Therapy; Road Engineering; Safety Engineering; Sanitary Engineering; Structural Architecture; Systems Analysis; Telecommunications Engineering.** *Mestrado*: **Administration; Construction Engineering; Cultural Studies; Information Technology; Law; Marketing.** *Doutorado*: **Administration; Information Technology.** Also MBA; Master of Laws (LL.M.); Postdoctoral Programme in Administration
Student Services: Library
Last Updated: 05/04/16

FUTURE FACULTY/FACULTY OF MANAGEMENT IN VOTUPORANGA

Faculdade Futura/Faculdade de Ciências Gerenciais em Votuporanga

Avenida Vale do Sol, 4876, Bairro Vale do Sol, Votuporanga, SP 15500-003
Tel: +55(17) 3405-1212
Fax: +55(17) 3405-1212
EMail: contato@faculdadefutura.com.br; kelly@academica-edu.com.br; nilson@faculdadefutura.com.br
Website: http://faculdadefutura.com.br

nilson@faculdadeftura.com.br: Nilson Roberto Domingos

Course
Accounting (Accountancy); **Administration** (Administration); **Human Resources Management** (Human Resources); **Logistics** (Transport Management); **Marketing** (Marketing); **Pedagogy** (Pedagogy); **Public Administration** (Public Administration)

History: Founded 2006.
Main Language(s) of Instruction: Portuguese
Degrees and Diplomas: *Tecnólogo*: **Human Resources; Marketing; Public Administration; Transport Management.** *Bacharelado*: **Accountancy; Administration.** *Licenciatura*: **Pedagogy.**
Last Updated: 10/06/15

GAMA AND SOUZA FACULTY

Faculdade Gama e Souza (FGS)

Rua Leopoldina Rego 502 Olária, Rio de Janeiro, Rio de Janeiro 21021521
Tel: +55(21) 2560-6884 +55(21) 2290-5959
Fax: +55(21) 3868-4513
EMail: gamaesouza@openlink.com.br
Website: http://www.gamaesouza.edu.br

Diretora: Peralva de Miranda Delgado

Course
Postgraduate Studies (Educational Administration; Special Education)

Campus
Campus I - Olaria (Accountancy; Administration; Economics; Education; Health Administration; Literature; Mathematics; Portuguese; Production Engineering; Safety Engineering); **Campus II - Avenida Brasil** (Business and Commerce; Computer Networks; Information Technology; Law; Marketing; Real Estate; Tourism); **Campus III - Bonsucesso** (Accountancy; Nursing; Physical Therapy); **Campus IV - Barra da Tijuca** (Administration; Environmental Engineering; Nursing; Physical Education; Physical Therapy; Production Engineering; Tourism); **Campus V - Recreio**

History: Founded 1998.
Main Language(s) of Instruction: Portuguese
Degrees and Diplomas: *Tecnólogo*; *Bacharelado*; *Licenciatura*; *Especialização/Aperfeiçoamento*: **Educational Administration; Special Education.**
Last Updated: 09/09/15

GAMMON FACULTIES

Faculdades Gammon
Rua Prefeito Jayme Monteiro, 791, Centro,
Paraguaçu Paulista, SP 19700-000
Tel: +55(18) 3361-9492
EMail: fundacao@funge.com.br
Website: http://www.faculdadesgammon.edu.br

Diretor: Edenis César de Oliveira

Course

Administration (Administration; Business Administration; Finance; Management); **Agronomy** (Agronomy; Animal Husbandry)

History: Founded as Escola Superior de Agronomia de Paraguaçú Paulista (ESSAP), 1974. ESAPP and the Faculty of Management Sciences (FACIG) merged to become Faculdade Gammon.

Degrees and Diplomas: *Bacharelado*

Student Services: IT Centre, Library
Last Updated: 24/09/15

GAMMON PRESBYTERIAN FACULTY

Faculdade Presbiteriana Gammon (FAGAMMON)
Praça Doutor Augusto Silva 616, Centro,
Lavras, Minas Gerais 37200000
Tel: +55(35) 6133-3821 +55(35) 6133-6114
Fax: +55(35) 821-6114
EMail: unigammon@gammon.br
Website: http://www.fagammon.edu.br

Diretor: Sergio Wagner de Oliveira

Course

Administration (Administration); **Computer Science** (Computer Science); **Physical Education** (Physical Education)

History: Founded 1990.

Main Language(s) of Instruction: Portuguese

Degrees and Diplomas: *Bacharelado*; *Licenciatura*; *Especialização/Aperfeiçoamento*

Student Services: Library
Last Updated: 04/06/15

GERALDO DI BIASE UNIVERSITY CENTRE

Centro Universitário Geraldo Di Biase (UGB)
Rua Deputado Geraldo Di Biase, 81, Aterrado,
Volta Redonda, Rio de Janeiro 27213-080
Tel: +55(24) 3345-1700
EMail: reitoria@ugb.edu.br
Website: http://www.ugb.edu.br

Reitor: Geraldo Di Biase Filho

Institute

Exact, Earth Sciences and Engineering - ICETE Barra do Piraí (Civil Engineering; Engineering; Mechanical Engineering; Production Engineering); **Exact, Earth Sciences and Engineering - ICETE Nova Iguaçu** *(Nova Iguaçu)* (Civil Engineering; Environmental Engineering; Production Engineering); **Health Sciences - ICS Barra do Pirai** (Biomedical Engineering; Nursing); **Social and Human Sciences - ICSH Barra do Piraí** (Accountancy; Administration; Social and Community Services); **Social and Human Sciences - ICSH Volta Redonda**

Higher Institute

Education - ISE Barra do Piraí (Biological and Life Sciences; Computer Science; English; History; Literature; Pedagogy; Physical Education; Portuguese; Theatre; Visual Arts); **Education - ISE Volta Redonda** (Biological and Life Sciences; Computer Science; English; Geography; History; Literature; Mathematics; Pedagogy; Portuguese; Spanish)

Course

Graduate Studies Barra do Piraí (Business Education; Educational Administration; Portuguese); **Graduate Studies Volta Redonda** (Architecture; Biochemistry; Business Education; Commercial Law; Contemporary History; Criminology; Data Processing; Ecology; Educational Administration; Educational Psychology; English; Environmental Studies; Finance; Geography; Geography (Human); Higher Education; History; Human Resources; Information Technology; Interior Design; Labour Law; Law; Literature; Mathematics Education; Microbiology; Natural Resources; Pedagogy; Portuguese; Public Administration; Religion; Safety Engineering; Small Business; Town Planning; Translation and Interpretation; Transport Management); **Technological Studies - NGT Barra do Piraí** (Environmental Management; Human Resources; Transport Management); **Technological Studies - NGT Volta Redonda** (Computer Networks; Environmental Management; Human Resources; Transport Management)

Further Information: Also Barra do Piraí and Nova Iguaçu campuses.

History: Founded 1967 as Fundação Educacional Rosemar Pimentel. Acquired present status and title 2005.

Main Language(s) of Instruction: Portuguese

Degrees and Diplomas: *Tecnólogo*; *Bacharelado*; *Licenciatura*; *Especialização/Aperfeiçoamento*: **Architecture; Civil Law; Contemporary History; Educational Administration; Educational Psychology; English; History; Labour Law; Law; Microbiology; Physical Education; Portuguese; Social Sciences; Town Planning; Translation and Interpretation.** *Mestrado*: **Business Administration.** Also MBA.

Student Services: Library
Last Updated: 27/08/15

GEREMÁRIO DANTAS FACULTY

Faculdade Geremário Dantas
Rua Cândido Benício, 159, Campinho,
Rio de Janeiro, RJ 21320-061
Tel: +55(21) 2108-7901
EMail: ouvidoria@fgd.edu.br; aquino@igd.com.br
Website: http://www.fgd.edu.br

Diretora Geral: Irmã Marisa Aquino

Coordenadora Acadêmica de Ensino: Vergília dos A. M. da Costa

Course

Graduate Studies (Educational Administration; Educational Psychology; Higher Education; Primary Education; Religious Education; Special Education); **Letters** (Literature; Portuguese; Spanish); **Pedagogy** (Pedagogy)

History: Founded 2004.

Main Language(s) of Instruction: Portuguese

Degrees and Diplomas: *Licenciatura*; *Especialização/Aperfeiçoamento*: **Educational Administration; Educational Psychology; Higher Education; Primary Education; Religious Education; Special Education.**

Student Services: IT Centre, Language Laboratory, eLibrary
Last Updated: 09/09/15

GETULIO VARGAS FOUNDATION

Fundação Getulio Vargas
Praia de Botafogo, 190, Rio de Janeiro 22250-900
Tel: +502 (21) 3799-5938
Website: http://portal.fgv.br

Presidente: Carlos Ivan Simonsen Leal

School

Applied Mathematics (Applied Mathematics); **Economics and Finance** (Economics; Finance); **Law** *(Rio de Janeiro)* (Law); **Public Administration and Business Studies** *(Brazilian)* (Administration; Business Administration; Finance; Marketing); **Social Sciences and History** (History; Social Sciences)

Further Information: Also campus in Sao Paulo

History: Founded 1944.

Main Language(s) of Instruction: Portuguese

Degrees and Diplomas: *Bacharelado*; *Licenciatura*; *Mestrado*: **Administration; Business Administration; Economics; Heritage Preservation; History; Law; Management; Mathematics.** *Doutorado*: **Administration; Economics; Heritage Preservation; History.**

Last Updated: 15/04/16

GRANBERY METHODIST FACULTY

Faculdade Metodista Granbery (FMG)
Rua Batista de Oliveira 1145, Centro,
Juiz de Fora, Minas Gerais 36010530
Tel: +55(32) 3215-1833
Fax: +55(32) 3213-4893
EMail: faculdade@granbery.edu.br
Website: http://www.granbery.edu.br

Diretora Geral: Elaine Lima de Oliveira

Course

Administration; **Information Systems** (Information Management); **Law**; **Pedagogy** (Education; Pedagogy); **Physical Education** (Physical Education)

History: Founded 1998.

Main Language(s) of Instruction: Portuguese

Degrees and Diplomas: *Bacharelado*; *Licenciatura*; *Especialização/Aperfeiçoamento*

Last Updated: 27/05/15

GUARULHOS UNIVERSITY

Universidade Guarulhos (UNG)
Praça Tereza Cristina, 1, Centro, Guarulhos,
São Paulo 07023-070
Tel: +55(11) 6464-1700 +55 (11) 2409-9222
Fax: +55(11) 6464-1727 +55(11) 2440-2030
EMail: ung@server.ung.br
Website: http://www.ung.br

Reitora: Luciane Lúcio Pereira
Tel: +55(11) 6464-1650 EMail: reitor@ung.br

International Relations: Maria Inês Nunes, Coordenação de Relações Internacionais
Tel: +55(11) 2464-1779 EMail: minunes@prof.ung.br

Unit

Guarulhos-Dutra Unit (Architecture; Art Education; Chemical Engineering; Civil Engineering; Electrical Engineering; Environmental Engineering; Foreign Languages Education; Graphic Design; Humanities and Social Science Education; Mathematics Education; Mechanical Engineering; Native Language Education; Pedagogy; Production Engineering; Town Planning; Veterinary Science)

Campus

Bonsucesso Campus (Administration; Pedagogy); **Guarulhos-Centro Campus** (Accountancy; Administration; Advertising and Publicity; Biological and Life Sciences; Biomedicine; Chemistry; Computer Science; Dentistry; Journalism; Law; Nursing; Nutrition; Pharmacy; Physical Education; Physical Therapy; Psychology; Science Education; Social and Community Services; Tourism); **Itaquá Campus** (Accountancy; Administration; Computer Science; Humanities and Social Science Education; Pedagogy; Social and Community Services); **SP-Centro Campus (Shopping Light)** (Accountancy; Administration; Computer Science; Foreign Languages Education; Humanities and Social Science Education; Mathematics Education; Native Language Education; Pedagogy)

History: Founded 1970 as Faculdade de Filosofia, Ciências e Letras 'Farias Brito'. Became Centros Integrados 'Farias Brito' 1982, and acquired present status and title 1986. A private institution.

Academic Year: February to December (February-June; August-December)

Admission Requirements: Secondary school certificate and entrance examination

Fees: 1443-7333 per semester (Brazilian Real)

Main Language(s) of Instruction: Portuguese

Degrees and Diplomas: *Tecnólogo*; *Bacharelado*; *Licenciatura*; *Especialização/Aperfeiçoamento*: **Advertising and Publicity; Business Education; Civil Law; Educational Administration; Higher Education Teacher Training; Labour Law; Law; Marketing; Private Law; Special Education.** *Mestrado*: **Dentistry; Earth Sciences; Nursing; Orthodontics.** *Doutorado*: **Dentistry; Nursing.** Also MBA

Student Services: Canteen, Careers Guidance, Cultural Activities, Facilities for disabled people, Health Services, Language Laboratory, Library, Nursery Care, Social Counselling, Sports Facilities

Publications: Revista Universidade Guarulhos

Publishing House: Editora Universidade Guarulhos

Last Updated: 05/04/16

HÉLIO ALONSO INTEGRATED FACULTIES

Faculdades Integradas Hélio Alonso (FACHA)
Rua Muniz Barreto 51, Botafogo,
Rio de Janeiro, Rio de Janeiro 22251090
Tel: +55(21) 2102-3100
EMail: secgeral@facha.br
Website: http://www.facha.edu.br

Diretor Geral: Paulo Alonso
EMail: presidencia@helioalonso.com.br

Course

Business Administration (International Business; Marketing); **Law** (Law); **Social Communication** (Advertising and Publicity; Journalism; Public Relations; Radio and Television Broadcasting); **Sports Management** (Sports Management); **Tourism** (Tourism)

Further Information: Also Centro campus and Meir campus

History: Founded 1972

Main Language(s) of Instruction: Portuguese

Accrediting Agency: Ministério da Educação

Degrees and Diplomas: *Bacharelado*; *Especialização/Aperfeiçoamento*. Also MBA

Student Services: Library

Last Updated: 24/06/15

HERMÍNIO OMETTO DE ARARRAS UNIVERSITY CENTRE

Centro Universitário Hermínio Ometto de Araras (UNIARARAS)
Avenida Dr. Maximiliano Baruto 500, Jardim Universitário,
Araras, São Paulo 13607-339
Tel: +55(19) 3543-1400
Fax: +55(19) 3543-1412
EMail: secretaria@uniararas.br
Website: http://www.uniararas.br

Reitor: José Antonio Mendes EMail: josemendes@uniararas.br

Area

Education (Chemistry; Mathematics; Pedagogy; Physics); **Engineering** (Engineering); **Health Sciences** (Acupuncture; Biology; Biomedicine; Dentistry; Nursing; Pharmacy; Physical Education; Physical Therapy); **Humanities** (Accountancy; Administration; Psychology); **Information Systems** (Information Sciences); **Technology** (Chemical Engineering; Computer Networks; Cosmetology; Environmental Management; Finance; Food Science; Human Resources; Industrial Management; Marketing; Safety Engineering; Transport Management)

Course

Graduate Studies *(Lato Sensu)* (Acupuncture; Agriculture; Alternative Medicine; Biological and Life Sciences; Biomedicine; Biotechnology; Business Administration; Cosmetology; Dentistry; Educational Administration; Educational Psychology; Educational Sciences; Finance; Food Technology; Gerontology; Haematology; Higher Education; Immunology; Information Technology; Molecular Biology; Nursing; Orthodontics; Orthopaedics; Pedagogy; Pharmacology; Pharmacy; Physical Therapy; Psychiatry and Mental Health; Public Health; Rehabilitation and Therapy; Science Education; Sports; Stomatology; Toxicology; Transport Management; Veterinary Science)

History: Founded 1973

Main Language(s) of Instruction: Portuguese

Degrees and Diplomas: *Tecnólogo*; *Bacharelado*; *Licenciatura*; *Especialização/Aperfeiçoamento*: **Acupuncture; Administration; Biotechnology; Business Administration; Clinical Psychology; Computer Engineering; Cosmetology; Education; Educational Administration; Educational Psychology; Finance; Health Administration; Higher Education Teacher Training; Human**

Resources; Industrial and Organizational Psychology; Information Technology; Labour Law; Law; Management; Marketing; Nursing; Orthodontics; Pharmacology; Pharmacy; Physical Therapy; Primary Education; Production Engineering; Psychology; Safety Engineering; Software Engineering; Special Education; Stomatology; Translation and Interpretation. *Mestrado*: **Biomedicine; Orthodontics.** Also MBA.

Student Services: Canteen, Library

Last Updated: 03/07/15

HIGHER EDUCATION ASSOCIATION OF PIAUÍ

Associação de Ensino Superior do Piauí (AESPI)

Rua Gov. Joca Pires 1000, Bairro de Fátima,
Teresina, Piauí 64046470
Tel: +55(86) 3233-6666
Fax: +55(86) 3232-7676
EMail: aespi@aespi.br; ouvidoria@aespi.br
Website: http://www.aespi.br

Director: Milton Ferreira de Oliveira

Pedagogical Coordinator: Marlia Socorro Lima Riedel

College

IEST *(Teresina)* (Accountancy; Advertising and Publicity; Law; Nursing; Pharmacy; Physical Therapy; Social Studies; Tourism); **Technology** (Computer Networks; Computer Science; Graphic Design; Management Systems; Multimedia; Systems Analysis)

School

Business *(FAT Teresina)* (Administration; Business Administration); **Data Processing** *(FPPD Piauiense)* (Computer Science; Data Processing)

Course

Modern Languages (English; Modern Languages; Portuguese; Translation and Interpretation)

Further Information: Also campus in São Cristóvão

History: Founded 1992.

Main Language(s) of Instruction: Portuguese

Degrees and Diplomas: *Tecnólogo*; *Bacharelado*

Student Services: IT Centre, Library, Sports Facilities

Last Updated: 08/06/15

HIGHER EDUCATION CENTRE OF AMAPÁ

Centro de Ensino Superior do Amapá (CEAP)

Rodovia Duca Serra, Via 17, n° 350, Alvorada,
Macapá, Amapá 68906720
Tel: +55(96) 3261-2133
Fax: +55(96) 3261-1401
EMail: ceap@ceap.br
Website: http://www.ceap.br

Diretor: Leonil de Aquino Pena Amanajas EMail: diretor@ceap.br

Vice-Director: José Claudio da Silva EMail: joseclaudio@ceap.br

Course

Accountancy (Accountancy); **Administration** (Administration); **Architecture and Town Planning** (Architecture; Town Planning); **Civil Engineering** (Civil Engineering); **Design** (Design); **Economics** (Economics); **Graduate Studies** (Business Administration; Design; Human Resources; Interior Design; Law; Public Administration); **Law** (Law); **Physical Education** (Physical Education); **Secretarial Studies** (Secretarial Studies)

History: Founded 1992.

Main Language(s) of Instruction: Portuguese

Degrees and Diplomas: *Bacharelado*; *Licenciatura*: **Physical Education.** *Especialização/Aperfeiçoamento*: **Accountancy; Business Administration; Human Resources; Interior Design; Labour Law; Law; Management; Media Studies; Public Administration.**

Student Services: Library

Last Updated: 17/06/15

HIGHER EDUCATION CENTRE OF CATALÃO

Centro de Ensino Superior de Catalão (CESUC)

Rua Prof. Paulo Lima, 100, Catalão, Goiás 75706420
Tel: +55(62) 3441-6200
Fax: +55(64) 3441-6200
EMail: cesuc@cesuc.br
Website: http://www.cesuc.br/

Director-General: Maria Eleonora de Oliveira Scalia

Director of Academic Affairs: Paulo Antônio de Lima

Faculty

Technology *(FATECA)* (Computer Science)

Course

Accountancy; **Administration** (Administration; Marketing); **Administration of Information System** (Information Management); **Graduate Studies** (Business Administration; Education; Engineering; Human Resources; Law; Management; Marketing; Production Engineering; Transport Management); **Law** (Law); **Physiotherapy**

History: Founded 1984.

Main Language(s) of Instruction: Portuguese

Degrees and Diplomas: *Bacharelado*; *Especialização/Aperfeiçoamento*: **Civil Law.** Also MBA degree (Finance, Accountancy, Management)

Student Services: Library

Last Updated: 10/06/15

HIGHER EDUCATION CENTRE OF CONSELHEIRO LAFAIETE

Centro de Ensino Superior de Conselheiro Lafaiete (CES-CL)

Rua Lopes Franco 1001, Carijós,
Conselheiro Lafaiete, Minas Gerais 36400-000
Tel: +55(31) 3762-0840
Fax: +55(31) 3761-2223
EMail: ces@ces-cl.edu.br
Website: http://www.ces-cl.edu.br

Diretor Geral: Antônio Efigênio Antunes
EMail: diretoria@ces-cl.edu.br

Secretária Geral: Maria Dalva Barbosa de Morais
EMail: ces@ces-cl.edu.br

Faculty

Chemical Engineering (Chemical Engineering); **Economic Science** *(FACEL)* (Accountancy; Economics); **Electrical Engineering** *(FACEC)* (Electrical Engineering); **Social Sciences** *(FACESA)* (Social Work)

History: Founded 2000.

Main Language(s) of Instruction: Portuguese

Degrees and Diplomas: *Bacharelado*: **Accountancy; Chemical Engineering; Electrical Engineering; Social Work.**

Student Services: Library

Last Updated: 12/06/15

HIGHER EDUCATION CENTRE OF FOZ DO IGUAÇU

Centro de Ensino Superior de Foz do Iguaçu (CESUFOZ)

Avenida Paraná 3695, Jardim Central,
Foz do Iguaçu, PR 85863-720
Tel: +55(45) 3520-1727
Fax: +55(45) 3520-1714
EMail: secretaria@cesufoz.br
Website: http://www.cesufoz.edu.br

Diretor Geral: Edson Gaspar EMail: direcao@cesufoz.br

Faculty

Economics and Data Processing *(FEPI)* (Computer Science; Data Processing; Economics); **Physical Education** *(FEFFI)* (Physical Education)

Course
Accountancy (Accountancy); **Administration** (Administration; Business Administration); **Advertising and Publicity** (Advertising and Publicity); **Civil Engineering** (Civil Engineering); **Computer Science** *(FEPI)* (Computer Science); **Law** (Law); **Nursing** (Nursing); **Pharmacy** (Pharmacy); **Physical Therapy** (Physical Therapy); **Production Engineering** (Production Engineering); **Psychology** (Psychology); **Tourism** (Tourism)

History: Founded 1993.

Main Language(s) of Instruction: Portuguese

Degrees and Diplomas: *Tecnólogo*; *Bacharelado*; *Licenciatura*: **Physical Education.** *Especialização/Aperfeiçoamento*: **Business Administration; Information Technology; Law; Safety Engineering.**

Student Services: Library

Last Updated: 28/07/15

HIGHER EDUCATION CENTRE OF JATAÍ

Centro de Ensino Superior de Jataí (CESUT)
Rua Santos Dumont 1200, Setor Oeste, Jataí, Goiás 75804-045
Tel: +55(64) 2102-1050 +55(64) 3631-2466
Fax: +55(64) 3631-2524
EMail: cesut@cesut.edu.br
Website: http://www.cesut.edu.br

President: Maria Amélia de Azevedo Lima

Director of Administration: Patrícia Macchione de Paula Maggioni

Faculty
Administration (Administration); **Law** (Law)

History: Founded 1994.

Main Language(s) of Instruction: Portuguese

Degrees and Diplomas: *Bacharelado*; *Especialização/Aperfeiçoamento*: **Agricultural Business; Human Resources; Labour Law; Marketing.**

Student Services: Library

Last Updated: 10/06/15

HIGHER EDUCATION CENTRE OF JUIZ DE FORA

Centro de Ensino Superior de Juiz de Fora (CES-JF)
Rua Halfeld 1179, Centro, Juiz de Fora,
Minas Gerais 36016000
Tel: +55(32) 3250-3800
Fax: +55(32) 3250-3842
EMail: cesjf@pucminas.cesjf.br
Website: http://www.cesjf.br

Reitor: Carlos Henrique Oliveira e Silva Passion
Tel: +55(32) 2102-6011 EMail: reitoriasec@cesjf.br

Director of Academic Affairs: Patricia Rodrigues Rezende de Souza

Department
Modern Languages (English; Portuguese)

Course
Advertising and Publicity (Advertising and Publicity); **Architecture and Town Planning** (Architecture; Town Planning); **Biology** (Biological and Life Sciences; Biology; Natural Sciences); **Computer Science** (Software Engineering); **Electrical Engineering** (Electrical Engineering); **Fashion Design** (Fashion Design); **Gastronomy** (Cooking and Catering); **Geography** (Geography); **History** (History); **Human Resourses** (Human Resources); **Interior Design** (Interior Design); **Journalism** (Advertising and Publicity; Communication Studies; Journalism; Media Studies); **Literature** (Literature); **Mathematics** (Mathematics); **Pedagogy** (Pedagogy); **Philosophy** (Philosophy); **Psychology** (Psychology); **Speech Therapy** (Speech Therapy and Audiology); **Telecommunications Engineering** (Telecommunications Engineering); **Theology** (Theology)

Further Information: Also Arnaldo Janssen and campus Verbum Divinum Campuses, St. Anthony Archdiocesan Seminary and a Culinary Cente

History: Founded 1972.

Main Language(s) of Instruction: Portuguese

Degrees and Diplomas: *Tecnólogo*; *Bacharelado*; *Licenciatura*; *Especialização/Aperfeiçoamento*; *Mestrado*: **Administration; Architecture; Biology; Electrical Engineering; Fashion Design; Interior Design; Philosophy; Software Engineering; Telecommunications Engineering; Town Planning.** Especialização in partnership with PUC Minas.

Student Services: Library

Last Updated: 15/06/15

HIGHER EDUCATION CENTRE OF UBERABA

Centro de Ensino Superior de Uberaba
Rua Ronan Martins Marques, 487, Santa Maria,
Uberaba, Minas Gerais 38050 600
Tel: +55(34) 3312-9897
EMail: cesube@cesube.edu.br
Website: http://www.cesube.edu.br

Diretor: Giovanna Aléxia Meireles EMail: dir.geral@fcetm.br

Coordenador Pedagógico: Reginaldo Pereira França Júnior
EMail: coord.pedagogica@fcetm.br

Course
Biology (Biology); **Civil Engineering** (Civil Engineering); **Education** (Adult Education; Education; Pedagogy; Primary Education; Secondary Education); **Environmental Management** *(Postgraduate Studies)* (Ecology; Environmental Management; Environmental Studies); **Geography** (Geography); **Physical Education** (Physical Education); **Social Science** (Social Sciences)

History: Founded 1999.

Main Language(s) of Instruction: Portuguese

Degrees and Diplomas: *Bacharelado*; *Licenciatura*; *Especialização/Aperfeiçoamento*: **Social Work.** Also MBA.

Student Services: Library

Last Updated: 16/06/15

HIGHER EDUCATION CENTRE OF VALENÇA

Centro de Ensino Superior de Valença (CESVA)
Rua Sargento Victor Hugo 161, Bairro Fátima,
Valença, Rio de Janeiro 27600000
Tel: +55(24) 2453-1888
Fax: +55(24) 2453-1888
EMail: ouvidoria@faa.edu.br
Website: http://www.faa.edu.br

Presidente: José Rogério Moura de Almeida Filho
EMail: direcaocesva@faa.edu.br

Diretor Geral: Antônio Celso Alves Pereira

Course
Arts and Humanities (Arts and Humanities; Literature; Philosophy); **Economics** (Economics); **Education** (Education; Pedagogy); **Graduate Studies** (Dentistry; Education; Law; Orthodontics; Periodontics; Physical Education; Physical Therapy; Veterinary Science); **History** (History); **Human Resources** (Human Resources); **Law** (Law); **Mathematics** (Mathematics); **Medicine** (Medicine); **Nursing** (Nursing); **Odontology** (Dentistry); **Portuguese** (Portuguese); **Systems Analysis** (Systems Analysis); **Veterinary Science** (Veterinary Science)

History: Founded 1966. Maintained by Fundação Educacional D. André Arcoverde - FAA.

Main Language(s) of Instruction: Portuguese

Degrees and Diplomas: *Bacharelado*; *Especialização/Aperfeiçoamento*: **Biomedicine; Cosmetology; Dentistry; Farm Management; Occupational Therapy; Orthodontics; Periodontics.** *Mestrado*: **Business Administration.** Also MBA.

Student Services: Library

Last Updated: 17/06/15

HIGHER EDUCATION FOUNDATION OF CLEVELANDIA

Fundação de Ensino Superior de Clevelândia

Rua Coronel Manoel Ferreira Bello, 270 - Centro, Caixa Postal 43, Clevelândia, PR 85530-000
Tel: +55(46) 3252-3399
Fax: +55(46) 3252-3399
EMail: danilo@fescpr.edu.br
Website: http://www.fescpr.edu.br

Diretor: Danilo Leão
VIce - Presidente: Humberto Passos

Course
Administration (Administration); **Geography** (Geography); **Pedagogy** (Pedagogy)
History: Founded 2001.
Main Language(s) of Instruction: Portuguese
Degrees and Diplomas: *Bacharelado*; *Licenciatura*: **Geography; Pedagogy.** *Especialização/Aperfeiçoamento*: **Special Education.** Also MBA
Student Services: Library
Last Updated: 25/03/16

HIGHER EDUCATION FOUNDATION OF OLINDA

Fundação de Ensino Superior de Olinda (FUNESO)

Campus Universitário da Funeso, s/n Jardim Fragoso, Olinda, Pernambuco 53060770
Tel: +55(81) 3439-1990
Fax: +55(81) 3439-3694
EMail: funeso@funeso.com.br
Website: http://www.funeso.com.br

Diretor Geral: Mário Marques de Santana
Diretora Acadêmica: Francisca Zuleide Duarte de Souza

Course
Biological Sciences (Biological and Life Sciences); **Business Administration** (Business Administration); **History** (History); **Literature** (Literature); **Mathematics** (Mathematics); **Nursing** (Nursing); **Pedagogy** (Pedagogy); **Speech Therapy and Audiology** (Speech Therapy and Audiology)
History: Founded 1971.
Main Language(s) of Instruction: Portuguese
Degrees and Diplomas: *Bacharelado*; *Licenciatura*; *Especialização/Aperfeiçoamento*; *Mestrado*: **Linguistics.**
Last Updated: 13/04/16

HIGHER EDUCATION INSTITUTE OF AMERICANA

Instituto de Ensino Superior de Americana (IESA)

Rua do Carpinteiro, 240/270 - Jardim Werner Plaas, Americana, São Paulo 13478-580
Tel: +55(19) 3478-1497
Website: http://www.iesam.edu.br/

Diretora Geral: Rosana Augusto
Coordenadora Geral: Natalia do Lago de Melo

Course
Accountancy (Accountancy); **Business Administration** (Business Administration); **Civil Engineering** (Civil Engineering); **Computer Science** (Computer Science); **Tourism** (Tourism)
History: Founded 1998
Main Language(s) of Instruction: Portuguese
Degrees and Diplomas: *Bacharelado*
Student Services: Library
Last Updated: 31/03/16

HIGHER EDUCATION INSTITUTE OF FORTALEZA

Instituto de Ensino Superior de Fortaleza

Rua Dona Leopoldina 912, Fortaleza, CE 60110-001
Tel: +502(85) 3226-6446
Fax: +502(85) 3221-1132
EMail: unice@unice.br
Website: http://www.unice.br

Diretora: Sylvia Helena Tartuce

Course
Accountancy (Accountancy); **Administration** (Administration); **Computer Networks** (Computer Networks); **Data Processing** (Data Processing); **Pharmacy** (Pharmacy); **Systems Analysis** (Computer Science); **Tourism** (Tourism)
Degrees and Diplomas: *Bacharelado*; *Especialização/Aperfeiçoamento*; *Mestrado*: **Business Administration.**
Last Updated: 15/04/16

HIGHER EDUCATION INSTITUTE OF ITAPIRA

Instituto de Ensino Superior de Itapira (IESI)

Avenida Rio Branco 99, Itapira, São Paulo 13970070
Tel: +55(19) 3863-5510
Fax: +55(19) 3863-4191
EMail: iesi@unip.br
Website: http://www.iesi.edu.br/

Diretor: William Zacariotto EMail: direcao.iesi@gmail.com
Coordenação Pedagógica: José Francisco Martinez EMail: josefrancisco.cp@gmail.com

Course
Accountancy (Accountancy); **Administration** (Administration; Business Administration); **Architecture and Town Planning** (Architecture; Town Planning); **Civil Engineering** (Civil Engineering); **Computer Science** (Computer Science); **Law** (Law); **Nursing** (Nursing); **Nutrition** (Nutrition); **Pedagogy** (Pedagogy); **Pharmacy** (Pharmacy); **Physical Education** (Physical Education); **Physiotherapy** (Physical Therapy); **Production Engineering** (Production Engineering); **Social Communication** (Advertising and Publicity); **Social Services** (Social and Community Services); **Tourism** (Tourism)
History: Founded 1999.
Degrees and Diplomas: *Bacharelado*; *Especialização/Aperfeiçoamento*: **Education; Educational Psychology; Health Administration; Higher Education; Law; Physical Therapy.** Also MBA
Student Services: Library
Last Updated: 31/03/16

HIGHER EDUCATION INSTITUTE OF TAUBATE

Instituto Taubaté de Ensino Superior (ITES)

Av. D. Pedro I, 3.575 - Jardim Eulália, Taubate, São Paulo
Tel: +55(12) 3635-4553
Fax: +55(12) 3635-4553
EMail: naotem@naotem.com.br
Website: http://www.ites.edu.br

Diretor: Izidro José de Paiva Medeiros

Course
Accountancy (Accountancy); **Administration** (Administration); **Advertisinng and Publicity** (Advertising and Publicity); **Computer Science** (Computer Science); **Nursing** (Nursing); **Nutrition** (Nutrition); **Pharmacy** (Pharmacy); **Physiotherapy** (Physical Therapy); **Tourism** (Tourism)
History: Founded 1999.
Main Language(s) of Instruction: Portuguese
Degrees and Diplomas: *Bacharelado*
Last Updated: 14/04/16

HIGHER EDUCATION INSTITUTE OF THE FUNLEC

Instituto de Ensino Superior da Funlec (IES FUNLEC)

Rua Coronel Calcido Arantes 322 Cachoeira II, Campo Grande, Mato Grosso do Sul 79040-450
Tel: +55(67) 3901-2878
Fax: +55(67) 3901-2872
EMail: secretaria.iesfcg@funlec.com.br
Website: http://www.funlec.com.br

Diretor Presidente: Luiz R oberto Pires

Course
Administration *(Bonito Campus)* (Administration); **Library Science** (Library Science); **Pedagogy** (Pedagogy); **Physical Education** (Physical Education)
Further Information: Also Bonito Campus.
History: Founded 1997.
Main Language(s) of Instruction: Portuguese
Degrees and Diplomas: *Bacharelado*
Last Updated: 31/03/16

HIGHER EDUCATION INSTITUTE OF THE PROVINCE OF PERNAMBUCO

Instituto Pernambuco de Ensino Superior (IPESU)
Rua São Miguel, 176, Afogados,
Pernambuco 50670-000
Tel: +55(81) 3472-8100
Website: http://www.ipes.edu.br

Diretora Geral: Ana Paula B. de Melo Oliveira Valença
Diretor Regional: Newton Roberto Gregório de Moraes

Course
Accountancy (Accountancy); **Administration** (Business Administration; Marketing); **Computer Science** (Computer Science); **Law** (Law); **Nursing** (Nursing); **Physiotherapy** (Physical Therapy); **Social Communication** (Advertising and Publicity); **Tourism** (Tourism)
History: Founded 2001.
Main Language(s) of Instruction: Portuguese
Degrees and Diplomas: *Bacharelado*
Student Services: Library
Last Updated: 12/04/16

HIGHER INSTITUTE OF THE COAST OF PARANA

Instituto Superior do Litoral do Paraná (ISULPAR)
Rua Coronel José Lobo 800, Costeira, Paranaguá
Paraná 83203-310
Tel: +55(41) 3423-3415 +55(41) 3424-9257
Fax: +55(41) 3423-3415
EMail: secretaria@isulpar.edu.br; gerenciasistemas@isulpar.edu.br; ouvidoria@isulpar.edu.br
Website: http://www.isulpar.com.br

Diretor de Graduação: Ivan de Medeiros Petry Maciel
Diretor Administrativo: Vilmar Fernandes da Silveir

Course
Administration (Administration); **Financial Management** (Finance); **Hospital Administration** (Health Administration); **Information Systems** (Information Technology); **Law** (Law); **Pedagogy** (Pedagogy); **Port Management** (Transport Management); **Postgraduate Studies** (Administration; Arts and Humanities; Education; Environmental Studies; Law; Technology; Tourism); **Social Communication** (Mass Communication)
History: Founded 2000.
Main Language(s) of Instruction: Portuguese
Degrees and Diplomas: *Tecnólogo*; *Bacharelado*; *Licenciatura*; *Especialização/Aperfeiçoamento*: **Administration; Art Education; Business Administration; Business Education; Civil Law; Constitutional Law; Criminology; Education of the Handicapped; Educational Administration; Environmental Studies; Finance; Fiscal Law; Geography (Human); Health Education; Hotel Management; Labour Law; Law; Management; Maritime Law; Marketing; Neurosciences; Political Sciences; Preschool Education; Primary Education; Private Law; Public Administration; Safety Engineering; Social and Community Services; Special Education; Tourism.** Also MBA in Transport Management
Student Services: IT Centre, Library, eLibrary
Last Updated: 14/04/16

HOLY SPIRIT METHODIST FACULTY

Faculdade Metodista do Espírito Santo
Rua Castelo Branco 1803, Centro,
Vila Velha, Espírito Santo 29100040
Tel: +55(27) 3200-4358
Fax: +55(27) 3399-5851
EMail: coordenacaoadm@metodistaes.edu.br
Website: http://www.metodistaes.edu.br

Diretor: Miguel Ângelo Três (1998-)
EMail: MiguelAngeloTres@metodistaes.edu.br
Vice Diretor: Hugo Luiz de Souza EMail: hsouza@univila.br

Faculty
Law (Law)

Course
Administration (Administration; International Business; Marketing); **Information Systems**; **Pedagogy** (Pedagogy); **Social Communication** (Advertising and Publicity); **Social Services** (Social and Community Services)
History: Founded 1998 incorporating the Faculdade de Ciências Econômicas e Administrativas de Vila Velha, the Faculdade de Vila Velha, the Faculdade de Ciências Sociais de Ibiraçu and the Faculdade de Direito de Vila Velha. Acquired present title through merger with Faculdades UNIVILA 2008.
Degrees and Diplomas: *Bacharelado*; *Especialização/Aperfeiçoamento*; *Mestrado*
Last Updated: 30/06/15

HORIZONTINA FACULTY

Faculdade Horizontina (FAHOR)
Unidade Centro (CFJL), Rua Buricá, 725,
Horizontina, RS 98920-000
Tel: +55(55) 3537-7750
EMail: fahor@fahor.com.br
Website: http://www.fahor.com.br

Diretor: Sedelmo Desbessel EMail: sedelmo@fahor.com.br
Vice-Diretor: Marcelo Blume EMail: marcelo@fahor.com.br

Course
Automation and Control Engineering (Automation and Control Engineering); **Economics** (Economics); **Mechanical Engineering** (Mechanical Engineering); **Postgraduate Studies** (Agricultural Business; Industrial Management; Management; Metal Techniques; Production Engineering; Safety Engineering); **Production Engineering** (Production Engineering)
Further Information: Also Arnoldo Schneider Campus
History: Founded 2001.
Main Language(s) of Instruction: Portuguese
Degrees and Diplomas: *Bacharelado*; *Especialização/Aperfeiçoamento*: **Metal Techniques; Safety Engineering.** Also MBA in Management, Industrial Management, Agricultural Business, Production Engineering
Student Services: IT Centre, Library
Last Updated: 07/09/15

IBESA FACULTY

Faculdade IBESA
Av. Menino Marcelo, s/n, Km2 - Serraria, Maceió, AL 57046
Tel: +55(82) 3221-5636
EMail: ibesa@ibesa.com.br
Website: http://www.ibesa.com.br

Diretora: Janaina Salmos

Course
Pegadogy (Education; Educational Psychology; Special Education); **Physical Education** (Physical Education; Sports); **Physical Therapy** (Physical Therapy)
History: Founded 1993 as Instituto Batista de Ensino Superior de Alagoas. Acquired present status 2002. Part of UNRIB group.
Fees: Postgraduate programmes: 200,00 - 350,00 (Brazilian Real)
Main Language(s) of Instruction: Portuguese

Degrees and Diplomas: *Bacharelado*: **Physical Education.** *Licenciatura*: **Physical Education.** *Especialização/Aperfeiçoamento*: **Educational Administration; Educational Psychology; Physical Education; Special Education.**

Student Services: Library

Last Updated: 29/03/16

IBGEN FACULTY

Faculdade IBGEN (IBGEN)

Rua Barão do Amazonas, 46, Petrópolis, Porto Alegre, RS 90670-000

Tel: +55(51) 3332-0202

Fax: +55(51) 3327-6620

EMail: ibgen@ibgen.com.br; tecnodohms@tecnodohms.org.br

Website: http://www.ibgen.com.br/novo

Diretor: Silvio Ceroni

College

Logistics (Transport Management)

Course

Administration (Business Administration); **Commercial Management** (Business and Commerce); **Computer Networks** (Computer Networks); **Finance** (Finance); **Human Resources Management** (Human Resources); **Information Systems** (Information Technology); **Information Technology Management** (Information Technology); **Law** (Law); **Management Processes** (Management); **Postgraduate Studies** (Business Administration; Clinical Psychology; Commercial Law; Health Administration; Human Resources; Industrial Engineering; Labour Law; Management; Marketing; Peace and Disarmament; Psychology; Safety Engineering; Service Trades; Transport Management); **Private Security** (Protective Services); **Psychology** (Psychology); **Systems for Internet** (Computer Science)

Main Language(s) of Instruction: Portuguese

Degrees and Diplomas: *Tecnólogo*; *Bacharelado*; *Especialização/Aperfeiçoamento*: **Clinical Psychology; Commercial Law; Industrial Engineering; Labour Law; Peace and Disarmament; Psychology; Safety Engineering.** Also MBA

Student Services: IT Centre, Library

Last Updated: 04/12/15

IBIRAPUERA UNIVERSITY

Universidade Ibirapuera (UNIB)

Avenida Interlagos, 1329, Chácara Flora, São Paulo 04661-100

Tel: +55(11) 5694-7900 +55(11) 5694-7935

Fax: +55(11) 5091-1108

EMail: ouvidoria@ibirapuera.edu.br; reitoria@ibirapuera.br; nucai@ibirapuera.edu.br

Website: http://www.ibirapuera.br

Reitor: Anderson José Campos de Andrade

Tel: +55(11) 5543-1911 EMail: reitoria@ibirapuera.br

Area

Business (Accountancy; Administration; Law); **Education** (Pedagogy; Physical Education); **Engineering** (Civil Engineering; Production Engineering); **Health Sciences** (Biomedicine; Dentistry; Nursing; Pharmacy; Physical Education; Physical Therapy; Psychology); **Professional/Technological Studies** (Finance; Human Resources; Marketing; Transport Management); **Technology** (Architecture; Computer Science; Town Planning)

History: Founded 1969.

Admission Requirements: Secondary school certificate and entrance examination

Main Language(s) of Instruction: Portuguese

Degrees and Diplomas: *Bacharelado*; *Licenciatura*; *Especialização/Aperfeiçoamento*: **Accountancy; Administration; Adult Education; Art Education; Business Administration; Business and Commerce; Civil Law; Dentistry; Education of the Handicapped; Educational Administration; Educational Psychology; Educational Technology; Finance; Health Sciences; Higher Education; Humanities and Social Science Education; Industrial and Organizational Psychology; Leadership; Literature; Management; Marketing; Portuguese; Primary Education; Public Health; Real Estate; Rehabilitation and Therapy; Religious Education; Science Education; Secretarial Studies; Special Education; Taxation; Teacher Training; Transport Management.** *Mestrado*: **Dentistry.** Also MBA

Student Services: Library

Last Updated: 05/04/16

ICESP FACULTIES

Faculdade ICESP (ICESP)

QE-11 - Área Especial C/D, Guará I, Brasília, DF 71020-631

Tel: +55(61) 3035-9500

Fax: +55(61) 3383-9524

EMail: unicesp@unicesp.edu.br

Website: http://www.icesp.br

Diretora Geral: Ana Angélica Gonçalves Paiva

Secretário Acadêmico: Claudio Amorim dos Santos

Course

Accountancy (Accountancy); **Administration** (Administration); **Advertising Production** (Advertising and Publicity); **Agronomy** (Agronomy); **Audiovisual Production** (Radio and Television Broadcasting); **Biomedicine** (Biomedicine); **Civil Aviation** (Air Transport); **Civil Engineering** (Civil Engineering); **English Literature** (Literature); **Environmental Management** (Environmental Management); **Financial Management** (Finance); **Human Resources Management** (Human Resources); **Journalism** (Journalism); **Law** (Law); **Marketing** (Marketing); **Nursing** (Nursing); **Pedagogy** (Pedagogy); **Postgraduate Studies** (Arts and Humanities; Business Administration; Communication Studies; Environmental Studies; Health Sciences; Information Technology; Law; Pedagogy; Psychology); **Radiology** (Radiology); **Spanish Literature** (Literature); **Technological Studies I** (Advertising and Publicity; Air Transport; Computer Networks; Information Management; Marketing; Radio and Television Broadcasting; Radiology; Systems Analysis); **Technological Studies II** (Environmental Management; Finance; Human Resources); **Veterinary Medicine** (Veterinary Science)

History: Founded 1995 as Faculdades Integradas ICESP (FACICESP). Acquired present status 2003 and title 2011.

Main Language(s) of Instruction: Portuguese

Degrees and Diplomas: *Tecnólogo*; *Bacharelado*; *Licenciatura*; *Especialização/Aperfeiçoamento*: **Accountancy; Biomedicine; Communication Studies; Educational Psychology; Environmental Studies; Finance; Foreign Languages Education; Health Sciences; Industrial and Organizational Psychology; Law; Management; Political Sciences; Radiology.** Also MBA

Student Services: Library

Last Updated: 02/12/15

IDC FACULTY

Faculdade IDC (IDC)

Rua Vicente da Fontoura, 1578, Bairro Partenon, Porto Alegre, RS 90640-002

Tel: +55(51) 3028-4888

EMail: idc@idc.org.br; paulobujes@idc.org.br

Website: https://www.idc.edu.br

Diretor-Geral: Domingos Roberto Colpo

Diretor Administrativo: Paulo Sérgio Postingher

Course

Law (Law); **Philosophy** (Philosophy); **Postgraduate Studies** (Civil Law; Commercial Law; Criminal Law; Labour Law; Protective Services; Public Law)

History: Founded 1962 as Instituto Social Cristão de Reforma de Estruturas – ISCRE. Acquired present title 1973. Acquired present status 2005.

Main Language(s) of Instruction: Portuguese

Degrees and Diplomas: *Bacharelado*; *Licenciatura*; *Especialização/Aperfeiçoamento*: **Civil Law; Commercial Law; Criminal Law; Labour Law; Protective Services; Public Law.**

Student Services: Library

Last Updated: 07/09/15

IGUAÇU UNIVERSITY - NOVA IGUAÇU

Universidade Iguaçu (UNIG)

Av. Abilio Augusto Távora, 2134, Nova Iguaçu,
Nova Iguaçu, Rio de Janeiro 26275-580
Tel: +55(21) 2765-4000 +55(21) 2765-4002
Fax: +55(21) 2765-4063
EMail: unig@unig.br; chancelaria@unig.br; proeg@unig.br; unigpi@gmail.com; marcelorosa@unig.br
Website: http://www.unig.br

Reitor: André Nascimento Monteiro
Tel: +55(21) 2765-4090 EMail: reitoria@unig.br

Pró-Reitoria Administrativa: José Carlos de Melo
Tel: +55(21) 2765-4084 EMail: proad@unig.br

Faculty

Biological and Health Sciences (FaCBS) (Biological and Life Sciences; Cosmetology; Dentistry; Environmental Management; Health Sciences; Medicine; Nursing; Pharmacy; Physical Education; Physical Therapy; Radiology; Veterinary Science); **Education and Letters (FAeL)** (English; Literature; Pedagogy; Portuguese); **Exact Sciences and Technology (FaCET)** (Civil Engineering; Computer Engineering; Mathematics Education; Metallurgical Engineering; Petroleum and Gas Engineering; Production Engineering; Safety Engineering); **Law and Applied Social Sciences (FaCJSA)** (Administration; Human Resources; Law; Marketing; Transport Management)

Further Information: Also University Hospital; Itaperuna Campus

History: Founded 1969 as Faculdade de Filosofia, Ciências e Letras; Incorporated other Faculties and acquired present status and title 1993. A private institution under the supervision of the Sociedade de Ensino Superior da Nova Iguaçu.

Academic Year: March to December

Admission Requirements: Secondary school certificate and competitive entrance examination

Main Language(s) of Instruction: Portuguese

Degrees and Diplomas: *Tecnólogo*; *Bacharelado*; *Licenciatura*; *Especialização/Aperfeiçoamento*: **Art Education; Business and Commerce; Civil Engineering; Civil Law; Clinical Psychology; Construction Engineering; Dentistry; Educational Administration; Educational and Student Counselling; Educational Psychology; Higher Education Teacher Training; Labour Law; Medical Technology; Medicine; Neurosciences; Nursing; Occupational Health; Orthodontics; Radiology; Sports Medicine.**

Student Services: Library

Publications: Revista Acta Biomédica Brasiliensia; Revista Conexão Acadêmica; Revista da Ciência e Tecnologia; Revista Eletrônica Saberes Múltiplos

Last Updated: 05/04/16

IMP INSTITUTE OF HIGHER EDUCATION

IMP de Ensino Superior (IMP)

CSG 09 Setor Sul, 15/16, Taguatinga, Brasília, DF 72035-509
Tel: +55(61) 3226_7955
EMail: otavio@weducacional.com.br

Diretor: Wellington Guimaraes

Course

Administration (Administration); **Letters (Portuguese)** (Arts and Humanities; Portuguese); **Philosophy** (Philosophy)

Main Language(s) of Instruction: Portuguese

Degrees and Diplomas: *Bacharelado*; *Licenciatura*

Last Updated: 15/04/16

INFÓRIUM FACULTY OF TECHNOLOGY

Faculdade Infórium de Tecnologia (FIT)

R. dos Timbiras, 1532, Funcionários,
Belo Horizonte, MG 30140-061
Tel: +55(31) 2103-2103
EMail: secretaria.geral@promove.net.br; angelica@unicesp.edu.br; diogo.goncalves@faculdadepromove.br
Website: http://www.faculdadepromove.br/bh

Diretor Geral: Dante Pires Cafaggi

Diretor Administrativo: Thiago Muniz

Programme

Information Technology (Information Technology); **Technological Studies** (Computer Networks; Cooking and Catering; Finance; Human Resources; Information Technology; Marketing; Transport Management)

Course

Administration (Administration); **Graduate Studies** (Accountancy; Business Administration; Business and Commerce; Cooking and Catering; Design; Finance; Higher Education; Human Resources; Information Management; Information Technology; Labour Law; Media Studies; Private Law; Public Law; Safety Engineering; Software Engineering; Transport Management); **Law** (Law); **Social Communication - Advertising and Publicity** (Advertising and Publicity; Mass Communication)

Further Information: Also João Pinheiro Campus.

History: Founded 1999 as Escola Técnica Infórium. Acquired present title and status 2003.

Main Language(s) of Instruction: Portuguese

Degrees and Diplomas: *Tecnólogo*; *Bacharelado*; *Especialização/Aperfeiçoamento*: **Business Administration; Information Technology; Software Engineering; Transport Management.** *Mestrado*: **Information Technology.** Also MBA in Cooking and Catering

Student Services: Library

Last Updated: 31/08/15

INGA FACULTY

Faculdade Ingá (UNINGA)

Rod. PR 317, 6114, Maringá, Paraná 87035-510
Tel: +55(44) 3225-5009
EMail: normas@uninga.br
Website: http://faculdadeinga.com.br

Diretor: Ricardo Benedito de Oliveira
EMail: diretoria@uninga.br

Course

Biology (Biology); **Biomedicine** (Biomedicine); **Dentistry** (Dentistry); **Medicine** (Medicine); **Nursing** (Nursing); **Nutrition** (Nutrition); **Pharmacy** (Pharmacy); **Physical Education** (Physical Education); **Physiotherapy** (Physical Therapy); **Psychology** (Psychology); **Social Services** (Social and Community Services); **Speech Therapy** (Speech Therapy and Audiology)

History: Founded 1999.

Main Language(s) of Instruction: Portuguese

Degrees and Diplomas: *Bacharelado*; *Licenciatura*; *Especialização/Aperfeiçoamento*; *Mestrado*

Student Services: Library

Last Updated: 05/05/15

INSAEOS FACULTY OF TECHNOLOGY

Faculdade de Tecnologia INSAEOS (INSAEOS)

Rua Mato Grosso, 408, São Cristóvão, Cascavel,
PR 85813-020
Tel: +55(45) 3322-0016
EMail: contato@insaeos.org.br
Website: http://www.insaeos.org.br

Course

Cooperative Management (Finance; Management; Marketing; Transport Management); **Postgraduate Studies** (Finance; Management)

History: Founded 2011.

Main Language(s) of Instruction: Portuguese

Degrees and Diplomas: *Tecnólogo*; *Especialização/Aperfeiçoamento*: **Finance; Management.**

Last Updated: 03/12/15

INSPER TEACHING AND RESEARCH INSTITUTE

INSPER Instituto de Ensino e Pesquisa (INSPER)
Rua Quatá, 300, Vila Olímpia, São Paulo, SP 04546-042
Tel: +55(11) 4504-2400 +55(11) 4504-2300
Fax: +55(11) 4504-2350
EMail: rogeriopc1@insper.edu.br; secretariaacademica@insper.edu.br
Website: http://www.insper.edu.br

Diretor Presidente: Marcos Lisboa
Diretora Acadêmica de Graduação: Carolina da Costa
Diretora de Desenvolvimento Institucional: Marcia Maria Nizzo de Moura

Course
Administration (Administration); **Computer Engineering** (Computer Engineering); **Economics** (Economics); **Mechanical Engineering** (Mechanical Engineering); **Mechatronics Engineering** (Electronic Engineering)
History: Founded 1987.
Main Language(s) of Instruction: Portuguese
Degrees and Diplomas: *Bacharelado*; *Mestrado*: **Administration; Economics.** *Doutorado*: **Industrial and Production Economics.** Also Executive MBA, Postgraduate Certificates, Advanced Program in Finance, Legal Master (LL.M.)
Last Updated: 15/04/16

INSTITUTE OF ADVANCED STUDIES OF BOITUVA

Instituto de Educação Superior de Boituva (FIB)
Rodovia SP 129, Km 14, Campo de Boituva, Boituva, SP 18550-000
Tel: +55(15) 3363-8120
Fax: +55(15) 3363-8120
EMail: nascimento@aasp.org.br; ckto@terra.com.br; academicosup@uniesp.edu.br
Website: http://fibsp.edu.br

Diretor: Fernando Costa

Course
Accounting (Accountancy); **Administration** (Administration); **Law** (Law); **Mathematics** (Mathematics); **Pedagogy** (Pedagogy)
Main Language(s) of Instruction: Portuguese
Degrees and Diplomas: *Bacharelado*; *Licenciatura*
Student Services: Library
Last Updated: 17/04/16

INSTITUTE OF APPLIED THEOLOGY

Instituto Superior de Teologia Aplicada (INTA)
Rua Coronel Antonio Rodrigues Magalhães, Bairro Dom Expedito Lopes, 359, Sobral, Ceará 62050-100
Tel: +55(88) 3112-3500 +55(88) 3614-3232
Fax: +55(88) 3614-3232
EMail: inta2@zipmail.com.br; diretoria@inta.edu.br
Website: http://www.inta.edu.br

Diretor-Presidente: Oscar Rodriguez Junior
Pró-Diretora Administrativa: Ingrid Soraya de Oliveira Sá
EMail: prodi@inta.edu.br

Area
Biological and Health Sciences (Biomedicine; Medicine; Nursing; Nutrition; Pharmacy; Physical Education; Physical Therapy; Veterinary Science); **Exact Sciences** (Architecture; Civil Engineering; Production Engineering; Protective Services; Town Planning); **Human Sciences** (History; Journalism; Law; Pedagogy; Social and Community Services; Theology)

Department
Distance Education (History; Pedagogy; Physical Education)

Course
PRODOC (Teacher Training)
History: Founded 1999.
Main Language(s) of Instruction: Portuguese
Degrees and Diplomas: *Tecnólogo*; *Bacharelado*; *Licenciatura*; *Especialização/Aperfeiçoamento*: **Alternative Medicine; Arts and Humanities; Biological and Life Sciences; Chemistry; Civil Law; Clinical Psychology; Community Health; Computer Networks; Data Processing; Dietetics; Educational Administration; Educational Psychology; English; Geography (Human); Gerontology; Health Administration; Health Sciences; History; Humanities and Social Science Education; Hygiene; Information Management; Information Technology; Labour Law; Marketing; Mass Communication; Mathematics Education; Media Studies; Midwifery; Native Language Education; Nursing; Nutrition; Occupational Health; Orthopaedics; Paediatrics; Pharmacy; Physical Therapy; Physics; Physiology; Preschool Education; Primary Education; Private Law; Psychiatry and Mental Health; Public Health; Rehabilitation and Therapy; Safety Engineering; Secondary Education; Small Business; Social and Community Services; Social Welfare; Software Engineering; Special Education; Sports; Sports Medicine; Toxicology.** *Mestrado*: **Biological and Life Sciences; Biotechnology.** Also MBA
Student Services: Library
Last Updated: 14/04/16

INSTITUTE OF EDUCATION AND CULTURE OF CUIABA

Instituto Cuiabá de Ensino e Cultura (ICEC)
R. Oswaldo da Silva Corrêa, 621 - Despraiado, Cuiabá, MT 78048-005
Tel: +55(65) 3927-3401
EMail: marcioacbarros@yahoo.com.br
Website: http://www.icec.edu.br

Diretor: Pedro Américo Frugoli

Course
Accountancy (Accountancy); **Administration** (Administration); **Civil Engineering** (Civil Engineering); **Computer Science** (Computer Networks; Computer Science); **Information Systems** (Information Technology); **Law** (Law); **Physiotherapy** (Physical Therapy); **Social Communication** (Advertising and Publicity); **Social Services** (Social and Community Services; Social Sciences); **Tourism** (Tourism)
History: Founded 2002.
Main Language(s) of Instruction: Portuguese
Degrees and Diplomas: *Tecnólogo*; *Bacharelado*
Student Services: Library
Last Updated: 30/03/16

INSTITUTE OF EDUCATION AND CULTURE OF MARANHAO

Instituto Maranhense de Ensino e Cultura (IMEC)
Av. São Marçal, 214, João Paulo, São Luís, MA 65071-680
Tel: +55(98) 3235-4762
EMail: marcioacbarros@yahoo.com.br
Website: http://www.suafaculdade.com.br/imec

Diretor Secretário: Regina Célia Bitencourt Reis Pinho

Course
Undergraduate Studies (Accountancy; Administration; Advertising and Publicity; Law; Tourism)
Further Information: Also Distance Education
History: Founded 2006.
Main Language(s) of Instruction: Portuguese
Degrees and Diplomas: *Bacharelado*
Student Services: eLibrary
Last Updated: 11/04/16

INSTITUTE OF EDUCATION OF BICAS

Instituto Superior de Educação de Bicas (ISEB)
Rua Áurea Aliada Pereira Lanha, 107, Centro, Bicas, MG 36600-000
Tel: +55(32) 3271-1043
EMail: isebfeap@hotmail.com
Website: http://www.faculdadebicas.adm.br/

Course
Pedagogy (Pedagogy)

Degrees and Diplomas: *Licenciatura*
Last Updated: 13/04/16

INSTITUTE OF EDUCATION OF IVOTI

Instituto Superior de Educaçao Ivoti (ISEI)

Rua Júlio Hauser n°171, Bairro 7 de Setembro, Ivoti, RS 93900-000
Tel: +55(51) 3563-8600 +55(51) 3563-8656
Fax: +55(51) 3563-8601
EMail: isei@isei.edu.br
Website: http://www.isei.edu.br

Diretor Geral: Manfredo Carlos Wachs

Diretor Administrativo: Cristiano Gestrich

Course
Education (Education); **Geography** (Pedagogy); **History** (History); **Letters - Portuguese** (Arts and Humanities; Portuguese); **Music** (Music); **Pedagogical Teacher Training** *(Special Programme)* (Teacher Training); **Portuguese and German Languages** (German; Portuguese)

History: Founded 1998, accredited 2002.

Main Language(s) of Instruction: Portuguese

Degrees and Diplomas: *Licenciatura*; *Especialização/Aperfeiçoamento*: **Education; Educational Administration; Educational and Student Counselling; Music; Neurosciences; Preschool Education.**

Student Services: Library
Last Updated: 14/04/16

INSTITUTE OF EDUCATION OF PARANA

Faculdade Instituto Superior de Educação do Paraná (FAINSEP)

Rua dos Gerânios, n° 1893, Borba Gato, Cianorte, PR 87060-010
Tel: +55(44) 3225-1197 +55(44) 3034-4488
EMail: fainsep@fainsep.edu.br
Website: http://www.fainsep.edu.br

Diretor Administrativo: Argemiro Aluísio Karling

Course
Pedagogy (Pedagogy); **Postgraduate Studies** (Education; Management)

History: Founded 2004.

Main Language(s) of Instruction: Portuguese

Degrees and Diplomas: *Licenciatura*; *Especialização/Aperfeiçoamento*: **Adult Education; Art Education; Business Education; Distance Education; Education; Educational Administration; Educational Psychology; Educational Sciences; Educational Technology; Environmental Studies; Law; Leadership; Management; Neurosciences; Pedagogy; Preschool Education; Public Administration; Special Education; Teacher Training.**

Student Services: Library, eLibrary
Last Updated: 13/04/16

INSTITUTE OF EDUCATION OF SAO PAULO - SINGULARIDADES

Instituto Superior de Educação de São Paulo - SINGULARIDADES

Deputado Lacerda Franco, 88, Pinheiros, São Paulo, SP 05418-000
Tel: +55(11) 3034-5445
EMail: singularidades@singularidades.com.br
Website: http://www.singularidades.com.br

Diretor Executivo: Miguel Thompson

Course
Letters (Humanities and Social Science Education; Native Language Education); **Mathematics** (Mathematics Education); **Pedagogy** (Pedagogy)

History: Founded 2001.

Main Language(s) of Instruction: Portuguese

Degrees and Diplomas: *Licenciatura*; *Especialização/Aperfeiçoamento*: **Art Education; Arts and Humanities; Bilingual and Bicultural Education; Child Care and Development; Educational Administration; Educational Sciences; Educational Technology; Portuguese; Preschool Education; Special Education; Sports; Translation and Interpretation.**

Student Services: Library
Last Updated: 13/04/16

INSTITUTE OF EDUCATION OF SERRA

Instituto Superior de Educação da Serra

Rua 1d Ue-I, Lote 02, 80, Setor Centro Industrial da Grande Vitória - CIVIT, CIVIT II, Serra, ES 29161-848
Tel: +55(27) 3322-6321
Fax: +55(27) 3321-7559
EMail: diretoria@doctum.edu.br
Website: www.doctum.edu.br

Diretor: Claudio Cezar Azevedo De Almeida Leitaob

Course
Undergraduate Studies (Biological and Life Sciences; Physical Education)

Degrees and Diplomas: *Licenciatura*
Last Updated: 12/04/16

INSTITUTE OF EDUCATION OF THE VALLEY OF THE JURUENA

Instituto Superior de Educação do Vale do Juruena (AJES)

Av. Gabriel Muller, 1065, módulo 01, Juína, MT 78320-000
Tel: +55(66) 3566-1875 +55(66) 3566-6172
EMail: secretaria@ajes.edu.br; gtomasini@ajes.edu.br; contato@pomini.or
Website: http://www.ajes.edu.br

Diretor: Clodis Antonio Menegaz EMail: clodis@ajes.edu.br

Course
Geography (Geography); **Letters** (Literature); **Mathematics** (Mathematics); **Pedagogy** (Pedagogy); **Physical Therapy** (Respiratory Therapy); **Psychology** (Psychology); **Social Services** (Social and Community Services); **Theology** (Theology)

History: Founded 2005.

Main Language(s) of Instruction: Portuguese

Degrees and Diplomas: *Bacharelado*; *Licenciatura*; *Especialização/Aperfeiçoamento*: **Developmental Psychology; Mathematics Education; Neurosciences; Public Health; Science Education; Special Education.**

Last Updated: 13/04/16

INSTITUTE OF HIGHER EDUCATION OF BAHIA

Instituto Baiano de Ensino Superior (IBES)

Av. Jorge Amado, 780, Imbuí, Salvador, BA
Tel: +55(71) 3496-4050
EMail: ibesbahia@yahoo.com.br
Website: http://www.ibes.edu.br

Diretor: Daniel Jorge dos Santos Branco Borges

Coordenadora Pedagogica: Paloma Martinez Veiga Branco

Course
Accountancy (Accountancy); **Administration** (Administration); **Computer Networks** (Computer Networks); **Computer Science** (Computer Science); **Law** (Law); **Nursing** (Nursing); **Pharmacy** (Pharmacy); **Physiotherapy** (Physical Therapy); **Social Communication** (Advertising and Publicity); **Social Service** (Social and Community Services); **Tourism** (Tourism)

History: Founded 2002.

Main Language(s) of Instruction: Portuguese

Degrees and Diplomas: *Bacharelado*: **Accountancy; Administration; Advertising and Publicity; Computer Networks; Computer Science; Law; Nursing; Pharmacy; Physical Therapy; Tourism.**

Student Services: Library
Last Updated: 25/03/16

INSTITUTE OF HIGHER EDUCATION OF ITAPETININGA

Instituto Itapetiningano de Ensino Superior (IIES)
Rua Isolina de Morais Rosa 727, Vila Nastri,
Itapetininga, São Paulo 18206-320
Tel: +55(15) 3275-8700
EMail: diretoria@ites.edu.br
Website: http://www.iies.edu.br

Diretora: Ana Paula Garcia Martins

Course
Accountancy (Accountancy); **Administration** (Administration; Marketing); **Advertising and Publicity** (Advertising and Publicity); **Law** (Law); **Pharmacy** (Pharmacy); **Physical Education** (Physical Education); **Physical Therapy** (Physical Therapy); **Production Engineering** (Production Engineering); **Social Services** (Social and Community Services); **Tourism** (Tourism)

History: Founded 1998.

Main Language(s) of Instruction: Portuguese

Degrees and Diplomas: *Bacharelado*

Student Services: Library
Last Updated: 11/04/16

INSTITUTE OF HIGHER EDUCATION OF JOÃO MONLEVADE

Instituto de Ensino Superior de João Monlevade (IES/FUNCEC)
Rua 16 24, Prédio 1, Vila Tanque,
João Monlevade, Minas Gerais 35930408
Tel: +55(31) 3852-4000 +55(31) 3852-4216
Fax: +55(31) 3852-4434
EMail: iesfuncec@funcec.br
Website: http://www.funcec.br

Diretor Geral: Alessandro Moreira Lima

Course
Accountancy; **Administration**; **Environmental Studies**; **Journalism** (Journalism); **Law**; **Literature** (Literature); **Pedagogy**

History: Founded 1972.

Main Language(s) of Instruction: Portuguese

Degrees and Diplomas: *Bacharelado*; *Especialização/ Aperfeiçoamento*
Last Updated: 18/04/16

INSTITUTE OF HIGHER EDUCATION OF MARANHÃO

Instituto de Estudos Superiores do Maranhão (IESMA)
Rua do Rancho, 110, Centro, São Luís, MA 65010-010
Tel: +55(98) 3334-6458
EMail: iiesma@iesma.com.br
Website: http://www.iesma.com.br

Diretor Geral: Abraão Marques Colins EMail: amcolins@elo.com.br

Vice-Diretor Geral/Diretor Acadêmico: Frei José Luís Leitão
EMail: academico@iesma.com.br

Course
Postgraduate Studies (Adult Education; Applied Linguistics; Canon Law; Education; Educational Administration; Educational and Student Counselling; Educational Psychology; Gerontology; Higher Education; Higher Education Teacher Training; History; Management; Philosophy; Religious Education; Special Education; Theology); **Undergraduate Studies** (Philosophy; Religious Studies; Theology)

History: Founded 1984 as Centro Teológico do Maranhão (CETEMA). Acquired present title 1999.

Main Language(s) of Instruction: Portuguese

Degrees and Diplomas: *Bacharelado*; *Licenciatura*; *Especialização/Aperfeiçoamento*: **Adult Education; Applied Linguistics; Canon Law; Education; Educational Administration; Educational and Student Counselling; Educational Psychology; Ethics; Gerontology; Higher Education Teacher Training; History; Management; Philosophy; Special Education; Theology.**

Student Services: Library
Last Updated: 04/04/16

INSTITUTE OF HIGHER EDUCATION OF MATO GROSSO

Instituto de Ensino Superior de Mato Grosso (IESMT)
Rua Santa Filomena, 621, Santa Marta, Cuiabá, MT
Tel: +55(65) 3621-3401
Website: http://www.suafaculdade.com.br/iesmt

Diretor Geral: Pedro Américo Frugoli

Course
Accountancy (Accountancy); **Administration** (Administration); **Law** (Law); **Mathematics** (Mathematics); **Nursing** (Nursing); **Production Engineering** (Production Engineering); **Social Communication** (Advertising and Publicity); **Social Services** (Social and Community Services); **Tourism** (Tourism)

Further Information: Also Distance Education

History: Founded 2007.

Main Language(s) of Instruction: Portuguese

Degrees and Diplomas: *Bacharelado*; *Licenciatura*
Student Services: Library
Last Updated: 01/04/16

INSTITUTE OF HIGHER EDUCATION OF NORTHERN RIO GRANDE

Instituto de Ensino Superior do Rio Grande do Norte (IESRN)
Av. Prudente de Morais, 4.890, Lagoa Nova, Natal, RN 59077-000
Tel: +55(84) 3234-3637
Website: http://www.suafaculdade.com.br/iesrn/index.asp

Diretora Geral: Josefa Iluminata de Macedo Borba
Tel: +55(84) 3234-3551 EMail: iluminataborba@yahoo.com.br

Course
Law (Law); **Social Services** (Social and Community Services)

History: Fouded 2005.

Main Language(s) of Instruction: Portuguese

Degrees and Diplomas: *Bacharelado*

Student Services: Library
Last Updated: 01/04/16

INSTITUTE OF HIGHER EDUCATION OF OLINDA

Instituto de Ensino Superior de Olinda
Av. Sigismundo Gonçalves, 375 Carmo, Olinda, PE
Tel: +55(81) 3429-4330
EMail: newton_moraes@uol.com.br
Website: http://www.suafaculdade.com.br/ieso

Diretor: Newton Roberto Gregório de Moraes

Course
Accountancy (Accountancy); **Administration** (Administration); **Law** (Law); **Social Communication** (Advertising and Publicity)

History: Founded 2002.

Main Language(s) of Instruction: Portuguese

Degrees and Diplomas: *Bacharelado*

Student Services: Library
Last Updated: 01/04/16

INSTITUTE OF HIGHER EDUCATION OF PIEDADE

Instituto de Ensino Superior de Piedade
Rua José Braz Moscow, n° 252, bairro Piedade,
Jaboatão dos Guararapes, PE 54410-390
Tel: +55(81) 3361-3844
Website: http://www.fape-pe.edu.br/FAPEIII/index.asp

Diretor: Newton Moraes

Course
Administration (Administration); **Social Communication** (Advertising and Publicity); **Tourism** (Tourism)
History: Founded 2002.
Main Language(s) of Instruction: Portuguese
Degrees and Diplomas: *Bacharelado*
Student Services: Library
Last Updated: 01/04/16

INSTITUTE OF HIGHER EDUCATION OF RONDÔNIA

Instituto de Ensino Superior de Rondônia (IESUR)
Avenida Capitão Sílvio 2738 - Fundos c/Rua Rio Negro, Ariquemes, Rondônia 78932000
Tel: +55(69) 3535-5005
Fax: +55(69) 3535-5008
EMail: iesur@faar.edu.br
Website: http://www.faar.edu.br

Diretor: Ivanilde José Rosique

Course
Administration (Administration; Business Administration); **Computer Science** (Computer Science); **Law** (Law); **Nursing** (Nursing); **Pharmacy** (Pharmacy); **Psychology** (Psychology)
History: Founded 2001.
Main Language(s) of Instruction: Portuguese
Degrees and Diplomas: *Bacharelado*; *Especialização/Aperfeiçoamento*: **Civil Law; Environmental Studies; Higher Education; Industrial and Organizational Psychology.**
Last Updated: 01/04/16

INSTITUTE OF HIGHER EDUCATION OF THE FUPESP

Instituto de Ensino Superior da Fupesp
Rua Aldo Moretti N°181, Jardim Ouro Negro, Paulínia, SP 13140-000
EMail: superint@fupespp.gov.br

Course
Administration (Administration)
History: Founded 2003.
Main Language(s) of Instruction: Portuguese
Degrees and Diplomas: *Bacharelado*
Last Updated: 31/03/16

INSTITUTE OF HIGHER EDUCATION OF THE GREATER FLORIANÓPOLIS

Instituto de Ensino Superior da Grande Florianópolis (IES)
Rua Vereador Walter Borges 424, Campinas, São José, Santa Catarina 88101030
Tel: +55(48) 3878-2000
Fax: +55(48) 3878-2000
EMail: adrivalgas.cgc@unip.br
Website: http://www.ies.edu.br

Diretor Geral: Samir Saliba Murad EMail: diretoria@ies.edu.br
Coordenação Pedagógica: Janaina Patricia Perez EMail: janainaperez.cp@unip.br

Course
Accountancy (Accountancy); **Administration** (Business Administration; Hotel Management; Human Resources; Information Management; Marketing); **Advertising** (Advertising and Publicity); **Civil Engineering** (Civil Engineering); **Computer Science** (Computer Science); **Law** (Law); **Nutricion** (Nutrition); **Pedagogy** (Pedagogy); **Physiotherapy** (Physical Therapy); **Production Engineering** (Production Engineering); **Social Services** (Social and Community Services); **Tourism** (Tourism)
History: Founded 1999.
Main Language(s) of Instruction: Portuguese
Degrees and Diplomas: *Bacharelado*; *Especialização/Aperfeiçoamento*: **Business Administration; Human Resources; Information Technology; Physical Education; Public Health.** Also MBA
Student Services: Library
Last Updated: 31/03/16

INSTITUTE OF PHILOSOPHY AND THEOLOGY OF GOIÁS

Instituto de Filosofia e Teologia de Goiás (IFITEG)
7a Avenida Quadra 531, Setor Leste Universitário, Goiânia, GO 74603-030
Tel: +55(62) 3218-3280 +55(62) 3920-1880
EMail: secretariageral@ifite.edu.br
Website: http://www.ifiteg.edu.br

Diretor Geral: Paulo Cézar Nunes de Oliveira

Course
Undergraduate Studies (Philosophy; Theology)
History: Founded 1982.
Main Language(s) of Instruction: Portuguese
Degrees and Diplomas: *Bacharelado*; *Licenciatura*
Student Services: eLibrary
Last Updated: 04/04/16

INSTITUTE OF SCIENCES AND HEALTH

Instituto de Ciências e Saúde (ICS)
Avenida Osmane Barbosa, 11,111, Montes Claros, MG 39404-006
Tel: +55(38) 2101-9268
Fax: +55(38) 2101-9292
EMail: halita.pimentel@funorte.edu.br; tania.raquel.muniz@hotmail.com; ruy.muniz@funorte.com.br
Website: http://www.funorte.com.br/index.php?option=com_content&view=article&id=98&Itemid=519

Diretor de Unidade/Campus São Luis: Ivanilde Soares Queiroz Almeida EMail: ivanilde.queiroz@funorte.edu.br

Course
Biomedicine (Biomedicine); **Dentistry** (Dentistry); **Medicine** (Medicine); **Nursing** (Nursing); **Nutrition** (Nutrition); **Phonoaudiology** (Speech Therapy and Audiology); **Physical Education** (Physical Education); **Physiotherapy** (Physical Therapy)
Main Language(s) of Instruction: Portuguese
Degrees and Diplomas: *Bacharelado*
Student Services: Library
Last Updated: 17/04/16

INSTITUTE OF SOCIAL AND HUMAN SCIENCES

Instituto de Ciências Sociais e Humanas (ICSH)
Rua 17, Quadra 47, Lotes 18/20, Jardim Oriente, Valparaíso, GO 72870-000
Tel: +55(61) 3627-2515
Fax: +55(61) 3627-2515
EMail: faleconosco@icsh.com.br; luizlukaspop@gmail.com
Website: www.icshvalparaiso.edu.br

Diretor Geral: Sérgio Bilotta

Course
Letters (Arts and Humanities); **Pedagogy** (Pedagogy); **Philosophy** (Philosophy)
Main Language(s) of Instruction: Portuguese
Degrees and Diplomas: *Licenciatura*; *Especialização/Aperfeiçoamento*: **Adult Education; African Studies; Art Education; Business Education; Education; Educational Administration; Educational Psychology; Ethics; Gender Studies; Health Education; Higher Education Teacher Training; Humanities and Social Science Education; Latin American Studies; Library Science; Literature; Management; Philosophy; Physical Education; Special Education; Teacher Training; Vocational Counselling.**
Student Services: IT Centre, Library, eLibrary
Last Updated: 17/04/16

INSTITUTE OF SOCIAL AND HUMAN SCIENCES OF JANUÁRIA

Instituto de Ciências Sociais e Humanas - Januária (INCISOH)

Praça Tiradentes 164, Centro, Januária, Minas Gerais 39480000
Tel: +55(38) 3621-1403
Fax: +55(38) 3621-2056
EMail: ceiva@soebras.edu.br
Website: http://www.incisoh.com.br/

Secretaria Geral: Maria Goret de Menezes Ferreira de Menezes Ferreira EMail: maria.goret@soebras.edu.br

Course
Administration (Administration); **Geography** (Geography); **History** (History); **Pedagogy** (Pedagogy; Teacher Training); **Portuguese Literature** (Portuguese); **Tourism** (Tourism)

History: Founded 1995.

Main Language(s) of Instruction: Portuguese

Degrees and Diplomas: *Bacharelado*: **Administration.** *Licenciatura*: **Geography; Pedagogy.**

Student Services: Library
Last Updated: 30/03/16

INTEGRATED ADVENTIST FACULTIES OF MINAS GERAIS

Faculdades Integradas Adventistas de Minas Gerais (FADMINAS)

Rua Joaquim Gomes Guerra N°590, Caixa Postal 144, Keneddy, Lavras, Minas Gerais 37200-000
Tel: +55(35) 3829-360
EMail: faculdade@fadminas.org.br
Website: http://www.fadminas.org.br

Diretor Geral: Luis Daniel Strumiello

Course
Accountancy (Accountancy); **Administration** (Administration); **Advertising and Publicity** (Advertising and Publicity); **Pedagogy** (Pedagogy)
History: Founded 1999.
Degrees and Diplomas: *Bacharelado*; *Especialização/Aperfeiçoamento*. Also MBA
Last Updated: 21/07/15

INTEGRATED FACULTIES OF ARACRUZ

Faculdades Integradas de Aracruz (FAACZ)

Rua Professor Berílio Basílio dos Santos, 180, Centro, Aracruz, ES 29194-910
Tel: +55(27) 3302-8000
Fax: +55(27) 3302-8001
EMail: secretaria@fsjb.edu.br
Website: http://www.faacz.com.br

Presidente: Celi Maria Guisso Cabral

Course
Accountancy (Accountancy); **Administration** (Administration); **Architecture and Urbanism** (Architecture; Town Planning); **Chemical Engineering** (Chemical Engineering); **Civil Engineering** (Civil Engineering); **Law** (Law); **Mechanical Engineering** (Mechanical Engineering); **Pedagogy** (Education; Pedagogy); **Production Engineering** (Production Engineering)

History: Founded 1989 as Faculdade de Ciências Humanas de Aracruz (FACHA). Acquired present status and title 2005.

Main Language(s) of Instruction: Portuguese

Accrediting Agency: Ministry of Education

Degrees and Diplomas: *Bacharelado*; *Licenciatura*; *Especialização/Aperfeiçoamento*: **Accountancy; Business Administration; Educational Psychology; Engineering; Environmental Engineering; Health Education; Management.** *Mestrado*: **Metal Techniques.** Also MBA

Student Services: Library
Last Updated: 21/10/15

INTEGRATED FACULTIES OF ARIQUEMES

Faculdades Integradas de Ariquemes (FIAR)

Avenida Guaporé 3577, Setor Institucional, Setor 6, Ariquemes, Rondônia 78932000
Tel: +55(69) 3536-1025
EMail: fiar@fiar.com.br
Website: http://www.fiar.com.br

Presidente: Nilton Elias de Sousa

Course
Accountancy (Accountancy); **Biology** (Biology); **Business Administration** (Business Administration); **Geography** (Geography); **History** (History); **Letters** (Literature); **Mathematics** (Mathematics); **Pedagogy** (Pedagogy); **Physical Education** (Physical Education); **Tourism** (Tourism)

History: Founded 1990.

Main Language(s) of Instruction: Portuguese

Degrees and Diplomas: *Bacharelado*; *Licenciatura*; *Especialização/Aperfeiçoamento*

Student Services: Library
Last Updated: 12/06/15

INTEGRATED FACULTIES OF BOTUCATU

Faculdades Integradas de Botucatu (UNIFAC)

Avenida Leonardo Villas Boas 351, Vila Nova Botucatu, Botucatu, SP 18608901
Tel: +55(14) 6821-2500
Fax: +55(14) 6821-2500
EMail: secretaria@unifac.com.br
Website: http://www.unifac.com.br

Diretora Geral: Cecília B. Pires Tavares de Anderlini (1997-) EMail: diretoria@unifac.com.br

Course
Accountancy (Accountancy); **Administration** (Administration); **Economics** (Economics); **Letters** (Literature); **Pedagogy**; **Physical Education** (Physical Education); **Social Services**; **Tourism** (Tourism)

History: Founded 1993.

Main Language(s) of Instruction: Portuguese

Degrees and Diplomas: *Bacharelado*; *Licenciatura*; *Especialização/Aperfeiçoamento*; *Mestrado*

Last Updated: 01/07/15

INTEGRATED FACULTIES OF CACOAL

Faculdades Integradas de Cacoal

Rua dos Esportes 1038, Incra, Cacoal, RO 78.976-215
Tel: +55(69) 3441-4503
Fax: +55(69) 3441-7002
EMail: unesc@unescnet.br
Website: http://www.unescnet.br

Diretor: Ismael Cury

Course
Accountancy (Accountancy); **Business Administration** (Business Administration); **Civil Engineering** (Civil Engineering); **Computer Science** (Computer Science); **Economics** (Economics); **Environmental Engineering** (Environmental Engineering); **Law** (Law); **Literature** (Literature); **Nutrition** (Nutrition); **Pedagogy** (Pedagogy); **Production Engineering** (Production Engineering); **Psychology** (Psychology); **Theology** (Theology)

History: Founded 1985.

Main Language(s) of Instruction: Portuguese

Degrees and Diplomas: *Bacharelado*; *Licenciatura*; *Especialização/Aperfeiçoamento*

Student Services: Library
Last Updated: 12/06/15

INTEGRATED FACULTIES OF CAMPO GRANDE

Faculdades Integradas Campo-Grandenses
Estrada da Caroba 685, Campo Grande,
Rio de Janeiro, Rio de Janeiro 23085590
Tel: +55(21) 3408-8485
EMail: feuc@feuc.br
Website: http://www.feuc.br

Presidente: Durval Neves da Silva

Course
Administration (Administration); **Computer Science** (Computer Science); **Geography** (Geography); **History** (History); **Letters** (Literature); **Mathematics** (Mathematics); **Pedagogy** (Pedagogy); **Social Sciences** (Social Sciences)

History: Founded 1960 as Faculdade de Filosofia de Campo Grande. Acquired present status and title 2005.

Main Language(s) of Instruction: Portuguese

Degrees and Diplomas: *Bacharelado*; *Licenciatura*; *Especialização/Aperfeiçoamento*. Also MBA
Last Updated: 12/06/15

INTEGRATED FACULTIES OF CARATINGA

Faculdades Integradas de Caratinga (FIC)
Rua João Pinheiro 147, Centro, Caratinga,
Minas Gerais 35300037
Tel: +55(33) 3321-2122
Fax: +55(33) 3321-1976
EMail: diretoria@doctum.com.br
Website: http://www.doctum.edu.br

Diretor: Cláudio Cézar Azevedo de Almeida Leitão

Course
Accountancy (Accountancy); **Architecture and Town Planning** (Architecture; Town Planning); **Computer Science** (Computer Science); **Engineering** (Civil Engineering; Electrical Engineering); **Law** (Law); **Social Services** (Social Work); **Tourism** (Tourism)

History: Founded 1972. Acquired present status and title 2000.

Main Language(s) of Instruction: Portuguese

Degrees and Diplomas: *Bacharelado*; *Especialização/Aperfeiçoamento*
Last Updated: 12/06/15

INTEGRATED FACULTIES OF CATAGUASES

Faculdades Integradas de Cataguases (FIC)
Rua Romualdo Menezes, s/n Menezes,
Cataguases, Minas Gerais 36773084
Tel: +55(32) 3421-3109
EMail: p.institucional@unis.edu.br
Website: http://www.unis.edu.br

Presidente: Stefano Barra Gazzola

Course
Administration (Administration); **Biology**; **Pedagogy** (Pedagogy); **Production Engineering** (Production Engineering)

History: Founded 1965.

Main Language(s) of Instruction: Portuguese

Degrees and Diplomas: *Bacharelado*; *Licenciatura*
Last Updated: 12/06/15

INTEGRATED FACULTIES OF CRUZEIRO

Faculdades Integradas de Cruzeiro (FIC)
Rua Dom Bosco 35, Centro, Cruzeiro, SP 12701250
Tel: +55(12) 3141 1600
EMail: diretoria.fic@hotmail.com
Website: http://www.faculdadefic.com.br

Diretora: Solange Alves de Souza Casemiro da Silva

Course
Administration (Administration); **Geography** (Geography); **History** (History); **Letters** (Literature); **Pedagogy** (Pedagogy)

History: Founded 1972.

Main Language(s) of Instruction: Portuguese

Degrees and Diplomas: *Bacharelado*; *Especialização/Aperfeiçoamento*
Last Updated: 23/10/15

INTEGRATED FACULTIES OF DIAMANTINO

Faculdades Integradas de Diamantino (FID)
Rua Almirante Batista das Neves 1112, Centro,
Diamantino, Mato Grosso 78400000
Tel: +55(65) 3336-1133
Fax: +55(65) 3336-2709
EMail: diretoriageral@fidedu.com.br
Website: http://www.fidedu.com.br

Diretor Geral: Geraldo Magela

Course
Accountancy (Accountancy); **Administration** (Administration); **Computer Science** (Computer Science); **Letters** (Literature); **Pedagogy** (Pedagogy)

History: Founded 1989.

Main Language(s) of Instruction: Portuguese

Degrees and Diplomas: *Bacharelado*; *Licenciatura*; *Especialização/Aperfeiçoamento*
Last Updated: 12/06/15

INTEGRATED FACULTIES OF ESPIRITO SANTO

Faculdades Integradas Espírito Santenses (FAESA I)
Av. Vitória, 2.220 - Monte Belo, Vitória,
Espirito Santo 29053-360
Tel: +55(27) 2122-4100
EMail: faesa@faesa.br
Website: http://portal.faesa.br

Diretor: Alexandre Nunes Theodoro (1990-)

Area
Administration (Accountancy; Administration); **Computer Science** (Computer Engineering; Computer Networks; Computer Science); **Design** (Fashion Design; Interior Design); **Education** (Biology; Chemistry; Pedagogy; Physical Education); **Engineering** (Automation and Control Engineering; Civil Engineering; Electrical Engineering; Environmental Engineering; Mechanical Engineering; Petroleum and Gas Engineering; Production Engineering); **Law** (Law); **Medical and Health Sciences** (Dentistry; Nursing; Nutrition; Occupational Therapy; Psychology; Speech Therapy and Audiology); **Social Communication** (Advertising and Publicity; Journalism; Radio and Television Broadcasting)

History: Founded 1972.

Main Language(s) of Instruction: Portuguese

Degrees and Diplomas: *Bacharelado*; *Especialização/Aperfeiçoamento*

Student Services: Library
Last Updated: 24/06/15

INTEGRATED FACULTIES OF FERNANDÓPOLIS

Faculdades integradas de Fernandópolis (FIFE)
Avenida Teotónio Vilela, s/n Campus Universitarió,
Fernandópolis, SP 15600-000
Tel: +55(17) 3465-0000
EMail: secretaria@fef.br; fef@fef.edu.br
Website: http://www.fef.br

Presidente: Paulo Sérgio do Nascimento

Diretor Acadêmico: Ocimar Antonio de Castro
EMail: ocimar.castro@fef.edu.br

Course
Accountancy (Accountancy); **Administration** (Accountancy; Administration; Marketing); **Aesthetics and Cosmetics** (Cosmetology); **Biology** (Biology; Science Education); **Biomedicine** (Biomedicine); **Chemistry** (Chemistry; Science Education); **Civil Engineering** (Civil Engineering); **Environmental Engineering and Health** (Environmental Engineering; Health Sciences); **Food**

Technology (Food Technology); **History** (History; Humanities and Social Science Education); **Information Systems** (Information Technology); **Journalism** (Journalism); **Letters** (Arts and Humanities; Humanities and Social Science Education); **Mathematics** (Mathematics; Mathematics Education); **Nursing** (Nursing); **Nutrition** (Nutrition); **Occupational Therapy** (Occupational Therapy); **Pedagogy** (Pedagogy); **Pharmacy** (Pharmacy); **Physical Education** (Physical Education); **Physiotherapy** (Physical Therapy); **Postgraduate Studies** (Accountancy; Clinical Psychology; Cosmetology; Educational Psychology; Management; Marketing; Real Estate; Safety Engineering; Sales Techniques; Speech Therapy and Audiology; Taxation; Transport Management); **Psychology** (Psychology); **Social Services** (Social and Community Services); **Speech Therapy** (Speech Therapy and Audiology)

History: Founded 1997

Main Language(s) of Instruction: Portuguese

Degrees and Diplomas: *Técnico de Nivel Medio*; *Tecnólogo*; *Bacharelado*; *Licenciatura*; *Especialização/Aperfeiçoamento*: **Clinical Psychology; Cosmetology; Educational Psychology; Real Estate; Safety Engineering; Speech Therapy and Audiology.** Also MBA

Student Services: Library

Last Updated: 08/02/16

INTEGRATED FACULTIES OF HUMAN SCIENCES, HEALTH AND EDUCATION OF GUARULHOS

Faculdades Integradas de Ciências Humanas, Saúde e Educação de Guarulhos

Rua Barão de Mauá 600, Centro, Guarulhos, São Paulo 07012040
Tel: +55(11) 6409-3533
Fax: +55(11) 6409 3533
EMail: documenta@fg.edu.br
Website: http://www.faculdadesdeguarulhos.edu.br

Diretora: Aparecida Najar

Course

Biology (Biology); **Business Administration** (Business Administration); **Geography** (Geography); **History** (History); **Letters** (Literature); **Mathematics** (Mathematics); **Nursing** (Nursing); **Pedagogy** (Pedagogy); **Physiotherapy** (Physical Therapy); **Psychology** (Psychology)

History: Founded 1971.

Main Language(s) of Instruction: Portuguese

Degrees and Diplomas: *Bacharelado*; *Licenciatura*; *Especialização/Aperfeiçoamento*

Last Updated: 12/06/15

INTEGRATED FACULTIES OF JACAREPAGUÁ

Faculdades Integradas de Jacarepaguá (FIJ)

Ladeira da Freguesia 196 Freguesia, Jacarepaguá, Rio de Janeiro, Rio de Janeiro 22760090
Tel: +55(21) 3392-6646
Fax: +55(21) 3392-6503
EMail: fij@fij.br
Website: http://www.fij.br

Diretor Acadêmico: Hercules Pereira

Course

Accountancy (Accountancy); **Administration** (Administration); **Computer Science** (Computer Science); **Environmental Engineering** (Environmental Engineering); **Nursing** (Nursing); **Physical Education** (Physical Education); **Tourism** (Tourism)

History: Founded 1973 as Faculdade Maria Magalhães Pinto. Acquired present status and title 1989.

Main Language(s) of Instruction: Portuguese

Degrees and Diplomas: *Bacharelado*; *Especialização/Aperfeiçoamento*

Student Services: Library

Last Updated: 12/06/15

INTEGRATED FACULTIES OF NAVIRAÍ

Faculdades Integradas de Naviraí (FINAV)

Rua Laurentino Pires de Arruda 220 Jardim Progresso, Naviraí, MS 79950000
Tel: +55(67) 8151-3008
Fax: +55(67) 461-2380
EMail: finav@terra.com.br
Website: http://www.finav.br

Diretor: Djalma Lino Gonçalves

Course

Accountancy *(FACINAV)* (Accountancy); **Administration** (Administration); **Geography** (Geography); **Literature** (Literature); **Pedagogy** (Pedagogy)

History: Founded 1987.

Main Language(s) of Instruction: Portuguese

Degrees and Diplomas: *Bacharelado*; *Especialização/Aperfeiçoamento*

Last Updated: 12/06/15

INTEGRATED FACULTIES OF OURINHOS

Faculdades Integradas de Ourinhos (FIO)

Rodovia BR153 Km339 + 400m, Bairro Água do Cateto, Ourinhos, São Paulo 19900011
Tel: +55(14) 3302-6400
Fax: +55(14) 3302-6401
EMail: secpedagogica@yahoo.com.br
Website: http://www.fio.edu.br

Diretor: Bianor Costa Freire Colchesqui

Course

Administration (Accountancy; Administration; Business Administration; International Business; Marketing; Public Administration); **Agronomy** (Agronomy); **Architecture and Town Planning** (Architecture; Town Planning); **Art Education** (Art Education; Fine Arts); **Biology** (Biology); **Geography** (Geography); **Information Systems** (Information Management); **Law** (Law); **Nursing** (Nursing); **Pedagogy** (Pedagogy); **Pharmacy** (Pharmacy); **Psychology** (Industrial and Organizational Psychology; Psychology); **Tourism** (Tourism); **Veterinary Science** (Veterinary Science)

History: Founded 1970.

Main Language(s) of Instruction: Portuguese

Degrees and Diplomas: *Bacharelado*; *Licenciatura*; *Especialização/Aperfeiçoamento*. Also MBA

Student Services: Library

Last Updated: 12/06/15

INTEGRATED FACULTIES OF PARANAIBA

Faculdades Integradas de Paranaíba (FIPAR)

Rua Maclino de Queiroz 270, Jardim Redentora, Paranaiba, MS 79500000
Tel: +55(17) 3668-1945
Fax: +55(17) 3668-1945
EMail: secretaria@fipar.edu.br
Website: http://www.fipar.edu.br

Diretora Geral: Edna Mendes de Medeiros

Course

Accountancy (Accountancy); **Administration** (Administration); **Computer Science** (Computer Science); **Law** (Law); **Letters** (Literature); **Pedagogy** (Pedagogy)

History: Founded 1995.

Main Language(s) of Instruction: Portuguese

Degrees and Diplomas: *Bacharelado*; *Especialização/Aperfeiçoamento*

Student Services: Library

Last Updated: 12/06/15

INTEGRATED FACULTIES OF PATOS

Faculdades Integradas de Patos (FIP)
R. Horácio Nóbrega, s/n - Belo Horizonte, Patos, PB 58704-000
Tel: +55(83) 3421-7300
EMail: ffmascarenhas@uol.com.br
Website: http://www.fiponline.com.br

Diretor: João Leuson Palmeira Gomes Alves

Course

Architecture and Town Planning (Architecture; Town Planning); **Biomedicine** (Biomedicine); **Computer Science** (Computer Science); **Dentistry** (Dentistry); **Economics** (Economics); **Geography**; **History** (History); **Journalism** (Journalism); **Law** (Law); **Literature** (Literature); **Nursing**; **Nutrition** (Nutrition); **Pedagogy** (Pedagogy); **Physical Education** (Physical Education); **Physiotherapy** (Physical Therapy); **Social Services** (Social and Community Services)

History: Founded 1967 as Faculdade de Ciências Econômicas de Patos.

Main Language(s) of Instruction: Portuguese

Degrees and Diplomas: *Bacharelado*; *Especialização/Aperfeiçoamento*

Student Services: Library
Last Updated: 12/06/15

INTEGRATED FACULTIES OF PONTA PORÃ

Faculdades Integradas de Ponta Porã (FIP)
Rua Tiradentes 349, Centro,
Ponta Porã, Mato Grosso do Sul 79900000
Tel: +55(67) 431-5851
EMail: faculdadesmagsul@terra.com.br
Website: http://www.fipmagsul.com.br

Diretora Geral: Alessandra Viegas Josgrilbert

Course

Administration (Administration; Marketing); **Law**

History: Founded 1997.

Main Language(s) of Instruction: Portuguese

Degrees and Diplomas: *Bacharelado*

Student Services: Library
Last Updated: 23/06/15

INTEGRATED FACULTIES OF RIBEIRÃO PIRES

Faculdades Integradas de Ribeirão Pires (FIRP)
Rua Coronel Oliveira Lima 3345 Parque Aliança,
Ribeirão Pires, São Paulo 09404000
Tel: +55(11) 4822-8520
Fax: +55(11) 4822-8521
EMail: firp@firp.edu.br
Website: http://www.firp.edu.br

Diretor: Jose Fernando Pinto da Costa
EMail: diretoria@firp.edu.br

Course

Business Administration (Business Administration; Finance); **History** (History); **Information Technology** (Information Technology); **Letters** (English; History; Portuguese); **Mathematics** (Mathematics); **Pedagogy** (Pedagogy); **Physical Education** (Physical Education)

History: Founded 1973 as Faculdade de Ciências e Letras de Ribeirão Pires. Acquired present status 2012.

Main Language(s) of Instruction: Portuguese

Degrees and Diplomas: *Bacharelado*; *Licenciatura*; *Especialização/Aperfeiçoamento*
Last Updated: 23/06/15

INTEGRATED FACULTIES OF SANTA CRUZ DE CURITIBA

Faculdades Integradas Santa Cruz de Curitiba (FARESC)
Rua Afiffe Mansur, 565, Novo Mundo, Curitibá, Paraná 81050-180
Tel: +55(41) 3346-1414
EMail: santacruz@santacruz.br
Website: http://www.santacruz.br

Diretor: José Antonio Soares (1997-)

Course

Accountancy (Accountancy); **Administration** (Administration); **Economics** (Economics); **Information Sciences** (Information Sciences); **Law** (Law); **Letters** (English; Literature; Portuguese); **Pedagogy** (Pedagogy); **Tourism** (Tourism)

History: Founded 1992.

Main Language(s) of Instruction: Portuguese

Degrees and Diplomas: *Bacharelado*; *Licenciatura*; *Especialização/Aperfeiçoamento*

Student Services: Library
Last Updated: 01/07/15

INTEGRATED FACULTIES OF SAO PAULO

Faculdades Integradas de São Paulo (FISP)
Rua Tagua N°:150 Liberdade, São Paulo, São Paulo 5688010
Tel: +55(11) 3758-3009
Fax: +55(11) 3758-7477
EMail: fisp@fisp.br
Website: http://www.fisp.br

Presidente: Marcelo Barbalho Cardoso

Area

Administration and Commerce (Accountancy; Administration; Economics; International Relations; Secretarial Studies); **Architecture, Art, Design and Fashion** (Architecture; Design; Fashion Design; Music; Town Planning); **Communication** (Advertising and Publicity; Journalism; Public Relations; Radio and Television Broadcasting); **Education** (History; Literature; Mathematics; Pedagogy; Social Sciences; Visual Arts); **Engineering** (Automation and Control Engineering; Civil Engineering; Electrical Engineering; Environmental Engineering; Mechanical Engineering; Petroleum and Gas Engineering); **Health Studies** (Art Therapy; Biological and Life Sciences; Biomedicine; Dentistry; Nursing; Nutrition; Pharmacy; Physical Education; Physical Therapy; Psychology; Speech Therapy and Audiology; Veterinary Science); **Law** (Law); **Social Sciences** (Social and Community Services); **Technology** (Computer Science)

History: Founded 1998.

Main Language(s) of Instruction: Portuguese

Degrees and Diplomas: *Bacharelado*; *Especialização/Aperfeiçoamento*; *Mestrado*. Also MBA
Last Updated: 23/07/15

INTEGRATED FACULTIES OF SÃO PEDRO

Faculdades Integradas São Pedro (FAESA)
Rodovia Serrafim Derenzi 3115, Inhanguetá,
São Pedro, Espirito Santo 29030-026
Tel: +55(27) 3331-4500
EMail: direcao@faesa.br
Website: http://www.faesa.br

Diretor Acâdemico: Juliano Silva Campana

Course

Advertising (Advertising and Publicity); **Architecture and Town Planning** (Architecture; Town Planning); **Biology** (Biology); **Dentistry** (Dentistry); **Engineering** (Automation and Control Engineering; Civil Engineering; Electrical Engineering; Mechanical Engineering); **Journalism** (Journalism); **Nursing** (Nursing); **Pedagogy** (Pedagogy); **Psychology** (Psychology)

History: Founded 1994.

Main Language(s) of Instruction: Portuguese

Degrees and Diplomas: *Bacharelado*; *Licenciatura*; *Especialização/Aperfeiçoamento*

Student Services: Library

Last Updated: 24/06/15

INTEGRATED FACULTIES OF TAQUARA

Faculdades Integradas de Taquara (FACCAT)

Avenida Oscar Martins Rangel 4500 - ERS 115,
Taquara, RS 95600000
Tel: +55(51) 3541-6600
Fax: +55(51) 3541-6626
EMail: faccat@faccat.br
Website: http://www.faccat.br

Diretor Geral: Delmar Henrique Backes

Course

Accountancy (Accountancy); **Administration** (Administration); **Computer Science** (Computer Science); **Design** (Design); **History** (History); **Literature** (Literature); **Management** (Management); **Mathematics** (Mathematics); **Nursing** (Nursing); **Pedagogy** (Pedagogy); **Production Engineering** (Production Engineering); **Psychology** (Psychology); **Social Communication** (Advertising and Publicity; Public Relations); **Tourism** (Tourism)

History: Founded 2001.

Main Language(s) of Instruction: Portuguese

Degrees and Diplomas: *Bacharelado*; *Licenciatura*; *Especialização/Aperfeiçoamento*; *Mestrado*

Student Services: Library

Last Updated: 08/07/15

INTEGRATED FACULTIES OF THE HEART OF JESUS

Faculdades Integradas Coração de Jesus (FAINC)

Rua Siqueira Campos, 483 – Centro, Santo André, SP 09020-240
Tel: +55(11) 4433-7477
EMail: wellington@fainc.com.br
Website: http://www.fainc.com.br

Diretor Geral: Wellington de Oliveira

Course

Administration (Administration); **Art Education** (Design; Fine Arts; Music; Theatre); **Library Studies** (Library Science); **Nutrition** (Nutrition); **Social Communication** (Advertising and Publicity)

History: Founded 1976.

Main Language(s) of Instruction: Portuguese

Degrees and Diplomas: *Bacharelado*; *Licenciatura*; *Especialização/Aperfeiçoamento*

Student Services: Library

Last Updated: 12/06/15

INTEGRATED FACULTIES OF THE VALLEY OF THE IVAI

Faculdades Integradas do Vale do Ivaí (UNIVALE)

Avenida Minas Gerais 651 Centro, Ivaiporã, Paraná 86870000
Tel: +55(43) 3472-1414
Fax: +55(43) 3472-1414
EMail: diretoria@univale.com.br
Website: http://www.univale.com.br

Diretora: Neila F. Estigarribia EMail: secuni@univale.com.br

Course

Accountancy (Accountancy); **Administration** (Administration); **Health Sciences** (Health Sciences); **Law** (Law); **Letters** (Literature); **Mathematics** (Mathematics); **Pedagogy** (Pedagogy); **Systems Analysis** (Systems Analysis)

History: Founded 1987.

Main Language(s) of Instruction: Portuguese

Degrees and Diplomas: *Bacharelado*; *Licenciatura*; *Especialização/Aperfeiçoamento*

Last Updated: 23/06/15

INTEGRATED FACULTIES OF TRÊS LAGOAS

Faculdades Integradas de Três Lagoas (AEMS)

Avenida Ponta Porã 2750, Distrito Industrial,
Três Lagoas, MS 79610320
Tel: +55(67) 2105-6060
Fax: +55(67) 2105-6056
EMail: aems@aems.com.br
Website: http://www.aems.com.br

Diretora Geral: Maria Lúcia Atique Gabriel (1998-)

Course

Accountancy (Accountancy); **Administration** (Administration); **Advertising** (Advertising and Publicity); **Agronomy** (Agronomy); **Architecture and Town Planning** (Architecture; Town Planning); **Biology** (Biology); **Biomedicine** (Biomedicine); **Engineering** (Chemical Engineering; Civil Engineering; Computer Engineering; Electrical Engineering; Production Engineering); **Environmental and Sanity Engineering** (Environmental Engineering; Sanitary Engineering); **Food Technology** (Food Technology); **Journalism** (Journalism); **Law** (Law); **Nursing** (Nursing); **Nutrition** (Nutrition); **Pedagogy** (Pedagogy); **Pharmacy** (Pharmacy); **Physical Education** (Physical Education); **Physiotherapy** (Physical Therapy); **Psychology** (Psychology); **Public Relations** (Public Relations); **Secretarial Studies** (Secretarial Studies); **Social Services** (Social and Community Services); **Tourism** (Tourism); **Veterinary Science** (Veterinary Science)

History: Founded 1994.

Main Language(s) of Instruction: Portuguese

Degrees and Diplomas: *Bacharelado*; *Licenciatura*; *Especialização/Aperfeiçoamento*. Also MBAs

Last Updated: 23/06/15

INTEGRATED FACULTIES OF UPIS

Faculdades Integradas da Upis (UPIS)

SEPS 712/912, Conj. A - Asa Sul, Brasília, DF 70390125
Tel: +55(61) 3445-6767
EMail: rodolpho@upis.br
Website: http://www.upis.br

Diretor Presidente: Vicente Nogueira Filho (1998-)

Course

Accountancy (Accountancy); **Administration** (Administration; Hotel Management; Marketing); **Agronomy** (Agronomy); **Computer Science** (Computer Science; Data Processing); **Economics** (Economics); **Geography** (Geography); **History** (History); **Secretarial Studies** (Secretarial Studies); **Tourism** (Tourism); **Veterinary Medicine** (Veterinary Science); **Zoology** (Zoology)

History: Founded 1971.

Main Language(s) of Instruction: Portuguese

Degrees and Diplomas: *Tecnólogo*; *Bacharelado*; *Especialização/Aperfeiçoamento*

Student Services: Library

Last Updated: 12/06/15

INTEGRATED FACULTIES OF VÁRZEA GRANDE

Faculdades Integradas de Várzea Grande (FIAVEC)

Rua Artur Bernades 525, Ipase,
Várzea Grande, Mato Grosso 78125100
Tel: +55(65) 3686-3730
Fax: +55(65) 3686-1902
EMail: secretaria@uninacional.com.br
Website: http://www.ive.edu.br

Diretor Geral: Charlie Rangel

Course

Pedagogy (Pedagogy; Preschool Education; Special Education)

History: Founded 2001.

Main Language(s) of Instruction: Portuguese

Degrees and Diplomas: *Licenciatura*; *Especialização/Aperfeiçoamento*

Student Services: Library

Last Updated: 23/06/15

INTEGRATED FACULTY OF ARAGUATINS

Faculdade Integrada de Araguatins (FAIARA)

Avenida Araguaia 1105 Centro, Araguatins, TO
EMail: faiara_febip@yahoo.com.br
Website: http://www.faiara.com.br

Course

Graduate Studies (Educational Technology; Public Administration); **Undergraduate Studies** (Business Administration; Literature; Pedagogy)

History: Founded 2004.

Main Language(s) of Instruction: Portuguese

Degrees and Diplomas: *Bacharelado*; *Licenciatura*. Also Post-graduate Diploma.
Last Updated: 06/05/15

INTEGRATED FACULTY OF BRAZIL

Faculdade Integrada do Brasil (FAIBRA)

Rua São Pedro, 880 Centro, Teresina, PI 64000-110
Tel: +55(86) 3223-0805
EMail: faibra@faibra.edu.br
Website: http://faibra.edu.br/v2

Diretor Geral: Marcizo Veimar
EMail: marcizoveimar@faibra.edu.br

Course

Pedagogy (Pedagogy)

History: Founded 2006.

Main Language(s) of Instruction: Portuguese

Degrees and Diplomas: *Bacharelado*; *Especialização/Aperfeiçoamento*
Last Updated: 06/05/15

INTEGRATED INSTITUTE OF HIGHER EDUCATION - EDUCATIONAL FOUNDATION OF THE NORTH EAST OF MINAS GERAIS

Instituto de Ensino Superior Integrado - Fundação Educacional Nordeste Mineiro (IESI/FENORD)

Rua Teodolindo Pereira 111, Campus - Bairro Grão Pará, Teófilo Otoni, Minas Gerais 39800-151
Tel: +55(33) 3522-2745
Fax: +55(33) 522-2745
EMail: fato@fenord.com.br
Website: http://www.fenord.com.br

Coordenador Geral: Gustavo Alves de Castro Pires
EMail: gustavo@fenord.com.br

Secretária Geral: Sandra Rodrigues do Nascimento
EMail: sandra@fenord.com.br

Course

Law (Law)

History: Founded 1990

Main Language(s) of Instruction: Portuguese

Degrees and Diplomas: *Bacharelado*

Student Services: Library

Publications: ÁGUIA ACADÊMICA: REVISTA CIENTIFICA DA FENORD; ÁGUIA: REVISTA CIENTIFICA DA FENORD
Last Updated: 04/04/16

INTEGRATED REGIONAL FACULTIES OF AVARÉ

Faculdades Integradas Regionais de Avaré (FIRA)

Praça Prefeito Romeu Bretas 163, Centro, Avaré, São Paulo 18700902
Tel: +55(14) 3711-1828
EMail: fies@frea.edu.br
Website: http://www.fira.edu.br

Presidente: Maria Lúcia Cabral de Freitas Visentin
EMail: direcaofira@frea.edu.br

Course

Arts (Art Education; Cultural Studies; Design; Education; Visual Arts); **Biology** (Biology); **Chemistry** (Chemistry); **History** (History); **Letters** (Literature; Philosophy); **Mathematics** (Mathematics); **Pedagogy** (Pedagogy); **Physical Education** (Physical Education)

History: Founded 1969 as Faculdade de Ciências e Letras de Avaré. Acquired present status and title 2001.

Main Language(s) of Instruction: Portuguese

Degrees and Diplomas: *Bacharelado*; *Licenciatura*; *Especialização/Aperfeiçoamento*

Student Services: Library
Last Updated: 24/06/15

INTEGRATION FACULTY - WESTERN ZONE

Faculdade Integração - Zona Oeste (FIZO)

Avenida Franz Voegeli 900, Vila Yara, Osasco, São Paulo 6020190
Tel: +55(11) 3681-0440
Fax: +55(11) 3681-0440
EMail: daex.aesa@unianhanguera.edu.br

Diretor Geral: Antonio Carbonari Netto

Course

Accountancy (Accountancy); **Administration**; **Law**; **Literature**; **Pedagogy** (Pedagogy); **Social Communication** (Advertising and Publicity; Journalism); **Teacher Training**; **Tourism** (Tourism)

History: Founded 1999.

Main Language(s) of Instruction: Portuguese

Degrees and Diplomas: *Bacharelado*; *Licenciatura*
Last Updated: 28/05/15

INTERMUNICIPAL FACULTY OF THE NORTHWEST OF PARANA

Faculdade Intermunicipal do Noroeste do Paraná (FACINOR)

Rua Mato Grosso 240, Loanda, PR 87900000
Tel: +55(44) 3425-1037
Fax: +55(44) 3425-1037
EMail: facinor@facinor.br
Website: http://www.facinor.br

Diretor: Agenor de Oliveira Duarte

Course

Administration (Administration); **Business Computing** (Business Computing); **Nursing** (Nursing); **Pedagogy** (Education; Pedagogy); **Physical Education** (Physical Education)

History: Founded 1999.

Main Language(s) of Instruction: Portuguese

Degrees and Diplomas: *Tecnólogo*; *Bacharelado*; *Licenciatura*
Last Updated: 22/05/15

INTERNATIONAL FACULTY OF THE DELTA

Faculdade Internacional do Delta (INTA)

Rua Bel Benjamin Constant, n° 540, Centro, Parnaíba, PI 64200-370
Tel: +55(86) 3322-5062
EMail: moses@sobral.org
Website: http://www.intafid.com.br/

Diretor Geral: Cleto Sandys Nascimento de Sousa

Course

Graduate Studies (Art Education; Biology; Business Administration; Business and Commerce; Civil Law; Computer Networks; Constitutional Law; Education; Educational Administration; Educational Psychology; Educational Technology; English; Health Administration; Health Sciences; Higher Education; History; Human Resources; Labour Law; Literacy Education; Literature; Marketing; Mathematics Education; Nutrition; Occupational Health; Physical Education; Physics; Physiology; Portuguese; Public Health; Rehabilitation and Therapy; Religious Education; Science Education; Social and Community Services; Social Policy; Sociology; Software Engineering; Spanish; Special Education; Sports; Tourism); **Undergraduate Studies** (History; Social and Community Services)

History: Founded 2008.

Degrees and Diplomas: *Bacharelado*; *Licenciatura*; *Especialização/Aperfeiçoamento*. Also Postgraduate diploma and MBA.

Last Updated: 22/05/15

INTESP FACULTY

Faculdade INTESP

Rua: Luiz de Souza Coelho, n°. 160, Ipaussu, São Paulo 18950000

Tel: +55(14) 3344-1157

Fax: +55(14) 3344-1157

EMail: intesp-eletrica@uol.com.br

Website: http://www.intesp.edu.br

Diretora: Maria Luiza Egreja Alves Lima

Course

Electrical Engineering (Electrical Engineering)

History: Founded 2001.

Main Language(s) of Instruction: Portuguese

Degrees and Diplomas: *Bacharelado*; *Especialização/Aperfeiçoamento*

Last Updated: 22/05/15

IPIRANGA INTEGRATED FACULTIES

Faculdades Integradas Ipiranga (FAINTIPI)

Avenida Almirante Barroso, 777, Belém, PA 66093-020

Tel: +55(91) 3344-0700

EMail: suely@ipirangaeducacional.com.br

Website: http://www.faculdadeipiranga.com.br

Diretora Geral: Suely Melo de Castro Menezes

Course

Graduate Studies (Accountancy; Business Administration; Development Studies; Education; Educational Administration; Educational Psychology; Educational Technology; Environmental Studies; Higher Education; History; Human Resources; Literacy Education; Mathematics Education; Pedagogy); **Undergraduate Studies** (Administration; Advertising and Publicity; Business and Commerce; Communication Studies; Computer Networks; Cosmetology; Graphic Design; Journalism; Management; Mathematics; Pedagogy; Portuguese; Public Administration; Tourism)

Further Information: Also Cabanagem campus.

Main Language(s) of Instruction: Portuguese

Degrees and Diplomas: *Tecnólogo*; *Bacharelado*; *Licenciatura*; *Especialização/Aperfeiçoamento*; *Mestrado*. Also MBA.

Last Updated: 08/07/15

IPUC FACULTY OF TECHNOLOGY

Faculdade de Tecnologia IPUC (FATIPUC)

Avenida Guilherme Schell, 5000, Centro, Canoas, RD 92310-022

Tel: +55(51) 2103-3000

EMail: ipuc@ipuc.com.br

Website: http://www.ipuc.com.br

Diretor: Francisco Dequi

Course

Grammar Neopedagogy *(Postgraduate)* (Grammar; Teacher Training); **Portuguese Language and Literature** (Literature; Portuguese); **Radiology** (Radiology)

History: Founded 1963.

Main Language(s) of Instruction: Portuguese

Degrees and Diplomas: *Tecnólogo*; *Licenciatura*; *Especialização/Aperfeiçoamento*: **Grammar.**

Last Updated: 31/08/15

ITABORAÍ FACULTY

Faculdade Itaboraí

Av. 22 de Maio 5300, Lj.10, Centro, Itaboraí, RJ 24800-000

Tel: +55(21) 2635-2212 +55(21) 3639-2600

Fax: +55(61) 3799-4910

EMail: andre.silveira@cnec.br; 0352.yohansesteves@cnec.br; ensinosuperior@cnec.br

Website: http://faculdadeitaborai.cnec.br

Diretor: André Stein da Silveira
EMail: 0352.direcao@cnec.br; andre.silveira@cnec.br

Secretaria: Magali Cardoso da Costa e Silva
EMail: magalisilva@cnecrj.com.br

Course

Business Administration (Business Administration); **Distance Mode Postgraduate Studies** (Educational Psychology; Educational Sciences; Environmental Studies; Pedagogy; Primary Education); **Distance Mode Undergraduate Studies** (Human Resources; Management; Pedagogy); **Law** (Law)

History: Founded 2006.

Main Language(s) of Instruction: Portuguese

Degrees and Diplomas: *Bacharelado*; *Licenciatura*; *Especialização/Aperfeiçoamento*: **Educational Psychology; Educational Sciences; Environmental Studies; Pedagogy; Primary Education.** Also MBA

Student Services: IT Centre, Library

Last Updated: 27/11/15

ITALIAN-BRAZILIAN UNIVERSITY CENTRE

Centro Universitario Ítalo-Brasileira (UNIÍTALO)

Avenida João Dias, 2046, Santo Amaro,
São Paulo, São Paulo 04724-003

Tel: +55(11) 5645-0099

Fax: +55(11) 5645-0103

EMail: secretariageral@italo.br

Website: http://www.italo.br

Reitor: Marcos Antônio Gagliardi Cascino EMail: reitor@uniitalo.it

Secretário Geral: Paulo Cesar Pereira

International Relations: Alfredo Grimaldi, Diretor de Relações Internacionais EMail: ri@italo.br

Course

Accountancy (Accountancy); **Administration** (Administration); **Arts and Humanities** (Arts and Humanities; English; Portuguese; Spanish); **Biological Sciences** (Biological and Life Sciences); **Computer Engineering** (Computer Engineering); **Geography** (Geography); **Graduate Studies** (Accountancy; Banking; Business Administration; Civil Law; Communication Studies; Education; Educational Administration; Educational Psychology; Environmental Studies; Finance; Health Administration; Human Rights; Industrial and Organizational Psychology; Marketing; Molecular Biology; Nursing; Nutrition; Pedagogy; Physical Education; Psychiatry and Mental Health; Real Estate; Rehabilitation and Therapy; Teacher Training; Theology); **Nursing** (Nursing); **Pedagogy** (Pedagogy); **Philosophy** (Philosophy); **Physical Education** (Physical Education); **Physiotherapy** (Physical Therapy); **Social Service** (Social and Community Services); **Sociology** (Sociology); **Visual Arts** (Visual Arts)

History: Founded 1972 as Faculdade Ítalo Brasileira. Acquired present status and title 2006.

Main Language(s) of Instruction: Portuguese

Degrees and Diplomas: *Bacharelado*; *Licenciatura*; *Especialização/Aperfeiçoamento*: **Accountancy; Acupuncture; Arts and Humanities; Business Administration; Clinical Psychology; Educational Administration; Educational Psychology; Gerontology; Health Administration; Linguistics; Literacy Education; Nursing; Philosophy; Physical Education; Public Health; Religious Studies; Teacher Training.** *Mestrado*: **Business Administration; Computer Engineering; Information Technology; Software Engineering.**

Student Services: Library

Last Updated: 04/08/15

IZABELA HENDRIX METHODIST UNIVERSITY CENTRE

Centro Universitário Metodista Izabela Hendrix (CEUNIH)

Rua da Bahia 2020, Praça da Liberdade,
Belo Horizonte, Minas Gerais 30160-012

Tel: +55(31) 3244-7200

Fax: +55(31) 3244-7250

EMail: paula.silva@izabelahendrix.edu.br

Website: http://www.izabelahendrix.edu.br

Diretor Geral e Reitor: Marcio de Moraes (2005-)

International Relations: Ana Clara Oliveira Santos Garner, Assessoria de Relações Internacionais- International Affairs Office EMail: ari@izabelahendrix.edu.br

Course

Accountancy (Accountancy); **Administration** (Administration); **Architecture and Urbanism** (Architecture; Town Planning); **Biological Sciences** (Biology); **Biomedicine** (Biomedicine); **Business and Management** (Business Administration; Management); **Civil Engineering** (Civil Engineering); **Communication** (Advertising and Publicity; Journalism); **Education** (Education; Pedagogy); **Environmental Engineering** (Environmental Engineering); **Environmental Management** (Environmental Management); **Interior Design** (Interior Design); **Law** (Law); **Marketing** (Marketing); **Music** (Music); **Nursing** (Nursing); **Nutrition** (Nutrition); **Phonaudiology** (Speech Therapy and Audiology); **Physical Education** (Physical Education); **Physiotherapy** (Physical Therapy); **Production Engineering** (Production Engineering); **Social Services** (Social and Community Services); **Theology** (Theology)

Further Information: Also Venda Nova Campus

History: Founded 1904 as Instituto Metodista Izabela Hendrix. Accredited as university centre 2002.

Admission Requirements: Secondary school certificate and entrance examination (Vestibular)

Fees: 2700 per annum (US Dollar)

Main Language(s) of Instruction: Portuguese

Degrees and Diplomas: *Tecnólogo*; *Bacharelado*; *Licenciatura*. Especialização in cooperation with São Paulo Methodist University.

Student Services: Cultural Activities, Facilities for disabled people, Library, Nursery Care, Social Counselling, Sports Facilities

Publications: A Tocha

Last Updated: 01/09/15

JESUIT FACULTY OF PHILOSOPHY AND THEOLOGY

Faculdade Jesuíta de Filosofia e Teologia (FAJE)

Avenida Doutor Cristiano Guimarães 2127 Planalto,
Belo Horizonte, Minas Gerais 31720300
Tel: +55(31) 3115-7000
Fax: +55(31) 3115-7015
EMail: faje@faculdadejesuita.edu.br
Website: http://www.faculdadejesuita.edu.br

Reitor: Álvaro Mendonça Pimentel
EMail: reitor@faculdadejesuita.edu.br

Department

Philosophy *(Ecclesiastical)*; **Theology** *(Ecclesiastical)*

Higher Institute

Education (Education; Philosophy)

History: Founded 1992. Acquired present title 2005.

Main Language(s) of Instruction: Portuguese

Degrees and Diplomas: *Bacharelado*; *Licenciatura*; *Especialização/Aperfeiçoamento*; *Mestrado*

Last Updated: 26/05/15

JOÃO CALVINO FACULTY

Faculdade João Calvino

Av. Clériston Andrade 3507, BR 242 – Loteamento Vila Nova,
Barreiras, BA 47806-180
Tel: +55(77) 3613-2914
EMail: contato@fjc-unirb.com.br
Website: http://fjc-unirb.com.br

Diretor: Flávio Morais Leite

Course

Philosophy (Anthropology; History; Philosophy; Sociology); **Theology** (Theology)

History: Founded 2000.

Main Language(s) of Instruction: Portuguese

Degrees and Diplomas: *Bacharelado*; *Licenciatura*; *Especialização/Aperfeiçoamento*

Last Updated: 10/07/15

JOHN PAUL II FACULTY

Faculdade João Paulo II (FAJOPA)

Rua Bartolomeu de Gusmão 531, Marília, SP 17506-280
Tel: +55(14) 3414-1965
EMail: sec.geral@fajopa.edu.br
Website: http://www.fajopa.edu.br

Diretor: Maurílio Alves Rodrigues (2008-)

Course

Philosophy (Philosophy); **Theology** (Theology)

History: Founded 2003.

Main Language(s) of Instruction: Portuguese

Degrees and Diplomas: *Bacharelado*; *Licenciatura*

Last Updated: 26/05/15

JOSÉ AUGUSTO VIEIRA FACULTY

Faculdade José Augusto Vieira (FJAV)

Praça Nossa Sra. Aparecida, 40, Bairro Cidade Nova, Lagarto, SE
Tel: +55(79) 3631-9210
EMail: fijav@marata.com.br
Website: http://www.unidom.com.br

Diretora Geral: Silmere Alves

Course

Accountancy (Accountancy); **Administration** (Administration); **Geography** (Geography); **History** (History); **Information Systems** (Computer Science); **Letters** (Literature); **Mathematics** (Mathematics); **Pedagogy** (Pedagogy); **Portuguese and English Literature** (Literature); **Production Engineering** (Production Engineering); **Social Services** (Social and Community Services)

History: Founded 2004.

Main Language(s) of Instruction: Portuguese

Degrees and Diplomas: *Bacharelado*; *Licenciatura*; *Especialização/Aperfeiçoamento*

Student Services: Library

Last Updated: 26/05/15

JOSÉ LACERDA JR FACULTY OF APPLIED SCIENCES

Faculdade José Lacerda Filho de Ciências Applicadas (FAJOLCA)

Avenida Francisco Alves de Souza 500, Centro,
Ipojuca, PE 55590000
Tel: +55(81) 3551-1221
Fax: +55(81) 3551-1370
EMail: secretaria@fajolca.edu.br
Website: http://www.fajolca.edu.br

Diretora: Lais da Fonseca Lacerda

Course

Accountancy (Accountancy); **Administration** (Administration); **Pedagogy** (Pedagogy)

History: Founded 1999.

Main Language(s) of Instruction: Portuguese

Degrees and Diplomas: *Bacharelado*; *Especialização/Aperfeiçoamento*

Last Updated: 26/05/15

KENNEDY FACULTIES

Faculdades Kennedy

Rua José Dias Vieira, 46, bairro Rio Branco,
Belo Horizonte, Minas Gerais 31535040
Tel: +55(31) 3408-2393 +55(31) 3408-2390
Fax: +55(31) 3408-2391
EMail: kennedy@gold.com.br
Website: http://www.kennedy.br/home

Diretor Geral: João Evangelista Alves de Paula (1996-)

Vice-Diretor Geral e Diretor Administrativo: Setembrino Lopes Filho

Faculty

Kennedy Faculty of Belo Horizonte (FKBH) (Environmental Engineering; Mechanical Engineering; Mining Engineering; Nursing;

Nutrition; Production Engineering; Road Transport; Safety Engineering); **Kennedy Faculty of Minais Gerais (FKMG)** (Electrical Engineering; Labour Law; Law)

School

Kennedy School of Engineering (Civil Engineering; Transport Management)

Course

Administration (Administration); **Computer Networks** (Computer Networks); **Events** (Public Relations); **Financial Management** (Finance); **Gastronomy** (Cooking and Catering); **Human Resources** (Human Resources); **Information Systems** (Information Technology); **Marketing** (Marketing); **Systems for Internet** (Computer Science)

History: Founded 1964 as Escola de Engenharia Civil Kennedy.

Main Language(s) of Instruction: Portuguese

Degrees and Diplomas: *Tecnólogo*; *Bacharelado*; *Especialização/Aperfeiçoamento*: **Accountancy; Business Administration; Business and Commerce; Civil Engineering; Civil Law; Design; E- Business/Commerce; Educational Administration; Finance; Higher Education; Industrial Management; Information Management; Information Technology; Labour Law; Management; Media Studies; Public Law; Safety Engineering; Software Engineering; Transport Management.** Also MBA in Cooking and Catering

Student Services: IT Centre, Library, Sports Facilities

Last Updated: 02/02/16

KURIOS FACULTY

Faculdade Kurios (FAK)

Avenida Dr. Argeu Gurgel B. Herbest 960,
Maranguape, Ceará 61940-000
Tel: +55(85)3341-0562
EMail: contato@fak.edu.br
Website: http://www.fak.edu.br

Diretor Geral: Augusto Ferreira da Silva Neto

Course

Accountancy (Accountancy); **Administration** (Administration); **Law** (Law); **Letters** (Literature); **Pedagogy** (Pedagogy); **Social Services** (Social and Community Services); **Theology** (Theology)

History: Founded 2002.

Main Language(s) of Instruction: Portuguese

Degrees and Diplomas: *Bacharelado*; *Licenciatura*; *Especialização/Aperfeiçoamento*

Last Updated: 26/05/15

LA SALLE FACULTY OF TECHNOLOGY - ESTRELLA

Faculdade de Tecnologia La Salle - Estrela (FACSALLE)

Rua Tiradentes, 401, Estrela, RS 95880-000
Tel: +55(51) 3720-2732
EMail: faleconosco.estrela@lasalle.edu.br;
marcos.corbellini@lasalle.edu.br
Website: http://lasalle.edu.br/faculdade/estrela

Diretor Geral: Marcos Corbellini

Diretora Administrativa: Cláudia Argiles da Costa

Course

Administration (Business Administration); **Postgraduate Studies** (Business Administration; Finance; Human Resources; Leadership; Management; Marketing; Sales Techniques); **Technological Studies** (Agricultural Business; Environmental Management; Finance; Human Resources; Management)

History: Founded 2006. Acquired current status 2009.

Main Language(s) of Instruction: Portuguese

Degrees and Diplomas: *Tecnólogo*; *Bacharelado*. Also MBA

Student Services: Academic Counselling, Canteen, IT Centre, Library, Sports Facilities

Last Updated: 03/12/15

LA SALLE UNIVERSITY CENTRE

Centro Universitário La Salle (UNILASALLE)

Avenida Victor Barreto, 2288, Centro,
Canoas, Rio Grande do Sul 92010-000
Tel: +55(51) 3476-8500
Fax: +55(51) 3472-3511
EMail: unilasalle@unilasalle.edu.br
Website: http://www.unilasalle.edu.br

Reitor: Paulo Fossatti EMail: reitoria@unilasalle.edu.br

Pró-Reitora Acadêmica: Vera Lúcia Ramirez

Faculty

Estrelas (Administration; Agricultural Business; Environmental Studies; Finance; Human Resources; Management; Marketing; Secretarial Studies; Tourism); **La Salle Caxias** (Management); **Lucas do Rio Verde** (Accountancy; Administration; Agricultural Business; Commercial Law; Industrial Management; Information Technology; Law; Pedagogy; Physical Education; Tourism); **Manaus** (Accountancy; Administration; Finance; Industrial Management; Information Technology; International Relations; Marketing; Physical Education)

Area

Linguistics and Literature, Arts (English; Portuguese; Spanish); **Applied Social Sciences** (Accountancy; Architecture; Economics; Law; Tourism; Town Planning); **Biological Sciences** (Biology); **Cultural Production and Design** (Graphic Design; Industrial Design); **Engineering** (Chemical Engineering; Civil Engineering; Computer Engineering; Engineering; Environmental Engineering; Production Engineering; Telecommunications Engineering); **Exact and Earth Sciences** (Chemistry; Computer Science; Mathematics; Physics); **Health Sciences** (Cosmetology; Health Sciences; Nursing; Physical Education; Physical Therapy); **Human Sciences** (Clinical Psychology; Educational Psychology; Geography; History; International Relations; Pedagogy; Psychology; Theology)

School

Business Administration (Business Administration; Finance; Human Resources; Management; Marketing; Transport Management)

Course

Hospitality and Leisure (Leisure Studies); **Information and Communication** (Computer Networks; Information Technology)

Further Information: Also Unilasalle Rio de Janeiro

History: Founded 1972 as Centro Educacional La Salle de Ensino Superior - CELES. Acquired present status and title 1998.

Admission Requirements: School Certificate (in Portuguese)

Main Language(s) of Instruction: Portuguese

Accrediting Agency: Ministry of Education.

Degrees and Diplomas: *Tecnólogo*; *Bacharelado*; *Licenciatura*; *Especialização/Aperfeiçoamento*: **Clinical Psychology; Law; Safety Engineering.** *Mestrado*: **Business Administration; Cultural Studies; Education; Environmental Studies; Health Sciences; Heritage Preservation; Law.** *Doutorado*: **Cultural Studies; Education; Heritage Preservation.** Also MBA.

Student Services: Academic Counselling, Canteen, Careers Guidance, Cultural Activities, Facilities for disabled people, Health Services, Language Laboratory, Library, Nursery Care, Social Counselling, Sports Facilities

Publications: Intervalo; Memória e Linguagens Culturais

Publishing House: Centro Editorial

Last Updated: 04/08/15

LA SALLE UNIVERSITY CENTRE OF RIO DE JANÉIRO

Centro Universitário La Salle Rio de Janeiro (UNILASALLE/RJ)

Rua Gastão Gonçalves 79, Santa Rosa, Niterói, RJ 24240-030
EMail: faleconosco.uni@lasalle.org.br
Website: http://unilasalle.edu.br/rj/a-rede-la-salle/

Reitor: Ignácio Lúcio Weschenfelder

Vice-Reitor e Pró-Reitor Acadêmico: Ronaldo Curi Gismondi

Area
Applied Social Sciences (Accountancy; International Relations; Social Sciences); **Exact and Earth Sciences** (Civil Engineering; Information Technology; Production Engineering); **Human Sciences** (Administration; History; Law; Pedagogy)

School
Business (Business Administration)

History: Founded 2002.

Main Language(s) of Instruction: Portuguese

Degrees and Diplomas: *Bacharelado*; *Especialização/Aperfeiçoamento*: **Commercial Law; Computer Engineering; Design; Educational Psychology; Law; Materials Engineering; Nutrition; Software Engineering.** *Mestrado*: **Business Administration.** Also MBA

Student Services: Library

Last Updated: 23/10/15

LATIN AMERICAN FACULTY OF EDUCATION

Faculdade Latino Americana de Educação (FLATED)
Rua Dona Leopoldina, 907 – Centro, Fortaleza, Ceará 60015051
Tel: +55(85) 3454-1299
EMail: diretoriacademica@flated.edu.br
Website: http://www.flated.edu.br

Diretor Geral: Celio Roberto da Silva

Course
Administration (Administration); **Pedagogy** (Pedagogy); **Tourism** (Tourism)

History: Founded 2000. Moved in 2004.

Main Language(s) of Instruction: Portuguese

Degrees and Diplomas: *Bacharelado*; *Licenciatura*; *Especialização/Aperfeiçoamento*

Last Updated: 26/05/15

LEMOS DE CASTRO FACULTY OF COMPUTER SCIENCE

Faculdade de Informática Lemos de Castro (FILC)
Rua Carolina Machado, 304,
Rio de Janeiro, Rio de Janeiro 21351-021
Tel: +55(21) 3390-0101 +55(21) 2450-1799
Fax: +55(21) 450-1666
EMail: filc@lemosdecastro.br; lemos@lemosdecastro.br
Website: http://www.faculdadelemosdecastro.edu.br/faculdade.asp

Diretor: Délio Torres de Castro

Course
Information Systems (Computer Engineering; Information Technology)

History: Founded 1999

Main Language(s) of Instruction: Portuguese

Degrees and Diplomas: *Bacharelado*. Also Postgraduate Programmes offered through distance mode by EaD UNIESP

Student Services: Library

Last Updated: 09/07/15

LIBERTAS INTEGRATED FACULTIES

Libertas Faculdades Integradas
Avenida Wenceslau Bras, 1018, Lagoinha,
São Sebastião do Paraíso, MG 37950-000
Tel: +55(35) 3531-1998
Fax: +55(35) 3531-1328
EMail: ceduc2008@hotmail.com
Website: http://www.libertas.edu.br

Presidente: José Carlos Marinzeck.

Course
Graduate Studies (Accountancy; Administrative Law; Business Administration; Computer Science; Finance; Health Administration; Public Health; Software Engineering); **Undergraduate Studies** (Accountancy; Administration; Information Sciences; Law; Nursing)

History: Founded 1970.

Main Language(s) of Instruction: Portuguese

Degrees and Diplomas: *Bacharelado*; *Especialização/Aperfeiçoamento*; *Mestrado*: **Business Administration; Finance; Law.**

Last Updated: 14/04/16

LIONS FACULTY

Faculdade Lions (FAC-LIONS)
Alameda dos Bambus, Qd.CL01 Lt.01 - Sítio de Recreio Mansões Bernardo Sayão, Goiânia, GO
Tel: +55(62) 3567-3480
EMail: diretor@faclions.com.br
Website: http://www.faclions.org

Diretor Geral: Ronaldo Nielson

Course
Administration (Administration); **Advertising** (Advertising and Publicity); **Hotel Management** (Hotel Management); **Law** (Law); **Tourism** (Tourism)

History: Founded 2002.

Main Language(s) of Instruction: Portuguese

Degrees and Diplomas: *Bacharelado*; *Especialização/Aperfeiçoamento*

Last Updated: 26/05/15

LOGOS THEOLOGICAL FACULTY OF HUMANITIES AND SOCIAL SCIENCES

Faculdade Teológica de Ciências Humanas e Sociais Logos (FAETEL)
Rua Padre Adelino, 700, Belenzinho, São Paulo, SP 03303-000
Tel: +55(11) 2081-4486
Fax: +55(11) 2081-5077
EMail: faetel@faetel.edu.br
Website: http://www.faetel.edu.br

Diretor Geral: Alcino Lopes de Toledo

Course
Graduate Studies (Educational Psychology; Higher Education; Religious Studies); **Undergraduate Studies** (Theology)

History: Founded 1983 as Faculdade de Educação Teológica.

Degrees and Diplomas: *Bacharelado*; *Licenciatura*; *Especialização/Aperfeiçoamento*

Last Updated: 08/07/15

LOURENÇO FILHO FACULTY

Faculdade Lourenço Filho (FLF)
Rua Barão do Rio Branco 2101, Centro, Fortaleza, Ceará 60025062
Tel: +55(85) 4009-6060
Fax: +55(85) 4009-6001
EMail: roberta@flf.edu.br
Website: http://www.flf.edu.br

Diretor Geral: Antônio Figueiras Lima Filho (1998-)

Course
Accountancy (Accountancy); **Administration** (Business Administration; Human Resources; International Business; Management); **Computer Science** (Computer Science); **Marketing** (Marketing); **Tourism** (Tourism)

Further Information: Also Faculty of Technology in Parangaba

History: Founded 1997.

Main Language(s) of Instruction: Portuguese

Degrees and Diplomas: *Bacharelado*; *Especialização/Aperfeiçoamento*: **Accountancy.** Also MBA

Last Updated: 27/05/15

LUCIANO FEIJÃO FACULTY

Faculdade Luciano Feijão (FLF)
Avenida Dom José 325 - Anexo B, Sobral, Ceará 62010-290
Tel: +55(88) 3611-3100
EMail: isabelpontes@lucianofeijao.com.br
Website: http://www.flucianofeijao.com.br

Diretor: Francisco Lúcio Pontes Feijão

Course

Administration (Administration); **Law** (Law); **Psychology** (Psychology); **Social Communication** (Communication Studies)

History: Founded 2004.

Main Language(s) of Instruction: Portuguese

Degrees and Diplomas: *Bacharelado*; *Especialização/Aperfeiçoamento*: **Law.** *Mestrado*: **Administration; Law.**

Student Services: Library

Last Updated: 27/05/15

LUSÍADA UNIVERSITY CENTRE

Centro Universitário Lusíada (UNILUS)

Armando de Salles Oliveira, 150, Boqueirão,
Santos, São Paulo 11050-071
Tel: +55(13) 3202-4500
Fax: +55(13) 3221-4488
EMail: unilus@lusiada.br
Website: http://www.lusiada.br

Reitor: Nelson Teixeira (1998-)

Course

Administration (Administration); **Biomedicine** (Biomedicine); **International Relations** (International Relations); **Medicine** (Medicine); **Nursing** (Nursing); **Nutrition** (Nutrition); **Pedagogy** (Pedagogy; Special Education); **Phonoaudiology** (Speech Therapy and Audiology); **Physical Education** (Physical Education); **Physical Therapy** (Physical Therapy); **Radiology** (Radiology); **Social and Community Services** (Social and Community Services); **Theatre** (Theatre)

History: Founded 1966.

Main Language(s) of Instruction: Portuguese

Degrees and Diplomas: *Tecnólogo*; *Bacharelado*; *Licenciatura*; *Especialização/Aperfeiçoamento*: **Acupuncture; Cardiology; Cosmetology; Educational Psychology; Fine Arts; Gynaecology and Obstetrics; Health Administration; International Relations; Marketing; Medical Technology; Nursing; Nutrition; Paediatrics; Physical Therapy; Public Health; Special Education; Surgery; Systems Analysis.** *Mestrado*: **Medicine.**

Student Services: Library

Last Updated: 27/08/15

LUTHERAN INSTITUTE AND EDUCATIONAL CENTRE - BOM JESUS

Instituto Superior e Centro Educacional Luterano - Bom Jesus (BOM JESUS/IELUSC)

Rua Princesa Isabel, 438, Centro, Joinville, SC 89201-270
Tel: +55(47) 3026-8000 +55(47) 3433-0155
Fax: +55(47) 3026-8090 +55(47) 3433-4737
EMail: ielusc@ielusc.br; paulo.aires@ielusc.br
Website: http://www.ielusc.br

Diretor Geral: Silvio Iung

Secretária Executiva: Marilia Jusi da Silva

Diretor do Ensino Superior: Paulo Aires

Course

Administration (Administration); **Advertising and Publicity** (Advertising and Publicity); **Journalism** (Journalism); **Nursing** (Nursing); **Nutrition** (Nutrition); **Phonoaudiology** (Speech Therapy and Audiology); **Physical Education** (Physical Education); **Postgraduate Studies** (Alternative Medicine; Gerontology; Mass Communication; Physical Education)

Further Information: Also 3 campuses in bairro Saguaçu

History: Founded 1995

Main Language(s) of Instruction: Portuguese

Degrees and Diplomas: *Bacharelado*; *Licenciatura*; *Especialização/Aperfeiçoamento*: **Alternative Medicine; Gerontology; Mass Communication; Physical Education.**

Student Services: Cultural Activities, Library, Sports Facilities

Last Updated: 14/04/16

LUTHERAN UNIVERSITY OF BRAZIL

Universidade Luterana do Brasil (ULBRA)

Avenida Farroupilha, 8001, Bairro São José,
Canoas, Rio Grande do Sul 92425-900
Tel: +55(51) 3477-4000
Fax: +55(51) 3477-1313
EMail: ulbra@ulbra.br; procinstitucional@ulbra.br
Website: http://www.ulbra.br

Reitor: Marcos Fernando Ziemer
Tel: +55(51) 477-2222 EMail: reitoria@ulbra.br

Pró-Reitor Acadêmico: Pedro Antonio González Hernández

Vice-Reitor: Ricardo Willy Rieth

Pró-Reitor de Planejamento e Administração: José Paulinho Brand

Faculty

Leonardo da Vinci Faculty - ULBRA (Administration)

Institute

Lutheran Institute of Higher Education of Porto Velho(ILES)/ ULBRA Porto Velho Unit (Administration; Electrical Engineering; Law; Physical Education; Production Engineering; Psychology)

Centre

Lutheran University Centre of Ji-Paraná (CEULJI/ULBRA) (Accountancy; Administration; Agronomy; Architecture; Biological and Life Sciences; Biomedicine; Information Technology; Journalism; Law; Nursing; Pharmacy; Physical Education; Physical Therapy; Social and Community Services; Town Planning; Veterinary Science); **Lutheran University Centre of Manaus (CEULM/ ULBRA)** (Administration; Architecture; Chemical Engineering; Civil Engineering; Electrical Engineering; Environmental Engineering; Law; Mechanical Engineering; Nursing; Psychology; Town Planning; Transport Management)

Course

Accounting (Accountancy); **Administration** (Administration); **Agronomy** (Agronomy); **Architecture and Urbanism** (Architecture; Town Planning); **Automotive Engineering** (Automotive Engineering); **Biological Sciences** (Biological and Life Sciences); **Biological Sciences** (Science Education); **Biomedicine** (Biomedicine); **Chemical Engineering** (Chemical Engineering); **Chemistry** (Science Education); **Civil Engineering** (Civil Engineering); **Computer Science** (Computer Science); **Cosmetology** (Cosmetology); **Dance** (Art Education); **Dentistry** (Dentistry); **Design** (Design); **Economics** (Economics); **Education in Organizations** (Education); **Electrical Engineering** (Electrical Engineering); **Environmental and Sanitary Engineering** (Environmental Engineering; Sanitary Engineering); **Geography** (Science Education); **History** (Humanities and Social Science Education); **History** (History); **Industrial Chemistry** (Industrial Chemistry); **Information Systems** (Information Technology); **Journalism** (Journalism); **Law** (Law); **Letters - English Language and Literature** (Foreign Languages Education; Humanities and Social Science Education); **Letters - Portuguese and Literature** (Humanities and Social Science Education; Native Language Education); **Mathematics** (Mathematics Education); **Mechanical Engineering** (Mechanical Engineering); **Medicine** (Medicine); **Nursing** (Nursing); **Pedagogy** (Pedagogy); **Pharmacy** (Pharmacy); **Physical Education** (Physical Education); **Physics** (Science Education); **Physiotherapy** (Physical Therapy); **Political Science** (Political Sciences); **Production Engineering** (Production Engineering); **Psychology** (Psychology); **Social Communication - Public Relations** (Mass Communication; Public Relations); **Social Communication, Publicity and Advertisement** (Advertising and Publicity; Mass Communication); **Social Sciences** (Humanities and Social Science Education); **Social service** (Social and Community Services); **Speech Therapy** (Speech Therapy and Audiology); **Theology** (Theology); **Trilingual Executive Secretariat** (Modern Languages; Secretarial Studies); **Veterinary Medicine** (Veterinary Science); **Visual Arts** (Art Education)

History: Founded 1964 as Canõas College of Administration Sciences, became University 1989. Maintained by the Comunidade Evangelica Luterana São Paulo.

Academic Year: March to December (March-July; August-December)

Admission Requirements: Secondary school certificate and entrance examination

Main Language(s) of Instruction: Portuguese

Degrees and Diplomas: *Tecnólogo*; *Bacharelado*; *Licenciatura*; *Especialização/Aperfeiçoamento*: **African Studies; Architecture; Arts and Humanities; Biomedicine; Civil Law; Civil Security; Clinical Psychology; Communication Studies; Computer Science; Cosmetology; Criminal Law; Criminology; Cultural Studies; Data Processing; Dental Technology; Dentistry; Education; Educational Administration; Educational and Student Counselling; Educational Psychology; Energy Engineering; Engineering; Environmental Management; Environmental Studies; Fashion Design; Finance; Fire Science; Gerontology; Gynaecology and Obstetrics; Health Sciences; Higher Education; Higher Education Teacher Training; History; Hygiene; Indigenous Studies; Industrial Design; International Business; Labour Law; Latin American Studies; Literature; Management; Marketing; Mathematics Education; Media Studies; Medicine; Orthodontics; Otorhinolaryngology; Pastoral Studies; Pathology; Peace and Disarmament; Pedagogy; Periodontics; Photography; Physical Education; Physiology; Plastic Surgery; Preschool Education; Production Engineering; Protective Services; Psychology; Public Health; Safety Engineering; Social Policy; Social Sciences; Social Welfare; Social Work; Software Engineering; Sports; Sports Management; Surgery; Technology; Transport Management; Veterinary Science; Vocational Counselling.** *Mestrado*: **Cell Biology; Dentistry; Education; Environmental Studies; Genetics; Health Sciences; Materials Engineering; Mathematics Education; Molecular Biology; Public Health; Science Education; Toxicology.** *Doutorado*: **Cell Biology; Dentistry; Education; Health Sciences; Mathematics Education; Molecular Biology; Science Education.**

Student Services: Academic Counselling, Canteen, Careers Guidance, Cultural Activities, Facilities for disabled people, Health Services, Library, Nursery Care, Social Counselling, Sports Facilities, eLibrary

Publications: Aletheia; Caesura; Logos; Opinio jure; Stomatos

Publishing House: Editora da Universidade Luterana do Brasil

Last Updated: 11/04/16

MACHADO DE ASSIS FACULTY

Faculdade Machado de Assis (FAMA)

Praça Marquês do Herval 4, Santa Cruz,
Rio de Janeiro, Rio de Janeiro 23510140
Tel: +55(21) 3395-5166
Fax: +55(21) 3395-0944
EMail: sap@famanet.br
Website: http://www.famanet.br

Diretor Geral: Rogério Leopoldo Rocha
EMail: diretorgeral@famanet.br

Course

Accountancy (Accountancy); **Administration** (Administration); **Letters** (Literature); **Mathematics** (Mathematics); **Tourism** (Tourism)

History: Founded 1998.

Main Language(s) of Instruction: Portuguese

Degrees and Diplomas: *Bacharelado*; *Licenciatura*; *Especialização/Aperfeiçoamento*; *Mestrado*

Student Services: Library

Last Updated: 27/05/15

MACHADO DE ASSIS INTEGRATED FACULTIES

Faculdades Integradas Machado de Assis (FEMA)

Rua Santos Dumont 820, Centro, Santa Rosa, RS 98900000
Tel: +55(55) 3511-3800
EMail: fema@fema.com.br
Website: http://www.fema.com.br

Diretor: Danilo Polacinski

Course

Accountancy (Accountancy); **Administration** (Administration; Human Resources); **Information Technology** (Information Management; Information Technology); **Law** (Law); **Social Services** (Social and Community Services)

History: Founded 1949 as Instituto Machado de Assis. Acquired present title and status 1961.

Main Language(s) of Instruction: Portuguese

Degrees and Diplomas: *Bacharelado*; *Especialização/Aperfeiçoamento*

Last Updated: 24/06/15

MACHADO SOBRINHO FACULTY

Faculdade Machado Sobrinho (FMS)

Rua Pedro Celeste s/n, Bairro Cruzeiro do Sul,
Juiz de Fora, Minas Gerais 36030140
Tel: +55(32) 3234-1436
Fax: +55(32) 3234-1444
EMail: secfac@machadosobrinho.com.br
Website: http://www.machadosobrinho.com.br

Diretor: José Luiz de Souza Botti

Course

Accountancy (Accountancy); **Administration** (Administration); **Pedagogy** (Pedagogy); **Production Engineering** (Production Engineering); **Psychology** (Psychology)

History: Founded 1969.

Main Language(s) of Instruction: Portuguese

Degrees and Diplomas: *Bacharelado*; *Especialização/Aperfeiçoamento*

Last Updated: 27/05/15

MACKENZIE PRESBYTERIAN UNIVERSITY

Universidade Presbiteriana Mackenzie (MACKENZIE)

Rua da Consolação 896, Campus São Paulo, Consolação,
São Paulo, São Paulo 01302-907
Tel: +55(11) 2114-8000 +55(11) 2114-8391 +55(11) 2114-1618
Fax: +55(11) 3214-3102 +55(11) 3259-6405
EMail: secgeral@mackenzie.br; acoi@mackenzie.br; procuradoria@mackenzie.br
Website: http://www.mackenzie.br

Reitor: Benedito Guimarães Aguiar Neto
Tel: +55(11) 2114-8170 EMail: reitoria@mackenzie.br

Vice-Reitor: Marco Tullio de Castro Vasconcelos

Faculty

Architecture and Urbanism (FAU) (Architecture; Design; Town Planning); **Computer Science and Information Technology (FCI)** (Computer Engineering; Computer Science; Electrical Engineering; Information Technology; Mathematics; Systems Analysis); **Law (FD)** (Law)

School

Engineering (EE) (Chemistry; Civil Engineering; Electrical Engineering; Materials Engineering; Mechanical Engineering; Physics; Production Engineering)

Centre

Applied Social Sciences (CCSA) (Accountancy; Administration; Economics; International Business); **Biological and Health Sciences (CCBS)** (Biological and Life Sciences; Cooking and Catering; Humanities and Social Science Education; Nutrition; Pharmacy; Physical Education; Physical Therapy; Psychology); **Communication and Letters (CCL)** (Advertising and Publicity; Arts and Humanities; Journalism); **Education, Philosophy and Theology (CEFT)** (Pedagogy; Philosophy; Theology)

History: Founded as College by American Presbyterian missionaries 1870. Became University and recognized by the State 1952. A private institution, under the jurisdiction of the Federal Government. Since 1961, affiliated to the Brazilian Presbyterian Church.

Academic Year: February to December (February-June; August-December)

Admission Requirements: Secondary school certificate and competitive entrance examination

Main Language(s) of Instruction: Portuguese

Degrees and Diplomas: *Tecnólogo*; *Bacharelado*: **Accountancy; Administration; Advertising and Publicity; Architecture; Arts and Humanities; Biological and Life Sciences; Chemistry; Civil Engineering; Computer Science; Design; Economics; Electrical Engineering; Information Technology; Journalism; Law; Materials Engineering; Mathematics; Mechanical Engineering; Nutrition; Pedagogy; Pharmacy; Philosophy; Physical Education; Physical Therapy; Physics; Production Engineering;**

Psychology; Theology; Town Planning. *Licenciatura*: **Pedagogy; Psychology.** *Especialização/Aperfeiçoamento*: **Accountancy; Administration; Architecture; Artificial Intelligence; Arts and Humanities; Business and Commerce; Civil Engineering; Civil Law; Communication Studies; Computer Science; Constitutional Law; Construction Engineering; Criminal Law; Data Processing; Educational Psychology; Educational Technology; Finance; Fiscal Law; Higher Education Teacher Training; Humanities and Social Science Education; Industrial and Organizational Psychology; Information Technology; Insurance; International Business; Labour Law; Law; Leadership; Literature; Management; Marketing; Neurosciences; Portuguese; Psychology; Public Administration; Religious Education; Safety Engineering; Sales Techniques; Service Trades; Structural Architecture; Systems Analysis; Town Planning; Transport Engineering; Transport Management.** *Mestrado*: **Accountancy; Architecture; Art History; Arts and Humanities; Business Administration; Business and Commerce; Computer Engineering; Cultural Studies; Developmental Psychology; Economics; Education; Electrical Engineering; Fine Arts; Law; Marketing; Materials Engineering; Nanotechnology; Political Sciences; Religious Studies; Surveying and Mapping; Town Planning.** *Doutorado*: **Architecture; Art History; Arts and Humanities; Business Administration; Computer Engineering; Cultural Studies; Developmental Psychology; Economics; Education; Electrical Engineering; Fine Arts; Law; Materials Engineering; Nanotechnology; Political Sciences; Surveying and Mapping; Town Planning.** Also MBA
Student Services: Academic Counselling, Canteen, Cultural Activities, Facilities for disabled people, Health Services, Library, Social Counselling, Sports Facilities
Publishing house: Gráfica Universitária
Last Updated: 07/04/16

MAGSUL FACULTIES

Faculdades Magsul
Avenida Presidente Vargas 725, Centro,
Ponta Porã, Mato Grosso do Sul 79904-616
Tel: +55(67) 3437-3804
Fax: +55(67) 3437-3850
EMail: magsul@pontapora.com.br
Website: http://magsul-ms.com.br/faculdade

Diretora Geral: Maria de Fatima Viegas Josgrilbert
Diretor Administrativo: Robison de Souza Josgrilbert
Tel: +55(67) 3437-3816
EMail: magsul@terra.com.br; faculdadesmagsul@terra.com.br

Programme
Law (Law)

Course
Accountancy (Accountancy); **Administration** (Administration); **Aesthetics and Cosmetics** (Aesthetics; Cosmetology); **Biological Sciences** (Biological and Life Sciences); **Pedagogy** (Pedagogy); **Physical Education** (Physical Education); **Postgraduate Studies** (Accountancy; Business Administration; Environmental Studies; Health Sciences; Higher Education Teacher Training; Physical Education; Teacher Training); **Visual Arts** (Visual Arts)
History: Founded 1986.
Main Language(s) of Instruction: Portuguese
Degrees and Diplomas: *Tecnólogo*; *Bacharelado*; *Licenciatura*; *Especialização/Aperfeiçoamento*: **Accountancy; Business Administration; Environmental Studies; Health Sciences; Higher Education Teacher Training; Physical Education; Teacher Training.**
Student Services: IT Centre, Library
Last Updated: 03/02/16

MARSHAL RONDON FACULTY

Faculdade Marechal Rondon (FMR)
Viscinal Dr Nilo Lisboa Chavasco 5000, Chacara Saltinho,
São Manuel, São Paulo 18650000
Tel: +55(14) 6841-3830
Fax: +55(14) 6841-3830
EMail: fmr@fmr.edu.br
Website: http://www.fmr.edu.br

Diretor: Eduardo Storópoli

Course
Accountancy (Accountancy); **Administration** (Administration); **Biomedicine** (Biomedicine); **Law** (Law); **Nursing** (Nursing); **Pharmacy** (Pharmacy); **Physical Education** (Physical Education); **Physiotherapy** (Physical Therapy); **Tourism** (Tourism)
History: Founded 2000.
Main Language(s) of Instruction: Portuguese
Degrees and Diplomas: *Bacharelado*; *Licenciatura*
Last Updated: 27/05/15

MARY AUXILIARY SALESIAN FACULTY

Faculdade Salesiana Maria Auxiliadora (FSMA)
Rua Monte Elisio s/n, Visconde de Araújo,
Macaé, Rio de Janeiro 27943180
Tel: +55(22) 2772-0010
Fax: +55(22) 2762-0358
EMail: secretaria@salesiana.edu.br
Website: http://www.salesiana.edu.br

Diretora Geral: Rosa Idália Pesca
EMail: irrosaidalia@insgmacae.com.br

Course
Administration (Administration); **Advertising** (Advertising and Publicity); **Chemical Engineering** (Chemical Engineering); **Computer Science** (Computer Science); **Environmental Engineering** (Environmental Engineering); **Journalism**; **Production Engineering** (Production Engineering); **Psychology** (Psychology)
History: Founded 2001.
Main Language(s) of Instruction: Portuguese
Degrees and Diplomas: *Bacharelado*; *Especialização/Aperfeiçoamento*. Also MBA
Last Updated: 10/06/15

MARY THE IMMACULATE INTEGRATED FACULTIES

Faculdades Integradas Maria Imaculada (FIMI)
Rua Paula Bueno, 240 - Centro, Mogi Guaçu, São Paulo 13423-514
Tel: +55(19) 3861-4066
EMail: secretaria@mariaimaculada.br
Website: http://www.mariaimaculada.br

Diretor: Rubens Scardua

Course
Aesthetics (Aesthetics); **Biomedicine** (Biomedicine); **Civil Engineering** (Civil Engineering); **Environmental Management** (Environmental Management); **History** (History); **Industrial Chemistry** (Industrial Chemistry); **Literature** (Literature); **Pedagogy** (Pedagogy); **Pharmacy** (Pharmacy); **Science** (Biology; Chemistry; Mathematics); **Social Services** (Social and Community Services)
History: Founded 1991 from the Faculties of Social Services of Piracicaba and Education, Science and Letters of Mogi Mirim.
Main Language(s) of Instruction: Portuguese
Degrees and Diplomas: *Bacharelado*; *Especialização/Aperfeiçoamento*
Student Services: Library
Last Updated: 24/06/15

MERCURIO FACULTY

Faculdade Mercúrio (FAMERC)
Rua Mercúrio 293 e 1.631, Rio de Janeiro,
RJ 21532-470
Tel: +55(21) 2474-8000
EMail: mercurio@faculdademercurio.edu.br
Website: http://www.famerc.com.br

Diretora: Nisia Fatima Sousa Gomes Gama

Course
Administration (Administration; Business Administration); **Information Systems** (Computer Science); **Physical Education** (Physical Education)
History: Founded 2001.

Main Language(s) of Instruction: Portuguese

Degrees and Diplomas: *Bacharelado*; *Licenciatura*

Last Updated: 05/06/15

METHODIST FACULTY OF SANTA MARIA

Faculdade Metodista de Santa Maria (FAMES)

Rua Doutor Turi 2003, Prédio Centro,
Santa Maria, Rio Grande do Sul 97050180
Tel: +55(55) 3028-7000
Fax: +55(55) 3028-7007
EMail: adriana@ipametodista.edu.br
Website: http://www.metodistadosul.edu.br/fames/capa/apresentacao.php

Diretora: Adriana Rivoire Menelli de Oliveira

Course

Accountancy (Accountancy); **Administration** (Administration); **Law**; **Physical Education**

History: Founded 1998.

Main Language(s) of Instruction: Portuguese

Degrees and Diplomas: *Bacharelado*; *Licenciatura*; *Especialização/Aperfeiçoamento*

Last Updated: 27/05/15

METHODIST UNIVERSITY CENTRE

Centro Universitário Metodista (IPA)

Rua Cel. Joaquim Pedro Salgado, 80, Bairro Rio Branco,
Porto Alegre, RS 90420-060
Tel: +55(51) 3316-1300
EMail: direcao.geral@metodistadosul.edu.br
Website: http://www.metodistadosul.edu.br/centro_universitario/capa/default.php

Reitor: Roberto Pontes da Fonseca
EMail: reitoria@metodistadosul.edu.br

Course

Accountancy (Accountancy); **Administration** (Administration); **Advertising** (Advertising and Publicity); **Analysis and Systems Development** (Systems Analysis); **Architecture and Urbanism** (Architecture; Town Planning); **Biological Sciences** (Biological and Life Sciences); **Biomedicine** (Biomedicine); **Civil Engineering** (Civil Engineering); **Computer Engineering** (Computer Engineering); **Education** (Education); **English** (English); **Fashion Design** (Fashion Design); **Graduate Studies** *(Stricto Sensu)* (Biological and Life Sciences; Rehabilitation and Therapy); **History** (History); **Hospital Administration** (Health Administration); **Interior Design** (Interior Design); **International Business** (International Business); **Journalism** (Journalism); **Law** (Law); **Mathematics** (Mathematics); **Music** (Music); **Nursing** (Nursing); **Nutrition** (Nutrition); **Occupational Therapy** (Occupational Therapy); **Pharmacy** (Pharmacy); **Philosophy** (Philosophy); **Phonoaudiology** (Speech Therapy and Audiology); **Physical Education** (Physical Education); **Physiotherapy** (Physical Therapy); **Portuguese** (Portuguese); **Production Engineering** (Production Engineering); **Psychology** (Psychology); **Social Service** (Social and Community Services); **Tourism** (Tourism)

Further Information: Also: Colégio Metodista Americano, Dona Leonor, DC Shopping, Instituto Metodista Centenário, Instituto União de Uruguaiana da Igreja Metodista.

Main Language(s) of Instruction: Portuguese

Degrees and Diplomas: *Bacharelado*; *Licenciatura*; *Especialização/Aperfeiçoamento*: **Art Education; Civil Law; Gerontology; Law; Music; Music Education; Occupational Health; Public Health; Safety Engineering; Sports.** *Mestrado*: **Human Resources.** Also MBA.

Last Updated: 27/08/15

METHODIST UNIVERSITY OF PIRACICABA

Universidade Metodista de Piracicaba (UNIMEP)

Campus Taquaral, Rodovia do Açúcar, km 156 (SP-308),
Piracicaba, São Paulo 13423-170
Tel: +55(19) 3124-1515
Fax: +55(19) 3124-1500
EMail: unimep@unimep.br; falecomreitor@unimep.br
Website: http://www.unimep.br

Reitor: Gustavo Jacques Dias Alvim
Tel: +55(19) 3124-1515 EMail: reitoria@unimep.br

Faculty

Communication and Computer Science (Advertising and Publicity; Cinema and Television; Computer Networks; Graphic Design; Information Technology; Journalism; Photography; Public Relations; Radio and Television Broadcasting); **Dentistry** *(Lins)* (Dentistry); **Engineering, Architecture and Town Planning** (Architecture; Automation and Control Engineering; Automotive Engineering; Chemical Engineering; Civil Engineering; Electrical Engineering; Food Technology; Industrial Chemistry; Industrial Engineering; Mathematics Education; Mechanical Engineering; Metallurgical Engineering; Production Engineering; Science Education; Town Planning); **Health Sciences** (Biological and Life Sciences; Health Sciences; Nursing; Nutrition; Pharmacy; Physical Education; Physical Therapy; Science Education); **Human Sciences** (Education; Educational Psychology; English; Foreign Languages Education; History; Literature; Music Education; Pedagogy; Philosophy; Portuguese; Psychology; Teacher Training; Translation and Interpretation); **Law** (Law); **Management and Business** (Accountancy; Administration; Cooking and Catering; Economics; Human Resources; Industrial Management; International Business; International Relations; Marketing; Transport Management)

Further Information: Also Santa Bárbara dOeste, Centro Piracicaba and Lins Cmapuses; Samaritan Evangelical Hospital. Senior Citizens University, Piracicaba Music School, Martha Watts Cultural Centre and several units and laboratories.

History: Founded 1881 as Primary School by the American Methodist Mission, became Faculdade de Ciências Econômicas, Contábeis e Administração de Emprêsas 1964. Faculty of Education added 1966 and Faculty of Law 1970. Became University with present structure 1975. An autonomous institution under the jurisdiction of the national Ministry of Education and Sports.

Academic Year: February to December (February-June; August-December)

Admission Requirements: Secondary school certificate and Entrance Examination.

Main Language(s) of Instruction: Portuguese

Degrees and Diplomas: *Tecnólogo*; *Bacharelado*; *Licenciatura*; *Especialização/Aperfeiçoamento*: **African Studies; Applied Mathematics; Automation and Control Engineering; Bioengineering; Business Administration; Civil Law; Commercial Law; Computer Networks; Educational Psychology; Engineering Management; Environmental Management; Environmental Studies; Fiscal Law; Health Sciences; Higher Education Teacher Training; Industrial Engineering; Interior Design; Laboratory Techniques; Labour Law; Latin American Studies; Literacy Education; Literature; Media Studies; Metallurgical Engineering; Modern Languages; Multimedia; Music Education; Neurosciences; Nursing; Nutrition; Physical Therapy; Physiology; Production Engineering; Psychology; Rehabilitation and Therapy; Safety Engineering; Sports; Translation and Interpretation; Vocational Counselling.** *Mestrado*: **Administration; Education; Law; Physical Education; Physical Therapy; Production Engineering; Sports.** *Doutorado*: **Administration; Education; Production Engineering; Sports.** Also MBA

Student Services: Canteen, Cultural Activities, Facilities for disabled people, Foreign Studies Centre, Health Services, Language Laboratory, Library, Social Counselling, Sports Facilities

Publications: Cadernos de Direito; Revista Brasileira de Educação Especial; Revista da Faculdade de Odontologia de Lins; Revista de Ciência e Tecnologia; Revista Impulso; Saúde em Revista

Publishing House: Editora UNIMEP

Last Updated: 05/04/16

METHODIST UNIVERSITY OF SÃO PAULO

Universidade Metodista de São Paulo (UMESP)

Rua Alfeu Tavares, 149, Rudge Ramos,
São Bernardo do Campo, São Paulo 09641-000
Tel: +55(11) 4366-5000
Fax: +55(11) 4366-5768
EMail: sgeral@metodista.br
Website: http://www.metodista.br

Reitor: Marcio de Moraes
Tel: +55(11) 4366-5510 EMail: marcio@metodista.br
Pró-Reitora de Graduação: Vera Lucia Gouvea Stivaletti

School

Communication, Education and Humanities (Advertising and Publicity; Arts and Humanities; Biological and Life Sciences; Computer Engineering; Education; Interior Design; Journalism; Marketing; Mass Communication; Mathematics; Multimedia; Pedagogy; Philosophy; Public Relations; Radio and Television Broadcasting; Religious Studies; Social Sciences); **Engineering, Technology and Information** (Automation and Control Engineering; Computer Engineering; Environmental Engineering; Environmental Management; Information Technology; Production Engineering; Sanitary Engineering; Software Engineering; Systems Analysis); **Management and Law** (Accountancy; Administration; Business and Commerce; Economics; Finance; Human Resources; Industrial Management; International Business; Law; Marine Transport; Marketing; Public Administration; Secretarial Studies; Transport Management); **Medical and Health Sciences** (Biomedicine; Cooking and Catering; Cosmetology; Dentistry; Health Administration; Health Sciences; Nursing; Pharmacy; Physical Education; Physical Therapy; Psychology; Veterinary Science); **Theology** (Theology)

Further Information: Also Veterinary Hospital; Planalto and Vergueiro Campuses

History: Founded 1970 as Methodist Institute of Higher Education, integrating Methodist School of Theology, founded 1938. Acquired present status and title 1997.

Academic Year: January to December

Admission Requirements: Secondary school certificate and entrance examination

Fees: 200-700 per month (US Dollar)

Main Language(s) of Instruction: Portuguese

Degrees and Diplomas: *Tecnólogo*; *Bacharelado*; *Especialização/Aperfeiçoamento*: **Aeronautical and Aerospace Engineering; Banking; Business Administration; Cell Biology; Communication Studies; Cosmetology; Dental Technology; Dentistry; Educational Psychology; Educational Sciences; English; Environmental Management; Finance; Health Administration; Health Sciences; History; Industrial and Organizational Psychology; Information Technology; Journalism; Laboratory Techniques; Law; Literacy Education; Literature; Management; Marketing; Mass Communication; Multimedia; Orthodontics; Pastoral Studies; Philosophy; Physical Therapy; Portuguese; Preschool Education; Primary Education; Production Engineering; Psychology; Public Relations; Safety Engineering; Secretarial Studies; Small Business; Town Planning; Transport Management; Veterinary Science.** *Mestrado*: **Administration; Education; Health Sciences; Mass Communication; Psychology; Religious Studies.** *Doutorado*: **Education; Health Sciences; Mass Communication; Psychology; Religious Studies.** Also MBA; Post-doctorate Degree (Pós-doutorado) in Administration, Religious Studies, Mass Communication

Student Services: Academic Counselling, Canteen, Careers Guidance, Cultural Activities, Library, Nursery Care, Sports Facilities

Publications: Jornal da Metodista

Last Updated: 06/04/16

METROPOLITAN FACULTY OF CAIEIRAS

Faculdade Metropolitana de Caieiras

Rua México 100, Caieiras, SP 07700-000
Tel: +55(11) 4445-4255
EMail: juridico@panelliarruda.com.br
Website: http://www.fmccaieiras.edu.br

Diretor: Wladimir Panelli

Course

Accountancy (Accountancy); **Administration** (Administration); **Law** (Law); **Pedagogy** (Pedagogy)

History: Founded 2005.

Main Language(s) of Instruction: Portuguese

Degrees and Diplomas: *Bacharelado*; *Licenciatura*; *Especialização/Aperfeiçoamento*; *Mestrado*

Last Updated: 28/05/15

METROPOLITAN FACULTY OF CAMAÇARI

Faculdade Metropolitana de Camaçari (FAMEC)

Avenida Eixo Urbano Central, s/n Prédio Centro,
Camaçari, BA 42800000
Tel: +55(71) 2101-3250
EMail: curriculos@famec.edu.br.
Website: http://www.famec.edu.br

Diretora: Celene Maria de Oliveira Santos (1998-)

Course

Administration (Administration); **Biology** (Biology); **Chemistry** (Chemistry); **Environmental Engineering** (Environmental Engineering); **Law** (Law); **Letters** (Literature); **Mathematics** (Mathematics); **Nursing** (Nursing); **Oceanography** (Marine Science and Oceanography); **Pedagogy** (Pedagogy); **Physics** (Physics); **Physiotherapy** (Physical Therapy); **Production Engineering** (Production Engineering); **Psychology** (Psychology); **Social Communication** (Public Relations); **Teacher Training** (Teacher Training)

History: Founded 1998.

Main Language(s) of Instruction: Portuguese

Degrees and Diplomas: *Bacharelado*; *Licenciatura*; *Especialização/Aperfeiçoamento*

Last Updated: 28/05/15

METROPOLITAN FACULTY OF THE AMAZON

Faculdade Metropolitana de Amazônia (FAMAZ)

Avenida Visconde de Souza Franco, n° 72, bairro Reduto (Doca, Belém, PA
Tel: +55(91) 3222-7560
EMail: ass@famaz.com.br
Website: http://www.famaz.edu.br

Diretora Geral: Adriana Letícia Barbosa dos Santos

Course

Accountancy (Accountancy); **Administration** (Administration); **Architecture and Town Planning** (Architecture; Town Planning); **Biomedicine** (Biomedicine); **Civil Engineering** (Civil Engineering); **Environmental Management** (Environmental Management); **Hospital Management** (Health Administration); **Law** (Law); **Medicine** (Medicine); **Nursing** (Nursing); **Physical Education** (Physical Education); **Production Engineering** (Production Engineering); **Social Services** (Social and Community Services)

History: Founded 2007.

Main Language(s) of Instruction: Portuguese

Degrees and Diplomas: *Bacharelado*; *Especialização/Aperfeiçoamento*

Student Services: Library

Last Updated: 28/05/15

METROPOLITAN UNIVERSITY CENTRE OF SÃO PAULO

Centro Universitário Metropolitano de São Paulo (FIG-UNIMESP)

Rua Dr. Sólon Fernandes, 155, Vila Rosalia,
Guarulhos, SP 07072-080
Tel: +55(11) 3544-0333
Fax: +55(11) 3544-0333
EMail: sec.geral@fig.br
Website: http://unimespfig.com.br/

Reitor: Antonio Darci Pannocchia

Pró-reitor Acadêmico: Eduardo Gimenes Romero

Course

Accountancy (Accountancy); **Administration** (Administration); **Art Education** (Art Education); **Biological Sciences** (Biological and Life Sciences); **Chemistry** (Chemistry); **Economics** (Economics); **Geography** (Geography); **History** (History); **Information Systems** (Information Technology); **Law** (Law); **Literature** (English; Literature; Portuguese; Spanish); **Mathematics** (Mathematics); **Nutrition** (Nutrition); **Pedagogy** (Pedagogy); **Philosophy** (Philosophy);

Physical Education (Physical Education); **Physics** (Physics); **Social Sciences** (Social Sciences)

History: Founded 1968.

Main Language(s) of Instruction: Portuguese

Degrees and Diplomas: *Tecnólogo*; *Bacharelado*; *Licenciatura*; *Especialização/Aperfeiçoamento*: **Civil Law; Clinical Psychology; Design; Education; Educational Psychology; Health Sciences.** *Mestrado*: **Business Administration; Finance.**

Student Services: Library

Last Updated: 01/09/15

METROPOLITAN UNIVERSITY OF SANTOS

Universidade Metropolitana de Santos (UNIMES)

Campus Bandeirante I, Rua da Constituição, n° 374, Vila Nova, Santos, São Paulo 11015-470

Tel: +55(13) 3226-3400

Fax: +55(13) 3235-2990

EMail: vera.raphaelli@unimes.com.br; renata5viegas@hotmail.com; elamarcilio@ig.com.br; mendesgd@yahoo.com.br

Website: http://www.unimes.br

Reitora: Renata de Siqueira Viegas (1996-)
EMail: reitoria@unimes.br

Pró-Reitor Acadêmica: Elaine Marcílio Santos

Course

Accountancy (Accountancy); **Administration** (Administration); **Dentistry** (Dentistry); **History** (Humanities and Social Science Education); **Law** (Law); **Mathematics** (Mathematics Education); **Medicine** (Medicine); **Nursing** (Nursing); **Pedagogy** (Pedagogy); **Physical Education** (Physical Education); **Veterinary Science** (Veterinary Science)

Further Information: Also Campus Bandeirante II (Encruzilhada), Campus Bandeirante III (Vila Nova), Campus Bandeirante IV Hospital Veterinário (Morro da Nova Cintra)

History: Founded 1996.

Admission Requirements: Secondary school certificate and entrance examination

Main Language(s) of Instruction: Portuguese

Degrees and Diplomas: *Tecnólogo*; *Bacharelado*; *Licenciatura*; *Especialização/Aperfeiçoamento*: **Dental Technology; Dentistry; Medicine; Orthodontics; Periodontics.** *Mestrado*: **Environmental Studies; Health Sciences; Primary Education.**

Student Services: Library

Publications: Acta Jurídica Unimes; Ágora - Revista Acadêmica de Formação de Professores; FACCE Review; Legalis Scientia; REVISTA - 08; Revista Higéi@; Revista Paidéi@

Last Updated: 06/04/16

MICHAELANGELO FACULTY

Faculdade Michelangelo

SCS Qd. 8 Bloco 'B' 60, 3° Andar, Shopping Venâncio 2000, Região Administrativa I, Brasília, DF 70333900

Tel: +55(61) 3323-4168

Fax: +55(61) 3225-1816

EMail: faculdade@fmichelangelo.com.br

Website: http://www.jk.edu.br

Diretor Geral: Stuart do Rêgo Barros Carício

Course

Accountancy (Accountancy); **Administration** (Administration); **Computer Science** (Computer Science); **History** (History); **Letters** (Literature); **Pedagogy** (Pedagogy); **Social Services** (Social and Community Services)

History: Founded 2000.

Main Language(s) of Instruction: Portuguese

Degrees and Diplomas: *Bacharelado*; *Licenciatura*; *Especialização/Aperfeiçoamento*; *Mestrado*

Last Updated: 26/06/15

MILTON CAMPOS FACULTIES

Faculdades Milton Campos (FAMC)

Campus I, Rua Milton Campos, 202, Vila da Serra, Nova Lima, MG 34000000

Tel: +55(31) 3289-1900

Fax: +55(31) 3286-1985

EMail: diretoriaadm@mcampos.br

Website: http://www.mcampos.br

Diretora: Lúcia Massara EMail: diretoria@mcampos.br

Vice-Diretora: Tereza Cristina Monteiro Mafra

Faculty

Accountancy (Accountancy); **Administration** (Administration); **Law** (Law)

Further Information: Also Campus II in Vila da Serra

History: Founded 1998. Maintained by CEFOS.

Main Language(s) of Instruction: Portuguese

Degrees and Diplomas: *Bacharelado*; *Especialização/Aperfeiçoamento*: **Accountancy; Civil Law; Criminal Law; Labour Law; Law; Notary Studies.** *Mestrado*: **Commercial Law; Law.**

Student Services: Library

Last Updated: 24/03/16

MOACYR SREDER BASTOS UNIVERSITY CENTRE

Centro Universitário Moacyr Sreder Bastos (UNIMSB)

Rua Engenheiro Trindade, 229, Campo Grande, Rio de Janeiro, Rio de Janeiro 23050-290

Tel: +55(21) 2413-5727

Fax: +55(21) 3394-4733

EMail: info@msb.br

Website: http://www.msb.br

Reitor: Mc. Catra EMail: reitor@msb.br

Pró-reitor Acadêmico: Ronaldinho Gaucho EMail: praa@msb.br

Course

Accountancy (Accountancy); **Administration** (Administration); **Arts and Humanities** (Arts and Humanities; English; Literature; Portuguese); **Geography** (Geography); **Graduate Studies** (Business Education; Civil Law; Computer Science; Criminal Law; Human Resources; Labour Law; Mathematics Education; Portuguese); **History** (History); **Information Systems** (Information Sciences); **Law** (Law); **Mathematics** (Mathematics); **Pedagogy** (Pedagogy); **Physical Education** (Physical Education); **Physical Therapy** (Physical Therapy); **Physics** (Physics); **Social Communication** (Communication Studies; Social Sciences); **Social Communication** (Advertising and Publicity)

History: Founded 1970, acquired present status 1997.

Academic Year: February to December

Admission Requirements: Secondary school certificate and entrance examination

Fees: 1240-2334 per semester (Brazilian Real)

Main Language(s) of Instruction: Portuguese

Degrees and Diplomas: *Bacharelado*; *Licenciatura*; *Especialização/Aperfeiçoamento*: **Business Education; Civil Law; Criminal Law; History; Labour Law; Mathematics Education; Physical Education; Portuguese.** *Mestrado*: **Business Administration.**

Student Services: Academic Counselling, Canteen, Careers Guidance, Language Laboratory, Library, Sports Facilities, eLibrary

Publications: Pró-Ciência; Redes

Last Updated: 01/09/15

MONTEIRO LOBATO FACULTY

Faculdade Monteiro Lobato (FATO)

Rua dos Andradas, 1180, Porto Alegre, RS 90020-007

Tel: +55(51) 3287-8000

EMail: monteirolobato@monteirolobato.com.br

Website: http://www.monteirolobato.edu.br

Diretor: Bruno Eizerik

Course
Accountancy (Accountancy); **Administration** (Administration); **Environmental Management** (Environmental Management); **Human Resources** (Human Resources); **Marketing** (Marketing); **Systems Analysis** (Computer Science)

History: Founded 2003.

Main Language(s) of Instruction: Portuguese

Degrees and Diplomas: *Bacharelado*; *Especialização/Aperfeiçoamento*. Also MBAs

Last Updated: 28/05/15

MONTENEGRO FACULTY

Faculdade Montenegro (FAM)
Avenida São Vicente de Paula n°462, Centro,
Ibicaraí, Bahia 45745-000
Tel: +55(73) 3242-2006
Fax: +55(73) 3242-1225
EMail: aemontenegro@ligmax.com.br
Website: http://www.faculdadesmontenegro.edu.br

Diretora Geral: Andréia Maria Barros Freitas
EMail: andreiafreitas@bol.com.br

Course
Executive Secretary (Secretarial Studies); **Pedagogy** *(FAEM)* (Pedagogy); **Physical Education** (Physical Education); **Post-graduate Studies** (Business Administration; Education; Health Sciences; Law); **Tourism** (Tourism)

History: Founded 1989.

Main Language(s) of Instruction: Portuguese

Degrees and Diplomas: *Bacharelado*: **Secretarial Studies; Tourism.** *Licenciatura*: **Pedagogy; Physical Education.** *Especialização/Aperfeiçoamento*: **Administrative Law; Advertising and Publicity; Biochemistry; Business and Commerce; Civil Law; Clinical Psychology; Community Health; Criminal Law; Educational Administration; Educational Psychology; English; Environmental Management; Environmental Studies; Fiscal Law; Foreign Languages Education; Gynaecology and Obstetrics; Health Administration; Health Sciences; Higher Education Teacher Training; Human Resources; Humanities and Social Science Education; Insurance; Law; Marketing; Mathematics Education; Native Language Education; Nursing; Pedagogy; Physical Education; Political Sciences; Portuguese; Preschool Education; Public Administration; Public Health; Public Law; Rehabilitation and Therapy; Religious Education; Religious Studies; Social and Community Services; Social Welfare; Social Work; Special Education; Sports; Sports Medicine; Tourism; Translation and Interpretation; Transport Management; Welfare and Protective Services.** Also MBA in Public Auditing.

Publications: Ação e Movimento; Diabetes; Enfermagem; Estética; Fisiologia do Exercício; Fisioterapia; Síndromes

Last Updated: 02/02/16

MONTES CLAROS FACULTY OF SCIENCE AND TECHNOLOGY

Faculdade de Ciência e Tecnologia de Montes Claros (FACIT)
Avenida Deputado Esteves Rodriguês, 1637, Centro,
Montes Claros, MG 39400-215
Tel: +55 (38) 2104-5777
EMail: femc@femc.edu.br
Website: http://www.facit.edu.br

Diretora Superintendente: Ângela Maria Carvalho Veloso

Coordenação Acadêmica: Gisele Figueiredo Braz
EMail: gisele@femc.edu.br

Course
Automation and Control Engineering (Automation and Control Engineering); **Chemical Engineering** (Chemical Engineering); **Civil Engineering** (Civil Engineering); **Computer Engineering** (Computer Engineering); **Electrical Engineering** (Electrical Engineering); **Mechanical Engineering** (Mechanical Engineering); **Production Engineering** (Production Engineering); **Telecommunications Engineering** (Telecommunications Engineering)

History: Founded 2002.

Main Language(s) of Instruction: Portuguese

Accrediting Agency: Ministry of Education

Degrees and Diplomas: *Bacharelado*; *Especialização/Aperfeiçoamento*: **Maintenance Technology; Safety Engineering.**

Student Services: Library

Last Updated: 19/10/15

MONTESSORI FACULTY OF SALVADOR

Faculdade Montessoriano de Salvador (FAMA)
Rua Abelardo Andrade de Carvalho, n°05 Boca do Rio,
Salvador, BA 41.706-710
Tel: +55(71) 3371-5643
EMail: fama@montessoriano.com.br
Website: http://www.montessoriano.com.br/faculdade

Diretor: Juraci Saraiva Matos

Course
Administration; **Pedagogy** (Pedagogy)

History: Founded 2005.

Main Language(s) of Instruction: Portuguese

Degrees and Diplomas: *Bacharelado*; *Especialização/Aperfeiçoamento*

Student Services: Library

Last Updated: 28/05/15

MORAES JÚNIOR -MACKENZIE RIO FACULTY

Faculdade Moraes Júnior-Mackenzie Rio (FMJ-MACKENZIE RIO)
Rua Buenos Aires 283, Centro,
Rio de Janeiro, Rio de Janeiro 20061003
Tel: +55(21) 2221-8200
EMail: ibc@ibc.br
Website: http://www.mackenzie-rio.edu.br

Diretor: Carlos Cesar Ferreira Vargas

Course
Accountancy (Accountancy); **Administration** (Administration); **Economics** (Economics); **Law** (Law)

History: Founded 1965.

Main Language(s) of Instruction: Portuguese

Degrees and Diplomas: *Bacharelado*; *Especialização/Aperfeiçoamento*

Last Updated: 28/05/15

MOURA LACERDA UNIVERSITY CENTRE

Centro Universitário Moura Lacerda (CUML)
Rua Padre Euclídes, 995, Campos Elíseos,
Ribeirão Preto, São Paulo 14085-420
Tel: +55(16) 2101-1010
Fax: +55(16) 2101-1024
EMail: reitoria@mouralacerda.edu.br
Website: http://www.mouralacerda.edu.br

Reitor: Denis Marcelo Lacerda dos Santos

Course
Accountancy (Accountancy); **Administration** (Administration); **Advertising and Publicity** (Advertising and Publicity); **Agronomy** (Agronomy); **Architecture and Town Planning** (Architecture; Town Planning); **Arts and Humanities** (Arts and Humanities; English; Literature; Portuguese; Spanish); **Civil Engineering** (Civil Engineering); **Computer Science** (Computer Science); **Economics** (Economics); **Electronic Engineering** (Electronic Engineering); **Fashion Design** (Fashion Design); **Fine Arts** (Fine Arts); **International Relations** (International Relations); **Law** (Law); **Mathematics** (Mathematics); **Pedagogy** (Pedagogy); **Philosophy** (Philosophy); **Physical Education** (Physical Education); **Production Engineering** (Production Engineering); **Veterinary Science** (Veterinary Science)

Further Information: Also Jaboticabal Campus

History: Founded 1923. Acquired present status 1997.

Main Language(s) of Instruction: Portuguese

Degrees and Diplomas: *Tecnólogo*; *Bacharelado*; *Licenciatura*; *Especialização/Aperfeiçoamento*: **Civil Engineering; Educational Psychology; Environmental Engineering; Higher Education; Safety Engineering; Translation and Interpretation; Veterinary Science.** *Mestrado*: **Business Administration; Education; Finance; Human Resources; Management.**

Student Services: Library

Last Updated: 01/09/15

MOZARTEUM FACULTY OF SAO PAULO

Faculdade Mozarteum de São Paulo (FAMOSP)

Rua Nova dos Portugueses 365, Santa Terezinha,
São Paulo, São Paulo 2462080
Tel: +55(11) 6236-0788
Fax: +55(11) 6236-0788
EMail: mozarteum@mozarteum.br
Website: http://www.mozarteum.br

Diretor: Ormando de Maria Colacioppo (1997-)

Course

Art Education (Art Education); **Business Administration** (Business Administration); **Music** (Music); **Pedagogy** (Pedagogy); **Singing** (Singing); **Theatre** (Theatre); **Visual Arts** (Visual Arts)

History: Founded 1973.

Main Language(s) of Instruction: Portuguese

Degrees and Diplomas: *Bacharelado*; *Licenciatura*; *Especialização/Aperfeiçoamento*

Last Updated: 29/05/15

MUSIC CONSERVATOIRE OF SÃO PAULO

Conservatório Dramático Musical de São Paulo (CDMSP)

Avenida São João 269, Centro, São Paulo,
São Paulo 01035-000
Tel: +55(11) 3337-2111
Fax: +55(11) 3223-9231
EMail: cdmsp@cdmsp.edu.br
Website: http://www.cdmsp.edu.br

Diretor: Julio da Cruz Navega Neto

Area

Music (Music)

History: Founded 1906.

Main Language(s) of Instruction: Portuguese

Degrees and Diplomas: *Bacharelado*

Last Updated: 15/09/15

NATIONAL INSTITUTE OF TELECOMMUNICATIONS

Instituto Nacional de Telecomunicações (INATEL)

Avenida João de Camargo 510 Centro,
Santa Rita do Sapucai, Minas Gerais 37540-000
Tel: +55(35) 3471-9200
Fax: +55(35) 3471-9314
EMail: inatel@inatel.br
Website: http://www.inatel.br

Diretor: Marcelo de Oliveira Marques

Course

Automation and Control Engineering (Automation and Control Engineering); **Biomedical Engineering** (Biomedical Engineering); **Computer Engineering** (Computer Engineering); **Computer Networks** (Computer Networks); **Electronic Engineering** (Electronic Engineering); **Telecommunications Engineering** (Telecommunications Engineering)

History: Founded 1965.

Main Language(s) of Instruction: Portuguese

Degrees and Diplomas: *Bacharelado*; *Especialização/Aperfeiçoamento*: **Automation and Control Engineering; Biomedical Engineering; Computer Engineering; Computer Networks; Electronic Engineering; Telecommunications Engineering.** *Mestrado*: **Telecommunications Engineering.**

Student Services: Library

Last Updated: 12/04/16

NATIONAL SCHOOL OF SECURITY

Escola Superior Nacional de Seguros (ESNS)

Rua Senador Dantas, 74, Subsolo, Loja, 2°, 3° e 4° andares,
Centro, Rio de Janeiro, RJ 20031-205
Tel: +55(21) 3380-1041/1044
Fax: +55(21) 3380-1446
EMail: graduacao@esns.org.br
Website: http://www.esns.org.br/

Diretor-Executivo: Renato Campos Martins Filho

Diretor Acadêmico: Mario Couro Soares Pinto

Course

Administration (Administration); **Security Management** (Insurance; Law)

Further Information: Units in Belo Horizonte, Blumenau, Brasília, Campinas, Curitiba, Goiânia, Porto Alegre, Recife, Ribeirão Preto, Salvador, Santos, São Paulo - Bela Vista, São Paulo – Paulista, Vitória. Also Distance Educaiton programmes

History: Founded 1971.

Main Language(s) of Instruction: Portuguese

Degrees and Diplomas: *Bacharelado*. Also MBA.

Student Services: Library

Last Updated: 29/09/15

NAZARENE FACULTY OF BRAZIL

Faculdade Nazarena do Brasil

Estrada da Rhodia, Km 15 em Barão Geraldo,
Campinas, SP 13085-000
Tel: +55(19) 3287-6053
EMail: contato@fnb.com.br
Website: http://www.fnb.edu.br

Diretor Geral: Ramon Santos da Costa

Course

Administration (Administration); **Music** (Music); **Pedagogy** (Pedagogy); **Theology** (Theology)

History: Founded 2008.

Main Language(s) of Instruction: Portuguese

Degrees and Diplomas: *Bacharelado*; *Licenciatura*

Student Services: Library

Last Updated: 29/05/15

NILTON LINS UNIVERSITY

Universidade Nilton Lins (UNINILTON LINS)

Av. Professor Nilton Lins, 3259, Parque das Laranjeiras, Flores,
Manaus, Amazonas 69058-030
Tel: +55(92) 3643-2000
Fax: +55(92) 3642-7742
EMail: uniniltonlins@niltonlins.br
Website: http://www.niltonlins.br

Reitora: Giselle Lins de Queiroz
Tel: +55 (92) 3643-2005 EMail: glins@niltonlins.br

Vice-Reitora: Carla Pedrosa
Tel: +55 (92) 3643-2115 EMail: karla@niltonlins.br

International Relations: Carlo Caitete, International Relations Officer Tel: +55 (92) 3643-2092 EMail: ccaitete@niltonlins.br

Area

Applied and Social Sciences (Accountancy; Administration; Advertising and Publicity; Journalism; Tourism); **Biological and Health Sciences** (Dentistry; Medicine; Nursing; Nutrition; Pharmacy; Physical Therapy; Speech Therapy and Audiology); **Engineering and Technology** (Architecture; Civil Engineering; Engineering; Environmental Engineering; Production Engineering; Town Planning); **Exact and Earth Sciences** (Veterinary Science); **Human and Social Sciences** (Law; Psychology; Social and

Community Services); **Technological Studies** (Computer Networks; Cooking and Catering; Environmental Management; Interior Design; Occupational Health; Petroleum and Gas Engineering; Safety Engineering; Transport Engineering)

Course

Graduate Studies (Accountancy; Aquaculture; Biology; Business and Commerce; Civil Security; Communication Studies; Environmental Management; Finance; Higher Education; Human Resources; Human Rights; Law; Physical Therapy; Production Engineering; Social Policy; Speech Therapy and Audiology; Transport Management)

History: Founded 1988 as Centro Universitário Nilton Lins. Acquired present title and status 2011.

Academic Year: January to December

Admission Requirements: Secondary School Certificate

Main Language(s) of Instruction: Portuguese

Degrees and Diplomas: *Tecnólogo*; *Bacharelado*; *Licenciatura*: **Biology; History; Literature; Mathematics; Pedagogy; Physical Education.** *Especialização/Aperfeiçoamento*: **Accountancy; Advertising and Publicity; Aquaculture; Architecture; Biology; Civil Law; Criminal Law; Distance Education; Educational Psychology; Gerontology; Haematology; Health Administration; Higher Education; Interior Design; International Business; International Relations; Labour Law; Nursing; Nutrition; Physical Education; Physical Therapy; Production Engineering; Public Administration; Social Sciences; Speech Therapy and Audiology; Surveying and Mapping; Tourism; Transport Management.** *Mestrado*: **Aquaculture; Biology.** *Doutorado*: **Aquaculture; Biology.** Alos MBA.

Student Services: Academic Counselling, Canteen, Facilities for disabled people, Health Services, Library, Nursery Care, Social Counselling, Sports Facilities

Last Updated: 02/09/15

NINTH OF JULY UNIVERSITY

Universidade Nove de Julho (UNINOVE)

Rua Vergueiro, 235, Liberdade, São Paulo, São Paulo 01504-001

Tel: +55(11) 2633-9000

Fax: +55(11) 6967-1195

EMail: uninove@uninove.br

Website: http://www.uninove.br

Reitor: Eduardo Storópoli (1997-)

Area

Communication and Tourism (Advertising and Publicity; Hotel Management; Journalism; Library Science; Public Relations; Radio and Television Broadcasting; Secretarial Studies; Tourism; Translation and Interpretation); **Computer Science** (Computer Networks; Computer Science; Data Processing; Information Technology; Software Engineering; Systems Analysis); **Education** (Art Education; Chemistry; Education; Educational Sciences; English; Higher Education; History; Mathematics; Pedagogy; Physical Education; Portuguese; Special Education); **Engineering and Architecture** (Architecture; Civil Engineering; Design; Electrical Engineering; Electronic Engineering; Graphic Design; Industrial Design; Mechanical Engineering; Production Engineering; Town Planning); **Health Sciences** (Biological and Life Sciences; Biomedicine; Cosmetology; Dentistry; Environmental Management; Nursing; Nutrition; Pharmacy; Physical Therapy; Psychology; Radiology; Science Education; Social and Community Services); **Law** (Law); **Management** (Accountancy; Administration; Business and Commerce; Economics; Finance; Human Resources; Industrial Management; International Business; Management; Marketing; Public Administration; Transport Management); **Medicine** (Medicine)

History: Founded 1997. Acquired present status and title 2008. Formerly known as Centro Universitário Nove de Julho (Ninth of July University Centre).

Main Language(s) of Instruction: Portuguese

Degrees and Diplomas: *Tecnólogo*; *Bacharelado*; *Licenciatura*; *Especialização/Aperfeiçoamento*: **Business Administration; Cardiology; Chemistry; Civil Engineering; Civil Law; Clinical Psychology; Commercial Law; Communication Studies; Community Health; Computer Networks; Computer Science; Construction Engineering; Cultural Studies; Data Processing; Dental Technology; Dentistry; Educational Psychology; Energy Engineering; Environmental Engineering; Finance; Fire Science; Food Science; Foreign Languages Education; Geological Engineering; Gerontology; Grammar; Health Administration; Health Education; Health Sciences; Higher Education Teacher Training; History; Hydraulic Engineering; Industrial and Organizational Psychology; Industrial Engineering; Information Technology; Linguistics; Literacy Education; Literature; Management; Mass Communication; Mathematics Education; Neurosciences; Nursing; Nutrition; Occupational Health; Oncology; Operations Research; Paediatrics; Pharmacy; Physical Therapy; Portuguese; Primary Education; Psychiatry and Mental Health; Psychology; Public Administration; Radiology; Respiratory Therapy; Safety Engineering; Social and Community Services; Social Policy; Software Engineering; Special Education; Statistics; Surgery; Town Planning.** *Mestrado*: **Administration; Biological and Life Sciences; Computer Science; Education; Educational Administration; Educational Sciences; Environmental Management; Health Administration; Health Sciences; Law; Management; Medicine; Production Engineering; Rehabilitation and Therapy; Sports Management; Urban Studies.** *Doutorado*: **Administration; Biological and Life Sciences; Computer Science; Education; Health Sciences; Medicine; Production Engineering; Rehabilitation and Therapy.** Also MBA; Postgraduate Professional Development Courses

Student Services: Library

Last Updated: 06/04/16

OBJETIVO FACULTY

Faculdade Objetivo

Rua 12 de Outubro, Quadra 64, Lote 02, Jardim Adriana, Rio Verde, GO 75906-577

Tel: +55(64) 3624-2600

EMail: atendimento@faculdadeobjetivo.com.br

Website: http://www.faculdadeobjetivo.com.br

Diretor Geral: Wellington Guimarães

Diretor Acadêmico: Getúlio Antônio de Freitas Filho

Course

Administration (Administration; Business Administration; Information Management; International Business; Marketing); **Agriculture Business** (Agricultural Business); **Law** (Law); **Nursing** (Nursing); **Pharmacy** (Pharmacy); **Physiotherapy** (Physical Therapy); **Social Communication** (Advertising and Publicity; Journalism); **Tourism** (Tourism)

History: Founded 1999.

Main Language(s) of Instruction: Portuguese

Degrees and Diplomas: *Bacharelado*; *Especialização/Aperfeiçoamento*: **Agricultural Business; Labour Law; Physical Therapy.** Also MBA

Student Services: Library

Last Updated: 01/04/16

OBJETIVO INSTITUTE OF EDUCATION AND RESEARCH

Instituto de Ensino e Pesquisa Objetivo (IEPO)

402 Sul - Conjunto 2 - Lotes 7 e 8 - Centro, Palmas, Tocantins 77103040

Tel: +55(63) 3232-7000

EMail: objfac@uol.com.br

Website: http://www.iepo.edu.br

Diretor: Ronaldo Roberto Filho (1998-)

Course

Administration (Administration); **Computer Science**; **Computer Science** (Computer Science); **Law** (Law); **Physiotherapy** (Physical Therapy); **Social Communication** (Advertising and Publicity); **Tourism** (Tourism)

History: Founded 1997.

Main Language(s) of Instruction: Portuguese

Degrees and Diplomas: *Tecnólogo*; *Bacharelado*
Student Services: Library
Last Updated: 30/03/16

OBJETIVO UNIFIED INSTITUTE OF HIGHER EDUCATION

Instituto Unificado de Ensino Superior Objetivo (IUESO)

Avenida T-02 1993, Setor Bueno, Goiânia, Goiás 74215010
Tel: +55(62) 3607-9000
Fax: +55(62) 3607-9025
EMail: objetivo@objetivo-goiania.br
Website: http://www.unilist.com.br/iueso/

Diretor: Eduardo Mendes Reed (1998-)

Course

Administration (Administration; Business Administration; Systems Analysis); **Architecture and Town Planning** (Architecture; Town Planning); **Computer Science** (Computer Science); **Engineering** (Civil Engineering; Electrical and Electronic Engineering; Engineering); **Law**; **Nursing** (Nursing); **Nutrition** (Nutrition); **Pedagogy** (Pedagogy); **Pharmacy** (Pharmacy); **Physiotherapy** (Physical Therapy); **Social Communication** (Communication Studies); **Speech Therapy and Audiology** (Speech Therapy and Audiology); **Tourism** (Tourism); **Veterinary Science** (Veterinary Science)

History: Founded 1988.

Main Language(s) of Instruction: Portuguese

Degrees and Diplomas: *Bacharelado*; *Licenciatura*; *Especialização/Aperfeiçoamento*: **Veterinary Science.**
Last Updated: 14/04/16

ORIGENES LESSA FACULTY

Faculdade Origenes Lessa (FACOL)

Rod. Osny Matheus, Km. 108, Centro,
Lencois Paulista, SP 18683-900
Tel: +55(14) 3269-3939
EMail: secretaria@facol.br
Website: http://www.facol.br

Diretor Geral: Marcelo de Paula Mascarenhas Ribeiro

School

Administration (Administration; Finance; Management); **Engineering** (Computer Science); **Sustainability** (Biotechnology; Environmental Management)

Course

Education (Educational Administration; Educational Psychology; Physical Education)

History: Founded 1999.

Main Language(s) of Instruction: Portuguese

Degrees and Diplomas: *Bacharelado*; *Licenciatura*; *Especialização/Aperfeiçoamento*
Student Services: Library
Last Updated: 26/06/15

OUR LADY OF APARECIDA FACULTY

Faculdade Nossa Senhora Aparecida (FANAP)

Avenida Pedro Luiz Ribeiro, Chácara Santo Antônio, Gleba 04, Conjunto Bela Morada, Aparecida de Goiânia, Goiás 74920-760
Tel: +55(62) 3277-1000
Fax: +55(62) 3277-1000
EMail: fanap@fanap.br
Website: http://www.fanap.br

Diretor Geral: Frederico Lucas EMail: frederico@fanap.br

Course

Accountancy (Accountancy); **Administration** (Administration); **Law** (Law); **Pedagogy** (Pedagogy); **Production Engineering** (Production Engineering)

History: Founded 1999.

Main Language(s) of Instruction: Portuguese

Degrees and Diplomas: *Bacharelado*; *Licenciatura*; *Especialização/Aperfeiçoamento*
Student Services: Library
Last Updated: 29/05/15

OUR LADY OF APARECIDA FACULTY OF PHILOSOPHY, SCIENCE AND LETTERS

Faculdade de Filosofia, Ciências e Letras Nossa Senhora Aparecida (FNSA)

Rua Jordão Borghetti, 1260, Centro, Sertãozinho, SP 14170-560
Tel: +55(16) 3946-4900
Fax: +55(16) 3945-3511
EMail: faculdade@semar.edu.br
Website: http://www.semar.edu.br

Diretor Geral: Carmen Lúcia Martins Ragazzi

Course

Administration (Administration); **Literature** (English; Literature; Portuguese); **Pedagogy** (Pedagogy)

History: Founded 2000.
Main Language(s) of Instruction: Portuguese
Degrees and Diplomas: *Bacharelado*; *Licenciatura*
Student Services: IT Centre, Library
Last Updated: 08/07/15

OUR LADY OF FATIMA FACULTY - FATIMA FACULTY

Faculdade Nossa Senhora De Fátima - Faculdade Fátima

Rua Alexandre Fleming, 454, Caxias do Sul, RS
Tel: +55(54) 3535-7300
EMail: direcao@faculdadefatima.com.br
Website: http://fatimaeducacao.com.br

Diretor: Cleciane Doncatto Simsen

Secretária Acadêmica: Márcia da Fonseca
EMail: marcia.fonseca@fatimaeducacao.com.br

Course

Administration (Administration); **Nursing** (Nursing); **Nutrition** (Nutrition); **Postgraduate Studies** (Alternative Medicine; Health Administration; Health Sciences; Human Resources; Nursing; Nutrition; Occupational Health; Public Health; Sports); **Speech Therapy** (Speech Therapy and Audiology)

History: Founded 2003.

Main Language(s) of Instruction: Portuguese
Degrees and Diplomas: *Técnico de Nivel Medio*; *Bacharelado*; *Especialização/Aperfeiçoamento*: **Alternative Medicine; Health Sciences; Nursing; Nutrition; Occupational Health; Public Health; Sports.** Also MBA in Health Administration and Human Resources
Student Services: Library
Last Updated: 09/09/15

OUR LADY OF FATIMA FRANCISCAN INSTITUTE OF EDUCATION

Instituto Superior de Educação Franciscano Nossa Senhora de Fátima

SGAS, Avenida W5, Quadra 906, Conjunto F, Lote 11/13, Asa Sul, Brasília, DF 70390-060
Tel: +55(61) 3442-8655 +55(61) 3442-8650
EMail: secretaria@uninacional.com.br; simaragui@bol.com.br
Website: http://www.institutofatima.edu.br

Diretora: Inês Alves Lourenço

Pró-Diretora Administrativa: Jacqueline Aparecida Guimarães Resende

Pró-Diretora Acadêmica e Vice-Diretora: Dinaura Tedesco Batista

Course

Letters (Portuguese) (Literature; Portuguese); **Managerial Processes** (Management); **Mathematics** (Mathematics); **Pedagogy** (Pedagogy); **Physics** (Physics); **Postgraduate Studies**

(Educational Administration; Educational and Student Counselling; Educational Psychology; Higher Education Teacher Training); **Systems Analysis** (Systems Analysis); **Systems Analysis and Development** (Systems Analysis)

History: Founded 2005.

Main Language(s) of Instruction: Portuguese

Degrees and Diplomas: *Tecnólogo*; *Licenciatura*; *Especialização/Aperfeiçoamento*: **Educational Administration; Educational and Student Counselling; Educational Psychology; Higher Education Teacher Training.**

Student Services: IT Centre, Library

Last Updated: 13/04/16

OUR LADY OF SION INSTITUTE OF EDUCATION

Instituto Superior de Educação Nossa Senhora de Sion (ISE - SION)

Alameda Presidente Taunay, 260, Batel, Curitiba, PR 80420-180

Tel: +55(41) 3019-6155 +55(41) 3019-6155 +55(41) 3077_6112

Fax: +55(41) 3224-1568

EMail: secretaria.ise@sioncuritiba.com.br; instituto@sion.arauc.br; faculdade@sioncuritiba.com.br

Website: http://www.isesion.edu.br

Diretora: Martha Marques

Diretora Administrativa: Tânia Cynthia Soares Calderari

Course

History (History); **Pedagogy** (Pedagogy); **Postgraduate Studies** (Cultural Studies; Curriculum; Education; Educational Psychology; Literacy Education)

History: Founded 2002.

Main Language(s) of Instruction: Portuguese

Degrees and Diplomas: *Licenciatura*; *Especialização/Aperfeiçoamento*: **Cultural Studies; Curriculum; Education; Educational Psychology; Literacy Education.**

Student Services: IT Centre, Library

Last Updated: 14/04/16

PADRE ALBINO INTEGRATED FACULTIES

Faculdades Integradas Padre Albino (FIPA)

Rua dos Estudantes, 225, Catanduva, São Paulo 15809-144

Tel: +55(17) 3311-3209

EMail: diretoriageral@fipa.com.br

Website: http://www.fipa.com.br

Diretor Geral: Nelson Jimenes

Course

Administration (Administration); **Biomedicine** (Biomedicine); **Law** (Law); **Medicine** (Medicine); **Nursing** (Nursing); **Pedagogy** (Pedagogy); **Physical Education** (Physical Education)

History: Founded 1968 as Faculdade de Medicina de Catanduva (FAMECA). Acquired present status and title 2007.

Main Language(s) of Instruction: Portuguese

Degrees and Diplomas: *Bacharelado*; *Licenciatura*; *Especialização/Aperfeiçoamento*

Student Services: Library

Last Updated: 24/06/15

PALOTINA FACULTY

Faculdade Palotina (FAPAS)

Av. Pres. Vargas, 115, Bairro Patronato, Santa Maria, RS 97020-001

Tel: +55(55) 3220-4575

EMail: fapas@fapas.edu.br

Website: http://www.fapas.edu.br

Diretor: Antônio Amélio Dalla Costa EMail: direcao@fapas.edu.br

Course

Administration (Administration); **Law** (Law); **Philosophy** (Philosophy); **Theology** (Theology)

History: Founded 2001.

Main Language(s) of Instruction: Portuguese

Degrees and Diplomas: *Bacharelado*; *Especialização/Aperfeiçoamento*

Student Services: Library

Last Updated: 29/05/15

PAN AMERICAN FACULTY

Faculdade Pan Americana (FPA)

Avenida João Paulo II, 801, Fatima, Capanema 68700-050

Tel: +55(91) 3462-4548

EMail: fpa@fpa.edu.br

Website: http://www.fpa.edu.br

Diretor Presidente: Dirceu Milani

Course

Literature (Literature; Portuguese); **Pedagogy** (Pedagogy); **Philosophy** (Philosophy); **Theology** (Theology)

History: Founded 1999.

Degrees and Diplomas: *Bacharelado*; *Licenciatura*; *Especialização/Aperfeiçoamento*. Also Postgraduate Diploma.

Student Services: Library

Last Updated: 29/05/15

PANAMERICAN FACULTY OF JI-PARANÁ

Faculdade Panamericana de Ji-Paraná

Rodovia RO 135, Km 01, Ji-Paraná, RO 78960-000

Tel: +55(69) 3903-1500

EMail: relacionamento@unijipa.edu.br

Website: http://www.unijipa.edu.br

Diretora: Rosângela Aparecida Silva

Course

Accountancy (Accountancy); **Architecture and Town Planning** (Architecture; Town Planning); **Business Administration** (Business Administration); **Nursing** (Nursing); **Pedagogy** (Pedagogy); **Pharmacy** (Pharmacy); **Psychology** (Psychology); **Social Service** (Social and Community Services)

History: Founded 2007.

Main Language(s) of Instruction: Portuguese

Degrees and Diplomas: *Bacharelado*; *Licenciatura*; *Especialização/Aperfeiçoamento*

Last Updated: 26/06/15

PARAIBANO INSTITUTE OF RENOVATED EDUCATION

Instituto Paraibano de Ensino Renovado (INPER)

Rua Afonso Barbosa, 2011, Jardim Marizópolis, João Pessoa, PB 58033-450

Tel: +55(83) 2106-9600

Website: http://www.asper.edu.br

Direção Geral: César Augusto S. Colque

Course

Postgraduate (Health Sciences; Law; Safety Engineering); **Undergraduate Studies** (Accountancy; Advertising and Publicity; Architecture; Business Administration; Civil Engineering; Computer Science; Information Sciences; Law; Nursing; Pedagogy; Pharmacy; Physical Therapy; Production Engineering; Tourism; Town Planning)

History: Founded 1986.

Degrees and Diplomas: *Tecnólogo*; *Bacharelado*; *Licenciatura*: **Pedagogy.** *Especialização/Aperfeiçoamento*: **Constitutional Law; Fiscal Law; Health Sciences; Law; Safety Engineering.**

Student Services: Library

Last Updated: 12/04/16

PASCHOAL DANTAS FACULTY

Faculdade Paschoal Dantas
Av. Afonso de Sampaio e Souza, 495 - Itaquera,
São Paulo, SP 08270-000
Tel: +55(11) 6741-5100
EMail: cpaschoald@uol.com.br
Website: http://www.faculdadepaschoaldantas.com.br

Diretor: Fábio Cardoso dos Santos

Course
Business Administration (Business Administration); **Civil Engineering** (Civil Engineering); **Gastronomy** (Cooking and Catering); **Mathematics** (Mathematics); **Nursing** (Nursing); **Pedagogy** (Pedagogy); **Theology** (Theology)

History: Founded 2008.

Main Language(s) of Instruction: Portuguese

Degrees and Diplomas: *Bacharelado*; *Licenciatura*; *Especialização/Aperfeiçoamento*

Student Services: Library
Last Updated: 02/06/15

PAUL VI FACULTY OF PHILOSOPHY AND THEOLOGY

Faculdade de Filosofia e Teologia Paulo VI
Av. Francisco Rodrigues Filho, 248, Mogilar,
Mogi das Cruzes, SP 08701-970
Tel: +55(11) 4790-5660
Fax: +55(11) 4790-6777
EMail: secretaria@faculdadepaulovi.com.br
Website: faculdadepaulovi.com.br

Diretor: Claudio Antonio Delfino
EMail: diretoria@faculdadepaulovi.com.br
Vice-Diretor: Ézio Bellini

Course
Philosophy (Philosophy); **Theology** (Theology)

History: Founded 2004.

Main Language(s) of Instruction: Portuguese

Degrees and Diplomas: *Bacharelado*; *Licenciatura*

Student Services: Library
Last Updated: 06/07/15

PAULUS FACULTY OF TECHNOLOGY AND COMMUNICATION

Faculdade Paulus de Tecnologia e Comunicação (FAPCOM)
Rua Major Maragliano 191, São Paulo, SP 04017-030
Tel: +55(11) 2139-8500
EMail: secretaria@fapcom.com.br
Website: http://www.fapcom.com.br

Diretor: Valdir José De Castro EMail: diretor@fapcom.com.br

Course
Philosophy (Philosophy); **Social Communication** (Advertising and Publicity; Journalism; Multimedia; Photography; Public Relations; Radio and Television Broadcasting)

History: Founded 2005.

Main Language(s) of Instruction: Portuguese

Degrees and Diplomas: *Bacharelado*; *Especialização/Aperfeiçoamento*

Student Services: Library
Last Updated: 03/06/15

PEDRO ROGÉRIO GARCIA FACULTY OF TECHNOLOGY

Faculdade de Tecnologia Pedro Rogério Garcia (FATTEP)
SC 283, Rodovia Pedro Rogério Garcia, n° 8,100, Bairro Fragosos,
Concórdia, SC 89700-000
Tel: +55(49) 3482-3850
Fax: +55(49) 3482-3850
EMail: marketing@fabet.com.br; luiscarlos@fabet.com.br;
vicente@fabet.com.br; marciac@fabet.com.br; marketing@f
Website: http://www.fattep.com.br

Diretor Geral: Luís Carlos Schaurich

Programme
Technical Studies (Administration; Automation and Control Engineering; Electronic Engineering; Heating and Refrigeration; Transport Management)

Course
Graduate Studies (Human Resources; Management; Transport Management); **Industrial Mechatonics** (Electronic Engineering; Industrial Engineering); **Logistics** (Transport Management); **Managerial Process** (Management)

History: Founded 2005.

Main Language(s) of Instruction: Portuguese

Degrees and Diplomas: *Técnico de Nivel Medio*; *Tecnólogo*. Also MBA in Transport Management

Student Services: IT Centre, Library
Last Updated: 31/08/15

PESTALOZZI FACULTIES

Faculdades Pestalozzi (ESEHA)
Estrada Caetano Monteiro 857, Pendotiba,
Niterói, Rio de Janeiro 24320570
Tel: +55(21) 2616-0937
EMail: eseha@nitnet.com.br
Website: http://www.pestalozzi.org.br

Diretora: Lizair de Moraes Guarino (1985-)

Course
Administration; **Dentistry** (Dentistry); **Occupational Therapy**; **Physiotherapy**; **Speech Therapy** (Speech Therapy and Audiology); **Visual Arts**

History: Founded 1985.

Main Language(s) of Instruction: Portuguese

Degrees and Diplomas: *Bacharelado*; *Especialização/Aperfeiçoamento*
Last Updated: 18/04/16

PHOENIX FACULTY OF HUMAN AND SOCIAL SCIENCES OF BRAZIL

Faculdade Phênix de Ciências Humanas e Sociais do Brasil
Avenida Goiás N°1/7Quadras 111 e 112, Centro,
Santo Antônio do Descoberto, GO 72900-000
Tel: +55(61) 3626-1209
EMail: phenix.assesb@ibest.com.br

Diretor: Moisés Dias da Silva

Course
Letters (Literature); **Philosophy** (Philosophy)
History: Founded 2006.

Main Language(s) of Instruction: Portuguese

Degrees and Diplomas: *Licenciatura*; *Especialização/Aperfeiçoamento*
Last Updated: 03/06/15

PIEMONTE FACULTY

Faculdade Piemonte (FAP)
Rua Cantiliano Rios, BA 417 Km 15 - Contornolândia,
Serrolândia, BA 44710-000
Tel: +55(74) 3631-2407
Fax: +55(74) 8126-6244
EMail: contato@fapbahia.com.br; antonia@facebahia.com;
ckto@terra.com.br; jc@facebahia.com; marcelo@facebahia.
Website: http://www.fapbahia.com.br

Diretor Geral: Dário Loureiro Guimarães

Diretora Acadêmica: Maria Antonia

Course
Administration (Administration); **Pedagogy** (Pedagogy); **Postgraduate Studies** (Adult Education; Educational Administration; Educational Psychology; Environmental Studies; Higher Education Teacher Training; Human Resources; Literature; Marketing;

Portuguese; Primary Education; Social Work; Special Education; Teacher Training)

History: Founded 2005. Formerly known as Faculdade de Educação Superior do Piemonte da Chapada - FESPC.

Main Language(s) of Instruction: Portuguese

Degrees and Diplomas: *Bacharelado*; *Licenciatura*; *Especialização/Aperfeiçoamento*: **Adult Education; Educational Administration; Educational Psychology; Environmental Studies; Higher Education Teacher Training; Human Resources; Literature; Marketing; Portuguese; Primary Education; Social Work; Special Education; Teacher Training.**

Student Services: Library, eLibrary

Last Updated: 02/07/15

PINHEIRO GUIMARÃES FACULTY

Faculdade Pinheiro Guimarães (FAPG)

Rua Silveira Martins 151 Catete,
Rio de Janeiro, Rio de Janeiro 22221000
Tel: +55(21) 2556-7995
Fax: +55(21) 2205-0797
EMail: secretaria@faculdadepinheiroguimaraes.edu.br
Website: http://www.faculdadepinheiroguimaraes.edu.br

Diretor: Armando Santos Pinheiro Guimarães
EMail: armandospg@facultadepinheiroguimaraes.edu.br

Course

Journalism (Journalism)

History: Founded 1996.

Main Language(s) of Instruction: Portuguese

Degrees and Diplomas: *Bacharelado*

Last Updated: 03/06/15

PIUS XII FACULTY

Faculdade Pio XII

Rua Bolivar de Abreu 48, Campo Grande, Cariacica, ES 29146-330
Tel: +55(27) 3343-2563
Fax: +55(27) 3343-2563
EMail: comunicacao@pioxii-es.com.br; faculdade@pioxii-es.com.br
Website: http://www.faculdade.pioxii-es.com.br

Diretor Geral: Luciano Villaschi Chibib

Faculty

Faculty of Biomedical Sciences of Espirito Santo - PIO XII - BIO (Biomedicine); **Faculty of Juridical Sciences of Espírito Santo - PIO XII - DIR** (Law); **Faculty of Social Studies of Espírito Santo - PIO XII** (Accountancy; Administration; Business Administration; International Business; Transport Management)

Course

Postgraduate Studies (Business Administration; Business and Commerce; Civil Law; Finance; Law; Management; Marketing; Radiology)

History: Founded 1998.

Main Language(s) of Instruction: Portuguese

Degrees and Diplomas: *Tecnólogo*; *Bacharelado*; *Especialização/Aperfeiçoamento*: **Accountancy; Civil Law; Management; Radiology.** Also MBAs

Last Updated: 10/12/15

POLYTECHNIC FACULTY OF CAMPINAS

Faculdade Politécnica de Campinas (POLICAMP)

Rua Luiz Otávio, 1281, Campinas, SP 13087-570
Tel: +55(19) 3756-2300
EMail: ckto@terra.com.br
Website: http://www.policamp.edu.br

Diretor: José Henrique Pereira Silva

Course

Undergraduate Studies (Accountancy; Administration; Automation and Control Engineering; Communication Studies; Computer Networks; Electronic Engineering; Information Sciences; International Business; Law; Marketing; Production Engineering; Systems Analysis; Transport Management)

History: Founded 2003.

Degrees and Diplomas: *Tecnólogo*; *Bachareladо*

Last Updated: 04/06/15

PONTIFICAL CATHOLIC UNIVERSITY OF CAMPINAS

Pontifícia Universidade Católica de Campinas (PUC-CAMPINAS)

Rodovia Dom Pedro I Km 136, s/n Parque das Universidades,
Campinas, São Paulo 130869-00
Tel: +55(19) 3343-7000
EMail: reitoria@puc-campinas.edu.br
Website: http://www.puc-campinas.br

Reitor: Angela de Mendonça Engelbrecht (2010-)
EMail: reitoria@puc-campinas.edu.br

Centre

Economics and Administration (Accountancy; Administration; Economics; International Business); **Exact Sciences, Environment and Technology** (Architecture; Chemistry; Civil Engineering; Computer Engineering; Computer Networks; Construction Engineering; Electrical Engineering; Environmental Engineering; Geography; Information Technology; Mathematics; Mathematics and Computer Science; Systems Analysis; Town Planning); **Human and Applied Sciences** (History; Law; Library Science; Pedagogy; Philosophy; Physical Education; Social and Community Services; Social Sciences; Theology); **Language and Communication** (Advertising and Publicity; Hotel Management; Journalism; Literature; Public Relations; Tourism; Visual Arts); **Life Sciences** (Biology; Dentistry; Medicine; Nursing; Nutrition; Occupational Therapy; Pharmacy; Physical Therapy; Psychology; Speech Therapy and Audiology)

Further Information: Also University hospital, 3 Health centres, Dentistry and Psychology clinics

History: Founded 1941 as Faculty of Philosophy, formally constituted as University and recognized by the State 1955. Raised to the rank of Catholic University 1955, and acquired present title 1972. A private university financially supported by 'Sociedade Campineira de Educação e Instrução'. The University is under the responsibilty of the Metropolitan Archbishop of Campinas, and is managed by its Grand Chancellor.

Academic Year: February to November (February-June; August-November)

Admission Requirements: Secondary school certificate and entrance examination

Fees: Vary according to courses

Main Language(s) of Instruction: Portuguese

Accrediting Agency: Brazilian Government Agency (CAPES)

Degrees and Diplomas: *Bacharelado*: **Accountancy; Administration; Advertising and Publicity; Architecture; Arts and Humanities; Biological and Life Sciences; Chemistry; Civil Engineering; Computer Engineering; Dentistry; Economics; Electrical Engineering; Environmental Engineering; Geography; History; Journalism; Law; Library Science; Medicine; Nursing; Nutrition; Occupational Therapy; Pharmacy; Philosophy; Physical Therapy; Psychology; Public Relations; Religion; Social Sciences; Social Work; Systems Analysis; Telecommunications Engineering; Theology; Tourism; Town Planning; Visual Arts.** *Licenciatura*: **Arts and Humanities; Biological and Life Sciences; Geography; History; Mathematics; Pedagogy; Philosophy; Physical Education; Physics; Psychology; Social Sciences; Special Education; Sports; Visual Arts.** *Mestrado*: **Clinical Psychology; Computer Networks; Education; Educational Psychology; Electrical Engineering; Ethics; Fine Arts; Health Sciences; Information Management; Library Science; Linguistics; Literature; Media Studies; Philosophy; Religious Studies; Telecommunications Engineering; Town Planning.** *Doutorado*: **Education; Psychology; Town Planning.**

Student Services: Academic Counselling, Canteen, Careers Guidance, Cultural Activities, Facilities for disabled people, Health Services, Nursery Care, Social Counselling, Sports Facilities

Publications: Cadernos da FACECA; Cadernos de Serviço Social; Cadernos do CCH; Comunicarte; Estudios de Psicologia; Humanitas; Óculum Ensaios; Phrónesis; Reflexão; Revista da Educação da

PUC-Campinas; Revista de Ciências Médicas; Revista de Estudos do Curso de Jornalismo; Revista de Letras; Revista de Nutrição; Revista Jurídica; Revista Notícia Bibliográfica e Histórica; Transinformação
Last Updated: 13/04/16

PONTIFICAL CATHOLIC UNIVERSITY OF MINAS

Pontifícia Universidade Católica de Minas (PUC MINAS)

Avenida Dom José Gaspar, 500, Coração Eucarístico,
Belo Horizonte, Minas Gerais 30535-610
Tel: +55(31) 3319-4915; +55(31) 3319-4200; +55(31) 3319-4226
Fax: +55(31) 3319-4225
EMail: central@pucminas.br
Website: http://www.pucminas.br

Reitor: Joaquim Giovani Mol Guimarães

Faculty

Law (Law)

Unit

Metropolitan Unit II - Contagem (Accountancy; Business Administration; Geography; Information Technology; International Business; Law; Social Work); **PUC/Minas - Arcos** *(PUC/Minas - Arcos)* (Advertising and Publicity; Business Administration; Communication Studies; Information Sciences; International Business; Journalism; Law; Psychology); **PUC/Minas - Poços de Caldas** (Architecture and Planning; Business Administration; Civil Engineering; Computer Science; Electrical Engineering; Law; Pedagogy; Physical Therapy; Psychology; Tourism; Veterinary Science); **PUC/Minas - São Gabriel** (Accountancy; Actuarial Science; Business Administration; Communication Studies; Computer Science; Information Sciences; Law; Management; Portuguese; Psychology; Social Sciences); **PUC/Minas - Serro** (Business Administration; Law); **PUC/Minas - Betim** (Biological and Life Sciences; Business Administration; English; Information Technology; Law; Mathematics; Nursing; Physical Therapy; Portuguese; Psychology; Veterinary Science)

School

Tourism (Tourism)

Higher School

Teacher Qualification (Teacher Training)

Department

Architecture and Urbanism (Architecture; Town Planning); **International Relations** (International Relations; Sociology); **Mathematics and Statistics** (Mathematics; Statistics); **Physics** (Physics); **Physics and Chemistry** (Chemistry; Physics); **Psychology** (Psychology); **Social Communication** (Advertising and Publicity; Journalism; Public Relations); **Social Work** (Social Work); **Sociology** (Sociology)

Institute

Biological and Health Sciences (Biological and Life Sciences; Dentistry; Nursing; Physical Therapy; Speech Therapy and Audiology); **Computer Science** (Computer Science; Information Sciences); **Economics and Management** (Accountancy; Business Administration; Economics); **Humanities** (English; Geography; History; Pedagogy; Philosophy; Portuguese; Religious Education; Special Education; Theology); **Polytechnic** (Automation and Control Engineering; Civil Engineering; Electrical Engineering; Electronic Engineering; Mechanical Engineering; Telecommunications Engineering)

History: Founded 1958, incorporating existing faculties and schools founded between 1943 and 1953. Title of Pontifical University conferred 1983.

Academic Year: February to November (February-June; August-November)

Admission Requirements: Senior high school certificate and entrance examination

Main Language(s) of Instruction: Portuguese

Degrees and Diplomas: *Bacharelado*; *Licenciatura*; *Especialização/Aperfeiçoamento*; *Mestrado*; *Doutorado*

Student Services: Academic Counselling, Canteen, Careers Guidance, Cultural Activities, Facilities for disabled people, Foreign Studies Centre, Health Services, Social Counselling, Sports Facilities

Publications: Arquitetura; Caderno de Estudos Jurídicos; Caderno de Geografia; Cadernos Cespuc de Pequisa; Econonomia e Gestão; Fronteira; Horizonte; Psicologia em Revista; Revista da Faculdade Mineira de Direito; Scripta
Last Updated: 14/04/16

PONTIFICAL CATHOLIC UNIVERSITY OF PARANÁ

Pontifícia Universidade Católica do Paraná (PUCPR)

Rua Imaculada Conceição 1155 Prado Velho,
Curitibá, Paraná 80215901
Tel: +55(41) 3271-1555
Fax: +55(41) 3271-1726
EMail: secretaria.geral@pucpr.br
Website: http://www.pucpr.br

Reitor: Waldemiro Gremski

Pro-Reitor de Administração: Paulo de Paula Baptista

School

Architecture and Design (Architecture; Fashion Design; Graphic Design; Industrial Design; Town Planning); **Business Studies** (Accountancy; Administration; Economics; Marketing; Tourism); **Communication and Arts** (Advertising and Publicity; Journalism; Music; Public Relations; Theatre); **Education and Humanities** (Chemistry; History; Literature; Mathematics; Pedagogy; Philosophy; Physics; Social Sciences; Theology); **Health, Agriculture and Biotechnology** (Agronomy; Biology; Biotechnology; Dentistry; Nursing; Nutrition; Pharmacy; Physical Education; Physical Therapy; Psychology; Veterinary Science); **Law** (Law); **Medicine** (Medicine); **Polytechnic** (Automation and Control Engineering; Civil Engineering; Computer Engineering; Computer Science; Electrical and Electronic Engineering; Environmental Engineering; Food Technology; Mechanical Engineering; Production Engineering)

Further Information: Also campuses in Londrina, Maringa, São José dos Pinhais, and Toledo

History: Founded 1959 incorporating institutions established between 1945 and 1956. Title of Pontifical University conferred 1985. A private institution under the supervision of the Sociedade Paranaense de Cultura and recognized by the Federal Government.

Academic Year: February to December

Admission Requirements: Secondary school certificate or foreign equivalent and entrance examination

Fees: 3732-15,108 per annum; Graduate, 2400-25,200 (Brazilian Real)

Main Language(s) of Instruction: Portuguese

Accrediting Agency: Ministry of Education

Degrees and Diplomas: *Bacharelado*; *Especialização/Aperfeiçoamento*; *Mestrado*: **Administration; Animal Husbandry; Computer Engineering; Computer Science; Dentistry; Education; Health Sciences; Human Rights; Law; Mechanical Engineering; Medicine; Philosophy; Production Engineering; Theology; Town Planning.** *Doutorado*: **Administration; Animal Husbandry; Computer Science; Dentistry; Education; Health Sciences; Law; Mechanical Engineering; Philosophy; Production Engineering; Theology; Town Planning.**

Student Services: Canteen, Careers Guidance, Cultural Activities, Health Services, Language Laboratory, Nursery Care, Social Counselling, Sports Facilities

Publications: Changer; Filosofia; Fisioterápia em Movimento; Psicologia Argumento

Publishing House: Editora Universitária Champagnat
Last Updated: 13/04/16

PONTIFICAL CATHOLIC UNIVERSITY OF RIO DE JANEIRO

Pontifícia Universidade Católica do Rio de Janeiro (PUC-RIO)

Rua Marquês de São Vicente 225, Gávea,
Rio de Janeiro, Rio de Janeiro 22453900
Tel: +55(21) 3114-1001
EMail: hortal@puc-rio.br
Website: http://www.puc-rio.br

Reitor: Josafá Carlos de Siqueira, S.J. EMail: josafa@puc-rio.br

Centre

Biological Sciences and Medicine (Biological and Life Sciences; Dentistry; Health Sciences; Medicine); **Science and Technology** (Chemistry; Civil Engineering; Computer Engineering; Computer Science; Electrical Engineering; Industrial Engineering; Materials Engineering; Mathematics; Mechanical Engineering; Metallurgical Engineering; Natural Sciences; Petroleum and Gas Engineering; Physics; Production Engineering; Technology; Telecommunications Engineering); **Social Sciences** (Advertising and Publicity; Business Administration; Cinema and Television; Communication Studies; Economics; Geography; History; Journalism; Law; Political Sciences; Social Sciences; Social Work; Sociology); **Theology and Humanities** (Architecture; Education; Fashion Design; Industrial Design; Media Studies; Philosophy; Psychology; Theology; Town Planning)

History: Founded 1940 by Cardinal D. Sebastião Leme and Father Leonel Franca, S.J. Acquired University status 1946. Title of Pontifical University conferred 1947. Under the supervision of the Society of Jesus and under the supreme authority of the Cardinal Archbishop of Rio de Janeiro as Grand Chancellor. Receives some financial support from the Federal Government.

Academic Year: March to December (March-July; August-December)

Admission Requirements: Secondary school certificate and entrance examination

Fees: 6000-11,000 per annum (Brazilian Real)

Main Language(s) of Instruction: Portuguese

Degrees and Diplomas: *Bacharelado*; *Licenciatura*; *Mestrado*: **Business Administration; Chemistry; Civil Engineering; Computer Science; Design; Economics; Education; Electrical Engineering; History; International Relations; Law; Linguistics; Literature; Mathematics; Measurement and Precision Engineering; Mechanical Engineering; Metallurgical Engineering; Modern Languages; Philosophy; Physics; Portuguese; Production Engineering; Psychology; Social Work; Theology.** *Doutorado*: **Business Administration; Chemistry; Civil Engineering; Computer Science; Design; Economics; Education; Electrical Engineering; Geography; History; Law; Linguistics; Literature; Mathematics; Mechanical Engineering; Metallurgical Engineering; Modern Languages; Philosophy; Physics; Portuguese; Production Engineering; Psychology; Theology.**

Student Services: Academic Counselling, Canteen, Careers Guidance, Cultural Activities, Health Services, Social Counselling, Sports Facilities

Publications: Contexto Internacional; Criatividade; Direito, Estado e Sociedade; Estudos em Design; Gavea; O que nos faz pensar; Psicologia Clínica; PUC-Ciência

Last Updated: 13/04/16

PONTIFICAL CATHOLIC UNIVERSITY OF RIO GRANDE DO SUL

Pontifícia Universidade Católica do Rio Grande do Sul (PUC-RS)

Avenida Ipiranga 6681, Partenon,
Porto Alegre, Rio Grande do Sul 90619-900
Tel: +55(51) 3320-3500
EMail: dircad@pucrs.br
Website: http://www.pucrs.br

Reitor: Joaquim Clotet (2005-)

International Relations: Silvana Souza Silveira
Tel: +55(51) 3320-3660
EMail: aaii@pucrs.br

Faculty

Administration, Accountancy and Economics *(Uruguaiana)* (Accountancy; Business Administration; Economics; Hotel Management; International Business; Management; Marketing; Tourism); **Aeronautical Sciences** (Aeronautical and Aerospace Engineering); **Architecture and Town Planning** (Architecture; Design; Landscape Architecture; Town Planning); **Arts** (Linguistics; Literature); **Bioscience** (Biology; Cell Biology; Genetics; Molecular Biology; Zoology); **Chemistry** (Chemistry; Industrial Chemistry); **Computer Science** (Computer Engineering; Computer Science); **Dentistry** (Dentistry); **Engineering** (Automation and Control Engineering; Chemical Engineering; Civil Engineering; Computer Engineering; Electrical and Electronic Engineering; Mechanical Engineering; Technology); **Law** *(Uruguaiana)* (Law); **Law** (Law); **Letters** (Arts and Humanities; Linguistics; Literature; Modern Languages); **Mathematics** (Mathematics); **Medicine** (Medicine); **Nursing, Nutrition and Physiotherapy** (Nursing; Nutrition; Physical Therapy); **Pharmacy** (Pharmacy); **Physical Education and Sports** (Physical Education; Sports); **Physics** (Physics); **Social Communications** (Communication Studies)

School

Humanities (Arts and Humanities; Geography; History; Pedagogy; Philosophy; Psychology; Social Sciences; Theology)

Institute

Bioethics; **Brain** (Neurology); **Cultural Studies** (Hispanic American Studies; Japanese; Music); **Environment** (Environmental Studies); **Geriatrics** (Gerontology); **Petroleum and Natural Resources** (Mineralogy; Petroleum and Gas Engineering); **Scientific and Technological Research** (Natural Sciences; Technology); **Toxicology and Pharmacology** (Pharmacy; Toxicology)

Further Information: Also São Lucas University Hospital. Portuguese for foreign students. Centre for Nature Preservation and Research. Viamão and Zona Norte campuses

History: Founded 1931 by the Marist Brothers as Faculty of Economics. Incorporated Faculties and Schools established 1939. Acquired University status 1948, became Pontifical University 1950. An independent institution.

Academic Year: March to December (March-July; August-December)

Admission Requirements: Secondary school certificate or foreign equivalent and competitive entrance examination

Fees: 1856-5433 per semester (20-35 per credit) (Brazilian Real)

Main Language(s) of Instruction: Portuguese

Degrees and Diplomas: *Bacharelado*: **Accountancy; Advertising and Publicity; Aeronautical and Aerospace Engineering; Agriculture; Animal Husbandry; Architecture; Arts and Humanities; Business Administration; Computer Science; Dentistry; Economics; Engineering; Geography; History; Journalism; Law; Mathematics; Medicine; Pedagogy; Pharmacy; Philosophy; Physics; Psychology; Public Relations; Social Sciences; Social Work; Systems Analysis; Tourism; Urban Studies; Veterinary Science.** *Licenciatura*: **Arts and Humanities; Biology; Chemistry; Geography; History; Mathematics; Pedagogy; Philosophy; Physics; Social Studies; Theology.** *Mestrado*: **Computer Science; Criminology; Dentistry; Education; Electrical Engineering; History; Law; Linguistics; Mass Communication; Medicine; Modern Languages; Paediatrics; Philosophy; Psychology; Social Work; Surgery; Zoology.** *Doutorado*: **Cell Biology; Computer Science; Criminal Law; Dentistry; Education; Gerontology; Health Sciences; History; Law; Linguistics; Materials Engineering; Medicine; Modern Languages; Molecular Biology; Paediatrics; Philosophy; Psychology; Social Sciences; Stomatology; Theology; Zoology.**

Student Services: Academic Counselling, Canteen, Careers Guidance, Cultural Activities, Facilities for disabled people, Health Services, Social Counselling, Sports Facilities

Publications: Análise; Biociência; Comunicações do Museu de Ciências e Tecnologia; Direito e Justiça; Divulgações do Museu de Ciências e Tecnologia; Educação; Estudos Ibero-Americanos; Letras de Hoje; Odontociência; Psico; Revista do FAMECO; Revista Medicina da PUCRS; Telecomunicação; Veritas

Publishing House: EDIPUCRS

Last Updated: 14/04/16

PONTIFICAL CATHOLIC UNIVERSITY OF SÃO PAULO

Pontifícia Universidade Católica de São Paulo (PUCSP)

Rua Monte Alegre 984, Perdizes, São Paulo, São Paulo 05014901
Tel: +55(11) 3670-8000
EMail: reitoria@pucsp.br
Website: http://www.pucsp.br

Reitora: Anna Maria Marques Cintra

Faculty
Economics, Administration, Accountancy and Acturial Studies (Accountancy; Actuarial Science; Administration; Economics); **Education** (Pedagogy); **Exact Sciences and Technology** (Biomedical Engineering; Computer Science; Electrical Engineering; Mathematics; Physics; Production Engineering); **Human and Health Sciences** (Physical Therapy; Psychology; Speech Therapy and Audiology); **Law** (Law); **Medicine and Health** (Medicine; Nursing); **Philosophy, Communication, Letters and Art** (Advertising and Publicity; Art Criticism; Art History; Communication Studies; Journalism; Literature; Multimedia; Philosophy; Secretarial Studies); **Social Sciences** (Geography; History; International Relations; Social Sciences; Social Work; Tourism); **Theology** (Theology)

Unit
Communication Problems (Communication Disorders)

Institute
Ageing Society Studies (Gerontology); **Language Research** (Linguistics); **Special Studies** *(Programmes for decentralized and disadvantaged areas)*; **Women's Studies** (Women's Studies)

Further Information: Also 3 University Hospitals. Programa Estudante-Convênio do Ministério das Relações Exteriores do Brasil

History: Founded 1946, incorporating extra Faculties, including Faculties of Science, Philosophy and Literature, founded 1908, by the Episcopate of the Province of São Paulo and recognized by Government decree. Title of Pontifical University conferred 1947. Academic structure reorganized 1976. Responsible to the Fundação São Paulo with the Cardinal Archbishop of São Paulo as Grand Chancellor.

Academic Year: February to December (February-June; August-December)

Admission Requirements: Secondary school certificate or foreign equivalent and entrance examination (Vestibular)

Fees: 850,28-2623,85 per month (Brazilian Real)

Main Language(s) of Instruction: Portuguese

Degrees and Diplomas: *Bacharelado*; *Licenciatura*; *Mestrado*: **Accountancy; Administration; Applied Linguistics; Communication Studies; Education; Gerontology; History; International Relations; Law; Literature; Philosophy; Portuguese; Psychology; Religion; Social Sciences; Social Studies; Sociology; Speech Therapy and Audiology; Theology.** *Doutorado*: **Administration; Communication Studies; Education; Experimental Psychology; History; International Relations; Law; Linguistics; Mathematics Education; Philosophy; Portuguese; Psychology; Religious Studies; Social and Community Services; Social Sciences; Speech Therapy and Audiology.**

Publications: Administração em diálogo; Cadernos de Administração; Cadernos Metrópole; Cadernos PUC Economia; Cognitio; Distúrbios da Comunicação; Educação Matemática Pesquisa; Estudos de Cinema; Hypnos; Natureza Humana; Projeto História; Psicologia da Educação; Psicologia Revista; PUC-SP Ciências Biológicas e do Ambiente

Publishing House: EDUC: Editora da Pontíficia Universidade Católica de São Paulo

Last Updated: 15/04/16

PORTUGUESE-BRAZILIAN FACULTY

Faculdade Luso-Brasileira (FALUB)

Avenida Congresso Eucarístico Internacional 01,
Carpina, PE 55815-150
Tel: +55(81) 3621-0668
EMail: maurifalub@crape.com.br
Website: http://www.falub.edu.br

Diretor Geral: Mauri Vieira Costa

Course
Accountancy (Accountancy); **Administration** (Administration); **Letters** (Literature); **Pedagogy** (Pedagogy)

History: Founded 2001.

Main Language(s) of Instruction: Portuguese

Degrees and Diplomas: *Bacharelado*; *Especialização/Aperfeiçoamento*

Last Updated: 27/05/15

PRESIDENT ANTÔNIO CARLOS UNIVERSITY

Universidade Presidente Antônio Carlos (UNIPAC)

Rua Monsenhor José Augusto 203 São José,
Barbacena, Minas Gerais 36205018
Tel: +55(32) 3339-4900 +55(32) 3693-8865
EMail: falecom@unipac.br
Website: http://www.unipac.br

Reitor: Bonifácio José Tamm de Andrada
Tel: +55(32) 3339-4901 EMail: reitoria@unipac.br

Vice-reitor Administrativo: Fábio Afonso Borges de Andrada
Tel: +55(32) 3339-4965 EMail: reitoria@unipac.br

International Relations: Giovanni Peres
Tel: +55(31) 3422-5044 EMail: giovanniperes@unipac.br

Unit
Aimorés Unit (Administration; Biological and Life Sciences; Business Administration; Civil Law; Educational Psychology; Environmental Management; Health Sciences; Law; Nursing; Pedagogy; Pharmacy; Physical Education; Public Administration; Public Law; Safety Engineering; Special Education; Systems Analysis); **Arcos Unit** (Pedagogy); **Barão de Cocais Unit** (Production Engineering); **Bocaiúva Unit** (Administration); **Carlos de Congonhas Unit** (Environmental Management; Human Resources; Transport Management); **Conselheiro Lafaiete Unit** (Administration; Automation and Control Engineering; Civil Engineering; Computer Engineering; Mechanical Engineering; Mining Engineering; Pedagogy; Physical Education; Production Engineering; Veterinary Science); **Elói Mendes Unit** (Pedagogy); **Itabira Unit** (Administration); **Itajubá Unit** (Nursing; Physical Education); **Perdões Unit** (Administration; Pedagogy); **Ribeirão das Neves Unit** (Pedagogy; Physical Education); **Sabará Unit** (Pedagogy); **São João Nepomuceno Unit** (Administration; Pedagogy); **São Lourenço Unit** (Pedagogy); **Vazante Unit** (Administration; Pedagogy); **Visconde do Rio Branco Unit** (Accountancy; Administration; Information Technology; Pedagogy)

Course
Accountancy (Accountancy); **Administration** (Administration); **Advertising and Publicity** (Advertising and Publicity); **Computer Science** (Computer Science); **Environmental Management** (Environmental Management); **Law** (Law); **Nursing** (Nursing); **Nutrition** (Nutrition); **Pedagogy** (Pedagogy); **Pharmacy** (Pharmacy); **Physical Education** (Physical Education); **Physical Therapy** (Physical Therapy); **Psychology** (Psychology)

Campus
Juiz de Fora Campus (Administration; Biomedicine; Environmental Management; Law; Medicine; Nutrition; Pharmacy; Physical Therapy; Veterinary Science)

History: Founded 1963. Acquired present status 1997.

Admission Requirements: Secondary school certificate and entrance examination

Main Language(s) of Instruction: Portuguese

Degrees and Diplomas: *Tecnólogo*; *Bacharelado*; *Licenciatura*; *Especialização/Aperfeiçoamento*: **Business Administration; Civil Engineering; Civil Law; Clinical Psychology; Educational Psychology; Energy Engineering; Environmental Management; Finance; Health Administration; Health Sciences; Law; Leadership; Mining Engineering; Nursing; Nutrition; Orthopaedics; Physical Therapy; Physiology; Psychiatry and Mental Health; Public Administration; Public Law; Rehabilitation and Therapy; Respiratory Therapy; Special Education; Sports; Telecommunications Engineering; Waste Management.** *Mestrado*: **Law; Nursing.**

Student Services: Library

Last Updated: 07/04/16

PRIMAVERA FACULTY CESPRI

Faculdade de Primavera CESPRI

Rua Diamantina Quadra 132, s/n Distrito de Primavera,
Rosana, São Paulo 19274-000
Tel: +55(18) 3284-1600 +55(18) 3284-2015
Fax: +55(18) 3284-1600
EMail: dircespri@uol.com.br
Website: http://www.cespri.com.br

Diretor: José Wanderley Correa da Silva

Programme

Distance Education *(EAD)* (Accountancy; Administration; Banking; Computer Science; Education; Educational Psychology; Finance; Health Education; Human Resources; Law; Marketing; Mathematics; Political Sciences; Psychoanalysis; Psychology; Telecommunications Engineering; Theology; Transport Management)

Course

Accountancy (Accountancy); **Administration** (Administration); **Environmental Management** (Environmental Management); **Occupational Safety** (Occupational Health); **Pedagogy** (Education; Educational Psychology; Pedagogy)

History: Founded 1999.

Main Language(s) of Instruction: Portuguese

Degrees and Diplomas: *Tecnólogo*; *Bacharelado*. Also MBA (distance education)

Student Services: Library

Last Updated: 07/09/15

PROCESSUS FACULTY

Faculdade Processus (PFD)

Avenida das Araucárias, 4400, Águas Claras,
Brasília, DF 71936-250
Tel: +55(61) 3563-3247 +55(61) 3562-6343
EMail: ouvidoria@institutoprocessus.com.br
Website: http://www.institutoprocessus.com.br

Diretora Geral: Claudine Fernandes de Araújo
EMail: claudine@institutoprocessus.com.br

Course

Graduate Studies (Commercial Law; Criminal Law; Labour Law; Portuguese; Public Law); **Undergraduate Studies** (Accountancy; Finance; Law; Public Administration; Secretarial Studies)

Further Information: Also Asa Sul and Planaltina campuses.

Degrees and Diplomas: *Tecnólogo*; *Bacharelado*; *Especialização/Aperfeiçoamento*. Also Postgraduate Diploma.

Student Services: Library

Last Updated: 04/06/15

PROFESSOR LUCIA DANTAS INSTITUTE OF EDUCATION

Instituto Superior de Educação Professora Lúcia Dantas (ISEL)

QNN 29 Área Especial A, Ceilândia Norte, Brasília, DF 72225-290
Tel: +55(61) 3964-6565
EMail: isel@ad1.br; secretaria@faculdadeisel.com.br; simaragui@bol.com.br
Website: http://www.faculdadeisel.com.br

Course

Educational Sciences (Educational Sciences)

Main Language(s) of Instruction: Portuguese

Degrees and Diplomas: *Licenciatura*; *Mestrado*: **Educational Sciences.**

Last Updated: 18/04/16

PROFESSOR MIGUEL ÂNGELO DA SILVA SANTOS FACULTY

Faculdade Professor Miguel Ângelo da Silva Santos (FEMASS)

R. Aluísio da Silva Gomes, 50, Granja dos Cavaleiros,
Macaé, RJ 27930-560
Tel: +55(22) 2796-2500
EMail: direcao.femass@macae.rj.gov.br
Website: http://www.macae.rj.gov.br/femass

Diretora Geral: Larissa Frossard Rangel Cruz
EMail: larissafrossard@macae.rj.gov.br

Course

Administration (Administration); **Information Systems** (Information Sciences); **Production Engineering** (Production Engineering)

History: Founded 2000.

Degrees and Diplomas: *Bacharelado*

Last Updated: 26/06/15

PROMOVE FACULTIES

Faculdades Promove

Av. João Pinheiro, 164, Belo Horizonte, Minas Gerais 30130180
Tel: +55(31) 2103-2103
Fax: +55(31) 2103-2103
EMail: faculdade@faculdadepromove.br
Website: http://www.faculdadepromove.br

Diretor Geral: Milton Cabral Moreira

Course

Administration (Administration; Marketing; Sports Management); **Law** *(Promove)* (Law); **Nursing**; **Social Communication** (Advertising and Publicity; Publishing and Book Trade)

Further Information: Also branch in Sete Lagoas

History: Founded 1999.

Main Language(s) of Instruction: Portuguese

Degrees and Diplomas: *Bacharelado*; *Especialização/Aperfeiçoamento*; *Mestrado*

Last Updated: 18/04/16

PROMOVE FACULTY OF JANAÚBA

Faculdade Promove de Janaúba

Rua da CODEVASF, 234, Vila São Vicente,
Janaúba, MG 39440-000
Tel: +55(38) 3821-3427 +55(38) 8428-9523
EMail: secretaria.promovejanauba@faculdadepromove.br; elaine.fagundes@unicesp.edu.br; thalita.pimentel@funort
Website: http://www.promovejanauba.com.br

Diretora: Marielle de Almeida Cavalcanti Araújo

Course

Administration (Administration); **Agribusiness** (Agricultural Business); **Geography** (Geography); **Letters (Portuguese/English)** (English; Literature; Portuguese); **Pedagogy** (Pedagogy)

History: Founded 2003 as Instituto Superior de Educação de Janaúba. Acquired current title 2011.

Main Language(s) of Instruction: Portuguese

Degrees and Diplomas: *Tecnólogo*; *Bacharelado*; *Licenciatura*

Student Services: eLibrary

Last Updated: 13/04/16

QUARESMA BI SOCIAL FACULTY

Faculdade Bi Social Quaresma

Avenida Frederico Ozannan N°: 6.000, loja 2.475 Maxi Shopping,
Jardim Florestal, Jundiaí, SP 13215-700
Tel: +55(11)4583-8300
EMail: antoniomotta@mail.com

Director: Carlos De Castro Magalhaes

Course

Accountancy (Accountancy); **Administration** (Administration); **Computer Science** (Computer Science); **Environmental Management** (Environmental Management); **Financial Management** (Finance); **Information Technology Management** (Information Technology); **Management** (Management); **Pedagogy** (Education; Pedagogy)

History: Founded 2004.

Main Language(s) of Instruction: Portuguese

Accrediting Agency: Ministry of Education

Degrees and Diplomas: *Bacharelado*

Last Updated: 01/10/15

QUEEN OF PEACE CATHOLIC FACULTY OF ARAPUTANGA

Faculdade Católica Rainha da Paz de Araputanga (FCARP)

Avenida 23 de Maio, N° 02, Araputanga, MT 78260-000
Tel: +55(65) 3261-1314
Fax: +55(65) 3261-2341
EMail: fcarp@fcarp.edu.br
Website: http://www.fcarp.edu.br

Diretora: Marilza Larranhagas da Cruz
EMail: diretoriageral@fcarp.edu.br

Diretora Adminisrativa: Eleuzamar Maria da Silva

Department
Accountancy (Accountancy); **Administration** (Administration); **Information Systems** (Computer Science); **Law** (Law); **Physical Education** (Physical Education)

History: Founded 1999.

Main Language(s) of Instruction: Portuguese

Accrediting Agency: Ministry of Education.

Degrees and Diplomas: *Bacharelado*; *Licenciatura*; *Especialização/Aperfeiçoamento*: **Human Resources.**

Student Services: Library
Last Updated: 06/10/15

RAIMUNDO MARINHO FACULTY

Faculdade Raimundo Marinho (FRM)

Avenida Durval de Góes Monteiro, 8501, Tabuleiro dos Martins, Maceió, AL 57200-000
Tel: +55(82) 3325-9574
EMail: contato@frm.edu.br
Website: http://www.frm.edu.br

Presidente: Lysia Ramalho Marinho

Course
Administration *(Penedo)* (Administration); **Law** (Law); **Nursing** (Nursing); **Pedagogy** (Pedagogy); **Social Service** (Social and Community Services)

Further Information: Also campus in Penedo

History: Founded 1999 as Faculdade de Ciências Sociais Aplicadas de Penedo (FCSAP). Merged with Faculdade de Formação de Professores (FFPP) and Faculdade de Ciências Jurídicas de Alagoas (FCJAL) 2010.

Main Language(s) of Instruction: Portuguese

Degrees and Diplomas: *Bacharelado*; *Licenciatura*; *Especialização/Aperfeiçoamento*. Also MBA.

Student Services: Library
Last Updated: 03/07/15

RAÍZES FACULTY

Faculdade Raízes (SER)

Rua Felipe dos Santos N°: 20, Jardim Eldorado, Anápolis, GO 75105-010
Tel: +55(62) 3099-5094
EMail: helia@unievangelica.edu.br
Website: http://www.faculdaderaizes.com.br/

Presidente: Geraldo Henrique Ferreira Espindola

Course
Law (Law)

History: Founded 2002.

Main Language(s) of Instruction: Portuguese

Degrees and Diplomas: *Bacharelado*

Student Services: Library
Last Updated: 10/07/15

REDENTOR FACULTY

Faculdade Redentor (FACREDENTOR)

Rodovia BR 356, número 25, Bairro Cidade Nova, Itaperuna, RJ 28300-000
Tel: +55 (22) 3811-0111
EMail: pi@redentor.edu.br
Website: http://www.redentor.edu.br/

Diretor: Heitor Antonio da Silva

Course
Administration (Administration); **Architecture and Town Planning** (Architecture; Town Planning); **Biological and Life Sciences** (Biological and Life Sciences); **Civil Engineering** (Civil Engineering); **Graduate Studies** (Acupuncture; Administration; Computer Networks; Education; Educational Administration; Educational and Student Counselling; Educational Psychology; Engineering Management; Environmental Management; Finance; Higher Education; Hotel Management; Law; Leisure Studies; Management; Medicine; Nursing; Public Administration; Safety Engineering; Social Policy; Software Engineering; Sports; Tourism); **Information Systems** (Information Sciences); **Law** (Law); **Mechanical Engineering** (Mechanical Engineering); **Nursing** (Nursing); **Nutrition** (Nutrition); **Phonoaudiology** (Speech Therapy and Audiology); **Physical Therapy** (Physical Therapy); **Production Engineering** (Production Engineering); **Social Service** (Social and Community Services)

Further Information: Also Campos and Paraiba do Sul campuses

History: Founded 2002.

Main Language(s) of Instruction: Portuguese

Degrees and Diplomas: *Bacharelado*; *Especialização/Aperfeiçoamento*. Also Postgraduate Diploma and MBA.

Last Updated: 05/06/15

REGES FACULTY OF OSVALDO CRUZ

Faculdade REGES de Osvaldo Cruz (FEOCRUZ)

Rua Chile, 501, Jardim das Bandeiras, Osvaldo Cruz, São Paulo 17700-000
Tel: +55(18) 3528-4706
Fax: +55(18) 3528-4706
EMail: osvaldocruz@reges.com.br; reges.denis@gmail.com
Website: http://reges.com.br/osvaldocruz

Presidente: José Gonzaga da Silva Neto

Course
Administration (Administration); **Graduate Studies** (Business Administration; Educational Psychology; Finance; Management; Marketing; Special Education); **Literature** (English; Literature; Portuguese); **Pedagogy** (Pedagogy)

History: Founded 1998 as Faculdade de Educação de Osvaldo Cruz. Acquired current title 2011.

Main Language(s) of Instruction: Portuguese

Degrees and Diplomas: *Bacharelado*; *Licenciatura*; *Especialização/Aperfeiçoamento*: **Educational Psychology; Special Education.** Also MBA in Finance, Managment.

Student Services: Library
Last Updated: 30/06/15

REGES FACULTY OF RIBEIRÃO PRETO

Faculdade REGES de Ribeirão Preto

R. Dr. Benjamim Anderson Stauffer, 801 – Jardim Botânico, Ribeirão Preto, SP 14021-617
Tel: +55(16) 2138-1868
EMail: diretoria@reges.com.br
Website: http://www.ribeiraopreto.cesd.br/

Presidente: José Gonzaga da Silva Neto

Course
Accountancy (Accountancy); **Administration** (Administration; Business Administration); **Computer Network** (Computer Networks); **Graduate Studies** (Accountancy; Business Administration; Finance; Health Administration; Human Resources; Marketing; Public Relations; Small Business); **Information System** (Computer Engineering)

History: Founded as Faculdade de Administração e Negócios em Ribeirão Preto.

Main Language(s) of Instruction: Portuguese

Degrees and Diplomas: *Bacharelado*; *Especialização/Aperfeiçoamento*: **Accountancy; Business Administration; Finance; Health Administration.**

Last Updated: 19/10/15

REGES FACULTY OF DRACENA

Faculdade Reges de Dracena (FCGD)

Rodovia Engenho Byron Azevedo Nogueira, s/n Km Zero Vila Barros, Dracena, São Paulo 17900-000
Tel: +55(18) 3821-9099
Fax: +55(18) 3821-9099
EMail: secretaria.dracena@reges.com.b
Website: http://reges.com.br/dracena

President: José Gonzaga Da Silva Neto

Vice-Presidente: Heron Fernando de Sousa Gonzaga

Course

Accountancy (Accountancy); **Administration** *(FCGD)* (Administration; Business Administration); **Law** (Law)

History: Founded 1995.

Main Language(s) of Instruction: Portuguese

Degrees and Diplomas: *Bacharelado*; *Especialização/Aperfeiçoamento*: **Accountancy; Business Administration; Finance; Human Resources; Marketing.** Also MBA.

Student Services: Library

Last Updated: 28/07/15

REGIONAL COMMUNITY UNIVERSITY OF CHAPECÓ

Universidade Comunitária Regional de Chapecó (UNOCHAPECÓ)

Av. Senador Attílio Fontana, 591-E, Efapi, Caixa Postal: 1141, Chapecó, Santa Catarina 89809-000
Tel: +55(49) 3321-8000 +55(49) 3321-8233
Fax: +55(49) 3321-8061
EMail: viceplan@unochapeco.edu.br
Website: http://www.unochapeco.edu.br

Reitor: Claudio Alcides Jacoski EMail: reitoria@unochapeco.edu.br

Vice-Reitor de Administração: José Alexandre de Toni
EMail: viceadm@unochapeco.edu.br

Area

Exact and Environmental Sciences (Agronomy; Architecture; Biological and Life Sciences; Chemical Engineering; Civil Engineering; Computer Science; Dairy; Electrical Engineering; Food Technology; Information Technology; Mathematics; Mechanical Engineering; Physics; Production Engineering; Town Planning; Veterinary Science); **Health Sciences** (Cooking and Catering; Dentistry; Medicine; Nursing; Nutrition; Pharmacy; Physical Education; Physical Therapy); **Human Sciences and Law** (Arts and Humanities; Bilingual and Bicultural Education; Law; Library Science; Literature; Natives Education; Pedagogy; Psychology; Religious Studies; Social and Community Services; Special Education; Visual Arts); **Social and Applied Sciences** (Accountancy; Administration; Advertising and Publicity; Design; Economics; Fashion Design; Graphic Design; Journalism; Marketing; Radio and Television Broadcasting; Software Engineering)

Further Information: Also São Lourenço and Xaxim Campuses

History: Founded 2002.

Main Language(s) of Instruction: Portuguese

Degrees and Diplomas: *Tecnólogo*; *Bacharelado*; *Licenciatura*; *Especialização/Aperfeiçoamento*: **Accountancy; Agriculture; Civil Law; Crop Production; Dentistry; Educational Administration; Fiscal Law; Food Science; Insurance; Journalism; Labour Law; Law; Mathematics Education; Microbiology; Psychoanalysis; Psychotherapy; Real Estate; Regional Planning; Safety Engineering; Surveying and Mapping; Taxation; Telecommunications Engineering; Waste Management.** *Mestrado*: **Accountancy; Administration; Education; Engineering Management; Environmental Studies; Health Sciences; Law; Regional Studies; Social Policy; Technology.** Also MBA

Student Services: Library

Last Updated: 30/03/16

REGIONAL FACULTY OF SERRANA

Faculdade Regional Serrana (FUNPAC)

BR 262 kM 110, São João de Viçosa, Venda Nova do Imigrante, ES 2937-5000
Tel: +55(28) 3546-6451
Fax: +55(28) 3546-6622
EMail: direcao@funpac.com.br

Diretor: Miguel Angelo Tres

Course

Administration (Administration); **Pedagogy** (Pedagogy); **Social Services** (Social and Community Services)

Main Language(s) of Instruction: Portuguese

Degrees and Diplomas: *Bacharelado*; *Licenciatura*

Last Updated: 25/06/15

REGIONAL INTEGRATED UNIVERSITY OF UPPER URUGUAI AND MISSIONS

Universidade Regional Integrada do Alto Uruguai e das Missões (URI)

Av. Sete de Setembro, 1558 - 2° e 3° andares, Caixa Postal: 290, Erechim, Rio Grande do Sul 99700-000
Tel: +55(54) 3522-1255
Fax: +55(54) 3522-1255
EMail: gabinete@reitoria.uri.br
Website: http://www.uri.reitoria.br

Reitor: Luiz Mario Silveira Spinelli
Tel: +55(54) 2107-1255 Ext.225
EMail: lmspinelli@reitoria.uri.br; gabinete@reitoria.uri.br

Pró-Reitor de Administração: Nestor Henrique de Cesaro
Tel: +55(54) 2107-1255 Ext.232
EMail: decesaros@reitoria.uri.br; pradm@reitoria.uri.br

Department

Agrarian Sciences (Agricultural Business; Agronomy); **Applied Social Sciences** (Accountancy; Administration; International Business; Social and Community Services; Tourism); **Biological Sciences** (Biology; Science Education); **Engineering and Computer Science** (Agricultural Engineering; Chemical Engineering; Civil Engineering; Computer Science; Electrical Engineering; Food Technology; Information Technology; Mechanical Engineering; Production Engineering); **Exact and Earth Sciences** (Architecture; Chemistry; Industrial Chemistry; Mathematics; Science Education; Town Planning); **Health Sciences** (Dentistry; Nursing; Pharmacy; Physical Education; Physical Therapy); **Human Sciences** (Educational Administration; Humanities and Social Science Education; Law; Preschool Education; Psychology; Theology); **Linguistics, Letters and Arts** (English; Foreign Languages Education; Literature; Native Language Education; Philosophy; Portuguese)

Further Information: Also Frederico Westphalen, Santo Ângelo and Santiago Campuses; São Luiz Gonzaga and Cerro Largo Extensions

History: Founded 1992.

Admission Requirements: Secondary school certificate and entrance examination

Main Language(s) of Instruction: Portuguese

Degrees and Diplomas: *Tecnólogo*; *Bacharelado*; *Licenciatura*; *Especialização/Aperfeiçoamento*: **Accountancy; Administration; Agriculture; Architecture; Civil Law; Clinical Psychology; Communication Studies; Computer Science; Education; Educational Administration; Educational Psychology; Energy Engineering; Environmental Studies; Finance; Foreign Languages Education; Health Sciences; Higher Education Teacher Training; Horticulture; Humanities and Social Science Education; Labour Law; Marketing; Medicine; Native Language Education; Natural Sciences; Nursing; Nutrition; Orthopaedics; Pharmacy; Physical Therapy; Preschool Education; Production Engineering; Psychiatry and Mental Health; Public Law; Social Policy; Sports.** *Mestrado*: **Arts and Humanities; Ecology; Education; Food Technology; Law; Management; Science Education; Technology Education.** *Doutorado*: **Food Technology.**

Last Updated: 11/04/16

REGIONAL UNIVERSITY CENTRE OF ESPIRITO SANTO DO PINHAL

Centro Regional Universitário de Espirito Santo do Pinhal (UNIPINHAL)

Avénida Hélio Vergueiro Leite, Jardim Universitário, Espirito Santo do Pinhal, São Paulo 13990-900
Tel: +55(19) 3651-9600 +55(19) 3651-9610
Fax: +55(19) 3651-9616
EMail: reitoriaadministrativa@unipinhal.edu.br
Website: http://www.unipinhal.edu.br/

Reitor: Eliseu Martins EMail: reitoria@unipinhal.edu.br

Programme

Accountancy (Accountancy; International Business); **Administration** (Administration; Human Resources); **Agricultural Engineering** (Agricultural Engineering); **Arts and Humanities** (Arts and Humanities; English; Portuguese); **Biological Sciences** (Biological and Life Sciences); **Biomedicine** (Biomedicine); **Computer Engineering** (Computer Engineering); **Computer Science** (Computer Science); **Environmental Engineering** (Environmental Engineering); **Hotel and Restaurant** (Cooking and Catering; Hotel and Restaurant); **Law** (Civil Law; Commercial Law; Law); **Logistics** (Transport Management); **Mechatronics Engineering** (Electronic Engineering; Mechanical Engineering); **Nursing** (Nursing); **Pharmacy** (Pharmacy); **Physical Education** (Physical Education); **Physical Therapy** (Physical Therapy); **Production Engineering** (Production Engineering); **Social Communication - Advertising and Publicity** (Advertising and Publicity); **Tourism** (Tourism); **Veterinary Science** (Veterinary Science)

History: Founded 1966.

Main Language(s) of Instruction: Portuguese

Degrees and Diplomas: *Tecnólogo*; *Bacharelado*; *Licenciatura*; *Especialização/Aperfeiçoamento*: **Communication Disorders; Gynaecology and Obstetrics; Pedagogy; Public Health; Social and Preventive Medicine.**

Last Updated: 22/06/15

REGIONAL UNIVERSITY OF THE NORTHWEST OF THE STATE OF RIO GRANDE DO SUL

Universidade Regional do Noroeste do Estado do Rio Grande do Sul (UNIJUI)

Caixa Postal 560, Rua do Comércio, 3000, Bairro Universitário, Ijui, Rio Grande do Sul 98700-000
Tel: +55(55) 3332-0200
Fax: +55(55) 3332-9100
EMail: eronitab@unijui.tche.br
Website: http://www.unijui.tche.br

Reitor: Martinho Luís Kelm EMail: reitoria@unijui.edu.br

Vice-Reitor de Administração: Laerde Sady Gehrke

Department

Administrative Sciences, Accountancy, Economics and Communication (DACEG) (Accountancy; Administration; Business Administration; Business and Commerce; Economics; Management); **Agrarian Studies (DEAG)** (Agriculture; Agronomy; Veterinary Science); **Exact Sciences and Engineering (DCEEng)** (Architecture; Chemical Engineering; Civil Engineering; Computer Science; Electrical Engineering; Mathematics; Mechanical Engineering; Town Planning); **Humanities and Education (DHE)** (English; Foreign Languages Education; History; Literature; Native Language Education; Pedagogy; Portuguese); **Juridical and Social Sciences (DCJS)** (Advertising and Publicity; Design; Journalism; Law; Mass Communication; Psychology); **Life Sciences (DCVida)** (Biological and Life Sciences; Cosmetology; Nursing; Nutrition; Pharmacy; Physical Education; Physical Therapy)

History: Founded 1957 as Faculty of Philosophy, Science and Letters. Acquired present status and title 1985. A private institution under the supervision of the Fundação de Integração, Desenvolvimento e Educação do Noroeste do Estado.

Academic Year: March to December (March-July; August-December)

Admission Requirements: Secondary school certificate and entrance examination

Fees: 3200 per semester (Brazilian Real)

Main Language(s) of Instruction: Portuguese

Degrees and Diplomas: *Tecnólogo*; *Bacharelado*; *Licenciatura*; *Especialização/Aperfeiçoamento*: **Accountancy; Business Administration; Civil Engineering; Cooking and Catering; Cosmetology; Environmental Management; Finance; Gerontology; Health Sciences; Hepatology; Higher Education Teacher Training; Industrial Engineering; Management; Nursing; Oncology; Pharmacy; Physical Therapy; Psychiatry and Mental Health; Real Estate; Safety Engineering; Telecommunications Services; Transport Management.** *Mestrado*: **Development Studies; Educational Sciences; Health Sciences; Law; Mathematics; Regional Studies.** *Doutorado*: **Development Studies; Educational Sciences; Mathematics; Regional Studies.** Also MBA

Student Services: Canteen, Health Services, Library, Sports Facilities

Publications: Ciência e Ambiente; Contexto e Educação; Direito em Debate; Espaços da Escola; Município e Saúde

Publishing House: SEDIGRAF-Serviços de Editoração e Gráfica

Last Updated: 11/04/16

RIO BRANCO INTEGRATED FACULTIES

Faculdades Integradas Rio Branco (FRB)

Av. José Maria de Faria, 111 - Lapa, São Paulo, São Paulo 05038-190
Tel: +55(11) 3879-3100
Fax: +55(11) 3611-7410
EMail: diretoriageral@riobrancofac.edu.br;
Website: http://www.riobrancofac.edu.br

Diretor Geral: Edman Altheman
EMail: edman@riobrancofac.edu.br

Course

Accountancy (Accountancy); **Administration** (Administration; Business Administration); **Design** (Design; Graphic Design; Multimedia); **Economics** (Economics); **Information Sciences** (Information Sciences); **International Relations** (International Relations); **Law** (Law); **Pedagogy** (Education; Pedagogy); **Production Engineering** (Production Engineering); **Social Communication** (Advertising and Publicity; Journalism; Radio and Television Broadcasting)

Further Information: Also Granja Vianna unit

History: Founded 2001.

Main Language(s) of Instruction: Portuguese

Degrees and Diplomas: *Bacharelado*; *Especialização/Aperfeiçoamento*. Also MBAs

Student Services: Library

Last Updated: 24/06/15

RIO DE JANEIRO SCHOOL OF LAW

Escola de Direito do Rio de Janeiro (FGV DIREITO RIO)

Praia de Botafogo, 190, 13° andar, Rio de Janeiro, RJ 22250-900
Tel: + 55(21) 3799-4608
Fax: + 55(21) 3799-5335
EMail: maria.freitas@fgv.br
Website: http://direitorio.fgv.br

Diretor: Joaquim Falcão

Vice-Diretor Executivo: Rodrigo Vianna

Course

Graduate Studies (Commercial Law; Fiscal Law; Law); **Law**

History: Founded 2002.

Main Language(s) of Instruction: Portuguese

Degrees and Diplomas: *Bacharelado*; *Especialização/Aperfeiçoamento*: **Commercial Law; Law.** *Mestrado*: **Law.**

Student Services: IT Centre, Library

Last Updated: 18/09/15

RIO SONO FACULTY

Faculdade Rio Sono (RISO)

Rua 04, 350, Centro, Pedro Afonso, TO 77710-000
Tel: +55(63) 3466-2432
EMail: secretaria@faculdaderiosono.edu.br
Website: http://www.faculdaderiosono.edu.br

Diretor Geral: Raymundo Costa Sales

Course

Administration (Administration); **Education** (Biology; Education; Educational Administration; Geography; Higher Education; History; Linguistics; Management; Organic Chemistry)

History: Founded 2005.

Degrees and Diplomas: *Tecnólogo*; *Bacharelado*; *Especialização/Aperfeiçoamento*

Last Updated: 25/06/15

RIO VERDE VALLEY UNIVERSITY

Universidade Vale do Rio Verde (UNINCOR)

Av. Castelo Branco, 82, Chácara das Rosas, Três Corações, Minas Gerais 37410-000
Tel: +55(35) 3239-1000 +55(35) 3239-1218 +55(35) 3239-1136
Fax: +55(35) 3239-1218 +55(35) 3239-1136
EMail: unincor@unincor.br; falecom@unincor.edu.br; rafaela.batista@unincor.edu.br
Website: http://www.unincor.br

Reitor: Gleicione Aparecida Dias Bagne de Souza
EMail: reitoria@unincor.br

Pró Reitora de Assuntos Administrativos: Viviane Barbosa

Vice-Reitor: Marcelo Junqueira Pereira

Unit

Belo Horizonte Unit (Dentistry; Medicine); **Betim Unit** (Administration; Industrial Management; Management; Nursing; Transport Management); **Caxambu Unit** (Law); **Pará de Minas** (Accountancy; Environmental Management; Management; Pedagogy; Physical Education; Radiology); **Pouso Alegre Unit** (Architecture; Education; Engineering; Management)

Course

Administration (Accountancy; Administration; Agronomy; Computer Science; Cosmetology; Dentistry; Environmental Engineering; Industrial Management; Law; Nursing; Nutrition; Pedagogy; Pharmacy; Physical Education; Psychology; Social and Community Services; Transport Management; Veterinary Science); **Distance Education (EAD)** (Administration; Architecture; Arts and Humanities; Civil Engineering; Human Resources; Marketing; Music; Pedagogy; Town Planning); **Post-graduate Studies** (Agriculture; Cultural Studies; Dentistry; Health Sciences; Law; Management; Veterinary Science)

Further Information: Also Belo Horizonte, Betim, Caxambu, Pará de Minas Campuses

History: Founded 1965 as Faculdade de Filosofia, Ciências e Letras de Três Corações, acquired present status and title 1998.

Admission Requirements: Secondary school certificate and entrance examination

Main Language(s) of Instruction: Portuguese

Degrees and Diplomas: *Bacharelado*; *Licenciatura*; *Especialização/Aperfeiçoamento*: **Accountancy; Animal Husbandry; Business and Commerce; Civil Engineering; Civil Law; Clinical Psychology; Commercial Law; Construction Engineering; Dental Technology; Dentistry; Educational Administration; Educational Psychology; Environmental Engineering; Environmental Management; Health Sciences; Horticulture; Hygiene; Industrial Management; Interior Design; Landscape Architecture; Marketing; Music Education; Orthodontics; Physical Therapy; Public Health; Safety Engineering; Soil Science; Sports; Veterinary Science.** *Mestrado*: **Arts and Humanities.** Also MBA

Student Services: Library

Last Updated: 08/04/16

RUI BARBOSA LUTHERAN FACULTY

Faculdade Luterana Rui Barbosa (FALURB)

Rua D. Pedro n° 1151. Caixa Postal: 04, Marechal Cândido Rondon, PR 85.960-000
Tel: +55(45) 3254-2175
EMail: falurb@falurb.edu.br
Website: http://www.falurb.edu.br

Diretor: Emerson Oditer Zielke

Course

Administration (Accountancy; Administration)

History: Founded 2002.

Main Language(s) of Instruction: Portuguese

Degrees and Diplomas: *Bacharelado*; *Mestrado*

Last Updated: 27/05/15

SAINT ANNA INSTITUTE OF EDUCATION

Instituto Superior de Educação SantÁna (IESSA)

Rua Senador Pinheiro Machado, 189, Centro, Ponta Grossa, PR 84010-310
Tel: +55(42) 3224-0301
EMail: contato@santanapos.com.br; secretaria@iessa.edu.br
Website: http://www.iessa.edu.br

Diretora Geral: Irmã Maria Aluísia Rhoden

Course

Executive Secretariat (Secretarial Studies); **Letters - Portuguese** (Arts and Humanities; Portuguese); **Logistics** (Transport Management); **Pedagogy** (Pedagogy); **Philosophy** (Philosophy); **Phonoaudiology** (Speech Therapy and Audiology); **Physical Education** (Physical Education); **Postgraduate Studies** (Engineering; Health Sciences; Management; Pedagogy; Psychology; Sports); **Psychology** (Psychology); **Sports** (Sports)

Main Language(s) of Instruction: Portuguese

Degrees and Diplomas: *Tecnólogo*; *Bacharelado*; *Licenciatura*; *Especialização/Aperfeiçoamento*: **Educational Psychology; Finance; Management; Neurosciences; Nursing; Psychology; Rehabilitation and Therapy; Software Engineering; Sports.** Also MBA

Student Services: Library

Last Updated: 14/04/16

SAINT ANNA UNIVERSITY CENTRE

Centro Universitário Sant'Anna

Avenida Tranquilo Gianini, 801, Saída 44 da Rodovia Santos Dumont, Salto, SP 13320-000
Tel: +55(11) 4028-1929
Fax: +55(11) 4028-1929
EMail: info@santanna.br
Website: http://www.unisantanna.br

Reitor: Leonardo Placucci

Course

Graduate Studies (Administration; Business Administration; Education; Engineering; Health Sciences; Literature); **Undergraduate Studies** (Accountancy; Administration; Advertising and Publicity; Biology; Civil Engineering; Computer Engineering; Computer Science; Dance; Economics; Electrical Engineering; Engineering; Geography; History; Journalism; Literature; Mathematics; Mechanical Engineering; Music; Nursing; Pedagogy; Physical Education; Physical Therapy; Production Engineering; Radio and Television Broadcasting; Theatre; Tourism)

History: Founded as Faculdade Sant' Anna de Salto. Acquired present title and status 1999.

Main Language(s) of Instruction: Portuguese

Degrees and Diplomas: *Bacharelado*; *Licenciatura*; *Especialização/Aperfeiçoamento*. Also MBA

Last Updated: 10/06/15

SAINT BENEDICT FACULTY OF BAHIA

Faculdade São Bento da Bahia

Avenida Sete de Setembro, 30/32, Centro, Salvador, BA 40060-001
Tel: +55(71) 3322-4746
EMail: faculdade@saobento.org
Website: http://www.saobento.org/Faculdade

Diretor: Gilberto Carvalho Martins
EMail: gilberto.martins@grupounidom.com.br

Course

Graduate Studies (Educational Administration; Educational Psychology; Heritage Preservation; Higher Education; History; Management; Philosophy; Portuguese; Psychology; Social Work; Theology); **Undergraduate Studies** (History; Philosophy; Psychology; Theology)

History: Founded 2002.

Main Language(s) of Instruction: Portuguese

Degrees and Diplomas: *Bacharelado*; *Licenciatura*; *Especialização/Aperfeiçoamento*

Last Updated: 10/06/15

SAINT CAMILO FACULTY - BAHIA

Faculdade São Camilo
Rua Visconde de Itaborai 102 Amaralina,
Salvador, Bahia 41900000
Tel: +55(71) 3205-3552
Fax: +55(71) 3240-1845
EMail: saocamilo@saocamilo-ba.br
Website: http://www.saocamilo-ba.br

Diretor Geral: Antônio Celso Pasquini

Course

Administration (Administration; Health Administration); **Biology** (Biology); **Nursing** (Nursing)

Further Information: Also branches in Rio de Janeiro, Minas Gerais, Espirito Santo, Rio Grande do Sul, Parana

History: Founded 1997.

Main Language(s) of Instruction: Portuguese

Degrees and Diplomas: *Bacharelado*; *Licenciatura*; *Especialização/Aperfeiçoamento*; *Mestrado*

Last Updated: 26/06/15

SAINT CAMILO FACULTY - BELO HORIZONTE

Faculdade São Camilo (FASC-MG)
Avenida Assis Chateaubriand, 218, Floresta,
Belo Horizonte, MG 30150-100
Tel: +55(31) 3308-6820
Fax: +55(31) 3308-6820
Website: http://www.saocamilo-mg.br

Diretor: Henrique Pinto dos Santos

Course

Graduate Studies (Accountancy; Anatomy; Biotechnology; Food Science; Gerontology; Health Administration; Industrial Design; Nursing; Nutrition; Occupational Health; Physical Therapy; Public Health; Radiology; Rehabilitation and Therapy); **Undergraduate Studies** (Administration; Radiology)

Further Information: Also Units in São Paulo; Espírito Santo; Bahia; Distrito Federal; Rio de Janeiro; Curitiba

Degrees and Diplomas: *Tecnólogo*; *Bacharelado*; *Especialização/Aperfeiçoamento*

Last Updated: 18/04/16

SAINT CAMILO FACULTY - RIO DE JANEIRO

Faculdade São Camilo - Rio de Janeiro
Rua Doutor Satamini 245, Prédio, Tijuca,
Rio de Janeiro, Rio de Janeiro 20270-233
Tel: +55(21) 2117-4200
Fax: +55(21) 2117-4246
EMail: atendimento@saocamilo-rj.br;
diretorgeral@saocamilo-rj.br;
elainepaiva@saocamilo-rj.br
Website: http://www.saocamilo-rj.br

Diretora Geral: Gilceia Maria Lodi
Tel: +55(21) 2117- 4208

Faculty

Luiza de Marillac Faculty of Nursing - FELM (Nursing); **São Camilo Faculy of Administration - FASC** (Business Administration; Health Administration)

History: Founded 1942.

Fees: Undergraduate, 438,24 per month for Business programmes and 685,24 per month for Nursing programmes (Brazilian Real)

Main Language(s) of Instruction: Portuguese

Degrees and Diplomas: *Bacharelado*; *Especialização/Aperfeiçoamento*: **Health Administration; Health Sciences; Industrial and Organizational Psychology; Nursing; Nutrition; Petroleum and Gas Engineering; Pharmacy; Public Health; Sports.** Also MBA

Last Updated: 10/12/15

SAINT CATHERINE FACULTY

Faculdade Santa Catarina (FASC)
Estrada do Arraial, 2740, Tamarineira, Recife, PE 52051-380
Tel: +55(81) 3334-1160
EMail: academicosup@uniesp.edu.br
Website: http://www.faculdadesantacatarina.com.br

Diretora Geral: Fernanda Pereira Tavares
EMail: fernanda.tavares@uniesp.edu.br

Course

Undergraduate Studies (Accountancy; Administration; Pedagogy)

History: Founded 2003.

Main Language(s) of Instruction: Portuguese

Degrees and Diplomas: *Bacharelado*; *Licenciatura*; *Especialização/Aperfeiçoamento*. Also MBA

Student Services: Library

Last Updated: 10/06/15

SAINT CECILIA FACULTY

Faculdade Santa Cecília (FASC)
Praça Barão do Rio Branco 59 Centro,
Pindamonhangaba, SP 12400280
Tel: +55(12) 3642-6496/
EMail: fascpinda@uol.com.br
Website: http://www.fascpinda.com.br

Diretora: Lenita de Azeredo Freitas

Course

Administration (Administration); **Art Education** (Design; Fine Arts; Theatre); **Financial Management** (Finance; Management); **Music** (Music)

History: Founded 1975 as Faculdade de Música Santa Cecília. Acquired present title and status 2000.

Main Language(s) of Instruction: Portuguese

Degrees and Diplomas: *Bacharelado*; *Licenciatura*; *Especialização/Aperfeiçoamento*

Last Updated: 02/07/15

SAINT CECÍLIA UNIVERSITY

Universidade Santa Cecília (UNISANTA)
Rua Oswaldo Cruz, 277, Boqueirão, Santos, São Paulo 11045-907
Tel: +55(13) 3202-7100
Fax: +55(13) 3234-5297
EMail: scecilia@unisanta.br; zuleika@unisanta.br
Website: http://www.unisanta.br

Reitora: Sílvia Ângela Texeira Penteado (1996-)
Tel: +55(13) 3232-4010 EMail: silvia@unisanta.br

Pró-Reitor Administrativo da Unisanta: Marcelo Pirilo Teixeira
EMail: marcelo@unisanta.br

Area

Applied Social Sciences (Accountancy; Administration; Advertising and Publicity; Journalism); **Biological Sciences** (Biological and Life Sciences; Science Education); **Engineering and Technology** (Architecture; Chemical Engineering; Civil Engineering; Computer Engineering; Electrical Engineering; Electronic Engineering; Information Technology; Mechanical Engineering; Petroleum and Gas Engineering; Production Engineering; Town Planning); **Health Sciences** (Dentistry; Pharmacy; Physical Education; Physical Therapy); **Human and Social Sciences** (Law; Pedagogy)

History: Founded 1961 as College, became Instituto Superior de Educação Santa Cecília 1969 and acquired present status and title 1996. A private Institution recognized by the Federal Government and administered by the Sociedade Universitária de Santos.

Academic Year: February to December (February-June; August-December)

Admission Requirements: Secondary school certificate and entrance examination

Main Language(s) of Instruction: Portuguese

Degrees and Diplomas: *Tecnólogo*; *Bacharelado*; *Licenciatura*; *Especialização/Aperfeiçoamento*: **Administrative Law; Constitutional Law; Dentistry; Education; Educational Psychology; Engineering; Gerontology; Health Administration; Insurance;**

Law; Physical Therapy; Preschool Education; Special Education; Transport Management. *Mestrado*: **Coastal Studies; Ecology; Marine Science and Oceanography; Mechanical Engineering.** Also MBA

Student Services: Cultural Activities, Library, Sports Facilities

Last Updated: 11/04/16

SAINT DOROTHY FACULTY OF PHILOSOPHY

Faculdade de Filosofia Santa Dorotéia (FFSD)
Rua Monsenhor Miranda, 86 - Centro,
Nova Friburgo, Rio de Janeiro 28610-230
Tel: +55(24) 2522-2900
Fax: +55(24) 2522-3930
EMail: diretoria@ffsd.br
Website: http://www.ffsd.br

Diretora: Celma Calvão da Silva (1998-) EMail: diretoria@ffsd.br

Course

Geography (Geography); **History** (History); **Literature** (Literature); **Literature and English** (English; Literature); **Literature and Portuguese** (Literature; Portuguese); **Literature, Portuguese and Spanish** (Literature; Portuguese; Spanish); **Pedagogy** (Pedagogy); **Science** (Natural Sciences); **Secretarial Studies** (Secretarial Studies); **Systems Analysis** (Systems Analysis)

History: Founded 1967.

Main Language(s) of Instruction: Portuguese

Degrees and Diplomas: *Tecnólogo*; *Bacharelado*; *Licenciatura*

Last Updated: 06/07/15

SAINT FRANCIS FACULTY OF BARREIRAS

Faculdade São Francisco de Barreiras (FASB)
BR 135 Km 01 n° 2341, Bairro Boa Sorte, Barreiras, BA 47805270
Tel: +55(77) 3613-8800
Fax: +55(77) 3613-8824
EMail: fasb@fasb.edu.br
Website: http://www.fasb.edu.br

Diretor: Tadeu Sergio Bergamo EMail: iaesb@fasb.edu.br

Course

Accountancy (Accountancy); **Administration** (Accountancy; Administration; International Business); **Agronomy** (Agronomy); **Biomedicine** (Biomedicine); **Law** (Law); **Nursing**; **Physical Education** (Physical Education); **Physiotherapy** (Physical Therapy); **Psychology** (Clinical Psychology; Educational Psychology; Industrial and Organizational Psychology; Psychology); **Systems Analysis** (Systems Analysis)

History: Founded 1999.

Main Language(s) of Instruction: Portuguese

Degrees and Diplomas: *Bacharelado*; *Licenciatura*; *Especialização/Aperfeiçoamento*. Also MBA

Student Services: Library

Last Updated: 10/06/15

SAINT FRANCIS FACULTY OF EDUCATION

Faculdade de Educação São Francisco (FAESF)
Rua Abilio Monteiro, 1751, Pedreiras, MA 65725-000
Tel: +55(99) 3626-5400
Fax: +55(99) 3642-1678
EMail: faesf@faesf.com.br; c.saofrancisco@zipmail.com.br
Website: http://www.faesf.com.br/novosite/site/home

Diretora Geral: Aldenôra Veloso Medeiros

Course

Accountancy (Accountancy); **Administration** (Administration); **Computer Science** (Computer Science); **Geography** (Geography); **Literature** (English; Literature; Portuguese); **Nursing** (Nursing); **Nutrition** (Nutrition); **Pedagogy** (Pedagogy); **Physical Education** (Physical Education); **Postgraduate Studies** (Accountancy; Educational Psychology; Environmental Management; Finance; Health Administration; Health Sciences; Higher Education Teacher Training; Midwifery; Nursing; Nutrition; Sports)

History: Founded 1990.

Main Language(s) of Instruction: Portuguese

Degrees and Diplomas: *Tecnólogo*; *Bacharelado*; *Licenciatura*; *Especialização/Aperfeiçoamento*: **Accountancy; Educational Psychology; Environmental Management; Finance; Food Science; Health Administration; Health Sciences; Higher Education Teacher Training; Management; Midwifery; Nursing; Social Policy; Sports.**

Student Services: Library, eLibrary

Last Updated: 01/07/15

SAINT FRANCIS FACULTY OF JUAZEIRO

Faculdade São Francisco de Juazeiro (FASJ)
Rua Paraíso, n° 800, Santo Antonio, Juazeiro, BA 48903-050
Tel: +55(74) 3611- 7672 +55(74) 3612-7579
EMail: dir.academica@fasj.edu.br
Website: http://www.fasj.edu.br

Diretora Academica: Ausinete França Santos
EMail: iaesb@fasb.edu.br

Course

Graduate Studies (Business Administration; Education; Physical Therapy); **Undergraduate Studies** (Accountancy; Administration; Advertising and Publicity; Physical Therapy)

Main Language(s) of Instruction: Portuguese

Degrees and Diplomas: *Bacharelado*; *Especialização/Aperfeiçoamento*

Last Updated: 11/06/15

SAINT FRANCIS OF ASSISI FACULTY

Faculdade São Francisco de Assis (FASFA)
Avenida Sertório, 253, Navegantes, Porto Alegre, RS 91020-001
Tel: +55(51) 3362-1771 +55(51) 3337-0428
EMail: secretaria@unifin.com.br
Website: http://www.unifin.com.br

Diretor: José Luiz dos Santos EMail: joseluiz@unifin.com.br

Course

Graduate Studies (Accountancy; Business Administration; Finance; Management; Marketing); **Undergraduate Studies** (Accountancy; Administration; Advertising and Publicity; Architecture; Civil Engineering; Computer Science; International Relations; Journalism; Law; Psychology; Town Planning)

History: Founded 2003.

Degrees and Diplomas: *Bacharelado*; *Especialização/Aperfeiçoamento*

Last Updated: 10/06/15

SAINT FRANCIS OF ASSISI SCHOOL

Escola Superior São Francisco de Assis (ESFA)
Rua Bernardino Monteiro, 700, Dois Pinheiros,
Santa Tereza, ES 29650-000
Tel: +55(27) 3259-3997
Fax: +55(27) 3259-3997
EMail: esfa@esfa.edu.br
Website: http://www.esfa.edu.br/

Diretor Geral: Clenilton Pereira EMail: diretor.geral@esfa.edu.br

Course

Biology (Biology); **Biomedicine** (Biomedicine); **Dentistry** (Dentistry); **Environmental Health** (Health Sciences); **Graduate Studies** (Environmental Studies; Pharmacology; Pharmacy; Physical Education; Sports); **Pharmacy** (Pharmacy); **Physical Education** (Physical Education); **Religious Studies** (Religious Studies); **Veterinary Science** (Veterinary Science)

History: Founded 1998. Acquired present title 2004.

Main Language(s) of Instruction: Portuguese

Degrees and Diplomas: *Bacharelado*; *Licenciatura*; *Especialização/Aperfeiçoamento*: **Environmental Studies; Law; Pharmacology; Pharmacy; Physical Education; Physical Therapy; Religious Studies; Sports.** Also MBA.

Student Services: Library

Last Updated: 24/09/15

SAINT FRANCIS UNIVERSITY

Universidade São Francisco (USF)

Avenida José de Souza Campos, 1547 - 11°, Edificio Norte, Sul Business Center, Campinas, São Paulo 13025320
Tel: +55(19) 3754-3300 +55(11) 4034-8269
Fax: +55(19) 3254-0490 +55(11) 4034-8007
EMail: secretariageral@saofrancisco.edu.br; nlegusf@usf.edu.br
Website: http://www.saofrancisco.edu.br

Reitor: Joel Alves de Sousa Júnior
EMail: reitoria@saofrancisco.edu.br

Pró-Reitor de Administração e Planejamento: Adriel de Moura Cabral

Programme

Advanced Management Program (AMP) *(Executive education programme of the ESADE Business School in Barcelona offered by FAE Centro Universitário de Curitiba)* (Business Administration; Leadership; Management)

Area

Biological and Health Sciences (Biomedicine; Dentistry; Health Sciences; Medicine; Nursing; Pharmacy); **Exact and Technological Sciences** (Architecture; Chemical Engineering; Civil Engineering; Computer Engineering; Electrical Engineering; Electronic Engineering; Environmental Engineering; Mathematics; Mechanical Engineering; Physical Therapy; Production Engineering; Sanitary Engineering; Town Planning); **Human and Applied Social Sciences** (Accountancy; Administration; Law; Pedagogy; Psychology; Social and Community Services)

Further Information: Also Teaching Hospital; Dental and Psychology Clinics

History: Founded 1976 as Faculdades Franciscanas under the supervision of the Third Order of Saint Francis of Assisi (Casa de Nossa Senhora da Paz). Acquired present status and title 1985.

Academic Year: February to December (February-June; August-December)

Admission Requirements: Secondary school certificate and entrance examination

Fees: Tuition, c. 370-2120 per month (Brazilian Real)

Main Language(s) of Instruction: Portuguese

Degrees and Diplomas: *Tecnólogo*; *Bacharelado*; *Licenciatura*; *Especialização/Aperfeiçoamento*: **Civil Law; Educational Psychology; Health Sciences; Orthodontics; Pharmacy; Psychiatry and Mental Health; Psychology; Safety Engineering.** *Mestrado*: **Education; Health Sciences; Psychology.** *Doutorado*: **Education; Health Sciences; Psychology.** Also MBA

Student Services: Academic Counselling, Canteen, Careers Guidance, Cultural Activities, Foreign Studies Centre, Health Services, Library, Social Counselling, Sports Facilities

Publications: Cadernos do IFAN; Educação e Ensino-USF; Horizontes; Lecta; Psico-USF

Last Updated: 11/04/16

SAINT HELENA FACULTY

Faculdade Santa Helena (FASH)

Rua Demócrito de Souza Filho N°: 452 - Madalena, Recife, Pernambuco 52110020
Tel: +55(81) 3797-6060
EMail: fsh@fsh.edu.br
Website: http://www.fsh.edu.br

Diretor: Marcelo Gustavo Cordeiro Pimentel

Course

Accountancy (Accountancy); **Administration** (Administration; Business Administration; Finance; Human Resources; Marketing); **Educational Management** (Educational Administration; Special Education)

History: Founded 1998.

Main Language(s) of Instruction: Portuguese

Degrees and Diplomas: *Bacharelado*; *Especialização/Aperfeiçoamento*; *Mestrado*

Last Updated: 10/06/15

SAINT JOSÉ FACULTY

Faculdades São José (FSJ)

Av. Santa Cruz, 580, Realengo, Rio de Janeiro, Rio de Janeiro 21710180
Tel: +55(21) 3107-8600 +55(21) 3159-1249
Fax: +55(21) 3332-0047
EMail: reitoria@saojose.br
Website: http://www.saojose.br

Diretor Geral: Antonio José Zaib (1997-)

Secretaria General: Glenda Campos

Course

Accountancy (Accountancy); **Administration** (Administration); **Biology** (Biology); **Computer Science** (Computer Science); **Dentistry** (Dentistry); **Law** (Law); **Pedagogy** (Pedagogy); **Physiotherapy** (Physical Therapy); **Tourism** (Tourism)

Graduate School

Commerce (Business and Commerce); **Education** (Education); **Health Sciences** (Health Sciences); **Law** (Law)

History: Founded 1980.

Main Language(s) of Instruction: Portuguese

Degrees and Diplomas: *Tecnólogo*; *Bacharelado*; *Licenciatura*; *Especialização/Aperfeiçoamento*: **Acupuncture; Administrative Law; Anatomy; Art Management; Business and Commerce; Business Education; Civil Law; Clinical Psychology; Criminal Law; Dental Technology; Dentistry; Educational Administration; Educational Psychology; Educational Sciences; Finance; Health Administration; Higher Education Teacher Training; Hotel Management; Labour Law; Law; Management; Marketing; Orthodontics; Private Law; Sales Techniques; Social Work; Special Education; Surgery; Transport Management.**

Student Services: Library

Last Updated: 03/02/16

SAINT JUDE THADDEUS FACULTY

Faculdade São Judas Tadeu (FSJT)

Rua Clarimundo de Melo 79 Encantado, Rio de Janeiro, Rio de Janeiro 20740321
Tel: +55(21) 3296-5000
Fax: +55(21) 2592-3493
EMail: sjtcpd@easynet.com.br
Website: http://www.sjt.com.br

Diretor Geral: Marcos Albuquerque Santana

Course

Administration (Accountancy; Administration; Business Administration; Environmental Management; Human Resources; Marketing; Tourism); **Pedagogy** (Education; Educational Psychology; Higher Education; Pedagogy; Primary Education)

History: Founded 1974.

Main Language(s) of Instruction: Portuguese

Degrees and Diplomas: *Bacharelado*; *Licenciatura*; *Especialização/Aperfeiçoamento*. Also MBAs

Last Updated: 11/06/15

SAINT JUDE THADDEUS INTEGRATED FACULTIES

Faculdades Integradas São Judas Tadeu (SJT)

Rua Dom Diogo de Souza 100, Cristo Redentor, Porto Alegre, Rio Grande do Sul 91350000
Tel: +55(51) 3340-7888
Fax: +55(51) 3340-2568
EMail: saojudas@saojudastadeu.com.br
Website: http://www.saojudastadeu.com.br

Diretora Acâdemica: Graciela Thisen

Course

Accountancy (Accountancy); **Administration** (Administration); **Law** (Law); **Pedagogy**; **Physical Education** (Physical Education)

History: Founded 1970.

Main Language(s) of Instruction: Portuguese

Degrees and Diplomas: *Bacharelado*; *Especialização/ Aperfeiçoamento*
Last Updated: 08/07/15

SAINT LOUIS FACULTY

Faculdade São Luiz (FSL)
Av das Comunidades, 233, Centro, Brusque, SC 88350-970
Tel: +55(47) 3396-7919
EMail: fsl@faculdadesaoluiz.edu.br
Website: http://www.faculdadesaoluiz.edu.br/

Diretor Geral: Claudio Marcio Piontkewicz

Course

Graduate Studies (Art Therapy; Business Administration); **Undergraduate Studies** (Administration; Philosophy)

History: Founded 2000.

Degrees and Diplomas: *Bacharelado*; *Especialização/Aperfeiçoamento*. Also MBA.
Last Updated: 11/06/15

SAINT LOUIS FACULTY OF JABOTICABAL

Faculdade São Luis de Jaboticabal (FESLJ)
Rua Floriano Peixoto, 839-873, Centro,
Jaboticabal, São Paulo 14870-370
Tel: +55(16) 3209-1800
Fax: +55(16) 3209-2120
EMail: saoluis@saoluis.br
Website: http://www.saoluis.br

Diretora: Iracê Miriam de Castro Martins (1973-)

Course

Accountancy (Accountancy); **Administration** (Administration); **Advertising and Publicity** (Advertising and Publicity); **Arts and Humanities** (Arts and Humanities; English; Literature; Portuguese); **Biological Sciences** (Biological and Life Sciences); **Geography** (Geography); **Graduate Studies** (Administrative Law; Art Education; Business Education; Community Health; Computer Science; Cultural Studies; Education of the Handicapped; Educational Administration; Educational Psychology; Environmental Studies; Health Administration; Health Education; Health Sciences; Human Resources; Labour Law; Law; Literacy Education; Literature; Management; Mathematics Education; Nursing; Occupational Health; Pedagogy; Portuguese; Preschool Education; Primary Education; Public Health; Special Education; Teacher Training); **History** (History); **Information Systems** (Information Technology); **Law** (Law); **Mathematics with Emphasis on Computer Sciences** (Computer Science; Mathematics); **Nursing** (Nursing); **Pedagogy** (Pedagogy); **Production Engineering** (Production Engineering); **Trilingual Executive Secretary** (Secretarial Studies); **Visual Arts** (Visual Arts)

History: Founded 1972. Formely known as Faculdade de Educação São Luis de Jaboticabal.

Main Language(s) of Instruction: Portuguese

Degrees and Diplomas: *Bacharelado*; *Licenciatura*; *Especialização/Aperfeiçoamento*: **Administrative Law; Art Education; Business Education; Community Health; Computer Education; Education of the Handicapped; Educational Administration; Educational Psychology; Environmental Studies; Health Education; Higher Education Teacher Training; Home Economics Education; Human Resources; Labour Law; Literacy Education; Management; Mathematics Education; Nursing; Occupational Health; Preschool Education; Primary Education; Special Education; Teacher Training.** Also MBA.

Student Services: Library
Last Updated: 01/07/15

SAINT LUCY FACULTY

Faculdade Santa Lúcia (FCACSL)
Rua Doutor Ulhoa Cintra, 351, Centro, Mogi-Mirim, SP 13800-970
Tel: +55(19) 3806-3996
EMail: santalucia@santalucia.br
Website: http://www.santalucia.br

Diretor: José Marcos Zanella Pinto

Course

Graduate Studies (Accountancy; Business Administration; Business and Commerce; Law; Management; Marketing; Transport Management); **Undergraduate Studies** (Accountancy; Administration; Information Sciences; Law; Social and Community Services)

History: Founded 1994.

Degrees and Diplomas: *Bacharelado*. Also MBA.
Last Updated: 10/06/15

SAINT MARCELINA FACULTY

Faculdade Santa Marcelina (FASM)
Rua Doutor Emílio Ribas 89, Perdizes,
São Paulo, São Paulo 5006020
Tel: +55(11) 3824-5800
Fax: +55(11) 3824-5818
EMail: fasm@fasm.edu.br
Website: http://www.fasm.edu.br

Diretora Geral: Irmã Valéria Araújo de Carvalho

Course

Accountancy *(Itaquera)* (Accountancy); **Administration** *(Itaquera)* (Administration); **Fashion Design** (Design; Fashion Design); **International Relations** (International Relations); **Music** (Music); **Nursing** *(Itaquera)* (Nursing); **Nutrition** *(Itaquera)* (Nutrition); **Physiotherapy** *(Itaquera)*; **Visual Arts** (Visual Arts)

Further Information: Also Unidade Itaquera

History: Founded 1981.

Main Language(s) of Instruction: Portuguese

Degrees and Diplomas: *Bacharelado*; *Especialização/Aperfeiçoamento*; *Mestrado*
Last Updated: 10/06/15

SAINT ÚRSULA UNIVERSITY

Universidade Santa Úrsula (USU)
Rua Fernando Ferrari, 75, Botafogo,
Rio de Janeiro, Rio de Janeiro 22231-040
Tel: +55(21) 2552-4750 +55(21) 2553-9681 +55(21) 2551-3150
Fax: +55(21) 2551-9049
EMail: usu@usu.br; elafags@gmail.com; paiva.rosita@gmail.com
Website: http://www.usu.br

Reitora: Elaine Fagundes Silva
Tel: +55(21) 2554-8036 EMail: reitoria@usu.br

Pró-Reitora Administrativa: Eliane Martins

Course

Administration (Administration); **Architecture and Urbanism** (Architecture; Town Planning); **Biological Sciences** (Biological and Life Sciences); **Civil Engineering** (Civil Engineering); **Electrical Engineering** (Electrical Engineering); **Law** (Law); **Mechanical Engineering** (Mechanical Engineering); **Production Engineering** (Production Engineering); **Psychology** (Psychology)

History: Founded 1939 by the Ursulines as Catholic Faculty of Education, Science and Letters. Acquired University status 1975. A private institution under the supervision of the Associação Universitária Santa Úrsula.

Academic Year: March to November (March-June; August-November)

Admission Requirements: Secondary school certificate and entrance examination

Main Language(s) of Instruction: Portuguese

Degrees and Diplomas: *Bacharelado*; *Licenciatura*; *Especialização/Aperfeiçoamento*: **Architectural Restoration; Cardiology; Endocrinology; Finance; Gynaecology and Obstetrics; Health Education; Heritage Preservation; Information Technology; International Business; Leadership; Management; Medicine; Physical Therapy; Plastic Surgery; Private Law; Psychoanalysis; Psychology; Publishing and Book Trade; Restoration of Works of Art; Rheumatology; Safety Engineering; Transport Management.** *Mestrado*: **Industrial Management.**

Student Services: Library

Publications: Espaço-Cadernos de Cultura; Série Documentos e Letra

Publishing House: Serviço Gráfico. Editora
Last Updated: 11/04/16

SAINT VINCENT FACULTY

Faculdade São Vicente (FASVIPA)
Rua Padre Soares Pinto N°314, Centro,
Pão de Açúcar, AL 57400-000
Tel: +55(82) 3624-1862
EMail: fasvipa@hotmail.com
Website: http://www.fasvipa.com.br

Diretor Geral: Alexandre Machado

Course
Graduate Studies (Business Administration; Education); **Undergraduate Studies** (Accountancy; Administration; Computer Science; Finance; International Business; Literature; Management; Marketing; Pedagogy; Physical Education; Transport Management)

Degrees and Diplomas: *Bacharelado*; *Licenciatura*; *Especialização/Aperfeiçoamento*
Last Updated: 11/06/15

SALESIAN FACULTY OF PINDAMONHANGABA

Faculdade Salesiana de Pindamonhangaba (FASP)
Rua São João Bosco, 873, Santana,
Pindamonhangaba, SP 12403-010
Tel: +55(12) 3645-3535
Fax: +55(12) 3642-1551
EMail: mrezende@unisal-lorena.br

Course
Administration (Administration); **Teacher Training** (Teacher Training)

Degrees and Diplomas: *Bacharelado*; *Licenciatura*; *Especialização/Aperfeiçoamento*
Last Updated: 25/06/15

SALESIAN FACULTY OF SANTA TERESA

Faculdade Salesiana de Santa Teresa (FSST)
Rua Dom Aquino, 1119, Centro, Corumbá, MS 79301-970
Tel: +55(67) 3234-2600
EMail: secretaria.executiva@steresa.org.br
Website: http://www.fsst.com.br

Diretor Geral: Slawomir Bronakowski

Course
Administration (Administration); **Economics** (Economics); **Law** (Law)

History: Founded 1998.
Main Language(s) of Instruction: Portuguese
Degrees and Diplomas: *Bacharelado*. Postgraduate diploma offered jointly with Universidade Católica Dom Bosco (UCDB virtual).
Last Updated: 09/06/15

SALESIAN FACULTY OF THE NORTH EAST

Faculdade Salesiana do Nordeste (FASNE)
Rua Dom Bosco 551, Boa Vista, Recife, Pernambuco 50070070
Tel: +55(81) 2129-5991
Fax: +55(81) 2129-5988
EMail: fasne@fasne.edu.br
Website: http://www.fasne.edu.br

Diretor Geral: João Carlos Ribeiro Rodrigues

Course
Accountancy (Accountancy); **Administration** (Administration); **Law** (Law); **Physical Education** (Physical Education)

History: Founded 2000.
Main Language(s) of Instruction: Portuguese
Degrees and Diplomas: *Bacharelado*; *Licenciatura*; *Especialização/Aperfeiçoamento*
Last Updated: 10/06/15

SALESIAN UNIVERSITY CENTRE OF SÃO PAULO

Centro Universitário Salesiano de São Paulo (UNISAL)
Av. de Cillo, n° 3.500, Americana, São Paulo 13467-600
Tel: +55(19) 3471-9700
Fax: +55(19) 3471-9716
EMail: secretaria.geral@unisal.br
Website: http://www.unisal.br

Reitor: Ronaldo Zacharias

Pró-Reitora de Ensino, Pesquisa e Pós-Graduação: Romane Fortes Bernardo

Course
Accountancy *(Americana/Maria Auxiliadora)* (Accountancy); **Administration** *(Americana/Maria Auxiliadora; Campinas/São José; Lorena/São Joaquim; São Paulo/Santa Teresinha)* (Administration); **Advertising and Publicity** *(Americana/Dom Bosco)* (Advertising and Publicity); **Automation and Control Engineering** *(Americana/Dom Bosco; Campinas/São José)* (Automation and Control Engineering); **Automotive Systems** *(Campinas/São José)* (Automotive Engineering); **Computer Science** *(Lorena/São Joaquim)* (Computer Science); **Electrical Engineering - Electronic Engineering** *(Campinas/São José)* (Electrical and Electronic Engineering); **Electrical Engineering - Telecommunciations Engineering** *(Campinas/São José)* (Electrical Engineering; Telecommunications Engineering); **Environmental Engineering** *(Americana/Dom Bosco)* (Environmental Engineering); **Fashion** *(Americana/Dom Bosco)* (Fashion Design); **Geography** *(Lorena/São Joaquim)* (Geography); **History** *(Lorena/São Joaquim)* (History); **Hotel Management** *(Lorena/São Joaquim)* (Hotel Management); **Industrial Automation** *(Campinas/São José)* (Automotive Engineering; Industrial Engineering); **Information Systems** *(Americana/Dom Bosco)* (Information Sciences); **Law** *(Americana/Maria Auxiliadora; Campinas/Liceu Salesiano; Lorena/São Joaquim; São Paulo/Santa Teresinha)* (Law); **Mathematics** *(Lorena/São Joaquim)* (Mathematics); **Pedagogy** *(Americana/Maria Auxiliadora; Lorena/São Joaquim; São Paulo/Santa Teresinha)* (Pedagogy); **Philosophy** *(Lorena/São Joaquim)* (Philosophy); **Postgraduate Lato Sensu** *(São Paulo/Santa Teresinha)* (Business and Commerce; Commercial Law; Education; Educational Administration; Educational and Student Counselling; International Law; Law; Marketing; Pedagogy); **Postgraduate Lato Sensu** *(Campinas/Liceu Salesiano)* (Civil Law; Commercial Law; Human Rights); **Postgraduate Lato Sensu** *(Lorena/São Joaquim)* (Biotechnology; Business and Commerce; Civil Law; Commercial Law; Educational Administration; Educational Psychology; Environmental Management; Environmental Studies; Finance; Industrial Management; Information Technology; International Business; Labour Law; Law; Management; Marketing; Mathematics Education; Psychoanalysis; Public Administration; Public Law; Rehabilitation and Therapy; Transport Management); **Postgraduate Lato Sensu** *(Campinas/São José)* (Accountancy; Agricultural Business; Automotive Engineering; Business and Commerce; Computer Science; Cultural Studies; Education; Educational Psychology; Electronic Engineering; Engineering; Finance; Gerontology; Health Administration; History; International Relations; Management; Marketing; Mechanical Engineering; Pedagogy; Philosophy; Production Engineering; Safety Engineering; Software Engineering; Telecommunications Engineering; Transport Management); **Postgraduate Lato Sensu** *(Americana/Maria Auxiliadora)* (Accountancy; Administrative Law; Business and Commerce; Civil Law; Communication Studies; Computer Networks; Criminal Law; Data Processing; Distance Education; Education; Educational Administration; Educational Psychology; Environmental Management; Finance; Information Technology; Labour Law; Law; Management; Marketing; Public Administration; Safety Engineering; Software Engineering; Systems Analysis; Transport Management); **Postgraduate Stricto Sensu** *(Lorena/São Joaquim)* (Law); **Postgraduate Stricto Sensu** *(Americana/Maria Auxiliadora)* (Administration; Education); **Psychology** *(Americana/Maria Auxiliadora; Lorena/São Joaquim)* (Psychology); **Social Services** *(Americana/Maria Auxiliadora)* (Social and Community Services); **Systems for Internet** *(Lorena/São Joaquim)* (Information Technology); **Theology** *(São Paulo/Pio Xi)* (Theology); **Tourism** *(Lorena/São Joaquim)* (Tourism)

History: Founded 1952. Acuired present title and status1993.

Degrees and Diplomas: *Tecnólogo*; *Bacharelado*; *Licenciatura*; *Especialização/Aperfeiçoamento*: **Automotive Engineering; Business Administration; Business and Commerce; Business Education; Civil Engineering; Civil Law; Commercial Law; Computer Engineering; Computer Science; Ecology; Education; Educational Administration; Educational Psychology; Electrical Engineering; Electronic Engineering; Environmental Engineering; Environmental Management; Finance; Gerontology; Health Administration; Higher Education Teacher Training; History; Human Resources; International Business; Judaic Religious Studies; Labour Law; Latin American Studies; Law;**

Literacy Education; Marketing; Mathematics Education; Mechanical Engineering; Neurosciences; Notary Studies; Pedagogy; Philosophy; Physical Education; Physical Therapy; Primary Education; Production Engineering; Psychiatry and Mental Health; Psychology; Public Law; Religious Education; Religious Studies; Safety Engineering; Software Engineering; Special Education; Telecommunications Engineering; Toxicology; Transport Management. *Mestrado*: **Business Administration; Education; Law.** Also MBA.

Student Services: Library

Last Updated: 03/09/15

SALGADO DE OLIVEIRA UNIVERSITY

Universidade Salgado de Oliveira (UNIVERSO)

Campus São Gonçalo, Rua Lambari, 10, Trindade, São Gonçalo, Rio de Janeiro 24456-570

Tel: +55(21) 2138-3432 +55(21) 2138-3459 +51(21) 2138-3440

EMail: universo@universo.edu.br

Website: http://www.universo.edu.br/portal/sao-goncalo

Reitora: Marlene Salgado de Oliveira (1997-)
Tel: +55(21) 2620-5206
EMail: reitoria@nt.universo.edu.br

Diretora Acadêmica: Maria José Soares
Tel: +55(21) 2138-4891
EMail: dir.academica@nt.universo.edu.br

Course

Accountancy (Accountancy); **Administration** (Administration); **Biological Sciences** (Biological and Life Sciences; Science Education); **Chemistry** (Chemistry; Science Education); **Civil Engineering** (Civil Engineering); **History** (History; Humanities and Social Science Education); **Information Systems** (Information Technology); **Law** (Law); **Letters** (Arts and Humanities); **Mathematics** (Mathematics; Mathematics Education); **Nursing** (Nursing); **Nutrition** (Nutrition); **Pedagogy** (Pedagogy); **Pharmacy** (Pharmacy); **Physical Education** (Physical Education); **Physical Therapy** (Physical Therapy); **Production Engineering** (Production Engineering)

Further Information: Also Goiânia, Juiz de Fora, Niterói, Campos, Belo Horizonte, Recife and Salvador Campuses

History: Founded 1976. Acquired present status 1993.

Admission Requirements: Secondary school certificate and entrance examination

Main Language(s) of Instruction: Portuguese

Degrees and Diplomas: *Tecnólogo*; *Bacharelado*; *Licenciatura*; *Especialização/Aperfeiçoamento*: **Administration; African American Studies; African Studies; Business and Commerce; Civil Engineering; Community Health; Criminal Law; Educational Administration; Educational Psychology; Environmental Management; History; Human Resources; Indigenous Studies; Latin American Studies; Nursing; Occupational Therapy; Physical Education; Physical Therapy; Rehabilitation and Therapy; Sports.** *Mestrado*: **History; Psychology; Sports.**

Student Services: Library, Sports Facilities

Last Updated: 11/04/16

SALVADOR INSTITUTE OF EDUCATION AND CULTURE

Instituto Salvador de Ensino e Cultura (ISEC)

Avenida Magalhães Neto, 571, Loteamento Aquarius, Pituba, Salvador, BA 41810-011

Tel: +55(71) 3496-4150

Course

Undergraduate Studies (Accountancy; Administration; Advertising and Publicity; Architecture; Computer Science; Information Technology; Law; Pedagogy; Physical Therapy; Tourism; Town Planning)

Degrees and Diplomas: *Tecnólogo*; *Bacharelado*; *Licenciatura*

Last Updated: 18/04/16

SANTA BARBARA FACULTY OF HIGHER EDUCATION

Faculdade de Ensino Superior Santa Barbara (FAESB)

Rua Onze de Agosto 2900, Tatuí, SP 18277-000

Tel: +55(15) 3259-3838 +55(15) 3259-2789

EMail: contato@faesb.edu.br; aejc@uol.com.br

Website: http://www.faesb.com.br/portal

Diretor: Antonio David Julian

Course

Accountancy (Accountancy); **Administration** (Administration); **Agricultural Engineering** (Agricultural Engineering); **Information Systems** (Information Technology); **Postgraduate Studies** (Business Administration; Education; Engineering; Health Sciences; Law)

History: Founded 2006.

Main Language(s) of Instruction: Portuguese

Degrees and Diplomas: *Bacharelado*; *Especialização/Aperfeiçoamento*: **Accountancy; Business Administration; Cardiology; Civil Law; Dietetics; Educational Administration; Educational Psychology; Finance; Gerontology; Gynaecology and Obstetrics; Health Sciences; Human Resources; Neurology; Nursing; Nutrition; Occupational Health; Paediatrics; Physical Therapy; Psychoanalysis; Public Administration; Public Health; Safety Engineering; Special Education; Surveying and Mapping; Taxation.** Also MBA in Human Resources, Health Administration

Student Services: Library

Last Updated: 03/07/15

SANTA CASA DE MISERICÓRDIA SCHOOL OF ADVANCED SCIENTIFIC STUDIES OF VITÓRIA

Escola Superior de Ciências da Santa Casa de Misericórdia de Vitória (EMESCAM)

Avenida Nossa Senhora da Penha, Santa Luiza, Vitória, Espirito Santo 29045-402

Tel: +55(27) 3334-3509

Fax: +55(27) 3334-3509

EMail: emescam@emescam.br

Website: http://www.emescam.br

Diretor: Flávio Takemi Kataoka

Vice-Diretor: Anna Maria Marreco

Course

Graduate Studies *(Lato Sensu)* (Genetics; Gerontology; Homeopathy; Medicine; Nephrology; Nursing; Nutrition; Oncology; Pharmacy; Physical Therapy; Public Health; Rehabilitation and Therapy; Social Policy; Toxicology); **Graduate Studies** (Development Studies; Social Policy); **Medicine** (Medicine); **Nursing** (Nursing); **Pharmacy** (Pharmacy); **Physiotherapy** (Physical Therapy); **Social Services** (Social and Community Services)

History: Founded 1968.

Main Language(s) of Instruction: Portuguese

Degrees and Diplomas: *Bacharelado*; *Especialização/Aperfeiçoamento*: **Development Studies; Gerontology; Medicine; Nursing; Pharmacy; Physical Therapy; Public Health; Social Policy; Toxicology.** *Mestrado*: **Development Studies; Social Policy.**

Student Services: Library

Last Updated: 25/09/15

SANTA CATARINA ASSOCIATION OF EDUCATION - GUILHERME GUIMBALA FACULTY

Associação Catarinense de Ensino - Faculdade Guilherme Guimbala (ACE)

Rua São José 490, Anita Garibaldi, Joinville, Santa Catarina 89202-010

Tel: +55(47) 3026-4000

Fax: +55(47) 3026-4000

EMail: ace@ace.br; ace@aceadm.com.br

Website: http://www.ace.br

Diretor: Petrônio Guimbala

Course

Education (Education); **Information Systems** (Information Sciences); **Law** (Civil Law; Commercial Law; Law); **Occupational Therapy** (Occupational Therapy); **Physical Therapy** (Physical Therapy); **Psychology** (Psychology)

History: Founded 1973.

Main Language(s) of Instruction: Portuguese

Degrees and Diplomas: *Bacharelado*; *Licenciatura*; *Especialização/Aperfeiçoamento*: **Civil Law; Law; Physical Therapy; Psychology; Rehabilitation and Therapy; Sports.** Also MBA

Student Services: Library, Sports Facilities

Last Updated: 05/06/15

SANTA MARCELINA FACULTY OF PHILOSOPHY, SCIENCE AND LETTERS

Faculdade de Filosofia, Ciências e Letras Santa Marcelina (FAFISM)

Praça Annina Bisegna, 40, Centro, Muriaé, Minas Gerais 36880-000

Tel: +55(32) 3721-1026

Fax: +55(32) 3722-4355

EMail: fafism@fafism.com.br

Website: http://www.fafism.com.br/faculdade.php

Diretora: Christina Maria Pastore (1995-)

Secretária: Neiza Matos Corrêa

Course

Biological Sciences (Biology); **Chemistry** (Chemistry); **Geography** (Geography (Human)); **History** (History); **Literature** (English; Literature; Portuguese); **Mathematics** (Mathematics); **Pedagogy** (Pedagogy); **Physics** (Physics); **Production Engineering** (Production Engineering); **Systems Analysis** (Systems Analysis)

History: Founded 1961.

Main Language(s) of Instruction: Portuguese

Degrees and Diplomas: *Tecnólogo*; *Licenciatura*. Also postgraduate courses offered by the Universidade Católica de Brasília through distance mode

Student Services: IT Centre, Library

Last Updated: 08/07/15

SANTA RITA OF CASSIA FACULTY OF ECONOMICS AND ADMINISTRATIVE SCIENCES

Faculdade de Ciências Econômicas e Administrativas Santa Rita de Cássia (FACEAS)

Avenida Jaçanã, 648, São Paulo, São Paulo 02273-001

Tel: +55(11) 2241-0777

Fax: +55(11) 2241-0777

EMail: santarita@santarita.br; storopoli@santarita.br

Website: http://www.santarita.br

Diretor: Anunciato Storopoli Neto (1996-)

Course

Accountancy (Accountancy); **Administration** (Business Administration); **Biomedicine** (Biomedicine); **Civil Engineering** (Civil Engineering); **Law** (Law); **Nursing** (Nursing); **Pedagogy** (Pedagogy); **Physical Education** (Physical Education); **Postgraduate Studies** (Accountancy; Business Administration; Civil Law; Commercial Law; Community Health; Educational Psychology; Finance; Higher Education Teacher Training; Human Resources; Psychoanalysis); **Technological Studies** (Finance; Human Resources; Marketing; Transport Management)

History: Founded 1994.

Main Language(s) of Instruction: Portuguese

Degrees and Diplomas: *Tecnólogo*; *Bacharelado*; *Licenciatura*; *Especialização/Aperfeiçoamento*: **Community Health; Educational Psychology; Higher Education Teacher Training; Psychoanalysis.** Also MBA

Last Updated: 03/12/15

SANTA TEREZINHA FACULTY

Faculdade Santa Terezinha (CEST)

Avenida Casemiro Júnior 12, Anil, São Luís, Maranhão 65045180

Tel: +55(98) 3213-8000

Fax: +55(98) 3213-8040

EMail: cest@cest.edu.br

Website: http://www.cest.edu.br

Diretor Geral: José Rodrigues Junior

Course

Administration (Administration); **Law** (Law); **Nursing** (Nursing); **Nutrition** (Nutrition); **Occupational Therapy** (Occupational Therapy); **Physiotherapy** (Physical Therapy); **Speech Therapy** (Speech Therapy and Audiology)

History: Founded 1998.

Main Language(s) of Instruction: Portuguese

Degrees and Diplomas: *Bacharelado*; *Especialização/Aperfeiçoamento*

Last Updated: 10/06/15

SÃO CAMILO UNIVERSITY CENTRE

Centro Universitário São Camilo

Avenida Nazaré 1501, Ipiranga, São Paulo, São Paulo 04263-200

Tel: +55(11) 2588-4000

Fax: +55(11) 6215-2361

EMail: info@scamilo.br

Website: http://www.scamilo.edu.br

Reitor: João Batista Gomes de Lima Tel: +55(11) 6169-4003

Course

Technical Studies (Nursing; Radio and Television Broadcasting); **Undergraduate Studies** (Biology; Biomedicine; Business Administration; Cooking and Catering; Health Administration; Medicine; Nursing; Nutrition; Occupational Therapy; Pedagogy; Pharmacy; Philosophy; Physical Therapy; Psychology; Radiology)

Further Information: Also Ipiranga 2 and Pompéia campuses.

History: Founded 1976, acquired present status 1997.

Academic Year: February-June; August-December

Admission Requirements: Secondary school certificate and entrance examination

Fees: 362.30-903.06 (Brazilian Real)

Main Language(s) of Instruction: Portuguese

Degrees and Diplomas: *Tecnólogo*; *Bacharelado*; *Licenciatura*; *Especialização/Aperfeiçoamento*: **Business Administration; Cooking and Catering; Education; Gerontology; Health Administration; Medical Technology; Medicine; Nutrition; Oncology; Pharmacy; Physical Therapy; Psychology; Public Health.** *Mestrado*: **Ethics; Health Sciences; Nursing; Nutrition.** *Doutorado*: **Ethics; Health Sciences.**

Student Services: Canteen, Cultural Activities, Facilities for disabled people

Publications: Cadernos - Centro Universitário São Camilo; O Mundo da Saúde

Last Updated: 03/09/15

SÃO CAMILO UNIVERSITY CENTRE - ESPÍRITO SANTO

Centro Universitário São Camilo - Espírito Santo (SÃO CAMILO-ES)

Rua São Camilo de Léllis, 01, Paraíso, Cachoeiro de Itapemirim, ES 29304-910

Tel: +55(28) 3526-5911

EMail: sg@saocamilo-es.br

Website: http://www.saocamilo-es.br/centrouniversitario/

Reitor: Francisco de Lélis Maciel

Vice-Reitor: Américo Pinho de Cristo

Course

Accountancy (Accountancy); **Administration** (Administration); **Biological Sciences** (Biology); **Chemistry** (Chemistry); **Engineering** (Civil Engineering; Environmental Engineering; Production

Engineering); **English Literature** (English; Literature); **Geography** (Geography); **Graduate Studies** (Accountancy; Business Administration; Communication Studies; Educational Psychology; Environmental Management; Ethics; Geography; Gerontology; Health Administration; Higher Education; History; Human Resources; Information Technology; International Business; Law; Marine Biology; Marketing; Mathematics Education; Nursing; Nutrition; Pedagogy; Physical Education; Physical Therapy; Portuguese; Public Health; Religious Education; Software Engineering); **History** (History); **Information Systems** (Information Technology); **Law** (Law); **Mathematics** (Mathematics); **Nursing** (Nursing); **Nutrition** (Nutrition); **Pedagogy** (Education; Pedagogy); **Pharmacy** (Pharmacy); **Physical Education** *(Licenciatura)* (Physical Education); **Physical Therapy** (Physical Therapy); **Physics** (Physics); **Portuguese Literature** (Portuguese); **Psychology** (Psychology); **Social Communication - Advertising** (Advertising and Publicity); **Social Communication - Journalism** (Journalism); **Technological Studies** (Petroleum and Gas Engineering; Systems Analysis; Tourism)

Further Information: Also São Camilo Campus II, São Camilo Vitória and Crato Training Centre.

History: Founded 1989.

Main Language(s) of Instruction: Portuguese

Degrees and Diplomas: *Tecnólogo*; *Bacharelado*; *Licenciatura*; *Especialização/Aperfeiçoamento*: **Business Administration; Civil Law; Clinical Psychology; Criminal Law; Education; Educational Psychology; Environmental Engineering; Finance; Gerontology; Health Administration; Higher Education; Human Resources; Law; Marketing; Mathematics Education; Nursing; Pharmacology; Physical Therapy; Public Health.** Also MBA.

Student Services: Library

Last Updated: 08/09/15

SÃO JOSÉ UNIVERSITY CENTRE OF ITAPERUNA

Centro Universitário São José de Itaperuna

Rua Major Porfírio Henriques, 41, Centro, Itaperuna, RJ 28300-000
Tel: +55(22) 3811-0700 +55(22) 99961-4885
Fax: +55(22) 3824-3202
EMail: unifsj@fsj.edu.br; fsj@fsj.edu.br; decom@fsj.edu.br
Website: http://fsj.edu.br/unifsj

Reitor: José Carlos Mendes Martins

Vice-Reitor Administrativo: Márcio de Oliveira Monteiro

Course

Accounting (Accountancy); **Administration** (Business Administration); **Biomedicine** (Biomedicine); **History** (History); **Letters - English** (Arts and Humanities; English); **Letters - Portuguese** (Arts and Humanities; Portuguese); **Letters - Spanish** (Arts and Humanities; Spanish); **Nursing** (Nursing); **Pharmacy** (Pharmacy); **Postgraduate Studies** (Business Administration; Finance; History; Human Resources; Linguistics; Literature; Political Sciences); **Psychology** (Psychology); **Sciences and Mathematics** (Mathematics; Performing Arts)

History: Founded 2001.

Main Language(s) of Instruction: Portuguese

Degrees and Diplomas: *Bacharelado*; *Licenciatura*; *Especialização/Aperfeiçoamento*: **History; Linguistics; Literature; Political Sciences.** Also MBA

Student Services: Library

Last Updated: 02/12/15

SÃO PAULO SCHOOL OF ECONOMICS

Escola de Economia de São Paulo (EESP)

Rua Itapeva, 474, 13° andar, Bela Vista, São Paulo, SP 01332-000
Tel: +55(11) 3799-3350
Fax: +55(11) 3799-3357
EMail: economia@fgv.br
Website: http://www.eesp.fgv.br/

Diretor: Yoshiaki Nakano EMail: nakano@fgv.br

Course

Economics (Agricultural Economics; Economics)

History: Founded 2004.

Main Language(s) of Instruction: Portuguese

Degrees and Diplomas: *Bacharelado*; *Mestrado*: **Economics.** *Doutorado*: **Economics.** Also MBA and Post-doctorate courses.

Last Updated: 18/09/15

SÃO PAULO SCHOOL OF LAW

Escola de Direito de São Paulo (FGV DIREITO SP)

Rua Rocha, 233, Bela Vista, São Paulo, SP 01330-000
Tel: +55(11) 3799-2222
Fax: +55(11) 3799-2233
EMail: direitogv@fgv.br
Website: http://direitosp.fgv.br/

Diretor: Oscar Vilhena Vieira EMail: oscar.vilhena@fgv.br

Vice-Diretor Administrativo: Paulo Clarindo Goldschmidt EMail: paulo.goldschmidt@fgv.br

Course

Law (Law)

History: Founded 2002.

Main Language(s) of Instruction: Portuguese

Degrees and Diplomas: *Bacharelado*; *Especialização/Aperfeiçoamento*: **Law.** *Mestrado*: **Law.**

Last Updated: 18/09/15

SATC FACULTY

Faculdade SATC (FASATC)

Rua Pascoal Meller, 73, Universitário, Criciúma, SC 88805-380
Tel: +55(48) 3431-7500
Fax: +55(48) 3431-7501
EMail: copefa@satc.edu.br
Website: http://www.portalsatc.com

Diretor Executivo: Fernando Luiz Zancan

Course

Graduate Studies (Business Administration; Design; Geology; Industrial Engineering; Management; Production Engineering; Public Administration; Surveying and Mapping); **Undergraduate Studies** (Automation and Control Engineering; Electrical Engineering; Graphic Design; Industrial Management; Journalism; Mechanical Engineering; Telecommunications Engineering)

History: Founded 2003.

Main Language(s) of Instruction: Portuguese

Degrees and Diplomas: *Tecnólogo*; *Bacharelado*; *Especialização/Aperfeiçoamento*; *Mestrado*. Also Postgraduate diploma.

Last Updated: 11/06/15

SCHOOL OF ADVERTISING AND MARKETING OF PORTO ALEGRE

Escola Superior de Propaganda e Marketing de Porto Alegre (ESPM)

Rua Guilherme Schel 350, Santo Antonio,
Porto Alegre, Rio Grande do Sul 90640-040
Tel: +55(51) 3218-1300
Fax: +55(51) 3219-1988
EMail: graduacao-rs@espm.br; cintra@espm.br
Website: http://www.espm.br

Presidente: Roberto Whitaker Penteado

International Relations: Rodrigo Cintra, Head EMail: cintra@espm.br

Course

Business Administration (Administration; Business Administration); **Design** (Design); **Film and Media Studies** (Film; Media Studies); **Graduate Studies** (Business Administration; Business and Commerce; Finance; Leadership; Marketing); **Information and Communication Technology** (Information Technology); **International Relations** (Business Administration; International Relations; Marketing); **Journalism** (Journalism); **Social Communication - Advertising and Publicity** (Advertising and Publicity)

Further Information: Also branches in Sao Paulo and Rio de Janeiro

History: Founded as São Paulo Art Museum School of Advertising 1951. 1999.

Main Language(s) of Instruction: Portuguese

Degrees and Diplomas: *Bacharelado*; *Especialização/Aperfeiçoamento*: **Agricultural Business; Business Administration; Business and Commerce; Design; Finance; Journalism; Leadership; Marketing.** *Mestrado*: **Communication Studies; Management; Marketing.** *Doutorado*: **Communication Studies; Management.** Also MBA.

Student Services: Health Services, IT Centre, Library, Residential Facilities

Last Updated: 26/11/15

SCHOOL OF AGRICULTURAL MEASUREMENT ENGINEERING

Escola de Engenharia de Agrimensura (EEA)
Avenida Joana Angélica, 1381, Nazaré, Bahia
Tel: +55(71) 2103-5922
Fax: +55(71) 3321-5694
EMail: euridez@hotmail.com
Website: http://www.eeemba.br

Diretor Presidente: Dirval Campos de Carvalho

Course

Agricultural Engineering (Agricultural Engineering; Surveying and Mapping)

Further Information: Also Brotas and Itabuna Unit.

History: Founded 1974.

Main Language(s) of Instruction: Portuguese

Degrees and Diplomas: *Bacharelado*; *Especialização/Aperfeiçoamento*

Last Updated: 22/09/15

SCHOOL OF APPLIED MATHEMATICS

Escola de Matemática Aplicada (EMAP-FGV)
Praia de Botafogo, 190, Rio de Janeiro, RJ 22250-900
Tel: +55(21) 3799-5917
EMail: emap@fgv.br; cirlei.oliveira@fgv.br
Website: http://emap.fgv.br

Diretora: Maria Izabel Camacho EMail: emap@fgv.br

Diretora Administrativa: Elisângela Santana Souza
Tel: +55(21) 3799-5917 EMail: elisangela.souza@fgv.br

Course

Applied Mathematics (Applied Mathematics)

History: Founded 2011.

Main Language(s) of Instruction: Portuguese

Degrees and Diplomas: *Bacharelado*; *Mestrado*: **Applied Mathematics.**

Last Updated: 01/12/15

SCHOOL OF BUSINESS ADMINISTRATION OF SAO PAULO

Escola de Administração de Empresas de São Paulo (EAESP-FGV)
Avenida 9 de Julho, 2029, Bela Vista,
São Paulo, São Paulo 01313-902
Tel: +55(11) 3799-7777
Fax: +55(11) 3284-1789
EMail: cri@fgv.br
Website: http://www.fgv.br/eaesp

Diretor: Luiz Artur Ledur Brito EMail: Luiz.Brito@fgv.br

Vice-Diretor: Tales Andreassi

Course

Business Administration (Accountancy; Administration; Business Administration; Business Computing; Economics; Finance; Human Resources; Marketing; Public Administration); **Graduate Studies** *(Stricto Sensu)* (Business Administration; Public Administration)

History: Founded 1963.

Main Language(s) of Instruction: Portuguese

Degrees and Diplomas: *Bacharelado*; *Especialização/Aperfeiçoamento*: **Business Administration; Finance; International Business; Public Administration.** *Mestrado*: **Administration; Management.** Also MBA.

Publications: RAE-Revista de Administração de Empresas

Last Updated: 17/09/15

SCHOOL OF ENVIRONMENTAL STUDIES

Escola Superior em Meio Ambiente (ESMA)
Rua 155 No 253, Bairro Bela Vista,
Iguatama, Minas Gerais 38910-000
Tel: +55(37) 3353-2222
Fax: +55(37) 3353-2110
EMail: esma@esma.edu.br; presidencia@esma.edu.br
Website: http://www.esma.edu.br

Presidente: Lucivane Lamounier Faria
EMail: presidencia@esma.edu.br

Course

Administration - Environmental Management (Administration; Environmental Management); **Biological Sciences** (Biological and Life Sciences); **Biomedicine** (Biomedicine)

History: Founded 1997.

Main Language(s) of Instruction: Portuguese

Degrees and Diplomas: *Bacharelado*; *Licenciatura*

Student Services: Library

Last Updated: 24/09/15

SCHOOL OF HEALTH SCIENCES

Escola Superior de Ciências da Saúde (ESCS)
SMHN Quadra 03, conjunto A, Bloco 1 Edifício Fepecs,
Brasília, DF 70710-907
Tel: +55 (61) 3326-9300
EMail: escs@saude.df.gov.br
Website: http://www.escs.edu.br/

Diretor Geral: Mourad Ibrahim Belaciano (2001-)

Course

Graduate Studies (Public Health); **Medicine** (Medicine); **Nursing** (Nursing)

History: Founded 2001.

Main Language(s) of Instruction: Portuguese

Degrees and Diplomas: *Bacharelado*; *Especialização/Aperfeiçoamento*

Student Services: Library

Last Updated: 25/09/15

SCHOOL OF MARKETING

Escola Superior de Marketing (ESM)
Rua Benfica, 126, Madalena, PE 50720-001
Tel: +55(81) 3081-0596
EMail: esm@escolademarketing.com.br
Website: http://www.escolademarketing.com.br

Diretor Geral: José Lavanère das Chagas Lemos

Diretora Acadêmica: Ana Carla Martins Lemos
EMail: diretoria.academica@escolademarketing.com.br

Course

Administration (Administration); **Advertising and Publicity** (Advertising and Publicity); **Commercial Management** (Business and Commerce); **Human Resources** (Human Resources); **Logistics** (Transport Management)

History: Founded 1974.

Main Language(s) of Instruction: Portuguese

Degrees and Diplomas: *Bacharelado*; *Especialização/Aperfeiçoamento*: **Business Administration; Design; Photography.** Also MBA.

Student Services: Library

Last Updated: 25/09/15

SCHOOL OF PUBLIC MINISTRY

Fundação Escola Superior do Ministério Público (FMP)

Rua Cel. Genuino, 421 - 6°, 7°, 8°, 9°, 10° e 12° andares, Porto Alegre, RS 90010-350

Tel: +55(51) 3027-6565

Fax: +55(51) 3027-6565

EMail: fmp@fmp.com.br; registro.academico@fmp.com.br

Website: http://www.fmp.edu.br/institucional/13/faculdade-de-direito

Diretor: Fábio Roque Sbardellotto

Faculty

Law (Law)

Course

Graduate Studies (Administrative Law; Law; Private Law; Public Administration)

History: Founded 2002.

Main Language(s) of Instruction: Portuguese

Degrees and Diplomas: *Bacharelado*; *Especialização/Aperfeiçoamento*: **Administrative Law; Law; Public Administration.** *Mestrado*: **Law.**

Student Services: Library

Publications: Bens Jurídicos Indisponíveis e Transindividuais; Revista da Faculdade de Direito; Revista Ibero-Americanos em Ciências Penais

Last Updated: 03/02/16

SCHOOL OF PUBLIC RELATIONS

Escola Superior de Relações Públicas (ESURP)

Avenida Conselheiro Rosa e Silva 839/773, Aflitos, Recife, Pernambuco 52020-220

Tel: +55(81) 3427-8600

Fax: +55(81) 3427-8620

EMail: direcao@esurp.edu.br

Website: http://www.esurp.edu.br

Diretora: Maria de Fátima Serrão Schuler Vilarôco

Course

Graduate Studies (Communication Studies; Environmental Engineering; Management; Marketing; Public Relations; Secretarial Studies); **Public Relations** (Public Relations); **Secretarial Studies** (Secretarial Studies)

History: Founded 1973.

Degrees and Diplomas: *Bacharelado*; *Especialização/Aperfeiçoamento*: **Communication Studies; Environmental Engineering; Management; Marketing; Public Relations; Secretarial Studies.**

Student Services: Library

Last Updated: 28/09/15

SCHOOL OF SOCIAL SCIENCES

Escola Superior de Ciências Sociais (FGV/CPDOC)

Praia de Botafogo, 190, 14° andar, Botafogo, Rio de Janeiro, RJ 22253-900

Tel: +55(21) 3799-5676 +55(21) 3799-5677

Fax: +55(21) 3799-5679

EMail: ri@fgv.br

Website: http://cpdoc.fgv.br/escs/

Coordenador: Alexandre Moreli EMail: alexandre.moreli@fgv.br

Course

Post-Graduate Studies (Business Administration; Cultural Studies; History; Political Sciences); **Undergraduate Studies** (Business Administration; Cultural Studies; Economics; History; International Relations; Law; Mathematics; Social Policy; Social Sciences)

Further Information: Also a branch in São Paulo

History: Founded 2005.

Main Language(s) of Instruction: Portuguese

Degrees and Diplomas: *Bacharelado*: **Social Sciences.** *Licenciatura*: **History.** *Especialização/Aperfeiçoamento*: **Business Administration; Film.** *Mestrado*: **Cultural Studies; History; Political Sciences.** *Doutorado*: **Cultural Studies; History; Political Sciences.** Also MBA in International Relations

Student Services: Library

Last Updated: 25/09/15

SCHOOL OF THE CITY - FACULTY OF ARCHITECTURE AND URBANISM

Escola da Cidade - Faculdade de Arquitetura e Urbanismo

Rua General Jardim, 65, Vila Buarque, São Paulo, SP 01223-011

Tel: +55(11) 3258-8108

Fax: +55(11) 3258-8108

EMail: escoladacidade@escoladacidade.edu.br

Website: http://www.escoladacidade.org/

Diretor: Ciro Pirondi

Course

Architecture and Urbanism (Architecture; Design; History; Urban Studies)

History: Founded 1996.

Degrees and Diplomas: *Bacharelado*; *Especialização/Aperfeiçoamento*

Student Services: IT Centre, Library

Last Updated: 16/09/15

SENAC FACULTY MINAS

Faculdade Senac Minas (FSM)

Rua das Paineiras, 1300, Jardim Eldorado, Contagem, MG 32310-400

Tel: +55(31) 3048-9365/3048-9365

Fax: +55(31) 3048-9801

EMail: janete.dias@mg.senac.br; raquel.amorim@mg.senac.br

Website: http://www.mg.senac.br/faculdade

Diretor: Marcio Mussy Toledo EMail: marcio.toledo@mg.senac.br

Secretária Escolar: Elke Cibele Silva Alves
EMail: elke@mg.senac.br

Faculty

SENAC Faculty Belo Horizonte Unit - FTS *(Belo Horizonte)* (Cooking and Catering; Finance; Human Resources; Management); **SENAC Faculty Contagem Unit - FSM** (Accountancy; Business Administration; Finance; Human Resources; Management; Safety Engineering); **SENAC Facutly Barbacena Unit - FTS** *(Barbacena)* (Hotel Management)

Course

Postgraduate Studies (Accountancy; Business Administration; Educational Administration; Finance; Hotel and Restaurant; Management; Public Administration; Transport Management)

Further Information: Also Unites in Araxá, Barbacena, Belo Horizonte, Conselheiro Lafaiete, Contagem, Coronel Fabriciano, Curvelo, Diamantina, Governador Valadares, Ipatinga, Itabira, Itabirito, Ituiutaba, Manhuaçu, Montes Claros, Patos de Minas, Pirapora, Pouso Alegre, Sete Lagoas, Três Marias, Uberaba e Uberlândia.

History: Founded 2004.

Main Language(s) of Instruction: Portuguese

Degrees and Diplomas: *Tecnólogo*; *Bacharelado*: **Accountancy; Business Administration.** Also MBA

Student Services: Library

Last Updated: 11/12/15

SENAC FACULTY OF TECHNOLOGY BLUMENAU

Faculdade de Tecnologia SENAC Blumenau (SENAC BLUMENAU)

Av. Brasil, 610 - Ponta Aguda, Blumenau, SC 89010-971

Tel: +55(47) 3035-9999 +(47) 8403-7128

Fax: +55(47) 3035-9988

EMail: marketing.blu@sc.senac.br

Website: http://portal.sc.senac.br/portal/WebForms/unidade.aspx?secao_id=60

Diretora: Elita Grosch Maba

Course
Graduate Studies (Industrial Management; Information Technology; Management; Multimedia; Transport Management); **Technical Studies** (Cosmetology; Human Resources; Marketing; Transport Management)
History: Founded 2004.
Main Language(s) of Instruction: Portuguese
Degrees and Diplomas: *Tecnólogo*; *Especialização/Aperfeiçoamento*: **Industrial Management; Information Technology; Management; Multimedia; Transport Management.**
Last Updated: 01/09/15

SENAC FACULTY OF TECHNOLOGY CHAPECÓ

Faculdade de Tecnologia SENAC Chapecó (SENAC CHAPECÓ)

Rua Castro Alves, 298E, Bairro São Cristóvão, Chapecó, SC 89803-110
Tel: +55(49) 3361-5000
Fax: +55(49) 3361-5000
EMail: chapeco@sc.senac.br
Website: http://portal.sc.senac.br/portal/WebForms/unidade.aspx?secao_id=64

Diretora: Silvana Marcon
EMail: silvanamarcon@sc.senac.br

Course
Distance Education (Computer Networks; Computer Science; Cosmetology; Taxation); **Project Management** *(Postgraduate)* (Management)
Main Language(s) of Instruction: Portuguese
Degrees and Diplomas: *Especialização/Aperfeiçoamento*: **Management.** Also Online Professional Certificates
Last Updated: 01/09/15

SENAC FACULTY OF TECHNOLOGY FEDERAL DISTRICT

Faculdade de Tecnologia SENAC Districto Federal (FAC SENAC DF)

Avenida SEUPS 703/903, lote A. Asa Sul, Brasília, DF 70390-039
Tel: +55(61) 3217-8821 +55(61) 3217-8814
Fax: +55(61) 3217-8811
EMail: antonia.rodrigues@senacdf.com.br; pesquisador@senacdf.com.br
Website: http://www.facsenac.edu.br

Diretora Geral: Antonia Maria Ribeiro Rodrigues
EMail: Antonia.Rodrigues@senacdf.com.br

Course
Commercial Management (Business and Commerce); **Graduate Studies** (Business and Commerce; Data Processing; Human Resources; Information Technology; Management; Real Estate; Software Engineering; Teacher Training; Transport Management); **Human Resources** (Human Resources); **Information Technology Management** (Information Technology); **Marketing** (Marketing); **Systems Analysis and Development** (Systems Analysis)
History: Founded 2007.
Main Language(s) of Instruction: Portuguese
Degrees and Diplomas: *Tecnólogo*; *Especialização/Aperfeiçoamento*: **Business and Commerce; Data Processing; Information Technology; Management; Real Estate; Software Engineering; Teacher Training; Transport Management.**
Student Services: Facilities for disabled people, IT Centre, Library
Last Updated: 01/09/15

SENAC FACULTY OF TECHNOLOGY FLORIANÓPOLIS

Faculdade de Tecnologia SENAC Florianópolis (SENAC FLORIANÓPOLIS)

Rua Silva Jardim, 360, Prainha, Florianópolis, SC 88020-200
Tel: +55(48) 3229-3200
Fax: +55(48) 3229-3200
EMail: florianopolis@sc.senac.br; ivanir@sc.senac.br
Website: http://www.sc.senac.br/open.php?outros=home&opc=009

Diretor: José Carlos Vieira

Course
Accountancy (Accountancy); **Distance Education** (Accountancy; Computer Science; Cooking and Catering; Cultural Studies; English; Ethics; Leadership; Management; Painting and Drawing; Portuguese; Psychology; Sales Techniques; Speech Studies); **Management** *(Postgraduate)* (Management)
History: Founded 2002.
Main Language(s) of Instruction: Portuguese
Degrees and Diplomas: *Tecnólogo*: **Accountancy.** *Especialização/Aperfeiçoamento*: **Management.**
Last Updated: 01/09/15

SENAC FACULTY OF TECHNOLOGY GOIÁS

Faculdade de Tecnologia SENAC Goiás (SENAC GOIÁS)

Avenida Independência, n° 1,002, Setor Leste Universitário, Goiânia, GO 74645-010
Tel: +55(62) 3524-4800
EMail: faculdadesenac@go.senac.br; lionisio@go.senac.br
Website: http://www.go.senac.br/faculdade/index.php

Diretor da Faculdade: Lionisio Pereira dos Santos Filho
EMail: lionisio@go.senac.br
Coordenador Administrativo: Rômulo Venâncio de Paiva
EMail: romulovenancio@go.senac.br

Course
Distance Education (Business and Commerce; Computer Science; Design; Education; Environmental Studies; Food Science; Management; Safety Engineering; Tourism); **Graduate Studies** (Business Computing; Computer Networks; Software Engineering); **Undergraduate Studies** (Business and Commerce; Computer Graphics; Environmental Management; Graphic Design; Information Management; Information Technology; Multimedia; Software Engineering)
History: Founded 2007.
Main Language(s) of Instruction: Portuguese
Degrees and Diplomas: *Tecnólogo*; *Especialização/Aperfeiçoamento*: **Computer Networks; Software Engineering.** Also distance mode programmes: Técnico de Ensino Médio, Tecnólogo, Bacharelado, Licenciatura in Pedagogy and Especialização in Teacher Training, Business Administration, Environmental Studies and Food Science offered through the university's distance education platform (SENAC EAD).
Student Services: Library
Last Updated: 01/09/15

SENAC FACULTY OF TECHNOLOGY JARAGUÁ DO SUL

Faculdade de Tecnologia SENAC Jaraguá do Sul (SENAC JARAGUÁ DO SUL)

Rua dos Imigrantes, 410, Vila Rau, Jaraguá do Sul, SC 89254-430
Tel: +55(47) 3275-8400
Fax: +55(47) 3275-8404
EMail: jaraguadosul@sc.senac.br; mauricio@sc.senac.br
Website: http://www.sc.senac.br/open.php?outros=home&opc=020

Diretor: Mauricio Anisio Ferreira

Course
Distance Education (Administration; Business Administration; Health Sciences; Leadership; Management; Marketing; Nursing; Occupational Health; Sales Techniques; Secretarial Studies; Speech Studies); **Graduate Studies** (Management); **Technical Studies** (Administration; Nursing; Occupational Health)
History: Founded 2008.
Main Language(s) of Instruction: Portuguese
Degrees and Diplomas: *Tecnólogo*; *Especialização/Aperfeiçoamento*: **Management.**
Last Updated: 01/09/15

SENAC FACULTY OF TECHNOLOGY CRICIÚMA

Faculdade de Tecnologia SENAC Criciúma (SENAC CRICIÚMA)

Rua General Lauro Sodré, 180, Comerciário, Criciúma, SC 88802-330
Tel: +55(48) 3437-9801
Fax: +55(48) 3437-9801
EMail: meneguetti@sc.senac.br
Website: http://portal.sc.senac.br/portal/WebForms/unidade.aspx?secao_id=66

Diretor: Rudney Raulino

Course

Postgraduate Studies (Business Administration; Fashion Design; Finance; Information Technology; Management; Marketing; Transport Management)

Main Language(s) of Instruction: Portuguese

Degrees and Diplomas: *Especialização/Aperfeiçoamento*: **Business Administration; Fashion Design; Finance; Information Technology; Management; Marketing; Transport Management.** Also MBA

Last Updated: 11/12/15

SENAC FACULTY OF TECHNOLOGY PELOTAS

Faculdade de Tecnologia SENAC Pelotas (SENAC PELOTAS)

Rua Gonçalves Chaves, 602, Centro, Pelotas, RS 96015-560
Tel: +55(53) 322-56918
EMail: fatecpelotas@senacrs.com.br; fatecsenacpelotas@senacrs.com.br
Website: http://portal.senacrs.com.br/unidades.asp?unidade=78

Diretora: Nara Beatriz Lópes Pires da Luz
EMail: nlpires@senacrs.com.br

Course

Computer Science (Computer Networks; Systems Analysis); **Graduate Studies** (Business and Commerce; Communication Studies; Leadership; Management; Marketing); **Management** (Human Resources; Management; Marketing)

History: Founded 2004.

Main Language(s) of Instruction: Portuguese

Degrees and Diplomas: *Tecnólogo*; *Especialização/Aperfeiçoamento*: **Business and Commerce; Leadership; Management; Marketing.**

Student Services: Library

Last Updated: 02/09/15

SENAC FACULTY OF TECHNOLOGY RIO DE JANEIRO

Faculdade de Tecnologia SENAC Rio de Janeiro (SENAC RJ)

Rua Santa Luzia, 735 - 2° Andar, Centro, Rio de Janeiro, Rio de Janeiro
Tel: +55(21) 2517-9232 +55(21) 2517-9231
Fax: +55(21) 2517-9284
EMail: graduacao@rj.senac.br
Website: http://www.rj.senac.br/unidades/faculdade-tecnologia-senac-rio

Diretora: Ana Alice Pinto

Course

Administration and Finance (Transport Management); **Design and Games** (Graphic Design); **Environment and Sustainability** (Environmental Management); **Graduate Studies** (Computer Engineering; International Business; Management; Media Studies; Software Engineering; Teacher Training); **Information Technology** (Information Technology; Software Engineering); **Tourism and Hospitality** (Hotel and Restaurant)

History: Founded 2002.

Main Language(s) of Instruction: Portuguese

Degrees and Diplomas: *Tecnólogo*; *Especialização/Aperfeiçoamento*: **Computer Engineering; Media Studies; Software Engineering; Teacher Training.** Also MBA in Management, Teacher Training, International Business.

Last Updated: 02/09/15

SENAC FACULTY OF TECHNOLOGY TUBARÃO

Faculdade de Tecnologia SENAC Tubarão (SENAC TUBARÃO)

Av. Marcolino Martins Cabral, 2100, Vila Moema, Tubarão, SC 88705-000
Tel: +55(48) 3632-2428
Fax: +55(48) 3626-5831
EMail: marisar@sc.senac.br
Website: http://portal.sc.senac.br/portal/WebForms/unidade.aspx?secao_id=81

Diretora: Marisa Martini Ramos

Course

Management *(Postgraduate)* (Management)

Further Information: Also distance education programmes

History: Founded 2004.

Main Language(s) of Instruction: Portuguese

Degrees and Diplomas: *Especialização/Aperfeiçoamento*: **Management.** Also MBA

Last Updated: 02/09/15

SENAC FACULTY PERNAMBUCO

Faculdade Senac Pernambuco (SENACPE)

Av. Visconde de Suassuna, n° 500, Santo Amaro, Recife, PE 50050-540
Tel: +55(81) 3413-6756
EMail: ouvidoriafaculdade@pe.senac.br
Website: http://www.faculdadesenacpe.edu.br/

Diretora Geral: Terezinha de Souza Ferraz Nunes

Course

Distance Postgraduate Education (Cultural Studies; Distance Education; Educational Administration; Environmental Management; Food Science; Information Technology; Retailing and Wholesaling; Visual Arts); **Graduate Studies** (Business and Commerce; Fashion Design; Higher Education; Public Relations); **Undergraduate Studies** (Administration; Fashion Design; Hotel and Restaurant; Public Relations; Service Trades)

History: Founded 1946.

Main Language(s) of Instruction: Portuguese

Degrees and Diplomas: *Tecnólogo*; *Bacharelado*; *Especialização/Aperfeiçoamento*

Last Updated: 11/06/15

SENAC RS FACULTY PORTO ALEGRE

Faculdade Senac Porto Alegre (FSPOA-SENAC/RS)

Rua Coronel Genuíno, 358, Centro, Porto Alegre, RS 90010-350
Tel: +55(51) 3212-4444
EMail: faculdadesenac@senacrs.com.br
Website: http://www.senacrs.com.br

Diretor Regional: José Paulo da Rosa
EMail: diretoria@senacrs.com.br

Course

Distance Postgraduate Studies (Cultural Studies; Distance Education; Educational Administration; Environmental Studies; Food Science; Information Technology; Retailing and Wholesaling; Visual Arts); **Graduate Studies** (Finance; Information Management); **Undergraduate Studies** (Administration)

History: Founded 1946.
Main Language(s) of Instruction: Portuguese
Degrees and Diplomas: *Bacharelado*; *Especialização/Aperfeiçoamento*
Last Updated: 11/06/15

SENAC UNIVERSITY CENTRE

Centro Universitário Senac (SENACSP)

Av. Engenheiro Eusébio Stevaux, 823, Santo Amaro,
São Paulo, São Paulo 04696-000
Tel: +55(11) 5682-7300
Fax: +55(11) 5682-7441
EMail: campussantoamaro@sp.senac.br
Website: http://www.sp.senac.br

Diretor: Luiz Francisco de A. Salgado

Course
Aesthetics (Aesthetics; Cosmetology); **Architecure and Town Planning** (Architecture; Town Planning); **Business Administration** (Accountancy; Business Administration; International Business; Management; Marketing); **Design** (Design); **Education** (Education); **Environmental Studies, Health Science** (Health Sciences; Occupational Health; Public Health); **Events and Lazer**; **Fashion** (Fashion Design); **Gastronomy** (Cooking and Catering); **Health Sciences and Wellness** (Nutrition; Physical Education); **Hotel and Tourism** (Hotel and Restaurant; Tourism); **Information Technology** (Information Technology)
Further Information: Also São Paulo State Units (Campos do Jordão, Águas de São Pedro, Araraquara, Araçatuba, Barretos, Bauru, Bebedouro, Botucatu, Campinas, Catanduva, Franca, Guaratinguetá, Itapetininga, Itapira, Itu, Jaboticabal, Jaú, Jundiaí, Limeira, Marília, Mogi Guaçu, Piracicaba, Presidente Prudente, Ribeirão Preto, Rio Claro, Santos, Sorocaba, São Carlos, São José do Rio Preto, São José dos Campos, São João da Boa Vista, Taubaté, Votuporanga) and Greater São Paulo Units (24 de Maio, Consolação, Francisco Matarazzo, Guarulhos, Itaquera, Jabaquara, Lapa Faustolo, Lapa Scipião, Lapa Tito, Nove de Julho, Osasco, Penha, Santa Cecília, Santana, Santo Amaro, Santo André, Tatuapé, Tiradentes, Vila Prudente).
History: Founded in 1946 as administrative commercial training centres. Previously individual faculties (Faculdade Senac de Ciências Exatas e Tecnologia; Faculdade Senac de Communicação e Artes; Faculdade Senac de Educação Ambiental; Faculdade Senac de Moda; Faculdade Senac de Turismo e Hotelaria de Águas de São Pedro; Faculdade Senac de Turismo e Hotelaria de Campos do Jordão; Faculdade Senac de Turismo e Hotelaria de São Paulo) merged to form current institution. Obtained current title and status 2004.
Academic Year: February to December
Admission Requirements: Undergraduate, Vestibular exam and High School Certificate; Postgraduate and Research Programmes, Entrance exam, interview and Undergraduate degree; Extension Programmes, Entrance exam and Undergraduate degree
Fees: 490,00 to 1.500,00 per month (Brazilian Real)
Main Language(s) of Instruction: Portuguese
Accrediting Agency: MEC
Degrees and Diplomas: *Tecnólogo*; *Bacharelado*; *Licenciatura*; *Especialização/Aperfeiçoamento*: **Accountancy; Acupuncture; Architectural and Environmental Design; Architecture; Banking; Business Administration; Cinema and Television; Computer Engineering; Computer Networks; Cosmetology; Dental Technology; Dentistry; Design; E- Business/Commerce; Education; Educational Administration; Environmental Studies; Fashion Design; Finance; Fine Arts; Health Administration; Health Sciences; Higher Education; Hotel Management; Human Resources; Information Technology; Interior Design; International Business; Journalism; Management; Marketing; Medicine; Multimedia; Orthodontics; Performing Arts; Periodontics; Pharmacy; Photography; Public Administration; Radio and Television Broadcasting; Safety Engineering; Social Sciences; Software Engineering; Stomatology; Technology Education.**
Student Services: Canteen, Careers Guidance, Foreign Studies Centre, Language Laboratory, Library, Nursery Care, Sports Facilities
Publications: INTERFACEHS
Last Updated: 08/09/15

SENAI ANTOINE SKAFF FACULTY OF TECHNOLOGY

Faculdade de Tecnologia SENAI Antoine Skaf (SENAI ANTOINE SKAF)

Avenida Paulista,1313 Cerqueira César,
São Paulo, São Paulo 01311923
Tel: +55(11) 3146-7698
EMail: spdesign@sp.senai.br
Website: http://www.sp.senai.br/spdesign

Course
Fashion Design (Fashion Design)
Degrees and Diplomas: *Especialização/Aperfeiçoamento*: **Fashion Design.**
Last Updated: 01/04/16

SENAI CETIND FACULTY OF TECHNOLOGY

Faculdade de Tecnologia SENAI CETIND (SENAI CETIND)

Avenida Luiz Tarquínio Pontes, 938, Aracuí,
Lauro de Freitas, BA 42700-000
Tel: +55(71) 3287-8201
Fax: +55(71) 3287-8249
EMail: falecomsenaicetind@cetind.fieb.org.br; sacsenai@fieb.org.br; tarsobrn@gmail.com
Website: http://portais.fieb.org.br/portal_faculdades/faculdade-cetind/apresentacao-cetind.html

Diretor: Alex Álisson Bandeira Santos

Course
Environmental Studies (Environmental Studies); **Postgraduate Studies** (Communication Studies; Environmental Engineering; Environmental Management; Environmental Studies; Health Sciences; Safety Engineering; Water Management)
Main Language(s) of Instruction: Portuguese
Degrees and Diplomas: *Tecnólogo*; *Especialização/Aperfeiçoamento*: **Communication Studies; Environmental Engineering; Environmental Management; Environmental Studies; Health Sciences; Safety Engineering; Water Management.**
Last Updated: 09/09/15

SENAI-CETIQT FACULTY

Faculdade SENAI-CETIQT (SENAI-CETIQT)

R. Magalhães Castro, 174 - Riachuelo,
Rio de Janeiro, Rio de Janeiro 20961-020
Tel: +55(21) 2582-1000
Fax: +55(21) 2241-0495
EMail: dg@cetiqt.senai.br
Website: http://www.cetiqt.senai.br

Diretor Geral: Henrique Paim

Course
Chemical Engineering (Chemical Engineering); **Design** (Design; Fashion Design; Textile Design); **Production Engineering** (Production Engineering); **Textile Engineering** (Textile Technology); **Visual Arts** (Visual Arts)
Further Information: Riachuelo and Barra campuses
History: Founded 1949 as Escola Técnica da Indústria Química e Têxtil.
Main Language(s) of Instruction: Portuguese
Degrees and Diplomas: *Bacharelado*; *Licenciatura*; *Especialização/Aperfeiçoamento*
Last Updated: 11/06/15

SENAI CIMATEC FACULTY OF TECHNOLOGY

Faculdade de Tecnologia SENAI CIMATEC (SENAI CIMATEC)

Avenida Orlando Gomes, 1845, Piatã, Salvador, BA 41650-010
Tel: +55(71) 3462-9580 +55(71) 3462-8517
EMail: falecomsenaicimatec@cimatec.fieb.org.br; miltoncruz54@hotmail.com; tarsobrn@gmail.com
Website: http://portais.fieb.org.br/portal_faculdades/faculdade-cimatec/apresentacao-cimatec.html

Gestor: Diretor Álisson Bandeira Santos

Secretaria Acadêmica: Maria Verônica da Rocha Bamberg

Course

Automation and Control Engineering (Automation and Control Engineering); **Automotive Engineering** (Automotive Engineering); **Chemical Engineering** (Chemical Engineering); **Civil Engineering** (Civil Engineering); **Computer Engineering** (Computer Engineering); **Electrical Engineering** (Electrical Engineering); **Graduate Studies** (Automation and Control Engineering; Automotive Engineering; Electrical Engineering; Energy Engineering; Engineering; Heating and Refrigeration; Industrial Design; Industrial Engineering; Industrial Management; Management; Metal Techniques; Metallurgical Engineering; Polymer and Plastics Technology; Transport Management); **Materials Engineering** (Materials Engineering); **Mechanical Engineering** (Mechanical Engineering); **Postgraduate Studies** (Design; Engineering; Environmental Studies; Food Science; Food Technology; Information Management; Public Health; Technology); **Production Engineering** (Production Engineering); **Professional Education** (Vocational Education); **Technological Studies** (Computer Networks; Environmental Management; Industrial Engineering; Metal Techniques; Safety Engineering; Systems Analysis; Transport Management)

Main Language(s) of Instruction: Portuguese

Degrees and Diplomas: *Tecnólogo*; *Bacharelado*; *Licenciatura*; *Especialização/Aperfeiçoamento*: **Automation and Control Engineering; Automotive Engineering; Construction Engineering; Environmental Management; Food Science; Food Technology; Heating and Refrigeration; Hygiene; Industrial Design; Information Management; Metal Techniques; Occupational Health; Petroleum and Gas Engineering; Polymer and Plastics Technology; Robotics; Safety Engineering; Telecommunications Engineering.** *Mestrado*: **Computer Graphics; Industrial Engineering; Industrial Management.** *Doutorado*: **Computer Graphics; Industrial Engineering.** Also MBA in Management, Industrial Management, Transport Management

Student Services: Library

Last Updated: 09/09/15

SENAI FACULTIES OF INDUSTRY

Faculdades da Indústria SENAI

Avenido Cândido de abreu, 200, centro cívico,
Curitiba, Paraná 80530-902
Tel: +55(45) 3220-5400
Website: www.pr.senai.br

Faculty

SENAI Cascavel Faculty of Industry *(Rua Heitor Stockler de França, 161 Jardim Maria Luiza, Cascavel (Paraná))* (Computer Science; Engineering); **SENAI Curitiba Faculty of Industry** *(Avenida Comendador Franco, 1341, Jardim Botânico, Curitiba (Paraná))* (Engineering); **SENAI Londrina Faculty of Industry** *(Rua Belém, 844, Centro, Londrina (Paraná))* (Engineering Management; Marketing); **SENAI Telemaco Borba Faculty of Industry** *(Avenida Presidente Kennedy, n° 66, Centro, Telêmaco Borba (Paraná))* (Engineering); **SENAI Toledo Faculty of Technology** *(Avenida Presidente Kennedy, n° 66, Centro, Telêmaco Borba (Paraná))* (Engineering; Food Technology)

Degrees and Diplomas: *Especialização/Aperfeiçoamento*: **Computer Science; Engineering; Food Technology.** *Mestrado*: **Engineering; Management.** Also MBA

Last Updated: 06/04/16

SENAI FACULTY OF ENVIRONMENTAL TECHNOLOGY

Faculdade Senai de Tecnologia Ambiental

Av. José Odorizzi, 1555, Assunção,
São Bernardo do Campo, SP 09861-000
Tel: +55(11) 4109-9499
EMail: senaimarioamato@sp.senai.br
Website: http://www.sp.senai.br/meioambiente

Course

Graduate Studies (Environmental Studies; Law); **Undergraduate Studies** (Environmental Engineering; Polymer and Plastics Technology)

History: Founded 1999.

Degrees and Diplomas: *Tecnólogo*; *Especialização/Aperfeiçoamento*

Last Updated: 11/06/15

SENAI FACULTY OF GRAPHIC TECHNOLOGY

Faculdade Senai de Tecnológia Gráfica

Rua Bresser 2315, Mooca, São Paulo, São Paulo 03162030
Tel: +55(11) 6097-6333
Fax: +55(11) 6097-6318
EMail: senaigrafica@sp.senai.br
Website: http://www.sp.senai.br

Diretor: Manoel Manteigas de Oliveira

Course

Graphic Design (Graphic Design; Printing and Printmaking)

History: Founded 1997.

Degrees and Diplomas: *Tecnólogo*; *Especialização/Aperfeiçoamento*

Last Updated: 11/06/15

SENAI FACULTY OF MECHATRONIC TECHNOLOGY

Faculdade Senai de Tecnológia Mecatrônica (SENAI)

Rua Niteroi 180, Centro, São Caetano do Sul, São Paulo 09510200
Tel: +55(11) 4228-3355
Fax: +55(11) 4228-3326
EMail: senaimecatronica@sp.senai.br
Website: http://www.sp.senai.br

Diretor Regional: Walter Vicioni Goncalves

Course

Engineering (Automation and Control Engineering; Computer Engineering; Electronic Engineering; Engineering; Industrial Engineering; Production Engineering; Robotics)

History: Founded 1999.

Degrees and Diplomas: *Tecnólogo*; *Especialização/Aperfeiçoamento*

Last Updated: 11/06/15

SENAI FACULTY OF TECHNOLOGY ANCHIETA

Faculdade de Tecnologia SENAI of Anchieta (SENAI ANCHIETA)

Rua Gandavo, 550, Vila Mariana, São Paulo, SP 04023-001
Tel: +55(11) 5908-9150
Fax: +55(11) 5908-9150
EMail: senaianchieta@sp.senai.br; adsilva@sp.senai.br
Website: http://eletronica.sp.senai.br

Diretor: Augusto Lins de Albuquerque Neto

Course

Electronic Systems for Control *(Postgraduate)* (Automation and Control Engineering; Electronic Engineering); **Industrial Electronics** (Electronic Engineering)

History: Founded 2008.

Main Language(s) of Instruction: Portuguese

Degrees and Diplomas: *Tecnólogo*; *Especialização/Aperfeiçoamento*: **Electronic Engineering.**

Student Services: Library

Last Updated: 02/09/15

SENAI FACULTY OF TECHNOLOGY OF BLUMENAU

Faculdade de Tecnologia SENAI Blumenau (SENAI BLUMENAU)

Rua São Paulo, 1147, Victor Konder, Blumenau, SC 89012-001
Tel: +55(47) 3321-9600
Fax: +55(47) 3321-9601
EMail: blumenau@sc.senai.br
Website: http://www.sc.senai.br

Diretor: Jacir Luiz Lenzi

Course
Computer Networks (Computer Networks); **Environmental Management** (Environmental Management); **Fashion Design** (Fashion Design); **Garment Production** (Textile Design); **Graduate Studies** (Business and Commerce; Communication Studies; Electronic Engineering; Fashion Design; Industrial Engineering; Information Management; Management; Water Management); **Industrial Automation** (Automation and Control Engineering; Industrial Engineering); **Industrial Mechatonics** (Electronic Engineering; Industrial Engineering); **Mechanical Manufacturing** (Industrial Engineering; Mechanical Engineering); **Systems Analysis and Development** (Computer Science; Systems Analysis); **Textile Production** (Textile Technology)

History: Founded 2001.

Main Language(s) of Instruction: Portuguese

Degrees and Diplomas: *Tecnólogo*; *Especialização/Aperfeiçoamento*: **Business and Commerce; Communication Studies; Electronic Engineering; Fashion Design; Industrial Engineering; Information Management; Management; Water Management.**
Last Updated: 02/09/15

SENAI FACULTY OF TECHNOLOGY OF CHAPECÓ

Faculdade de Tecnologia SENAI Chapecó (SENAI CHAPECÓ)

Rua Frei Bruno 201 E Jardim América, Chapecó, SC 89808-400
Tel: +55(49) 3321-7300
Fax: +55(49) 3321-7336
EMail: chapeco@sc.senai.br
Website: http://sc.senai.br/cursos-senai/faculdade/chapeco

Diretora: Ivânia Biazussi Thomas
Tel: +55(49) 3321-7300 EMail: ivania@sc.senai.br

Course
Engineering (Automation and Control Engineering); **Food Science** (Food Science); **Industrial Handling** (Technology)

Degrees and Diplomas: *Tecnólogo*; *Especialização/Aperfeiçoamento*: **Automation and Control Engineering.**
Last Updated: 01/04/16

SENAI FACULTY OF TECHNOLOGY OF FLORIANÓPOLIS

Faculdade de Tecnologia SENAI Florianopolis (SENAI FLORIANOPOLIS)

Rodovia SC 401, n° 3730, Saco Grande,
Florianópolis, Santa Catarina 88032005
Tel: +55(48) 3239-5800
Fax: +55(42) 3239-5802
EMail: florianopolis@sc.senai.br
Website: http://www.sc.senai.br

Diretor: João Roberto Lorenzett

Course
Computer Networks (Computer Networks); **Graduate Studies** (Automation and Control Engineering; Business Administration; Construction Engineering; Educational Administration; Environmental Management; Food Science; Industrial Management; Information Management; Information Technology; Management; Service Trades; Software Engineering); **Industrial Automation** (Automation and Control Engineering); **Management Processes** (Management); **Systems Analysis and Development** (Systems Analysis); **Technical Studies** (Automation and Control Engineering; Communication Arts; Computer Science; Maintenance Technology; Safety Engineering; Software Engineering)

History: Founded 1998.

Main Language(s) of Instruction: Portuguese

Degrees and Diplomas: *Técnico de Nivel Medio*; *Tecnólogo*; *Especialização/Aperfeiçoamento*: **Automation and Control Engineering; Industrial Management; Information Management; Information Technology; Software Engineering.** Also MBA in Business Administration, Construction Engineering, Management, Service Trades, Educational Administration, Industrial Management, Environmental Management, Food Science, Information Technology.
Last Updated: 03/09/15

SENAI FACULTY OF TECHNOLOGY OF JOINVILLE

Faculdade de Tecnologia SENAI Joinville (SENAI JOINVILLE)

Rua Arno Waldemar Döhler, 957, Zona Industrial Norte,
Joinville, Santa Catarina 89219-510
Tel: +55(47) 3441-7600 +55(47) 3441-7700
Fax: +55(47) 3441-7740
EMail: joinville@joinville.senai.br
Website: http://www.sc.senai.br/siteinstitucional/servicos/unidade/index/cidade/16/pgcursoaberto/2/

Diretora: Hildegarde Schlupp

Programme
Industrial Mechatonics (Electronic Engineering; Industrial Engineering)

Course
Computer Networks (Computer Networks); **Graduate Studies** (Electronic Engineering; Industrial Engineering; Industrial Management); **Mechanical Engineering** (Mechanical Engineering); **Systems Analysis and Development** (Systems Analysis); **Technical Studies** (Automation and Control Engineering; Building Technologies; Clothing and Sewing; Computer Science; Cooking and Catering; Electronic Engineering; Fashion Design; Maintenance Technology; Mechanical Engineering; Occupational Health; Polymer and Plastics Technology; Transport Management)

History: Founded 2001.

Main Language(s) of Instruction: Portuguese

Degrees and Diplomas: *Técnico de Nivel Medio*; *Tecnólogo*; *Especialização/Aperfeiçoamento*: **Electronic Engineering; Industrial Engineering; Industrial Management.** Also MBA
Last Updated: 03/09/15

SENAI FACULTY OF TECHNOLOGY OF MANAGEMENT DEVELOPMENT

Faculdade de Tecnologia SENAI de Desenvolvimento Gerencial (FATESG)

Rua 227-A, n° 95, Setor Leste Universitário,
Goiânia, GO 74610-155
Tel: +55(62) 3269-1200
Fax: +55(62) 3269-1233
EMail: fatesg.senai@sistemafieg.org.br
Website: http://www.senaigo.com.br

Diretor: Dario Queija de Siqueira EMail: dario@sistemafieg.org.br
Secretária Acadêmica: Herla Cristina Honório de Oliveira

Course
Computer Networks (Computer Networks); **Graduate Studies** (Agricultural Management; Building Technologies; Business Administration; Clothing and Sewing; Computer Networks; Construction Engineering; Environmental Management; Industrial Chemistry; Industrial Engineering; Industrial Maintenance; Industrial Management; Information Technology; International Business; Management; Safety Engineering; Telecommunications Engineering; Transport Management); **Systems Analysis and Development** (Systems Analysis); **Technical Studies** (Administration; Computer Networks; Telecommunications Services; Transport Management)

History: Founded 2005.

Main Language(s) of Instruction: Portuguese

Degrees and Diplomas: *Técnico de Nivel Medio*; *Tecnólogo*; *Especialização/Aperfeiçoamento*: **Agricultural Management; Building Technologies; Business Administration; Clothing and Sewing; Computer Networks; Construction Engineering; Environmental Management; Industrial Chemistry; Industrial Engineering; Industrial Maintenance; Industrial Management; Information Technology; International Business; Management; Safety Engineering; Telecommunications Engineering; Transport Management.** Also MBA.

Student Services: IT Centre, Library
Last Updated: 03/09/15

SENAI FACULTY OF TECHNOLOGY OF PORTO ALEGRE

Faculdade de Tecnologia SENAI de Porto Alegre (FATEC SENAI)

Avenida Assis Brasil, 8450, Sarandi, Porto Alegre, RS 91140-000
Tel: +55(51) 3347-8400
Fax: +55(51) 3347-8435
EMail: faculdadesenai@senairs.org.br; marcio.torres@senairs.org.br
Website: http://www.senairs.com.br/faculdade

Diretora: Adriana Rivoire Menelli de Oliveira
EMail: adriana.menelli@senairs.org.br

Administrative Officer: Juneia Kingeski
EMail: juneia.kingeski@fiergs.org.br

Course
Computer Networks (Computer Networks); **Embedded Systems** (Computer Engineering); **Graduate Studies** (Automation and Control Engineering; Computer Networks; Educational Technology; Energy Engineering; Robotics); **Industrial Automation** (Automation and Control Engineering; Industrial Engineering); **Systems Analysis and Development** (Systems Analysis); **Technical Studies** (Computer Graphics; Computer Networks; Electronic Engineering; Software Engineering); **Telecommunications Engineering** (Telecommunications Engineering)

History: Founded 2006.

Main Language(s) of Instruction: Portuguese

Degrees and Diplomas: *Técnico de Nivel Medio*; *Tecnólogo*; *Especialização/Aperfeiçoamento*: **Automation and Control Engineering; Computer Networks; Educational Technology; Energy Engineering; Robotics.**
Student Services: IT Centre, Library
Last Updated: 03/09/15

SENAI FACULTY OF TECHNOLOGY OF SÃO PAULO

Faculdade de Tecnologia SENAI São Paulo (SENAI SÃO PAULO)

Avenida Paulista,1313 Cerqueira César,
São Paulo, São Paulo 01311923
Tel: +55(11) 3528-2000
EMail: faleconosco@sesisenaisp.org.br
Website: http://www.sp.senai.br

Diretor Regional SENAI-SP: Walter Vicioni Gonçalves

School
SENAI "Armando de Arruda Pereira" *(Rua Santo André, 400 (Boa Vista - São Caetano do Sul))* (Automation and Control Engineering; Business Administration); **SENAI "Horácio Augusto da Silveira"** *(Rua Tagipuru, 242 (Barra Funda - São Paulo))* (Food Science); **SENAI "Antonio Adolpho Lobbe"** *(Rua Cândido Padim, 25 - Vila Prado (Vila Carlos - São Carlos))* (Automation and Control Engineering); **SENAI "Conde José Vicente de Azevedo"** *(Rua Moreira de Godói, 226 (Ipiranga - São Paulo))* (Mechanical Engineering); **SENAI "Engenheiro Adriano José Marchini"** *(Rua Correia de Andrade, 232 (Brás - São Paulo))* (Fashion Design); **SENAI "Francisco Matarazzo"** *(Rua Correia de Andrade, 232 (Brás - São Paulo))* (Fashion Design); **SENAI "Gaspar Ricardo Júnior"** *(Praça Roberto Mange, 30 (Santa Rosália - Sorocaba))* (Mechanical Engineering); **SENAI "Mariano Ferraz"** *(Rua Jaguaré Mirim, 71 (Vila Leopoldina))* (Automation and Control Engineering); **SENAI "Nadir Dias de Figueiredo"** *(Rua Ari Barroso, 305 (Presidente Altino - Osasco))* (Metallurgical Engineering); **SENAI "Roberto Mange"** *(Rua Pastor Cícero Canuto de Lima, 71 (São Bernardo - Campinas))* (Mechanical Engineering); **SENAI "Roberto Simonsen"** *(Rua Monsenhor Andrade, 298 (Brás -São Paulo))* (Electronic Engineering; Mechanical Engineering); **SENAI "Theobaldo de Nigris"** *(Rua Bresser, 2315 (Mooca - São Paulo))* (Graphic Design; Information Sciences); **SENAI Escola "Anchieta"** *(Rua Gandavo, 550 (Vila Mariana - São Paulo))* (Electronic Engineering); **SENAI Escola "Mariano Ferraz"** *(Rua Jaguaré Mirim, 71 (Vila Leopoldina - São Paulo))* (Energy Engineering); **SENAI Escola "Mario Amato"** *(Av. José Odorizzi, 1.555 (Assunção - São Bernardo do Campo))* (Business Administration; Environmental Management; Polymer and Plastics Technology)

Further Information: Also 78 units in Brazil.

Degrees and Diplomas: *Especialização/Aperfeiçoamento*: **Automation and Control Engineering; Business Administration; Electronic Engineering; Energy Engineering; Environmental Management; Fashion Design; Food Science; Information Sciences; Mechanical Engineering; Metallurgical Engineering; Polymer and Plastics Technology.**
Last Updated: 06/04/16

SERRA DOS ORGÃOS UNIVERSITY CENTRE

Centro Universitario Serra dos Orgãos (UNIFESO)

Avenida Alberto Torres 111 Alto,
Teresópolis, Rio de Janeiro 25964-000
Tel: +55(21) 2641-7000
EMail: dirger@feso.br
Website: http://www.unifeso.edu.br/

Reitora: Verônica Santos Albuquerque
EMail: reitoria@unifeso.edu.br

Course
Accountancy (Accountancy); **Administration** (Administration); **Biological Sciences** (Biology); **Civil Engineering** (Civil Engineering); **Computer Science** (Computer Science); **Environmental Engineering** (Environmental Engineering); **Law** (Law); **Mathematics** (Mathematics); **Medicine** (Medicine); **Nursing** (Nursing); **Odontology** (Dentistry); **Pedagogy** (Pedagogy); **Pharmacy** (Pharmacy); **Physical Therapy** (Physical Therapy); **Production Engineering** (Production Engineering); **Veterinary Science** (Veterinary Science)

Further Information: Also Quinta do Paraíso, FESO PRO ARTE and HCTCO campuses.

History: Founded 1970.

Main Language(s) of Instruction: Portuguese

Degrees and Diplomas: *Bacharelado*; *Licenciatura*; *Especialização/Aperfeiçoamento*: **Dentistry; Gynaecology and Obstetrics; Nursing; Orthodontics; Physical Therapy; Public Health.** Also MBA.
Last Updated: 09/09/15

SERRANA REGIONAL FACULTY OF EDUCATION

Faculdade de Educação Regional Serrana

Br 262 Km 110 s/n, Distrito de São João de Viçosa,
Conceição do Castelo, ES 29370-000
Tel: +55(28) 3546-6451
EMail: direcao@funcap.com.br

Diretor: Hugo Luis de Souza

Course
Pedagogy (Pedagogy)

History: Founded 2001

Main Language(s) of Instruction: Portuguese

Degrees and Diplomas: *Licenciatura*
Last Updated: 01/07/15

SEVERINO SOMBRA UNIVERSITY

Universidade Severino Sombra (USS)

Av. Expedicionário Oswaldo de Almeida Ramos, n° 280, Centro,
Vassouras, Rio de Janeiro 27700-000
Tel: +55(24) 2471-8200
Fax: +55(24) 2471-2223
EMail: reitoria@uss.br
Website: http://www.uss.br

Reitor: Marco Antonio Soares de Souza (2012-)
Tel: +55(24) 2471-2223 EMail: reitor@uss.br

Superintendência Administrativa e Financeira: Yolanda de Souza Capute

International Relations: Ana Paula de Almeida, General Coordinator, Setor de Relações Internacionais
Tel: +55(24) 2471-8378 EMail: relacoes.internacionais@uss.br

Course
Administration (Administration); **Chemical Engineering** (Chemical Engineering); **Civil Engineering** (Civil Engineering); **Computer Engineering** (Computer Engineering); **Dentistry** (Dentistry); **Electrical Engineering** (Electrical Engineering); **Environmental and Sanitary Engineering** (Environmental Engineering; Sanitary Engineering); **Medicine** (Medicine); **Nursing** (Nursing); **Pedagogy** (Pedagogy); **Pharmacy** (Pharmacy); **Physiotherapy** (Physical Therapy); **Production Engineering** (Production Engineering); **Psychology** (Psychology); **Veterinary Medicine** (Veterinary Science)

Campus
Maricá Campus (Administration)

Further Information: Also University Hospital

History: Founded 1968.

Admission Requirements: Secondary school certificate and entrance examination

Main Language(s) of Instruction: Portuguese

Degrees and Diplomas: *Bacharelado*; *Licenciatura*; *Especialização/Aperfeiçoamento*: **Dentistry; Nursing; Production Engineering; Safety Engineering.** *Mestrado*: **Environmental Studies; History; Mathematics Education.** Also MBA

Student Services: Academic Counselling, Canteen, Careers Guidance, Cultural Activities, Facilities for disabled people, Health Services, Library, Nursery Care, Social Counselling, Sports Facilities

Publications: Caminhos da Historia; Revista do Mestrado de História

Last Updated: 11/04/16

SILVA AND SOUZA INTEGRATED FACULTIES

Faculdades Integradas Silva e Souza (FISS)

Estrada dos Três Rios 385,
Rio de Janeiro, Rio de Janeiro 22745-004
Tel: +55(21)) 2456-2069
EMail: silvaesouza@silvaesouza.com.br

Diretor: Anley Sleiman da Costa

Course
Architecture and Town Planning (Architecture; Town Planning); **Environmental Engineering** (Environmental Engineering); **Safety Engineering** *(Tijuca Unit)* (Safety Engineering)

History: Founded 1971.

Main Language(s) of Instruction: Portuguese

Degrees and Diplomas: *Bacharelado*; *Especialização/Aperfeiçoamento*; *Mestrado*

Last Updated: 30/06/15

SIMONSEN INTEGRATED FACULTIES

Faculdades Integradas Simonsen (FEFIS)

Rua Ibitiuva 151, Padre Miguel,
Rio de Janeiro, Rio de Janeiro 21715400
Tel: +55(21) 2406-6464
Fax: +55(21) 2406-6464
EMail: simonsen@simonsen.br
Website: http://www.simonsen.br

Diretor Geral: Celso Murilo Menezes da Costa

Course
Accountancy (Accountancy); **Administration** (Administration); **Geography** (Geography); **History** (History); **Law** (Law); **Letters** (Literature); **Pedagogy** (Pedagogy)

History: Founded 1971.

Main Language(s) of Instruction: Portuguese

Degrees and Diplomas: *Bacharelado*; *Licenciatura*; *Especialização/Aperfeiçoamento*

Last Updated: 24/06/15

SOARES DE OLIVEIRA INTEGRATED FACULTIES

Faculdades Integradas Soares de Oliveira (FISO)

Avenida Vinte e Nove 783, Térreo, Centro,
Barretos, São Paulo 14780350
Tel: +55(17) 3321-5733
Fax: +55(17) 3321-5733
EMail: faleconosco@fiso.edu.br
Website: http://fiso.edu.br

Diretor Geral: Milton Diniz Soares de Oliveira (1998-)
EMail: aceb@soaresoliveira.br

Faculty
Pedagogy (Pedagogy)

Course
Accountancy (Accountancy)

History: Founded 1973. Formerly known as Faculdade de Educação 'Antonio Augusto Reis Neves'.

Degrees and Diplomas: *Licenciatura*; *Especialização/Aperfeiçoamento*

Last Updated: 08/07/15

SOCIAL FACULTY OF BAHIA

Faculdade Social da Bahia (FSBA)

Av. Oceânica, n° 2717, Ondina, Salvador, BA 40170-010
Tel: +55(71) 4009-2840 +55(71) 4009-2841
EMail: extensao@faculdadesocial.edu.br
Website: http://www.fsba.edu.br

Diretora Geral: Rita Margareth Passos

Course
Graduate Studies (Communication Studies; Education; Educational Psychology; Human Resources; Industrial and Organizational Psychology; Journalism; Management; Nursing; Physical Education; Physical Therapy; Psychology; Public Health; Rehabilitation and Therapy; Sports; Urology); **Undergraduate Studies** (Administration; Advertising and Publicity; Journalism; Law; Pedagogy; Physical Education; Physical Therapy; Psychology)

Further Information: Also Unidade Macapá I Unidade Macapá II Unidade Macapá III Unidade Senta Pua Unidade Adhemar de Barros Unidade Oceânica

History: Founded 2001.

Main Language(s) of Instruction: Portuguese

Degrees and Diplomas: *Bacharelado*; *Licenciatura*; *Especialização/Aperfeiçoamento*. Also MBA.

Last Updated: 12/06/15

SOCIESC FACULTY

Faculdade Sociesc

Rua Salvatina Feliciano dos Santos 525, Itacurubi,
Florianópolis, Santa Catarina 88034-600
Tel: +55(48) 3239-4700
Fax: +55(48) 3334-6437
EMail: unica@sociesc.com.br, sociescfln@sociesc.org.br
Website: http://www.sociesc.org.br/pt/unica

Diretor Geral: Sandro Murilos Santos

Course
Accountancy (Accountancy; Business Administration); **Administration** (Administration; Business Administration; Business and Commerce; Human Resources; Management; Marketing); **Civil Engineering** (Civil Engineering); **Electrical Engineering** (Electrical Engineering); **Graduate Studies** (Accountancy; Architecture; Business Administration; Business and Commerce; Management; Marketing; Real Estate; Safety Engineering; Software Engineering)

History: Founded 1998 as Centro de Educação Superior – UNICA. Acquired present title 2013.

Main Language(s) of Instruction: Portuguese

Degrees and Diplomas: *Bacharelado*; *Especialização/Aperfeiçoamento*; *Mestrado*: **Mechanical Engineering; Production Engineering.**

Student Services: Library

Last Updated: 04/11/15

HIGHER EDUCATION INSTITUTE OF BLUMENAU

INSTITUTO BLUMENAUENSE DE ENSINO SUPERIOR

Rua Pandiá Calógeras, 272, Blumenau 89010-350
Tel: +502(47) 2111-2900
EMail: secretaria.ibes@sociesc.org.br
Website: http://www.sociesc.org.br/pt/ibes

Reitor: Marcos Holz

Course
Accountancy (Accountancy); **Administration** (Administration); **Advertisinng and Publicity** (Advertising and Publicity); **Civil Engineering** (Civil Engineering); **Electrical Engineering** (Electrical Engineering); **Journalism** (Journalism); **Law** (Law); **Psychology** (Psychology)

History: Founded 2000.

Degrees and Diplomas: *Bacharelado*; *Especialização/Aperfeiçoamento*; *Mestrado*: **Business Administration; Engineering.**

SOCIESC FACULTY OF BALNEÁRIO CAMBORIÚ

FACULDADE SOCIESC DE BALNEÁRIO CAMBORIÚ

Rua Santa Catarina, 151, Balneário Camboriú, SC 88339-005
Tel: +502(47) 3366-7201
EMail: secretaria.flc@sociesc.org.br
Website: http://www.sociesc.org.br/pt/flc/?&lng=2

Diretor: Vicente Otávio Martins de Resende

Course
Accountancy (Accountancy); **Administration** (Administration)

History: Founded 2005.

Main Language(s) of Instruction: Portuguese

Degrees and Diplomas: *Bacharelado*

TUPY FACULTY OF TECHNOLOGY - CURITIBA

FACULDADE DE TECNOLOGIA TUPY - CURITIBA

BR 116 Km 106,5 - nr. 18.805, Linha Verde, Bairro Pinheirinho, Curitiba, PR 81690-300
Tel: +502(41) 3296-0132
Website: http://www.sociesc.org.br/pt/ftt-curitiba/index.php

Diretor: Gilberto Paulo Zluhan

Course
Administration (Administration); **Automation and Control Engineering** (Automation and Control Engineering); **Chemical Engineering** (Chemical Engineering); **Civil Engineering** (Civil Engineering); **Electrical Engineering** (Electrical Engineering); **Mechanical Engineering** (Mechanical Engineering); **Polymers** (Polymer and Plastics Technology); **Production Engineering** (Production Engineering)

History: Founded 2004.

Main Language(s) of Instruction: Portuguese

Degrees and Diplomas: *Bacharelado*

TUPY UNIVERSITY CENTRE

CENTRO UNIVERSITARIO TUPY

Rua Albano Schmidt, 3333, Joinville, SC 89206-001
Tel: +502(47) 3461-0172

Reitor: Sandro Murilo Santos

Course
Accountancy (Accountancy); **Administration** (Administration); **Architecture and Town Planning** (Architecture; Town Planning); **Automation and Control Engineering** (Automation and Control Engineering); **Chemical Engineering** (Chemical Engineering); **Civil Engineering** (Civil Engineering); **Computer Engineering** (Computer Engineering); **Economics** (Economics); **Electrical Engineering** (Electrical Engineering); **Information Systems** (Computer Science); **Law** (Law); **Materials Engineering** (Materials Engineering); **Mechanical Engineering** (Mechanical Engineering); **Metallurgical Engineering** (Metallurgical Engineering); **Pedagogy** (Pedagogy); **Production Engineering** (Production Engineering)

History: Founded as Instituto Superior Tupy. Acquired present status and title 2013.

Degrees and Diplomas: *Bacharelado*; *Licenciatura*; *Especialização/Aperfeiçoamento*; *Mestrado*: **Mechanical Engineering; Production Engineering.**

SOGIPA FACULTY OF PHYSICAL EDUCATION

Faculdade SOGIPA de Educação Física
Rua Barão do Cotegipe N°: 415, São João, Porto Alegre, RS 90540-020
Tel: +55(51)) 3371.2690
EMail: secretaria@faculdadesogipa.edu.br
Website: http://www.faculdadesogipa.edu.br/

Diretor Geral: Roberto Plentz

Course
Graduate Studies (Sports; Sports Management); **Physical Education** (Physical Education)

History: Founded 1867 as Sociedade Alemã de Ginástica. Acquired present status and title 2008.

Degrees and Diplomas: *Bacharelado*; *Especialização/Aperfeiçoamento*. Also MBA

Student Services: Library
Last Updated: 12/06/15

SOUZA LIMA FACULTY OF MUSIC

Faculdade de Música Souza Lima (FMSL)
Rua José Maria Lisboa, 745, São Paulo, SP 01423-001
Tel: +55(11) 3884-9149
Fax: +55(11) 3884-7611
EMail: faculdade@souzalima.com.br
Website: http://www.souzalima.com.br

Diretor Geral: Antonio Mario da Silva Cunha

Course
Music (Music)
Further Information: Also Alphaville, Moema, 9 de Julho and Ribeirão Preto Units

History: Founded 2010.

Main Language(s) of Instruction: Portuguese

Degrees and Diplomas: *Tecnólogo*; *Bacharelado*
Last Updated: 03/12/15

SOUZA MARQUES FACULTIES

Faculdades Souza Marques
Avenida Ernani Cardoso 335/345 Cascadura, Rio de Janeiro, Rio de Janeiro 21310310
Tel: +55(21) 2128-4900
Fax: +55(21) 350-5981
EMail: ftesm@ism.com.br
Website: http://www.souzamarques.br/2006/index.php

Diretor: Francisco Michel

School
Medicine *(EMSM)* (Medicine)

Course
Accountancy (Accountancy); **Administration** *(FCCASM)* (Accountancy; Administration); **Biology** (Biology); **Chemistry** (Chemistry); **Civil Engineering**; **Letters** (Literature); **Mechanical Engineering** (Mechanical Engineering); **Nursing** *(EESM)* (Nursing); **Pedagogy**
History: Founded 1985.

Degrees and Diplomas: *Bacharelado*; *Licenciatura*; *Especialização/Aperfeiçoamento*
Last Updated: 18/04/16

SPEI FACULTIES

Faculdades SPEI
Rua Cruz Machado, 525, Centro, Curitibá, Paraná 80410-170
Tel: +55(41) 3321-3131
Fax: +55(41) 3321-3131
EMail: spei@spei.br
Website: http://www.spei.br

Presidente: Ailton Renato Dörl EMail: ailton@spei.br

Course

Accountancy (Accountancy); **Administration** (Administration; Business and Commerce; Human Resources); **Information System** (Computer Science; Information Technology); **Logistics** (Transport Management)

History: Founded 1983

Main Language(s) of Instruction: Portuguese

Degrees and Diplomas: *Tecnólogo*; *Bacharelado*

Student Services: Library

Last Updated: 24/03/16

STELLA MARIS INTEGRATED FACULTIES OF ANDRADINA

Faculdades Integradas Stella Maris de Andradina (FISMA)
Rua Amazonas 571, Stella Maris, Andradina, São Paulo 16901-160
Tel: +55(18) 3702-3702
EMail: fisma@fea.br
Website: http://www.fea.br

Diretora: Cristina Lacerda Soares Petrarolha Silva
EMail: petrarolha@fea.br

Course

Agronomy (Agronomy); **Biotechnology** (Biotechnology); **Physical Education** (Physical Education); **Systems Analysis** (Data Processing; Systems Analysis)

History: Founded 1977.

Main Language(s) of Instruction: Portuguese

Degrees and Diplomas: *Bacharelado*; *Licenciatura*; *Especialização/Aperfeiçoamento*

Student Services: Library

Last Updated: 26/06/15

STRONG SCHOOL OF ADMINISTRATION AND MANAGEMENT

Escola Superior de Administração e Gestão Strong (STRONG ESAGS)
Av. Industrial, 1455, Santo André, SP 09090-030
Tel: +55(11) 4433-6161
EMail: esag@esag.edu.br
Website: http://www.esags.edu.br

Diretora: Regina Célia Alem Jorge Socolowski

Course

Accountancy (Accountancy); **Administration** (Administration); **Advertising and Publicity** (Advertising and Publicity); **Economics** (Economics)

Further Information: Also Unit in Santos

History: Founded 2000. Affiliated to Fundação Getúlio Vargas.

Main Language(s) of Instruction: Portuguese

Degrees and Diplomas: *Bacharelado*; *Especialização/Aperfeiçoamento*: **Administration; Business Administration; Management.** Also MBA

Student Services: IT Centre, Library

Last Updated: 24/09/15

TÁHIRIH FACULTY

Faculdade Táhirih (FT)
Rua Leonora Armstrong, n°09, Bloco A, São José IV, Manaus, AM 69084-598
Tel: +55(92) 3249-9500 +55(92) 3249-9503
Fax: +55(92) 3648-5545
EMail: adcam@adcam.org.br
Website: http://www.adcam.org.br

Diretora: Suzan Sami Ramos

Course

Undergraduate Studies (Administration; Pedagogy; Social and Community Services)

History: Founded 2002.

Degrees and Diplomas: *Bacharelado*; *Licenciatura*

Last Updated: 17/07/15

TAMANDARÉ FACULTY

Faculdade Tamandaré (FAT)
Rua T-53 n° 1336 Setor Bueno, Goiânia, GO 74210-030
Tel: +55(62) 3946-2248
Fax: +55(62) 3946-2248
EMail: faculdadetamandare@hotmail.com
Website: http://www.faculdadetamandare.com.br

Diretor administrativo: Augusto Cezar Casseb

Course

Undergraduate Studies (Administration; Computer Engineering; Computer Science; Marketing; Physical Therapy; Sales Techniques)

History: Founded 2004.

Main Language(s) of Instruction: Portuguese

Degrees and Diplomas: *Bacharelado*

Last Updated: 07/07/15

TEACHING AND RESEARCH CENTRE OF MACHADO

Centro Superior de Ensino e Pesquisa de Machado (CESEP)
Av Dr Athayde Pereira de Souza 730, Machado, Minas Gerais 37750-000
Tel: +55(35) 3295-9500
Fax: +55(35) 3295-9540
EMail: secretaria@fem.com.br
Website: http://www.fem.com.br

Diretor Presidente: Guilherme Bernardes

Administrative Officer: Francisco Edson Iannuzzi
EMail: gerenciaadm@fem.com.br

Course

Accountancy (Accountancy); **Administration** (Administration); **Agronomy** (Agronomy); **Biology** (Biology); **Computer Networks** (Computer Networks); **Environmental Management** (Environmental Management); **Forestry** (Forestry); **History** (History); **Literature** (English; Literature); **Marketing** (Marketing); **Mathematics** (Mathematics); **Nursing** (Nursing); **Nutrition** (Nutrition); **Pedagogy** (Education; Pedagogy; Teacher Training); **Physical Education** (Physical Education); **Social Services** (Social Policy)

Further Information: Also a campus in São Lourenço.

History: Founded 1968.

Main Language(s) of Instruction: Portuguese

Degrees and Diplomas: *Tecnólogo*; *Bacharelado*; *Licenciatura*; *Especialização/Aperfeiçoamento*

Student Services: Library

Last Updated: 22/06/15

TECHNOLOGICAL INSTITUTE OF APPLIED SOCIAL AND HEALTH SCIENCES OF OUR LADY HELP OF CHRISTIANS EDUCATIONAL CENTRE

Instituto Tecnológico e das Ciências Sociais Aplicadas e da Saúde do Centro Educacional Nossa Senhora Auxiliadora (ITCSAS/CENSA)

Rua Salvador Correa, 139, Centro,
Campos dos Goytacazes, RJ 28035-310
Tel: +55(22) 2726-2727
Fax: +55(22) 2726-2720
EMail: ise-censa@censanet.com.br
Website: http://www.isecensa.edu.br/

Diretora Geral: Suraya Benjamin Chaloub

Course

Undergraduate Studies (Administration; Architecture; Mechanical Engineering; Nursing; Physical Education; Physical Therapy; Production Engineering; Psychology)

History: Founded 2002.

Main Language(s) of Instruction: Portuguese

Degrees and Diplomas: *Bacharelado*; *Licenciatura*; *Especialização/Aperfeiçoamento*; *Mestrado*: **Business Administration.**

Last Updated: 14/04/16

TECHNOLOGICAL INSTITUTE OF CARATINGA

Instituto Tecnológico de Caratinga (ITC)

Praça Cesário Alvim, 110, 5° andar, Centro,
Caratinga, MG 35300-036
Tel: +55(33) 3322-6321 +55(33) 3322-6322 +55(33) 9912-9787
Fax: +55(33) 3321-7559
EMail: diretoria@doctum.edu.br
Website: http://faculdadesja.com.br/faculdades/instituto-tecnologico-de-caratinga-itc

Reitor: Cláudio Cezar. Azevedo de Almeida Leitão

Course

Administration (Administration); **Architecture** (Architecture); **Civil Engineering** (Civil Engineering); **Electrical Engineering** (Electrical Engineering); **Environmental Engineering** (Environmental Engineering)

Degrees and Diplomas: *Bacharelado*

Last Updated: 14/04/16

TERESA OF AVILA INTEGRATED FACULTIES - LORENA

Faculdades Integradas Teresa d'Avila - Lorena (FATEA)

Avenida Peixoto de Castro 539, Vila Celeste,
Lorena, São Paulo 12606580
Tel: +55(12) 2124-2831
EMail: direcao@fatea.br
Website: http://www.fatea.br

Diretor Geral: Wellington de Oliveira

Course

Administration (Administration; Advertising and Publicity; Business Administration; Finance; Human Resources; Public Relations); **Art Education** (Art Education; Fine Arts); **Biology** (Biology); **Computer Science** (Computer Science); **Decoration** (Interior Design); **Industrial Design** (Industrial Design); **Letters** (Literature); **Library Science** (Library Science); **Nursing** (Nursing); **Pedagogy** (Pedagogy); **Social Communication** (Advertising and Publicity; Journalism; Radio and Television Broadcasting)

History: Founded 1975.

Main Language(s) of Instruction: Portuguese

Degrees and Diplomas: *Bacharelado*; *Especialização/Aperfeiçoamento*

Last Updated: 24/06/15

TIBIRIÇÁ INTEGRATED FACULTIES

Faculdades Integradas Tibiriçá (FIT)

Rua Líbero Badaró, 616 (Prédio 1) Centro,
São Paulo, São Paulo 01008-000
Tel: +55(11) 3105-5155 +55(11) 9924-42438
Fax: +55(11) 3105-5155
EMail: fati@fati.br; victor@grupoeducamais.com.br

Diretor: Davi Chermann

Course

Accountancy (Accountancy); **Administration** (Administration); **Computer Science** (Computer Science); **Letters - English** (English; Literature); **Pedagogy** (Pedagogy)

History: Founded 1972.

Main Language(s) of Instruction: Portuguese

Degrees and Diplomas: *Tecnólogo*; *Bacharelado*; *Licenciatura*

Last Updated: 02/02/16

TRIÂNGULO MINEIRO FACULTY

Faculdade Triângulo Mineiro (FTM)

Avenida Geraldo Alves Tavares 1980, Campus Universitario,
Ituiutaba, Minas Gerais 38302134
Tel: +55(34) 3269-8200
Fax: +55(34) 3269-8200
EMail: ftm@ftm.edu.br
Website: http://www.ftm.edu.br

Diretor: Domingos Sávio Gonçalves EMail: savio@ftm.edu.br

Course

Accountancy (Accountancy); **Administration** (Administration); **Social Communication** (Advertising and Publicity)

History: Founded 1970 as Escola Superior de Administração de Empresas de Ituiutaba (EAEI).Acquired present status and title 2002.

Main Language(s) of Instruction: Portuguese

Degrees and Diplomas: *Bacharelado*; *Especialização/Aperfeiçoamento*

Student Services: Library

Last Updated: 03/07/15

TRIÂNGULO UNIVERSITY CENTRE

Centro Universitário do Triângulo (UNITRI)

Av. Nicomedes Alves dos Santos, 4545, Bairro Gávea,
Uberlândia, Minas Gerais 38411-106
Tel: +55(34) 4009-9053
Fax: +55(34) 4009-9125
EMail: cpa@unitri.edu.br
Website: http://www.unitri.edu.br

Reitora: Marlene Salgado de Oliveira
Tel: +55(34) 4009-9041 EMail: reitoria@unitri.edu.br

Vice-Reitor: José Maria Mina

Course

Accountancy (Accountancy); **Administration** (Administration); **Advertising and Publicity** (Advertising and Publicity); **Architecture and Urbanism** (Architecture and Planning; Town Planning); **Biology** (Biology); **Civil Engineering** (Civil Engineering); **Computer Science** (Computer Science); **Fashion Design** (Fashion Design); **Graduate Studies** (Accountancy; Agricultural Business; Business Administration; Business and Commerce; Data Processing; Educational Sciences; Finance; History; Hotel Management; Journalism; Marketing; Nursing; Pedagogy; Physical Therapy; Safety Engineering; Software Engineering; Tourism); **Information Systems** (Information Sciences); **Journalism** (Journalism); **Journalism** (Journalism; Social Sciences); **Law** (Law); **Literature** (English; Literature; Portuguese); **Nursing** (Nursing); **Nutrition** (Nutrition); **Odontology** (Dentistry); **Pedagogy** (Pedagogy); **Pharmacy** (Pharmacy); **Physical Education** (Physical Education); **Physical Therapy** (Physical Therapy); **Production Engineering** (Production Engineering); **Psychology** (Psychology); **Technological Studies** (Aesthetics; Agricultural Business; Business Administration; Cinema and Television; Civil Security; Computer Networks; Cooking and Catering; Finance; Software Engineering; Transport Management); **Tourism and Hotel Management** (Hotel and Restaurant; Service Trades; Tourism); **Veterinary Science** (Veterinary Science)

Further Information: Also campus in Araguari.
History: Founded 1990. Acquired present status 1997.
Main Language(s) of Instruction: Portuguese
Accrediting Agency: Ministry of Education.
Degrees and Diplomas: *Tecnólogo*; *Bacharelado*; *Licenciatura*; *Especialização/Aperfeiçoamento*: **Accountancy; Clinical Psychology; Computer Engineering; Crop Production; Data Processing; Educational Psychology; Human Resources; Management; Nursing; Nutrition; Physical Therapy.**
Student Services: Library
Last Updated: 16/07/15

TUPY FACULTY OF TECHNOLOGY - SÂO BENTO DO SUL

Faculdade de Tecnologia TUPY - Sâo Bento do Sul
Rua Hans Dieter Schmidt, 950, São Bento do Sul, SC 89283-105
Tel: +502 (47) 3626-2222

Diretor: Luiz Fernando Bublitz

Course

Accountancy (Accountancy); **Administration** (Administration); **Architecture and Town Planning** (Architecture; Town Planning); **Automation and Control Engineering** (Automation and Control Engineering); **Civil Engineering** (Civil Engineering); **Computer Engineering** (Computer Engineering); **Economics** (Economics); **Electrical Engineering** (Electrical Engineering); **Law** (Law); **Materials Engineering** (Materials Engineering); **Production Engineering** (Production Engineering)
History: Founded 2003.
Main Language(s) of Instruction: Portuguese
Degrees and Diplomas: *Bacharelado*
Last Updated: 15/04/16

TUPY HIGHER INSTITUTE OF FLORIANÓPOLIS

Instituto Superior Tupy de Florianópolis (IST FLORIANÓPOLIS)
Rua Salvatina Feliciana dos Santos, 525, Itacorubi, Florianópolis, SC 88034-001
Tel: +55(48) 3239-4700
Fax: +55(48) 3239-4700
EMail: unica@sociesc.org.br
Website: http://www.sociesc.org.br/pt/unica/

Course

Production Engineering (Production Engineering)

UNA FACULTY OF BETIM

Faculdade Una de Betim (UNA)
Av. Gov. Valadares, 640, Centro, Betim, MG 32510-260
Tel: +55(31) 3235-7300 +55(31) 3515-1008 +55(31) 3319-9226
EMail: reitoria@una.br; regulatorio@animaeducacao.com.br
Website: https://www.una.br/unidade/faculdade-una-de-betim
Diretor: Átila Simões da Cunha

Course

Accounting (Accountancy); **Administration** (Administration); **Aesthetics and Cosmetics** (Cosmetology); **Biological Sciences - Betim** (Biological and Life Sciences); **Chemical Engineering** (Chemical Engineering); **Civil Engineering** (Civil Engineering); **Environmental and Sanitary Engineering** (Environmental Engineering; Sanitary Engineering); **Human Resources** (Human Resources); **Information Systems** (Information Technology); **Interor Design** (Interior Design); **Law** (Law); **Logistics** (Transport Management); **Managerial Processes** (Management); **Pedagogy** (Pedagogy); **Quality Management** (Safety Engineering)
Main Language(s) of Instruction: Portuguese
Degrees and Diplomas: *Tecnólogo*; *Bacharelado*; *Licenciatura*
Student Services: Library
Last Updated: 15/04/16

UNIÃO BUSINESS SCHOOL

Faculdade União (UBS)
Rua Frei Mont, 445, Vila Aricanduva, São Paulo, SP 03505-010
Tel: +55(11) 2092-3777
Fax: +55(11) 2092-3777
EMail: uniao@faculdadeuniao.edu.br
Website: http://www.faculdadeuniao.edu.br/
Diretora: Edna Aparecida Vieira dos Santos

Course

Graduate Studies (Business and Commerce; Finance; Human Resources; Management; Marketing); **Undergraduate Studies** (Administration)
Further Information: Also Av. Paulista and Penha units.
Degrees and Diplomas: *Bacharelado*. Also Postgraduate Diploma.
Last Updated: 18/04/16

ÚNICA FACULTY OF CONTAGEM

Faculdade Única de Contagem (FUNIC)
Rua Professor Sigefredo Marques, 341, Estância do Hibisco, Contagem, MG 32017-590
Tel: +55(31) 2519-5100 +55(800) 724-2300
Fax: +55(31) 2519-5100
EMail: diretoria@unicacontagem.com.br
Website: http://www.unipaccontagem.com.br/paginainterna.aspx?cd=8

Course

Administration (Administration); **Commercial Management** (Business and Commerce); **Nursing** (Nursing); **Pedagogy** (Pedagogy); **Systems Analysis and Development** (Systems Analysis)
Main Language(s) of Instruction: Portuguese
Degrees and Diplomas: *Tecnólogo*; *Bacharelado*; *Licenciatura*
Student Services: Library
Last Updated: 15/04/16

ÚNICA FACULTY OF IPATINGA

Faculdade Única de Ipatinga (FUNIP)
Rua Salermo, 299, Bethânia, Ipatinga, MG 35164-779
Tel: +55(31) 2109-2300 +55(800) 724-2300 +55(31) 8489-3225
Fax: +55(31) 2109-2300
EMail: diretoria@unicaipatinga.com.br
Website: http://www.unipacvaledoaco.com.br

Diretor Executivo: Walter Teixeira dos Santos Jr

Course

Accounting (Accountancy); **Administration** (Administration); **Automation and Control Engineering** (Automation and Control Engineering); **Biomedicine** (Biomedicine); **Building Technologies** (Building Technologies); **Chemical Engineering** (Chemical Engineering); **Civil Engineering** (Civil Engineering); **Computer Science** (Computer Science); **Environmental Engineering** (Environmental Engineering); **Information Systems** (Information Technology); **Nursing** (Nursing); **Pharmacy** (Pharmacy); **Phonoaudiology** (Speech Therapy and Audiology); **Physical Education** (Physical Education); **Physical Education** (Sports); **Production Engineering** (Production Engineering); **Psychology** (Psychology); **Social Service** (Social and Community Services)
Main Language(s) of Instruction: Portuguese
Degrees and Diplomas: *Tecnólogo*; *Bacharelado*; *Licenciatura*
Last Updated: 15/04/16

ÚNICA FACULTY OF TIMÓTEO

Faculdade Única de Timóteo (FUNIT)
Av. Ary Barroso, 765, Serenata, Timóteo, MG 35180-442
Tel: +55(31) 3849-9150 +55(31) 8489-2711
Fax: +55(31) 3849-9150
EMail: diretoria@unicatimoteo.com.br
Website: http://www.unipacvaledoaco.com.br/paginainterna.aspx?cd=321

Course

Administration (Administration); **Human Resources** (Human Resources)

History: Founded 2006.
Main Language(s) of Instruction: Portuguese
Degrees and Diplomas: *Tecnólogo*; *Bacharelado*
Last Updated: 15/04/16

UNIFAE UNIVERSITY CENTRE

UniFAE Centro Universitário (UNIFAE)
Rua 24 de Maio 135, 5° Andar, Centro, Curitibá, Paraná 80230-090
Tel: +55(41) 2105-1450
Fax: +55(41) 2105-4195
EMail: pro.reitoria@fae.edu
Website: http://www.fae.edu

Reitor: Nelson José Hilesheim (2007-)
Tel: +55 (41) 2105-4122
EMail: nelsonh@bomjesus.br; reitoria@fae.edu

Secretary-General: Vicente Keller
Tel: +55 (41) 2105-4154 EMail: vkeller@fae.edu

International Relations: Areta Galat, International Relations Officer Tel: +55 (41) 2105-4444 EMail: aretagallat@fae.edu

Programme

Accountancy (Accountancy); **Administration** (Administration); **Economics** (Economics); **Environmental Engineering**; **Industrial Design** (Industrial Design); **International Business**; **Law** (Law); **Mechanical Engineering**; **Production Engineering** (Production Engineering); **Psychology** (Psychology); **Social Communication** (Advertising and Publicity)

Further Information: Also Cristo Rei Campus

History: Founded 1957. Previously known as Faculdades Bom Jesus. 1998 became FAE Business School. Acquired current title and status 2005.

Main Language(s) of Instruction: Portuguese

Accrediting Agency: Ministry of Education and Culture (MEC)

Degrees and Diplomas: *Tecnólogo*: **Computer Engineering; Finance; Human Resources; Marketing; Transport Management.** *Bacharelado*: **Accountancy; Administration; Economics; Environmental Engineering; Industrial Design; International Business; Law; Mass Communication; Philosophy; Production Engineering.** *Especialização/Aperfeiçoamento*; *Mestrado*

Student Services: Academic Counselling, Canteen, Careers Guidance, Foreign Studies Centre, Health Services, Language Laboratory, Social Counselling, Sports Facilities

Publications: FAE Business; Scintilla
Last Updated: 18/04/16

UNIFIED FACULTIES OF TEÓFILO OTONI

Faculdades Unificadas de Teófilo Otoni (FUTO)
Rua Gustavo Leonardo, 1,127, São Jacinto, Teófilo Otoni, MG 39800-000
Tel: +55(33) 3529-3157 +55(33) 3529-3150 +55(33) 3322-6321
Fax: +55(33) 3321-7559
EMail: morgana@doctum.edu.br; heloisa@doctum.edu.br
Website: http://www.doctum.edu.br/hotsite/?id=522

Diretor: Claudio Cezar Azevedo de Almeida Leitao
EMail: diretoria@doctum.edu.br

Direção Administrativa: Katiane Lemos
EMail: katiane@doctum.edu.br

Direção Acadêmica: Humberto Pereira Gomes
EMail: humberto@doctum.edu.br

Course

Accounting (Accountancy); **Administration** (Administration); **Architecture and Urbanism** (Architecture; Town Planning); **Biological Sciences** (Biological and Life Sciences); **Civil Engineering** (Civil Engineering); **Electrical Engineering** (Electrical Engineering); **Environmental Engineering** (Environmental Engineering); **Information Systems** (Information Technology); **Law** (Law); **Pedagogy** (Pedagogy); **Physics** (Physics); **Production Engineering** (Production Engineering); **Psychology** (Psychology); **Social Service** (Social and Community Services)

History: Founded 2002. A regional unit of the Doctum educational network.
Main Language(s) of Instruction: Portuguese
Degrees and Diplomas: *Bacharelado*; *Licenciatura*
Last Updated: 15/04/16

UNIGRAN CAPITAL FACULTY

Faculdade UNIGRAN Capital
Rua Abrão Júlio Rahe, 325, Monte Castelo, Campo Grande, MS 79010-190
Tel: +55(67) 3389-3302
Fax: +55(67) 3389-3389
EMail: direcaounigrancapital@unigran.br
Website: http://www.unigrancapital.com.br

Diretor Geral: Newton Luiz Medina Carvalho
EMail: direcaounigrancapital@unigran.br

Course

Accountancy (Accountancy); **Administration** (Administration); **Biomedicine** (Biomedicine); **Nursing** (Nursing); **Physical Education** (Physical Education); **Psychology** (Psychology)

History: Founded 2007.
Main Language(s) of Instruction: Portuguese
Degrees and Diplomas: *Bacharelado*; *Licenciatura*; *Especialização/Aperfeiçoamento*. Also Postgraduate Diploma.
Last Updated: 03/07/15

UNILAGOS FACULTY

Faculdade Unilagos
Rua Saldanha Marinho, 85, Mangueirinha, PR 85540-000
Tel: +55(46) 3243-1371
EMail: secretaria@unilagos.com.br
Website: http://www.unilagos.com.br

Diretora Geral: Marlene Graminho

Course

Undergraduate Studies (Administration; Mathematics; Pedagogy; Social and Community Services; Visual Arts)

Main Language(s) of Instruction: Portuguese
Degrees and Diplomas: *Tecnólogo*; *Bacharelado*; *Licenciatura*; *Especialização/Aperfeiçoamento*. Also Postgraduate Diploma.
Student Services: Library
Last Updated: 03/07/15

UNINOVAFAPI UNIVERSITY CENTRE

Centro Universitário UNINOVAFAPI (NOVAFAPI)
Rua Vitorino Orthiges Fernandes 6123, Bairro do Uruguai, Teresina, Piauí 64000000
Tel: +55(86) 2106-0700
Fax: +55(86) 2106-0740
EMail: novafapi@novafapi.com.br
Website: http://www.novafapi.com.br

Reitora: Cristina Maria Miranda de Sousa

Course

Administration (Administration); **Architecture and Town Planning** (Architecture; Town Planning); **Biomedicine** (Biomedicine); **Civil Engineering** (Civil Engineering); **Dentistry** (Dentistry); **Law** (Law); **Medicine** (Medicine); **Nursing** (Nursing); **Nutrition** (Nutrition); **Physical Education** (Physical Education); **Physiotherapy** (Physical Therapy); **Production Engineering** (Production Engineering); **Speech Therapy** (Speech Therapy and Audiology)

History: Founded 2001 as Faculdade NOVAFAPI. Acquired present status and title 2012.
Main Language(s) of Instruction: Portuguese
Degrees and Diplomas: *Bacharelado*; *Especialização/Aperfeiçoamento*; *Mestrado*
Last Updated: 29/05/15

UNION OF FACULTIES OF THE GREAT LAKES

União das Faculdades dos Grandes Lagos (UNILAGO)

Rua Eduardo Nielsen 960, Jardim Aeroporto,
São José do Rio Preto, São Paulo 15001970
Tel: +55(17) 3203-6166
Fax: +55(17) 3203-6154
EMail: unilago@unilago.com.br
Website: http://www.unilago.com.br

Diretora Geral: Maria Lúcia Atique Gabriel (1998-)

Course

Accountancy (Accountancy); **Administration** (Administration); **Advertising** (Advertising and Publicity); **Agronomy** (Agronomy); **Architecture and Town Planning** (Architecture; Town Planning); **Biological Sciences** (Biological and Life Sciences); **Biomedicine** (Biomedicine); **Chemical Engineering** (Chemical Engineering); **Civil Engineering** (Civil Engineering); **Computer Engineering** (Computer Engineering); **Electrical Engineering** (Electrical Engineering); **Environmental Engineering** (Environmental Engineering); **Food Processing** (Food Technology); **Information Systems**; **Journalism** (Journalism); **Law** (Law); **Literature** (Literature); **Medicine** (Medicine); **Nursing** (Nursing); **Nutrition** (Nutrition); **Pedagogy** (Pedagogy); **Pharmacy** (Pharmacy); **Physical Education** (Physical Education); **Physiotherapy** (Physical Therapy); **Production Engineering** (Production Engineering); **Psychology** (Psychology); **Public Relations** (Public Relations); **Secretarial Studies** (Secretarial Studies); **Social Services** (Social and Community Services); **Tourism**; **Translation and Interpretation** (Literature; Translation and Interpretation); **Veterinary Science** (Veterinary Science)

History: Founded 1990 as Faculdades da Associação de Ensino Superior. Acquired present status and title 1997.

Main Language(s) of Instruction: Portuguese

Degrees and Diplomas: *Bacharelado*; *Especialização/Aperfeiçoamento*

Student Services: Library

Last Updated: 14/04/16

UNION OF SCHOOLS OF PARAÍSO

União de Escolas Superiores Paraíso (UNIESP)

Av Jose Pio de Oliveira, 10, Bairro Jardim Cidade Industrial,
São Sebastião do Paraíso, MG 37950-000
Tel: +55(800) 771-2242
Website: http://www.uniesp.edu.br/uniesp.asp

Diretor-Presidente: José Fernando Pinto da Costa

History: Founded 1999.

Main Language(s) of Instruction: Portuguese

Last Updated: 14/12/15

FACULTY CENTRE OF SAO PAULO

FACULDADE CENTRO PAULISTANO

Rua Álves Penteado 208/216, Largo do Café,
São Paulo, SP 01012-905
Tel: +55(11) 2173-4722
EMail: ckto@terra.com.br
Website: www.uniesp.edu.br

Presidente: José Fernando Pinto da Costa
EMail: fernando.costa@uniesp.edu.br

Diretor – Centro Novo: José Erivam Silveira Filho

Course

Accountancy (Accountancy); **Administration** (Administration); **Letters** (English; Literature; Portuguese); **Pedagogy** (Pedagogy); **Social Communication** (Advertising and Publicity)

History: Founded 2008.

Main Language(s) of Instruction: Portuguese

Degrees and Diplomas: *Bacharelado*; *Licenciatura*

Student Services: Library

FACULTY OF AMAMBAI

FACULDADE DE AMAMBAI (FIAMA)

Rua Pe. Anchieta, 202, Vila Copacabana, Amambai, MS 79990-000
Tel: +55(67) 3481-1355
Fax: +55(67) 3481-1355
EMail: atendimento@fiama.edu.br
Website: http://www.uniesp.edu.br/fiama/

Diretor: Wantuir Smaniotto

Course

Accountancy (Accountancy); **Administration** (Administration; Business Administration); **Pedagogy** (Education; Pedagogy)

History: Founded 1998.

Main Language(s) of Instruction: Portuguese

Accrediting Agency: Ministry of Education

Degrees and Diplomas: *Bacharelado*; *Licenciatura*

Student Services: Library

FACULTY OF BIRIGUI

FACULDADE BIRIGUI (FABI)

Rua João Escanhuela 133, Birigui, SP 16204-142
Tel: +55(18) 3642-7808
Fax: +55(18) 3642-7808
EMail: mantenedora@uniesp.edu.br
Website: http://www.uniesp.edu.br/birigui

Direito: Eldir Paulo Scarpim EMail: eldir.scarpim@uniesp.edu.br

Secretário Acadêmico: Cleber José Zanettii

Course

Accountancy (Accountancy); **Administration** (Administration); **Geography** (Geography); **History** (History); **Law** (Law); **Mathematics** (Mathematics); **Modern Languages** (English; Literature; Portuguese; Spanish); **Pedagogy** (Education; Pedagogy); **Visual Arts** (Visual Arts)

History: Founded 2001.

Main Language(s) of Instruction: Portuguese

Accrediting Agency: Ministry of Education

Degrees and Diplomas: *Bacharelado*; *Licenciatura*

Student Services: Library

FACULTY OF DUQUE DE CAXIAS

FACULDADE DE DUQUE DE CAXIAS

Rua Pedro Correia, 318, Vila Meriti, Duque de Caxia, RJ 25020-160
Tel: +55(21) 2782-8278
Fax: +55(21) 2782-8278
EMail: rosane.cordeiro@uniesp.edu.br; ckto@terra.com.br; academicosup@uniesp.edu.br
Website: http://www.faculdadededuquedecaxias.edu.br

President: Fernando Costa

Course

Administration (Business Administration); **Information Systems** (Information Technology); **Nursing** (Nursing); **Social Services** (Social and Community Services)

History: Founded 1997.

Main Language(s) of Instruction: Portuguese

Degrees and Diplomas: *Bacharelado*

FACULTY OF EDUCATION AND MANAGEMENT SCIENCES OF SÃO PAULO

FACULDADE DE EDUCAÇÃO E CIÊNCIAS GERENCIAIS DE SÃO PAULO (FECG-SP)

Rua Santa Crescência, 443, Butantã, São Paulo, SP 05524-020
Tel: +55(11) 3752-2000
Fax: +55(11) 3752-2000
EMail: ckto@terra.com.br; academicosup@uniesp.edu.br
Website: http://www.uniesp.edu.br/fecg

Presidente: Fernando Costa EMail: fernando.costa@uniesp.edu.br

Course
Accounting (Accountancy); **Administration** (Business Administration); **Pedagogy** (Pedagogy)
Main Language(s) of Instruction: Portuguese
Degrees and Diplomas: *Bacharelado*; *Licenciatura*

FACULTY OF EDUCATION AND MANAGERIAL SCIENCES OF SUMARÉ

FACULDADE DE EDUCAÇÃO E CIÊNCIAS GERENCIAIS DE SUMARÉ (FECGS)

Rua José Maria Miranda, 480, Centro, Sumaré, SP 13170-001
Tel: +55(19) 3873-4028
Fax: +55(19) 3883-1893
EMail: fernando.costa@uniesp.edu.br; ckto@terra.com.br; academicosup@uniesp.edu.br
Website: http://www.uniesp.edu.br/fecgs

Diretor Geral: Paulo Roberto de Lima
EMail: paulo.lima@uniesp.edu.br

Course
Accounting (Accountancy); **Administration** (Business Administration); **Commercial Management** (Business and Commerce; Management); **Financial Management** (Finance; Management); **Human Resources Management** (Human Resources; Management); **International Business** (International Business); **Marketing** (Marketing); **Pedagogy** (Pedagogy)
History: Founded 1995.
Main Language(s) of Instruction: Portuguese
Degrees and Diplomas: *Tecnólogo*; *Bacharelado*; *Licenciatura*

FACULTY OF EDUCATION OF ASSISI

FACULDADE DE EDUCAÇÃO DE ASSIS (FAEDA)

Av. Dr. Dória, n° 260, Vila Ouro Verde 19816-230
Tel: +55(18) 3302-2552
Fax: +55(18) 3302-2552
EMail: secretariafac@ieda.edu.br
Website: http://www.ieda.edu.br

Diretor Geral: Heber Ricardo da Silva
Coordenadora do Curso: Luciana Cavalcante de Assis
EMail: luciana.assis@uniesp.edu.br

Course
Accountancy (Accountancy); **Administration** (Administration; Management); **Education** (Education); **Physical Education** (Physical Education)
History: Founded 1970 as Escola de Educação Física de Assis. Maintained by Instituto Educacional de Assis (IEDA). IEDA joined the EDUCATIONAL GROUP UNIESP, 2014.
Main Language(s) of Instruction: Portuguese
Degrees and Diplomas: *Bacharelado*; *Licenciatura*: **Education; Physical Education.**
Student Services: Library

FACULTY OF HORTOLÂNDIA

FACULDADE DE HORTOLÂNDIA

Avenida Santana, 1070, Jardim Amanda I, Hortolândia, SP 13188-000
Tel: +55(19) 3865-8320
Fax: +55(19) 3865-8322
EMail: academicosup@uniesp.edu.br
Website: http://www.faculdadedehortolandia.edu.br

Diretor: Andre Luiz Padovani
EMail: andre.padovani@uniesp.edu.br

Course
Accounting (Accountancy); **Administration** (Business Administration); **Information Systems** (Information Technology); **Logistics** (Transport Management); **Pedagogy** (Pedagogy); **Production Engineering** (Production Engineering); **Social Services** (Social and Community Services)
History: Founded 2000.
Main Language(s) of Instruction: Portuguese
Degrees and Diplomas: *Tecnólogo*; *Bacharelado*
Student Services: Canteen, IT Centre, Library

FACULTY OF MANAGEMENT OF BARÃO DE JUNDIAÍ

FACULDADE DE CIÊNCIAS GERENCIAIS BARÃO DE JUNDIAÍ (FCG)

Rua Senador Fonseca, 1182, Jundiaí, SP 13201-017
Tel: +55(11) 4522-2212
Fax: +55(11) 4522-2212
EMail: ckto@terra.com.br; academicosup@uniesp.edu.br
Website: http://www.uniesp.edu.br/fcg

Course
Accounting (Accountancy); **Administration** (Administration)
History: Founded 2006.
Main Language(s) of Instruction: Portuguese
Degrees and Diplomas: *Bacharelado*: **Accountancy; Administration.**
Student Services: eLibrary

FACULTY OF MARILIA

FACULDADE DE MARÍLIA (FAMAR)

Rua Vinte e Quatro de Dezembro, 1251, Alto Cafezal, Marília, SP 17504-010
Tel: +55(14) 3402-8900 +55(14) 3402-8910
Fax: +55(14) 3402-8910
EMail: fernando@uniesp.edu.br; ckto@terra.com.br; academicosup@uniesp.edu.br
Website: http://www.faculdadedemarilia.edu.br

Presidente: Fernando Costa

Course
Administration (Business Administration); **Pedagogy** (Pedagogy)
History: Founded 2011.
Main Language(s) of Instruction: Portuguese
Degrees and Diplomas: *Bacharelado*; *Licenciatura*

FACULTY OF MIRANDÓPOLIS

FACULDADE DE MIRANDÓPOLIS (FAM)

Avenida São Paulo, 965, Bairro Nogara, Mirandópolis, SP 16800-000
Tel: +55(18) 3701-9110
Fax: +55(18) 3701-9110
EMail: gisele.marconato@uniesp.edu.br; ckto@terra.com.br; academicosup@uniesp.edu.br; jose.codonho@uniesp.edu
Website: http://www.faculdadedemirandopolis.edu.br

Diretor Geral: Marco Antonio Ferreira Matheus

Course
Administration (Business Administration); **Pedagogy** (Pedagogy); **Social Services** (Social and Community Services)
History: Founded 1999.
Main Language(s) of Instruction: Portuguese
Degrees and Diplomas: *Bacharelado*; *Licenciatura*

FACULTY OF MONTE ALTO

FACULTE DE MONTE ALTO (FMA)

Rua Wady Elias, 191, Jardim Alvorada, Monte Alto, São Paulo 15910-000
Tel: +55(16) 3242-7399
Fax: +55(16) 3242-1213
EMail: ckto@terra.com.br; academicosup@uniesp.edu.br
Website: http://www.fan.edu.br

Diretora: Flavia Petra Melara Benatti
Secretária Acadêmica: Naiara Thimótheo

Course
Administration (Business Administration); **Pedagogy** (Pedagogy); **Post-graduate Studies** *(Distance Mode)* (Arts and Humanities; Education; Finance; Law; Management)

History: Founded 1995. Acquired present status 2001.

Main Language(s) of Instruction: Portuguese

Degrees and Diplomas: *Bacharelado*; *Licenciatura*; *Especialização/Aperfeiçoamento*: **Administrative Law; Business Administration; Commercial Law; Educational Administration; Educational Psychology; Environmental Management; Finance; Health Administration; Labour Law; Management; Marketing; Mathematics Education; Native Language Education; Preschool Education; Public Administration; Special Education; Teacher Training.**

Student Services: IT Centre, Library

FACULTY OF SOROCABA

FACULDADE DE SOROCABA

Rua Doutor Álvaro Soares, 550, Centro, Sorocaba, SP 18010-191
Tel: +55(15) 3211-8335 +55(15) 2173-4760
Fax: +55(15) 3211-8335 +55(15) 2173-4762
EMail: ckto@terra.com.br
Website: http://www.faculdadedesorocaba.edu.br

Diretor: Demetrius Abrão Bigaran
EMail: demetrius.bigaran@uniesp.edu.br

Course
Accounting (Accountancy); **Administration** (Business Administration); **Pedagogy** (Pedagogy)

History: Founded 2005.

Main Language(s) of Instruction: Portuguese

Degrees and Diplomas: *Bacharelado*; *Licenciatura*

FACULTY OF SÃO PAULO - NEW CENTRE

FACULDADE DE SÃO PAULO - CENTRO NOVO (FASP)

Rua Conselheiro Crispiniano, 120, Centro,
São Paulo, SP 01037-000
Tel: +55(11) 3155-7770 +55(11) 3297-9865
Fax: +55(11) 3297-9865
EMail: fernando.costa@uniesp.edu.br; ckto@terra.com.br;
academicosup@uniesp.edu.br
Website: http://www.faculdadedesaopaulo.edu.br/centronovo/index.asp

Diretor: José Erivam Silveira Filho

Diretor Adjunto: Sérgio Ávila Rizo

Course
Biological Sciences (Biological and Life Sciences); **Geography** (Geography; Geography (Human)); **History** (History); **Letters** (English; Foreign Languages Education; Humanities and Social Science Education; Literature; Native Language Education; Portuguese); **Mathematics** (Mathematics); **Nursing** (Nursing); **Pedagogy** (Pedagogy); **Physical Education** (Physical Education)

History: Founded 2000.

Main Language(s) of Instruction: Portuguese

Degrees and Diplomas: *Bacharelado*; *Licenciatura*

Student Services: IT Centre, Library

FACULTY OF SÃO ROQUE

FACULDADE DE SÃO ROQUE (FAEV)

Avenida Varangüera, 623, Jardim Bela Vista,
São Roque, SP 18132-340
Tel: +55(11) 4784-9199 +55(11) 4784-9111
Fax: +55(11) 4784-9111
EMail: ckto@terra.com.br; academicosup@uniesp.edu.br
Website: http://www.faculdadedesaoroque.edu.br/index.asp

Diretor: Fernando Costa

Course
Administration (Business Administration); **Law** (Law)

History: Founded 2002.

Main Language(s) of Instruction: Portuguese

Degrees and Diplomas: *Bacharelado*

FACULTY OF TAQUARITINGA

FACULDADE DE TAQUARITINGA (FTGA)

Fazenda Contendas, s/n, Zona Rural, Taquaritinga, SP 15900-000
Tel: +55(16) 3253-8660
Fax: +55(16) 3253-8660
EMail: valeria.mantovani@uniesp.edu.br; ckto@terra.com.br;
academicosup@uniesp.edu.br
Website: http://www.faculdadedetaquaritinga.edu.br

Diretor Geral: Osmar Bueno de Morais

College
Biological Sciences (Biological and Life Sciences; Science Education)

Course
Administration (Business Administration); **Information Systems** (Information Technology); **Nursing** (Nursing); **Nutrition** (Nutrition); **Pedagogy** (Pedagogy); **Pharmacy** (Pharmacy); **Physical Education** (Physical Education); **Physical Therapy** (Physical Therapy)

History: Founded 2007.

Main Language(s) of Instruction: Portuguese

Degrees and Diplomas: *Bacharelado*; *Licenciatura*

FACULTY OF VARGEM GRANDE PAULISTA

FACULDADE DE VARGEM GRANDE PAULISTA

Estrada Planalto, 174 - Km 41,5, Rodovia Raposo Tavares,
Vargem Grande Paulista, SP 06730-000
Tel: +55(11) 4158-9199
Fax: +55(11) 4158-9199
EMail: fernando.costa@uniesp.edu.br; ckto@terra.com.br;
academicosup@uniesp.edu.br
Website: http://www.faculdadedevargemgrande.edu.br

Diretor Geral: Ludmila Covallero Renck

Secretária Acadêmica: Fabrícia Lenotti

College
Letters (English; Literature; Portuguese)

Course
Pedagogy (Pedagogy)

History: Founded 1998.

Main Language(s) of Instruction: Portuguese

FACULTY OF VINHEDO

FACULDADE DE VINHEDO (FV)

Avenida João Pescarini, 568, Jardim Trevisan,
Vinhedo, São Paulo 13280-000
Tel: +55(19) 3826-4644
Fax: +55(19) 3886-6144
EMail: kelsen.ferreira@uniesp.edu.br; ckto@terra.com.br;
academicosup@uniesp.edu.br
Website: http://www.fv.edu.br

Diretor: Kelsen Ricardo Ferreira Pinto

Course
Administration (Administration); **Information Systems** (Computer Science); **Letters** (Literature; Portuguese); **Pedagogy** (Pedagogy); **Physical Education** (Physical Education); **Tourism** (Tourism)

History: Founded 2000.

Fees: 7,698-8,076 per semester (Brazilian Real)

Main Language(s) of Instruction: Portuguese

Degrees and Diplomas: *Bacharelado*; *Licenciatura*

FACULTY OF THE SOUTH WEST OF SAO PAULO

FACULDADE SUDOESTE PAULISTANO (FASUP)

Avenida Professor Francisco Morato 1900, Butantã, São Paulo, SP 05512200
Tel: +55(11) 3721-5243
Fax: +55(11) 3721-8926
EMail: fasup@fasup.edu.br
Website: http://www.uniesp.edu.br/fasup/faculdade.asp

Diretora: Simone Della Torre

Course

Administration (Accountancy; Administration); **Letters** (Literature); **Pedagogy** (Pedagogy)

History: Founded 1997.

Main Language(s) of Instruction: Portuguese

Degrees and Diplomas: *Bacharelado*; *Especialização/Aperfeiçoamento*

FIPECAFI FACULTY

FACULDADE FIPECAFI (FIPECAFI)

Rua Maestro Cardim, 1,170, Bela Vista, São Paulo, SP 01323-001
Tel: +55(11) 2184-2000
Fax: +55(11) 2184-2001
EMail: fipecafi@fipecafi.org; mbasecretaria@fipecafi.org
Website: http://www.fipecafi.org

Diretor-Presidente: Welington Rocha (2015-)

Diretor Administrativo/Financeiro: Carlos Alberto Pereira

Course

Accounting *(Distance Mode)* (Accountancy); **Accounting** *(Presential Mode)* (Accountancy); **Postgraduate Studies** (Accountancy; Banking; Finance; Insurance; Taxation)

History: Founded 1974. Maintained by the Fundação Instituto de Pesquisas Contábeis, Atuariais e Financeiras.

Main Language(s) of Instruction: Portuguese

Degrees and Diplomas: *Bacharelado*; *Especialização/Aperfeiçoamento*: **Accountancy; Banking; Finance.** *Mestrado*: **Accountancy; Finance.** Also MBA

Student Services: Library

FLEMING FACULTY

FACULDADE FLEMING (SEF)

Rua Luiz Otávio, 1281, Taquaral, Campinas, SP 13090-110
Tel: +55(19) 3756-2300
Fax: +55(19) 3744-4010
EMail: fleming@setanet.com.br; ckto@terra.com.br
Website: http://www.faculdadefleming.edu.br

Diretora Geral: Elizanita Sassi Pugliesi

Secretário Acadêmico: Roberto Mauro Duarte

Course

Accountancy (Accountancy); **Administration** (Administration); **Letters** (Foreign Languages Education; Literature; Native Language Education); **Pedagogy** (Pedagogy)

History: Founded 1999.

Main Language(s) of Instruction: Portuguese

Degrees and Diplomas: *Bacharelado*; *Licenciatura*

Student Services: Library

GUARÁ ORGANISATION OF EDUCATION

ORGANIZAÇÃO GUARÁ DE ENSINO (OGE)

Avenida Pedro de Toledo, 195, Vila Paraíba, Guaratinguetá, SP 12515-690
Tel: +55(12) 3123-3123
Fax: +55(12) 3123-3123
EMail: oge@oge.edu.br; ckto@terra.com.br; academicosup@uniesp.edu.br
Website: http://www.oge.edu.br

Diretora Geral: Érica Barbosa Joslin
EMail: erica.joslin@uniesp.edu.br

Faculty

Faculty of Economics and Administrative Sciences of Guaratinguetá (FACEAG) (Administration); **Faculty of Education of Guaratinguetá (FACEG)** (Education)

History: Founded 1973.

Main Language(s) of Instruction: Portuguese

Degrees and Diplomas: *Bacharelado*; *Licenciatura*

Student Services: IT Centre, Library

INTEGRATED FACULTIES OF NOVA ANDRADINA

FACULDADES INTEGRADAS DE NOVA ANDRADINA (FINAN)

Av. Antonio Joaquim de Moura Andrade, 910, Centro, Nova Andradina, MS 79750-000
Tel: +55(67) 3441-6700
Fax: +55(67) 3441-1991
EMail: finan@finan.com.br; lauroandrey1969@gmail.com; ivolim.mc@gmail.com
Website: http://www.uniesp.edu.br/finan

Diretor: Henrique Barros

Faculty

Nova Andradina Faculty of Accountancy *(FACINAN)* (Accountancy; Law; Production Engineering); **Nova Andradina Faculty of Administration** *(FANOVA)* (Agriculture; Business Administration); **Nova Andradina Faculty of Education** *(FENA)* (Pedagogy)

History: Founded 1999.

Main Language(s) of Instruction: Portuguese

Degrees and Diplomas: *Tecnólogo*; *Bacharelado*; *Licenciatura*

INTEGRATED FACULTY OF HIGHER EDUCATION OF COLINAS

FACULDADE INTEGRADA DE ENSINO SUPERIOR DE COLINAS (FIESC)

Rua Dom Manoel, 1297, Novo Planalto, Colinas do Tocantins, TO 77760-000
Tel: +55(63) 3476-1855
Fax: +55(63) 3476-1855
EMail: fiesc@fecolinas.edu.br; ckto@terra.com.br; academicosup@uniesp.edu.br
Website: http://www.uniesp.edu.br/fiesc

Diretora Geral: Marisete Tavares Ferreira
EMail: marisete.tavares@hotmail.com

Course

Accountancy (Accountancy); **Geography** (Geography); **History** (History); **International Business** (International Business); **Law** (Law); **Nursing** (Nursing); **Occupational Safety** (Safety Engineering); **Pedagogy** (Pedagogy); **Psychology** (Psychology); **Social Services** (Social Welfare)

History: Founded 1999.

Main Language(s) of Instruction: Portuguese

Degrees and Diplomas: *Tecnólogo*; *Bacharelado*; *Licenciatura*

UNISSA FACULTY OF SARANDI

FACULDADE UNISSA DE SARANDI (UNISSA)

Rua Machado de Assis, s/n Jardim Universitário, Sarandi, PR 87111970
Tel: +55(44) 3264-6000
Fax: +55(44) 3264-6000
EMail: academicosup@uniesp.edu.br
Website: http://www.uniesp.edu.br/sarandi

Diretora Geral: Fátima Regina Selleri

Course

Accountancy (Accountancy); **Administration** (Accountancy; Administration); **Geography** (Geography); **Pedagogy** (Pedagogy)

History: Founded 1999.

Main Language(s) of Instruction: Portuguese

Degrees and Diplomas: *Bacharelado*; *Licenciatura*; *Especialização/Aperfeiçoamento*

Student Services: Library

UNION OF THE AMERICAS FACULTY

Faculdade União das Américas

Avenida Tarquínio Joslin Santos 1000, Jardim Universitário das Américas, Foz do Iguaçu, PR 85870400

Tel: +55(45) 2105-9000

Fax: +55(45) 2105-9033

EMail: uniamerica@uniamerica.br

Website: http://www.uniamerica.br

Course

Accountancy (Accountancy); **Administration** (Administration); **Architecture and Town Planning** (Architecture; Town Planning); **Biology** (Biology); **Biomedicine** (Biomedicine); **Civil Engineering** (Civil Engineering); **Electrical Engineering** (Electrical Engineering); **Environmental Engineering** (Environmental Engineering); **History** (History); **Nursing** (Nursing); **Nutrition** (Nutrition); **Pedagogy** (Pedagogy); **Pharmacy** (Pharmacy); **Physical Education** (Physical Education); **Physiotherapy** (Physical Therapy); **Production Engineering** (Production Engineering); **Psychology** (Psychology); **Radiology** (Radiology); **Social Service** (Social and Community Services)

History: Founded 2001.

Degrees and Diplomas: *Bacharelado*; *Licenciatura*; *Especialização/Aperfeiçoamento*; *Mestrado*

Last Updated: 25/06/15

UNIRONDON UNIVERSITY CENTRE

Centro Universitário Cândido Rondon – UNIRONDON

Avenida Beira Rio 3001, Jardim Europa, Cuiabá, Mato Grosso 78065780

Tel: +55(65) 3316-4000

Fax: +55(65)3634-1881

EMail: ouvidoria.unirondon@kroton.com.br

Website: http://www.unirondon.br

Diretor: Rogério Boscoli

Tel: +11(65) 3316-4024 +11(65) 3316-4078

Coordenação Acadêmica: Alceu Vidotti

Course

Accountancy (Accountancy); **Administration** (Administration); **Advertising and Publicity** (Advertising and Publicity); **Biology** *(Licenciatura)* (Biology); **Biomedicine** (Biomedicine); **Business and Commerce** (Business and Commerce); **Computer Science** (Computer Science); **Environmental Management** (Environmental Management); **Finance** (Finance); **Journalism** (Journalism); **Law** (Law); **Nursing** (Nursing); **Pedagogy** *(Licenciatura)* (Pedagogy); **Radiology** (Radiology); **Technological Studies** (Business and Commerce; Finance; Information Management; Public Administration; Radiology; Real Estate; Systems Analysis); **Tourism** (Tourism)

Further Information: Also Distance Education.

History: Founded 2004.

Main Language(s) of Instruction: Portuguese

Degrees and Diplomas: *Tecnólogo*; *Bacharelado*; *Licenciatura*; *Especialização/Aperfeiçoamento*: **Education; Engineering; Health Sciences; Human Resources; Law; Technology.** Also MBA.

Last Updated: 29/06/15

UNITED FACULTIES OF THE NORTH OF MINAS

Faculdades Unidas do Norte de Minas (FUNORTE)

Avenida Osmane Barbosa 11.111 JK, Montes Claros, Minas Gerais 39404006

Tel: +55(38) 2101-9292

Fax: +55(38) 2101-9268

EMail: contato@funorte.edu.br

Website: http://www.funorte.com.br

Diretora Acadêmica da Soebras: Thalita Pimentel Nunes

EMail: thalita.pimentel@funorte.edu.br

Institute

Health Sciences *(ICS)* (Biomedicine; Dentistry; Medicine; Nursing; Nutrition; Physical Education; Physical Therapy; Speech Therapy and Audiology)

Course

Administration (Administration); **Aesthetics and Cosmetology** (Cosmetology); **Biomedical Engineering** (Biomedical Engineering); **Civil Engineering** (Civil Engineering); **Electrical Engineering** (Electrical Engineering); **Food Processing** (Food Technology); **Geography** (Geography); **History** (History); **Journalism** (Journalism); **Law** (Law); **Mechanichal Engineering** (Mechanical Engineering); **Pedagogy** (Pedagogy); **Pharmacy** (Pharmacy); **Portuguese** (Portuguese); **Psychology** (Psychology); **Social Services** (Social and Community Services); **Teacher Training** (Teacher Training); **Veterinary Science** (Veterinary Science)

Further Information: AAlso branches in São Paulo

History: Founded 1997. Acquired present status 2000. Maintained by Educational Association of Brazil (SOEBRAS).

Main Language(s) of Instruction: Portuguese

Degrees and Diplomas: *Bacharelado*; *Especialização/Aperfeiçoamento*: **Dentistry; Education; Educational Psychology; Law; Medicine; Pedagogy.** *Mestrado*

Student Services: Library

Last Updated: 24/03/16

UNITED FACULTIES OF THE VALLEY OF ARAGUAIA

Faculdades Unidas do Vale do Araguaia

Rua Moreira Cabral, 1,000, Domingos Mariano, Barra do Garças, MT 78600-000

Tel: +55(65) 3401-1602

Fax: +55(65) 3401-1602 +55(65) 3401-1212

EMail: contato@univar.edu.br; univar@univar.edu.br

Website: http://www.univar.edu.br

Diretor Presidente: Marcelo Antôncio Fuster Soler (1997-)

Course

Accountancy (Accountancy); **Administration** (Administration); **Aesthetics and Cosmetics** (Aesthetics; Cosmetology); **Agronomy** (Agronomy); **History** (History); **Nursing** (Nursing); **Nutrition** (Nutrition); **Odontology** (Dentistry); **Pedagogy** (Pedagogy); **Pharmacy** (Pharmacy); **Physical Education** (Physical Education); **Physiotherapy** (Physical Therapy); **Postgraduate Studies** (Biological and Life Sciences; Community Health; Educational Psychology; Finance; Higher Education Teacher Training; Management; Microbiology; Social Policy; Social Work; Software Engineering); **Psychology** (Psychology); **Social Services** (Social and Community Services); **Systems Analysis and Development** (Systems Analysis); **Veterinary Medicine** (Veterinary Science)

History: Founded 1992

Main Language(s) of Instruction: Portuguese

Degrees and Diplomas: *Tecnólogo*; *Bacharelado*; *Licenciatura*; *Especialização/Aperfeiçoamento*: **Biological and Life Sciences; Community Health; Educational Psychology; Finance; Higher Education Teacher Training; Management; Microbiology; Social Policy; Social Work; Software Engineering.**

Student Services: Library

Last Updated: 03/02/16

UNITED FACULTY OF SUZANO

Faculdade Unida de Suzano (UNISUZ)

Rua José Correia Gonçalves 57, Centro, Suzano, São Paulo 08675130

Tel: +55(11) 4746-7300

EMail: diretoria@unisuz.com.br

Website: http://www.unisuz.edu.br

Diretor Geral: Benedito Luiz Franco

Course

Accountancy (Accountancy); **Administration** (Administration); **Finance** (Finance); **Information Systems** (Computer Science); **Law** (Law); **Letters** (Literature); **Marketing** (Marketing);

Mathematics (Mathematics); **Pedagogy** (Pedagogy); **Physical Education** (Physical Education); **Real Estate** (Real Estate)

History: Founded 2000.

Main Language(s) of Instruction: Portuguese

Degrees and Diplomas: *Bacharelado*; *Licenciatura*; *Especialização/Aperfeiçoamento*

Last Updated: 03/07/15

UNITED FACULTY OF VITÓRIA

Faculdade Unida de Vitória

Rua Engenheiro Fábio Ruschi, n° 161, Bento Ferreira, Vitória, ES 29050-670
Tel: +55(27) 3325-2071
EMail: contato@faculdadeunida.com.br
Website: http://www.faculdadeunida.com.br

Diretor Geral: Wanderley Pereira da Rosa

Course

Graduate Studies (Bible; Family Studies; Nursing; Pharmacology; Philosophy; Psychoanalysis; Religious Studies; Sports); **Undergraduate Studies** (Theology)

History: Founded 1997 as Faculdade Teológica Unida - FTU. Acquired present title 2007.

Main Language(s) of Instruction: Portuguese

Degrees and Diplomas: *Bacharelado*; *Especialização/Aperfeiçoamento*; *Mestrado*

Last Updated: 03/07/15

UNIVATES UNIVERSITY CENTRE

Centro Universitário Univates (UNIVATES)

Rua Avelino Tallini, 171-B. Universitário, Lajeado, RS 95900-000
Tel: +55(51) 3714-7000
Fax: +55(51) 3714-7001
EMail: campus@univates.br, linhadireta@univates.br
Website: http://www.univates.br

Reitor: Ney José Lazzari EMail: nlazzari@univates.br

Vice-Reitor: Carlos C. da S. Cyrne

International Relations: Isabel Körbes Scapini
EMail: aaii@univates.br

Course

Graduate Studies (Biotechnology; Business Administration; Education; Engineering; Environmental Studies; Natural Sciences); **Undergraduate Studies** (Accountancy; Agricultural Management; Biomedicine; Business Administration; Business and Commerce; Chemical Engineering; Civil Engineering; Commercial Law; Computer Engineering; Dance; Design; Ecology; Education; Electrical Engineering; Environmental Engineering; Fashion Design; Finance; Food Technology; Health Sciences; History; Industrial Chemistry; Industrial Management; International Relations; Journalism; Labour Law; Law; Management; Marketing; Mechanical Engineering; Modern Languages; Oncology; Pedagogy; Photography; Physical Education; Physical Therapy; Physiology; Production Engineering; Rehabilitation and Therapy; Safety Engineering; Software Engineering; Special Education; Tourism; Water Management)

History: Founded 1972. Acquired present status 1997.

Academic Year: March to December (March-July; August-December)

Admission Requirements: Secondary education certificate and entrance examination

Main Language(s) of Instruction: Portuguese

Accrediting Agency: Federal Ministry of Education

Degrees and Diplomas: *Bacharelado*; *Licenciatura*; *Especialização/Aperfeiçoamento*: **Business Administration; Human Resources; Management; Marketing; Safety Engineering.** *Mestrado*: **Biotechnology; Education; Environmental Studies; Science Education.** *Doutorado*: **Environmental Studies.** Also Teaching Qualification

Student Services: Academic Counselling, Canteen, Careers Guidance, Cultural Activities, Language Laboratory, Library, Social Counselling, Sports Facilities

Publications: Estudio y Debate

Last Updated: 09/09/15

UNIVERSITY CENTRE OF EDUCATIONAL FOUNDATION OF BARRETOS

Centro Universitario da Fundação Educational De Barretos (UNIFEB)

Avenida Professor Roberto Frade Monte 389, Bairro Aeroporto, Barretos, São Paulo 14783-226
Tel: +55(17) 3322-6411
Fax: +55(17) 3322-6205
EMail: reitoria@feb.br
Website: http://www.unifeb.edu.br

Reitor: Reginaldo da Silva EMail: reitoria@feb.br

Pró-Reitora de Graduação: Sissi Kawai Marcos
EMail: prograd@feb.br

Course

Administration (Administration); **Agronomy** (Agronomy); **Biology** (Biology); **Chemical Engineering** (Chemical Engineering); **Chemical Technology** (Industrial Chemistry); **Chemistry** (Chemistry); **Civil Engineering** (Civil Engineering); **Electrical Engineering** (Electrical Engineering); **Environmental Engineering** (Environmental Engineering); **Graduate Studies** *(Lato Sensu)* (Civil Law; Computer Networks; Criminal Law; Finance; Labour Law; Rehabilitation and Therapy; Safety Engineering; Social Policy; Surgery); **Graduate Studies** *(Stricto Sensu)* (Dentistry); **Information Systems** (Information Sciences); **Law** (Law); **Mathematics** (Mathematics); **Mechanical Engineering** (Mechanical Engineering); **Odontology** (Dentistry); **Pedagogy** (Pedagogy; Teacher Training); **Pharmacy** (Pharmacy); **Physical Education** (Physical Education); **Physics** (Physics); **Production Engineering** (Production Engineering); **Social Services** (Social and Community Services); **Zootechniccs** (Animal Husbandry)

History: Founded 1996

Main Language(s) of Instruction: Portuguese

Accrediting Agency: Ministry of Education.

Degrees and Diplomas: *Bacharelado*; *Licenciatura*; *Especialização/Aperfeiçoamento*: **Civil Law; Computer Networks; Dentistry; Finance; Higher Education Teacher Training; Information Technology; Labour Law; Law; Management; Mathematics; Orthodontics; Periodontics; Pharmacy; Preschool Education; Primary Education; Social and Community Services; Special Education.** *Mestrado*

Last Updated: 17/07/15

UNIVERSITY CENTRE OF THE STATE OF PARÁ

Centro Universitário do Estado do Pará (CESUPA)

Avenida Nazaré 630, Nazaré, Belém, Pará 66035-170
Tel: +55(91) 4009-2100
Fax: +55(91) 4009-2116
EMail: cesupa@cesupa.br
Website: http://www.cesupa.br

Reitor: João Paulo do Valle Mendes

Vice-Reitor: Sérgio Fiuza de Mello Mendes

Area

Applied Social Sciences (Accountancy; Administration; Advertising and Publicity; Business Administration; Human Resources; Information Technology; Law; Management; Marketing); **Environmental, Biological and Health Sciences** (Biology; Dentistry; Environmental Studies; Medicine; Nursing; Nutrition; Pharmacy; Physical Therapy); **Exact Sciences and Technology** (Computer Networks; Computer Science; Data Processing; Industrial Engineering; Information Sciences; Production Engineering; Systems Analysis)

Further Information: Also José Malcher, Almirante Barroso, Alcindo Cacela campuses.

History: Founded as University Centre of Pará,1986. Acquired present title and status 2002.

Main Language(s) of Instruction: Portuguese

Accrediting Agency: Ministry of Education.

Degrees and Diplomas: *Tecnólogo*; *Bacharelado*; *Licenciatura*; *Especialização/Aperfeiçoamento*: **Civil Law; Education; Law; Nutrition; Pharmacy.** *Mestrado*: **Health Sciences; Law.**

Student Services: IT Centre, Library

Last Updated: 10/07/15

UNIVERSITY CENTRE OF UNITED METROPOLITAN FACULTIES

Centro universitário das faculdades metropolitanas Unidas (FMU)

Campus Liberdade, Avenida Liberdade 654, São Paulo, São Paulo 1508010

Tel: +55(11) 3132-3000 +55(11) 3346-6200 +55(11) 3346-6221

Fax: +55(11) 3209-4589

EMail: relacionamento.candidato@fmu.br; depto_normas@fmu.br

Website: http://www.fmu.br

Reitora: Sara Pedrini Martins EMail: gabinete_reitoria@fmu.br

Secretária Geral: Aline Alves de Andrade

Area

Architecture, Arts, Design and Fashion (Architecture; Art Management; Design; Fashion Design; Graphic Design; Industrial Design; Interior Design; Marketing; Music; Photography; Town Planning); **Communication** (Advertising and Publicity; Communication Studies; Journalism; Marketing; Mass Communication; Multimedia; Public Relations; Radio and Television Broadcasting); **Distance Education** (Accountancy; Banking; Business Administration; Business and Commerce; Civil Law; Commercial Law; E-Business/Commerce; Educational Administration; Educational Psychology; Energy Engineering; Finance; Foreign Languages Education; Higher Education Teacher Training; Human Resources; Information Technology; International Business; Labour Law; Law; Marketing; Mass Communication; Nursing; Occupational Health; Petroleum and Gas Engineering; Portuguese; Preschool Education; Public Administration; Public Health; Real Estate; Sales Techniques; Social Work; Software Engineering; Transport Management); **Education** (Art Education; Education; Educational Administration; Educational Psychology; English; Foreign Languages Education; Higher Education Teacher Training; History; Humanities and Social Science Education; Latin American Studies; Mathematics Education; Neurosciences; Pedagogy; Portuguese; Preschool Education; Special Education; Translation and Interpretation); **Engineering** (Automation and Control Engineering; Civil Engineering; Construction Engineering; Electrical Engineering; Engineering; Environmental Engineering; Maintenance Technology; Mechanical Engineering; Petroleum and Gas Engineering; Production Engineering; Safety Engineering; Sanitary Engineering; Statistics; Telecommunications Engineering); **Health** (Aesthetics; Art Therapy; Biological and Life Sciences; Biomedicine; Cosmetology; Dentistry; Embryology and Reproduction Biology; Environmental Studies; Health Sciences; Microbiology; Nursing; Nutrition; Pharmacy; Physical Education; Physical Therapy; Psychology; Rehabilitation and Therapy; Speech Therapy and Audiology; Veterinary Science); **Law** (Civil Law; Commercial Law; Criminal Law; Fiscal Law; Labour Law; Law; Private Law); **Management and Commerce** (Accountancy; Administration; Banking; Business Administration; Business and Commerce; Business Education; Cooking and Catering; E-Business/Commerce; Economics; Environmental Management; Finance; Hotel Management; International Business; International Relations; Management; Marketing; Public Administration; Public Relations; Real Estate; Sales Techniques; Secretarial Studies; Tourism; Transport Management); **Social Services** (Social and Community Services; Social Work); **Technology** (Computer Engineering; Computer Networks; Computer Science; Information Management; Information Technology; Management; Software Engineering)

Further Information: Also following Campuses: Itaim Bibi, Liberdade, Morumbi, Ponte Estaiada, Santo Amaro, Vergueiro, Vila Mariana I and II; HOVET - Veterinary Hospital; Advanced Teaching Units (Polos)

History: Founded 1968.

Main Language(s) of Instruction: Portuguese

Degrees and Diplomas: *Tecnólogo*; *Bacharelado*; *Licenciatura*; *Especialização/Aperfeiçoamento*: **Architecture; Art Education; Art Therapy; Biomedicine; Business Administration; Business Education; Cinema and Television; Civil Law; Commercial Law; Communication Studies; Criminal Law; Design; E-Business/Commerce; Economics; Educational Administration; Educational Psychology; Educational Sciences; Embryology and Reproduction Biology; Energy Engineering; Environmental Engineering; Fiscal Law; Foreign Languages Education; Graphic Design; Health Administration; Health Education; Health Sciences; Higher Education Teacher Training; History; Humanities and Social Science Education; Information Technology; Interior Design; Journalism; Labour Law; Latin American Studies; Law; Maintenance Technology; Management; Marketing; Mass Communication; Microbiology; Midwifery; Music; Neurosciences; Nursing; Nutrition; Occupational Health; Oncology; Orthopaedics; Paediatrics; Petroleum and Gas Engineering; Physical Education; Physiology; Portuguese; Preschool Education; Primary Education; Private Law; Public Health; Radio and Television Broadcasting; Radiology; Rehabilitation and Therapy; Safety Engineering; Social Work; Software Engineering; Special Education; Sports; Sports Management; Taxation; Translation and Interpretation.** *Mestrado*: **Administration; Business Administration; Commercial Law; Health Sciences; Journalism; Town Planning.** Also MBA and Master of Business Information System (MBIS)

Student Services: Library

Last Updated: 02/02/16

UNIVERSITY CENTRE FACEX

Centro Universitário FACEX (UNIFACEX)

Rua Orlando Silva, 2897 - Capim Macio, Natal, Rio Grande do Norte 59080-020

Tel: +55(84) 3235-1415

Fax: +55(84) 3235-1433

EMail: secretaria@facex.com.br; callcenter@facex.com.br

Website: http://www.facex.com.br/superior

Reitor: Raymundo Gomes Vieira EMail: vieira@facex.com.br

Pró-Reitor Acadêmico: Ronald Fábio de Paiva Campo

Pró-Reitora Administrativa: Candysse Medeiros de Figueiredo

Course

Accountancy (Accountancy); **Administration** (Administration); **Architecture and Urbanism** (Architecture; Town Planning); **Biology** (Biology); **Civil Engineering** (Civil Engineering); **Graduate Studies** (Business Administration; Education; Environmental Studies; Health Sciences; Law; Management); **Law** (Law); **Nursing** (Nursing); **Nutrition** (Nutrition); **Pedagogy** (Pedagogy); **Physical Education** (Physical Education); **Production Engineering** (Production Engineering); **Psychology** (Psychology); **Secretarial Studies** (Secretarial Studies); **Social Services** (Social and Community Services); **Technological Studies** (Business and Commerce; Computer Networks; Finance; Hotel Management; Human Resources; Information Technology; International Business; Marketing; Petroleum and Gas Engineering; Public Administration; Transport Management); **Tourism** (Tourism)

Further Information: Also Campus Imaculada Conceição

History: Founded 1981. Formerly known as Faculdade de Ciências, Cultura e Extensão do Rio Grande do Norte.

Main Language(s) of Instruction: Portuguese

Degrees and Diplomas: *Tecnólogo*; *Bacharelado*; *Licenciatura*; *Especialização/Aperfeiçoamento*: **Accountancy; Civil Law; Education of the Handicapped; Educational Psychology; Environmental Studies; Gerontology; Health Education; Health Sciences; Higher Education Teacher Training; Labour Law; Law; Management; Microbiology; Nursing; Occupational Health; Parasitology; Pharmacology; Protective Services; Public Administration; Public Health; Social and Community Services; Special Education; Toxicology.** Also MBA in Business Administration, Media Studies, Management, Finance, Taxation, Marketing

Student Services: Library

Last Updated: 26/06/15

UNIVERSITY CENTRE OF ANÁPOLIS

Centro Universitário de Anápolis (UNIEVANGÉLICA)

Avenida Universitária Km. 3,5, Cidade Universitária, Anápolis, Goiás 75070-290

Tel: +55(62) 3310-6600

Fax: +55(62) 3318-1120

EMail: unievangelica@unievangelica.edu.br; helia@unievangelica.edu.br

Website: http://www.unievangelica.edu.br

Chancellor: Geraldo Henrique Ferreira Espíndola

Provost: Carlos Hassel Mendes da Silva

Course

Administration (Administration); **Biology** (Biology); **Civil Engineering** (Civil Engineering); **Computer Science** (Computer Science); **Information Systems** (Information Management); **Law** (Law); **Mathematics** (Mathematics); **Mechanical Engineering** (Mechanical Engineering); **Medicine** (Medicine); **Modern Languages** (English; Portuguese; Spanish); **Nursing** (Nursing); **Odontology** (Dentistry); **Pedagogy** (Pedagogy); **Pharmacy** (Pharmacy); **Physical Education** (Physical Education); **Physical Therapy** (Physical Therapy); **Technological Studies** (Cosmetology; Graphic Design; Maintenance Technology; Radiology; Transport Management)

History: Founded 1961. Supported by Evangelical Education Association (AEE). Acquired present title 2004.

Main Language(s) of Instruction: Portuguese

Accrediting Agency: Ministry of Education.

Degrees and Diplomas: *Tecnólogo*; *Bacharelado*; *Licenciatura*; *Especialização/Aperfeiçoamento*: **Accountancy; Business Administration; Civil Law; Clinical Psychology; Criminal Law; Dentistry; Education; Educational Psychology; Environmental Management; Environmental Studies; Finance; Food Technology; Foreign Languages Education; Health Sciences; Higher Education Teacher Training; Human Rights; Information Technology; Labour Law; Law; Management; Marketing; Mathematics Education; Nursing; Occupational Therapy; Orthodontics; Pedagogy; Pharmacology; Pharmacy; Physical Therapy; Primary Education; Production Engineering; Safety Engineering; Taxation.** *Mestrado*: **Environmental Studies; Social Sciences; Technology.** Also MBA.

Student Services: Library

Last Updated: 01/07/15

UNIVERSITY CENTRE OF ARARAQUARA

Centro Universitário de Araraquara (UNIARA)

Rua Carlos Gomes, n.° 1338, Centro,
Araraquara, São Paulo 14801-340
Tel: +55(16) 3201-7100
Fax: +55(16) 3232-1921
EMail: uniara@uniara.com.br; marketing@uniara.com.br
Website: http://www.uniara.com.br

Reitor: Luiz Felipe Cabral Mauro (1997-)

Pró-Reitoria Administrativa: Fernando Soares Mauro

Course

Administration (Administration); **Advertising and Publicity** (Advertising and Publicity); **Agronomy** (Agronomy); **Architecture and Urbanism** (Architecture; Town Planning); **Bioenergetic Engineering** (Bioengineering; Energy Engineering); **Biology** (Biology); **Biomedicine** (Biomedicine); **Civil Engineering** (Civil Engineering); **Computer Engineering** (Computer Engineering); **Design** (Design; Fashion Design); **Economics** (Economics); **Electrical Engineering** (Electrical Engineering); **Graduate Studies** (Business Administration; Civil Law; Commercial Law; Computer Science; Criminal Law; Development Studies; Ecology; Environmental Management; Finance; Gerontology; Human Resources; Industrial Management; International Business; International Relations; Labour Law; Law; Management; Marketing; Nutrition; Orthodontics; Physical Education; Physical Therapy; Production Engineering; Safety Engineering; Sports; Surgery; Tourism); **Information Systems** (Information Sciences); **Journalism** (Journalism); **Law** (Law); **Mechatronics Engineering** (Electronic Engineering; Mechanical Engineering); **Medicine** (Medicine); **Nursing** (Nursing); **Nutrition** (Nutrition); **Occupational Therapy** (Occupational Therapy); **Odontology** (Dentistry); **Pedagogy** (Education; Pedagogy); **Pharmacy** (Pharmacy); **Physical Education** (Physical Education); **Physical Therapy** (Physical Therapy); **Production Engineering** (Production Engineering); **Psychology** (Psychology); **Technological Studies** (Business Administration; Computer Science; Cosmetology; Fashion Design; Finance; Human Resources; Marketing)

History: Founded 1968. Acquired present status 1997.

Academic Year: February to December

Admission Requirements: Secondary school certificate and SAT examination (vestibular)

Main Language(s) of Instruction: Portuguese

Accrediting Agency: Ministry of Education.

Degrees and Diplomas: *Tecnólogo*; *Bacharelado*; *Licenciatura*; *Especialização/Aperfeiçoamento*: **Acupuncture; Business Administration; Cosmetology; Dentistry; Environmental Studies; Finance; Gerontology; Human Resources; Management; Nutrition; Physical Therapy; Psychology.** *Mestrado*: **Biotechnology; Dentistry; Education; Environmental Studies; Orthodontics; Production Engineering; Regional Studies.** *Doutorado*: **Biotechnology; Environmental Studies; Regional Studies.** Also MBA.

Student Services: Canteen, Cultural Activities, Facilities for disabled people, Health Services, Library

Publications: Revista UNIARA

Last Updated: 02/07/15

UNIVERSITY CENTRE OF BARRA MANSA

Centro Universitário de Barra Mansa (UBM)

Rua Vereador Pinho de Carvalho, 267, Centro,
Barra Mansa, Rio de Janeiro 27330-550
Tel: +55(24) 3325-0222
Fax: +55(24) 3323-3690
EMail: ubm@ubm.br, secretaria.geral@ubm.br
Website: http://www.ubm.br

Reitor: Leandro Álvaro Chaves
Tel: +55(24) 3325-0222 EMail: reitor@ubm.br

Pro-Reitor Administration: Feres Osrraia Nader
Tel: +55(24) 3325-0222 EMail: pro.adm@ubm.br

Course

Accountancy (Accountancy); **Administration** (Administration); **Arts and Humanities** (Arts and Humanities; English; Journalism; Spanish); **Automation and Control Engineering** (Automation and Control Engineering); **Biological and Life Sciences** (Biological and Life Sciences); **Computer Engineering** (Computer Graphics; Computer Networks; Data Processing; Software Engineering); **Computer Science** (Computer Science); **Educational Sciences** (Pedagogy); **Engineering** (Civil Engineering; Electrical Engineering; Mechanical Engineering; Petroleum and Gas Engineering; Production Engineering); **Geography** (Geography (Human)); **Graduate Studies** (Acupuncture; Art Education; Art History; Biological and Life Sciences; Communication Studies; Data Processing; Dietetics; Economics; Education; Educational Administration; Electronic Engineering; English; Environmental Management; Environmental Studies; Finance; Gerontology; History; Human Resources; Industrial and Organizational Psychology; Industrial Management; Information Technology; Literature; Management; Marketing; Mathematics Education; Mechanical Engineering; Nursing; Nutrition; Philosophy; Physical Education; Physical Therapy; Portuguese; Public Administration; Public Health; Rehabilitation and Therapy; Spanish; Statistics; Theatre; Transport Management); **History** (History); **Law** (Private Law; Public Law); **Mathematics** (Mathematics); **Music** (Music); **Nursing** (Nursing); **Nutrition** (Nutrition); **Pedagogy** (Pedagogy; Teacher Training); **Pharmacy** (Pharmacy); **Physical Education** (Physical Education); **Physical Therapy** (Physical Therapy); **Psychology** (Psychology); **Social Communication** (Communication Studies); **Technological Studies** (Environmental Management; Human Resources; Industrial Management; Safety Engineering; Tourism; Transport Management); **Veterinary Medicine** (Veterinary Science); **Visual Arts** (Painting and Drawing; Photography; Sculpture)

Further Information: Also Cicuta Campus.

History: Founded 1961.

Academic Year: February to December

Admission Requirements: High School Diploma and Vestibular (university entrance exam)

Main Language(s) of Instruction: Portugese

Accrediting Agency: Ministry of Education.

Degrees and Diplomas: *Tecnólogo*; *Bacharelado*; *Licenciatura*; *Especialização/Aperfeiçoamento*: **Accountancy; Acupuncture; Art Education; Art History; Biological and Life Sciences; Business Administration; Communication Studies; Community Health; Data Processing; Dietetics; Education; Educational Administration; Educational Psychology; Electronic**

Engineering; English; Environmental Management; Environmental Studies; Gerontology; History; Human Resources; Industrial and Organizational Psychology; Industrial Management; Information Technology; Literature; Management; Marketing; Mathematics Education; Mechanical Engineering; Nursing; Nutrition; Philosophy; Physical Education; Physical Therapy; Public Law; Spanish; Theatre; Transport Management. Also MBA.

Student Services: Academic Counselling, Canteen, Cultural Activities, Facilities for disabled people, Health Services, Language Laboratory, Library, Sports Facilities

Publications: Caderno de Cultura Referencia; Revista Cientifica

Last Updated: 03/07/15

UNIVERSITY CENTRE OF BRASILIA

Centro Universitário de Brasília (UNICEUB)
Eqn. 707/907 Conjunto C, Campus do CEUB, Asa Norte, Brasília, DF 70790-075
Tel: +55(61) 3966-1200
Fax: +55(61) 3273-0503
EMail: central.atendimento@uniceub.br
Website: http://www.uniceub.br

Reitor: Getúlio Américo Moreira Lopes

Pró-Reitora Acadêmica: Elizabeth Regina Lopes Manzur

Course

Accountancy (Accountancy); **Administration** (Administration); **Advertising and Publicity** (Advertising and Publicity); **Architecture and Urbanism** (Architecture; Urban Studies); **Arts and Humanities** (Arts and Humanities); **Biology** (Biology); **Biomedicine** (Biomedicine); **Civil Engineering** (Civil Engineering); **Communication and Marketing** (Communication Studies; Marketing); **Computer Engineering** (Computer Engineering); **Computer Science** (Computer Science); **Geography** (Geography); **Graduate Studies** (Commercial Law; Communication Studies; Criminal Law; Environmental Studies; Genetics; Higher Education; History; Immunology; Information Technology; International Relations; Labour Law; Law; Management; Marketing; Physical Therapy; Portuguese; Psychoanalysis; Psychology; Public Health; Public Law; Social Studies; Software Engineering); **History** (History); **International Relations** (International Relations); **Journalism** (Journalism); **Law** (Law); **Nursing** (Nursing); **Nutrition** (Nutrition); **Pedagogy** (Pedagogy); **Physical Education** (Physical Education); **Physical Therapy** (Physical Therapy); **Psychology** (Psychology); **Technological Studies** (Management; Systems Analysis)

Further Information: Also Distance Education

History: Founded 1968 as Centro de Ensino Unificado de Brasília. Acquired present title and status 1990.

Main Language(s) of Instruction: Portuguese

Accrediting Agency: Ministry of Education.

Degrees and Diplomas: *Tecnólogo*; *Bacharelado*; *Licenciatura*; *Especialização/Aperfeiçoamento*: **Business Administration; Civil Engineering; Commercial Law; Communication Studies; Environmental Studies; Higher Education Teacher Training; History; Information Technology; Journalism; Labour Law; Law; Management; Marketing; Physical Therapy; Psychoanalysis; Psychology; Software Engineering; Transport Management.** *Mestrado*: **Law; Psychology.** *Doutorado*: **Law.** Also MBA

Student Services: Library

Last Updated: 03/07/15

UNIVERSITY CENTRE OF BRUSQUE

Centro Universitário de Brusque (UNIFEBE)
Rua Dorval Luz 123, Bairro Santa Terezinha, PO Box 1501, Brusque, Santa Catarina 88352-400
Tel: +55(47) 3211-7000
Fax: +55(47) 3211-7000
EMail: reitoria@unifebe.edu.br
Website: http://www.unifebe.edu.br

Rector: Günther Lother Pertschy (2011-)
EMail: reitoria@unifebe.edu.br

Vice-reitor: Alessandro Fazzino
Tel: +55(47) 3211-7231 EMail: vice@unifebe.edu.br

Course

Accountancy (Accountancy); **Administration** (Administration); **Business Administration** (Business Administration); **Commercial Management** (Management); **Fashion Design** (Fashion Design); **Graduate Studies** (Business Administration; Fashion Design; Textile Design); **History** (History); **Industrial Process Technology-Electromechanics** (Hydraulic Engineering; Industrial Engineering); **Information Sciences** (Information Sciences); **Law** (Law); **Literature** (Literature); **Logistics** (Transport Management); **Pedagogy** (Pedagogy); **Physical Education** (Physical Education); **Production Engineering** (Production Engineering); **Real Estate** (Real Estate); **Textile Production** (Textile Technology)

History: Founded 1973. Acquired present status 2003.

Academic Year: February to December

Admission Requirements: Secondary school diploma and entrance examination

Main Language(s) of Instruction: Portuguese

Accrediting Agency: Ministry of Education.

Degrees and Diplomas: *Tecnólogo*; *Bacharelado*; *Licenciatura*; *Especialização/Aperfeiçoamento*: **Business Administration.** Also MBA.

Student Services: Academic Counselling, Canteen, Facilities for disabled people

Publications: Revista da Unifebe

Last Updated: 06/07/15

UNIVERSITY CENTRE OF CARATINGA

Centro Universitário de Caratinga (UNEC)
Avenida Moacyr de Mattos 87, 1° Andar, Centro, Caratinga, Minas Gerais 35300-047
Tel: +55(33) 3329-4500
EMail: vestibular@funec.br
Website: http://www.unec.edu.br

Reitor: Antônio Fonseca da Silva
Tel: +55(33) 3329-4509 EMail: reitoria@funec.br

Course

Accountancy (Accountancy); **Actuarial Sciences** (Actuarial Science); **Administrative Sciences** (Administration); **Arts and Humanities** (Arts and Humanities; English; French; Portuguese; Spanish); **Biological Sciences** (Biological and Life Sciences); **Chemistry** (Chemistry); **Civil Engineering** (Civil Engineering); **Economics** (Economics); **Fonaudiology** (Speech Therapy and Audiology); **Geography** (Geography); **Graduate Studies** *(Lato Sensu)* (Business Administration; Educational Psychology; Environmental Management; Environmental Studies; Health Sciences; Nutrition; Pharmacology; Physical Education; Public Health; Rehabilitation and Therapy); **Healt and Environmental Engineering** (Environmental Engineering); **History** (History); **Industrial and Technological Production Engineering** (Production Engineering); **Information Systmes** (Information Technology); **Mathematics** (Mathematics); **Medicine** (Medicine); **Nursing** (Nursing); **Nutrition** (Nutrition); **Pedagogy** (Pedagogy); **Pharmacy** (Pharmacy); **Phsyical Therapy** (Physical Therapy); **Physical Education** (Physical Education); **Physics** (Physics); **Psychology** (Psychology); **Religious Studies** (Religious Studies); **Teacher Training** (Teacher Training)

History: Founded 1963 as FUNEC. Acquired present status 2009.

Main Language(s) of Instruction: Portuguese

Accrediting Agency: Ministry of Education.

Degrees and Diplomas: *Bacharelado*; *Licenciatura*; *Especialização/Aperfeiçoamento*: **Business Administration; Educational Psychology; Environmental Management; Environmental Studies; Finance; Health Sciences; Nutrition; Physical Therapy; Psychiatry and Mental Health; Public Administration; Public Health; Rehabilitation and Therapy.** *Mestrado*: **Environmental Studies.**

Student Services: Library

Last Updated: 06/07/15

UNIVERSITY CENTRE OF CERRADO PATROCÍNIO

Centro Universitário do Cerrado Patrocínio (UNICERP)

Av. Liria Terezinha Lassi Capuano 466, Campus Universitário, Patrocínio, Minas Gerais 38740-000
Tel: +55(34) 3839-3737
Fax: +55(34) 3839-3737
EMail: unicerp@unicerp.edu.br
Website: http://www.unicerp.edu.br

Reitora: Iêda Pereira de Magalhães Martins
EMail: reitoria@unicerp.edu.br

Course

Accountancy (Accountancy); **Administration** (Administration); **Agribusiness** (Agricultural Business); **Agronomy** (Agronomy); **Biology** (Biological and Life Sciences); **Information Systems** (Information Sciences); **Interior Design** (Interior Design); **Literature** (Literature); **Mathematics** (Mathematics); **Nursing** (Nursing); **Nutrition** (Nutrition); **Pedagogy** (Education; Pedagogy); **Phonoaudiology** (Speech Therapy and Audiology); **Physical Education** (Physical Education); **Physiotherapy** (Physical Therapy); **Psychology** (Psychology)

History: Founded 1997 as Faculdades Integradas de Patrocínio. Acquired present status and title 2005.

Main Language(s) of Instruction: Portuguese

Accrediting Agency: Ministry of Education.

Degrees and Diplomas: *Tecnólogo*; *Bacharelado*; *Licenciatura*; *Especialização/Aperfeiçoamento*: **Accountancy; Business Administration; Environmental Studies; Finance.**

Student Services: Library

Last Updated: 09/07/15

UNIVERSITY CENTRE OF ESPIRITO SANTO

Centro Universitário do Espirito Santo (UNESC)

Av. Fioravante Rossi, 2930, Bairro Martinelli, Colatina, Espírito Santo 29703-900
Tel: +55(27) 3723-3000 +55(27) 2101-3000
Fax: +55(27) 3723-3000 +55(27) 2101-3000
EMail: revista@unesc.br; fchiepe@unesc.br
Website: http://www.unesc.br

Reitor: Pergentino de Vasconcelos Junior

Course

Accountancy (Accountancy); **Administration** (Administration); **Architecure and Town Planning** (Town Planning); **Civil Engineering** (Civil Engineering); **Cosmetology** (Cosmetology); **Design** (Fashion Design; Interior Design); **Electrical Engineering** (Electrical Engineering; Telecommunications Engineering); **Graduate Studies** (Accountancy; Business Administration; Civil Law; Commercial Law; Computer Networks; Criminal Law; Gerontology; Health Administration; Health Sciences; Higher Education; Industrial and Organizational Psychology; Labour Law; Nutrition; Physical Therapy; Public Health; Public Law; Software Engineering; Water Management); **Information Systems** (Information Technology); **Law** (Law); **Mechanical Engineering** (Mechanical Engineering); **Medicine** (Medicine); **Nursing** (Nursing); **Nutrition** (Nutrition); **Pedagogy** (Pedagogy); **Pharmacy** (Pharmacy); **Physical Education** *(Bacharelado & Licenciatura)* (Physical Education); **Physical Therapy** (Physical Therapy); **Teacher Training** (Teacher Training); **Veterinary Medicine** (Veterinary Science)

Further Information: Also Campus in Serra.

History: Founded 1997. Acquired present status 2000.

Main Language(s) of Instruction: Portuguese

Accrediting Agency: Ministry of Education.

Degrees and Diplomas: *Tecnólogo*; *Bacharelado*; *Licenciatura*; *Especialização/Aperfeiçoamento*: **Civil Law; Higher Education Teacher Training; Law.** *Mestrado*: **Business Administration; Health Sciences.** Also MBA.

Student Services: Library

Last Updated: 10/07/15

UNIVERSITY CENTRE OF FINE ARTS OF SAO PAULO

Centro Universitário Belas Artes de São Paulo (FEBASP)

Rua Dr. Álvaro Alvin, 76 Vila Mariana, São Paulo, São Paulo 4018-010
Tel: +55(11) 5576-7300
Fax: +55(11) 5549-7985
EMail: paulo.cardim@belasartes.br
Website: http://www.belasartes.br

Reitor: Paulo Antonio Gomes Cardim
EMail: paulo.cardim@belasartes.br

Course

Advertising and Publicity (Advertising and Publicity); **Architecture and Town Planning** (Architecture; Town Planning); **Fashion Design** (Fashion Design); **Graduate Studies** (Architecture; Ceramic Art; Cinema and Television; Communication Studies; Design; Display and Stage Design; Educational Administration; Higher Education; Human Rights; International Relations; Museum Studies; Photography; Public Relations; Video); **Graphic Design** (Graphic Design); **Interior Design** (Interior Design); **International Relations** (International Relations); **Public Relations** (Public Relations); **Radio and TV** (Radio and Television Broadcasting); **Teacher Training** (Teacher Training); **Visual Arts** (Visual Arts)

History: Founded 1925. Acquired present status and title 2002.

Main Language(s) of Instruction: Portuguese

Degrees and Diplomas: *Bacharelado*; *Licenciatura*; *Especialização/Aperfeiçoamento*: **Architectural Restoration; Art History; Cinema and Television; Design; Fashion Design; Film; Landscape Architecture; Museum Studies; Painting and Drawing; Town Planning.**

Student Services: Library

Last Updated: 24/06/15

UNIVERSITY CENTRE OF FORMIGA

Centro Universitario de Formiga (UNIFORMG)

Avenida Dr. Arnaldo de Senna 328, Bairro Água Vermelha, Formiga, Minas Gerais 37570-000
Tel: +55(37) 3329-1400
EMail: uniformg@uniformg.edu.br
Website: http://www.uniformg.edu.br

Reitor: Marco Antonio de Souza Leão
EMail: reitor@uniformg.edu.br

Course

Accountancy (Accountancy); **Administration** (Administration); **Agricultural Engineering** (Agricultural Engineering); **Architecture and Urbanism** (Architecture; Town Planning); **Arts and Humanities** (Arts and Humanities; English; Portuguese); **Biological Science** (Biological and Life Sciences); **Biomedicina** (Biomedicine); **Chemical Engineering** (Chemical Engineering); **Chemistry** (Chemistry); **Civil Engineering** (Civil Engineering); **Computer Science** (Computer Science); **Environmental Engineering** (Environmental Engineering); **Graduate Studies** (Accountancy; Business Administration; Marketing); **Health Administration** (Health Administration); **Law** (Law); **Library Science** (Library Science); **Marketing** (Marketing); **Nursing** (Nursing); **Nutrition** (Nutrition); **Pedagogy** (Pedagogy); **Physical Education** *(Licenciatura)* (Physical Education); **Physical Therapy** (Physical Therapy); **Production Engineering** (Production Engineering); **Social Service** (Social and Community Services); **Veterinary Science** (Veterinary Science)

History: Founded 1974.

Main Language(s) of Instruction: Portuguese

Accrediting Agency: Ministry of Education.

Degrees and Diplomas: *Bacharelado*; *Licenciatura*; *Especialização/Aperfeiçoamento*: **Business Administration; Human Resources; Management; Marketing.** Also MBA.

Student Services: Library

Last Updated: 06/07/15

UNIVERSITY CENTRE OF GOIAS

Centro Universitário de Goiás (UNI-ANHANGÜERA)
Av. João Candido de Oliveira, N° 115, Cidade Jardim,
Goiânia, Goiás 74423-115
Tel: +55(62) 3246-1404
Fax: +55(62) 3246-1444
EMail: anhanguera@anhanguera.edu.br
Website: http://www.anhanguera.edu.br

Reitor: Jovenny Sebastião Cândido de Oliveira

Vice-Reitor: Raymar Leite Santos

Course

Accountancy (Accountancy); **Administration** (Administration; Public Administration); **Advertising and Publicity** (Advertising and Publicity); **Agronomy** (Agricultural Business; Agricultural Engineering; Agronomy); **Architecture and Town Planning** (Architecture; Town Planning); **Biological Sciences** (Biological and Life Sciences); **Business Administration** (Business Administration; Human Resources; Information Technology); **Chemistry** (Chemistry); **Civil Engineering** (Civil Engineering); **Computer Engineering** (Computer Engineering); **Economics** (Economics); **Electrical Engineering** (Electrical Engineering); **Law** (Law); **Pedagogy** (Education; Pedagogy); **Pharmacy** (Pharmacy); **Transport Management** (Transport Management)

History: Founded 1973 as Faculdade Anhangüera. Acquired present status and title 2004.

Main Language(s) of Instruction: Portuguese

Accrediting Agency: Ministry of Education.

Degrees and Diplomas: *Tecnólogo*; *Bacharelado*; *Licenciatura*; *Especialização/Aperfeiçoamento*: **Accountancy; Business Administration; Civil Law; Criminal Law; Finance; Human Resources; Labour Law; Law; Management; Public Law.** *Mestrado.* Also MBA.

Student Services: Library

Last Updated: 06/07/15

UNIVERSITY CENTRE OF ITAJUBÁ

Centro Universitário de Itajubá (FEPI)
Avenida Doutor Antônio Braga Filho 687, Varginha,
Itajubá, Minas Gerais 37501-002
Tel: +55(35) 3629-8400
Fax: +55(35) 3629-8400
EMail: universitas@fepi.br
Website: http://www.fepi.br

Reitora: Cidélia Maria Barbosa Lima EMail: reitoria@fepi.br

Pró-Reitoria Acadêmica: Magda Cristina Nascimento Rochael EMail: proreitoria.acad@fepi.br

Course

Automation and Control Engineering (Automation and Control Engineering); **Biological Sciences** (Biological and Life Sciences); **Civil Engineering** (Civil Engineering); **Cosmetology** (Cosmetology); **Electrical Engineering** (Electrical Engineering); **Industrial Automation** (Automation and Control Engineering); **Information Systems** (Information Sciences; Information Technology); **Law** (Law); **Mechanical Engineering** (Mechanical Engineering; Metal Techniques); **Mechanical Equipment and Maintenance** (Mechanical Equipment and Maintenance); **Modern Languages** (English; Portuguese); **Pedagogy** (Pedagogy; Teacher Training); **Pharmacy** (Pharmacy); **Physical Education** (Physical Education); **Physical Therapy** (Physical Therapy); **Production Engineering** (Production Engineering); **Psychology** (Psychology); **Veterinary Medicine** (Veterinary Science)

Further Information: Also Brasópolis, Borda da Mata and Natércia Units.

History: Founded 1965.

Main Language(s) of Instruction: Portuguese

Degrees and Diplomas: *Tecnólogo*; *Bacharelado*; *Licenciatura*; *Especialização/Aperfeiçoamento*: **Business Administration; Clinical Psychology; Educational Administration; Higher Education Teacher Training; Human Resources; Law; Physical Therapy; Safety Engineering.** Also MBA.

Last Updated: 07/07/15

UNIVERSITY CENTRE OF JALES

Centro Universitário de Jales (UNIJALES)
Avenida Francisco Jales 1851, Centro, Jales, São Paulo 15700-000
Tel: +55(17) 3622-1620
EMail: unijales@unijales.edu.br
Website: http://www.unijales.edu.br

Reitor: Silvio Luiz Lofego

Vice-Reitora Acadêmica: Maria Christina F. S. Bernardo

Course

Accountancy (Accountancy); **Administration** (Administration); **Arts and Humanities** (Arts and Humanities; Portuguese; Spanish); **Arts and Humanities** (Arts and Humanities; English; Portuguese); **Biological and Life Sciences** (Biological and Life Sciences); **Geography** (Geography); **Graduate Studies** (Accountancy; Agriculture; Business Administration; Dance; Education; Educational Administration; Educational Psychology; English; Environmental Management; Finance; Fine Arts; History; Information Management; Information Sciences; Literature; Mathematics Education; Music; Physical Education; Portuguese; Public Administration; Public Health; Social and Community Services; Spanish; Sports; Sports Management); **History** (History); **Information Systems** (Information Sciences); **Mathematics** (Mathematics); **Nursing** (Nursing); **Pedagogy** (Pedagogy); **Pharmacy** (Pharmacy); **Physical Education** (Physical Education); **Physical Therapy** (Physical Therapy); **Social Services** (Social and Community Services); **Tourism** (Tourism); **Visual Arts - Art Education** (Art Education; Visual Arts)

History: Founded 1970.

Main Language(s) of Instruction: Portuguese

Accrediting Agency: Ministry of Education.

Degrees and Diplomas: *Bacharelado*; *Licenciatura*; *Especialização/Aperfeiçoamento*: **Administration; Art Education; Business Administration; Computer Networks; Cosmetology; Educational Administration; Educational Psychology; Environmental Management; Finance; Higher Education Teacher Training; History; Human Resources; Literature; Mathematics Education; Music Education; Nursing; Oncology; Pedagogy; Physical Education; Portuguese; Public Administration; Public Health; Social Sciences; Special Education.** Also MBA.

Student Services: Library

Last Updated: 07/07/15

UNIVERSITY CENTRE OF JOÃO PESSOA

Centro Universitário de João Pessoa (UNIPE)
Campus do Unipê BR 230 - Km 22, Água Fria,
João Pessoa, Paraíba 58053-000
Tel: +55(83) 2106-9200
Fax: +55(83) 3231-1130
EMail: info@unipe.br
Website: http://www.unipe.br

Reitor: Ana Flávia Pereira da Fonseca
Tel: +55(83) 2106-9202/9240 EMail: reitoria@unipe.br

Pró-Reitoria de Ensino de Graduação: Paulo de Tarso Costa Henriques EMail: preg@unipe.br

Course

Accountancy (Accountancy); **Administration** (Administration); **Architecture and Town Planning** (Architecture; Town Planning); **Civil Engineering** (Civil Engineering); **Computer Science** (Computer Science); **Fashion Design** (Fashion Design); **Fonaudiology** (Speech Therapy and Audiology); **Graduate Studies** *(MBA)* (Business Administration; Computer Science); **Information Technology Management** (Information Technology); **Law** (Law); **Medicine** (Medicine); **Nursing** (Nursing); **Odontology** (Dentistry); **Physical Education** (Physical Education); **Physical Therapy** (Physical Therapy); **Psychology** (Psychology); **Systems for Internet** (Computer Science)

Further Information: Also distance Education

History: Founded 1997.

Main Language(s) of Instruction: Portuguese

Accrediting Agency: Ministry of Education.

Degrees and Diplomas: *Tecnólogo*; *Bacharelado*; *Especialização/Aperfeiçoamento*: **Accountancy; Administrative Law;**

Architecture; Civil Law; Clinical Psychology; Commercial Law; Computer Engineering; Criminal Law; Criminology; Dentistry; Educational Administration; Educational Research; Environmental Studies; Fashion Design; Information Technology; Interior Design; International Law; International Relations; Labour Law; Law; Nursing; Periodontics; Physical Education; Physical Therapy; Psychoanalysis; Psychology; Public Health; Public Law; Safety Engineering; Social and Preventive Medicine; Software Engineering; Speech Therapy and Audiology; Sports; Stomatology; Town Planning. *Mestrado*: **Law.** Also MBA.

Student Services: Library

Last Updated: 08/07/15

UNIVERSITY CENTRE OF LAVRAS

Centro Universitário de Lavras (UNILAVRAS)

Rua Padre José Poggel, 506, Centenário, Minas Gerais 37200000
Tel: +55(800) 283-2833
EMail: reitoria@unilavras.edu.br
Website: http://www.unilavras.edu.br

Reitora: Christiane Amaral Lunkes Argenta

Diretor Geral: Paulo Toshio Abe

Course

Architecture and Town Planning (Architecture; Town Planning); **Biology** (Biology); **Business and Commerce** (Business and Commerce); **Civil Engineering** (Civil Engineering); **Graduate Studies** (Biological and Life Sciences; Chemistry; Pedagogy; Teacher Training); **Industrial Chemistry** (Industrial Chemistry); **Law** (Law); **Nursing** (Nursing); **Nutrition** (Nutrition); **Odontology** (Dentistry); **Pedagogy** (Pedagogy); **Pharmacy** (Pharmacy); **Physiotherapy** (Physical Therapy); **Production Engineering** (Production Engineering); **Psychology** (Psychology)

History: Founded 1968.

Main Language(s) of Instruction: Portuguese

Degrees and Diplomas: *Tecnólogo*; *Bacharelado*; *Licenciatura*; *Especialização/Aperfeiçoamento*: **Business Administration; Dentistry; Finance; Management; Orthodontics; Public Administration; Safety Engineering.**

Student Services: Library

Last Updated: 08/07/15

UNIVERSITY CENTRE OF LESTE MINAS GERAIS

Centro Universitário do Leste de Minas Gerais (UNILESTEMG)

Av Tancredo de Almeida Neves, 3500, Bairro Universitário, Coronel Fabriciano, Minas Gerais 35170-056
Tel: +55(31) 3846-5500
Fax: +55(31) 3846-5524
EMail: unilestemg@unilestemg.br
Website: http://www.unilestemg.br

Reitor: Genésio Zeferino da Silva Filho
Tel: +55(31) 3846-7901 EMail: reitoria@unilestemg.br

School

Business Administration (Accountancy; Administration; Advertising and Publicity; Business Administration; Journalism); **Educational and Arts and Humanity** (English; Geography; History; Literature; Pedagogy; Philosophy; Portuguese); **Engineering** (Automation and Control Engineering; Chemical Engineering; Civil Engineering; Computer Networks; Computer Science; Electrical Engineering; Environmental Engineering; Materials Engineering; Mechanical Engineering; Metallurgical Engineering; Production Engineering); **Health Sciences** (Biological and Life Sciences; Health Sciences; Nursing; Nutrition; Pharmacy; Physical Education; Physical Therapy; Psychology); **Law** (Law)

Course

Graduate Studies *(Especialização)* (Accountancy; Administration; Architecture; Art Management; Automation and Control Engineering; Biological and Life Sciences; Biomedicine; Business Administration; Business and Commerce; Business Education; Clinical Psychology; Communication Studies; Dental Technology; Ecology; Education; Educational Administration; Educational Psychology; Engineering; English; Environmental Management; Finance; Gerontology; Health Administration; Higher Education; Human Resources; Industrial and Organizational Psychology; Industrial Engineering; Law; Literacy Education; Literature; Marketing; Mathematics Education; Metal Techniques; Metallurgical Engineering; Nursing; Nutrition; Orthodontics; Pedagogy; Periodontics; Pharmacology; Physical Therapy; Psychiatry and Mental Health; Psychoanalysis; Psychology; Public Administration; Public Health; Public Law; Safety Engineering; Sports; Telecommunications Engineering; Transport Management; Water Management)

Further Information: Also Ipatinga Campus and Distance Education.

History: Founded 1972. Acquired present title and Status 2000.

Academic Year: February to December

Admission Requirements: High school diploma

Fees: 3,000 per semester (depending on course) (Brazilian Real)

Main Language(s) of Instruction: Portuguese

Accrediting Agency: Ministry of Education.

Degrees and Diplomas: *Tecnólogo*; *Bacharelado*; *Licenciatura*; *Especialização/Aperfeiçoamento*: **Clinical Psychology; Dentistry; Ecology; Educational Psychology; Environmental Management; Industrial Engineering; Industrial Management; Law; Literacy Education; Maintenance Technology; Metal Techniques; Nursing; Periodontics; Pharmacology; Physical Therapy; Psychology; Public Health; Safety Engineering.** *Mestrado*: **Business Administration; Industrial Engineering.** Also MBA.

Student Services: Academic Counselling, Canteen, Cultural Activities, Facilities for disabled people, Health Services, Language Laboratory, Library, Social Counselling, Sports Facilities

Publications: Doxa (Scientific Journal)

Last Updated: 10/07/15

UNIVERSITY CENTRE OF LINS

Centro Universitário de Lins (UNILINS)

Avenida Nicolau Zarvos, 1925, Jardim Aeroporto, Lins, São Paulo 16401-371
Tel: +55(14) 3533-3200
Fax: +55(14) 3533-3248
EMail: unilins@unilins.edu.br
Website: http://www.unilins.edu.br

Reitor: Milton Batista Nizato EMail: reitoria@unilins.edu.br

Vice-Reitor: Hamilton Luiz de Souza

Course

Administration (Administration); **Architecture and Town Planning** (Architecture; Town Planning); **Automation and Control Engineering - Mechatronics** (Automation and Control Engineering); **Civil Engineering** (Civil Engineering); **Computer Engineering** (Computer Engineering); **Electronic Engineering** (Electronic Engineering); **Electrotechnical Engineering** (Electrical and Electronic Engineering; Electronic Engineering); **Environmental Engineering** (Environmental Engineering); **Executive Secretarial Studies** (Secretarial Studies); **Graduate Studies** (Advertising and Publicity; Agricultural Business; Automation and Control Engineering; Business Administration; Computer Science; Environmental Studies; Health Sciences; Higher Education; Human Resources; Industrial Chemistry; Information Sciences; International and Comparative Education; Law; Safety Engineering; Social Policy; Social Work; Structural Architecture; Surveying and Mapping; Transport Engineering); **Health Sciences** (Health Sciences); **Information Systems** (Information Sciences); **Marketing** (Marketing); **Nursing** (Nursing); **Social Services** (Social and Community Services)

History: Founded 1964, acquired present status 2001.

Main Language(s) of Instruction: Portuguese

Degrees and Diplomas: *Tecnólogo*; *Bacharelado*; *Especialização/Aperfeiçoamento*: **Agricultural Business; Automation and Control Engineering; Banking; Business Administration; Civil Engineering; Computer Engineering; Educational Technology; Environmental Management; Finance; Forestry; Human Resources; Industrial Chemistry; Management; Marketing; Road Engineering; Social Sciences; Surveying and Mapping; Transport Management.** Also MBA.

Student Services: Academic Counselling, Canteen, Careers Guidance, Cultural Activities, Facilities for disabled people, Foreign

Studies Centre, Health Services, Language Laboratory, Library, Nursery Care, Social Counselling, Sports Facilities

Publications: Estudos e Pesquisas; Jornal de Olho na Fundação; Revista Científica

Last Updated: 08/07/15

UNIVERSITY CENTRE OF NORTHERN SÃO PAULO

Centro Universitário do Norte Paulista (UNORP)

Rua Ipiranga, 3460, Jardim Alto Rio Preto,
São José do Rio Preto, São Paulo 15020-040
Tel: +55(17) 3203-2500
Fax: +55(17) 3203-2515
EMail: deluca@unorp.br
Website: http://www.unorp.br

Reitor: Eudes Quintino de Oliveira Junior
EMail: eudesojrreitor@unorp.br

Pró-Reitor Acadêmico: José Luiz Falótico Corrêa
EMail: joseluiz@unorp.br

Course

Accountancy (Accountancy); **Administration** (Administration); **Agronomy** (Agronomy); **Architecture and Urbanism** (Architecture; Town Planning); **Arts and Humanities** (Arts and Humanities; English; Portuguese; Spanish; Translation and Interpretation); **Biological and Life Sciences** (Biological and Life Sciences); **Biomedicine** (Biomedicine); **Chemical Engineering** (Chemical Engineering); **Civil Engineering** (Civil Engineering); **Computer Engineering** (Computer Engineering); **Computer Science** (Computer Science); **Cosmetology** (Cosmetology); **Design** (Design; Graphic Design; Interior Design); **Electrical Engineering** (Electrical Engineering); **Finance** (Finance); **Gastronomy and Events** (Cooking and Catering); **Graduate Studies** (Accountancy; Administration; Agriculture; Civil Law; Communication Studies; Criminal Law; Curriculum; Dental Technology; Dentistry; Education; Finance; Forensic Medicine and Dentistry; Health Sciences; Higher Education; Human Resources; Labour Law; Marketing; Orthodontics; Pedagogy; Periodontics; Physical Education; Physical Therapy; Portuguese; Psychology; Public Administration; Radiology; Special Education; Stomatology; Tourism); **Information Systems** (Information Sciences); **Journalism** (Journalism; Mass Communication); **Labour Safety Engineering** (Safety Engineering); **Law** (Law); **Marketing** (Marketing); **Nursing** (Nursing); **Nutrition** (Nutrition); **Occupational Therapy** (Occupational Therapy); **Odontology** (Dentistry); **Pedagogy** (Education; Teacher Training); **Pharmacy** (Pharmacy); **Phonoaudiology** (Speech Therapy and Audiology); **Physical Education** (Physical Education); **Physiotherapy** (Physical Therapy); **Production Engineering** (Production Engineering); **Psychology** (Psychology); **Telecommunications Engineering** (Telecommunications Engineering); **Veterinary Science** (Veterinary Science)

History: Founded 1972 as Faculdade Riopretense de Filosofia, Ciências e Letras, acquired present status and title 1996.

Academic Year: February to December

Admission Requirements: Secondary school certificate

Main Language(s) of Instruction: Portuguese

Degrees and Diplomas: *Tecnólogo*; *Bacharelado*; *Licenciatura*; *Especialização/Aperfeiçoamento*: **Civil Law; Criminal Law; Dental Technology; Dentistry; Forensic Medicine and Dentistry; Law; Orthodontics; Periodontics; Stomatology.**

Student Services: Canteen, Cultural Activities, Facilities for disabled people, Library, Sports Facilities

Publications: Leia Já

Last Updated: 15/07/15

UNIVERSITY CENTRE OF PATOS DE MINAS

Centro Universitário de Patos de Minas (UNIPAM)

Rua Major Gote, 808, Bairro Caiçaras,
Patos de Minas, Minas Gerais 38702-054
Tel: +55(34) 3823-0300 +55(34) 3822-1599
Fax: +55(34) 3822-1312
EMail: assessoria.educacional@unipam.edu.br
Website: http://www.unipam.edu.br

Reitor: Milton Roberto de Castro Teixeira

Vice-Reitor: Fernando Dias da Silva

Course

Accountancy (Accountancy); **Administration** (Administration); **Advertising and Publicity** (Advertising and Publicity); **Agricultural Business** (Agricultural Business); **Agronomy** (Agronomy); **Architecture and Town Planning** (Architecture; Town Planning); **Arts and Humanities** (Arts and Humanities; Literature); **Biological Sciences** (Biological and Life Sciences); **Business and Commerce** (Business and Commerce); **Chemcial Engineering** (Chemical Engineering); **Chemistry** (Chemistry); **Civil Engineering** (Civil Engineering); **Environmental Engineering** (Environmental Engineering); **Executive Secretarial Studies** (Secretarial Studies); **History** (History); **Information Systems** (Information Sciences); **Journalism** (Journalism); **Law** (Law); **Mathematics** (Mathematics); **Mechanical Engineering** (Mechanical Engineering); **Medicine** (Medicine); **Nursing** (Nursing); **Nutrition** (Nutrition); **Pedagogy** (Pedagogy); **Pharmacy** (Pharmacy); **Physical Education** (Physical Education); **Physical Therapy** (Physical Therapy); **Physics** (Physics); **Production Engineering** (Production Engineering); **Psychology** (Psychology); **Veterinary Science** (Veterinary Science); **Zootechnics** (Zoology)

History: Founded 2001.

Main Language(s) of Instruction: Portuguese

Accrediting Agency: Ministry of Education.

Degrees and Diplomas: *Tecnólogo*; *Bacharelado*; *Licenciatura*; *Especialização/Aperfeiçoamento*: **Accountancy; Business Administration; Clinical Psychology; Constitutional Law; Educational and Student Counselling; Educational Psychology; Environmental Management; Health Sciences; Law; Management; Physical Therapy; Psychology; Software Engineering; Soil Management.** Also postgraduate studies

Student Services: Library

Last Updated: 19/06/15

UNIVERSITY CENTRE OF RIO GRANDE DO NORTE

Centro Universitário do Rio Grande do Norte (UNI-RN)

Rua Prefeita Eliane Barros 2000, Tirol,
Natal, Rio Grande do Norte 59014540
Tel: +55(84) 211-8688 +55(84) 215-2917
Fax: +55(84) 211-8688
EMail: farn@farn.br
Website: http://www.farn.br

Reitor: Daladier Pessoa Cunha Lima (1999-)

Course

Accountancy (Accountancy); **Administration** (Administration); **Civil Engineering** (Civil Engineering); **Computer Science** (Computer Science); **Law** (Law); **Marketing** (Marketing); **Nursing** (Nursing); **Nutrition** (Nutrition); **Physical Education** (Physical Education); **Physiotherapy** (Physical Therapy); **Psychology** (Psychology); **Social Services** (Social and Community Services)

History: Founded 1998 as Faculdade Natalense Para o Desenvolvimento do Rio Grande do Norte.

Main Language(s) of Instruction: Portuguese

Degrees and Diplomas: *Bacharelado*; *Licenciatura*; *Especialização/Aperfeiçoamento*; *Mestrado*

Last Updated: 29/05/15

UNIVERSITY CENTRE OF SETE LAGOAS - UNIFEMM

Centro Universitario de Sete Lagoas - UNIFEMM

Av. Marechal Castelo Branco 2765, Santo Antônio,
Sete Lagoas, Minas Gerais 35701242
Tel: +55(31) 2106-2106
Fax: +55(31) 2106-2101
EMail: comunicacao@unifemm.edu.br
Website: http://www.unifemm.edu.br

Diretor: Antônio Fernandino de Castro Bahia Filho
EMail: falecomreitor@unifemm.edu.br

Pró-Reitor Acadêmico: José Hamilton Ramalho

Course

Accountancy (Accountancy); **Administration** (Administration); **Arts and Humanities** (Arts and Humanities; English; Literature; Portuguese; Spanish); **Biological Sciences** (Biological and Life Sciences); **Civil Engineering** (Civil Engineering); **Economic Sciences** (Economics); **Environmental Engineering** (Environmental Engineering); **Geography** (Geography); **History** (History); **Human Resources** (Human Resources); **Industrial Production** (Industrial Engineering); **Information Management** (Information Management); **Law** (Law); **Mathematics** (Mathematics); **Metallurgical Engineering** (Metallurgical Engineering); **Nursing** (Nursing); **Nutrition** (Nutrition); **Pedagogy** (Pedagogy); **Physical Education** (Physical Education); **Physics** (Physics); **Production and Engineering** (Production Engineering); **Public Administration** (Public Administration); **Social Services** (Social Sciences); **Surveying and Mapping** (Surveying and Mapping); **Transport Management** (Transport Management)

History: Founded 1999 as Faculdades FEMM. Acquired present status and title 2006.

Main Language(s) of Instruction: Portuguese

Accrediting Agency: Ministry of Education.

Degrees and Diplomas: *Tecnólogo*; *Bacharelado*; *Licenciatura*; *Especialização/Aperfeiçoamento*: **Agronomy; Commercial Law; Finance; Public Law; Rehabilitation and Therapy; Taxation.** *Mestrado*: **Biotechnology.**

Student Services: Library

Last Updated: 08/07/15

UNIVERSITY CENTRE OF THE ARAXA PLATEAU

Centro Universitário do Planalto de Araxá (UNIARAXÁ)

Av. Ministro Olavo Drummond, 5, São Geraldo,
Araxa, Minas Gerais 38180-129
Tel: +55(34) 3669-2000
Fax: +55(34) 3669-2002
EMail: uniaraxa@uniaraxa.edu.br
Website: http://www.uniaraxa.edu.br

Reitor: Válter Gomes EMail: reitoria@uniaraxa.edu.br

Pró-Reitor de Administração e Planejamento: Wendel Rodrigo de Almeida

Institute

Applied Social Science, Exact and Earth Sciences (Business Administration; Computer Science; Human Resources; Marketing; Pedagogy); **Engineering**; **Health, Agricultural and Human Sciences** (Biological and Life Sciences; Biology; Nursing; Physical Education; Physical Therapy)

History: Founded 1999 as Faculdades Integradas do Alto Paranaíba, following merger of the Faculdade de Filosofia do Alto Paranaíba, the Faculdade de Ciências Gerenciais do Alto Paranaíba and the Faculdade de Direito do Alto Paranaíba. Acquired present status and title 2002.

Main Language(s) of Instruction: Portuguese

Degrees and Diplomas: *Tecnólogo*; *Bacharelado*; *Licenciatura*; *Especialização/Aperfeiçoamento*: **Banking; Business Administration; Civil Law; Data Processing; Higher Education Teacher Training; Human Resources; Management; Physical Therapy.**

Student Services: Library

Last Updated: 10/07/15

UNIVERSITY CENTRE OF THE DEVELOPMENT OF THE CENTRE WEST

Centro Universitário de Desenvolvimento do Centro Oeste (UNIDESC)

Km. 16 da BR-040, Luziania, GO 72870-000
Tel: +55(61) 3878-3100
EMail: unidesc@unidesc.edu.br; secretariageral@unidesc.edu.br
Website: http://www.unidesc.com

Reitor: Luiz Pinto Fernandes

Course

Accountancy (Accountancy); **Administration** (Administration); **Arts and Humanities** (Education; English; Linguistics; Literature; Portuguese; Teacher Training); **Biological Sciences** (Biological and Life Sciences); **Biomedicine** (Biomedicine); **Executive Secretarial Studies** (Secretarial Studies); **Fashion Design** (Fashion Design); **History** (History); **Information System** (Information Sciences); **Law** (Law); **Mathematics** (Mathematics); **Nursing** (Nursing); **Pedagogy** (Pedagogy; Teacher Training); **Pharmacy** (Pharmacy); **Physical Education** (Physical Education); **Physical Therapy** (Physical Therapy); **Radiology** (Radiology); **Veterinary Medicine** (Veterinary Science)

Further Information: Also campus in Valparaíso de Goiás.

History: Founded 1990.

Main Language(s) of Instruction: Portuguese

Accrediting Agency: Ministry of Education.

Degrees and Diplomas: *Tecnólogo*; *Bacharelado*; *Licenciatura*; *Especialização/Aperfeiçoamento*: **Business Administration; Criminal Law; Finance; Health Administration; Higher Education Teacher Training; Labour Law; Marketing; Portuguese.** Also MBA

Student Services: Library

Last Updated: 06/07/15

UNIVERSITY CENTRE OF THE EDUCATIONAL FOUNDATION OF GUAXUPÉ

Centro Universitário da Fundação Educacional Guaxupé (UNIFEG)

Avenida Dona Floriana 463, Centro,
Guaxupé, Minas Gerais 37800-000
Tel: +55(35) 3551-5267
Fax: +55(35) 3551-5267
EMail: secretaria@unifeg.edu.br
Website: http://www.unifeg.edu.br

Reitor: Reginaldo Arthuis

Pro-Rector Academic: Antonio Carlos Pereira

Course

Accountancy (Accountancy); **Achitecture and Town Planning** (Architecture; Town Planning); **Administration** (Administration); **Advertising and Publicity** (Advertising and Publicity); **Arts and Humanities - Portuguese/English** (English; Portuguese); **Biological Sciences** (Biological and Life Sciences); **Chemical Engineering** (Chemical Engineering); **Computer Science** (Computer Science); **Environmental Engineering** (Environmental Engineering; Environmental Studies); **Industrial Chemistry** (Industrial Chemistry); **Journalism** (Journalism); **Law** (Law); **Nursing** (Nursing); **Pedagogy** (Education; Pedagogy; Primary Education; Teacher Training); **Philosophy** (Philosophy); **Physical Education** (Physical Education); **Physical Therapy** (Physical Therapy); **Production and Quality Engineering** (Production Engineering; Safety Engineering); **Social Services** (Social and Community Services)

History: Founded 1965.

Main Language(s) of Instruction: Portuguese

Accrediting Agency: Ministry of Education.

Degrees and Diplomas: *Bacharelado*; *Licenciatura*; *Especialização/Aperfeiçoamento*: **Civil Law; Clinical Psychology; Computer Graphics; Criminal Law; Family Studies; Human Resources; Labour Law; Marketing.** Also MBA.

Student Services: Library

Last Updated: 01/07/15

UNIVERSITY CENTRE OF THE FEDERAL DISTRICT PLATEAU - UNIPLAN

Centro Universitário Planaltodo Distrito Federal - Uniplan (UNIPLAN)

Avenida Pau Brasil, lote 02 s/n, Águas Claras,
Brasília, DF 70390-130
Tel: +55 (61) 345-9100
EMail: marcioacbarros@yahoo.com.br
Website: http://www.uniplandf.edu.br

Reitor: Yugo Okida

Director: Geraldo Magela

Course

Accountancy (Accountancy); **Administration** (Administration); **Advertising and Publicity** (Advertising and Publicity); **Architecture and Urbanism** (Architecture; Town Planning); **Automation and Control Engineering** (Automation and Control Engineering); **Business Administration** (Accountancy; Business Administration); **Civil Engineering** (Civil Engineering); **Communication and Digital Illustration** (Communication Arts; Graphic Design; Media Studies); **Computer Science** (Computer Science); **Corporate Communication** (Communication Studies); **Design** (Fashion Design; Interior Design); **Event Management** (Management); **Graphic Design** (Graphic Design); **History** (History); **Hospital Management** (Health Administration); **Human Resources** (Human Resources); **Information Technology Management** (Information Technology); **International Business** (International Business); **Law** (Law); **Marketing Management** (Management; Marketing); **Multimedia** (Multimedia); **Nursing** (Nursing); **Nutrition** (Nutrition); **Pedagogy** (Pedagogy); **Pharmacy** (Pharmacy); **Phonoaudiology** (Speech Therapy and Audiology); **Physical Education** (Physical Education); **Physical Therapy** (Physical Therapy); **Portuguese** (Portuguese); **Production Engineering** (Production Engineering); **Real Estate** (Real Estate); **Social Communication** (Advertising and Publicity); **Spanish** (Spanish); **Sports Management** (Sports Management); **Tourism** (Tourism)

History: Founded 1995.

Main Language(s) of Instruction: Portuguese

Degrees and Diplomas: *Tecnólogo*; *Bacharelado*; *Licenciatura*; *Especialização/Aperfeiçoamento*: **Communication Studies; Educational Psychology; Higher Education; Law; Public Health.** *Mestrado*: **Business Administration; Finance; Health Administration; Human Resources; Transport Management.**

Student Services: Library

Last Updated: 02/09/15

UNIVERSITY CENTRE OF THE FEI

Centro Universitário da FEI (UNIFEI)

Avenida Humberto de Alencar, Castelo Branco 3972, Assunção, São Bernardo do Campo, São Paulo 09850 901

Tel: +55(11) 4353-2900

Fax: +55(11) 4109-5994

EMail: info_fei@fei.edu.br; internacional@fei.edu.br

Website: http://www.fei.edu.br

Reitor: Fábio do Prado

Department

Administration (Administration; Management); **Chemical Engineering** (Chemical Engineering); **Civil Engineering** (Civil Engineering); **Computer Science** (Computer Science; Mathematics); **Electrical Engineering** (Electrical Engineering); **Mathematics** (Mathematics); **Mechanical Engineering** (Mechanical Engineering); **Metallurgical and Materials Engineering** (Materials Engineering; Metallurgical Engineering); **Production Engineering** (Production Engineering); **Social and Juridical Sciences** (Law; Social and Community Services); **Textile Engineering** (Textile Technology)

Course

Graduate Studies (Accountancy; Administration; Automation and Control Engineering; Automotive Engineering; Business Administration; Chemistry; Energy Engineering; Environmental Management; Finance; Health Administration; Heating and Refrigeration; Human Resources; Industrial Management; Information Technology; International Business; Management; Marketing; Mechanics; Metallurgical Engineering; Occupational Health; Safety Engineering; Textile Design; Transport and Communications; Transport Management)

Further Information: Also campus Liberdade.

History: Founded 1945. Acquired present title and status 2002.

Admission Requirements: Secondary school certificate, certificate of regularity for military obligation (for Brazilians)

Main Language(s) of Instruction: Portuguese

Accrediting Agency: Ministry of Education.

Degrees and Diplomas: *Bacharelado*; *Especialização/Aperfeiçoamento*: **Aeronautical and Aerospace Engineering; Automation and Control Engineering; Automotive Engineering; Building Technologies; Business Administration; Chemical Engineering; Civil Engineering; Electrical Engineering; Environmental Management; Health Administration; Heating and Refrigeration; Human Resources; Management; Management Systems; Marketing; Production Engineering; Textile Technology; Town Planning; Transport Management.** *Mestrado*: **Chemical Engineering; Electrical Engineering; Management; Mechanical Engineering.** *Doutorado*: **Electrical Engineering; Management.**

Student Services: Academic Counselling, Careers Guidance, Library, Sports Facilities

Last Updated: 01/07/15

UNIVERSITY CENTRE OF THE GRANDE DOURADOS REGION

Centro Universitário da Grande Dourados (UNIGRAN)

Rua Balbina de Matos, 2121, Jardim Universitário, Dourados, Mato Grosso do Sul 79824 900

Tel: +55(67) 3411-4141

Fax: +55(67) 3411-4167

EMail: webmaster@unigran.br

Website: http://www.unigran.br

Reitora: Rosa Maria d'Amato de Déa (1996-) EMail: rosa@unigran.br

Administração: Valdir da Costa Pereira EMail: adm@unigran.b

Faculty

Administration and Accountancy (Accountancy; Administration; Advertising and Publicity; Agricultural Business; Civil Engineering; Journalism); **Education** (Education; Visual Arts); **Exact and Earth Sciences** (Agronomy; Architecture; Computer Science; Town Planning); **Law** (Law; Social and Community Services)

School

Biological and Health Sciences (Biological and Life Sciences; Biomedicine; Dentistry; Earth Sciences; Nursing; Pharmacy; Physical Education; Physical Therapy; Psychology; Veterinary Science)

Course

Distance Education (Accountancy; Administration; Advertising and Publicity; Agricultural Business; Arts and Humanities; Business and Commerce; Educational Psychology; Environmental Management; Higher Education; Information Sciences; Modern Languages; Pedagogy; Real Estate; Social and Community Services; Systems Analysis; Theology); **Technological Studies** (Advertising and Publicity; Agriculture; Cosmetology; Interior Design)

History: Founded 1976, Acquired present status and title 1998.

Academic Year: February to December

Admission Requirements: Secondary school certificate and entrance examination

Main Language(s) of Instruction: Portuguese

Degrees and Diplomas: *Bacharelado*; *Licenciatura*; *Especialização/Aperfeiçoamento*: **Accountancy; Business Administration; Educational Administration; Educational Psychology; Environmental Management; Health Administration; Higher Education Teacher Training; Human Resources; Preschool Education; Primary Education; Safety Engineering; Special Education.** Also postgraduate courses.

Student Services: Academic Counselling, Canteen, Careers Guidance, Facilities for disabled people, Library, Nursery Care, Sports Facilities

Publications: Revista Jurídica

Last Updated: 01/07/15

UNIVERSITY CENTRE OF THE MAUÁ INSTITUTE OF TECHNOLOGY

Centro Universitário do Instituto Mauá de Tecnologia (CEUN-IMT)

Praça Mauá 1, Mauá, São Caetano do Sul, São Paulo 09580-900

Tel: +55(11) 4239-3000

Fax: +55(11) 4239-3131

EMail: cp@maua.br

Website: http://www.maua.br

Reitor: José Carlos de Souza Jr. Tel: +55(11) 4329-3022

Course

Administration (Administration); **Chemical Engineering** (Chemical Engineering); **Civil Engineering** (Civil Engineering); **Design** (Design; Industrial Design); **Electrical Engineering** (Electrical Engineering); **Engineering** (Engineering); **Environmental Management** (Environmental Management); **Food Engineering** (Food Technology); **Information Technology Management** (Information Technology); **Marketing** (Marketing); **Mechanical Engineering** (Mechanical Engineering); **Mechanical Production Engineering** (Production Engineering); **Process Management** (Management)

Campus

Automation and Control Engineering (Automation and Control Engineering); **São Paulo** (Administration)

Further Information: Also São Paulo Campus

History: Founded as Mauá Engineering School in 1962. Acquired present status 2000.

Academic Year: February to December (February-June; August-December)

Admission Requirements: High school certificate and entrance examination

Main Language(s) of Instruction: Portuguese

Accrediting Agency: Ministry of Education.

Degrees and Diplomas: *Tecnólogo*; *Bacharelado*; *Especialização/Aperfeiçoamento*: **Administration; Civil Engineering; Design; Electronic Engineering; Environmental Management; Food Technology; Management; Marketing; Materials Engineering; Petroleum and Gas Engineering; Transport Management.** *Mestrado*: **Automation and Control Engineering; Business Administration; Chemical Engineering; Civil Engineering; Electronic Engineering.** Also MBA.

Student Services: Academic Counselling, Canteen, Careers Guidance, Library, Sports Facilities

Last Updated: 10/07/15

UNIVERSITY CENTRE OF THE OCTÁVIO BASTOS EDUCATION FOUNDATION

Centro Universitário Fundação de Ensino Octávio Bastos (UNIFEOB)

Rua General Osório 433, Centro,
São João da Boa Vista, São Paulo 13870-000
Tel: +55(19) 3634-3300
Fax: +55(19) 3634-3328
EMail: ouvidoria@unifeob.edu.br
Website: http://www.unifeob.edu.br

Reitor: João Otávio Bastos Junqueira

Pró-Reitor Acadêmico: José Roberto Almeida Junqueira (2012-)

Course

Accountancy (Accountancy); **Administration** (Administration; Public Administration); **Angricular Engineering** (Agricultural Engineering); **Architecture and Town Planning** (Architecture; Town Planning); **Arts and Humanities** (Arts and Humanities); **Biology** (Biology); **Chemistry** (Chemistry); **Civil Engineering** (Civil Engineering); **Geography** (Geography); **History** (History); **Human Resources** (Human Resources); **Information Systems** (Information Sciences); **Law** (Law); **Marketing** (Marketing); **Mathematics** (Mathematics); **Nursing** (Nursing); **Pedagogy** (Pedagogy); **Philosophy** (Philosophy); **Physical Therapy** (Physical Therapy); **Physics** (Physics); **Safety Engineering** (Safety Engineering); **Social Sciences** (Social Sciences); **Transport Management** (Transport Management); **Veterinary Science** (Veterinary Science)

History: Founded 2001.

Main Language(s) of Instruction: Portuguese

Accrediting Agency: Ministry of Education.

Degrees and Diplomas: *Tecnólogo*; *Bacharelado*; *Licenciatura*; *Especialização/Aperfeiçoamento*: **Business Administration; Education; Veterinary Science.**

Student Services: Library

Last Updated: 27/07/15

UNIVERSITY CENTRE OF THE SANTO ANDRÉ FOUNDATION

Centro Universitário Fundação Santo André (CUFSA)

Avenida Príncipe de Gales 821, Bairro Príncipe de Gales,
Santo André, São Paulo 09060-650
Tel: +55(11) 4979-3300
Fax: +55(11) 4990-2048
EMail: fsa@fsa.br
Website: http://www.fsa.br

Reitor: José Amilton de Souza EMail: reitoria@fsa.br

Pró-Reitor de Administração e Planejamento: Verenice P. Garcia

Faculty

Economics and Administration *(Faeco)* (Accountancy; Administration; Economics; Health Administration; International Relations); **Engineering** *(Faeng - Eng. Celso Daniel)* (Computer Engineering; Electronic Engineering; Engineering; Environmental Engineering; Materials Engineering; Mechanical Engineering; Production Engineering); **Philosophy, Science and Letters** *(Fafil)* (Biology; Chemistry; Computer Science; English; Geography; History; Information Sciences; Literature; Mathematics; Pedagogy; Physics; Portuguese; Social Sciences)

Course

Graduate Studies (Administration; Banking; Business Administration; Communication Studies; Distance Education; Education; Educational Psychology; Electronic Engineering; Energy Engineering; Engineering; Environmental Management; Finance; Geography; Health Administration; History; Information Sciences; Information Technology; International Business; International Relations; Journalism; Linguistics; Literature; Management; Marketing; Mathematics Education; Mechanical Engineering; Public Law; Safety Engineering; Science Education; Social Sciences; Software Engineering; Special Education; Statistics; Telecommunications Engineering; Transport Management)

History: Founded 1962. Acquired present status 2000.

Main Language(s) of Instruction: Portuguese

Accrediting Agency: Ministry of Education.

Degrees and Diplomas: *Bacharelado*; *Licenciatura*; *Especialização/Aperfeiçoamento*: **Automation and Control Engineering; Education; Educational Psychology; English; Geography; History; Law; Linguistics; Literature; Mathematics Education; Portuguese; Safety Engineering.** *Mestrado*: **Business Administration.** Also MBA.

Student Services: Academic Counselling, Canteen, Careers Guidance, Language Laboratory, Library, Nursery Care

Last Updated: 31/07/15

UNIVERSITY CENTRE OF THE SOUTH OF MINAS

Centro Universitário do Sul de Minas (UNIS-MG)

Avenida Cel. José Alves, 256, Vila Pinto,
Varginha, Minas Gerais 37010-540
Tel: +55(35) 3219-5000
Fax: +55(35) 3219-5251
EMail: unis@unis.edu.br
Website: http://portal.unis.edu.br

Reitor: Stéfano Barra Gazzola

Course

Accountancy (Accountancy); **Administration** (Administration; International Business); **Agronomy** (Agronomy); **Architecture and Town Planning** (Architecture; Town Planning); **Automation and Control Engineering** (Automation and Control Engineering); **Biomedicine** (Biomedicine); **Civil Engineering** (Civil Engineering); **Computer Science** (Computer Science; Systems Analysis); **Cosmetology** (Cosmetology); **Electrical Engineering** (Electrical Engineering); **Mechanical Engineering** (Mechanical Engineering); **Nursing** (Nursing); **Nutrition** (Nutrition); **Pedagogy** (Pedagogy); **Physical Education** (Physical Education); **Physical Therapy** (Physical Therapy); **Production Engineering** (Production Engineering); **Social Communication - Advertising and Publicity** (Advertising and Publicity); **Social Communication - Journalism**

(Journalism); **Social Services** (Social and Community Services); **Transport Management** (Transport Management)

Further Information: Also campuses in Cabo Verde, Nova Resende, Silvianópolis and Três Pontas and Distance Education Programumes.

History: Founded 1996.

Main Language(s) of Instruction: Portuguese

Degrees and Diplomas: *Tecnólogo*; *Bacharelado*; *Licenciatura*; *Especialização/Aperfeiçoamento*: **Educational Administration; Educational and Student Counselling; Educational Psychology; Law; Mathematics Education; Music; Music Education; Nursing; Public Administration.** *Mestrado*: **Business Administration.** Also Postgraduate Studies and MBA.

Student Services: Library
Last Updated: 16/07/15

UNIVERSITY CENTRE OF THE STATE OF SAO PAULO

Centro Universitário Paulistano (UNIPAULISTANA)
Rua Madre Cabrini 38, Vila Mariana,
São Paulo, São Paulo 04020001
Tel: +55(11) 5549-3033 +55(11) 5549-3035
Fax: +55(11) 5549-3033 +55(11) 5549-3049
EMail: unipaulistana@unipaulistana.edu.br
Website: http://www.unipaulistana.edu.br

Reitor: Clóvis Benedito Rosa

Secretária Acadêmica: Maria Messias Martins Braga
EMail: secretaria@unipaulistana.edu.br

Course

Accountancy (Accountancy); **Administration** (Administration); **Architecture and Urbanism** (Architecture; Town Planning); **Biological Sciences** (Biology); **Chemistry** (Chemistry); **Information Systems** (Information Management); **Letters** (English; Literature; Portuguese); **Mathematics** (Mathematics); **Mechanical Engineering** (Mechanical Engineering); **Nursing** (Nursing); **Pedagogy** (Pedagogy); **Production Engineering** (Production Engineering); **Psychology** (Psychology); **Technological Studies** (Business and Commerce; Computer Networks; Finance; Health Administration; Human Resources; Occupational Health; Public Administration; Systems Analysis; Transport Management)

History: Founded 1972.

Main Language(s) of Instruction: Portuguese

Degrees and Diplomas: *Tecnólogo*; *Bacharelado*; *Licenciatura*; *Especialização/Aperfeiçoamento*: **Administration; Educational Administration; Management; Psychology; Religion.**

Student Services: Library
Last Updated: 02/09/15

UNIVERSITY CENTRE OF VÁRZEA GRANDE

Centro Universitário de Várzea Grande (UNIVAG)
Av. Dom Orlando Chaves, 2655 Bairro Cristo Rei,
Várzea Grande, Mato Grosso 78118-900
Tel: +55(65) 3688-6000
Fax: +55(65) 3685-6000
EMail: univag@univag.com.br
Website: http://www.univag.com.br

Diretor Geral: Dráuzio Antônio Medeiros (1986-)

Course

Accountancy (Accountancy); **Administration** (Administration; Business Administration; International Business; Management; Marketing); **Agronomy** (Agricultural Business; Agronomy); **Arts and Humanities** (Arts and Humanities; Geography (Human); History; Philosophy; Sociology); **Biological Sciences** (Biological and Life Sciences); **Biomedicine** (Biomedicine); **Cosmetology** (Cosmetology); **Electrical Engineering** (Electrical Engineering); **Environmental Engineering** (Environmental Engineering); **Food Engineering** (Food Technology); **Graduate Studies** (Administration; Biotechnology; Botany; Business Education; Communication Studies; Data Processing; Higher Education; Information Technology; Labour Law; Law; Literacy Education; Management; Mathematics; Molecular Biology; Pharmacology; Political Sciences; Portuguese; Preschool Education; Public Administration; Public Health; Speech Therapy and Audiology; Zoology); **Information Systems** (Information Sciences); **Law** (Law); **Literature** (Literature); **Mathematics** (Mathematics; Mathematics and Computer Science); **Nursing** (Nursing); **Odontology** (Dentistry); **Pedagogy** (Pedagogy); **Pharmacy** (Pharmacy); **Phonaudiology** (Speech Therapy and Audiology); **Physical Education** (Physical Education); **Physical Therapy** (Physical Therapy); **Psychology** (Psychology); **Social Communication** (Communication Studies; Social Sciences); **Social Services** (Social and Community Services); **Tourism** (Tourism)

History: Founded 1989

Main Language(s) of Instruction: Portuguese

Degrees and Diplomas: *Tecnólogo*; *Bacharelado*; *Licenciatura*; *Especialização/Aperfeiçoamento*: **Agricultural Business; Banking; Civil Law; Commercial Law; Environmental Studies; Fiscal Law; Genetics; Gerontology; Health Sciences; Higher Education Teacher Training; Human Resources; Information Technology; Labour Law; Management; Molecular Biology; Private Law; Public Health; Safety Engineering.** *Mestrado*: **Business Administration.** Also MBA.

Student Services: Library
Last Updated: 09/07/15

UNIVERSITY CENTRE OF VILA VELHA

Centro Universitário Vila Velha (UVV)
Rua Commissário José Dantas de Melo, 21, Boa Vista,
Vila Velha, Espírito Santo 29102-920
Tel: +55(27) 3421-2001
Fax: +55(27) 3320-2029
EMail: uvv@uvv.br
Website: http://www.uvv.br

Reitor: Manoel Ceciliano Salles de Almeida

International Relations: Tarina Macedo, Associate Director International Affairs Tel: +55(27) 3320-2032 EMail: tarina@uvv.br

Course

Graduate Studies (Business Administration; Cooking and Catering; Cosmetology; Law; Photography); **Technological Studies** (Cooking and Catering; Cosmetology; Environmental Studies; Fashion Design; Human Resources; Industrial Design; Marine Transport; Occupational Health; Petroleum and Gas Engineering; Transport Management); **Undergraduate Studies** (Accountancy; Administration; Advertising and Publicity; Animal Husbandry; Architecture; Biological and Life Sciences; Biology; Chemical Engineering; Civil Engineering; Dentistry; Education; Electrical Engineering; Environmental Studies; Geology; Information Technology; International Relations; Journalism; Law; Marketing; Mechanical Engineering; Medicine; Nursing; Nutrition; Pedagogy; Performing Arts; Petroleum and Gas Engineering; Pharmacy; Physical Education; Physical Therapy; Production Engineering; Psychology; Speech Therapy and Audiology; Town Planning; Veterinary Science)

Further Information: Also N. Sra da Penha, Praia da Costa, Vitória and Guaçuí campuses.

History: Founded 1976.

Admission Requirements: Secondary school certificate and entrance examination (Vestibular)

Fees: 6,000 per annum; 3,000 per semester (Brazilian Real)

Main Language(s) of Instruction: Portuguese

Accrediting Agency: Ministry of Education

Degrees and Diplomas: *Tecnólogo*; *Bacharelado*; *Especialização/Aperfeiçoamento*: **Business Administration; Clinical Psychology; Cooking and Catering; Cosmetology; Finance; Human Resources; International Business; Management; Marketing; Mass Communication; Photography; Public Law; Safety Engineering; Transport Management.** *Mestrado*: **Animal Husbandry; Ecology; Pharmacy; Political Sciences; Protective Services; Social Sciences.** *Doutorado*: **Ecology.** Also MBA.

Student Services: Academic Counselling, Canteen, Careers Guidance, Cultural Activities, Facilities for disabled people, Health Services, Language Laboratory, Library, Nursery Care, Sports Facilities

Publications: Scientia
Last Updated: 09/09/15

UNIVERSITY CENTRE OF VOLTA REDONDA

Centro Universitário de Volta Redonda (UNIFOA)

Avenida Paulo Erlei Alves Abrantes, 1325, Três Poços,
Volta Redonda, Rio de Janeiro 27240-560
Tel: +55(24) 3340-8400
Fax: +55(24) 3340-8404
EMail: unifoa@foa.org.br
Website: http://www.unifoa.edu.br

Reitora: Claudia Yamada Utagawa

Secretária-geral: Daiana Biassa Chalate Lima

Course

Accountancy (Accountancy); **Administration** (Administration); **Advertising and Publicity** (Advertising and Publicity); **Biological Sciences** (Biological and Life Sciences; Biotechnology); **Civil Engineering** (Civil Engineering); **Design** (Design; Industrial Design); **Electrical Engineering** (Electrical Engineering); **Environmental Engineering** (Environmental Engineering); **Graduate Studies** *(Stricto Sensu)* (Environmental Management; Health Sciences; Materials Engineering); **Graduate Studies** *(Lato Sensu)* (Accountancy; Business and Commerce; Civil Law; Communication Studies; Comparative Literature; Computer Networks; Computer Science; Dental Technology; Dentistry; Education; Finance; Higher Education; Industrial Engineering; Industrial Management; Information Technology; Linguistics; Management; Mechanical Engineering; Nursing; Nutrition; Occupational Health; Physical Therapy; Psychiatry and Mental Health; Public Health; Radiology; Rehabilitation and Therapy; Safety Engineering; Sports; Surgery); **History** (History); **Information Systems** (Computer Science); **Journalism** (Journalism); **Law** (Law); **Literature** (Literature); **Mechanical Engineering** (Mechanical Engineering); **Medicine** (Medicine); **Nursing** (Nursing); **Nutrition** (Nutrition); **Odontology** (Dentistry); **Physical Education** (Physical Education); **Physical Therapy** (Physical Therapy); **Production Engineering** (Production Engineering); **Social Service** (Social Sciences)

Further Information: Also Aterrado, Colina, Vila, and Tangerinal campuses.

History: Founded 1968.

Main Language(s) of Instruction: Portuguese

Accrediting Agency: Ministry of Education.

Degrees and Diplomas: *Tecnólogo*; *Bacharelado*; *Licenciatura*; *Especialização/Aperfeiçoamento*: **Acupuncture; Cosmetology; Dentistry; Environmental Studies; Health Administration; Industrial Maintenance; Management; Mechanical Equipment and Maintenance; Microbiology; Nutrition; Orthodontics; Periodontics; Photography; Physical Education; Physical Therapy; Public Law; Radiology; Sports.** *Mestrado*: **Health Sciences; Materials Engineering.**

Last Updated: 09/07/15

UNIVERSITY CENTRE OF VOTUPORANGA

Centro Universitário de Votuporanga (UNIFEV)

Rua Pernambuco 4196, Centro,
Votuporanga, São Paulo 15500-006
Tel: +55(17) 3405-9999
Fax: +55(17) 3422-4510
EMail: faleconosco@fev.edu.br; ate@fev.edu.br
Website: http://www.unifev.edu.br

Reitor: Marcelo Ferreira Lourenço

Course

Accountancy; **Administration**; **Advertising and Publicity** (Advertising and Publicity); **Architecture and Urbanism** (Architecture; Town Planning); **Biological Sciences**; **Biomedicine** (Biomedicine); **Chemistry**; **Clothing Production** (Clothing and Sewing); **Commercial Management** (Business and Commerce); **Computer Engineering** (Computer Engineering); **Cooking and Catering** (Cooking and Catering); **Education** (Education); **Electrical and Electronic Engineering** (Electrical and Electronic Engineering); **Electrical Engineering** (Electrical Engineering); **Environmental Management** (Environmental Management); **Furniture Production** (Furniture Design); **Geography** (Geography); **Hospitality** (Hotel and Restaurant); **Human Resources**; **Industrial Production**; **Information Systems**; **Journalism**; **Law** (Law); **Literature**; **Logistics**; **Marketing** (Marketing); **Mathematics** (Mathematics); **Mechanical Fabrication**; **Multimedia Production**; **Nursing**; **Nutrition** (Nutrition); **Pharmacy** (Pharmacy); **Physical Education**; **Physical Therapy** (Physical Therapy); **Physics** (Physics); **Physics** (Physics); **Postgradute Studies**; **Psychology** (Psychology); **Quality Management** (Safety Engineering); **Social Work**; **Sugarcane Production** (Agriculture)

Further Information: Also Cidade Universitária campus.

History: Founded 1966. Acquired present status and title 1997.

Main Language(s) of Instruction: Portuguese

Accrediting Agency: Ministry of Education.

Degrees and Diplomas: *Tecnólogo*; *Bacharelado*; *Licenciatura*; *Especialização/Aperfeiçoamento*: **Automation and Control Engineering; Computer Engineering; Constitutional Law; Construction Engineering; Education; Educational Psychology; Environmental Studies; Health Sciences; Higher Education Teacher Training; Industrial and Organizational Psychology; Interior Design; Linguistics; Literature; Mathematics Education; Nursing; Nutrition; Pharmacology; Physical Education; Physical Therapy; Preschool Education; Primary Education; Psychology; Safety Engineering; Social and Community Services; Software Engineering.** *Mestrado*: **Business Administration.** Also MBA.

Last Updated: 09/07/15

UNIVERSITY OF CAXIAS DO SUL

Universidade de Caxias do Sul (UCS)

Rua Francisco Getúlio Vargas, 1130,
Caxias do Sul, Rio Grande do Sul 95070-560
Tel: +55(54) 3218-2100
EMail: informa@ucs.br
Website: http://www.ucs.br

Reitor: Evaldo Antonio Kuiava EMail: reitoria@ucs.br

Diretor Acadêmico: Cesar Augusto Bernardi
EMail: cesar.bernardi@ucs.br

Pró-Reitor Acadêmico: Marcelo Rossato EMail: mrossato@ucs.br

Vice-Reitor: Odacir Deonisio Graciolli EMail: odgracio@ucs.br

Centre

Biological and Health Sciences (Agronomy; Biological and Life Sciences; Cosmetology; Dance; Medicine; Nutrition; Pharmacy; Physical Education; Physical Therapy; Radiology; Science Education; Veterinary Science); **Exact Sciences and Technology** (Automation and Control Engineering; Automotive Engineering; Chemical Engineering; Chemistry; Civil Engineering; Computer Engineering; Computer Science; Dentistry; Electrical Engineering; Environmental Engineering; Food Technology; Information Technology; Materials Engineering; Mathematics Education; Mechanical Engineering; Physics; Polymer and Plastics Technology; Production Engineering; Science Education; Systems Analysis); **Humanities and Educational Sciences** (English; Foreign Languages Education; Geography (Human); History; Humanities and Social Science Education; Native Language Education; Pedagogy; Philosophy; Portuguese; Psychology; Secretarial Studies; Social and Community Services; Sociology; Spanish; Special Education); **Juridical Sciences** (Law); **Social Sciences** (Accountancy; Administration; Advertising and Publicity; Business Administration; Business and Commerce; Cooking and Catering; Economics; Finance; Human Resources; Industrial Management; International Business; Journalism; Library Science; Management; Marketing; Photography; Public Relations; Real Estate; Tourism)

Course

Arts and Architecture (Architecture; Art Education; Design; Fashion Design; Interior Design; Music; Town Planning; Visual Arts)

Campus

Farroupilha University Campus (Accountancy; Administration; Human Resources; Law); **Guaporé University Campus** (Administration; Law); **Hortênsias Region University Campus** *(Canela)* (Accountancy; Administration; Hotel Management; Law; Management; Nutrition; Public Relations; Tourism); **Nova Prata University Campus** (Accountancy; Administration; Business Administration; Law); **Vacaria University Campus** (Accountancy; Administration; Agronomy; Information Technology; Law; Pedagogy; Physical Education); **Vale do Caí University Campus** *(São Sebastião do Caí)* (Accountancy; Administration; Law); **Vinhedos Region**

University Campus *(Bento Gonçalves)* (Accountancy; Administration; Architecture; Arts and Humanities; Biological and Life Sciences; Business Administration; Civil Engineering; Computer Science; Design; Electrical Engineering; Electronic Engineering; Geography (Human); Graphic Design; Humanities and Social Science Education; Industrial Design; Information Technology; International Business; Law; Mechanical Engineering; Native Language Education; Pedagogy; Physical Education; Portuguese; Production Engineering; Psychology; Science Education; Tourism; Town Planning)

History: Founded 1967, incorporating previously existing Faculties. A private Institution constituted as a Foundation and recognized by the Federal Government.

Academic Year: March to December (March-July; August-December)

Admission Requirements: Secondary school certificate and entrance examination

Main Language(s) of Instruction: Portuguese

Degrees and Diplomas: *Tecnólogo*; *Bacharelado*; *Licenciatura*; *Especialização/Aperfeiçoamento*: **Accountancy; Agricultural Business; Banking; Behavioural Sciences; Biological and Life Sciences; Business Administration; Business and Commerce; Business Education; Child Care and Development; Clinical Psychology; Cognitive Sciences; Education of the Handicapped; Educational Administration; Educational Sciences; Educational Technology; Ethics; Fiscal Law; Forensic Medicine and Dentistry; Health Sciences; Human Resources; Human Rights; Industrial and Production Economics; Industrial Management; Information Management; Labour Law; Literature; Management; Marketing; Nursing; Oncology; Pharmacy; Preschool Education; Psychiatry and Mental Health; Psychotherapy; Public Health; Safety Engineering; Sales Techniques; Special Education; Taxation; Town Planning; Writing.** *Mestrado*: **Arts and Humanities; Biotechnology; Business Administration; Education; Environmental Engineering; Environmental Studies; Health Sciences; History; Hotel and Restaurant; Law; Materials Engineering; Mathematics Education; Mechanical Engineering; Philosophy; Production Engineering; Science Education; Tourism.** *Doutorado*: **Arts and Humanities; Biotechnology; Business Administration; Education; Hotel and Restaurant; Materials Engineering; Tourism.** Also MBA

Student Services: Library

Publications: Revista Chronos

Publishing House: Editora da Universidade de Caxias do Sul

Last Updated: 30/03/16

UNIVERSITY OF CRUZ ALTA

Universidade de Cruz Alta (UNICRUZ)

Campus Universitário Dr. Ulysses Guimarães, Rodovia Municipal Jacob Della Méa, Km 5.6 - Parada Benito,
Cruz Alta, Rio Grande do Sul 98020-290
Tel: +55(55) 3321-1500
Fax: +55(55) 3321-1500
EMail: reitoria@unicruz.edu.br
Website: http://www.unicruz.edu.br

Reitora: Patrícia Dall'Agnol Bianchi EMail: reitoria@unicruz.edu.br

Pró-Reitor de Administração: Carlos Eduardo Moreira Tavares EMail: pradm@unicruz.edu.br

Faculty

Health and Agricultural Sciences (Agronomy; Biomedicine; Cosmetology; Environmental Engineering; Nursing; Pharmacy; Physical Education; Physical Therapy; Sanitary Engineering; Veterinary Science)

Centre

Social and Human Sciences (Accountancy; Administration; Architecture; Arts and Humanities; Civil Engineering; Computer Science; English; Law; Pedagogy; Portuguese; Production Engineering; Spanish; Town Planning)

History: Founded 1964. Acquired present status and title 1993.

Academic Year: March to December (March-June; August-December)

Admission Requirements: Secondary school certificate and entrance examination

Main Language(s) of Instruction: Portuguese

Degrees and Diplomas: *Bacharelado*; *Licenciatura*; *Especialização/Aperfeiçoamento*: **Cattle Breeding; Communication Studies; Computer Science; Cosmetology; Environmental Management; Marketing; Oncology; Town Planning.** *Mestrado*: **Animal Husbandry; Development Studies; Health Sciences; Horticulture; Rural Studies.**

Student Services: Library

Last Updated: 05/04/16

UNIVERSITY OF FORTALEZA

Universidade de Fortaleza (UNIFOR)

Av. Washington Soares, 1321, Edson Queiroz,
Fortaleza, Ceará 60811-905
Tel: +55(85) 3477-3000
Fax: +55(85) 3477-3055
EMail: reitoria@unifor.br
Website: http://www.unifor.br

Reitora: Fátima Maria Fernandes Veras (2009-)
Tel: +55(85) 477-3001 EMail: reitoria@unifor.br

Vice-Reitor de Administração: José Maria Gondim Felismino Júnior

Centre

Communication and Management (Accountancy; Administration; Advertising and Publicity; Economics; Hotel Management; International Business; Journalism; Media Studies; Radio and Television Broadcasting; Theatre; Tourism; Visual Arts); **Health Sciences** (Dentistry; Health Sciences; Medicine; Nursing; Occupational Therapy; Pharmacy; Physical Education; Physical Therapy; Psychology; Speech Therapy and Audiology)); **Juridical Sciences** (Law); **Technological Sciences** (Architecture; Automation and Control Engineering; Civil Engineering; Computer Engineering; Computer Science; Electrical Engineering; Electronic Engineering; Environmental Engineering; Mechanical Engineering; Production Engineering; Sanitary Engineering; Telecommunications Engineering; Town Planning)

History: Founded 1973. Under the supervision of the Fundação Edson Queiroz. A private Institution recognized by the Federal Government.

Academic Year: February to December (February-July; August-December)

Admission Requirements: Secondary school certificate and entrance examination

Main Language(s) of Instruction: Portuguese

Degrees and Diplomas: *Bacharelado*: **Accountancy; Administration; Architecture; Civil Engineering; Computer Science; Dentistry; Economics; Electrical Engineering; Information Sciences; Law; Mechanical Engineering; Nursing; Occupational Therapy; Pedagogy; Pharmacy; Physical Education; Physical Therapy; Psychology; Social Sciences; Speech Therapy and Audiology; Tourism.** *Especialização/Aperfeiçoamento*: **Administrative Law; Architecture; Architecture and Planning; Automation and Control Engineering; Behavioural Sciences; Civil Engineering; Civil Law; Commercial Law; Constitutional Law; Construction Engineering; Criminal Law; Educational Psychology; Energy Engineering; Engineering; Environmental Management; Environmental Studies; Fiscal Law; Geological Engineering; Gerontology; Health Administration; Health Sciences; Industrial and Organizational Psychology; Industrial Engineering; Information Management; Information Technology; International Law; Labour Law; Law; Neurosciences; Notary Studies; Nursing; Nutrition; Occupational Health; Oncology; Peace and Disarmament; Pharmacy; Physical Therapy; Physiology; Private Law; Production Engineering; Psychiatry and Mental Health; Psychology; Public Health; Public Law; Rehabilitation and Therapy; Respiratory Therapy; Road Transport; Safety Engineering; Speech Therapy and Audiology; Sports; Surgery; Telecommunications Engineering.** *Mestrado*: **Administration; Business Administration; Computer Science; Constitutional Law; Dentistry; Law; Medicine; Nursing; Peace and Disarmament; Psychology; Public Health; Town Planning.** *Doutorado*: **Biotechnology; Business**

Administration; Computer Science; Constitutional Law; Psychology; Public Health. Also MBA

Student Services: Library, Nursery Care, Sports Facilities

Publications: Pensar; Revista do Centro de Ciências Administrativas; Revista do Centro de Ciências da Saúde; Revista Humanidades; Revista Tecnologia

Publishing House: Gráfica Unifor

Last Updated: 30/03/16

UNIVERSITY OF GRANDE RIO

Universidade do Grande Rio (UNIGRANRIO)

Rua Prof. José de Souza Herdy, 1160, Jardim Vinte e Cinco de Agosto, Duque de Caxias, Rio de Janeiro 25071-200

Tel: +55(21) 3219-4040 +55(21) 2672-7813

Fax: +55(21) 3219-4040 +55(21) 2671-4248

EMail: unirelacionamento@unigranrio.com.br; faleconosco@unigranrio.edu.br; daa@unigranrio.com.br

Website: http://www.unigranrio.br

Reitor: Arody Cordeiro Herdy EMail: reitoria@unigranrio.com.br

Pró-Reitor de Administração Acadêmica: Carlos de Oliveira Varella

School

Education, Science, Letters, Arts and Humanities (History; Literature; Mathematics; Pedagogy; Theology; Visual Arts); **Health Sciences** (Biology; Cosmetology; Dentistry; Health Sciences; Medicine; Nursing; Nutrition; Pharmacy; Physical Education; Physical Therapy; Radiology; Veterinary Science); **Science and Technology** (Architecture; Chemical Engineering; Chemistry; Civil Engineering; Computer Networks; Environmental Management; Information Technology; Petroleum and Gas Engineering; Production Engineering; Systems Analysis; Town Planning); **Social and Applied Sciences** (Accountancy; Advertising and Publicity; Business Administration; Fashion Design; Finance; Graphic Design; Human Resources; Journalism; Law; Marketing; Secretarial Studies; Social and Community Services; Social Sciences; Transport Management)

Further Information: Also following units: Rio de Janeiro (Lapa, Silva Jardim, Magé, São João de Meriti, Macaé, Nova Iguaçu, Barra da Tijuca, Carioca Shopping, Colégio Casimiro de Abreu, Irajá, Penha, Santa Cruz da Serra), Palhoça (Fatenp Unit) and Grupo Unigranrio (CAP - Colégio de Aplicação Unigranrio, PDC - Policlínica de Saúde)

History: Founded 1972 as Faculdades Unidas Grande Rio. Acquired present status and title 1994.

Main Language(s) of Instruction: Portuguese

Degrees and Diplomas: *Tecnólogo*; *Bacharelado*; *Licenciatura*; *Especialização/Aperfeiçoamento*: **Biological and Life Sciences; Business Administration; Cardiology; Dental Technology; Dentistry; Dermatology; Educational and Student Counselling; Embryology and Reproduction Biology; Environmental Engineering; Gynaecology and Obstetrics; Health Sciences; Industrial and Organizational Psychology; Laboratory Techniques; Labour Law; Law; Nursing; Nutrition; Oncology; Ophthalmology; Paediatrics; Pharmacology; Pharmacy; Physical Therapy; Physiology; Radiology; Rehabilitation and Therapy; Religious Education; Religious Studies; Social Policy; Sports; Surgery; Transport Management.** *Mestrado*: **Arts and Humanities; Biomedicine; Business Administration; Cultural Studies; Dentistry; Health Education; Primary Education.** Also MBA

Student Services: Library, eLibrary

Student Numbers *2014-2015*: Total: c. 18,000

Last Updated: 01/03/16

UNIVERSITY OF ITAÚNA

Universidade de Itaúna (UI)

Rodovia MG 431 - Km 45 (Trevo Itaúna/Pará de Minas), Caixa Postal 100, Itaúna, Minas Gerais 35680-142

Tel: +55(37) 3249-3000 +55(37) 3249-3033

Fax: +55(37) 3249-3062 +55(37) 3249-3031

EMail: uit@uit.br; uitreitor@hotmail.com

Website: http://www.uit.br

Reitor: Faiçal David Freire Chequer (1998-)
Tel: +55(37) 3249-3003

Vice-Reitor: Irineu Carvalho de Macedo

Pró-Reitor Administrativo e Financeiro: Matozinho Ferreira Barbosa

Course

Accounting (Accountancy); **Administration** (Administration); **Architecture and Urbanism** (Architecture; Town Planning); **Biological Sciences** (Biological and Life Sciences); **Chemistry** (Chemistry); **Civil Engineering** (Civil Engineering); **Computer Science** (Computer Science); **Dentistry** (Dentistry); **Electronic Engineering** (Electronic Engineering); **Law** (Law); **Mechanical Engineering** (Mechanical Engineering); **Medicine** (Medicine); **Nursing** (Nursing); **Nutrition** (Nutrition); **Pedagogy** (Pedagogy); **Pharmacy** (Pharmacy); **Physical Education** (Physical Education); **Physical Therapy** (Physical Therapy); **Production Engineering** (Production Engineering)

Further Information: Also Almenara campus

History: Founded 1965, acquired present status and title 1997.

Admission Requirements: Secondary school certificate and entrance examination

Main Language(s) of Instruction: Portuguese

Degrees and Diplomas: *Tecnólogo*; *Bacharelado*; *Licenciatura*; *Especialização/Aperfeiçoamento*: **Orthodontics.** *Mestrado*: **Law.**

Student Services: Canteen, Library, Sports Facilities

Last Updated: 30/03/16

UNIVERSITY OF JOSÉ DO ROSÁRIO VELLANO

Universidade José do Rosário Vellano (UNIFENAS)

Rod. MG 179, Km 0, Campus Universitário, Alfenas, Minas Gerais 37130-000

Tel: +55(35) 3299-3000 +55(35) 3299-3257

Fax: +55(35) 3299-3800

EMail: unifenas@unifenas.br; alfenas@unifenas.br

Website: http://www.unifenas.br

Reitora: Maria do Rosário Araújo Valeno (2008-)
Tel: +55(35) 3299-3157 EMail: unifenas@unifenas.br

Diretor Financeiro: Paulo Tadeu Barroso Salles
Tel: +55(35) 3299-3148 EMail: paulo.salles@unifenas.br

Pró-Reitor Acadêmico: Mário Sérgio Oliveira Swerts

Pró-Reitora Administrativo-Financeira: Larissa Araújo Velano Dozza

International Relations: Sebastião M. Franco de Carvalho
Tel: +55(35) 3299-3257 EMail: unifenas@unifenas.br

Course

Accounting (Accountancy); **Administration** (Administration); **Administration FGV** (Administration); **Agronomy** (Agronomy); **Biomedicine** (Biomedicine); **Civil Engineering** (Civil Engineering); **Computer Science** (Computer Science); **Dentistry** (Dentistry); **Law** (Law); **Medicine** (Medicine); **Nursing** (Nursing); **Nutrition** (Nutrition); **Pedagogy** (Pedagogy); **Pharmacy** (Pharmacy); **Physical Education** (Physical Education); **Psychology** (Psychology); **Veterinary Medicine** (Veterinary Science)

Campus

Belo Horizonte (Administration; Biomedicine; Law; Medicine; Nursing); **Campos Belos Campus** (Law); **Divinópolis Campus** (Biomedicine; Physical Therapy); **Varginha** (Dentistry; Psychology)

Further Information: Also Alzira Velano Universitarian Hospital

History: Founded 1972 as Faculdades Integradas da Região de Alfenas, became Universidade de Alfenas 1988. Under the supervision of the Fundação de Ensino e Tecnologia de Alfenas. Acquired present title 2002.

Academic Year: February to December (February-June; August-December)

Admission Requirements: Secondary school certificate and entrance examination

Main Language(s) of Instruction: Portuguese

Accrediting Agency: Conselho Nacional de Educação; Conselho Estadual de Educação de Minas Gerais; Fundação CAPES

Degrees and Diplomas: *Bacharelado*; *Licenciatura*; *Especialização/Aperfeiçoamento*: **Behavioural Sciences; Biomedicine; Biotechnology; Civil Law; Cognitive Sciences; Community Health; Cosmetology; Criminal Law; Dermatology; Education; Educational Sciences; Environmental Engineering; Gerontology; Health Administration; Health Sciences; Labour Law; Law; Nursing; Nutrition; Occupational Health; Orthodontics; Orthopaedics; Pharmacy; Physical Therapy; Physiology; Preschool Education; Psychoanalysis; Public Administration; Public Health; Rehabilitation and Therapy; Safety Engineering; Sanitary Engineering; Special Education; Sports; Sports Medicine; Surgery; Toxicology; Translation and Interpretation.** *Mestrado*: **Agriculture; Animal Husbandry; Health Education; Zoology.** *Doutorado*: **Animal Husbandry.** Also MBA

Student Services: Academic Counselling, Canteen, Careers Guidance, Cultural Activities, Facilities for disabled people, Health Services, Library, Social Counselling, Sports Facilities

Last Updated: 05/04/16

UNIVERSITY OF PARANÁ

Universidade Paranaense (UNIPAR)

Praça Mascarenhas de Moraes, 4282, Centro,
Umuarama, Paraná 87502-210
Tel: +55(44) 3621-2828
Fax: +55(44) 3621-2830
EMail: degpa@unipar.br; degedu@unipar.br; avaliacao@unipar.br
Website: http://www.unipar.br

Reitor: Carlos Eduardo Garcia
Tel: +55(44) 621-2828 EMail: carlos@unipar.br; reitoria@unipar.br

Diretoria Executiva de Gestão de Planejamento Acadêmico: Sônia Regina da Costa Oliveira EMail: degpa@unipar.br

Vice-Reitor Chanceler: Candido Garcia EMail: candido@unipar.br

Unit

Cascavel Unit (Accountancy; Administration; Architecture; Biomedicine; Civil Engineering; Cosmetology; Dentistry; Fashion Design; History; Information Technology; Law; Mathematics; Nursing; Psychology; Town Planning); **Cianorte Unit** (Accountancy; Administration; Architecture; Cosmetology; Fashion Design; Law; Management; Physical Education; Science Education; Systems Analysis; Town Planning); **Francisco Beltrão Unit** (Accountancy; Administration; Architecture; Biological and Life Sciences; Civil Engineering; Cosmetology; Dentistry; History; Information Technology; Law; Nursing; Nutrition; Pharmacy; Physical Education; Psychology; Town Planning); **Guaíra Unit** (Administration; Civil Engineering; Cosmetology; Environmental Studies; Law; Nursing; Pedagogy; Systems Analysis); **Paranavaí Unit** (Administration; Architecture; Civil Engineering; Cosmetology; Information Technology; Law; Pharmacy; Town Planning); **Toledo Unit** (Accountancy; Administration; Architecture; Biological and Life Sciences; Civil Engineering; Cosmetology; Law; Pharmacy; Physical Education; Physical Therapy; Systems Analysis; Town Planning); **Umuarama Unit** (Accountancy; Administration; Advertising and Publicity; Agricultural Engineering; Architecture; Business and Commerce; Civil Engineering; Cosmetology; Dentistry; Fashion Design; Industrial Chemistry; Information Technology; Law; Mechanical Engineering; Nursing; Nutrition; Pedagogy; Pharmacy; Physical Education; Psychology; Science Education; Town Planning; Veterinary Science)

Further Information: Campuses at Toledo, Guaíra, Paranavaí, Cianorte and Cascavel. Also Veterinary Hospital

History: Founded 1972 as Faculty of Umuarama, became Faculdades Integradas de Umurama 1990 incorporating already existing faculties. Acquired present status and title 1993.

Admission Requirements: Secondary school certificate and entrance examination

Main Language(s) of Instruction: Portuguese

Degrees and Diplomas: *Tecnólogo*; *Bacharelado*; *Licenciatura*; *Especialização/Aperfeiçoamento*: **Animal Husbandry; Archaeology; Architecture; Art Management; Cinema and Television; Civil Law; Clinical Psychology; Construction Engineering; Cosmetology; Dental Technology; Dermatology; Education of the Handicapped; Educational Psychology; Environmental Management; Environmental Studies; Fashion Design; Heritage Preservation; History; Information Technology; Interior Design; Management; Microbiology; Notary Studies; Oncology; Orthodontics; Peace and Disarmament; Pharmacology; Pharmacy; Plant and Crop Protection; Plastic Surgery; Primary Education; Psychoanalysis; Psychology; Public Health; Safety Engineering; Social and Community Services; Social Policy; Social Psychology; Software Engineering; Sports; Telecommunications Engineering.** *Mestrado*: **Agriculture; Alternative Medicine; Animal Husbandry; Biotechnology; Private Law.** *Doutorado*: **Agriculture; Animal Husbandry; Biotechnology.** Also MBA; Combined Licenciatura and Bacharelado, 4-5 yrs, in Physical Education, Psychology, Industrial Chemistry

Student Services: Academic Counselling, Canteen, Careers Guidance, Cultural Activities, Facilities for disabled people, Health Services, Language Laboratory, Library, Social Counselling, Sports Facilities, eLibrary

Publications: Akropolis - Revista de Ciências Humanas da UNIPAR; Arquivos de Ciências da Saúde da UNIPAR; Arquivos de Ciências Veterinárias e Zoologia da UNIPAR; Revista de Ciências Empresariais da UNIPAR; Revista de Ciências Jurídicas e Sociais da UNIPAR

Last Updated: 06/04/16

UNIVERSITY OF PASSO FUNDO

Universidade de Passo Fundo (UPF)

Campus I - Km 171 - BR 285, São José,
Passo Fundo, Rio Grande do Sul 99052-900
Tel: +55(54) 3316-8100
Fax: +55(54) 3316-8125
EMail: informacoes@upf.br
Website: http://www.upf.tche.br

Reitor: José Carlos Carles de Souza (2014-) EMail: reitoria@upf.br

Vice-Reitor Administrativo: Agenor Dias de Meira Júnior
Tel: +55(54) 3316-8105 EMail: vradm@upf.br

Faculty

Agronomy and Veterinary Medicine (FAMV) (Agronomy; Veterinary Science); **Arts and Communication (FAC)** (Advertising and Publicity; Graphic Design; Journalism; Music; Musical Instruments; Singing; Visual Arts); **Dentistry (FO)** (Dentistry); **Economics, Administration and Accounting (FEAC)** (Accountancy; Administration; Agricultural Business; Economics; Human Resources; International Business; Transport Management); **Education (FAED)** (Fashion Design; Pedagogy; Social and Community Services); **Engineering and Architecture (FEAR)** (Architecture; Chemical Engineering; Civil Engineering; Electrical Engineering; Environmental Engineering; Food Technology; Industrial Design; Mechanical Engineering; Production Engineering; Town Planning); **Law (FD)** (Law); **Medicine (FM)** (Medicine); **Physical Education and Physiotherapy (FEFF)** (Physical Education; Physical Therapy)

Institute

Biological Sciences (ICB) (Biological and Life Sciences; Cosmetology; Nursing; Nutrition; Pharmacy; Speech Therapy and Audiology); **Exact Sciences and Geosciences (ICEG)** (Chemistry; Computer Engineering; Computer Science; Geography; Information Technology; Mathematics; Physics; Systems Analysis); **Philosophy and Humanities (IFCH)** (English; History; Literature; Philosophy; Portuguese; Psychology; Secretarial Studies; Spanish)

Research Centre

Economics, Administration and Accountancy (CEPEAC) (Administration; Economics); **Food (CEPA)** (Food Science)

Research Unit

UPFTec (Technology)

Further Information: Branches at Carazinho, Casca, Lagoa Vermelha, Palmeira das Missões, Soledade and Sarandi; Veterinary Hospital; Museums

History: Founded 1968 incorporating Faculty of Law, established 1956 and Faculties of Philosophy and Political Science, established 1957. A private institution recognized by the federal government.

Academic Year: March to December (March-July; August-December)

Admission Requirements: Secondary school certificate and entrance examination

Main Language(s) of Instruction: Portuguese

Degrees and Diplomas: *Tecnólogo*; *Bacharelado*; *Licenciatura*; *Especialização/Aperfeiçoamento*: **Accountancy; Archaeology; Art Therapy; Civil Law; Criminal Law; Cultural Studies; Educational Administration; Fashion Design; Industrial Design; Insurance; Interior Design; Journalism; Labour Law; Management; Orthopaedics; Plant and Crop Protection; Production Engineering; Safety Engineering; Taxation.** *Mestrado*: **Administration; Agronomy; Biological and Life Sciences; Civil Engineering; Computer Science; Dentistry; Education; Environmental Engineering; Environmental Studies; Food Technology; Gerontology; History; Law; Literature; Mathematics Education; Mechanical Engineering; Production Engineering; Science Education.** *Doutorado*: **Agronomy; Civil Engineering; Dentistry; Education; Environmental Engineering; History; Literature.** Also MBA

Student Services: Academic Counselling, Canteen, Careers Guidance, Cultural Activities, Language Laboratory, Library, Sports Facilities

Publications: Cesta Básica; Espaço Pedagógico; Justiça do Direito; Revista da Faculdade de Odontologia; Revista de Filosofia e Ciências Humanas; Teoria e Evidência Econômica

Publishing House: Gráfica e Editora UPF

Last Updated: 31/03/16

UNIVERSITY OF RIBEIRÃO PRÊTO

Universidade de Ribeirão Prêto (UNAERP)

Av. Costábile Romano, 2,201, Ribeirania,
Ribeirão Preto, São Paulo 14096-900
Tel: +55(16) 3603-7000 +55(800) 771-8388
Fax: +55(16) 3603-7073 +55(16) 3603-7005
EMail: unaerp@unaerp.br
Website: http://www.unaerp.br

Reitora: Elmara Lúcia de Oliveira Bonini Corauci (1997-)
Tel: +55(16) 3603-6815
EMail: ecorauci@unaerp.br; elbonini@unaerp.br

International Relations: Teobaldo Rivas
Tel: +55(16) 3603-7087 EMail: trivas@unaerp.br

Area

Exact Sciences (Chemical Engineering; Civil Engineering; Computer Engineering; Production Engineering; Systems Analysis); **Health Sciences** (Dentistry; Health Sciences; Medicine; Nursing; Nutrition; Pharmacy; Physical Education; Physical Therapy; Psychology); **Human Sciences** (Accountancy; Administration; Advertising and Publicity; Architecture; International Business; International Relations; Journalism; Law; Music; Pedagogy; Social and Community Services; Town Planning); **Technology** (Biological and Life Sciences; Transport Management)

Further Information: Also Guarujá Campus

History: Founded 1924. A private institution under the jurisdiction of the Associação de Ensino de Ribeirão Prêto.

Academic Year: February to June and August to December

Admission Requirements: Secondary school certificate and entrance examination

Main Language(s) of Instruction: Portuguese

Accrediting Agency: Ministério da Educação (MEC)

Degrees and Diplomas: *Técnico de Nivel Medio*; *Tecnólogo*; *Bacharelado*; *Licenciatura*; *Especialização/Aperfeiçoamento*: **Automation and Control Engineering; Cosmetology; Data Processing; Dental Hygiene; Dentistry; Educational Psychology; Health Administration; Information Technology; Laboratory Techniques; Medicine; Nursing; Orthodontics; Pathology; Pharmacy; Physical Education; Physical Therapy; Psychiatry and Mental Health; Radiology; Rehabilitation and Therapy; Safety Engineering; Sports.** *Mestrado*: **Biotechnology; Dentistry; Education; Environmental Engineering; Health Sciences; Law.** *Doutorado*: **Biotechnology; Dentistry; Environmental Engineering.** Also MBA; Medical Residencies

Student Services: Academic Counselling, Canteen, Cultural Activities, Facilities for disabled people, Health Services, Language Laboratory, Library, Social Counselling, Sports Facilities

Last Updated: 31/03/16

UNIVERSITY OF SANTA CRUZ DO SUL

Universidade de Santa Cruz do Sul (UNISC)

Avenida Independência 2293, Bairro Universitário,
Santa Cruz do Sul, Rio Grande do Sul 96815-900
Tel: +55(51) 3717-7300
Fax: +55(51) 3717-1855
EMail: info@unisc.br
Website: http://www.unisc.br

Reitor: Carmen Lúcia de Lima Helfer
Tel: +55(51) 3717-7303
EMail: reitoria@unisc.br

Pró-Reitor de Administração: Dorivaldo Brites de Oliveira
Tel: +55(51) 3717-7351
EMail: proad@unisc.br

Vice-Reitor: Eltor Breunig

International Relations: Cristiana Verônica Mueller, Coordenadora, Assuntos Internacionais e Interinstitucionais
Tel: +55(51) 3717-7314
EMail: cmueller@unisc.br; aai@unisc.br

Department

Accountancy (Accountancy); **Administrative Sciences** (Administration); **Biology and Pharmacy** (Biology; Pharmacy); **Chemistry and Physics** (Chemistry; Physics); **Computer Science** (Computer Science); **Economics** (Agricultural Engineering; Economics); **Education** (Education); **Engineering, Architecture and Agrarian Sciences** (Agriculture; Architecture; Engineering; Town Planning); **History and Geography** (Geography; History); **Human Sciences** (Philosophy; Social and Community Services); **Law** (Law); **Liberal Arts** (Arts and Humanities; English; Modern Languages; Native Language; Spanish); **Mathematics** (Mathematics); **Nursing and Odontology** (Dentistry; Nursing); **Physical Education and Health Sciences** (Health Sciences; Physical Education); **Psychology** (Psychology); **Social Communication** (Advertising and Publicity; Journalism; Mass Communication)

Research Centre

Accountancy *(CEC)* (Accountancy); **Administration** *(CEPAD)* (Business Administration); **Archaeology** *(CEPA)* (Archaeology); **Economics** *(CEPE)* (Economics); **Innovation and Technology Transfer** *(NIIT)* (Technology); **Law** *(CEPEJUR)* (Law); **Linguistics and Literature** *(CEPELL)* (Linguistics; Literature); **Regional Development** *(CEPEDER)* (Development Studies)

History: Founded 1964, incorporating existing Faculties, acquired present status and title 1993. A communitary non Governmental Institution administered by the Santa Cruz do Sul Pro-Instruction Association.

Academic Year: March to November (March-July; August-November)

Admission Requirements: Competitive entrance examination

Main Language(s) of Instruction: Portuguese

Degrees and Diplomas: *Tecnólogo*; *Bacharelado*; *Licenciatura*; *Especialização/Aperfeiçoamento*: **Automation and Control Engineering; Biological and Life Sciences; Civil Law; Construction Engineering; Cooking and Catering; Fiscal Law; Labour Law; Management; Multimedia; Notary Studies; Nutrition; Peace and Disarmament; Pharmacy; Physical Therapy; Private Law; Public Law; Sports; Taxation; Toxicology; Vocational Education.** *Mestrado*: **Administration; Arts and Humanities; Development Studies; Education; Environmental Engineering; Health Sciences; Industrial Engineering; Law.** *Doutorado*: **Development Studies; Education; Environmental Engineering; Law.** Also MBA

Student Services: Academic Counselling, Canteen, Careers Guidance, Cultural Activities, Facilities for disabled people, Foreign Studies Centre, Health Services, Language Laboratory, Library, Nursery Care, Social Counselling, Sports Facilities

Publications: Ágora; Barbarói; Caderno de Pesquisa-Série Botânica; Estudos do CEPA; Estudos do CEPE; REDES; Reflexão e Ação; Revista do Direito; SIGNO; Tecno-lógica

Publishing House: Editora da Universidade de Santa Cruz do Sul (EDUNISC)

Last Updated: 31/03/16

UNIVERSITY OF SANTO AMARO

Universidade de Santo Amaro (UNISA)

Rua Professor Enéas de Siqueira Neto, 340 - Jardim das Imbuias - Sto. Amaro, São Paulo, São Paulo 04829-300
Tel: +55(11) 5545-8800
Fax: +55(11) 5522-7844
EMail: sdutra@unisa.br; institucional@unisa.br
Website: http://www.unisa.br

Reitora: Margareth Rose Priel

Secretária Geral: Vera Lucia Barreto Moreira

International Relations: Luciane Lucio Pereira
Tel: +55(11) 2141-8676
EMail: international@unisa.br

Area

Biological and Health Sciences/Agricultural and Earth Sciences (Biological and Life Sciences; Biology; Biomedicine; Dentistry; Medicine; Nursing; Pharmacy; Physical Education; Physical Therapy; Psychology; Veterinary Science); **Exact Sciences** (Chemical Engineering; Chemistry; Civil Engineering; Economics; Environmental Engineering; Information Technology; Production Engineering); **Humanities and Social Sciences** (Accountancy; Administration; Advertising and Publicity; Architecture; Arts and Humanities; Geography (Human); History; Journalism; Law; Pedagogy; Public Relations; Radio and Television Broadcasting; Social and Community Services; Town Planning); **Technological Studies** (Advertising and Publicity; Business and Commerce; Communication Studies; Cosmetology; Environmental Management; Finance; Human Resources; Industrial Management; Information Technology; International Business; Management; Marketing; Public Administration; Safety Engineering; Transport Management)

Further Information: Also Teaching Hospital; Veterinary Hospital. Dental Clinic. Psychology Clinic

History: Founded 1968 as Faculdades de Santo Amaro. Acquired present status and title 1994. A private Institution.

Academic Year: February to December

Admission Requirements: Secondary school certificate (Vestibular) and entrance examination

Fees: 4200-18,000 per annum (Brazilian Real)

Main Language(s) of Instruction: Portuguese

Accrediting Agency: Ministry of Education and Culture

Degrees and Diplomas: *Tecnólogo*; *Bacharelado*; *Licenciatura*; *Especialização/Aperfeiçoamento*: **Accountancy; Advertising and Publicity; Archaeology; Art Therapy; Clinical Psychology; Communication Studies; Cultural Studies; Dental Technology; Dentistry; Development Studies; Educational and Student Counselling; Educational Psychology; Educational Sciences; Environmental Management; Environmental Studies; Forest Management; Grammar; Health Administration; Health Sciences; History; Human Rights; Industrial and Organizational Psychology; Industrial Management; Laboratory Techniques; Labour Law; Literacy Education; Management; Mining Engineering; Natural Resources; Neurosciences; Nursing; Occupational Therapy; Orthodontics; Periodontics; Petroleum and Gas Engineering; Pharmacy; Physical Education; Physical Therapy; Portuguese; Production Engineering; Psychology; Public Health; Safety Engineering; Small Business; Social and Community Services; Social and Preventive Medicine; Social Policy; Social Psychology; Social Studies; Special Education; Veterinary Science.** *Mestrado*: **Arts and Humanities; Dental Technology; Dentistry; Health Sciences; Veterinary Science.** Also MBA; Medical and Multidisciplinary Residencies; Aprimoramento (Postgraduate Capacity Building Programme) in Veterinary Medicine; Postgraduate Professional Development Programmes

Student Services: Academic Counselling, Canteen, Cultural Activities, Facilities for disabled people, Health Services, Library, Social Counselling, Sports Facilities

Publications: Biological; Direito; Humanas; Verbum

Publishing House: Editora UNISA

Last Updated: 31/03/16

UNIVERSITY OF SOROCABA

Universidade de Sorocaba (UNISO)

Rodóvia Raposo Tavares s/n km 92,5, Jardim Novo Eldorado, Sorocaba, São Paulo 18023-000
Tel: +55(15) 2101-7000
Fax: +55(15) 2101-7112
EMail: uniso@uniso.br
Website: http://www.uniso.br

Reitor: Fernando de Sá Del Fiol EMail: fernando.fiol@prof.uniso.br

Pró-Reitor Administrativo: Rogério Augusto Profeta
EMail: rogerio.profeta@uniso.br

Pró-Reitor Acadêmico: José Martins de Oliveira Jr.
EMail: jose.oliveira@prof.uniso.br

Centre

Agricultural Sciences (Agronomy; Veterinary Science); **Applied Social Sciences** (Accountancy; Administration; Advertising and Publicity; Architecture; Design; Economics; Hotel Management; International Business; Journalism; Law; Public Relations; Town Planning); **Biological and Health Sciences** (Biological and Life Sciences; Biotechnology; Nursing; Nutrition; Occupational Therapy; Pharmacy; Physical Education; Physical Therapy); **Engineering** (Automation and Control Engineering; Bioengineering; Biotechnology; Chemical Engineering; Civil Engineering; Computer Engineering; Electrical Engineering; Environmental Engineering; Food Technology; Materials Engineering; Mechanical Engineering; Production Engineering); **Exact and Earth Sciences** (Chemistry; Computer Science; Industrial Chemistry; Information Technology; Mathematics; Physics); **Human Sciences** (Geography (Human); History; International Relations; Pedagogy; Philosophy; Psychology); **Linguistics, Letters and Arts** (Dance; English; Literature; Music; Portuguese; Spanish; Theatre; Visual Arts); **Technological Studies** (Business and Commerce; Cattle Breeding; Cooking and Catering; Cosmetology; Fashion Design; Finance; Graphic Design; Hotel and Restaurant; Human Resources; Industrial Management; Interior Design; Management; Marketing; Public Relations; Safety Engineering; Software Engineering; Transport Management)

Further Information: Also Seminário and Trujillo Campuses

History: Founded 1951, became Faculdade de Filosofia, Ciências e Letras 1954 and acquired present status and title 1994.

Academic Year: February-June; August-December

Admission Requirements: Secondary school certificate and entrance examination

Fees: c. 3000 per semester (Brazilian Real)

Main Language(s) of Instruction: Portuguese

Accrediting Agency: Ministry of Education

Degrees and Diplomas: *Bacharelado*; *Licenciatura*; *Especialização/Aperfeiçoamento*: **Construction Engineering; Educational Psychology; Environmental Management; Oncology; Paediatrics; Production Engineering; Town Planning.** *Mestrado*: **Communication Studies; Cultural Studies; Education; Environmental Engineering; Pharmacy.** *Doutorado*: **Education; Pharmacy.** Also MBA

Student Services: Academic Counselling, Canteen, Facilities for disabled people, Foreign Studies Centre, Health Services, Language Laboratory, Library, Nursery Care, Social Counselling, Sports Facilities

Publications: Quaestio - Revista de Estudos de Educação; Revista de Estudos Universitários; Tríade: Revista de Comunicação, Cultura e Mídia; €CO$: Revista de Estudos em Economia

Last Updated: 31/03/16

UNIVERSITY OF SOUTH SANTA CATARINA

Universidade do Sul de Santa Catarina (UNISUL)

Avenida José Acácio Moreira 787, Dehon, Tubarão, Santa Catarina 88704-900
Tel: +55(48) 3621-3000
Fax: +55(48) 3621-3036
EMail: unisul@unisul.br; gabinete@unisul.br
Website: http://www.unisul.br

Reitor: Sebastião Salésio Herdt
EMail: reitor@unisul.br; salesio.herdt@unisul.br

Vice Reitor: Mauri Luiz Heerdt EMail: Mauri.heerdt@unisul.br

Secretária-Geral: Mirian Maria de Medeiros

Unit

Araranguá *(Tubarão Campus)* (Accountancy; Business Administration; Business and Commerce; Finance; Geography (Human); History; Law; Nursing); **Braço do Norte** *(Tubarão Campus)* (Accountancy; Business Administration; Finance; International Business; Law; Management; Veterinary Science); **Florianópolis** *(Grande Florianópolis Campus)* (Architecture; Business Administration; Computer Science; Design; Fashion Design; Information Technology; International Relations; Law; Management; Psychology; Town Planning); **Içara** *(Tubarão Campus)* (Business Administration; Finance; Law; Social and Community Services); **Pedra Branca** *(Grande Florianópolis Campus)* (Accountancy; Advertising and Publicity; Business Administration; Cinema and Television; Civil Engineering; Computer Science; Cooking and Catering; Cosmetology; Dentistry; Electrical Engineering; Environmental Engineering; Finance; Information Technology; Journalism; Law; Marketing; Medicine; Nursing; Nutrition; Physical Education; Physical Therapy; Production Engineering; Psychology; Sanitary Engineering; Social Work); **Tubarão** *(Tubarão Campus)* (Accountancy; Advertising and Publicity; Agronomy; Architecture; Automation and Control Engineering; Biological and Life Sciences; Business Administration; Business and Commerce; Chemical Engineering; Chemistry; Civil Engineering; Computer Networks; Computer Science; Cooking and Catering; Cosmetology; Dentistry; Electrical Engineering; Fashion Design; Finance; Food Technology; Geography (Human); History; Information Technology; International Relations; Journalism; Law; Literature; Management; Marketing; Mathematics; Medicine; Nursing; Nutrition; Pedagogy; Pharmacy; Physical Education; Physical Therapy; Physics; Portuguese; Psychology; Social and Community Services; Town Planning; Veterinary Science); **UnisulVirtual** (Accountancy; Aeronautical and Aerospace Engineering; Agricultural Business; Business Administration; Business and Commerce; Civil Security; Communication Studies; Criminology; Economics; Environmental Management; Human Resources; Industrial Management; Information Technology; International Business; Law; Management; Marketing; Mathematics; Mathematics Education; Multimedia; Pedagogy; Philosophy; Public Administration; Tourism; Transport and Communications; Transport Management)

History: Founded 1964 as Instituto Municipal de Ensino Superior, acquired present status and title 1989.

Academic Year: March to December (March-July; August-December)

Admission Requirements: Secondary school certificate and entrance examination

Fees: 9,000 per annum (Brazilian Real)

Main Language(s) of Instruction: Portuguese

Degrees and Diplomas: *Tecnólogo*; *Bacharelado*; *Licenciatura*; *Especialização/Aperfeiçoamento*: **Accountancy; Business Administration; Civil Security; E- Business/Commerce; Environmental Management; Finance; Fiscal Law; Government; Haematology; Health Administration; Health Sciences; Information Management; Information Technology; International Business; Labour Law; Law; Management; Marketing; Mass Communication; Military Science; Nursing; Nutrition; Physical Education; Protective Services; Psychiatry and Mental Health; Public Administration; Safety Engineering; Social Policy; Social Psychology; Social Welfare; Software Engineering; Sports; Sports Management; Taxation; Transport Management.** *Mestrado*: **Business Administration; Education; Health Sciences; Linguistics.** *Doutorado*: **Health Sciences; Linguistics.** Also MBA

Student Services: Academic Counselling, Careers Guidance, Cultural Activities, Language Laboratory, Library, Nursery Care, Social Counselling, Sports Facilities

Publications: Cadernos da Integração; Gestão Empresarial; Linguagem em (Dis)curso; Revista Episteme; Revista Juridíca da Unisul

Last Updated: 29/02/16

UNIVERSITY OF THE CAMPANHA REGION

Universidade da Região da Campanha (URCAMP)

Av. Tupy Silveira, 2099, Bagé, Rio Grande do Sul 96400-110

Tel: +55(53) 3242-8244

Fax: +55(53) 3242-8898

EMail: Reitora@urcamp.edu.br

Website: www.urcamp.tche.br

Reitor: Lia Maria Herzer Quintana
Tel: +55(532) 42-8244 EMail: reitor@urcamp.edu.br

Pró-reitor Administrativo: Aurelino Brites Rocha
EMail: aurelinorocha@ucamp.edu.br

Vice-reitora: Núbia Juliani EMail: nubiajuliani@gmail.com

Centre

Applied Social Sciences (CCSA) (Accountancy; Administration; Advertising and Publicity; Economics; Journalism; Law); **Educational and Applied Human Sciences (CCEHA)** (Biology; Humanities and Social Science Education; Pedagogy; Physical Education; Science Education); **Exact and Environmental Sciences (CCEA)** (Agronomy; Architecture; Civil Engineering; Environmental Management; Information Technology; Town Planning); **Health Sciences (CCS)** (Nursing; Nutrition; Pharmacy; Physical Therapy; Psychology; Veterinary Science)

Further Information: Campuses at Alegrete, Caçapava do Sul, Dom Pedrito, Sant'Ana do Livramento, São Borja, Itaqui and São Gabriel. Also University Hospital

History: Founded 1955.

Admission Requirements: Secondary school certificate and entrance examination

Main Language(s) of Instruction: Portuguese

Degrees and Diplomas: *Bacharelado*; *Licenciatura*; *Especialização/Aperfeiçoamento*: **Agricultural Management; Art Management; Business Administration; Business and Commerce; Community Health; Computer Networks; Educational and Student Counselling; Educational Psychology; Environmental Management; Environmental Studies; Higher Education Teacher Training; Petroleum and Gas Engineering; Regional Planning; Social Psychology; Sports.**

Student Services: Canteen

Last Updated: 30/03/16

UNIVERSITY OF THE REGION OF JOINVILLE

Universidade da Região de Joinville (UNIVILLE)

Rua Paulo Malschitzki, 10, Zona Industrial Norte,
Joinville, Santa Catarina 89219-710

Tel: +55(47) 3461-9000

Fax: +55(47) 3473-0131

EMail: univille@univille.br

Website: http://www.univille.edu.br

Reitora: Sandra Aparecida Furlan
Tel: +55(47) 3461-9011 EMail: reitoria@univille.br

Vice-Reitor: Alexandre Cidral
Tel: +55(47) 3461-9182 EMail: vicereitoria@univille.br

Pró-reitor de Administração: Cleiton Vaz
Tel: +55(47) 3461-9007 EMail: proadm@univille.br

International Relations: Jurema Tomelin Barg, Assessora de Relações Internacionais
Tel: +55(47) 3461-9051
EMail: internacional@univille.br; mobilidade@univille.br

Course

Accountancy (Accountancy); **Advertising and Publicity** (Advertising and Publicity); **Architecture** (Architecture); **Biological and Life Sciences** (Biological and Life Sciences); **Business Administration** (Business Administration); **Business and Commerce** (Business and Commerce); **Chemical Engineering** (Chemical Engineering); **Civil Engineering** (Civil Engineering); **Cooking and Catering** (Cooking and Catering); **Dentistry** (Dentistry); **Design** (Design); **Economics** (Economics); **Electrical Engineering** (Electrical Engineering); **Environmental Engineering** (Environmental Engineering); **Environmental Studies** (Environmental Studies); **Fashion Design** (Fashion Design); **Finance** (Finance); **History** (History); **Information Technology** (Information Technology); **Interior Design** (Interior Design); **International Business** (International Business); **Law** (Law); **Letters** (Arts and Humanities); **Marine Biology** (Marine Biology); **Marine Transport** (Marine Transport); **Mechanical Engineering** (Mechanical Engineering); **Medicine** (Medicine); **Nursing** (Nursing); **Pedagogy** (Pedagogy); **Pharmacy** (Pharmacy); **Photography** (Photography); **Physical Education** (Physical Education); **Production Engineering** (Production Engineering); **Psychology** (Psychology); **Sanitary Engineering** (Sanitary Engineering); **Science Education** (Science

Education); **Software Engineering** (Software Engineering); **Town Planning** (Town Planning); **Transport Management** (Transport Management); **Visual Arts** (Visual Arts)

Further Information: Also São Bento do Sul Campus, São Francisco do Sul and Centro Units; Distance Education courses offered

History: Founded 1967. Acquired present status 1996. A Municipal Institution.

Admission Requirements: Secondary school certificate and entrance examination

Main Language(s) of Instruction: Portuguese

Degrees and Diplomas: *Tecnólogo*; *Bacharelado*; *Licenciatura*; *Especialização/Aperfeiçoamento*: **Archaeology; Art History; Business and Commerce; Civil Law; Commercial Law; Consumer Studies; Cooking and Catering; Design; Economics; Educational Administration; Educational Psychology; Finance; Health Administration; Human Resources; Industrial Management; Management; Marketing; Mass Communication; Neurosciences; Physical Education; Production Engineering; Psychoanalysis; Public Administration; Safety Engineering; Sanitary Engineering; Special Education; Sports; Taxation; Tourism; Transport Management.** *Mestrado*: **Cultural Studies; Design; Education; Environmental Studies; Health Sciences; Production Engineering; Social Studies.** *Doutorado*: **Environmental Studies; Health Sciences.** Also MBA

Student Services: Academic Counselling, Canteen, Careers Guidance, Facilities for disabled people, Nursery Care, Sports Facilities

Last Updated: 30/03/16

UNIVERSITY OF THE RIO DOS SINOS VALLEY

Universidade do Vale do Rio dos Sinos (UNISINOS)
Av. Unisinos, 950, Bairro Cristo Rei,
São Leopoldo, Rio Grande do Sul 93022-750
Tel: +55(51) 3591-1122
Fax: +55(51) 3590-8289 +55(51) 3590-8208
EMail: atendimento@unisinos.br; intercambio@unisinos.br; elianam@unisinos.br
Website: http://www.unisinos.br

President: Marcelo Fernandes de Aquino (2006-)

Pró-Reitor de Administração: João Zani

Pró-Reitor Acadêmico: Pedro Gilberto Gomes

International Relations: Cristiano Richter, Director of Business and International Affairs
Tel: +55(51) 3590-8237
EMail: engrichter@unisinos.br; nri@unisinos.br

School

Creative Industry (Advertising and Publicity; Cooking and Catering; Design; Fashion Design; Graphic Design; Industrial Design; Journalism; Marketing; Multimedia; Photography; Public Relations; Radio and Television Broadcasting; Sound Engineering (Acoustics)); **Health Sciences** (Biomedicine; Cooking and Catering; Health Sciences; Nursing; Pharmacy; Physical Education; Physical Therapy; Psychology); **Humanities** (Arts and Humanities; Biology; Education; History; International Relations; Mathematics; Philosophy; Physical Education; Physics; Social and Community Services; Social Sciences); **Law** (Law); **Management and Commerce** (Accountancy; Business Administration; Economics; Finance; Health Administration; Human Resources; International Business; International Relations; Leadership; Management; Marketing; Transport Management); **Polytechnics** (Architecture; Automation and Control Engineering; Biology; Biomedical Engineering; Chemical Engineering; Civil Engineering; Computer Engineering; Computer Graphics; Computer Science; Electrical Engineering; Electronic Engineering; Energy Engineering; Environmental Engineering; Environmental Management; Food Technology; Geology; Industrial Management; Information Management; Information Technology; Materials Engineering; Mathematics; Mechanical Engineering; Physics; Production Engineering; Surveying and Mapping; Systems Analysis; Town Planning)

History: Founded 1954 as Faculdade de Filosofia, Ciências e Letras. A private Institution under the supervision of the Society of Jesus. Acquired present status 1969, and recognized 1983. Reorganized with a structure comprising centres for Professional Education.

Academic Year: February to December (February-July; August-December)

Admission Requirements: Secondary school certificate and entrance examination

Fees: c. 1,093,97 per subject, per semester (Brazilian Real)

Main Language(s) of Instruction: Portuguese

Degrees and Diplomas: *Tecnólogo*; *Bacharelado*; *Licenciatura*; *Especialização/Aperfeiçoamento*: **Administration; Administrative Law; Architecture; Arts and Humanities; Behavioural Sciences; Business Administration; Civil Engineering; Civil Law; Cognitive Sciences; Commercial Law; Community Health; Computer Engineering; Construction Engineering; Cooking and Catering; Criminal Law; Design; Distance Education; Educational Administration; Educational Psychology; Fiscal Law; Foreign Languages Education; Furniture Design; Gerontology; Graphic Design; Gynaecology and Obstetrics; Health Administration; Health Sciences; History; Hotel and Restaurant; Information Technology; Insurance; International Relations; Journalism; Labour Law; Landscape Architecture; Law; Mass Communication; Mathematics Education; Medicine; Midwifery; Music; Notary Studies; Nursing; Nutrition; Occupational Health; Oncology; Philosophy; Physical Therapy; Polymer and Plastics Technology; Preschool Education; Psychiatry and Mental Health; Psychology; Psychotherapy; Public Administration; Public Health; Public Law; Radio and Television Broadcasting; Rehabilitation and Therapy; Safety Engineering; Sanitary Engineering; Social Work; Software Engineering; Special Education; Sports; Sports Medicine; Surveying and Mapping; Taxation; Town Planning; Transport Engineering.** *Mestrado*: **Accountancy; Applied Linguistics; Architecture; Biology; Business Administration; Business and Commerce; Civil Engineering; Commercial Law; Computer Science; Design; Economics; Education; Educational Administration; Electrical Engineering; Food Science; Geology; History; Law; Management; Mass Communication; Mechanical Engineering; Nursing; Nutrition; Philosophy; Production Engineering; Psychology; Public Health; Social Sciences; Town Planning.** *Doutorado*: **Accountancy; Applied Linguistics; Biology; Business Administration; Computer Science; Education; Geology; History; Law; Mass Communication; Philosophy; Production Engineering; Psychology; Public Health; Social Sciences.** Also MBA, MBE e Pós-MBA

Student Services: Academic Counselling, Canteen, Careers Guidance, Cultural Activities, Facilities for disabled people, Health Services, Language Laboratory, Library, Nursery Care, Social Counselling, Sports Facilities

Publications: Acta Biologica Leopoldensia; Arquitetura Unisinos; Ciências Sociais da Unisinos; Controvérsia; Educação Unisinos; Entrelinhas; Estudos Jurídicos; Estudos Tecnológicos-Engenharia; Filosofia Unisinos; Fronteiras; História Unisinos; Perspectiva Econômica; Revista AV; Revista BASE; Revista Calidoscopio; Revista GAEA; Scientia; Verso e Reverso

Publishing House: UNISINOS Press; UNISINOS Publishing House

Academic Staff *2014-2015*: Total 1,108
Student Numbers *2014-2015*: Total 31,383
Last Updated: 29/02/16

UNIVERSITY OF THE SACRED HEART

Universidade do Sagrado Coração (USC)
Rua Irmã Arminda, Jardim Brasil, Bauru, São Paulo 17011-160
Tel: +55(14) 3235-7000
Fax: +55(14) 3235-7325
EMail: centraldeatendimento@usc.br; dicom@usc.br
Website: http://www.usc.br

Reitora: Irmã Susana de Jesus Fadel
Tel: +55(14) 2107-7005 EMail: reitoria@usc.br

Pró-Reitora Administrativa: Irmã Maria Inês Périco

Secretária Geral: Gesiane Monteiro Branco Folkis

International Relations: Daniel Freire e Almeida, Diretor do Departamento de Relações Internacionais
Tel: +55(14) 2107-7194 EMail: ird@usc.br

Area

Applied Social Sciences (Accountancy; Administration; Advertising and Publicity; Architecture; Cooking and Catering; Design; Fashion Design; Human Resources; International Relations; Journalism; Public Relations; Town Planning); **Exact Sciences** (Agricultural Engineering; Chemical Engineering; Chemistry; Civil Engineering; Computer Engineering; Computer Science; Electrical Engineering; Environmental Engineering; Mathematics; Production Engineering; Sanitary Engineering; Science Education); **Health Sciences** (Biological and Life Sciences; Biomedicine; Cosmetology; Dentistry; Health Sciences; Nursing; Nutrition; Occupational Therapy; Pharmacy; Physical Therapy; Science Education); **Human Sciences** (Art Education; Arts and Humanities; English; History; Music; Music Education; Performing Arts; Philosophy; Portuguese; Psychology; Translation and Interpretation)

Further Information: Also Clinics: Physiotherapy; Dental; Psychology; Speech Therapy

History: Founded 1953 as Faculdade de Filosofia, Ciências e Letras do Sagrado Coração de Jesus. Acquired present status 1986. A private Catholic institution under the supervision of the Instituto das Apóstolas do Sagrado Coração.

Academic Year: February to December (February-June; August-December)

Admission Requirements: Secondary school certificate and entrance examination (Vestibular)

Main Language(s) of Instruction: Portuguese

Degrees and Diplomas: *Tecnólogo*; *Bacharelado*; *Licenciatura*; *Especialização/Aperfeiçoamento*: **Anthropology; Business Administration; Communication Studies; Community Health; Cultural Studies; Dance; Dental Technology; Education; Educational Psychology; English; Foreign Languages Education; Forensic Medicine and Dentistry; Health Sciences; History; Information Management; Information Technology; Interior Design; International Business; Laboratory Techniques; Literature; Marketing; Nutrition; Orthopaedics; Pharmacy; Philosophy; Physical Therapy; Portuguese; Psychiatry and Mental Health; Psychology; Public Health; Radiology; Rehabilitation and Therapy; Respiratory Therapy; Social Psychology; Software Engineering; Special Education; Theatre.** *Mestrado*: **Dentistry; Environmental Engineering; Environmental Studies; Oral Pathology; Physical Therapy.** *Doutorado*: **Oral Pathology.** Also MBA

Student Services: Academic Counselling, Canteen, Careers Guidance, Cultural Activities, Facilities for disabled people, Health Services, Library, Social Counselling, Sports Facilities

Publications: Cadernos de Divulgação Cultural; Revista Mimesis; Revista Salusvita

Publishing House: Editora do Sagrado Coração - EDUSC

Last Updated: 23/02/16

UNIVERSITY OF THE SANTA CATARINA PLATEAU

Universidade do Planalto Catarinense (UNIPLAC)

Av. Castelo Branco, n°170, Bairro Universitário,
Lages, Santa Catarina 88509-900
Tel: +55(49) 3251-1022
Fax: +55(49) 3251-1051
EMail: uniplac@uniplac.net; pesqinst@uniplaclages.edu.br
Website: http://www.uniplac.net

Reitor: Luiz Carlos Pfleger
Tel: +55(49) 3251-1003
EMail: gabinetedoreitor@uniplaclages.edu.br

Department

Applied Social Sciences (Accountancy; Administration; Cosmetology; Journalism; Pedagogy; Physical Education; Social and Community Services; Social Sciences); **Biological and Health Sciences** (Biological and Life Sciences; Biomedicine; Dentistry; Health Sciences; Medicine; Nursing; Physical Education; Physical Therapy; Psychology); **Exact and Technological Sciences** (Architecture; Automation and Control Engineering; Chemistry; Civil Engineering; Electrical Engineering; Information Technology; Mathematics; Mechanical Engineering; Natural Sciences; Production Engineering; Technology; Town Planning); **Human Sciences, Letters and Arts** (Arts and Humanities; English; Geography (Human); History; Interior Design; Literature; Music; Portuguese; Visual Arts); **Law** (Law)

History: Founded 1998.

Main Language(s) of Instruction: Portuguese

Degrees and Diplomas: *Bacharelado*; *Licenciatura*; *Especialização/Aperfeiçoamento*: **Accountancy; Civil Law; Community Health; Dentistry; Human Resources; Labour Law; Orthopaedics; Physical Therapy; Political Sciences; Portuguese; Production Engineering; Psychology; Public Health; Respiratory Therapy; Safety Engineering; Social Psychology; Software Engineering; Sports Medicine.** *Mestrado*: **Education; Environmental Studies; Health Sciences.** Also MBA; Medical Residencies

Student Services: Library

Last Updated: 01/04/16

UNIVERSITY OF THE SAPUCAI VALLEY

Universidade do Vale do Sapucai (UNIVÁS)

Av. Cel. Alfredo Custódio de Paula, 320,
Pouso Alegre, Minas Gerais 37550-000
Tel: +55(35) 3449-877 +55(35) 3449-9211
Fax: +55(35) 3449-9211
EMail: reitoria@univas.edu.br; facimpa@univas.edu.br
Website: http://www.univas.edu.br

Reitor: Carlos de Barros Laraia

Course

Accountancy (Accountancy); **Administration** (Administration); **Advertising and Marketing** (Advertising and Publicity; Marketing); **Biological Sciences** (Biological and Life Sciences); **Gastronomy** (Cooking and Catering); **History** (History); **Human Resources** (Human Resources); **Industrial Management** (Industrial Management); **Letters** (Arts and Humanities); **Medicine** (Medicine); **Nursing** (Nursing); **Pedagogy** (Pedagogy); **Pharmacy** (Pharmacy); **Physical Education** (Physical Education); **Physiotherapy** (Physical Therapy); **Postgraduate Studies** (Administration; Biological and Life Sciences; Education; Engineering; Food Science; Health Administration; Health Sciences; Linguistics; Medicine; Nutrition; Public Health; Rehabilitation and Therapy; Social Sciences; Teacher Training); **Production Engineering** (Production Engineering); **Psychology** (Psychology)

Further Information: Also Fatima Unit

History: Founded 1964 as Fundação Universidade do Vale do Sapucaí. Acquired present status and title 1999.

Main Language(s) of Instruction: Portuguese

Degrees and Diplomas: *Bacharelado*; *Especialização/Aperfeiçoamento*: **Education; Educational Administration; Educational Psychology; Food Science; Health Administration; Health Sciences; Hygiene; Microbiology; Nutrition; Occupational Health; Orthopaedics; Physical Education; Physical Therapy; Public Administration; Rehabilitation and Therapy; Respiratory Therapy; Safety Engineering.** *Mestrado*: **Biology; Education; Health Sciences; Linguistics.** *Doutorado*: **Linguistics.** Also MBA

Last Updated: 05/02/16

UNIVERSITY OF THE STATE OF RIO GRANDE DO NORTE

Universidade do Estado do Rio Grande do Norte (UERN)

Rua Almino Afonso 478, Sede da Reitoria, Centro,
Mossoró, Rio Grande do Norte 59610210
Tel: +55(84) 3315-2139
Fax: +55(84) 3315-2108
EMail: daa@unigranrio.com.br
Website: http://www.uern.br

Reitor: Pedro Fernandes Ribeiro Neto (2013-)
EMail: reitoria@uern.br

Pró-Reitor de Administração: Anderson Fernandes
Tel: +55(84) 3315-2116
EMail: gab.proad@uern.br; proad@uern.br

International Relations: Marcelo Melo da Costa, Diretor de Relações Internacionais e Interinstitucionais
Tel: +55(84) 3316-0794 EMail: daint@uern.br

Faculty

Arts and Humanities (Arts and Humanities; English; Literature; Music; Portuguese; Spanish); **Economics** (Accountancy; Administration; Economics; Environmental Management; Tourism); **Education** (Education; Pedagogy); **Exact and Natural Sciences** (Biology; Chemistry; Computer Science; Mathematics; Natural Sciences; Physics; Science Education); **Health Sciences** (Health Sciences; Medicine); **Law** (Law); **Nursing** (Nursing); **Philosophy and Social Sciences** (Advertising and Publicity; Geography; History; Humanities and Social Science Education; Journalism; Mass Communication; Philosophy; Radio and Television Broadcasting; Social Sciences); **Physical Education** (Physical Education); **Social Work** (Social Work)

Further Information: Also Advanced Campuses in Assu, Pau dos Ferros, Patu, Natal, Caicó

History: Founded 1968.

Academic Year: March to December (March-June; August-December)

Admission Requirements: Secondary school certificate and entrance examination

Main Language(s) of Instruction: Portuguese

Degrees and Diplomas: *Bacharelado*; *Licenciatura*; *Especialização/Aperfeiçoamento*: **Accountancy; Administrative Law; Child Care and Development; Education; Health Administration; Human Rights; Labour Law; Management; Media Studies; Nursing; Physical Education; Teacher Training; Welfare and Protective Services.** *Mestrado*: **Arts and Humanities; Biochemistry; Computer Science; Economics; Education; Health Sciences; Labour Law; Molecular Biology; Natural Sciences; Physics; Regional Planning; Rural Planning; Social Sciences; Social Work; Teacher Training; Town Planning.** *Doutorado*: **Arts and Humanities; Biochemistry; Molecular Biology.** Also Medical Residencies; Inter-institutional Doctorate courses in: Geography (DINTER) - UFPE; Business Administration (DINTER) - UFERSA/PUC/PR; Law (DINTER) - UFERSA/UNB; Education (DINTER) - UERJ.

Student Services: Library

Last Updated: 18/02/16

UNIVERSITY OF THE STATE OF SÃO PAULO

Universidade Paulista (UNIP)

Rua Doutor Bacelar 1212, Mirandópolis,
São Paulo, São Paulo 04026002
Tel: +55(11) 577-3184 +55(11) 577-4000
Fax: +55(11) 275-1541
Website: http://www.unip.br

Reitor: João Carlos Di Genio
Tel: +55(11) 5586-4031 EMail: reitoria@unip.br

Vice-Reitor de Planejamento, Administração e Finanças: Fábio Romeu de Carvalho

Institute

Exact Sciences and Technology (ICET) (Aeronautical and Aerospace Engineering; Architecture; Automation and Control Engineering; Chemical Engineering; Civil Engineering; Computer Engineering; Computer Science; Electrical Engineering; Electronic Engineering; Industrial Design; Information Technology; Mathematics; Mathematics Education; Mechanical Engineering; Production Engineering; Telecommunications Engineering; Town Planning); **Health Sciences (ICS)** (Animal Husbandry; Biological and Life Sciences; Biomedicine; Cosmetology; Dentistry; Health Administration; Nursing; Nutrition; Pharmacy; Physical Education; Physical Therapy; Radiology; Speech Therapy and Audiology; Veterinary Science); **Human Sciences (ICH)** (Cooking and Catering; Educational Sciences; Fashion Design; Hotel Management; Pedagogy; Psychology; Secretarial Studies; Social and Community Services; Tourism); **Social Sciences and Communication (ISC)** (Accountancy; Administration; Advertising and Publicity; Economics; International Relations; Journalism; Law; Marketing; Mass Communication; Translation and Interpretation)

Further Information: Also 6 campuses in other cities in the State of São Paulo

History: Founded 1972 as Instituto Unificado Paulista de Ensino Superior. Acquired present status 1988.

Academic Year: February to December

Admission Requirements: Secondary school certificate and entrance examination

Main Language(s) of Instruction: Portuguese

Degrees and Diplomas: *Tecnólogo*; *Bacharelado*; *Licenciatura*; *Especialização/Aperfeiçoamento*: **Acupuncture; Administration; African Studies; Agricultural Business; Alternative Medicine; Anatomy; Art Therapy; Automation and Control Engineering; Cognitive Sciences; Community Health; Computer Engineering; Cosmetology; Criminal Law; Dental Technology; Dentistry; Ecology; Educational Psychology; Electrical Engineering; Electronic Engineering; Embryology and Reproduction Biology; Energy Engineering; English; Environmental Management; Fire Science; Fiscal Law; Food Science; Gerontology; Graphic Design; Gynaecology and Obstetrics; Health Administration; Health Sciences; Higher Education Teacher Training; History; Human Rights; Industrial and Organizational Psychology; Industrial Engineering; Insurance; Interior Design; Labour Law; Latin American Studies; Law; Literature; Maintenance Technology; Marketing; Mathematics Education; Medicine; Midwifery; Nursing; Nutrition; Oncology; Oral Pathology; Orthodontics; Paediatrics; Pedagogy; Petroleum and Gas Engineering; Pharmacy; Physical Education; Physical Therapy; Physiology; Political Sciences; Portuguese; Private Law; Production Engineering; Psychiatry and Mental Health; Psychoanalysis; Psychology; Psychotherapy; Public Health; Radiology; Real Estate; Rehabilitation and Therapy; Safety Engineering; Social Problems; Social Psychology; Software Engineering; Speech Therapy and Audiology; Sports; Stomatology; Telecommunications Engineering; Translation and Interpretation; Veterinary Science.** *Mestrado*: **Administration; Dentistry; Environmental Studies; Mass Communication; Production Engineering.** *Doutorado*: **Dentistry; Mass Communication; Production Engineering.** Also MBA, MBC, DBA

Student Services: Academic Counselling, Canteen, Careers Guidance, Nursery Care, Sports Facilities

Publishing house: Centro de Recursos Educacionais (CERED)

Last Updated: 06/04/16

UNIVERSITY OF THE VALLEY OF ITAJAÍ

Universidade do Vale do Itajaí (UNIVALI)

Rua Uruguai, 458, Centro, Itajaí, Santa Catarina 88302-901
Tel: +55(47) 3341-7500 +55(47) 3341-7575
Fax: +55(47) 3341-7577
EMail: falecom@univali.br; ouvidoria@univali.br
Website: http://www.univali.br

Reitor: Mário Cesar dos Santos (2010-)
EMail: reitoria@univali.br; reitormcs@univali.br

Vice-Reitoria de Planejamento e Desenvolvimento Institucional: Carlos Alberto Tomelin

Campus

Camboriú (Aesthetics; Architecture; Business Administration; Computer Graphics; Cooking and Catering; Cosmetology; Design; Fashion Design; Graphic Design; Hotel and Restaurant; Human Resources; Industrial Design; Interior Design; International Relations; Law; Marketing; Pedagogy; Tourism; Town Planning); **Center - Biguaçu** (Accountancy; Business Administration; Law; Pedagogy; Physical Education); **Florianópolis** (Advertising and Publicity; Aesthetics; Architecture; Computer Graphics; Cosmetology; Graphic Design; Interior Design; Photography; Town Planning); **Itajaí** (Accountancy; Advertising and Publicity; Biological and Life Sciences; Biomedicine; Business Administration; Chemical Engineering; Civil Engineering; Computer Engineering; Computer Science; Dentistry; Electrical Engineering; Environmental Engineering; History; Information Technology; International Business; International Relations; Journalism; Law; Literature; Marine Science and Oceanography; Marine Transport; Marketing; Mathematics; Mechanical Engineering; Medicine; Music; Naval Architecture; Nursing; Nutrition; Pedagogy; Pharmacy; Photography; Physical Education; Physical Therapy; Portuguese; Production Engineering; Psychology; Public Relations; Radio and Television Broadcasting; Sanitary Engineering; Special Education; Speech Therapy and Audiology; Transport Management; Visual Arts); **Kobrasol - San Jose** (Business Administration; Computer Science; Human Resources; Law); **Tijucas** (Business Administration; Law; Pedagogy)

Further Information: Also Pequeno Anjo University Hospital

History: Founded 1989, incorporating previously existing faculties. Under the supervision of the Municipal authorities.
Academic Year: February to December (February-June; July-December)
Admission Requirements: Secondary school certificate or equivalent and entrance examination
Main Language(s) of Instruction: Portuguese
Degrees and Diplomas: *Bacharelado*; *Licenciatura*; *Especialização/Aperfeiçoamento*: **Administrative Law; Alternative Medicine; Business Administration; Civil Law; Commercial Law; Communication Studies; Constitutional Law; Dental Technology; Design; Environmental Studies; Fashion Design; Furniture Design; International Business; Journalism; Labour Law; Landscape Architecture; Law; Management; Marketing; Notary Studies; Pharmacy; Plastic Surgery; Production Engineering; Public Law; Radio and Television Broadcasting; Real Estate; Safety Engineering; Social Welfare; Software Engineering; Taxation; Textile Design; Tourism.** *Mestrado*: **Business Administration; Computer Science; Environmental Engineering; Environmental Studies; Health Sciences; Hotel and Restaurant; International Business; Law; Management; Pharmacy; Public Administration; Tourism; Transport Management.** *Doutorado*: **Business Administration; Environmental Engineering; Environmental Studies; Hotel and Restaurant; Law; Pharmacy; Tourism.** Also MBA
Student Services: Academic Counselling, Canteen, Careers Guidance, Health Services, Language Laboratory, Library, Social Counselling, Sports Facilities
Publications: Novos Estudos Jurídicos; Turismo Visão e Ação
Publishing House: Editora da UNIVALI
Last Updated: 29/02/16

UNIVERSITY OF THE VALLEY OF PARAIBA

Universidade do Vale do Paraíba (UNIVAP)
Av. Shishima Hifumi, n° 2911, Bairro Urbanova,
São José dos Campos, São Paulo 12244-000
Tel: +55(12) 3947-1000 +55(12) 3947-1056
Fax: +55(12) 3949-1334
EMail: gabinete@univap.br
Website: http://www.univap.br

Reitor: Jair Candido de Melo
Tel: +55(12) 3947-1056 EMail: gabinete@univap.br

Vice-Reitora: Sandra Maria Fonseca da Costa
Tel: +55(12) 3947-1056 EMail: gabinete@univap.br

International Relations: Antonio de Souza Teixeira Jr
Tel: +55(12) 3947-1036 EMail: texjr@univap.br

Faculty

Applied Social Sciences and Communication (Accountancy; Administration; Advertising and Publicity; Cooking and Catering; Fashion Design; Journalism; Mass Communication; Radio and Television Broadcasting); **Education and Arts** (Art Education; Biological and Life Sciences; Chemistry; Humanities and Social Science Education; Mathematics Education; Pedagogy; Physical Education; Science Education); **Engineering, Architecture and Town Planning** (Aeronautical and Aerospace Engineering; Architecture; Civil Engineering; Electrical and Electronic Engineering; Environmental Engineering; Materials Engineering; Town Planning); **Health Sciences** (Biomedicine; Cosmetology; Dentistry; Health Sciences; Nursing; Nutrition; Physical Therapy; Radiology; Social Work); **Law** (Law)
Further Information: Also campus at Urbanova
History: Founded 1954.
Academic Year: February to November
Admission Requirements: Secondary school certificate and entrance examination
Fees: 1,000 per semester (US Dollar)
Main Language(s) of Instruction: Portuguese
Degrees and Diplomas: *Tecnólogo*; *Bacharelado*; *Licenciatura*; *Especialização/Aperfeiçoamento*: **Biological and Life Sciences; Business Administration; Clinical Psychology; Dentistry; Educational Psychology; Environmental Management; Finance; Gerontology; Human Resources; Human Rights; Industrial and Organizational Psychology; Journalism; Latin American Studies; Marketing; Mass Communication; Midwifery; Neurology; Nursing; Orthopaedics; Physical Therapy; Psychoanalysis; Safety Engineering; Special Education.** *Mestrado*: **Astronomy and Space Science; Bioengineering; Biological and Life Sciences; Biomedical Engineering; Materials Engineering; Physics; Regional Planning; Town Planning.** *Doutorado*: **Astronomy and Space Science; Biomedical Engineering; Physics; Regional Planning; Town Planning.**
Student Services: Academic Counselling, Canteen, Cultural Activities, Language Laboratory, Nursery Care, Sports Facilities
Publications: Revista UNIVAP
Last Updated: 23/02/16

UNIVERSITY OF THE WEST OF SAO PAULO

Universidade do Oeste Paulista (UNOESTE)
Rua José Bongiovani 700, Cidade Universitária, Campus
Universitário, Presidente Prudente, São Paulo 19050-900
Tel: +55(18) 3229-1000
Fax: +55(18) 3229-1013
EMail: unoeste@apec.unoeste.br
Website: http://www.unoeste.br

Diretor Geral: Ana Cristina de Oliveira Lima
Tel: +55(18) 3229-1000

Pró-reitor Administrativo: Guilherme de Oliveira Lima Carapeba

Faculty

Agriculture (Agriculture; Animal Husbandry); **Dentistry** (Dentistry); **Engineering** (Civil Engineering); **Health Sciences** (Health Sciences; Physical Therapy; Psychology); **Informatics** (Computer Engineering; Computer Science); **Law, Administration and Accountancy** (Accountancy; Administration; Law); **Medicine** (Medicine); **Pharmacy and Biochemistry** (Biochemistry; Pharmacy); **Sciences, Letters, and Education** (Arts and Humanities; Education; Mathematics and Computer Science; Natural Sciences); **Social Communication** (Mass Communication)
Further Information: reitoria@unoeste.br; proacad@unoeste.br; rsantana@unoeste
History: Founded 1972. Under the supervision of the Associação Prudentina de Educação e Cultura.
Academic Year: February to December (February-June; August-December)
Admission Requirements: Secondary school certificate and entrance examination
Main Language(s) of Instruction: Portuguese
Degrees and Diplomas: *Bacharelado*; *Licenciatura*; *Especialização/Aperfeiçoamento*: **Aesthetics; Animal Husbandry; Architecture; Biological and Life Sciences; Biotechnology; Cardiology; Civil Engineering; Civil Law; Clinical Psychology; Commercial Law; Community Health; Computer Engineering; Crop Production; Cultural Studies; Development Studies; Economics; Educational Administration; Educational Psychology; Energy Engineering; Environmental Studies; Food Science; Food Technology; Forestry; Gerontology; Graphic Design; Gynaecology and Obstetrics; Health Administration; Health Sciences; History; Hygiene; Interior Design; Journalism; Laboratory Techniques; Labour Law; Law; Literature; Medicine; Microbiology; Nursing; Nutrition; Occupational Health; Occupational Therapy; Oncology; Orthodontics; Pharmacology; Pharmacy; Physical Education; Physical Therapy; Physiology; Primary Education; Psychiatry and Mental Health; Psychoanalysis; Psychology; Public Health; Radiology; Social Psychology; Social Sciences; Software Engineering; Soil Science; Special Education; Speech Therapy and Audiology; Sports; Toxicology; Transport Engineering; Veterinary Science.** *Mestrado*: **Agronomy; Animal Husbandry; Education; Environmental Studies; Regional Planning.** *Doutorado*: **Agronomy; Animal Husbandry; Pathology; Physiology.** Also MBA
Student Services: Library
Publications: Scientific Magazine
Last Updated: 19/02/16

UNIVERSITY OF UBERABA

Universidade de Uberaba (UNIUBE)
Av. Guilherme Ferreira, 217, Bairro Centro,
Uberaba, Minas Gerais 38010-200
Tel: +55(34) 3319-6600 +55(34) 3319-8800
Fax: +55(34) 3314-8910
EMail: uniube@uniube.br
Website: http://www.uniube.br

Reitor: Marcelo Palmério (1996-)
Tel: +55(34) 3311-8811 EMail: marcelo.palmerio@uniube.br
Superintendente: Alaor Vilela
Tel: +55(34) 3321-6600 EMail: alaor.vilela@uniube.br
International Relations: José Neto
EMail: jose.peres@uniube.br

Area

Agricultural Sciences (Veterinary Science); **Applied Social Sciences** (Accountancy; Administration; Advertising and Publicity; Architecture; Journalism; Law; Mass Communication; Town Planning); **Computer Science** (Information Technology); **Engineering** (Chemical Engineering; Civil Engineering; Computer Engineering; Electrical Engineering; Environmental Engineering; Production Engineering); **Health Sciences** (Dentistry; Medicine; Nursing; Pharmacy; Physical Education; Physical Therapy); **Human Sciences and Education** (Pedagogy; Physical Education; Psychology); **Humanities** (Accountancy); **Technological Studies** (Agricultural Business; Environmental Management; Finance; Human Resources; Interior Design; Safety Engineering)

Campus

Uberlândia Campus (Accountancy; Administration; Agricultural Business; Civil Engineering; Computer Engineering; Electrical Engineering; Environmental Engineering; Environmental Management; Finance; Human Resources; Law; Pedagogy; Production Engineering; Safety Engineering)

Further Information: Also Aeroporto and Rondon Campuses; Araxá Unit; Veterinary Hospital

History: Founded 1647 as Faculdade de Odontologia do Triângulo Mineiro. Acquired present status and title 1988.

Academic Year: February to December

Admission Requirements: Secondary school certificate and entrance examination

Main Language(s) of Instruction: Portuguese

Degrees and Diplomas: *Tecnólogo*; *Bacharelado*: **Accountancy; Administration; Advertising and Publicity; Architecture; Chemical Engineering; Civil Engineering; Computer Engineering; Computer Science; Dentistry; Electrical Engineering; Environmental Engineering; Information Technology; Journalism; Law; Medicine; Nursing; Pharmacy; Physical Education; Physical Therapy; Production Engineering; Safety Engineering; Town Planning; Veterinary Science.** *Licenciatura*: **Pedagogy; Psychology.** *Especialização/Aperfeiçoamento*: **Civil Engineering; Civil Law; Commercial Law; Construction Engineering; Educational Administration; Educational Sciences; Electronic Engineering; Environmental Management; Fiscal Law; Health Administration; Health Sciences; Industrial Engineering; Labour Law; Microbiology; Pharmacy; Physical Therapy; Primary Education; Psychoanalysis; Psychology; Respiratory Therapy; Safety Engineering; Software Engineering.** *Mestrado*: **Animal Husbandry; Chemical Engineering; Dentistry; Education; Veterinary Science.** Also MBA

Student Services: Canteen, Careers Guidance, Cultural Activities, Facilities for disabled people, Health Services, Language Laboratory, Library, Sports Facilities

Publications: Jornal Revelação; Revista Profissão Docente

Last Updated: 01/04/16

UNIVERSITY OF WEST SANTA CATARINA

Universidade do Oeste de Santa Catarina (UNOESC)

Rua Getúlio Vargas, 2125, Flor da Serra,
Chapecó, Santa Catarina 89600-000
Tel: +55(49) 3551-2000 +55(49) 3551-2098
Fax: +55(49) 3551-2004
EMail: reitoria@unoesc.edu.br
Website: http://www.unoesc.edu.br

Reitor: Aristides Cimadon
Tel: +55(49) 3551-2000 EMail: reitor@unoesc.edu.br

Diretor Executivo: Alciomar Antônio Marin

Area

Exact Sciences and Technology (Bioengineering; Chemical Engineering; Chemistry; Civil Engineering; Computer Engineering; Computer Science; Electrical Engineering; Energy Engineering; Information Technology; Mechanical Engineering; Physics; Production Engineering; Systems Analysis); **Humanities** (Accountancy; Advertising and Publicity; Architecture; Arts and Humanities; Business Administration; Design; Geography (Human); History; Human Resources; Law; Management; Marketing; Music; Pedagogy; Portuguese; Special Education; Town Planning; Visual Arts); **Life Sciences** (Agricultural Engineering; Agronomy; Animal Husbandry; Biological and Life Sciences; Biomedicine; Biotechnology; Cosmetology; Dentistry; Environmental Engineering; Food Technology; Nursing; Nutrition; Pharmacy; Physical Education; Physical Therapy; Sanitary Engineering; Veterinary Science)

History: Founded 1968. A Municipal institution.

Admission Requirements: Secondary school certificate and entrance examination

Main Language(s) of Instruction: Portuguese

Degrees and Diplomas: *Bacharelado*; *Licenciatura*; *Especialização/Aperfeiçoamento*: **Advertising and Publicity; Architecture; Art Education; Art Therapy; Automation and Control Engineering; Civil Law; Clinical Psychology; Computer Engineering; Construction Engineering; Criminal Law; Dairy; Dentistry; Ecology; Education; Educational Psychology; Finance; Food Science; Food Technology; Gerontology; Health Sciences; Human Resources; Hygiene; Interior Design; Labour Law; Landscape Architecture; Management; Marketing; Mass Communication; Nursing; Nutrition; Paper Technology; Pharmacy; Preschool Education; Primary Education; Psychology; Rehabilitation and Therapy; Safety Engineering; Special Education; Sports Management; Structural Architecture; Taxation; Transport Management.** *Mestrado*: **Administration; Biological and Life Sciences; Biotechnology; Education; Health Sciences; Law; Natural Sciences.** Also MBA

Student Services: Canteen, Library

Last Updated: 19/02/16

URUBUPUNGÁ INTEGRATED FACULTIES

Faculdades Integradas Urubupungá (FIU)

Avenida Coronel Jonas Alves de Mello 1660,
Térreo Centro, Pereira Barreto, SP 15370-000
Tel: +55(18) 3704-4242
Fax: +55(18) 3704-4222
EMail: fiu@fiu.com.br
Website: http://www.fiu.com.br

Presidente: Candido Pinheiro Dias Júnior

Diretor Executivo: João de Altayr Domingues

Course

Accountancy (Accountancy); **Administration** (Administration); **Aesthetics and Cosmetics** (Aesthetics; Cosmetology); **Chemical Engineering** (Chemical Engineering); **Letters - English** (Arts and Humanities; English); **Pedagogy** (Pedagogy); **Philosophy** (Philosophy); **Postgraduate Studies** (Business Administration; Clinical Psychology; Educational Administration; Educational Psychology; Higher Education Teacher Training; Human Resources; Literacy Education; Marketing; Protective Services; Public Administration; Social and Community Services; Special Education)

History: Founded 1995 as Faculdade de Ciências Administrativas e Contábeis Urubupungá (FACCUR). Acquired current title following merger with Faculdade de Educação, Ciências e Letras Urubupungá (FECLU) 1999.

Fees: From 338 to 872 per month (Brazilian Real)

Main Language(s) of Instruction: Portuguese

Degrees and Diplomas: *Técnico de Nivel Medio*; *Bacharelado*: **Accountancy; Administration; Chemical Engineering.** *Licenciatura*: **Arts and Humanities; English; Pedagogy; Philosophy.** *Especialização/Aperfeiçoamento*: **Business Administration; Clinical Psychology; Educational Administration; Educational Psychology; Higher Education Teacher Training; Human Resources; Literacy Education; Marketing; Protective Services; Public Administration; Social and Community Services; Special Education.**

Student Services: Library

Last Updated: 02/02/16

VALLEY OF THE RIO DOCE UNIVERSITY

Universidade Vale do Rio Doce (UNIVALE)
Campus Armando Vieira, Rua Juiz de Paz José Lemos, 279, Bairro Vila Bretas, Cx. Postal 295,
Governador Valadares, Minas Gerais 35030-260
Tel: +55(33) 3279-5200 +55(33) 3279-5500
Fax: +55(33) 3279-5503
EMail: fpf@univale.br; denise.chaves@univale.br
Website: http://www.univale.br

Reitor: José Geraldo Lemos Prata EMail: reitoria@univale.br

Pró-Reitora Acadêmica: Lissandra Lopes Coelho Rocha

School
UNIVALE-ETEIT Technical School

Centre
Communication and Humanities (Accountancy; Administration; Advertising and Publicity; Journalism; Law; Public Administration); **Health Sciences** (Dentistry; Nursing; Nutrition; Pharmacy; Physical Education; Physical Therapy; Psychology); **Licenciatura Degree** (Humanities and Social Science Education; Pedagogy; Physical Education); **Science and Technology** (Agricultural Business; Agronomy; Civil Engineering; Electrical Engineering; Environmental Engineering; Information Technology; Production Engineering)

Further Information: Also Armando Vieira and Antônio Rodrigues Coelho Campuses

History: Founded 1967.

Admission Requirements: Secondary school certificate and entrance examination

Main Language(s) of Instruction: Portuguese

Degrees and Diplomas: *Técnico de Nivel Medio*; *Tecnólogo*; *Bacharelado*: **Accountancy; Agronomy; Architecture; Dentistry; Electrical Engineering; Environmental Engineering; Journalism; Law; Nursing; Pharmacy; Physical Education; Physical Therapy; Production Engineering; Psychology; Public Administration; Town Planning.** *Licenciatura*: **Arts and Humanities; Pedagogy; Physical Education.** *Especialização/Aperfeiçoamento*: **Dentistry.** *Mestrado*: **Biological and Life Sciences; Regional Studies.**
Last Updated: 11/04/16

VASCO DE GAMA FACULTY

Faculdade Vasco de Gama
Avenida Vasco da Gama 2787 A, Salvador, BA 40240-090
Tel: +55(71) 3261-1658
EMail: lhaba14@hotmail.com
Website: http://www.faculdadevascodagama.com.br

Diretor: Luiz Henrique de Jesus Almeida

Course
Accountancy (Accountancy); **Administration** (Administration); **Social Communication** (Advertising and Publicity); **Social Pedagogy** (Pedagogy); **Social Services** (Social and Community Services); **Tourism** (Tourism)

History: Founded 2005.

Main Language(s) of Instruction: Portuguese

Degrees and Diplomas: *Bacharelado*; *Especialização/Aperfeiçoamento*; *Mestrado*
Last Updated: 18/04/16

VASCONCELLOS AND SOUZA FACULTY

Faculdade Vasconcellos e Souza
Avenida Anchieta, 50, Centro, Anchieta, ES 29230-000
Tel: +55(28) 3536-1799
EMail: ivs@anchietaonline.com.br

Director President: Cleomar Wolffgram

Course
Pedagogy (Pedagogy)

History: Founded 2007.

Main Language(s) of Instruction: Portuguese

Degrees and Diplomas: *Licenciatura*
Last Updated: 15/04/16

VERA CRUZ INSTITUTE OF EDUCATION

Instituto Superior de Educação Vera Cruz (ISE VERA CRUZ)
Rua Baumann 73, São Paulo, SP 05318-000
Tel: +55(11) 3838-5992 +55(11) 3838-5998
Fax: +55(11) 3838-5991 +55(11) 3838-5999
EMail: instituto@veracruz.edu.br; eventos@veracruz.edu.br; secretaria.instituto@veracruz.edu.br
Website: http://site.veracruz.edu.br/inicio/instituto

Course
Pedagogy (Pedagogy); **Postgraduate Studies** (Education; Literacy Education; Literature; Pedagogy; Preschool Education; Writing)
Main Language(s) of Instruction: Portuguese
Degrees and Diplomas: *Licenciatura*; *Especialização/Aperfeiçoamento*: **Education; Literature; Pedagogy; Preschool Education; Writing.**
Student Services: Library, Sports Facilities
Last Updated: 14/04/16

VICENTINA FACULTY

Faculdade Vicentina
Rua Jaime Reis, 531A - São Francisco, Curitiba, PR 80510-020
Tel: +55(41) 3079-7716
EMail: direcao@favic.com.br
Website: http://www.faculdadevicentina.com.br

Reitor: André Marmilicz

Course
Philosophy (Philosophy); **Theology** (Theology)

History: Founded 2006.

Main Language(s) of Instruction: Portuguese

Degrees and Diplomas: *Bacharelado*; *Especialização/Aperfeiçoamento*
Last Updated: 23/10/15

VITORIA ASSOCIATION OF HIGHER EDUCATION

Associação Vitoriana de Ensino Superior (FAVI)
Avenida Nossa Senhora da Penha, 1800, Barro Vermelho, Vitoria, Espírito Santo
Tel: +55(27) 3421-1500
Website: http://www.favi.br

FACULTY OF ACCOUNTANCY OF VITORIA
FACULDADE VITORIANA DE CIÊNCIAS CONTÁBEIS (FVCC)
Avenida Nossa Senhora da Penha 1800, Barro Vermelho, Vitória, Espirito Santo 29045400
Tel: +55(27) 325-0244
Fax: +55(27) 324-1500
EMail: favi@favi.com.br
Website: http://www.favi.br

Diretor: Geraldo Magela Alves

Course
Accountancy (Accountancy)
History: Founded 1990.
Main Language(s) of Instruction: Portuguese
Degrees and Diplomas: *Bacharelado*

FACULTY OF TECHNOLOGY OF VITORIA

FACULDADE VITORIANA DE TECNOLOGIA (FAVI)

Avenida Nossa Senhora da Penha 1800, Barro Vermelho, Vitória, Espirito Santo 29045400
Tel: +55(27) 3325-0244
Fax: +55(27) 324-1500
EMail: alves.geraldomagela@gmail.com

Diretor: Geraldo Magela Alves

Course
Information Systems (Computer Science; Information Technology)
History: Founded 1986
Main Language(s) of Instruction: Portuguese
Degrees and Diplomas: *Bacharelado*

INSTITUTE OF HIGHER EDUCATION AND ADVANCED TRAINING OF VITORIA

INSTITUTO DE ENSINO SUPERIOR E FORMAÇÃO AVANÇADA DE VITÓRIA (IESFAVI)

Avenida Nossa Senhora da Penha 1800, Vermelho, Vitória, Espírito Santo 29045400
Tel: +55(27) 3325-0244
Fax: +55(27) 3324-1500
EMail: favi@favi.br
Website: http://www.favi.br/IESFAVI/index.asp

Diretor: Rodrigo Cambará Arantes Garcia de Paiva
EMail: direcao@favi.br

Course

Administration (Administration; Hotel Management; Human Resources; International Business; Marketing; Systems Analysis); **Computer Science** (Computer Science); **Law** (Law); **Pedagogy** (Pedagogy); **Physiotherapy** (Physical Therapy); **Psychology** (Psychology); **Social Communication** (Communication Studies); **Tourism** (Tourism)

History: Founded 2000.

Main Language(s) of Instruction: Portuguese

Degrees and Diplomas: *Tecnólogo*; *Bacharelado*

WENCESLAU BRAZ NURSING SCHOOL

Escola de Enfermagem Wenceslau Braz (EEWB)

Avenida Cesário Alvim, 566, Centro, Itajubá, Minas Gerais 37500000
Tel: +55(35) 3622-0930
Fax: +55(35) 3622-1043
EMail: eewb@eewb.br
Website: http://www.eewb.br

Vice-Diretora: Lucyla Junqueira Carneiro

Course

Nursing (Nursing)

History: Founded 1954.

Main Language(s) of Instruction: Portuguese

Degrees and Diplomas: *Bacharelado*; *Especialização/Aperfeiçoamento*: **Nursing.**

Student Services: IT Centre, Library

Last Updated: 21/09/15

WRITER OSMAN DA COSTA LINS FACULTY

Faculdade Escritor Osman da Costa Lins (FACOL)

Rua do Estudante 85, Barrio Universitario, Vitória, PE 55612650
Tel: +55(81) 3523-0604
Fax: +55(81) 3523-0012
EMail: contato@facol.net
Website: http://www.facol.net

Diretor Geral: Paulo Roberto Leite de Arruda

Course

Accountancy (Accountancy); **Administration** (Administration); **Civil Engineering** (Civil Engineering); **Computer Science** (Computer Science); **Dentistry** (Dentistry); **Law** (Law); **Nursing** (Nursing); **Pedagogy** (Pedagogy); **Physical Education** (Physical Education); **Physiotherapy** (Physical Therapy); **Tourism** (Tourism)

History: Founded 1999 as Faculdade Escritor Osman da Costa Lins. Acquired present status and title 2001.

Main Language(s) of Instruction: Portuguese

Degrees and Diplomas: *Bacharelado*; *Licenciatura*; *Especialização/Aperfeiçoamento*

Student Services: Library

Last Updated: 07/07/15

ZACARIAS DE GÓES FACULTY

Faculdade Zacarias de Góes

Rua A Loteamento Jardim Grimaldi s/n, Valença, BA 45400-000
Tel: +55(75) 3641-6217
EMail: vitorino.coor@fazag.com.br
Website: http://www.fazag.edu.br

Diretor Geral: Vitorino Ferreira de Souza Filho

Area

Exact Sciences (Accountancy; Computer Science); **Health** (Nursing; Physical Therapy); **Human Sciences** (Administration; Literature; Pedagogy; Physical Education; Tourism)

History: Founded 2002.

Main Language(s) of Instruction: Portuguese

Degrees and Diplomas: *Bacharelado*; *Licenciatura*

Last Updated: 17/07/15

ZUMBI DOS PALMARES FACULTY

Faculdade Zumbi dos Palmares (FAZP)

Av. Santos Dumont, 843, Armênia, São Paulo, SP 01101-000
Tel: +55(11) 3229-4590
EMail: vestibular@zumbidospalmares.edu.br
Website: http://www2.zumbidospalmares.edu.br

Reitor: José Vicente

Course

Administration (Administration); **Law** (Law); **Pedagogy** (Pedagogy); **Social Communication** (Advertising and Publicity)

History: Founded 2000.

Main Language(s) of Instruction: Portuguese

Degrees and Diplomas: *Bacharelado*

Last Updated: 21/07/15

Brunei Darussalam

STRUCTURE OF HIGHER EDUCATION SYSTEM

Description:

To enter tertiary level education, students must have completed 'A' level courses with adequate and relevant passes. Tertiary education is provided by universities, one Polytechnic, institutes, and colleges. It is offered at both public and private institutions.

Stages of studies:

University level first stage: *Bachelor's degree*
The first stage of higher education leads, after studies lasting four years, to the Bachelor's degree.

University level second stage: *Master's degree*
A Master's degree is conferred after one to two years' study beyond the Bachelor's degree.

University level third stage: *Doctorate*
PhD degrees are conferred after a minimum of three years' study.

ADMISSION TO HIGHER EDUCATION

Admission to university-level studies:

Name of secondary school credential required: Brunei Cambridge General Certificate of Education Advanced Level

For entry to: All undergraduate programmes

Alternatives to credentials: "A" level equivalents such as the International Baccalaureate or a pass in year 1 or an undergraduate programme from a recognized university abroad.

Foreign students admission:

Definition of foreign student: Foreign students are non-Bruneian citizens residing in Brunei or students directly arriving from abroad and/or students holding a green identity card enrolled in any of the ITB academic programmes and universities in Brunei Darussalam.

Entry regulations: Successful applicants must have a valid travel document (passport) with a valid visa to enter Brunei Darussalam. Once registered as a university student, he/she is required to have a valid student pass issued by the Brunei Immigration and Registration Department and any overseas qualifications must be approved by the Brunei Darussalam National Accreditation Council. (MKPK).

To apply for a scholarship from the Government, applicants can contact:
- Brunei Darussalam Embassies/ High Commissions in the capitals of ASEAN Member countries;
- Commonwealth agencies in the student's home country;
- Scholarships and Training Unit, Permanent Secretary Office, Ministry of Education;

or look at the website of the Ministry of Foreign Affairs and Trade.

Health requirements: Foreign students are required to pass a medical fitness test with a certified government doctor.

Language proficiency: Foreign students must have either a grade Jayyid grade or above for Islamic language programmes or a "O" level in Malay language for Malay medium programmes or a "O" level in English language for English medium programmes or TOEFL 550 or IELTS 6.5.

RECOGNITION OF STUDIES

Quality assurance system:

The Brunei Darussalam National Accreditation Council, a unit under the Ministry of Education, is in charge of assessing the qualifications awarded by local and overseas higher education institutions/universities.

NATIONAL BODIES

Kementerian Pendidikan (Ministry of Education)

Minister: Suyoi bin Osman
Permanent Secretary, Higher Education: Haji Junaidi bin Haji Abdul Rahman
Bandar Seri Bagawan
Tel: +673(2) 381133
Fax: +673(2) 380880
EMail: jalil.mail@moe.edu.bn
WWW: http://www.moe.gov.bn
Role of national body: Responsible for all levels of education.

Sistem Pengambilan Pusat Institusi Pengajian Tinggi - HECAS (Higher Education Centralised Admission System)

Bandar Seri Bagawan
WWW: http://www.hecas.edu.bn/hecasportal
Role of national body: To process applications for undergraduate programmes at higher education institutions in Brunei Darussalam and government scholarships to study abroad.

Majlis Kebangsaan Pengiktirafan Kelulusan - MKPK (Brunei Darussalam National Accreditation Council)

Old Airport Road
Berakas 3510
Tel: +673(2) 380036
Fax: +673(2) 381238
EMail: mkpk@moe.edu.bn
WWW: http://moe.gov.bn/secretariat-of-brunei-darussalam-national-accreditation-council/
Role of national body: To assess and ascertain the value and status of qualifications

Data for academic year: 2013-2014
Source: IAU from the Website of the Ministry of Education and "Brunei Darussalam Education Statistics 2012", Ministry of Education, 2013. Bodies 2016.

INSTITUTIONS

PUBLIC INSTITUTIONS

BRUNEI INSTITUTE OF TECHNOLOGY

Institut Teknologi Brunei (ITB)
Jalan Tungku Link, Gadong BE 1410
Tel: +673(2) 461020
Fax: +673(2) 461035/6
EMail: enquiry@itb.edu.bn
Website: http://www.itb.edu.bn

Acting Vice Chancellor: Hjh Zohrah binti Haji Sulaiman

Faculty
Business and Computing (Accountancy; Business Computing; Computer Graphics; Computer Networks; Computer Science; E-Business/Commerce; Finance; Marketing); **Engineering** (Chemical Engineering; Civil Engineering; Electrical and Electronic Engineering; Mechanical Engineering; Petroleum and Gas Engineering; Telecommunications Engineering)

Centre
Communication, Teaching and Learning (CCTL)

History: Founded 1986.
Main Language(s) of Instruction: Malay, English
Degrees and Diplomas: *Diploma/Certificate*; *Bachelor's Degree*
Last Updated: 16/07/13

SERI BEGAWAN RELIGIOUS TEACHERS UNIVERSITY COLLEGE

Kolej Universiti Perguruan Ugama Seri Begawan (KUPU SB)
KM 2, Jalan Raja Isteri Pengiran Anak Saleha, Bandar Seri Begawan BA 2111
Tel: +673 (2) 225227
Fax: +673 (2) 225226
EMail: info@kupu-sb.edu.bn
Website: http://www.kupu-sb.edu.bn

Ra'es: Hajah Masnon binti Haji Ibrahim
Tel: +673(2) 225227 ext 101 EMail: raes@kupu-sb.edu.bn

Acting Registrar, Treasurer: Anak Haji Damit Baharuddin bin Pengiran Anak Safiuddin

Faculty
Education (Education); **Shariah** (Islamic Law); **Ushuluddin** (Islamic Studies)

Centre
Core Knowledge; **Multimedia and Technology**; **Postgraduate Studies and Research**; **Research Understanding Waljama'ah Sunni**

History: Founded 2007.
Main Language(s) of Instruction: Malay

Degrees and Diplomas: *Diploma/Certificate*: **Religious Education.** *Bachelor's Degree*: **Religious Education.**
Last Updated: 04/12/13

SULTAN SHARIF ALI ISLAMIC UNIVERSITY

Universiti Islam Sultan Sharif Ali (UNISSA)
Spg 347, Jalan Pasar Baharu, Gadong,
Bandar Seri Begawan BE 1310
Tel: +673 2462000
Fax: +673 2462233 - +673 2462244
EMail: info@unissa.edu.bn
Website: http://www.unissa.edu.bn

Deputy Rector/Acting Rector: Haji Amiruddin Alam Shah bin Pg Anak Haji Ismail Tel: +673 2462000 EMail: rektor@unissa.edu.bn

Registrar: Haji Tarip bin Mat Yassin
Tel: +673 2462204 EMail: hatamaya@unissa.edu.bn

Faculty
Arabic Language and Islamic Civilisation (Arabic; Islamic Studies); **Business and Management Sciences** (Business and Commerce; Management); **Shariah and Law** (Islamic Law); **Usuluddin** (Islamic Studies)

Centre
Madhhab Shafi'i Research Centre (MSRC); **Postgraduate Studies and Research (CPSR)**; **Promotion of Knowledge and Language Learning**

History: Founded 2007.

Main Language(s) of Instruction: Malay, English

Degrees and Diplomas: *Bachelor's Degree*: **Arabic; Finance; Islamic Studies.** *Master's Degree*: **Arabic; Banking; Finance; Islamic Studies.** *Ph.D.*: **Arabic; Islamic Studies.**

Student Services: Careers Guidance, Social Counselling, Sports Facilities
Last Updated: 04/12/13

UNIVERSITY OF BRUNEI DARUSSALAM

Universiti Brunei Darussalam (UBD)
Tungku Link Road, Gadong BE 1410
Tel: +673(2) 463-001
Fax: +673(2) 461-003
EMail: admi@admin.ubd.edu.bn
Website: http://www.ubd.edu.bn

Vice-Chancellor: Hj Zulkarnain bin Haji Hanafi
Tel: +673(2) 460-957
EMail: chanclry@admin.ubd.edu.bn; hihd@admin.ubd.edu.bn

Bursar/Acting Registrar & Secretary: Dayang Rubiah binti Haji Yacub EMail: registr@admin.ubd.edu.bn

International Relations: Abby Tan Chee Hong
Tel: +673(2) 463-062 EMail: ioenquiry@admin.ubd.edu.bn

Faculty
Arts and Social Sciences (FASS) (Anthropology; Applied Linguistics; Arts and Humanities; English; Environmental Studies; Geography; History; Linguistics; Literature; Malay; Social Sciences; Sociology); **Business, Economics and Policy Studies (FBEPS)** (Accountancy; Business Administration; Economics; Finance; Management; Political Sciences; Public Administration); **Integrated Technologies (FIT)** (Engineering); **Science** (Applied Physics; Biology; Chemistry; Computer Science; Engineering; Geology; Mathematics; Natural Sciences; Petroleum and Gas Engineering; Physics)

Institute
Asian Studies (IAS) (Asian Studies); **Biodiversity and Environmental Research (IBER)** (Environmental Studies); **Education (SHBIE, Sultan Hassanal Bolkiah)** (Art Education; Education; Educational Psychology; Mathematics Education; Native Language Education; Preschool Education; Science Education; Social Sciences; Teacher Training); **Health Sciences (Pengiran Anak Puteri Rashidah Sa'adatul Bolkiah)** (Biomedicine; Medicine; Midwifery; Nursing); **Islamic Studies (SOASCIS, Sultan Omar 'Ali Saifuddien)** (Arabic; Islamic Law; Islamic Studies); **Leadership, Innovation and Advancement (ILIA)** (Leadership; Management); **Policy Studies** (Public Law)

Section
Student Affairs

Academy
Brunei Studies (Asian Studies)

Centre
Centre for Student with Diverse Learning Needs (Special Education); **Continuing Education (CEC)** (Continuing Education); **e-Government Innovation (eG.InC)** (Information Technology; Public Administration); **Information Communication Technology** (Computer Networks; Computer Science; Information Technology; Telecommunications Engineering); **Islamic Banking, Finance and Management** (Banking; Finance; Management); **Language** (Chinese; Filipino; German; Korean; Malay; Spanish); **UBD/IBM** (Asian Studies; Energy Engineering; Environmental Studies; Finance; Food Science)

History: Founded 1985.

Academic Year: August to May (August-December; January-May)

Admission Requirements: General Certificate of Education (GCE) 'A' levels, International Baccalaureate (I.B.), or equivalent

Fees: 3000-4000 per annum; graduate, c. 10,000 (Brunei Dollar)

Main Language(s) of Instruction: Malay, English, Arabic

Degrees and Diplomas: *Bachelor's Degree*; *Master's Degree*: **Arts and Humanities; Business Administration; Computer Science; Crop Production; Economics; Education; Energy Engineering; Finance; Health Sciences; Management; Public Law; Social Sciences.** *Ph.D.*: **Arts and Humanities; Asian Studies; Business and Commerce; Education; Health Sciences; Islamic Studies; Natural Sciences; Social Sciences.**

Student Services: Foreign Studies Centre, IT Centre, Library
Last Updated: 02/01/14

Bulgaria

STRUCTURE OF HIGHER EDUCATION SYSTEM

Description:

Higher education is provided by higher schools - universities, specialized higher schools (academies, institutes etc.) and independent colleges. Some universities and colleges are private. Higher education is regulated by the 1995 Law on Higher Education (latest amendment 2010) and the Law for the Development of Academic Staff (May 2010).

Stages of studies:

University level first stage: *Bakalavr (Bachelor)*
This stage of higher education lasts for at least four years of regular study of at least 240 credits and leads to the Bachelor's degree (Bakalavr) in many fields. It is a first cycle degree according to the Bologna process and corresponds to level 6 in the EQF and to level 5A in ISCED-97. This is a degree created by the Higher Education Act of 1995. However, there are some fields where the Bachelor does not exist and where studies lead directly to the second stage of studies (Master's degree level) e.g. Law, Medicine, Dental Medicine, Pharmacy, Architecture, and Veterinary Medicine.

University level second stage: *Magistr (Master)*
This stage of study accounts for at least 300 credits and lasts for five to six years of regular study following secondary education or one year after a Bachelor's degree. Students must (usually) complete a thesis and pass a state examination. It is a second cycle degree according to the Bologna process and corresponds to level 7 in the EQF and to level 5A in ISCED-97. The former Diplom za Visse Obrazovanie, awarded before the 1995 law, is officially regarded as equivalent to the Master's.

University level third stage: *Doktor (Doctor)*
This stage is the third cycle of the higher education system and leads to the title of Doctor. It corresponds to level 8 in the EQF and to level 6 in ISCED-97. It is obtained on the basis of individual research and after the defence of a thesis. It replaces the former Kandidat na Naukite (Candidate of Sciences). The Higher Education Act of 1995 grants all Kandidat na Naukite holders the same rights as a holder of a Doctor's degree.

ADMISSION TO HIGHER EDUCATION

Admission to university-level studies:

Name of secondary school credential required: Diploma za Sredno Obrazovanie

Numerus clausus: Yes

Other requirements: For less demanded specialities, candidates may enrol on the basis of document submission, graded according to academic record.

Foreign students admission:

Definition of foreign student: Students who are not Bulgarian citizens.

Quotas: Quotas are defined each year according to the needs of the higher education institutions.

Admission requirements: Foreign students must hold a Secondary School Leaving Certificate equivalent to the Bulgarian Secondary School Leaving Certificate and must be officially admitted by the Ministry of Education and Science.

Entry regulations: Candidates should have a valid passport or a visa and be recommended by qualified persons and institutions in their home country.

Language proficiency: A pre-university year of studies in the Bulgarian language is required. Examinations take place after 1 year of studies in the Bulgarian language at the Institute for Foreign Students.

RECOGNITION OF STUDIES

Quality assurance system:

Bulgarian higher education institutions, NACID (Nacionalen centar za informacia i dokumentacia), Bulgarian scientific organisations, and competent recognition authorities in the respective regulated professions are all responsible for recognition.

Bodies dealing with recognition:

Natzionalen tzentar za informatzia i dokmentatzia (National Centre for Information and Documentation)

Executive Director: Vanya Grashkina
52 A, Dr. GM Dimitrov Blvd.
Sofia 1125
Tel: +359(2) 817-3824
Fax: +359(2) 971-3120
EMail: nacid@nacid-bg.net; naric@nacid.bg
WWW: http://www.nacid.bg

Special provisions for recognition:

Recognition for university level studies: All Bulgarian higher education institutions for access to their university level programmes.

For access to advanced studies and research: All Bulgarian scientific organisations and higher education institutions for access to their advanced studies/research programsmes. NACID for Master's degree holders, wishing to be admitted to PhD studies in scientific organisations which are not HEIs.

For exercising a profession: NACID (Nacionalen centar za informacia i dokumentacia) for facilitating access to the non-regulated segment of the labour market. Competent recognition authorities in the respective regulated professions - for the regulated segment of the labour market.

NATIONAL BODIES

Ministerstvo na obrazovanieto i naukata (Ministry of Education and Science)

Minister: Meglena Kuneva
2A, Knyaz Dondukov Bld.
Sofia 1000
Tel: +359(2) 921-7799
Fax: +359(2) 988-2485
WWW: http://www.mon.bg

Role of national body: Executive body in charge of the implementation of the national higher education policy.

Bulgarian Rectors' Conference

President: Dimitar Grekov
c/o Agrarian University
12, Mendeleev Bld.
Plovdiv 4000
Tel: +359(32) 633-232
Fax: +359(32) 633-242
EMail: rector@au-plovdiv.bg
WWW: http://www.au-plovdiv.bg

Natzionalna agentzia za ozeniavane i akreditatzia - NAOA (National Evaluation and Accreditation Agency)

Chairman: Boyan Biolchev
General Secretary: Mila Nencheva Penelova
125 Tsarigradsko shose Blvd, bl. 5,fl. 4, north wing
Sofia 1113
Tel: +359(2) 807-7811
Fax: +359(2) 971-068
EMail: info@neaa.government.bg
WWW: http://www.neaa.government.bg

Role of national body: NEAA is the specialized national body for quality assurance, evaluation and accreditation of the activities of Higher Education Institutions: teaching, research, artistic, etc. that correspond to their specific features. There are two types of accreditation: institutional accreditation and programme accreditation (for all educational degrees). NEAA developed and adopted evaluation and accreditation criteria in accordance with the Higher Education Act and adopted state requirements. NEAA also evaluates projects for the establishing or transforming of higher schools or colleges and their main units, as well as the opening of new specialities.

Data for academic year: 2014-2015
Source: IAU from the National Center for Information and Documentation (NACID), Sophia, 2014. Bodies 2016.

INSTITUTIONS

PUBLIC INSTITUTIONS

ACADEMY OF ECONOMICS D.A. TSENOV - SVISHTOV

D.A. Čenov Stopanska akademija - Svištov
2 Emanuil Cakarov Str., 5250 Svištov
Tel: +359(631) 66-201
Fax: +359(631) 87-355
EMail: rectorat@uni-svishtov.bg
Website: http://www.uni-svishtov.bg

Rector: Velichko Adamov
Tel: +359(631) 66-200 EMail: rector@uni-svishtov.bg

Vice Rector of Students' Policy and Academic Development: Teodora Dimitrova Tel: +359(631) 66-205

International Relations: Tanya Gorcheva, Director, Centre for International Cooperation and Projects
Tel: +359(631) 66-440 EMail: gorcheva@uni-svishtov.bg

Faculty
Economic Accounting (Accountancy; Economic History; Mathematics; Physical Education; Sports; Statistics); **Finance** (Banking; Economics; Finance; Foreign Languages Education; Insurance; Social Welfare); **Industrial and Commercial Business** (Agricultural Economics; Business Administration; Business and Commerce; Ecology; History; Industrial Management; Law; Philosophy; Sociology; Tourism); **Management and Marketing** (Business Administration; Business Computing; International Economics; International Relations; Management; Marketing)

Further Information: Branches in Loveč, Plovdiv, Botevgrad, College of Economics and Management, Svishtov

History: Founded 1936, as Higher Institute of Finance and Economics, acquired present status and title 1995.

Academic Year: September to June (September-December; February-June)

Admission Requirements: Secondary school certificate (Diploma za zavarsheno sredno obrazovanie), and entrance examination

Fees: c. 40 per semester (Bulgarian Lev)

Main Language(s) of Instruction: Bulgarian

Accrediting Agency: National Agency for Evaluation and Accreditation; Lloyd Register Quality Assurance

Degrees and Diplomas: *Bakalavr*, *Magistr*: **Accountancy; Agricultural Business; Banking; Business Administration; Business and Commerce; Business Computing; Economics; Finance; Health Administration; Industrial and Organizational Psychology; Insurance; International Business; Management; Marketing; Public Administration; Regional Planning; Statistics; Tourism.** *Doktor*: **Business Administration.**

Student Services: Academic Counselling, Canteen, Cultural Activities, Health Services, IT Centre, Sports Facilities

Publications: Business Management; Economic World Library; Narodostopanski Archiv

Publishing House: 'D. Čenov' Publishing House
Last Updated: 25/02/15

ACADEMY OF MUSIC, DANCE AND FINE ARTS

Akademija za muzikalno i tanzovo izkustvo (ADMFA)
str. "Todor Samodumov" n°2, pk 783, 4000 Plovdiv
Tel: +359(32) 601-441
Fax: +359(32) 632-467
EMail: office@artacademyplovdiv.com
Website: http://www.artacademyplovdiv.com

Rector: Vasilev Milcho
Tel: +359(32) 601-442 +359(32) 628-312
EMail: m.vasilev@artacademyplovdiv.com; office@artacademyplovdiv.com

Vice-Rector: Julia Kuyumdzhieva
Tel: +359(32) 601-463
EMail: kujumdziev@artacademyplovdiv.com

Faculty
Fine Arts (Design; Fine Arts; Visual Arts); **Music Education** (Music Education); **Musical Folklore and Choreograpy** (Dance; Music; Musical Instruments; Musicology)

History: Founded 1964 as Pedagogical Faculty, became Pedagogical Institute of Music 1972. Acquired present status and title 1995.

Academic Year: September to May (September-December; February-May)

Admission Requirements: Secondary school certificate (Diploma za zavarsheno sredno obrazovanie) and entrance examination

Main Language(s) of Instruction: Bulgarian

Degrees and Diplomas: *Bakalavr*, *Magistr*: **Art Education; Art Management; Art Therapy; Clothing and Sewing; Computer Graphics; Conducting; Dance; Display and Stage Design; Fashion Design; Fine Arts; Graphic Design; Jazz and Popular Music; Media Studies; Multimedia; Music Education; Music Theory and Composition; Musical Instruments; Musicology; Painting and Drawing; Photography; Public Relations; Religious Art; Religious Music; Sculpture; Singing; Sound Engineering (Acoustics).**

Student Services: Canteen, Careers Guidance, Cultural Activities, Health Services, Library, Residential Facilities, Sports Facilities
Last Updated: 13/02/15

AGRICULTURAL UNIVERSITY

Agraren Universitet (AU)
12 Mendeleev Boulevard, 4000 Plovdiv
Tel: +359(32) 654-200
Fax: +359(32) 633-157
EMail: info@au-plovdiv.bg
Website: http://www.au-plovdiv.bg

Rector: Hristina Yancheva
Tel: +359(32) 634-300
EMail: rector@au-plovdiv.bg; christina@au-plovdiv.bg

Administrative Manager: Velichko Rodopski
Tel: +359(32) 654-313 EMail: Velichko_rodopski@abv.bg

International Relations: Nelly Nencheva, Vice Rector Education and International Relations
Tel: +359(32) 654-301 EMail: bencheva@gmail.com

Faculty

Agronomy *("Saint Dimitrius of Thessaloniki")* (Agronomy; Animal Husbandry; Biochemistry; Botany; Crop Production; Farm Management; Plant and Crop Protection; Soil Science); **Economics** (Accountancy; Agricultural Business; Agricultural Economics; Computer Science; Management; Marketing; Statistics; Tourism); **Horticulture and Viticulture** (Agricultural Equipment; Fruit Production; Geology; Horticulture; Viticulture); **Plant Protection and Agroecology** (Agriculture; Biotechnology; Chemistry; Ecology; Entomology; Environmental Management; Microbiology; Plant and Crop Protection; Plant Pathology)

Department

Languages and Sport (Bulgarian; Modern Languages; Physical Education; Sports)

Further Information: Experimental fields - 185 ha, Experimental Wine-cellar

History: Founded 1945 as Higher Institute of Agriculture, acquired present status and title 2001.

Academic Year: September to June

Admission Requirements: Secondary school certificate (Diploma za zavarsheno sredno obrazovanie), or foreign equivalent

Fees: 2,500 for preparatory course; 1,250-625 per semester for foreign students with dual citizenship (Euro)

Main Language(s) of Instruction: Bulgarian

Accrediting Agency: National Evaluation and Accreditation Agency

Degrees and Diplomas: *Bakalavr, Magistr.* **Accountancy; Agricultural Business; Agricultural Equipment; Agricultural Management; Agriculture; Animal Husbandry; Apiculture; Biological and Life Sciences; Biotechnology; Botany; Business Administration; Crop Production; Economics; Environmental Management; Farm Management; Finance; Floriculture; Horticulture; Interior Design; Irrigation; Landscape Architecture; Management; Meat and Poultry; Pharmacy; Plant and Crop Protection; Protective Services; Soil Conservation; Tourism; Viticulture.** *Doktor.* **Agricultural Business; Agricultural Economics; Agricultural Management; Animal Husbandry; Apiculture; Biology; Biotechnology; Chemistry; Crop Production; Ecology; Environmental Management; Floriculture; Fruit Production; Genetics; Horticulture; Meat and Poultry; Physiology; Plant and Crop Protection; Plant Pathology; Sericulture; Soil Science; Vegetable Production; Viticulture.** Some Master's Degree Programmes are conducted in English Language (Biotechnology, Agriculture and Rural Planning)

Student Services: Canteen, Careers Guidance, IT Centre, Library, Residential Facilities, Sports Facilities

Publications: Scientific Works

Academic Staff *2014-2015*: Total: c. 150
Student Numbers *2014-2015*: Total: c. 3,500
Last Updated: 12/02/15

INTERNATIONAL BUSINESS SCHOOL

Meždunarodno vische biznes učiliše (IBS)
14 Gurko Str., 2140 Botevgrad
Tel: +359 723-688-12
Fax: +359 723-688-13
EMail: info@ibsedu.bg
Website: http://www.ibsedu.bg

Rector: Ruslan Penchev
Tel: +359 723-688-12 EMail: rpenchev@ibsedu.bg

Vice-Rector: Teodora Georgieva
Tel: +359 723-688-18 EMail: tgeorgieva@ibsedu.bg

International Relations: Nadya Gaydarska-Kirilova, Director Development and International Relations Department
Tel: +359(2) 987-0292 EMail: ngaydarska@ibsedu.bg

Programme

Accountancy (Accountancy); **Accountancy and Audit** *(Graduate)* (Accountancy); **Business Administration** (Business Administration); **Business Administration** *(in English)* (Business Administration); **Business Administration** *(Graduate)* (Business Administration); **Business Finance** *(Graduate)* (Finance); **Entrepreneurship and Innovation** *(Graduate)* (Management); **Health Care Management** *(Graduate)* (Health Administration); **Information Management** *(Graduate)* (Information Management); **International Economic Relations** (International Economics); **Internet Marketing** *(Graduate)* (E- Business/Commerce; Marketing); **Logistics** *(Graduate)* (Transport Management); **Marketing and Communications** (Advertising and Publicity; Marketing; Public Relations; Sales Techniques); **Music Business** *(Graduate)* (Art Management; Business Administration); **Project Management** *(Graduate)* (Management); **Public Sector Management** *(Graduate)* (Public Administration); **Taxation and Management** *(Graduate)* (Management; Taxation); **Tourism** (Tourism); **Tourism Management** *(Graduate)* (Tourism)

History: Founded 1991. Acquired present status 2002.

Fees: Bachelor's programmes, 700 per semester; Bachelor's programme in English, 1,350 per semester; Master's programmes, 750 per semester (Bulgarian Lev)

Main Language(s) of Instruction: Bulgarian, English

Accrediting Agency: National Agency for Assessment and Accreditation

Degrees and Diplomas: *Bakalavr; Magistr.* **Accountancy; Art Management; Business Administration; Finance; Information Management; Insurance; Management; Marketing; Public Administration; Taxation; Tourism; Transport Management.** *Doktor.* **Agricultural Management; Economics; Industrial Management; Management; Tourism.**

Student Services: Careers Guidance, Library
Last Updated: 24/02/15

MEDICAL UNIVERSITY PROF. DR. PARASKEV STOYANOV - VARNA

Prof. Dr. Paraskev Stoyanov Medicinski universitet - Varna (MEDICAL UNIVERSITY OF VARNA)
55, Marin Drinov Str., 9002 Varna
Tel: +359(52) 677-050
Fax: +359(52) 650-019
EMail: uni@mu-varna.bg; international_relations@mu-varna.bg
Website: http://mu-varna.bg

Rector: Krasimir Ivanov (2012-)
Tel: +359(52) 225-622 EMail: rektor@mu-varna.bg

Vice Rector Educational Affairs: Albena Kerekovska

International Relations: Aneta Dokova, Director of the International Relations Office
Tel: +359(52) 677-019 EMail: dokova@mu-varna.bg

Faculty

Dentistry (Dentistry); **Medicine** (Anatomy; Embryology and Reproduction Biology; Histology; Medicine; Orthopaedics; Pathology; Physiology); **Pharmacy** (Pharmacy); **Public Health** (Health Administration; Health Sciences; Public Health)

College

Medicine *(Šoumen, Dobrič)* (Medicine)

Further Information: Also University Hospitals (St Marina, St Anna)

History: Founded 1961 as Higher Institute of Medicine, acquired present status 1995.

Academic Year: September to June (September-December; February-June)

Admission Requirements: Secondary school certificate (Diploma za zavarsheno sredno obrazovanie)

Fees: 8,000 per anum; Ph.D., 5,000 per annum (Euro)

Main Language(s) of Instruction: Bulgarian, English

Degrees and Diplomas: *Profesionalen Bakalavr.* **Cosmetology; Medical Auxiliaries; Medical Technology; Ophthalmology; Public Health; Rehabilitation and Therapy; Treatment Techniques.** *Bakalavr.* **Health Administration; Midwifery; Nursing.**

Magistr: **Dentistry; Health Administration; Medicine; Nursing; Pharmacy; Public Health.** *Doktor*: **Anaesthesiology; Anatomy; Biochemistry; Cardiology; Cell Biology; Community Health; Dentistry; Dermatology; Endocrinology; Forensic Medicine and Dentistry; Gastroenterology; Genetics; Gynaecology and Obstetrics; Haematology; Histology; Hygiene; Laboratory Techniques; Management; Medicine; Microbiology; Nephrology; Neurology; Occupational Health; Oncology; Ophthalmology; Organic Chemistry; Orthopaedics; Otorhinolaryngology; Paediatrics; Pathology; Pharmacology; Pharmacy; Physical Therapy; Physiology; Pneumology; Psychiatry and Mental Health; Psychology; Radiology; Rehabilitation and Therapy; Social and Preventive Medicine; Surgery; Toxicology; Urology; Venereology; Virology.** Also programmes conducted in English: Undergraduate level (Doctor of Medicine (MD) and Dentistry (DMD)) and graduate level (Master's Degree in Public Health).

Student Services: Academic Counselling, Canteen, Careers Guidance, Health Services, Library, Social Counselling, Sports Facilities

Publications: Biomedical Reviews; Scripta Scientifica Medica

Last Updated: 12/02/15

MEDICAL UNIVERSITY - PLEVEN

Medicinski universitet - Pleven (MUPL)

1, Sv. Kliment Ohridski Str., 5800 Pleven

Tel: +359(64) 884-101

Fax: +359(64) 801-603

EMail: rector@mu-pleven.bg

Website: http://www.mu-pleven.bg/

Rector: Slavcho Tomov
Tel: +359(64) 800-728
EMail: rector@mu-pleven.bg

Vice-Rector of Education: Margarita Alexandrova
Tel: +359(64) 884-130
EMail: vice_rector_edu@mu-pleven.bg

International Relations: Savelina Popovska, Head, International Cooperation Department
Tel: +359(64) 884-169
EMail: katiakovach@gmail.com; iro@mu-pleven.bg

Faculty

Health Care (Health Sciences; Orthopaedics; Rehabilitation and Therapy); **Medicine** (Medicine); **Public Health** (Forensic Medicine and Dentistry; Health Administration; Health Education; Information Technology; Medical Parasitology; Medicine; Occupational Health; Occupational Therapy; Physical Therapy; Psychiatry and Mental Health; Psychology; Public Health; Rehabilitation and Therapy; Social and Preventive Medicine)

College

Medical Sciences (Medicine)

Department

Language and Specialized Training (Bulgarian; English; French; German; Latin; Natural Sciences)

Further Information: Branches in Rousse and Véliko Turnovo for the Medical College. Also Institute Hospital

History: Founded 1974 as independent Institute.

Academic Year: September to May (September-December; February-May)

Admission Requirements: Secondary school certificate (Diploma za zavarsheno sredno obrazovanie) or foreign equivalent and entrance examination. One year preparatory courses in Bulgarian language for foreign students. For students of the Faculty of Nursing - Speciality 'Management of Nursing Care', Diploma from a medical college and a minimum of 5 years of practice in health institutions

Fees: 3,000-7,000 per annum (Euro)

Main Language(s) of Instruction: Bulgarian, English

Accrediting Agency: Ministry of Education and Science; National Evaluation and Accreditation Agency

Degrees and Diplomas: *Bakalavr*: **Health Administration; Midwifery; Nursing.** *Magistr*: **Health Administration; Medicine; Public Health.** *Doktor*: **Cardiology; Epidemiology; Medical Parasitology; Medicine; Paediatrics; Surgery; Urology.**

Student Services: Academic Counselling, Canteen, Careers Guidance, Health Services, Library, Residential Facilities, Social Counselling, Sports Facilities

Academic Staff *2014-2015*	**TOTAL**
FULL-TIME	**360**
STAFF WITH DOCTORATE	
FULL-TIME	**60**
Student Numbers *2014-2015*	
All (Foreign included)	**2,044**
FOREIGN ONLY	**275**

Last Updated: 24/02/15

MEDICAL UNIVERSITY - PLOVDIV

Medicinski Universitet - Plovdiv

15A Vassil Aprilov Str., 4002 Plovdiv

Tel: +359(32) 443-839

Fax: +359(32) 442-194

EMail: vicer_ms@meduniversity-plovdiv.bg

Website: http://www.meduniversity-plovdiv.bg

Rector: Stefan Stoilov Kostianev (2003-)
Tel: +359(32) 602-507 EMail: rector@meduniversity-plovdiv.bg

Vice-Rector of Educational Activity: Maria Petrova Kukleva
Tel: +359(32) 602-478 EMail: vicer_ud@meduniversity-plovdiv.bg

International Relations: Mariana Atanasova Murdjeva, Vice-Rector of International Relations and Project Activity
Tel: +359(32) 602-201 EMail: vicer_ms@meduniversity-plovdiv.bg

Faculty

Dentistry (Dental Technology; Dentistry; Orthodontics; Periodontics; Surgery); **Medicine** (Biological and Life Sciences; Medicine); **Pharmacy** (Immunology; Microbiology; Pharmacy); **Public Health** (Anthropology; Economics; Epidemiology; Ethics; Health Administration; Hygiene; Law; Psychology; Public Health; Statistics)

College

Medicine (Dental Technology; Laboratory Techniques; Medical Auxiliaries; Medical Technology; Midwifery; Nursing; Nutrition; Public Health; Radiology; Rehabilitation and Therapy)

Department

Languages and Specialized Training (Bulgarian; Modern Languages; Natural Sciences)

Further Information: Also Teaching Hospitals

History: Founded 1945.

Academic Year: September to July (September-January; February-July)

Admission Requirements: Secondary school certificate (Diploma za zavarsheno sredno obrazovanie) and entrance examination

Main Language(s) of Instruction: Bulgarian

Degrees and Diplomas: *Bakalavr*: **Health Administration; Midwifery; Nursing.** *Magistr*: **Dentistry; Health Administration; Medicine; Pharmacy.** *Doktor*: **Medicine.** Also Professional Degree (3yrs)

Student Services: Academic Counselling, Canteen, Health Services, Social Counselling, Sports Facilities

Publications: Folia Medica

Last Updated: 24/02/15

MEDICAL UNIVERSITY - SOFIA

Medicinski universitet - Sofia

15, Akad. Ivan Geshov Blvd., Sofia

Tel: +359(2) 915-2149

Fax: +359(2) 953-1174

EMail: glavsec@mu-sofia.bg

Website: http://mu-sofia.bg

Rector: Vanyo Mitev
Tel: +359(2) 952-3791 EMail: rector@mu-sofia.bg

Vice Rector for Academic Affairs: Carolina Doshev Lubomirova

International Relations: Radomir Ljubomirov Ugrinov, Vice Rector for International Integration and Project Financing

Faculty
Medicine (Anatomy; Biochemistry; Biology; Chemistry; Histology; Medicine; Microbiology; Pathology; Pharmacology; Physics; Physiology; Surgery); **Pharmacy** (Pharmacy); **Public Health** (Public Health)

College
Medicine *(Sofia)* (Medicine)

Centre
Languages and Student Sports (Anatomy; Biochemistry; Biology; Bulgarian; Physiology; Sports)

Campus
Medicine *(Vratsa)* (Medicine)

Further Information: Also 13 university hospitals.

History: Founded 1917 as a Faculty of Medicine at Sofia University, became independent 1950 as Medical Academy with departments of Medicine and Dentistry, joined by the Department of Pharmacy 1951. Acquired present status 2006.

Academic Year: September to June (September-January; February-June)

Admission Requirements: Secondary school certificate (Diploma za zavarsheno sredno obrazovanie) or recognized foreign equivalent

Main Language(s) of Instruction: Bulgarian

Degrees and Diplomas: *Bakalavr*, *Magistr*: **Dentistry; Medicine; Pharmacy.** *Doktor*: **Medicine.**

Student Services: Canteen, Careers Guidance, Health Services, IT Centre, Library, Residential Facilities, Sports Facilities

Publications: Acta Medica Bulgarica

Academic Staff *2014-2015*	**TOTAL**
FULL-TIME	**1,969**
Student Numbers *2014-2015*	
All (Foreign included)	c. **4,000**
FOREIGN ONLY	**800**

Last Updated: 24/02/15

NATIONAL ACADEMY FOR THEATRE AND FILM ARTS KRUSTYO SARAFOV

Nacionalna akademia za teatralno i filmovo izkustvo "Krustyo Sarafov" (NATFIZ/NATFA)

PO Box 100, 108A, G. S. Rakovski St., 1000 Sofia
Tel: +359(2) 9231-351
Fax: +359(2) 989-7389
EMail: natfiz@bgcict.acad.bg
Website: http://natfiz.bg

Rector: Lubomir Halatchev
Tel: +359(2) 9231-225
EMail: lubo_halatchev@yahoo.com; rector.office@natfiz.bg

Academic Affairs Officer: Aneliya Tsvetkova

International Relations: Krasimira Ivanova, International Relations Expert Tel: +359(2) 9231-232 EMail: info_natfiz@yahoo.com

Faculty
Performing Arts (Acting; Display and Stage Design; Performing Arts; Theatre); **Screen Arts** (Cinema and Television; Film; Photography; Video)

History: Founded 1948 as Higher Institute of Theatrical Art, acquired present status and title 1995. A State Institution.

Academic Year: October to June (October-January; February-June)

Admission Requirements: Secondary school certificate (Diploma za zavarsheno sredno obrazovanie)

Fees: National: Bachelor, 725-1,450 per semester; Master, 775-3,500 per semester; Ph.D., 1,650 per annum (Bulgarian Lev), International: Bachelor, 3,500-8,000 per annum; Master, 4,500-6,000 per annum; Ph.D., 8,000 per annum in full-time mode and 4,000 per annum in part-time mode (US Dollar)

Main Language(s) of Instruction: Bulgarian

Accrediting Agency: National Agency for Evaluation and Accreditation

Degrees and Diplomas: *Bakalavr*: **Arts and Humanities; Fine Arts; Performing Arts.** *Magistr*: **Cinema and Television; Film; Performing Arts; Theatre.** *Doktor*: **Acting; Art Criticism; Cinema and Television; Computer Graphics; Film; Photography; Theatre; Visual Arts.**

Student Services: Canteen, Library, Residential Facilities

Last Updated: 25/02/15

NATIONAL ACADEMY OF ARTS

Nacionalna hudojestvena akademija (NAA)

1 Šipka Str., 1000 Sofia
Tel: +359(2) 988-1702
Fax: +359(2) 987-8064
EMail: art_academy@yahoo.com
Website: http://nha.bg/

Rector: Antoaneta Markova
Tel: +359(2) 988-1701 EMail: amarkova@nha.bg

Head, Educational Department: Svilena Mateeva
Tel: +359(2) 988-1702 EMail: s.mateeva@nha.bg

International Relations: Mitko Dinev, Head, International Department
Tel: +359(2) 987-8177 +359(2) 987-3328
EMail: art_academy@yahoo.com

Faculty
Applied Arts (Ceramic Art; Design; Display and Stage Design; Fashion Design; Fine Arts; Glass Art; Industrial Design; Metal Techniques; Restoration of Works of Art; Textile Design); **Fine Arts** (Art Education; Art History; Communication Arts; Education; Fine Arts; Graphic Arts; Painting and Drawing; Printing and Printmaking; Psychology; Sculpture; Visual Arts)

History: Founded 1896 as Higher School of Drawing (Fine Arts), acquired present title 1921. A State institution.

Academic Year: October to June (October-January; February-June)

Admission Requirements: Secondary school certificate (Diploma za zavarsheno sredno obrazovanie) and entrance examination

Fees: National: 148-197 per annum (Euro), International: 3,000-4,000, specialisations, 400 per month, Bulgarian language course, 2,000 per annum (Euro)

Main Language(s) of Instruction: Bulgarian

Accrediting Agency: National Agency for Evaluation and Accreditation

Degrees and Diplomas: *Bakalavr*: **Fine Arts.** *Magistr*: **Advertising and Publicity; Art Education; Art Therapy; Ceramic Art; Communication Arts; Computer Graphics; Design; Display and Stage Design; Fashion Design; Fine Arts; Glass Art; Graphic Design; Handicrafts; Heritage Preservation; Industrial Design; Interior Design; Packaging Technology; Painting and Drawing; Photography; Printing and Printmaking; Psychology; Restoration of Works of Art; Sculpture; Textile Design; Visual Arts; Weaving.** *Doktor*: **Fine Arts.** Also Professional qualification certificate, following specialisations

Student Services: Academic Counselling, Cultural Activities, Health Services, Language Laboratory, Library, Residential Facilities, Social Counselling, Sports Facilities

Publications: Art and Critique Journal

Student Numbers *2014-2015*: Total: c. 1,000

Last Updated: 25/02/15

NATIONAL ACADEMY OF MUSIC PROF. PANČO VLADIGEROV

Natsionalna muzikalna akademija "Prof. Pančo Vladigerov" (NMA)

94 Evlogi Georgiev Blvd., 1505 Sofia
Tel: +359(2) 442-197
Fax: +359(2) 944-1454
EMail: info@nma.bg
Website: http://nma.bg/

Rector: Dimitar Momtchilov Tel: +359(2) 943-4862

Vice-Rector: Pravda Atanasova Goranova Tel: +359(2) 944-1449

International Relations: Petya Kissimova Tel: +359(2) 4409-783

Faculty

Instruments (Musical Instruments); **Theory, Composition and Conducting** (Conducting; Music Theory and Composition; Musicology; Sound Engineering (Acoustics)); **Vocal Studies** (Dance; Jazz and Popular Music; Opera; Singing)

History: Founded 1921 as Bulgarian State Conservatory, became National Academy of Music in 1995, acquired present status and title 2006.

Academic Year: September to June

Admission Requirements: Secondary school certificate (Diploma za zavarsheno sredno obrazovanie), and competitive entrance examination

Fees: National: 600-800 per annum (Bulgarian Lev), International: For Foreign students (non-EU): Undergraduate, 4,000 per annum; Master, 6,600 per annum. For Foreign students (EU and EEA): 600-700 Bulgarian Lev per semester (Euro)

Main Language(s) of Instruction: Bulgarian, English

Accrediting Agency: National Agency for Evaluation and Accreditation

Degrees and Diplomas: *Bakalavr*; *Magistr*: **Art Management; Art Therapy; Conducting; Jazz and Popular Music; Journalism; Music Education; Music Theory and Composition; Musical Instruments; Musicology; Opera; Singing; Sound Engineering (Acoustics); Theatre.** Also Postgraduate Qualifications in Opera, Conducting and Music.

Student Services: Academic Counselling, Canteen, Careers Guidance, Foreign Studies Centre, Health Services, Language Laboratory, Library, Residential Facilities

Last Updated: 12/02/15

NATIONAL SPORTS ACADEMY VASSIL LEVSKI

Nacionalna sportna akademija "Vassil Levski" (NSA)

Studentski grad, 1700 Sofia
Tel: +359(2) 401-2345
Fax: +359(2) 629-007
EMail: intrelations@nsa.bg
Website: http://nsa.bg

Rector: Pencho Geshev
Tel: +359(2) 400-7504 EMail: rector@nsa.bg; p_geshev@nsa.bg

Vice-Rector of Education: Nikolay Izov
Tel: +359(2) 400-7505 EMail: nikolay.izov@gmail.com

International Relations: Daniela Dasheva, Vice-Rector of Research, Project and International Affairs
Tel: +359(2) 400-7505
EMail: dani_dash@yahoo.com; dasheva@nsa.bg

Faculty

Coaches (Biochemistry; Physiology; Sports; Sports Management); **Physiotherapy** (Physical Therapy; Rehabilitation and Therapy; Sports; Sports Medicine); **Teachers** (Anatomy; Pedagogy; Psychology; Sociology; Sports)

History: Founded 1942 as Higher Institute of Physical Culture, acquired present status and title 1995.

Academic Year: September to June

Admission Requirements: Secondary school certificate (Diploma za zavarsheno sredno obrazovanie), and a year of preparation course in the Language Training Centre

Fees: National: 350-840 per annum (Bulgarian Lev), International: 3,200-4,000 per annum (Euro)

Main Language(s) of Instruction: Bulgarian

Accrediting Agency: National Agency for Evaluation and Accreditation

Degrees and Diplomas: *Bakalavr*: **Physical Education; Physical Therapy; Sports.** *Magistr*: **Health Sciences; Journalism; Performing Arts; Physical Education; Physical Therapy; Psychology; Sports.** *Doktor*: **Physical Education; Physical Therapy; Sports.**

Student Services: Academic Counselling, Canteen, Health Services, IT Centre, Language Laboratory, Library, Residential Facilities, Social Counselling, Sports Facilities

Publications: NSA International Annual Scientific Conference; Sport and Science

Last Updated: 25/02/15

PLOVDIV UNIVERSITY PAISSII HILENDARSK

Plovdivski universitet "Paisii Hilendarski" (PU)

"Tzar Assen" str. 24, 4000 Plovdiv
Tel: +359(32) 261-363
Fax: +359(32) 635-049
EMail: pduniv@uni-plovdiv.bg; webmaster@uni-plovdiv.bg
Website: http://www.uni-plovdiv.bg

Rector: Zapryan Kozlydzov
Tel: +359(32) 631-449 +359(32) 261-222
EMail: rector@uni-plovdiv.bg

Vice-Rector, Study and Publishing Activities: Zhorheta Cholakova Tel: +359(32) 261-248
EMail: tcholakova@uni-plovdiv.bg

International Relations: Nadya Kaneva, International Cooperation Officer
Tel: +359(32) 261-363
EMail: nadya@uni-plovdiv.bg; ir@uni-plovdiv.bg

Faculty

Biology (Behavioural Sciences; Biological and Life Sciences; Biology; Biotechnology; Chemistry; Computer Science; Ecology; English; Environmental Management; Environmental Studies; Molecular Biology; Tourism); **Chemistry** (Analytical Chemistry; Chemistry; Ecology; English; Marketing; Physics); **Economics and Social Sciences** (Business Administration; Economics; Finance; International Economics; Marketing; Political Sciences); **History and Philosophy** (Anthropology; Archaeology; Arts and Humanities; Economics; Ethnology; History; Philosophy; Sociology; Theology); **Law** (Law); **Mathematics and Computer Science** (Applied Mathematics; Business Computing; Computer Graphics; Educational Administration; Information Technology; Mathematics; Mathematics and Computer Science; Software Engineering); **Pedagogy** (Acting; Advertising and Publicity; Art Education; Education; Education of the Socially Disadvantaged; Foreign Languages Education; Graphic Design; Humanities and Social Science Education; Jazz and Popular Music; Music Education; Musical Instruments; Pedagogy; Physical Education; Preschool Education; Primary Education; Psychology; Special Education; Sports; Technology Education; Theatre); **Philology** (Applied Linguistics; Bulgarian; Business Administration; Central European Studies; Chinese; Czech; English; French; Greek; Hebrew; History; Information Technology; Italian; Korean; Linguistics; Marketing; Philology; Polish; Russian; Serbocroatian; Slavic Languages; Spanish; Turkish); **Physics** (Information Technology; Laser Engineering; Management; Materials Engineering; Physical Engineering; Physics; Polymer and Plastics Technology; Telecommunications Engineering)

College

Khardzali *(Liuben Karavelov)* (Biology; Bulgarian; Business Administration; English; Environmental Studies; Foreign Languages Education; History; Preschool Education; Primary Education; Tourism); **Smolyan** (Behavioural Sciences; Biology; Bulgarian; Ecology; Educational Administration; English; Foreign Languages Education; History; Information Technology; Marketing; Mathematics; Primary Education; Tourism); **Smolyan Technical** (Automotive Engineering; Computer Engineering; Energy Engineering; Mechanical Engineering; Telecommunications Engineering)

Further Information: Also Technical College in the town of Smolyan and affiliated College in Smolyan and Kardzhali.

History: Founded 1961 as Teacher Training Institute, acquired present status and title 1972. A State institution with the right of autonomy.

Academic Year: September to June (September-December; February-June)

Admission Requirements: Secondary school certificate (diploma za zavarsheno sredno obrazovanie), and entrance examination

Fees: National: 1,500 per annum for applicants with double citizenship, one of which is Bulgarian; Part-time students, 2,000-3,000 (Euro), International: 3,000 per annum (Euro)

Main Language(s) of Instruction: Bulgarian

Accrediting Agency: National Agency for Evaluation and Accreditation

Degrees and Diplomas: *Bakalavr*; *Magistr*: **Accountancy; Advertising and Publicity; Analytical Chemistry; Applied Chemistry; Archiving; Biochemistry; Biological and Life Sciences; Biology; Biotechnology; Bulgarian; Business Administration; Chemistry; Communication Studies; Computer Science; Cultural Studies; Ecology; Education; Electronic Engineering; Energy Engineering; English; Environmental Management; Ethnology; Finance; Genetics; German; Heritage Preservation; History; Human Resources; Industrial Chemistry; Information Management; Information Technology; International Business; International Relations; Journalism; Laser Engineering; Law; Linguistics; Literature; Management; Mathematics; Mathematics Education; Media Studies; Microbiology; Modern Languages; Molecular Biology; Organic Chemistry; Orthodox Theology; Parasitology; Physics; Protective Services; Public Administration; Public Relations; Russian; Science Education; Slavic Languages; Social Studies; Telecommunications Engineering; Tourism.** *Doktor*: **Administration; Administrative Law; Analytical Chemistry; Anthropology; Biochemistry; Biological and Life Sciences; Botany; Bulgarian; Cell Biology; Chemistry; Civil Law; Comparative Literature; Computer Science; Criminal Law; Cultural Studies; Ecology; Economics; Education; Electrical Engineering; English; Ethnology; Genetics; German; Industrial Chemistry; Inorganic Chemistry; International Relations; Labour Law; Law; Linguistics; Literature; Management; Mathematics; Microbiology; Molecular Biology; Organic Chemistry; Physical Chemistry; Physics; Physiology; Private Law; Public Law; Romance Languages; Science Education; Slavic Languages; Social Welfare; Sociology; Zoology.** Also Postgraduate Qualifications in Chemistry

Student Services: Academic Counselling, Canteen, Careers Guidance, IT Centre, Language Laboratory, Library, Sports Facilities

Publications: Naučni Trudove

Publishing House: University Publishing House

Academic Staff *2014-2015*	**TOTAL**
FULL-TIME	c. **550**
Student Numbers *2014-2015*	
All (Foreign included)	c. **8,000**

Part-time students, 5,000.

Last Updated: 13/02/15

RUSE UNIVERSITY ANGEL KANČEV

Rusenski universitet "Angel Kančev" (RU)

8 Studentska str., 7017 Ruse

Tel: +359(82) 888-467

Fax: +359(82) 845-708

EMail: secretary@uni-ruse.bg

Website: http://www.uni-ruse.bg

Rector: Hristo Beloev (2007-)
Tel: +359(82) 888-465
EMail: rector@uni-ruse.bg; hbeloev@uni-ruse.bg

Secretary-General: Tania Grozeva
Tel: +359(82) 888-258 EMail: gl-sec@ru.acad.bg

International Relations: Todorka Todorova
EMail: cicm@ru.acad.bg

Faculty

Agro-industry (Agricultural Equipment; Chemical Engineering; Ecology; Hydraulic Engineering; Industrial Design; Maintenance Technology; Mechanics; Thermal Engineering; Transport Management); **Business and Management** (Business Administration; Economics; European Studies; International Relations; Management); **Electrical and Electronic Engineering and Automation** (Automation and Control Engineering; Computer Engineering; Electrical and Electronic Engineering; Power Engineering; Telecommunications Engineering); **Law** (Criminal Law; Law; Modern Languages; Private Law; Public Law); **Mechanical and Manufacturing Engineering** (Materials Engineering; Mechanical Engineering; Mechanics; Production Engineering); **Natural Sciences and Education** (Arts and Humanities; Bulgarian; Computer Science; History; Literature; Mathematics; Pedagogy; Psychology); **Public Health and Health Care** (Applied Mathematics; Health Sciences; Physical Education; Public Health; Sports; Statistics); **Transport** (Automotive Engineering; Machine Building; Mechanics; Physics; Transport and Communications; Transport Engineering)

Further Information: Branches in Razgrad and Silistra

History: Founded 1946 as Higher Technical School, acquired present status and title 1995.

Academic Year: September to June (September-January; February-June)

Admission Requirements: Secondary school certificate (Diploma za zavarsheno sredno obrazovanie) and entrance examination

Fees: National: 180-230 per annum (Bulgarian Lev), International: 1,800-2,400 per annum (Euro)

Main Language(s) of Instruction: Bulgarian

Accrediting Agency: Bureau Veritas Quality International (BVQI); National Agency for Evaluation and Accreditation

Degrees and Diplomas: *Bakalavr*; *Magistr*: **Agriculture; Automation and Control Engineering; Business Administration; Education; Electrical and Electronic Engineering; Law; Management; Mechanical Engineering; Natural Sciences; Production Engineering; Public Health; Transport and Communications.** *Doktor*: **Administration; Agricultural Engineering; Agricultural Equipment; Hydraulic Engineering; Industrial Engineering; Management; Thermal Engineering.**

Student Services: Canteen, Careers Guidance, Cultural Activities, Foreign Studies Centre, Health Services, IT Centre, Language Laboratory, Library, Residential Facilities, Social Counselling, Sports Facilities

Publications: Nauchni Trudove

Publishing House: Pečantna Baza

Academic Staff *2014-2015*: Total 500
STAFF WITH DOCTORATE: Total 300

Student Numbers *2014-2015*: Total: c. 10,000

Last Updated: 13/02/15

SHUMEN UNIVERSITY KONSTANTIN PRESLAVSKI

Šumenski universitet "Episcop Konstantin Preslavski"

115, Universitetska St., 9700 Šoumen

Tel: +359(54) 830-495

Fax: +359(54) 830-371

EMail: int.rel@shu-bg.net; pr@shu-bg.net

Website: http://www.shu-bg.net

Rector: Margarita Georgieva (2007-)
Tel: +359(54) 830-350, Ext.101 EMail: rector@shu.bg

Vice-Rector of Educational Affairs: Zhivko Zhekov
Tel: +359(54) 830-495 EMail: jekovj@shu-bg.net

International Relations: Rumyana Todorova, Vice-Rector of Research and International Relations
Tel: +359(54) 830-360
EMail: r_todorova@shu-bg.net; r_todorova@yahoo.com

Faculty

Education (Art Education; Pedagogy); **Humanities** (Arts and Humanities; Bulgarian; English; German; History; Modern Languages; Philology; Theology); **Mathematics and Computer Science** (Computer Science; Economics; Mathematics); **Natural Sciences** (Biology; Chemistry; Physics); **Technical Sciences** (Technology)

College

Dobrich (Computer Science; Foreign Languages Education; Information Technology; Mathematics and Computer Science; Plant and Crop Protection; Preschool Education; Primary Education)

Department

Information Qualification and Lifelong Learning (Educational Sciences; Pedagogy)

Centre

Astronomy (Astronomy and Space Science)

History: Founded 1971 as Higher Pedagogical Institute, acquired present status and title 1996.

Academic Year: September to June (September-December; February-June)

Admission Requirements: Secondary school certificate (Diploma za zavarsheno sredno obrazovanie)

Fees: Doctorate, 800 per annum (Bulgarian Lev)

Main Language(s) of Instruction: Bulgarian

Accrediting Agency: National Agency for and Assessment and Accreditation

Degrees and Diplomas: *Profesionalen Bakalavr*; *Bakalavr*; *Magistr*: **Accountancy; Advertising and Publicity; Archaeology; Art Education; Art Management; Astrophysics; Automation and Control Engineering; Bulgarian; Business Administration; Chemistry; Computer Engineering; Computer Science; Ecology; Economics; Education of the Socially Disadvantaged; Educational Administration; English; Environmental Management; Finance; Geological Engineering; German; Heritage Preservation; History; Information Sciences; Journalism; Linguistics; Mass Communication; Mathematics; Mathematics and Computer Science; Mathematics Education; Music Education; Natural Sciences; Organic Chemistry; Pedagogy; Philology; Physics; Plant and Crop Protection; Preschool Education; Primary Education; Public Relations; Religion; Russian; Social and Community Services; Software Engineering; Special Education; Telecommunications Engineering; Theology; Tourism; Turkish.** *Doktor*: **Archaeology; Architecture and Planning; Art Education; Astrophysics; Automation and Control Engineering; Bulgarian; Computer Education; Computer Engineering; Computer Networks; Computer Science; Ecology; Educational Administration; Educational Sciences; Environmental Management; Foreign Languages Education; Geology; Germanic Languages; History; Humanities and Social Science Education; Journalism; Linguistics; Literature; Mathematics; Mathematics Education; Medieval Studies; Music Education; Native Language Education; Organic Chemistry; Pedagogy; Physical Education; Protective Services; Russian; Science Education; Slavic Languages; Special Education; Surveying and Mapping; Technology Education; Telecommunications Engineering; Theology; Turkish.**

Student Services: Careers Guidance, Language Laboratory, Library, Residential Facilities, Sports Facilities

Publications: Acta Scientifica Naturalis

Publishing House: Konstantin Preslavski Publishing House

Academic Staff *2014-2015*: Total: c. 400

Student Numbers *2014-2015*: Total: c. 7,000

Last Updated: 25/02/15

SOFIA UNIVERSITY ST. KLIMENT OHRIDSKI

Sofiiski universitet "Sv. Kliment Ohridski" (SU)

15 Tsar Osvoboditel Blvd., 1504 Sofia
Tel: +359(2) 930-8200
Fax: +359(2) 946-0255
EMail: rectorsoffice@admin.uni-sofia.bg
Website: http://www.uni-sofia.bg

Rector: Ivan Ilchev
Tel: +359(2) 987-3996
EMail: rector@uni-sofia.bg; rectorsoffice@admin.uni-sofia.bg

Vice-Rector of Education: Milena Stefanova
Tel: +359(2) 9308-595 EMail: stefanova@vice-rector.uni-sofia.bg

International Relations: Tatyana Tsaneva, Head, International Relations Department and ERASMUS Administrative Coordinator
Tel: +359(2) 944-6423 EMail: ttsaneva@admin.uni-sofia.bg

Faculty

Biology (Animal Husbandry; Anthropology; Biochemistry; Biological and Life Sciences; Biology; Biophysics; Biotechnology; Botany; Cell Biology; Ecology; Embryology and Reproduction Biology; Environmental Studies; Genetics; Histology; Inorganic Chemistry; Limnology; Marine Biology; Microbiology; Molecular Biology; Organic Chemistry; Physiology; Plant Pathology; Zoology); **Chemistry and Pharmacy** (Analytical Chemistry; Chemistry; Inorganic Chemistry; Organic Chemistry; Pharmacy; Physical Chemistry; Polymer and Plastics Technology; Thermal Physics); **Classical and Modern Philology** (American Studies; Classical Languages; English Studies; Foreign Languages Education; German; Germanic Studies; Modern Languages; Philology; Romance Languages; Scandinavian Languages; Spanish); **Economics and Business Administration** (Business Administration; Economics); **Education** (Education; Educational Administration; Pedagogy); **Geology and Geography** (Geography; Geology; Tourism); **History** (Ancient Civilizations; Archaeology; Archiving; Central European Studies; History; Modern History); **Journalism and Mass Communication** (Journalism; Mass Communication; Printing and Printmaking; Public Relations; Publishing and Book Trade; Radio and Television Broadcasting); **Law** (Administrative Law; Civil Law; Constitutional Law; Criminal Law; History of Law; International Law; International Relations; Law); **Mathematics and Informatics** (Applied Mathematics; Computer Education; Computer Graphics; Computer Science; Information Technology; Mathematics; Mathematics Education; Statistics; Systems Analysis); **Medicine** (Medicine); **Philosophy** (Aesthetics; Cultural Studies; Developmental Psychology; Educational Psychology; Ethics; Experimental Psychology; Information Sciences; Library Science; Logic; Philosophical Schools; Philosophy; Political Sciences; Psychology; Public Administration; Social Psychology; Sociology); **Physics** (Applied Physics; Astronomy and Space Science; Atomic and Molecular Physics; Electronic Engineering; Geophysics; Laser Engineering; Meteorology; Microelectronics; Nuclear Physics; Optics; Physics; Power Engineering; Radiophysics; Solid State Physics; Thermal Physics); **Preschool and Primary School Education** (Preschool Education; Primary Education); **Slavic Studies** (Ancient Civilizations; Bulgarian; Central European Studies; Eastern European Studies; Educational Sciences; Literature; Native Language Education; Russian; Slavic Languages); **Theology** (Bible; Canon Law; Christian Religious Studies; History of Religion; New Testament; Orthodox Theology; Theology)

Department

Information and In-Service Training of Teachers (Teacher Training); **Language Learning** (Bulgarian; Modern Languages); **Sports** (Physical Education; Sports)

Further Information: Also Regional Centre of Distance Education

History: Founded 1888 as Higher School of Education with one Faculty, reorganized as University 1904 and acquired present title 1905 with the number of Faculties increasing to seven by 1938. Reorganized 1944, when the Faculties of Medicine and Agriculture were detached from the University and established as separate Institutions. Acquired present title and status 2004. A State Institution.

Academic Year: September to June (September-December; February-June)

Admission Requirements: Secondary school certificate (diploma za zavarsheno sredno obrazovanie) and entrance examination

Fees: National: 3,100-3,300 per annum (except in Medicine and Pharmacy, 4,650); Doctoral degree programmes, 5,500 per annum in full-time mode and 2,750 per annum in part-time mode (Euro), International: 3,850 per annum; Doctoral degree programmes, 6,500 per annum in full-time mode and 3,300 per annum in part-time mode (Euro)

Main Language(s) of Instruction: Bulgarian, English

Accrediting Agency: National Agency for Evaluation and Accreditation

Degrees and Diplomas: *Bakalavr*; *Magistr*: **Biology; Chemistry; Classical Languages; Education; Geography; Geology; History; Journalism; Law; Mass Communication; Mathematics and Computer Science; Medicine; Modern Languages; Pharmacy; Philology; Philosophy; Physics; Preschool Education; Primary Education; Slavic Languages; Theology.** *Doktor*: **Administrative Law; Aesthetics; African Languages; Anaesthesiology; Analytical Chemistry; Ancient Books; Ancient Civilizations; Anthropology; Applied Mathematics; Archaeology; Archiving; Astronomy and Space Science; Astrophysics; Biochemistry; Biology; Biophysics; Botany; Bulgarian; Business Computing; Cardiology; Cell Biology; Chemistry; Civil Law; Classical Languages; Computer Education; Computer Science; Constitutional Law; Criminal Law; Criminology; Crystallography; Demography and Population; Documentation Techniques; Earth Sciences; Ecology; Educational Psychology; Educational Sciences; English; Entomology; Environmental Management; Ethics; Ethnology; Finnish; Folklore; Foreign**

Languages Education; Genetics; Geochemistry; Geography; Geography (Human); Geology; Geophysics; German; History of Law; Humanities and Social Science Education; Hungarian; Industrial and Production Economics; Industrial Management; Information Sciences; Information Technology; Inorganic Chemistry; International Law; International Relations; Journalism; Labour Law; Latin; Law; Library Science; Literature; Logic; Management; Marine Science and Oceanography; Mathematics; Mathematics Education; Mechanics; Medicine; Medieval Studies; Meteorology; Microbiology; Mineralogy; Modern History; Molecular Biology; Mongolian; Native Language Education; Nuclear Physics; Operations Research; Organic Chemistry; Orthopaedics; Paleontology; Pedagogy; Persian; Petrology; Philology; Philosophy; Physical Chemistry; Physics; Physiology; Political Sciences; Prehistory; Primary Education; Private Law; Psychology; Public Law; Radiophysics; Science Education; Slavic Languages; Social Psychology; Social Work; Sociology; Solid State Physics; South and Southeast Asian Languages; Special Education; Statistics; Surgery; Surveying and Mapping; Teacher Training; Theology; Translation and Interpretation; Turkish; Virology; Water Management; Water Science; Zoology.

Student Services: Academic Counselling, Canteen, Careers Guidance, Cultural Activities, Health Services, Language Laboratory, Library, Nursery Care, Residential Facilities, Social Counselling, Sports Facilities

Publishing house: University Printing House

Last Updated: 25/02/15

SOUTH-WEST UNIVERSITY NEOFIT RILSKI

Yugo-zapaden universitet "Neofit Rilski" (SWU)

66 Ivan Michailov st., 2700 Blagoevgrad

Tel: +359(73) 885-505

Fax: +359(73) 885-516

EMail: info@aix.swu.bg; admission@swu.bg

Website: http://www.swu.bg

Rector: Ivan Mirchev
Tel: +359(73) 885-501 EMail: mirchev@swu.bg

Vice Rector of Educational Activities: Trayan Popkochev
Tel: +359(73) 831-562 EMail: vr_edu@swu.bg

International Relations: Georgieva Dobrinka, Head, International Relations Office Tel: +359(73) 588-599 EMail: iroffice@swu.bg

Faculty

Arts (Acting; Art Education; Cinema and Television; Cultural Studies; Dance; Fashion Design; Industrial Design; Music Education; Performing Arts; Photography; Singing; Theatre); **Economics** (Accountancy; Business Administration; Finance; Management; Marketing; Tourism); **Law and History** (Administration; Administrative Law; Anthropology; Business Administration; Civil Law; Constitutional Law; Criminal Law; Criminology; Finance; Health Administration; History; International Law; International Relations; Law; Medicine; Pedagogy; Psychology; Public Administration; Public Law; Public Relations; Religious Studies; Social Policy; Sociology); **Mathematics and Natural Sciences** (Chemistry; Computer Engineering; Computer Science; Ecology; Environmental Studies; Geography; Inorganic Chemistry; Mathematics Education; Organic Chemistry; Pedagogy; Physics; Teacher Training); **Pedagogy** (Educational Administration; Humanities and Social Science Education; Modern Languages; Pedagogy; Physical Education; Physical Therapy; Preschool Education; Primary Education; Psychology; Social and Community Services; Social Psychology; Special Education; Sports; Technology Education); **Philology** (Applied Linguistics; Bulgarian; English; Foreign Languages Education; Modern Languages; Philology; Slavic Languages); **Philosophy** (Community Health; Philosophy; Political Sciences; Psychotherapy; Social and Community Services; Social Work; Speech Therapy and Audiology); **Public Health and Sports** (Physical Therapy; Public Health; Social Sciences; Speech Therapy and Audiology; Sports)

College

Technology (Electronic Engineering; Mechanical Engineering; Telecommunications Engineering; Textile Technology)

Further Information: Branches in Kjustendil, Dupnica, Targovište, Smoljan

History: Founded 1976 as an affiliate faculty of Sofia St. Kliment Ohridski University, reorganized as Higher Institute of Education 1983, an independent Institution. Acquired present status and title 1995. Acquired institutional accreditation 2001.

Academic Year: September to June (September-January; February-June)

Admission Requirements: Secondary Education Diploma in Bulgarian (Diploma za zavarsheno sredno obrazovanie); Diploma from High School, translated and legalized in Bulgarian Language

Fees: 2,500-3,500 per annum (Euro)

Main Language(s) of Instruction: Bulgarian

Accrediting Agency: National Agency for Evaluation and Accreditation

Degrees and Diplomas: *Profesionalen Bakalavr, Bakalavr, Magistr.* **Anthropology; Archaeology; Bulgarian; Business Administration; Chemistry; Computer Science; Cultural Studies; Dance; Earth Sciences; Economics; Educational Administration; Film; Fine Arts; Foreign Languages Education; History; Journalism; Law; Linguistics; Management; Mathematics; Modern Languages; Music; Pedagogy; Philosophy; Physics; Political Sciences; Psychology; Public Health; Public Relations; Rehabilitation and Therapy; Secondary Education; Slavic Languages; Social Work; Sociology; Sports; Teacher Training; Theatre; Tourism; Translation and Interpretation.** *Doktor.* **Administrative Law; Ancient Books; Ancient Civilizations; Applied Mathematics; Archaeology; Archiving; Art Education; Banking; Bulgarian; Cinema and Television; Civil Law; Computer Education; Computer Engineering; Computer Networks; Computer Science; Criminal Law; Criminology; Cultural Studies; Dance; Documentation Techniques; Ecology; Educational Administration; Educational Psychology; Educational Sciences; English; Environmental Management; Film; Finance; Geography; German; History; Industrial and Organizational Psychology; Industrial and Production Economics; Industrial Management; Information Technology; Inorganic Chemistry; Insurance; International Law; International Relations; Linguistics; Literature; Management; Mathematics; Mathematics Education; Modern History; Music Education; Operations Research; Organic Chemistry; Pedagogy; Performing Arts; Philosophy; Physical Education; Political Sciences; Preschool Education; Primary Education; Psychology; Public Relations; Science Education; Slavic Languages; Social Welfare; Social Work; Sociology; Special Education; Speech Therapy and Audiology; Surveying and Mapping; Technology Education; Tourism.** Some programmes offered in English

Student Services: Academic Counselling, Canteen, Careers Guidance, Cultural Activities, Foreign Studies Centre, Health Services, Language Laboratory, Library, Residential Facilities, Social Counselling, Sports Facilities

Publications: South-West Pages

Publishing House: University Publishing House

Student Numbers *2014-2015*: Total: c. 14,000

Last Updated: 27/02/15

IAU ST. CYRIL AND ST. METHODIUS UNIVERSITY OF VÉLIKO TARNOVO

Vélikoturnovski universitet Sv. Sv. Kiril i Metodi (VTU)

2 Teodossi Turnovski Str., 5003 Véliko Turnovo

Tel: +359(62) 618-221

Fax: +359(62) 628-023

EMail: mbox@uni-vt.bg

Website: http://www.uni-vt.bg

Rector: Plamen Anatoliev Legkostup (2007-)
Tel: +359(62) 620-189 EMail: rector@uni-vt.bg

Vice-Rector for Academic Affairs: Petko Stefanov Petkov
Tel: +359(62) 618-215 EMail: p.petkov@uni-vt.bg

International Relations: Bagrelia Borissova, Vice-Rector for European Integration and International Cooperation
Tel: +359(62) 618-247 EMail: b.borisova@uni-vt.bg

Faculty

Economics (Accountancy; Business Administration; Economics; Finance; Foreign Languages Education; International Business;

International Economics; Library Science; Management; Marketing; Social and Community Services; Tourism); **Education** (Computer Education; Computer Science; Education; Foreign Languages Education; Information Technology; Mathematics; Mathematics Education; Music Education; Pedagogy; Physical Education; Preschool Education; Primary Education; Psychology; Social Psychology; Sports); **Fine Arts** (Fine Arts; Graphic Arts; Graphic Design; Painting and Drawing; Visual Arts); **History** (Archaeology; Geography; History; Medieval Studies); **Law** (Law); **Mathematics and Informatics** (Computer Science; Information Technology; Mathematics); **Modern Languages** (Applied Linguistics; Bulgarian; Central European Studies; Classical Languages; English; English Studies; French; French Studies; German; Germanic Studies; Information Sciences; Library Science; Linguistics; Literature; Oriental Languages; Philology; Romance Languages; Russian; Slavic Languages); **Orthodox Theology** (Bible; Orthodox Theology; Religious Art; Theology); **Philosophy** (Cultural Studies; Foreign Languages Education; Philosophy; Political Sciences; Psychology; Sociology)

College

Education *(Pleven)* (Bulgarian; Business Administration; Education; Environmental Studies; Finance; Geography; Geography (Human); History; Philosophy; Preschool Education; Primary Education); **Education** *(Vratza)* (Education)

History: Founded 1963 as Teacher Training Institute, acquired present status and title 1971. A State Institution.

Academic Year: September to June (September-December; February-June)

Admission Requirements: Secondary school certificate (diploma za zavarsheno sredno obrazovanie) and entrance examination

Fees: 2,200 full-time per annum; 1,300 part-time per annum (Euro)

Main Language(s) of Instruction: Bulgarian

Accrediting Agency: National Agency for Evaluation and Accreditation

Degrees and Diplomas: *Bakalavr*; *Magistr*; *Doktor*. **Administrative Law; Ancient Civilizations; Archaeology; Art Education; Bulgarian; Catholic Theology; Civil Law; Communication Arts; Computer Science; Constitutional Law; Contemporary History; Criminal Law; Design; Economics; Educational Administration; Ethnology; Fine Arts; Folklore; Foreign Languages Education; French; Geography; Geography (Human); Germanic Languages; Graphic Design; Greek; History; History of Law; Humanities and Social Science Education; Industrial and Production Economics; Industrial Management; Law; Linguistics; Literature; Mathematics Education; Medieval Studies; Modern History; Music Education; Native Language Education; Painting and Drawing; Pastoral Studies; Pedagogy; Philosophy; Physical Education; Political Sciences; Preschool Education; Psychology; Religious Art; Sculpture; Slavic Languages; Social Psychology; Sociology; Special Education; Sports; Teacher Training; Theology; Translation and Interpretation.** Also Teaching Qualifications; Some Master's Degree Programmes conducted in English and Russian Languages.

Student Services: Academic Counselling, Canteen, Careers Guidance, Health Services, Language Laboratory, Library, Nursery Care, Residential Facilities, Sports Facilities

Publications: Archives of Historical and Geographical Research; Epohi; Pedagogičeski Almanač; Proglass; Trudove na VTU Kiril i Metodii

Publishing House: University Publishing House

Last Updated: 27/02/15

TECHNICAL UNIVERSITY OF GABROVO

Tehničeski universitet Gabrovo (TUG)
4 Hadji Dimitar Str., 5300 Gabrovo
Tel: +359(66) 827-777
Fax: +359(66) 801-155
EMail: info@tugab.bg
Website: http://www.tugab.bg

Rector: Raycho Todorov Ilarionov
Tel: +359(66) 801-144 EMail: rector@tugab.bg; ilar@tugab.bg

Vice-Rector, Academic Affairs: Petar Kolev Petrov
Tel: +359(66) 800-265
EMail: petrov_p_tu@abv.bg; gencheva@tugab.bg

International Relations: Tsvetelina Alexandrova Gankova, Vice-Rector, International Cooperation and Public Relations
Tel: 359(66) 800-671
EMail: gankova@tugab.bg; igencheva@tugab.bg

Faculty

Economics (Business and Commerce; Economics; Industrial Management; Marketing; Public Administration; Social Work); **Electrical Engineering and Electronics** (Automation and Control Engineering; Computer Engineering; Electrical and Electronic Engineering; Environmental Engineering; Power Engineering; Telecommunications Engineering); **Mechanical and Precision Engineering** (Environmental Engineering; Hydraulic Engineering; Industrial Design; Industrial Engineering; Instrument Making; Machine Building; Materials Engineering; Measurement and Precision Engineering; Mechanical Engineering; Power Engineering; Textile Technology)

Department

Language and Specialized Training (Bulgarian; Educational Sciences; English; German; History; Literature; Mathematics; Physical Education; Physics; Russian; Sports)

History: Founded 1964 as Higher Institute of Mechanical and Electrical Engineering, acquired present status and title 1995.

Academic Year: September to July

Admission Requirements: Secondary school certificate (Diploma za zavarsheno sredno obrazovanie) and entrance examination

Fees: National: Bachelor, 2,200 per annum; Master, 2,400 per annum (Euro), International: 3,000 per annum (Euro)

Main Language(s) of Instruction: Bulgarian

Accrediting Agency: National Evaluation and Accreditation Agency

Degrees and Diplomas: *Bakalavr*: **Business Administration; Engineering; Social Sciences.** *Magistr*: **Automation and Control Engineering; Automotive Engineering; Computer Engineering; Electrical Engineering; Electronic Engineering; Engineering; Environmental Management; Hydraulic Engineering; Industrial Engineering; Industrial Management; Laser Engineering; Management; Materials Engineering; Measurement and Precision Engineering; Mechanical Engineering; Power Engineering; Public Administration; Safety Engineering; Social Work; Telecommunications Engineering; Textile Design; Textile Technology.** *Doktor*: **Automation and Control Engineering; Computer Engineering; Computer Networks; Electrical Engineering; Electronic Engineering; Hydraulic Engineering; Industrial Engineering; Machine Building; Materials Engineering; Measurement and Precision Engineering; Mechanical Engineering; Mechanics; Microelectronics; Power Engineering; Telecommunications Engineering; Textile Technology.**

Student Services: Academic Counselling, Canteen, Careers Guidance, Cultural Activities, Health Services, Language Laboratory, Library, Residential Facilities, Social Counselling, Sports Facilities

Publications: Journal of the Technical University of Gabrovo; Proceedings from Conferences

Publishing House: University Publishing House

Academic Staff *2013-2014*: Total 24

Last Updated: 25/02/15

TECHNICAL UNIVERSITY OF SOFIA

Tehničeski universitet Sofija (TUS)
8 Kliment Ohridski Str., 1000 Sofia
Tel: +359(2) 8623-073
Fax: +359(2) 8683-215
EMail: office_tu@tu-sofia.bg
Website: http://www.tu-sofia.bg

Rector: Georgi Slavchev Mihov
Tel: +359(2) 965-2450
EMail: rector@tu-sofia.bg; mdench@tu-sofia.bg

Vice-Rector for Learning Activity, Quality and Accreditation: Valentin Dimitrov
Tel: +359(2) 965-2560
EMail: idakov@tu-sofia.bg; sevdalina@tu-sofia.bg

International Relations: Valeri Markov Mladenov, Vice-Rector for International Integration and Public Relations
Tel: +359(2) 965-2131
EMail: valerim@tu-sofia.bg; verginia@tu-sofia.bg

Faculty

Applied Mathematics and Informatics (Applied Mathematics; Computer Science); **Automatics** (Automation and Control Engineering; Electrical Engineering; Production Engineering; Systems Analysis); **Computer Systems and Control** (Computer Engineering; Computer Science); **Electrical Engineering** (Electrical Engineering); **Electrical Engineering** *(In French)* (Electrical Engineering); **Electronic Engineering and Technology** (Chemistry; Microelectronics; Power Engineering; Technology); **Electronics and Automation - Plovdiv** (Automation and Control Engineering; Electronic Engineering); **Engineering** *(In English)* (Engineering); **Engineering and Pedagogy - Sliven** (Automation and Control Engineering; Computer Engineering; Electrical Engineering; Information Technology; Machine Building); **Engineering Education and Industrial Management** *(In German)* (Industrial Management; Technology Education); **Industrial Technology** (Industrial Engineering); **Management** (Economics; Industrial Engineering; Industrial Management); **Mechanical Engineering** (Automation and Control Engineering; Mechanical Engineering; Production Engineering); **Mechanical Engineering - Plovdiv** (Mechanical Engineering); **Power Engineering and Power Machines** (Heating and Refrigeration; Hydraulic Engineering; Nuclear Engineering; Power Engineering; Textile Technology; Thermal Engineering); **Telecommunications** (Telecommunications Engineering; Telecommunications Services); **Transport** (Air Transport; Automotive Engineering; Railway Transport; Transport and Communications)

Department

Applied Physics (Applied Physics); **Foreign Languages and Applied Linguistics** (Applied Linguistics; Linguistics; Modern Languages); **Physical Education and Sports** (Physical Education; Sports)

History: Founded 1945. Acquired present status and title 1995.

Academic Year: September to June (September-January; February-June)

Admission Requirements: Secondary school certificate and entrance examination

Fees: National: 200 per annum (Bulgarian Lev), International: 3,000 per annum (US Dollar)

Main Language(s) of Instruction: Bulgarian

Degrees and Diplomas: *Profesionalen Bakalavr*, *Bakalavr*, *Magistr*: **Aeronautical and Aerospace Engineering; Applied Mathematics; Automation and Control Engineering; Automotive Engineering; Business Administration; Business Computing; Computer Engineering; Computer Science; Education; Electrical Engineering; Electronic Engineering; Environmental Engineering; Industrial Management; Information Technology; Management; Measurement and Precision Engineering; Mechanical Engineering; Power Engineering; Production Engineering; Public Administration; Telecommunications Engineering; Telecommunications Services; Transport Management.** *Doktor*: **Applied Mathematics; Artificial Intelligence; Automation and Control Engineering; Automotive Engineering; Computer Engineering; Computer Graphics; Computer Science; Economics; Educational Sciences; Electrical Engineering; Electronic Engineering; Heating and Refrigeration; Hydraulic Engineering; Industrial Management; Information Management; Laser Engineering; Management; Materials Engineering; Mathematics; Measurement and Precision Engineering; Mechanical Engineering; Mechanics; Metal Techniques; Microelectronics; Nuclear Engineering; Optical Technology; Power Engineering; Production Engineering; Robotics; Safety Engineering; Telecommunications Services; Transport and Communications; Transport Engineering; Transport Management.**

Student Services: Academic Counselling, Canteen, Careers Guidance, Health Services, Language Laboratory, Library, Residential Facilities, Sports Facilities

Publications: Annals of the Technical University of Sofia

Publishing House: Izdatelstvo i Pechatna baza

Academic Staff *2014-2015*	**TOTAL**
FULL-TIME	c. **800**
FOREIGN ONLY	**1400**

Last Updated: 25/02/15

PLOVDIV BRANCH

25 Tsanko Diustabanov St, 4000 Plovdiv
Tel: +359(32) 659-558 +359(32) 659-555
Fax: +359(32) 626-600 +359(32) 626-886
EMail: branch@tu-plovdiv.bg
Website: http://www.tu-plovdiv.bg/

Director: Michail Petrov
Tel: +359(32) 626-886 EMail: mpetrov@tu-plovdiv.bg

Vice Rector: Valyo Nikolov EMail: vnikolov@tu-plovdiv.bg

International Relations: Lalka Boteva, Public and International Relations Officer
Tel: +359(32) 659-541 EMail: boteva@tu-plovdiv.bg

Faculty

Electronics and Automatics (Automation and Control Engineering; Computer Engineering; Electrical Engineering; Electronic Engineering; Laser Engineering; Optical Technology; Physical Education; Sports); **Mechanical Engineering** (Aeronautical and Aerospace Engineering; Chemistry; Industrial Management; Instrument Making; Mathematics; Mechanical Engineering; Mechanics; Physics; Transport Engineering)

Department

Special Training (Banking; Business Administration; Computer Graphics; Computer Networks; Electrical Engineering; Finance; Food Technology; International Economics; International Relations; Law; Management; Mathematics; Mechanical Engineering; Metal Techniques; Nuclear Engineering; Pedagogy; Physics; Power Engineering; Private Law; Safety Engineering; Telecommunications Engineering)

History: Founded 1945, acquired present status and title 1986. An independent legal entity since 1990;

Main Language(s) of Instruction: Bulgarian

Degrees and Diplomas: *Bakalavr*, *Magistr*: **Aeronautical and Aerospace Engineering; Automation and Control Engineering; Computer Engineering; Electrical Engineering; Electronic Engineering; Graphic Design; Industrial Engineering; Instrument Making; Mechanical Engineering; Printing and Printmaking; Transport Engineering.**

Student Services: Canteen, IT Centre, Library, Residential Facilities

SLIVEN BRANCH

59 Burgasko Šose Bvd., 8800 Sliven
Tel: +359(44) 66-77-09
EMail: umo.sliven@gmail.com; priem.sliven@gmail.com
Website: http://www.tu-sliven.com/

Director: Milko Yordanov (2014-)

Faculty

Engineering and Pedagogy (Chemistry; Education; Electrical and Electronic Engineering; Heating and Refrigeration; Management; Mathematics; Mechanical Engineering; Mechanics; Physics)

History: Founded 1986.

Fees: National: Undergraduate, 160 per semester; Graduate, 325 per semester; Doctorate, 680 per annum (Bulgarian Lev), International: 1,500 per semester (Euro)

Main Language(s) of Instruction: Bulgarian

Degrees and Diplomas: *Profesionalen Bakalavr*, *Bakalavr*, *Magistr*: **Automation and Control Engineering; Automotive Engineering; Computer Engineering; Electrical Engineering; Energy Engineering; Heating and Refrigeration; Machine Building; Mechanical Engineering; Transport Engineering.** *Doktor*: **Automation and Control Engineering; Business Administration; Energy Engineering; Machine Building; Materials Engineering; Mechanical Engineering; Mechanics; Production Engineering; Public Administration.**

Student Services: Careers Guidance, IT Centre, Library

TECHNICAL UNIVERSITY OF VARNA

Tehničeski universitet Varna (TU-VARNA)
1 Studentska Str., Vassil Levski district, 9010 Varna
Tel: +359(52) 302-444
Fax: +359(52) 302-771
EMail: rector@tu-varna.acad.bg
Website: http://www.tu-varna.acad.bg

Rector: Rosen Vassilev
EMail: rector@tu-varna.bg; rsnvasilev@tu-varna.bg

Vice Rector Academic Affairs: Maria Marinova
Tel: +359(52) 302-447
EMail: m_i_marinova@tu-varna.bg; m_i_m@abv.bg

International Relations: Hristo Skulev, Head of International Relations EMail: fs_centre@tu-varna.acad.bg; skulev@tu-varna.bg

Faculty

Automation and Computing (Applied Mathematics; Artificial Intelligence; Automation and Control Engineering; Computer Networks; Mathematics and Computer Science); **Electrical Engineering** (Electrical Engineering; Power Engineering); **Electronic Engineering** (Electronic Engineering; Telecommunications Engineering); **Marine Sciences and Ecology** (Ecology; Engineering Management; Marine Science and Oceanography; Marine Transport; Nautical Science); **Mechanical Engineering** (Building Technologies; Industrial Design; Machine Building; Metal Techniques); **Shipbuilding** (Building Technologies; Heating and Refrigeration; Marine Engineering; Naval Architecture; Physical Education; Sports; Thermal Engineering)

College

Technical Studies (Automation and Control Engineering; Information Technology; Mechanical Engineering; Transport Engineering); **Technology** *(Dobrudzha)* (Agricultural Engineering; Automation and Control Engineering; Electronic Engineering; Information Technology; Maintenance Technology; Mechanical Engineering)

Department

Mathematics and Foreign Languages (Mathematics; Modern Languages)

History: Founded 1962 as Institute of Mechanical and Electrical Engineering, acquired present status and title 1995.

Academic Year: September to July

Admission Requirements: Secondary school certificate (Diploma za zavarsheno sredno obrazovanie) and entrance examination

Fees: 500-2,094 per annum (Bulgarian Lev)

Main Language(s) of Instruction: Bulgarian

Accrediting Agency: National Agency for Evaluation and Accreditation

Degrees and Diplomas: *Profesionalen Bakalavr*; *Bakalavr*; *Magistr*: **Automotive Engineering; Business Computing; Chemical Engineering; Computer Engineering; Computer Networks; Crop Production; Electrical Engineering; Electronic Engineering; Heating and Refrigeration; Industrial Engineering; Industrial Management; Information Technology; Machine Building; Marine Transport; Mechanical Engineering; Naval Architecture; Occupational Health; Optical Technology; Social Policy; Social Work; Software Engineering; Sports; Telecommunications Engineering; Transport Engineering.** *Doktor*: **Automation and Control Engineering; Automotive Engineering; Computer Engineering; Computer Networks; Electrical Engineering; Electronic Engineering; Energy Engineering; Industrial Management; Machine Building; Marine Transport; Materials Engineering; Mechanical Engineering; Naval Architecture; Power Engineering; Safety Engineering; Social Policy; Social Psychology; Social Work; Telecommunications Engineering; Transport Management.** Also Diplom za Visše Obrazovanie 5 yrs

Student Services: Canteen, Careers Guidance, Foreign Studies Centre, Health Services, Library, Residential Facilities, Sports Facilities

Publications: Acta Universitatis Pontica Euxinus

Publishing House: Printing House (Pečatna Baza)

Last Updated: 26/02/15

TODOR KABLESHKOV UNIVERSITY OF TRANSPORT

Vische transportno utchilichte "Todor Kablechkov"
58 Geo Milev Str., 1574 Sofia
Tel: +359(2) 970-9211 +359(2) 970-9230
Fax: +359(2) 970-9242 +359(2) 970-9407
EMail: office@vtu.bg
Website: http://www.vtu.bg/

Rector: Peter Kolev Kolev
Tel: +359(2) 970-9240 EMail: rector@vtu.bg; petarkolev@vtu.bg

Vice Rector of Academic Affairs: Rumen Kostadinov Uluchev
Tel: +359(2) 970-9406 EMail: ruluchev@vtu.bg

International Relations: Daniela Dimitrova Todorova, Vice-Rector, Research and International Relations
Tel: +359(2) 9709-335 EMail: dtodorova@vtu.bg

Faculty

Machinery and Construction Technologies in Transport (Building Technologies; Machine Building; Mechanical Engineering; Transport and Communications; Transport Engineering); **Telecommunications and Electrical Equipment in Transport** (Computer Science; Electrical Engineering; Mathematics; Physics; Power Engineering; Telecommunications Engineering); **Transport Management** (Arts and Humanities; Machine Building; Transport Economics; Transport Management)

History: Founded 1922. Renamed Todor Kableshkov Higher Military School of Transport 1984. Demilitarized and renamed as Todor Kableshkov Higher School of Transport 2000.

Fees: 2,500 per annum in full-time mode; 1,500-1,800 per annum in part-time mode (Euro)

Main Language(s) of Instruction: Bulgarian

Accrediting Agency: National Assessment and Accreditation Agency

Degrees and Diplomas: *Profesionalen Bakalavr*; *Bakalavr*; *Magistr*: **Air Transport; Automation and Control Engineering; Computer Engineering; Computer Graphics; Economics; Electrical Engineering; Electronic Engineering; Machine Building; Marine Transport; Mechanical Engineering; Small Business; Telecommunications Engineering; Transport and Communications; Transport Economics; Transport Engineering; Transport Management.** *Doktor*: **Automation and Control Engineering; Automotive Engineering; Building Technologies; Civil Engineering; Computer Networks; Construction Engineering; Electrical Engineering; Machine Building; Maintenance Technology; Materials Engineering; Mechanical Engineering; Mechanics; Power Engineering; Railway Transport; Safety Engineering; Telecommunications Engineering; Transport Engineering.**

Last Updated: 27/02/15

IAU TRAKIA UNIVERSITY

Trakiyski universitet
Studentski Grad, 6000 Stara Zagora
Tel: +359(42) 699-213
Fax: +359(42) 672-009
EMail: academic@uni-sz.bg; intern@uni-sz.bg
Website: http://www.uni-sz.bg

Rector: Ivan Stankov
Tel: +359(42) 670-204 EMail: rector@uni-sz.bg

Secretary-General: Tsonka Kasnakova
Tel: +359(42) 699-205 EMail: kasnakova@uni-sz.bg

International Relations: Veselina Gadjeva, Vice-Rector
Tel: +359(42) 673-004 EMail: vgadjeva@mf.uni-sz.bg

Faculty

Agriculture *(with experimental station)* (Agricultural Engineering; Agronomy; Animal Husbandry; Aquaculture; Ecology; Fishery); **Economics** (Agricultural Economics; Banking; Economics; Finance; Regional Planning; Rural Studies); **Education** (Education; Pedagogy); **Medicine** *(with University Hospital)* (Medicine; Social and Community Services; Social Welfare; Social Work); **Veterinary Medicine** *(with Clinics)* (Veterinary Science)

College

Medicine *(Stara Zagora)* (Nursing; Rehabilitation and Therapy); **Technology** *(Yambol)* (Agricultural Equipment; Automation and Control Engineering; Electronic Engineering; Food Technology; Machine Building; Maintenance Technology; Textile Technology)

Department

Information and In-service Teacher Training (Art Education; Computer Education; Foreign Languages Education; Humanities and Social Science Education; Literacy Education; Mathematics Education; Music Education; Native Language Education; Physical Education; Preschool Education; Primary Education; Secondary Education; Teacher Trainers Education; Technology Education)

Campus

Haskovo (Midwifery; Nursing)

Further Information: University Hospital; Preparatory courses for foreign students; Experimental Farm; Training-Experimental Base(Medicine), Haskovo

History: Founded 1995, incorporating the former Higher Institute of Medicine and Higher Institute of Animal Production and Veterinary Medicine. Three Medical Colleges affiliated to Trakia University 1997.

Academic Year: September to July (September-December; February-July)

Admission Requirements: Secondary school certificate (zrelostno svidetelstvo), or equivalent

Fees: National: 460-950 per annum (Bulgarian Lev), International: 1,000-5,200 per annum (Euro)

Main Language(s) of Instruction: Bulgarian

Accrediting Agency: National Agency for Evaluation and Accreditation

Degrees and Diplomas: *Profesionalen Bakalavr*: **Medical Auxiliaries; Rehabilitation and Therapy.** *Bakalavr*: **Agricultural Economics; Agriculture; Economics; Education; Engineering; Health Administration; Industrial Management; Midwifery; Nursing; Social Work; Teacher Training; Technology.** *Magistr*: **Agronomy; Animal Husbandry; Ecology; Economics; Environmental Management; Health Administration; Medicine; Social Work; Veterinary Science.** *Doktor*: **Cardiology; Ecology; Economics; Educational Sciences; Endocrinology; Environmental Management; Gynaecology and Obstetrics; Health Administration; Hygiene; Immunology; Management; Microbiology; Occupational Health; Pathology; Physical Therapy; Psychology; Rehabilitation and Therapy; Special Education; Surgery; Veterinary Science.** Also Postgraduate Certificate in Animal Husbandry

Student Services: Academic Counselling, Canteen, Careers Guidance, Cultural Activities, Foreign Studies Centre, Health Services, IT Centre, Language Laboratory, Library, Nursery Care, Residential Facilities, Social Counselling, Sports Facilities

Publications: Agricultural Science and Technology; Bulgarian Journal of Veterinary Medicine; Trakia Journal of Sciences

Last Updated: 26/02/15

UNIVERSITY OF ARCHITECTURE, CIVIL ENGINEERING AND GEODESY

Universitet po Arhitektura, Stroitelstvo i Geodezia (UACEG)

1 Hristo Smirnenski Blvd., 1046 Sofia
Tel: +359(2) 963-5245
Fax: +359(2) 865-6863
EMail: aceadm@uacg.bg
Website: http://www.uacg.bg

Rector: Krasimir Petrov
Tel: +359(2) 963-5245 EMail: k_petrov_fhe@uacg.bg

Vice-Rector for Academic Affairs: Nedyalko Ivanov Bonchev
Tel: +359(2) 963-2892 EMail: nedialko_far@uacg.bg

International Relations: Boyan Milchev Georgiev, Vice-Rector
Tel: +359(2) 963-5245
EMail: boyangeo_far@uacg.bg; aceint@uacg.bg

Faculty

Architecture (Architecture; Architecture and Planning; Interior Design; Landscape Architecture; Regional Planning; Rural Planning; Town Planning); **Geodesy** (Engineering; Geological Engineering; Soil Science; Surveying and Mapping); **Hydraulic Engineering** (Civil Engineering; Environmental Engineering; Hydraulic Engineering; Irrigation; Waste Management; Water Management); **Structural Engineering** (Building Technologies; Construction Engineering; Structural Architecture); **Transportation Engineering** (Railway Engineering; Road Engineering; Transport Engineering)

Department

Applied Linguistics and Physical Education (Applied Linguistics; Physical Education)

Centre

Open and Continuing Education *(COCE)* (Business Administration; Business and Commerce; Civil Engineering; Computer Engineering; Computer Science; Construction Engineering; Engineering Drawing and Design; International Business; International Economics; International Law; International Relations; Management; Real Estate; Systems Analysis)

History: Founded 1942 as Higher Technical School, reorganized as State Polytechnic 1945 and as Higher Institute of Civil Engineering 1953. Became Higher Institute of Architecture and Civil Engineering (VIAS) 1977 and University of Architecture, Civil Engineering and Geodesy 1990. Acquired present status 1995.

Academic Year: September to June (September-January; February-June)

Admission Requirements: Secondary school certificate (diploma za zavarsheno sredno obrazovanie)

Fees: National: 155 per semester (Bulgarian Lev), International: 2,000 for the preparatory year; 3,000 per annum for full time course (Euro)

Main Language(s) of Instruction: Bulgarian, German, English

Accrediting Agency: National Agency for Evaluation and Accreditation

Degrees and Diplomas: *Bakalavr*, *Magistr*: **Architectural Restoration; Architecture; Art Criticism; Civil Engineering; Earth Sciences; Geological Engineering; Hydraulic Engineering; Irrigation; Real Estate; Seismology; Structural Architecture; Town Planning; Transport Engineering; Water Management.** *Doktor*: **Architecture; Civil Engineering; Geology.**

Student Services: Canteen, Health Services, IT Centre, Library, Residential Facilities, Sports Facilities

Publishing house: Printing House of UACEG

Academic Staff *2014-2015*	**TOTAL**
FULL-TIME	**364**
PART-TIME	**212**
STAFF WITH DOCTORATE	
FULL-TIME	**310**
Student Numbers *2014-2015*	
All (Foreign included)	c. **5,000**
FOREIGN ONLY	**350**

Part-time students, 490.

Last Updated: 26/02/15

UNIVERSITY OF CHEMICAL TECHNOLOGY AND METALLURGY

Himiko-tehnologičen i metalurgičen universitet (UCTM)

University Boulevard, 8, 1756 Sofia
Tel: +359(2) 816-3120
Fax: +359(2) 868-5488
EMail: rectorat@uctm.edu; m.dicheva@uctm.edu
Website: http://www.uctm.edu

Rector: Mitko Georgiev (2011-)
Tel: +359(2) 81-63-100 EMail: uctm.rector@uctm.edu

Vice-Rector for Academic Affairs: Nikolai Dishovski
Tel: +359(2) 81-63-101 +359(2) 81-63-221
EMail: dishov@uctm.edu

International Relations: Margarita Koleva, International Cooperation Officer Tel: +359(2) 8163-111 EMail: rectorat@uctm.edu

Faculty

Chemical Systems Engineering (Automation and Control Engineering; Biotechnology; Chemical Engineering; Ecology;

Environmental Studies; Industrial Management; Information Technology); **Chemical Technology** (Chemical Engineering; Inorganic Chemistry; Leather Techniques; Paper Technology; Polymer and Plastics Technology; Textile Technology; Wood Technology); **Metallurgy and Material Sciences** (Materials Engineering; Metallurgical Engineering)

Department

Chemical Sciences (Analytical Chemistry; Chemistry; Inorganic Chemistry; Organic Chemistry; Physical Chemistry); **Humanitarian Sciences** (Arts and Humanities; Bulgarian; English; French; German; Modern Languages; Physical Education; Russian; Sports); **Physics-mathematical and Tehnical sciences** (Computer Science; Electronic Engineering; Mathematics; Mechanics; Physics)

History: Founded 1953 as Institute of Chemical Technology, acquired present status and title 1995.

Academic Year: September to June

Admission Requirements: Secondary school certificate (Diploma za zavarsheno sredno obrazovanie), and entrance examination (chemistry or mathematics)

Main Language(s) of Instruction: Bulgarian

Accrediting Agency: National Agency for Evaluation and Accreditation

Degrees and Diplomas: *Bakalavr*; *Magistr*: **Automation and Control Engineering; Biochemistry; Biotechnology; Business Administration; Chemical Engineering; Energy Engineering; Environmental Engineering; Environmental Management; Industrial Chemistry; Industrial Management; Information Technology; Inorganic Chemistry; Leather Techniques; Materials Engineering; Metal Techniques; Metallurgical Engineering; Nanotechnology; Organic Chemistry; Packaging Technology; Paper Technology; Polymer and Plastics Technology; Printing and Printmaking; Safety Engineering; Textile Technology.** *Doktor*: **Agricultural Economics; Agricultural Management; Artificial Intelligence; Automation and Control Engineering; Biochemistry; Biotechnology; Chemical Engineering; Computer Science; Data Processing; Educational Research; Electrical Engineering; Electronic Engineering; Energy Engineering; Fire Science; Higher Education; Industrial Engineering; Industrial Management; Inorganic Chemistry; Leather Techniques; Materials Engineering; Mechanics; Metal Techniques; Metallurgical Engineering; Organic Chemistry; Paper Technology; Petroleum and Gas Engineering; Polymer and Plastics Technology; Rubber Technology; Safety Engineering; Solid State Physics; Textile Technology; Thermal Engineering; Water Science.** Some subjects taught in German, French and English

Student Services: IT Centre, Library, Residential Facilities, Sports Facilities

Publications: Journal of the University of Chemical Technology and Metallurgy

Student Numbers *2014-2015*: Total: c. 4,000

Last Updated: 13/02/15

UNIVERSITY OF ECONOMICS - VARNA

Ikonomičeski universitet, Varna (UE-VARNA)

77 Kniaz Boris I Blvd., 9002 Varna
Tel: +359(52) 660-212 +359(52) 660-325
Fax: +359(52) 235-680
EMail: int_relations@ue-varna.bg
Website: http://www.ue-varna.bg

Rector: Plamen Blagov Iliev
Tel: +359(52) 609-565 EMail: rector@ue-varna.bg

Vice-Rector for Academic Affairs: Evgeni Petrov Stanimirov
Tel: +359(52) 643-361 EMail: stanimirov@ue-varna.bg

International Relations: Violeta Janeva Dimitrova, Vice-Chancellor, International Co-operation and Public Relations
Tel: +359(52) 643-363
EMail: violeta_dimitrova@mail.ue-varna.bg; int_relations@ue-varna.bg

Faculty

Economics (Agricultural Economics; Business Administration; Business and Commerce; Economics; Industrial and Production Economics; Real Estate; Transport Economics); **Finance and Accountancy** (Accountancy; Finance); **Information Technologies** (Business Computing; Computer Science; Econometrics; Statistics); **Management** (International Business; International Economics; Management; Marketing; Tourism)

College

Tourism (European Languages; Hotel and Restaurant; International Economics; Leisure Studies; Slavic Languages; Tourism)

Department

Foreign Languages (European Languages; Modern Languages; Slavic Languages)

History: Founded 1920 as Higher School of Commerce, acquired present status and title 1994.

Academic Year: September to May (September-December; February-May)

Admission Requirements: Secondary school certificate (Diploma za zavarsheno sredno obrazovanie), and entrance examination

Fees: National: 200-260 per annum; Graduate, 650-800 per semester (Bulgarian Lev), International: 2,500 (US Dollar)

Main Language(s) of Instruction: Bulgarian

Accrediting Agency: National Agency for Evaluation and Accreditation

Degrees and Diplomas: *Bakalavr*: **Computer Science; Economics; Management.** *Magistr*: **Accountancy; Advertising and Publicity; Agricultural Business; Banking; Business Administration; Business Computing; Computer Science; Economics; Finance; International Business; Management; Mass Communication; Public Administration; Real Estate; Sales Techniques; Transport Management.** *Doktor*: **Accountancy; Agricultural Economics; Agricultural Management; Banking; Business Administration; Business Computing; Demography and Population; Economics; Finance; Industrial and Production Economics; Industrial Management; Insurance; Management; Marketing; Statistics; Tourism.**

Student Services: Academic Counselling, Canteen, Careers Guidance, Cultural Activities, Health Services, Library, Nursery Care, Social Counselling, Sports Facilities

Publishing house: University Publishing House

Last Updated: 13/02/15

UNIVERSITY OF FOOD TECHNOLOGIES

Universitet po hranitelni technologii (UFT)

26 "Maritza" Blvd., 4000 Plovdiv
Tel: +359(32) 643-005 +359(32) 642-738
Fax: +359(32) 644-102
EMail: uht@uft-plovdiv.bg; intoffice@uft-plovdiv.bg
Website: http://uft-plovdiv.bg/

Rector: Kolyo Dinkov
Tel: +359(32) 643-005 EMail: rector_uft@uft-plovdiv.bg

Vice-Rector for Academic Affairs: Albena Stoyanova
Tel: +359(32) 643-008 EMail: vicerector_edu@uft-plovdiv.bg

International Relations: Nikolay Menkov, Vice Rector of International Affairs and Public Relations
Tel: +359(32) 643-033 EMail: vicerector_inter@uft-plovdiv.bg

Faculty

Economics (Business Administration; Economics; Industrial and Production Economics; Tourism); **Technical** (Automation and Control Engineering; Computer Engineering; Electrical and Electronic Equipment and Maintenance; Engineering; Heating and Refrigeration; Mechanical Engineering); **Technology** (Analytical Chemistry; Biochemistry; Biotechnology; Dairy; Food Technology; Heating and Refrigeration; Inorganic Chemistry; Microbiology; Oenology; Plant and Crop Protection; Technology)

Department

Language Training (Modern Languages); **Physical Education and Sports** (Physical Education; Sports)

Centre

Francophone Training (Food Technology; Technology Education)

Sector

Scientific Research (Food Science)

History: Founded 1953 as Higher Institute of Food and Flavour Industries, acquired present title and status 2003.

Academic Year: September to May (September-December; February-May)

Admission Requirements: Secondary school certificate (Diploma za zavarsheno sredno obrazovanie)

Fees: Bachelor, 2,500-3,500 per annum; Master, 2,500-3,500 per annum; Ph.D., 3,000-4,000; Bulgarian or English Language Training Course, 2,500 per annum (Euro)

Main Language(s) of Instruction: Bulgarian, English

Accrediting Agency: National Evaluation and Accreditation Agency

Degrees and Diplomas: *Bakalavr*: **Agricultural Business; Automation and Control Engineering; Biotechnology; Brewing; Computer Engineering; Cooking and Catering; Dairy; Dietetics; Ecology; Engineering; Environmental Engineering; Environmental Management; Food Science; Food Technology; Heating and Refrigeration; Horticulture; Hotel and Restaurant; Industrial Management; Machine Building; Meat and Poultry; Nutrition; Tourism; Viticulture.** *Magistr*: **Agricultural Business; Agricultural Economics; Automation and Control Engineering; Biotechnology; Brewing; Business Administration; Business Computing; Computer Engineering; Cooking and Catering; Cosmetology; Ecology; Energy Engineering; Environmental Management; Food Science; Food Technology; Heating and Refrigeration; Horticulture; Hotel and Restaurant; Industrial Management; Machine Building; Management; Meat and Poultry; Packaging Technology; Safety Engineering; Viticulture.** *Doktor*: **Analytical Chemistry; Biochemistry; Biotechnology; Computer Engineering; Cooking and Catering; Cosmetology; Dairy; Electrical Engineering; Food Science; Food Technology; Fruit Production; Heating and Refrigeration; Horticulture; Industrial Engineering; Inorganic Chemistry; Management; Meat and Poultry; Microbiology; Organic Chemistry; Physical Chemistry.**

Student Services: Academic Counselling, Canteen, Careers Guidance, Health Services, Language Laboratory, Library, Residential Facilities, Social Counselling, Sports Facilities

Publications: Scientific Works of UFT

Last Updated: 26/02/15

UNIVERSITY OF FORESTRY - SOFIA

Lesotehničeski universitet - Sofia (LTU/UF)

10 St. Kliment Ohridski Blvd., 1756 Sofia

Tel: +359(2) 962-5997

Fax: +359(2) 622-830

EMail: zhelev@ltu.bg

Website: http://www.ltu.bg

Chancellor: Vesselin Stamenov Brezin
Tel: +359(2) 962-5997 EMail: rektor@ltu.bg; brezin@ltu.bg

Vice Chancellor, Student Affairs: Ivan Paligorov
Tel: +359(2) 91-907-420 EMail: ipaligorov@abv.bg

International Relations: Petar Stoyanov Zhelev, Vice Chancellor, Accreditation, International Integration and Public Relations
Tel: +3559(2) 862-1682
EMail: peter_zhelev@abv.bg; zhelev@ltu.bg

Faculty

Agronomy (Agriculture; Agronomy; Crop Production; Forest Biology; Horticulture); **Business Administration** (Business Administration; Economics; Industrial Management; Marketing); **Ecology and Landscape Architecture** (Ecology; Landscape Architecture; Plant Pathology); **Forest Industry** (Forest Economics; Forest Management; Forestry; Furniture Design; Wood Technology); **Forestry** (Forest Management; Forest Products; Forestry; Soil Science); **Veterinary Medicine** (Veterinary Science)

Further Information: Also Scientific Research Department

History: Founded 1925 as Forestry Department of Sofia University 'St. Kliment Ochridski', reorganized as Higher Technical Institute of Forestry, an autonomous institution. Acquired present status and title 1995.

Academic Year: October to June

Fees: 3,000 per annum

Main Language(s) of Instruction: Bulgarian

Degrees and Diplomas: *Bakalavr*, *Magistr*: **Business Administration; Crop Production; Ecology; Environmental Management; Food Technology; Forestry; Furniture Design; Interior Design; Landscape Architecture; Plant and Crop Protection; Tourism; Veterinary Science.** *Doktor*: **Agricultural Equipment; Agriculture; Animal Husbandry; Architecture; Automation and Control Engineering; Biochemistry; Business Computing; Ecology; Economics; Fishery; Forest Management; Forestry; Genetics; Geology; Industrial Management; Landscape Architecture; Management; Mechanical Engineering; Plant and Crop Protection; Sericulture; Soil Science; Surveying and Mapping; Vegetable Production; Veterinary Science; Viticulture; Wood Technology.**

Student Services: Canteen, Cultural Activities, IT Centre, Language Laboratory, Library

Publications: Forestry Ideas; Management and Sustainable Development; Woodworking and Furniture Production

Publishing House: Publishing Division

Last Updated: 24/02/15

UNIVERSITY OF MINING AND GEOLOGY ST. IVAN RILSKI

Minno-geoložki universitet "Sv. Ivan Rilski" (MGU)

Studentski Grad, "prof. Boyan Kamenov" Street,
1700 Sofia

Tel: +359(2) 806-0300

Fax: +359(2) 962-5931

EMail: staf@mgu.bg

Website: http://www.mgu.bg

Rector: Lyuben Ivanov Totev
Tel: +359(2) 806-0201 EMail: rector@mgu.bg

Vice-Rector for Education: Vyara Georgieva Pozhidaeva
Tel: +359(2) 806-0202 EMail: vpojidaeva@abv.bg

International Relations: Stefka Dimitrova Pristavova, Vice-rector for International Cooperation and Projects
Tel: +359(2) 806-0252 EMail: stprist@mgu.bg

Faculty

Geoexploration (Ecology; Environmental Management; Geology; Geophysics; Petroleum and Gas Engineering); **Mining Electromechanics** (Automation and Control Engineering; Electrical Engineering; Mining Engineering; Petroleum and Gas Engineering); **Mining Technology** (Industrial Management; Mineralogy; Mining Engineering; Surveying and Mapping)

Department

Humanities (Arts and Humanities)

History: Founded 1953. Acquired present status and title 2005.

Academic Year: September to July

Admission Requirements: Secondary school certificate (Diploma za zavarsheno sredno obrazovanie), and entrance examination

Fees: 1,650-3,300 per annum (Euro)

Main Language(s) of Instruction: Bulgarian, English

Accrediting Agency: National Agency for Evaluation and Accreditation

Degrees and Diplomas: *Bakalavr*, *Magistr*: **Biotechnology; Civil Engineering; Computer Engineering; Computer Science; Construction Engineering; Ecology; Electrical Engineering; Energy Engineering; Environmental Management; Geological Engineering; Geology; Geophysics; Industrial Engineering; Mineralogy; Mining Engineering; Petroleum and Gas Engineering; Petrology; Surveying and Mapping; Waste Management; Water Management.** *Doktor*: **Geology; Mining Engineering.**

Student Services: Academic Counselling, Canteen, Facilities for disabled people, Foreign Studies Centre, Health Services, Language Laboratory, Nursery Care, Social Counselling, Sports Facilities

Publications: Annual of the University of Mining and Geology "St. Ivan Rilski"

Publishing House: University Publishing House

Last Updated: 25/02/15

UNIVERSITY OF NATIONAL AND WORLD ECONOMY

Universitet za nacionalno i svetovno stopanstvo (UNWE)

Studentski Grad 'Hristo Botev', 1756 Sofia
Tel: +359(2) 819-5211
Fax: +359(2) 962-3903
EMail: secretary@unwe.acad.bg; international@unwe.bg
Website: http://www.unwe.bg

Rector: Statty Stattev
Tel: +359(2) 819-5515 EMail: rectorss@unwe.bg

First Vice-Rector and Vice-Rector on Education in EQD of Bachelor: Ognian Georgiev Simeonov
Tel: +359(2) 962-3473 EMail: osimeonov@unwe.bg

Faculty

Applied Informatics and Statistics (Business Computing; Communication Studies; Econometrics; Information Technology; Statistics); **Business** (Agricultural Business; Business Administration; Economics; Real Estate); **Economics of Infrastructure** (Communication Studies; Economics; Media Studies; Transport Economics); **Finance and Accountancy** (Accountancy; Finance); **General Economics** (Economics; Human Resources; Social Policy; Sociology); **International Economics and Politics** (International Business; International Relations; Political Sciences); **Law** (Criminal Law; Law; Private Law; Public Law); **Management and Administration** (Business Administration; Management; Marketing; Public Administration; Regional Studies)

Further Information: Also affiliated branch (Economics and Management) in Haskovo

History: Founded 1947 as Higher Institute of Economics, acquired present status and title 1995.

Academic Year: October to June (October-January; March-June)

Main Language(s) of Instruction: Bulgarian

Accrediting Agency: National Agency for Evaluation and Accreditation

Degrees and Diplomas: *Bakalavr*, *Magistr*: **Accountancy; Business Administration; Economics; Finance; Health Administration; Insurance; International Business; International Economics; Journalism; Management; Marketing; Media Studies; Public Administration; Transport Management.** *Doktor*: **Econometrics; Economics; Statistics.** Joint Master's Degree Programmes with Universite du Littoral Cote d'Opale (France) and Nottingham Trent University (United Kingdom)

Student Services: Canteen, Health Services, IT Centre, Library, Residential Facilities, Sports Facilities

Publications: Alternativi; Ikonomist; Trudove

Publishing House: University Publishing House 'Stopanstvo'. University Press

Last Updated: 26/02/15

UNIVERSITY OF STRUCTURAL ENGINEERING AND ARCHITECTURE LYUBEN KARAVELOV

Vische stroitelno utchilichte "Juben Karavelov" (VSU)

175 Suhodolska Str., 1373 Sofia
Tel: +359(2) 802-9100 +359(2) 802-9191
Fax: +359(2) 802-9001
EMail: vsu@vsu.bg
Website: http://www.vsu.bg

Rector: Radan Ivanovo
Tel: +359(2) 802-9191 EMail: rector@vsu.bg

Vice-Rector for Academic Affairs: Margarita Nikolova Khamova
Tel: +359(2) 802-9110 EMail: zrector@vsu.bg

International Relations: Neli Yordanova, International Cooperation Officer Tel: +359(2) 802-9188 EMail: intoffice.vsu@gmail.com

Faculty

Architecture (Architecture); **Construction Engineering** (Civil Engineering; Construction Engineering)

History: Founded 1928 as Professional School for Army Corps' Engineers. HSCE was transformed from a military into a civilian state institution of higher education. Acquired present title and status 2000.

Fees: National: Bachelor, 660-800 per annum; Master, 660-1,800 per annum; Ph.D., 400 per annum (Bulgarian Lev), International: Bachelor, 1,500-3,000 per annum; Master, 1,500-2,000 per annum; Ph.D., 3,000 per annum (Euro)

Main Language(s) of Instruction: Bulgarian, English

Accrediting Agency: National Evaluation and Accreditation Agency (NAOA)

Degrees and Diplomas: *Profesionalen Bakalavr*, *Bakalavr*, *Magistr*: **Architecture; Civil Engineering.** *Doktor*: **Civil Engineering.**

Student Services: Canteen, Residential Facilities, Sports Facilities

Last Updated: 26/02/15

UNIVERSITY PROF. DR. ASSEN ZLATAROV - BURGAS

Prof. Dr. Assen Zlatarov Universitet - Burgas (BTU)

1 Prof. Jakimov Str., 8010 Burgas
Tel: +359(56) 860-041
Fax: +359(56) 880-249
EMail: office@btu.bg
Website: http://www.btu.bg

Rector: Petko Petkov Stoyanov
Tel: +359(56) 716-560 EMail: rector@btu.bg

Vice-Rector for Academic Affairs: Pertanka Pipeva Todorova Dimitrova Tel: +359(56) 716-508 EMail: ppipeva@abv.bg

International Relations: Magdalena Sabeva Mitkova, Vice-Rector for International Cooperation Studies
Tel: +359(56) 716-481 EMail: mmitkova@btu.bg

Faculty

Natural Sciences (Analytical Chemistry; Chemistry; Ecology; Environmental Studies; Inorganic Chemistry; Mathematics; Natural Sciences; Organic Chemistry; Physics); **Social Sciences** (Accountancy; Bulgarian; Business Administration; Computer Science; Economics; Education; Foreign Languages Education; Industrial Management; Information Technology; Management; Marketing; Natural Sciences; Pedagogy; Preschool Education; Primary Education; Production Engineering; Psychology; Social Sciences; Tourism); **Technical Sciences** (Biotechnology; Chemical Engineering; Hydraulic Engineering; Inorganic Chemistry; Materials Engineering; Organic Chemistry)

College

Medicine (Medical Auxiliaries; Medicine; Nursing; Rehabilitation and Therapy); **Technical Studies** (Computer Engineering; Electrical and Electronic Engineering; Marketing; Mechanical Engineering; Mechanical Equipment and Maintenance; Technology; Transport Engineering); **Tourism** (Hotel Management; Tourism)

Department

Teaching of Foreign Languages (English; Foreign Languages Education; French; Slavic Languages)

Section

Research

History: Founded 1963 as Higher Institute of Chemical Technology, acquired present status and title 1995.

Academic Year: October to June

Admission Requirements: Secondary school certificate (Diploma za zavarsheno sredno obrazovanie)

Fees: 2,800 per annum (Euro)

Main Language(s) of Instruction: Bulgarian and English

Accrediting Agency: National Evaluation and Accreditation Agency

Degrees and Diplomas: *Profesionalen Bakalavr*: **Computer Engineering; Electrical Engineering; Electronic Engineering; Management; Marketing; Mechanical Engineering; Medical Auxiliaries; Nursing; Rehabilitation and Therapy; Transport and Communications; Transport Engineering.** *Bakalavr*: **Biotechnology; Bulgarian; Business Administration; Chemical Engineering; Chemistry; Computer Networks; Ecology; Education of the Socially Disadvantaged; Environmental Management; Foreign Languages Education; Humanities and Social Science Education; Industrial Management; Inorganic**

Chemistry; Marketing; Materials Engineering; Native Language Education; Nursing; Occupational Therapy; Organic Chemistry; Preschool Education; Primary Education; Rehabilitation and Therapy; Tourism. *Magistr*: **Art Management; Biotechnology; Bulgarian; Business Administration; Business Computing; Chemical Engineering; Chemistry; Communication Studies; Computer Engineering; Computer Science; Ecology; Economics; Electrical Engineering; Electronic Engineering; Engineering Drawing and Design; Environmental Studies; Finance; Food Technology; Health Administration; Human Resources; Humanities and Social Science Education; Industrial Chemistry; Industrial Design; Industrial Management; Inorganic Chemistry; International Business; Management; Marketing; Materials Engineering; Native Language Education; Natural Resources; Organic Chemistry; Petroleum and Gas Engineering; Polymer and Plastics Technology; Preschool Education; Primary Education; Public Administration; Public Relations; Science Education; Secondary Education; Special Education; Tourism.** *Doktor*

Student Services: Academic Counselling, Canteen, Careers Guidance, Foreign Studies Centre, Health Services, IT Centre, Language Laboratory, Library, Nursery Care, Residential Facilities, Sports Facilities, eLibrary

Academic Staff *2014-2015*: Total: c. 320

Last Updated: 13/02/15

VARNA FREE UNIVERSITY CHERNORIZETS HRABAR

Varnenski svoboden universitet "Chernorizeth Hrarbar" (VFU)

"Chaika" Resort Complex, 9007 Varna
Tel: +359(52) 359-513
Fax: +359(52) 357-066
EMail: admission@vfu.bg
Website: http://www.vfu.bg

President: Anna Nedyalkova (1997-) EMail: vfu_president@vfu.bg

Vice-Rector for Academic Affairs: Galya Gercheva
Tel: +359(52) 357-066
EMail: gercheva@vfu.bg; rector_vfu@vfu.bg

International Relations: Nikolay Dragoev, Head, International Admissions Centre EMail: dragoev@vfu.bg

Faculty

Architecture (Architecture; Arts and Humanities; Construction Engineering; Fine Arts; Urban Studies); **International Economics and Administration** (Administration; Computer Science; Information Technology; International Economics; Management; Political Sciences); **Law** (Economics; Law; Protective Services; Psychology)

Department

Foreign Language Teaching (Bulgarian; English; French; German; Latin; Modern Languages; Russian; Spanish)

Further Information: Also Campus in Smolyan

History: Founded 1991, officially recognized 1995.

Academic Year: October to June (October-January; February-June)

Admission Requirements: Secondary school certificate (Diploma za zavarsheno sredno obrazovanie)

Fees: National: 2,000-2,500 per annum (Euro), International: Bachelor, 1,000-2,000 per annum full-time and 800-1,750 per annum part-time; Master, 1,200-2,400 per annum; Ph.D., 3,100 full-time, 2,700 part-time (Euro)

Main Language(s) of Instruction: Bulgarian, English

Accrediting Agency: National Evaluation and Accreditation Agency (NEAA)

Degrees and Diplomas: *Bakalavr*, *Magistr*: **Administration; Architecture; Art Management; Civil Engineering; Civil Security; Computer Science; Dance; Economics; Fashion Design; International Law; Law; Management; Political Sciences; Protective Services; Psychology; Public Health.** *Doktor*: **Administrative Law; Architectural and Environmental Design; Architecture; Building Technologies; Civil Engineering; Civil Law; Civil Security; Computer Science; Constitutional Law; Construction Engineering; Criminal Law; Criminology; Dance; Developmental Psychology; Economics; Educational Psychology; Fire Science; Forensic Medicine and Dentistry; Industrial and Production Economics; Industrial Management; Information Technology; Interior Design; International Economics; International Law; International Relations; Landscape Architecture; Management; Political Sciences; Psychology; Public Law; Safety Engineering; Structural Architecture; Town Planning.**

Student Services: Academic Counselling, Canteen, Cultural Activities, Facilities for disabled people, Health Services, Language Laboratory, Nursery Care, Sports Facilities

Publications: Science Almanach

Last Updated: 27/02/15

PRIVATE INSTITUTIONS

AMERICAN UNIVERSITY IN BULGARIA

Amerikanski universitet v Bulgaria (AUBG)

1 Georgi Izmirliev Sq., 2700 Blagoevgrad
Tel: +359(73) 888-111
Fax: +359(73) 888-344
EMail: admissions@aubg.edu
Website: http://www.aubg.bg

President: Kevin J. Aspegren
Tel: +359(73) 888-307
EMail: president@aubg.bg; aspergren@aubg.bg

Registrar: Tanya Markova
Tel: +359(73) 888-221 EMail: tania@aubg.bg; registrar@aubg.bg

International Relations: Pavlina Pavlova, Coordinator, International Student Services
Tel: +359(73) 888-519 EMail: pavlinap@aubg.edu

Department

Arts, Languages and Literature (Arts and Humanities; English; Fine Arts; Literature; Modern Languages; Philosophy; Religion; Writing); **Business** (Business Administration); **Computer Science** (Computer Science; Information Technology); **Economics** (Economics); **History and Civilizations** (American Studies; Anthropology; European Studies; History; Philosophy; Religion); **Journalism and Mass Communication** (Journalism; Mass Communication); **Mathematics and Science** (Mathematics); **Political Science and European Studies** (European Studies; International Relations; Political Sciences; Psychology; Sociology)

Further Information: Also Branch in Bălţi (Moldova)

History: Founded in 1991. First American-style liberal arts institution in Eastern Europe, established as a joint venture between the US and Bulgarian governments, the Open Society Institute and the University of Maine

Academic Year: August to May (August-December; January-May)

Admission Requirements: College Board SAT Examination. TOEFL test (minimum 550)

Fees: c. 10,800 per annum (US Dollar)

Main Language(s) of Instruction: English

Accrediting Agency: New England Association of Schools and Colleges (NEASC); National Agency for Evaluation and Accreditation

Degrees and Diplomas: *Bakalavr*: **Business Administration; Computer Science; Economics; European Studies; History; Information Technology; International Relations; Journalism; Mass Communication; Mathematics.** *Magistr*: **Business Administration.** Executive MBA program (a 16 month program) offered by AUBG's Elieff Center for Education and Culture in Sofia and recognized by the US.

Student Services: Academic Counselling, Canteen, Careers Guidance, Facilities for disabled people, Health Services, Language Laboratory, Library, Residential Facilities, Social Counselling, Sports Facilities

Academic Staff *2013-2014*	**TOTAL**
FULL-TIME	**74**

Student Numbers *2013-2014*	
All (Foreign included)	**1,041**
FOREIGN ONLY	**300**

Last Updated: 12/02/15

BURGAS FREE UNIVERSITY

Burgaski svoboden universitet (BFU)
62 San Stefano Street, 8001 Burgas
Tel: +359(56) 900-501 +359(56) 900-400 +359(56) 900-418
Fax: +359(56) 813-905
EMail: bfu@bfu.bg; darina@bfu.bg
Website: http://www.bfu.bg

Rector: Galya Hristozova
Tel: +359(56) 900-507 EMail: hristozova@bfu.bg

Vice-Rector for Academic Affairs and Accreditation: Evelina Dineva Tel: +359(56) 900-506
EMail: dineva@bfu.bg

International Relations: Valya Pavlova, International Relations Officer Tel: +359(56) 900-520 EMail: valia@bfu.bg

Faculty

Business Studies (Accountancy; Business Administration; Finance; Management; Marketing); **Computer Science and Engineering** (Business Computing; Computer Engineering; Computer Networks; Computer Science; Electrical and Electronic Engineering; Industrial Management; Technology); **Humanities** (Bulgarian; English; Journalism; Philology; Primary Education; Public Relations; Social Work); **Legal Studies** (Administrative Law; Civil Law; Commercial Law; Constitutional Law; Criminal Law; European Union Law; Fiscal Law; History of Law; International Law; International Relations; Labour Law; Law; Political Sciences; Public Administration; Public Law)

Further Information: Also Foreign Languages Centre. Centre for Telematics and Information Support. Multimedia Centre for Teaching Foreign Languages. 7 Centres for Further Education

History: Founded 1991 by the Burgas Academic Association. Acquired status of Higher Educational Institution by the Act of the Great National Assembly.

Academic Year: October to June (October-January; February-June)

Admission Requirements: Secondary school certificate (diploma za zavarsheno sredno obrazovanie) or recognized foreign equivalent and entrance examination

Fees: National: 620,000 per semester; Part-time 500,000 (Bulgarian Lev), International: 3,200 per annum (Euro)

Main Language(s) of Instruction: Bulgarian

Accrediting Agency: National Evaluation and Accreditation Agency

Degrees and Diplomas: *Bakalavr*; *Magistr*. **Administration; Automation and Control Engineering; Computer Engineering; Computer Science; Economics; Electrical Engineering; Electronic Engineering; Information Sciences; Law; Management; Mass Communication; Psychology; Social Work; Telecommunications Engineering.** *Doktor*: **Computer Science; Social Work.**

Student Services: Academic Counselling, Canteen, Cultural Activities, IT Centre, Language Laboratory, Library, Social Counselling, Sports Facilities, eLibrary

Publications: Burgas Free University Annual; Conference Proceedings; Electronic Journal Computer Science and Communications; Journal BUSINESS DIRECTIONS (Journal Biznes Posoki); Journal CONTEMPORARY HUMANITARISTICS (Journal Suvremenna Humanitaristika); Journal of Legal Studies; Student Research Conference Proceedings

Publishing House: University Publishing House

Last Updated: 12/02/15

COLLEGE OF TELECOMMUNICATIONS AND POST - SOFIA

Kolej po telekomunikatsii I pochti-Sofia
1 Akad. Stefan Mladenov Str., 1700 Sofia
Tel: +359(2) 86-22-893
Fax: +359(2) 80-62-227
EMail: info@hctp.acad.bg
Website: http://www.hctp.acad.bg/

Rector: Dimitar Radev
Tel: +359(2) 862-2893 EMail: rector@hctp.acad.bg

Vice Chancellor: Emilia Saranova
Tel: +359(2) 80-62-178
EMail: saranova@hctp.acad.bg; vicerector@hctp.acad.bg

International Relations: Anna Otsetova, Head of the International Relations Office
Tel: +359(2) 806-21-24 EMail: aotsetova@hctp.acad.bg

Department

Fundamental Training (Computer Networks; Software Engineering; Telecommunications Engineering); **Information Technology and Modeling** (Information Technology); **Management in Communications** (Management; Telecommunications Engineering); **Telecommunication Technologies** (Computer Networks; Computer Science; Electrical Engineering; Electronic Engineering; English); **Wireless Communications and Broadcasting** (Communication Studies; Computer Engineering; Computer Networks; Information Sciences; Radio and Television Broadcasting)

History: Founded 1922.

Main Language(s) of Instruction: Bulgarian

Accrediting Agency: National Agency for Assessment and Accreditation Agency (NEAA)

Degrees and Diplomas: *Bakalavr*: **Administration; Computer Engineering; Management; Telecommunications Engineering.**

Student Services: Careers Guidance, Residential Facilities, Sports Facilities

Last Updated: 12/02/15

EUROPEAN COLLEGE OF ECONOMICS AND MANAGEMENT

Evropejski kolej po iknomika i upravlenie (ECEM)
18 Zadruga Str., Krim 1, 4004 Plovdiv
Tel: +359(32) 672-362
Fax: +359(32) 677-004
EMail: info@ecem.org
Website: http://www.ecem.org

Rector: Tsvetan Kotzev EMail: kotsev@ecem.org

Vice-Rector: Veselin Lulanski
EMail: loulanski@ecem.org

Programme

Accounting and Control (Accountancy); **Administration and Management** *(Master Programmes - Varna "Free University" (VSU))* (Banking; Finance; International Business; Management; Marketing); **Business Administration** (Business Administration); **Economics** *(Master Programmes - Varna "Free University" (VSU))* (Banking; Finance; International Business; Marketing); **Management of Tourism Services** (Management; Tourism); **Marketing** (Marketing)

History: Founded 2001.

Main Language(s) of Instruction: Bulgarian

Degrees and Diplomas: *Bakalavr*, *Magistr*. **Administration; Economics; Management.** The Master's Degree Programmes are jointly offered with Varna "Free University".

Student Services: Careers Guidance, Sports Facilities

Publications: "Science and Business" Magazine

Last Updated: 12/02/15

EUROPEAN POLYTECHNIC UNIVERSITY

"23 "Sv. sv. Kiril i Metodiy" str., 2300 Pernik
Tel: +359(76) 600-773
Fax: +359(76) 605-207
EMail: office@epu.bg
Website: http://epu.bg

Rector: Ivan Petkov Tel: +359(76) 600-773
EMail: rector@epu.bg

International Relations: Nikolay Andreev, Head, International Office Tel: +359(76) 600-773 EMail: nikolay.andreev@epu.bg

Department

Architectural Design, Theory and History of Architecture (Architectural and Environmental Design; Architecture); **Communication and Computer Technology** (Computer Engineering; Telecommunications Engineering); **Construction of Buildings and**

Facilities, Building Materials and Technology (Building Technologies; Construction Engineering); **Economics, Management and Administration** (Administration; Economics; Management); **Green Energetics** (Energy Engineering); **Mechanics and Mathematics** (Mathematics; Mechanics); **Psychology** (Psychology)

Further Information: International Centre in Istanbul and Kosovo

History: Founded 2010.

Fees: Undergraduate, 750-1,500 per semester; Graduate, 1,000-2,000 per semester (Euro)

Main Language(s) of Instruction: English

Accrediting Agency: National Evaluation and Accreditation Agency

Degrees and Diplomas: *Bakalavr*, *Magistr*: **Architectural and Environmental Design; Architectural Restoration; Architecture; Business Administration; Computer Engineering; Computer Networks; Educational Administration; Energy Engineering; Management; Public Administration; Safety Engineering; Structural Architecture; Telecommunications Engineering.** International Dual Bachelor's Degree Programmes in Psychology and Business Administration with Moscow Humanitarian Economic Institute

Student Services: IT Centre, Library

Last Updated: 12/02/15

NEW BULGARIAN UNIVERSITY

Nov Bulgarski Universitet (NBU)

21 Montevideo Str., 1618 Sofia
Tel: +359(2) 811-0482
Fax: +359(2) 811-0248
EMail: info@nbu.bg
Website: http://www.nbu.bg

Rector: Plamen Bochkov
Tel: +359(2) 811-247
EMail: pbochkov@nbu.bg

Executive Director: George Tekev
Tel: +359(2) 811-0223
EMail: gtekev@nbu.bg

International Relations: Alisa Stoynova, Director
Tel: +359(2) 811-0482
EMail: astoynova@nbu.bg

Department

Anthropology (Anthropology; Arts and Humanities; Comparative Religion; East Asian Studies; History of Religion; Social Policy; Social Studies; Sociology); **Archaeology** (Archaeology; Prehistory); **Architecture** (Architecture); **Art Studies and History of Culture** (Art History; Fine Arts); **Business Administration** (Accountancy; Banking; Business Administration; Business and Commerce; Finance; Labour and Industrial Relations; Management; Management Systems; Marketing; Statistics; Taxation; Tourism); **Cinema, Advertising and Show Business** (Advertising and Publicity; Cinema and Television; Film; Graphic Design; Painting and Drawing; Performing Arts; Photography; Video; Visual Arts); **Cognitive Science and Psychology** (Clinical Psychology; Cognitive Sciences; Communication Disorders; Communication Studies; Developmental Psychology; Experimental Psychology; Psychoanalysis; Psychology; Social Psychology; Social Sciences); **Design** (Fashion Design; Glass Art; Interior Design; Textile Design); **Economics** (Economics); **English Studies** (English; English Studies); **Fine Arts** (Art Management; Ceramic Art; Design; Fashion Design; Fine Arts; Painting and Drawing; Sculpture; Textile Design); **Health and Social Work** (Health Sciences; Social Work); **History** (Central European Studies; Contemporary History; Heritage Preservation; History; History of Societies; Modern History); **Informatics** (Applied Mathematics; Artificial Intelligence; Business Computing; Computer Engineering; Computer Graphics; Computer Science; Information Management; Information Technology; Medical Technology; Software Engineering; Systems Analysis; Technology); **Law** (Administrative Law; Canon Law; Civil Law; Commercial Law; Comparative Law; Constitutional Law; Criminal Law; European Union Law; Fiscal Law; History of Law; Human Rights; International Law; Justice Administration; Labour Law; Law); **Mass Communication** (Advertising and Publicity; Communication Arts; Information Sciences; Journalism; Mass Communication; Media Studies; Multimedia; Public Relations; Radio and Television Broadcasting); **Mediterranean and Eastern Studies** (Ancient Civilizations; Comparative Religion; History; History of Religion; Jewish Studies; Medieval Studies; Mediterranean Studies; Oriental Studies; Tourism); **Modern Bulgarian Studies** (Bulgarian; Cultural Studies; Linguistics; Literature; Native Language; Slavic Languages); **Music** (Conducting; Dance; Folklore; Jazz and Popular Music; Music; Music Education; Music Theory and Composition; Musical Instruments; Musicology; Opera; Performing Arts; Singing); **National and International Security** (Protective Services); **Natural Sciences** (Natural Sciences); **Philosophy and Sociology** (Philosophy; Sociology); **Political Science** (Comparative Politics; European Studies; International Relations; Political Sciences); **Public Administration** (Public Administration); **Public Administration** (Administration; Art Management; Government; Institutional Administration; Management; Public Administration; Social and Community Services; Welfare and Protective Services); **Romanic studies and German studies** (German; Germanic Studies; Romance Languages); **Telecommunications** (Postal Services; Telecommunications Engineering); **Theatre** (Acting; Conducting; Dance; Display and Stage Design; Theatre)

Centre

Human Relations *(Bulgarian)* (Psychology; Psychotherapy; Social Welfare; Welfare and Protective Services); **Semiotic Studies** *(South-Eastern European)* (Aesthetics; Ethics; Gender Studies; Linguistics; Logic; Metaphysics; Philosophical Schools; Philosophy; Psycholinguistics; Speech Studies; Writing); **Social Practices** (Leadership; Political Sciences)

History: Founded 1990. Acquired present status 1991. A private Institution.

Academic Year: October to July

Admission Requirements: Secondary school certificate (Diploma za zavarsheno sredno obrazovanie) or foreign equivalent, and competitive entrance examination

Fees: National: Undergraduate, 1,100 per annum; Graduate, 1,650 per annum (Bulgarian Lev), International: Undergraduate, 1,200-2,700 per annum; Graduate, 1,500-2,700 per annum (Euro)

Main Language(s) of Instruction: Bulgarian, English

Accrediting Agency: National Agency for Evaluation and Accreditation

Degrees and Diplomas: *Bakalavr*, *Magistr*: **Accountancy; Advertising and Publicity; Agricultural Business; American Studies; Ancient Civilizations; Anthropology; Archaeology; Architecture; Banking; Bulgarian; Business Administration; Ceramic Art; Cinema and Television; Clinical Psychology; Cognitive Sciences; Communication Arts; Computer Graphics; Cultural Studies; Developmental Psychology; Display and Stage Design; English Studies; Environmental Studies; European Studies; Fashion Design; Film; Finance; Foreign Languages Education; Glass Art; Graphic Design; Health Administration; History; Hotel Management; Human Resources; Insurance; Interior Design; International Business; International Relations; Journalism; Law; Leadership; Literature; Management; Mass Communication; Media Studies; Mediterranean Studies; Multimedia; Music; Painting and Drawing; Philosophy; Photography; Political Sciences; Protective Services; Public Administration; Public Relations; Rehabilitation and Therapy; Social Psychology; Social Work; Sociology; Software Engineering; Sound Engineering (Acoustics); Speech Therapy and Audiology; Telecommunications Engineering; Theatre; Tourism; Visual Arts; Writing.** *Doktor*: **Anthropology; Archaeology; Bulgarian; Business Administration; Cinema and Television; Civil Law; Communication Studies; Computer Science; Criminal Law; Design; English; Finance; Fine Arts; Foreign Languages Education; Government; History; International Economics; Literature; Mass Communication; Mediterranean Studies; Philosophy; Political Sciences; Private Law; Protective Services; Psychology; Public Administration; Sociology; Telecommunications Engineering; Theatre; Translation and Interpretation; Visual Arts.**

Student Services: Academic Counselling, Canteen, Foreign Studies Centre, Health Services, Language Laboratory, Social Counselling, Sports Facilities

Publications: 'Sledva'; Proceedings 'Archaeology'; Proceedings 'Mass Communication'

Last Updated: 13/02/15

UNIVERSITY OF AGRIBUSINESS AND RURAL DEVELOPMENT

Visshe uchilishte po agrobiznes i razvitie na regionite (UARD)

78, Dunav Blvd., 4003 Plovdiv
Tel: +359(32) 960-360
Fax: +359(32) 960-406
EMail: uard@uard.bg
Website: http://uard.bg/

Rector: Dimitar Dimitrov
Tel: +359(32) 966-360 EMail: rector@uard.bg

Vice Rector Educational Activities and International Cooperation: Mariana Ivanova
Tel: +359(32) 960-356 EMail: mivanova@uard.bg

International Relations: Miglena Kazashka, International Relations Officer Tel: +359(32) 966-811 EMail: uard@uard.bg

Faculty

Economics and Management (Development Studies; Economics; Finance; Information Management; Information Technology; Management; Regional Studies; Tourism)

Department

Agribusiness and General Science (Agricultural Business; Technology)

Institute

Regional Studies (Agricultural Business; Agricultural Management; Business Administration; Development Studies; Economics; Information Technology; Management; Regional Studies; Rural Studies; Tourism)

Further Information: Veliko Tarnovo and Ruse branches

History: Founded 1992.

Main Language(s) of Instruction: Bulgarian

Degrees and Diplomas: *Bakalavr*: **Business Administration; Economics; Finance; Information Management; Management.** *Magistr*: **Accountancy; Administration; Advertising and Publicity; Agricultural Business; Agricultural Economics; Agricultural Management; Art Management; Banking; Business Administration; Finance; Information Management; Management; Marketing; Tourism.**

Student Services: Careers Guidance, Library

Publications: New Knowledge Journal of Science

Publishing House: Academic Publishing House

Last Updated: 26/02/15

UNIVERSITY OF FINANCE, BUSINESS AND ENTREPRENEURSHIP

Vische utchilichte po zastrahovane i finansi (VUZF)

29 Panajot Volov Str., Sofia
EMail: vazov@vuzf.bg
Website: http://www.vuzf.bg

President: Grigorii Vazov
Tel: +359(2) 401-5803 EMail: vazov@vuzf.bg

Executive Director: Radostin Vazov
Tel: +359(2) 401-5809 EMail: vazov_rado@vuzf.bg

Programme

Audit and Risk Management *(Graduate)* (Business Administration; Insurance); **Banking** *(Graduate)* (Banking); **Corporate Social Responsibility and Financial Management** *(in partnership with The UN Global Compact)* (Business Administration; Finance); **Entrepreneurship and Finance** *(Graduate - in partnership with Cisco Entrepreneurs Institute)* (Finance; Management); **Finance** *(Graduate)* (Finance); **Finance** (Finance); **Financial Management and Marketing** *(Graduate)* (Finance; Marketing); **Financial Management and Marketing** (Finance; Marketing); **Leadership, Management and Finance** *(in partnership with Embient)* (Finance; Leadership; Management)

History: Founded 2002.

Fees: National: 550-1,100 per annum (Euro), International: 1,600-2,500 per annum (Euro)

Main Language(s) of Instruction: Bulgarian, English

Degrees and Diplomas: *Bakalavr*, *Magistr*: **Accountancy; Banking; Business Administration; Economics; Finance; Industrial and Organizational Psychology; Insurance; Management; Marketing; Welfare and Protective Services.** Also Joint Programmes with the University of Sheffield: Bachelor in Business Administration (Finance and Accounting; Management; Marketing); and Master's Degree in: Marketing and Mass Communication; Marketing, Advertising and Public Relations; Business Administration, Technology and Innovation; Banking and Finance.

Student Services: Library

Publishing house: University Publishing House

Last Updated: 25/02/15

UNIVERSITY OF LIBRARY STUDIES AND INFORMATION TECHNOLOGIES - SOFIA

Universitet po Bibliotekoznanie i Informacionni Technologii - Sofia (ULSIT)

119 Tzarigradsko Chausee Bvld., 1784 Sofia
Tel: +359(2) 971-8068
Fax: +359(2) 970-8583
EMail: unibit@unibit.bg
Website: http://www.unibit.bg

Rector: Stoyan Denchev
Tel: +359(2) 971-8052 EMail: s.denchev@unibit.bg

Vice-Rector for Academic Affairs: Ivanka Pavlova
Tel: +359(2) 970-8580 EMail: i.pavlova@unibit.bg

International Relations: Irena Peteva, Vice-Rector, Scientific Research and International Cooperation
Tel: +359(2) 970-8585 EMail: i.peteva@unibit.bg

Faculty

Information Sciences (Computer Science; Information Sciences; Information Technology; Protective Services); **Library Studies and Cultural Heritage** (Heritage Preservation; Library Science)

History: The University of Library Studies and Information Technologies (ULSIT) is a state university, renamed by Parliament Decree on 29th Nov. 2010 after the Specialized Higher School of Library Studies and Information Technologies, voted as such in 2004. Throughout the years it was respectively: Established - 18th September 1950 by Government Decree as the State Library Institute and later renamed as The College of Library Studies by Parliament Decree.

Main Language(s) of Instruction: Bulgarian

Degrees and Diplomas: *Profesionalen Bakalavr*, *Bakalavr*, *Magistr*: **Advertising and Publicity; Business Administration; E-Business/Commerce; Information Sciences; Information Technology; Library Science; Media Studies; Tourism.** *Doktor*: **Information Sciences; Library Science; Mass Communication.**

Student Services: IT Centre, Library

Academic Staff *2014-2015*: Total: c. 150

Student Numbers *2014-2015*: Total: c. 2,000

Last Updated: 26/02/15

Burkina Faso

STRUCTURE OF HIGHER EDUCATION SYSTEM

Description:

Higher education is provided by universities and several higher education institutions, both public and private, the latter since 2004. Public universities are autonomous institutions under the jurisdiction of the Ministère des Enseignements secondaire, supérieur et de la Recherche scientifique. In 1996, the Institut universitaire de Technologie, the Institut de Développement rural and the Ecole supérieure d'Informatique were transferred to Bobo-Dioulasso to constitute the Centre universitaire Polytechnique de Bobo-Dioulasso which is now the Université Polytechnique de Bobo-Dioulasso. In 1996-97, the Institut des Sciences de l'Education was transferred to Koudougou and is now called the Université de Koudougou. The Universities of Ouaga II, Fada N'Gourma and Ouahigouya were created in 2007 and 2010.

Stages of studies:

University level first stage: *Premier cycle*

The first stage of university studies leads to the Diplôme d'Etudes universitaires générales (DEUG) after two years. In Health Sciences, the first stage leads to the premier cycle d'études médicales (PCEM) and, at the Institut universitaire de Technologie, it leads to the Diplôme universitaire de Technologie (DUT). The new Licence, a degree awarded after three years' study, is progressively being introduced.

University level second stage: *Deuxième cycle*

The second stage leads after one year to the Licence. One year after the Licence, the Maîtrise may be obtained in some fields. In Medicine, the second stage lasts for four years. In Engineering, it leads after three years' further study to the Diplôme d'Ingénieur. The Master, a degree awarded after two years' study after the new Licence is progressively being introduced.

University level third stage: *Troisième cycle*

The third stage leads after one year to the Diplôme d'Etudes supérieures spécialisées (DESS) and to the Diplôme d'Etudes approfondies (DEA), and after two years following the DEA, to the Doctorat de troisième Cycle. After three to five years following the DEA, the Doctorat or the Doctorat d'Etat is conferred in some fields of study. In Medicine, the Doctorat d'Etat en Médecine is awarded after one further year following the four-year second cycle. The new Doctorat, a degree awarded after three years' study and research after the Master is progressively being introduced.

ADMISSION TO HIGHER EDUCATION

Admission to university-level studies:

Name of secondary school credential required: Baccalauréat

Other requirements: Secondary school certificate (baccalauréat) or recognized equivalent; an entrance examination may also be required.

Foreign students admission:

Admission requirements: Foreign students must hold the Baccalauréat or its equivalent or sit for a special entrance examination.

Entry regulations: Conditions vary according to relations with the country of origin.

Language proficiency: Students must have a good command of French.

NATIONAL BODIES

Ministère de l'Enseignement supérieur, de la Recherche scientifique et de l'Innovation (Ministry of Higher Education, Research and Innovation)

Minister: Filiga Michel Sawadogo

03 BP 7047

Ouagadougou

Tel: +226 5033-7334
WWW: http://www.mess.gov.bf

Data for academic year: 2012-2013
Source: IAU from the website of the Ministry of Secondary and Higher Education and IBE, 2012. Bodies 2016.

INSTITUTIONS

PUBLIC INSTITUTIONS

INTERNATIONAL CENTRE FOR RESEARCH-DEVELOPMENT OF ANIMAL HUSBANDRY IN SUBHUMID ZONES

Centre international de Recherche-Développement sur l'Elevage en Zone subhumide (CIRDES)
01 BP 454, Bobo-Dioulasso 01
Tel: +226 20-97-20-53
Fax: +226 20-97-23-20
EMail: cirdes@ird.bf
Website: http://www.cirdes.org

Directrice Générale: Valentine C. Yapi-Gnaoré (2011-)
EMail: dgcirdes@fasonet.bf

Research Unit
Animal Husbandry and Environment *(UREEN)* (Animal Husbandry; Biotechnology; Epidemiology; Parasitology); **Animal Production** *(URPAN)* (Animal Husbandry); **Parasitology** *(URBIO)* (Epidemiology; Parasitology)

History: Founded 1991.

Degrees and Diplomas: *Diplôme d'Etudes supérieures spécialisées*; *Diplôme d'Etudes approfondies*; *Doctorat de troisième Cycle*. Also postgraduate training at MSc and PhD levels

Publications: La Lettre du CIRDES; Rapport d'Activité scientifique

Last Updated: 19/07/12

INTERNATIONAL INSTITUTE FOR WATER AND ENVIRONMENTAL ENGINEERING

Institut international d'Ingénierie de l'Eau et de l'Environnement (2IE)
01 BP 594, Rue de la Science, Ouagadougou 01
Tel: +226 50-49-28-00
Fax: +226 50-49-28-01
EMail: 2ie@2ie-edu.org; desa@2ie-edu.org
Website: http://www.2ie-edu.org

Directeur Général: Paul Giniès
Tel: +226 50-49-28-14
EMail: pal.ginies@eieretsher.org; dg@2ie-edu.org

Directeur, Administration et Finance: Jacques Muhet
EMail: jacques.andre.muhet@eier.org

International Relations: Abibou Ciss

Programme
Agricultural Engineering (Agricultural Engineering); **Civil Engineering** (Civil Engineering); **Computer Science** (Computer Science); **Environmental Engineering** (Environmental Engineering); **Hydraulic Engineering** (Hydraulic Engineering); **Industrial and Energy Engineering** (Energy Engineering; Industrial Engineering); **Sanitary Engineering** (Sanitary Engineering); **Water Management** (Water Management)

Further Information: Branch in Kamboinse.

History: Founded 1968. Acquired present status and title after merger between Ecole inter-Etats d'Ingénieurs de l'Equipement rural and Ecole inter-Etats des Techniciens supérieurs de l'Hydraulique et de l'Equipement rural. Known as Groupe EIER-ETSHER until 2006.

Main Language(s) of Instruction: French

Degrees and Diplomas: *Licence*: **Civil Engineering; Construction Engineering; Hydraulic Engineering; Water Management.** *Diplôme d'Ingénieur*: **Engineering.** *Doctorat d'Etat*: **Environmental Studies; Water Science.** Also Master and Master spécialisé

Student Services: Academic Counselling, Canteen, Cultural Activities, Health Services, Language Laboratory, Social Counselling, Sports Facilities

Publications: Sud Sciences et Technologie

Last Updated: 19/07/12

NATIONAL SCHOOL FOR ADMINISTRATION AND MAGISTRACY

Ecole nationale d'Administration et de Magistrature (ENAM)
03 B.P. 7024, Ouagadougou 03
Tel: +226 50-31-42-64
Fax: +226 50-30-66-11
EMail: enam@cenatrin.bf
Website: http://www.enam.gov.bf

Directeur: Moctar Tall

Programme
Communication (Communication Studies); **Management** (Management); **National Economy** (Economics); **Political Science** (Political Sciences); **Public Administration** (Public Administration); **Public Finance** (Finance); **Social Sciences** (Social Sciences)

Centre
Centre de Formation du Personnel de Bureau *(CFPB)* (Accountancy; Administration)

History: Founded 1960. Formerly 'Ecole Nationale d'Administration' (ENA). Acquired present status and title 2002.

Admission Requirements: Entrance exam and: Brevet d'Etudes du Premier Cycle de l'Enseignement Secondaire for Basic cycle C, Baccalauréat de l'Enseignement Secondaire for Medium cycle B, Maîtrise for Superior cycle A.

Main Language(s) of Instruction: French

POLYTECHNIC UNIVERSITY OF BOBO-DIOULASSO

Université Polytechnique de Bobo-Dioulasso (UPB)
01 B.P. 1091, Bobo-Dioulasso 01
Tel: +226 20-98-06-35
Fax: +226 20-97-25-77
EMail: info@univ-bobo.bf
Website: http://www.univ-bobo.bf

Président: George Anicet Ouédraogo (2012-)
Tel: +226 20-97-05-57 EMail: oga@fasonet.bf

Secretary General: Abdou Rahamane Sawadogo
EMail: abdouraso@yahoo.fr

International Relations: Irenée Somda, Director
Tel: +226 70 28-66-35 EMail: ireneesomda@yahoo.fr

Higher School
Computer Science *(ESI)* (Computer Science; Mathematics; Statistics)

Institute

Exact and Applied Sciences *(ISEA)* (Applied Mathematics; Applied Physics; Mathematics; Physics); **Life and Natural Science** *(ISNV)* (Agronomy; Biological and Life Sciences); **Medical Science** *(INSSA)* (Entomology; Medicine; Parasitology); **Rural Development** *(IDR)* (Agricultural Economics; Agriculture; Animal Husbandry; Forestry; Rural Studies; Social Studies; Sociology); **Technology** *(IUT)* (Electrical Engineering; Management; Mechanical Engineering; Mechanical Equipment and Maintenance; Secretarial Studies; Technology)

History: Founded 1995 as Centre universitaire polytechnique de Bobo-Dioulasso. Acquired present status 2002.

Academic Year: October to July

Admission Requirements: Secondary school certificate (baccalauréat)

Fees: (CFA Francs): 15,000 per annum; foreign students 200,500 per annum

Main Language(s) of Instruction: French

Accrediting Agency: Ministère des Enseignements Secondaire, Supérieur et de la Recherche Scientifique (MESSRS)

Degrees and Diplomas: *Diplôme universitaire de Technologie*: **Accountancy; Business and Commerce; Finance.** *Licence*: **Civil Engineering.** *Diplôme d'Ingénieur*: **Agronomy; Animal Husbandry; Computer Science; Forestry; Sociology.** *Diplôme d'Etudes approfondies*; *Doctorat de troisième Cycle*: **Agronomy; Computer Engineering; Forestry; Health Sciences; Veterinary Science.**

Student Services: Canteen, Health Services, Social Counselling, Sports Facilities

Last Updated: 20/07/12

UNIVERSITY OF KOUDOUGOU

Université de Koudougou (UK)

BP 376, Koudougou
Tel: +226 50-44-01-22
Fax: +226 50-44-01-19
EMail: info@univ-koudougou.bf
Website: http://www.univ-koudougou.bf/

Président: Bila Gérard Segda EMail: segbilge@yahoo.fr

Vice-Président: Missa Barro

Secrétaire Général: M. Sompougdou

Unit

Economics and Management *(SEG)* (Agricultural Economics; Economics; Environmental Studies; Management); **Languages and Humanities** *(LSH)* (Geography (Human); History; Literature; Psychology)

School

Teacher Training *(ENS)* (Education; Educational Administration; Educational and Student Counselling; Pedagogy; Physical Education; Secondary Education; Teacher Training; Technology Education)

Institute

Technology *(IUT)* (Accountancy; Business Administration; Finance; Hotel Management; Secretarial Studies)

Centre

Centre de Pédagogie Universitaire *(CPU)* (Education; Educational Sciences)

History: Founded 2005 incorporating the Ecole Normale Supérieure de Koudougou (ENSK).

Main Language(s) of Instruction: French

Accrediting Agency: Ministère des Enseignements secondaire, supérieur et de la Recherche scientifique (MESSRS)

Degrees and Diplomas: *Licence*; *Maîtrise*. Also Certificat d'aptitude au professorat

Last Updated: 19/07/12

UNIVERSITY OF OUAGA II

Université Ouaga II (UO2)

BP 417, Ouagadougou 12
Tel: +226 50-36-99-60
EMail: univ_ouaga2@yahoo.fr
Website: http://www.elearningouaga2.net

Président: Stanislas Ouaro (2007-)

Unit

Economics and Management *(UFR/SEG)* (Economics; Management); **Law and Political Science** *(UFR/SPJ)* (Law; Political Sciences)

History: Founded 2007.

Fees: (CFA Francs) 853,000 (License); 965,000 (Master 1); 1,550,000 (Master 2)

Main Language(s) of Instruction: French

Accrediting Agency: Ministère des Enseignements Secondaire, Supérieur et de la Recherche Scientifique (MESSRS)

Degrees and Diplomas: *Licence*: **Management.** *Master*: **International Business; Management; Marketing.**

Last Updated: 20/07/12

UNIVERSITY OF OUAGADOUGOU

Université de Ouagadougou (UO)

B.P. 7021, Ouagadougou 03
Tel: +226 50 30-70-64/65
Fax: +226 50 30-72-42
EMail: info@univ-ouaga.bf
Website: http://www.univ-ouaga.bf

Président: Karifa Bayo
Tel: +226 50 30-16-36
EMail: president@univ-ouaga.bf; karifabayo@yahoo.fr

Faculty

Applied and Exact Sciences (Applied Mathematics; Chemistry; Computer Science; Mathematics; Physics); **Health Sciences** (Dentistry; Health Sciences; Medical Technology; Medicine; Pharmacy); **Humanities** (Arts and Humanities; Geography (Human); History; Philosophy; Psychology; Sociology); **Languages, Arts and Communication** (African Studies; Arts and Humanities; Communication Studies; Cultural Studies; English; Fine Arts; German; Journalism; Linguistics; Literature; Modern Languages); **Life and Earth Sciences** (Biochemistry; Biological and Life Sciences; Earth Sciences; Geology; Microbiology; Physiology; Plant and Crop Protection)

Institute

Arts and Crafts *(IBAM)* (Accountancy; Banking; Business and Commerce; Computer Networks; Finance; Insurance; Secretarial Studies); **Demography** *(ISSP)* (Demography and Population); **Media, Information and Communication** *(IPERMIC)* (Communication Studies; Information Technology; Journalism)

Further Information: Other campus in Bobo-Dioulasso

History: Founded 1965 as Ecole normale supérieure, became Centre d'Enseignement supérieur 1969. Acquired present title and status 1974. Reorganized 1985, 1991 and 1997. An autonomous institution under the jurisdiction of the Ministry of Education and Culture.

Academic Year: September to June (September-December; January-March; April-June)

Admission Requirements: Secondary school certificate (baccalauréat) or recognized equivalent and entrance examination

Main Language(s) of Instruction: French

Accrediting Agency: Ministère des Enseignements Secondaire, Supérieur et de la Recherche Scientifique (MESSRS)

Degrees and Diplomas: *Diplôme d'Etudes universitaires générales*; *Diplôme universitaire de Technologie*; *Licence*; *Diplôme d'Etudes supérieures spécialisées*; *Maîtrise*; *Diplôme d'Etudes approfondies*; *Doctorat d'Etat en Médecine*: **Medicine.** *Doctorat d'Etat*; *Doctorat de troisième Cycle*: **Chemistry; Economics; Linguistics; Mathematics.** *Certificat d'Etudes spécialisées*: **Surgery.**

Student Services: Canteen, Cultural Activities, Health Services, Social Counselling, Sports Facilities

Publications: Annales de l'Ecole supérieure des Lettres et des Sciences humaines; Annales de l'Université (Série A: Sciences humaines et sociales, Série B: Sciences exactes); Bulletin du Laboratoire universitaire pour la Tradition orale; La Revue du CEDRES; Revue Burkinabe de Droit

Publishing House: Direction des Presses Universitaires (DPU)

Last Updated: 20/07/12

Burundi

STRUCTURE OF HIGHER EDUCATION SYSTEM

Description:

Public higher education is mainly provided by the University of Burundi and a Teachers' Training School (ENS). Several private higher education institutions exist. Passing the secondary-school leaving certificate conditions entrance in both types of higher education provision. To enter the University of Burundi or to benefit from a scholarship, students also have to pass a State examination (Examen d'Etat).

Stages of studies:

University level first stage: *Premier cycle*

The first stage of study leads to the Bachelier degree and lasts for three years.

University level second stage: *Second cycle*

A further two years' study beyond the Bachelier degree leads to the Maîtrise.

University level third stage: *Troisième cycle*

A Doctorat is conferred in three years following upon the Maîtrise.

ADMISSION TO HIGHER EDUCATION

Admission to university-level studies:

Name of secondary school credential required: Diplôme de fin des Humanités

Minimum score/requirement: Varies according to year

Name of secondary school credential required: Examen d'Etat

Foreign students admission:

Admission requirements: Foreign students must have followed seven years' general secondary education or hold a technician's diploma.

Entry regulations: They must hold a visa and a residence permit.

Language proficiency: Good knowledge of French

RECOGNITION OF STUDIES

Bodies dealing with recognition:

Commission Nationale d'Equivalence des Diplômes

PO Box 1990
Bujumbura

Special provisions for recognition:

Recognition for university level studies: The holder of a foreign credential must submit to the "Commission d'Equivalence des Diplômes" the following data: curriculum vitae specifying the duration of the training abroad; total number of hours of all the training modules; contents of training programmes; methods of assessment, and certified copy of the original credential.

For access to advanced studies and research: Same as above.

NATIONAL BODIES

Ministère de l'Enseignement Supérieur et de la Recherche Scientifique (Ministry of Higher Education and Scientific Research)

Minister: Janviere Ndirahisha
PO Box 1990
Bujumbura
Role of national body: Central administration and coordination body.

Data for academic year: 2012-2013
Source: IAU from documentation, 2012. Bodies 2016.

INSTITUTIONS

PUBLIC INSTITUTIONS

HIGHER INSTITUTE OF BUSINESS ADMINISTRATION

Institut supérieur de Gestion des Entreprises (ISGE)
BP 2450, Bujumbura
Tel: +257(22) 224698
EMail: isgebi@yahoo.com

Directeur général: François Nibizi (2011-)
Tel: +257(22) 221785 EMail: nibifranc@yahoo.fr

Directeur adjoint: Deo Nshimirimana Tel: +257(22) 214875

Institute
Business Management (Management; Marketing); **Finance and Accounting** (Accountancy; Finance)

History: Founded 1987. Acquired current status 1990.

Academic Year: January - November

Main Language(s) of Instruction: French, English for some business classes

Degrees and Diplomas: *Bachelier*, *Maîtrise*

Student Services: Academic Counselling, Careers Guidance, Language Laboratory, Social Counselling

Academic Staff *2012-2013*	MEN	WOMEN	TOTAL
FULL-TIME	3	2	5
Student Numbers *2012-2013*			
All (Foreign included)	255	130	**385**

Distance students, 70.
Last Updated: 06/04/12

HOPE AFRICA UNIVERSITY

Université Espoir d'Afrique
BP 238, Bujumbura
Tel: +(257) 22-23-7973
Website: http://hopeafricauniversity.org/

Rector: Elie Buconyori

Faculty
Arts and Sciences (Biochemistry; Biological and Life Sciences; Clinical Psychology; Communication Studies; Computer Science; Holy Writings; Psychology; Social Psychology; Social Work; Theology); **Business and Professional Studies** (Accountancy; Banking; Business Administration; Economics; Information Management; Law; Marketing; Political Sciences); **Educational Sciences** (Education; Foreign Languages Education; Mathematics Education; Science Education; Special Education); **Engineering and Technology** (Civil Engineering; Mining Engineering; Rural Planning; Telecommunications Engineering; Town Planning); **Health Sciences** (Anaesthesiology; Dentistry; Medicine; Midwifery; Nursing; Ophthalmology; Psychiatry and Mental Health; Public Health)

History: Created 2003.

Degrees and Diplomas: *Bachelier*, *Doctorat en Médecine*; *Maîtrise*: **Civil Engineering; Education; Law; Nursing; Rural Planning; Theology; Town Planning.**

Last Updated: 21/01/14

UNIVERSITY OF BURUNDI

Université du Burundi
Blvd. de l'UPRONA, BP 1550, Bujumbura
Tel: +257(22) 222-059
Fax: +257(22) 223-288
EMail: rectorat@ub.edu.bi
Website: http://www.ub.edu.bi

Recteur: Gaston Hakiza
Tel: +257(21) 9838
EMail: recteurub@ub.edu.bi; gahakiza@yahoo.fr

Vice-Recteur: Samuel Bigawa
EMail: vicerecteurub@ub.edu.bi; samuelbigawa@yahoo.fr

Faculty
Agronomy (Agronomy); **Applied Sciences** (Applied Chemistry; Applied Mathematics; Applied Physics; Natural Sciences); **Arts and Humanities** (African Languages; Arts and Humanities; English; French; Geography; History; Literature); **Economics and Administration** (Administration; Economics); **Law** (Law); **Medicine** (Medicine); **Psychology and Education Sciences** (Education; Psychology); **Science** (Mathematics and Computer Science; Natural Sciences)

Institute
Pedagogy (Pedagogy); **Physical Education and Sports** (Physical Education; Sports)

Higher Institute
Agriculture *(Gitega)* (Agriculture); **Commerce** (Business and Commerce)

History: Founded 1960, incorporating the Institut agronomique du Rwanda-Urundi, previously Faculty of Agriculture of the Université officielle du Congo Belge founded 1958 and the Centre universitaire Rumuri founded 1960. Title of Université officielle de Bujumbura adopted 1964, acquired present title 1977. Largely financed by the State.

Academic Year: October to July (October-December; January-April; April-July)

Admission Requirements: Secondary school certificate (Certificat d'Humanités complètes) or foreign equivalent

Main Language(s) of Instruction: French

Accrediting Agency: Ministère de l'Enseignement Supérieur et de la Recherche Scientifique (Ministry of Higher Education and Scientific Research)

Degrees and Diplomas: *Bachelier*. **Administration; Agriculture; Arts and Humanities; Business and Commerce; Civil Engineering; Economics; Education; Journalism; Law; Medicine;**

Physical Education; Psychology; Social Studies; Teacher Training. *Doctorat en Médecine*: **Medicine.** *Maîtrise*: **Agricultural Economics; Agriculture; Agronomy; Civil Engineering; Management Systems; Mathematics; Physics.**

Publications: Revue de l'Université (Séries: Sciences humaines; Sciences exactes, naturelles, et médicales)

Last Updated: 27/07/12

PRIVATE INSTITUTIONS

LIGHT UNIVERSITY OF BUJUMBURA

Université Lumière de Bujumbura (ULBU)
BP 1368, Campus Mutanga Nord, Bujumbura
Tel: +257(22) 235-549
Fax: +257(22) 229-275
EMail: ulbu@cbinf.com
Website: http://ulbu.bi

Recteur: Gérard Nkunzimana
Tel: +257(22) 23 55 49 EMail: genkunzimana@yahoo.fr

Vice-Recteur: Charles Kabwigiri Tel: +257(22) 259-001

Faculty
Business Administration (Business Administration); **Communication** (Cinema and Television; Communication Studies); **Computer Science** (Computer Science); **Law** (Law); **Management** (Management); **Theology** (Theology)

Further Information: Also Kinindo Campus

History: Founded 2000.

Academic Year: October to July (October-December; January-March; April-July)

Admission Requirements: High School Diploma

Main Language(s) of Instruction: French, English

Accrediting Agency: Ministry of National Education

Degrees and Diplomas: *Bachelier*: **Business Administration; Clinical Psychology; Communication Arts; Computer Engineering; International Relations; Law.** also Masters in Business Management, Law, Gender and Institutions, Development Management.

Student Services: Academic Counselling, Canteen, Cultural Activities, Foreign Studies Centre, Language Laboratory, Social Counselling, Sports Facilities

Last Updated: 27/07/12

UNIVERSITY OF LAKE TANGANYIKA

Université du Lac Tanganyika (ULT)
Q. KIGOBE, BP 5403, Mutanga
Tel: +257(22) 243-645
Fax: +257(22) 246-843
EMail: webmaster@ult.bi
Website: http://ult.bi

Recteur: Evariste Ngayimpenda EMail: ngayevariste@yahoo.fr

Faculty
Applied Economics and Management; **Computer Science** (Computer Science); **Law** (Law); **Political, Social and Administrative Sciences** (Administration; Political Sciences; Social Sciences)

History: Founded 2000.

Main Language(s) of Instruction: French

Degrees and Diplomas: *Bachelier*, *Maîtrise*

Last Updated: 27/07/12

UNIVERSITY OF NGOZI

Université de Ngozi
BP 137, Ngozi, Bujumbura 2900
Tel: +257(22) 302-259; +257(22) 243-816
Fax: +257(22) 302-259
EMail: info@univ-ngozi.org
Website: http://www.univ-ngozi.org/

Recteur: Apollinaire Bangayimbaga
Tel: +257(79) 957-447 EMail: bangaapo@yahoo.es

Vice-Recteur: Bonaventure Bangurambona
EMail: bbangur@yahoo.fr

Faculty
Agronomy (Accountancy; Agricultural Economics; Agricultural Equipment; Agricultural Management; Agriculture; Agronomy; Animal Husbandry; Biochemistry; Biology; Botany; Chemistry; Economics; Entomology; Food Technology; Forestry; Genetics; Geography; Geology; Inorganic Chemistry; Limnology; Mathematics; Mechanics; Meteorology; Microbiology; Mineralogy; Physics; Physiology; Sociology; Soil Science; Statistics; Surveying and Mapping; Water Science; Zoology); **Arts and Humanities** (Arts and Humanities; Computer Science; Grammar; Greek (Classical); Latin; Linguistics; Literature; Philosophy; Phonetics; Psychology; Social Sciences; Sociology; Spanish; Swahili; Translation and Interpretation; Writing); **Law, Economics and Administration** *(FDSEA)*; **Mathematics and Computer Science** (Accountancy; Computer Engineering; Computer Networks; Computer Science; Electrical and Electronic Engineering; Physics; Software Engineering; Statistics; Technology; Telecommunications Engineering); **Medicine** *(FM)*

Institute
Health Sciences (Anaesthesiology; Anatomy; Biochemistry; Cardiology; Cell Biology; Chemistry; Child Care and Development; Dermatology; Dietetics; Endocrinology; English; Epidemiology; French; Gastroenterology; Genetics; Gynaecology and Obstetrics; Haematology; Health Administration; Health Education; Histology; Hygiene; Immunology; Laboratory Techniques; Microbiology; Molecular Biology; Nephrology; Neurology; Nursing; Nutrition; Ophthalmology; Otorhinolaryngology; Paediatrics; Pathology; Pharmacology; Philosophy; Physical Therapy; Physiology; Pneumology; Psychiatry and Mental Health; Psychology; Radiology; Rheumatology; Stomatology)

History: Founded 1999.

Admission Requirements: Secondary school certificate

Fees: (Burundi Francs): from 350,000 to 500,000 per annum (500 US$ for foreign students)

Main Language(s) of Instruction: French, English

Accrediting Agency: Ministère de l'Enseignement Supérieur et de la Recherche Scientifique (Ministry of Higher Education and Scientific Research)

Degrees and Diplomas: *Bachelier*: **Business and Commerce; Economics; Health Sciences; Law; Translation and Interpretation.** *Doctorat en Médecine*: **Medicine.** *Maîtrise*: **Agronomy; Computer Science.**

Student Services: Academic Counselling, Health Services, Social Counselling, Sports Facilities

Last Updated: 25/07/12

UNIVERSITY OF THE GREAT LAKES

Université des Grands Lacs (UGL)
BP 2310, Bujumbura
Tel: +257(22) 244-544
EMail: info@ugl.bi
Website: http://www.ugl.bi/

Recteur: Herménégilde Ndoricimpa

International Relations: Nicodème Niyongabo

Faculty
Administration and Business Management (Administration; Business Administration); **Computer** (Computer Science); **Education** (Education); **Law** (Law); **Psychology and Education Sciences** (Psychology)

History: Founded 2000.

Degrees and Diplomas: *Bachelier*, *Maîtrise*

Academic Staff *2011-2012*: Total 15
Student Numbers *2011-2012*: Total 2,464
Last Updated: 27/07/12

Cabo Verde

STRUCTURE OF HIGHER EDUCATION SYSTEM

Description:

Higher education is provided by universities (universidades) and polytechnics (institutos superiores and escolas superiores) that can be public or private.

Stages of studies:

University level first stage: *Licenciatura*
The first stage leads to the Licenciatura after 3 to 4 years' study.

University level second stage: *Mestrado*
The second stage leads to the Mestrado after one and 1/2 to two years' further study beyond the Licenciatura.

University level third stage: *Doutoramento*
The third stage leads to the Doutoramento.

ADMISSION TO HIGHER EDUCATION

Admission to university-level studies:

Name of secondary school credential required: Curso complementar do ensino secundario
For entry to: Universities and Institutes

RECOGNITION OF STUDIES

Bodies dealing with recognition:

Comissão Nacional de Equivalências (National Commission of Equivalencies)

Ministerio de Educação e Desporto
C.P. 111
Praia
WWW: http://www.minedu.gov.cv/index.php/o-sistema-educativo/87-med/o-sistema-educativo/119-comissao-nacional-de-equivalencias

NATIONAL BODIES

Ministério da Educação e Desporto

Minister: Fernanda Maria de Brito Marques
Palacio do Governo-Varzea
BP 111
Praía-Santiago
Tel: +238 261-0510
Fax: +238 261-5873
EMail: cci.mees@palgov.gov.cv
WWW: http://www.minedu.gov.cv

Data for academic year: 2012-2013
Source: IAU from the website of the Ministry of Education and Higher Education, 2012. Bodies 2016.

INSTITUTIONS

PUBLIC INSTITUTIONS

NATIONAL INSTITUTE OF AGRICULTURAL RESEARCH AND DEVELOPMENT/ AGRICULTURAL TRAINING CENTRE

Instituto Nacional de Investigação e Desenvolvimento Agrário/ Centro de Formação Agrária (INIDA)
Endereço São Jorge do orgãos, C.P. 84, Praia
Tel: +238 71-11-47
Fax: +238 71-11-33
EMail: inida@inida.gov.cv
Website: http://www.inida.cv

Presidente: Aline Rendall Monteiro (2011-)
EMail: alirendall@yahoo.com.br; arendall@inida.gov.cv

Department
Agricultural Business and Rural Sociology (Agricultural Business; Rural Studies; Sociology); **Agriculture, Forestry and Fishery** (Agriculture; Fishery; Forestry); **Environmental Studies** (Biological and Life Sciences; Environmental Studies; Soil Science; Water Science)

History: Founded 1979 as Centro de Estudos Agrários. Became Instituto Nacional de investigação Agrária (INIA) 1985. Acquired present title 1992.

Degrees and Diplomas: Professional degrees (Técnicos Profissionais; Técnicos Médios; Bacharéis)

UNIVERSITY OF CAPE VERDE

Universidade de Cabo Verde (UNI-CV)
Praça Antonio Loreno, CP: 379-C, Praia, Santiago
Tel: +238 261-99-04
Fax: +238 261-26-60
EMail: reitoria@adm.unicv.edu.cv; administracao@adm.unicv.edu.cv
Website: http://www.unicv.edu.cv

Rector: Judite Nascimento
EMail: Judite.nascimento@adm.unicv.edu.cv

Administrador: Elizabeth Coutinho
EMail: elizabeth.coutinho@adm.unicv.edu.cv

International Relations: Albino Luciano Silva, Head of International and Cooperation Department
EMail: albino.silva@adm.unicv.edu.cv

School
Agricultural and Environmental Sciences (Agricultural Equipment; Agricultural Management; Animal Husbandry; Computer Science; Environmental Studies; Food Science; Forestry; Mathematics; Regional Planning; Rural Planning; Social Work; Statistics; Tropical Agriculture; Water Science); **Business and Government** (Accountancy; Administration; Business and Commerce; Economics; Finance; Human Resources; Human Rights; Labour Law; Management; Marketing; Mass Communication; Private Law; Public Law; Real Estate; Secretarial Studies; Social Work; Statistics; Teacher Training; Tourism)

Department
Engineering and Marine Sciences (Automation and Control Engineering; Biological and Life Sciences; Chemistry; Civil Engineering; Computer Engineering; Computer Science; Electrical and Electronic Engineering; Environmental Engineering; Fishery; Heating and Refrigeration; Industrial Engineering; Information Technology; Instrument Making; Laboratory Techniques; Leather Techniques; Maintenance Technology; Marine Engineering; Marine Science and Oceanography; Marine Transport; Maritime Law; Materials Engineering; Mathematics; Measurement and Precision Engineering; Mechanical Engineering; Physical Engineering; Physics; Statistics; Telecommunications Engineering; Transport Management); **Science and Technology** (Biological and Life Sciences; Biomedical Engineering; Biomedicine; Chemical Engineering; Chemistry; Civil Engineering; Computer Engineering; Computer Science; Demography and Population; Electrical and Electronic Engineering; Food Science; Gerontology; Industrial Engineering; Laboratory Techniques; Mathematics; Medical Auxiliaries; Medical Technology; Orthopaedics; Physical Engineering; Physics; Psychiatry and Mental Health; Public Health; Statistics; Teacher Training; Treatment Techniques); **Social Sciences and Humanities** *(DCSH)* (African Studies; Anthropology; Art History; Communication Studies; Comparative Literature; Cultural Studies; Education; Educational Sciences; English; European Studies; French; History; Linguistics; Literature; Modern Languages; Music; Philosophy; Portuguese; Psychology; Social Sciences; Teacher Training; Translation and Interpretation; Writing)

History: Founded 2006. Incorporated the Instituto Superior de Educação (ISE), the Instituto Superior de Engenharia e Ciências do Mar (ISECMAR) and the Instituto Nacional de Administração e Gestão (INAG) 2008.

Academic Year: September to June (September-December; January-March; April-June)

Admission Requirements: High school diploma and entrance examination

Main Language(s) of Instruction: Portuguese

Accrediting Agency: Ministry of Higher Education, Science and Innovation

Degrees and Diplomas: *Licenciatura*: **Bioengineering; Biological and Life Sciences; Chemical Engineering; Civil Engineering; Communication Arts; Computer Engineering; Earth Sciences; Geography; Mathematics; Multimedia; Nursing; Regional Planning.** *Mestrado*: **Agronomy; Business and Commerce; Computer Engineering; Education; Energy Engineering; Finance; Heritage Preservation; Law; Mathematics; Natural Resources; Public Administration; Public Health; Surveying and Mapping; Tourism.** *Doutoramento*. Also Professional Degrees (14-18 months)

Student Services: Academic Counselling, Canteen, Careers Guidance, Cultural Activities, Facilities for disabled people, Language Laboratory, Social Counselling, Sports Facilities

Publications: Scientific Journal of Cape Verdean Studies

Publishing House: Edicões Uni-CV (Uni-CV Press)

Academic Staff *2011-2012*	MEN	WOMEN	**TOTAL**
FULL-TIME	–	–	**233**
PART-TIME	–	–	**271**
STAFF WITH DOCTORATE			
FULL-TIME	35	17	**52**
Student Numbers *2011-2012*			
All (Foreign included)	–	–	**4,433**

Last Updated: 10/12/12

PRIVATE INSTITUTIONS

HIGHER INSTITUTE OF ECONOMICS AND BUSINESS

Instituto Superior de Ciências Económicas e Empresariais (ISCEE)
Rua 5 de Julho n° 32, Praia 136
Tel: +238 260-21-00
Fax: +238 261-31-64
EMail: iscee@cvtelecom.cv
Website: http://www.iscee.edu.cv

Administradora Geral: Helena Rebelo Rodrigues
Tel: +238 232-60-88 EMail: helenarebelorodrigues@gmail.com

Programme
Accountancy (Accountancy); **Management** (Business Administration; Management); **Marketing** (Marketing)

Further Information: Also in São Vicente

History: Founded 1991.

Main Language(s) of Instruction: Portuguese

Degrees and Diplomas: *Licenciatura*: **Accountancy; Management; Marketing; Tourism.** *Mestrado*: **Accountancy; Management.**
Last Updated: 31/07/12

INSTITUTE OF LAW AND SOCIAL SCIENCES

Instituto Superior de Ciências Jurídicas e Sociais (ISCJS)
Fazenda, CP 212, Praia, São Tiago
Tel: +238 262-79-38
Fax: +238 261-89-47
EMail: iscjs.org@gmail.com
Website: http://www.iscjs.edu.cv

Presidente: José Pina Delgado

Course

Economics; **International Relations and Diplomacy**; **Law**; **Social Services**

History: Founded 2009.

Main Language(s) of Instruction: Portuguese

Degrees and Diplomas: *Licenciatura*
Last Updated: 31/07/12

INTERCONTINENTAL UNIVERSITY OF CAPE VERDE

Universidade Intercontinental de Cabo Verde (UNICA)
Avenida de Santiago, n° 1/Palmarejo, Praia, Santiago
Tel: +268 261-77-76
EMail: unica.cv@gmail.com

Reitor: Daniel Medina

Course

Clinical Analyses and Public Health; **Nursery**; **Pharmacy**; **Physiotherapy**; **Sport**

History: Founded 2009.

Main Language(s) of Instruction: Portuguese

Degrees and Diplomas: *Licenciatura*
Last Updated: 31/07/12

JEAN PIAGET UNIVERSITY OF CAPE VERDE

Universidade Jean Piaget de Cabo Verde
Caixa Postal 775, Campus Universitário da Cidade da Praía, Palmarejo Grande, Praia
Tel: +238 262-90-85 +238 260-90-00
Fax: +238 262-90-89 +238 260-90-20
EMail: info@unipiaget.cv
Website: http://www.unipiaget.cv

Reitor: Jorge Sousa Brito EMail: jsb@unipiaget.cv

Administrador Geral: Luis Filipe Lopes Tavares EMail: eft@unipiaget.cv

Course

Aerobiological Analysis *(Postgraduate)* (Biology); **Architecture** (Architecture); **Art Education** (Art Education); **Business Administration** *(Postgraduate)* (Business Administration); **Business Computing** (Business Computing); **Civil Engineering** (Civil Engineering); **Clinical Analysis** *(Postgraduate)* (Laboratory Techniques); **Clinical Analysis and Public Health** (Public Health); **Communication Sciences** (Communication Studies); **Computer Engineering** *(Postgraduate)* (Computer Engineering); **Ecology and Development Studies** (Development Studies; Ecology); **Economics and Management** (Economics; Management); **Educational Sciences** (Educational Sciences); **Food Technology** (Food Technology); **Hotel Management and Tourism** (Hotel Management; Tourism); **Law** (Law); **Pharmacotherapeutic Accompanying** (Pharmacology); **Pharmacy** (Pharmacy); **Physiotherapy** (Alternative Medicine); **Portuguese Language Teaching** *(Postgraduate)* (Portuguese); **Psychology** (Psychology); **Public and Autocratic Administration** (Public Administration); **Social Work** (Social Work); **Sociology** (Sociology); **Systems Engineering and Computer Engineering** (Computer Engineering; Computer Science; Systems Analysis)

History: Founded 2001.

Academic Year: October-July (October-February; March-July)

Main Language(s) of Instruction: Portuguese

Degrees and Diplomas: *Licenciatura*: **Architecture; Business Computing; Chemistry; Civil Engineering; Communication Arts; Computer Engineering; Economics; Educational Sciences; English; Hotel Management; Management; Mathematics; Nursing; Pharmacy; Physics; Portuguese; Psychology; Social Work; Sociology; Tourism.** *Mestrado*: **Accountancy; Business Administration; Computer Engineering; Finance.** *Doutoramento*
Last Updated: 31/07/12

LUSOPHONE UNIVERSITY OF CAPE VERDE

Universidade Lusofona de Cabo Verde (ULCV)
Chã de Cricket, Ex-Zona Militar, Mindelo, São Vicente
Tel: +238 231-50-15
EMail: infoulcv@ulusofona.pt
Website: http://www.ulusofona.edu.cv/

Reitora: Iva Cabral

Course

Accountancy, Administration and Audit (Accountancy; Administration); **Business Administration** (Business Administration); **Communication Sciences** (Communication Studies); **Computer Engineering** (Computer Engineering); **Design** (Design); **Hotel and Tourist Companies Management** (Hotel Management; Tourism); **Law** (Law); **Psychology** (Psychology); **Social Services** (Social and Community Services)

History: Founded 2009.

Main Language(s) of Instruction: Portuguese

Degrees and Diplomas: *Licenciatura*
Last Updated: 31/07/12

UNIVERSITY INSTITUTE OF ART, TECHNOLOGY AND CULTURE

Instituto Universitário de Arte, Tecnologia e Cultura (M_EIA)
Liceu Velho, Caixa Postal 190, Mindelo, São Vicente
Tel: +238 231-25-84
EMail: M_EIA@gmail.com
Website: http://meia-instituto.info

Reitoria: Leão Lopes

Course

Design (Design); **Visual Arts** (Visual Arts)

Laboratory

Architecture and Urban Design; **Communication Design**; **Sound and Images**

History: Founded 2009.

Main Language(s) of Instruction: Portuguese

Degrees and Diplomas: *Licenciatura*
Last Updated: 31/07/12

UNIVERSITY OF MINDELO

Universidade do Mindelo
CP 648, Rua Patrice Lumumba, Mindelo - São Vicente
Tel: +238 232-68-10
Fax: +238 232-51-32
EMail: uni-mindelo@sapo.cv
Website: http://uni.uni-mindelo.edu.cv/

President: Albertino Graça EMail: gracalbertino@hotmail.com

Head, Academic and Administrative Services: João Dias

Department

Languages, Literature and Cultural Studies (Cultural Studies; Literature; Modern Languages); **Law** (Law); **Science and Technology** (Natural Sciences; Technology); **Social Sciences and Education** (Education; Social Sciences)

History: Founded 2003. Acquired present title and status 2010. Formerly named 'Instituto de Ensino Superior Isidoro da Graça' (IESIG).

Academic Year: September to July (September-February; March-July)

Main Language(s) of Instruction: Portuguese

Degrees and Diplomas: *Licenciatura*; *Mestrado*

Last Updated: 21/06/12

UNIVERSITY OF SANTIAGO

Universidade de Santiago (US)

Rua António Hopffer de Almada, Ed Prestige 2° Andar, Assomada, Ilha de Santiago

Tel: +238 265-42-00

Fax: +238 265-24-79

EMail: sec.geral@us.edu.cv

Reitor: Gabriel Antonio Monteiro Fernandes

EMail: gabriel.fernandes@us.edu.cv

Course

Accountancy (Accountancy); **Biological Sciences and Mathematics** (Biological and Life Sciences; Mathematics); **Business Administration** (Business Administration); **Computer Engineering** (Computer Engineering); **Economics** (Economics); **Education Sciences** (Educational Sciences); **French Studies** (French Studies); **Geography and Land Management** (Geography); **History** (History); **History and Geography** (Geography; History); **Information and Communication Technologies** (Communication Studies; Information Technology); **Law**; **Nursery** (Nursing); **Philosophy** (Philosophy); **Portuguese and English** (English; Portuguese); **Portuguese and French** (French; Portuguese); **Social Communication - Journalism** (Journalism); **Social Service and Public Policy** (Social and Community Services); **Sociology** (Sociology)

History: Founded 2009

Main Language(s) of Instruction: Portuguese

Degrees and Diplomas: *Licenciatura*

Last Updated: 31/07/12

Cambodia

STRUCTURE OF HIGHER EDUCATION SYSTEM

Description:

Higher education is the third level (3rd Phumasekar) of education. It falls under the responsibility of the Ministry of Education, Youth and Sport. It is composed of two types of institutions: universities and institutes that can be public or private.

Stages of studies:

University level first stage: *Bachelor's degree*
Degree awarded in a large variety of disciplines and normally awarded after 4 years' study or longer in medical fields.

University level second stage: *Master's degree*
Degree awarded after two-years' study following upon a Bachelor's degree.

University level third stage: *Doctoral degree*
Degree awarded after three years' study.

ADMISSION TO HIGHER EDUCATION

Admission to university-level studies:

Name of secondary school credential required: Baccalauréat

Admission requirements: Yes

Foreign students admission:

Definition of foreign student: Students who are not Cambodian and are studying in Cambodia.

Quotas: Based on MOU with other countries.

Admission requirements: Meet criteria of MOU. Students should have credentials that are equivalent to the Baccalauréat.

Entry regulations: Visas and financial guarantees.

Language proficiency: The national language of instruction is Khmer but English is also used in most higher education institutions

RECOGNITION OF STUDIES

Quality assurance system:

The Accreditation Committee was created to develop the standards of education and to assess higher education quality.

NATIONAL BODIES

Ministry of Education, Youth and Sports

Minister: Hang Chuon Naron
80, Norodom Blvd
Phnom Penh
Tel: +855(23) 210134
Fax: +855(23) 210134
EMail: info@moeys.gov.kh
WWW: http://www.moeys.gov.kh

Supreme National Council for Education
No. 208A, Norodom Blvd., Sangkat Tonle Basak, Khan Chamkarmon
Phnom Penh
Tel: +855(23) 722870
Fax: +855(23) 722870
EMail: admin@snec.gov.kh
WWW: http://www.snec.gov.kh
Role of national body: Responsible for educational policy before the Royal Government.

Accreditation Committee of Cambodia
Building of the Office of the Council of Ministers, 41 Russian Federation Blvd
Phnom Penh
Tel: +855(23) 224620
EMail: info@acc.gov.kh
WWW: http://www.acc.gov.kh

Data for academic year: 2013-2014
Source: IAU from Ministry of Education, Youth and Sport website, 2013. Bodies 2016.

INSTITUTIONS

PUBLIC INSTITUTIONS

CAMBODIAN UNIVERSITY OF HEALTH SCIENCES

Sakal Vityalay Vitya Sas Sokha Phibal (UHS)
73 Monivong Boulevard, Sangkat Sras Chak, Khan Daun, Phnom Penh
Tel: +855(23) 430-559
Fax: +855(23) 430-186
EMail: info@uhs.edu.kh
Website: http://uhs.edu.kh/

Rector: Vonthanak Saphonn (2012-) Tel: +855(23) 430-715

Vice-Rector: Sophanna Youk
Tel: +855(23) 430-715 EMail: sophanna@univ-sante.edu.kh

International Relations: Tharith Seang, Director, International Relations and Cooperation
Tel: +855(23) 430-732 EMail: tharith_seang@univ-sante.edu.kh

Faculty
Dentistry (Dentistry); **Medicine** (Medicine); **Pharmacology** (Pharmacology; Pharmacy)

School
Nursing (Nursing)

History: Founded 1946 as School for Medical Officers; became Faculty of Medicine, Pharmacy and Dentistry in 1980. Acquired current status and title 2001.

Admission Requirements: Secondary school certificate (baccalauréat)

Fees: (US Dollars): 850 - 1200 per annum

Main Language(s) of Instruction: Khmer, French and English

Accrediting Agency: Ministry of Education, Youth and Sport

Degrees and Diplomas: *Bachelor's Degree/Licence*: **Dentistry; Medicine; Nursing; Pharmacy.** *Master's Degree*; *Doctoral Degree*

Student Services: Canteen, Language Laboratory, Nursery Care

CHEA SIM UNIVERSITY OF KAMCHAYMEAR (CSKU)

GPO Box 865, No.152 Norodom Blvd, Phnom Penh 12302
Tel: +855(23) 210-743
EMail: info@csuk.edu.kh
Website: http://www.csuk.edu.kh/

Rector: Uk Thaun

Faculty
Agriculture (Agricultural Management; Agriculture; Agronomy; Rural Planning); **Management** (Accountancy; Human Resources; Marketing)

Further Information: Also campuses in Kampong Cham and Prey Veng.

History: Founded 1993 as Sakal Vityalay ved Maharishi (Maharishi Vedic University) by agreement between the Ministry of Education, Youth and Sports and Australian Aid for Cambodia Fund (AACF) to provide education to rural youth. Acquired current title 2008.

Academic Year: October to July (October-March; April-July)

Admission Requirements: Entrance examination

Main Language(s) of Instruction: Khmer

Accrediting Agency: Ministry of Education, Youth and Sport

Degrees and Diplomas: *Bachelor's Degree/Licence*: **Agriculture; Management.** *Master's Degree*: **Agriculture; Business Administration.**

Student Services: Academic Counselling, Careers Guidance, Health Services, Social Counselling, Sports Facilities

Last Updated: 30/06/14

CHENLA UNIVERSITY

No.43 St.231, Phnom Penh 12159
Tel: +855(23) 883-269
EMail: info@chenla-edu.org
Website: http://www.clu.edu.kh

Faculty
Arts, Humanities and Languages (English; History; Indic Languages); **Education** (Education); **Health Care** (Medical Technology; Midwifery; Nursing; Physical Therapy); **Mathematics and Science** (Biology; Chemistry; Information Technology; Mathematics; Physics); **Social Sciences** (Accountancy; Banking; Finance; Law; Management; Marketing)

History: Founded 2007.

Accrediting Agency: Ministry of Education, Youth and Sport

Degrees and Diplomas: *Bachelor's Degree/Licence*; *Master's Degree*

Last Updated: 30/06/14

CITY UNIVERSITY

N° 6A, Yothapol Khemarak Phoumin (St. 271), Phnom Penh 12102
EMail: cu_education@yahoo.com

History: Founded 2005.

Accrediting Agency: Ministry of Education, Youth and Sport

Degrees and Diplomas: *Bachelor's Degree/Licence*; *Master's Degree*

ECONOMICS AND FINANCE INSTITUTE (EFI)

N° 60 Daun Penh (St. 92), Phnom Penh
Tel: +855(23) 430-556 +855(23) 428-624
Fax: +855(23) 430-168
EMail: efi@camnet.com.kh
Website: http://www.efi.edu.kh

Director: Seng Sreng

Programme

Economics (Economics); **Finance** (Finance)

History: Founded 2002.

Accrediting Agency: Ministry of Economy and Finance

Degrees and Diplomas: *Bachelor's Degree/Licence*; *Master's Degree*

Last Updated: 30/06/14

MEAN CHEY UNIVERSITY

No 5 National Road, Sangkat Teuk Thla,
Sisophon, Banteay Mean Chey
EMail: info@mcu.edu.kh
Website: http://www.mcu.edu.kh/

Rector: Sam Nga

Faculty

Agriculture and Food Processing (Agricultural Engineering; Agriculture; Agronomy; Environmental Management; Environmental Studies; Natural Resources; Veterinary Science); **Business Management** (Accountancy; Banking; Finance; Management; Marketing); **Humanities, Arts and Languages** (English; History; Japanese; Korean; Literature; Native Language; Thai Languages); **Science and Technology** (Biology; Chemistry; Civil Engineering; Electrical Engineering; Information Technology; Mathematics; Physics); **Social Science and Community Development** (Economics; Educational Sciences; Law; Philosophy; Political Sciences; Public Administration; Sociology)

History: Founded 2007.

Accrediting Agency: Ministry of Education, Youth and Sport

Degrees and Diplomas: *Bachelor's Degree/Licence*; *Master's Degree*

Student Services: Library

Last Updated: 01/07/14

NATIONAL INSTITUTE OF BUSINESS (NIB)

Street 217 (Monireth Blvd.), Sangkart Steung Mean Chey,
Khan Mean Chey, Phnom Penh 12202
Tel: +855(23) 424-591
Fax: +855(23) 430-810
EMail: nib@everyday.com.kh
Website: http://www.nib.edu.kh

Director: Ly Sothea

Department

Accounting (Accountancy); **Banking and Finance** (Banking; Finance); **English Language** (English); **Management** (Management); **Sales and Marketing** (Marketing; Retailing and Wholesaling)

Further Information: Traditional and Open Learning Institution

History: Founded 1979 as School of Central Commercial Technique. Acquired present status and title 2001.

Main Language(s) of Instruction: Khmer

Accrediting Agency: Ministry of Labour and Vocational Training

Degrees and Diplomas: *Bachelor's Degree/Licence*; *Master's Degree*: **Business Administration.**

Last Updated: 01/07/14

NATIONAL TECHNICAL TRAINING INSTITUTE (NTTI)

Russian Boulevard, Sangkat Teukthla, Khan Sen Sok,
Phnom Penh 12102
Tel: +855(23) 883-039
Fax: +855(23) 883-039
EMail: info@ntti.edu.kh
Website: http://www.ntti.edu.kh/

Director: Yok Sothy EMail: sothy.yok@ntti.edu.kh

Department

Civil Engineering (Civil Engineering; Engineering); **Electrical and Electronic Engineering** (Electrical and Electronic Engineering); **Information Technology** (Information Technology)

History: Founded 1999.

Accrediting Agency: Ministry of Labour and Vocational Training

Degrees and Diplomas: *Bachelor's Degree/Licence*; *Master's Degree*: **Civil Engineering; Electrical Engineering.**

Last Updated: 01/07/14

NATIONAL UNIVERSITY OF MANAGEMENT

Sakal Vityalay Cheath Kroup Krorng (NUM)

St.96 Christopher Howes, Khan Daun Penh, Phnom Penh
Tel: +855(23) 427-105
Fax: +855(23) 427-105
EMail: num@num.edu.kh
Website: http://num.edu.kh/

Rector: Hor Peng

Faculty

Economics (Economics); **Finance and Accountancy** (Accountancy; Finance); **Information Technology** (Business Computing; Information Technology); **Law** (Law); **Management** (Business Administration; International Business; Management; Marketing); **Tourism** (Tourism)

History: Created 1983 as National Institute of Management. Acquired present status and title 2004.

Admission Requirements: High School Certificate

Fees: (USD): 4,000 per annum

Main Language(s) of Instruction: Khmer

Accrediting Agency: Ministry of Education, Youth and Sport

Degrees and Diplomas: *Bachelor's Degree/Licence*: **Business Administration.** *Master's Degree*: **Business Administration; Finance.** *Doctoral Degree*: **Business Administration.** Also certificate

Last Updated: 01/07/14

PREAH SIHANOUK RAJA BUDDHIST UNIVERSITY

Ministry of Cults and Religions, Preah Sisowath Quay, Sangkat Chey Chum Neas, Khan Daun Penh, Phnom Penh 12206
Tel: +855(23) 722-699 +855(23) 725-099
Fax: +855(23) 725-699

Faculty

Education and Information Technology (Education; Information Technology); **Khmer Literature** (Literature); **Pasi-Sanskrit and Foreign Languages** (Modern Languages; Sanskrit); **Philosophy and Religions** (Philosophy; Religion)

History: Founded 1954. Acquired present status 2006.

Accrediting Agency: Ministry of Cults and Religions

Degrees and Diplomas: *Bachelor's Degree/Licence*; *Master's Degree*

Last Updated: 26/04/11

ROYAL ACADEMY OF CAMBODIA

PO Box 2070, Phnom Penh 12102
Tel: +855(23) 890-180 +855(23) 884-523
Fax: +855(23) 221-408 +855(23) 884-523
EMail: info@rac-academy.edu.kh
Website: http://www.rac-academy.edu.kh

Director: Khlot Thyda

Institute

Biology, Medicine and Agriculture (Agriculture; Biology; Dentistry; Ecology; Fishery; Forestry; Medicine; Pharmacy; Water Management; Water Science); **Culture and Fine Arts** (Archaeology; Architecture; Cultural Studies; Fine Arts); **Humanities and Social Sciences** (Anthropology; Business and Commerce; Economics; Education; Ethics; Ethnology; Geography; History; Law; Management; Philosophy; Political Sciences; Psychology; Religion; Sociology; Urban Studies); **National Language** (Linguistics; Literature; Native Language; Translation and Interpretation); **Science and Technology** (Chemistry; Food Technology; Information Technology; Mathematics; Physics; Statistics; Technology)

History: Founded 1999.

Accrediting Agency: Council of Ministers

Degrees and Diplomas: *Master's Degree*; *Doctoral Degree*

Last Updated: 01/07/14

ROYAL UNIVERSITY OF AGRICULTURE

Sakal Vityalay Phum Min Kasi Kam (RUA)
PO Box 2696, Dongkor District, Phnom Penh 12401
Tel: +855(23) 219-829
Fax: +855(23) 219-690
EMail: rua@camnet.com.kh
Website: http://www.rua.edu.kh/

Rector: Ngo Bunthan

Faculty

Agricultural Economics and Rural Development (Agricultural Business; Agricultural Economics; Rural Planning); **Agricultural Technology and Management** (Agricultural Engineering; Agricultural Equipment; Agricultural Management); **Agro-Industry** (Food Science; Harvest Technology); **Agronomy** (Agronomy; Crop Production; Horticulture; Plant and Crop Protection; Soil Science); **Animal Science and Veterinary Science** (Animal Husbandry; Veterinary Science); **Fisheries** (Fishery); **Forestry** (Forestry); **Land Management and Administration** (Farm Management)

History: Founded 1964. Acquired present status 1999.

Admission Requirements: High School Certificate

Fees: (US Dollars): 370 per annum

Main Language(s) of Instruction: Khmer

Accrediting Agency: Ministry of Education, Youth and Sport

Degrees and Diplomas: *Bachelor's Degree/Licence*; *Master's Degree*; *Doctoral Degree*

Publications: Agriculture Magazine

Last Updated: 01/07/14

ROYAL UNIVERSITY OF LAW AND ECONOMICS

Mohavityalay Netesas neng Vecheasas sethakech (RULE)
Monivong Boulevard, District Tonle Basac, Khan Chamkamon, Phnom Penh
Tel: +855(23) 211-565
Fax: +855(12) 564-094
EMail: rector@rule.edu.kh
Website: http://www.rule.edu.kh

Rector: Luy Channa

Faculty

Economics and Management (Accountancy; Banking; Economics; Finance); **Informatic Economics** (Business Computing; Economics); **Law** (Civil Law; Constitutional Law; Criminal Law; History of Law; International Law; Labour Law; Public Law); **Public Administration** (Public Administration)

History: Founded 1949 as National Institute of Law, Politics and Economics. Acquired present status and title 2003.

Accrediting Agency: Ministry of Education, Youth and Sport

Degrees and Diplomas: *Bachelor's Degree/Licence*; *Master's Degree*

Last Updated: 01/07/14

ROYAL UNIVERSITY OF PHNOM PENH

Sakal Vityalay Phoum min Phnom Penh (RUPP)
Russian Federation Boulevard Khan Tuol Kork, Phnom Penh 12156
Tel: +855(12) 811-925
Fax: +855(23) 880-116
EMail: secretary@upp.edu.kh
Website: http://www.rupp.edu.kh

President: Lao Chhiv Eav (2005-)

Faculty

Development Studies (Development Studies); **Engineering** (Bioengineering; Computer Engineering; Electronic Engineering; Information Technology; Telecommunications Engineering); **Science** (Biology; Chemistry; Computer Science; Environmental Studies; Mathematics; Physics); **Social Sciences and Humanities** (Communication Studies; Geography; History; Literature; Media Studies; Philosophy; Psychology; Sociology; Tourism)

Institute

Foreign Languages (Chinese; English; French; Japanese; Korean)

History: Founded 1960 incorporating Faculties established between 1955 and 1959. A State institution responsible to the Ministry of Education, Youth and Sports. Acquired present status and title 1988.

Academic Year: September to June (September-January; February-June)

Admission Requirements: Secondary school certificate (baccalauréat), and entrance examination

Main Language(s) of Instruction: Khmer, French, English

Accrediting Agency: Ministry of Education, Youth and Sport

Degrees and Diplomas: *Bachelor's Degree/Licence*; *Master's Degree*

Student Services: Health Services, Library

Last Updated: 01/07/14

SVAY RIENG UNIVERSITY

National Road N° 1, Chek Commune, Svay Rieng City
Tel: +855(44) 715-776
Fax: +855(44) 715-778
EMail: info@sru.edu.kh
Website: http://www.sru.edu.kh

Rector: Saravuth Tum

Faculty

Agriculture (Agronomy; Rural Planning; Veterinary Science); **Arts, Humanities and Foreign Languages** (Arts and Humanities; English); **Business Administration** (Accountancy; Banking; Business Administration; Finance; Management; Marketing); **Science and Technology** (Business Computing; Computer Science; Mathematics); **Social Sciences** (Public Administration)

History: Founded 2005.

Main Language(s) of Instruction: Khmer and English

Accrediting Agency: Ministry of Education, Youth and Sport

Degrees and Diplomas: *Bachelor's Degree/Licence*; *Master's Degree*

Student Services: Library

Last Updated: 02/07/14

UNIVERSITY OF BATTAMBANG

National Road No 5, Prek Preah Sdech Commune, Battambang, Battambang
Tel: +855(53) 952-905
Fax: +855(53) 952-905
EMail: info@ubb.edu.kh
Website: http://www.ubb.edu.kh/

Rector: Sieng Emtotim

Faculty

Agriculture and Food Processing (Agriculture; Animal Husbandry; Aquaculture; Food Science; Food Technology; Horticulture; Veterinary Science; Zoology); **Arts, Humanities and Education** (Arts and Humanities; Biology; Chemistry; Cultural Studies; Education; Indic Languages; Mathematics; Physics); **Business**

Administration and Tourism (Accountancy; Business Administration; Finance; Management; Marketing; Tourism); **Science and Technology** (Civil Engineering; Engineering; Information Technology; Nuclear Engineering); **Sociology and Community Development** (Agricultural Business; Economics; Law; Rural Studies; Social Sciences)

Institute

Foreign Languages

History: Created 2007.

Accrediting Agency: Ministry of Education, Youth and Sport

Degrees and Diplomas: *Bachelor's Degree/Licence*; *Master's Degree*

Student Services: Library

Last Updated: 02/07/14

PRIVATE INSTITUTIONS

ANGKOR UNIVERSITY

Borey Seang Nam, Phum Khna, Khum Chreav, Srok Siem Reap, Siem Reap

Tel: +855(92) 256-086

Fax: +855(63) 760-340

EMail: info@angkor.edu.kh

Website: http://www.angkor.edu.kh/

Rector: Neak Oknha Seang Nam

Programme

Accountancy and Finance (Accountancy; Finance); **Computer Science and Technology** (Computer Science; Technology); **Education and Manegement** (Educational Administration); **Foreign Languages** (Modern Languages); **Management** (Management); **Marketing** (Marketing); **Tourism and Hospitality** (Tourism)

History: Founded 2004.

Fees: (US Dollars): Undergraduate, 360 per annum; Master programme, 750 per annum

Accrediting Agency: Ministry of Education, Youth and Sport

Degrees and Diplomas: *Bachelor's Degree/Licence*; *Master's Degree*; *Doctoral Degree*

Last Updated: 30/06/14

ASIA EURO UNIVERSITY

Sakal Vityalay Asia Euro (AEU)

832 ABCD, Kampuchea Krom Blvd., Sangkat Teuk Laak I, Khan Toul Kork, Phnom Penh

Tel: +855(17) 797-799 +855(23) 998-124

EMail: info@aeu.edu.kh

Website: http://www.aeu.edu.kh/

Rector: Duong Leang

Faculty

Arts, Humanities and Languages (English); **Business** (Accountancy; Business Administration; Management); **Economics** (Banking; Economics; Finance); **Hotel Management and Tourism** (Hotel Management; Tourism); **Law and Political Science** (International Relations; Law; Political Sciences; Public Administration)); **Science And Information Technology** (Computer Networks; Computer Science)

History: Founded 2002 as Asia Euro Institute. Acquired present status and title 2005. Former name "Mohavityalay Asia Euro".

Main Language(s) of Instruction: Khmer

Accrediting Agency: Ministry of Education, Youth and Sport

Degrees and Diplomas: *Bachelor's Degree/Licence*; *Master's Degree*; *Doctoral Degree*: **Business Administration; Economics; Finance; International Relations; Law; Political Sciences.** Also Associate Degree.

Student Services: Library

Last Updated: 01/07/14

BUILD BRIGHT UNIVERSITY (BBU)

Samdech Sothearos (St. 3) Grey building, riverside near Samdech Hun Sen Park, Phnom Penh 12301

Tel: +855(23) 987 700

Fax: +855(23) 987 900

EMail: info@bbu.edu.kh

Website: http://www.bbu.edu.kh

President: Diep Seiha

Faculty

Arts, Humanities and Languages (Education; English; Journalism; Mass Communication; Modern Languages); **Business Management** (Accountancy; Banking; Business Administration; Finance; Human Resources); **Engineering and Architecture** (Architecture; Civil Engineering; Electrical and Electronic Engineering); **Law and Social Sciences** (Law; Social Sciences); **Science and Technology** (Computer Networks; Computer Science; Information Technology); **Tourism and Hospitality**

Further Information: Also study centres in Siem Reap, Sihanouk, Ratanakiri, Battambang, Takeo, Banteay Meanchey, and Stung Treng.

History: Founded 2000.

Main Language(s) of Instruction: Laotian

Accrediting Agency: Ministry of Education, Youth and Sport

Degrees and Diplomas: *Bachelor's Degree/Licence*; *Master's Degree*; *Doctoral Degree*

Last Updated: 30/06/14

CAMBODIAN MEKONG UNIVERSITY

Mohavityalay Mekong Kampochea (CMU)

#9B, Street 271, Sangkat Tek Thla, Khan Sen Sok, Phnom Penh 12102

Tel: +855(23) 882-211

Fax: +855(23) 88 01 48

EMail: info@mekong.edu.kh

Website: http://www.mekong.edu.kh/

Chancellor: Ich Seng

Faculty

Arts, Humanities and Foreign Languages (American Studies; Arts and Humanities; Chinese; Education; English; Japanese; Modern Languages); **Economics** (Banking; Economics; Finance; Rural Planning); **Law** (Commercial Law; Law); **Management and Tourism** (Accountancy; Hotel Management; Human Resources; International Business; Management; Marketing; Real Estate; Tourism); **Science and Technology** (Architecture; Civil Engineering; Computer Science; Technology); **Social Sciences** (Leadership; Management; Social Sciences)

History: Founded 2003.

Main Language(s) of Instruction: Khmer

Accrediting Agency: Ministry of Education, Youth and Sport

Degrees and Diplomas: *Bachelor's Degree/Licence*; *Master's Degree*; *Doctoral Degree*: **Business Administration; Development Studies; Economics; Law; Management; Political Sciences; Public Administration.**

Student Services: Library

Last Updated: 01/07/14

CAMBODIAN UNIVERSITY FOR SPECIALTIES (CUS)

N° 43 Street 231 Psar Doum Kor, Phnom Penh 12159

Tel: +855(23) 350-828

EMail: info@cus.edu.kh

Website: http://www.cus.edu.kh

President: Sokhom Sdoueng

Faculty

Arts, Humanities and Linguistics (English; Geography; History; Native Language); **Business Administration and Economics** (Accountancy; Advertising and Publicity; Banking; Business Administration; Economics; Finance; Hotel Management; Human Resources; International Business; Management; Marketing; Rural Planning; Tourism); **Engineering** (Civil Engineering; Computer Engineering; Computer Networks; Electrical and Electronic Engineering); **Science and Technology** (Biology; Chemistry; Computer

Science; Information Technology; Mathematics; Physics); **Social Science and Law** (Private Law; Public Law)

Further Information: Also campuses in Kampong Cham, Siem Reap and Battambang.

History: Founded 2001 as Cambodian Institute for Specialties. Acquired present title 2004.

Accrediting Agency: Ministry of Education, Youth and Sport

Degrees and Diplomas: *Bachelor's Degree/Licence*; *Master's Degree*; *Doctoral Degree*: **Business Administration; Educational Sciences; Law; Social Sciences.**

Last Updated: 02/07/14

CHAMROEUN UNIVERSITY OF POLY-TECHNOLOGY (CUP)

88, St. 150, Sangkat Toul Svayprey I, Khan Chamkarmon, Phnom Penh 12308
Tel: +855(23) 987-795
Fax: +855(23) 987-695
EMail: info@cup.edu.kh
Website: http://www.cup.edu.kh/

Rector: Chea Chamroeun

Faculty

Business and Finance (Business Administration; Finance); **Foreign Languages** (Modern Languages); **Law** (Law)

History: Founded 2002.

Main Language(s) of Instruction: Khmer

Accrediting Agency: Ministry of Education, Youth and Sport

Degrees and Diplomas: *Bachelor's Degree/Licence*; *Master's Degree*; *Doctoral Degree*

HUMAN RESOURCES UNIVERSITY

Building 2, Street 163, Sangkat Olympic, Khan Chamkamorn, Phnom Penh
Tel: +855(23) 987 826
EMail: info@hru.edu.kh
Website: http://www.hru.edu.kh

Rector: Seng Phally

Faculty

Arts, Humanities and Languages (Arts and Humanities; Cultural Studies; English; Geography (Human); Literature); **Business Management and Tourism** (Accountancy; Banking; Business Administration; Finance; Management; Marketing; Tourism); **Law and Political Science** (Law; Political Sciences)

History: Created 2005.

Accrediting Agency: Ministry of Education, Youth and Sport

Degrees and Diplomas: *Bachelor's Degree/Licence*; *Master's Degree*; *Doctoral Degree*: **Business Administration; Education.**

Last Updated: 02/07/14

IIC UNIVERSITY OF TECHNOLOGY (IICUT)

Building 650, National Road 2, Sankat Chak Angre Krom, Khan Mean Chey, Phnom Penh
Tel: +855(23) 425-148
Fax: +855(23) 425-149
EMail: info@iic.edu.kh
Website: http://www.iic.edu.kh

Rector: Chan Than Chhuon

International Relations: Chee Seng Leow, Program Director
Tel: +60(1) 6977 4993 EMail: drleowcs@iic.edu.kh

Faculty

Arts, Humanities and Linguistics (Chinese; Communication Studies; English; Japanese); **Commerce** (Business and Commerce); **Economics** (Economics); **Mathematics and Science** (Computer Science; Information Technology; Mathematics); **Social Science** (Political Sciences; Public Administration)

Graduate Department

Graduate *(The IIC University of Technology offers a unique experience to graduates, including the opportunity to work with leading academics and with some of the very best libraries, laboratories, museums and collections worldwide)* (Agriculture; Architecture and Planning; Arts and Humanities; Business Administration; Education; Engineering; Fine Arts; Health Sciences; Home Economics; Information Sciences; Law; Mathematics and Computer Science; Natural Sciences; Performing Arts; Religion; Service Trades; Social Sciences; Technology; Transport and Communications; Welfare and Protective Services)

History: Founded 2008 through the evolution of International Institute of Cambodia, founded in 1999.

Admission Requirements: The minimum entrance requirements for each type of programme are normally as follows: A degree or equivalent qualification and experience. Master's degree A first or upper second class honours (2:1) degree from a Cambodia university or a non-UK equivalent in a subject appropriate to the programme to be followed. PhD Normally a taught master's degree with merit or a non-Cambodia equivalent in a subject appropriate to the research to be undertaken. The most appropriate supervisor for your work will be allocated with particular reference to your research proposal. Any offer of a place would depend on: The quality and feasibility of research proposal Academic qualifications, and relevant professional or other experience, if appropriate. The ability of the department to provide adequate and appropriate supervision an interview with the department, unless there are exceptional circumstances which prevent this

Main Language(s) of Instruction: English, Cambodian, Chinese

Accrediting Agency: Ministry of Education, Youth and Sport

Degrees and Diplomas: *Bachelor's Degree/Licence*; *Master's Degree*: **Business Administration.** *Doctoral Degree*: **Agriculture; Architecture and Planning; Arts and Humanities; Business Administration; Education; Engineering; Health Sciences; Home Economics; Information Sciences; Law; Mathematics and Computer Science; Natural Sciences; Performing Arts; Religion; Service Trades; Social Sciences; Technology; Transport and Communications; Welfare and Protective Services.**

Student Services: Academic Counselling, Canteen, Careers Guidance, Cultural Activities, Foreign Studies Centre, IT Centre, Language Laboratory, Library, Residential Facilities, Social Counselling, Sports Facilities, eLibrary

Publications: Journal of Productivity Management

Academic Staff *2014-2015*	MEN	WOMEN	TOTAL
FULL-TIME	10	15	**25**
PART-TIME	20	10	**30**
STAFF WITH DOCTORATE			
FULL-TIME	5	3	c. **8**
FOREIGN ONLY	–	–	**50**

Distance students, 50.

Last Updated: 29/10/14

INSTITUTE OF TECHNOLOGY OF CAMBODIA

Vitya Satan Bachek Vichea Kampuchea (ITC)
PO Box 86, Pochentong Boulevard, Phnom Penh
Tel: +855(23) 880-370 +855(11) 878-207
Fax: +855(23) 880-369
EMail: info@itc.edu.kh
Website: http://www.itc.edu.kh

Director: Sackona Phoeurng

Director of Administration: San Penh

Department

Chemical Engineering and Food Technology (Chemical Engineering; Food Technology); **Civil Engineering** (Civil Engineering); **Computer Science** (Computer Science); **Energy and Electrical Engineering** (Electrical Engineering; Energy Engineering); **Mechanical and Industrial Engineering** (Industrial Engineering; Mechanical Engineering); **Rural Engineering** (Agricultural Engineering)

History: Founded 1964.

Main Language(s) of Instruction: Khmer, French, English.

Accrediting Agency: Ministry of Education, Youth and Sport

Degrees and Diplomas: *Bachelor's Degree/Licence*; *Master's Degree*. Also professional degree (Engineer and Higher Technician)

INTERNATIONAL UNIVERSITY (IU)

Building 89-91-93 & 95, St.1011-1984, Sangkat, Phnom Penh 12150
Tel: +855(23) 881-623
EMail: info@iu.edu.kh
Website: http://www.iu.edu.kh/

President: Uon Sabo EMail: iusabo@yahoo.com

Faculty
Agriculture and Rural Development (Agricultural Economics; Agronomy; Development Studies; Rural Planning); **Business and Economics** (Accountancy; Banking; Business Administration; Economics; Finance; Hotel Management; Marketing; Tourism); **Dentistry** (Dentistry; Orthodontics; Surgery); **Humanities and Social Sciences** (Arts and Humanities; English); **Law** (Commercial Law; International Law; Law; Private Law; Public Law); **Medicine and Pediatrics** (Medicine; Paediatrics); **Nursing Sciences** (Homeopathy; Midwifery; Nursing; Physical Therapy); **Pharmacy** (Pharmacy); **Science and Technology** (Architecture; Biochemistry; Civil Engineering; Computer Science; Electrical and Electronic Engineering; Energy Engineering; Environmental Management; Information Technology; Microbiology; Surveying and Mapping); **Social Sciences and Journalism** (Journalism; Social Sciences)

History: Founded 2002.

Main Language(s) of Instruction: Khmer, English

Accrediting Agency: Ministry of Education, Youth and Sport

Degrees and Diplomas: *Bachelor's Degree/Licence*; *Master's Degree*: **Civil Engineering; Commercial Law; Computer Engineering; Construction Engineering; Educational Administration; English; Environmental Management; Finance; Hotel Management; Human Resources; International Business; International Law; International Relations; Literature; Management; Public Health; Sociology; Tourism.** *Doctoral Degree*: **Business Administration; Civil Engineering; Natural Sciences; Philosophy; Public Administration.** Also Associate Degree.

Student Services: Library
Last Updated: 01/07/14

KHEMARAK UNIVERSITY

Sihanouk Boulevard, Building D, Phnom Penh
Tel: +855(23) 223-415
EMail: khemarak_university@yahoo.com
Website: http://www.khemarak.edu.kh

Rector: Sok Touch

Faculty
Agricultural Science and Rural Development (Agriculture; Rural Planning; Rural Studies); **Business Administration and Tourism** (Accountancy; Banking; Business Administration; Finance; Hotel Management; Management; Marketing; Tourism); **Educational Science** (Biology; Chemistry; Educational Administration; English; Geography; History; Literature; Mathematics; Native Language; Philosophy; Physics); **Humanities, Art and Linguistics** (Fine Arts; Linguistics; Psychology; Sociology); **Law and Economic Science** (Economics; Law); **Political Science and International Relations** (International Relations; Political Sciences); **Science, Technology and Information Science** (Computer Networks; Computer Science; Information Sciences; Information Technology; Mathematics)

History: Founded 2004.

Main Language(s) of Instruction: Khmer

Accrediting Agency: Ministry of Education, Youth and Sport

Degrees and Diplomas: *Bachelor's Degree/Licence*; *Master's Degree*; *Doctoral Degree*
Last Updated: 01/07/14

NORTON UNIVERSITY

Sakal Vityalay Norton (NU)

St. Keo Chenda, Sangkat Chroy Changva, Khan Russey Keo, Phnom Penh
Tel: +855(12) 900-222 +855(23) 982-177 +855(23) 982-166
Fax: +855(23) 211-273
EMail: info@norton.edu.kh
Website: http://www.norton-u.com

Rector: Chan Sok Khieng EMail: khieng_cvt@norton-u.com
Vice-Rector: Vannthoeun Ung EMail: vannthoeun@gmail.com

College
Arts, Humanities and Languages (English; Translation and Interpretation); **Science** (Architecture; Bridge Engineering; Civil Engineering; Computer Networks; Computer Science; Electrical and Electronic Engineering; Interior Design; Road Engineering; Town Planning); **Social Sciences** (Social Sciences)

School
Graduate Studies (Business Administration; English; Information Technology; Management)

Further Information: Also Branch in Phnom Penh (Banana Centre).

History: Founded 1996.

Academic Year: October to June (October-January; March-June)

Admission Requirements: Secondary school certificate baccalauréat

Main Language(s) of Instruction: Khmer, English

Accrediting Agency: Ministry of Education, Youth and Sport

Degrees and Diplomas: *Bachelor's Degree/Licence*; *Master's Degree*: **Business Administration; Development Studies; English; Information Technology.**

Student Services: Canteen, Language Laboratory

Publications: Norton's Academic Research
Last Updated: 01/07/14

PANNASASTRA UNIVERSITY OF CAMBODIA (PUC)

No.92-94, Sothearos Blvd., Phnom Penh 12207
Tel: +855(23) 990-153
Fax: +855(23) 218-909
EMail: info@puc.edu.kh
Website: http://www.puc.edu.kh/

President: Kol Pheng

Faculty
Architecture and Design (Architecture; Design; Interior Design); **Arts, Letters and Humanities** (Anthropology; Archaeology; Arts and Humanities; Asian Studies; English; History; Music; Musicology; Philosophy; Religion; Southeast Asian Studies); **Business and Economics** (Accountancy; Banking; Business Administration; Economics; Finance; Tourism); **Communication and Media Arts** (Communication Arts; Communication Studies; Journalism; Media Studies); **Education** (Curriculum; Education; Educational Administration); **Law and Public Affairs** (Comparative Law; Human Rights; International Law; Law); **Mathematics, Sciences and Engineering** (Architecture; Civil Engineering; Computer Engineering; Computer Science; Environmental Engineering; Interior Design); **Social Sciences and International Relations** (Development Studies; International Relations; Peace and Disarmament; Political Sciences; Social Sciences)

History: Founded 1997.

Fees: (US Dollars): 160-1250 per term

Main Language(s) of Instruction: English

Accrediting Agency: Ministry of Labour and Vocational Training

Degrees and Diplomas: *Bachelor's Degree/Licence*; *Master's Degree*; *Doctoral Degree*
Last Updated: 01/07/14

PNOMH PENH INTERNATIONAL UNIVERSITY (PPIU)

Building 36, St. 169, Sangkat Veal Vong, Khan 7 Makara, Phnom Penh 12253
Tel: +855(23) 999-908 +855(23) 999-907
EMail: info@ppiu.edu.kh
Website: http://www.ppiu.edu.kh

Rector: Tep Kolap

Faculty
Business and Tourism (Accountancy; Management; Marketing; Tourism); **Educational Sciences** (English); **Law and Economics**

(Banking; Economics; Finance; Law; Public Administration); **Science and Information Technology** (Computer Science; Information Management; Telecommunications Engineering)

History: Founded 2006 as a result of merger of the International Institute of Cambodia and the ASEAN University.

Fees: (US Dollars): Undergraduate, 390 per annum; graduate, 1,000-2,400

Main Language(s) of Instruction: Khmer

Accrediting Agency: Ministry of Labour and Vocational Training

Degrees and Diplomas: *Bachelor's Degree/Licence*; *Master's Degree*; *Doctoral Degree*: **Banking; Economics; Finance; Management; Marketing; Tourism.**

Last Updated: 01/07/14

SETEC UNIVERSITY (SETECU)

92, Russian Blvd, Khan Toul Kork, Phnom Penh 12102
Tel: +855(23) 880-612 +855(12) 395-190
EMail: info@setecu.com

Director: Sokveng Ngoun

Faculty

Information Technology (Business Administration; Computer Networks; Data Processing; Information Technology; Management); **Management Systems** (Business Administration; Computer Networks; English; Management Systems; Multimedia; Software Engineering)

Programme

Design (Design)

History: Founded 2002.

Main Language(s) of Instruction: Khmer

Accrediting Agency: Ministry of Education, Youth and Sport

Degrees and Diplomas: *Bachelor's Degree/Licence*: **Business Administration; Computer Engineering; Computer Science; Engineering; Management Systems; Multimedia; Software Engineering.** *Master's Degree*: **Computer Networks; Data Processing; Engineering; Information Technology; Management.** Also Associate Degree.

UNIVERSITY OF CAMBODIA

P.O. Box 166, 143-145, Preah Norodom Boulevard, Phnom Penh 12000
Tel: +855(23) 993-274 +855(23) 993-275 +855(23) 993-276
Fax: +855(23) 993-284 +855(23) 994940
EMail: info@uc.edu.kh
Website: http://www.uc.edu.kh/

President: Kao Kim Hourn EMail: uc_president@uc.edu.kh

College

Arts and Humanities (American Studies; Asian Studies; Communication Studies; Fine Arts; Journalism; Linguistics; Modern Languages; Performing Arts; Philosophy; Religious Studies); **Education** (Education; Educational Administration; Foreign Languages Education; Pedagogy); **Law** (International Law; Law; Private Law; Public Law); **Management** (Accountancy; Banking; Business Administration; Economics; Finance; Human Resources; International Business; Management; Marketing; Tourism); **Science and Technology** (Computer Science; Electronic Engineering; Information Technology; Technology; Telecommunications Engineering); **Social Sciences** (Development Studies; History; International Relations; Peace and Disarmament; Political Sciences; Public Administration)

History: Founded 2003.

Academic Year: September to September (September-January; February-June; June-September)

Main Language(s) of Instruction: English

Accrediting Agency: Ministry of Education, Youth and Sports. Accredited by the Accreditation Committee of Cambodia

Degrees and Diplomas: *Bachelor's Degree/Licence*; *Master's Degree*; *Doctoral Degree*

Last Updated: 02/07/14

UNIVERSITY OF MANAGEMENT AND ECONOMICS

Vitya Satan Krap Krang ning Sethakek (UME)
PO Box 303, Battambang, Battambang
Tel: +855(53) 952-160 +855(17) 868-386 +855(12) 723-794
Fax: +855(53) 953-160
EMail: umecambodia@gmail.com
Website: http://www.ume.edu.kh/

President: Tun Pheakdey EMail: tunume@gmail.com

School

Agriculture and Rural Development (Agriculture; Agronomy; Rural Planning; Rural Studies); **Arts, Humanities and Foreign Languages** (English; Translation and Interpretation); **Engineering and Architecture** (Architecture; Engineering); **Law and Economics** (Economics; Law; Private Law; Public Law); **Management and Tourism** (Accountancy; Banking; Finance; Human Resources; International Business; Tourism); **Science and Technology** (Computer Networks; Computer Science; Information Technology)

Further Information: Also campuses in Posat, Kampot, Sihanukville, Kampong Cham and Banteay Meanchey.

History: Founded 2000 as Institute of Management and Economics. Acquired present status and title 2005.

Main Language(s) of Instruction: Khmer

Accrediting Agency: Ministry of Education, Youth and Sport

Degrees and Diplomas: *Bachelor's Degree/Licence*; *Master's Degree*

UNIVERSITY OF PUTHISASTRA

55, St 180, Sangkat Boeung Raing, Khan Daun Penh, Phnom Penh
Tel: +855(23) 220-476 +855(16) 707-855 +855(17) 803-806
EMail: info@puthisastra.edu.kh
Website: http://www.puthisastra.edu.kh

Faculty

Arts and Humanities (English; Social Studies; Translation and Interpretation); **Economics and Business** (Banking; Business Administration; Economics; Finance; Management; Marketing); **Law** (Law); **Rural Development and Agriculture** (Agricultural Economics; Agriculture; Natural Resources; Plant and Crop Protection; Rural Planning; Rural Studies); **Science and Technology** (Computer Science; Information Technology; Technology)

History: Created 2007.

Accrediting Agency: Ministry of Education, Youth and Sport

Degrees and Diplomas: *Bachelor's Degree/Licence*; *Master's Degree*

Last Updated: 02/07/14

UNIVERSITY OF SOUTH EAST ASIA (USEA)

In front of Angkor High School, Siem Reap City
Tel: +855(63) 690-1696 +855(12) 428-889 +855(12) 886-476
EMail: info@usea.edu.kh
Website: http://www.usea.edu.kh

Rector: Sein Sovanna

Faculty

Arts, Humanities, and Languages (Educational Psychology; English; History; Linguistics; Literature; Pedagogy; Philosophy; Teacher Training; Translation and Interpretation; Writing); **Economics, Business and Tourism** (Accountancy; Banking; Business Administration; Business and Commerce; Economics; Finance; Hotel Management; International Business; Management; Tourism); **Science and Technology** (Civil Engineering; Computer Science; Data Processing; Information Technology; Mathematics; Software Engineering); **Social Science and Law** (Commercial Law; Criminal Law; International Law; International Relations; Law; Political Sciences; Private Law; Public Administration; Public Law)

History: Founded 2006.

Accrediting Agency: Ministry of Education, Youth and Sport

Degrees and Diplomas: *Bachelor's Degree/Licence*; *Master's Degree*
Last Updated: 02/07/14

VANDA INSTITUTE (VIA)

N° 216-218 Mao Tse Toung (St. 245), Phnom Penh 12306
Tel: +855(23) 213-563
EMail: vanda@camnet.com.kh
Website: http://www.vanda.edu.kh/

Director: Vanda Heng

Programme

Accountancy (Accountancy); **Political Science** (Political Sciences)

History: Founded 2001.

Main Language(s) of Instruction: Khmer

Accrediting Agency: Ministry of Education, Youth and Sport

Degrees and Diplomas: *Bachelor's Degree/Licence*: **Accountancy.** *Master's Degree*: **Accountancy.**

WESTERN UNIVERSITY (WU)

3, Street 528, Sangkat Boeungkok I, Khan Toul Kork, Phnom Penh
Tel: +855(23) 990-699
Fax: +855(23) 990-699
EMail: info@western.edu.kh
Website: http://www.western.edu.kh

Principal: Lauren Te

Department

Business Administration (Business Administration); **Computer Science** (Computer Science); **Economics** (Economics); **Engineering** (Engineering); **English** (English); **Hotel and Tourism** (Hotel Management; Tourism); **Law** (Law); **Public Administration and Policy** (Public Administration)

History: Founded 2003.

Accrediting Agency: Ministry of Education, Youth and Sport

Degrees and Diplomas: *Bachelor's Degree/Licence*; *Master's Degree*; *Doctoral Degree*: **Business Administration; Economics; Law; Political Sciences; Public Administration.**

Student Services: Library

Last Updated: 02/07/14

Cameroon

STRUCTURE OF HIGHER EDUCATION SYSTEM

Description:

Higher education is mainly provided by universities, specialized institutions and schools. The Minister in charge of higher education takes final policy decisions regarding universities, although each university has a governing council. Councils are responsible for personnel recruitment. The creation of departments, degrees, courses and changes in regulations must receive ministerial consent. Each university receives a budget from the State. The University of Buea is headed by a Vice-Chancellor who is appointed by the government and who, in turn, is chair of the Administrative Council. Other public universities are headed by a Rector. The Presidents of the Administrative Councils of Yaoundé I and II, Dschang, Ngaoundéré, and Douala Universities and the pro-chancellor of Buea University are nominated. Several higher education institutions do not fall directly under the Ministry of Higher Education, but the Minister must ascertain that they meet academic standards. Some are directly run by other Ministries or belong to the private sector.

Stages of studies:

University level first stage: *Premier cycle*
The Licence or Bachelor's degree are obtained after three years' study.

University level second stage: *Deuxième cycle*
The Master is conferred after a further two years' study following the Licence/Bachelor's degree. In Medicine, the Diplôme de Docteur en Médecine is conferred after six years.

University level third stage: *Troisième cycle*
A Doctorat or Doctor of Philosophy (PhD) degree is conferred 3 years after the Master's degree.

ADMISSION TO HIGHER EDUCATION

Admission to university-level studies:

Name of secondary school credential required: Baccalauréat/General Certificate of Education Advanced Level

Admission requirements: Entrance Examination

Foreign students admission:

Definition of foreign student: Non-Cameroonian, non-member of CEMAC (Central African Economic Community).

Admission requirements: Foreign students must hold a Baccalauréat or its equivalent, a scientific Baccalauréat or a General Certificate of Education Advanced Level or the Higher School Certificate and have passed the competitive examination of one of the schools.

Entry regulations: Visa, residence permit

Health requirements: Medical assistance is offered free of charge at the university.

Language proficiency: Good knowledge of French or English. Language and orientation courses are offered.

RECOGNITION OF STUDIES

Quality assurance system:

The State is responsible for the higher education policy and its implementation. Private higher education institutions have to be authorized to open, registered to deliver courses and approved to grant national diplomas. Evaluations are compulsory for both public and private institutions.

NATIONAL BODIES

Ministère de l'Enseignement Supérieur (Ministry of Higher Education)

Minister: Jacques Fame Ndongo
BP 1739
Yaoundé
Tel: +237 2222-2983
Fax: +237 2222-9724
EMail: cab@minesup.gov.cm; sg@minesup.gov.cm
WWW: http://www.minesup.gov.cm

Data for academic year: 2012-2013
Source: IAU from the website of the Ministry of Higher Education and World Data on Education 2010/2011, UNESCO-IBE, 2012. Bodies 2016.

INSTITUTIONS

PUBLIC INSTITUTIONS

INSTITUTE OF STATISTICS AND APPLIED ECONOMICS

Institut sous-régional de Statistique et d'Economie appliquée (ISSEA)
BP 294, Yaoundé, Centre
Tel: +237 2222 01 34
Fax: +237 2222 95 21
EMail: isseacemac@yahoo.fr
Website: http://www.issea-cemac.org

Directeur général: Leoncio Feliciano Esono Nze Oyana
EMail: lfesono@hotmail.com

Programme
Continuing Education and Research in Applied Statistics and Economics; **Initial Training in Applied Statistics and Economics** (Economics; Statistics)

History: Founded 1961. Acquired present status 1984.

Academic Year: October to June

Admission Requirements: First and second cycles, Secondary school leaving certificate with scientific major (Baccalauréat scientifique); 3rd cycle, Licence

Fees: (CFA Francs): Free for citizens from the Communauté Économique et Monétaire de l'Afrique Centrale (CEMAC); 1 m. for others

Main Language(s) of Instruction: French

Accrediting Agency: CEMAC Commission

Degrees and Diplomas: *Brevet de Technicien Supérieur*: **Statistics.** *Diplôme d'Ingénieur de Conception*: **Economics; Statistics.**

Student Services: Careers Guidance, Sports Facilities

Last Updated: 20/09/12

INTERNATIONAL INSTITUTE OF INSURANCE

Institut International des Assurances (IIA)
BP 1575, Yaounde, Centre
Tel: +237 2220 71 52
Fax: +237 2220 71 51
EMail: iia@iiacameroun.com; iia@cm.refer.org
Website: http://www.iiayaounde.com/

Directeur général: Roger J. R. Dossou-Yovo
EMail: dg@iiacameroun.com

Directeur administratif et financier: Luc Ze Ndong
EMail: daf@iiacameroun.com

International Relations: Paul Sarr, Directeur des Etudes
EMail: de@iiacameroun.com

Programme
Insurance Management and Studies *(International)* (Insurance)

History: Founded 1972. Acquired present status 1992.

Academic Year: December to November

Admission Requirements: DEUG for cycle II, MSTA; Master for cycle III, DESSA

Main Language(s) of Instruction: French

Degrees and Diplomas: *Master*: **Insurance; Management.** MTA and DESSA

Student Services: Canteen, Cultural Activities, Health Services, Sports Facilities

Publications: Afrique Assurance

Last Updated: 20/09/12

NATIONAL ADVANCED SCHOOL OF POST AND TELECOMMUNICATIONS

Ecole nationale supérieure des Postes et Télécommunications (ENSPT)
route Joseph Tchooungui Akoa BP, Yaoundé, Centre
Tel: +237 22 23 26 42
Fax: +237 22 23 50 05
Website: http://www.enspt.net/

Director: Jean-Marie Dongo (2010-) Tel: +237 2222-37-23

Department
Communications (Communication Studies); **Electronics, Computer Science and Telematics** (Computer Science; Electronic Engineering); **Financing and Accountancy Services** (Accountancy; Finance); **General Studies**; **Local Networks** (Telecommunications Engineering); **Post Management** (Postal Services); **Technology and Electronics** (Electronic Engineering; Technology); **Telecommunications** (Telecommunications Engineering); **Transmissions and Radio Communications** (Radio and Television Broadcasting)

History: Founded 1969 as Ecole Fédérale des Postes et Télécommunications. Acquired present status and title 1982.

Fees: 200,000 to 500,000 per annum (CFA Franc BEAC)

Main Language(s) of Instruction: French

Degrees and Diplomas: *Diplôme d'Ingénieur de Conception*; *Master*

Student Services: Cultural Activities, Language Laboratory, Sports Facilities

Last Updated: 20/09/12

NATIONAL INSTITUTE OF YOUTH AND SPORT

Institut national de la Jeunesse et des Sports (INJS)
BP 1016, Yaoundé, Centre
Tel: +237 22 23 08 35
EMail: infos@injs-yaounde.org
Website: http://injs-yaounde.org/

Directeur: Daniel Ngoa Nguele

Division

Animation Science and Techniques (Leisure Studies); **Physical and Sport Sciences and Techniques** (Physical Education; Sports); **Specialized Studies** (Special Education)

Department

Administration and Management (Administration; Management); **Andragogy**; **Educational Technology** (Educational Technology); **Physical Education** (Physical Education); **Psychopedagogy** (Pedagogy; Psychology); **Recreation** (Leisure Studies); **Sports Education** (Sports)

Research Centre

Adult Education (Adult Education); **High Level Sports** (Sports); **Sports Medicine** (Sports Medicine)

History: Founded 1960.

Main Language(s) of Instruction: French

Accrediting Agency: Ministère des Sports et de l'Education Physique

Degrees and Diplomas: *Master*. Also Diplôme de Conseiller Principal de Jeunesse et d'Animation (DCPJA); Diplôme de Conseiller de Jeunesse et d'Animation (DCJA); Certificat d'aptitude au Professorat d'Education Physique et Sportive I (CAPEPS I); Certificat d'aptitude au Professorat d'Education Physique et Sportive II (CAPEPS II)

Student Services: Sports Facilities

Last Updated: 20/09/12

NATIONAL SCHOOL OF ADMINISTRATION AND MAGISTRACY

Ecole nationale d'Administration et de Magistrature (ENAM)
BP 7171, Yaoundé, Centre
Tel: +237 2222 91 95
Fax: +237 2222 92 13
EMail: infos@enam.cm
Website: http://www.enam.cm

Directeur Général: Linus Toussaint Mendjana (2012-)
Tel: +237 2222 08 13

Division

Administration (Administration; Labour and Industrial Relations; Social Welfare); **Finance** (Accountancy; Finance; Taxation); **Information and Communications Technology** (Communication Studies; Information Technology); **Legal Administration** (Justice Administration)

Centre

Research and Documentation (Documentation Techniques; Library Science)

History: Founded 1959. Acquired present status 1995. Its mission is to train top-ranking civil servants and carry out applied research in order to develop government services and the judiciary.

Admission Requirements: Secondary school certificate (baccalauréat) or equivalent and competitive entrance examination for Brevet; Undergraduate degree for Diploma course; Master's degree in Magistracy for Legal Administration

Fees: (CFA Francs): 120,000 per annum

Main Language(s) of Instruction: French, English

Accrediting Agency: Ministry of Public Service and Administrative Reform

Degrees and Diplomas: Brevet de l'ENAM (1 yr), Diplôme de l'ENAM (2 yrs)

Student Services: Academic Counselling, Canteen, Careers Guidance, Health Services, Language Laboratory, Social Counselling, Sports Facilities

Publications: Journal de l'ENAM

Last Updated: 20/09/12

NATIONAL SCHOOL OF PUBLIC WORKS

Ecole nationale supérieure des Travaux publics (ENSTP)
BP 510, Yaoundé, Centre 510
Tel: +237 2223-09-44
Fax: +237 2222-18-16
Website: http://www.enstp.cm

Directeur: George Elambo Nkeng (2000-)
EMail: gnkeng@yahoo.com

Directeur Adjoint: Jean-Pierre Mebenga
EMail: jeanpierre_mebenga@yahoo.fr

International Relations: Roger Blaise Limaleba, Chef de la cellule de Coopération, des Stages et des Évaluations
EMail: rlimaleba@yahoo.fr

Department

Civil Engineering (Civil Engineering); **Rural Engineering** (Rural Planning); **Surveying** (Surveying and Mapping); **Urban Planning** (Town Planning)

History: Founded 1970 as Ecole Nationale de Technologie (ENAT). Acquired present title and status 1982.

Academic Year: Oct to March; April to Sept

Admission Requirements: Baccalauréats scientifiques et techniques/Secondary school certificate (GCE Advanced Level)

Fees: 235,000 per annum, Ingénieur; 185,000 per annum, Technicien supérieur; 900,000 per annum, Master (CFA Franc BEAC)

Main Language(s) of Instruction: French, English

Accrediting Agency: Ministère des Travaux Publics

Degrees and Diplomas: *Brevet de Technicien Supérieur*; *Diplôme d'Ingénieur de Conception*; *Master*. Diplôme d'Ingénieur des Travaux: Civil Engineering; Rural Engineering; Surveying; Town Planning (3 yrs); Diplôme d'Ingénieur Manager (2 yrs)

Student Services: Academic Counselling, Health Services, Language Laboratory, Social Counselling, Sports Facilities

Academic Staff *2012-2013*	**TOTAL**
FULL-TIME	**50**
PART-TIME	**20**
STAFF WITH DOCTORATE	
FULL-TIME	**15**
Student Numbers *2012-2013*	
All (Foreign included)	**1,115**
FOREIGN ONLY	**15**

Distance students, 325.

Last Updated: 22/11/13

UNIVERSITY OF BUEA (UB)

PO Box 63, Buéa, South West Province
Tel: +237 33 32 21 34
Fax: +237 33 32 27 60
Website: http://www.ubuea.net/

Vice-Chancellor: Pauline Nalova Lyonga Egbe (2012-)
Tel: +237 33 32 27 06

Registrar: Samson N. Abangma

International Relations: Victor Julius Ngoh, Deputy Vice-Chancellor, Research and Cooperation EMail: ngohvictor@hotmail.com

Faculty

Arts (English; French; History; Linguistics; Performing Arts); **Education** (Curriculum; Education; Educational Administration; Educational Psychology); **Health Sciences** (Health Sciences; Laboratory Techniques; Medicine; Nursing; Surgery); **Science** (Biochemistry; Botany; Chemistry; Environmental Studies; Geology; Mathematics; Microbiology; Physics; Zoology); **Social and Management Sciences** (Accountancy; Anthropology; Banking; Economics; Finance; Gender Studies; Geography; Journalism; Law; Management; Mass Communication; Political Sciences; Sociology; Women's Studies)

School

Translation and Interpretation *(ASTI)* (Translation and Interpretation)

History: Founded 1985 as University Centre of Buea. Acquired present status and title 1993.

Academic Year: October to July (October-February; March-July)

Admission Requirements: Secondary school certificate and competitive entrance examination. Bachelor's Degree or recognized equivalent for School of Translation and Interpretation

Main Language(s) of Instruction: English

Accrediting Agency: Ministère de l'Enseignement Supérieur

Degrees and Diplomas: *Bachelor's Degree/Licence*: **Fine Arts; Gender Studies; Law; Medical Technology; Medicine; Nursing; Surgery; Women's Studies.** *Master*: **Fine Arts.** *Doctor of Philosophy/Doctorat*: **Economics; Law; Linguistics.**

Student Services: Academic Counselling, Canteen, Health Services, Language Laboratory, Social Counselling, Sports Facilities

Publications: Epasa Moto; Journal of Applied Social Sciences

Last Updated: 03/09/12

UNIVERSITY OF DOUALA

Université de Douala (UDLA)

BP 2701, Douala, Littoral
Tel: +237 33 40 11 26
Fax: +237 33 40 11 26
EMail: infos.udla@univ-douala.com
Website: http://www.univ-douala.com

Recteur: François-Xavier Etoa (2015-)

International Relations: Hélène Ntone Kouo, Vice-Recteur chargé de la Recherche et des Relations avec le Monde des Entreprises

Faculty

Arts and Humanities *(FLSH)* (African Languages; African Studies; Arts and Humanities; Bilingual and Bicultural Education; English; French; German; History; Literature; Philosophy; Spanish); **Economics and Applied Management** *(FSEGA)* (Econometrics; Economic and Finance Policy; Economics; Finance; Management; Marketing; Mathematics); **Industrial Engineering** *(FGI)* (Industrial Engineering); **Law and Political Science** *(FSJP)* (Law; Political Sciences; Private Law; Public Law); **Medicine and Pharmacy** *(FMSP)* (Biochemistry; Biology; Medicine; Pharmacy; Sports); **Science** *(FS)* (Biology; Chemistry; Computer Science; Mathematics; Natural Sciences; Physics)

School

Economics and Commerce *(ESSEC, Advanced Studies)* (Business and Commerce; Economics); **Teacher Training in Technical Education** *(ENSET, Advanced Studies)* (Teacher Trainers Education; Technology Education)

Institute

Fine Arts *(IBA)* (Fine Arts); **Fisheries Science** *(ISH)* (Fishery); **Technology** *(IUT)* (Accountancy; Biology; Business Administration; Business and Commerce; Civil Engineering; Computer Science; Electrical and Electronic Engineering; Industrial Engineering; Secretarial Studies; Telecommunications Engineering)

History: Founded 1977 as Centre Universitaire. Previously part of the University of Yaoundé. Acquired present status and title 1993.

Academic Year: October to July (October-December; January-March; April-July)

Admission Requirements: Competitive entrance examination following secondary school certificate (baccalauréat)

Fees: (CFA Francs): c. 50,000 per annnum; foreign students, c. 300,000-1m

Main Language(s) of Instruction: French, English

Accrediting Agency: Ministère de l'Enseignement Supérieur

Degrees and Diplomas: *Brevet de Technicien Supérieur*; *Diplôme universitaire de Technologie*; *Bachelor's Degree/Licence*; *Docteur en Médecine*: **Medicine; Pharmacy.** *Master*: **Economics; Fine Arts; Law; Management; Political Sciences.** *Doctor of Philosophy/Doctorat*: **Administration; African Languages; Bioengineering; Communication Studies; Comparative Literature; Economics; English; French; Geography; German; History; Industrial Engineering; Philosophy; Physics; Political Sciences; Private Law; Public Law; Sociology; Spanish.**

Student Services: Academic Counselling, Canteen, Cultural Activities, Health Services, Social Counselling, Sports Facilities

Last Updated: 03/09/12

UNIVERSITY OF DSCHANG

Université de Dschang (UDS)

BP 96, Dschang, West
Tel: +237 33 45 13 81
Fax: +237 33 45 13 81
EMail: contact@univ-dschang.org
Website: http://www.univ-dschang.org

Recteur: Roger Tsafack Nanfosso (2015-)
EMail: udsrectorat@univ-dschang.org

Faculty

Agronomy and Agricultural Sciences *(FASA)* (Agricultural Engineering; Agriculture; Animal Husbandry; Biotechnology; Forestry; Rural Studies; Soil Science; Veterinary Science; Water Management; Water Science); **Arts and Humanities** *(FLSH)* (African Studies; Arts and Humanities; French; Geography (Human); German; History; Italian; Linguistics; Philosophy; Psychology; Sociology; Spanish); **Economics and Management** *(FSEG)* (Agricultural Business; Economic and Finance Policy; Economics; Management); **Law and Political Science** *(FSJP)* (Human Rights; Law; Political Sciences; Private Law; Public Law); **Science** *(FS)* (Biochemistry; Chemistry; Earth Sciences; Geology; Mathematics and Computer Science; Natural Sciences; Physics)

Institute

Fine Arts *(Foumban)* (Fine Arts); **Technology** *(IUT Fotso Victor de Bandjoun (Koung-Khi))* (Business and Commerce; Civil Engineering; Computer Engineering; Electrical and Electronic Engineering; Secretarial Studies; Technology)

Further Information: Also in Bambui, Belabo, Ebolowa, Maroua and Nkolbisson.

History: Founded 1977 as Centre Universitaire. Previously part of the University of Yaoundé. Acquired present status and title 1993.

Academic Year: October to July (October-March; March-July)

Admission Requirements: Secondary school certificate (baccalauréat), or foreign equivalent at Advanced 'A' level. General Certificate of Education

Fees: (CFA Francs): 50, 000 per annum; Foreign students, 500,000-1m. per annum

Main Language(s) of Instruction: French, English

Accrediting Agency: Ministère de l'Enseignement Supérieur

Degrees and Diplomas: *Brevet de Technicien Supérieur*; *Diplôme universitaire de Technologie*: **Agriculture.** *Bachelor's Degree/Licence*; *Master*: **Economics; Law; Literature.** *Doctor of Philosophy/Doctorat*: **Agronomy.**

Student Services: Academic Counselling, Canteen, Careers Guidance, Cultural Activities, Facilities for disabled people, Health Services, Language Laboratory, Sports Facilities

Publications: Jeune Afrique Economique; Le Flamboyant

Last Updated: 03/09/12

UNIVERSITY OF MAROUA

Université de Maroua (UMA)

Diamaré, Extrème-Nord
Tel: 237 7726 29 57
Website: http://www.citi.cm/maroua

Recteur: Edward Oben Ako (2008-)

Secrétaire Général: Halidou Mohamadou

School

Advanced Teacher Training *(ENS)* (Arabic; Chemistry; Chinese; Computer Science; Earth Sciences; Educational Sciences; English Studies; French Studies; Geography; German; History; Italian; Literature; Mathematics; Nautical Science; Philosophy; Physics; Spanish)

Higher Institute

Sahel *(ISS)* (Agriculture; Architecture; Building Technologies; Cattle Breeding; Computer Networks; Energy Engineering; Environmental Studies; Fine Arts; Heritage Preservation; Social Sciences; Textile Technology; Water Management)

History: Founded 2008.

Main Language(s) of Instruction: French

Accrediting Agency: Ministère de l'Enseignement Supérieur

Degrees and Diplomas: *Bachelor's Degree/Licence*; *Docteur en Médecine*; *Master*

Student Services: Canteen, Health Services, Sports Facilities

Last Updated: 21/09/12

UNIVERSITY OF NGAOUNDÉRÉ

Université de Ngaoundéré (UNDERE)

BP 454, Ngaoundéré, Adamaoua

Tel: +237 22 19 01 95

Fax: +237 22 25 40 01

Website: http://www.univ-ndere.cm/

Recteur: Paul Henri Amvam Zollo (2003-)

EMail: phamvam@yahoo.fr

Secrétaire Général: Rémy Sylvestre Bouelet Ivaha Mbembe

Faculty

Arts and Humanities *(FALSH)* (African Studies; Anthropology; Arts and Humanities; Cultural Studies; Demography and Population; Development Studies; Environmental Studies; Geography (Human); History; International Relations; Literature; Modern Languages; Museum Studies; Psychology; Regional Planning; Social Sciences; Social Studies; Sociology; Tourism; Town Planning; Translation and Interpretation); **Economics and Management** *(FSEG)* (Accountancy; Banking; Economics; Finance; Human Resources; Insurance; International Economics; Management; Marketing); **Law and Political Science** *(FSJP)* (Commercial Law; Economic and Finance Policy; Finance; International Law; International Relations; Law; Political Sciences; Private Law; Public Law); **Science** *(FS)* (Biological and Life Sciences; Biology; Biomedicine; Chemistry; Civil Engineering; Earth Sciences; Electrical Engineering; Environmental Studies; Food Science; Geology; Mathematics and Computer Science; Mechanical Engineering; Medicine; Mining Engineering; Natural Sciences; Nutrition; Pharmacy; Physics)

School

Agro-Industry *(ESAI)* (Agronomy; Food Science; Food Technology; Industrial Chemistry; Nutrition); **Geology and Mining Prospecting** *(EGEM)* (Geology; Mining Engineering; Petroleum and Gas Engineering); **Veterinary Medicine and Animal Science** *(ESMV)* (Anatomy; Animal Husbandry; Histology; Microbiology; Parasitology; Pathology; Pharmacy; Physiology; Veterinary Science)

Institute

Technology *(IUT)* (Computer Science; Electrical and Electronic Engineering; Food Technology; Heating and Refrigeration; Maintenance Technology; Mechanical Engineering; Technology)

Centre

Information and Communications Technologies (Communication Studies; Information Technology)

History: Founded 1977 as Centre Universitaire, acquired present status and title 1993. A State Institution.

Academic Year: October to July (October-February; March-July)

Admission Requirements: Secondary school certificate (baccalauréat), or foreign equivalent at Advanced ('A') level

Fees: (CFA Francs): Foreign students, undergraduate, 300,000-600,000 per annum; postgraduate, 3m.-5m

Main Language(s) of Instruction: French, English

Accrediting Agency: Ministère de l'Enseignement Supérieur

Degrees and Diplomas: *Diplôme universitaire de Technologie*: **Biology; Chemistry; Computer Engineering; Industrial Maintenance.** *Bachelor's Degree/Licence*: **Arts and Humanities; Economics; Food Science; Law; Management; Political Sciences.** *Diplôme d'Ingénieur de Conception*: **Animal Husbandry; Food Technology; Veterinary Science.** *Master*: **Arts and Humanities; Economics; Food Science; Law; Management; Political Sciences.** *Doctor of Philosophy/Doctorat*: **Arts and Humanities; Food Science; Geography; Management.**

Student Services: Academic Counselling, Canteen, Health Services, Social Counselling, Sports Facilities

Publications: Annales de la FALSH

Last Updated: 20/09/12

UNIVERSITY OF YAOUNDÉ I

Université de Yaoundé I (UY I)

BP 337, Yaoundé, Centre

Tel: +237 22 22 13 20

EMail: cuti@uy1.uninet.cm

Website: http://www.uy1.uninet.cm/

Recteur: Maurice Aurélien Sosso (2012-)

EMail: sossomaurice@yahoo.fr

Secrétaire général: Jean-Emmanuel Pondi

Tel: +237 2222-15-23 EMail: jepondi2009@yahoo.fr

International Relations: Emmanuel Tonye, Vice-recteur, Recherche, Coopération, et Relations avec le Monde des Entreprises EMail: tonyee@hotmail.com

Faculty

Arts, Letters and Social Sciences *(FALSH)* (African Languages; African Studies; Anthropology; Archaeology; Art History; Arts and Humanities; Behavioural Sciences; English; Fine Arts; French; Geography (Human); German; History; Italian; Linguistics; Performing Arts; Philosophy; Psychology; Sociology; Spanish); **Medicines and Biomedical Studies** *(FSMB)* (Alternative Medicine; Anaesthesiology; Anatomy; Biochemistry; Biology; Biomedicine; Cardiology; Dentistry; Dermatology; Diabetology; Endocrinology; Epidemiology; Forensic Medicine and Dentistry; Gastroenterology; Gerontology; Gynaecology and Obstetrics; Haematology; Health Administration; Hepatology; Medical Auxiliaries; Medical Parasitology; Medical Technology; Medicine; Microbiology; Midwifery; Nephrology; Neurology; Oncology; Ophthalmology; Optometry; Orthopaedics; Otorhinolaryngology; Paediatrics; Parasitology; Pathology; Pharmacology; Pharmacy; Physiology; Plastic Surgery; Pneumology; Podiatry; Psychiatry and Mental Health; Public Health; Radiology; Rehabilitation and Therapy; Rheumatology; Surgery; Tropical Medicine; Urology; Venereology; Virology); **Science** *(FS)* (Agrobiology; Applied Chemistry; Applied Physics; Biochemistry; Biology; Botany; Computer Science; Earth Sciences; Ecology; Environmental Management; Geology; Inorganic Chemistry; Mathematics; Multimedia; Natural Resources; Natural Sciences; Organic Chemistry; Parasitology; Pest Management; Petrology; Physics; Physiology; Plant and Crop Protection; Seismology; Statistics; Waste Management; Wildlife; Zoology)

School

Polytechnic *(Ecole Nationale Supérieure Polytechnique (ENSP))* (Chemistry; Civil Engineering; Computer Engineering; Electrical Engineering; Engineering; Industrial Engineering; Mathematics; Mechanical Engineering; Technology; Telecommunications Engineering; Urban Studies); **Teacher Training** *(Ecole normale supérieure (ENS))* (Biology; Chemistry; Economics; Education; Educational Sciences; English; Foreign Languages Education; French; Geography; Geology; History; Mathematics Education; Philosophy; Physics; Secondary Education; Teacher Training)

Centre

Biotechnology (Biotechnology); **Information Technology** (Information Technology)

Further Information: School of Distance Learning (Virtual University)

History: Founded 1962, replacing the Institut national d'Etudes supérieures, founded 1961. Acquired present status and title 1993. A State institution.

Academic Year: October to August (October-February; March-August)

Admission Requirements: Secondary school certificate (baccalauréat) or foreign equivalent, and entrance examination (for Teacher Training, Medicine and Engineering)

Fees: (CFA Francs): 50,000 per annum; foreign students, 600,000 per annum for Science and Technology; 300,000 for foreign students in Arts and Education

Main Language(s) of Instruction: French, English

Accrediting Agency: Ministère de l'Enseignement Supérieur

Degrees and Diplomas: *Bachelor's Degree/Licence*: **Arts and Humanities; Economics; Law.** *Diplôme d'Ingénieur de Conception*: **Engineering.** *Docteur en Médecine*: **Medicine.** *Master, Doctor of Philosophy/Doctorat*

Student Services: Academic Counselling, Canteen, Cultural Activities, Facilities for disabled people, Health Services, Language Laboratory, Nursery Care, Social Counselling, Sports Facilities

Publications: Annales de la FALSH; Annales de la FS

Academic Staff *2011/2012*	MEN	WOMEN	TOTAL
FULL-TIME	789	483	**1,272**
PART-TIME	61	33	**94**
STAFF WITH DOCTORATE			
FULL-TIME	510	209	**719**
Student Numbers *2011-2012*			
All (Foreign included)	22,560	25,720	**48,280**

Last Updated: 06/08/12

UNIVERSITY OF YAOUNDÉ II

Université de Yaoundé II (UY II)
B.P. 1365, Yaoundé, Centre
Tel: +237 2219 30 41
Fax: +237 7799 14 23
EMail: contact@universite-yde2.org
Website: http://www.universite-yde2.org/

Recteur: Ibrahima Adamou (2015-)

Secrétaire générale: Lisette Elomo Ntonga
Tel: +237 2219 30 42
EMail: lisette.elomo-ntonga@universite-yde2.org

International Relations: Mol Nang, Vice-recteur, Recherche, de la Coopération et des Relations avec le monde des entreprises

Faculty

Economics and Management *(FSEG)* (Economics; Management); **Law and Political Science** *(FSJP)* (Law; Political Sciences)

Higher School

Information and Communication Technologies *(ESSTIC)* (Information Sciences; Journalism; Mass Communication; Radio and Television Broadcasting)

Institute

Demographic Training and Research *(IFORD)* (Demography and Population); **International Relations** *(IRIC)* (Banking; Finance; International Relations; Marketing)

Further Information: Also campus in Soa

History: Founded 1993.

Academic Year: October to July (October-December; January-March; April-July)

Admission Requirements: Secondary school certificate (baccalauréat) or foreign equivalent, and entrance examination

Main Language(s) of Instruction: French, English

Accrediting Agency: Ministère de l'Enseignement Supérieur

Degrees and Diplomas: *Diplôme universitaire de Technologie*: **Information Technology; Journalism.** *Bachelor's Degree/Licence*: **Economics; Law.** *Master*: **Economics; International Relations; Law.** *Doctor of Philosophy/Doctorat*: **International Relations; Law.**

Student Services: Canteen, Careers Guidance, Health Services, Social Counselling, Sports Facilities

Last Updated: 20/09/12

PRIVATE INSTITUTIONS

ADVANCED INSTITUTE OF MANAGEMENT

Institut supérieur de Management (ISMA)
BP 5739, Douala, Littoral
Tel: +237 3343-12-51
Fax: +237 3343-12-59
EMail: isma@ismacameroun.com
Website: http://www.ismacameroun.com/

Président Directeur Général: Bob Ngamoe
EMail: ngamoeb@yahoo.fr

Programme

Commerce (Business and Commerce); **Management** (Management)

History: Founded 1998.

Main Language(s) of Instruction: French

Degrees and Diplomas: *Brevet de Technicien Supérieur*; *Bachelor's Degree/Licence*; *Master*

Last Updated: 01/08/12

CATHOLIC UNIVERSITY OF CENTRAL AFRICA

Université catholique d'Afrique Centrale (UCAC)
BP 11628, Yaoundé, Centre
Tel: +237 22 23 74 00
Fax: +237 22 23 74 02
Website: http://www.apdhac.org/ucac.html

Recteur: Christian Mofor (2005-)
Tel: +237 2223 74 01
EMail: recteuruca@camnet.cm; recteur@uca.ac

Vice-recteur: Richard Filakota

Faculty

Philosophy (Philosophy); **Social Sciences and Management** (Accountancy; Computer Science; Economics; Law; Management; Political Sciences; Social Sciences); **Theology** (Theology)

School

Nursing (Nursing)

Department

Canon Law (Canon Law)

Higher Institute

Technology *(IST/Pointe-Noire (Congo))* (Industrial Maintenance)

Research Group

Artificial Intelligence and Management Sciences *(GRIAGES)* (Artificial Intelligence; Management); **Business and Culture** *(GREC)* (Business Administration; Cultural Studies)

Further Information: Also in Douala and Pointe-Noire (Congo)

History: Founded 1989, opened 1991.

Academic Year: October to June (October-February; March-June)

Admission Requirements: Secondary school certificate (baccalauréat), or foreign equivalent

Main Language(s) of Instruction: French

Degrees and Diplomas: *Brevet de Technicien Supérieur*: **Industrial Maintenance.** *Diplôme universitaire de Technologie*: **Business and Commerce; Marketing.** *Bachelor's Degree/Licence*: **Business Administration; Business and Commerce; Human Resources; Law; Management; Philosophy.** *Diplôme d'Ingénieur de Conception*: **Industrial Maintenance.** *Master*: **Accountancy; Anthropology; Business and Commerce; Canon Law; Finance; Human Rights; International Relations; Theology.** *Doctor of Philosophy/Doctorat*: **Human Rights.**

Student Services: Academic Counselling, Canteen, Health Services, Social Counselling, Sports Facilities

Publications: Cahiers de l'UCAC

Publishing House: Presses de l'UCAC (PUCAC)

Last Updated: 03/09/12

COSENDAI ADVENTIST UNIVERSITY

Université Adventiste Cosendai
BP 04, Nanga-Eboko, Centre
Tel: +237 77 39 89 88
EMail: contact@uacosendai-edu.net
Website: http://www.uacosendai-edu.net/

Rector: Joseph I. Masinda
Tel: +237 7755-95-54 EMail: cosendai_rectorat@yahoo.fr

Faculty

Educational Sciences (Educational Sciences); **Health Sciences** (Health Sciences); **Management and Computer Science** (Computer Science; Management); **Theology** (Theology)

History: Founded in 1996. Acquired present status 2002.

Admission Requirements: Baccalauréat

Main Language(s) of Instruction: French, English

Accrediting Agency: Ministry of Higher Education; Adventist Accrediting Association

Degrees and Diplomas: *Bachelor's Degree/Licence*: **Business Administration; Computer Science; Educational Sciences; Nursing; Theology.**

Student Services: Academic Counselling, Canteen, Careers Guidance, Health Services, Nursery Care, Sports Facilities

Last Updated: 03/09/12

HIGHER INSTITUTE OF TECHNOLOGY AND INDUSTRIAL DESIGN

Institut supérieur des Technologies et du Design Industriel (ISTDI)

BP 3001, Douala, Littoral
Tel: +237 3300-13-92
Fax: +237 3347-33-55
EMail: istdi@yahoo.fr
Website: http://www.istdi.net

Président: Paul Guimezap (2001-)
Tel: +237 9991-92-91 EMail: guimezapp@yahoo.fr

Secrétaire Général: Cyrille Meukaleuni
Tel: +237 5524-68-92 EMail: meukaleuni@yahoo.fr

International Relations: Martine Guimezap, Attachée de direction
Tel: +237 9968-21-60 EMail: guimemart@yahoo.fr

Programme

Business and Commerce and Management; **Engineering**; **Industrial Design** (Industrial Design; Wood Technology); **Technology** (Information Technology)

History: Founded 2001.

Admission Requirements: Secondary school certificate (baccalauréat) and entrance examination

Fees: (CFA Francs): from 425,000 to 1,235,000

Main Language(s) of Instruction: French

Accrediting Agency: Ministère de l'Enseignement Supérieur

Degrees and Diplomas: *Brevet de Technicien Supérieur*, *Bachelor's Degree/Licence*; *Master*

Student Services: Academic Counselling, Canteen, Careers Guidance, Foreign Studies Centre, Language Laboratory, Sports Facilities

Last Updated: 27/07/12

HIGHER SCHOOL OF SCIENCE AND TECHNIQUES

Ecole supérieure des Sciences et Techniques (ESSET)

Ndogbong - BP 13244, Douala, Littoral
Tel: +237 33 43 38 93
EMail: esset.douala@camnet.cm

Directeur: Robert Womonou

School

Commerce and Management (Accountancy; Business Administration; Business Computing; Insurance; International Business; Secretarial Studies); **Industry and Technology** (Electrical Engineering; Electronic Engineering; Industrial Engineering; Maintenance Technology; Technology)

History: Founded 1997. Acquired present status 2002.

Admission Requirements: Baccalauréat

Fees: (CFA Francs): 260,000-1,500,000 per annum

Main Language(s) of Instruction: French and English

Degrees and Diplomas: *Brevet de Technicien Supérieur*, *Bachelor's Degree/Licence*; *Diplôme d'Ingénieur de Conception*; *Master*. Also Mastère spécialisé

Student Services: Academic Counselling, Canteen, Careers Guidance, Foreign Studies Centre, Health Services, Language Laboratory, Sports Facilities

Last Updated: 27/07/12

HIGHER SIANTOU INSTITUTE

Institut Siantou Supérieur (ISS)

BP 04, Yaoundé, Centre
Tel: +237 2230-62-71
EMail: vsiantou@yahoo.fr
Website: http://siantou.net/

Président Général: Lucien Wandou Siantou (1991-)
EMail: vsiantou@yahoo.fr

Department

Accountancy (Accountancy); **Banking and Finance** (Banking; Finance); **Communication** (Communication Studies; Journalism; Photography); **Computer Engineering** (Computer Engineering); **French Studies** (French Studies); **Hotel Management** (Hotel Management); **Insurance** (Insurance); **Law** (Law); **Marketing** (Marketing); **Mathematics** (Mathematics); **Mechanical Engineering** (Mechanical Engineering); **Secretarial Studies** (Secretarial Studies)

Higher Institute

Commerce and Business Administration *(ISCGS)* (Accountancy; Banking; Business Administration; Computer Engineering; Finance; Human Resources); **Technologies** *(ISTS)* (Civil Engineering; Computer Engineering; Mechanics; Telecommunications Engineering)

Further Information: Also in Biteng campus (ISCG, ISTS).

History: Founded 1991.

Academic Year: September to May (September-February; February-May)

Fees: 235,000 per annum, Ingénieurs; 185,000 per annum, Techniciens Supérieurs; 900,000 per annum, Masters (CFA Franc BEAC)

Main Language(s) of Instruction: French, English

Degrees and Diplomas: *Brevet de Technicien Supérieur*, *Bachelor's Degree/Licence*; *Master*. Also Diplôme Supérieur d'Étude Professionnels (D.S.E.P)

Student Services: Canteen, Health Services, Sports Facilities

Last Updated: 01/08/12

PANAFRICAN INSTITUTE FOR DEVELOPMENT IN CENTRAL AFRICA

Institut panafricain pour le Développement en Afrique Centrale (IPD-AC/PAID-CA)

BP 4078, Douala, Littoral
Tel: +237 3340-37-70
Fax: +237 3340-30-68
EMail: ipdac_ong@yahoo.fr; info@ipd-ac.org
Website: http://www.paidafrica.org/ipd-ac/

Directeur: Romuald Pial Mezala (2011-)
Tel: +237(77) 44-16-11 EMail: romuald_pial@hotmail.com

Institute

Panafrican Development (Adult Education; African Studies; Development Studies; Library Science; Natural Resources; Rural Studies)

History: Founded 1965, IPD-AC contributes to the development of regions through training, research and practical action, counselling, publication and institution development.

Academic Year: October to September

Admission Requirements: Secondary school certificate or equivalent

Main Language(s) of Instruction: French

Degrees and Diplomas: *Bachelor's Degree/Licence*: **Development Studies; Environmental Management; Environmental Studies; Natural Resources.** *Master*: **Development Studies; Environmental Studies; Regional Studies.** Also Certificat de fin de Formation, 1-7 months

Student Services: Academic Counselling, Canteen, Health Services, Sports Facilities

Last Updated: 01/08/12

PROTESTANT UNIVERSITY OF CENTRAL AFRICA

Université protestante d'Afrique Centrale (UPAC)
BP 4011, Yaoundé, Centre
Tel: +237 22 21 26 90
Fax: +237 22 20 53 24
EMail: rectorat@upac-edu.org
Website: http://www.upac-edu.org

Rector: Timothée Bouba Mbima (2012-)
Tel: +237 7774-54-46 EMail: rectorat@upac-edu.org

Secrétaire Général: Maurice Kouam EMail: sg@upac-edu.org

Faculty

Information and Communication Technology *(FTIC)* (Communication Studies; Information Technology); **Medicine and Human Welfare** *(FMBEH)* (Medicine); **Protestant Theology and Religious Sciences** *(FTPSR)* (Protestant Theology; Religious Studies); **Social Sciences and International Relations** *(FSSRI)* (International Relations; Social Sciences)

History: Founded 1962. Previously known as Faculté de Théologie protestante de Yaoundé (Faculty of Protestant Theology). Acquired present status 2007.

Admission Requirements: Baccalauréat; Licence

Main Language(s) of Instruction: French

Accrediting Agency: Ministère de l'Enseignement Supérieur

Degrees and Diplomas: *Bachelor's Degree/Licence*: **Development Studies; Peace and Disarmament; Theology.** *Master*: **Development Studies; Peace and Disarmament; Theology.** *Doctor of Philosophy/Doctorat*: **Theology.**

Student Services: Academic Counselling, Canteen, Careers Guidance, Health Services, Sports Facilities
Last Updated: 03/09/12

SAINT MONICA UNIVERSITY

PO Box 132, Buea, SW
Tel: +237(669) 999-801
EMail: contact@stmonicauniversity.com
Website: http://www.smuedu.org

President: Januarius Jingwa Asongu (2013-)
EMail: asongu@stmonicauniversity.com

International Relations: Joseph Forsuh Nfor Muyamah, Director of International Education
EMail: international@stmonicauniversity.com

School

Arts, Education and Humanities (Arts and Humanities; Education); **Business and Public Policy** (Business Administration; Public Administration); **Health and Human Services** (Medical Auxiliaries; Medical Technology; Nursing); **Science, Engineering and Technology** (Agriculture; Engineering; Technology)

History: Created 2009. Acquired current title and status 2012.

Accrediting Agency: Ministère de l'Enseignement Supérieur/Ministry of Higher Education

Degrees and Diplomas: *Bachelor's Degree/Licence*; *Master*; *Doctor of Philosophy/Doctorat*: **Business Administration; Education; Philosophy; Public Administration; Public Health; Theology.**

Academic Staff *2015-2016*	**TOTAL**
FULL-TIME	**56**
PART-TIME	**41**
Student Numbers *2015-2016*	
All (Foreign included)	**904**

Last Updated: 18/12/15

UNIVERSITY COLLEGE OF TECHNOLOGY BUEA (UCT)

PMB 63, Buéa, South West Region
Tel: +237 33 09 36 78
Fax: +237 33 35 11 77
EMail: info@uctbuea.cm
Website: http://www.uctbuea.cm/

President: Ebot Ntui Ogork (2004-)
EMail: cobmate@gmail.com

Registrar: Paul Arrey Abunaw
Tel: +237 33 00 97 21 EMail: registrar@uctbuea.com

International Relations: Eric Kami
EMail: international@uctbuea.com

School

Business Computing and Contemporary Management (Actuarial Science; Agricultural Engineering; Banking; Business Administration; Economics; Environmental Management; Film; Finance; Insurance; International Relations; Management; Marketing; Mass Communication; Public Administration; Tourism; Transport Management); **Engineering & Technology** (Architectural and Environmental Design; Civil Engineering; Computer Engineering; Electrical and Electronic Engineering; Energy Engineering; Industrial Engineering; Mechanical Engineering; Petroleum and Gas Engineering)

Institute

Professional Training

Higher Institute

Technology

History: Created 2004. Acquired current status 2008.

Academic Year: October to July

Fees: (CFA Francs): 300,000 - 400,000

Main Language(s) of Instruction: English

Accrediting Agency: Ministry of Higher Education

Degrees and Diplomas: *Bachelor's Degree/Licence*: **Engineering; Technology.** *Master*. Also Advanced Professional Diploma (1 yr) and Higher Professional Diploma (2 yrs)

Student Services: Academic Counselling, Canteen, Careers Guidance, Foreign Studies Centre, Health Services, Language Laboratory, Social Counselling, Sports Facilities
Last Updated: 01/08/12

UNIVERSITY INSTITUTE OF GULF

Institut Universitaire du Golfe (ESG-ISTA-ISA) (IUG)
BP 12 489, Douala, Littoral
Tel: +237 3337-50-58
Fax: +237 3342-89-02
EMail: info@esg-ista-isa-univ.com
Website: http://www.iug-univ.com

Directeur général: Louis-Marie Djambou
Tel: +237 3343-04-52 EMail: lmdacf@yahoo.fr

Directeur des Affaires Administratives et Financières: Marie Rolette Wako EMail: desiree200570@yahoo.fr

International Relations: Emile Kemassi, Directeur de l'Académie de la recherche et de la Coopération
Tel: +237 9989 52 17 EMail: edkemasi@yahoo.fr

School

Management *(ESG (Ecole Supérieur de Gestion))* (Accountancy; Banking; Business and Commerce; Business Computing; Communication Studies; Human Resources; International Business; Management; Secretarial Studies; Transport Management)

Institute

Health Sciences *(ISA (Institut Supérieur des Sciences Appliquées))* (Biomedicine; Health Sciences; Nursing; Physical Therapy); **Industry and Technology** *(ISTA (Institut Supérieur des Technologies Avancées)* (Automotive Engineering; Computer Engineering; Electronic Engineering; Heating and Refrigeration; Industrial Engineering; Industrial Maintenance; Technology; Telecommunications Engineering)

History: Founded 1993 as Ecole supérieure de Gestion (ESG). Acquired present title 2011 by merging of ESG, ISTA (Institut Supérieur des Technologies Avancées) and ISA (Institut Supérieur des Sciences Appliquées).

Academic Year: September-July

Admission Requirements: Baccalauréat; General Certificate Education; Advanced Level

Fees: 250,000-400,000 (depending on degrees) (CFA Franc BEAC)

Main Language(s) of Instruction: French, English

Degrees and Diplomas: *Brevet de Technicien Supérieur*; *Bachelor's Degree/Licence*; *Master*. Also High National Diploma (HDN) 2yrs; Diplôme Supérieur d'Etudes Professionnelles (DSEP) 2 yrs

Student Services: Academic Counselling, Canteen, Careers Guidance, Cultural Activities, Facilities for disabled people, Foreign Studies Centre, Health Services, Language Laboratory, Nursery Care, Social Counselling, Sports Facilities

Academic Staff *2011-2012*	MEN	WOMEN	TOTAL
FULL-TIME	24	6	**30**
PART-TIME	114	26	**140**
STAFF WITH DOCTORATE			
FULL-TIME	3	–	**3**
Student Numbers *2011-2012*			
All (Foreign included)	3,025	2,475	**5,500**
FOREIGN ONLY	8	24	**32**

Last Updated: 29/06/12

Canada

STRUCTURE OF HIGHER EDUCATION SYSTEM

Description:

In Canada, education is the responsibility of each province and territory. For specific information about each provincial and territorial education system, consult CICIC's Web site at [http://education.cicic.ca] or the WHED profile of the province or territory of Canada.

The Council of Ministers of Education, Canada (CMEC), is an intergovernmental body founded in 1967 by ministers of education and provides leadership in education at the pan-Canadian and international levels and contributes to the exercise of the exclusive jurisdiction of provinces and territories over education. CMEC is governed by the Agreed Memorandum on a Council of Ministers of Education, Canada, approved by all members. All 13 provinces and territories are members. You will find the names of the ministries/departments responsible for education in the provinces and territories of Canada at [http://cicic.ca/1301/Ministries-Departments-responsible-for-education-in-Canada/index.canada].

ADMISSION TO HIGHER EDUCATION

Foreign students admission:

Definition of foreign student: Foreign (international) students are students who are neither Canadian citizens nor permanent residents of Canada, and are enrolled full time in a recognized academic, professional or vocational training course of study at a university, college or other educational institution in Canada.

Admission requirements: Each institution may vary in its international admission requirements. Institutions may require the following documentation: official academic transcripts (some institutions may require them to be translated into English or French), proof of your country's equivalent of a Canadian secondary school or high school education, and completion of English or French Language requirements as requested by the institution.

Entry regulations: Before you come to study in Canada, you will need: a "Study Permit" if the programme of study you will be admitted to is longer than six months in duration, regardless of the length of your stay in Canada; a letter of acceptance from the school of your choice; proof that you have enough money to pay for school fees, living expenses and return transportation for yourself and any family members who come with you to Canada; to establish that you will return home at the end of your studies; to pass a medical exam if required; to be a law abiding citizen with no criminal record and not be a risk to the security of Canada and to qualify as a temporary resident in Canada, including holding a temporary resident visa (required for citizens of many countries). A small number of students do not require a Study Permit by virtue of their status in Canada (e.g. diplomats and their children); students should contact the nearest overseas Canadian diplomatic mission to confirm procedures and requirements.

Health requirements: Most education institutions require international students to buy health insurance in addition to their tuition fees; those that do not will require proof of independent health insurance coverage. Medical examinations are not required by institutions but may be required by Citizenship and Immigration Canada (CIC) for students from a number of countries.

Language proficiency: Students must be proficient in English or French. Many universities offer second language upgrading courses.

RECOGNITION OF STUDIES

Quality assurance system:

A brief description of Canada's post-secondary institutions and their quality assurance mechanisms is available at: [http://cicic.ca/1264/An-overview/index.canada] and [http://education.cicic.ca].

Bodies dealing with recognition:

Alliance canadienne des services d'évaluation des diplômes - ACSED (Alliance of Credential Evaluation Services of Canada - ACESC)

Coordonnateur, CICDI/Coordinator, CICIC: Natasha Sawh
Agent d'information/Information Officer: Michael Ringuette
95 St Clair Avenue West, Suite 1106
Toronto M4V 1N6
Tel: +1(416) 962-9725
Fax: +1(416) 962-2800
WWW: http://www.canalliance.org

Centre d'information canadien sur les diplômes internationaux - CICDI (Canadian Information Centre for International Credentials - CICIC)

Coordonnateur, CICDI/Coordinator, CICIC: Natasha Sawh
Agent d'information/Information Officer: Michael Ringuette
95 St Clair Avenue West, Suite 1106
Toronto M4V 1N6
Tel: +1(416) 962-9725
Fax: +1(416) 962-2800
WWW: http://cicic.ca

NATIONAL BODIES

Ministères responsables de l'Education au Canada (Ministries/Departments responsible for Education in Canada)

WWW: http://cicic.ca/1301/Ministries-Departments-responsible-for-education-in-Canada/index.canada

Conseil des Ministres de l'Education (Canada) - CMEC (Council of Ministers of Education, Canada)

directrice générale/Executive Director: Chantal C. Beaulieu
Coordonnatrice, International/Coordinator, International Programmes: Antonella Manca-Mangoff
95 St Clair Avenue West, Suite 1106
Toronto, ON M4V 1N6
Tel: +1(416) 962-8100
Fax: +1(416) 962-2800
EMail: information@cmec.ca
WWW: http://cmec.ca

Bureau canadien de l'Education internationale - BCEI (Canadian Bureau for International Education - CBIE)

President and CEO: Karen McBride
Director, Corporate Affairs: Leah Nord
1550 - 220 Laurier Avenue West
Ottawa, ON K1P 5Z9
Tel: +1(613) 237-4820
Fax: +1(613) 237-1160
EMail: info@cbie.ca
WWW: http://cbie.ca

Association des Registraires des Universités et Collèges du Canada - ARUCC (Association of Registrars of the Universities and Colleges of Canada)

President: Andrew Arida
Secretary-Treasurer: Kam Holland
WWW: http://www.arucc.ca

Association des Universités de l'Atlantique (Association of Atlantic Universities)
President: Ray Ivany
Executive Director: Peter Halpin
Suite 403, 5657 Spring Garden Road
Halifax, Nova Scotia B3J 3R4
Tel: +1(902) 425-4230
Fax: +1(902) 425-4233
EMail: info@atlanticuniversities.ca
WWW: http://atlanticuniversities.ca
Role of national body: Membership organization representing the university communities of New Brunswick, Newfoundland and Labrador, Nova Scotia and Prince Edward Island.

Association des Universités de la Francophonie canadienne - AUFC
Directrice générale: Jocelyne Lalonde
223, rue Main
Ottawa, Ontario K1S 1C4
Tel: +1(613) 244-7837
EMail: info@aufc.ca
WWW: http://www.aufc.ca
Role of national body: Membership organization of French-speaking universities.

Collèges et Instituts Canada - CICan (Colleges and Institutes Canada)
President and CEO: Denise Amyot
701 - 1 Rideau Street
Ottawa, ON K1N 8S7
Tel: +1(613) 746-2222
Fax: +1(613) 746-6721
EMail: info@collegesinstituts.ca
WWW: http://www.collegesinstitutes.ca
Role of national body: Membership organization of Canadian colleges and cegeps (formerly ACCC)

Universités Canada (Universities Canada)
Chairperson: Elizabeth Cannon
President and CEO: Paul Davidson
Director of Research and International Relations: Gail Bowkett
1710-350 Albert Street
Ottawa, ON K1R 1B1
Tel: +1(613) 563-1236
Fax: +1(613) 563-9745
EMail: info@univcan.ca
WWW: http://www.univcan.ca
Role of national body: To foster and promote the interests of higher education and university research.

Polytechnics Canada
Chief Executive Officer: Nobina Robinson
Suite 1410, 130 Albert Street
Ottawa, ON K1P 5G4
Tel: +1(613) 656-1541
Fax: +1(616) 594-2917
EMail: info@polytechnicscanada.ca
WWW: http://www.polytechnicscanada.ca

The U4 League
WWW: http://www.u4league.ca
Role of national body: Acadia, Bishop's, Mount Allison, and St. Francis Xavier universities have formed an alliance called the U4 League. It is a cooperative initiative to promote and extend our common objectives of providing students from across Canada and around the world with a high quality, undergraduate university education in a residential setting.

Université Virtuelle Canadienne - UVC (Canadian Virtual University - CVU)

Tel: +1(780) 421-2540
EMail: info@oui-iohe.org
WWW: http://www.cvu-uvc.ca
Role of national body: Canadian Virtual University (CVU) is an association of public Canadian universities specializing in online and distance education, and collaborating to increase access to quality assured university education.

Data for academic year: 2014-2015
Source: IAU from the Canadian Information Centre for International Credentials (CICIC), a unit of the Council of Ministers of Education, Canada (CMEC), November 2014. Bodies 2016.

Canada - Alberta

STRUCTURE OF HIGHER EDUCATION SYSTEM

Description:

Higher education in Canada is the constitutional responsibility of the provinces. There are several types of institutions providing post secondary education in Alberta.

Stages of studies:

University level first stage: *Baccalaureate degree/First Professional degree*

Bachelor's degree programmes are offered at institutions that have received approval from the ministry responsible for advanced education. Institutions must meet specific quality requirements before they can offer degrees. Approved under graduate degree programmes are currently offered at the University of Alberta, University of Calgary, University of Lethbridge, Athabasca University, Alberta College of Art & Design, Grant MacEwan University, Mount Royal University, NAIT, SAIT, Ambrose University College, Concordia University College of Alberta, The King's University College, St. Mary's University, Canadian University College and one private institution. Most under graduate study leads to a "General" Bachelor's degree or an "Honours" or specialized degree (4 years and prescribed subject concentration). Degrees are normally titled in broad descriptive groups, e.g. Bachelor of Arts (B.A.) and Bachelor of Science (B.Sc.). In addition, there are other professional degree programmes that typically require specific high school prerequisites and four years of study, e.g. Bachelor of Science in Nursing (B.Sc.N.), Bachelor of Commerce (B.Comm.) and Bachelor of Education (B.Ed.). Applied Bachelor's degrees are also offered at 9 public colleges and polytechnical institutions. First- and second-year university transfer courses and programmes are also offered by most public colleges. As well, first professional degree programmes require prerequisite university studies followed by additional years of professional training, e.g. three years for a Juris Doctor (J.D.) and four years for Doctor of Medicine (M.D.) and Doctor of Dental Surgery (D.D.S.) degrees.

University level second stage: *Masters Degree*

The Master's degree normally requires at least two years of study after completion of a Bachelor's degree or equivalent. A Master's degree may bethesis- or course-based, with some professional programmes consisting of nonthesis options. Examples of Masters' degrees include the M.A., M.Sc., M.Ed., and MBA.

University level third stage: *Doctorate Degree*

The Doctoral degree is the highest academic qualification awarded in Alberta; it comprises the third stage of university level studies. This degree normally requires at least 3 to 6 years of study after the Bachelor's degree. The submission and defence of a major thesis (dissertation) are the principal requirements, and supplemental course work is usually required. The degree "Doctor of Philosophy" (Ph.D.) is the designation most commonly used to signify the Doctorate. It is a generic title applicable to degrees in most disciplines (the Doctorate should not be confused with certain first professional degrees, e.g. Doctor of Medicine, Doctor of Dental Surgery).

ADMISSION TO HIGHER EDUCATION

Admission to university-level studies:

Alternatives to credentials: Post secondary institutions and private vocational providers determine specific programme based admission requirements. Admission requirements for mature (adult) students may vary by institution and by programme. Prior learning assessment and recognition (PLAR) may be used to determine credit or advanced standing for specific courses.

Other requirements: Admission averages required to enter an under graduate programme, vary by institution, faculty, and programme. Admission to programmes that have enrolment limits may require competitive marks higher than the minimum admission requirements set out in the academic calendar. Mature applicants who do not meet normal admission requirements may be considered with differing qualifications. Competency in English is required of foreign students. Prospective students should consult the institution(s) of their choice for further details on admission.

Foreign students admission:

Definition of foreign student: Foreign (international) students are students who are neither Canadian citizens nor permanent residents of Canada, andare enrolled full-time in a recognized academic, professional or vocational training, or English as a Second Language programme of study at a university, college or other educational institution in Canada.

Admission requirements: Each institution may vary in its international admission requirements. Contact the International Education or Admissions Office at the institution for specific details. Generally, institutions may require the following documentation: official academic transcripts translated into English (some institutions may require official transcripts be notarized, proof of your country's equivalent of a Canadian secondary school or high school education, and completion of English Language requirements as requested by the institution.

Entry regulations: As of June 1, 2014, Citizenship and Immigration Canada (CIC) implemented new federal regulations regarding study permits for international students. All international students must obtain a study permit for a program that is longer than six months, or for a program shorter than six months if it has an integrated and mandatory work component. Study permits for international students will be granted only for study at Designated Learning Institutions (DLI), with designated education programs or training providers in Canada. To accept and enrol international students, Alberta learning institutions and training providers must be designated eligible by the Ministry of Alberta Innovation and Advanced Education (IAE). In addition; students will require: the letter of introduction that students received from the visa office when their study permit was approved (this letter contains the study permit reference number); a letter of acceptance from the school of your choice (that contains the designated learning institution number); proof that you have enough money to pay for school fees, living expenses and return transportation for yourself and any family members who come with you to Canada; toe stablish that you will return home at the end of your studies; to pass a medical exam if required; to be a law abiding citizen with no criminal record and not be a risk to the security of Canada and to qualify as a temporary resident in Canada, including holding a temporary resident visa (required for citizens of many countries). A small number of students do not require a Study Permit by virtue of their status in Canada (e.g. diplomats and their children); students should contact their home country embassy in Canada to confirm this requirement. See also http://www.cic.gc.ca/english/study/.

Health requirements: Most education institutions require international students to buy health insurance in addition to their tuition fees; those that do not will require proof of independent health insurance coverage. Medical examinations are not required by institutions but may be required by Citizenship and Immigration Canada for students from a number of countries. Those intending to study and reside in Alberta for at least 12 months are eligible for free Alberta Health Care Insurance Plan (AHCIP) coverage for the period of their studies. Coverage begins on the date of arrival in Alberta, provided registration validation requirements are met.

Language proficiency: Each institution's language requirements will vary but most institutions will require students to demonstrate English language proficiency (by presenting specific test results); otherwise students will be required to enrol in an English as a second language course if they have not met specific requirements. Contact the International Education or Admissions Office at the institution for specific details.

RECOGNITION OF STUDIES

Quality assurance system:

Approval of degree programmes under the Post-secondary Learning Act and the Approval of Programmes of Study Regulation follows a two-stage review process once the Minister receives a proposal. Stage 1 is a system coordination review of the proposed programme by the Ministry to make a determination of the need for the programme and how it fits with other programmes currently offered within Alberta's post-secondary system. Stage 2 is a quality review enacted if the Minister forwards the proposal to the Campus Alberta Quality Council. The Campus Alberta Quality Council (CAQC) is an arms-length quality assurance agency that reviews all proposals for new degrees to be offered in Alberta. It also monitors all new degree programmes.

Bodies dealing with recognition:

International Qualifications Assessment Service (IQAS)

9th Floor, 108 Street Building
9942 - 108 Street
Edmonton T5K 2J5
Tel: +1(780) 427-2655
Fax: +1(780) 422-9734
WWW: http://work.alberta.ca/iqas

PROVINCIAL BODIES

Alberta Advanced Education

Minister of Advanced Education: Marlin Schmidt
403 Legislature Building, 10800 - 97 Avenue
Edmonton, AB T5K 2B6
Canada
Tel: +1(780) 427-5777
EMail: studyinalberta.ps@gov.ab.ca
WWW: http://iae.alberta.ca/post-secondary/international

Role of national body: To provide the leadership, services and coordination necessary for the efficient development and functioning of an effective and responsive post-secondary learning system.

Campus Alberta Quality Council (CAQC)

Director of Secretariat: Marilyn Patton
8th Floor, Commerce Place
10155 - 102 Street
Edmonton, Alberta T5J 4L5
Canada
Tel: +1(780) 427-8921
Fax: +1(780) 427-4185
EMail: caqc@gov.ab.ca
WWW: http://caqc.gov.ab.ca

Role of national body: To advance the quality of the post-secondary system in Alberta, and to review the quality and recommend degree programmes for approval, and monitor the quality of degree programmes within the post-secondary system.

Alberta Council on Admissions and Transfer (ACAT)

11th Floor, Commerce Place
10155 - 102 Street
Edmonton, Alberta T5J 4L5
Canada
Tel: +1(780) 422-9021
Fax: +1(780) 422-3688
EMail: acat@gov.ab.ca
WWW: http://www.transferalberta.ca

Role of national body: To provide leadership and oversight regarding learner pathways and mobility in the advanced learning system, working cooperatively with stakeholders to support admissions and transfer and the improvement of educational opportunities for Alberta students.

Data for academic year: 2014-2015

Source: IAU from the Canadian Information Centre for International Credentials (CICIC), a unit of the Council of Ministers of Education, Canada (CMEC), on behalf of the Alberta Innovation and Advanced Education, October 2014. Bodies 2016.

INSTITUTIONS

PUBLIC INSTITUTIONS

ALBERTA COLLEGE OF ART AND DESIGN (ACAD)

1407-14 Avenue, Calgary, Alberta T2N 4R3
Tel: +1(403) 284-7600
Fax: +1(403) 289-6682
EMail: admissions@acad.ca
Website: http://www.acad.ca

President and CEO: Daniel Doz (2010-) Tel: +1(403) 284-7670

Associate Vice President, Research and Academic Affairs: Alison Miyauchi

Programme
Design (Design); **Fine Arts** (Ceramics and Glass Technology; Crafts and Trades; Design; Jewellery Art; Painting and Drawing; Printing and Printmaking; Sculpture); **Liberal Studies** (Art History; Arts and Humanities; English; Social Sciences); **Media Arts and Digital Technologies** (Electronic Engineering)

History: Founded 1926.

Fees: National: Canadian Citizen + Permanent Resident Students: 5,191 per annum (Canadian Dollar), International: International Students: 14,815 per annum (Canadian Dollar)

Main Language(s) of Instruction: English

Degrees and Diplomas: *Baccalauréat/Bachelor's Degree*: **Design; Fine Arts.** *Master's Degree*: **Fine Arts.**

Student Services: Library

Student Numbers *2014*: Total 1,238
Last Updated: 19/01/15

ATHABASCA UNIVERSITY (AU)

1 University Drive, Athabasca, Alberta T9S 3A3
Tel: +1(780) 675-6100
Fax: +1(780) 675-6450
Website: http://www.athabascau.ca

Interim President: Peter MacKinnon (2014-)
EMail: peter.mackinnon@athabascau.ca

Vice-President, Academic: Cindy Ives
EMail: cindyi@athabascau.ca

Faculty
Business (Accountancy; Business Administration; E- Business/ Commerce; Finance; Human Resources; Leadership; Marketing); **Graduate Studies** (Business Administration; Distance Education; Educational Sciences; Educational Technology; Health Sciences; Heritage Preservation; Information Sciences; Law; Management; Nursing; Psychology); **Health Disciplines** (Health Sciences; Nursing; Psychology); **Humanities and Social Sciences** (Anthropology; Art History; Arts and Humanities; Canadian Studies; Communication Studies; Criminal Law; Cultural Studies; Education; Educational Sciences; English; Environmental Studies; Film; French; Gender Studies; Geography (Human); German; Government; Health Administration; Heritage Preservation; History; Human Resources; Indigenous Studies; International Studies; Labour and Industrial Relations; Labour Law; Law; Literature; Music; Philosophy; Political Sciences; Psychology; Public Administration; Religious Studies; Social and Community Services; Sociology; Spanish; Women's Studies; Writing); **Science and Technology** (Astronomy and Space Science; Biology; Chemistry; Computer Engineering; Computer Science; Environmental Studies; Geography; Geology; Health Sciences; Information Sciences; Laboratory Techniques; Mathematics; Nutrition; Physics; Software Engineering; Statistics)

Further Information: Traditional and Open Learning Institution. Also Learning Centres in Edmonton and Calgary and Centre for Innovative Management (CIM) in St. Albert.

History: Founded 1970. An open, distance education university funded by the Department of Advanced Education of the government of Alberta. Accepted first students 1973, and received permanent self-governing status under the Alberta University Act 1978.

Academic Year: No terms. Admission is granted all year round in undergraduate programmes

Admission Requirements: Minimum age is 16 years old

Fees: (Can. Dollars): Undergraduate programmes, canadians permanent Residents of Alberta, 646 for a 3 credit course; For Canadian residents outside Alberta, per course, 751 (for Senior Canadian, 414/519 for a 3-credit course). Foreign students, 971 for a 3-credit course

Main Language(s) of Instruction: English

Degrees and Diplomas: *Baccalauréat/Bachelor's Degree*; *Maîtrise/Master's Degree*: **Business Administration; Distance Education; Health Sciences; Information Sciences; Nursing; Psychology.** *Doctorat/Doctoral Degree*: **Business Administration; Distance Education.** Also Post-Baccalaureate Diploma, 2,5 yrs.

Student Services: Academic Counselling, Canteen, Facilities for disabled people, Library

Publications: Bridging the Distance; Profiles in Research

Academic Staff *2013-2014*: Total 1,350
Student Numbers *2013-2014*: Total: c. 40,000
Last Updated: 19/01/15

GRANT MACEWAN UNIVERSITY

PO Box 1796, 10050 MacDonald Drive, Edmonton, Alberta T5J 2P2
Tel: +1(780) 497-5040
Fax: +1(780) 497-5001
EMail: info@macewan.ca
Website: http://www.macewan.ca

President: David W. Atkinson
Tel: +1(780) 497-5400 EMail: AtkinsonD@MacEwan.ca

Faculty
Arts and Science (Anthropology; Arts and Humanities; Biological and Life Sciences; Chemistry; Chinese; Classical Languages; Computer Science; Earth Sciences; Economics; English; French; German; Greek (Classical); History; Japanese; Latin; Mathematics; Philosophy; Physics; Political Sciences; Psychology; Sociology; Spanish; Statistics); **Fine Arts and Communications** (Art Management; Communication Studies; Design; Display and Stage Design; Fine Arts; Jazz and Popular Music; Journalism; Music; Musical Instruments; Theatre; Writing); **Health and Community Studies** (Acupuncture; Child Care and Development; Criminal Law; Gerontology; Health Sciences; Law; Nursing; Occupational Therapy; Physical Therapy; Police Studies; Rehabilitation and Therapy; Social Work; Special Education; Speech Therapy and Audiology)

School
Business (Accountancy; Business Administration; Business and Commerce; Human Resources; Information Technology; Insurance; Law; Leadership; Library Science; Management; Public Relations)

History: Founded 1971 as Grant MacEwan College. Acquired present title 2009.

Fees: Bachelor's degree, domestic students, 134-305 per credit depending on programmes. international Students: 520 per credit (Canadian Dollar)

Degrees and Diplomas: *Grade appliquée/Applied Degree*; *Baccalauréat/Bachelor's Degree*: **Arts and Humanities; Business and Commerce; Child Care and Development; Communication Studies; Music; Nursing.**

Student Services: Academic Counselling, Canteen, Careers Guidance, Health Services, Library, Residential Facilities, Sports Facilities

Student Numbers *2013-2014*: Total: c. 14,000
Last Updated: 20/01/15

LAKELAND COLLEGE

5707 College Drive, Vermillion, Alberta T9X 1K5
Tel: +1(780) 853-8400
Fax: +1(780) 853-7355
EMail: admissions@lakelandcollege.ca
Website: http://www.lakelandcollege.ca

President and Chief Executive Officer: Tracy Edwards (2014-) Tel: +1(780) 853-8400 Ext. 510 EMail: tracy@tracyedwards.ca

Vice President Academic: Alice Wainwright-Stewart EMail: maureen.lehmann@lakelandcollege.ca

Programme

Academic Upgrading (Adult Education); **Agricultural Sciences** (Agricultural Business; Agriculture; Animal Husbandry; Cattle Breeding; Crop Production; Veterinary Science; Zoology); **Business** (Accountancy; Agricultural Business; Business Administration; Finance; Management; Real Estate); **Continuing Education** (Agriculture; Fire Science; Health Sciences; Social and Community Services); **Energy and Petroleum Technology** (Energy Engineering; Polymer and Plastics Technology; Power Engineering); **Environmental Sciences** (Ecology; Environmental Management; Fishery; Tourism; Wildlife); **Fire and Emergency** (Fire Science; Protective Services); **Health and Wellness** (Nursing; Physical Therapy); **Human Services** (Child Care and Development; Education); **Interior Design** (Interior Design); **Tourism** (Tourism); **Trades and Technology** (Electrical Engineering; Metal Techniques; Service Trades; Technology)

Further Information: Also Lloydminster Campus and online Courses and Programs

History: Founded 1973.

Main Language(s) of Instruction: English

Degrees and Diplomas: *Baccalauréat/Bachelor's Degree*: **Agriculture; Arts and Humanities; Business and Commerce; Education; Food Science; Medical Technology; Nursing; Nutrition; Social Work.** Applied Bachelor's degree, 2-3 yrs post-diploma programme; Bachelor's degree (professional), 4 yrs.

Student Services: Canteen, Facilities for disabled people, Health Services, Library, Residential Facilities, Sports Facilities

Student Numbers *2013-2014*: Total 2,000
Last Updated: 20/01/15

LETHBRIDGE COLLEGE

300 College Drive South, Lethbridge, Alberta T1K 1L6
Tel: +1(403) 320-3200
Fax: +1(403) 320-1461
EMail: info@lethbridgecollege.ca
Website: http://www.lethbridgecollege.ca

President and Chief Executive Officer: Paula Burns Tel: +1(403) 320-3209 EMail: president@lethbridgecollege.ca

Vice President Academic: Stuart Cullum

Area

Academic Upgrading & Transition Programs (Biology; Chemistry; English; Mathematics; Physics); **Agriculture and Science** (Agricultural Equipment; Agriculture; Biotechnology; Fishery; Wildlife); **Alternative Energy** (Energy Engineering); **Apprenticeships** (Automotive Engineering; Cooking and Catering; Metal Techniques); **Automotives and Mechanics** (Agricultural Equipment; Automotive Engineering); **Business and Administration** (Administration; Business Administration; Information Technology; Management); **Communications and Media** (Communication Arts; Multimedia); **Computing and Information Technology** (Communication Arts; Computer Science; Information Technology; Multimedia; Surveying and Mapping); **Criminal Justice and Law** (Criminal Law; Fire Science; Law; Police Studies); **Culinary Arts and Hospitality** (Business Administration; Cooking and Catering); **Design** (Civil Engineering; Communication Arts; Computer Science; Design; Fashion Design; Information Technology; Interior Design; Marketing; Multimedia); **Education** (Preschool Education; Special Education); **Engineering** (Civil Engineering; Engineering; Surveying and Mapping); **Environment** (Biotechnology; Environmental Studies; Fishery; Natural Resources; Wildlife); **Fitness and Recreation** (Management; Sports); **Health** (Biotechnology; Health Sciences; Nursing); **Human Services** (Child Care and Development; Preschool Education; Rehabilitation and Therapy; Special Education); **Humanities, Psychology and Sociology** (Child Care and Development; Law; Police Studies); **Languages and English as a Second Language** (English); **Marketing** (Business Administration); **Outdoor Careers** (Energy Engineering; Environmental Studies; Fishery; Natural Resources; Wildlife); **Science** (Biotechnology); **Trades** (Agricultural Equipment; Automotive Engineering; Energy Engineering; Metal Techniques); **Transportation** (Agricultural Equipment; Automotive Engineering)

Further Information: Traditional and Open Learning Institution

History: Founded 1957 as Lethbridge Community College.

Degrees and Diplomas: *Baccalauréat/Bachelor's Degree*: **Nursing.** Applied bachelor's degree (professional), 4 yrs; Bachelor of Nursing in partnership with University of Lethbridge, 4 yrs.

Student Services: Library, Residential Facilities, Sports Facilities
Last Updated: 20/01/15

MEDICINE HAT COLLEGE (MHC)

299 College Drive S.E., Medicine Hat, Alberta T1A 3Y6
Tel: +1(403) 529-3811 +1(866) 282-8394
Fax: +1(403) 504-3517
EMail: info@acd.mhc.ab.ca
Website: http://www.mhc.ab.ca

President and CEO: Denise K. Henning Tel: +1(403) 529-3801

Vice-President, Academic: Linda Schwatrz-Trivett Tel: +1(403) 529-3802 EMail: lschwartz@mhc.ab.ca

Division

Adult Development (Adult Education; Biology; Chemistry; Computer Science; English; Mathematics; Physics); **Arts** (Arts and Humanities; Child Care and Development; Communication Studies; Criminal Law; Education; Fine Arts; Journalism; Law; Police Studies; Preschool Education; Social Work; Visual Arts); **Arts and Education** (Adult Education; Communication Studies; Criminal Law; Education; Educational Administration; Fine Arts; Journalism; Law; Police Studies; Preschool Education; Tourism); **Business and Enterprise** (Administration; Business Administration; Business and Commerce; Communication Studies; Management; Marketing; Tourism); **International Education** (English); **Science and Health** (Business Computing; Chiropractic; Computer Graphics; Computer Science; Dental Hygiene; Dentistry; Engineering; Environmental Studies; Health Sciences; Information Technology; Laboratory Techniques; Leadership; Medicine; Nursing; Nutrition; Occupational Therapy; Optometry; Paramedical Sciences; Pharmacy; Physical Therapy; Power Engineering; Social Work; Speech Therapy and Audiology; Tourism; Veterinary Science); **Trades and Technology** (Metal Techniques; Service Trades; Technology)

Further Information: Also Brooks Campus.

History: Founded 1965 as Medicine Hat Junior College. Acquired present title 1969.

Degrees and Diplomas: *Baccalauréat/Bachelor's Degree*: **Business Administration.** Bachelor's degree with University of Alberta, University of Calgary and Athabasca University; Bachelor of Professional Arts with Athabasca University. Bachelor of Business Administration (BBA) degree in partnership with Mount Royal University (MRU)

Student Services: Health Services, Language Laboratory, Library, Residential Facilities, Sports Facilities

Student Numbers *2012-2013*: Total 2,422
Last Updated: 20/01/15

MOUNT ROYAL UNIVERSITY

4825 Mount Royal Gate, SW, Calgary, Alberta T3E 6K6
Tel: +1(403) 440-6111
Fax: +1(403) 240-6339
EMail: admissions@mtroyal.ca
Website: http://www.mtroyal.ca/

President: David Docherty (2011-) Tel: +1(403) 440-6393 EMail: president@mtroyal.ca

Provost and Vice-President, Academic: Kathryn Shailer Tel: +1(403) 440-6858

International Relations: Lorna Smith, Director, International Education
Tel: +1(403) 440-5100
EMail: LSmith@mtroyal.ca; international@mtroyal.ca

Faculty

Arts (Anthropology; Art History; Arts and Humanities; Canadian Studies; Chinese; Classical Languages; Economics; English; French; German; Greek (Classical); History; Interior Design; Italian; Japanese; Latin; Linguistics; Modern Languages; Philosophy; Political Sciences; Psychology; Religious Studies; Romance Languages; Social Policy; Sociology; Spanish; Women's Studies); **Communication Studies** (Information Management; Journalism; Music; Public Relations; Radio and Television Broadcasting; Theatre); **Continuing Education and Extention** (Accountancy; Adult Education; Arabic; Business Administration; Child Care and Development; Chinese; Cinema and Television; Communication Studies; Computer Science; Data Processing; Design; English; Environmental Management; Film; Finance; French; German; Health Sciences; Human Resources; Insurance; Italian; Japanese; Leadership; Management; Marketing; Occupational Therapy; Petroleum and Gas Engineering; Photography; Physical Therapy; Police Studies; Portuguese; Public Relations; Real Estate; Rehabilitation and Therapy; Russian; Small Business; Spanish; Toxicology; Transport and Communications; Video; Visual Arts; Writing; Yoga); **Health and Community Studies** (Business Administration; Child Care and Development; Criminal Law; Forensic Medicine and Dentistry; Health Sciences; Nursing; Physical Education; Psychiatry and Mental Health; Rehabilitation and Therapy; Social Work; Tourism); **Science and Technology** (Biological and Life Sciences; Chemistry; Computer Science; Earth Sciences; Engineering; Environmental Studies; Information Sciences; Mathematics; Physics); **Teaching and Learning** (Education)

School

Business *(Bissett)* (Accountancy; Business Administration; Finance; Human Resources; Insurance; International Business; Management; Marketing)

Institute

International Education/Languages Institute (Arabic; Chinese; Communication Studies; English; French; German; Italian; Japanese; Modern Languages; Portuguese; Russian; Spanish)

Centre

Child Well-Being (Child Care and Development); **Iniskim** (Indigenous Studies)

Conservatory

Music *(Mount Royal)* (Jazz and Popular Music; Music; Music Theory and Composition; Musical Instruments; Singing)

Further Information: Also Institute for Scholarship of Teaching and Learning; Centre for Child Well-Being; Also Holy Cross and Springbank campuses.

History: Founded 1910 as Mount Royal College. Acquired present title 2009.

Admission Requirements: Secondary school certificate or recognized foreign equivalent; interview for some programmes

Fees: Canadian/resident students, degree program (five courses), 6,400 per year; International students, degree program (five courses), 12,800 per annum (Canadian Dollar)

Main Language(s) of Instruction: English

Degrees and Diplomas: *Baccalauréat/Bachelor's Degree*: **Anthropology; Computer Science; Criminal Law; Education; English; Health Education; History; Midwifery; Natural Sciences; Nursing; Physical Education; Psychology; Sociology; Spanish.** Also Advanced Certificates and Diploma (Aviation, Broadcasting; Social Work)

Student Services: Academic Counselling, Canteen, Careers Guidance, Cultural Activities, Facilities for disabled people, Health Services, Language Laboratory, Library, Nursery Care, Social Counselling, Sports Facilities

Academic Staff *2013-2014*	**TOTAL**
FULL-TIME	**405**
PART-TIME	**447**
Student Numbers *2013-2014*	
All (Foreign included)	**12,577**

Last Updated: 20/01/15

NORTHERN ALBERTA INSTITUTE OF TECHNOLOGY (NAIT)

11762-106 Street N.W., Edmonton, Alberta T5G 2R1
Tel: +1(780) 471-6248
Fax: +1(780) 471-8490
EMail: registrar@nait.ca
Website: http://www.nait.ca/

President and CEO: Glenn Feltham
Tel: +(780) 471-7704 EMail: president@nait.ca

Provost and Vice President Academic: Neil Fassina
EMail: academichub@nait.ca

Programme

Academic Upgrading (Business Administration; Engineering; Technology); **Animal Studies** (Business Administration; Veterinary Science); **Building Construction and Design** (Architecture; Building Technologies; Civil Engineering; Construction Engineering; Graphic Design; Interior Design; Materials Engineering; Mechanical Engineering); **Business Administration** *(JR Shaw (JRSSB))* (Accountancy; Banking; Business Administration; Finance; Human Resources; Management; Marketing); **Engineering and Applied Sciences** (Aeronautical and Aerospace Engineering; Architecture; Biological and Life Sciences; Biomedical Engineering; Building Technologies; Chemical Engineering; Computer Engineering; Computer Networks; Construction Engineering; Design; Electrical Engineering; Electronic Engineering; Energy Engineering; Engineering Management; Environmental Studies; Forestry; Geological Engineering; Instrument Making; Interior Design; Laboratory Techniques; Materials Engineering; Nanotechnology; Petroleum and Gas Engineering; Surveying and Mapping; Telecommunications Engineering); **Health and Safety** (Biomedical Engineering; Dental Technology; Dentistry; Laboratory Techniques; Medical Technology; Medicine; Occupational Therapy; Physical Therapy; Radiology; Respiratory Therapy; Sports; Veterinary Science); **Hospitality and Culinary Arts** (Cooking and Catering; Hotel and Restaurant); **Information Technology and Electronics** (Aeronautical and Aerospace Engineering; Computer Engineering; Computer Networks; Electrical Engineering; Electronic Engineering; Graphic Arts; Information Technology; Photography; Radio and Television Broadcasting; Telecommunications Engineering); **Mechanical and Industrial** (Aeronautical and Aerospace Engineering; Automotive Engineering; Building Technologies; Instrument Making; Mechanical Engineering; Petroleum and Gas Engineering; Power Engineering); **Media and Design** (Communication Arts; Graphic Arts; Media Studies; Photography; Radio and Television Broadcasting); **Recreation and Outdoors** (Landscape Architecture; Marine Transport; Sports)

School

Sustainable Building and Environmental Management *((SSBEM))* (Biological and Life Sciences; Chemical Engineering; Energy Engineering; Geological Engineering; Landscape Architecture; Surveying and Mapping; Water Management); **Trades** (Aeronautical and Aerospace Engineering; Automotive Engineering; Business Administration; Marine Transport; Power Engineering; Service Trades)

History: Founded 1962.

Main Language(s) of Instruction: English

Degrees and Diplomas: *Baccalauréat/Bachelor's Degree*: **Accountancy; Business Administration; Finance; Industrial Management; Information Technology.** Also Diploma

Student Services: Library, Sports Facilities

Academic Staff *2010-2011*: Total: c. 3,300

Last Updated: 21/01/15

OLDS COLLEGE (OCCI)

4500-50th Street, Olds, Alberta T4H 1R6
Tel: +1(403) 556-8281 +1(800) 661-6537
Fax: +1(403) 556-4711
EMail: info@oldscollege.ca
Website: http://www.oldscollege.ca

President: H.J. Thompson

Area

Agriculture (Agricultural Business; Finance; Management); **Animal Sciences** (Animal Husbandry; Veterinary Science); **Business** (Administration; Business Administration); **Fashion** (Marketing); **Horticulture** (Horticulture; Management); **Hospitality and Food Services** (Brewing; Hotel and Restaurant; Meat and Poultry; Tourism); **Land and Environment** (Environmental Studies; Natural Resources; Water Management); **Trades** (Agricultural Equipment; Agriculture; Metal Techniques; Service Trades)

Further Information: Also Calgary Campus.

History: Founded 1913.

Main Language(s) of Instruction: English

Degrees and Diplomas: *Baccalauréat/Bachelor's Degree*. Also Diploma

Student Services: Health Services, Library, Residential Facilities, Sports Facilities

Last Updated: 21/01/15

RED DEER COLLEGE (RDC)

P.O. Box 5005, 100 College Blvd., Red Deer, Alberta T4N 5H5
Tel: +1(403) 342-3300
Fax: +1(403) 340-8940
EMail: inquire@rdc.ab.ca
Website: http://rdc.ab.ca

President: Joel Ward (2009-) Tel: +1(403) 342-3233

Programme

Certificates and Diplomas (Acting; Administration; Automotive Engineering; Business Administration; Child Care and Development; Computer Networks; Finance; Health Sciences; Laboratory Techniques; Music; Nursing; Performing Arts; Pharmacy; Service Trades; Social Work; Software Engineering; Sports; Theatre; Visual Arts)

School

Arts and Sciences (Anthropology; English; French; History; Political Sciences; Psychology; Sociology; Spanish); **Business** *(Donald)* (Accountancy; Business Administration; Finance; International Business; Management; Marketing); **Continuing Education** (Accountancy; Business Administration; Computer Science; Information Technology; Leadership; Marketing; Service Trades; Social Work); **Creative Arts** (Film; Music; Theatre; Visual Arts); **Education** *(University of Alberta)* (Education); **Health Science** (Nursing); **Trades and Technology** (Electrical and Electronic Engineering; Mechanical Engineering; Technology)

Further Information: Also Continuing Education and Distance Learning

History: Founded 1963.

Degrees and Diplomas: *Baccalauréat/Bachelor's Degree*. Also Certificates and Diploma.s; Bachelor's degree offered in collaboration with Athabasca University, University of Alberta and University of Calgary.

Student Numbers *2014-2015*: Total 7,500

Last Updated: 21/01/15

SOUTHERN ALBERTA INSTITUTE OF TECHNOLOGY (SAIT)

1301-16 Avenue N.W., Calgary, Alberta T2M 0L4
Tel: +1(403) 284-7248 +1(877) 284-7248
Fax: +1(403) 284-8940
EMail: international@sait.ca
Website: http://www.sait.ca

President and CEO: David Ross (2013-) Tel: +1(403) 284-8581

Interim Vice President, Academic: Lee Haldeman

School

Business (Accountancy; Business Administration; Finance; Information Management; Law; Management; Marketing); **Construction** (Architecture; Civil Engineering; Design; Surveying and Mapping); **Energy** *(MacPhail)* (Automation and Control Engineering; Chemical Engineering; Electrical Engineering; Environmental Engineering; Laboratory Techniques; Petroleum and Gas Engineering; Power Engineering); **Health and Public Safety** (Dentistry; Health Sciences; Information Technology; Medical Technology; Medicine; Pharmacy; Radiology; Rehabilitation and Therapy; Respiratory Therapy); **Hospitality and Tourism** (Cooking and Catering; Hotel and Restaurant; Tourism); **Information and Communications Technologies** (Electronic Engineering; Film; Information Sciences; Information Technology; Journalism; Library Science; Media Studies; Radio and Television Broadcasting; Video); **Manufacturing and Automation** (Automation and Control Engineering; Mechanical Engineering; Metal Techniques); **Transportation** (Aeronautical and Aerospace Engineering; Automotive Engineering; Business Administration; Railway Transport)

Further Information: Also Mayland Heights Campus and Art Smith Aero Centre for Training and Technology.

History: Founded 1916, as the Provincial Institute of Technology and Art (PITA). Renamed the Southern Alberta Institute of Technology (SAIT) 1960. Rebranded as SAIT Polytechnic in 2004.

Main Language(s) of Instruction: English

Degrees and Diplomas: *Baccalauréat/Bachelor's Degree*: **Accountancy; Management.** Also Diplomas. Bachelor's degree (professional), 4 yrs; Applied Bachelor's degree, 2 yrs following diploma.

Student Services: Library, Sports Facilities

Last Updated: 21/01/15

UNIVERSITY OF ALBERTA (U OF A)

114 St. 89 Avenue, Edmonton, Alberta T6G 2E1
Tel: +1(780) 492-3111
Fax: +1(780) 492-7172
EMail: admissions.international@ualberta.ca
Website: http://www.ualberta.ca

President and Vice-Chancellor: David H. Turpin (2015-)
EMail: president@ualberta.ca

Faculty

Agricultural, Life and Environmental Sciences (Agricultural Business; Agricultural Economics; Animal Husbandry; Ecology; Food Science; Food Technology; Forest Biology; Forest Economics; Forest Management; Horticulture; Natural Resources; Nutrition; Soil Science; Veterinary Science; Wildlife); **Arts** (African Studies; Ancient Civilizations; Anthropology; Arabic; Art History; Arts and Humanities; Comparative Literature; Criminology; Cultural Studies; Danish; Design; East Asian Studies; Economics; English; Environmental Studies; Film; Fine Arts; Folklore; French; German; History; Hungarian; Indic Languages; Information Sciences; International Studies; Italian; Linguistics; Literature; Mathematics; Medieval Studies; Middle Eastern Studies; Modern Languages; Music; Music Theory and Composition; Musicology; Norwegian; Peace and Disarmament; Persian; Philosophy; Polish; Political Sciences; Portuguese; Psychology; Religious Studies; Russian; Singing; Slavic Languages; Sociology; Spanish; Swahili; Swedish; Technology; Theatre; Translation and Interpretation; Visual Arts; Women's Studies); **Education** (Education; Educational Psychology; Educational Sciences; Natives Education; Physical Education; Primary Education; Secondary Education); **Engineering** (Biomedical Engineering; Chemical Engineering; Civil Engineering; Computer Engineering; Electrical Engineering; Engineering; Environmental Engineering; Materials Engineering; Mechanical Engineering; Mining Engineering; Petroleum and Gas Engineering); **Extension** (Acupuncture; Administration; Adult Education; Business Administration; Chinese; Communication Studies; Continuing Education; English; Fine Arts; French; German; Government; Human Resources; Information Management; Information Technology; Insurance; Japanese; Management; Natural Resources; Occupational Health; Painting and Drawing; Spanish; Statistics; Writing); **Graduate Studies and Research** (Agricultural Economics; Agriculture; Ancient Civilizations; Anthropology; Applied Linguistics; Arts and Humanities; Biochemistry; Biological and Life Sciences; Biomedical Engineering; Business Administration; Canadian Studies; Cell Biology; Chemical Engineering; Chemistry; Civil Engineering; Communication Studies; Comparative Law; Computer Engineering; Computer Science; Cultural Studies; Dentistry; Design; Earth Sciences; East Asian Studies; Ecology; Economics; Education; Educational Psychology; Educational Sciences; Electrical Engineering; Engineering; English; Environmental Engineering; Environmental Studies; Fine Arts; Food Science; French; Genetics; German; Gynaecology and Obstetrics; Health Education; Health Sciences; History; Immunology;

Information Sciences; Italian; Laboratory Techniques; Latin American Studies; Law; Library Science; Linguistics; Materials Engineering; Mathematics; Mechanical Engineering; Medicine; Microbiology; Modern Languages; Music; Natural Resources; Neurosciences; Nursing; Nutrition; Occupational Therapy; Oncology; Ophthalmology; Paediatrics; Pathology; Pharmacology; Pharmacy; Philosophy; Physical Education; Physical Therapy; Physics; Physiology; Political Sciences; Primary Education; Psychiatry and Mental Health; Psychology; Public Health; Radiology; Rehabilitation and Therapy; Religious Studies; Russian; Secondary Education; Slavic Languages; Sociology; Spanish; Speech Therapy and Audiology; Statistics; Surgery; Technology; Telecommunications Engineering; Theatre; Translation and Interpretation); **Law** (Law); **Medicine and Dentistry** (Anaesthesiology; Biochemistry; Biomedical Engineering; Cell Biology; Dental Hygiene; Dentistry; Genetics; Gynaecology and Obstetrics; Immunology; Laboratory Techniques; Medicine; Microbiology; Oncology; Ophthalmology; Paediatrics; Pathology; Pharmacology; Physiology; Psychiatry and Mental Health; Public Health; Radiology; Surgery); **Native Studies** (Native American Studies); **Nursing** (Nursing); **Pharmacy and Pharmaceutical Sciences** (Pharmacy); **Physical Education and Recreation** (Physical Education; Physical Therapy; Sports; Tourism); **Rehabilitation Medicine** (Occupational Therapy; Physical Therapy; Rehabilitation and Therapy; Speech Therapy and Audiology); **Science** (Biological and Life Sciences; Chemistry; Computer Science; Earth Sciences; Mathematics; Psychology; Statistics)

College

St. Joseph's (Ethics; Philosophy; Religious Education; Theology); **St. Stephen's** (Art Therapy; Pastoral Studies; Psychology; Theology)

School

Business *(Alberta)* (Accountancy; Business Administration; Economics; Finance; Information Sciences; Law; Management; Marketing; Operations Research; Statistics); **Library and Information Studies** (Information Sciences; Library Science); **Public Health** (Behavioural Sciences; Epidemiology; Health Sciences; Occupational Health; Public Health)

Campus

Augustana (Biology; Chemistry; Classical Languages; Computer Science; Development Studies; Economics; English; Environmental Studies; Fine Arts; French; Geography; German; Greek (Classical); History; Latin; Management; Mathematics; Modern Languages; Music; Physical Therapy; Physics; Political Sciences; Psychology; Religion; Scandinavian Languages; Social Sciences; Sociology; Spanish; Sports; Theatre; Visual Arts); **Saint-Jean** (Agriculture; Animal Husbandry; Arts and Humanities; Biological and Life Sciences; Business Administration; Canadian Studies; Earth Sciences; Ecology; Economics; Education; Engineering; Environmental Studies; History; Literature; Mathematics; Modern Languages; Natural Sciences; Nursing; Physics; Political Sciences; Primary Education; Psychology; Secondary Education; Sociology; Soil Management; Teacher Training)

Further Information: Also St. Joseph's College and St. Stephen's College for Theological Education. Campuses: North Campus and South Campus, Augustana, Saint-Jean (French-language campus), Enterprise Square

History: Founded 1908.

Academic Year: September to April (September-December; January-April); Spring and Summer sessions available

Admission Requirements: Secondary school certificate or recognized foreign equivalent; post secondary transcrits; English language proficiency

Main Language(s) of Instruction: French, English

Degrees and Diplomas: *Baccalauréat/Bachelor's Degree*; *Maîtrise/Master's Degree*: **Business Administration; Education; Engineering; Finance; Law; Library Science.** *Doctorat/Doctoral Degree*: **Biological and Life Sciences; Chemistry; Computer Science; Earth Sciences; Education; Engineering; French; German; Italian; Law; Linguistics; Literature; Mathematics; Nursing; Physics; Psychology; Public Health; Romance Languages; Slavic Languages; Spanish; Translation and Interpretation.** Also combined degree programmes, 4-5 yrs; Executive MBA, 2 yrs. Doctor of Dental Surgery

Student Services: Academic Counselling, Careers Guidance, Health Services, Library, Social Counselling, Sports Facilities

Last Updated: 21/01/15

UNIVERSITY OF CALGARY (U OF C)

2500 University Drive North West, Calgary, Alberta T2N 1N4
Tel: +1(403) 220-5110
Fax: +1(403) 282-8413
EMail: uofcinfo@ucalgary.ca
Website: http://www.ucalgary.ca

President: Elizabeth Cannon (2010-2015)
Tel: +1(403) 220-5617 EMail: president@ucalgary.ca

Provost and Vice-President (Academic): Dru Marshall
Tel: +1(403) 220-5464 EMail: provost@ucalgary.ca

International Relations: Janaka Ruwanpura, Vice-Provost (International) Tel: +1(403) 220-3672 EMail: vpi@ucalgary.ca

Faculty

Arts (African Studies; Anthropology; Archaeology; Art Education; Canadian Studies; Communication Studies; Cultural Studies; Dance; Development Studies; Earth Sciences; East Asian Studies; Economics; English; French; Geography; German; Greek (Classical); Heritage Preservation; History; Indigenous Studies; International Relations; International Studies; Italian; Latin; Latin American Studies; Law; Linguistics; Media Studies; Museum Studies; Music; Philosophy; Political Sciences; Psychology; Religious Studies; Slavic Languages; Sociology; Spanish; Technology; Theatre; Urban Studies; Women's Studies); **Environmental Design** (Architecture; Design; Environmental Studies); **Graduate Studies** (Anthropology; Archaeology; Architecture; Arts and Humanities; Astronomy and Space Science; Biochemistry; Biological and Life Sciences; Biomedical Engineering; Business Administration; Cardiology; Chemical Engineering; Chemistry; Civil Engineering; Communication Studies; Computer Engineering; Computer Science; Continuing Education; Design; Earth Sciences; East Asian Studies; Economics; Education; Electrical Engineering; Energy Engineering; Engineering; English; Environmental Engineering; Fine Arts; French; Gastroenterology; Geography; German; Germanic Studies; Greek (Classical); History; Immunology; Italian; Latin; Law; Linguistics; Mathematics; Mechanical Engineering; Medicine; Microbiology; Military Science; Molecular Biology; Music; Natural Sciences; Neurosciences; Nursing; Petroleum and Gas Engineering; Philosophy; Physical Therapy; Physics; Political Sciences; Psycholinguistics; Psychology; Religious Studies; Respiratory Therapy; Slavic Languages; Social and Preventive Medicine; Social Work; Sociology; Spanish; Statistics; Surveying and Mapping; Theatre; Veterinary Science); **Kinesiology** (Anatomy; Health Sciences; Pedagogy; Physical Therapy; Physiology; Rehabilitation and Therapy); **Law** (Law); **Nursing** (Nursing); **Nursing - Qatar** *(Qatar)* (Nursing); **Science** (Astronomy and Space Science; Biological and Life Sciences; Chemistry; Computer Science; Earth Sciences; Environmental Studies; Mathematics; Nanotechnology; Natural Sciences; Physics; Statistics); **Social Work** (Social Work); **Veterinary Medicine** (Veterinary Science)

Unit

Continuing Education (English)

School

Business *(Haskayne)* (Accountancy; Business Administration; Business and Commerce; Finance; Hotel and Restaurant; Human Resources; Information Sciences; International Business; Management; Marketing; Operations Research; Tourism); **Education** *(Werklund)* (Education; Psychology; Teacher Training); **Engineering** *(Schulich)* (Bioengineering; Biomedical Engineering; Chemical Engineering; Civil Engineering; Computer Engineering; Electrical Engineering; Engineering; Environmental Engineering; Mechanical Engineering; Petroleum and Gas Engineering; Software Engineering; Surveying and Mapping); **Medicine** *(Cumming)* (Anatomy; Biochemistry; Cardiology; Cell Biology; Genetics; Gynaecology and Obstetrics; Health Sciences; Laboratory Techniques; Medicine; Microbiology; Molecular Biology; Neurosciences; Oncology; Paediatrics; Pathology; Pharmacology; Physiology; Psychiatry and Mental Health; Radiology; Rehabilitation and Therapy; Surgery; Veterinary Science)

Institute

Advanced Policy Research; **Biocomplexity and Informatics** (Biology; Molecular Biology); **Biogeoscience** (Biological and Life Sciences; Biology; Botany; Earth Sciences; Ecology; Environmental Engineering; Environmental Management; Environmental Studies; Geography; Neurosciences; Surveying and Mapping; Wildlife);

Bone and Joint Health *(McCaig)* (Medicine; Rheumatology); **Gender Research** (Gender Studies); **Humanities** *(Calgary)* (Arts and Humanities); **Professional Communication** *(IPC)* (Communication Studies; Cultural Studies); **Quantum Information Science** (Applied Mathematics; Computer Science; Physics); **Space Research** (Astronomy and Space Science); **Sustainable Energy, Environment and Economy** (Economics; Energy Engineering; Environmental Studies); **United States Policy Research** (Economics; International Relations; Political Sciences)

Centre

Advanced Technologies of Life Sciences *(CAT)* (Biological and Life Sciences; Biomedicine; Health Sciences; Veterinary Science); **Alberta Global Forum** (Communication Studies; Cultural Studies); **Bioengineering Research and Education** *(CBRE)* (Bioengineering); **Environmental Engineering Research and Education** *(CEERE)* (Energy Engineering; Environmental Engineering); **Gifted Education** (Special Education); **Health and Policy Studies** *(CHAPS)* (Public Health); **Information Security and Cryptography** (Computer Science; Mathematics); **Innovation Studies** *(THECIS)*; **Innovative Technology** *(Calgary - CCIT)*; **Institutional Research Information Services Solution** *(IRISS)* (Information Sciences); **Mathematics in Life Sciences** (Biological and Life Sciences; Ecology; Mathematics; Medicine); **Microsystems Engineering** *(CME)* (Engineering); **Military and Strategic Studies** *(CMSS)* (Military Science); **Pipeline Engineering** *(PEC)* (Mechanical Engineering; Petroleum and Gas Engineering); **Public Interest Accounting** *(CPIA)* (Accountancy); **Risk Studies** (Management); **Social Work Research and Development** (Social Work); **Study of Higher Education** *(Canadian)* (Higher Education); **World Tourism Education and Research** (Tourism)

Research Centre

Fine Arts *(CRFA)* (Fine Arts); **Informatics** (Computer Science); **Language** (Linguistics; Modern Languages); **Latin American** *(LARC)* (Latin American Studies)

Further Information: Also Consortium for Research in Elastic Wave Exploration Seismology

History: Founded 1960 as University of Alberta at Calgary, and acquired present status and title 1966.

Academic Year: September to June (September-December; January-April; May-June). Also Summer Session (July-August)

Admission Requirements: Secondary school certificate or recognized foreign equivalent

Fees: Undergraduate programmes, 667.93 per course for Canadian students and 1,927.72 per course for International students, except Medicine, 1,489.36 per course; Law, 6,485.59 for 6 courses for Canadian students and 20,400.67 for 6 courses for International students. Graduate programmes, 5,439.90-5,561.28 per programme for Canadian students except MBA, 11,148.36; for international students, 12,347.34 per programme, except MBA, 24,598.68 (Canadian Dollar)

Main Language(s) of Instruction: English

Degrees and Diplomas: *Baccalauréat/Bachelor's Degree*; *Maîtrise/Master's Degree*; *Doctorat/Doctoral Degree*: **Astronomy and Space Science; Biochemistry; Biomedicine; Chemical Engineering; Civil Engineering; Communication Studies; Community Health; Computer Science; Economics; Education; Educational and Student Counselling; Educational Research; Engineering; English; Environmental Engineering; Film; Geography; Greek (Classical); History; Immunology; Latin; Linguistics; Management; Mathematics; Mechanical Engineering; Media Studies; Microbiology; Molecular Biology; Music; Neurosciences; Petroleum and Gas Engineering; Philosophy; Physical Therapy; Physics; Political Sciences; Production Engineering; Psychology; Religious Studies; Social Work; Sociology; Statistics; Veterinary Science.** Also Combined Degree Programmes (Bachelor/Master), 5 yrs; Postgraduate Medical Education; MBA

Student Services: Academic Counselling, Canteen, Careers Guidance, Facilities for disabled people, Foreign Studies Centre, Health Services, Language Laboratory, Nursery Care, Social Counselling, Sports Facilities

Publications: Arctic; Ariel; Canadian Ethnic Studies; Canadian Journal of Law and Society; Canadian Journal of Philosophy; Canadian Review of American Studies; Classical Views/Echos du Monde Classique; Grove; International Journal of Drama and Theatre; Journal of Child and Youth Care; Journal of Comparative Family Studies; Journal of Educational Thought; Journal of Military and Strategic Studies

Publishing House: The University of Calgary Press

Last Updated: 22/01/15

UNIVERSITY OF LETHBRIDGE (U OF L)

4401 University Drive, Lethbridge, Alberta T1K 3M4
Tel: +1(403) 329-2111
Fax: +1(403) 329-5159
EMail: inquiries@uleth.ca
Website: http://www.uleth.ca

President and Vice-Chancellor: Mike Mahon (2010-)
Tel: +1(403) 329-2201
EMail: mike.mahon@uleth.ca; President@uleth.ca

Provost and Vice-President (Academic): Andrew Hakin
Tel: +1(403) 329-2202 EMail: hakin@uleth.ca

Faculty

Arts and Science (Agriculture; Anthropology; Archaeology; Art History; Biochemistry; Biological and Life Sciences; Biotechnology; Canadian Studies; Chemistry; Computer Science; Dentistry; Economics; Engineering; English; Environmental Studies; Food Science; French; Geography; German; History; Journalism; Law; Mathematics; Medicine; Museum Studies; Music; Native American Studies; Neurosciences; Nutrition; Optometry; Painting and Drawing; Philosophy; Physical Education; Physical Therapy; Physics; Political Sciences; Psychology; Regional Studies; Religious Studies; Social Sciences; Social Work; Sociology; Spanish; Surveying and Mapping; Theatre; Urban Studies; Veterinary Science; Women's Studies; Writing); **Education** (Curriculum; Education; Educational and Student Counselling; Educational Psychology; Special Education); **Fine Arts** (Art History; Display and Stage Design; Fine Arts; Media Studies; Museum Studies; Music; Performing Arts; Theatre); **Graduate Studies** (Arts and Humanities; Education; Educational and Student Counselling; Fine Arts; Health Sciences; Leadership; Management; Music; Philosophy); **Health Sciences** (Health Sciences; Nursing; Public Health; Toxicology); **Management** *(Edmonton)* (Accountancy; Business Administration; Finance; Human Resources; International Business; Management; Marketing); **Management** *(Calgary)* (Accountancy; Government; International Business; Management); **Management** *(Lethbridge)* (Management)

Further Information: Also Language Centre providing non-credit programmes in English as a Second Language, and University level writing

History: Founded 1967.

Academic Year: September to August (September-December; January-April; May-August)

Admission Requirements: Secondary school certificate or recognized foreign equivalent, with 65% or equivalent average (actual cut-off may vary from year to year depending on space available and demand)

Main Language(s) of Instruction: English

Degrees and Diplomas: *Baccalauréat/Bachelor's Degree*; *Maîtrise/Master's Degree*: **Computer Science; Education; Fine Arts; Management; Music; Natural Sciences; Psychology.** *Doctorat/Doctoral Degree*: **Behavioural Sciences; Earth Sciences; Molecular Biology; Neurosciences; Physics.** Also combined degree programmes (Bachelor in a chosen degree, and a Bachelor of Education), 5 yrs; Post-Diploma Bachelor's degree, 2yrs; Pre-Professional Transfer Programmes

Student Services: Academic Counselling, Canteen, Careers Guidance, Cultural Activities, Facilities for disabled people, Health Services, Language Laboratory, Social Counselling, Sports Facilities

Publications: Performing Arts Preview

Student Numbers *2014-2015*	MEN	WOMEN	**TOTAL**
All (Foreign included)	3,406	4,653	**8,059**
FOREIGN ONLY	–	–	**888**

Last Updated: 27/01/15

PRIVATE INSTITUTIONS

AMBROSE UNIVERSITY

610, 833-4th Avenue SW, Calgary, Alberta T2P 3T5
Tel: +1(403) 410-2000
Fax: +1(403) 571-2556
EMail: enrolment@ambrose.edu
Website: http://www.ambrose.edu/

President: Gordon T. Smith

Vice-President Academic: Paul Spilsbury

Programme
Arts and Science (Arts and Humanities; Behavioural Sciences; Business Administration; English; History; Literature; Music)

School
Ministry (Cultural Studies; Religious Education; Religious Studies; Theology); **Theology** *(Chinese)* (Theology)

History: Founded 1921 (NUC) and 1941 (AUC). Joined on same campus 2003. Started offering common programs 2006. Previously known as Alliance and Nazarene University College. Became Ambrose University College, 2007. Acquired present title and status 2014

Main Language(s) of Instruction: English

Degrees and Diplomas: *Baccalauréat/Bachelor's Degree*; *Master's Degree*: **Christian Religious Studies; Religious Studies; Theology.**

Student Services: Academic Counselling, Canteen, Library, Residential Facilities, Sports Facilities

Student Numbers *2014-2015*: Total 800

Last Updated: 19/01/15

CANADIAN UNIVERSITY COLLEGE (CUC)

5415 College Avenue, Lacombe, Alberta T4L 2E5
Tel: +1(403) 782-3381 +1(800) 661-8129
Fax: +1(403) 782-3170
EMail: info@cauc.ca; admissions@cauc.ca
Website: http://cauc.ca/

President: Mark Haynal EMail: mhaynal@cauc.ca

Vice-President, Student Services: Stacy Hunter
EMail: shunter@cauc.ca

Division
Arts (Art History; Ceramic Art; Design; English; French; History; Music; Painting and Drawing; Philosophy; Political Sciences; Religious Studies; Spanish); **Science** (Behavioural Sciences; Biochemistry; Biology; Chemistry; Computer Science; Engineering; Geology; Mathematics; Physical Education; Physics; Psychology; Social Work; Sociology)

School
Business (Accountancy; Business Administration; Human Resources; International Business; Management); **Education** (Art Education; Business Education; Education; Foreign Languages Education; Mathematics Education; Music Education; Native Language Education; Physical Education; Primary Education; Religious Studies; Science Education; Secondary Education; Social Studies)

History: Founded 1907 as Alberta Seventh-day Adventist secondary school. The Board of Trustees authorized the establishment of a junior college 1919. Became known as Canadian Union College and statred offering its first four-year programme in Theology 1947. Acquired present title 1997.

Main Language(s) of Instruction: English

Degrees and Diplomas: *Baccalauréat/Bachelor's Degree*: **Behavioural Sciences; Biology; Business Administration; Education; English; International Studies; Music; Psychology; Religious Studies.** Bachelor's degree (Professional), 4 years.

Student Services: Library, Sports Facilities

Last Updated: 19/01/15

CONCORDIA UNIVERSITY COLLEGE OF ALBERTA (CUCA)

7128 Ada Boulevard, Edmonton, Alberta T5B 4E4
Tel: +1(780) 479-8481
Fax: +1(780) 477-1033
EMail: admits@concordia.ab.ca
Website: http://concordia.ab.ca

President: Gerald S. Krispin
Tel: +1(780) 479-9236 EMail: gerald.krispin@concordia.ab.ca

Vice-President, Academics and Provost: Richard Willie
Tel: +1(780) 479-9215 EMail: richard.willie@concordia.ab.ca

Faculty
Arts (Art History; Arts and Humanities; English; Greek (Classical); Hebrew; History; Modern Languages; Music; Nursing; Philosophy; Political Sciences; Psychology; Religious Studies; Sociology; Theatre; Writing); **Continuing Education** (Accountancy; Behavioural Sciences; Biological and Life Sciences; Chemistry; Computer Science; Economics; English; Environmental Studies; Finance; Fine Arts; History; Management; Marketing; Mathematics; Musical Instruments; Nursing; Physics; Psychology; Social Studies; Spanish; Writing); **Education** (Education); **Graduate Studies** (Bible; Christian Religious Studies; Information Management; Information Sciences); **Professional Education** (Management; Public Health); **Science** (Biology; Chemistry; Earth Sciences; Environmental Studies; Forensic Medicine and Dentistry; Health Sciences; Mathematics and Computer Science; Physics)

History: Founded 1921. Became a degree-granting university 1987.

Academic Year: September to April (September-December; January-April). Also Spring/Summer Session (May-August)

Admission Requirements: Secondary school certificate or recognized foreign equivalent, including International Baccalaureate and Advanced Placement

Fees: Undergraduate programmes, 280 per credit; 3,500 per semester; Mandatory Fees (full-time), 685,50 per semester; International Student Fee, 602 per credit or 6,525 per semester (Canadian Dollar)

Main Language(s) of Instruction: English

Accrediting Agency: Government of Alberta - Post-Secondary Learning Act (Alberta); Association of Universities and Colleges of Canada

Degrees and Diplomas: *Baccalauréat/Bachelor's Degree*; *Maîtrise/Master's Degree*: **Bible; Christian Religious Studies; Information Technology.**

Student Services: Academic Counselling, Canteen, Careers Guidance, Facilities for disabled people, Library, Residential Facilities, Social Counselling, Sports Facilities

Last Updated: 19/01/15

ST. MARY'S UNIVERSITY

14500 Bannister Road SE, Calgary, Alberta T2X 1Z4
Tel: +1(403) 531-9130
Fax: +1(403) 531-9136
EMail: info@stmu.ca
Website: http://www.stmu.ca

President: Gerry Turcotte Tel: +1(403) 254-3701

Vice-President Academic and Dean: Mark Charlton
Tel: +1(403) 254-3771 EMail: Mark.Charlton@stmu.ca

Programme
Biological Sciences (Biological and Life Sciences); **Business/ Management** (Business Administration; Management); **Catholic Educators** (Educational Administration; Religious Education); **English** (English); **General Studies** (Arts and Humanities; Natural Sciences); **History** (History); **Psychology** (Psychology)

History: Founded 1986 as Mark Charlton. Became St. Mary's University College, 2004. Acquired present status and title 2014

Academic Year: September to June

Admission Requirements: Secondary school certificate or recognized equivalent

Fees: National: Domestic Students: Bachelor of Arts: 6,405 per annum. Bachelor of Education: 8,880 (Canadian Dollar),

International: Bachelor of Arts:12,810; Bachelor of Education: 17,760 (Canadian Dollar)

Main Language(s) of Instruction: English

Degrees and Diplomas: *Baccalauréat/Bachelor's Degree*: **Arts and Humanities; Education; English; Psychology.** Bachelor of Arts in English, 4yrs; Bachelor of Education (Elementary), 2 yr after degree programme.

Student Services: Academic Counselling, Canteen, Facilities for disabled people, Sports Facilities

Publications: Salvia; Sight Lines

Publishing House: St. Mary's University College Press
Last Updated: 21/01/15

THE KING'S UNIVERSITY COLLEGE (TKUC)

9125-50 Street North West, Edmonton, Alberta T6B 2H3
Tel: +1(780) 465-3500
Fax: +1(780) 465-3534
EMail: general-info@kingsu.ca; registrar@kingsu.ca
Website: http://www.kingsu.ca

President: Melanie J. Humphreys (2013-)
EMail: president@kingsu.ca
Vice-President Academic: Hank Bestman

Faculty

Arts (Art History; Display and Stage Design; English; History; Media Studies; Music; Music Theory and Composition; Musical Instruments; Musicology; Painting and Drawing; Philosophy; Singing; Theatre; Theology); **Education** (Education; Primary Education; Secondary Education); **Natural Sciences** (Astronomy and Space Science; Biology; Chemistry; Computer Science; Mathematics; Natural Sciences; Physics); **Social Sciences** (Business and Commerce; Economics; Geography; Management; Physical Education; Political Sciences; Psychology; Social Sciences; Sociology)

Programme

Interdisciplinary Studies (Communication Arts; Economics; Environmental Studies; History; Political Sciences; Social Sciences)

Further Information: Also Study Abroad programmes: American, China, Latin American, Middle East, Dutch, Russian Studies Programmes; Los Angeles Film Studies Center; Oxford Honors Programme; Oxford Summer School Programme; Summer Institute of Journalism and others

History: Founded 1979 as The King's College. A private, co-educational Christian liberal arts institution offering undergraduate degrees accredited by the Government of Alberta since 1987. Acquired present title 1993.

Academic Year: September to April (September-December; January-April)

Admission Requirements: Secondary school certificate with minimum 60% average in prescribed courses or recognized foreign equivalent. Proficiency in oral and written English. If English is applicant's second language, TOEFL score of 580+, or computer-based score of 237+, or IELTS score of 6.5. Requirements may include acceptable performance in entrance tests, such as ACT and SAT

Fees: Tuition, 6696 per annum; Bachelor of Education, 6810; Student fees, 305 (Canadian Dollar)

Main Language(s) of Instruction: English

Accrediting Agency: Private Colleges Accreditation Board (Alberta); Association of Universities and Colleges in Canada; Council for Christian Colleges and Universities

Degrees and Diplomas: *Baccalauréat/Bachelor's Degree*. Bachelor's degree (professional), 4 yrs.

Student Services: Academic Counselling, Canteen, Careers Guidance, Facilities for disabled people, Library, Social Counselling, Sports Facilities
Last Updated: 21/01/15

Canada - British Columbia

STRUCTURE OF HIGHER EDUCATION SYSTEM

Description:

Higher education in Canada is the constitutional responsibility of the provinces. British Columbia's public post-secondary education system includes 25 public institutions: 11 universities, 11 colleges and 3 institutes. Universities in B.C. offer an array of undergraduate degree programmes and a range of programmes at the graduate level. Some also offer courses and programmes in trades, vocational and career technical studies leading to certificates and diplomas, as well as developmental programmes that prepare adult learners for post-secondary studies. Some universities undertake original and applied research in a range of disciplines, while others undertake applied research and scholarly activities in support of their programming. Colleges offer developmental programmes that prepare adult learners for post-secondary studies, as well as courses and programmes in trades, vocational, career technical and academic studies leading to certificates, diplomas, associate degrees and applied baccalaureate degrees. Institutes are organized according to career, vocational and technical specialties, covering a variety of occupations. They may offer credentials from certificates to degrees. One institute has an Aboriginal focus. All public post-secondary institutions are governed by boards comprised of provincially-appointed members and members elected by faculty, staff and students. Government also supports pre-employment, apprenticeship and vocational programmes. Private or out of province public institutions must receive authorization through provincial legislation in order to offer or grant degrees, or use the word "university" to indicate that an educational programme is available. 17 private post-secondary institutions (including two out of province public institutions) have legislative authority to offer and grant academic degrees and 14 private post-secondary institutions have legislative authority to offer and grant theological degrees. 349 private career training institutions offer certificate and diploma programmes in trades, technology, and vocational fields of study. In addition, there are a large number of private institutions operating in British Columbia that offer programmes such as language training, non-degree theological or recreational courses. These institutions are not required to register with PCTIA as they do not offer career training as defined in the Act; however, they may register on a voluntary basis.

Stages of studies:

University level first stage: Bachelor's degree

In B.C., universities, colleges and institutes all offer programming that leads to baccalaureate degrees. In the case of colleges, it is typically the first two years of a baccalaureate degree, as well as some applied baccalaureate degrees (e.g., Bachelor of Business Administration). Most undergraduate study leads to a "General" Bachelor's degree (minimum three years) or an "Honours" degree (4 years and prescribed subject concentration). Degrees are normally titled in broad descriptive groups, e.g. B.A. and B.Sc. Arts and Sciences programmes which consist of courses in the liberal arts, humanities, social or physical sciences. A two-year Associate degree in Arts and Science provides two-year transfer to the public universities. The first stage also includes undergraduate Diplomas (1-3 years of study) and short (up to 1 year) special Certificate programmes; these may enable entry to degree programmes and are frequently given in close cooperation with professional bodies. In addition, the first stage includes other professional programmes that typically require no university level prerequisites and four years of study, e.g. Bachelor of Science in Nursing, Bachelor Business Administration and Bachelor of Education. First stage includes first professional degree programmes requiring prerequisite university studies (generally a baccalaureate degree) followed by three years for a Bachelor of Law (LL.B.) while others, e.g. Doctor of Medicine (M.D.) and Doctor of Veterinary Medicine (D.V.M.), normally require four years.

University level second stage: Master's degree

The Master's degree normally requires at least one year's study after a Bachelor's degree or equivalent. Most Master's programmes, e.g. in Business Administration, require at least two years. A thesis is usually required, often course work as well. Examples are: M.A., M.Sc., M.Ed., and MBA.

University level third stage: Doctoral degrees

A Doctoral degree is the highest academic qualification and comprises the third stage of university level studies. This degree normally requires at least three years of study after the Master's degree; the submission and defence of a dissertation are the principal requirements, and supplemental course work is usually also required. The degree "Doctor of Philosophy" (Ph.D.) is the designation most commonly used to signify the doctoral degrees. There are also doctoral programmes in professional areas that typically use the term "Doctorate". Doctoral degree-holders frequently use the title "Dr." (Doctoral degrees should not be confused with certain first professional degrees in the Health Sciences, e.g. Medicine, Veterinary Medicine and Dentistry). In B.C., Doctoral degrees are limited to 5 of the 11 public universities. Doctoral degrees in professional studies are becoming more common for third level studies in specific professional fields such as Doctor of Education (Ed.D).

ADMISSION TO HIGHER EDUCATION

Admission to university-level studies:

Alternatives to credentials: Post-secondary institutions set their own admission policies.

Numerus clausus: Post-secondary institutions set their own admissions policies.

Other requirements: Minimum score: Generally, at least C+ (67-72%). Proof of proficiency in the language of instruction. Some post-secondary institutions provide remedial courses or a transitional year programme, and most seek to admit a proportionately equitable mix of qualified applicants.

Foreign students admission:

Definition of foreign student: Foreign (International) Students are students who are not Canadian citizens, refugees or permanent residents of Canada, and are enrolled full time or part time in recognized academic, professional or vocational training, or English or French as a Second Language programme or courses at a university, college or other educational institution in Canada.

Admission requirements: Students applying to any post-secondary programme in B.C. must meet the admission requirements of the specific institution. Students should contact the International Education or Admissions Office at the institution for specific details.

Entry regulations: Students applying for study permits through Citizenship and Immigration Canada must now have a letter of acceptance from a Designated Learning Institution [http://www.cic.gc.ca/english/study/study-institutions-list.asp]. A study permit is not needed for short-term courses or programmes of study of six months or less. Students may enrol in short-term programmes at any post-secondary institution, regardless of whether or not it is designated; if they are from a non-visa-exempt country, they must have a valid visitor visa. Students wishing to get a study permit for studies of six months or less must attend a Designated Learning Institution. A small number of students do not require a study permit by virtue of their status in Canada (e.g. diplomats and their children).

Additional guidelines for foreign (international) students coming to study in Canada on study permits - before students come to study in Canada, they will need:

• a valid passport or travel document;

• the letter of introduction they received from the visa office when their study permit was approved; which contains their study permit reference number;

• a letter of acceptance from the institution where they have been granted permission to study;

• proof that they have enough money to pay for school fees, living expenses and return transportation for themselves and any family members that come with them to Canada;

• a valid temporary resident visa (required for citizens of many countries); and,

• letters of reference or any other documents recommended by the visa office where they applied for the study permit.

Students must also be able to satisfy an immigration officer that they will leave Canada at the end of their authorized stay.

Health requirements: Medical examinations are required by Citizenship and Immigration Canada for students who plan to study in Canada longer than six months if they will be studying and working in a school, hospital, day-care centre or other facility where it is important to protect public health, or if they have lived in certain countries or territories temporarily or in the year prior to the date they want to enter Canada. Students should consult a visa office near them if they are unsure if they require a medical exam.

Medical insurance is required for all students while they are in Canada. In B.C., basic health-care insurance coverage begins three months after they arrive in the province and apply to the B.C. Medical Services Plan (MSP). Basic MSP health-care insurance covers things like visiting the doctor and going to the hospital. Students must have enough private health-care insurance to cover their entire stay in B.C. for shorter programmes (less than six months) or to cover the waiting period prior to receiving MSP coverage.

Language Proficiency: Students may need to demonstrate competence in the English language, generally by achieving a specified minimum score on an IELTS, TOEFL or other English proficiency test. Students should contact the International Education or Admissions Office at the institution for specific details.

RECOGNITION OF STUDIES

Quality assurance system:

Public post-secondary institutions have senates, education councils or other similar bodies which include appointed administration and elected student and faculty representatives. These bodies oversee academic matters, such as admission standards, curriculum and grading. The Private Career Training Institutions Agency offers a voluntary accreditation process to registered private career training institutions in which institutions undergo a more rigorous quality assurance process, including demonstrating they meet certain institutional and quality standards. The Degree Quality Assessment Board (the Board) reviews and makes recommendation to the Minister on new degree programmes, use of the word "university" in British Columbia.

Bodies dealing with recognition:

Degree Quality Assessment Board - DQAB

PO Box 9177, Stn Prov Govt
Victoria V8W 9H8
Tel: +1(250) 387-5163
WWW: http://www.aved.gov.bc.ca/degree-authorization/

International Credential Evaluation Service - ICES

British Columbia Institute of Technology
3700 Willingdon Avenue
Burnaby V5G 3H2
Tel: +1(604) 432-8800
Fax: +1(604) 435-7033
EMail: icesinfo@bcit.ca
WWW: http://www.bcit.ca/ices/

Special provisions for recognition:

Recognition for university level studies: Post-secondary institutions establish their own admissions criteria and make their own admissions decisions in response to individual applications. Any restrictions on admissions are determined by each institution based on given available teaching and other resources. Universities and other post-secondary institutions regularly assess and make decisions on foreign academic credentials for admission purposes. Additionally, the Canadian Information Centre for International credentials (CICIC) provides information and guidance on the assessment and recognition of international academic credentials.

For access to advanced studies and research: Post-secondary institutions establish their own admissions criteria and make their own admissions decisions in response to individual applications. Any restrictions on admissions are determined by each institution based on given available teaching and other resources.

For exercising a profession: Access to most professions is governed by provincial and/or federal statutes and is restricted to Canadian citizens or immigrants accepted as permanent residents. Applicants must meet examination and/or practical training requirements set by the relevant professional body or provincial or federal licensing board. The International Credential Evaluation Service (ICES) has service agreements with over 90 affiliations comprised of regulated professional organizations, government agencies and educational institutions in Canada. A formal ICES assessment provides recognition and credits for individuals to purse their career and to studies in Canada with minimal disruption or loss of previous educational and work experiences.

PROVINCIAL BODIES

Ministry of Advanced Education

Minister: Andrew Wilkinson

PO Box 9884 Stn Prov Govt

Victoria, BC V8W 9T6

Canada

Tel: + 1(250) 356-0179

Fax: + 1(250) 952-0260

EMail: AVED.GeneralInquiries@gov.bc.ca

WWW: http://www2.gov.bc.ca/gov/content/governments/organizational-structure/ministries-organizations/ministries/advanced-education

BC Council on Admissions and Transfer - BCCAT

Executive Director: Robert Fleming

709-555 Seymour Street

Vancouver, BC V6B 3H6

Canada

Tel: + 1(604) 412-7700

Fax: + 1(604) 683-0576

EMail: info@bccat.bc.ca

WWW: http://www.bccat.ca

Role of national body: To develop, in cooperation with the various institutions of post-secondary education, policies that will facilitate successful admission and transfer of students within the British Columbia post-secondary education system.

Private Career Training Institutions Agency - PCTIA

Registrar and Chief Executive Officer: Monica Lust

203 - 1155 West Pender St

Vancouver, BC V6E 2P4

Canada

Tel: + 1(604) 569-0033

Fax: + 1(778) 945-0606

EMail: info@pctia.bc.ca

WWW: http://pctia.bc.ca

Role of national body: The Private Career Training Institutions Agency is a not-for-profit corporation which operates at arm's length from government.

On April 17, 2014, the BC Government announced that PCTIA would be dissolved and its functions transferred into Government under the authority of the Ministry of Advanced Education. This will provide a regulatory approach that is consistent with other Canadian jurisdictions. Transition into Government is dependent on introduction of new legislation. Government's objectives for the change are:

• to strengthen quality assurance for private institutions;

• improve recognition of BC credentials overseas;

• lower student loan default rates in the sector; and,

• streamline designation and administrative processes currently managed by both PCTIA (Registration and Accreditation of private career training institutions) and the Ministry of Advanced Education (Student Financial Assistance Designation and Education Quality Assurance).

Data for academic year: 2014-2015

Source: IAU from the Canadian Information Centre for International Credentials (CICIC), a unit of the Council of Ministers of Education, Canada (CMEC), on behalf of the Ministry of Advanced Education, October 2014. Bodies 2016.

INSTITUTIONS

PUBLIC INSTITUTIONS

BRITISH COLUMBIA INSTITUTE OF TECHNOLOGY (BCIT)

3700 Willingdon Avenue, Burnaby, British Columbia V5G 3H2
Tel: + 1(604) 434-5734
Fax: + 1(604) 434-6243
EMail: international@bcit.ca
Website: http://www.bcit.ca

President: Kathy Kinloch (2014-) EMail: kkinloch@bcit.ca

School

Business (Accountancy; Business Administration; Communication Studies; Design; Finance; Human Resources; Information Technology; Insurance; International Business; Journalism; Management; Marketing; Media Studies; Radio and Television Broadcasting; Real Estate; Sales Techniques; Tourism); **Computing and Academic Studies** (Accountancy; Chemistry; Computer Networks; Computer Science; Criminology; English; Forensic Medicine and Dentistry; History; Information Technology; Literature; Mass Communication; Mathematics; Philosophy; Physics; Political Sciences; Sociology; Software Engineering); **Construction and the Environment** (Architecture; Building Technologies; Civil Engineering; Construction Engineering; Design; Ecology; Electrical Engineering; Energy Engineering; Engineering; Environmental Engineering; Fishery; Heating and Refrigeration; Interior Design; Metal Techniques; Mining Engineering; Natural Resources; Structural Architecture; Surveying and Mapping; Technology; Wildlife; Wood Technology); **Energy** (Automation and Control Engineering; Chemical Engineering; Computer Graphics; Electrical Engineering; Electronic Engineering; Energy Engineering; Fire Science; Heating and Refrigeration; Industrial Engineering; Machine Building; Mechanical Engineering; Petroleum and Gas Engineering; Polymer and Plastics Technology; Power Engineering; Robotics; Technology Education; Telecommunications Engineering); **Health Sciences** (Biomedical Engineering; Biotechnology; Cardiology; Food Technology; Genetics; Health Administration; Health Sciences; Laboratory Techniques; Medical Technology; Nursing; Occupational Health; Public Health; Radiology; Rehabilitation and Therapy); **Transportation** (Aeronautical and Aerospace Engineering; Automotive Engineering; Crafts and Trades; Maintenance Technology; Marine Engineering; Marine Transport; Railway Transport; Technology; Transport and Communications)

Further Information: Also Downtown Campus, Marine Campus, Aerospace Technology Campuses, Great Northern Way Campus and Satellite Locations (Burnaby, Surrey, North Vancouver, Langley, Kelowna, Coquitlam, Maple Ridge).

History: Founded 1961. Merged with Pacific Vocational Institute 1986 and amalgamated with Pacific Marine Training 1994. Acquired Polytechnic status 2004.

Fees: For Canadian students, Full-time degree programme tuition fees, 2,396-2,755; Technology programmes, 2,121-2,890 per term. For International students, degree programmes, 7,876-9,636; Technology programmes, 6,536-16,897 (Canadian Dollar)

Degrees and Diplomas: *Certificat et diplôme/Certificate and diploma*; *Grade associé/Associate Degree*; *Bachelor's Degree*; *Master's Degree*: **Building Technologies; Engineering.** Bachelor of Technology (Professional), 4 yrs; Advanced diploma and Advanced speciality certificate.

Student Services: Academic Counselling, Canteen, Careers Guidance, Facilities for disabled people, Library, Social Counselling, Sports Facilities

Last Updated: 22/01/15

CAMOSUN COLLEGE

3100 Foul Bay, Victoria, British Columbia V8P 5J2
Tel: + 1(250) 370-3000
Fax: + 1(250) 370-3551
EMail: inted@camosun.ca
Website: http://camosun.ca/

President: Peter Lockie (2014-) EMail: smedleyr@camosun.ca

School

Access; **Arts and Science** (Anthropology; Asian Studies; Biology; Biotechnology; Chemistry; Communication Studies; Criminology; English; Environmental Engineering; Geography; Geophysics; Health Sciences; Journalism; Mathematics; Music; Pacific Area Studies; Physics; Political Sciences; Psycholinguistics; Radio and Television Broadcasting; Social Sciences; Social Work; Sociology; Visual Arts); **Business** (Business Administration); **Health and Human Services** (Child Care and Development; Dental Hygiene; Dental Technology; Health Sciences; Medical Auxiliaries; Nursing; Pharmacy; Social and Community Services); **Trades and Technology** (Automotive Engineering; Civil Engineering; Computer Science; Cooking and Catering; Crafts and Trades; Electrical Engineering; Electronic Engineering; Horticulture; Maintenance Technology; Mechanical Engineering; Metal Techniques; Nautical Science; Wood Technology)

Campus

Interurban

History: Founded 1971.

Degrees and Diplomas: *Certificat et diplôme/Certificate and diploma*; *Grade associé/Associate Degree*; *Baccalauréat/Bachelor's Degree*

Last Updated: 22/01/15

CAPILANO UNIVERSITY

2055 Purcell Way, Vancouver, British Columbia V7J 3H5
Tel: + 1(604) 986-1911
Fax: + 1(604) 984-4985
EMail: admissions@capilanou.ca
Website: http://www.capilanou.ca

President: Kris Bulcroft (2010-) EMail: kbulcroft@capilanou.ca

Programme

Business and Professional Studies (Accountancy; Business Administration; Business and Commerce; Communication Studies; Human Resources; International Business; Law; Management; Marketing; Public Administration; Tourism); **Fine and Applied Arts** (Acting; Art Therapy; Cinema and Television; Conducting; Design; Jazz and Popular Music; Media Studies; Music; Painting and Drawing; Performing Arts; Textile Design; Theatre; Video; Visual Arts); **Health and Education** (Art Therapy; Education; Health Sciences; Nursing; Preschool Education; Rehabilitation and Therapy; Special Education); **Liberal Arts** (Anthropology; Art History; Behavioural Sciences; Chinese; Criminology; Economics; English; French; Geography; German; History; Japanese; Linguistics; Philosophy; Political Sciences; Psychology; Sociology; Spanish; Women's Studies); **Science and Technology** (Astronomy and Space Science; Biology; Chemistry; Computer Science; Design; Engineering; Geography; Geology; Mathematics; Physical Education; Physics; Statistics); **Tourism and Outdoor Recreation** (Tourism)

Further Information: Also Squamish and Sunshine Coast Campuses.

History: Founded 1968 as Capilano College. Acquired present title and status 2008.

Main Language(s) of Instruction: English

Degrees and Diplomas: *Certificat et diplôme/Certificate and diploma*; *Grade associé/Associate Degree*; *Bachelor's Degree*: **Behavioural Sciences; Business Administration; Cinema and Television; Communication Studies; Design; Law; Music; Performing Arts; Tourism.**

Academic Staff *2014*: Total 785

Student Numbers *2014*: Total 7,000

Last Updated: 22/01/15

DOUGLAS COLLEGE

P.O. Box 2503, New Westminster, British Columbia V3L 5B2
Tel: + 1(604) 527-5400
Fax: + 1(604) 527-5095
EMail: regoffice@douglascollege.ca
Website: http://www.douglascollege.ca/

President: Kathy Denton (2010-)
EMail: daileyl@douglascollege.ca

Interim Vice President, Academic and Provost: Thor Borgford
EMail: borgfordt@douglascollege.ca

Faculty

Child, Family and Community Studies (Business Administration; Child Care and Development; Criminology; Nursing; Physical Education; Physical Therapy; Psychology; Rehabilitation and Therapy; Sports Management; Urban Studies); **Commerce and Business Administration** (Accountancy; Business Administration; Business and Commerce; Computer Science; Finance; Hotel Management; Information Sciences; Management; Marketing); **Health Sciences** (Health Sciences; Nursing); **Language, Literature and Performing Arts** (Communication Studies; English; Literature; Modern Languages; Music; Performing Arts); **Science and Technology** (Biology; Building Technologies; Chemistry; Earth Sciences; Ecology; Environmental Studies; Mathematics; Natural Sciences; Physical Education; Technology)

Further Information: Traditional and Open Learning Institution

Fees: National: 95.80 per credit (Canadian Dollar), International: 510 per credit (Canadian Dollar)

Degrees and Diplomas: *Certificat et diplôme/Certificate and diploma*; *Baccalauréat/Bachelor's Degree*: **Accountancy; Finance; Home Economics; Nursing; Physical Education; Psychology.**

Student Services: Careers Guidance, Library, Sports Facilities

Last Updated: 22/01/15

EMILY CARR UNIVERSITY OF ART AND DESIGN (ECUAD)

1399 Johnston Street, Granville Island,
Vancouver, British Columbia V6H 3R9
Tel: +1(604) 844-3800 +1(800) 832-7788
Fax: +1(604) 844-3801
EMail: admissions@ecuad.ca
Website: http://www.ecuad.ca/

President and Vice Chancellor: Ron Burnett
Tel: +1(604) 844-3890 EMail: rburnett@ecuad.ca

Vice-President (Finance and Administration): Michael Clifford
Tel: +1(604) 844-3851 Ext.3851
EMail: mclifford@ecuad.ca

Faculty

Culture and Community (English; Film; Media Studies; Social and Community Services; Video; Visual Arts); **Design and Dynamic Media** (Design; Visual Arts); **Graduate Studies** (Design; Fine Arts; Media Studies; Visual Arts); **Visual Art and Material Practice** (Art History; Ceramic Art; Fine Arts; Media Studies; Painting and Drawing; Sculpture; Visual Arts)

History: Founded 1925. Acquired university status 2008. Formerly known as Emily Carr Institute of Art and Design.

Fees: National: Tuition fees for Canadian students, 378,84 for a 3-credit class (Canadian Dollar), International: 1,351.98 for a 3-credit class (Canadian Dollar)

Main Language(s) of Instruction: English

Degrees and Diplomas: *Baccalauréat/Bachelor's Degree*; *Maîtrise/Master's Degree*: **Design; Visual Arts.**

Student Services: Academic Counselling, Facilities for disabled people, Library, Residential Facilities

Student Numbers *2014-2015*: Total 1,700
Last Updated: 27/01/15

JUSTICE INSTITUTE OF BRITISH COLUMBIA

715 McBride Boulevard,
New Westminster, British Columbia V3L 5T4
Tel: +1(604) 525-5422
Fax: +1(604) 528-5518
EMail: register@jibc.ca
Website: http://www.jibc.ca/

President: Michel Tarko (2012-)

Vice President, Academic: Laureen Styles

School

Criminal Justice and Security (Civil Security; Criminal Law; Police Studies); **Health, Community and Social Justice** (Health Sciences; Indigenous Studies; Leadership; Protective Services; Psychology); **Public Safety** (Fire Science; Peace and Disarmament; Protective Services)

History: Founded 1978.

Main Language(s) of Instruction: English

Accrediting Agency: BC EQA (BC Education Quality Assurance)

Degrees and Diplomas: *Bachelor's Degree*: **Law; Welfare and Protective Services.** Also Graduate Certificates

Student Services: Academic Counselling

Student Numbers *2014-2015*: Total: c. 28,000
Last Updated: 27/01/15

KWANTLEN POLYTECHNIC UNIVERSITY

12666 - 72nd Avenue, Surrey, British Columbia V3W 2M8
Tel: +1(604) 599-2100
Fax: +1(604) 599-2086
EMail: studentinfo@kpu.ca
Website: http://www.kpu.ca/

President and Vice-Chancellor: Alan Davis (2012-)
Tel: +1(604) 599-2078
EMail: alan.davis@kwantlen.ca; keri.vangerven@kpu.ca

Registrar: Robert Hensley
Tel: +1(604) 599-2018 EMail: robert.hensley@kpu.ca

Faculty

Academic and Career Advancement *(formerly College of Qualifying Studies)* (Adult Education; Child Care and Development; Communication Studies; English); **Arts** (Anthropology; Art History; Arts and Humanities; Asian Studies; Ceramic Art; Chinese; Criminology; English; Fine Arts; French; Geography; German; History; Indic Languages; Japanese; Journalism; Linguistics; Mathematics; Media Studies; Modern Languages; Music; Musical Instruments; Painting and Drawing; Philosophy; Political Sciences; Psychology; Sculpture; Singing; Sociology; Spanish; Special Education; Visual Arts; Writing); **Health** (Gerontology; Health Sciences; Nursing; Psychiatry and Mental Health; Special Education); **Science and Horticulture** (Astronomy and Space Science; Biology; Chemistry; Engineering; Environmental Studies; Horticulture; Landscape Architecture; Mathematics; Physics; Psychology); **Trades and Technology** (Automotive Engineering; Building Technologies; Electrical Engineering; Maintenance Technology; Metal Techniques; Technology)

School

Business (Accountancy; Administration; Business Administration; Business Computing; Communication Studies; Computer Science; Economics; Human Resources; Information Sciences; Information Technology; Law; Leadership; Management; Marketing; Public Relations); **Design** *(Chip and Shannon Wilson)* (Design; Fashion Design; Graphic Design; Interior Design)

Further Information: Also Richmond, Langley and Cloverdale campuses. International Student Exchange Programme

History: Founded 1981 as Kwantlen University College, acquired present status and title 2008.

Academic Year: September to August (September-December; January-April; May-August)

Admission Requirements: Secondary school certificate or recognized foreign equivalent

Fees: Open admission and selective entry Programmes, Tuition 121.15 per credit for Canadian students and 450.00 per credit for international students; Fixed term and full-time continuous intake programmes, 105.50 per week for Canadian students and 450.00 per week for International students; For other programmes, 121.15-181.66 per credit for Canadian students and 450.00 per credit for International students (Canadian Dollar)

Main Language(s) of Instruction: English

Accrediting Agency: Government of British Columbia

Degrees and Diplomas: *Certificat et diplôme/Certificate and diploma*; *Grade associé/Associate Degree*; *Bachelor's Degree*: **Accountancy; Biology; Business Administration; Design;**

English; Fashion Design; Fine Arts; Graphic Design; Health Sciences; History; Information Technology; Journalism; Leadership; Management; Marketing; Mathematics; Music; Nursing; Physics; Political Sciences; Psychology; Sociology.

Student Services: Academic Counselling, Canteen, Careers Guidance, Facilities for disabled people, Library, Social Counselling, Sports Facilities

Last Updated: 27/01/15

NORTH ISLAND COLLEGE

2300 Ryan Road, Courtenay, British Columbia V9N 8N6
Tel: + 1(250) 334-5000
Fax: + 1(250) 334-5018
EMail: study@nic.bc.ca
Website: http://www.nic.bc.ca

President and CEO: John Bowman (2013-)
EMail: john.bowman@nic.bc.ca

Programme

Arts and Sciences (Criminology); **Business** (Accountancy; Business Administration; Management; Marketing); **Community Care** (Child Care and Development; Preschool Education); **Fine Arts and Design** (Design; Fine Arts; Jewellery Art); **Health Care** (Health Sciences; Nursing); **Tourism and Hospitality** (Hotel and Restaurant; Tourism); **Trades and Technology** (Maintenance Technology; Metal Techniques; Technology)

Further Information: Campbell River Campus; Comox Valley Campus; Port Alberni Campus and Mount Waddington Regional Campus

History: Founded 1975.

Main Language(s) of Instruction: English

Degrees and Diplomas: *Associate Degree*; *Bachelor's Degree*: **Business Administration; Management; Marketing; Nursing.**

Student Services: Academic Counselling

Last Updated: 27/01/15

OKANAGAN COLLEGE (OUC)

3333 University Way, Kelowna, British Columbia V1V 1V7
Tel: + 1(250) 862-5472
Fax: + 1(250) 862-5439
EMail: admission@okanagan.bc.ca
Website: http://www.okanagan.bc.ca/

President: Jim Hamilton EMail: jhamilton@okanagan.bc.ca

Vice President Education: Andrew Hay
EMail: ahay@okanagan.bc.ca

Faculty

Adult Continuing Education *(Adult Basic Education (ABE), Adult Special Education (ASE), Extension Services)*; **Arts** (Anthropology; Arts and Humanities; Economics; English; Fine Arts; Geography; History; Modern Languages; Philosophy; Political Sciences; Psychology; Sociology); **Education** (Education); **Engineering Technologies** (Air Transport; Civil Engineering; Computer Networks; Electrical Engineering; Electronic Engineering; Engineering; Mechanical Engineering; Technology; Telecommunications Engineering; Water Management); **Health and Social Development** (Health Sciences; Medical Auxiliaries; Nursing; Preschool Education; Primary Education; Social Work); **Industrial Trades and Services** (Business and Commerce; Cooking and Catering; Industrial and Production Economics; Industrial Maintenance; Industrial Management; Metal Techniques); **Science** (Astronomy and Space Science; Biology; Chemistry; Computer Science; Earth Sciences; Environmental Studies; Mathematics; Natural Sciences; Physics; Statistics)

School

Business (Accountancy; Administration; Business Administration; Business and Commerce; Finance; Hotel Management; Human Resources; Marketing)

Further Information: Also campuses in Armstrong, Oliver, Revelstoke, Summerland, Penticton, Salmon Arm, and Vernon.

History: Founded 1965 as Okanagan College, acquired present status and title 1995.

Academic Year: September to May (September-December; January-May). Also 2 Summer Sessions (May-June; July-August)

Admission Requirements: Secondary school certificate

Fees: c. 3350 per semester (Canadian Dollar)

Main Language(s) of Instruction: English

Accrediting Agency: Government of British Columbia; Association of Universities and Colleges of Canada

Degrees and Diplomas: *Grade associé/Associate Degree*: **Fine Arts.** *Baccalauréat/Bachelor's Degree*: **Accountancy; Business Administration; Computer Science; Education; Finance; Fine Arts; Hotel and Restaurant; Human Resources; Information Sciences; Nursing; Social Work; Tourism; Wood Technology.**

Student Services: Academic Counselling, Canteen, Careers Guidance, Facilities for disabled people, Health Services, IT Centre, Language Laboratory, Nursery Care, Social Counselling, Sports Facilities

Publishing house: OUC Press

Last Updated: 27/01/15

ROYAL ROADS UNIVERSITY (RRU)

2005 Sooke Road, Victoria, British Columbia V9B 5Y2
Tel: + 1(250) 391-2511 + 1(800) 788-8028
Fax: + 1(250) 391-2500
EMail: registrar@royalroads.ca
Website: http://www.royalroads.ca

President, Vice-Chancellor: Allan Cahoon (2007-)
Tel: + 1(250) 391-2517 EMail: allan.cahoon@royalroads.ca

Vice President, Academic and Provost: Stephen Grundy
Tel: + 1(250) 391-2545

Programme

Interdisciplinary Studies (Leadership; Management; Social Sciences)

School

Business (Business Administration; Business and Commerce; Human Resources; International Business; Management; Tourism); **Communication and Culture** (Communication Studies; Educational Administration; Educational Technology); **Environment and Sustainability** (Communication Studies; Education; Environmental Management; Environmental Studies); **Leadership Studies** (Leadership); **Peace and Conflict Management** (Computer Science; Criminology; Law; Peace and Disarmament; Philosophy; Political Sciences; Public Administration; Safety Engineering; Social Work; Sociology); **Tourism and Hospitality Management** (Hotel Management; Tourism)

Institute

Values-Based Leadership *(Todd Thomas)* (Leadership)

Centre

Applied Leadership and Management (Development Studies; Health Administration; Human Resources; Leadership; Management); **Continuing Studies** (Business Administration; Communication Studies; Computer Science; Cultural Studies; Ecology; Education; Environmental Management; Environmental Studies; Fine Arts; Horticulture; Leadership; Performing Arts; Teacher Training; Tourism; Visual Arts; Writing); **Entrepreneurial Studies** *(Eric C. Douglass)* (Business Administration); **Health Leadership and Research** (Health Administration); **Livelihoods and Ecology** (Ecology; Forest Products; Natural Resources); **Robert Bateman** (Environmental Studies; Fine Arts)

History: Founded 1995 by the Government of British Columbia. The institution offers a blend of web-based and classroom courses, or online only.

Academic Year: September to August

Fees: Doctoral Programs, 79,460; Graduate Programs, 21,630-39,450 for domestic students and 27,830-45,650 for international students; Undergraduate Programs, 13,056-17,680 for domestic students or 26,624-35,360 for international students; (Canadian Dollar)

Main Language(s) of Instruction: English

Accrediting Agency: AUCC; WARUCC

Degrees and Diplomas: *Certificat et diplôme/Certificate and diploma*; *Baccalauréat/Bachelor's Degree*; *Maîtrise/Master's Degree*: **Business Administration; Education; Educational Administration; Environmental Studies; Higher Education; Leadership; Management; Peace and Disarmament; Protective**

Services; Tourism. *Doctorat/Doctoral Degree*: **Social Sciences.** Also Graduate Diploma and Graduate Certificate

Student Services: Academic Counselling, Canteen, Careers Guidance, Facilities for disabled people, Health Services, Library, Social Counselling, Sports Facilities

Last Updated: 27/01/15

SIMON FRASER UNIVERSITY (SFU)

8888 University Drive, Burnaby, British Columbia V5A 1S6
Tel: +1(778) 782-3111
EMail: international@sfu.ca
Website: http://www.sfu.ca

President and Vice-Chancellor: Andrew Petter (2010-)
Tel: +1(778) 782-4641 EMail: Petter@sfu.ca

Vice-President, Academic and Provost: Jon Driver
Tel: +1(778) 782-3925 EMail: vpacad@sfu.ca

International Relations: Philip Steenkamp, Vice-President of External Relations Tel: +1(778) 782-9328

Faculty

Applied Sciences (Artificial Intelligence; Automation and Control Engineering; Biomedical Engineering; Computer Engineering; Computer Graphics; Computer Science; Data Processing; Electronic Engineering; Engineering; Geography; Mechanical Engineering; Microelectronics; Multimedia; Physical Engineering; Software Engineering; Surveying and Mapping); **Arts and Social Sciences** (Ancient Civilizations; Anthropology; Archaeology; Arts and Humanities; Asian Studies; Canadian Studies; Chinese; Cognitive Sciences; Criminology; Cultural Studies; Economics; English; Film; Gender Studies; German; Gerontology; Greek; Greek (Classical); History; International Studies; Japanese; Labour and Industrial Relations; Latin American Studies; Linguistics; Literature; Medieval Studies; Modern History; Modern Languages; Native American Studies; Persian; Philosophy; Political Sciences; Portuguese; Psychology; Religion; Social Sciences; Sociology; Spanish; Urban Studies; Women's Studies); **Business Administration** (Accountancy; Business Administration; Engineering Management; Finance); **Communication, Art and Technology** (Communication Studies; Computer Science; Cultural Studies; Dance; Design; Film; Fine Arts; Media Studies; Music; Music Theory and Composition; Musical Instruments; Political Sciences; Publishing and Book Trade; Technology; Theatre; Visual Arts); **Education** (Art Education; Curriculum; Education; Educational and Student Counselling; Educational Psychology; Educational Sciences; Educational Technology; English; Foreign Languages Education; Indigenous Studies; Mathematics; Natives Education; Physical Education; Secondary Education; Special Education; Teacher Training); **Environment** (Development Studies; Environmental Management; Environmental Studies; Geography; Geography (Human); Natural Resources; Surveying and Mapping; Urban Studies); **Health Sciences** (Behavioural Sciences; Biology; Chemistry; Epidemiology; Health Administration; Health Sciences; Molecular Biology; Occupational Health; Psychiatry and Mental Health; Public Health; Social and Preventive Medicine; Statistics; Toxicology); **Science** (Actuarial Science; Applied Mathematics; Applied Physics; Behavioural Sciences; Biochemistry; Biological and Life Sciences; Biology; Biophysics; Business Administration; Cell Biology; Chemistry; Computer Science; Earth Sciences; Ecology; Environmental Studies; Forestry; Geology; Health Education; Management; Marine Science and Oceanography; Mathematical Physics; Mathematics; Molecular Biology; Neurosciences; Nuclear Physics; Nutrition; Physical Therapy; Physics; Physiology; Rehabilitation and Therapy; Sports; Statistics; Toxicology)

Further Information: Also campuses in Surrey and Vancouver

History: Founded 1963. First students enrolled 1965. A downtown Vancouver campus (Simon Fraser University at Vancouver) opened 1989. Programmes at this campus focus on the advanced recurring educational needs of the urban population. The Surrey campus (Simon Fraser University Surrey) opened its doors in 2002 offering undegraduate and graduate programmes including innovative cohort programmes: Tech One, Science Year One and Explorations.

Academic Year: January to December (January-April; May-August; September-December)

Admission Requirements: Secondary school certificate or recognized foreign equivalent

Fees: Undergraduate tuition fee, 173.91-231.88 per unit for domestic students or 654.94-734.91 per unit for international students; Graduate tuition fees: Research programmes full-time fee, 1,728.80 per term or 5,186.40 per year, as of Fall 2014 (Canadian Dollar)

Main Language(s) of Instruction: English

Degrees and Diplomas: *Certificat et diplôme/Certificate and diploma*; *Baccalauréat/Bachelor's Degree*; *Maîtrise/Master's Degree*: **Computer Science; Economics; Education; Environmental Studies; Health Sciences; Natural Sciences.** *Doctorat/Doctoral Degree*: **Computer Science; Economics; Education; Environmental Studies; Health Sciences; Natural Sciences.** Also Honour Bachelor's degree; Executive MBA; Double-Degree Programme.

Student Services: Academic Counselling, Canteen, Careers Guidance, Facilities for disabled people, Foreign Studies Centre, Health Services, Language Laboratory, Library, Nursery Care, Sports Facilities

Publications: International History Review; Journal of Computational Intelligence

Last Updated: 27/01/15

THE UNIVERSITY OF BRITISH COLUMBIA (UBC)

2329 West Mall, Vancouver, British Columbia V6T 1Z4
Tel: +1(604) 822-2211
Fax: +1(604) 822-5055
EMail: student.information@ubc.ca; international.reception@ubc.ca
Website: http://www.ubc.ca

Interim President: Martha Piper
Tel: +1(604) 822-8300 EMail: presidents.office@ubc.ca

Provost and Vice-President Academic, pro tem: Angela Redish
EMail: provost.vpa@ubc.ca

International Relations: Helen Pennant, Executive Director, International Affairs
EMail: helen.pennant@ubc.ca; ubcintl@interchange.ubc.ca

Faculty

Applied Science (Architecture; Bioengineering; Biomedical Engineering; Chemical Engineering; Civil Engineering; Computer Engineering; Design; Electrical Engineering; Engineering; Environmental Engineering; Geological Engineering; Landscape Architecture; Materials Engineering; Mechanical Engineering; Mining Engineering; Nursing; Physical Engineering); **Arts** (Anthropology; Archiving; Art History; Arts and Humanities; Asian Studies; Central European Studies; Eastern European Studies; Economics; English; Film; Fine Arts; French; Gender Studies; Geography; History; Information Sciences; Italian; Journalism; Linguistics; Museum Studies; Music; Philosophy; Political Sciences; Psychology; Religious Studies; Social Work; Sociology; Spanish; Theatre; Visual Arts; Women's Studies; Writing); **Commerce and Business Administration** (Accountancy; Behavioural Sciences; Business Administration; Business and Commerce; Economics; Finance; Human Resources; Information Sciences; Law; Marketing; Operations Research; Real Estate; Transport Management); **Continuing Studies** (Business Administration; Chinese; Cooking and Catering; Development Studies; English; French; French Studies; Health Administration; Italian; Japanese; Law; Management; Marketing; Multimedia; Psychology; Spanish; Technology); **Creative and Critical Studies** *(Okanagan Campus)* (Art History; Cultural Studies; English; French; Spanish; Visual Arts); **Dentistry** (Biological and Life Sciences; Dentistry; Health Sciences; Oral Pathology); **Education** (Curriculum; Education; Educational and Student Counselling; Educational Psychology; Educational Sciences; Foreign Languages Education; Literacy Education; Physical Education; Teacher Training); **Forestry** (Forest Management; Forest Products; Forestry; Wood Technology); **Graduate Studies** (Adult Education; Agricultural Economics; Ancient Civilizations; Anthropology; Archaeology; Architecture; Archiving; Art Education; Art History; Asian Studies; Astronomy and Space Science; Biochemistry; Bioengineering; Biomedical Engineering; Botany; Business Administration; Cell Biology; Chemical Engineering; Chemistry; Civil Engineering; Classical Languages; Computer Engineering; Computer Science; Cultural Studies; Curriculum; Dentistry; Development Studies; Economic History; Economics; Education; Educational Administration; Educational Sciences; Educational Technology; Electrical Engineering;

English; Environmental Management; Environmental Studies; Film; Fine Arts; Foreign Languages Education; Forestry; French; Gender Studies; Genetics; Geography; Geological Engineering; Geology; Geophysics; Germanic Studies; Health Administration; Health Sciences; Higher Education; History; Home Economics Education; Humanities and Social Science Education; Hygiene; Immunology; Information Sciences; Journalism; Landscape Architecture; Law; Library Science; Linguistics; Literacy Education; Literature; Marine Science and Oceanography; Materials Engineering; Mathematics; Mathematics Education; Measurement and Precision Engineering; Mechanical Engineering; Media Studies; Medical Technology; Medicine; Meteorology; Microbiology; Mining Engineering; Molecular Biology; Music; Music Education; Natural Resources; Neurosciences; Nursing; Nutrition; Occupational Health; Occupational Therapy; Oncology; Pacific Area Studies; Pathology; Pharmacology; Pharmacy; Philosophy; Physical Education; Physical Engineering; Physical Therapy; Physics; Political Sciences; Preschool Education; Psychology; Public Health; Rehabilitation and Therapy; Religious Studies; Science Education; Social Work; Sociology; Software Engineering; Soil Science; Spanish; Special Education; Speech Therapy and Audiology; Statistics; Surgery; Technology Education; Theatre; Women's Studies; Writing; Zoology); **Land and Food Systems** (Agricultural Economics; Biology; Botany; Ecology; Food Science; Health Sciences; Nutrition; Soil Science; Zoology); **Law** (Law); **Medicine** (Anaesthesiology; Biochemistry; Cardiology; Cell Biology; Dermatology; Endocrinology; Gastroenterology; Genetics; Gynaecology and Obstetrics; Haematology; Immunology; Laboratory Techniques; Medicine; Midwifery; Molecular Biology; Nephrology; Occupational Health; Occupational Therapy; Oncology; Ophthalmology; Orthodox Theology; Paediatrics; Pathology; Pharmacology; Physical Therapy; Physiology; Psychiatry and Mental Health; Public Health; Radiology; Rehabilitation and Therapy; Respiratory Therapy; Rheumatology; Speech Therapy and Audiology; Surgery; Urology); **Pharmaceutical Sciences** (Pharmacy); **Science** (Astronomy and Space Science; Botany; Chemistry; Computer Science; Earth Sciences; Immunology; Marine Science and Oceanography; Mathematics; Microbiology; Physics; Statistics; Zoology)

College

Health Disciplines (Health Sciences; Public Health); **Interdisciplinary Studies** (Applied Mathematics; Asian Studies; Biotechnology; Computer Graphics; Computer Science; Environmental Management; Environmental Studies; Ethics; European Studies; Fishery; Forest Economics; Gender Studies; Genetics; International Relations; Molecular Biology; Multimedia; Natural Resources; Neurosciences; Oncology; Pacific Area Studies; Peace and Disarmament; Public Health; Regional Planning; Statistics; Women's Studies)

School

Arts and Sciences *(Irving K. Barber)* (Biochemistry; Biology; Earth Sciences; Environmental Studies)

Further Information: Also Okanagan Campus. UBC is affiliated with several research institutes, centres, organizations, and hospitals, many of which are located on the university's main Point Grey campus. Details available at: http://www.ubc.ca/affiliated/index.html

History: Founded 1908 and incorporated by the Provincial Government. Admitted first students 1915 and moved to its present location at Point Grey 1925. The University operates under the authority of the University Act of the Province of British Columbia (RSBC, 1979), and is the second largest University in Canada.

Academic Year: September to August (September-December; January-April). Also Summer session (May-July; July-August)

Admission Requirements: Secondary school certificate or recognized foreign equivalent

Fees: National: Undergraduate Degree programmes for Canadian Citizens or Permanent Residents: 4,890.30-7,245.90 per annum (Canadian Dollar), International: International Students: 26,399.10-30,798.95 (depending on programmes)

Main Language(s) of Instruction: English

Degrees and Diplomas: *Certificat et diplôme/Certificate and diploma*; *Baccalauréat/Bachelor's Degree*; *Maîtrise/Master's Degree*; *Doctorat/Doctoral Degree*: **Anthropology; Art History; Asian Studies; Biological and Life Sciences; Chemistry; Civil Engineering; Computer Engineering; Curriculum; Dentistry; Economics; Education; Educational Administration; Educational Sciences; Electrical Engineering; English; Food Science; Forestry; International and Comparative Education; Medicine; Psychology.** Also Certificates in Advanced Studies (Library, Archival and Information Studies) and Diplomas (Accountancy, Administration, Art History, Applied Creative Non-Fiction, Piano Studies, Computer Science, Education, Film Studies, Forestry, Linguistics, Aquaculture, Meteorology, Periodontics, Translation, Urban Land Economics); Also Combined Programmes and Dual Degrees.

Student Services: Academic Counselling, Canteen, Careers Guidance, Facilities for disabled people, Foreign Studies Centre, Health Services, Language Laboratory, Library, Nursery Care, Social Counselling, Sports Facilities

Publications: Asia Pacific Report; B.C. Studies; BC Asian Review; Canadian Journal of Civil Engineering; Canadian Journal of Family Law; Canadian Literature; Canadian Yearbook of International Law; Journal of Business Administration; Pacific Affairs; PRISM International; Studies in Medieval and Renaissance History; University of British Columbia Law Review

Publishing House: University of British Columbia Press

Academic Staff *2014-2015*	**TOTAL**
FULL-TIME	**15,253**
Student Numbers *2014-2015*	
All (Foreign included)	**59,659**
FOREIGN ONLY	**11965**

Last Updated: 27/01/15

THOMPSON RIVERS UNIVERSITY (TRU)

Box 3010, 900 McGill Road, Kamloops, British Columbia V2C 0C8
Tel: +1(250) 828-5000
Fax: +1(250) 828-5006
EMail: admissions@tru.ca
Website: http://www.tru.ca

President and Vice-Chancellor: Alan Shaver (2010-)
Tel: +1(250) 828-5001 EMail: president@tru.ca

Vice-President, Administration and Finance: Matt Milovick (2013-) Tel: +1(250) 828-5012 EMail: mmilovick@tru.ca

Provost and Vice-President Academic: Ulrich Scheck
EMail: Provost@tru.ca

International Relations: Baihua Chadwick, Associate Vice President, International and CEO Global Operations
Tel: +1(250) 828-1902

Faculty

Adventure, Culinary Arts and Tourism (Cooking and Catering; Food Science; Hotel Management; Sports; Sports Management; Tourism); **Arts** (Anthropology; Canadian Studies; Chinese; Economics; English; Fine Arts; French; Geography; German; History; Japanese; Journalism; Modern Languages; Performing Arts; Philosophy; Political Sciences; Psychology; Sociology; Spanish; Theatre; Visual Arts); **Human, Social and Educational Development** (Distance Education; Education; Foreign Languages Education; Physical Education; Preschool Education; Primary Education; Social Work; Special Education); **Law** (Law); **Science** (Animal Husbandry; Architectural and Environmental Design; Astronomy and Space Science; Automation and Control Engineering; Biological and Life Sciences; Biology; Cell Biology; Chemistry; Computer Engineering; Computer Science; Design; Ecology; Electronic Engineering; Engineering; Engineering Drawing and Design; Fine Arts; Geology; Mathematics; Molecular Biology; Natural Resources; Physics; Respiratory Therapy; Statistics; Telecommunications Engineering)

School

Business and Economics *(SoBE)* (Accountancy; Business Administration; Computer Science; Economics; Finance; Human Resources; International Business; Management; Marketing); **Nursing** (Health Sciences; Nursing); **Trades and Technology** (Horticulture; Metal Techniques; Service Trades; Technology; Water Management)

Further Information: Also Williams Lake Campus.

History: Founded 1970 as Cariboo College. Named the University College of the Cariboo (UCC) 1992. Acquired present status and title 2004.

Academic Year: September to August (September-December; January-April; May-August)

Admission Requirements: Secondary school certificate or recognized foreign equivalent; English Language Assessment Test, TOEFL or IELTS for students whose first language is not English

Fees: Canadian citizens, 120.33 per credit; Master of Business Administration, 561.13/credit; Master of Education, 457.77 per credit; Master of Science, 1,987.33/semester. International Students, Undergraduate: 7,900/semester. Master of Business Administration: 849.19 per credit. Master of Education: 875.85/credit. Master of Science: 5,838.99/semester (US Dollar)

Main Language(s) of Instruction: English

Degrees and Diplomas: *Certificat et diplôme/Certificate and diploma*; *Grade associé/Associate Degree*; *Baccalauréat/Bachelor's Degree*; *Maîtrise/Master's Degree*: **Business Administration; Education; Environmental Studies.**

Student Services: Academic Counselling, Canteen, Careers Guidance, Cultural Activities, Facilities for disabled people, Foreign Studies Centre, Health Services, Library, Nursery Care, Residential Facilities, Social Counselling, Sports Facilities

Last Updated: 27/01/15

UNIVERSITY OF NORTHERN BRITISH COLUMBIA (UNBC)

3333 University Way, Prince George, British Columbia V2N 4Z9
Tel: + 1(250) 960-5555
Fax: + 1(250) 960-5791
EMail: registrar-info@unbc.ca
Website: http://www.unbc.ca

President: Daniel J. Weeks
Tel: + 1(250) 960-5600 EMail: president@unbc.ca

Vice-President Administration: Eileen Bray
Tel: + 1(250) 960-5541 EMail: Eileen.Bray@unbc.ca

College

Arts, Social and Health Sciences (Anthropology; Canadian Studies; Community Health; Economics; Education; English; Health Sciences; History; Indigenous Studies; International Studies; Native Language; Nursing; Political Sciences; Psychology; Rehabilitation and Therapy; Social Work; Women's Studies); **Science and Management** (Accountancy; Business Administration; Chemistry; Computer Science; Ecology; Environmental Engineering; Environmental Management; Environmental Studies; Finance; Geography; Human Resources; International Business; Leisure Studies; Marketing; Mathematics; Physics; Tourism)

Programme

Continuing Studies (Christian Religious Studies; Forest Management; Human Resources; Management; Music Education; Occupational Health; Surveying and Mapping; Wildlife); **Graduate Studies** (Anthropology; Biology; Business Administration; Chemistry; Community Health; Computer Science; Economics; Education; English; Environmental Studies; Forestry; Gender Studies; Geography; Health Sciences; History; Indigenous Studies; International Studies; Leadership; Mathematics; Natural Resources; Nursing; Physics; Political Sciences; Psychology; Rehabilitation and Therapy; Social Work; Special Education; Tourism); **Northern Medical** (Anaesthesiology; Cardiology; Dermatology; Epidemiology; Ethics; Gynaecology and Obstetrics; Health Sciences; Law; Medicine; Ophthalmology; Orthopaedics; Paediatrics; Pharmacology; Psychiatry and Mental Health; Surgery)

Further Information: Also following campuses: Northwest (Prince Rupert), Peace River-Liard (Fort St. John) and South-Central (Quesnel).

History: Founded 1990.

Academic Year: September to May (September-December; January-May)

Admission Requirements: Successful completion of an academic grade 12 programme (65% average)

Fees: Tuition for undergraduate studies, 151.28 per credit hour; Foreign students, 529.47 per credit hour. Graduate studies, 864-922.18 per semester; MBA, 6,494.60 per semester (Canadian Dollar)

Main Language(s) of Instruction: English

Accrediting Agency: Association of Universities and Colleges of Canada

Degrees and Diplomas: *Certificat et diplôme/Certificate and diploma*; *Baccalauréat/Bachelor's Degree*: **Business and Commerce; Education; Fine Arts; Health Sciences; Nursing; Social Work.** *Maîtrise/Master's Degree*: **Business Administration; Community Health; Economics; Education; Environmental Studies; Health Sciences; History; International Studies; Mathematics and Computer Science; Natural Resources; Nursing; Sociology.** *Doctorat/Doctoral Degree*: **Environmental Studies; Health Sciences; Natural Resources; Psychology.**

Student Services: Academic Counselling, Canteen, Careers Guidance, Cultural Activities, Facilities for disabled people, Foreign Studies Centre, Health Services, IT Centre, Language Laboratory, Library, Nursery Care, Social Counselling, Sports Facilities

Last Updated: 27/01/15

UNIVERSITY OF THE FRASER VALLEY (UFV)

33844 King Road, Abbotsford, British Columbia V2S 7M8
Tel: + 1(604) 504-7441
Fax: + 1(604) 855-7614
EMail: info@ufv.ca
Website: http://www.ufv.ca/

President: Mark Evered (2009-)
Tel: + 1(604) 854-4608 EMail: jill.smith@ufv.ca

Vice-President, Academic and Provost: Eric Davis
Tel: + 1(604) 864-4630 EMail: eric.davis@ufv.ca

International Relations: David McGuire, Executive Director of International Education Department
Tel: + 1(604) 854-4544 EMail: international@ufv.ca

Faculty

Access and Continuing Studies (Accountancy; Business Administration; Child Care and Development; Communication Studies; Computer Science; Dentistry; Education; English; Environmental Studies; Foreign Languages Education; Health Sciences; Horticulture; Human Resources; Law; Library Science; Management; Modern Languages; Nursing; Photography; Publishing and Book Trade; Service Trades; Technology; Writing); **Applied and Technical Studies** (Agriculture; Air Transport; Architectural and Environmental Design; Automotive Engineering; Cooking and Catering; Electrical Engineering; Electronic Engineering; Jewellery Art; Metal Techniques; Technology; Wood Technology); **Health Sciences** (Medical Auxiliaries; Nursing; Physical Therapy); **Professional Studies** (Accountancy; Administration; Adult Education; Agricultural Management; Air Transport; Business Administration; Child Care and Development; Dental Hygiene; Dental Technology; Health Sciences; Information Technology; Library Science; Management; Marketing; Nursing; Preschool Education; Service Trades; Social and Community Services; Social Work; Teacher Trainers Education); **Science** (Biology; Chemistry; Computer Science; Engineering; Geography; Mathematics; Physical Education; Physical Therapy; Physics; Statistics)

College

Arts (Chinese; Communication Studies; Criminal Law; Criminology; Cultural Studies; Economics; English; Fashion Design; French; Geography; Graphic Design; History; Indic Languages; Japanese; Journalism; Media Studies; Modern Languages; Native Language; Philosophy; Political Sciences; Psychology; Russian; Social Studies; Spanish; Theatre; Visual Arts)

School

Graduate Studies (Criminal Law; Social Work)

Further Information: Also campuses and locations in Abbotsford, Chilliwack, Mission, Hope and Agassiz, and a growing presence in Chandigarh, India.

History: Founded 1974 as Fraser Valley College, a two-year community college. Became the University College of the Fraser Valley (UCFV) 1991. Acquired university status and present title 2008.

Academic Year: September to August (September-December; January-April; May-August)

Fees: Tuition, 123.78 per credit; Some programmes (Dental Hygiene, Nursing, Teacher Education) have special fees 2,706-

18,041 per programme. Graduate studies, 509.23 per credit (Canadian Dollar)

Main Language(s) of Instruction: English

Accrediting Agency: British Columbia Ministry of Advanced Education; Canadian Bureau of International Education (CBIE); British Columbia Centre of International Education (BCCIE); Association of Universities and Colleges of Canada (AUCC); Association of Canadian Colleges (ACC)

Degrees and Diplomas: *Certificat et diplôme/Certificate and diploma*; *Grade associé/Associate Degree*; *Baccalauréat/Bachelor's Degree*; *Maîtrise/Master's Degree*: **Criminal Law.** Also Honours Bachelor's degree.

Student Services: Academic Counselling, Canteen, Facilities for disabled people, Foreign Studies Centre, Language Laboratory, Social Counselling, Sports Facilities

Student Numbers *2013-2014*: Total: c. 15,000

Last Updated: 27/01/15

UNIVERSITY OF VICTORIA (UVIC)

P.O. Box 1700, STN CSC, Victoria, British Columbia V8W 2Y2
Tel: +1(250) 721-7211
Fax: +1(250) 721-7212
EMail: admsinfo@uvic.ca
Website: http://www.uvic.ca

President and Vice-Chancellor: Jamie Cassels
Tel: +1(250) 721-7002 EMail: pres@uvic.ca

Vice-President Academic and Provost: Valerie S. Kuehne (2014-) Tel: +1(250) 721-7013 EMail: provost@uvic.ca

Faculty

Education (Education; Health Education; Natives Education; Physical Education; Primary Education; Secondary Education; Teacher Training); **Engineering** (Computer Engineering; Computer Science; Electrical Engineering; Engineering; Mechanical Engineering; Software Engineering); **Fine Arts** (Art History; Fine Arts; Music; Music Education; Music Theory and Composition; Musical Instruments; Painting and Drawing; Photography; Sculpture; Theatre; Video; Visual Arts; Writing); **Graduate Studies** (Anthropology; Applied Linguistics; Art History; Asian Studies; Astronomy and Space Science; Biochemistry; Biology; Business Administration; Chemistry; Child Care and Development; Computer Engineering; Computer Science; Curriculum; Economics; Educational Psychology; Electrical Engineering; English; Environmental Studies; French; Geography; Germanic Studies; Greek (Classical); History; Indigenous Studies; Information Sciences; Italian; Latin; Law; Leadership; Linguistics; Marine Science and Oceanography; Mathematics; Mechanical Engineering; Microbiology; Music; Nursing; Pacific Area Studies; Peace and Disarmament; Philosophy; Physical Education; Physics; Political Sciences; Psychology; Public Administration; Russian; Social and Community Services; Social Work; Sociology; Spanish; Statistics; Theatre; Visual Arts; Writing); **Human and Social Development** (Child Care and Development; Indigenous Studies; Information Sciences; Nursing; Peace and Disarmament; Public Administration; Public Health; Social Policy; Social Work); **Humanities** (Asian Studies; English; Ethics; European Studies; Film; French; German; Germanic Studies; Greek (Classical); History; Indigenous Studies; Italian; Latin; Linguistics; Medieval Studies; Mediterranean Studies; Pacific Area Studies; Philosophy; Religious Studies; Slavic Languages; Social Studies; Spanish; Women's Studies; Writing); **Law** (Law); **Science** (Astronomy and Space Science; Biochemistry; Biology; Chemistry; Earth Sciences; Marine Science and Oceanography; Mathematics; Microbiology; Physics; Statistics); **Social Sciences** (Anthropology; Economics; Environmental Studies; Geography; Political Sciences; Psychology; Social Sciences; Sociology)

Division

Continuing Studies (Adult Education; Arts and Humanities; Business Administration; Canadian Studies; Community Health; Computer Science; Continuing Education; Dentistry; Distance Education; English; Environmental Management; Fine Arts; Foreign Languages Education; French; Health Sciences; Heritage Preservation; Indigenous Studies; Museum Management; Native Language; Occupational Health; Public Relations; Tourism); **Medical Sciences** (Medicine; Neurosciences)

School

Business *(Peter B. Gustavson)* (Business Administration; Business and Commerce; International Business; Management)

Institute

Climate Solutions *(Pacific)*; **Coastal and Oceans Research**; **Dispute Resolution**; **Integrated Energy Systems** *(IESVic)*

Centre

Aboriginal Health Research; **Addictions Research of B.C.**; **Advanced Materials and Related Technology** *(CAMTEC)*; **Aging**; **Asia-Pacific Initiatives** *(CAPI)*; **Biomedical Research**; **Co-operative and Community-Based Economy**; **Forest Biology**; **Global Studies; Studies in Religion and Society**; **Youth and Society**

Laboratory

Automation, Communication and Information Systems Research *(LACIR)*

History: Founded 1903 as Victoria College in affiliation with McGill University, acquired present status and title 1963.

Academic Year: September to August (September-December; January-April; May-August)

Admission Requirements: Secondary school certificate or recognized foreign equivalent

Fees: Undergraduate Tuition, 317.74 per unit; international students, 1,028.12 per unit. Graduate tuition fees, 1,650.08 for Canadian students and 1,963.44 for International students. Exceptions: MBA, for Canadian students, 3,552.78 per term for daytime programme and 2,368.52 for evening programme; for international students 3,866.16 per term for daytime programme 2,577.44 per term for evening programme; Master's degrees in Global Business, Community Development, Health Informatics, Public Health and Double Degree Nursing and Health Information, 2,000-6,000 per term for Candian students and 2,380-7,666.68 for international students. Graduate diploma and certificates, 612-750 for Canadian students and 726.24-1,000 for International students (Canadian Dollar)

Main Language(s) of Instruction: English

Degrees and Diplomas: *Certificat et diplôme/Certificate and diploma*; *Baccalauréat/Bachelor's Degree*; *Maîtrise/Master's Degree*; *Doctorat/Doctoral Degree*: **Anthropology; Art History; Astronomy and Space Science; Biochemistry; Biology; Business Administration; Chemistry; Child Care and Development; Computer Engineering; Computer Science; Curriculum; Earth Sciences; Economics; Educational Administration; Educational Psychology; Electrical Engineering; English; Environmental Studies; Geography; Germanic Languages; Greek; Health Sciences; History; Law; Linguistics; Marine Science and Oceanography; Mathematics; Mechanical Engineering; Microbiology; Music; Neurosciences; Nursing; Philosophy; Physical Education; Political Sciences; Psychology; Public Administration; Romance Languages; Slavic Languages; Sociology.** Also MBA; Honours Bachelor's degree; Concurrent degree programmes (JD/Master of Business Administration, JD/Master of Public Administration, JD/BCL (Civil Law Degree Graduates)).

Student Services: Academic Counselling, Canteen, Careers Guidance, Cultural Activities, Facilities for disabled people, Foreign Studies Centre, Health Services, Library, Nursery Care, Social Counselling, Sports Facilities

Last Updated: 27/01/15

VANCOUVER ISLAND UNIVERSITY

900 Fifth Street, Nanaimo, British Columbia V9R 5S5
Tel: +1(250) 753-3245
Fax: +1(250) 755-8725
EMail: info@viu.ca
Website: http://www.viu.ca/

President and Vice-Chancellor: Ralph Nilson
Tel: +1(250) 740-6102 EMail: Ralph.Nilson@viu.ca

Vice-President, Administration and Finance: Shelley Legin
Tel: +1(250) 740-6231

Vice-President Academic and Provost: David Witty (2010-)
Tel: +1(250) 740-6436 EMail: Michelle.Champagne@viu.ca

International Relations: Graham Pike, Dean, International Programmes
Tel: + 1(250) 740-6311
EMail: Graham.Pike@viu.ca; worldviu@viu.ca

Faculty

Adult and Continuing Education (Animal Husbandry; Business Administration; Communication Studies; Fire Science; Forestry; Health Administration; Management; Marine Engineering; Psychiatry and Mental Health; Service Trades; Technology)

Programme

Natural Resources Extension (Environmental Studies; Fishery; Geology; Water Science)

Area

Art, Design and Performing Arts (Fine Arts; Graphic Design; Interior Design; Jazz and Popular Music; Music; Theatre; Visual Arts); **Business and Management** (Business Administration; Health Administration; Hotel and Restaurant; Leisure Studies; Management; Sports Management; Tourism); **Career and Academic Preparation** (Biology; Chemistry; Computer Science; Education; English; History; Mathematics; Natural Sciences; Physics; Psychology; Technology; Writing); **Education** (Education; Leadership; Special Education); **English-as-a-Second-Language** *(ESL)* (English); **First Nations** (Child Care and Development; Forestry; Natives Education; Sports Management); **Health** (Dental Hygiene; Dentistry; Health Administration; Health Sciences; Nursing); **High School Equivalency** *(ABE)* (Biology; Chemistry; Computer Science; Education; English; History; Mathematics; Natural Sciences; Physics; Psychology; Writing); **Human Services** (Child Care and Development; Horticulture; Leadership; Preschool Education; Social and Community Services; Special Education); **Humanities and Social Sciences** (Anthropology; Arts and Humanities; Biology; Business Administration; Chemistry; Computer Science; Criminology; Development Studies; Earth Sciences; Economics; English; Environmental Management; Geography; Graphic Design; History; Indigenous Studies; International Economics; Mathematics; Media Studies; Natural Resources; Philosophy; Physical Education; Political Sciences; Psychology; Romance Languages; Sociology; Theatre; Visual Arts; Welfare and Protective Services; Women's Studies; Writing); **Online/Distance Courses** (Biology; Business Computing; Child Care and Development; Energy Engineering; English; Geology; Gerontology; Health Administration; Journalism; Media Studies; Physical Education; Sports; Tourism; Writing); **Science and Technology** (Aquaculture; Biology; Chemistry; Computer Science; Earth Sciences; Engineering; Fishery; Forest Products; Geography; Horticulture; Information Technology; Mathematics; Natural Resources; Physics; Psychology); **Tourism, Recreation and Hospitality** (Hotel and Restaurant; Leisure Studies; Sports Management; Tourism); **Trades and Applied Technology** (Automotive Engineering; Business Computing; Cooking and Catering; Electrical Engineering; Heating and Refrigeration; Information Technology; Marine Transport; Metal Techniques; Road Engineering; Service Trades; Sports; Technology)

Further Information: Also campuses in Cowichan, Parksville - Qualicum, Powell River.

History: Founded 1969 as Malaspina College. Renamed Malaspina University-College 1989. Acquired present title 2008. A comprehensive university-college serving the central Vancouver Island region.

Academic Year: September to May (September-December; January-May). Also Summer Session (May-August)

Admission Requirements: Secondary school certificate or equivalent. TOEFL test for foreign students with score of min. 550

Fees: National: Undegraduate:136.51 per semester credit hour; MBA program: 19,632.35 (Canadian Dollar), International: MBA program: 31,500.00 (Canadian Dollar)

Main Language(s) of Instruction: English

Accrediting Agency: Association of Universities and Colleges of Canada (AUCC)

Degrees and Diplomas: *Certificat et diplôme/Certificate and diploma; Grade associé/Associate Degree; Baccalauréat/Bachelor's Degree; Maîtrise/Master's Degree*: **Business Administration; Education; Educational Administration; Leisure Studies; Parks and Recreation; Special Education.**

Student Services: Academic Counselling, Canteen, Careers Guidance, Facilities for disabled people, Foreign Studies Centre, Health Services, Language Laboratory, Library, Nursery Care, Social Counselling, Sports Facilities

Academic Staff *2013-2014*	**TOTAL**
FULL-TIME	**2,000**
Student Numbers *2013-2014*	
All (Foreign included)	**16,000**
FOREIGN ONLY	**1800**

Last Updated: 06/02/15

PRIVATE INSTITUTIONS

ACSENDA SCHOOL OF MANAGEMENT - VANCOUVER

9th Floor – 1090 West Pender,
Vancouver, British Colombia V6E 2N7
Tel: + 1(604) 430-5111
Website: http://www.acsenda.com/

President and Vice Chancellor: Lindsay Redpath (2014-)

Programme

Business Administration (Business Administration)

History: Founded 2003 as Sprott Shaw Degree College, acquired present title and status 2013.

Main Language(s) of Instruction: English

Accrediting Agency: BC Minister of Advanced Education

Degrees and Diplomas: *Bachelor's Degree*: **Accountancy; Business Administration; Hotel and Restaurant; International Business; Management.** Also Post Graduate Certificate and Post Graduate Diploma (Accounting, Human Resources)

Student Services: Library, Sports Facilities

Last Updated: 16/01/15

PACIFIC COAST UNIVERSITY FOR WORKPLACE HEALTH SCIENCES

4755 Cherry Creek Road, Port Alberni V9Y 0A7
Tel: + 1 778-421-0821
Fax: + 1 778-421-0823
EMail: education@pcu-whs.ca
Website: http://www.pcu-whs.ca/

President: Wolfgang Zimmermann

Vice-President Academic and Dean: Lynn Shaw
EMail: lynn.shaw@pcu-whs.ca

Programme

Disability Management (Welfare and Protective Services)

Further Information: Also online programs

History: Founded 2011.

Main Language(s) of Instruction: English

Degrees and Diplomas: *Bachelor's Degree*: **Welfare and Protective Services.**

Student Services: Academic Counselling, Facilities for disabled people, Library

Last Updated: 03/02/15

QUEST UNIVERSITY CANADA (QUC)

3200 University Blvd., Squamish, British Columbia V8B 0N8
Tel: + 1(604) 898-0800
Fax: + 1(604) 815-0829
EMail: info@questu.ca
Website: http://www.questu.ca

President: Peter Englert EMail: peter.englert@questu.ca

Faculty

Arts and Sciences (Arts and Humanities; History; Literature; Mathematics; Music; Natural Sciences; Philosophy; Visual Arts)

Academic Year: September-April

Fees: 28,000 per Academic Year (Canadian Dollar)

Main Language(s) of Instruction: English

Accrediting Agency: British Columbia Ministry of Advanced Education

Degrees and Diplomas: *Baccalauréat/Bachelor's Degree*: **Arts and Humanities.**

Student Services: Academic Counselling, Canteen, Careers Guidance, Facilities for disabled people, Health Services, Language Laboratory, Social Counselling, Sports Facilities

Academic Staff *2012-2013*	MEN	WOMEN	TOTAL
FULL-TIME	41	37	**78**
PART-TIME	2	4	**6**
STAFF WITH DOCTORATE			
FULL-TIME	21	8	**29**
Student Numbers *2012-2013*			
All (Foreign included)	215	205	**420**
FOREIGN ONLY	–	–	**201**

Part-time students, 35.

Last Updated: 08/04/13

THE ART INSTITUTE OF VANCOUVER (AI VANCOUVER)

2665 Renfrew Street, Vancouver, British Columbia V5M 0A7
Tel: +1 604.683.9200
EMail: aivadm@aii.edu
Website: http://artinstitutes.edu/vancouver

Area

Culinary Art (Cooking and Catering); **Design** (Computer Graphics; Design; Fashion Design; Graphic Design; Interior Design); **Fashion** (Fashion Design; Marketing; Textile Design); **Media Arts** (Film; Graphic Design; Photography; Video)

History: Founded 2004.

Accrediting Agency: Accrediting Council for Independent Colleges and Schools (ACICS)

Degrees and Diplomas: *Certificate/Diploma*; *Bachelor's Degree*: **Art Management; Design; Graphic Design; Interior Design.**

Student Services: Library, Sports Facilities

Last Updated: 03/02/15

TRINITY WESTERN UNIVERSITY (TWU)

Work 7600 Glover Road, Langley, British Columbia V2Y 1Y1
Tel: +1(604) 888-7511
Fax: +1(604) 513-2061
EMail: admissions@twu.ca
Website: http://www.twu.ca

President: Bob Kuhn (2014-)
Tel: +1(604) 888-7511, Ext.2021 EMail: president@twu.ca

Provost: Robert Wood
Tel: +1(604) 513-2121 Extension 3203 EMail: wood@twu.ca

International Relations: Mark Charlton, International Liaison Officer Tel: +1(604) 888-7511, Ext. 3120 EMail: charlton@twu.ca

Faculty

Humanities and Social Sciences (Arts and Humanities; Bible; Canadian Studies; Chinese; Christian Religious Studies; Cultural Studies; English; Environmental Studies; European Studies; French; Geography; German; History; International Studies; Japanese; Linguistics; Literature; Missionary Studies; Modern Languages; Philosophy; Political Sciences; Psychology; Religious Studies; Russian; Social Studies; Sociology; Spanish); **Natural and Applied Sciences** (Biology; Biotechnology; Chemistry; Computer Science; Engineering; Environmental Studies; Mathematics; Physics)

Programme

ACTS Seminaries (Applied Linguistics; Christian Religious Studies; Holy Writings; Religion; Social Problems; Theology)

School

Business (Accountancy; Business Administration; Communication Studies; Finance; Human Resources; International Business; Leadership; Management; Marketing; Sports Management); **Education** (Art Education; Education; Humanities and Social Science Education; Leadership; Mathematics Education; Native Language Education; Primary Education; Science Education; Secondary Education; Teacher Training); **Graduate Studies** (Bible; Business Administration; English; Foreign Languages Education; History; Leadership; Linguistics; Nursing; Philosophy; Psychology); **Human Kinetics, Sport, and Leisure Management** (Leisure Studies; Physical Education; Physical Therapy; Sports; Sports Management); **Nursing** (Nursing); **The Arts, Media and Culture** (Acting; Art History; Communication Arts; Communication Studies; Design; Handicrafts; Leadership; Media Studies; Music; Music Education; Musical Instruments; Painting and Drawing; Photography; Printing and Printmaking; Religious Music; Sculpture; Theatre; Writing)

Further Information: Also Extension Campuses: the Laurentian Leadership Centre in Ottawa, TWU Bellingham in Bellingham, Richmond Campus (Richmond, BC), Crows Nest Ecological Research Area on Salt Spring Island; Also Irish, American, Latin American, and Russian Studies Programmes. Oxford Summer School Programme. Los Angeles Film Studies Centre.

History: Founded 1962 as Trinity Junior College, became Trinity Western College 1972, and acquired present status and title 1985.

Academic Year: September to April (September-December; January-April); Interweave: End-April to Mid-May, and August. Also Summer Session (May-August)

Admission Requirements: Secondary school certificate or recognized foreign equivalent

Fees: c. 7,500 per semester (Canadian Dollar)

Main Language(s) of Instruction: English

Degrees and Diplomas: *Certificat et diplôme/Certificate and diploma*; *Baccalauréat/Bachelor's Degree*; *Maîtrise/Master's Degree*: **Bible; Business Administration; Christian Religious Studies; Education; English; International Business; Leadership; Linguistics; Management; Missionary Studies; Nursing; Psychology; Religion; Special Education; Theology.** Also concurrent programme to obtain a Bachelor of Arts or a Bachelor of Science degree at the same time as a Bachelor of Education degree in five years; Also Honours Bachelor's degree; Post-degree Bachelor's degree Programme in Education, 2 yrs.

Student Services: Academic Counselling, Canteen, Careers Guidance, Facilities for disabled people, Health Services, Library, Residential Facilities, Social Counselling, Sports Facilities

Student Numbers *2014-2015*: Total 4,000

Last Updated: 27/01/15

UNIVERSITY CANADA WEST (UCW)

Suite 100 – 626 West Pender Street,
Vancouver, British Columbia V6B 1V9
Tel: +1(604) 915-9607
Fax: +1(604) 638-0339
EMail: info@ucanwest.ca; registrar@ucanwest.ca
Website: http://www.ucanwest.ca

President and Vice Chancellor: Arthur Coren

Vice President Academic: Lindsay Redpath

Programme

English as a Second Language (English); **Graduate degree** (Business Administration); **Online degree** (Business Administration; Business and Commerce; Communication Studies; Media Studies); **Undergraduate degree** (Business and Commerce; Communication Studies; Media Studies)

Further Information: Also online programmes

History: Founded 2004.

Fees: National: Canadian students, undergraduate fee, 636 per course and graduate fee, 2,160 per course (Canadian Dollar), International: Undergraduate fee, 1,575 per course and graduate fee, 2,160 per course (Canadian Dollar)

Main Language(s) of Instruction: English

Accrediting Agency: Ministry of Advanced Education and Labour Market Development.

Degrees and Diplomas: *Baccalauréat/Bachelor's Degree*; *Maîtrise/Master's Degree*: **Business Administration.** Also accelerated MBA programme, 2 yrs; Degree Completion programme to obtain a Bachelor's degree.

Student Services: Academic Counselling, Canteen, Facilities for disabled people, Health Services, Nursery Care, Sports Facilities

Last Updated: 27/01/15

Canada - Manitoba

STRUCTURE OF HIGHER EDUCATION SYSTEM

Description:

Higher education in Canada is the constitutional responsibility of the provinces. The main types of institutions providing higher education in Manitoba are universities, university colleges and colleges. The colleges provide diverse technical and vocational programmes leading to a certificate or diploma, and also offer Baccalaureate degrees with an applied focus, while the universities are degree-granting institutions. The one university college in the province offers degrees, certificates and diplomas. Colleges, university colleges and universities in Manitoba are independently administered institutions with full autonomy on admissions and all other academic matters. The governing bodies of universities and the university college are a mixture of provincial and institutional representatives and the college boards are all composed of provincial representatives. In addition to the public post secondary institutions and various government-supported re-employment, apprenticeship and other vocational programmes there are also numerous private vocational or career training institutions.

Stages of studies:

University level first stage: Baccalauréat/Bachelor's degree

There are four public universities in Manitoba which offer undergraduate degree programmes; the University of Manitoba, the University of Winnipeg and Brandon University offer programmes in English, while the Université de Saint-Boniface is a French language institution. Most undergraduate study in Manitoba leads to a "General" Bachelor's degree (minimum 3 years) or an "Honours" degree (4 years and prescribed subject concentration). Degrees are normally titled in broad descriptive groups, e.g. B.A. and B.Sc. Universities also offer undergraduate diplomas (1 to 2 years of study) and short (up to 1 year) certificate programmes. Certificate programmes may enable entry to degree programmes and are frequently given in close cooperation with professional bodies. The undergraduate stage includes professional programmes that require no university-level prerequisites such as the Bachelor of Social Work (BSW) and the Bachelor of Commerce (B.Comm) and others that have prerequisite university studies such as the Bachelor of Law (LL.B) or a Doctor of Medicine (M.D.). In Manitoba, a Bachelor of Education degree is offered either as a five-year concurrent programme or a two-year after degree programme, which requires a three-year undergraduate degree prior to entering the programme. Manitoba has one private religious university which receives public funds, the Canadian Mennonite University (CMU). CMU offers one certificate programme, as well as Bachelor's and Master's level degrees. Programmes offered include general Arts, Music and Theology. These programmes are accepted for university transfer where agreements exist with Manitoba universities. Graduates of CMU have gone on to complete graduate studies in Canada and internationally. In Manitoba, there are three partially funded private degree-granting religious institutions; Providence College and Seminary, Steinbach Bible College and Booth University College. These colleges are special purpose institutions which offer certificates, diplomas and degrees, as well as seminary studies. General Arts, Science and some Religion programmes are accepted for university transfer where agreements exist with Manitoba universities. Graduates of private religious colleges in Manitoba have gone on to complete graduate studies in Canada and internationally.

University level second stage: Maîtrise/Master's degree

Most graduate work is done at the University of Manitoba, although Brandon University, Université de Saint-Boniface and the University of Winnipeg offer a limited number of Master's programmes. The Master's degree normally requires from one to two years' study after a four year Bachelor's degree or an Honours degree. A thesis or comprehensive examination is usually required in addition to course work. Examples are: M.A., M.Sc., M.Ed., MBA.

University level third stage: Doctorat/Doctorate

The Doctorate is the highest academic qualification awarded by Canadian universities and it comprises the third stage of university-level studies. This degree normally requires at least five years of study after the Bachelor's degree; the submission and defence of a major thesis (dissertation) are the principal requirements, and supplemental course work is usually also required. The degree "Doctor of Philosophy" (Ph.D.) is the designation most commonly used to signify the Doctorate. It is a generic title, applicable to degrees in most disciplines (the Doctorate should not be confused with certain first professional degrees in the Health Sciences, e.g. Medicine, Veterinary Medicine and Dentistry). The University of Manitoba is the only doctoral degree-granting institution in Manitoba.

ADMISSION TO HIGHER EDUCATION

Admission to university-level studies:

Alternatives to credentials: Universities set their own admission policies and requirements. These do not involve separate entrance examinations, and usually include flexibility for mature students, i.e. applicants aged 21 or more, who have not completed secondary school.

Numerus clausus: Universities limit enrolment in professional programmes because of the number of allotted seats based on anticipated demand in the workforce as estimated by the professional bodies, e.g. Medicine. Percentage of students admitted varies with size of applicant pool. Order of preference: provincial residents, those of other provinces, and foreign students (in Medicine, about 25% of applicants across Canada are admitted).

Other requirements: Admission to some professional programmes (e.g. Medicine, Dentistry, Law) requires previous university education. Specific admission requirements may vary by field of study and by university and may include such factors as interviews and references.

Foreign students admission:

Definition of foreign student: Foreign (International) students are students who are neither Canadian citizens nor permanent residents of Canada, and are enrolled full-time in a recognized academic, professional or vocational training course at a university, college or other educational institution in Canada.

Admission requirements: Institutions have their own policies on international students. The universities will accept international students on a pre-established list of high school equivalents. As well, students must provide proof of English language proficiency if the student's first language is not English (or French if attending CUSB). This may be done through various internationally accepted tests. A lack of proficiency in English or French will also be taken into account by the Canadian Immigration Office in the evaluation of the application.

Entry regulations: Before you come to study in Canada, you will need: a "Study Permit" if the programme of study you will be admitted to is longer than six months in duration, regardless of the length of your stay in Canada; a letter of acceptance from the school of your choice; proof that you have enough money to pay school fees and living expenses; to establish that you will return home at the end of your studies; to pass a medical exam if required; and to qualify as a temporary resident in Canada, including holding a temporary resident visa (required for citizens of many countries). A small number of students do not require a Study Permit by virtue of their status in Canada (e.g. diplomats and their children).

Health requirements: Most education institutions require international students to buy health insurance in addition to their tuition fees; those that do not will require proof of independent health insurance coverage. Medical examinations are not required by institutions but are required by Citizenship and Immigration Canada for students from many countries. Free Manitoba Medical Insurance is provided if students hold a valid study permit and reside in Manitoba for at least 6 consecutive months.

RECOGNITION OF STUDIES

Quality assurance system:

Learn about quality assurance practices for postsecondary institutions at [http://www.cicic.ca/1201/Quality-assurance-practices-for-postsecondary-institutions-in-Manitoba/index.canada].

Bodies dealing with recognition:

Ministère de l'Éducation et de l'Enseignement supérieur du Manitoba (Department of Education and Advanced Learning)

162 Legislative Building
Winnipeg R3C 0V8
Tel: +1(204) 945-3744

Fax: +1(204) 945-4261
EMail: mgi@gov.mb.ca
WWW: http://www.edu.gov.mb.ca

Special provisions for recognition:

Recognition for university level studies: Universities establish their own admissions criteria and make their own admissions decisions in response to individual applications. Any restrictions on admission are determined by the institutions themselves, given available teaching and other resources, but in a few instances are a result of government policy. For restricted programmes, priority is usually given to provincial residents first, other Canadian residents, then international students.
Additionally, the Canadian Information Centre for International Credentials (CICIC) provides information and guidance on the assessment and recognition of international academic credentials.

For access to advanced studies and research: In general, none. However, some high cost, limited enrolment programmes, e.g. Medicine and Dentistry, limit enrolment to Canadian citizens.

For exercising a profession: For each profession, anyone who has not obtained their credentials within Canada must meet specified educational, experience and language requirements and pass registration examinations. A special programme gives immigrants who are foreign-trained professionals improved access to acquiring Canadian experience by creating new full-time positions in certain areas for up to one year.

PROVINCIAL BODIES

Ministère de l'Éducation et de l'Enseignement supérieur du Manitoba (Department of Education and Advanced Learning)

Ministre/Minister: James Allum
162 Legislative Building
Winnipeg, MB R3C 0V8
Canada
Tel: +1(204) 945-3744
Fax: +1(204) 945-4261
EMail: mgi@gov.mb.ca
WWW: http://www.edu.gov.mb.ca

Role of national body: Manitoba Education and Advanced Learning (MEAL) is charged with the overall responsibility for Manitoba's system of postsecondary education and advanced learning. It is also the department responsible for the elementary/secondary education system in the province.

Data for academic year: 2014-2015

Source: IAU from the Canadian Information Centre for International Credentials (CICIC), a unit of the Council of Ministers of Education, Canada (CMEC), on behalf of the Manitoba Department of Education and Advanced Learning, November 2014. Bodies 2016.

INSTITUTIONS

PUBLIC INSTITUTIONS

BRANDON UNIVERSITY (BU)

270 18th Street, Brandon, Manitoba R7A 6A9
Tel: +1(204) 728-9520
Fax: +1(204) 726-4573
EMail: admissions@brandonu.ca
Website: http://www.brandonu.ca

President and Vice-Chancellor: Gervan Fearon
EMail: president@brandonu.ca

Vice-President Academic and Provost (Acting): Heather Duncan

International Relations: Anita Allan, Coordinator, Office of International Activities
Tel: +1(204) 727-7479 EMail: allan@brandonu.ca

Faculty

Arts (Anthropology; Archaeology; Business Administration; Ceramic Art; Classical Languages; Design; Economics; English; French; Gender Studies; German; Greek (Classical); History; Indigenous Studies; Italian; Latin; Linguistics; Modern Languages; Native Language; Painting and Drawing; Philosophy; Political Sciences; Religion; Rural Planning; Sociology; Spanish; Theatre; Visual Arts;

Women's Studies; Writing); **Education** (Curriculum; Education; Educational Administration; Educational and Student Counselling; Educational Psychology; Music Education; Physical Education; Special Education; Teacher Training); **Graduate Studies** (Education; Music; Nursing; Rural Planning); **Health Studies** (Health Sciences; Nursing; Psychiatry and Mental Health; Psychology); **Music** (Jazz and Popular Music; Music; Music Education; Music Theory and Composition; Musical Instruments); **Science** (Agriculture; Astronomy and Space Science; Biology; Chemistry; Computer Science; Dentistry; Environmental Studies; Geography; Geology; Mathematics and Computer Science; Medicine; Optometry; Pharmacy; Physics; Psychology; Safety Engineering; Veterinary Science)

History: Founded 1899 as Brandon College, affiliated with the University of Manitoba, acquired present status and title 1967.

Academic Year: September to April (September-December; January-April). Also Spring/Summer Session (May-August)

Admission Requirements: Secondary school certificate or recognized foreign equivalent, including International Baccalaureate

Fees: Undergraduate Canadian students, 323.55-357.90 (for 3 credit hours depending on programmes). Graduate: 494.10-648 (3 credit hours) (Canadian Dollar)

Main Language(s) of Instruction: English

Degrees and Diplomas: *Certificat et diplôme universitaire/University certificate and diploma*; *Baccalauréat/Baccalaureate*; *Maîtrise/Master's Degree*: **Education; Environmental Studies; Music; Nursing; Rural Studies.** *Diplôme et certificat de 2e cycle/Graduate Diploma and Certificate*: **Education.** Also Honours Bachelor's degree, 4 yrs; Concurrent Bachelor's degree programmes, B.Ed./and another degree, 5 yrs; Pre-professional degree programmes.

Student Services: Academic Counselling, Careers Guidance, Facilities for disabled people, Library

Publications: Canadian Journal of Native Studies; Community Report; Peace Research: The Canadian Journal of Peace Studies

Last Updated: 17/02/15

THE UNIVERSITY OF WINNIPEG (UWINNIPEG)

515 Portage Avenue, Winnipeg, Manitoba R3B 2E9
Tel: +1(204) 786-7811
Fax: +1(204) 786-8656
EMail: info@uwinnipeg.ca
Website: http://uwinnipeg.ca/

President and Vice-Chancellor: Annette Trimbee (2014-)
Tel: +1(204) 786-9214 EMail: president@uwinnipeg.ca

Provost and Vice-President, Academic: Neil Besner
Tel: +1(204) 988-7104 EMail: n.besner@uwinnipeg.ca

Faculty

Arts (Classical Languages; Communication Studies; Criminal Law; Cultural Studies; East Asian Studies; English; Film; French; Gender Studies; German; Greek (Classical); History; Indigenous Studies; Italian; Latin; Literature; Modern Languages; Philosophy; Physical Therapy; Political Sciences; Psychology; Religion; Sociology; Spanish; Sports; Theatre; Women's Studies; Writing); **Business and Economics** (Business Administration; Economics; Finance); **Education** (Business Education; Education; Natives Education; Teacher Training); **Science** (Anthropology; Biochemistry; Biology; Chemistry; Computer Science; Engineering; Environmental Studies; Geography; Mathematics; Physics; Psychology; Statistics)

Division

Continuing Education (Arabic; Art Management; Business Computing; Chinese; Computer Science; Data Processing; Education; French; German; Hindi; Human Resources; Indigenous Studies; Information Technology; Italian; Japanese; Korean; Leadership; Management; Marketing; Portuguese; Public Relations; Russian; Software Engineering; Spanish)

Programme

Pre-Professional Studies (Architecture; Chiropractic; Dental Hygiene; Dentistry; Engineering; Journalism; Law; Medical Technology; Medicine; Occupational Therapy; Optometry; Pharmacy; Physical Therapy; Respiratory Therapy; Social Work; Veterinary Science)

Centre

Theology *(United Centre for Theological Studies (UCTS))* (Pastoral Studies; Religion; Theology)

Further Information: Also 23 Academic Units, Centres, and Chairs: see http://www.uwinnipeg.ca/index/faculty-academic

History: Founded 1871 as Manitoba College by the Presbyterian Church and Wesley College by the Methodist Church 1877. Merged and became United Colleges 1938. Acquired present status and title 1967.

Academic Year: September to August (September-December; January-April; May-August)

Admission Requirements: Secondary school certificate or recognized foreign equivalent

Fees: National: Undergraduate: 330.30- 380.25 per 3 credit hours; Master Degree Programs: 5,954.60 per annum (Canadian Dollar), International: Undergraduate:1,416.90 per 3 credit hours. Master Degree Programs: 12,307.80 per annum

Main Language(s) of Instruction: English

Degrees and Diplomas: *Certificat et diplôme universitaire/University certificate and diploma*; *Baccalauréat/Bachelor's Degree*; *Maîtrise/Master's Degree*: **Computer Science; Cultural Studies; Development Studies; Environmental Studies; Family Studies; Indigenous Studies; Political Sciences; Social Problems; Theology.** Alo integrated Bachelor's degree of Education and Arts or Science, 5 yrs; After degree Bachelor's degree of Education programme, 2 yrs following undergraduate degree; Joint Master's Programmes with the University of Manitoba.

Student Services: Academic Counselling, Canteen, Careers Guidance, Cultural Activities, Facilities for disabled people, Health Services, Library, Nursery Care, Social Counselling, Sports Facilities

Academic Staff *2014-2015*	**TOTAL**
FULL-TIME	**350**
PART-TIME	c. **570**
Student Numbers *2014-2015*	
All (Foreign included)	c. **10,000**
FOREIGN ONLY	**1000**

Last Updated: 19/02/15

UNIVERSITY COLLEGE OF THE NORTH (UCN)

55 UCN Drive, Thompson, Manitoba R8N 1L7
Tel: +1(204) 677-6450
Fax: +1(866) 677-6450
EMail: admissions@ucn.ca
Website: http://www.ucn.ca

President and Vice-Chancellor: Konrad Jonasson

Faculty

Arts, Business and Science (Arts and Humanities; Business Administration; Natural Sciences); **Education** *(Kenanow)* (Education; Preschool Education); **Health** (Nursing); **Trades and Technology** (Electrical and Electronic Equipment and Maintenance; Industrial Maintenance; Maintenance Technology; Mechanical Equipment and Maintenance; Wood Technology)

Centre

Adult Learning

Further Information: Also The Pas Campus. Traditional and Open Learning Institution

History: Founded 2004.

Main Language(s) of Instruction: English

Degrees and Diplomas: *Baccalauréat/Baccalaureate*

Student Services: IT Centre

Academic Staff *2014-2015*: Total 300

Student Numbers *2014-2015*: Total 2,400

Last Updated: 19/02/15

IAU UNIVERSITY OF MANITOBA (UM)

66 Chancellors Circle, Winnipeg, Manitoba R3T 2N2
Tel: +1(204) 474-8880
Fax: +1(204) 474-7536
EMail: admissions@umanitoba.ca
Website: http://www.umanitoba.ca

President and Vice-Chancellor: David T. Barnard (2008-)
Tel: +1(204) 474-9345 EMail: president@umanitoba.ca

Vice President (Academic) and Provost: Joanne Keselman
Tel: + 1(204) 474-8889 EMail: Joanne.Keselman@ad.umanitoba.ca

International Relations: Rhonda Friesen, Manager, International Relations
EMail: Rhonda.Friesen@umanitoba.ca; international_students@umanitoba.ca

International Relations: Jay Doering, Associate Vice President (Partnerships) EMail: Jay.Doering@umanitoba.ca

Faculty

Agricultural and Food Sciences (Agricultural Business; Agricultural Economics; Agriculture; Animal Husbandry; Bioengineering; Biomedicine; Botany; Entomology; Environmental Engineering; Food Science; Soil Science; Veterinary Science); **Architecture** (Architectural and Environmental Design; Architecture; Design; Interior Design; Landscape Architecture; Town Planning); **Arts** (Adult Education; Anthropology; Arts and Humanities; Asian Studies; Canadian Studies; Catholic Theology; Central European Studies; Classical Languages; Criminology; Cultural Studies; Development Studies; Eastern European Studies; Economics; English; Film; French; Gender Studies; German; Greek (Classical); History; Icelandic; Indigenous Studies; Italian; Jewish Studies; Judaic Religious Studies; Labour and Industrial Relations; Labour Law; Latin; Latin American Studies; Leadership; Linguistics; Medieval Studies; Modern History; Philosophy; Political Sciences; Psychology; Religion; Slavic Languages; Sociology; Spanish; Theatre; Women's Studies); **Dentistry** (Biology; Community Health; Dental Hygiene; Dentistry; Oral Pathology; Surgery); **Education** (Adult Education; Continuing Education; Education; Foreign Languages Education); **Engineering** (Aeronautical and Aerospace Engineering; Bioengineering; Civil Engineering; Computer Engineering; Design; Electrical Engineering; Engineering; Industrial Engineering; Mechanical Engineering); **Environment, Earth, and Resources** *(Clayton H. Riddell)* (Environmental Management; Environmental Studies; Geography; Geology; Geophysics; Natural Resources); **Graduate Studies** (Agricultural Business; Agricultural Economics; Anatomy; Animal Husbandry; Anthropology; Architectural and Environmental Design; Architecture and Planning; Astronomy and Space Science; Biochemistry; Bioengineering; Biological and Life Sciences; Biology; Botany; Canadian Studies; Cell Biology; Chemistry; Civil Engineering; Classical Languages; Community Health; Computer Engineering; Computer Science; Curriculum; Dentistry; Economics; Education; Educational Administration; Educational Psychology; Electrical Engineering; English; Entomology; Environmental Studies; Family Studies; Film; Fine Arts; Food Science; French; Genetics; Geography; Geology; German; Greek; Health Sciences; History; Icelandic; Immunology; Indigenous Studies; Interior Design; Italian; Landscape Architecture; Latin; Law; Linguistics; Management; Mathematics; Mathematics and Computer Science; Mechanical Engineering; Medical Auxiliaries; Microbiology; Music; Natural Resources; Nursing; Nutrition; Occupational Therapy; Oncology; Orthodontics; Pathology; Peace and Disarmament; Periodontics; Pharmacology; Pharmacy; Philosophy; Physical Therapy; Physics; Physiology; Political Sciences; Psychology; Public Administration; Public Health; Rehabilitation and Therapy; Religion; Slavic Languages; Social Sciences; Social Work; Sociology; Soil Science; Spanish; Statistics; Surgery; Textile Design; Theatre; Town Planning; Zoology); **Human Ecology** (Family Studies; Nutrition; Textile Design); **Kinesiology and Recreation Management** (Leisure Studies; Physical Education; Physical Therapy; Sports); **Law** *(Robson Hall)* (Administrative Law; Civil Law; Commercial Law; Constitutional Law; Criminal Law; History of Law; Law; Private Law; Public Law); **Music** *(Marcel A. Desautels)* (Art History; Jazz and Popular Music; Music; Music Education; Music Theory and Composition; Musical Instruments; Singing); **Science** (Actuarial Science; Astronomy and Space Science; Biochemistry; Biological and Life Sciences; Biotechnology; Chemistry; Computer Science; Genetics; Mathematics; Microbiology; Physics; Psychology; Statistics); **Social Work** (Social Work)

Unit

Aerospace Materials Engineering Facility (Aeronautical and Aerospace Engineering); **Crystallography and Mineralogy Research Facility** (Crystallography; Mineralogy); **Digital Image Analysis Facility**; **Nuclear Magnetic Resonance (NMR) Facility** (Nuclear Engineering); **Regional Materials and Surface Characterization Facility** *(Manitoba)* (Materials Engineering)

Division

Extended Education (Anthropology; Architecture; Arts and Humanities; Business Administration; Earth Sciences; Ecology; Engineering; English; Environmental Studies; Food Science; Geology; Indigenous Studies; Management; Modern Languages; Music; Native Language Education; Natural Resources; Natural Sciences; Nursing; Nutrition; Physics; Slavic Languages; Social Work; Sports; Sports Management; Writing)

College

Medicine (Anaesthesiology; Anatomy; Biochemistry; Cell Biology; Clinical Psychology; Community Health; Genetics; Gynaecology and Obstetrics; Health Education; Immunology; Medicine; Microbiology; Ophthalmology; Otorhinolaryngology; Paediatrics; Pharmacology; Physiology; Psychiatry and Mental Health; Radiology; Surgery); **Nursing** (Health Sciences; Nursing; Oncology); **Pharmacy** (Pharmacy)

Programme

University 1 (Accountancy; Agricultural Business; Agriculture; Anthropology; Applied Mathematics; Architectural and Environmental Design; Architecture; Art History; Arts and Humanities; Asian Studies; Astronomy and Space Science; Biological and Life Sciences; Biotechnology; Business Administration; Canadian Studies; Catholic Theology; Chemistry; Classical Languages; Computer Science; Dental Hygiene; Dentistry; Ecology; Economics; Education; Engineering; English; Entomology; Environmental Studies; Family Studies; Film; Fine Arts; Food Science; French; Gender Studies; Genetics; Geography; Geology; Geophysics; German; Greek (Classical); Health Sciences; History; Hungarian; Icelandic; Indigenous Studies; Italian; Jewish Studies; Labour and Industrial Relations; Latin; Law; Leisure Studies; Linguistics; Management; Marketing; Mathematics; Medicine; Microbiology; Music; Native Language; Natural Resources; Nursing; Nutrition; Occupational Therapy; Pharmacy; Philosophy; Physical Education; Physical Therapy; Physics; Polish; Political Sciences; Portuguese; Psychology; Religion; Respiratory Therapy; Russian; Slavic Languages; Social Work; Sociology; Spanish; Statistics; Textile Design; Theatre; Veterinary Science; Women's Studies)

School

Agriculture (Agriculture; Crop Production; Fruit Production; Horticulture; Landscape Architecture; Vegetable Production); **Art** (Art History; Ceramic Art; Fine Arts; Graphic Design; Painting and Drawing; Photography; Printing and Printmaking; Sculpture; Video); **Business** *(I.H. Asper)* (Business Administration; Finance; Human Resources; Management; Marketing; Small Business); **Dental Hygiene** (Dental Hygiene); **Medical Rehabilitation** (Health Sciences; Occupational Therapy; Physical Therapy; Rehabilitation and Therapy; Respiratory Therapy)

Institute

Cardiovascular Sciences (Cardiology); **Humanities** (Arts and Humanities); **Industrial Mathematical Sciences** (Mathematics); **Legal Research** (Law); **Theoretical Physics** *(with University of Winnipeg)* (Physics); **Transport** (Transport and Communications)

Centre

Aging (Gerontology); **Agri-food Research in Health and Medicine** *(Canadian)* (Food Science); **Architectural Structures and Technology** *(C.A.S.T.)* (Architecture); **Breast Cancer Research and Diagnosis** *(Great-West Life Manitoba)* (Oncology); **Cell Biology** *(Manitoba)* (Cell Biology); **Defence and Security Studies** (Protective Services); **Earth Observation Science** *(CEOS)* (Earth Sciences); **Functional Foods and Nutraceuticals** *(RCFFN)* (Food Science); **Global Public Health** (Public Health); **Globalization and Cultural Studies** (Cultural Studies); **Health Policy** *(Manitoba)* (Health Sciences); **Hellenic Civilization** (Ancient Civilizations); **Human Models of Disease**; **Internet Innovation** (Information Technology); **Livestock and the Environment** *(Manitoba)* (Animal Husbandry); **Nursing and Health Research** *(MCNHR)* (Health Sciences; Nursing); **Professional and Applied Ethics** (Ethics); **Proteomics and Systems Biology** *(Manitoba)* (Biology); **Research and Treatment of Atherosclerosis** (Medicine; Rehabilitation and Therapy)

Laboratory

Applied Electromagnetics (Electrical Engineering); **Structural Engineering** *(W.R. McQuade)* (Engineering)

Research Centre

Aboriginal Health (Health Sciences); **Data** *(Manitoba)* (Data Processing); **Grain Storage** *(Canadian Wheat Board)* (Agriculture); **Higher Education and Development** *(CHERD)* (Development Studies; Higher Education); **RESOLVE** *(Prairie Research Network on Family Violence)* (Family Studies; Social Problems); **Spinal Cord** (Medicine)

Research Group

Aquatic Biology (Biology); **Community Acquired Infections** (Community Health); **Composite Materials and Structures** (Materials Engineering); **Developmental Health** (Health Sciences); **Mood and Anxiety Disorders** (Psychology); **Psychiatric Neuroimaging** (Psychiatry and Mental Health)

Research Institute

Health, Leisure and Human Performance (Health Sciences; Leisure Studies; Sports)

Further Information: Also Fort Garry Campus, Bannatyne Campus; William Norrie Centre; University of Manitoba Downtown: Aboriginal Education Centre (hosting the Division of Extended Education); National Centre for Livestock and Environment, agricultural research farm at Carman; field stations at Delta Marsh on Lake Manitoba, Star Lake in the Whiteshell, and Wallace Lake in eastern Manitoba.

History: Founded 1877 on the model of the University of London, as an examining and degree-conferring body. Appointed the first Professors 1904.

Academic Year: September to April, Regular Session; May to June, Intersession; July to August, Summer-Day Session; May to July, Summer-Evening Session

Admission Requirements: Secondary school certificate or recognized foreign equivalent

Fees: National: Undergraduate: 77.90 -142.95 per credit hour depending on programs. Masters and PhD programmes: 4,455.70 per annum (Canadian Dollar), International: Undergraduate:272.65-500.35 per credit hour depending on programs. Mastersand PhD programmes: 8,911.40 per annum (Burundi Franc)

Main Language(s) of Instruction: English

Degrees and Diplomas: *Certificat et diplôme universitaire/University certificate and diploma*; *Baccalauréat/Bachelor's Degree*; *Maîtrise/Master's Degree*; *Diplôme et certificat de 2e cycle/Graduate Diploma and Certificate*; *Doctorat/Doctoral Degree*: **Anatomy; Astronomy and Space Science; Botany; Cell Biology; Civil Engineering; Community Health; Computer Engineering; Economics; Education; Electrical Engineering; English; Entomology; Film; Food Science; French; Geography; Geology; Health Sciences; History; Immunology; Indigenous Studies; Linguistics; Management; Mechanical Engineering; Microbiology; Natural Resources; Natural Sciences; Nursing; Nutrition; Peace and Disarmament; Pharmacology; Pharmacy; Physics; Physiology; Psychology; Religion; Social Work; Sociology; Soil Science; Spanish; Statistics; Theatre; Zoology.** Bachelor of Medicine: awarded concurrently to Medicine students who choose a research option

Student Services: Academic Counselling, Canteen, Careers Guidance, Cultural Activities, Facilities for disabled people, Foreign Studies Centre, Health Services, IT Centre, Language Laboratory, Library, Nursery Care, Social Counselling, Sports Facilities

Academic Staff *2014-2015*	**TOTAL**
FULL-TIME	c. 4,800
Student Numbers *2014-2015*	
All (Foreign included)	c. 29,800
FOREIGN ONLY	2170

Last Updated: 18/02/15

ST. ANDREW'S COLLEGE (UNIVERSITY OF MANITOBA)

29 Dysart Road, Winnipeg, Manitoba R3T 2M7
Tel: +1(204) 474-8895
Fax: +1(204) 474-7624
EMail: st_andrews@umanitoba.ca
Website: http://www.umanitoba.ca/colleges/st_andrews/

Principal (Acting): Roman Bozyk

Faculty

Theology (Religion; Religious Music; Theology)

History: St. Andrew's College is an institution of the Ukrainian Orthodox Church of Canada.

Degrees and Diplomas: *Certificat et diplôme universitaire/University certificate and diploma*; *Baccalauréat/Bachelor's Degree*; *Maîtrise/Master's Degree*: **Theology.**

ST. JOHN'S COLLEGE (UNIVERSITY OF MANITOBA)

92 Dysart Road, Winnipeg, Manitoba R3T 2M5
Tel: +1(204) 474-8531
Fax: +1(204) 474-7610
EMail: stjohns_college@umanitoba.ca
Website: http://www.umanitoba.ca/colleges/st_johns/

Warden and Vice-Chancellor: Chris Trott
Tel: +1(204) 474-8529 EMail: trottcg@cc.umanitoba.ca

Bursar and Executive Assistant to the Warden: Ivan Froese
Tel: +1(204) 474-8533 EMail: froesei@cc.umanitoba.ca

Faculty

Architecture, Interior Design (Architecture; Interior Design); **Education** (Education); **Environment, Earth, and Resources** (Biology; Chemistry; Geography); **Theology** (Bible; Religion; Theology)

School

Art (Fine Arts; Performing Arts); **Music** (Music)

Department

Anthropology (Anthropology); **Economics** (Economics); **English** (English; Literature); **History** (History); **Political Studies** (Political Sciences); **Sociology** (Indigenous Studies; Sociology)

Institute

Anglican Ministry (Protestant Theology)

History: Founded 1866.

Main Language(s) of Instruction: English

Degrees and Diplomas: *Certificat et diplôme universitaire/University certificate and diploma*; *Baccalauréat/Bachelor's Degree*; *Maîtrise/Master's Degree*; *Doctorat/Doctoral Degree*. Also Advanced Certificate, 3 yrs.

Student Services: Library, Residential Facilities

ST. PAUL'S COLLEGE (UNIVERSITY OF MANITOBA)

70 Dysart Road, Winnipeg, Manitoba R3T 2M6
Tel: +(204) 474-8575
Fax: +(204) 474-7620
EMail: stpauls@umanitoba.ca
Website: http://www.umanitoba.ca/colleges/st_pauls/

Rector: Chrisopher J. Adams Tel: +(204) 474-8581
EMail: Rector.StPaulsCollege@umanitoba.ca

Centre

Catholic Studies *(Jesuit)* (Catholic Theology; Christian Religious Studies); **Peace and Justice** *(Arthur V. Mauro)* (Peace and Disarmament)

History: Founded 1926.

Main Language(s) of Instruction: English

Degrees and Diplomas: *Baccalauréat/Bachelor's Degree*; *Maîtrise/Master's Degree*; *Doctorat/Doctoral Degree*

UNIVERSITY OF SAINT-BONIFACE

Université de Saint-Boniface (CUSB)

200, avenue de la Cathédrale, Saint-Boniface, Manitoba R2H 0H7
Tel: +1(204) 233-0210
Fax: +1(204) 237-3240
EMail: stad@ustboniface.mb.ca
Website: http://www.ustboniface.ca

Recteur: Gabor Csepregi (2014-) Tel: +1(204) 233-0210 Ext.318

Secrétaire Général: Stéphane Dorge
Tel: +1(204) 237-1818 Ext.408

International Relations: Robin Rooke, Coordonnatrice, Bureau international
Tel: +1(204) 237-1818 Ext.503
EMail: international@cusb.ca; rrooke@ustboniface.mb.ca

Faculty

Arts (Anthropology; Arts and Humanities; Canadian Studies; Economics; English; French; Geography (Human); German; History; Literature; Mathematics; Modern Languages; Philosophy; Political Sciences; Psychology; Religious Studies; Social Sciences; Sociology; Spanish); **Business Administration** (Business Administration; Human Resources; International Business; Labour and Industrial Relations; Management; Marketing); **Education** (Curriculum; Education; Educational Administration; Educational and Student Counselling; Literacy Education; Native Language Education; Primary Education; Secondary Education); **Sciences** (Biochemistry; Chemistry; Computer Science; Mathematics; Microbiology; Physics; Statistics; Zoology); **Social Services** (Social and Community Services)

Programme

Continuing Education (French; Spanish); **Distance Education** (Canadian Studies; Computer Science; Education; Translation and Interpretation)

School

Technical and Professional (Business Administration; Computer Science; Health Sciences; Multimedia; Nursing; Preschool Education; Tourism); **Translation** (English; French; Translation and Interpretation)

History: Founded 1818. An affiliated college of the University of Manitoba.

Main Language(s) of Instruction: French

Degrees and Diplomas: *Certificat et diplôme universitaire/University certificate and diploma*; *Baccalauréat/Bachelor's Degree*; *Maîtrise/Master's Degree*: **Canadian Studies; Curriculum; Education; Educational Administration; Educational and Student Counselling; Literacy Education; Special Education.** Cooperation with Manitoba University for the following programmes: PhD in Dentistry; Doctor of Medecine; Bachelor in Pharmacy, Rehabilitation and Therapy,

Student Services: Cultural Activities, Library, Residential Facilities, Sports Facilities

Last Updated: 18/02/15

PRIVATE INSTITUTIONS

BOOTH UNIVERSITY COLLEGE

447 Webb Place, Winnipeg, Manitoba R3B 2P2
Tel: +1(204) 947-6701 +1(877) 942-6684
Fax: +1(204) 942-3856
EMail: admissions@boothuc.ca
Website: http://www.boothuc.ca/

President: Donald E. Burke
Tel: +1(204) 924-4871 EMail: president@boothuc.ca

Programme

Behavioural Sciences (Behavioural Sciences); **Business Administration** (Business Administration); **Christian Studies** *(Certificate Programme)* (Christian Religious Studies); **English and Film** (English; Film); **General Studies** (Arts and Humanities; Natural Sciences); **Liberal Arts** *(Certificate Programme)* (Arts and Humanities); **Psychology** (Psychology); **Religion** (Religion); **Social Work** (Social Work)

Further Information: Traditional and Open Learning Institution

History: Created 1982 as William and Catherine Booth College. Acquired current title and status 2010.

Fees: National: 260 per credit hour. 3900 per semester (Canadian Dollar), International: 9,800 per annum (Canadian Dollar)

Main Language(s) of Instruction: English

Degrees and Diplomas: *Certificat et diplôme universitaire/University certificate and diploma*; *Baccalauréat/Bachelor's Degree*: **Behavioural Sciences; Business Administration; English; Film; Psychology; Religion; Social Work.** Bachelor's degree (professional), 4 yrs.

Student Services: Library, Residential Facilities
Last Updated: 17/02/15

CANADIAN MENNONITE UNIVERSITY (CMU)

500 Shaftsbury Boulevard, Winnipeg, Manitoba R3P 2N2
Tel: +1(204) 487-3300
Fax: +1(204) 487-3858
EMail: info@cmu.ca
Website: http://www.cmu.ca/

President: Cheryl Pauls (2012-)
EMail: cpauls@cmu.ca

Vice-President Academic: Gordon Zerbe

International Relations: Paul Kroeker, Dean of International Programs EMail: pkroeker@cmu.ca

College

Menno Simons *(http://www.mscollege.ca/. Menno Simons College is located on the campus of The University of Winnipeg)* (Arts and Humanities; Development Studies; International Studies; Peace and Disarmament)

Programme

Biblical and Theological Studies (Bible; Christian Religious Studies; Religion; Theology); **Biology** (Anatomy; Biological and Life Sciences; Biology; Physiology); **Chemistry** (Chemistry; Physical Chemistry); **Communications and Media** (Communication Studies; Graphic Design; Journalism; Mass Communication; Media Studies; Political Sciences; Radio and Television Broadcasting); **Computer Science** (Computer Science); **Counselling Studies** (Psychology; Social Sciences); **Economics** (Economics; International Business; International Economics); **English** (English; Literature; Writing); **Geography** (Environmental Studies; Geography; Geography (Human)); **Graduate Studies** (Christian Religious Studies; Theology); **History** (History); **Intercultural Studies** (Social Sciences); **International Development Studies** (Development Studies; Economics; Religion; Rural Studies); **Languages** (French; German; Greek; Hebrew; Spanish); **Mathematics** (Mathematics); **Music** (Art Therapy; Music; Musical Instruments; Musicology); **Music Therapy** (Art Therapy; Music); **Peace and Conflict Transformation Studies** (Peace and Disarmament); **Philosophy** (Metaphysics; Philosophy); **Physics** (Physics); **Political Studies** (Development Studies; History; Human Rights; Media Studies; Philosophy; Political Sciences); **Preprofessional Studies** (Agriculture; Dentistry; Ecology; Education; Law; Medicine; Nursing; Pharmacy; Physical Education; Rehabilitation and Therapy; Social Work); **Psychology** (Behavioural Sciences; Psychology); **Social Sciences** (Anthropology; Social and Community Services; Social Sciences); **Sociology** (Media Studies; Philosophy; Social Welfare; Sociology); **Theatre, Film, and Art** (Art History; Film; Literature; Theatre)

School

Business and Organizational Administration *(Redekop)* (Accountancy; Administration; Business Administration; Finance; Human Resources; International Business; Leadership; Management; Small Business)

Graduate School

Theology (Theology)

History: Founded 1998 through the amalgamation of three colleges: Mennonite Brethren Bible College/Concord College (est. 1944); Canadian Mennonite Bible College (est. 1947); and Menno Simons College (est. 1989). CMU is affiliated withThe University of Winnipeg.

Fees: National: Undergraduate and graduate studies, 699 per 3 credit hour course (or 5,592 for 24 credit hours). Graduate Studies: 723 per 3 credit hour course (Canadian Dollar), International: 10,173 per annum (Canadian Dollar)

Degrees and Diplomas: *Certificat et diplôme universitaire/University certificate and diploma*; *Baccalauréat/Bachelor's Degree*; *Maîtrise/Master's Degree*: **Theology.** *Diplôme et certificat de 2e cycle/Graduate Diploma and Certificate*. Students who complete programs at Menno Simons College, a collage of CMU, graduate with a Bachelor of Arts from the University of Winnipag.

Student Services: Library, Residential Facilities

Publications: Direction; Peace Research Journal; Vision
Last Updated: 17/02/15

PROVIDENCE UNIVERSITY COLLEGE AND THEOLOGICAL SEMINARY

10 College Crescent, Otterburne, Manitoba R0A 1G0
Tel: +1(204) 433-7488
Fax: +1(204) 433-7158
EMail: info@prov.ca
Website: http://www.providenceuc.ca/

President: David H. Johnson (2013-)
EMail: David.Johnson@prov.ca

International Relations: Debi van Duin, International Student Services Coordinator

Programme

Aviation (Air Transport); **Business Administration** (Accountancy; Business Administration; Commercial Law; Economics; Finance; Human Resources; Management; Marketing); **Church Ministries** (Christian Religious Studies; Theology); **Communications and Media** (Journalism; Mass Communication; Media Studies; Photography; Radio and Television Broadcasting; Writing); **Field Education** (Christian Religious Studies); **Humanities** (Arts and Humanities; Bible; English; History; Music; Music Theory and Composition; Musical Instruments; Musicology; Philosophy; Theatre; Theology); **Integrative Vocational Studies**; **Intercultural Studies** (Anthropology; Cultural Studies; Protestant Theology; Religion; Theology); **Mathematics** (Mathematics); **Music** (Art Therapy; Jazz and Popular Music; Music; Music Education; Musical Instruments; Religious Music; Singing); **Pre-Professional Studies** (Agriculture; Architecture; Dental Hygiene; Dentistry; Ecology; Education; Engineering; Environmental Studies; Fine Arts; Law; Management; Medicine; Music; Natural Resources; Natural Sciences; Nursing; Pharmacy; Physical Education; Rehabilitation and Therapy; Social Work); **Seminary** (Christian Religious Studies; Foreign Languages Education; Psychology; Religion; Theology); **Social Sciences** (Anthropology; Bible; Psychology; Social Sciences; Sociology; Theology); **Social Work** (Social Work); **Sociology** (Social Sciences; Sociology); **Teaching English to Speakers of Other Languages** *(TESOL)* (English; Foreign Languages Education); **Theatre** (Acting; Theatre); **Worship Studies** (Bible; Communication Studies; Fine Arts; Leadership; Music; Theology); **Youth Leadership** (Leadership)

Department

Biblical and Theological Studies (Bible; Theology)

Institute

English Language *(ELI)* (English)

History: Founded 1925 as Winnipeg Bible School. Became Winnipeg Bible Institute and College of Theology 1949. Formed Theological Seminary 1972. Became Providence College and Theological Seminary 1992. Acquired present title and Status 2011.

Academic Year: September to June (September-December; January-June)

Admission Requirements: High School Certificate or equivalent with 28 credits.

Fees: National: Undergraduate: Canadian and US Students, 3705 per semester. Graduate: 5775 (Canadian Dollar), International: Undergraduate:5205 per semester. Graduate: 7275 (Canadian Dollar)

Main Language(s) of Instruction: English

Accrediting Agency: Association of Biblical Higher Education (ABHE); TESOL program is accredited by TESL Canada.

Degrees and Diplomas: *Certificat et diplôme universitaire/University certificate and diploma*; *Baccalauréat/Bachelor's Degree*; *Maîtrise/Master's Degree*: **Christian Religious Studies; Education; Missionary Studies; Pastoral Studies; Theology.** *Doctorat/Doctoral Degree*: **Pastoral Studies.** Also Honours Bachelor's degree, 4 yrs.

Student Services: Academic Counselling, Canteen, Careers Guidance, Language Laboratory, Library, Sports Facilities

Publications: Didaskalia
Last Updated: 18/02/15

Canada - New Brunswick

STRUCTURE OF HIGHER EDUCATION SYSTEM

Description:

Higher education in Canada is the constitutional responsibility of the provinces. The two main types of institutions providing higher education are universities and colleges, which provides diverse technical and vocational programmes usually leading to a Certificate or Diploma. The former are degree-granting institutions, while the latter are not (although some offer university-level transfer courses). Besides various government support pre-employment, apprenticeship and other vocational programmes, there are also several private training organizations operating in New Brunswick (which are required to register under the Private Occupational Training Act). Universities are independently administered institutions with full autonomy on admissions and all other academic matters. New Brunswick provides funding to four public universities. Private universities do not receive government funding. There are three not-for-profit private chartered institutions operating in the Province. In 2001, New Brunswick adopted the Degree Granting Act, allowing private for-profit institutions to confer university degrees. Currently, two institutions; Yorkville University and the University of Fredericton are designated to confer specific degree programmes.

Stages of studies:

University level first stage: *Bachelor's degree*
Most undergraduate study leads to a "general" Bachelor's degree (minimum 3 years) or an "Honours" degree (4 years and prescribed subject concentration). Degrees are normally titled in broad descriptive groups, e.g. B.A. and B.Sc. The first stage also includes undergraduate diplomas (1-3 years of study) and short (up to 1 year) special Certificate programmes; these may enable entry to degree programmes and are frequently given in close cooperation with professional bodies. In addition, the first stage includes other professional programmes that typically require no university-level prerequisites and 4 years of study, e.g. Bachelor of Science in Nursing (B.Sc.N) and Bachelor of Commerce (B.Comm.) and also first- and second-year university transfer programmes offered by provincially-supported community colleges.

University level second stage: *Master's degree*
The Master's degree normally requires at least one year's study after an Honours Bachelor's degree or equivalent. Some Master's programmes, e.g. in Business Administration, necessitate at least 2 years. A thesis is usually required, often course work as well. Examples are: M.A., M.Sc., M.Ed., MBA. Besides graduate level Diplomas (considered as intermediate between the Bachelor's or first professional degree and the Master's degree), the second stage also includes first professional degree programmes requiring prerequisite university studies - followed by perhaps 3 years for a Bachelor of Law (LL.B.) or typically 2 years for a Bachelor of Education (B.Ed.) while a few others normally require 4 years.

University level third stage: *Doctorate degree*
The Doctorate is the highest qualification awarded by Canadian universities and (in all provinces except Quebec) it comprises the third stage of university-level studies. This degree normally requires at least 3 years of study after the Bachelor's degree; the submission and defence of a major thesis (dissertation) are the principal requirements, and supplemental course work is usually also required. The degree "Doctor of Philosophy" (Ph.D.) is the designation most commonly used to signify the Doctorate. It is a generic title, applicable to degrees in most disciplines (the Doctorate should not be confused with certain first professional degrees in the Health Sciences, e.g. Medicine, Veterinary Medicine and Dentistry). Universities may choose to allow a PhD graduate to pursue Post-Doctoral studies which do not lead to another degree and may be combined with entrance-level professorial responsibilities.

ADMISSION TO HIGHER EDUCATION

Foreign students admission:

Definition of foreign student: Foreign (International) Students are students who are neither Canadian citizens nor permanent residents of Canada, and are enrolled full-time in a recognized academic, professional or vocational training course at a university, college or other educational institution in Canada.

Quotas: There is a quota applied at institutional and provincial level.

Admission requirements: Generally, as for domestic students, a high school diploma or equivalent will be required.

Entry regulations: Before you come to study in Canada, you will need: a "Study Permit" if the programme of study you will be admitted to is longer than six months in duration, regardless of the length of your stay in Canada; a letter of acceptance from the school of your choice; proof that you have enough money to pay for school fees and living expenses; to establish that you will return home at the end of your studies; to pass a medical exam if required; and to qualify as a temporary resident in Canada, including holding a temporary resident visa (required for citizens of many countries). A small number of students do not require a Study Permit by virtue of their status in Canada (e.g. diplomats and their children).

Health requirements: Most education institutions require international students to buy health insurance in addition to their tuition fees; those that do not will require proof of independent health insurance coverage. Medical examinations are not required by institutions but are required by Citizenship and Immigration Canada for students from many countries.

Language proficiency: A lack of proficiency in English or French will be taken into account by the Canadian immigration office in the evaluation of the application.

RECOGNITION OF STUDIES

Quality assurance system:

All four public universities consider possible transfer credit for applicable coursework completed at New Brunswick community colleges. However, the transfer potential of many college programmes is limited by their vocational and specialized character.

Special provisions for recognition:

Recognition for university level studies: Universities establish their own admissions criteria and make their own admissions decisions in response to individual applications. Any restrictions on admission are determined by the institutions themselves, given available teaching and other resources, but in a few instances are results of government policy.

For access to advanced studies and research: In general none. However, if in some high cost or limited enrolment programmes, e.g. Law and Education, qualified applicants outnumber available enrolment capacity, then most universities will establish special admissions committees and provide for proportionately more Canadians than foreign applicants to be admitted.

For exercising a profession: In general none. For each profession, both Canadians and non-Canadians who studied abroad have to meet specified educational and experience requirements, and usually pass registration examinations. Non-Canadians may sometimes also need to pass language tests. Access to most professions is governed by provincial and/or federal statutes and is restricted to Canadian citizens or immigrants accepted as permanent residents. In addition to professional studies, applicants must also meet examination and/or practical training requirements set by the relevant professional body.

PROVINCIAL BODIES

Ministère de l'Éducation postsecondaire, de la Formation et du Travail (Department of Post-Secondary Education,Training and Labour)

Minister/Ministre: Francine Landry
Chestnut Complex
P.O. Box 6000
Fredericton, NB E3B 5H1
Canada
Tel: +1(506) 453-2597
Fax: +1(506) 453-3618
EMail: dpetlinfo@gnb.ca
WWW: http://www.gnb.ca/post-secondary

Commission de l'Enseignement supérieur des Provinces maritimes - CESPM (Maritime Provinces Higher Education Commission - MPHEC)

Chief Executive Officer/Directrice générale: Mireille Duguay
82 Westmorland Street, Suite 401, P.O. Box 6000
Fredericton, NB E3B 5H1
Canada
Tel: +1(506) 453-2844
Fax: +1(506) 453-2106
EMail: mphec@mphec.ca
WWW: http://www.mphec.ca

Role of national body: Advisory body to assist the three Maritime provinces (N.B., N.S., P.E.I.) and institutions in achieving a more efficient and effective utilization of resources.

Data for academic year: 2014-2015

Source: IAU from The Canadian Information Centre for International Credentials (CICIC), a unit of the Council of Ministers of Education, Canada (CMEC), on behalf of the New Brunswick Department of Post-Secondary Education,Training and Labour, November 2014. Bodies 2016.

INSTITUTIONS

PUBLIC INSTITUTIONS

MOUNT ALLISON UNIVERSITY (MTA)

62 York Street, Sackville, New Brunswick E4L 1E2
Tel: +1(506) 364-2269
Fax: +1(506) 364-2272
EMail: admissions@mta.ca
Website: http://www.mta.ca

President: Robert Campbell (2006-)
Tel: +1(506) 364-2300 EMail: rcampbell@mta.ca

Provost and Vice-President Academic and Research: Karen R. Grant Tel: +1(506) 364-2622 EMail: kgrant@mta.ca

Faculty

Arts (American Studies; Ancient Civilizations; Canadian Studies; Classical Languages; English; Fine Arts; French; French Studies; German; Germanic Studies; Greek (Classical); Hispanic American Studies; History; Japanese; Latin; Literature; Modern Languages; Music; Music Education; Music Theory and Composition; Musical Instruments; Philosophy; Psychology; Religious Studies; Spanish; Theatre; Women's Studies); **Science** (Air Transport; Biochemistry; Biology; Chemistry; Cognitive Sciences; Computer Networks; Computer Science; Environmental Studies; Geography; Mathematics; Mathematics and Computer Science; Physics; Psychology; Software Engineering); **Social Science** (Anthropology; Business and Commerce; Economics; Environmental Studies; Geography (Human); International Relations; Meteorology; Political Sciences; Social Sciences; Sociology)

History: Founded 1839 as Mount Allison Wesleyan Academy, became degree-granting Mount Allison Wesleyan College 1858, and acquired present status and title 1886. Although conducted on a non-sectarian basis, the University is a Church-related institution (United Church of Canada). As such, it is interested in the all-round development of students.

Academic Year: September to April (September-December; January-April)

Admission Requirements: Secondary school certificate or recognized foreign equivalent

Fees: National: Full-Time tuition fees, 7,465 per annum (Canadian Dollar), International: Full-Time tuition fees: 16,420 per annum (Canadian Dollar)

Main Language(s) of Instruction: English

Degrees and Diplomas: *Certificat et diplôme universitaire/University certificate and diploma*; *Baccalauréat/Bachelor's Degree*; *Maîtrise/Master's Degree*: **Biochemistry; Biology; Chemistry.**

Student Services: Academic Counselling, Canteen, Careers Guidance, Cultural Activities, Facilities for disabled people, Health Services, IT Centre, Language Laboratory, Library, Nursery Care, Social Counselling, Sports Facilities

Publications: About Canada; Josiah Wood Lectures

Last Updated: 20/02/15

UNIVERSITY OF MONCTON

Université de Moncton

Campus de Moncton, 18, avenue Antonine-Maillet,
Moncton, New Brunswick E1A 3E9
Tel: +1(506) 858-4000
Fax: +1(506) 858-4379
EMail: info@umoncton.ca
Website: http://www.umoncton.ca

Recteur et Vice-Chancelier: Raymond Théberge (2012-)
Tel: +1(506) 858-4111 EMail: recteur@umoncton.ca

Secrétaire générale: Lynne M. Castonguay
Tel: +1(506) 858-4106 EMail: lynne.castonguay@umoncton.ca

International Relations: Marie-Linda Lord, Vice-rectrice aux affaires étudiantes et internationales Tel: +1(506) 858-4826

Faculty

Administration (Accountancy; Administration; Business Administration; Finance; International Business; Management; Marketing); **Arts and Social Sciences** (Arts and Humanities; Economics; English; French; Geography; German; Gerontology; Health Administration; History; Interior Design; Linguistics; Literature; Music; Philosophy; Political Sciences; Public Administration; Religious Studies; Social Sciences; Social Work; Sociology; Spanish; Theatre; Translation and Interpretation; Visual Arts); **Educational Sciences** (Education; Educational and Student Counselling; Educational Psychology; Educational Sciences; Primary Education; Secondary Education); **Engineering** (Civil Engineering; Electrical Engineering; Engineering; Industrial Engineering; Mechanical Engineering; Technology); **Forestry** *(Edmundston)* (Forestry); **Health Sciences and Community Services** (Family Studies; Food Science; Gerontology; Health Sciences; Leisure Studies; Nursing; Nutrition; Physical Education; Physical Therapy; Psychology; Social and Community Services; Tourism); **Law** (Administrative Law; Civil Law; Commercial Law; Law; Public Law); **Sciences** (Astronomy and

Space Science; Biochemistry; Biological and Life Sciences; Biology; Chemistry; Computer Science; Laboratory Techniques; Mathematics; Physics; Radiology; Respiratory Therapy; Statistics)

Further Information: Also Edmunston and Shippagan campuses, where students can complete the first-cycle of their studies.

History: Founded 1864 as Saint Joseph College, acquired present status and title 1963. The University now has 3 campuses: Campus de Moncton, Campus d'Edmunston and Campus de Shippagan.

Academic Year: May to April (May-August; September-December; January-April)

Admission Requirements: Secondary school certificate or recognized foreign equivalent

Fees: National: 5 604 per annum (Canadian Dollar), International: 10 270 per annum (Canadian Dollar)

Main Language(s) of Instruction: French

Degrees and Diplomas: *Baccalauréat/Bachelor's Degree*; *Maîtrise/Master's Degree*: **Business Administration; Education; Engineering; Environmental Studies; Family Studies; French; History; Law; Natural Sciences; Nursing; Nutrition; Public Administration; Social Work.** *Doctorat/Doctoral Degree*: **Biological and Life Sciences; Education; French; Linguistics; Psychology.** For Bachelor of Common Law, LLB, Degree courses are either 3 yrs full-time following First Degree, by course of instruction, dissertion and examination, or for approved Civil Law graduates of a Canadian University, 2 sem. full-time; Also combined programmes, Master in Business Administration/Bachelor of Law, Master in Public Administration/Bachelor of Law, Master in Environmental Studies/ Bachelor of Law (all in 4 yrs).

Student Services: Academic Counselling, Careers Guidance, Library, Sports Facilities

Publications: Le Bulletin; Le Prisme
Last Updated: 23/02/15

UNIVERSITY OF NEW BRUNSWICK (UNB)

P.O. Box 4400, Fredericton, New Brunswick E3B 5A3
Tel: +1(506) 453-4666
Fax: +1(506) 453-4599
EMail: registrar@unb.ca
Website: http://www.unb.ca

President and Vice-Chancellor: Eddy Campbell (2009-)
Tel: +1(506) 453-4567 EMail: president@unb.ca

Vice-President, Finance and Corporate Services: Karen Cunningham Tel: +1(506) 453-4797

Faculty

Arts *(Saint John Campus)* (Clinical Psychology; Communication Studies; Comparative Literature; Economics; English; French; History; Information Sciences; Linguistics; Philosophy; Political Sciences; Psychology; Social Sciences; Sociology; Spanish; Sports); **Arts** (Ancient Civilizations; Anthropology; Arabic; Archaeology; Chinese; Classical Languages; Cultural Studies; Development Studies; Economics; English; Film; French; German; Germanic Studies; Greek (Classical); History; Japanese; Latin American Studies; Law; Literature; Modern Languages; Multimedia; Music; Philosophy; Political Sciences; Psychology; Russian; Social Problems; Sociology; Spanish; Theatre; Women's Studies; Writing); **Business** *(Saint John Campus)* (Accountancy; Business Administration; E-Business/Commerce; Hotel and Restaurant; Management; Tourism); **Business Administration** (Business Administration; Engineering Management; Human Resources; Public Administration; Sports Management); **Computer Science** (Computer Science; Information Sciences; Software Engineering); **Education** (Adult Education; Art Education; Curriculum; Education; Educational Administration; Educational and Student Counselling; Foreign Languages Education; Humanities and Social Science Education; Literacy Education; Mathematics Education; Physical Education; Preschool Education; Science Education); **Engineering** (Chemical Engineering; Civil Engineering; Computer Engineering; Electrical Engineering; Engineering; Engineering Management; Forestry; Geological Engineering; Management; Mechanical Engineering; Software Engineering; Surveying and Mapping); **Forestry and Environmental Management** (Engineering; Environmental Management; Forestry); **Kinesiology** (Physical Therapy; Sports; Sports Management); **Law** (Administrative Law; Civil Law; Commercial Law; Constitutional Law; Criminal Law; Law); **Nursing** (Nursing); **Science** (Biology; Chemistry; Computer Science; Geochemistry; Geology; Mathematics; Physics; Psychology; Statistics); **Science, Applied Science and Engineering** *(Saint John Campus)* (Biology; Chemistry; Computer Science; Engineering; Health Sciences; Marine Biology; Mathematics; Nursing; Statistics)

College

Extended Learning (Administration; Adult Education; Business Administration; Education; Film; French; Health Sciences; Human Resources; Leadership; Management; Nursing; Rehabilitation and Therapy; Social Problems; Software Engineering; Spanish; Women's Studies); **Renaissance** (Economics; Leadership; Philosophy; Political Sciences); **Saint John** *(Saint John Campus)* (Cultural Studies; English)

Institute

Biomedical Engineering (Biomedical Engineering); **Canadian Rivers** *(Fredericton and Saint John campuses)*; **Micmac - Maliseet**

Centre

Applied Statistics (Statistics); **Coastal Studies and Aquaculture** *(Saint John campus)* (Aquaculture; Coastal Studies); **Construction Technology Centre Atlantic, Inc.** *(CTCA)* (Construction Engineering); **Criminal Justice Studies** *(Saint John campus)* (Criminal Law); **Early Childhood**; **Educational Administration** *(New Brunswick)* (Educational Administration); **Electronic Commerce** *(Saint John campus)* (E- Business/Commerce); **Electronic Text** (Electronic Engineering); **Enhanced Teaching and Learning**; **Geodetic Engineering** *(CCGE)* (Surveying and Mapping); **Information Technology** *(ITC)* (Information Technology); **International Business and Entrepreneurship** (International Business; Management); **Management Development and Information** *(Saint John campus)* (Management); **Nuclear Energy Research, Inc.** (Nuclear Engineering); **Planetary and Space Science** (Astronomy and Space Science); **Promotion of Instructional Technology** (Educational Technology); **Property Studies**; **Second Language Education** (Foreign Languages Education); **Study of War and Society** *(Gregg)* (Peace and Disarmament); **Wood Science and Technology** (Forest Products; Wood Technology)

Laboratory

Acoustics and Vibration (Sound Engineering (Acoustics)); **Advanced Computational Research and ACEnet** (Computer Science); **Advanced Machining**; **Advanced Plastics Manufacturing** (Polymer and Plastics Technology); **Architectural, Engineering and Construction Interactive Collaboration** (Architecture; Construction Engineering; Engineering); **Bio Signals** (Biological and Life Sciences); **Canadian Rivers Institute Research Facility** *(Saint John campus)*; **Computer Applications** (Computer Science); **Entomology** (Entomology); **Flow-Induced Vibration**; **Fluid Mechanics** (Mechanics); **Forest and Conservation Genomics and Biotechnology** (Biotechnology; Forest Management); **Forest Engineering/Geotechnical** *(Gillan)* (Forestry; Geological Engineering); **Geodetic Research** (Surveying and Mapping); **Geographic Information Systems** *(GIS)* (Surveying and Mapping); **Heat Transfer** (Heating and Refrigeration); **High-Resolution X-ray Microtomography** *(Micro-CT)*; **Integrated Forest Management** (Forest Management); **Magnetic Resonance Imaging**; **Manufacturing and Processing**; **Motion Analysis**; **Network Security**; **Nuclear Radiation** (Nuclear Engineering); **Robotics and Mechanisms** (Robotics); **Soils and Environmental Quality** (Environmental Management; Soil Conservation); **Stable Isotopes in Nature**; **Thermal Analysis Unit** (Thermal Engineering); **Threat-Material Detection**; **Tree Physiology/Biochemistry** (Biochemistry; Physiology)

Research Centre

Atlantic Cooperative Wildlife Ecology Research Network (Ecology; Wildlife); **CADMI Microelectronics, Inc.** (Microelectronics); **Environment and Sustainable Development** (Environmental Studies); **Environment and Sustainable Development** (Environmental Studies); **Family Violence** *(Muriel McQueen Fergusson)* (Social Problems); **Forest Watershed** *(NEXFOR/BOWATER)*; **Noncommutative Geometry and Topology** (Mathematics); **Pulp and Paper Research and Education** *(Dr. Jack McKenzie Limerick)* (Paper Technology); **Youth, Science, Teaching and Learning - CRYSTAL Atlantique** *(NSERC CRYSTAL)*

Research Group

Artificial Intelligence (Artificial Intelligence); **Automated Reasoning** (Automation and Control Engineering); **Canadian**

observatory on the justice system response to intimate partner violence *(SSHRC Cluster)*; **Energy Conversion Engineering** (Energy Engineering); **Greater Fundy Ecosystem Project**; **Groundwater Studies** (Water Science); **Health and Education** *(HERG)* (Education; Health Sciences); **Industrial City in Transition: A Cultural and Environmental Inventory of Greater Saint John** *(SSHRC CURA)* (Environmental Studies); **Labour History in New Brunswick Project** *(SSHRC CURA)*; **Materials** (Materials Engineering); **Ocean Mapping Group** (Surveying and Mapping); **Parallel/Distributed Processing**; **Population Ecology**; **Sustainable Power** (Power Engineering); **Transportation** (Transport and Communications); **UNB/Bhutan Project**

Research Institute

Chronic Illness (Health Sciences); **Social Policy** *(CRISP)* (Social Policy)

Research Unit

Fish and Wildlife *(NB Cooperative)* (Biology; Forestry; Wildlife)

Chair

Construction Engineering and Management *(M. Patrick Gillin)* (Construction Engineering; Management); **Environmental Design Engineering** *(NSERC)* (Environmental Engineering); **Highway Construction and Pavement Research** *(D.C. Campbell)* (Civil Engineering); **Nuclear Engineering** *(NSERC/NB Power/AECL)* (Nuclear Engineering); **Ocean Mapping** (Surveying and Mapping); **Power Plant Engineering** *(NB Power)* (Power Engineering); **Regional Economics** *(Vaughan)* (Economics); **Technology Management and Entrepreneurship** *(J. Herbert Smith/ACOA)* (Engineering Management); **Wildlife Ecology** *(NSERC/CWS Research)* (Ecology; Wildlife); **Women and the Law** *(Mary Louise Lynch)* (Law)

Further Information: Also Saint John campus.

History: Founded 1785 as Provincial Academy of Liberal Arts and Sciences; incorporated by Royal Charter 1828 as King's College. Acquired present title 1859. Saint John campus founded 1964. New Brunswick Teachers College incorporated 1973.

Academic Year: September to April (September-December; January-April)

Admission Requirements: Secondary school certificate or recognized foreign equivalent

Fees: National: 6,187 per annum (Canadian Dollar), International: International Differential Fee: 7,493 (Canadian Dollar)

Main Language(s) of Instruction: English

Degrees and Diplomas: *Certificat et diplôme universitaire/University certificate and diploma*; *Baccalauréat/Bachelor's Degree*; *Maîtrise/Master's Degree*: **Business Administration.** *Doctorat/Doctoral Degree*: **Biology; Chemical Engineering; Chemistry; Computer Engineering; Computer Science; Earth Sciences; Electrical Engineering; English; Surveying and Mapping.** Also concurrent degree programmes: Bachelor of Arts/Bachelor of Science (BA/BCS), 5 yrs and Bachelor of Arts/Bachelor of Computer Science (BA/BSc), 5 yrs; Professional development certificate programmes.

Student Services: Academic Counselling, Canteen, Careers Guidance, Cultural Activities, Facilities for disabled people, Foreign Studies Centre, Health Services, Language Laboratory, Nursery Care, Residential Facilities, Social Counselling, Sports Facilities

Publications: Acadiensis (Historical journal of the Atlantic Provinces); Canadian Journal of Regional Science; Journal of Conflict Studies; Qwerty; The Fiddlehead

Last Updated: 02/03/15

PRIVATE INSTITUTIONS

CRANDALL UNIVERSITY

333 Gorge Road, Box 6004, Moncton, New Brunswick NB E1C 9L7
Tel: +1(506) 858-8970
Fax: +1(506) 858-9694
EMail: admissions@crandallu.ca
Website: http://www.crandallu.ca

President: Bruce G. Fawcett (2012-)
Tel: +1(506) 858-8970 Ext. 107 EMail: president@crandallu.ca

Registrar: Sheldon MacLeod
Tel: +1(506) 858-8970 Ext. 103
EMail: sheldon.macleod@crandallu.ca

Programme

Arts (Bible; Communication Studies; English; History; Management; Psychology; Religious Studies; Sociology); **Business** (Business Administration; Management); **Certificate** (Christian Religious Studies; English; Leadership); **Continuing Education** (Literacy Education; Management); **Education** (Education; Literacy Education); **Off-Site Study** (American Studies; Education; Environmental Studies; Film; Latin American Studies; Middle Eastern Studies; Russian); **Science** (Biology)

History: Founded 1949 as the United Baptist Bible Training School, both a Bible College and a High School. In transition as the emphasis changed to a post high school program, it became a Bible College and a Christian Junior Liberal Arts College 1968. Changed its name to Atlantic Baptist College 1970. Started offering Bachelor's degree in the early 1980s. Changed its name to Atlantic Baptist University 1996. Acquired present title 2009.

Fees: National: Bachelor programmes: BA, BBA, BSc: 7,630.00. BEd: 7,920.00 per annum (Canadian Dollar), International: International Student – differential: 3,000.00 per annum (Canadian Dollar)

Main Language(s) of Instruction: English

Degrees and Diplomas: *Certificat et diplôme universitaire/University certificate and diploma*; *Baccalauréat/Baccalaureate*; *Maîtrise/Master's Degree*: **Education; Management.** Bachelor's degree (professional), 4 yrs.

Student Services: Library, Residential Facilities

Last Updated: 20/02/15

KINGSWOOD UNIVERSITY

P.O. Box 5125, 26 Western Street,
Sussex, New Brunswick E4E 1E6
Tel: +1(506) 432-4400
Fax: +1(506) 432-4425
EMail: admissions@kingswood.edu
Website: http://www.kingswood.edu/

President: Mark Gorveatte (2010-)
EMail: president@kingswood.edu

Division

Biblical and Theological Studies (Bible; Theology); **General Education** (Education; English; History; Natural Sciences; Philosophy; Psychology; Sociology); **Professional Studies** (Christian Religious Studies; Missionary Studies; Religious Education)

History: Founded 1945 as Holiness Bible Institute. Became Bethany Bible College in 1947. Acquired present title and status 2011.

Main Language(s) of Instruction: English

Degrees and Diplomas: *Baccalauréat/Baccalaureate*: **Education; Theology.** *Maîtrise/Master's Degree*: **Pastoral Studies.**

Academic Staff *2014-2015*: Total: c. 30

Student Numbers *2014-2015*: Total: c. 300

Last Updated: 20/02/15

ST. STEPHEN'S UNIVERSITY (SSU)

8 Main Street, St Stephen, New Brunswick E3L 3E2
Tel: +1(506) 466-1781
Fax: +1(506) 466-1783
EMail: ssu@ssu.ca
Website: http://www.ssu.ca

President: Robert J. Cheatley

Programme

International Studies (International Studies); **Liberal Arts** (Ancient Civilizations; Arts and Humanities; History; International Studies; Literature; Philosophy; Psychology; Religious Studies); **Ministry** (Theology)

History: Founded 1975.

Fees: Bachelor of Arts/international studies programmes, 5,500 per term; Ministry module programmes, 3,000 per module (Canadian Dollar)

Main Language(s) of Instruction: English

Degrees and Diplomas: *Certificat et diplôme universitaire/University certificate and diploma*: **Missionary Studies.** *Baccalauréat/Bachelor's Degree*: **Arts and Humanities; International Studies; Psychology.** *Maîtrise/Master's Degree*: **Missionary Studies.** Also Bachelor of Arts Honours.

Student Numbers *2014-2015*: Total: c. 120

Last Updated: 20/02/15

UNIVERSITY OF FREDERICTON

371 Queen Street, Suite 101, Fredericton, New Brunswick E3B 1B1
Tel: + 1(506) 454-6232
Fax: + 1(506) 455-1675
EMail: Info@UFred.ca
Website: http://www.ufred.ca/

Director and President: Don Roy

Provost: Kenneth Green

School

Applied Occupational Health Specialties (Occupational Health); **Business** (Business Administration; Criminal Law; Leadership)

Institute

Professional Learning (Environmental Engineering; Environmental Management; Industrial Design; Leadership; Rehabilitation and Therapy; Safety Engineering)

History: The University of Fredericton is a completely online university.

Fees: 19,000 for MBA programme and 24,500 for Executive MBA programme (Canadian Dollar)

Main Language(s) of Instruction: English

Accrediting Agency: The Province of New Brunswick in Canada.

Degrees and Diplomas: *Maîtrise/Master's Degree*: **Business Administration.** Also Professional diploma

Student Services: IT Centre

Last Updated: 23/02/15

YORKVILLE UNIVERSITY

1149 Smythe Street, Fredericton, New Brunswick E3B 3H4
Tel: + 1(506) 454-1220 + 1(866) 838-6542
Fax: + 1(506) 454-1221
EMail: info@yorkvilleu.ca
Website: http://www.yorkvilleu.ca

President: Rick Davey

Vice President, Academic: Ron McDonald

Bursar: Anna E. Jelavic EMail: ajelavic@yorkvilleu.ca

Faculty

Behavioural Sciences (Behavioural Sciences; Psychology; Social Problems; Toxicology); **Business** (Business Administration); **Education** (Education)

Further Information: Traditional and Open Learning Institution

History: Founded 2003. Acquired present status 2004.

Fees: Bachelor of Business Administration: 355 (per credit hour). Master of Education and Master of Arts in Counselling Psychology: 560 (per credit hour) (Canadian Dollar)

Main Language(s) of Instruction: English

Accrediting Agency: New Brunswick Department of Education

Degrees and Diplomas: *Baccalauréat/Baccalaureate*: **Business Administration.** *Maîtrise/Master's Degree*: **Adult Education; Psychology.** Also Post-graduate Diploma, 2-3 semesters following Master's degree.

Student Services: Library

Last Updated: 02/03/15

Canada - Newfoundland & Labrador

STRUCTURE OF HIGHER EDUCATION SYSTEM

Description:

Higher education in Canada is the constitutional responsibility of the provinces. In Newfoundland and Labrador, the institutions providing higher education are the provincially supported Memorial University of Newfoundland (MUN, categorized as a comprehensive university), and the College of the North Atlantic (CNA), which provides diverse technical and career-oriented certificate, apprenticeship and diploma programmes. As an affiliate of MUN, the Marine Institute (MI) provides training in all aspects of fisheries and marine technology. MUN is a full degree granting institution, while CNA is not (although it does offer university level transfer courses). MUN is an autonomous institution largely dependent on government for funding, whereas CNA is an agent of the crown. Besides MUN and CNA, there are also 25 provincially registered private training institutions which also provide technical and career oriented certificates and diplomas. Queen's College, a theology school, is a private not-for-profit institution, affiliated with MUN, and with the power to grant degrees qualifying recipients for ordination. Adult Basic Education (ABE) is a high school equivalency programme for adults who did not complete high school, and is part of the NL higher education system offered through the community college, private training institutions and community organizations.

Stages of studies:

University level first stage: *Baccalauréat/Bachelor's degree*
Most undergraduate study leads to a "General" (Pass) Bachelor's degree (4 years of full time study) or an "Honours" degree (additional year) as well as professional degrees in areas such as Business Administration, Engineering, Medicine, Nursing, Pharmacy, and Social Work. Degrees are normally titled in broad descriptive groups, e.g. B.A., B.Sc., B.N. The first stage also includes undergraduate diplomas (1-3 years of study) and short (up to 1 year) special certificate programmes. The Marine Institute of Memorial University offers Bachelor's degrees in Maritime Studies and Technology. In addition, first year university transfer courses are offered by CNA.

University level second stage: *Maîtrise/Master's degree*
The Master's degree normally requires at least one year's study after a Bachelor's (Honours) degree or equivalent. Some Master's programmes, e.g. Business Administration, necessitate at least two years. A thesis is usually required supplemented by course work. Examples are: M.A., M.Sc., M.Ed., MBA. Besides graduate level diplomas (considered as intermediate between the Bachelor's or first professional degree and the Master's degree), the second stage also includes first professional degree programmes requiring prerequisite university studies (e.g. Doctor of Medicine (M.D.)). The Marine Institute of Memorial University offers a Master's degree in Maritime Studies, Technology Management, and Maritime Management.

University level third stage: *Doctorat/Doctorate degree*
The Doctorate is the highest academic qualification awarded by Canadian universities and (in all provinces except Quebec) it comprises the third stage of university level studies. This degree normally requires at least three years of study after the Master's degree; the submission and defence of a major thesis (dissertation); along with supplemental course work. The degree "Doctor of Philosophy" (Ph.D.) is the designation that is most commonly used to signify the Doctorate, although other designations exist (e.g., the degree of Doctor of Psychology (Psy.D.)). The doctoral degree is a generic title, applicable to degrees in most disciplines (the Doctorate should not be confused with certain first professional degrees in the Health Sciences, e.g. Medicine (M.D.), Veterinary Medicine and Dentistry).

ADMISSION TO HIGHER EDUCATION

Admission to university-level studies:

Alternatives to credentials: Secondary School Diploma. Alternatives: Memorial University sets admission policies and requirements for various categories of applicants including local high school students; high schools students from other Canadian provinces and abroad; mature students (aged 21 or more); Adult Basic Education (ABE) students; senior citizens (aged 60 or more); and transfer students.

Numerus clausus: There is a numerus clausus at institutional level.

Other requirements: At least 70% overall average in select high school courses. Proof of proficiency in the language of instruction.

Foreign students admission:

Definition of foreign student: Foreign (International) Students are students who are neither Canadian citizens nor permanent residents of Canada and are enrolled full-time in a recognized academic, professional or vocational training course at a university, college or other educational institution in Canada.

Quotas: Neither MUN nor CNA set quotas for international students. Students are advised that admission to certain professional programmes (e.g. MUN Pharmacy) is highly competitive and selective. In some cases, priority is given to applicants who are bona fide residents of Newfoundland and Labrador.
Private training institutions are also involved in foreign student education and have their own admissions and quota policies for these students.

Admission requirements: Generally, as for domestic students, a high school diploma or equivalent will be required.

Entry regulations: Before you come to study in Canada, you will need: a "Study Permit" if the programme of study you will be admitted to is longer than six months in duration, regardless of the length of your stay in Canada; a letter of acceptance from the school of your choice; proof that you have enough money to pay school fees and living expenses; to establish that you will return home at the end of your studies; to pass a medical exam if required; and to qualify as a temporary resident in Canada, including holding a temporary resident visa (required for citizens of many countries). A small number of students do not require a Study Permit by virtue of their status in Canada (e.g. diplomats and their children). More at http://www.cic.gc.ca/english/study/

Health requirements: Most education institutions require international students to buy health insurance in addition to their tuition fees; those that do not will require proof of independent health insurance coverage. Medical examinations are not required by institutions but are required by Citizenship and Immigration Canada for students from many countries.

Language proficiency: Both MUN and CNA require the Test of English as a Foreign Language (TOEFL) - minimum mark is 550 (written) or 213 (computer-based).

RECOGNITION OF STUDIES

Quality assurance system:
MUN: Before making a regulation providing for a new course of study or a change in an existing course of study, the Senate will refer to the appropriate faculty council and appropriate faculty of affiliated colleges or institutions for consideration. University programmes are accredited and reviewed by accrediting bodies where appropriate (e.g., nursing, medicine, etc).
CNA: The Board of Governors must assess the education and training needs of the Province and of the region in respect of which CNA is responsible for providing educational services, as those needs are perceived by community committees, local organizations, private citizens or other groups.
MUN and CNA have agreements that enable students to obtain transfer credit for some courses/programmes. All private training institutions must be registered, the superintendent of private training institutions reviews and approves every course of study prior to registration of the institutions, and the provincial government conducts yearly inspections. Provincial Apprenticeship and Certification Board accredits apprenticeship programmes offered by both public colleges and private training institutions to ensure standards are consistent across institutions delivering provincial curriculum.

Bodies dealing with recognition:

Ministère de l'Enseignement postsecondaire et des Compétences avancées de Terre-Neuve-et-Labrador (Newfoundland and Labrador Department of Advanced Education and Skills)

PO Box 8700
St. John's A1B 4J6
Tel: +1(709) 729-2480
Fax: +1(709) 729-6996
EMail: aesweb@gov.nl.ca
WWW: http://aes.gov.nl.ca

PROVINCIAL BODIES

Ministère de l'Enseignement postsecondaire et des Compétences avancées de Terre-Neuve-et-Labrador (Newfoundland and Labrador Department of Advanced Education and Skills)

Ministre/Minister: Gerry Byrne
PO Box 8700
St. John's, NL A1B 4J6
Canada
Tel: +1(709) 729-2480
Fax: +1(709) 729-6996
EMail: aesweb@gov.nl.ca
WWW: http://aes.gov.nl.ca

Role of national body: The Department of Advanced Education and Skills is responsible for the post-secondary education and skills training, and adult literacy.

Data for academic year: 2014-2015

Source: IAU from the Canadian Information Centre for International Credentials (CICIC), a unit of the Council of Ministers of Education, Canada (CMEC), on behalf of the Newfoundland and Labrador Department of Advanced Education and Skills, November 2014. Bodies 2016.

INSTITUTION

PUBLIC INSTITUTION

MEMORIAL UNIVERSITY OF NEWFOUNDLAND (MUN)

P.O. Box 4200, St John's, Newfoundland A1C 5S7
Tel: +1(709) 864-8000
Fax: +1(709) 864-4569
EMail: info@mun.ca
Website: http://www.mun.ca

President and Vice-Chancellor: Gary Kachanoski (2010-)
Tel: +1(709) 864-8212 EMail: president@mun.ca

Vice-President, Administration and Finance: Kent Decker
Tel: +1(709) 737-8217 EMail: vpadmin@mun.ca

International Relations: Sonja Knutson, Acting Director, International Centre Tel: +1(709) 864-3288 EMail: sknutson@mun.ca

Faculty

Arts (Ancient Civilizations; Anthropology; Archaeology; Arts and Humanities; Asian Religious Studies; Bible; Canadian Studies; Communication Studies; Constitutional Law; Criminal Law; Cultural Studies; Economics; English; Ethics; European Studies; Film; Folklore; Foreign Languages Education; French; Gender Studies; Geography; German; Greek (Classical); History; History of Law; History of Religion; Indigenous Studies; International Law; Islamic Theology; Judaic Religious Studies; Latin; Law; Linguistics; Literature; Medieval Studies; Music; New Testament; Philosophy; Police Studies; Political Sciences; Psychology; Regional Studies; Religious Studies; Russian; Sociology; Spanish; Theatre; Women's Studies); **Business Administration** (Business Administration; Business and Commerce; International Business; Labour and Industrial Relations; Management); **Education** (Adult Education; Computer Education; Curriculum; Education; Foreign Languages Education; French; Higher Education; Humanities and Social Science Education; Information Technology; Leadership; Literacy Education; Mathematics Education; Music; Music Education; Native Language Education; Natives Education; Primary Education; Psychology; Science Education; Secondary Education; Special Education; Teacher Training); **Engineering and Applied Science** (Civil Engineering; Computer Engineering; Electrical Engineering; Engineering; Engineering Management; Environmental Engineering; Mechanical Engineering; Naval Architecture; Petroleum and Gas Engineering); **Medicine** (Anaesthesiology; Biomedicine; Cardiology; Community Health; Epidemiology; Genetics; Gynaecology and Obstetrics; Immunology; Laboratory Techniques; Medicine; Nephrology; Neurosciences; Oncology; Orthopaedics; Paediatrics; Pathology; Psychiatry and Mental Health; Public Health; Radiology; Surgery); **Science** (Aquaculture; Atomic and Molecular Physics; Behavioural Sciences; Biochemistry; Biology; Chemistry; Cognitive Sciences; Computer Science; Earth Sciences; Environmental Studies; Food Science; Geography; Geology; Geophysics; Marine Biology; Marine Science and Oceanography; Mathematics; Physics; Psychology; Social Psychology; Statistics)

Division

Lifelong Learning (Accountancy; Business Administration; Communication Studies; Computer Networks; Criminology;

Development Studies; Human Resources; Insurance; Leadership; Library Science; Management; Marketing; Public Administration; Public Relations; Regional Studies; Robotics; Transport and Communications; Writing)

College

Queen's *(http://www.queenscollegemun.ca)* (Bible; History of Religion; New Testament; Pastoral Studies; Religion; Theology)

School

Graduate Studies (Administration; Ancient Civilizations; Anthropology; Aquaculture; Archaeology; Arts and Humanities; Asian Religious Studies; Atomic and Molecular Physics; Behavioural Sciences; Bible; Biochemistry; Biology; Business Administration; Cardiology; Chemistry; Christian Religious Studies; Civil Engineering; Cognitive Sciences; Computer Engineering; Computer Science; Conducting; Curriculum; Earth Sciences; Economics; Education; Electrical Engineering; Engineering; Engineering Management; English; Environmental Engineering; Environmental Management; Environmental Studies; Epidemiology; Ethics; Ethnology; Experimental Psychology; Fishery; Folklore; Food Science; Foreign Languages Education; French Studies; Genetics; Geography; Geology; Geophysics; German; Greek (Classical); Health Sciences; Higher Education; History; History of Religion; Immunology; Information Technology; Inorganic Chemistry; Islamic Theology; Labour and Industrial Relations; Latin; Leadership; Linguistics; Literature; Management; Marine Biology; Marine Engineering; Marine Science and Oceanography; Mathematics; Mechanical Engineering; Medicine; Music; Music Education; Musical Instruments; Musicology; Naval Architecture; Neurosciences; New Testament; Nursing; Oncology; Organic Chemistry; Parks and Recreation; Performing Arts; Petroleum and Gas Engineering; Pharmacy; Philosophy; Physical Therapy; Physics; Physiology; Political Sciences; Psychology; Public Health; Religious Studies; Social Psychology; Social Work; Sociology; Sports; Statistics; Women's Studies); **Human Kinetics and Recreation** (Administration; Curriculum; Parks and Recreation; Physical Education; Physical Therapy; Physiology; Psychology); **Music** (Art History; Conducting; Music; Music Education; Music Theory and Composition; Musical Instruments; Musicology); **Nursing (Western Regional)** (Nursing); **Pharmacy** (Pharmacy); **Social Work** (Social Work)

Department

Distance Education and Learning Technologies (Anthropology; Biology; Business Administration; Criminology; Curriculum; Earth Sciences; Economics; Education; Educational and Student Counselling; Educational Psychology; Engineering; English; Folklore; French; German; Higher Education; Law; Leadership; Leisure Studies; Library Science; Linguistics; Marine Engineering; Marine Science and Oceanography; Mathematics; Music; Nursing; Parks and Recreation; Philosophy; Physical Education; Physical Therapy; Police Studies; Political Sciences; Psychology; Public Administration; Regional Studies; Religious Studies; Russian; Social Work; Sociology; Spanish; Sports; Statistics; Technology; Women's Studies)

Institute

Labrador (Anthropology; Archaeology; English; Geography; Linguistics; Meteorology; Social Work); **Marine** *(http://www.mi.mun.ca/)* (Aquaculture; Fishery; Marine Science and Oceanography; Marine Transport; Natural Resources; Petroleum and Gas Engineering; Safety Engineering); **Social and Economic Research** *(ISER)* (Economics; Social Sciences)

Laboratory

Language *(Digital Language Centre)* (Classical Languages; Danish; English; French; German; Greek (Classical); Irish; Italian; Latin; Linguistics; Russian; Spanish)

Research Centre

Ocean Engineering (Marine Engineering); **Study of Music, Media, and Place** *((MMaP))* (Media Studies; Music)

Campus

Sir Wilfred Grenfell (Arts and Humanities; Biology; Business Administration; Chemistry; Cultural Studies; Earth Sciences; English; Environmental Studies; Fine Arts; History; Mathematics; Natural Resources; Nursing; Physics; Primary Education; Psychology; Social Studies; Theatre; Tourism; Visual Arts)

Further Information: Traditional and Open Learning Institution. Also affiliation with 4 major Teaching Hospitals (Eastern Health, Central Health, Western Health, Labrador-Grenfell Health). Other campuses: Grenfell Campus in Corner Brook, Harlow (in Essex, England), Labrador Institute (Happy Valley-Goose Bay).

History: Founded 1925 as Memorial University College. Awarded degree-granting status and present title 1949. The only degree-granting post-secondary institution in the Province of Newfoundland and Labrador.

Academic Year: September to August (September-December; January-April; May-August); also 6-week inter-session and 6-week summer session.

Admission Requirements: Secondary school certificate or recognized foreign equivalent, with minimum of 70% average. Proof of proficiency in English language

Fees: National: Undergraduate tuition on Saint John's campus, 2,550 for two semesters (30 credit-hours). Program fee per semester: Graduate Diploma: 323. Master's: 733. PhD and PsyD: 683 (Canadian Dollar), International: Undergraduate tuition: 8,800 for two semesters (30 credit-hours). Program fee per semester: Graduate Diploma: 420. Master's: 953. PhD and PsyD: 887 (Canadian Dollar)

Main Language(s) of Instruction: English

Degrees and Diplomas: *Certificat et diplôme universitaire/University certificate and diploma*; *Baccalauréat/Bachelor's Degree*; *Baccalauréat spécialisé/Bachelor's Degree - Honours*; *Maîtrise/Master's Degree*; *Diplôme et certificat de 2e cycle/Graduate Diploma and Certificate*; *Doctorat/Doctoral Degree*: **Anthropology; Archaeology; English; Ethnology; Geography; History; Linguistics; Philosophy; Sociology.** also Executive MBA

Student Services: Academic Counselling, Canteen, Careers Guidance, Cultural Activities, Facilities for disabled people, Health Services, Language Laboratory, Nursery Care, Social Counselling, Sports Facilities

Publications: Canadian Folklore/Folklore canadien; Culture and Tradition; International Journal of Maritime History; Labour/Le Travail; Newfoundland Quarterly; Regional Languages Studies; Research Directory

Publishing House: University Printing Services

Academic Staff *2010-2011*: Total 950

Student Numbers *2011-2012*: Total: c. 19,000

Last Updated: 06/02/15

Canada - Northwest Territories

STRUCTURE OF HIGHER EDUCATION SYSTEM

Description:

The Department of Education, Culture and Employment is responsible for postsecondary education in the Northwest Territories. It does not have its own university, though the Department contributes financially to students from the Territory pursuing university studies elsewhere in Canada. Aurora College provides postsecondary education and offers academic (including university transfer courses), business, trades (pre-employment and apprenticeship), career development, technical and vocational training programmes usually leading to a Certificate or Diploma. The College can grant degrees but has not to date. It has full autonomy on admissions and all other academic matters. The Boards of Governors are appointed by the Department of Education, Culture and Employment.

Stages of studies:

University level first stage:

Many of the courses in the College Diploma programmes are eligible for transfer credit with universities and professional associations across Canada. The College also offers selected university credit courses through its campuses. Aurora College offers a Bachelor in Science of Nursing in partnership with the University of Victoria. In addition, it offers a Licensed Practical Nurse programme that prepares students for the Canadian Practical Nurse Registration Examinations and a Community Health Representative programme.

ADMISSION TO HIGHER EDUCATION

Foreign students admission:

Definition of foreign student: Foreign (International) Students are students who are neither Canadian citizens nor permanent residents of Canada and are enrolled full-time in a recognized academic, professional or vocational training course at a university, college or other educational institution in Canada.

Admission requirements: Generally, as for domestic students, a high school diploma or equivalent will be required. A lack of proficiency in English or French will be taken into account by the Canadian Immigration Office in the evaluation of the application.

Entry regulations: Before you come to study in Canada, you will need: a "Study Permit" if the programme of study you will be admitted to is longer than six months in duration, regardless of the length of your stay in Canada; a letter of acceptance from the school of your choice; proof that you have enough money to pay school fees and living expenses; to establish that you will return home at the end of your studies; to pass a medical exam if required; and to qualify as a temporary resident in Canada, including holding a temporary resident visa (required for citizens of many countries). A small number of students do not require a Study Permit by virtue of their status in Canada (e.g. diplomats and their children).

Health requirements: Most education institutions require international students to buy health insurance in addition to their tuition fees; those that do not will require proof of independent health insurance coverage. Medical examinations are not required by institutions but are required by Citizenship and Immigration Canada for students from many countries.

RECOGNITION OF STUDIES

Quality assurance system:

See http://www.cicic.ca/573/quality-assurance-NT.canada

PROVINCIAL BODIES

Ministère de l'Éducation, de la Culture et de l'Emploi des Territoires du Nord-Ouest (Northwest Territories Department of Education, Culture and Employment)

Minister/Ministre: Alfred Moses
PO Box 1320
Yellowknife, NT X1A 2L9
Canada
Tel: +1(867) 920-3059
Fax: +1(867) 873-0456
EMail: ecepublicaffairs@gov.nt.ca
WWW: http://www.ece.gov.nt.ca
Role of national body: To coordinate the development and delivery of career programmes and services for adult education and training and postsecondary education.

Data for academic year: 2014-2015
Source: IAU from Canadian Information Centre for International Credentials (CICIC),Council of Ministers of Education of Canada (CMEC) on behalf of the Northwest Territories Department of Education, Culture and Employment, November 2014. Bodies 2016.

Canada - Nova Scotia

STRUCTURE OF HIGHER EDUCATION SYSTEM

Description:

Higher education in Canada is the constitutional responsibility of the Provinces. The three main types of institutions are universities, community college and private career colleges. The universities are independent, degree granting institutions, with full autonomy on admission policies and all other academic matters. The Nova Scotia Community College (NSCC) provides a variety of post-secondary programmes usually leading to a Certificate or Diploma. It is a self-governing institution operating under the direction of a board of governors with a mandate to meet the Province's occupational training needs. The NSCC is accountable to government for matters of public concern, such as the appropriate use of tax dollars, admissions policy and tuition. Private career colleges are independently operated for profit business institutions that operate under regulations established by the province.

Stages of studies:

University level first stage: *Baccalauréat/Bachelor's degree*

University level education in Nova Scotia is delivered through 11 publicly supported degree-granting institutions. Some of the Province's degree-granting institutions are highly specialized; others offer a broader range of undergraduate and graduate programmes. General undergraduate degrees at most universities in Nova Scotia require a minimum of 3 years of full-time study. Honours degrees, involving a higher level of concentration in the honours discipline and a higher level of academic performance generally require 4 years of full-time study. Most universities also offer diploma and certificate programmes in various specialized fields. These vary in length depending on the program and the institution.

University level second stage: *Maîtrise/Master's degree*

The Master's degree may take one or two years after an Honours degree (or equivalent) depending on the field of study. Some programmes require both course work and a thesis, while others require only course work. Degrees awarded include Master of Arts, Master of Science, Master of Business Administration and Master of Education. This stage also includes graduate level, or intermediate, diplomas (between a Bachelor's degree and a Master's degree).

University level third stage: *Doctorat/Doctorate degree (Ph.D.)*

The Doctorate is the highest qualification awarded by Canadian universities and, in all provinces except Quebec, it comprises the third stage of university-level studies. This degree normally requires at least three years of study beyond a Bachelor's degree and the submission and defence of a dissertation. Course work is also usually required. The degree "Doctor of Philosophy" (Ph.D.). is a designation most commonly used to signify the Doctorate.

ADMISSION TO HIGHER EDUCATION

Admission to university-level studies:

Alternatives to credentials: Students are sometimes admitted with "mature student status". Prior learning assessment practices are also being introduced as an alternative means of assessing applicants.

Other requirements: 60% average in final year of secondary school studies in 5 appropriate academic subjects (most programmes have minimum grade point average). Universities set their admissions policies. Highly selective programmes require admissions qualifications that are higher than specified minimum. Proof of proficiency in language of instruction may be required. Some universities offer remedial courses or preparatory programmes.

Foreign students admission:

Definition of foreign student: Foreign (International) Students are students who are neither Canadian citizens nor permanent residents of Canada, and are enrolled full-time in a recognized academic, professional or vocational training course at a university, college or other educational institution in Canada.

Admission requirements: Generally, as for domestic students, a high school diploma or equivalent will be required. A lack of proficiency in English or French will be taken into account by the Canadian immigration office in the evaluation of the application.

Entry regulations: Before you come to study in Canada, you will need: a "Study Permit" if the programme of study you will be admitted to is longer than six months in duration, regardless of the length of your stay in Canada; a letter of acceptance from the school of your choice; proof that you have enough money to pay school fees and living expenses; to establish that you will return home at the end of your studies; to pass a medical exam if required; and to qualify as a temporary resident in Canada, including holding a temporary resident visa (required for citizens of many countries). A small number of students do not require a "Study Permit" by virtue of their status in Canada (e.g. diplomats and their children).

Health requirements: Most education institutions require international students to buy health insurance in addition to their tuition fees; those that do not will require proof of independent health insurance coverage. Medical examinations are not required by institutions but are required by Citizenship and Immigration Canada for students from many countries.

RECOGNITION OF STUDIES

Quality assurance system:

The Maritime Provinces Higher Education Commission (MPHEC) assesses programme quality through a quality assurance process for new programmes and monitors the institutions to ensure a quality assurance process is in place for existing programmes. Individual educational institutions are responsible for recognition/accreditation for credit transfer. As a result, practices vary by institution and programme. In general, the institutions use information from a variety of sources to assess academic credentials.

Bodies dealing with recognition:

Ministère du Travail et de l'Éducation postsecondaire de la Nouvelle-Écosse (Nova Scotia Department of Labour and Advanced Education)

PO Box 697
Halifax B3J 2T8
Tel: +1(902) 424-6647
Fax: +1(902) 424-0575
EMail: MIN_LAE@gov.ns.ca
WWW: http://www.gov.ns.ca/lae

Special provisions for recognition:

Recognition for university level studies: In general none. Universities establish their own admissions criteria and make their own admissions decisions in response to individual applications. Any restrictions on admission are determined by the institutions themselves, given available teaching and other resources, but in a few instances are a result of government policy. Priority is usually given to provincial residents first, other Canadian residents, then foreign students.
Additionally, the Canadian Information Centre for International Credentials (CICIC) provides information and guidance on the assessment and recognition of international academic credentials.

For access to advanced studies and research: In general none. However, if in some high cost, limited enrolment programmes, e.g. medicine and dentistry, qualified applicants outnumber available enrolment capacity, then most universities will establish special admissions committees and provide for proportionately more domestic than foreign applicants to be admitted.

For exercising a profession: In general none. For each profession, both Canadians and non-Canadians who studied abroad have to meet specified educational and experience requirements, and usually pass registration examinations. Non-Canadians may sometimes also need to pass language tests.

PROVINCIAL BODIES

Ministère du Travail et de l'Éducation postsecondaire de la Nouvelle-Écosse (Nova Scotia Department of Labour and Advanced Education)

Ministre/Minister: Kelly Regan
PO Box 697
Halifax, NS B3J 2T8
Canada
Tel: +1(902) 424-6647
Fax: +1(902) 424-0575
EMail: MIN_LAE@gov.ns.ca
WWW: http://www.gov.ns.ca/lae

Conseil des Rectrices et Recteurs des Universités de la Nouvelle-Écosse (Council of Nova Scotia University Presidents - CONSUP)

Chairperson: Allister Surette
Suite 403, 5657 Spring Garden Road
Halifax, NS B3J 3R4
Canada
Tel: +1(902) 425-4230
Fax: +1(902) 425-4233
WWW: http://www.atlanticuniversities.ca/about-aau/council-nova-scotia-university-presidents-consup

Private Colleges Association of Nova Scotia

1577 Barrington Street
Halifax, NS B3J 1Z7
Canada

Data for academic year: 2014-2015

Source: IAU from the Canadian Information Centre for International Credentials (CICIC), a unit of the Council of Ministers of Education, Canada (CMEC), on behalf of the Nova Scotia Department of Labour and Advanced Education, November 2014. Bodies 2016.

INSTITUTIONS

PUBLIC INSTITUTIONS

ACADIA UNIVERSITY

15 University Avenue, Wolfville, Nova Scotia B4P 2R6
Tel: +1(902) 542-2201 +1(902) 585-2201
Fax: +1(902) 585-7224
EMail: agi@acadiau.ca
Website: http://www.acadiau.ca

President and Vice-Chancellor: Ray Ivany (2009-)
Tel: +1(902) 585-1218 EMail: president@acadiau.ca

Vice-President, Academic (Acting): Robert Perrins

Faculty
Arts (Ancient Civilizations; Art Therapy; Canadian Studies; Comparative Religion; Economics; English; Environmental Studies; French; German; Greek (Classical); Histology; History; Latin; Literature; Modern Languages; Music; Music Education; Music Theory and Composition; Musical Instruments; Musicology; Philosophy; Political Sciences; Singing; Sociology; Spanish; Theatre; Women's Studies); **Professional Studies** (Accountancy; Biology; Business Administration; Education; Marketing; Music Education; Nutrition; Parks and Recreation; Physical Therapy; Primary Education; Secondary Education; Technology Education); **Pure and Applied Science** (Biology; Chemistry; Computer Science; Dietetics; Earth Sciences; Engineering; Environmental Studies; Mathematics; Nutrition; Physics; Psychology; Statistics); **Theology** (Bible; Christian Religious Studies; History of Religion; New Testament; Religion; Religious Education; Religious Studies; Theology)

Department
Graduate Studies (Biology; Chemistry; Computer Science; Education; Educational Sciences; English; Geology; Mathematics; Parks and Recreation; Political Sciences; Psychology; Social Sciences; Sociology; Statistics; Surveying and Mapping)

Academy
Environment *(Arthur Irving)* (Environmental Studies)

Laboratory
Chemical Analysis and Bio-imaging *(CABL)* (Biological and Life Sciences; Chemistry); **Environmental Biogeochemistry** (Chemistry); **Eukaryotic Microbiology and Parasitology** (Microbiology; Parasitology); **Inorganic Photophysics and Biological Sciences** (Biological and Life Sciences; Physics); **Investigating Ultra-trace Organic Contaminants in the Environment**; **Photosciences**; **Plant Developmental Morphology and Systematics**; **Psychomotor Behaviour**

Research Centre
Analytical Research on the Environment *(CARE)* (Environmental Studies); **Estuarine Research** *(ACER)* (Coastal Studies); **Lifestyle Studies** *(CoLS)*; **Mathematical Modelling and Computation**

(ACMMaC) (Mathematics); **Media** *(AMC)* (Media Studies); **Microstructural Analysis** *(ACMA)*; **Northeast Asia** *(NEARC)* (Asian Studies); **Organizational Research and Development** *(COR&D)*; **Sensory Research of Food** *(CSRF)* (Food Technology); **Social and Business Entrepreneurship** (Business Administration; Management); **Study of Ethnocultural Diversity** *(ACSED)* (Cultural Studies; Ethnology); **Wildlife and Conservation Biology** (Biology; Wildlife)

Research Unit

K.C. Irving Environmental Science Centre and Harriet Irving Botanical Gardens (Botany; Environmental Studies)

History: Founded 1838 as Queen's College by the Nova Scotia Baptist Education Society, became Acadia College 1841. Incorporated 1891 by act of the Nova Scotia legislature with the powers of a university. Acquired present title 1891.

Academic Year: September to April (September-December; January-April)

Admission Requirements: Secondary school certificate or recognized foreign equivalent, including International Baccalaureate

Fees: National: Undergraduate, 3102.50-6205 per term for Nova Scotia residents. 3613,50-7521 (Non Nova Scotia residents). Masters programmes, 3,934- 6163 per annum for Nova Scotia residents. 7185 per annum for Canadian Students (Non Residents of Nova Scotia) (Canadian Dollar), International: Undergraduate 7,495-15,535 per term; Masters Programmes: 15,136 per annum (Canadian Dollar)

Main Language(s) of Instruction: English

Degrees and Diplomas: *Baccalauréat/Bachelor's Degree*; *Maîtrise/Master's Degree*: **Christian Religious Studies.** *Doctorat/Doctoral Degree*: **Religion.** Also Bachelor with Honours in Business Administration, Recreation Management and Kynesiology, 4 yrs. Also inter-university doctoral programme (PhD) in Educational Studies, 14 months, jointly offered with Mount Saint Vincent University and St. Francis Xavier University.

Student Services: Library, Sports Facilities

Publications: Acadia Connections

Last Updated: 03/03/15

CAPE BRETON UNIVERSITY (CBU)

P.O.Box 5300, 1250 Grand Lake Road,
Sydney, Nova Scotia B1P 6L2
Tel: +1(902) 539-5300 +1(888) 959-9995
Fax: +1(902) 562-0119
EMail: registrar@cbu.ca
Website: http://www.cbu.ca

President and Vice-Chancellor: David Wheeler
Tel: 1+(902) 563-1333 EMail: david_wheeler@cbu.ca

Vice-President, Student Services and Registrar: Alexis Manley
Tel: +1(902) 563-1650 EMail: registrar@cbu.ca

International Relations: Terry Gibbs, Director, Centre for International Studies Tel: +1(902) 563-1274 EMail: terry_gibbs@cbu.ca

Programme

Online Education (Engineering; Environmental Studies; Hotel and Restaurant; Industrial Engineering; Protective Services; Public Administration; Public Health; Social and Community Services; Tourism)

School

Arts and Social Sciences (Anthropology; Business Administration; Celtic Languages and Studies; Communication Studies; Cultural Studies; English; Environmental Studies; Fine Arts; Folklore; French; Health Sciences; Heritage Preservation; History; Literature; Management; Media Studies; Modern Languages; Musicology; Native American Studies; Native Language; Philosophy; Physical Education; Political Sciences; Psychology; Public Administration; Religious Studies; Social and Community Services; Social Sciences; Sociology; Spanish; Theatre; Women's Studies); **Business** *(Shannon)* (Accountancy; Business Administration; Development Studies; Economics; Finance; Hotel and Restaurant; Human Resources; Law; Marketing; Tourism); **Graduate and Professional Studies** (Art Education; Arts and Humanities; Biology; Business Administration; Chemistry; Curriculum; Education; Educational and Student Counselling; Educational Technology; Health Sciences; Information Technology; Mathematics; Microbiology; Nursing; Nutrition; Occupational Health; Public Health; Secondary Education; Social Sciences); **Science and Technology** (Agriculture; Automation and Control Engineering; Bioengineering; Biology; Chemical Engineering; Chemistry; Civil Engineering; Computer Engineering; Computer Science; Electrical Engineering; Electronic Engineering; Engineering; Environmental Studies; Geology; Industrial Engineering; Mathematics; Mechanical Engineering; Metallurgical Engineering; Mining Engineering; Petroleum and Gas Engineering; Physical Therapy; Physics; Psychology; Technology)

Institute

Alexander Graham Bell; **Beaton** (Cultural Studies; Economics; Environmental Studies; History; Industrial and Production Economics; Labour and Industrial Relations; Political Sciences; Religious Studies; Rural Studies; Social Studies); **Community Economic Development** *(CED)* (Development Studies); **Development of Energy and Sustainability** (Energy Engineering); **Ecosystem Research** *(Bras d'Or)* (Ecology); **Human Values and Technology** *(Tompkins)* (Technology); **Integrative Science and Health** *(IISH)*; **Louisbourg** (Education); **Small and Medium-sized Enterprise** *(SMEI)* (Small Business); **Tourism Development** *(International)* (Tourism)

Centre

Cape Breton Studies (Celtic Languages and Studies; Ethnology; Folklore; Music; Musicology); **Children's Rights** (Human Rights); **International Studies**; **Natural History** (Biological and Life Sciences; Botany; Natural Sciences); **Philosophy and Religion** *(PAR)* (Philosophy; Religion); **Religion and Society** *(Abraham)* (Christian Religious Studies; Islamic Theology; Judaic Religious Studies; Religion); **Small Business Development** *(SBDC)* (Small Business); **Sustainability in Energy and the Environment** *(CSEE)* (Energy Engineering; Environmental Studies)

Group

Petroleum Applications of Wireless Systems *(PAWS)* (Petroleum and Gas Engineering)

Research Centre

Marketing (Marketing)

Further Information: Also Campus in Cairo (Canadian International College Egypt); Study Abroad and Exchange programmes (Contact Diane Toomey. Tel: +1(902) 563-1278; E-mail: diane_toomey@cbu.ca)

History: Founded 1974 by amalgamation of Saint Francis Xavier University's former Sydney campus (1951) and Nova Scotia Eastern Institute of Technology (1968). Acquired present status and title 2005.

Academic Year: September to August (September-December; January-April; May-August)

Admission Requirements: Secondary school certificate or recognized foreign equivalent, including International Baccalaureate; TOEFL score of 550

Fees: (Can. Dollars): Undergraduate Courses, 566-620,50 per 3 credit course (Nova Scotia students and Out-of-Province Canadian Students receive a bursary the Province of Nova Scotia to be applied against tuition respectively in the amount of 128.30 and 26.10 per three credit course; International Students, 1,132 per 3 credit course or equivalent. Graduate tuition fees, 1,184 per 3 credit course for Canadian students and 1,750 per 3 credit course for International students

Main Language(s) of Instruction: English

Degrees and Diplomas: *Baccalauréat/Bachelor's Degree*; *Maîtrise/Master's Degree*. Also joint Bachelor of Arts Community Studies/Bachelor of Business Administration (BACS/BBA) degree program; Pre-MBA Program for International Students; Honours Bachelor's degree; two year programme for graduates with a relevant Bachelor's Degree or Technology Programme (first year of a joint 2-year post-diploma program is also offered in French in partnership with the Bathurst campus of the New Brunswick Community College).

Student Services: Academic Counselling, Canteen, Careers Guidance, Cultural Activities, Facilities for disabled people, Health Services, Nursery Care, Social Counselling, Sports Facilities

Publishing house: CBU Press

Academic Staff *2010-2011*	**TOTAL**
FULL-TIME	**100**
PART-TIME	**50**
STAFF WITH DOCTORATE	
FULL-TIME	c. **80**
Student Numbers *2010-2011*	
All (Foreign included)	c. **3,500**
FOREIGN ONLY	**400**

Last Updated: 13/02/13

DALHOUSIE UNIVERSITY (DAL)

1236 Henry Street, Halifax, Nova Scotia B3H 4R2
Tel: +1(902) 494-2211
Fax: +1(902) 494-2319
EMail: admissions@dal.ca
Website: http://www.dal.ca

President and Vice-Chancellor: Richard Florizone
Tel: +1(902) 494-2511

Provost and Vice-President, Academic: Carolyn Watters
EMail: carolyn.watters@dal.ca

Faculty

Agriculture (Agricultural Business; Agricultural Economics; Agriculture; Food Science); **Architecture and Planning** (Architecture and Planning; Arts and Humanities; Building Technologies; Design; Environmental Management; History; Landscape Architecture; Technology; Town Planning); **Arts and Social Sciences** (Acting; Ancient Civilizations; Anthropology; Arabic; Business Administration; Canadian Studies; Chinese; Cognitive Sciences; Contemporary History; Development Studies; Display and Stage Design; Engineering; English; Environmental Studies; European Studies; Film; French; Gender Studies; German; Greek (Classical); Health Sciences; History; Italian; Journalism; Latin; Law; Linguistics; Literature; Modern History; Music; Philosophy; Political Sciences; Religious Studies; Russian; Sociology; Spanish; Theatre; Women's Studies; Writing); **Computer Science** (Computer Science); **Dentistry** (Dental Hygiene; Dental Technology; Dentistry; Oral Pathology; Orthodontics; Periodontics; Surgery); **Engineering** (Bioengineering; Biomedical Engineering; Chemical Engineering; Civil Engineering; Computer Engineering; Electrical Engineering; Engineering; Environmental Engineering; Food Science; Food Technology; Industrial Engineering; Materials Engineering; Mathematics; Mechanical Engineering; Mining Engineering; Petroleum and Gas Engineering); **Graduate Studies** (Agriculture; Anatomy; Ancient Civilizations; Anthropology; Architecture; Architecture and Planning; Biochemistry; Bioengineering; Biology; Biomedical Engineering; Biophysics; Business Administration; Chemical Engineering; Chemistry; Civil Engineering; Communication Disorders; Computer Engineering; Computer Science; Dental Technology; Dentistry; Development Studies; E- Business/Commerce; Earth Sciences; Economics; Electrical Engineering; Engineering; English; Environmental Engineering; Environmental Management; Environmental Studies; Finance; Food Science; Food Technology; French; German; Greek (Classical); Health Administration; Health Sciences; History; Immunology; Industrial Engineering; Information Management; Journalism; Latin; Law; Leisure Studies; Management; Marine Science and Oceanography; Materials Engineering; Mathematics; Mechanical Engineering; Medicine; Meteorology; Microbiology; Mining Engineering; Molecular Biology; Musicology; Neurosciences; Nursing; Occupational Therapy; Ophthalmology; Pathology; Periodontics; Petroleum and Gas Engineering; Pharmacology; Pharmacy; Philosophy; Physical Education; Physical Therapy; Physics; Physiology; Political Sciences; Psychology; Public Administration; Public Health; Rehabilitation and Therapy; Social Work; Sociology; Speech Therapy and Audiology; Statistics); **Health Professions** (Communication Disorders; Health Administration; Health Sciences; Leisure Studies; Nursing; Occupational Therapy; Ophthalmology; Pharmacy; Physical Therapy; Social Work); **Law** (Civil Law; Comparative Law; Constitutional Law; Criminal Law; International Law; Law; Maritime Law; Public Law); **Management** (Business Administration; Business and Commerce; E- Business/Commerce; Environmental Management; Finance; Information Management; Information Sciences; Library Science; Management; Natural Resources; Public Administration); **Medicine** (Anaesthesiology; Anatomy; Biochemistry; Biomedical Engineering; Biophysics; Cardiology; Dermatology; Endocrinology; Epidemiology; Ethics; Gastroenterology; Gerontology; Gynaecology and Obstetrics; Haematology; Immunology; Medicine; Microbiology; Molecular Biology; Nephrology; Neurology; Oncology; Ophthalmology; Orthopaedics; Otorhinolaryngology; Paediatrics; Pathology; Pharmacology; Physical Therapy; Physiology; Plastic Surgery; Psychiatry and Mental Health; Public Health; Radiology; Rehabilitation and Therapy; Respiratory Therapy; Rheumatology; Surgery; Urology); **Science** (Biochemistry; Biology; Chemistry; Earth Sciences; Economics; Environmental Studies; Immunology; Marine Biology; Marine Science and Oceanography; Mathematics; Meteorology; Microbiology; Molecular Biology; Neurosciences; Physics; Psychology; Statistics)

College

Continuing Education (Adult Education; Engineering; English; Environmental Management; Fire Science; Information Technology; Leadership; Management; Occupational Health; Peace and Disarmament; Safety Engineering; Small Business; Writing)

Further Information: Also Teaching Hospitals

History: Founded 1818. Acquired present status 1997 by merging with Technical University of Nova Scotia.

Academic Year: September to June (September-December; January-April; May-June). Also Summer Sessions (July-August)

Admission Requirements: Secondary school certificate or recognized foreign equivalent, including International Baccalaureate

Main Language(s) of Instruction: English

Degrees and Diplomas: *Baccalauréat/Bachelor's Degree*; *Maîtrise/Master's Degree*; *Doctorat/Doctoral Degree*. Also Honours Bachelor's degree; Dual/Combined Degrees: Master of Library and Information Studies/Master of Public Administration, Master of Library and Information Studies/Master of Resource and Environmental Studies, Master of Library and Information Studies/Bachelor of Laws, Master of Public Administration/Bachelor of Laws

Student Services: Academic Counselling, Canteen, Careers Guidance, Cultural Activities, Facilities for disabled people, Foreign Studies Centre, Health Services, Language Laboratory, Nursery Care, Social Counselling, Sports Facilities

Publishing house: Dalhousie University Press

Academic Staff *2014-2015*: Total 1,100
Student Numbers *2014-2015*: Total 18,500
Last Updated: 03/03/15

MOUNT SAINT VINCENT UNIVERSITY (MSVU)

166 Bedford Highway, Halifax, Nova Scotia B3M 2J6
Tel: +1(902) 457-6788 +1(902) 457-6117
Fax: +1(902) 457-6498
EMail: admissions@msvu.ca
Website: http://www.msvu.ca

President and Vice-Chancellor: Ramona Lumpkin (2010-)
Tel: +1(902) 457-6131 EMail: johnann.leblanc@msvu.ca

Vice-President, Administration: Elizabeth Church
Tel: +1(902) 457-6116 EMail: elizabeth.church@msvu.ca

International Relations: Paula Barry, Manager, International Education Centre
Tel: +1(902) 457-6130 EMail: paula.barry@msvu.ca

Faculty

Arts and Science (Anthropology; Biology; Canadian Studies; Chemistry; Communication Studies; Computer Science; Cultural Studies; Economics; English; French; German; History; Library Science; Linguistics; Mathematics; Modern Languages; Peace and Disarmament; Philosophy; Physics; Political Sciences; Psychology; Religious Studies; Social Policy; Sociology; Spanish; Statistics; Women's Studies; Writing); **Education** (Continuing Education; Curriculum; Education; Educational Psychology; Literacy Education; Primary Education; Secondary Education; Teacher Training); **Professional Studies** (Business Administration; Child Care and Development; Family Studies; Gerontology; Hotel and Restaurant; Information Technology; Nutrition; Public Relations; Tourism)

Programme

Distance Learning and Continuing Education (Business Administration; Child Care and Development; Educational Psychology; English; Hotel and Restaurant; Marketing; Psychology; Public Relations; Religious Studies; Tourism; Women's Studies)

Further Information: Also Study Abroad Programmes. Branch in Ontario

History: Founded 1873 as an academy. The Nova Scotia legislature granted Mount Saint Vincent College status to confer degrees 1925, making it the only independent Women's college in the British Commonwealth. Became Mount Saint Vincent University 1966. Current charter was approved to transfer ownership of the University from Sisters of Charity to the Board of Governors 1988.

Academic Year: September to April (September-December; January-April)

Admission Requirements: Secondary school certificate or recognized foreign equivalent

Fees: National: Undergraduate tuition fee, 624.85-658.85 per course; Graduate courses (excluding certain school psychology courses), 857.20. School Psychology (GSPY), 907.20 per course (Canadian Dollar), International: International students have to pay 613.81 per course in addition to regular tuition fees

Main Language(s) of Instruction: English

Degrees and Diplomas: *Baccalauréat/Bachelor's Degree*; *Maîtrise/Master's Degree*: **Communication Studies; Education; Family Studies; Gender Studies; Nutrition; Public Relations.** *Doctorat/Doctoral Degree.* Also inter-university doctoral programme (PhD) in Educational Studies, 14 months, jointly offered with Acadia University and St. Francis Xavier University.

Student Services: Academic Counselling, Canteen, Careers Guidance, Health Services, Language Laboratory, Nursery Care, Social Counselling, Sports Facilities

Publications: Atlantis (A Women's Studies Journal)

Academic Staff *2014-2015*	**TOTAL**
FULL-TIME	**250**
PART-TIME	c. **150**
Student Numbers *2014-2015*	
All (Foreign included)	c. **4,050**

Last Updated: 04/03/15

NSCAD UNIVERSITY (NSCAD)

5163 Duke Street, Halifax, Nova Scotia B3J 3J6
Tel: +1(902) 444-9600
Fax: +1(902) 425-2420
EMail: admissions@nscad.ca
Website: http://nscad.ca

President: Dianne Taylor-Gearing
Tel: +1(902) 494-8114 EMail: president@nscad.ca

Registrar: Shawna Garrett
Tel: +1(902) 494-8129 EMail: registrar@nscad.ca

International Relations: John Mabley, Vice President, University Relations
Tel: +1(902) 444-7223 EMail: universityrelations@nscad.ca

Division

Craft (Ceramic Art; Fine Arts; Handicrafts; Jewellery Art; Textile Design); **Design** (Design); **Fine Arts** (Fine Arts; Painting and Drawing; Printing and Printmaking; Sculpture); **Foundation Studies** (Computer Science; Design; Film; Metal Techniques; Painting and Drawing; Photography; Printing and Printmaking; Video; Visual Arts; Wood Technology); **Historical and Critical Studies** (Art History); **Media Arts** (Film; Fine Arts; Media Studies; Photography; Video; Visual Arts)

School

Extended Studies (Art Management; Ceramic Art; Computer Graphics; Computer Science; Design; Fashion Design; Fine Arts; Glass Art; Graphic Arts; Jewellery Art; Painting and Drawing; Paper Technology; Photography; Printing and Printmaking; Sculpture; Textile Design); **Graduate Studies** (Ceramic Art; Design; Film; Fine Arts; Handicrafts; Jewellery Art; Painting and Drawing; Performing Arts; Photography; Printing and Printmaking; Sculpture; Textile Design; Video)

History: Founded 1887 as Victoria School of Art and Design, became Nova Scotia College of Art 1925 and Nova Scotia College of Art and Design 1969. An independent institution of higher education. Students may also arrange to take courses at Dalhousie University and at other universities in Halifax. Acquired current title and status 2003.

Academic Year: September to April (September-December; January-April). Also Summer session, May to August

Admission Requirements: Secondary school certificate or recognized foreign equivalent

Fees: 772.50 per 3 credit tuition (per semester) (Canadian Dollar)

Main Language(s) of Instruction: English

Accrediting Agency: Association of Universities and Colleges of Canada (AUCC)

Degrees and Diplomas: *Baccalauréat/Bachelor's Degree*; *Maîtrise/Master's Degree*: **Design; Fine Arts.** Also Professional certificates.

Student Services: Academic Counselling, Careers Guidance, Social Counselling

Last Updated: 04/03/15

SAINT-ANNE UNIVERSITY

Université Sainte-Anne
1695, Route 1, Pointe-de-l'Eglise,
Nova Scotia BOW 1MO
Tel: +1(902) 769-2114
Fax: +1(902) 769-2930
EMail: admission@usainteanne.ca
Website: http://www.usainteanne.ca

President and Vice-Chancellor: Allister Surette
Tel: +1(902) 769-2114, Ext. 300
EMail: Allister.Surette@usainteanne.ca

Vice President – Academics and Research: Kenneth Deveau
Tel: +1(902) 769-2114, Ext. 7307
EMail: Kenneth.Deveau@usainteanne.ca

Faculty

Arts and Sciences (Canadian Studies; Education; English; Foreign Languages Education; French; Health Sciences; History; Primary Education; Public Health; Secondary Education; Social and Community Services; Translation and Interpretation); **Professional Programmes** (Accountancy; Business Administration; Education; English; Foreign Languages Education; French; Humanities and Social Science Education; International Business; Marketing; Mathematics Education; Native Language Education; Primary Education; Science Education; Secondary Education; Transport Management)

Programme

Customized Language Training Services *(Non-credited courses)* (Chinese; English; French; Spanish)

School

French Immersion (Foreign Languages Education; French)

Centre

Acadian (Canadian Studies)

Research Centre

Education (Education); **Minority Health** (Health Sciences); **Orality of Francophone minority of America** *(Coframi)* (Folklore)

Research Group

Acadian Studies *(GREA)* (Canadian Studies)

Further Information: Also campuses in Halifax, Petit-de-Grat, Saint-Joseph-du-Moine and Tusket.

History: Founded as College Sainte-Anne 1890 by Mgr. Blanche and the Fathers of the Congregation of Jesus and Mary (Eudists). Incorporated 1892 by an Act of the Nova Scotia legislature, and endowed with the power of conferring degrees. Acquired present title 1977.

Academic Year: September to June (September-December; January-April; May-June)

Admission Requirements: Secondary school certificate or recognized foreign equivalent. Acceptable knowledge of the French language necessary

Fees: National: Undergraduate tuition, 636 per 3 credit-course. Master of Education, 852 per 3 credit-course (Canadian Dollar),

International: Undergraduate tuition 882 per 3 credit-course. Master of Education: 1 083 per 3 credit-course

Main Language(s) of Instruction: French

Degrees and Diplomas: *Baccalauréat/Bachelor's Degree*; *Maîtrise/Master's Degree*: **Education.** Some Baccalauréat degrees in Business Administration are offered in 2 years in collaboration with the Collège communautaire du Nouveau-Brunswick (CCNB); Integrated programme: Baccalauréat ès arts/Baccalauréat en éducation, 5 years.

Student Services: Academic Counselling, Canteen, Careers Guidance, Cultural Activities, Facilities for disabled people, Library, Nursery Care, Sports Facilities

Publications: Revue de l'Université Sainte-Anne

Publishing House: Les Presses de l'Université Sainte-Anne

Last Updated: 02/03/15

SAINT MARY'S UNIVERSITY

923 Robie Street, Halifax, Nova Scotia B3H 3C3
Tel: +1(902) 420-5400
Fax: +1(902) 420-5561
EMail: info@smu.ca
Website: http://smu.ca/

President: J. Colin Dodds (2000-)
Tel: +1(902) 420-5401
EMail: president@smu.ca; colin.dodds@smu.ca

Vice President, Administration: Gabrielle Morrison
Tel: +1(902) 420-5409 EMail: gabe.morrison@smu.ca

Vice-President, Academic and Research: David Gauthier

Faculty

Arts (Ancient Civilizations; Anthropology; Asian Studies; Business Administration; Canadian Studies; Chinese; Classical Languages; Criminology; Development Studies; Economics; English; Film; French; Gender Studies; Geography; German; Greek (Classical); Hispanic American Studies; History; Irish; Japanese; Latin; Linguistics; Mathematics; Modern Languages; Philosophy; Political Sciences; Psychology; Religious Studies; Sociology; Spanish; Theology; Women's Studies); **Education** (Education; Foreign Languages Education; Linguistics; Mathematics Education; Teacher Training); **Graduate Studies and Research** *(FGSR)* (Astronomy and Space Science; Business Administration; Canadian Studies; Criminology; Development Studies; Finance; Gender Studies; History; Industrial and Organizational Psychology; Management; Philosophy; Psychology; Religious Studies; Theology; Women's Studies); **Science** (Applied Physics; Astronomy and Space Science; Astrophysics; Biology; Chemistry; Computer Science; Engineering; Environmental Studies; Forensic Medicine and Dentistry; Geography; Geology; Industrial and Organizational Psychology; Mathematics; Mathematics Education; Physics; Psychology)

Division

Continuing Education (Accountancy; Business Administration; Canadian Studies; Chinese; Communication Studies; Finance; Forensic Medicine and Dentistry; Hispanic American Studies; Human Resources; Human Rights; Japanese; Leadership; Linguistics; Management; Mathematics Education; Peace and Disarmament; Spanish; Writing)

Programme

Co-operative Education (Accountancy; Anthropology; Biology; Business Administration; Business Computing; Chemistry; Computer Science; Economics; Environmental Studies; Finance; Geography; Geology; Human Resources; Information Technology; International Business; Labour and Industrial Relations; Management; Marketing; Mathematics; Psychology; Small Business); **Coastal CURA** (Coastal Studies); **English as a Second Language** (English; Foreign Languages Education)

School

Business *(Sobey)* (Accountancy; Business Administration; Computer Science; Economics; Finance; Human Resources; Information Sciences; Information Technology; International Business; Labour and Industrial Relations; Management; Marketing)

Department

Engineering (Bioengineering; Chemical Engineering; Civil Engineering; Electrical Engineering; Engineering; Environmental Engineering; Industrial Engineering; Mechanical Engineering; Metallurgical Engineering; Mining Engineering)

Institute

Computational Astrophysics *(ICA)* (Astrophysics)

Centre

Atlantic Metropolis *(Immigration, Integration and Cultural Diversity)*; **Electron Microscopy Centre** *(EMC)*; **Ethics and Public Affairs** *(Canadian)* (Ethics); **Excellence in Accounting and Reporting for Co-operatives** *(CEARC)* (Accountancy); **Leadership Excellence** (Leadership); **Occupational Health and Safety** *(CN)* (Occupational Health); **Regional Geochemistry** *(Saint Mary's University)* (Geochemistry); **Spirituality and the Workplace**; **Students with Disabilities** *(Atlantic)*; **Study of Sport and Health** (Health Sciences; Sports)

Research Centre

ACEnet (Computer Science); **Astronomical Observatory** *(Burke-Gaffney)* (Astronomy and Space Science); **Community Based Environmental Monitoring Network** *(CBEMN)* (Environmental Management); **Environmental Analysis and Remediation** *(CEAR)* (Environmental Studies); **Maritime Provinces Spatial Analysis** *(MP_SpARC)*

Research Institute

Gorsebrook (Canadian Studies; Regional Studies)

Further Information: Affiliated to Atlantic School of Theology

History: Founded 1802 as Saint Mary's College, acquired present status and title 1841. From 1970, a public, non-denominational institution.

Academic Year: September to April (September-December; January-April). Also Summer Semesters.

Admission Requirements: Secondary school certificate or recognized foreign equivalent; TOEFL test for foreign students

Fees: National: Undergraduate: 539-701 per half credit (3 credit hours) course for Canadian students (though the Nova Scotia University Student Bursary reduces the cost) (Canadian Dollar), International: Undergraduate: 1217.40-1379.40 per half credit (3 credit hours) course (Canadian Dollar)

Main Language(s) of Instruction: English

Degrees and Diplomas: *Baccalauréat/Bachelor's Degree*; *Maîtrise/Master's Degree*; *Doctorat/Doctoral Degree*: **Astronomy and Space Science; Business Administration; Industrial and Organizational Psychology; International Studies; Management.** Also Bachelor of Arts (Honours) degree; Executive MBA, 18 months; Accelerated MBA, 12-28 months; MBA-CMA, 24 months; Professional certificates.

Student Services: Academic Counselling, Careers Guidance, Facilities for disabled people, Health Services, Library, Nursery Care, Social Counselling, Sports Facilities

Publications: Maroon and White; The Times

Academic Staff *2014-2015*	**TOTAL**
FULL-TIME	**c. 500**
Student Numbers *2014-2015*	
All (Foreign included)	**c. 7,465**
FOREIGN ONLY	**1580**

Last Updated: 04/03/15

ST. FRANCIS XAVIER UNIVERSITY (STFX)

P.O. Box 5000, Antigonish, Nova Scotia B2G 2W5
Tel: +1(902) 863-3300
Fax: +1(902) 867-5153
EMail: admit@stfx.ca
Website: http://www.stfx.ca

President and Vice-Chancellor: Kent MacDonald (1996-)
Tel: +1(902) 867-2188 EMail: kdmacdon@stfx.ca

Academic Vice President and Provost: Leslie MacLaren
EMail: avp@stfx.ca

Registrar: Fred Rosmanitz
Tel: +1(902) 867-2160 EMail: registr@stfx.ca

Faculty

Arts (Adult Education; Ancient Civilizations; Anthropology; Aquaculture; Asian Religious Studies; Bible; Canadian Studies; Catholic Theology; Celtic Languages and Studies; Christian Religious Studies; Classical Languages; Development Studies; Economics; English; Fine Arts; French; German; Greek (Classical); History; Jazz and Popular Music; Latin; Literature; Modern Languages; Music; Music Theory and Composition; Philosophy; Political Sciences; Psychology; Religious Studies; Sociology; Spanish; Women's Studies); **Business** *(Gerald Schwartz)* (Accountancy; Business Administration; Business Computing; Computer Science; Economics; Finance; Information Sciences; Information Technology; Leadership; Management; Marketing; Software Engineering); **Education** (Continuing Education; Curriculum; Education; French; Leadership; Literacy Education; Pedagogy; Physical Education; Primary Education; Secondary Education); **Science** (Aquaculture; Biology; Chemistry; Computer Science; Earth Sciences; Engineering; Environmental Studies; Mathematics; Nursing; Nutrition; Physical Education; Physical Therapy; Physics; Statistics)

Programme

Climate Science *(CREATE Training Programs)* (Meteorology); **Graduate Studies** (Adult Education; Biology; Celtic Languages and Studies; Chemistry; Computer Science; Earth Sciences; Education; Physics)

Institute

Coady International (Adult Education; Development Studies; Finance; Health Sciences; Leadership; Natural Resources)

Laboratory

Aquatic Plant Resources *(McLachlan)* (Plant and Crop Protection); **Behavioural Neuroscience** *(Dr. Karen Brebner and Dr. John McKenna)* (Behavioural Sciences; Neurosciences); **Comparative Biomechanics**; **Food Research** *(FRL)*; **Infant Action and Cognition**; **Infant Development** (Child Care and Development); **Invertebrate Neuroethology**; **Marine Ecology** (Ecology); **Parent and Child Interaction** (Child Care and Development); **SafetyNET-Rx Research**; **X-CELL Analytical Service**

Research Centre

ACEnet *(Atlantic Computational Excellence Network)* (Computer Science); **Culture and Human Development** *(CRCHD)*; **Environmental Sciences** *(ESRC)* (Environmental Studies); **Health Literacy in Rural Nova Scotia Research Project** (Health Sciences); **TPI [physics]** (Physics)

History: Founded 1853 as St. Francis Xavier College, Seminary 1855. Full university powers conferred by the province of Nova Scotia 1866.

Academic Year: September to May (September-December; January-May)

Admission Requirements: Secondary school certificate or recognized foreign equivalent

Fees: National: 5,702 per annum for Nova Scotia Students, 6,724 for Non-Nova Scotia Students, International: 6,985 per annum (Canadian Dollar)

Main Language(s) of Instruction: English, French, Scottish Gaelic

Degrees and Diplomas: *Baccalauréat/Bachelor's Degree*; *Maîtrise/Master's Degree*: **Adult Education; Biology; Celtic Languages and Studies; Chemistry; Computer Science; Earth Sciences; Education.** Also Honours Bachelor's degree programmes; inter-university doctoral programme (PhD) in Educational Studies, 14 months, jointly offered with Acadia University and Mount Saint Vincent University.

Student Services: Academic Counselling, Canteen, Careers Guidance, Cultural Activities, Facilities for disabled people, Foreign Studies Centre, Health Services, Language Laboratory, Library, Nursery Care, Social Counselling, Sports Facilities

Last Updated: 04/03/15

UNIVERSITY OF KING'S COLLEGE

University of King's College (KING'S)
6350 Coburg Road, Halifax, Nova Scotia B3H 2A1
Tel: +1(902) 422-1271
Fax: +1(902) 423-3357
EMail: admissions@ukings.ns.ca
Website: http://www.ukings.ns.ca

President and Vice-Chancellor: George Cooper (2012-)
Tel: +1(902) 422-1271, Ext. 120

Registrar Acting): Jim Fitzpatrick
Tel: +1(902) 422-1271, Ext. 122 EMail: bursar@ukings.ca

College

Arts and Science (Arts and Humanities; Natural Sciences)

School

Journalism (Journalism)

Department

Contemporary Studies *(CSP)* (Contemporary History); **Early Modern Studies** (History); **History of Science and Technology**

Further Information: King's and Dalhousie University have shared a campus and many facilities since King's moved to Halifax in 1920.

History: Founded 1789 at Windsor, Nova Scotia, established by provincial statute and granted a Royal Charter by King George III 1802. Associated with Dalhousie University.

Academic Year: September to May (September-December; January-May)

Admission Requirements: Secondary school certificate or recognized foreign equivalent

Fees: National: Science & Bachelor of Journalism honours tuition 770.10 per 1/2 credit course. Arts tuition: 678.60. Bachelor of Journalism: 8,623.80 per annum. Master of Journalism: 7,539.60 per annum (Canadian Dollar), International: International students will be charged the international student differential fee each term, summer 4,224 and fall 4,224 (Canadian Dollar)

Main Language(s) of Instruction: English

Degrees and Diplomas: *Baccalauréat/Bachelor's Degree*: **Fine Arts; Journalism; Music.** *Maîtrise/Master's Degree*: **Fine Arts; Journalism.**

Student Services: Academic Counselling, Canteen, Careers Guidance, Cultural Activities, Facilities for disabled people, Foreign Studies Centre, Health Services, Library, Residential Facilities, Social Counselling, Sports Facilities

Last Updated: 04/03/15

Canada - Nunavut

STRUCTURE OF HIGHER EDUCATION SYSTEM

Description:

The Department of Education is responsible for the legislation governing the provision of post secondary education programming in Nunavut while Nunavut Arctic College is responsible for the delivery of postsecondary education programming.

Although Nunavut does not have a university, Nunavut Arctic College, the only postsecondary institution in Nunavut, offers a variety of certificate, diploma, trades and university transfer programmes as well as two degree programmes in partnership with the University of Regina and Dalhousie University. Programme areas include Teacher Education, Nursing, Career Development, Environmental Technology and Management Studies. A Master of Education degree is also available through a partnership with the University of Prince Edward Island, St. Francis Xavier University, Nunavut Arctic College and the Department of Education. Programmes vary in length from eight weeks (trades programmes) to two years, but generally speaking, certificate programmes involve one year of full time studies, and diploma programmes two years. In addition, Nunavut Arctic College provides adult basic education, skills development courses, trades training and contract training on behalf of local employers. Nunavut Arctic College has an established process to allow students to apply for course credits for previous learning and work experience. Nunavut Arctic College has transfer arrangements with a number of institutions in the south, including McGill University, Dalhousie University, Athabasca University, University of Manitoba and numerous Alberta institutions through their membership in the Alberta Council on Admissions and Transfer.

Stages of studies:

University level first stage: *Post-Secondary Programmes*

Many of the courses in the college diploma programmes are eligible for transfer credit with universities and professional associations throughout Canada. As well, the college offers selected university courses and programmes through agreements with approved degree granting institutions. Nunavut-based students can attend other post-secondary institutions within and outside of Canada.

ADMISSION TO HIGHER EDUCATION

Admission to university-level studies:

Alternatives to credentials: Mature students not meeting the academic requirements – will demonstrate that they are 19 years or older and have been out of the K-12 school system for a minimum of one year; provide at least 2 letters of reference from persons able to assess the candidate's ability to proceed with post-secondary studies; provide a personal letter outlining the grounds for requesting mature student status; provide official transcripts documents showing formal and informal academic qualifications; and information about related work experience. An interview man be required.

Numerus clausus: This applies to International and Out of Territory Students: acceptance of non-resident applicant will be limited by the maximum student capacity of the programme, the number of qualified applications received from Nunavut residents, and specific programme language requirements.

Foreign students admission:

Definition of foreign student: Foreign (International) students are students who are neither Canadian citizens nor permanent residents of Canada and are enrolled full-time in a recognized academic, professional or vocational training course at a university, college or other educational institution in Canada.

Admission requirements: Generally, as for domestic students, a high school diploma or equivalent will be required. A lack of proficiency in English or French will be taken into account by the Canadian Immigration Office in the evaluation of the application.

Entry regulations: Before you come to study in Canada, you will need: a "Study Permit" if the programme of study you will be admitted to is longer than six months in duration, regardless of the length of your stay in Canada; a letter of acceptance from the school of your choice; proof that you have enough money to pay school fees and living expenses; to establish that you will return home at the end of your studies; to pass a medical exam if required; and to qualify as a temporary resident in Canada, including holding a temporary resident visa (required for citizens of many countries). A small number of students do not require a Study Permit by virtue of their status in Canada (e.g. diplomats and their children).

Health requirements: Most education institutions require international students to buy health insurance in addition to their tuition fees; those that do not will require proof of independent health insurance coverage. Medical examinations are not required by institutions but are required by Citizenship and Immigration Canada for students from many countries.

RECOGNITION OF STUDIES

Quality assurance system:

The college has established its own academic evaluation policies, academic probation, attendance policies and policies relating to student conduct.

PROVINCIAL BODIES

Ministère de l'Éducation (Department of Education)

Ministre/Minister: Paul Aarulaaq Quassa
Sous-ministre/Deputy Minister: Kathy Okpik
PO Box 1000, Station 910, 2nd Floor Sivummut Building
Iqaluit, NU X0A 0H0
Canada
Tel: +1(867) 975-5600
Fax: +1(867) 975-5605
EMail: info.edu@gov.nu.ca
WWW: http://www.gov.nu.ca/education

Collège de l'arctique du Nunavut (Nunavut Arctic College)

Président/President: Peter Ma
President's Office, PO Box 609, Building 961
Iqaluit, NU X0A 0H0
Canada
Tel: +1 (867) 975-2540
Fax: +1 (867) 975-2549
EMail: registrar@arcticcollege.ca
WWW: http://www.arcticcollege.ca

Data for academic year: 2014-2015

Source: IAU from the Canadian Information Centre for International Credentials (CICIC), a unit of the Council of Ministers of Education, Canada (CMEC), on behalf of the Nunavut Department of Education, November 2014. Bodies 2016.

Canada - Ontario

STRUCTURE OF HIGHER EDUCATION SYSTEM

Description:

Higher education in Canada is constitutionally the responsibility of the provinces. There are 19 provincially assisted universities and the Ontario College of Arts and Design and 24 provincially assisted colleges of applied arts and technology (CAATs).

Universities are degree granting institutions. Each institution has an Act of the Legislative Assembly and operates independently, determines its own academic and admissions policies, programmes and staff appointments. Several privately funded degree granting institutions also exist in Ontario. CAATs provide technical and vocational programmes usually leading to a Certificate or Diploma. In addition to certificate and diploma programmes, CAATs may also apply to the Minister of Training, Colleges and Universities for consent to offer a degree programme in an applied area of study. A combination of theory and applied skills training makes up the four year college applied degree programme model, which also includes a compulsory paid work term.

Pursuant to the Post-secondary Education Choice and Excellence Act 2000 (PSECE Act), all institutions – Ontario or out-of-province, public or private for-profit or not-for-profit – require either an act of the Legislative Assembly of Ontario or the consent of the Minister of Training, Colleges and Universities to offer and/or advertise a degree, programs or part of a program leading to a degree, or to call themselves a university or to advertise using the word "university" in Ontario. The act also allows CAATs to apply for a ministerial consent to offer a baccalaureate degree in an applied area of study. The act also enshrines in legislation the Post-secondary Education Quality Assessment Board. The Board is responsible for providing recommendations to the Minister on the academic rigour and institutional soundness of new degree granting proposals. The Board has established criteria against which it assesses applications for a Minister's consent prior to making its recommendations to the Minister for consideration.

The College Compensation and Appointments Council, a provincial government agency, appoints the governing bodies of the CAATs.

Besides various government supported pre-employment and apprenticeship programs, there are also many private career colleges which are required to register and have their vocational programs approved by the Ministry of Training, Colleges and Universities under the Private Career Colleges Act, 2005.

Stages of studies:

University level first stage: *Baccalauréat/Bachelor's degree*

Most undergraduate study leads to a "General" Bachelor's Degree (minimum three years) or a "specialized" degree (four years and prescribed subject concentration). Degrees are normally titled in broad descriptive groups, e.g. Bachelor of Arts (B.A.) and Bachelor of Science (B.Sc.) The first stage also includes the undergraduate Diploma (one to three years of study) and short (up to one year) special certificate programmes; these may enable entry to degree programmes and are frequently given in close cooperation with professional bodies. In addition, the first stage includes other professional programmes that typically require no university level prerequisites and four years of study, e.g. Bachelor of Science in Nursing (B.Sc.N.), Bachelor of Commerce (B.Comm.). Finally, the Royal Military College of Canada, operated by the Federal Department of National Defence, is located in Kingston.

University level second stage: *Maîtrise/Master's degree*

The Master's Degree normally requires at least one year of study after a specialized Bachelor's Degree or equivalent. Most Master's programmes, e.g. in Business Administration, require two years of study. A thesis and course work are usually required. Graduate level Diplomas are considered an intermediate between a Bachelor's degree or first professional degree and the Master's Degree). The second stage also includes first professional degree programmes that demand prerequisite university studies e.g. professional Baccalaureate programmes (Bachelor of Law (LL.B.) and clinical Doctorates (Doctor of Medicine (M.D.); Doctor of Dental Surgery (DDS).

University level third stage: *Doctorat/Doctorate*

The research Doctorate is the highest academic qualification awarded by Ontario universities and it comprises the third stage of university-level studies. This degree normally requires at least three years of study after the

Bachelor's Degree; the submission and defence of a major thesis (dissertation) are the principal requirements, and supplemental course work is usually also required. The degree "Doctor of Philosophy" (Ph.D.) is the designation most commonly used to signify the Doctorate. It is a generic title, applicable to degrees in most disciplines. (The research Doctorate should not be confused with the "clinical" Doctorate, which is a first professional degree awarded in certain health science disciplines, e.g., M.D. in Medicine, D.D.S. in Dentistry and D.V.M. in Veterinary Medicine).

ADMISSION TO HIGHER EDUCATION

Admission to university-level studies:

Alternatives to credentials: Varying credentials for mature students.

Other requirements: Overall average of 60% and six Grade 12 university (U) or university/college (M) courses. Universities and/or programmes often have additional specific requirements.

Foreign students admission:

Definition of foreign student: Foreign (International) Students are students who are neither Canadian citizens nor permanent residents of Canada, and are enrolled full-time in a recognized academic, professional or vocational training course at a university, college or other educational institution in Canada.

Quotas: Generally no. However, in a small number of professional programmes, there are limits to enrolment.

Admission requirements: Generally, as for domestic students, a high school diploma or equivalent will be required. A lack of proficiency in English or French will be taken into account by the Canadian Immigration Office in the evaluation of the application.

Entry regulations: Before an international students can come to study in Canada, he or she will need: a "Study Permit" if the programme of study the individual is admitted to is longer than six months in duration, regardless of the length of your stay in Canada. In order to obtain a study permit, the student must provide: a letter of acceptance from the postsecondary institution; proof of enough money to pay school fees and living expenses; confirmation that the student will return home at the end of his of her studies; passing a medical exam if required; and qualification as a temporary resident in Canada, including holding a temporary resident visa (required for citizens of many countries). A small number of students do not require a Study Permit by virtue of their status in Canada (e.g. diplomats and their children).

Health requirements: Most education institutions require international students to buy health insurance in addition to their tuition fees; those that do not will require proof of independent health insurance coverage. Medical examinations are not required by institutions but are required by Citizenship and Immigration Canada for students from many countries.

RECOGNITION OF STUDIES

Quality assurance system:

There are more than 100 provincial standards which set the expected outcomes for college programs. The Ontario College Quality Assurance Service (OCQAS) implements and manages the self-regulatory quality assurance mechanism for Ontario's publicly supported colleges through the Credentials Validation Service (CVS) and the Program Quality Assurance Process Audit (PQAPA). The CVS ensures that all proposed new or modified certificate and diploma level programs of instruction conform to provincial standards. The PQAPA independently audits, on a cyclical basis, the colleges' quality assurance policies and procedures.

Once a university program receives approval from the University's Senate, the Undergraduate Program Review Audit Committee of the Council of Ontario Universities (reviews undergraduate programs only), and Ontario Council of Graduate Studies (reviews graduate programs only) review and approve the program proposal. Also, Multi-Year Accountability Agreements (MYAAs) are bilateral agreements signed by the executive heads of all publicly-supported colleges and universities and the government. The agreements outline the government's goals and commitments for access, quality and accountability, and the system-level measures and indicators that will be used to demonstrate clear and tangible results for the increased investment in postsecondary education.

Bodies dealing with recognition:

Ministère de la Formation et des Collèges et Universités de l'Ontario (Ontario Ministry of Training, Colleges and Universities)

14th Floor, Mowat Block, 900 Bay Street
Toronto M7A 1L2
Tel: +1(416) 325-2929
Fax: +1(416) 325-6348
EMail: information.met@ontario.ca
WWW: http://www.tcu.gov.on.ca

Commission d'Evaluation de la Qualité de l'Education postsecondaire - CEQEP (Postsecondary Education Quality Assessment Board - PEQAB)

Président/Chair: Maureen J. Morton
900 Bay Street, 23rd Floor, Mowat Block
Toronto M7A 1L2
Tel: +1 (416) 212-1230
Fax: +1 (416) 212-6620
EMail: peqab@ontario.ca
WWW: http://www.peqab.ca

Comparative Education Service - CES (Comparative Education Service)

University of Toronto School of Continuing Studies, 162 St. George Street
Toronto M5S 2E9
Tel: (+1) 416-978-2400
Fax: (+1) 416-978-2185
EMail: ces.info@utoronto.ca
WWW: http://learn.utoronto.ca/ces

Service canadien d'Evaluation de Documents scolaires internationaux (International Credential Assessment Service of Canada - ICAS)

Ontario AgriCentre, 100 Stone Rd. West, Suite/Bureau 102
Guelph N1G 5L3
Tel: (+1) 519-763-7282
Fax: (+1) 519-763-6964
EMail: info@icascanada.ca
WWW: http://www.icascanada.ca

World Education Services, Canada - WES

2 Carlton Street, Suite/Bureau 1400
Toronto M5B 1J3
Tel: (+1) 416-972-0070
Fax: (+1) 416-972-9004
EMail: contactca@wes.org
WWW: http://www.wes.org/ca/

Special provisions for recognition:

Recognition for university level studies: In general none. Universities establish their own admissions criteria and make their own admissions decisions in response to individual applications.
Additionally, the Canadian Information Centre for International Credentials (CICIC) provides information and guidance on the assessment and recognition of international academic credentials.
For access to advanced studies and research: In general none.

For exercising a profession: In general, none. Both Canadians and non-Canadians who studied abroad have to meet specified educational, experience and language requirements, and usually pass registration examinations. The Comparative Education Service (CES), International Credential Assessment Service of Canada (ICAS) and World Education Services - Canada (WES) assess foreign qualifications relating to numerous professions. Access to most professions is governed by provincial and/or federal statutes and is generally restricted to Canadian citizens or immigrants accepted as permanent residents. Applicants must also meet examination and/or practical training requirements set by the relevant professional body or provincial or federal licensing board.

PROVINCIAL BODIES

Ministère de la Formation et des Collèges et Universités de l'Ontario (Ontario Ministry of Training, Colleges and Universities)

Ministre/Minister: Reza Moridi
14th Floor, Mowat Block, 900 Bay Street
Toronto, ON M7A 1L2
Canada
Tel: +1(416) 325-2929
Fax: +1(416) 325-6348
EMail: information.met@ontario.ca
WWW: http://www.tcu.gov.on.ca

Role of national body: The Ministry of Training, Colleges and Universities is responsible for: developing policy directions for universities and colleges of applied arts and technology; planning and administering policies related to basic and applied research in this sector; authorizing universities to grant degrees; distributing funds allocated by the provincial legislature to colleges and universities; providing financial assistance programmes for post-secondary school students; defining courses of study at faculties of education; and registering private career colleges.

IAU Conseil ontarien de la Qualité de l'Enseignement supérieur (Higher Education Quality Council of Ontario - HEQCO)

Président/President: Harvey P. Weingarten
1 Yonge Street, Suite 2402
Toronto, ON M5E 1E5
Canada
Tel: +1(416) 212-3893
Fax: +1(416) 212-3899
EMail: info@heqco.ca
WWW: http://www.heqco.ca

Role of national body: Created through the Higher Education Quality Council of Ontario Act, 2005, HEQCO is an arm's-length agency of the Government of Ontario that brings evidence-based research to the continued improvement of the postsecondary education system in Ontario. As part of its mandate, HEQCO evaluates the postsecondary sector and provides policy recommendations to the Minister of Training, Colleges and Universities to enhance the access, quality and accountability of Ontario's colleges and universities.

Collèges Ontario (Colleges Ontario)

President and CEO: Linda Franklin
20 Bay Street, Suite 1600, Box 88
Toronto, ON M5J 2N8
Canada
Tel: +1(647) 258-7670
Fax: +1(647) 258-7699
EMail: savage@collegesontario.org
WWW: http://www.collegesontario.org

Role of national body: Advocacy and marketing association of the 24 Colleges of Applied Arts and Technology of Ontario.

Conseil des Universités de l'Ontario (Council of Ontario Universities)

President and CEO: David Lindsay
180 Dundas St West, Suite 1100
Toronto, ON M5G 1Z8
Canada
Tel: +1(416) 979-2165
Fax: +1(416) 979-8635
WWW: http://www.cou.on.ca

Role of national body: The Council provides services to its University members and the community including research advocacy, communication and public affairs, and the central processing of university applications. The Council is comprised of Ontario University Presidents and is the primary advocacy group for the public university system.

Data for academic year: 2014-2015

Source: IAU from the Canadian Information Centre for International Credentials (CICIC), a unit of the Council of Ministers of Education, Canada (CMEC), on behalf of the Ontario Ministry of Training, Colleges and Universities, November 2014. Bodies 2016.

INSTITUTIONS

PUBLIC INSTITUTIONS

ALGONQUIN COLLEGE

1385 Woodroffe Avenue, Ottawa, Ontario K2G 1V8
Tel: +1(613) 727-4723
Fax: +1(613) 727-7684
EMail: international@ algonquincollege.com; registrar@algonquincollege.com
Website: http://www.algonquincollege.com/

President: Cheryl Jensen

Vice President Academic: Claude Brulé (2012-)
EMail: brulec@algonquincollege.com

College

Algonquin *(Ottawa Valley)* (Administration; Arts and Humanities; Business Administration; Computer Science; Cooking and Catering; Forest Products; Nursing; Police Studies; Preschool Education; Social and Community Services)

School

Advanced Technology (Aeronautical and Aerospace Engineering; Architecture; Biotechnology; Civil Engineering; Computer Engineering; Computer Science; Construction Engineering; Data Processing; Electrical Engineering; Information Technology; Mechanical Engineering; Microelectronics; Surveying and Mapping; Telecommunications Engineering; Water Management); **Business** (Accountancy; Administration; Business Administration; Finance; Human Resources; International Business; Law; Management; Marketing; Small Business); **General Arts and Science** (Communication Studies; Design; Environmental Studies; Health Sciences; Media Studies; Music; Nursing; Service Trades; Social and Community Services; Technology); **Health and Community Studies** (Dental Hygiene; Leisure Studies; Museum Studies; Nursing; Physical Therapy; Preschool Education; Respiratory Therapy; Social Work; Sports); **Hospitality and Tourism** (Cooking and Catering; Food Science; Hotel and Restaurant; Nutrition; Service Trades; Tourism); **Media and Design** (Advertising and Publicity; Graphic Design; Horticulture; Information Technology; Interior Design; Journalism; Media Studies; Multimedia; Music; Painting and Drawing; Photography; Public Relations; Radio and Television Broadcasting; Software Engineering; Theatre; Writing); **Transportation and Building Trades** (Automotive Engineering; Heating and Refrigeration; Maintenance Technology; Metal Techniques; Service Trades)

Institute

Algonquin College Heritage (Administration; Social Work); **Language** (English; Modern Languages); **Police and Public Safety** (Police Studies; Protective Services; Social and Community Services; Veterinary Science)

Centre

Algonquin Centre for Construction Excellence *(Ottawa)* (Architecture and Planning; Engineering); **Career and Academic Access** (Health Sciences)

Further Information: Traditional and Open Learning Institution; Also Perth and Pembroke campuses.

History: Founded 1957.

Main Language(s) of Instruction: English

Degrees and Diplomas: *Certificat et diplôme/Certificate and diploma*; *Baccalauréat/Bachelor's Degree*; *Diplôme et certificat de 2e cycle/Graduate Diploma and Certificate*. Bachelor's degree (professional), Advanced Diploma, 3 yrs.

Student Services: Academic Counselling, Library, Residential Facilities, Sports Facilities

Academic Staff *2014-2015*	**TOTAL**
FULL-TIME	**1,265**
PART-TIME	**1,820**
Student Numbers *2014-2015*	
All (Foreign included)	**19,000**

Last Updated: 05/03/15

BRESCIA UNIVERSITY COLLEGE

1285 Western Road, London, Ontario N6G 1H2
Tel: +1(519) 432-8353
Fax: +1(519) 858-5137
EMail: brescia@uwo.ca
Website: http://www.brescia.uwo.ca/

Principal: Colleen Hanycz (2008-)
Tel: +1(519) 432-8353 Ext. 28263 EMail: chanycz@uwo.ca

Vice Principal and Academic Dean: Donna Rogers
Tel: +1(519) 432-8353 Ext. 28263 EMail: donna.rogers@uwo.cac

Division

Arts and Humanities (English; French; French Studies; Linguistics; Literature; Philosophy; Religious Education; Religious Studies); **Food and Nutritional Sciences** (Dietetics; Food Science; Food Technology; Nutrition); **Social Sciences** (Accountancy; Administration; Anthropology; Canadian Studies; Finance; History; Human Resources; Leadership; Management; Political Sciences; Psychology; Public Administration; Social Sciences); **Sociology and Family Studies** (Development Studies; Family Studies; Sociology)

Programme

Graduate Studies (Food Science; Nutrition); **Health Sciences** (Health Sciences; Public Health); **Kinesiology** (Physical Therapy; Sports); **Pre-University** (Biology; Canadian Studies; Chemistry; English; French; Geography; Leadership; Mathematics; Religious Studies; Sociology; Spanish)

History: Founded 1919 as Brescia Hall. Became a separately incorporated not-for-profit corporation 2001. Acquired present title 2001. Brescia University College is affiliated with Western University, the third-largest university in the province.

Fees: National: 6,234.35 per annum (Canadian Dollar), International: 11,856 per annum (Canadian Dollar)

Main Language(s) of Instruction: English

Degrees and Diplomas: *Certificat et diplôme universitaire/University certificate and diploma*: **Development Studies.** *Baccalauréat/Bachelor's Degree*; *Maîtrise/Master's Degree*: **Food Science; Nutrition.**

Student Services: Canteen, Health Services, IT Centre, Library

Last Updated: 05/03/15

BROCK UNIVERSITY (BROCK U)

500 Glenridge Avenue, Saint Catharines, Ontario L2S 3A1
Tel: +1(905) 688-5550
Fax: +1(905) 688-2789
EMail: international@brocku.ca
Website: http://brocku.ca

President and Vice-Chancellor: Jack N. Lightstone
Tel: +1(905) 688-5550, Ext. 3333 EMail: president@brocku.ca

Provost and Vice-President, Academic: Neil McCartney
Tel: +1(905) 688-5550 Ext. 4121
EMail: nmccartney@brocku.ca

International Relations: John Kaethler, Director, International Services and Programs Abroad Tel: +1(905) 688-5550 Ext. 3732
EMail: international@brocku.ca

Faculty

Applied Health Sciences (Dental Hygiene; Health Sciences; Leisure Studies; Nursing; Parks and Recreation; Pharmacy; Physical Education; Physical Therapy; Public Health; Sports; Sports Management); **Education** (Adult Education; Education; Educational Sciences; Natives Education; Preschool Education; Teacher Training); **Graduate Studies** (Accountancy; Aesthetics; Ancient Civilizations; Applied Linguistics; Biological and Life Sciences; Biotechnology; Business Administration; Chemistry; Child Care and Development; Classical Languages; Comparative Literature; Computer Science; Cultural Studies; Earth Sciences; Economics; Education; Educational Sciences; English; Folklore; Geography; Greek (Classical); Health Sciences; History; Latin; Management; Mathematics; Philosophy; Physics; Political Sciences; Psychology; Rehabilitation and Therapy; Sociology; Statistics); **Humanities** (Aesthetics; Ancient Civilizations; Applied Linguistics; Art History; Arts and Humanities; Canadian Studies; Classical Languages; Communication Disorders; Comparative Literature; Computer Science; Cultural Studies; English; Fine Arts; Foreign Languages Education; French; French Studies; Greek (Classical); History; Italian; Latin; Latin American Studies; Literature; Medieval Studies; Modern History; Modern Languages; Multimedia; Music; Performing Arts; Philosophy; Portuguese; Spanish; Speech Therapy and Audiology; Theatre; Visual Arts; Writing); **Mathematics and Science** (Biochemistry; Biological and Life Sciences; Biomedicine; Biophysics; Biotechnology; Chemistry; Computer Networks; Computer Science; Earth Sciences; Education; Geology; Mathematics; Mathematics and Computer Science; Neurosciences; Oenology; Physics; Viticulture); **Social Sciences** (Child Care and Development; Communication Studies; Cultural Studies; Economics; Environmental Studies; Film; Folklore; Geography; Geography (Human); Information Technology; International Relations; Labour and Industrial Relations; Media Studies; Neurosciences; Philosophy; Political Sciences; Psychology; Public Administration; Public Law; Rehabilitation and Therapy; Social Psychology; Social Sciences; Sociology; Surveying and Mapping; Tourism; Women's Studies)

School

Business *(Goodman)* (Accountancy; Administration; Business Administration; Management)

Institute

Cool Climate Oenology and Viticulture (Oenology; Viticulture); **Electrophysiological Research** (Biological and Life Sciences; Physical Education; Physical Therapy; Psychology)

Centre

Aboriginal Education and Research *(Tecumseh)* (Natives Education); **Digital Humanities** (Arts and Humanities; History; Literature; Modern Languages); **Healthy Development** (Physical Education; Sports); **Muscle Metabolism and Biophysics** (Biophysics; Physical Education; Public Health); **Sport Capacity** (Sports)

Research Centre

Lifespan Development *(Jack and Nora Walker)*; **Niagara Community Observatory** (Regional Studies)

Research Institute

Humanities (Arts and Humanities); **Youth Studies** *(BRIYS)*

Further Information: Also Hamilton campus.

History: Founded 1964.

Academic Year: Fall/Winter Session: September to April (September-December; January-April); Spring Session: May to June; Summer Session: July to August

Admission Requirements: Secondary school certificate or recognized foreign equivalent

Fees: National: Undergraduate tuition, 6,352.65-8,068.10 per annum for Canadian students and students. Graduate tuition, 2,250.08- 2,861.88 per term for Canadian students (Canadian Dollar), International: Undergraduate tuition, 19,938.50 per annum. Graduate tuition: 6,662.70. PhD in Education, 6,662.70; PhD in Arts or Science, 6,580.03 per term (Canadian Dollar)

Main Language(s) of Instruction: English

Accrediting Agency: Ministry of Training, Colleges and Universities of Ontario

Degrees and Diplomas: *Certificat et diplôme universitaire/University certificate and diploma*; *Baccalauréat/Bachelor's Degree*; *Baccalauréat spécialisé/Bachelor's Degree - Honours*; *Maîtrise/Master's Degree*; *Doctorat/Doctoral Degree*: **Arts and Humanities; Education; Natural Sciences.** Also Concurrent degrees in 5 yrs: Bachelor of Arts (Honours)/Bachelor of Education (Intermediate/Senior); Bachelor of Arts Child and Youth Studies (Honours)/Bachelor of Education (Primary/Junior); Bachelor of Arts - Integrated Studies (Honours)/Bachelor of Education (Junior/Intermediate); Bachelor of Physical Education (Honours)/Bachelor of Education (Intermediate/Senior); Bachelor of Physical Education (Honours)/Bachelor of Education (Junior/Intermediate); Bachelor of Science (Honours)/Bachelor of Education (Intermediate/Senior); Bachelor of Science - Integrated Studies (Honours)/Bachelor of Education (Junior/Intermediate).

Student Services: Academic Counselling, Canteen, Careers Guidance, Cultural Activities, Facilities for disabled people, Foreign Studies Centre, Health Services, Language Laboratory, Library, Nursery Care, Social Counselling, Sports Facilities

Publications: Research Directory; Surgite

Publishing House: Block Press

Academic Staff *2014-2015*: Total 594
Student Numbers *2014-2015*: Total 18,824
Last Updated: 05/03/15

CARLETON UNIVERSITY (CU)

1125 Colonel By Drive, Ottawa, Ontario K1S 5B6
Tel: +1(613) 520-7400
Fax: +1(613) 520-7858
EMail: info@carleton.ca
Website: http://www.carleton.ca/

President and Vice-Chancellor: Roseann O'Reilly Runte (2008-)
Tel: +1(613) 520-3801
EMail: presidents_office@carleton.ca

Provost and Vice-President (Academic): Peter Ricketts
Tel: +1(613) 520-3806 EMail: provost@carleton.ca

International Relations: Kimberly Matheson, Vice-President (Research and International)
Tel: +1(613) 520-3570 EMail: vpri@carleton.ca

Faculty

Arts and Social Sciences (African Studies; Ancient Civilizations; Anthropology; Applied Linguistics; Arabic; Art History; Arts and Humanities; Canadian Studies; Child Care and Development; Chinese; Classical Languages; Cognitive Sciences; Communication Studies; Comparative Literature; Cultural Studies; Education; English; Environmental Studies; Film; Folklore; Foreign Languages Education; French; Gender Studies; Geography; German; Greek (Classical); Hebrew; History; Human Rights; Italian; Japanese; Jazz and Popular Music; Latin; Linguistics; Literature; Modern Languages; Music; Natives Education; Philosophy; Portuguese; Psychology; Religion; Russian; Social Problems; Sociology; Spanish; Surveying and Mapping; Women's Studies); **Engineering and Design** (Aeronautical and Aerospace Engineering; Architecture; Biomedical Engineering; Civil Engineering; Computer Engineering; Design; Electrical Engineering; Electronic Engineering; Energy Engineering; Engineering; Engineering Management; Environmental Engineering; Industrial Design; Information Technology; Materials Engineering; Mechanical Engineering; Software

Engineering; Telecommunications Engineering; Town Planning); **Graduate and Postdoctoral Affairs** (Aeronautical and Aerospace Engineering; Anthropology; Applied Linguistics; Applied Mathematics; Architecture; Art History; Biology; Biomedical Engineering; Business Administration; Canadian Studies; Chemistry; Civil Engineering; Cognitive Sciences; Communication Studies; Computer Engineering; Computer Science; Cultural Studies; Earth Sciences; Economics; Electrical and Electronic Engineering; Electrical Engineering; Energy Engineering; Engineering Management; English; Environmental Engineering; Environmental Studies; European Studies; Film; French; Gender Studies; Geography; Health Administration; History; Industrial Design; International Studies; Journalism; Law; Management; Materials Engineering; Mathematics; Mechanical Engineering; Music; Neurosciences; Peace and Disarmament; Philosophy; Physics; Political Sciences; Psychology; Public Administration; Religion; Russian; Social Work; Sociology; Statistics; Welfare and Protective Services; Women's Studies); **Public Affairs** (Asian Studies; Communication Studies; Criminal Law; Criminology; Economics; European Studies; Journalism; Law; Political Sciences; Public Administration; Russian; Social Work); **Science** (Biochemistry; Biological and Life Sciences; Biology; Business Computing; Chemistry; Computer Networks; Computer Science; Earth Sciences; Environmental Studies; Ethics; Forensic Medicine and Dentistry; Health Sciences; Information Sciences; Information Technology; Mathematics; Natural Sciences; Neurosciences; Physics; Software Engineering; Statistics; Technology)

School
Business *(Sprott)* (Accountancy; Business Administration; Business and Commerce; Engineering Management; Finance; Information Sciences; International Business; Management; Marketing)

Institute
Ottawa Medical Physics *(OMPI)*

Centre
Community Innovation *(3CI)*; **Conflict Education and Research** *(CCER)* (Peace and Disarmament); **European Studies** *(CES)* (European Studies); **Indigenous Research, Culture, Language and Education** *(CIRCLE)* (Indigenous Studies); **Intelligence and Security Studies** *(CCISS)* (Protective Services); **International Migration and Settlement Studies** (Demography and Population); **Public History** *(CCPH)* (History); **Research and Education on Women and Work** *(CREWW)* (Education); **Security and Defence Studies** *(CSDS)* (Military Science); **Social and Cultural Analysis** *(Duncombe)* (Cultural Studies; Social Studies); **Study of Stress Processes and Stress Management** (Health Sciences); **Survey** *(CUSC)*; **Trade Policy and Law** *(CTPL)* (Law); **Transnational Cultural Analysis** *(CTCA)* (Cultural Studies); **Treaty Compliance** *(CCTC)*; **Values and Ethics** *(COVE)* (Ethics); **Visualization and Simulation** *(VSIM)*; **Voluntary Sector Research and Development** *(CVSRD)*

Research Centre
Broadband Communications and Wireless Systems *(BCWS)* (Telecommunications Engineering); **Carleton Immersive Media Studio** *(CIMS)* (Media Studies); **Geomatics and Cartographic** *(GCRC)* (Surveying and Mapping); **Sustainable Energy** *(CSERC)* (Energy Engineering); **Technology Innovation** (Technology)

Research Institute
Ottawa-Carleton Bridge *(OCBRI)*

Research Unit
Innovation, Science and Environment Policy *(CRUISE)*

Further Information: Also a number of Study Abroad programmes as part of student/faculty exchange programmes. Contact Carleton International for further information

History: Founded 1942, incorporated as Ottawa Association for the Advancement of Learning, 1943, and reorganized as Carleton College 1952. Acquired present status and title 1957.

Academic Year: September to May (September-December; January-May). Also Summer Session (May-August)

Admission Requirements: Secondary school certificate or recognized foreign equivalent

Fees: National: Undegraduate, 5967.35-8,509.35. Graduate, 2,303.16-3,912.16 per term (Canadian Dollar), International: Undegraduate tuition,16,857.35-19,681.35 per annum; Graduate: 5,121.16-8,560.16 per term

Main Language(s) of Instruction: English

Degrees and Diplomas: *Certificat et diplôme universitaire/University certificate and diploma*; *Baccalauréat/Bachelor's Degree*; *Baccalauréat spécialisé/Bachelor's Degree - Honours*; *Maîtrise/Master's Degree*; *Diplôme et certificat de 2e cycle/Graduate Diploma and Certificate*; *Doctorat/Doctoral Degree*: **Anthropology; Architecture; Biology; Chemistry; Civil Engineering; Computer Engineering; Computer Science; Electrical Engineering; Engineering; English; Environmental Engineering; Ethics; Geography; International Business; Law; Linguistics; Management; Mathematics; Mechanical Engineering; Physics; Political Sciences; Psychology; Social Work; Sociology.** Some Master's and Doctorates degree are offered through an Ottawa-Carleton Joint Institute.

Student Services: Academic Counselling, Canteen, Careers Guidance, Cultural Activities, Facilities for disabled people, Health Services, Language Laboratory, Library, Nursery Care, Social Counselling, Sports Facilities

Publishing house: Carleton University Press

Academic Staff *2014-2015*	**TOTAL**
FULL-TIME	**841**
Student Numbers *2014-2015*	
All (Foreign included)	**27,823**

Part-time students, 4,866.

Last Updated: 05/03/15

CENTENNIAL COLLEGE

P.O. Box 631, Station A, Toronto, Ontario M1K 5E9
Tel: +1(416) 289-5000
Fax: +1(416) 439-7358
EMail: international@centennialcollege.ca
Website: http://www.centennialcollege.ca/

President: Ann Buller (2004-)
Tel: +1(416) 289-5289 EMail: ABuller@centennialcollege.ca

School
Advancement (Arts and Humanities; Biology; Chemistry; English; Logic; Mathematics; Natural Sciences; Social Sciences); **Business** (Accountancy; Administration; Business Administration; Finance; Human Resources; International Business; Law; Marketing); **Communications, Media and Design** (Advertising and Publicity; Design; Film; Fine Arts; Journalism; Media Studies; Radio and Television Broadcasting); **Community and Health Studies** (Child Care and Development; Food Science; Health Sciences; Leisure Studies; Nursing; Nutrition; Occupational Therapy; Paramedical Sciences; Pharmacy; Physical Therapy; Preschool Education; Social and Community Services; Social Work); **Continuing Education at Centennial College** (Accountancy; Administration; Adult Education; Aesthetics; Automotive Engineering; Behavioural Sciences; Business Administration; Business Computing; Chinese; Computer Networks; Computer Science; Data Processing; Design; Education; Electrical Engineering; English; Finance; Food Science; Foreign Languages Education; French; French Studies; Gerontology; Health Administration; Human Resources; Information Technology; Insurance; International Business; Labour and Industrial Relations; Law; Leadership; Management; Marketing; Mechanics; Nursing; Oncology; Ophthalmology; Paramedical Sciences; Preschool Education; Psychology; Public Relations; Real Estate; Rehabilitation and Therapy; Safety Engineering; Sales Techniques; Small Business; Software Engineering; Spanish; Technology; Toxicology; Translation and Interpretation; Transport Management; Writing); **Engineering Technology and Applied Science** *(SETAS)* (Architecture; Automation and Control Engineering; Biomedical Engineering; Biotechnology; Computer Engineering; Computer Networks; Design; Electrical Engineering; Electronic Engineering; Energy Engineering; Environmental Engineering; Heating and Refrigeration; Industrial Engineering; Laboratory Techniques; Maintenance Technology; Mechanical Engineering; Microbiology; Robotics; Software Engineering); **Hospitality, Tourism and Culinary Arts** (Cooking and Catering; Hotel Management; Tourism); **Transportation** (Air Transport; Automotive Engineering; Maintenance Technology; Mechanics; Road Transport; Safety

Engineering; Transport and Communications; Transport Management)

History: Founded 1966.

Fees: National: Post-Secondary Programs, c. 2,320 for two semesters for domestic students and. Bachelor of Science in Nursing (BScN), c. 5,300 for two semesters for domestic students and. Applied Degree Programmes, 5,710-6,394,50 for two semesters for domestic students, International: c.10,400 for two semesters. c.14,375 for two semesters. Bachelor of Science in Nursing (BScN), c.16,160 for two semesters for International students (Canadian Dollar)

Main Language(s) of Instruction: English

Degrees and Diplomas: *Certificat et diplôme/Certificate and diploma*; *Baccalauréat/Bachelor's Degree*; *Diplôme et certificat de 2e cycle/Graduate Diploma and Certificate*

Student Services: Library

Last Updated: 06/03/15

CONESTOGA COLLEGE

299 Doon Valley Drive, Kitchener, Ontario N2G 4M4
Tel: +1(519) 748-5220
Fax: +1(519) 748-3505
EMail: geninfo@conestogac.on.ca
Website: http://conestogac.on.ca/

President: John Tibbits (1987-)
Tel: +1(519) 748-5220 Ext. 3500 EMail: jtibbits@conestogac.on.ca

Programme

Postgraduate Studies (Accountancy; Computer Science; Environmental Engineering; Finance; Human Resources; Information Management; Information Technology; Journalism; Management; Marketing; Media Studies; Paramedical Sciences; Police Studies; Preschool Education; Public Relations; Wood Technology)

School

Business and Hospitality (Accountancy; Administration; Business Administration; Cooking and Catering; Finance; Health Administration; Hotel and Restaurant; Insurance; International Business; Management; Marketing; Public Administration; Retailing and Wholesaling; Service Trades; Social and Community Services; Tourism); **Career and Academic Access** (Business Administration; Design; Engineering; Interior Design); **Engineering and Information Technology** (Architecture; Automation and Control Engineering; Business Administration; Civil Engineering; Computer Engineering; Computer Networks; Computer Science; Construction Engineering; Design; Electrical Engineering; Electronic Engineering; Energy Engineering; Environmental Engineering; Information Technology; Interior Design; Mechanical Engineering; Media Studies; Metal Techniques; Robotics; Software Engineering; Technology; Telecommunications Engineering; Wood Technology); **Health and Life Sciences and Community Services** (Biotechnology; Computer Science; Criminal Law; Dietetics; Fire Science; Health Sciences; Law; Leisure Studies; Nursing; Occupational Therapy; Paramedical Sciences; Police Studies; Preschool Education; Respiratory Therapy; Social and Community Services; Social Work; Sports); **Liberal Studies** (Air Transport; Applied Mathematics; Arts and Humanities; Behavioural Sciences; Social Sciences); **Media and Design** (Advertising and Publicity; Communication Studies; Design; Graphic Design; Interior Design; Journalism; Marketing; Media Studies; Public Relations; Radio and Television Broadcasting; Visual Arts); **Trades and Apprenticeship** (Automotive Engineering; Construction Engineering; Cooking and Catering; Electrical Engineering; Maintenance Technology; Mechanical Engineering; Metal Techniques; Power Engineering)

Institute

Language *(Conestoga Language)* (English)

Further Information: Also Guelph, Waterloo, Stratford, Cambridge and Ingersoll campuses.

History: Founded 1967.

Fees: National: 2,300-9,720 for two semesters (Canadian Dollar), International: International Student Tuition, 9,800-12,500 for two semesters

Main Language(s) of Instruction: English

Degrees and Diplomas: *Certificat et diplôme/Certificate and diploma*; *Baccalauréat/Bachelor's Degree*. Applied Bachelor's degree (professional), 4 yrs; Bachelor's degree (profeesional) in Nursing, 4 yrs; Advanced College Diploma,

Student Services: Library, Nursery Care, Residential Facilities

Student Numbers *2013 30000*: Total 11,000

Last Updated: 06/03/15

DOMINICAN UNIVERSITY COLLEGE

Collège universitaire dominicain

96, Empress Avenue, Ottawa, Ontario K1R 7G3
Tel: +1(613) 233-5696
Fax: +1(613) 233-6064
EMail: info@udominicaine.ca
Website: http://www.udominicaine.ca/

President: Maxime Allard Tel: +1(613) 233-5696 poste 319

Registrar: Ousmane Diallo
Tel: +1(613) 233-5696 EMail: registraire@udominicaine.ca

Vice-président des études: Jean-François Méthot Allard

Faculty

Philosophy (Philosophy); **Theology** (Theology)

Institute

Pastoral Theology (Pastoral Studies; Theology)

History: Founded 1967, previously established 1900 as 'Studium Generale' of the Order of Friars Preachers in Canada. A private university institution incorporated in the Province of Ontario since 1909. Previously known as the Collège Dominicain de Philosophie et de Théologie (Dominican College of Philosophy and Theology).

Academic Year: September to April (September-December; January-April). Also Summer Session (July)

Admission Requirements: 1 yr study in a Faculty of Arts of a recognized university, or foreign equivalent

Fees: National: Undergraduate tuition, 4 330 per annum. Graduate tuition, 6 975 per annum (Canadian Dollar), International: Full -time undergraduate tuition, 8 700 per annum. Full-time graduate, 11 300 per annum (Canadian Dollar)

Main Language(s) of Instruction: French, English

Degrees and Diplomas: *Certificat et diplôme universitaire/University certificate and diploma*; *Baccalauréat/Bachelor's Degree*; *Maîtrise/Master's Degree*: **Philosophy.** *Doctorat/Doctoral Degree*: **Philosophy.**

Student Services: Library

Publications: Koinônia

Last Updated: 06/03/15

FANSHAWE COLLEGE

P.O. Box 7005, 1001 Fanshawe College Boulevard, London, Ontario N5Y 5R6
Tel: +1(519) 452-4430
Fax: +1(519) 452-4420
EMail: registrar@fanshawec.ca
Website: http://fanshawec.ca/

President: Peter Devlin Tel: +1(519) 452-4200

School

Applied Science and Technology (Biotechnology; Electrical Engineering; Electronic Engineering; Environmental Engineering; Heating and Refrigeration; Industrial Engineering; Laboratory Techniques; Mechanical Engineering; Metal Techniques; Technology); **Building Technology** (Architecture; Building Technologies; Civil Engineering; Construction Engineering; Technology); **Business** *(Lawrence Kinlin)* (Accountancy; Business Administration; Communication Studies; Finance; Health Administration; Human Resources; Insurance; International Business; Law; Leadership; Management; Marketing; Public Relations); **Contemporary Media** (Communication Studies; Film; Fine Arts; Journalism; Media Studies; Multimedia; Photography; Public Relations; Radio and Television Broadcasting; Theatre); **Design** (Fashion Design; Graphic Design; Horticulture; Interior Design; Landscape Architecture; Marketing; Surveying and Mapping; Town Planning); **Health Sciences and Nursing** (Anaesthesiology; Dental Hygiene; Dentistry; Health

Sciences; Nursing; Paramedical Sciences; Pharmacy; Respiratory Therapy; Sports; Treatment Techniques); **Human Services** (Behavioural Sciences; Child Care and Development; Development Studies; Law; Leadership; Leisure Studies; Police Studies; Preschool Education; Protective Services; Social Work); **Information Technology** (Administration; Business Administration; Computer Science; Information Management; Law; Software Engineering); **Language and Liberal Studies** (Accountancy; Administration; Agricultural Equipment; Anaesthesiology; Architecture; Automotive Engineering; Behavioural Sciences; Biotechnology; Business Administration; Business Computing; Child Care and Development; Cinema and Television; Civil Engineering; Communication Studies; Computer Science; Construction Engineering; Cooking and Catering; Dental Hygiene; Dentistry; Development Studies; Electrical Engineering; Electronic Engineering; English; Environmental Engineering; Fashion Design; Film; Finance; Fine Arts; Food Science; Graphic Design; Health Sciences; Heating and Refrigeration; Horticulture; Hotel Management; Human Resources; Industrial Engineering; Information Management; Information Sciences; Insurance; Interior Design; International Business; Journalism; Laboratory Techniques; Landscape Architecture; Law; Leadership; Leisure Studies; Maintenance Technology; Management; Marketing; Mechanical Engineering; Media Studies; Medical Technology; Metal Techniques; Multimedia; Nursing; Nutrition; Paramedical Sciences; Pharmacy; Photography; Police Studies; Power Engineering; Preschool Education; Public Relations; Radio and Television Broadcasting; Respiratory Therapy; Service Trades; Social Work; Sports; Surveying and Mapping; Technology; Telecommunications Engineering; Theatre; Tourism; Town Planning); **Motive Power Technology** (Agricultural Equipment; Automotive Engineering; Maintenance Technology; Technology); **Tourism and Hospitality** (Cooking and Catering; Hotel and Restaurant; Hotel Management; Nutrition; Tourism)

Centre

Digital and Performance Arts (Computer Graphics; Design; Display and Stage Design; Graphic Design)

Further Information: Also Simcoe/Norfolk Regional Campus, St. Thomas/Elgin Campus, Strathroy Centre, Woodstock/Oxford Regional Campus, Tillsonburg Centre.

History: Founded 1967.

Fees: National: Bachelor's and Collaborative Degree Programmes: c. 5,000 per annum or 2,500 per semester (Canadian Dollar), International: 2,168.34-12,411.54 per term depending on programmes (Canadian Dollar)

Main Language(s) of Instruction: English

Degrees and Diplomas: *Certificat et diplôme/Certificate and diploma*; *Baccalauréat/Bachelor's Degree*; *Diplôme et certificat de 2e cycle/Graduate Diploma and Certificate*: **Human Resources.** Applied Bachelor's degree (professional), 4 yrs; College Advanced Diploma, 3 yrs.

Student Numbers *2014-2015*: Total 17,350
Last Updated: 09/03/15

GEORGE BROWN COLLEGE (GBC)

P.O. Box 1015, Station B, Toronto, Ontario M5T 2T9
Tel: +1(416) 415-2000
Fax: +1(416) 415-4993
EMail: info@gbrownc.on.ca; international@georgebrown.ca
Website: http://www.georgebrown.ca/

President: Anne Sado
Tel: +1(416) 415-5000 Ext. 4471
EMail: asado@georgebrown.ca

School

Accounting and Finance (Accountancy; Finance); **Chef** (Cooking and Catering); **Computer Technology** (Computer Engineering; Mechanical Engineering); **Construction Management** *(Angelo Del Zotto)* (Architecture; Construction Engineering); **Design** (Dance; Design; Fashion Design; Jewellery Art; Performing Arts; Theatre); **Fashion Studies** (Fashion Design); **Health and Wellness** (Behavioural Sciences; Dental Hygiene; Dental Technology; Dentistry; Health Administration; Health Sciences; Medical Technology; Nursing); **Hospitality and Tourism Management** (Hotel and Restaurant; Tourism); **Human Resources** (Human Resources); **Immigrant and Transitional Education** (Educational and Student Counselling; English; Teacher Training); **Management** (Accountancy; Business Administration; Finance; Human Resources; International Business; Management; Marketing; Sports Management); **Marketing** (Marketing); **Nursing** *(Sally Horsfall Eaton)* (Nursing)

Centre

Community Services and Early Childhood (Preschool Education; Social and Community Services; Special Education); **Continuous Learning** (Arabic; Business Administration; Chinese; Communication Studies; Computer Science; Cooking and Catering; Cosmetology; Electronic Engineering; English; Fashion Design; Film; French; German; Greek; Health Sciences; Hotel and Restaurant; Information Technology; Interior Design; Italian; Japanese; Jewellery Art; Management; Mechanical Engineering; Nursing; Photography; Portuguese; Protective Services; Russian; Service Trades; Social and Community Services; Spanish; Technology; Transport Management; Visual Arts); **Preparatory and Liberal Studies** (Arts and Humanities; Cooking and Catering; Health Sciences; Hotel and Restaurant; Natural Sciences; Social and Community Services; Special Education)

Further Information: Traditional and Open Learning Institution

History: Founded 1967.

Main Language(s) of Instruction: English

Degrees and Diplomas: *Certificat et diplôme/Certificate and diploma*; *Diplôme et certificat de 2e cycle/Graduate Diploma and Certificate.* Applied Bachelor's degree (professional), 4 yrs; Postgraduate programme, 1-4 semesters.

Academic Staff *2010-2011*	**TOTAL**
FULL-TIME	**1,216**
PART-TIME	**1,862**
Student Numbers *2010-2011*	
All (Foreign included)	**70,956**
FOREIGN ONLY	**2070**

Last Updated: 09/03/15

GEORGIAN COLLEGE

1 Georgian Drive, Barrie, Ontario L4M 3X9
Tel: +1(705) 728-1968
Fax: +1(705) 722-5123
EMail: inquire@georgiancollege.ca
Website: http://www.georgiancollege.ca/

President: MaryLynn West-Moynes (2012-)
Tel: +1(705) 728-1968 Ext. 1248

Programme

Aboriginal Studies (Development Studies; Natives Education); **Automotive Studies** (Business Administration; Management; Marketing; Mechanical Engineering); **Aviation Studies** (Air Transport); **Business Studies** (Accountancy; Administration; Advertising and Publicity; Air Transport; Business Administration; Hotel Management; Human Resources; International Business; Law; Management; Marketing; Tourism); **Community Studies** (Administration; Child Care and Development; Dental Hygiene; Dentistry; Development Studies; Environmental Engineering; Justice Administration; Natives Education; Paramedical Sciences; Physical Therapy; Police Studies; Preschool Education; Social Work; Technology; Toxicology; Veterinary Science); **Computer Studies** (Computer Engineering; Computer Networks; Computer Science); **Design and Visual Art Studies** (Advertising and Publicity; Design; Fine Arts; Graphic Design; Interior Design; Jewellery Art; Photography; Visual Arts); **Health Studies** (Communication Disorders; Dental Hygiene; Dentistry; Health Administration; Health Sciences; Nursing; Optometry; Paramedical Sciences; Physical Therapy; Toxicology; Veterinary Science); **Hospitality, Tourism and Recreation Studies** (Cooking and Catering; Hotel Management; Leisure Studies; Management; Tourism); **Skilled Trades and Apprenticeships** (Heating and Refrigeration; Maintenance Technology; Mechanics; Metal Techniques; Service Trades; Technology); **Social Sciences and Humanities** (Anthropology; Arts and Humanities; Gerontology; History; Law; Political Sciences; Psychology; Social Sciences; Social Work; Sociology); **Transportation Studies** (Business Administration; Marine Engineering; Marketing; Mechanical Engineering); **University and Graduate Studies** (Business Administration; Communication Disorders; Computer

Networks; Human Resources; International Business; Jewellery Art; Management; Nursing; Paramedical Sciences; Police Studies; Rehabilitation and Therapy; Social Work; Toxicology)

School

Engineering Technology (Architecture; Automation and Control Engineering; Automotive Engineering; Civil Engineering; Electrical Engineering; Marine Engineering; Mechanical Engineering; Power Engineering; Service Trades; Technology); **Environmental Studies** (Environmental Engineering; Environmental Studies)

Further Information: Also Orillia, Owen Sound, Midland, Muskoka, Orangeville and South Georgian Bay campuses

History: Founded 1967.

Fees: National: 1,958.68- 10,360.32 per annum, International: 6,738.35-18,197.90 per annum

Main Language(s) of Instruction: English

Degrees and Diplomas: *Certificat et diplôme universitaire/University certificate and diploma*; *Baccalauréat/Bachelor's Degree*. Bachelor's degree (professional), 4 yrs, offered in association with Laurentian University; Applied Bachelor's degree (professional), 4 yrs; Bachelor's degree in Nursing in association with Georgian College/York University; Postgraduate diplomas, 1-2 yrs following a two-year college diploma or university degree.

Student Services: Residential Facilities

Last Updated: 09/03/15

HUMBER COLLEGE

205 Humber College Boulevard, Toronto,
Ontario M9W 5L7
Tel: +1(416) 675-3111
Fax: +1(416) 675-2427
EMail: enquiry@humber.ca
Website: http://www.humber.ca/

President: Chris Whitaker Tel: +1(416) 675-6622 Ext. 4853

School

Applied Technology (Civil Engineering; Computer Engineering; Computer Networks; Design; Electrical Engineering; Electronic Engineering; Heating and Refrigeration; Horticulture; Industrial Design; Interior Design; Landscape Architecture; Maintenance Technology; Management; Mechanical Engineering; Service Trades; Telecommunications Engineering); **Business** (Accountancy; Business Administration; Cosmetology; E- Business/Commerce; Finance; Human Resources; International Business; Law; Management; Marketing; Public Administration; Tourism); **Creative and Performing Arts** (Acting; Jazz and Popular Music; Music; Publishing and Book Trade; Theatre; Writing); **Health Sciences** (Health Sciences; Medicine; Nursing; Occupational Health; Paramedical Sciences; Pharmacy; Preschool Education); **Hospitality, Recreation and Tourism** (Cooking and Catering; Hotel Management; Leisure Studies; Nutrition; Physical Therapy; Sports; Sports Management; Tourism); **Liberal Arts and Sciences** (Arts and Humanities; English); **Media Studies and Information Technology** (Advertising and Publicity; Computer Graphics; Film; Graphic Design; Information Technology; Journalism; Media Studies; Multimedia; Photography; Public Relations; Radio and Television Broadcasting; Visual Arts); **Social and Community Services** (Child Care and Development; Criminal Law; Police Studies; Social and Community Services)

Further Information: Traditional and Open Learning Institution. Also Humber Lakeshore and Humber Orangeville Campuses.

History: Founded 1967. Acquired present status 2003.

Main Language(s) of Instruction: English

Degrees and Diplomas: *Certificat et diplôme universitaire/University certificate and diploma*; *Baccalauréat/Bachelor's Degree*; *Diplôme et certificat de 2e cycle/Graduate Diploma and Certificate*. Applied Bachelor's degree (professional), 4 yrs; Bachelor's degree (professional), 4yrs; Bachelor's degree in Nursing in collaboration with the University of New Brunswick, 4 yrs; Advanced Diplomas, 6 semesters.

Student Services: Library, Residential Facilities

Student Numbers *2014-2015 56000*: Total: c. 19,000

Last Updated: 09/03/15

LA CITÉ COLLEGE OF APPLIED ARTS AND TECHNOLOGY

Le Collège d'arts appliqués et de technologie La Cité
801, promenade de l'aviation, Ottawa, Ontario K1K 4R3
Tel: +1(613) 742-2483
Fax: +1(613) 742-2483
EMail: info@lacitec.on.ca; admissions@LaCitec.on.ca
Website: http://www.lacitec.on.ca/

Presidente: Lise Bourgeois (2010-)
Tel: +1(613) 742-2483 Ext. 2000

Programme

Preparatory Studies (Arts and Humanities; Biology; Chemistry; Communication Studies; English; Ethics; Mathematics; Philosophy; Physics; Psychology)

Area

Administration (Administration; Business Administration; Finance; Law; Marketing; Sales Techniques); **Arts and Design** (Fine Arts; Graphic Design; Interior Design; Photography); **Communication** (Advertising and Publicity; Public Relations); **Construction and Mechanics** (Automotive Engineering; Building Technologies; Electrical Engineering; Heating and Refrigeration; Mechanical Engineering; Metal Techniques; Technology); **Electronics** (Electronic Engineering); **Esthetics and Hairdressing** (Cosmetology; Service Trades); **Forestry and Environment** (Environmental Engineering; Forestry); **Health Sciences** (Biotechnology; Dental Hygiene; Dentistry; Health Sciences; Medical Auxiliaries; Paramedical Sciences; Physical Therapy; Physiology; Respiratory Therapy); **Hospitality** (Cooking and Catering; Hotel and Restaurant); **Housing and Town Planning** (Architecture; Civil Engineering); **Human Sciences** (Behavioural Sciences; Gerontology; Social Work; Special Education); **Informatics** (Computer Engineering; Computer Networks; Computer Science; Information Technology); **Media** (Journalism; Radio and Television Broadcasting); **Security** (Civil Security; Fire Science; Police Studies; Protective Services); **Tourism and Leisure** (Service Trades; Tourism)

Further Information: Also Hawkesbury and Alphonse-Desjardins campuses, and online programmes

History: Founded 1990.

Fees: National: first year, 1158,77 per term; second year, 1145,16 per term; third year, 1134,73 per term, International: 12 600 per annum (Canadian Dollar)

Main Language(s) of Instruction: English

Degrees and Diplomas: *Certificat et diplôme/Certificate and diploma*; *Baccalauréat/Bachelor's Degree*: **Biotechnology.** Applied Bachelor's degree (professional), 4 yrs; Postgraduate diploma, a further 1-2 yrs following college diploma or first university degree. Joint Bachelor of Nursing with Ottawa University

Student Services: Library

Last Updated: 06/03/15

LAKEHEAD UNIVERSITY

955 Oliver Road, Thunder Bay, Ontario P7B 5E1
Tel: +1(807) 343-8110
Fax: +1(807) 343-8023
EMail: info@lakeheadu.ca
Website: http://www.lakeheadu.ca

President and Vice-Chancellor: Brian Stevenson (2010-)
Tel: +1(807) 343-8200 EMail: bstevens@lakeheadu.ca

Vice-President Administration and Finance: Kathy Pozihun
Tel: +1(807) 343-8383

Faculty

Business Administration (Accountancy; Business Administration; Business and Commerce; Finance; Human Resources; Information Sciences; Labour and Industrial Relations; Marketing; Secretarial Studies); **Education** (Communication Studies; Curriculum; Ecology; Education; English; Fine Arts; Foreign Languages Education; French; Gerontology; History; Human Resources; Information Technology; Leadership; Native Language Education; Natives Education; Natural Sciences; Parks and Recreation; Physical Therapy; Psychology; Religious Education; Special Education; Teacher Training; Women's Studies); **Engineering** (Automation and Control Engineering; Chemical Engineering; Civil Engineering;

Computer Engineering; Electrical Engineering; Engineering; Environmental Engineering; Mechanical Engineering; Software Engineering); **Graduate Studies** (Automation and Control Engineering; Biology; Biotechnology; Business Administration; Chemistry; Computer Engineering; Computer Science; Economics; Education; Educational Sciences; Electrical Engineering; English; Environmental Engineering; Environmental Studies; Forestry; Geology; Gerontology; Health Sciences; History; Management; Mathematics; Nursing; Physical Therapy; Physics; Psychology; Public Health; Social Work; Sociology; Tourism; Women's Studies); **Health and Behavioural Sciences** (Behavioural Sciences; Gerontology; Health Sciences; Nursing; Physical Therapy; Psychology; Public Health; Social Work); **Natural Resources Management** (Botany; Ecology; Entomology; Environmental Management; Fire Science; Fishery; Forestry; Genetics; Management; Natural Resources; Pathology; Soil Science; Water Science; Wildlife; Wood Technology); **Science and Environmental Studies** (Anthropology; Biology; Chemistry; Computer Science; Economics; Environmental Studies; Geography; Geology; Information Technology; Mathematics; Molecular Biology; Physics; Water Science); **Social Sciences and Humanities** (Classical Languages; English; Finnish; French; German; Greek (Classical); History; Indigenous Studies; Italian; Latin; Modern Languages; Music; Musical Instruments; Nordic Studies; Parks and Recreation; Philosophy; Political Sciences; Singing; Social Sciences; Sociology; Spanish; Tourism; Visual Arts; Women's Studies)

Programme

Biorefining Research Initiative; **Biotechnology Research** (Biotechnology)

School

Medicine *(Northern Ontario - NOSM)* (Anaesthesiology; Gerontology; Gynaecology and Obstetrics; Health Sciences; Medicine; Orthopaedics; Paediatrics; Psychiatry and Mental Health; Public Health; Social and Preventive Medicine; Surgery)

Institute

Globalization and Culture *(Advanced)* (Cultural Studies); **Social History** *(Lakehead)* (History)

Centre

Analytical Services *(LUCAS)* (Archaeology; Environmental Studies; Forensic Medicine and Dentistry; Forest Products; Forestry; Mineralogy; Molecular Biology; Paleontology; Soil Science; Toxicology); **Application of Resource Information Systems** (Information Sciences); **Excellence for Children and Adolescents with Special Needs** (Education of the Handicapped); **Health Care Ethics** (Ethics; Health Sciences); **Northern Studies** (Nordic Studies)

Research Centre

Education and Research on Aging and Health (Gerontology; Health Sciences); **Rural and Northern Health** (Health Sciences); **Safe Driving** (Road Transport); **Tourism and Community Development** *(Lakehead University)* (Social and Community Services; Tourism)

Further Information: Also Orillia Campus.

History: Founded 1946 as Lakehead Technical Institute, became Lakehead College of Arts, Science and Technology 1956 and acquired present status and title 1965.

Academic Year: September to April (September-December; January-April)

Admission Requirements: Ontario secondary school diploma (OSSD) or equivalent

Fees: National: Range from 5,735 to 6,968 for degree programs (Canadian Dollar), International: Range from: 17,750 to 18,250 for degree programs (Canadian Dollar)

Main Language(s) of Instruction: English

Degrees and Diplomas: *Baccalauréat/Bachelor's Degree*; *Baccalauréat spécialisé/Bachelor's Degree - Honours*; *Maîtrise/Master's Degree*: **Business Administration; Engineering; English; Environmental Studies; Forestry; Health Sciences; Mathematics and Computer Science; Natural Sciences; Psychology; Social Work; Sociology.** *Diplôme et certificat de 2e cycle/Graduate Diploma and Certificate*: **Health Sciences; Nursing; Physical Therapy.** *Doctorat/Doctoral Degree*: **Biotechnology; Chemistry; Clinical Psychology; Computer Engineering; Education; Electrical Engineering; Forestry; Psychology.**

Student Services: Academic Counselling, Canteen, Careers Guidance, Cultural Activities, Facilities for disabled people, Foreign Studies Centre, Health Services, Library, Social Counselling, Sports Facilities

Publications: Agora; Publications of the Faculties

Publishing House: In-House Publishing

Last Updated: 16/03/15

LAURENTIAN UNIVERSITY

Université Laurentienne (LU)

935 Ramsey Lake Road, Sudbury, Ontario P3E 2C6

Tel: +1(705) 675-1151 +1(800) 461-4030

Fax: +1(705) 675-4891

EMail: admissions@laurentian.ca; international@laurentian.ca

Website: http://laurentian.ca

President: Dominic Giroux (2009-)
Tel: +1(705) 675-1151 Ext. 3410
EMail: president@laurentian.ca; dominicgiroux@laurentian.ca

Vice-President Academic and Provost: Robert Kerr
Tel: +1(705) 675-1151 Ext. 3438

International Relations: Melissa Keeping, Director, Laurentian International
Tel: +1(705) 675-1151 Ext. 1556
EMail: mkeeping@laurentian.ca; international@laurentian.ca

Faculty

Arts (Ancient Civilizations; Archaeology; Classical Languages; Communication Studies; Computer Science; English; Ethics; Ethnology; Fine Arts; Folklore; French; French Studies; Greek (Classical); History; Indigenous Studies; Italian; Latin; Literature; Mathematics; Mathematics and Computer Science; Media Studies; Modern Languages; Music; Native American Studies; Native Language; Philosophy; Religion; Religious Studies; Spanish; Speech Therapy and Audiology; Theatre; Women's Studies); **Education** (Education; Educational Administration; Educational Sciences; Health Education; Physical Education); **Health** (Health Sciences; Midwifery; Nursing; Speech Therapy and Audiology); **Management** *(Some Programmes are offered at Georgian College (Barrie) and St-Lawrence College (Kingston))* (Accountancy; Business Administration; Business and Commerce; Economics; Finance; Human Resources; Management; Marketing; Public Administration; Sports Management); **Medicine** (Health Sciences; Midwifery; Nursing; Physical Therapy; Psychology; Social Work; Sports); **Science, Engineering and Architecture** (Anthropology; Archaeology; Architecture; Behavioural Sciences; Biochemistry; Biology; Biomedicine; Chemical Engineering; Chemistry; Civil Engineering; Computer Science; Earth Sciences; Ecology; Engineering; Environmental Studies; Ethnology; Forensic Medicine and Dentistry; Geography; Geology; Mathematics; Mechanical Engineering; Mineralogy; Mining Engineering; Neurosciences; Physics; Psychology; Radiology; Rehabilitation and Therapy; Surveying and Mapping; Zoology); **Social Sciences** (Anthropology; Earth Sciences; Economics; Geography (Human); Geology; Gerontology; Health Sciences; History; Labour and Industrial Relations; Law; Political Sciences; Psychology; Public Health; Social Sciences; Sociology)

Unit

Cooperative Freshwater Ecology *(CFEU)* (Ecology)

School

Mines *(Goodman)* (Mining Engineering)

Institute

Franco-Ontarien *(IFO)*; **International Economic Policy** *(IEPI)* (International Economics); **Northern Ontario Research and Development** *(INORD)* (Regional Studies); **Sport Marketing** *(ISM)* (Marketing; Sports Management)

Laboratory

Elliot Lake Research Field Station (Environmental Studies; Inorganic Chemistry; Soil Science); **Laurentian University Mining Automation** *(LUMAL)* (Mining Engineering)

Research Centre

Association francophone pour le savoir *((ACFAS), Sudbury Section)* (French); **Geomechanics** *(GRC)* (Mining Engineering); **Human Development** *(CRHD)* (Administration; Business and Commerce; Geology; Indigenous Studies; Nursing; Philosophy;

Psychology; Social Work; Sociology); **Humanities Research and Creativity** (Cultural Studies; Education; Fine Arts; History; Literature; Modern Languages; Music; Philosophy; Political Sciences); **Interdisciplinarity Research in Human Sciences** *(International - ICIRHS)* (Social Sciences); **Interdisciplinary Research in Law** *(International - ICIRL)* (Law); **Mineral Exploration** *(MERC)* (Earth Sciences; Geology); **Mining Materials** *(CIMMR)* (Mining Engineering); **Occupational Safety and Health** *(CROSH)* (Occupational Health); **Rural and Northern Health Research** *(CRaNHR)* (Health Sciences); **Social Justice and Policy** *(CRSJP)* (Social Policy); **Sudbury Neutrino Observatory** *(SNO)* (Astrophysics)

Research Group

Mining Innovation, Rehabilitation and Applied Research Corporation *(MIRARCO)* (Environmental Management; Mining Engineering)

Further Information: Also Barrie Campus. Online and Distance Education.

History: Founded 1960 as a non-denominational bilingual institution offering courses in both French and English.

Academic Year: September to April (September-December; January-April)

Admission Requirements: Ontario secondary school diploma (OSSD) including a minimum of 6 Ontario Academic Courses (OAC's) with minimun overall average of 70%

Fees: Undergraduate, 6,796.20 -8,875.00 (30 credits) for Canadian students. Master: 2,256.40-3,208.20 per 6 credits (Canadian Dollar)

Main Language(s) of Instruction: English, French

Degrees and Diplomas: *Certificat et diplôme universitaire/University certificate and diploma*; *Baccalauréat/Bachelor's Degree*; *Maîtrise/Master's Degree*; *Doctorat/Doctoral Degree*: **Arts and Humanities; Ecology; Geology; Molecular Biology; Natural Resources; Natural Sciences.**

Student Services: Academic Counselling, Canteen, Careers Guidance, Cultural Activities, Facilities for disabled people, Health Services, Library, Nursery Care, Social Counselling, Sports Facilities

Publishing house: Laurentian Press

Academic Staff *2014-2015*: Total 355

Student Numbers *2014-2015*: Total 9,500

Last Updated: 26/03/15

HUNTINGTON UNIVERSITY

935 Ramsey Lake Road, Sudbury, Ontario P3E 2C6
Tel: + 1(705) 673-4126 + 1(800) 461-6366
Fax: + 1(705) 673-6917
EMail: info@huntingtonuniversity.com
Website: http://www.huntingtonu.ca/

President and Vice-Chancellor: Kevin McCormick (2006-)
Tel: + 1(705) 673-4126, Ext.209
EMail: hupresident@huntingtonu.ca

Registrar, Executive Assistant and Secretary to the Board of Regents: Karen McBain EMail: kmcbain@huntingtonu.ca

Programme

Communication Studies (Communication Studies; Mass Communication); **Ethics** (Ethics; Philosophy; Religious Studies); **Gerontology** (Gerontology); **Graduate Studies** (Pastoral Studies); **Religious Studies** (Christian Religious Studies; Religion; Religious Studies); **Theology** (Theology)

History: Founded 1960 as a federated university of Laurentian University

Main Language(s) of Instruction: English

Degrees and Diplomas: *Certificat et diplôme universitaire/University certificate and diploma*: **Ethics.** *Baccalauréat/Bachelor's Degree*; *Maîtrise/Master's Degree*: **Pastoral Studies.** Also Honours Bachelor's degree in Communication Studies, 4 yrs.

Student Services: Library

Student Numbers *2010-2011*: Total 2,300

MCMASTER UNIVERSITY

1280 Main Street West, Hamilton, Ontario L8S4L8
Tel: + 1(905) 525-9140
Fax: + 1(905) 521-1504
EMail: univsec@mcmaster.ca
Website: http://mcmaster.ca

President and Vice-Chancellor: Patrick Deane (2010-)
Tel: + 1(905) 525 9140 Ext.24340 EMail: president@mcmaster.ca

Provost and Vice-President (Academic): David S. Wilkinson
Tel: + 1(905) 525-9140 Ext. 24301 EMail: provost@mcmaster.ca

Faculty

Engineering (Biomedical Engineering; Business Computing; Chemical Engineering; Civil Engineering; Computer Engineering; Electrical Engineering; Electronic Engineering; Engineering; Engineering Drawing and Design; Engineering Management; Materials Engineering; Mechanical Engineering; Physics; Production Engineering; Software Engineering; Technology); **Health Sciences** (Anaesthesiology; Behavioural Sciences; Biochemistry; Biomedicine; Cardiology; Endocrinology; Epidemiology; Gastroenterology; Gerontology; Gynaecology and Obstetrics; Haematology; Health Sciences; Immunology; Medical Auxiliaries; Medicine; Microbiology; Molecular Biology; Nephrology; Neurology; Neurosciences; Nursing; Occupational Therapy; Oncology; Ophthalmology; Orthopaedics; Otorhinolaryngology; Paediatrics; Pathology; Physical Therapy; Plastic Surgery; Psychiatry and Mental Health; Radiology; Rehabilitation and Therapy; Respiratory Therapy; Rheumatology; Social and Preventive Medicine; Statistics; Surgery; Urology); **Humanities** (Acting; Ancient Civilizations; Archaeology; Art History; Asian Studies; Cinema and Television; Cognitive Sciences; Communication Studies; Comparative Literature; Cultural Studies; English; Film; Fine Arts; French; Gender Studies; German; Greek (Classical); History; Italian; Japanese; Latin; Linguistics; Literature; Modern Languages; Multimedia; Music; Music Education; Musical Instruments; Painting and Drawing; Peace and Disarmament; Performing Arts; Philology; Philosophy; Polish; Printing and Printmaking; Russian; Sculpture; Spanish; Theatre; Women's Studies); **Science** (Astronomy and Space Science; Behavioural Sciences; Biochemistry; Biology; Biomedicine; Biophysics; Cell Biology; Chemistry; Earth Sciences; Ecology; Environmental Studies; Geochemistry; Geography; Geography (Human); Mathematics; Neurosciences; Physical Therapy; Physics; Psychology; Radiology; Statistics; Water Science); **Social Sciences** (Accountancy; Anthropology; Archaeology; Asian Religious Studies; Behavioural Sciences; Bible; Business Administration; Christian Religious Studies; Cognitive Sciences; Cultural Studies; Earth Sciences; Economics; Environmental Studies; Experimental Psychology; Finance; Geography (Human); Gerontology; Health Sciences; International Business; International Relations; International Studies; Islamic Theology; Judaic Religious Studies; Labour and Industrial Relations; Linguistics; Neurosciences; Political Sciences; Psychology; Public Administration; Religious Studies; Social Problems; Social Psychology; Social Sciences; Social Work; Sociology; Water Science)

College

Mc Master Divinity College (Religion; Theology)

Programme

Arts and Science; **Indigenous Studies**

School

Business *(DeGroote)* (Accountancy; Business Administration; Business and Commerce; Engineering Management; Finance; Human Resources; Information Sciences; Management; Marketing); **Graduate Studies** (Ancient Civilizations; Anthropology; Astronomy and Space Science; Behavioural Sciences; Biochemistry; Biology; Biomedicine; Business Administration; Chemical Engineering; Chemistry; Civil Engineering; Classical Languages; Cognitive Sciences; Communication Studies; Computer Engineering; Cultural Studies; Earth Sciences; Economics; Electrical Engineering; Engineering; Engineering Management; English; French; Gender Studies; Geography; Gerontology; Greek (Classical); Health Administration; Health Sciences; History; Labour and Industrial Relations; Latin; Materials Engineering; Mathematics; Mechanical Engineering; Media Studies; Medical Technology; Metal Techniques; Neurosciences; Nuclear Engineering; Nursing; Occupational Therapy; Philosophy; Physical Therapy; Physics; Political Sciences;

Psychology; Rehabilitation and Therapy; Religious Studies; Social Sciences; Social Work; Sociology; Software Engineering; Statistics; Surveying and Mapping)

Institute
Applied Radiation Sciences *(McMaster - McIARS)*; **Automotive Research and Technology** *(McMaster - MacAUTO)* (Automotive Engineering); **Confucius** (Asian Studies; Chinese); **Energy Studies** *(McMaster)* (Energy Engineering); **Globalization and the Human Condition**; **Molecular Biology and Biotechnology** *(McMaster)* (Biotechnology; Molecular Biology); **Polymer Production Technology** *(McMaster)* (Polymer and Plastics Technology); **Respiratory Health** *(Firestone)* (Respiratory Therapy); **Transportation and Logistics** *(McMaster)* (Transport and Communications; Transport Management); **Water, Environment and Health** *((UNU-INWEH))* (Environmental Studies; Health Sciences; Water Science)

Centre
Ancient DNA *(McMaster)*; **Child Studies** *(Offord)* (Child Care and Development); **Climate Change** *(McMaster)* (Meteorology); **Emerging Device Technologies** (Technology); **Evaluation of Medicines** (Medicine); **Functional Genomics** (Genetics); **Gene Therapeutics** (Genetics); **Health Economics and Policy Analysis** (Economics); **Microbial Chemical Biology** (Biology); **Minimal Access Surgery** (Surgery); **Peace Studies** (Peace and Disarmament); **Probe Development and Commercialization**; **Spatial Analysis**; **Statistics Canada Research Data** (Statistics); **Surgical Invention and Innovation** (Surgery)

Research Centre
Antimicrobial; **Bertrand Russell**; **Childhood Disability** *(CanChild)* (Rehabilitation and Therapy); **eBusiness** *(McMaster - MeRC)* (E- Business/Commerce); **Gerontological Health** *(R. Samuel McLaughlin)* (Gerontology); **Henderson**; **Management of Innovation and New Technology** (Engineering Management; Technology); **Medical Imagining Informatics** *(MIIRC@M)* (Medical Technology); **Network for Evaluation of Education and Training Technologies** (Educational Technology); **Promotion of Women's Health** (Women's Studies); **Pulp and Paper** *(McMaster)* (Paper Technology); **Steel** (Metal Techniques); **Surgical Outcomes** (Surgery)

Research Institute
Child Health *(McMaster)* (Health Administration); **Infectious Disease** *(Michael G. DeGroote)* (Epidemiology); **Manufacturing** *(McMaster)* (Production Engineering); **Materials** *(Brockhouse)* (Materials Engineering); **Population Health** (Public Health); **Quantitative Studies in Economics and Population** (Demography and Population; Economics)

Further Information: Also Teaching Hospitals

History: Founded 1887 in Toronto and located in Hamilton 1930. A non-denominational private foundation.

Academic Year: September to April (September-December; January-April)

Admission Requirements: Secondary school certificate or recognized foreign equivalent

Main Language(s) of Instruction: English

Degrees and Diplomas: *Baccalauréat/Bachelor's Degree*; *Baccalauréat spécialisé/Bachelor's Degree - Honours*: **Music.** *Maîtrise/Master's Degree*: **Arts and Humanities; Business Administration; Engineering; Health Sciences; Natural Sciences; Social Sciences.** *Diplôme et certificat de 2e cycle/Graduate Diploma and Certificate*: **Gender Studies; Health Administration; Nuclear Engineering; Nursing; Women's Studies.** *Doctorat/Doctoral Degree*

Student Services: Library, Sports Facilities

Publications: Journal of the Bertrand Russell Archives; Library Research News; McMaster Nuclear Reactor Research Report; McMaster Times; McMaster University Medical Centre Report; Research Bulletin

Academic Staff *2014-2015*: Total 1,413
Student Numbers *2014-2015*: Total 30,117
Last Updated: 27/03/15

NIAGARA COLLEGE

P.O. Box 1005, 300 Woodlawn Road, Welland, Ontario L3C 7L3
Tel: +1(905) 735-2211 Ext. 7559
Fax: +1(905) 736-6000
EMail: info@niagaracollege.ca
Website: http://www.niagaracollege.ca/

President: Daniel J. Patterson
Tel: +1(905) 641-2252 Ext. 4040
EMail: dpatterson@niagaracollege.ca

Area
Academic and General Studies (Arts and Humanities; Behavioural Sciences; Design; Health Sciences; Literacy Education; Media Studies; Natural Sciences; Psychology; Social and Community Services); **Administrative Studies** (Administration; Health Administration; Information Management; Law); **Business and Entrepreneurship** (Accountancy; Business Administration; Hotel and Restaurant; Human Resources; International Business; Leadership; Management; Marketing; Military Science; Occupational Health; Safety Engineering; Sales Techniques; Small Business; Transport Management); **Community Studies** (Adult Education; Behavioural Sciences; Child Care and Development; Gerontology; Leisure Studies; Preschool Education; Psychology; Rehabilitation and Therapy; Social and Preventive Medicine; Social Work); **Computer Studies and Computer Engineering Technology** (Computer Engineering; Computer Networks; Computer Science; Software Engineering); **Construction Studies** (Civil Engineering; Construction Engineering); **Culinary Studies** *(Canadian and Food and Wine Institute)* (Cooking and Catering; Food Technology); **Electrical and Electronics Studies** (Electrical Engineering; Electronic Engineering); **Environmental Studies** (Energy Engineering; Environmental Engineering; Environmental Management; Surveying and Mapping); **Health Studies** (Dental Hygiene; Dentistry; Health Sciences; Nursing; Occupational Therapy; Paramedical Sciences; Pharmacy; Physical Therapy; Rehabilitation and Therapy; Sports); **Horticulture and Agribusiness** (Horticulture; Landscape Architecture; Viticulture); **Hospitality and Tourism** (Hotel and Restaurant; Tourism); **Language Studies** (English; French; Spanish); **Mechanical Studies** (Mechanical Engineering; Mechanics); **Media and Design** (Acting; Cinema and Television; Computer Science; Design; E- Business/Commerce; Film; Fine Arts; Graphic Design; Journalism; Media Studies; Photography; Public Relations; Radio and Television Broadcasting; Writing); **Motive Power Automotive Studies** (Automotive Engineering; Maintenance Technology); **Photonics Studies** (Engineering; Laser Engineering); **Policing and Security** (Justice Administration; Law; Police Studies; Social and Community Services); **Skilled Trades, Apprenticeships and Pre-Apprenticeships** (Automotive Engineering; Cooking and Catering; Metal Techniques; Service Trades); **Spa and Salon Studies** (Cosmetology; Service Trades); **Welding Studies** (Metal Techniques); **Winery, Viticulture and Brewery Studies** (Brewing; Management; Marketing; Viticulture)

Further Information: Also Niagara College NOTL Campus.

History: Founded 1967.

Main Language(s) of Instruction: English

Degrees and Diplomas: *Certificat et diplôme/Certificate and diploma*; *Baccalauréat/Bachelor's Degree*: **International Business.** *Diplôme et certificat de 2e cycle/Graduate Diploma and Certificate*

Student Services: Library

Last Updated: 27/03/15

NIPISSING UNIVERSITY (NU)

100 College Drive, Box 5002, North Bay, Ontario P1B 8L7
Tel: +1(705) 474-3450
Fax: +1(705) 474-1947
EMail: nuinfo@nipissingu.ca
Website: http://www.nipissingu.ca

President and Vice-Chancellor: Michael DeGagné
Tel: +1(705) 474-3461 Ext. 4286
EMail: cherylz@nipissingu.ca

Vice-President, Finance, Administration and Strategic Capital Investments: Vicky Paine-Mantha
Tel: +1(705) 474-3450 Ext. 4289 EMail: vickyp@nipissingu.ca

International Relations: Marie-Andrée Labelle, Secretary, International Student Support Services and Programs
Tel: +1(705) 474-3461 Ext. 4321
EMail: marieandreel@nipissingu.ca

Faculty

Applied and Professional Studies (Accountancy; Administration; Business Administration; Business and Commerce; Cell Biology; Child Care and Development; Commercial Law; Criminal Law; Criminology; Development Studies; Economics; English; Family Studies; Finance; Health Sciences; History; Human Resources; Information Sciences; International Business; Law; Management; Marketing; Mathematics; Medieval Studies; Molecular Biology; Nursing; Occupational Health; Philosophy; Small Business; Social Welfare; Statistics); **Arts and Science** (Adult Education; Ancient Civilizations; Art History; Arts and Humanities; Biology; Classical Languages; Computer Science; Cultural Studies; Education; English; Environmental Management; Environmental Studies; Family Studies; Fine Arts; Gender Studies; Geography; Geography (Human); Greek (Classical); Health Education; History; Human Rights; Indigenous Studies; Latin; Literature; Mathematics; Mathematics and Computer Science; Natives Education; Neurosciences; Painting and Drawing; Philosophy; Physical Education; Physical Therapy; Political Sciences; Psychology; Religion; Sculpture; Social Sciences; Social Work; Sociology; Surveying and Mapping; Writing)

School

Education *(Schulich)* (Adult Education; Education; Health Education; Natives Education; Physical Education; Primary Education; Secondary Education)

Institute

Applied Social Research *(IASR)* (Social Studies)

Research Centre

Education and the Arts *(Northern Canadian - NORCCREA)* (Education)

Further Information: Also Muskoka and Brantford regional campuses.

History: Founded 1967 as University College affiliated with Laurentian University, acquired present status 1992.

Academic Year: September to April (September-December; January-April). Also Spring and Summer Sessions (Early May-Late June; July-Mid August)

Admission Requirements: Ontario secondary school diploma (OSSD) with minimum overall average of 60% in at least 6 Academic Credits, or recognized foreign equivalent. All student visa applicants or landed immigrant applicants for admission to Faculty of Arts and Science whose first or mother tongue is not English must supply proof of proficiency in English. TOEFL test with minimum score of 550 or MELAB with minimum score of 90%

Main Language(s) of Instruction: English

Degrees and Diplomas: *Certificat et diplôme universitaire/University certificate and diploma*; *Baccalauréat/Bachelor's Degree*; *Maîtrise/Master's Degree*: **Education; Environmental Studies; History; Mathematics.** *Doctorat/Doctoral Degree*: **Education.**

Student Services: Academic Counselling, Canteen, Careers Guidance, Facilities for disabled people, Health Services, Library, Residential Facilities, Social Counselling, Sports Facilities

Publications: Nipissing Review

Academic Staff *2010-2011*	**TOTAL**
FULL-TIME	**149**
Student Numbers *2010-2011*	
All (Foreign included)	**4,838**

Part-time students, 1,051.
Last Updated: 27/03/15

OCAD UNIVERSITY (OCAD)

100 McCaul Street, Toronto, Ontario M5T 1W1
Tel: +1(416) 977-6000
Fax: +1(416) 977-6006
EMail: admissions@ocadu.ca
Website: http://www.ocad.ca

President: Sara Diamond
Tel: +1(416) 977-6000 Ext. 300 EMail: sdiamond@ocad.ca

Vice-President, Academic: Christine Bovis-Cnossen
Tel: +1(416) 977-6000 Ext. 427 EMail: cboviscnossen@ocadu.ca

International Relations: Susan Kemp, Coordinator, International Student Services and tudent Mobility/Exchange
Tel: +1(416) 977-6000 Ext. 293 EMail: international@ocad.ca

Faculty

Art (Art Criticism; Fine Arts; Media Studies; Painting and Drawing; Photography; Printing and Printmaking; Sculpture); **Design** (Advertising and Publicity; Ceramic Art; Design; Graphic Design; Handicrafts; Industrial Design; Jewellery Art; Painting and Drawing); **Liberal Studies** (Arts and Humanities; English; Mathematics; Natural Sciences; Social Sciences; Technology; Visual Arts)

Programme

Aboriginal Visual Culture (Indigenous Studies; Visual Arts); **Alternative Studies** (Design; Fine Arts); **English Language** (English); **Graduate Studies** (Advertising and Publicity; Art Criticism; Art History; Design; Fine Arts; Media Studies)

Course

Continuing Studies (Art History; Design; Multimedia; Painting and Drawing; Photography; Sculpture); **DFI (Digital Futures Initiative)** (Media Studies; Multimedia); **Interdisciplinary Studies** (Media Studies; Technology; Visual Arts)

History: Founded 1876 as the Ontario School of Art. Became Ontario College of Art and Design, 1996. Aquired present title and status 2010.

Main Language(s) of Instruction: English

Degrees and Diplomas: *Baccalauréat/Bachelor's Degree*; *Maîtrise/Master's Degree*: **Design; Fine Arts; Media Studies.** *Diplôme et certificat de 2e cycle/Graduate Diploma and Certificate*: **Fine Arts.**

Student Services: Library, Sports Facilities

Academic Staff *2014-2015*: Total 250
Student Numbers *2014-2015*: Total 4,827
Last Updated: 27/03/15

QUEEN'S UNIVERSITY (QUEEN'S)

99 University Avenue, Kingston, Ontario K7L 3N6
Tel: +1(613) 533-2000
Fax: +1(613) 533-6300
EMail: admissn@post.queensu.ca
Website: http://queensu.ca

Principal and Vice-Chancellor: Daniel Woolf (2009-)
Tel: +1(613) 533-2201 EMail: Principal@Queensu.ca

Registrar: John Metcalfe Tel: +1(613) 533-2045

International Relations: Kathy O'Brien, Associate Vice-Principal, International EMail: kathy.obrien@queensu.ca

Faculty

Arts and Science (Anatomy; Ancient Civilizations; Arabic; Archaeology; Art History; Asian Religious Studies; Astronomy and Space Science; Bible; Biochemistry; Biological and Life Sciences; Biology; Cell Biology; Chemistry; Chinese; Classical Languages; Cognitive Sciences; Computer Science; Design; Development Studies; Economics; English; Environmental Studies; Ethics; Film; Fine Arts; French Studies; Gender Studies; Geography; Geography (Human); Geological Engineering; Geology; German; Greek; Greek (Classical); Health Education; Health Sciences; Hebrew; Heritage Preservation; History; History of Religion; Immunology; Italian; Japanese; Jewish Studies; Latin; Linguistics; Literature; Mathematics; Mathematics and Computer Science; Media Studies; Microbiology; Music; Music Education; Music Theory and Composition; Musical Instruments; Musicology; Painting and Drawing; Pharmacology; Philosophy; Physical Education; Physical Engineering; Physical Therapy; Physics; Physiology; Political Sciences; Psychology; Religious Studies; Sociology; Software Engineering; Spanish; Statistics; Surveying and Mapping; Theatre; Theology; Toxicology); **Education** (Education; Natives Education; Primary Education; Teacher Training); **Engineering and Applied Science** (Chemical Engineering; Chemistry; Civil Engineering; Computer Engineering; Electrical Engineering; Engineering; Geological Engineering; Materials Engineering; Mathematics; Mechanical Engineering; Mining Engineering; Physics); **Health Sciences**

(Anaesthesiology; Anatomy; Biochemistry; Cardiology; Cell Biology; Endocrinology; Epidemiology; Ethics; Gastroenterology; Gerontology; Gynaecology and Obstetrics; Haematology; Health Sciences; Immunology; Medicine; Microbiology; Molecular Biology; Nephrology; Neurology; Nursing; Occupational Therapy; Oncology; Ophthalmology; Otorhinolaryngology; Paediatrics; Pathology; Pharmacology; Physical Therapy; Physiology; Plastic Surgery; Psychiatry and Mental Health; Public Health; Radiology; Rehabilitation and Therapy; Respiratory Therapy; Rheumatology; Surgery; Toxicology; Urology); **Law** (Civil Law; Commercial Law; Comparative Law; Constitutional Law; Criminal Law; Economics; European Union Law; Fiscal Law; Human Rights; International Law; Labour Law; Law; Private Law; Public Law)

School

Business (Accountancy; Business Administration; Business and Commerce; Data Processing; Economics; Finance; Human Resources; Information Sciences; International Business; Labour and Industrial Relations; Leadership; Management; Marketing; Operations Research; Small Business; Statistics; Taxation); **Graduate Studies** (Anatomy; Archaeology; Art History; Astronomy and Space Science; Biochemistry; Biology; Biomedical Engineering; Business Administration; Cell Biology; Chemical Engineering; Chemistry; Civil Engineering; Classical Languages; Computer Engineering; Computer Science; Cultural Studies; Development Studies; Economics; Education; Electrical Engineering; Engineering; English; Environmental Studies; Epidemiology; French Studies; Gender Studies; Geography; Geological Engineering; Geology; German; Greek (Classical); Health Sciences; Heritage Preservation; History; Immunology; Labour and Industrial Relations; Latin; Law; Management; Materials Engineering; Mathematics; Mechanical Engineering; Microbiology; Mining Engineering; Molecular Biology; Neurosciences; Nursing; Occupational Therapy; Oncology; Pathology; Pharmacology; Philosophy; Physical Engineering; Physical Therapy; Physics; Physiology; Political Sciences; Psychology; Public Administration; Public Health; Regional Planning; Rehabilitation and Therapy; Religious Studies; Sociology; Statistics; Town Planning; Toxicology); **Religion** (Asian Religious Studies; Christian Religious Studies; Islamic Theology; Religious Studies; Theology)

Institute

Energy and Environmental Policy *(Queen's)* (Energy Engineering; Environmental Engineering); **Intergovernmental Relations** (International Relations); **Study of Economic Policy** *(John Deutsch)* (Economic and Finance Policy)

Centre

Advanced Materials and Manufacturing *(Queen's RMC)* (Materials Engineering; Production Engineering); **Biological Communication** (Biological and Life Sciences); **Geoengineering** (Geological Engineering); **Health Services and Policy Research** (Health Administration); **Industrial Relations** (Labour and Industrial Relations); **International Relations** (International Relations); **Manufacturing of Advanced Ceramics and Nanomaterials** (Ceramics and Glass Technology; Nanotechnology); **Monieson** (Economics; Human Resources; Management); **Neuroscience Studies** (Neurosciences); **Obesity Research and Education** (Dietetics); **Studies in Primary Care** (Health Sciences); **Study of Democracy** (Political Sciences); **Surveillance Studies**; **Water and the Environment** (Environmental Studies; Water Science)

Laboratory

High Performance Computing Virtual *(HPCVL)* (Computer Engineering)

Research Centre

Fuell Cell *(Queen's -RMC/FCRC)*; **Human Mobility** (Demography and Population); **Southern African** (African Studies); **Sudbury Neutrino Observatory**

Research Institute

Cancer (Oncology)

Further Information: Also Branch in British Columbia. Also distance education courses.

History: Founded 1841 by Royal Charter issued by Queen Victoria. Modelled on the University of Edinburgh, Scottish academic influences have helped to mould its character. A national institution privately endowed and privately controlled.

Academic Year: September to April (September-December; January-April)

Admission Requirements: Secondary school certificate or recognized foreign equivalent

Fees: (Can. Dollars): Undergraduate tuition, 5,135-13,170 per annum (18,228 for Medical studies programmes) for Canadian students and 17,135-26,504.50 per annum (65,000 for Medical studies programmes) for International students. Graduate tuition, 6,258-9,054 per annum for Canadian students and 9,883-18,300 per annum for International students. MBA, 65,000 for Canadian students and 70,000 for International students

Main Language(s) of Instruction: English

Degrees and Diplomas: *Certificat et diplôme universitaire/University certificate and diploma*; *Baccalauréat/Bachelor's Degree*; *Baccalauréat spécialisé/Bachelor's Degree - Honours*; *Maîtrise/Master's Degree*: **Business Administration.** *Diplôme et certificat de 2e cycle/Graduate Diploma and Certificate*; *Doctorat/Doctoral Degree.* Executive MBA, 16 months; Dual Degree Programme (5 yrs), allowing students to complete degrees from two different Faculties or Schools concurrently at Queen's University; Double degree: Master of Management - Global Management degree/master's degree from one of Queen's University's international business school partners.

Student Services: Academic Counselling, Canteen, Careers Guidance, Cultural Activities, Facilities for disabled people, Foreign Studies Centre, Health Services, Language Laboratory, Library, Nursery Care, Social Counselling, Sports Facilities

Publications: Inventory of Research in Progress; Queen's Quarterly

Publishing House: McGill-Queen's University Press

Academic Staff *2014-2015*	**TOTAL**
FULL-TIME	**3,014**
Student Numbers *2014-2015*	
All (Foreign included)	**24,582**
FOREIGN ONLY	**1413**

Part-time students, 2,927.

Last Updated: 27/03/15

ROYAL MILITARY COLLEGE OF CANADA

Royal Military College of Canada/Collège militaire royal du Canada (RMCC)

P.O. Box 17000, Station Forces, Kingston,
Ontario K7K 7B4
Tel: + 1(613) 541-6000
Fax: + 1(613) 542-3565
EMail: liaison@rmc.ca
Website: http://www.rmc.ca

Principal: Harry James Kowal (2013-)
Tel: + 1(613) 541-6000 Ext. 3880
EMail: principals.office@rmc.ca

Registrar: Raymond Stouffer Tel: + 1(613) 541-6000 Ext. 6302

Faculty

Arts (Business Administration; Economics; French; French Studies; History; Leadership; Linguistics; Military Science; Political Sciences; Psychology; Social Sciences); **Engineering** (Aeronautical and Aerospace Engineering; Chemical Engineering; Civil Engineering; Computer Engineering; Electrical Engineering; Engineering; Materials Engineering; Mechanical Engineering); **Science** (Astronomy and Space Science; Chemical Engineering; Chemistry; Computer Science; Marine Science and Oceanography; Materials Engineering; Mathematics; Mathematics and Computer Science; Physics; Sound Engineering (Acoustics))

Division

Continuing Studies *(DCS)* (Business Administration; Chemistry; Computer Science; Economics; English; French; History; Mathematics; Military Science; Physics; Political Sciences; Psychology); **Graduate Studies and Research** (Business Administration; Chemical Engineering; Chemistry; Civil Engineering; Computer Engineering; Computer Science; Electrical Engineering; Environmental Engineering; Environmental Studies; Materials Engineering; Mathematics; Mechanical Engineering; Military Science; Nuclear Engineering; Physics; Protective Services; Software Engineering)

Centre

Language (English; French; Modern Languages)

History: Founded 1876.

Academic Year: September to April (September-December; January-April)

Fees: National: Undergraduate tuition, 2,780-3,710.per term for Canadian students; Graduate tuition, 2,780-3,165 per term for Canadian students. MBA, c. 4,500 per term (Canadian Dollar), International: Undergraduate tuition, 8,750- 9,000 per term. Graduate studies, 6,200 -6,700 per term. MBA, c. 11,400 per term (Canadian Dollar)

Main Language(s) of Instruction: English

Degrees and Diplomas: *Certificat et diplôme universitaire/University certificate and diploma*; *Baccalauréat/Bachelor's Degree*; *Maîtrise/Master's Degree*: **Business Administration; Protective Services; Public Administration.** *Doctorat/Doctoral Degree*: **Protective Services.** Also Honours Bachelor's degree, 4 yrs.

Student Services: Library, Sports Facilities

Last Updated: 27/03/15

RYERSON UNIVERSITY

350 Victoria Street, Toronto, Ontario M5B 2K3
Tel: +1(416) 979-5000
Fax: +1(416) 979-5221
EMail: inquiries@acs.ryerson.ca
Website: http://ryerson.ca

Interim President: Mohamed Lachemi
EMail: mlachemi@ryerson.ca

International Relations: Marsha McEachrane, Director, RI and International Liaison Officer
Tel: +1(416) 979-5000 Ext. 6995 EMail: mmceachr@ryerson.ca

Faculty

Arts (Arts and Humanities; Business and Commerce; Criminal Law; Cultural Studies; Economics; English; Finance; French; Geography; Geography (Human); Government; History; International Economics; International Studies; Literature; Management; Philosophy; Political Sciences; Psychology; Public Administration; Religion; Social Sciences; Sociology); **Communication and Design** (Acting; Communication Arts; Communication Studies; Dance; Design; Fashion Design; Film; Interior Design; Journalism; Media Studies; Photography; Radio and Television Broadcasting; Theatre); **Community Services** (Child Care and Development; Food Science; Health Administration; Information Management; Midwifery; Nursing; Nutrition; Occupational Health; Public Health; Rehabilitation and Therapy; Rural Planning; Social Work; Town Planning); **Engineering, Architecture and Science** (Aeronautical and Aerospace Engineering; Applied Mathematics; Architecture; Biology; Biomedical Engineering; Chemical Engineering; Chemistry; Civil Engineering; Computer Engineering; Computer Science; Electrical Engineering; Engineering; Engineering Management; Industrial Engineering; Mathematics; Mechanical Engineering; Natural Sciences; Physics)

School

Graduate Studies *(Yeates)* (Aeronautical and Aerospace Engineering; Applied Mathematics; Architecture; Business Administration; Chemical Engineering; Civil Engineering; Communication Studies; Computer Engineering; Computer Networks; Computer Science; Construction Engineering; Cultural Studies; Demography and Population; Economics; Electrical Engineering; Engineering Management; Environmental Management; Fashion Design; Finance; International Economics; Journalism; Literature; Mechanical Engineering; Media Studies; Molecular Biology; Nursing; Nutrition; Philosophy; Photography; Physics; Preschool Education; Psychology; Public Administration; Social Policy; Social Work; Surveying and Mapping; Town Planning); **Management** *(Ted Rogers)* (Accountancy; Business Administration; Business Computing; Commercial Law; Economics; Finance; Hotel and Restaurant; Human Resources; Information Technology; International Business; Management; Marketing; Tourism)

Institute

Innovation and Technology Management *(IITM)* (Engineering Management); **Management and Technology** *(Diversity)* (Management; Technology); **Privacy and Cyber Crime** *(PCCI)* (Criminology); **Study of Corporate Social Responsibility** *(Ryerson - CSR)* (Sociology)

Centre

Communication *(Rogers)* (Communication Studies); **Food Security** (Food Science); **Learning Technologies** (Educational Technology); **Research Data** (Data Processing); **Study of Commercial Activity** (Business and Commerce); **Urban Energy** (Energy Engineering); **Voluntary Sector Studies** (Management; Public Administration; Social Work)

Laboratory

Analytical Centre *(Ryerson University)*; **Electric Drive Applications and Research** *(LEDAR)* (Electrical Engineering); **Experiential Design and Gaming Environments** *(EDGE)* (Software Engineering); **Human Factors Engineering** (Safety Engineering); **Human Factors in Amusement Safety** *(THRILL)* (Safety Engineering); **Network-Centric Applied Research Team** *(NCART)* (Computer Science; Information Sciences); **Propulsion Research Facility** (Aeronautical and Aerospace Engineering); **Robotics and Manufacturing Automation** (Automation and Control Engineering; Robotics); **Science of Music, Auditory Research and Technology** *(SMART)* (Music)

Research Centre

Caribbean *(Ryerson)* (Caribbean Studies); **GTA Forum - Planning; Human Factors in Amusement Safety** (Safety Engineering); **Immigration and Settlement** *(Joint Centre of Excellence for Research)* (Demography and Population); **Interdisciplinary Human Factors** (Safety Engineering); **Progressive Research Portal** *(sponsored by the CAW-Sam Gindin Chair in Social Justice and Democracy)*; **Social Reporting Network** *(Ryerson)* (Social Studies); **Toronto Region Statistics Canada** (Data Processing; Statistics)

Research Group

Signal Analysis *(SAR)* (Electrical Engineering)

Research Institute

International (International Business)

Research Laboratory

Heat Transfer (Heating and Refrigeration); **Infoscape** (Media Studies); **Multimedia** *(Ryerson University)* (Multimedia)

Chair

Management of Technological Change in Retailing (Engineering Management; Retailing and Wholesaling)

History: Founded 1948 as Ryerson Institute of Technology, became Ryerson Polytechnic Institute 1963 and acquired present status and title 1993. Ryerson combines a traditional focus on theory with career-oriented emphasis on applicable skills-through laboratory work, field trips, outside projects, work experience, internships, regular contact with business and industry and work experience in the professional community.

Academic Year: September to April (September-December; January-April). Also 2 seven week summer sessions

Admission Requirements: If graduating with OACs, most Ryerson programmes/schools encourage 70% or higher in six OACs, or equivalent, and include the required subject prerequisite within these averages. If graduating under the new curriculum effective 2003, most Ryerson programmes/schools encourage 70% or higher in a minimum of six Grade 12 U or U/C credits, and include the required subject prerequisite within these averages. Applicants from a country where English is not the first language, or where English is an official language but not the first language are required to provide proof of English proficiency at a satisfactory level. Eligibility for admission will be based on an assessment of academic and, when applicable, non-academic factors, such as audition, admission essay, interview, portfolio, etc. For the Diploma of Arts Programme and the pre-University Studies option, the minimum requirements is the OSSD.

Fees: Undergraduate fees, 5,758.15- 8,267.88 per annum for Canadian students and 17,498.19-19,148.43 per annum for International students; Master's degree, 4,785.03 per annum (Communication and Culture) to 19,479.30 per annum (MBA and Computer Networks) for Canadian students and 16,159.83-34,097.25 per annum for International students; PhD, 4,785.03 per annum (Communication and Culture) to 8,014.68 per annum (Engineering) for

Canadian students and 16,159.86 to 17,295.27 per annum for International students (Canadian Dollar)

Main Language(s) of Instruction: English

Degrees and Diplomas: *Certificat et diplôme universitaire/University certificate and diploma*; *Baccalauréat/Bachelor's Degree*; *Maîtrise/Master's Degree*; *Diplôme et certificat de 2e cycle/Graduate Diploma and Certificate*; *Doctorat/Doctoral Degree*: **Aeronautical and Aerospace Engineering; Biomedical Engineering; Chemical Engineering; Civil Engineering; Communication Studies; Computer Engineering; Computer Science; Cultural Studies; Economics; Electrical Engineering; Industrial Engineering; Mechanical Engineering; Molecular Biology; Political Sciences; Psychology.** PhD and Master's degree in Communication and Culture are jointly offered with York University.

Student Services: Academic Counselling, Canteen, Careers Guidance, Cultural Activities, Facilities for disabled people, Health Services, Library, Nursery Care, Social Counselling, Sports Facilities

Publications: Eyeopener (during school year); Forum (during school year); Night Views (during school year); Ryerson Magazine; Ryersonian (during semester)

Academic Staff *2014-2015*	TOTAL
FULL-TIME	2,700

Student Numbers *2014-2015*	
All (Foreign included)	38,950
FOREIGN ONLY	680

Last Updated: 27/03/15

SENECA COLLEGE

1750 Finch Avenue East, North York, Ontario M2J 2X5
Tel: +1(416) 491-5050
Fax: +1(416) 493-3958
EMail: admissions@senecacollege.ca
Website: http://senecacollege.ca/

President: David Agnew
Tel: +1(416) 491-5050 Ext. 77001
EMail: president@senecacollege.ca

Section

Visual Arts (Advertising and Publicity; Graphic Design; Media Studies; Photography; Public Relations; Radio and Television Broadcasting; Visual Arts)

Sector

Academic Studies (Arts and Humanities; English; Natural Sciences; Technology); **Accounting** (Accountancy; Business Administration; Finance); **Administration** (Administration; Business Administration; Finance; International Business; Marketing); **Advertising** (Advertising and Publicity); **Analyst** (Accountancy; Business Administration; Computer Engineering; Computer Science; Information Technology; Marketing; Software Engineering; Transport Management); **Animal Care** (Veterinary Science); **Animation** (Visual Arts); **Aviation/Pilot** (Air Transport); **Business** (Accountancy; Business Administration; Finance; Human Resources; Insurance; International Business; Management; Marketing; Small Business; Transport Management); **CNC Programming** (Mechanical Engineering); **Communications** (Advertising and Publicity; Communication Studies; Film; Information Technology; Journalism; Library Science; Media Studies; Radio and Television Broadcasting; Visual Arts); **Community Service** (Child Care and Development; Fire Science; Gerontology; Leisure Studies; Preschool Education; Social Work); **Computers** (Computer Engineering; Computer Networks; Data Processing; Electronic Engineering; Visual Arts); **Customs** (Taxation; Transport Management); **Die Design** (Mechanical Engineering); **Early Childhood Education** (Child Care and Development; Preschool Education); **Education** (Arts and Humanities; English); **Electronics** (Computer Engineering; Electronic Engineering); **Emergency Services** (Fire Science); **Engineering/Technology** (Air Transport; Building Technologies; Civil Engineering; Computer Science; Electronic Engineering; Engineering; Fire Science; Mechanical Engineering); **Environmental Studies** (Civil Engineering; Environmental Engineering; Environmental Studies; Mechanical Engineering); **Esthetics/Spa** (Cosmetology); **Fashion** (Fashion Design); **Finance** (Accountancy; Business Administration; Finance); **Fire Alarm Inspection** (Fire Science; Technology); **Fire Fighter** (Fire Science; Technology); **Fire Investigation** (Fire Science; Technology); **Fire Prevention Officer** (Fire Science; Technology); **General Machinist** (Mechanical Engineering); **Government Service** (Administration; Business Administration; Finance; Justice Administration; Law; Public Administration); **Graphic Design** (Graphic Design); **Health Sciences** (Chemical Engineering; Nursing; Optometry; Rehabilitation and Therapy); **Human Resources** (Business Administration; Human Resources); **Illustration** (Painting and Drawing); **Insurance** (Business Administration; Finance; Insurance); **Landscaping/Horticulture** (Horticulture; Landscape Architecture); **Law/Legal Services** (Justice Administration; Law; Police Studies); **Life Skills/ Employment Preparation** (Adult Education; Vocational Education); **Logistics** (Taxation; Transport Management); **Machine Design** (Machine Building; Mechanical Engineering); **Management** (Business Administration; Civil Engineering; Computer Networks; Finance; Fire Science; Management; Mechanical Engineering; Software Engineering); **Marketing** (Advertising and Publicity; Business Administration; Marketing); **Media** (Journalism; Media Studies; Radio and Television Broadcasting); **Mould Design** (Mechanical Engineering); **Mould Maker** (Mechanical Engineering); **Networking** (Automation and Control Engineering; Computer Engineering; Computer Networks; Computer Science; Electronic Engineering); **Photography** (Photography); **Policing** (Police Studies); **Preparatory Programs**; **Programming** (Computer Engineering; Computer Science; Data Processing); **Public Administration** (Justice Administration; Public Administration); **Recreation/Parks** (Environmental Management; Landscape Architecture; Leisure Studies); **Sales/Merchandising** (Advertising and Publicity; Business Administration; Cosmetology; Design; Graphic Design; Management; Marketing; Sales Techniques; Small Business; Visual Arts); **Science/Research** (Biotechnology; Forensic Medicine and Dentistry; Laboratory Techniques; Pharmacy); **Skilled Trades** (Mechanical Engineering); **Social Services** (Gerontology; Social Work); **Sprinkler Design** (Fire Science); **Technical** (Communication Studies; Data Processing); **Technician/Technology** (Biotechnology; Building Technologies; Chemical Engineering; Civil Engineering; Computer Networks; Fire Science; Laboratory Techniques; Mechanical Engineering); **Therapeutic Recreationist** (Rehabilitation and Therapy); **Tool and Die** (Mechanical Engineering); **Tourism/Leisure Services** (Hotel and Restaurant; Leisure Studies; Tourism)

Further Information: Also Buttonville, Jane, King, Markham, Newham, York and Community campuses.

History: Founded 1966.

Main Language(s) of Instruction: English

Degrees and Diplomas: *Certificat et diplôme/Certificate and diploma*; *Baccalauréat/Bachelor's Degree*; *Diplôme et certificat de 2e cycle/Graduate Diploma and Certificate*. Collaborative Bachelor's degree in Nursing with York University; Advanced Diploma, 3yrs.
Last Updated: 27/03/15

SHERIDAN COLLEGE INSTITUTE OF TECHNOLOGY AND ADVANCED LEARNING

1430 Trafalgar Road, Oakville, Ontario L6H 2L1
Tel: +1(905) 845-9430
Fax: +1(905) 815-4002
Website: http://www.sheridancollege.ca

President: Jeff Zabudsky (2009-)
Tel: +1(905) 845-9430 Ext. 4020
EMail: jeff.zabudsky@sheridanc.on.ca

Provost and Vice President, Academic: Mary Preece
EMail: mary.preece@sheridanc.on.ca

Faculty

Animation, Arts and Design (Art History; Ceramic Art; Communication Arts; Computer Graphics; Crafts and Trades; Design; Film; Fine Arts; Glass Art; Information Technology; Interior Design; Journalism; Media Studies; Painting and Drawing; Performing Arts; Photography; Radio and Television Broadcasting; Sculpture; Theatre; Visual Arts); **Applied Health and Community Studies** (Anatomy; Animal Husbandry; Arts and Humanities; Behavioural Sciences; Biology; Business Administration; Chemistry; Cosmetology; Education; English; Health Sciences; Mathematics; Pharmacy; Physiology; Preschool Education; Rehabilitation and Therapy; Social and Community Services; Social Sciences); **Applied**

Science and Technology (Architecture; Chemical Engineering; Chemistry; Computer Engineering; Computer Networks; Computer Science; Data Processing; Electrical Engineering; Electronic Engineering; Environmental Management; Information Sciences; Information Technology; Laboratory Techniques; Mechanical Engineering; Metal Techniques; Multimedia; Safety Engineering; Software Engineering; Systems Analysis; Technology; Telecommunications Engineering); **Humanities and Social Sciences** (Anthropology; Arts and Humanities; Biology; Chemistry; Communication Studies; Criminology; English; Mathematics; Social Sciences; Sociology)

School

Business *(Pilon)* (Accountancy; Administration; Advertising and Publicity; Banking; Business Administration; Finance; Human Resources; International Business; Law; Management; Marketing; Tourism)

Further Information: Traditional and Open Learning Institution. Also Davis and Mississauga campuses and Oakville Skills Training Centre.

History: Founded 1967.

Fees: (Canadian Dollar): Full-Time Tuition Fee, 1,135-1,160 per Term

Degrees and Diplomas: *Grade appliquée/Applied Degree*; *Certificat et diplôme universitaire/University certificate and diploma*; *Baccalauréat/Bachelor's Degree*; *Diplôme et certificat de 2e cycle/ Graduate Diploma and Certificate.* Also advanced diploma, 2-3 yrs.

Student Services: Library, Sports Facilities

Last Updated: 27/03/15

ST. JEROME'S UNIVERSITY (UNIVERSITY OF WATERLOO) (SJU)

290 Westmount Road, North, Waterloo, Ontario N2L 3G3
Tel: +1(519) 884-8110
Fax: +1(519) 884-5759
EMail: webmaster@usjc.uwaterloo.ca
Website: http://www.sju.ca

President and Vice-Chancellor: Katherine Bergman (2012-)
Tel: +1(519) 884-8111, Ext.28245

Vice President Academic and Dean: Scott Kline
EMail: scott.kline@uwaterloo.ca

Faculty

Arts (Accountancy; Anthropology; Arts and Humanities; Business Administration; Classical Languages; Communication Studies; Computer Science; Criminology; Development Studies; Eastern European Studies; Economics; English; Family Studies; Fine Arts; French Studies; Gender Studies; Geography; German; Greek (Classical); History; Human Resources; International Business; Latin; Latin American Studies; Law; Medieval Studies; Music; Philosophy; Political Sciences; Psychology; Religious Studies; Russian; Social Sciences; Sociology; Spanish; Speech Studies; Statistics; Theatre; Women's Studies); **Mathematics** (Accountancy; Business Administration; Computer Science; Insurance; Mathematics; Mathematics and Computer Science)

Programme

Interdisciplinary (Cognitive Sciences; Criminology; Development Studies; East Asian Studies; Economics; Family Studies; Fine Arts; Gender Studies; Human Resources; International Studies; Jewish Studies; Law; Management; Medieval Studies; Peace and Disarmament; Performing Arts; Religion; Religious Music; Speech Studies; Women's Studies); **Master of Catholic Thought** (Catholic Theology)

Further Information: Also 3 affiliated colleges

History: Founded 1865 as St. Jerome's College, acquired present status and title 1959. Federated to University of Waterloo.

Academic Year: September to August (September-December; January-April; May-August)

Fees: National: First-year tuition (2 academic terms/8 months), c. 6,100 (Canadian Dollar), International: First-year tuition (2 academic terms/8 months), c. 21,000 (Canadian Dollar)

Main Language(s) of Instruction: English

Degrees and Diplomas: *Baccalauréat/Bachelor's Degree*; *Maîtrise/Master's Degree*: **Christian Religious Studies.** Degrees are offered by the University of Waterloo. Also Honours Bachelor's degree, 4 yrs; Double Degrees in 5 yrs jointly offered by University of Waterloo and Wilfred Laurier University: Business Administration/ Computer Science; Business Administration and Mathematics.

Student Services: Academic Counselling, Canteen, Cultural Activities, Facilities for disabled people, Health Services, Nursery Care, Social Counselling, Sports Facilities

Last Updated: 30/03/15

TRENT UNIVERSITY

1600 West Bank Drive, Peterborough, Ontario K9J 7B8
Tel: +1(705) 748-1011
Fax: +1(705) 748-1246
EMail: communications@trentu.ca
Website: http://trentu.ca

President and Vice-Chancellor: Leo Groarke
Tel: +1(705) 748-1090 EMail: leogroarke@trentu.ca

Provost and Vice-President, Academic: Gary Boir
Tel: +1(705) 748-1011 Ext. 7695 EMail: provost@trentu.ca

International Relations: Michael Allcott, Director, international Programmes
Tel: +1(705) 748-1314 EMail: michaelallcott@trentu.ca

Unit

Trail Studies *(Trent-Fleming)* (Economics; Education; Environmental Studies; Health Sciences; Heritage Preservation; Parks and Recreation; Tourism)

Programme

Biochemistry and Molecular Biology (Biochemistry; Molecular Biology); **Business Administration** (Business Administration; Development Studies; Human Resources; Management); **Chemical Physics** (Chemistry; Physics); **Computing and Physics** (Computer Science; Physics); **Concurrent Teacher Education** *(Queen's-Trent)* (Art Education; Computer Education; Foreign Languages Education; Humanities and Social Science Education; Mathematics Education; Native Language Education; Science Education; Teacher Training); **Degree Completion Options** *(for Students at Ontario Community Colleges)* (Biology; Business Administration; Chemistry; Computer Science; Environmental Studies; Information Technology; Natural Resources); **Diploma Studies** (Canadian Studies; Development Studies; Environmental Studies; Indigenous Studies; Native Language; Natives Education); **Ecological Restoration** (Ecology); **Emphasis** (Agriculture; Anthropology; Archaeology; Ethics; Food Science; International Economics; International Studies; Law; Linguistics; Medieval Studies; Modern History; Museum Studies; Nordic Studies; Political Sciences; Surveying and Mapping; Teacher Training); **Environmental Chemistry** (Chemistry; Environmental Studies); **Environmental Resource Science/Studies** *(ERS)* (Chemistry; Ecology; Environmental Studies; Indigenous Studies; Natural Resources); **Forensic Science** (Biology; Chemistry; Computer Science; Forensic Medicine and Dentistry; Physics; Political Sciences; Psychology; Sociology); **Indigenous Environmental Studies** *(IES)* (Environmental Studies; Indigenous Studies); **International Development Studies** (Cultural Studies; Development Studies; Economics; Environmental Studies; Gender Studies; History; Political Sciences; Social Problems; Social Studies); **International Political Economy** (International Economics); **International Students, Study Abroad** *(Trent International)* (Business Administration; Development Studies; Economics; Education; Forensic Medicine and Dentistry; Natural Sciences; Nursing; Social Sciences); **Professional Studies** (Business Administration; Education; Forensic Medicine and Dentistry; Nursing; Teacher Training); **Psychology** (Cognitive Sciences; Developmental Psychology; Neurosciences; Psychology); **Special Programs and Opportunities** *(including Trent-Fleming Joint Programmes)* (Teacher Training)

School

Education and Professional Learning (Art Education; Computer Education; Education; Foreign Languages Education; Natives Education; Science Education; Teacher Training); **Graduate Studies** (Ancient Civilizations; Anthropology; Astronomy and Space Science; Biological and Life Sciences; Canadian Studies; Chemistry; Classical Languages; Computer Science; Cultural Studies;

Economics; Engineering; English; Environmental Studies; Geography; Greek (Classical); History; Indigenous Studies; Latin; Materials Engineering; Mathematics; Natural Resources; Physics; Political Sciences; Psychology); **Nursing** *(Trent/Fleming)* (Anatomy; Microbiology; Nursing; Pharmacology; Physiology)

Department

Ancient History and Classics (Ancient Civilizations; Archaeology; Classical Languages; Greek (Classical); Latin; Literature; Theatre); **Anthropology** (Anthropology; Archaeology; Biology; Cultural Studies; Linguistics); **Astronomy and Physics** (Astronomy and Space Science; Physics); **Biology** (Biology; Health Sciences); **Canadian Studies** (Canadian Studies); **Chemistry** (Analytical Chemistry; Biochemistry; Chemistry; Inorganic Chemistry; Organic Chemistry; Physical Chemistry); **Computing and Information Systems** *(COIS)* (Computer Science; Information Technology; Software Engineering); **Cultural Studies** (Comparative Literature; Cultural Studies; Film; Literature; Media Studies; Music; Social Sciences; Theatre; Visual Arts); **Economics** (Econometrics; Economics; Finance; International Business; Labour and Industrial Relations; Mathematics; Statistics); **English Literature** (English; Literature); **Geography** (Earth Sciences; Geography; Geography (Human); Meteorology; Natural Sciences; Soil Conservation; Soil Management; Surveying and Mapping; Town Planning; Water Science; Wildlife); **History** (History); **Indigenous Studies** (Indigenous Studies; Native American Studies; Native Language; Natives Education); **Mathematics** (Computer Science; Economics; Finance; Mathematical Physics; Mathematics; Statistics); **Modern Languages and Literatures** (French; German; Hispanic American Studies; Linguistics; Literature; Modern Languages); **Philosophy** (Ethics; Philosophy); **Politics** (Political Sciences); **Sociology** (Sociology); **Women's Studies** (Women's Studies)

Centre

Community-Based Education *(Trent)* (Education); **Kawartha World Issues** (Education)

Campus

Oshawa (Anthropology; English; Environmental Studies; History; Literature; Natural Resources; Psychology; Sociology)

Further Information: Also Oshawa campus.

History: Founded 1963 as an independent university with full degree-granting powers by an Act of the Ontario legislature which received Royal Assent in April 1963. Accepted first students 1964. Teaching takes the form of tutorial and seminar work in small groups. Undergraduates are expected to do considerable academic work outside term.

Academic Year: September to April (September-December; January-April)

Admission Requirements: Secondary school certificate or recognized foreign equivalent

Main Language(s) of Instruction: English

Degrees and Diplomas: *Certificat et diplôme universitaire/University certificate and diploma*; *Baccalauréat/Bachelor's Degree*; *Maîtrise/Master's Degree*; *Doctorat/Doctoral Degree*: **Canadian Studies; Cultural Studies; Environmental Studies; Indigenous Studies.** Also Trent-Queen's (various disciplines) Ph.D./M.A./M.Sc. Through an agreement with Queen's University in Kingston, Trent faculty may undertake the supervision and instruction of students enrolled for Masters or Ph.D. degrees at Queen's here at Trent University. Master of Materials Science offered jointly with the University of Ontario Institute of Technology.

Student Services: Academic Counselling, Canteen, Careers Guidance, Cultural Activities, Facilities for disabled people, Health Services, Nursery Care, Residential Facilities, Sports Facilities

Publications: Journal of Canadian Studies

Academic Staff *2010-2011*	MEN	WOMEN	**TOTAL**
FULL-TIME	143	96	**239**
PART-TIME	–	–	**70**
STAFF WITH DOCTORATE			
FULL-TIME	–	–	**238**
Student Numbers *2010-2011*			
All (Foreign included)	2,734	4,940	**7,674**
FOREIGN ONLY	325	163	**488**

Part-time students, 1,311.

Last Updated: 30/03/15

UNIVERSITY OF GUELPH (U OF G)

50 Stone Road East, Guelph, Ontario N1G 2W1
Tel: +1(519) 824-4120
Fax: +1(519) 766-94881
EMail: univsec@uoguelph.ca
Website: http://uoguelph.ca

President and Vice-Chancellor: Franco J. Vaccarino
Tel: +1(519) 824-4120 Ext. 52200 EMail: president@uoguelph.ca

Provost and Vice-President (Academic): Serge Desmarais
Tel: +1(519) 824-4120 Ext. 53845

College

Agriculture *(Ontario (OAC))* (Agricultural Economics; Agriculture; Animal Husbandry; Botany; Environmental Studies; Food Science; Horticulture; Landscape Architecture; Meat and Poultry; Plant and Crop Protection; Rural Planning; Rural Studies; Safety Engineering); **Arts** (Art History; Caribbean Studies; Classical Languages; English; European Studies; Fine Arts; French; French Studies; German; Greek (Classical); History; Italian; Latin; Latin American Studies; Literature; Modern Languages; Music; Philosophy; Spanish; Theatre; Visual Arts); **Biological Science** (Biological and Life Sciences; Biology; Biomedicine; Biophysics; Cell Biology; Health Sciences; Molecular Biology; Neurosciences; Nutrition; Sports; Toxicology); **Business and Economics** (Agricultural Business; Business Administration; Business and Commerce; Economics; Environmental Studies; Finance; Hotel and Restaurant; Human Resources; Leadership; Management; Marketing; Public Administration; Real Estate; Tourism); **Physical and Engineering Science** (Applied Mathematics; Bioengineering; Biological and Life Sciences; Biology; Biomedical Engineering; Biophysics; Chemistry; Computer Engineering; Computer Science; Earth Sciences; Engineering; Environmental Engineering; Environmental Studies; Forest Biology; Geology; Hydraulic Engineering; Information Sciences; Mathematics; Mechanical Engineering; Meteorology; Natural Resources; Physics; Statistics); **Social and Applied Human Sciences** (Anthropology; Child Care and Development; Clinical Psychology; Cognitive Sciences; Criminal Law; Development Studies; Earth Sciences; Environmental Studies; Family Studies; Geography; Industrial and Organizational Psychology; Neurosciences; Nutrition; Political Sciences; Psychology; Public Administration; Social Problems; Social Psychology; Social Sciences; Sociology; Surveying and Mapping); **Veterinary Science** *(Ontario)* (Biology; Biomedical Engineering; Epidemiology; Immunology; Medicine; Microbiology; Parasitology; Pathology; Public Health; Veterinary Science)

Programme

Graduate Studies (Agricultural Economics; Agriculture; Animal Husbandry; Anthropology; Aquaculture; Biology; Biomedical Engineering; Biophysics; Business Administration; Caribbean Studies; Cell Biology; Chemistry; Computer Science; Criminal Law; Criminology; Development Studies; Economics; Engineering; English; European Studies; Family Studies; Fine Arts; Food Science; Food Technology; French Studies; Geography; Health Sciences; History; Hydraulic Engineering; Landscape Architecture; Latin American Studies; Leadership; Literature; Management; Marketing; Mathematics; Meat and Poultry; Medicine; Molecular Biology; Natural Resources; Neurosciences; Nutrition; Philosophy; Physics; Political Sciences; Psychology; Public Health; Rural Planning; Rural Studies; Safety Engineering; Sociology; Statistics; Theatre; Toxicology; Veterinary Science; Visual Arts; Writing); **Research** *(U of G/OMAFRA enhanced partnership)* (Agriculture; Food Science); **University of Guelph-Humber** (Business Administration; Child Care and Development; Law; Media Studies; Physical Therapy; Psychology; Social and Community Services)

Institute

Biodiversity *(Ontario)* (Molecular Biology); **Comparative Cancer Investigation** (Oncology); **Ichthyology** *(Axelrod)* (Marine Biology); **Robotics and Intelligent Systems** (Artificial Intelligence; Robotics); **Turfgrass** *(Guelph - GTI)* (Horticulture)

Centre

Advanced Analysis (Biological and Life Sciences; Physics); **Agri-Technology Commercialization** (Agricultural Engineering; Energy Engineering; Waste Management); **Agricultural Renewable Energy and Sustainability** (Agricultural Engineering; Energy Engineering); **Aquaculture** (Aquaculture); **Arthritis Network Core Facility** *(Canadian)* (Rheumatology); **Bioproducts Discovery and**

Development (Biological and Life Sciences); **Co-operative Wildlife Health** *(Canadian)* (Wildlife); **Couple and Family Therapy** (Social Problems); **Electrochemical Technology** (Chemical Engineering; Electronic Engineering); **Families, Work and Well-being**; **Food Safety Network** (Food Technology; Safety Engineering); **Food Technology** *(Guelph - GFTC)* (Food Technology); **Genetic Improvement of Livestock** (Animal Husbandry; Genetics); **Genomics Facility/Advanced Analysis** (Genetics); **Health and Performance** (Health Sciences; Sports Medicine); **Land and Water Stewardship** (Soil Management; Water Management); **Landscape Architecture Community Outreach** (Landscape Architecture); **Language and Literacy Research Network** *(Canadian)* (Education); **Mathematics of Information Technology and Complex Systems** (Information Technology; Mathematics); **Nuclear Magnetic Resonance** (Nuclear Physics); **Nutrition Modelling** (Nutrition); **Organization and Management Solution** (Human Resources; Psychology); **Poultry Welfare** (Meat and Poultry); **Psychological Services** (Psychology); **Public Health and Zoonoses** (Public Health); **Rural Wastewater** *(Ontario)* (Water Management); **Study of Animal Welfare** *(Campbell)* (Welfare and Protective Services); **Urban Systems Environment Design** (Environmental Engineering; Town Planning); **Veterinary Teaching Hospital** (Veterinary Science); **Water Safety and Security** *(AquaSanitas)* (Public Health; Water Management); **Weather Innovation** (Meteorology)

Group

Advanced Foods and Materials Network *(AFMNet)* (Biological and Life Sciences; Ethics; Food Science; Law); **Bioconversion Network** (Energy Engineering; Environmental Engineering)

Laboratory

Advanced Robotics and Intelligent Systems (Artificial Intelligence; Automation and Control Engineering; Robotics); **Aqualab** *(Hagen)* (Aquaculture; Biology; Ecology; Physiology; Toxicology); **Laboratory Services** (Food Technology)

Research Centre

Agricultural Trade Policy and Competitive Research Network *(Canadian)* (Agricultural Business); **Arboretum Gene Bank** (Botany; Genetics); **Business Development Office** (Business Administration); **Controlled Environment Systems** (Environmental Studies); **International Leadership** (Leadership); **Metals in the Human Environment** (Environmental Studies); **Neutrino Observatory** *(Sudbury)* (Nuclear Engineering); **Pollination Initiative** *(Canadian)* (Biological and Life Sciences; Ecology; Entomology); **Shared Hierarchical Academic Research Computing Network** *(SHARCNET)* (Business Computing; Computer Science); **Transgenic Plant** *(Guelph)* (Botany; Genetics)

Research Institute

Food Safety *(Canadian - CRIFS)* (Food Technology; Safety Engineering)

Research Unit

Human Nutraceutical (Dietetics)

Further Information: Also Ontario Veterinary College Teaching Hospital. Affiliated with Collège d'Alfred, Kemptville College and Ridgetown College. Overseas study semesters in: London; Cracow; India; Latin America and Paris. 66 Study Abroad programmes in 27 countries. Open Learning Bureau offers Continuing Education, Open Learning Programmes, Distance Education and English as a Scond Language (ESL) University Preparation Programmes.

History: Founded 1964 comprising 3 colleges previously affiliated with the University of Toronto (Ontario Veterinary College, Ontario Agricultural College and Macdonald Institute).

Academic Year: September-December; January-April; May-August

Admission Requirements: Ontario Secondary School Diploma (OSSD), or equivalent

Main Language(s) of Instruction: English

Degrees and Diplomas: *Certificat et diplôme universitaire/University certificate and diploma*; *Baccalauréat/Bachelor's Degree*; *Maîtrise/Master's Degree*; *Diplôme et certificat de 2e cycle/Graduate Diploma and Certificate*; *Doctorat/Doctoral Degree*

Student Services: Academic Counselling, Canteen, Careers Guidance, Cultural Activities, Facilities for disabled people, Foreign Studies Centre, Health Services, Language Laboratory, Library, Nursery Care, Social Counselling, Sports Facilities

Publications: Research Magazine

Last Updated: 30/03/15

UNIVERSITY OF ONTARIO INSTITUTE OF TECHNOLOGY (UOIT)

2000 Simcoe Street North, Oshawa, Ontario L1H 7K4
Tel: +1(905) 721-8668
Fax: +1(905) 721-3178
EMail: admissions@uoit.ca
Website: http://uoit.ca

President and Vice-Chancellor: Tim McTiernan
Tel: +1(905) 721-8668 Ext. 3212 EMail: president@uoit.ca

Provost and vice-president, Academic: Deborah Saucier
Tel: +1(905) 721-8668 Ext. 3147 EMail: provost@uoit.ca

Faculty

Business and Information Technology (Accountancy; Business Administration; Business and Commerce; E- Business/Commerce; Finance; Human Resources; Information Technology; International Business; Management; Marketing; Transport Management); **Education** (Computer Education; Education; Mathematics Education; Science Education; Teacher Training); **Energy Systems and Nuclear Science** (Energy Engineering; Engineering; Health Sciences; Nuclear Engineering; Power Engineering; Safety Engineering); **Engineering and Applied Science** (Automotive Engineering; Electrical Engineering; Energy Engineering; Engineering; Mechanical Engineering; Nuclear Engineering; Production Engineering; Software Engineering); **Health Sciences** (Community Health; Dental Hygiene; Haematology; Health Sciences; Information Management; Laboratory Techniques; Microbiology; Nursing; Occupational Therapy; Pharmacy; Physical Therapy; Respiratory Therapy); **Science** (Applied Mathematics; Biological and Life Sciences; Chemistry; Computer Science; Forensic Medicine and Dentistry; Management; Materials Engineering; Mathematics; Physics); **Social Science and Humanities** (Arts and Humanities; Business and Commerce; Communication Studies; Constitutional Law; Criminology; Health Sciences; Human Rights; Labour Law; Law; Marketing; Media Studies; Police Studies; Social Policy; Social Sciences; Technology)

History: Founded 2002.

Fees: National: Undergraduate, 5,901.78-9,003.12 per annum for Canadian students (Canadian Dollar), International: Undergraduate,17,112.60-21,396.40 per annum (Canadian Dollar)

Main Language(s) of Instruction: English

Degrees and Diplomas: *Baccalauréat/Bachelor's Degree*; *Baccalauréat spécialisé/Bachelor's Degree - Honours*; *Maîtrise/Master's Degree*: **Business Administration; Criminology; Education; Engineering; Natural Sciences; Psychology.** *Diplôme et certificat de 2e cycle/Graduate Diploma and Certificate*; *Doctorat/Doctoral Degree*: **Computer Engineering; Computer Science; Electrical Engineering; Engineering; Materials Engineering; Mechanical Engineering; Nuclear Engineering; Psychology.** Also Concurrent BSc/BEd Five Year Teacher Education Programme, 5 yrs

Last Updated: 30/03/15

UNIVERSITY OF OTTAWA

University of Ottawa/Université d'Ottawa (UOTTAWA)
550 rue Cumberland, pièce 212, Ottawa, Ontario K1N 6N5
Tel: +1(613) 562-5700
Fax: +1(613) 562-5323
EMail: infoservice@uOttawa.ca
Website: http://www.uottawa.ca

President: Allan Rock (2008-)
Tel: +1(613) 562-5809
EMail: president@uOttawa.ca; recteur@uottawa.ca

Vice-President Academic and Provost: Christian Detellier
EMail: vpacademic@uOttawa.ca

International Relations: Gary Slater, Associate Vice-President Academic (International)
Tel: +1(613) 562-5800 Ext. 1450 EMail: avp-intl@uOttawa.ca

Faculty

Arts (Arabic; Art History; Art Management; Asian Studies; Canadian Studies; Celtic Languages and Studies; Classical Languages;

Communication Studies; Conducting; English; English Studies; Environmental Studies; Ethics; Film; Fine Arts; Foreign Languages Education; French Studies; Geography; German; Greek (Classical); History; Indigenous Studies; Information Sciences; Italian; Jewellery Art; Journalism; Latin; Latin American Studies; Linguistics; Medieval Studies; Modern History; Music; Music Education; Philosophy; Political Sciences; Psycholinguistics; Public Relations; Religious Studies; Russian; Sociology; Spanish; Surveying and Mapping; Theatre; Translation and Interpretation; Visual Arts; Women's Studies; Writing); **Education** (Canadian Studies; Cultural Studies; Education; Educational Administration; Educational and Student Counselling; Health Education; Higher Education; Literacy Education; Natives Education; Teacher Training; Technology Education; Women's Studies); **Engineering** (Aeronautical and Aerospace Engineering; Bioengineering; Biomedical Engineering; Chemical Engineering; Civil Engineering; Computer Engineering; Computer Science; E- Business/Commerce; Electrical Engineering; Engineering; Engineering Management; Environmental Engineering; Information Technology; Mechanical Engineering; Software Engineering); **Graduate and Postdoctoral Studies** (Administration; Anthropology; Behavioural Sciences; Biochemistry; Biology; Biomedical Engineering; Business Administration; Canadian Studies; Canon Law; Cell Biology; Chemical Engineering; Chemistry; Civil Engineering; Classical Languages; Communication Studies; Computer Engineering; Computer Science; Conducting; Criminology; Development Studies; E- Business/Commerce; Earth Sciences; Economic History; Economics; Education; Electrical Engineering; Engineering Management; English; Environmental Engineering; Epidemiology; Ergotherapy; Ethics; Fine Arts; French Studies; Genetics; Geography; Government; Greek; Health Administration; Health Education; Health Sciences; Higher Education; History; Immunology; Information Sciences; Information Technology; International Relations; Latin; Law; Linguistics; Management; Materials Engineering; Mathematics; Mechanical Engineering; Medical Technology; Medicine; Medieval Studies; Microbiology; Modern History; Molecular Biology; Music; Music Education; Neurosciences; Nursing; Pathology; Peace and Disarmament; Philosophy; Physical Therapy; Physics; Political Sciences; Production Engineering; Psychology; Public Administration; Public Health; Rehabilitation and Therapy; Religious Education; Religious Studies; Slavic Languages; Social and Community Services; Social Work; Sociology; Software Engineering; Spanish; Speech Therapy and Audiology; Statistics; Theatre; Theology; Toxicology; Translation and Interpretation; Visual Arts; Women's Studies); **Health Sciences** (Biophysics; Health Sciences; Leisure Studies; Nursing; Occupational Therapy; Parks and Recreation; Physical Therapy; Physiology; Psychology; Public Health; Social Sciences; Speech Therapy and Audiology; Sports; Sports Management); **Law** (Civil Law; Environmental Studies; Human Rights; International Law; Labour Law; Law); **Medicine** (Anaesthesiology; Biochemistry; Cardiology; Cell Biology; Community Health; Dermatology; Endocrinology; Epidemiology; Gastroenterology; Genetics; Gerontology; Gynaecology and Obstetrics; Haematology; Immunology; Laboratory Techniques; Medicine; Microbiology; Molecular Biology; Nephrology; Neurology; Oncology; Ophthalmology; Otorhinolaryngology; Paediatrics; Pathology; Physical Therapy; Plastic Surgery; Psychiatry and Mental Health; Public Health; Radiology; Rehabilitation and Therapy; Respiratory Therapy; Rheumatology; Surgery; Urology); **Science** (Biochemistry; Biological and Life Sciences; Biology; Biomedicine; Chemical Engineering; Chemistry; Computer Science; Earth Sciences; Economics; Environmental Studies; Geology; Geophysics; Mathematics; Pharmacy; Physics; Science Education; Statistics; Toxicology); **Social Sciences** (Anthropology; Civil Law; Clinical Psychology; Criminology; Development Studies; Economics; Experimental Psychology; French; Gerontology; Government; Human Rights; International Economics; International Studies; Law; Modern Languages; Peace and Disarmament; Political Sciences; Psychology; Public Administration; Social and Community Services; Social Sciences; Social Work; Sociology; Women's Studies)

School

Management *(Telfer)* (Accountancy; Business Administration; Business and Commerce; E- Business/Commerce; Finance; Health Administration; Human Resources; International Business; Leadership; Management; Marketing)

Department

Professional Training Service (Communication Studies; Grammar; Management; Writing)

Institute

Brain and Mind *(University of Ottawa)* (Behavioural Sciences; Neurosciences); **Canadian Studies** (Canadian Studies); **Environment** (Environmental Studies); **Medical Devices Innovation** (Medical Technology); **Official Languages and Bilingualism** *(OLBI)* (English; French; Modern Languages); **Population Health** (Public Health); **Prevention of Crime** *(IPC)* (Criminal Law; Criminology; Police Studies); **Science, Society and Policy** *(ISSP)*; **Systems Biology** *(Ottawa)* (Biology); **Women's Studies** (Women's Studies)

Centre

Advanced Research in Environmental Genomics *(CAREG)* (Genetics); **Catalysis Research and Innovation**; **Environmental Law and Global Sustainability** (Environmental Studies; Law); **Environmental Microbiology** *(CREM)* (Microbiology); **Governance** (Government); **Hazard Mitigation and Emergency Management** (Safety Engineering); **Human Rights Research and Education** (Human Rights); **Interdisciplinary Research on Citizenship and Minorities** *(CIRCEM)*; **International Policy Studies** *(CIPS)* (International Studies); **Law, Technology and Society** (Law; Technology); **Neural Dynamics** (Neurosciences); **Neuromuscular Disease** *(University of Ottawa)* (Medicine; Neurology; Pathology)

Research Centre

Accounting *(CGA)* (Accountancy); **Biopharmaceuticals and Biotechnology** (Biotechnology; Pharmacy); **Educational and Community Services** *(CRECS)* (Education; Social and Community Services); **Emerging Pathogens** *(University of Ottawa)* (Epidemiology); **French Canadian Culture** (Canadian Studies; French Studies); **Photonics** (Electrical and Electronic Engineering); **Sport in Canadian Society** (Sports); **Tax** *(CGA)* (Taxation)

Further Information: Also 6 Teaching Hospitals

History: Founded 1848 as College of Bytown, became College of Ottawa 1933. Acquired present status and title 1965.

Academic Year: September to August (September-December; January-April; May-August)

Admission Requirements: Senior secondary school diploma, or recognized foreign equivalent

Main Language(s) of Instruction: French, English

Accrediting Agency: Association Canadienne des Orthophonistes et Audiologistes (ACOA), Health Services Administration (ACEHSA), American Psychological Association

Degrees and Diplomas: *Certificat et diplôme universitaire/University certificate and diploma*; *Baccalauréat/Bachelor's Degree*; *Baccalauréat spécialisé/Bachelor's Degree - Honours*; *Maîtrise/Master's Degree*; *Diplôme et certificat de 2e cycle/Graduate Diploma and Certificate*; *Doctorat/Doctoral Degree*: **Arts and Humanities; Education; Educational and Student Counselling; Engineering; Epidemiology; Health Sciences; Law; Management; Natural Sciences; Social Sciences; Theology.** Also Ottawa-Carleton Joint Programs (Doctorate)

Student Services: Academic Counselling, Canteen, Careers Guidance, Cultural Activities, Facilities for disabled people, Foreign Studies Centre, Health Services, Language Laboratory, Library, Nursery Care, Social Counselling, Sports Facilities

Publishing house: Presses de l'Université d'Ottawa/University of Ottawa Press

Last Updated: 30/03/15

SAINT PAUL UNIVERSITY

SAINT PAUL UNIVERSITY/UNIVERSITÉ SAINT PAUL
223 Main Street, Ottawa, Ontario K1S 1C4
Tel: + 1(613) 236-1393 + 1(800) 637-685
Fax: + 1(613) 782-3005
EMail: info@ustpaul.ca
Website: http://www.ustpaul.ca

Rectrice: Chantal Beauvais (2009-)
Tel: + 1(613) 236-1393 EMail: rectrice-rector@ustpaul.ca

Registrar/Registraire: Claudette Dubé-Socqué
Tel: + 1(613) 236-1393 EMail: csocque@ustpaul.ca

Vice-Rector Academic and Research: Jean-Marc Barrette

Faculty

Canon Law (Administration; Canon Law); **Human Sciences** (Communication Studies; Peace and Disarmament; Psychology;

Religious Studies); **Philosophy** (Arts and Humanities; Ethics; Philosophy; Theology); **Theology** (Christian Religious Studies; Ethics; Missionary Studies; Pastoral Studies; Religion; Religious Education; Religious Studies; Theology)

Institute

Eastern Christian Studies *(Metropolitan Andrey Sheptytsky)* (Christian Religious Studies)

Centre

Ethics (Ethics); **Lonergan** (Business Administration; Ethics; Peace and Disarmament; Religion); **Women and Christian Traditions** (Bible; Ethics; History; Pastoral Studies; Psychology; Religion; Theology)

Research Centre

Conflict (Peace and Disarmament); **Religious History of Canada** (History of Religion)

History: Founded 1848 as College of Byton. A Federated institution whose degree-granting authority is held in abeyance with the University of Ottawa.

Academic Year: September to April (September-December; January-April). Also Summer Session

Admission Requirements: Secondary school certificate or recognized equivalent

Fees: National: Full time Canadian students, Undergraduate tuiton, 2,344.97 per semester. Graduate tuition, 2,500.11 per semester (Canadian Dollar), International: Full time International student, Undergraduate tuiton, 5,895.46 per semester. Graduate tuition, 5,955.24 per semester

Main Language(s) of Instruction: French, English

Degrees and Diplomas: *Certificat et diplôme universitaire/University certificate and diploma*; *Baccalauréat/Bachelor's Degree*; *Baccalauréat spécialisé/Bachelor's Degree - Honours*: **Theology.** *Maîtrise/Master's Degree*: **Canon Law; Religious Education; Theology.** *Diplôme et certificat de 2e cycle/Graduate Diploma and Certificate*: **Canon Law.** *Doctorat/Doctoral Degree*: **Canon Law; Peace and Disarmament; Social Psychology; Theology.** Also Honours Bachelor's degree programmes; Ecclesiastical Programmes (Bachelor's degree, Licenciate and Doctorate) in Philosophy.

Student Services: Academic Counselling, Canteen, Careers Guidance, Facilities for disabled people, Library, Social Counselling, Sports Facilities

Publications: Locos; Mission, Revue des Sciences de la Mission; Pastoral Sciences-Sciences pastorales; Studia Canonica; Theoforum

Publishing House: Novalis

UNIVERSITY OF TORONTO (U OF T)

563 Spadina Crescent, Toronto, Ontario M5S 2J7
Tel: +1(416) 978-2011
Fax: +1(416) 978-7022
EMail: ut.info@utoronto.ca
Website: http://utoronto.ca

President: Meric Gertler (2013-)
Tel: +1(416) 978-2121 EMail: president@utoronto.ca

Vice-President and Provost: Cheryl Regehr
Tel: +1(416) 978-4865 EMail: provost@utoronto.ca

International Relations: Vinitha Gengatharan, Director, International Relations
Tel: +1(416) 978-8828
EMail: international.relations@utoronto.ca; vinitha.gengatharan@utoronto.ca

Faculty

Applied Science and Engineering (Aeronautical and Aerospace Engineering; Applied Chemistry; Bioengineering; Biomedical Engineering; Chemical Engineering; Civil Engineering; Computer Engineering; Electrical Engineering; Energy Engineering; Engineering; Environmental Engineering; Industrial Engineering; Materials Engineering; Mechanical Engineering; Mining Engineering; Nanotechnology); **Architecture, Landscape, and Design** *(John H. Daniels)* (Architecture; Design; Landscape Architecture); **Arts and Science** (Actuarial Science; African Studies; American Studies; Anthropology; Archaeology; Architecture; Art History; Artificial Intelligence; Arts and Humanities; Asian Religious Studies; Asian Studies; Astronomy and Space Science; Astrophysics; Biology; Business and Commerce; Canadian Studies; Caribbean Studies; Cell Biology; Celtic Languages and Studies; Chemistry; Christian Religious Studies; Cinema and Television; Classical Languages; Communication Studies; Comparative Literature; Computer Science; Criminology; East Asian Studies; Ecology; Economics; Electrical Engineering; English; Environmental Studies; Ethics; Eurasian and North Asian Languages; European Studies; Finance; Fine Arts; Foreign Languages Education; French; French Studies; Gender Studies; Genetics; Geography; Geology; German; Government; Greek (Classical); Health Sciences; History; Human Resources; Hungarian; Immunology; Indigenous Studies; Inorganic Chemistry; International Economics; International Law; International Relations; International Studies; Italian; Jewish Studies; Korean; Labour and Industrial Relations; Latin; Latin American Studies; Law; Linguistics; Literature; Materials Engineering; Mathematics; Medieval Studies; Modern History; Multimedia; Optics; Pacific Area Studies; Peace and Disarmament; Philosophy; Physics; Political Sciences; Polymer and Plastics Technology; Portuguese; Psychiatry and Mental Health; Psychology; Public Administration; Publishing and Book Trade; Religion; Russian; Slavic Languages; Sociology; South Asian Studies; Spanish; Statistics; Theatre; Urban Studies; Visual Arts; Women's Studies; Writing; Zoology); **Dentistry** (Anaesthesiology; Dental Technology; Dentistry; Oral Pathology; Orthodontics; Periodontics; Surgery); **Forestry** (Ecology; Environmental Studies; Forest Biology; Forest Economics; Forest Management; Forestry); **Information** (Information Sciences; Museum Studies); **Law** (Commercial Law; Constitutional Law; Environmental Studies; International Law; Law); **Medicine** (Anaesthesiology; Biochemistry; Biology; Biomedical Engineering; Biophysics; Community Health; Genetics; Gynaecology and Obstetrics; Health Administration; Health Sciences; Immunology; Laboratory Techniques; Medical Auxiliaries; Medical Technology; Medicine; Nutrition; Occupational Health; Occupational Therapy; Oncology; Ophthalmology; Otorhinolaryngology; Paediatrics; Pathology; Pharmacology; Physical Therapy; Physiology; Psychiatry and Mental Health; Public Health; Radiology; Rehabilitation and Therapy; Speech Therapy and Audiology; Surgery; Toxicology); **Music** (Jazz and Popular Music; Music; Music Education; Music Theory and Composition; Musical Instruments; Musicology; Opera; Singing); **Nursing** *(Lawrence S. Bloomberg)* (Anaesthesiology; Health Sciences; Nursing); **Pharmacy** *(Leslie L. Dan)* (Chemistry; Molecular Biology; Pharmacy); **Physical Education and Health** (Health Education; Physical Education); **Social Work** *(Factor-Inwentash)* (Administration; Development Studies; Family Studies; Gerontology; Social Problems; Social Work; Welfare and Protective Services)

College

Emmanuel College of Victoria University *(http://www.emmanuel.utoronto.ca/Page21.aspx)* (Pastoral Studies; Religion; Religious Education; Religious Music; Theology); **Knox** *(http://www.knox.utoronto.ca/why-knox/)* (Bible; Christian Religious Studies; Religion; Religious Studies; Theology); **Regis** *(http://www.regiscollege.ca/- Jesuit Faculty of Theology at the University of Toronto)* (Christian Religious Studies; Philosophy; Religion; Theology); **St. Augustine's Seminary** (Philosophy; Religion; Religious Education; Theology)

Programme

Transitional Year *(TYP)* (Arts and Humanities; English; Literature; Social Sciences)

School

Continuing Studies (Accountancy; Advertising and Publicity; Arabic; Architecture; Business Administration; Chinese; Communication Studies; E- Business/Commerce; English; Environmental Studies; Finance; French; German; Germanic Languages; Greek; Health Sciences; Human Resources; Italian; Japanese; Korean; Latin; Law; Leadership; Literature; Management; Marketing; Music; Persian; Philosophy; Polish; Portuguese; Public Relations; Religion; Romanian; Russian; Spanish; Translation and Interpretation; Turkish; Vietnamese; Visual Arts; Writing); **Global Affairs** *(Munk)* (American Studies; Asian Studies; Eurasian and North Asian Languages; European Studies; Hungarian; International Relations; International Studies; Korean; Latin American Studies; Pacific Area Studies; Peace and Disarmament; Russian; South Asian Studies); **Graduate Studies** (Accountancy; Adult Education; Aeronautical and Aerospace Engineering; Ancient Civilizations; Anthropology; Applied Chemistry; Architecture; Art History; Asian Studies; Astronomy and Space Science; Astrophysics; Biochemistry; Biology; Biomedical Engineering; Biophysics; Biotechnology; Cell Biology; Chemical Engineering; Chemistry; Cinema and Television; Civil Engineering; Classical Languages; Communication Studies; Community Health; Comparative Literature; Computer Engineering; Computer Science; Criminology; Cultural Studies; Curriculum; Dentistry; Design; Developmental Psychology; East Asian Studies; Ecology; Economics; Education; Educational Administration; Educational and Student Counselling; Educational Psychology; Electrical Engineering; English; Environmental Engineering; Environmental Studies; Ethics; Ethnology; Eurasian and North Asian Languages; European Studies; Finance; Foreign Languages Education; Forest Management; Forestry; French; Gender Studies; Genetics; Geography; Geology; German; Germanic Languages; Gerontology; Government; Greek (Classical); Health Administration; Health Sciences; Higher Education; History; Human Resources; Immunology; Indigenous Studies; Industrial Engineering; Information Sciences; International Relations; International Studies; Italian; Jewish Studies; Labour and Industrial Relations; Landscape Architecture; Latin; Law; Linguistics; Literature; Management; Materials Engineering; Mathematics; Mechanical Engineering; Medical Technology; Medicine; Medieval Studies; Middle Eastern Studies; Museum Studies; Music; Musical Instruments; Neurosciences; Nursing; Nutrition; Occupational Health; Occupational Therapy; Optics; Pacific Area Studies; Pathology; Pharmacology; Pharmacy; Philosophy; Philosophy of Education; Physical Therapy; Physics; Physiology; Political Sciences; Primary Education; Psychology; Public Administration; Public Health; Radiology; Rehabilitation and Therapy; Religion; Russian; Secondary Education; Slavic Languages; Social Welfare; Social Work; Sociology; South Asian Studies; Spanish; Speech Therapy and Audiology; Statistics; Town Planning; Toxicology; Visual Arts; Women's Studies); **Management** *(Joseph L. Rotman)* (Business Administration; Business and Commerce; Finance; Management); **Public Health** *(Dalla Lana)* (Behavioural Sciences; Community Health; Epidemiology; Health Sciences; Nutrition; Occupational Health; Psychiatry and Mental Health; Public Health; Social and Preventive Medicine; Statistics); **Public Policy and Governance** (Government; Public Administration; Social Policy)

Institute

Aerospace Studies (Aeronautical and Aerospace Engineering); **Asian** (Asian Studies); **Biomaterials and Biomedical Engineering** *(IBBME)* (Biomedical Engineering; Materials Engineering); **Child Study** *(ICS)* (Child Care and Development); **Cinema Studies** (Cinema and Television); **Communication and Culture** *(UTM)* (Communication Studies; Cultural Studies); **Drug Research** (Pharmacology); **Education** *(Ontario)* (Adult Education; Child Care and Development; Curriculum; Development Studies; Education; Educational Administration; Educational and Student Counselling; Educational Psychology; Foreign Languages Education; Higher Education; Philosophy of Education; Primary Education; Psychology; Secondary Education; Sociology; Teacher Training; Technology Education); **Emerging Communication Technology** (Biotechnology; Electronic Engineering; Information Technology; Nanotechnology; Optics); **European Studies** (European Studies); **Knowledge Media Design** *(KMDI)* (Media Studies); **Lassonde** (Geological Engineering; Geology); **Life Course and Aging** (Gerontology; Health Sciences; Psychology; Social Sciences); **Medical Science** *(IMS)* (Communication Studies; Ethics; Medicine; Radiology); **Music** *(Canadian)* (Music); **Optical Sciences** (Optics); **Policy Analysis** (Economics; Social Policy); **Risk Management** (Insurance); **Theoretical Astrophysics** *(Canadian - CITA)* (Astrophysics); **Theoretical Astrophysics** *(Canadian)* (Astrophysics); **Women's Studies and Gender Studies** (Gender Studies; Women's Studies)

Centre

Aboriginal Studies (Indigenous Studies); **Academic Retiree**; **Bioethics** *(Joint)* (Ethics); **Cellular and Biomolecular Research** *(Terrence Donnelly)* (Cell Biology; Molecular Biology); **Cities** (Development Studies; Urban Studies); **Comparative Literature** (Comparative Literature); **Criminology** (Criminology); **Diaspora and Transnational Studies** (Geography (Human)); **Economics and Public Affairs** (Economics); **Environment** (Environmental Studies); **Ethics** (Ethics); **European, Russian and Eurasian Studies** (Eurasian and North Asian Languages; European Studies; Russian); **Forensic Science** (Forensic Medicine and Dentistry); **Global Affairs** *(Munk)* (American Studies; Asian Studies; Eastern European Studies; European Studies; Germanic Studies; International Studies; Latin American Studies; Pacific Area Studies; South Asian Studies; Southeast Asian Studies); **Global Change Science**; **Health Promotion** (Health Sciences); **History and Philosophy of Science and Technology** (History; Philosophy); **Humanities** *(Jackman)* (Arts and Humanities); **Industrial Relations and Human Resources** (Human Resources; Labour and Industrial Relations); **Innovation Law and Policy** *(CILP)* (Law); **International Health** (Health Sciences); **International Studies** (International Studies); **Medieval Studies** (Medieval Studies); **Molecular Medicine** *(McLaughlin)* (Medicine; Molecular Biology); **Neurobiology of Stress** *(UTSC)* (Neurosciences); **Nuclear Engineering** (Nuclear Engineering); **Peace and Conflict Studies** *(Trudeau)* (Peace and Disarmament); **Pulp and Paper** (Paper Technology); **Quantum Information and Quantum Control** *(CQIQC)* (Chemistry; Computer Science; Electrical Engineering; Materials Engineering; Mathematics; Physics); **Reformation and Renaissance Studies** (Modern History); **Research in Neurodegenerative Diseases** (Neurology); **Research in Women's Health** (Health Sciences); **Sexual Diversity Studies** (Gender Studies); **South Asian Studies** (South Asian Studies); **Study of Drama** *(Graduate)* (Theatre); **Study of France and the Francophone World** (French; French Studies); **Study of Pain** (Health Sciences); **Study of Religion** (Religion); **Study of United States** (American Studies); **Urban and Community Studies** (Social and Community Services; Urban Studies); **Urban Health Initiatives** (Health Sciences); **Urban Schooling** *(OISE/UT)* (Education); **Wilson** *(Faculty of Medicine)* (Medicine); **Women's Studies in Education** *(OISE/UT)* (Education; Women's Studies)

Research Institute

Dental (Dentistry); **Mathematical Science** *(Fields)* (Mathematics)

Campus

University of Toronto Mississauga (Accountancy; Ancient Civilizations; Anthropology; Arabic; Art History; Astronomy and Space Science; Behavioural Sciences; Biochemistry; Biology; Biotechnology; Business and Commerce; Canadian Studies; Cell Biology; Chemistry; Chinese; Cinema and Television; Commercial Law; Communication Studies; Computer Science; Criminal Law; Criminology; Cultural Studies; Earth Sciences; Ecology; Economics; English; Environmental Management; Environmental Studies; Finance; Fine Arts; French; French Studies; Gender Studies; Geography; Geology; German; Hindi; History; Human Resources; Information Sciences; Information Technology; International Relations; Italian; Labour and Industrial Relations; Latin; Law; Linguistics; Logic; Management; Marketing; Mathematical Physics; Mathematics; Molecular Biology; Neurology; Paleontology; Performing Arts; Persian; Philosophy; Physics; Physiology; Political Sciences; Psychology; Religion; Sanskrit; Science Education; Sociology; Spanish; Statistics; Surveying and Mapping; Theatre; Visual Arts; Women's Studies; Writing); **University of Toronto Scarborough** (Anthropology; Arabic; Art History; Arts and Humanities; Astronomy and Space Science; Astrophysics; Biochemistry; Biological and Life Sciences; Biology; Business Administration; Cell Biology; Chemistry; Chinese; Cognitive Sciences; Computer Science; Ecology; Economics; English; Environmental Engineering; Environmental Studies; Geography; Health Sciences; Hindi; History; Information Technology; International Studies; Journalism; Latin; Linguistics; Management; Mathematics; Media Studies; Microbiology; Modern Languages; Molecular Biology; Music; Neurosciences; Performing Arts; Philosophy; Political Sciences; Psychology; Public Administration; Religion; Sanskrit; Social Sciences; Sociology; South and Southeast Asian Languages; Spanish; Statistics; Teacher Training; Urban Studies; Visual Arts; Women's Studies)

Further Information: Also Mississauga and Scarborough campuses.

History: Founded as King's College at York 1827 by Royal Charter, in close collaboration with the Church of England. Became secularized and acquired present title 1849. University of St. Michael's College and Victoria University entered into federation with the University 1890, Trinity College was federated 1904. The University has 8 colleges: Innis, New, St. Michael's, Trinity, University, Victoria, Woodsworth.

Academic Year: September to August (September-December; January-May; May-June; July-August)

Admission Requirements: Secondary school certificate or recognized foreign equivalent

Fees: National: Undergraduate tuition, 6,040 to 12,980 per annum depending on the program. Graduate tuition, 7,115-44,834 per annum depending on the programme (Canadian Dollar), International: Undergraduate students: 35,280 -39,580 per annum depending on the program.Graduate students:18,620 to 51,293 depending on the programme (Canadian Dollar)

Main Language(s) of Instruction: English

Degrees and Diplomas: *Certificat et diplôme universitaire/University certificate and diploma*; *Baccalauréat/Bachelor's Degree*; *Maîtrise/Master's Degree*; *Diplôme et certificat de 2e cycle/Graduate Diploma and Certificate*; *Doctorat/Doctoral Degree*. Also Concurrent Teacher Education Programmes; Collaborative Programmes (multidisciplinary programs that involve a wide range of graduate departments across the institution); Combined Programmes, two degree programmes within a reduced timeframe of four years (Juris Doctor and the Master of Information; Combined Doctor of Medicine/Doctor of Philosophy Programme); Professional Master's degree programmes in Health Sciences.

Student Services: Academic Counselling, Canteen, Careers Guidance, Cultural Activities, Facilities for disabled people, Foreign Studies Centre, Health Services, Language Laboratory, Library, Nursery Care, Social Counselling, Sports Facilities

Publishing house: University of Toronto Press

Academic Staff *2014-2015*	**TOTAL**
FULL-TIME	**13,239**
Student Numbers *2014-2015*	
All (Foreign included)	**84,556**
FOREIGN ONLY	**14409**

Last Updated: 30/03/15

UNIVERSITY OF ST. MICHAEL'S COLLEGE (USMC)

81 St. Mary Street, Toronto, Ontario M5S 1J4
Tel: + 1(416) 926-1300
Fax: + 1(416) 926-7276
EMail: usmc.presidentsoffice@utoronto.ca
Website: http://stmikes.utoronto.ca/

President: Anne Anderson (2009-)
Tel: + 1(416) 926-7147 EMail: anne.anderson@utoronto

Faculty

Theology *(Graduate Studies)* (Christian Religious Studies; Ecology; Leadership; Religion; Religious Education; Theology)

Division

Continuing Education (Leadership; Religion; Social Work)

Programme

Book and Media Studies (Media Studies; Publishing and Book Trade); **Celtic Studies** (Archaeology; Celtic Languages and Studies; Cultural Studies; Fine Arts; Folklore; Irish; Literature; Music); **Christianity and Culture** (Christian Religious Studies; Cultural Studies); **Medieval Studies** (Medieval Studies); **Religious Education** (Religious Education)

Institute

Canadian Catholic Bioethics (Ethics); **Mediaeval Studies** *(Pontifical)* (Medieval Studies)

Further Information: Students registered at St Michael's College have full access to all of the more than 2,000 courses offered in over 300 programs by the Faculty of Arts and Science of the University of Toronto.

History: Founded 1852 as St. Michael's College, acquired present status and title 1958. A Federated University of the University of Toronto.

Academic Year: September to April (September-December; January-April). Also Summer Sessions (May-June; July-August)

Admission Requirements: Secondary school certificate or recognized foreign equivalent

Fees: Basic degree fees, 518.50 per course for Canadian students and 1,393 per course for international students. Advanced degree fees, 1,021-9,197 per annum, foreign students (Theology), 2,322-13,938 per annum (Canadian Dollar)

Main Language(s) of Instruction: English

Degrees and Diplomas: *Certificat et diplôme universitaire/University certificate and diploma*; *Baccalauréat/Bachelor's Degree*; *Maîtrise/Master's Degree*: **Religion; Theology.** *Diplôme et certificat de 2e cycle/Graduate Diploma and Certificate*; *Doctorat/Doctoral Degree*: **Theology.** Also Concurrent Education programme in Religious Education that enables students to study simultaneously for a Bachelor of Arts degree (with a major in Christianity and Culture) and a Bachelor of Education, 5 yrs; joint degree programmes (MDiv/MRE and MDiv/MA) 4 yrs; Non-degree certificates.

Student Services: Academic Counselling, Facilities for disabled people, Library, Social Counselling

Publications: Medieval Studies; Original texts, documents and commentaries regularly edited and published in field of Medieval research

UNIVERSITY OF TRINITY COLLEGE

6 Hoskin Avenue, Toronto, Ontario M5S 1H8
Tel: + 1(416) 978-2522
Fax: + 1(416) 978-2797
EMail: registrar@trinity.utoronto.ca
Website: http://www.trinity.utoronto.ca

Provost and Vice-Chancellor: Mayo Moran
Tel: + 1(416) 978-2689
EMail: provost@trinity.utoronto.ca; mayo.moranatsignutoronto.ca

Registrar: Nelson De Melo
Tel: + 1(416) 946-7614
EMail: demeloatsigntrinity.utoronto.ca; registrar@trinity.utoronto.ca

Faculty

Divinity (Christian Religious Studies; Religion; Religious Music; Theology)

Programme

Ethics, Society, and Law *(Interdisciplinary)* (Anthropology; Classical Languages; Criminology; Economics; Ethics; Geography; Law; Philosophy; Political Sciences; Religion; Sociology); **Immunology** *(Interdisciplinary)* (Immunology); **Independent Studies**; **International Relations** *(Interdisciplinary)* (Economics; History; International Relations; Political Sciences); **International Relations/Peace and Conflict Studies** *(Joint specialist degree)* (International Relations; Peace and Disarmament)

History: Founded 1852 as Trinity College, the Church of England University in Canada. Became a Federated University of the University of Toronto 1904.

Academic Year: September to August (September-December; January-April; May-August)

Admission Requirements: Secondary school certificate or recognized foreign equivalent

Fees: National: 3,196-3,250 per annum (Canadian Dollar), International: Foreign students, 8,000-10,000 per annum

Main Language(s) of Instruction: English

Degrees and Diplomas: *Certificat et diplôme universitaire/University certificate and diploma*; *Baccalauréat/Bachelor's Degree*; *Maîtrise/Master's Degree*: **Theology.** *Doctorat/Doctoral Degree*: **Theology.**

Student Services: Academic Counselling, Facilities for disabled people, Library, Social Counselling

Publications: Trinity University Review

VICTORIA UNIVERSITY

73 Queen's Park Crescent, Toronto, Ontario M5S 1K7
Tel: + 1(416) 585-4508
Fax: + 1(416) 585-4584
EMail: applytovic@utoronto.ca
Website: http://www.vicu.utoronto.ca

President and Vice-Chancellor: Paul W. Gooch
Tel: + 1(416) 585-4511
EMail: vic.president@utoronto.ca; paul.gooch@utoronto.ca

Registrar: Susan McDonald
Tel: +1(416) 585-4405
EMail: vic.registrar@utoronto.ca; s.mcdonald@utoronto.ca

International Relations: Caitriona Brennan, Coordinator, International Student Life and Study Abroad
Tel: +1(416) 585-4582 EMail: vic.international@utoronto.ca

College

Emmanuel (Asian Religious Studies; Bible; History of Religion; Islamic Studies; New Testament; Pastoral Studies; Religion; Religious Education; Religious Music; Theology); **Victoria** (Architecture; Cinema and Television; Communication Studies; Comparative Literature; Education; Ethics; History; Linguistics; Literature; Logic; Modern History; Music; Philosophy; Political Sciences; Religious Studies; Teacher Training; Theatre; Visual Arts)

History: Founded 1836 as Upper Canada Academy at Cobourg, granted degree-conferring power as Victoria College 1841. Became a Federated University of the University of Toronto 1892.

Academic Year: September to August (September-December; January-April; May-August)

Admission Requirements: Secondary school certificate or recognized foreign equivalent

Fees: (Can. Dollars): 1,160.37 per course; foreign students, 4,051.37; graduate, 11,400-27,000 per annum; graduate for foreign students, 16,800-37,839 per annum

Main Language(s) of Instruction: English

Degrees and Diplomas: *Certificat et diplôme universitaire/University certificate and diploma*; *Baccalauréat/Bachelor's Degree*; *Baccalauréat spécialisé/Bachelor's Degree - Honours*; *Maîtrise/Master's Degree*; *Doctorat/Doctoral Degree*

Student Services: Academic Counselling, Canteen, Facilities for disabled people, Library, Sports Facilities

Publications: The annual Senator Keith Davey Lecture

WYCLIFFE COLLEGE

5 Hoskin Avenue, Toronto, Ontario M5S 1H7
Tel: +1(416) 946-3535
Fax: +1(416) 979-0471
EMail: wycliffe.registrar@utoronto.ca
Website: http://www.wycliffecollege.ca/

Principal: George Sumner
Tel: +1(416) 946-3521 EMail: george.sumner@utoronto.ca

Registrar: Marie Soderlund
Tel: +1(416) 946-3530 EMail: wycliffe.registrar@utoronto.ca

Programme

Advanced Degree (Religion; Theology); **Basic Degree** (Christian Religious Studies; Religion; Theology)

History: Founded 1877.

Fees: Basic degree tuition fees, 597 per course for Canadian students (Canadian Dollar)

Main Language(s) of Instruction: English

Degrees and Diplomas: *Maîtrise/Master's Degree*; *Diplôme et certificat de 2e cycle/Graduate Diploma and Certificate*; *Doctorat/Doctoral Degree*

Student Services: Facilities for disabled people

UNIVERSITY OF WATERLOO (UW)

200 University Avenue West, Waterloo, Ontario N2L 3G1
Tel: +1(519) 888-4567
Fax: +1(519) 888-8009
EMail: registrar@uwaterloo.ca
Website: http://uwaterloo.ca

President and Vice-Chancellor: Feridun Hamdullahpur (2010-)
Tel: +1(519) 888-4567 Ext. 32202 EMail: president@uwaterloo.ca

Vice-President Academic and Provost: Ian Orchard (2014-)
EMail: provost@uwaterloo.ca

International Relations: Nello Angerilli, Associate Vice President, International Tel: +1(519) 888-4567 Ext. 35466

Faculty

Applied Health Sciences (Gerontology; Health Sciences; Leisure Studies; Parks and Recreation; Physical Therapy; Public Health); **Arts** (Accountancy; Acting; Ancient Civilizations; Anthropology; Archaeology; Art History; Art Management; Ceramic Art; Chinese; Classical Languages; Communication Studies; Criminology; Development Studies; Dutch; East Asian Studies; Eastern European Studies; Economics; English; Family Studies; Film; Finance; Fine Arts; French; French Studies; Gender Studies; German; Germanic Languages; Germanic Studies; Government; Greek (Classical); History; International Economics; Italian; Japanese; Jewish Studies; Latin; Latin American Studies; Law; Leadership; Literature; Media Studies; Medieval Studies; Music; Painting and Drawing; Peace and Disarmament; Philosophy; Polish; Political Sciences; Psychology; Religious Music; Religious Studies; Russian; Slavic Languages; Social Work; Sociology; Spanish; Speech Studies; Taxation; Theatre; Women's Studies; Writing); **Engineering** (Architecture; Automation and Control Engineering; Biomedical Engineering; Biotechnology; Chemical Engineering; Civil Engineering; Computer Engineering; Electrical Engineering; Electronic Engineering; Energy Engineering; Engineering; Engineering Management; Environmental Engineering; Fire Science; Geological Engineering; Management; Mechanical Engineering; Microwaves; Nanotechnology; Safety Engineering; Software Engineering); **Environment** (Design; Development Studies; Ecology; Economics; Environmental Management; Environmental Studies; Geography; Natural Resources; Political Sciences; Regional Planning; Sociology; Statistics; Surveying and Mapping; Tourism; Town Planning; Waste Management; Water Management); **Mathematics** (Actuarial Science; Applied Mathematics; Computer Science; Finance; Mathematical Physics; Mathematics; Mathematics and Computer Science; Software Engineering; Statistics); **Science** (Astronomy and Space Science; Astrophysics; Biochemistry; Biology; Biophysics; Biotechnology; Cell Biology; Chemistry; Earth Sciences; Ecology; Environmental Studies; Genetics; Geochemistry; Geological Engineering; Geology; Geophysics; Mathematical Physics; Microbiology; Molecular Biology; Optics; Optometry; Pharmacology; Pharmacy; Physics; Physiology; Toxicology)

College

Conrad Grebel University *(Affiliated cf: (https://uwaterloo.ca/grebel/))* (Arts and Humanities; Bible; Christian Religious Studies; English; Fine Arts; History; Music; New Testament; Peace and Disarmament; Philosophy; Religious Studies; Sociology; Theology); **Renison University** *(Affiliated)* (Asian Studies; Chinese; Development Studies; Japanese; Korean; Psychology; Social Work; Sociology); **St. Jerome's University** *(Affiliated)* (Accountancy; Anthropology; Business Administration; Catholic Theology; Christian Religious Studies; Classical Languages; Cognitive Sciences; Communication Studies; Criminology; Development Studies; East Asian Studies; Eastern European Studies; Economics; English; Family Studies; Finance; Fine Arts; French Studies; Gender Studies; Geography; German; Greek (Classical); History; Human Resources; Insurance; International Studies; Italian; Jewish Studies; Latin; Latin American Studies; Law; Management; Mathematics; Mathematics and Computer Science; Medieval Studies; Music; Peace and Disarmament; Performing Arts; Philosophy; Political Sciences; Psychology; Religious Music; Religious Studies; Russian; Sociology; Spanish; Speech Studies; Theatre; Women's Studies); **St. Paul's University** *(Affiliated)* (Canadian Studies; Development Studies; English; Indigenous Studies; International Studies; Philosophy; Psychology; Religious Studies; Sociology)

Institute

Advanced Information Technology *(Nortel Networks - NNI)* (Information Technology); **Biochemistry and Molecular Biology** (Biochemistry; Molecular Biology); **Computer Research** *(ICR)* (Computer Science); **Groundwater Research** *(Waterloo - WIGR)* (Water Science); **Innovation Research** *(IIR)* (Management; Technology); **Insurance and Pension Research** *(IIPR)* (Insurance); **Nanotechnology** *(Waterloo)* (Nanotechnology); **Polymer Research** *(IPR)* (Polymer and Plastics Technology); **Quantum Computing** *(IQC)* (Computer Science); **Risk Research** *(IRR)* (Insurance); **Sustainable Energy** *(Waterloo - WISE)* (Energy Engineering); **Water** (Actuarial Science; Applied Mathematics; Biology; Chemical Engineering; Chemistry; Civil Engineering; Computer Science; Earth Sciences; Economics; Electronic Engineering; Engineering; Environmental Engineering; Environmental Management; Environmental Studies; Geography; Hydraulic

Engineering; Mechanical Engineering; Natural Resources; Statistics; Water Science)

Centre

Accounting Research and Education *(CARE)* (Accountancy); **Advanced Materials Joining** (Materials Engineering); **Advanced Studies in Finance** *(CASF)* (Finance); **Advancement of Co-operative Education** *(Waterloo - WatCACE)* (Education); **Advancement of Trenchless Technologies at Waterloo** *(CATT)* (Technology); **Applied Cryptographic Research** *(CACR)* (Mathematics and Computer Science); **Arts and Technology** *(Canadian - CCAT)* (Arts and Humanities; Technology); **Atmospheric Sciences** *(Waterloo)* (Earth Sciences; Environmental Studies); **Automotive Research** *(Waterloo - WatCAR)* (Automotive Engineering); **Business, Entrepreneurship and Technology** *(Conrad - CBET)* (Business Administration; Management; Technology); **Computational Mathematics in Industry and Commerce** *(CCMIC)* (Business Computing; Mathematics and Computer Science); **Contact Lens Research** *(CCLR)* (Optical Technology); **Control of Emerging Contaminants** (Environmental Studies); **Ecosystem Resilience and Adaptation** *(ERA)* (Ecology; Environmental Management); **Education in Mathematics and Computing** *(CEMC)* (Computer Education; Mathematics Education); **German Studies** *(Waterloo)* (German; Germanic Studies); **Heritage Resource** (Heritage Preservation); **Mental Health Research** *(CMHR)* (Psychiatry and Mental Health); **Pavement and Transportation Technology** *(CPATT)* (Transport Engineering); **Survey Research** *(SRC)* (Actuarial Science; Statistics); **Teaching Excellence** *(CTE)* (Teacher Training); **Theoretical Neuroscience** (Neurosciences)

Research Institute

Aging *(Schlegel - UW/RIA)* (Gerontology); **Insurance, Securities and Quantitative Finance** *(Waterloo - WatRISQ)* (Finance; Insurance)

Further Information: Also Cambridge, Kitchener, and Stratford satelite campuses.

History: Founded 1957 as Waterloo College Associate Faculties in association with Waterloo College (a Liberal Arts College operated by the Lutheran Church, later Waterloo Lutheran University, now Wilfrid Laurier University). Acquired present status and title 1959. The University of Waterloo Act was updated 1972.

Academic Year: September to August (September-December; January-April; May-August)

Admission Requirements: Ontario Secondary school Diploma or recognized Canadian or foreign equivalent

Main Language(s) of Instruction: English

Accrediting Agency: Association of Universities and Colleges of Canada; Ontario Council of Graduate Studies

Degrees and Diplomas: *Certificat et diplôme universitaire/University certificate and diploma*; *Baccalauréat/Bachelor's Degree*; *Baccalauréat spécialisé/Bachelor's Degree - Honours*; *Maîtrise/Master's Degree*; *Diplôme et certificat de 2e cycle/Graduate Diploma and Certificate*; *Doctorat/Doctoral Degree*

Student Services: Academic Counselling, Canteen, Careers Guidance, Cultural Activities, Facilities for disabled people, Foreign Studies Centre, Health Services, Language Laboratory, Library, Nursery Care, Social Counselling, Sports Facilities

Publications: The New Quarterly

Academic Staff *2014-2015*	**TOTAL**
FULL-TIME	**1,139**
Student Numbers *2014-2015*	
All (Foreign included)	**35,900**

Part-time students, 2,549.

Last Updated: 30/03/15

UNIVERSITY OF WESTERN ONTARIO (UWO)

1151 Richmond Street, London, Ontario N6A 3K7
Tel: + 1(519) 661-2111
Fax: + 1(519) 661-3388
EMail: reg_admissions@uwo.ca
Website: http://www.uwo.ca

President and Vice-Chancellor: Amit Chakma (2009-)
Tel: + 1(519) 661-3106 EMail: achakma@uwo.ca

Provost and Vice-President (Academic): Janice Deakin
Tel: + 1(519) 661-3110 Ext. 83110 EMail: provostvpa@uwo.ca

Faculty

Arts and Humanities (Arabic; Archaeology; Art Criticism; Art History; Arts and Humanities; Classical Languages; Communication Studies; Comparative Literature; Cultural Studies; English; Ethics; Film; Fine Arts; French; French Studies; Gender Studies; German; Greek (Classical); Hindi; History; Italian; Japanese; Korean; Latin; Linguistics; Literature; Mediterranean Studies; Modern Languages; Museum Studies; Philology; Philosophical Schools; Philosophy; Portuguese; Russian; Spanish; Speech Studies; Women's Studies; Writing); **Education** (Curriculum; Education; Educational Psychology; Educational Sciences; Leadership; Natives Education; Primary Education; Secondary Education; Special Education; Technology Education); **Engineering** (Chemical Engineering; Civil Engineering; Computer Engineering; Electrical Engineering; Electronic Engineering; Engineering; Environmental Engineering; Mechanical Engineering; Software Engineering); **Health Sciences** (Communication Disorders; Communication Studies; Health Sciences; Nursing; Occupational Therapy; Physical Therapy; Rehabilitation and Therapy); **Information and Media Studies** (Folklore; Information Sciences; Jazz and Popular Music; Journalism; Library Science; Media Studies); **Law** (Civil Law; Commercial Law; Comparative Law; International Law; Law; Private Law); **Music** *(Don Wright)* (Art History; Jazz and Popular Music; Music; Music Education; Music Theory and Composition; Musical Instruments; Musicology; Opera; Performing Arts; Singing); **Science** (Actuarial Science; Anatomy; Applied Mathematics; Astronomy and Space Science; Biochemistry; Biological and Life Sciences; Biology; Biophysics; Cell Biology; Chemistry; Computer Science; Earth Sciences; Environmental Studies; Genetics; Geology; Geophysics; Immunology; Inorganic Chemistry; Materials Engineering; Mathematics; Mathematics and Computer Science; Microbiology; Organic Chemistry; Pathology; Pharmacology; Physics; Software Engineering; Statistics; Zoology); **Social Science** (Air Transport; American Studies; Anthropology; Archaeology; Canadian Studies; Cognitive Sciences; Criminology; Cultural Studies; Demography and Population; Economics; Ethnology; Finance; Gender Studies; Geography; History; Indigenous Studies; International Economics; International Relations; Jewish Studies; Latin American Studies; Linguistics; Management; Neurosciences; Philosophy; Political Sciences; Psychoanalysis; Psycholinguistics; Social Sciences; Sociology; Surveying and Mapping; Urban Studies; Women's Studies)

College

Brescia University (Anthropology; Development Studies; Dietetics; English; Family Studies; Food Science; Food Technology; French; Health Sciences; History; Leadership; Management; Nutrition; Philosophy; Physical Therapy; Political Sciences; Psychology; Religious Studies; Sociology); **Huron University** *(Affiliated)* (Asian Studies; Business Administration; Chinese; Economics; English; French; French Studies; History; International Studies; Japanese; Jewish Studies; Management; Philosophy; Political Sciences; Psychology; Religious Studies; Theology); **King's University** *(Affiliated)* (Business Administration; Economics; English; Film; French; History; Italian; Literature; Mathematics; Modern Languages; Peace and Disarmament; Philosophy; Political Sciences; Psychology; Religious Studies; Social Work; Sociology; Spanish; Writing)

Programme

London Regional Cancer *(Affiliated)* (Oncology)

School

Business *(Richard Ivey)* (Business Administration; Finance; Leadership; Management); **Graduate and Postdoctoral Studies** (Actuarial Science; American Studies; Anatomy; Anthropology; Applied Mathematics; Art History; Astronomy and Space Science; Biochemistry; Bioengineering; Biology; Biomedical Engineering; Biophysics; Business Administration; Cell Biology; Chemical Engineering; Chemistry; Civil Engineering; Classical Languages; Communication Disorders; Communication Studies; Comparative Literature; Computer Engineering; Computer Science; Demography and Population; Economics; Education; Electrical Engineering; English; Environmental Engineering; Environmental Studies; Epidemiology; Ethnology; Film; Fine Arts; Folklore; Food Science; French; Geography; Geology; Geophysics; Greek (Classical); Health Sciences; History; Immunology; Information Sciences; Jazz and Popular Music; Journalism; Latin; Law; Library Science;

Linguistics; Management; Materials Engineering; Mathematics; Mechanical Engineering; Media Studies; Medicine; Microbiology; Music; Neurosciences; Nuclear Engineering; Nursing; Nutrition; Occupational Therapy; Orthodontics; Pathology; Pharmacology; Philosophy; Physical Therapy; Physics; Physiology; Political Sciences; Production Engineering; Psychology; Public Administration; Rehabilitation and Therapy; Social Work; Sociology; Spanish; Statistics; Theology; Toxicology; Visual Arts; Women's Studies); **Medicine and Dentistry** *(Schulich)* (Anaesthesiology; Anatomy; Biochemistry; Biology; Biomedical Engineering; Biophysics; Cell Biology; Dentistry; Engineering; Epidemiology; Gynaecology and Obstetrics; Immunology; Medicine; Microbiology; Neurology; Neurosciences; Oncology; Ophthalmology; Orthodontics; Otorhinolaryngology; Paediatrics; Pathology; Pharmacology; Physiology; Psychiatry and Mental Health; Rehabilitation and Therapy; Statistics; Surgery; Toxicology)

Research Institute

Lawson Health *(Affiliated)* (Health Sciences); **Robarts** (Dentistry; Engineering; Medicine)

Further Information: Also two Teaching Hospitals: St. Joseph's Health Care London.

History: Founded 1878 as The Western University of London, Ontario. Acquired present status and title 1923.

Academic Year: September to April (September-December; January-April); summer session, May to August

Admission Requirements: Secondary school certificate or recognized foreign equivalent. Specific requirements according to programme

Main Language(s) of Instruction: English

Accrediting Agency: Association of Universities and Colleges of Canada

Degrees and Diplomas: *Certificat et diplôme universitaire/University certificate and diploma*; *Baccalauréat/Bachelor's Degree*; *Maîtrise/Master's Degree*; *Doctorat/Doctoral Degree*: **Arts and Humanities; Business Administration; Education; Engineering; Fine Arts; Information Sciences; Law; Medicine; Music; Natural Sciences; Social Sciences.** Also Dual degrees (Concurrent degrees and Combined Degrees); Professional programmes and professional graduate programmes.

Student Services: Academic Counselling, Canteen, Careers Guidance, Cultural Activities, Facilities for disabled people, Foreign Studies Centre, Health Services, Language Laboratory, Nursery Care, Social Counselling, Sports Facilities

Publications: Academic Calendar; Publications on the history of the University

Academic Staff *2014-2015*: Total: c. 1,400

Student Numbers *2014-2015*: Total: c. 27,300

Last Updated: 30/03/15

HURON UNIVERSITY COLLEGE (HURON)

1349 Western Road, London, Ontario N6G 1H3
Tel: +1(519) 438-7224
Fax: +1(519) 438-3938
EMail: huron@uwo.ca
Website: http://huronuc.ca/

Principal: Stephen McClatchie (2011-)
Tel: +1(519) 438-7224 Ext. 237 EMail: smcclatchie@huron.uwo.ca

Chief Administrative Officer: Neil Carruthers
Tel: +1(519) 438-7224 Ext. 285

Faculty

Arts and Social Science (Accountancy; Administration; Asian Studies; Business Administration; Chinese; Economics; English; Finance; French; French Studies; History; Human Resources; International Studies; Japanese; Jewish Studies; Management; Mathematics; Philosophy; Political Sciences; Psychology; Religion; Sociology; Writing); **Theology** (Religious Studies; Theology)

History: Founded 1863 as Huron College. An affiliated institution of The University of Western Ontario. Acquired present status and title 2000.

Academic Year: September to May (September-December; January-May)

Main Language(s) of Instruction: English

Degrees and Diplomas: *Baccalauréat/Bachelor's Degree*; *Maîtrise/Master's Degree*. Also Honours Bachelor's degree, 4 yrs; Honors Bachelor in Business Administration (HBA) with Honors Specialization in Global Development studies/Globalization Studies/Global Culture Studies, 5 yrs.

Student Services: Academic Counselling, Canteen, Careers Guidance, Cultural Activities, Foreign Studies Centre, Health Services, Language Laboratory, Library, Sports Facilities

UNIVERSITY OF WINDSOR

401 Sunset Avenue, Windsor, Ontario N9B 3P4
Tel: +1(519) 253-3000 +1(519) 253-4232
Fax: +1(519) 973-7050
EMail: registr@uwindsor.ca
Website: http://uwindsor.ca

President and Vice-Chancellor: Alan Wildeman (2008-)
Tel: +1(519) 253-3000 Ext. 2000 EMail: president@uwindsor.ca

Provost and Vice-President, Academic: Douglas Kneale
Tel: +1(519) 253-3000 Ext. 4242 EMail: ivag@uwindsor.ca

Faculty

Arts and Social Sciences (Acting; Anthropology; Arabic; Art History; Art Management; Art Therapy; Arts and Humanities; Classical Languages; Communication Studies; Criminology; Cultural Studies; English; Film; Fine Arts; Foreign Languages Education; French; French Studies; German; Greek (Classical); History; Italian; Latin; Latin American Studies; Literature; Media Studies; Music; Music Theory and Composition; Musical Instruments; Philosophy; Political Sciences; Psychology; Social and Community Services; Social Work; Sociology; Spanish; Theatre; Visual Arts; Women's Studies); **Education** (Curriculum; Education; Educational Administration; Educational Sciences; Primary Education; Secondary Education; Teacher Training); **Engineering** (Automotive Engineering; Civil Engineering; Computer Engineering; Electrical Engineering; Engineering; Environmental Engineering; Industrial Engineering; Materials Engineering; Mechanical Engineering); **Graduate Studies** (Biochemistry; Biological and Life Sciences; Business Administration; Chemistry; Civil Engineering; Communication Studies; Computer Science; Criminology; Data Processing; Earth Sciences; Economics; Education; Electrical Engineering; English; Environmental Engineering; Environmental Studies; History; Industrial Engineering; Management; Materials Engineering; Mathematics; Mechanical Engineering; Nursing; Philosophy; Physical Therapy; Physics; Political Sciences; Production Engineering; Psychology; Social Work; Sociology; Statistics; Visual Arts); **Human Kinetics** (Physical Therapy; Sports; Sports Management); **Law** (Civil Law; Constitutional Law; Criminal Law; International Law; Law); **Nursing** (Health Sciences; Nursing); **Science** (Behavioural Sciences; Biochemistry; Biological and Life Sciences; Biology; Biotechnology; Chemistry; Cognitive Sciences; Computer Science; Earth Sciences; Econometrics; Economics; Environmental Studies; Information Technology; Mathematics; Mathematics and Computer Science; Mathematics Education; Neurosciences; Physics; Software Engineering; Statistics)

School

Business *(Odette)* (Accountancy; Business Administration; Business and Commerce; Business Computing; Finance; Human Resources; Industrial Management; International Business; Management; Marketing; Transport Management); **Medicine and Dentistry - Windsor Program** *(Schulich -)* (Dentistry; Medicine)

Institute

Diagnostic Imaging Research (Medical Technology); **Environmental Research** *(Great Lakes - GLIER)* (Environmental Studies); **North American Public Health** *(NAPHI - collaboration with Wayne State University)* (Public Health)

Centre

Automotive Research and Development (Automotive Engineering); **Business Advancement and Research** (Business Administration); **Canadian Aquatic Invasive Species Network** *(CAISN)* (Environmental Studies); **Catalysis and Materials Research** (Materials Engineering); **Community Based Research and Development** (Data Processing; Psychiatry and Mental Health); **Contemporary Studies in Accounting and Finance** *(Odette)*

(Accountancy; Finance); **Excellence** *(AUTO21 Network)* (Automotive Engineering); **Executable Specifications of Grammars** (Grammar); **History of Health Communication - Cultures of Health** (Communication Studies; Health Sciences); **Imaging Research and Advanced Materials Characterization** (Engineering; Materials Engineering); **Intelligent Manufacturing Systems** (Production Engineering); **Inter-Faculty Programmes** (Arts and Humanities; Criminology; Environmental Studies; Forensic Medicine and Dentistry); **Lake Erie Millennium Network** (Ecology; Environmental Studies); **Materials and Surface Science** (Materials Engineering); **Smart Community Innovation**; **SpeechWeb Project** (Computer Science); **Statistical Consulting, Research and Learning Services** (Statistics); **Studies in Social Justice** (Human Rights); **Teaching and Learning** (Education; Teacher Training)

Course

Distance Education (Accountancy; Art Management; Business Administration; Canadian Studies; Cell Biology; Economics; Finance; French; Genetics; International Law; Mathematical Physics; Microbiology; Public Administration; Sociology; Theatre)

Group

Developmental Group on Aging (Gerontology); **Signal and Information Processing** (Automation and Control Engineering; Computer Engineering; Electrical Engineering; Engineering; Robotics; Telecommunications Engineering)

Laboratory

Clean Diesel Engine (Mechanical Engineering); **Computer Vision and Sensing Systems** (Computer Science); **Multi-purpose Environmental Modelling Facility** *(MEMF Lab)* (Environmental Studies)

Research Centre

Canadian-American (American Studies; Canadian Studies); **Data** *(Windsor)* (Data Processing); **Integrated Microsystems** (Computer Engineering; Electrical Engineering; Engineering); **Management of Intelligent Enterprise Systems, Security and Assurance** *(ARC-MIE)* (E- Business/Commerce; Insurance); **Reasoning, Argumentation and Rhetoric** (Communication Studies; Speech Studies); **Study of Violence against Women** *(Health)* (Women's Studies)

Research Group

Animal Cognition (Zoology); **Feminist** (Women's Studies); **Humanities** (Arts and Humanities); **Light Metals Casting Technology** (Metal Techniques); **Operational** *(ORG)* (Operations Research); **Problem Gambling** (Behavioural Sciences); **Tribology of Lightweight Materials** (Materials Engineering); **Vehicle Dynamics and Control** (Automotive Engineering)

Research Institute

Fluid Dynamics (Physics)

History: Founded 1857 as Assumption College, reorganized as Assumption University of Windsor 1953, affiliated with the Faculty of Arts and Science of University of Western Ontario 1919-1956. Acquired present title 1962.

Academic Year: September to April (September-November; January-April)

Admission Requirements: Secondary school certificate or recognized foreign equivalent

Main Language(s) of Instruction: English

Degrees and Diplomas: *Certificat et diplôme universitaire/University certificate and diploma*; *Baccalauréat/Bachelor's Degree*; *Maîtrise/Master's Degree*; *Diplôme et certificat de 2e cycle/Graduate Diploma and Certificate*; *Doctorat/Doctoral Degree*. Also concurrent programmes with Bachelor of Education; Combined Bachelor's degrees; Honours Bachelor's degrees and Combined Honours Bachelor's degrees, 4 yrs.

Student Services: Academic Counselling, Canteen, Facilities for disabled people, Foreign Studies Centre, Health Services, Language Laboratory, Library, Sports Facilities

Publications: Catalogue of Research and Scholarly Activity

Academic Staff *2014-2015*: Total 524

Student Numbers *2014-2015*: Total 16,092

Last Updated: 30/03/15

WILFRID LAURIER UNIVERSITY (WLU)

75 University Avenue West, Waterloo, Ontario N2L 3C5
Tel: +1(519) 884-1970
Fax: +1(519) 886-9351
EMail: webmaster@wlu.ca; chooselaurier@wlu.ca
Website: http://www.wlu.ca

President and Vice-Chancellor: Max Blouw (2007-)
Tel: +1(519) 884-0710 Ext. 2443 EMail: mknechtelbell@wlu.ca

Vice-President: Academic and Provost: Deborah MacLatchy
Tel: +1(519) 884-0710 Ext. 2248

Faculty

Arts (American Studies; Ancient Civilizations; Anthropology; Arabic; Archaeology; Asian Religious Studies; Christian Religious Studies; Classical Languages; Communication Studies; Cultural Studies; English; Environmental Studies; Film; French; Gender Studies; Geography; German; Greek; Greek (Classical); History; International Studies; Islamic Studies; Islamic Theology; Italian; Judaic Religious Studies; Latin; Literature; Medieval Studies; Mediterranean Studies; Middle Eastern Studies; Modern Languages; Philosophy; Political Sciences; Religion; Social Sciences; Sociology; Spanish; Women's Studies); **Education** (Education; Primary Education; Secondary Education; Teacher Training); **Graduate Studies** (Ancient Civilizations; Art Therapy; Biology; Business Administration; Chemistry; Communication Studies; Criminology; Cultural Studies; Economics; Education; English; Finance; Geography; Government; History; International Studies; Management; Mathematics; Philosophy; Physical Therapy; Political Sciences; Psychology; Religion; Religious Studies; Social Work; Sociology; Theology); **Music** (Art History; Art Therapy; Music; Music Education; Music Theory and Composition; Musical Instruments); **Science** (Analytical Chemistry; Biochemistry; Biology; Chemistry; Computer Science; Health Sciences; Inorganic Chemistry; Materials Engineering; Mathematics; Organic Chemistry; Physical Chemistry; Physical Education; Physical Therapy; Physics; Psychology); **Social Work** (Indigenous Studies; Social Work)

College

Waterloo Lutheran Seminary (Religious Studies; Theology)

School

Business and Economics *(Laurier)* (Accountancy; Business Administration; Economics; Finance; Human Resources; Management; Marketing; Operations Research); **International Affairs** *(Balsillie)* (Government; International Studies; Public Administration)

Institute

Study of Contemporary Africa *(Tshepo)* (African Studies); **Water Science** *(Laurier)* (Water Science)

Centre

Community Research, Learning and Action *(CCRLA)* (Social and Community Services; Welfare and Protective Services); **Executive Development** *(Laurier)* (Finance; Leadership; Marketing; Technology; Transport Management); **Northwest Territories Partnership** *(Laurier)* (Environmental Studies); **Strategic Leadership** (Leadership); **Study of Nascent Entrepreneurship and the eXploitation of Technology** *(NeXt)* (Management)

Research Centre

Cold Regions *(CRRC)* (Regional Studies); **International Migration** (Demography and Population)

Campus

Brantford (Child Care and Development; Contemporary History; Criminology; Education; Engineering Management; Health Administration; Health Sciences; Human Rights; Journalism; Law; Leadership; Psychology; Social Studies)

Further Information: Also Waterloo Lutheran Seminary. Kitchener, Brantford, Toronto and Chongqing, China campuses.

History: Founded 1911 as Evangelical Lutheran Seminary of Canada, became Water College of Arts 1925, reorganized Waterloo Lutheran University 1960, and acquired present status and title 1973.

Academic Year: September to August (September-December; January-April; May-August)

Admission Requirements: Secondary school certificate or recognized foreign equivalent

Main Language(s) of Instruction: English

Degrees and Diplomas: *Certificat et diplôme universitaire/University certificate and diploma*; *Baccalauréat/Bachelor's Degree*; *Baccalauréat spécialisé/Bachelor's Degree - Honours*; *Maîtrise/Master's Degree*; *Diplôme et certificat de 2e cycle/Graduate Diploma and Certificate*; *Doctorat/Doctoral Degree*

Student Services: Academic Counselling, Canteen, Careers Guidance, Cultural Activities, Facilities for disabled people, Foreign Studies Centre, Health Services, Language Laboratory, Library, Social Counselling, Sports Facilities

Publishing house: WLU Press

Academic Staff *2014-2015*: Total: c. 700

Student Numbers *2014-2015*: Total 19,000

Last Updated: 30/03/15

YORK UNIVERSITY (YORK U)

4700 Keele Street, Toronto, Ontario M3J 1P3
Tel: + 1(416) 736-2100
Fax: + 1(416) 736-5700
EMail: infoserv@yorku.ca
Website: http://www.yorku.ca

President and Vice-Chancellor: Mamdouh Shoukri (2007-)
Tel: + 1(416) 736-5200
EMail: mshoukri@yorku.ca; president@yorku.ca

Vice-President Academic and Provost: Rhonda Lenton
Tel: + 1(416) 736-5280 Ext. 5528 EMail: vpacad@yorku.ca

International Relations: Marilyn Lambert-Drache, Associate Vice-President Tel: + 1(416) 736-5280 EMail: avpi@yorku.ca

Faculty

Education (Education; Environmental Studies; Higher Education; Jewish Studies; Mathematics Education; Preschool Education; Primary Education; Secondary Education; Special Education; Teacher Training); **Environmental Studies** *(FES)* (Environmental Studies); **Fine Arts** (Art History; Cinema and Television; Dance; Design; Film; Fine Arts; Music; Theatre; Visual Arts); **Graduate Studies** (Accountancy; Acting; Administration; Anthropology; Applied Linguistics; Art History; Art Management; Arts and Humanities; Asian Studies; Astronomy and Space Science; Biology; Business Administration; Caribbean Studies; Chemistry; Civil Security; Communication Studies; Computer Engineering; Computer Science; Cultural Studies; Dance; Demography and Population; Design; Development Studies; Earth Sciences; Economics; Education; Engineering; English; Environmental Studies; Ethics; European Studies; Film; French Studies; Geography; Germanic Studies; Health Sciences; Hebrew; Higher Education; History; Human Resources; Information Technology; International Studies; Jewish Studies; Latin American Studies; Law; Leadership; Linguistics; Management; Mathematics; Mathematics Education; Music; Neurosciences; Nursing; Philosophy; Physics; Political Sciences; Psychology; Public Administration; Real Estate; Rehabilitation and Therapy; Safety Engineering; Social Sciences; Social Studies; Social Work; Sociology; Statistics; Technology; Theatre; Translation and Interpretation; Visual Arts; Women's Studies); **Health** (Behavioural Sciences; Clinical Psychology; Developmental Psychology; Health Administration; Health Sciences; Neurosciences; Nursing; Physical Therapy; Physiology; Psychology; Rehabilitation and Therapy; Social Psychology; Sports Management); **Liberal Arts and Professional Studies** (Accountancy; Administration; Advertising and Publicity; African Studies; Amerindian Languages; Ancient Civilizations; Anthropology; Applied Linguistics; Arabic; Arts and Humanities; Bible; Business Administration; Canadian Studies; Caribbean Studies; Child Care and Development; Chinese; Classical Languages; Cognitive Sciences; Communication Studies; Criminology; Cultural Studies; Development Studies; East Asian Studies; Economics; English; Ethics; Ethnology; European Studies; Finance; Foreign Languages Education; French; French Studies; Gender Studies; Geography; German; Germanic Studies; Greek; Greek (Classical); Health Sciences; Hebrew; Hindi; History; Human Resources; Human Rights; Indic Languages; Indigenous Studies; Information Technology; International Studies; Italian; Japanese; Jewish Studies; Journalism; Korean; Labour and Industrial Relations; Latin; Latin American Studies; Law; Linguistics; Management; Marketing; Modern Languages; Philosophy; Polish; Political Sciences; Portuguese; Public Administration; Public Relations; Publishing and Book Trade; Radio and Television Broadcasting; Real Estate; Religious Studies; Russian; Safety Engineering; Social Sciences; Social Studies; Social Work; Sociology; South Asian Studies; Spanish; Swahili; Technology; Transport Management; Urban Studies; Women's Studies; Writing); **Science** (Astronomy and Space Science; Biological and Life Sciences; Biology; Chemistry; Mathematics; Natural Sciences; Physics; Statistics; Technology)

School

Business *(Schulich)* (Business Administration; Finance; International Business; Management; Marketing; Public Administration); **Engineering** *(Lassonde)* (Astronomy and Space Science; Biochemistry; Biology; Biomedicine; Biophysics; Biotechnology; Business Computing; Chemistry; Computer Engineering; Computer Science; Earth Sciences; Engineering; Environmental Studies; Geography; Geological Engineering; Mathematics and Computer Science; Mathematics Education; Meteorology; Multimedia; Physics; Software Engineering; Surveying and Mapping; Technology); **Law** *(Osgoode Hall)* (Comparative Law; Fiscal Law; International Law; Justice Administration; Law)

Institute

City (Urban Studies); **Health Research** *(YIHR)* (Health Sciences); **Research and Innovation in Sustainability** *(IRIS)* (Environmental Studies); **Science and Technology Studies** *(iSTS)* (Arts and Humanities; Social Sciences; Technology); **Social Research** *(ISR)* (Social Studies)

Centre

Asian Research *(YCAR)* (Asian Studies); **Atmospheric Chemistry** *(CAC)* (Meteorology); **Canadian Studies** *(Robarts)* (Canadian Studies); **CERIS - The Ontario Metropolis Project** *(Centre of Excellence)* (Demography and Population); **Education and Community** *(YCEC)* (Education); **Feminist Research** *(CFR)* (Women's Studies); **German and European Studies** *(Canadian - CCGES)* (European Studies; Germanic Studies); **International and Security Studies** *(YCISS)* (International Studies; Welfare and Protective Services); **Jewish Studies** *(Israel and Golda Koschitzky - CJS)* (Jewish Studies); **Practical Ethics** *(CPE)* (Ethics); **Public Policy and Law** *(YCPPL)* (Public Administration; Public Law); **Refugee Studies** *(CRS)* (Demography and Population); **Transnational Human Rights, Crime and Security** *(Jack and Mae Nathanson)* (Criminology; Human Rights; Protective Services); **Vision Research** *(CVR)* (Ophthalmology)

Research Centre

Biomolecular Interactions *(CRBI)* (Molecular Biology); **Child and Youth Research** *(LaMarsh)* (Child Care and Development); **Earth and Space Science** *(CRESS)* (Astronomy and Space Science; Earth Sciences; Robotics); **Language Contact** *(CRLC)* (Demography and Population; History; Linguistics; Musicology; Political Sciences; Psychology; Sociology); **Latin America and the Caribbean** *(CERLAC)* (Caribbean Studies; Latin American Studies); **Mass Spectrometry** *(CRMS)* (Chemistry); **Muscle Health** *(MHRC)* (Health Sciences; Sports); **Work and Society** *(CRWS)* (Labour and Industrial Relations)

Research Institute

Global Migrations of African People *(Harriet Tubman)* (Demography and Population); **Learning Technologies** *(IRLT)* (Educational Technology)

Campus

Glendon (Business Administration; Canadian Studies; Communication Studies; Economics; English; Environmental Studies; Foreign Languages Education; French Studies; Health Sciences; International Studies; Law; Linguistics; Mathematics; Philosophy; Phonetics; Political Sciences; Psychology; Sociology; Spanish; Theatre; Translation and Interpretation; Women's Studies; Writing)

Further Information: Also Glendon campus, Miles S. Nadal Management Centre and Osgoode Professional Development Centre.

History: Founded 1959. Established originally as affiliate of University of Toronto, the University moved to Glendon campus 1961. The University has 4 campuses in the City of Toronto.

Academic Year: September to April (September-December; January-April). Summer Session: May-August

Admission Requirements: Ontario Secondary School Diploma (OSSD), or equivalent. A minumum of six Grade 12 U or M courses, including Grade 12 U English, all Faculty prerequisites and at least one Grade 12 U or M course from one of the following disciplines: Canadian and World Studies; Classical Languages and International Languages; French; Mathematics; Social Sicence and Humanities; or native Studies. Additional requirements for many programmes. Francophone applicants can present 12U French (FRA4U, FEF4U, or FIF4U). Combination of U and M courses and OACs accepted. Early conditional admission if strong grade 11 finals and/or interim Grade 12 results.

Fees: (Can. Dollars): Undergraduate programmes, 6,003-8,473 per annum; International students, 16,403-17,944

Main Language(s) of Instruction: English

Degrees and Diplomas: *Certificat et diplôme universitaire/University certificate and diploma*; *Baccalauréat/Bachelor's Degree*; *Maîtrise/Master's Degree*; *Diplôme et certificat de 2e cycle/Graduate Diploma and Certificate*; *Doctorat/Doctoral Degree*. Also certificates and diploma programmes, offered through affiliated Colleges Centennial College and Seneca College); the Faculty of Education offers a 4-yr Concurrent co registered BEd degree, a Concurrent co registered program in Jewish Teacher Education and a Concurrent co registered BEd (French) degree and a full-time and part-time Consecutive BEd programme running over an extended academic year; the school of Law offers combined programmes (Juris Doctor and Master of Business Administration, Environmental Studies, Philosophy, Law or Bachelor of Civil Law); the Business school also offers a 2-yr MBA programme in India, an Executive MBA, combined Master's degree in Business Administration/Fine Arts/Arts and Business and Law (MBA/Juris Doctor) in 3-4 yrs; the Faculty of Science and Engineering offers an International Bachelor of Science (exchange agreements in 32 countries).

Student Services: Academic Counselling, Canteen, Careers Guidance, Facilities for disabled people, Foreign Studies Centre, Health Services, Language Laboratory, Library, Nursery Care, Social Counselling, Sports Facilities

Publications: Canada Watch; Canadian Woman Studies Journal

Academic Staff *2014-2015*: Total: c. 7,000

Student Numbers *2014-2015*: Total: c. 53,000

Last Updated: 30/03/15

PRIVATE INSTITUTIONS

CANADIAN MEMORIAL CHIROPRACTIC COLLEGE (CMCC)

6100 Leslie Street, Toronto, Ontario M2H 3J1
Tel: +1(416) 482-2340 +1(800) 463-2923
Fax: +1(416) 646-1114
EMail: admissions@cmcc.ca
Website: http://cmcc.ca/

President: David Wickes

Programme

Chiropractic and Clinical Education (Chiropractic)

History: Founded 1945.

Fees: 2658 per annum (Canadian Dollar)

Degrees and Diplomas: *Certificat et diplôme/Certificate and diploma*. Four year Doctor of Chiropractic (DC) Degree Program. Master of Science, Advanced Professional Practice (Clinical Sciences) program of the Anglo-European College of Chiropractic (AECC), validated by Bournemouth University, UK

Last Updated: 05/03/15

INSTITUTE FOR CHRISTIAN STUDIES

100–229 College Street, Toronto, Ontario M5T 1R4
Tel: +1(416) 979-2331 +1(888) 326-5347
Fax: +1(416) 979-2332
EMail: info@icscanada.edu
Website: http://www.icscanada.edu/

President: Doug Blomberg
Tel: +1(416) 979-2331 Ext. 235 EMail: DBlomberg@icscanada.edu

Registrar: Jeffrey Hocking
Tel: +1(416) 979-2331 Ext. 290 EMail: JeffreyH@icscanada.edu

Programme

Philosophy (Aesthetics; Anthropology; Bible; Ethics; Philosophy; Theology); **Worldview Studies** *(MWS)* (Bible; Education; Philosophy)

Research Centre

Philosophy, Religion and Social Ethics (Ethics; Philosophy; Religion)

Further Information: Also Distance Education programmes.

History: Founded 1967.

Main Language(s) of Instruction: English

Degrees and Diplomas: *Maîtrise/Master's Degree*: **Philosophy.** *Doctorat/Doctoral Degree*: **Philosophy.**

Student Services: Library

Last Updated: 10/03/15

REDEEMER UNIVERSITY COLLEGE

777 Garner Road East, Ancaster, Ontario L9K 1J4
Tel: +1(905) 648-2131 +1(800) 263-6467
Fax: +1(905) 648-2134
EMail: adm@redeemer.ca
Website: http://redeemer.ca

President: Hubert R. Krygsman (2010-)
Tel: +1(905) 648-2131 Ext.4218 EMail: hkrygsman@redeemer.ca

Provost and Vice-President (Academic): Doug Needham
Tel: +1(905) 648-2131 Ext.4204 EMail: dneedham@redeemer.ca

Department

Arts (Fine Arts); **Biology** (Biology); **Business and Economics** (Business and Commerce; Economics); **Chemistry** (Chemistry); **Classical Studies** (Classical Languages); **Computer Science** (Computer Science); **Dutch** (Dutch); **Education** (Education); **English** (English); **Environmental Studies** (Environmental Studies); **French** (French); **Geography** (Geography); **History** (History); **Horticulture** (Horticulture); **Mathematics** (Mathematics); **Music** (Music); **Philosophy** (Philosophy); **Physical Education** (Education; Physical Education; Social Sciences); **Physics** (Physics); **Political Science** (Political Sciences); **Psychology** (Psychology); **Religion and Theology** (Arts and Humanities; Religion; Theology); **Social Work** (Social Work); **Sociology** (Sociology); **Spanish** (Spanish); **Theatre Arts** (Theatre)

Centre

Advanced Studies for Faith and Science (Natural Sciences; Religious Studies); **Christian Philosophy** (Christian Religious Studies)

History: Founded 1982 as Redeemer College by Charter from the Ontario Provincial Government, acquired present status and title 2000.

Academic Year: September to April (September-December; January-April)

Admission Requirements: Secondary school certificate or recognized foreign equivalent, with a minimum average of 65%. Grade 12 U/M courses. Some special students admissions allowed

Fees: 15,162 per annum (Canadian Dollar)

Main Language(s) of Instruction: English

Degrees and Diplomas: *Baccalauréat/Bachelor's Degree*: **Art History; Arts and Humanities; Education; Fine Arts; Natural Sciences.**

Student Services: Academic Counselling, Facilities for disabled people, Health Services, Library, Residential Facilities, Social Counselling, Sports Facilities

Publications: Images

Academic Staff *2013*	**TOTAL**
FULL-TIME	**46**
PART-TIME	**61**
Student Numbers *2013*	
All (Foreign included)	**910**

Last Updated: 30/03/15

ST. LAWRENCE COLLEGE (SLC)

100 Portsmouth Avenue, Kingston, Ontario K7L 5A6
Tel: +1(613) 544-5400
Fax: +1(613) 545-3923
EMail: dreamit@sl.on.ca; international@sl.on.ca
Website: http://stlawrencecollege.ca/

President and CEO: Glenn Vollebregt

School

Applied Arts (Adult Education; English; Fine Arts; Journalism; Mathematics; Music; Performing Arts; Visual Arts); **Business** (Accountancy; Administration; Advertising and Publicity; Business Administration; Graphic Design; Human Resources; Marketing); **Community Services** (Behavioural Sciences; Preschool Education; Psychology; Social Work); **Computer and Engineering Technology** (Automation and Control Engineering; Civil Engineering; Computer Networks; Energy Engineering; Thermal Engineering); **Graphic Design** (Graphic Design); **Health and Science** (Biotechnology; Health Administration; Laboratory Techniques; Medical Technology; Nursing; Veterinary Science); **Hospitality** (Hotel and Restaurant; Tourism); **Justice Studies** (Administration; Law; Police Studies; Social and Community Services); **Skilled Trades and Apprenticeships** (Automotive Engineering; Cooking and Catering; Mechanical Engineering; Metal Techniques; Service Trades)

Further Information: Also Brockville and Cornwall campuses.

History: Founded 1967.

Main Language(s) of Instruction: English

Degrees and Diplomas: *Certificat et diplôme/Certificate and diploma*; *Baccalauréat/Bachelor's Degree*: **Psychology.** *Diplôme et certificat de 2e cycle/Graduate Diploma and Certificate*: **Behavioural Sciences; Communication Disorders; Health Administration; Marketing; Transport Management.** Also, Bachelor's degree in Business Administration and Nursing from Laurentian University; College Advanced diploma, 3yrs.

Student Services: Academic Counselling, Canteen, Careers Guidance, IT Centre, Library, Nursery Care, Residential Facilities, Sports Facilities

Last Updated: 30/03/15

TYNDALE UNIVERSITY COLLEGE AND SEMINARY

25 Ballyconnor Court, Willowdale, Ontario M2M 4B3
Tel: +1(416) 226-6380 +1(877) 896-3253
Fax: +1(416) 226-6746
EMail: contact@tyndale.ca; admissions@tyndale.ca
Website: http://tyndale.ca/

President: Gary V. Nelson EMail: GNelson@Tyndale.ca

Programme

Business Administration (Accountancy; Business Administration; Economics; Finance; Marketing); **Business Administration - International Development** (Accountancy; Business Administration; Finance; International Business; Management); **Christian Studies** (Christian Religious Studies); **Education** (Education; Primary Education; Secondary Education; Teacher Training); **English** (English; Literature); **Graduate Studies** (Bible; Christian Religious Studies; History of Religion; Leadership; Missionary Studies; Pastoral Studies; Religion; Theology); **History** (History); **Human Services - Early Childhood Education Track** (Child Care and Development; Preschool Education); **Human Services - Social Service Work Track** (Social and Community Services; Social Work); **Linguistics** (Bible; English; Linguistics; Literature; Philosophical Schools; Psychology); **Philosophy** (Ethics; Philosophy); **Psychology** (Behavioural Sciences; Psychology; Social Psychology); **Religious Education** (Pastoral Studies; Religion; Religious Education); **Religious Studies** (Bible; Religion; Religious Studies; Theology)

History: Founded 1894. Obtained current status 2003.

Fees: (Canadian Dollar): Undergraduate tuition, 1,296 per course (12,960 per annum); Graduate tuition, 1,113 per course (10,017 per annum)

Accrediting Agency: Association for Biblical Higher Education (ABHE)

Degrees and Diplomas: *Certificat et diplôme/Certificate and diploma*; *Baccalauréat/Bachelor's Degree*: **Education; Religious Education.** *Baccalauréat spécialisé/Bachelor's Degree - Honours*: **Bible; Business Administration; English; History; Philosophy; Psychology; Theology.** *Maîtrise/Master's Degree*: **Religion; Theology.** *Diplôme et certificat de 2e cycle/Graduate Diploma and Certificate*; *Doctorat/Doctoral Degree*: **Missionary Studies.**

Student Services: Residential Facilities, Sports Facilities

Last Updated: 30/03/15

Canada - Prince Edward Island

STRUCTURE OF HIGHER EDUCATION SYSTEM

Description:

Higher education in Canada is the constitutional responsibility of the provinces. The two main institutions providing higher education on PEI are the University of Prince Edward Island and Holland College; the latter provides diverse technical and vocational programmes usually leading to a Certificate or Diploma. The University, independently administered with full autonomy on admissions and academic matters, offers mainly undergraduate degrees and houses the regional Atlantic Veterinary College. UPEI also offers postgraduate studies in Education, Science, Biology and Chemistry with the Master of Education in Leadership and Learning, the Master of Science in Biology and the Master of Science in Chemistry programmes having recently been added to its delivery options. The Atlantic Veterinary College provides undergraduate, graduate and continuing education in the field of Veterinary Medicine. Holland College provides technical and vocational programmes leading to a Certificate or Diploma. Besides various pre-employment, apprenticeship and vocational programmes, there are 13 private vocational or career training colleges registered with the PEI Department of Innovation and Advanced Learning. French post-secondary education programmes are delivered through Collège l'Acadie.

Stages of studies:

University level first stage: Bachelor's degree

The courses offered by the University of Prince Edward Island lead to degrees in Arts, Science, Business Administration, Engineering, Education, Music, Veterinary Medicine and Nursing.

University level second stage: Master's degree

In 1999, UPEI was granted the authority to offer graduate level degrees. Since then, a Master of Education in Leadership and Learning (M.Ed), a Master of Science in Biology, a Master of Science in Chemistry, a Master of Arts in Island Studies, a Master of Applied Health Services Research, a Master of Nursing and a Master of Business Administration have been added to its offerings. In addition to the above mentioned programmes, UPEI offers a Master of Science (M.Sc.) programme through the Atlantic Veterinary College (which also primarily serves the other three Atlantic provinces of Nova Scotia, New Brunswick and Newfoundland, as well as international students). The first class was accepted in 1986 and about 50 students are admitted each year. The M.Sc. degree normally requires two years of training after an appropriate first degree.

University level third stage: Ph.D. degree

PhDs available at UPEI in Educational Studies; Molecular and Macromolecular Sciences, and Environmental Sciences. Following the completion of the four-year Doctorate of Veterinary Medicine (DVM), some students continue on to also complete a Master's degree or PhD in Veterinary Medicine. The DVM programme, while often considered at doctoral level, is an initial degree programme and is provided through the Atlantic Veterinary College, which serves (primarily) the other three Atlantic Provinces.

ADMISSION TO HIGHER EDUCATION

Admission to university-level studies:

Alternatives to credentials: The University of PEI sets its own admission policies and requirements. These do not involve separate entrance examinations, and usually include flexibility for mature students, i.e. applicants aged 21 who have been out of school for three years. Prior learning assessment and recognition (PLAR) and GED testing ares generally recognized.

Other requirements: Admission to university programmes usually includes attaining a certain average in high school and completion of certain academic subjects, besides holding a Gr. 12 certificate. Admission to some professional programmes (e.g. Medicine) may require previous university education. Specific admission requirements may vary by field of study and by university (and may include interviews and references).

Foreign students admission:

Definition of foreign student: Foreign (International) Students are students who are neither Canadian citizens nor permanent residents of Canada, and are enrolled full-time in a recognized academic, professional or vocational training course at a university, college or other educational institution in Canada.

Quotas: There are quotas at the institutional level for some programmes.

Admission requirements: Generally, as for domestic students, a high school diploma or equivalent will be required. A lack of proficiency in English or French will be taken into account by the Canadian Immigration Office in the evaluation of the application. UPEI: International students must submit documents which prove that their qualifications are comparable to Canadian applicants. High school admission requirements include: successful completion of final examinations with an overall average of at least 65% or a standing of A, B, or C in at least five subjects. For BA, BBA: English, Mathematics, and three acceptable academic electives; for BSc: English, Mathematics, two Sciences and one acceptable academic elective. There are special requirements for Nursing, Education, Radiography, and Veterinary Medicine programmes. The same subject cannot be counted more than once when taken at more than one level (Advanced or Ordinary level). Students must have 12 years of elementary and secondary education and Senior Secondary Certificate, Higher School Certificate or matriculation as defined by home institution. Students are usually required to pass one of the following English language proficiency tests with a score at or above the acceptable minimum. TOEFL: 550 minimum on paper based test, or 213 minimum on computer based test; MELAB: 80 minimum; IELTS: 6,5 minimum - with a minimum of 6.0 in each category; and Can TEST: 4.5 minimum.

Entry regulations: Before you come to study in Canada, you will need: a "Study Permit" if the programme of study you will be admitted to is longer than six months in duration, regardless of the length of your stay in Canada; a letter of acceptance from the school of your choice; proof that you have enough money to pay for school fees and living expenses; to establish that you will return home at the end of your studies; to pass a medical exam if required; and to qualify as a temporary resident in Canada, including holding a temporary resident visa (required for citizens of many countries). A small number of students do not require a Study Permit by virtue of their status in Canada (e.g. diplomats and their children).

Health requirements: Most education institutions require international students to buy health insurance in addition to their tuition fees; those that do not will require proof of independent health insurance coverage. Medical examinations are not required by institutions but are required by Citizenship and Immigration Canada for students from many countries.

Language proficiency: English language proficiency tests with a score at or above the acceptable minimum. TOEFL: 550 minimum on paper based test, or 213 minimum on computer based test; MELAB: 80 minimum; IELTS: 6,5 minimum with a minimum of 6.0 in each category; and Can TEST: 4.5 minimum.

RECOGNITION OF STUDIES

Quality assurance system:

Maritime Provinces Higher Education Commission reviews degree programmes at UPEI as a quality assurance measure. Holland College is ISO 9001:9008 certified and offers a student warranty guaranteeing that students will meet employers' needs or will be offered retraining.

Bodies dealing with recognition:

Department of Innovation and Advanced Learning

Shaw Building, 5th Floor, 105 Rochford Street, P.O. Box 2000
Charlottetown C1A 7N8
Tel: + 1(902) 368-4240
Fax: + 1(902) 368-4242
WWW: http://www.gov.pe.ca/ial

Special provisions for recognition:

Recognition for university level studies: In general, none. The University of PEI establishes its own admission criteria and makes decisions in response to individual applications. Any restrictions on admission are determined by the University, given available teaching and other resources, but in a few instances are a result of government policy.

Additionally, the Canadian Information Centre for International Credentials (CICIC) provides information and referral services to individuals and organizations on mobility and academic credential recognition.

For access to advanced studies and research: Admission to the Atlantic Veterinary College (which has only postgraduate programmes) at the University of Prince Edward Island is mainly restricted to Canadian citizens and permanent residents of the four Atlantic provinces (New Brunswick, Newfoundland, Nova Scotia and Prince Edward Island). However, there is a quota set for international students each year.

For exercising a profession: In general, none. For each profession, both Canadian and non-Canadians who studied abroad have to meet specified educational and experience requirements, and usually pass registration examinations. Non-Canadians may sometimes also need to pass a language test. Access to most professions is governed by provincial and/or federal statutes and is restricted to Canadian citizens or immigrants accepted as permanent residents. Usually, applicants must also meet examination and/or practical training requirements set by the relevant professional body or provincial or federal licensing board.

PROVINCIAL BODIES

Department of Innovation and Advanced Learning

Minister: Richard E. Brown
Shaw Building, 5th Floor, 105 Rochford Street, P.O. Box 2000
Charlottetown, PE C1A 7N8
Canada
Tel: +1(902) 368-4240
Fax: +1(902) 368-4242
WWW: http://www.gov.pe.ca/ial

Role of national body: Provincial government department responsible for post-secondary and continuing education including the funding arrangements for UPEI, Holland College, College l'Acadie and the administration of the Private Training Schools Act. Representative of the Department sits on the board of Holland College, College l'Acadie and the Maritime Provinces Higher Education Commission.

Data for academic year: 2014-2015

Source: IAU from the Canadian Information Centre for International Credentials (CICIC), a unit of the Council of Ministers of Education, Canada (CMEC), on behalf of the Prince Edward Island Department of Innovation and Advanced Learning, November 2014. Bodies 2016.

INSTITUTION

PUBLIC INSTITUTION

UNIVERSITY OF PRINCE EDWARD ISLAND (UPEI)

550 University Avenue,
Charlottetown, Prince Edward Island C1A 4P3
Tel: +1(902) 566-0439
Fax: +1(902) 566-0795
EMail: registrar@upei.ca
Website: http://www.upei.ca

President and Vice-Chancellor: Alaa Abd-El-Aziz (2011-)
Tel: +1(902) 566-0400 EMail: president@upei.ca

Vice-President Academic: Christian Lacroix (2014-)

Faculty

Arts (Ancient Civilizations; Anthropology; Arts and Humanities; Asian Studies; Canadian Studies; Classical Languages; Development Studies; Economics; English; Environmental Studies; Fine Arts; French; German; Greek (Classical); History; Island Studies; Journalism; Latin; Modern Languages; Music; Music Education; Philosophy; Political Sciences; Psychology; Public Administration; Religious Studies; Sociology; Spanish; Theatre; Women's Studies; Writing); **Education** (Adult Education; Education; Human Resources; International and Comparative Education; Leadership; Library Science; Natives Education); **Graduate Studies** (Business Administration; Education; Environmental Studies; Health Sciences; Island Studies; Leadership; Management; Materials Engineering; Molecular Biology; Veterinary Science); **Science** (Biology; Business Administration; Chemistry; Computer Science; Engineering; Environmental Studies; Family Studies; Information Technology; Mathematics; Nutrition; Physics; Psychology; Radiology; Statistics; Veterinary Science); **Veterinary** *(Atlantic Veterinary College's - AVC)* (Anaesthesiology; Animal Husbandry; Biomedicine; Cardiology; Cell Biology; Endocrinology; Environmental Studies; Epidemiology; Health Administration; Health Sciences; Immunology; Microbiology; Molecular Biology; Neurosciences; Parasitology; Pathology; Physiology; Public Health; Surgery; Toxicology; Veterinary Science; Virology; Zoology)

School

Business (Accountancy; Business Administration; Hotel and Restaurant; International Business; Management; Tourism); **Nursing** (Nursing)

History: Founded 1969, a public, non-denominational university, formed by the merger of 2 institutions of higher learning, Prince of Wales College (founded 1834) and Saint Dunstan's University (founded 1855). Faculty of Veterinary Science established 1986.

Academic Year: September to April (September-December; January-April)

Admission Requirements: Secondary school certificate or recognized foreign equivalent

Fees: National: Undergraduate programme: 5,520 per annum. Master of Business: 32,640 per 2 year programme. PhD in Educational Studies: 11,124 per 3 year programme (Canadian Dollar), International: Undergraduate programme: 6,428 per annum. Master of Business 32,640 per 2 year programme + 6,428 per year (This amount is paid in addition to full-time graduate student tuition) (Canadian Dollar)

Main Language(s) of Instruction: English

Degrees and Diplomas: *Certificat et diplôme/Certificate and diploma*; *Baccalauréat/Bachelor's Degree*; *Maîtrise/Master's Degree*: **Business Administration; Education; Health Sciences; Island Studies; Natural Sciences; Nursing; Veterinary Science.** *Doctorat/Doctoral Degree*: **Education; Veterinary Science.** Also Honours Bachelor's degrees, 4 yrs; Executive-Style MBA, 23 months-6 yrs; Accelerated Bachelor of Business Administration, 3 yrs; Professional programmes in Business Administration and through the Centre for Life-Long Learning; Accelerated programme in Nursing, 2 yrs.

Student Services: Academic Counselling, Canteen, Careers Guidance, Cultural Activities, Health Services, Library, Nursery Care, Social Counselling, Sports Facilities

Student Numbers *2013*: Total 4,336

Last Updated: 06/02/15

Canada - Quebec

STRUCTURE OF HIGHER EDUCATION SYSTEM

Description:

Higher education in Canada, as well as primary, secondary, vocational or technical education, are the constitutional responsibility of the provinces. In Quebec, higher education is delivered by two main types of institutions: colleges and universities. The Collèges d'enseignement général et professionnel (CEGEPs) offer two different types of programmes: 2-year pre-university programmes leading to university and 3-year technical programmes mainly for entry into the labour market. There are 48 public CEGEPs (43 French-speaking and 5 English-speaking) located in large and medium cities of the province. There are also 25 private subsidized institutions under the responsibility of the Ministère de l'Éducation, du Loisir et du Sport (18 French-speaking; 3 English-speaking; 4 French-English-speaking). Some institutions are under the responsibility of other Ministries such as music conservatories or agricultural institutes. The programmes offered by these institutions are approved by the Ministère de l'Éducation, du Loisir et du Sport (MELS). There are also 32 private colleges under licence of the MELS. There are 18 universities organized as follows: 3 English-speaking degree-granting universities (McGill, Concordia and Bishop's); 15 French-speaking degree-granting universities (Laval, Montréal, École Polytechnique de Montréal,École des Hautes Études Commerciales de Montréal, Sherbrooke and the 10 institutions related to the Université du Québec network hereby located in the main cities of the province (Université du Québec à Montréal, Université du Québec à Rimouski, Université du Québec à Chicoutimi, Université du Québec à Trois Rivières, Université du Québec en Outaouais, Université du Québec en Abitibi Témiscamingue, École nationale d'administration publique, École de technologie supérieure, Institut national de la recherche scientifique, Télé-université). Except for the Université du Québec, created by an Act of the National Assembly of Quebec, each other institution has a private charter. Although the Québec government provides a major portion of their funding, these institutions operate independently in all academic matters (admission, programs of study, evaluation, management, staffing).

Stages of studies:

University level first stage: Baccalauréat/Bachelor's degree
In Québec, the undergraduate university level usually leads to a Bachelor's degree after 3 or 4 years of study (Teacher Education, Engineering, Medicine). In English-universities, a bachelor programme can include a major and one minor or a choice of 3 certificates. Universities also offer short programmes, recognized by an undergraduate certificate.

University level second stage: Maîtrise/Master's degree
In Québec, the graduate university level usually leads to a Master's degree normally requiring 2 years of study and a dissertation after a Bachelor's degree. Universities also offer short one-year programmes recognized by a Diplôme d'études supérieures spécialisées (advanced graduate diploma). Graduate students include medical residents whose clinical training period may vary by specialty, with a minimum of 2 years.

University level third stage: Doctorat/Ph.D./Doctorate
Post-graduate studies lead to a PhD, requiring 3 years of study after the Master's degree and the submission of a major thesis (doctoral dissertation).

ADMISSION TO HIGHER EDUCATION

Admission to university-level studies:

Alternatives to credentials: Universities set their own admission policies and requirements. These do not involve separate entrance examinations, and usually include flexibility for mature students, i.e. applicants aged 21 or more, who have not completed secondary school. Quebec universities have introduced "prior learning assessments" (PLA) in considering admission to some degree programmes.

Numerus clausus: Universities decree numerus clausus in some programmes, mainly in the health sector. In medicine, a numerus clausus is decided by the Government, including a quota for foreign students.

Foreign students admission:

Definition of foreign student: Foreign (International) Students are students who are neither Canadian citizens nor permanent residents of Canada, and are enrolled full-time in a recognized academic, professional or vocational training course at a university, college or other educational institution in Canada.

Entry regulations: Before you come to study in Quebec, you will need: a "Certificat d'acceptation du Québec (CAQ)" from the Ministère de l'Immigration, de la Diversité et de l'Inclusion du Québec (MIDI); a "Study Permit" from Citizenship and Immigration Canada (CIC) if the programme of study you will be admitted to is longer than six months in duration, regardless of the length of your stay in Canada; a letter of acceptance from the school of your choice; proof that you have enough money to pay school fees and living expenses; to establish that you will return home at the end of your studies; to pass a medical exam if required; and to qualify as a temporary resident in Canada, including holding a temporary resident visa (required for citizens of many countries). A small number of students do not require a Study Permit by virtue of their status in Canada (e.g. diplomats and their children).

Health requirements: Quebec requires foreign students to provide proof of health insurance. The universities offer a health insurance policy to foreign students. Medical examinations are not required by institutions but are required by Citizenship and Immigration Canada for students from many countries.

Language proficiency: Universities offer language training programmes.

RECOGNITION OF STUDIES

Quality assurance system:

Recognition of studies is given by colleges (public and private) and by universities. For some professional bodies, additional requirements have to be met.

Bodies dealing with recognition:

Ministère de l'Immigration, de la Diversité et de l'Inclusion du Québec, Direction du courrier, de l'encaissement et de l'évaluation comparative (Ministère de l'Immigration, de la Diversité et de l'Inclusion du Québec, Direction du courrier, de l'encaissement et de l'évaluation comparative)

285 rue Notre-Dame Ouest, 4e étage
Montréal H2Y 1T8
Tel: (+1) 514-864-9191
Fax: (+1) 877-864-9191
WWW: http://www.immigration-quebec.gouv.qc.ca/fr/education/evaluation-comparative/index.html

Special provisions for recognition:

Recognition for university level studies: In general, no special requirement. Universities establish their own admissions criteria and make their own admissions decisions in response to individual applications. Any restrictions on admission are determined by the institutions themselves, given available teaching and other resources. Additionally, the Canadian Information Centre for International Credentials (CICIC) provides information and guidance on the assessment and recognition of international academic credentials.

For access to advanced studies and research: In general, no special requirements.

For exercising a profession: In Québec, adequate knowledge of French is required to practice any profession. The Office des professions and the Office de la langue française are responsible for the tests administered to candidates who come from outside Québec. Access to most professions is governed by provincial status and is restricted to Canadian citizens or immigrants accepted as permanent residents.

PROVINCIAL BODIES

Ministère de l'Education, du Loisir et du Sport

Minister/Ministre: Sébastien Proulx
Ministre responsable de l'Enseignement supérieur: Hélène David
1035, rue De La Chevrotière, 28e étage

Québec, Québec G1R 5A5
Canada
Tel: +1(418) 643-7095
Fax: +1(418) 646-6561
WWW: http://www.mels.gouv.qc.ca
Role of national body: To direct, promote and develop postsecondary, college and university education, including scientific research and development.

Commission d'Evaluation de l'Enseignement collégial

President: Céline Durand
800, place d'Youville, 18° étage
Québec, Québec G1R 5P4
Canada
Tel: +1(418) 643-9938
Fax: +1(418) 643-9019
EMail: info@ceec.gouv.qc.ca
WWW: http://www.ceec.gouv.qc.ca
Role of national body: To act as an independent government organization whose evaluation mandate covers most aspects of college education, with special emphasis on student achievement and programmes of studies. Legislation attributes to the Commission the power to evaluate and make recommendations, as well as to exercise a declaratory power.

Conseil supérieur de l'Education

Secretary-General: Lucie Bouchard
1175, avenue Lavigerie, bureau 180
Québec, Québec G1V 5B2
Canada
Tel: +1(418) 643-3850
Fax: +1(418) 644-2530
EMail: panorama@cse.gouv.qc.ca
WWW: http://www.cse.gouv.qc.ca
Role of national body: To advise the Minister on the status of education and university research and needs in this area.

Association des Collèges privés du Québec

President: Michel April
Director-General: Pierre L'Heureux
1940, boulevard Henri-Bourassa Est
Montréal, Québec H2B 1S2
Canada
Tel: +1(514) 880-8890
Fax: +1(514) 381-4086
EMail: acpq@acpq.net
WWW: http://www.acpq.net/
Role of national body: To act as the voice of 20-plus private subsidized colleges in order to promote education at college level.

Bureau de Coopération interuniversitaire - BCI

President: Guy Breton
500, rue Sherbrooke Ouest, bureau 200
Montréal, Québec H3A 3C6
Canada
Tel: +1(514) 288-8524
Fax: +1(514) 288-0554
EMail: info@crepuq.qc.ca
WWW: http://www.crepuq.qc.ca
Role of national body: Originally known as CREPUQ (Conférence des recteurs et des principaux des universités du Québec), the Bureau acts as the voice of Quebec's universities, facilitates cooperation and information-sharing among universities, and coordinates assessment activities on study programmes.

Fédération des Cégeps

President: Marie-France Bélanger
500, boulevard Crémazie Est
Montréal, Québec H2P 1E7
Canada
Tel: +1(514) 381-8631
Fax: +1(514) 381-2263
EMail: comm@fedecegeps.qc.ca
WWW: http://www.fedecegeps.qc.ca
Role of national body: To promote education at the college level, and more specifically in the general and vocational colleges known as CEGEPs; the Fédération is the voice of 48 public CEGEPS in Québec.

Data for academic year: 2014-2015
Source: IAU from the Canadian Information Centre for International Credentials (CICIC), a unit of the Council of Ministers of Education, Canada (CMEC), on behalf of the Ministère de l'Enseignement supérieur, de la Recherche et de la Science du Québec, November 2014. Bodies 2016.

INSTITUTIONS

PUBLIC INSTITUTIONS

BISHOP'S UNIVERSITY (BU)

2600 College St., Sherbrooke, Québec J1M 1Z7
Tel: +1(819) 822-9600
Fax: +1(819) 822-9661
EMail: liaison@ubishops.ca; admissions@ubishops.ca
Website: http://www.ubishops.ca

Principal and Vice-Chancellor: Michael Goldbloom (2008-)
Tel: +1(819) 822-9600 Ext. 2611 EMail: principal@ubishops.ca

Registrar: Hans Rouleau Tel: +1(819) 822-9600 Ext. 2676

International Relations: Diane Mills, Coordinator of International Students
Tel: +1(819) 822-9600 Ext. 2616 EMail: diane.mills@ubishops.ca

Division
Humanities (Art History; Arts and Humanities; Canadian Studies; Classical Languages; English; Film; Fine Arts; French Studies; German; Greek (Classical); History; Italian; Japanese; Jazz and Popular Music; Latin; Modern Languages; Music; Music Theory and Composition; Painting and Drawing; Philosophy; Religion; Sculpture; Spanish; Theatre; Writing); **Natural Sciences and Mathematics** (Biochemistry; Biology; Chemistry; Computer Science; Environmental Studies; Information Technology; Mathematics; Natural Sciences; Physics); **Social Sciences** (Criminology; Economics; Environmental Studies; Geography; Gerontology; International Economics; International Studies; Political Sciences; Psychology; Social Sciences; Sociology)

Programme
Collaborative Studies *(BU/UdeS)* (Arts and Humanities; Chemical Engineering; Civil Engineering; Engineering); **Multidisciplinary Studies** (Business and Commerce; Environmental Studies; Information Technology; International Studies; Medicine; Social Studies; Sports)

School
Business *(Williams)* (Accountancy; Business Administration; Finance; Human Resources; International Business; Management; Marketing); **Continuing Education** (English; Fine Arts; Italian; Museum Studies; Painting and Drawing; Photography; Sculpture); **Education** (Art Education; Curriculum; Education; English; Foreign Languages Education; French; Humanities and Social Science Education; Leadership; Mathematics Education; Music Education; Native Language Education; Primary Education; Science Education; Secondary Education; Spanish; Teacher Training)

Centre
Entrepreneurship *(Dobson-Lagassé)* (Management)

Group
Modélisation en Imagerie, Vision et Réseaux de neurones (Neurosciences); **Plato** (Philosophy)

Research Centre
Eastern Townships (Regional Studies)

Research Group
Multi-scale Climate and Environmental Change (Environmental Studies; Meteorology); **Psychological Health and Well-being** (Health Sciences; Psychology)

Research Unit
Crossing Borders Research Cluster (African Studies); **Modern History of Europe and Africa** (Modern History); **Stellar Astrophysics and Relativity Research Cluster** (Astrophysics)

Chair
Representation of Algebras *(Maurice Auslander)* (Mathematics)

Further Information: Also Knowlton and St. Lambert campuses.

History: Founded 1843 as Bishop's College, constituted as a university by Royal Charter with power to confer degrees 1853.

Academic Year: September to April (September-December; January-April). Also 2 Summer Sessions (May-August)

Admission Requirements: Collegial Diploma (DEC), or recognized foreign equivalent

Fees: National: Tuition Fees for Quebec residents, 75.77 per credit; Tuition Fees for Out-of-province residents, 221.06 per credit; (Canadian Dollar), International: International fees, 511.26-570.91 per credit (Canadian Dollar)

Main Language(s) of Instruction: English

Degrees and Diplomas: *Certificat et diplôme universitaire/University certificate and diploma*; *Baccalauréat/Bachelor's Degree*; *Diplôme d'études supérieures spécialisées/Graduate Advanced Diploma*; *Maîtrise/Master's Degree*: **Education; Leadership.** Also Honours Bachelor's degree; double majors in Liberal Arts combined with everything from Fine Art to Biology, from Music to Modern Languages, in Secondary Education and Music, and Education and a teaching discipline; Double-degree programme leading simultaneously to two Bachelor's degrees: a B.A. in Liberal Arts from Bishop's University (taught in English), and a B.Ing. (either Civil or Chemical Engineering), from the Université de Sherbrooke (taught in French).

Student Services: IT Centre, Library, Sports Facilities

Publications: Bishop's Collects

Student Numbers *2014-2015*: Total 2,756
Last Updated: 20/03/15

CONCORDIA UNIVERSITY

1455 Maisonneuve Blvd. West, Montréal, Québec H3G 1M8
Tel: +1(514) 848-2424
Fax: +1(514) 848-4546
Website: http://www.concordia.ca

President and Vice-Chancellor: Alan Shepard (2012-)
Tel: +1(514) 848-2424, Ext. 4849 EMail: president@concordia.ca

Provost and VP, Academic Affairs: Benoit-Antoine Bacon
EMail: theprovost@concordia.ca

International Relations: William W. Cheaib, Interim Associate Vice-President, International
Tel: +1(514) 848-2424, Ext. 5429
EMail: William.Cheaib@concordia.ca

Faculty

Arts and Science (Actuarial Science; Adult Education; Ancient Civilizations; Anthropology; Applied Linguistics; Applied Mathematics; Arabic; Archaeology; Arts and Humanities; Behavioural Sciences; Biochemistry; Biology; Biophysics; Biotechnology; Canadian Studies; Cell Biology; Chemistry; Child Care and Development; Chinese; Classical Languages; Communication Studies; Cultural Studies; Ecology; Economics; Education; Educational Sciences; Educational Technology; English; Environmental Studies; Finance; Foreign Languages Education; French; French Studies; Gender Studies; Genetics; Geography; German; Greek (Classical); Histology; History; Italian; Jewish Studies; Journalism; Latin; Leisure Studies; Linguistics; Literature; Mathematics; Mathematics Education; Media Studies; Molecular Biology; Neurosciences; Philosophy; Physical Therapy; Physics; Physiology; Political Sciences; Preschool Education; Primary Education; Psychology; Public Administration; Rehabilitation and Therapy; Religion; Sociology; South Asian Studies; Spanish; Statistics; Theology; Town Planning; Translation and Interpretation; Urban Studies; Western European Studies; Women's Studies; Writing); **Engineering and Computer Science** (Aeronautical and Aerospace Engineering; Civil Engineering; Computer Engineering; Computer Networks; Computer Science; Construction Engineering; Electrical Engineering; Engineering; Environmental Engineering; Industrial Engineering; Information Sciences; Mechanical Engineering; Safety Engineering; Software Engineering); **Fine Arts** (Art Education; Art History; Art Therapy; Ceramic Art; Dance; Design; Display and Stage Design; Film; Fine Arts; Gender Studies; Jazz and Popular Music; Music; Music Theory and Composition; Musical Instruments; Painting and Drawing; Photography; Printing and Printmaking; Sculpture; Sound Engineering (Acoustics); Theatre)

School

Business *(John Molson)* (Accountancy; Administration; Business Administration; Economics; Finance; Human Resources; Information Management; Insurance; International Business; Management; Marketing); **Canadian Irish Studies** (Irish); **Extended Learning** (Business Administration; Human Resources; Marketing); **Graduate Studies** (Accountancy; Administration; Adult Education; Aeronautical and Aerospace Engineering; Anthropology; Applied Linguistics; Art Education; Art History; Art Therapy; Arts and Humanities; Biochemistry; Biology; Biotechnology; Business Administration; Chemistry; Child Care and Development; Civil Engineering; Communication Studies; Computer Engineering; Computer Networks; Computer Science; Construction Engineering; Cultural Studies; Economics; Education; Educational Sciences; Educational Technology; Electrical Engineering; English; Environmental Engineering; Environmental Studies; Film; Fine Arts; Genetics; Geography; History; Industrial Engineering; Information Sciences; Jewish Studies; Journalism; Literature; Management; Mathematics; Mathematics Education; Mechanical Engineering; Media Studies; Musical Instruments; Philosophy; Physics; Political Sciences; Psychology; Public Administration; Religion; Safety Engineering; Social Sciences; Sociology; Software Engineering; Spanish; Theology; Translation and Interpretation; Urban Studies)

Institute

Canadian Jewish Studies *(Concordia)* (Jewish Studies); **Cooperative education** (Accountancy; Acting; Applied Mathematics; Art History; Biochemistry; Business Administration; Chemistry; Civil Engineering; Computer Science; Construction Engineering; Design; Economics; Electrical Engineering; Environmental Engineering; Finance; Fine Arts; French Studies; Human Resources; Industrial Engineering; Information Sciences; International Business; Management; Marketing; Mathematics; Mechanical Engineering; Physics; Safety Engineering; Software Engineering; Statistics); **Community Entrepreneurship and Development** (Development Studies; Management); **Genocide and Human Rights Studies** *(Montreal)* (Human Rights); **Political Economy** *(Karl Polanyi)* (Political Sciences); **Research/Creation In Media Arts and Technologies** *(Hexagram-Concordia)* (Media Studies); **Studies in Canadian Art** *(Gail and Stephen A. Jarislowsky)* (Fine Arts)

Centre

Advanced Vehicle Engineering *(Concordia)* (Automotive Engineering); **Arts in Human Development** (Art Therapy; Fine Arts); **Biological Applications of Mass Spectrometry** (Biological and Life Sciences); **Broadcasting Studies** *(Concordia)* (Radio and Television Broadcasting); **Building Studies** (Building Technologies); **Composites** *(Concordia)* (Materials Engineering); **Continuing Education** (Business Administration; Communication Studies; Computer Science; Photography; Public Relations; Visual Arts); **Ethnographic Research and Exhibition in the Aftermath of Violence** (Human Rights; Museum Studies); **Innovation in Business Finance** *(Desjardins)* (Finance); **Investment and Trading** (Business Administration); **JMSB Executive** (Accountancy; Business Administration; Finance; Leadership; Management; Marketing); **Multidisciplinary Business Research** (Business Administration); **Oral History and Digital Storytelling** (History); **Pattern Recognition and Machine Intelligence** (Artificial Intelligence); **Recherche en Développement Humain** (Development Studies); **Signal Processing and Communications** (Computer Science); **Structural and Functional Genomics** (Genetics); **Studies in Behavioural Neurobiology** (Behavioural Sciences; Biology; Neurosciences); **Study of Learning and Performance** (Higher Education; Preschool Education; Primary Education; Secondary Education); **Sustainable Enterprise** *(David O'Brien)* (Management); **Technoculture, Art and Games** (Computer Science; Literature)

Course

eConcordia (Accountancy; Business Administration; Chemistry; Christian Religious Studies; Communication Studies; Computer Science; Criminal Law; Cultural Studies; Economics; Ethics; Finance; Fine Arts; Human Rights; Information Management; Information Technology; Law; Leisure Studies; Management; Marketing; Mathematics; Political Sciences; Protective Services; Real Estate; Religion; Social Studies; Sociology; Statistics; Taxation; Urban Studies)

Group

Hardware Verification (Computer Engineering); **NanoScience** (Nanotechnology)

Research Centre

Business Process Innovations *(Bell)* (Business Administration); **InterNeg** (Business Administration); **Molecular Modeling** (Molecular Biology)

Research Group

New Rural Economy 2 *(Concordia Rural)* (Economics; Rural Studies)

Research Unit

High Performance Computer Cluster Platform (Computer Science); **Solar Buildings Research Network** (Energy Engineering)

Further Information: Also Loyola Campus

History: Founded 1974 by the merger of Sir George Williams University, founded 1948, and Loyola College of Montreal, incorporated 1896.

Academic Year: Regular session, September to April (September-December; January-April); summer session, May to August).

Admission Requirements: Diploma of Collegial Studies (DEC) following successful completion of a 2-year pre-university course at a CEGEP (Collège d'Enseignement général et professionnel), or recognized equivalent

Fees: National: Undergraduate tuition, 2,224.20 per Fall and Winter term for Canadian, Quebec Resident; 6,234.90 per Fall and Winter term for Canadian, Non-Quebec Resident. (Amounts are based on attendance for the Faculty of Arts and Science during the fall and winter terms) (Canadian Dollar), International: US and international students, 16,692. (These amounts are based on attendance for the Faculty of Arts and Science during the fall and winter terms.) (Canadian Dollar)

Main Language(s) of Instruction: English

Degrees and Diplomas: *Certificat et diplôme universitaire/University certificate and diploma*; *Baccalauréat/Bachelor's Degree*; *Diplôme d'études supérieures spécialisées/Graduate Advanced Diploma*; *Maîtrise/Master's Degree*: **Computer Science; Economics; Education; Engineering; English; Natural Sciences; Social Sciences.** *Doctorat/Doctoral Degree*: **Art Education; Art History; Biology; Building Technologies; Business Administration; Civil Engineering; Communication Studies; Computer Engineering; Computer Science; Economics; Education; Electrical Engineering; English; Environmental Studies; Film; Geography; Industrial Engineering; Mathematics; Mechanical Engineering; Physics; Political Sciences; Psychology; Religion; Social Sciences; Statistics; Urban Studies; Video.** Also Honours degrees; Accelerated MBA, 1-2 yrs; Executive MBA, 20 months.

Student Services: Canteen, Library, Residential Facilities, Sports Facilities

Publications: Arts and Sciences' Connections; Concordia Journal; Concordia University Magazine; Engineering and Computer Science Faculty Quarterly; President's Report

Academic Staff *2014-2015*	**TOTAL**
FULL-TIME	**984**
PART-TIME	**755**
Student Numbers *2014-2015*	
All (Foreign included)	**43,752**

Last Updated: 20/03/15

LAVAL UNIVERSITY

Université Laval

2325, rue de l'Université, Québec, Québec G1V 0A6
Tel: + 1(418) 656-2131 + 1(418) 656-3333
Fax: + 1(418) 656-5920
EMail: info@ulaval.ca
Website: http://www.ulaval.ca

Recteur: Denis Brière (2007-)
Tel: + 1(418) 656-2272 EMail: Denis.Briere@rec.ulaval.ca

Secrétaire générale: Monique Richer
EMail: Monique.Richer@sg.ulaval.ca

International Relations: Bernard Garnier, Vice-recteur aux études et aux activités internationales
EMail: Bernard.Garnier@vre.ulaval.ca

Faculty

Agriculture and Food Sciences (Agricultural Business; Agricultural Economics; Agricultural Engineering; Agriculture; Agronomy; Animal Husbandry; Biology; Botany; Dietetics; Environmental Engineering; Food Science; Food Technology; Forest Products; Microbiology; Nutrition; Soil Science; Zoology); **Arts** (Ancient Civilizations; Archaeology; Archiving; Art History; Arts and Humanities; Chinese; Cinema and Television; Classical Languages; Communication Studies; English; English Studies; Ethnology; Foreign Languages Education; French; German; Grammar; Greek (Classical); History; Information Sciences; International Studies; Italian; Japanese; Journalism; Latin; Linguistics; Literature; Modern Languages; Museum Studies; Portuguese; Public Relations; Russian; Spanish; Terminology; Theatre; Translation and Interpretation; Writing); **Business Administration** (Accountancy; Business Administration; E- Business/Commerce; Finance; Information Management; Information Sciences; Insurance; International Business; Management; Marketing; Occupational Health; Real Estate; Small Business; Tourism); **Dentistry** (Dental Hygiene; Dentistry; Gerontology; Surgery); **Education** (Education; Educational Administration; Educational and Student Counselling; Educational Psychology; Educational Technology; Health Education; Humanities and Social Science Education; Mathematics Education; Native Language Education; Pedagogy; Physical Education; Primary Education; Science Education; Secondary Education; Sports; Technology Education; Vocational Education); **Forestry, Goegraphy and Geomatics** (Environmental Studies; Forest Biology; Forest Management; Forestry; Geography; Meteorology; Rural Studies; Surveying and Mapping; Urban Studies; Wood Technology); **Graduate Studies**; **Law** (Commercial Law; Environmental Studies; International Law; Law; Notary Studies); **Medicine** (Anaesthesiology; Anatomy; Biochemistry; Biomedicine; Cardiology; Cell Biology; Cognitive Sciences; Community Health; Endocrinology; Epidemiology; Ergotherapy; Gender Studies; Gynaecology and Obstetrics; Immunology; Medicine; Microbiology; Molecular Biology; Neurology; Neurosciences; Ophthalmology; Otorhinolaryngology; Paediatrics; Pathology; Physical Therapy; Physiology; Plastic Surgery; Psychiatry and Mental Health; Public Health; Radiology; Rehabilitation and Therapy; Social and Preventive Medicine; Speech Therapy and Audiology; Surgery; Toxicology; Urology); **Music** (Music; Music Education; Religious Music); **Nursing** (Cardiology; Community Health; Nursing); **Pharmacy** (Epidemiology; Pharmacology; Pharmacy); **Philosophy** (Ethics; Philosophy); **Planning, Architecture and Visual Arts** (Architecture; Art Education; Fine Arts; Graphic Design; Regional Planning; Town Planning; Visual Arts); **Science and Engineering** (Actuarial Science; Aeronautical and Aerospace Engineering; Biochemistry; Biology; Biotechnology; Chemical Engineering; Chemistry; Civil Engineering; Computer Engineering; Computer Science; Earth Sciences; Electrical Engineering; Engineering; Geological Engineering; Geology; Hydraulic Engineering; Industrial Engineering; Marine Science and Oceanography; Materials Engineering; Mathematics; Mechanical Engineering; Metallurgical Engineering; Microbiology; Mining Engineering; Natural Sciences; Optics; Physical Engineering; Physics; Polymer and Plastics Technology; Software Engineering; Statistics); **Social Sciences** (Anthropology; Clinical Psychology; Criminology; Cultural Studies; Economics; Gerontology; Human Resources; International Relations; Labour and Industrial Relations; Management; Mathematics; Philosophy; Political Sciences; Psychology; Public Administration; Social and Community Services; Social Sciences; Sociology; Women's Studies); **Theology and Religious Studies** (Classical Languages; Ethics; Hebrew; Oriental Languages; Pastoral Studies; Religious Studies; Sanskrit; Theology)

Programme

Continuous Education (Accountancy; Agricultural Management; Bible; Biotechnology; Computer Science; Development Studies; Educational Administration; English Studies; Ethics; Finance; Food Science; French; Geography; German; Grammar; Greek (Classical); History of Religion; Human Resources; Industrial Engineering; Information Management; Information Technology; International Business; International Law; Journalism; Latin; Law; Leadership; Management; Music; Occupational Health; Ophthalmology; Pastoral Studies; Pharmacy; Philosophy; Portuguese; Public Relations; Publishing and Book Trade; Real Estate; Religion; Religious Studies; Russian; Small Business; Social Psychology; Software Engineering; Statistics; Surveying and Mapping; Theology; Tourism; Toxicology; Vocational Education; Writing); **Distance Education** (Agrobiology; Animal Husbandry; Business Administration; Cognitive Sciences; Communication Studies; Computer Science; Cultural Studies; E- Business/Commerce; Ethnology; Food Technology; Forestry; French; Geography; Gerontology; Health Sciences; Horticulture; Information Sciences; Information Technology; Insurance; Law; Nutrition; Philosophy; Political Sciences; Religious Practice; Small Business; Theology)

Institute

International Studies *(Québec)* (International Studies)

Laboratory

'Mont Mégantic' Observatory *(OMM)*

Research Centre

Aboriginal Studies and Research *(CIERA)*; **Agricultural Economics** *(CREA)* (Agricultural Economics; Agronomy); **Algebric Mathematics Calculation** *(Interuniversity Centre, CICMA)* (Mathematics); **Brain, Behaviour and Neuropsychiatry** *(CRCN)* (Behavioural Sciences; Neurology; Psychiatry and Mental Health); **Cancer** *(CRC)* (Oncology); **Catalysis and Interfaces Properties** *(CERPIC)* (Organic Chemistry); **Concrete Technology** *(Interuniversity Research, CRIB)* (Building Technologies); **Education and Work Life** *(Interuniversity Research, CRIEVAT)*; **Energy Metabolism** *(CREME)* (Physiology); **Forestry Biology** *(CRBF)* (Forest Biology); **Geomatics** *(CRG)* (Surveying and Mapping); **Horticulture** *(CRH)* (Horticulture); **Infectiology** *(CRI)* (Epidemiology); **Language Planning** *(International Research Centre, CIRAL)* (Linguistics; Modern Languages); **Languages, Arts and Popular**

Francophone Traditions of North America *(CELAT)* (Canadian Studies; Cultural Studies; Folklore; French Studies; Modern Languages); **Macromolecules Sciences and Engineering** *(CERSIM)* (Molecular Biology); **Milk Science and Technology** *(STELA)* (Dairy; Technology); **Molecular Endocrinology and Oncology** *(CREMO)* (Endocrinology; Oncology); **Network Organisation Technologies** *(CENTOR)* (Computer Networks; Telecommunications Engineering); **Nordic Studies**; **Optics, Photonics and Laser** (Laser Engineering; Optics); **Protein, Function and Structure Engineering** *(CREFSIP)* (Physical Engineering); **Quebec Literature and Culture** *(Interuniversity Research; CRILCQ)* (Canadian Studies; Cultural Studies; Literature); **Quebec Studies** *(Interuniversity Centre, CIEQ)* (Canadian Studies; Cultural Studies; Social Sciences); **Regional Planning and Development** *(CRAD)* (Regional Planning; Rural Planning; Town Planning); **Rehabilitation and Social Integration** (Psychology; Rehabilitation and Therapy; Social Work); **Reproduction Biology** *(CRBR)* (Embryology and Reproduction Biology); **Research and Intervention on Academic Success** *(CRIRES)* (Educational Sciences); **Risk, Economic Policies and Employment** *(Interuniversity Research, CIRPEE)* (Economics; Finance); **Training and Teaching Professions** *(Interuniversity Research Centre (CRIFPE))* (Teacher Trainers Education; Teacher Training); **Violence Against Women and Family Violence** (Gender Studies; Women's Studies); **Youth and Families at Risk** *(JEFAR)* (Social Work)

Research Group

Finite Element Methods *(Interdisciplinary Research Group, GIREF)* (Engineering; Mathematics); **Health Respiratory** *(GESER)* (Health Sciences); **Oral Ecology** *(GREB)* (Oral Pathology); **Psychosocial Inadaptation of the Child** *(GRIP)* (Child Care and Development; Educational Psychology); **Quebec Oceanographic Research** *(Interuniversity Group, Quebec-Ocean)* (Marine Science and Oceanography)

Further Information: Also 9 Teaching Hospitals. French courses for foreign students. 386 programmes. International, Work-Study and Entrepeneurial profiles integrated into many programmes.

History: Founded 1663 as Grand Séminaire de Québec. Granted royal Charter 1852. Granted a new charter by the Assemblée Nationale du Québec 1970; modified 1991. Financed by a Provincial Grant.

Academic Year: September to August (September-December; January-April; May-August)

Admission Requirements: Diploma of Collegial Studies (DEC) following successful completion of a 2-year pre-university course at a CEGEP (Collège d'Enseignement général et professionnel), or recognized equivalent

Fees: National: Undergraduate, 294,57 per course (3 credits) for Québec residents. 730,44 for other Canadian students (Canadian Dollar), International: Undergraduate,1601,04-1928,52 per course (3 credits) (Canadian Dollar)

Main Language(s) of Instruction: French

Degrees and Diplomas: *Certificat et diplôme universitaire/University certificate and diploma*; *Baccalauréat/Bachelor's Degree*; *Diplôme d'études supérieures spécialisées/Graduate Advanced Diploma*; *Maîtrise/Master's Degree*: **Business Administration; Education; Engineering; Health Sciences; Information Technology; Law; Natural Sciences; Public Health; Social Sciences.** *Doctorat/Doctoral Degree*: **Agricultural Economics; Art History; Cinema and Television; Literature; Music; Music Education; Performing Arts; Psychology; Theatre.** Also M.B.A.; Undergraduate and graduate microprogrammes.

Student Services: Academic Counselling, Canteen, Careers Guidance, Cultural Activities, Facilities for disabled people, Foreign Studies Centre, Health Services, Language Laboratory, Library, Nursery Care, Social Counselling, Sports Facilities

Publishing house: Presses de l'Université Laval

Academic Staff *2014-2015*	**TOTAL**
FULL-TIME	**2,500**
PART-TIME	**100**
STAFF WITH DOCTORATE	
FULL-TIME	c. **1,310**
Student Numbers *2014-2015*	
All (Foreign included)	c. **48,000**
FOREIGN ONLY	**4000**

Last Updated: 26/03/15

MCGILL UNIVERSITY

845 Sherbrooke Street West, Montréal, Québec H3A 2T5
Tel: +1(514) 398-4455
EMail: admissions@mcgill.ca
Website: http://www.mcgill.ca

Principal and Vice-Chancellor: Suzanne Fortier (2013-)

University Registrar and Executive Director, Enrolment Services: Kathleen Massey
Tel: +1(514) 398-3672 EMail: kathleen.massey@mcgill.ca

International Relations: Rose Goldstein, Vice-Principal, Research and International Relations
Tel: +1(514) 398-2995 EMail: rose.goldstein@mcgill.ca

Faculty

Agricultural and Environmental Sciences (Agricultural Economics; Agriculture; Animal Husbandry; Biochemistry; Bioengineering; Biological and Life Sciences; Biology; Botany; Dietetics; Ecology; Entomology; Environmental Engineering; Environmental Studies; Farm Management; Food Science; Food Technology; Forestry; Meteorology; Microbiology; Molecular Biology; Natural Resources; Nutrition; Soil Management; Soil Science; Tropical Agriculture; Water Management; Wildlife); **Arts** (African Studies; American Studies; Anthropology; Art History; Arts and Humanities; Canadian Studies; Caribbean Studies; Catholic Theology; Cinema and Television; Classical Languages; Cognitive Sciences; Communication Studies; Development Studies; East Asian Studies; Economics; Educational Psychology; English; French; Gender Studies; German; Greek (Classical); History; Italian; Jewish Studies; Labour and Industrial Relations; Latin; Latin American Studies; Linguistics; Literature; Middle Eastern Studies; Philosophy; Political Sciences; Religion; Russian; Slavic Languages; Social Work; Sociology; Spanish; Statistics; Women's Studies); **Dentistry** (Dentistry; Oral Pathology; Surgery); **Education** (Education; Educational and Student Counselling; Educational Psychology; Educational Sciences; Family Studies; Foreign Languages Education; Health Education; Human Resources; Indigenous Studies; Information Sciences; Jewish Studies; Leadership; Library Science; Music Education; Natives Education; Pedagogy; Physical Education; Physical Therapy; Physiology; Primary Education; Psychology; Secondary Education; Special Education; Teacher Training); **Engineering** (Architecture; Bioengineering; Biomedical Engineering; Chemical Engineering; Civil Engineering; Computer Engineering; Computer Science; Electrical Engineering; Energy Engineering; Engineering; Environmental Engineering; Hydraulic Engineering; Materials Engineering; Mechanical Engineering; Mechanics; Mining Engineering; Nanotechnology; Power Engineering; Software Engineering; Structural Architecture; Telecommunications Engineering; Town Planning; Transport Engineering); **Law** (Air and Space Law; Civil Law; Comparative Law; Environmental Studies; Ethics; European Union Law; Human Rights; International Law; Law; Private Law); **Management** (Accountancy; Business Administration; Health Administration; Industrial Management; Leadership; Management); **Medicine** (Anaesthesiology; Anatomy; Biochemistry; Biomedical Engineering; Cardiology; Cell Biology; Communication Disorders; Communication Studies; Dermatology; Endocrinology; Epidemiology; Gastroenterology; Genetics; Gerontology; Gynaecology and Obstetrics; Haematology; Immunology; Medicine; Microbiology; Nephrology; Neurology; Nursing; Occupational Health; Occupational Therapy; Oncology; Ophthalmology; Orthopaedics; Otorhinolaryngology; Paediatrics; Pathology; Pharmacology; Physical Therapy; Physiology; Plastic Surgery; Psychiatry and Mental Health; Radiology; Respiratory Therapy; Rheumatology; Social Studies; Statistics; Surgery; Urology); **Religious Studies** (Asian Religious Studies; Bible; Christian Religious Studies; Ethics; History of Religion; New Testament; Philosophy; Religion; Religious Studies; Theology); **Science** (Applied Mathematics; Astronomy and Space Science; Biochemistry; Biological and Life Sciences; Biology; Cell Biology; Chemistry; Clinical Psychology; Computer Science; Earth Sciences; Environmental Studies; Experimental Psychology; Geography; Geophysics; Immunology; Marine Science and Oceanography; Mathematics; Meteorology; Microbiology; Molecular Biology; Natural Sciences; Neurosciences; Physics; Psychology; Software Engineering; Statistics)

College

Montréal Diocesan Theological College (Ethics; History of Religion; New Testament; Pastoral Studies; Philosophy; Religion; Religious Education; Religious Studies; Theology); **Presbyterian**

College (Christian Religious Studies; History of Religion; Holy Writings; New Testament; Religion; Theology); **United Theological College (UTC)** *((UTC))* (Bible; Christian Religious Studies; Ethics; History of Religion; New Testament; Pastoral Studies; Philosophy; Religion; Religious Studies; Theology)

Programme

Graduate and Postdoctoral Studies (Agricultural Economics; Agriculture; Anatomy; Anthropology; Architecture; Art History; Astronomy and Space Science; Biochemistry; Bioengineering; Biology; Biomedical Engineering; Biotechnology; Botany; Business Administration; Cell Biology; Chemical Engineering; Chemistry; Civil Engineering; Classical Languages; Communication Disorders; Communication Studies; Computer Engineering; Computer Science; Dentistry; Development Studies; Dietetics; Earth Sciences; East Asian Studies; Economics; Education; Educational and Student Counselling; Educational Psychology; Electrical Engineering; English; Environmental Engineering; Environmental Studies; Epidemiology; Ethics; European Studies; Food Science; French; Gender Studies; Genetics; Geography; German; Greek (Classical); History; Immunology; Information Sciences; Islamic Studies; Italian; Jewish Studies; Latin; Law; Linguistics; Literature; Management; Marine Science and Oceanography; Materials Engineering; Mechanical Engineering; Mechanics; Medical Technology; Meteorology; Microbiology; Mining Engineering; Music; Natural Resources; Neurosciences; Nursing; Nutrition; Occupational Health; Occupational Therapy; Oncology; Otorhinolaryngology; Parasitology; Pathology; Pharmacology; Philosophy; Physical Education; Physical Therapy; Physics; Physiology; Polish; Psychiatry and Mental Health; Psychology; Religious Studies; Russian; Slavic Languages; Social Studies; Social Work; Sociology; Spanish; Statistics; Surgery; Town Planning; Tropical Agriculture; Women's Studies; Zoology)

School

Music *(Schulich)* (Jazz and Popular Music; Music; Music Education; Music Theory and Composition; Musical Instruments; Musicology; Singing)

Centre

Continuing Education (Accountancy; Business Administration; Education; English; Finance; French; Health Sciences; Human Resources; Information Technology; Insurance; International Business; Leadership; Management; Marketing; Operations Research; Public Relations; Social Work; Spanish; Taxation; Translation and Interpretation; Transport Management)

Further Information: For additional information see website. Also online courses.

History: Founded 1821 as University of McGill College. A corporation created by Royal Charter granted by the United Kingdom Crown and exercised through the Governor-General as 'visitor'.

Academic Year: September to April (September-December; January-April)

Admission Requirements: Diploma of Collegial Studies (DEC) following successful completion of a 2-year pre-university course at a CEGEP (Collège d'Enseignement général et professionnel) in Quebec, or high school diploma with university entrance

Fees: (Can. Dollars): Undergraduate tuition, Quebec Students, 2,067.90-4,825.10 per annum; non-Quebec Canadians, 5,667.60-13,224.40 per annum; international students, 14,461.80-37,705.50 per annum. Graduate tuition, Quebec Students, 2,067.90 per annum; non-Quebec Canadians, 2,067.90-5,667.60 per annum; international students, 12,975.60-14,461.80 per annum

Main Language(s) of Instruction: English (Students may write term papers and exams in French)

Accrediting Agency: Association of Universities and Colleges of Canada

Degrees and Diplomas: *Certificat et diplôme universitaire/University certificate and diploma*; *Baccalauréat/Bachelor's Degree*; *Diplôme d'études supérieures spécialisées/Graduate Advanced Diploma*; *Maîtrise/Master's Degree*; *Doctorat/Doctoral Degree*. Also Honours Bachelor's degree; Concurrent degree programmes in Science and Education; Joint Bachelor's degree programmes in Law and Business Administration/Social Work; Joint PhD McGill/Université de Montreal Programme in Social Work; MBA, Executive MBA; MBA in Japan.

Student Services: Academic Counselling, Facilities for disabled people, Health Services, Language Laboratory, Nursery Care, Social Counselling, Sports Facilities

Publications: McGill International Journal of Sustainable Development Law and Policy; McGill Journal of Education; McGill Journal of Law and Health; McGill Journal of Medicine; McGill Law Journal

Publishing House: McGill-Queen's University Press

Academic Staff *2010-2011*	**TOTAL**
FULL-TIME	**1,627**
STAFF WITH DOCTORATE FULL-TIME	**1,538**
Student Numbers *2010-2011*	
All (Foreign included)	**36,531**
FOREIGN ONLY	**7294**

Part-time students, 6,776.

Last Updated: 04/09/13

NATIONAL INSTITUTE OF SCIENTIFIC RESEARCH (UNIVERSITY OF QUEBEC)

Institut national de la Recherche scientifique (Université du Québec) (INRS)

490, rue de la Couronne, Québec, Québec G1K 9A9

Tel: + 1(418) 654-4677

Fax: + 1(418) 654-3876

EMail: communications@adm.inrs.ca

Website: http://www.inrs.ca/

Rector: Daniel Coderre
Tel: + 1(418) 654-2505 EMail: daniel.coderre@adm.inrs.ca

Vice Rector, Research and Academic Affairs: Yves Bégin
Tel: + 1(418) 654-2512 EMail: yves.begin@adm.inrs.ca

International Relations: Dalida Poirier, Director, Department of Planning, International Affairs
Tel: + 1(450) 686-5670 EMail: dalida.poirier@adm.inrs.ca

Centre

Energy, Materials and Telecommunications *(Varennes)* (Optics; Physics; Telecommunications Engineering); **INRS - Armand Frappier** *(Laval)* (Biological and Life Sciences; Food Science; Health Sciences; Public Health); **Urbanization, Culture and Society** (Cultural Studies; Demography and Population; Urban Studies); **Water, Earth and Environment** (Earth Sciences; Environmental Studies; Forestry; Soil Science; Water Science)

History: Founded 1969. A Postgraduate Research Institute constituent of the University of Quebec.

Academic Year: Summer semester (May to August); Autumn semester (September to December); Winter semester (January to April)

Admission Requirements: University degree at Bachelor level for Master's level programmes; Master's degree for doctoral programmes.

Fees: 1213.10 per semester (Canadian Dollar)

Main Language(s) of Instruction: French

Accrediting Agency: Ministère de l'Enseignement supérieur, de la Recherche, de la Science et de la Technologie du Québec.

Degrees and Diplomas: *Diplôme d'études supérieures spécialisées/Graduate Advanced Diploma*; *Maîtrise/Master's Degree*: **Demography and Population; Earth Sciences; Energy Engineering; Health Sciences; Immunology; Materials Engineering; Microbiology; Telecommunications Engineering; Urban Studies; Virology; Water Science.** *Doctorat/Doctoral Degree*: **Biology; Demography and Population; Earth Sciences; Energy Engineering; Immunology; Materials Engineering; Telecommunications Engineering; Urban Studies; Virology; Water Science.**

Academic Staff *2013-2014*	**TOTAL**
FULL-TIME	**150**
STAFF WITH DOCTORATE FULL-TIME	**c. 150**
Student Numbers *2013-2014*	
All (Foreign included)	**c. 752**
FOREIGN ONLY	**339**

Last Updated: 20/03/15

TÉLÉ-UNIVERSITÉ (TÉLUQ)

455, rue du Parvis, Québec, Québec G1K 9H6
Tel: +1(418) 657-2262
Fax: +1(418) 657-2094
EMail: info@teluq.ca
Website: http://www.teluq.ca/

Directrice générale: Ginette Legault (2013-)
Tel: +418 657-2747, Ext. 5201 EMail: Ginette.Legault@teluq.ca

Unit

Education (Adult Education; Distance Education; Education; Educational Technology; Information Technology); **Humanities, Arts and Communications** (Canadian Studies; Communication Studies; Developmental Psychology; English; Foreign Languages Education; French; Literature; Media Studies; Philosophy; Psychiatry and Mental Health; Psychology; Public Relations; Social Psychology; Social Sciences; Sociology; Spanish; Statistics; Translation and Interpretation); **Science and Technology** (Computer Science; Environmental Studies; Information Technology; Natural Resources; Software Engineering; Wildlife)

School

Administration (Accountancy; Administration; Business Administration; Development Studies; E- Business/Commerce; Finance; Health Administration; Human Resources; Insurance; Labour and Industrial Relations; Management; Marketing; Occupational Health; Social Sciences; Tourism)

Further Information: Also Montréal campus.

History: Founded 1972. Part of the University of Québec network.

Main Language(s) of Instruction: French

Degrees and Diplomas: *Certificat et diplôme universitaire/University certificate and diploma*; *Baccalauréat/Bachelor's Degree*; *Diplôme d'études supérieures spécialisées/Graduate Advanced Diploma*; *Maîtrise/Master's Degree*; *Doctorat/Doctoral Degree*: **Computer Science.**

Student Services: Academic Counselling, Careers Guidance, Facilities for disabled people, Library, Sports Facilities
Last Updated: 25/03/15

UNIVERSITY OF MONTREAL

Université de Montréal (UDEM)

C.P. 6128, succursale Centre-ville, Montréal, Québec H3C 3J7
Tel: +1(514) 343-6111
Fax: +1(514) 343-5976
EMail: dcr@umontreal.ca
Website: http://www.umontreal.ca

Recteur/Rector: Guy Breton (2010-)
Tel: +1(514) 343-6776
EMail: recteur@umontreal.ca; guy.breton@umontreal.ca

Secrétaire général: Alexandre Chabot
Tel: +1(514) 343-6800 EMail: alexandre.chabot@umontreal.ca

International Relations: Guy Lefebvre, Vice-rectrice aux relations internationales, à la Francophonie
Tel: +1(514) 343-6488 EMail: guy.lefebvre@umontreal.ca

Faculty

Arts and Sciences (Ancient Civilizations; Anthropology; Arabic; Art History; Arts and Humanities; Biochemistry; Biological and Life Sciences; Catalan; Chemistry; Chinese; Communication Studies; Comparative Literature; Computer Science; Criminology; Demography and Population; Economics; Educational Psychology; Educational Technology; English; Film; French; Geography; German; Germanic Studies; Greek; History; Information Sciences; Italian; Japanese; Labour and Industrial Relations; Library Science; Linguistics; Literature; Mathematics; Medieval Studies; Modern Languages; Operations Research; Philosophy; Physics; Political Sciences; Portuguese; Psychology; Social Sciences; Social Work; Sociology; Spanish; Statistics; Translation and Interpretation); **Continuing Education** (Advertising and Publicity; Child Care and Development; Communication Studies; Community Health; Computer Science; Criminology; Foreign Languages Education; French; Gerontology; Health Administration; Health Sciences; Journalism; Labour and Industrial Relations; Law; Management; Multimedia; Psychiatry and Mental Health; Public Relations; Rehabilitation and Therapy; Social and Community Services; Social Problems; Translation and Interpretation; Writing); **Dentistry** (Biochemistry; Biomedicine; Community Health; Dental Technology; Dentistry; Immunology; Microbiology; Neurology; Orthodontics; Public Health; Stomatology); **Education** (Education; Educational Administration; Educational Psychology; Educational Sciences; Foreign Languages Education; French; International and Comparative Education; Mathematics Education; Physical Education; Preschool Education; Primary Education; Religious Education; Science Education; Secondary Education; Special Education; Teacher Training); **Environmental Design** (Architectural and Environmental Design; Architecture; Design; Industrial Design; Interior Design; Landscape Architecture; Software Engineering; Town Planning); **Graduate and Postdoctoral Studies** (Actuarial Science; Administration; Anaesthesiology; Anthropology; Architecture; Archiving; Art History; Arts and Humanities; Bible; Biochemistry; Biological and Life Sciences; Biology; Biomedical Engineering; Biomedicine; Cell Biology; Chemistry; Civil Law; Classical Languages; Clinical Psychology; Commercial Law; Communication Studies; Community Health; Comparative Literature; Computer Science; Conducting; Criminology; Curriculum; Demography and Population; Dentistry; Development Studies; E- Business/Commerce; Economics; Education; Educational Administration; Educational Psychology; English; English Studies; Environmental Management; Environmental Studies; Ethics; Film; Fiscal Law; Forensic Medicine and Dentistry; French; Genetics; Geography; German; Germanic Studies; Greek (Classical); Health Administration; Health Education; Health Sciences; Higher Education; History; Immunology; Information Sciences; Information Technology; International Economics; International Law; International Studies; Labour and Industrial Relations; Latin; Law; Library Science; Linguistics; Literature; Mathematics; Mathematics and Computer Science; Microbiology; Molecular Biology; Museum Studies; Music; Music Theory and Composition; Musical Instruments; Neurosciences; Notary Studies; Nursing; Nutrition; Occupational Health; Optometry; Oral Pathology; Paediatrics; Pathology; Pharmacology; Pharmacy; Philosophy; Physical Therapy; Physics; Physiology; Political Sciences; Psychology; Public Health; Radiology; Rehabilitation and Therapy; Religious Studies; Safety Engineering; Secondary Education; Social Sciences; Social Work; Sociology; Software Engineering; Spanish; Special Education; Speech Studies; Speech Therapy and Audiology; Statistics; Surveying and Mapping; Teacher Training; Theology; Town Planning; Toxicology; Translation and Interpretation; Veterinary Science; Virology); **Law** (Administrative Law; Civil Law; Commercial Law; Constitutional Law; Criminal Law; Fiscal Law; International Law; Labour Law; Law; Notary Studies); **Medicine** (Anaesthesiology; Biochemistry; Biomedicine; Cardiology; Community Health; Dermatology; Endocrinology; Gastroenterology; Genetics; Gerontology; Gynaecology and Obstetrics; Haematology; Health Administration; Immunology; Medicine; Microbiology; Molecular Biology; Nephrology; Neurology; Nutrition; Occupational Health; Oncology; Ophthalmology; Paediatrics; Pathology; Pharmacology; Physical Therapy; Physiology; Plastic Surgery; Psychiatry and Mental Health; Public Health; Radiology; Rehabilitation and Therapy; Respiratory Therapy; Rheumatology; Speech Therapy and Audiology; Surgery; Toxicology; Urology; Virology); **Music** (Art History; Conducting; Music; Music Theory and Composition; Musical Instruments; Musicology; Singing); **Nursing** (Cardiology; Health Administration; Health Education; Health Sciences; Nephrology; Nursing); **Pharmacy** (Biological and Life Sciences; Epidemiology; Pharmacology; Pharmacy); **Theology and Religious Studies** (Bible; Christian Religious Studies; Community Health; Ethics; Islamic Studies; Religious Studies; Theology); **Veterinary Medicine** (Biomedicine; Epidemiology; Food Technology; Immunology; Microbiology; Pathology; Pharmacology; Toxicology; Veterinary Science; Virology)

School

Optometry (Biomedicine; Neurosciences; Ophthalmology; Optometry; Paediatrics; Physiology; Psychology; Rehabilitation and Therapy); **Public Health** (Public Health)

Department

Kinesiology (Ethics; Health Education; Physical Education; Physical Therapy; Physiology)

Further Information: Also Laval Campus

History: Founded 1878 as a branch of Laval University. Became autonomous 1919 and acquired present status and title 1967. A public institution. The largest French-speaking university outside France.

Academic Year: September to August (September-December; January-April; May-August)

Admission Requirements: Diploma of Collegial Studies (DEC) following successful completion of a 2-year pre-university course at a CEGEP (Collège d'enseignement général et professionnel), or recognized equivalent

Fees: National: Quebec residents: Undergraduate, 75,77 per credit for; Graduate studies:1, 136,55 (15 crédits). Non-Quebec Canadian Students: Undergraduate, 221,06 per credit. Graduate: 3 315,90 per term (Canadian Dollar), International: Undergraduate: 75,77- 673,79 per credit depending on programmes. Master's: 7 668,90 per term. PhD, 6 885,65 per term

Main Language(s) of Instruction: French, English

Degrees and Diplomas: *Certificat et diplôme universitaire/University certificate and diploma*; *Baccalauréat/Bachelor's Degree*; *Diplôme d'études supérieures spécialisées/Graduate Advanced Diploma*; *Maîtrise/Master's Degree*; *Doctorat/Doctoral Degree*: **Adult Education; Anthropology; Architecture; Architecture and Planning; Arts and Humanities; Biochemistry; Bioengineering; Biology; Biomedicine; Chemistry; Communication Studies; Computer Science; Criminology; Demography and Population; Economics; Educational Administration; Educational Psychology; Educational Testing and Evaluation; English; French; Geography; German; History; Industrial Management; Information Sciences; International and Comparative Education; Law; Library Science; Linguistics; Literature; Mathematics; Microbiology; Molecular Biology; Music; Neurosciences; Nutrition; Optometry; Pathology; Pedagogy; Pharmacology; Philosophy; Physical Therapy; Physics; Political Sciences; Psychology; Public Health; Rehabilitation and Therapy; Religious Studies; Social Sciences; Sociology; Spanish; Statistics; Theology; Translation and Interpretation; Veterinary Science; Virology.** Also Honours Bachelor's degree; Joint degrees (Combined Honours Mathematics and Computer science; Combined programmes in Law; Postdoctoral fellows in Nursing.

Student Services: Academic Counselling, Canteen, Careers Guidance, Cultural Activities, Facilities for disabled people, Health Services, Library, Nursery Care, Social Counselling, Sports Facilities

Publications: Cahiers d'histoire; Circuit, revue nord-américaine de musique du XXe siècle; Forum; META, Journal des Traducteurs/ Translator's Journal; Revue juridique Thémis; Sociologie et Sociétés

Publishing House: University Press (Les Presses de l'Université de Montréal)

Last Updated: 24/03/15

HEC MONTRÉAL (HEC)

3000, chemin de la Côte-Sainte-Catherine,
Montréal, Québec H3T 2A7
Tel: +1(514) 340-6000
Fax: +1(514) 340-6411
EMail: registraire.info@hec.ca
Website: http://www.hec.ca

Director: Michel Patry
Tel: +1(514) 340-6300 EMail: michel.patry@hec.ca

Secrétaire général: Federico Pasin
Tel: +1(514) 340-6752 EMail: federico.pasin@hec.ca

Department

Accounting Studies (Accountancy; Administration; Business Administration; Finance; Fiscal Law; Management; Taxation); **Finance** (Finance); **Human Resources Management** *(GRH)* (Business Administration; Human Resources; Management); **Information Technology** (Business Administration; Business Computing; E- Business/Commerce; Information Technology); **International Business** (Business Administration; International Business; Management); **Logistics and Operations Management** *(GOL)* (Management; Transport Management); **Management** (Administration; Art Management; Business Administration; Environmental Management; Management); **Marketing** (Administration; Business Administration; Business and Commerce; Management; Marketing; Retailing and Wholesaling; Sales Techniques); **Quantitative Methods for Management Development** *(MQG)* (Administration; Finance; Management; Transport Management)

Institute

Applied Economics *(IEA)* (Administration; Economics; Finance)

Centre

Computerization of Organizations *(Francophone - CEFRIO)* (Computer Science); **Financial Information** *(International Watch)* (Finance); **House of Technology for Training and Learning** *(MATI Montreal)* (Educational Technology); **Humanism, Management and Globalization** (Management); **International Association for Research in Entrepreneurship and SMEs** *(AIREPME)* (Management; Small Business); **International Business Families** *(McGill - HEC Montreal)* (International Business); **Logistics hub** (Transport Management); **Productivity and Prosperity** (Economics); **Promotion of Excellence in Municipal Management** (Management); **Studies in Management of Financial Services Cooperatives** *(Desjardins)* (Finance; Management); **Studies of Business Processes** *(CMA International)* (Business Administration)

Group

Strategy as Practice Study (Management); **Women, Management and Organizations** (Management)

Laboratory

ERPsim (Business Administration)

Research Centre

Analysis on Organizations *(Interuniversity - CIRANO)* (Management); **Creation Management and Transfer** *(Mosaic)* (Management); **E-Finance** (Finance); **Enterprise Networks, Logistics and Transportation** *(Interuniversity - CIRRELT)* (Transport and Communications; Transport Management); **Families in Business** (Business Administration); **Globalization and Work** *(Interuniversity - CRIMT)* (International Economics); **Healthcare Management Hub** (Health Administration); **Life Cycle of Products, Processes and Services** *(Interuniversity - CIRAIG)* (Business Administration); **Organizational Transformation** *(CETO)* (Management); **Quantitative Economics** *(Interuniversity - CIREQ)* (Economics); **Risk, Economic Policies and Employment** *(Interuniversity - CIRPEE)* (Economics); **Social Innovations** *(CRISES)* (Welfare and Protective Services); **Work, Health and Organizational Effectiveness** *(CRITEOS)* (Management)

Research Group

CHAIN (Transport Management); **Decision Analysis** *(GERAD)* (Management; Operations Research); **Education and Research on Management and Environment** *(GERM)* (Environmental Studies; Management); **Information Systems** *(GReSI)* (Information Sciences); **International Affairs** *(GRAI)* (International Business); **Non-profit, Community and Cultural Organizations** (Management); **Organizations Strategy** *(STRATEGOS)* (Management); **Sustainable Development** *(Interdisciplinary - GRIDD-HEC)* (Development Studies); **Use, Development and Transfer of Management Knowledge** (Management)

Chair

Arts Management *(Carmelle and Rémi Marcoux)* (Art Management); **Commercial Space and Customer Service Management** (Business and Commerce; Management); **Data Mining** (Data Processing); **E-Commerce** *(RBC Financial Group)* (E- Business/Commerce); **Entrepreneurship** *(Rogers–J.-A.-Bombardier)* (Management); **Ethical Management** (Management); **Game Theory and Management** (Management); **Governance and Forensic Accounting** (Accountancy; Government); **International Economics and Governance** (Government; International Economics); **International Strategic Management** *(Walter-J.-Somers)* (Management); **Leadership** *(Pierre-Péladeau)* (Leadership); **Learning and Teaching Technologies in Management Education** (Educational Technology); **Monetary Policy and Financial Markets** (Finance); **Research in Distribution Management** *(Canada)* (Transport Management); **Research in Information Technology Implementation and Management** *(Canada)* (Information Management; Information Technology); **Research in Information Technology in Health Care** *(Canada)* (Information Technology); **Research in Logistics and Transportation** *(Canada)* (Transport and Communications; Transport Management); **Research in Management of Employee Commitment and Performance** *(Canada)* (Management); **Research in Risk Management** *(Canada)* (Insurance); **Research in Strategic Management in Pluralistic Settings** *(Canada)* (Management); **Retailing** *(Omer DeSerres)* (Retailing and Wholesaling); **Small and Medium-size Business Development and Succession** (Small Business); **Strategic Management of**

Information Technology (Information Technology; Management); **Supply Management** (Transport Management)

Further Information: Exchange Programme (Passeport pour le Monde)

History: Founded 1907 as Ecole des Hautes Etudes Commerciales de Montréal. Acquired present name 2002. Affiliated to the University of Montreal.

Academic Year: September to July (September-December; January-May; May-July)

Admission Requirements: Depending on programmes; information available from the institution

Fees: National: BBA: 75,77 per credit for Quebec-resident students, 221,06 per credit for Non-Quebec-resident students. Master's degree, 76,77 per credit for Quebec-resident students. 221,06 for Non-Quebec-resident students. PhD, 75,77 per credit (Residents and Non-residents of Québec) (Canadian Dollar), International: BBA: 604,68 per credit. Maste's degree: 551,26 per credit. PhD Administration: 459,04 per credit

Main Language(s) of Instruction: French, English, Spanish

Accrediting Agency: AMBA (The Association of MBA's - UK); European Quality Improvement System (EQUIS) of the European Foundation for Management Development (EFMD); AACSB International (United States)

Degrees and Diplomas: *Certificat et diplôme universitaire/University certificate and diploma*; *Baccalauréat/Bachelor's Degree*; *Diplôme d'études supérieures spécialisées/Graduate Advanced Diploma*; *Maîtrise/Master's Degree*: **Administration; Business Administration.** *Doctorat/Doctoral Degree*: **Administration.** Also joint EMBA offered by McGill's Desautels Faculty of Management and HEC Montreal

Student Services: Academic Counselling, Canteen, Careers Guidance, Cultural Activities, Facilities for disabled people, Foreign Studies Centre, Health Services, Language Laboratory, Library, Nursery Care, Social Counselling, Sports Facilities

Publications: Assurances; Gestion (Revue internationale); International Journal of Arts Management; International Management

Student Numbers *2014-2015*: Total 13,046

POLYTECHNIC SCHOOL OF MONTREAL

ECOLE POLYTECHNIQUE DE MONTRÉAL

Case postale 6079, succ. Centre-ville, Montréal, Québec H3C 3A7
Tel: + 1(514) 340-4711
Fax: + 1(514) 340-5836
EMail: registraire@polymtl.ca
Website: http://www.polymtl.ca/

Directeur général: Christophe Guy (2007-)
Tel: + 1(514) 340-4943
EMail: christophe.guy@polymtl.ca; direction.generale@polymtl.ca

Registraire: Stéphanie de Celles
Tel: + 1(514) 340-4711 Ext. 4324
EMail: stephanie.decelles@polymtl.ca; registraire@polymtl.ca

Directeur des affaires académiques et internationales: Pierre G. Lafleur

International Relations: Line Dubé, Directrice, Bureau des relations internationales (BRIN)
Tel: + 1(514) 340-4711 poste
EMail: line.dube@polymtl.ca; brin@polymtl.ca

Department

Biomedical Engineering (Biomedical Engineering); **Chemical Engineering** (Biomedical Engineering; Biotechnology; Chemical Engineering; Energy Engineering; Engineering Management; Environmental Engineering; Paper Technology; Pharmacology; Polymer and Plastics Technology); **Civil, Geological and Mining Engineering** (Civil Engineering; Construction Engineering; Environmental Engineering; Geological Engineering; Mining Engineering; Transport Engineering); **Computer Engineering** (Computer Engineering; Computer Networks; Information Technology; Multimedia; Software Engineering); **Electrical Engineering** (Aeronautical and Aerospace Engineering; Automation and Control Engineering; Computer Engineering; Electrical Engineering; Energy Engineering; Engineering Management; Management; Microelectronics; Microwaves; Software Engineering; Telecommunications Engineering); **Engineering Physics** (Biomedical Engineering; Engineering; Nanotechnology; Nuclear Engineering; Physical Engineering); **Mathematics and Industrial Engineering** (Applied Mathematics; Engineering Management; Industrial Design; Industrial Engineering; Mathematics; Production Engineering; Safety Engineering; Transport Management); **Mechanical Engineering** (Aeronautical and Aerospace Engineering; Materials Engineering; Mechanical Engineering; Metallurgical Engineering)

Centre

Applied Research on Polymers and Composites (Polymer and Plastics Technology); **Characterization and Microscopy of Materials** *((CM)2)* (Metallurgical Engineering); **Continuing Education** (Aeronautical and Aerospace Engineering; Biomedical Engineering; Building Technologies; Civil Engineering; Construction Engineering; Development Studies; Display and Stage Design; Electrical Engineering; Engineering; Fire Science; Industrial Design; Industrial Engineering; Mechanical Engineering; Operations Research; Polymer and Plastics Technology; Production Engineering; Safety Engineering; Technology; Water Management); **Northern Engineering** *(CINEP)* (Engineering; Meteorology); **Research in Computational Thermochemistry** *(CRCT)* (Chemical Engineering; Safety Engineering); **Research in Radiofrequency Electronics** *(CREER)* (Electronic Engineering; Telecommunications Engineering); **Risque et Performance** (Industrial Engineering; Safety Engineering); **Water Treatment Technologies and Processes** *(Research, Development and Validation)* (Waste Management; Water Management)

Group

Experimental and numerical engineering water flow *(GENIE EAU)* (Hydraulic Engineering; Safety Engineering); **Mechanical Components Analysis** *(GACM)* (Mechanical Engineering); **Nuclear Analysis** (Nuclear Engineering); **Ptidej** (Software Engineering); **Regroupement Québécois sur les Matériaux de Pointe** *(RQMP)* (Materials Engineering); **URPEI** (Chemical Engineering)

Laboratory

BioMEMS (Mechanical Engineering; Microelectronics); **Bio-performance Analysis and Innovation** (Biomedical Engineering); **Broadband Networks** *(Broadlab)* (Electrical Engineering); **Complex Applications Design and Implementation** (Computer Engineering); **Distributed open reliable systems analysis** *(DORSAL)* (Computer Engineering; Software Engineering); **Electrical Energy** (Electrical Engineering); **Environmental Engineering** (Environmental Engineering); **Epitaxy and Characterization of Compound Semiconductors** (Electronic Engineering; Physical Engineering); **Fiber Optics** (Physical Engineering); **Fluid Dynamics** *(LADYF)* (Hydraulic Engineering; Mechanics); **Functional Coating and Surface Engineering** (Physical Engineering); **Hydrogeology and Mining Environment** (Geological Engineering; Hydraulic Engineering); **LASEM** (Electrical Engineering); **Laser Processing** *(LPL)* (Laser Engineering); **Magnetics** (Physical Engineering); **Material Surface Analysis** *(LASM)* (Materials Engineering; Nanotechnology; Physical Engineering); **Micro and Nano Systems** (Microelectronics; Nanotechnology); **Microfabrication** (Physical Engineering); **Multi-scale Mechanics** (Mechanics); **NanoRobotics** (Nanotechnology; Robotics); **Nanostructures** (Nanotechnology); **Networking and Digital Geometry** *(MAGNU)* (Computer Engineering); **Neurotechnology** *(Polystim)* (Electrical Engineering); **New Materials for Energy and Electrochemistry** (Chemistry; Electronic Engineering; Energy Engineering; Materials Engineering); **Optoelectronics** (Physical Engineering); **Photo Acoustic Spectroscopy and Laser-Ultrasonics** *(PASLU)* (Laser Engineering; Physical Engineering); **Polynov** (Chemical Engineering); **Robotics** *(Ecole Polytechnique Montreal)* (Robotics); **SCRIBENS** (Electrical Engineering; Neurosciences); **SLOWPOKE** (Physical Engineering); **Software Engineering** (Software Engineering); **Spectroscopy of Materials and Nanostructures** (Materials Engineering; Nanotechnology); **Thermalhydraulics** (Nuclear Engineering)

Research Centre

Biomedical Science and Technologies *(GRSTB)* (Biomedical Engineering; Biomedicine); **Entreprise Networks, Logistics and Transportation** *(Interuniversity -CIRRELT)* (Transport and Communications; Transport Management); **IDEA** (Aeronautical and Aerospace Engineering); **Life Cycle of Products, Processes and**

Services *(Interuniversity - CIRAIG)* (Chemical Engineering; Industrial Design); **Microsystems Strategic Alliance** *(RESMIQ)* (Electrical Engineering); **Microwaves and Space Electronics** *(Advanced - POLY-GRAMES)* (Electronic Engineering; Microwaves); **Process Engineering - Biorefinery** *(CRIP)* (Chemical Engineering; Heating and Refrigeration; Petroleum and Gas Engineering); **SQUIRREL** (Software Engineering); **Technology for Training and Learning** *(Roland-Giguère House)* (Educational Technology)

Research Group

Computational Engineering *(GRMIAO)* (Computer Engineering); **Decision Analysis** *(GERAD)* (Industrial Engineering; Mathematics; Operations Research); **MADITUC** (Civil Engineering); **Microelectronics and Microsystems** *(GR2M)* (Microelectronics); **Networking and Mobile Computing** *(GRIM)* (Computer Engineering; Computer Networks); **Perception and Robotics** *(GRPR)* (Robotics); **PolyPhotonic** (Electrical Engineering; Physical Engineering); **Product Development and Manufacturing** *(GRDFP)* (Mechanical Engineering; Production Engineering); **Structural Engineering** *(GRS)* (Civil Engineering; Safety Engineering); **Thin Film Physics and Technology** *(GCM)* (Physical Engineering)

Research Laboratory

Mobile Computing and Networking *(LARIM)* (Computer Engineering; Computer Networks); **Tightness Testing** *(TTRL)* (Mechanical Engineering); **Virtual Manufacturing** (Mechanical Engineering)

Research Unit

Energy Efficiency and Sustainable Development of the Forest Biorefinery (Chemical Engineering; Environmental Engineering; Paper Technology)

Chair

Drinking Water Treatment *(NSERC Industrial)* (Water Management); **Environment and Mine Wastes Management** *(NSERC-Polytechnique-UQAT Industrial)* (Mining Engineering; Waste Management; Water Management); **Fluid-Structure Interaction** *(BWC/AECL/NSERC Industrial)* (Mechanical Engineering); **Liquid Composite Molding Technological Network** *(RTMFLOT Software)* (Mechanical Engineering); **Methodology for Life Cycle Assessment** *(Industrial International)* (Chemical Engineering); **Next Generations Mobile Networking Systems** *(NSERC/Ericsson Industrial)* (Computer Engineering); **Nuclear Engineering** *(Hydro-Quebec Industrial)* (Nuclear Engineering); **Process Integration in the Pulp and Paper Industry** *(NSERC Environmental Design - I3P)* (Environmental Engineering; Paper Technology); **Research on Low Cost Composite Manufacturing for Automotive Applications** *(NSERC/GM Canada Industrial)* (Automotive Engineering; Production Engineering); **Research in Advanced Microelectronic Systems Architecture and Development** *(Canada)* (Microelectronics); **Research in Analysis, Characterization and Multidisciplinary Design Optimization of Complex Systems** *(Canada)* (Mechanical Engineering); **Research in Applied Metabolic Engineering** *(Canada)* (Chemical Engineering); **Research in Cartilage Tissue Engineering** *(Canada)* (Biomedical Engineering); **Research in Earthquake Resistance Design and Construction of Steel Structures** *(Canada)* (Civil Engineering); **Research in Ergonomic Intervention for the Prevention and Rehabilitation of Musculoskeletal Disorders** *(Canada - MSD)* (Industrial Engineering; Rehabilitation and Therapy); **Research in Fabricating Microsystems and Advanced Materials** *(Canada)* (Aeronautical and Aerospace Engineering; Automotive Engineering); **Research in Future Intelligent Radio-frequency Metamaterials** *(Canada)* (Electrical and Electronic Engineering); **Research in Future Photonics Systems** *(Canada)* (Materials Engineering; Technology); **Research in High Performance Composite Design and Manufacturing** (Mechanical Engineering); **Research in Hybrid Biomaterials for Innovative Regenerative Technologies** *(NSERC Piramal Industrial)* (Biomedical Engineering; Chemical Engineering); **Research in International Project Management** *(Jarislowsky/SNC-Lavalin)* (Management); **Research in Large Transportation Network Optimization** *(Canada)* (Applied Mathematics); **Research in Materials Micro/Nanoengineering Using Lasers** *(Canada)* (Materials Engineering); **Research in Mechanobiology of the Pediatric Musculoskeletal System** (Bioengineering); **Research in Micro/Nanosystem Development, Construction and Validation** *(Canada)* (Robotics); **Research in Microbial Contaminant Dynamics in Source Waters** *(Canada)* (Environmental Engineering; Water Science); **Research in Radio Frequency and Millimetric Wave Engineering** *(Canada)* (Electrical Engineering; Electronic Engineering); **Research in Smart Medical Devices** *(Canada - SMD)* (Biomedical Engineering; Electrical and Electronic Equipment and Maintenance; Electronic Engineering; Information Technology); **Research In Software Change and Evolution** *(Canada)* (Information Technology); **Research in Software Patterns and Patterns of Software** (Software Engineering); **Research in Spine Biomechanics** *(NSERC/Medtronic Industrial)* (Biomedical Engineering); **Research in the Theory, Manufacturing and Applications of Photonic Crystals** *(Canada)* (Electrical and Electronic Engineering); **Research on Evaluation and Implementation of Sustainability in Transportation** *(MOBILITÉ Chair)* (Transport Engineering); **Research on innovations CAO/MAO in orthopedic engineering** *(Canada)* (Biomedical Engineering); **Research on Materials and Films for smart, Safe and Sustainable Packaging** *(NSERC/Saputo/Excel-Pac Industrial)* (Packaging Technology; Safety Engineering); **Research on Protein-enhanced biomaterials** *(Canada)* (Chemical Engineering); **Research on Technology Management** *(Canada)* (Industrial Engineering; Mathematics); **Sciences and Engineering Academic Teaching** (Engineering; Science Education)

History: Founded 1873.

Academic Year: September to August (September-December; January-April; May-August)

Admission Requirements: Diplôme d'études collégiales (DEC) in Sciences. Baccalauréat français (Serie S)

Main Language(s) of Instruction: French

Degrees and Diplomas: *Baccalauréat/Bachelor's Degree*; *Diplôme d'études supérieures spécialisées/Graduate Advanced Diploma*; *Maîtrise/Master's Degree*; *Doctorat/Doctoral Degree*: **Aeronautical and Aerospace Engineering; Biomedical Engineering; Chemical Engineering; Civil Engineering; Computer Engineering; Energy Engineering; Industrial Engineering; Mathematics; Mechanical Engineering; Metallurgical Engineering; Mining Engineering; Physical Engineering.** Graduate diploma programmes are called "Microprogrammes" and can be achieved in 3-6 terms.

Student Services: Academic Counselling, Canteen, Careers Guidance, Cultural Activities, Facilities for disabled people, Health Services, Nursery Care, Social Counselling, Sports Facilities

Student Numbers *2014-2015*: Total: c. 7,000

UNIVERSITY OF QUEBEC

Université du Québec (UQ)

475, rue du Parvis, Québec, Québec G1K 9H7
Tel: +1(418) 657-3551
Fax: +1(418) 657-2132
EMail: communications@uquebec.ca
Website: http://www.uquebec.ca

Présidente: Sylvie Beauchamp (2009-2014)
Tel: +1(418) 657-4301
EMail: sylvie.beauchamp@uquebec.ca; presidence@uquebec.ca

Secrétaire général: André G. Roy (2009-)
Tel: +1(418) 657-4307
EMail: andre.g.roy@uquebec.ca; sg@uquebec.ca

History: Founded 1968 by an Act of the National Assembly of the Province of Quebec, the University is the Province's first public university but it is self-governing and reports to the State each year. The University of Quebec groups 10 institutions (6 comprehensive universities, 1 research institute and 2 schools and 1 distance education institution Télé-université (TÉLUQ)). The traditional university organization by Faculties and Schools has been replaced by a structure composed of 3 elements: Departments, Modules and Research Centres. The Module is responsible for administration of First Degree programmes (1er cycle) while Departments and Research Centres (concerned with higher Degrees) are respectively responsible for teaching and research of any given discipline.

Academic Year: September to April

Admission Requirements: Diploma of Collegial Studies (DEC) following successful completion of 2 yrs pre-university course at a

CEGEP (Collège d'Enseignement général et professionnel), or recognized equivalent

Main Language(s) of Instruction: French

Degrees and Diplomas: *Certificat et diplôme universitaire/University certificate and diploma*; *Baccalauréat/Bachelor's Degree*; *Diplôme d'études supérieures spécialisées/Graduate Advanced Diploma*; *Maîtrise/Master's Degree*; *Doctorat/Doctoral Degree*. Also Attestation d'études de premier, deuxième et troisième cylces, and Doctorat de premier cycle.

Student Services: Library

Publishing house: Presses de l'Université du Québec

Last Updated: 25/03/15

ENGINEERING SCHOOL - ETS

ECOLE DE TECHNOLOGIE SUPÉRIEURE (ETS)

1100, rue Notre-Dame Ouest, (angle Peel), Montréal, Québec H3C 1K3
Tel: +1(514) 396-8800
Fax: +1(514) 396-8950
EMail: admission@etsmtl.ca
Website: http://www.etsmtl.ca

Directeur général: Pierre Dumouchel
Tel: +1(514) 396-8802 EMail: pierre.dumouchel@etsmtl.ca

Direction des affaires académiques et des relations avec l'industrie: Jean-Luc Fihey
Tel: +1(514) 396-8806 EMail: jean-luc.fihey@etsmtl.ca

Department

Automated Production Engineering (Automation and Control Engineering; Operations Research; Production Engineering; Sanitary Engineering; Transport Management); **Construction Engineering** (Bridge Engineering; Construction Engineering; Engineering Management; Environmental Engineering; Hydraulic Engineering); **Electrical Engineering** (Electrical Engineering; Energy Engineering; Microelectronics; Telecommunications Engineering); **Mechanical Engineering** (Aeronautical and Aerospace Engineering; Energy Engineering; Engineering; Industrial Management; Mechanical Engineering; Production Engineering; Safety Engineering); **Software Engineering and Information Technologies** (Engineering Management; Information Technology; Software Engineering)

Centre

Thermal Technology/Technologie thermique *(CTT)* (Thermal Engineering)

Laboratory

Computer Systems Architecture *(LASI)* (Computer Engineering); **Control and Robotics/Commande et de robotique** *(CoRo)* (Automation and Control Engineering; Robotics); **Design and Control of Production Systems/Conception et contrôle des systèmes de production** *(C2SP)* (Production Engineering); **Management Networks and Telecommunications/Gestion des réseaux informatiques et de télécommunications** *(LAGRIT)* (Computer Networks; Telecommunications Engineering); **Multimedia Communication in Telepresence/Communication multimédia en téléprésence** *(Synchromedia)* (Multimedia; Telecommunications Engineering); **Pavement, Roads and Bituminous Materials/Chaussées, routes et enrobés bitumineux** *(LUCREB)* (Road Engineering); **Production Technologies Integration/Intégration des technologies de production** *(LITP)* (Production Engineering); **Products, Processes, and Systems Engineering** *(P2SEL)* (Engineering); **Semantics and Cognitive Engineering** *(LiNCS)* (Cognitive Sciences); **Shape Memory Alloys and Intelligent Systems/Alliages à mémoire et les systèmes intelligents** *(LAMSI)* (Artificial Intelligence); **Stress Analysis by Finite Element and Testing/Analyse des contraintes par éléments finis et expérimentation** *(ACEFE)* (Mechanical Engineering); **Telecommunications and Microelectronics Integration/Communications et d'intégration de la microélectronique** *(LACIME)* (Microelectronics; Telecommunications Engineering)

Research Centre

Advanced Research in Telecommunications/Recherche avancée en télécommunications *(COMunity/COMunité)* (Telecommunications Engineering); **Development and Research on Structures and Rehabilitation/Développement et recherche en structures et réhabilitation** *(DRSR)* (Bridge Engineering; Civil Engineering); **Experimental Station of Pilot Processes in Environment/Station expérimentale des procédés pilotes en environnement** *(STEPPE)* (Environmental Engineering); **Machine Dynamics, Structures and Processes/Dynamique des machines, des structures et des procédés** *(DYNAMO)* (Mechanical Engineering); **Occupational Safety/Sécurité du travail** *(EREST)* (Safety Engineering)

Research Group

Avionic and Navigation (Air Transport); **Development and Applied Research in Environmental Modeling/Développement et en recherche appliquée à la modélisation environnementale** *(DRAME)* (Environmental Engineering); **Integration and Sustainable Development in Built Environment/Intégration et développement durable en environnement bâti** *(GRIDD)* (Development Studies); **Power Electronics and Industrial Control/Electronique de puissance et commande industrielle** *(GREPCI)* (Automation and Control Engineering; Electronic Engineering; Industrial Engineering; Power Engineering); **Production of Francis Turbine Shroud Ring/Fabrication de couronnes de turbine Francis** (Hydraulic Engineering)

Research Laboratory

Active Control, Avionics and Aeroservoelasticity/Commande active, avionique et aéroservoélasticité *(LARCASE)* (Aeronautical and Aerospace Engineering); **Imagery and Orthopedics/Imagerie et orthopédie** *(LIO)* (Medical Technology; Orthopaedics); **Multimedia** *(LABMULTIMEDIA)* (Multimedia); **Software Engineering Management/Génie logiciel** *(GELOG)* (Software Engineering)

History: Founded 1974. An Engineering School, part of the University of Quebec network specialized in applied engineering and technology. Cooperative education system with work-study programme.

Academic Year: September to August (September-December; January-April; May-August)

Admission Requirements: Diploma of Collegial Studies (DEC) following successful completion of 3-year pre-university course in physical technology or technology of computer-controlled systems, at a CEGEP (Collège d'Enseignement général et professionnel) in Quebec, or recognized equivalent

Fees: National: Undergraduate tuition, (12 credits): 1,126.21 per term for Quebec Resident Canadian Students; 2,730.49 for Non-Quebec Resident Canadian Students; 6,913.33 for International students (Canadian Dollar), International: Undergraduate tuition, (12 credits): 6,913.33 per term (Canadian Dollar)

Main Language(s) of Instruction: French

Degrees and Diplomas: *Certificat et diplôme universitaire/University certificate and diploma*; *Baccalauréat/Bachelor's Degree*; *Diplôme d'études supérieures spécialisées/Graduate Advanced Diploma*; *Maîtrise/Master's Degree*; *Doctorat/Doctoral Degree*: **Engineering; Medical Technology.**

Student Services: Academic Counselling, Canteen, Careers Guidance, Facilities for disabled people, Library, Residential Facilities, Social Counselling, Sports Facilities

Publications: L'ETS @ 360°

Academic Staff *2014-2015*: Total 190

Student Numbers *2014-2015*: Total 8,000

NATIONAL SCHOOL OF PUBLIC ADMINISTRATION

ECOLE NATIONALE D'ADMINISTRATION PUBLIQUE (ENAP)

555, boul. Charest Est, Québec, Québec G1K 9E5
Tel: +1(418) 641-3000
Fax: +1(418) 641-3060
EMail: info@enap.ca; brelquebec@enap.ca
Website: http://www.enap.ca

Directeur général: Nelson Michaud (2011-)
Tel: +1(418) 641-3000, Ext. 6500

Directeur de l'administration et secrétaire général par intérim: Jean-Pierre Mailhot

Programme

Second-Cycle Studies (Communication Studies; Finance; Government; Health Administration; Human Resources; Information

Sciences; Information Technology; International Business; Management; Public Administration; Urban Studies); **Third-Cycle Studies** (Management; Public Administration)

Further Information: Also Branches in Montréal, Gatineau, Saguenay and Trois-Rivières. On-line short second-cycle programme in Public Management.

History: Founded 1969. A Postgraduate Constituent School of the University of Quebec.

Academic Year: August to June (August-December; January-April; May-June)

Admission Requirements: Diploma of Collegial Studies (DEC) following successful completion of a 2-year pre-university course at a CEGEP (Collège d'Enseignement général et professionnel), or recognized equivalent

Fees: National: 227,31 per 3 credits for Quebec-resident Canadian students and 324,03 per 3 credit for non-Quebec resident (Canadian Dollar), International: 324,03 per 3 credits (Canadian Dollar)

Main Language(s) of Instruction: French

Degrees and Diplomas: *Diplôme d'études supérieures spécialisées/Graduate Advanced Diploma*; *Maîtrise/Master's Degree*; *Doctorat/Doctoral Degree*: **Management; Public Administration.** Also short degree programmes.

Student Services: Academic Counselling, Careers Guidance, Facilities for disabled people, Library, Social Counselling, Sports Facilities

UNIVERSITY OF QUEBEC ABITIBI-TEMISCAMINGUE

Université du Québec en Abitibi-Témiscamingue (UQAT)

445 boul. de l'Université, Rouyn-Noranda, Québec J9X 5E4
Tel: +1(819) 762-0971
Fax: +1(819) 797-4727
EMail: information@uqat.ca
Website: http://uqat.ca

Rectrice: Johanne Jean (2004-)
Tel: +1(819) 762-0971 poste 2248
EMail: Johanne.Jean@uqat.ca

Secrétaire général: Guy Lemire
Tel: +1(819) 762-0971 poste 2265
EMail: Guy.Lemire@uqat.ca

Area

Applied Sciences (Biology; Computer Science; Electronic Engineering; Engineering; Environmental Studies; Forest Management; Forestry; Geological Engineering; Geology; Information Technology; Mechanical Engineering; Mining Engineering; Multimedia); **Creation and New Media** (Cinema and Television; Computer Science; Fine Arts; Multimedia; Visual Arts); **Education** (Art Education; Education; Educational Administration; Fine Arts; Foreign Languages Education; Painting and Drawing; Pedagogy; Preschool Education; Primary Education; Secondary Education; Vocational Education); **First Peoples** (Cultural Studies; Indigenous Studies); **Health Sciences** (Anaesthesiology; Cardiology; Health Sciences; Nursing; Occupational Health; Rehabilitation and Therapy); **Human and Social Development** (Art Therapy; Development Studies; Educational Psychology; Indigenous Studies; Peace and Disarmament; Psychology; Social Sciences; Social Work); **Management Sciences** (Accountancy; Administration; Business Administration; Development Studies; Finance; Health Administration; Human Resources; Management)

Further Information: Also following campuses: Amos, La Sarre, Mont-Laurier, Barraute-Senneterre, Val-d'Or, Chibougamau, Lebel-sur-Quévillon, Matagami-Radisson, Ville-Marie; Station de recherche du lac-Duparquet.

History: Active from 1970 as Services universitaires dans le Nord-Ouest québécois, reorganized as Direction des études universitaires dans l'Ouest québécois 1972, as Centre d'études universitaires dans l'Ouest québécois 1976, as Centre d'études universitaires en Abitibi-Témiscamingue 1981 and acquired present status and title 1983, a Constituent University of the University of Quebec.

Academic Year: September to August (September-December; January-April; May-August)

Admission Requirements: Diploma of Collegial Studies (DEC) following successful completion of a 2-year pre-university course at a CEGEP (Collège d'Enseignement général et professionnel), or recognized equivalent.

Fees: National: Undergraduate tuition, 359,5 per course (3 credits) for Quebec residents; 795,40 per course for other Canadian students. Graduate tuition, 405,76-1 627,52 per course for Quebec residents; 841,63-3,806,87 per course for other Canadian students (Canadian Dollar), International: Undergraduate tuition,1 844,95 per course (3 credits). Graduate tuition, 1,712,23-8,159,87 per course (Canadian Dollar)

Main Language(s) of Instruction: French

Degrees and Diplomas: *Certificat et diplôme universitaire/University certificate and diploma*; *Baccalauréat/Bachelor's Degree*; *Diplôme d'études supérieures spécialisées/Graduate Advanced Diploma*; *Maîtrise/Master's Degree*; *Doctorat/Doctoral Degree*: **Environmental Studies; Health Sciences.** Also undergraduate and graduate short programmes (microprogrammes).

Student Services: Academic Counselling, Canteen, Careers Guidance, Facilities for disabled people, Library, Residential Facilities, Social Counselling, Sports Facilities

Academic Staff *2010-2011*: Total: c. 420

Student Numbers *2010-2011*: Total: c. 3,500

Distance students, 800.

Last Updated: 26/03/15

UNIVERSITY OF QUEBEC AT CHICOUTIMI

Université du Québec à Chicoutimi (UQAC)

555, boulevard de l'Université, Chicoutimi, Québec G7H 2B1
Tel: +1(418) 545-5011 +1(800) 463-9880
Fax: +1(418) 545-5012
EMail: Info_Programmes@uqac.ca
Website: http://uqac.ca

Recteur: Martin Gauthier
Tel: +1(418) 545-5011 Ext. 5509 EMail: Martin_Gauthier@uqac.ca

International Relations: Gravel Marc, Secrétaire Exécutif du Comité de gestion de l'international
Tel: +1(418) 545-5011 Ext. 5240 EMail: Marc_Gravel@uqac.ca

Department

Applied Science (Civil Engineering; Computer Engineering; Earth Sciences; Electrical Engineering; Engineering; Geological Engineering; Geology; Mechanical Engineering; Meteorology); **Arts and Letters** (Art Education; Art History; Arts and Humanities; Cinema and Television; Design; Fine Arts; Foreign Languages Education; French; Linguistics; Literature; Modern Languages; Spanish; Theatre; Video; Writing); **Basic Sciences** (Biology; Chemistry; Environmental Studies; Natural Resources; Natural Sciences); **Computer Science and Mathematics** (Computer Science; Information Technology; Mathematics); **Economics and Administrative Sciences** (Accountancy; Administration; Air Transport; Business Administration; Economics; Health Sciences; Hotel and Restaurant; Human Resources; Management; Marketing; Transport Management); **Educational Sciences** (Education; Educational Administration; Educational Sciences; Foreign Languages Education; Humanities and Social Science Education; Mathematics Education; Preschool Education; Primary Education; Psychology; Secondary Education; Special Education; Vocational Education); **Health Sciences** (Community Health; Health Education; Health Sciences; Industrial and Organizational Psychology; Nursing; Physical Education; Physical Therapy; Psychiatry and Mental Health; Psychology); **Humanities** (African Studies; Anthropology; Archaeology; Archiving; Arts and Humanities; Communication Studies; Development Studies; Ethics; Geography; Government; Health Education; History; Indigenous Studies; International Studies; Medicine; Nursing; Philosophy; Physical Education; Political Sciences; Regional Planning; Regional Studies; Religious Studies; Social Work; Sociology; Tourism; Toxicology)

Centre

Studies on Mineral Resources *(CERM)* (Mineralogy)

Research Centre

Atmospheric Icing and Engineering of Electrical Networks *(International Agency)* (Electrical Engineering; Meteorology)

Research Group

Creation and Community (Development Studies); **Informatics** *(GRI)* (Computer Science); **Process Engineering and Systems** *(GRIPS)* (Engineering Management); **Regional Response** *(GRIR)* (Regional Studies); **Renewable Energy and the Impact of Northern Climate** *(GREEN)* (Natural Resources); **Renewable Resources in the Boreal** *(GR 3 MB)* (Natural Resources); **Wood Thermotransformation** *(GRTB)* (Wood Technology)

Research Laboratory

Ambient Intelligence for Recognition of Activities *(LIAR)* (Household Management); **Computer and Office** *(ENBI)* (Business Computing; Computer Science); **Ethics** *(LARIEP)* (Ethics); **Organizational Governance** *(LARIGO)* (Government)

Research Unit

Commercial Boreal Forest *(Consortium)* (Forest Management); **Educational Research** *(Regional Consortium - RRAC)* (Educational Sciences); **Mineral Exploration** *(Consortium - CONSOREM)* (Mineralogy); **Native American** *(Consortium)* (Native American Studies)

Further Information: Also Research Laboratories, and Research Centers.

History: Founded 1969. A Constituent University of the University of Quebec.

Academic Year: September to August (September-December; January-April; May-August)

Admission Requirements: Diploma of Collegial Studies (DEC) following successful completion of a 2-year pre-university course at a CEGEP (Collège d'Enseignement général et professionnel), or recognized equivalent

Main Language(s) of Instruction: French

Degrees and Diplomas: *Certificat et diplôme universitaire/University certificate and diploma*; *Baccalauréat/Bachelor's Degree*; *Diplôme d'études supérieures spécialisées/Graduate Advanced Diploma*; *Maîtrise/Master's Degree*; *Doctorat/Doctoral Degree*

Student Services: Academic Counselling, Canteen, Careers Guidance, Cultural Activities, Facilities for disabled people, Health Services, IT Centre, Language Laboratory, Library, Social Counselling, Sports Facilities

Publications: Protee

Last Updated: 25/03/15

UNIVERSITY OF QUEBEC AT MONTREAL

Université du Québec à Montréal (UQAM)

C.P. 8888, Succursale Centre-ville, Montréal, Québec H3C 3P8

Tel: +1(514) 987-3000

Fax: +1(514) 987-7906

EMail: admission@uqam.ca; general@uqam.ca

Website: http://www.uqam.ca

Recteur: Robert Proulx

Tel: +1(514) 987-3080 EMail: proulx.robert@uqam.ca

Secrétaire-général: Normand Petitclerc

Tel: +1(514) 987-3046 EMail: petitclerc.normand@uqam.ca

International Relations: Sylvain St-Amant, Directeur, Service des Relations internationales

Tel: +1(514) 987-7969 EMail: st-amand.sylvain@uqam.ca

Faculty

Arts (Architectural and Environmental Design; Architecture; Archiving; Art History; Communication Arts; Dance; Design; Education; Environmental Studies; Fine Arts; French; Geography; Graphic Design; Heritage Preservation; History; Information Management; Information Sciences; Jazz and Popular Music; Literature; Media Studies; Museum Studies; Music; Music Education; Performing Arts; Political Sciences; Regional Planning; Surveying and Mapping; Theatre; Tourism; Urban Studies; Visual Arts); **Communication** (Arabic; Asian Religious Studies; Asian Studies; Chinese; Cinema and Television; Communication Studies; Cultural Studies; French; German; Italian; Japanese; Journalism; Marketing; Mass Communication; Media Studies; Modern Languages; Portuguese; Public Relations; Radio and Television Broadcasting; Russian; Spanish); **Educational Sciences** (Adult Education; Education; Educational Sciences; Foreign Languages Education; French; Grammar; Mathematics Education; Pedagogy; Special Education); **Political Science and Law** (Administration; Communication Studies; International Law; International Relations; International Studies; Labour Law; Law; Political Sciences; Private Law; Public Administration; Social Sciences; Women's Studies); **Sciences** (Actuarial Science; Biochemistry; Biological and Life Sciences; Biology; Chemistry; Computer Networks; Computer Science; Earth Sciences; Ecology; Environmental Studies; Ergotherapy; Geology; Health Education; Industrial Design; Mathematics; Mathematics Education; Meteorology; Microelectronics; Natural Resources; Physical Education; Physical Therapy; Physiology; Preschool Education; Software Engineering; Statistics; Telecommunications Engineering); **Social Sciences** (Ancient Civilizations; Cognitive Sciences; Gender Studies; Geography; Geography (Human); Gerontology; Grammar; History; Linguistics; Medieval Studies; Philosophy; Psychology; Religious Studies; Social Sciences; Social Work; Sociology; Surveying and Mapping; Women's Studies)

School

Management *(ESG UQAM)* (Accountancy; Administration; Business Administration; Business Computing; Communication Studies; Cooking and Catering; E- Business/Commerce; Economics; Ethics; Fashion Design; Finance; Hotel and Restaurant; Hotel Management; Human Resources; Industrial Management; Information Sciences; Information Technology; Insurance; International Business; Leadership; Leisure Studies; Management; Marketing; Multimedia; Operations Research; Public Administration; Real Estate; Road Transport; Safety Engineering; Sales Techniques; Small Business; Statistics; Taxation; Tourism; Town Planning; Transport and Communications; Transport Management; Urban Studies)

Higher School

Fashion (Fashion Design; Industrial Management)

Institute

Cognitive Sciences *((ISC))*; **Environmental Sciences** *((ISE))* (Environmental Studies); **Feminist Research and Studies** *((IREF))* (Gender Studies; Women's Studies); **Health and Society** (Health Sciences; Occupational Health); **The Montreal Institute of International Studies** *((IEIM))* (International Studies)

Centre

International Center for Tourism Education and Research *((CIFORT))* (Tourism); **Research on Immigration, Ethnicity and Citizenship** *((CRIEC))* (International Relations; Political Sciences); **Studies and Research on Brazil** *((CERB))* (Latin American Studies)

Research Centre

Biological Interactions between Health and the Environment *(CINBIOSE)*; **BIOMED** (Biochemistry; Biomedical Engineering; Physiology); **Cognition Neuroscience** *(CNC)*; **Computer Mathematics and Combinatory Laboratory** *(LACIM)* (Applied Mathematics; Mathematics and Computer Science); **CRILICQ** (Canadian Studies; Cultural Studies; Literature); **Differential Geometry and Topology** *(CIRGET)*; **Environment Toxicology** *(TOXEN)* (Environmental Studies; Public Health; Toxicology); **FIGURA**; **Forestry Research** *(CEF)* (Ecology; Forest Management; Forest Products); **Geochemistry and Geodynamics** *(GEOTOP-UQAM-McGill)* (Environmental Studies; Geochemistry; Geophysics; Marine Science and Oceanography; Meteorology); **Globalization and International Studies** *(CEIM)*; **Humanities, Arts and Traditions** *(CELAT)*; **Interdisciplinary Center for Research on Diversity in Quebec** *((CRIDAQ))*; **Limnology and Marine Environment Research** *(GRIL)* (Environmental Management; Limnology; Marine Biology; Marine Science and Oceanography); **Mediatic Arts** *(CIAM)* (Fine Arts; Technology); **Regional Climate Modelling** *(ESCER)* (Meteorology); **Risk, Economic Policies and Employment** (Econometrics; Economic and Finance Policy); **Science and Technology** *(CIRST)* (History; Information Management; Social Studies; Technology); **Social Innovations** *(CRISES)* (Consumer Studies; Economic and Finance Policy; Labour and Industrial Relations; Public Administration; Social and Community Services)

Research Group

Continental Integration *((GRIC))*; **International and Comparative Consumer Law** *((GREDICC))* (International Law); **Mining Activities in Africa** *((GRAMA))* (Mining Engineering); **Political Imaginaries in Latin America** *((GRIPAL))* (Latin American Studies)

Chair

Aesthetics and Poetics *((CEP))* (Aesthetics); **Canada Research Chair in Environmental Education** *((ERE))* (Environmental

Studies); **Cognitive Science** (Computer Science; Linguistics; Philosophy; Psychology); **Education and Health** (Education; Health Sciences); **Globalization, Citizenship and Democracy** *((MCD))* (Political Sciences); **International Law and Globalization** *((CEDIM))* (International Law); **Network of UNESCO Chairs in Communications** *(ORBICOM)* (Communication Studies); **Public Relations and Marketing Communications** *((CRPCM))* (Marketing; Public Relations); **Quebec and Canadian Studies** *((CREQC))* (Canadian Studies); **Social Economy** *(CES)* (Economic and Finance Policy; Social Problems); **Social Responsibility and Sustainable Development** *((CRSDD))* (Development Studies; Ethics; Social Problems); **Socioterritorial Conflict and Local Governance** (Development Studies; Government); **Strategic and Diplomatic Studies** *(Raoul-Dandurand)* (Comparative Politics; International Economics; International Relations); **Tourism** *(Transat)* (Tourism); **UNESCO Chair for the Study of the Philosophical Foundations of Justice and Democratic Society** (Philosophy); **UNESCO Chair in Communication and technology for the development** (Communication Studies; Information Sciences; Information Technology; Media Studies); **UNESCO Chair in Global Environmental Change** (Environmental Studies); **Urban Heritage** (Ecology; Urban Studies)

Further Information: Also 4 regional campuses in Laval, Lanaudière, Longueuil and Ouest-de-l'île and a large number of research institutes, chairs and centres.

History: Founded 1969, incorporating 5 existing institutions. The University gained 'associate university' status in the University of Quebec network 1989, giving it greater autonomy.

Academic Year: September to April (September-December; January-April)

Admission Requirements: Diploma of Collegial Studies (DEC) following successful completion of a 2-year pre-university course at a CEGEP (Collège d'Enseignement général et professionnel), or recognized equivalent (13 years of study); if only 12, one year of transition courses (30 credits) before admission to bachelor's programme; or 22 years of age and appropriate experience or basic university studies

Main Language(s) of Instruction: French

Accrediting Agency: Association of Universities and Colleges of Canada (AUCC); European Foundation for Management Development (EQUIS); Conférence des Recteurs et des Principaux des Universités du Québec (CREPUQ)

Degrees and Diplomas: *Certificat et diplôme universitaire/University certificate and diploma*; *Baccalauréat/Bachelor's Degree*; *Diplôme d'études supérieures spécialisées/Graduate Advanced Diploma*: **Accountancy; Adult Education; Architecture; Art Education; Computer Engineering; Educational Administration; Finance; Information Technology; Management; Music; Special Education; Theatre.** *Maîtrise/Master's Degree*; *Doctorat/Doctoral Degree*: **Administration; Art History; Biochemistry; Biology; Chemistry; Communication Studies; Computer Science; Earth Sciences; Economics; Education; Environmental Studies; Fine Arts; Law; Linguistics; Mathematics; Museum Studies; Philosophy; Political Sciences; Psychology; Religion; Social Work; Sociology; Urban Studies.**

Student Services: Academic Counselling, Canteen, Careers Guidance, Cultural Activities, Facilities for disabled people, Foreign Studies Centre, Language Laboratory, Library, Social Counselling, Sports Facilities

Academic Staff *2014-2015*	**TOTAL**
FULL-TIME	**1,162**
Student Numbers *2014-2015*	
All (Foreign included)	**43,703**
FOREIGN ONLY	**3564**

Last Updated: 25/03/15

UNIVERSITY OF QUEBEC AT RIMOUSKI

Université du Québec à Rimouski (UQAR)

C.P. 3300, succ. A, 300, allée des Ursulines,
Rimouski, Québec G5L 3A1
Tel: + 1(418) 723-1986
Fax: + 1(418) 724-1525
EMail: uqar@uqar.ca
Website: http://www.uqar.ca

Recteur: Jean-Pierre Ouellet
Tel: + 1(418) 724-1410 EMail: recteur@uqar.ca

Secrétaire générale: Cathy-Maude Croft
Tel: + 1(418) 724-1416 EMail: secgen@uqar.ca

Unit

Educational Sciences *(Lévis Campus)* (Adult Education; Education; Educational Administration; Educational Psychology; Educational Sciences; Foreign Languages Education; Pedagogy; Preschool Education; Secondary Education); **Educational Sciences** *(Rimouski Campus)* (Education; Educational Administration; Educational Psychology; Educational Sciences; Preschool Education; Primary Education; Secondary Education; Vocational Education); **Management Sciences** *(Rimouski Campus)* (Accountancy; Administration; Biology; Computer Science; E- Business/Commerce; Electrical Engineering; Electronic Engineering; Finance; Geography; Human Resources; Management; Marine Transport; Marketing; Mechanical Engineering; Natural Resources; Taxation); **Management Sciences** *(Lévis Campus)* (Accountancy; Administration; Business Administration; Finance; Human Resources; Management; Marine Transport; Marketing; Taxation)

Department

Arts and Humanities (Arts and Humanities; Cultural Studies; English; Ethics; French; History; Literature; Writing); **Biology, Chemistry and Geography** (Biology; Chemistry; Ecology; Environmental Studies; Geography; Marine Science and Oceanography; Physiology; Wildlife); **Mathematics, Computer Science and Engineering** (Computer Science; E- Business/Commerce; Electrical Engineering; Electronic Engineering; Energy Engineering; Engineering; Ethics; Management; Marine Science and Oceanography; Mathematics; Mechanical Engineering; Telecommunications Engineering); **Nursing** (Community Health; Health Sciences; Nursing; Psychiatry and Mental Health); **Psychology and Social Work** (Communication Studies; Psychology; Social Sciences; Social Work); **Societies, Territories and Development** (Development Studies; Public Administration; Regional Studies; Rural Studies; Social Problems; Social Studies)

Institute

Marine Science *(Rimouski - ISMER)* (Biology; Computer Science; Ecology; Electrical Engineering; Environmental Studies; Geography; Marine Science and Oceanography; Mechanical Engineering; Physiology; Wildlife)

Research Centre

Forestry *(Multiregional)* (Forestry); **Marine and Island Environments** *(CERMIM - Affiliated)* (Environmental Studies); **Northern Studies** *(NEC)* (Environmental Studies); **Québec Aquaculture Network** *(RAQ)* (Aquaculture); **Quebec-Ocean** (Marine Science and Oceanography); **Spatial Development** *(CRTD)* (Development Studies)

Research Group

Ethics *(ETHOS)* (Ethics); **Learning and Socialization** *(APPSO)* (Science Education); **Northern Environments** *(BOREAS)* (Environmental Studies); **Regional Development of Eastern Quebec** *(GRIDEQ - Interdisciplinary)* (Development Studies)

Research Laboratory

Biotechnology and Environmental Chemistry *(CRAB)* (Biotechnology; Chemistry; Environmental Studies); **Health in the Region** *(LASER)* (Health Sciences); **Production** *(PRL)* (Production Engineering); **Wind** *(LREE)* (Energy Engineering; Power Engineering)

Further Information: Also campus in Lévis. Research Centres, Groups, Laboratories and Chairs

History: Founded as Centre d'Etudes universitaires de Rimouski, 1969. Acquired present status and title 1973. A Constituent University of the University of Quebec. Campus in Lévis.

Academic Year: September to June (September-December; January-April; May-June)

Admission Requirements: Diploma of Collegial Studies (DEC) following successful completion of a 2-year pre-university course at a CEGEP (Collège d'Enseignement général et professionnel), or recognized equivalent

Main Language(s) of Instruction: French

Accrediting Agency: Association of Universities and Colleges of Canada (AUCC); ADARUQ

Degrees and Diplomas: *Certificat et diplôme universitaire/University certificate and diploma*; *Baccalauréat/Bachelor's Degree*; *Diplôme d'études supérieures spécialisées/Graduate Advanced*

Diploma: **Accountancy; Educational Administration; Ethics; Human Resources; Marine Science and Oceanography; Public Administration.** *Maîtrise/Master's Degree*: **Arts and Humanities; Business Administration; Education; Engineering; Geography; History; Literature; Marine Science and Oceanography; Natural Sciences; Nursing.** *Doctorat/Doctoral Degree*: **Arts and Humanities; Biology; Education; Environmental Studies; Marine Science and Oceanography; Regional Studies.**

Student Services: Academic Counselling, Canteen, Careers Guidance, Facilities for disabled people, Library, Social Counselling, Sports Facilities

Student Numbers *2014-2015*: Total 7,200

Last Updated: 25/03/15

UNIVERSITY OF QUEBEC AT TROIS-RIVIÈRES

Université du Québec à Trois-Rivières (UQTR)

3351, boul. des Forges, C.P. 500, Trois-Rivières, Québec G9A 5H7

Tel: +1(819) 376-5011

Fax: +1(819) 376-5210

EMail: rectorat@uqtr.ca

Website: http://uqtr.ca

Rectrice: Nadia Ghazzali
Tel: +1(819) 376-5000 EMail: Nadia.Ghazzali@uqtr.ca

International Relations: Jacques E. Brisoux, Directeur
Tel: +1(819) 376-5001 EMail: dci@uqtr.ca

School

Engineering (Chemical Engineering; Computer Engineering; Electrical Engineering; Engineering; Industrial Engineering; Mechanical Engineering); **French** *(International)* (French)

Department

Accounting Studies (Accountancy); **Biomedicine** (Biochemistry; Biology; Biomedicine; Biophysics; Biotechnology; Cell Biology; Chemistry; Ecology; Environmental Studies; Midwifery); **Chemical Engineering** (Chemical Engineering); **Chemistry, Biochemistry and Physics** (Biochemistry; Chemistry; Computer Science; Materials Engineering; Physics); **Chiropractic** (Chiropractic); **Educational Sciences** (Education; Educational Administration; Educational Sciences; Mathematics Education; Native Language Education; Pedagogy; Primary Education; Science Education; Secondary Education; Technology Education); **Electrical and Computer Engineering** (Computer Engineering; Electrical Engineering; Energy Engineering); **Environmental Sciences** (Environmental Studies; Geography; Meteorology; Natural Resources; Surveying and Mapping); **Humanities** (Canadian Studies; History); **Humanities and Social Communication** (Arts and Humanities; Communication Studies; French Studies; Literature; Writing); **Industrial Engineering** (Engineering; Industrial Engineering; Occupational Health); **Leisure Studies, Culture and Tourism** (Cultural Studies; Leisure Studies; Tourism); **Management Science** (Administration; Business Administration; Finance; Human Resources; Labour and Industrial Relations; Management; Marketing; Operations Research; Protective Services; Small Business); **Mathematics and Computer Science** (Applied Mathematics; Computer Science; Mathematics; Mathematics and Computer Science; Mathematics Education); **Mechanical Engineering** (Mechanical Engineering); **Modern Languages and Translation** (English; Modern Languages; Spanish; Translation and Interpretation); **Nursing** (Nursing; Psychiatry and Mental Health; Public Administration); **Occupational Therapy** (Health Sciences; Occupational Therapy); **Philisophie and Arts** (Aesthetics; Art Education; Art History; Fine Arts; Glass Art; Philosophy; Theatre; Visual Arts); **Physical Activity Sciences** (Health Sciences; Physical Education; Physical Therapy; Podiatry); **Psychoeducation** (Educational Psychology; Social Psychology); **Psychology** (Gerontology; Psychology); **Speech Theraphy** (Speech Theraphy and Audiology)

Laboratory

"Family-School-Community and Transversal Skills"; **Political and Cultural Analyses**; **Professional Integration in Teaching**; **Teaching of Media Studies** (Media Studies); **Vertebral Illnesses**

Research Centre

Pulp and Paper (Paper Technology); **Quebec Studies** *(Interdisciplinary)* (Canadian Studies; Regional Studies)

Research Group

Aquatics (Aquaculture); **Cellular and Molecular Biopathologies** (Cell Biology; Molecular Biology; Pathology); **Child and Family Development** (Child Care and Development; Family Studies); **Communication and Speech** (Communication Studies; Speech Studies); **Energy and Biomolecular Information** (Biomedical Engineering; Energy Engineering); **Industrial Electronics** (Electronic Engineering)

Research Institute

Hydrogen; **Small and Medium Business** (Business Administration; Small Business)

Research Laboratory

Business Performances (Business Administration); **French Youth Literatures of America** (Literature); **Gerontology** (Gerontology); **Mental Deficiencies** *(LARIDI)* (Psychiatry and Mental Health); **Mental Health** (Psychiatry and Mental Health); **Neurosciences** (Neurosciences); **Transdisciplinary and Interdisciplinary Studies and Research in Education** (Educational Research); **Visual Arts** (Visual Arts)

History: Founded 1969. A Constituent University of the University of Quebec.

Academic Year: September to August (September-December; January-April; May-August)

Admission Requirements: Diploma of Collegial Studies (DEC) following successful completion of a 2-year pre-university course at a CEGEP (Collège d'Enseignement général et professionnel), or recognized equivalent

Main Language(s) of Instruction: French

Degrees and Diplomas: *Certificat et diplôme universitaire/University certificate and diploma*; *Baccalauréat/Bachelor's Degree*; *Diplôme d'études supérieures spécialisées/Graduate Advanced Diploma*; *Maîtrise/Master's Degree*; *Doctorat/Doctoral Degree*: **Administration; Biomedicine; Canadian Studies; Cell Biology; Education; Educational Psychology; Energy Engineering; Engineering; Environmental Engineering; Materials Engineering; Modern Languages; Molecular Biology; Neurosciences; Oncology; Philosophy; Psychology.**

Student Services: Academic Counselling, Canteen, Careers Guidance, Facilities for disabled people, Health Services, Language Laboratory, Library, Nursery Care, Social Counselling, Sports Facilities

Last Updated: 26/03/15

UNIVERSITY OF QUEBEC IN OUTAOUAIS

Université du Québec en Outaouais (UQO)

283, boulevard Alexandre-Taché, C.P. 1250, succursale Hull, Gatineau, Québec J8X 3X7

Tel: +1(819) 595-3900 +1(800) 567-1283

Fax: +1(819) 595-3924

EMail: registraire@uqo.ca

Website: http://www.uqo.ca

Recteur: Denis Harrisson (2015-)
Tel: +1(819) 595-3910 EMail: rectorat@uqo.ca

Secrétaire général: André J. Roy
Tel: +1(819) 595-3965 EMail: andre.roy@uqo.ca

School

Image Arts *(Multidisciplinary)* (Graphic Design; Museum Studies; Painting and Drawing; Visual Arts)

Department

Accounting Studies (Accountancy; Business Administration; Finance; Management); **Administrative Sciences** (Administration; Commercial Law; Finance; Management; Marketing; Public Relations); **Computer and Engineering** (Computer Engineering; Computer Science; Information Management; Information Sciences; Information Technology); **Educational Psychology and Psychology** (Educational and Student Counselling; Educational Psychology; Psychology); **Educational Sciences** (Art Education; Education; Educational Administration; Educational Sciences; Educational Technology; Preschool Education; Primary Education; Secondary Education); **Industrial Relations** (Human Resources; Industrial and Organizational Psychology; Labour and Industrial Relations; Occupational Health); **Language Studies** (Foreign Languages Education; Linguistics; Modern Languages; Translation and

Interpretation); **Natural Sciences** (Biology; Environmental Studies; Forest Management; Natural Resources); **Nursing** (Nursing); **Social Sciences** (Communication Studies; Development Studies; Geography; History; Media Studies; Museum Studies; Occupational Health; Political Sciences; Social Sciences; Sociology); **Social Work** (Development Studies; Social Work)

Further Information: Also Saint-Jérôme campus and a large number of research units.

History: Founded 1970 as Services universitaires dans le nord-ouest québécois, reorganized several times and acquired present status and title 2002. A Constituent University of the University of Quebec.

Academic Year: September to August (September-December; January-April; May-August)

Admission Requirements: Undergraduate programmes, Diploma of Collegial Studies (DEC) following successful completion of a 2-year pre-university course at a CEGEP (Collège d'enseignement général et professionnel), or recognized equivalent

Fees: National: Undergraduate Programs, 15 credits, 1427.39 per term for Québec residents; 3 435.89 per term for other Canadian students; Second cycle programmes tuition, 852.29 per term for Québec residents; 1,932.20 per term for other Canadian students; c. 4,583 per term for international students. Third cycle programmes tuition, 1,265.87 per term for Québec residents; 3,065.72 per term for other Canadian students; c. 4,580 per term for international students (Canadian Dollar), International: Undergraduate Programs, 15 credits, c.7 768.79 per term for international students

Main Language(s) of Instruction: French. Some graduate programmes in English

Degrees and Diplomas: *Certificat et diplôme universitaire/University certificate and diploma*; *Baccalauréat/Bachelor's Degree*; *Diplôme d'études supérieures spécialisées/Graduate Advanced Diploma*; *Maîtrise/Master's Degree*: **Biology; Business Administration; Economics; Education; Educational Psychology; Human Resources; Information Sciences; Information Technology; Linguistics; Management; Museum Studies; Nursing; Secondary Education; Social Work.** *Doctorat/Doctoral Degree*: **Business Administration; Education; Industrial Management; Information Technology; Psychology; Social Sciences.** Also undergraduate and graduate short programmes.

Student Services: Academic Counselling, Canteen, Careers Guidance, Cultural Activities, Facilities for disabled people, Library, Nursery Care, Residential Facilities, Social Counselling, Sports Facilities

Publications: Savoir Outaouais

Publishing House: Presses de l'Université du Québec

Academic Staff *2014-2015*	**TOTAL**
FULL-TIME	635
PART-TIME	370
STAFF WITH DOCTORATE	
FULL-TIME	140
Student Numbers *2014-2015*	
All (Foreign included)	6,360
FOREIGN ONLY	237

Last Updated: 26/03/15

UNIVERSITY OF SHERBROOKE

Université de Sherbrooke (UDES)
2500, boul. de l'Université, Sherbrooke, Québec J1K 2R1
Tel: +1(819) 821-7686 +1(800) 267-8337
Fax: +1(819) 821-7966
EMail: information@usherbrooke.ca
Website: http://www.usherb.ca

Rectrice: Luce Samoisette (2009-)
Tel: +1(819) 821-8280 EMail: rectrice@usherbrooke.ca

Secrétaire générale, vice-rectrice aux relations internationales et vice-rectrice à la vie étudiante: Jocelyne Faucher

Directrice du Service des communications: Lucie Frenière
Tel: +1(819) 821-7388 EMail: Lucie.Freniere@USherbrooke.ca

International Relations: Adel El Zaïm, Directeur général, Relations internationales EMail: Adel.Elzaim@usherbrooke.ca

Faculty

Administration (Accountancy; Administration; Business Administration; Economics; Finance; Human Resources; Information Sciences; Management; Management Systems; Marketing); **Arts and Humanities** (Arts and Humanities; Communication Studies; Comparative Literature; Economics; English; Ethics; French; Geography; Gerontology; History; Music; Philosophical Schools; Political Sciences; Psychology; Social and Community Services; Social Sciences; Social Work; Surveying and Mapping); **Education** (Adult Education; Educational Administration; Educational and Student Counselling; Educational Psychology; Pedagogy; Preschool Education; Primary Education; Secondary Education; Special Education); **Engineering** (Aeronautical and Aerospace Engineering; Biotechnology; Chemical Engineering; Civil Engineering; Computer Engineering; Electrical Engineering; Electronic Engineering; Mechanical Engineering); **Law** (Civil Law; International Law; Law; Notary Studies); **Medicine and Health Sciences** (Anaesthesiology; Anatomy; Biochemistry; Cardiology; Cell Biology; Community Health; Endocrinology; Environmental Studies; Gastroenterology; Gynaecology and Obstetrics; Haematology; Immunology; Medicine; Microbiology; Nephrology; Neurology; Nursing; Oncology; Ophthalmology; Otorhinolaryngology; Paediatrics; Pathology; Pharmacology; Physiology; Pneumology; Psychiatry and Mental Health; Public Health; Radiology; Rehabilitation and Therapy; Rheumatology; Surgery; Toxicology); **Physical Education and Sports** (Physical Education; Physical Therapy; Sports); **Religious Studies** (Ethics; Indigenous Studies; Pastoral Studies; Philosophy; Religious Studies; Theology); **Sciences** (Biochemistry; Biology; Chemistry; Computer Science; Mathematics; Natural Sciences; Physics)

Programme

Performa (Education; Educational and Student Counselling; Higher Education; Teacher Training; Vocational Education)

Institute

Entrepreneurship (Management); **Pharmacology** *(Sherbrooke)* (Pharmacology); **Research on Educational Practice** (Educational Sciences)

Centre

Business (Business Administration); **Continuing Education** (Administration; Arts and Humanities; Business Administration; Chinese; Communication Studies; Computer Science; Education; Educational Administration; Engineering; Engineering Management; Environmental Studies; Ethics; Health Sciences; Information Technology; Law; Management; Medicine; Multimedia; Natural Sciences; Political Sciences; Rehabilitation and Therapy; Sports; Theology); **Environmental Training** (Environmental Management; Environmental Studies); **Monitoring of the Environment and Sustainable Development** *(Observatory)* (Development Studies; Environmental Management; Environmental Studies); **Research and Training in Disability Prevention** (Rehabilitation and Therapy); **Training in Gerontology** (Gerontology)

History: Founded 1954. Recognized as a Catholic University through a decree 1957.

Academic Year: September to August (September-December; January-April; May-August)

Admission Requirements: Diploma of Collegial Studies (DEC) following successful completion of a 2-year pre-university course at a CEGEP (Collège d'Enseignement général et professionnel), or recognized equivalent

Fees: Undergraduate level, 8 563,65 per trimester in the following sectors: medicine, peripheral medicine, paramedic medicine, arts, pure science, applied sciences. All other sectors at the undergraduate level and master's level 7 668,90 per trimester. Doctoral level, 6 885,60 per trimester (Canadian Dollar)

Main Language(s) of Instruction: French

Degrees and Diplomas: *Certificat et diplôme universitaire/University certificate and diploma*; *Baccalauréat/Bachelor's Degree*; *Diplôme d'études supérieures spécialisées/Graduate Advanced Diploma*; *Maîtrise/Master's Degree*: **Arts and Humanities; Business Administration; Engineering; Health Sciences; Law; Natural Sciences.** *Doctorat/Doctoral Degree*: **Administration; Biochemistry; Biology; Biomedicine; Chemical Engineering; Chemistry; Civil Engineering; Clinical Psychology; Computer Engineering; Economics; Education; Educational Psychology; Electrical Engineering; French; Genetics; Gerontology; Health Sciences; History; Immunology; Law; Linguistics; Literature;**

Mathematics; Mechanical Engineering; Microbiology; Molecular Biology; Neurosciences; Pharmacology; Philosophy; Physical Education; Physics; Physiology; Psychology; Religious Studies; Surveying and Mapping; Translation and Interpretation. Also Diploma in Environmental Management; Combined Bachelor's degree programmes (Law and Business/biological and Life Sciences); Post-doctoral floows in Law; MBA.

Student Services: Academic Counselling, Canteen, Careers Guidance, Cultural Activities, Facilities for disabled people, Foreign Studies Centre, Health Services, Library, Nursery Care, Residential Facilities, Social Counselling, Sports Facilities

Academic Staff *2014-2015*	**TOTAL**
FULL-TIME	c. 6,882
Student Numbers *2014-2015*	
All (Foreign included)	c. 40,000
FOREIGN ONLY	1600

Last Updated: 24/03/15

PRIVATE INSTITUTION

INSTITUTE OF THEOLOGICAL TRAINING OF MONTREAL

Institut de Formation Théologique de Montréal (IFTM)

2065, rue Sherbrooke Ouest, Montréal, Québec H3H 1G6
Tel: +1(514) 935-1169
Fax: +1(514) 935-5497
EMail: info@iftm.ca
Website: http://www.iftm.ca/

Recteur: Kaufmann Jaroslaw
Tel: +1(514) 935-1169 Poste 202 EMail: recteur@iftm.ca

Directeur des études: Jorge Pacheco
Tel: +1(514) 935-1169 Poste 203 EMail: dir.etudes@iftm.ca

Department

Canon Law (Canon Law); **Pastoral Studies** (Pastoral Studies); **Philosophy** (Philosophy); **Theology** (Bible; Theology)

History: Founded 1840 as Grand Seminary of Montreal. Became headquarters of the Faculty of Theology 1878. Attached to the Université Laval of Quebec it was then recognised as a Faculty of the University of Montreal as of 1920. Affiliated to the Faculty of Theology of the Pontifical University of Latran as of 1979 an to the Faculty of Philosophy of the Pontifical University of Latran as of 1986. The Centre for Theological Formation was transformed into an Institute was 1988 and acquired present title 1995. Granted the right to offer civil degrees 1998. Acquired autonomy 2009.

Fees: National: Undergraduate programmes, 87 per credit for Canadian student resident of Quebec. 185 per credit for Canadian student non-resident of Quebec (Canadian Dollar), International: 330 per credit (Canadian Dollar)

Main Language(s) of Instruction: French

Degrees and Diplomas: *Certificat et diplôme universitaire/University certificate and diploma*; *Baccalauréat/Bachelor's Degree*; *Diplôme d'études supérieures spécialisées/Graduate Advanced Diploma*; *Maîtrise/Master's Degree*: **Theology.**

Student Services: Library

Last Updated: 20/03/15

Canada - Saskatchewan

STRUCTURE OF HIGHER EDUCATION SYSTEM

Description:

Higher education in Canada is the constitutional responsibility of the provinces. In Saskatchewan, the Ministry of Advanced Education has responsibility for higher education. The higher (post-secondary) education system includes two universities with four federated and seven affiliated colleges; Saskatchewan Polytechnic (SP),the Saskatchewan Indian Institute of Technologies (SIIT), Dumont Technical Institute (DTI), seven regional colleges and one inter provincial college under Alberta legislation, Lakeland College; the Saskatchewan Apprenticeship and Trade Certification Commission (SATCC); and many private vocational schools. The universities grant undergraduate and graduate degrees in the professions, Arts, Sciences, and Humanities. SP and SIIT deliver a wide range of Certificate and Diploma skill training programmes intended to lead directly to employment. SATCC contracts SP and other training institutions to deliver apprenticeship and technical training. Regional Colleges, located throughout the province in seven distinct geographic regions, broker university and SP credit courses, and other courses, through contracts with the credit granting institutions. The universities are autonomous institutions, governed by boards and responsible for their own administrative, academic, and financial affairs in accordance with the respective university Acts. SP, SATCC, and the regional colleges operate at arm's length from government under their own boards of directors and trustees, respectively. SIIT operates under the legislated authority of the Federation of Saskatchewan Indian Nations (FSIN). All parts of the higher education system are governed by acts of the provincial legislature. The Gabriel Dumont Institute of Native Studies and Applied Research Inc. (GDI) is the official education, research and development arm of the Métis Nation - Saskatchewan. GDI is affiliated with the University of Saskatchewan and the University of Regina and federated with SP. Its programs include the Saskatchewan Urban Native Teacher Education Program (SUNTEP), a four year, fully accredited Bachelor of Education program. The Dumont Technical Institute arm of GDI is responsible for Adult Basic Education, skills training, vocational and cultural programs. The Gabriel Dumont College arm of GDI offers the first two years of a Bachelor of Arts and Science degree. The Northern Teacher Education Program and Northern Professional Access College (NORTEP/PAC) is an off-campus institution that is accredited by the University of Saskatchewan and the University of Regina (and First Nations University of Canada). NORTEP/PAC currently offers four degree programs in Northern Saskatchewan; the four-year Bachelor of Education (B.Ed.) program; Education students may attend a fifth year and obtain a Bachelor of Arts (B.A.) as well; a Master's Program (M.ED) in Curriculum and Instruction; and NORPAC offers three years of university arts and sciences courses designed to prepare Northerners for entry into the two universities or other post-secondary programs.

Stages of studies:

University level first stage: *Bachelor's degree*

Most undergraduate study leads to a Bachelor's degree (minimum 3 or 4 years) or an "Honours" degree (minimum 4 years) with a major subject concentration. Degrees are normally labelled in broad descriptive groups such as Bachelor of Arts (B.A.) and Bachelor of Science (B.Sc.). The first stage also includes undergraduate Diplomas (1-3 years of study) and short (up to 1 year) special Certificate programs, frequently in close cooperation with professional bodies. Undergraduate professional programs that require no university level pre-requisites, such as Bachelor of Commerce (B.Com.), and Bachelor of Education (B.Ed.), require 4 years of study. Some first and second year university courses are offered by the universities off campus through provincially supported regional colleges, GDI, NORTEP/PAC, and SP.

University level second stage: *Master's degree*

The Master's degree normally requires two years of study after a Bachelor's degree or equivalent. A thesis and course-work are usually required. Examples are: Master of Arts (M.A.), Master of Science (M.Sc.), Master of Education (M.Ed.), and Master of Business Administration (MBA). There are also graduate-level Diplomas (considered intermediate between the Bachelor's or first professional degree and the Master's degree). Second stage programs also includes first professional degree programs requiring one to two years of prerequisite university studies, followed by three to four years, such as Bachelor of Law (LL.B.), Doctor of Medicine (M.D.) and Doctor of Veterinary Medicine (D.V.M.).

University level third stage: *Doctorate*

The Doctorate is the highest academic qualification awarded by universities and comprises the third stage of university level studies. This degree normally requires at least 3 years of study after the Master's degree; the submission and defence of a major thesis (dissertation) are the principal requirements, and supplemental course work. Doctor of Philosophy" (Ph.D.) is the generic title used to signify the Doctorate degrees in most disciplines. (The Doctorate should not be confused with titles attributed to certain first professional degrees in the health sciences, such as Medicine, Veterinary Medicine and Dentistry).

ADMISSION TO HIGHER EDUCATION

Admission to university-level studies:

Alternatives to credentials: SP offers mature adult admission for applicants, 19 years of age or older, who do not meet the usual entrance requirements. They may be admitted on the basis of probable success established through interviews and aptitude/ability tests.

Universities set their own admission policies and requirements. Some provision is made for special admission procedures such as mature students (e.g. 22 years of age or older) or probationary entrance for students who do not meet established academic entrance criteria. Some university faculties or colleges select only the most qualified applicants. Admission to some professional programs requires previous university education. Both universities and SP adhere to Recognition of Prior Learning practices and plan to expand upon this initiative (e.g. 2 + 2 program offerings internationally).

Numerus clausus: Each institution may have differing policies and should be contacted individually to inquire.

Other requirements: Admission requirements for entry into university programs will vary by each program and change from time to time.

Foreign students admission:

Definition of foreign student: Foreign (International) Students are students who are neither Canadian citizens nor permanent residents of Canada, and are enrolled in a recognized academic, professional or vocational training course at a university, college or other educational institution in Canada, The federal government, in cooperation with the provincial governments, will designate which institutions qualify.

Quotas: Each postsecondary institution should be contacted individually to inquire about this.

Admission requirements: As with domestic students, requirements will vary by program. Each institution should be contacted individually to inquire about requirements.

Entry regulations: Before you come to study in Canada, you will need: a Study Permit unless your program of study is six months or less and can be completed within six months. To obtain a Study Permit you must meet the following requirements: have received an original acceptance letter from a university in Saskatchewan; be able to provide proof of enough money to pay for tuition and living costs for you and any accompanying family members; be able to prove that you will return to your home country after completing studies at a university in Saskatchewan; pass a medical examination if required; and meet other visitor requirements, including a visa if required. You must be a law abiding citizen with no criminal record and be of no risk to the security of Canada. You may have to provide a police certificate (it is not required for all countries). A small number of students do not require a Study Permit by virtue of their status in Canada (e.g. diplomats and their children).

Health requirements: International students attending the universities in Saskatchewan, are entitled to Provincial Health Coverage for no additional cost. Medical examinations are not required by institutions but are required by Citizenship and Immigration Canada for students from many countries.

Language proficiency: All applicants must demonstrate an appropriate level of proficiency in the English language: TOEFL: Internet based – overall 0f 80; computer based – 213; paper based – 550; IELTS: band score of 6.5; CanTest: Listening – 4.5, reading – 4.5, Writing – 4.0; MELAB – 85; CAEL – 60; CELT - 60.

RECOGNITION OF STUDIES

Quality assurance system:

There are formalized credit transfer agreements between the universities and their federated or affiliated colleges and between Saskatchewan Polytechnic (SP) and the two universities in selected program areas such as Nursing, Engineering and Commerce, as well as universities in other provinces.

Bodies dealing with recognition:

International Qualifications Assessment Service - IQAS

9th floor, 9942 108 Street
Edmonton T5K 2J5
Tel: (+1) 780-427-2655
Fax: (+1) 780-422-9734
WWW: http://work.alberta.ca/iqas

Special provisions for recognition:

Recognition for university level studies: In general, none. Universities establish their own criteria for recognition of studies in their institutions.
Additionally, the Canadian Information Centre for International Credentials (CICIC) provides information and guidance on the assessment and recognition of international academic credentials.
For access to advanced studies and research: Applications from international students are not accepted for undergraduate study in Medicine, Physical Therapy or Veterinary Medicine at the University of Saskatchewan. No restrictions are imposed by the University of Regina.
For exercising a profession: For each profession, both Canadian and non-Canadians who studied abroad have to meet specified educational and experience requirements, and usually pass registration examinations. Non-Canadians whose first language is not English, may sometimes also need to pass language testing. Access to most professions is governed by provincial and/or federal statutes and is restricted to Canadian citizens or immigrants accepted as permanent residents. Applicants must also meet examination and/or practical training requirements set by the relevant professional body or provincial or federal licensing board.

PROVINCIAL BODIES

Ministère de l'Enseignement supérieur de la Saskatchewan (Saskatchewan Ministry of Advanced Education)

Ministre/Minister: Scott Moe
Legislative Building, 2405 Legislative Drive
Regina, SK S4S 0B3
Canada
Tel: +1(306) 787-0341
Fax: +1(306) 798-0263
EMail: aeeinquiry@gov.sk.ca
WWW: http://www.saskatchewan.ca/government/government-structure/ministries/advanced-education
Role of national body: Fosters the development of an educated, skilled and productive workforce in partnership with the private sector, education institutions and community organizations. Aims to recruit and retain more international students and to help First Nations and Métis learners to expand their workforce participation.

Saskatchewan Higher Education Quality Assurance Board - SHEQAB

Chair: Ronald Bond
Ministry of Advanced Education, 1120-2010 12th Avenue
Regina, SK S4P 0M3
Canada
Tel: (+1) 306-787-1782
EMail: info@quality-assurance-sk.ca
WWW: http://www.quality-assurance-sk.ca

Role of national body: Established by the Ministry of Advanced Education to oversee a quality assurance process that ensures new degree programs in the province meet high quality standards.

Data for academic year: 2014-2015
Source: IAU from The Canadian Information Centre for International Credentials (CICIC), a unit of the Council of Ministers of Education, Canada (CMEC), on behalf of the Saskatchewan Ministry of Advanced Education, November 2014. Bodies 2016.

INSTITUTIONS

PUBLIC INSTITUTIONS

UNIVERSITY OF REGINA (U OF R)

3737 Wascana Parkway, Regina, Saskatchewan S4S 0A2
Tel: +1(306) 585-4111
Fax: +1(306) 337-2525
EMail: admissions@uregina.ca; international.admissions@uregina.ca
Website: http://www.uregina.ca

President and Vice-Chancellor: Vianne Timmons
Tel: +1(306) 585-4382 EMail: The.President@uregina.ca

Provost and Vice-President (Academic): Thomas Chase
Tel: +1(306) 585-4384 EMail: Provost@uregina.ca

International Relations: Shahnora Mustafayeva, International Relations and Partnerships Specialist
EMail: international.relations@uregina.ca

Faculty
Arts (Anthropology; Asian Studies; Business Administration; Classical Languages; Cultural Studies; Development Studies; Economics; English; Environmental Studies; European Studies; French; French Studies; Gender Studies; Geography; History; Indigenous Studies; International Studies; Journalism; Latin American Studies; Law; Linguistics; Medieval Studies; Philosophy; Police Studies; Political Sciences; Psychology; Religious Studies; Social Studies; Sociology; Women's Studies); **Business Administration** (Accountancy; Finance; Human Resources; International Business; Management; Marketing; Small Business); **Education** (Adult Education; Education; Humanities and Social Science Education; Natives Education; Preschool Education; Primary Education; Secondary Education); **Engineering and Applied Science** (Electronic Engineering; Environmental Engineering; Industrial Engineering; Petroleum and Gas Engineering; Software Engineering); **English as a Second Language (ESL)** (English); **Fine Arts** (Acting; Art History; Ceramic Art; Film; Fine Arts; Music; Music Education; Music Theory and Composition; Painting and Drawing; Printing and Printmaking; Sculpture; Theatre; Video); **Graduate Studies and Research** (Arts and Humanities; Biochemistry; Biology; Business Administration; Computer Science; Education; Engineering; Fine Arts; Geography; Health Sciences; Mathematics; Natural Sciences; Physical Therapy; Physics; Psychology; Social Work; Statistics); **Kinesiology and Health Studies** (Gerontology; Physical Therapy; Public Health; Sports; Sports Management); **Nursing** (Nursing); **Science** (Actuarial Science; Biochemistry; Biology; Cell Biology; Chemistry; Computer Science; Ecology; Geography; Geology; Mathematics; Molecular Biology; Physics; Statistics); **Social Work** (Social Work)

College
Campion *(http://campioncollege.ca/)* (Arts and Humanities; Fine Arts; Natural Sciences); **First Nations University of Canada** *(http://www.fnuniv.ca)* (Business Administration; Environmental Studies; Health Sciences; Indigenous Studies; Natural Sciences; Public Administration); **Luther** *(http://luthercollege.edu)* (Arts and Humanities; Fine Arts; Natural Sciences); **Northern Teacher Education Program/Northern Professional Access College** *(http://www.nortep-nopac.sk.ca)* (Education; Health Sciences; Medicine; Natural Sciences; Physics; Veterinary Science)

Institute
French (French); **Native Studies and Applied Research** *(Gabriel Dumont. (http://www.gdins.org))* (Adult Education; Indigenous Studies)

Graduate School
Public Policy *(Johnson-Shoyama)* (Political Sciences)

Further Information: Also Federated Colleges (Campion College, Luther College and the First Nations University of Canada)

History: Founded 1911 as Regina College, Reorganized 1925 as University of Saskatchewan, 1959 as University of Saskatchewan, Regina Campus, and acquired present status and title 1974.

Academic Year: From Septembe to August (September-December; January-April; May-August)

Admission Requirements: Secondary school certificate or recognized foreign equivalent. For individual course requirements, please see website.

Main Language(s) of Instruction: English

Degrees and Diplomas: *Baccalauréat/Bachelor's Degree*: **Business Administration; Computer Science; Education; Engineering; Fine Arts; Nursing; Physical Therapy; Social Work.** *Maîtrise/Master's Degree*: **Business Administration; Computer Science; Education; Engineering; Fine Arts; Nursing; Physical Therapy; Social Work.** *Doctorat/Doctoral Degree*: **Biochemistry; Biology; Chemistry; Clinical Psychology; Computer Science; Education; Engineering; Geology; Health Sciences; Mathematics; Physical Therapy; Physics; Statistics.** Also Combined Degree BA/Badm, BA/BEd (French), Bachelor of Education/ Bachelor of Science; Honours Bachelor's degree; Advanced Certificates (Undergraduate); Professional Certificate Programmes.

Student Services: Academic Counselling, Canteen, Careers Guidance, Cultural Activities, Facilities for disabled people, Foreign Studies Centre, Health Services, IT Centre, Language Laboratory, Library, Nursery Care, Social Counselling, Sports Facilities

Publications: Policy and Practice in Education; Prairie Forum

Academic Staff *2012-2013*	**TOTAL**
FULL-TIME	**484**
PART-TIME	**348**
STAFF WITH DOCTORATE	
FULL-TIME	**c. 386**
Student Numbers *2012-2013*	
All (Foreign included)	**13,155**

Last Updated: 04/02/15

UNIVERSITY OF SASKATCHEWAN (U OF S)

107 Administration Place, Saskatoon, Saskatchewan S7N 5A2
Tel: +1(306) 966-4343
Fax: +1(306) 975-1026
EMail: registrar@usask.ca
Website: http://www.usask.ca

Vice-Chancellor: Peter Stoicheff (2015-)
EMail: uofspresident@usask.ca

Provost and Vice-President Academic (Interim): Ernie Barber
EMail: provost@usask.ca

International Relations: Diane Martz, Director, International Research and Partnerships EMail: uofsinternational@usask.ca

College

Agriculture and Bioresources (Agricultural Business; Agricultural Economics; Agriculture; Agronomy; Animal Husbandry; Biochemistry; Biotechnology; Botany; Chemistry; Computer Science; Crop Production; Ecology; Environmental Studies; Food Science; Forestry; Genetics; Horticulture; Meat and Poultry; Microbiology; Molecular Biology; Natural Resources; Nutrition; Physics; Physiology; Plant and Crop Protection; Plant Pathology; Social Sciences; Soil Science; Veterinary Science); **Arts and Science** (Amerindian Languages; Anatomy; Ancient Civilizations; Anthropology; Archaeology; Art History; Astronomy and Space Science; Biochemistry; Biology; Biotechnology; Cell Biology; Chemistry; Computer Science; Criminology; Cultural Studies; Economics; English; Environmental Studies; Fine Arts; Food Science; French; Gender Studies; Geography; Geology; Geophysics; German; Greek (Classical); Hebrew; History; Indigenous Studies; International Studies; Latin; Law; Linguistics; Literature; Mathematical Physics; Mathematics; Medieval Studies; Modern History; Modern Languages; Music; Music Education; Native American Studies; Pharmacology; Philosophy; Physical Engineering; Physics; Physiology; Political Sciences; Psychology; Public Administration; Regional Planning; Religion; Religious Studies; Russian; Sanskrit; Slavic Languages; Social Sciences; Sociology; Spanish; Statistics; Theatre; Town Planning; Toxicology; Women's Studies); **Briercrest College and Seminary** (Arts and Humanities; Business Administration; Christian Religious Studies; Education; Holy Writings; Music; Pastoral Studies; Religion; Religious Music; Theology); **Dentistry** (Dentistry); **Education** (Curriculum; Education; Educational Psychology; Educational Technology; Music Education; Natives Education; Physical Education; Primary Education; Secondary Education; Special Education; Teacher Training); **Emmanuel and St. Chad** (Bible; Christian Religious Studies; Ethics; History of Religion; Protestant Theology; Religion; Religious Studies; Theology); **Engineering** (Agricultural Engineering; Bioengineering; Chemical Engineering; Civil Engineering; Computer Engineering; Electrical Engineering; Engineering; Environmental Engineering; Geological Engineering; Mechanical Engineering; Physical Engineering); **Graduate Studies and Research** (Accountancy; Agricultural Economics; Agricultural Engineering; Agriculture; Anaesthesiology; Anatomy; Animal Husbandry; Anthropology; Archaeology; Art History; Biochemistry; Bioengineering; Biology; Biomedicine; Botany; Business Administration; Cell Biology; Chemical Engineering; Chemistry; Civil Engineering; Community Health; Computer Engineering; Computer Science; Cultural Studies; Curriculum; Economics; Education; Educational Administration; Educational Psychology; Electrical Engineering; English; Environmental Engineering; Environmental Management; Environmental Studies; Epidemiology; Finance; Fine Arts; Food Science; Gender Studies; Geography; Geological Engineering; Geology; Gynaecology and Obstetrics; Health Sciences; History; Immunology; Indigenous Studies; International Business; Laboratory Techniques; Law; Linguistics; Management; Mathematics; Meat and Poultry; Mechanical Engineering; Microbiology; Music; Native American Studies; Natural Resources; Neurological Therapy; Nursing; Nutrition; Oncology; Paediatrics; Pathology; Pharmacology; Pharmacy; Philosophy; Physical Engineering; Physical Therapy; Physics; Physiology; Political Sciences; Psychiatry and Mental Health; Psychology; Public Administration; Public Health; Rehabilitation and Therapy; Religion; Sociology; Soil Science; Special Education; Statistics; Surgery; Theatre; Toxicology; Veterinary Science; Women's Studies; Writing); **Horizon College and Seminary** *(http://www.horizon.edu)* (Christian Religious Studies; Missionary Studies; Pastoral Studies; Religious Studies; Theology); **Kinesiology** (Nutrition; Physical Education; Physical Therapy; Physiology; Psychology; Sports); **Law** (Law); **Lutheran Theological Seminary** *(http://www.usak.ca/stu/luther)* (Bible; Classical Languages; Greek (Classical); History of Religion; Holy Writings; New Testament; Protestant Theology; Theology); **Medicine** (Anaesthesiology; Anatomy; Biochemistry; Biomedicine; Cardiology; Cell Biology; Community Health; Epidemiology; Gynaecology and Obstetrics; Health Sciences; Immunology; Information Technology; Laboratory Techniques; Medical Technology; Medicine; Microbiology; Neurosciences; Occupational Therapy; Oncology; Ophthalmology; Paediatrics; Pathology; Pharmacology; Physical Therapy; Physiology; Psychiatry and Mental Health; Public Health; Radiology; Rehabilitation and Therapy; Speech Therapy and Audiology; Surgery); **Northern Teacher Education Program/ Northern Professional Access College** *(http://nortep-norpac.sk.ca/)* (Education; English; Indigenous Studies; Medicine; Native Language; Natural Sciences; Physics; Veterinary Science); **Nursing** (Nursing); **Pharmacy and Nutrition** (Biotechnology; Economics; Epidemiology; Molecular Biology; Nanotechnology; Nutrition; Pharmacy; Toxicology); **St. Andrew's** *(http://www.usask.ca/stu/standrews/)* (Bible; Ethics; Holy Writings; Pastoral Studies; Religion; Religious Education; Theology); **St. Peter's** (Art History; Arts and Humanities; Business Administration; Business and Commerce; Fine Arts; History; International Business; Philosophy; Physical Education; Physical Therapy; Psychology; Sports; Writing); **St. Thomas More** *(http://stmcollege.ca)* (Anthropology; Archaeology; Arts and Humanities; English; French; History; Natural Sciences; Philosophy; Political Sciences; Psychology; Slavic Languages; Sociology); **Veterinary Medicine** *(Western)* (Biomedicine; Microbiology; Pathology; Veterinary Science)

School

Business *(Edwards)* (Accountancy; Business Administration; Business and Commerce; Finance; Human Resources; International Business; Management; Marketing); **Environment and Sustainability** (Arts and Humanities; Education; Engineering; Environmental Management; Environmental Studies; Law; Natural Resources; Natural Sciences); **Physical Therapy** (Physical Therapy); **Public Health** (Anthropology; Biological and Life Sciences; Biology; Business Administration; Chemistry; Computer Science; Dentistry; Epidemiology; Health Administration; Health Sciences; Immunology; Medicine; Microbiology; Native American Studies; Nursing; Nutrition; Pharmacy; Physical Therapy; Psychology; Public Health; Social Sciences; Sociology; Statistics; Veterinary Science)

Institute

Native Studies and Applied Research *(Gabriel Dumont (Also affiiated to Universiy of Regina). http://gdins.org)* (Adult Education; Indigenous Studies)

Centre

Continuing and Distance Education *(CCDE)* (Adult Education; Agriculture; Business Administration; Chinese; Design; Ecology; Educational Psychology; English; Environmental Studies; Fine Arts; Foreign Languages Education; French; German; Horticulture; Indigenous Studies; Japanese; Leadership; Mathematics; Music; Music Education; Spanish; Special Education)

Graduate School

Public Policy *(Johnson-Shoyama)* (Health Administration; International Business; Public Administration)

Further Information: Teaching Hospital. Study Abroad programmes.

History: Founded 1907.

Academic Year: September to June (September-December; January-April; May-June). Also summer session (July-August)

Admission Requirements: Secondary school certificate or recognized equivalent. Proof of English proficiency

Fees: National: Undergraduate, 549.00 -1,201.50 per 3 credit unit class. Masters and Doctoral programs: 3,729.00 per annum (Canadian Dollar), International: Undergraduate, 1,427.40-3,123.90 per 3 credit unit class. Masters and Doctoral programs: 5,593.50 per annum

Main Language(s) of Instruction: English

Degrees and Diplomas: *Certificat et diplôme universitaire/University certificate and diploma*; *Baccalauréat/Bachelor's Degree*: **Agricultural Business; Agriculture; Arts and Humanities; Biological and Life Sciences; Business Administration; Chemistry; Computer Science; Education; Engineering; Mathematics.** *Maîtrise/Master's Degree*: **Accountancy; Agricultural Economics; Animal Husbandry; Anthropology; Archaeology; Biochemistry; Bioengineering; Biology; Business Administration; Chemical Engineering; Chemistry; Civil Engineering; Community Health; Computer Engineering; Cultural Studies; Curriculum; Economics; Educational Administration; Educational Psychology; Educational Technology; Electrical Engineering; English; Environmental Studies; Epidemiology; Finance; Fine Arts; Food Science; French; Gender Studies; Geography; Geology; Health Sciences; History; Indigenous Studies; Law; Linguistics; Marketing; Mathematics; Mathematics and Computer Science; Mechanical Engineering; Microbiology; Music; Nursing; Nutrition; Pharmacology; Pharmacy; Physical Therapy; Physiology; Plant Pathology; Political Sciences; Psychology; Public Administration; Public**

Health; Sociology; Soil Science; Special Education; Veterinary Science; Water Management; Women's Studies; Writing. *Doctorat/Doctoral Degree*: **Agricultural Economics; Anatomy; Animal Husbandry; Biochemistry; Biology; Cell Biology; Chemical Engineering; Chemistry; Civil Engineering; Community Health; Computer Engineering; Computer Science; Educational Administration; Electrical Engineering; English; Food Science; Geology; Health Sciences; History; Immunology; Mathematics; Mechanical Engineering; Microbiology; Nursing; Nutrition; Pharmacology; Pharmacy; Physical Engineering; Physiology; Psychology; Social and Community Services; Soil Science; Statistics; Toxicology; Veterinary Science.**

Student Services: Academic Counselling, Canteen, Careers Guidance, Cultural Activities, Facilities for disabled people, Foreign Studies Centre, Health Services, Language Laboratory, Library, Nursery Care, Social Counselling, Sports Facilities

Academic Staff *2014-2015*	**TOTAL**
FULL-TIME	**1,059**
PART-TIME	**47**
STAFF WITH DOCTORATE	
FULL-TIME	**888**
Student Numbers *2014-2015*	
All (Foreign included)	**20,953**

Last Updated: 05/02/15

BRIERCREST COLLEGE AND SEMINARY

510 College Drive, Caronport S0H 0S0
Tel: +1(306) 756-3200
Fax: +1(306)756-5500
EMail: academicservices@briercrest.ca
Website: http://www.briercrest.ca/

President: Michael B. Pawelke (2013-)
Tel: +1(306) 756-3285 EMail: president@briercrest.ca

Programme

Arts and Humanities (Arts and Humanities; Economics; English; Fine Arts; History; Literature; Mathematics; Philosophy; Social Sciences); **Biblical Studies** (Bible; Greek (Classical); Theology); **Business Administration** (Accountancy; Administration; Business Administration; Finance; Human Resources; Information Management; Leadership; Management; Marketing; Operations Research); **Christian Ministry** (Bible; Family Studies; Pastoral Studies; Psychology; Religion; Religious Music; Theology); **Church and Culture** (Bible; Christian Religious Studies; History of Religion; Religious Studies; Theology); **Education** (Education; Foreign Languages Education; History; Humanities and Social Science Education; Music Education; Physical Education; Primary Education); **Global Studies**; **Music** (Art History; Music; Music Education; Musical Instruments; Religious Music; Singing); **Social Sciences** (Administration; Anthropology; Native American Studies; Psychology; Social Sciences; Sociology); **Theology** (Technology); **Youth Ministry** (Bible; Pastoral Studies; Psychology; Sociology; Theology)

Further Information: Traditional and Distance Education. Also Seminary

History: Founded 1935 as Briecrest Bible Institute. Earned full accrediaion 1976. Acquired present title 1982. Affiliated with University of Saskachewan.

Fees: Tuition per 3 credit hour courses: 918 ($306/credit) (Canadian Dollar)

Main Language(s) of Instruction: English

Accrediting Agency: The Association for Biblical Higher Education (ABHE). Association of Theological Schools in the United States and the Canada (ATS)

Degrees and Diplomas: *Bachelor's Degree*: **Arts and Humanities; English; History.** *Master's Degree*: **Bible; Christian Religious Studies; Family Studies; Holy Writings; Leadership; Management; Missionary Studies; New Testament; Pastoral Studies; Psychology; Theology.**

Student Services: Canteen, Library

Canada - Yukon

STRUCTURE OF HIGHER EDUCATION SYSTEM

Description:

The Department of Education has responsibility for post-secondary education in Yukon. It does not have its own university, though the Department contributes financially to students from the Yukon pursuing university studies elsewhere in Canada. In June 1990, Yukon College became a board governed community college. To serve people across the territory, Yukon College has a main campus, Ayamdigut, and 11 community campuses. Yukon College is the only public institution providing post-secondary education and offers first and second year university transfer, vocational, technical, academic upgrading and other programmes usually leading to a certificate or diploma. Most of the university transfer courses offered at Yukon College are articulated through the British Columbia Council on Admissions and Transfer (BCCAT). All colleges and universities in BC participate in BCCAT. Further, the College is negotiating a similar agreement with the Alberta Council on Admissions and Transfer (ACAT). Although Yukon College holds the rights to offer degrees, to date it has not introduced its own degree, however the college is planning on introducing its own degree and post-degree programs in 2017. The College has full autonomy on admissions and all other academic matters. A permanent board of governors was appointed in 1990. Three Bachelor's degree programmes, accredited by other universities, are offered at Yukon College: the Yukon Native Teacher Education Programme, and a Bachelor of Social Work, both programmes are offered in partnership with the University of Regina, and a Bachelor of Northern Environmental and Conservation Science in partnership with the University of Alberta are a part of the core delivery at Yukon College. In addition, through a partnership with University of Alaska Southeast, Yukon College offers a Master in Public Administration. The College has provided several instructors in the programme as well as additional curricular support in northern and First Nations content. The Department's Advanced Education Branch licenses private trade/vocational schools located in Yukon that deliver vocational, business, or professional programmes. Apprenticeship training is administered by the Department's Advanced Education Branch.

Stages of studies:

University level first stage:

University level first–stage studies in the Yukon includes general arts, science and business administration courses offered by Yukon College. Almost all of the courses are articulated through BCCAT. Certificates and diplomas in this area include circumpolar studies, general studies, heritage and culture, liberal arts, northern studies, northern outdoor and environmental studies, northern First Nation studies, northern justice and criminology, northern science, visual arts, and women's and gender studies. In addition, Yukon College has several course specific and block transfers with universities across the country for students completing a certificate or diploma.

University level second stage:

For the second stage university-level (degree programmes), Yukon College offers four degree programmes. The degree programmes include: the Yukon Native Teacher Education Programme, offered in conjunction with the University of Regina, leads to a four year Bachelor of Education degree; the Bachelor of Social Work degree which is also delivered in partnership with University of Regina and leads to a four-year degree; and a Bachelor of Environmental and Conservation Science through a partnership with the University of Alberta (this also leads to a four-year degree). Students may also complete a degree in circumpolar studies through participation in the University of the Arctic. Yukon College offers one master program by distance through the University of Alaska Southeast –the Master's of Public Administration.

ADMISSION TO HIGHER EDUCATION

Admission to university-level studies:

Admission requirements: Secondary School Diploma may not be required.

Other requirements: No general entrance exams; however, depending on their level of high school completion, students may need to write the Canadian Achievement Test, the GED or the Language Proficiency Index.

Foreign students admission:

Definition of foreign student: International students must be here on a study permit or less than six months on a visitor visa. They must be enrolled full-time in a recognized academic, career or vocational training program at Yukon College.

Admission requirements: Vary by program, with all requiring a level of English proficiency, and some requiring math or science proficiency. Some programs have additional entrance requirements. See [http://yukoncollege.yk.ca/programs] and [http://yukoncollege.yk.ca/international/] for complete information.

Entry regulations: See Citizenship and Immigration Canada's Web site at [http://www.cic.gc.ca/english/study/index.asp].

Health requirements: Yukon College requires proof of independent health insurance coverage.

Language proficiency: For international students coming to Canada, Yukon College requires them to write iBT TOEFL, IELTS or CLBPT. Yukon College also offers English as a Second Language programs.

RECOGNITION OF STUDIES

Quality assurance system:

Yukon College has formal transfer credit arrangements through British Columbia Council on Admissions and Transfer (BCCAT) and Alberta Council on Admissions and Transfer (ACAT). In addition, Yukon College has several program or course specific transfer arrangements with colleges and universities across the country.

PROVINCIAL BODIES

Ministère de l'Éducation (Department of Education)

Minister of Education/Ministre de l'Éducation: Doug Graham
PO Box 2703
Whitehorse, YK Y1A 2C6
Canada
Tel: + 1(867) 667-5141
Fax: + 1(867) 393-6254
EMail: contact.education@gov.yk.ca
WWW: http://education.gov.yk.ca

Data for academic year: 2014-2015

Source: IAU from The Canadian Information Centre for International Credentials (CICIC), a unit of the Council of Ministers of Education, Canada (CMEC), on behalf of the Yukon Department of Education, October 2014. Bodies 2016.

INSTITUTION

PUBLIC INSTITUTION

YUKON COLLEGE

P.O. Box 2799, 500 College Drive, Whitehorse, Yukon Y1A 5K4
EMail: kbarnes@yukoncollege.yk.ca
Website: http://www.yukoncollege.yk.ca

President: Karen Barnes (2011-)
EMail: kbarnes@yukoncollege.yk.ca

Vice President Academic and Student Service: Deborah Bartlette EMail: dbartlette@yukoncollege.yk.ca

School

Health, Education and Human Services (Education; Health Sciences; Social Work; Welfare and Protective Services); **Liberal Arts** (Arts and Humanities; Public Administration); **Management, Tourism and Hospitality** (Hotel and Restaurant; Management; Tourism)

History: Founded 1963.

Fees: National: Resident of Canada or Alaska: 112/credit, 336/three-credit course (Canadian Dollar), International: 3,690-5,200 depending on programmes (Canadian Dollar)

Main Language(s) of Instruction: English

Degrees and Diplomas: *Bachelor's Degree*: **Education; Nordic Studies; Public Administration; Social Work.**

Student Services: IT Centre, Library, Sports Facilities

Student Numbers *2014-2015*: Total 1,223

Last Updated: 04/03/15

Central African Republic

STRUCTURE OF HIGHER EDUCATION SYSTEM

Description:

Postsecondary education is offered at the Université de Bangui, which is made up of faculties, institutes and a Higher Teacher Training College (Ecole normale supérieure). The Administrative Council, which is presided over by the Minister of Higher Education and Research implements the University's development plan set out by the government. The University Council, presided over by the Rector of the university, approves proposed official documents to be submitted to higher authorities. It is consulted about the regulations, organization and programme of study.

Stages of studies:

University level first stage: *Premier cycle*

The first cycle lasts for two years. Admission is based on the Baccalauréat. It leads to the Diplôme d'Etudes universitaires générales (DEUG).

University level second stage: *Deuxième cycle*

The second cycle lasts for one year after the DEUG and leads to the Licence. In Engineering, the Diplôme d'Ingénieur is conferred after a minimum of four years' study. A further two years after the Licence leads to the Master I/II. In Medicine, a Doctorate is awarded after six years of study.

ADMISSION TO HIGHER EDUCATION

Admission to university-level studies:

Name of secondary school credential required: Baccalauréat

NATIONAL BODIES

Ministère de l'Enseignement supérieur et de la Recherche scientifique (Ministry of Higher Education and Research)

Minister: Gisèle Bedan
PO Box 35
Bangui

Data for academic year: 2009-2010

Source: IAU from World Data on Education 2006/07, International Bureau of Education (IBE); Base Curie, Ministère des Affaires étrangères et européennes, France, and documentation, 2009. Bodies, 2015.

INSTITUTIONS

PUBLIC INSTITUTIONS

NATIONAL SCHOOL FOR ADMINISTRATION AND MAGISTRACY

Ecole nationale d'Administration et de Magistrature (ENAM)

BP 1045, Bangui
Tel: +236(61) 08-94 +236(61) 04-88
Fax: +236(61) 27-77 +236(61) 20-78

Directeur Général: Henri-Lactare Gbénénoui

Programme

Administration and Magistracy (Administration; Economics; Finance; International Relations; Justice Administration; Law)

History: Founded 1962.
Last Updated: 22/06/12

UNIVERSITY OF BANGUI

Université de Bangui

BP 1450, Avenue des Martyrs, Bangui
Tel: +236(61) 20-05
Fax: +236(61) 78-90
EMail: info@univ-bangui.info
Website: http://www.univ-bangui.net

Recteur: Georgette Florence Koyt (2011-)
EMail: recteur@univ-bangui.info; gfdkoyt@gmail.com

Vice-Recteur: Joachin Rouauld

Faculty

Arts and Humanities *(FLSH)* (Anthropology; Arts and Humanities; Communication Studies; Educational Sciences; English; Geography (Human); History; Information Sciences; Modern Languages; Philosophy; Social Sciences; Sociology; Spanish); **Health Sciences**

(FACSS) (Anaesthesiology; Biomedicine; Community Health; Gynaecology and Obstetrics; Health Education; Health Sciences; Laboratory Techniques; Medicine; Midwifery; Nursing; Paediatrics; Public Health; Social Work; Surgery); **Law and Political Science** *(FSJP)* (International Relations; Law; Private Law; Public Law); **Law, Economics and Management** *(FSEG)* (Economics; Management; Rural Planning); **Science** *(F-Sciences)* (Biology; Chemistry; Geology; Mathematics and Computer Science; Physics; Science Education)

Higher School

Teacher Training *(Ecole nationale supérieure (ENS))* (Agricultural Education; Agricultural Engineering; Agriculture; Arts and Humanities; Biological and Life Sciences; Cattle Breeding; Earth Sciences; Educational and Student Counselling; Educational Psychology; English; Forestry; Geography; Geography (Human); History; Mathematics; Mathematics Education; Modern Languages; Pedagogy; Physics; Primary Education; Secondary Education; Teacher Training)

Institute

Applied Linguistics *(ILA)* (African Languages; Applied Linguistics); **Business Management** *(IUGE)* (Business Administration)

Higher Institute

Rural Development *(ISDR)* (Cattle Breeding; Forestry; Rural Studies; Water Management); **Technology** *(IST)* (Building Technologies; Civil Engineering; Computer Engineering; Geological Engineering; Industrial Engineering; Mining Engineering; Technology)

Further Information: Also 9 research centres and 6 laboratories.

History: Founded 1969. Formerly Institut d'Etudes juridiques of the Fondation de l'Enseignement supérieur en Afrique centrale. Acquired present status 1985.

Academic Year: September to June (September-December; January-March; April-June)

Admission Requirements: Secondary school certificate (Baccalauréat) or special entrance examination

Main Language(s) of Instruction: French

Degrees and Diplomas: *Diplôme universitaire de Technologie*: **Agriculture; Civil Engineering; Computer Science; Geology; Industrial Engineering; Management; Mining Engineering.** *Certificat d'Aptitude pédagogique à l'Enseignement secondaire*; *Licence*: **Arts and Humanities; Development Studies; Economics; Law; Management; Mathematics; Natural Sciences; Physics; Rural Planning.** *Diplôme d'Ingénieur*; *Doctorat en Médecine*: **Medicine.** *Master I/II*: **Arts and Humanities; Economics; Law.**

Student Services: Canteen, Cultural Activities, Nursery Care, Social Counselling, Sports Facilities

Publications: Annales; Revue d'Histoire et d'Archéologie Centrafricaine

Last Updated: 23/07/12

Chad

STRUCTURE OF HIGHER EDUCATION SYSTEM

Description:

Higher education is provided by both public and private universities, higher institutes and specialized schools.

Stages of studies:

University level first stage: *Premier cycle*

Since 2010, with the introduction of the three-tier (LMD) system, the first stage lasts for three years and leads to a Licence.

University level second stage: *Deuxième cycle*

Since 2010, with the introduction of the three-tier (LMD) system, the second stage lasts for two years and leads to a Master.

University level third stage: *Troisième cycle*

Since 2010, with the introduction of the three-tier (LMD) system, doctoral schools are being created. They lead to a Doctorat after 3 years of study. The University of N'Djamena awards a Doctorate in Medicine after seven years of study.

ADMISSION TO HIGHER EDUCATION

Admission to university-level studies:

Name of secondary school credential required: Baccalauréat

Alternatives to credentials: Special entrance examination to the university instead of secondary school certificate

Foreign students admission:

Admission requirements: Foreign students should hold the Baccalauréat or an equivalent qualification or pass the special entrance examination to the University.

Entry regulations: Students should have a visa for entrance to Chad and a residence permit.

Health requirements: None

Language proficiency: Good knowledge of French or Arabic is required.

RECOGNITION OF STUDIES

Bodies dealing with recognition:

Commission d'Admission de l'Université de N'Djaména

PO Box 1117
Avenue Mobutu
N'Djaména
Tel: +235(51) 4444
Fax: +235(51) 4033
EMail: rectorat@intnet.td

NATIONAL BODIES

Ministère de l'Enseignement supérieur et de la Recherche scientifique (Ministry of Higher Education and Research)

Minister: Makaye Hassan Taisso
N'Djamena

Tel: +235 2251 6158
Fax: +235 2251 4243
Role of national body: The Ministry is responsible for the elaboration, coordination, implementation, follow-up of the Government's higher education policy for the public and the private sectors.

Data for academic year: 2012-2013
Source: IAU from the University of N'Djamena, 2007, and documentation, 2012. Bodies 2016.

INSTITUTIONS

PUBLIC INSTITUTIONS

ADAM BARKA UNIVERSITY OF ABÉCHÉ

Université Adam Barka d'Abéché (UNABA)
BP 1173 Route de N'Djamena, Abéché, Ouaddaï
Tel: +235(6) 200-005
Fax: +235(6) 98078
EMail: unaba@intnet.td
Website: http://univ-abeche.com

Recteur: Moustapha Mahamat Ali (2008-)

Faculty
Arts and Humanities *(FALASH)* (Arts and Humanities); **Health Sciences** *(FASS)* (Health Sciences); **Law and Economics** *(FADSE)* (Economics; Law); **Science and Techniques** (Chemistry; Geology; Mathematics; Natural Sciences; Physics)

History: Founded 2003.

Main Language(s) of Instruction: French

Accrediting Agency: Ministry of Higher Education, Research and Vocational Training

Degrees and Diplomas: *Diplôme d'Etudes universitaires générales*; *Licence*; *Maîtrise/Master*

Student Services: Sports Facilities

Last Updated: 03/08/12

MOUNDOU UNIVERSITY

Université de Moundou (UDM)
BP 206, Moundou, Logone Occidental
Tel: +235(251) 81-01
Fax: +235(251) 40-33
Website: http://univ-moundou.org

Recteur: Djarangar Djitta Issa (2012-)
EMail: djarangar@yahoo.fr

Vice-Recteur chargé des enseignements: Miandiguem Demoyel Maïport

Secrétaire Général: Alhadj Djabarna Zakaria

Faculty
Arts and Humanities *(FLASH)* (Geography; Philosophy); **Business Techniques and Sciences** *(FASTE)* (Accountancy; Business Administration; Human Resources; Management); **Exact and Applied Sciences** *(FASEA)* (Applied Chemistry; Computer Networks); **Law and Social Sciences** *(FADSS)* (Banking; Law)

History: Founded 2002. Formely named 'Institut Universitaire des Techniques d'Entreprise de Moundou' (IUTEM). Acquired present title and status 2008.

Main Language(s) of Instruction: French

Accrediting Agency: Ministry of Higher Education, Research and Vocational Training

Degrees and Diplomas: *Licence*; *Maîtrise/Master*

Last Updated: 03/08/12

NATIONAL HIGH SCHOOL OF CIVIL ENGINEERING

Ecole nationale Supérieure des Travaux publics (ENSTP)
BP 60, N'Djaména
Tel: +235(252) 3420
EMail: entp@intnet.td

Directeur: Koina Rodoumta (1965-)
Tel: +235 66 29 66 03 EMail: koina@yahoo.fr

Directeur des Etudes: Savaissel Hinamari Tel: +235 66 29 94 20

Higher School
Civil Engineering (Bridge Engineering; Civil Engineering; Construction Engineering; Road Engineering)

History: Founded 1965. Formerly "Ecole Nationale des Travaux Publics" (ENTP). Acquired present status 2012.

Academic Year: October to June

Admission Requirements: Baccalauréat (scientific sections: C, D, E, F)

Main Language(s) of Instruction: French

Degrees and Diplomas: *Licence*: **Civil Engineering.** *Diplôme d'Ingénieur*: **Civil Engineering.**

Student Services: Academic Counselling, Canteen, Careers Guidance, Foreign Studies Centre, Health Services, Social Counselling, Sports Facilities

Publications: Gamma

Academic Staff *2011-2012*	MEN	WOMEN	TOTAL
STAFF WITH DOCTORATE			
FULL-TIME	5	–	5
Student Numbers *2011-2012*			
All (Foreign included)	275	26	301

Last Updated: 11/12/12

NATIONAL SCHOOL OF ADMINISTRATION AND MAGISTRACY

Ecole Nationale d'Administration et de Magistrature (ENAM)
BP 758, N'Djaména
Tel: +235(251) 4097
Fax: +235(251) 4356
Website: http://enam-tchad.org/

Department
Administration (Administration; Business Administration); **Diplomacy Studies** (International Relations); **Finance and Economy** (Economics; Finance; Taxation); **Justice Administration**; **Law** (Law); **Technical Studies** (Technology)

History: Founded 1963.

Academic Year: October to July

Admission Requirements: Baccalauréat; DEUG; Licence and entrance examination.

Main Language(s) of Instruction: French

Accrediting Agency: Primature (Presidency)

Degrees and Diplomas: 1st cycle: Attaché d'administration (2 yrs); 2nd cycle: Administrateur civil de 2ème classe (2 yrs); 3rd cycle: Inspecteur d'administration générale (2 yrs)

Student Services: Health Services, Language Laboratory, Sports Facilities

Last Updated: 06/08/12

SARH UNIVERSITY

Université de Sarh
BP 105, Sarh, Moyen Chari
Tel: +235(268) 1097

Recteur: Ahmat Charfadine (2012-)

Directeur général: Hougoto Nguemadjingaye

Faculty

Agronomy *(IUSAES)* (Agronomy)

Programme

Environmental Sciences (Environmental Studies)

History: Founded 1997. Acquired present title and status 2010. Formely named 'Institut des Sciences Agronomiques et de l'Environnement de Sarh', now a faculty of the University.

Main Language(s) of Instruction: French

Accrediting Agency: Ministry of Higher Education, Research and Vocational Training

Degrees and Diplomas: *Diplôme d'Ingénieur*

Last Updated: 06/08/12

TEACHER TRAINING SCHOOL

Ecole Normale Supérieure de N'Djaména (ENS)
BP 60, N'Djaména
Tel: +235(51) 4487
Fax: +235(51) 4550
EMail: lssed@intnet.td

Department

Teacher Trainers Education; **Teacher Training for Primary Education** (Education; Educational Administration; Educational Psychology; Primary Education); **Teacher Training for Secondary Education** (Administration; Arabic; Biology; Chemistry; Curriculum; Education; Educational Technology; English; French; Geography; Geology; History; Mathematics; Physics; Secondary Education); **Teacher Training for Technical and Professional Education** (Accountancy; Administration; Finance; Management)

History: Founded 1992. Formerly 'Institut supérieur des Sciences de l'Education (ISSED)'. Acquired present status and title 2011.

Accrediting Agency: Ministry of Higher Education, Research and Vocational Training

Degrees and Diplomas: *Licence*; *Maîtrise/Master*

Last Updated: 06/08/12

UNIVERSITY INSTITUTE OF SCIENCE AND TECHNOLOGY OF ABÉCHÉ

Institut universitaire des Sciences et Techniques d'Abéché (IUSTA)
BP 130, Abéché, Ouaddaï
Tel: +235 6 625 12 90
Website: http://iusta-tchad.org/index.html

Directeur Général: Maloum Soultan

Directeur Adjoint: Désiré Allaissem

Secrétaire Général: Issa Youssouf

Department

Biomedical and Pharmaceutical Sciences (Biomedicine; Pharmacy); **Electrical and Mechanical Engineering** (Computer Science; Electrical Engineering; Mechanical Engineering); **Industrial Computing and Management** (Computer Science; Industrial Management); **Livestock Techniques** (Cattle Breeding)

History: Founded 1997.

Admission Requirements: Secondary school certificate (baccalauréat) and entrance examination.

Main Language(s) of Instruction: French, Arabic

Accrediting Agency: Ministry of Higher Education and Research

Degrees and Diplomas: *Licence*; *Diplôme d'Ingénieur*; *Maîtrise/Master*: **Animal Husbandry; Electrical Engineering; Mechanical Engineering.**

Last Updated: 06/08/12

IAU UNIVERSITY OF N'DJAMENA

Université de N'Djaména (UNDJ/UNDT)
BP 1117, Avenue Mobutu, N'Djaména
Tel: +235 22-51-44-44
Fax: +235 22-51-40-33
EMail: info@undt.info
Website: http://www.univ-ndjamena.org/

Recteur: Ali Abdelrhamane Haggar Mahamat Saleh (2012-)
EMail: rector@undt.info

Vice-Recteur, Chargé des enseignements: Tchago Bouimon

Chef de Service de Relations publiques et protocole: Mahamat Saleh Ali
Tel: +235 66-28-48-61 +235 99-58-17-73
EMail: mahamatsaleh86@yahoo.fr

International Relations: Ali Adoum, Directeur des Affaires académiques

Faculty

Arts and Humanities (Arabic; Arts and Humanities; Communication Studies; English; Geography; History; Linguistics; Modern Languages; Philosophy; Social Sciences; Sociology); **Exact and Applied Sciences** (Biology; Chemistry; Computer Science; Geology; Hydraulic Engineering; Mathematics; Paleontology; Physics); **Health Sciences** (Biological and Life Sciences; Gynaecology and Obstetrics; Medicine; Paediatrics; Public Health; Surgery); **Law and Economics** (Economics; Law; Management; Private Law; Public Law)

Institute

Rural Planning *(Observatoire Foncier du Tchad)* (Natural Resources; Rural Planning; Social Sciences; Soil Management)

History: Founded 1971 as University of Chad comprising institutions that were formerly part of the Fondation de l'Enseignement supérieur en Afrique Centrale. Acquired present status and title 1994.

Academic Year: October to June (October-February; March-June).

Admission Requirements: Secondary school certificate (baccalauréat).

Fees: (CFA Francs): 40,000 per annum

Main Language(s) of Instruction: French, Arabic, English (Distance programmes).

Accrediting Agency: Ministry of Higher Education and Research

Degrees and Diplomas: *Diplôme d'Etudes universitaires générales*: **Arts and Humanities.** *Licence*: **Arts and Humanities; Law.** *Diplôme d'Ingénieur*: **Engineering; Technology.** *Doctorat en Médecine*: **Medicine.** *Maîtrise/Master*: **Arts and Humanities; Law.** Also Licence Professionnelle, Maîtrise Professionnelle and Certificates. Master in Law, Arts and Humanities, 5 yrs.

Student Services: Academic Counselling, Canteen, Cultural Activities, Health Services, Nursery Care, Sports Facilities

Publications: Annales de l'Universite de N'Djaména

Academic Staff *2010-2011*	MEN	WOMEN	**TOTAL**
FULL-TIME	–	–	**411**
Student Numbers *2010-2011*			
All (Foreign included)	7,039	1,396	**8,435**
FOREIGN ONLY	–	–	**48**

Last Updated: 06/04/12

UNIVERSITY POLYTECHNIC INSTITUTE OF MONGO

Institut universitaire polytechnique de Mongo (IUPM)
BP 4377, Route d'Aboudéa, Mongo, Guera
Tel: +235(51) 8064
EMail: iupm@intnet.td

Directeur: Mahamat Barka (2003-) EMail: mt_barka@yahoo.fr

Department

Basic Sciences (Natural Sciences); **Chemical Engineering** (Chemical Engineering); **Civil Engineering** (Civil Engineering);

Geology (Geology); **Industrial Maintenance** (Industrial Maintenance); **Mechanical Engineering** (Mechanical Engineering)

History: Founded 2002.

Main Language(s) of Instruction: French

Degrees and Diplomas: *Licence*; *Diplôme d'Ingénieur*

PRIVATE INSTITUTION

KING FAISAL UNIVERSITY

Université Roi Fayçal (URF)

BP 582, N'Djaména
Tel: +56 (235) 253 0289
Fax: +56 (235) 251 9004
EMail: info@urfchad.org

Recteur: Abderahmane Oumar Almahy

Faculty
Management and Economics (Economics; Management); **Modern Languages** (Arabic)

College
Educational Sciences (Pedagogy); **Law** (Law)

School
Computer Engineering and Information Technology (Computer Engineering; Information Technology); **Graduate Studies**

Higher Institute
Health Science and Technology (Health Sciences)

History: Founded 1992.

Main Language(s) of Instruction: Arabic, French

Degrees and Diplomas: *Maîtrise/Master*

Student Services: Language Laboratory

Last Updated: 12/12/12

Chile

STRUCTURE OF HIGHER EDUCATION SYSTEM

Description:

Higher education is provided by universities, professional institutes and technical training centres. All have tuition fees. Only universities can deliver academic degrees.The Higher Education Division of the Ministry of Education is responsible for planning and implementing policies and funds allocation in higher education. The main coordinating bodies are the Council of Rectors of Chilean Universities (Consejo de Rectores de Universidades Chilenas) which coordinates the traditional state and private universities which were created before the 1980s reform and those derived from these, and the Council for Higher Education (Consejo Superior de Educación) which is responsible for the assessment and accreditation of other private universities. Tuition-free higher education for students from the poorest families was granted in 2016.

Stages of studies:

University level first stage: *Licenciatura*

The four- to six-year Licenciatura is the main academic degree at the undergraduate level.

University level second stage: *Magister/Doctorado*

Students holding the Licenciatura or the Professional title may be awarded a Magister degree after one to two years' further study. The Doctorado takes between three and five years usually beyond the Magister. Candidates must submit a thesis.

ADMISSION TO HIGHER EDUCATION

Admission to university-level studies:

Name of secondary school credential required: Licencia de Educación Media

Admission requirements: Prueba de Selección Universitaria (PSU)

Foreign students admission:

Admission requirements: Foreign students must have completed their secondary education to be admitted to university. Each higher education institution is free to set up its entrance requirements for foreign students.

RECOGNITION OF STUDIES

Quality assurance system:

The national system of higher education quality assurance provided by the National Accreditation Committee (CNA) was put into place in 2006. The CNA is responsible for licensing, institutional accreditation, course/programme accreditation, and information.

NATIONAL BODIES

Ministerio de Educación (Ministry of Education)

Minister: Adriana Delpiano Puelma

Head, Higher Education Division: Francisco Javier Martínez Concha

Dirección Av. Libertador Bernardo O'Higgins 1371

Santiago

Tel: +56 2 2406 6000

EMail: consultas@mineduc.cl

WWW: http://www.mineduc.cl

Role of national body: Development of education at all levels. At higher education level, responsible for policy development and implementation, allocation of higher education public funds, and student financial support.

Comisión Nacional de Acreditación - CNA (National Accreditation Commission)

Executive Secretary: Paula Beale Sepúlveda
Santa Lucía 360, Piso 6
Santiago
Tel: +56 2 2620 1100
Fax: +56 2 2620 1120
EMail: amiranda@cnachile.cl
WWW: https://www.cnachile.cl/

Consejo de Rectores de Universidades Chilenas - CRUCH (Chilean University Rectors' Conference)

Executive Director: Teresa Marshall Infante
Alameda 1371, piso 4
Santiago
Tel: +56 2 2426 8620
Fax: +56 2 2426 8626
EMail: cruch@consejoderectores.cl
WWW: http://www.consejoderectores.cl
Role of national body: The Chilean University Rectors' Conference is a legal entity created in 1954 as the coordination body for public universities. It is chaired by the Minister of Education.

Consejo Nacional de Educación - CNED (National Council for Education)

Executive Secretary: Fernanda Valdés
Marchant Pereira 844
Providencia
Santiago
Tel: +56 2 2341 3412
WWW: http://www.cned.cl/
Role of national body: Independent public body in charge of the accreditation of higher education institutions.

Data for academic year: 2015-2016
Source: IAU from the website of the Ministry of Education, Chile, the 2009 Education Law (http://www.leychile.cl/Navegar?idNorma=1006043&idParte=0&idVersion=2009-09-12), and NUFFIC's Education System Chile (https://www.nuffic.nl/en/library/education-system-chile.pdf), 2015.

INSTITUTIONS

PUBLIC INSTITUTIONS

ARTURO PRAT UNIVERSITY

Universidad Arturo Prat
Avenida Arturo Prat 2120, Iquique
Tel: +56(57) 2526-000
EMail: admision@unap.cl
Website: http://www.unap.cl

Rector: Gustavo Soto Bringas

Vicerrectora Académica: Veronica Maria Frias Pistono
EMail: mfrias@unap.cl

Faculty
Arts and Humanities (Arts and Humanities; Bilingual and Bicultural Education; Education; English; Mathematics Education; Physical Education; Physics; Preschool Education; Primary Education; Science Education; Sociology; Spanish; Translation and Interpretation); **Business Administration** (Accountancy; Administration; Business Administration; Business and Commerce; Computer Science; Economics; Information Management; Information Sciences; Management; Marketing; Tourism); **Engineering and Architecture** (Architecture; Civil Engineering; Computer Engineering; Computer Science; Electronic Engineering; Engineering; Environmental Engineering; Industrial Engineering; Metallurgical Engineering; Mineralogy; Mining Engineering; Safety Engineering); **Health Sciences** (Chemistry; Dentistry; Health Sciences; Nursing; Pharmacy; Physical Therapy; Psychology; Speech Therapy and Audiology); **Natural and Renewable Resources** (Agronomy; Aquaculture; Arid Land Studies; Biology; Biotechnology; Fishery; Marine Biology; Marine Science and Oceanography)

School
Law and Political Sciences (Law; Political Sciences; Social Work)

Campus
Antofagasta (Business Administration; Business and Commerce; English; International Business; Marketing; Mining Engineering; Safety Engineering; Spanish; Translation and Interpretation); **Arica** (Architecture; Business Administration; Engineering; Safety Engineering); **Calama** (Architecture; Business Administration; Safety Engineering); **Santiago** (Administration; Business Administration; English; Human Resources; Marketing; Mining Engineering; Safety Engineering; Spanish; Translation and Interpretation); **Victoria** (Agriculture; Business Administration; Computer Science; Law; Marketing; Nursing; Physical Therapy; Preschool Education; Psychology; Safety Engineering)

Further Information: Also Institutes and Research Centres

History: Founded 1967. Previously regional branch of University of Chile and Instituto Profesional. A State institution.

Academic Year: March to December (March-July; August-December)

Admission Requirements: Secondary school certificate (Licencia de Educación Media) and entrance examination

Main Language(s) of Instruction: Spanish

Degrees and Diplomas: *Técnico de Nivel Superior*, *Licenciatura*: **Biotechnology; Education; Law; Marine Science and Oceanography; Social Work; Sociology; Teacher Training.** *Título Profesional*: **Accountancy; Agricultural Engineering; Biology; Biotechnology; Business Administration; Education; Engineering; Law; Management; Nursing; Social Work.** *Post- título/ Diploma*: **Communication Studies; English; Genetics; Mathematics Education; Modern Languages; Pedagogy; Visual Arts.** *Magister*: **Administration; Arid Land Studies; Business Administration; Clinical Psychology; Computer Science; English; Environmental Management; Finance; Fishery; Health Administration; Higher Education Teacher Training; Human Resources; International Business; Marketing; Physical Education; Public Administration; Secondary Education; Social Work; Sports.** *Doctorado*: **Arid Land Studies; Chemistry.**

Publications: Colosos de Iquique; Nuestro Norte

Publishing House: University Press

Last Updated: 30/12/15

METROPOLITAN UNIVERSITY OF EDUCATIONAL SCIENCES

Universidad Metropolitana de Ciencias de la Educación (UMCE)

Casilla 1487, Avenida José Pedro Alessandri 774,
Santiago 7760197
Tel: +56(2) 2241-2400
Fax: +56(2) 2241-2723
EMail: contacto@umce.cl
Website: http://www.umce.cl

Rector: Jaime Espinoza Araya (2009-)
Tel: +56(2) 2241-2408 EMail: rector@umce.cl

Secretario General: Ramiro Baldomar Aguilar

International Relations: José Martínez Armesto
Tel: +56(2) 2241-2528

Faculty

Arts and Physical Education (Arts and Humanities; Music Education; Painting and Drawing; Physical Education; Physical Therapy; Sculpture; Sports; Sports Management); **Basic Sciences** (Biology; Chemistry; Entomology; Natural Sciences; Physics); **History, Geography, and Letters** (Arts and Humanities; Classical Languages; English; French; Geography; German; History); **Philosophy and Education** (Education; Pedagogy; Philosophy; Preschool Education; Religion; Special Education; Teacher Training)

Further Information: Campuses in Defder (Santiago) and Rancagua. Regional Branch in Graneros

History: Founded 1986. Previously Institute of Education of University of Chile (1889) and Academia Superior de Ciencias Pedagógicas (1980). A State institution.

Academic Year: March to December (March-July; August-December)

Admission Requirements: Secondary school certificate (Licencia de Educación Media) and entrance examination

Main Language(s) of Instruction: Spanish

Accrediting Agency: National Accreditation Commission (CNA)

Degrees and Diplomas: *Técnico de Nivel Medio*; *Licenciatura*; *Magister*: **Curriculum; Educational Administration; Educational Testing and Evaluation; English; Entomology; Greek (Classical); Latin; Literature; Pedagogy; Physical Education; Special Education.** *Doctorado*: **Education.**

Student Services: Academic Counselling, Careers Guidance, Cultural Activities, Health Services, Library, Nursery Care, Social Counselling, Sports Facilities

Publications: Acta Entomológica Chilena; Dimensión Histórica de Chile; Revista Contextos; Revista Educación Física Chile; Revista Limes

Last Updated: 19/01/16

METROPOLITAN UNIVERSITY OF TECHNOLOGY

Universidad Tecnológica Metropolitana (UTEM)

Dieciocho no 161, Santiago
Tel: +56(2) 2787-7500
Fax: +56(2) 2696-2946
EMail: relint@utem.cl
Website: http://www.utem.cl

Rector: Luis Pinto Faverio
Tel: +56(2) 2787-7541 EMail: rectoria@utem.cl

Secretario General: Patricio Bastías Román
Tel: +56(2) 2787-7547 EMail: secgral@utem.cl

Faculty

Administration and Economics (Accountancy; Administration; Agricultural Management; Business Administration; Documentation Techniques; Economic and Finance Policy; Economics; Finance; Human Resources; Industrial Management; International Business; International Economics; Library Science; Management; Tourism; Transport Engineering); **Construction and Regional Planning** (Architecture; Civil Engineering; Construction Engineering; Environmental Engineering; Regional Planning; Safety Engineering; Town Planning); **Engineering** (Agricultural Engineering; Civil Engineering; Computer Engineering; Computer Science; Electrical Engineering; Electronic Engineering; Engineering; Industrial Engineering; Information Technology; Measurement and Precision Engineering; Mechanical Engineering; Safety Engineering; Surveying and Mapping; Transport Engineering; Wood Technology); **Humanities and Social Communication Technology** (Communication Studies; Humanities and Social Science Education; Industrial Design; Social Work); **Natural Sciences, Mathematics and Environmental Studies** (Biotechnology; Chemical Engineering; Chemistry; Environmental Studies; Food Technology; Industrial Chemistry; Mathematics and Computer Science; Natural Sciences)

History: Founded 1981 as Professional Institute of Santiago, acquired present status and title 1993.

Academic Year: March to December

Admission Requirements: Secondary school certificate (Licencia de Educación Média) and entrance examination (Prueba de Selección Universitaria)

Main Language(s) of Instruction: Spanish

Accrediting Agency: National Accreditation Commission (CNA)

Degrees and Diplomas: *Licenciatura*; *Título Profesional*; *Post-título/Diploma*; *Magister*: **Nuclear Engineering.**

Student Services: Academic Counselling, Canteen, Careers Guidance, Cultural Activities, Health Services, Language Laboratory, Library, Social Counselling, Sports Facilities

Publications: Revista Trilogía

Last Updated: 20/01/16

PROFESSIONAL INSTITUTE IPG

Instituto Profesional IPG

General Salvo 20, Providencia, Santiago
Tel: +56(2) 2836-7900
EMail: admisionprovidencia@ipg.cl
Website: http://www.ipg.cl

Rector: Ricardo Sobarzo Zambrano

Vicerrector Académico: Ulises Toledo Nickels

School

Education, Sports and Society (Education; Educational Psychology; Physical Education; Preschool Education; Social Sciences; Sports); **Health Sciences** (Health Sciences; Nursing; Physical Therapy); **Management and Communication** (Administration; Business Administration; Cooking and Catering; Management); **Technology and Industrial Process** (Civil Engineering; Computer Science; Construction Engineering; Industrial Engineering; Maintenance Technology; Safety Engineering; Technology)

Further Information: Also Rancagua, Arauco, Panguipulli, and Concepción Branches

History: Founded 1983.

Admission Requirements: High School Diploma (Licencia de Educación Media)

Main Language(s) of Instruction: Spanish

Accrediting Agency: National Accreditation Commission (CNA)

Degrees and Diplomas: *Técnico de Nivel Superior*, *Título Profesional*

Last Updated: 05/01/16

UNIVERSITY OF ANTOFAGASTA

Universidad de Antofagasta (UA)

Avenida Angamos 601, Casilla 170, Antofagasta

Tel: +56(55) 600-822-1010

Website: http://www.uantof.cl

Rector: Luis Alberto Loyola Morales

Vicerrector Académico: Hernán Sagua Franco

Faculty

Basic Sciences *(Coloso)* (Chemistry; Mathematics; Natural Sciences; Physics); **Education** (Education; Mathematics Education; Modern Languages; Physical Education; Preschool Education; Science Education; Special Education); **Engineering** *(Coloso)* (Chemical Engineering; Chemistry; Electrical and Electronic Engineering; Electrical Engineering; Electronic Engineering; Engineering; Industrial Engineering; Measurement and Precision Engineering; Mechanical Engineering; Mining Engineering; Systems Analysis); **Health Sciences** *(Coloso)* (Biochemistry; Health Sciences; Medical Technology; Medicine; Nursing; Nutrition; Occupational Therapy; Paediatrics; Parasitology; Public Health; Rehabilitation and Therapy; Speech Therapy and Audiology); **Judicial Sciences** *(Coloso)* (Law); **Marine Studies and Natural Resources** *(Coloso)* (Agriculture; Aquaculture; Ecology; Environmental Studies; Fishery; Food Science; Marine Science and Oceanography; Natural Resources; Natural Sciences); **Medicine and Dentistry** (Dentistry; Gynaecology and Obstetrics; Medicine); **Social Sciences, Art and Humanities** *(Coloso)* (Arts and Humanities; Business Administration; Graphic Arts; Graphic Design; Music; Pedagogy; Private Administration; Psychology; Public Administration; Social Sciences; Social Work; Welfare and Protective Services)

Institute

Anthropology (Anthropology); **Natural Sciences** *(Alexander Von Humboldt)* (Ecology; Marine Science and Oceanography; Natural Sciences); **Renewable Natural Resources** *(Coloso)* (Natural Resources)

Further Information: Also Coloso and Área Clínica campuses

History: Founded 1981, incorporating previous regional branches at Antofagasta of the University of Chile and the Technical State University.

Academic Year: March to December (March-July; August-December)

Admission Requirements: Secondary school certificate (Licencia de Educación Media) and entrance examination

Main Language(s) of Instruction: Spanish

Accrediting Agency: National Accreditation Commission (CNA)

Degrees and Diplomas: *Técnico de Nivel Superior*; *Licenciatura*: **Administration; Education; Engineering; Health Sciences.** *Título Profesional*; *Magister*: **Applied Mathematics; Biomedicine; Biotechnology; Ecology; Educational Administration; Energy Engineering; Engineering; Environmental Studies; Maintenance Technology; Mining Engineering; Occupational Therapy; Public Health; Social Sciences.** *Doctorado*: **Biology; Cell Biology; Marine Biology; Mining Engineering; Molecular Biology.** Also Especialización programmes in Medicine and Dentistry

Student Services: Health Services, Language Laboratory, Library, Social Counselling, Sports Facilities

Publications: Estudios Oceanológicos; Innovación

Last Updated: 13/01/16

UNIVERSITY OF ATACAMA

Universidad de Atacama (UDA)

Casilla 240, Avenida Copayapu 485, Copiapó

Tel: +56(52) 2206-500

Fax: +56(52) 2206-504

EMail: admision2015@uda.cl

Website: http://www.uda.cl

Rector: Celso Arias Mora EMail: celso.arias@uda.cl

Vicerrector Académico: Jorge Valdivia D.

Faculty

Engineering (Business and Commerce; Computer Science; Engineering; Geology; Industrial Engineering; Marketing; Metallurgical Engineering; Mining Engineering); **Health Sciences** (Child Care and Development; Dietetics; Gynaecology and Obstetrics; Health Sciences; Nursing; Nutrition; Physical Therapy); **Humanities and Education** (Arts and Humanities; Education; English; Physical Education; Preschool Education; Spanish); **Law** (Law; Private Law; Public Law); **Natural Sciences** (Biology; Chemistry; Earth Sciences; Health Education; Marine Science and Oceanography; Natural Sciences; Nursing; Physics)

Institute

Technology (Automation and Control Engineering; Business Administration; Civil Engineering; Computer Engineering; Computer Networks; Industrial Maintenance; Instrument Making; Metallurgical Engineering; Technology)

Further Information: Campuses in Caldera, Vallenar, Los Andes and Santiago

History: Founded 1857 as School of Mining and became regional branch of State Technical University 1947. Became independent and acquired present status and title 1981. An autonomous institution financially supported by the State. Teacher education started in the Normal School of Copiapó 1905.

Academic Year: March to December (March-June; August-December)

Admission Requirements: Secondary school certificate (Licencia de Educación Media) and entrance examination

Main Language(s) of Instruction: Spanish

Accrediting Agency: National Accreditation Commission (CNA)

Degrees and Diplomas: *Licenciatura*; *Título Profesional*: **Engineering; Geology; Law.** *Magister*: **Computer Engineering; Computer Science; Law; Metallurgical Engineering.**

Student Services: Library

Publications: Revista de Ingeniera

Publishing House: Editorial de la Universidad de Atacama

Last Updated: 13/01/16

UNIVERSITY OF BÍO BÍO

Universidad del Bio Bío (UBB)

Avenida Collao 1202, Casilla 5-C, Concepción

Tel: +56(41) 3111-258

EMail: sregistro@ubiobio.cl

Website: http://www.ubiobio.cl

Rector: Héctor Gaete Feres EMail: hgaete@ubiobio.cl

Prorrectora: Gloria Gómez Vera EMail: ggomez@ubiobio.cl

Faculty

Architecture, Construction and Design (Architecture; Building Technologies; Construction Engineering; Design; Graphic Design; Industrial Design; Visual Arts); **Business Administration** (Accountancy; Administration; Business Administration; Commercial Law; Computer Engineering; Computer Science; Information Sciences; Marketing; Sanitary Engineering); **Education and Humanities** (Arts and Humanities; Communication Studies; Education; Educational Sciences; English; Geography; History; Pedagogy; Preschool Education; Primary Education; Social Sciences; Social Work; Spanish; Translation and Interpretation); **Engineering** (Civil Engineering; Electrical and Electronic Engineering; Engineering; Engineering Management; Forestry; Industrial Engineering; Mechanical Engineering; Wood Technology); **Health and Food Science** *(Chillán)* (Food Science; Health Sciences; Nutrition); **Science** (Chemistry; Computer Science; Mathematics; Natural Sciences; Physics; Statistics)

School

Nursing (Nursing)

Further Information: Also Chillán Campus

History: Founded 1988 and incorporated Instituto Profesional de Chillán.

Academic Year: March to December (March-July; August-December)

Admission Requirements: Secondary school certificate (Licencia de Enseñanza Media) or recognized equivalent, and entrance examination

Main Language(s) of Instruction: Spanish

Accrediting Agency: National Accreditation Commission (CNA)

Degrees and Diplomas: *Licenciatura*: **Teacher Training.** *Título Profesional*: **Accountancy; Architecture; Business Administration; Civil Engineering; Computer Science; Engineering; Food Technology; Forestry; Graphic Design; Nutrition; Wood Technology.** *Magister*: **Biology; Business Administration; Chemistry; Computer Science; Construction Engineering; Ecology; Education; Educational Administration; Food Technology; Health Sciences; Industrial Engineering; Mathematics; Natural Sciences; Nutrition; Physics; Western European Studies; Wood Technology.** *Doctorado*: **Applied Mathematics; Architecture and Planning; Education; Food Technology; Town Planning; Wood Technology.**

Student Services: Academic Counselling, Cultural Activities, Health Services, Language Laboratory, Library, Nursery Care, Social Counselling, Sports Facilities

Publications: Maderas: Ciencia y Tecnologia; Teoría

Last Updated: 18/01/16

UNIVERSITY OF CHILE

Universidad de Chile

Avenida Bernardo O'Higgins 1058, Casilla 10-D, Santiago
Tel: +56(2) 678-2000
Fax: +56(2) 678-1012
Website: http://www.uchile.cl

Rector: Ennio Vivaldi Véjar

Vicerrectoría de Asuntos Académicos: Rosa Devés Alessandri
EMail: vicerrectoria.academica@uchile.cl

Faculty

Agriculture (Agricultural Engineering; Agriculture; Agronomy; Animal Husbandry; Aquaculture; Biotechnology; Crop Production; Food Science; Food Technology; Forestry; Fruit Production; Natural Resources; Nutrition; Veterinary Science); **Architecture and Town Planning** (Architecture; Design; Geography; Graphic Design; Industrial Design; Landscape Architecture; Regional Planning; Rural Planning; Social Welfare; Town Planning); **Arts** (Art History; Art Management; Art Therapy; Arts and Humanities; Ceramic Art; Computer Education; Dance; Engraving; Heritage Preservation; Jewellery Art; Multimedia; Music; Music Education; Music Theory and Composition; Musicology; Painting and Drawing; Photography; Restoration of Works of Art; Sculpture; Sound Engineering (Acoustics); Textile Design; Theatre; Visual Arts); **Chemistry and Pharmacy** (Biochemistry; Chemistry; Food Science; Pharmacy); **Dentistry** (Dental Technology; Dentistry; Oral Pathology; Periodontics); **Economics and Administration** (Accountancy; Administration; Business Administration; Economics; Finance; Management; Public Administration); **Forestry and Nature Conservation** (Environmental Studies; Forestry; Natural Resources); **Law** (Commercial Law; Fiscal Law; International Law; Law; Private Law; Public Law); **Medicine** (Biochemistry; Biological and Life Sciences; Biology; Biophysics; Child Care and Development; Diabetology; Dietetics; Epidemiology; Ethics; Gerontology; Gynaecology and Obstetrics; Haematology; Health Administration; Medicine; Nursing; Occupational Therapy; Otorhinolaryngology; Paediatrics; Physical Therapy; Psychiatry and Mental Health; Public Health; Social and Preventive Medicine; Speech Therapy and Audiology; Statistics; Urology); **Philosophy and Humanities** (Arts and Humanities; Cognitive Sciences; English; English Studies; Ethics; Ethnology; History; Latin American Studies; Linguistics; Literature; Media Studies; Metaphysics; Philosophy; Spanish); **Physics and Mathematics** (Applied Mathematics; Astronomy and Space Science; Automation and Control Engineering; Biomedical Engineering; Biotechnology; Business Administration; Chemical Engineering; Civil Engineering; Computer Engineering; Construction Engineering; Econometrics; Electrical Engineering; Engineering; Environmental Engineering; Geology; Geophysics; History; Hydraulic Engineering; Industrial Engineering; Materials Engineering; Mathematics; Mechanical Engineering; Metallurgical Engineering; Mining Engineering; Multimedia; Physics; Structural Architecture; Transport Engineering); **Science** (Biology; Biotechnology; Chemistry; Ecology; Environmental Studies; Mathematics; Molecular Biology; Natural Sciences; Physics); **Social Sciences** (Anthropology; Archaeology; Communication Studies; Computer Education; Curriculum; Development Studies; Education; Gerontology; Journalism; Preschool Education; Psychology; Social Sciences; Sociology); **Veterinary Medicine and Stockraising** (Animal Husbandry; Cattle Breeding; Meat and Poultry; Social and Preventive Medicine; Veterinary Science)

Institute

Communication and Image (Communication Studies); **International Studies** (American Studies; International Relations; International Studies); **Nutrition and Food Technology** *(Postgraduate (INTA))* (Food Science; Food Technology; Genetics; Nutrition; Public Health); **Public Affairs** (American Studies; International Relations; Political Sciences; Public Administration)

Further Information: Also Clinical Hospital

History: Founded 1738 by Philip V of Spain as Universidad de San Felipe. Replaced by present institution 1839, present title adopted 1842. Acquired present autonomous status 1931.

Academic Year: March to December (March-July; August-December)

Admission Requirements: Secondary school certificate (Licencia de Educación Media) and entrance examination

Main Language(s) of Instruction: Spanish

Degrees and Diplomas: *Licenciatura*: **Accountancy; Agriculture; Animal Husbandry; Anthropology; Architecture; Art History; Biochemistry; Biology; Business Administration; Chemical Engineering; Chemistry; Dentistry; Design; Economics; Education; Engineering; Fine Arts; Food Science; Forestry; Geography; Geology; Geophysics; Gynaecology and Obstetrics; History; Industrial Engineering; Law; Literature; Materials Engineering; Mathematics; Mechanical Engineering; Medical Technology; Medicine; Midwifery; Mining Engineering; Modern Languages; Music; Music Theory and Composition; Musical Instruments; Natural Sciences; Nursing; Nutrition; Occupational Therapy; Painting and Drawing; Performing Arts; Pharmacology; Pharmacy; Philosophy; Physical Therapy; Physics; Psychology; Public Administration; Sculpture; Social Sciences; Sociology; Speech Therapy and Audiology; Theatre; Veterinary Science.** *Título Profesional*: **Accountancy; Acting; Administration; Agronomy; Animal Husbandry; Anthropology; Architecture; Biochemistry; Biology; Business Administration; Ceramic Art; Chemical Engineering; Chemistry; Civil Engineering; Computer Engineering; Dance; Dentistry; Design; Education; Electrical Engineering; Fine Arts; Food Science; Forestry; Geography; Geology; Graphic Design; Industrial Design; Industrial Engineering; Journalism; Law; Materials Engineering; Mechanical Engineering; Medical Technology; Medicine; Midwifery; Mining Engineering; Nursing; Nutrition; Occupational Therapy; Performing Arts; Pharmacy; Photography; Physical Therapy; Psychology; Sculpture; Sociology; Speech Therapy and Audiology; Surgery; Veterinary Science; Wood Technology.** *Post- título/Diploma*: **Dentistry; Medicine; Pharmacy; Veterinary Science.** *Magister*: **Agriculture; Animal Husbandry; Anthropology; Applied Mathematics; Aquaculture; Archaeology; Arts and Humanities; Astronomy and Space Science; Biochemistry; Biology; Business Administration; Chemistry; Civil Law; Clinical Psychology; Commercial Law; Computer Science; Criminal Law; Cultural Studies; Curriculum; Economics; Education; Educational Psychology; English; Environmental Management; Environmental Studies; Finance; Fiscal Law; Food Science; Genetics; Geography; Health Sciences; History; Human Resources; Immunology; Information Technology; International Law; Latin American Studies; Law; Linguistics; Literature; Marketing; Mathematics; Mechanics; Medical Technology; Medicine; Meteorology; Microbiology; Mineralogy; Music Theory and Composition; Musicology; Natural Resources; Neurosciences; Nutrition; Pharmacology; Philosophy; Physics; Psychology; Public Health; Regional Studies; Seismology; Social Psychology; Sociology; Soil Science; Spanish; Theatre; Town Planning; Urban Studies; Veterinary Science; Visual Arts; Water Science.** *Doctorado*: **Astronomy and Space Science; Biochemistry; Biology; Biomedical Engineering; Biotechnology; Business Administration; Chemical Engineering; Chemistry; Computer Engineering; Computer Science; Ecology; Economics;**

Electrical Engineering; Engineering; Geology; Latin American Studies; Law; Literature; Materials Engineering; Mathematics; Microbiology; Mining Engineering; Molecular Biology; Natural Sciences; Pharmacology; Philosophy; Physics; Psychology; Social Sciences.
Student Services: Library
Publications: Anales de la Universidad de Chile; Anuario Astronómico; Bizantion Nea Hellas; Boletín Chileno de Parasitología; Boletín de Filología; Boletín Interamericano de Educación Musical; Comentarios sobre la Situación Económica; Cuadernos de Ciencia Política; Cuadernos de Historia; Desarrollo Rural; Estudios Internacionales; Ocupación y Desocupación Encuesta nacional; Política; Publicaciones Científicas-INTA; Revista Chilena de Antropología; Revista Chilena de Historia del Derecho; Revista Chilena de Humanidades; Revista de Derecho Económico; Revista de Derecho Público; Revista de Filosofía; Revista Economía y Administración; Revista Musical Chilena; Revista Psiquiátrica Clínica; Taller de Coyuntura; Terra Aridae; Tralka
Publishing House: Editorial Universitaria
Last Updated: 17/12/15

UNIVERSITY OF LA SERENA

Universidad de La Serena (ULS)
Av. Raul Bitran Nachary n°1305, La Serena
Tel: +56(51) 2225-179
Website: http://www.userena.cl

Rector: Nibaldo Avilés Pizarro
Tel: +56(51) 2204-439 EMail: rectoria1@userena.cl
Secretario General: Calixto Veas Gaz Tel: +56(51) 2204-334
Vicerrector Académico: Jorge Catalán Ahumada

Faculty

Economics and Social Sciences (Economics; Social Sciences); **Engineering** (Architecture; Civil Engineering; Computer Engineering; Construction Engineering; Engineering; Environmental Engineering; Food Technology; Industrial Engineering; Mechanical Engineering; Mechanics; Mining Engineering; Natural Resources); **Humanities** (Business and Commerce; Design; Educational Administration; English; Music Education; Philosophy; Primary Education; Psychology; Spanish; Special Education; Teacher Training; Translation and Interpretation); **Science** (Agricultural Engineering; Arid Land Studies; Biology; Chemistry; Computer Education; Mathematics; Mathematics and Computer Science; Natural Sciences; Nursing; Physics; Science Education)
Further Information: Also campuses in Coquimbo and Ovalle
History: Founded 1981 via the fusion of two regional campuses of the University of Chile, and State Technical University.
Academic Year: March to December (March-July; August-December)
Admission Requirements: Secondary school certificate (Licenciade Educación Media) and entrance examination: Academic Aptitude Test
Main Language(s) of Instruction: Spanish
Accrediting Agency: National Accreditation Commission (CNA)
Degrees and Diplomas: *Licenciatura*: **Education; Engineering; Journalism; Nursing; Psychology.** *Título Profesional*: **Architecture; Education; Engineering; Journalism; Nursing.** *Magister*: **Business and Commerce; Education; Latin American Studies; Mining Engineering; Psychology.** *Doctorado*: **Education.**
Student Services: Academic Counselling, Canteen, Cultural Activities, Facilities for disabled people, Health Services, Library, Nursery Care, Social Counselling, Sports Facilities
Publications: Actas Colombinas; Geoespacios; Investigación y Desarrollo; Logos; Temas de Educación
Last Updated: 14/01/16

UNIVERSITY OF MAGALLANES

Universidad de Magallanes (UMAG)
Avenida Bulnes 01855, Punta Arenas
Tel: +56(61) 2207-000
Fax: +56(61) 2207-123
EMail: gino.casassa@umag.cl
Website: http://www.umag.cl

Rector: Juan Oyarzo Pérez (2014-)
Tel: +56(61) 2207-161 EMail: juan.oyarzo@umag.cl
Vicerrector Académica: José Maripani Maripani
Tel: +56(61) 2207-173 EMail: jose.maripani@umag.cl

Faculty

Economics and Law (Economics; Law); **Engineering** (Architecture; Chemical Engineering; Civil Engineering; Computer Engineering; Construction Engineering; Electrical Engineering; Electronic Engineering; Food Technology; Mechanical Engineering; Safety Engineering); **Humanities, Health and Social Sciences** (Education; Health Sciences; Humanities and Social Science Education; Medicine; Nursing; Occupational Therapy; Pedagogy; Physical Therapy; Psychology; Social Work); **Science** (Agricultural Engineering; Aquaculture; Biology; Forestry; Marine Biology; Mathematics; Natural Resources; Physics)

School

Technology (Accountancy; Education; Nursing; Tourism)

Institute

Patagonia (Archaeology; Botany; Geology; History; Paleontology; Zoology)
Further Information: University Campus in Puerto Natales
History: Founded 1961 and attached to the State Technical University, and became its regional branch 1964. Became institute of professional studies 1981 and acquired present status and title 1981. Institute of Patagonia Studies, formerly private research institution, incorporated 1985. An autonomous institution financed by the State.
Academic Year: March to December (March-July; July-December)
Admission Requirements: Secondary school certificate (Licencia de Educación Media) and entrance examination (national selection)
Main Language(s) of Instruction: Spanish
Accrediting Agency: National Accreditation Commission (CNA)
Degrees and Diplomas: *Licenciatura*: **Accountancy; Biology; Business and Commerce; Economics; Education; Engineering; Law; Nursing; Occupational Therapy; Physical Therapy; Social and Community Services.** *Post- título/Diploma*; *Magister*: **Arctic Studies; Chemistry; Curriculum; Electrical Engineering; Environmental Management; Management; Natural Resources; Social Sciences.** *Doctorado*: **Organic Chemistry.**
Student Services: Academic Counselling, Canteen, Careers Guidance, Cultural Activities, Health Services, Language Laboratory, Library, Nursery Care, Social Counselling, Sports Facilities
Publications: Anales del Instituto de la Patagonia; Austrouniversitario
Last Updated: 14/01/16

UNIVERSITY OF PLAYA ANCHA

Universidad de Playa Ancha (UPLA)
Avda. González de Hontaneda 855, Valparaíso
Tel: +56(32) 2205-580
Fax: +56(32) 2205-832
EMail: maedo@upla.cl
Website: http://www.upla.cl

Rector: Patricio Sanhueza Vivanco
Tel: +56(32) 2205-109 EMail: mbaxman@upla.cl
Secretario General: Jorge Sánchez Valencia
Tel: +56(32) 2205-173 EMail: jsanchez@upla.cl

Faculty

Educational Sciences (Computer Education; Education; Educational Administration; Educational and Student Counselling; Educational Sciences; Educational Testing and Evaluation; Pedagogy; Preschool Education; Primary Education; Special Education; Technology Education; Vocational Education); **Engineering** (Computer Engineering; Computer Science; Environmental Engineering; Industrial and Production Economics; Industrial Engineering); **Fine Arts** (Art Education; Art History; Computer Graphics; Graphic Design; Music; Music Education; Painting and Drawing; Sculpture; Technology Education; Theatre; Visual Arts); **Health Sciences** (Nursing; Occupational Therapy; Physical Therapy; Speech Therapy and Audiology); **Humanities** (Arts and Humanities; English; French; German; History; Linguistics; Literature; Philosophy;

Spanish; Tourism; Translation and Interpretation); **Natural and Exact Sciences** (Biology; Chemistry; Geography; Mathematics; Mathematics Education; Natural Sciences; Physics; Statistics); **Physical Education and Sports** (Physical Education; Sports)

Institute

Adult Education *(Ignacio Domeyko)* (Accountancy; Analytical Chemistry; Computer Science; Law)

Further Information: Also Distance Education. Study abroad programmes. Courses for foreign students. Regional Centre in San Felipe

History: Founded 1948 as Instituto Pedagógico, Valparaíso, became an Institute of the University of Chile 1955. Acquired present status and title 1981.

Academic Year: March to December (March-July; July-December)

Admission Requirements: Secondary school certificate (Licencia de Educación Media) and entrance examination

Main Language(s) of Instruction: Spanish

Accrediting Agency: National Accreditation Commission (CNA)

Degrees and Diplomas: *Licenciatura*; *Post- título/Diploma*: **Adult Education; Cultural Studies; Educational and Student Counselling; Mathematics Education.** *Magister*: **Adult Education; Art Education; Communication Studies; Computer Education; Educational Administration; Environmental Studies; Library Science; Linguistics; Literature; Physical Education; Preschool Education; Science Education; Sports; Vocational Education.** *Doctorado*: **Educational Administration; Educational Sciences; Spanish.**

Student Services: Academic Counselling, Canteen, Careers Guidance, Cultural Activities, Health Services, Nursery Care, Social Counselling, Sports Facilities

Publications: Diálogos Educacionales; Nueva Revista del Pacífico; Revista Ciencia de la Actividad Física; Revista Orientación Educacional

Publishing House: Editorial Puntangoles

Last Updated: 14/01/16

UNIVERSITY OF SANTIAGO DE CHILE

Universidad de Santiago de Chile (USACH)

Avenida Libertador Bernardo O'Higgins 3363,
Estación Central, Santiago
Tel: +56(2) 2718-4900
EMail: rectoria@usach.cl
Website: http://www.usach.cl

Rector: Juan Manuel Zolezzi Cid (2006-)
Tel: +56(2) 2718-0010 EMail: rectoria@usach.cl

Secretario General: Gustavo Robles
Tel: +56(2) 2718-0006 EMail: grobles@usach.cl

International Relations: Maria Fernanda Contreras
Tel: +56(2) 2718-0042 EMail: mfcontreras@usach.cl

Faculty

Administration and Economics (Accountancy; Administration; Business Administration; Economics; Finance; Human Resources; Management; Public Administration; Taxation); **Chemistry and Biology** (Biochemistry; Biological and Life Sciences; Biology; Chemistry; Environmental Studies; Microbiology); **Engineering** (Automation and Control Engineering; Chemical Engineering; Civil Engineering; Computer Engineering; Construction Engineering; Electrical Engineering; Engineering; Environmental Engineering; Geography; Heating and Refrigeration; Industrial Engineering; Materials Engineering; Measurement and Precision Engineering; Mechanical Engineering; Metallurgical Engineering; Mining Engineering; Telecommunications Engineering); **Humanities** (Arts and Humanities; Education; Educational Sciences; English; History; Journalism; Latin American Studies; Linguistics; Literature; Modern Languages; Philosophy; Psychology; Sports; Translation and Interpretation); **Medical Sciences** (Gynaecology and Obstetrics; Medicine; Nursing); **Sciences** (Computer Education; Computer Science; Mathematics; Mathematics and Computer Science; Mathematics Education; Natural Sciences; Physics; Statistics); **Technology** (Advertising and Publicity; Agricultural Business; Agricultural Management; Food Technology; Graphic Design; Industrial Engineering; Industrial Maintenance; Technology)

School

Architecture (Architecture)

History: The University's roots go back to the founding of the School of Arts and Trades in 1849 and the Schools of Mining in Copiapó, La Serena and Antofagasta. Later, Industrial Schools were founded in Southern cities and all these institutions became branches of the Universidad Técnica del Estado (State Technical University), founded in 1947. Acquired present title in 1981. An autonomous institution financed by the State.

Academic Year: March to December (March-July; August-December)

Admission Requirements: Secondary school certificate (Licencia de Educación Media) and national entrance examination (Prueba de selección universitaria (PSU))

Fees: PhD in Engineering: 842.000 per semester (c. US$ 1.600) (Chilean Peso)

Main Language(s) of Instruction: Spanish

Accrediting Agency: National Accreditation Commission (CNA)

Degrees and Diplomas: *Licenciatura*: **Accountancy; Administration; Advertising and Publicity; Agricultural Business; Applied Physics; Architecture; Biochemistry; Chemistry; Communication Studies; Economics; Education; Engineering; Food Science; Gynaecology and Obstetrics; Linguistics; Mathematics; Medicine; Psychology.** *Magister*: **Accountancy; Administration; Architecture; Biotechnology; Business Administration; Chemical Engineering; Chemistry; Clinical Psychology; Communication Studies; Computer Engineering; Cultural Studies; Design; Economics; Education; Educational Psychology; Electrical Engineering; Engineering; Engineering Management; Environmental Management; Environmental Studies; Finance; Fine Arts; Food Technology; Gender Studies; Geological Engineering; History; Human Resources; Industrial Engineering; International Relations; International Studies; Linguistics; Literature; Mathematics Education; Mechanical Engineering; Philosophy; Political Sciences; Psychology; Psychotherapy; Public Administration; Safety Engineering; Social Sciences; Taxation; Telecommunications Engineering.** *Doctorado*: **American Studies; Automation and Control Engineering; Biotechnology; Chemistry; Computer Engineering; Engineering; Engineering Management; Food Technology; Materials Engineering; Mathematics; Microbiology; Physics.** Also MBA

Student Services: Academic Counselling, Canteen, Careers Guidance, Cultural Activities, Facilities for disabled people, Health Services, IT Centre, Language Laboratory, Library, Social Counselling, Sports Facilities

Publications: Revista Contribuciones

Publishing House: Editorial Universidad de Santiago

Last Updated: 15/01/16

UNIVERSITY OF TALCA

Universidad de Talca (UTALCA)

Dos Norte 685, Talca
Tel: +56(71) 2200-200
Fax: +56(71) 2200-103
EMail: rrii@utalca.cl
Website: http://www.utalca.cl

Rector: Álvaro Rojas Marín EMail: arojas@utalca.cl

Secretaria General: María Fernanda Vásquez Palma
Tel: +56(71) 2200-110

International Relations: Carolina Torres Del Campo
EMail: cartorres@utalca.cl

Faculty

Agronomy *(Experimental Station Panguilemo)* (Agricultural Business; Agricultural Economics; Agricultural Management; Agriculture; Agronomy; Crop Production; Food Science; Fruit Production; Horticulture; Soil Science; Water Science); **Architecture, Music and Design** (Architectural and Environmental Design; Architecture; Architecture and Planning; Industrial Design; Music; Regional Planning); **Economics and Business** (Accountancy; Business Administration; Business and Commerce; Economics; Human Resources; International Business; Management); **Educational Sciences** (Curriculum; Education; Educational

Administration; Educational Research; Educational Sciences; Higher Education; Staff Development); **Engineering** *(Curicó)* (Bioengineering; Computer Engineering; Electronic Engineering; Engineering; Industrial Engineering; Mechanical Engineering); **Forestry** (Environmental Studies; Forest Management; Forest Products; Forestry; Wood Technology); **Health Sciences** (Dentistry; Medical Technology; Medicine; Physical Therapy; Speech Therapy and Audiology); **Law and Social Sciences** (Criminal Law; History of Law; Human Rights; International Law; Justice Administration; Labour Law; Notary Studies; Private Law; Public Law); **Psychology** (Psychology)

Institute

Chemistry of Natural Resources (Analytical Chemistry; Chemistry; Natural Resources; Organic Chemistry); **Humanities** *(Abate Juan Ignacio Molina)* (Art Criticism; Art History; Arts and Humanities; Contemporary History; Ethics; Latin American Studies; Literature; Philosophical Schools; Regional Studies; Social Sciences; Women's Studies); **Mathematics and Physics** (Mathematics; Pedagogy; Physics; Statistics); **Technological** *(Colchagua)* (Oenology); **Vegetal Biology and Biotechnology** (Agrobiology; Biochemistry; Biology; Biotechnology; Botany; Entomology; Molecular Biology)

Further Information: Also Santiago, Curico and Linares campuses

History: Founded 1981, incorporating regional branches of the University of Chile and University of Santiago de Chile. A State institution.

Academic Year: March to December (March-July; August-December)

Admission Requirements: Secondary school certificate (Licencia de Educación Media) and entrance examination

Main Language(s) of Instruction: Spanish

Accrediting Agency: National Accreditation Commission (CNA)

Degrees and Diplomas: *Licenciatura*: **Accountancy; Agriculture; Architecture; Dentistry; Design; Education; Forest Products; Forestry; Industrial Engineering; Information Technology; Law; Medical Technology; Music; Psychology.** *Título Profesional*; *Post- título/Diploma*: **Dentistry; Orthodontics.** *Magister*: **Agricultural Business; Biomedicine; Biotechnology; Business Administration; Criminal Law; Ecology; Education; Educational Administration; Environmental Studies; Horticulture; International Business; Labour Law; Law; Literature; Management; Mathematics; Microbiology; Psychology; Public Administration; Taxation; Visual Arts.** *Doctorado*: **Agricultural Engineering; Agriculture; Arts and Humanities; Engineering; Law; Mathematics; Natural Sciences.** Also joint Master of Laws programs with University of Valencia and University Pompeu Fabra (Spain), and joint Master and PhD programs in Agricultural Science with University of Göttingen, (Germany)

Student Services: Academic Counselling, Canteen, Careers Guidance, Cultural Activities, Facilities for disabled people, Foreign Studies Centre, Health Services, Language Laboratory, Library, Nursery Care, Social Counselling, Sports Facilities

Publications: Lus et Praxis; Panorama Socioeconómico; Revista Acontecer; Serie "Cuadernos Regionales"; Universum

Publishing House: Editorial Universidad de Talca

Last Updated: 15/01/16

UNIVERSITY OF TARAPACÁ

Universidad de Tarapacá (UTA)

General Velásquez 1775, Casilla 7-D, Arica

Tel: +56(58) 2205-100

EMail: rrii@uta.cl; mesacentral@uta.cl

Website: http://www.uta.cl

Rector: Arturo Flores Franulić EMail: recstgo@uta.cl

Faculty

Agronomy (Agronomy; Crop Production; Water Management); **Education and Humanities** (Applied Linguistics; Archaeology; Arts and Humanities; Communication Studies; Curriculum; Education; Educational Administration; Educational and Student Counselling; English; Geography; History; Physical Education; Preschool Education; Primary Education; Secondary Education; Spanish; Sports); **Engineering** (Computer Engineering; Electrical and Electronic Engineering; Engineering; Industrial Engineering; Mechanical Engineering); **Health Sciences** (Gynaecology and Obstetrics; Health Sciences; Medical Technology; Midwifery; Nursing; Nutrition; Physical Therapy; Radiology); **Sciences** (Biological and Life Sciences; Biology; Chemistry; Environmental Studies; Mathematics; Mathematics and Computer Science; Natural Sciences; Physics); **Social Sciences And Law** (Anthropology; Archaeology; Heritage Preservation; Law; Philosophy; Psychology; Social Sciences; Social Work; Tourism)

School

Business Administration (Accountancy; Administration; Business Administration; Business and Commerce; Economics; Finance; Human Resources; Information Sciences; International Business; Management; Marketing; Public Administration); **Electrical and Electronic Engineering** (Electrical and Electronic Engineering); **Industrial, Computer and Systems Engineering** (Computer Engineering; Industrial Engineering); **Mechanical Engineering** (Mechanical Engineering); **Virtual Technology Education** (Information Technology; Multimedia)

Further Information: Campuses in Velásquez, Saucache and Azapa

History: Founded 1981, incorporating Instituto Profesional de Conandes de Arica, a regional branch of Universidad de Chile and Universidad del Norte. An autonomous institution.

Academic Year: March to January (March-July; August-January)

Admission Requirements: Secondary school certificate (Licencia de Educación Media) or equivalent, and entrance examination (Prueba de Selección Académica)

Main Language(s) of Instruction: Spanish

Accrediting Agency: National Accreditation Commission (CNA)

Degrees and Diplomas: *Técnico de Nivel Superior*: **Administration; Business and Commerce; Design; Law; Painting and Drawing.** *Licenciatura*; *Título Profesional*: **Accountancy; Agronomy; Engineering; Law; Medical Technology; Midwifery; Nursing; Pedagogy; Psychology.** *Post- título/Diploma*: **Administration; Business and Commerce.** *Magister*: **Communication Studies; Distance Education; Education; Engineering; English; Environmental Studies; Higher Education Teacher Training; History; Linguistics; Literature; Mathematics; Multimedia; Radiology; Software Engineering.** *Doctorado*: **Anthropology; Archaeology; Mathematics.**

Student Services: Academic Counselling, Canteen, Careers Guidance, Cultural Activities, Health Services, Language Laboratory, Nursery Care, Social Counselling, Sports Facilities

Publications: Chungara; Dialogo Andino; Idesia; Limite; Revista Facultad de Ingeniería

Last Updated: 15/01/16

UNIVERSITY OF THE FRONTIER

Universidad de la Frontera (UFRO)

Avenida Francisco Salazar 01145, Casilla 54-D, Temuco

Tel: +56(45) 2325-000

Fax: +56(45) 2592-822

EMail: comunicaciones@ufrontera.cl

Website: http://www.ufro.cl

Rector: Sergio Bravo Escobar Tel: +56(45) 2325-090

Vicerrector Académico: Rubén Leal Riquelme
Tel: +56(45) 2325-065 EMail: ruben.leal@ufrontera.cl

Faculty

Agronomy and Forestry (Agricultural Engineering; Agriculture; Agronomy; Biotechnology; Forestry; Natural Resources); **Dentistry** (Dentistry); **Education, Social Sciences and Humanities** (Arts and Humanities; Civics; Communication Studies; Development Studies; Education; Educational Testing and Evaluation; Geography; History; Journalism; Literature; Mathematics Education; Modern Languages; Physical Education; Psychology; Regional Studies; Science Education; Social and Community Services; Social Sciences; Social Work; Sociology; Sports); **Engineering and Science** (Agricultural Engineering; Chemical Engineering; Chemistry; Civil Engineering; Computer Engineering; Construction Engineering; Economics; Electrical Engineering; Electronic Engineering; Engineering; Environmental Engineering; Food Science; Food Technology; Industrial Engineering; Mathematics; Mechanical Engineering; Natural Resources; Natural Sciences; Physics;

Statistics); **Law and Business** (Accountancy; Administration; Business Administration; Economics; Law; Management); **Medicine** *(Edificio de la Salud)* (Dentistry; Dietetics; Epidemiology; Gender Studies; Gynaecology and Obstetrics; Medical Technology; Medicine; Nursing; Nutrition; Paediatrics; Physical Therapy; Psychology; Public Health; Social Work; Speech Therapy and Audiology)

Institute

Agro-industry (Agricultural Business; Agronomy; Food Technology; Molecular Biology; Soil Science); **Computer Education** (Computer Education; Educational Sciences; Information Technology); **Environmental Studies** (Environmental Studies); **Local and Regional Development** (Regional Planning); **Native Studies** (Native American Studies; Natives Education)

Campus

Malleco (Administration; Education; Primary Education); **Pucon** (Administration; Communication Studies; Education; Mathematics Education; Modern Languages; Nursing; Tourism)

Further Information: Also Teaching Hospitals. Postgraduate specialization programme for foreign students. 2 university campuses in Temuco: Andrés Bello and Ciencas de La Salud

History: Founded 1981, incorporating the former branches of Universidad de Chile and Universidad Técnica del Estado in Temuco.

Academic Year: March to December (March-July; August-December)

Admission Requirements: Secondary school certificate (Licencia de Educación Media) and entrance examination

Main Language(s) of Instruction: Spanish

Accrediting Agency: National Accreditation Commission (CNA)

Degrees and Diplomas: *Licenciatura*; *Título Profesional*: **Civil Engineering; Dentistry; Engineering; Medicine.** *Magister*: **Biotechnology; Communication Studies; Computer Engineering; Dentistry; Education; Electrical Engineering; Family Studies; Mathematics; Mathematics Education; Mechanical Engineering; Natural Resources; Physical Education; Physics; Psychology; Social Psychology; Social Sciences; Vocational Education.** *Doctorado*: **Bioengineering; Cell Biology; Educational Sciences; Mathematics; Molecular Biology; Natural Resources; Psychology; Social Sciences.** Also Especialista in Dentistry, Medicine, Nursing, Midwifery, and Software Engineering

Student Services: Academic Counselling, Canteen, Cultural Activities, Facilities for disabled people, Health Services, Library, Nursery Care, Social Counselling, Sports Facilities

Publications: Educación y Humanidades; International Journal of Morphology; Lengua Literatura Mapuche; Memoria Institucional; Revista Chilena de Anatomía; Revista Chilena de Ciencias Médico-Biológicas; Revista Cubo (Mathematics); Revista Investigaciones en Educatión; Revista Nuestra Muestra; Vertientes UFRO

Publishing House: Ediciones Universidad de La Frontera

Last Updated: 13/01/16

UNIVERSITY OF THE LAKES

Universidad de Los Lagos

Casilla 933, Av. Fuchslocher 1305, Osorno

Tel: +56(64) 333-000

Fax: +56(64) 239-517

EMail: secretariageneral@ulagos.cl

Website: http://www.ulagos.cl

Rector: Óscar Garrido Álvarez
Tel: +56(64) 2237-116 EMail: rectoria@ulagos.cl

Secretaria General: Diana Kiss de Alejandro
Tel: +56(64) 2333-012 EMail: dkiss@ulagos.cl

International Relations: Julio E. Crespo, Director
Tel: +56(64) 2333-590 EMail: jcrespo@ulagos.cl

Department

Administration and Economics (Accountancy; Administration; Economics; Public Administration; Tourism); **Aquaculture and Marine Resources** (Aquaculture; Marine Biology); **Architecture and Design** (Architecture; Design); **Basic Sciences** (Natural Sciences); **Education** (Communication Studies; Computer Education; Education; Geography; History; Mathematics Education; Media Studies; Preschool Education; Translation and Interpretation); **Exact Sciences** (Mathematics; Natural Sciences; Physics); **Food Science and Technology** (Food Science; Food Technology); **Government and Business** *(Puerto Montt)* (Administration; Business Administration; Business and Commerce; Government; Political Sciences; Public Administration); **Health Sciences** (Health Sciences); **Humanities and Fine Arts** (Arts and Humanities; Design; Fine Arts); **Natural Resources and Environment** *(Puerto Montt)* (Agricultural Engineering; Civil Engineering; Environmental Studies; Natural Resources); **Physical Education** (Physical Education); **Social Sciences** (Educational Psychology; Social Sciences; Social Work)

Centre

Computer Science (Computer Science); **English Translation** (English; Translation and Interpretation); **Limnology** *(Puyehue)* (Limnology)

Conservatory

Music (Music)

Further Information: Campuses in Puerto Montt and Santiago. Also a location in Chiloé

History: Founded 1964 as Universidad Técnica del Estado. Acquired present status and title 1993.

Academic Year: March to December (March-July; August-December)

Admission Requirements: Secondary school certificate and entrance examination

Main Language(s) of Instruction: Spanish

Accrediting Agency: National Accreditation Commission (CNA)

Degrees and Diplomas: *Licenciatura*; *Título Profesional*; *Post-título/Diploma*; *Magister*: **Business Administration; Education; Educational Sciences; History; Latin American Studies; Mathematics Education; Regional Studies; Social Sciences.** *Doctorado*: **Mathematics Education; Natural Resources; Natural Sciences; Social Sciences.**

Student Services: Academic Counselling, Canteen, Cultural Activities, Facilities for disabled people, Health Services, Library, Nursery Care, Social Counselling, Sports Facilities

Publications: Alpha; Biota; Cuadernos de Historia y Cultura de Aysén; Francachela

Publishing House: Editorial Universidad de Los Lagos

Last Updated: 21/01/16

UNIVERSITY OF VALPARAÍSO

Universidad de Valparaíso (UV)

Blanco 951, Valparaíso

Tel: +56(32) 250-7000

EMail: secretaria.rectoria@uv.cl

Website: http://www.uv.cl

Rector: Aldo Valle Acevedo
Tel: +56(32) 2507-103 EMail: rector@uv.cl

Secretario General: Osvaldo Corrales Jorquera
EMail: osvaldo.corrales@uv.cl

Faculty

Architecture (Architecture; Cinema and Television; Civil Engineering; Construction Engineering; Design; Theatre; Tourism); **Dentistry** (Dental Technology; Dentistry; Oral Pathology; Orthodontics; Periodontics; Stomatology); **Economics and Administration** *(Viña del Mar)* (Accountancy; Administration; Business and Commerce; Economics; Finance; Hotel and Restaurant; Human Resources; Industrial Engineering; International Business; Management; Marketing; Public Administration); **Engineering** (Biomedical Engineering; Civil Engineering; Construction Engineering; Engineering; Environmental Engineering; Industrial Engineering; Marine Engineering); **Humanities** (Arts and Humanities; History; Latin American Studies; Music; Philosophy; Sociology); **Law and Social Sciences** (Arts and Humanities; Hispanic American Studies; History; Humanities and Social Science Education; Law; Logic; Philosophy; Social Sciences; Social Work); **Marine Science and Natural Resources** *(Viña del Mar)* (Marine Science and Oceanography; Natural Resources); **Medicine** (Chemistry; Gynaecology and Obstetrics; Medicine; Nursing; Nutrition; Paediatrics; Pharmacy; Psychology; Speech Therapy and Audiology); **Pharmacy** (Pharmacy); **Science** (Biological and Life Sciences; Biomedical

Engineering; Biomedicine; Chemistry; Computer Science; Mathematics; Meteorology; Natural Sciences; Neurosciences; Physics; Statistics)

History: Founded 1911 as regional branch of the University of Chile. Became an independent institution 1981.

Academic Year: March to December (March-July; August-December)

Admission Requirements: Secondary school certificate and entrance examination

Main Language(s) of Instruction: Spanish

Accrediting Agency: National Accreditation Commission (CNA)

Degrees and Diplomas: *Licenciatura*; *Título Profesional*; *Post-título/Diploma*: **Civil Law; Constitutional Law; Dentistry; Educational Psychology; English; Fiscal Law; Geological Engineering; Gynaecology and Obstetrics; Health Sciences; International Law; Labour Law; Latin American Studies; Medicine; Orthodontics; Pharmacy; Public Health; Social Psychology; Special Education; Stomatology; Surgery.** *Magister*: **Architectural and Environmental Design; Astrophysics; Biology; Biomedical Engineering; Biomedicine; Cell Biology; Clinical Psychology; Dentistry; Dietetics; Engineering; Environmental Engineering; Environmental Studies; Epidemiology; Finance; Gerontology; Health Sciences; Heritage Preservation; History; Human Resources; Industrial and Organizational Psychology; Management; Marine Science and Oceanography; Marine Transport; Marketing; Mathematics; Molecular Biology; Natural Resources; Nursing; Nutrition; Oral Pathology; Orthodontics; Paediatrics; Periodontics; Pharmacy; Philosophy; Public Administration; Regional Planning; Social Psychology; Speech Therapy and Audiology; Statistics.** *Doctorado*: **Astrophysics; Chemistry; Law; Marine Science and Oceanography; Mathematics; Natural Resources; Neurosciences; Social Sciences; Statistics.** Also Especialidades in Medicine and Dentistry

Student Services: Academic Counselling, Canteen, Careers Guidance, Cultural Activities, Health Services, Library, Nursery Care, Social Counselling, Sports Facilities

Publications: Revista de Biología Marina y Oceanografía; Revista de Ciencias Económicas y Administrativas; Revista de Ciencias Sociales; Revista de la Facultad de Odontología; Revista Facultad de Arquitectura

Publishing House: Sello Editorial Universidad de Valparaíso. Editorial Escuela de Derecho (EDEVAL)

Last Updated: 18/01/16

PRIVATE INSTITUTIONS

ADOLFO IBÁÑEZ UNIVERSITY

Universidad Adolfo Ibáñez (UAI)

Avenida Diagonal Las Torres 2640, Peñalolén, Santiago
Tel: +56(32) 2331-1000
EMail: info@uai.cl
Website: http://www.uai.cl

Rector: Andrés Benítez Pereira EMail: andres.benitez@uai.cl

Secretarío General: Agustin Ántola
Tel: +56(32) 503-824 EMail: agustin.antola@uai.cl

International Relations: Agustín Julio, Secretarío Académico - Estudiantes extranjeros EMail: rrii@uai.cl

Faculty

Arts and Humanities (Arts and Humanities; Education; Fine Arts; History; Journalism; Literature; Philosophy); **Engineering** (Civil Engineering; Computer Engineering; Engineering; Industrial Engineering; Mathematics); **Law** (Commercial Law; Criminal Law; Labour Law; Law; Private Law; Public Law)

School

Business (Agricultural Business; Business Administration; Business and Commerce; Economics; Engineering Management; Finance; Human Resources; International Business; Management; Marketing); **Government** (Government); **Journalism** (Journalism); **Psychology** (Business Administration; Business and Commerce; Clinical Psychology; Design; Finance; Human Resources; Industrial and Organizational Psychology; Marketing; Media Studies; Psychology; Social Psychology)

Institute

Political Economy (Economics; Political Sciences)

Further Information: Also branches in Viña del Mar, Pdte. Errázuriz and Miami

History: Founded 1953 as Business School of Valparaíso, acquired present status and title 1989.

Academic Year: March to December (March-July; August-December)

Admission Requirements: Secondary school certificate (Licencia de Educación Media) and entrance examination

Main Language(s) of Instruction: Spanish

Accrediting Agency: National Accreditation Commission (CNA)

Degrees and Diplomas: *Bachiller*: **Arts and Humanities.** *Licenciatura*: **Arts and Humanities; Business Administration; Engineering; Law.** *Título Profesional*: **Industrial Engineering.** *Magister*: **Art History; Arts and Humanities; Business Administration; Business and Commerce; Clinical Psychology; Communication Studies; Criminal Law; Finance; History; Industrial and Organizational Psychology; Industrial Engineering; Labour Law; Law; Literature; Management; Public Law; Taxation.** *Doctorado*: **Business Administration; Engineering; Finance; Industrial Engineering; Management; Political Sciences; Systems Analysis.** Also MBA

Student Services: Canteen, Careers Guidance, Language Laboratory, Library, Sports Facilities

Publications: Notebook on Law

Last Updated: 07/01/16

ADVENTIST UNIVERSITY OF CHILE

Universidad Adventista de Chile (UNACH)

Km. 12 camino a Tanilvoro, Las Mariposas, Chillán, Chillán 3780000, Ñuble
Tel: +56(42) 243-3500
Fax: +56(42) 243-3501
EMail: contacto@unach.cl
Website: http://www.unach.cl

Rector: Ricardo A. González
Tel: +56(42) 243-3505 EMail: rectoria@unach.cl

Vicerrector Académico: Ramón Pérez
Tel: +56(42) 243-3600 EMail: viceacademica@unach.cl

Vicerrector Financiero: Uziel Alvarado
Tel: +56(42) 243-3583 EMail: viceadministrativa@unach.cl

Vicerrector de Desarrollo Estudiantil: Antonio Parra
Tel: +56(42) 243-3570 EMail: viceestudiantil@unach.cl

Secretaria General: Lilian Schmied
Tel: +56(42) 243-3504 EMail: secretariageneral@unach.cl

Faculty

Education and Social Sciences (Biology; English; History; Mathematics and Computer Science; Music Education; Physical Education; Preschool Education; Primary Education; Social Work; Spanish); **Engineering and Trade** (Accountancy; Agronomy; Business Administration; Computer Engineering; Electronic Engineering; Food Technology; Telecommunications Engineering); **Health Sciences** (Medical Auxiliaries; Nursing; Psychology); **Theology** (Theology)

History: The historical background of the UnACh goes back to 1906, when the first Adventist College was created near the city of Temuco in Chile. The purpose was to prepare missionaries and teachers to support the Seventh-day Adventist Church in the country. In 1990 the Seventh-day Church created the Universidad Adventista de Chile, the UnACh offers 20 undergraduate academic programs and 4 graduate programs.

Academic Year: March to December

Admission Requirements: Secondary school certificate (Licencia de Enseñanza Media), an interview with the program director and entrance examination.

Fees: National: Between 1.202.040 and 2.756.000 (per annum, according to the program) (Chilean Peso), International: Between 1,740 and 3,987 approximately (US Dollar)

Main Language(s) of Instruction: Spanish

Accrediting Agency: National Accreditation Commission (CNA)

Degrees and Diplomas: *Licenciatura*: **Agronomy; Business Administration; Computer Engineering; Education; Food Technology; Nursing; Psychology; Social Work; Theology.** *Título Profesional*: **Accountancy; Agronomy; Biology; Business Administration; Computer Engineering; Electronic Engineering; English; History; Mathematics and Computer Science; Medical Auxiliaries; Music Education; Nursing; Physical Education; Preschool Education; Primary Education; Psychology; Social Work; Spanish; Telecommunications Engineering; Theology.** *Magister*: **Administration; Education; Public Health; Religious Education.**

Student Services: Academic Counselling, Canteen, Careers Guidance, Cultural Activities, Facilities for disabled people, Health Services, IT Centre, Language Laboratory, Library, Nursery Care, Residential Facilities, Social Counselling, Sports Facilities, eLibrary

Publications: Pulso Docente; Revista Kathedra

Last Updated: 04/01/16

AGRICULTURAL TRAINING INSTITUTE ADOLFO MATTHEI

Instituto Profesional Agrario Adolfo Matthei

Avenida René Soriano N° 2615, Osorno
Tel: +56(64) 211-671
Fax: +56(64) 311-676
EMail: info@amatthei.cl
Website: http://www.amatthei.cl

Director Presidente: Luis Momberg Bórquez
Tel: +56(64) 311-672

Director Vicepresidente: Alfredo Matthei Neumann

Programme

Agricultural Business (Agricultural Business); **Agricultural Engineering** (Agricultural Engineering; Agriculture; Agronomy); **Agricultural Technology** (Agriculture); **Forestry** (Forestry)

Further Information: Also Meteorological Station

History: Founded 1932 as Escuela Superior de Agricultura de Osorno. Acquired present status and title 1981.

Academic Year: February to August (February-March; April-August)

Main Language(s) of Instruction: Spanish

Degrees and Diplomas: *Técnico de Nivel Superior*, *Título Profesional*

Student Services: Library

Last Updated: 17/12/15

AIEP PROFESSIONAL INSTITUTE

Instituto Profesional AIEP

Avenida Santa Maria 729, Santiago
Tel: +56(600) 450-1500
EMail: comunicaciones@aiep.cl
Website: http://www.aiep.cl

Rector: Fernando Martínez Santana
EMail: Fernando.Martinez@aiep.cl

Secretario Académico: Carlos Silva Sánchez

School

Aesthetics (Aesthetics; Cosmetology); **Business** (Accountancy; Administration; Business Administration; International Business; Sales Techniques); **Communication Studies** (Communication Studies; Public Relations; Radio and Television Broadcasting); **Construction and Civil Works** (Architectural and Environmental Design; Civil Engineering; Construction Engineering; Safety Engineering; Surveying and Mapping); **Costume Design** (Fashion Design); **Design and Advertising** (Advertising and Publicity; Design); **Food, Hospitality and Tourism** (Cooking and Catering; Hotel and Restaurant; Tourism); **Health Sciences** (Dental Technology; Gynaecology and Obstetrics; Health Sciences; Medical Technology; Nursing); **Information Technology** (Computer Engineering; Computer Networks; Information Technology; Multimedia; Systems Analysis); **Social Development** (Social Sciences; Social Work; Special Education); **Sound Engineering and Television** (Radio and Television Broadcasting; Sound Engineering (Acoustics)); **Sports** (Sports; Sports Management)

Further Information: Also 19 branches all over the country (Calama, Antofagasta, La Serena, Viña del Mar, Rancagua, San Fernando, Curicó, Concepción, Puerto Montt, Valparaíso...)

History: Founded 1989.

Admission Requirements: High School Diploma.

Main Language(s) of Instruction: Spanish

Degrees and Diplomas: *Técnico de Nivel Superior*, *Título Profesional*

Last Updated: 18/12/15

ALBERTO HURTADO UNIVERSITY

Universidad Alberto Hurtado (UAH)

Almirante Barroso 6, Casilla 14446, Correo 21,
Santiago, Región Metropolitana
Tel: +56(2) 692-0200
Fax: +56(1) 692-0216
EMail: uah@uahurtado.cl
Website: http://www.uahurtado.cl

Rector: Fernando Montes Matte, S.J.

Secretario General: José Miguel Burmeiste

International Relations: Sebastián Kaufmann, Vicerrector Integración y Director de la Dirección de Cooperación Internacional

Faculty

Economics and Business (Administration; Business Administration; Business and Commerce; Economics; Finance; Leadership); **Education** (Educational Administration; Primary Education; Secondary Education); **Law** (Law); **Philosophy and Humanities** (Arts and Humanities; Ethics; Literature; Philosophy; Spanish); **Social Sciences** (Communication Studies; Ethics; International Relations; Journalism; Political Sciences; Regional Studies; Social Sciences; Social Work; Sociology; Theology)

School

Psychology (Psychology)

History: Founded 1997.

Admission Requirements: Secondary school certificate (Licencia de Educación Media)

Main Language(s) of Instruction: Spanish

Accrediting Agency: National Accreditation Commission (CNA)

Degrees and Diplomas: *Bachiller*: **Arts and Humanities; Mass Communication; Philosophy.** *Licenciatura*: **Arts and Humanities; Business and Commerce; Mass Communication; Philosophy.** *Título Profesional*: **Engineering Management; Journalism; Law; Mass Communication; Primary Education; Psychology; Secondary Education; Social Work; Sociology.** *Post- título/Diploma*: **Arts and Humanities; Economics; Education; Journalism; Law; Literature; Mass Communication; Philosophy; Psychology; Social Sciences.** *Magister*: **Anthropology; Business Administration; Clinical Psychology; Economics; Education; Educational Sciences; English; Ethics; Foreign Languages Education; Government; History; Human Resources; Latin American Studies; Law; Literature; Mathematics Education; Musicology; Philosophy; Protective Services; Psychology; Social Psychology; Social Sciences; Sociology.** *Doctorado*: **Education; Philosophy; Social Work; Sociology.** Also Diplomados and MBA. PhD in Social Work, joint degree delivered in partnership with Boston College

Student Services: Academic Counselling, Careers Guidance, Foreign Studies Centre, Library, Social Counselling, Sports Facilities

Publications: Ethos; Persona y Sociedad; Revista de Análisis Económico

Last Updated: 07/01/16

ANDRÉS BELLO UNIVERSITY

Universidad Andrés Bello

Avenida República 237-252, Santiago
Tel: +56(2) 661-8001
Fax: +56(2) 671-1936
EMail: info@unab.cl
Website: http://www.unab.cl

Rector: Jose Rodriguez Perez

Secretario General: Fernando Castro Azofeifa

Faculty

Architecture and Design *(Casona de Las Condes)* (Advertising and Publicity; Architectural and Environmental Design; Architecture; Construction Engineering; Design; Fashion Design; Graphic Design; Journalism; Textile Design; Visual Arts); **Dentistry** (Dentistry); **Ecology and Natural Resources** (Aquaculture; Ecology; Environmental Engineering; Marine Biology; Marine Science and Oceanography; Natural Resources; Tourism; Veterinary Science); **Economics and Trade** (Accountancy; Administration; Economics; Engineering Management; Finance; Human Resources; International Business; Marketing; Taxation); **Engineering** (Civil Engineering; Computer Engineering; Construction Engineering; Engineering; Industrial Engineering); **Humanities and Education** (Arts and Humanities; Education; History; Journalism; Literature; Philosophy; Psychology; Social Sciences); **Law** (Law); **Medicine** (Anaesthesiology; Biochemistry; Cardiology; Chemistry; Dietetics; Gynaecology and Obstetrics; Health Sciences; Medical Technology; Medicine; Orthopaedics; Pharmacy; Surgery); **Nursing** (Nursing); **Rehabilitation Science** (Occupational Therapy; Physical Therapy; Rehabilitation and Therapy; Speech Therapy and Audiology)

Programme

Liberal Arts (Arts and Humanities; Fine Arts; Natural Sciences)

Further Information: Study Abroad Programmes with the University of Reno, Nevada. Also Casona de las Condes and Viña del Mar campuses

History: Founded 1988. Incorporated Universidad Maritima de Chile 2008.

Academic Year: March to December (March-July; August-December)

Admission Requirements: Secondary school certificate (Licencia de Educación Media) and entrance examination

Main Language(s) of Instruction: Spanish

Accrediting Agency: National Accreditation Commission (CNA)

Degrees and Diplomas: *Bachiller*; *Licenciatura*; *Título Profesional*: **Communication Studies; Educational Psychology; Mathematics Education; Modern Languages; Social Work.** *Magister*: **Business Administration; Business and Commerce; Computer Science; Curriculum; Dentistry; Education; Educational Administration; English; Environmental Management; Finance; Health Administration; Higher Education Teacher Training; History; Human Resources; Industrial Engineering; International Business; Literature; Management; Marketing; Mathematics Education; Nursing; Occupational Therapy; Oral Pathology; Orthopaedics; Physical Education; Preschool Education; Public Administration; Public Health; Rehabilitation and Therapy; Social Sciences; Speech Therapy and Audiology; Sports; Sports Management; Taxation; Tourism; Transport Management.** *Doctorado*: **Astrophysics; Atomic and Molecular Physics; Biotechnology; Medicine; Molecular Biology; Nursing; Physics; Psychoanalysis; Veterinary Science.** Also Especialización in Medecine and Diplomado

Student Services: Library

Last Updated: 08/01/16

ARCOS PROFESSIONAL INSTITUTE

Instituto Profesional ARCOS

Santo Domingo 789, Barrio Bellas Artes, Santiago

Tel: +56(2) 2365-7000

EMail: arcos@arcos.cl

Website: http://www.arcos.cl

Rector: José Sanfuentes

School

Cinema and Audiovisual Communication (Cinema and Television); **Communication and Cultural Studies** (Communication Studies; Cultural Studies); **Design and Multimedia** (Design; Graphic Design; Multimedia); **Photography** (Photography); **Sound** (Sound Engineering (Acoustics)); **Theatre** (Theatre)

History: Founded 1981.

Admission Requirements: High School Diploma. Entrance examination and interview.

Main Language(s) of Instruction: Spanish

Accrediting Agency: National Accreditation Commission (CNA)

Degrees and Diplomas: *Técnico de Nivel Superior*, *Título Profesional*

Student Services: Library

Last Updated: 18/12/15

AUSTRAL UNIVERSITY OF CHILE

Universidad Austral de Chile (UACH)

Independencia 641, Valdivia, Valdivia

Tel: +56(63) 2221500

Fax: +56(63) 2293812

EMail: urinternacionales@uach.cl

Website: http://www.uach.cl

Rector: Óscar Galindo Villarroel

Tel: +56(63) 2221960 EMail: rectoria@uach.cl

International Relations: Patricia Burgos H., Directora

EMail: patricia.burgos@uach.cl

Faculty

Agriculture (Agricultural Economics; Agricultural Management; Agriculture; Animal Husbandry; Dairy; Food Science; Food Technology; Nutrition; Rural Planning; Rural Studies; Soil Science; Vegetable Production); **Arts and Architecture** (Architecture; Music; Visual Arts); **Economics and Administration** (Accountancy; Business Administration; Economics; Management; Statistics; Tourism); **Engineering** (Architecture; Business Computing; Computer Engineering; Construction Engineering; Electronic Engineering; Engineering; Industrial Engineering; Information Technology; Mechanical Engineering; Naval Architecture; Safety Engineering; Sound Engineering (Acoustics); Systems Analysis); **Forestry and Natural Resources** (Forest Management; Forest Products; Forestry; Natural Resources; Wood Technology); **Law and Social Sciences** (Administration; Justice Administration; Latin American Studies; Law; Safety Engineering; Social Sciences); **Medicine** (Dentistry; Gynaecology and Obstetrics; Medical Technology; Medicine; Midwifery; Nursing; Occupational Therapy; Physical Therapy; Psychiatry and Mental Health; Psychology); **Philosophy and Humanities** (Anthropology; Arts and Humanities; Communication Studies; Development Studies; Education; Educational Administration; Family Studies; Hispanic American Studies; History; Information Technology; Journalism; Linguistics; Literature; Mathematics Education; Philosophy; Physics; Preschool Education; Social Sciences); **Science** (Biochemistry; Biology; Botany; Cell Biology; Chemistry; Ecology; Genetics; Geography; Geology; Limnology; Marine Biology; Mathematics; Microbiology; Molecular Biology; Natural Sciences; Pharmacy; Physics; Water Science); **Veterinary Science** (Anatomy; Animal Husbandry; Food Technology; Pathology; Veterinary Science; Zoology)

Campus

Patagonia (Education; Engineering; Technology; Tourism); **Puerto Montt** (Aquaculture; Industrial Engineering; Natural Sciences; Speech Therapy and Audiology)

History: Founded 1954. A private institution financed by the government.

Academic Year: March to December (March-July; August-December)

Admission Requirements: Secondary school certificate (Licencia de Educación Media) or recognized equivalent, and entrance examination. Also Certificate of Spanish Language Proficiency

Main Language(s) of Instruction: Spanish

Accrediting Agency: National Accreditation Commission (CNA)

Degrees and Diplomas: *Técnico de Nivel Superior*, *Licenciatura*: **Accountancy; Agricultural Engineering; Animal Husbandry; Anthropology; Biological and Life Sciences; Business Administration; Civil Engineering; Computer Science; Construction Engineering; Electronic Engineering; Food Technology; Foreign Languages Education; Forestry; Health Sciences; Journalism; Law; Management; Marine Biology; Marine Engineering; Mechanical Engineering; Medicine; Midwifery; Naval Architecture; Pharmacy; Sound Engineering (Acoustics); Veterinary Science.** *Título Profesional*: **Music.** *Magister*: **Agricultural Engineering; Animal Husbandry; Arts and Humanities; Biochemistry; Botany; Business Administration; Communication Arts; Communication Studies; Dairy; Ecology;**

Economics; Education; English; Environmental Management; Forest Management; Genetics; Horticulture; Immunology; Law; Linguistics; Literature; Management; Materials Engineering; Mechanical Engineering; Medicine; Natural Sciences; Nursing; Paleontology; Philosophy; Physics; Physiology; Plant and Crop Protection; Regional Planning; Rural Planning; Sound Engineering (Acoustics); Spanish; Technology Education; Tourism; Veterinary Science; Water Science; Zoology. *Doctorado*: **Agriculture; Animal Husbandry; Aquaculture; Cell Biology; Cultural Studies; Ecology; Forestry; Linguistics; Literature; Marine Biology; Medicine; Microbiology; Molecular Biology; Natural Resources; Veterinary Science.**

Student Services: Academic Counselling, Canteen, Facilities for disabled people, Foreign Studies Centre, Health Services, Language Laboratory, Library, Nursery Care, Social Counselling, Sports Facilities

Publications: Agrosur; Archivos de Medicina Veterinaria; Bosque; Cuadernos de Cirugía; Estudios Filológicos; Estudios Pedagógicos; Medio Ambiente; Revista Austral de Ciencias Sociales; Revista de Derecho

Last Updated: 04/01/16

AUTONOMOUS UNIVERSITY OF CHILE

Universidad Autónoma de Chile (UAS)

Avenida Alemania 01090, Temuco

Tel: +56(45) 2895-000

EMail: admision@uas.cl

Website: http://www.uas.cl

Rector: Teodoro Ribera Neumann EMail: rector@uas.cl

Vicerrector Académico: Jaime Torralba Cubillos

International Relations: Osvaldo Ramírez Castro
EMail: oramirez@uas.cl

Faculty

Architecture and Contruction (Architecture; Civil Engineering; Construction Engineering); **Business Administration** (Accountancy; Business Administration; Business and Commerce); **Education** (Education; Preschool Education); **Engineering** (Computer Engineering; Engineering; Industrial Engineering); **Health Sciences** (Dentistry; Health Sciences; Medicine; Nursing; Occupational Therapy; Physical Therapy; Speech Therapy and Audiology); **Law** (Law); **Social Sciences and Humanity** (Social and Community Services; Social Sciences; Welfare and Protective Services)

Further Information: Also Santiago, Providencia, and Talca Campuses

History: Founded 1989. Formerly known as Universidad Autónoma del Sur.

Admission Requirements: Secondary school certificate (Licencia de Educación Media)

Main Language(s) of Instruction: Spanish

Accrediting Agency: National Accreditation Commission (CNA)

Degrees and Diplomas: *Técnico de Nivel Superior*; *Licenciatura*; *Título Profesional*; *Magister*: **American Studies; Biology; Biomedicine; Business Administration; Development Studies; Engineering; Health Administration; Higher Education Teacher Training; Law; Neurosciences; Public Administration; Social Work.** *Doctorado*: **Biomedicine; History; Law.** Also Especialización in Dentistry, and Diplomados

Student Services: Library

Last Updated: 08/01/16

BERNARDO O'HIGGINS UNIVERSITY

Universidad Bernardo O'Higgins (UBO)

Avenida Viel 1497, Santiago 8370993

Tel: +56(2) 2477-4100

EMail: comunicaciones.ubo@ubo.cl

Website: http://www.ubo.cl

Rector: Claudio Ruff Escobar EMail: rector@ubo.cl

International Relations: Virginie Delalande, Vicerrectoria de Desarrollo, Directora de Extensión y Relaciones Interinstitucionales
EMail: virginie.delalande@ubo.cl

Faculty

Engineering (Business Administration; Civil Engineering; Computer Engineering; Environmental Engineering; Industrial Engineering; Safety Engineering; Surveying and Mapping); **Faculty of Health, Sport and Recreation** (Dietetics; Medical Technology; Nursing; Occupational Therapy; Physical Therapy; Speech Therapy and Audiology); **Human Sciences and Education** (English; Geography; History; Pedagogy; Physical Education; Preschool Education; Primary Education; Psychology; Secondary Education; Sports); **Law and Social Communication** (Journalism; Law; Public Relations)

History: Created and was established as private foundation non-profit, by deed, the March 1, 1990 in Santiago. Bernardo O'Higgins University is dedicated to the academic training institution, research and dissemination of knowledge, contributing to the spiritual, cultural and economic development of the country to prepare graduates and qualified professionals in different areas of knowledge. According to its values ã *and* principles facilitates the education of their children in an atmosphere of discipline, respect and tolerance. Also, within its objectives, the University promotes research, creation, preservation and transmission of universal knowledge in the field of science and the humanities.

Admission Requirements: PSU average score in Language and Mathematics or score according to weight provided by Universidad Bernardo O'Higgins. Besides the PSU results, applicants must present the following documents: Academic transcript; High school diploma; Identity card The entry score for each program is calculated according to the PSU score or the corresponding polynomial and according to the minimal score required for each program.

Fees: National: 2,000,000 (Chilean Peso), International: 3.000 (US Dollar)

Main Language(s) of Instruction: Spanish

Accrediting Agency: CNA-Chile

Degrees and Diplomas: *Técnico de Nivel Superior*; *Licenciatura*; *Título Profesional*; *Magister*: **Biology; Business Administration; Chemistry; Education; Law; Management.**

Student Services: Academic Counselling, Canteen, Careers Guidance, Cultural Activities, Facilities for disabled people, Foreign Studies Centre, Health Services, IT Centre, Language Laboratory, Library, Nursery Care, Social Counselling, Sports Facilities, eLibrary

Academic Staff *2014-2015*	MEN	WOMEN	TOTAL
FULL-TIME	69	47	**116**
PART-TIME	213	188	**401**
STAFF WITH DOCTORATE			
FULL-TIME	56	25	**81**
Student Numbers *2014-2015*			
All (Foreign included)	2,400	2,600	**5,000**
FOREIGN ONLY	30	28	**58**

Last Updated: 04/01/16

CARLOS CASANUEVA PROFESSIONAL INSTITUTE

Instituto Profesional Carlos Casanueva (ICC)

Londres 46, Santiago

Tel: +56(2) 222-9207

Fax: +56(2) 634-3672

EMail: admission@carloscasanueva.cl

Website: http://www.carloscasanueva.cl

Rectora: Maria Josefina Bilbao Mendezona

Presidente del Directorio: Víctor Aguilera Vásquez

Secretaria General: María del Carmen González Urroz

Programme

Business Administration (Business Administration; Marketing); **Early Childhood Education** (Preschool Education); **Health Sciences** (Physical Therapy); **Human and Social Development** (Development Studies; Family Studies; Social Sciences); **Library Science and Information Management** (Information Management; Library Science); **Naturopathy** (Alternative Medicine); **Nursing** (Nursing); **Psychopedagogy** (Educational Psychology; Psychology); **Risks Prevention** (Safety Engineering); **Social Work** (Social Work)

History: Founded 1993, acquired present status and title 1997.

Admission Requirements: High School Diploma
Main Language(s) of Instruction: Spanish
Accrediting Agency: CNA - Chile
Degrees and Diplomas: *Técnico de Nivel Superior*; *Titulo Profesional*
Last Updated: 18/12/15

CATHOLIC UNIVERSITY OF CHILE

Pontificia Universidad Católica de Chile (UC)
Avenida Libertador Bernardo O'Higgins 340, Santiago
Tel: +56(2) 2354-4000
Website: http://www.uc.cl

Presidente: Ignacio Sánchez Diaz EMail: rectoria@uc.cl
Secretaria General: María Elena Pimstein
Académico Vicepresidente: Juan Agustín Larraín Correa
EMail: jlarraic@uc.cl

Faculty

Agronomy and Forestry Engineering (Agricultural Economics; Agriculture; Agronomy; Animal Husbandry; Cattle Breeding; Forestry; Fruit Production; Oenology; Plant and Crop Protection; Vegetable Production; Zoology); **Architecture, Design and Urban Studies** (Architecture; Design; Environmental Studies; Industrial Design; Rural Planning; Town Planning; Urban Studies); **Arts and Humanities** (Acting; Arts and Humanities; Music; Painting and Drawing; Singing; Theatre); **Biological Sciences** (Biochemistry; Biological and Life Sciences; Biology; Cell Biology; Ecology; Genetics; Marine Biology; Microbiology; Molecular Biology; Natural Resources; Physiology); **Chemistry** (Chemistry; Natural Sciences; Pharmacy); **Communication Studies** (Communication Studies; Journalism; Social Psychology); **Economics and Administration** (Administration; Business Administration; Economic and Finance Policy; Economics; Finance; Public Administration); **Education** (Computer Education; Curriculum; Education; Educational Administration; Educational Sciences; Educational Technology; Media Studies; Pedagogy; Preschool Education; Special Education; Vocational Counselling; Vocational Education); **Engineering** (Civil Engineering; Construction Engineering; Engineering; Engineering Management; Safety Engineering; Structural Architecture); **History, Geography, and Political Science** (Environmental Studies; European Studies; Geography; Hispanic American Studies; History; International Relations; Political Sciences); **Law** (Commercial Law; Constitutional Law; Criminology; Law; Public Law); **Letters** (Arts and Humanities; English; Linguistics; Literature; Philology); **Mathematics** (Mathematics; Mathematics and Computer Science; Natural Sciences; Statistics); **Medicine** (Anaesthesiology; Cardiology; Dermatology; Ethics; Gerontology; Gynaecology and Obstetrics; Medicine; Nephrology; Neurology; Nursing; Nutrition; Oncology; Ophthalmology; Orthopaedics; Paediatrics; Pathology; Public Health; Radiology; Social and Preventive Medicine; Surgery); **Philosophy** (Literature; Philosophy); **Physics** (Astronomy and Space Science; Astrophysics; Natural Sciences; Physics); **Social Sciences** (Adult Education; Educational Psychology; Family Studies; Psychology; Psychotherapy; Social Sciences; Social Work; Sociology); **Theology** (Theology)

Further Information: Branch in Villarrica. University Hospitals

History: Founded 1888 by decree of Archbishop of Santiago. Recognized by Pope Leo XIII 1889; became Pontifical University 1930. A private, autonomous institution, with degrees recognized by Chilean Law. Financially supported by State subsidy and tuition fees.

Academic Year: March to December (March-July; August-December)

Admission Requirements: Secondary school certificate (Licencia de Educación Media) and entrance examination

Main Language(s) of Instruction: Spanish

Accrediting Agency: National Accreditation Commission (CNA); AACSB (USA); MEXA (MERCOSUR) RIBA (United Kingdom); ABET (USA); AAMC (USA) ACEJMC (USA)

Degrees and Diplomas: *Bachiller*: **Philosophy; Religious Studies; Theology.** *Licenciatura*: **Aesthetics; Agriculture; Architecture; Arts and Humanities; Biochemistry; Biology; Chemistry; Economics; Education; Engineering; Environmental Management; Fine Arts; Geography; History; Law; Management; Mathematics; Medicine; Music; Philosophy; Physics; Psychology; Religious Studies.** *Titulo Profesional*: **Biochemistry; Business Administration; Design; Economics; Engineering; Geography; Journalism; Law; Medicine; Nursing; Psychology; Social Work; Translation and Interpretation.** *Magister*: **Business Administration; Economics; Finance; Human Resources; Public Administration.** *Doctorado*: **Agriculture; Architecture; Astrophysics; Biology; Cell Biology; Chemical Engineering; Chemistry; Civil Engineering; Communication Studies; Computer Engineering; Ecology; Economics; Education; Electrical Engineering; Fine Arts; Genetics; Geography; Health Sciences; History; Industrial Engineering; Law; Linguistics; Literature; Mathematics; Mechanical Engineering; Medicine; Microbiology; Molecular Biology; Natural Sciences; Neurosciences; Philosophy; Physics; Physiology; Political Sciences; Psychology; Sociology; Statistics; Theology; Transport Management; Urban Studies.**

Student Services: Academic Counselling, Canteen, Careers Guidance, Cultural Activities, Facilities for disabled people, Foreign Studies Centre, Health Services, Language Laboratory, Library, Social Counselling, Sports Facilities

Publications: Aisthesis; Anales de Educación; Anales de Teología; Apuntes de Ingeniería; Apuntes de Teatro; Arq (Arquitectura); Biología Pesquera; Boletín de la Escuela de Medicina; Ciencia e Investigación Agraria; Ciencia Política; Cuadernos de Economía; Ediciones Gráficas; Filosofía; Historia; Letras; Monografías Biológicas; Notas Matemáticas; Revista Chilena de Derecho; Revista Eure; Revista Geografía; Revista Universitaria; Serie de Estudios Sociológicos; Teología y Vida; Trabajo Social

Publishing House: Editorial Universidad Católica
Last Updated: 06/01/16

CATHOLIC UNIVERSITY OF MAULE

Universidad Católica del Maule
Avenida San Miguel 3605, Casilla 617, Talca
Tel: +56(71) 2203-100
EMail: info@ucm.cl
Website: http://www.ucdelmaule.cl

Rector: Diego Durán Jara (2012-)
Tel: +56(71) 2203-309 EMail: rector@ucm.cl

Secretario General: Patrick Gatica Mandiola
Tel: +56(71) 2203-312 EMail: sgeneral@ucm.cl

Faculty

Agrarian Sciences and Forestry *(Curicó)* (Agriculture; Agronomy; Forestry); **Basic Sciences** (Mathematics and Computer Science; Natural Sciences); **Education** (Computer Education; Curriculum; Education; Educational Administration; English; Native Language Education; Physical Education; Preschool Education; Special Education); **Engineering** (Civil Engineering; Computer Engineering; Construction Engineering; Engineering; Industrial Engineering); **Health Sciences** (Dietetics; Health Sciences; Nursing; Nutrition; Physical Therapy; Psychology; Public Health); **Medicine** (Medicine); **Religious and Philosophical Sciences** (Philosophy; Religious Studies; Theology); **Social Sciences and Economics** (Accountancy; Business Administration; Business and Commerce; Economics; Management; Social Sciences; Social Work; Sociology)

Institute

General Studies (Arts and Humanities; English; Literature; Natural Sciences; Philosophy; Social Sciences; Theology)

Further Information: Campuses Nuestra Señora del Carmen (Curicó), Campus San Isidro (Curicó)

History: Founded 1991. A private institution financially supported by the State.

Admission Requirements: Secondary school certificate (Licencia de Educación Media)

Main Language(s) of Instruction: Spanish

Accrediting Agency: National Accreditation Commission (CNA)

Degrees and Diplomas: *Titulo Profesional*; *Post- titulo/Diploma*; *Magister*: **Agriculture; Computer Science; Curriculum; Educational Administration; English; Higher Education Teacher Training; Mathematics Education; Nursing; Philosophy; Physical Therapy; Science Education; Special Education;**

Theology; Vocational Education. *Doctorado*: **Education; Physical Education.** Also Especialidades in Medicine and Health Sciences

Student Services: Library

Last Updated: 11/01/16

CATHOLIC UNIVERSITY OF TEMUCO

Universidad Católica de Temuco

Avenida Alemania 0211, Casilla 15-D, Temuco 4780000, Cautín
Tel: +56(45) 2205-428
EMail: uctemuco@uctemuco.cl
Website: http://www.uctemuco.cl

Rector: Aliro Bórquez Ramirez EMail: rector@uctemuco.cl

Secretario General: Marcela Alarcón Momberg
Tel: +56(45) 2205-685 EMail: secgral@uctemuco.cl

International Relations: David Figueroa Hernández, Prorrector
Tel: +52(45) 205-280 EMail: ver@uctemuco.cl

Faculty

Arts and Humanities *(Campus Menchaca Lira)* (Architecture; Art Management; Arts and Humanities; Design; English; Graphic Design; Industrial Design; Painting and Drawing; Spanish; Translation and Interpretation; Visual Arts); **Education** *(San Francisco)* (Bilingual and Bicultural Education; Education; English; Foreign Languages Education; Mathematics Education; Modern Languages; Native Language Education; Physical Education; Preschool Education; Primary Education; Science Education; Secondary Education; Special Education); **Engineering** *(San Francisco)* (Business and Commerce; Chemical Engineering; Civil Engineering; Computer Engineering; Engineering; Engineering Management; Environmental Engineering; Geological Engineering; Industrial Engineering); **Health Sciences** (Dietetics; Health Sciences; Medical Technology; Nutrition; Occupational Therapy; Physical Therapy; Speech Therapy and Audiology); **Law** (Law); **Natural Resources** *(Campus Norte)* (Agronomy; Animal Husbandry; Aquaculture; Biological and Life Sciences; Environmental Studies; Geography; Geology; Natural Resources; Veterinary Science); **Social Sciences** *(Campus San Francisco)* (Anthropology; Archaeology; Political Sciences; Psychology; Public Administration; Social Sciences; Social Work; Sociology); **Technology** (Agriculture; Aquaculture; Business Administration; Computer Networks; Construction Engineering; Environmental Studies; Preschool Education; Sports; Surveying and Mapping; Telecommunications Engineering; Tourism)

Institute

Theology *(San Francisco Campus)* (Catholic Theology; Religious Education; Theology; Vocational Education)

Centre

Social and Cultural Studies *(CES, San Francisco)* (Cultural Studies; Social Studies); **Sustainable Development** *(CDS, Campus San Francisco)* (Development Studies)

Further Information: Also Juan Pablo, San Francisco, Luis Rivas Del Canto, Menchaka Lira Campuses

History: Founded 1959 as University Schools of La Frontera. Incorporated to the Pontificial Catholic University in Chile 1974, as a regional branch. Acquired present status and title 1991. A private institution financially supported by the State.

Academic Year: March to January

Admission Requirements: Secondary School Certificate and University Selection Test (PSU)

Main Language(s) of Instruction: Spanish

Accrediting Agency: National Accreditation Committee (CNA)

Degrees and Diplomas: *Técnico de Nivel Superior*: **Forestry; Water Science.** *Licenciatura*: **Agronomy; Animal Husbandry; Bilingual and Bicultural Education; Biological and Life Sciences; Catholic Theology; Civil Engineering; Computer Engineering; Education; English; Environmental Engineering; Foreign Languages Education; Forestry; Law; Mathematics Education; Modern Languages; Native Language Education; Natural Resources; Preschool Education; Primary Education; Religious Education; Secondary Education; Social Work; Special Education; Veterinary Science; Vocational Education; Water Science.** *Título Profesional*: **Agricultural Engineering; Animal Husbandry; Art Management; Bilingual and Bicultural Education; Biological and Life Sciences; Business and Commerce; Catholic Theology; Civil Engineering; Computer Engineering; Design; Education; English; Environmental Engineering; Foreign Languages Education; Forestry; Law; Modern Languages; Natural Resources; Painting and Drawing; Political Sciences; Religious Education; Social Work; Sociology; Special Education; Translation and Interpretation; Visual Arts; Vocational Education.** *Post- título/Diploma*: **Agriculture; Catholic Theology; Computer Science; Environmental Studies; Family Studies; Forestry; Human Resources; Law; Management; Mathematics Education; Modern Languages; Native Language; Religious Education; Social Sciences; Social Work; Special Education; Teacher Training; Veterinary Science.** *Magister*: **Anthropology; Bilingual and Bicultural Education; Education; Educational Administration; Environmental Engineering; Environmental Studies; Foreign Languages Education; Law; Mathematics Education; Native Language Education; Preschool Education; Primary Education; Secondary Education; Social Work; Special Education; Teacher Training.**

Student Services: Academic Counselling, Cultural Activities, Facilities for disabled people, Health Services, Language Laboratory, Library, Nursery Care, Social Counselling, Sports Facilities

Last Updated: 08/01/16

CATHOLIC UNIVERSITY OF THE HOLY CONCEPTION

Universidad Católica de la Santísima Concepción (UCSC)

Alonso de Ribera 2850, Concepción 4070129
Tel: +56(41) 2345-000
Fax: +56(41) 2745-001
EMail: ucsc@ucsc.cl
Website: http://www.ucsc.cl

Rector: Christian Schmitz Vaccaro
Tel: +56(41) 2345-011 EMail: rectoria@ucsc.cl

Secretaria General: Teresa Lobos del Fierro
Tel: +56(41) 2345-014 EMail: tlobos@ucsc.cl

International Relations: Alfredo Garcia Luarte, Director
Tel: +56(41) 2345-050 EMail: agarcia@ucsc.cl

Faculty

Communication, History and Social Sciences (Communication Studies; History; Journalism; Social Sciences); **Economics and Management** (Accountancy; Business and Commerce; Economics; Management); **Education** (Education); **Engineering** (Civil Engineering; Computer Engineering; Electrical Engineering; Engineering; Fishery; Industrial Engineering; Transport Engineering); **Law** (Criminal Law; Law); **Medicine** (Dietetics; Medical Technology; Medicine; Nursing; Nutrition; Physical Therapy); **Science** (Chemistry; Marine Biology)

Institute

Technology (Agriculture; Automation and Control Engineering; Construction Engineering; Cooking and Catering; Finance; Industrial Engineering; Industrial Maintenance; Maintenance Technology; Nursing; Preschool Education; Tourism; Transport Management); **Theology** (Theology)

Further Information: Campuses at San Andres and Santo Domingo

History: Founded 1991. Extends the academic activities of the Pontifical Catholic University of Chile. A private institution financially supported by the State.

Academic Year: March to December

Admission Requirements: Secondary school certificate. National Selection test. Test of specific knowledge according to speciality

Main Language(s) of Instruction: Spanish

Accrediting Agency: National Accreditation Committee (CNA); CLAEP (for Journalism)

Degrees and Diplomas: *Licenciatura*: **Business and Commerce; Engineering; Journalism; Law; Medicine; Natural Sciences; Teacher Training.** *Título Profesional*; *Magister*: **Applied Linguistics; Applied Mathematics; Business Administration; Civil Engineering; Communication Studies; Community Health; Computer Education; Criminal Law; Education; Educational**

Psychology; Educational Sciences; Family Studies; Finance; Higher Education Teacher Training; Mathematics Education; Multimedia; Nutrition; Public Health; Special Education; Surveying and Mapping; Taxation. Also MBA and Diplomado

Student Services: Academic Counselling, Careers Guidance, Cultural Activities, Health Services, Language Laboratory, Library, Nursery Care, Social Counselling, Sports Facilities

Publications: Civil Engineering Magazine; Law Magazine; Legete; Philosophy Magazine; Rexe; Theology Magazine

Last Updated: 08/01/16

CATHOLIC UNIVERSITY OF THE NORTH

Universidad Católica del Norte (UCN)

Avenida Angamos 0610, Casilla 1280, Antofagasta

Tel: +56(55) 2355000

EMail: contacto@ucn.cl

Website: http://www.ucn.cl

Rector: Jorge Tabilo (2013-)
Tel: +56(55) 2355-002 EMail: jtabilo@ucn.cl

Secretaria General: Fernando Orellana (2014-)
Tel: +56(55) 2355-065 EMail: forellana@ucn.cl

Vicerrector Académico: Rodrigo Alda (2013-)
Tel: +56(55) 2355-004 EMail: ralda@ucn.cl

Vicerrectora de Investigación y Desarrollo Tecnológico: Maria Cecilia Hernández (2013-)
Tel: +56(55) 2355-031 EMail: mhernan@ucn.cl

Vicerrectora de Asuntos Económicos y Administrativos: Jacqueline Fuentes (2013-)
Tel: +56(55) 2355-006 EMail: jafuente@ucn.cl

Vicerrector de Sede Coquimbo: Francisco Correa (2015-)
Tel: +56(51) 2209-891 EMail: fcorrea@ucn.cl

International Relations: Dania Trista, Directora Relaciones Institucionales Tel: +56(55) 2222-6216 EMail: dtrista@ucn.cl

Faculty

Architecture, Civil Construction and Civil Engineering (Architecture; Civil Engineering; Construction Engineering); **Economics and Administration** (Accountancy; Administration; Business and Commerce; Economics; Management); **Engineering and Geological Science** (Chemical Engineering; Civil Engineering; Computer Engineering; Computer Science; Engineering; Environmental Engineering; Geology; Industrial Engineering; Metallurgical Engineering); **Humanities** (Arts and Humanities; Journalism; Law; Philosophy; Psychology; Religious Studies; Theology); **Law** (Law); **Marine Science** *(Coquimbo)* (Aquaculture; Marine Biology; Marine Science and Oceanography); **Medicine** (Biomedicine; Medicine; Public Health); **Science** (Astronomy and Space Science; Chemistry; Computer Education; Environmental Studies; Mathematics; Mathematics and Computer Science; Mathematics Education; Natural Sciences; Pharmacy; Physics; Statistics)

School

Commercial Engineering *(Coquimbo)* (Business and Commerce); **Journalism** (Information Sciences; Journalism; Mass Communication); **Psychology** (Psychology); **Theology** *(Coquimbo)* (Theology)

Institute

Applied Economics *(Regional)* (Economics); **Archeological Research** (Anthropology; Archaeology); **Astronomy** (Astronomy and Space Science)

Centre

Distance Education (Distance Education)

Further Information: Also Coquimbo, Santiago and San Pedro de Atacama campuses

History: Founded 1956. UCN gives its contribution to the world through its professionals trained in the various disciplines of knowledge, at the light of an education characterized by incorporating the principles of Christian Humanism and Social Vocation.

Academic Year: March to December (March-July; August-December)

Admission Requirements: Secondary school certificate (Licencia de Educación Media) and entrance examination (PSU). Special admissions for professionals and foreign students.

Fees: National: c. 3.700.000 per annum (Chilean Peso), International: c. 5.300 per annum (US Dollar)

Main Language(s) of Instruction: Spanish

Accrediting Agency: National Accreditation Commission (CNA)

Degrees and Diplomas: *Licenciatura*: **Architecture; Business Administration; Chemistry; Communication Arts; Computer Science; Engineering; Law; Marine Science and Oceanography; Mathematics; Physics; Psychology; Secondary Education.** *Título Profesional*: **Accountancy; Engineering; Geology.** *Post- título/Diploma*; *Magister*; *Doctorado*

Student Services: Academic Counselling, Canteen, Careers Guidance, Cultural Activities, Facilities for disabled people, Foreign Studies Centre, Health Services, IT Centre, Language Laboratory, Library, Nursery Care, Residential Facilities, Social Counselling, Sports Facilities, eLibrary

Publications: Boletín de Educación; Revista de Derecho; Revista de Matemáticas: Proyecciones; Revista Norte; Revista Vertientes; Tercer Milenio

Publishing House: Imprenta Universidad Católica del Norte

Last Updated: 11/01/16

CATHOLIC UNIVERSITY OF VALPARAÍSO

Pontificia Universidad Católica de Valparaíso (UCV)

Avenida Brasil 2950, Casilla 4059, Valparaíso

Tel: +56(32) 273-000

Fax: +56(32) 273-183

EMail: info@ucv.cl

Website: http://www.ucv.cl

Rector: Claudio Raffo Elórtegui EMail: rector@ucv.cl

Secretario General: Juan Carlos Morales Gentina
Tel: +56(32) 2273221 EMail: secgnral@ucv.cl

Faculty

Agronomy and Food Science *(Quillota)* (Agronomy; Food Science); **Architecture and Town Planning** *(Viña del Mar)* (Architecture; Graphic Design; Industrial Design; Town Planning); **Economics and Administration** (Accountancy; Administration; Business Administration; Business and Commerce; Economics; Journalism; Management; Social and Community Services; Social Work); **Engineering** (Bioengineering; Chemical Engineering; Civil Engineering; Computer Engineering; Computer Networks; Construction Engineering; Electrical Engineering; Electronic Engineering; Engineering; Engineering Management; Industrial Engineering; Marine Engineering; Marine Science and Oceanography; Materials Engineering; Mechanical Engineering; Metallurgical Engineering; Production Engineering; Transport Engineering); **Marine Science and Geography** (Aquaculture; Food Science; Geography; Marine Science and Oceanography; Natural Resources); **Philosophy and Education** *(Viña del Mar)* (Applied Linguistics; Computer Education; Curriculum; Education; Education of the Handicapped; Educational Administration; History; Linguistics; Literacy Education; Literature; Music Education; Native Language; Pedagogy; Philosophy; Physical Education; Preschool Education; Psychology; Social Sciences; Spanish; Special Education; Translation and Interpretation; Writing); **Science** (Biochemistry; Biology; Chemistry; Industrial Chemistry; Mathematics; Medical Technology; Optics; Physical Therapy; Physics; Statistics)

School

Law (Law; Social Sciences); **Theology** (Christian Religious Studies; Ethics; Religious Studies; Theology)

Further Information: Also courses for foreign students. Branches in Viña del Mar, Quilpué and Quillota

History: Founded 1928, recognized by official decree 1929. Recognized as Catholic university by the Holy See 1961. A private institution financially supported by the State.

Academic Year: March to December (March-July; August-December)

Admission Requirements: High School Diploma (Licencia de Educación Media) or foreign equivalent, and entrance examination

Main Language(s) of Instruction: Spanish

Accrediting Agency: National Accreditation Commission (CNA)

Degrees and Diplomas: *Bachiller*: **Fine Arts; Natural Sciences; Religious Studies.** *Licenciatura*: **Agronomy; Architecture;**

Biochemistry; Biology; Business Administration; Business and Commerce; Chemistry; Economics; Engineering; History; Law; Literature; Mathematics; Music; Philosophy; Physics; Religious Studies; Spanish. *Título Profesional*: **Accountancy; Agronomy; Architecture; Bioengineering; Biology; Business Administration; Chemical Engineering; Chemistry; Civil Engineering; Communication Studies; Computer Engineering; Computer Science; Construction Engineering; Education; Electrical Engineering; Electronic Engineering; English; Fishery; Food Technology; Geography; Graphic Design; History; Industrial Chemistry; Industrial Design; Industrial Engineering; Journalism; Law; Marine Science and Oceanography; Mathematics; Mechanical Engineering; Mining Engineering; Music; Natural Sciences; Optics; Philosophy; Physical Education; Physical Therapy; Physics; Preschool Education; Primary Education; Psychology; Religious Studies; Social Sciences; Social Work; Spanish; Special Education; Statistics; Translation and Interpretation; Transport Engineering.** *Post- título/Diploma*: **Accountancy; Administration; Business Administration; Communication Studies; Computer Science; Educational Administration; Educational Psychology; Electrical Engineering; English; Finance; Industrial Engineering; International Relations; Justice Administration; Mathematics Education; Metallurgical Engineering; Physics; Public Administration; Science Education; Taxation; Transport Engineering; Writing.** *Magister*: **Accountancy; Agriculture; Applied Linguistics; Architecture; Biochemistry; Biology; Business Administration; Chemical Engineering; Chemistry; Communication Studies; Computer Engineering; Construction Engineering; Criminal Law; Design; Education; Electrical Engineering; Engineering; Environmental Engineering; Environmental Studies; Finance; Food Technology; History; Industrial Engineering; International Relations; Law; Leadership; Literature; Management; Marine Science and Oceanography; Mathematics; Mathematics Education; Microbiology; Philosophy; Physics; Science Education; Social Work; Spanish; Statistics; Transport Engineering; Transport Management; Water Management.** *Doctorado*: **Aquaculture; Biochemistry; Biotechnology; Chemistry; Computer Engineering; History; Industrial Engineering; Linguistics; Literature; Mathematics; Mathematics Education; Philosophy; Physics; Psychology.**

Student Services: Library

Publications: Monografías Históricas; Revista de Derecho; Revista de Estudios Histórico-Jurídico; Revista de Investigaciones Marinas; Revista Facultad de Ingeniería; Revista Filosofica; Revista Geográfica; Revista Perspectiva Educacional; Revista Signos

Publishing House: Ediciones Universitarias de Valparaíso

Last Updated: 06/01/16

CATHOLIC UNIVERSITY SILVA HENRÍQUEZ

Universidad Católica Silva Henríquez (UCSH)
General Jofré 462, Casilla 28, Correo 22, Santiago
Tel: +56(2) 2460-1100
EMail: universidad@ucsh.cl
Website: http://www.ucsh.cl

Rector: Jorge Baeza Correa
Tel: +56(2) 2460-1102 EMail: rector@ucsh.cl

Vicerrector de Administración y Finanzas: Guillermo Escobar Alaniz

Faculty

Education (Art Education; Education; English; Geography; History; Mathematics Education; Pedagogy; Physical Education; Preschool Education; Primary Education; Science Education; Spanish; Special Education; Vocational Education); **Health Sciences** (Health Sciences); **Religious Studies and Philisophy** (Philosophy; Religious Studies); **Social Science, Law and Economics** (Accountancy; Administration; Business and Commerce; Economics; Law; Psychology; Social Sciences; Social Work; Sociology)

Further Information: Also Lo Canas Campus and San Isidoro site.

History: Founded 1991 from former Instituto Profesional de Estudios Superiores Blas Cañas, acquired present title 1993.

Academic Year: March to December (March-July; July-December)

Admission Requirements: Secondary school certificate (Licencia de Educación Media) and Prueba de Aptitud Académica. Some courses require additional examinations

Main Language(s) of Instruction: Spanish

Accrediting Agency: National Accreditation Commission (CNA)

Degrees and Diplomas: *Licenciatura*; *Post- título/Diploma*; *Magister*: **Education; Social and Community Services.**

Student Services: Canteen, Health Services, Library, Social Counselling, Sports Facilities

Publications: Bulletin of Literature and Linguistics; Bulletin of Philosophy; Educational Forum; Journal of Religious Sciences; OIKOS; Research Series; Sociological Topics

Last Updated: 11/01/16

CENTRAL UNIVERSITY OF CHILE

Universidad Central de Chile
Toesca 1783, Casilla 285-V, Correo 21, Santiago 8370178, Región Metropolitana
Tel: +56(2) 2582-6000
Fax: +56(2) 2582-6109
Website: http://www.ucentral.cl

Rector: Santiago Gonzalez Larrain
Tel: +56(2) 2582-6078 EMail: rector@ucentral.cl

Secretario General: Omar Ahumada Mora
Tel: +56(2) 2582-6029 EMail: oahumada@ucentral.cl

International Relations: Eliana Abad, National and International Relations Director EMail: eabad@ucentral.cl

Faculty

Architecture, Urban Planning and Landscape Architecture (Architectural Restoration; Architecture; Landscape Architecture; Regional Planning; Rural Planning; Structural Architecture; Town Planning); **Communication Studies** (Advertising and Publicity; Communication Arts; Communication Studies; Information Management; Information Technology; Journalism; Marketing; Mass Communication; Media Studies; Multimedia; Public Relations; Radio and Television Broadcasting); **Economics and Public Administration** (Accountancy; Administration; Agricultural Business; Banking; Business Administration; Business and Commerce; Business Computing; Economics; Farm Management; Finance; Human Resources; Industrial Management; International Business; Leadership; Management; Management Systems; Public Administration; Small Business; Taxation); **Educational Sciences** (Bilingual and Bicultural Education; Continuing Education; Curriculum; Educational Administration; Educational and Student Counselling; Educational Research; Educational Sciences; Educational Testing and Evaluation; Foreign Languages Education; Higher Education; Humanities and Social Science Education; Mathematics Education; Pedagogy; Physical Education; Preschool Education; Primary Education; Science Education; Secondary Education; Special Education; Teacher Trainers Education; Teacher Training); **Law and Social Sciences** (Administrative Law; Civil Law; Commercial Law; Comparative Law; Constitutional Law; Criminal Law; Fiscal Law; History of Law; Human Rights; International Law; Justice Administration; Labour Law; Law; Private Law; Public Law); **Physics and Mathematics** (Civil Engineering; Computer Engineering; Computer Networks; Construction Engineering; Data Processing; Industrial Engineering; Mathematics; Physics; Software Engineering); **Political Science and Public Administration** (Comparative Politics; Demography and Population; Development Studies; Economic and Finance Policy; Economic History; Economics; Government; Industrial and Production Economics; International Economics; International Relations; International Studies; Political Sciences; Public Administration; Regional Planning; Rural Studies; Urban Studies); **Social Sciences** (Behavioural Sciences; Clinical Psychology; Cognitive Sciences; Comparative Sociology; Developmental Psychology; Educational Psychology; Family Studies; History of Societies; Psychoanalysis; Psychology; Psychometrics; Social and Community Services; Social Policy; Social Problems; Social Psychology; Social Sciences; Social Studies; Social Welfare; Social Work; Sociology; Vocational Counselling)

Institute

Cognitive Development *(International)*; **Elementary Education** *(International)* (Preschool Education; Teacher Training); **Public Management** (Administration; Comparative Politics; Government; Institutional Administration; Political Sciences; Private Administration; Public Administration)

Further Information: Also La Serena, Antofagasta campuses

History: Founded 1983. Became autonomous 1993.

Academic Year: March to January

Admission Requirements: Secondary school certificate (Licencia de Educación Media); PAA (Academic Aptitude Test) and entrance examination

Main Language(s) of Instruction: Spanish

Accrediting Agency: National Accreditation Commission (CNA)

Degrees and Diplomas: *Licenciatura*; *Post- título/Diploma*: **Agricultural Business; Business and Commerce; Civil Engineering; Commercial Law; Communication Studies; Design; Education; Educational Administration; Educational Psychology; English; Environmental Studies; Ethics; Finance; Higher Education; Landscape Architecture; Management; Marketing; Modern Languages; Natural Sciences; Peace and Disarmament; Political Sciences; Psychoanalysis; Psychology; Public Administration; Public Health; Road Engineering; Social and Community Services; Social Sciences; Surveying and Mapping; Welfare and Protective Services.** *Magister*: **Architecture; Computer Science; Construction Engineering; Criminal Law; Criminology; Design; Education; Educational Administration; Educational and Student Counselling; Educational Sciences; Higher Education Teacher Training; Information Technology; Law; Management; Preschool Education; Public Administration; Public Health; Science Education; Social Problems; Special Education.**

Student Services: Academic Counselling, Canteen, Careers Guidance, Cultural Activities, Facilities for disabled people, Health Services, Language Laboratory, Social Counselling, Sports Facilities

Publications: Diseño Urbano y Paisaje (Digital Version); Ingenería al Día (Printed Version); Perspectivas (Printed Version); Revista Central de Sociología (Printed and Digital Version); Revista de Derecho (Printed Version); Revista de Educación Básica (Printed Version); Revista Ecoengen (Printed Version); Revista Enfoques (Printed Version); Revista Mesa Redonda (Printed Version); Revista Motricidad y Persona (Printed Version); Revista Sociedad y Conocimiento (Printed Version); Rumbos TS (Printed Version)

Last Updated: 12/01/16

CIISA TECHNOLOGICAL INSTITUTE

Instituto de Ciencias Tecnológicas CIISA

Avenida República 20 y 40, Santiago

Tel: +56(2) 2663-7801

EMail: admision@ciisa.cl

Website: http://www.ipciisa.cl

Rector: Arturo Fuentes Espinosa

Vicerrector Académico: Christian Quezada Ruíz

Programme

Automation (Automation and Control Engineering); **Computer Engineering** (Computer Engineering; Computer Networks; Computer Science; Systems Analysis)

Further Information: Also Santa Lucía and Alameda Campuses

History: Founded 1975, acquired present status 1990.

Admission Requirements: High School Diploma (Licencia de Educación Media)

Main Language(s) of Instruction: Spanish

Accrediting Agency: National Accreditation Commission (CNA)

Degrees and Diplomas: *Título Profesional*: **Automation and Control Engineering; Computer Engineering; Computer Networks.**

Student Services: Library

Last Updated: 18/12/15

DIEGO PORTALES UNIVERSITY

Universidad Diego Portales (UDP)

Manuel Rodríguez Sur 415, Santiago 8370179

Tel: +56(2) 22676-2000

Fax: +56(2) 22676-2112

EMail: admision@udp.cl

Website: http://www.udp.cl

Rector: Carlos Peña (2006-)
Tel: +56(2) 676-2131 EMail: carlos.pena@udp.cl

Vicerrector Academico: Cristóbal Marín Correa
Tel: +56(2) 676-2116 EMail: cristobal.marin@udp.cl

International Relations: Gabriel Libedinsky
Tel: +56(2) 676-8307
EMail: gabriel.libedinsky@udp.cl; internacional@mail.udp.cl

Faculty

Architecture, Design and Fine Arts (Architecture; Design; Fine Arts; Graphic Design; Industrial Design; Visual Arts); **Communication and Literature** (Advertising and Publicity; Communication Studies; Journalism; Literature); **Economics and Business Administration** (Accountancy; Business Administration; Economics; Finance; Human Resources; Marketing); **Education** (Education; English; History; Preschool Education; Primary Education; Social Sciences; Spanish; Special Education); **Engineering** (Business Computing; Civil Engineering; Computer Engineering; Computer Science; Construction Engineering; E-Business/Commerce; Engineering; Industrial Engineering; Information Technology; Statistics; Telecommunications Engineering); **Health Sciences and Dentistry** (Dentistry; Health Sciences; Medical Technology; Nursing; Ophthalmology; Optometry; Physical Therapy; Radiology); **Law** (Commercial Law; Justice Administration; Law; Social Sciences); **Medicine** (Medicine); **Psychology** (Psychology); **Social Sciences and History** (History; Political Sciences; Social Sciences; Sociology)

Further Information: Regional Branch in Temuco

History: Founded 1982, acquired autonomous status 1993. A private institution.

Academic Year: March to December

Admission Requirements: Secondary school certificate; National university admission test and interviews

Main Language(s) of Instruction: Spanish

Accrediting Agency: National Accreditation Commission (CNA)

Degrees and Diplomas: *Licenciatura*; *Post- título/Diploma*: **Anaesthesiology; Education; Law; Medicine; Nursing; Psychiatry and Mental Health; Psychology; Surgery.** *Magister*: **Administration; Civil Law; Clinical Psychology; Communication Studies; Criminal Law; Economics; Educational Administration; Educational Testing and Evaluation; Engineering; Finance; Fiscal Law; Government; Human Resources; Human Rights; International Law; Landscape Architecture; Latin American Studies; Law; Marketing; Neurosciences; Philosophy; Political Sciences; Psychology; Publishing and Book Trade; Social Psychology; Social Sciences.** *Doctorado*: **Education; Higher Education; Law; Philosophy; Political Sciences; Psychology.** Also joint MBA programs with Pompeu Fabra University (Spain)

Student Services: Academic Counselling, Careers Guidance, Cultural Activities, Facilities for disabled people, Language Laboratory, Library, Nursery Care, Social Counselling, Sports Facilities

Last Updated: 18/01/16

DR. VIRGINIO GÓMEZ PROFESSIONAL INSTITUTE

Instituto Profesional Dr. Virginio Gómez (IPVG)

Arturo Prat 196, Concepción

Tel: +56(41) 279-3400

EMail: vtallia@virginiogomez.cl

Website: http://www.virginiogomez.cl

Rector: Claudio Sáez Fuentes EMail: csaez@virginiogomez.cl

Vicerrector Académico: René Lagos Cuitiño
EMail: rlagos@virginiogomez.cl

School

Basic Sciences and Humanities (Arts and Humanities; Natural Sciences); **Construction and Risk Prevention** (Civil Engineering; Construction Engineering; Safety Engineering); **Health and Education** (Dental Hygiene; Laboratory Techniques; Nursing; Rehabilitation and Therapy; Special Education); **Industrial Technology** (Electrical and Electronic Engineering; Industrial Engineering; Maintenance Technology; Mechanical Engineering; Mining

Engineering; Technology; Telecommunications Engineering); **Management and Information Technology** (Administration; Business Administration; Business and Commerce; Computer Science; Information Technology; Management)

Further Information: Also campuses in Chillán and Los Angeles

History: Founded 1988, Institute maintains co-operation agreements with the Universidad de Concepción.

Admission Requirements: Licencia de Enseñanza Media

Main Language(s) of Instruction: Spanish

Degrees and Diplomas: *Técnico de Nivel Superior*, *Título Profesional*: **Engineering.**

Last Updated: 31/12/15

DUOCUC PROFESSIONAL INSTITUTE

Instituto Profesional DuocUC (DUOCUC)
Dario Urzúa 2100, Santiago
Tel: +56(2) 2235-2546
EMail: info@duoc.cl
Website: http://www.duoc.cl

Rector: Ricardo Paredes Molina

Vicerrector Académico: Andrés Villela C.

International Relations: Rodrigo Nuñez R., Director of International Relations EMail: rnunez@duoc.cl

School

Business and Administration (Accountancy; Business Administration; International Business; Marketing); **Communication Studies** (Acting; Advertising and Publicity; Communication Studies; Fashion Design; Graphic Design; Hotel Management; Industrial Design; Tourism); **Construction Engineering** (Architectural and Environmental Design; Civil Engineering; Construction Engineering; Safety Engineering; Surveying and Mapping); **Design** (Design); **Engineering** (Automation and Control Engineering; Automotive Engineering; Computer Engineering; Computer Networks; Electrical and Electronic Engineering; Engineering; Industrial Engineering); **Health Sciences** (Health Sciences); **Information Technology and Telecommunications** (Computer Engineering; Computer Science; Information Technology; Telecommunications Engineering); **Natural Resources** (Agricultural Engineering; Environmental Engineering; Natural Resources); **Tourism** (Cooking and Catering; Hotel Management; Tourism)

Further Information: Also 16 campuses all over the region (Valparaíso, Viña del Mar, Concepción, Antonio Varas, Alameda, San Carlos de Apoquindo and more)

History: Founded 1968. Acquired present title and status 1982.

Main Language(s) of Instruction: Spanish

Accrediting Agency: National Accreditation Commission (CNA)

Degrees and Diplomas: *Técnico de Nivel Superior*, *Título Profesional*

Student Services: Library

Academic Staff *2014-2015*: Total 3,876
Student Numbers *2014-2015*: Total 93,584
Last Updated: 04/01/16

EATRI PROFESSIONAL INSTITUTE

Instituto Profesional EATRI
Avenida Condell 451, Providencia, Santiago
Tel: +56(2) 2223-1089
Fax: +56(2) 2269-2990
EMail: contacto@eatri.cl
Website: http://www.eatri.cl

Rectora (Acting): Violeta Morgado Segura

Director Académico: Max Guillermo Colillán Martínez

Programme

Translation and Interpretation (English; French; German; Portuguese; Spanish; Translation and Interpretation)

History: Founded 1970.

Admission Requirements: Licencia de Enseñanza Media

Main Language(s) of Instruction: Spanish

Accrediting Agency: Comisión Nacional de Acreditación

Degrees and Diplomas: *Título Profesional*: **Translation and Interpretation.**

Student Services: Library

Last Updated: 03/01/16

ESUCOMEX PROFESSIONAL INSTITUTE

Instituto Profesional ESUCOMEX
Ejército Libertador 91, Providencia, Santiago
Tel: +56(2) 2367-9700
EMail: info@esucomex.cl
Website: http://www.esucomex.cl

Rector: Cristóbal Silva Labbé

Vicerrector Académico: Oscar Iriani Montes

School

Administration (Accountancy; Business Administration; Business and Commerce; Finance; Human Resources; International Business; Secretarial Studies; Transport Management); **Construction Engineering** (Architectural and Environmental Design; Construction Engineering; Industrial Design; Interior Design; Safety Engineering); **Engineering** (Computer Engineering; Computer Science; Industrial Engineering; Information Technology; Mining Engineering; Systems Analysis)

History: Founded 1989.

Admission Requirements: High School Certificate (Licencia de Educación Media)

Main Language(s) of Instruction: Spanish

Accrediting Agency: National Accreditation Commission (CNA)

Degrees and Diplomas: *Técnico de Nivel Superior*, *Título Profesional*

Last Updated: 05/01/16

FEDERICO SANTA MARÍA TECHNICAL UNIVERSITY

Universidad Técnica Federico Santa María
Avenida España 1680, Casilla 110-V, Valparaíso
Tel: +56(32) 2654-000
Fax: +56(32) 2797-501
EMail: dgc@usm.cl
Website: http://www.utfsm.cl

Rector: Darcy Fuenzalida
Tel: +56(32) 2654-140 EMail: darcy.fuenzalida@usm.clnospam

Secretario General: Jerome Mac Auliffe
Tel: +56(32) 2654-264 EMail: jerome.mac-auliffe@usm.clnospam

Department

Architecture (Architecture); **Business and Commerce** (Business Administration; Business and Commerce); **Chemical and Enviromental Engineering** (Chemical Engineering; Environmental Engineering); **Chemistry** (Chemistry; Environmental Engineering; Industrial Chemistry; Natural Sciences); **Civil Engineering** (Civil Engineering; Construction Engineering); **Computer Engineering** (Computer Engineering; Computer Science; Information Management; Software Engineering); **Electrical Engineering** (Civil Engineering; Electrical Engineering); **Electronic Engineering** (Automation and Control Engineering; Computer Science; Electronic Engineering; Telecommunications Engineering); **Humanities** (Arts and Humanities); **Industrial Engineering** (Industrial Engineering); **Mathematics** (Mathematics); **Mechanical Engineering** (Mechanical Engineering; Production Engineering); **Metallurgical and Materials Engineering** (Civil Engineering; Materials Engineering; Metallurgical Engineering); **Physical Education, Sports and Recreation** (Leisure Studies; Physical Education; Sports); **Physics** (Physics); **Product Design** (Design)

Academy

Aeronautics *(Santiago)* (Aeronautical and Aerospace Engineering)

Campus

Concepción (Chemistry; Construction Engineering; Electrical Engineering; Mechanical Engineering); **Guayaquil** (Business Administration; Economics; Graphic Design; International Business; Management; Marketing); **Rancagua** (Civil Engineering; Industrial

Engineering; Management); **San Joaquín** (Arts and Humanities; Chemical Engineering; Chemistry; Computer Engineering; Electrical Engineering; Environmental Studies; Mathematics; Mechanical Engineering; Parks and Recreation; Physical Education; Physics; Sports); **Santiago** (Aeronautical and Aerospace Engineering; Arts and Humanities; Chemical Engineering; Chemistry; Civil Engineering; Computer Engineering; Electrical Engineering; Environmental Engineering; Industrial Engineering; Mathematics; Mechanical Engineering; Parks and Recreation; Physical Education; Physics; Sports); **Viña del Mar** (Chemistry; Computer Engineering; Construction Engineering; Design; Electrical Engineering; Environmental Studies; Mechanical Engineering; Natural Sciences); **Vitacura** (Aeronautical and Aerospace Engineering; Chemistry; Industrial Engineering; Mathematics; Physical Education; Physics; Sports)

History: Founded 1932 as a private institution, endowed by Federico Santa María Carrera. Recognized by the State as technical university 1935. Mainly financed by the government, but enjoying administrative and academic autonomy.

Academic Year: March to January (March-June; July-November; November-January)

Admission Requirements: Secondary education (Licencia Secundaria) and entrance examination

Main Language(s) of Instruction: Spanish

Accrediting Agency: National Accreditation Commission (CNA)

Degrees and Diplomas: *Licenciatura*: **Chemistry; Mathematics; Physics.** *Título Profesional*: **Architecture; Chemistry; Engineering.** *Magister*: **Aeronautical and Aerospace Engineering; Business Administration; Chemical Engineering; Chemistry; Civil Engineering; Computer Engineering; Electrical Engineering; Electronic Engineering; Engineering; Industrial Engineering; Information Technology; Management; Mathematics; Metallurgical Engineering; Natural Sciences; Physics.** *Doctorado*: **Biotechnology; Chemistry; Computer Engineering; Electrical Engineering; Electronic Engineering; Mathematics; Mechanical Engineering; Physics.** Also MBA a further 2 yrs

Student Services: Cultural Activities, Library

Publications: Gestión Tecnológica; Scientia

Last Updated: 20/01/16

FINISTERRAE UNIVERSITY

Universidad FinisTerrae (UFT)

Avenida Pedro de Valdivia 1509, Providencia, Santiago
Tel: +56(2) 420-7100
Fax: +56(2) 420-7600
EMail: fterrae@finisterrae.cl
Website: http://www.finisterrae.cl

Rector: Cristian Nazer A.

Secretario General: Roberto Salim-Hanna S.

Faculty

Architecture and Design (Architectural and Environmental Design; Architecture; Design); **Arts** (Acting; Engraving; Fine Arts; Painting and Drawing; Sculpture; Visual Arts); **Business Administration and Economics** (Business Administration; Economics; Hotel and Restaurant); **Civil Engineering** (Civil Engineering); **Communication Studies and Humanities** (Advertising and Publicity; Communication Studies; History; Journalism; Literature; Theatre); **Dentistry** (Dentistry); **Education and Family Studies** (Education; Family Studies; Preschool Education; Primary Education; Religious Education; Secondary Education); **Law** (Commercial Law; Law; Public Law); **Medicine** (Dietetics; Health Sciences; Medicine; Nursing; Nutrition; Psychology); **Social Sciences** (Communication Studies; History; Journalism; Social Sciences)

History: Founded 1981, acquired autonomous status 1996.

Academic Year: March to December (March-July; August-December)

Admission Requirements: Secondary school certificate (Licencia de Educación Media), Prueba de Aptitud Académica and interview

Main Language(s) of Instruction: Spanish

Accrediting Agency: National Accreditation Commission (CNA)

Degrees and Diplomas: *Licenciatura*; *Título Profesional*; *Post-título/Diploma*: **Dentistry; Education; Law.** *Magister*: **Business Administration; Curriculum; Dentistry; Education; Health Sciences; Heritage Preservation; Literature; Mathematics Education; Physical Therapy; Public Law; Religious Education; Visual Arts.** Also MBA

Student Services: Academic Counselling, Canteen, Cultural Activities, Health Services, Language Laboratory, Social Counselling, Sports Facilities

Publications: Alas y Raíces; Finis Terrae Review; Revista de Derecho; Teatrae

Last Updated: 18/01/16

GUILLERMO SUBERCASEAUX INSTITUTE OF BANKING STUDIES

Instituto de Estudios Bancarios Guillermo Subercaseaux

Agustinas 1476 piso 8, Santiago
Tel: +56(2) 2469-4000
Fax: +56(2) 2499-4091
EMail: ieb@ieb.cl
Website: http://www.ieb.cl

Rector: Mario Merino G. Merino G.

International Relations: Fernando Saavedra D., Vicerrector Académico

Programme

Accountancy (Accountancy); **Business Administration** (Business Administration); **Finance** (Banking; Finance)

Further Information: Also virtual campus and branches in Rancagua, Concepción, Temuco, Viña del Mar

History: Founded 1929.

Admission Requirements: High School Certificate (Licencia de Educación Media)

Main Language(s) of Instruction: Spanish

Accrediting Agency: National Accreditation Commission (CNA)

Degrees and Diplomas: *Técnico de Nivel Superior*, *Título Profesional*. Also Especialización

Last Updated: 05/01/16

LA ARAUCANA PROFESSIONAL INSTITUTE

Instituto Profesional La Araucana

Ejército 171, Santiago
Tel: +56(2) 427-1000
Fax: +56(2) 427-1027
EMail: info@iplaaraucana.cl
Website: http://www.iplaaraucana.cl

Rector: Edmundo Durán Vallejos

Vicerrectora Académico: Isabel Gómez Rojas

School

Business Administration (Accountancy; Business Administration; Finance; Hotel and Restaurant; Hotel Management; Human Resources; International Business; Tourism); **Health Sciences** (Dietetics; Health Sciences; Nursing; Nutrition; Sports); **Humanities and Social Science** (Education; Educational Psychology; Preschool Education; Social and Community Services; Special Education); **Production and Engineering** (Agricultural Engineering; Aquaculture; Computer Networks; Computer Science; Construction Engineering; Industrial Engineering; Information Technology; Mining Engineering; Safety Engineering; Telecommunications Engineering; Viticulture)

Further Information: Regional Branches in La Serena, Curicó, Concepción, Temuco, Osorno, Puerto Montt, Melipilla, San Bernardo, Vina del Mar, Los Angeles and Castro

History: Founded 1988.

Admission Requirements: Secondary school certificate

Main Language(s) of Instruction: Spanish

Accrediting Agency: Comisión Nacional de Acreditación (CNA)

Degrees and Diplomas: *Técnico de Nivel Superior*, *Título Profesional*

Student Services: Library

Last Updated: 23/12/15

LATIN AMERICAN PROFESSIONAL INSTITUTE OF FOREIGN TRADE

Instituto Profesional Latinoamericano de Comercio Exterior (IPLATEX)
Av. Compañia N° 2015, Providencia, Santiago
Tel: +56(2) 24812664
EMail: contacto@iplacex.cl; admisionsantiago@iplacex.cl
Website: http://www.iplacex.cl

Rector: Gonzalo Tomarelli Tomarelli
Vicerrector Académico: Giovanni Pinedo

School
Business and Trade (Accountancy; Business Administration; International Business); **Computer Science** (Computer Engineering; Computer Science; Systems Analysis); **Construction Engineering** (Construction Engineering; Safety Engineering; Surveying and Mapping); **Education** (Educational Psychology; Preschool Education; Special Education); **Health Sciences** (Dietetics; Nursing; Nutrition; Physical Therapy); **Social Sciences** (Public Administration; Social Sciences; Social Work); **Tourism** (Cooking and Catering; Tourism)

Further Information: Also Distance Education campus and branches in Copiapó, and Talca
History: Founded 1990.
Admission Requirements: High School Diploma (Licencia de Educación Media)
Main Language(s) of Instruction: Spanish
Accrediting Agency: National Accreditation Commission (CNA)
Degrees and Diplomas: *Técnico de Nivel Superior*; *Título Profesional*
Student Services: Library
Last Updated: 05/01/16

LIBERATOR OF THE ANDES PROFESSIONAL INSTITUTE

Instituto Profesional Libertador de Los Andes
Membrillar 360, Los Andes
Tel: +56(34) 2595600
EMail: ipla@ipla.cl
Website: http://www.ipla.cl

Rector: José Lazcano

Programme
Business Administration and Human Resource (Business Administration; Human Resources; Management); **Computer Engineering** (Computer Engineering; Computer Networks; Software Engineering); **Early Childhood Education** (Preschool Education); **Environmental and Safety Engineering** (Environmental Engineering; Safety Engineering); **Psychopedagogy** (Educational Psychology); **Public Administration** (Public Administration); **Social Services** (Social and Community Services)

Further Information: Also branch in Valparaíso
History: Founded 1981.
Admission Requirements: High School Diploma (Licencia de Educación Media)
Main Language(s) of Instruction: Spanish
Accrediting Agency: National Accreditation Commission (CNA)
Degrees and Diplomas: *Técnico de Nivel Superior*, *Título Profesional*
Last Updated: 05/01/16

LOS LEONES PROFESSIONAL INSTITUTE

Instituto Profesional Los Leones
Arturo Prat 386, Alonzo de Ovalle 1546, Santiago
Tel: +56(2) 632-1573
Fax: +56(2) 632-1698
EMail: ipleones@ctcreuna.cl
Website: http://www.ipleones.cl

Rector: Fernando Vicencio Silva
Vicerrector Académico: Emilio Gautier

Programme
Accountancy (Accountancy); **Advertising and Publicity** (Advertising and Publicity; Marketing); **Business Administration** (Business Administration); **Construction Engineering** (Civil Engineering; Construction Engineering); **Graphic Design** (Graphic Design); **Marketing** (Marketing); **Photography** (Photography); **Psychopedagogy** (Educational Psychology); **Public Relations** (Public Relations); **Social Services** (Social and Community Services); **Theatre** (Theatre)

Further Information: Also a branch in Viña del Mar
History: Founded 1990.
Admission Requirements: High School Diploma (Licencia de Enseñanza Media)
Main Language(s) of Instruction: Spanish
Degrees and Diplomas: *Título Profesional*
Last Updated: 06/01/16

MAYOR UNIVERSITY

Universidad Mayor
San Pío X 2422, Providencia, Santiago
Tel: +56(2) 2328-1000
Website: http://www.umayor.cl

Rector: Rubén Covarrubias Giordano (1998-)
Tel: 328-1114 EMail: rector@umayor.cl
Vicerrector Académico: René Salamé Martin
International Relations: René Lara, Director
EMail: rene.lara@umayor.cl

Faculty
Agriculture and Forestry *(Santiago and Temuco Campuses)* (Agriculture; Agronomy; Forestry; Veterinary Science); **Architecture, Design and Contruction** *(Santiago and Temuco Branch)* (Architecture; Construction Engineering; Design; Industrial Design; Interior Design); **Art** *(Santiago Branch)* (Theatre); **Dentistry** *(Santiago and Temuco Branches)* (Dentistry); **Economics and Business Administration** *(Santiago/Temuco Branches and Online Campus)* (Accountancy; Business Administration; Business and Commerce; Economics; Finance; Marketing); **Education** *(Santiago Branch)* (Education; Educational Psychology; English; Music Education; Parks and Recreation; Pedagogy; Physical Education; Primary Education; Secondary Education; Special Education; Sports); **Engineering** *(Santiago/Temuco Branches and Online campus)* (Civil Engineering; Computer Science; Electronic Engineering; Engineering; Industrial Engineering; Information Technology; Telecommunications Engineering); **Law and Social Sciences** *(Temuco and Santiago Campuses)* (Law; Social Sciences); **Medicine** *(Santiago and Temuco Campuses)* (Clinical Psychology; Dentistry; Dietetics; Educational Psychology; Gynaecology and Obstetrics; Health Sciences; Industrial and Organizational Psychology; Medical Technology; Medicine; Nursing; Nutrition; Occupational Therapy; Physical Therapy; Psychology; Psychotherapy; Speech Therapy and Audiology); **Science** *(Santiago Branch)* (Biotechnology; Geology)

School
Public Administration *(Santiago Branch and Online Campus)* (Public Administration); **Sociology** *(Santiago Branch)* (Sociology)

Institute
Art and Audiovisual Technology *(Santiago Branch)* (Cinema and Television; Computer Graphics); **Communication and New Technology** *(Santiago Branch)* (Communication Studies; Journalism)

Conservatory
Music *(Vespucio Campus/Santiago)* (Music; Music Education; Musical Instruments)

Further Information: Also Temuco Brach
History: Founded 1988, acquired present status 1996.
Academic Year: March to December (March-July; August-December)
Admission Requirements: Secondary school certificate (Licencia de Educación Media), and PSU, national examination test
Main Language(s) of Instruction: Spanish
Accrediting Agency: National Accreditation Committee (CNA)

Degrees and Diplomas: *Licenciatura*; *Título Profesional*; *Post-título/Diploma*: **Dentistry.** *Magister*: **Agronomy; Architecture; Business Administration; Business and Commerce; Clinical Psychology; Commercial Law; Communication Studies; Criminal Law; Design; Educational Psychology; Educational Sciences; Environmental Studies; Finance; Fine Arts; Gerontology; Health Administration; Health Sciences; Horticulture; Human Resources; Industrial and Organizational Psychology; Law; Marketing; Medicine; Midwifery; Music; Nursing; Nutrition; Pedagogy; Physical Education; Physical Therapy; Political Sciences; Psychology; Psychotherapy; Public Health; Special Education; Sports Medicine; Veterinary Science.** *Doctorado*: **Natural Sciences.** Also MBA and Diplomado

Student Services: Canteen, Careers Guidance, Cultural Activities, Health Services, Language Laboratory, Library, Sports Facilities

Last Updated: 19/01/16

PROFESSIONAL INSTITUTE MODERN SCHOOL OF MUSIC AND DANCE

Instituto Profesional Escuela Moderna de Música y Danza

Luis Pasteur 5303, Vitacura, Santiago
Tel: +56(2) 2365-1818
Fax: +56(2) 195-393
EMail: info@emoderna.cl
Website: http://www.emoderna.cl

Rector: Vivien Wurman Shapiro

Director Académico: Guillermo S. Rifo

Programme

Dance (Dance); **Music** (Music; Music Theory and Composition; Musical Instruments; Singing)

Further Information: Also branch in Viña del Mar and Bellavista Cultural Center

History: Founded 1988.

Main Language(s) of Instruction: Spanish

Accrediting Agency: National Accreditation Commission (CNA)

Degrees and Diplomas: *Título Profesional*

Last Updated: 05/01/16

PROFESSIONAL INSTITUTE OF CHILE

Instituto Profesional de Chile (IPCHILE)

República 285, Santiago
Tel: +56(2) 685-0800
EMail: admision@ipdechile.cl
Website: http://www.ipdechile.cl

Rector: Jorge Narbona Lemus EMail: jorge.narbona@ipchile.cl

Vicerrectora de Administración y Finanzas: Anamari Martínez Elortegui

Programme

Communication (Communication Studies); **Education** (Pedagogy; Preschool Education; Primary Education); **Health and Physical Activities** (Nursing; Nutrition; Occupational Therapy; Physical Education; Speech Therapy and Audiology; Sports)

School

Arts and Humanity (Advertising and Publicity; Design; Education; Educational Psychology; Graphic Design; Justice Administration; Preschool Education; Primary Education; Radio and Television Broadcasting; Social Work; Sound Engineering (Acoustics)); **Business Administration** (Business Administration; Business and Commerce; Cooking and Catering; Finance; Human Resources; International Business; Marketing; Public Relations; Tourism); **Engineering** (Automation and Control Engineering; Civil Engineering; Computer Engineering; Computer Networks; Construction Engineering; Electrical and Electronic Engineering; Electrical Engineering; Electronic Engineering; Energy Engineering; Industrial Engineering; Mechanical Engineering; Safety Engineering); **Mining** (Metallurgical Engineering; Mining Engineering)

Further Information: Also branches in La Serena, Rancagua, Temuco, and San Joaquín

History: Founded 1985.

Main Language(s) of Instruction: Spanish

Accrediting Agency: National Accreditation Commission (CNA)

Degrees and Diplomas: *Técnico de Nivel Superior*, *Título Profesional*

Student Services: Library

Last Updated: 18/12/15

SAINT THOMAS PROFESSIONAL INSTITUTE AND TECHNICAL TRAINING CENTRE

Instituto Profesional y Centro de Formación Técnica Santo Tomás

Zenteno 234, Santiago
Tel: +56(2) 495-7000
Fax: +56(2) 697-1200
EMail: ipst_stgo@santotomas.cl
Website: http://www.santotomas.cl

Rector: Juan Pablo Guzmán Aldunate

Programme

Administration (Administration; Tourism); **Communication Studies** (Communication Studies; Multimedia); **Computer Science** (Computer Science); **Dentistry** (Dentistry); **Design** (Design); **Education** (Education; Special Education); **Engineering and Construction** (Construction Engineering; Safety Engineering); **Health Sciences** (Health Sciences; Nursing); **Law** (Law); **Mining Engineering** (Chemical Engineering; Industrial Chemistry; Mining Engineering); **Natural Resources** (Natural Resources); **Social Sciences** (Criminology; Social and Community Services; Social Work); **Sports** (Sports); **Tourism and Gastronomy** (Cooking and Catering; Tourism)

Further Information: Also 22 branches all over the country (Arica, Iquique, Antofagasta, Copiapó, La Serena, Ovalle, Viña del Mar, Santiago, Rancagua, Curicó, Talca, Chillán, Concepción, Los Ángeles, Temuco, Valdivia, Osorno, Puerto Montt y Punta Arenas and more

History: Founded 2001.

Admission Requirements: High School Diploma (Licencia de Enseñanza Media)

Main Language(s) of Instruction: Spanish

Accrediting Agency: National Accreditation Commission (CNA)

Degrees and Diplomas: *Técnico de Nivel Superior*, *Título Profesional*

Last Updated: 06/01/16

SAN SEBASTIÁN UNIVERSITY

Universidad San Sebastián (USS)

Calle Cruz 1577, Concepción
Tel: +56(41) 2400-100
Fax: +56(41) 2400-102
EMail: admision@uss.cl
Website: http://www.uss.cl

Rector: Hugo Lavados Montes

Secretario General: Luis Camilo De la Maza De la Maza

Faculty

Architecture and Art (Architectural and Environmental Design; Architectural Restoration; Architecture; Graphic Design; Industrial Design; Landscape Architecture; Regional Planning; Town Planning); **Dentistry** (Dental Hygiene; Dental Technology; Dentistry; Oral Pathology; Orthodontics; Periodontics; Radiology); **Economics and Business** (Accountancy; Administration; Business Administration; Business Computing; Economics; Finance; Human Resources; Industrial Management; International Business; Leadership; Management; Management Systems; Small Business); **Education Sciences** (Curriculum; Education of the Handicapped; Educational Sciences; Educational Testing and Evaluation; Foreign Languages Education; Humanities and Social Science Education; Pedagogy; Physical Education; Preschool Education; Primary Education; Science Education; Secondary Education; Teacher Training); **Engineering and Technology** (Bioengineering; Biomedical Engineering; Biotechnology; Civil Engineering; Computer Engineering; Computer Networks; Energy Engineering; Environmental Engineering; Industrial Engineering; Safety Engineering; Telecommunications Engineering); **Health Sciences** (Dietetics; Medical Parasitology; Nutrition; Occupational Therapy; Pharmacy;

Physical Therapy; Speech Therapy and Audiology); **Law** (Administrative Law; Civil Law; Commercial Law; Constitutional Law; Criminal Law; Fiscal Law; International Law; Justice Administration; Labour Law; Law; Maritime Law; Public Law); **Medicine** (Gynaecology and Obstetrics; Medicine); **Nursing** (Nursing); **Physical Education** (Physical Education); **Psychology** (Psychology); **Science** (Biochemistry; Chemistry; Health Sciences; Pharmacy); **Social Sciences and Humanity** (Clinical Psychology; Educational Psychology; Industrial and Organizational Psychology; Journalism; Social Work; Sociology); **Veterinary Medicine** (Animal Husbandry; Aquaculture; Cattle Breeding; Veterinary Science)

Further Information: Also branches in Valdivia, Santiago, and De la patagonia

History: Founded 1989, acquired autonomous status 2001.

Academic Year: March to December (March-July; August-December)

Admission Requirements: Secondary school certificate (Licencia de Enseñanza Media) and university entrance examination, Prueba de Selección a la Universidad (PSU).

Main Language(s) of Instruction: Spanish

Accrediting Agency: National Accreditation Commission (CNA)

Degrees and Diplomas: *Licenciatura*: **Architecture; Biochemistry; Design; Education; Engineering; Medical Technology; Nursing; Nutrition; Pharmacy; Physical Therapy; Speech Therapy and Audiology.** *Título Profesional*: **Animal Husbandry; Architecture; Dentistry; Design; Education; Engineering; Medical Technology; Medicine; Nursing; Nutrition; Pharmacy; Physical Therapy; Psychology; Social Work; Speech Therapy and Audiology; Veterinary Science.** *Magister*: **Education; Health Administration; Management; Social Sciences.** Also Diplomado

Student Services: Academic Counselling, Canteen, Careers Guidance, Cultural Activities, Facilities for disabled people, Health Services, Language Laboratory, Library, Social Counselling, Sports Facilities

Publications: Biological Sciences; Cuadranos de Trabajo Social; Materia Arquitectura; Revista de Derecho; Revista SCEMUSS

Publishing House: Ediciones Universidad San Sebastiá

Last Updated: 19/01/16

SANTO TOMÁS UNIVERSITY

Universidad Santo Tomás (UST)

Avenida Ejército Libertador 146, Santiago
Tel: +56(2) 2362-5000
Fax: +56(2) 2360-1376
EMail: rectoria@santotomas.cl
Website: http://www.santotomas.cl

Rector: Jaime Vatter Gutiérrez (2015-)
Tel: +56(2) 2362-4905 EMail: rectoria@santotomas.cl

Secretario General: Patricio Cepeda Silva Tel: +56(2) 2362-4950

Faculty

Economics and Business (Accountancy; Business Administration; Business and Commerce; Economics; Management); **Education** (Education; English; Physical Education; Primary Education; Special Education); **Engineering** (Civil Engineering; Engineering; Geological Engineering; Mining Engineering); **Health Sciences** (Dietetics; Health Sciences; Medical Technology; Nursing; Nutrition; Occupational Health; Ophthalmology; Optometry; Physical Therapy; Speech Therapy and Audiology); **Law** (Law); **Natural Resouces and Veterinary Science** (Agriculture; Agronomy; Forestry; Natural Resources; Soil Science; Veterinary Science); **Science** (Biotechnology; Natural Sciences); **Social Sciences** (Psychology; Social Sciences; Social Work)

School

Communication Studies (Communication Studies; Journalism; Public Relations)

Institute

Sports (Physical Education; Sports)

Further Information: Also 14 branches across the country

History: Founded 1988. A private institution under the supervision of the Corporación Santo Tomás.

Academic Year: March to December

Admission Requirements: Secondary school certificate (Licencia de Educación Media), and entrance examination

Main Language(s) of Instruction: Spanish

Accrediting Agency: National Accreditation Commission (CNA)

Degrees and Diplomas: *Licenciatura*; *Título Profesional*

Student Services: Canteen, Facilities for disabled people, Health Services, Language Laboratory, Library, Social Counselling

Publications: IUS Publicum; Law Faculty Journal

Last Updated: 20/01/16

SCHOOL OF CHARTERED ACCOUNTANTS OF SANTIAGO PROFESSIONAL INSTITUTE

Instituto Profesional Escuela de Contadores Auditores de Santiago

Avenida Providencia 2640, Piso 3, Santiago
Tel: +56(2) 2597-5000
Fax: +56(2) 2231-4996
EMail: info@ecas.cl
Website: http://www.ecas.cl

Rector: Rodrigo Cerón Prandi EMail: rceron@ecas.cl

Directora Académica: Alicia Navarro Cabeza

Department

Accountancy (Accountancy); **Administration** (Administration); **Auditing** (Accountancy); **Computer Science** (Computer Science); **Finance and Economics** (Economics; Finance); **Law** (Law); **Mathematics** (Mathematics); **Social Sciences** (Social Sciences); **Sports** (Sports); **Statistics** (Statistics); **Taxation** (Fiscal Law; Taxation)

Further Information: Also Hernando de Aguirre Campus

History: Founded 1981.

Admission Requirements: High School Diploma (Licencia de enseñanza media)

Main Language(s) of Instruction: Spanish

Accrediting Agency: National Accreditation Commission (CNA)

Degrees and Diplomas: *Título Profesional*

Student Services: Library

Last Updated: 05/01/16

TECHNOLOGICAL UNIVERSITY OF CHILE INACAP

Universidad Tecnológica de Chile INACAP

Av. Vitacura 10.151, Vitacura, Santiago
Tel: +56(2) 2472-3000
EMail: informaciones@inacap.cl
Website: http://www.inacap.cl

Rector: Gonzalo Vargas Otte

Secretarío General: Luis Eduardo Prieto Fernandez de Castro

International Relations: José Joaquín Valenzuela P., Director
EMail: jjvalenzuela@inacap.cl

Area

Arts and Humanities and Education (Arts and Humanities; Education; Educational Psychology; English; Music Education; Social Work; Spanish); **Business and Administration** (Accountancy; Business Administration; Finance; Human Resources; Marketing); **Construction Engineering** (Construction Engineering); **Electrical and Electronical Engineering** (Electrical Engineering; Electronic Engineering; Sound Engineering (Acoustics)); **Health Sciences** (Dietetics; Health Sciences; Nursing; Nutrition; Physical Therapy); **Industrial Engineering** (Industrial Engineering)

Further Information: Also 26 branches across the country

History: Founded 1966 as Technical Training Agency, became Institute 1988. Formerly known as Universidad Tecnológica Vicente Pérez Rosales. Acquired present status 2005.

Academic Year: March to December

Admission Requirements: Secondary school certificate (Licencia de Educación Media) and entrance examination

Main Language(s) of Instruction: Spanish

Accrediting Agency: National Accreditation Commission (CNA)

Degrees and Diplomas: *Bachiller*; *Licenciatura*; *Título Profesional*: **Computer Science; Cooking and Catering; Electrical Engineering; Hotel and Restaurant; Hotel Management; Industrial Management; Management; Occupational Therapy.** *Magister*: **Business Administration; Computer Engineering; Construction Engineering; Development Studies; Higher Education; Information Technology.** Also Diplomado

Student Services: Careers Guidance, Cultural Activities, Social Counselling

Last Updated: 20/01/16

UNIVERSITY ACADEMY OF CHRISTIAN HUMANISM

Universidad Academia de Humanismo Cristiano

Condell 506, Providencia, Santiago

Tel: +56(2) 2787-8000

EMail: admision@academia.cl

Website: http://www.academia.cl

Rector: José Bengoa Cabello EMail: rectoria@academia.cl

Secretarío General: Luis Rivera Contreras
EMail: estudios@academia.cl

Faculty

Arts (Dance; Music; Music Theory and Composition; Performing Arts; Theatre); **Education** (Education; Educational Research; History; Pedagogy; Preschool Education; Teacher Training); **Social Sciences** (Anthropology; Development Studies; Geography; History; International Relations; Journalism; Political Sciences; Psychology; Public Administration; Social Sciences; Social Studies; Social Work; Sociology)

School

Accountancy (Accountancy; Business and Commerce); **Commercial Engineering** (Business and Commerce); **Computer Engineering** (Computer Engineering)

Further Information: Also Brasil Campus in Huérfanos

History: Founded 1975 as Academia de Humanismo Cristiano, became autonomous private university 1988.

Academic Year: March to January (March-August; August-January)

Admission Requirements: Secondary school certificate (Licencia de Educación Media) and entrance examination

Main Language(s) of Instruction: Spanish

Accrediting Agency: National Accreditation Commission (CNA)

Degrees and Diplomas: *Bachiller*; *Licenciatura*: **Cinema and Television.** *Post- título/Diploma*: **Communication Studies; Education; Educational and Student Counselling; Modern Languages; Social Sciences; Social Work; Teacher Training.** *Magister*: **Anthropology; Education; Public Administration; Social Sciences; Social Work; Sociology.** *Doctorado*: **Education.**

Student Services: Library

Last Updated: 07/01/16

UNIVERSITY FOR DEVELOPMENT

Universidad del Desarrollo (UDD)

Av. La Plaza 700, San Carlos de Apoquindo, Las Condes, Santiago

Tel: +56(2) 2327-9110

EMail: internacional@udd.cl

Website: http://www.udd.cl

Rector: Federico Valdés Lafontaine Tel: +56(2) 2327-9159

Secretario General: Gonzalo Rioseco Martínez
Tel: +56(2) 2327-9159

International Relations: Carla Jiménez, Director
Tel: +56(2) 2327-9480 EMail: carlajimenez@udd.cl

Faculty

Architecture and Art (Architecture; Design; Film; Fine Arts; Graphic Design; Theatre); **Communications** (Advertising and Publicity; Journalism); **Economics and Business** (Business Administration; Business and Commerce; Economics; Management; Marketing); **Education** (Education; Modern Languages; Pedagogy; Preschool Education; Primary Education); **Engineering** (Civil Engineering; Engineering; Engineering Management; Industrial Engineering; Mining Engineering)); **Government** (Government; Political Sciences); **Law** *(Santiago)* (Law); **Medicine** *(Clinica Alemana-UDD Santiago)* (Dentistry; Dietetics; Medical Technology; Medicine; Nursing; Nutrition; Physical Therapy; Speech Therapy and Audiology); **Psychology** (Psychology)

Institute

Humanities (Arts and Humanities; Economics; Law; Literature; Mathematics)

Further Information: Also 5 campuses in Santiago and Concepción and 18 Research Centers

History: Founded 1990.

Main Language(s) of Instruction: Spanish

Accrediting Agency: National Accreditation Commission (CNA)

Degrees and Diplomas: *Licenciatura*; *Post- título/Diploma*: **Anaesthesiology; Anatomy; Arts and Humanities; Cardiology; Civil Law; Clinical Psychology; Commercial Law; Communication Studies; Dental Technology; Dentistry; Educational Psychology; Gynaecology and Obstetrics; Health Administration; Mathematics; Medicine; Modern Languages; Neurological Therapy; Neurology; Oral Pathology; Orthodontics; Orthopaedics; Paediatrics; Periodontics; Radiology; Radiophysics; Rehabilitation and Therapy; Social Sciences; Surgery.** *Magister*: **Accountancy; Administration; Arts and Humanities; Business Administration; Clinical Psychology; Commercial Law; Communication Studies; Computer Engineering; Construction Engineering; Curriculum; Design; Education; Educational Administration; Educational Psychology; Educational Testing and Evaluation; Engineering; Environmental Management; Ethics; Finance; Health Administration; Health Sciences; Human Resources; Industrial Engineering; Law; Marketing; Mining Engineering; Nursing; Physical Therapy; Political Sciences; Psychology; Psychotherapy; Rehabilitation and Therapy; Theatre.** *Doctorado*: **Medicine; Social Sciences.**

Student Services: Library

Student Numbers *2014-2015*: Total 16,544

Last Updated: 18/01/16

UNIVERSITY OF CONCEPCIÓN

Universidad de Concepción

Victor Lamas No 1290, Casilla 160-C, Correo 3, Concepción 41

Tel: +56(41) 204-246

Fax: +56(41) 227-455

Website: http://www.udec.cl

Rector: Sergio Lavanchy Merino (1998-)
Tel: +56(41) 2204-246 EMail: slavanc@udec.cl; rector@udec.cl

Secretario General: Rodolfo Walter Diaz
Tel: +56(41) 2204-297 EMail: secretariogeneral@udec.cl

Faculty

Agricultural Engineering (Agricultural Engineering; Agricultural Equipment; Irrigation); **Agronomy** *(Chillán)* (Agronomy; Animal Husbandry; Soil Science; Vegetable Production); **Architecture, Town Planning and Geography** (Architecture; Geography; Town Planning); **Arts and Humanities** (Applied Linguistics; Arts and Humanities; Engraving; Ethics; Fine Arts; Hispanic American Studies; History; Linguistics; Literature; Modern Languages; Painting and Drawing; Philosophy; Sculpture; Spanish; Theatre; Translation and Interpretation); **Biological Sciences** (Biochemistry; Biological and Life Sciences; Microbiology; Pharmacology; Physiology); **Chemistry** (Chemistry; Geology); **Dentistry** (Dentistry; Orthodontics; Periodontics); **Economics and Administration** (Accountancy; Administration; Business and Commerce; Economics; Environmental Management; Environmental Studies; Human Resources; International Business); **Education** (Art Education; Biology; Chemistry; Computer Education; Education; Educational Administration; Educational Sciences; Foreign Languages Education; Geography; History; Humanities and Social Science Education; Mathematics Education; Music Education; Philosophy; Physical Education; Physics; Preschool Education; Science Education; Social Work; Spanish; Special Education); **Engineering** (Aeronautical and Aerospace Engineering; Chemical Engineering; Civil Engineering; Computer Engineering; Computer Science; Electrical Engineering; Electronic Engineering; Engineering; Environmental

Engineering; Hydraulic Engineering; Industrial Engineering; Mechanical Engineering; Metallurgical Engineering; Production Engineering); **Environmental Sciences** (Environmental Engineering; Environmental Studies; Regional Planning; Water Management); **Forestry** (Forestry); **Law and Social Sciences** (Administration; Law; Political Sciences; Social Sciences); **Medicine** (Community Health; Gender Studies; Gerontology; Gynaecology and Obstetrics; Medicine; Nursing; Psychiatry and Mental Health; Psychotherapy; Speech Therapy and Audiology; Surgery; Toxicology); **Oceanography and Natural Sciences** (Biology; Botany; Fishery; Marine Biology; Marine Science and Oceanography; Natural Sciences; Zoology); **Pharmacy** (Biochemistry; Chemistry; Child Care and Development; Dietetics; Pharmacology; Pharmacy); **Physics and Mathematics** (Astronomy and Space Science; Mathematics; Mathematics and Computer Science; Physics; Statistics); **Social Sciences** (Communication Studies; Educational Psychology; Human Resources; Journalism; Psychology; Social and Community Services; Social Policy; Social Sciences; Social Work; Sociology); **Veterinary Medicine** *(Chillán)* (Cattle Breeding; Food Technology; Hygiene; Veterinary Science)

Unit

Academic *(Los Angeles)* (Food Science; Food Technology; Forestry; Surveying and Mapping)

Centre

Environmental Sciences *(Eula-Chile)* (Environmental Management; Environmental Studies)

Further Information: Also Chillán and Los Angeles Campuses

History: Founded 1920 as a private institution and recognized by the State 1980. Financed from State subsidies.

Academic Year: March to December (March-August; August-December)

Admission Requirements: Secondary school certificate (Licencia de Educación Media) or recognized equivalent, and entrance examination (PAA)

Main Language(s) of Instruction: Spanish

Degrees and Diplomas: *Bachiller*, *Título Profesional*: **Accountancy; Education; Forestry; Nursing; Surveying and Mapping.** *Magister*: **Agricultural Engineering; Agronomy; Biochemistry; Botany; Business Administration; Chemical Engineering; Chemistry; Civil Engineering; Clinical Psychology; Computer Education; Computer Engineering; Dentistry; Development Studies; Economics; Education; Educational Administration; Educational Sciences; Electrical Engineering; Engineering; English; Environmental Management; Environmental Studies; Family Studies; Fiscal Law; Fishery; Forestry; Geography; Government; Health Education; Health Sciences; Human Resources; Immunology; Industrial Engineering; Information Technology; Marine Science and Oceanography; Mathematics; Meat and Poultry; Mechanical Engineering; Metallurgical Engineering; Microbiology; Mining Engineering; Natural Resources; Nursing; Nutrition; Pharmacy; Physical Education; Physics; Physiology; Political Sciences; Private Law; Psychology; Social Sciences; Social Work; Soil Science; Statistics; Toxicology; Veterinary Science; Welfare and Protective Services; Zoology.** *Doctorado*: **Agronomy; Analytical Chemistry; Biology; Botany; Cell Biology; Chemical Engineering; Chemistry; Computer Engineering; Computer Science; Education; Electrical Engineering; Energy Engineering; Environmental Management; Environmental Studies; Forestry; Geology; Hispanic American Studies; Irrigation; Linguistics; Literature; Marine Science and Oceanography; Materials Engineering; Mathematics; Metallurgical Engineering; Microbiology; Molecular Biology; Natural Resources; Nursing; Physics; Psychiatry and Mental Health; Psychology; Veterinary Science; Water Management; Water Science.** Also MBA, Diplomado and Especializacion in Medicine and Dentistry

Student Services: Academic Counselling, Canteen, Careers Guidance, Cultural Activities, Facilities for disabled people, Health Services, Language Laboratory, Nursery Care, Social Counselling, Sports Facilities

Publications: Acta Literaria; Agro-Cienca; Atenea; Gayana (4 series); Informe Económico Regional; Paidieia; R.L.A.; Revista de Derecho; Revista de Enfermería; Revista de Historia

Publishing House: Editorial Universidad de Concepción

Last Updated: 13/01/16

UNIVERSITY OF THE ANDES

Universidad de los Andes (UANDES)

Monseñor Álvaro del Portillo 12445, Las Condes, Santiago

Tel: +56(2) 2618-1000

EMail: info@uandes.cl

Website: http://www.uandes.cl

Rector: José Antonio Guzmán C.

Secretario General: Luis Alejandro Silva I.

Faculty

Communication Studies (Communication Studies; Journalism; Linguistics; Literature; Media Studies; Philosophy; Social Sciences); **Economics and Business Administration** (Business Administration; Business and Commerce; Economics; Management; Marketing; Social and Community Services); **Education** (Child Care and Development; Educational Sciences; Linguistics; Literature; Mathematics; Natural Sciences; Pedagogy; Preschool Education; Primary Education; Secondary Education; Social Sciences); **Engineering and Applied Science** (Construction Engineering; Electrical Engineering; Engineering; Industrial Engineering; Mathematics; Physics; Science Education); **Law** (Canon Law; Civil Law; Commercial Law; Constitutional Law; International Law; Labour Law; Law); **Medicine** (Dietetics; Gynaecology and Obstetrics; Medicine; Nutrition; Occupational Therapy; Ophthalmology; Orthopaedics; Paediatrics; Psychiatry and Mental Health; Speech Therapy and Audiology; Surgery); **Nursing and Obstetrics** (Gynaecology and Obstetrics; Nursing); **Odontology** (Dental Technology; Oral Pathology; Periodontics; Stomatology); **Philosophy and Humanities** (Arts and Humanities; History; Literature; Philosophy)

School

Nursing (Health Administration; Health Sciences; Nursing; Philosophy; Public Health); **Psychology** (Clinical Psychology; Educational Psychology; Psychology; Social Psychology); **Service Management** (Arts and Humanities; Business Administration; Science Education; Service Trades)

Institute

Family Studies (Family Studies); **History** (Art History; Education; Heritage Preservation; History)

History: Founded 1989. Acquired present status 2001.

Admission Requirements: Secondary school certificate (Licencia de Educación Media) and national entrance examination (PSU)

Main Language(s) of Instruction: Spanish

Accrediting Agency: National Accreditation Commission (CNA)

Degrees and Diplomas: *Bachiller*: **Mathematics and Computer Science; Natural Sciences.** *Licenciatura*: **Business Administration; Dentistry; Education; Engineering; Journalism; Medicine; Psychology.** *Título Profesional*; *Post- título/Diploma*: **Dentistry; Education; Educational and Student Counselling; English; Family Studies; Health Administration; Law; Mathematics Education; Medicine; Natural Resources; Nursing; Philosophy; Psychology.** *Magister*: **Commercial Law; Communication Arts; Dentistry; Educational Administration; Educational Psychology; Engineering; Engineering Management; English; Epidemiology; Family Studies; Fiscal Law; Health Administration; Heritage Preservation; History; Law; Mathematics Education; Nursing; Philosophy; Psychology; Transport Engineering.** *Doctorado*: **Biomedicine; Communication Studies; History; Law; Philosophy.** Also MBA

Student Services: Academic Counselling, Canteen, Cultural Activities, Facilities for disabled people, Language Laboratory, Library, Social Counselling, Sports Facilities

Last Updated: 14/01/16

UNIVERSITY OF THE PACIFIC

Universidad del Pacífico (UPACIFICO)

Avenida Las Condes 11121, Las Condes, Santiago

Tel: +56(2) 2862-5315

Fax: +56(2) 2862-5318

EMail: info@upacifico.cl

Website: http://www.upacifico.cl

Rector: Gilberto Zárate Barrera

International Relations: Pablo Ortúzar Muñoz, Director
Tel: +56(2) 2862-5232 EMail: portuzar@upacifico.cl

Faculty

Business and Management (Accountancy; Business Administration; Business and Commerce; Management; Marketing; Tourism); **Communication Studies** (Advertising and Publicity; Communication Studies; Journalism; Media Studies; Multimedia; Music; Photography; Public Relations); **Design** (Fashion Design; Graphic Design; Interior Design); **Humanities and Education** (Pedagogy; Psychology; Social Work)

School

Agronomy (Agriculture; Agronomy; Veterinary Science); **Health Science** (Dietetics; Health Sciences; Nursing; Nutrition); **Technical Training** (Business Administration; Computer Graphics; Computer Science; Photography; Social Work; Sports)

Further Information: Also Las Condes and Melipilla Campuses

History: Founded 1976 as Escuela de Publicidad de Chile, became Instituto Profesional del Pacífico in 1982. Acquired present status 1990.

Academic Year: March to December (March-July; August-December)

Admission Requirements: Secondary School Certificate (Licencia de Educación Media), and entrance examination

Main Language(s) of Instruction: Spanish

Accrediting Agency: National Accreditation Commission (CNA)

Degrees and Diplomas: *Técnico de Nivel Superior*, *Licenciatura*: **Business Administration; Journalism; Preschool Education; Social Work.** *Título Profesional*: **Multimedia; Photography.** *Post-título/Diploma*: **Advertising and Publicity; Family Studies; Graphic Design; Social Problems.** *Magister*: **Clinical Psychology; Family Studies; International Business; Marketing; Social Problems.** Also Titulo Universitario (4 yrs) in Advertising/Graphic Design; Public Relations; Textile and Fashion; Media

Student Services: Academic Counselling, Canteen, Careers Guidance, Cultural Activities, Foreign Studies Centre, Language Laboratory, Library, Social Counselling, Sports Facilities

Publications: Revista de Comunicaciones

Last Updated: 18/01/16

VIÑA DEL MAR UNIVERSITY

Universidad de Viña del Mar (UVM)
Diego Portales 90, Recreo, Viña del Mar 2580022
Tel: +56(32) 2462-400
Website: http://www.uvm.cl

Rector: Juan Pablo Prieto Cox
Tel: +56(32) 2462-420/21 EMail: rectoria@uvm.cl

Secretaria General: Paz Valenzuela Céspedes
EMail: rectoria@uvm.cl

International Relations: Carlos Ramírez Sánchez, Vicerrector de Internacionalización y Vinculación Tel: +56(32) 2462-740

School

Agricultural Sciences (Agriculture; Agronomy); **Architecture and Design** (Architecture; Design); **Business Administration** (Accountancy; Business Administration; Business and Commerce; Hotel Management; International Business; Tourism); **Communications** (Journalism; Multimedia; Public Relations); **Education** (Education; Educational Psychology; Foreign Languages Education; Literacy Education; Native Language Education; Physical Education; Preschool Education; Primary Education); **Engineering** (Civil Engineering; Computer Engineering; Construction Engineering; Engineering; Environmental Management; Industrial Engineering; Natural Resources; Safety Engineering); **Health Sciences** (Dentistry; Dietetics; Medical Technology; Nursing; Nutrition; Physical Therapy; Speech Therapy and Audiology; Veterinary Science); **Law and Social Sciences** (Law; Psychology; Social Sciences; Social Work; Sociology); **Veterinary Medicine** (Veterinary Science)

Further Information: Campuses also in Rodelillo, Miraflores, and San Felipe.

History: Founded 1989.

Academic Year: March to December (March-July; August-December)

Admission Requirements: Secondary school certificate (Licencia de Educación Media) or foreign equivalent and entrance examination

Main Language(s) of Instruction: Spanish

Accrediting Agency: National Accreditation Commission (CNA)

Degrees and Diplomas: *Licenciatura*: **Accountancy; Business Administration; Civil Engineering; Construction Engineering; Educational Psychology; Foreign Languages Education; Law; Psychology; Safety Engineering; Social Work.** *Post-título/Diploma*: **Business Administration; Dentistry; Design; Health Administration; Health Sciences; Management.** *Magister*: **Environmental Management; Management; Marketing; Regional Planning; Sports Management; Town Planning.**

Last Updated: 18/01/16

WILHELM VON HUMBOLDT GERMAN PROFESSIONAL INSTITUTE

Instituto Profesional Alemán Wilhelm von Humboldt
Casilla 125 – Correo 30, Nuestra Señora del Rosario 1120, Vitacura, Santiago 765-0682
Tel: +56(2) 2449-0800
Fax: +56(2) 2449-0801
EMail: info@lbi.cl
Website: http://www.lbi.cl

Rector: Alban Schraut EMail: rector@lbi.cl

Vicerrectora Académica: Tanja Olbrich
EMail: dir.academica@lbi.cl

Programme

Education (Education; Pedagogy; Preschool Education; Primary Education)

History: Founded 1988.

Admission Requirements: University Selection Test (PSU), German language test.

Fees: 270.000 per semerster (US Dollar)

Main Language(s) of Instruction: Spanish, German

Degrees and Diplomas: *Título Profesional*. Under agreement with the University San Sebastián, LBI also provides Bachelor of Education.

Student Services: Library

Last Updated: 18/12/15

China

STRUCTURE OF HIGHER EDUCATION SYSTEM

Description:

The State is responsible for the overall planning of higher education. Higher education consists of regular higher education, adult higher education and technical and vocational education and training. The academic degree system is divided into three levels. Since 1992, there have been private universities.

Stages of studies:

University level first stage: *Undergraduate education*

This stage aims at enabling students to master the basic theory, knowledge, skills and know-how and acquiring the capacity for practical and research work in their field of study. Students following these courses are awarded a Bachelor's degree after four years of study.

University level second stage: *Graduate education*

This stage aims at enabling students to master firm basic theory, systematic knowledge, skills, techniques and know-how and acquiring the capacity for practical and scientific research work in their field. Students following these courses are awarded a Master's degree after two to three years' study following a Bachelor's degree and taking the National Entrance Test for MA/MS candidates, and the defence of a thesis.

University level third stage: *Doctoral education*

Students following these courses are awarded a Doctor's degree.

ADMISSION TO HIGHER EDUCATION

Admission to university-level studies:

Name of secondary school credential required: General Ability Test

Admission requirements: National Matriculation Test

Foreign students admission:

Admission requirements: Foreign students must abide by Chinese laws and decrees, comply with the rules and regulations of the universities and colleges where they study, and respect Chinese customs. Undergraduate students should possess a degree equivalent to the Chinese high school diploma and be under 30 years of age. Master degree students should possess a degree equivalent to the Chinese Bachelor's degree and be under 35 years of age. The Candidate's diploma needs to be evaluated and accredited. Doctor's degree students should possess a degree equivalent to the Chinese Master degree and be under 40 years of age. They must be recommended by two full or associate professors and approved by the university where they want to study. Some tests administered by the Chinese Embassy in the country of the applicant might have to be taken.

Language proficiency: Students must pass the Chinese Proficiency Test.

RECOGNITION OF STUDIES

Quality assurance system:

The Higher Education Evaluation Center of the Ministry of Education is responsible for the evaluation of the first cycle of higher education. The Academic Degree Committee of the Ministry of Education is responsible for the evaluation of second and third cycles of higher education.

Bodies dealing with recognition:

China Academic Degrees and Graduate Education Information - CDGDC

B17 Tongfang Scientific Building, No. 1 Wangzhuang Road, Haidian District
Beijing 100083
Tel: +86(10) 8237-8812
Fax: +86(10) 8237-9482
EMail: bgs@cdgdc.edu.cn
WWW: http://www.cdgdc.edu.cn

NATIONAL BODIES

Ministry of Education

Minister: Yuan Guiren
No. 37 Damucang Hutong, Xidan
Beijing 100816
Tel: +86(10) 6609-6114
EMail: english@moe.edu.cn
WWW: http://www.moe.edu.cn
Role of national body: To draw up strategies, policies and plans for educational reform and development; and to draft relevant rules and regulations, and supervise their implementation.

Ministry of Science and Technology

Minister: Gang Wan
15B, Fuxing Road
Beijing 100862
WWW: http://www.most.gov.cn/eng

China Education Association for International Exchange - CEAIE

President: Zhang Xinsheng
Secretary-General: Sheng Jianxue
No. 37, Damucang Hutong, Xicheng District
Beijing 100816
Tel: +86(10) 6641-6080
Fax: +86(10) 6641-1885
EMail: secretariat@ceaie.edu.cn
WWW: http://www.ceaie.edu.cn
Role of national body: Nationwide not-for-profit organization affiliated to the Ministry of Education in charge of international educational exchanges and cooperation.

China Academic Degrees and Graduate Education Information - CDGDC

Director-General: Li Jun
B17 Tongfang Scientific Building, No. 1 Wangzhuang Road, Haidian District
Beijing 100083
Tel: +86(10) 8237-8812
Fax: +86(10) 8237-9482
EMail: bgs@cdgdc.edu.cn
WWW: http://www.cdgdc.edu.cn
Role of national body: CDGDC constructs and administrates the National Academic Degrees and Graduate Education Data Center. It is also a consultative committee on issues related to academic degrees and graduate education.

Data for academic year: 2013-2014
Source: IAU from the website of the Ministry of Education, 2014. Bodies 2016.

INSTITUTIONS

AGRICULTURAL UNIVERSITY OF HEBEI (AUH)

289 Lingyusi Sreet, Baoding, Hebei Province 071001
Tel: +86(312) 7521823
Fax: +86(312) 7521217
EMail: fauh@hebau.edu.cn
Website: http://www.hebau.edu.cn

President: Wang Zhigang Tel: +86(312) 2091286

College

Adult Education (Adult Education); **Agronomy** (Agronomy); **Animal Science and Technology** (Animal Husbandry; Technology; Zoology); **Arts** (Fine Arts); **Basic Sciences** (Chemistry; Mathematics; Physics); **Economics and Trade** (Business and Commerce; Economics); **Food Science & Technology** (Food Science; Technology); **Foreign Languages** (English; Japanese); **Forestry** (Forestry); **Humanities Adult Education** (Adult Education; Arts and Humanities); **Information Science and Technology** (Information Sciences; Information Technology); **Knowledge and Practice**; **Landscape Architecture and Tourism** (Landscape Architecture; Tourism); **Life Sciences** (Biochemistry; Biological and Life Sciences; Botany; Molecular Biology; Pharmacology); **Mechanical and Electrical Engineering** (Electrical Engineering; Mechanical Engineering); **Modern Science and Technology** (Technology); **Natural Resources and Environment Sciences** (Environmental Studies; Natural Resources); **Ocean** (Aquaculture; Marine Biology; Marine Science and Oceanography); **Plant Protection, Gardening, Forestry and Tourism** (Forestry; Landscape Architecture; Plant and Crop Protection; Tourism); **Rural Development** (Rural Planning); **Technical and Vocational Education** (Vocational Education); **Traditional Chinese Veterinary Medicine** (Traditional Eastern Medicine; Veterinary Science); **Urban and Rural Construction** (Building Technologies; Rural Studies; Urban Studies)

School

Business (Business and Commerce); **Postgraduate**

Further Information: Also campuses in Qinghuangdao, Huanghua, Dingzhou.

History: Founded 1902. Acquired present status 1958.

Academic Year: September to July

Admission Requirements: Graduation from senior high school and entrance examination

Fees: (Yuan): 16,000-27,000 per annum

Main Language(s) of Instruction: Chinese

Accrediting Agency: Ministry of Education; Hebei Provincial Education Department

Degrees and Diplomas: *Zhuanke*; *Xueshi Xuewei*; *Shuoshi Xuewei*; *Boshi*: **Agricultural Economics; Agricultural Management; Agronomy; Botany; Crop Production; Plant Pathology.**

Student Services: Academic Counselling, Canteen, Careers Guidance, Cultural Activities, Health Services, Language Laboratory, Nursery Care, Social Counselling, Sports Facilities

Publications: Academic Journal; Academic Journal on Forestry; Education in Agriculture and Forestry of Hebei; Hebei Village and Town Construction; Scientific and Technical Development in Rural Areas

Last Updated: 20/11/12

ANHUI AGRICULTURAL UNIVERSITY (AHAU)

130 West Changjiang Road, Hefei, Anhui Province 230036
Tel: +86(551) 2823720
Fax: +86(551) 5120833
EMail: ioff@ahau.edu.cn
Website: http://www.ahau.edu.cn

President: Xiaochun Wan
Tel: +86(551) 2843266 EMail: president@ahau.edu.cn

School

Agronomy (Agriculture; Agronomy; Plant and Crop Protection); **Animal Science** (Animal Husbandry; Aquaculture; Fishery; Veterinary Science); **Continuing Education** (Arts and Humanities; Economics; Engineering; Environmental Engineering; Law; Management); **Economics and Technology** (Automation and Control Engineering; Biological and Life Sciences; Business and Commerce; Computer Science; English Studies; Finance; Landscape Architecture; Law); **Economics and Trade** *(Detached)* (Finance; International Business); **Engineering** (Agricultural Equipment; Information Technology; Machine Building); **Foreign Languages** (English; Japanese); **Forestry and Landscape Architecture** (Forestry; Landscape Architecture; Town Planning; Wood Technology); **Horticulture** (Horticulture); **Humanities and Social Sciences** (Law; Literature; Social Sciences); **Information and Computer Science** (Business Computing; Computer Science; Technology; Telecommunications Engineering); **Life Science** (Biological and Life Sciences; Biology; Biophysics; Microbiology; Sericulture; Traditional Eastern Medicine); **Light Industry and Art Design** (Design; Packaging Technology; Textile Design; Textile Technology); **Management** (Agricultural Economics; Management); **Modern AG Technology and Management** (Agricultural Engineering; Agricultural Management); **Natural Sciences** (Applied Chemistry; Computer Science; Information Sciences); **Plant Protection** (Agricultural Engineering; Biotechnology; Environmental Engineering; Environmental Studies; Plant and Crop Protection); **Resources and Environment** (Agriculture; Ecology; Environmental Engineering; Environmental Studies; Meteorology; Natural Resources; Soil Science); **Senior Vocational Education** (Accountancy; Agricultural Economics; Agricultural Engineering; Agronomy; Animal Husbandry; Bioengineering; Biotechnology; English; Forestry; Horticulture; Information Sciences; Japanese; Sericulture; Social Sciences); **Tea and Food Technology** (Food Technology)

Department

Physical Education (Physical Education)

History: Founded 1928 as Agricultural College of Anhui National University. Acquired present name 1995.

Academic Year: September to July (September-January; March-July)

Admission Requirements: Local students: admission tests by National Testing Centre; Overseas students: previous diploma or degree

Main Language(s) of Instruction: Chinese

Accrediting Agency: Anhui Educational Department

Degrees and Diplomas: *Zhuanke*; *Xueshi Xuewei*: **Engineering; Fine Arts; Management; Medicine.** *Shuoshi Xuewei*: **Engineering; Management; Medicine.** *Boshi*: **Animal Husbandry; Crop Production; Microbiology.**

Student Services: Academic Counselling, Canteen, Careers Guidance, Cultural Activities, Foreign Studies Centre, Health Services, Language Laboratory, Nursery Care, Sports Facilities

Publications: Journal of Agricultural Statistics; Journal of Anhui Agricultural University; Journal of Biomathematics

Last Updated: 23/11/12

ANHUI MEDICAL UNIVERSITY (AHMU)

81 Meishan Road, Hefei, Anhui Province 230032
Tel: +86(551) 2813965
Fax: +86(551) 2813965
EMail: ayddwsj@ahmu.edu.cn
Website: http://www.ahmu.edu.cn

President: Zhang Xuejun (2006-)
Tel: +86(551) 5161002 EMail: ayzxj@vip.sina.com

College

Clinical Medicine (Medicine; Nursing; Pharmacology; Pharmacy; Public Health)

School

First School of Clinical Medicine (Laboratory Techniques; Medicine; Psychiatry and Mental Health; Psychology; Rehabilitation and Therapy); **General Education** (Computer Science; Foreign Languages Education; Linguistics; Literature; Physical Education);

Humanities and Social Science (Arts and Humanities; Social Sciences); **International Education** (Foreigners Education; International Relations); **Life Science** (Biology; Biomedical Engineering; Physics); **Medical Sciences** (Medicine); **Pharmacy** (Pharmacology; Pharmacy; Traditional Eastern Medicine); **Public Health** (Child Care and Development; Epidemiology; Hygiene; Public Health; Toxicology); **Public Health Administration** (Health Administration; Public Health); **School of Adult and Continuing Education** (Adult Education; Continuing Education); **Stomatology** (Stomatology)

History: Founded 1926 as Shangai Southeast Medical College. Moved to Huaiyuan Country 1949, Anhui Province and moved 1952 to Hefei to become Anhui Medical College. Acquired present title 1996.

Main Language(s) of Instruction: Chinese

Accrediting Agency: Ministry of Education

Degrees and Diplomas: *Xueshi Xuewei*; *Shuoshi Xuewei*; *Boshi*: **Medicine; Pharmacology.**

Publications: Chinese Rural Health Service Management Magazine; Journal of Anhui Medical University; Journal of Clinical Medicine and Pathology; Journal of Clinical Orthopedics; Journal of Disease Control; Journal of Lungs; Journal of Nursing; Journal of Ophthalmology; Journal of Surgery

Last Updated: 26/11/12

ANHUI NORMAL UNIVERSITY (AHNU)

1 Renmin Road, Wuhu, Anhui Province 241003
Tel: +86(553) 5910027
Fax: +86(553) 3839452
EMail: president@mail.ahnu.edu.cn
Website: http://www.ahnu.edu.cn

President: Lun Wang

College

Chemistry and Materials Science (Chemistry); **History and Society** (History; Sociology); **Land Resources and Tourism** (Natural Resources; Tourism); **Liberal Arts** (Arts and Humanities); **Physics and Electronic Information** (Electronic Engineering; Physics)

School

Adult Education (Adult Education); **Economics and Management** (Economics; Management); **Environmental Science** (Environmental Studies); **Foreign Studies** (English; Foreign Languages Education; French; Japanese; Literature; Russian); **Life Sciences** (Biological and Life Sciences)

Department

Administration (Administration); **Chinese Language and Literature** (Chinese); **Computer Science** (Computer Science); **Economics** (Economics); **Education** (Education); **Educational Technology** (Educational Technology); **Electronic and Information Engineering** (Electronic Engineering; Information Technology); **Geography** (Geography); **Journalism** (Journalism); **Law** (Law); **Mathematics** (Mathematics); **Sociology** (Sociology)

Institute

International Education (Foreigners Education); **Media** (Media Studies); **Physical Education** (Physical Education); **Politics and Law Institute** (Law; Political Sciences)

Academy

Fine Arts (Fine Arts); **Music** (Music)

Research Centre

Analytical Test (Chemistry); **Anatomy** (Anatomy); **Basic Education** (Education); **Environmental Science** (Environmental Studies); **Examination** (Educational Testing and Evaluation); **Higher Education** (Higher Education)

Research Institute

Biology (Biology); **Chinese Language** (Chinese); **Classics** (Archaeology; Art History; History; Linguistics; Literature; Philosophy); **Computer Science** (Computer Science); **Educational Sciences** (Educational Sciences); **Geography** (Geography); **Organic Chemistry** (Organic Chemistry); **Sociology** (Sociology); **Traditional Culture** (Cultural Studies)

History: Founded 1928 as National Anhui University. Acquired present status 1970 and present title 1972. Under the jurisdiction of the National Education Commission and of the Provincial Government.

Academic Year: September to July (September-January; February-July)

Admission Requirements: Graduation from senior middle school and entrance examination

Main Language(s) of Instruction: Chinese

Accrediting Agency: Ministry of Education

Degrees and Diplomas: *Xueshi Xuewei*; *Shuoshi Xuewei*; *Boshi*

Publications: Journal of Anhui Normal University; Learning Chinese; Mathematics for Middle School Students; Middle School Chemistry; Moral Education Research

Last Updated: 21/01/13

ANHUI POLYTECHNIC UNIVERSITY

Beijing Middle Road, Wuhu, Anhui Province 241000
Tel: +86(553) 2871201
Fax: +86(553) 2871091
Website: http://www.ahpu.edu.cn

President: Wang Xueqian

International Relations: Ma Jian

School

Adult Education (Adult Education); **Career Technology** (Technology)

Department

Applied Mathematics and Physics (Applied Mathematics; Applied Physics); **Art and Design** (Industrial Design; Interior Design); **Biochemical Engineering** (Bioengineering; Chemical Engineering; Food Science; Food Technology); **Computer Science and Engineering** (Computer Engineering; Computer Science); **Electrical Engineering** (Automation and Control Engineering; Electrical Engineering; Electronic Engineering; Information Technology); **Foreign Languages** (Modern Languages); **Humanities and Social Science** (Humanities and Social Science Education); **Management Engineering** (Business Administration; Industrial Engineering); **Mechanical Engineering** (Automation and Control Engineering; Engineering Drawing and Design; Engineering Management; Materials Engineering; Mechanical Engineering); **Physical Education** (Physical Education); **Textile Engineering and Clothes Design** (Design; Textile Technology)

History: Founded 1935 as a Spanish Catholic private vocational school. Formerly known as Anhui University of Technology and Science. Acquired present title 2007.

Main Language(s) of Instruction: Chinese

Degrees and Diplomas: *Xueshi Xuewei*; *Shuoshi Xuewei*

Last Updated: 22/01/13

ANHUI SCIENCE AND TECHNOLOGY UNIVERSITY (ASHTU)

Eastern Suburb of Bengbu, Fengyang, Anhui Province 233100
Tel: +86(550) 6732001
Fax: +86(550) 6733165
EMail: mayer123321@163.com
Website: http://www.ahstu.edu.cn/

President: Shen Taiji

College

Animal Science (Animal Husbandry; Hygiene; Traditional Eastern Medicine; Veterinary Science); **Engineering** (Electronic Engineering; Food Science; Machine Building; Mechanical Engineering; Nutrition; Transport Engineering); **Foreign Languages** (English); **Life Science** (Bioengineering; Biology; Environmental Engineering; Horticulture; Landscape Architecture); **Literature and Laws** (Law; Literature; Public Law); **Management** (Accountancy; Business Administration; Business and Commerce; Finance; Management; Marketing; Rural Planning); **Plant Science** (Agriculture; Agronomy; Farm Management); **Sciences** (Chemistry; Computer Science)

Department

Physical Education (Physical Education)

History: Founded 1950 as North Anhui Advanced Agriculture and Forestry School. Formerly known as Anhui Agrotechnical Teachers College.

Main Language(s) of Instruction: Chinese

Accrediting Agency: Ministry of Education

Degrees and Diplomas: *Xueshi Xuewei*

Student Services: Sports Facilities

Publications: Journal of Anhui Science & Technology University

Last Updated: 23/11/12

ANHUI UNIVERSITY (AHU)

No. 111 Jiulong Road, Hefei, Anhui Province 230601
Tel: +86(551)63861610
Fax: +86(551) 63861610
EMail: xum@ahu.edu.cn
Website: http://www.ahu.edu.cn

President: Huang Dekuan

International Relations: Xu Ming

School

Adult Education (Adult Education); **Arts** (Chinese; History; Journalism; Philosophy); **Chemistry and Chemical Engineering** (Applied Chemistry; Chemical Engineering; Chemistry); **Economics** (Accountancy; Business Administration; Economics; Finance; International Business); **Electrical Engineering and Information Science** (Automation and Control Engineering; Computer Science; Electrical Engineering; Information Sciences; Technology); **Foreign Studies** (English; Russian); **Law** (Law); **Life Science** (Biological and Life Sciences; Biology); **Management** (Archiving; Library Science; Management; Public Administration); **Mathematics and Physics** (Mathematics; Physics); **Teacher Training** (Computer Science; English; Military Science; Physical Education)

Research Institute

Ancient Books Collation and Publication (Ancient Books); **Applied Chemistry** (Applied Chemistry); **Artificial Intelligence** (Artificial Intelligence); **Automation** (Automation and Control Engineering); **Chinese Language and Sinology** (Chinese; Cultural Studies; South Asian Studies); **Computer Application and Recognition Technology** (Computer Science); **Demography** (Demography and Population); **Economic Development** (Economics); **Electronics and Communication Technologies** (Electronic Engineering; Telecommunications Engineering); **Oceanic Literature** (Literature); **Polymer Material** (Polymer and Plastics Technology); **Russian Studies** (Eastern European Studies)

Further Information: Also Hospital; courses for foreign students

History: Founded 1928.

Academic Year: September to July

Admission Requirements: Graduation from senior middle school and entrance examination

Main Language(s) of Instruction: Chinese, English

Degrees and Diplomas: *Xueshi Xuewei*; *Shuoshi Xuewei*; *Boshi*

Publications: Ancient Book Studies; Anhui Population; Anhui University Journal; Russian Studies

Publishing House: Anhui University Publishing House

Last Updated: 21/01/13

ANHUI UNIVERSITY OF ARCHITECTURE (AIAI)

856 Jinzhai Road, Baohe District, Hefei,
Anhui Province 230022
Tel: +86(551) 3313028
Fax: +86(551) 3517457
Website: http://www.aiai.edu.cn/

President: Cheng Hua EMail: ch@aiai.edu.cn

College

Continuing Education (Continuing Education)

School

Adult Education (Adult Education); **Architecture** (Architecture; Design; Landscape Architecture; Town Planning); **Civil Engineering** (Civil Engineering; Mechanical Engineering); **Electronic and Information Engineering** (Computer Engineering; Electronic Engineering); **Environmental Engineering** (Environmental Engineering; Irrigation; Natural Resources; Water Management); **Materials and Chemical Engineering** (Chemical Engineering; Materials Engineering)

Department

Arts (Design); **Electromechanical Engineering** (Automation and Control Engineering; Electrical Engineering; Mechanical Engineering); **Foreign Language Studies** (English); **Law and Politics** (Human Resources; Law); **Management Engineering** (Accountancy; Business Administration; Engineering Management; Finance; Marketing); **Mathematics and Physics** (Applied Physics; Computer Science; Information Sciences)

History: Founded 1958 as Anhui Institute of Architecture.

Main Language(s) of Instruction: Chinese

Accrediting Agency: Ministry of Education

Degrees and Diplomas: *Xueshi Xuewei*; *Shuoshi Xuewei*: **Architecture; Civil Engineering; Environmental Engineering; Environmental Studies.**

Last Updated: 23/11/12

ANHUI UNIVERSITY OF FINANCE AND ECONOMICS (AUFE)

255 Hongye Road, Bengbu, Anhui Province 233041
Tel: +86(552) 3170010
Fax: +86(552) 3170010
EMail: wsb@aufe.edu.cn
Website: http://www.aufe.edu.cn

President: Ding Zhongming

International Relations: Sun Xuebin

Faculty

Law (Law)

School

Accountancy (Accountancy); **Business** (Business and Commerce); **Economics** (Economics); **Finance** (Finance); **Finance and Public Administration** (Finance; Public Administration); **Foreign Languages** (Foreign Languages Education); **Information Engineering** (Information Technology); **International Economics and Trade** (International Economics); **Literature, Art and Media** (Media Studies); **Management** (Management); **Politics** (Political Sciences); **Statistics and Applied Economics** (Economics; Statistics)

Research Centre

Accounting Financial Development (Accountancy; Finance); **Consumer's Behavior** *(RCCB)* (Consumer Studies); **Enterprise Information Management** (Private Administration; Public Administration); **Entrepreneurship and Business Growth** *(RCEBG)* (Business and Commerce); **International Law and International Tax Law** (International Law; Taxation); **Logistics and Supply Chain Management** (Transport Management); **Rural Public Policies** *(RCRPP)* (Rural Studies); **SOE Management** *(RCSM)* (Public Administration)

Research Institute

Applied Mathematics (Applied Mathematics); **Applied Statistics** (Statistics); **Circulation of Economic Research** (Business and Commerce); **Company Economy** (Economics); **Cotton Project** (Crop Production; Textile Technology); **Economies at County Level** (Economics; Public Administration); **Government and Nonprofit organization Accounting** (Accountancy; Government; Institutional Administration); **History and Culture** *(HCRI)* (Cultural Studies; History); **Modern Finance** *(RIMF)* (Finance); **Rural Economic and Social Development** (Development Studies; Rural Studies); **Trade and Industry Development** *(RITID)* (Business and Commerce)

History: Founded 1959 as Anhui Commercial Institute. Renamed Anhui University of Finance and Trade 1978. Acquired present title 2004.

Main Language(s) of Instruction: Chinese

Degrees and Diplomas: *Xueshi Xuewei*; *Shuoshi Xuewei*

Student Services: Sports Facilities

Publications: Finance and Trade Research

Last Updated: 21/01/13

ANHUI UNIVERSITY OF SCIENCE AND TECHNOLOGY (AUST)

Shungeng Road 168, Huainan, Anhui Province 232001
Tel: +86(554) 6668842
Fax: +86(554) 6668927
EMail: xiaoban@aust.edu.cn
Website: http://www.aust.edu.cn

President: Yan Shilong

Faculty

Education (Education); **Science** (Applied Mathematics; Applied Physics; Computer Engineering; Information Technology; Mathematics; Mechanics; Physics)

College

Foreign Languages (Modern Languages); **Humanities and Social Sciences** (Humanities and Social Science Education)

School

Advanced Professional Technology Education (Technology Education); **Chemical Engineering** (Chemical Engineering); **Civil Engineering and Architecture** (Architecture; Civil Engineering); **Computer Science and Engineering** (Computer Science; Engineering Management); **Earth and Environment** (Environmental Engineering; Natural Resources); **Economics and Management** (Economics; Management); **Electrical and Information Engineering** (Electrical Engineering); **Materials Science and Engineering** (Materials Engineering); **Mechanical Engineering** (Mechanical Engineering); **Medicine** (Medicine)

Institute

Energy and Safety (Energy Engineering; Safety Engineering); **Surveying and Mapping** (Surveying and Mapping)

History: Founded 2002 as a merger of East China Coal Medical College and Huainan Chemical Engineering College.

Main Language(s) of Instruction: Chinese

Degrees and Diplomas: *Xueshi Xuewei*; *Shuoshi Xuewei*; *Boshi*
Last Updated: 21/01/13

ANHUI UNIVERSITY OF TECHNOLOGY (AHUT)

59 Lake Road East, Ma'anshan, Anhui Province 240302
Tel: +86(555) 2311691
Fax: +86(555) 2473747
EMail: xiaoban@ahut.edu.cn; foreign@ahut.edu.cn
Website: http://www.ahut.edu.cn

President: Cen Yuwan

College

Continuing Education (Continuing Education)

School

Arts and Law (Law; Literature; Management; Public Administration; Social Sciences); **Chemistry and Chemical Engineering** (Applied Chemistry; Chemical Engineering; Polymer and Plastics Technology); **Civil Engineering and Architecture** (Architecture; Civil Engineering); **Computer Science** (Computer Networks; Computer Science; Software Engineering); **Economics** (Economics; Finance; International Business; Statistics); **Electrical Engineering and Information** (Automation and Control Engineering; Electrical Engineering); **Foreign Languages** (Modern Languages); **Management** (Accountancy; Business Administration; Finance; Marketing); **Management Science and Engineering** (Management Systems); **Materials Science and Engineering** (Materials Engineering); **Mathematics and Physics** (Mathematics; Physics); **Mechanical Engineering** (Automotive Engineering; Industrial Design; Mechanical Engineering); **Metallurgy and Resources** (Metallurgical Engineering; Thermal Engineering)

History: Founded 1977 as Ma'anshan School of Iron and Steel Industry. Renamed East China University of Metallurgy 1985. Acquired present title 2000.

Main Language(s) of Instruction: Chinese

Degrees and Diplomas: *Xueshi Xuewei*; *Shuoshi Xuewei*; *Boshi*

Publications: Journal
Last Updated: 22/01/13

ANHUI UNIVERSITY OF TRADITIONAL CHINESE MEDICINE (AHTCM)

103 Meishan Road, Hefei, Anhui Province 230038
Tel: +86(551) 5169289
Fax: +86(551) 2819950
EMail: azywb@yahoo.com.cn
Website: http://www.ahtcm.edu.cn

President: Wang Jian
International Relations: Zhang Si-hong

School

Acupuncture and Osteology (Acupuncture; Alternative Medicine; Osteopathy); **Continuing Education** (Continuing Education); **Integrated Traditional Chinese and Western Medicine** (Medicine; Traditional Eastern Medicine); **Medical Economics and Management** (Economics; Health Administration; Management); **Medical Information Technology** (Information Technology); **Nursing** (Nursing); **Pharmacy** (Pharmacology; Pharmacy); **Traditional Chinese Medicine** (Traditional Eastern Medicine)

Department

Social Sciences (Social Sciences)

History: Founded 1959 as Anhui Advanced School of Traditional Chinese Medicine. Acquired present title 1976.

Admission Requirements: High school diplomas or certificates. Chinese proficiency test

Main Language(s) of Instruction: Chinese and Chinese Mandarin

Degrees and Diplomas: *Xueshi Xuewei*: **Acupuncture; Computer Science; Information Management; International Business; International Economics; Medicine; Nursing; Pharmacology; Pharmacy; Psychology; Traditional Eastern Medicine.** *Shuoshi Xuewei*: **Acupuncture; Gynaecology and Obstetrics; Health Sciences; History; Literature; Medicine; Orthopaedics; Paediatrics; Pharmacology; Pharmacy; Surgery; Traditional Eastern Medicine.**

Last Updated: 22/01/13

ANQING NORMAL UNIVERSITY

128 Linghu South Road, Anqing, Anhui Province 246011
Tel: +86(556) 5500789
Fax: +86(556) 5500789
EMail: waish@aqtc.edu.cn
Website: http://www.aqtc.edu.cn/

President: Zhu Shiqun

School

Chemistry and Chemical Industry (Chemical Engineering; Chemistry); **Computer and Information** (Communication Studies; Computer Science; Information Management); **Economics Management** (Economics; International Business; Marketing); **Education** (Educational Technology; Journalism; Preschool Education; Psychology); **Environmental Resources** (Environmental Studies; Geography); **Foreign Languages** (English; French); **Humanities** (Arts and Humanities; Chinese; Journalism); **Humanities and Society** (History; Humanities and Social Science Education; Social Work); **Law and Politics** (Law; Political Sciences); **Life Science** (Biological and Life Sciences); **Mathematics** (Applied Mathematics; Mathematics; Science Education); **Music** (Music; Opera); **Painting** (Design; Leisure Studies; Painting and Drawing); **Physical Education** (Physical Education); **Physics and Electronic Engineering** (Automation and Control Engineering; Electronic Engineering; Physics)

History: Founded 1928 as Anhui University and then Anqing Teachers College. Acquired present title 1980.

Main Language(s) of Instruction: Chinese

Degrees and Diplomas: *Xueshi Xuewei*
Last Updated: 24/01/13

ANSHAN NORMAL UNIVERSITY

43 Ping'an Street, Tiedong District,
Anshan, Liaoning Province 114005
Tel: +86(412) 5847025
Fax: +86(412) 5847019
EMail: webmaster@mail.asnc.edu.cn
Website: http://www.asnc.edu.cn/

President: Song Hui

College

Liberal Arts (History; Linguistics; Literature; Mathematics; Philosophy; Psychology; Science Education); **Physical Science and Technology** (Physics)

School

Business (Accountancy; Economics; Finance; Law); **Education Science and Technology** (Education); **Health** (Midwifery; Nursing; Pharmacy; Traditional Eastern Medicine); **Music** (Music); **Social Development** (Social and Community Services)

Department

Foreign Languages (English); **Physical Education** (Physical Education); **Politics and History** (History; Political Sciences)

Institute

Chemistry and Life Sciences (Chemistry); **Mathematics and Information Science** (Applied Mathematics; Computer Science; Mathematics; Technology)

Academy

Fine Arts (Performing Arts; Visual Arts)

Centre

Computing (Computer Engineering)

History: Founded 1958 as Anshan Teachers College. Acquired present title 1993.

Main Language(s) of Instruction: Chinese

Degrees and Diplomas: *Xueshi Xuewei*
Last Updated: 24/01/13

BAICHENG NORMAL COLLEGE

9 Zhongxing Dong Road, Baicheng, Jilin Province 137000
Tel: +86(436) 3243802
Fax: +86(436) 3223381
EMail: teachinbaicheng@hotmail.com
Website: http://www.bcsfxy.com

President: Ren Feng-Chun

Department

Biology (Biology); **Chemistry** (Chemistry); **Chinese Languages and Literature** (Chinese); **Civil Engineering** (Civil Engineering); **Computer Science** (Computer Science); **Economics and Management** (Economics; Management); **Education Sciences** (Education; Educational Sciences); **Fine Arts** (Fine Arts); **Foreign Languages and Literature** (Modern Languages); **Geography** (Geography); **History** (History); **Mathematics** (Mathematics); **Mechanical and Electronic Engineering** (Electronic Engineering; Mechanical Engineering); **Music** (Music); **Physical Education** (Physical Education); **Physics** (Physics); **Politics and Law** (Law; Political Sciences)

History: Founded 1958. Acquired present title 2000.

Main Language(s) of Instruction: Chinese

Degrees and Diplomas: *Xueshi Xuewei*
Last Updated: 21/03/13

BAOJI UNIVERSITY OF ARTS AND SCIENCES

No. 1 Hi-Tech Avenue, Baoji, Shaanxi Province 721013
Tel: +86(917) 3566366
EMail: webmaster@bjwlxy.edu.cn
Website: http://www.bjwlxy.cn
President: Wang Zhigang

Department

Chemistry and Chemical Engineering (Chemical Engineering; Chemistry); **Chinese and Literature** (Chinese; Literature); **Computer Science** (Computer Science); **Economic Management** (Management); **Education** (Education); **Electromechanical Engineering** (Electronic Engineering; Mechanical Engineering); **Electronic and Electrical Engineering** (Electrical and Electronic Engineering); **Fine Arts** (Fine Arts); **Foreign Languages and Literature** (English; Modern Languages); **Geography and Environmental Economics** (Economics; Environmental Studies); **History** (History); **Mathematics** (Applied Mathematics; Mathematics); **Music** (Music); **Philosophy** (Philosophy; Social Sciences; Teacher Trainers Education); **Physical Education** (Physical Education); **Physics** (Physics); **Politics and Law** (Law; Political Sciences)

History: Founded 1958 as Baoji University. Baoji Teachers College 1978. Acquired present title 1992.

Main Language(s) of Instruction: Chinese

Degrees and Diplomas: *Xueshi Xuewei*
Last Updated: 08/02/13

BEIFANG UNIVERSITY OF NATIONALITIES

204 North Wenchang Road, New District,
Yinchuan, Ningxia Province 750021
Tel: +86(951) 2066335
Fax: +86(951) 2066992
EMail: bfmdzs@163.com
Website: http://www.nwsni.edu.cn

President: Xie Yujie

International Relations: Yang Ming

Department

Chinese (Chinese); **Computer Science**; **Electronic Engineering and Information Technology** (Electronic Engineering; Information Technology); **History** (History); **Law** (Law); **Management** (Management); **Modern Languages**

History: Founded 1984.

Degrees and Diplomas: *Xueshi Xuewei*; *Shuoshi Xuewei*
Last Updated: 22/11/12

BEIHANG UNIVERSITY (BUAA)

37 XueYuan Road, HaiDian District, Beijing 100083
Tel: +86(10) 82317658
EMail: webmaster@buaa.edu.cn
Website: http://www.buaa.edu.cn

President: Huai Jinpeng

School

Advanced Engineering (Engineering); **Aeronautical Science and Engineering** (Aeronautical and Aerospace Engineering); **Applied Technology** *(BUAA-Haidan)* (Technology); **Astronautics** (Astronomy and Space Science); **Automation Science and Electrical Engineering** (Automation and Control Engineering; Electrical Engineering); **Computer Science and Engineering** (Computer Engineering; Computer Science; Engineering); **Continuing Education** (Continuing Education); **Distant Learning** (Distance Education); **Economics and Management** (Economics; Management); **Electronic Information Engineering** (Electronic Engineering); **Flying** (Aeronautical and Aerospace Engineering); **Humanities and Social Sciences** (Arts and Humanities; Social Sciences); **Instrumentation Science and Opto-electronics Engineering** (Instrument Making; Optical Technology); **Jet Propulsion** (Aeronautical and Aerospace Engineering; Thermal Engineering); **Law** (Law); **Materials Science and Engineering** (Materials Engineering); **Mechanical Engineering and Automation** (Automation and Control Engineering; Mechanical Engineering); **Science** (Natural Sciences); **Software** (Software Engineering); **Vocational Techniques** (Vocational Education)

Department

Automobile Engineering (Automotive Engineering); **Biological Engineering** (Bioengineering); **Civil Engineering** (Civil Engineering); **Foreign Languages** (Modern Languages); **Project Systems Engineering** (Computer Engineering)

History: Founded as Beijing Institute of Aeronautics 1952. Renamed Beijing University of Aeronautics and Astronautics 1988. Acquired present title 2002.

Academic Year: September to July (September-January; February-July)

Admission Requirements: Graduation from senior middle school and entrance examination

Main Language(s) of Instruction: Chinese

Accrediting Agency: Ministry of Industry and Information Technology

Degrees and Diplomas: *Xueshi Xuewei*; *Shuoshi Xuewei*

Publications: Acta Aeronautica et Astronautica Sinica; Acta Materiae Compositae Sinica; Aerospace Knowledge; China Aeronautical Education; Journal of Aerospace Power; Journal of Beijing University of Aeronautics and Astronautics; Journal of Engineering Graphics; Model World

Publishing House: BUAA Publishing House

Last Updated: 11/02/13

BEIHUA UNIVERSITY

No. 3999 Huashan Road, Jilin, Jilin Province 132013
Tel: +86(432) 4683797
Fax: +86(432) 4602163
EMail: bhoffice@beihua.edu.cn
Website: http://www.beihua.edu.cn

President: Liu Hezhong

College

Adult and Continuing Education (Adult Education; Continuing Education); **Basic Medicine** (Medical Technology; Medicine; Nursing; Social and Preventive Medicine); **Chemistry and Biology** (Biology; Chemistry); **Education Science** (Educational Technology; Primary Education; Psychology); **Electrical and Information Engineering** (Automation and Control Engineering; Electrical Engineering; Information Technology); **Fine Arts** (Fine Arts); **Foreign Languages** (English; Japanese); **Forestry** (Civil Engineering; Forestry; Horticulture; Painting and Drawing; Transport Engineering); **History and Culture** (Cultural Studies; History); **International Education and Exchange** (International and Comparative Education); **Law** (Law; Political Sciences); **Mathematics** (Mathematics); **Mechanical Engineering** (Industrial Design; Mechanical Engineering); **Medical Test** (Medical Technology); **Music** (Music); **Nursing** (Nursing); **Pharmacy** (Pharmacy); **Physical Education** (Physical Education); **Physics** (Physics); **Software** (Software Engineering); **Stomatology** (Stomatology); **Transportation and Civil Engineering** (Civil Engineering; Transport Engineering)

School

Chinese Language and Culture (Chinese); **Computer Science and Technology** (Computer Science); **Economic Management** (Economics; Management); **Public Health** (Public Health)

History: Founded 1999 by the combination of Jilin Teacher's college, Jilin Medical College, Jilin Forestry College and Jilin Electrification Academy.

Main Language(s) of Instruction: Chinese

Degrees and Diplomas: *Xueshi Xuewei*; *Shuoshi Xuewei*

Publications: Beihua University Journal

Last Updated: 11/02/13

BEIJING DANCE ACADEMY

19 Minzuxudaxue Nanlu, Haidian District, Beijing 100081
Tel: +86(10) 68935695
Fax: +86(10) 68411605
Website: http://www.bda.edu.cn

President: Wang Zhuanliang

Department

Ballet (Dance); **Chinese Folk Dance** (Dance; Folklore); **Chinese National Dance Drama** (Dance; Theatre); **Choreography** (Dance; Music Theory and Composition); **Dance Study** (Dance); **Social Education of Music and Dance** (Dance; Music)

History: Founded 1954 as Beijing Dance School. Acquired present title 1978.

Main Language(s) of Instruction: Chinese

Degrees and Diplomas: *Xueshi Xuewei*; *Shuoshi Xuewei*

Last Updated: 21/03/13

BEIJING ELECTRONIC SCIENCE AND TECHNOLOGY INSTITUTE

7 Fufeng Road, Fengtai District, Beijing 100070
Tel: +86(10) 63740588
Fax: +86(10) 63742726
Website: http://www.besti.edu.cn/

Department

Computer Application (Computer Science); **Computer Science and Technology** (Computer Science); **Electronic Information Engineering** (Electronic Engineering; Information Technology); **Telecommunication Engineering** (Telecommunications Engineering)

History: Founded 1981 as Beijing Electronic Science and Technology School. Acquired present title 1992.

Main Language(s) of Instruction: Chinese

Degrees and Diplomas: *Xueshi Xuewei*

Last Updated: 21/03/13

BEIJING FILM ACADEMY (BFA)

4 Xitucheng Road, Haidian District, Beijing 100088
Tel: +86(10) 8204-5433
Fax: +86(10) 8204-3731
EMail: ao.is@bfa.edu.cn
Website: http://www.bfa.edu.cn

Head: Zhang Huijun

School

Animation; **Continue Education** (Continuing Education); **International** (Foreigners Education); **Performing Arts** (Theatre); **Photography** (Photography)

Department

Basic Education (Education); **Cinematography** (Cinema and Television); **Directing** (Cinema and Television); **Film and TV** (Cinema and Television); **Film Studies** (Cinema and Television); **Fine Arts** (Fine Arts); **Graduate**; **Management** (Management); **Screenwriting** (Cinema and Television; Writing); **Sound Recording** (Sound Engineering (Acoustics)); **Technology** (Technology)

History: Founded 1953 as Beijing Film School. Acquired present title 1956.

Main Language(s) of Instruction: Chinese

Degrees and Diplomas: *Xueshi Xuewei*; *Shuoshi Xuewei*; *Boshi*: **Cinema and Television.**

Student Services: Canteen, Health Services

Last Updated: 21/02/13

BEIJING FOREIGN STUDIES UNIVERSITY (BFSU)

2 Xisanhuan Beilu, Haidian District, Beijing 100089
Tel: +86(10) 88816215
Fax: +86(10) 88813144
EMail: bwxzb@bfsu.edu.cn
Website: http://www.bfsu.edu.cn

President: Han Zhen

College

Continuing Education *(CEC)* (Continuing Education); **Training** (Teacher Training)

School

Asian and African Studies (African Studies; Asian Studies); **Chinese Language and Literature** (Chinese; Literature); **English and International Studies** (English; International Studies); **English for Specific Purposes** *(SESP)* (English); **European Languages and Cultures** *(SELC)* (European Languages); **International Business** (International Business); **International Relations and Diplomacy** (International Relations); **Law** (Law); **Philosophy and Social Sciences** (Philosophy; Social Sciences); **Russian** (Russian)

Department

Afro-Asian Languages (African Languages; Oriental Languages); **Arabic** (Arabic); **Computer Science** (Computer Science); **French** (French); **German** (German); **Japanese** (Japanese); **Physical**

Education (Physical Education); **Social Sciences** (Social Sciences); **Spanish and Portuguese** (Portuguese; Spanish)

Institute

Online Education (Distance Education)

Centre

Japanese Studies (Japanese)

Graduate School

Translation and Interpretation (Translation and Interpretation)

History: Founded 1941 as Yan'an School of Foreign Languages. Renamed Beijing Foreign Languages Institute 1949. Merger with Beijing Russian Institute 1959. Acquired present status and title 1994. A "Project 211" and "Project 985" university.

Academic Year: September to July (September-January; February-July)

Admission Requirements: Graduation from senior middle school and entrance examination

Main Language(s) of Instruction: Chinese, English, German, French, Russian, Arabic

Accrediting Agency: Ministry of Education

Degrees and Diplomas: *Xueshi Xuewei*; *Shuoshi Xuewei*; *Boshi*: **Comparative Literature; Cultural Studies; Foreign Languages Education; Linguistics; Literature; Translation and Interpretation.**

Student Services: Academic Counselling, Canteen, Careers Guidance, Foreign Studies Centre, Health Services, Language Laboratory, Nursery Care, Social Counselling, Sports Facilities

Publications: English Learning; Foreign Language Teaching and Research; Foreign Literatures; Russian Art and Literature; Russian Learning

Last Updated: 21/02/13

BEIJING FORESTRY UNIVERSITY (BJFU)

Qinghua East Road 35, Haidian District, Beijing 100083
Tel: +86(10) 62554411
Fax: +86(10) 62555276
EMail: service@bjfu.edu.cn
Website: http://www.bjfu.edu.cn

President: Song Weiming

College

Environmental Science and Engineering (Environmental Studies; Water Management); **Information Science and Technology** (Information Sciences); **Material Science and Technology** (Forest Products; Packaging Technology; Wood Technology); **Science** (Applied Mathematics; Electronic Engineering; Information Technology; Mathematics); **Vocational Training and Adult Education**

School

Economics and Management (Economics; Management); **Foreign Languages** (Modern Languages); **Humanities and Social Sciences** (Arts and Humanities; Social Sciences); **Landscape Architecture** (Landscape Architecture); **Soil and Water Conservation** (Water Science); **Technology** (Automation and Control Engineering; Electrical Engineering; Industrial Design; Machine Building)

History: Founded 1952 as Beijing Forestry College. Merger of the Landscape Architecture Department of Beijing Agricultural University and the Architecture Department of Tsinghua University 1956.

Academic Year: February to January (February-July; September-January)

Admission Requirements: Graduation from senior middle school and entrance examination

Main Language(s) of Instruction: Chinese

Accrediting Agency: Ministry of Education

Degrees and Diplomas: *Xueshi Xuewei*; *Shuoshi Xuewei*; *Boshi*

Student Services: Academic Counselling, Careers Guidance, Language Laboratory, Nursery Care, Social Counselling, Sports Facilities

Publications: Journal of Beijing Forestry University; Journal of Beijing Forestry University-Social Sciences

Last Updated: 21/02/13

BEIJING INFORMATION SCIENCE AND TECHNOLOGY UNIVERSITY (BISTU)

12 East Road, Qinghe Xiaoying - HaiDian District, Beijing 100192
Tel: +86(10) 62939325
Fax: +86(10) 62843757
EMail: webmaster@bistu.edu.cn
Website: http://www.bistu.edu.cn/

President: Liu Gonghui

School

Automation (Automation and Control Engineering); **Computer Science** (Computer Science); **Economics and Management** (Economics; Management); **Electrical and Mechanical Engineering** (Electrical Engineering; Mechanical Engineering); **Foreign Studies** (International Business; Modern Languages); **Humanities and Social Sciences** (Arts and Humanities; Social Sciences); **Political Theory and Education** (Education; Political Sciences); **Sciences** (Science Education)

Department

Graduate Students; **Physical Education** (Physical Education)

Centre

Computing (Computer Science); **Mechatronics Practice** (Electronic Engineering; Mechanical Engineering)

History: Founded 1986 by the merger of Beijing Institute of Machinery and Beijing Information Technology Institute. Acquired present title 2004.

Main Language(s) of Instruction: Chinese

Degrees and Diplomas: *Xueshi Xuewei*; *Shuoshi Xuewei*
Last Updated: 25/02/13

BEIJING INSTITUTE OF FASHION TECHNOLOGY (BIFT)

No.2 Yinghua Road, Chaoyang District, Beijing 100029
Tel: +86(10) 64288257
Fax: +86(10) 64210959
EMail: dyb@bift.edu.cn
Website: http://www.bift.edu.cn
President: Liu Yuanfeng

Division

Basic Courses (Education); **Social Science** (Education; Social Sciences)

School

Art and Design (Arts and Humanities; Design); **Business** (Business and Commerce); **Clothing and Art Business** (Clothing and Sewing; Textile Design); **Continuing Education** (Continuing Education); **Higher Vocational Education** (Vocational Education); **Industrial Design and Information Engineering** (Industrial Design; Information Technology); **Materials Science and Engineering** (Materials Engineering)

Department

Foreign Language (English); **Plastic Arts** (Design; Painting and Drawing)

Centre

Computer Science Teaching (Computer Education)

History: Founded 1959 as Beijing Institute of Textile Technology. Acquired present title 2008.

Main Language(s) of Instruction: Chinese

Degrees and Diplomas: *Xueshi Xuewei*; *Shuoshi Xuewei*
Last Updated: 11/03/13

BEIJING INSTITUTE OF GRAPHIC COMMUNICATION (BIGC)

25 Xinghua North Road, Daxing District, Beijing 102600
Tel: +86(10) 60261002 +86(10) 60261010
EMail: waiban@bigc.edu.cn
Website: http://www.bigc.edu.cn
President: Wang Yongsheng

Division

Basic Sciences (Science Education); **Physical Education** (Physical Education); **Social Sciences** (Education; Social Sciences)

College

Art and Design (Design); **Continued Education** (Continuing Education); **Information and Mechanical Engineering** (Information Technology; Mechanical Engineering)); **Printing and Packaging Engineering** (Packaging Technology; Printing and Printmaking); **Publishing Communication Management** (Communication Studies; Publishing and Book Trade); **Vocational Technology** (Technology; Vocational Education)

Research Centre

Aesthetics (Aesthetics); **Printing and Packaging Material Technology** (Packaging Technology; Printing and Printmaking); **Publishing and Communication** (Communication Studies; Publishing and Book Trade)

History: Founded 1978 as Department of Graphic Arts of Beijing Culture College. Renamed Beijing Institute of Printing 1978.

Main Language(s) of Instruction: Chinese

Degrees and Diplomas: *Xueshi Xuewei*; *Shuoshi Xuewei*

Last Updated: 11/03/13

BEIJING INSTITUTE OF PETROCHEMICAL TECHNOLOGY (BIPT)

Daxing, Beijing 102600
Tel: +86(10) 69244752 +86(10) 69244373
Fax: +86(10) 69241846
EMail: biptweb@bipt.edu.cn
Website: http://www.bipt.edu.cn

President: Guo Wenli

College

Chemical Engineering (Chemical Engineering); **Continuing Education** (Continuing Education); **Economics and Management** (Accountancy; International Economics; Management; Marketing); **Humanities and Social Sciences** (Arts and Humanities; Social Sciences); **Information Engineering** (Automation and Control Engineering; Computer Science; Electrical Engineering); **Material Science and Engineering** (Materials Engineering); **Mechanical Engineering** (Mechanical Engineering)

Department

Foreign Languages (English); **Mathematics and Physics** (Mathematics; Physics); **Physical Education** (Physical Education)

Centre

Engineering Education (Education; Engineering)

History: Founded 1978 as Beijing Petrochemical Junior College. Acquired present title 1992.

Main Language(s) of Instruction: Chinese

Degrees and Diplomas: *Xueshi Xuewei*

Last Updated: 11/03/13

BEIJING INSTITUTE OF TECHNOLOGY (BIT)

5 South Zhongguancun Street, Haidian District, Beijing 100081
Tel: +86(10) 68914247
Fax: +86(10) 68468035
EMail: service@bit.edu.cn
Website: http://www.bit.edu.cn/

President: Haiyan Hu (2007-) EMail: president@bit.edu.cn

School

Aerospace Engineering (Aeronautical and Aerospace Engineering); **Automation** (Automation and Control Engineering); **Chemical Engineering and the Environment** *(SCEE)* (Applied Chemistry; Chemical Engineering; Environmental Studies); **Chemistry** (Chemistry); **Computer Science** (Computer Science); **Design and Arts** (Design; Fine Arts); **Education** (Education); **Foreign Languages** (Modern Languages); **Graduate Studies**; **Information and Electronics** (Electronic Engineering; Information Technology); **Law** (Law); **Life Science** (Biological and Life Sciences); **Management and Economics** (Economics; Management); **Materials Science and Engineering** *(SMSE)* (Materials Engineering); **Mechatronical Engineering** (Automotive Engineering; Mechanical Engineering); **Optoelectronics** (Electronic Engineering; Optometry); **Physics** (Physics); **Software** (Software Engineering)

History: Founded 1940 as Yan'an Academy of Natural Sciences. Acquired present title 1951.

Main Language(s) of Instruction: Chinese, English

Degrees and Diplomas: *Xueshi Xuewei*; *Shuoshi Xuewei*; *Boshi*

Student Services: Academic Counselling, Canteen, Careers Guidance, Cultural Activities, Health Services, Nursery Care, Social Counselling, Sports Facilities

Publications: Journal Beijing Institute of Technology; Optical Engineering

Publishing House: Beijing Institute of Technology Press

Last Updated: 11/03/13

BEIJING INTERNATIONAL STUDIES UNIVERSITY (BISU)

Ding Fu Zhuang Nan Li 1#, Chaoyang District, Beijing 100024
Tel: +86(10) 65778564
Fax: +86(10) 65762520
EMail: webmaster@bisu.edu.cn
Website: http://www.bisu.edu.cn/

President: Zhou Lie

School

Applied English (English); **Chinese** (Chinese); **English Language Literature and Culture** (English Studies); **German** (German); **International Communication** (Communication Studies; International Studies); **International Economics and Trade** (Finance; International Business; International Economics; Marketing); **Japanese Language Literature and Culture** (Japanese); **Law and Politics** (Law; Political Sciences); **Tourism Management** (Hotel Management; Marketing; Tourism)

Department

Arabic (Arabic); **French and Italian** (French; Italian); **Korean** (Korean); **Russian** (Russian); **Spanish and Portuguese** (Portuguese; Spanish)

History: Founded 1964 as Beijing Second Foreign Languages Institute. Acquired present title 2002.

Main Language(s) of Instruction: Chinese

Degrees and Diplomas: *Xueshi Xuewei*; *Shuoshi Xuewei*

Student Services: Academic Counselling, Canteen, Careers Guidance, Foreign Studies Centre, Language Laboratory, Social Counselling, Sports Facilities

Publications: Journal of Beijing Second Foreign Languages Institute

Last Updated: 11/03/13

BEIJING JIAOTONG UNIVERSITY (BJTU)

No. 3 Shang Yuan Cun, Hai Dian District, Beijing 100044
Tel: +86(10) 51688312
Fax: +86(10) 62255671
EMail: wsc@bjtu.edu.cn
Website: http://www.njtu.edu.cn

President: Ning Bin

School

Architecture and Design (Architecture; Design); **Civil Engineering and Architecture** (Architecture; Civil Engineering; Construction Engineering; Environmental Engineering; Railway Engineering; Structural Architecture); **Computer and Information Technology** (Computer Engineering; Information Technology); **Economics and Management** (Accountancy; Business Administration; Economics; Industrial Management; Information Technology; Management); **Electrical Engineering** (Electrical Engineering; Energy Engineering; Power Engineering); **Electronics and Information Engineering** (Automation and Control Engineering; Electronic Engineering; Information Management; Information Sciences); **Foreign Languages and Mass Communication** (Communication Studies; Foreign Languages Education); **Humanities and Social Sciences** (Arts and Humanities; English; Foreign Languages Education; Law; Modern Languages; Physical Education; Social Sciences); **Mechanical, Electronic and Control Engineering** (Automation and Control Engineering; Electronic Engineering; Materials

Engineering; Measurement and Precision Engineering; Mechanical Engineering; Power Engineering); **Science** (Chemistry; Environmental Engineering; Mathematics; Optical Technology; Physics); **Software Engineering** (Software Engineering); **Traffic and Transportation** (Transport and Communications; Transport Engineering)

History: Founded 1896 as Peking Railway Training School of Postal Ministry of Qing Dynasty. Renamed Northern Jiaotong University 1950. Acquired present title 2003.

Academic Year: September to July (September-February; March-July)

Admission Requirements: Graduation from senior middle school and entrance examination

Main Language(s) of Instruction: Chinese

Accrediting Agency: Ministry of Education

Degrees and Diplomas: *Xueshi Xuewei*; *Shuoshi Xuewei*; *Boshi*

Publications: Higher Education Research; Journal of Beijing Jiatong University

Last Updated: 11/03/13

BEIJING LANGUAGE AND CULTURE UNIVERSITY (BLCU)

15 Xueyuan Road, Haidian District, Beijing 100083
Tel: +86(10) 62311348
Fax: +86(10) 62311228
EMail: waisshi2@blcu.edu.cn
Website: http://www.blcu.edu.cn

President: Xiao Zhang EMail: xiaozhang@blcu.edu.cn

College

Advanced Chinese Training (Chinese); **Chinese Language Studies** *(for foreign students)* (Chinese; Cultural Studies); **Foreign Languages** (Arabic; English; French; German; Japanese; Korean; Spanish); **Humanities and Social Sciences** (Humanities and Social Science Education); **Information Science** (Information Sciences); **Intensive Chinese Education** (Chinese)

School

International Business (International Business)

Department

Continuing Education (Continuing Education); **Physical Education** (Physical Education); **Predeparture Training**

Centre

English Education; **Overseas Test**

History: Founded 1962. Acquired present status and title 1996.

Main Language(s) of Instruction: Chinese

Degrees and Diplomas: *Xueshi Xuewei*; *Shuoshi Xuewei*; *Boshi*

Student Services: Canteen

Publications: Chinese Culture Research; Chinese Learning; Chinese Teaching in the World; Higher Education Research BLCU; Language Teaching and Linguistic Studies; Teaching and Research

Last Updated: 11/03/13

BEIJING NORMAL UNIVERSITY (BNU)

19 Xinjiekou Wai Street, Xicheng District, Beijing 100875
Tel: +86(10) 62208106
Fax: +86(10) 62200823
EMail: info@bnu.edu.cn
Website: http://www.bnu.edu.cn

President: Dong Qi

Faculty

Education (Adult Education; Curriculum; Educational Research; Educational Technology; Higher Education; Pedagogy; Preschool Education; Special Education; Vocational Education)

College

Chemistry (Analytical Chemistry; Applied Chemistry; Chemistry; Inorganic Chemistry; Organic Chemistry; Physical Chemistry); **Chinese Language and Culture** (Chinese; Linguistics); **Global Change and Earth System Science** (Geography; Geography (Human); Regional Planning; Town Planning); **Information Science and Technology** (Computer Science; Information Management; Information Technology; Software Engineering); **Nuclear Science and Technology** (Nuclear Engineering); **Philosophy and Sociology** (Philosophy; Sociology); **Physical Education and Sports Science** (Physical Education; Sports); **Resource Sciences and Technology** (Geography; Geography (Human); Natural Resources; Safety Engineering; Surveying and Mapping); **Water Sciences** (Water Science)

School

Arts and Communication (Cinema and Television; Dance; Design; Film; Fine Arts; Musicology; Radio and Television Broadcasting); **Chinese Ancient Books and Traditional Culture** (Ancient Books); **Chinese Language and Literature** (Chinese; Literature); **Continuing Education and Teacher Training** (Continuing Education; Teacher Training); **Economics and Business Administration** (Business Administration; Economics); **Economics and Resource Management** (Economics); **Environment** (Environmental Management; Environmental Studies); **Foreign Languages and Literatures** (English; Japanese; Modern Languages; Russian); **Geography** (Geography); **History** (Archaeology; History; Museum Studies); **Law** (Criminal Law; International Law; Law); **Life Sciences** (Biochemistry; Biological and Life Sciences; Biology; Biotechnology; Botany; Cell Biology; Ecology; Genetics; Molecular Biology; Physiology; Soil Conservation; Water Management; Wildlife; Zoology); **Management** (Administration; Human Resources; Information Management; Management; Public Administration); **Marxism Studies** (Political Sciences); **Mathematical Sciences** (Applied Mathematics; Automation and Control Engineering; Mathematics; Statistics); **Psychology** (Psychology); **Social Development and Public Policy** (Public Administration; Social Sciences)

Department

Astronomy (Astronomy and Space Science); **Physics** (Physics)

Institute

Agricultural Education and Development (Agricultural Education); **Basic Education Research** *(Capital Institute)* (Education); **Chinese Information Processing** (Information Management); **Cultural and Creative Industry** (Cultural Studies); **Economics of Education** *(Capital Institute)* (Economics; Education); **Educational Policy** (Educational Administration); **Higher Education** (Higher Education); **Mathematics and Mathematics Education** (Mathematics; Mathematics Education); **Medicine** (Medicine); **National Assessment of Education Quality**; **National Educational Testing and Evaluation** (Educational Testing and Evaluation); **Publishing Science** *(Universities' Confederated Institute)* (Publishing and Book Trade)

Academy

Beijing Cultural Development (Cultural Studies); **Disaster Reduction and Emergency Management** (Safety Engineering)

Centre

Analytical and Testing; **Literary Theory and Criticism**; **Study of Folk Custom, Ancient Codes and Records and Characters** (Folklore)

Laboratory

Cognitive Neuroscience and Learning (Cognitive Sciences; Neurosciences)

Research Centre

Basic Education Curriculum (Curriculum)

History: Founded 1902. Acquired present status 1949.

Academic Year: September to July (September-January; February-July)

Admission Requirements: Graduation from high school and entrance examination

Main Language(s) of Instruction: Chinese

Accrediting Agency: Ministry of Education

Degrees and Diplomas: *Xueshi Xuewei*; *Shuoshi Xuewei*; *Boshi*

Student Services: Academic Counselling, Canteen, Careers Guidance, Cultural Activities, Foreign Studies Centre, Health Services, Language Laboratory, Nursery Care, Social Counselling, Sports Facilities

Publications: Comparative Education Review; Foreign Language Teaching in Schools; Journal of Psychological Development and

Education; Journal of Beijing Normal University; Journal of Beijing Normal University; Journal of Historiography; Journal of Subject Education; Journal of Teacher's Education; Russian Literature

Publishing House: BNU Press
Last Updated: 21/03/13

BEIJING SPORT UNIVERSITY (BSU)

Beidajie Street, Zhongguancun Village, Haidian District, Beijing 100084
Tel: +86(10) 62989244
Fax: +86(10) 62989297
EMail: isc@bsu.edu.cn
Website: http://www.bsu.edu.cn

President: Yang Hua

College
Management (Management); **Physical Education** (Physical Education); **Sport Science** (Sports); **Sports Coaching** (Sports); **Wushu** (Sports)

School
Continuing Education (Continuing Education); **Graduate**

Department
Foreign Languages (Foreign Languages Education); **Sport Journalism and Communication** (Journalism; Sports); **Sport Performance**

History: Founded 1953 as Central Sports Institute. Renamed Beijing Institute of Physical Education 1956. Acquired present title 1993.

Main Language(s) of Instruction: Chinese

Degrees and Diplomas: *Xueshi Xuewei*; *Shuoshi Xuewei*; *Boshi*: **Physical Education; Sports; Sports Medicine.**

Publications: Journal of Beijing Sport University; Physical Education in Chinese School
Last Updated: 21/03/13

BEIJING TECHNOLOGY AND BUSINESS UNIVERSITY (BTBU)

11/33 Fucheng Road, Haidian District, Beijing 100048
Tel: +86(10) 68904774
Fax: +86(10) 68417834
EMail: fao@btbu.edu.cn
Website: http://www.btbu.edu.cn

President: Tan Xiangyong

School
Accountancy; **Art and Communication** (Communication Arts; Fine Arts); **Business** (Business and Commerce); **Computer and Information Engineering** (Computer Engineering; Information Technology); **Continuing Education** (Continuing Education); **Economics** (Economics); **Foreign Languages** (English); **Law** (Law); **Material Science and Mechanical Automation** (Materials Engineering; Mechanical Engineering); **Science** (Biotechnology; Chemistry; Cosmetology; Laboratory Techniques; Mathematics; Physics)

Department
Physical Education and Art Education (Art Education; Physical Education)

History: Founded 1950 as Beijing Institute of Business. Acquired present title and status after merger with Beijing Institute of Light Industry 1999.

Main Language(s) of Instruction: Chinese

Degrees and Diplomas: *Xueshi Xuewei*; *Shuoshi Xuewei*

Publications: Journal of Beijing Institute of Business; Journal of Beijing Institute of Light Industry
Last Updated: 21/03/13

BEIJING UNION UNIVERSITY (BUU)

97 Beisihuan East Road, Chao Yang District, Beijing 100101
Tel: +86(10) 64930059
Fax: +86(10) 64930059
Website: http://www.buu.edu.cn

President: Lu Zhenyang

College
Advertising (Advertising and Publicity); **Applied Arts and Science** (Archiving; Biotechnology; Computer Science; History; Law; Urban Studies); **Applied Science and Technology** (Applied Chemistry; Applied Mathematics; Applied Physics; Technology); **Automation** (Automation and Control Engineering); **Biochemical Engineering** (Biochemistry; Engineering); **Business** (Business and Commerce); **Continuing Education** (Continuing Education); **Information Technology** (Information Technology); **International Education** (International and Comparative Education); **Management** (Management); **Mechanical and Electrical Engineering** (Electrical Engineering; Mechanical Engineering); **Special Education** (Special Education); **Teacher Training** *(Vocational-Technical)* (Teacher Training); **Tourism** (Tourism)

History: Founded 1978.

Main Language(s) of Instruction: Chinese

Degrees and Diplomas: *Xueshi Xuewei*

Student Services: Canteen, Health Services

Publications: Journal of Beijing Union University
Last Updated: 21/03/13

BEIJING UNIVERSITY OF AGRICULTURE (BUA)

7 Beinong Road, Changping, Beijing 102206
Tel: +86(10) 80799313
Fax: +86(10) 80799004
Website: http://www.bac.edu.cn/

President: Younian Wang

College
Animal Science and Technology (Animal Husbandry; Veterinary Science); **Basic Science**; **Biological Science and Engineering** (Biological and Life Sciences); **Computer and Information Engineering** (Computer Engineering; Information Technology); **International** (Foreigners Education); **Plant Science and Technology** (Agriculture; Plant Pathology); **Urban and Rural Development** (Rural Studies; Urban Studies)

School
Continuing Education (Continuing Education)

Department
Arts and Law (Arts and Humanities; Law); **Economics and Trade** (Business and Commerce; Economics); **Food Science and Engineering** (Food Science; Food Technology); **Physical Education** (Physical Education)

History: Founded 1956 as Beijing Agricultural School. Acquired present title 1978.

Main Language(s) of Instruction: Chinese

Degrees and Diplomas: *Xueshi Xuewei*; *Shuoshi Xuewei*
Last Updated: 21/03/13

BEIJING UNIVERSITY OF CHEMICAL TECHNOLOGY (BUCT)

15 Beisanhuan East Road, Chaoyang District, Beijing 100029
Tel: +86(10) 64434755
Fax: +86(10) 64423610
EMail: news@buct.edu.cn
Website: http://www.buct.edu.cn

President: Wang Zihao

School
Chemical Engineering (Biochemistry; Chemical Engineering); **Economic Management** (Economics; Management); **Further Education** (Accountancy; Automation and Control Engineering; Chemical Engineering; Computer Science; English; Environmental Engineering; Finance; Law; Management; Marketing); **Humanities and Law** (Humanities and Social Science Education; Law); **Information Science and Technology** (Information Sciences); **Materials Science and Engineering** (Materials Engineering; Polymer and Plastics Technology); **Mechanical and Electrical** (Electrical Engineering; Mechanical Engineering); **Science** (Applied Chemistry; Chemistry; Computer Science; Electronic Engineering;

Mathematics; Physics); **Vocational Education** (Computer Networks; Computer Science; Design; English; Multimedia; Technology)

History: Founded 1958 as Beijing Institute of Chemical Technology. Acquired present name 1994 following merger of Beijing Institute of Chemical Technology and Beijing Institute of Administrative Cadres.

Academic Year: September to July (September-January; February-July)

Admission Requirements: Graduation from senior middle school and entrance examination

Main Language(s) of Instruction: Chinese

Degrees and Diplomas: *Xueshi Xuewei*; *Shuoshi Xuewei*; *Boshi*

Student Services: Academic Counselling, Canteen, Careers Guidance, Cultural Activities, Health Services, Nursery Care, Social Counselling, Sports Facilities

Publications: Learned Journal of BUCT; Research of College Education

Last Updated: 22/03/13

BEIJING UNIVERSITY OF CHINESE MEDICINE (BUCM)

11 Bei San Huan Dong Lu, ChaoYang District, Beijing 100029
Tel: +86(10) 64286322
Fax: +86(10) 64220858
EMail: isbucm@bucm.edu.cn
Website: http://www.bucm.edu.cn

President: Gao Sihua

School

Acupuncture, Moxibustion and Tuina (Acupuncture); **Chinese Materia Medica** (Chemistry; Mathematics; Pharmacology; Physics); **Continuing Education** (Continuing Education); **Distance Education** (Distance Education); **Graduate**; **Humanities** (Arts and Humanities); **International** (International and Comparative Education); **Nursing** (Nursing); **Pre-Clinical Medicine** (Medicine; Traditional Eastern Medicine); **Traditional Chinese Nursing** (Nursing)

Further Information: Also 3 Affiliated Hospitals, 4 Teaching Hospitals and 18 Hospitals for externs

History: Founded 1956 as Beijing College of Traditional Chinese Medicine. Acquired present title 1993. Incorporated Beijing College of Acupuncture, Orthopedics and Traumatology 2000.

Academic Year: September to July (September-January; February-July)

Admission Requirements: Graduation from senior middle school and entrance examination

Main Language(s) of Instruction: Chinese

Degrees and Diplomas: *Xueshi Xuewei*; *Shuoshi Xuewei*; *Boshi*: **Medicine.**

Student Services: Academic Counselling, Careers Guidance, Cultural Activities, Health Services, Social Counselling, Sports Facilities

Publications: Education of Chinese Medicine; Journal of Beijing University of Chinese Medicine

Last Updated: 22/03/13

BEIJING UNIVERSITY OF CIVIL ENGINEERING AND ARCHITECTURE (BUCEA)

1 Zhanlanlu, Xicheng District, Beijing 100044
Tel: +86(10) 68322507
Fax: +86(10) 68322899
EMail: nic@bucea.edu.cn
Website: http://www.bucea.edu.cn/

President, Party Secretary: Quian Jun
EMail: qianjun@bucea.edu.cn

School

Architecture and Urban Planning (Architecture; Urban Studies); **Civil Engineering and Traffic Engineering** (Civil Engineering); **Economics and Management Engineering** (Economics; Management); **Electricity and Information Engineering** (Electrical Engineering; Information Technology); **Environment and Energy Engineering** (Energy Engineering; Environmental Engineering); **Geomatics and Urban Information** (Geophysics; Urban Studies); **Humanity and Law** (Humanities and Social Science Education; Law); **Mechanical-electronic and Automobile Engineering** (Automotive Engineering; Electronic Engineering; Mechanical Engineering)

History: Founded 1936 as Beijing Senior Vocational Industry School-Civil Engineering Section. Acquired present status and title 1977. Formerly Beijing Institute of Civil Engineering and Architecture.

Main Language(s) of Instruction: Chinese

Degrees and Diplomas: *Xueshi Xuewei*; *Shuoshi Xuewei*

Last Updated: 11/03/13

BEIJING UNIVERSITY OF POSTS AND TELECOMMUNICATIONS (BUPT)

10 Xitucheng Road, Haidian District, Beijing 100876
Tel: +86(10) 62282639
Fax: +86(10) 62281942
EMail: lzli@bupt.edu.cn
Website: http://www.bupt.edu.cn

President: Chen Junliang

School

Automation (Automation and Control Engineering); **Computer Science** (Computer Science); **Continuing Education** (Continuing Education); **Digital Media and Design Arts** (Computer Graphics; Design); **Economics and Management** (Economics; Management); **Electronic Engineering** (Electronic Engineering); **Humanities, Law and Economics** (Arts and Humanities; Economics; Law); **Information and Communication Engineering** (Communication Studies; Information Technology); **International** (International Studies); **Languages** (Modern Languages); **Management and Humanities** (Arts and Humanities; Management); **Network Education** (Computer Networks); **Public Policy and Management** (Public Administration); **Science** (Mathematics; Physics); **Software Engineering** (Software Engineering); **Telecommunications Engineering** (Telecommunications Engineering)

Institute

Information Photonics and Optical Communications (Optical Technology); **National**

Further Information: Branch at Fuzhou. Also Chinese courses for foreign students

History: Founded 1955 as Beijing Institute of Posts and Telecommunications. Renamed University 1993.

Academic Year: September to July (September-January; March-July)

Admission Requirements: Graduation from senior middle school and national unified entrance examination

Main Language(s) of Instruction: Chinese

Accrediting Agency: Ministry of Posts and Telecommunications

Degrees and Diplomas: *Xueshi Xuewei*; *Shuoshi Xuewei*; *Boshi*

Student Services: Academic Counselling, Canteen, Careers Guidance, Cultural Activities, Health Services, Nursery Care, Social Counselling, Sports Facilities

Publications: Higher Education Research; Journal of Beijing University of Posts and Telecommunications; Journal of China's Post and Telecommunications Higher Education; Journal of Human Studies

Publishing House: The University Press

Last Updated: 22/03/13

BEIJING UNIVERSITY OF TECHNOLOGY (BJUT)

100 Pingleyuan, Chaoyang District, Beijing 100124
Tel: +86(10) 67391465
Fax: +86(10) 67392319
EMail: beijingtech@bjut.edu.cn
Website: http://www.bjut.edu.cn

President: Guo Guangsheng

College
Applied Sciences (Applied Mathematics; Applied Physics; Statistics); **Architecture and Civil Engineering** (Architecture; Bridge Engineering; Civil Engineering; Hydraulic Engineering; Railway Engineering; Road Engineering; Structural Architecture; Transport Engineering); **Architecture and Urban Planning** *(CAUP)* (Architecture; Industrial Design; Town Planning); **Art and Design** (Fashion Design; Industrial Design; Media Studies); **Computer Science** (Artificial Intelligence; Computer Networks; Computer Science; Software Engineering); **Electronic Information and Control Engineering** (Automation and Control Engineering; Electronic Engineering); **Environmental and Energy Engineering** (Energy Engineering; Environmental Engineering; Heating and Refrigeration); **Foreign Languages** (English; Japanese; Korean; Modern Languages); **Humanities and Social Sciences** (Arts and Humanities; Chinese; Economics; History; Law; Pedagogy; Philosophy; Psychology; Social Sciences; Sociology); **Life Sciences and Bioengineering** (Bioengineering; Biological and Life Sciences); **Materials Science and Engineering** (Automation and Control Engineering; Engineering; Materials Engineering); **Mechanical Engineering and Applied Electronic Technology** (Electronic Engineering; Machine Building; Mechanical Engineering; Technology)

School
Economics and Management (Economics; Management); **Software Engineering** (Software Engineering)

Institute
Laser Engineering *(ILE)* (Laser Engineering); **Microstructure and Property of Advanced Materials** (Materials Engineering); **Recycling Economy** (Environmental Management)

History: Founded 1960 as Beijing Polytechnic University. Acquired present tilte and status 2000.

Academic Year: September to July (September-January; February-July)

Admission Requirements: Graduation from senior middle school and National Entrance Examination for Universities and Colleges

Main Language(s) of Instruction: Chinese

Accrediting Agency: Beijing Municipality, Beijing Education Commission

Degrees and Diplomas: *Xueshi Xuewei*; *Shuoshi Xuewei*; *Boshi*

Student Services: Academic Counselling, Canteen, Careers Guidance, Cultural Activities, Foreign Studies Centre, Health Services, Language Laboratory, Nursery Care, Sports Facilities

Last Updated: 22/03/13

BEIJING WUZI UNIVERSITY (BWU)

1 Fue Street, Tongzhou District, Beijing 101149
Tel: +86(10) 89634412
Fax: +86(10) 89534661
Website: http://www.bwu.edu.cn

President: Wang Xudong

School
Business (Business and Commerce); **Economics** (Business Administration; Economics; Finance; Management); **Foreign Languages and Cultures** (English); **Information Technology** (Information Technology); **Labour Science and Law** (Labour and Industrial Relations; Law); **Logistics** (Marketing; Production Engineering)

History: Founded 1980 as Beijing Materials Institute. Acquired present status and title 2005.

Academic Year: September to July

Accrediting Agency: Beijing Municipal Government

Degrees and Diplomas: *Xueshi Xuewei*; *Shuoshi Xuewei*: **Business and Commerce; Engineering; Industrial and Production Economics; Management.**

Student Services: Canteen

Last Updated: 22/03/13

BENGBU MEDICAL COLLEGE

801 Huaihe River, Bengbu, Anhui Province 233003
Tel: +86(552) 3063243
Fax: +86(552) 3063243
Website: http://www.bbmc.edu.cn

President: Zhu Yan

Department
Biological Science (Biological and Life Sciences); **Clinical Medicine** (Medicine); **Laboratory Medicine** (Laboratory Techniques); **Medical Imaging** (Radiology); **Nursing** (Nursing); **Pharmacy** (Pharmacy); **Preventive Medicine** (Social and Preventive Medicine)

History: Founded 1958. Acquired present title 1974.

Main Language(s) of Instruction: Chinese

Degrees and Diplomas: *Xueshi Xuewei*; *Shuoshi Xuewei*

Last Updated: 22/03/13

BINZHOU MEDICAL UNIVERSITY

522, Huanghe Sanlu, Bincheng District, Binzhou, Shandong 256603
Tel: +86(535) 3256054
Fax: +86(535) 3322752
EMail: binwang001@yahoo.com.cn
Website: http://www.bzmc.edu.cn

President: Yuan Junping

Department
Basic Medicine (Medicine); **Clinical Medicine** (Medicine); **Handicapped** (Education of the Handicapped; Medicine); **Nursing** (Nursing); **Stomatology** (Stomatology)

History: Founded 1974 as Beizhen Medical College. Acquired present title 1983.

Main Language(s) of Instruction: Chinese

Degrees and Diplomas: *Xueshi Xuewei*; *Shuoshi Xuewei*

Last Updated: 22/03/13

BOHAI UNIVERSITY

19, Keji Road, New Songshan District,
Jinzhou, Liaoning Province 121013
Tel: +86(416) 3400015
Fax: +86(416) 2822546
EMail: bhu@bhu.edu.cn
Website: http://www.bhu.edu.cn

President: Qin Qiu-tian

College
International Exchanges (International Relations); **Liberal Arts** (History; Political Sciences); **Marxism** (Political Sciences)

School
Finance and Commerce (Business and Commerce; Finance); **Graduate; Law** (Law); **Management** (Management); **Mathematics and Physics** (Mathematics; Physics)

Department
Chemistry and Food Safety (Chemistry; Food Science); **Chinese Language and Literature** (Chinese; Literature); **Fine Arts** (Fine Arts); **Journalism** (Journalism); **Sports** (Sports)

Institute
Adult Education (Adult Education); **Foreign Languages** (Foreign Languages Education); **Information Science and Technology** (Information Technology); **New Energy** (Energy Engineering); **Tourism Studies** (Tourism)

History: Founded 1950 as Jinzhou Teachers College. Acquired present status and title 2003.

Main Language(s) of Instruction: Chinese

Degrees and Diplomas: *Xueshi Xuewei*; *Shuoshi Xuewei*

Last Updated: 27/03/13

CAPITAL INSTITUTE OF PHYSICAL EDUCATION

North Third Ring Road, Beijing 100191
Tel: +86(10) 82099007
EMail: wanggaohua@cupes.edu.cn
Website: http://www.cupes.edu.cn

President: Zhong Bing Shu

College
Leisure and Social Science Sports (Sports); **Management and Communication** (Sports Management); **Sports Science and Health** (Sports Medicine)
School
International Education (International and Comparative Education); **Martial Arts and Performing** (Sports)
Institute
Physical Education and Training (Physical Education)

History: Founded 1956 as Beijing Sports School, became Beijing Teachers College of Physical Education 1960. Acquired present title 2000.

Main Language(s) of Instruction: Chinese

Degrees and Diplomas: *Xueshi Xuewei*: **Sports.** *Shuoshi Xuewei*: **Sports.**

Last Updated: 25/02/14

CAPITAL MEDICAL UNIVERSITY

10 Xitoutiao, Youanmen, Fengtai District, Beijing 100069
Tel: +86(10) 83911000
Fax: +86(10) 83911029
EMail: webmaster@ccmu.edu.cn
Website: http://www.ccmu.edu.cn/

President: Lu Zhaofeng

School
Basic Medical Sciences (Medicine); **Biochemical and Pharmaceutical Sciences** (Biochemistry; Chemistry; Pharmacology); **Biomedical Engineering** (Biomedical Engineering); **Health Administration and Education** (Health Administration; Health Education); **Nursing** (Nursing); **Public Health and Family Medicine** (Public Health); **Traditional Chinese Medicine** (Traditional Eastern Medicine); **Yan Jing Medical** (Medicine)

History: Founded 1960 as Beijing Second Medical College, became Institute 1985, and acquired present title 1994.

Academic Year: September to July (September-January; February-July)

Admission Requirements: Graduation from senior middle school and entrance examination

Main Language(s) of Instruction: Chinese, English

Degrees and Diplomas: *Xueshi Xuewei*: **Medicine.** *Shuoshi Xuewei*: **Medicine.** *Boshi*: **Medicine.**

Last Updated: 25/02/14

CAPITAL NORMAL UNIVERSITY

105 Xisanhuan Beilu, Beijing 100037
Tel: +86(10) 689026512
Fax: +86(10) 68416837
EMail: info@mail.cnu.edu.cn
Website: http://www.cnu.edu.cn

President: Liu Xincheng

College
Adult Education (Adult Education); **Fine Arts** (Fine Arts); **Foreign Languages**; **Information Engineering** (Computer Science); **International Education**; **Life Sciences**; **Music** (Music); **Political Science and Law**; **Primary Education** (Primary Education)
School
Continuing Education; **Educational Sciences** (Education; Pedagogy; Preschool Education; Psychology); **International Education**
Department
Chemistry (Chemistry); **Educational Technology** (Educational Technology); **Mathematics** (Mathematics); **Physics**
Research Institute
Culture of Calligraphy of China (Painting and Drawing)

History: Founded 1954 as Beijing Teachers College. Merged with Beijing Teachers College of Foreign Languages. Acquired present status and title 1992.

Degrees and Diplomas: *Xueshi Xuewei*; *Shuoshi Xuewei*; *Boshi*

Publications: Capital Normal University Journal

CAPITAL UNIVERSITY OF ECONOMICS AND BUSINESS

Flower-Town, Fengtai District, Beijing 100070
Tel: +86(10) 83952828
Fax: +86(10) 83952818
EMail: xcb@cueb.edu.cn
Website: http://www.cueb.edu.cn/English/index.htm

President: Wang Jiaqiong (2010-)

School
Accountancy (Accountancy); **Business Administration** (Administration; Advertising and Publicity; Business Administration; Human Resources; Information Management; International Business; Management; Marketing; Public Administration; Tourism); **Engineering** (Engineering; Engineering Management; Environmental Engineering; Industrial Engineering; Safety Engineering); **Humanities** (Arts and Humanities; Social Work); **Labour Economics** (Economics; Natural Resources); **Public Finance** (Banking; Finance)

History: Founded 1956. A merger of the Beijing College of Economics and the Beijing Trade and Finance Institute. Acquired present title 1995.

Degrees and Diplomas: *Xueshi Xuewei*; *Shuoshi Xuewei*; *Boshi*

Publications: Beijing Economic Outlook; Journal of Capital University of Economics and Business; Population and Economics; Research on Economics and Management

CENTRAL ACADEMY OF DRAMA (CCAD)

Dongmianhua Hutong 39, Dongcheng District, Beijing 100710
Tel: +86(10) 640 35626
Fax: +86(10) 640 16479
EMail: zhongxi@zhongxi.cn
Website: http://www.zhongxi.cn

President: Xiang Xu (2003-) Tel: +86(10) 640 17573

Vice-President: Libin Liu Tel: +86(10) 640 18301

International Relations: Shaoyu Zhou, Head of Foreign Affairs Office Tel: +86(10) 640 35626 EMail: wsci@chntheatre.edu.cn

Department
Directing; **Drama Literature** *(Playwriting; Drama Studies)* (Ancient Civilizations; History; Literature; Modern History; Writing); **Performing**; **Stage Art** (Art Management; Design; Display and Stage Design; Fine Arts; Painting and Drawing; Visual Arts); **Stage Management**; **TV Arts** *(production, management, advertisement, direction)* (Cinema and Television; Film; Information Sciences; Mass Communication; Performing Arts; Radio and Television Broadcasting; Video)

History: Founded 1950 as Lu Xun Art College in Yan' an. Merged with Art Faculty of North China University and Nanking National Academy of Drama.

Academic Year: September to June

Admission Requirements: High school certificate

Fees: (Yuan): Undergraduates, 1,600 per term; post-graduates, 2,000 per term

Main Language(s) of Instruction: Chinese

Degrees and Diplomas: *Xueshi Xuewei*; *Shuoshi Xuewei*: **Arts and Humanities; Cinema and Television; Display and Stage Design; Literature; Performing Arts; Theatre.** *Boshi*: **Arts and Humanities; Cinema and Television; Literature; Performing Arts; Theatre.** Also Continuous Study programmes (1 yr) in all fields of study

Student Services: Academic Counselling, Canteen, Careers Guidance, Foreign Studies Centre, Health Services, Language Laboratory, Nursery Care, Social Counselling, Sports Facilities

Publications: Drama

CENTRAL ACADEMY OF FINE ARTS

No.8 Hua Jia Di Nan St, Chaoyang District, Beijing 100015
Tel: +86(10) 64380464
Fax: +86(10) 65134140
EMail: xujia@cafa.edu.cn
Website: http://www.cafa.edu.cn/channel.asp?id=10

President: Pan Gongkai

School

Architecture (Architecture); **Chinese Painting**; **City Design**; **Design** (Design); **Fine Art**; **Humanities** (Art Education; Art History; Art Management; Heritage Preservation; Restoration of Works of Art)

History: Founded 1918 as Beijing School of Fine Arts, acquired present title 1950.

Degrees and Diplomas: *Xueshi Xuewei*; *Shuoshi Xuewei*; *Boshi*

Publications: Art Research; World Art

CENTRAL CHINA NORMAL UNIVERSITY (CCNU)

100, 152 Luoyu Road, Wuhan, Hubei Province 430079
Tel: +86(27) 87673048
Fax: +86(27) 87875696
EMail: www@ccnu.edu.cn
Website: http://www.ccnu.edu.cn

President: Yang Zongkai

College

Chemistry (Analytical Chemistry; Applied Chemistry; Chemistry; Inorganic Chemistry; Organic Chemistry; Physical Chemistry)

School

Computer Science (Computer Science; Software Engineering); **Economics and Management** (Economics; International Economics); **Education** (Education; Preschool Education; Psychology; Special Education); **Fine Arts** (Design; Fine Arts; Painting and Drawing); **Foreign Languages** (English; Japanese; Linguistics; Literature; Russian; Translation and Interpretation); **History and Culture** (Cultural Studies; Heritage Preservation; History); **Law** (Administrative Law; Commercial Law; Constitutional Law; Criminal Law; International Law); **Literature** (Chinese; Literature; Radio and Television Broadcasting; Theatre); **Mathematics** (Applied Mathematics; Mathematics; Statistics); **Physics** (Physics); **Political Science and Law** (Law; Philosophy; Political Sciences)

History: Founded 1903 as Wen-hua Academy. In 1951, the public Huazhong University came into being after the Pedagogical College of Zhongyuan University merged with Huazhong University. Then it was reorganized into Huazhong Higher Normal School in 1952 and later renamed Huazhong Teachers College in 1953. Acquired present status and title 1985.

Academic Year: September to July

Admission Requirements: Graduation from senior high school or foreign equivalent, and entrance examination

Main Language(s) of Instruction: Chinese

Accrediting Agency: Ministry of Education

Degrees and Diplomas: *Xueshi Xuewei*; *Shuoshi Xuewei*; *Boshi*

Student Services: Academic Counselling, Canteen, Careers Guidance, Cultural Activities, Foreign Studies Centre, Health Services, Language Laboratory, Nursery Care, Social Counselling, Sports Facilities

Publications: Correspondence Studies of Higher Education; Education and Economics; Educational Research and Experiment; Foreign Literature Studies; Teaching and Research of Chinese Language

Publishing House: CCNU University Press

Last Updated: 26/11/12

CENTRAL CONSERVATORY OF MUSIC

43 Baojia Street, Xicheng District, Beijing 100031
Tel: +86(10) 66412585
Fax: +86(10) 66412138
EMail: contactus@ccom.edu.cn
Website: http://www.ccom.edu.cn

President: Wang Cizhao

International Relations: Jiang Xiaoai

Department

Chinese Traditional Musical Instrument Performance; **Composition** (Music; Music Theory and Composition); **Conducting** (Conducting); **Electronic Music** (Music); **History of Western Music** (Art History); **Instrument Making and Repairing** (Instrument Making); **Keyboard Instrument Performance** (Musical Instruments); **Music Education** (Music Education); **Musicology** (Musicology); **Voice and Opera** (Opera; Singing); **Wind and String Instrument Performance** (Musical Instruments)

History: Founded 1950.

Degrees and Diplomas: *Xueshi Xuewei*; *Shuoshi Xuewei*; *Boshi*

Publications: Journal of Central Conservatory of Music

CENTRAL INSTITUTE FOR CORRECTIONAL POLICE (CICP)

103 Seventy-one Road, Baoding, Hebei 071000
Website: http://www.cicp.edu.cn/

President: Wangheng Qin

Department

Basic Course Teaching and Research (Accountancy; Behavioural Sciences; Computer Networks; Computer Science; Data Processing; Economics; Management; Marketing; Police Studies; Science Education; Software Engineering; Statistics); **Continuing Education**; **Detention Management** (Protective Services); **Information Management** (Computer Science; Information Management; Information Technology; Management); **Law** (Administrative Law; Civil Law; Commercial Law; Constitutional Law; Criminal Law; Criminology; History of Law; International Law; Law; Police Studies; Protective Services; Psychology; Public Law); **Marxism-Leninism Teaching and Research** (Political Sciences); **Modern Educational technology** (Educational Technology); **Police Management** (Police Studies); **Police Sports Teaching and Research** (Sports); **Training**

Institute

Prison Inmates Science (Protective Services)

Centre

Detention Theoretical Research (Protective Services); **Theoretical Study Prisons**

Research Centre

Prison Investigative Technology (Protective Services; Technology)

History: Founded 1956. Under the Ministry of Justice.

Main Language(s) of Instruction: Chinese

Degrees and Diplomas: *Xueshi Xuewei*

Student Services: Sports Facilities

Publications: China Prison Journal

Academic Staff *2012-2013*: Total 314
Student Numbers *2012-2013*: Total 6,336
Last Updated: 24/10/13

CENTRAL SOUTH FORESTRY UNIVERSITY

Zhuzhou, Hunan Province 412006
Tel: +86(733) 8703331
Fax: +86(773) 8703331
Website: http://www.csfu.edu.cn

President: Su Xiancai

International Relations: Liu Yuan

Faculty

Architectural Engineering (Structural Architecture); **Economics and Trade** (Economics); **Industry**; **Resources and Environment** (Environmental Studies; Natural Resources)

Department

Foreign Languages (Modern Languages); **Law** (Law)

History: Founded 1958, acquired present title 1964.

Degrees and Diplomas: *Xueshi Xuewei*; *Shuoshi Xuewei*

Publications: CSFU Journal

CENTRAL SOUTH UNIVERSITY

88 Xiangyalu, Changsha, Hunan Province 410078
Tel: +86(731) 4805210
Fax: +86(731) 4471339
EMail: admis@mail.csu.edu.cn
Website: http://www.csu.edu.cn

School

Art (Fine Arts); **Business** (Business Administration); **Chemistry and Chemical Engineering** (Chemical Engineering; Chemistry); **Chinese Language and Literature**; **Civil Engineering and Architecture**; **Energy and Power Engineering** (Energy Engineering; Power Engineering); **Foreign Languages** (Modern Languages); **Fundamental Medicine** (Medicine); **Geoscience and Environmental Engineering**; **Information Science and Engineering**; **Law** (Law); **Material Science and Engineering** (Engineering; Materials Engineering); **Mathematical Sciences and Computer Technology** (Mathematics and Computer Science); **Mechanical and Electrical Engineering**; **Medical Technology** (Medical Technology); **Metallurgical Science and Engineering** (Engineering; Metallurgical Engineering); **Nursing**; **Pharmaceutical Sciences** (Pharmacy); **Physics and Technology**; **Political Science and Executive Administration**; **Public Health** (Public Health); **Resources and Safety Engineering**; **Resources Processing and Bioengineering** (Bioengineering); **Stomatology**; **Traffic and Transport** (Transport and Communications)

History: Founded 1914 as Central South University of Technology, merged with Changsha Railway University and Hunan Medical University 2000.

Academic Year: August to July (August-January; February-July)

Admission Requirements: Graduation from senior middle school and entrance examination

Main Language(s) of Instruction: Chinese, English

Degrees and Diplomas: *Xueshi Xuewei*; *Shuoshi Xuewei*; *Boshi*

CENTRAL UNIVERSITY OF FINANCE AND ECONOMICS (CUFE)

39th South College Road, Haidan District, Beijing 100081
Tel: +86(10) 62288335
Fax: +86(10) 62288982
EMail: lxs@cufe.edu.cn
Website: http://www.cufe.edu.cn

President: Wang Guangqian (2002-) Tel: +86(10) 62288117

International Relations: Cai Caishii

School

Accountancy (Accountancy; Finance); **Adult Education** (Adult Education); **Applied Mathematics** (Applied Mathematics); **Business** (Business Administration; Human Resources; Management; Marketing); **Culture and Communication** (Cultural Studies); **Economics** (Business Administration; Economics; Marketing; Statistics); **Finance** (Finance); **Foreign Languages** (Modern Languages); **Government Administration** (Government); **Information** (Information Sciences); **Insurance** (Insurance); **Law** (Law); **Management** (Management); **Marxism** (Political Sciences); **Public Finance** (Economic and Finance Policy; Finance; Government; Management; Public Administration); **Social Development** (Social Studies); **Sports Economics and Management** (Sports; Sports Management); **Statistics** (Statistics); **Taxation** (Taxation)

Department

Banking (Banking; Finance); **Chinese**; **Investments Economics**

History: Founded 1949 as Central School of Taxation, acquired present title 1996 and status 2000.

Admission Requirements: Graduation from high school and entrance examination

Fees: (Yuan): c. 4,500 per annum

Main Language(s) of Instruction: Chinese

Accrediting Agency: Ministry of Education

Degrees and Diplomas: *Xueshi Xuewei*: **Accountancy; Banking; Information Technology; Insurance; Law; Management; Taxation.** *Shuoshi Xuewei*: **Banking; Information Technology; Insurance; Management.** *Boshi*: **Accountancy; Banking.**

Student Services: Academic Counselling, Canteen, Careers Guidance, Cultural Activities, Foreign Studies Centre, Health Services, Language Laboratory, Nursery Care, Social Counselling, Sports Facilities

Publications: Journal of Central University of Finance and Economics

CHANG'AN UNIVERSITY

Xi'an, Shaanxi Province 710064
Tel: +86(29) 2338114
Fax: +86(29) 5261532
EMail: president@chd.edu.cn
Website: http://www.xahu.edu.cn

President: Ma Jian

International Relations: Zhang Wei

College

Foreign Languages (English; French; German; Japanese; Russian); **Geological Engineering and Geomatics** (Geological Engineering; Geophysics); **Highway** (Road Engineering); **Science** (Applied Mathematics; Applied Physics; Chemistry; Engineering Drawing and Design; Mechanical Engineering)

School

Automotive (Automotive Engineering; Transport Engineering); **Civil Engineering** (Automation and Control Engineering; Civil Engineering; Construction Engineering; Electrical Engineering; Engineering Management); **Economics and Management** (Economics; Management); **Humanities and Social Sciences** (Advertising and Publicity; Art Education; Chinese; Law; Political Sciences; Public Administration); **Information** (Information Sciences)

Institute

Environmental Science (Environmental Studies)

History: Founded 2000 following merger of Xi'an Highway University (founded 1951), Xi'an Engineering University (founded 1953) and North-western Architecture Engineering Institute.

Degrees and Diplomas: *Xueshi Xuewei*; *Shuoshi Xuewei*; *Boshi*

Publications: Journal of Chang'an University; Journal of China Highway and Transportation Engineering

CHANGCHUN INSTITUTE OF TECHNOLOGY

395 Kuanping Road, Changchun, Jilin Province 130012
Tel: +86(431) 5955991
Fax: +86(431) 5955991
EMail: webmaster@ccit.edu.cn
Website: http://www.ccit.edu.cn

College

Software Engineering (Software Engineering)

Department

Applied Chemistry (Applied Chemistry); **Architecture** (Architecture); **Business Management** (Business Administration; Management); **Civil Engineering** (Civil Engineering); **Continuing Education**; **Electronic Engineering** (Electronic Engineering); **Energy and Power Engineering** (Energy Engineering; Power Engineering); **Environmental Engineering** (Environmental Engineering); **Foreign Languages** (Modern Languages); **Industrial Design** (Industrial Design); **Information Engineering** (Information Technology); **Land Resources** (Natural Resources); **Management Engineering** (Management); **Mechanical Engineering**; **Physical Education** (Physical Education); **Social Science**; **Water Conservation Engineering** (Hydraulic Engineering; Water Management)

History: Founded 2000.

Degrees and Diplomas: *Xueshi Xuewei*

CHANGCHUN NORMAL UNIVERSITY

3 Jichang Highway (North), Changchun, Jilin Province 130032
Tel: +86(431) 7915263 Ext 3023
Fax: +86(431) 4711779
EMail: cnuice@163.com
Website: http://www.cncnc.edu.cn

President: Zhao Lixing

International Relations: Tian Chunde Tel: +86(431) 4711779

Department
Biology (Biology); **Chemistry** (Chemistry); **Chinese** (Chinese; Literature); **Fine Arts** (Fine Arts); **Foreign Languages** (English; Modern Languages); **Geography** (Geography); **History** (History); **Mathematics** (Mathematics); **Music** (Music); **Physical Training** (Physical Education); **Physics** (Physics); **Politics** (Political Sciences)

History: Founded 1978.

Degrees and Diplomas: *Xueshi Xuewei*

CHANGCHUN UNIVERSITY

6543 Weixing Road, Changchun, Jilin Province 130022
Tel: +86(431) 5387435
Fax: +86(431) 5387435
Website: http://www.ccu-edu.cn/

President: Zhang Deijang

College
Aviation (Aeronautical and Aerospace Engineering; Electrical Engineering); **Biological Sciences and Technology** (Automotive Engineering; Biotechnology; Food Technology; Landscape Architecture); **Computer Science and Technology** (Computer Networks; Computer Science; Software Engineering); **Economics** (Economics; International Business); **Electronic Information and Engineering** (Automation and Control Engineering; Electrical and Electronic Equipment and Maintenance; Electronic Engineering); **Fine Arts** (Design; Painting and Drawing); **Foreign Languages and Literature**; **Humanities** (Administration; Chinese; Cultural Studies; Literature; Political Sciences; Special Education); **International** *(Raffles-CU)*; **Machine Engineering** (Automation and Control Engineering; Industrial Design; Industrial Engineering; Machine Building); **Management**; **Music** (Music); **Science** (Applied Mathematics; Applied Physics; Computer Science; Educational Technology; Mathematics); **Software** (Computer Networks; Software Engineering)

Research Institute
Applied Technology (Technology); **Biological Engineering** (Bioengineering); **Scientific and Technological Development in Higher Education**

History: Founded 1987. Merged with Jilin University of Science and Technology, Jilin Specialized School of Mechanical and Electrical Engineering, Changchun Specialized School of Foreign Languages and Changchun Vocational University.

Degrees and Diplomas: *Xueshi Xuewei*

Publications: Journal of Changchun University

CHANGCHUN UNIVERSITY OF CHINESE MEDICINE

39 Gongnong Street, Changchun, Jilin Province 130021
Tel: +86(431) 5955911 +86(431) 5956499
Fax: +86(431) 5958760
EMail: liumiao_66@hotmail.com
Website: http://www.ccucm.edu.cn

President: Sui Dianjun

International Relations: Song Bailin Tel: +86(431) 5940940

Department
Acupuncture, Moxibustion and Osteology Nursing (Acupuncture; Health Sciences; Nursing); **Chinese Medical Science** (Traditional Eastern Medicine); **Traditional Chinese Medicine** (Medicine; Traditional Eastern Medicine)

History: Founded 1958 as Changchun College of Traditional Chinese Medicine.

Degrees and Diplomas: *Xueshi Xuewei*; *Shuoshi Xuewei*; *Boshi*

CHANGCHUN UNIVERSITY OF SCIENCE AND TECHNOLOGY

7 Weixing Road, Changchun, Jilin Province 130022
Tel: +86(431) 5386407
Fax: +86(431) 5303278
EMail: webmaster@cust.edu.cn
Website: http://www.cust.edu.cn

President: Yu Huadong

International Relations: Zhang Qifang

School
Biological and Medical Engineering (Bioengineering; Biomedical Engineering); **Chemistry and Environmental Engineering**; **Chinese Literature** (Chinese; Literature); **Computer Science and Technology** (Computer Science); **Economics and Management** (Economics; Management); **Electronics and Information Engineering** (Computer Engineering; Electronic Engineering); **Foreign Languages** (Modern Languages); **Law** (Law); **Life Sciences and Technology**; **Material and Chemical Industry**; **Mechatronical Engineering**; **Photoelectric Engineering**; **Science** (Applied Chemistry; Applied Mathematics; Applied Physics; Chemical Engineering; Materials Engineering; Optical Technology)

History: Founded 1958 as Changchun Institute of Optics and Precision Instruments. Acquired present title 2002.

Main Language(s) of Instruction: Chinese

Degrees and Diplomas: *Xueshi Xuewei*; *Shuoshi Xuewei*; *Boshi*

Publications: Journal of Changchun Institute of Optics and Precision Instruments; Research in Higher Education

CHANGCHUN UNIVERSITY OF TECHNOLOGY

17 Yan'an Road, Changchun,
Jilin Province 130012
Tel: +86(431) 5955521
Website: http://www.ccut.edu.cn/

President: Du Lizheng

International Relations: Xiao Ning

School
Computer Science and Engineering (Computer Engineering; Computer Science); **Humanities** (Arts and Humanities); **Management** (Management); **Mechanical Engineering** (Mechanical Engineering); **Modern Languages** (Modern Languages); **Rural Planning** (Rural Planning)

Department
Applied Sciences (Applied Chemistry; Applied Mathematics; Applied Physics); **Automation and Electronic Engineering** (Automation and Control Engineering; Electronic Engineering); **Chemical Engineering** (Chemical Engineering); **Materials Engineering** (Materials Engineering); **Metallurgical Engineering**; **Textile Engineering** (Textile Technology); **Transport Engineering** (Transport Engineering)

History: Founded 1952 as Changchun School of Automotive Technology. Renamed Jilin Institute of Science and Technology 1961 and Jilin Institute of Technology 1962. Acquired present title 2002.

Degrees and Diplomas: *Xueshi Xuewei*; *Shuoshi Xuewei*

CHANGSHA UNIVERSITY

21 Hongshanmiao, Kaifu District,
Changsha, Hunan Province 410003
Tel: +86(731) 425 4372
Fax: +86(731) 425 0583
EMail: wsb@ccsu.cn
Website: http://www.ccsu.cn

Department
Applied Chemistry and Environmental Science (Applied Chemistry; Environmental Studies); **Applied Physics and Electronic Technology** (Applied Physics; Electronic Engineering); **Arts** (Fine Arts); **Computer Science and Technology** (Computer Science; Technology); **Economics and Management** (Economics; Management); **Engineering** (Engineering); **Foreign Languages** (Modern Languages); **Humanities** (Art Criticism); **Mathematics and Information Science** (Information Sciences; Mathematics); **Physical Education** (Physical Education); **Politics and Law** (Law; Political Sciences)

History: Create 1983.

Degrees and Diplomas: *Xueshi Xuewei*

CHANGSHA UNIVERSITY OF SCIENCE AND TECHNOLOGY

9 Chiling Road, Changsha, Hunan Province 410077
Tel: +86(731) 2617768
EMail: study@csust.edu.cn
Website: http://www.csust.edu.cn

President: Yan Guoliang

International Relations: Tu Heping

Department

Engineering (Engineering); **Humanities** (Arts and Humanities); **Science** (Natural Sciences); **Social Sciences** (Social Sciences)

History: Founded 2002 following merger of Changsha University of Electric Power (founded 1956) and Changsha Communications University (founded 1956).

Degrees and Diplomas: *Xueshi Xuewei*; *Shuoshi Xuewei*; *Boshi*

CHANGZHI MEDICAL COLLEGE

46 Yanan Nanku, Changzhi, Shanxi Province 046000

President: Wang Yongjin

Department

Clinical Medicine (Medicine); **Medical X-ray and Imaging**; **Nursing** (Nursing)

History: Founded 1946 as Changzhi Nursing School. Acquired present title 1986.

Degrees and Diplomas: *Xueshi Xuewei*

CHANGZHOU INSTITUTE OF TECHNOLOGY

3 Changcheng Road, Changzhou, Jiangsu Province 213002
Tel: +86(519) 5210282 +86(519) 5210284
Fax: +86(519) 5210282
EMail: bgs@oa.czu.cn
Website: http://www.czu.cn

President: Ma Shushan

International Relations: Yu Xinhuai

Division

Foundation Studies; **Social Sciences** (Social Sciences)

Department

Civil Engineering (Civil Engineering); **Computer Application Engineering** (Computer Engineering); **Economic Management** (Economics; Management); **Electrical Engineering** (Electrical Engineering); **Languages and Literature** (Literature; Modern Languages); **Mechanical Engineering** (Mechanical Engineering); **Quality Technology Engineering**

History: Founded 1978 as Changzhou Industrial College. Changed its title 2003. Previously known as Changzhou College of Industrial Technology.

Degrees and Diplomas: *Xueshi Xuewei*

CHANGZHOU UNIVERSITY

Beiyun Road, Changzhou, Jiangsu Province 213016
Tel: +86(519) 3290140
Fax: +86(519) 3290011
EMail: jlc@jpu.edu.cn
Website: http://eng.jpu.edu.cn

President: Pu Yuzhong

College

Huaide

School

Business Administration (Accountancy; Business Administration; Industrial Design; Information Management; International Business; International Economics; Marketing); **Chemical Engineering** (Applied Chemistry; Bioengineering; Chemical Engineering; Organic Chemistry); **Computer Science and Technology** (Automation and Control Engineering; Computer Science; Telecommunications Engineering); **Environmental and Safety Engineering** (Environmental Engineering; Safety Engineering; Water Management); **Foreign Languages** (English; Japanese); **Humanities, Law and Art** (Design; Industrial Design; Law; Political Sciences; Social Sciences; Social Work); **Information Science** (Applied Mathematics; Applied Physics; Electronic Engineering; Information Sciences); **Materials Science and Engineering** (Materials Engineering; Metallurgical Engineering; Polymer and Plastics Technology); **Materials Science and Engineering** (Materials Engineering; Metallurgical Engineering; Polymer and Plastics Technology); **Mechanical and Energy Engineering** (Automation and Control Engineering; Energy Engineering; Petroleum and Gas Engineering; Thermal Engineering); **Petrochemical Engineering** (Applied Chemistry; Chemical Engineering; Organic Chemistry); **Petroleum Engineering** (Building Technologies; Petroleum and Gas Engineering; Thermal Engineering); **Pharmaceutical Engineering and Life Sciences** (Bioengineering; Biotechnology; Medicine; Nursing; Pharmacology)

History: Founded 1978 as Jiangsu Institute of Chemical Technology. Became Jiangsu Institute of Petrochemical Technology. Renamed Jiangsu Polytechnic University in 2002. Acquired present title 2010.

Main Language(s) of Instruction: Chinese

Degrees and Diplomas: *Xueshi Xuewei*

Last Updated: 30/11/12

CHENGDE MEDICAL COLLEGE

Chengde, Hebei Province 067000
Tel: +86(314) 2065269
Fax: +86(314) 2064089
Website: http://china786.com/Chendge%20Medical%20College/index.htm

President: Jin Yongde

International Relations: Hu Shidong

Department

Biomedical Engineering (Biomedical Engineering); **Clinical Medicine** (Medicine); **Nursing** (Nursing); **Psychology** (Psychology); **Traditional Chinese Medicine** (Traditional Eastern Medicine); **Traditional Chinese Pharmacy** (Pharmacy)

History: Founded 1945 as Health School of the Jidong Region. Acquired present status and title 1982.

Degrees and Diplomas: *Xueshi Xuewei*; *Shuoshi Xuewei*

CHENGDU SPORT UNIVERSITY

2 Tiyuan Road, Chengdu, Sichuan Province 610041
Tel: +86(28) 5593292
Fax: +86(28) 5582752
EMail: kycswp@263.net
Website: http://www.cdsu.edu.cn/en/indexe.asp

President: Zhou Xikuan

International Relations: Li Guodong

Faculty

Athletic Sports (Sports); **Economics and Management** (Economics; Management; Statistics); **Foreign Languages**; **Journalism**; **Physical Education**; **Sports Medicine**; **Wu Shu**

Further Information: Also Hang Kong Gang Campus

History: Founded 1942 as Sichuan Standing Junior Sports College. Chengdu Sport Polytechnic 1950, Chengdu Institute of Physical Education 1956.

Degrees and Diplomas: *Xueshi Xuewei*; *Shuoshi Xuewei*; *Boshi*

CHENGDU UNIVERSITY

Shiling Town, Chengdu, Sichuan Province 610081
Tel: +86(28) 3389284
Fax: +86(28) 3337939
EMail: faocdu@cdu.edu.cn
Website: http://www.cdu.edu.cn

President: Zhang Rixin

International Relations: Yang Meijin

Faculty

Art (Art Education); **Bio-industry**; **Continuing Education** (Continuing Education); **Economics, Political Science and Law** (Economics; Law; Political Sciences); **Electronic and Information**

Engineering (Computer Engineering; Electronic Engineering); **Fine Arts** (Fine Arts); **Foreign Languages and Culture** (Cultural Studies; Modern Languages); **Industrial Manufacturing**; **Information Science and Technology**; **International Education**; **Literature and Journalism**; **Management** (Management); **Medicine and Nursing**; **Normal Education** (Education); **Preschool Education**; **Software Industry**; **Tourism and Cultural Industry** (Cultural Studies; Tourism); **Urban and Rural Construction** (Construction Engineering)

History: Founded 1978.

Main Language(s) of Instruction: Chinese

Degrees and Diplomas: *Xueshi Xuewei*

CHENGDU UNIVERSITY OF INFORMATION TECHNOLOGY

3 Block, Renminnan Road, Chengdu, Sichuan Province 610041
Tel: +86(28) 5533523
Fax: +86(28) 5553580
EMail: wsb@cuit.edu.cn
Website: http://www.cuit.edu.cn

President: Duan Tingyang

International Relations: Tan Jiansheng

Division

Arts (Chinese; English; Literature); **Business** (Accountancy; E-Business/Commerce; Finance; Human Resources; International Business; Marketing; Public Administration); **Engineering** (Automation and Control Engineering; Biomedical Engineering; Computer Engineering; Computer Networks; Electrical Engineering; Electronic Engineering; Environmental Engineering; Microelectronics; Software Engineering; Telecommunications Engineering); **Law** (Law; Social Work); **Science** (Information Technology; Mathematics; Optics; Statistics)

History: Founded 1951. Acquired present title 2000. Previously known as Chengdu Institute of Meteorology.

Main Language(s) of Instruction: Chinese

Degrees and Diplomas: *Xueshi Xuewei*; *Shuoshi Xuewei*

CHENGDU UNIVERSITY OF TECHNOLOGY

1 Dongsanlu Erxianqiao, Chengdu, Sichuan Province 610059
Tel: +86(28) 84078960 +86(28) 84079488
Fax: +86(28) 84077099
EMail: lsg@cdut.edu.cn; yhd@cdut.edu.cn
Website: http://www.cdut.edu.cn

College

Applied Nuclear Technology and Automation Engineering; **Commerce** (Accountancy; Business Administration; Economics; Finance; Tourism); **Communication Science and Art**; **Continuing Education**; **Earth Sciences** (Earth Sciences; Information Technology; Rural Planning; Tourism; Town Planning); **Energy Resources** (Geology; Petroleum and Gas Engineering); **Environment and Civil Engineering** (Architecture; Civil Engineering; Construction Engineering; Environmental Engineering; Geological Engineering); **Foreign Languages and Cultures** (Cultural Studies; English; Japanese; Modern Languages); **Information Engineering** (Computer Engineering; Electronic Engineering; Geophysics; Information Technology; Physics); **Information Management** (Computer Science; E-Business/Commerce; Information Sciences; Management; Mathematics); **Materials and Bioengineering**; **Network Education**

School

Humanities and Law (Administration; Arts and Humanities; Law; Political Sciences; Public Administration; Social Sciences; Teacher Training)

Institute

Tourism and Hospitality *(Sino-Australian)*

History: Founded 1956 as Chengdu College of Geology. Acquired present title in 1993. Incorporated Sichuan Commercial College and the Training Institute for Staff Members of Non-Ferrous Metal Geological Institutions 2001.

Admission Requirements: Graduation from high school and national university entrance examination

Fees: (Yuan): 4,000-17,000 (tuition fees) according to field of study

Accrediting Agency: Department of Education of Sichuan Provincial Government

Degrees and Diplomas: *Xueshi Xuewei*: **Accountancy; Acting; Advertising and Publicity; Applied Chemistry; Automation and Control Engineering; Bioengineering; Business Administration; Chemistry; Civil Engineering; Computer Science; Design; Economics; Electrical Engineering; Electronic Engineering; English; Environmental Engineering; Finance; Geochemistry; Geography; Geology; Geophysics; Human Resources; Hydraulic Engineering; Industrial Design; Information Management; Information Sciences; Information Technology; International Business; International Economics; Japanese; Landscape Architecture; Law; Literature; Management; Marketing; Natural Resources; Nuclear Engineering; Petroleum and Gas Engineering; Public Administration; Rural Planning; Sociology; Town Planning.** *Shuoshi Xuewei*: **Analytical Chemistry; Anthropology; Applied Chemistry; Applied Mathematics; Chemical Engineering; Computer Engineering; Computer Science; Environmental Engineering; Environmental Studies; Finance; Foreign Languages Education; Geochemistry; Geography; Geological Engineering; Geology; Geophysics; Human Resources; Information Technology; Linguistics; Management; Marketing; Mathematics; Mineralogy; Mining Engineering; Natural Sciences; Nuclear Engineering; Paleontology; Petroleum and Gas Engineering; Philosophy; Safety Engineering; Surveying and Mapping; Technology.** *Boshi*: **Anthropology; Civil Engineering; Environmental Studies; Geochemistry; Geological Engineering; Geology; Geophysics; Information Technology; Mineralogy; Mining Engineering; Nuclear Engineering; Paleontology; Petroleum and Gas Engineering; Surveying and Mapping.**

Student Services: Academic Counselling, Canteen, Careers Guidance, Health Services, Language Laboratory, Nursery Care, Social Counselling, Sports Facilities

Publications: Computing Techniques for Geophysical and Geochemical Exploration; Journal of Chengdu University of Technology (Natural Science); Journal of Chengdu University of Technology (Social Science); Journal of Geological Hazards and Environmental Preservation; Journal of Mineralogy and Petrology; Scientific and Technological Management of Land and Resources

CHENGDU UNIVERSITY OF TRADITIONAL CHINESE MEDICINE

37 Shierqiao Road, Chengdu, Sichuan Province 610075
Tel: +86(28) 7768611
Fax: +86(28) 7763471
EMail: wsc@cdutcm.edu.cn
Website: http://www.cdutcm.edu.cn

President: Li Mingfu

International Relations: Huang Qingxian

School

Acupuncture and Moxibustion (Acupuncture; Traditional Eastern Medicine); **Clinical Medicine**; **Continuing Education**; **International Education**; **Medicine** (Medicine); **Pharmacy**

History: Founded 1956 as Chengdu College of Traditional Chinese Medicine, acquired present title 1995.

Degrees and Diplomas: *Xueshi Xuewei*; *Shuoshi Xuewei*; *Boshi*

Publications: Guide of Chinese Medicine Information; Journal of Chengdu University of Traditional Chinese Medicine; Journal of Educational Science

CHIFENG UNIVERSITY

Airport Road, Chifeng, Inner Mongolia 024000
Tel: +86(476) 2205811
Fax: +86(476) 8810068

History: Founded 1958. Acquired present title 2003, following merger with Chifeng Teachers Training College for Nationalities, Chifeng College of Education and Chifeng Branch of Inner Mongolian TV University.

Degrees and Diplomas: *Xueshi Xuewei*

CHINA ACADEMY OF ART

218 Nanshan Road, Hangzhou, Zhejiang Province 310002
Tel: +86(571) 7038237
Fax: +86(571) 7070039
EMail: caafao@caa.edu.cn
Website: http://www.chinaacademyofart.com/

President: Xu Jiang

Department

Art History and Theory (Art History); **Environmental Design** (Architectural and Environmental Design); **Fashion and Textile Design** (Fashion Design); **Industrial Design and Ceramics** (Ceramic Art; Design); **Oil Painting** (Painting and Drawing); **Print-Making** (Printing and Printmaking); **Sculpture** (Sculpture); **Traditional Chinese Painting** (Painting and Drawing); **Visual Communication and Design** (Communication Arts; Design)

History: Founded 1928 as National Academy of Art. Renamed China Academy of Art 1993.

Degrees and Diplomas: *Xueshi Xuewei*; *Shuoshi Xuewei*; *Boshi*

CHINA AGRICULTURAL UNIVERSITY

2 Yuanmingyuan West Road, Haidian District, Beijing 100094
Tel: +86(10) 62892736
Fax: +86(10) 62891055
EMail: cauie@cau.edu.cn
Website: http://www.cau.edu.cn

President: Jiang Shuren
International Relations: Wang Jingguo

School

Adult Education (Adult Education); **Agricultural Development** (Agriculture); **Animal Science and Technology** (Technology; Zoology); **Basic Science and Technology** (Natural Sciences; Technology); **Biology** (Biology); **Continuing Education**; **Economics** (Economics); **Electronic and Electrical Power Engineering** (Electrical and Electronic Engineering; Electronic Engineering); **Food Science** (Food Science); **Humanities and Social Sciences** (Arts and Humanities; Social Sciences); **Hydraulic and Civil Engineering** (Civil Engineering; Hydraulic Engineering); **Management** (Management); **Mechanical Engineering** (Mechanical Engineering); **Plant Sciences and Technology** (Agronomy; Botany; Entomology; Pathology; Plant and Crop Protection; Plant Pathology); **Resources and Environment** (Environmental Studies; Natural Resources); **Vehicle Engineering** (Automotive Engineering); **Veterinary Medicine** (Veterinary Science)

History: Founded 1905 as Agricultural Section of Jingshi Daxuetang. Merged with Beijing Agricultural Engineering University. Acquired present title 1995.

Academic Year: September to July (September-January; February-July)

Admission Requirements: Graduation from senior middle school and national entrance examination

Fees: (Yuan): c. 1,600-1,800 per annum

Main Language(s) of Instruction: Chinese

Accrediting Agency: Ministry of Agriculture

Degrees and Diplomas: *Xueshi Xuewei*; *Shuoshi Xuewei*; *Boshi*

Student Services: Academic Counselling, Canteen, Health Services, Nursery Care, Sports Facilities

Publications: Acta Phytopathologica Sinica (in Latin); Chinese Journal of Animal Sciences; Chinese Journal of Veterinary Medicine; Journal of Agricultural Biotechnology; Journal of China Agricultural University; Journal of Plant Pathology

Publishing House: Publishing House of CAU

CHINA CRIMINAL POLICE UNIVERSITY (CCPU)

83 Tawan Street, Huanguu District,
Shenyang, Liaoning Province 110035
Tel: +86(24) 86982416
Fax: +86(24) 86723000
Website: http://www.ccpc.edu.cn/

President: Wang Siquan

Department

Criminal Investigation (Criminology); **Economic Crime Investigation**; **Forensic Medicine** (Forensic Medicine and Dentistry); **Forensic Science and Technology** (Forensic Medicine and Dentistry); **Police Physical Training** (Physical Education); **Social Sciences**

History: Founded 1949 as Northeast Public Security Officer School. Acquired present title 1981.

Degrees and Diplomas: *Xueshi Xuewei*; *Shuoshi Xuewei*

Student Services: Sports Facilities

Publications: China Criminal Police; China Criminal Police Journal; China Criminal Police Review

CHINA FOREIGN AFFAIRS UNIVERSITY

24 Zhanlan Road, Xicheng District, Beijing 100037
Tel: +86(10) 68323894
Fax: +86(10) 68348664
EMail: zhuliqu@cfau.edu.cn
Website: http://www.cfau.edu.cn

President: Wu Jianmin

Department

Basic Education (Education); **Diplomatic Studies** (International Relations); **English and International Studies** (English; International Studies; Modern Languages); **Foreign Languages**; **International Economics** (International Economics); **International Law** (International Law)

History: Founded 1955. Became Institute of International Relations 1958 and Foreign Affairs College 1961. Acquired present title 2000.

Degrees and Diplomas: *Xueshi Xuewei*; *Shuoshi Xuewei*; *Boshi*

Publications: Journal of Foreign Affairs College

CHINA JILIANG UNIVERSITY

Xueyuan Street, Xiasha Higher Education Park,
Hangzhou, Zhejiang Province 310034
Tel: +86(571) 86836028
EMail: iecd@cjlu.edu.cn
Website: http://english.cjlu.edu.cn/newslist.php?type=4

President: Zhuang Songling

College

Foreign Languages; **Humanities and Social Sciences**; **Information Engineering**; **Law** (Law); **Life Sciences**; **Management** (Accountancy; Business Administration; Engineering; Information Management; International Business; Management; Marketing); **Mechatronics Engineering**; **Metrological Technology & Engineering** (Measurement and Precision Engineering; Power Engineering; Safety Engineering; Thermal Engineering); **Physical Education and Military Training** (Physical Education); **Science** (Applied Mathematics; Applied Physics; Computer Science; Materials Engineering; Mathematics; Microelectronics)

History: Founded 1978 as China Institute of Metrology.

Degrees and Diplomas: *Xueshi Xuewei*; *Shuoshi Xuewei*

CHINA MEDICAL UNIVERSITY

92 North Second Road, Heping District,
Shenyang, Liaoning Province 110001
Tel: +86(24) 23875539
Fax: +86(24) 23875539
EMail: mikezxh885@yahoo.com.cn
Website: http://www.cmu.edu.cn

President: Qun Zhao

Faculty

Forensic Medicine (Forensic Medicine and Dentistry)

College

Basic Medical Sciences (Anatomy; Biochemistry; Bioengineering; Biophysics; Cell Biology; Chemistry; Embryology and Reproduction Biology; Genetics; Histology; Immunology; Mathematics; Medicine; Pathology; Pharmacology; Physical Education; Physics; Physiology); **Clinical Medicine I** (Medicine; Nursing); **Clinical Medicine II**; **Clinical Medicine III**

School

Adult Education; **Public Health** (Child Care and Development; Nutrition; Occupational Health; Public Health; Statistics; Toxicology); **Stomatology** (Orthodontics; Stomatology)

History: Founded 1931 as Health School of Chinese Workers' and Peasants' Red Army. Merged with National Shenyang Medical College and Liaoning Medical University 1948. Acquired present title 1940. Moved to Shenyang 1948.

Academic Year: September to July (September-January; February-July)

Main Language(s) of Instruction: Chinese

Degrees and Diplomas: *Xueshi Xuewei*; *Shuoshi Xuewei*; *Boshi*

Student Services: Health Services, Sports Facilities

Publications: Advance in Anatomy Science; Chinese Journal of Health Statistics; Chinese Journal of Medical Image; Chinese Journal of Practical Ophthalmology; Journal of China Medical University; Journal of Diabetes; Journal of First Aid in Paediatrics; Journal of Practical Rural Medicine; Paediatrics Fascicule Foreign Medicine; Progress in Japanese Medicine

Publishing House: China Medical University Press

CHINA PHARMACEUTICAL UNIVERSITY

24 Tongjiaxiang, Nanjing, Jiangsu Province 210009
Tel: +86(25) 3213611
Fax: +86(25) 3213611
Website: http://www.cpu.edu.cn

President: Wu Xiaoming

International Relations: Lü Qingrong

School

Chinese Traditional Pharmacy (Pharmacy; Traditional Eastern Medicine); **Continuing Education**; **International Pharmaceutical Business** (International Business); **Life Science and Technology** (Biochemistry; Biomedical Engineering; Biotechnology; Marine Biology; Microbiology; Molecular Biology; Pharmacology); **Pharmacy** (Pharmacy)

History: Founded 1936 as National Pharmaceutical School. Acquired present title 1986.

Degrees and Diplomas: *Xueshi Xuewei*; *Shuoshi Xuewei*; *Boshi*

Publications: China Pharmaceutics Yearbook; Journal of China Pharmaceutical University; Pharmaceutical Education Journal on Progress in Pharmaceutical Science

CHINA THREE GORGES UNIVERSITY (CTGU)

11 Tiyuchang Road, Yichang, Hubei Province 443000
Tel: +86(717) 6461202
Fax: +86(717) 6454495
EMail: dir@ctgu.edu.cn
Website: http://www.ctgu.edu.cn

President: Jianlin Li (2001-)

College

Chemistry and Life Science; **Civil and Hydroelectric Engineering**; **Clinical Medicine** *(Second)* (Medicine); **Clinical Medicine** *(First)*; **Economics and Management**; **Electrical Engineering and Information Technology**; **Foreign Languages** (English; Literature; Modern Languages); **International Communication** (Communication Studies); **Mechanical and Material Engineering**; **Medical Science**; **Nursing Science** (Nursing); **Performing and Fine Arts** (Fine Arts; Performing Arts); **Physical Education and Sports** (Physical Education; Sports); **Political Science and Law** (Law; Political Sciences); **Science**; **Vocational Technology** (Technology)

Laboratory

Construction and Management in Hydroelectric Engineering (Construction Engineering; Electrical Engineering; Hydraulic Engineering; Management)

Research Centre

Biological Engineering (Bioengineering); **Three Gorges Culture and Economic and Social Development** (Cultural Studies; Development Studies; Economics)

History: Founded 2000 following merger of University of Hydraulic and Electric Engineering/Yichang and Hubei Sanxia University.

Admission Requirements: Secondary school certificate or equivalent

Fees: Registration fees, 40; tuition fees, undergraduate, 1,800-2,000 per annum; postgraduate, 1,300-1,800 per annum (US Dollar)

Main Language(s) of Instruction: Chinese

Degrees and Diplomas: *Xueshi Xuewei*; *Shuoshi Xuewei*

Student Services: Health Services, Sports Facilities

Publications: Journal of Three Gorges University; Practical Medicine Further Study Notes

CHINA UNIVERSITY OF GEOSCIENCES

485 Lumo Lu, Hongshan District, Wuhan, Hubei Province 430074
Tel: +86(27) 87482986
Fax: +86(27) 87481364
EMail: ljzhang@cug.edu.cn
Website: http://www.cugb.edu.cn

President: Yanxin Wang

School

Energy Resources; **Engineering and Technology** (Automation and Control Engineering; Civil Engineering; Machine Building; Safety Engineering); **Gem Studies** (Jewellery Art); **Geophysics and Geoinformation Systems**; **Geosciences and Resources** (Geochemistry; Geology); **Humanities and Economic Management** (Accountancy; Commercial Law; E-Business/Commerce; Industrial Management; Information Management; Law; Marketing; Tourism); **Information Technology** (Information Technology); **Marine Science** (Marine Science and Oceanography); **Materials Science and Technology** (Materials Engineering); **Water Resources and Environmental Science** (Water Science)

Department

Foreign Language (English; Modern Languages); **Land Science** (Surveying and Mapping)

History: Founded 1952 as Wuhan College of Geology, acquired present title 1987.

Main Language(s) of Instruction: Chinese

Degrees and Diplomas: *Xueshi Xuewei*; *Shuoshi Xuewei*; *Boshi*

Publications: Earth Sciences Journal; Gemstone and Gemmology; Information on Geological Science and Technology; Liberal Arts and Management; Modern Higher Education Research

CHINA UNIVERSITY OF GEOSCIENCES (BEIJING)

29 Xueyuan Lu, Beijing 100083
Tel: +86(10) 82321080
Fax: +86(10) 82321006
Website: http://www.cugb.edu.cn

President: Wu Ganguo

International Relations: Wan Xiaoqiao

Faculty

Earth Sciences and Resources (Earth Sciences; Natural Resources)

College

Adult Education

School

Energy Resources (Energy Engineering; Petroleum and Gas Engineering); **Engineering and Technology** (Automation and Control Engineering; Civil Engineering; Engineering; Production Engineering; Safety Engineering; Technology); **Gem Studies** (Jewellery Art; Materials Engineering); **Geophysics and Geoinformation Systems** (Automation and Control Engineering; Geophysics; Technology); **Geosciences and Resources** (Geochemistry; Geology); **Humanities and Economic Management** (Accountancy; Arts and Humanities; Business Administration; Commercial Law; E-Business/Commerce; Industrial Management; Information Management; Law; Management; Marketing; Tourism); **Information Technology** (Applied Mathematics; Automation and Control Engineering; Computer Science; Electronic Engineering;

Information Technology; Mathematics); **Marine Science** (Marine Science and Oceanography); **Materials Science and Engineering** (Materials Engineering); **Network**; **Software** (Software Engineering); **Water Resources and Environmental Science** (Environmental Engineering; Hydraulic Engineering; Water Science)

Department
Foreign Languages (English; Modern Languages); **Land Science**; **Physical Education** (Physical Education)

History: Founded 1952 as Beijing College of Geology, acquired present title 1987.

Degrees and Diplomas: *Xueshi Xuewei*; *Shuoshi Xuewei*; *Boshi*

Publications: China Geological Education; Foreign References on Prospecting Engineering; Geological Frontiers; Geological Hazards and Prevention; Modern Geology

CHINA UNIVERSITY OF MINING AND TECHNOLOGY

Nanhu Campus, Xuzhou, Jiangsu Province 2211116
Tel: +86(516) 8359-0256
Fax: +86(516) 8359-0255
EMail: msca@cumt.edu.cn
Website: http://www.cumt.edu.cn

President: Ge Shirong

International Relations: Zhenkang Zhang
EMail: zhangzk@cumt.edu.cn

College
Adult Education (Accountancy; Business Administration; Civil Engineering; Computer Science; Design; E-Business/Commerce; English; International Business; International Economics; Law; Management; Marketing); **International Education and Student Exhange**; **Science and Technology** (Automation and Control Engineering; Chemical Engineering; Civil Engineering; Electrical Engineering; Geological Engineering; Marketing; Mechanical Engineering; Mining Engineering; Safety Engineering; Technology; Tourism); **Xuhai College** (Administration; Automation and Control Engineering; Banking; Chinese; Civil Engineering; Computer Science; English; Finance; Fire Science; International Business; International Economics; Literature; Management; Marketing; Materials Engineering; Measurement and Precision Engineering; Mechanical Engineering; Native Language; Power Engineering; Safety Engineering; Technology; Thermal Engineering)

School
Architecture and Civil Engineering; **Art and Design**; **Chemical Engineering and Technology** (Applied Chemistry; Bioengineering; Chemical Engineering; Mining Engineering; Technology); **Computer Science and Technology** (Computer Science; Information Sciences; Information Technology; Technology); **Environmental Science and Spatial Informatics**; **Foreign Studies** (English; German); **Information and Electrical Engineering**; **Literature, Law and Politics** (Administration; Chinese; Law; Literature; Native Language; Radio and Television Broadcasting; Social Work); **Management** (Accountancy; Banking; Business Administration; E-Business/Commerce; Finance; Human Resources; International Business; International Economics; Management; Marketing); **Materials Science and Engineering**; **Mechatronic Engineering**; **Mining and Safety Engineering** (Fire Science; Industrial Engineering; Mining Engineering; Safety Engineering; Transport and Communications); **Physical Education** (Physical Education; Sports); **Resources and Geosciences** (Biomedical Engineering; Environmental Management; Geological Engineering; Geophysics; Hydraulic Engineering; Rural Planning; Town Planning; Water Science); **Science** (Applied Mathematics; Applied Physics; Computer Science; Information Sciences; Mathematics; Mechanical Engineering; Optical Technology)

History: Founded 1909 as Jiaozuo Institute of Roads and Mines. Merged with Beijing Coal Administration Institute. Ministry of Coal Industry. Acquired present title 1988.

Academic Year: September to July

Admission Requirements: School certificate and entrance examination

Fees: (Yuan): c. 8,000-12,000 per annum

Main Language(s) of Instruction: Chinese, English

Accrediting Agency: Ministry of Education

Degrees and Diplomas: *Xueshi Xuewei*; *Shuoshi Xuewei*; *Boshi*

Student Services: Academic Counselling, Canteen, Careers Guidance, Cultural Activities, Facilities for disabled people, Foreign Studies Centre, Health Services, Language Laboratory, Nursery Care, Social Counselling, Sports Facilities

Publications: Coal Mine World; Higher Education Research; Meitian Higher Education; Mine Pressure and Roof Management

Publishing House: CUMT Publishing House

CHINA UNIVERSITY OF PETROLEUM (EAST CHINA) (UPC)

No. 66, Changjiang West Road, Huangdao District, Qingdao 266580
Tel: +86(546) 8392248
Fax: +86(546) 8392253
EMail: netnews@upc.edu.cn
Website: http://www.upc.edu.cn/

President: Shan Honghong Tel: +86(546) 8392601

Unit
Chemical Engineering and Technology *(postdoctoral)* (Chemical Engineering; Technology); **Geological Resources and Geological Engineering** *(Postdoctoral)* (Geological Engineering; Geology); **Petroleum and Gas Engineering** *(Postdoctoral)* (Petroleum and Gas Engineering)

College
Chemistry and Chemical Engineering (Chemical Engineering; Chemistry; Environmental Engineering); **Computer and Communication Engineering** (Computer Science; Mathematics and Computer Science; Telecommunications Engineering; Transport and Communications); **Economics and Management** (Administration; Economics; Management); **Electrical and Mechanical Engineering** (Electrical and Electronic Engineering; Mechanical Engineering); **Information and Control Engineering** (Automation and Control Engineering; Information Management); **Net-based Education**; **Petroleum Engineering** (Petroleum and Gas Engineering); **Petroleum Resources and Information Sciences** (Geology; Geophysics); **Storage and Transportation and Construction Engineering** (Architecture and Planning; Construction Engineering; Service Trades; Transport Engineering)

Programme
Accountancy (Accountancy)

School
Adult Education; **Advanced Vocational** (Vocational Education); **Graduate**

Centre
Bitumen Technology (Chemistry); **Chemistry Engineering Technology in Oil Fields** (Chemical Engineering; Petroleum and Gas Engineering); **Software Engineering for Petroleum Engineering** (Petroleum and Gas Engineering; Software Engineering)

Laboratory
Chemistry Teaching Base for Engineering Courses *(National)* (Chemistry; Teacher Training); **Drilling Engineering** (Production Engineering); **Heavy Oil Processing** (Chemistry); **Oil and Oil Well Engineering** (Petroleum and Gas Engineering; Production Engineering); **Oil Reservoir Geology** (Geology); **Oil Storage and Transport** (Store Management; Transport Management); **Petroleum Geophysical Exploration** (Geophysics; Petroleum and Gas Engineering); **Petroleum Machinery Engineering** (Mechanical Engineering); **Petroleum Well-logging** (Geology; Petroleum and Gas Engineering)

Research Centre
Environmental Engineering (Environmental Engineering); **Non-asbestos Abrasive Materials** (Materials Engineering); **Oil and Gas Catalysis** (Chemistry; Petroleum and Gas Engineering); **Oil and Gas Processing Technology** (Petroleum and Gas Engineering)

Further Information: Also campus in Dongying.

History: Founded 1953 as Beijing Petroleum Institute, became East China Petroleum Institute 1969. Acquired present status and title 2005.

Academic Year: September to July (September-January; February-July)

Admission Requirements: Graduation from senior middle school and entrance examination

Fees: (Yuan): 3,800-7,000 per annum according to major

Main Language(s) of Instruction: Chinese

Accrediting Agency: Ministry of Education

Degrees and Diplomas: *Xueshi Xuewei*: **Economics; Engineering; Law; Literature; Management.** *Shuoshi Xuewei*: **Engineering; Law; Literature; Management.** *Boshi*: **Engineering.**

Student Services: Academic Counselling, Canteen, Careers Guidance, Cultural Activities, Facilities for disabled people, Foreign Studies Centre, Health Services, Language Laboratory, Nursery Care, Social Counselling, Sports Facilities

Publications: Higher Education; Journal of the University of Petroleum (Natural Sciences and Social Sciences Editions)

Publishing House: University of Petroleum Publishing House

CHINA UNIVERSITY OF PETROLEUM - BEIJING

18 Fuxue Road, Changping, Beijing 102249
Tel: +86(10) 8973 3266
Fax: +86(10) 6970 0644
EMail: overseas@cup.edu.cn
Website: http://www.cup.edu.cn

President: Laibin Zhang (2005-)
Tel: +86(10) 8973 3334 EMail: zhanglb@cup.edu.cn

Director, International Relations: Xudong Sun
Tel: +86(10) 8973 3477 EMail: sxudong@cup.edu.cn

International Relations: Xiaoqing Liu, International Affairs Officer
Tel: +86(10) 8973 1677

Faculty

Chemical Engineering (Chemical Engineering; Energy Engineering; Environmental Engineering); **Geosciences**; **Mechanical and Electronic Engineering** (Automation and Control Engineering; Electronic Engineering; Materials Engineering; Mechanical Engineering; Safety Engineering); **Petroleum Engineering** (Civil Engineering; Petroleum and Gas Engineering)

School

Business Administration (Accountancy; Business Administration; Finance; International Business; Management; Marketing)

Department

Computer Science (Computer Engineering); **Foreign Languages** (Linguistics; Modern Languages); **Humanities** (Classical Languages; Literature; Philosophy); **Mathematics and Physics** (Mathematics; Physics); **Physical Education**

History: Founded 1953 as Beijing Petroleum Institute, acquired present title and status 2005.

Academic Year: September to July

Main Language(s) of Instruction: Chinese

Accrediting Agency: Ministry of Education

Degrees and Diplomas: *Xueshi Xuewei*; *Shuoshi Xuewei*; *Boshi*

Student Services: Academic Counselling, Canteen, Careers Guidance, Facilities for disabled people, Foreign Studies Centre, Health Services, Language Laboratory, Nursery Care, Social Counselling, Sports Facilities

Publications: Palaeogeology; Petroleum Science

CHINA UNIVERSITY OF POLITICAL SCIENCE AND LAW

25 Xitucheng Road, Haidian District, Beijing 100088
Tel: +86(10) 62229863
Fax: +86(10) 62228804
EMail: oice@cupl.edu.cn
Website: http://www.cupl.edu.cn

President: Xu Xianming

School

American and Comparative Law (Comparative Law; Law); **Business** (Business Administration); **Civil, Commercial and Economic Laws**; **Continuing Education**; **Criminal and Judicatory Law** (Criminal Law; Criminology); **Foreign Languages** (English; French; German; Italian; Japanese; Modern Languages; Russian); **German and Comparative Law** (Comparative Law; Law); **Graduate**; **Humanities** (Chinese; Journalism; Literature; Philosophy); **Law** (Law); **Political Science and Public Administration** (Political Sciences; Public Administration); **Sociology** (Sociology)

Institute

Comparative Law (Comparative Law); **Globalization and Global Issues**

History: Founded 1952 as Beijing Political Science and Law College. Acquired present title 1983.

Main Language(s) of Instruction: Chinese

Degrees and Diplomas: *Xueshi Xuewei*; *Shuoshi Xuewei*; *Boshi*

Publications: Administrative Law Research; Comparative Law Research; Journal of Central Leadership Institute of Politics and Law; Tribune of Political Science and Law

CHINA WEST NORMAL UNIVERSITY

1 ShiDa Road, Nanchong, Sichuan Province 637002
Tel: +86(817) 2568017
Fax: +86(817) 2314331
EMail: oice@cwnu.edu.cn
Website: http://www.cwnu.edu.cn

President: Chen Ning EMail: cning60@hotmail.com

College

Chemistry and Chemical Engineering (Chemical Engineering; Chemistry); **Chinese Language and Literature** (Chinese; Literature); **Land and Resources** (Environmental Studies; Geography; Rural Planning; Town Planning); **Life Sciences** (Biological and Life Sciences; Biology); **Mathematics and Information** (Applied Mathematics; Information Management; Mathematics); **Physical Education** (Physical Education)

School

Business (Business Administration); **Computer Science** (Computer Science); **Educational Science and Technology** (Education; Educational Technology; Pedagogy; Preschool Education; Primary Education); **Foreign Languages** (Modern Languages); **History and Culture** (Cultural Studies; History); **Journalism and Communication** (Communication Studies; Journalism); **Law** (Law); **Management** (Management); **Marxism** (Political Sciences); **Physics and Electrical Information** (Electrical Engineering; Physics); **Politics and Administration** (Administration; Political Sciences)

Department

Fine Arts (Fine Arts); **Music** (Music)

History: Founded 1946 as Northern Sichuan Agriculture and Industry College, acquired present title 2003.

Degrees and Diplomas: *Xueshi Xuewei*; *Shuoshi Xuewei*

CHINA YOUTH UNIVERSITY FOR POLITICAL SCIENCES

25 Xisanhuan North Road, Beijing 100089
Tel: +86(10) 68475409
Fax: +86(10) 68475649
EMail: cycp5@263.net
Website: http://cms.cyu.edu.cn

President: Zhou Qiang

International Relations: Zhang Qinghong

Department

Economic Management (Management); **Journalism** (Journalism); **Law** (Law); **Social Work** (Social Work); **Youth Work**

History: Founded 1985 as Central School of China Youth League. Formerly known as China Youth College for Political Sciences.

Degrees and Diplomas: *Xueshi Xuewei*; *Shuoshi Xuewei*

CHINESE ACADEMY OF MEDICAL SCIENCES AND PEKING UNION MEDICAL COLLEGE

9 Dongdan Santiao, Beijing 100730
Tel: +86(10) 65249442
Fax: +86(10) 65124876
EMail: bgs@ibms.pumc.edu.cn
Website: http://www.pumc.edu.cn

President: Depei Liu

School

Basic Medicine (Anatomy; Biochemistry; Biology; Biomedical Engineering; Biophysics; Cell Biology; Embryology and Reproduction Biology; Endocrinology; Epidemiology; Genetics; Gerontology; Haematology; Histology; Immunology; Medicine; Microbiology; Molecular Biology; Nutrition; Paediatrics; Parasitology; Pathology; Pharmacology; Physiology; Pneumology; Psychology; Rheumatology; Statistics; Traditional Eastern Medicine); **Clinical Medicine** (Anaesthesiology; Cardiology; Dentistry; Gynaecology and Obstetrics; Medicine; Oncology; Ophthalmology; Otorhinolaryngology; Radiology; Surgery); **Continuing Education**; **Graduate Studies**; **Nursing** (Nursing); **Public Health** (Public Health)

History: Founded 1917as Peking Union Medical College. Merged with Chinese Academy of Medical Sciences (CAMS).

Degrees and Diplomas: *Xueshi Xuewei*; *Shuoshi Xuewei*; *Boshi*

Publications: Chinese Medical Sciences Journal

Last Updated: 25/01/13

CHINESE PEOPLE'S PUBLIC SECURITY UNIVERSITY

Muxudi, Xicheng District, Beijing 100038
Tel: +86(10) 63404433-2126
Fax: +86(10) 63260301

President: Sun Zhongguo

International Relations: Song Qiang

Programme

Modern Languages (Modern Languages); **Welfare and Protective Services** (Civil Security; Criminology; Police Studies)

History: Founded 1948 as North China Public Security Cadre School. Merged with Chinese People's Police Officers' University and Chinese People's Public Security University. Acquired present title 1984.

Degrees and Diplomas: *Xueshi Xuewei*; *Shuoshi Xuewei*

Publications: Modern World Choice; Public Security Education; Public Security University Journal

CHONGQING JIAOTONG UNIVERSITY

No. 66 Xuefudadao, Nanan district,
Chongqing, Sichuan Province 400074
Tel: +86(23) 62651999
Fax: +86(23) 62650387
EMail: waiban@cquc.edu.cn
Website: http://www.cquc.edu.cn

President: Boming Tang

School

Adult Education

Department

Automotive Engineering (Automotive Engineering); **Bridge Engineering** (Bridge Engineering); **Computer and Information Engineering** (Computer Engineering; Information Technology); **Finance and Economics** (Economics; Finance); **Foreign Languages** (Modern Languages); **Highway Engineering** (Civil Engineering; Road Engineering); **Management** (Management); **River and Ocean Engineering** (Marine Engineering; Water Management)

History: Founded 1951 as Southwest Jiaotong College, acquired present title 1978.

Degrees and Diplomas: *Xueshi Xuewei*; *Shuoshi Xuewei*; *Boshi*

Publications: Applied Mathematics & Mechanics; Journal

CHONGQING NORMAL UNIVERSITY

12 Tianchen Road, Shapingba,
Chongqing, Sichuan Province 400047
Tel: +86(23) 65362739
Fax: +86(23) 65316566
EMail: interoff@cqnu.edu.cn
Website: http://www.cqnu.edu.cn

President: Qin Zhiren

International Relations: Hu Lang

Department

Art and Design (Design; Fine Arts); **Biology** (Biology); **Chemistry** (Chemistry); **Chinese Language and Literature** (Chinese); **Economics, Politics and Law** (Economics; Law; Political Sciences); **Foreign Languages** (English); **Geography** (Geography); **History** (History); **Management of Modern Information** (Information Management); **Mathematics and Computer** (Computer Science; Mathematics); **Photographic Engineering**; **Physics and Information Technology** (Information Technology; Physics); **Tourism**

History: Founded 1953 as Chongqing Teachers College. Acquired present status and title 1978.

Degrees and Diplomas: *Xueshi Xuewei*; *Shuoshi Xuewei*

CHONGQING TECHNOLOGY AND BUSINESS UNIVERSITY

Wugongli, Nan'an District, Chongqing, Sichuan Province 400067
Tel: +86(23) 62804306
Fax: +86(23) 62803515
EMail: wshch@ctbu.edu.cn

President: Wang Chongju

International Relations: Chen Quanfu

Department

Accountancy (Accountancy); **Administration** (Administration); **Commercial Planning** (Business and Commerce); **Computer Engineering**; **Economics** (Economics); **Finance and Investment** (Finance); **Graphic Arts** (Graphic Arts); **Law** (Law); **Tourism Administration** (Tourism)

Further Information: Also campus in Jiangbei

History: Founded 1962 as Chongqing Finance and Commerce School. Acquired present title following merge of two former colleges, Yuzhou University and Chongqing Institute of Commerce..

Degrees and Diplomas: *Xueshi Xuewei*; *Shuoshi Xuewei*

CHONGQING THREE GORGES UNIVERSITY

780 Shalong Road, Wanzhou,
Chongqing, Sichuan Province 404000
Tel: +86(23) 58102298
Fax: +86(23) 58124510
EMail: pxd1998@163.com
Website: http://www.sanxiau.net/english/index.htm

President: Wu Tieqing

International Relations: Ding Jiadi

Department

Architectural Engineering (Structural Architecture); **Biochemistry** (Biochemistry); **Business Administration** (Business Administration); **Chinese** (Chinese); **Computer Science** (Computer Science); **Economics** (Economics); **Electrical Engineering** (Electrical Engineering); **English** (English); **Fine Arts** (Fine Arts); **Social Sciences** (Social Sciences); **Sports** (Sports)

History: Founded 1994.

Main Language(s) of Instruction: Chinese

Degrees and Diplomas: *Xueshi Xuewei*

CHONGQING UNIVERSITY (CQU)

174 Shazhengjie, Shapingba, Chongqing, Sichuan Province 400044
Tel: +86(23) 65102391
Fax: +86(23) 65106656
EMail: fao101@cqu.edu.cn
Website: http://www.cqu.edu.cn

President: Li Xiaohong Tel: +86(23) 65102349

College
Architecture and Construction (Architecture; Construction Engineering; Design); **Automation** (Automation and Control Engineering); **Business Administration and Economics** (Accountancy; Business Administration; Economics; Finance; Information Management; Management; Marketing); **Chemistry and Chemical Engineering** (Chemical Engineering; Chemistry); **Computer Science** (Computer Science; Engineering); **Electrical Engineering** (Electrical Engineering); **Foreign Languages** (Linguistics; Literature; Modern Languages; Translation and Interpretation); **Material Science and Engineering** (Materials Engineering; Metallurgical Engineering); **Mathematics and Physics** (Mathematics; Physics); **Mechanical Engineering** (Mechanical Engineering); **Optical and Electronic Engineering** (Electronic Engineering; Optical Technology); **Resources and Environmental Engineering** (Environmental Engineering; Natural Resources); **Telecommunications Engineering** (Telecommunications Engineering); **Thermal Power Engineering** (Thermal Engineering); **Trade and Law** (Commercial Law; Economics)

Academy
Film *(Meishi)* (Film)

History: Founded 1929. Merged with Chongqing Jianzhu University and Chongqing Architectural College 2000.

Academic Year: September to July

Admission Requirements: Matriculation Examination Score above 550 on average

Fees: (Yuan): 4,500-15,000

Main Language(s) of Instruction: Chinese, English

Degrees and Diplomas: *Xueshi Xuewei*; *Shuoshi Xuewei*; *Boshi*

Student Services: Academic Counselling, Canteen, Careers Guidance, Cultural Activities, Facilities for disabled people, Foreign Studies Centre, Health Services, Language Laboratory, Nursery Care, Social Counselling, Sports Facilities

Publications: Chongqing University Journal; Chongqing University Journal

Publishing House: Chongqing University Publishing House

CHONGQING UNIVERSITY OF MEDICAL SCIENCES

1 Yixue Yuan Road, Chongqing, Sichuan Province 400016
Tel: +86(23) 68809229
Fax: +86(23) 68809229
EMail: cqumsfao@mail.cqums.edu.cn

President: Jin Xianqing

International Relations: Tang Haiqig

Faculty
Family Planning (Family Studies); **Laboratory Medicine** (Laboratory Techniques; Medicine)

School
Adult Education; **Basic Medical Sciences** (Medicine); **Clinical Medicine** (Medicine); **Clinical Medicine II** (Medicine); **Paediatrics** (Paediatrics); **Social Sciences** (Social Sciences)

Department
Preventive Medicine (Social and Preventive Medicine)

History: Founded 1956 as Chongqing Medical College, acquired present title 1956.

Degrees and Diplomas: *Xueshi Xuewei*; *Shuoshi Xuewei*; *Boshi*

Publications: ACTA University Sciences Medicine Chongqing; Journal of Hepatology; Journal of Ultrasonic Medicine

CHONGQING UNIVERSITY OF POSTS AND TELECOMMUNICATIONS

Huang Jieya, Nan'an District, Chongqing, Sichuan Province 400065
Tel: +86(23) 62461002
Fax: +86(23) 62461882
EMail: gjc@cqupt.edu.cn
Website: http://www.cqupt.edu.cn/

President: Chen Liuting

Department
Computer Science and Technology (Computer Science); **Information and Computational Science** (Computer Science; Information Sciences); **Management Engineering** (Engineering Management); **Modern Languages** (Modern Languages); **Postal Engineering** (Postal Services; Telecommunications Engineering; Telecommunications Services); **Radio Communications Engineering** (Telecommunications Engineering); **Social Sciences** (Social Sciences); **Telecommunication Engineering** (Telecommunications Engineering)

History: Founded 1959 as Posts and Telecommunications School. Acquired present status 1980.

Degrees and Diplomas: *Xueshi Xuewei*; *Shuoshi Xuewei*

CHONGQING UNIVERSITY OF TECHNOLOGY (CQUT)

4 Xingsheng Road, Yangjiaping, Jiulongpo District, Chongqing, Sichuan Province 400050
Tel: +86(23) 68777496
Fax: +86(23) 68820848
Website: http://cj.cqut.edu.cn/Default.aspx

President: Xiaohui Shi

College
Business and Information (Business Administration)

School
Accountancy (Accountancy); **Adult Education** (Adult Education); **Biological Engineering** (Bioengineering); **Business Administration** (Business Administration); **Computer Science and Engineering** (Computer Engineering; Computer Science); **Economics and Trade** (Business Administration; Economics); **Electronic Information and Automation**; **Foreign Languages** (Modern Languages); **Humanities and Social Sciences**; **Material Science and Engineering**; **Mathematics and Science** (Mathematics; Natural Sciences)

Institute
Automobile *(Chongqing)* (Automotive Engineering)

History: Founded 1950 as Chongqing Technological University. Formerly known as Chongqing Institute of Technology. Acquired present status and title 2009.

Main Language(s) of Instruction: Chinese

Degrees and Diplomas: *Xueshi Xuewei*; *Shuoshi Xuewei*

CIVIL AVIATION FLIGHT UNIVERSITY OF CHINA

Guanghan, Sichuan Province 618307
Tel: +86(838) 5182117
Fax: +86(838) 5191777
EMail: wsb@cafuc.edu.cn
Website: http://www.cafuc.edu.cn/structure/NewWeb/index

President: Zheng Xiaoyong

International Relations: Gong Jianyu

Department
Aircraft Oparation; **Airline Transport Communication Services** (Air Transport); **Aviation Engineering**; **English** (English); **Social Sciences**

Centre
Aero-Engine Maintenance Training; **Flight Simulator Training**

History: Founded 1956 as CCAC Aviation School. Acquired present title 1987.

Degrees and Diplomas: *Xueshi Xuewei*; *Shuoshi Xuewei*

CIVIL AVIATION UNIVERSITY OF CHINA

100 Xunhai Road, Dongli District, Tianjin, Tianjin Province 300300
Tel: +86(22) 24960647
Fax: +86(22) 24960647
EMail: cauciad@cauc.edu.cn
Website: http://www.cauc.edu.cn

President: Wu Tongshui

College

Aeronautical Mechanics and Avionics Engineering; **Air Traffic Management** (Air Transport); **Computer Science and Technology** (Computer Science); **Flight**; **Humanities and Social Sciences** (English; Law; Modern Languages; Social Sciences); **Management** (Accountancy; Business Administration; Finance; Industrial Engineering; Management); **Safety Science and Engineering**; **Science** (Chemistry; Computer Science; Physics); **Transport Engineering** (Transport Engineering)

Department

Physical Education (Physical Education)

History: Founded 1951 as CAAC Training School. Acquired present status and title 1981.

Degrees and Diplomas: *Xueshi Xuewei*; *Shuoshi Xuewei*

COMMUNICATION UNIVERSITY OF CHINA (CUC)

1 East Street, Dingfuzhuang, Chaoyang District, Beijing 100024
Tel: +86(10) 65779773
Fax: +86(10) 65779138
EMail: jishuqing@cuc.edu.cn
Website: http://www.cuc.edu.cn

President: Jinan Liu

College

Advertising (Advertising and Publicity)

School

Animation; **Computer and Software** (Computer Science; Software Engineering); **Information Engineering** (Engineering; Information Sciences); **Literature** (Literature); **Media Management** (Management; Media Studies); **Presentation Art**; **Science** (Natural Sciences); **Social Sciences** (Social Sciences); **Television and Journalism** (Journalism; Radio and Television Broadcasting)

History: Founded 1954. Formerly Beijing Broadcasting University. Acquired present title 2004 following merger with China University of Mining and Technology (Beijing).

Academic Year: March to January (March-July; September-January)

Fees: (US Dollars): 1,900-3,600 per annum

Main Language(s) of Instruction: Chinese

Degrees and Diplomas: *Xueshi Xuewei*; *Shuoshi Xuewei*; *Boshi*

Student Services: Academic Counselling, Canteen, Careers Guidance, Cultural Activities, Foreign Studies Centre, Health Services, Language Laboratory, Nursery Care, Social Counselling, Sports Facilities

Publications: Modern Communications

Publishing House: BBU Press

DALIAN JIAOTONG UNIVERSITY

794 Huanghe Road, Dalian, Liaoning Province 116028
Tel: +86(411) 4604323 Ext. 2799
Fax: +86(411) 4629614
EMail: xinxi@djtu.edu.cn
Website: http://www.djtu.edu.cn

President: Ge Jiping

School

Art; **Electronics and Information Engineering** (Electrical Engineering; Electronic Engineering; Information Sciences; Technology); **Environmental and Chemical Engineering**; **Foreign Languages**; **Management** (Management); **Materials Science and Engineering** (Engineering; Materials Engineering); **Mechanical Engineering** (Mechanical Engineering); **Science** (Mathematics and Computer Science; Natural Sciences); **Traffic and Transport** (Architecture; Civil Engineering; Road Engineering; Road Transport; Transport Engineering; Transport Management)

Institute

International (International Studies); **Software** (Software Engineering)

History: Founded 1956 as Dalian Engine Vehicle Production School. Acquired present title 2004.

Degrees and Diplomas: *Xueshi Xuewei*; *Shuoshi Xuewei*; *Boshi*

DALIAN MARITIME UNIVERSITY (DMU)

1 Linghai Road, Dalian, Liaoning Province 116026
Tel: +86(411) 84729259
Fax: +86(411) 84727395
EMail: fsodmu@hotmail.com
Website: http://www.dlmu.edu.cn

President: Wang Zuwen (2004-)
Tel: +86(411) 84723311 EMail: wangaw@dlmu.edu.cn

Registrar: Youtao Zhao Tel: +86(411) 84729341

International Relations: Bin Xu, Director, International Cooperation and Communication

College

Automation and Electrical Engineering; **Computer Science and Technology** (Computer Engineering; Computer Science; Software Engineering); **Continuing Education**; **Economics and Management**; **Electromechanics and Materials Engineering** (Automation and Control Engineering; Machine Building; Marine Engineering; Materials Engineering); **Environmental Science and Engineering** (Environmental Engineering; Environmental Studies; Nautical Science); **Foreign Languages** (English; Japanese); **Humanities and Social Sciences**; **Information Engineering** (Electronic Engineering; Information Sciences; Information Technology; Telecommunications Engineering); **Law** (International Economics; International Law; Labour Law; Law); **Marine Engineering**; **Mathematics** (Computer Science; Information Sciences; Mathematics); **Navigation** (Nautical Science); **Physics**; **Postgraduate Studies**; **Specialised Degree Education**; **Transportation and Logistics**

Research Centre

Automation Engineering; **Global Navigation Satellite**; **Globalisation and Foreign Language Teaching**; **IMO Conventions**; **Logistics System Engineering**

Research Institute

Antenna; **Automation and Control Engineering**; **Circuit and System**; **Communication Electronics**; **Electronic Infomation Technology Education and Application**; **Environmental Biology**; **Environmental Engineering**; **Image Information Processing**; **Information System Engineering**; **International Shipping Human Resource**; **International Trade and Multinational Investment**; **Maritime Mobile Communications**; **Mobile Communications**; **Nautical Science and Technology**; **Ocean Exploration and Management**; **Optoelectronics Information Engineering**; **Optoelectronics Technology**; **Port and Shipping**; **Road and Bridge Engineering**; **Tourism Planning**; **Transportation Economics**; **Transportation Planning**; **Waterway Transportation Acts**

History: Founded 1953, incorporating Shanghai Nautical College, Northeast Navigation College, and Fujian Navigation School. Became a key maritime university 1960.

Academic Year: March to January (March-July; September-January)

Admission Requirements: Graduation from senior middle school and national college entrance examination

Fees: (US Dollars): 2,500 per annum

Main Language(s) of Instruction: Chinese, English

Accrediting Agency: Norwegian Classification Society; China Maritime Safety Administration; Ministry of Communication

Degrees and Diplomas: *Xueshi Xuewei*: **Economics; Fine Arts; Law; Management; Technology.** *Shuoshi Xuewei*: **Economics; Law; Management; Technology.** *Boshi*: **Law; Technology.** Also Professional Diplomas

Student Services: Academic Counselling, Canteen, Careers Guidance, Cultural Activities, Facilities for disabled people, Foreign Studies Centre, Health Services, Language Laboratory, Nursery Care, Social Counselling, Sports Facilities

Publications: Higher Maritime Education; Journal of Dalian Maritime University; Nautical Laws of China; World Shipping Journal

Publishing House: Dalian Maritime University Press

DALIAN MEDICAL UNIVERSITY

465 Zhongshan Road, Shahekou District,
Dalian, Liaoning Province 116027
Tel: +86(411) 4672546
Fax: +86(411) 4672546
EMail: admin@dlmedu.edu.cn
Website: http://www.dlmedu.edu.cn

President: Jiang Chao

College

Basic Medical Sciences (Anatomy; Biochemistry; Embryology and Reproduction Biology; Histology; Hygiene; Medicine; Microbiology; Molecular Biology; Parasitology; Pathology; Pharmacology; Physiology); **Cosmetology** (Cosmetology; Plastic Surgery); **Health Administration** (Health Administration); **Stomatology** (Stomatology)

School

Adult Education

Department

Clinical Pharmacy (Pharmacy); **Medical Laboratory Tests and Analysis** (Laboratory Techniques; Medical Technology); **Obstetrics and Gynaecology** (Gynaecology and Obstetrics); **Oral Medicine** (Medicine); **Photography** (Photography)

Further Information: Also 3 Affiliated Teaching Hospitals.

History: Founded 1947 as Guandong Medical college. Became Dalian University Medical College 1949, Dalian Medical College 1950, Zunyi Medical College 1969, and Dalian Medical College 1978. Acquired present title 1994.

Degrees and Diplomas: *Xueshi Xuewei*; *Shuoshi Xuewei*; *Boshi*

Publications: Journal of Dalian Medical University

DALIAN NATIONALITIES UNIVERSITY

18 Liaohe Wet Road, Dalian Economic and Technical Development Zone, Dalian, Liaoning Province 116600
Tel: +86(411) 7612616
Fax: +86(411) 7618179
EMail: office@dlnu.edu.cn
Website: http://www.dlnu.edu.cn

Faculty

Architecture (Architecture); **Chemical Engineering** (Chemical Engineering); **Electronic and Computer Engineering** (Computer Engineering; Electronic Engineering); **Electronics and Accountancy** (Accountancy; Electronic Engineering); **Industrial Design** (Industrial Design); **International Economics** (International Economics); **Management** (Management); **Mechanical Engineering and Computer Science** (Computer Science; Mechanical Engineering); **Modern Languages** (Modern Languages)

Department

General Studies; **Social Sciences** (Social Sciences)

DALIAN OCEAN UNIVERSITY (DOU)

52 Heshijao Street, Dalian, Liaoning Province 116023
Tel: +86(411) 4660163
Fax: +86(411) 4660163
EMail: iecd@dlou.edu.cn
Website: http://www.dlfu.edu.cn

President: Yao Jie

Department

Aquaculture (Aquaculture); **Civil Engineering** (Civil Engineering); **Electronic Engineering** (Electronic Engineering); **Management** (Management); **Marine Fisheries** (Fishery); **Mechanical Engineering** (Mechanical Engineering)

History: Founded 1952 as Northeast Fisheries Technical School. Formerly known as Dalian Fisheries Academy in 1958, Dalian Fisheries University in 1978. Acquired present name and title 2010.

Main Language(s) of Instruction: Chinese

Degrees and Diplomas: *Xueshi Xuewei*; *Shuoshi Xuewei*

Last Updated: 21/11/14

DALIAN POLYTECHNIC UNIVERSITY

1 Qinggongyuan, Dalian, Liaoning Province 116034
Tel: +86(411) 86324486
Fax: +86(411) 86323647
Website: http://www.dlili.edu.cn/

President: Xiao Zhengyang

International Relations: Chen Yang

School

Artistic Design (Design); **Textile and Fashion** (Fashion Design; Textile Design)

Department

Automation (Automation and Control Engineering); **Chemical Engineering** (Chemical Engineering); **Economics**; **Food Engineering and Bioengineering** (Bioengineering; Food Technology); **Materials Science and Engineering** (Materials Engineering); **Mechanical Engineering** (Mechanical Engineering); **Modern Languages**

History: Founded 1958 as Shenyang Institute of Light Industry. Became Dalian Institute of Light Industry 1970. Acquired present title 2007.

Degrees and Diplomas: *Xueshi Xuewei*; *Shuoshi Xuewei*

DALIAN UNIVERSITY

Dalian Economic and Technology Development Zone,
Dalian, Liaoning Province 116622
Tel: +86(411) 87300952
Fax: +86(411) 87403963
EMail: office@dalianu.com
Website: http://202.199.158.1/old/eng/index.htm

President: Xiaopeng Wei

International Relations: Hongtao Wang Tel: +86(411) 87402135

College

Adult Education (Teacher Training); **Bioengineering** (Bioengineering; Biological and Life Sciences); **Economics and Administration** (Accountancy; Business Administration; Economics; Management; Marketing); **English Language**; **Fine Arts** (Fine Arts); **Humanities** (Arts and Humanities; History; Law; Linguistics; Literature; Philosophy; Psychology; Social Sciences); **Information Technology** (Computer Science; Electrical and Electronic Engineering; Information Technology; Library Science; Mathematics); **International Cultural Exchange** (Cultural Studies); **International studies**; **Japanese Language and Culture** (Japanese; Linguistics; Teacher Training); **Medicine** (Dentistry; Medicine; Nursing; Pharmacy); **Music**; **Physical Education** (Physical Education); **Teacher Training** (Teacher Training); **Tourism** (Tourism); **Women** (Women's Studies)

Department

Chemical Engineering (Chemical Engineering); **Civil Engineering** (Architecture; Civil Engineering; Industrial Engineering); **Mechanical Engineering** (Mechanical Engineering); **Physics** (Physics)

Centre

Advanced Designing Technology (Computer Graphics); **Gender Studies** (Gender Studies)

History: Founded 1987. Merged with College of Teachers, College of Engineering and Medical College in 1995.

Academic Year: September to February; March to August

Admission Requirements: National Entrance Examination

Fees: (Yuan) 4,000-16,000 per annum

Main Language(s) of Instruction: Chinese

Accrediting Agency: Ministry of Education

Degrees and Diplomas: *Xueshi Xuewei*; *Shuoshi Xuewei*. Also 3 yr University Diploma

Student Services: Academic Counselling, Canteen, Careers Guidance, Cultural Activities, Facilities for disabled people, Foreign Studies Centre, Health Services, Language Laboratory, Nursery Care, Social Counselling, Sports Facilities

Publications: Journal of Dalian University

DALIAN UNIVERSITY OF FOREIGN LANGUAGES

94 Yan'an Road, Zhongshan District,
Dalian, Liaoning Province 116002
Tel: +86(441) 2801220 +86(441) 2801297
Fax: +86(441) 2639958
Website: http://www.dlufl.edu.cn

President: Sun Yuhua

School

Chinese Studies (Chinese); **Cultural Communications** (Communication Studies); **English Studies** (English); **International Art and Design** (Design); **International Tourism and Hospitality Management** (Tourism); **Japanese Studies** (Japanese); **Software** (Software Engineering)

Department

French (French); **German** (German); **Korean** (Korean); **Russian Studies** (Russian)

History: Founded 1964 as Dalian Japanese Language Institute. Acquired present title 1978.

Degrees and Diplomas: *Xueshi Xuewei*; *Shuoshi Xuewei*

DALIAN UNIVERSITY OF TECHNOLOGY

2 Linggong Road, Ganjingzi District,
Dalian, Liaoning Province 116023
Tel: +86(411) 84708702
Fax: +86(411) 84708704
EMail: office@dlut.edu.cn
Website: http://www.dlut.edu.cn

President: Ou Jinping Tel: +86(411) 84708936

School

Adult Education; **Architecture and Fine Arts**; **Chemical Engineering** (Chemical Engineering; Chemistry; Environmental Engineering; Polymer and Plastics Technology); **Civil and Hydraulic Engineering** (Architecture; Civil Engineering; Hydraulic Engineering); **Electronics and Information Engineering** (Automation and Control Engineering; Computer Science; Electronic Engineering; Information Technology); **Environmental and Biological Science and Technology**; **Foreign Languages** (Modern Languages); **Humanities and Social Sciences** (Engineering; Law; Linguistics; Media Studies; Philosophy; Political Sciences; Public Administration; Social Sciences); **International Cultural Exchange** (Cultural Studies); **Management** (Business Administration; Information Management; Management); **Mechanical Engineering** (Mechanical Engineering); **Naval Architectural Engineering** (Marine Engineering; Naval Architecture; Power Engineering); **Software Engineering**

Department

Applied Mathematics (Applied Mathematics); **Electromagnetic Engineering** (Mechanics); **Materials Engineering** (Materials Engineering); **Mechanics** (Mechanics); **Physics** (Physics); **Power Engineering**

Further Information: Also 4 national key laboratories; Coastal and Offshore Engineering; Material Surface Modification by Laser, Ionand Electronic beams; Fine Chemical Engineering; Structural Analyses for Industrial Equipment

History: Founded 1949 as School of Engineering of Dalian University, became independent as Dalian Institution of Technology 1950. Acquired present name 1988

Admission Requirements: Score of 565 in National College Entrance Exam

Main Language(s) of Instruction: Chinese

Accrediting Agency: Ministry of Education

Degrees and Diplomas: *Xueshi Xuewei*; *Shuoshi Xuewei*; *Boshi*

Student Services: Academic Counselling, Canteen, Careers Guidance, Cultural Activities, Facilities for disabled people, Health Services, Language Laboratory, Nursery Care, Social Counselling, Sports Facilities

Publications: Computational Mechanics; Journal; Journal of Dalian University of Technology; Mathematics Study and Review

Publishing House: Dalian University of Technology Press

DONGBEI UNIVERSITY OF FINANCE AND ECONOMICS

217 Jianshan Street, Dalian, Liaoning Province 116025
Tel: +86(411) 4691811
Fax: +86(411) 4691811
EMail: dufe@dufe.edu.cn
Website: http://www.dufe.edu.cn

President: Yu Yang

International Relations: Wang Tiejun

School

Accountancy (Accountancy); **Chinese Language and Culture** *(International)* (Chinese; Cultural Studies); **Continuing Education** (Banking; Economics; Ethics; Law; Management; Statistics); **Hotel Management** (Hotel Management); **Industrial and Commercial Management** (Industrial Management); **Public Finance and Taxation** (Finance; Taxation)

History: Founded 1952 as Dongbei College of Finance and Economics.

Degrees and Diplomas: *Xueshi Xuewei*; *Shuoshi Xuewei*; *Boshi*

Publications: Journal of Dongbei University of Finance and Economics; Research in Problems of Finance and Economics

DONGHUA UNIVERSITY

1882 Yan-An Road West, Shanghai, Shanghai 200051
Tel: +86(21) 62373678
Fax: +86(21) 62194722
EMail: ices@dhu.edu.cn
Website: http://www.dhu.edu.cn

President: Xu Mingzhi

International Relations: Shen Bai yao

School

Adult Education (Adult Education); **Business and Management** *(Glorious Sun)* (Accountancy; Business Administration; Business and Commerce; E-Business/Commerce; Information Management; International Economics; Management; Marketing); **Business and Management** *(Glorious Sun)* (Business Administration; Management); **Chemistry and Chemical Engineering** (Applied Chemistry; Bioengineering; Chemical Engineering; Chemistry; Textile Technology); **Computer Science and Technology** (Computer Science); **Environmental Science and Engineering** (Construction Engineering; Environmental Engineering; Heating and Refrigeration); **Fashion and Art Design** (Fashion Design; Industrial Design); **Foreign Languages** (English; Japanese; Modern Languages); **Humanities** (Administration; Arts and Humanities; Law; Public Administration; Public Relations); **Information Science and Technology** (Computer Science; Electronic Engineering; Information Sciences; Information Technology; Technology; Telecommunications Engineering); **Material Science and Engineering** (Inorganic Chemistry; Materials Engineering; Optical Technology; Optics; Polymer and Plastics Technology); **Mechanical Engineering** (Automation and Control Engineering; Industrial Design; Mechanical Engineering); **Network Education**; **Science** (Applied Mathematics; Applied Physics; Mathematics; Natural Sciences); **Textile** (Information Technology; Textile Technology)

Institute

Fashion (Fashion Design)

Centre

Modern Education Technology (Educational Technology; Multimedia)

Campus

Wuxi (Accountancy; Business Administration; Computer Science; E-Business/Commerce; Information Management; Marketing; Technology)

History: Founded 1951 as China Textile University, acquired present title and status 1999.

Academic Year: September to July (September-January; February-July)

Fees: (Yuan): 5,000-10,000 per annum; foreign students, US$ 1,800-4,500

Degrees and Diplomas: *Xueshi Xuewei*; *Shuoshi Xuewei*; *Boshi*

Publications: Journal of Donghua University; Textile Education

EAST CHINA INSTITUTE OF TECHNOLOGY

14 Xuefu Road, Linchuan, Fuzhou, Fujian Province 344000
Tel: +86(794) 8268345
Fax: +86(794) 8258345
Website: http://www.ecit.edu.cn/

President: Liu Qingcheng

International Relations: Cao Shuanglin

Department

Applied Chemistry (Applied Chemistry); **Business and Management** (Business Administration; Management); **Engineering** (Engineering); **English** (English); **Geoscience** (Geology); **Information Sciences** (Information Sciences); **Materials Science and Engineering** (Materials Engineering); **Survey Engineering** (Surveying and Mapping)

History: Founded 1956 as Taigu Geological College. Previously known as East China Institute of Geology. Acquired present title and status 2002.

Degrees and Diplomas: *Xueshi Xuewei*; *Shuoshi Xuewei*

EAST CHINA JIAOTONG UNIVERSITY

Changbei Open and Developing District,
Nanchang, Jiangxi Province 330013
Tel: +86(791) 7046910
Fax: +86(791) 7046924
EMail: xqb@ecjtu.jx.cn
Website: http://www.ecjtu.jx.cn

President: Lei Xiaoyan Tel: +86(791) 7046001

School

Adult Education (Economics; Engineering; Technology); **Basic Science** (Applied Chemistry; Applied Physics; Computer Graphics; Software Engineering); **Civil Engineering and Architecture** (Architecture; Bridge Engineering; Civil Engineering; Environmental Engineering; Mechanical Engineering; Railway Engineering; Transport Engineering); **Economics and Management** (Accountancy; Banking; Economics; Finance; International Business; Management); **Electrical and Electronic Engineering** (Automation and Control Engineering; Electrical and Electronic Engineering; Electrical Engineering); **Information Engineering**; **Mechanical and Electrical Engineering** (Electrical Engineering; Electronic Engineering; Industrial Management; Mechanical Engineering); **Professional Technology** (Technology); **Social Science and Chinese Language** (Chinese; Law; Social Sciences; Social Work)

Department

Foreign Languages (Modern Languages); **Physical Education** (Physical Education); **Social Sciences** (Arts and Humanities; Philosophy; Social Sciences)

Centre

Family Education and Female Research (Family Studies; Women's Studies); **Modern Education and Technology** (Education; Technology)

Research Centre

Civil Engineering (Civil Engineering); **Mechanical Engineering** (Mechanical Engineering); **Transportation and Economics** (Economics; Transport Management)

Further Information: Also University Hospital

History: Founded 1971.

Academic Year: September to July (September-January; March-July)

Admission Requirements: Graduation from senior middle school and entrance examination

Fees: (Yuan): c. 6,000 per annum

Main Language(s) of Instruction: Chinese

Degrees and Diplomas: *Xueshi Xuewei*: **Accountancy; Architectural and Environmental Design; Architecture; Automation and Control Engineering; Bridge Engineering; Civil Engineering; Economics; Electronic Engineering; Engineering; English; Environmental Engineering; Human Resources; Industrial Design; Information Management; International Business; Mechanical Engineering; Software Engineering.** *Shuoshi Xuewei*: **Accountancy; Computer Engineering; Industrial Management; Labour and Industrial Relations; Machine Building; Mechanical Engineering; Statistics; Transport Engineering.**

Student Services: Academic Counselling, Careers Guidance, Health Services, Language Laboratory, Nursery Care, Social Counselling, Sports Facilities

Publications: Journal of East China Jiatong University

EAST CHINA NORMAL UNIVERSITY

3663 Zhongshan Road North, Shanghai, Shanghai 200062
Tel: +86(21) 62572289
Fax: +86(21) 62570590
EMail: eoffice@admin.ecnu.edu.cn
Website: http://www.ecnu.edu.cn

President: Lizhong Yu Tel: +86(21) 62574476

School

Educational Administration (Educational Administration); **Educational Sciences** (Curriculum; Education; Educational Technology; Physical Education; Psychology); **Graduate**; **Humanities** (Advertising and Publicity; Arts and Humanities; Chinese; History; Journalism; Literature; Music; Philosophy; Political Sciences; Radio and Television Broadcasting); **Preschool and Special Education** (Preschool Education; Special Education)

Further Information: Also c. 50 research centres and institutes

History: Founded 1951. Merged with Shanghai Preschool Teacher Junior College, Shanghai Institute of Education and Shanghai Second Institute of Education. Acquired present title 1980.

Academic Year: September to July

Admission Requirements: Graduation from senior middle school and entrance examination

Degrees and Diplomas: *Xueshi Xuewei*; *Shuoshi Xuewei*; *Boshi*

Publications: East Europe and Middle Asia Today; English Teaching and Research in Elementary and Secondary Schools; Journal of East China Normal University; Psychological Science; Research on Ideology and Politics; Research on Literature and Art Theory; Research on World Geography

Publishing House: University Press

EAST CHINA UNIVERSITY OF POLITICS AND LAW

1575 Wanghangdu Road, Shanghai, Shanghai 200042
Tel: +86(21) 62512497
Fax: +86(21) 62137121
EMail: ecuplnews@ecupl.edu.cn
Website: http://www.ecupl.edu.cn

President: He Qinhua

School

Business; **Criminal Justice** (Criminal Law); **Economic Law** (Commercial Law); **Foreign Languages** (Modern Languages); **Humanities**; **Intellectual Property**; **International Law** (International Law); **Law** (Law); **Politics and Public Administration** (Political Sciences; Public Administration)

Department

Sociology (Sociology)

History: Founded 1952 as St. John's University, acquired present status 1979.

Degrees and Diplomas: *Xueshi Xuewei*; *Shuoshi Xuewei*; *Boshi*

Publications: Journal of East China Institute of Politics and Law; Science of Law

EAST CHINA UNIVERSITY OF SCIENCE AND TECHNOLOGY

China Meilang Road, Shanghai, Shanghai 200237
Tel: +86(21) 64252760
Fax: +86(21) 64250735
EMail: baohua@ecust.edu.cn
Website: http://www.ecust.edu.cn

President: Qian Xuhong

College

Technology *(Sino-German)* (Technology)

School

Art, Design and Media; **Bioengineering** (Applied Chemistry; Biochemistry; Bioengineering); **Business** (Accountancy; Business Administration; Business and Commerce; Economics; International Economics; Management); **Chemical Engineering** (Chemical Engineering; Petroleum and Gas Engineering); **Chemistry and Molecular Engineering** (Chemistry; Molecular Biology; Pharmacology; Pharmacy); **Continuing Education**; **Foreign Languages**; **Humanities** (Administration; Arts and Humanities; Industrial Design; Modern Languages; Sociology); **Information Sciences and Engineering** (Automation and Control Engineering; Computer Science; Electronic Engineering; Engineering; Information Sciences; Information Technology); **Law** (Law); **Materials Engineering** (Inorganic Chemistry; Materials Engineering; Polymer and Plastics Technology); **Mechanical and Power Engineering** (Mechanical Engineering; Power Engineering); **Resource and Environmental Engineering** (Environmental Engineering; Natural Resources); **Science** (Mathematics; Physics); **Social and Public Administration**

History: Founded 1952 as East China Institute of Chemical Technology, acquired present title 1980, incorporating previously existing departments of Chiaotung, Tatung, Aurora, Soochow and Kiangnan Universities.

Academic Year: September to July (September-February; February-July)

Admission Requirements: Graduation from senior middle school and entrance examination

Main Language(s) of Instruction: Chinese

Accrediting Agency: State Education Commission

Degrees and Diplomas: *Xueshi Xuewei*; *Shuoshi Xuewei*; *Boshi*

Publications: Journal of Functional Polymers

FOSHAN UNIVERSITY

18 Jiangwan First Road, Foshan, Guangdong Province 528000
Tel: +86(757) 2713853
Fax: +86(757) 2713853
EMail: ieo@fosu.edu.cn
Website: http://www.fosu.edu.cn

President: Zou Cairong

International Relations: Lin Zhi

Faculty

Physical Education (Physical Education)

School

Business; **Educational Sciences**; **Environment and Civil Engineering**; **Life Sciences** (Biological and Life Sciences); **Literature and Arts** (Ceramic Art; Chinese; Design; English; Literature); **Mechanical and Electronic Engineering** (Applied Physics; Automation and Control Engineering; Communication Studies; Mechanical Engineering); **Medical** (Medicine); **Politics and Law** (Law; Political Sciences); **Science**

History: Founded 1955. Acquired present status 2005 after merging with Foshan Medical College and Foshan College of Education.

Degrees and Diplomas: *Xueshi Xuewei*

FUDAN UNIVERSITY

220 Handan Road, Shanghai, Shanghai 200433
Tel: +86(21) 65642260
Fax: +86(21) 65649524
EMail: xjshi@fudan.edu.cn
Website: http://www.fudan.edu.cn

President: Wang Shenghong

International Relations: Shen Dingli

School

Economics (Economics; Finance; International Business; International Economics); **Humanities** (Arts and Humanities; Chinese; Cultural Studies; History; Literature; Modern Languages; Philosophy); **Journalism** (Journalism); **Law** (International Law; International Relations; Law; Sociology); **Life Sciences** (Biochemistry; Biological and Life Sciences; Biophysics; Environmental Studies; Genetics; Microbiology; Physiology); **Management** (Accountancy; Finance; International Business; Management; Statistics); **Medicine**; **Nursing** (Nursing); **Pharmacy** (Pharmacy); **Public Health** (Public Health); **Technology** (Computer Science; Materials Engineering; Mechanical Engineering; Technology)

Department

Chemistry (Chemistry); **Environmental Science and Engineering** (Engineering; Environmental Studies); **Mathematics** (Mathematics); **Physics** (Physics); **Polymer Science** (Polymer and Plastics Technology)

History: Founded 1905 as Fudan College. Merged with Shanghai Medical University 2000.

Academic Year: September to July (two semesters)

Admission Requirements: Graduation from senior middle school and entrance examination

Main Language(s) of Instruction: Chinese, English

Degrees and Diplomas: *Xueshi Xuewei*; *Shuoshi Xuewei*; *Boshi*

Publications: Chinese Annual of Mathematics; Fudan Natural Sciences Journal; Fudan Social Sciences Journal; Mathematics Annals; Research and Developmental Management; Rhetoric; World Economic Forum

FUJIAN AGRICULTURE AND FORESTRY UNIVERSITY

Jinshan, Fuzhou, Fujian Province 350002
Tel: +86(591) 3789208
Fax: +86(591) 3741251
EMail: fafufao@126.com
Website: http://www.fjau.edu.cn

President: Zheng Jingui

International Relations: Zhu Pengfei

School

Adult Education; **Animal Science** (Zoology); **Crop Science** (Agronomy; Crop Production); **Economics and Trade** (Agriculture; Business and Commerce; Commercial Law; Economics; Finance; Management)

Department

Food Science (Food Science); **Fundamental Subjects**; **Horticulture** (Horticulture); **Land and Environmental Science** (Environmental Studies); **Mechanical and Electrical Engineering** (Electrical Engineering; Mechanical Engineering); **Plant Protection** (Plant and Crop Protection)

History: Founded 1936 as Private Agricultural College of Fukien Christian University and Fukien Provincial Agricultural College. Renamed Fujian Agricultural University 1994. Acquired present title 2000, following merger with Fujian College of Forestry and Fujian Provincial Agricultural College.

Degrees and Diplomas: *Xueshi Xuewei*; *Shuoshi Xuewei*; *Boshi*

Publications: Entomological Journal of East China; Journal; Sugarcane; Wuyi Science Journal

FUJIAN MEDICAL UNIVERSITY

88 Jiaotong Road, Fuzhou, Fujian Province 350004
Tel: +86(591) 22862315
EMail: setup@mail.fjmu.edu.cn
Website: http://www.fjmu.edu.cn

President: Chen Liying

International Relations: Xu Huiyuan

Department

Medicine (Medicine); **Nursing** (Nursing); **Preventive Medicine** (Social and Preventive Medicine); **Stomatology** (Stomatology)

History: Founded 1937 as Fujian Provincial Medical School, acquired present title 1996.

Degrees and Diplomas: *Xueshi Xuewei*; *Shuoshi Xuewei*; *Boshi*

Publications: Journal of Fujian Medical University; Study of Higher Medical Education

FUJIAN NORMAL UNIVERSITY

8 Shangsan Road, Canshan District,
Fuzhou, Fujian Province 350007
Tel: +86(591) 3412820
Fax: +86(591) 3442840
EMail: fjw@fli.com.cn
Website: http://www.fjtu.edu.cn

President: Zeng Minyong (1996-) Tel: +86(591) 3440179

International Relations: Huang Jiahua Tel: +86(591) 3412820

School

Adult Education; **Arts** (Arts and Humanities; Fine Arts; Music); **Biological Engineering** (Bioengineering; Biology; Microbiology); **Chinese Studies** *(International)* (Administration; Chemistry; Chinese; Computer Science; Education; Educational Technology; Geography; History; Literature; Mathematics; Physical Education; Physics; Sociology; Tourism; Urban Studies); **Foreign Languages** (English; Japanese; Modern Languages; Translation and Interpretation); **Law and Economics** (Economics; Law; Political Sciences)

Research Institute

Polymer (Polymer and Plastics Technology)

Further Information: Also Teaching Hospital. Courses for foreign students

History: Founded 1907 as school, acquired present status and title 1972.

Academic Year: September to June (September-February; March-June)

Admission Requirements: Graduation from senior middle school and entrance examination

Degrees and Diplomas: *Xueshi Xuewei*: **Fine Arts; History; Law.** *Shuoshi Xuewei*; *Boshi*

Publications: Chinese and Foreign Education; Chinese World; Chinese World; Education of China and Foreign Countries; Fujian Foreign Language; Fujian Geography; Fujian Secondary School Mathematics; Journal

FUJIAN UNIVERSITY OF TRADITIONAL CHINESE MEDICINE

282 Wusilu, Fuzhou, Fujian Province 350003
Tel: +86(591) 7842528
Fax: +86(591) 7852754
EMail: hwxy@fjtcm.edu.cn
Website: http://www.fjtcm.edu.cn

President: Du Jian

International Relations: Li Candong

School

Overseas Education

Department

Acupuncture and Massage (Acupuncture); **Medicine** (Medicine); **Nursing** (Nursing); **Postgraduate**; **Social Sciences** (Social Sciences); **Traditional Chinese Medicine** (Orthopaedics; Traditional Eastern Medicine)

History: Founded 1953 as Fuzhou Teaching School.

Degrees and Diplomas: *Xueshi Xuewei*; *Shuoshi Xuewei*; *Boshi*

Publications: Higher Education and Research of TCM; Journal of Fujian TCM University

FUYANG TEACHERS COLLEGE

Qinghe Road, Fuyang, Anhui Province 236032
Tel: +86(558) 2262882
Fax: +86(558) 2263670
Website: http://www.fync.edu.cn/ch2008/index.html

President: Liu Shengzhen

International Relations: Yin Zhanyin

Department

Biology; **Chemistry** (Chemistry); **Chinese Language and Literature** (Chinese); **Computer Science** (Computer Science); **Fine Arts** (Fine Arts); **History**; **Mathematics** (Mathematics); **Modern Languages** (Modern Languages); **Music** (Music); **Physical Education** (Physical Education); **Physics** (Physics); **Political Science and Law** (Law; Political Sciences)

Degrees and Diplomas: *Xueshi Xuewei*; *Shuoshi Xuewei*

Last Updated: 22/11/12

FUZHOU UNIVERSITY

2 Xue Yuan Road, University Town,
Fuzhou, Fujian Province 350002
Tel: +86(591) 22866099
EMail: faomail@fzu.edu.cn
Website: http://www.fzu.edu.cn

President: Wu Minsheng

College

Adult Education (Accountancy; Architecture; Automation and Control Engineering; Banking; Business and Commerce; Chemical Engineering; Computer Science; Electronic Engineering; English; Finance; Secretarial Studies); **Architecture** (Architecture); **Chemistry and Chemical Engineering** (Chemical Engineering; Chemistry); **Civil Engineering** (Civil Engineering; Industrial Engineering; Structural Architecture); **Industrial Arts**; **Management** (Management)

School

Adult Education; **Arts and Crafts** (Crafts and Trades; Fine Arts); **Civil Engineering** (Architecture; Civil Engineering); **Foreign Languages** (English; Modern Languages); **Management** (Management); **Materials Science and Engineering** (Engineering; Materials Engineering)

Department

Accountancy (Accountancy); **Arts and Crafts** (Crafts and Trades; Handicrafts); **Biological and Food Engineering** (Biology; Food Technology); **Chemistry** (Chemistry); **Computer Science and Technology** (Computer Science; Technology); **Electrical Engineering** (Electrical Engineering); **Electronics and Applied Physics** (Applied Physics; Electronic Engineering); **Environmental and Resources Engineering** (Environmental Engineering; Natural Resources); **Finance and Banking** (Banking; Finance); **Humanities and Social Sciences** (Arts and Humanities; Chinese; Cultural Studies; Social Sciences); **Hydraulic Engineering** (Hydraulic Engineering); **Management** (Management); **Materials Science and Engineering** (Materials Engineering); **Mathematics** (Mathematics); **Mechanical Engineering** (Mechanical Engineering); **Radio Engineering** (Telecommunications Engineering); **Trade** (Business and Commerce)

Section

Bioelectric Chemistry (Chemistry); **Biomedical Engineering** (Biomedical Engineering); **Chemical Engineering** (Chemical Engineering); **Finance Supporting Systems** (Finance); **Geology** (Geology); **Hydraulics** (Hydraulic Engineering); **Industrial Computers and Systems** (Industrial Engineering); **Irrigation and Hydropower** (Hydraulic Engineering; Irrigation); **Microcomputer Applications** (Computer Science)

History: Founded 1958.

Academic Year: September to July (September-January; February-July)

Admission Requirements: Graduation from senior middle school and entrance examination

Main Language(s) of Instruction: Chinese

Degrees and Diplomas: *Xueshi Xuewei*; *Shuoshi Xuewei*; *Boshi*

Publications: Annals of Differential Equations; Fouzhou University Paper; Journal of Fuzhou University; Studies of Higher Education; Yearbook of Differential Equations

Publishing House: Fuzhou University Press

GANNAN MEDICAL UNIVERSITY

1, Yixueyuan Road, Ganzhou, Jiangxi Province 314000
Tel: +86(797) 8223090
Fax: +86(797) 8223812
Website: http://www.gnmc.net.cn/bumen/gjxy/gmu.html

President: Chen Fangrong

International Relations: Xu Feng

College
International Education (Anaesthesiology; Nursing; Ophthalmology)

School
Basic Medicine (Medicine; Pharmacy); **Clinical Medicine** *(Second)*; **Clinical Medicine** *(First)* (Anaesthesiology; Medicine; Nursing); **Social Sciences and Humanities**

Degrees and Diplomas: *Xueshi Xuewei*; *Shuoshi Xuewei*

GANNAN NORMAL UNIVERSITY

53 Hongqi Road, Ganzhou, Jiangxi Province 341000
Tel: +86(797) 8223690
Fax: +86(797) 8227700
EMail: gnnu1958@yahoo.com.cn
Website: http://www.gntc.net.cn

President: Xiao Dingzhi

International Relations: Liu Ruigui

Department
Chemistry; **Chinese** (Chinese); **Economics and Law** (Economics; Law); **Fine Arts**; **Information Management** (Information Management); **Mathematics**; **Modern Languages** (Modern Languages); **Physical Education** (Physical Education); **Physics**

Degrees and Diplomas: *Xueshi Xuewei*; *Shuoshi Xuewei*

GANSU AGRICULTURAL UNIVERSITY (GAU)

N° 1 Yingmen Village, Anning District,
Lanzhou, Gansu Province 730070
Tel: +86(931) 7632459
Fax: +86(931) 7631125
EMail: faogau@gsau.edu.cn
Website: http://www.gsau.edu.cn

President: Di Wang Tel: +86(931) 7631140

International Relations: Hui-zhen Qiu
Tel: +86(931) 7631492 EMail: hzqiu@gsau.edu.cn

College
Agronomy (Agronomy; Crop Production; Farm Management; Horticulture); **Animal Science and Technology** (Animal Husbandry; Aquaculture); **Economy Management** (Banking; Economics; Finance); **Extended Education** (Education); **Food Science and Engineering** (Biotechnology; Food Science; Food Technology); **Foreign Languages** (English); **Grassland Sciences**; **Humanities** (Arts and Humanities); **Information Sciences and Technology** (Computer Engineering; Computer Science; Information Sciences; Information Technology); **Life Science and Technology** (Biotechnology); **Physical Education** (Physical Education); **Resources and Environmental Sciences** (Environmental Engineering; Environmental Management; Natural Resources); **Science** (Applied Chemistry; Chemistry; Mathematics; Physics); **Technology** (Agricultural Engineering; Agricultural Equipment; Automation and Control Engineering; Hydraulic Engineering; Water Management); **Veterinary Medicine** (Veterinary Science)

Chair
Forestry (Forestry; Landscape Architecture; Soil Conservation; Water Management)

History: Founded 1946 as National Veterinary College. Acquired present status 1958.

Academic Year: September to July (two semesters)

Admission Requirements: Graduation from senior middle school and entrance examination

Fees: (Yuan): 3,000-4,000 per annum

Main Language(s) of Instruction: Chinese

Accrediting Agency: Gansu Province Department of Education

Degrees and Diplomas: *Xueshi Xuewei*: **Agricultural Equipment; Agriculture; Agronomy; Animal Husbandry; Business and Commerce; Computer Science; Economics; Environmental Management; Food Science; Food Technology; Forestry; Horticulture; Hydraulic Engineering; Plant and Crop Protection; Veterinary Science.** *Shuoshi Xuewei*: **Agronomy; Animal Husbandry; Botany; Forestry; Horticulture; Plant and Crop Protection; Veterinary Science.** *Boshi*: **Agronomy; Animal Husbandry; Botany; Veterinary Science.**

Student Services: Canteen, Foreign Studies Centre, Health Services, Nursery Care, Sports Facilities

Publications: Journal of Gansu Agricultural University; Journal of Grassland and Turf

GANSU COLLEGE OF TRADITIONAL CHINESE MEDICINE

35 Dinxi Road, Lanzhou, Gansu Province 730000
Tel: +86(931) 8619986
Fax: +86(931) 8627950
EMail: wsc@gszy.edu.cn
Website: http://www.gszy.edu.cn

Dean: Zhang Shiqing

International Relations: Wang Daokun

Department
Acupuncture and Osteology; **Chinese Botany** (Botany); **Traditional Chinese Medicine** (Traditional Eastern Medicine); **Traditional Tibetan Medicine** (Traditional Eastern Medicine)

Degrees and Diplomas: *Xueshi Xuewei*; *Shuoshi Xuewei*

GANSU INSTITUTE OF POLITICAL SCIENCE AND LAW

2 Annin West Road, Lanzhou, Gansu Province 730070
Tel: +86(931) 7601586
Fax: +86(931) 7678037
EMail: sun@gsli.edu.cn
Website: http://www.gsli.edu.cn

President: Wang Suyuan

Department
Administration (Administration); **Art** (Fine Arts); **Civil Security** (Civil Security); **Commercial Law** (Commercial Law); **Information Science and Technology** (Information Sciences; Information Technology); **Law** (Law); **Management** (Management)

History: Founded 1984.

Main Language(s) of Instruction: Chinese

Degrees and Diplomas: *Xueshi Xuewei*; *Shuoshi Xuewei*

GRADUATE SCHOOL OF CHINESE ACADEMY OF AGRICULTURAL SCIENCES

12 Zhongguancun Nandajie, Beijing 100081
Tel: +86(10) 62152115; +86(10) 68918848
Fax: +86(10) 68975643
EMail: studyincaas@caas.net.cn; international@caas.net.cn
Website: http://www.gscaas.net.cn/

Party Secretary, Executive Vice-President: Hanhui Peng

Vice-President: Dennis Lau Yue

Programme
Agriculture (Agriculture); **Engineering** (Engineering); **Management Science** (Management); **Natural Sciences** (Natural Sciences)

History: Founded 1979.

Fees: National: Master, 30,000; PhD, 40,000 (Yuan Renminbi), International: Master, 30,000; PhD, 40,000 (Yuan Renminbi)

Main Language(s) of Instruction: Chinese

Accrediting Agency: State Council

Degrees and Diplomas: *Shuoshi Xuewei*: **Agricultural Engineering; Agricultural Management; Animal Husbandry; Biology; Crop Production; Ecology; Environmental Engineering; Food Science; Forest Management; Horticulture; Information Sciences; Plant and Crop Protection; Soil Science; Veterinary Science.** *Boshi*: **Animal Husbandry; Biology; Crop Production; Ecology; Forest Management; Horticulture; Plant and Crop Protection; Soil Science; Veterinary Science.**

Student Services: Health Services, Library, Residential Facilities

Last Updated: 18/06/14

GUANGDONG MEDICAL COLLEGE (GDMC)

2 Wenmin East Road, Xiashan,
Zhanjiang, Guangdong Province 524023
Tel: +86(759) 2388505
Fax: +86(759) 2284104
EMail: gdmcbgs@gdmc.edu.cn
Website: http://www.gdmc.edu.cn

President: Zhou Keyuan
Tel: +86(759) 2388601 EMail: pres@gdmc.edu.cn

Department

Clinical Medicine (Medicine); **Laboratory Medicine**

Further Information: Also 3 Affiliated Hospitals

History: Founded 1958 as Zhanjiang Branch of the Sun Yat-sen Medical College, acquired present title 1992.

Main Language(s) of Instruction: Chinese

Degrees and Diplomas: *Xueshi Xuewei*; *Shuoshi Xuewei*

Student Services: Academic Counselling, Canteen, Careers Guidance, Cultural Activities, Health Services, Social Counselling, Sports Facilities

Publications: Journal of Guangdong Medical College

GUANGDONG OCEAN UNIVERSITY

East Huguangyan, Zhanjiang, Guangdong Province 524088
Tel: +86(759) 2284448
Fax: +86(759) 2284448
EMail: fao@gdou.edu.cn
Website: http://www.gdou.edu.cn/english/index_en.htm

President: He Zhen

Faculty

Agriculture (Agronomy; Animal Husbandry; Biotechnology; Horticulture; Veterinary Science; Zoology); **Art** (Dance; Design; Fine Arts; Music); **Arts** (Arts and Humanities); **Economic Management** (Business Administration; Economics; Finance; International Business; International Economics; Public Administration); **Engineering** (Energy Engineering; Marine Engineering; Mechanical Engineering); **Fishery** (Aquaculture; Bioengineering; Fishery; Food Technology; Marine Science and Oceanography); **Foodstuff Technology** (Food Technology); **Foreign Studies** (International Studies); **Information Technology** (Information Technology); **Law** (Law); **Navigation** (Nautical Science); **Physical Education** (Physical Education); **Politics and Executive Studies** (Political Sciences; Sociology); **Science** (Natural Sciences); **Software** (Software Engineering)

School

Engineering (Engineering)

History: Founded 1997 as Zhanjiang Ocean University, acquired present status and title 2005.

Degrees and Diplomas: *Xueshi Xuewei*; *Shuoshi Xuewei*

GUANGDONG PHARMACEUTICAL UNIVERSITY

Baogang Haizhu District, Guangzhou, Guangdong Province 510224
Tel: +86(20) 84449735
Fax: +86(20) 84449735
Website: http://www.at0086.com/GZPU/College.aspx?c=626

President: Ren Liang

International Relations: Zhang Zhong

School

Basic Courses; **Clinical Medicine** (Medicine); **Continuing Education** (Continuing Education); **Food Science and Engineering** (Food Science); **Life Science and Biopharmacy** (Biological and Life Sciences); **Medical Business** (Health Administration); **Medical Information Engineering** (Data Processing); **Pharmacy** (Pharmacy); **Preventive Medicine** (Social and Preventive Medicine); **Public Health** (Public Health); **Traditional Chinese Medicine** (Traditional Eastern Medicine)

Degrees and Diplomas: *Xueshi Xuewei*; *Shuoshi Xuewei*; *Boshi*
Last Updated: 17/02/14

GUANGDONG POLYTECHNIC NORMAL UNIVERSITY

293 Zhonghshan Road, Tianhe, Shipai,
Guangzhou, Guangdong Province 510633
Tel: +86(20) 38265465
Fax: +86(20) 38256600
EMail: gpnuwsb@163.com
Website: http://www.gdin.edu.cn

President: Wang Lefu

International Relations: Ding Li

School

Administration (Administration); **Automatization** (Automation and Control Engineering; Electrical Engineering); **Chinese Language and Literature** (Chinese); **Computer Science** (Computer Science; E-Business/Commerce; Mathematics; Software Engineering); **Economics and Trade**; **Education** (Education); **Educational Technology** (Education; Educational Technology; Vocational Education); **Electronics Information Engineering** (Computer Science; Electronic Engineering; Software Engineering); **Finance and Economics** (Economics; Finance); **Foreign Languages** (Modern Languages); **Mechanics and Electronics** (Electronic Engineering; Mechanical Engineering); **Nationalities** (Social Sciences); **Politics and Law**

History: Founded 1958. Acquired present status 1998.

Main Language(s) of Instruction: Chinese

Degrees and Diplomas: *Xueshi Xuewei*; *Shuoshi Xuewei*

GUANGDONG UNIVERSITY OF BUSINESS STUDIES

21 Luntou Road, Guangzhou, Guangdong Province 510320
Tel: +86(20) 84096080
Fax: +86(20) 84096140
EMail: guangtuanchen@hotmail.com
Website: http://www.gdcc.edu.cn

College

Accountancy; **Administration**; **Economics and Statistics** (Administration; Economics; Statistics); **Finance** (Finance); **Foreign Languages** (Modern Languages); **Humanities and Communication**; **Information** (Information Management); **Law** (Law); **Taxation and Public Finance** (Taxation); **Tourism and Environment**

Degrees and Diplomas: *Xueshi Xuewei*; *Shuoshi Xuewei*

GUANGDONG UNIVERSITY OF FOREIGN STUDIES

2 Baiyun Dadaon, Guangzhou, Guangdong Province 510420
Tel: +86(20) 36207007
Fax: +86(20) 86627367
Website: http://www.gdufs.edu.cn

President: Sui Sui Guangjun Guangjun (2008-)
Tel: +86(20) 36207009

Vice-President: Chen Jianping
Tel: +86(20) 36207039 EMail: io@mail.gdufs.edu.cn

Faculty

Asian Languages and Culture (Cultural Studies; Indonesian; Japanese; Korean; Thai Languages; Vietnamese); **English Language and Culture** (American Studies; Cultural Studies; English; English Studies; Linguistics; Tourism; Translation and Interpretation); **European Languages and Culture** (Cultural Studies; French; French Studies; German; Germanic Studies; Italian; Russian; Spanish); **International Communication** (Chinese; English; Foreigners Education; Management; Media Studies; Secretarial Studies)

College

Continuing Education; **Information Science and Technology** (Information Technology; Software Engineering; Statistics); **International** (International Studies)

School

English for Business; **International Trade and Economics** (Business and Commerce; English; Finance; International Business;

International Economics); **Legal Studies** (English; International Business; Law); **Management**; **Politics and Public Administration** (Administration; Management; Public Administration; Social Sciences)

Department

Chinese for International Students (Chinese); **Physical Education**

Institute

English Language Education

History: Founded 1965 and incorporated the Guangzhou Institute of Foreign Languages and Guangzhou Institute of Foreign Trade 1995.

Academic Year: September to July (September-January; February-July)

Admission Requirements: Graduation from senior middle school and entrance examination

Fees: (Yuan): 4,500 per annum

Main Language(s) of Instruction: Chinese

Accrediting Agency: Department of Education of the Guangdong Provincial Government

Degrees and Diplomas: *Xueshi Xuewei*: **Economics; Foreign Languages Education; Law; Literature.** *Shuoshi Xuewei*: **Foreign Languages Education; Linguistics; Literature.** *Boshi*: **French; Linguistics.**

Student Services: Academic Counselling, Canteen, Careers Guidance, Cultural Activities, Foreign Studies Centre, Health Services, Language Laboratory, Nursery Care, Social Counselling, Sports Facilities

Publications: Higher Education Research on Foreign Students; International Economics and Trade Research; Modern Foreign Languages

Publishing House: University Publishing House

GUANGDONG UNIVERSITY OF SCIENCE AND TECHNOLOGY (GUST)

the West Lake Road 99, Dongguan, Guangdong 523083
Tel: +86(769) 86211555 +86(769) 86211666 +86(769) 86211999
Fax: +86(769) 86211818
EMail: zsgdst@126.com
Website: http://www.gdst.cc/

President: Wang Guojian EMail: gkyzxx@163.com

Department

Applied English (Applied Linguistics; English); **Art** (Fine Arts); **Computer Science** (Computer Science); **Continuing Education**; **Finance** (Finance); **Ideological and Political Theory Teaching** (Political Sciences); **Management** (Management); **Mechanical and Electrical Engineering** (Electrical Engineering; Mechanical Engineering)

History: Founded 2003.

Main Language(s) of Instruction: Chinese

Degrees and Diplomas: *Xueshi Xuewei*

Academic Staff *2012-2013*: Total: c. 600

Student Numbers *2012-2013*: Total: c. 13,000

Last Updated: 12/11/13

GUANGDONG UNIVERSITY OF TECHNOLOGY

729 East Dongfeng Road,
Guangzhou, Guangdong Province 510080
Tel: +86(20) 87617779
Fax: +86(20) 87302737
EMail: wsc@gdut.edu.cn
Website: http://www.gdut.edu.cn

President: Zhang Xiangwei

International Relations: Wei Guihui

Faculty

Applied Mathematics (Applied Mathematics); **Automation** (Automation and Control Engineering; Electrical Engineering); **Chemical Engineering and Light Industry** (Chemical Engineering); **Computer** (Computer Science); **Construction** (Construction Engineering); **Electro-mechanical Engineering** (Electronic Engineering; Mechanical Engineering); **Environmental Science and Engineering** (Environmental Engineering; Environmental Studies); **Information Engineering** (Information Technology); **Materials and Energy** (Energy Engineering; Materials Engineering); **Physics and Optoelectronic Engineering** (Physics)

School

Arts Design (Fashion Design; Fine Arts; Visual Arts); **Business** (Business Administration); **Continuing Education**; **Economics and Management** (Economics; Management); **Foreign Languages** (Modern Languages); **Liberal Arts and Law** (Law; Social Work)

History: Founded 1958. Merged with Guangdong Institute of Technology, Guangdong Mechanical College and East South China Construction College.

Degrees and Diplomas: *Xueshi Xuewei*; *Shuoshi Xuewei*; *Boshi*

Publications: Industrial Engineering; Journal of Guangdong University of Technology

GUANGXI ARTS INSTITUTE

7 Jiaoyu Road, Nanning,
Guangxi Zhuang Province 530022
Tel: +86(711) 5313138
Fax: +86(711) 5312637
EMail: gxaiied@yahoo.cn
Website: http://www.gxai.edu.cn

President: Huang Gesheng

International Relations: Xuan Si

College

Dance (Dance); **Design** (Design; Fashion Design); **Film and Television** (Cinema and Television; Film); **Fine Arts** (Fine Arts; Painting and Drawing; Printing and Printmaking; Sculpture; Visual Arts); **Humanities** (Humanities and Social Science Education); **Music** (Music; Music Theory and Composition; Musical Instruments)

School

Adult Education (Adult Education)

Academy

Chinese Painting *(Guilin)* (Painting and Drawing)

History: Founded 1938.

Main Language(s) of Instruction: Chinese

Degrees and Diplomas: *Xueshi Xuewei*; *Shuoshi Xuewei*

Publications: Exploration in Arts

Last Updated: 30/10/12

GUANGXI MEDICAL UNIVERSITY (GMU)

22 Shuangyong Road, Nanning,
Guangxi Zhuang Province 530021
Tel: +86(771) 5352512 +86(771) 5359031
Fax: +86(771) 5352523
EMail: gxmu1934@263.net
Website: http://www.gxmu.edu.cn

President: Zhao Jinmin (2012-)

College

Adult Education (Dermatology; Gynaecology and Obstetrics; Medicine; Nursing; Rehabilitation and Therapy); **Basic Medical Studies** (Anatomy; Cell Biology; Electronic Engineering; Embryology and Reproduction Biology; Genetics; Immunology; Information Technology; Mathematics; Medical Technology; Medicine; Microbiology; Molecular Biology; Parasitology; Physics; Physiology); **Foreign Languages** (English; Modern Languages); **Nursing** (Nursing); **Pharmacy** (Pharmacology; Pharmacy)

School

Clinical Sciences I *(I)* (Cardiology; Medicine; Otorhinolaryngology; Paediatrics; Surgery); **Clinical Sciences II** (Medicine); **Graduate Studies; Humanities and Management** (Arts and Humanities; Biomedical Engineering; Health Administration; Management; Public Administration; Social Work); **Oncology** (Oncology); **Public**

Health (Epidemiology; Health Administration; Hygiene; Information Management; Nutrition; Occupational Health; Public Health; Rehabilitation and Therapy; Social and Preventive Medicine; Statistics; Toxicology); **Stomatology** (Stomatology)

Department
Medical Laboratory (Laboratory Techniques; Medicine); **Sports** (Sports)

Institute
International Education (English; Medicine)

Research Centre
Transnational Medicine (Medicine)

Further Information: 21 secondary colleges; 11 affiliated hospitals, including 9 non-affiliated hospitals; Post-doctoral research stations

History: Founded 1934, acquired present status 1996.

Academic Year: September to July

Admission Requirements: Graduation from senior middle school and entrance examination

Fees: (Yuan): 21,250 per annum

Main Language(s) of Instruction: Chinese, English (Master Programme)

Accrediting Agency: Guangxi Education Bureau

Degrees and Diplomas: *Xueshi Xuewei*; *Shuoshi Xuewei*; *Boshi*. Also postdoctoral programmes in clinical medicine, basic medicine, public health and preventive medicine, pharmacy.

Student Services: Academic Counselling, Canteen, Careers Guidance, Cultural Activities, Foreign Studies Centre, Health Services, Language Laboratory, Nursery Care, Social Counselling, Sports Facilities

Publications: Abstracts of Tumor Diseases; Journal of Coloproctocological Surgery; Journal of GMU

Academic Staff *2011-2012*: Total 1,044
Student Numbers *2011-2012*: Total: c. 11,000
Last Updated: 11/02/13

GUANGXI NORMAL UNIVERSITY (GXNU)

15 Yucai Road, Guilin,
Guangxi Zhuang Province 541004
Tel: +86(773) 5812081
Fax: +86(773) 2825850
EMail: info@mailbox.gxnu.edu.cn
Website: http://www.gxnu.edu.cn

President: Liang Jieshan (2002-)
Tel: +86(773) 5812081 +86(773) 5846185

International Relations: Xu Deqiang

College
Chemistry and Chemical Engineering (Analytical Chemistry; Biochemistry; Chemical Engineering; Chemistry; Industrial Chemistry; Inorganic Chemistry; Organic Chemistry; Physical Chemistry; Polymer and Plastics Technology; Science Education); **Computer Science and Information Engineering** (Computer Engineering; Computer Science; Information Technology); **Design**; **Electronic Engineering** (Automation and Control Engineering; Electronic Engineering; Mechanical Engineering; Software Engineering; Telecommunications Engineering); **Environmental and Resource Sciences** (Environmental Studies; Natural Resources); **Foreign Languages** (English; Modern Languages); **History, Culture and Tourism** (Cultural Studies; History; Tourism); **Liberal Arts** (Applied Linguistics; Arts and Humanities; Chinese; Foreign Languages Education; History; Linguistics; Literature; Philology; Secondary Education; Secretarial Studies); **Lijiang** *(Independent Institute)*; **Physical Science and Technology** (Physics; Science Education; Technology); **Vocational and Technical Teachers** (Vocational Education)

School
Design (Art Education; Design; Industrial Design; Multimedia; Visual Arts); **Economics and Management** (Economics; Management); **Educational Sciences** (Curriculum; Education; Educational Psychology; Educational Sciences; Educational Technology; Higher Education; Pedagogy; Preschool Education; Primary Education); **Law** (Administrative Law; Constitutional Law; International Law; Law; Social Welfare; Social Work; Sociology); **Life Sciences** (Biological and Life Sciences; Biotechnology; Ecology); **Marxism** (Political Sciences); **Mathematical Sciences** (Mathematics); **Political Sciences and Administration** (Administration; Political Sciences; Public Administration)

Institute
Physical Education (Physical Education; Sports)

Academy
Fine Arts (Art History; Fine Arts; Painting and Drawing); **Music** (Music)

Further Information: King City and Yanshan Campuses

History: Founded 1932 as Guangxi Provincial Normal School. Changed name to Guangxi Provincial Guilin Teachers College 1942 and then National Guilin Teachers College 1943. Relocated to Nanning and renamed National Nanning Teachers College 1946. Moved back to Guilin and merged with Guangxi University 1950. Became Guangxi Teachers College after merger with Guangxi university was undone 1953. Acquired present title 1983.

Main Language(s) of Instruction: Chinese

Degrees and Diplomas: *Xueshi Xuewei*; *Shuoshi Xuewei*; *Boshi*

Student Services: Sports Facilities

Publications: Journal of Guangxi Normal University; Oriental Literature Series

Academic Staff *2012-2013*	**TOTAL**
FULL-TIME	**1,417**
Student Numbers *2012-2013*	
All (Foreign included)	c. **35,112**
FOREIGN ONLY	**10000**

Distance students, 1200.
Last Updated: 11/02/13

GUANGXI TEACHERS EDUCATION UNIVERSITY (GXTC)

19 Mingxiu East Road, Nanning,
Guangxi Zhuang Province 530001
Tel: +86(711) 3126960
Fax: +86(711) 3126960
EMail: iro@gxtc.edu.cn; gxtcwb@public.nn.gx.cn
Website: http://www.gxtc.edu.cn

President: Liu Muren

International Relations: Huang Dou

College
Art and Design (Art Education; Art History; Design; Fine Arts; Painting and Drawing); **Chemistry and Life Science** (Applied Chemistry; Biological and Life Sciences; Chemistry; Organic Chemistry; Polymer and Plastics Technology; Science Education); **Computer and Information Engineering** (Computer Engineering; Computer Science; Information Technology); **Continuing Education**; **Economics and Management** (Economics; Human Resources; Management; Marketing; Public Administration; Tourism; Transport Management); **International Culture and Education** (Applied Linguistics; Chinese; Linguistics; Literature); **Journalism and Mass Communication** (Journalism; Mass Communication); **Natural Resources and Environmental Sciences** (Environmental Management; Environmental Studies; Geography; Geography (Human); Human Rights; Natural Resources; Surveying and Mapping; Town Planning); **Physics and Electronic Engineering** (Electrical Engineering; Electronic Engineering; Information Technology; Physics; Telecommunications Engineering); **Political Sciences and Law** (Law; Political Sciences); **Primary Education** (Primary Education); **Sports** (Sports)

School
Educational Sciences (Educational Sciences); **Music and Dance** (Dance; Music)

Department
Liberal Arts (Arts and Humanities; Chinese; Literature); **Mathematics** (Mathematics)

Institute
Foreign Languages (Cultural Studies; English; Foreign Languages Education; Japanese; Literature; Modern Languages; Translation and Interpretation)

Centre
Information Network (Information Sciences)

History: Founded as Guangxi Secondary Teacher Training College and renamed Guangxi Teachers Training College 1953. Incorporated Guangxi University for Nationalities 1960. Separated from the Guangxi University for Nationalities 1963. Renamed Guangxi College of Education 1967. Changed name to Nanning Teachers College 1979. Acquired present status and title 2003.

Main Language(s) of Instruction: Chinese

Degrees and Diplomas: *Xueshi Xuewei*; *Shuoshi Xuewei*

Publications: Intangible Cultural Heritage

Academic Staff *2012-2013*	**TOTAL**
FULL-TIME	793
STAFF WITH DOCTORATE	
FULL-TIME	139
Student Numbers *2012-2013*	
All (Foreign included)	29,279
FOREIGN ONLY	537

Last Updated: 11/02/13

GUANGXI UNIVERSITY (GXU)

10 Xixiangtang Road, Nanning, Guangxi Zhuang Province 530004
Tel: +86(771) 3238638 +86(771) 3821264
Fax: +86(771) 3237734
EMail: gjc@gxu.edu.cn
Website: http://www.gxu.edu.cn

President: Tang Jiliang
Tel: +86(771) 3232111 EMail: xiaoban@gxu.edu.cn

International Relations: Yang Lin
Tel: +86(771) 3235228 EMail: gjc@gxu.edu.cn; lxs@gxu.edu.cn

College
Agriculture (Agricultural Engineering; Agricultural Equipment; Agriculture; Agronomy; Animal Husbandry; Aquaculture; Environmental Studies; Horticulture; Natural Resources; Plant and Crop Protection; Veterinary Science); **Animal Science and Technology** (Animal Husbandry); **Business** (Accountancy; Agricultural Management; Business Administration; Economics; Finance; Forest Economics; Information Management; International Business; International Economics; Management; Tourism); **Chemistry and Chemical Engineering** (Applied Chemistry; Bioengineering; Chemical Engineering; Chemistry); **Civil Engineering and Architectire** (Architecture; Civil Engineering); **Computer Science and Electronic Information** (Computer Science; Electronic Engineering; Information Technology); **Continuing Education**; **Culture and Mass Communication** (Cultural Studies; Mass Communication); **Electrical Engineering** (Electrical Engineering); **Foreign Languages** (English; Japanese; Literature; Modern Languages); **Forestry** (Forestry); **International Education**; **Law** (Law); **Liberal Arts** *(Xingjian)* (Arts and Humanities; Journalism; Mass Communication; Philosophy); **Life Sciences and Technology** (Biological and Life Sciences; Natural Sciences); **Light Industry and Food Engineering** (Food Science; Food Technology; Production Engineering); **Mathematics and Information Sciences** (Applied Mathematics; Information Sciences; Information Technology; Mathematics); **Mechanical Engineering** (Machine Building; Mechanical Engineering); **Physical Education** (Physical Education); **Physical Science and Technology** (Physics); **Political Sciences** (Political Sciences); **Public Management** (Public Administration); **Resource and Environment** (Environmental Studies); **Sino-Canadian International Studies** (Development Studies; Economics; English)

Department
Arts (Cinema and Television; Theatre); **Education** (Agricultural Education; Education; Maintenance Technology; Technology)

Further Information: Also 61 research institutes

History: Founded 1928. Merged with Guangxi Agricultural University 1997.

Main Language(s) of Instruction: Chinese, English

Degrees and Diplomas: *Xueshi Xuewei*; *Shuoshi Xuewei*; *Boshi*. Also MBA

Publications: Guangxi Agricultural and Biological Science; Journal of Guangxi University

Academic Staff *2011-2012*: Total 1,824
Student Numbers *2011-2012*: Total 24,205
Last Updated: 12/02/13

GUANGXI UNIVERSITY FOR NATIONALITIES

188, East Daxue Road, Nanning, Guangxi Zhuang Province 530006
Tel: +86(711) 3260111
Fax: +86(711) 3262052
Website: http://www.gxun.edu.cn

President: He Longqun

International Relations: Wei Jinhai

College
Physical Education and Health Sciences (Health Sciences; Physical Education); **Physics and Electronic Engineering** (Automation and Control Engineering; Computer Networks; Electronic Engineering; Physics; Telecommunications Engineering)

School
Arts (Aesthetics; Chinese; Linguistics; Literature; Publishing and Book Trade); **Business** (Business Administration; E-Business/Commerce; International Business; Marketing); **Chemistry and Ecology Engineering** (Chemical Engineering; Chemistry; Ecology; Engineering); **Educational Science** (Educational Sciences; Teacher Training); **Ethnology and Sociology** (Ethnology; History; Psychology; Social Work; Sociology); **Fine Arts** (Music; Radio and Television Broadcasting); **Foreign Languages** (English; French; Indonesian; Malay; Modern Languages; Thai Languages; Vietnamese); **Law** (Criminal Law; Law); **Management** (Archiving; Business Administration; Library Science; Management; Public Administration); **Mathematics and Computer Science** (Computer Science; Mathematics); **Political Science and International Studies** (International Studies; Political Sciences)

History: Founded 1952 as Guangxi Institute. Acquired present status and title 2006.

Main Language(s) of Instruction: Chinese

Degrees and Diplomas: *Xueshi Xuewei*; *Shuoshi Xuewei*
Last Updated: 31/10/12

GUANGXI UNIVERSITY OF FINANCE AND ECONOMICS (GXUFE)

Ming Xiu Road 100, Nanning, Guangxi 530003
Website: http://www.gxufe.cn/www/myweb/home.cdi

President: Hongjian XI

College
Business Administration (Business Administration); **Cultural Communication** (Communication Studies; Cultural Studies; Journalism; Literature; Mass Communication); **Foreign Languages** (English; French; Japanese; Modern Languages; Thai Languages; Translation and Interpretation; Vietnamese); **Information and Statistics** (Computer Engineering; Computer Networks; Computer Science; E-Business/Commerce; Information Management; Information Sciences; Information Technology; Mathematics; Media Studies; Software Engineering; Statistics); **Vocational and Technical Education** (Technology Education; Vocational Education)

School
Law (Civil Law; Commercial Law; International Law; Law)

Department
Ideological and Political Theory (Political Sciences); **Management Science and Engineering** (Engineering; Management); **Physical Education** (Physical Education)

Institute
Accounting and Auditing (Accountancy); **Economy and Trade** (Agricultural Economics; Business Administration; Economics; Environmental Management; International Business; International

Economics; Regional Planning; Rural Planning); **Finance and Insurance** (Finance; Insurance); **Finance and Public Administration** (Finance; Labour and Industrial Relations; Management; Public Administration; Public Relations; Social Welfare; Taxation); **International Education** (Accountancy)

History: Founded 2004 through merger of College of Finance by the Guangxi and Guangxi Commercial College.

Main Language(s) of Instruction: Chinese

Degrees and Diplomas: *Xueshi Xuewei*

Academic Staff *2012-2013*: Total 874
Student Numbers *2012-2013*: Total 19,686
Last Updated: 12/11/13

GUANGXI UNIVERSITY OF TECHNOLOGY

268 Donghuan Road, Liuzhou,
Guangxi Zhuang Province 5455005
Tel: +86(772) 2687357
EMail: gxutgjc@126.com
Website: http://www.admissions.cn/gxut/en7.html

President: Li Dewei

Department

Arts and Design (Design; Fine Arts); **Automobile Engineering** (Automotive Engineering); **Biological and Chemical Engineering** (Bioengineering; Chemical Engineering); **Civil Engineering** (Civil Engineering); **Computer Engineering** (Computer Engineering); **Electronic Information and Control Engineering** (Automation and Control Engineering; Information Technology); **Finance and Economics** (Economics; Finance); **Foreign Languages and Literature** (Literature; Modern Languages); **Information and Computer Science** (Computer Science); **Management** (Management); **Mechanical Engineering** (Mechanical Engineering); **Social Sciences** (Social Sciences)

History: Founded 1958. In 1982 Guangxi Light Industry College, Guangxi Mechanical Engineering College and Guangxi Institute of Petroleum and Chemical Engineering merged.

Admission Requirements: Senior high school graduate or above 2. passed HSK-3 or Chinese language test organized by GXUT

Main Language(s) of Instruction: Chinese

Degrees and Diplomas: *Xueshi Xuewei*; *Shuoshi Xuewei*
Last Updated: 31/10/12

GUANGXI UNIVERSITY OF TRADITIONAL CHINESE MEDICINE (GXTCMU)

179 Mingxiu Dong Road,
Nanning, Guangxi Zhuang Province 530001
Tel: +86(711) 3137401 +86(711) 3148091
Fax: +86(711) 3135812
EMail: FIE@gxtcmu.edu.cn
Website: http://www.gxtcmu.edu.cn/

President: Tang Nong EMail: tangnong@gxtcmu.edu.cn

International Relations: Huang Cenhan

College

Acupuncture and Moxibustion (Acupuncture; Physical Therapy; Traditional Eastern Medicine); **Adult Education** (Medicine; Traditional Eastern Medicine); **Basic Medical Studies** *(Preclinical Medicine)* (Medicine); **Humanities and Social Sciences** (Arts and Humanities; Chinese; Cultural Studies; Health Administration; Public Administration; Social Sciences); **Medicine** *(Sainz)* (Medicine); **Medicine** *(Zhuang)* (Medicine); **Nursing** (Nursing); **Pharmacy** (Marketing; Pharmacology; Pharmacy); **Vocational and Technical Studies**

School

Clinical Medicine *(Ruikang)* (Medicine); **Clinical Medicine I** (Medicine); **Graduate Studies** (Acupuncture; Anatomy; Chemistry; Gynaecology and Obstetrics; Literature; Medicine; Orthopaedics; Paediatrics; Pharmacology; Pharmacy; Physical Therapy; Surgery; Traditional Eastern Medicine)

Institute

International Education; **Traumatology** (Orthopaedics)

Further Information: 10 affiliated hospitals (over 2,600 beds); postdoctoral research station

History: Founded 1956 as Guangxi Traditional Chinese Medical School. Acquired present title 1964. Incorporated Nanning Medical College 1970. Acquired present title 2012.

Fees: (Yuan): Undergraduate studies, 16,400 per annum; Postgraduate studies, 22,400 per annum

Main Language(s) of Instruction: Chinese

Degrees and Diplomas: *Xueshi Xuewei*; *Shuoshi Xuewei*

Academic Staff *2011-2012*: Total: c. 2,800
Student Numbers *2011-2012*: Total: c. 15,000
Last Updated: 12/02/13

GUANGZHOU ACADEMY OF FINE ARTS

257 East Changgang Road,
Guangzhou, Guangdong Province 510261
Tel: +86(20) 84017740; +86(20) 20) 84429572
Fax: +86(20) 84497083
EMail: zsb@gzarts.edu.cn
Website: http://www.gzarts.edu.cn/english/index.htm

President: Ming Li

International Relations: Wang Yuesheng, Vice-President

College

Design (Architectural and Environmental Design; Design; Fashion Design; Furniture Design; Graphic Design; Industrial Design)

Department

Fine Arts (Art Education; Art History; Painting and Drawing; Photography; Printing and Printmaking; Sculpture); **Traditional Chinese Painting** (Painting and Drawing)

History: Founded 1953, as Central South China Fine Arts School, Acquired present name 1958.

Degrees and Diplomas: *Xueshi Xuewei*; *Shuoshi Xuewei*
Last Updated: 15/02/13

GUANGZHOU MEDICAL UNIVERSITY

195, Dongfengxi Road, Guangzhou,
Guangdong Province 510182
Tel: +86(20) 81340481
EMail: gmuinoffice@163.com
Website: http://www.gzhmc.edu.cn

President: Zhong Nanshan

International Relations: Zhou Yuhong

School

Basic Science (Bioengineering; Biotechnology; Laboratory Techniques; Medicine; Pharmacology); **Health Management** (Law; Management; Marketing; Psychology); **Nursing** (Nursing); **Public Health** (Community Health; Epidemiology; Medicine; Statistics; Toxicology)

Research Institute

Cancer (Oncology); **Cardiovascular Disease** *(Guangzhou)* (Cardiology); **Chemical Carcinogenesis** (Chemistry); **Humanities and Social Sciences** (Arts and Humanities; Social Sciences); **Neuroscience** (Neurosciences); **Obstetrics and Gynaecology** (Gynaecology and Obstetrics); **Orthopaedics** *(Guangzhou)* (Orthopaedics); **Respiratory Diseases** (Pneumology); **Snake Venom** *(Guangzhou)* (Toxicology)

History: Founded 1958.

Main Language(s) of Instruction: Chinese

Degrees and Diplomas: *Xueshi Xuewei*; *Shuoshi Xuewei*; *Boshi*

Publications: Journal of Guangzhou Medical University; Journal of Modern Medical Bioengineering; Medical Ethics of China

Last Updated: 31/10/12

GUANGZHOU SPORT UNIVERSITY (GIPE)

1268, Middle Guangzhou Avenue,
Guangzhou, Guangdong Province 510500
Tel: +86(20) 87553731
Fax: +86(20) 87553785
EMail: linw2312@hotmail.com
Website: http://www.gipe.edu.cn

Department

Adult Education (Adult Education); **Economics** (Economics); **Kinesiology and Science** (Physical Therapy); **Literature** (Literature); **Physical Education** (Physical Education); **Sociology of Sports** (Sociology; Sports); **Sports** (Sports); **Sports Management** (Sports Management)

Further Information: Also Campus in Shenshen.

History: Founded 1958. Formerly known as Guangzhou Physical Education Institute.

Main Language(s) of Instruction: Chinese

Accrediting Agency: Ministry of Education; National Sports Bureau

Degrees and Diplomas: *Xueshi Xuewei*; *Shuoshi Xuewei*

Student Services: Canteen, Sports Facilities

Publications: Academic Guangzhou Institute of Physical Education

Academic Staff *2011-2012*: Total: c. 700
Student Numbers *2011-2012*: Total: c. 8,000
Last Updated: 18/02/13

GUANGZHOU UNIVERSITY

248 Guangyuan Zhonglu,
Guangzhou, Guangdong Province 510405
Tel: +86(20) 39366230
Fax: +86(20) 39366236
EMail: zhaosb@gzhu.edu.cn
Website: http://english.gzhu.edu.cn

President: Jian-she Yu

International Relations: Zhong Xiandong

School

Architecture and Urban Planning (Architecture; Environmental Studies; Landscape Architecture; Town Planning); **Biological Engineering** (Bioengineering; Biology; Biotechnology); **Business** (Business Administration; Economics); **Chemistry and Chemical Engineering** (Chemical Engineering; Chemistry); **Civil Engineering** (Building Technologies; Civil Engineering; Structural Architecture); **Computer Science and Education Software** (Computer Science; Software Engineering); **Education** (Education; Teacher Training); **Electro-mechanical Engineering** (Automation and Control Engineering; Electrical Engineering; Electronic Engineering; Mechanical Engineering); **Environmental Engineering** (Environmental Engineering); **Fine Art and Design** (Design; Fine Arts); **Foreign Studies** (International Studies); **Humanities** (Arts and Humanities; Chinese; Communication Studies; History); **International Education** (International Studies); **Journalism and Communication** (Communication Studies; Journalism); **Law** (Ethics; Law; Management; Political Sciences; Social Sciences); **Music and Dance** (Dance; Music); **Physical Education** (Physical Education); **Public Administration** (Public Administration); **Tourism** *(Sino-French)* (Tourism)

History: Founded 2000, following merger of Guangzhou Normal University, South China Institute of Construction, Guangzhou University, Guangzhou Junior Teachers' College, and Guangzhou Institute of Education.

Main Language(s) of Instruction: Chinese

Degrees and Diplomas: *Xueshi Xuewei*; *Shuoshi Xuewei*; *Boshi*

Last Updated: 31/10/12

GUANGZHOU UNIVERSITY OF CHINESE MEDICINE

12 Jichang Road, Guangzhou, Guangdong Province 510405
Tel: +86(20) 86593715
Fax: +86(20) 86593715
EMail: xwsc@gzhtcm.edu.cn
Website: http://www.gzhtcm.edu.cn

President: Xu Zhiwei

School

Acupuncture and Massage (Acupuncture; Physical Therapy); **Basic Medicine** (Medicine); **Chinese Pharmacology** (Pharmacology; Traditional Eastern Medicine); **Clinical Medicine** (Medicine); **Continuing Education** (Continuing Education); **Management** (Management); **Traditional Chinese Medicine** *(Affiliated)*

Department

Nursing (Nursing); **Social Sciences** (Social Sciences)

History: Founded 1956 as Guangzhou College of Traditional Chinese Medicine, acquired present title 1995.

Degrees and Diplomas: *Xueshi Xuewei*; *Shuoshi Xuewei*; *Boshi*

Publications: Education Survey of Traditional Chinese Medicine; Journal of Guangzhou University of Traditional Chinese Medicine; New Journal of Traditional Chinese Medicine; Traditional Chinese Drug Research

Last Updated: 31/10/12

GUILIN MEDICAL UNIVERSITY

109 Huancheng Road, Guilin, Guangxi Zhuang Province 541001
Tel: +86(773) 2822194
Fax: +86(773) 2822194
EMail: cie@glmc.edu.cn
Website: http://www.glmc.edu.cn

President: Lei Xun

Programme

Biotechnology (Biotechnology); **Clinical Medicine** (Medicine); **Medical Laboratory** (Analytical Chemistry; Biochemistry; Parasitology; Pathology; Pharmacology; Statistics; Surgery); **Nursing** (Nursing); **Oral Medicine** (Anatomy; Embryology and Reproduction Biology; Histology; Immunology; Microbiology); **Pharmacy** (Pharmacy); **Pharmacy** (Pharmacy); **Preventive Medicine** (Anatomy; Dermatology; Gynaecology and Obstetrics; Histology; Nutrition; Occupational Health; Parasitology; Pathology; Pharmacology; Physiology; Psychiatry and Mental Health; Venereology)

History: Founded 1935 as Guilin Advanced Nurse Midwives School, renamed Guilin Medical School in 1958, and in 1987 it was promoted Guilin Medical University.

Admission Requirements: Completion of higher school education

Main Language(s) of Instruction: Chinese

Degrees and Diplomas: *Xueshi Xuewei*

Last Updated: 31/10/12

GUILIN UNIVERSITY OF ELECTRONIC TECHNOLOGY (GUET)

1 Jinji Road, Guilin, Guangxi Zhuang Province 541004
Tel: +86 (773) 5841372
Fax: +86(773) 5815683
EMail: oic@gliet.edu.cn
Website: http://www.at0086.com/GUETC

President: Zhao Yanlin

Faculty

Management (Accountancy; Business Administration; E-Business/Commerce; Finance; Industrial Engineering; International Business; Marketing; Public Administration); **Computer & Control** (Automation and Control Engineering; Computer Networks; Computer Science; Information Technology; Multimedia; Software Engineering); **Design** (Design; Industrial Design); **Electronic Engineering** (Automation and Control Engineering; Electronic Engineering; Environmental Engineering; Optical Technology); **Foreign Studies** (English); **Information & Communications** (Information Technology; Microelectronics; Telecommunications Engineering); **Informational Material Science & Engineering** (Automation and Control

Engineering; Materials Engineering); **Law** (Government; Law); **Mathematics & Computing Science** (Applied Mathematics; Computer Science; Statistics); **Mechanical and Electrical Engineering** (Architectural and Environmental Design; Automation and Control Engineering; Machine Building; Mechanical Engineering; Microelectronics; Transport Engineering)

History: Founded 1960 as Guilin Mechanical Faculty. Re-named "Guilin Institute of Electronic Technology" 1980. Acquired present status and title 2006.

Admission Requirements: Senior high school education

Main Language(s) of Instruction: Chinese

Degrees and Diplomas: *Xueshi Xuewei*; *Shuoshi Xuewei*; *Boshi*

Last Updated: 31/10/12

GUILIN UNIVERSITY OF TECHNOLOGY (GUT)

12 Jian'gan Road, Guilin, Guangxi Zhuang Province 541004
Tel: +86 (773) 5895613
Fax: +86 (773) 5895613
EMail: cie@glite.edu.cn
Website: http://www.gutedu.cn

President: Zhang Xuehong

College

Adult Continuing Education (Continuing Education); **Applied Science** (Applied Chemistry; Applied Mathematics; Applied Physics); **Arts** (Design; Fine Arts; Jewellery Art); **Chemistry and Bioengineering** (Bioengineering; Chemistry); **Civil Engineering** (Civil Engineering); **Computer Science and Engineering** (Computer Engineering; Computer Science); **Earth Sciences** (Earth Sciences; Geological Engineering; Geology); **Environment Science and Engineering** (Environmental Engineering; Environmental Studies); **Foreign Studies** (International Studies); **Humanities and Social Sciences** (Arts and Humanities; Social Sciences); **Materials Science and Engineering** (Materials Engineering); **Mechanical and Control Engineering** (Automation and Control Engineering; Mechanical Engineering); **Tourism** (Tourism)

School

Management (Management); **Professional Development**

Further Information: University Clinic

History: Founded 1956 as Guilin College of Technology. Acquired present status and title 1997.

Academic Year: September to January; March to July

Admission Requirements: Senior High School Diploma

Accrediting Agency: Ministry of Education

Degrees and Diplomas: *Xueshi Xuewei*; *Shuoshi Xuewei*

Last Updated: 31/10/12

GUIYANG COLLEGE OF TRADITIONAL CHINESE MEDICINE

1 Shidong Road, Guiyang, Guizhou Province 550002
Tel: +86(851) 5928633
Fax: +86(851) 5926551
EMail: hsz@gyctcm.edu.cn

President: Jun Shenfeng

International Relations: Ying Shenghai

Programme

Traditional Chinese Medicine (Traditional Eastern Medicine)

History: Founded 1965 as the Guiyang College of Traditional Chinese Medicine.

Main Language(s) of Instruction: Chinese

Degrees and Diplomas: *Xueshi Xuewei*; *Shuoshi Xuewei*; *Boshi*

Last Updated: 31/10/12

GUIYANG MEDICAL UNIVERSITY

4 Beijing Road, Guiyang, Guizhou Province 550004
Tel: +86(851) 6783850
Fax: +86(851) 6783850
EMail: tina@publicl.gy.gz.cn
Website: http://www.gmc.edu.cn

President: Ren Xilin

International Relations: He Keyong

School

Clinical Medicine (Medicine); **Medical Laboratory** (Medical Technology); **Pharmacy** (Pharmacy); **Preventive Medicine** (Social and Preventive Medicine); **Social Sciences** (Social Sciences)

Degrees and Diplomas: *Xueshi Xuewei*; *Shuoshi Xuewei*

GUIYANG UNIVERSITY (GYU)

103 Jianlongdong Road, Guiyang, Guizhou 550005
Tel: +86(851) 5400755
Fax: +86(851) 5402889
EMail: gyncscl@126.com; gyxydwxcb5400708@163.com
Website: http://www.gyu.cn/

President: Zhen Qian Gong

Department

Biology and Environmental Engineering (Agronomy; Bioengineering; Biology; Environmental Engineering; Landscape Architecture; Pharmacology); **Chinese Language and Literature** (Chinese; Journalism; Literature; Publishing and Book Trade; Radio and Television Broadcasting); **Fine Arts** (Architectural and Environmental Design; Design; Fine Arts; Graphic Design; Painting and Drawing; Textile Design; Visual Arts); **Foreign Languages** (English; Foreign Languages Education; Primary Education; Secondary Education); **Mathematics** (Applied Mathematics; Information Sciences; Mathematics; Mathematics and Computer Science); **Music** (Music; Music Theory and Composition; Musical Instruments; Musicology; Performing Arts); **Physical Education** (Physical Education; Sociology; Sports); **Physics and Electronic Information Science** (Electronic Engineering; Information Sciences; Information Technology; Physics); **Politics and Pedagogy** (Pedagogy; Political Sciences; Social Work)

History: Founded 2004 through merger of Guiyang Normal College and Jinzhu University.

Main Language(s) of Instruction: Chinese

Degrees and Diplomas: *Xueshi Xuewei*

Academic Staff *2012-2013*: Total 581

Student Numbers *2012-2013*: Total: c. 11,000

Last Updated: 13/11/13

GUIZHOU MINZU UNIVERSITY (GZMU)

Huaxi District, Guiyang, Guizhou Province 550025
Tel: +86(851) 3610498
Fax: +86(851) 3610498
Website: http://www.gzmu.edu.cn/

President: Dahua Wu

College

Administration (Administration; Educational Administration); **Adult-Education** (Adult Education); **Broadcasting Media** (Media Studies; Radio and Television Broadcasting); **Business Administration** (Accountancy; Business Administration; E-Business/Commerce; Economics; Finance; Management; Marketing); **Chemistry and Environmental Science** (Chemistry; Environmental Studies); **Computer and Information Engineering** (Computer Engineering; Information Technology); **Construction and Engineering** (Construction Engineering; Engineering); **Ethnology and Sociology** (Ethnology; Sociology); **Fine Arts** (Architecture and Planning; Fashion Design; Fine Arts; Folklore; Painting and Drawing); **Foreign Languages** (English; Foreign Languages Education; Japanese; Native Language Education); **Humanities and Sciences** (Arts and Humanities; Natural Sciences); **Literature** (Literature); **Marx-Leninism** (Political Sciences); **Music and Dance** (Dance; Music; Musicology); **Physical and Health Education** (Health Education; Physical Education); **Polytechnic** (Applied Mathematics; Applied Physics; Computer Science; Information Sciences; Mathematics; Statistics); **Prep-Education** (Education); **Tourism and Steward** (Hotel Management; Tourism)

School

Law (Law)

Graduate School

Graduate Studies (Chinese; Criminal Law; Economics; Ethnology; Law; Literature; Mathematics; Sociology; Statistics)

History: Founded 1951. Formerly known as Guizhou Institute for Nationalities or Guizhou Nationalities University.

Main Language(s) of Instruction: Chinese

Degrees and Diplomas: *Xueshi Xuewei*; *Shuoshi Xuewei*: **Chinese; Criminal Law; Economics; Ethnology; Law; Literature; Mathematics; Sociology; Statistics.**

Academic Staff *2012-2013*: Total 1,152

Student Numbers *2012-2013*: Total: c. 18,000

Last Updated: 21/11/13

GUIZHOU NORMAL COLLEGE (GZNC)

115 Gaoxin Road, Wudang District, Guiyang,
Guiyang, Guizhou 550018
Tel: +86(851) 5815957 +86(851) 6205886
EMail: gzncdwjl@gmail.com
Website: http://www.gznc.edu.cn/

President: Li Cunxiong

School

Arts (Dance; Fine Arts; Music; Performing Arts); **Chemistry and Life Sciences** (Analytical Chemistry; Applied Chemistry; Biochemistry; Biological and Life Sciences; Biology; Biotechnology; Botany; Chemical Engineering; Chemistry; Ecology; Environmental Studies; Genetics; Immunology; Inorganic Chemistry; Microbiology; Natural Resources; Organic Chemistry; Pedagogy; Pharmacology; Pharmacy; Physical Chemistry; Physiology; Plant Pathology; Psychology; Science Education; Zoology); **Chinese Language and Literature** (Advertising and Publicity; Aesthetics; Chinese; Communication Studies; Comparative Literature; Education; Educational Technology; English; Journalism; Linguistics; Literature; Mass Communication; Native Language Education; Psychology; Radio and Television Broadcasting; Sports; Writing); **Continuing Education** (Adult Education; Continuing Education; Educational Administration; Primary Education; Secondary Education; Teacher Training); **Economics and Political Science** (Economics; Educational Administration; International Relations; Philosophy; Political Sciences; Secondary Education); **Educational Sciences** (Education; Educational Administration; Educational Psychology; Educational Sciences; Preschool Education); **Foreign Languages and Literature** (Engineering Management; Foreign Languages Education; Literature; Modern Languages; Primary Education; Secondary Education); **Geography and Tourism** (Agriculture; Ecology; Economics; English; Environmental Studies; Finance; Geography; Geography (Human); Geology; Human Resources; Management; Marketing; Measurement and Precision Engineering; Meteorology; Microbiology; Physiology; Psychology; Soil Conservation; Surveying and Mapping; Tourism; Water Management); **History and Social Science** (Archaeology; Contemporary History; History; History of Religion; Modern History; Social Sciences); **Mathematics and Computer Science** (Applied Mathematics; Computer Engineering; Computer Science; Data Processing; Information Technology; Mathematics; Mathematics and Computer Science; Multimedia; Operations Research); **Physical Education Sciences** (Anatomy; Biochemistry; Hygiene; Physical Education; Physiology; Psychology; Sports; Sports Management); **Physics and Electronic Sciences** (Artificial Intelligence; Electronic Engineering; Information Sciences; Information Technology; Mathematics; Mechanics; Optical Technology; Optics; Pedagogy; Physical Education; Physics; Robotics; Science Education); **Vocational Technical Education** (Advertising and Publicity; Architectural and Environmental Design; Graphic Design; Tourism)

Department

Marxism and Leninism Instruction

Institute

Foreign Languages Education (English; Foreign Languages Education)

History: Founded 1978. Acquired present status 2009.

Fees: (Yuan): Tuition for international students, 6,000 per term

Main Language(s) of Instruction: Chinese

Degrees and Diplomas: *Xueshi Xuewei*

Academic Staff *2012-2013*: Total 790

Last Updated: 18/11/13

GUIZHOU NORMAL UNIVERSITY

116 BaoshanBeiLu, Guiyang, Guizhou Province 550001
Tel: +86(851) 6701140
Fax: +86(851) 6766891
EMail: wsc@gznu.edu.cn
Website: http://e.gznu.edu.cn/

President: Pengcheng Wu Tel: +86(851) 6897028

College

Qiushi (Teacher Training)

School

Adult Education (Adult Education)

Department

Biology (Biology); **Chemistry and Material Sciences** (Chemistry; Materials Engineering); **Chinese Language and Literature** (Chinese; Literature); **Economics and Management** (Economics; Management); **Education** (Education; Educational Psychology; Educational Sciences); **Fine Arts and Music** (Fine Arts; Music); **Foreign Languages** (English; Japanese; Modern Languages; Russian); **Geographic and Environmental Sciences** (Environmental Engineering; Geography; Geography (Human); Geology); **History and Politics** (History; Political Sciences); **International Tourism and Culture** (Anthropology; Cultural Studies; Tourism); **Law** (Law); **Life Sciences** (Biological and Life Sciences); **Materials and Architectural Engineering** (Architecture; Materials Engineering); **Mathematics and Computer Science** (Mathematics and Computer Science); **Mechanical and Electrical Engineering** (Electrical Engineering; Mechanical Engineering); **Physical Education** (Physical Education); **Vocational Technology**

History: Founded 1941 as Guiyang Teachers College, acquired present status 1985.

Admission Requirements: Graduation from high school and entrance examination

Main Language(s) of Instruction: Chinese

Accrediting Agency: Ministry of Education

Degrees and Diplomas: *Xueshi Xuewei*; *Shuoshi Xuewei*; *Boshi*

Student Services: Canteen, Careers Guidance, Health Services, Nursery Care, Sports Facilities

Publications: Journal of Guizhou Normal University; Journal of Guizhou Normal University

Last Updated: 18/02/13

GUIZHOU UNIVERSITY

Huaxi, Guiyang, Guizhou Province 550025
Tel: +86(851) 8292178
Fax: +86(851) 3621956
EMail: fa.myxie@gzu.edu.cn
Website: http://www.gzu.edu.cn

President: Qiang Zheng

International Relations: Yinghua Wang, Director
Tel: +86(851) 8290342 EMail: yhwang@gzu.edu.cn

College

Agriculture (Agronomy; Farm Management; Horticulture; Plant and Crop Protection); **Arts** (Dance; Design; Fine Arts; Music; Painting and Drawing; Sculpture; Theatre); **Chemical Engineering** (Bioengineering; Chemical Engineering; Food Science; Materials Engineering; Pharmacology); **Civil Engineering and Building Construction** (Architecture; Civil Engineering; Construction Engineering; Hydraulic Engineering; Industrial Design; Landscape Architecture; Town Planning; Transport Engineering); **Computer Science and Information Technology** (Computer Networks; Information Technology); **Continuing Education** (Continuing Education); **Economics** (Accountancy; E-Business/Commerce; Economics; Finance; Marketing); **Electrical Engineering** (Electrical Engineering); **Forestry** (Forestry; Soil Conservation; Water Management); **Humanities** (Arts and Humanities; Chinese; Cultural Studies; History; Journalism; Literature; Modern Languages; Philosophy; Tourism); **International Studies** (English; Japanese; Literature); **Law** (Administration; Law; Political Sciences; Social Work); **Life Sciences** (Biotechnology; Ecology; Environmental Studies; Food Technology; Pharmacy); **Management** (Administration; Agricultural Equipment; Human Resources; Industrial

Management; Library Science; Management; Tourism); **Materials and Metallurgical Engineering** (Materials Engineering; Metal Techniques); **Mechanical Engineering and Automation** (Agricultural Engineering; Agricultural Equipment; Automation and Control Engineering; Industrial Engineering; Mechanical Engineering); **Mingde**; **Mining** (Construction Engineering; Mineralogy; Mining Engineering; Safety Engineering; Surveying and Mapping); **Peoples Armed Forces** (Management; Military Science); **Resource and Environment Engineering** (Building Technologies; Civil Engineering; Construction Engineering; Environmental Engineering; Geological Engineering; Hydraulic Engineering); **Science** (Applied Chemistry; Applied Mathematics; Chemistry; Computer Science; Information Sciences; Natural Sciences; Physics); **Science and Technology** (Technology); **Vocational Education** (Administration; Automation and Control Engineering; Business Administration; Chinese; Civil Engineering; Computer Engineering; E-Business/Commerce; English; Information Technology; Mechanical Engineering; Teacher Training; Tourism); **Zoology** (Aquaculture; Veterinary Science; Zoology)

History: Founded 1902 as Guizhou Institute of Higher Learning. Merged with Guizhou People's University 1993, Guizhou Agricultural College, Guizhou Institute of Arts and Guizhou Agricultural Cadre-Training School 1997. Acquired present title after merging with Guizhou University of Technology, 2004.

Academic Year: September to June (September-February; March-June)

Admission Requirements: Graduation from senior middle school and entrance examination

Main Language(s) of Instruction: Chinese

Degrees and Diplomas: *Xueshi Xuewei*; *Shuoshi Xuewei*; *Boshi*

Publications: Journal of Guizhou University; Journal of Guizhou University; Journal of Guizhou University

Publishing House: University Publishing House

Academic Staff *2011-2012*: Total: c. 4,200

Student Numbers *2011-2012*: Total: c. 62,000

Last Updated: 18/02/13

GUIZHOU UNIVERSITY OF FINANCE AND ECONOMICS

276 Luchongguan Rd., Yunyan District,
Guiyang, Guizhou Province 550004
Tel: +86(851) 6903811
EMail: yb@mail.gzife.edu.cn
Website: http://www.gufe.edu.cn/web/english

President: Zgong Yongxing

International Relations: Li Hua

School

Accountancy (Accountancy); **Arts** (Design; Musicology; Singing); **Business** (Accountancy; Business Administration; Computer Science; E-Business/Commerce; Finance; Fiscal Law; Human Resources; International Business; International Economics; Law; Management; Marketing; Statistics); **Business Administration** (Business Administration; Human Resources; Management; Marketing); **Economics** (Economics); **Education Administration** (Educational Administration; Educational Technology; Psychology); **Finance** (Banking; Finance; Insurance); **Finance and Taxation** (Finance; Taxation); **Foreign Languages** (English; Translation and Interpretation); **Information** (Computer Networks; Computer Science; E-Business/Commerce; Information Management; Software Engineering); **International Economics** (Economics; International Business); **Mathematics and Statistics** (Applied Mathematics; Mathematics; Statistics); **Resource and Environmental Management** (Demography and Population; Regional Planning; Town Planning); **Tourism Management** (Hotel Management; Tourism)

History: Founded 1958. Acquired present status and title 2012.

Main Language(s) of Instruction: Chinese

Degrees and Diplomas: *Xueshi Xuewei*, *Shuoshi Xuewei*

Last Updated: 18/11/13

HAIKOU COLLEGE OF ECONOMICS (HKC)

Guilin Yang universities, Haikou, Hainan 571127
Tel: +86(898) 65733552
Fax: +86(898) 65733552
EMail: xybgs@hkc.edu.cn
Website: http://www.hkc.edu.cn/

Department

Hotel Management (Hotel and Restaurant; Hotel Management); **Musical Performances** (Dance; Music; Performing Arts); **Radio and Television Broadcasting** (Radio and Television Broadcasting); **Sports** (Sports); **Tourism Management** (Tourism); **transportation (aviation transportation** (Air Transport; Transport Management)

History: Founded 1974 as Haikou Economic Vocational Technical College. Acquired present status and title 2008.

Fees: (Yuan): Tuition, 6,900-19,500

Main Language(s) of Instruction: Chinese

Degrees and Diplomas: *Xueshi Xuewei*

Last Updated: 22/11/13

HAINAN MEDICAL UNIVERSITY

No. 3, College Road, Longhua District,
Haikou City, Hainan Province 570102
Tel: +86(898) 66893760
Fax: +86(898) 66893760
Website: http://www.hainmc.edu.cn/

President: Jiao Jiege

School

Basic Medical Science (Medicine); **Clinical Medicine** (Medicine); **Dental Sciences** (Dentistry); **Humanities and Social Sciences** (Arts and Humanities; Social Sciences); **International Education** (Education); **Medical Management** (Health Administration); **Nursing** *(International)* (Nursing); **Pharmaceutical Sciences** (Pharmacology; Pharmacy); **Public Health Sciences** (Public Health); **Traditional Chinese Medicine** (Traditional Eastern Medicine); **Tropical and Laboratory** (Laboratory Techniques; Tropical Medicine)

Department

Foreign Languages (Modern Languages); **Information Technology** (Information Technology); **Physical Education** (Physical Education)

History: Founded 1951 following the merger of Haiqiang Medical Vocational School (created in 1947) and the Medical College of Hainan University (established in 1948). Acquired present title 1993.

Main Language(s) of Instruction: Chinese

Degrees and Diplomas: *Xueshi Xuewei*

Last Updated: 16/11/12

HAINAN NORMAL UNIVERSITY

99 South Longkun Road, Haikou, Hainan Province 571158
Tel: +86(898) 65884843
Fax: +86(898) 5883035
EMail: hsddb@hainnu.edu.cn
Website: http://www.hainnu.edu.cn

President: Han Changri

College

Chemistry and Chemical Engineering (Applied Chemistry; Chemical Engineering; Chemistry); **Chinese Language and Literature** (Chinese; Communication Studies; History; Journalism; Literature); **Economics and Management** (Accountancy; Economics; Finance; Management); **Educational Sciences** (Education; Preschool Education; Psychology); **Foreign Languages** (English); **Geography and Tourism** (Geography; Tourism; Town Planning); **Information Science and Technology** (E-Business/Commerce; Educational Technology; Information Technology; Software Engineering); **Life Sciences** (Biological and Life Sciences; Biology; Biotechnology); **Mathematics and Statistics** (Computer Science; Mathematics; Statistics); **Physical Education** (Physical Education; Sports); **Physics and Electronic Engineering** (Automation and Control Engineering; Electronic Engineering; Physics); **Political Science**

and Law (Law; Political Sciences); **Primary Education** (Primary Education)

Department

Social Science (Social Sciences)

Academy

Fine Arts (Art Education; Fine Arts; Painting and Drawing)

Conservatory

Music (Dance; Music; Musical Instruments)

History: Founded 1949 as Hainan Teachers College. Acquired present status and title 2007.

Main Language(s) of Instruction: Chinese

Degrees and Diplomas: *Xueshi Xuewei*; *Shuoshi Xuewei*

Last Updated: 16/11/12

HAINAN UNIVERSITY

58 Renmin Road, Haikou, Hainan Province 570228
Tel: +86(898) 6259705
Fax: +86(898) 6258369
EMail: cicehn@126.com
Website: http://www.hainu.edu.cn

President: Li Jianbao

School

Engineering (Agricultural Engineering; Architecture; Bioengineering; Chemical Engineering; Civil Engineering; Electrical Engineering; Food Science; Information Technology; Materials Engineering; Mechanical Engineering); **Humanities** (Advertising and Publicity; Arts and Humanities; Chinese; Cinema and Television; Dance; English; Fine Arts; Japanese; Literature; Music; Russian; Theatre); **Social Sciences** (Accountancy; Business Administration; Civil Law; Commercial Law; Economics; Finance; International Law; Law; Marketing; Political Sciences; Public Administration; Public Law; Tourism); **Tropical Agriculture and Life Science** (Agronomy; Aquaculture; Biochemistry; Botany; Crop Production; Environmental Studies; Forestry; Horticulture; Marine Science and Oceanography; Molecular Biology; Plant and Crop Protection; Soil Science; Wildlife)

History: Founded 1958. Merged with South China University of Tropical Agriculture 2007.

Admission Requirements: High school diploma or equivalent

Main Language(s) of Instruction: Chinese

Degrees and Diplomas: *Xueshi Xuewei*; *Shuoshi Xuewei*; *Boshi*

Publications: School Journal of Hainan University; School Journal of Hainan University

Last Updated: 16/11/12

HANDAN COLLEGE (HDC)

Hanshan College Road 530, Handan, Hebei 056005
Website: http://www.hdc.edu.cn/

College

Arts (Dance; Design; Fine Arts; Graphic Design; Music; Musical Instruments; Painting and Drawing; Singing); **Biological Sciences** (Biological and Life Sciences); **Chemistry** (Chemistry); **Chinese** (Chinese); **Continuing Education**; **Education** (Education); **Foreign Languages** (English; Modern Languages); **Geography and Tourism** (Geography; Tourism); **History** (History); **Information Engineering** (Information Technology); **Law and Political Sciences** (Law; Political Sciences); **Mathematics** (Mathematics); **Physics and Electrical Engineering** (Electrical Engineering; Physics); **Social Sciences** (Social Sciences)

Institute

Media (Media Studies); **Software** (Software Engineering); **Sports** (Sports); **Tai Chi Cultural Studies** *(Handan)* (Cultural Studies)

Main Language(s) of Instruction: Chinese

Degrees and Diplomas: *Xueshi Xuewei*

Academic Staff *2012-2013*: Total 925

Student Numbers *2012-2013*: Total 12,682

Last Updated: 22/11/13

HANGZHOU DIANZI UNIVERSITY

Hangzhou, Zhejiang Province 310018
Tel: +86(571) 86915076
Fax: +86(571) 86915183
EMail: foreign2@hziee.edu.cn
Website: http://www.hdu.edu.cn/english/

President: Xue Anke

School

Automation (Automation and Control Engineering; Electrical Engineering); **Computer Science** (Computer Science); **Electronics and Information** (Electronic Engineering; Information Technology; Optical Technology); **Finance and Economics** (Accountancy; Finance; International Business; Management; Statistics); **Foreign Languages** (English); **Humanities** (Law; Publishing and Book Trade; Sociology); **Management** (Business Administration; E-Business/Commerce; Human Resources; Information Management; Marketing); **Mechanical and Electronic Engineering** (Electronic Engineering; Environmental Engineering; Industrial Design; Mechanical Engineering); **Science** (Applied Physics; Computer Science; Mathematics); **Software** (Educational Technology; Software Engineering); **Telecommunications Engineering** (Telecommunications Engineering)

History: Founded 1956 as Hangzhou School of Aviation. Renamed Hangzhou Institute of Electronic Engineering 1980. Acquired present title 2004.

Main Language(s) of Instruction: Chinese

Degrees and Diplomas: *Xueshi Xuewei*; *Shuoshi Xuewei*; *Boshi*

Last Updated: 16/11/12

HANGZHOU NORMAL UNIVERSITY (HNU)

No.58, Haishu Rd, Cangqian, Yuhang District,
Hangzhou, Zhejiang 311121
Tel: +86(571) 28869670 +86(571) 28868671
Fax: +86(571) 28869670
Website: http://www.hznu.edu.cn/

President: Ye Gaoxiang

Faculty

Basic Medicine *(Graduate)* (Anatomy; Embryology and Reproduction Biology; Histology)

School

Business *(Alibaba)* (Business Administration; Business and Commerce; E-Business/Commerce; International Business; Marketing); **Clinical Medicine** (Medicine; Stomatology); **Economics and Political Science** (Economics; Philosophy; Political Sciences; Social Welfare; Social Work); **Educational Science** (Cognitive Sciences; Curriculum; Educational Administration; Educational Psychology; Educational Sciences; Educational Technology; Higher Education; Management; Neurosciences; Preschool Education; Primary Education; Psychology; Teacher Training); **Elementary Education** (Art Education; Preschool Education; Primary Education); **Fine Arts** (Architectural and Environmental Design; Design; Fine Arts; Painting and Drawing; Video); **Foreign Languages** (Applied Linguistics; English; Japanese; Linguistics; Literature); **Hangzhou International School of Ani-com** (Design; Fine Arts; Visual Arts); **Health Care Administration** (Health Administration; Health Sciences; Marketing; Pharmacology; Public Administration; Social and Preventive Medicine); **Humanities** (Applied Linguistics; Arts and Humanities; Chinese; Economics; Foreign Languages Education; History; Linguistics; Literature; Management; Philology); **Information Science and Engineering** (Computer Education; Computer Science; Electronic Engineering; Information Sciences; Information Technology; Software Engineering); **Law** (Civil Law; Commercial Law; Criminal Law; Law); **Life Science and Environmental Science** (Biological and Life Sciences; Biology; Biotechnology; Botany; Environmental Studies; Food Science; Genetics; Safety Engineering; Zoology); **Material Science, Chemistry and Chemical Engineering** (Analytical Chemistry; Applied Chemistry; Chemical Engineering; Chemistry; Inorganic Chemistry; Materials Engineering; Organic Chemistry; Pharmacology; Physical Chemistry; Polymer and Plastics Technology); **Music** (Art Education; Dance; Music; Music Theory and Composition; Musical Instruments; Musicology; Performing Arts; Visual Arts); **Nursing** (Nursing); **Physical Education and Health** (Health Sciences; Leisure Studies; Physical Education; Sports); **Science** (Applied

Mathematics; Applied Physics; Biology; Computer Science; Ecology; Information Sciences; Mathematics; Molecular Biology; Natural Sciences; Physical Therapy; Physics; Science Education; Statistics)

Institute

Hangzhou Institute of Service Engineering (Computer Engineering); **Service Engineering** *(Hangzhou)* (Electronic Engineering; Information Technology)

Academy

Art Education *(Graduate)* (Fine Arts)

Further Information: Also Xiasha Campus, Wenyi Campus, Gudangwan Campus, Yuhuangshan Campus.

History: Founded 1908 as as Zhejiang Dual-Level Normal School. Renamed as Hangzhou Teachers College 1978. Merged with Hangzhou School of Education and Hangzhou Senior Medical School before acquireing present title 2007.

Main Language(s) of Instruction: Chinese

Degrees and Diplomas: *Xueshi Xuewei*; *Shuoshi Xuewei*: **Anatomy; Arts and Humanities; Biological and Life Sciences; Chemical Engineering; Chemistry; Computer Engineering; Economics; Education; English; Environmental Studies; Fine Arts; Health Administration; Japanese; Law; Materials Engineering; Mathematics; Music; Nursing; Physical Education; Physics; Sports.** *Boshi*: **Social and Preventive Medicine.**

Academic Staff *2011-2012*: Total: c. 860

Student Numbers *2012-2013*: Total: c. 21,600

Last Updated: 22/11/13

HANKOU UNIVERSITY

Cultural Avenue No. 299, Wuhan, Jiangxia
Website: http://www.hkxy.edu.cn/

President: Wu Chung-shu

College

Continuing Education *(International)*; **General Education**; **Liberal Arts** (Arts and Humanities)

School

Economics (Economics); **Electrical Engineering and Automation** (Automation and Control Engineering; Electrical Engineering); **Electrical Engineering and Automation, Electronic Information and Communication Engineering, Optoelectronics and Precision Machinery** (Electronic Engineering; Information Technology; Measurement and Precision Engineering; Optometry; Telecommunications Engineering); **Foreign Languages** (Modern Languages); **Information Science and Technology** (Information Sciences; Information Technology); **Law** (Law); **Management** (Management); **Music, Art and Design** (Design; Fine Arts; Music)

Institute

Tourism Studies (Tourism)

History: Founded 2000 as Central China Normal University Hankou Branch. Acquired present status 2011.

Main Language(s) of Instruction: Chinese

Degrees and Diplomas: *Xueshi Xuewei*

Academic Staff *2012-2013*: Total: c. 600

Last Updated: 25/11/13

HANSHAN NORMAL UNIVERSITY

Qiaodong, Chaozhou, Guangdong Province 521041
Tel: +86(768) 2523275 +86(768) 2525005
Fax: +86(768) 2522194
EMail: hs_xyb@hstc.edu.cn
Website: http://www.hstc.edu.cn

President: Lunlun Lin

Vice-President: Sanpang Chen

Department

Arts and Design (Design; Fine Arts; Painting and Drawing); **Biology** (Biology); **Economics** (Economics; Finance; Management); **Education** (Education; Science Education; Teacher Training); **Environmental and Chemical Applied Technology** (Chemical Engineering; Chemistry; Environmental Engineering); **Fine Arts** (Ceramic Art); **Foreign Language** (English); **Geography and Tourism Management** (Geography; Tourism); **History** (History); **Language and Literature** (Chinese; Literature); **Mathematics and Information Technology** (Computer Science; Information Technology; Mathematics); **Music** (Music); **Physical Education** (Physical Education); **Physics and Electronic Engineering** (Electronic Engineering; Physics); **Political Science and Law** (Law; Political Sciences)

History: Founded 1903.

Degrees and Diplomas: *Xueshi Xuewei*

Academic Staff *2011-2012*: Total: c. 16,000

Student Numbers *2011-2012*: Total: c. 1,000

Last Updated: 19/02/13

HARBIN CAMBRIDGE UNIVERSITY

Ha Ping Road, No. 239, XiangFang, Harbin, Heilongjiang
Tel: +86(451) 86615811 +86(451) 86615811
Website: http://www.jqu.net.cn/

College

Adult Education (Architectural and Environmental Design; Design; Landscape Architecture; Maintenance Technology; Microelectronics; Preschool Education; Technology); **Business Administration** (Business Administration); **Education** (Education); **Foreign Languages** (English; Japanese; Korean; Modern Languages)

School

International Cultural Exchange

Department

Basic Education; **Ideological and Political Education** (Political Sciences); **Physical Education** (Physical Education)

Institute

Art (Architectural and Environmental Design; Communication Arts; Fashion Design; Fine Arts; Industrial Design; Photography; Textile Design; Video; Visual Arts); **Automotive Electrical and Mechanical Engineering** (Automotive Engineering; Electrical Engineering; Mechanical Engineering); **Computer Engineering** (Computer Engineering); **Electrical and Electronic Engineering** (Electrical and Electronic Engineering)

Main Language(s) of Instruction: Chinese

Degrees and Diplomas: *Xueshi Xuewei*

Academic Staff *2012-2013*: Total 517

Student Numbers *2012-2013*: Total: c. 9,300

Last Updated: 25/11/13

HARBIN ENGINEERING UNIVERSITY

Wenmiao Street, Nangang District, Harbin, Heilongjiang Province
Tel: +86(451) 2519213
Fax: +86(451) 2530010
EMail: weilin@hrbeu.edu.cn
Website: http://www.hrbeu.edu.cn/

President: Zhigang Liu EMail: liuzhigang@hrbeu.edu.cn

College

Aerospace and Civil Engineering (Aeronautical and Aerospace Engineering; Civil Engineering; Environmental Engineering); **Automation** (Aeronautical and Aerospace Engineering; Automation and Control Engineering; Biomedical Engineering; Electrical Engineering); **Computer Science and Technology** (Computer Science; Information Sciences; Software Engineering); **Economics and Management** (Accountancy; Business Administration; E-Business/Commerce; Economics; Educational Administration; Finance; International Economics; Management); **Humanities and Social Sciences** (Law; Political Sciences; Psychology; Public Administration; Sociology); **Information and Communication Engineering** (Communication Studies; Electronic Engineering; Microelectronics; Optical Technology); **Material Science and Chemical Engineering** (Applied Chemistry; Chemical Engineering; Environmental Engineering; Materials Engineering); **Mechanical and Electrical Engineering** (Electrical Engineering; Industrial Design; Mechanical

Engineering); **Nuclear Science and Technology** (Nuclear Engineering); **Power and Energy Engineering** (Energy Engineering; Environmental Engineering; Heating and Refrigeration; Marine Engineering; Power Engineering; Thermal Engineering); **Science** (Applied Mathematics; Computer Science; Mathematics; Optical Technology); **Shipbuilding Engineering** (Marine Engineering; Naval Architecture); **Underwater Acoustics** (Sound Engineering (Acoustics); Water Science)

Department

Foreign Languages (English; French; German; Japanese; Korean; Modern Languages; Russian); **Physical Education** (Physical Education)

History: Founded 1953 as Harbin Military Engineering Academy, acquired present title 1994.

Main Language(s) of Instruction: Chinese

Degrees and Diplomas: *Xueshi Xuewei*; *Shuoshi Xuewei*; *Boshi*

Publications: Applied Science and Technology; Journal of Harbin Engineering University

Last Updated: 16/11/12

HARBIN HUADE UNIVERSITY

Limin Development Zone, Institute of Road 5, Harbin 150025
Tel: +86(451) 88128600
Website: http://www.hrbhuade.net/

President: Gu Deku

School

Architecture and Civil Engineering (Architecture; Building Technologies; Civil Engineering; Construction Engineering; Measurement and Precision Engineering; Structural Architecture); **Arts and Media** (Architectural and Environmental Design; Clothing and Sewing; Communication Arts; Design; Fashion Design; Industrial Design; Radio and Television Broadcasting; Textile Design; Visual Arts); **Economics and Management** (Economics; Human Resources; International Economics; Management; Marketing); **Electronic and Information Engineering** (Automation and Control Engineering; Computer Science; Electrical Engineering; Electronic Engineering; Information Management; Information Sciences; Information Technology; Software Engineering; Telecommunications Engineering); **Foreign Language** (English; Foreign Languages Education; Modern Languages; Russian); **Liberal Arts** (Economics; Health Sciences; Mathematics; Modern History; Physics; Political Sciences; Sports; Statistics); **Mechanical and Electrical Engineering** (Electrical Engineering; Mechanical Engineering)

Degrees and Diplomas: *Xueshi Xuewei*

Academic Staff *2012-2013*: Total: c. 600

Last Updated: 26/11/13

HARBIN INSTITUTE OF FINANCE

Harbin Finance College, Harbin, Heilongjiang
Website: http://www.hrbfu.edu.cn/

President: Deng Fuqing

College

Accountancy (Accountancy); **Business English** (English); **Computer Science** (Computer Engineering; Computer Networks; Computer Science; E-Business/Commerce; Information Management; Software Engineering); **Finance** (Finance; International Business; International Economics); **Ideological and Political Theory** (Contemporary History; History; Modern History; Political Sciences); **Investment Insurance** (Finance; Insurance; Management); **Law** (Fiscal Law; Law); **Management** (Management; Marketing; Statistics; Taxation); **Research Foundation**; **Sports Teaching and Research for the Armed Forces** (Physical Education; Sports)

History: Founded 2000. Acquired present status and title 2010.

Main Language(s) of Instruction: Chinese

Degrees and Diplomas: *Xueshi Xuewei*

Academic Staff *2012-2013*: TOTAL 567

Last Updated: 26/11/13

HARBIN INSTITUTE OF TECHNOLOGY (HIT)

92 West Dazhi Street, Nangang District,
Harbin, Heilongjiang Province 150001
Tel: +86(451) 86413483
EMail: president@hit.edu.cn
Website: http://www.hit.edu.cn

President: Shuguo Wang
Tel: +86(451) 6415886 EMail: president@hit.edu.cn

International Relations: Hongbo Fan, Director
Tel: +86(451) 86418080 EMail: fanhb@hit.edu.cn

School

Architecture (Architecture); **Astronautics** (Aeronautical and Aerospace Engineering; Automation and Control Engineering; Electronic Engineering; Mechanical Engineering; Telecommunications Engineering); **Chemical Engineering and Technology** (Chemical Engineering; Technology); **Civil Engineering** (Civil Engineering); **Computer Science and Technology** (Computer Engineering; Computer Science); **Continuing Education**; **Economy and Management** (Business Administration; Economics; Finance; International Business; Management); **Electrical Engineering and Automation** (Automation and Control Engineering; Automotive Engineering; Electrical Engineering; Mechanical Engineering); **Electronics and Information Technology** (Electronic Engineering; Information Technology; Telecommunications Engineering); **Energy Engineering** (Automation and Control Engineering; Automotive Engineering; Energy Engineering; Hydraulic Engineering); **Food Science** (Food Science); **Foreign Languages** (Cultural Studies; English; Japanese; Russian); **Humanities and Social Sciences** (Arts and Humanities; Economics; Modern Languages; Philosophy; Political Sciences; Social Sciences; Sociology); **Law** (Law); **Life Science and Technology** (Biology; Biomedical Engineering); **Materials Engineering** (Materials Engineering; Metal Techniques); **Mechanical and Electrical Engineering** (Electrical Engineering; Measurement and Precision Engineering; Mechanical Engineering); **Media Technology and Art** (Media Studies); **Municipal and Environmental Engineering** (Environmental Engineering; Town Planning); **Science** (Applied Chemistry; Applied Physics; Biological and Life Sciences; Engineering; Mathematics; Natural Sciences); **Softaware** (Software Engineering); **Transport Engineering** (Transport Engineering)

Further Information: Also courses for foreign students

History: Founded 1920, as Sino-Russian Technical School of Harbin. Acquired present title 1938. Harbin University of Civil Engineering and Architecture incorporated 2000.

Academic Year: February to January (February-July; September-January)

Admission Requirements: Graduation from senior middle school and entrance examination

Main Language(s) of Instruction: English, Russian, Japanese

Degrees and Diplomas: *Xueshi Xuewei*; *Shuoshi Xuewei*; *Boshi*

Student Services: Academic Counselling, Canteen, Careers Guidance, Cultural Activities, Health Services, Social Counselling, Sports Facilities

Publications: Higher Education Forum; Journal of HIT; Material Science and Technology

Academic Staff *2011-2012*: Total: c. 2,900
Student Numbers *2011-2012*: Total: c. 42,700
Last Updated: 19/02/13

HARBIN MEDICAL UNIVERSITY

157 Baojian Road, Nangang District,
Harbin, Heilongjiang Province 150086
Tel: +86(451) 86669485
Fax: +86(451) 87085974
EMail: international@ems.hrbmu.edu.cn; iohmu@yahoo.cn
Website: http://www.hrbmu.edu.cn

President: Yang Baofeng
Tel: +86(451) 87086250 EMail: harbinmedical@gmail.com

School

Basic Medicine (Anatomy; Embryology and Reproduction Biology; Hispanic American Studies; Medicine; Microbiology; Pharmacology;

Physiology); **Health Management** (Health Administration); **Nursing** (Nursing); **Pharmacy** (Pharmacy); **Public Health** (Public Health); **Stomatology** (Stomatology)

Department

Bioinformatics (Biomedical Engineering); **Humanities and Social Sciences** (Arts and Humanities; Social Sciences); **Sport** (Sports)

Further Information: Also Campus in Daqing

History: Founded 1926 as Harbin Medical College.

Fees: (Yuan): Bachelor: 28,000 per annum (foreign students)

Main Language(s) of Instruction: Chinese

Degrees and Diplomas: *Xueshi Xuewei*; *Shuoshi Xuewei*; *Boshi*
Last Updated: 19/02/13

HARBIN NORMAL UNIVERSITY (HNU)

50 Hexinglu, Nangang District,
Harbin, Heilongjiang Province 150080
Tel: +86(451) 6315015
Fax: +86(451) 6305382
Website: http://www.hrbnu.edu.cn

President: Xuanzhang Wang Tel: +86(451) 6376293

Programme

Administration (Administration); **Chemistry** (Chemistry); **Chinese Language and Literature** (Ancient Books; Chinese); **Education** (Education; Teacher Training); **Fine Arts** (Fine Arts); **Foreign Languages** (English; Japanese; Literature; Russian; Slavic Languages); **Forestry Engineering** (Forestry); **Geography** (Geography); **History** (History); **Life Science and Technology** (Biology); **Mathematics** (Mathematics); **Music** (Music); **Northeast Asian Economics** (Economics); **Physical Education** (Physical Education); **Physics and Electronic Engineering** (Electronic Engineering; Physics); **Political Education** (Political Sciences); **Psychology** (Psychology); **Social Science and Tourism Management** (Social Sciences; Tourism); **Software** (Software Engineering)

History: Founded 1951, acquired present status 1980.

Admission Requirements: Graduation from senior middle school and entrance examination

Main Language(s) of Instruction: Chinese

Accrediting Agency: Ministry of Education

Degrees and Diplomas: *Xueshi Xuewei*; *Shuoshi Xuewei*

Student Services: Academic Counselling, Canteen, Careers Guidance, Cultural Activities, Foreign Studies Centre, Health Services, Language Laboratory, Nursery Care, Social Counselling, Sports Facilities

Publications: Heilongjiang; Natural Science Journal of Harbin Normal University; The Northern Forum
Last Updated: 20/02/13

HARBIN UNIVERSITY

9 Xufusidaojie, Harbin, Heilongjiang Province 150086
Tel: +86(451) 6688516
Fax: +86(451) 6677510
Website: http://www.hrbu.edu.cn

Department

Biology (Biology); **Chemistry** (Chemistry); **Chinese** (Chinese); **Computer Science** (Computer Science); **Construction Engineering** (Construction Engineering); **Crafts and Trades** (Crafts and Trades); **Food Technology** (Food Technology); **Geography** (Geography); **History**; **Management**; **Mathematics**; **Mechanics** (Mechanics); **Modern Languages** (Modern Languages); **Music** (Music); **Physical Education** (Physical Education); **Physics**; **Political Science** (Political Sciences); **Secretarial Studies**; **Textile Design**

History: Founded 1997.

HARBIN UNIVERSITY OF COMMERCE

No. 1 Xuehai Street, Songbei District,
Harbin, Heilongjiang Province 150028
Tel: +86(451) 84892000
Fax: +86(451) 4601086
EMail: YZS@hrbcu.edu.cn
Website: http://www.hljcu.edu.cn

President: Liu Dequan

College

Medicine (Medicine)

School

Accountancy (Accountancy; Finance; Management); **Basic Science** (Applied Mathematics; Chinese; Journalism; Literature; Mathematics); **Computer and Information Engineering** (Computer Engineering; Computer Science; E-Business/Commerce; Electronic Engineering; Management; Software Engineering); **Design and Art** (Design; Graphic Design; Industrial Design; Interior Design; Packaging Technology); **Economics** (Economics; International Business; Statistics); **Energy and Civil Engineering** (Building Technologies; Civil Engineering; Engineering Management; Heating and Refrigeration; Power Engineering; Thermal Engineering; Transport Engineering); **Finance** (Finance); **Finance and Public Administration** (Finance; Public Administration; Taxation); **Food Engineering** (Bioengineering; Chemistry; Environmental Engineering; Food Science; Food Technology); **Foreign Languages** (English; Modern Languages; Russian); **International Education** (International and Comparative Education); **Law** (Commercial Law; Law; Social Work); **Management** (Business Administration; Management); **Marxism** (Political Sciences); **Pharmacy** (Pharmacology; Pharmacy; Traditional Eastern Medicine); **Physical Education** (Physical Education; Sports); **Tourism and Cuisine** (Cooking and Catering; Tourism); **Vocational and Technical Education** (Accountancy; Business Administration; Cooking and Catering; Economics; Food Science; Management; Marketing; Nutrition; Software Engineering; Tourism)

History: Founded 1952 as Heilongjiang Commercial University. Acquired present title 2000.

Main Language(s) of Instruction: Chinese

Degrees and Diplomas: *Xueshi Xuewei*; *Shuoshi Xuewei*; *Boshi*

Publications: Commercial Research; Journal of Harbin University of Commerce; Journal of Harbin University of Commerce
Last Updated: 19/11/12

HARBIN UNIVERSITY OF SCIENCE AND TECHNOLOGY

52 Xuefu Road, Harbin, Heilongjiang Province 150080
Tel: +86(451) 86390081 +86(451) 86390114
Fax: +86(451) 86390866
EMail: wzgl@hrbust.edu.cn
Website: http://www.hrbust.edu.cn/

President: Li Dayong

Vice-President: Dawei Meng

School

Adult and Continuing Education (Adult Education; Continuing Education); **Applied Sciences** (Applied Chemistry; Applied Physics; Computer Science; Electronic Engineering; Information Technology); **Architecture and Civil Engineering** (Architecture; Civil Engineering); **Art** (Design; Fine Arts; Painting and Drawing); **Automation** (Automation and Control Engineering); **Chemistry and Environmental Engineering** (Chemistry; Environmental Engineering); **Computer Science** (Computer Science); **Economics** (Economics); **Electrical and Electronic Engineering** (Automation and Control Engineering; Electrical and Electronic Engineering; Information Technology); **Foreign Languages** (English; Japanese; Korean; Russian); **Graduate Studies**; **International Culture and Education** (Business Administration; Chinese); **Law** (Law); **Management** (Accountancy; Business Administration; Economics; International Economics; Management; Marketing); **Materials Science and Engineering** (Engineering; Inorganic Chemistry; Materials Engineering; Polymer and Plastics Technology); **Measurement–Control Technology and Communications Engineering** (Measurement and Precision Engineering; Safety Engineering; Telecommunications Engineering); **Mechanical and Power Engineering** (Automation and Control Engineering; Industrial Design; Machine Building; Mechanical Engineering; Power Engineering); **Reserve Officers**; **Software** (Software Engineering)

Campus

Rongcheng

History: Founded 1995 following merger of Harbin University of Science and Technology, Harbin Institute of Electrical Engineering and Harbin Higher Industrial Vocational College.

Academic Year: September to July (September-January; February-July)

Admission Requirements: Graduation from senior middle school and entrance examination

Main Language(s) of Instruction: Chinese

Accrediting Agency: Ministry of Machinery and Electronics

Degrees and Diplomas: *Xueshi Xuewei*; *Shuoshi Xuewei*; *Boshi*

Publications: Journal of Electric Machines and Control; Journal of Science and Technology; Journal of Science-Technology and Management

Last Updated: 20/02/13

HE'S UNIVERSITY

Surabaya Street 66, Dongling District, Shenyang, Liaoning 110163
Tel: +86(24) 88059778 +86(24) 88059798
Fax: +86(24) 88053142
Website: http://www.he-edu.com/

President: He Wei

Department

Art and Design (Advertising and Publicity; Design; Fine Arts; Visual Arts); **Clinical Medicine** (Biology; Embryology and Reproduction Biology; Gynaecology and Obstetrics; Histology; Immunology; Medicine; Paediatrics); **Management** (Management; Marketing; Public Administration); **Medical Imaging** (Medical Technology; Radiology); **Nursing** (Anatomy; Biochemistry; Nursing; Pathology; Physiology); **Optometry** (Ophthalmology; Optical Technology; Optometry); **Pharmacy** (Health Sciences; Medicine; Pharmacology; Pharmacy; Toxicology; Traditional Eastern Medicine)

Centre

Professional Training (Nutrition; Ophthalmology; Optical Technology; Optometry; Psychology)

Further Information: Affiliated Eye Hospital

History: Founded 1999 as Shenyang Medical College - School of Optometry Ho. Transofrmed into Ho Shenyang Medical College of Visual Science 2004.

Main Language(s) of Instruction: Chinese

Degrees and Diplomas: *Xueshi Xuewei*

Student Numbers *2012-2013*: Total: c. 6,000

Last Updated: 29/11/13

HEBEI ACADEMY OF FINE ARTS (HBAFA)

No.44 Fuxi St Xinle, Shijiazhuang, Hebei 050700
Tel: +86(311) 88651148
Fax: +86(311) 88596160
EMail: dongfangbgsh@126.com
Website: http://www.hbafa.com/

President: Zhongyi Zhen

College

Fashion (Fashion Design)

School

Animation (Visual Arts); **Continuing Education**; **Industrial Design** (Industrial Design); **Visual Arts** (Visual Arts)

Institute

Calligraphy (Painting and Drawing); **Environmental Art** (Architectural and Environmental Design); **International Education**; **Media** (Media Studies); **Urban Design** (Design)

Academy

Fine Arts (Fine Arts)

Main Language(s) of Instruction: Chinese

Degrees and Diplomas: *Xueshi Xuewei*

Last Updated: 27/11/13

HEBEI COLLEGE OF SCIENCE AND TECHNOLOGY

1956 South Second Ring Road, Baoding, Hebei 071000
Website: http://www.hbkjxy.cn

President: Wang Xin

Department

Architectural Engineering (Civil Engineering; Management; Structural Architecture); **Automotive Engineering** (Automation and Control Engineering; Automotive Engineering; Maintenance Technology; Marketing; Metal Techniques; Transport Engineering); **Economic Management** (Accountancy; Business Administration; Business Computing; Cooking and Catering; E-Business/Commerce; Economics; Finance; Food Technology; Hotel and Restaurant; Hotel Management; Insurance; Management; Nutrition; Safety Engineering; Tourism; Transport Management); **Information and Arts** (Advertising and Publicity; Architectural and Environmental Design; Communication Arts; Computer Networks; Computer Science; Design; Electronic Engineering; Graphic Design; Information Technology; Nursing; Software Engineering; Technology; Visual Arts); **Mechanical Engineering** (Automation and Control Engineering; Electrical Engineering; Industrial Design; Mechanical Engineering; Power Engineering; Production Engineering); **Public Course** (English; Mathematics; Sports)

History: Founded 1991.

Main Language(s) of Instruction: Chinese

Degrees and Diplomas: *Xueshi Xuewei*

Academic Staff *2012-2013*: Total: c. 500

Student Numbers *2012-2013*: Total: c. 8,000

Last Updated: 27/11/13

HEBEI FINANCE UNIVERSITY

3188 North Main Street, Baoding, Hebei 071051
Tel: +86(312) 3338101
Fax: +86(312) 3338102
Website: http://www.hbcf.edu.cn/

President: Zunhou Chen

Department

Accountancy (Accountancy); **Basic Education**; **Continuing Education**; **Economic and Trade** (Business Administration; Economics); **Finance** (Finance); **Foreign Language Teaching** (Foreign Languages Education); **Foreign Languages and Commerce** (Business Administration; Business and Commerce; English; Management; Modern Languages); **Information Management and Engineering** (Information Management; Information Technology); **Insurance** (Insurance); **International Education**; **Law** (Law); **Management** (Management); **Physical Education** (Physical Education; Sports); **Social Sciences** (Social Sciences)

Institute

International Financial Services Outsourcing (Finance)

History: Founded 1952 as Hebei Institute of Finance Banking School of Baoding. Upgraded into College 1984. Renamed Baoding Finance College 1991. Acquired present status and title 2007.

Main Language(s) of Instruction: Chinese

Degrees and Diplomas: *Xueshi Xuewei*

Academic Staff *2012-2013*: Total 598

Student Numbers *2012-2013*: Total 11,993

Last Updated: 27/11/13

HEBEI INSTITUTE OF ARCHITECTURE AND CIVIL ENGINEERING

33 Jiangguo Road, Zhangjiakou, Hebei Province 075024
Tel: +86(313) 2050803
Fax: +86(313) 20106I26
EMail: netcenter@hebiace.edu.cn
Website: http://www.hebiace.edu.cn

Président: Cong Liu

Department
Architecture (Architecture); **Basic Sciences** (Mathematics; Physics); **Civil Engineering** (Civil Engineering); **Computer Science** (Computer Science); **Construction Engineering** (Construction Engineering; Town Planning); **Engineering Management** (Engineering Management); **Foreign Languages** (English); **Machinery and Electricity** (Electrical Engineering; Machine Building); **Mechanical Engineering** (Automation and Control Engineering; Industrial Engineering; Mechanical Engineering); **Physical Education** (Physical Education); **Social Sciences** (Social Sciences)

History: Founded 1950, acquired present name 1978.

Degrees and Diplomas: *Xueshi Xuewei*

Last Updated: 20/02/13

HEBEI INSTITUTE OF COMMUNICATIONS

Security Police, Xinhua Road on the 8th,
Shijiazhuang, Hebei 050071
Tel: +86(311) 8510068 +86(311) 885100699
Website: http://www.hebic.cn/

College
Vocational and Technical Studies

School
Art Design (Design); **Continuing Education**; **Film** (Film); **Journalism and Communication** (Journalism; Mass Communication; Radio and Television Broadcasting)

Department
Art (Fine Arts); **Chinese** (Chinese); **Foreign Languages** (English; Modern Languages; Portuguese; Spanish); **Information Technology** (Computer Engineering; Computer Networks; Computer Science; Information Management; Information Technology; Multimedia); **Management** (Management); **Music** (Music); **Performing** (Performing Arts; Theatre); **Physical Education** (Physical Education)

Institute
Outsourcing

Academy
Animation (Visual Arts); **Dance** (Dance)

History: Founded 2000.

Main Language(s) of Instruction: Chinese

Degrees and Diplomas: *Xueshi Xuewei*

Student Numbers *2012-2013*: Total 15,000

Last Updated: 27/11/13

HEBEI INSTITUTE OF PHYSICAL EDUCATION

No.82 Xuefu Rd, Shijiazhuang, Hebei Province 050041
Tel: +86(311) 85337626
Fax: +86(311) 85336296
EMail: intl@mail.hepec.edu.cn
Website: http://www.hepec.edu.cn

President: Sun Banjun

Faculty
English (English); **Human Sports and Exercise Science** (Physical Education; Sports); **Physical Education** (Physical Education); **Social Sports** (Sports); **Traditional Sports** (Sports)

School
Sports (Sports)

History: Founded 1984.

Main Language(s) of Instruction: Chinese

Degrees and Diplomas: *Xueshi Xuewei*

Last Updated: 19/11/12

HEBEI MEDICAL UNIVERSITY

361 Xinshi South Road, Shijiazhuang, Hebei Province 050091
Tel: +86(311) 86265043
EMail: webmaster@hebmu.edu.cn
Website: http://www.hebmu.edu.cn/

Vice-Chancellor: Bin Cong

Department
Acupuncture and Massage (Acupuncture); **Anaesthesiology** (Anaesthesiology); **Basic Medical Sciences** (Medicine); **Clinical Medicine** (Medicine); **Dental Surgery** (Stomatology); **Foreign Languages** (English); **Forensic Medicine** (Forensic Medicine and Dentistry); **Medical Imaging** (Medical Technology; Medicine); **Nursing** (Nursing); **Pharmacology** (Pharmacology); **Preventive Medicine** (Medicine); **Public Health** (Public Health; Social and Preventive Medicine); **Social Sciences and Humanities** (Arts and Humanities; Social Sciences); **Traditional Chinese Clinical Medicine** (Acupuncture; Pharmacology; Traditional Eastern Medicine)

Further Information: Also six affiliated hospitals

History: Founded 1894. Merged with Hebei College of Traditional Chinese Medicine and Shijiazhuang Medical College.

Main Language(s) of Instruction: Chinese

Degrees and Diplomas: *Xueshi Xuewei*; *Shuoshi Xuewei*; *Boshi*

Publications: Journal of Hebei Medical University

Academic Staff *2011-2012*	**TOTAL**
FULL-TIME	c. **7,100**
Student Numbers *2011-2012*	
All (Foreign included)	c. **25,600**
FOREIGN ONLY	**400**

HEBEI NORMAL UNIVERSITY

No.20 Road East of 2nd Ring South, Yuhua District,
Shijiazhuang, Hebei Province 050024
Tel: +86(311) 80789793
EMail: HNUIO@sina.com
Website: http://io.hebtu.edu.cn:8080/inter_en/index.php

President: Jiang Chunlan

College
Business (Accountancy; Economics; Human Resources; Information Management; International Business); **Chemistry and Material Science** (Applied Chemistry; Chemistry; Science Education); **Chinese Language and Literature** (Chinese; Linguistics; Literature); **Education** (Educational Administration; Educational Sciences; Preschool Education; Psychology); **Fine Arts and Design** (Design; Fine Arts; Sculpture; Visual Arts); **Foreign Languages** (English; Japanese; Modern Languages; Russian; Spanish); **History and Culture** (Archaeology; Cultural Studies; History); **Huihua** (Arts and Humanities; Biology; Chemistry; Chinese; Fine Arts; Mathematics; Modern Languages; Physics; Psychology); **Information Technology** (Computer Science; E-Business/Commerce; Educational Technology; Information Technology); **Law and Politics** (Law; Political Sciences); **Life Sciences** (Animal Husbandry; Biochemistry; Biology; Botany; Cell Biology; Genetics; Molecular Biology); **Mathematics and Information Science** (Applied Mathematics; Computer Science; Mathematics); **Music** (Dance; Music; Music Theory and Composition; Musicology); **Physical Education** (Physical Education; Sports); **Physics and Information Engineering** (Computer Networks; Electronic Engineering; Physics); **Public Administration** (Public Administration); **Resources and Environment** (Environmental Studies; Geography; Natural Resources); **Software** (Software Engineering); **Vocational Education and Technology** (Automotive Engineering; Electrical Engineering; Mechanical Engineering)

School
Journalism and Communication (Advertising and Publicity; Cinema and Television; Journalism; Radio and Television Broadcasting)

Department
Tourism (Cooking and Catering; Hotel and Restaurant; Tourism)

History: Founded 1902 as school. Acquired present status and title 1996 following merge of Hebei Teachers University, Hebei Teachers College, Hebei Education Institute established in 1952 and Hebei Vocational and Technological College. Under the jurisdiction of the Provincial Government.

Academic Year: August to July (August-January; February-July)

Admission Requirements: Graduation from high school and entrance examination

Main Language(s) of Instruction: Chinese

Degrees and Diplomas: *Xueshi Xuewei*; *Shuoshi Xuewei*; *Boshi*
Publications: Journal of Hebei Normal University; Social Sciences Information of Higher Learning Institution; Thought and Wisdom
Last Updated: 22/11/12

HEBEI NORMAL UNIVERSITY FOR NATIONALITIES (HBUN)

Higher Education Park, Chengde, Hebei 067000
Tel: +86(314) 2370999
Website: http://www.hbun.net/

President: Jian Wang (2003-)

Department

Biology (Biology); **Chemistry** (Chemistry); **Chinese** (Chinese); **Fine Arts** (Fine Arts); **Foreign Languages** (Modern Languages); **Law and Political Sciences** (Law; Political Sciences); **Mathematics and Computer Science** (Mathematics and Computer Science); **Music** (Music); **Physical Education** (Physical Education); **Physics** (Physics); **Primary Education** (Primary Education); **Public Course**; **Social Sciences** (Social Sciences); **Tourism Management** (Management; Tourism)

History: Founded 1907 as a Law School. Upgraded into Chengde Teachers College 1959. Acquired present title and status 2010.

Main Language(s) of Instruction: Chinese

Degrees and Diplomas: *Xueshi Xuewei*

Academic Staff *2012-2013*: Total 545
Last Updated: 27/11/13

HEBEI NORMAL UNIVERSITY OF SCIENCE AND TECHNOLOGY

360 West Hebei Street, Qinhuangdao, Hebei, Hebei Province 066004
Tel: +86(335) 8076537
Fax: +86(335) 8076005
Website: http://w3.hevttc.edu.cn/hevttc/

President: Xin Yanhuai

Department

Agronomy (Agricultural Management; Agronomy; Plant and Crop Protection); **Animal Science** (Zoology); **Architecture** (Architecture); **Art Design** (Design; Visual Arts); **Business Administration** (Accountancy; Business Administration); **Chemistry** (Chemistry); **Chinese Language and Literature** (Chinese; Literature); **Civil Engineering** (Civil Engineering); **Computer Science** (Computer Science); **Economy and Trade** (Business and Commerce; Economics); **Food Engineering** (Food Technology); **Foreign Languages** (English); **Horticulture** (Horticulture); **Law** (Law); **Life Science** (Biological and Life Sciences); **Mathematics and Physics** (Mathematics; Physics); **Mechanics and Electronics** (Electronic Engineering; Mechanical Engineering); **Physical Education** (Physical Education); **Social Sciences** (Social Sciences)

History: Founded 1941 as Changli Agro-vocational School. Merged with Qinhuangdao Coal-Industry Management School. Acquired present title 2003.

Degrees and Diplomas: *Xueshi Xuewei*

Publications: Journal of Hebei Normal Normal University of Science and Technology; Journal of Normal University of Science and Technology

Academic Staff *2011-2012*: Total 1,200
STAFF WITH DOCTORATE: Total 710
Student Numbers *2011-2012*: Total: c. 24,000
Last Updated: 21/02/13

HEBEI NORTH UNIVERSITY

14 Changqing Road, Zhangjiakou, Hebei Province 075000
Tel: +86(313) 8032544
Fax: +86(313) 8032544
EMail: gulinu888@yahoo.com.cn
Website: http://www.hebeinu.org.cn

President: Zhang Li

College

Adult Education (Adult Education); **Agronomy and Horticulture** (Agronomy; Horticulture); **First Clinical Medicine** (Medicine); **Foreign Languages** (English); **Literature** (Chinese; Literature); **Medical** (Medicine); **Medical Technology** (Anaesthesiology; Nursing; Radiology); **Science** (Natural Sciences); **Second Clinical Medicine** (Medicine); **Veterinary Medicine** (Animal Husbandry; Veterinary Science)

Further Information: Also clinical hospital

History: Founded 2003 through merger between Zhangjiakou Medical College (founded 1945), Zhangjiakou Teachers Training College and Zhangjiakou Advanced Postsecondary Agronomy School.

Main Language(s) of Instruction: Chinese

Degrees and Diplomas: *Xueshi Xuewei*; *Shuoshi Xuewei*
Last Updated: 19/11/12

HEBEI UNITED UNIVERSITY

46 Xinhua Xidao, Tangshan, Hebei Province 063009
Tel: +86(315) 2592044
EMail: international@heuu.edu.cn
Website: http://international.heuu.edu.cn/

President: Yuan Juxiang

College

Arts (Ceramic Art; Design; Fine Arts; Industrial Design; Industrial Engineering; Painting and Drawing); **Chemical Engineering** (Biotechnology; Chemical Engineering); **Chinese Medicine** (Medicine); **Civil and Architectural Engineering** (Architecture; Civil Engineering; Transport Engineering; Water Management); **Clinical Medicine** (Medicine); **Continuing Education** (Continuing Education); **Economics** (Economics; Finance; International Business); **Electrical Engineering** (Automation and Control Engineering; Electrical Engineering); **Elementary Medicine** (Medicine); **Foreign Languages** (Modern Languages); **Humanities and Law** (Arts and Humanities; Law); **Information Engineering** (Electronic Engineering; Information Sciences; Information Technology; Marine Engineering); **International Education** (International and Comparative Education); **Jitang** (Biotechnology; English; Law; Nursing; Pharmacy; Radiology; Traditional Eastern Medicine); **Life Sciences** (Biological and Life Sciences; Biotechnology; Genetics); **Management** (Management); **Materials Science and Engineering** (Materials Engineering); **Mechanical Engineering** (Automation and Control Engineering; Industrial Design; Industrial Engineering; Mechanical Engineering; Packaging Technology); **Metallurgy and Energy** (Energy Engineering; Metallurgical Engineering; Power Engineering; Thermal Engineering); **Mining Engineering** (Mining Engineering); **Nursing and Rehabilitation** (Nursing; Rehabilitation and Therapy); **Pharmaceutical Sciences** (Pharmacology; Pharmacy); **Psychology** (Psychology); **Public Health** (Child Care and Development; Community Health; Epidemiology; Health Administration; Nutrition; Occupational Health; Public Health; Toxicology); **Science** (Natural Sciences); **Stomatology** (Oral Pathology; Orthodontics; Stomatology; Surgery); **Transportation and Mapping** (Surveying and Mapping; Transport and Communications)

School

Graduate Studies

Department

Physical Education (Physical Education)

History: Founded 1958 as Tangshan Metallurgical College. Acquired present title and status following merger between Hebei Polytechnic University and North China Coal Medical College.

Main Language(s) of Instruction: Chinese

Degrees and Diplomas: *Xueshi Xuewei*; *Shuoshi Xuewei*
Last Updated: 19/11/12

HEBEI UNIVERSITY

No.180, Wusidong Road, Baoding, Hebei Province 071002
Tel: +86(312) 5079533
Fax: +86(312) 5022648
EMail: webmaster@mail.hbu.edu.cn
Website: http://www.hbu.edu.cn

President: Wang Hongrui

International Relations: Guo Xianting

School

Commerce and Business Administration (Business Administration; Business and Commerce); **Computer Science** (Computer Science); **Economics** (Economics); **Electronic Engineering** (Electronic Engineering); **Foreign Languages** (Modern Languages)

Further Information: Also branch in Qinhuangdao City

History: Founded 1921as Tianjin Technology and Business University. Acquired present title 1960.

Academic Year: August to July (August-January; March-July)

Admission Requirements: Graduation from senior middle school and entrance examination

Main Language(s) of Instruction: Chinese

Degrees and Diplomas: *Xueshi Xuewei*; *Shuoshi Xuewei*; *Boshi*

Publications: Bulletin of Physics; Hebei Higher Education Study; Hebei Science and Technology Library Journal; Japanese Study; Journal of Hebei University

Publishing House: Hebei University Press

Last Updated: 19/11/12

HEBEI UNIVERSITY OF ECONOMICS AND BUSINESS

XueFu Road Number 47, Shijiazhuang, Hebei province 050061
Tel: +86(311) 7655607
EMail: huebfao@heuet.edu.cn
Website: http://www.heuet.edu.cn

President: Wang Ying

Department

Banking (Banking); **Commerce** (Business and Commerce); **Economics** (Economics); **Finance** (Finance); **Food Engineering** (Food Technology); **Foreign Languages** (Japanese; Modern Languages); **Foreign Trade** (International Business); **Industrial and Business Management** (Business Administration; Industrial Management); **Labour and Personnel Management** (Staff Development); **Public Relations and Secretarial Studies** (Public Relations; Secretarial Studies); **Statistics** (Statistics)

History: Founded 1995. Merged with Hebei Institute of Economics and Trade, Hebei Institute of Finance and Economics and Hebei Higher Training School of Commerce.

Main Language(s) of Instruction: Chinese

Degrees and Diplomas: *Xueshi Xuewei*; *Shuoshi Xuewei*

Publications: Economy and Management; Journal of Hebei University of Economics and Trade

Last Updated: 20/11/12

HEBEI UNIVERSITY OF ENGINEERING

Guangming South Street 199, Handan, Hebei Province 056038
Tel: +86(310) 8579017
EMail: sunny@yahoo.com.cn
Website: http://www.hebeu.edu.cn/en/index.html

President: Zhanzhou Liu

School

Agriculture (Agriculture; Horticulture; Veterinary Science; Zoology); **Architecture** (Architecture; Town Planning); **Civil Engineering** (Civil Engineering; Materials Engineering; Transport Engineering); **Economics and Management** (Accountancy; Business Administration; Economics; International Business; International Economics; Management); **Equipment and Manufacturing** (Materials Engineering); **Humanities** (Chinese; English; Law; Literature); **Information Sciences and Electrical Engineering** (Automation and Control Engineering; Computer Science; Electrical Engineering; Electronic Engineering; Information Sciences); **Mechanical and Electrical Engineering** (Automation and Control Engineering; Electrical Engineering; Industrial Design; Mechanical Engineering); **Medicine** (Laboratory Techniques; Medicine; Nursing); **Resources** (Geography; Mining Engineering; Natural Resources; Rural Planning; Town Planning); **Science** (Applied Chemistry; Applied Physics; Computer Science; Natural Sciences); **Urban Construction** (Building Technologies; Environmental Engineering; Water Management); **Water Resources and Hydropower** (Hydraulic Engineering; Power Engineering; Thermal Engineering; Water Science)

History: Founded 2003 following the amalgamation of Hebei Institute of Architectural Science and Technology, North China Institute of Water Conservancy and Hydro-electric Power, Handan Medicine College and Handan Agriculture College. Acquired present title 2006.

Main Language(s) of Instruction: Chinese

Degrees and Diplomas: *Xueshi Xuewei*; *Shuoshi Xuewei*

Last Updated: 20/11/12

HEBEI UNIVERSITY OF SCIENCE AND TECHNOLOGY

70 East Yuhua Road, Shijiazhuang, Hebei Province 050018
Tel: +86(311) 88623762
Fax: +86(311) 81668197
EMail: waiban@hebust.edu.cn
Website: http://www.hebust.edu.cn

President: Hexu Sun

International Relations: Zhanzhong Jin, Vice-President

School

Animation; **Architecture Engineering** (Architectural and Environmental Design; Civil Engineering); **Biological Science and Engineering** (Bioengineering; Biological and Life Sciences; Biotechnology; Food Science); **Chemical and Pharmaceutical Engineering** (Chemical Engineering; Chemistry; Pharmacy); **Continuing Education**; **Economics and Management** (Business Administration; E-Business/Commerce; Finance; Industrial Engineering; Management; Marketing); **Electrical Engineering** (Automation and Control Engineering; Electrical Engineering); **Environmental Engineering** (Environmental Engineering; Safety Engineering; Water Science); **Fine Art** (Design; Sound Engineering (Acoustics)); **Foreign Languages** (English); **Graduate Studies**; **Information Science and Engineering** (Computer Networks; Computer Science; Information Technology; Software Engineering); **Liberal Art and Laws** (Chinese; Journalism; Law; Literature; Social Work); **Materials Engineering** (Materials Engineering); **Mechanical Engineering** (Industrial Design; Mechanical Engineering); **Polytechnic** (Engineering); **Sciences** (Applied Mathematics; Applied Physics; Engineering; Information Sciences; Mathematics; Mechanical Engineering); **Textile Engineering** (Textile Design; Textile Technology)

History: Founded 1996 by incorporating former Hebei Institute of Chemical Technology and Light Industry, Hebei Institute of Mechano-Electric Engineering and Hebei Textile Staff and Workers University.

Main Language(s) of Instruction: Chinese

Degrees and Diplomas: *Xueshi Xuewei*

Publications: Hebei Industrial Science & Technology; Higher Education Study; Journal of Hebei University of Science and Technology

Last Updated: 21/02/13

HEBEI UNIVERSITY OF TECHNOLOGY (HUT)

No 8 Guangrongdao Dingzigu, Hong Qiao District,
Tianjin, Tianjin Province 300130
Tel: +86(22) 26564069
Fax: +86(22) 26545303
EMail: fao@hebut.edu.cn
Website: http://www.hebut.edu.cn

President: Qiang Li

School

Architecture and Artistic Design (Architecture; Industrial Design; Town Planning); **Chemical Engineering** (Applied Chemistry; Automotive Engineering; Chemical Engineering; Mechanical Engineering; Safety Engineering); **Civil Engineering** (Bridge Engineering; Civil Engineering; Construction Engineering; Geological Engineering; Road Engineering; Transport Engineering); **Computer Science and Engineering** (Computer Networks; Computer Science; Software Engineering); **Continuing Education**; **Electrical Engineering and Automation** (Automation and Control Engineering; Biomedical Engineering; Electrical Engineering; Power Engineering); **Energy and Environmental Engineering** (Energy Engineering; Environmental Engineering; Heating and Refrigeration; Thermal Engineering); **Foreign Languages** (English; French;

Japanese; Modern Languages); **Humanities and Law** (Arts and Humanities; Labour and Industrial Relations; Law; Political Sciences); **Information** (Communication Studies; Data Processing; Electronic Engineering; Information Management; Information Technology); **Management** (Business Administration; Economics; Finance; Industrial Engineering; Industrial Management; Information Management; International Business; International Economics; Management; Marketing); **Materials Science and Engineering** (Materials Engineering; Physics); **Mechanical Engineering** (Automation and Control Engineering; Automotive Engineering; Measurement and Precision Engineering; Mechanical Engineering); **Science** (Applied Mathematics; Applied Physics; Computer Science; Information Sciences; Mathematics)

History: Founded 1903, acquired present status and title 1995.

Admission Requirements: Senior high school certificate and National College entrance examination

Main Language(s) of Instruction: Chinese

Accrediting Agency: Ministry of Education; State Education Commission

Degrees and Diplomas: *Xueshi Xuewei*; *Shuoshi Xuewei*; *Boshi*

Student Services: Canteen, Careers Guidance, Foreign Studies Centre, Health Services, Sports Facilities

Publications: Journal of Hebei University of Technology

Last Updated: 20/11/12

HECHI UNIVERSITY (HCNU)

Longjiang Road 42, Yizhou, Guangxi 546300
Website: http://www.hcnu.edu.cn/

President: Lang Yao-Xiu

College

Computer and Information Engineering (Computer Science; Information Technology); **Foreign Languages** (English; Modern Languages); **Physics, Mechanical and Electrical Engineering** (Electrical Engineering; Mechanical Engineering; Physics)

School

Mathematics and Statistics (Mathematics; Statistics)

Department

Chemical and Biological Engineering (Bioengineering; Chemical Engineering); **Continuing Education**; **Economics and Management** (Economics; Management); **Ideological and Political Theory Teaching** (Political Sciences); **Politics and History and Culture** (Cultural Studies; History; Political Sciences); **Teacher Education** (Teacher Training)

Institute

Art (Fine Arts); **Literature and Media** (Media Studies); **Sports** (Sports)

Degrees and Diplomas: *Xueshi Xuewei*

Academic Staff *2012-2013*: Total: c. 450

Student Numbers *2012-2013*: Total: c. 9,500

Last Updated: 27/11/13

HEFEI NORMAL UNIVERSITY (HNU)

Jinzhai Road No. 327, Hefei, Anhui 230061
Website: http://xy.hftc.edu.cn/index.html

President: Xian-liang Wu

College

Liberal Arts (Arts and Humanities); **Teacher Education** (Teacher Training)

School

Economics and Management (Economics; Management); **Electronic and Information Engineering** (Electronic Engineering; Information Technology); **Mathematics** (Mathematics; Statistics)

Department

Chemistry and Chemical Engineering (Chemical Engineering; Chemistry); **College English** (English; Foreign Languages Education; Secondary Education); **Computer Science and Technology** (Computer Engineering; Computer Science); **Continuing Education**; **Foreign Language** (Modern Languages); **Ideological and Political Theory Teaching** (Political Sciences); **Life Sciences** (Biological and Life Sciences); **Music** (Music); **Physical Education** (Physical Education; Sports); **Public Computer** (Computer Science)

Institute

Media Arts (Media Studies)

History: Founded 1955 as Anhui Institute of Education. Acquired present status and title 2007.

Main Language(s) of Instruction: Chinese

Degrees and Diplomas: *Xueshi Xuewei*

Academic Staff *2012-2013*: Total 667

Student Numbers *2012-2013*: Total 13,221

Last Updated: 27/11/13

HEFEI UNIVERSITY

373 Huangshan Road, Hefei, Anhui Province 230022
Tel: +86(551) 2158005
Fax: +86(551) 2158147
EMail: yzxx@hfuu.edu.cn
Website: http://www.hfuu.edu.cn/

President: Cai Jingmin

Deputy-Secretary: Yang Li

College

Continuing Education (Continuing Education)

Department

Art and Design (Design; Fine Arts); **Biological and Environmental Engineering** (Biological and Life Sciences; Environmental Engineering); **Building Engineering** (Building Technologies); **Chemical Engineering** (Chemical Engineering); **Chinese Language and Literature** (Chinese; Literature); **Computer Engineering** (Computer Engineering); **Economics** (Economics); **Education** (Education); **Electronic and Electrical Engineering** (Electrical and Electronic Engineering); **Foreign Languages and Literature** (English; Literature); **Information Technology** (Information Technology); **Materials Engineering** (Materials Engineering); **Mathematics and Physics** (Mathematics; Physics); **Mechanical Engineering** (Mechanical Engineering); **Physical Education** (Physical Education); **Political Sciences** (Political Sciences); **Tourism** (Tourism)

Institute

International Education

History: Founded 1980. Acquired present title 2002 following merger of Hefei Union University and Hefei Education College.

Degrees and Diplomas: *Xueshi Xuewei*; *Shuoshi Xuewei*

Publications: Hefei Union University Journal

Academic Staff *2011-2012*: Total: c. 900

Student Numbers *2011-2012*: Total: c. 14,000

Last Updated: 21/02/13

HEFEI UNIVERSITY OF TECHNOLOGY

193 Tunxi Road, Hefei, Anhui Province 230009
Tel: +86 (551) 4658410
Fax: +86 (551) 4658410
EMail: webmaster@hfut.edu.cn
Website: http://www.hfut.edu.cn

President: Congwei Xu

School

Architecture and Arts (Architecture; Design; Town Planning); **Biotechnology and Food Engineering** (Agricultural Engineering; Agricultural Equipment; Bioengineering; Biotechnology; Food Science; Food Technology); **Chemical Engineering** (Applied Chemistry; Chemical Engineering; Pharmacy); **Civil Engineering** (Architectural and Environmental Design; Civil Engineering; Hydraulic Engineering; Water Science); **Computer and Information** (Computer Networks; Computer Science; Information

Technology); **Electrical Engineering and Automation** (Automation and Control Engineering; Biomedical Engineering; Electrical Engineering); **Finance and Economics** (Economics; Finance); **Humanities** (Advertising and Publicity; Arts and Humanities; Economics; English; Finance; International Economics; Law; Political Sciences); **Machinery and Automobile Engineering** (Automation and Control Engineering; Automotive Engineering; Industrial Design; Industrial Engineering; Machine Building; Power Engineering; Transport Engineering); **Management** (Accountancy; Business Administration; E-Business/Commerce; Information Management; Tourism); **Materials Science and Engineering** (Materials Engineering; Metallurgical Engineering); **Resources and Environment** (Environmental Engineering; Natural Resources); **Science** (Applied Mathematics; Applied Physics; Electronic Engineering; Mathematics and Computer Science; Microelectronics; Natural Sciences)

History: Founded 1945 as Bengbu Advanced Industry Vocational School. Acquired present title 1958 and incorporated Anhui Institute of Technology 1997.

Degrees and Diplomas: *Xueshi Xuewei*; *Shuoshi Xuewei*; *Boshi*

Publications: Journal of Hefei University of Technology

Last Updated: 20/11/12

HEIHE UNIVERSITY

Cooperation Zone, Heihe,
Heilongjiang 164300
Tel: +86(456) 8222907 +86(456) 8222832
Fax: +86(456) 8223750
Website: http://www.hhxy.edu.cn/

President: Xianmin Sun

Department

Chinese Language and Literature (Chinese; Literature); **Computer Science and Information Engineering** (Computer Engineering; Computer Networks; Computer Science; Information Technology; Telecommunications Engineering); **Economic Management** (Economics; Management); **Education** *(Comparative Education Research Institute)* (Education); **English** (English); **Fine Arts** (Fine Arts); **History and Culture Tourism** (History; Tourism); **Ideological and Political Theory Teaching and Research** (Political Sciences); **Mathematics** (Mathematics); **Music** (Music); **Physical Chemistry** (Physical Chemistry); **Physical Education** (Physical Education); **Russian Department** *(Russian Centre)* (Russian)

Institute

History and Culture *(Heilongjiang River)* (Cultural Studies; History); **Youth** (Preschool Education)

Centre

Continuing Education *(Heihe Radio and Television University)*; **Higher Education Research and Evaluation** *(FIPP)* (Educational Research; Higher Education); **International Cooperation Center for Education**

Further Information: Theory Research Institute TRIZ (Theory of Inventive Problem Solving); 4 research institutes: Institute of Russian Affairs, Sino-Russian Comparative Pedagogical Institute, History and Culture of Heilongjiang River Valley Research Institute and the Environmental Art Research Institute.

History: Founded 1960 as Heihe Normal College. Successively known as Heihe Normal School, the Preparatory Office of Heihe Normal University, the Heihe Branch of Qiqihar Normal University, and the Heihe Branch of Qiqihar University. Acquired current title in 2004.

Main Language(s) of Instruction: Chinese

Degrees and Diplomas: *Xueshi Xuewei*

Student Services: Sports Facilities

Academic Staff *2012-2013*	**TOTAL**
FULL-TIME	389
Student Numbers *2012-2013*	
All (Foreign included)	c. 7,000
FOREIGN ONLY	81

Last Updated: 28/11/13

HEILONGJIANG BAYI AGRICULTURAL UNIVERSITY

Mishan, Heilongjiang Province 158308
Tel: +86(453) 5070010
Fax: +86(453) 5070015
EMail: skywang2006@yahoo.com.cn
Website: http://www.hlau.cn

President: Xu Mei

International Relations: Liu Fengjun

College

Accountancy (Accountancy; Finance); **Agronomy** (Agriculture; Agronomy; Crop Production; Horticulture; Landscape Architecture; Plant and Crop Protection); **Animal Science and Technology** (Computer Science; Food Science; Social Sciences; Veterinary Science; Zoology); **Economics and Management** (Accountancy; Agricultural Economics; Business and Commerce; Economics; Human Resources; Management; Marketing); **Engineering** (Agricultural Engineering; Architectural and Environmental Design; Automation and Control Engineering; Civil Engineering; Construction Engineering; Engineering; Industrial Design); **Food Science and Technology** (Food Science; Food Technology); **Humanities and Social Sciences** (Administration; Chinese; English; Japanese; Political Sciences; Public Administration; Russian; Social Work); **Information Science and Technology** (Automation and Control Engineering; Computer Science; Electrical Engineering; Information Technology); **Life Sciences** (Bioengineering; Biological and Life Sciences; Biotechnology; Microbiology; Pharmacy); **Science** (Chemistry; Computer Science; Mathematics; Physics); **Vocational &Technical Training** (Accountancy; Computer Science; Crop Production; Technology; Veterinary Science)

History: Founded 1958 as HeiLongJiang August First Land Reclamation University.

Academic Year: March to January (March-July; September-January)

Admission Requirements: Graduation from senior middle school

Main Language(s) of Instruction: Chinese

Accrediting Agency: Department of Agriculture

Degrees and Diplomas: *Xueshi Xuewei*; *Shuoshi Xuewei*; *Boshi*

Publishing house: Nong Da Press

Last Updated: 20/11/12

HEILONGJIANG EAST UNIVERSITY

331 Xuefu Road, Nangang District,
Harbin, Heilongjiang Province 150086
Tel: +86(451) 86673244
Fax: +86(451) 86653600
EMail: yzbgs@mail.dfxy.net; liuoe@126.com
Website: http://www.dfxy.net

Department

Arts and Design (Design; Fine Arts); **Computer Science and Electrical Engineering** (Computer Engineering; Computer Science; Electrical Engineering); **Construction Engineering** (Construction Engineering); **Economics and Trade** (Business and Commerce; Economics); **Electrical and Mechanical Engineering** (Electrical and Electronic Engineering; Mechanical Engineering); **Food Engineering and Environmental Engineering** (Food Technology); **Foreign Language** (English; Japanese; Korean; Russian); **Humanities and Social Sciences** (Arts and Humanities; Social Sciences); **Management** (Accountancy; Management; Tourism)

History: Founded 1993. Acquired present title 1995.

Degrees and Diplomas: *Xueshi Xuewei*

HEILONGJIANG INSTITUTE OF SCIENCE AND TECHNOLOGY

32 Nanxing Street, Jiguan District,
Jixi, Heilongjiang Province 158105
Tel: +86(453) 2385022
Fax: +86(453) 2385022
EMail: shuchun@hr.hl.cn
Website: http://www.usth.edu.cn

President: Xing Zhongguang
International Relations: Sun Guoyu

Department

Automotive Engineering; **Civil Engineering** (Civil Engineering); **Computer Engineering**; **Economics** (Economics); **Natural Resources and Environemental Engineering** (Environmental Engineering; Natural Resources); **Social Sciences** (Social Sciences)

History: Founded 1981 as Heilongjiang Mining Institute. Acquired present status and title 2000.

Degrees and Diplomas: *Xueshi Xuewei*

HEILONGJIANG INSTITUTE OF TECHNOLOGY

Harbin market area Hongqi Street 999, Harbin, Heilongjiang 150050
Tel: +86(451) 88028000
Fax: +86(451) 57678811
Website: http://www.hljit.edu.cn/

President: Tian Zhanghong (2011-)

College

Adult Education (Automotive Engineering; Civil Engineering; Surveying and Mapping); **Vocational and Technical Studies** (Accountancy; Automation and Control Engineering; Civil Engineering; Computer Science; Electronic Engineering; Hotel Management; Maintenance Technology; Mechanical Engineering; Production Engineering; Surveying and Mapping; Town Planning)

School

Art and Design (Design; Fine Arts); **Automotive and Traffic Engineering** (Automotive Engineering; Transport Engineering); **Civil Engineering and Architecture** (Architecture; Civil Engineering); **Computer Science and Technology** (Computer Engineering; Computer Science); **Economics and Management** (Economics; Management); **Electrical and Information Engineering** (Electrical Engineering; Information Technology); **Foreign Languages** (English; Japanese; Modern Languages; Russian); **Humanities and Social Sciences** (Arts and Humanities; Media Studies; Social Sciences; Social Work); **Materials and Chemical Engineering** (Chemical Engineering; Materials Engineering); **Mathematics** (Mathematics); **Mechanical Engineering** (Mechanical Engineering); **Surveying Engineering** (Surveying and Mapping)

Department

Ideological and Political Theory Teaching and Research (Political Sciences); **Public Sports Teaching and Research** (Physical Education; Sports)

Centre

Engineering Training (Engineering)

Further Information: Also West Campus and North Campus

Degrees and Diplomas: *Xueshi Xuewei*

Academic Staff *2012-2013*: Total: c. 830

Student Numbers *2012-2013*: Total: c. 14,200
Last Updated: 28/11/13

HEILONGJIANG INTERNATIONAL UNIVERSITY (HIU)

Normal South Road, Limin Development Zone,
Harbin, Heilongjiang 150025
Tel: +86(451) 88121011
Website: http://www.hiu.edu.cn/

President: Ying Liu

Department

Applied Business Studies (Accountancy; Business Administration; Finance; International Business; Transport Management); **Arts** (Architectural and Environmental Design; Design; Fine Arts; Graphic Design; Visual Arts); **Chinese Language and Literature** (Chinese; Japanese; Korean; Literature; Russian); **Foreign Language and Literature** (English; Literature; Modern Languages); **Informatics and Science** (Applied Mathematics; Computer Engineering; Computer Science; Mathematics; Mathematics and Computer Science); **Second Foreign Language** (Foreign Languages Education; Japanese; Russian); **Western Languages** (English; French; Modern Languages; Spanish)

Main Language(s) of Instruction: Chinese

Degrees and Diplomas: *Xueshi Xuewei*

Student Services: Language Laboratory

Student Numbers *2012-2013*: Total 8,333
Last Updated: 28/11/13

HEILONGJIANG UNIVERSITY

74 Xuefu Road, Harbin, Heilongjiang Province 150080
Tel: +86(451) 86609033
Fax: +86(451) 86608114
EMail: fsoffice@gmail.com
Website: http://www.hlju.edu.cn

President: Yi Junqing
International Relations: Zhang Xiaoguang

School

Chemistry and Chemical Engineering (Chemical Engineering; Chemistry); **Economics** (Accountancy; Economics; International Economics); **Foreign Languages** (English; Modern Languages; Oriental Languages; Russian); **International Cultural Education** (International and Comparative Education); **Law** (Commercial Law; Economics; Law); **Vocational** (Automation and Control Engineering; Bioengineering; Chinese; Computer Science; Electronic Engineering; History; Information Management; Mathematics; Philosophy)

History: Founded 1941 as Russian Military School, acquired present status and title 1958 and incorporated Harbin Institute of Foreign Languages 1972. Under the jurisdiction of the Provincial Government.

Academic Year: September to July (September-January; March-July)

Admission Requirements: Graduation from senior middle school and entrance examination

Main Language(s) of Instruction: Chinese

Degrees and Diplomas: *Xueshi Xuewei*; *Shuoshi Xuewei*; *Boshi*

Publications: Higher Education Studies; Journal of Foreign Languages; Journal of Natural Sciences

Academic Staff *2011-2012*	**TOTAL**
FULL-TIME	**c. 3,200**

Student Numbers *2011-2012*	
All (Foreign included)	**c. 30,000**
FOREIGN ONLY	**600**

HEILONGJIANG UNIVERSITY OF CHINESE MEDICINE

24 Heping Road, Harbin, Heilongjiang Province 150040
Tel: +86(451) 82193620
Fax: +86(451) 82112786
EMail: khxoffice@hljucm.net
Website: http://www.hljucm.net/

President: Kuang Haixue (2003-)

School

Acupuncture and Massage (Acupuncture); **Adult Education**; **Basic Medicine** (Medicine); **Clinical Medicine** (Orthopaedics); **Humanities and Management** (Arts and Humanities; Management); **Marxism** (Political Sciences); **Pharmacy** (Pharmacy)

Institute

International Education; **Traditional Chinese Medicine** (Traditional Eastern Medicine)

History: Founded 1959 as Heilongjiang Provincial Advanced College for Medical Staff. Acquired present status 1996.

Main Language(s) of Instruction: Chinese

Degrees and Diplomas: *Xueshi Xuewei*; *Shuoshi Xuewei*; *Boshi*

Publications: Information on Traditional Chinese Medicine; Journal of Acupuncture Clinic; Journal of Traditional Medicine

Academic Staff *2011-2012*: Total: c. 2,500
Student Numbers *2011-2012*: Total: c. 15,000
Last Updated: 25/02/13

HEILONGJIANG UNIVERSITY OF FINANCE AND ECONOMICS (HUFE)

School Zone, Limin Road, No 99, Harbin, Heilongjiang
Tel: +86(451) 85911666
EMail: HUFE2013@163.com
Website: http://www.hfu.edu.cn/

School

Accountancy (Accountancy); **Computer and Information Engineering** (Computer Engineering; Information Technology); **Economics** (Economics); **Foreign Languages** (English; Modern Languages); **Humanities and Arts** (Arts and Humanities); **Management** (Management)

History: Formerly know as Harbin Deqiang College of Commerce.

Main Language(s) of Instruction: Chinese

Degrees and Diplomas: *Xueshi Xuewei*

Academic Staff *2012-2013*: Total 518
Student Numbers *2012-2013*: Total: c. 11,300
Last Updated: 25/11/13

HENAN AGRICULTURAL UNIVERSITY

95 Wenhua Road, Zhengzhou, Henan Province 450002
Tel: +86(371) 63555685
Fax: +86(371) 63555578
EMail: oliver_xing@henau.edu.cn
Website: http://www.henau.edu.cn

President: Wang Yanling

College

Agronomy (Agronomy; Genetics; Plant Pathology; Soil Science); **Animal Husbandry and Veterinary Science** (Animal Husbandry; Veterinary Science; Zoology); **Economics and Management** (Economics; Management); **Food Technology** (Food Technology); **Foreign Languages** (Modern Languages); **Forestry and Horticulture** (Environmental Management; Forestry; Horticulture; Landscape Architecture); **Humanities and Law** (Arts and Humanities; Foreign Languages Education; Law; Social Sciences); **Information and Management Science** (Information Management; Information Sciences); **International Education** (International and Comparative Education); **Life Sciences** (Biological and Life Sciences); **Mechanical and Electronic Engineering** (Agricultural Equipment; Electronic Engineering; Information Management; Mechanical Engineering; Rural Planning); **Physical Education** (Physical Education); **Plant Protection** (Plant and Crop Protection); **Resources and Environment** (Environmental Studies; Natural Resources); **Rural Development and Management** (Management; Rural Planning); **Science** (Chemistry; Physics); **Tobacco**

History: Founded 1912 as Henan Public Agricultural Specialized School. Acquired present title 1984.

Main Language(s) of Instruction: Chinese

Degrees and Diplomas: *Xueshi Xuewei*; *Shuoshi Xuewei*; *Boshi*

Publications: Acta Agriculturae Universitie Henanensis
Last Updated: 22/11/12

HENAN INSTITUTE OF ENGINEERING (HNIE)

No.1 Zhongshan North Road, Longhu Town, Xinzheng, Zhengzhou, Henan 451191
Tel: +86(371) 62508001 +86(371) 62508888
Fax: +86(371) 62508801
EMail: hngcxcb@163.com
Website: http://www.haue.edu.cn/

President: Wenkai Liu

School

Software Engineering (Software Engineering)

Department

Accounting Science (Accountancy; Business Computing; Finance); **Arts Design** (Architectural and Environmental Design; Design; Fine Arts; Visual Arts); **Business Administration** (Business Administration; Human Resources; Marketing; Transport Management); **Civil Engineering** (Civil Engineering; Construction Engineering; Engineering Management; Heating and Refrigeration; Surveying and Mapping); **Computer Science and Engineering** (Computer Engineering; Computer Science; Information Management; Software Engineering); **Continuing Education**; **Economics and Trade** (Business Administration; Economics; Finance; Hotel Management; International Business; International Economics; Tourism); **Electrical Information and Engineering** (Automation and Control Engineering; Electrical Engineering; Electronic Engineering; Information Technology; Telecommunications Engineering); **Fashion Design and Engineering** (Fashion Design); **Foreign Language** (English; Literature; Modern Languages; Translation and Interpretation; Writing); **Human and Social Sciences** (Administration; Arts and Humanities; Law; Secretarial Studies; Social and Community Services; Social Sciences); **Management Science and Engineering** (E-Business/Commerce; Engineering; Information Management; Management); **Materials and Chemical Engineering** (Chemical Engineering; Materials Engineering; Packaging Technology; Polymer and Plastics Technology; Printing and Printmaking); **Mathematics and Physics Science** (Computer Science; Information Technology; Mathematics; Physics); **Mechanical Engineering** (Automation and Control Engineering; Automotive Engineering; Electrical Engineering; Machine Building; Maintenance Technology; Materials Engineering; Mechanical Engineering; Production Engineering); **Physical Education** (Physical Education); **Resources and Environment Engineering** (Biotechnology; Environmental Engineering; Geological Engineering; Natural Resources; Town Planning); **Safety Science and Engineering** (Mining Engineering; Safety Engineering); **Textiles Engineering** (Electrical Engineering; Mechanical Engineering; Textile Technology)

Institute

International Education

Further Information: Also North campus and South Campus (located in Xinzheng)

History: Founded 2007.

Main Language(s) of Instruction: Chinese

Degrees and Diplomas: *Xueshi Xuewei*

Academic Staff *2012-2013*: Total: c. 960
Student Numbers *2012-2013*: Total: c. 25,000
Last Updated: 28/11/13

HENAN INSTITUTE OF SCIENCE AND TECHNOLOGY (HIST)

Eastern HuaLan Avenue, Xinxiang, Henan 453003
Website: http://www.hist.edu.cn/

President: Lian Wang Qing
Tel: +86(373) 3040395 EMail: xzbgs@hist.edu.cn

College

Animal Science (Veterinary Science; Zoology); **Economics and Management** (Accountancy; Business Administration; Economics; Human Resources; Information Management; Information Technology; International Economics; Management; Marketing); **Fashion** (Fashion Design; Technology Education); **Fine Arts** (Fashion Design; Fine Arts; Music; Painting and Drawing); **Foreign Languages** (English; Literature; Modern Languages); **Higher Vocational and Technical** (Accountancy; Animal Husbandry; Architectural and Environmental Design; Automation and Control Engineering; Biotechnology; Computer Education; Computer Engineering; Computer Networks; Computer Science; Crop Production; Electrical Engineering; Electronic Engineering; English; Horticulture; Interior Design; Machine Building; Maintenance Technology; Marketing; Public Relations; Secretarial Studies; Tourism; Town Planning; Veterinary Science); **Life Science and Technology** (Agronomy; Bioengineering; Biological and Life Sciences; Biotechnology; Crop Production); **Marxism Education** (History; Political Sciences); **Mathematical Sciences** (Applied Mathematics; Computer Science; Finance; Mathematics; Mathematics and Computer Science; Statistics); **Mechanical and Electrical Engineering** (Automation and Control Engineering; Electrical Engineering; Electronic Engineering; Engineering Drawing and Design; Mechanical

Engineering); **Resources and Environmental Sciences** (Agriculture; Entomology; Environmental Studies; Natural Resources)

School

Chemistry and Chemical Engineering (Analytical Chemistry; Applied Chemistry; Chemical Engineering; Chemistry; Inorganic Chemistry; Organic Chemistry; Pharmacology; Physical Chemistry); **Educational Sciences** (Educational Sciences); **Food Science** *(SFS)* (Food Science; Food Technology; Nutrition; Safety Engineering; Tourism); **Grammar** (Chinese; Law); **Horticulture and Landscape** (Architecture; Ecology; Forestry; Horticulture; Landscape Architecture; Town Planning); **Information Engineering** (Computer Science; Information Technology); **Physical Education** *(PES)* (Physical Education; Sports)

Institute

Software (Computer Engineering; Computer Networks; Computer Science; Multimedia; Software Engineering)

Academy

New Academy (Agriculture; Bioengineering; Chemical Engineering; Chinese; Economics; Education; Electrical Engineering; Engineering; Fine Arts; Food Science; Food Technology; Information Technology; Law; Literature; Management; Mechanical Engineering; Modern Languages; Natural Sciences; Physical Education; Political Sciences; Town Planning)

History: Founded 1949. Succesively known as Pingyuan Agricultural College, BaiQuan Agricultural Junior College and Henan Normal Institute of Vocational Technology, it acquired present title 2004.

Main Language(s) of Instruction: Chinese

Degrees and Diplomas: *Xueshi Xuewei*; *Shuoshi Xuewei*: **Applied Mathematics; Atomic and Molecular Physics; Biochemistry; Botany; Ecology; Food Science; Food Technology; Instrument Making; Management; Materials Engineering; Mechanical Engineering; Mechanics; Molecular Biology; Organic Chemistry; Physical Chemistry; Physics.**

Academic Staff *2012-2013*: Total: c. 1,550
Student Numbers *2012-2013*: Total: c. 31,000
Last Updated: 28/11/13

HENAN NORMAL UNIVERSITY

46 East of Construction Road, Xinxiang, Henan Province 453007
Tel: +86(373) 3383000
EMail: president@htu.cn
Website: http://www.htu.cn/english

President: Zhang Yawei

College

Chemistry and Environmental Sciences (Chemical Engineering; Chemistry; Environmental Engineering); **Economics and Management** (Economics; Industrial Management; International Business; Marketing); **Life Sciences** (Aquaculture; Biochemistry; Biological and Life Sciences; Biotechnology; Botany; Cell Biology; Genetics; Microbiology; Molecular Biology; Zoology)); **Literature** (Chinese; Literature; Radio and Television Broadcasting); **Mathematics and Information Sciences** (Information Sciences; Mathematics); **Physical Education** (Physical Education); **Physics and Information Engineering** (Educational Technology; Electronic Engineering; Physics); **Politics and Management Science** (Management; Political Sciences); **Politics and Management Science** (Management; Political Sciences); **Social Development** (Social Studies)

Department

Computer Science (Computer Science); **Fine Arts** (Computer Graphics; Fine Arts; Metal Techniques; Painting and Drawing; Photography; Sculpture); **Law** (Civil Law; Commercial Law; Criminal Law; Law); **Music** (Dance; Music)

History: Founded 1923 as Zhongzhou University. Acquired present title 1985.

Main Language(s) of Instruction: Chinese

Degrees and Diplomas: *Xueshi Xuewei*; *Shuoshi Xuewei*

Publications: Journal of Hernan Normal University
Last Updated: 22/11/12

HENAN POLYTECHNIC UNIVERSITY

No.2001, Century Avenue, Jiaozuo City, Henan Province 454003
Tel: +86(391) 2930003
Fax: +86(391) 2923353
EMail: President@hpu.edu.cn
Website: http://www.hpu.edu.cn/english/NewsEvents.asp

President: Wang Shao-an

School

Electrical Engineering and Automation (Automation and Control Engineering; Electrical Engineering); **Civil Engineering** (Civil Engineering); **Computer Science and Technology** (Computer Science); **Economic Management** (Economics); **Energy Science and Engineering** (Energy Engineering); **Humanities and Social Sciences** (Arts and Humanities; Social Sciences); **Materials Science and Engineering** (Materials Engineering); **Mathematics and Information Science** (Information Sciences; Mathematics); **Mechanics and Power Engineering** (Mechanical Engineering; Power Engineering); **Resources and Environmental Engineering** (Environmental Engineering; Natural Resources); **Safety Science and Engineering** (Safety Engineering); **Surveying and Land Information Engineering** (Surveying and Mapping)

Department

Foreign Languages (Modern Languages); **Physical Education** (Physical Education); **Physics and Chemistry** (Chemistry; Physics)

History: Founded 1909 as Jiaozuo Coal Mining School. Acquired present title 2004.

Main Language(s) of Instruction: Chinese

Degrees and Diplomas: *Xueshi Xuewei*; *Shuoshi Xuewei*; *Boshi*
Last Updated: 22/11/12

HENAN UNIVERSITY (HNU)

85 Minglun Street, Kaifeng, Henan Province 475001
Tel: +86(378) 2862311 +86(378) 2825161
Fax: +86(378) 8857224 +86(378) 2861029
EMail: hnufao@public.zz.ha.cn
Website: http://www.henu.edu.cn

President: Lou Yuangong

School

Arts (Dance; Fine Arts; Musical Instruments; Musicology; Singing; Theatre; Visual Arts); **Chemistry and Chemical Engineering** (Chemical Engineering; Chemistry; Materials Engineering); **Chinese Language and Literature** (Chinese; Communication Studies; Literature); **Civil Engineering and Architecture** (Architecture; Civil Engineering; Design; Structural Architecture); **Distance and Continuing Education** (Continuing Education; Distance Education); **Economics** (Economics; Management); **Foreign Languages** (English; Japanese; Literature; Modern Languages; Russian; Translation and Interpretation); **History and Culture** (Archaeology; History; Museum Studies; Tourism); **International Education** (Accountancy; Bioengineering; Computer Science; Information Management; International Business); **Journalism and Communication** (Advertising and Publicity; Journalism; Media Studies; Publishing and Book Trade; Radio and Television Broadcasting); **Law** (Law); **Life Sciences** (Biological and Life Sciences); **Management** (Management); **Mathematics and Information Science** (Applied Mathematics; Computer Science; Mathematics); **Medicine** (Dentistry; Medicine); **Nursing** (Nursing); **People's Arms Academy** (Military Science); **Philosophy & Public Administration** (Administration; Philosophy; Political Sciences; Public Administration); **Physics and Electronics** (Computer Networks; Electronic Engineering; Information Technology; Physics); **Software** (Computer Networks; Computer Science; Multimedia; Software Engineering)

History: Founded 1912, acquired present title 2000.

Academic Year: September to July

Admission Requirements: Graduation from senior middle school and entrance examination

Fees: (Yuan): c. 12,000 per annum

Main Language(s) of Instruction: Chinese, English

Accrediting Agency: Henan Provincial Government

Degrees and Diplomas: *Xueshi Xuewei*; *Shuoshi Xuewei*; *Boshi*

Student Services: Academic Counselling, Canteen, Careers Guidance, Foreign Studies Centre, Health Services, Language Laboratory, Nursery Care, Social Counselling, Sports Facilities

Publications: Chemistry Study; Foreign Languages and Literature; History Monthly; Journal of Henan; Mathematics Quaterly; Mind World

Publishing House: Henan University Press

Last Updated: 22/11/12

HENAN UNIVERSITY OF ECONOMICS AND LAW

PO Box 15, 80 Wenhua Road, Zhengzhou, Henan Province 450002
Tel: +86(371) 63522938
Fax: +86(371) 63522938
Website: http://www.huel.edu.cn

President: Xiaojian Li
Tel: +86(371) 63519666 EMail: xjli@huel.edu.cn

Department

Economics (Economics; Finance; Fiscal Law; International Business; International Economics; Statistics; Taxation); **Engineering** (Computer Science); **Law** (Law; Sociology); **Literature** (Advertising and Publicity; Design; English; Fine Arts; Modern Languages; Radio and Television Broadcasting); **Management** (Accountancy; Agricultural Business; Business Administration; E-Business/Commerce; Engineering Management; Finance; Human Resources; Information Management; International Business; Management; Marketing; Public Administration; Real Estate; Tourism); **Science** (Computer Science; Geography; Mathematics; Town Planning)

History: Founded 2010 following merger between former Henan University of Finance and Economics (HUFE, founded in 1983) and Henan Administrative Institute of Politics and Law (founded in 1984).

Main Language(s) of Instruction: Chinese

Degrees and Diplomas: *Xueshi Xuewei*; *Shuoshi Xuewei*

Academic Staff *2011-2012*: Total 1,800
STAFF WITH DOCTORATE: Total 450
Student Numbers *2011-2012*: Total: c. 25,000
Last Updated: 25/02/13

HENAN UNIVERSITY OF SCIENCE AND TECHNOLOGY (HUST)

48, Xiyuan Road, Luoyang, Henan Province 471003
Tel: +86(379) 64231879
EMail: fao@mail.haust.edu.cn
Website: http://www.haust.edu.cn/

President: Wang Jianji

School

Agriculture (Agriculture; Agronomy; Biotechnology; Environmental Studies; Natural Resources); **Animal Science and Technology** (Animal Husbandry; Technology; Veterinary Science); **Art and Design** (Design; Fine Arts; Industrial Design; Packaging Technology); **Chemical Engineering and Pharmaceutics** (Chemical Engineering; Pharmacology; Pharmacy); **Economics** (Economics); **Electronic Information Engineering** (Automation and Control Engineering; Computer Science; Electronic Engineering; Information Sciences); **Food and Bioengineering** (Bioengineering; Food Science); **Foreign Languages** (English; Japanese; Modern Languages); **Forensic Medicine** (Forensic Medicine and Dentistry); **Forestry** (Forestry; Landscape Architecture; Plant and Crop Protection); **Humanities** (Arts and Humanities; Chinese; History; Literature); **Law** (Law); **Management** (Accountancy; Business Administration; E-Business/Commerce; Information Management; Management; Marketing; Tourism); **Material Science and Engineering** (Materials Engineering; Metallurgical Engineering); **Mathematics and Statistics** (Mathematics; Statistics); **Mechatronics Engineering** (Electronic Engineering; Mechanical Engineering); **Medical Technology and Engineering** (Engineering; Medical Technology); **Medicine** (Medicine; Nursing; Pharmacy); **Physical Education** (Physical Education); **Physics and Engineering** (Applied Physics; Engineering; Physics); **Schematizing and Architectural Engineering** (Architecture; Civil Engineering; Construction Engineering); **Vehicle and Motive Power Engineering** (Agricultural Engineering; Agricultural Equipment; Automotive Engineering; Power Engineering; Thermal Engineering; Transport and Communications)

History: Founded 1952 as Luoyang Institute of Technology. Acquired present status and title 2002 following merge with Luoyang Medical School and Luoyang Agricultural School.

Main Language(s) of Instruction: Chinese

Degrees and Diplomas: *Xueshi Xuewei*; *Shuoshi Xuewei*

Last Updated: 23/11/12

HENAN UNIVERSITY OF TECHNOLOGY

140 Songshan Road, Zhengzhou, Henan Province 450052
Tel: +86(371) 7447915
EMail: dec@haut.edu.cn
Website: http://www.admissions.cn/haut/

President: Wang Lumin

Department

Bioengineering (Bioengineering); **Chemistry and Chemical Engineering** (Chemical Engineering; Chemistry); **Civil Engineering** (Civil Engineering); **Computer Science and Technology** (Computer Science; Technology); **Economics and Commerce** (Business and Commerce; Economics); **Food Science and Technology** (Food Science; Food Technology); **Industrial and Commercial Management** (Industrial Management); **Mechanical Engineering** (Mechanical Engineering); **Modern Languages** (Modern Languages)

History: Founded 2004 on the basis of the amalgamation of Zhengzhou Institute of Technology and Zhengzhou Polytechnic Institute.

Main Language(s) of Instruction: Chinese

Degrees and Diplomas: *Xueshi Xuewei*; *Shuoshi Xuewei*

Last Updated: 23/11/12

HENAN UNIVERSITY OF TRADITIONAL CHINESE MEDICINE

1 Jinshui Road, Zhengzhou, Henan Province 450008
Tel: +86(371) 65945879
Fax: +86(371) 65944307
EMail: dbyb@hactcm.edu.cn
Website: http://www.hactcm.edu.cn/

President: Yuling Zheng

Department

Acupuncture-Moxibustion and Massage (Acupuncture); **Adult Education**; **Basic Medicine** (Medicine); **Chinese Pharmacology** (Pharmacology); **Foreign Languages** (English); **Humanities** (Administration; Arts and Humanities; Physical Education; Political Sciences; Psychology); **Information Engineering** (Information Technology); **International Education**; **Nursing** (Nursing); **Orthopedics and Traumatology** (Orthopaedics); **Science of the Five Sense Organs** (Health Sciences); **Traditional Chinese Medicine** (Traditional Eastern Medicine)

Further Information: Also 6 affiliated hospitals and 12 research institutes

History: Founded 1954 as Henan School for TCM Continuing Education. Acquired present title 1958.

Main Language(s) of Instruction: Chinese

Degrees and Diplomas: *Xueshi Xuewei*; *Shuoshi Xuewei*; *Boshi*

Academic Staff *2011-2012*: Total: c. 2,500
Last Updated: 25/02/13

HENAN UNIVERSITY OF URBAN CONSTRUCTION (HNCJ)

XIn Chen Area, Ming Yue Road, Pingdingshan, Henan 467036
EMail: admin@hncj.edu.cn
Website: http://hncj.edu.cn/

President: Liuan Kong

School
Architectural Environment and Energy Engineering (Building Technologies; Construction Engineering; Energy Engineering; Petroleum and Gas Engineering; Power Engineering; Thermal Engineering); **Bioengineering** (Bioengineering; Biological and Life Sciences; Biotechnology); **Business Administration** (Business Administration; Marketing; Social Welfare; Tourism); **Chemistry and Chemical Engineering** (Chemical Engineering; Chemistry; Materials Engineering; Polymer and Plastics Technology); **Civil and Materials Engineering** (Architecture and Planning; Building Technologies; Civil Engineering; Construction Engineering; Materials Engineering; Mechanics; Structural Architecture); **Computer Science and Engineering** (Computer Engineering; Computer Networks; Computer Science; Information Management; Multimedia); **Construction Engineering Management** (Construction Engineering; Engineering Management; Real Estate); **Continuing Education** (Construction Engineering; Town Planning); **Electrical Engineering and Automation** (Automation and Control Engineering; Computer Engineering; Electrical Engineering; Electronic Engineering; Power Engineering; Software Engineering); **Environment and Municipal Engineering** (Environmental Engineering; Environmental Studies; Safety Engineering; Water Management); **Foreign Languages** (Applied Linguistics; English; Modern Languages); **Law and Political Sciences** (Law; Political Sciences); **Mathematics and Physics** (Applied Mathematics; Applied Physics; Finance; Mathematics; Physics); **Software** (Computer Engineering; Computer Graphics; Computer Networks; Information Management; Information Technology; Software Engineering); **Survey Engineering** (Computer Science; Geography; Information Technology; Real Estate; Soil Management; Surveying and Mapping); **Traffic Engineering** (Bridge Engineering; Road Engineering; Transport and Communications; Transport Economics); **Urban Planning and Architecture** (Architecture; Town Planning)

Department
Physical Education (Physical Education; Sports)

History: Founded 2000 as Henan Urban Construction College though merger between Pingdingshan Urban Environmental Protection School (founded 1983) and Henan Urban Construction College (formerly the Henan branch of Wuhan Urban Construction University, founded 1985). Acquired present title 2008.

Main Language(s) of Instruction: Chinese

Degrees and Diplomas: *Xueshi Xuewei*

Student Services: Sports Facilities

Academic Staff *2012-2013*: Total: c. 850

Student Numbers *2012-2013*: Total: c. 18,700

Last Updated: 28/11/13

HENGSHUI UNIVERSITY

Hengshui, Hebei
Website: http://www.hsnc.edn/hsnc/index.html

President: Wangshou Zhong

Faculty
Chemical Engineering (Applied Chemistry; Chemical Engineering; Chemistry; Materials Engineering; Polymer and Plastics Technology); **Electronic and Information Engineering** (Electronic Engineering; Information Technology; Multimedia; Physics); **Literature and Communication** (Advertising and Publicity; Chinese; Literature; Radio and Television Broadcasting); **Mathematics and Computer Science** (Applied Mathematics; Computer Engineering; Computer Science; Mathematics; Mathematics and Computer Science); **Music** (Dance; Music; Musical Instruments; Musicology); **Physical Education** (Physical Education; Sports; Sports Management)

College
Education (Education; Psychology)

School
Economics and Management (Economics; Human Resources; Information Management; Information Technology; International Business; International Economics; Management); **Foreign Languages** (Chinese; English; International Studies; Japanese; Modern Languages); **Life Sciences** (Biological and Life Sciences; Biology; Biotechnology; Ecology; Environmental Engineering; Landscape Architecture)

Academy
Fine Arts (Architectural and Environmental Design; Communication Arts; Design; Fine Arts; Visual Arts)

History: Founded 1923 as National Civilized Unit College.

Main Language(s) of Instruction: Chinese

Degrees and Diplomas: *Xueshi Xuewei*

Academic Staff *2012-2013*: Total: c. 560

Student Numbers *2012-2013*: Total: c. 10,000

Last Updated: 29/11/13

HENGYANG NORMAL UNIVERSITY

167 Huangbai Road, Hengyang, Hunan Province 421008
Tel: +86(734) 8484904
Fax: +86(734) 8485971
EMail: hnkdz@yahoo.com.cn
Website: http://www.hynu.edu.cn/index.jsp

President: Liu Peilin

Department
Chemistry and Materials Science (Chemistry; Materials Engineering); **Chinese** (Chinese); **Computer Science** (Computer Science); **Economy and Law** (Economics; Law); **Educational Sciences** (Educational Sciences); **Fine Arts** (Design; Fine Arts; Painting and Drawing); **Foreign Languages** (English); **Life Sciences** (Biochemistry; Biological and Life Sciences; Botany; Molecular Biology; Zoology); **Mathematics and Computer Science** (Mathematics and Computer Science); **Music** (Music); **Physical Education** (Physical Education); **Physics and Information Science** (Communication Studies; Information Technology; Physics); **Resources and Environment and Tourism Managemen** (Environmental Studies; Geography; Rural Planning; Tourism; Town Planning)

Institute
Nanyue (Art Education; Economics; Education; History; Law; Literature; Management; Natural Sciences)

History: Founded 1904 as Hunan Government Authorized Teachers' Academy. Hengyang Teachers College 1958. Merged with Hengyang Educational Training College 1999 and Hunan Third Teacher Training School 2001.

Main Language(s) of Instruction: Chinese

Degrees and Diplomas: *Xueshi Xuewei*

Publications: Journal of Hengyang Normal University; Journal of Wang Chuanshan Studies

Last Updated: 23/11/12

HEXI UNIVERSITY

846 Ring Road, Zhangye, Gansu 734000
EMail: dangban@hxu.edu.cn
Website: http://www.hxu.edu.cn/

President: Ren-Yi Liu

College
Agriculture and Biotechnology (Agriculture; Biotechnology); **Chemistry and Chemical Engineering** (Chemical Engineering; Chemistry); **Foreign Languages** (English; Modern Languages); **History and Culture and Tourism** (Cultural Studies; History; Tourism); **Liberal Arts** (Arts and Humanities; Chinese; Literature; Native Language Education; Writing); **Physics and Mechanical and Electrical Engineering** (Electrical and Electronic Engineering; Mechanical Engineering; Physics)

School
Civil Engineering (Civil Engineering); **Economics and Management** (Accountancy; Business Administration; Economics; Finance; Management; Transport Management); **Information Technology and Media** (Information Technology; Media Studies); **Mathematics and Statistics** (Mathematics; Statistics); **Music** (Music; Music Education; Musical Instruments); **Political Sciences and Law** (Law; Political Sciences)

Department
Teacher Education (Teacher Training)

Institute
Sports (Sports)

Academy
Fine Arts (Fine Arts; Painting and Drawing)

History: Founded 1958 as Zhangye Teachers College. Transformed into Zhangye Teachers College 1959. Closed down between 1962 and 1978. Incorporated Zhangye Agriculture School and Zhangye Vocational School 2000. Acquired present title 2001.

Main Language(s) of Instruction: Chinese

Degrees and Diplomas: *Xueshi Xuewei*

Academic Staff *2012-2013*: Total 844
Student Numbers *2012-2013*: Total 12,449
Last Updated: 29/11/13

HEZE UNIVERSITY

2269 University Avenue, Heze, Shandong 274015
Tel: +86(530) 5529585
Website: http://www.hezeu.edu.cn/

President: Yu Zhang Yu

Faculty
Law (Law)

School
Mechanical Engineering *(Chiang Chen)* (Automation and Control Engineering; Electronic Engineering; Materials Engineering; Mechanical Engineering)

Department
Chinese Language and Literature (Advertising and Publicity; Chinese; Journalism; Literature; Radio and Television Broadcasting); **Economics** (Accountancy; E-Business/Commerce; Economics; Management; Marketing; Statistics; Transport Management); **Education** (Education; Psychology); **Fine Arts** (Fine Arts); **Foreign Languages** (English; Modern Languages); **Landscape Engineering** (Landscape Architecture); **Life Sciences** (Biochemistry; Biological and Life Sciences; Genetics; Microbiology; Molecular Biology; Zoology); **Music** (Music; Music Theory and Composition; Musical Instruments; Singing); **Pharmaceutical Engineering** (Engineering; Pharmacy); **Physical Education** (Physical Education); **Preschool Education** (Preschool Education); **Primary Education** (Primary Education); **Resources and Environment** (Environmental Studies; Geography; Geography (Human); Horticulture; Natural Resources; Town Planning); **Social Sciences** (History; Political Sciences; Social Sciences)

History: Founded 1949 as Shandong and Henan area second Normal School, later known as Provincial Normal School of Heze plain. Renamed First Normal Heze, Shandong Province 1952. Transfromed into Heze Teachers College 1958. Refounded as New Heze Teachers College 2002 after merger between Heze Teachers College, Heze Education College, Heze Radio and Television University and incorporated Heze Normal College and Heze agricultural school. Acquired present status and title 2004.

Main Language(s) of Instruction: Chinese

Degrees and Diplomas: *Xueshi Xuewei*

Academic Staff *2012-2013*: Total 1,327
Student Numbers *2012-2013*: Total: c. 16,800
Last Updated: 29/11/13

HEZHOU UNIVERSITY (HZU)

Hezhou Lim Road 147, Hezhou, Guangxi 542899
Tel: +86(774) 5228600
Fax: +86(774) 5228605
Website: http://www.hzu.gx.cn/

President: Wu Guoquan

College
Chemical and Biological Engineering (Applied Chemistry; Bioengineering; Biotechnology; Chemistry; Construction Engineering; Food Science; Food Technology; Safety Engineering; Science Education); **Computer Science and Information Engineering** (Computer Science; Information Technology); **Foreign Languages** (American Studies; Chinese; English; English Studies; Modern Languages; Tourism; Translation and Interpretation); **Mechanical and Electronic Engineering** (Electronic Engineering; Mechanical Engineering); **Science** (Applied Mathematics; Construction Engineering; Mathematics; Mathematics Education); **Teacher Education** (Teacher Training)

School
Economics and Management (Accountancy; Business Administration; Business Computing; Economics; Finance; International Business; International Economics; Management; Tourism); **Marxism** (Political Sciences)

Institute
Art (Architectural and Environmental Design; Clothing and Sewing; Fashion Design; Fine Arts; Photography; Textile Design); **Culture and Media** (Advertising and Publicity; Art Management; Chinese; Cultural Studies; Literature; Media Studies; Radio and Television Broadcasting; Sociology); **Sports** (Sports)

History: Founded 1943.

Main Language(s) of Instruction: Chinese

Degrees and Diplomas: *Xueshi Xuewei*; *Shuoshi Xuewei*: **Construction Engineering.**

Academic Staff *2012-2013*: Total 825
Student Numbers *2012-2013*: Total 9,769
Last Updated: 29/11/13

HOHAI UNIVERSITY (HHU)

1 Xikang Road, Nanjing, Jiangsu Province 210098
Tel: +86(25) 83723124
Fax: +86(25) 83735375
EMail: hohai@hhu.edu.cn
Website: http://www.hhu.edu.cn

President: Wang Cheng

Division
International Cooperation and Education

College
Civil and Transportation Engineering (Transport Engineering); **Computer and Information Engineering** (Computer Science; Software Engineering; Telecommunications Engineering); **Energy and Electrical Engineering** (Automation and Control Engineering; Electronic Engineering; Energy Engineering); **Environment** (Chemistry; Ecology; Environmental Studies; Hydraulic Engineering; Waste Management); **Foreign Languages and Cultures** (English; French; German; Japanese; Literature; Russian; Translation and Interpretation); **Harbour,Coastal and Offshore Engineering** (Coastal Studies; Marine Engineering; Marine Science and Oceanography); **Mechanical and Electronic Engineering** (Industrial Design; Materials Engineering; Mechanical Engineering; Metallurgical Engineering; Power Engineering; Thermal Engineering); **Science** (Applied Physics; Computer Science; Mathematics; Physics; Water Science); **Water Conservation and Hydropower Engineering** (Hydraulic Engineering; Power Engineering; Thermal Engineering; Water Science)

School
Business (Accountancy; Business Administration; E-Business/Commerce; Economics; Finance; Management; Marketing)

Department
Physical Education (Physical Education)

History: Founded 1915 as Hohai Civil Engineering School and known as the East China Technical University of Water Resources from 1952 to 1985 when Hohai University was resumed. A key university under the jurisdiction of the Ministry of Education.

Academic Year: September to July (September-February; February-July)

Admission Requirements: Graduation from senior middle school or equivalent and entrance examination

Main Language(s) of Instruction: Chinese, English

Accrediting Agency: International Cooperation and Education Division, Ministry of Education

Degrees and Diplomas: *Xueshi Xuewei*: **Economics; Education; Engineering; English; Law; Management.** *Shuoshi Xuewei*: **Economics; Engineering; Law; Management.** *Boshi*: **Economics; Engineering; Management.**

Student Services: Academic Counselling, Canteen, Cultural Activities, Foreign Studies Centre, Health Services, Language Laboratory, Nursery Care, Social Counselling, Sports Facilities

Publishing house: Hohai Publishing House

Last Updated: 23/11/12

HOHHOT MONGOLIA UNIVERSITY FOR NATIONALITIES

56 North Road, Xincheng District, Hohhot, Inner Mongolia 010051
EMail: nm_hong@163.com
Website: http://www.imnc.edu.cn/

President: Bai Changming

Department

Chinese Language and Literature (Chinese; Literature); **Computer Science** (Computer Engineering; Computer Science); **Economics** (Economics); **Education** (Education; Preschool Education); **Environmental Engineering** (Environmental Engineering); **Fine Arts** (Art Education; Fine Arts; Painting and Drawing); **Foreign Language** (Applied Linguistics; English; Japanese; Modern Languages); **Law** (Law); **Management** (Management; Public Administration); **Marxist-Leninist Teaching and Research** (Political Sciences); **Mathematics** (Mathematics); **Media** (Journalism; Media Studies); **Mongolian Language and Literature** (Literature; Mongolian; Translation and Interpretation); **Music** (Dance; Music; Music Education; Musicology); **Physical Education** (Physical Education)

Main Language(s) of Instruction: Chinese

Degrees and Diplomas: *Xueshi Xuewei*

Publications: Mongolian Studies Journal

Academic Staff *2012-2013*: Total 322

Student Numbers *2012-2013*: Total: c. 4,000

Last Updated: 29/11/13

HONGHE UNIVERSITY

No.1 Nanhu Lake North Road, Mengzi, Yunnan Province 661100
Tel: +86(873) 3694865
Fax: +86(873) 3694865
EMail: kittywangfei@gmail.com; pengjuan1213@hotmail.com

College

Foreign Languages (Modern Languages); **Humanities** (Administration; Advertising and Publicity; Chinese; History; Journalism; Literature; Native Language; Political Sciences); **Life Sciences and Technology** (Biological and Life Sciences; Technology); **Physical Education** (Leisure Studies; Physical Education; Sports); **Science** (Chemistry; Metallurgical Engineering; Physics); **Teacher Education** (Preschool Education; Primary Education; Science Education)

School

Art (Design; Painting and Drawing); **Business** (Business Administration; International Business; International Economics; Management; Transport Management); **Engineering** (Automotive Engineering; Computer Science; Educational Technology; Electrical Engineering; Mechanical Engineering); **International Relations** (Chinese; Thai Languages; Vietnamese); **Mathematics** (Applied Mathematics; Computer Science; Information Sciences; Mathematics); **Music**; **Politics** (Political Sciences)

History: Founded 2003 following merger of Mengzi Teachers' College and Yunnan Radio and Television University Honghe Branch School.

Main Language(s) of Instruction: Chinese

Degrees and Diplomas: *Xueshi Xuewei*

Last Updated: 23/11/12

HUAIBEI NORMAL UNIVERSITY

100 Donghshan Road, Huaibei, Anhui Province 235000
Tel: +86(5611) 3090967
Fax: +86(5611) 3090518
EMail: jpl@hbcnc.edu.cn
Website: http://www.hbcnc.edu.cn

President: Lei Wang

Department

Biology (Biology); **Chemistry** (Chemistry); **Chinese Language and Literature** (Chinese; Literature); **Computer Science** (Computer Science); **Education** (Education); **Fine Arts** (Fine Arts); **History** (History); **Mathematics** (Mathematics); **Modern Languages** (Modern Languages); **Music** (Music); **Physical Education** (Physical Education); **Physics** (Physics); **Political Science and Law** (Law; Political Sciences)

History: Founded 1974 as as Anhui Normal University at Huaibei. Became Huaibei Coal Industry Teachers College 1978. Acquired present title 2010.

Main Language(s) of Instruction: Chinese

Accrediting Agency: Ministry of Coal Industry

Degrees and Diplomas: *Xueshi Xuewei*; *Shuoshi Xuewei*

Last Updated: 23/11/12

HUAIHAI INSTITUTE OF TECHNOLOGY

9 Cangwu Road, Lianyungang, Jiangsu Province 222005
Tel: +86(518) 85895018
Fax: +86(518) 85806171
EMail: xiaojiehan@hotmail.com
Website: http://www.hhit.edu.cn

President: Weilong Yan

College

Donggang

School

Law (Law)

Department

Architecture (Architecture); **Art** (Fine Arts; Industrial Design); **Business** (Accountancy; Business Administration; Management; Marketing); **Chemical Engineering** (Chemical Engineering); **Chinese Language and Literature** (Chinese; Literature); **Civil Engineering** (Civil Engineering); **Computer Engineering** (Computer Engineering); **Electronic Engineering** (Electronic Engineering); **Food Technology** (Food Technology); **Foreign Languages** (English); **Humanities** (Arts and Humanities); **International Exchange** (International Relations); **Marine Science and Technology** (Aquaculture; Marine Engineering; Marine Science and Oceanography); **Mechanical Engineering** (Automation and Control Engineering; Mechanical Engineering); **Science** (Mathematics; Physics); **Surveying and Mapping Engineering** (Surveying and Mapping)

History: Founded 1985 as part of Huaihai University.In May 1998, January 2000, and August 2002 respectively, Jiangsu Salt Industry School, Lianyungang Ocean School, and Lianyungang College of Chemical Technology were merged into the institute.

Degrees and Diplomas: *Xueshi Xuewei*; *Shuoshi Xuewei*

Publications: Journal of Huaihai Institute of Technology(Natural Sciences Edition)

Academic Staff *2011-2012*: Total: c. 1,600

Student Numbers *2011-2012*: Total: c. 20,000

Last Updated: 26/02/13

HUAIHUA UNIVERSITY (HHU)

612 Yingfeng East Road, Huaihua, Hunan 418008
Tel: +86(745) 2851001 +86(745) 2852542
Fax: +86(745) 2851305 +86(745) 2854961
Website: http://www.hhtc.edu.cn/

President: Lukas Tam

Department

Art (Arts and Humanities); **Art and Design** (Design; Fine Arts; Industrial Design); **Business Administration** (Business Administration; Transport Management); **Chemistry and Chemical Engineering** (Chemical Engineering; Chemistry; Pharmacy; Science Education); **Chinese Language and Literature** (Chinese; Journalism; Literature; Radio and Television Broadcasting); **Computer Science and Technology** (Computer Engineering; Computer Science); **Economics** (Economics; International Business; International Economics); **Education** (Education; Preschool Education; Primary Education); **Foreign Language and Literature** (Literature; Modern Languages); **Human Education** (Education; Public Administration); **Life Science** (Bioengineering; Biological and Life Sciences; Landscape Architecture); **Mathematics and Applied Mathematics** (Applied Mathematics; Computer Science; Information Sciences; Mathematics); **Music** (Dance; Music; Music Education); **Physical Education** (Physical Education; Sports); **Physics and Electronic Information Science** (Electronic Engineering; Information Sciences; Information Technology; Physics; Radio and Television Broadcasting; Telecommunications Engineering); **Politics and Law** (Law; Political Sciences)

History: Founded 1985 as Huaihua Teachers College. Acquired present status and title 2002.

Main Language(s) of Instruction: Chinese

Degrees and Diplomas: *Xueshi Xuewei*

Academic Staff *2012-2013*: Total: c. 1,000
Student Numbers *2012-2013*: Total: c. 20,400
Last Updated: 02/12/13

HUAINAN NORMAL UNIVERSITY (HNNU)

Dongshan Road (West), Huainan, Anhui 232038
Tel: +86(554) 6863615 +86(554) 6863600
Fax: +86(554) 6863612
EMail: ybmsk@hnnu.edu.cn
Website: http://www.hnnu.edu.cn/

President: Cao Jie Wang

College

Electrical and Information Engineering (Automation and Control Engineering; Electrical Engineering; Electronic Engineering; Information Technology; Mechanical Engineering; Telecommunications Engineering); **Physics and Electronic Information Engineering** (Electronic Engineering; Information Sciences; Information Technology; Optical Technology; Physics)

School

Business Administration (Accountancy; Business Administration; E-Business/Commerce; Finance; International Business; International Economics; Management; Marketing)

Department

Chemistry and Chemical Engineering (Chemical Engineering; Chemistry; Materials Engineering); **Chinese and Media and Communications** (Advertising and Publicity; Chinese; Journalism; Literature; Mass Communication; Media Studies); **Computer and Information Engineering** (Computer Engineering; Computer Networks; Information Technology; Multimedia); **Education and Science** (Education; Educational Technology; Preschool Education; Primary Education; Psychology); **Fine Arts** (Advertising and Publicity; Architectural and Environmental Design; Art History; Communication Arts; Design; Fine Arts; Graphic Arts; Painting and Drawing; Photography; Visual Arts); **Foreign Languages** (English; Modern Languages); **Life Sciences** (Bioengineering; Biological and Life Sciences; Biotechnology; Food Technology; Horticulture; Safety Engineering); **Marxism** (Administration; Law; Philosophy; Political Sciences); **Mathematics and Computer Science** (Applied Mathematics; Information Sciences; Information Technology; Mathematics and Computer Science); **Music** (Music; Musical Instruments; Musicology); **Political Science and Law** (Administration; Commercial Law; Criminology; International Law; Law; Management; Political Sciences; Public Administration; Social Psychology; Social Work; Sociology); **Sports** (Leisure Studies; Physical Education; Sports)

History: Founded 1958 as Teachers College. Closed down between 1962 and 1977. Merged with Huainan Teachers College and Huainan Institute of Education 1999. Acquired present status and title 2000.

Main Language(s) of Instruction: Chinese

Degrees and Diplomas: *Xueshi Xuewei*

Academic Staff *2012-2013*: Total 709
Student Numbers *2012-2013*: Total 17,174
Last Updated: 02/12/13

HUAIYIN INSTITUTE OF TECHNOLOGY

1 Meicheng Rd, Huaiyin, Jiangsu Province 223001
Tel: +86(517) 83559103
EMail: faoffice@mail.hyit.edu.cn
Website: http://eng.hyit.edu.cn

President: Zhu Hanqing

Faculty

Architecture and Civil Engineering (Architecture; Civil Engineering); **Artistic Design** (Design); **Computer Engineering** (Computer Engineering; Computer Networks; Information Technology; Software Engineering; Telecommunications Engineering); **Economics and Management** (Economics; Management); **Electronic and Electrical Engineering** (Electrical Engineering; Electronic Engineering); **Foreign Languages** (English; Modern Languages); **Humanities** (Arts and Humanities; Public Administration; Social Work); **Life Sciences and Chemical Engineering** (Biological and Life Sciences; Biotechnology; Chemical Engineering; Food Science; Horticulture; Landscape Architecture); **Mathematics and Physics** (Mathematics; Physics); **Mechanical Engineering** (Automation and Control Engineering; Mechanical Engineering; Metallurgical Engineering); **Transport Engineering** (Transport Engineering)

College

Jianghuai (Accountancy; Automation and Control Engineering; Bioengineering; Civil Engineering; Computer Science; Electrical Engineering; English; Finance; International Business; Machine Building)

Department

Physical Education (Physical Education)

History: Founded 1958. Acquired present title 2002.

Main Language(s) of Instruction: Chinese

Degrees and Diplomas: *Xueshi Xuewei*

Last Updated: 14/12/12

HUAIYIN TEACHERS UNIVERSITY

71 Jiaotong Road, Huaiyin, Jiangsu Province 223001
Tel: +86(517) 3522010
Fax: +86(517) 3942349
EMail: nic@hytc.edu.cn
Website: http://www.hytc.edu.cn

President: Chen Fasong

International Relations: Mao Zonggang

School

Chemistry and Chemical Engineering (Applied Chemistry; Chemical Engineering; Chemistry; Environmental Studies); **Economics and Management** (Accountancy; Economics; Insurance; International Business; Management; Marketing); **Educational Administration** (Educational Administration); **Educational Science** (Preschool Education; Primary Education; Psychology); **Fine Arts** (Design; Fine Arts); **History, Culture and Tourism** (History; Social Work; Tourism); **Life Sciences** (Bioengineering; Biology; Biotechnology); **Mathematics** (Applied Mathematics; Computer Science; Mathematics; Statistics); **Urban and Environmental Science** (Environmental Management; Geography; Real Estate; Rural Planning; Town Planning)

Department

Chinese Language and Literature (Chinese; Literature); **Computer Science** (Computer Networks; Computer Science; Software Engineering); **Music** (Dance; Music); **Physical Education** (Physical Education); **Physics** (Optical Technology; Physics); **Politics and Public Administration** (Political Sciences; Public Administration)

History: Founded 1958 as Huaiyin Teacher Training College, acquired present name 1997.

Main Language(s) of Instruction: Chinese

Degrees and Diplomas: *Xueshi Xuewei*

Last Updated: 23/11/12

HUANGGANG NORMAL UNIVERSITY

No.146, Xingang 2 Road, Huangzhou, Hubei Province 438000
Tel: +86(713) 8616627
Fax: +86(713) 8616901
EMail: wlzx@hgnu.edu.cn
Website: http://www.hgnc.net

President: Peng Ye EMail: yepeng@hgnc.edu.cn

School

Business (Business Administration; Business and Commerce; Management; Marketing); **Chemichal Engineering** (Chemical Engineering; Chemistry); **Chemistry and Life Science** (Biological and Life Sciences; Chemistry); **Chinese Language and Literature** (Chinese; Literature); **Educational Sciences and Technology** (Educational Sciences; Educational Technology); **Fine Arts** (Fine Arts); **Foreign Studies** (English); **Further Education**; **International Education**; **Mathematics and Computer Science** (Mathematics; Mathematics and Computer Science); **Media Studies** (Communication Studies; Journalism; Media Studies); **Music** (Music); **Physical Education** (Physical Education); **Physical Sience and Technology** (Physics); **Political Science and Law** (Law; Political Sciences)

History: Founded 1905 as Huangzhou Teachers Training School, acquired present status 1978 and title 1999.

Degrees and Diplomas: *Xueshi Xuewei*

Academic Staff *2011-2012*: Total: c. 1,200

Student Numbers *2011-2012*: Total: c. 15,000

Last Updated: 26/02/13

HUANGHE S & T COLLEGE (HHSTU)

Navigation Road No. 94, Zhengzhou, Henan
Tel: +86(371) 68782596
Fax: +86(371) 68784554
Website: http://www.hhstu.edu.cn/

President: Yang Xuemei

College

Applied Technology (Technology); **Foreign Languages** (Business Administration; English; Japanese; Modern Languages); **Nationalities**

School

Business (Accountancy; Business Administration; E-Business/Commerce; Economics; Management); **Distance and Continuing Education** (Adult Education); **International Dance Studio**; **Journalism and Communication** (Journalism; Mass Communication; Media Studies; Photography; Radio and Television Broadcasting); **Medicine** (Laboratory Techniques; Medicine; Nursing; Pharmacy; Rehabilitation and Therapy; Sports Medicine); **Music** (Art Management; Dance; Music; Music Education; Music Theory and Composition; Musical Instruments; Singing); **Transportation** (Automotive Engineering; Maintenance Technology; Transport and Communications)

Department

Art and Design (Design; Fine Arts); **Foreign Language Teaching** (Foreign Languages Education); **Information Engineering** (Information Technology); **Public Art Education** (Art Education); **Public Physical Education** (Physical Education); **Social Sciences** (Social Sciences)

Institute

Information Engineering (Information Technology); **Private Education** (Education); **Sports** (Physical Education; Sports); **Yellow River Technology Training** *(Professional)* (Accountancy; Architecture; Automotive Engineering; Computer Engineering; Construction Engineering; English; Machine Building; Nursing; Software Engineering; Telecommunications Engineering)

Research Institute

Economic (Economics); **Nano Functional Materials** (Materials Engineering; Nanotechnology)

Further Information: Also Afiliated High School of Science and Technology and Affiliated College of Technology

History: Founded 1984. Acquired present status 2000.

Main Language(s) of Instruction: Chinese

Degrees and Diplomas: *Xueshi Xuewei*

Academic Staff *2012-2013*	**TOTAL**
FULL-TIME	**1,235**
PART-TIME	**559**
Student Numbers *2012-2013*	
All (Foreign included)	c. **25,000**

Last Updated: 02/12/13

HUANGHUAI UNIVERSITY (HHU)

6 Kaiyuan Road, Zhumadian, Henan 463000
Tel: +86(396) 2853503 +86(396) 2879226
Fax: +86(396) 2853115 +86(396) 2879226
EMail: nic@huanghuai.edu.cn; hhbgs@huanghuai.edu.cn; huanghuaigj@gmail.com
Website: http://www.huanghuai.edu.cn/

Chancellor: Jie Xiaolei

College

Animation (Design; Literature; Painting and Drawing; Visual Arts); **Architecture and Civil Engineering** (Architecture; Civil Engineering; Engineering Management; Environmental Engineering; Rural Planning; Structural Architecture; Town Planning); **Art and Design** (Architectural and Environmental Design; Design; Fine Arts; Graphic Design; Visual Arts); **Culture and Media** (Chinese; Cultural Studies; International Studies; Media Studies; Radio and Television Broadcasting); **International College** (Accountancy; Business Computing; Computer Engineering; Finance; Management; Marketing; Nursing; Software Engineering; Visual Arts); **Software Technology** *(Vocational)* (Computer Engineering; Computer Networks; Multimedia; Software Engineering; Visual Arts)

Department

Bioengineering (Animal Husbandry; Bioengineering; Horticulture; Landscape Architecture; Zoology); **Chemistry and Chemical Engineering** (Applied Chemistry; Chemical Engineering; Chemistry); **Economic Management** (E-Business/Commerce; Economics; International Business; International Economics; Management; Marketing; Tourism); **Electronic Science and Engineering** (Automotive Engineering; Electronic Engineering; Energy Engineering; Maintenance Technology); **Foreign Languages and Literature** (English; Foreign Languages Education; Literature; Modern Languages); **Information Engineering** (Computer Engineering; Computer Networks; Computer Science; Electronic Engineering; Information Technology; Telecommunications Engineering); **Mathematical Sciences** (Applied Mathematics; Computer Science; Information Technology; Mathematics; Mathematics Education; Primary Education); **Music Performance** (Dance; Music; Musical Instruments; Singing); **Nursing** (Nursing); **Physical Education** (Physical Education; Sociology; Sports); **Social Management** (Political Sciences; Public Administration; Welfare and Protective Services)

History: Merged 2004 with Zhumadian Teachers College, Central Plains Vocational Technical College, and Zhumadian Institute of Forestry.

Main Language(s) of Instruction: Chinese

Degrees and Diplomas: *Xueshi Xuewei*

Student Services: Canteen

Academic Staff *2012-2013*: Total: c. 1,100

Student Numbers *2012-2013*: Total: c. 18,000

Last Updated: 02/12/13

HUANGSHAN UNIVERSITY (HSU)

Tunxi, Huangshan, Anhui 245041
Tel: +86(559) 2546600
Fax: +86(559) 2546611
EMail: iec@hsu.edu.cn
Website: http://www.hsu.edu.cn/

President: Wang Jianli

College

Architecture Engineering (Architecture; Civil Engineering; Construction Engineering; Rural Planning; Structural Architecture; Town Planning); **Arts** (Archaeology; Graphic Design; Industrial Design; Music; Radio and Television Broadcasting; Visual Arts); **Chemistry and Chemical Engineering** (Applied Chemistry; Chemical Engineering; Chemistry; Materials Engineering; Pharmacy); **Economic Management** (Accountancy; Economics; Finance; International Business; International Economics; Management; Marketing; Public Administration); **Education Science** (Educational Psychology; Preschool Education; Primary Education); **Foreign Languages** (English; Japanese; Modern Languages); **Liberal Arts** (Chinese; Cultural Studies; Film; International Studies; Literature; Management; Theatre); **Life and Environment Science** (Biological and Life Sciences; Biotechnology; Environmental Studies; Food Science; Food Technology; Forestry; Horticulture); **Mathematics and Statistics** (Applied Mathematics; Mathematics; Statistics); **Mechanics, Electronics and Information Engineering** (Automation and Control Engineering; Computer Engineering; Computer Science; Electronic Engineering; Information Sciences; Information Technology; Mechanical Engineering; Optical Technology; Software Engineering); **Physical Education** (Leisure Studies; Physical Education; Sports; Sports Management); **Tourism** (Cooking and Catering; Hotel Management; Human Resources; Nutrition; Tourism)

History: Founded 1978 as Huizhou Teacher's College. Renamed Huangshan Junior College 1997. Acquired present status and title 2002.

Main Language(s) of Instruction: Chinese

Degrees and Diplomas: *Xueshi Xuewei*

Student Services: Language Laboratory

Student Numbers *2012-2013*: Total: c. 17,000

Last Updated: 02/12/13

HUAQIAO UNIVERSITY

Quanzhou, Fujian Province 362021
Tel: +86(595) 2680680
Fax: +86(595) 2686969
EMail: xzbgs@hqu.edu.cn
Website: http://www.hqu.edu.cn

President: Qiu Jin

College

Architecture (Architecture; Landscape Architecture; Town Planning); **Business Administration** (Business Administration; Finance; Human Resources; Management; Marketing); **Chemical Engineering** (Bioengineering; Biotechnology; Chemical Engineering; Environmental Engineering; Environmental Studies; Horticulture; Pharmacology); **Chinese Language and Culture** (Chinese; Cultural Studies); **Civil Engineering** (Civil Engineering; Construction Engineering; Engineering Management; Geological Engineering; Structural Architecture; Water Science); **Commerce** (Banking; E-Business/Commerce; Economics; Finance; International Business; Management); **Computer Science and Technology** (Computer Networks; Computer Science; Software Engineering); **Fine Arts** (Design; Fine Arts); **Foreign Languages** (English; Japanese; Modern Languages); **Humanities** (Advertising and Publicity; Chinese; Literature; Radio and Television Broadcasting); **Humanities and Public Administration** (Administration; Public Administration); **Information Science and Engineering** (Applied Physics; Automation and Control Engineering; Electrical Engineering; Electronic Engineering; Telecommunications Engineering); **Law** (Law); **Mathematical Science** (Applied Mathematics; Computer Science; Information Sciences; Mathematics); **Mechanical Engineering and Automation** (Automation and Control Engineering; Automotive Engineering; Industrial Design; Materials Engineering; Mechanical Engineering); **Music and Dance** (Dance; Music); **Sports** (Sports); **Tourism** (Tourism)

History: Founded 1960, mainly for students from Hong Kong, Macau, Taiwan, and for Overseas Chinese students in other countries.

Academic Year: February to January (February-July; September-January)

Admission Requirements: Graduation from senior middle school and entrance examination

Main Language(s) of Instruction: Chinese

Degrees and Diplomas: *Xueshi Xuewei*; *Shuoshi Xuewei*; *Boshi*

Student Services: Canteen, Careers Guidance, Cultural Activities, Health Services, Language Laboratory, Sports Facilities

Publications: Journal of Huaqiao University

Last Updated: 26/11/12

HUAZHONG AGRICULTURAL UNIVERSITY (HAU)

No.1,Shizishan Street · Hongshan District,
Wuhan, Hubei Province 430070
Tel: +86(27) 87282027
Fax: +86(27) 87384670
EMail: fao@hzau.edu.cn
Website: http://www.hzau.edu.cn

President: Deng Xiuxin

College

Adult Education (Adult Education); **Animal Husbandry and Veterinary Medicine** (Animal Husbandry; Food Science; Genetics; Veterinary Science); **Economics and Management/Land Management** (Accountancy; Agricultural Economics; Agriculture; Business Administration; Business and Commerce; Economics; Forestry; International Business; Management); **Engineering and Technology** (Agricultural Engineering; Electrical and Electronic Engineering; Engineering; Mechanical Engineering); **Fishery** (Aquaculture; Fishery); **Food Science and Technology** (Food Science; Food Technology; Microbiology; Molecular Biology); **Horticulture and Forestry Sciences** (Forestry; Horticulture; Landscape Architecture; Vegetable Production); **Humanities and Social Sciences** (Advertising and Publicity; Arts and Humanities; Human Resources; Law; Marketing; Social Sciences; Social Work; Sociology); **Life Sciences and Technology** (Biochemistry; Bioengineering; Biological and Life Sciences; Biotechnology; Microbiology); **Plant Sciences and Technology** (Agronomy; Plant and Crop Protection); **Resources and Environment** (Crop Production; Environmental Engineering; Environmental Studies; Soil Science); **Science** (Applied Chemistry; Applied Physics; Computer Science; Information Sciences; Mathematics)

School

Foreign Languages and Literature (English; Literature; Modern Languages)

History: Founded 1898. Acquired present title 1952.

Academic Year: September to June (September-December; February-June)

Main Language(s) of Instruction: Chinese, English

Accrediting Agency: Ministry of Education

Degrees and Diplomas: *Xueshi Xuewei*; *Shuoshi Xuewei*; *Boshi*

Student Services: Academic Counselling, Canteen, Careers Guidance, Cultural Activities, Foreign Studies Centre, Health Services, Language Laboratory, Nursery Care, Social Counselling, Sports Facilities

Publications: Huazhong Agricultural University Journal; Huazhong Agricultural University Journal

Last Updated: 26/11/12

HUAZHONG UNIVERSITY OF SCIENCE AND TECHNOLOGY (HUST)

1037 Luo Yu Road, Wuhan, Hubei Province 430074
Tel: +86(27) 87542157
Fax: +86(27) 87547063
EMail: haoli@hust.edu.cn
Website: http://www.hust.edu.cn

President: Li President Peigen

College

Medicine *(Tongji)* (Forensic Medicine and Dentistry; Nursing)

School

Architecture and Town Planning (Architectural and Environmental Design; Architecture; Urban Studies); **Civil Engineering**

and Mechanics (Bridge Engineering; Civil Engineering; Engineering Management; Mechanics; Road Engineering; Transport Engineering); **Computer Science and Technology** (Computer Science; Technology); **Distance and Continuing Education** (Continuing Education; Distance Education); **Economics** (Economics; Finance; International Business; International Economics; Regional Planning; Rural Planning); **Electrical and Electronic Engineering** (Automation and Control Engineering; Electrical and Electronic Engineering; Engineering; Power Engineering); **Energy and Power Engineering** (Chemical Engineering; Energy Engineering; Heating and Refrigeration; Mechanical Engineering; Power Engineering; Thermal Engineering); **Environmental Science and Engineering** (Environmental Engineering; Environmental Studies); **Hydropower and Information Engineering** (Hydraulic Engineering; Information Technology; Water Science); **Journalism and Information Communications** (Advertising and Publicity; Communication Studies; Journalism; Radio and Television Broadcasting); **Law** (Law); **Life Science and Technology** (Biological and Life Sciences; Biomedical Engineering; Biotechnology; Technology); **Materials Science and Engineering** (Automation and Control Engineering; Engineering; Heating and Refrigeration; Materials Engineering; Metallurgical Engineering); **Mechanical Science and Engineering** (Automation and Control Engineering; Electronic Engineering; Engineering; Industrial Design; Mechanical Engineering; Technology); **Medicine and Health Management** (Health Administration; Medicine); **Naval Architecture and Ocean Engineering** (Marine Engineering; Naval Architecture); **Pharmacy** (Pharmacy; Traditional Eastern Medicine); **Public Administration** (Public Administration); **Software Engineering** (Software Engineering)

History: Founded 1953 as Huazhong Institute of Technology. Merged with Tongji Medical University (founded 1907), Wuhan Urban Construction Institute (founded 1954) and Wuhan Science and Technology Vocational College (founded 1968) to form the new HUST 2000.

Admission Requirements: Senior middle school certificate and entrance examination

Main Language(s) of Instruction: Chinese

Accrediting Agency: Ministry of Education; Ministry of Public Health; Ministry of Construction and Ministry of Science and Technology

Degrees and Diplomas: *Xueshi Xuewei*: **Medicine.** *Shuoshi Xuewei*; *Boshi*

Student Services: Academic Counselling, Canteen, Careers Guidance, Cultural Activities, Foreign Studies Centre, Health Services, Language Laboratory, Nursery Care, Social Counselling, Sports Facilities

Publications: Applied Medicine; China Higher Medical Education; China Medical Abstract; Chinese Journal of Clinical Gastroenterology; Chinese Journal Rehabilitation; Deutsche Medizin; Journal of Clinical Cardiology; Journal of Clinical Otorhinolaryngology; Journal of Clinical Urology; Journal of Haematology; Journal of Higher Education; Journal of Huazhong University of Science and Technology; Journal of Huazhong University of Science and Technology; Journal of Nursing; Journal of Tongji Medical College; Journal of Wuhan Urban Construction Institute; New Architecture; Roentgenpraxis

Publishing House: Huazhong University of Science & Technology Press

Last Updated: 26/11/12

HUBEI INSTITUTE OF AUTOMOBILE INDUSTRY

Jyaoyukou, Shiyan, Hubei Province 442002
Tel: +86(719) 8238444
Fax: +86(719) 8260748
EMail: wlzx@huat.edu.cn

President: Liu Kaiming

International Relations: Zhang Jingbo

Department

Automotive Engineering (Automotive Engineering); **Industrial and Electrical Engineering**; **Materials Engineering** (Materials Engineering); **Mechanics** (Mechanics); **Modern Languages** (Modern Languages); **Social Sciences**

History: Founded 1972 as Workers University of Dongfeng Motor Company, acquired present name 1983.

Degrees and Diplomas: *Xueshi Xuewei*; *Shuoshi Xuewei*

HUBEI INSTITUTE OF FINE ARTS

374 Zhongshan Road, Wuchang District,
Wuhan, Hubei Province 430060
Tel: +86(27) 81317000
Fax: +86(27) 81317011
Website: http://www.hifa.edu.cn/

President: Xu Yongmin

Department

Aesthetics (Aesthetics); **Apparel Design** (Design); **Art Education** (Art Education); **Chinese Painting** (Painting and Drawing); **Design** (Design); **Environmental Art Design** (Design; Environmental Management); **Fashion Design** (Fashion Design); **Industrial Design** (Industrial Design); **Mural Painting and Mixed Media Painting** (Painting and Drawing); **Oil Painting** (Painting and Drawing); **Printmaking** (Printing and Printmaking); **Sculpture** (Sculpture); **Visual Communication Design** (Design; Visual Arts); **Watercolor Painting** (Painting and Drawing)

History: Founded 1920 as Wuchang School of Fine Arts, acquired present status and title 1985.

Main Language(s) of Instruction: Chinese

Degrees and Diplomas: *Xueshi Xuewei*; *Shuoshi Xuewei*. School signed a joint training doctoral agreement with other Colleges and Universities

Academic Staff *2011-2012*: Total: c. 500

Student Numbers *2011-2012*: Total: c. 7,000

Last Updated: 26/02/13

HUBEI NORMAL UNIVERSITY

11, Cihu Road, Huangchi, Hubei Province 435002
Tel: +86(714) 6525179 +86(714) 6519012
Fax: +86(714) 6575993
EMail: admissions@hbnu.edu.cn
Website: http://www.hbnu.edu.cn

President: Chunlan Jiang

College

Arts and Science (Arts and Humanities; Natural Sciences); **Chemistry and Environmental Engineering** (Chemistry; Environmental Engineering); **Chinese Language and Literature** (Chinese; Literature); **Computer Science and Technology** (Computer Science); **Continuing Education**; **Economics and Management** (Economics; Management); **Educational Science** (Educational Sciences); **Fine Arts** (Design; Fine Arts; Industrial Design); **Foreign Studies** (English; Japanese); **History and Culture** (Cultural Studies; History; Social Work; Tourism); **International**; **Life Sciences** (Biological and Life Sciences); **Mathematics and Statistics** (Mathematics; Statistics); **Music** (Music); **Physics and Electronic Science** (Electronic Engineering; Physics)

Department

Control Science and Engineering (Automation and Control Engineering; Electrical Engineering); **Geography** (Geography); **Physical Education** (Physical Education; Sports); **Political Science** (Political Sciences)

History: Founded 1973 as Central China Normal University Huangshi Branch, acquired present name 1985.

Main Language(s) of Instruction: Chinese

Degrees and Diplomas: *Xueshi Xuewei*; *Shuoshi Xuewei*

Academic Staff *2011-2012*: Total: c. 1,300

Student Numbers *2011-2012*: Total: c. 20,000

Last Updated: 26/02/13

HUBEI POLYTECHNIC UNIVERSITY (HBPU)

16, Guilin Road, Huangshi, Hubei 435003
Tel: +86(714) 6353390
Fax: +86(714) 6350612
EMail: wlzx@hbpu.edu.cn
Website: http://www.hbpu.edu.cn/

President: Li Wang

College

Chemical and Materials Engineering (Applied Chemistry; Biochemistry; Bioengineering; Chemical Engineering; Inorganic Chemistry; Materials Engineering); **Economics and Management** (Accountancy; Business Administration; E-Business/Commerce; Economics; Finance; International Business; International Economics; Management; Marketing; Transport Management); **Environmental Engineering** (Environmental Engineering; Environmental Management; Environmental Studies; Hydraulic Engineering; Safety Engineering; Water Management); **Foreign Languages** (Applied Linguistics; Business Administration; English; Modern Languages; Musicology); **International** (Accountancy; Automation and Control Engineering; Electrical Engineering; Marketing; Mechanical Engineering; Production Engineering); **Teachers** (Art Education; Chinese; Literature; Music Education; Musicology; Preschool Education; Primary Education); **Vocational and Technical Studies**

School

Civil Engineering (Bridge Engineering; Civil Engineering; Management; Road Engineering; Structural Architecture); **Computer Science** (Computer Engineering; Computer Networks; Computer Science; Software Engineering); **Continuing Education** *(Zikaoban)*; **Mathematics** (Applied Physics; Mathematics; Mathematics and Computer Science); **Mechanical Engineering** (Automation and Control Engineering; Automotive Engineering; Electronic Engineering; Materials Engineering; Mechanical Engineering; Production Engineering; Transport Engineering); **Medicine** (Laboratory Techniques; Medical Technology; Medicine; Nursing; Pharmacy)

Department

Humanities and Social Sciences (Arts and Humanities; Social Sciences); **Sports** (Sports)

Institute

Art (Architectural and Environmental Design; Clothing and Sewing; Communication Arts; Dance; Display and Stage Design; Fashion Design; Industrial Design; Music; Music Education; Musicology; Textile Design; Textile Technology; Visual Arts); **Electrical and Electronics Engineering** (Automation and Control Engineering; Electrical and Electronic Engineering; Electrical Engineering; Electronic Engineering; Information Technology; Railway Transport; Telecommunications Engineering)

Centre

Environmental Engineering Experimental Teaching Demonstration (Environmental Engineering; Science Education); **Fashion Design and Engineering Experimental Teaching** (Art Education; Fashion Design; Textile Technology); **IT and Application of Experimental Teaching** (Computer Education; Information Technology); **Mechanical Basic Experimental Teaching Demonstration** (Mechanics)

Laboratory

Pollution Control and Repair *(Hubey Key Mining Environment)* (Environmental Management; Mining Engineering)

Research Centre

The Middle Reaches of the Yangtze River Mining Development (Cultural Studies; Economics; Mining Engineering; Social Studies)

History: Founded 1975 as Huangshi Industrial Secondary School. Renamed Wuhan University of Technology, Huangshi Branch 1981. Became Huangshi Polytechnical College 1991 after merging with Huangshi Professional College. Became Huangshi Institute of Technology 2004 after merging with Huangshi Teacher Training College. Acquired present title 2011.

Main Language(s) of Instruction: Chinese

Degrees and Diplomas: *Xueshi Xuewei*

Academic Staff *2012-2013*: Total 956
STAFF WITH DOCTORATE: Total 110
Student Numbers *2012-2013*: Total: c. 20,000
Distance students, 6000.
Last Updated: 02/12/13

HUBEI UNIVERSITY

11 Xueyuan Road, Wuchang, Wuhan, Hubei Province 430062
Tel: +86(27) 86717841
Fax: +86(27) 86814263
EMail: international@hubu.edu.cn
Website: http://www.hubu.edu.cn

President: Jianmin Xiong

Faculty

Arts (Chinese; Mass Communication; Media Studies); **Business** (Accountancy; Business Administration; Engineering Management; Finance; Hotel Management; International Business; Tourism); **Chemistry and Chemical Engineering** (Chemical Engineering; Chemistry); **Creative Art** (Design; Fine Arts; Music); **Education** (Education; Educational Psychology; Public Administration); **Foreign Languages and Literature** (English; French; Japanese; Literature); **History and Culture** (Architecture and Planning; History); **Life Sciences** (Bioengineering; Biological and Life Sciences; Ecology; Environmental Engineering); **Material Science and Engineering** (Materials Engineering; Physical Chemistry; Polymer and Plastics Technology); **Mathematics and Computer Science** (Computer Science; Information Technology; Mathematics); **Philosophy** (Philosophy); **Physical Education** (Physical Education; Sports); **Physics and Electronic Engineering** (Electronic Engineering; Physics); **Politics, Law and Public Administration** (Law; Political Sciences; Public Administration); **Resource and Environment** (Environmental Engineering; Geography)

Department

Chu-cai *((Hubei Talents))*

History: Founded 1931 as Hubei Institute of Education. Acquired present status and title 1984.

Academic Year: February to January (February-June; September-January)

Admission Requirements: Graduation from senior middle school and entrance examination

Degrees and Diplomas: *Xueshi Xuewei*; *Shuoshi Xuewei*; *Boshi*

Student Services: Academic Counselling, Canteen, Careers Guidance, Cultural Activities, Health Services, Nursery Care, Social Counselling, Sports Facilities

Publications: Hubei University Journal; Middle-school Chinese Education; Middle-school Mathematics Education

Academic Staff *2011-2012*: Total: c. 2,000
Student Numbers *2011-2012*: Total: c. 20,000
Last Updated: 26/02/13

HUBEI UNIVERSITY FOR NATIONALITIES

39 Xueyuan Road, Enshi, Hubei Province 445000
Tel: +86(718) 8437495
EMail: rogerluo1973@163.com
Website: http://www.hbmy.edu.cn

President: Dai Xiaoming

School

Biological Science and Technology (Bioengineering; Food Science; Forestry; Horticulture; Town Planning; Wildlife); **Chemistry and Environmental Engineering** (Applied Chemistry; Chemical Engineering; Chemistry; Environmental Studies); **Economics and Law** (Accountancy; Finance; International Economics; Law; Marketing; Political Sciences); **Education** (Education); **Fine Arts** (Dance; Design; Fine Arts; Music); **Foreign Languages** (English; Japanese; Modern Languages); **Information Engineering** (Automation and Control Engineering; Computer Science; Electronic Engineering; Information Technology); **Laws** (Administration; Law; Political Sciences; Social Studies; Sociology); **Literature and Communication** (Chinese; Journalism; Literature; Publishing and Book Trade; Radio and Television Broadcasting); **Marxism Studies** (Political Sciences); **Medical Science** (Medicine; Nursing; Pharmacy; Traditional Eastern Medicine); **Physical Education** (Physical Education); **Science** (Applied Mathematics; Computer Science; Electronic Engineering; Mathematics; Mechanical Engineering; Physics)

History: Founded 1938 as branch of United Rural Teaching School of Hubei Province, acquired present status and title 1989.

Main Language(s) of Instruction: Chinese
Degrees and Diplomas: *Xueshi Xuewei*; *Shuoshi Xuewei*
Last Updated: 26/11/12

HUBEI UNIVERSITY OF CHINESE MEDICINE

110 Yunjiaqiao, Wuchang, Wuhan, Hubei Province 430061
Tel: +86(27) 88852621
Fax: +86(27) 88852621
Website: http://www1.hbtcm.edu.cn
President: Hua Wang

School
Adult Education (Adult Education)

Department
Acupuncture, Moxibustion and Orthopaedics (Acupuncture; Orthopaedics); **Pharmacology** (Pharmacology); **Traditional Chinese Medicine** (Traditional Eastern Medicine)

History: Founded 1959 as Hubei Provincial Traditional Chinese Medicine Advanced Training School. Acquired present status and title 2003.
Main Language(s) of Instruction: Chinese
Degrees and Diplomas: *Xueshi Xuewei*; *Shuoshi Xuewei*; *Boshi*
Publications: Hepatic Disease Journal of the Combination of TCM and Western Medicine; Hubei Journal of TCM; Journal of Hubei College of TCM
Last Updated: 26/11/12

HUBEI UNIVERSITY OF ECONOMICS (HBUE)

No.8 Yangqiao Lake Avenue, Hidden Dragon, Island Development Zone, Jiangxia, Wunhan 430205
EMail: hbjjxyacca@163.com
Website: http://www.hbue.edu.cn/
President: Lv Zhongmei EMail: x001@hbue.edu.cn

Faculty
Law (Law; Social Work)

College
Finance and Public Administration (Finance; Insurance; International Business; Public Administration); **Foreign Languages** (English; Modern Languages); **Logistics and Engineering Management** (Transport Engineering; Transport Management)

School
Accountancy (Accountancy; Finance); **Information Management** (Computer Engineering; Computer Networks; E-Business/Commerce; Information Management; Software Engineering); **Journalism and Communication** (Chinese; Journalism; Mass Communication; Writing); **Tourism and Hotel Management** (Cooking and Catering; Hotel Management; Nutrition; Tourism)

Department
Continuing Education; **Economics** (Economic and Finance Policy; Economics); **Electronic Engineering** (Electronic Engineering; Information Technology; Telecommunications Engineering); **Ideological and Political Theory** (Political Sciences); **Physical Education** (Leisure Studies; Physical Education; Sports)

Institute
Art (Advertising and Publicity; Architectural and Environmental Design; Design; Fine Arts; Graphic Design); **Business Administration** (Business Administration; Human Resources; Marketing); **Finance** (Finance); **International Education**; **Management Technology** (Accountancy; Arts and Humanities; Computer Science; Electronic Engineering; Finance); **Statistics** (Applied Mathematics; Mathematics; Statistics)

Academy
International Trade (International Business; International Economics)

History: Founded 2002 following merger of Hubei Commercial College, Wuhan Finance College and Hubei Institute for Planning Personnel Management.
Main Language(s) of Instruction: Chinese
Degrees and Diplomas: *Xueshi Xuewei*

Academic Staff *2012-2013*: Total 796
STAFF WITH DOCTORATE: Total 1
Student Numbers *2012-2013*: Total 17,022
Last Updated: 03/12/13

HUBEI UNIVERSITY OF EDUCATION (HUE)

East Lake New Technology Development Zone, Gaoxin Road, No. 129, Wuhan, Hubei 430205
Website: http://www.hue.edu.cn/
President: Hu Zhongjun

College
Vocational Studies *(Wuhan)* (Accountancy; Architecture; Automotive Engineering; Economics; Electrical Engineering; Electronic Engineering; Engineering; Information Technology; Management; Mechanical Engineering; Media Studies; Modern Languages; Tourism)

School
Arts (Fine Arts; Music); **Chemistry and Life Sciences** (Biological and Life Sciences; Chemistry); **Computer Science** (Computer Engineering; Computer Science; E-Business/Commerce; Educational Technology; Information Management; Information Technology; Multimedia; Software Engineering); **Continuing Education**; **Economics and Management** (Economics; Hotel Management; Insurance; International Business; International Economics; Management; Marketing; Tourism; Transport Management); **Educational Sciences** (Educational Sciences); **International Education**; **Liberal Arts** (Arts and Humanities); **Mathematics and Econometrics** (Econometrics; Mathematics; Statistics); **Physical Education** (Physical Education); **Physics and Electrics information** (Electrical Engineering; Mechanical Engineering; Physics); **Political Sicences and Law** (Law; Political Sciences)

Department
Accountancy (Accountancy; Business Computing; Finance); **Architecture and Building Materials** (Architecture; Construction Engineering; Materials Engineering); **BTN Department** *(Hubei Province Education Training Centre)* (Teacher Training); **Jijiao** *(Continuing Education Center of Hubei Primary and Secondary School Tteachers, Hubei Teacher Qualification Centre)* (Teacher Training); **Teaching and Research** *(Hubei Provincial Education Research)* (Teacher Training)

Centre
Teacher Quality Training *(Teacher Development Centre)* (Teacher Training)

History: Founded 1931 as Hubei Provincial Institute of Education. Tranformed into Hubei Industrial School and moved to current location 2003. Acquired present status and title 2007.
Main Language(s) of Instruction: Chinese
Degrees and Diplomas: *Xueshi Xuewei*
Publications: Contemporary Economy; Friends of the Teacher; Journal of Hubei University of Education; Yushu Wai Learning

Academic Staff *2012-2013*: Total: c. 800
Student Numbers *2012-2013*: Total: c. 16,000
Last Updated: 03/12/13

HUBEI UNIVERSITY OF MEDICINE (HBMU)

25 South Peoples' Road, Shiyan, Hubei Province 442000
Tel: +86(719) 8891088
Website: http://www.hbmu.edu.cn/
President: Tu Han

Department
Anaesthesiology (Anaesthesiology); **Clinical Medicine** (Medicine); **Health Administration** (Health Administration); **Medical Imaging** (Medical Technology); **Medical Laboratory** (Laboratory Techniques); **Nursing** *(international)* (Nursing); **Nursing** (Nursing); **Oral Medicine** (Oral Pathology; Orthodontics; Periodontics; Stomatology); **Pharmacy** (Pharmacy); **Rehabilitation and Therapy** (Rehabilitation and Therapy)
Further Information: Also affiliated hospital

History: Founded 1965 as Yunyang Branch of Wuhan Medical College. Changed its name to Yunyang Medical College, Tongji Medical University 1985. Renamed Yunyang Medical College 1994. Acquired present title 2010.

Main Language(s) of Instruction: Chinese

Degrees and Diplomas: *Xueshi Xuewei*; *Shuoshi Xuewei*

Publications: Journal of Yunyang Medical College

Academic Staff *2011-2012*: Total 908

STAFF WITH DOCTORATE: Total 214

Student Numbers *2011-2012*: Total: c. 7,783

Last Updated: 01/02/13

HUBEI UNIVERSITY OF POLICE (HBPA)

Jiefang Road, No. 86, Wuhan, Hubei 430034
Tel: +86(27) 3421017
Website: http://www.hbpa.edu.cn/

President: Cao Shiquan

Faculty

Law (Administrative Law; Civil Law; Commercial Law; Criminal Law; International Law; Law)

Department

Combat Training (Police Studies); **Ideological and Political Education** (Political Sciences); **Information Technology** (Computer Science; Information Technology); **International Police Studies** (Police Studies); **Investigation** (Police Studies); **Police Battle** (Police Studies); **Police Studies**; **Public Administration** (Public Administration; Transport Management); **Public Base Courses** (Chemistry; Physics; Psychology); **Security Management System** (Protective Services)

History: Founded 2002 as Hubei Police Academy on the basis of the Hubei Province Public Security School (founded 1949) and Hubei Province Public Security School (founded 1976), later repectively known as Hubei Zhongnan University of Economics and Law, and University of Joint Naval Engineering Undergraduate Education. Acquired present status 2006.

Main Language(s) of Instruction: Chinese

Degrees and Diplomas: *Xueshi Xuewei*

Academic Staff *2012-2013*: Total 263

Student Numbers *2012-2013*: Total 2,347

Last Updated: 03/12/13

HUBEI UNIVERSITY OF SCIENCE AND TECHNOLOGY (HBUST)

88, Xianning Avenue, Xianning, Hubei Province 437100
Tel: +86(715) 8260538
Fax: +86(715) 8260538
EMail: wlglzx@hbust.com.cn
Website: http://www.enxnc.com.cn/

President: Wu Ji-liang (2011-) Tel: +86(715) 8260584

International Relations: Du Shengfu

Unit

Ideological and Political Theory Course (Political Sciences)

College

Arts (Design; Fine Arts; Musicology); **Basic Medical Studies** (Medicine; Social and Preventive Medicine); **Chemistry and Life Sciences** (Biological and Life Sciences; Chemistry); **Computer Science and Technology** (Computer Engineering; Computer Networks; Computer Science); **Education** (Education; Primary Education; Psychology); **Electronic and Information Engineering** (Automation and Control Engineering; Electrical Engineering; Electronic Engineering; Information Sciences; Information Technology; Nuclear Engineering; Physics); **Foreign Language** (English; Modern Languages); **Nursing** (Nursing); **Pharmacy** (Pharmacology; Pharmacy); **Resources and Environmental Science** (Engineering Management; Geography; Natural Resources)

School

Biomedical Engineering (Biomedical Engineering); **Clinical Medicine** (Medical Technology); **Continuing Education**; **Economics and Management** (Business Administration; Economics; Finance; Management); **Facial Medicine** (Medicine; Optometry; Oral Pathology); **Mathematics and Statistics** (Applied Mathematics; Mathematics; Statistics)

Institute

Humanities (Arts and Humanities; Chinese; Foreign Languages Education; History; Literature); **Physical Education** (Physical Education; Sports)

Centre

E'nan Cultural Studies (Asian Studies); **Mental Health Education and Research** (Psychiatry and Mental Health); **Non-Power Nuclear Technology Research and Development** (Nuclear Engineering)

Research Centre

Soil and Water Resources *(Middle Reaches of the Yangtze River)* (Natural Resources; Soil Science; Water Science)

Research Institute

Pharmaceutical (Pharmacology)

History: Founded 2002 as Xianning College through merger of Xianning Medical College and Xianning Teachers College. Acquired present title 2011.

Main Language(s) of Instruction: Chinese

Degrees and Diplomas: *Xueshi Xuewei*

Publications: Journal of Xianning Medical College

Academic Staff *2011-2012*: Total 1,200

STAFF WITH DOCTORATE: Total 41

Student Numbers *2011-2012*: Total: c. 14,000

Distance students, 4000.

Last Updated: 21/01/13

HUBEI UNIVERSITY OF TECHNOLOGY

Nanhu, Wuhan, Hubei Province 430068
Tel: +86(27) 88034023
Fax: +86(27) 88034023
EMail: international@mail.hubpu.edu.cn
Website: http://io.hbut.edu.cn/en/intro.asp

President: Pan Anfu

International Relations: Pan Shaobo

Department

Bioengineering (Bioengineering); **Civil Engineering**; **Electrical Engineering and Computer Science** (Computer Science; Electrical Engineering); **Industrial and Commercial Management** (Industrial Management; Management); **Mechanical Engineering** (Mechanical Engineering); **Social Sciences** (Social Sciences)

Institute

Design (Design)

History: Founded 1958 as Hubei Institute of Light Industry, renamed Hubei Polytechnic University. Acquired present title 2004.

Degrees and Diplomas: *Xueshi Xuewei*; *Shuoshi Xuewei*

Last Updated: 03/12/13

HUIZHOU UNIVERSITY (HZU)

Guangdong Yanda Road 46, Huizhou, Guangdong 516007
Tel: +86(752) 2529260
Fax: +86(752) 2529489
EMail: fao@hzu.edu.cn
Website: http://www.hzu.edu.cn/

President: Peng Yonghong

Department

Architecture and Civil Engineering (Architecture; Civil Engineering; Engineering Management); **Biological Science** (Bioengineering; Biological and Life Sciences; Horticulture; Science Education); **Chemical Engineering** (Applied Chemistry; Chemical Engineering; Industrial Chemistry; Polymer and Plastics Technology); **Chinese**

Language (Chinese; Foreign Languages Education; Journalism; Literature; Radio and Television Broadcasting); **Computer Science** (Computer Engineering; Computer Networks; Computer Science; Software Engineering); **Economics and Management** (Economics; Finance; International Business; International Economics; Management; Marketing; Transport Management); **Electronic Engineering** (Automation and Control Engineering; Electrical Engineering; Electronic Engineering; Information Technology; Physics); **Fine Arts** (Architectural and Environmental Design; Art Education; Design; Fine Arts); **Foreign Languages** (English; Foreign Languages Education; Japanese; Modern Languages); **Ideological and Political Education** (Political Sciences); **Mathematics** (Applied Mathematics; Information Management; Information Technology; Mathematics; Mathematics Education); **Music** (Music; Music Education; Musicology); **Physical Education** (Physical Education; Sports); **Political Science and Law** (Administration; History; Humanities and Social Science Education; Law; Political Sciences); **Textiles and Clothing Manufacture** (Clothing and Sewing; Design; Fashion Design; Textile Design; Textile Technology); **Tourism** (Earth Sciences; Tourism)

History: Founded 1921 as Guangzhou Municipal Normal School, a campus of Guangzhou Yue Xiu Academy of Classical Learning. Moved to the Huiyang Fenghu Academy of Learning and renamed Guangdong Provincial Huizhou Normal School 1945. Succesively renamed Guangdong Huizhou Normal School 1949, Huiyang Normal School 1959, Huiyang Prefecture Normal School 1970, Huiyang Teachers College 1978. Incorporated the Huizhou Education Faculty 1986 and later merged with Northwestern Textile Polytechnic University. Acquired present status and title 1993.

Main Language(s) of Instruction: Chinese

Degrees and Diplomas: *Xueshi Xuewei*

Academic Staff *2012-2013*: Total 748

Student Numbers *2012-2013*: Total 16,144

Last Updated: 03/12/13

HULUNBUIR COLLEGE

83 Xuefu Road, Hailar, Hulunbuir, Inner Mongolia 021008
Tel: +86(470) 8259118
Fax: +86(470) 8259380
EMail: mxh-hlr@163.com
Website: http://www.hlbrc.cn/

President: Zhu Yudong

Department

Architecture Engineering (Structural Architecture); **Arts** (Fine Arts); **Biology** (Biological and Life Sciences); **Chinese** (Chinese); **Computer Science** (Computer Science); **Continuing Education** (Continuing Education); **Economic Management** (Economics; Management); **Education** (Education); **Foreign Language** (English; Russian); **Mathematics** (Mathematics); **Mongolian** (Mongolian); **Music** (Music); **Physical Education** (Physical Education); **Physics** (Physics); **Politics and History** (History; Political Sciences); **Public Administration and Law** (Law; Public Administration); **Tourism and Geography** (Geography; Tourism)

History: Founded 1997

Degrees and Diplomas: *Xueshi Xuewei*

HUNAN AGRICULTURAL UNIVERSITY

Furong District, Changsha, Hunan Province 410128
Tel: +86(731) 4618060
Fax: +86(731) 4612870
EMail: principal@hunau.net
Website: http://www.hunau.net/en

President: Zhou Qingming

College

Agriculture (Agriculture; Agronomy; Plant and Crop Protection); **Animal Science and Technology** (Animal Husbandry; Aquaculture; Zoology); **Biosafety Science and Technology** (Biotechnology; Entomology; Microbiology; Plant Pathology); **Bioscience and Biotechnology** (Bioengineering; Biotechnology; Ecology); **Business** (Accountancy; Business Administration; International Business; Management; Marketing); **Economics** (Economics; Finance; Management); **Engineering** (Agricultural Engineering; Automotive Engineering; Engineering Management; Mechanical Engineering; Water Science); **Food Science and Technology** (Food Science; Food Technology); **Foreign Languages** (English; Japanese); **Horticulture and Landscape** (Horticulture; Landscape Architecture; Vegetable Production); **Humanities and Social Sciences** (Labour and Industrial Relations; Law; Political Sciences; Public Administration; Sociology); **Information Science and Technology** (Computer Science; E-Business/Commerce; Information Technology); **National Research and Environment** (Agriculture; Environmental Engineering; Environmental Studies; Soil Science); **Science** (Applied Chemistry; Applied Physics; Computer Science); **Sport and Art** (Design; Physical Education; Sports); **Vocational Education and Technology**

History: Founded 1951 as Hunan Agricultural College, acquired present title 1994.

Main Language(s) of Instruction: Chinese

Degrees and Diplomas: *Xueshi Xuewei*; *Shuoshi Xuewei*; *Boshi*

Publications: Crop Research; Journal of Hunan Agricultural University

Last Updated: 27/11/12

HUNAN CITY UNIVERSITY (HNCU)

Yingbin Road, 518 No, Yiyang, Hunan 413000
Tel: +86(737) 6353036
Fax: +86(737) 6353036
Website: http://www.hncu.net/

President: Li Jianhua

College

Architecture and Urban Planning (Architecture; Town Planning); **Art and Design** (Advertising and Publicity; Architectural and Environmental Design; Communication Arts; Design; Fine Arts; Interior Design; Landscape Architecture; Multimedia; Packaging Technology; Painting and Drawing; Visual Arts); **Chemical and Environmental Engineering** (Chemical Engineering; Environmental Engineering); **Communication and Electronic Engineering** (Electronic Engineering; Telecommunications Engineering); **Foreign Languages** (English; Foreign Languages Education; Modern Languages; Western European Studies); **Information Science and Engineering** (Computer Education; Computer Engineering; Computer Networks; Information Sciences; Information Technology); **Liberal Arts** (Advertising and Publicity; Arts and Humanities; Chinese; Literature; Secretarial Studies); **Management** (Management); **Mathematics and Computer Science** (Mathematics and Computer Science); **Municipal and Surveying Engineering** (Surveying and Mapping)

School

Civil Engineering (Civil Engineering); **Marxism** (Political Sciences); **Music** (Music)

Institute

Sports (Sports)

History: Founded 2002 through merger of Yiyang Teachers College and Hunan Urban Construction College.

Main Language(s) of Instruction: Chinese

Degrees and Diplomas: *Xueshi Xuewei*

Academic Staff *2012-2013*: Total 850

Student Numbers *2012-2013*: Total 16,450

Last Updated: 04/12/13

HUNAN FIRST NORMAL UNIVERSITY (HFNU)

1015 Fenglin 3rd Rd, Yuelu District, Changsha, Hunan 410205
Tel: +86(731) 5150619 +86(731) 5136572
EMail: hnysxcb@126.com; hnfnc@126.com
Website: http://www.hnfnu.edu.cn/

President: Peng Xiaoqi Tel: +86(731) 88228210

Department

Chinese (Chinese; Journalism; Literature; Radio and Television Broadcasting); **Economic Management** (Accountancy; Economics; Finance; International Business; International Economics; Management; Tourism); **Educational Sciences** (Educational Sciences; Primary Education); **Fine Arts** (Fine Arts); **Foreign Language**

Teaching (English; Foreign Languages Education); **Foreign Languages** (English; Modern Languages); **Ideological and Political Theory Teaching Department** (Management; Political Sciences; Social Sciences); **Information Science and Engineering** (Computer Networks; Computer Science; Electronic Engineering; Information Sciences; Information Technology; Telecommunications Engineering); **Mathematics** (Mathematics); **Music** (Music); **Physical Education** (Physical Education)

Centre

Public Experiment Management (Management)

History: Founded 1903 as Hunan Normal School. Became Public Hunan First Normal School 1912. Upgraded into a three-year normal college 2000. Acquired present status and title 2008.

Main Language(s) of Instruction: Chinese

Degrees and Diplomas: *Xueshi Xuewei*. Also 3-year undergraduate programmes

Academic Staff *2012-2013*	**TOTAL**
FULL-TIME	**639**
PART-TIME	**150**

Student Numbers *2012-2013*	
All (Foreign included)	**10,272**

Last Updated: 04/12/13

HUNAN INSTITUTE OF ENGINEERING (HIE)

Fuxing Road, No. 88, Xiangtan, Hunan 411104
Tel: +86(731) 58688500
Fax: +86(731) 58688109
Website: http://www.hnie.edu.cn/

President: Liu Fan

Faculty

Science (Natural Sciences)

College

Applied Technology (Technology); **Art and Design** (Design; Fine Arts); **Chemistry and Chemical Engineering** (Chemical Engineering; Chemistry); **Foreign Languages** (English; Modern Languages); **Humanities** (Arts and Humanities)

School

Architecture and Engineering (Architecture; Engineering); **Economics and Management** (Economics; Management); **Electrical Engineering and Information** (Electrical Engineering); **Mechanical Engineering** (Mechanical Engineering)

Department

Adult Education (Engineering); **Physical Education** (Physical Education)

Institute

Computer Science (Computer Science; Telecommunications Engineering); **International Education**; **Textile and Apparel** (Textile Design; Textile Technology)

Centre

Engineering Training (Engineering)

History: Founded 1951. Acquired present status and title 2000 following merger of Xiangtan Institute of Machinery and Electricity Technology and Hunan Textile College.

Main Language(s) of Instruction: Chinese

Degrees and Diplomas: *Xueshi Xuewei*

Academic Staff *2012-2013*: Total 726

Student Numbers *2012-2013*: Total 20,789

Last Updated: 04/12/13

HUNAN INSTITUTE OF HUMANITIES, SCIENCE AND TECHNOLOGY (HUHST)

Diwing Road, Loudi, Hunan 417000
Tel: +86(738) 8325700
Fax: +86(738) 8372887
Website: http://www.huhst.edu.cn/

President: Liu Yun

Department

Chemistry and Materials Engineering (Chemistry; Materials Engineering; Polymer and Plastics Technology); **Chinese Language and Literature** (Chinese; Literature; Secretarial Studies); **Communication and Control Engineering** (Automation and Control Engineering; Electronic Engineering; Information Technology; Mechanical Engineering; Production Engineering; Telecommunications Engineering); **Computer Science and Technology** (Computer Engineering; Computer Networks; Computer Science; Software Engineering); **Continuing Education**; **Economics and Management** (E-Business/Commerce; Economics; Finance; Management; Marketing; Tourism); **Educational Sciences** (Educational Psychology; Educational Sciences; Humanities and Social Science Education; Preschool Education); **Fine Arts** (Design; Fine Arts; Painting and Drawing); **Foreign Language** (English; Foreign Languages Education; Modern Languages); **Life Sciences** (Agriculture; Biological and Life Sciences; Biotechnology; Food Science; Food Technology); **Mathematics and Applied Mathematics** (Applied Mathematics; Computer Science; Information Sciences; Mathematics); **Music** (Dance; Music; Musicology); **Physical Education** (Physical Education; Sports); **Physics and Information Technology** (Information Sciences; Information Technology; Physics; Power Engineering; Thermal Engineering); **Political Sciences and Law** (Law; Political Sciences)

History: Founded 1978.

Main Language(s) of Instruction: Chinese

Degrees and Diplomas: *Xueshi Xuewei*

Student Services: Sports Facilities

Academic Staff *2012-2013*	**TOTAL**
FULL-TIME	**710**
STAFF WITH DOCTORATE	
FULL-TIME	**43**

Student Numbers *2012-2013*	
All (Foreign included)	**13,583**

Part-time students, 7,800.

Last Updated: 04/12/13

HUNAN INSTITUTE OF SCIENCE AND TECHNOLOGY

Xueyuan road, Yueyang City, Hunan Province 414006
Tel: +86(73) 8640001
Fax: +86(73) 8640000
EMail: yuanban302@126.com
Website: http://www.hnist.cn

President: Wei Chenglong

College

Chemistry and Chemical Engineering (Applied Chemistry; Chemical Engineering; Chemistry); **Chinese Language and Literature** (Chinese; Literature); **Civil Engineering and Architecture** (Architecture; Civil Engineering; Engineering Management); **Computer Science** (Computer Science); **Economics and Management** (Accountancy; Business and Commerce; E-Business/Commerce; Human Resources; Industrial Management; International Business; International Economics; Tourism); **Fine Arts** (Design; Fine Arts); **Foreign Languages and Literature** (English; Korean); **Information and Communication Engineering** (Automation and Control Engineering; Communication Studies; Information Technology); **Journalism and Communication** (Advertising and Publicity; Journalism); **Mathematics** (Applied Mathematics; Computer Science; Mathematics); **Mechanical Engineering** (Electronic Engineering; Machine Building; Mechanical Engineering); **Music** (Dance; Music; Music Education); **Physical Science Education** (Physics); **Physics and Electronics Information** (Electronic Engineering; Physics); **Political Science and Law** (Law; Political Sciences; Public Administration)

History: Founded by Americans as Lakeside University. Renamed Yueyang Normal College 1999. Acquired present title 2003 and present status 2008.

Degrees and Diplomas: *Xueshi Xuewei*; *Shuoshi Xuewei*

Last Updated: 22/11/12

HUNAN INSTITUTE OF TECHNOLOGY (HNPU)

18, Heng Hua Road, Chu Hui District, Hengyang, Hunan
EMail: webmaster@hnpu.edu.cn
Website: http://www.hnpu.edu.cn/

President: Zhang Li

College
Art and Design (Design; Fine Arts); **Computer and Information Science** (Computer Science; Information Sciences); **Construction Engineering** (Construction Engineering); **Economics and Management** (Economics; Management); **Materials and Chemical Engineering** (Chemical Engineering; Materials Engineering); **Safety and Environmental Engineering** (Environmental Engineering; Safety Engineering)

School
Electrical and Information Engineering (Electrical Engineering; Information Technology); **Foreign Languages** (English; Modern Languages); **Mechanical Engineering** (Mechanical Engineering)

Department
Continuing Education; **Ideological and Political Theory Teaching and Research** (Political Sciences); **Mathematics Teaching** (Mathematics Education); **Physical Education** (Physical Education)

Centre
Network Information

History: Founded 1975.
Main Language(s) of Instruction: Chinese
Degrees and Diplomas: *Xueshi Xuewei*

Academic Staff *2012-2013*: Total: c. 700
Student Numbers *2012-2013*: Total: c. 18,000
Last Updated: 04/12/13

HUNAN INTERNATIONAL ECONOMICS UNIVERSITY (HIEU)

Lugu Development Zone, Chansha, Hunan 410205
Tel: +86(731) 8100988
Fax: +86(731) 8101999
Website: http://www.hunaneu.com/

Programme
Art and Design (Design; Fine Arts); **Aviation Services** (Air Transport); **Business Management** (Business Administration; Management); **Commerce** (Business and Commerce); **Computer Science** (Computer Science); **Electronic Engineering** (Electronic Engineering); **Foreign Languages** (English; Modern Languages); **Golf Management** (Sports Management); **Logistics Management.** (Transport Management)

History: Founded 1997.
Main Language(s) of Instruction: Chinese
Degrees and Diplomas: *Xueshi Xuewei*

Student Numbers *2012-2013*: Total: c. 27,800
Last Updated: 04/12/13

HUNAN NORMAL UNIVERSITY

36 Lushan Road, Yuelu Disctrict,
Changsha, Hunan Province 410081
Tel: +86(731) 88872245
Fax: +86(731) 88854711
EMail: oiec@hunnu.edu.cn
Website: http://www.hunnu.edu.cn

President: Liu Xiangrong
Tel: +86(731) 88872201 EMail: xzmail@hunnu.edu.cn

College
Chemistry and Chemical Engineering (Chemical Engineering; Chemistry); **Chinese Language and Culture** *(International)* (Chinese; Cultural Studies); **Educational Sciences** (Curriculum; Education; Educational Psychology; Educational Sciences; Educational Technology; Higher Education; Pedagogy; Preschool Education); **Fine Arts** (Design; Fine Arts); **Foreign Languages** (English; Japanese; Literature; Modern Languages; Russian); **History and Culture** (Cultural Studies; History); **Law** (Civil Law; Commercial Law; International Law; Law); **Liberal Arts** (Arts and Humanities; Chinese; History; Linguistics; Literature); **Life Sciences** (Biochemistry; Biological and Life Sciences; Biology; Botany; Genetics; Microbiology; Molecular Biology; Zoology); **Mathematics and Computer Science** (Computer Science; Mathematics); **Medicine** (Medicine; Nursing; Pharmacy); **Music** (Dance; Music; Musicology); **Physical Education** (Physical Education); **Physics and Information Science** (Information Sciences; Physics); **Polytechnic** (Design; Electronic Engineering; Fashion Design; Industrial Design; Mechanical Engineering); **Public Administration** (Administration; Demography and Population; Ethics; Philosophy; Political Sciences; Public Administration; Sociology); **Resource and Environment Studies** (Environmental Studies; Geography; Natural Resources); **Tourism** (Tourism); **Vocational Studies** (Clothing and Sewing; Electrical and Electronic Engineering)

School
Business (Administration; Economics; Finance; Management; Real Estate); **Journalism and Communication** (Communication Studies; Journalism)

History: Founded 1938 as National Teachers College, acquired present title 1984.
Main Language(s) of Instruction: Chinese
Degrees and Diplomas: *Xueshi Xuewei*; *Shuoshi Xuewei*; *Boshi*
Publications: Natural Science Journal of Hunan Normal University; Social Science Journal of Hunan Normal University

Academic Staff *2011-2012*	**TOTAL**
FULL-TIME	c. **1,000**
Student Numbers *2011-2012*	
All (Foreign included)	c. **32,000**
FOREIGN ONLY	**300**

Last Updated: 27/02/13

HUNAN UNIVERSITY

Yuelu District, Changsha, Hunan Province 410082
Tel: +86(731) 88821364
Fax: +86(731) 88821364
EMail: xiaoban@hnu.cn
Website: http://www.hnu.edu.cn/

President: Yueyu Zhao

College
Architecture (Architecture); **Chinese Language and Literature** (Chinese; Literature); **Civil Engineering** (Civil Engineering); **Electrical and Information Engineering** (Electrical Engineering; Information Technology); **Environmental Science and Engineering** (Environmental Engineering); **Finance and Statistics** (Finance; Statistics); **Foreign Languages** (English; Literature); **Information Science and Engineering** (Computer Engineering; Computer Science; Information Technology; Software Engineering; Telecommunications Engineering); **Journalism and Communication** (Communication Studies; Film; Journalism; Radio and Television Broadcasting); **Law** (Law); **Marxist Studies** (Political Sciences); **Material Science and Engineering** (Materials Engineering); **Mathematics and Econometrics** (Applied Mathematics; Econometrics); **Mechanical and Automotive Engineering** (Automotive Engineering; Mechanical Engineering); **Physical Education** (Physical Education)

School
Biology (Biological and Life Sciences; Biology); **Business Administration** (Accountancy; Business Administration; International Business); **Chemistry and Chemical Engineering** (Chemical Engineering; Chemistry); **Design** (Design); **Economics and Trade** (Business and Commerce; Economics); **Physics and Microelectronics** (Microelectronics; Physical Therapy)

Institute
Educational Sciences (Education; Educational Sciences)

Academy
Yuelu

History: Founded 926 as Yuelu Academy's Foundation. Reconstructed into Hunan Higher School in 1903. Merged with Hunan

University of Finance and Economics and renamed Hunan University, 1926.

Academic Year: September to July

Admission Requirements: Graduation from senior middle school

Main Language(s) of Instruction: Chinese

Degrees and Diplomas: *Xueshi Xuewei*; *Shuoshi Xuewei*; *Boshi*

Publications: Journal of Hunan University; Research of Higher Education for Mechanical Industry

Academic Staff *2011-2012*: Total: c. 4,600

Student Numbers *2011-2012*: Total: c. 30,000

Last Updated: 27/02/13

HUNAN UNIVERSITY OF ARTS AND SCIENCE

170 Dongting Road, Changde, Hunan Province 415000
Tel: +86(736) 7277716
Fax: +86(736) 7283046
Website: http://www.huas.cn

President: Li Dazhi

College

Chemistry and Chemical Engineering (Chemical Engineering; Chemistry); **Civil Engineering** (Civil Engineering; Construction Engineering; Town Planning); **Computer Science and Technology** (Computer Engineering; Computer Science); **Continuing Education**; **Economy and Management** (Economics; Management); **Electrical and Information Engineering** (Electrical Engineering; Information Technology); **Fine Arts** (Design; Fine Arts); **Foreign Studies** (English); **Furong**; **History and Culture** (Cultural Studies; History); **Law** (Law); **Life Science** (Biological and Life Sciences); **Mathematics and Computer Science** (Applied Mathematics; Mathematics; Mathematics and Computer Science); **Mechanical Engineering** (Automation and Control Engineering; Mechanical Engineering; Mechanics); **Music** (Music); **Physical Engineering** (Physical Engineering); **Physics and Electronics** (Electronic Engineering; Physics); **Tourism, Resources and Environment Science** (Environmental Studies; Natural Resources; Tourism)

History: Changed its title 2003, previously known as Changde Teachers College.

Main Language(s) of Instruction: Chinese

Degrees and Diplomas: *Xueshi Xuewei*

Academic Staff *2011-2012*: Total: c. 800

Student Numbers *2011-2012*: Total: c. 14,000

Last Updated: 27/02/13

HUNAN UNIVERSITY OF CHINESE MEDICINE

Xiangzui Rd. Hanpu Science & Education District, Changsha, Hunan Province 410208
Tel: +86(731) 88458266
Fax: +86(731) 88458261
EMail: hncstcm@hotmail.com; hukal2011@hotmail.com
Website: http://www.hnctcm.edu.cn/

President: Liao Duanfang

School

Acupuncture, Moxibustion and Tuina (Acupuncture); **Adult Education** (Cultural Studies); **Basic Medical Sciences** (Medicine); **Chinese and Western Medicine** (Medicine; Traditional Eastern Medicine); **Clinical Medicine** *(First)* (Medical Technology; Medicine; Otorhinolaryngology; Stomatology; Surgery); **Clinical Medicine** *(Second)* (Medicine; Ophthalmology; Osteopathy; Otorhinolaryngology; Surgery); **Continuing Education**; **Culture, Information Technology and Management** (Cultural Studies; Information Technology; Management); **Humanities, Information Technology** (Arts and Humanities; Information Technology); **International Education** (English); **Medicine** (Medicine; Rehabilitation and Therapy; Traditional Eastern Medicine); **Nursing** (Nursing); **Pharmacy** (Pharmacy; Traditional Eastern Medicine)

History: Founded 1934 as Hunan Chinese Medicine Specialization School, acquired present title 1960.

Main Language(s) of Instruction: Chinese

Degrees and Diplomas: *Xueshi Xuewei*; *Shuoshi Xuewei*; *Boshi*

Publications: Journal of Hunan College of TCM; Medicine Food Research

Academic Staff *2011-2012*: Total: c. 1,200

Student Numbers *2011-2012*: Total: c. 20,000

Last Updated: 27/02/13

HUNAN UNIVERSITY OF COMMERCE

569 Yuelu, Changsha, Hunan Province 410205
Tel: +86(731) 8869018
Fax: +86(731) 8882487
EMail: zsb@hnbc.com.cn
Website: http://www.hnuc.edu.cn

President: Tang Weibing

School

Accountancy (Accountancy; Finance); **Arts Design** (Advertising and Publicity; Communication Arts; Communication Studies; Design); **Business Administration** (Business Administration; Business and Commerce; Human Resources; Marketing); **Chinese Language and Literature** (Chinese; Literature; Publishing and Book Trade); **Computer and Electronic Engineering** (Computer Engineering; Electronic Engineering); **Finance** (Banking; Finance; Insurance); **Foreign Languages** (English; Modern Languages); **Law** (Civil Law; Commercial Law; Criminal Law; Law); **Public Administration** (Public Administration; Social Work); **Tourism Management** (Tourism)

Department

Physical Education (Physical Education)

Academy

Economy and Trade (Economics; International Business)

History: Founded by the merging of Hunan Commercial School and Hunan Business Management School. Formerly known as Hunan College of Commerce.

Main Language(s) of Instruction: Chinese

Degrees and Diplomas: *Xueshi Xuewei*

Last Updated: 28/11/12

HUNAN UNIVERSITY OF FINANCE AND ECONOMICS (HUFE)

139 Fenglin Road, Yuelu District, Changsha, Hunan 410205
Tel: +86(731) 88811032 +86(731) 88811907
Fax: +86(731) 88811907
EMail: hufe-728@hotmail.com
Website: http://www.hufe.edu.cn/

Department

Accounting (Accountancy); **Basic Knowledge**; **Business Administration** (Business Administration; Human Resources; International Business; International Economics; Marketing); **Engineering Management** (Engineering Management); **Finance** (Finance); **Foreign Languages** (Modern Languages); **Information Management** (Computer Engineering; Computer Science; Information Management); **Laws and Public Administration** (Law; Public Administration); **Physical Education** (Physical Education); **Political Theories** (Political Sciences)

History: Founded 1933 as Housheng Accounting Institute. Acquired present title 2010.

Main Language(s) of Instruction: Chinese

Degrees and Diplomas: *Xueshi Xuewei*. Also 3-year undergraduate diploma programmes

Academic Staff *2012-2013*: Total 531

Student Numbers *2012-2013*: Total: c. 10,000

Last Updated: 05/12/13

HUNAN UNIVERSITY OF SCIENCE AND ENGINEERING

Yang Zi Tang Road, 130, Lingling District, Yongzhou, Hunan 425100
Tel: +86(746) 6381425 +86(746) 6382796
Fax: +86(746) 6381287 +86(746) 6382796
EMail: fao_huse@aliyun.com
Website: http://www.huse.cn/

President: Chen Hong

Department

Chinese Language and Literature (Chinese; Literature); **Computer and Communication Engineering** (Computer Engineering; Data Processing; Telecommunications Engineering); **Foreign Language and Literature** (English; Literature; Modern Languages); **Information Technology and Education** (Educational Technology; Information Technology); **Law** (Criminal Law; History of Law; Law); **Mathematics and Computer Science** (Computer Science; Mathematics; Mathematics and Computer Science)

Main Language(s) of Instruction: Chinese

Degrees and Diplomas: *Xueshi Xuewei*

Last Updated: 05/12/13

HUNAN UNIVERSITY OF SCIENCE AND TECHNOLOGY

Shimatou, Yuhu District, Xiangtan, Hunan Province 411201
Tel: +86(732) 8290011 +86(732) 8291452
Fax: +86(732) 8291454
EMail: enghunan@126.com
Website: http://www.hnust.cn

President: Tian Yinhua

International Relations: Xiong Muqing, Director of Foreign Affairs Office

School

Adult Education and Vocational Technology (Adult Education; Vocational Education); **Architecture and Urban Planning** (Architecture; Town Planning); **Arts** (Fine Arts); **Business** (Business Administration); **Chemistry and Chemical Technology** (Chemical Engineering; Chemistry); **Civil Engineering** (Civil Engineering); **Computer Science and Engineering** (Computer Engineering; Computer Science); **Education** (Education); **Energy and Safety Engineering** (Energy Engineering; Safety Engineering); **Foreign Studies** (Modern Languages); **Human Studies** (Arts and Humanities); **Information and Electrical Engineering** (Electronic Engineering; Information Technology); **Law** (Law); **Life Science** (Biological and Life Sciences); **Mathematics and Computer Science** (Mathematics and Computer Science); **Physical Education and Sports** (Physical Education; Sports); **Physics** (Physics); **Technology** (Technology)

History: Founded 2003 following merger of Xiangtan Polytechnic University and Xiangtan Normal University.

Main Language(s) of Instruction: Chinese

Degrees and Diplomas: *Xueshi Xuewei*; *Shuoshi Xuewei*

Publications: Forum on Higher Education; Journal of Hunan University of Science and Technology; Journal of Hunan University of Science and Technology; Xiangtan Normal University; Xiangtan Normal University

Last Updated: 28/11/12

HUNAN UNIVERSITY OF TECHNOLOGY

Wenhua Road, Zhuzhou, Hunan Province 412008
Tel: +86(733) 8182936
EMail: hut4330@126.com
Website: http://www.hut.edu.cn

President: Wang Hanqing

Vice-President: Cao Xing Tel: +86(731) 22182185

College

Packaging Technology *(Zhongshan)* (Business Administration; Design; Marketing; Packaging Technology)

School

Industrial Design (Industrial Design); **International Education** (Chinese); **Law** (Law)

Department

Adult Education; **Civil Engineering** (Civil Engineering); **Communication** (Communication Studies); **Computer Engineering** (Computer Engineering); **Economics and Management** (Business and Commerce; Economics; Human Resources; Management); **Electronic Engineering** (Electronic Engineering); **Information and Computing Science** (Computer Engineering; Information Technology); **Mechanical Engineering** (Mechanical Engineering); **Packaging Technology and Printing** (Design; Packaging Technology; Printing and Printmaking); **Physical Education** (Physical Education); **Sciences** (Advertising and Publicity; Computer Science; Design; Fashion Design; Packaging Technology); **Social Sciences** (Social Sciences)

Institute

Foreign Languages (English)

History: Founded 1979 as Zhouzhou College. Became Zhuzhou Institute of Technology. Acquired present status 1986 and name 1989.

Degrees and Diplomas: *Xueshi Xuewei*; *Shuoshi Xuewei*

Academic Staff *2011-2012*: Total: c. 2,500

Student Numbers *2011-2012*: Total: c. 34,000

Last Updated: 28/02/13

HUNAN WOMEN'S UNIVERSITY (HWU)

160, Zhongyi Road, Changsha, Hunan 410004
Tel: +86(731) 82825950 +86(731) 82825012
Fax: +86(731) 82825950
EMail: faohwu@163.com
Website: http://www.hnnd.com.cn/

President: Luo Ting

Department

Accounting (Accountancy; Finance; Management); **Art and Performance** (Dance; Music; Music Education; Musical Instruments; Performing Arts); **Art Design** (Communication Arts; Design; Fine Arts; Textile Design; Visual Arts); **Continuing Education** (Business Administration; Home Economics; Nursing; Secretarial Studies); **Economic Management** (Economics; Human Resources; International Business; International Economics; Management; Marketing; Transport Management); **Education and Law** (Education; Law; Preschool Education; Social Work; Sports); **Foreign Language** (Applied Linguistics; English; Foreign Languages Education; Japanese); **Information Technology** (Computer Engineering; Computer Science; E-Business/Commerce; Information Management); **Literature and Media** (Chinese; Linguistics; Literature; Media Studies; Radio and Television Broadcasting; Secretarial Studies); **Physical Education Teaching** (Physical Education; Sports); **Tourism Management** (Air Transport; Hotel Management; Tourism)

Further Information: Also 11 Research Institutes and Centres

History: Founded 1985.

Main Language(s) of Instruction: Chinese

Degrees and Diplomas: *Xueshi Xuewei*

Academic Staff *2012-2013*: Total: c. 500

Student Numbers *2012-2013*: Total: c. 8,000

Last Updated: 05/12/13

HUZHOU TEACHERS COLLEGE

China Road, Huzhou, Zhejiang 313000
Tel: +86(572) 2321071
Website: http://www.hutc.zj.cn/

President: Hu Jian Zhang

Faculty

Fine Arts (Architectural and Environmental Design; Art Education; Communication Arts; Design; Fashion Design; Fine Arts; Industrial Design; Textile Design; Visual Arts); **Liberal Arts** (Advertising and Publicity; Arts and Humanities; Chinese; Journalism; Literature; Modern Languages); **Life Sciences** (Biological and Life Sciences)

School
Business Administration (Business Administration; E-Business/Commerce; International Business; International Economics; Marketing; Transport Management); **Medicine** (Medicine); **Nursing** (Nursing); **Science, Information and Engineering** (Automation and Control Engineering; Computer Networks; Computer Science; Electronic Engineering; Information Technology; Mechanical Engineering); **Social Development and Management** (Administration; Development Studies; History; Social Sciences; Tourism); **Teacher Education** (Educational Psychology; Educational Research; Educational Technology; Preschool Education; Primary Education; Psychology; Teacher Training)

Department
Physical Education (Physical Education; Sports); **Political Science** (Contemporary History; Modern History; Political Sciences)

Institute
Foreign Languages (English; Japanese; Modern Languages)

History: Founded 1915 as County Municipal Teachers Training Institute. Approved by the Ministry of Education. Merged with Huzhou Huzhou Normal School 1999 and with Huzhou Health School 2005. Acquired present status 2005.

Main Language(s) of Instruction: Chinese

Degrees and Diplomas: *Xueshi Xuewei*

Academic Staff *2012-2013*: Total 616

STAFF WITH DOCTORATE: Total 250

Student Numbers *2012-2013*: Total: c. 18,000

Distance students, 4800.

Last Updated: 05/12/13

HUZHOU UNIVERSITY

1 Xueshi Road, Huzhou, Zhejiang Province 313000
Tel: +86(572) 2321566
Fax: +86(572) 2321566
EMail: xcb@hutc.zj.cn
Website: http://www.hutc.zj.cn

President: Zhangjian Hu

School
Arts (Design; Music; Painting and Drawing); **Education Sciences and Technology** (Education; Educational Psychology; Educational Sciences; Educational Technology; Preschool Education; Primary Education); **Foreign Languages** (English; Japanese); **Humanities** (Chinese; History; Political Sciences); **Information Engineering** (Computer Science; Information Technology); **Law and Business** (Business Administration; E-Business/Commerce; International Business; Law; Tourism); **Life Sciences** (Chemistry); **Medicine** (Medicine; Traditional Eastern Medicine); **Physical Education** (Physical Education); **Sciences** (Mathematics; Physics)

History: Founded as Huzhou Teachers College 1958. Moved to its present campus site 1997. Acquired present title 1999.

Main Language(s) of Instruction: Chinese

Degrees and Diplomas: *Xueshi Xuewei*

Academic Staff *2011-2012*: Total: c. 14,000

Student Numbers *2011-2012*: Total: c. 4,000

Last Updated: 28/02/13

INNER MONGOLIA AGRICULTURAL UNIVERSITY

306 Zhaowu Dalu, Hohhot, Inner Mongolia 010018
Tel: +86(471) 4309331
Fax: +86(471) 4308933
EMail: imaulyb@imau.edu.cn
Website: http://www.imau.edu.cn

President: Changyou Li

International Relations: Lin Yubao

College
Agronomy (Agricultural Engineering; Agronomy; Horticulture; Plant and Crop Protection); **Animal Science and Medicine** (Animal Husbandry; Aquaculture; Veterinary Science); **Bioengineering** (Bioengineering; Biotechnology); **Computer Science and Information Engineering** (Computer Engineering; Computer Science; Information Management); **Ecology and Environmental Science** (Ecology; Environmental Studies; Rural Planning; Soil Science; Town Planning); **Economics and Management** (Agricultural Economics; Business Administration; E-Business/Commerce; Economics; Finance; Management); **Food Science and Engineering** (Food Science; Packaging Technology); **Foreign Languages** (English); **Forestry** (Forestry); **Forestry Engineering** (Forestry; Wood Technology); **Mechanical and Electrical Engineering** (Automation and Control Engineering; Electrical Engineering; Industrial Design; Mechanical Engineering); **Science** (Applied Chemistry; Statistics); **Social Sciences** (Administration; Law; Social Work); **Vocational Technology** (Accountancy; Agronomy; Business Administration; Civil Engineering; Computer Science; Finance; Food Science; Marketing; Tourism; Veterinary Science); **Water Conservation and Civil Engineering** (Architecture; Civil Engineering; Environmental Engineering; Hydraulic Engineering; Water Science)

History: Founded 1952 as Inner Mongolia College of Animal Husbandry and Veterinary Science, acquired present title 1999. Merged with Inner Mongolia Forestry College.

Main Language(s) of Instruction: Chinese

Degrees and Diplomas: *Xueshi Xuewei*; *Shuoshi Xuewei*; *Boshi*

Publications: Journal of Inner Mongolia Agricultural University; Resources and Environment in Arid Areas

Last Updated: 28/11/12

INNER MONGOLIA FINANCE AND ECONOMICS COLLEGE (IMFEC)

185 North Second Ring Road, Hohhot, Inner Mongolia 010070
Tel: +86(471) 3661025
Fax: +86(471) 651 2517
EMail: sunnyzhangyuping@163.com
Website: http://www.imfec.edu.cn/

President: Yamin Zhang (2006-)
Tel: +86(471) 366 1193 EMail: zym@imfec.edu.cn

College
Business (International Business; International Economics; Management; Marketing); **Business Administration** (Business Administration; Human Resources; Transport Management); **Finance and Taxation** (Finance; Taxation); **Foreign Language** (English; Modern Languages); **Humanities** (Chinese; Literature; Mongolian); **Statistics and Mathematics** (Applied Mathematics; Business Computing; Computer Science; Information Technology; Statistics); **Vocational Education**

School
Accountancy (Accountancy; Finance; Management); **Continuing Education**; **Economics** (Economics); **Law** (Commercial Law; International Law; Law); **Marxism** (Political Sciences); **MBA Education** (Business Administration); **Public Administration** (Public Administration); **Resources and Environment Economics** (Economics; Environmental Studies; Natural Resources)

Department
Physical Education (Physical Education)

Institute
Computer Information Management (Computer Networks; Computer Science; E-Business/Commerce; Information Management; Information Technology; Software Engineering); **Finance** (Finance); **International Education**; **Tourism Studies** (Cooking and Catering; Hotel Management; Tourism)

History: Inner Mongolia Finance and Economics College was founded in 1960. It started undergraduate education in 1979. Authorized to award Master's degrees in 2005.

Academic Year: September - December; March - June

Admission Requirements: Ranking in the top 10% of the national college entrance examination.

Main Language(s) of Instruction: Mongolian, Chinese

Accrediting Agency: State Education Commission of the People's Republic of China

Degrees and Diplomas: *Xueshi Xuewei*; *Shuoshi Xuewei*. Also MBA

Student Services: Academic Counselling, Canteen, Careers Guidance, Cultural Activities, Facilities for disabled people, Foreign Studies Centre, Health Services, Language Laboratory, Social Counselling, Sports Facilities

Publications: Journal of Inner Monglia College of Finance and Economics

Academic Staff *2011-2012*: Total 975

STAFF WITH DOCTORATE: Total 206

Student Numbers *2011-2012*: Total: c. 22,000

Last Updated: 28/02/13

INNER MONGOLIA MEDICAL UNIVERSITY (IMMU)

5 Xinhua Street, Huhhot, Inner Mongolia 010059
Tel: +86(471) 6965120 +86(471) 6967406
Fax: +86(471) 6965120
EMail: webmaster@immc.edu.cn
Website: http://www.immc.edu.cn

President: Du Mao Lin EMail: dumaolin1959@126.com

College

Medicine (Medicine); **Mongolia Medical Studies** (Medicine); **Nursing** (Health Sciences; Nursing)

School

Basic Medical Studies (Medicine); **Continuing Education**; **Foreign Languages** (English; Modern Languages); **Graduate Studies** (Medicine); **Pharmacy** (Pharmacy); **Public Health** (Public Health)

Department

Ideological and Political Theory Teaching and Research (Political Sciences); **Physical Education** (Physical Education)

Institute

Computer and Information Science (Computer Science; Information Sciences); **Health Administration** (Health Administration); **International Education** (Medicine)

Further Information: Also Ordos Branch 16 teaching units; 5 affiliated hospitals; 22 clinical teaching hospitals and 54 other professional practice teaching base in the region peripheral

History: Founded 1956.

Main Language(s) of Instruction: Chinese

Degrees and Diplomas: *Xueshi Xuewei*; *Shuoshi Xuewei*

Academic Staff *2011-2012*	**TOTAL**
FULL-TIME	**782**
STAFF WITH DOCTORATE	
FULL-TIME	**164**
Student Numbers *2011-2012*	
All (Foreign included)	c. **14,060**
FOREIGN ONLY	**80**

Last Updated: 28/02/13

INNER MONGOLIA NORMAL UNIVERSITY (IMNU)

Xincheng, Huhhot, Inner Mongolia 010022
Tel: +86(471) 4964444 Ext. 2515
Fax: +86(471) 4964887
EMail: help@imnu.edu.cn; Imast@vip.163.com
Website: http://www.imnu.edu.cn

President: Yang Yijiang

College

Chemistry and Environmental Science (Analytical Chemistry; Chemistry; Environmental Studies; Inorganic Chemistry; Materials Engineering; Organic Chemistry; Physical Chemistry; Science Education); **Geographical Science** (Computer Science; Geography; Geography (Human); Natural Resources; Rural Planning; Surgery; Town Planning); **Life Science and Technology** (Biological and Life Sciences; Biology; Biotechnology; Ecology); **Modern Design and Art** *(International)* (Communication Arts; Design; Fashion Design; Fine Arts; Interior Design); **Physics and Electronic Information** *(CPEI)* (Electronic Engineering; Information Technology; Materials Engineering; Optics; Physics; Science Education)

School

Foreign Language Education (English; Japanese; Modern Languages; Russian); **History and Culture** (Archaeology; Contemporary History; Cultural Studies; History; Humanities and Social Science Education; Management; Modern History; Museum Studies); **People's Armed Forces** (Hotel Management; Military Science; Nutrition); **Tourism** (Air Transport; Hotel Management; Music; Tourism)

Centre

International Exchange Service *(IESC)*

History: Founded 1952 as Inner Mongolia Teachers College, acquired present title 1982.

Main Language(s) of Instruction: Chinese and Mongolian

Degrees and Diplomas: *Xueshi Xuewei*; *Shuoshi Xuewei*; *Boshi*

Publications: Journal of Inner Mongolia Normal University

Academic Staff *2011-2012*	**TOTAL**
FULL-TIME	c. **1,500**
Student Numbers *2011-2012*	
All (Foreign included)	c. **30,000**
FOREIGN ONLY	**400**

Last Updated: 27/02/13

INNER MONGOLIA UNIVERSITY

235 West College Road, Huhhot, Inner Mongolia 010021
Tel: +86(471) 4992241 +86(471) 4992278
Fax: +86(471) 4992084
EMail: ndxcb@imu.edu.cn
Website: http://www.imu.edu.cn

President: B. LianJi Tel: +86(471) 4992238

College

Arts (Dance; Design; Music; Painting and Drawing); **Chemistry and Chemical Engineering** (Chemical Engineering; Chemistry); **Computer Science** (Computer Science); **Economics and Management** (Economics; Industrial Management; International Economics); **Electronic Information Engineering** (Information Technology); **Environment and Resources** (Ecology; Environmental Studies; Natural Resources); **Ethnology and Sociology** (Ethnology; Sociology); **Foreign Languages** (Modern Languages); **History and Tourism Culture** (Cultural Studies; History; Tourism); **Law** (Law); **Liberal Arts and Journalism** (Arts and Humanities; Journalism; Publishing and Book Trade); **Life Sciences** (Bioengineering; Biological and Life Sciences; Biology; Biotechnology); **Mathematics** (Mathematics); **Mongolian Studies** (Asian Studies; Mongolian); **Philosophy** (Philosophy); **Physical Science and Technology** (Physics; Technology); **Public Administration** (Public Administration); **Software** (Software Engineering); **Transportation** (Transport and Communications)

School

Chemistry and Chemical Industry (Chemistry; Industrial Chemistry); **Computer Science** (Computer Science); **Continuing Education**; **Economics** (Accountancy; Economics; Finance; Industrial Management; Management); **Foreign Languages**; **Humanities** (Chinese; History; Journalism; Literature; Philosophy; Tourism); **International Education**; **Law**; **Life Sciences**; **Mongolian Studies** (History; Journalism; Literature; Mongolian); **Professional and Vocational Education** (Civil Engineering; Engineering Management; Mechanical Engineering; Transport Engineering); **Public Management** (Management; Political Sciences); **Science and Engineering**

Institute

High Polymer Science; **Inner Mongolia Natural Resources** (Natural Resources); **Modern and Contemporary History**; **Mongolian Culture**; **Mongolian History**; **Mongolian Language**; **Neighbouring Countries**

Centre
Biological Engineering; **Experimental Animal Research** (Animal Husbandry; Veterinary Science; Zoology)

History: Founded 1957.

Academic Year: September to July (September-January; February-July)

Admission Requirements: School certificate

Fees: (US Dollars): 1,500-2,500

Main Language(s) of Instruction: Chinese, English, Mongolian

Degrees and Diplomas: *Xueshi Xuewei*: **Accountancy; Administration; Applied Chemistry; Automation and Control Engineering; Bioengineering; Biological and Life Sciences; Biology; Biotechnology; Chemical Engineering; Chemistry; Chinese; Civil Engineering; Communication Arts; Computer Science; Dance; Design; Ecology; Economics; Electronic Engineering; Engineering Management; English; Environmental Studies; Ethnology; Finance; History; Human Resources; Industrial Management; Information Management; Information Technology; International Business; International Economics; Japanese; Journalism; Law; Literature; Management; Mathematics; Mechanical Engineering; Mongolian; Music; Music Theory and Composition; Painting and Drawing; Performing Arts; Philosophy; Physics; Public Relations; Radio and Television Broadcasting; Russian; Singing; Social Sciences; Technology; Transport and Communications.** *Shuoshi Xuewei*: **Ancient Languages; Applied Mathematics; Artificial Intelligence; Asian Studies; Biophysics; Botany; Business Administration; Business and Commerce; Chinese; Civil Law; Commercial Law; Computer Engineering; Computer Science; Ecology; Economics; Electronic Engineering; Environmental Studies; Ethnology; History; Inorganic Chemistry; Linguistics; Literature; Management; Mathematics; Microbiology; Modern Languages; Operations Research; Organic Chemistry; Oriental Languages; Physical Chemistry; Physics; South Asian Studies; Zoology.** *Boshi*: **Applied Mathematics; Biochemistry; Biophysics; Botany; Ecology; History; Literature; Oriental Languages; Physics; South Asian Studies; Zoology.**

Student Services: Academic Counselling, Careers Guidance, Cultural Activities, Foreign Studies Centre, Health Services, Nursery Care, Sports Facilities

Publications: Journal of Inner Mongolia University

Last Updated: 29/11/12

INNER MONGOLIA UNIVERSITY FOR THE NATIONALITIES (IMUN)

22 Huolinhe Street, Tongliao, Inner Mongolia 028043
Tel: +86(475) 8282292 +86(475) 8282544
Fax: +86(475) 8232937
EMail: support@imun.edu.cn; nmgxiuquan@126.com
Website: http://www.imun.edu.cn/

President: Jiang Guishi Tel: +86(475) 8313367

International Relations: Liu Yunfeng

College
Computer Science and Technology (Computer Science; Information Technology); **International Exchange**; **Mongolia Medical Education** (Medicine); **Nursing** (Nursing); **Tourism and Aviation Services** (Air Transport; Management)

School
Adult Education; **Agronomy** (Agronomy); **Animal Science and Technology** (Animal Husbandry; Technology); **Chemistry and Chemical Engineering** (Chemical Engineering; Chemistry); **Economics and Management** (Economics; Management); **Education** (Education); **Foreign Languages** (English; Modern Languages); **Liberal Arts** (Arts and Humanities); **Life Sciences** (Biological and Life Sciences); **Marxism** (Political Sciences); **Mathematics** (Mathematics); **Mechanical Engineering** (Mechanical Engineering); **Medicine** (Medicine); **Physics and Electronic Information** (Electronic Engineering; Information Technology; Physics); **Political Sciences, Law and History** (History; Law; Political Sciences)

Department
Foreign Language (English; Modern Languages); **Physical Education** (Physical Education)

Institute
Media (Media Studies); **Mongolian Studies** (Asian Studies; Mongolian); **Physical Education** (Physical Education)

Academy
Fine Arts (Fine Arts); **Music** (Music)

History: Founded 1958 as Inner Mongolia College of Traditional Mongolian Medicine. Acquired present title and status 2000 following merger with Zhelimu Animal Husbandry College.

Degrees and Diplomas: *Xueshi Xuewei*; *Shuoshi Xuewei*

Last Updated: 27/02/13

INNER MONGOLIA UNIVERSITY OF SCIENCE AND TECHNOLOGY (IMUST)

7 Aerding Street, Kun District, Baotou, Inner Mongolia 014010
Tel: +86(472) 2107107
Fax: +86(472) 2124408
EMail: webmaster@imust.cn
Website: http://www.imust.cn

President: Lee Bao

School
Architecture and Civil Engineering (Architecture; Civil Engineering); **Art and Design** (Design; Fine Arts); **Arts and Law** (Arts and Humanities; Law); **Chemistry and Chemical Engineering** (Chemical Engineering; Chemistry); **Continuing Education**; **Economics and Management** (Economics; Management); **Energy and Environmental Engineering** (Energy Engineering; Environmental Engineering); **Foreign Languages** (English; Modern Languages); **Graduate Studies**; **Information Engineering** (Information Technology); **International Education**; **Marxism** (Political Sciences); **Materials and Metallurgical Engineering** (Materials Engineering; Metallurgical Engineering); **Mathematics and Biological Engineering** (Bioengineering; Mathematics); **Mechanical Engineering** (Mechanical Engineering); **Mining Engineering** (Mining Engineering); **Vocational and Technical Education**

Department
Physical Education (Physical Education)

Institute
Coal (Mining Engineering); **Rare Earth** (Earth Sciences)

Centre
Engineering Training (Engineering)

Research Centre
Technology (Technology)

Research Institute
Biological Engineering and Technology (Bioengineering; Biotechnology); **Higher Education** (Higher Education); **Mining and Metallurgical Engineering** (Metallurgical Engineering; Mining Engineering)

History: Founded 1956 as Baotou Iron and Steel Colleges. changed name to Institute of Baotou following merger with construction engineering schools 1958. Renamed Baotou Iron and Steel Institute 1960. Placed under governance of the Inner Mongolia Autonomous Region 1998. Acquired present title 2003.

Main Language(s) of Instruction: Chinese

Degrees and Diplomas: *Xueshi Xuewei*; *Shuoshi Xuewei*

Student Services: Sports Facilities

Academic Staff *2011-2012*: Total 1,400
Student Numbers *2011-2012*: Total 25,000
Last Updated: 27/02/13

INNER MONGOLIA UNIVERSITY OF TECHNOLOGY (IMUT)

221 Aimin Road, Huhhot, Inner Mongolia 010062
Tel: +86(475) 6510939
Fax: +86(475) 6503298
EMail: zsb@imut.edu.cn
Website: http://www.imut.edu.cn

President: Xing Yongmin

School
Architecture (Architecture); **Chemical Engineering** (Chemical Engineering); **Civil Engineering** (Civil Engineering); **Electrical and Power Engineering** (Electrical Engineering; Power Engineering); **Energy and Power Engineering** (Energy Engineering; Power Engineering); **Foreign Languages** (English; Modern Languages); **Humanities** (Arts and Humanities); **Information Engineering** (Information Technology); **International Business** (International Business); **International Education**; **Light Industry and Textile** (Industrial Engineering; Textile Technology); **Management** (Management); **Materials Science and Engineering** (Materials Engineering); **Mechanical Engineering** (Mechanical Engineering); **Mining** (Mining Engineering); **Science** (Natural Sciences); **Sports** (Sports)

Institute
Marxism (Political Sciences)

Centre
Engineering Training (Engineering)

Further Information: 3 campuses: Xincheng Campus, Jinchuan Campus and Junggar Campus; Also 54 research institutes

History: Founded 1951 as Inner Mongolia Engineering College on the basis of the Suiyuan Provincial Technical School. Initially under direct administration of the Ministry of Mechanical Industry and the Ministry of Agricultural Machinery, the college has been subordinated to Inner Mongolia Autonomous Region 1983. Acquired present title 1993.

Main Language(s) of Instruction: Chinese

Degrees and Diplomas: *Xueshi Xuewei*; *Shuoshi Xuewei*; *Boshi*. Also MBA

Publications: Journal of Inner Mongolia University of Technology

Academic Staff *2011-2012*	**TOTAL**
FULL-TIME	**1,430**

Student Numbers *2011-2012*	
All (Foreign included)	**27,000**
FOREIGN ONLY	**139**

Last Updated: 27/02/13

INSTITUTE OF DISASTER PREVENTION (IDP)

East Yanjiao, Beijing, Hebei 101601
Tel: +86(10) 61598807
Fax: +86(10) 61598807
EMail: international@cidp.edu.cn
Website: http://www.fzxy.edu.cn/

President: Bo Jingshan

Department
Disaster Information Engineering (Computer Education; Computer Engineering; Computer Networks; Computer Science; Information Technology; Multimedia; Software Engineering); **Disaster Prevention Apparatus** (Automation and Control Engineering; Electrical Engineering; Industrial Engineering; Telecommunications Engineering); **Disaster Prevention Engineering** (Construction Engineering; Engineering Management; Seismology); **Earthquake Science** (Geography; Geophysics; Information Technology; Seismology); **Economic Management** (Accountancy; Business Administration; Economics; Finance; Insurance; International Business; Management); **Foreign Language** (American Studies; English; English Studies; Modern Languages); **Fundamental Courses** (Chinese; English; Mathematics; Physical Education; Physics; Political Sciences); **Humanities and Social Sciences** (Advertising and Publicity; Arts and Humanities; Communication Arts; Design; Secretarial Studies; Social Sciences); **Physical Education** (Physical Education; Sports)

Graduate Department
Disaster Prevention Science and Technology (Geological Engineering; Geology; Geophysics; Safety Engineering; Seismology)

History: Founded 1975 as State Seismological Bureau. Upgraded into College of Seismology Techniques 1985. Renamed College of Disaster Prevention Technique 1992 and Institute of Disaster-Prevention Science and Technology 2006. Acquired present title 2009.

Main Language(s) of Instruction: Chinese

Degrees and Diplomas: *Xueshi Xuewei*; *Shuoshi Xuewei*: **Safety Engineering; Seismology.**

Academic Staff *2012-2013*: Total 418
STAFF WITH DOCTORATE: Total 30

Last Updated: 05/12/13

JIAMUSI UNIVERSITY

No.188 Xuefu Street, Jiamusi, Heilongjiang Province 154007
Tel: +86(454) 8781844
Fax: +86(454) 8793612
EMail: jmsu_icec@163.com
Website: http://www.jmsu.org/

President: Meng Xiangcai

College
Adult Education (Adult Education)

School
Applied Technology (Computer Science; E-Business/Commerce; Information Technology; Real Estate); **Architectural Engineering** (Architecture; Civil Engineering); **Basic Medicine** (Medicine); **Economics and Management** (Accountancy; Business Administration; International Economics; Management; Marketing); **Educational Sciences** (Educational Psychology; Educational Technology; Preschool Education); **ElectronicTechnology and Computer Science** (Computer Science; Electrical Engineering; Telecommunications Engineering); **Foreign Languages** (English; Japanese; Korean; Russian); **Humanities** (Chinese; History; Literature; Political Sciences); **Life Sciences** (Biological and Life Sciences); **Mechanical Engineering** (Agricultural Engineering; Industrial Design; Machine Building; Mechanical Engineering; Power Engineering); **Pharmaceutical Sciences** (Chemical Engineering; Pharmacology; Pharmacy); **Physical Education** (Physical Education); **Stomatology** (Stomatology)

Department
Materials Science and Engineering (Automation and Control Engineering; Materials Engineering; Metal Techniques; Metallurgical Engineering)

Academy
Fine Arts (Art Education; Design; Fine Arts; Painting and Drawing)

History: Founded 1947

Main Language(s) of Instruction: Chinese

Degrees and Diplomas: *Xueshi Xuewei*; *Shuoshi Xuewei*

Publications: Journal of Natural Sciences; Journal of Social Sciences

Last Updated: 29/11/12

JIANGHAN UNIVERSITY

18 Jiangda Road, Wuhan, Hubei Province 430010
Tel: +86(27) 82622241
Fax: +86(27) 82631533
EMail: jdwb@public.wh.hb.cn
Website: http://www.jhun.edu.cn

President: Yan Weidong

School
Art (Fine Arts); **Business** (Accountancy; Management; Tourism); **Chemistry and Environmental Engineering** (Chemical Engineering; Environmental Engineering); **Foreign Languages** (English; Literature; Modern Languages); **Golf** (Sports); **Health Technology** (Health Sciences); **Humanities** (Applied Linguistics; Chinese; Linguistics; Literature); **Life Sciences** (Genetics); **Mathematics and Computer Science** (Mathematics and Computer Science); **Medicine** (Medicine; Pathology; Surgery; Traditional Eastern Medicine); **Physical Education** (Physical Education); **Physics and Information Engineering** (Applied Physics; Automation and Control Engineering); **Politics and Law** (Law; Political Sciences)

History: Founded 1980. In 2001, it merged with HUST Hankou branch and Wuhan Worker's Medical College.

Main Language(s) of Instruction: Chinese

Degrees and Diplomas: *Xueshi Xuewei*

Publications: Journal of Jianghan University

Last Updated: 29/11/12

JIANGNAN UNIVERSITY (JU)

1800 Lihu Avenue, Wuxi, Jiangsu Province 214122

Tel: +86(510) 85913660 +86(510) 85913623 +86(510) 85913625

Fax: +86(510) 85913622

EMail: international@jiangnan.edu.cn

Website: http://www.jiangnan.edu.cn

President: Chen Jian Tel: +86(510) 85913660

International Relations: Zhong Fang, Director, International Office EMail: fzhong@jiangnan.edu.cn

College

Lambton (Accountancy; Business Administration; Computer Engineering; Computer Science; Information Management; Information Technology; Marketing; Telecommunications Engineering)

School

Art (Dance; Design; Fine Arts; Musicology); **Biotechnology** (Biological and Life Sciences; Biotechnology; Environmental Engineering); **Business** (Accountancy; Business Administration; Finance; Human Resources; International Business; International Economics; Tourism; Transport Management); **Chemical Engineering and Materials Engineering** (Applied Chemistry; Chemical Engineering; Materials Engineering; Polymer and Plastics Technology); **Chinese Language and Literature** (Chinese; Cinema and Television; Literature; Theatre); **Communication and Control Engineering** (Advertising and Publicity; Architectural and Environmental Design; Art History; Automation and Control Engineering; Communication Arts; Design; Electronic Engineering; Industrial Design; Information Management; Information Technology; Telecommunications Engineering); **Continuing Education and E-learning** (Accountancy; Administration; Bioengineering; Business and Commerce; Chinese; Computer Science; Food Science; Food Technology; Industrial Management; Information Technology; International Business; International Economics; Law; Literature; Management); **Design** (Advertising and Publicity; Architecture; Design; Industrial Design; Visual Arts); **Digital Media** (Computer Engineering; Computer Graphics; Computer Science; Design; Media Studies; Visual Arts); **Education** (Education; Educational Psychology; Educational Technology; Pedagogy; Primary Education); **Environmental and Civil Engineering** (Civil Engineering; Engineering Management; Environmental Engineering); **Food Science and Technology** (Animal Husbandry; Biotechnology; Food Science; Food Technology; Safety Engineering); **Foreign Studies** (English; Japanese); **Information Technology** (Computer Engineering; Computer Science; Information Management; Information Technology; Media Studies; Printing and Printmaking); **International Education** (Accountancy; Animal Husbandry; Applied Chemistry; Architecture; Automation and Control Engineering; Bioengineering; Biotechnology; Business Administration; Chemical Engineering; Chinese; Cinema and Television; Civil Engineering; Computer Science; Dance; Design; Electrical Engineering; Electronic Engineering; Engineering Management; English; Finance; Food Science; Food Technology; Industrial Design; Industrial Engineering; Information Sciences; Information Technology; International Business; International Economics; Japanese; Law; Linguistics; Literature; Materials Engineering; Mechanical Engineering; Media Studies; Nursing; Optical Technology; Packaging Technology; Pharmacy; Sociology; Telecommunications Engineering; Textile Design; Textile Technology; Theatre; Visual Arts); **Law and Politics** (Administration; Law; Political Sciences; Social Work; Sociology); **Mechanical Engineering** (Automation and Control Engineering; Mechanical Engineering; Packaging Technology); **Medicine and Pharmaceuticals** (Biochemistry; Microbiology; Nursing; Pharmacy); **Physical Education** (Physical Education; Sports); **Science** (Applied Linguistics; Applied Mathematics; Applied Physics; Computer Science; Information Sciences; Information Technology; Mathematics; Optical Technology; Optics; Physics); **Textile and Clothing** (Clothing and Sewing; Textile Design; Textile Technology)

History: Founded 1958 as Sanjiang Normal UNiversity. Renamed Wuxi College of Light Industry 1958 and Wuxi University of Light Industry 1995. Merged with Jiangnan College and Wuxi Teachers College. Acquired present title 2001.

Degrees and Diplomas: *Xueshi Xuewei*; *Shuoshi Xuewei*; *Boshi*: **Agricultural Engineering; Applied Chemistry; Automation and Control Engineering; Chemical Engineering; Environmental Engineering; Food Science; Food Technology; Information Technology; Leather Techniques; Marine Science and Oceanography; Natural Resources; Nutrition; Packaging Technology; Safety Engineering.**

Publications: Higher Education Research Report; Journal of Wuxi University of Light Industry

Academic Staff *2011-2012*	**TOTAL**
FULL-TIME	**1,568**
Student Numbers *2011-2012*	
All (Foreign included)	c. **30,000**
FOREIGN ONLY	**450**

Part-time students, 7,000. **Distance students,** 15000.

Last Updated: 27/02/13

JIANGSU NORMAL UNIVERSITY (XZNU)

101 Shanghai Road, Xuzhou, Jiangsu Province 221116

Tel: +86(516) 83403023

Fax: +86(516) 83403320

EMail: office@jsnu.edu.cn

Website: http://www.xznu.edu.cn

President: Ping Ren

International Relations: Guan Jidong

College

Chemistry and Chemical Engineering (Chemical Engineering; Chemistry); **Education Sciences** (Educational Sciences); **Electrical Engineering and Automation** (Automation and Control Engineering; Electrical Engineering); **Foreign Languages** (English; Modern Languages); **Historical Culture and Tourism** (Cultural Studies; History; Tourism); **Language Sciences** (Chinese; Modern Languages); **Law and Political Sciences** (Law; Political Sciences); **Liberal Arts** (Arts and Humanities); **Liberal Arts** (Arts and Humanities); **Mechanical and Electrical Engineering** (Electrical Engineering; Mechanical Engineering); **Physical and Electronic Engineering** (Electronic Engineering; Physics); **Urban and Environmental Sciences** (Environmental Studies; Urban Studies)

School

Continuing Education; **Economics** (Economics); **International Business** (International Business); **Life Sciences** (Biological and Life Sciences); **Management** (Management); **Marxism** (Political Sciences); **Media and Film** (Film; Media Studies); **Music** (Music)

Institute

Computer Science and Technology (Computer Science); **Mathematics and Statistics** (Mathematics; Statistics); **Physical Education** (Physical Education); **Surveying and Mapping** (Surveying and Mapping)

Academy

Fine Arts (Art Education; Design; Fine Arts; Painting and Drawing)

History: Founded 1957 as Jiangsu Teachers College. Moved to north Xuzhou and merged with Xuzhou Teachers College 1959. Renamed Xuzhou Normal University 1996. Acquired present title 2011.

Main Language(s) of Instruction: Chinese

Degrees and Diplomas: *Xueshi Xuewei*; *Shuoshi Xuewei*

Publications: Higher Education Research; Journal of Xuzhou Normal University

Academic Staff *2011-2012*: Total 1,365

STAFF WITH DOCTORATE: Total 34

Student Numbers *2011-2012*: Total 24,914

Last Updated: 25/01/13

JIANGSU POLICE INSTITUTE (JSPI)

Pukou District, No. 48 Shifosi Sannomiya, fff, Jiangsu 210031

EMail: info@jspi.edu.cn

Website: http://www.jspi.cn/

President: Wu Yue Zhang EMail: wyz@jspi.edu.cn

Faculty
Law (Law)

Department
Higher Education Research (Higher Education); **Ideological and Political Theory Teaching and Research** (Political Sciences); **Investigation** (Police Studies); **Police Sports Teaching and Research** (Physical Education; Sports); **Public Security Management** (Protective Services); **Public Security Science and Technology** (Protective Services); **Security Management System** (Protective Services)

Centre
Modern Educational Technology *(Campus Network Management Centre)* (Educational Technology)

Research Centre
Modern Policing (Police Studies)

Degrees and Diplomas: *Xueshi Xuewei*

Academic Staff *2012-2013*: Total 395

Student Numbers *2012-2013*: Total: c. 5,700
Last Updated: 05/12/13

JIANGSU UNIVERSITY

301 Xuefu Road, Zhenjiang, Jiangsu Province 212013
Tel: +86(511) 88792208
EMail: ieecisr@ujs.edu.cn
Website: http://www.ujs.edu.cn

President: Shouqi Yuan

Faculty
Civil and Mechanical Engineering (Civil Engineering; Mechanical Engineering); **Science** (Applied Mathematics; Computer Science; Mathematics; Physics)

College
Adult Education (Adult Education); **Teacher Training** (Teacher Training)

School
Humanities and Law (Arts and Humanities; Law); **Arts** (Design; Fine Arts; Industrial Design); **Automotive and Traffic Engineering** (Automotive Engineering; Road Transport); **Chemistry and Chemical Engineering** (Biochemistry; Chemical Engineering; Chemistry); **Computer Science and Telecommunications Engineering** (Computer Science; Telecommunications Engineering); **Electrical and Information Engineering** (Agricultural Engineering; Automation and Control Engineering; Biology; Biomedical Engineering; Electrical Engineering); **Energy and Power Engineering** (Energy Engineering; Power Engineering); **Environment** (Environmental Engineering; Environmental Studies; Marine Science and Oceanography; Safety Engineering); **Finance and Economics** (Accountancy; Economics; Finance; Insurance; International Business; International Economics; Statistics); **Food and Biological Engineering** (Bioengineering; Biotechnology; Food Science; Food Technology); **Foreign Languages** (English; Japanese; Linguistics); **Management** (Business Administration; Industrial Engineering; Management; Marketing); **Marxism** (Political Sciences); **Material Science and Technology** (Materials Engineering; Technology); **Medical Science and Laboratory Medicine** (Anatomy; Embryology and Reproduction Biology; Haematology; Histology; Immunology; Pathology; Pharmacology; Physiology); **Pharmacy** (Pharmacology; Pharmacy); **Teacher Education** (Education; Educational Technology; Teacher Training)

Further Information: Also College in Jingjiang.

History: Founded 1902 as Sanjiang Normal School. Acquired present status 2001 following merger of Jiangsu University of Science and Technology, Zhenjiang Teacher's College, and Zhenjiang Medical College.

Academic Year: September to June

Admission Requirements: Graduation from High School and HSK Certificate

Fees: (US Dollars): 1,800 per annum

Main Language(s) of Instruction: English, Chinese

Degrees and Diplomas: *Xueshi Xuewei*; *Shuoshi Xuewei*; *Boshi*. Also Post-Doctor Degree.

Student Services: Academic Counselling, Careers Guidance, Cultural Activities, Health Services, Nursery Care, Social Counselling, Sports Facilities

Publications: Journal of Jiangsu
Last Updated: 30/11/12

JIANGSU UNIVERSITY OF SCIENCE AND TECHNOLOGY

2 Huanchen Road, Zhenjiang, Jiangsu Province 212003
Tel: +86(511) 4401002
Fax: +86(511) 4421823
EMail: Office@just.edu.cn
Website: http://www.just.edu.cn/

President: Wu Liren
International Relations: Liu Wenfu

Department
Electronics and Information Sciences (Electronic Engineering; Information Sciences); **Engineering Management** (Engineering Management); **Mechanical Engineering** (Mechanical Engineering); **Naval Architecture** (Naval Architecture); **Social Sciences** (Social Sciences); **Welding and Materials Science** (Materials Engineering)

History: Founded 1933 as Shanghai Dagong Private Vocational School 1953 as Shanghai Shipbuilding School. Also previously known as Eastern China Shipbuilding Institute. Renamed Jiangsu University of Science and Technology 2004 following the merging of Jiangsu Jianghai Trade School in 1999 and Silkworm Industry Institute of CAAS in 2000.

Degrees and Diplomas: *Xueshi Xuewei*; *Shuoshi Xuewei*; *Boshi*
Last Updated: 30/11/12

JIANGXI AGRICULTURAL UNIVERSITY

Meiling, Nanchang, Jiangxi Province 330045
Tel: +86(791) 83813345
EMail: zhxm889@yahoo.com.cn
Website: http://www.jxau.edu.cn

President: Liu Yibei

International Relations: Wang Jinxiang

College
Engineering (Bioengineering; Chemical Engineering; Civil Engineering; Energy Engineering; Engineering; Environmental Engineering; Software Engineering); **Forestry** (Forestry); **Land Resources and Environment** (Rural Planning)

School
Agriculture (Agronomy; Horticulture; Plant and Crop Protection); **Animal Science and Technology** (Animal Husbandry; Aquaculture; Veterinary Science); **Economics and Trade** (Accountancy; E-Business/Commerce; Economics; Finance; International Economics; Management)

History: Founded 1940 as Agricultural School of the National Zhongzheng University. Acquired present title 1980.

Academic Year: September to July (September-January; February-July)

Admission Requirements: Graduation from senior middle school and entrance examination

Main Language(s) of Instruction: Chinese

Degrees and Diplomas: *Xueshi Xuewei*; *Shuoshi Xuewei*

Publications: Acta Agriculturae Universitatis Jiangxiensis; Jiangxi Plant Protection
Last Updated: 30/11/12

JIANGXI INSTITUTE OF FASHION TECHNOLOGY

Xiang Tang Ecnomic Development Area, Nanchang, Jiangxi 330201
Tel: +86(577) 0791 85055769

President: Chen Wanlong

Department
Apparel Accessories Arts (Textile Design); **Apparel Engineering** (Textile Technology); **Art Design** (Design; Fine Arts); **Clothing Commerce and Trade** (Business and Commerce); **Fashion Design** (Fashion Design); **Fashion Design and Management** (Management; Marketing)

Section
Common Teaching

History: Founded 1991. Acquired present status 2011. Formerly known as Jiangxi Institute of Clothing.

Main Language(s) of Instruction: Chinese

Degrees and Diplomas: *Xueshi Xuewei*

Last Updated: 06/12/13

JIANGXI NORMAL UNIVERSITY (JXNU)

Nanchang, Jiangxi Province 330027
Tel: +86(791) 8506180
Fax: +86(791) 8502744
EMail: iedept@sina.com
Website: http://www.jxnu.edu.cn

President: Mei Guoping (2011-)

College
Chemical Engineering (Chemical Engineering); **Communication Career Development Research Center** (Communication Studies); **Computer and Information Engineering** *(Computing Centre)* (Computer Engineering; Computer Science; Information Technology); **Education** (Education); **Elementary Education** (Primary Education); **Foreign Languages** (English; Modern Languages); **Geography and Environmental Science** (Environmental Studies; Geography); **Historical Culture and Tourism** (Cultural Studies; History; Tourism); **Liberal Arts** (Arts and Humanities); **Mathematics and Information Science** (Information Sciences; Mathematics); **Physics and Communication Electronics** (Electronic Engineering; Physics)

School
Business *(MBA Education Center)* (Business Administration); **Continuing Education**; **Finance** (Finance); **Life Sciences** (Biological and Life Sciences); **Marxism** (Political Sciences); **Psychology** (Psychology); **Science and Technology** (Natural Sciences; Technology); **Software** (Software Engineering)

Institute
International Education; **Physical Education** (Physical Education); **Politics and Law** (Law; Political Sciences); **Urban Construction** (Construction Engineering; Town Planning)

Academy
Fine Arts (Fine Arts); **Music** (Music)

Further Information: 3 campuses: Lake Yaohu Campus, Lake Qingshanhu Campus and Gongqing City Campus; 3 Post-doctoral research stations; c. 30 Research Institutes

History: Founded 1940 as hongzheng University. Changed name to Nanchang University 1949 and Jiangxi Normal Academy 1953. Acquired present status and title 1983. Merged with Jiangxi Banking School 2003. Under the jurisdiction of the Provincial Government.

Academic Year: September to July (September-January; March-July)

Admission Requirements: Graduation from senior middle school and entrance examination

Main Language(s) of Instruction: Chinese

Degrees and Diplomas: *Xueshi Xuewei*; *Shuoshi Xuewei*; *Boshi*

Publications: Study of Higher Education Administration; Study of Middle School Mathematics

Publishing House: University Printing House

Academic Staff *2011-2012*: Total: c. 1,860

Last Updated: 26/02/13

JIANGXI POLICE COLLEGE

Hing Wan Road, No. 1666, Xinjian County, Nanchang, Jianxi
Tel: +86(791) 88673013
Website: http://www.jxga.com/

President: Cheng Xiaobai

Department
Criminal Science and Technology (Criminology); **Economic Crime Investigation** (Police Studies); **English (Foreign Police)** (English; Police Studies); **Information Security** (Information Management); **Investigation** (Police Studies); **Law** (Law); **Law and Order** (Law; Police Studies); **Security Prevention Engineering** (Protective Services; Safety Engineering); **Sports** (Sports); **Transport Management** (Transport Management)

History: Founded 1951 as Jiangxi Public Security. Closed down between 1968 and 1972. Acquired present status and title 2010.

Main Language(s) of Instruction: Chinese

Degrees and Diplomas: *Xueshi Xuewei*

Academic Staff *2012-2013*: Total 322

Student Numbers *2012-2013*: Total: c. 2,100

Last Updated: 06/12/13

JIANGXI SCIENCE AND TECHNOLOGY NORMAL UNIVERSITY (JXSTNU)

Yuping W Street, Qingshanhu, Nanchang,
Jiangxi 330029
Website: http://www.jxstnu.cn/

President: Guo Jiezhong

Unit
Vocational Teacher Training Base (Vocational Education)

College
Art and Design (Design; Fine Arts); **Chemistry and Chemical Engineering** (Applied Chemistry; Chemical Engineering; Chemistry); **Communications and Electronics** (Electronic Engineering; Telecommunications Engineering); **Economics and Management** (Accountancy; Business Administration; E-Business/Commerce; Economics; International Business; Management); **Education** (Education); **Foreign Languages** (English; Modern Languages); **History and Culture** (Cultural Studies; History); **Law** (Law); **Liberal Arts** (Arts and Humanities); **Life Sciences** (Biological and Life Sciences); **Materials, Electrical and Mechanical Engineering** (Electrical Engineering; Materials Engineering; Mechanical Engineering); **Mathematics and Computer Science** (Computer Science; Mathematics; Mathematics and Computer Science); **Pharmacy** (Pharmacy)

School
Architecture and Engineering (Architecture; Structural Architecture); **Business** (Business Administration; E-Business/Commerce; International Business; International Economics; Marketing; Transport Management); **Music** (Music)

Department
Continuing Education

Institute
International Education; **Sports** (Sports); **Tourism Studies** (Tourism)

Research Department
Social Science (Social Sciences)

Further Information: Also 3 research institutes and departments

History: Founded 1977as Nanchang Branch of Jiangxi Normal University. Renamed Nanchang Teachers College 1984. Acquired present title 2012.

Main Language(s) of Instruction: Chinese

Degrees and Diplomas: *Xueshi Xuewei*; *Shuoshi Xuewei*: **Applied Chemistry; Business Administration; Chemistry; Dance; Design; Fine Arts; Music; Pharmacy; Vocational Education.**

Academic Staff *2012-2013*: Total 1,316

Student Numbers *2012-2013*: Total 1,316

Last Updated: 06/12/13

JIANGXI UNIVERSITY OF FINANCE AND ECONOMICS (JUFE)

169, East Shuanggang Road, Xialuo, Changbei District, Nanchang, Jiangxi Province 330013
Tel: +86(791) 3816418
Fax: +86(791) 3805665
EMail: oec@jxufe.edu.cn
Website: http://www.jxufe.edu.cn

President: Qiao Wang
Tel: +86(791) 83816602 EMail: xiaoban@jxufe.edu.cn

International Relations: Changhe Zhu, Coordinator, Office of International Cooperation and Exchange
Tel: +86(791) 83807960 EMail: jxguy@163.com

College
Modern Economics and Management (Economics; Management)

School
Accountancy (Accountancy); **Art** (Fine Arts); **Business Administration** (Business Administration); **Continuing Education**; **Economics** (Economics; Engineering Management; Real Estate); **Finance and Statistics** (Finance; Statistics); **Foreign Languages** (English; Modern Languages); **Humanities** (Arts and Humanities); **Information Management** (Information Management); **International Economics and Trade** (International Business; International Economics); **International Education**; **Law** (Law); **Marxism** (Political Sciences); **MBA** (Business Administration); **Physical Education** (Physical Education); **Software and Communication Engineering** (Software Engineering; Telecommunications Engineering); **Taxation and Public Administration** (Public Administration; Taxation); **Tourism and Urban Management** (Tourism; Town Planning); **Vocational Education**

Further Information: Also over 20 research institutes

History: Founded 1923 as School of Finance and Economics of Jiangxi Province. Merged with Jiangnan Cadres' Institute of Finance and Management. Acquired present title 1996.

Main Language(s) of Instruction: Chinese

Degrees and Diplomas: *Xueshi Xuewei*; *Shuoshi Xuewei*; *Boshi*: **Economics.** Also 4 postdoctoral programmes

Publications: Contemporary Finance; Journal of Jiangxi University of Finance and Economics

Academic Staff *2011-2012*: Total 1,395
STAFF WITH DOCTORATE: Total 478
Student Numbers *2011-2012*: Total: c. 39,000
Last Updated: 26/02/13

JIANGXI UNIVERSITY OF SCIENCE AND TECHNOLOGY (JUST)

86 Hongqi Avenue, Ganzhou, Jiangxi Province 341000
Tel: +86(797) 8312013
Fax: +86(797) 8312107
EMail: jxust@mail.jxust.cn
Website: http://www.jxust.cn

President: Ye Rensun

School
Materials and Chemical Engineering (Bioengineering; Chemical Engineering; Materials Engineering; Metallurgical Engineering); **Architectural and Surveying and Mapping Engineering** (Construction Engineering; Environmental Engineering; Rural Planning; Surveying and Mapping; Town Planning; Water Management); **Continuing Education**; **Economics and Management** (Accountancy; Economics; Finance; Information Technology; Management; Marketing; Real Estate; Software Engineering); **Foreign Studies** (English; International Studies; Japanese; Modern Languages); **Information Engineering** (Computer Networks; Computer Science; Optical Technology); **Liberal Arts and Law** (Advertising and Publicity; Arts and Humanities; Design; Industrial Design; Law; Media Studies; Political Sciences; Public Administration); **Mechanical and Electronic Engineering** (Automation and Control Engineering; Electronic Engineering; Industrial Engineering; Mechanical Engineering; Transport Engineering); **Resources and Environmental Engineering** (Environmental Engineering; Geological Engineering; Mineralogy; Mining Engineering; Safety Engineering); **Science** (Applied Mathematics; Computer Science; Information Technology; Mathematics; Natural Sciences; Sports); **Software** (Software Engineering)

History: Founded 1958 as Jiangxi Metallurgic Institute, acquired present name 2004.

Fees: (Yuan): c. 4,000 per annum

Main Language(s) of Instruction: Chinese

Accrediting Agency: Jiangxi Provincial Government

Degrees and Diplomas: *Xueshi Xuewei*; *Shuoshi Xuewei*; *Boshi*

Publications: Jiangxi University of Science and Technology Academic Periodical

Last Updated: 30/11/12

JIANGXI UNIVERSITY OF TECHNOLOGY (JXUT)

Jiangxi Yao Lake Park, Nanchang, Jiangxi 330098
Tel: +86(400) 1698888
Website: http://www.jxut.edu.cn/

President: Wang Hai EMail: zfwang@yahoo.com

College
Art and Design (Design; Fine Arts); **Automotive Engineering** (Automotive Engineering); **Information Engineering** (Computer Engineering; Information Technology); **Nursing** (Nursing)

School
Civil Engineering (Civil Engineering); **Management** (Management); **Mechanical Engineering** (Mechanical Engineering)

Department
Ideological and Political Theory Teaching (Political Sciences); **Science Teaching** (Science Education); **Sports** (Sports)

Institute
Culture and Media (Cultural Studies; Media Studies); **Finance** (Finance); **Foreign Languages** (English; Japanese; Modern Languages)

Academy
Music and Dance (Dance; Music)

Centre
Engineering Training (Engineering)

Further Information: Also 8 research institutes

History: Founded 1994 as a secondary vocational school. Became Jiangxi Southeast Training Institute 1996. Acquired present status and renamed Jiangxi Blue Sky University 2005. Acquired present title.

Main Language(s) of Instruction: Chinese

Degrees and Diplomas: *Xueshi Xuewei*

Student Services: Sports Facilities

Academic Staff *2012-2013*: Total: c. 2,000
Student Numbers *2012-2013*: Total: c. 46,000
Last Updated: 06/12/13

JIANGXI UNIVERSITY OF TRADITIONAL CHINESE MEDICINE

56 Yangming Road, Nanchang, Jiangxi Province 330006
Tel: +86(791) 6820664
Fax: +86(791) 6820664
EMail: jzied@163.com
Website: http://www.jxtcmi.com

President: Fu Ke Gang

Department
Acupuncture and Traumatology (Acupuncture); **Pharmacology** (Pharmacology); **Traditional Chinese Medicine** (Traditional Eastern Medicine)

History: Founded 1959.

Main Language(s) of Instruction: Chinese

Degrees and Diplomas: *Xueshi Xuewei*; *Shuoshi Xuewei*

Last Updated: 04/12/12

JIAXING UNIVERSITY (ZJXU)

56 Yuexiu Road (South), Jiaxing, Zhejiang Province 314001
Tel: +86(573) 83641233
Fax: +86(573) 83641210
EMail: yvetyin@126.com

President: Xu Xianmin EMail: sjxz@mail.zjxu.edu.cn

College

Adult Education (E-Business/Commerce); **Architectural and Civil Engineering** (Architectural and Environmental Design; Architecture; Civil Engineering; Management; Structural Architecture); **Biology and Chemical Engineering** (Bioengineering; Biology; Chemical Engineering; Environmental Engineering; Materials Engineering); **Business** (Accountancy; Business Administration; Finance; Human Resources; Marketing); **Economics** (Economics; Finance; International Business; International Economics); **Electromechanics Engineering** (Automation and Control Engineering; Electrical Engineering; Electronic Engineering; Industrial Engineering; Measurement and Precision Engineering; Mechanical Engineering; Production Engineering); **Foreign Languages** (English; Japanese; Modern Languages); **Garment and Art Design** (Design; Textile Design; Textile Technology); **Literature and Law** (Chinese; Foreign Languages Education; Law; Literature); **Mathematics and Information Engineering** (Applied Mathematics; Computer Science; Information Management; Information Sciences; Mathematics; Statistics); **Medicine** (Medicine; Nursing); **Nanhu** (International Business; International Economics)

Campus

Pinghu (Accountancy; Computer Graphics; English; Japanese; Preschool Education; Primary Education; Textile Design)

Further Information: Also Liangling campus

History: Created 2000 through merger of Jiaxing Junior College and Zhejiang Junior College of Economics.

Main Language(s) of Instruction: Chinese

Degrees and Diplomas: *Xueshi Xuewei*; *Shuoshi Xuewei*. Also 2-year specialized programmes; The Master's degree programmes are jointly offered with Changzhou University, Jiangxi University of Science and Technology, and Zhejiang Normal University.

Academic Staff *2011-2012*	**TOTAL**
FULL-TIME	**1,000**
STAFF WITH DOCTORATE FULL-TIME	c. **200**
Student Numbers *2011-2012*	
All (Foreign included)	c. **24,000**
FOREIGN ONLY	**100**

Last Updated: 26/02/13

JIAYING UNIVERSITY (JYU)

Meizigang, Eastern District, Meizhou, Guangdong Province 514015
Tel: +86(753) 2357776
Fax: +86(753) 2354276
EMail: fao@jyu.edu.cn
Website: http://www.jyu.edu.cn

President: Zhou Chi (2009-)

Department

Architecture (Architecture); **Biology** (Biology); **Chemistry** (Chemistry); **Chinese and Literature** (Chinese); **Computer Science** (Computer Science); **Economics and Finance** (Economics; Finance); **Electronics** (Electronic Engineering); **Fine Arts** (Fine Arts); **Foreign Languages** (Modern Languages); **Geography** (Geography); **Mathematics** (Mathematics); **Physical Education** (Physical Education); **Physics** (Physics); **Politics and Law** (History; Law; Political Sciences)

History: Founded 1913 as Jiaying Teachers College, acquired present title 1988.

Academic Year: September to July

Admission Requirements: Graduation from senior middle school and entrance examination

Main Language(s) of Instruction: Chinese

Degrees and Diplomas: *Zhuanke*; *Xueshi Xuewei*

Publications: Jiaying University Journal

Academic Staff *2011-2012*	**TOTAL**
FULL-TIME	**1,150**
STAFF WITH DOCTORATE FULL-TIME	**85**
Student Numbers *2011-2012*	
All (Foreign included)	**21,791**

Part-time students, 11,943.

Last Updated: 26/02/13

JILIN AGRICULTURAL SCIENCE AND TECHNOLOGY COLLEGE

Jilin Economic and Technological Development Zone, Jilin, Jilin 132101
EMail: www.jlnku.com@163.com
Website: http://www.jlnku.com/

College

Animal Science (Zoology); **Arts and Science** (Arts and Humanities; Natural Sciences); **Biology Engineering** (Bioengineering); **Chinese Medicine** (Traditional Eastern Medicine); **Economics and Management** (Economics; Management); **Food Engineering** (Food Technology); **Foreign Languages** (English; Modern Languages); **Information Science** (Information Sciences); **Mechanical Engineering** (Mechanical Engineering); **Plant Science** (Botany); **Veterinary Mecicine** (Veterinary Science); **Vocational and Technology Education** (Technology Education; Vocational Education)

Department

Civil Engineering (Civil Engineering); **Physical Education** (Physical Education); **Social Sciences** (Social Sciences)

History: Founded 1907 as a secondary school. Renamed as Agricultural School of Jilin Province 1953. Merged with North China University 2001 to form the North China Institute of Agricultural Technology university. Merged with Jilin Special College 2004 and upgraded into Jilin Institute of Agricultural Science and Technology.

Main Language(s) of Instruction: Chinese

Degrees and Diplomas: *Xueshi Xuewei*

Academic Staff *2012-2013*: Total 534

STAFF WITH DOCTORATE: Total 183

Student Numbers *2012-2013*: Total 11,246

Last Updated: 06/12/13

JILIN AGRICULTURAL UNIVERSITY (JLAU)

Changchun, Jilin Province 130118
Tel: +86(431) 4531646
Fax: +86(431) 4531646
EMail: info@jlau.edu.cn
Website: http://www.jlau.edu.cn

President: Qin Guixin (2008-)

College

Agricultural Economics and Management (Agricultural Economics; Agricultural Management); **Animal Science and Technology** (Animal Husbandry; Technology); **Chinese Herbal Medicines** (Alternative Medicine; Traditional Eastern Medicine); **Engineering and Technology** (Engineering; Technology); **Foreign Languages** (English; Modern Languages); **Humanities** (Arts and Humanities); **Life Science, Food Science and Engineering** (Biological and Life Sciences; Engineering; Food Science; Food Technology); **Marxism** (Political Sciences); **Resources and Environmental Sciences** (Environmental Studies; Natural Resources)

Department

Military Sports (Sports)

Institute

Horticulture (Horticulture)

Centre

Teaching and Management (Educational Administration; Teacher Training)

History: Founded as college 1948. Acquired present status and title 1959, incorporating previously existing agricultural colleges. Under the jurisdiction of the Provincial Government.

Academic Year: September to July (September-January; March-July)

Admission Requirements: Graduation from senior middle school and entrance examination

Main Language(s) of Instruction: Chinese

Degrees and Diplomas: *Xueshi Xuewei*; *Shuoshi Xuewei*; *Boshi*. Also 7 postdoctoral programmes

Publications: Higher Education Study; Journal of Jilin Agricultural University; Mycology Sinica

Publishing House: JAU Publishing House

Academic Staff *2011-2012*: Total 1,851

Student Numbers *2011-2012*: Total: c. 18,000

Last Updated: 25/02/13

JILIN ANIMATION INSTITUTE (JAI)

No.168 Boshi Road High-Tech Industry Development Zone, Changchun, Jilin 130012
Tel: +86(431) 87021971 +86(431) 87021917
Fax: +86(431) 87021913
EMail: jldh2000@sina.com
Website: http://www.jldh.com.cn/

President: Zheng Liguo

School

Advertisement (Advertising and Publicity; Business Administration; Design; Management; Marketing; Photography; Video); **Animation and Cartoon** (Painting and Drawing; Visual Arts); **Cutlutral Industry Management** (Art Management); **Design** (Design); **Foreign Languages Education** (English; Modern Languages); **Game** (Multimedia; Visual Arts); **Ideological and Political Theory Teaching** (Political Sciences); **Media Studies** (Media Studies); **Public Basic Education** (Arts and Humanities); **Television Drama** (Radio and Television Broadcasting)

Research Centre

Games Engineering (Software Engineering; Visual Arts)

Research Institute

Animation (Visual Arts)

Further Information: Also Shuangyang Campus

History: Founded 2000.

Main Language(s) of Instruction: Chinese

Degrees and Diplomas: *Xueshi Xuewei*

Academic Staff *2012-2013*: Total: c. 550

Student Numbers *2012-2013*: Total: c. 10,300

Last Updated: 09/12/13

JILIN BUSINESS AND TECHNOLOGY COLLEGE

1606 Haoyue Rd, Lvyuan, Changchun, Jilin 130062
Website: http://www.jlbtc.edu.cn/

President: Jian-Dong Yang

College

Bioengineering (Bioengineering); **Business** (Business Administration); **Food Engineering** (Food Technology); **Foreign Languages** (English; Modern Languages); **Taxation** (Taxation)

School

Business Administration (Business Administration); **Finance** (Finance); **Information Engineering** (Information Technology); **Tourism** (Tourism)

Department

Continuing Education; **Ideological and Political Theory Research and Education** (Political Sciences); **Sports** (Sports)

Institute

Higher Education (Higher Education); **Media Arts** (Communication Arts; Media Studies)

Centre

Modern Education and Information Technology (Education; Educational Technology; Information Technology); **Teaching Abilities Development** (Teacher Training)

Main Language(s) of Instruction: Chinese

Degrees and Diplomas: *Xueshi Xuewei*

Academic Staff *2012-2013*: Total 665

Student Numbers *2012-2013*: Total 13,413

Last Updated: 09/12/13

JILIN COLLEGE OF THE ARTS

11 Ziyou Street, Changchun, Jilin Province 130021
Tel: +86(431) 5643767
EMail: jlart@263.net
Website: http://www.jlart.edu.cn

Director: Chunfang Guo

Department

Dance (Dance); **Design** (Design); **Fine Arts** (Painting and Drawing; Sculpture); **Music** (Music); **Theatre** (Theatre)

History: Founded 1958 as Jilin Technological Academy of the Arts. Acquired present title 2000.

Main Language(s) of Instruction: Chinese

Degrees and Diplomas: *Xueshi Xuewei*; *Shuoshi Xuewei*; *Boshi*

Last Updated: 04/12/12

JILIN HUAQIAO FOREIGN LANGUAGES INSTITUTE

3658 Jingyue Street, Changchun, Jilin Province 130117
Tel: +86(431) 4533550 +86(431) 4533627
Fax: +86(431) 4533598
EMail: hqjilin@yahoo.com.cn
Website: http://www.huabridge.com

President: Yang Fan

School

Applied (English; Italian; Korean; Portuguese; Russian; Spanish)

Department

Chinese (Chinese); **German** (German); **Japanese** (Japanese)

History: Founded 1995.

Main Language(s) of Instruction: Chinese

Degrees and Diplomas: *Xueshi Xuewei*

Last Updated: 04/12/12

JILIN INSTITUTE OF ARCHITECTURE AND CIVIL ENGINEERING

27 Hongqi Road, Changchun, Jilin Province 130021
Tel: +86(431) 5935075
Fax: +86(431) 5914478
EMail: faojiae@public.jl.cc.cn
Website: http://www.jliae.edu.cn/newjliae/stylenew111.htm

President: Yin Jun

International Relations: Zhang Wei

Department

Architecture (Architecture); **Civil Engineering** (Civil Engineering); **Construction Engineering** (Construction Engineering); **Road and Highway Engineering** (Road Engineering); **Town Planning** (Town Planning)

History: Founded 1956.

Main Language(s) of Instruction: Chinese

Degrees and Diplomas: *Xueshi Xuewei*; *Shuoshi Xuewei*

Last Updated: 05/12/12

JILIN INSTITUTE OF CHEMICAL TECHNOLOGY

45 Chengde Street, Jilin, Jilin Province 132022
Tel: +86(432) 3093625
Fax: +86(431) 3093625
EMail: jhxy@public.jl.jl.cn
Website: http://www.jlict.edu.cn

President: Gao Weiping

Department
Automation Engineering (Automation and Control Engineering); **Chemical Engineering** (Chemical Engineering); **Chemical Equipment and Machinery** (Machine Building); **Environmental Engineering** (Environmental Engineering); **Fine Chemical Engineering** (Chemical Engineering)

History: Founded 1958 as Jilin Mechanical and Electrical Technological School, acquired present status and title 1978.

Main Language(s) of Instruction: Chinese

Degrees and Diplomas: *Xueshi Xuewei*
Last Updated: 05/12/12

JILIN MEDICAL COLLEGE (JLMU)

Jilin 5th Avenue, Jilin, Jilin 132013
EMail: jlyyxytsg@sina.com
Website: http://www.jlmpc.cn/

President: Suiwan Lin (2004-)

College
Basic Medical Studies (Medicine); **Clinical Medicine** (Anaesthesiology; Dermatology; Gynaecology and Obstetrics; Medicine; Ophthalmology; Otorhinolaryngology; Paediatrics; Pathology; Rehabilitation and Therapy; Surgery; Venereology); **Dental Imaging System** (Dental Technology); **Nursing** (Nursing); **Pharmacy** (Pharmacy)

School
Public Health (Public Health)

Institute
Humanities and Social Sciences (Arts and Humanities; Contemporary History; Educational Psychology; Ethics; Law; Modern History; Political Sciences; Social Sciences)

Academy
Laboratory Techniques (Laboratory Techniques)

Further Information: 465 affiliated hospitals

History: Founded 1952 as Liaoning Anshan Medical School. Renamed Air Force Health School 1961, Air Force Military School 1975, Air Force Medical College 1986, Fourth Military Medical University, Jilin Military Medical College 1999. Aquired present title 2004.

Main Language(s) of Instruction: Chinese

Degrees and Diplomas: *Xueshi Xuewei*

Academic Staff *2012-2013*: Total 568
Student Numbers *2012-2013*: Total: c. 9,000
Last Updated: 09/12/13

JILIN NORMAL UNIVERSITY

8 Shida Road, Tiexi District, Siping, Jilin Province 136000
Tel: +86(434) 3290040
Fax: +86(434) 3290363
EMail: wsc@jlnu.edu.cn
Website: http://www.jlnu.edu.cn/english/english/e11.htm

President: Zhang Baijun

College
Administration (Administration; Human Resources; Management; Public Administration); **Audiovisual Education** (Education); **Biology** (Biology); **Chemistry** (Chemistry; Inorganic Chemistry); **Chinese Language and Literature** (Chinese; Literature); **Computer Science** (Computer Science; Technology); **Economics** (International Business; International Economics); **Education** (Education; Preschool Education; Psychology; Teacher Training); **Environment Engineering** (Environmental Engineering); **Fine Arts** (Design; Fine Arts); **Foreign Languages and Literature** (English; Japanese; Literature; Modern Languages; Russian); **Information Engineering** (Information Technology); **Mathematics** (Mathematics); **Music** (Music); **Physical Education** (Physical Education); **Physics** (Physics); **Politics and Law** (Law; Political Sciences); **Tourism and Geography** (Geography; Information Technology; Tourism)

History: Founded 1953 as Siping Teachers College. Acquired present title 2002.

Academic Year: September to July (September-February; March-July)

Admission Requirements: Senior High School Graduation Diploma; international students have to pass the Chinese Certificate Examination (HSK); no certificate is required for language training students

Fees: (US Dollar): four years programme, 1,600 per annum; language training, 1,300 per annum; short programme (4 weeks), 200, plus 40 for each extra week

Degrees and Diplomas: *Xueshi Xuewei*; *Shuoshi Xuewei*
Last Updated: 05/12/12

JILIN POLICE COLLEGE

Changchun, Jilin 130000
Website: http://www.jljcxy.com/

President: Zhang Zhaoduan (2008-)

Programme
Applied English (Applied Linguistics; English); **Art Design** (Design; Fine Arts); **Chinese Language and Literature** (Chinese; Literature); **Computer Science and Technology** (Computer Engineering; Computer Science); **Financial Management** (Finance; Management); **Insurance** (Insurance); **Korean** (Korean); **Law** (Law); **Marketing** (Marketing); **Science of Investigation** (Police Studies); **Science of Public Security** (Civil Security); **Transport Management Engineering** (Transport Engineering; Transport Management)

Further Information: Jingyue and Leshan campuses

History: Founded 1949 as Jilin Province Public Security Cadre's School. Upgraded into Jilin Public Security Academy 1985. Renamed Jilin Public Security Academy 1993. Acquired present status and title 2010.

Main Language(s) of Instruction: Chinese

Degrees and Diplomas: *Xueshi Xuewei*

Academic Staff *2012-2013*: Total 306
Student Numbers *2012-2013*: Total: c. 6,000
Last Updated: 09/12/13

JILIN TEACHERS INSTITUTE OF ENGINEERING AND TECHNOLOGY

3050 Kaixuan Road, Changchun, Jilin Province 130052
Tel: +86(431) 2938664
Fax: +86(431) 2938664
EMail: baolong7@126.com
Website: http://www.jltiet.net

College
Business Management (Business Administration); **Clothing Engineering** (Clothing and Sewing); **Continuing Education** (Continuing Education); **Cultural Media** (Cultural Studies; Media Studies); **Electrical Engineering** (Electrical Engineering); **Fine Arts** (Fine Arts); **Food Engineering** (Food Technology); **Foreign Languages** (Modern Languages); **Information Engineering** (Information Technology); **Mechatronic Engineering** (Electronic Engineering; Mechanical Engineering)

Department
Basic Courses (Gender Studies); **Biological Engineering** (Bioengineering); **Foreign Languages** (Modern Languages); **Physical Education** (Physical Education); **Social Science**

History: Founded 1979 as Jilin Mechanics Normal University. Acquired present title 2002.

Main Language(s) of Instruction: Chinese

Degrees and Diplomas: *Xueshi Xuewei*; *Shuoshi Xuewei*

Publications: Journal of Jilin Teachers Institute of Engineering and Technology

Last Updated: 05/12/12

JILIN UNIVERSITY

2699 Qianjin Street, Changchun, Jilin Province 130012
Tel: +86(431) 5166571
Fax: +86(431) 5166570
EMail: dbliu@jlu.edu.cn
Website: http://www.jlu.edu.cn

President: Yuanyuan Li

Division

Agriculture (Animal Husbandry; Economics; Industrial Arts Education; Management; Plant and Crop Protection; Veterinary Science); **Arts and Humanities** (Arts and Humanities; Fine Arts; Modern Languages; Philosophy; Physical Education; Sociology); **Engineering** (Agricultural Engineering; Automotive Engineering; Biology; Engineering; Management; Materials Engineering; Mechanical Engineering; Transport and Communications; Transport Engineering); **Geosciences** (Construction Engineering; Earth Sciences; Natural Resources); **Health Sciences** (Dentistry; Medicine; Nursing; Pharmacy; Public Health); **Information Sciences** (Computer Engineering; Computer Science; Electronic Engineering; Information Sciences; Telecommunications Engineering); **Science** (Biological and Life Sciences; Chemistry; Mathematics; Physics); **Social Sciences** (Administration; Business and Commerce; Economics; Law; Social Sciences)

History: Founded 1946 as Northeast Administration Institute. Merged with Harbin University 1948. Became People's University 1950. Incorporated Jilin University of Technology (founded 1955), Norman Bethune University of Medical Sciences (founded 1939), Changchun University of Science and Technology (founded 1951) and Changchun Institute of Posts and Telecommunications (founded 1947) and acquired present status 2000.

Academic Year: September to July (September-January; February-July)

Admission Requirements: Graduation from senior middle school and entrance examination

Main Language(s) of Instruction: Chinese

Accrediting Agency: State Education Commission

Degrees and Diplomas: *Xueshi Xuewei*; *Shuoshi Xuewei*; *Boshi*

Publications: Chemical Research in Chinese Universities; Chemistry Journal for Institutions of Higher Learning; Higher Education Research and Practice; Jilin University Natural Science Journal; Journal of Demography; Journal of Historical Studies; Legal System and Social Development; Legality and Social Development; Mathematics of Northeast China; Modern Japanese Economy; Northeast Asia Forum

Publishing House: Jilin University Press

Last Updated: 05/12/12

JILIN UNIVERSITY OF FINANCE AND ECONOMICS

3699 Jingyue Street, Changchun, Jilin Province 130117
Tel: +86(431) 84539078
Fax: +86(431) 84539077
EMail: nic@jlufe.edu.cn
Website: http://www.ctu.cc.jl.cn/

President: Song Donglin

School

Accounting (Accountancy); **Applied Mathematics** (Actuarial Science; Applied Mathematics); **Business Administration** (Business Administration; Human Resources; Management; Marketing; Tourism; Transport Management); **Economics** (Economics); **Finance** (Accountancy; Finance; Insurance); **Foreign Languages** (Applied Linguistics; English; Japanese; Koran; Linguistics); **International Economics and Trade** (Business and Commerce; International Business; International Economics); **International Exchange** *(Jointly operated with Charles Sturt University, Australia)* (Accountancy; E-Business/Commerce; Finance; International Business); **Journalism and Media** (Journalism); **Law** (Civil Law; Commercial Law; Law); **Management Science and Information Engineering** (Computer Science; E-Business/Commerce; Engineering Management; Information Management); **Public Administration** (Agricultural Economics; Agricultural Management; Labour and Industrial Relations; Public Administration); **Statistics** (Economics; Statistics); **Taxation** (Finance; Taxation)

History: Founded 1948 as Northeast Bank College, became Changchun Taxation College 1992 and acquired current title 2010.

Degrees and Diplomas: *Xueshi Xuewei*; *Shuoshi Xuewei*

Last Updated: 26/08/13

JIMEI UNIVERSITY (JMU)

Jimei Schools Village, 185 Yinjiang Rd., Jimei District, Xiamen, Fujian Province 361021
Tel: +86(592) 6181097
Fax: +86(592) 6180120
EMail: faojmu@jmu.edu.cn
Website: http://www.jmu.edu.cn

President: Wenjin Su

College

Arts (Art Education; Design; Fine Arts; Music); **Bioengineering** (Bioengineering; Environmental Engineering; Food Science; Food Technology; Microbiology); **Computer Science & Engineering** (Computer Science; Software Engineering); **Fisheries** (Aquaculture; Fishery); **Information Engineering** (Computer Science; Electronic Engineering; Information Management; Information Technology); **Mechanical Engineering** (Mechanical Engineering; Thermal Engineering); **Physical Education** (Physical Education; Sports); **Science** (Applied Physics; Geography; Information Management; Mathematics); **Teacher Training** (Educational Technology; Pedagogy; Teacher Training)

School

Business Administration (Accountancy; Business Administration; Information Management; Marketing; Tourism); **Computer Science and Engineering**; **Foreign Languages** (English; Japanese); **Foreign Languages** (English; Japanese); **Political Science and Law** (Law; Political Sciences; Social Work)

Institute

Finance and Economics (Accountancy; Banking; Economics; Finance; Taxation); **Marine Engineering** (Marine Engineering; Naval Architecture); **Navigation** (Marine Transport; Nautical Science; Transport Engineering)

History: Founded 1913 as Jimei Normal School. Acquired present title 1994 following merger between Jimei Navigation Institute, Xiamen Fisheries College, Fujian Physical Education College, Finance and Economics Institute of Fujian and Jimei Teachers College.

Academic Year: September to July

Main Language(s) of Instruction: Chinese

Degrees and Diplomas: *Xueshi Xuewei*; *Shuoshi Xuewei*

Student Services: Canteen, Cultural Activities, Health Services, Language Laboratory, Sports Facilities

Publications: Journal of Jimei University

Last Updated: 05/12/12

JINAN UNIVERSITY

Shipai, Guangzhou, Guangdong Province 510632
Tel: +86(20) 85220085
Fax: +86(20) 85221395
EMail: omba@jnu.edu.cn
Website: http://www.jnu.edu.cn

President: Hu Jun

College

Tourism *(Shenzhen)* (Tourism); **Arts** (Cinema and Television; Fine Arts; Music); **Chinese Language and Culture** (Chinese; Cultural Studies; Linguistics); **Economics** (Economics; Finance; Information Management; International Business; International Economics; Law; Taxation); **Economics** (Economics; Finance; International Business; International Economics; Statistics; Taxation); **Education** (Adult Education); **Electrical & Information** (Automation and Control Engineering; Computer Science; Electrical Engineering; Information

Technology; Packaging Technology; Software Engineering); **Foreign Studies** (English; Japanese; Linguistics; Literature; Modern Languages); **Information Science and Technology** (Computer Networks; Computer Science; Electronic Engineering; Information Management; Information Technology; Mathematics; Software Engineering); **Intellectual Property** (American Studies; Cultural Studies; International Relations; Political Sciences; Southeast Asian Studies); **Journalism and Communication** (Advertising and Publicity; Journalism; Radio and Television Broadcasting); **Liberal Arts** (Chinese; History; Literature); **Life Science and Technology** (Analytical Chemistry; Bioengineering; Biology; Biomedical Engineering; Chemistry; Ecology; Genetics; Immunology; Microbiology; Molecular Biology; Organic Chemistry; Zoology); **Pharmacy** (Biomedical Engineering; Pharmacy; Traditional Eastern Medicine); **Science and Engineering** (Architecture; Civil Engineering; Environmental Engineering; Environmental Studies; Food Science; Materials Engineering; Mechanical Engineering; Optical Technology; Physics)

School

Humanities (Administration; Advertising and Publicity; Chinese; Journalism; Law; Literature); **International Business** (Business Administration; Finance; International Business; International Economics; Marketing); **Law** (Administrative Law; Civil Law; Commercial Law; Constitutional Law; Criminal Law; International Law); **Management** (Accountancy; Business Administration; Management; Marketing; Public Administration; Tourism); **Medicine** (Haematology; Medicine; Nursing; Ophthalmology; Stomatology); **Translation Studies** (Translation and Interpretation)

Further Information: Also Teaching Hospital

History: Founded 1906 as Jinan School. Became university 1927. Mainly opened to Chinese students coming from abroad, to students from Hong Kong, Macau, Taiwan, and Chinese students of foreign nationality.

Academic Year: September to July (September-January; February-July)

Admission Requirements: Graduation from senior middle school and entrance examination

Main Language(s) of Instruction: Chinese

Accrediting Agency: Office of Overseas Chinese Affairs of the State Council; State Education Commission

Degrees and Diplomas: *Xueshi Xuewei*; *Shuoshi Xuewei*; *Boshi*

Publications: Chinese Pathology and Pathophysiology Periodical; Jinan Education; Journal of Jinan University; Southeast Asian Studies

Last Updated: 14/12/12

JINGCHU UNIVERSITY OF TECHNOLOGY (JUT)

Xiangshan Road 33, Jingmen, Hubei 448000
Website: http://www.jcut.edu.cn/

President: Wu Linzhang

College

Adult Education; **Biological Engineering** (Bioengineering); **Computer Engineering** (Computer Engineering); **Economics and Management** (Economics); **Electronic and Information Engineering** (Electronic Engineering; Information Technology); **Foreign Languages** (English; Modern Languages); **Humanities and Social Sciences** (Arts and Humanities; Social Sciences); **Mathematics** (Mathematics); **Mechanical Engineering** (Mechanical Engineering); **Teachers** (Teacher Training)

School

Medicine (Medicine)

Department

Sports (Sports)

Institute

Art (Fine Arts); **Chemical and Pharmaceutical Studies** (Chemistry; Pharmacology); **International Studies**; **New Rural Technology** (Agricultural Equipment)

Main Language(s) of Instruction: Chinese

Degrees and Diplomas: *Xueshi Xuewei*

Academic Staff *2012-2013*: Total: c. 1,000

Student Numbers *2012-2013*: Total: c. 18,000

Last Updated: 09/12/13

JINGDEZHEN CERAMIC INSTITUTE

Eastern Suburb, Jingdezhen, Jiangxi Province 333001
Tel: +86(798) 8449200
Fax: +86(798) 8441837
EMail: oyxscn@vip.sina.com
Website: http://www.jci.edu.cn

President: Chou Jianer

School

Art and Design (Archaeology; Ceramic Art; Design; Fine Arts; Industrial Design; Sculpture); **Business Administration** (Business Administration; E-Business/Commerce; Finance; Marketing); **Information Engineering** (Computer Science); **Materials Science and Engineering** (Environmental Engineering; Materials Engineering); **Mechanical and Electronic Engineering** (Automation and Control Engineering; Electronic Engineering; Mechanical Engineering; Microelectronics)

Department

Foreign Languages (English; Japanese; Modern Languages); **Physical Education** (Physical Education); **Social Sciences** (Aesthetics; Literature; Political Sciences; Social Sciences); **Thermal Engineering** (Thermal Engineering)

Institute

Science & Technology and Art (Administration; Engineering; Fine Arts; Law; Modern Languages)

History: Founded 1909 as School of Ceramics. Acquired present status and title 1958.

Main Language(s) of Instruction: Chinese

Degrees and Diplomas: *Xueshi Xuewei*; *Shuoshi Xuewei*

Last Updated: 14/12/12

JINGGANGSHAN UNIVERSITY

Academy Road, 28, Tsing district, Ji'an, Jiangxi 343009
Tel: +86(796) 8103282
Website: http://www.jgsu.edu.cn/

President: Zhang Taicheng

College

Architecture and Engineering (Architecture; Civil Engineering); **Chemistry and Chemical Engineering** (Chemical Engineering; Chemistry); **Clinical Medicine** (Medicine); **Commercial Studies** (Business Administration; Economics); **Education** (Education); **Electronic and Information Engineering** (Computer Science; Electronic Engineering; Information Technology); **Foreign Languages** (English; Foreign Languages Education; Modern Languages); **Humanities** (Arts and Humanities; Chinese; History; Journalism); **Life Sciences** (Biological and Life Sciences); **Mathematics** (Mathematics; Physics); **Mechanical Engineering** (Automation and Control Engineering; Biomedical Engineering; Electrical and Electronic Engineering; Electrical Engineering; Mechanical Engineering; Production Engineering); **Medicine** (Medicine; Oral Pathology; Pathology); **National Defense** (Military Science); **Nursing** (Nursing)

School

Marxism (Political Sciences); **Political Science and Law** (Law; Political Sciences; Social Work)

Institute

Art (Fine Arts; Music); **Sports** (Physical Education)

Academy

Training

Further Information: Affiliated Hospital

History: Jinggangshan Normal College, Jinggangshan Medical College and Technical College merged to form Jinggangshan College. Acquired present title 2007.

Main Language(s) of Instruction: Chinese

Degrees and Diplomas: *Xueshi Xuewei*; *Shuoshi Xuewei*: **Social Work.**

Academic Staff *2012-2013*: Total 1,092

Student Numbers *2012-2013*: Total: c. 17,000

Last Updated: 09/12/13

JINING MEDICAL COLLEGE (JNMC)

Hehua Road 16, Beihu New District,
Jining, Shandong Province 272067
Tel: +86(537) 3616022
Fax: +86(537) 3616777
EMail: admin@jiningmedicalcollege.com
Website: http://www.jnmc.edu.cn

President: Bai Bo

International Relations: Qin Jianzhong

School

Basic Medicine (Medicine); **Clinical Medicine** (Medicine); **Continuing Education**; **Information Engineering** (Information Technology); **Management** (Management); **Mental Health** (Psychiatry and Mental Health); **Nursing** (Nursing); **Pharmacy** (Pharmacy); **Public Health** (Public Health)

Department

Biological Sciences (Biological and Life Sciences); **Foreign Language Teaching** (English; Foreign Languages Education; Modern Languages); **Medical Imaging** (Medical Technology); **Social Sciences** (Social Sciences); **Stomatology** (Stomatology)

Further Information: Also Rizhao campus

History: Founded 1952 as Jining Secondary Medical Practitioner School, acquired present status and name 1987.

Main Language(s) of Instruction: Chinese

Degrees and Diplomas: *Xueshi Xuewei*; *Shuoshi Xuewei*

Academic Staff *2011-2012*: Total: c. 598

Student Numbers *2011-2012*: Total: c. 13,500

Last Updated: 25/02/13

JINING TEACHERS COLLEGE

Wulanchabu Street 59, Jining, Inner Mongolia
EMail: jnszwlzx@163.Com; jnszxcb@163.com
Website: http://www.jntc.nm.cn/

President: Tan Fugui

Department

Biology (Political Sciences); **Chemistry** (Chemistry); **Chinese** *(Zheng Shiji)* (Chinese); **Computer Science** (Computer Science); **Fine Arts** (Fine Arts); **Foreign Languages** (English; Modern Languages); **Ideological and Political** (Political Sciences); **Mathematics** (Mathematics); **Mongolian** (Mongolian); **Music** (Music); **Physical Education** (Physical Education); **Physics** (Physics); **School Teachers Training** (Primary Education)

Main Language(s) of Instruction: Chinese

Degrees and Diplomas: *Xueshi Xuewei*

Academic Staff *2012-2013*: Total 495

Student Numbers *2012-2013*: Total: c. 10,022

Last Updated: 09/12/13

JINING UNIVERSITY

Xingtan Road, 1, Shandong, Qufu 273155
Tel: +86(537) 3196001
EMail: xcb@jnxy.edu.cn
Website: http://www.jnxy.edu.cn/

President: Lvling Chang

School

Primary Education (Primary Education)

Department

Chemistry and Chemical Engineering (Chemical Engineering; Chemistry); **Chinese** (Chinese; Literature); **Computer Science** (Computer Science); **Culture and Communication** (Communication Studies; Cultural Studies); **Economics and Management** (Economics; Management); **Education** (Education); **Fine Arts** (Fine Arts); **Foreign Language Teaching** (Foreign Languages Education); **Foreign Languages** (English; Modern Languages); **Life Sciences and Engineering** (Bioengineering; Biological and Life Sciences); **Mathematics** (Mathematics); **Music** (Music); **Physical Education** (Physical Education); **Physics and Information Engineering** (Information Technology; Physics); **Social Sciences** (Social Sciences)

History: Founded 1951 as Jining Teachers College. Acquired present title and status 2007.

Main Language(s) of Instruction: Chinese

Degrees and Diplomas: *Xueshi Xuewei*

Academic Staff *2012-2013*: Total 826

STAFF WITH DOCTORATE: Total 52

Student Numbers *2012-2013*: Total 15,055

Last Updated: 10/12/13

JINLING INSTITUTE OF TECHNOLOGY (JIT)

99 Hongjing Ave, Jiangning District, Nanjing, Jiangsu 211169
Tel: +86(25) 86188966
Fax: +86(25) 86188966
EMail: zjc@jit.edu.cn
Website: http://www.jit.edu.cn/

President: Ying Nie EMail: xzxx@jit.edu.cn

Faculty

International Education

College

Further Education; **Longpan**

School

Animal Science and Technology (Zoology); **Architecture Engineering** (Architecture; Civil Engineering; Structural Architecture); **Arts** (Design; Fashion Design; Fine Arts; Visual Arts); **Business** (Accountancy; Business Administration; Economics; Finance; International Business; International Economics; Management; Marketing; Transport Management); **Computer Science and Technology** (Computer Engineering; Computer Networks; Computer Science; Educational Technology; Electronic Engineering; Information Technology; Software Engineering; Telecommunications Engineering); **Foreign Languages** (English; Modern Languages); **Horticulture** (Agricultural Engineering; Agriculture; Biotechnology; Horticulture; Landscape Architecture); **Humanities and Social Sciences** (Arts and Humanities; Literature; Public Administration; Secretarial Studies; Social Sciences; Tourism); **Ideology and Politics Teaching** (Political Sciences); **Materials Engineering** (Materials Engineering); **Mechanical and Electrical Engineering** (Automation and Control Engineering; Automotive Engineering; Electrical Engineering; Mechanical Engineering)

Department

Fundamental Courses

Further Information: Also Mufu and Baixia Campus

History: Founded 2002 following merger of Nanjing Polytechnic University and Nanjing Agricultural College.

Main Language(s) of Instruction: Chinese

Degrees and Diplomas: *Xueshi Xuewei*

Academic Staff *2012-2013*: Total: c. 900

Student Numbers *2012-2013*: Total: c. 19,000

Last Updated: 10/12/13

JINZHONG UNIVERSITY

Yuci Yuen Street, Jinzhong, Shanxi 030600
EMail: jzxy@sxjztc.edu.cn
Website: http://www.sxjztc.edu.cn/

President: Sun Jianzhong

College

Foreign Languages (English; Modern Languages); **Liberal Arts** (Arts and Humanities; Journalism; Literature; Writing); **Vocational and Technical Education** (Technology Education; Vocational Education)

School

Biological Science and Technology (Biological and Life Sciences; Biotechnology); **Chemistry and Chemical Engineering** (Chemical Engineering; Chemistry); **Computer Science and Technology** (Computer Engineering; Computer Networks; Computer Science;

Software Engineering); **Economics and Management** (Economics; Management); **Education Science and Technology** (Education; Educational Technology); **Mathematics** (Applied Mathematics; Information Sciences; Mathematics; Mathematics and Computer Science); **Mechanical Engineering** (Automation and Control Engineering; Electronic Engineering; Mechanical Engineering; Production Engineering); **Music** (Dance; Music; Musical Instruments; Singing); **Physics and Electronic Engineering** (Electronic Engineering; Physics); **Politics and History** (History; Political Sciences); **Tourism Management** (Management; Tourism)

Department
Continuing Education; **Distance Education**

Institute
Public Administration (Public Administration); **Sports** (Sports)

Academy
Fine Arts (Architectural and Environmental Design; Design; Fine Arts)

History: Founded 1958. Closed down between 1962 and 1978. Merged with Jinzhong College of Education to form regional Jinzhong Teachers College 1998.

Main Language(s) of Instruction: Chinese

Degrees and Diplomas: *Xueshi Xuewei*

Academic Staff *2012-2013*: Total 732

STAFF WITH DOCTORATE: Total 30

Student Numbers *2012-2013*: Total: c. 12,000

Distance students, 7000.

Last Updated: 10/12/13

JISHOU UNIVERSITY (JSU)

120, South Renmin Road, Jishou, Hunan Province 416000
Tel: +86(743) 8551001
Fax: +86(743) 8551001
EMail: XYZH@jsu.edu.cn; office@jsu.edu.cn
Website: http://www.jsu.edu.cn

President: You Jun EMail: president@jsu.edu.cn

College
Adult Education; **Business** (Business Administration); **Chemistry and Industrial Chemistry** (Chemistry; Industrial Chemistry); **Foreign Languages** (English; Modern Languages); **International Exchange**; **Literature and Journalism** (Journalism; Literature); **Living resources and Environment Science** (Environmental Studies; Natural Resources); **Mathematics and Computer Science** (Computer Science; Mathematics); **Medicine** (Medicine); **Music and Dance** (Dance; Music); **Physical Education** (Physical Education); **Physics Science and Information Engineering** (Information Technology; Physics); **Zhangjiajie**

Department
English (English); **Fine Art** (Fine Arts); **Gardens** (Horticulture); **History** (History); **Information and Automatisation** (Automation and Control Engineering; Information Sciences); **Law** (Law); **Modern Education Technology** (Educational Technology); **Politics and Public Management** (Political Sciences; Public Administration); **Preparatory course**

Laboratory
Key

Further Information: Also Central Laboratory with 9 Research Institutes. Courses for foreign students

History: Founded 1958, acquired present status 1978.

Academic Year: February to January (February-July; September-January)

Degrees and Diplomas: *Xueshi Xuewei*

Publications: Journal of Jishou University (Natural Sciences Edition); Journal of Jishou University (Social Sciences Edition)

Academic Staff *2011-2012*: Total: c. 600

Student Numbers *2011-2012*: Total: c. 24,000

Last Updated: 25/02/13

JIUJIANG UNIVERSITY

551 Qianjin Donglu, Jiujiang, Jiangxi Province 332005
Tel: +86(792) 831-4451
Fax: +86(792) 833-7982
EMail: fao@jju.edu.cn; jjuxb@jju.edu.cn
Website: http://www.jju.edu.cn

Faculty
Accounting (Accountancy; Business Computing; Finance; Management; Statistics; Taxation); **Art** (Art Education; Design; Fine Arts; Music Education; Musicology); **Business** (Business Administration; E-Business/Commerce; Human Resources; International Business; Marketing; Transport Management); **Chemical Science and Engineering** (Applied Chemistry; Chemical Engineering; Chemistry; Organic Chemistry); **Chinese Literature and Communication** (Advertising and Publicity; Chinese; Cinema and Television; Literature; Multimedia; Secretarial Studies); **Civil Engineering and Urban Construction** (Architecture and Planning; Civil Engineering; Real Estate; Town Planning); **Clinical Medicine** (Medicine); **Foreign Languages** (English; Japanese); **Information Science and Technology** (Computer Science; Educational Technology; Information Management; Information Sciences; Information Technology; Software Engineering); **Law** (Law); **Life Sciences and Biological Engineering** (Aquaculture; Biological and Life Sciences; Biomedical Engineering; Biotechnology; Geography; Pharmacy); **Material Science and Engineering** (Materials Engineering); **Mechanical Engineering** (Automation and Control Engineering; Automotive Engineering; Mechanical Engineering); **Nursing** (Nursing); **Political and Public Management** (History; Public Administration); **Science and Mathematics** (Applied Mathematics; Applied Physics; Information Sciences; Mathematics; Mathematics Education); **Sports** (Physical Education; Sports); **Tourism** (Hotel Management; Tourism)

College
Medicine (Alternative Medicine; Anaesthesiology; Dentistry; Health Administration; Medical Technology; Medicine; Pharmacy)

History: Founded 1901 as Danforth Hospital Nursing School. Acquired current name and status 2000.

Degrees and Diplomas: *Xueshi Xuewei*

Last Updated: 07/01/13

KAILI UNIVERSITY

3 Kaiyuan Road, Economic Development Zone,
Kaili, Guizhou 556011
Tel: +86(855) 8503572
EMail: klxyxcb@163.com
Website: http://www.kluniv.cn/

College
Environment and Life Sciences (Biological and Life Sciences; Environmental Studies); **Information Engineering** (Computer Engineering; Information Sciences; Information Technology)

School
Architecture and Civil Engineering (Architecture; Civil Engineering; Construction Engineering); **Chemistry and Materials Engineering** (Chemical Engineering; Chemistry; Materials Engineering); **Continuing Education**; **Economics and Management** (Economics; Management); **Educational Sciences** (Education); **Foreign Languages** (English; Japanese; Linguistics; Modern Languages; Tourism); **Humanities** (Arts and Humanities; Chinese; Literature; Philology); **Marxism** (Political Sciences); **Mathematics** (Mathematics); **Music** (Dance; Music; Musicology); **Physical Education** (Physical Education; Sports); **Physics and Electronic Engineering** (Electronic Engineering; Physics); **Tourism** (Geography; Hotel Management; Insurance; Management; Tourism)

Institute
International Education

History: Founded 1958. Renamed Southeast Teachers College in 1959. Acquired present status and title 2006.

Main Language(s) of Instruction: Chinese

Degrees and Diplomas: *Xueshi Xuewei*

Academic Staff *2012-2013*: Total 760

STAFF WITH DOCTORATE: Total 16

Student Numbers *2012-2013*: Total 10,348

Last Updated: 10/12/13

KASHGAR TEACHERS COLLEGE

463 Kuonanaizheerbage Road,
Kashgar, Xinjiang Uygur Province 844000
Tel: +86(998) 2822996
Fax: +86(998) 2825144
EMail: yixia0110@163.com
Website: http://www.kstc.edu.cn

President: Abdurahman Amad

International Relations: Jiang Jizhao

Department

Chemistry (Chemistry); **Chinese Language and Literature** (Chinese; Literature); **Fine Arts** (Fine Arts); **Mathematics** (Mathematics); **Modern Languages** (Modern Languages); **Physical Education** (Physical Education); **Physics** (Physics); **Political Science and History** (History; Political Sciences)

History: Founded 1962 as Kashgar Teachers Training School, acquired present name 1978.

Degrees and Diplomas: *Xueshi Xuewei*; *Shuoshi Xuewei*

KUNMING MEDICAL UNIVERSITY

191 West Renmin Road, Kunming, Yunnan Province 650031
Tel: +86(871) 5332571
Fax: +86(871) 5332571
EMail: faokmu@vip.km169.net
Website: http://www.kmmc.edu.cn

President: Jiang Runsheng

School

Basic Medical Sciences (Medicine); **Clinical Medicine** (Medicine); **Clinical Oncology** (Oncology); **Forensic Medicine** (Forensic Medicine and Dentistry); **Humanities and Social Sciences** (Arts and Humanities; Social Sciences); **Nursing** (Nursing); **Pharmaceutical Sciences** (Pharmacy); **Public Health** (Public Health); **Stomatology** (Dentistry; Oral Pathology; Stomatology)

Institute

Health Sciences (Health Sciences); **Higher Medical Education** (Medicine); **Neurosciences** (Neurosciences)

Research Centre

Biomedical Engineering (Bioengineering)

History: Founded 1937 as Medical School of Yunnan University.

Main Language(s) of Instruction: Chinese

Degrees and Diplomas: *Xueshi Xuewei*; *Shuoshi Xuewei*; *Boshi*

Last Updated: 07/01/13

KUNMING UNIVERSITY

Kunming Economic and Technological Development Zone, 2,
Pudong New Road, Kunming, Yunnan 650214
Website: http://www.kmu.edu.cn/

President: Jiangyong Wen

College

Agriculture (Agriculture); **Automation and Control Engineering** (Automation and Control Engineering; Mechanical Engineering; Production Engineering); **Medicine** (Medicine; Nursing); **Teacher Education** (Teacher Training)

School

Construction Engineering (Architecture; Civil Engineering; Construction Engineering); **Economics, Management and Social Sciences** (Business Administration; Economics; Human Resources; International Business; International Economics; Management; Social Sciences); **Foreign Languages** (English; Modern Languages); **Humanities** (Arts and Humanities; Chinese; Literature); **Management** (Management); **Music** (Music)

Department

Chemical Science and Technology (Chemical Engineering; Chemistry); **Information Technology** (Computer Engineering; Computer Science; Information Technology); **Life Science and Technology** (Biological and Life Sciences; Biotechnology); **Mathematics** (Actuarial Science; Applied Mathematics; Finance; Mathematics); **Physical Education** (Physical Education); **Physical Science and Technology** (Physical Engineering; Physics); **Rural and Public Education** (Education; Educational Technology; Foreign Languages Education; Health Education; Humanities and Social Science Education; Physical Education; Political Sciences; Preschool Education; Science Education)

Institute

Art and Design (Architectural and Environmental Design; Design; Fine Arts; Graphic Design); **Tourism Studies** (Cooking and Catering; Nutrition; Tourism)

History: Founded 1978 as Kunming Teacher College. Merged with Kunming Institute of Education 1998. Merged with Normal School in Kunming, Kunming Normal Children. Acquired present status and title 2000. Merged with Kunming Light Industry School, Urban and Rural Construction Schools and Kunming Lixin University 2003.

Main Language(s) of Instruction: Chinese

Degrees and Diplomas: *Xueshi Xuewei*

Academic Staff *2012-2013*: Total: c. 1,000

Student Numbers *2012-2013*: Total: c. 17,000

Last Updated: 10/12/13

KUNMING UNIVERSITY OF SCIENCE AND TECHNOLOGY (KUST)

68 Wenchang Road, 121 Street,
Kunming, Yunnan Province 650093
Tel: +86(871) 5144184
Fax: +86(871) 5198622
EMail: wsc@kmust.edu.cn
Website: http://www.kmust.edu.cn

President: Rong Zhou (2003-) EMail: zre@kmust.edu.cn

Chairman of the University Committee: Yulin He
EMail: ylhe@kmust.edu.cn

International Relations: Gang Deng, Director
EMail: iep@kmust.edu.cn

Faculty

Applied Technology (Technology); **Arts** (Advertising and Publicity; Design; English; Fine Arts; Publishing and Book Trade); **Biological and Chemical Engineering** (Automation and Control Engineering; Biology; Chemical Engineering; Energy Engineering; Engineering Management; Food Science; Food Technology); **Civil and Architectural Engineering** (Architecture; Civil Engineering; Mechanical Engineering; Natural Resources; Town Planning); **Electrical Engineering** (Automation and Control Engineering; Electrical Engineering; Hydraulic Engineering; Power Engineering; Thermal Engineering; Water Management); **Environmental Science and Engineering** (Chemical Engineering; Environmental Engineering; Natural Resources); **Information Engineering and Automation** (Automation and Control Engineering; Computer Engineering); **Land Resource Engineering** (Environmental Engineering; Geography; Mining Engineering; Natural Resources; Rural Planning; Safety Engineering; Surveying and Mapping); **Management and Economics** (Accountancy; Business Administration; Economics; Finance; International Business; International Economics; Management; Marketing); **Materials and Metallurgical Engineering** (Materials Engineering; Metallurgical Engineering); **Mechanical and Electrical Engineering** (Automation and Control Engineering; Electrical Engineering; Industrial Design; Industrial Engineering; Mechanical Engineering; Packaging Technology); **Science** (Computer Science; Electronic Engineering; Information Technology); **Transport Engineering** (Transport Engineering)

School

Graduate Studies

History: Founded 1954 as Kunming Institute of Technology. Changed its name to Kunming University of Science and Technology 1995. Acquired present status following amalgamation with Yunnan Polytechnic University 1999.

Academic Year: March to January (March-July; September-January)

Admission Requirements: National College Entrance Examination or equivalent

Main Language(s) of Instruction: Chinese. Some courses in English, French, German

Accrediting Agency: Ministry of Education

Degrees and Diplomas: *Zhuanke*; *Xueshi Xuewei*; *Shuoshi Xuewei*; *Boshi*

Student Services: Academic Counselling, Canteen, Careers Guidance, Foreign Studies Centre, Health Services, Language Laboratory, Nursery Care, Social Counselling, Sports Facilities

Publications: Journal of KUST; Newsletter of KUST

Last Updated: 07/01/13

LANGFANG TEACHERS COLLEGE

100 West Aimin Street, Langfang,
Hebei Province 065000
Tel: +86(316) 2188211
EMail: lftcadmin@126.com
Website: http://www.lfsfxy.org.cn

President: Li Yanrui

School

Architecture Engineering (Architectural and Environmental Design; Civil Engineering); **Chemistry and Materials Science** (Chemistry; Materials Engineering); **Economics** (E-Business/Commerce; Economics; Finance; Insurance; International Business; Marketing); **Education** (Education; Preschool Education; Primary Education; Psychology); **Fine Arts** (Advertising and Publicity; Design; Fine Arts; Furniture Design; Sculpture); **Foreign Languages** (English; Japanese; Modern Languages); **Life Sciences** (Biological and Life Sciences; Biotechnology; Food Science; Food Technology; Nutrition); **Literature** (Chinese; Cinema and Television; Cultural Studies; Journalism; Literature; Theatre); **Management** (Accountancy; Business Administration; Finance; Hotel Management; Human Resources; Management); **Mathematics and Information Science** (Applied Mathematics; Computer Engineering; Computer Networks; Computer Science; Mathematics; Software Engineering); **Music** (Dance; Music Education; Musicology); **Physical Education** (Physical Education); **Physics and Electronic Information** (Automation and Control Engineering; Communication Studies; Educational Technology; Electronic Engineering; Physics); **Social Development** (History; Law; Social Work)

History: Founded 1946 as Elementary Teachers School of Anci District. Merged with Hebei Vocational and Technical College 2005.

Main Language(s) of Instruction: Chinese

Degrees and Diplomas: *Xueshi Xuewei*

Publications: Journal of Langfang Teacher's College

Last Updated: 07/01/13

LANZHOU CITY UNIVERSITY (LCU)

11, Jiefang Road, Anning District, Lanzhou,
Gansu 730070
Tel: +86(931) 7601062
Fax: +86(931) 7601062
Website: http://www.lzcu.edu.cn/

President: Wang Rufeng

College

Automotive Engineering *(Northern)* (Automotive Engineering); **Bailie Engineering and Technology** (Engineering; Technology); **Bailie International Studies**; **Chemistry and Environmental Science** (Chemistry; Environmental Studies); **Child Care Teachers**; **Education** (Education); **Foreign Languages** (English; Modern Languages); **Information Engineering** (Information Technology); **Liberal Arts** (Arts and Humanities); **Vocational and Technical Studies** *(Bailie)*

School

Management (Law; Management; Political Sciences; Social Work); **Marxism** (Political Sciences); **Mathematics** (Mathematics); **Music** (Music; Musical Instruments); **Petroleum Engineering** *(Bailie)* (Petroleum and Gas Engineering)

Department

Continuing Education

Institute

Media (Media Studies); **Sports** (Sports); **Urban Economy and Tourism Culture** (Tourism; Urban Studies)

Academy

Fine Arts (Art Education; Fine Arts; Landscape Architecture)

History: Founded 2006.

Main Language(s) of Instruction: Chinese

Degrees and Diplomas: *Xueshi Xuewei*

Academic Staff *2012-2013*: Total 809

STAFF WITH DOCTORATE: Total 253

Student Numbers *2012-2013*: Total 14,458

Last Updated: 11/12/13

LANZHOU JIAOTONG UNIVERSITY (LZJTU)

88 West Anning Road, Lanzhou, Gansu Province 730070
Tel: +86(931) 4938030
Fax: +86(931) 7667661
EMail: shunli@mail.lzjtu.cn
Website: http://www.lzjtu.edu.cn/

President: Ren Enen

School

Architecture and Urban Planning (Architecture; Town Planning); **Art and Design** (Design; Fine Arts); **Automatization and Electrical Engineering** (Automation and Control Engineering; Electrical Engineering); **Chemical and Biological Engineering** (Bioengineering; Chemical Engineering); **Civil Engineering** (Civil Engineering); **Continuing Education** (Continuing Education); **Economics and Management** (Business Administration; Economics; Management); **Electronics and Information Engineering** (Electronic Engineering; Information Technology); **Environmental and Municipal Engineering** (Environmental Engineering; Environmental Studies); **Foreign Languages** (English; Modern Languages); **International Joint Education**; **Mathematics, Physics and Software Engineering** (Mathematics; Physics; Software Engineering); **Mechatronic Engineering** (Electronic Engineering; Mechanical Engineering); **Traffic and Transportation** (Transport and Communications)

Department

Chinese Language (Chinese); **Physical Education** (Physical Education); **Social Science** (Social Sciences)

Further Information: Also 73 research centers and institutes; 5 Technical and Engineering Centers

History: Founded 1958 as Lanzhou Railway University, through combination of departments and sections from Tangshan Railway Institute (the present Southwest Jiaotong University) and Beijing Railway Institute (the present Beijing Jiaotong University. Acquired present status and title 2003.

Main Language(s) of Instruction: Chinese

Degrees and Diplomas: *Xueshi Xuewei*; *Shuoshi Xuewei*; *Boshi*

Academic Staff *2011-2012*: Total 2,300

STAFF WITH DOCTORATE: Total 80

Student Numbers *2011-2012*: Total: c. 30,000

Last Updated: 25/02/13

LANZHOU UNIVERSITY (LZU)

222, South Tianshui Road, Lanzhou, Gansu Province 730000
Tel: +86(931) 8612850 +86(931) 8912076
Fax: +86(931) 8617355 +86(931) 8617355
EMail: news@lzu.edu.cn
Website: http://www.lzu.edu.cn

President: Zhou Xuhong (2006-)

International Relations: Yu Yajia, Director, Office of International Cooperation and Exchange Tel: +86(931) 8912076

College

Cuiying Honors

School

Arts (Fine Arts); **Atmospheric Sciences** (Meteorology); **Basic Medical Sciences** (Medicine); **Chemistry and Chemical Engineering** (Chemical Engineering; Chemistry); **Chinese Language and Literature** (Chinese; Literature); **Civil Engineering and Mechanics** (Civil Engineering; Mechanics); **Clinical Medical Studies** (Medicine); **Continuing Education**; **Earth and Environmental Sciences** (Earth Sciences; Environmental Studies); **Economics** (Economics); **Education** (Education); **Foreign Languages and Literature** (Applied Linguistics; French; German; Japanese; Linguistics; Literature; Modern Languages; Russian; Translation and Interpretation); **Geological Sciences and Mineral Resources** (Geological Engineering; Mineralogy); **Higher Vocational Education**; **History and Culture** (Cultural Studies; History); **Information Science and Engineering** (Information Sciences; Information Technology); **International Cultural Exchange**; **Journalism and Communication** (Journalism; Mass Communication); **Law** (Law); **Life Sciences** (Biological and Life Sciences); **Management** (Administration; Business Administration; Management); **Marxism** (Political Sciences); **Mathematics and Statistics** (Mathematics; Statistics); **Network Education**; **Nuclear Science and Technology** (Nuclear Engineering; Nuclear Physics); **Pastoral Agriculture Science and Technology** (Agriculture); **Pharmacy** (Pharmacy); **Philosophy and Sociology** (Philosophy; Sociology); **Physical Science and Technology** (Physics); **Politics and Administration** (Administration; Political Sciences); **Public Health** (Public Health); **Stomatology** (Stomatology)

Department

Sports Teaching and Research (Sports)

Laboratory

Agriculture Grassland Agro Ecosystem *(Ministry of Agriculture)* (Agriculture); **Applied Organic Chemistry** *(SKLAOC)* (Applied Chemistry; Organic Chemistry); **Arid and Grassland Ecology** *(Ministry of Education)* (Arid Land Studies; Ecology); **Magnetism and Magnetic Materials** *(Ministry of Education)* (Materials Engineering; Physics); **Mechanics on Disaster and Environment in Western China** *((Chinese Ministry of Education)* (Environmental Studies; Safety Engineering); **Western China's Environmental Systems** *(Ministry of Education)* (Environmental Studies)

Research Centre

Studies of Ethnic Minorities in Northwest China (Ethnology)

Research Institute

Dunhuang Studies (Asian Studies; Religion)

Research School

Arid Environment and Climate Change (Arid Land Studies; Geography; Meteorology)

Further Information: Also First Satellite Campus, Second Satellite Campus, Yuzhong Campus, Medical Campus, Pastoral Science Campus; 2 Affiliated Hospitals and 1 University Hospital

History: Founded 1909 as Gansu Law and Politics School. Became Lanzhou Sun Yat-sen University 1928. Acquired present title 1946. Merged with the former Gansu Grassland Ecological Institute 2002 and with Lanzhou Medical School 2004.

Admission Requirements: Graduation from senior middle school and national entrance examination

Main Language(s) of Instruction: Chinese

Accrediting Agency: Ministry of Education; Gansu Provincial Education Commission

Degrees and Diplomas: *Xueshi Xuewei*; *Shuoshi Xuewei*; *Boshi*. Also MBA and Executive MBA; Post-doctoral Research Programmes

Student Services: Academic Counselling, Canteen, Cultural Activities, Foreign Studies Centre, Health Services, Language Laboratory, Nursery Care, Social Counselling, Sports Facilities

Publications: Journal of Lanzhou University (Medical Sciences); Journal of Lanzhou University (Natural Sciences); Journal of Lanzhou University (Social Sciences)

Publishing House: Lanzhou University Press

Last Updated: 22/02/13

LANZHOU UNIVERSITY OF FINANCE AND ECONOMICS (LUFE)

418 Duanjiatan Street, Lanzhou, Gansu Province 730020
Tel: +86(931) 8493093
Fax: +86(931) 8660024
EMail: roman@lzcc.edu.cn
Website: http://www.lzcc.edu.cn

President: Lu Zhaoxin

International Relations: Xiao Huaiyun

School

Accountancy (Accountancy; Business Computing; Finance); **Adult Education**; **Arts** (Design; Display and Stage Design; Fashion Design; Fine Arts; Music; Musical Instruments; Performing Arts; Singing; Visual Arts)

History: Founded 1951 as Gansu Staff Finance and Economics College. Became Lanzhou Commercial College and then Lanzhou University of Finance and Economics.

Main Language(s) of Instruction: Chinese

Degrees and Diplomas: *Xueshi Xuewei*; *Shuoshi Xuewei*

Last Updated: 22/02/13

LANZHOU UNIVERSITY OF TECHNOLOGY (LUT)

85 Langongping Street, Qilihe District,
Lanzhou, Gansu Province 730050
Tel: +86(931) 2976037 +86(931) 2976038
Fax: +86(931) 2975037
EMail: gdrsc@lut.cn; international@lut.cn
Website: http://yuanxi.lut.cn/english

Division

Physical Education and Research (Physical Education)

College

Software *(Vocational and Technical)* (Software Engineering)

School

Civil Engineering (Architectural and Environmental Design; Civil Engineering; Engineering Management; Water Management); **Computer Communication** (Computer Engineering; Computer Science; Information Technology; Telecommunications Engineering); **Continuing Education**; **Designing Art** (Architecture; Design; Fine Arts; Industrial Design; Town Planning); **Electric Engineering and Information Engineering** (Automation and Control Engineering; Electrical and Electronic Engineering; Electrical Engineering; Electronic Engineering; Information Sciences; Information Technology); **Energy and Power Engineering** (Automation and Control Engineering; Energy Engineering; Instrument Making; Power Engineering; Thermal Engineering); **Foreign Languages** (English; Japanese; Modern Languages); **Humanities** (Administration; Arts and Humanities; Law); **International Economics and Management** (Accountancy; Business Administration; Finance; Human Resources; Information Management; Information Sciences; International Business; International Economics; Management; Marketing; Tourism); **Life Science and Engineering** (Bioengineering; Biological and Life Sciences; Food Science; Food Technology); **Material Science and Engineering** (Materials Engineering; Metallurgical Engineering; Polymer and Plastics Technology); **Mechanical and Electronical Engineering** (Automation and Control Engineering; Electronic Engineering; Industrial Engineering; Machine Building; Mechanical Engineering; Packaging Technology; Production Engineering; Textile Technology); **Modern Network Education**; **Petrochemical Engineering** (Applied Chemistry; Chemical Engineering; Petroleum and Gas Engineering; Safety Engineering); **Science** (Applied Physics; Mechanical Engineering; Mechanics; Natural Sciences); **Technology Engineering** (Engineering; Technology)

Centre

MBA Education (Business Administration); **Mechanical Engineering Teaching and Practice** (Mechanical Engineering)

History: Founded 1919 as Gansu Provincial Polytechnic School. Renamed Gansu University of Technology 1958. Placed under the jurisdiction of the Ministry of Machine Building Industry and the Provincial Government 1998. Acquired present status and title 2003.

Academic Year: September to July (September-January; March-July)

Admission Requirements: Graduation from senior middle school and entrance examination

Main Language(s) of Instruction: Chinese

Accrediting Agency: Ministry of Machine Building Industry

Degrees and Diplomas: *Xueshi Xuewei*; *Shuoshi Xuewei*; *Boshi*. Also MBA; Post-doctoral studies in engineering

Publications: Journal

Academic Staff *2011-2012*: Total: c. 1,506
Student Numbers *2011-2012*: Total: c. 38,000
Last Updated: 22/02/13

LESHAN NORMAL UNIVERSITY

778 Binhe Rd, Shizhong, Leshan, Sichuan 614000
Tel: +86(833) 2276393 +86(833) 2276399
Fax: +86(833) 2276022
Website: http://www.lstc.edu.cn/

President: Luo Dayu

College

Chemistry (Applied Chemistry; Chemical Engineering; Chemistry; Environmental Studies; Industrial Engineering; Science Education); **Computer Science** (Computer Engineering; Computer Networks; Computer Science; Software Engineering); **Educational Sciences** (Education; Educational Sciences); **Fine Arts** (Fine Arts); **Foreign Languages** (English; Modern Languages); **Law and Public Administration** (Law; Public Administration); **Life Sciences** (Biological and Life Sciences); **Literature and Journalism** (Journalism; Literature); **Mathematics and Information Science** (Information Sciences; Mathematics; Mathematics and Computer Science); **Physics and Electronic Engineering** (Electronic Engineering; Physics); **Political Sciences** (Political Sciences); **Tourism and Economic Management** (Economics; Management; Tourism)

School

Music (Dance; Music; Musical Instruments)

Institute

Sports (Physical Education; Sports)

Degrees and Diplomas: *Xueshi Xuewei*

Academic Staff *2012-2013*: Total: c. 1,200
Student Numbers *2012-2013*: Total: c. 14,600
Last Updated: 11/12/13

LIAOCHENG UNIVERSITY (LCU)

34 Wenhua Road, Liaocheng, Shandong Province 252000
Tel: +86(635) 8238155
Fax: +86(635) 8238040
EMail: xzxx@lcu.edu.cn
Website: http://www.lcu.edu.cn/

President: Song Yiqiao

School

Agriculture (Agriculture; Animal Husbandry; Food Science; Food Technology; Horticulture; Landscape Architecture; Plant and Crop Protection; Veterinary Science); **Architecture and Civil Engineering** (Architecture; Civil Engineering); **Automobile and Transportation Engineering** (Automotive Engineering; Mechanical Engineering; Transport and Communications; Transport Engineering); **Business** (Business Administration; Economics; Industrial and Production Economics; International Business; International Economics; Law); **Chemistry and Chemical Engineering** (Analytical Chemistry; Applied Chemistry; Chemical Engineering; Chemistry; Inorganic Chemistry; Organic Chemistry; Physical Chemistry; Polymer and Plastics Technology); **Computer Science** (Computer Education; Computer Networks; Computer Science; E-Business/Commerce; Information Management; Information Sciences; Information Technology; Software Engineering); **Educational Science** (Curriculum; Developmental Psychology; Education; Educational Psychology; Educational Sciences; Pedagogy; Primary Education; Public Administration); **Environment and Planning** (Curriculum; Environmental Studies; Geography; Regional Planning; Science Education; Surveying and Mapping; Town Planning); **Fine Arts** (Design; Fine Arts; Painting and Drawing; Visual Arts); **Foreign Languages** (Applied Linguistics; English; Japanese; Korean; Linguistics); **History and Culture** (Cultural Studies; History; Tourism); **Law** (Law); **Life Science** (Bioengineering; Biological and Life Sciences; Botany; Cell Biology; Science Education); **Literature** (Chinese; Curriculum; Humanities and Social Science Education; Literature; Philology; Radio and Television Broadcasting; Secretarial Studies; Teacher Training); **Management** (Administration; Human Resources; Labour and Industrial Relations; Management; Social Studies); **Materials Science and Engineering** (Materials Engineering); **Mathematical Sciences** (Accountancy; Applied Mathematics; Computer Science; Information Sciences; Mathematics; Mathematics Education); **Media Technology** (Communication Arts; Curriculum; Educational Technology; Media Studies; Radio and Television Broadcasting; Teacher Training); **Music** (Music; Performing Arts); **Pharmacy** (Biological and Life Sciences; Chemistry; Pharmacy); **Physical Education** (Curriculum; Physical Education; Sports; Teacher Trainers Education); **Physics Science and Information Engineering** (Electronic Engineering; Information Sciences; Information Technology; Optics; Physics; Safety Engineering; Telecommunications Engineering); **Politics and Marxism** (Curriculum; Philosophy; Political Sciences)

History: Founded 1974 as Liaocheng Branch of Shandong Normal College. Renamed Liaocheng Teachers CollegeAcquired present status and title 2002.

Main Language(s) of Instruction: Chinese

Degrees and Diplomas: *Xueshi Xuewei*; *Shuoshi Xuewei*

Student Services: Sports Facilities

Academic Staff *2011-2012*: Total 2,150
STAFF WITH DOCTORATE: Total 354
Student Numbers *2011-2012*: Total: c. 31,000
Last Updated: 21/02/13

LIAONING FINANCE AND TRADE COLLEGE

Xingcheng, Higher Education Park, Liaoning, Liaoning 125105
Tel: +86(429) 5418666
EMail: lncmxy@126.com
Website: http://www.lncmxy.com/

Department

Accountancy (Accountancy); **Arts and Design** (Design; Fine Arts); **Economics** (Economics); **Foreign Languages** (English); **Physical Education** (Physical Education); **Teacher Training** (Teacher Training); **Tourism** (Tourism)

Degrees and Diplomas: *Xueshi Xuewei*
Last Updated: 04/12/13

LIAONING MEDICAL UNIVERSITY

40 Section 3, Songpo Road, Linghe District,
Jinzhou, Liaoning 121001
Tel: +86(416) 4673073
Fax: +86(416) 4673528
EMail: cie@jzmu.edu.cn
Website: http://www.lnmu.edu.cn

President: Huanjiu Xi

Administrative Officer: Lizhou Zhang

International Relations: Meng Jie

College

International Education (International and Comparative Education)

Department

Animal Science and Veterinary Science (Veterinary Science; Zoology); **Clinical Medicine** (Medicine); **Medicine** (Medicine); **Nursing** (Nursing); **Otorhinolaryngology** (Otorhinolaryngology); **Pharmacy** (Pharmacy)

Further Information: University hospital

History: Founded 1946 as Liaoji Military Area Hygiene School, became Jinzhou Medical University 1958. Acquired present title 2006.

Admission Requirements: Graduation from senior middle school or recognized equivalent

Fees: (Yuan): 4,800

Main Language(s) of Instruction: Chinese, English

Accrediting Agency: Ministry of Education

Degrees and Diplomas: *Xueshi Xuewei*: **Medicine.** *Shuoshi Xuewei*: **Medicine.** *Boshi*: **Anatomy.**

Student Services: Academic Counselling, Canteen, Careers Guidance, Cultural Activities, Foreign Studies Centre, Health Services, Language Laboratory, Nursery Care, Sports Facilities

Last Updated: 18/12/12

LIAONING NORMAL UNIVERSITY (LNNU)

850 Huanghe Avenue, Dalian, Liaoning 116029
Tel: +86(411) 4121181 Ext. 8366
Fax: +86(411) 4121181 Ext. 8562
EMail: dwhy@dl.cn
Website: http://www.lnnu.edu.cn

President: Qu Qingbiao (2010-)

College

Education *(International)* (Chinese; Education); **Haihua**; **International Business** *(LNU-MSU)* (International Business)

School

Chemistry and Chemical Engineering (Chemical Engineering; Chemistry); **Chinese Language and Literature** (Arts and Humanities; Chinese); **Computer Science and Information Technology** (Computer Science; Information Technology); **Continuous Education**; **Education** *(Tianjiabing Academy)* (Education); **Film and Television Art** (Cinema and Television; Film); **Fine Arts** (Fine Arts); **Foreign Languages** (English; Modern Languages); **History Culture and Tourism** (History; Tourism); **Law** (Law); **Life Science** (Biological and Life Sciences); **Management** (Management); **Mathematics** (Mathematics); **Music** (Music); **Physical Education** (Physical Education); **Physics and Electronic Technology** (Electronic Engineering; Physics); **Political Science and Administration** (Administration; Political Sciences); **Urban and Environmental Sciences** (Environmental Studies)

Higher School

Junior High School *(Attached to LNU)*; **Senior High School** *(Attached to LNU)*

Centre

Australian Studies (Pacific Area Studies)

Further Information: Also 3 post-doctoral research stations

History: Founded 1951 as Luda Teachers Junior School. Renamed Dalian Teachers School in 1953. Transformed into Dalian Teachers College 1958 and Liaoning Teachers College 1960. Acquired present title 1983.

Main Language(s) of Instruction: Chinese

Degrees and Diplomas: *Xueshi Xuewei*; *Shuoshi Xuewei*; *Boshi*

Publications: Educational Science; Journal of Liaoning Normal University

Academic Staff *2011-2012*: Total: c. 1,000
Student Numbers *2011-2012*: Total: c. 18,000
Last Updated: 21/02/13

LIAONING TECHNICAL UNIVERSITY (LNTU)

47 Zhonghua Road, Haizhou District, Fuxin, Liaoning 123000
Tel: +86(418) 3351111
Fax: +86(418) 2823977
EMail: lntu@chinatefl.com
Website: http://www.lntu.edu.cn

President: Yishan Pan (2008-)

Faculty

Science (Natural Sciences)

College

Applied Technology (Technology); **Business Administration** (Business Administration); **Electronic Information Engineering** (Electronic Engineering; Information Technology); **Environmental Science and Engineering** (Environmental Engineering; Environmental Studies); **Mapping and Geographic Sciences** (Geography; Surveying and Mapping); **Materials Engineering** (Materials Engineering); **Mechanics and Mechanical Engineering** (Mechanical Engineering; Mechanics); **Media and Art** (Fine Arts; Media Studies); **Security Science and Engineering** (Safety Engineering)

School

Architecture and Civil Engineering (Architecture; Civil Engineering); **Civil and Transportation** (Civil Engineering; Transport Engineering); **Continuing Education**; **Economics and Management** (Business Administration; Economics; Management); **Electrical and Control Engineering** (Automation and Control Engineering; Electrical Engineering); **Foreign Languages** (English; Modern Languages); **Graduate Studies**; **Innovative Practice**; **Marketing Management** (Management; Marketing); **Mechanical Engineering** (Mechanical Engineering); **Mines** (Mining Engineering); **Physical Education** (Physical Education); **Public Management and Law** (Law; Public Administration); **Software Engineering** (Software Engineering)

Department

Basic Teaching; **Ideological and Political Theory Teaching and Research** (Political Sciences); **Military Teaching** (Military Science)

Institute

Mining and Technology (Mining Engineering; Technology)

Further Information: Also Huludao Campus

History: Founded 1963 as Fuxin Coalmine Institute. Became Fuxin Mining Institute 1978. Incorporated Fushun Mining Institute, Liaoning Coalmine Teachers Institute and Jixi Mining Institute. Acquired present title 1996.

Main Language(s) of Instruction: Chinese

Degrees and Diplomas: *Xueshi Xuewei*; *Shuoshi Xuewei*; *Boshi*. Also MBA

Publications: EI Chinese Academic Journal (CD); Journal of Liaoning Technical University (Natural Science Edition); Journal of Liaoning Technical University (Social Science Edition)

Academic Staff *2011-2012*: Total 1,700
STAFF WITH DOCTORATE: Total 240
Student Numbers *2011-2012*: Total 41,487
Last Updated: 08/02/13

LIAONING UNIVERSITY (LNU)

66 Chongshan Zhonglu, Huanggu District,
Shenyang, Liaoning 110036
Tel: +86(24) 62202135 +86(24) 62202503 +86(24) 62202490
Fax: +86(24) 62202710
EMail: zsk@lnu.edu.cn; studyinlnu@yahoo.com.cn
Website: http://wwwen.lnu.edu.cn

President: Cheng Wei

Faculty

Environment Science (Environmental Studies); **History** (History); **Life Sciences** (Biological and Life Sciences); **Mathematics** (Mathematics); **Physics** (Physics)

College

Adult Education (Adult Education); **Business** *(Asia-Australia)* (Business Administration); **Business Administration** (Business Administration); **Chemical Science and Engineering** (Chemical Engineering; Chemistry); **Cultural Propagation** (Cultural Studies); **Economics** (Economics); **Foreign Languages** (English; Modern Languages); **Foreign Students**; **Higher Professional Techniques**; **Information Science and Technology** (Information Sciences; Information Technology); **International Economics** (International Economics); **Law** (Law); **Philosophy and Public Administration** (Philosophy; Public Administration); **Radio, Film and Television** (Cinema and Television; Film; Radio and Television Broadcasting); **Training Self-Study Students of Humanities and Professional Techniques**

Further Information: Also University Hospital; 38 laboratories and more than 110 teaching and research sections; 3 mobile stations for post-doctoral studies

History: Founded 1958, incorporating the Northeastern Economy and Accounting College, Shenyang Teachers College, and Shenyang Institute of Russian.

Academic Year: February to January (February-July; August-January)

Admission Requirements: Secondary school certificate and entrance examination

Fees: (Yuan): Chinese language student, 13,000 per annum; Undergraduate programmes, 15,000 per annum; Master's Degree programmes, 20,000 per annum; Ph. D programmes, 26000 per annum

Main Language(s) of Instruction: Chinese

Degrees and Diplomas: *Xueshi Xuewei*; *Shuoshi Xuewei*; *Boshi*. Also MBA

Publications: Journal of Japanese Studies; Journal of Korean Studies; Journal of Liaoning University; Journal of Population Research

Publishing House: Liaoning University Press

Academic Staff *2011-2012*: Total 1,116

Student Numbers *2011-2012*: Total: c. 18,700

Last Updated: 08/02/13

LIAONING UNIVERSITY OF INTERNATIONAL BUSINESS AND ECONOMICS

Lushun Economic Development Zone, Dallian,
Dalian, Liaoning 116052
Tel: +86(411) 86208715
Fax: +86(411) 86209388
EMail: wanglonglong@gmail.com
Website: http://www.ulet.edu.cn

Course

Finance and Economics (Economics; Finance; International Economics); **Foreign Languages and Literature** (English; Japanese; Literature); **Inoformation Technology and Information Management** (Computer Engineering; Information Management; Information Technology; Software Engineering); **Management** (Accountancy; Business Administration; Information Management; International Business; Management; Secretarial Studies); **Tourism** (Tourism)

History: Founded 1964. Acquired present title and status 2005.

Accrediting Agency: Ministry of Education

Degrees and Diplomas: *Xueshi Xuewei*

Publications: Journal of Liaoning International Business

Last Updated: 03/10/13

LIAONING UNIVERSITY OF PETROLEUM AND CHEMICAL TECHNOLOGY (LUPCT)

1 Dandong Road, Fushun, Liaoning 113001
Tel: +86(24) 56865005
Fax: +86(24) 56860766
EMail: shxw@lnpu.edu.cn
Website: http://www.lnpu.edu.cn/

President: Li Ping (2004-)
Tel: +86(413) 56860588 EMail: liping@lnpu.edu.cn

Faculty

Science (Natural Sciences)

College

Chemistry and Materials Science (Chemistry; Materials Engineering); **Computer and Telecommunications Engineering** (Computer Engineering; Telecommunications Engineering); **Environmental and Biological Engineering** (Bioengineering; Environmental Engineering); **Information and Control Engineering** (Automation and Control Engineering; Information Sciences); **Mining Engineering** (Mining Engineering); **Vocational and Technical Education** (Technology Education; Vocational Education)

School

Continuing Education; **Economics and Management** (Business Administration; Economics; Management); **Foreign Languages** (English; Modern Languages); **Marxism** (Political Sciences); **Mechanical Engineering** (Mechanical Engineering)

Institute

Energy *(Shun-Hua)* (Energy Engineering); **International Education**; **Oil and Gas Engineering** (Petroleum and Gas Engineering); **Petrochemical Technology** (Petroleum and Gas Engineering); **Physical Education** (Physical Education; Sports)

History: Founded 1950 as Dalian Petroleum Industry School. 1953. Moved to Fushun and renamed Fushun Petroleum Institute 1958. Renamed Liaoning Shihua University 2002.

Admission Requirements: Secondary school certificate

Main Language(s) of Instruction: Chinese

Degrees and Diplomas: *Xueshi Xuewei*; *Shuoshi Xuewei*; *Boshi*. The Doctor's Degree are offered through joint training programmes; Also MBA

Academic Staff *2011-2012*	**TOTAL**
FULL-TIME	**1,547**
Student Numbers *2011-2012*	
All (Foreign included)	c. **23,430**
FOREIGN ONLY	**100**

Last Updated: 08/02/13

LIAONING UNIVERSITY OF SCIENCE AND TECHNOLOGY

185 Qianshan Middle Rd, Anshan, Liaoning 114051
Tel: +86(412) 5928000
Fax: +86(412) 5928012
EMail: ustl@ustl.edu.cn
Website: http://www.ustl.edu.cn/

Chancellor: Sun Qiubo

School

Chemical Engineering (Chemical Engineering); **Civil Engineering** (Civil Engineering); **Natural Resources** (Machine Building; Natural Resources); **Software Engineering** (Software Engineering)

Department

Electronic and Information Technology (Electronic Engineering; Information Technology); **Materials and Metallurgical Engineering** (Materials Engineering; Metallurgical Engineering)

Centre

Mechanical and Automation Engineering (Automation and Control Engineering; Mechanical Engineering)

Degrees and Diplomas: *Xueshi Xuewei*; *Shuoshi Xuewei*; *Boshi*

Last Updated: 04/12/13

LIAONING UNIVERSITY OF TECHNOLOGY

169 Shiying Street, Guta District, Jinzhou, Liaoning 121001
Tel: +86(416) 4198745 +86(416) 4199704
Fax: +86(416) 4142701
EMail: iclitjz@mail.jzptt.ln.cn
Website: http://www.lnit.edu.cn/

President: Son Hui

International Relations: Chen Qingfu

Department

Architecture (Architecture); **Chemical Engineering** (Chemical Engineering); **Civil Engineering** (Civil Engineering); **Design** (Design); **Economics and Administration** (Administration; Economics); **Information Sciences and Engineering** (Engineering; Information Sciences); **Machine Building and Automotive Engineering** (Automotive Engineering; Machine Building); **Materials Engineering** (Materials Engineering); **Modern Languages** (English); **Physical Education** (Physical Education); **Political Science** (Political Sciences)

History: Founded 1951 as Technical School, acquired present status 1960 and name 1997. Liaoning Institute of Technology

Main Language(s) of Instruction: Chinese

Degrees and Diplomas: *Xueshi Xuewei*; *Shuoshi Xuewei*

Academic Staff *2011-2012*: Total: c. 480
Student Numbers *2011-2012*: Total: c. 18,000
Last Updated: 21/02/13

LIAONING UNIVERSITY OF TRADITIONAL CHINESE MEDICINE (LNUTCM)

Chongshan Eastern Road, Huanggu District, Shenyang, Liaoning 110847
Tel: +86(24) 31207286 +86(24) 31207283 +86(24) 31207282
Fax: +86(24) 31207284
EMail: lnutcm1958@yahoo.com.cn; lnutcmiec@yahoo.com.cn
Website: http://www.lnutcm.edu.cn

President: Yang Kuan Lin

College
Acupuncture and Tuina (Acupuncture; Alternative Medicine; Physical Therapy; Traditional Eastern Medicine); **Basic Medical Science** (Medicine); **Economics and Management** (Economics; Finance; Law; Management; Marketing; Pharmacy; Public Administration; Transport Management); **Foreign Languages** (English; Japanese; Modern Languages; Russian); **Information Engineering** (Chemistry; Computer Science; Information Management; Information Sciences; Information Technology; Mathematics; Physics); **International Education**; **Nursing** (English; Medicine; Nursing; Traditional Eastern Medicine)

Department
Affiliated Hospital *(I)* (Gynaecology and Obstetrics; Medicine; Otorhinolaryngology; Paediatrics; Surgery); **Affiliated Hospital** *(II)* (Cardiology; Dermatology; Gynaecology and Obstetrics; Immunology; Medicine; Ophthalmology; Orthopaedics; Otorhinolaryngology; Respiratory Therapy; Rheumatology; Surgery); **Affiliated Hospital** *(IV)* (Gynaecology and Obstetrics; Medicine; Otorhinolaryngology; Paediatrics; Surgery)

Further Information: Also 4 indirectly affiliated hospitals; 40 clinical teaching hospitals; 2 experimental and teaching centers; 3 research institutes; 6 research divisions

History: Founded 1958 as Liaoning College of Traditional Chinese Medicine. Merged with Liaoning Research Institute of TCM, Liaoning Staff Medical School 1997. Merged with Liaoning Research School of Basic Medicine 2000. Acquired present title and status 2006.

Main Language(s) of Instruction: Chinese

Degrees and Diplomas: *Xueshi Xuewei*; *Shuoshi Xuewei*; *Boshi*. Also post-doctoral programmes

Publications: TCM Correspondence Magazine

Student Numbers *2010-2011*: Total: c. 10,000
Last Updated: 08/02/13

LINYI UNIVERSITY

The Middle Part of Shuangling Road, Linyi, Shandong 276005
Tel: +86(539) 8766196
Fax: +86(539) 8766198
EMail: sc@lyu.edu.cn; wsc@lyu.edu.cn
Website: http://www.lyu.edu.cn/

President: Han Yanming

School
Architecture (Architecture); **Automobile Engineering** (Automotive Engineering); **Business** (Business Administration); **Chemistry and Chemical Engineering** (Chemical Engineering; Chemistry); **Chinese Language and Literature** (Chinese; Literature); **Education** (Education; Educational Sciences); **Fine Arts** (Fine Arts); **Foreign Languages** (English; Modern Languages); **Information** (Information Sciences); **Law** (Law); **Life Science** (Biological and Life Sciences); **Logistics** (Transport Management); **Maxism** (Political Sciences); **Mechanical Engineering** (Mechanical Engineering); **Media** (Media Studies); **Music** (Music); **Physical Education** (Physical Education); **Resources and Environment** (Environmental Studies; Natural Resources)

Department
Mathematics (Mathematics)

History: Founded 1941.

Fees: (Yuan): Tuition, 6,000 per semester

Main Language(s) of Instruction: Chinese

Degrees and Diplomas: *Xueshi Xuewei*

Student Services: Language Laboratory

Academic Staff *2012-2013*	**TOTAL**
FULL-TIME	c. **1,900**
Student Numbers *2012-2013*	
All (Foreign included)	c. **35,000**
FOREIGN ONLY	**100**

Last Updated: 12/12/13

LISHUI UNIVERSITY

1, Xueyuan Road, Lishui, Zhejiang 323000
Tel: +86(578) 2271072 +86(578) 2271288 +86(578) 2271710
Fax: +86(578) 2134306 +86(578) 2271602
EMail: ygljshen@126.com
Website: http://lsu.edu.cn/

President: Zhou Xiang Zhe

College
Adult and Continuing Education; **Art** (Design; Fine Arts; Landscape Architecture; Musicology; Photography); **Business** (Business Administration; E-Business/Commerce; Finance; International Business; International Economics; Tourism); **Ecology** (Ecology; Horticulture); **Education** (Education; Foreign Languages Education; Physical Education; Preschool Education; Primary Education); **Engineering** (Automation and Control Engineering; Civil Engineering; Computer Engineering; Electronic Engineering; Engineering; Information Technology; Mechanical Engineering; Production Engineering); **Liberal Arts** (Arts and Humanities; Chinese; English; Literature); **Medicine** (Dentistry; Medicine; Nursing; Oral Pathology); **Science** (Applied Chemistry; Applied Mathematics; Biological and Life Sciences; Chemical Engineering; Chemistry; Computer Science; Information Sciences; Mathematics; Natural Sciences; Physics)

History: Founded 2004.

Main Language(s) of Instruction: Chinese

Degrees and Diplomas: *Xueshi Xuewei*

Academic Staff *2013-2014*: Total 724
Student Numbers *2013-2014*: Total: c. 11,700
Last Updated: 12/12/13

LIUPANSHUI NORMAL COLLEGE (LNU)

Liupanshui, Guizhou 553004
Tel: +86(858) 8602133
EMail: lpssfxy@163.com
Website: http://www.lpssy.edu.cn

Department
Adult Education; **Art** (Fine Arts; Handicrafts; Music; Musical Instruments; Painting and Drawing; Singing); **Chemistry** (Chemistry; Industrial Chemistry; Science Education); **Chinese** (Chinese; Literature; Native Language Education); **Education Science** (Education; Preschool Education; Primary Education); **Environmental and Chemical Engineering** (Chemical Engineering; Environmental Engineering); **Foreign Language and Literature** (Cultural Studies; English; Literature; Modern Languages; Translation and Interpretation); **History and Social Culture Science** (History); **Ideological and Political Theory Course Teaching** (Political Sciences); **Life Sciences** (Biological and Life Sciences; Biology; Biotechnology; Geography; Science Education); **Mathematics** (Applied Mathematics; Mathematics; Mathematics Education); **Physical Education** (Health Sciences; Physical Education; Psychology; Sports); **Physics and Electronic Science** (Applied Physics; Electronic Engineering; Physics; Science Education); **Political Education and Law** (History; Law; Political Sciences); **Resources and Mining Engineering** (Automation and Control Engineering; Chemical Engineering; Engineering Management; Mining Engineering; Natural Resources; Safety Engineering)

Section
Public English Teaching (English)

History: Founded 1978 as Liupanshui Teachers College. Acquired present status and title 2009.

Main Language(s) of Instruction: Chinese

Degrees and Diplomas: *Xueshi Xuewei*

Student Services: Language Laboratory

Academic Staff *2011-2012*: Total 487

Student Numbers *2011-2012*: Total: c. 5,200

Last Updated: 12/12/13

LONGDONG UNIVERSITY

137 Nandajie, Xifeng District, Qingyang,
Gangsu 74500
Tel: +86(934) 8632312
Fax: +86(934) 8632822
Website: http://www.ldxy.edu.cn/

Department

Arts (Art Education); **Biology** (Biology); **Chinese and Literature** (Chinese; Literature); **Civil Engineering and Architecture** (Architecture; Civil Engineering); **Economics and Management** (Economics; Management); **Education** (Adult Education; Education; Primary Education); **Engineering** (Computer Engineering; Electrical Engineering; Electronic Engineering; Energy Engineering; Engineering; Information Technology; Mechanical Engineering); **English and Literature** (English; Literature); **History** (History); **Mathematics and Statistics** (Mathematics; Statistics); **Music** (Music); **Physical Education** (Physical Education); **Political Sciences and Law** (Law; Political Sciences)

History: Founded 1978 as Qingyang Teachers College. Merged with Qingyang Institute of Agricultural Science and Qingyang Agricultural Schools, 2001. Acquired present title and Status 2003.

Degrees and Diplomas: *Xueshi Xuewei*

Academic Staff *2012-2013*: Total 738

Student Numbers *2012-2013*: Total 15,715

Last Updated: 02/12/13

LONGYAN UNIVERSITY

1 Dongxiao Rd. N, Xinluo District, Longyan,
Fujian 364012
Tel: +86(597) 2795053
Fax: +86(597) 2795053
EMail: lyun@lyun.edu.cn
Website: http://www.lyun.edu.cn/

President: Ze Yu Lee

College

Chemistry and Materials Science (Applied Chemistry; Chemistry; Materials Engineering); **Economics and Management** (Economics; Management; Marketing; Tourism); **Foreign Languages** (Applied Linguistics; English; Foreign Languages Education; Japanese; Modern Languages); **Humanities and Education** (Arts and Humanities; Chinese; Education; Journalism; Literature; Musicology; Psychology); **Life Science** (Biological and Life Sciences; Biology; Biotechnology; Veterinary Science); **Mathematics and Computer Science** (Applied Mathematics; Computer Engineering; Computer Science; Information Sciences; Mathematics; Mathematics and Computer Science); **Physics, Mechanical and Electrical Engineering** (Automation and Control Engineering; Electrical Engineering; Electronic Engineering; Information Technology; Mechanical Engineering; Physics); **Resource Engineering** (Furniture Design; Geological Engineering; Mining Engineering; Natural Resources; Surveying and Mapping; Wood Technology)

School

Continuing Education

Department

Art (Fine Arts); **Ideological and Political Theory Teaching and Research** (Political Sciences); **Physical Education** (Physical Education)

History: Founded 1958 as Longyan Higher Normal College. Renamed Fujian Resources Industrial School 2001. Acquired present status and title 2004.

Main Language(s) of Instruction: Chinese

Degrees and Diplomas: *Xueshi Xuewei*

Academic Staff *2012-2013*: Total: c. 600

Student Numbers *2012-2013*: Total: c. 7,500

Last Updated: 12/12/13

LUDONG UNIVERSITY

184 Shixue Road, Zhifu District, Yantai,
Shandong 264025
Tel: +86(535) 6013012
Fax: +86(535) 6011042
EMail: lxs@ldu.edu.cn
Website: http://www.ytnc.edu.cn

President: Liu Dawen

Department

Biology (Biology); **Chemistry** (Chemistry); **Chinese Language and Literature**; **Fine Arts**; **Geography**; **History**; **International Studies** (International Studies); **Law, Political Science and Economics** (Economics; Law; Political Sciences); **Mathematics and Computer Sciences** (Computer Science; Mathematics); **Modern Languages** (Modern Languages); **Music** (Music); **Physical Education**; **Physics** (Physics); **Psychology and Education**

History: Founded 1958 as Yantai Normal College, became Yantai Normal University and acquired present status and title 2006.

Fees: (US Dollars): 1700-6400 per annum, depending on subjects

Main Language(s) of Instruction: Chinese

Degrees and Diplomas: *Xueshi Xuewei*; *Shuoshi Xuewei*. Also Associate Degree (Literature)

LULIANG UNIVERSITY

38 Binhebei Donglu, Luliang, Shanxi 033000
Tel: +86(358) 8248710
Fax: +86(358) 8249976
EMail: xzb@llhc.edu.cn
Website: http://www.llhc.edu.cn/

School

Architecture (Architecture); **Arts** (Fine Arts; Music); **Chemistry** (Chemistry); **Chinese** (Chinese); **Computer Engineering** (Computer Engineering; Software Engineering); **Cultural Studies** (Cultural Studies); **Economics** (Economics); **Education** (Education; Preschool Education); **Engineering** (Chemical Engineering; Civil Engineering; Electronic Engineering; Food Science; Mechanical Engineering; Mining Engineering); **English** (English); **History** (History); **Life Science** (Biological and Life Sciences); **Mathematics** (Mathematics); **Physical Education** (Physical Education); **Physics** (Physics); **Politics and Law** (Law; Political Sciences); **Social Sciences** (Journalism; Psychology; Social Sciences)

History: Founded 1984 as Luliang Normal College, merged with Luliang Polytechnic College. Acquired present title 2010

Degrees and Diplomas: *Xueshi Xuewei*

Last Updated: 30/09/13

LUOYANG INSTITUTE OF SCIENCE AND TECHNOLOGY

90 Luolong King City Avenue, Luoyang,
Henan 471023
EMail: yld@lit.edu.cn
Website: http://www.lit.edu.cn

Department

Administration (Administration); **Economics** (Economics); **Engineering** (Engineering); **Fine Arts** (Fine Arts); **Law** (Law); **Science** (Natural Sciences)

Further Information: Also 2 other campuses

History: Founded 1980. Became Luoyang Institute of Science and Technology by merging of Luoyang College of Technology and Luoyang University in March 2007.

Degrees and Diplomas: *Xueshi Xuewei*

Last Updated: 29/10/13

LUXUN ACADEMY OF FINE ARTS

19 Sanhao Street, Helping District,
Shenyang, Liaoning Province 110003
Tel: +86(24) 23892467
Fax: +86(24) 23929750
EMail: lmwsb@lumei.edu.cn
Website: http://www.lumei.edu.cn/

President: Wei Ershen

Department
Chinese Painting (Painting and Drawing); **Cultural Communication and Management** (Communication Disorders; Cultural Studies; Management); **Environmental Art Design** (Design; Environmental Studies); **History of Art** (Art History); **Industrial Design** (Industrial Design); **Oil Painting** (Painting and Drawing); **Photography** (Photography); **Printmaking** (Printing and Printmaking); **Sculpture** (Sculpture); **Textile and Fashion Design** (Fashion Design; Textile Design); **Visual Communication Art Design** (Design; Visual Arts)

Centre
Art Culture (Art Education)

Further Information: Also a campus in Dalian

History: Founded 1938 as Luxun College of Arts, acquired present status and title 1958.

Degrees and Diplomas: *Xueshi Xuewei*; *Shuoshi Xuewei*
Last Updated: 31/10/12

LUZHOU MEDICAL COLLEGE

3 Zhongshan Road, Luzhou, Sichuan Province 646000
Tel: +86(83) 3163998
Fax: +86(83) 3162557
EMail: iceo@lzmc.edu.cn
Website: http://www.lzmc.edu.cn

President: Ma Yuerong

Dean: Liao Bin

College
Nursing (Nursing); **Pharmacy** (Pharmacy)

School
Continuing Education; **Public Health** (Public Health)

Department
Clinical Medicine (Laboratory Techniques; Medical Technology; Medicine; Physical Therapy); **Dentistry** (Dentistry); **Foreign Languages** (English); **Law** (Law); **Medicine** (Anaesthesiology; Epidemiology; Medicine; Neurology); **Otolaryngology** (Otorhinolaryngology); **Physiology** (Physiology); **Social Sciences** (Social Sciences); **Sport** (Sports); **Surgery** (Surgery); **Traditional Chinese Medicine** (Traditional Eastern Medicine)

Institute
Vascular Medicine (Cardiology)

Further Information: The college has 3 affiliated hospitals

History: Founded 1951 as Southern Sichuan Secondary School for Medical Practitioners, acquired present status 1959 and title 1978.

Degrees and Diplomas: *Xueshi Xuewei*; *Shuoshi Xuewei*; *Boshi*

Academic Staff *2011-2012*	**TOTAL**
FULL-TIME	c. **1,170**
Student Numbers *2011-2012*	
All (Foreign included)	c. **14,000**
FOREIGN ONLY	**300**

Last Updated: 10/01/13

MINJIANG UNIVERSITY

1 Wenxianlu, Daxuecheng, Fujian Fuzhou 350108
Tel: +86(591) 83761109
Fax: +86(591) 83761127
EMail: mjuoffice@mju.edu.cn
Website: http://www1.mju.edu.cn

President: Yang Bin

School
Adult Education; **Arts** (Arts and Humanities); **Chemistry and Chemical Engineering** (Chemical Engineering; Chemistry); **Chinese** (Chinese); **Clothing and Art Engineering** (Fashion Design; Textile Technology); **Computer Science** (Computer Science); **Economics and Finance** (Economics; Finance); **Foreign Languages** (English; Foreign Languages Education); **Geography** (Geography); **History** (History); **Management** (Management); **Mathematics** (Mathematics); **Physical Siences and Electronic and Information Engineering** (Electronic Engineering; Information Technology; Physics); **Political Sciences and Sociology** (Political Sciences; Sociology); **Tourism** (Tourism)

History: Founded 2002, after merging of Fuzhou Teacher Training College and Minjiang Vocational University

Degrees and Diplomas: *Xueshi Xuewei*
Last Updated: 17/07/13

MINZU UNIVERSITY OF CHINA

27 South Zhongguancun Street, Haidian District,
Beijing 100081
Tel: +86(10) 68933350 +86(10) 68932847
Fax: +86(10) 68933982
EMail: gjj1@cun.edu.en
Website: http://eng.muc.edu.cn/

President: Chen Li

College
Art (Fine Arts); **Dance** (Dance); **Economics** (Economics; Finance; International Business; International Economics); **Education** (Education); **Ethnology and Sociology** (Archaeology; Ethnology; Law; Museum Studies; Sociology); **Foreign Languages** (English; Italian; Japanese; Korean; Modern Languages; Russian; Translation and Interpretation); **History** (History); **Information Engineering** (Information Technology); **International Education** (Chinese); **Law** (Law); **Life Science and Environmental Sciences** (Alternative Medicine; Biology; Botany; Chemistry; Ecology; Environmental Studies); **Literature, Journalism and Communication Studies** (Communication Studies; Journalism; Literature); **Management** (Accountancy; Business Administration; Human Resources; Management; Marketing; Public Administration); **Marxism and Leninism** (Political Sciences); **Music** (Music); **Science** (Natural Sciences)

Department
Kazakh Language and Literature (Literature; Slavic Languages); **Korean Language and Literature** (Korean; Literature); **Language and Literature of Chinese Ethnic Minorities** (Asian Studies; Chinese; Literature); **Minority Languages and Literature** (Literature; Native Language Education); **Mongolian** (Mongolian); **Philosophy and Religion** (Philosophy; Religion); **Uygur Language and Literature** (Asian Studies; Native Language)

Research College
Tibetan Studies

History: Founded 1941 as Yan'an Institute for Nationalities. Became The Central University for Nationalities in 1993. Acquired current title 2008.

Degrees and Diplomas: *Xueshi Xuewei*; *Shuoshi Xuewei*; *Boshi*
Last Updated: 06/03/12

MUDANJIANG MEDICAL UNIVERSITY

3 Tongxiang Road, Mudanjiang, Heilongjiang 157011
Tel: +86(453) 6526156 Ext. 3218
Fax: +86(453) 6531054
EMail: mdjmu2006@163.com
Website: http://www.mdjmu.cn

Department
Clinical Medicine (Anaesthesiology; Medicine; Nursing; Paediatrics; Pharmacy; Public Health; Traditional Eastern Medicine); **Medical Imaging**

History: Founded 1958 as Mudanjiang Medical School, became Mudanjiang Medical College,1986.

Degrees and Diplomas: *Xueshi Xuewei*

Academic Staff *2012*: Total 2,300

Student Numbers *2012*: Total 10,000

Last Updated: 03/10/13

MUDANJIANG NORMAL UNIVERSITY

19 Wenhua Street, Xingzhong Road,
Mundanjiang, Heilongjiang Province 157422
Tel: +86(453) 6534206
Fax: +86(453) 6511203
EMail: ybz@mail.mdjnu.com
Website: http://www.mdjnu.cn

President: Xiu Pengyue

International Relations: Chen Jingwen

Department

Biology (Biology); **Chemistry** (Chemistry); **Chinese Language and Literature** (Chinese; Literature); **Computer Science and Technology** (Computer Science; Information Technology); **Electronic Engineering, Information Sciences and Technology** (Electronic Engineering; Information Sciences; Information Technology); **Fine Arts** (Design; Fine Arts); **Information and Computer Science** (Computer Science; Information Technology); **Management** (Business Administration; Tourism); **Mathematics** (Mathematics); **Modern Languages**; **Physical Education** (Physical Education); **Physics** (Physics); **Political Science and Law** (Law; Political Sciences); **Science Education** (Science Education)

History: Founded 1958 as branch school of Northeast Agriculture College, became Mudanjiang Teachers College 1970.

Degrees and Diplomas: *Xueshi Xuewei*; *Shuoshi Xuewei*

Last Updated: 07/11/12

NANCHANG HANGKONG UNIVERSITY (NCHU)

173 Shanghai Road, Nanchang,
Jiangxi Province 330009
Tel: +86(791) 8224596
Fax: +86(791) 8213248
Website: http://www.nchu.edu.cn/

President: Liu Gaohang

International Relations: Luo Liming

College

Mathematics and Information Sciences (Information Sciences; Mathematics)

School

Arts and Art Design (Arts and Humanities; Design); **Automation** (Automation and Control Engineering); **Civil Engineering** (Civil Engineering); **Economics and Management** (Economics; Management); **Further Education**; **Humanities and Law** (Arts and Humanities; Law); **Navy** (Nautical Science); **Physical Education** (Physical Education); **Scientific Technology** (Technology); **Software Engineering** (Software Engineering); **Vocational and Technical Education** (Technology Education; Vocational Education)

Department

Aeronautic and Mechanical Engineering (Aeronautical and Aerospace Engineering; Mechanical Engineering); **Applied Engineering** (Engineering); **Computer Science** (Computer Science); **Electronic and Information Engineering** (Electronic Engineering; Information Technology); **Environment and Chemical Engineering** (Chemical Engineering; Environmental Engineering); **Foreign Language** (English); **Materials Engineering** (Materials Engineering); **Military Science and Physical Education** (Military Science; Physical Education); **Social Sciences** (Social Sciences)

History: Founded 1952 as Hankou Aerotechnical School, became Nanchang Institute of Aeronautical Technology, 1978, acquired present status and name, 2007. Also known as Nanchang University of Aeronautics

Degrees and Diplomas: *Xueshi Xuewei*; *Shuoshi Xuewei*

Academic Staff *2011-2012*: Total: c. 1,170

Student Numbers *2011-2012*: Total 18,675

Last Updated: 10/01/13

NANCHANG INSTITUTE OF TECHNOLOGY (NIT)

289 Tianxiang Dadao, High-tech Developping Zone,
Nanchang, Jiangxi 330099
Tel: +86(791) 8307915
Fax: +86(791) 8307948
Website: http://www.nit.edu.cn

Director: Jin Zhinong

Faculty

Arts (Fine Arts); **Civil Engineering** (Civil Engineering); **Computer Science and Technology** (Computer Science; Technology); **Ecological Environment** (Ecology; Environmental Studies); **Electrical and Electronic Engineering** (Electrical and Electronic Engineering); **Foreign Languages** (English; Foreign Languages Education); **Humanities and Social Sciences** (Arts and Humanities; Social Sciences); **Management Engineering** (Management); **Mechanics and Power Engineering** (Mechanical Engineering; Power Engineering); **Science** (Natural Sciences); **Software Engineering** (Software Engineering); **Water Conservacy** (Water Science)

School

Adults Education; **International Education**

History: Founded 1958 as Nanchang College of Water Conservancy and Hydropower. Became Nanchang Junior College of Hydraulic Engineering, 1993. Acquired present status and title 2004.

Degrees and Diplomas: *Xueshi Xuewei*

Last Updated: 21/10/13

NANCHANG INSTITUTE OF TECHNOLOGY (NIT)

901 Yingxiong Avenue, Economical Developed Zone,
Nanchang, Jiangxi 330013
Tel: +86(791) 3865376
Fax: +86(791) 3865376
EMail: nclg@nut.edu.cn
Website: http://www.nclg.com.cn

Principal: Li Xianyu

Department

Aeronautical Engineering (Aeronautical and Aerospace Engineering); **Arts** (Fine Arts); **Biological and Ecological Environment** (Biological and Life Sciences; Ecology); **Civil Engineering and Architecture** (Architecture; Civil Engineering); **Computer Science** (Computer Science; Information Technology); **Economics and Management** (Advertising and Publicity; Economics; Management); **Electrical and Electronic Engineering** (Electrical Engineering; Electronic Engineering; Information Sciences; Mechanical Engineering); **Foreign Languages and Literature** (English; Foreign Languages Education; Literature); **Journalism and Mass Media** (Journalism; Mass Communication); **Nursing** (Nursing); **Physical Education** (Physical Education); **Political Sciences and Law** (Law; Political Sciences); **Psychology** (Psychology)

History: Founded 1999 as Jiangxi Aerospace and Technology College. Acquired present status and title, 2005.

Degrees and Diplomas: *Xueshi Xuewei*

Academic Staff *2012*: Total: c. 1,400

Student Numbers *2012*: Total: c. 25,000

Last Updated: 18/10/13

NANCHANG UNIVERSITY

235 Nanjing Donglu, Nanchang,
Jiangxi Province 330047
Tel: +86(791) 83969099
Fax: +86(791) 83969069
EMail: newncu@ncu.edu.cn
Website: http://www.ncu.edu.cn

President: Wenbin Zhou Tel: +86(791) 8305001

International Relations: Mingyong Xie, Vice-President

College

Gong Qing

School
Architecture (Architecture); **Basic Medical Science** (Medicine); **Chemistry and Materials Science** (Chemistry); **Civil Engineering** (Civil Engineering); **Computer and Information** (Computer Science; Information Technology); **Economics and Administration** (Accountancy; Administration; Economics; International Economics); **Electric and Automation Engineering** (Automation and Control Engineering; Electrical Engineering); **Electronic Information Engineering** (Electronic Engineering); **Environmental and Chemical Engineering**; **Foreign Language Studies**; **Humanities** (Arts and Humanities); **Journalism, Culture and Art** (Cultural Studies; Journalism); **Life Sciences and Food Engineering** (Aquaculture; Biological and Life Sciences; Biology; Food Science); **Mathematics and Physics** (Mathematics; Physics); **Mechanical and Electronic Engineering** (Electronic Engineering; Mechanical Engineering); **Paediatrics** (Paediatrics); **Physical Education and Military Training** (Military Science; Physical Education); **Politics and Law** (Administration; Law; Political Sciences); **Social Sciences** (Social Sciences)

Department
Medical Imaging (Medical Technology); **Preventive Medicine** (Medicine); **Stomatology** (Stomatology)

Institute
Sino-French Business Administration (Business Administration)

Further Information: Also 93 Laboratories and five campuses: Qian-Hu Main campus; Qingshan-Hu; Dong-Hu; Poyang-Hu and Fuzhou campus

History: Founded 1940 as Zhongzheng University. Acquired present name and status 1993 when the top two universities of Jiangxi Province Jiangxi University and Jiangxi Industrial University merged. NCU entered a new era of development when it merged with Jiangxi Medical College in August 2005

Academic Year: September to July (September-February; March-July)

Admission Requirements: Graduation from senior middle school and entrance examination

Main Language(s) of Instruction: Chinese, English

Accrediting Agency: Ministry of Education; General Political Department

Degrees and Diplomas: *Xueshi Xuewei*; *Shuoshi Xuewei*; *Boshi*

Student Services: Academic Counselling, Canteen, Careers Guidance, Cultural Activities, Foreign Studies Centre, Health Services, Language Laboratory, Social Counselling, Sports Facilities

Publications: Higher Education Reform; Journal of Nanchang University

Publishing House: Nanchang University Editorial Office

Academic Staff *2012*: Total 4,638

Student Numbers *2012*: Total 65,703

Last Updated: 19/11/12

NANJING AGRICULTURAL UNIVERSITY

1 Weigang, Nanjing, Jiangsu Province 210095
Tel: +86(25) 84892424
Fax: +86(25) 84395708
EMail: ietc@njau.edu.cn
Website: http://www.njau.edu.cn

President: Zhiming Yan
Tel: +86(25) 84395366 EMail: xb@njau.edu.cn

International Relations: Hongsheng Zhang
EMail: ietc@njau.edu.cn

Faculty
Agriculture (Agronomy; Forestry; Plant and Crop Protection; Rural Studies); **Animal Science and Technology** (Animal Husbandry; Fishery; Zoology); **Economics and Management** (Accountancy; Agricultural Business; Agricultural Management; Economics; Finance; International Economics; Management); **Engineering** (Agricultural Engineering; Agricultural Equipment; Automation and Control Engineering; Engineering; Industrial Design; Industrial Engineering); **Food Science and Technology** (Bioengineering; Food Science; Food Technology); **Foreign Studies** (English; Japanese; Linguistics; Literature); **Horticulture** (Chinese; Horticulture; Landscape Architecture); **Humanities and Social Sciences** (Law; Public Administration; Social Sciences; Sociology; Tourism); **Information Science and Technology** (Computer Science; Information Management; Information Technology); **International Education**; **Life Sciences** (Biotechnology; Microbiology; Molecular Biology); **Plant Protection** (Ecology; Plant and Crop Protection); **Public Administration** (Labour Law; Public Administration; Rural Planning; Social Welfare; Town Planning); **Resources and Environmental Sciences** (Agriculture; Environmental Studies; Microbiology; Natural Resources; Soil Science); **Science** (Computer Science; Information Sciences); **Veterinary Medicine** (Veterinary Science)

History: Founded 1952 as Agricultural College of Nanjing University. Acquired present title 1984.

Degrees and Diplomas: *Xueshi Xuewei*; *Shuoshi Xuewei*; *Boshi*

Publications: Animal Husbandry and Veterinary Medicine; China Agricultural Education Information; History of China's Agriculture; Journal of Nanjing Agricultural University

Last Updated: 19/11/12

NANJING AUDIT UNIVERSITY

77 Beiwei Road, Nanjing, Jiangsu Province 210029
Tel: +86(25) 6618619
Fax: +86(25) 6618619
EMail: nsyb@public1.ptt.js.cn
Website: http://www.nau.edu.cn

President: Wang Jiaxin

International Relations: Yu Su

College
Jinshen

School
Accountancy (Accountancy); **Administration** (Administration; Adult Education; Vocational Education); **International Auditing** (Accountancy; International Business); **Law and Politics** (Law; Political Sciences)

Department
Applied Mathematics (Applied Mathematics); **Chinese as a Foreign Language** (Chinese); **Economics** (Business and Commerce; Economics); **Finance** (Finance); **Foreign languages** (Foreign Languages Education); **Information Sciences** (Information Sciences); **Management** (Management); **Physical Education** (Physical Education)

History: Founded 1983 as Nanjing Finance and Trade College, acquired present status and name 1987. Previously known as Nanjing Audit Institute.

Main Language(s) of Instruction: Chinese

Degrees and Diplomas: *Xueshi Xuewei*; *Shuoshi Xuewei*

NANJING FORESTRY UNIVERSITY

159 Longpan Road, Nanjing, Jiangsu Province 210037
Tel: +86(25) 85412431
Fax: +86(25) 85412589
EMail: nfu@njfu.edu.cn
Website: http://www.njfu.edu.cn

President: Fuliang Cao

International Relations: Wang Qingyu
EMail: interpro@njfu.com.cn

College
Applied Technology (Technology); **Automotive and Traffic Engineering** (Automotive Engineering); **Civil Engineering** (Civil Engineering); **Economics and Management** (Economics; Management); **Forest Resources and Environment** (Environmental Studies; Forestry); **Landscape Architecture** (Landscape Architecture)

School
Arts and Design (Design; Fine Arts); **Chemical Engineering** (Chemical Engineering); **Humanities and Social Sciences** (Arts and Humanities; Social Sciences); **Information Science and Technology** (Information Sciences; Information Technology); **Vocational Education** (Civil Engineering; Forestry)

Department
Ideological and Political Theory Teaching (Political Sciences); **Physical Education** (Physical Education)
Institute
Electronic and Mechanical Engineering (Electronic Engineering; Mechanical Engineering); **Furniture and Industrial Design** (Furniture Design; Industrial Design); **Wood Science and Technology** (Wood Technology)
Graduate School
Continuing Education

History: Founded 1952 as Nanjing Institute of Forestry, acquired present status and title 1985.

Academic Year: September to July (September-January; February-July)

Admission Requirements: Graduation from high school and entrance examination

Main Language(s) of Instruction: Chinese

Accrediting Agency: Ministry of Forestry

Degrees and Diplomas: *Xueshi Xuewei*; *Shuoshi Xuewei*; *Boshi*

Publications: China Forestry Science and Technology; Forestry Energy Conservation Technique; Journal of Nanjing Forestry University

Publishing House: Nanjing Forestry University Press
Last Updated: 23/11/12

NANJING INSTITUTE OF PHYSICAL EDUCATION

8 Linggusi Road, Nanjing, Jiangsu Province 210014
Tel: +86(25) 84432317
Fax: +86(25) 84431552

President: Hua Hongxing

International Relations: Xin Li

Department
Athletics (Sports); **Physical Education** (Physical Education); **Sports** (Sports)
History: Founded 1956 as Nanjing Sports School, acquired present status and name 1958.
Degrees and Diplomas: *Xueshi Xuewei*; *Shuoshi Xuewei*
Last Updated: 07/01/13

NANJING INSTITUTE OF TECHNOLOGY

Philip King's Road, Jiangning Science Park 1,
Nanjing, Jiangsu Province 211167
Tel: +86(25) 58003988
EMail: zsb@njit.edu.cn
Website: http://www.njit.edu.cn

President: Chen Xiaohu

Vice-President: Wu Jianhua

School
Architecture and Civil Engineering (Architecture; Civil Engineering); **Art and Design** (Design; Fine Arts); **Automation** (Automation and Control Engineering); **Communications Engineering** (Telecommunications Engineering); **Computer Engineering** (Computer Engineering); **Continuing Education** (Continuing Education); **Economics and Management** (Economics; Management); **Materials Engineering** (Materials Engineering); **Mechanical Engineering** (Mechanical Engineering); **Power Engineering** (Electrical Engineering; Energy Engineering; Power Engineering); **Vehicle Engineering** (Automotive Engineering)
Department
Energy and Power Engineering (Energy Engineering; Power Engineering); **Environmental Engineering** (Environmental Engineering); **Foreign Languages; Humanities and Social Sciences** (Arts and Humanities; Social Sciences); **Physical Education** (Physical Education); **Sports** (Sports)
Institute
Connie

Centre
Electricity Simulation and Control Engineering (Automation and Control Engineering; Electrical Engineering); **Engineering** (Engineering); **Manufacturing Technology** (Technology)
History: Founded 2000.
Degrees and Diplomas: *Xueshi Xuewei*
Last Updated: 09/01/13

NANJING MEDICAL UNIVERSITY

140 Hanzhong Road, Nanjing, Jiangsu Province 210029
Tel: +86(25) 86862020
Fax: +86(25) 86862799
EMail: waishi@njmu.edu.cn
Website: http://www.njmu.edu.cn

President: Qi Chen EMail: qchen@njmu.edu.cn

International Relations: Xu Shan, Director
EMail: xushan@njmu.edu.cn

School
Basic Medical Sciences (Anatomy; Biochemistry; Medicine; Modern Languages; Molecular Biology; Pharmacology; Pharmacy; Physical Education); **Clinical Medicine** *(Fourth)* (Medicine); **Clinical Medicine** *(Third)* (Medicine); **Clinical Medicine** *(Gulou)* (Medicine); **Clinical Medicine** *(Second)* (Medicine); **Clinical Medicine** *(First)* (Medicine); **Continuing and Higher Vocational Technical Education** (Vocational Education); **Foreign Language** (English); **Medical Policy and Management** (Health Administration; Management); **Nursing** (Nursing); **Pharmacy** (Pharmacy); **Public Health** (Public Health); **Stomatology** (Stomatology)
History: Founded 1934 as Jiangsu Medical College, became Nanjing Medical College 1957, and acquired present status and title 1993.

Academic Year: September to July (September-January; February-July)

Admission Requirements: Graduation from senior middle school and entrance examination

Main Language(s) of Instruction: Chinese

Degrees and Diplomas: *Xueshi Xuewei*; *Shuoshi Xuewei*; *Boshi*

Publications: Journal Nanjin Medical University
Last Updated: 09/01/13

NANJING NORMAL UNIVERSITY

1 Wenyuan Road, Nanjing, Jiangsu Province 210046
Tel: +86(25) 85898060
EMail: sun@njnu.edu.cn
Website: http://www.njnu.edu.cn

President: Yongzhong Song

College
Chinese Studies *(International)* (Chinese); **Teacher Education** (Teacher Trainers Education)
School
Business Administration (Business Administration); **Chemistry and Materials Science** (Chemistry; Materials Engineering); **Chinese Language and Literature** (Chinese; Literature; Secretarial Studies); **Computer Science** (Computer Science); **Dynamics Engineering** (Engineering); **Economics and Law** (Economics; Industrial Management; Law; Political Sciences); **Education** (Education; Educational Sciences; Preschool Education; Psychology); **Electrical and Electronic Engineering** (Electrical and Electronic Engineering); **Fine Arts** (Fine Arts); **Foreign Languages and Cultures** (English; Japanese; Modern Languages; Russian); **Geography** (Earth Sciences; Geography; Tourism); **International Culture and Education** (Cultural Studies; International Studies); **Jingling** *(For Women)* (Women's Studies); **Journalism and Communications** (Communication Studies; Journalism; Mass Communication); **Life Sciences** (Biological and Life Sciences); **Mathematics** (Mathematics); **Music** (Music); **Physical Education** (Physical Education); **Physical Science and Technology** (Physics; Technology); **Public Administration** (Public Administration); **Social Development** (Development Studies; Social Studies)
History: Founded 1902 as Sanjinag Normal Academy, acquired present status and title 1984.

Academic Year: February to January (February-June; September-January)

Admission Requirements: Graduation from senior middle school and entrance examination

Fees: (US Dollars): Foreign students, c. 1,800-4,000

Degrees and Diplomas: *Xueshi Xuewei*; *Shuoshi Xuewei*; *Boshi*

Student Services: Academic Counselling, Canteen, Careers Guidance, Cultural Activities, Health Services, Nursery Care, Social Counselling, Sports Facilities

Publications: Fine Arts Education in China; Journal of Nanjing Normal University; References for Educational Research

Publishing House: Nanjing Normal University Publishing House

NANJING UNIVERSITY (NJU)

22 Hankou Road, Nanjing, Jiangsu Province 210093
Tel: +86(25) 83393186
Fax: +86(25) 83302728
EMail: xzbgs@nju.edu.cn
Website: http://www.nju.edu.cn/

President: Chen Jun Tel: +86(25) 3595219

Secretary-General: Xingcheng Hang
Tel: +86(25) 3592503 EMail: hangxingo@nju.edu.cn

International Relations: Chenfeng Huang
Tel: +86(25) 3593326 EMail: huang@nju.edu.cn

Division
Ideological and Political Theories (Political Sciences)

School
Astronomy and Space Sciences (Astronomy and Space Science); **Atmospheric Sciences** (Meteorology); **Business** (Accountancy; Business Administration; Economics; Finance; Human Resources; Industrial Management; Insurance; International Economics; Management; Marketing); **Foreign Studies** (English; French; German; International Business; Japanese; Korean; Russian; Spanish); **Geographic and Oceanographic Sciences** (Geography; Marine Science and Oceanography); **Jinling**; **Stomatology** (Stomatology)

Department
Acoustics and Engineering (Sound Engineering (Acoustics)); **Architecture** (Architecture); **Automatic Control and System Engineering** (Automation and Control Engineering; Systems Analysis); **Basic Medicine** (Medicine); **Biochemistry** (Biochemistry); **Biological Science and Technology** (Biology); **Biomedical Engineering** (Biomedical Engineering); **Chemical Engineering** (Chemical Engineering); **Chemistry** (Chemistry); **Chinese Studies** (Chinese); **Clinical Medical Sciences** (Medicine); **Communication Engineering** (Information Technology; Telecommunications Engineering); **Communication Studies** (Communication Studies); **Computer Science and Technology** (Computer Science; Technology); **Decision-Making Policy** (Leadership; Management); **Documentation** (Documentation Techniques; Information Sciences); **Drama, Film and Television** (Cinema and Television; Theatre); **Earth Sciences** (Earth Sciences); **Economic Law** (Law); **Economics** (Economics); **Electronic Science and Engineering** (Electronic Engineering); **Embedded Technology** (Technology); **Energy Science and Engineering** (Energy Engineering); **Environmental Engineering** (Environmental Engineering); **Environmental Sciences** (Environmental Studies); **Foreign Languages and Literature** (Literature; Modern Languages); **Geological Engineering and Information Technology** (Geological Engineering; Information Technology); **Highpolymer Science and Engineering** (Polymer and Plastics Technology); **History** (History); **Hydrosciences** (Hydraulic Engineering); **Information Management** (Information Management); **Information System Engineering** (Information Technology); **International Business Management** (Business Administration; International Business); **International Economic Law** (International Law); **International Economy and Trade** (Economics; International Economics); **Journalism** (Journalism); **Land and Marine Sciences** (Marine Science and Oceanography); **Law** (Law); **Linguistics** (Linguistics); **Literature** (Literature); **Materials Science and Engineering** (Materials Engineering); **Mathematics** (Mathematics); **Micro-Electronics and Photoelectronics** (Electronic Engineering); **Personnel Management and Social Security** (Human Resources; Social Welfare); **Philosophy** (Philosophy); **Physics** (Physics; Solid State Physics); **Political Sciences** (Political Sciences); **Psychology** (Psychology); **Public Administration** (Public Administration); **Quantum Electronics and Optical Engineering** (Optical Technology); **Social Work and Social Policy** (Social Policy; Social Work); **Sociology** (Sociology); **Software Engineering** (Software Engineering); **Urban and Regional Planning** (Regional Planning; Town Planning; Urban Studies); **Urban Planning and Design** (Design; Town Planning)

Institute
Education (Education)

Academy
Fines Arts (Fine Arts)

Centre
Model Animal Research (Zoology); **Sino-American Culture** (Cultural Studies)

Research Institute
Chinese Cultural Studies (Chinese; Cultural Studies; Literature; Modern Languages)

History: Founded 1902.

Academic Year: September to July (September-January; February-July)

Admission Requirements: Graduation from senior middle school and entrance examination

Main Language(s) of Instruction: Chinese

Accrediting Agency: State Education Commission

Degrees and Diplomas: *Xueshi Xuewei*; *Shuoshi Xuewei*; *Boshi*

Student Services: Academic Counselling, Canteen, Careers Guidance, Cultural Activities, Foreign Studies Centre, Health Services, Nursery Care, Sports Facilities

Publications: Approximation Theory and Its Application; Computer Science; Contemporary Foreign Literature; Geology of Higher Education; Humanities and Social Sciences; Inorganic Chemistry; Mathematics of Higher Education; Natural Sciences; Progress in Physics; Research on Higher Education; Review of Mathematics

Publishing House: Nanjing University Press

Last Updated: 27/12/12

NANJING UNIVERSITY OF AERONAUTICS AND ASTRONAUTICS

29 Yudao Street, Nanjing, Jiangsu Province 210016
Tel: +86(25) 84892440
Fax: +86(25) 84891512
EMail: icedao@nuaa.edu.cn
Website: http://ice.nuaa.edu.cn

President: Zhu Di (2009-) EMail: office@nuaa.edu.cn

College
Advanced Vocational Education (Automotive Engineering; Computer Engineering; English; Maintenance Technology; Mechanical Equipment and Maintenance; Vocational Education); **Aerospace Engineering**; **Automation Engineering** (Automation and Control Engineering); **Civil Aviation** (Aeronautical and Aerospace Engineering); **Economics and Management** (Economics; Management); **Energy and Power Engineering** (Automotive Engineering; Energy Engineering; Mechanical Engineering; Power Engineering); **Humanities and Social Sciences** (Arts and Humanities; Economics; English; Japanese; Journalism; Law; Media Studies; Philosophy; Political Sciences; Social Sciences); **Information Science and Technology** (Computer Science; Electronic Engineering; Information Sciences; Information Technology); **Material Science and Engineering** (Applied Chemistry; Engineering; Materials Engineering); **Mechanical Engineering** (Mechanical Engineering); **Natural Science** (Applied Physics; Mathematics; Natural Sciences)

Further Information: Also campuses in Minggugong and Jiangjunlu

History: Founded 1952 as Nanjing Aeronautical Institute, acquired present title 1993.

Degrees and Diplomas: *Xueshi Xuewei*; *Shuoshi Xuewei*; *Boshi*

Publications: Journal of DATA Acquisition and Processing; Journal of NUAA; Journal of Vibration Engineering; Journal of Vibration Measurement and Diagnosis

Last Updated: 11/01/13

NANJING UNIVERSITY OF FINANCE AND ECONOMICS

128 Tielu Bei Jie, Nanjing, Jiangsu Province 210003
Tel: +86(25) 83494933
EMail: foreignaffairs@njue.edu.cn
Website: http://www.njue.edu.cn

President: Xu Congcai

International Relations: Hou Lijun

School

Economics (Economics); **Accountancy** (Accountancy); **Economics** (Economics); **Finance** (Finance; Insurance); **Food Science and Engineering** (Engineering; Food Science); **Information Engineering** (Computer Science; Information Management; Technology); **International Economics and Commerce** (Business and Commerce; International Economics); **Law** (Law; Social Work); **Marketing and Logistics Management** (Marketing; Transport Management); **Public Finance and Taxation** (Finance; Taxation)

Department

Applied Mathematics (Applied Mathematics); **Artistic Design** (Design; Fine Arts); **Business Administration** (Business Administration; Human Resources; Management; Tourism); **Foreign Languages** (English); **Humanities and Social Sciences** (Arts and Humanities; Social Sciences); **Physical Education** (Physical Education)

History: Founded 1956 as Nanjing University of Economics. Acquired present title 2003.

Degrees and Diplomas: *Xueshi Xuewei*

Publications: Journal of Nanjing University of Economics

Last Updated: 14/01/13

NANJING UNIVERSITY OF INFORMATION SCIENCE AND TECHNOLOGY

114 Pancheng New Street, Pukou District,
Nanjing, Jiangsu Province 210044
Tel: +86(25) 7010085
Fax: +86(25) 7010085
EMail: qihao@nuist.edu.cn
Website: http://www.nuist.edu.cn

President: Li Lianshui

International Relations: Ye Qihao

College

Adult Education; **Binjiang**; **Professional Training** *(Technical)*

Department

Applied Meteorology; **Atmospheric Sciences** (Meteorology); **Chinese Language and Literature**; **Computer Science and Technology**; **Economics and Trade** (Business and Commerce; Economics); **Electronic Engineering** (Computer Engineering; Electronic Engineering); **Environmental Science and Engineering**; **Foreign Languages**; **Information Management**; **Law** (Law); **Mathematics**; **Physical Education**; **Physics** (Physics); **Public Administration** (Management; Public Administration); **Resource, Environment and City-rural Planning** (Environmental Studies; Rural Planning; Town Planning); **Spatial Information Science** (Aeronautical and Aerospace Engineering)

Academy

Yue Jian (Political Sciences)

History: Founded 1960 as Meteorological College of Nanjing University. Renamed Nanjing Institute of Meteorology 1963. Acquired present title 2004.

Main Language(s) of Instruction: Chinese

Degrees and Diplomas: *Xueshi Xuewei*; *Shuoshi Xuewei*; *Boshi*

NANJING UNIVERSITY OF POSTS AND TELECOMMUNICATIONS (NUPT)

66 Xin Mofan Malu, Nanjing, Jiangsu Province 210003
Tel: +86(25) 83492393
Fax: +86(25) 83492349
EMail: wb@njupt.edu.cn
Website: http://www.njupt.edu.cn

President: Zheng Yang (2006-)

College

Automation (Automation and Control Engineering); **Electronic Engineering** (Electronic Engineering); **Opto-Electronic Engineering** (Electronic Engineering; Optical Technology); **Telecommunications and Information Engineering** (Information Technology; Telecommunications Engineering)

School

Computer Science and Technology (Computer Science; Technology); **Continuing Education** (Technology); **Economics and Management** (Economics; Management); **Foreign Languages** (Foreign Languages Education); **Geography and Biology** (Biological and Life Sciences; Geography); **Humanities and Social Sciences** (Arts and Humanities; Social Sciences); **Materials Engineering** (Materials Engineering); **Media and Arts** (Arts and Humanities; Media Studies); **Natural Sciences** (Natural Sciences); **Software Engineering** (Software Engineering)

Department

Physical Education (Physical Education)

Further Information: Also two campuses: Xianlin District and Sanpailou District

History: Founded 1942 as Nanjing Postal College, became Nanjing Institute of Posts and Telecommunications1958, acquired present title 2005.

Main Language(s) of Instruction: Chinese

Degrees and Diplomas: *Xueshi Xuewei*; *Shuoshi Xuewei*; *Boshi*

Publications: Journal of Nanjing University of Posts and Telecommunications

Academic Staff *2011-2012*: Total 1,622
Student Numbers *2011-2012*: Total 16,771
Last Updated: 11/01/13

NANJING UNIVERSITY OF SCIENCE AND TECHNOLOGY (NUST)

200 Xiaolingwei, Nanjing, Jiangsu Province 210094
Tel: +86(25) 84432727
Fax: +86(25) 84431622
EMail: sunjing@njust.edu.cn
Website: http://www.njust.edu.cn

President: Xiaofeng Wang Tel: +86(25) 84315204

School

Automation (Automotive Engineering); **Chemical Engineering** (Applied Chemistry; Chemical Engineering; Chemistry; Energy Engineering; Environmental Engineering; Explosive Engineering; Materials Engineering; Safety Engineering); **Computer Science and Technology** (Computer Science; Technology); **Design and Communication** (Communication Studies; Design; Journalism); **Economics and Management** (Economics; Human Resources; International Business; Management; Management Systems; Marketing); **Electronic Engineering and Optoelectronic Technology** (Electronic Engineering; Microelectronics; Microwaves; Optical Technology; Telecommunications Engineering); **Environment and Biological Engineering** (Bioengineering; Biological and Life Sciences; Environmental Engineering; Environmental Studies); **Foreign Studies**; **Humanities and Social Sciences** (Arts and Humanities; Labour and Industrial Relations; Law; Public Administration; Sociology); **Mechanical Engineering** (Aeronautical and Aerospace Engineering; Automotive Engineering; Electronic Engineering; Industrial Design; Machine Building; Measurement and Precision Engineering; Mechanical Engineering; Robotics); **Power Engineering** (Laser Engineering; Measurement and Precision Engineering; Mechanics; Power Engineering; Thermal Engineering); **Science** (Applied Mathematics; Applied Physics; Civil Engineering; Mechanics; Statistics)

History: Founded 1953 as Artillery Technology Institute. Acquired present title 1993.

Academic Year: September to July

Admission Requirements: Graduation from senior middle school and national entrance examinations

Fees: (Yuan): 2,700-4,600

Main Language(s) of Instruction: Chinese, English

Accrediting Agency: Jiangsu Education Bureau

Degrees and Diplomas: *Xueshi Xuewei*; *Shuoshi Xuewei*; *Boshi*: **Engineering.**

Student Services: Academic Counselling, Canteen, Careers Guidance, Cultural Activities, Health Services, Sports Facilities

Publications: Journal of Nanjing University of Science and Technology; Journal of Nanjing University of Science and Technology

Last Updated: 21/12/12

NANJING UNIVERSITY OF TECHNOLOGY

5 Xinmofan Road, Nanjing, Jiangsu Province 210009
Tel: +86(25) 3587667
Fax: +86(25) 3211323
EMail: cie@njut.edu.cn
Website: http://www.njut.edu.cn

President: Huang Wei

International Relations: Karen Jin, International Programs Coordinator Tel: +86(25) 83587060 EMail: karenjm@njut.edu.cn

College

Automation and Electrical Engineering (Automation and Control Engineering; Electrical Engineering); **Biothechnology and Pharmaceutical Engineering** (Biotechnology; Pharmacy); **Chemistry and Chemical Engineering** (Chemical Engineering; Chemistry); **Civil Engineering** (Civil Engineering); **Continued Education**; **Continuing Education**; **Economics and Management** (Economics; Management); **Electronics and Information Engineering** (Electrical and Electronic Engineering; Information Technology); **Energy Engineering** (Energy Engineering); **Environment** (Environmental Engineering); **Food Science and Light Industry** (Food Science); **Foreign Studies** (English; German; Japanese); **Geomatics Engineering** (Surveying and Mapping); **Industrial and Artistic Design** (Design; Industrial Design); **International Education**; **Law and Administrative Management** (Administration; Law); **Materials Science and Engineering** (Materials Engineering; Polymer and Plastics Technology); **Mechanical and Power Engineering** (Mechanical Engineering; Power Engineering); **Pharmaceutical Sciences** (Pharmacy); **Political Education** (Education); **Pujiang College**; **Sciences** (Applied Chemistry; Applied Mathematics; Applied Physics; Computer Science; Information Sciences; Organic Chemistry); **Transportation Science and Engineering** (Transport Engineering); **Urban Construction and Safety Engineering** (Construction Engineering; Fire Science; Safety Engineering; Town Planning)

Department

Physical Education (Physical Education)

History: Founded 1958. Renamed Nanjing University of Chemical Technology 1995. Acquired present title and status 2001 following merger with Nanjing Institute of Architectural and Civil Engineering.

Main Language(s) of Instruction: Chinese

Degrees and Diplomas: *Xueshi Xuewei*; *Shuoshi Xuewei*; *Boshi*

Publications: Higher Education Research

Academic Staff *2012-2013*: Total: c. 2,800

Student Numbers *2012-2013*: Total: c. 26,000

Last Updated: 26/12/12

NANJING UNIVERSITY OF TRADITIONAL CHINESE MEDICINE

138 Xianlin Road, Nanjing, Jiangsu Province 210046
Tel: +86(25) 85811079
Fax: +86(25) 85811078
EMail: wsc@njutcm.edu.cn
Website: http://www.njutcm.edu.cn

President: Mianhua Wu

International Relations: Guicheng Huang, Director Tel: +86(25) 85811080 EMail: hgc@njutcm.edu.cn

College

Basic Medical Science (Medicine); **First Clinical Medicine** (Medicine); **Foreign Languages**; **Second Clinical Medicine** (Acupuncture; Medicine; Occupational Health)

School

Management (Management); **Nursing** (Nursing); **Pharmacy** (Pharmacy); **Psychology** (Psychology)

Department

Humanities and Social Sciences (Arts and Humanities; Social Sciences)

Institute

Information Technology (Information Technology)

History: Founded 1955 as Jiangsu School for Continuing Study of Traditional Chinese Medicine. Acquired present title 1995.

Degrees and Diplomas: *Xueshi Xuewei*; *Shuoshi Xuewei*; *Boshi*

Publications: Journal of TCM

Last Updated: 26/12/12

NANJING UNIVERSITY OF THE ARTS

No.74, Beijing West Road, Nanjing, Jiangsu Province 210013
Tel: +86(25) 3312350
Fax: +86(25) 3733746
EMail: nylxs@njarti.edu.cn
Website: http://www.njarti.edu.cn

President: Jianping Zou (2008-)

International Relations: Lihua Qiu, Vice President

College

Adult Education; **Cultural Industry** (Cultural Studies); **Dance** (Dance); **Design** (Design; Graphic Design; Industrial Design); **Fine Arts** (Fine Arts; Painting and Drawing; Sculpture); **Humanities** (Literature; Modern Languages; Political Sciences; Sports); **Industrial Design** (Industrial Design); **International Education**; **Media** (Media Studies); **Movie and Television** (Film; Radio and Television Broadcasting); **Music** (Music; Music Education; Musicology); **Pop Music** (Jazz and Popular Music; Music); **Summit** (Art Management; Dance; Graphic Design; Interior Design; Opera); **Vocational Education**

History: Founded 1912 as Shanghai Chinese Art College, became Nanjing Arts Institute 1958.

Main Language(s) of Instruction: Chinese

Degrees and Diplomas: *Xueshi Xuewei*; *Shuoshi Xuewei*; *Boshi*

Publications: Garden of Arts

Last Updated: 20/11/12

NANJING XIAOZHUANG UNIVERSITY

41 Beiwei Road, Nanjing, Jiangsu Province 210017
Tel: +86(25) 86569129
Fax: +86(25) 86614926
EMail: yuanzhang@njxzc.edu.cn
Website: http://www.njxzc.edu.cn

Programme

Arts and Humanities (Chinese; English; History); **Education** (Education; Physical Education; Preschool Education); **Fine and Performing Arts** (Design; Fine Arts; Music); **Mathematics and Computer Science** (Computer Science; Mathematics); **Natural Sciences** (Biological and Life Sciences; Geography; Physics); **Radio and Television Broadcasting** (Radio and Television Broadcasting); **Social Sciences** (Social Sciences); **Welfare and Protective Services** (Environmental Studies; Natural Resources; Social Work)

History: Founded 1927. Acquired present status 2003.

Degrees and Diplomas: *Xueshi Xuewei*

NANKAI UNIVERSITY

94 Weijin Road, Nankai District, Tianjin, Tianjin Province 300071
Tel: +86(22) 23508229
Fax: +86(22) 23502990
EMail: exchange@nankai.edu.cn
Website: http://www.nankai.edu.cn

President: Gong Ke (2011-)
Tel: +86(22) 23508632 +86(22) 23501631

Vice-President: Naijia Guan EMail: guanj@nankai.edu.cn

International Relations: Haiyan Gao, Director, Office for International Academic Exchanges
EMail: gaohaiyan@nankai.edu.cn; nkexchange@gmail.com

College

Chemistry (Chemistry; Organic Chemistry; Physical Chemistry; Polymer and Plastics Technology); **Chinese Language and Culture** (Ancient Civilizations; Chinese; Cultural Studies; Oriental Studies); **Environmental Sciences and Engineering** (Environmental Engineering; Environmental Studies); **Foreign Languages** (English; Modern Languages); **History** (History); **Information Sciences and Technology** (Computer Science; Information Sciences; Information Technology); **Life Sciences** (Biological and Life Sciences; Biology); **Software** (Software Engineering); **TEDA** (International Business; International Economics)

School

Applied Physics *(TEDA)* (Applied Physics); **Biotechnology** *(TEDA)* (Biochemistry; Molecular Biology); **Business Administration** (Accountancy; Business Administration; Finance; Human Resources; Management; Marketing); **Economics** (Economics); **Government** *(Zhou En Lai)* (International Relations; Political Sciences; Public Administration; Social Policy; Social Psychology; Social Work); **Law** (Law); **Literature** (Literature); **Mathematical Sciences** (Mathematics); **Medicine** (Medicine); **Modern Distance Education**; **Pharmacy** (Pharmacy); **Philosophy** (Philosophy); **Physics** (Physics)

Institute

Japanese Studies (Japanese)

History: Founded 1919. Incorporated the former Tianjin Institute of Foreign Trade 1994.

Academic Year: September to July (September-January; February-July)

Admission Requirements: Graduation from senior middle school and entrance examination

Fees: (Yuan): c. 4,000 per annum

Main Language(s) of Instruction: Chinese

Accrediting Agency: Ministry of Education

Degrees and Diplomas: *Xueshi Xuewei*; *Shuoshi Xuewei*; *Boshi*

Student Services: Academic Counselling, Canteen, Careers Guidance, Cultural Activities, Facilities for disabled people, Foreign Studies Centre, Health Services, Language Laboratory, Nursery Care, Social Counselling, Sports Facilities

Publications: Higher Education; Nankai Business Review; Nankai Economic Research; Nankai Journal (Natural Sciences and Social Sciences Editions)

Publishing House: Nankai University Press

Academic Staff *2011-2012*: Total: c. 4,300
Student Numbers *2011-2012*: Total: c. 23,000
Last Updated: 14/01/13

NANTONG UNIVERSITY

19 Qixiu Road, Nantong, Jiangsu Province 226001
Tel: +86(513) 85012000
Fax: +86(513) 85012255
EMail: xiaozhang@ntu.edu.cn
Website: http://english.ntu.edu.cn/index.htm

President: Xiaosong Gu EMail: xsgu@ntu.edu.cn

School

Business (Business Administration; Business and Commerce); **Chemistry and Chemical Engineering** (Chemical Engineering; Chemistry); **Computer Science and Technology** (Computer Science; Technology); **Education** (Education); **Electrical Engineering** (Electrical Engineering); **Electronics and Information Science** (Electronic Engineering; Information Sciences); **Fine Arts and Design** (Design; Fine Arts); **Foreign Studies**; **Further Education**; **Geography** (Geography); **Humanities** (Arts and Humanities); **Law and Politics** (Law; Political Sciences); **Life Sciences** (Biological and Life Sciences); **Mechanical Engineering** (Mechanical Engineering); **Medicine** (Medicine); **Nursing** (Nursing); **Public Administration** (Public Administration); **Public Health** (Public Health); **Sciences** (Natural Sciences); **Sports Science** (Sports; Sports Management); **Textile and Clothing** (Architecture; Textile Design); **Xinglin**

Department

Navigation Medicine (Medicine); **Neurosciences** (Neurosciences)

History: Founded in 1912 as Nantong Medical College. Merged with Nantong Institute of Technology and Nantong Teachers College in 2004, when obtained current title and status.

Admission Requirements: Undergraduate, High School Diploma or equivalent; Postgraduate, Bachelor's degree or equivalent.

Fees: (Yuan): Home students, 160,000 per annum; Foreign students, 16,000 - 25,000 per annum

Accrediting Agency: Ministry of Education

Degrees and Diplomas: *Xueshi Xuewei*; *Shuoshi Xuewei*; *Boshi*

Publications: Journals of Nantong University

Last Updated: 14/01/13

NANYANG INSTITUTE OF TECHNOLOGY

Changjiang Road 80, Nanyang, Henan
Tel: +86(37) 84231841
Fax: +86(37) 84230415
Website: http://www.nyist.edu.cn

Vice-Chancellor: Liu Rongying

International Relations: Yao Xiyuan Tel: +86(37) 84231879

Department

Economics (Economics); **Education** (Education); **Engineering** (Computer Engineering; Electrical and Electronic Engineering; Engineering); **Law** (Law); **Literature**; **Management** (Management); **Medicine** (Medicine); **Science** (Natural Sciences)

History: Founded 1987.

Last Updated: 04/11/13

NANYANG NORMAL UNIVERSITY

Nanyang, Henan
EMail: gjjy@nynu.edu.cn
Website: http://www.nynu.edu.cn

School

Agriculture (Agriculture); **Arts and Humanities** (Arts and Humanities); **Chemistry** (Chemistry); **Chinese Literature** (Chinese; Literature; Theatre); **Economics and Management** (Business Administration; Economics; International Economics; Management; Transport Management); **Education** (Education; Teacher Trainers Education); **Engineering** (Engineering); **Environmental Science and Tourism** (Environmental Engineering; Surveying and Mapping; Tourism); **Fine Art** (Fine Arts); **Foreign Language** (English; Japanese); **History and Culture** (Cultural Studies; History); **Journalism and Communication** (Communication Studies; Journalism; Radio and Television Broadcasting); **Law** (Law); **Life Science and Technology** (Bioengineering; Biological and Life Sciences; Technology); **Mathematics and Statistics** (Mathematics; Mathematics and Computer Science; Statistics); **Physics and Electronic Engineering** (Electrical Engineering; Physics); **Politics and Public Management** (Administration; Political Sciences; Public Administration); **Science**

Degrees and Diplomas: *Xueshi Xuewei*; *Shuoshi Xuewei*

Publications: Academic Forum of Nandu; Nanyang Normal University Academic Journal

Academic Staff *2012*: Total 1,400
STAFF WITH DOCTORATE: Total 780
Student Numbers *2012*: Total: c. 23,000
Last Updated: 04/11/13

NATIONAL ACADEMY OF CHINESE THEATRE ARTS (NACTA)

400 Wanquansi, Fengtai District, Beijing 100073
Tel: +86(10) 63351063
Fax: +86(10) 63351063
EMail: international@nacta.edu.cn
Website: http://www.nacta.edu.cn

President: Du Changsheng

Department

Chinese Traditional Opera *(Graduates Studies)* (Chinese; Cinema and Television; Literature; Music; Musicology; Painting and Drawing; Theatre); **Continuing Education** (Continuing Education); **Directing** (Conducting); **Dramatic Writing** (Writing); **General Education** (Chinese; Education; English; Ethics; Philosophy; Political Sciences); **Music** (Music; Opera); **New Media Arts**; **Performing Arts** (Musical Instruments; Performing Arts); **Physical Training** (Physical Education); **Stage Design** (Display and Stage Design)

History: Founded 1950 as Chinese Traditional Opera School. Acquired present title 1978.

Degrees and Diplomas: *Xueshi Xuewei*; *Shuoshi Xuewei*

Last Updated: 15/01/13

NEIJIANG NORMAL UNIVERSITY

705 Dongtonglu, Neijiang, Sichuan 641112
Tel: +86(832) 2341562
Fax: +86(832) 2341206
Website: http://www.njtc.edu.cn

President: Xie Feng

School

Literature and Journalism (Chinese; Journalism; Literature; Radio and Television Broadcasting)

Department

Chemistry and Life Sciences (Biological and Life Sciences; Chemistry); **Computer Sciences** (Computer Science; Information Sciences); **Economics and Management** (Economics; Management); **Education** (Education; Preschool Education); **Electronic and Information Sciences** (Electronic Engineering; Information Sciences); **Fine Arts** (Fine Arts); **Foreign Languages** (English); **Geography and Natural Resources** (Geography; Natural Resources); **Mathematics** (Applied Mathematics; Mathematics); **Music** (Music); **Physical Education** (Physical Education); **Politics, Law and History** (History; Law; Political Sciences)

History: Founded 1958 as Neijiang Teachers Training College.

Degrees and Diplomas: *Xueshi Xuewei*

Last Updated: 22/11/13

NINGBO DAHONGYING UNIVERSITY (NDU)

Ningbo, Zhejiang 315175
Tel: +86(574) 88052277
Website: http://www.nbdhyu.edu.cn/

College

Adult Education; **Mechanical and Electronic Engineering** (Automation and Control Engineering; Electrical Engineering; Hydraulic Engineering; Industrial Design; Machine Building; Measurement and Precision Engineering; Mechanical Engineering); **Software** (Computer Engineering; Computer Science; Software Engineering)

Programme

Electronic and Information (Computer Science; Electronic Engineering; Information Sciences; Mathematics)

School

Economics and Management (Business Administration; Economics; Finance; Information Management; Information Sciences; International Economics; Marketing; Transport Management); **Foreign Languages** (English; Japanese); **Humanity** (Advertising and Publicity; Design; Fine Arts; Journalism; Radio and Television Broadcasting)

Department

Social Sciences (Social Sciences)

Further Information: Also a campus in new zone of Hangzhou Bay

History: Founded 1997.

Degrees and Diplomas: *Xueshi Xuewei*

Student Numbers *2013*: Total: c. 17,000

Last Updated: 16/10/13

NINGBO UNIVERSITY

818 Fenghua Road, Jiangbei District,
Ningbo, Zhejiang Province 315211
Tel: +86(574) 87600249
Fax: +86(574) 87604338
EMail: wsc@nbu.edu.cn
Website: http://www.nbu.edu.cn

President: Yan Luguang Tel: +86(574) 87600253

Vice-President: Nie Qiuhua Tel: +86(574) 87600252

International Relations: Chen Yujuan
Tel: +86(574) 87600271 EMail: shelly@nbu.edu.cn

Faculty

Architectural Engineering, Civil Engineering and Environment (Architecture; Civil Engineering; Environmental Engineering; Geography (Human); Surveying and Mapping; Town Planning; Urban Studies); **Arts** (Art Management; Arts and Humanities; Design; Fine Arts; Music; Musicology; Performing Arts); **Business** (Business Administration; Economics); **Education** (Education; Educational Sciences); **Foreign Languages** (Arts and Humanities; French; Japanese; Modern Languages); **Information Sciences and Engineering** (Engineering; Information Sciences; Mass Communication; Mechanical Engineering; Telecommunications Engineering); **Law** (Commercial Law; Criminal Law; Law); **Liberal Arts and Communication** (Arts and Humanities; Chinese; Communication Studies; History; Literature; Modern Languages); **Life Science and Biotechnology** (Biological and Life Sciences; Biotechnology); **Marine Science** (Marine Science and Oceanography); **Maritime** (Marine Transport; Naval Architecture); **Materials and Chemical Engineering** (Chemical Engineering; Materials Engineering; Polymer and Plastics Technology); **Physical Education** (Physical Education; Sports; Sports Management); **Sciences** (Chemistry; Mathematics; Mathematics and Computer Science; Natural Sciences; Physics)

College

Continuing Education (Continuing Education); **Elementary Education** (Primary Education); **International**; **Science and Technology** (Engineering; Technology)

School

Graduate Studies; **Medicine** (Epidemiology; Health Administration; Medicine; Microbiology; Molecular Biology; Pharmacology; Surgery)

Further Information: Also courses for foreign students

History: Founded 1986. Incorporated Ningbo Teacher's College and Zhejiang Aquatic Products Institute 1996.

Academic Year: August to July (August-January; February-July)

Admission Requirements: Graduation from senior middle school and entrance examination

Main Language(s) of Instruction: Chinese

Accrediting Agency: Department of Education of Zhejiang Province

Degrees and Diplomas: *Xueshi Xuewei*; *Shuoshi Xuewei*

Student Services: Academic Counselling, Canteen, Careers Guidance, Cultural Activities, Foreign Studies Centre, Health Services, Language Laboratory, Nursery Care, Social Counselling, Sports Facilities

Publications: Journal of Ningbo University

Last Updated: 15/01/13

NINGDE NORMAL UNIVERSITY

No.98-1 Jiaochengnanlu, Jiaocheng District, Ningde,
Fujian 352100
Tel: +86(593) 2952906
Fax: +86(593) 2952906

President: Lin Yuexin

Vice President: Lin Shou

Department

Administration and Engineering (Administration; Engineering); **Biology** (Biology); **Chemistry** (Chemistry); **Chinese** (Chinese); **Computer Science** (Computer Science); **Elementary Education** (Primary Education); **English** (English); **Law** (Law); **Mathematics**

(Mathematics); **Physical Education** (Physical Education); **Physics** (Physics); **Politics Education** (Political Sciences); **Tourism** (Tourism)

History: Founded 1958 as Fu'an Teachers College. Acquired present title and status 2010.

Degrees and Diplomas: *Xueshi Xuewei*

Student Numbers *2013*: Total: c. 6,000
Last Updated: 16/10/13

NINGXIA MEDICAL UNIVERSITY

692, Shengli Street, Yinchuan, Ningxia Province 750004
Tel: +86(951) 4091732
Fax: +86(951) 4071296
EMail: admission@nxmc.info
Website: http://www.ningxiamedical.com/

President: Sun Tao

International Relations: Han Xiaobao
Tel: 86(951) 6980038
EMail: nxadmission@yahoo.com.cn

Department

Basic Science Research Education; **Clinical Medicine** (Dermatology; Endocrinology; Epidemiology; Forensic Medicine and Dentistry; Gastroenterology; Gynaecology and Obstetrics; Medicine; Neurology; Ophthalmology; Oral Pathology; Orthodontics; Orthopaedics; Otorhinolaryngology; Paediatrics; Psychiatry and Mental Health; Surgery; Urology); **Marxism Theory and Political Education** (Political Sciences); **Medical Radiology and Anesthesia** (Anaesthesiology; Radiology); **Nursing** (Nursing); **Pharmacology** (Pharmacology); **Public Sanitation** (Public Health; Social and Preventive Medicine); **Secondary Specialized Education** (Secondary Education; Special Education); **Stomatology** (Stomatology); **Traditional Chinese Medicine** (Traditional Eastern Medicine)

Institute

Cardiovascular Disease (Cardiology)

Centre

Experimental Animal

Laboratory

Molecular Biology (Molecular Biology)

Research Institute

Family Planning (Public Health); **Medical Science** (Medicine); **Neurology** (Neurology); **Oncology** (Oncology)

History: Founded 1958. Acquired present title and status 2008.

Fees: (Yuan): 115,000 for International MBBS courses (5 yrs)

Main Language(s) of Instruction: Chinese

Degrees and Diplomas: *Xueshi Xuewei*; *Shuoshi Xuewei*; *Boshi*: **Medicine; Public Health.**

Student Numbers *2012-2013*: Total: c. 26,000
Last Updated: 15/01/13

NINGXIA TEACHERS UNIVERSITY

161 Wenhuaxiang, Guyuan,
Ningxia, Ningxia Hui Autonomous Region 756000
Tel: +86(954) 2079453
Fax: +86(954) 2025672
Website: http://www.nxtu.cn

Department

Arts (Art Education); **Chinese** (Chinese; Literature); **Education** (Education); **Engineering** (Engineering); **Foreign Languages and Literature** (English; Literature); **History** (History); **Law** (Law); **Medical Science** (Medical Technology); **Science** (Chemistry; Mathematics; Physics)

History: Founded 1978 as Guyan Teachers Training College. Acquired present title and status 2005.

Degrees and Diplomas: *Xueshi Xuewei*; *Shuoshi Xuewei*
Last Updated: 02/12/13

NINGXIA UNIVERSITY

489 Helanshan West Road, Xinshi District,
Yinchuan, Ningxia Province 750021
Tel: +86(951) 2077800
Fax: +86(951) 2077740
EMail: dwhjzx@nxu.edu.cn
Website: http://www.nxu.edu.cn

President: He Jianguo

School

Adult Education (Adult Education); **Agriculture** (Agriculture); **Biological Science** (Biological and Life Sciences); **Chemistry and Chemical Engineering** (Chemical Engineering; Chemistry); **Civil Engineering and Water Conservation** (Civil Engineering; Water Management); **Distance Education** (Distance Education); **Economics and Management** (Economics; Management); **Educational Sciences** (Educational Sciences); **Fine Arts** (Fine Arts); **Foreign Languages and Cultures** (Modern Languages); **Humanities** (Arts and Humanities); **Mathematics and Computer** (Computer Science; Mathematics); **Mechanical Engineering** (Mechanical Engineering); **Music** (Music); **Physical Education** (Physical Education); **Physics and Electronic Information Engineering** (Electronic Engineering; Information Technology; Physics); **Politics and Law** (Law; Political Sciences); **Resources and Environment** (Environmental Studies; Natural Resources); **Xinhua**

History: Founded 1958. Merged with Ningxia Institute of Engineering and Yinchuan Teachers Training College 1997, and with Ningxia Agricultural College 2002.

Degrees and Diplomas: *Xueshi Xuewei*; *Shuoshi Xuewei*; *Boshi*

Publications: Higher Education Research of Ningxia University; Journal of Ningxia University

Academic Staff *2011-2012*: Total: c. 2,700
Student Numbers *2011-2012*: Total: c. 30,000
Last Updated: 15/01/13

NORTH CHINA ELECTRIC POWER UNIVERSITY (NCEPU)

Zhuxinzuhuang, Dewai, Beijing, Hebei Province 10206
Tel: +86(10) 61772074
Fax: +86(10) 80793074
EMail: admission@ncepu.edu.cn; icd@ncepu.edu.cn
Website: http://www.ncepu.edu.cn/

President: Liu Jizhen

School

Business Administration (Accountancy; Business and Commerce; Finance; Human Resources; Management); **Computer Science and Technology** (Computer Engineering; Computer Science; Software Engineering; Technology); **Control Engineering** (Automation and Control Engineering; Mechanical Engineering); **Electrical and Electronic Engineering** (Electrical and Electronic Engineering; Electronic Engineering); **Energy and Power Engineering** (Energy Engineering; Power Engineering; Thermal Engineering); **Environment Engineering** (Environmental Engineering); **Foreign Language** (English); **Human and Social Science** (Arts and Humanities; Law; Political Sciences; Public Administration; Social Sciences); **Mathematical and Physical Science** (Mathematics; Physics); **Nuclear Science and Engineering** (Nuclear Engineering); **Renewable Energy** (Energy Engineering; Environmental Engineering); **Science and Technology** (Engineering; Technology)

Further Information: Also a campus in Baoding

History: Founded 1958 as Beijing Electric Power Institute. Merged with North China Institute of Electric Power and Beijing Power Engineering and Economics Institute. Acquired present status 1995. Affiliated with the State Power Corporation of China.

Academic Year: September to July

Admission Requirements: Graduation from high school and entrance examination

Fees: (Yuan): Bachelor: 22000 per annum for foreign students

Main Language(s) of Instruction: Chinese

Degrees and Diplomas: *Xueshi Xuewei*; *Shuoshi Xuewei*; *Boshi*

Student Services: Academic Counselling, Canteen, Careers Guidance, Cultural Activities, Foreign Studies Centre, Health Services, Language Laboratory, Nursery Care, Social Counselling, Sports Facilities

Publications: Higher Education of Electric Power; Higher Education Theory and Practice; Journal of North China Electric Power University

Academic Staff *2011-2012*: Total: c. 27,000
Student Numbers *2011-2012*: Total: c. 1,700
Last Updated: 15/01/13

NORTH CHINA INSTITUTE OF AEROSPACE ENGINEERING

133 Aimin Donglu, Langfang, Hebei 065000
Tel: +86(316) 2083201
Fax: +86(316) 2232540
EMail: gao@nciae.edu.en
Website: http://www.nciae.edu.cn

President: Guo Tieliang

Department

Accounting and Finance (Accountancy; Finance); **Computer Science and Engineering** (Computer Engineering; Computer Science); **Construction Engineering** (Architecture; Construction Engineering); **Economic Management** (Economics; Management); **Electronic Engineering** (Automation and Control Engineering; Electrical Engineering; Electronic Engineering); **Foreign Languages** (English; Foreign Languages Education); **Materials Engineering** (Industrial Design; Materials Engineering; Metal Techniques); **Mechanical Engineering** (Aeronautical and Aerospace Engineering; Measurement and Precision Engineering; Mechanical Engineering); **Social Sciences** (Law; Nursing; Social Work)

History: Founded as Langfang Precision Machinery School; acquired present title 1985.

Degrees and Diplomas: *Xueshi Xuewei*
Last Updated: 30/09/13

NORTH CHINA INSTITUTE OF SCIENCE AND TECHNOLOGY

P.O. Box 206, East Yanjiao, Beijing 101601
Tel: +86(10) 61591417
Fax: +86(10) 61591963
EMail: office@ncist.edu.cn
Website: http://www.ncist.edu.cn

President: Yang Gengyu

School

Adult Education; **Safety and Engineering** (Mining Engineering; Safety Engineering)

Department

Architectural Engineering (Civil Engineering; Construction Engineering; Engineering; Heating and Refrigeration; Real Estate); **Basic Curriculum** (Computer Science; Information Sciences); **Computer Science and Technology** (Computer Science); **Electronics and Information Engineering** (Automation and Control Engineering; Electronic Engineering; Industrial Engineering; Information Technology; Telecommunications Engineering); **Environment** (Chemical Engineering; Environmental Engineering); **Foreign Languages** (English; Modern Languages); **Literature and Laws** (Law; Literature); **Management** (Accountancy; Business Administration; E-Business/Commerce; Economics; Hotel Management; International Economics; Marketing; Tourism); **Mechanical and Electronic Engineering** (Electronic Engineering; Mechanical Engineering); **Physical Education** (Physical Education)

History: Founded 1984 as a branch school of Beijing Coal Management Institute in Yanjiao. Became North China Mining College 1994. Acquired present title and status 2002.

Degrees and Diplomas: *Xueshi Xuewei*. Also non-degree programs

Publications: Journal of North China Institute of Science and Technology
Last Updated: 16/01/13

NORTH CHINA UNIVERSITY OF TECHNOLOGY

No.5 Jinyuanzhuang Road, Shijingshan District, Beijing 100041
Tel: +86(10) 88803237
Fax: +86(10) 88803581
EMail: fao@ncut.edu.cn; admission@ncut.edu.cn
Website: http://www.ncut.edu.cn

President: Wang Xiaochun Tel: +86(10) 68874420

International Relations: Xu Mei

College

Architecture and Civil Engineering (Architecture; Civil Engineering); **Art** (Advertising and Publicity; Design; Industrial Design); **Continuing Education**; **Economics and Management** (Business Administration; Economics; Management); **Humanities and Law** (Arts and Humanities; Chinese; English; Japanese; Law; Literature); **Information Engineering** (Engineering; Information Technology); **Marxist Theory Education** (Political Sciences); **Mechanical and Electrical Engineering** (Electrical Engineering; Mechanical Engineering); **Sciences** (Chemistry; Mathematics; Physics; Statistics)

History: Founded 1946 as Beijing State Senior Polytechnic High School, became Beijing Metallurgical Institute of Mechanical and Electrical Engineering 1978. Acquired present title 1985.

Academic Year: September to July (September-February; March-July)

Admission Requirements: Graduation from senior middle school and entrance examination

Main Language(s) of Instruction: Chinese

Accrediting Agency: Central and Beijing Municipal Governments

Degrees and Diplomas: *Xueshi Xuewei*; *Shuoshi Xuewei*

Student Services: Academic Counselling, Canteen, Careers Guidance, Cultural Activities, Health Services, Nursery Care, Social Counselling, Sports Facilities

Publications: Journal of North China University of Technology

Publishing House: University Printing House
Last Updated: 16/01/13

NORTH CHINA UNIVERSITY OF WATER RESOURCES AND ELECTRIC POWER (NCWU)

20 Zhenghua Street, Zhengzhou, Henan Province 450011
Tel: +86(371) 5727655 Ext. 3430
Fax: +86(371) 5729645
EMail: hbsyzs@ncwu.edu.cn

President: Lin Jinsong
Vice-President: Handong Liu
International Relations: Cui Yunhao

Faculty

Civil Engineering (Architecture; Civil Engineering; Design; Mechanical Engineering; Town Planning; Urban Studies); **Dynamic Engineering** (Electrical Engineering; Power Engineering); **Economics** (Accountancy; Economics; Industrial Engineering; Information Management; International Economics); **Environmental Engineering** (Architectural and Environmental Design; Environmental Engineering; Fire Science; Water Management); **Foreign Languages** (English); **Geothechnical Engineering** (Civil Engineering; Environmental Engineering; Geological Engineering; Geology; Hydraulic Engineering); **Information Engineering** (Computer Science; Information Technology); **Law** (Law); **Mathematics and Computer Science** (Computer Science; Mathematics; Statistics); **Mechanical Engineering** (Automation and Control Engineering; Automotive Engineering; Materials Engineering; Mechanical Engineering); **Water Conservation Engineering** (Hydraulic Engineering; Water Management; Water Science)

History: Founded 1951 as Beijing University Water Conservancy and Electric Power, acquired present name 1978.

Main Language(s) of Instruction: Chinese

Degrees and Diplomas: *Xueshi Xuewei*; *Shuoshi Xuewei*
Last Updated: 16/01/13

NORTH SICHUAN MEDICAL COLLEGE

234# Fujiang Road, Nanchong, Sichuan Province 637007
Tel: +86(817) 2242632
Fax: +86(817) 2242600
EMail: fao@nsmc.edu.cn
Website: http://www.nsmc.edu.cn/en/

President: Kang Jian

International Relations: Hu Hongyi

Department

Anesthesiology (Anaesthesiology); **Biomedical Engineering** (Biomedical Engineering); **Clinical Medicine**; **Forensic Medicine** (Forensic Medicine and Dentistry); **Health Administration** (Health Administration); **Laboratory Medicine** (Medical Technology); **Medical Imaging** (Radiology); **Nursing** (Nursing); **Optometry and Ophthalmology** (Ophthalmology); **Social Science** (English; Social Sciences); **Stomatology** (Stomatology); **Traditional Chinese and Western medicine** (Medicine; Traditional Eastern Medicine)

History: Founded 1951 as North Sichuan Nursing School, acquired present status and title 1985.

Main Language(s) of Instruction: Chinese

Degrees and Diplomas: *Xueshi Xuewei*

Last Updated: 16/01/13

NORTH UNIVERSITY OF CHINA

3 Xueyuan Road, Taiyuan, Shanxi Province 030051
Tel: +86(351) 3921209
Fax: +86(351) 4048163
EMail: webmaster@nuc.edu.cn
Website: http://www.nuc.edu.cn

President: Liu Youzhi (2012-)

School

Chemical Engineering and Environment (Chemical Engineering; Environmental Engineering; Safety Engineering); **Continuing Education** (Continuing Education); **Economics and Management** (Economics; Management); **Electronic and Computer Science and Technology** (Computer Networks; Computer Science; Electronic Engineering); **Graduate Studies**; **Humanities and Social Sciences** (Administration; Arts and Humanities; Communication Studies; Foreign Languages Education; Journalism; Law; Political Sciences); **Information and Communication Engineering** (Communication Studies; Electrical and Electronic Engineering; Electrical Engineering; Information Technology); **Materials Science and Engineering** (Materials Engineering; Production Engineering); **Mechanical Engineering and Automation** (Automation and Control Engineering; Industrial Engineering; Mechanical Engineering); **Mechatronic Engineering** (Automation and Control Engineering; Automotive Engineering; Electronic Engineering; Mechanical Engineering); **Science** (Chemistry; Mathematics; Mechanical Engineering; Physics); **Software** (Software Engineering); **Sports and Arts** (Art Education; Music; Sports)

History: Founded 1940 as Taihang Technical School. Renamed North China Institute of Technology 1993. Acquired present title 2001.

Main Language(s) of Instruction: Chinese

Degrees and Diplomas: *Xueshi Xuewei*; *Shuoshi Xuewei*; *Boshi*

Last Updated: 17/01/13

NORTHEAST AGRICULTURAL UNIVERSITY

59 Mucai Street, Xiangfang District,
Harbin, Heilongjiang Province 150030
Tel: +86(451) 55190114
EMail: neauxcb@126.com
Website: http://www.neau.edu.cn

President: Xu Mei

College

Art (Design; Music; Musical Instruments; Visual Arts); **Continuing Education**; **Graduate Studies**; **Law** (Civil Law; Commercial Law; Criminal Law; Law); **Physical Education** (Physical Education)

School

Administration (Administration); **Agriculture** (Agriculture; Agronomy; Biology; Environmental Studies; Plant and Crop Protection); **Animal Science and Technology** (Animal Husbandry; Aquaculture; Cattle Breeding; Technology); **Applied Technology** (Agricultural Education); **Economics and Management** (Accountancy; Agricultural Management; Business Administration; Business and Commerce; Economics; Finance; Insurance; International Economics; Management; Marketing; Rural Planning); **Engineering** (Agricultural Engineering; Agricultural Equipment; Civil Engineering; Computer Science; Engineering; Engineering Management); **Food Science** (Biochemistry; Food Science; Molecular Biology); **Horticulture** (Horticulture); **Humanities and Social Sciences** (Chinese; Development Studies; English; Human Resources; Japanese; Russian; Social Sciences; Social Work; Tourism); **Life Sciences** (Biochemistry; Biological and Life Sciences; Biotechnology; Botany; Microbiology; Molecular Biology); **Professional Technology** (Technology); **Resources and Environment** (Ecology; Environmental Studies; Rural Planning; Soil Conservation; Soil Science; Surveying and Mapping; Town Planning); **Science** (Applied Chemistry; Biophysics; Computer Science; Information Sciences); **Town Planning** (Town Planning); **Veterinary Science** (Biological and Life Sciences; Veterinary Science); **Water Conservancy and Construction** (Civil Engineering; Construction Engineering; Electrical Engineering; Water Management)

History: Founded 1948 as Northeast Agricultural College. Merged with Heilongjiang Provincial Agricultural Administrators' Training College. Acquired present title 1994.

Academic Year: September to July (September-January; March-July)

Admission Requirements: Graduation from high school

Main Language(s) of Instruction: Chinese

Degrees and Diplomas: *Xueshi Xuewei*; *Shuoshi Xuewei*; *Boshi*

Student Services: Academic Counselling, Cultural Activities, Health Services, Nursery Care, Social Counselling, Sports Facilities

Publications: Journal of Northeast Agricultural University; Research on Fishing Economics and Soybean Technology

Publishing House: Northeast Agricultural University Publishing House

NORTHEAST DIANLI UNIVERSITY

169 Changchun Road, Jilin, Jilin Province 132012
Tel: +86(432) 64806433
Fax: +86(432) 64884186
EMail: ddy@mail.nedu.edu.cn
Website: http://www.nedu.edu.cn

President: Li Guoqing Tel: +86(432) 64806458

School

Arts (Arts and Humanities; Design; Fashion Design; Industrial Design); **Automation Engineering** (Automation and Control Engineering); **Chemical Engineering** (Applied Chemistry; Chemical Engineering); **Civil Engineering** (Civil Engineering); **Economics and Management** (Accountancy; Business Administration; Engineering Management; International Economics); **Electrical Engineering** (Electrical Engineering; Power Engineering); **Energy and Power Engineering** (Energy Engineering; Nuclear Engineering; Power Engineering; Thermal Engineering); **Foreign Languages** (English; Japanese); **Information Technology** (Computer Science; Information Management; Information Technology; Software Engineering); **Mechanical Engineering** (Electronic Engineering; Mechanical Engineering); **Physical Education** (Leisure Studies; Physical Education; Sports); **Power Transmission and Distribution Technology** (Power Engineering); **Science** (Mathematics; Physics); **Social Sciences** (Social Sciences)

Department

Media Technology and Transmission (Film; Media Studies; Radio and Television Broadcasting)

History: Founded 1949. In 1978 name changed to Northeast China Institute of Electric Power Engineering. Acquired present name and status 2005.

Academic Year: September to July (September-January; March-July)

Admission Requirements: Finished 12-year or above education

Fees: (Yuan): Chinese Language Students:10,400 per annum; Undergraduates:17,000/annum; Master:19,000/annum; PhD: 22,000/annum, Registration Fee: 400; Insurance fee: 600/annum

Degrees and Diplomas: *Xueshi Xuewei*; *Shuoshi Xuewei*; *Boshi*

Student Services: Careers Guidance

Academic Staff *2011-2012*: Total: c. 18,000

Last Updated: 18/01/13

NORTHEAST FORESTRY UNIVERSITY (NEFU)

26 Hexing Road, Harbin, Heilongjiang Province 150040
Tel: +86(451) 82192015 +86(451) 82192020
Fax: +86(451) 82110148
EMail: daifang@nefu.edu.cn
Website: http://www.nefu.edu.cn

President: Yang Chuanping Tel: +86(451) 2190131

College

Civil Engineering (Civil Engineering; Construction Engineering; Engineering Management; Town Planning); **Continuing Education** (Continuing Education); **Electromechanical Engineering** (Computer Engineering; Electrical Engineering; Electronic Engineering; Mechanical Engineering; Transport and Communications); **Engineering and Technology** (Forestry; Industrial Engineering; Packaging Technology; Technology); **Foreign Languages** (English; Modern Languages); **Forest Economics and Management** (Accountancy; Economics; Finance; Forestry; Management; Statistics; Taxation); **Forestry** (Bioengineering; Environmental Studies; Food Science; Forest Biology; Forest Products; Zoology); **Humanities and Law** (Administration; Advertising and Publicity; Arts and Humanities; Law; Political Sciences; Social Sciences); **Information and Computer Engineering** (Computer Engineering; Computer Science; Information Management); **Landscape Architecture** (Landscape Architecture); **Life Sciences** (Biological and Life Sciences); **Material Science and Engineering** (Materials Engineering); **Sciences** (Applied Chemistry; Applied Mathematics; Applied Physics; Computer Science; Education; Information Sciences); **Traffic**; **Wildlife Resources** (Biological and Life Sciences; Forestry; Tourism; Wildlife)

Department

Marxism (Political Sciences); **Physical Education** (Physical Education)

History: Founded 1952.

Academic Year: March to February (March-July; September-February)

Admission Requirements: Graduation from senior middle school and entrance examination

Fees: (US Dollars): 1,500-3,000 per annum

Main Language(s) of Instruction: Chinese

Accrediting Agency: Foreign Affairs Office

Degrees and Diplomas: *Xueshi Xuewei*; *Shuoshi Xuewei*; *Boshi*

Student Services: Academic Counselling, Canteen, Cultural Activities, Foreign Studies Centre, Health Services, Language Laboratory, Nursery Care, Sports Facilities

Publications: Bulletin of Botanical Research; China Forestry Business; Chinese Wildlife; Forest Engineering; Forest Fire Prevention; Journal of Forestry Research (in English); Journal of Northeast Forestry University

Publishing House: Northeast Forestry University Press

Last Updated: 18/01/13

NORTHEAST NORMAL UNIVERSITY

5268 Renmin Street, Changchun, Jilin Province 130024
Tel: +86(431) 85099754
EMail: efly@nenu.edu.cn
Website: http://www.nenu.edu.cn

President: Liu Yichun (2012-)

School

Business (Business Administration; International Business); **Chemistry** (Chemistry); **Chinese Language and Literature** (Chinese; Literature); **Computer Science and Information Technology** (Computer Science; Information Technology); **Economics** (Economics); **Education** (Education); **Ethnic Education** (Ethnology); **Fine Arts** (Fine Arts); **Foreign Languages** (English; Literature; Modern Languages); **History and Culture** (Cultural Studies; History); **Life Sciences** (Biological and Life Sciences); **Long Distance and Continuing Education**; **Mathematics and Statistics** (Mathematics; Statistics); **Media Science** (Media Studies); **Music** (Music); **Physical Education** (Physical Education); **Physics** (Physics); **Politics and Law** (Law; Political Sciences); **Software** (Software Engineering); **Urban and Environmental Science** (Environmental Studies; Urban Studies)

Institute

International Relations and Marxism

History: Founded 1946. Acquired present title 1980.

Main Language(s) of Instruction: Chinese

Degrees and Diplomas: *Xueshi Xuewei*; *Shuoshi Xuewei*; *Boshi*

Publications: Journal of Ancient Civilization; Journal of International Studies; Journal of Molecular Science; Journal of Northeast Normal University

Academic Staff *2011-212*: Total: c. 24,500

Student Numbers *2011-2012*: Total: c. 1,480

Last Updated: 21/01/13

NORTHEAST PETROLEUM INSTITUTE

Daqing City Development Road 199, Daqing, Heilongjiang 163318
Tel: +86(459) 4653391
Fax: +86(459) 4653380
Website: http://www.dqpi.edu.cn

President: Yang Xiaolong

Department

Architectural Engineering (Structural Architecture); **Automation and Control Engineering** (Automation and Control Engineering); **Computer Science** (Computer Science); **Economics** (Economics); **Electronic Engineering** (Electronic Engineering); **Foreign Languages** (Modern Languages); **Mathematics** (Mathematics); **Petroleum and Gas Engineering** (Chemical Engineering; Mechanical Engineering; Petroleum and Gas Engineering); **Social Sciences** (Social Sciences)

History: Founded 1960 as Northeastern Petroleum Institute. Formerly known as Daqing Petroleum Institute.

Main Language(s) of Instruction: Chinese

Degrees and Diplomas: *Xueshi Xuewei*; *Shuoshi Xuewei*; *Boshi*

Publications: Journal of Daqing Petroleum Institute

NORTHEAST PETROLEUM UNIVERSITY (NEPU)

Hi-Tech Development Zone, Daqing, Heilongjiang 163318
Tel: +86 (459) 650-3662
Fax: +86 (459) 650-3380
EMail: zsb007@126.com
Website: http://www.dqpi.edu.cn/

President: Yang Liu

Faculty

Arts (Arts and Humanities); **Economics** (Economics); **Engineering** (Chemical Engineering; Engineering; Petroleum and Gas Engineering); **Law** (Law); **Management** (Management); **Pedagogy** (Pedagogy); **Science** (Natural Sciences)

History: Founded 1960, as Northeast Petroleum Institute, renamed Daqing Petroleum Institute 1975. Acquired present title and status 2010.

Admission Requirements: High School Diploma

Degrees and Diplomas: *Xueshi Xuewei*; *Shuoshi Xuewei*; *Boshi*

Last Updated: 03/10/13

NORTHEASTERN UNIVERSITY (NEU)

No. 3-11 Wen Hua Road, Heping District,
Shenyang, Liaoning Province 110004
Tel: +86(24) 83685590
EMail: webmaster@mail.neu.edu.cn
Website: http://www.neu.edu.cn

President: Ding Lieyun

College
Business Administration (Accountancy; Business Administration; Finance; Industrial Engineering; International Business; Management; Marketing); **Foreign Studies** (English; Japanese); **Humanities and Law** (Administration; Arts and Humanities; International Law; Law); **Information Science and Engineering** (Automation and Control Engineering; Biomedical Engineering; Computer Engineering; Computer Science; Electronic Engineering; Information Management; Information Sciences; Information Technology; Management Systems; Measurement and Precision Engineering); **Materials and Metallurgy** (Materials Engineering; Metal Techniques; Metallurgical Engineering; Thermal Engineering); **Mechanical Engineering and Automation** (Automation and Control Engineering; Hydraulic Engineering; Mechanical Engineering); **Resources and Civil Engineering** (Civil Engineering; Environmental Engineering; Mining Engineering; Natural Resources; Safety Engineering); **Science** (Applied Chemistry; Applied Mathematics; Applied Physics; Mathematics and Computer Science; Natural Resources; Physics)

School
Distance Education (Business and Commerce; Finance; Software Engineering); **Fine Arts** (Design; Fine Arts; Music)

Centre
Automation Engineering Research *(National)* (Automation and Control Engineering); **Computer Software Research** *(National)* (Computer Science; Software Engineering)

History: Founded 1923. Acquired present status and title 1950 and incorporated Shenyang Institute of Gold Technology (founded 1952).

Academic Year: September to July (September-January March-July)

Admission Requirements: Graduation from high school and entrance examination

Main Language(s) of Instruction: Chinese

Degrees and Diplomas: *Xueshi Xuewei*; *Shuoshi Xuewei*; *Boshi*

Student Services: Canteen, Careers Guidance, Foreign Studies Centre, Health Services, Language Laboratory, Nursery Care, Sports Facilities

Publications: Basic Automation; Control and Decision; Journal of Northeastern University; Metallurgical Economy and Management; Software Engineers

Publishing House: Northeastern University Press

Last Updated: 21/01/13

NORTHWEST A & F UNIVERSITY (NWSUAF)

3 Taicheng Road, Yangling, Shaanxi 712100
Tel: +86(29) 87082857
Fax: +86(29) 87082892
EMail: ipo@nwsuaf.edu.cn
Website: http://www.nwsuaf.edu.cn

President: Sun Qixin Tel: +86(29) 87082812

Vice-President: Zhao Zhong

International Relations: Jun Luo, Director
Tel: +86(29) 87082891 EMail: luojun@nwsuaf.edu.cn

College
Agronomy (Agronomy; Botany; Crop Production); **Animal Science and Technology** (Biology; Horticulture; Veterinary Science; Zoology); **Economics and Management** (Accountancy; Agricultural Economics; Agricultural Management; Business and Commerce; Business Computing; Economics; Finance; Forestry; Industrial Management; International Business; Natural Resources); **Food Science and Engineering** (Food Science); **Foreign Languages** (English); **Forestry** (Forestry; Landscape Architecture; Wildlife; Wood Technology); **Horticulture** (Agricultural Engineering; Floriculture; Horticulture); **Humanities** (Arts and Humanities); **Information Engineering** (Computer Engineering; Computer Science; Information Management; Information Technology; Software Engineering; Systems Analysis); **Innovative Experiment**; **Life Science** (Biological and Life Sciences); **Mechanical and Electronic Engineering** (Agricultural Equipment; Automation and Control Engineering; Electronic Engineering; Industrial Design; Information Technology; Mechanical Engineering; Packaging Technology; Production Engineering); **Oenology** (Oenology); **Physical Education** (Physical Education); **Plant Protection** (Pharmacology; Plant and Crop Protection); **Resources and Environment** (Ecology; Environmental Engineering; Environmental Studies; Hydraulic Engineering; Information Technology; Natural Resources; Rural Planning; Soil Conservation; Town Planning; Water Management); **Science** (Applied Chemistry; Applied Mathematics; Biophysics; Computer Science); **Veterinary Science** (Veterinary Science); **Vocational and Adult Education** (Adult Education); **Water Resources and Architectural Engineering** (Architecture and Planning; Water Management)

Institute
Ideological and Political Education (Political Sciences); **Soil and Water Conservation** (Soil Conservation; Water Management)

History: Founded as school 1934. Merger between Northwest Agricultural University and Northwest Forestry University. Acquired present status and title 1999.

Academic Year: September to July (September-January; February-July)

Admission Requirements: Graduation from senior middle school and entrance examination

Main Language(s) of Instruction: Chinese

Accrediting Agency: Ministry of Education

Degrees and Diplomas: *Xueshi Xuewei*; *Shuoshi Xuewei*; *Boshi*

Student Services: Academic Counselling, Canteen, Careers Guidance, Cultural Activities, Health Services, Language Laboratory, Nursery Care, Social Counselling, Sports Facilities

Publications: Agricultural Research in Arid Area; Forestry Science and Technology in Shaanxi Province; Journal of Insect Classification; Journal of Northwest Agriculture; Journal of Northwest Forestry College; Journal of Northwest Plant; Journal of Northwest Sci-University of Agriculture and Forestry, Social Science and Natural Sciences; Journal of Soil and Water Conservation; Journal of Wheat Crop; Livestock Ecology; Magazine of Animal Husbandry and Veterinary Medicine; Northwest Water Resource and Irrigation Works; Northwest Water Resource and Irrigation Works; Progress of Animal Medicine; Soil and Water Conservation Bulletin; Soil and Water Conservation Bulletin; Study of Soil and Water Conservation; Village Economy in Shaanxi Province

Academic Staff *2011-2012*: Total 4,672
Student Numbers *2011-2012*: Total 27,100
Last Updated: 21/01/13

NORTHWEST NORMAL UNIVERSITY

967 East Anning Road, Hanning District,
Lanzhou, Gansu Province 730070
Tel: +86(931) 7971114
Fax: +86(931) 7661274
EMail: wlzx@nwnu.edu.cn
Website: http://www.nwnu.edu.cn

President: Wang Jiayi

College
Chemistry and Chemical Engineering (Chemical Engineering; Chemistry); **Chinese Language and Litterature** (Chinese; Literature); **Communication Studies** (Communication Studies); **Computer Science and Engineering** (Computer Engineering; Computer Science); **Continuing Education**; **Economics** (Accountancy; Economics; Management); **Education** (Curriculum; Education; Educational Sciences); **Educational Technology** (Educational Technology); **Fine Arts** (Fine Arts); **Foreign Languages and Literature** (English; Literature; Modern Languages); **Geography and Environmental Science** (Environmental Studies; Geography); **History and Culture** (Cultural Studies; History); **Life Sciences** (Biological and Life Sciences); **Marxism** (Political Sciences); **Mathematics and Statistics** (Mathematics; Statistics); **Music** (Music); **Physical Education** (Physical Education); **Physics and Electronic Engineering** (Electronic Engineering; Physics); **Psygohology** (Psychology); **Social Development and Public Management** (Development Studies; Public Administration; Social Studies); **Teacher Training**; **Tourism** (Tourism)

School
Business Administration (Business Administration); **Dance** (Dance); **Graduate Studies**; **Law** (Law)

History: Founded 1902 as National Beijing Teachers University. Acquired present title 1998.

Degrees and Diplomas: *Xueshi Xuewei*; *Shuoshi Xuewei*

Publications: Journal of Northwest Normal University

Academic Staff *2011-2012*: Total 2,547
Student Numbers *2011-2012*: Total 35,200
Last Updated: 22/01/13

NORTHWEST UNIVERSITY

1 Taibai Road, Xi'an, Shaanxi Province 710048
Tel: +86(29) 8302344
Fax: +86(29) 8303511
EMail: OIP@nwu.edu.cn
Website: http://www.nwu.edu.cn

President: Fang Guanghua

Vice-President: Zhang Yunxiang

School
Adult Education (Adult Education); **Arts** (Chinese; Design; Film; Literature; Mass Communication; Radio and Television Broadcasting); **Chemical Engineering** (Chemical Engineering); **Culture and Museology** (Archaeology; Cultural Studies; History; Museum Studies); **Economics and Management** (Accountancy; Business Administration; Business and Commerce; Economics; Management; Tourism); **Foreign Languages** (English; Japanese); **International Cultural Exchange**; **Journalism and Mass Communication** (Advertising and Publicity; Journalism; Mass Communication); **Law** (Law); **Life Sciences** (Biological and Life Sciences; Biotechnology); **Public Administration** (Archiving; Library Science; Public Administration)

Department
Applied Social Sciences (Finance; Philosophy; Social Sciences; Social Work); **Chemistry** (Applied Chemistry; Chemistry); **Computer Science** (Computer Science); **Electronic Science** (Electronic Engineering; Information Technology); **Environmental Science** (Environmental Engineering; Environmental Studies); **Geology** (Geochemistry; Geology); **Mathematics** (Applied Mathematics; Information Sciences; Mathematics); **Physics** (Applied Physics; Physics); **Urban Studies and Resource Science** (Environmental Management; Rural Planning; Town Planning; Urban Studies)

History: Founded 1902 as Shaanxi College and assumed its present name in 1912. It was renamed National Northwest University in 1923, and called National Xi'an Provisional University after the merger with National Beiping University, Beiping Normal University, Beiyang College of Engineering and other institutions.

Degrees and Diplomas: *Xueshi Xuewei*; *Shuoshi Xuewei*; *Boshi*

Publications: Journal of Analytical Chemistry; Journal of Higher Education Studies; Journal of Modern Physics; Journal of the Northwest University; Journal of Theoretical Mathematics and Applied Mathematics

NORTHWEST UNIVERSITY FOR NATIONALITIES

1 Xibeixincun, Lanzhou, Gansu Province 730030
Tel: +86(931) 2938060
EMail: maqing@xbmu.edu.cn
Website: http://www.xbmu.edu.cn

President: Jin Yasheng

International Relations: Ma Qing

Faculty
Chemical Engineering (Chemical Engineering); **Civil Engineering** (Civil Engineering); **Computer Science and Information Engineering** (Computer Science; Information Technology); **Continuing and Vocational Education**; **Economics and Management** (Economics; Management); **Electrical Engineering** (Electrical Engineering); **Fine Arts** (Fine Arts); **Foreign Languages** (English; Modern Languages); **History and Civilization** (History); **Law** (Law); **Life Science and Engineering** (Biological and Life Sciences; Engineering); **Linguistics, Culture and Communication** (Communication Studies; Cultural Studies; Linguistics); **Medicine** (Medicine); **Modern Educational Technology** (Educational Technology); **Mongolian Language & Culture** (Mongolian); **Physical Education** (Physical Education); **Social Anthropology & Folklore** (Anthropology; Folklore)

Institute
Overseas Ethnic Documents Institute

Academy
The Chinese Academy of National Information Technology (Information Technology)

Research Department
The Teaching and Research Department of Marxist Theory and Morality (Political Sciences)

Research Institute
Islamic Culture (Islamic Studies); **The Gesar Research Institute** (Philology)

History: Founded 1950 as Northweast University College. Also known as Northwest Minorities University. Acquired present title and status 2003.

Degrees and Diplomas: *Xueshi Xuewei*; *Shuoshi Xuewei*; *Boshi*

Publications: Journal of Northwest Minorities University; Northwest Minorities Research

NORTHWEST UNIVERSITY OF POLITICS AND LAW

300 South Chang'an Road, Xi'an, Shaanxi Province 710063
Tel: +86(29) 88182226
Fax: +86(29) 85262185
EMail: xcb@nwupl.cn
Website: http://www.nwupl.cn/

President: Yu Jia

School
Administrative Law (Administrative Law); **Civil and Commercial Law** (Civil Law; Commercial Law); **Continuing Education** (Continuing Education); **Criminal Law** (Criminal Law); **Economic Law** (Commercial Law; Economics); **Foreign Languages** (English); **Graduate Studies**; **International Law** (International Law); **Journalism and Communications** (Communication Studies; Journalism); **Law** (Law); **Marxist Education** (Political Sciences); **Philosophy and Social Development** (Development Studies; Philosophy; Social Sciences); **Politics and Public Management** (Political Sciences; Public Administration); **Public Security** (Civil Security)

Department
Physical Education (Physical Education)

Further Information: Also campuses in Yanta and Chang'an districs

History: Founded 1937 as as Northern Shaanxi School of Politics and Law. Renamed Northwest Institute of Politics and Law, 1958. Acquired present title 2006.

Main Language(s) of Instruction: Chinese

Degrees and Diplomas: *Xueshi Xuewei*; *Shuoshi Xuewei*
Last Updated: 23/01/13

NORTHWESTERN POLYTECHNICAL UNIVERSITY (NPU)

127 Youyixilu, Xi'an, Shaanxi Province 710072
Tel: +86(29) 88492267
Fax: +86(29) 88491544
EMail: fao@nwpu.edu.cn
Website: http://www.nwpu.edu.cn

President: Jiang Chengyu (2001-) EMail: jiangcy@nwpu.edu.cn

Secretary: Ye Jinfu

International Relations: Tang Hong
Tel: +86(29) 8494379 EMail: tanghong@nwpu.edu.cn

School
Aeronautics (Aeronautical and Aerospace Engineering; Air Transport; Automation and Control Engineering; Mechanical

Engineering); **Astronautics** (Aeronautical and Aerospace Engineering; Astronomy and Space Science; Automation and Control Engineering); **Automation** (Automation and Control Engineering; Computer Engineering; Electrical Engineering; Measurement and Precision Engineering); **Computer Science and Engineering** (Computer Engineering; Computer Science; E-Business/Commerce; Information Technology; Microelectronics; Software Engineering); **Electronics and Information** (Electrical Engineering; Information Technology); **Humanities, Economics and Law** (Arts and Humanities; Economics; Law); **Life Science** (Astronomy and Space Science; Biological and Life Sciences; Biology; Biomedical Engineering; Biotechnology); **Management** (Accountancy; Business Administration; Economics; Engineering Management; Information Technology; Management); **Marine Engineering** (Automation and Control Engineering; Electronic Engineering; Environmental Engineering; Marine Engineering; Mechanical Engineering; Sound Engineering (Acoustics); Telecommunications Engineering); **Materials Science and Engineering** (Materials Engineering); **Mechanics, Civil Engineering & Architecture** (Architecture; Civil Engineering; Mechanical Engineering); **Mechatronic Engineering** (Electrical Engineering; Mechanical Engineering); **Natural and Applied Sciences** (Applied Chemistry; Applied Mathematics; Applied Physics; Natural Sciences); **Power and Energy** (Aeronautical and Aerospace Engineering; Power Engineering; Thermal Engineering)

History: Founded 1938, as Northwest Institute of Engineering incorporating previously existing engineering colleges, institutes and departments. Acquired new title and status 1958.

Academic Year: September to July (September-January; February-July)

Admission Requirements: Graduation from senior middle school and entrance examination

Main Language(s) of Instruction: Chinese

Accrediting Agency: Commission of Science, Technology and Industry

Degrees and Diplomas: *Xueshi Xuewei*; *Shuoshi Xuewei*; *Boshi*

Student Services: Canteen, Cultural Activities, Foreign Studies Centre, Health Services, Language Laboratory, Sports Facilities

Publications: International Journal of Plant Engineering and Management; University Journal

Publishing House: NPU Press

Academic Staff *2011-2012*: Total 28,363
Student Numbers *2011-2012*: Total 3,500
Last Updated: 23/01/13

OCEAN UNIVERSITY OF CHINA

5 Yushan Road, Qingdao, Shandong Province 266003
Tel: +86(532) 82032872
Fax: +86(532) 82032799
EMail: lpx@ouc.edu.cn
Website: http://www.ouc.edu.cn/english/

President: Dexing Wu (2005-)

College

Chemistry and Chemical Engineering (Applied Chemistry; Chemical Engineering; Chemistry; Marine Engineering); **Chinese Language and Culture** (Chinese; Cultural Studies; Literature; Native Language); **Economics** (Economics); **Engineering** (Automation and Control Engineering; Civil Engineering; Engineering; Mechanical Engineering; Naval Architecture); **Environmental Science and Engineering** (Environmental Engineering; Environmental Studies); **Fishery** (Fishery); **Food Science and Engineering** (Food Science); **Foreign Languages** (English; French; German; Japanese; Korean; Modern Languages); **Information Science and Engineering** (Information Sciences; Information Technology); **International Education** (Cultural Studies; International Studies; Modern Languages); **Liberal Arts, Journalism and Communication** (Chinese; Communication Studies; Journalism; Literature); **Life Sciences and Technology** (Aquaculture; Ecology; Fishery; Food Science; Food Technology; Marine Biology); **Management** (Accountancy; Business Administration; E-Business/Commerce; Management; Marketing; Tourism); **Marine Geo-Science** (Coastal Studies; Marine Biology; Marine Science and Oceanography); **Materials Science and Engineering** (Materials Engineering); **Mathematics** (Mathematics); **Physical and Environmental Oceanography** (Applied Physics; Environmental Studies; Marine Science and Oceanography; Meteorology)

School

Law and Political Sciences (Administration; Law; Political Sciences); **Medicine and Pharmaceutics** (Medicine; Pharmacy)

Further Information: Subcampus in Maidao district; research institutes and laboratories

History: Founded 1924 as Private Qingdao University, became Shandong College of Oceanology 1959. Renamed Ocean University of Qingdao 1988. Acquired present title 2002.

Academic Year: September to July (September-January; February-July)

Admission Requirements: Graduation from senior middle school and entrance examination

Main Language(s) of Instruction: Chinese

Accrediting Agency: Ministry of Education

Degrees and Diplomas: *Xueshi Xuewei*; *Shuoshi Xuewei*; *Boshi*

Publications: Journal of Higher Education Studies; Journal of Ocean University

Publishing House: Ocean University of Qingdao Publishing House

Last Updated: 23/01/13

PANZHIHUA UNIVERSITY (PZHU)

Xue Yuan Road, Eastern District,
Panzhihua, Sichuan Province 617000
Tel: +86(812) 3371007
Fax: +86(812) 3371000
EMail: pzhxywsc@163.com
Website: http://www.panzhihua-university.com

President: Liu Guoqin

International Relations: He Yongbing

School

Art (Fine Arts); **Chemistry and Biology Engineering** (Bioengineering; Chemistry); **Civil Engineering** (Civil Engineering); **Computer Science** (Computer Science); **Economics and Administration** (Administration; Economics); **Electromechanical Engineering** (Electrical Engineering; Mechanical Engineering); **Engineering Technology** (Engineering; Technology); **Foreign Languages and Cultures** (Cultural Studies; Modern Languages); **Further Education** (Education); **Humanities and Social Sciences** (Arts and Humanities; Social Sciences); **Information and Electrical Engineering** (Electrical Engineering; Information Technology); **Medical Science** (Medicine)

Department

Materials Engineering (Materials Engineering); **Physical Education** (Physical Education)

History: Founded 1984.

Degrees and Diplomas: *Xueshi Xuewei*

Last Updated: 24/01/13

PEKING UNION MEDICAL COLLEGE (PUMC)

9 Dongdan Santioao, Dongcheng District, Beijing 100730
Tel: +86(10) 65105934
Fax: +86(10) 65253447
EMail: international@pumc.edu.cn
Website: http://pumc.edu.cn

President: Yixin Zeng

School

Adult Education; **Basic Medicine** (Biochemistry; Biomedical Engineering; Biotechnology; Cell Biology; Embryology and Reproduction Biology; Epidemiology; Genetics; Histology; Immunology; Medicine; Pathology; Pharmacology; Physiology; Social and Preventive Medicine); **Clinical Medicine** (Medical Technology; Medicine); **Nursing** (Nursing)

Further Information: Also Research Institutes and Research Centers

History: Founded 1917.

Degrees and Diplomas: *Shuoshi Xuewei*; *Boshi*

Last Updated: 17/07/13

PEKING UNIVERSITY (PKU)

5 Yiheyyuan Road, Haidan District, Beijing 100871
Tel: +86(10) 62751230
Fax: +86(10) 62751233
EMail: oir@pku.edu.cn; study@pku.edu.cn
Website: http://www.pku.edu.cn

President: Jianhua Lin (2015-)

College

Chemistry (Analytical Chemistry; Chemistry; Inorganic Chemistry; Physical Chemistry; Polymer and Plastics Technology); **Environmental Science and Engineering** (Environmental Engineering; Environmental Studies); **Urban and Environmental Sciences** (Ecology; Environmental Studies; Geography; Geography (Human); Regional Planning; Urban Studies)

School

Archaeology and Museology (Archaeology; Museum Studies); **Arts** (Arts and Humanities; Film; Fine Arts; Musicology; Radio and Television Broadcasting); **Business** *(HSBC)* (Business Administration); **Chinese as a Second Language**; **Earth and Space Sciences** (Aeronautical and Aerospace Engineering; Earth Sciences; Geochemistry; Geology; Mineralogy; Natural Resources); **Economics** (Economics; Finance; Insurance; International Business; International Economics); **Electronics Engineering and Computer Science** (Computer Science; Electronic Engineering); **Foreign Languages** (Arabic; English Studies; French Studies; Germanic Studies; Oriental Languages; Russian; South and Southeast Asian Languages); **Government** (Economics; Government; Political Sciences; Public Administration); **International Studies** (International Business; International Relations; International Studies; Political Sciences); **Journalism and Communication** (Advertising and Publicity; Communication Studies; Information Technology; Journalism); **Law** (Civil Law; Commercial Law; Criminal Law; History of Law; International Law; Law); **Life Sciences** (Biological and Life Sciences; Biology; Biotechnology; Ecology); **Management** *(Guanghua)* (Accountancy; Business Administration; Finance; Information Technology; Management; Marketing; Transport Management); **Marxism** (Political Sciences); **Mathematical Sciences** (Actuarial Science; Computer Engineering; Computer Science; Information Sciences; Mathematics; Statistics); **Physics** (Atomic and Molecular Physics; Nuclear Physics; Optics; Physics; Radiophysics; Solid State Physics; Sound Engineering (Acoustics)); **Software and Microelectronics** (Microelectronics; Software Engineering); **Transnational Law** (Law); **Yuanpei**

Department

Chinese Language and Literature (Chinese; Linguistics; Literature); **History** (Ancient Civilizations; History); **Information Management** (Information Management; Information Sciences; Library Science); **Philosophy** (Aesthetics; Ethics; Logic; Philosophy; Religious Studies); **Physical Education** (Physical Education); **Psychology** (Psychology); **Sociology** (Administration; Anthropology; Demography and Population; Environmental Studies; Political Sciences; Public Administration; Regional Studies; Rural Studies; Social Work; Sociology; Urban Studies)

Institute

Advanced Technology (Technology); **Astronomy and Astrophysics** *(Kavil)* (Astronomy and Space Science; Astrophysics); **Computer Science and Technology** (Computer Science; Microelectronics; Technology); **Molecular Medicine** (Medicine); **Population Research** (Demography and Population); **Social Science Survey** (Social Sciences)

Centre

Economic Research (Economics)

Graduate School

Education (Education; Educational Administration; Educational Technology); **ShenZhen** *(ShenZhen)*

Further Information: Also 232 research labs and centers

History: Founded 1898 as Metropolitan University. Reorganized 1952. Merged with Beijing Medical University 1999.

Academic Year: September to July (September-February; March-July)

Admission Requirements: Graduation from senior middle school and entrance examination

Main Language(s) of Instruction: Chinese

Degrees and Diplomas: *Xueshi Xuewei*; *Shuoshi Xuewei*; *Boshi*

Student Services: Academic Counselling, Canteen, Careers Guidance, Cultural Activities, Facilities for disabled people, Foreign Studies Centre, Health Services, Language Laboratory, Nursery Care, Social Counselling, Sports Facilities

Publications: Journal of Peking University; Natural Sciences Journal; Peking University Law Journal; Philosophy and Social Sciences Journal

Publishing House: Peking University Press

Last Updated: 25/01/13

PUTIAN UNIVERSITY

1133 Xueyuan Road, Chengxiang District, Putian, Fujian 351100
Tel: +86(594) 2692440
Fax: +86(594) 2692367
Website: http://www.ptu.edu.cn/

President: Li Yongcang

School

Art and Crafts (Fine Arts; Handicrafts); **Business** (Business Administration); **Civil Engineering** (Civil Engineering); **Culture and Communication** (Chinese; Journalism); **Environmental and Biological Engineering** (Bioengineering; Environmental Engineering); **Foreign Languages** (Modern Languages); **Information Engineering** (Computer Engineering); **Management** (Management); **Mathematics** (Mathematics); **Mechanical and Electrical Engineering** (Electrical Engineering; Mechanical Engineering); **Music** (Music); **Nursing** (Nursing); **Pharmaceutical Sciences and Medical Technology** (Medical Technology; Pharmacy); **Physical Education** (Physical Education)

History: Created 2002

Degrees and Diplomas: *Xueshi Xuewei*

Last Updated: 20/10/15

QIANNAN NORMAL COLLEGE FOR NATIONALITIES

Longshan Dadao, Development Zone, Duyun,
Qiannan, Guizhou 55800
Tel: +86(854) 8737011
Fax: +86(854) 8737012
EMail: qnsybgs@sgmtu.edu.cn
Website: http://www.sgmtu.edu.cn/

President: Shi Pei Hua

Programme

Administration (Administration); **Agriculture Management and Forestry** (Agricultural Management; Forestry); **Chemistry** (Chemical Engineering; Chemistry); **Chinese Language and Literature** (Chinese; Literature); **Computer Science and Technology** (Computer Engineering; Computer Science); **English** (English); **History** (History); **Ideology and Political Sciences** (Political Sciences); **Information and Computation Science** (Computer Science; Information Sciences); **Law and Economics** (Economics; Law); **Mathematics and Applied Mathematics** (Applied Mathematics; Mathematics); **Physical Education** (Physical Education); **Physics** (Physics); **Preschool Educaion** (Preschool Education)

History: Founded 2000.

Degrees and Diplomas: *Xueshi Xuewei*

Last Updated: 27/11/13

QINGDAO AGRICULTURAL UNIVERSITY

Chunyang Road, Laiyang, Shandong Province 266109
Tel: +86(532) 86080222
EMail: iao@qau.edu.cn
Website: http://en.qau.edu.cn

President: Li Baodu

College

Animal Science and Veterinary Medicine (Animal Husbandry; Veterinary Science); **Architectural Engineering** (Architectural and Environmental Design; Civil Engineering); **Botany Science and Technology** (Agronomy; Botany; Crop Production); **Communication** (Communication Studies); **Continuing Education**;

Economics (Agricultural Economics; Economics); **Electromechanical Engineering** (Agricultural Engineering; Automation and Control Engineering; Electrical Engineering; Machine Building); **Environmental Arts** (Environmental Management; Horticulture; Landscape Architecture); **Fishery** (Aquaculture; Fishery); **Food Science and Engineering** (Food Science; Food Technology); **Foreign Languages** (English; French; Japanese; Korean; Russian); **Haidu**; **Horticulture** (Horticulture); **Humanities and Social Sciences** (Philosophy; Political Sciences; Public Administration; Social Sciences; Social Studies; Writing); **Information Sciences and Engineering** (Information Management; Information Sciences); **Life Sciences** (Biochemistry; Biotechnology; Botany; Genetics; Zoology); **Management**; **Plant Protection** (Plant and Crop Protection; Plant Pathology); **Resources and Environment** (Environmental Studies; Natural Resources); **Science** (Mathematics; Natural Sciences; Physics)

Department

Physical Education (Physical Education)

History: Founded 1951 as Laiyang Agricultural School, acquired present status and title 1977.

Main Language(s) of Instruction: Chinese

Degrees and Diplomas: *Xueshi Xuewei*; *Shuoshi Xuewei*

Last Updated: 25/01/13

QINGDAO TECHNOLOGICAL UNIVERSITY

11 Fushun Road, Qingdao, Shandong Province 266033
Tel: +86(532) 85071068
Fax: +86(532) 85071098
EMail: wshb@qtech.edu.cn
Website: http://www.qtech.edu.cn

President: Yi Chuijie

International Relations: Liu Xuming

School

Architecture (Architecture; Environmental Engineering; Rural Planning; Rural Studies; Town Planning; Urban Studies); **Arts** (Arts and Humanities); **Automotive Engineering** (Automation and Control Engineering; Automotive Engineering); **Business** (Accountancy; E-Business/Commerce; Finance; International Business; Management; Marketing); **Civil Engineering** (Civil Engineering); **Communications and Electronic Engineering** (Communication Studies; Electronic Engineering); **Computer Engineering** (Computer Engineering); **Economics and Trade** (Economics; International Economics; Service Trades; Statistics); **Environmental and Municipal Engineering** (Architectural and Environmental Design; Environmental Engineering; Environmental Studies; Water Management); **Foreign Languages** (English); **Humanities and Social Sciences** (Advertising and Publicity; Social Work); **Management** (Industrial Engineering; Information Management; Information Technology; Management; Natural Resources; Transport Management); **Mechanical Engineering** (Automation and Control Engineering; Computer Graphics; Industrial Design; Instrument Making; Mechanical Engineering; Production Engineering); **Sciences** (Applied Mathematics; Information Sciences; Mathematics); **Vehicle and Traffic Engineering** (Automotive Engineering)

History: Founded 1952 as Qingdao Institute of Architecture and Engineering. Acquired present status and title 2004.

Degrees and Diplomas: *Xueshi Xuewei*; *Shuoshi Xuewei*; *Boshi*

Last Updated: 25/01/13

QINGDAO UNIVERSITY

308 Ningxia Road, Qingdao, Shandong Province 266071
Tel: +86(532) 85953863
Fax: +86(532) 85953085
EMail: oip@qdu.edu.cn
Website: http://www.qdu.edu.cn

President: Wan Anmin

College

Arts, Music and Performance (Fine Arts; Music; Performing Arts); **Automation Engineering** (Automation and Control Engineering; Electrical Engineering); **Chemical Engineering** (Chemical Engineering; Chemistry); **Chinese Language and Culture** (Chinese; Literature); **Continuing Education**; **Economics** (Economics); **Fine Arts, Painting and Sculpture** (Fine Arts; Painting and Drawing; Sculpture); **Foreign Languages and Literature** (English; French; German; Japanese; Korean; Literature); **Haier Software** (Software Engineering); **Information Engineering** (Computer Science; Information Technology); **International Business** (Accountancy; Finance; International Business; Management; Marketing); **Law** (Law); **Literature** (Chinese; Journalism; Literature; Media Studies); **Mechanical Engineering** (Electrical Engineering; Mechanical Engineering); **Medicine** (Anaesthesiology; Anatomy; Dermatology; Embryology and Reproduction Biology; Gynaecology and Obstetrics; Histology; Medicine; Neurology; Nutrition; Oncology; Otorhinolaryngology; Paediatrics; Pathology; Pharmacology; Surgery); **Natural Sciences** (Biology; Biotechnology; Chemistry; Electronic Engineering; Environmental Studies; Geography; Information Sciences; Mathematics; Physics); **Textile and Clothing** (Chemistry; Fashion Design; Fine Arts; Textile Design); **Tourism** (Tourism)

Department

History (History); **Philosophy** (Philosophy)

History: Founded 1985. Merged with Shandong Textile Engineering College, Qingdao Medical College and Qingdao Teachers College 1993.

Academic Year: September to July (September-January; February-July)

Admission Requirements: Graduation from senior middle school and entrance examination

Main Language(s) of Instruction: Chinese

Degrees and Diplomas: *Xueshi Xuewei*; *Shuoshi Xuewei*; *Boshi*

Publications: Journal of Qingdao University

Last Updated: 25/01/13

QINGDAO UNIVERSITY OF SCIENCE AND TECHNOLOGY

69 Songling Road,Laoshan District,
Qingdao, Shandong Province 266061
Tel: +86(532) 84023322
Fax: +86(532) 88956566
EMail: ieco@qust.edu.cn
Website: http://www.qust.edu.cn

President: Lianxiang Ma

Faculty

Technical *(Chinese-German)* (Technology)

College

Arts (Fine Arts); **Automation Electrical Engineering** (Automation and Control Engineering; Electrical Engineering); **Chemical Engineering** (Chemical Engineering); **Chemistry and Molecular Engineering** (Chemistry); **Communication and Cartoon** (Communication Studies; Film); **Economics and Management** (Economics; Management); **Electromechanical Engineering** (Electronic Engineering; Mechanical Engineering); **Environmental and Safety Engineering** (Environmental Engineering; Safety Engineering); **Foreign Languages** (English; German; Japanese; Korean; Russian); **Information Sciences and Technology** (Information Sciences; Technology); **Materials Science and Engineering** (Materials Engineering); **Mathematical Science and Physics** (Mathematics; Physics); **Physical Education** (Physical Education); **Political Science and Law** (Law; Political Sciences); **Polymer Science and Engineering** (Polymer and Plastics Technology)

School

Information and Control Engineering (Automation and Control Engineering; Computer Science; Information Technology; Technology)

Further Information: Also campuses in Laoshan, Sifang, and Gaomi

History: Founded 1950 as Shenyang Senior Vocational School of Light Industry. Renamed Qingdao Institute of Chemical Technology 1984. Acquired present title and status 2002.

Main Language(s) of Instruction: Chinese

Degrees and Diplomas: *Xueshi Xuewei*; *Shuoshi Xuewei*; *Boshi*

Academic Staff *2011-2012*: Total 1,452

Student Numbers *2011-2012*: Total 25,000

Last Updated: 25/01/13

QINGHAI NORMAL UNIVERSITY

38 Wusi Xilu, Xining, Qinghai Province 810008
Tel: +86(971) 6107640
Fax: +86(971) 6150977
EMail: webmaster@qhnu.edu.cn
Website: http://www.qhnu.edu.cn

President: Dong Jiaping

School

Computer Science (Computer Science)

Department

Arts and Humanities (Arts and Humanities); **Biology** (Biology); **Chemistry** (Chemistry); **Chinese Language and Literature** (Chinese); **Economics and Management** (Economics; Management); **Education** (Education); **Fine Arts** (Arts and Humanities; Fine Arts); **Foreign Languages** (Modern Languages); **History** (History); **Ideology and Political Studies** (Political Sciences); **Journalism and Communication** (Communication Studies; Journalism); **Life Sciences and Geography** (Biological and Life Sciences; Geography); **Mathematics** (Mathematics); **Music** (Music); **Physics** (Physics); **Political Studies and Law** (Law; Political Sciences)

Institute

Physical Education (Physical Education)

History: Founded 1956 as Qinghai Normal School, became college 1958. Acquired present status and title 1984.

Academic Year: August to July (August-January; March-July)

Admission Requirements: Graduation from senior middle school and entrance examination

Main Language(s) of Instruction: Chinese

Accrediting Agency: Ministry of Education and the Provincial Government.

Degrees and Diplomas: *Xueshi Xuewei*; *Shuoshi Xuewei*

Publications: Journal of Qinghai Normal University

Last Updated: 29/01/13

QINGHAI UNIVERSITY

97 Ningzhang Road, Chengbei District,
Xining, Qinghai Province 810016
Tel: +86(971) 5310410
Fax: +86(971) 5310031
EMail: qhuoffice@qhu.edu.cn; hfq@public.xn.qh.cn
Website: http://www.qhu.edu.cn/

President: Liang Xidong Tel: +86(971) 5310033

Secretary: Zhengxiao Qiao

College

Adult Education (Adult Education); **Agriculture and Animal Husbandry** (Agriculture; Animal Husbandry; Forestry; Veterinary Science); **Civil Engineering** (Civil Engineering); **Finance and Economics** (Economics; Finance); **Mechanical Engineering** (Mechanical Engineering); **Medicine** (Medicine)

Institute

Adult Education (Architecture; Economics; Social Sciences; Water Management); **Chemical Technology** (Applied Chemistry; Chemical Engineering); **Hydraulic and Electric Engineering** (Electrical Engineering; Hydraulic Engineering)

History: Founded 1958. Acquired present status 1987. Merged with Qinghai Animal Husbandry and Veterinary Science College 1997, and with Qinghai Medical College 2004.

Academic Year: September to July (September-February, March-July)

Admission Requirements: Graduation from senior middle school and entrance examination

Fees: (Yuan): c. 3,000 per annum

Main Language(s) of Instruction: Chinese

Degrees and Diplomas: *Xueshi Xuewei*; *Shuoshi Xuewei*; *Boshi*

Student Services: Academic Counselling, Canteen, Careers Guidance, Cultural Activities, Health Services, Language Laboratory, Nursery Care, Social Counselling, Sports Facilities

Publications: Journal of Medical College; Journal of Qinghai University; Qinghai Journal of animal husbandry and veterinary medicine

Last Updated: 29/01/13

QINGHAI UNIVERSITY FOR NATIONALITIES

3 Bayi Middle Road, Xining, Qinghai Province 810007
Tel: +86(971) 8802722
Fax: +86(971) 8176888
EMail: webmaster@qhmu.edu.cn
Website: http://www.qhmu.edu.cn

President: He Feng

Faculty

Chemistry and Life Sciences (Biological and Life Sciences; Chemistry); **Economy and Management** (Economics; Management); **Law** (Law); **Mathematics** (Mathematics); **Tibetology** (Tibetan)

Department

Chinese Language and Literature (Chinese; Literature); **Computer Science and Technology** (Computer Science); **Electronic and Information Science and Technology** (Electronic Engineering; Information Sciences; Information Technology); **Fine Arts** (Fine Arts); **Foreign Languages** (Modern Languages); **Mongolian** (Mongolian); **Social Sciences** (Social Sciences)

History: Founded 1949 as a class for cadres, acquired present status and title 1956.

Degrees and Diplomas: *Xueshi Xuewei*; *Shuoshi Xuewei*; *Boshi*

Student Numbers *2012-2013*: Total: c. 12,000

Last Updated: 29/01/13

QIQIHAR MEDICAL UNIVERSITY

333, Bukui Street, Jianhua District,
Qiqihar, Heilongjiang Province 161006
Tel: +86(452) 2663515
Fax: +86(452) 2663515
EMail: xiaoqianangle@163.com
Website: http://english.qqhrmu.cn/

President: Jicheng Liu

School

Basic Medicine (Embryology and Reproduction Biology; Genetics; Physiology); **Medical Technology** (Laboratory Techniques; Medical Technology); **Mental Health** (Psychiatry and Mental Health); **Nursing** (Nursing); **Pharmacy** (Pharmacy); **Public Health** (Public Health)

History: Founded 1946.

Main Language(s) of Instruction: Chinese

Degrees and Diplomas: *Xueshi Xuewei*

Academic Staff *2012-2013*: Total: c. 3,500

Student Numbers *2012-2013*: Total: c. 15,000

Last Updated: 29/01/13

QIQIHAR UNIVERSITY

42, Wenhua Street, Qiqihar, Heilongjiang Province 161006
Tel: +86(452) 2712809
Fax: +86(452) 2712809
EMail: sss@mail.qqhru.edu.cn
Website: http://www.qqhru.edu.cn

President: Liqun Ma

School

Vocational Technical

Department

Arts (Arts and Humanities); **Chemistry and Chemical Engineering** (Chemical Engineering; Chemistry); **Communication and Electronic Engineering** (Electronic Engineering; Telecommunications Engineering); **Computer and Control Engineering** (Automation and Control Engineering; Computer Engineering); **Economics and Management** (Economics; Management);

Education and Communication (Communication Studies; Education); **Foreign Languages** (Modern Languages); **Higher Professional Technology** (Technology); **Humanities** (Arts and Humanities); **Information Sciences and Mechanical Engineering** (Automation and Control Engineering; Computer Science; Electrical Engineering; Information Sciences; Mechanical Engineering); **Libraries**; **Life Sciences and Engineering** (Biological and Life Sciences; Engineering; Food Science); **Light industry and Textile** (Textile Design); **Literature and History** (Chinese; History; Literature; Political Sciences); **Materials Engineering** (Materials Engineering); **Mechanical Engineering** (Mechanical Engineering); **Physical Education** (Physical Education); **Science** (Geography; Mathematics; Physics); **Social Sciences** (Social Sciences)

Centre

Network and Audio-visual Education (Computer Graphics)

History: Founded 1995. Merged with Qiqihar Teachers College and Qiqihar Light Industry Institute.

Degrees and Diplomas: *Xueshi Xuewei*; *Shuoshi Xuewei*

Publications: Journal of Qiqihar University

Academic Staff *2012-2013*: Total: c. 1,400

Student Numbers *2012-2013*: Total: c. 29,000

Last Updated: 29/01/13

QUFU NORMAL UNIVERSITY

1 Jingxuan West Road, Qufu, Shandong Province 273165
Tel: +86(537) 4456157
Fax: +86(537) 4455878
EMail: lxqsd@mail.qfnu.edu.cn
Website: http://www.qfnu.edu.cn

President: Yanqi Ren

School

Adult Education; **Confucius Culture** (Philosophy); **Education** (Education; Educational Sciences); **Vocational Technical Education** (Technology)

Department

Administration (Administration); **Agriculture** (Agriculture); **Chemistry and Chemical Engineering** (Chemical Engineering; Chemistry); **Chinese Ancient Literature** (Chinese; Literature); **Economics** (Economics); **Engineering** (Electrical Engineering; Optical Technology); **Foreign Languages** (English); **Geography** (Geography); **History and Culture** (Cultural Studies; History); **Information Technology and Communication** (Information Technology; Telecommunications Engineering); **Law** (Law); **Liberal Arts** (Arts and Humanities); **Mathematics and Science** (Applied Mathematics; Mathematics; Mathematics and Computer Science); **Music** (Music); **Physical Education** (Physical Education); **Physics** (Physics); **Political and Social Development** (Development Studies; Political Sciences; Psychology)

Further Information: Also a campus in Rizhao

History: Founded 1955 as Shanghai Teachers' School, acquired present status and title 1985.

Academic Year: September to July

Admission Requirements: Graduation from senior middle school and entrance examination

Fees: None

Main Language(s) of Instruction: Chinese

Degrees and Diplomas: *Xueshi Xuewei*; *Shuoshi Xuewei*; *Boshi*

Publications: Journal of High School Mathematics; Journal of Modern Chinese; Journal of Qilu Publication; Journal of Qufu Normal University

Last Updated: 30/01/13

QUJING NORMAL UNIVERSITY

Xishan Development Zone, Qujing, Yunnan 6550141
EMail: xjzx@qjnu.edu.cn
Website: http://www.qjnu.edu.cn/

Chancellor: Jiang Li

Department

Chemistry and Life Sciences (Biological and Life Sciences; Chemistry); **Chinese** (Chinese); **Fine Arts** (Fine Arts); **History and Demography** (History); **Information and Computer Science**; **Mathematics** (Mathematics); **Music and Dance** (Dance; Music); **Physical Education** (Physical Education); **Physics** (Physics)

History: Founded 1993 as Qujing Teachers College. Acquired present name and status 2000, after merging of Qujing Teachers College, Qujing Education College and Qujing Secondary Normal School.

Degrees and Diplomas: *Xueshi Xuewei*

Last Updated: 27/11/13

RENMIN UNIVERSITY OF CHINA

59 Zhongguancun Street, Beijing 100872
Tel: +86(10) 62511081
Fax: +86(10) 62515329
EMail: rmdxxb@ruc.edu.cn
Website: http://www.ruc.edu.cn

President: Ji Baocheng

International Relations: Tang Zhong
Tel: +86(10) 82509513 EMail: international@ruc.edu.cn

School

Agricultural Economics and Rural Development (Agricultural Economics; Real Estate; Regional Planning; Rural Planning; Rural Studies); **Arts** (Arts and Humanities); **Business** (Accountancy; Economics; Management); **Chinese Classics** (Chinese); **Continuing Education**; **Economics** (Economics); **Education and Training** (Education); **Environment and Natural Resources** (Environmental Studies; Natural Resources); **Finance** (Finance); **Fine Arts**; **Foreign Languages** (Modern Languages); **History** (History); **Information** (Computer Science; Information Management); **Information Resource Management** (Administration; Archiving; Information Management; Library Science); **International Studies** (Asian Studies; Eastern European Studies; European Studies; International Economics; International Relations; Political Sciences; Social Studies); **Journalism** (Communication Studies; Journalism); **Labour and Human Resources** (Human Resources; Labour and Industrial Relations); **Law** (Civil Law; Commercial Law; Criminal Law); **Literary Studies** (Arts and Humanities; Comparative Literature; Linguistics; Literature); **Marxism Studies** (Political Sciences); **Natural Sciences** (Chemistry; Physics; Psychology); **Philosophy** (Ethics; Philosophy; Religious Studies); **Public Administration** (Economics; Education; Finance; Human Resources; Management; Public Administration; Real Estate; Regional Planning; Safety Engineering; Taxation; Urban Studies); **Sociology and Population Studies** (Anthropology; Demography and Population; Development Studies; Gerontology; Social Studies; Sociology); **Statistics** (Statistics); **Teaching Chinese as a Foreign Language** (Chinese; Foreign Languages Education)

Department

Physical Education (Physical Education)

Institute

Qing History (History)

History: Founded 1937 as Shaan Bei Public School.

Academic Year: September to July

Admission Requirements: Graduation from senior middle school and national entrance examination

Fees: (US Dollars): Foreign students, 2,676-3,920 per annum

Main Language(s) of Instruction: Chinese

Degrees and Diplomas: *Xueshi Xuewei*; *Shuoshi Xuewei*; *Boshi*. Also postdoctoral programmes

Student Services: Academic Counselling, Canteen, Careers Guidance, Cultural Activities, Facilities for disabled people, Health Services, Nursery Care, Social Counselling, Sports Facilities

Publications: Economic Theory and Business Management; Journal of Renmin University of China; Population Research; Studies in Qing History; Teaching and Research

Publishing House: China Renmin University Press

Last Updated: 30/01/13

SANDA UNIVERSITY

2727 Jinhai Road, Pudong, Shanghai 201209
Tel: +86(21) 50210894
Fax: +86(21) 50210895
Website: http://www.sandau.edu.cn/

President: Li Jin

Vice-President: Zhang Zengtai

International Relations: Hua Hua

College

Arts and Humanities (Arts and Humanities; Journalism); **Engineering** (Electrical and Electronic Engineering; Engineering; Mechanical Engineering; Nautical Science; Transport Engineering); **Fashion Design** (Fashion Design); **Foreign Languages** (English; Japanese; Spanish); **Information Science and Technology** (Computer Science; Information Sciences; Information Technology); **International Medicine and Technology** (Medicine); **Management** (Management; Tourism); **Public Education** (Education)

School

Business Administration (Accountancy; Business Administration; International Relations; Law; Marketing)

Institute

Medical Technology (Medical Technology; Nursing; Rehabilitation and Therapy)

Further Information: Also a campus in Jiashan

History: Founded 1992.

Accrediting Agency: Shanghai Municipal Education Commission

Degrees and Diplomas: *Xueshi Xuewei*

Academic Staff *2011*	**TOTAL**
FULL-TIME	**580**
PART-TIME	**240**
Student Numbers *2011*	
All (Foreign included)	**11,130**

Last Updated: 07/10/13

SANJIANG UNIVERSITY (SJU)

310 Long Xi Rd, Tiexinqiao, Yuhuatai District,
Nanjing, JiangSu 210012
Tel: +86(25) 5289-7027
Fax: +86(25) 5235-4928
EMail: lin_chao@sju.js.cn
Website: http://www.sju.js.cn/

President: Dong Xinhua

International Relations: Huang Keming, Director
Tel: +86(25) 5289-7027

College

Computer Science and Engineering (Computer Science; Engineering; Technology); **Cultural Industry Management** (Industrial Management); **Electrical and Automatic Engineering** (Automation and Control Engineering; Electrical Engineering); **Liberal Arts**

School

Mechanical Engineering (Mechanical Engineering); **Tourism Management** (Tourism)

Department

Architecture (Architecture); **Business Administration** (Business Administration; Management); **Chinese** (Chinese); **Economics** (Economics); **English** (English); **Japanese** (Japanese); **Law** (Law); **Tourism** (Tourism)

Institute

Art (Fine Arts); **Civil Engineering** (Civil Engineering); **Electronic Engineering** (Electronic Engineering); **International Education** (Education); **Landscape and Horticulture** (Horticulture; Landscape Architecture); **Vocational and Technical Training** (Technology)

History: Founded as Sanjiang Colege. Acquired present title and status 2002.

Academic Year: August to June

Degrees and Diplomas: *Xueshi Xuewei*

Last Updated: 15/10/13

SANMING UNIVERSITY

25 Jingdong Road, Sanming, Fujian 365004
Tel: +86 (598) 8398956
Fax: +86 (598) 8399217
Website: http://www.smxy.com/

Vice President: Jian Liu

Department

Arts (Fine Arts); **Chemistry and Biological Engineering** (Bioengineering; Chemistry); **Chinese** (Chinese); **Civil Construction Engineering** (Civil Engineering; Construction Engineering); **Economics; Management** (Economics; Management); **Foreign Languages** (English; Foreign Languages Education); **Mathematics and Computer Science** (Computer Science; Mathematics); **Physical Education** (Physical Education); **Physics, Mechanical and Electrical Engineering** (Electrical Engineering; Mechanical Engineering; Physics); **Politics and Law** (Law; Political Sciences); **Teachers Training** (Teacher Training)

History: Founded 1999 as Sanming College. Acquired present title and status 2004.

Degrees and Diplomas: *Xueshi Xuewei*

Last Updated: 18/10/13

SHAANXI FASHION ENGINEERING INSTITUTE

Symphony Metro West Ham, Xi'an, Shaanxi 712046
Tel: +86(29) 38114111
Fax: +86(29) 38114112
Website: http://www.sxfu.org/

President: Wang Pengfei

College

Civil Engineering (Civil Engineering); **Economics and Management** (Economics; Management); **Foreign Languages** (English); **Information Technology** (Information Technology); **Jewelery Art** (Jewellery Art); **Pharmacy** (Pharmacy)

Department

Political Sciences (Political Sciences)

Institute

Clothing Art (Fashion Design)

History: Founded 1994 as Shaanxi Engineering College. Became Shaanxi College of Fashion 2002.

Degrees and Diplomas: *Xueshi Xuewei*

Last Updated: 04/12/13

SHAANXI INSTITUTE OF INTERNATIONAL TRADE & COMMERCE

Shaanxi University Park, Xianyang, Shaanxi 712046
Tel: +86(29) 33814519
Fax: +86(29) 33811620
Website: http://www.csiic.com/

School

Business (Business Administration); **Continuing Education**; **Culture and Arts** (Cultural Studies; Fine Arts); **Information Technology and Engineering** (Information Technology); **Jewelry and Clothing** (Clothing and Sewing; Jewellery Art); **Medicine** (Medicine)

Institute

Finance and Accounting (Accountancy; Finance); **International Economics** (International Economics)

Degrees and Diplomas: *Xueshi Xuewei*

Student Numbers *2012-2013*: Total: c. 15,000

Last Updated: 27/11/13

SHAANXI NORMAL UNIVERSITY

199 South Chang'an Road, Xi'an, Shaanxi Province 710062
Tel: +86(29) 85308114
EMail: wsc@snnu.edu.cn
Website: http://www.snnu.edu.cn

President: Fang Yu

Vice-President: Zhao Bin

College
Arts (Fine Arts); **Chemistry and Materials Science** (Chemistry; Materials Engineering); **Chinese Literature** (Chinese; Literature); **Chinese Studies** *(International)*; **Computer Science** (Computer Science); **Distance Education**; **Educational Sciences** (Education; Educational Administration; Preschool Education; Psychology); **Ethnic Education** (Ethnology); **Food Engineering and Nutritional Science** (Food Technology; Nutrition); **Foreign Languages** (English; Japanese; Linguistics; Literature; Modern Languages; Russian); **Further Education**; **History and Civilization** (History); **International Business** (Commercial Law; Economics; International Business; Management); **Life Sciences** (Biological and Life Sciences); **Mathematics and Information Science** (Information Sciences; Mathematics); **Music** (Music); **News and Media** (Media Studies); **Physics and Information Technology** (Information Technology; Physics); **Political Economy** (Economics; Philosophy; Political Sciences); **Psychology** (Psychology); **Science and Engineering** (Engineering; Natural Sciences); **Sport** (Physical Education; Sports); **Teachers' and Administrators' Training** (Teacher Training); **Tourism and Environment** (Environmental Studies; Geography; Tourism)

Department
Humanity and Social Science (Arts and Humanities; Social Sciences)

History: Founded 1944 as Shaanxi Provincial Teachers College, acquired present status and title 1960.

Academic Year: September to July (September-January; March-July)

Admission Requirements: Graduation from senior middle school and entrance examination

Fees: None

Main Language(s) of Instruction: Chinese

Accrediting Agency: State Education Commission

Degrees and Diplomas: *Xueshi Xuewei*; *Shuoshi Xuewei*; *Boshi*. Also Certificate, 1-2 yrs

Publications: Journal of Shaanxi Normal University; Philosophy and Science

Publishing House: Shaanxi Normal University Press

Last Updated: 31/01/13

SHAANXI UNIVERSITY OF CHINESE MEDICINE

Shiji Avenue, Xianyang, Xianyang, Shaanxi 712046
Tel: +86(29) 38185000
Fax: +86(29) 38185070
EMail: snucm@163.com
Website: http://www.sntcm.edu.cn

President: Yongxue Zhou

Department
Acupuncture and Moxibustion (Acupuncture); **Chinese-Western Medicine** (Medicine; Oncology; Paediatrics; Surgery; Traditional Eastern Medicine); **Clinical Medicine** (Medical Technology; Medicine); **Continuing Education**; **English** (English); **Human Science**; **Medical Techniques** (Medical Technology); **Nursing** (Nursing); **Pharmacology** (Pharmacology); **Physical Education** (Physical Education); **Public Health** (Public Health); **Social Sciences** (Social Sciences); **Traditional Chinese Medicine** (Traditional Eastern Medicine); **Treatment Techniques** (Treatment Techniques)

History: Founded 1959 as Shaanxi College of Traditional Chinese Medicine.

Degrees and Diplomas: *Xueshi Xuewei*; *Shuoshi Xuewei*

Last Updated: 30/01/13

SHAANXI UNIVERSITY OF SCIENCE AND TECHNOLOGY

6 Xuefu Road, Weiyang District, Xi'an, Shaanxi Province 710021
Tel: +86(29) 86168058
EMail: oice@sust.edu.cn
Website: http://www.sust.edu.cn

President: Yu Zhaijing

School
Chemistry and Chemical Engineering (Chemical Engineering; Chemistry); **Life Science and Engineering** (Biochemistry; Bioengineering; Engineering; Food Science; Food Technology; Pharmacology; Traditional Eastern Medicine); **Light Industry and Energy** (Energy Engineering; Environmental Engineering; Heating and Refrigeration; Paper Technology; Power Engineering); **Materials Science and Engineering** (Chemical Engineering; Materials Engineering; Physical Chemistry); **Mechanical and Electrical Engineering** (Automation and Control Engineering; Electrical Engineering; Industrial Design; Mechanical Engineering; Transport Engineering); **Resource and Environment** (Environmental Engineering; Industrial Design; Leather Techniques; Natural Resources); **Science** (Applied Mathematics; Applied Physics; Computer Science; Information Technology)

History: Founded 1958 as Beijing Institute of Light Industry. Renamed Shaanxi University of Science and Technology 2002.

Degrees and Diplomas: *Xueshi Xuewei*; *Shuoshi Xuewei*; *Boshi*

Last Updated: 31/01/13

SHAANXI UNIVERSITY OF TECHNOLOGY

Hedongdian, Hanzhong, Shaanxi Province 723003
Tel: +86(916) 2296374 Ext. 2211
Fax: +86(916) 2296407
EMail: gjc@snut.edu.cn
Website: http://www.snut.edu.cn/

President: He Ning

International Relations: Wei Shuiyi

School
Arts (Design; Fine Arts; Musicology); **Bioscience and Engineering** (Bioengineering; Food Technology); **Chemistry and Environmental Science**; **Economics and Law** (Economics; Human Resources; Law; Management; Political Sciences); **Liberal Arts** (Chinese; Journalism; Radio and Television Broadcasting; Secretarial Studies); **Materials Science and Engineering** (Automation and Control Engineering; Materials Engineering; Metallurgical Engineering); **Mechanical Engineering** (Mechanical Engineering); **Sports Sciences** (Physical Education; Sports)

History: Founded 1978 as Shaanxi Institute of Technology. Acquired present status 2001 following merger of Hanzhong Teacher's College and Shaanxi Institute of Technology.

Degrees and Diplomas: *Xueshi Xuewei*; *Shuoshi Xuewei*

SHANDONG AGRICULTURAL UNIVERSITY

61 Daizong Street, Tai'an, Shandong Province 271018
Tel: +86(538) 8242297
Fax: +86(538) 8226399
EMail: wugw@sdau.edu.cn
Website: http://www.sdau.edu.cn

President: Fujiang Wen Tel: +86(538) 8242291

College
Agronomy (Agronomy; Natural Resources; Plant and Crop Protection; Traditional Eastern Medicine); **Animal Science and Technology** (Animal Husbandry; Aquaculture; Veterinary Science; Zoology); **Chemistry and Material Science** (Applied Chemistry; Chemical Engineering; Chemistry); **Continuing Education**; **Economics and Management** (Accountancy; Agricultural Business; Business and Commerce; Economics; Finance; Information Management; Rural Planning); **Farm Management** (Farm Management); **Food Science and Engineering** (Food Science; Food Technology; Oenology); **Foreign Languages** (English; Japanese; Russian); **Forestry** (Forestry; Landscape Architecture; Sericulture; Soil Conservation; Water Management); **Horticulture** (Agricultural Engineering; Horticulture); **Humanities and Law** (Administration; Law; Secretarial Studies); **Hydrology and Civil Engineering** (Architectural and Environmental Design; Bridge Engineering; Civil Engineering; Hydraulic Engineering; Road Engineering; Structural Architecture; Water Management; Wood Technology); **Information Science and Engineering** (Computer Networks; Computer Science; Mathematics); **International Exchanges** (Accountancy; Business Administration; Food Science; International Economics); **Life Sciences** (Biochemistry; Bioengineering; Biological and Life Sciences; Biotechnology; Cell Biology; Microbiology; Molecular

Biology); **Marxism** (Political Sciences); **Mechanical and Electronic Engineering** (Agricultural Engineering; Agricultural Equipment; Automation and Control Engineering; Electronic Engineering; Mechanical Engineering); **Physical Education and Arts** (Musicology; Physical Education); **Plant Protection** (Forest Biology; Forestry; Pharmacology; Plant and Crop Protection); **Resources and Environment Studies** (Environmental Engineering; Environmental Management; Environmental Studies; Natural Resources; Soil Science; Surveying and Mapping)

Further Information: Also 2 Experimental Farms. Teaching Hospital

History: Founded 1906 as Shandong Agricultural and Forestry School of Higher Learning. Acquired present title 1983, incorporating Shandong Agricultural College, Agricultural College of Shandong University, Agricultural Institute of Qilu University and the Horticulture Departments of Jinling University and Nanjing University.

Degrees and Diplomas: *Xueshi Xuewei*; *Shuoshi Xuewei*; *Boshi*. Also postgraduate Diplomas

Publications: Journal of Shandong Agricultural University; Research of Agricultural Higher Education; Shandong Animal Husbandry and Veterinary Science; Shandong Nongda Bao; Translation Series on New Agricultural Techniques and Methods

Academic Staff *2012-2013*: Total 2,598

Student Numbers *2012-2013*: Total 31,000

Last Updated: 31/01/13

SHANDONG INSTITUTE OF BUSINESS AND TECHNOLOGY (SDIBT)

191 BinHai Road, Yantai, Shandong Province 264005
Tel: +86(535) 6904023
Fax: +86(535) 6904244
EMail: yzmail@sdibt.edu.cn
Website: http://www.sdibt.edu.cn

President: Qu Jianxin

International Relations: Zhang Yiqiang

College

Higher Applied Technology *(Sino-Canada)* (Technology); **Information and Electronic Engineering** (Electronic Engineering; Information Technology); **International Business** (International Business); **Mathematics and Information Sciences** (Information Sciences; Mathematics)

School

Accountancy (Accountancy); **Adults Education**; **Business Administration** (Accountancy; Business Administration); **Computer** *(Sino-Singapore)* (Computer Science); **Economics** (Economics; Industrial Management); **International Exchanges**; **Law** (Law); **Management Science and Engineering** (Engineering Management; Management; Marketing); **Public Management** (Public Administration); **Statistics** (Statistics)

Department

Foreign Studies and Literature (Literature; Modern Languages); **Social Sciences** (Social Sciences); **Sports** (Sports)

History: Founded 1985 as China Coal Economic College. Acquired present title 2003.

Main Language(s) of Instruction: Chinese

Degrees and Diplomas: *Xueshi Xuewei*

Academic Staff *2011-2012*: Total 18,600

Student Numbers *2011-2012*: Total 1,000

Last Updated: 01/02/13

SHANDONG JIANZHU UNIVERSITY

Fengming Road, Jinan, Shandong Province 250101
Tel: +86(531) 86362000
Fax: +86(531) 86367302
EMail: international@sdjzu.edu.cn
Website: http://wwm.sdjzu.edu.cn/index0.php

President: Chong-jie Wang

College

Adult Education; **Foreign Languages** (English; Modern Languages); **Law and Political Science** (Law; Political Sciences); **Science** (Mathematics; Physics)

School

Civil Engineering (Civil Engineering); **Art** (Fine Arts); **Business** (Business Administration); **Computer Science and Technology** (Computer Science; Technology); **Electrical and Mechanical Engineering** (Electronic Engineering; Mechanical Engineering); **Heat Energy Engineering** (Energy Engineering; Heating and Refrigeration); **Information and Electrical Engineering** (Electrical Engineering; Information Sciences); **Management Engineering** (Engineering Management); **Materials Science and Engineering** (Materials Engineering); **Public Works and Environmental Engineering** (Environmental Engineering; Public Administration)

Department

Physical Education (Physical Education; Sports)

Institute

Architecture and Urban Planning (Architecture; Architecture and Planning)

History: Founded 1956 as Jinan Urban Construction School. Renamed Shandong Institute of Architecture and Engineering 1978.

Degrees and Diplomas: *Xueshi Xuewei*; *Shuoshi Xuewei*

Student Numbers *2011-2012*: Total: c. 21,000

Last Updated: 05/02/13

SHANDONG JIAOTONG UNIVERSITY

5 Jiaoxiao Road, Tianqiao District, Jinan, Shandong 250023
Tel: +86(531) 80687816
EMail: international_sdjtu@126.com
Website: http://www.sdjtu.edu.cn/

President: Lu Lin

Vice President: Zhang Cheng

International Relations: Michelle Lee, Director

College

Continual Education; **Vocational Technical**

School

Automotive Engineering (Automotive Engineering); **Civil Engineering** (Architecture; Civil Engineering); **Finance and Economics** (Economics; Finance); **Foreign Studies** (English; Japanese; Russian); **Humanity and Law** (Arts and Humanities; Design; Fine Arts; Law); **Information Sciences and Electrical Engineering** (Electrical Engineering; Information Sciences); **International** *(Northern)*; **Management** (Management); **Marine Engineering** (Marine Engineering); **Material and Elecrical Engineering** (Electrical Engineering; Materials Engineering); **Mechanical Engineering** (Mechanical Engineering); **Science** (Computer Science; Information Technology); **Transport Engineering** (Transport Engineering)

Department

Physical Education (Physical Education); **Social Sciences** (Social Sciences)

History: Founded 1958 as Shandong Communications College. Acquired present title and status 2002.

Academic Staff *2012*: Total 1,200

Student Numbers *2012*: Total 17,300

Last Updated: 24/10/13

SHANDONG NORMAL UNIVERSITY (SDNU)

88 East Wenhua Road, Jinan, Shandong Province 250014
Tel: +86(531) 86180015
Fax: +86(531) 86180954
EMail: sie@sdnu.edu.cn
Website: http://www.sdnu.edu.cn/

President: Zhao Yanxiu

Vice-President: Shaohua Wang

College

Chemistry, Chemical Engineering and Materials Science (Chemical Engineering; Chemistry; Materials Engineering); **Chinese Language and Literature** (Chinese; Literature); **Culture and Social Development** (Cultural Studies; Development Studies); **Education** (Education); **English Teaching** (English); **Fine Arts** (Fine Arts); **Foreign Languages** (English; Japanese; Korean; Literature; Modern Languages; Russian); **Information Management** (Information Management); **Law** (Law; Political Sciences); **Life Sciences** (Biological and Life Sciences; Biology); **Mathematics** (Mathematics); **Music** (Music); **Physical Education** (Physical Education); **Physics and Electronics** (Electronic Engineering; Physics); **Population, Resource and Environment** (Demography and Population; Environmental Studies)

School

International Exchanges; **Psychology** (Psychology)

History: Founded 1950 as Shandong Teachers College. Acquired present title 1981.

Academic Year: September to July (September-January; March-July)

Admission Requirements: Graduation from senior middle school and entrance examination

Fees: (US Dollars): Foreign students, c. 1,600-2,900 per annum

Main Language(s) of Instruction: Chinese

Degrees and Diplomas: *Xueshi Xuewei*; *Shuoshi Xuewei*; *Boshi*

Student Services: Academic Counselling, Canteen, Careers Guidance, Cultural Activities, Health Services, Nursery Care, Social Counselling, Sports Facilities

Publications: China Population, Resources and Environment; Journal of Foreign Languages; Journal of Shandong Normal University

Last Updated: 05/02/13

SHANDONG POLYTECHNIC UNIVERSITY (SPU)

Daxue Road, Western University Science Park,
Jinan, Shandong Province 250100
Tel: +86(531) 89631666 Ext. 226
Fax: +86(531) 89631111
EMail: Internationaloffice@sdili.edu.cn
Website: http://english.spu.edu.cn/

Administrative Officer: Zheng Zhong
Tel: +86(531) 89631016 EMail: guojichu@hotmail.com

Department

Administration of Public Affairs (Administration; Law; Public Administration); **Art Design** (Industrial Chemistry; Photography; Visual Arts); **Chemical Engineering** (Applied Chemistry; Chemical Engineering; Pharmacology); **Electronic Information and Control Engineering** (Automation and Control Engineering; Electrical and Electronic Engineering; Industrial Design); **Food and Biology Engineering** (Bioengineering; Food Technology); **Foreign Languages** (English; Japanese); **Industrial Design** (Industrial Design); **Information Science and Technology** (Computer Engineering; Information Sciences; Information Technology; Mathematics; Optics; Telecommunications Engineering); **Inorganic Materials** (Inorganic Chemistry; Materials Engineering; Polymer and Plastics Technology); **International Economy and Trade** (Accountancy; Finance; Human Resources; Information Management; International Economics; Marketing); **Light Chemistry and Environmental Engineering** (Chemical Engineering; Environmental Engineering; Environmental Studies); **Light Industry Engineering** (Environmental Engineering; Forest Products; Paper Technology; Printing and Printmaking); **Machinery and Automobile Engineering** (Automotive Engineering; Machine Building); **Mechanical Engineering** (Automation and Control Engineering; Industrial Design; Mechanical Engineering)

History: Founded 1948 as Jiaodong Industry School, in Jiaodong Military Area. Became Shandong Institute of Light Industry,1978.

Degrees and Diplomas: *Xueshi Xuewei*; *Shuoshi Xuewei*

Academic Staff *2011-2012*: Total 21,404

Student Numbers *2011-2012*: Total 1,140

Last Updated: 01/02/13

SHANDONG SPORT UNIVERSITY

10600 Century Avenue, Jinan, Shandong Province 250102
Tel: +86(531) 89655015
EMail: info@sdpei.edu.cn
Website: http://www.sdpei.edu.cn

President: Han Dong

International Relations: Liu Wei

Department

Arts (Dance); **Physical Education** (Physical Education); **Social Sciences** (Social Sciences); **Sports** (Sports); **Wushu** (Sports)

History: Founded 1958. Formerly known as Shandong Institute of Physical Education.

Degrees and Diplomas: *Xueshi Xuewei*; *Shuoshi Xuewei*

Last Updated: 05/02/13

SHANDONG UNIVERSITY (SDU)

27 South Shanda Road, Jinan, Shandong Province 250100
Tel: +86(531) 88364853
Fax: +86(531) 88565051
EMail: ipo@sdu.edu.cn
Website: http://www.sdu.edu.cn

President: Xu Xianming
Tel: +86(531) 88364953 EMail: president@sdu.edu.cn

College

English (English); **International Education**; **Physical Education** *(Qianfoshan)* (Physical Education); **Software** *(Software Park)* (Software Engineering)

School

Chemistry and Chemical Engineering (Analytical Chemistry; Applied Chemistry; Chemical Engineering; Chemistry; Inorganic Chemistry; Organic Chemistry; Physical Chemistry); **Civil Engineering** *(Qianfoshan)* (Architecture; Architecture and Planning; Civil Engineering; Construction Engineering; Geological Engineering; Hydraulic Engineering; Mechanical Engineering; Water Management; Water Science); **Computer Science and Technology** *(Software Park)* (Computer Engineering; Computer Science); **Control Science and Engineering** *(Qianfoshan)* (Automation and Control Engineering); **Economics** (Economics); **Electrical Engineering** *(Qianfoshan)* (Automation and Control Engineering; Electrical Engineering; Electronic Engineering); **Energy and Power Engineering** *(Qianfoshan)* (Energy Engineering; Heating and Refrigeration; Machine Building; Mechanical Engineering; Thermal Engineering; Thermal Physics); **Environmental Science and Engineering** (Environmental Engineering; Environmental Studies); **Fine Arts** *(Hongliaou)* (Fine Arts); **Foreign Languages and Literature** *(Hongliaou)* (English; French; German; Japanese; Korean; Russian); **History and Culture** (Archaeology; Archiving; History); **Information Science and Engineering** (Information Sciences; Information Technology); **Law** *(Hongliaou)* (Civil Law; Commercial Law; International Law; Law); **Life Sciences** (Biological and Life Sciences); **Literature and Journalism** (Chinese; Comparative Literature; Fine Arts; Journalism; Linguistics; Literature; Philology); **Management** (Management); **Marxism** (Political Sciences); **Materials Science and Engineering** *(Qianfoshan)* (Chemistry; Machine Building; Materials Engineering; Mechanics; Physics); **Mathematics and System Sciences** (Applied Mathematics; Computer Science; Information Sciences; Mathematics; Operations Research; Statistics; Systems Analysis); **Mechanical Engineering** *(Qianfoshan)* (Automation and Control Engineering; Automotive Engineering; Chemical Engineering; Electronic Engineering; Industrial Design; Mechanical Engineering); **Medicine** *(Baotuquan)* (Medicine); **Nursing** *(Baotuquan)* (Nursing); **Pharmacy** *(Baotuquan)* (Pharmacy); **Philosophy and Social Development** (Development Studies; Philosophy; Social Sciences); **Physics** (Chemistry; Electronic Engineering; Materials Engineering; Microelectronics; Physics); **Political Science and Public Administration** (Administration; Education; International Studies; Political Sciences; Social Sciences); **Public Health** *(Baotuquan)* (Child Care and Development; Environmental Studies; Epidemiology; Health Administration; Health Sciences; Hygiene; Laboratory Techniques; Medicine; Nutrition; Occupational Health; Public Health; Social and Preventive Medicine; Statistics; Toxicology); **Stomatology** *(Baotuquan)* (Stomatology)

Institute
Literature History and Philosophy (Literature; Philosophy)

Centre
Economic Research (Economics)

Campus
Xinglongsham *(Undergraduate)* (Automation and Control Engineering; Civil Engineering; Electrical Engineering; Energy Engineering; Materials Engineering; Mechanical Engineering; Power Engineering)

History: Founded 1901. Merged with Shandong Medical University and Shandong University of Technology (former) 2000.

Academic Year: August to June (August-January; February-June)

Admission Requirements: Graduation from senior middle school and entrance examination

Main Language(s) of Instruction: Chinese and English

Accrediting Agency: Degree Committee of the State Council of China; Ministry of Education

Degrees and Diplomas: *Xueshi Xuewei*; *Shuoshi Xuewei*; *Boshi*

Student Services: Academic Counselling, Canteen, Careers Guidance, Cultural Activities, Foreign Studies Centre, Health Services, Language Laboratory, Nursery Care, Social Counselling, Sports Facilities

Publications: Issues of Contemporary Socialism; Literature, History and Philosophy; Shandong University Journal; Studies of Folklore; Studies of Zhouyi; Young Thinker

Publishing House: Shandong University Publishing House

Student Numbers *2011-2012*: Total: c. 51,700
Last Updated: 05/02/13

SHANDONG UNIVERSITY OF ART AND DESIGN

23 Qianfu Shan East Road, Jinan, Shandong Province 250014
Tel: +86(531) 89626168
Fax: +86(531) 89626166
EMail: kangwang59@sdada.edu.cn
Website: http://www.sdada.edu.cn/

President: Pan Lusheng

School
Applied Design (Design; Interior Design); **Architecture and Landscape Design** (Architecture; Interior Design; Landscape Architecture); **Arts and Humanities** (Arts and Humanities); **Continuing Education** (Continuing Education); **Digital Art and Communication** (Cinema and Television; Communication Arts; Film; Photography); **Fashion Design** (Fashion Design); **Fine Arts** (Fine Arts; Painting and Drawing; Sculpture); **Industrial Design** (Industrial Design); **Modern Handicraft Arts** (Handicrafts); **Visual Communication Design** (Advertising and Publicity; Graphic Design; Visual Arts)

History: Founded 1973 as Shandong School of Arts and Crafts, acquired present status and tile 1994. Formerly known as Shandong Institute of Industrial Arts.

Degrees and Diplomas: *Xueshi Xuewei*; *Shuoshi Xuewei*
Last Updated: 05/02/13

SHANDONG UNIVERSITY OF ARTS

91 East Wenhua Road, Jinan, Shandong Province 250014
Tel: +86(531) 86423601
Fax: +86(531) 86423203
Website: http://www.sdca.edu.cn/

President: Zhang Zhimin (2000-) EMail: sdysxyyb@163.com

International Relations: Shaoli Hu, Director of Foreign Affairs
Tel: +86(531) 86423246 EMail: hushaoli@sdca.edu.cn

School
Adult Education; **Arts and Humanities** (Advertising and Publicity; Arts and Humanities; Printing and Printmaking); **Dance** (Dance); **Design** (Design); **Digital Art and Communication** (Communication Arts; Film; Multimedia; Photography; Radio and Television Broadcasting); **Fine Arts** (Fine Arts; Jewellery Art; Painting and Drawing; Sculpture); **International Art Exchange and Creative Design** (Design; Fine Arts; International Relations); **International Design** (Design); **Music** (Music); **Theatre** (Theatre); **Traditional Opera** (Opera); **Vocational Education**

Further Information: Also a campus in Changqing

History: Founded 1958 as Shandong Arts Training School. Renamed Shandong Arts College 1978. Acquired present status and title 2001, following merger with Shandong Traditional Opera School.

Academic Year: September to July

Admission Requirements: Professional examination

Main Language(s) of Instruction: Chinese

Accrediting Agency: Committee of Academic Degrees of Shandong College of Arts and Shandong Provincial Office of Academic Degrees; Shangdong Provincial Education Department

Degrees and Diplomas: *Xueshi Xuewei*; *Shuoshi Xuewei*

Student Services: Academic Counselling, Canteen, Careers Guidance, Cultural Activities, Foreign Studies Centre, Health Services, Language Laboratory, Nursery Care, Social Counselling, Sports Facilities

Publications: Oilu Realm of Arts

Student Numbers *2011-2012*: Total: c. 7,500
Last Updated: 05/02/13

SHANDONG UNIVERSITY OF FINANCE AND ECONOMICS

40 Shungeng Road, Jinan, Shandong Province 250014
Tel: +86(531) 82911306
EMail: info@sdfi.edu.cn
Website: http://www.sdufe.edu.cn/

President: Yun Liu Xing

School
Accounting (Accountancy); **Banking** (Banking); **Business Administration** (Management); **Computer and Information Engineering** (Computer Engineering; Information Technology); **Economics** (Economics); **Finance** (Banking; Finance); **Finance Taxation and Public Administration** (Finance; Public Administration; Taxation); **Foreign Languages** (Modern Languages); **International Economics and Trade** (International Economics); **Physical Education** (Physical Education); **Statistics and Mathematics** (Mathematics; Statistics)

Further Information: Also Yanshan, Mingshui, East School campuses

History: Founded 1986 as Finance College, became Shandong University of Finance, 1992. Merged with Shandong Economic University, acquired present status and title 2011.

Admission Requirements: High school certificate or equivalent; Hanyu Shuiping Kaoshi (HSK) 3 grade or equivalent level in chinese language.

Fees: (Yuan): registration fee, 200; undergraduate studies, 13,000 per annum; Master's degree 16,000 per annum; further studies, 12,000 per annum; short-term further studies, 2,500 per 4 weeks or less

Main Language(s) of Instruction: Chinese

Degrees and Diplomas: *Xueshi Xuewei*; *Shuoshi Xuewei*

Academic Staff *2011-2012*: Total: c. 1,320
Student Numbers *2011-2012*: Total: c. 33,000
Last Updated: 06/02/13

SHANDONG UNIVERSITY OF POLITICAL SCIENCE AND LAW (SUPL)

63, East Jiefang Road, Jinan, Shandong 250014
EMail: xxhbgs@sdupsl.edu.cn
Website: http://www.sdupsl.edu.cn/

President: Li Yufu

School
Law (Law); **Business** (Business Administration; Management); **Civil and Commercial Law** (Civil Law; Commercial Law); **Criminal Justice** (Law); **Economic and Trade Law** (Commercial Law)

Department
Foreign Languages (Foreign Languages Education); **Informaion Sciences and Technology** (Information Sciences; Information Technology); **Journalism and Communication Studies** (Communication Studies; Journalism); **Physical Education** (Physical Education); **Political Science and Administration** (Administration; Political Sciences)

Academy
Police (Police Studies)

Degrees and Diplomas: *Xueshi Xuewei*
Last Updated: 25/10/13

SHANDONG UNIVERSITY OF SCIENCE AND TECHNOLOGY

579 Qianwangang Road, Qingdao, Shandong Province 266510
Tel: +86(532) 86057717
Fax: +86(532) 86057187
EMail: liuxue@sdust.edu.cn
Website: http://en.sdust.edu.cn/

President: Tingqi Ren
Tel: +86(532) 86057059 EMail: sustxb@sdust.edu.cn

College
Arts and Design (Design; Fine Arts); **Chemical and Environmental Engineering** (Chemical Engineering; Environmental Engineering); **Civil Engineering and Architecture** (Architecture; Civil Engineering); **Continuing Education**; **Economics and Management** (Economics; Management); **Foreign Languages** (Modern Languages); **Geomatics** (Geology); **Geoscience and Technology** (Earth Sciences; Geology); **Humanities and Law** (Arts and Humanities; Law); **Information and Electrical Engineering** (Electrical Engineering); **Information Science and Technology** (Information Sciences; Information Technology); **Materials Science and Engineering** (Materials Engineering); **Mechanical and Electronic Engineering** (Electronic Engineering; Mechanical Engineering); **Natural Resources and Environmental Engineering** (Environmental Engineering; Natural Resources); **Science** (Chemistry; Mathematics; Physics); **Science and Technology** *(Taishan)* (Natural Sciences; Technology)

Further Information: Also campuses in Tai'an and Jinan

History: Founded 1958 as Shandong Technical College of Coal Industry. Merged with Shandong Institute of Mining and Technology 1999.

Main Language(s) of Instruction: Chinese

Degrees and Diplomas: *Xueshi Xuewei*; *Shuoshi Xuewei*; *Boshi*

Academic Staff *2011-2012*: Total: c. 2,900

Student Numbers *2011-2012*: Total: c. 46,000
Last Updated: 06/02/13

SHANDONG UNIVERSITY OF TECHNOLOGY (SDUT)

12 Zhangzhou Road, Zibo, Shandong Province 255049
Tel: +86(533) 2786727
Fax: +86(533) 2780944
EMail: international@sdut.edu.cn
Website: http://www.sdut.edu.cn

President: Xinyi Zhang

School
Architecture Engineering (Civil Engineering; Surveying and Mapping; Town Planning); **Chemical Engineering** (Chemical Engineering); **Computer Science and Technology** (Computer Engineering; Computer Science); **Distance Education** (Distance Education); **Economics** (Economics; Finance; International Economics); **Electrical and Electronic Engineering** (Automation and Control Engineering; Electrical Engineering; Electronic Engineering); **Engineering Technology** (Educational Sciences; Electronic Engineering; Engineering Management; Mechanical Engineering); **Fine Arts** (Fine Arts); **Foreign Languages** (English; Japanese; Modern Languages); **Law** (Administration; Law; Political Sciences; Sociology); **Life Sciences and Technology** (Biological and Life Sciences); **Light Industry and Agricultural Engineering** (Agricultural Engineering; Automation and Control Engineering; Food Science; Industrial Design); **Literature and Media Dissemination** (Advertising and Publicity; Chinese; History; Literature); **Machinery Engineering** (Machine Building; Mechanical Engineering; Metal Techniques); **Management** (Accountancy; Business Administration; Industrial Engineering; Information Management; Management); **Materials Science and Engineering** (Materials Engineering); **Mathematics and Information Science** (Information Sciences; Mathematics; Statistics); **Music** (Music); **National Defense Education**; **Physical Education** (Physical Education); **Physics** (Physics); **Resources and Environmental Engineering** (Environmental Engineering; Environmental Studies); **Traffic and Vehicle Engineering** (Automotive Engineering; Power Engineering; Thermal Engineering; Transport Engineering)

Department
Computer Teaching (Computer Education); **English** (English); **Marxism** (Political Sciences)

History: Founded 1949 as Shandong Provincial Industrial School. Renamed Shandong Institute of Engineering 1951. Acquired present title and status 2001 following merger with Zibo University.

Academic Year: September to July (September-February; March-July)

Admission Requirements: Graduation from senior middle school and entrance examination

Main Language(s) of Instruction: Chinese

Degrees and Diplomas: *Xueshi Xuewei*; *Shuoshi Xuewei*; *Boshi*

Publications: Journal of Shandong University of Technology (Edition of Natural Sciences); Journal of Shandong University of Technology (Edition of Social Sciences)
Last Updated: 06/02/13

SHANDONG UNIVERSITY OF TRADITIONAL CHINESE MEDICINE

53 Jingshi Road, Jinan, Shandong Province 250014
Tel: +86(531) 2968823
Fax: +86(531) 2968823
EMail: sutcm@public.jn.sd.cn
Website: http://www.sdutcm.edu.cn

School
Acupuncture and Moxibustion (Acupuncture); **Clinical Medicine** (Medicine); **Combined Chinese and Western Clinical Medicine** (Medicine; Traditional Eastern Medicine); **Herbal Promotion and Marketing** (Marketing); **Nursing** (Nursing); **Physical Education** (Physical Education); **Rehabilitation and Therapy** (Rehabilitation and Therapy); **Traditional Chinese Medicine** (Traditional Eastern Medicine)

Department
Biomedical Engineering (Biomedical Engineering); **English** (English); **Law** (Law); **Osteotraumatology** (Osteopathy)

History: Founded 1958 as Shandong College of Traditional Chinese Medicine, acquired present title 1996.

Fees: (Yuan): 23,000-38,000 per annum depending on Degree programs

Degrees and Diplomas: *Xueshi Xuewei*; *Shuoshi Xuewei*; *Boshi*

Publications: Shandong Magazine of TCM

Student Numbers *2011-2012*: Total: c. 18,700
Last Updated: 06/02/13

SHANDONG WANJIE MEDICAL UNIVERSITY

Economic and Technological Development zone; Boshan district, Zibo, Shandong 255213
Tel: +86(533) 4619600
EMail: wanjiemedicaluniversity@live.cn
Website: http://www.wjmu.net/

President: Kuang Yizhen

International Relations: Zhang Lu, Director

Programme
Chinese (Chinese)

School
Basic Medicine (Medicine); **Medical Humanities** (Medicine); **Adult Education** (Adult Education); **Clinical Medicine** (Medicine); **Clinical Medicine for the Handicapped** (Medicine); **Nursing** (Nursing); **Stomatology** (Stomatology)

Fees: (Dollars): 2000 per annum for foreign students

Degrees and Diplomas: *Xueshi Xuewei*; *Shuoshi Xuewei*: **Anatomy; Embryology and Reproduction Biology; Histology; Immunology; Pathology; Physiology; Stomatology.**

Publications: Hospital Statistics; Wanjie Medical University Transactions

Last Updated: 28/10/13

SHANDONG WOMEN'S UNIVERSITY

Jinan, Shandong

President: Fan Suhua

Department
Arts (Fine Arts); **Business Administration** (Business Administration); **Computer Science and Technology** (Computer Science; Technology); **Engineering** (Engineering); **English** (English); **Law** (Law); **Literature** (Literature); **Preschool Education** (Preschool Education); **Social Work** (Social Work); **Tourism Management** (Tourism)

History: Founded 1952 as Shandong Women's Cadres School, 1995 the university was renamed China Women's University Shandong Branch. Acquired present title and status, 2010.

Degrees and Diplomas: *Xueshi Xuewei*

Last Updated: 29/10/13

SHANDONG XIE HE UNIVERSITY

No.6277 Jiqinglu, Licheng District, Jihan, Shandong 250109
Tel: +86(531) 88795666
Website: http://www.sdxiehe.com/

Party Secretary: Wanggui Yun

International Relations: Sheng Zhenwen Tel: +86(531) 81307137

Department
Architecture and Engineering (Architecture; Civil Engineering); **Basic Courses** (Arts and Humanities); **Computer Science and Technology** (Computer Engineering; Computer Science); **Economics and Management** (Economics; Management); **Electromechanical Engineering** (Electronic Engineering; Mechanical Engineering); **Further Education**; **Humanities Education** (Education); **Medicine** (Medicine); **Nursing** (Nursing)

Accrediting Agency: Chinese Ministry of Education

Degrees and Diplomas: *Xueshi Xuewei*

Student Services: Nursery Care

Last Updated: 29/10/13

SHANDONG YINGCAI UNIVERSITY

2 Yingcai Rd, Licheng, Jinan, Shandong 250104
Tel: +86(531) 88253033
Fax: +86(531) 88257501
Website: http://www.ycxy.com/Index.html

President: Xia Jiting

Vice President: Liu Cuilan

International Relations: Liu Cungang, Director
Tel: +86(531) 88253033 EMail: lcg66@yahoo.com

School
Agriculture (Agriculture); **Art and Design** (Design; Fine Arts); **Business Administration** (Business Administration); **Civil Engineering** (Civil Engineering); **Computer Science and Information Technology** (Computer Science; Information Technology); **Economics and Management** (Economics; Management); **Foreign Languages** (Foreign Languages Education); **Humanities and Law** (Arts and Humanities; Law); **Machinery and Automation Engineering** (Automation and Control Engineering; Machine Building); **Medicine and Healthcare** (Health Sciences; Medicine); **Preschool Education** (Preschool Education)

History: Founded 1998.

Degrees and Diplomas: *Xueshi Xuewei*

Student Numbers *2012*: Total 36,000

Last Updated: 28/10/13

SHANDONG YOUTH UNIVERSITY OF POLITICAL SCIENCE

31699 Jingshi East Rd, Licheng, Jinan, Shandong 250014
Tel: +86(531) 58997373
EMail: wyx@sdyu.edu.cn
Website: http://wyxy.sdyu.edu.cn/

College
English (English); **Foreign Languages** (Arabic; French; German; Japanese; Korean; Spanish)

School
Culture and Communication Studies (Communication Studies; Cultural Studies); **Dance** (Dance); **Design Art** (Design); **Economics** (Economics); **Information Engineering** (Information Technology); **Management** (Management)

Department
Continuing Education; **International Trade** (International Business); **Political Sciences and Law** (Law; Political Sciences); **Youth Training**

History: ounded 1987.

Degrees and Diplomas: *Xueshi Xuewei*

Last Updated: 28/10/13

SHANGHAI BUSINESS SCHOOL

123 Fengpu Ave., Fen Xian, Shanghai, Shanghai 201400
Tel: +86(21) 64870020
Fax: +86(21) 64288497; +86-21) 67105438
EMail: lxsb@sbs.edu.cn
Website: http://www.sbs.edu.cn

President: Zhu Guohong

Division
Art and Design (Design; Fine Arts); **Computer and Electronic Engineering** (Computer Engineering; E-Business/Commerce; Electronic Engineering); **Ecology and Tourism** (Ecology; Horticulture; Hotel Management; Tourism); **Finance and Accountancy** (Accountancy; Finance; Taxation); **Food Technology** (Food Science); **Foreign Languages** (Economics; English; Japanese; Korean); **International Economics and Trade** (International Economics); **Journalism and Media** (Journalism; Media Studies); **Law and Politics** (Law; Political Sciences); **Management** (Management; Retailing and Wholesaling; Transport Management)

Further Information: Also Xuhui Campus, 2271 West Zhong Shan Rd, Shanghai

History: Founded as Shangai Commercial Polytechnic, 1998, acquired present status and title 2004.

Student Numbers *2012*: Total: c. 10,000

Last Updated: 07/10/13

SHANGHAI CONSERVATORY OF MUSIC (SCOM)

20 Fenyang Road, Shanghai, Shanghai 200031
Tel: +86(21) 64312000
Fax: +86(21) 64310305
EMail: wb@shcmusic.edu.cn
Website: http://www.shcmusic.edu.cn

President: Shuya Xu

International Relations: Zhang Xianping
EMail: shcmfso@yahoo.com

Department
Arts Administration (Art Management); **Chinese Traditional Instruments** (Musical Instruments); **Composition** (Music Theory and Composition); **Conducting** (Conducting); **General Education** (Political Sciences; Social Sciences); **Modern Instrumental Music** (Music; Musical Instruments); **Music Education** (Music Education);

Music Engineering (Music; Sound Engineering (Acoustics)); **Musical Theater**; **Musicology** (Musicology); **Orchestral Instruments** (Musical Instruments); **Piano** (Musical Instruments); **Traditional Instruments** (Musical Instruments); **Voice Opera** (Opera)

History: Founded 1927 as National Conservatory of Music, acquired present name 1956.

Degrees and Diplomas: *Xueshi Xuewei*; *Shuoshi Xuewei*; *Boshi*

Last Updated: 07/02/13

SHANGHAI CUSTOMS COLLEGE

5677 Huaxia Xilu, Pudong, Shanghai 201204
Tel: +86(21) 28992899
Fax: +86(21) 33907157
Website: http://shanghai_edu.customs.gov.cn

President: Jianguo Xiao

International Relations: Shujie Zhang
EMail: shujiezhang@customs.gov.cn

Programme

Customs (English; International Law; Taxation; Transport Management)

History: Founded in 1953 as Shanghai Junior College of Customs. Acquired present title 2007.

Degrees and Diplomas: *Xueshi Xuewei*; *Shuoshi Xuewei*

Last Updated: 07/10/13

SHANGHAI DIANJI UNIVERSITY

Jiangchuang Road No.690, Minhang District, Shanghai 200240
Tel: +86(21) 64300980
EMail: international@sdju.edu.cn
Website: http://www.sdju.edu.cn

President: Xia Jianguo

School

Advanced Vocational Technology (Technology); **Arts and Science** (Cultural Studies; Economics; History; International Economics; Law; Mathematics; Philosophy; Physics; Political Sciences; Writing); **Automotive Engineering** (Automotive Engineering); **Economics and Management** (Economics; Engineering Management; Finance; Industrial Engineering; International Economics; Management; Marketing; Transport Management); **Electrical Engineering** (Automation and Control Engineering; Electrical Engineering; Power Engineering); **Electronic Engineering and Information Science** (Computer Science; Electronic Engineering; Information Technology; Software Engineering; Telecommunications Engineering); **Foreign Languages** (English; German); **International Education** (Automation and Control Engineering; Automotive Engineering; Computer Engineering; Electrical Engineering; International Business; Mechanical Engineering); **Mechanical Engineering** (Electronic Engineering; Industrial Design; Mechanical Engineering)

History: Created 1953

Degrees and Diplomas: *Xueshi Xuewei*

Academic Staff *2011-2012*: Total: c. 900

Student Numbers *2011-2012*: Total: c. 10,800

Last Updated: 06/02/13

SHANGHAI FINANCE UNIVERSITY

995 Shangchuan Road, Pudong, Shanghai 201209
Tel: +86(21) 68680725
Fax: +86(21) 68680725
EMail: jzzb@shfc.edu.cn
Website: http://www.shfc.edu.cn

President: Chu Minwei

International Relations: Ming Zheng, Director

School

Accounting (Accountancy); **Business Administration** (Business Administration); **Continuing Education**; **Information Management** (Computer Engineering; Computer Science; E-Business/Commerce; Information Management); **Insurance** (Insurance); **International Economics and Trades** (International Business; International Economics; International Studies); **International Exchange** (Finance; International Business; Technology); **International Finance** (Finance; Insurance); **Political Science and Law** (Law; Political Sciences); **Public Economics and Administration** (Administration; Economics; Finance; Public Administration)

Department

Applied Mathematics (Applied Mathematics); **Arts and Humanities** (Design); **Foreign Languages** (English); **Physical Education** (Physical Education)

Further Information: Also a campus in Puxi

History: Founded 1952 as Shanghai Banking School. Became Shanghai Finance School 1960, changed its name to Shanghai Finance College,1987. Acquired present title 2003.

Main Language(s) of Instruction: Chinese

Degrees and Diplomas: *Xueshi Xuewei*

Last Updated: 06/02/13

SHANGHAI INSTITUTE OF TECHNOLOGY (SIT)

120 Caobao Road, Shanghai, Shanghai 200235
Tel: +86(21) 64941159
Fax: +86(21) 34141355
EMail: inter@sit.edu.cn
Website: http://www.sit.edu.cn

President: Guanzhong Lu (2004-)
Tel: +86(21) 64945020 EMail: pd@sit.edu.cn

Vice-President: Ye Yinzhong

International Relations: Shichang Zhu, Director, International Relations Tel: +86(21) 60873673 EMail: ic@sit.edu.cn

School

Art and Design (Design; Painting and Drawing); **Chemical and Environmental Engineering** (Applied Chemistry; Chemical Engineering; Environmental Engineering; Pharmacology); **Computer Science and Information Technology** (Computer Science; Information Technology; Software Engineering); **Continuing Education** (Continuing Education); **Ecological Technology and Engineering** (Ecology); **Economics and Management** (Economics; Management); **Electrical and Electronic Engineering** (Electrical and Electronic Engineering); **Foreign Languages** (English); **Humanities** (Arts and Humanities; Political Sciences); **Materials Science and Engineering** (Materials Engineering); **Mechanical Engineering** (Automation and Control Engineering; Automotive Engineering; Mechanical Engineering); **Perfume and Aroma Technology** (Biology; Biotechnology; Chemical Engineering; Food Science); **Rail Transportation** (Railway Engineering); **Science** (Mathematics; Physics); **Urban Construction and Safety Engineering** (Architectural and Environmental Design; Building Technologies; Civil Engineering; Environmental Engineering; Power Engineering; Safety Engineering; Thermal Engineering); **Vocational Studies** (Electronic Engineering; Mechanical Engineering)

Department

Physical Education (Physical Education)

Further Information: Also a campus in Fengxian

History: Created in 2000 following a merger between Shanghai College of Metallurgy, Shanghai College of Chemistry and Shanghai College of Light Industry.

Admission Requirements: Undergraduate programmes: National Matriculation Test; Masters programmes: Graduate Candidate Test

Main Language(s) of Instruction: Chinese

Accrediting Agency: Ministry of Education

Degrees and Diplomas: *Xueshi Xuewei*: **Applied Chemistry; Automation and Control Engineering; Business and Commerce; Chemistry; Civil Engineering; Fine Arts; Management; Mechanical Engineering; Modern Languages; Pharmacology; Safety Engineering.** *Shuoshi Xuewei*: **Applied Chemistry.**

Student Services: Academic Counselling, Canteen, Careers Guidance, Cultural Activities, Facilities for disabled people, Foreign Studies Centre, Health Services, Language Laboratory, Nursery Care, Social Counselling, Sports Facilities

Publications: Journal of Shanghai Institute of Technology

Publishing House: SIT Press

Last Updated: 07/02/13

SHANGHAI INTERNATIONAL STUDIES UNIVERSITY (SISU)

550 Dalian Road, Shanghai, Shanghai 200083
Tel: +86(21) 35372867
EMail: fao@shisu.edu.cn
Website: http://www.shisu.edu.cn

President: Cao Deming (2006-)

College

Adult Education (Adult Education); **International Cultural Exchange** (Chinese; Cultural Studies); **International Finance and Trade** (Business and Commerce; Finance; International Business)

School

International Business (Business Administration; International Business; Public Relations); **International Finance and Commerce** (Accountancy; Economics; Finance); **International Journalism** (Journalism); **Japanese Cultural and Economic Studies** (Japanese); **Law** (International Relations; Law; Political Sciences); **Media and Communications** (Communication Studies; Journalism; Media Studies); **Oriental Studies** (Arabic; Hebrew; Hindi; Indonesian; Korean; Oriental Studies; Persian; Thai Languages; Turkish; Vietnamese)

Department

English Language and Literature (English; Literature); **European Studies** (Dutch; Greek; Italian; Portuguese; Spanish); **French** (French); **German** (German); **Russian** (Russian)

Graduate Institute

Interpretation and Translation (Translation and Interpretation)

History: Founded 1949 as Shanghai Russian College. Acquired present status and title 1994.

Academic Year: September to July (September-February; February-July)

Admission Requirements: Graduation from senior middle school and entrance examination

Main Language(s) of Instruction: Chinese

Accrediting Agency: State Commission of Education

Degrees and Diplomas: *Xueshi Xuewei*; *Shuoshi Xuewei*; *Boshi*. Also Advanced Teacher Training qualification

Publications: Arab World; Comparative Literature in China; Foreign Language World; Journal of Foreign Languages; Media in Foreign Language Instruction; Russian Teaching in China

Publishing House: Shanghai Foreign Language Education Press; Shanghai Foreign Language Audio-Visual Publishing House

Academic Staff *2011-2012*: Total: c. 10,400

Student Numbers *2011-2012*: Total: c. 1,050

SHANGHAI JIANQIAO UNIVERSITY

1500-1700 Kangqiao Road, Pudong, Shanghai 201315
Tel: +86(21) 68191299
Fax: +86(21) 58137900
EMail: dwjl@mail.gench.com.cn
Website: http://www.gench.edu.cn

Vice-President: Qingyun Huang

College

Art Design (Design; Fine Arts); **Foreign Languages** (English); **Information Technology** (Information Technology); **Journalism and Communication** (Communication Studies; Journalism); **Mechanical and Electronic Engineering** (Electronic Engineering; Mechanical Engineering)

School

Business School (Business Administration)

Department

Nursing (Nursing)

History: Founded 2000.

Fees: (Yuan): 8000-10,000 per semester depending on program

Degrees and Diplomas: *Xueshi Xuewei*

Academic Staff *2012-2013*: Total: c. 800

Student Numbers *2012-2013*: Total: c. 9,800

Last Updated: 07/10/13

SHANGHAI JIAO TONG UNIVERSITY

800 Dongchuan Road, Shanghai, Shanghai 200240
Tel: +86(21) 54740000
Fax: +86(21) 62817613
EMail: iso@sjtu.edu.cn
Website: http://www.sjtu.edu.cn/

President: Zhang Jie Tel: +86(21) 62932448

International Relations: Xu Jun Tel: +86(21) 34206750

College

Economics and Management *(Antai)* (Economics; Management)

School

Aeronautics and Astronautics (Aeronautical and Aerospace Engineering; Astronomy and Space Science); **Agriculture and Biology** (Agriculture; Biology); **Biomedical Engineering** (Biology); **Chemistry and Chemical Engineering** (Applied Chemistry; Chemical Engineering; Chemistry; Materials Engineering; Polymer and Plastics Technology); **China Europe International Business** (International Business); **Civil Engineering and Mechanics; Continuing Education** (Continuing Education); **Electronic, Information and Electrical Engineering** (Automation and Control Engineering; Computer Networks; Computer Science; Electronic Engineering; Engineering; Information Technology); **Entrepreneurship and Innovation** (Business Administration); **Environmental Sciences and Engineering** (Environmental Engineering; Environmental Studies); **Foreign Languages** (English; Japanese; Modern Languages); **Humanities** (Aesthetics; Anthropology; History; Literature); **International and Public Affairs** (International Relations; Public Administration); **International Education; Law** *(KoGuan)* (Law); **Life Sciences and Biotechnology** (Biological and Life Sciences; Biotechnology); **Management** (Accountancy; Finance; Hotel Management; Industrial Management; Management); **Marxism** (Political Sciences); **Materials Science and Engineering** (Materials Engineering); **Mechanical Engineering** (Automation and Control Engineering; Mechanical Engineering; Nuclear Engineering); **Media and Design** (Design; Media Studies); **Medicine** (Medicine); **Microelectronics** (Microelectronics); **Naval Architecture,Ocean and Civil Engineering** (Civil Engineering; Marine Engineering; Naval Architecture); **Pharmacy** (Pharmacy); **Science** (Applied Mathematics; Applied Physics; Mathematics); **Software** (Software Engineering); **Techniques**

Department

Mathematics (Mathematics); **Physical Education** (Physical Education); **Physics** (Physics)

Institute

Finance (Finance)

Further Information: Also campuses in Xuhui, Fahua, Shangzhong, Qibao, Luwan campuses

History: Founded 1896 as Nanyang Public School, became Jiaotong University 1921, and acquired present title 1959.

Academic Year: September to July (September-February; February-July)

Degrees and Diplomas: *Xueshi Xuewei*; *Shuoshi Xuewei*; *Boshi*

Publications: Academic Journal of Shanghai Jiaotong University; Chinise Journal of Somatic Science; Journal of Shanghai Jiaotong University; Systems Engineering Theory Methodology Applications

Academic Staff *2011-2012*	**TOTAL**
FULL-TIME	**c. 3,000**
Student Numbers *2011-2012*	
All (Foreign included)	**c. 34,400**
FOREIGN ONLY	**1600**

Last Updated: 07/02/13

SHANGHAI LIXIN UNIVERSITY OF COMMERCE

2800 Wenxiang Road, Songjiang District,
Shanghai, Shanghai 201620
Tel: +86(21) 67705200
Fax: +86(21) 67705109
EMail: iec2008@lixin.edu.com
Website: http://www.lixin.edu.cn/

President: Haiyan Tang

School

Business Administration (Accountancy; Business Administration; Finance; International Economics; Management); **Law** (Law); **Literature, Arts** (Chinese; Fine Arts; Literature); **Science and Engineering** (Engineering; Natural Sciences)

Further Information: Also Xuhui Campus

History: Founded 1928.

Admission Requirements: High School Diploma

Fees: (RMB): 18,000- 20,000 per year depending on programs

Accrediting Agency: Shanghai Municipal Government

Degrees and Diplomas: *Xueshi Xuewei*

Last Updated: 15/10/13

SHANGHAI MARITIME UNIVERSITY

1550 Haigang Avenue, Shanghai, Shanghai 201306
Tel: +86(21) 38282000
Fax: +86(21) 38284166
EMail: iec@shmtu.edu.cn
Website: http://www.shmtu.edu.cn

President: Youfang Huang

College

Arts and Sciences (Administration; Design; Industrial Design; Mathematics; Physical Education; Physics; Social Sciences); **Continuing Education**; **Foreign Languages** (English; Linguistics); **Information Engineering** (Information Technology); **Logistics Engineering** (Transport Engineering); **Merchant Marine** (Electrical Engineering; Marine Engineering; Marine Transport); **Ocean Environment and Engineering** (Marine Engineering; Marine Science and Oceanography); **Technology** (Technology); **Transport and Communications** (Transport and Communications; Transport Engineering; Transport Management)

School

Economics & Management (Accountancy; Economics; Finance; International Business; Management; Tourism; Transport Management); **Law** (Law)

Institute

Marine Science and Engineering (Marine Engineering; Marine Science and Oceanography)

Academy

Scientific Research (Engineering Management; Transport Engineering)

Further Information: The University has four campuses: Lingang, Minsheng, East and Haihua

History: Founded 1909 as Wosong Merchant Marine College, acquired present title and status 1959.

Academic Year: February to January (February-July; September-January)

Fees: (Yuan): 20,000 per annum for Bachelor's degree

Main Language(s) of Instruction: Chinese

Degrees and Diplomas: *Xueshi Xuewei*; *Shuoshi Xuewei*; *Boshi*

Student Services: Canteen, Careers Guidance, Cultural Activities, Health Services, Nursery Care, Sports Facilities

Publications: Journal of Shanghai Maritime University; Maritime Transport Information; Ocean Shipping Business; Shipping Management

Last Updated: 07/02/13

SHANGHAI NORMAL UNIVERSITY (SHNU)

100 Guilin Road, Shanghai, Shanghai 200234
Tel: +86(21) 64322493
Fax: +86(21) 64701661
EMail: xwzx_yy@shtu.edu.cn
Website: http://www.shnu.edu.cn

President: Minxuan Zhang

International Relations: Li Meizhen

College

Architectural and Civil Engineering (Architecture; Civil Engineering); **Business** (Business Administration; Economics; Human Resources; Insurance; Management); **Chinese Studies** *(International)* (Chinese); **Education, Law and Politics** (Economics; Education; Educational Administration; Educational Psychology; Educational Technology; Law; Pedagogy; Political Sciences; Preschool Education; Primary Education; Science Education; Social Work); **Film and Television Art** *(Xie Jin)* (Film; Radio and Television Broadcasting); **Finance** (Finance); **Fine Arts** (Design; Fine Arts; Sculpture); **Foreign Languages** (English; French; Japanese; Modern Languages); **Humanities and Communications** (Acting; Advertising and Publicity; Arts and Humanities; Chinese; Communication Studies; Cultural Studies; Journalism; Literature; Media Studies; Musicology; Printing and Printmaking); **Information, Mechanical and Electronic Engineering** (Automation and Control Engineering; Electrical Engineering; Electronic Engineering; Engineering; Information Sciences; Information Technology; Mechanical Engineering); **Life and Environmental Sciences** (Biological and Life Sciences; Biology; Chemistry; Environmental Studies; Geography; Horticulture); **Marxism** (History; Political Sciences); **Mathematics and Science** (Applied Chemistry; Applied Mathematics; Biological and Life Sciences; Biophysics; Chemistry; Computer Science; Environmental Studies; Geography; Information Sciences; Mathematics; Mathematics and Computer Science; Physics; Psychology; Statistics); **Music** (Music); **Philosophy** (Philosophy); **Physical Education** (Physical Education); **Women's Culture** (Women's Studies)

School

Further Education (Chemical Engineering; Electronic Engineering; Mechanical Engineering; Structural Architecture; Technology)

Institute

Tourism *(Shanghai)* (Hotel Management; Tourism)

History: Founded 1954 as Shangai Teacher Training College. Merged with Shanghai Teachers College of Technology 1994 and with Shangai Higher Normal College 1997. Acquired present title and status 1997.

Degrees and Diplomas: *Xueshi Xuewei*; *Shuoshi Xuewei*; *Boshi*

Publications: Journal of Shanghai Teachers University

Last Updated: 07/02/13

SHANGHAI OCEAN UNIVERSITY

Lingang New City, Shanghai City Loop No. 999,
Shanghai, Shanghai 201306
Tel: +86(21) 61900296
Fax: +86(21) 61900000
EMail: xzxx@shou.edu.cn
Website: http://www.shou.edu.cn/

President: Yingjie Pan Tel: +86(21) 65684287

College

Continuing Education (Technology); **Economics and Management** (Economics; Finance; International Business; International Economics; Management; Marketing); **Engineering** (Automation and Control Engineering; Industrial Engineering; Marine Engineering); **Fisheries and Life Science** (Aquaculture; Biological and Life Sciences; Fishery); **Foreign Languages** (English; Japanese); **Humanities** (Administration; Arts and Humanities; Literature; Public Administration; Sports); **Information Technology** (Applied Mathematics; Computer Science; Information Management; Information Technology); **Vocational and Technical**

Department

Social Sciences (Social Sciences)

Institute
Food Science (Chemistry; Food Science; Food Technology; Heating and Refrigeration); **Marine Science** (Marine Science and Oceanography)

History: Founded 1912 as Fishery School of Jiangsu Province, became college 1952. Became Shanghai Fisheries University and acquired present status and title 2008.

Academic Year: September to July (September-February; February-July)

Admission Requirements: Graduation from senior middle school and entrance examination

Main Language(s) of Instruction: Chinese

Accrediting Agency: Ministry of Agriculture

Degrees and Diplomas: *Xueshi Xuewei*; *Shuoshi Xuewei*; *Boshi*

Publications: Journal of Fisheries of China Society; Journal of Shanghai Fisheries University

Last Updated: 07/02/13

SHANGHAI OPEN UNIVERSITY (SHOU)

195 Zhengfa Rd, Yangpu, Shanghai, Shanghai 200433
Website: http://www.shtvu.edu.cn

President: Jiang Hong (2012-)

Programme
Economics (Business Administration; Finance); **Mechanical Electrical Engineering** (Electrical Engineering; Mechanical Engineering); **Public Safety Management** (Safety Engineering); **Software Engineering** (Software Engineering)

History: Founded 1960 as Shanghai Television University. Acquired present title 2012.

Degrees and Diplomas: *Xueshi Xuewei*

Last Updated: 07/02/13

SHANGHAI THEATRE ACADEMY

630 Huashan Road, Shanghai, Shanghai 200040
Tel: +86(21) 62482920
Fax: +86(21) 62482646
EMail: yzxx@sta.edu.cn
Website: http://www.sta.edu.cn/

President: Sheng Hang

Department
Acting (Theatre); **Directing** (Theatre); **Dramatic Literature** (Literature); **Stage Design** (Display and Stage Design); **Television Arts** (Cinema and Television)

History: Founded 1945, acquired present title 1956.

Degrees and Diplomas: *Xueshi Xuewei*; *Shuoshi Xuewei*; *Boshi*

Publications: Theatre Art

Last Updated: 07/02/13

SHANGHAI UNIVERSITY

99 Shangda Road, Baoshan, Shanghai, Shanghai 200444
Tel: +86(21) 56331839
Fax: +86(21) 56333187
EMail: International@oa.shu.edu.cn
Website: http://www.shu.edu.cn/

President: Hongjie Luo

College
Advanced Professional Studies; **Automobile** *(Bashi)* (Automotive Engineering); **Continuing Education**; **International Exchange** (Bioengineering; Chinese; Design; Finance; International Business; International Economics; Tourism; Transport Management); **Science** (Chemistry; Mathematics; Physics)

School
Communications and Information Engineering (Biomedical Engineering; Communication Studies; Electronic Engineering; Information Technology); **Computer Engineering and Science** (Computer Engineering; Mathematics and Computer Science; Software Engineering); **Digital Arts** (Design; Film; Industrial Design; Radio and Television Broadcasting); **Economics** (Economics); **Environmental and Chemical Engineering** (Architecture; Chemical Engineering; Civil Engineering; Environmental Engineering; Environmental Studies; Structural Architecture); **Film and Television Arts and Technology** (Cinema and Television; Journalism); **Fine Arts** (Fine Arts); **Foreign Languages** (English; Japanese; Modern Languages); **Intellectual Property**; **International Business and Administration** (Administration; Business Administration; Economics; International Business; Management); **International Exchange** (International Relations); **Law** (Law); **Liberal Arts** (Anthropology; Archiving; Arts and Humanities; Chinese; Folklore; History; Literature; Sociology); **Life Sciences** (Biological and Life Sciences); **Management** (Management); **Materials Science and Engineering** (Electronic Engineering; Engineering; Materials Engineering; Molecular Biology); **Mechatronic Engineering and Automation** (Automation and Control Engineering; Electronic Engineering; Industrial and Organizational Psychology; Mechanical Engineering); **Physical Education** (Physical Education); **Social Sciences** (Social Sciences); **Sociology and Political Sciences** (Political Sciences; Sociology); **Technology** *(Sino-European)* (Technology)

Department
Civil Engineering (Civil Engineering); **Library, Information and Archives** (Archiving; Information Management; Library Science)

Institute
Intellectual Property; **Language and Commerce** *(Sydney Institute)* (Business and Commerce; Modern Languages)

Centre
MBA (Business Administration)

Further Information: Also Yanchang Campus at Yanchang District, and Jiading Campus at Jiading District

History: Founded 1994. Merged with Shanghai University of Technology, Shanghai University of Science and Technology and Shanghai Junior College of Science and Technology.

Academic Year: September to July

Admission Requirements: Graduation from senior middle school and entrance examination

Fees: (Yuan): 21000-42000 per annum depending on programs

Main Language(s) of Instruction: Chinese

Degrees and Diplomas: *Xueshi Xuewei*; *Shuoshi Xuewei*; *Boshi*

Publications: Shanghai University Journal

Academic Staff *2011-2012*	**TOTAL**
FULL-TIME	**2,890**
Student Numbers *2011-2012*	
All (Foreign included)	**37,800**
FOREIGN ONLY	**3000**

Last Updated: 08/02/13

SHANGHAI UNIVERSITY OF ELECTRIC POWER

2103 Pingliang Road, Shanghai, Shanghai 200090
Tel: +86(21) 65458500
Fax: +86(21) 65432514
EMail: cieoffice@shiep.edu.cn
Website: http://www.shiep.edu.cn/

President: Hexing Li (2011-)

College
Electrical Engineering (Electrical Engineering); **Energy and Mechanical Engineering** (Automation and Control Engineering; Chemistry; Environmental Engineering; Mechanical Engineering; Thermal Engineering; Water Science); **Foreign Languages** (English; Japanese); **International College**; **Management and Humanities** (Business Administration; Information Management; International Business; Public Administration)

School
Economics and Management (Economics; Management)

Department
Automation Engineering; **Electronic and Information Engineering** (Electronic Engineering; Information Technology); **Environmental and Chemical Engineering** (Chemical Engineering; Environmental Engineering); **Mathematics and Physics**;

Mathematics and Physics (Mathematics; Physics); **Social Sciences** (Social Sciences); **Sports** (Sports)

Institute

Adult Education; **Computer Science and Technology** (Computer Engineering; Computer Science)

History: Founded 1951 as Shanghai Electrical schools. Acquired present title and status 1985.

Degrees and Diplomas: *Xueshi Xuewei*; *Shuoshi Xuewei*

Last Updated: 08/02/13

SHANGHAI UNIVERSITY OF ENGINEERING SCIENCE

350 Xianxia Road, Shanghai, Shanghai 200336
Tel: +86(21) 62759779
Fax: +86(21) 62758481
EMail: gcd@sues.edu.cn
Website: http://www.sues.edu.cn

President: Wang Hong

College

Fundamental Studies (Automation and Control Engineering; Electronic Engineering; International Economics)

School

Advanced Technician (Technology); **Air Transportation** (Air Transport); **Art and Design** (Advertising and Publicity; Design; Fine Arts); **Automotive Engineering** (Automotive Engineering); **Chemistry and Chemical Engineering** (Chemical Engineering; Chemistry); **Electrical and Electronic Engineering** (Automation and Control Engineering; Computer Science; Electrical Engineering; Electronic Engineering); **Fashion Technology** (Chemical Engineering; Fashion Design; Textile Design); **Management** (Banking; Business Administration; Economics; Finance; Information Management; Management); **Materials Engineering** (Materials Engineering); **Mechanical Engineering** (Automation and Control Engineering; Mechanical Engineering; Thermal Engineering); **Multimedia** *(Sino-Korean)* (Multimedia); **Social Science**; **Urban Rail Transportation** (Railway Engineering; Transport and Communications; Transport Engineering); **Vocational Education**

Department

Sports (Sports)

Institute

Fashion Design *(Sino-French)* (Fashion Design)

Further Information: Also a campus in Xianxia

History: Founded 1978, acquired present title 1986.

Academic Year: February to January (February-July; September-January)

Admission Requirements: Graduation from senior middle school and entrance examination

Main Language(s) of Instruction: Chinese

Degrees and Diplomas: *Xueshi Xuewei*

Publications: Journal of Shanghai University of Engineering Science

Last Updated: 08/02/13

SHANGHAI UNIVERSITY OF FINANCE AND ECONOMICS (SUFE)

777 Guodinglu, Shanghai, Shanghai 200433
Tel: +86(21) 65903560
Fax: +86(21) 65361958
EMail: ices@mail.shufe.edu.cn
Website: http://www.shufe.edu.cn

President: Liming Fan Tel: +86(21) 65904384

Vice-President: Hua Fang Tel: +86(21) 65904536

International Relations: Yamin Jin
Tel: +86(21) 65904899 EMail: jinym@mail.shufe.edu.cn

School

Accountancy (Accountancy; Finance); **Continuing Education** (Continuing Education); **Economics** (Economics); **Finance** (Finance); **Humanities** (Arts and Humanities; Chinese; Journalism; Sociology); **Information Management and Engineering** (Computer Science; E-Business/Commerce; Information Management; Information Technology); **International Business Administration** (Business Administration; International Business); **International Culture Exchange** (Chinese); **Law** (Administrative Law; Civil Law; Fiscal Law; Law); **MBA** (Business Administration); **Public Economy and Administration** (Economics; Finance; Management; Public Administration)

Department

Applied Mathematics (Applied Mathematics; Computer Science; Mathematical Physics; Statistics); **Foreign Languages** (English; Japanese); **Information Management** (Information Management); **Mathematics** (Mathematics); **Physical Education** (Physical Education); **Statistics** (Statistics)

Institute

International Professional Education (Economics; Finance)

Research Institute

Marxism (Political Sciences)

Further Information: Also campuses at North Zhongshan Road, Wuchuan Road and Wudong Road

History: Founded 1917 as Commerce Department of Nanjing Teachers' College, became Institute 1950, and acquired present status and title 1985.

Academic Year: February to January (February-July; September-January)

Admission Requirements: Graduation from senior middle school and entrance examination

Main Language(s) of Instruction: Chinese

Accrediting Agency: Ministry of Education

Degrees and Diplomas: *Xueshi Xuewei*; *Shuoshi Xuewei*; *Boshi*

Student Services: Academic Counselling, Careers Guidance, Cultural Activities, Health Services, Sports Facilities

Publications: Cai Jing Research; Foreign Economy Management; SUFE Academic Journal

Publishing House: University Publishing House

Last Updated: 08/02/13

SHANGHAI UNIVERSITY OF INTERNATIONAL BUSINESS AND ECONOMICS

1900 Wenxiang Road, Songjiang, Shanghai,
Shanghai 201620
Tel: +86(21) 67703024
EMail: xb@shift.edu.cn
Website: http://www.shift.edu.cn/

President: Sun Haiming

International Relations: Wang Xingsun, Vice-President
Tel: +86(21) 67703025

School

Accountancy (Accountancy); **Business** (Business Administration); **Business Information Management** (Information Management; Information Technology; Statistics); **Continuing Education**; **Finance** (Finance); **Foreign Languages** (English; French; Japanese; Linguistics; Modern Languages); **International Studies** (Chinese; International Studies); **Law** (Law); **Management** (Management); **Tourism and Event Management** (Management; Tourism); **WTO Research and Education** (International Business; International Economics); **WTO Research and Education** (International Business; International Law; Modern Languages)

History: Founded 1960 as Shanghai Institute of Foreign Trade (SIFT). Acquired present title and status, 2013.

Academic Year: February to September

Fees: (US Dollars): Undergraduate, 1,380 per semester; postgraduate, 1,600

Accrediting Agency: Ministry of Education (MOE)

Degrees and Diplomas: *Xueshi Xuewei*; *Shuoshi Xuewei*

Last Updated: 07/10/13

SHANGHAI UNIVERSITY OF SPORT

399 Chang Hai Road, Shanghai, Shanghai 200438
Tel: +86(21) 51253000
Fax: +86(21) 51253096
EMail: wsc@sus.edu.cn
Website: http://www.sus.edu.cn/web/sus/index

President: Yao Songping

School
Continuing Education; **Economics and Management** (Economics; Management); **Kinesiology** (Physical Therapy); **Martial Arts** *(Wushu)*; **Physical Education and Sports Coaching** (Physical Education; Sports); **Sports and Humanities** (Arts and Humanities; Sports; Sports Management)

Department
Leisure and Recreation (Leisure Studies; Parks and Recreation); **Physical Education** (Physical Education; Sports)

History: Founded 1952 as East China Institute of Physical Education, acquired present title 1956.

Main Language(s) of Instruction: Chinese

Degrees and Diplomas: *Xueshi Xuewei*; *Shuoshi Xuewei*; *Boshi*

Last Updated: 11/02/13

SHANGHAI UNIVERSITY OF TRADITIONAL CHINESE MEDICINE

1200 Cailun Road, Pudong New District,
Shanghai, Shanghai 201203
Tel: +86(21) 51322222
Fax: +86(21) 51322276
EMail: oversea@shtcm.com
Website: http://www.shutcm.com/english/

President: Xinghai He Tel: +86(21) 64037208

School
Basic Medical Sciences (Medicine); **Nursing** (Nursing); **Traditional Chinese Medicine** (Medicine; Pharmacy; Traditional Eastern Medicine)

Department
Acupuncture and Moxibustion (Acupuncture); **Chinese Pharmacology** (Pharmacology)

History: Founded 1956.

Admission Requirements: Graduation from senior middle school and entrance examination

Degrees and Diplomas: *Xueshi Xuewei*; *Shuoshi Xuewei*; *Boshi*

Student Services: Academic Counselling, Canteen, Careers Guidance, Cultural Activities, Foreign Studies Centre, Health Services, Language Laboratory, Social Counselling, Sports Facilities

Publications: ACTA Universitae Traditionis Medicalis Sinensis Pharmacologiae Shanghai; ET Academiae Traditionis Medicalis Sinensis Pharmacologiae Shanghai; Journal of Shanghai Traditional Chinese Medicine

Publishing House: University Publishing House

Student Numbers *2011-2012*: Total: c. 9,000

Last Updated: 11/02/13

SHANGQIU INSTITUTE OF TECHNOLOGY

235 Suiyang Dadao, Shangqiu, Henan 476000
Tel: +86(370) 2692888
Fax: +86(370) 2692884
Website: http://www.sstvc.com/

President: Gao Qing-min

School
Civil Engineering (Civil Engineering); **Information and Electronic Engineering** (Electronic Engineering; Information Technology); **Management** (Accountancy; Management; Marketing); **Mechanical Engineering** (Mechanical Engineering); **Media and Modern Art** (Fine Arts; Media Studies); **Nursing** (Nursing)

Department
Basic Teaching (Education; Physical Education)

History: Founded 1994.

Degrees and Diplomas: *Xueshi Xuewei*

Last Updated: 04/12/13

SHANGQIU NORMAL UNIVERSITY (SNU)

No. 55 Pingyuan Road, Shangqiu, Henan 476000
Tel: +86(370) 2586878
Fax: +86(370) 2586896
Website: http://www.sqnc.edu.cn/

Programme
Architecture and Civil Engineering (Architecture; Civil Engineering); **Biology** (Biology); **Chemistry** (Chemistry); **Chinese Language and Literature** (Chinese; Literature); **Computer Science** (Computer Science); **Economics and Management** (Economics; Management); **Education** (Education); **Foreign Languages** (English); **History** (History); **Journalism and Communication Studies** (Communication Studies; Journalism); **Law** (Law); **Mathematics** (Mathematics); **Music** (Music); **Physical Education** (Physical Education); **Physics** (Physics); **Political Sciences** (Political Sciences)

History: Founded as Shangqiu Teachers' College.

Degrees and Diplomas: *Xueshi Xuewei*

Last Updated: 13/11/13

SHANGQIU UNIVERSITY

Beihai Road 66, Shangqiu, Henan 476113
Tel: +86(370) 3167111
EMail: shangqiu.university@yahoo.cn
Website: http://www.hnhyedu.net/

President: Hou Chunlai

International Relations: Jiang, Deputy Director

Faculty
Administration (Administration)

College
Electronic and Information Technology (Electrical and Electronic Engineering; Information Technology)

School
Business Administration (Business Administration; Business and Commerce)

Department
Computer Science and Technology (Computer Engineering; Computer Science); **Foreign Languages** (English); **Landscape Architecture** (Landscape Architecture); **Liberal Arts** (Journalism); **Media and Arts** (Fine Arts; Media Studies); **Political Sciences** (Political Sciences)

Institute
Physical Education (Physical Education)

Degrees and Diplomas: *Xueshi Xuewei*

Last Updated: 13/11/13

SHANGRAO NORMAL UNIVERSITY

Zhimin Road 85, Shangrao, Jiangxi 344001
Tel: +86(793) 815 0671
EMail: wlzx@sru.jx.cn
Website: http://www.sru.jx.cn/

President: Liu Hesheng

College
Art and Design (Design; Fine Arts); **Chemistry and Chemical Engineering** (Chemical Engineering; Chemistry); **Continuing Education**; **Economics and Management** (Economics; Management); **Education and Science** (Education; Natural Sciences); **Foreign Languages** (English; Foreign Languages Education); **History, Geography and Tourism** (Geography; History; Tourism); **Life Sciences** (Biological and Life Sciences); **Literature and Journalism and Communication** (Communication Studies; Journalism; Literature); **Physical Education** (Physical Education); **Physics and Electronic Engineering** (Electronic Engineering; Physics)

Institute
Mathematics and Computer Science (Computer Science; Mathematics); **Politics and Law** (Law; Political Sciences)

Academy
Music and Dance (Dance; Music)

History: Founded in 1958 as Shangrao Normal Junior College. Acquired present title and status 2000.

Degrees and Diplomas: *Xueshi Xuewei*

Publications: Journal of Shangrao Normal University

Academic Staff *2012*: Total: c. 970

Last Updated: 24/10/13

SHANTOU UNIVERSITY (STU)

243 Daxue Road, Shantou, Guangdong Province 515063
Tel: +86(754) 86503821
Fax: +86(754) 86500050
EMail: icd@stu.edu.cn
Website: http://www.stu.edu.cn

President: Xiaohu Xu EMail: o_xzxx@stu.edu.cn

Provost: Peihua Gu

Faculty
Engineering (Civil Engineering; Computer Engineering; Electronic Engineering; Engineering; Mechanical Engineering); **Law** (Law); **Liberal Arts** (Arts and Humanities; Chinese; English); **Science** (Biology; Mathematics; Natural Sciences; Physics)

College
Veritas

School
Art and Design *(Cheung Kong)* (Arts and Humanities; Design); **Business** (Accountancy; Business Administration; International Business); **Continuing Education** (Continuing Education); **Journalism and Communication** *(Cheung Kong)* (Advertising and Publicity; Communication Arts; Journalism); **Medicine** (Medicine; Nursing)

Department
Physical Education (Physical Education); **Social Sciences** (Social Sciences)

Centre
Chinese Language Training (Chinese); **English** (English)

Further Information: Also 5 Affiliated Hospitals

History: Founded 1981. Under the jurisdiction of the Provincial authorities.

Academic Year: September to July (September-January; February-July)

Admission Requirements: Graduation from high school

Main Language(s) of Instruction: Chinese

Degrees and Diplomas: *Xueshi Xuewei*; *Shuoshi Xuewei*; *Boshi*

Student Services: Academic Counselling, Canteen, Careers Guidance, Cultural Activities, Facilities for disabled people, Foreign Studies Centre, Health Services, Language Laboratory, Nursery Care, Social Counselling, Sports Facilities

Student Numbers *2011-2012*: Total 9,450

Last Updated: 11/02/13

SHANXI AGRICULTURAL UNIVERSITY

Taigu, Shanxi Province 030801
Tel: +86(351) 6288221
Fax: +86(351) 6288303
EMail: info@sxau.edu.cn
Website: http://www.sxau.edu.cn

Chancellor: Chang-Sheng Dong

International Relations: Bingxiang Fan
Tel: +86(354) 6288304 EMail: fanbingxiang@yahoo.com

College
Adult Education; **Agromnomy** (Agriculture; Agronomy; Plant and Crop Protection); **Animal Science and Technology** (Animal Husbandry; Veterinary Science; Zoology); **Arts and Sciences** (Arts and Humanities; Natural Sciences); **Engineering** (Agricultural Engineering; Engineering); **Food Engineering** (Food Science; Food Technology); **Forestry and Environmental Sciences** (Environmental Engineering; Forestry); **Horticulture** (Horticulture); **Information Sciences and Engineering** (Information Sciences; Information Technology); **Life Sciences** (Biological and Life Sciences); **Modern Technology** (Technology); **Public Administration** (Public Administration); **Resources and Environment** (Environmental Studies; Natural Resources)

School
Graduate Studies; **Information** (Information Sciences)

Department
Physical Education (Physical Education)

Institute
Economics and Trade (Business and Commerce; Economics)

History: Founded 1907 as Oberlin Shanxi Memorial School. Acquired present title 1979.

Degrees and Diplomas: *Xueshi Xuewei*; *Shuoshi Xuewei*; *Boshi*

Publications: Journal of Shanxi Agricultural University

Academic Staff *2012-2012*: Total 1,600

Student Numbers *2011-2012*: Total 20,000

Last Updated: 11/02/13

SHANXI DATONG UNIVERSITY (SDU)

Yudong, Dantong, Shanxi 037009
Tel: +86(352) 7158248
Fax: +86(352) 6090248
Website: http://www.sxdtdx.edu.cn

President: Wang Shouyi

School
Agriculture (Agriculture; Bioengineering); **Arts** (Design; Fine Arts; Music); **Business Administration** (Accountancy; Business Administration; Marketing; Tourism); **Chemistry and Chemical Engineering** (Applied Chemistry; Chemical Engineering; Chemistry); **Educational Sciences and Technology** (Computer Networks; Educational Sciences; Educational Technology; Primary Education; Psychology); **Engineering** (Automation and Control Engineering; Civil Engineering; Engineering; Mechanical Engineering; Mining Engineering); **Foreign Languages** (English); **Literature and History** (Chinese; History; Journalism; Literature; Philosophy); **Mathematics and Computer Science** (Applied Mathematics; Computer Science; Mathematics; Statistics); **Medicine** (Medicine; Nursing; Pharmacology; Traditional Eastern Medicine); **Physical Education** (Physical Education); **Physics and Electronics Science** (Electronic Engineering; Optical Technology; Physics); **Political and Law** (Law; Political Sciences)

History: Founded 2006, by merging of Yanbei Teachers College, DaTong Medica College, Datong Vocational and Technical College and Shanxi Industry Polytechnic College.

Main Language(s) of Instruction: Chinese

Degrees and Diplomas: *Xueshi Xuewei*

Academic Staff *2012-2013*: Total 1,400

Student Numbers *2012-2013*: Total 22,000

Last Updated: 01/10/13

SHANXI MEDICAL UNIVERSITY

56 Xinjian South Road, Taiyuan, Shanxi Province 030001
Tel: +86(351) 4135479
Fax: +86(351) 4135207
EMail: web@sxmu.edu.cn
Website: http://www.sxmu.edu.cn

President: Zhiguang Duan

International Relations: Xiuyun Li

College
Continuing Education (Continuing Education); **First Clinical Medicine** (Medicine); **Forensic Medicine** (Forensic Medicine and Dentistry); **Humanities and Social Sciences** (Arts and Humanities; Social Sciences); **Jinci**; **Medicine (Fenyang)** (Medicine); **Nursing** (Nursing); **Pharmacy** (Pharmacy); **Pre-Clinical Medicine** (Medicine); **Professional and Technical**; **Public Health** (Public Health); **Second Clinical Medicine** (Medicine)

School
Basic Medicine (Medicine)

Department
Anaesthesiology (Anaesthesiology); **Computer Education** (Computer Science); **Foreign Languages** (Modern Languages); **Medical Imaging** (Medical Technology); **Paediatrics** (Paediatrics); **Postgraduate Studies**; **Stomatology** (Stomatology)

Further Information: Also Sim-hospital of Clinical Skills Education

History: Founded 1919 as Shanxi Medical College, acquired present title 1996.

Academic Year: September to July

Admission Requirements: National entrance examination

Main Language(s) of Instruction: Chinese

Degrees and Diplomas: *Xueshi Xuewei*: **Medicine.** *Shuoshi Xuewei*: **Medicine.** *Boshi*: **Medicine.**

Student Services: Canteen, Careers Guidance, Health Services, Sports Facilities

Publications: Journal of Shanxi Medical University

Last Updated: 11/02/13

SHANXI NORMAL UNIVERSITY

1 Gonyuan Jie, Linfen, Shanxi Province 041004
Tel: +86(357) 2051084
Fax: +86(357) 2051083
EMail: waisc2@163.com
Website: http://www.sxnu.edu.cn

President: Haishun Wu

International Relations: Yaning Liu

School
Foreign Languages (English; Japanese; Modern Languages)

Institute
Art (Art Education; Design; Fine Arts; Painting and Drawing); **Biological Technology and Engineering** (Agronomy; Bioengineering; Biotechnology; Civil Engineering; Construction Engineering; Electronic Engineering; Food Science; Horticulture; Zoology); **Chemistry and Materials Science** (Applied Chemistry; Chemistry); **City and Environmental Science** (Environmental Management; Environmental Studies; Geography); **Economics** (Economics; Management); **Education and Psychology** (Education; Preschool Education; Psychology); **Educational Technology** (Educational Technology); **Educational Technology** (Educational Technology); **History and Tourist Culture** (History; Tourism); **Life and Science** (Bioengineering; Biological and Life Sciences; Biotechnology; Botany); **Literature** (Chinese; Literature; Publishing and Book Trade); **Management** (Management); **Mathematics and Computer Science** (Applied Linguistics; Mathematics; Mathematics and Computer Science); **Music** (Music); **Physical Education** (Physical Education); **Physics and Information Engineering** (Computer Science; Physics); **Politics and Law** (Law; Political Sciences); **Traditional Opera and Historical Relics** (History; Opera)

History: Founded 1958 as Normal Training College of Southern Shanxi. Acquired present title 1984.

Main Language(s) of Instruction: Chinese

Degrees and Diplomas: *Xueshi Xuewei*; *Shuoshi Xuewei*

Publications: Journal of Shanxi Teachers University

Last Updated: 11/02/13

SHANXI TECHNOLOGY AND BUSINESS COLLEGE

City Dock, City Road No. 99, Taiyuan, Shanxi
Website: http://www.sxtbu.net

President: Niu Sanpin

School
Accountancy (Accountancy); **Architecture** (Architecture); **Art Design** (Design); **Business Administration** (Business Administration); **Continuing Education** (Continuing Education); **Finance** (Finance); **General Education** (Education); **Information Technology** (Information Technology); **Media** (Media Studies); **Music** (Music); **Tourism and Hotel Management** (Hotel Management; Tourism)

Department
Ideological and Political Education (Political Sciences); **Physical Education** (Physical Education)

History: Founded 2004, as former Shanxi Vocational Education College of Technology and Business. Acquired present status 2011.

Degrees and Diplomas: *Xueshi Xuewei*

Student Numbers *2012*: Total 10,236

Last Updated: 01/10/13

SHANXI UNIVERSITY (SXU)

92 Wucheng Rd, Taiyuan, Shanxi Province 030006
Tel: +86(351) 7010255
Fax: +86(351) 7011981
EMail: maxx@sxu.edu.cn
Website: http://www.sxu.edu.cn

President: Suotang Jia Tel: +86(351) 7011311

International Relations: Guo-dong Yu, Director of Foreign Office Tel: +85(351) 7011583

College
Fine Arts (Design; Fine Arts; Painting and Drawing); **Music** (Music; Music Theory and Composition); **Physical Education** (Physical Education); **Physics and Electronic Engineering** (Electronic Engineering; Physics)

School
Chemistry and Engineering (Chemistry; Engineering); **Chinese Language and Literature** (Chinese; Comparative Literature; Literature); **Economics** (Economics); **Education Science** (Educational Sciences); **Environmental Science and Resources** (Environmental Studies; Natural Resources); **Foreign Languages** (English Studies; Linguistics; Literature; Modern Languages; Russian); **Law** (Administrative Law; Commercial Law; Constitutional Law; International Law; Law); **Life Science and Technology** (Biological and Life Sciences; Technology); **Management** (Management); **Philosophy and Sociology** (Philosophy; Sociology); **Political Science and Public Administration** (Political Sciences; Public Administration)

Department
Computer Science (Computer Science); **Foreign Language (for Non Majors)** (English; French; German; Japanese; Russian); **History** (History); **Mathematics** (Mathematics)

History: Founded 1902. Acquired present status 1949.

Academic Year: August to July

Admission Requirements: Secondary school certificate; entrance examination

Fees: (Yuan):14,000-20,000 per annum depending on programs

Main Language(s) of Instruction: Chinese

Accrediting Agency: Ministry of Education; Education Commission of Shanxi Province

Degrees and Diplomas: *Xueshi Xuewei*; *Shuoshi Xuewei*; *Boshi*

Student Services: Academic Counselling, Canteen, Careers Guidance, Cultural Activities, Facilities for disabled people, Foreign Studies Centre, Health Services, Language Laboratory, Nursery Care, Social Counselling, Sports Facilities

Academic Staff *2011-2012*: Total 1,982

Student Numbers *2011-2012*: Total 23,757

Last Updated: 11/02/13

SHANXI UNIVERSITY OF FINANCE AND ECONOMICS

696 Wucheng Road, Taiyuan, Shanxi Province 030006
Tel: +86(351) 7111895
Fax: +86(351) 7111895
EMail: waishiban@sxufe.edu.com
Website: http://www.sxufe.edu.cn/english/index.htm

President: Yuan Meisheng (2005-)

Faculty
International Exchange

College
Hua Shang; **Zhong De**

School
Accountancy (Accountancy); **Business Administration** (Accountancy; Engineering Management; Hotel Management; Labour and Industrial Relations; Management; Tourism); **Business Foreign Languages** (Modern Languages); **Continuing Education**; **Economics** (Economics; Statistics); **Finance** (Banking; Finance); **Information Management** (Information Management); **International Trade** (International Business); **Law** (Administrative Law; Law); **Management Science and Engineering** (Engineering; Management); **Public Management** (Public Administration); **Statistics** (Statistics); **Vocational Skills**

Department
Applied Mathematics (Applied Mathematics); **Cultural Communication** (Cultural Studies); **Environmental Economics** (Economics; Environmental Management); **Marxist Theory** (Political Sciences); **Physical Education** (Physical Education); **Tourism Administration** (Tourism)

Centre
MBA

History: Founded 1951, acquired present status and title 1997.

Degrees and Diplomas: *Xueshi Xuewei*; *Shuoshi Xuewei*

Last Updated: 12/02/13

SHANXI UNIVERSITY OF TRADITIONAL CHINESE MEDICINE

89 Jinci Road, Taiyuan, Shanxi Province 030024
Tel: +86(351) 2272240
Fax: +86(351) 2272240
EMail: sxgjzx88@yahoo.com.cn
Website: http://www.sxtcm.com

President: Ran Zhou

Administrative Officer: Sun Wei Tel: +86(351) 6684481

International Relations: Xueli Zhao, Director
Tel: +86-130-68043195 EMail: sxgizx88@yahoo.com.cn

Department
Acupuncture and Moxibustion (Acupuncture); **Nursing** (Nursing); **Traditional Chinese Medicine** (Pharmacology; Traditional Eastern Medicine)

Further Information: Also correspondence course

History: Founded 1989.

Admission Requirements: Secondary school certificate, English and Chinese

Fees: (US Dollars): Undergraduates: 2300 per annum

Main Language(s) of Instruction: Chinese and English

Degrees and Diplomas: *Xueshi Xuewei*

Student Services: Academic Counselling, Canteen, Careers Guidance, Cultural Activities, Facilities for disabled people, Foreign Studies Centre, Health Services, Language Laboratory, Nursery Care, Social Counselling, Sports Facilities

Publications: Journal of Shanxi College of Traditional Medicine

Academic Staff *2011-2012*: Total 287

Student Numbers *2011-2012*: Total 4,266

Last Updated: 12/02/13

SHAOGUAN UNIVERSITY

Daxue Road, Zhenjiang District,
Shaoguan, Guangdong Province 512005
Tel: +86(751) 8120021
Fax: +86(751) 8120025
EMail: sguio@sgu.edu.cn
Website: http://www.sgu.edu.cn

President: Zeng Zheng

College
Economics and Management (Economics; Management); **International**; **Shaozhou Normal Branch** (Teacher Training)

School
Agricultural Science and Technology (Agricultural Engineering; Agriculture); **Arts** (Fine Arts); **Biological Science** (Biological and Life Sciences); **Chemistry and Environmental Engineering** (Chemistry; Environmental Engineering); **Computer Science** (Computer Science); **Education** (Education; Teacher Training); **Food Science and Technology** (Food Science; Food Technology); **Foreign Languages** (English; Modern Languages); **Law** (Law); **Literature** (Chinese; Literature); **Mathematics and Information Sciences** (Information Sciences; Mathematics); **Medicine** (Medicine); **Music** (Music); **Physics and Mechanical and Electrical Engineering** (Electrical Engineering; Mechanical Engineering; Physical Therapy); **Politics and Public Affairs** (Political Sciences; Public Administration); **Tourism and Geography** (Geography; Tourism)

Institute
Physical Education (Physical Education)

History: Founded 1989.

Degrees and Diplomas: *Xueshi Xuewei*

Last Updated: 12/02/13

SHAOXING UNIVERSITY

5 Huancheng West Road, Shaoxing, Zhejiang Province 312000
Tel: +86(575) 8064138
Fax: +86(575) 8067917
EMail: intl@usx.edu.cn
Website: http://english.usx.edu.cn

President: Feifan Ye (2008-)

College
Shangyu *(Diploma Programs)* (Accountancy; Education; English; Hotel Management; Music)

School
Calligraphy *(Lanting)*; **Chemistry and Chemical Engineering** (Applied Chemistry; Chemical Engineering; Chemistry; Pharmacy); **Economics and Management** (Accountancy; Business Administration; Economics; International Business; Management); **Education** (Education; Educational Psychology; Preschool Education; Primary Education); **Engineering** (Automation and Control Engineering; Civil Engineering; Computer Science; Mechanical Engineering; Telecommunications Engineering); **Fine Arts** (Design; Fine Arts); **Foreign Languages** (English; Japanese); **Humanities** (Chinese); **Law** (Law; Political Sciences; Public Administration); **Life Sciences** (Biological and Life Sciences; Environmental Studies; Science Education); **Mathematics, Physics and Information Sciences** (Applied Mathematics; Computer Science; Electrical Engineering; Information Technology; Mathematics; Physics); **Medicine** (Medical Technology; Medicine; Nursing); **Music** (Music); **Sports Science** (Physical Education; Sports); **Textile Engineering and Apparel Design** (Textile Design; Textile Technology)

Further Information: Also 2 other campuses: Lanting Campus and Shangyu Campus

History: Founded 1980 as Shaoxing Teachers Training College, merged with Shaoxing College 1995. Acquired present status and title 1996.

Degrees and Diplomas: *Xueshi Xuewei*

Last Updated: 12/02/13

SHAOYANG UNIVERSITY

Liziyuan, Daxiang District, Shaoyang, Hunan 422000
Tel: +86(739) 5431794
Fax: +86(739) 5431794
Website: http://www.hnsyu.net/

President: Tan Jingxing

Department

Agronomy (Agronomy); **Art and Design** (Design; Fine Arts; Music); **Economics** (Accountancy; Economics); **Education** (Education; Physical Education); **Engineering** (Chemical Engineering; Computer Engineering; Electrical Engineering; Energy Engineering; Engineering; Food Science; Information Technology; Mechanical Engineering; Power Engineering; Technology); **History** (History); **Language and Literature** (Chinese; Literature; Modern Languages); **Law** (Law); **Literature** (Literature); **Management** (Management; Marketing); **Medicine** (Medicine); **Philosophy** (Philosophy); **Science** (Chemistry; Geography; Mathematics; Natural Sciences; Physics); **Sociology** (Political Sciences; Sociology); **Urban Construction** (Civil Engineering; Town Planning)

History: Founded 1958 as Shaoyang Teachers College. Acquired present title and status 2002 by merging of Shaoyang Vocational College and Shaoyang Teachers Training College.

Degrees and Diplomas: *Xueshi Xuewei*; *Shuoshi Xuewei*: **Food Technology.**

Publications: Journal of Shaoyang University

Academic Staff *2012-2013*: Total: c. 800
Student Numbers *2012-2013*: Total: c. 15,000
Last Updated: 22/11/13

SHENGDA ECONOMICS, TRADE AND MANAGEMENT COLLEGE

1 Zhongshan South Road, Longhu Town, Xinzheng, Zhengzhou, Henan 451191
Tel: +86(371) 62436336
Fax: +86(371) 62577766
EMail: shengdafao@yahoo.com.cn
Website: http://www.shengda.edu.cn/

President: Muyue Cui

Vice President: Jie Zhang

Division

Education (Education); **English for Non-Majors** (English); **Physical Education** (Physical Education)

Department

Accountancy (Accountancy); **Business Administration** (Business Administration); **Chinese Literature and Law** (Chinese; Law; Literature); **Fine Arts** (Fine Arts; Music; Performing Arts); **Foreign Languages and Literature** (English; Japanese; Literature); **Information Management** (Information Management); **International Economics and Trade** (Finance; International Economics); **Marketing** (Marketing)

History: Founded 1994, jointly by Guangxing Culture and Education Fund and Zhengzhou University. Since April 2011, Shengda became independent from its mother college, Zhengzhou University.

Degrees and Diplomas: *Xueshi Xuewei*
Last Updated: 18/11/13

SHENYANG AEROSPACE UNIVERSITY

37 Daoyi South Avenue, Daoyi Development District, Shenyang, Liaoning Province 110136
Tel: +86(24) 89724298
Fax: +86(24) 89724298
EMail: admission@sau.edu.cn
Website: http://www.sau.edu.cn/

President: Wang Wei

International Relations: Richard Chen, Dean
Tel: +86(24) 89724898 EMail: richardchen@sau.edu.cn

School

Aerodynamics and Energy Engineering (Energy Engineering); **Aerospace Engineering** (Aeronautical and Aerospace Engineering); **Airforce Officials Training** (Air and Space Law; Air Transport); **Auto Control** (Automation and Control Engineering); **Civil Aviation and Safety Engineering** (Safety Engineering); **Computer Science** (Computer Science); **Design Art** (Design; Engineering Drawing and Design); **Economics and Management** (Economics; Management); **Electronics Information Engineering** (Computer Engineering; Electronic Engineering); **Foreign Languages** (Modern Languages); **Material Science and Engineering** (Materials Engineering); **Mechanical and Electrical Engineering** (Electrical Engineering; Mechanical Engineering; Mechanics); **Northern Software** (Software Engineering); **Science** (Natural Sciences)

History: Founded 1952 as Shenyang Aeronautical Engineering School. Became Shenyang Institute of Aeronautical Engineering in 1978. Acquired present title and status 2010.

Degrees and Diplomas: *Xueshi Xuewei*; *Shuoshi Xuewei*
Last Updated: 12/02/13

SHENYANG AGRICULTURAL UNIVERSITY

120 Dongling Road, Shenyang, Liaoning Province 100866
Tel: +86(24) 88421031
Fax: +86(24) 88417416
EMail: international@syau.edu.cn
Website: http://www.syau.edu.cn

President: Zhang Yu-Long

International Relations: E. Jian Tel: +86(24) 88487084

College

Biological Science and Technology (Biological and Life Sciences; Biotechnology; Botany); **Horticulture** (Horticulture); **Information and Electrical Engineering** (Electrical Engineering; Information Technology)

School

Agricultural Engineering (Agricultural Engineering; Agricultural Equipment; Water Science); **Agronomy** (Agronomy; Plant and Crop Protection); **Animal Husbandry and Veterinary Medicine** (Animal Husbandry; Aquaculture; Veterinary Science); **Economics and Trade** (Agricultural Management; Business Administration; Economics; Management; Tourism); **Forestry** (Forestry); **Land and Environment** (Environmental Engineering; Environmental Studies; Microbiology; Water Management)

History: Founded 1952 as Shenyang Agricultural College acquired present title 1985.

Degrees and Diplomas: *Xueshi Xuewei*; *Shuoshi Xuewei*; *Boshi*

Publications: Journal of Shenyang Agricultural University

Academic Staff *2011-2012*: Total: c. 1,800
Student Numbers *2011-2012*: Total: c. 20,000
Last Updated: 12/02/13

SHENYANG CONSERVATORY OF MUSIC

61 Sanhao Street, Heping District, Shenyang, Liaoning Province 110003
Tel: +86(24) 23892223
Fax: +86(24) 23891655
Website: http://www.sycm.com.cn/

President: Hui Liu

Department

Chinese Traditional Instruments (Musical Instruments); **Composition** (Music Theory and Composition); **Dance** (Dance); **Music Education** (Music Education); **Musicology** (Musicology); **Singing** (Singing); **Wind and String Instruments** (Musical Instruments)

History: Founded 1938 as Luxun Academy of Arts, acquired present status and title 1958.

Degrees and Diplomas: *Xueshi Xuewei*; *Shuoshi Xuewei*
Last Updated: 12/02/13

SHENYANG INSTITUTE OF ENGINEERING

18, Puchang Road, Shenbei New Distric,
Shenyang, Liaoning Province 110136
Tel: +86(24) 31975555
Website: http://www.sie.edu.cn

International Relations: Lou Yuying, Director
Tel: +86(24) 31975301 EMail: lisa@sie.edu.cn

School
Adult Education

Department
Automation and Control Engineering (Automation and Control Engineering); **Electrical Engineering** (Electrical Engineering); **Energy and Power Engineering** (Energy Engineering; Power Engineering); **English** (English); **Information Engineering** (Information Technology); **Management Engineering** (Management); **Mechanical Engineering** (Mechanical Engineering); **Political Science and Law** (Law; Political Sciences); **Technology and Economics** (Economics; Technology)

History: Founded 2003 through merger of Shenyang Junior College of Electric Power and Liaoning Vocational College of Commerce.

Degrees and Diplomas: *Xueshi Xuewei*

Academic Staff *2011-2012*: Total 939
Student Numbers *2011-2012*: Total 15,000
Last Updated: 12/02/13

SHENYANG JIANZHU UNIVERSITY (SJZU)

9, Hunnan East Road, Hunnan New District,
Shenyang, Liaoning Province 110168
Tel: +86(24) 24692693
Fax: +86(24) 24692696
EMail: wb@sjzu.edu.cn
Website: http://www.sjzu.edu.cn/

Director: Jun Wang
International Relations: M. Yu EMail: yujin@sjzu.edu.cn

School
Architecture and Urban Planning (Architecture; Construction Engineering; Town Planning; Water Management); **Civil and Environmental Engineering** (Building Technologies; Civil Engineering; Environmental Engineering); **Vocational and Technical** (Vocational Education)

Department
Civil Engineering (Civil Engineering; Safety Engineering; Surveying and Mapping); **Design Art** (Advertising and Publicity; Design; Industrial Design); **Foreign Languages** (English); **Humanities and Law** (Arts and Humanities; Law); **Information and Control Engineering** (Information Sciences; Information Technology); **Management** (Accountancy; Engineering Management; Law; Management); **Material Science and Engineering** (Materials Engineering; Polymer and Plastics Technology); **Physical Education** (Physical Education); **Social Sciences** (Social Sciences); **Traffic and Mechanical Engineering** (Mechanical Engineering; Transport Engineering); **Urban Construction** (Town Planning; Urban Studies)

Institute
Technology (Technology)

History: Founded 1948 as Shenyang Architectural and Civil Engineering Institute. Acquired present title and status 2004.

Fees: (US Dollars): Tuition, undergraduate, 1,700 per annum, graduate, 2,500

Accrediting Agency: National Education Department

Degrees and Diplomas: *Xueshi Xuewei*; *Shuoshi Xuewei*
Last Updated: 13/02/13

SHENYANG LIGONG UNIVERSITY

6, Nanping center Road, Hunnan New District,
Shenyang, Liaoning Province 110159
Tel: +86(24) 24686047
Fax: +86(24) 24686029
EMail: webmaster@mail.sylu.edu.cn
Website: http://www.sylu.edu.cn

President: Jun Liu (2011-)

School
Art and Design (Industrial Design); **Automotive Engineering** (Automation and Control Engineering); **Computer Science** (Computer Science); **Continuing Education**; **Economics and Management** (E-Business/Commerce; Economics; Finance; International Economics; Management; Marketing); **Electronic Engineering** (Electronic Engineering); **Engineering Management** (Engineering Management); **Environmental and Chemical Engineering** (Chemical Engineering; Environmental Engineering); **Information Science and Engineering** (Information Sciences; Information Technology); **International Education** (Chinese); **Law** (Law; Political Sciences); **Materials Engineering** (Materials Engineering); **Mechanical Engineering** (Mechanical Engineering); **Modern Languages** (English; Modern Languages; Russian); **Science** (Computer Science; Information Sciences; Optical Technology)

History: Founded 1953 as Northeast China Industrial School. Acquired present status and title 2004.

Main Language(s) of Instruction: Chinese

Degrees and Diplomas: *Xueshi Xuewei*; *Shuoshi Xuewei*; *Boshi*

Academic Staff *2011-2012*: Total: c. 1,900
Student Numbers *2011-2012*: Total: c. 36,200
Last Updated: 13/02/13

SHENYANG MEDICAL COLLEGE

146 Huanghe North Street, Shenyang, Liaoning Province 110034
Tel: +86(24) 62215776
Fax: +86(24) 62215656
EMail: shenyiyuanban@symc.edu.cn
Website: http://www.symc.edu.cn/

President: Ling Xiaochu
International Relations: Li Min

College
Vocational and Technical Studies

School
Adult Education; **Ophtalmology and Optics** (Ophthalmology; Optical Technology; Optics); **Public Health** (Health Administration; Public Health)

Department
Basic Medicine (Medicine); **Clinical Medicine** (Medicine); **Foreign Language**; **Nursing** (Nursing); **Preventive Medicine** (Social and Preventive Medicine); **Social Sciences** (Social Sciences); **Sports** (Sports); **Stomatology** (Stomatology)

Centre
Information Technology (Information Technology)

History: Founded 1949 as nursing school, acquired present status and title 1987.

Degrees and Diplomas: *Xueshi Xuewei*; *Shuoshi Xuewei*
Last Updated: 13/02/13

SHENYANG NORMAL UNIVERSITY

253 Huanghe North Street, Shenyang, Liaoning Province 110031
Tel: +86(24) 86574288
Fax: +86(24) 86574225
EMail: synugj04@163.com
Website: http://www.synu.edu.cn/

President: Zhao Dayu
Tel: +86(24) 86592023 EMail: zhaodayu@synu.edu.cn
Vice-President: Min Xia

International Relations: Wu Yulun
Tel: +86(24) 86574276 EMail: yulunwu@163.com

College

Arts and Design (Design; Painting and Drawing; Visual Arts); **Chemistry and Life Sciences** (Biological and Life Sciences; Chemistry); **Drama Art** (Acting; Theatre); **Educational Sciences** (Educational Sciences); **Educational Technology** (Educational Technology); **Foreign Languages** (English; French; German; Japanese; Literature; Modern Languages; Russian); **International Business** (Economics; International Business); **International Education** (Chinese; Tourism); **Law** (Law); **Liberal Arts** (Chinese; Literature); **Management** (Management); **Marxism** (Political Sciences); **Mathematics and Systematic Science** (Computer Science; Mathematics); **Music** (Music); **Physical Science and Technology** (Physics; Technology); **Sociology** (Sociology); **Software** (Software Engineering); **Sports** (Sports); **Teachers Professional Development** (Pedagogy; Preschool Education; Primary Education; Science Education); **Tourism Management** (Tourism); **Vocational and Technical**

History: Founded 1951 as Northeastern College of Education, became Shenyang Normal College in 1953. Merged with Liaoning College of Education and acquired present status 2002.

Academic Year: From August to July

Main Language(s) of Instruction: Chinese

Degrees and Diplomas: *Xueshi Xuewei*; *Shuoshi Xuewei*

Student Services: Academic Counselling, Canteen, Careers Guidance, Foreign Studies Centre, Health Services, Language Laboratory, Nursery Care, Sports Facilities

Academic Staff *2011-2012*	**TOTAL**
FULL-TIME	c. **1,600**
Student Numbers *2011-2012*	
All (Foreign included)	c. **25,000**
FOREIGN ONLY	**320**

Last Updated: 13/02/13

SHENYANG PHARMACEUTICAL UNIVERSITY

103 Wenhua Road, Shenhe District,
Shenyang, Liaoning Province 110016
Tel: +86(24) 23986072
Fax: +86(24) 23891576
EMail: master@syphu.edu.cn
Website: http://www.syphu.edu.cn

President: Wu Chunfu

School

Adult Education; **Basic Courses**; **Business Administration** (Business Administration); **Pharmaceutical Engineering** (Pharmacology); **Pharmacy** (Pharmacy); **Traditional Chinese Medicine** (Pharmacology; Traditional Eastern Medicine); **Vocational Technology**

History: Founded 1931 as Medical School of the Red Army. Acquired present name 1994.

Degrees and Diplomas: *Xueshi Xuewei*; *Shuoshi Xuewei*; *Boshi*

Publications: Journal of Shenyang Pharmaceutical University

Academic Staff *2011-2012*: Total: c. 1,000
Student Numbers *2011-2012*: Total: c. 7,000
Last Updated: 13/02/13

SHENYANG SPORT UNIVERSITY

36 Jinqiansong East Road, Sujiatun District,
Shenyang, Liaoning Province 110102
Tel: +86(24) 89166623
Fax: +86(24) 86893614
EMail: zhaoning@163.com
Website: http://www.syty.edu.cn

President: Yuqing Wang

Department

Chinese Traditional Martial Art (Sports); **Kinesiology** (Physical Therapy); **Management** (Management; Public Administration; Sports Management); **Physical Education** (Physical Education); **Sports Humanities**

History: Founded 1954 as Northeast Institute of Physical Education, acquired present title 1956.

Degrees and Diplomas: *Xueshi Xuewei*; *Shuoshi Xuewei*

Last Updated: 13/02/13

SHENYANG UNIVERSITY

21 Wanghua South Street, Dadong District,
Shenyang, Liaoning Province 110044
Tel: +86(24) 88502777-1
Fax: +86(24) 88523363
Website: http://www.syu.edu.cn

President: Tieheng Sun

School

Agriculture (Agriculture; Horticulture); **Architectural and Environmental Engineering** (Architectural and Environmental Design); **Economics** (Economics; International Business); **Education** (Education; Educational Psychology; Pedagogy; Primary Education); **Engineering** (Civil Engineering; Computer Engineering; Environmental Engineering; Food Technology; Information Technology; Mechanical Engineering); **Foreign Languages** (Korean); **Higher Vocational Technology** (Technology); **Law** (Law); **Liberal Arts** (Design; Fine Arts; Industrial Chemistry; Literature; Music; Musicology); **Management** (Accountancy; Management; Tourism); **Sciences** (Bioengineering; Biotechnology; Chemistry; Geography; Mathematics; Natural Sciences; Physics); **Tourism**

History: Founded 1980.

Degrees and Diplomas: *Xueshi Xuewei*; *Shuoshi Xuewei*

Publications: Journal of Shenyang University

Academic Staff *2011-2012*: Total: c. 1,200
Student Numbers *2011-2012*: Total: c. 30,000

SHENYANG UNIVERSITY OF CHEMICAL TECHNOLOGY

11 Aigong South Street, Tiexi District,
Shenyang, Liaoning Province 110142
Tel: +86(24) 89388462
Fax: +86(24) 89381026
EMail: syict@syict.edu.cn
Website: http://www.syuct.edu.cn/

President: Yu Jun Pang

Department

Applied Chemistry (Applied Chemistry); **Chemical Engineering, Environment and Biological Engineering** (Bioengineering; Chemical Engineering; Environmental Engineering); **Computer Science and Engineering** (Computer Engineering; Computer Science); **Economics and Management** (Economics; Management); **Engineering Management** (Engineering Management); **Foreign Languages** (English); **Materials Science and Technology** (Industrial Design; Materials Engineering; Polymer and Plastics Technology); **Mathematics and Physics** (Mathematics; Physics); **Mechanical Engineering** (Mechanical Engineering); **Physical Education** (Physical Education)

History: Founded 1952 as school of chemical industry, became Shenyang Institute of Chemical Technology 1958. Acquired present status and name 2010.

Degrees and Diplomas: *Xueshi Xuewei*; *Shuoshi Xuewei*

Last Updated: 12/02/13

SHENYANG UNIVERSITY OF TECHNOLOGY

111, Shenliao West Road, Shenyang, Liaoning Province 110178
Tel: +86(24) 25415365
Fax: +86(24) 25411629
EMail: webmaster@sut.edu.cn
Website: http://eng.sut.edu.cn

President: Li Rongde Tel: +86(24) 25415365

School
Advanced Vocational Technology (Technology); **Basic Science**; **Business and Commerce** (Business and Commerce); **Economics** (Accountancy; Administration; Business Administration; Business and Commerce; Economics; Engineering Management; Finance; International Business; International Economics); **Electrical Engineering** (Automation and Control Engineering; Electrical Engineering; Machine Building); **Engineering** (Engineering); **Foreign Languages** (English; Modern Languages; Russian); **Information Sciences and Engineering** (Automation and Control Engineering; Computer Science; Electrical and Electronic Equipment and Maintenance; Engineering; Information Sciences; Measurement and Precision Engineering; Telecommunications Engineering); **International Education** (Chinese); **Literature and Law** (International Relations; Law; Literature); **Management** (Management); **Materials Science and Engineering** (Engineering; Materials Engineering; Metal Techniques); **Mechanical Engineering** (Automation and Control Engineering; Electronic Engineering; Graphic Design; Industrial Design; Industrial Engineering; Mechanical Engineering; Production Engineering); **Petrochemical Engineering** (Petroleum and Gas Engineering); **Science** (Mathematics and Computer Science; Natural Sciences); **Software** (Software Engineering)

Department
Architecture and Civil Engineering (Architecture; Civil Engineering); **Physical Education** (Physical Education)

Further Information: Also a campus in Hongwei

History: Founded 1949, acquired present status and title 1985.

Degrees and Diplomas: *Xueshi Xuewei*; *Shuoshi Xuewei*; *Boshi*

Publications: Academic Journal of Shenyang University of Technology

Last Updated: 13/02/13

SHENZHEN UNIVERSITY

Nanhai Ave 3688, Shenzhen, Guangdong Province 518060
Tel: +86(755) 26536108
Fax: +86(755) 26534940
EMail: szufao@szu.edu.cn
Website: http://www.szu.edu.cn

President: Qingquan Li Tel: +86(755) 26534375

Vice-President: Xing Miao
Tel: +86(755) 26558382 EMail: xingmiao@szu.edu.cn

International Relations: Ruan Shuangchen, Vice-President
Tel: +86(755) 26536108

College
Arts (Advertising and Publicity; Chinese; Communication Studies; Japanese; Modern Languages; Tourism); **Normal** (Teacher Training); **Physics Science and Technology** (Physics); **Software** (Software Engineering)

School
Adult Education; **Architecture and Town Planning** (Architectural and Environmental Design; Architecture; Civil Engineering; Town Planning); **Art and Design** (Design); **Chemistry and Chemical Engineering** (Chemical Engineering; Chemistry); **Civil Engineering** (Civil Engineering); **Economics** (Accountancy; Business and Commerce; Economics; Finance; International Business); **Electronic Science and Technology** (Electronic Engineering; Optical Technology); **Foreign Languages** (Modern Languages); **Golf Management** (Sports; Sports Management); **Information Engineering** (Computer Engineering; Electronic Engineering; Information Technology); **Law** (Law; Sociology); **Life Sciences** (Biological and Life Sciences); **Management** (Management; Public Administration); **Mass Communication** (Mass Communication); **Material Science** (Materials Engineering); **Mathematics and Computer Science** (Mathematics and Computer Science); **Mechatronics and Control Engineering** (Automation and Control Engineering; Electronic Engineering; Mechanical Engineering); **Medicine** (Medicine); **Optoelectronics Engineering** (Electronic Engineering; Optical Technology)

Department
Social Sciences (Social Sciences)

History: Founded 1983.

Academic Year: September to July (September-February; March-July)

Admission Requirements: Graduation from senior middle school and entrance examination

Fees: (Yuan): c. 5,000

Main Language(s) of Instruction: Chinese

Accrediting Agency: Ministry of Education

Degrees and Diplomas: *Xueshi Xuewei*; *Shuoshi Xuewei*; *Boshi*

Student Services: Canteen, Careers Guidance, Cultural Activities, Foreign Studies Centre, Health Services, Language Laboratory, Nursery Care, Sports Facilities

Publications: Journal of Shenzhen University; World Architecture Review

Academic Staff *2011-2012*: Total: c. 29,000
Student Numbers *2011-2012*: Total: c. 1,500
Last Updated: 14/02/13

SHIHEZI UNIVERSITY

Beisi Road, Shihezi, Xinjiang Uygur Province 832003
Tel: +86(993) 2058053
Fax: +86(993) 2017247
EMail: webmaster@shzu.edu.cn
Website: http://www.shzu.edu.cn/structure/index

President: Huixing He

Director of Academic Affairs: Wang Weixin
Tel: +86(993) 2058037 EMail: wwx_mac@shzu.edu.cn

College
Agronomy (Agronomy); **Animal Science** (Zoology); **Chemistry and Chemical Engineering** (Chemical Engineering; Chemistry); **Engineering** (Engineering); **Foreign Languages** (English; Russian); **Information Sciences** (Information Sciences); **Medicine** (Nursing; Pharmacy); **Pharmacy** (Pharmacy); **Politics and Law** (Law; Political Sciences); **Teachers Training** (Biology; Chemistry; Chinese; Education; Fine Arts; Geography; Mathematics; Modern Languages; Physics); **Water Architecture and Civil Engineering** (Civil Engineering; Water Management)

School
Business (Business Administration); **Economics and Management** (Accountancy; Business and Commerce; Economics; Management); **Life Sciences** (Biological and Life Sciences); **Marxism** (Political Sciences); **Mechanical Electrical Engineering** (Electrical Engineering; Mechanical Engineering)

Institute
Arts (Chinese; Design; Fine Arts; Literature; Radio and Television Broadcasting); **Food Science** (Food Science; Food Technology); **Physical Education** (Physical Education)

History: Founded 1949 as Shihezi Agricultural College. Merged with Shihezi Medical College (founded 1949). Acquired present status and title 1996.

Degrees and Diplomas: *Xueshi Xuewei*; *Shuoshi Xuewei*

Last Updated: 14/02/13

SHIJIAZHUANG TIEDAO UNIVERSITY (STDU)

No.17 North 2nd-Ring East Road,
Shijiazhuang, Hebei Province 050043
Tel: +86(311) 87935052
Fax: +86(311) 87935052
EMail: exchangecentre@stdu.edu.cn
Website: http://www.stdu.edu.cn/

President: Yue Zurun

International Relations: Song Jin EMail: guojichu@stdu.edu.cn

School
Civil Engineering (Civil Engineering); **Electronics and Information** (Electronic Engineering; Telecommunications Engineering); **Further Education**; **Higher Vocational Education**; **Humanities** (Arts and Humanities); **Information Sciences and Technology** (Information Sciences; Information Technology); **Materials Engineering** (Materials Engineering); **Mechanical Engineering**

(Mechanical Engineering); **Postgraduates**; **Transport Engineering** (Transport Engineering)

Department

Accountancy (Accountancy); **Architecture and Arts Design** (Architecture; Design); **Economics and Management** (Economics; Management); **Electronic Engineering** (Electronic Engineering); **Machine Building** (Machine Building)

History: Founded 1950 as Railway Engineering College, became Shijiazhuang Railway Institute 1984. Acquired present name 2010.

Fees: (Yuan): 16,000- 19,000 par annum, depending on programs

Degrees and Diplomas: *Xueshi Xuewei*; *Shuoshi Xuewei*; *Boshi*

Student Numbers *2011-2012*: Total: c. 1,400

Last Updated: 14/02/13

SHIJIAZHUANG UNIVERSITY

Everest Hi-Tech Development Zone, 288 Main Street, Shijiazhuang, Hebei 050035

EMail: admin@sjzc.edu.cn

Website: http://www.sjzc.edu.cn/

President: Wang Junhua

College

Education (Education); **Foreign Languages and Literature** (English; Literature)

School

Computer Science (Computer Science); **Mathematics and Information Sciences** (Information Sciences; Mathematics); **Resources and Environment Studies** (Environmental Studies; Natural Resources)

Department

Continuing Education (Adult Education); **Economics and Management** (Economics; Management); **Education** (Education); **History and Cultural Studies** (Cultural Studies; History); **Law and Political Sciences** (Law; Political Sciences); **Marxism** (Political Sciences); **Music** (Music); **Physical Edication** (Physical Education; Sports); **Physics; Electronic and Information Engineering** (Electronic Engineering; Information Technology; Physics)

Institute

Chemical Engineering (Chemical Engineering); **Literature and Media** (Literature; Media Studies)

Academy

Fine Arts (Fine Arts)

Degrees and Diplomas: *Xueshi Xuewei*

Last Updated: 04/12/13

SHIJIAZHUANG UNIVERSITY OF ECONOMICS

136 East Huai'an Road, Yuhua district, Shijiazhuang, Hebei Province 050031

Tel: +86(311) 86033811

Fax: +86(311) 87208114

EMail: xywmail@sjzue.edu.cn

Website: http://www.sjzue.edu.cn

President: Hao Dongheng

Department

Accountancy (Accountancy); **Applied Economics** (Economics); **Business Administration** (Business Administration); **Economics** (Economics); **Humanities and Law** (Arts and Humanities; Law); **Information Technology** (Information Technology); **Natural Resources and Environmental Engineering** (Environmental Engineering; Natural Resources)

History: Founded 1971 as Hebei College of Geology, acquired present title 1996.

Degrees and Diplomas: *Xueshi Xuewei*; *Shuoshi Xuewei*

Academic Staff *2011-2012*: Total: c. 1,200

Student Numbers *2011-2012*: Total: c. 24,000

Last Updated: 14/02/13

SHOUGANG INSTITUTE OF TECHNOLOGY

155, Fushi Road, Shijingshan District, Beijing 100144

Tel: +86(10) 59805990

Fax: +86(10) 59805999

EMail: sggxy@sgit.edu.cn

Website: http://www.sgit.edu.cn

President: Wang Chuanxue

Department

Adult Education; **Architecture and Environmental Protection Engineering** (Architectural and Environmental Design; Civil Engineering; Design; Environmental Engineering; Metal Techniques); **Basic Education** (English; Mathematics); **Computer Science** (Computer Science); **Economic Administration** (Accountancy; Administration; International Economics; Management); **Electromechanichal Engineering** (Automation and Control Engineering; Electrical Engineering; Materials Engineering; Mechanical Engineering)

History: Founded 1978 as a branch of Beijing Instiute of Iron and Steel. Acquired present title 2004.

Fees: (Yuan): 25,000 per annum

Degrees and Diplomas: *Xueshi Xuewei*

Last Updated: 17/07/13

SIAS INTERNATIONAL UNIVERSITY

168 Renmin East Road, Xinzheng, Henan Province 451150

Tel: +86(371) 6260 5536

Fax: +86(371) 6260 5536

EMail: iced@sias.edu.cn

Website: http://www.sias.edu.cn/

Chairman: Shawn Chen

Tel: +86(371) 6260 6641 EMail: sqfang@hotmail.com

International Relations: Fang Wen Chang, Director, International Relations Office

Tel: +86(371) 6260 5536 EMail: sqfang@hotmail.com

School

Art Design (Design; Fine Arts); **Basic Education** (Education); **Business** (Accountancy; Business and Commerce; Economics; Management); **Chinese Language and Culture** (Chinese); **Electronics and Information Engineering** (Electronic Engineering; Information Technology); **Foreign Languages** (English; Japanese; Translation and Interpretation); **International Education** (Business Administration; English; Finance; International Business); **Law** (Law); **Music** (Music); **Nursing** (Nursing); **Physical Education** (Physical Education)

History: Created 1998.

Fees: (Yuan):12,000 - 14,000 per annum depending on programs

Degrees and Diplomas: *Xueshi Xuewei*

Academic Staff *2011-2012*: Total: c. 1,100

Student Numbers *2012-2013*: Total 16,000

Last Updated: 11/03/13

SICHUAN AGRICULTURAL UNIVERSITY (SAU)

36 Xinkang Road, Ya'an, Sichuan Province 625014

Tel: +86(835) 2882233

Fax: +86(835) 2883166

EMail: aumdwsb@sicau.edu.cn

Website: http://www.sicau.edu.cn

President: Youliang Zheng

School

Agriculture (Agriculture; Environmental Studies; Genetics; Microbiology; Plant and Crop Protection; Soil Science); **Animal Science and Technology** (Animal Husbandry; Veterinary Science; Zoology); **Economics and Trade** (Business Administration; Business and Commerce; Economics; Finance); **Engineering** (Automation and Control Engineering; Computer Science; Engineering; Food Science; Mechanical Engineering; Physics); **Forestry and Horticulture** (Forestry; Horticulture); **Vocational Technology** (Technology)

Further Information: Also Chengdu Campus in Wenjiang District, and Dujiangyan Campus in Dujiangyan City

History: Founded 1906 as Sichuan Tong Sheng Agricultural School, acquired present title 1985.

Academic Year: September to July

Admission Requirements: Graduation from senior middle school and entrance examination

Main Language(s) of Instruction: Chinese

Degrees and Diplomas: *Xueshi Xuewei*; *Shuoshi Xuewei*; *Boshi*

Publications: Journal of Sichuan Agricultural University

Academic Staff *2011-2012*: Total 1,300

Student Numbers *2011-2012*: Total 26,000

Last Updated: 14/02/13

SICHUAN CONSERVATORY OF MUSIC (SCCM)

6 Xinsheng Road, Chengdu, Sichuan Province 610021
Tel: +86(28) 85430876 +86(28) 85430297
Fax: +86(28) 85430712
EMail: scyyxy@mail.sc.cninfo.net; sccmws@126.com
Website: http://www.sccm.cn/

President: Ao Changqun

International Relations: Yang Jianzhong

College

Fine Arts *(Chengdu)*; **Opera and Art Management** (Art Management; Opera); **Theatre and Movie and TV Play Literature** (Literature; Radio and Television Broadcasting; Theatre)

Department

Chinese Traditional Music (Folklore; Music); **Composition** (Music Theory and Composition); **Dance** (Dance); **Mass Media** (Mass Communication); **Music Education** (Music Education); **Musicology** (Musicology); **Piano** (Musical Instruments); **Singing** (Singing); **Theatre** (Theatre); **Wind and String Instruments** (Musical Instruments)

Academy

Pop Music Academy (Music)

Centre

Adult Education

History: Founded 1939 as Sichuan Provincial School of Drama and Music, acquired present status and title 1959.

Fees: (Yuan): Secondary school student, 15,000 per annum; three-year college student and undergraduate, 21,000; master degree, 27,000 or 10,000 per term; general advanced-study student,18,000

Degrees and Diplomas: *Xueshi Xuewei*; *Shuoshi Xuewei*

Last Updated: 14/02/13

SICHUAN FINE ARTS INSTITUTE

108 Huangjiaoping, Jiulongpo District,
Chongqing, Sichuan Province 400053
Tel: +86(23) 86181008
Fax: +86(23) 68514451
EMail: info@scfai.edu.cn
Website: http://www.scfai.edu.cn/

President: Luo Zhongli

International Relations: Thomas Kuang

College

Continuous Education and Advanced Vocational Art Studies

School

Fashion Design (Fashion Design)

Department

Architecture Art (Architecture); **Art Education** (Art Education); **Art History and Theory** (Art Criticism; Art History); **Chinese Traditional Painting** (Chinese; Painting and Drawing); **Crafts and Design**; **Design** (Design); **Fine Arts** (Fine Arts); **Landscape Architecture**; **Oil Painting** (Painting and Drawing); **Photography and Video** (Photography; Video); **Printmaking** (Printing and Printmaking); **Sculpture** (Sculpture)

History: Founded 1939 as Chengdu Arts School, acquired present status 1950 and name 1959.

Admission Requirements: Equivalent to Chinese senior high school certificate

Fees: (Yuan): long-term, 10,000 per annum; short-term, 450 per week

Degrees and Diplomas: *Xueshi Xuewei*; *Shuoshi Xuewei*

Last Updated: 14/02/13

SICHUAN INTERNATIONAL STUDIES UNIVERSITY

33 Zhuangzhi Road, Shapingba,
Chongqing, Sichuan Province 400031
Tel: +86(23) 65385238
Fax: +86(23) 65385875
EMail: webmaster@sisu.edu.cn
Website: http://www.sisu.edu.cn

Vice-President: Keyong Li (2001-) Tel: +86(23) 65385815

Vice-President: Yanan LI Tel: +86(23) 65385219

International Relations: Chun Zhao Tel: +86(23) 65380010

College

Chengdu (Chinese; English; Journalism); **International Cultural Exchange** *(ICEC)* (Chinese; English; Journalism); **Vocational and Technical Education** (Foreign Languages Education; Home Economics; International Business; Marketing; Secretarial Studies; Tourism)

School

Applied Foreign Languages (French; German; Russian); **International Law and Business** (Economics; English; International Business; International Law; Law)

Department

English (English; International Relations; Translation and Interpretation); **French** (French); **German** (German; Translation and Interpretation); **Japanese** (Japanese; Translation and Interpretation); **Postgraduate**; **Russian** (Russian; Translation and Interpretation); **Social Sciences** (Social Sciences); **Sports** (Sports)

Institute

Adult Education

Centre

Audiovisual Studies (Cinema and Television); **Computer** (Computer Science)

History: Founded 1950, acquired present status 1952.

Academic Year: September to July (September-January; February-July)

Admission Requirements: Graduation from high school and entrance examination

Fees: None

Main Language(s) of Instruction: Chinese

Degrees and Diplomas: *Zhuanke*; *Xueshi Xuewei*; *Shuoshi Xuewei*. Also Certificates (2 yrs)

Student Services: Academic Counselling, Canteen, Cultural Activities, Health Services, Nursery Care, Social Counselling, Sports Facilities

Publications: World Children's Literature

SICHUAN NORMAL UNIVERSITY

5 Jing'an Road, Jinjiang District,
Chengdu, Sichuan Province 610066
Tel: +86(28) 4770706
Fax: +86(28) 4761103
EMail: scsdxcb@sicnu.edu.cn
Website: http://www.sicnu.edu.cn

President: Zhou Jieming

Department

Arts (Arts and Humanities; Design; Industrial Design); **Chemistry** (Chemistry); **Chinese for Foreigners** (Chinese; Literature); **Computer Science** (Computer Science; Information Technology); **Economics and Management** (Economics; Management); **Education** (Education); **Educational Sciences** (Educational Sciences); **Engineering** (Automation and Control Engineering; Electrical

Engineering; Engineering); **Film and Television** (Cinema and Television; Film; Radio and Television Broadcasting); **Foreign Languages** (Modern Languages); **Geography** (Geography); **History and Tourism** (History; Tourism); **Journalism and Communication** (Communication Studies; Information Sciences; Journalism); **Law** (Law; Political Sciences); **Life Sciences** (Biology); **Marxist Theories** (Philosophy; Political Sciences); **Mathematics and Software Science** (Mathematics; Software Engineering); **Music and Painting** (Music; Painting and Drawing); **Physical Education** (Physical Education); **Physics and Electrical Engineering** (Electrical Engineering; Physics); **Teacher Training** (Teacher Training); **Tourism** (Tourism)

Academy
Dance (Dance)

Centre
Business Administration (Business Administration)

History: Founded as college 1952, acquired present status and title 1986. Under the jurisdiction of Sichuan Provincial Authorities.

Academic Year: August to June (August-December; January-June)

Admission Requirements: Graduation from senior middle school and entrance examination

Main Language(s) of Instruction: Chinese

Degrees and Diplomas: *Xueshi Xuewei*; *Shuoshi Xuewei*

Publications: Journal of Sichuan Normal University; Teaching and Management Research

Academic Staff *2011-2012*: Total: c. 3,000
Student Numbers *2011-2012*: Total: c. 35,000
Last Updated: 15/02/13

SICHUAN UNIVERSITY

24 South Section 1, Yihuan Road,
Chengdu, Sichuan Province 610065
Tel: +86(28) 85407199 +86(28) 85405773
Fax: +86(28) 85405773
EMail: wsc@scu.edu.cn
Website: http://www.scu.edu.cn

President: Heping Xie
Tel: +86(28) 8540 3116 EMail: president@scu.edu.cn

College
Architecture and Environment (Architecture; Civil Engineering; Environmental Engineering; Environmental Studies; Mechanical Engineering); **Arts** (Fine Arts); **Business** (Business Administration); **Chemical Engineering** (Chemical Engineering); **Chemistry** (Applied Chemistry; Chemistry); **Computer Science** (Computer Science); **Economics** (Economics; Finance; Taxation); **Electrical Engineering and Information Technology** (Electrical Engineering; Information Technology); **Electronics and Information Engineering** (Electronic Engineering; Information Sciences); **Foreign Languages** (English; French; German; Modern Languages; Russian; Spanish); **History and Culture** (Cultural Studies; History; Tourism); **Hydraulic Engineering** (Hydraulic Engineering); **Law** (Law); **Life Sciences** (Bioengineering; Biological and Life Sciences; Biology); **Light Industry, Textile and Food Engineering** (Engineering; Food Science; Textile Technology); **Literature and Journalism** (Journalism; Literature); **Manufacturing Science and Engineering** (Mechanical Engineering; Production Engineering); **Material Science and Engineering** (Materials Engineering; Polymer and Plastics Technology); **Mathematics** (Applied Mathematics; Mathematics); **Medicine** *(West China)* (Medicine); **Pharmacy** *(West China)* (Pharmacy); **Physical Education** (Physical Education); **Physics and Technology** (Applied Physics; Physics; Technology); **Political Sciences** (Political Sciences); **Polymer Science and Engineering** (Polymer and Plastics Technology); **Preclinical and Forensic Medicine** *(West China)* (Forensic Medicine and Dentistry; Medicine); **Public Administration** (Public Administration); **Public Health** *(West China)* (Public Health); **Software Engineering** (Software Engineering); **Stomatology** (Stomatology)

Further Information: Also Huaxi and Jiang'an Campuses and University Hospital

History: Founded 1896 as East-West School. Merged with Chengdu University of Science and Technology and West China University of Medical Sciences in 1995 as Sichuan Union University. In 2000 the name of the merged university changed back to Sichuan University.

Admission Requirements: High School Diploma

Fees: (Yuan): 14,500-37,000 per annum depending on faculty and degree

Main Language(s) of Instruction: Chinese

Degrees and Diplomas: *Xueshi Xuewei*; *Shuoshi Xuewei*; *Boshi*

Publications: Journal of Sichuan University
Last Updated: 15/02/13

SICHUAN UNIVERSITY FOR NATIONALITIES

15th Wenhua Road Guza, Kangding, Sichuan 626001
Tel: +86(836) 2856168
Fax: +86(836) 2856196
EMail: lcp@scun.edu.cn
Website: http://www.scun.edu.cn

President: Li Jiping

Dean: Can Wu Lee

Department
Business Administration (Business Administration); **Chinese Language** (Chinese); **Computer Science** (Computer Science; Mathematics and Computer Science); **Economics and Management** (Economics; Management); **Education** (Educational Administration; Primary Education; Teacher Training); **English** (English); **Environmental and Life Sciences** (Biological and Life Sciences; Environmental Studies); **Fine Arts** (Fine Arts); **Law** (Law); **Mathematics** (Mathematics); **Music and Folk Dance** (Dance; Music); **Physical Education** (Physical Education); **Tibetan Language and Literature** (Literature; Tibetan); **Tourism and Vocational Education** (Tourism; Vocational Education)

History: Founded 1985 as Kangding Teachers College. Acquired present title and status 2009.

Degrees and Diplomas: *Xueshi Xuewei*
Last Updated: 26/11/13

SICHUAN UNIVERSITY OF ARTS AND SCIENCE

400 Nanbalu, Dazhou, Sichuan 63500
Tel: +86(818) 2760540
Fax: +86(818) 2760295
Website: http://www.sasu.edu.cn

President: Meng Zhaohuai

Department
Arts (Fine Arts); **Chemistry** (Chemistry); **Chinese Language and Literature** (Chinese; Literature); **Educational Sciences and Technology** (Educational Sciences; Educational Technology); **Engineering** (Engineering); **Foreign Languages** (English); **Mathematics** (Mathematics); **Music** (Music); **Physics and Electronic Engineering** (Electronic Engineering; Physics); **Social Sciences** (Social Sciences)

History: Founded 1976.

Degrees and Diplomas: *Xueshi Xuewei*

Academic Staff *2012-2013*: Total: c. 500
Student Numbers *2012-2013*: Total: c. 8,000
Last Updated: 26/11/13

SICHUAN UNIVERSITY OF SCIENCE AND ENGINEERING

Zigong, Sichuan Province 643000
Tel: +86(571) 88165512
Fax: +86(571) 88165698
Website: http://www.suse.edu.cn

President: Huanglin Zeng

Department
Architectural and Civil Engineering (Architecture; Civil Engineering); **Arts** (Fine Arts; Industrial Design); **Automation and Electrical Engineering** (Automation and Control Engineering; Electrical Engineering); **Bioengineering** (Bioengineering; Biotechnology); **Economics and Management** (Economics;

Management); **Electronic Engineering and Information Technology** (Electronic Engineering; Information Technology); **Engineering Management** (Engineering Management); **Foreign Languages** (English); **Law** (Law); **Materials Science and Chemical Engineering** (Chemical Engineering; Materials Engineering); **Mechanical Engineering** (Mechanical Engineering); **Physical Education** (Physical Education); **Physics**; **Political Sciences** (Political Sciences)

History: Founded 1965 as East China University of Chemical Technology. Acquired present title 2003 following merger of Sichuan Institute of Light Industry and Chemical Technology, Zigong Teachers College, Zigong Polytechnic College and Zigong Institute of Education.

Degrees and Diplomas: *Xueshi Xuewei*; *Shuoshi Xuewei*

Academic Staff *2011-2012*: Total: c. 1,600

Student Numbers *2011-2012*: Total: c. 25,000

Last Updated: 15/02/13

SOOCHOW UNIVERSITY (SUDA)

1, Shizi Street, Suzhou, Jiangsu Province 215006
Tel: +86(512) 65112308
Fax: +86(512) 65221028
EMail: mail@suda.edu.cn; t_huangxing@suda.edu.cn
Website: http://www.suda.edu.cn

President: Zhu Xiulin Tel: +86(512) 65112798

Vice-President: Zhang Xueguang Tel: +86(512) 65113042

International Relations: Huang Xing, Director of International Office Tel: +86(512) 671-63702 EMail: t_huangxing@suda.edu.cn

College

Applied Technology (Accountancy; Arts and Humanities; Business Administration; Computer Science; Economics; Electrical Engineering; Electronic Engineering; Fashion Design; Mechanical Engineering; Modern Languages; Tourism); **Chemistry, Chemical Engineering and Material Science** *(CCEMS)* (Analytical Chemistry; Applied Chemistry; Chemical Engineering; Chemistry; Inorganic Chemistry; Materials Engineering; Organic Chemistry; Physical Chemistry; Polymer and Plastics Technology); **Communication** *(Phoenix)* (Journalism; Mass Communication; Media Studies; Radio and Television Broadcasting); **Iron and Steel** *(Shagang)* (Metallurgical Engineering); **Medicine** (Anaesthesiology; Anatomy; Animal Husbandry; Biochemistry; Biological and Life Sciences; Biology; Biomedicine; Biotechnology; Cardiology; Dermatology; Ecology; Embryology and Reproduction Biology; Endocrinology; Epidemiology; Forensic Medicine and Dentistry; Gastroenterology; Genetics; Gerontology; Gynaecology and Obstetrics; Haematology; Health Sciences; Histology; Hygiene; Immunology; Laboratory Techniques; Medical Technology; Medicine; Microbiology; Molecular Biology; Neurology; Nursing; Nutrition; Oncology; Ophthalmology; Otorhinolaryngology; Paediatrics; Pathology; Pharmacology; Pharmacy; Physical Therapy; Psychology; Public Health; Radiology; Rehabilitation and Therapy; Social and Preventive Medicine; Sports Medicine; Stomatology; Surgery; Toxicology; Traditional Eastern Medicine; Venereology); **Textile and Clothing Engineering** (Clothing and Sewing; Energy Engineering; Engineering; Industrial Chemistry; Materials Engineering; Textile Design; Textile Technology); **Wenzheng** (Economics; Engineering; Law; Literature; Management; Natural Sciences)

School

Architecture and Urban Environment *(Gold Mantis)* (Architecture; Architecture and Planning; Entomology; Heritage Preservation; Horticulture; Interior Design; Landscape Architecture; Pest Management; Town Planning); **Arts** (Art Education; Communication Arts; Design; Fine Arts; Multimedia; Music; Music Education; Textile Design; Visual Arts); **Business, Finance and Securities** *(Dongwu)* (Accountancy; Banking; E-Business/Commerce; Economics; Finance; International Business; International Economics; Management; Marketing); **Computer Science and Technology** (Computer Engineering; Computer Networks; Computer Science; Engineering; Information Management; Information Technology; Management; Software Engineering); **Education** (Curriculum; Education; Educational Administration; Educational Psychology; Educational Sciences; Educational Technology; Higher Education; Pedagogy); **Electronics and Information** (Electrical Engineering; Electronic Engineering; Information Technology; Microelectronics; Telecommunications Engineering); **Foreign Languages** (Applied Linguistics; English; Foreign Languages Education; French; German; Japanese; Korean; Linguistics; Literature; Modern Languages; Russian; Spanish; Translation and Interpretation); **Humanities** (Aesthetics; Applied Linguistics; Arts and Humanities; Chinese; Cinema and Television; Comparative Literature; Curriculum; Film; Linguistics; Literature; Pedagogy; Philology; Theatre); **Law** *(Kenneth Wang)* (Administrative Law; Civil Law; Commercial Law; Comparative Law; Constitutional Law; Criminal Law; History of Law; International Law; Law; Private Law; Public Law); **Mathematical Sciences** (Applied Mathematics; Biology; Mathematics; Mathematics and Computer Science; Mathematics Education; Operations Research; Statistics); **Mechanical and Electrical Engineering** (Automation and Control Engineering; Automotive Engineering; Electrical Engineering; Industrial Engineering; Materials Engineering; Measurement and Precision Engineering; Mechanical Engineering); **Overseas Education** (Chinese; Economics); **Physical Education** (Physical Education; Sports); **Physical Science, Technology and Energy** (Automation and Control Engineering; Chemistry; Energy Engineering; Information Technology; Measurement and Precision Engineering; Optical Technology; Optics; Physics; Power Engineering; Structural Architecture; Technology); **Political Science and Public Administration** (Administration; Business Administration; Human Resources; Management; Philosophy; Political Sciences; Public Administration; Public Relations; Social Sciences; Transport Management; Urban Studies); **Social Science** (Archiving; History; Information Management; Information Sciences; Library Science; Social Studies; Social Work; Sociology; Tourism; Welfare and Protective Services); **Urban Rail Transportation** (Automation and Control Engineering; Automotive Engineering; Electrical Engineering; Engineering Management; Railway Engineering; Structural Architecture; Transport and Communications; Transport Engineering)

Further Information: Also post-doctoral research stations.

History: Founded 1900. Merged with Suzhou College of Sericulture 1995, Suzhou Institute of Silk Technology 1997 and Suzhou Medical College 2000.

Academic Year: September to July (September-January; February-July)

Admission Requirements: Graduation from senior middle school and entrance examination

Fees: (Yuan): c. 14,000 per annum

Main Language(s) of Instruction: Chinese

Accrediting Agency: State Commission of Education

Degrees and Diplomas: *Xueshi Xuewei*; *Shuoshi Xuewei*; *Boshi*

Student Services: Academic Counselling, Canteen, Careers Guidance, Foreign Studies Centre, Health Services, Language Laboratory, Nursery Care, Social Counselling, Sports Facilities

Publications: Foreign Silk; Soochow University Journal

Publishing House: Soochow University Press

Academic Staff *2012-2013*	**TOTAL**
FULL-TIME	c. **1,640**
Student Numbers *2012-2013*	
All (Foreign included)	c. **50,000**
FOREIGN ONLY	**2000**

Last Updated: 07/11/12

SOUTH-CENTRAL UNIVERSITY FOR NATIONALITIES (SCNU)

708 Minyuan Road, Hongshan District,
Wuhan, Hubei Province 430074
Tel: +86(27) 87800443
Fax: +86(27) 87800443
Website: http://www.scuec.edu.cn

President: Li Jinlin (2012-)

International Relations: Du Zhangwei Tel: +86(27) 87807805

School

Art and Design (Art History; Design; Fine Arts; Graphic Design; Painting and Drawing; Visual Arts); **Biological Science and Medical Engineering** (Biological and Life Sciences; Biomedical Engineering; Information Technology; Medical Technology); **Chemistry**

and Materials Science (Analytical Chemistry; Applied Chemistry; Chemistry; Inorganic Chemistry; Materials Engineering; Organic Chemistry; Physical Chemistry; Polymer and Plastics Technology; Water Management); **Computers** (Automation and Control Engineering; Computer Engineering; Computer Networks; Computer Science; Software Engineering); **Continuing Education** (Chinese; Computer Science; Economics; English; Law; Literature; Management; Social Work; Technology); **Economics** (Economics; Finance; Insurance; International Economics); **Electronics and Information Engineering** (Electronic Engineering; Information Sciences; Information Technology; Optical Technology; Physics; Telecommunications Engineering); **Ethnology and Sociology** (Ethnology; Sociology); **Foreign Languages** (English; French; German; Japanese; Korean; Modern Languages; Translation and Interpretation); **Law** (Administrative Law; Civil Law; Constitutional Law; Criminal Law; International Law; Law; Philosophy; Political Sciences; Public Administration); **Life Sciences** (Biochemistry; Bioengineering; Biological and Life Sciences; Biology; Biotechnology; Cell Biology; Chemistry; Ecology; Food Technology; Genetics; Microbiology; Molecular Biology; Safety Engineering); **Literature, Journalism and Communication** (Advertising and Publicity; Applied Linguistics; Chinese; Communication Studies; Comparative Literature; Journalism; Linguistics; Literature; Mass Communication; Philology; Radio and Television Broadcasting); **Management** (Accountancy; Business Administration; E-Business/Commerce; Finance; Human Resources; Information Management; Information Sciences; Management; Marketing; Tourism); **Marxist Studies** (Political Sciences); **Mathematics and Statistics** (Mathematics; Mathematics and Computer Science; Statistics); **Music and Dance** (Art History; Dance; Folklore; Music); **Pharmaceutical Sciences** (Biology; Chemistry; Pharmacy); **Preparatory Education** (Chemistry; Chinese; Computer Science; Cultural Studies; English; Geography; History; Literature; Mathematics; Philosophy; Physics; Political Sciences); **Public Policy and Management** (Public Administration); **Sports Science and Physical Education** (Physical Education; Sports)

Centre

Computer Teaching and Experiment (Computer Science; Electrical and Electronic Engineering; Physics; Software Engineering)

History: Founded 1951 as Central College for Nationalities. Acquired present title 2003. One of the 13 higher education institutes for ethnic groups in China.

Fees: (Yuan): c. 3,000

Main Language(s) of Instruction: Chinese

Accrediting Agency: Commission for Nationalities

Degrees and Diplomas: *Xueshi Xuewei*; *Shuoshi Xuewei*; *Boshi*

Student Services: Academic Counselling, Canteen, Careers Guidance, Cultural Activities, Foreign Studies Centre, Health Services, Language Laboratory, Nursery Care, Social Counselling, Sports Facilities

Publications: Higher Education for Nationalities; Journal of South Central University for Nationalities

Publishing House: University Press

Academic Staff *2012-2013*: Total 1,240
STAFF WITH DOCTORATE: Total 168
Last Updated: 08/11/12

SOUTH CHINA AGRICULTURAL UNIVERSITY

Wushan, Guangzhou, Guangdong Province 510642
Tel: +86(20) 85511299 Ext. 2342
Fax: +86(20) 85511299 Ext. 2344
EMail: xcb@scau.edu.cn
Website: http://www.scau.edu.cn

President: Chen Xiaoyang
EMail: sec@scau.edu.cn; xychen@scau.edu.cn

Vice-Chancellor, Administration: Lu Huazhong
EMail: huazlu@scau.edu.cn

Faculty

Science (Applied Chemistry; Applied Mathematics; Applied Physics; Mathematics and Computer Science; Natural Sciences)

College

Agronomy (Agriculture; Agronomy); **Animal Husbandry** (Animal Husbandry); **Economics and Management** (Economics; Management); **Engineering** (Engineering); **Foreign Languages** (English; Japanese; Modern Languages); **Forestry** (Forest Products; Forestry; Landscape Architecture; Tourism; Town Planning; Wood Technology); **Horticulture** (Horticulture); **Natural Resources and Environment** (Environmental Studies; Natural Resources); **Pearl River**; **Veterinary Medicine** (Veterinary Science)

School

Arts (Advertising and Publicity; Communication Arts; Design; Display and Stage Design; Fashion Design; Fine Arts; Industrial Design; Music; Performing Arts; Radio and Television Broadcasting; Textile Design; Visual Arts); **Continuing Education** (Continuing Education); **Humanities and Law** (Arts and Humanities; Law); **information sciences** (Information Sciences); **Life Sciences** (Biological and Life Sciences); **Public Administration** (Public Administration); **Water Conservation and Civil Engineering** (Agricultural Engineering; Bridge Engineering; Civil Engineering; Energy Engineering; Environmental Engineering; Hydraulic Engineering; Irrigation; Road Engineering; Soil Science; Water Management)

Department

Ideological and Political Theory Teaching (Political Sciences); **Sports** (Physical Education; Sports)

Institute

Food Science (Bioengineering; Food Science; Food Technology; Safety Engineering); **International Education**

History: Founded 1909 as Lingnan Agricultural School and Guagdong Agricultural School, acquired present status and title 1984. Under the jurisdiction of the Ministry of Agriculture and the Provincial Government.

Academic Year: September to July (September-January; March-July)

Admission Requirements: Graduation from senior middle school and entrance examination

Main Language(s) of Instruction: Chinese

Accrediting Agency: Ministry of Agriculture

Degrees and Diplomas: *Xueshi Xuewei*; *Shuoshi Xuewei*; *Boshi*

Publications: Journal of South China Agricultural University
Last Updated: 08/11/12

SOUTH CHINA NORMAL UNIVERSITY (SCNU)

Shipai, Guangzhou, Guangdong Province 510631
Tel: +86(20) 85211065
Fax: +86(20) 85212131
EMail: wsh3@scnu.edu.cn
Website: http://www.scnu.edu.cn

President: Liu Ming EMail: wsh3@scnu.edu.cn

Director: Xiao Hua

International Relations: Shen Liling, Head, International Exchange Division EMail: wsh3@scnu.edu.cn

College

Liberal Arts (Chinese; Linguistics; Literature; Publishing and Book Trade); **Nanhai** (Accountancy; Administration; Applied Mathematics; Chinese; Computer Engineering; Computer Networks; Computer Science; Economics; Educational Technology; Electronic Engineering; English; Finance; French; Information Sciences; Law; Literature; Management; Mathematics; Political Sciences; Software Engineering); **Network Education** (Accountancy; Administration; Business Administration; Chinese; Computer Science; Hotel Management; Human Resources; Law; Literature; Musicology; Preschool Education; Primary Education; Transport Management)

School

Basic Educational Training and Research (Education; Primary Education; Secondary Education); **Chemistry and Environment** (Chemistry; Environmental Engineering; Environmental Studies); **Computer Science** (Computer Networks; Computer Science; Software Engineering); **Continuing Education** (Adult Education); **Economics and Management** (Accountancy; E-Business/Commerce; Economics; Finance; Human Resources; Information

Management; Information Sciences; International Economics; Transport Management); **Educational Information Technology** (Educational Technology; Information Management; Information Technology; Mass Communication; Photography); **Foreign Languages and Culture** (English; Japanese; Literature; Modern Languages; Russian); **Law** (Law); **Life Science** (Bioengineering; Biological and Life Sciences; Biotechnology); **Mathematics** (Applied Mathematics; Computer Science; Information Sciences; Mathematics; Statistics); **Physics and Telecommunications Engineering** (Electronic Engineering; Information Sciences; Information Technology; Materials Engineering; Physics; Science Education; Telecommunications Engineering); **Political Sciences and Administration** (Administration; Political Sciences; Public Administration); **Public Administration** (Educational Administration; Government; Management; Public Administration); **Sports** (Physical Education; Sociology; Sports); **Tourism Management** (Management; Tourism)

Institute

Biophotonics (Biological and Life Sciences; Physics); **Cultural Studies** *(International)* (Asian Studies; Chinese; Cultural Studies); **Educational Sciences** (Education; Educational Psychology; Educational Sciences; Pedagogy; Preschool Education; Primary Education; Psychology); **Geography** (Computer Science; Geography; Town Planning); **History and Culture** (Cultural Studies; History); **Information and Optoelectronic Science** (Electronic Engineering; Information Sciences; Information Technology; Optical Technology; Telecommunications Engineering); **Optoelectronic Materials and Technology** (Electronic Engineering; Optical Technology)

Academy

Fine Arts (Communication Arts; Design; Fine Arts; Industrial Design; Media Studies); **Music** (Dance; Music; Performing Arts; Singing); **Zengcheng** (Accountancy; Computer Science; Design; E-Business/Commerce; Economics; Engineering; English; Finance; Fine Arts; German; Information Management; Information Sciences; Information Technology; International Business; International Economics; Japanese; Law; Literature; Management; Tourism; Transport Management)

Centre

Economic Studies *(South China)* (Economics)

Laboratory

Aquatic Health and Aquaculture Safety (Aquaculture; Marine Science and Oceanography; Safety Engineering); **Biotechnology for Plant Development** (Biotechnology; Plant and Crop Protection); **Ecology and Environmental Science** (Ecology; Environmental Studies); **Electrochemical Energy Storage and Power Generation Technology** (Chemical Engineering; Electronic Engineering; Energy Engineering; Power Engineering); **Electroluminescent Optoelectronic Devices** (Electronic Engineering; Optical Technology); **Laser Life Science** (Biological and Life Sciences; Laser Engineering); **Mental Health and Cognitive Science** (Cognitive Sciences; Psychiatry and Mental Health); **Quantum Information Technology** (Information Technology); **Traditional Chinese Medicine and Photonic Technology** (Alternative Medicine; Physics; Technology)

Research Centre

Computer Networks and Information Systems Engineering Technology (Computer Engineering; Computer Networks; Information Sciences; Technology); **Emergency Technology** (Technology); **LED Industrial Research and Development** (Industrial Engineering; Physics); **Lingnan Culture** (Cultural Studies); **Modern Educational** (Educational Sciences); **Physical Fitness and Health** *(National)* (Health Sciences; Physical Education; Sports); **Psychology** (Psychology); **Services Engineering Technology** (Computer Science; Service Trades; Technology); **Systems Science and Systems Management** (Management Systems)

Further Information: Also Language and Culture Training Centre for foreign students; post-doctoral research stations.

History: Founded 1933 as Teachers College, Xiangqin University. Acquired present title 1982.

Academic Year: November to June (November-January; February-June)

Admission Requirements: Graduation from senior middle school and entrance examination

Degrees and Diplomas: *Xueshi Xuewei*; *Shuoshi Xuewei*; *Boshi*

Publications: Chinese Language and Literature; Journal of South China Normal University; Moral Education for Primary Schools

Academic Staff *2010-2011*	**TOTAL**
FULL-TIME	c. **2,800**
Student Numbers *2010-2011*	
All (Foreign included)	c. **32,430**
FOREIGN ONLY	**380**

Last Updated: 09/11/12

SOUTH CHINA UNIVERSITY OF TECHNOLOGY (SCUT)

371 Wushan Road, Guangzhou, Guangdong Province 510641
Tel: +86(20) 87114470 +86(20) 87110009
Fax: +86(20) 87110206 +86(20) 85516386
EMail: scuta04@scut.edu.cn; j2xb@scut.edu.cn; zhk@scut.edu.cn
Website: http://www.scut.edu.cn

President: Yingjun Wang
Tel: +86(20) 8711008 EMail: yyli@scut.edu.cn

International Relations: Yiwu Hu
Tel: +86(20) 87110973 EMail: flywhu@scut.edu.cn

School

Architecture (Architectural and Environmental Design; Architecture; Landscape Architecture; Structural Architecture; Town Planning); **Arts** (Art Education; Dance; Music; Musical Instruments; Musicology; Performing Arts; Singing); **Automation Science and Engineering** (Automation and Control Engineering; Computer Engineering; Computer Networks; Information Technology); **Bioscience and Bioengineering** (Biochemistry; Bioengineering; Biological and Life Sciences; Biomedical Engineering; Biotechnology; Engineering; Genetics; Microbiology; Molecular Biology; Physiology); **Business Administration** (Accountancy; Business Administration; Economics; Human Resources; Industrial Engineering; Industrial Management; Management; Marketing; Transport Management); **Chemistry and Chemical Engineering** (Applied Chemistry; Chemical Engineering; Chemistry; Energy Engineering); **Civil and Transport Engineering** (Civil Engineering; Marine Engineering; Mechanics; Naval Architecture; Transport Engineering; Water Management); **Computer Science and Engineering** (Computer Engineering; Computer Networks; Computer Science; Software Engineering); **Economics and Commerce** (Business Administration; E-Business/Commerce; Economics; Engineering; Finance; Insurance; International Business; International Economics; Tourism; Transport and Communications; Transport Engineering); **Electric Power** (Automation and Control Engineering; Electrical Engineering; Industrial Engineering; Power Engineering; Thermal Engineering); **Electronic and Information Engineering** (Electrical and Electronic Engineering; Electronic Engineering; Information Technology; Microelectronics; Microwaves; Optical Technology; Physics; Solid State Physics; Telecommunications Engineering); **Environmental Science and Engineering** (Environmental Engineering; Environmental Studies; Water Management); **Foreign Languages** (Applied Linguistics; English; German; Japanese; Linguistics; Modern Languages; Russian); **Ideology and Politics** (Political Sciences); **Journalism and Communication** (Advertising and Publicity; Aesthetics; Communication Arts; Journalism; Mass Communication; Media Studies; Philosophy; Publishing and Book Trade); **Law** (Civil Law; Commercial Law; Criminal Law; Economics; History of Law; Law); **Light Chemistry and Food Science** (Chemical Engineering; Food Science; Food Technology; Industrial Engineering; Paper Technology; Safety Engineering); **Materials Science and Engineering** (Biomedical Engineering; Ceramics and Glass Technology; Materials Engineering; Optical Technology; Polymer and Plastics Technology); **Mechanical and Automotive Engineering** (Automation and Control Engineering; Automotive Engineering; Chemical Engineering; Electronic Engineering; Energy Engineering; Industrial Engineering; Materials Engineering; Measurement and Precision Engineering; Mechanical Engineering; Power Engineering; Safety Engineering; Thermal Engineering; Transport Engineering); **Physical Education** (Physical Education; Sports); **Public Administration** (Administration; Educational Administration; Public Administration); **Sciences** (Applied Mathematics; Applied Physics; Computer Science; Electrical Engineering; Information Technology;

Mathematics; Mathematics and Computer Science; Physics; Statistics); **Software Engineering** (Software Engineering)

Further Information: Also Guangzhou Higher Education Mega Center Campus.

History: Founded 1952 as South China Institute of Technology. Acquired present title 1988.

Academic Year: September to July (September-February; March-July)

Admission Requirements: High school diploma

Fees: (Yuan): 21,580 per annum

Main Language(s) of Instruction: Chinese

Accrediting Agency: Ministry of Education

Degrees and Diplomas: *Xueshi Xuewei*; *Shuoshi Xuewei*; *Boshi*. Also Graduate Professional Degrees; MBA; Executive MBA.

Student Services: Academic Counselling, Canteen, Careers Guidance, Cultural Activities, Facilities for disabled people, Foreign Studies Centre, Health Services, Language Laboratory, Nursery Care, Social Counselling, Sports Facilities

Academic Staff *2012-2013*	**TOTAL**
FULL-TIME	c. **2,300**
Student Numbers *2012-2013*	
All (Foreign included)	**91,893**
FOREIGN ONLY	**1672**

Last Updated: 14/11/12

SOUTHEAST UNIVERSITY (SEU)

2 Sipailou, Nanjing, Jiangsu Province 210096
Tel: +86(25) 3792412
Fax: +86(25) 3615736
EMail: admission@seu.edu.cn; oic@seu.edu.cn
Website: http://www.seu.edu.cn

President: Hong Yi Tel: +86(25) 83792215

International Relations: Shi Lanxin, Head, Office for International Cooperation Tel: +86(25) 83792412

College

Chien-Shiung Wu; **Continuing Education** (Continuing Education); **Integrated Circuits** (Computer Engineering; Electronic Engineering); **International Students** (International Studies); **Software Engineering** (Software Engineering)

School

Architecture (Architecture); **Arts** (Design; Fine Arts; Industrial Design); **Automation** (Automation and Control Engineering); **Basic Medical Sciences** (Medicine); **Biological Science and Medical Engineering** (Biological and Life Sciences; Biomedical Engineering); **Chemistry and Chemical Engineering** (Chemical Engineering; Chemistry; Industrial Chemistry); **Civil Engineering** (Bridge Engineering; Building Technologies; Civil Engineering; Construction Engineering; Environmental Engineering; Mechanical Engineering; Real Estate; Structural Architecture); **Communication and Transportation** (Telecommunications Engineering; Transport Economics); **Computer Science and Engineering** (Computer Engineering; Computer Science); **Economic and Management** (Accountancy; Business Administration; Business and Commerce; Economics; Engineering; Finance; International Business; International Economics; Management; Vocational Education); **Electrical Engineering** (Automation and Control Engineering; Electrical Engineering); **Electronic Science and Engineering** (Electronic Engineering); **Energy and Environment** (Energy Engineering; Power Engineering; Thermal Engineering); **Foreign Languages** (English; Literature; Modern Languages); **Humanities** (Arts and Humanities; Chinese; Economics; Literature; Philosophy; Political Sciences; Public Administration; Tourism); **Information Science and Engineering** (Electronic Engineering; Information Sciences; Information Technology); **Instrument Science and Engineering** (Instrument Making; Measurement and Precision Engineering); **Law** (Commercial Law; Law); **Material Science and Engineering** (Materials Engineering); **Mechanical Engineering** (Automation and Control Engineering; Materials Engineering; Mechanical Engineering); **Medicine** (Medicine); **Preclinic Medical Studies** (Laboratory Techniques; Medical Technology; Medicine; Nursing; Social and Preventive Medicine); **Public Health** (Epidemiology; Food Science; Health Sciences; Hygiene; Insurance; Nutrition; Occupational Health; Public Health; Statistics); **Science** (Applied Mathematics; Applied Physics; Mathematics; Mathematics and Computer Science; Physics)

Research Institute

Preventive Medicine (Social and Preventive Medicine); **Railway Station and Occupational Health** (Hygiene; Occupational Health; Railway Engineering); **Systems Engineering** (Engineering; Systems Analysis)

Further Information: Also post-doctoral research stations.

History: Founded 1902 as Sanjiang Normal College, before evolving into Nanjing Higher Normal School, National Southeast University and National Central University. Transformed into Nanjing Institute of Technology 1952. Acquired present title 1988. Merged with Nanjing Railway Medical College, Nanjing College of Communications and Nanjing Geological School 2000.

Main Language(s) of Instruction: Chinese

Degrees and Diplomas: *Xueshi Xuewei*; *Shuoshi Xuewei*; *Boshi*

Publications: Southeast University Journal of Higher Education

Academic Staff *2011-2012*: Total: c. 6,000
Student Numbers *2011-2012*: Total: c. 27,000
Last Updated: 20/11/12

SOUTHERN MEDICAL UNIVERSITY
Nanfang Yike Daxue (FIMMU)

Shatai Lu, Baiyun Qu, Guangzhou 510515
Tel: +86(20) 6164-0114 +86(135) 7051-5378
Fax: +86(135) 7051-5362
EMail: xzgz@smu.edu.cn; nanfang.admission@gmail.com; mbbs@fimmu.com
Website: http://www.fimmu.com/

President: Yu Yanhong (2013-)

School

Basic Medical Sciences (Medicine); **Biomedical Engineering** (Biomedical Engineering); **Biotechnology** (Biotechnology); **Clinical Medicine 1** (Medicine); **Clinical Medicine 2** (Medicine); **Continuing Education**; **Experimental Medicine and Laboratory Techniques** (Laboratory Techniques; Medicine); **Foreign Studies** (International Studies; Modern Languages); **Humanities and Social Sciences** (Arts and Humanities; Social Sciences); **Medical Technology** (Medical Technology); **Nursing** (Nursing); **Pharmaceutical Sciences** (Pharmacy); **Public Administration** (Public Administration); **Public Health and Tropical Medicine** (Public Health; Tropical Medicine); **Traditional Chinese Medicine** (Traditional Eastern Medicine)

Department

Sports (Sports)

Institute

Genetic Engineering (Bioengineering; Genetics)

Further Information: 7 affiliated hospitals and 16 schools or colleges

History: Founded 1951 as First Military Medical University. Handed over to the local government of Guangdong Province and acquired present title 2004.

Main Language(s) of Instruction: Chinese

Degrees and Diplomas: *Xueshi Xuewei*; *Shuoshi Xuewei*: **Medicine.** *Boshi*: **Medicine.**

Student Services: Sports Facilities

Academic Staff *2012-2013*: Total: c. 1,100
Student Numbers *2012-2013*: Total 15,514
Last Updated: 09/09/13

SOUTHWEST FORESTRY UNIVERSITY (SWFU)

300 Bailongsi, Kunming, Yunnan Province 650224
Tel: +86(871) 3863211 +86(871) 3863954 +86(871) 3862829
Fax: +86(871) 5637217
EMail: oicswfc@swfc.edu.cn
Website: http://www.swfc.edu.cn

President: Liu Huimin

International Relations: Li Maobiao

Faculty

Conservation Biology (Animal Husbandry; Biology; Environmental Management; Fire Science; Forestry; Protective Services; Welfare and Protective Services; Wildlife; Zoology); **Economics and Management** (Accountancy; Agricultural Economics; Agricultural Management; Business Administration; Development Studies; Economics; Forest Economics; Forest Management; Management); **Ecotourism** (Ecology; Environmental Studies; Information Sciences; Information Technology; Natural Resources; Parks and Recreation; Tourism); **Landscape Architecture** (Design; Fine Arts; Horticulture; Landscape Architecture; Rural Planning; Town Planning; Urban Studies); **Natural Resources** (Agronomy; Biotechnology; Botany; Computer Science; Food Science; Food Technology; Forest Management; Forestry; Genetics; Information Sciences; Natural Resources; Surveying and Mapping; Wildlife); **Transportation, Machinery and Civil Engineering** (Agricultural Engineering; Automation and Control Engineering; Automotive Engineering; Civil Engineering; Electronic Engineering; Forestry; Industrial Design; Machine Building; Mechanical Engineering; Production Engineering; Transport Engineering); **Wood Science and Technology** (Chemical Engineering; Design; Forest Management; Forest Products; Interior Design; Packaging Technology; Wood Technology)

Unit

Biodiversity Conservation in Southwest Region of China *(SFA Key Lab)* (Biological and Life Sciences; Environmental Management; Environmental Studies)

College

Continuing Education and College of Forestry Vocational Education (Arts and Humanities; Biological and Life Sciences; Chinese; Civil Engineering; Computer Science; English; Environmental Engineering; Environmental Studies; Forest Economics; Forest Management; Forestry; Information Sciences; Landscape Architecture; Law; Machine Building; Natural Resources; Tourism; Transport Engineering; Wood Technology)

Department

Computer and Information Sciences (Computer Engineering; Computer Graphics; Computer Science; Electronic Engineering; Information Sciences); **Environmental Sciences and Engineering** (Agriculture; Arid Land Studies; Ecology; Environmental Engineering; Environmental Management; Environmental Studies; Water Management); **Foreign Languages** (Chinese; English; Literature; Modern Languages); **Fundamental Courses** (Applied Chemistry; Computer Science; Information Sciences; Physical Education); **Humanities and Social Sciences** (Arts and Humanities; Chinese; Law; Literature; Public Administration; Social Sciences)

Institute

Modern Forestry and Engineering (Agricultural Engineering; Forestry); **Urban Forestry and Urban-Rural Planning** (Forestry; Rural Planning); **Wood Sciences and Technology** (Agricultural Engineering; Forestry; Wood Technology)

Centre

Biodiversity and Nature Conservation (Biological and Life Sciences; Environmental Management; Environmental Studies); **Social Forestry and Mountain Development** *(Yunan)* (Agriculture; Forestry; Social Work)

Laboratory

Early Warning and Control of Forest Disasters *(Yunnan Provincial Key Lab)* (Forest Management; Forestry; Safety Engineering); **Forest Resources Conservation and Utilization in Southwestern Mountainous Area** *(Key Laboratory)* (Forest Products; Forestry; Natural Resources); **Landscaping Plants and Ornamental Horticulture** *(Yunnan Provincial Key Lab)* (Horticulture; Landscape Architecture); **Silviculture in the Southwestern Mountainous Areas** *(Yunnan Provincial Key Lab)* (Environmental Management; Forestry; Natural Resources)

Research Centre

Biotic Materials *(Yunnan Provincial Key Engineering research Centre)* (Chemistry; Forest Products; Forestry; Production Engineering; Wood Technology); **Education and Human Resources** *(Base of the Floriculture Association of China)* (Education; Human Resources); **Education Reform and Development** (Education); **National Plateau Wetland** (Biological and Life Sciences; Education; Environmental Engineering; Environmental Management; Environmental Studies; Health Sciences; Information Sciences); **Wood Bio-fuel Resources** (Natural Resources; Wood Technology); **'3S' Technology** *(Yunnan Provincial Key Engineering Research Centre)* (Agricultural Engineering; Data Processing; Forestry; Software Engineering; Telecommunications Engineering)

Research Institute

Bamboo and Rattan (Agriculture); **National Parks** (Environmental Studies); **Wood Engineering** (Agricultural Engineering; Wood Technology)

History: Founded as the Department of Forestry in Yunnan University in 1939. Became separate institution and acquired present title 1978 following the establishment and merger of Kunming College of Agriculture and Forestry and Yunnan Forestry College, and affiliated with China's Ministry of Forestry. Acquired predent title 1983.

Main Language(s) of Instruction: Chinese

Degrees and Diplomas: *Xueshi Xuewei*; *Shuoshi Xuewei*. Also higher professional and vocational education programmes.

Academic Staff *2011-2012*: Total 1,027

Student Numbers *2011-2012*: Total 12,463

Last Updated: 20/11/12

SOUTHWEST JIAOTONG UNIVERSITY (SWJTU)

Chengdu High-tech Zone West Park,
Chengdu, Sichuan Province 611756
Tel: +86(28) 87600114
Fax: +86(28) 7605147
EMail: fad@home.swjtu.edu.cn
Website: http://www.swjtu.edu.cn

President: Chen Chunyang

School

Architecture (Architecture); **Arts and Communications** (Advertising and Publicity; Arts and Humanities; Chinese; Communication Arts; Communication Studies; Dance; Design; Film; Fine Arts; Industrial Design; Literature; Mass Communication; Music; Musicology; Painting and Drawing; Radio and Television Broadcasting); **Civil Engineering** (Civil Engineering; Computer Science; Geography; Surveying and Mapping); **Economics and Business Administration** (Accountancy; Business Administration; E-Business/Commerce; Economics; Finance; Information Management; Information Sciences; Tourism); **Electrical Engineering** (Automation and Control Engineering; Electrical Engineering; Information Technology); **Foreign Languages** (African Languages; Applied Linguistics; Arabic; Chinese; English; European Languages; Foreign Languages Education; French; German; Hindi; Japanese; Linguistics; Modern Languages; South and Southeast Asian Languages; Spanish; Translation and Interpretation); **Geological Science and Environmental Engineering** (Environmental Engineering; Environmental Studies; Fire Science; Forestry; Geological Engineering; Geology; Surveying and Mapping); **Information Science and Technology** (Automation and Control Engineering; Computer Engineering; Computer Networks; Computer Science; Information Sciences; Information Technology; Software Engineering; Telecommunications Engineering); **Life Sciences and Engineering** (Biochemistry; Bioengineering; Biological and Life Sciences; Biology; Pharmacology; Pharmacy; Traditional Eastern Medicine); **Mao Yisheng**; **Material Science and Engineering** (Architectural and Environmental Design; Architecture and Planning; Automation and Control Engineering; Biomedical Engineering; Engineering; Environmental Management; Landscape Architecture; Materials Engineering; Natural Resources; Tourism; Town Planning); **Mathematics** (Applied Mathematics; Computer Science; Information Sciences; Mathematics; Mathematics and Computer Science; Operations Research; Statistics); **Mechanical Engineering** (Automotive Engineering; Industrial Engineering; Information Technology; Measurement and Precision Engineering; Mechanical Engineering; Power Engineering; Production Engineering; Transport Engineering); **Mechanics and Engineering** (Mechanical Engineering; Mechanics; Systems Analysis); **Physical Science and Technology** (Applied Physics; Atomic and Molecular Physics; Information Sciences; Information Technology; Nuclear

Physics; Optics; Physics; Radiophysics; Sound Engineering (Acoustics); Technology); **Political Sciences** (Administration; Law; Political Sciences); **Public Administration** (Administrative Law; Civil Law; Commercial Law; Constitutional Law; Criminal Law; Economics; Health Administration; History of Law; International Business; International Economics; International Law; International Relations; Public Administration; Real Estate; Welfare and Protective Services); **Traffic and Logistics** (Transport and Communications; Transport Engineering; Transport Management); **Zhan Tianyou**

Department

Physical Education (Physical Education; Sociology; Sports)

Centre

Psychological Research and Counseling (Psychology); **Training for Modern Industrial Technology** (Industrial Engineering)

Research Institute

Tangshan

Further Information: Also post-doctoral research stations; Guri Campus in Emeishan City.

History: Founded 1896 as Imperial Chinese Railway College, acquired present title 1972.

Fees: (Yuan): Tuition fee, 16,500-20,000 per annum for undergraduate programmes; 20,000-25,000 per annum undergraduate tuition; 25,000-30,000 per annum undergraduate tuition

Main Language(s) of Instruction: Chinese, English

Degrees and Diplomas: *Xueshi Xuewei*; *Shuoshi Xuewei*; *Boshi*

Student Services: Academic Counselling, Canteen, Careers Guidance, Foreign Studies Centre, Health Services, Language Laboratory, Nursery Care, Social Counselling, Sports Facilities

Publications: Journal of Southwest Jiaotong University; Journal of Transportation Engineering and Information

Academic Staff *2011-2012*: Total: c. 2,500

Student Numbers *2011-2012*: Total: c. 40,000

Last Updated: 21/11/12

SOUTHWEST PETROLEUM UNIVERSITY

Xindu Avenue 8#, Xindu District,
Chengdu, Sichuan Province 637001
Tel: +86(28) 83032308
EMail: swpuaa@swpu.edu.cn
Website: http://www.swpi.edu.cn

President: Du Zhimin

College

Applied Technology (Technology); **Arts** (Arts and Humanities)

School

Arts and Law (Law); **Chemistry and Chemical Engineering** (Chemical Engineering; Chemistry; Environmental Engineering; Safety Engineering); **Civil Engineering and Architecture** (Architecture; Civil Engineering); **Computer Science** (Computer Science; Information Technology); **Economics and Management** (Business Administration; Economics; Management; Marketing); **Electronics and Information Engineering** (Electronic Engineering; Information Technology); **Material Science and Engineering** (Automation and Control Engineering; Chemical Engineering; Chemistry; Energy Engineering; Materials Engineering; Physical Chemistry; Polymer and Plastics Technology); **Mechanical and Electrical Engineering** (Electrical Engineering; Machine Building; Management; Mechanical Engineering); **Political Science** (Political Sciences); **Resources and Environmental Engineering** (Environmental Engineering; Geochemistry; Geography; Geological Engineering; Geology; Information Technology; Mineralogy; Natural Resources; Paleontology; Surveying and Mapping); **Science** (Applied Mathematics; Applied Physics; Computer Science; Information Sciences; Information Technology; Mathematics and Computer Science; Natural Sciences; Petroleum and Gas Engineering)

Department

Foreign Languages (Applied Linguistics; English; Foreign Languages Education; Linguistics; Modern Languages)

Institute

Petroleum Engineering (Petroleum and Gas Engineering); **Physical Education** (Physical Education; Sports)

Academy

Continuing Education and Networking (Law; Modern Languages; Petroleum and Gas Engineering)

Centre

Engineering Training (Engineering)

Further Information: Also University Hospital; post-doctoral programmes.

History: Founded 1958 as Sichuan Petroleum Institute. Renamed Southwest Petroleum Institute title 1970. Gained university status 2003 and officially acquired present title 2005.

Main Language(s) of Instruction: Chinese

Degrees and Diplomas: *Xueshi Xuewei*; *Shuoshi Xuewei*; *Boshi*

Publications: Journal of Southwest Petroleum Institute

Academic Staff *2011-2012*	**TOTAL**
FULL-TIME	c. **2,250**
Student Numbers *2011-2012*	
All (Foreign included)	c. **27,650**
FOREIGN ONLY	**560**

Last Updated: 21/11/12

SOUTHWEST UNIVERSITY (SWU)

No. 2, innate Road, Beibei District,
Chongqing, Sichuan Province 400715
Tel: +86(23) 68250773
Fax: +86(23) 68863805
EMail: efoffice@swu.edu.cn; fstudent@swu.edu.cn
Website: http://www.swu.edu.cn/english/index.html

President: Zhang Weiguo (2011-)

International Relations: Wang Jing
Tel: +86(23) 68254388 EMail: Jing67@swnu.edu.cn

Faculty

Education (Adult Education; Education; Educational Administration; Educational Psychology; Educational Sciences; Educational Technology; Higher Education; Leadership; Pedagogy; Preschool Education; Primary Education; Science Education; Special Education; Vocational Education)

Unit

Psychology (Psychology)

College

Agronomy and Biotechnology (Agronomy; Biotechnology; Development Studies; Floriculture; Rural Studies); **Animal Science and Technology** (Animal Husbandry; Aquaculture; Veterinary Science); **Applied Technology** (Technology); **Chinese Language and Literature** (Chinese; Film; Foreign Languages Education; Literature; Modern Languages; Theatre); **Culture and Social Development** (Cultural Studies; Social Studies; Social Welfare; Social Work); **Engineering** (Agricultural Engineering; Agricultural Equipment; Automation and Control Engineering; Automotive Engineering; Civil Engineering; Electronic Engineering; Energy Engineering; Environmental Engineering; Industrial Design; Machine Building); **Food Science** (Food Science; Food Technology; Packaging Technology; Safety Engineering); **Foreign Languages** (English; Japanese; Modern Languages); **Horticulture and Landscape Architecture** (Horticulture; Landscape Architecture; Town Planning); **Liberal Arts** (Chinese; Literature); **Material Science and Engineering** (Materials Engineering; Physics); **Physics and Technology/ Electronic Information Engineering** (Electronic Engineering; Information Technology; Physics; Science Education; Telecommunications Engineering); **Resources and Environment** (Arid Land Studies; Environmental Engineering; Environmental Management; Environmental Studies; Forestry; Natural Resources; Soil Conservation; Soil Science; Water Management; Water Science)

School

Chemistry and Chemical Engineering (Analytical Chemistry; Applied Chemistry; Chemical Engineering; Chemistry); **Computer Science and Information Sciences** (Automation and Control Engineering; Computer Networks; Computer Science; E-Business/

Commerce; Information Sciences; Information Technology; Software Engineering); **Economics and Management** (Accountancy; Business Administration; Economics; Farm Management; Finance; Forest Management; Human Resources; International Business; International Economics; Management; Marketing; Tourism); **Law** (Law); **Life Sciences** (Aquaculture; Biochemistry; Bioengineering; Biological and Life Sciences; Cell Biology; Genetics; Microbiology); **Marxism** (Political Sciences); **Mathematics and Statistics** (Applied Mathematics; Mathematics; Statistics); **Pharmacy and Chinese Medicine** (Biology; Chemistry; Pharmacology; Pharmacy; Traditional Eastern Medicine); **Textile and Garment** (Clothing and Sewing; Textile Design; Textile Technology); **Yucai** *(Independent two Academy)*

Institute

Biotechnology (Biotechnology; Sericulture); **Geographical Sciences** (Environmental Studies; Geography; Natural Resources; Rural Planning; Surveying and Mapping; Town Planning); **History and Culture** *(National)* (Cultural Studies; Ethnology; History); **News and Media** (Journalism; Mass Communication; Media Studies; Radio and Television Broadcasting); **Physical Education** (Physical Education; Sports); **Plant Protection** (Chemistry; Plant and Crop Protection); **Political Science and Public Administration** (Administration; Philosophy; Political Sciences; Public Administration)

Academy

Fine Arts (Design; Fine Arts; Sculpture); **Music** (Dance; Music; Musicology; Performing Arts)

Further Information: Also post-doctoral research stations.

History: Founded 1950, acquired present name 2005 through the merger of Southwest China Normal University and Southwest Agricultural University.

Fees: (Yuan): Undergraduate tuition fees, 15,000-19,000 per annum; Master's degree, 22,000 per annum; Doctoral degree, 30,000 per annum

Main Language(s) of Instruction: Chinese, English

Degrees and Diplomas: *Xueshi Xuewei*; *Shuoshi Xuewei*; *Boshi*. Also postdoctoral programmes.

Publications: Higher Education Research; Journal of Southwest China Normal University

Academic Staff *2011-2012*	**TOTAL**
FULL-TIME	c. 2,600

Student Numbers *2011-2012*	
All (Foreign included)	c. 80,000

Part-time students, 30,000.

Last Updated: 22/11/12

SOUTHWEST UNIVERSITY FOR NATIONALITIES

16, 4th Section, Yihuan Nanlu, Chengdu, Sichuan Province 610041
Tel: +86(28) 5522042 +86(28) 5522282
Fax: +86(28) 5523220
EMail: jwc@swun.edu.cn
Website: http://www.swun.edu.cn/swun/

Principal: Zhao Xin-Yu

Unit

Preparatory Education

College

Adult Education (Adult Education); **Arts** (Fine Arts); **Chemistry and Environmental Protection** (Chemistry; Environmental Engineering; Environmental Management); **Computer Science and Technology** (Computer Engineering; Computer Science); **Economics** (Economics; Finance); **Electrical and Information Engineering** (Electrical Engineering; Information Technology); **Foreign Languages** (Modern Languages); **Life Sciences and Technology** (Biological and Life Sciences); **Network Education**; **Tibetan Studies** (Asian Studies; Native Language); **Tourism, History and Culture** (Cultural Studies; History; Tourism); **Yi Studies** (Native Language)

School

Hotel Management *(Maruika)* (Hotel Management); **Law** (Law; Management); **Literature, Journalism and Communication** (Communication Studies; Journalism; Literature); **Management** (Management); **Political Science** (Political Sciences); **Sociology and Psychology** (Psychology; Sociology); **Urban Planning and Architecture** (Architecture; Town Planning)

Institute

International Education (International Studies); **Physical Education** (Physical Education; Sports)

Research Institute

Southwest

Further Information: Also Univerity Hospital.

History: Founded 1951 as Southwest Institute for Nationalities. Acquired present title 2003.

Main Language(s) of Instruction: Chinese

Degrees and Diplomas: *Xueshi Xuewei*; *Shuoshi Xuewei*; *Boshi*. Also postdoctoral programmes.

Academic Staff *2011-2012*: Total: c. 1,800

Last Updated: 22/11/12

SOUTHWEST UNIVERSITY OF POLITICAL SCIENCE AND LAW (SWUPL)

301, Baosheng Ave, Huixing Street, Yubei District,
Chongqing, Sichuan Province 400031
Tel: +86(23) 65342111
Fax: +86(23) 65316074
EMail: xzdxsc@126.com; international@swupl.edu.cn
Website: http://www.swupl.edu.cn

President: Fu Zitang
Tel: +86(23) 67258207 EMail: xzxb@supsl.cn

School

Administrative Law (Administrative Law; Constitutional Law; History of Law); **Applied Law** (Criminal Law; Environmental Studies; Law); **Civil and Commercial law** (Civil Law; Commercial Law); **Criminal investigation** (Criminology); **Economic Law** (Economics; Environmental Studies; Law; Natural Resources); **Economics** (Economics); **Foreign Languages** (Applied Linguistics; English; French; Japanese; Linguistics; Modern Languages; Russian; Translation and Interpretation); **International Law** (International Law; Private Law; Public Law); **Journalism and Communication** (Communication Studies; Journalism; Mass Communication; Radio and Television Broadcasting); **Juris Master** (Law); **Law** (Civil Law; Criminal Law; Justice Administration; Law); **Management** (Accountancy; Administration; Business Administration; Finance; Human Resources; Labour and Industrial Relations; Management; Marketing; Political Sciences); **Marxism** (Ethics; History; Philosophy; Political Sciences); **Politics and Public Administration** (Administration; Political Sciences; Public Administration); **Stilwell** *(International - SIS)* (English; International Economics)

Further Information: Also post-doctorate mobile stations.

History: Founded 1953 through merger of the Political Science and Law departments of Chongqing University and Sichuan University, the Law departments of Chongqing Finance and Economy College, and of Guizhou University and Yunnan University. Accredited as a key university by the State Council 1978. The administration of the University was transferred from the Ministry of Justice to the Chongqing municipality 2000. Was awarded "excellent undergraduate education" distinction by the Ministry of Education 2007. Became a key university co-administrated by Ministry of Education and Chongqing Municipality.

Academic Year: September to July (September-January; February-July)

Admission Requirements: Graduation from senior middle school and entrance examination

Fees: (Yuan): c. 3,500 per annum

Main Language(s) of Instruction: Chinese, English

Accrediting Agency: Education Committee of Chongqing Municipality Government

Degrees and Diplomas: *Xueshi Xuewei*; *Shuoshi Xuewei*; *Boshi*

Student Services: Academic Counselling, Canteen, Careers Guidance, Cultural Activities, Foreign Studies Centre, Health Services,

Language Laboratory, Nursery Care, Social Counselling, Sports Facilities

Publications: Law Journal of SUPSL; Modern Law Science

Academic Staff *2011-2012*	**TOTAL**
FULL-TIME	**1,157**
PART-TIME	**264**
Student Numbers *2011-2012*	
All (Foreign included)	**23,750**

Last Updated: 23/11/12

SOUTHWEST UNIVERSITY OF SCIENCE AND TECHNOLOGY (SWUST)

59 Qinglong Road, Mianyang,
Sichuan Province 621010
Tel: +86(816) 6089963
Fax: +86(816) 6089126
EMail: fao@swust.edu.cn
Website: http://www.swust.edu.cn/

President: Xiao Zhengxue

International Relations: Zhong Wenqiao

College

Adult Education (Adult Education); **Newtork Education** (Education)

School

Applied Technology (Technology); **Chinese Literature and Arts** (Arts and Humanities; Chinese; Communication Arts; Design; Journalism; Literature; Mass Communication; Music; Musicology; Performing Arts; Radio and Television Broadcasting); **Civil Engineering and Architecture** (Architectural and Environmental Design; Architecture; Civil Engineering; Management; Mechanical Engineering; Structural Architecture; Town Planning); **Computer Science** (Computer Science; Information Management; Information Technology; Software Engineering); **Economics and Management** (Accountancy; Business Administration; E-Business/Commerce; Economics; Information Management; Information Sciences; International Business; International Economics; Management; Marketing; Public Administration); **Environmental Resources and Engineering** (Computer Science; Environmental Engineering; Geography; Geological Engineering; Mining Engineering; Safety Engineering; Surveying and Mapping; Transport Engineering); **Foreign Languages Education** (English; Japanese; Modern Languages); **Information Engineering** (Automation and Control Engineering; Biomedical Engineering; Electronic Engineering; Information Sciences; Telecommunications Engineering); **Law** (Administration; Law; Political Sciences; Psychology); **Life Science and Engineering** (Agriculture; Bioengineering; Biological and Life Sciences; Biotechnology; Engineering; Food Science; Food Technology; Horticulture; Pharmacy; Zoology); **Manufacturing Science and Engineering** (Automation and Control Engineering; Design; Industrial Design; Industrial Engineering; Production Engineering); **Materials Science and Engineering** (Applied Chemistry; Materials Engineering; Physics); **National Defence Science and Technology** (Applied Chemistry; Environmental Engineering; Information Technology; Nuclear Engineering; Nuclear Physics; Radiophysics); **Science** (Applied Mathematics; Applied Physics; Computer Science; Information Sciences; Information Technology; Mathematics; Mathematics and Computer Science)

Department

Physical Education (Physical Education)

Research Centre

CIMS; **Information Technology** (Information Technology); **Nano Technology Research and Development** (Nanotechnology); **Water Treatment and Pollution Control** (Waste Management; Water Management)

Research Institute

Applied Chemistry (Applied Chemistry); **Architecture and Building Materials Design** (Architecture; Building Technologies); **Computer Application Technology** (Computer Science; Information Technology); **Computer Technology** (Computer Science; Information Technology); **Engineering Technology** *(Mianyang Huanxing)* (Engineering; Technology); **Enterprise Management and Development** (Management); **Food Science and Technology** (Food Science; Food Technology); **Higher Education** (Higher Education); **Land and Resources Utilization** (Soil Management); **Law** (Law); **Mechanical-Electronic Technology** (Electronic Engineering; Mechanical Engineering); **Mineral Materials and Application** (Mineralogy); **New Materials** (Materials Engineering); **New-type Building Materials** (Building Technologies; Materials Engineering); **Nonmetallic Mineral** (Mineralogy); **Regional Economy** (Economics; Regional Studies); **Rice** (Agriculture); **Wheat** (Agriculture)

Research Laboratory

Automation (Automation and Control Engineering); **Building Materials** (Building Technologies; Materials Engineering); **Computer Network Technology** (Computer Networks); **EDA**; **Electronic Technology** (Electronic Engineering); **Materials** (Materials Engineering); **Wind Tunnel** (Aeronautical and Aerospace Engineering)

Further Information: Also university hospital.

History: Founded 1952 as Chongqing Architectural Engineering School School. Renamed Sichuan Institute of Building Materials and acquired the right to grant Bachelor degrees 1978. Renamed Southwest Institute of Technology 1993. Merged with Mianyang College of Economy and Technology and acquired current title 2000. One of 14 key universities receiving State's special support in western China.

Main Language(s) of Instruction: Chinese

Accrediting Agency: State Commission of Science Technology and Industry for National Defense and the Sichuan Provincial People's government

Degrees and Diplomas: *Xueshi Xuewei*; *Shuoshi Xuewei*; *Boshi*. Ph.D. are joint programs offered with the Chinese Academy of Engineering Physics

Student Services: Canteen, Social Counselling, Sports Facilities

Academic Staff *2011-2012*: Total 2,300

Student Numbers *2011-2012*: Total 29,000

Last Updated: 23/11/12

SOUTHWESTERN UNIVERSITY OF FINANCE AND ECONOMICS (SWUFE)

55 Guanghuacun, Chengdu, Sichuan Province 610074
Tel: +86(28) 7352227
Fax: +86(28) 7352040
EMail: ig@swufe.edu.cn
Website: http://www.swufe.edu.cn

President: Zhao Dewu

International Relations: Jing Guang

School

Accountancy (Accountancy); **Business Administration** (Business Administration); **Continuing Education** *(Distance)*; **E-Commerce** (E-Business/Commerce); **Economic Information Engineering** (Economics; Engineering; Information Technology); **Economical Mathematics** (Economics; Mathematics); **Economics** (Economics); **Finance** (Finance); **Foreign Languages of Economics and Trade** (Business Administration; Economics; English; Modern Languages); **General Education** (Education); **Humanities** (Arts and Humanities); **Insurance** (Insurance); **International Business** (International Business; International Economics); **Law** (Law); **Marxism** (Political Sciences); **Public Administration** (Public Administration); **Public Finance and Taxation** (Finance; Taxation); **Securities and Futures**; **Statistics** (Statistics)

Department

International Studies (International Studies)

Centre

MBA Education (Business Administration)

Research Department

Physical Education (Physical Education)

Research Institute

Economics and Management (Economics; Management)

Further Information: Also Liulin Campus; 3 mobile post-doctoral stations.

History: Founded 1952 as Sichuan Institute of Finance and Economics. Acquired present status and title 1985. Governed by the People's Bank of China (PBC) untill 2000, when the governance was transferred to the Ministry of Education. A key university under direct administration from the Ministry of Education.

Main Language(s) of Instruction: Chinese

Degrees and Diplomas: *Xueshi Xuewei*; *Shuoshi Xuewei*; *Boshi*. Also MBA and Executive MBA.

Student Services: Sports Facilities

Publications: Science of Finance and Economics

Academic Staff *2011-2012*	**TOTAL**
FULL-TIME	**1,057**
PART-TIME	**691**
Student Numbers *2011-2012*	
All (Foreign included)	c. **22,000**

Last Updated: 23/11/12

SUIHUA UNIVERSITY (SHXY)

No 18 Huanghe Road, Suihua, Hei Longjiang
Tel: +86(455) 8308268 +86(455) 8301068
Fax: +86(455) 8308268
EMail: shxywaishichu@126.com
Website: http://www.shxy.net/

President: Zhuang Yan

College

Art and Design (Design; Fine Arts); **Bio-systems Engineering and Food Science** (Biochemistry; Bioengineering; Biotechnology; Food Science; Food Technology; Microbiology; Nutrition; Pharmacology); **Business Management** (Business Administration; E-Business/Commerce; Finance; Insurance; Management; Marketing; Transport Management); **Computer Science and Technology** (Automation and Control Engineering; Computer Engineering; Computer Graphics; Computer Science; Data Processing; Information Technology; Software Engineering); **Foreign Languages** (Computer Science; English; French; Japanese; Linguistics; Literature; Modern Languages; Russian; Translation and Interpretation); **Literature and Media** (Chinese; Comparative Literature; Cultural Studies; Journalism; Literature; Media Studies; Writing); **Mathematics and Information Science** (Applied Mathematics; Information Management; Information Sciences; Mathematics; Mathematics and Computer Science; Statistics); **Physical Education** (Physical Education)

Department

Education (Education; Educational Technology; Preschool Education; Psychology; Special Education; Teacher Training); **Electronic Engineering** (Electrical and Electronic Engineering; Electrical Engineering; Electronic Engineering; Information Technology; Physics); **Ideological Policy Teaching and Research** (Ethics; History; Law; Political Sciences); **Music** (Music; Music Education; Musical Instruments; Musicology; Singing); **Pharmaceutical and Chemical Engineering** (Analytical Chemistry; Applied Chemistry; Chemical Engineering; Chemistry; Inorganic Chemistry; Organic Chemistry; Pharmacy; Physical Chemistry); **Tourism and Resource Management** (Environmental Engineering; Geography; Natural Resources; Rural Studies; Tourism; Transport Management; Urban Studies)

History: Founded 1953 as Suihua Normal School. Renamed Suihua Normal Institution 1978. Acquired present status and title 2004.

Fees: (Yuan): Tuition, 5,200-6,200 per semester

Main Language(s) of Instruction: Chinese

Degrees and Diplomas: *Xueshi Xuewei*

Academic Staff *2012-2013*	**TOTAL**
FULL-TIME	**508**
Student Numbers *2012-2013*	
All (Foreign included)	**9,633**
FOREIGN ONLY	**12**

Last Updated: 14/10/13

SUN YAT-SEN UNIVERSITY (SYSU)

135 Xingangxilu, Guangzhou, Guangdong Province 510275
Tel: +86(20) 84112828
Fax: +86(20) 84039173
EMail: adpo01@zsu.edu.cn
Website: http://www.sysu.edu.cn

President: Ningsheng Xu (2010-) EMail: stsxns@mail.sysu.edu.cn

Executive Vice-president: Jiarui Xu
Tel: +86(20) 84111585 EMail: xjr@mail.sysu.edu.cn

International Relations: Fukang Xie, Director, Office of International Cooperation and Exchange
Tel: +86(20) 84111896 EMail: adeao@sysu.edu.cn

Faculty

English Education (English; Foreign Languages Education)

Unit

University General Education (Education)

College

Liberal Arts (Arts and Humanities); **Lingnan** (Business Administration; Economics; Finance; Insurance; International Business; Management; Taxation; Transport Management); **Yat-sen**

School

Asian-Pacific Studies (Asian Studies; Pacific Area Studies); **Business** (Accountancy; Business Administration; E-Business/Commerce; Economics; Finance; Human Resources; Management; Marketing; Tourism); **Cancer** *(Sun Yat-sen University)* (Oncology); **Chemistry and Chemical Engineering** (Analytical Chemistry; Chemical Engineering; Chemistry; Inorganic Chemistry; Materials Engineering; Organic Chemistry; Physical Chemistry; Polymer and Plastics Technology); **Chinese as a Second Language** (Chinese; Foreign Languages Education); **Communication and Design** (Communication Arts; Design; Journalism; Mass Communication; Media Studies; Radio and Television Broadcasting; Visual Arts); **Continuing Education** *(Online Education)*; **Education** (Education); **Engineering** (Engineering); **Environmental Science and Engineering** (Environmental Engineering; Environmental Studies); **Foreign Languages** (English; Modern Languages); **Geography and Planning** (Geography; Rural Planning); **Humanities** (Arts and Humanities; Chinese; History; Philosophy); **Information Management** (Information Management); **Information Science and Technology** (Information Sciences; Information Technology); **Intellectual Property** (Private Law); **International Business** *(IBS)* (Accountancy; Business Administration; Economics; Finance; International Business; Marketing; Taxation; Transport Management); **International Studies** (International Studies); **Law** (Law); **Life Sciences** (Biological and Life Sciences); **Marine Sciences** (Marine Science and Oceanography); **Mathematics and Computational Science** (Mathematics and Computer Science); **Medicine** *(Zhongshan)* (Medicine); **Mobile Information Engineering** (Information Technology; Telecommunications Engineering); **Nursing** (Nursing); **Pharmaceutical Science** (Pharmacy); **Physics and Engineering** (Engineering; Physics); **Public Health** (Public Health); **Sociology and Anthropology** (Anthropology; Sociology); **Software** (Software Engineering); **Stomatology, Hospital of Stomatology** *(Guanghua - Affiliated)* (Stomatology); **Tourism Management** (Management; Tourism)

Department

Earth Science (Earth Sciences); **Psychology** (Psychology); **Social Science Education** (Humanities and Social Science Education)

Institute

Advanced Studies in Humanities (Arts and Humanities); **Nuclear Engineering and Technology** *(Sino-French)* (Nuclear Engineering; Technology)

Academy

Entrepreneurship (Management)

Centre

Ophthalmology *(Zhongshan)* (Ophthalmology)

Further Information: 4 campuses: Guangzhou South Campus, Guangzhou North Campus, Guangzhou East Campus, and Zhuhai Campus; Also 39 postdoctoral research stations; 6 affiliated hospitals

History: Founded 1924 as Guangdong University. Renamed Zhongshan University 1926. Acquired present title and status 2001, following merger with Sun Yat-Sen University of Medical Sciences.

Academic Year: September to July (September-February; March-July)

Admission Requirements: Graduation from senior middle school and entrance examination

Fees: (Yuan): c. 5,000 per annum

Main Language(s) of Instruction: Chinese

Accrediting Agency: Ministry of Education

Degrees and Diplomas: *Xueshi Xuewei*; *Shuoshi Xuewei*; *Boshi*. Also MBA, Executive MBA and Executive Development (EDP) programmes.

Student Services: Academic Counselling, Canteen, Careers Guidance, Foreign Studies Centre, Health Services, Language Laboratory, Nursery Care, Sports Facilities

Publications: Acta Scientiarum Naturalium Universitatis Sunyatseni; Anatomy Research (In Chinese); Chinese Journal of Cancer; Chinese Journal of Gastrointestinal Surgery (In Chinese); Chinese Journal of Microsurgery (In Chinese); Chinese Journal of Nephrology (In Chinese); Chinese Journal of Nervous and Mental Diseases (In Chinese); Cultural Heritage; Diagnostic Imaging and Interventional Radilogy (In Chinese); Eye Science; Family Doctor General Practice (In Chinese); Journal of Public Administration (In Chinese); Journal of Sun Yat-Sen University Social Science Edition; Journal of Tropical Medicine (In Chinese); Lingnan Journal of Emergency Medicine (In Chinese); Lingnan Mordern Clinics in Surgery; Modern Clinical Nursing (In Chinese); Modern Computer (In Chinese); Modern Philosophy; New Medicine (In Chinese); Organ Transplantation (In Chinese); South China Journal of Economics (In Chinese); South China Population; Studies in Logic

Publishing House: Sun Yat-Sen University Press

Academic Staff *2011-2012*	**TOTAL**
FULL-TIME	c. **6,691**
Student Numbers *2011-2012*	
All (Foreign included)	c. **82,871**
FOREIGN ONLY	**1642**

Part-time students, 3,715. **Distance students,** 15893.

Last Updated: 23/11/12

SUZHOU UNIVERSITY OF SCIENCE AND TECHNOLOGY (SUST)

1701 Binhe Road, Suzhou, Jiangsu Province 215011
Tel: +86(512) 68255226
Fax: +86(512) 68242298
EMail: wsc@mail.usts.edu.cn
Website: http://web.usts.edu.cn/english/index.htm

President: Chen Zhigang

Department

Applied Maths (Applied Mathematics; Computer Science; Information Sciences; Mathematics); **Applied Physics** (Applied Physics; Physics); **Architecture** (Architecture; Design; Interior Design; Landscape Architecture; Town Planning); **Biology** (Biological and Life Sciences; Biology; Biotechnology); **Chemistry and Chemical Engineering** (Applied Chemistry; Chemical Engineering; Chemistry); **Chinese** (Chinese; Radio and Television Broadcasting); **Civil Engineering** (Civil Engineering; Materials Engineering; Mechanical Engineering; Transport Engineering); **Communication Science and Technology** (Communication Studies; Educational Technology); **Education** (Education; Educational Psychology); **Electronics and Information Engineering** (Computer Science; Electronic Engineering; Information Sciences; Information Technology); **Environmental Science and Engineering** (Environmental Engineering; Environmental Studies; Irrigation; Water Management); **Fine Arts** (Design; Fine Arts; Graphic Design); **Foreign Languages** (English; Japanese; Modern Languages); **History and Sociology** (History; Social Work; Sociology); **Management** (Business Administration; Management; Marketing; Tourism); **Music** (Music); **Physical Education** (Physical Education); **Political Science and Public Administration** (Human Resources; Political Sciences; Public Administration; Social Welfare; Welfare and Protective Services); **Urban and Environmental Science** (Environmental Management; Environmental Studies; Geography; Information Technology; Natural Resources; Rural Planning; Urban Studies)

Centre

Basic Lab; **Computer** (Computer Science)

Further Information: Three campuses: Jiangfeng, Shihu and Tianping.

History: Founded 2001 through the merging of the former Suzhou Institute of Urban Construction and nvironmental Protection and the former Suzhou Railway Teachers College.

Main Language(s) of Instruction: Chinese

Degrees and Diplomas: *Xueshi Xuewei*; *Shuoshi Xuewei*

Academic Staff *2011-2012*: Total 833
Student Numbers *2011-2012*: Total 13,837
Last Updated: 26/11/12

TAIHU UNIVERSITY OF WUXI (THXY)

Nanjing, Jiangsu
Tel: +86(510) 85502763
Fax: +86(510) 85502663
Website: http://www.thxy.org/

President: Jin Qiuping

Department

Arts (Fine Arts); **Civil Engineering** (Civil Engineering); **Economics and Management** (Economics; International Business; International Economics; Management); **Information Technology and Mechanical Engineering** (Information Technology; Mechanical Engineering); **Languages and Law** (English; Law; Modern Languages); **Medicine** (Medicine)

History: Founded 2002 as Jiangnan University

Main Language(s) of Instruction: Chinese

Degrees and Diplomas: *Xueshi Xuewei*

Student Services: Sports Facilities

Last Updated: 15/10/13

TAISHAN MEDICAL UNIVERSITY (TSMC)

Chang Cheng Road, Hi-Tech Development Zone, Taian, Shandong Province 271016
Tel: +86(538) 6222034 +86(538) 6229956 +86(538) 6236359
Fax: +86(538) 6222505
EMail: info@taishanmedicaluniversity
Website: http://www.taishanmedicaluniversity.com

President: Jiafu Wang
Tel: +86(538) 6222002 +86(538) 6229902
EMail: jfwang@tsmc.edu.cn

International Relations: Shouliang Wang
EMail: shouliangwang@hotmail.com

Programme

Acupuncture *(Short Term)* (Acupuncture); **Anatomy and Histoembryology** *(Postgraduate)* (Anatomy; Embryology and Reproduction Biology; Histology); **Chinese** *(Short Term)* (Chinese); **Chinese Painting** *(Short Term)* (Painting and Drawing); **Clinical Medicine** *(Undergraduate)* (Medicine); **Epidemiology and Health Statistics** *(Postgraduate)* (Epidemiology; Health Sciences; Public Health; Statistics); **Geriatrics** *(Postgraduate)* (Gerontology); **Gynaecology and Obstetrics** *(Postgraduate)* (Gynaecology and Obstetrics); **Imagining and Nuclear Medicine** *(Postgraduate)* (Medical Technology); **Immunology** *(Postgraduate)* (Immunology); **Internal Medicine** *(Postgraduate)* (Medicine); **Laboratary Medicine** *(Undergraduate)* (Laboratory Techniques; Medicine); **Martial Arts** *(Short Term)* (Sports); **Massage** *(Short Term)* (Physical Therapy); **Medical Imagining** *(Undergraduate)* (Medical Technology); **Neuro Biology** *(Postgraduate)* (Biology; Neurology); **Neurology** *(Postgraduate)* (Neurology); **Nursing** *(Undergraduate)* (Nursing); **Nursing** *(Postgraduate)* (Nursing); **Oncology** *(Postgraduate)* (Oncology); **Pathogeny Biology** *(Postgraduate)* (Biology; Pathology); **Pathology and Pathophysiology** *(Postgraduate)* (Pathology; Physiology); **Pharmacology** *(Postgraduate)* (Pharmacology); **Pharmacy** *(Undergraduate)* (Pharmacy); **Shadow Boxing** *(Short Term)* (Sports); **Sports Medicine** *(Postgraduate)* (Sports

Medicine); **Surgery** *(Postgraduate)* (Surgery); **Traditional Chinese Medicine** *(Short Term)* (Traditional Eastern Medicine)

History: Founded 1974 as the Loude Branch College of Shandong Medical College and then was moved to Taian City 1979. Renamed Taian Branch College of Shandong Medical College. Acquried present title 1981.

Fees: (Yuan): Undergraduate Programmes Tution Fee, 19,000 per annum for foreign students and 11,000 per annum for chinese students; Master Programmes Tution Fee, 21,000 per annum for foreign students and 19,000 per annum for chinese students

Main Language(s) of Instruction: English and Chinese

Degrees and Diplomas: *Xueshi Xuewei*; *Shuoshi Xuewei*

Academic Staff *2011-2012*	**TOTAL**
FULL-TIME	1,100
PART-TIME	c. 400
Student Numbers *2011-2012*	
All (Foreign included)	13,000

Last Updated: 26/11/12

TAISHAN UNIVERSITY (TSU)

Yingbin Middle Road, Tai'an, Shandong 271021
Tel: +86(538) 6715597
Fax: +86(538) 6715521
EMail: ws5597@126.com; webmaster@tsu.edu.cn
Website: http://www.tsu.edu.cn/

President: Qin Menghua (2013-)

School

Biology and Brewing Engineering (Biological and Life Sciences; Biology; Biotechnology; Viticulture); **Business** (Business Administration; Finance; International Business; International Economics; Management; Marketing); **Chemistry and Chemical Engineering** (Applied Chemistry; Chemical Engineering; Chemistry; Environmental Studies; Materials Engineering; Pharmacology; Polymer and Plastics Technology); **Fine Arts** (Architectural and Environmental Design; Clothing and Sewing; Communication Arts; Fashion Design; Fine Arts; Visual Arts); **Foreign Languages** (English; Japanese; Modern Languages); **History and Social Development** (Cultural Studies; Heritage Preservation; History; Museum Studies; Social Sciences; Social Welfare); **Ideological and Political Education** (Political Sciences); **Information Science and Technology** (Automation and Control Engineering; E-Business/Commerce; Information Sciences; Information Technology; Software Engineering); **Literature and Communication** (Advertising and Publicity; Chinese; Communication Studies; Foreign Languages Education; Literature; Radio and Television Broadcasting); **Management** (Administration; Human Resources; Management; Public Administration; Transport Engineering); **Mathematics and Statistics** (Applied Chemistry; Applied Mathematics; Computer Science; Information Sciences; Mathematics; Statistics); **Mechanical and Engineering** (Automation and Control Engineering; Civil Engineering; Industrial Design; Mechanical Engineering; Production Engineering); **Physics and Electronic Engineering** (Electronic Engineering; Information Sciences; Information Technology; Optical Technology; Physics; Telecommunications Engineering); **Sports** (Physical Education; Sports; Sports Management); **Teachers Education** (Educational Administration; Preschool Education; Primary Education; Psychology); **Tourism** (Geography; Geography (Human); Rural Studies; Tourism; Urban Studies)

Conservatory

Music (Dance; Music; Musical Instruments; Musicology)

Further Information: Also South Campus

History: Founded 1958. Acquired present status 2002.

Fees: (Yuan): Tuition fee for Associate degrees in Liberal arts 17,000 per annum; Science, 20,000 per annum; Fine arts and Sports, 22,000 per annum. Tuition fee for Undergraduate degrees in Liberal arts 18,000 per annum; Science, 21,000 per annum; Fine arts and Sports, 24,000 per annum

Main Language(s) of Instruction: Chinese

Degrees and Diplomas: *Xueshi Xuewei*. Also Associate degree and professional training programmes

Student Services: Language Laboratory, Sports Facilities

Student Numbers *2012-2013*: Total: c. 17,800

Last Updated: 15/10/13

TAIYUAN INSTITUTE OF TECHNOLOGY (TIT)

Yingxinjie Street, Taiyuan City, Shanxi Province 030008
Tel: +86(351) 3566078
Fax: +86(351) 3566078
EMail: paulzhangxiaobin@yahoo.com.cn; zhangxiaobinpaul@yahoo.com.cn
Website: http://210.31.100.5/english/

Department

Adult Education (Adult Education); **Advanced Vocational Education** (Vocational Education); **Automation Engineering** (Automation and Control Engineering); **Chemical engineering** (Chemical Engineering); **Computer Science** (Computer Science); **Economical and Law Management** (Economics; Law; Management); **Electronic Engineering** (Electronic Engineering); **Environmental Engineering** (Environmental Engineering); **Financial Management** (Finance); **Foreign Language** (Cultural Studies; English; European Studies; Foreign Languages Education; International Business; Linguistics; Literature; Modern Languages; Tourism); **Materials engineering** (Materials Engineering); **Mechanical Engineering** (Mechanical Engineering); **Science** (Natural Sciences); **Social Sciences** (Social Sciences); **Sports** (Sports)

Degrees and Diplomas: *Xueshi Xuewei*

Last Updated: 16/10/13

TAIYUAN NORMAL UNIVERSITY (TYNU)

189, Nanneihuanjie, Taiyuan, Shanxi Province 030012
Tel: +86(351) 4120436
Fax: +86(351) 4165215 +86(351) 4120436
EMail: abing226@163.com; sdsywsb@public.ty.sx.cn
Website: http://www.tynu.edu.cn/

President: Liang Ji

College

Jiaxi xingerke *(Sino-Canadian Selkirk)* (Applied Linguistics; Chinese; English; Foreign Languages Education; International Business; Tourism); **Urban and Tourism** (Architectural and Environmental Design; Geography; Surveying and Mapping; Tourism; Town Planning)

Department

Basic Education (Teacher Training); **Biology** (Biological and Life Sciences; Biology; Biotechnology); **Chemistry** (Applied Chemistry; Chemistry); **Computer Science** (Computer Engineering; Computer Science); **Dance** (Dance); **Economics** (Economics); **Education** (Education; Educational Psychology; Preschool Education); **Fine Arts** (Design; Fine Arts; Visual Arts); **Foreign Languages** (English); **History** (History); **Liberal Arts** (Chinese; Literature); **Mathematics** (Applied Mathematics; Computer Science; Information Sciences; Mathematics; Mathematics and Computer Science); **Music** (Music; Music Theory and Composition; Musicology); **Physical Education** (Physical Education); **Physics** (Science Education); **Politics** (Law; Political Sciences; Public Administration); **Social Sciences** (Political Sciences; Social Sciences)

Centre

Computer (Computer Science)

History: Founded 1958 as Taiyuan Teachers College. Acquired present title 1999, following merger with Normal College of Shanxi University and Shanxi Educational Institute.

Main Language(s) of Instruction: Chinese

Degrees and Diplomas: *Xueshi Xuewei*

Publications: Taiyuan Normal University (Social Sciences); Taiyuan Normal University (Social Sciences), teaching and management

Academic Staff *2012-2013*: Total 745

STAFF WITH DOCTORATE: Total 76

Student Numbers *2012-2013*: Total 12,527

Distance students, 5022.

Last Updated: 28/01/13

TAIYUAN UNIVERSITY OF SCIENCE AND TECHNOLOGY (TYUST)

138 Waliu Road, Taiyuan, Shanxi Province 030024
Tel: +86(351) 6222521 Ext. 145
Fax: +86(351) 6220233
EMail: fao@tyust.edu.cn
Website: http://www.tyust.edu.cn/

President: Guo Yongyi

International Relations: Chai Yuesheng, Director, Office of International Relations Tel: +86(351) 6998162 EMail: fao@tyust.edu.cn

College

Huake

School

Adult Education; **Applied Science** (Applied Physics; Chemical Engineering; Chemistry; Computer Science; Information Sciences; Mathematics; Mechanics; Physics; Production Engineering); **Chemistry and Bioengineering** (Bioengineering; Chemistry); **Computer Science and Technology** (Computer Science; Information Management; Information Technology); **Economics and Management** (Accountancy; Administration; Business and Commerce; E-Business/Commerce; Economics; Industrial Engineering; Information Management; International Economics; Management; Marketing); **Electronic Information Engineering** (Automation and Control Engineering; Electronic Engineering; Telecommunications Engineering); **Engineering** *(Yun Cheng Campus)* (Automation and Control Engineering; Electrical Engineering; Engineering; Environmental Engineering; Machine Building; Materials Engineering; Measurement and Precision Engineering; Mechanics; Power Engineering); **Material Science and Engineering** (Automation and Control Engineering; Environmental Engineering; Environmental Studies; Materials Engineering; Safety Engineering); **Mechanical and Electronic Engineering** (Electronic Engineering; Machine Building; Mechanical Engineering); **Vocational Education**

Department

Arts; **Foreign Languages** (English; Modern Languages); **Humanity and Social Science** (Arts and Humanities; Social Sciences); **Law** (Law); **Physical Education** (Physical Education)

History: Founded 1952 as Taiyuan Machine Manufacturing School. 1998. Acquired present status and name 2004.

Main Language(s) of Instruction: Chinese

Degrees and Diplomas: *Xueshi Xuewei*; *Shuoshi Xuewei*; *Boshi*

Last Updated: 26/11/12

TAIYUAN UNIVERSITY OF TECHNOLOGY (TUT)

79 West Yingze Street, Taiyuan, Shanxi Province 030024
Tel: +86(305) 6010360
Fax: +86(305) 6041142
EMail: xiaoban@tyut.edu.cn
Website: http://www.tyut.edu.cn

President: Zhang Wendong Tel: +86(351) 6018818

International Relations: Li Jingbao

College

Arts (Administration; Applied Linguistics; Arts and Humanities; Engineering; English; Law; Linguistics; Modern Languages; Political Sciences); **Architecture and Civil Engineering** (Architecture; Bridge Engineering; Civil Engineering; Safety Engineering; Soil Science; Structural Architecture; Town Planning); **Business Administration** (Accountancy; Administration; Business Administration; Economics; Engineering Management; International Business; International Economics; Management; Marketing); **Chemistry and Chemical Engineering** (Applied Chemistry; Biochemistry; Chemical Engineering; Chemistry; Industrial Engineering; Mechanics; Physical Chemistry; Physics; Polymer and Plastics Technology); **Computer Engineering and Software** (Computer Engineering; Software Engineering); **Electrical and Power Engineering** (Automation and Control Engineering; Electrical Engineering; Electronic Engineering; Energy Engineering; Power Engineering; Thermal Engineering); **Environmental Science and Engineering** (Construction Engineering; Environmental Engineering; Environmental Studies; Heating and Refrigeration; Irrigation; Water Management; Water Science); **Fiber Textile and Weaving Arts** (Design; E-Business/Commerce; Industrial Design; Painting and Drawing; Photography; Visual Arts); **Further Education**; **Information Engineering** (Automation and Control Engineering; Electrical Engineering; Electronic Engineering; Information Technology; Telecommunications Engineering); **International Education and Exchange**; **Materials Science and Engineering** (Automation and Control Engineering; Chemistry; Materials Engineering; Metallurgical Engineering; Physics; Polymer and Plastics Technology); **Mechanical Engineering** (Automation and Control Engineering; Automotive Engineering; Electronic Engineering; Industrial Design; Mechanical Engineering); **Mining Engineering** (Computer Science; Environmental Engineering; Information Technology; Mineralogy; Mining Engineering; Natural Resources; Safety Engineering; Surveying and Mapping; Town Planning); **Modern Science and Technology** (Natural Sciences; Technology); **Postgraduate Studies**; **Sciences** (Applied Mathematics; Applied Physics; Biomedical Engineering; Computer Science; Electronic Engineering; Information Sciences; Information Technology; Mathematics; Mathematics and Computer Science; Measurement and Precision Engineering; Mechanics; Optical Technology; Physics); **Sports** (Physical Education; Sports); **Vocational Education** (Vocational Education); **Water Conservancy Science and Engineering** (Agricultural Economics; Electrical Engineering; Hydraulic Engineering; Natural Resources; Water Management; Water Science)

Further Information: Also 6 post-doctorate research centers.

History: Founded as College of Shanxi University 1902. Became independent institute 1953. Acquired present status and title 1984. Incorporated Shanxi Mining College 1997. Under the jurisdiction of the Provincial Government.

Academic Year: September to July (September-January; February-July)

Admission Requirements: Graduation from senior middle school and entrance examination

Main Language(s) of Instruction: Chinese

Degrees and Diplomas: *Xueshi Xuewei*; *Shuoshi Xuewei*; *Boshi*. Also dual-degrees; Master-PhD joint programmes; Post-doctorate programmes.

Publications: Journal of Taiyuan University of Technology

Academic Staff *2011-2012*: Total: c. 2,010
Student Numbers *2011-2012*: Total: c. 26,000
Last Updated: 26/11/12

TAIZHOU UNIVERSITY (TZC)

Economic Exploitation Zone of Linhai, Taizhou, Zhejiang 317000
Tel: +86(576) 5137003 +86(576) 88661988
Fax: +86(576) 5137088
EMail: webmaster@tzc.edu.cn; wsb@tzc.edu.cn
Website: http://www.tzc.edu.cn/

President: Wang Gang Tel: +86(576) 88661960

School

Arts (Fine Arts); **Civil Engineering and Architecture** (Architecture; Civil Engineering); **Economy and Trade Management** (Business Administration; Economics); **Foreign Languages** (English; Modern Languages); **Humanities** (Arts and Humanities); **Life Science** (Biological and Life Sciences); **Mathematics and Information Engineering** (Information Technology; Mathematics); **Mechanical Engineering** (Mechanical Engineering); **Medicine** (Medicine); **Pharmaceutical and Chemical Engineering** (Chemical Engineering; Pharmacology); **Physical Culture** (Physical Education); **Physics and Electronic Engineering** (Electronic Engineering; Physics); **Teachers Education** (Teacher Training)

Department

Adult Education (Adult Education); **Ideological Studies** (Political Sciences)

History: Founded 1907.

Fees: (Yuan): 8,000 per annum for international students; 10,000 per annum for chinese students

Main Language(s) of Instruction: Chinese

Degrees and Diplomas: *Xueshi Xuewei*

Academic Staff *2012-2013*: Total 800
STAFF WITH DOCTORATE: Total 100
Student Numbers *2012-2013*: Total: c. 15,000
Last Updated: 18/10/13

TANGSHAN COLLEGE

Hebei University of West Road No. 9,
Tangshan, Hebei Province 063000
Tel: +86(315) 2792191 +86(315) 2792198 +86(315) 2792199
Fax: +86(315) 2792159
EMail: tsc@tsc.edu.cn
Website: http://www.tsc.edu.cn

Dean: Liu Xuedong (2012-)

Department

Arts (Arts and Humanities); **Civil Engineering** (Civil Engineering); **Computer Science and Information Technology** (Computer Science; Information Technology); **Continuing Education**; **Economics and Management** (Economics; Management); **Electrical Engineering and Mechanical Engineering** (Electrical Engineering; Mechanical Engineering); **Environmental Engineering and Chemical Engineering** (Chemical Engineering; Environmental Engineering); **Foreign Languages** (Chinese; English; Foreign Languages Education; Japanese; Modern Languages); **Grammar** (Grammar); **Information Engineering** (Engineering; Information Technology); **Physical Education** (Physical Education); **Social Sciences** (Social Sciences)

Further Information: 3 campuses in the South, North, East. A traditional and distance learning institution.

History: Founded 1956 as Tangshan Adult College of Technology. Renamed Tangshan City Amateur Institute of Technology 1957. Changed name to the Workers' University in Tangshan City 1988. Acquired present title 1992. Received approval from the Ministry of Education 2002.

Fees: (Yuan) 3,500-7,000 per annum

Main Language(s) of Instruction: Chinese, English

Degrees and Diplomas: *Xueshi Xuewei*

Academic Staff *2011-2012*	**TOTAL**
FULL-TIME	c. **980**
Student Numbers *2011-2012*	
All (Foreign included)	c. **15,740**

Part-time students, 2,400.
Last Updated: 27/11/12

TANGSHAN NORMAL UNIVERSITY (TSNU)

156 Janshebei Road, Tangshan, Hebei Province 063000
Tel: +86(315) 2039727
Fax: +86(315) 2039727
EMail: webmaster@tstc.edu.cn
Website: http://www.tstc.edu.cn

Dean: Fan Yongsheng

Department

Agronomy (Agronomy); **Biological and Life Sciences** (Biology); **Chemistry** (Chemistry); **Chinese Literature** (Chinese; Literature); **Computer Science and Technology** (Computer Engineering; Computer Science); **Economics** (Economics); **Education** (Education); **English** (English); **Fine Arts** (Fine Arts); **Law** (Law); **Management** (Management); **Mathematics and Information Science** (Information Sciences; Mathematics); **Music** (Music); **Physical Education** (Physical Education; Sports); **Physics** (Physics); **Politics and History** (History; Political Sciences); **Social Science** (Social Sciences)

Further Information: Two campuses: Daxuedao Campus and Xueyuanlu Campus.

History: Founded 1956 as Tangshan Speeded-up Teachers Academy College. Acquired present title 2000. Previously known as Tangshan Teachers College.

Main Language(s) of Instruction: Chinese

Degrees and Diplomas: *Zhuanke*; *Xueshi Xuewei*

Publications: Journal of Tangshan Teachers College

Academic Staff *2011-2012*: Total 966
Student Numbers *2011-2012*: Total: c. 16,000
Last Updated: 28/11/12

TARIM UNIVERSITY

Alar, Xinjiang Uygur Province 843300
Tel: +86(997) 4682653 +86(997) 4680609
Fax: +86(997) 4680643
EMail: waheli@taru.edu.cn; scq926@hotmail.com; maming2005@tom.com
Website: http://www.taru.edu.cn/

President: Xinming Li (2002-) Tel: +86(997) 4680601

Vice-President: Heli Wang Tel: +86(997) 4680717

International Relations: Yongzhong Su Tel: +86(997) 4680609

College

Advanced Vocational Training; **Animal Science** (Zoology); **Arts and Humanities** (Arts and Humanities); **Economics and Management** (Economics; Management); **Information Engineering** (Computer Engineering; Information Technology); **Life science** (Biological and Life Sciences); **Mechanic and Electrical Engineering** (Agricultural Engineering; Electrical Engineering; Mechanical Engineering); **Plant Science** (Botany; Crop Production; Horticulture); **Water Conservancy and Architecture Engineering** (Structural Architecture; Water Management)

Further Information: Also 10 research Institutes.

History: Founded 1958 as Tarim University of Agricultural Reclamation. Acquired present title 2004.

Academic Year: September to July (September-January; March-July)

Admission Requirements: Secondary school certificate and entrance examination

Fees: (Yuan): c. 3,000-4,000 per annum

Main Language(s) of Instruction: Chinese

Accrediting Agency: Education Bureau of Government of Xingjiang Uygur Autonomous Region; Ministry of Education

Degrees and Diplomas: *Xueshi Xuewei*; *Shuoshi Xuewei*

Student Services: Academic Counselling, Canteen, Careers Guidance, Cultural Activities, Health Services, Language Laboratory, Nursery Care, Sports Facilities

Publications: Journal of Tarim Agricultural University

Academic Staff *2011-2012*: Total: c. 690
Student Numbers *2011-2012*: Total: c. 13,000
Last Updated: 29/11/12

THE CHINA CONSERVATORY (CCMUSIC)

Deshengmenwai Sizhuyuan, Dewai, Chaoyang District, Beijing 100101
Tel: +86(10) 64874884
Fax: +86(10) 64872695
EMail: zyywb@yahoo.com.cn
Website: http://www.ccmusic.edu.cn/

President: Zhao Talimu

International Relations: Zhao Wen

Department

Arts Administration (Art Management); **Chinese Instruments** (Musical Instruments); **Composition** (Music; Music Theory and Composition); **Conducting** (Conducting); **Music Education** (Music Education); **Musicology** (Musicology); **Orchestral Instrument** (Music; Musical Instruments); **Piano** (Musical Instruments); **Voice and Opera** (Opera; Singing)

History: Founded 1964.

Fees: (Yuan): Undergraduate programmes, 32,000 per annum; Master's Degree programmes, 38,000 per annum; PhD programmes, 42,000 per annum

Main Language(s) of Instruction: Chinese

Degrees and Diplomas: *Xueshi Xuewei*; *Shuoshi Xuewei*: **Musicology.** *Boshi*

Academic Staff *2011-2012*: Total: c. 300
Last Updated: 29/11/12

TIANJIN ACADEMY OF FINE ARTS

No.4 Tianwei Road, Hebei District, Tianjin, Tianjin Province 300141
Tel: +86(22) 26241505
Fax: +86(22) 26241505
EMail: master@tjarts.edu.cn; master@tjarts.edu.cn
Website: http://www.tjarts.edu.cn

President: Jiang Lu

School

Contemporary Art (Communication Arts; Design; Fine Arts; Mass Communication; Multimedia; Painting and Drawing; Photography; Visual Arts); **Design** (Architectural and Environmental Design; Design; Fashion Design; Industrial Design; Visual Arts); **Plastic Art** (Fine Arts; Graphic Arts; Painting and Drawing; Sculpture); **Traditional Chinese Painting** (Graphic Arts; Painting and Drawing; Visual Arts)

Department

Art History and Theory (Art History)

History: Founded 1906 as Normal School, acquired present status and title 1980.

Main Language(s) of Instruction: Chinese

Degrees and Diplomas: *Xueshi Xuewei*; *Shuoshi Xuewei*

Academic Staff *2011-2012*	**TOTAL**
FULL-TIME	c. **200**
Student Numbers *2011-2012*	
All (Foreign included)	c. **3,650**
FOREIGN ONLY	**30**

Last Updated: 29/11/12

TIANJIN AGRICULTURAL UNIVERSITY (TJAU)

No.22, Jinjing Street, Xiqing District, Tianjin, Tianjin Province 300384
Tel: +86(22) 23781315
Fax: +86(22) 23781315
EMail: yuanzhang@tjau.edu.cn; waishiyong@yahoo.cn
Website: http://www.tjau.edu.cn/

Dean: Xing Kezhi

Faculty

Arts and Humanities (Accountancy; Arts and Humanities; English; Human Resources; International Business; International Economics; Marketing; Tourism)

College

Vocational Studies

Department

Adult Education; **Agronomy** (Agricultural Management; Agriculture; Agronomy; Animal Husbandry; Forest Economics; Forest Management; Forestry; Genetics; Plant and Crop Protection; Veterinary Science); **Basic Science** (Applied Chemistry; Bioengineering; Biological and Life Sciences; Chemistry; English; Environmental Studies; Mathematics; Natural Sciences; Physics); **Computer Science** (Computer Science; Information Management; Information Sciences; Information Technology; Software Engineering); **Electrical and Mechanical Engineering** (Agricultural Engineering; Agricultural Equipment; Electrical Engineering; Measurement and Precision Engineering; Mechanical Engineering); **Fishery** (Aquaculture; Fishery); **Food Science** (Food Science; Food Technology; Safety Engineering); **Horticulture** (Horticulture; Landscape Architecture); **Hydraulic Engineering** (Hydraulic Engineering; Water Management; Water Science); **Physical Education** (Physical Education; Sports)

History: Founded 1976 in in Wuqing County. Moved to current location 1985. Incorporated with Urban and Rural Economy School of Tianjin 2002.

Fees: (Yuan): Undergraduate tuition fee, 14,000 per annum; Master's degree tuition fee, 18,000 per annum

Main Language(s) of Instruction: Chinese

Degrees and Diplomas: *Xueshi Xuewei*; *Shuoshi Xuewei*

Student Services: Sports Facilities

Academic Staff *2011-2012*	**TOTAL**
FULL-TIME	**590**
PART-TIME	c. **100**
Student Numbers *2011-2012*	
All (Foreign included)	c. **11,000**

Last Updated: 29/11/12

TIANJIN FOREIGN STUDIES UNIVERSITY (TFSU)

No.117, MaChang Road, HeXi District, Tianjin, Tianjin Province 300204
Tel: +86(22) 23280875
Fax: +86(22) 23282410
EMail: foreignexperts@tjfsu.edu.cn; foreignstudents@tjfsu.edu.cn
Website: http://www.tjfsu.edu.cn

President: Xiu Gang

International Relations: Zhang Jintong

School

Educational Technology and Information (Computer Networks; Educational Technology; Information Technology; Multimedia); **International Exchange** *(SIE)* (Applied Linguistics; Chinese; Linguistics; Literature; Phonetics); **Law** (International Law; Law)

Department

Asian and African Studies (African Studies; Arabic; Asian Studies; Korean; Swahili; Translation and Interpretation); **Athletics and Physical Education** (Physical Education; Sports); **Chinese Culture and Communications** (Advertising and Publicity; Chinese; Communication Studies; Cultural Studies; Journalism; Linguistics; Literature; Mass Communication); **Continuing Education**; **English Studies** (English; English Studies); **European Studies** (European Studies; French; German; Italian; Portuguese; Russian; Spanish); **Graduate Studies** (Applied Linguistics; Arabic; Chinese; Comparative Literature; Economics; English; French; German; International Economics; Italian; Japanese; Korean; Linguistics; Literature; Management; Modern Languages; Philology; Philosophy; Political Sciences; Portuguese; Russian; Spanish; Translation and Interpretation); **International Business** (Accountancy; Computer Networks; E-Business/Commerce; Economics; Finance; Human Resources; International Business; International Economics; Management; Marketing); **Japanese** (Asian Studies; Japanese); **Requisite Courses** (Arts and Humanities; Computer Science; English; French; German; Japanese; Mathematics; Psychology)

Centre

Foreign Languages Education (English; Foreign Languages Education)

History: Founded 1974 though merger of the Tianjin Foreign Languages School and Tianjin Teachers' College (today known as Tianjin Normal University).

Fees: (Yuan): Undergraduate tuition fees, 14,600 per annum; Postgraduate tuition fees, 18,600 per annum

Main Language(s) of Instruction: Chinese

Degrees and Diplomas: *Xueshi Xuewei*; *Shuoshi Xuewei*

Student Services: Sports Facilities

Publications: Journal of Tianjin Foreign Studies University; World Culture

Student Numbers *2011-2012*: Total: c. 10,000
Last Updated: 29/11/12

TIANJIN INSTITUTE OF URBAN CONSTRUCTION (TJUCI)

Xiqing District, Tianjin, Tianjin Province 300384
Tel: +86(22) 23792015
EMail: zyz@tjuci.edu.cn; president@tjuci.edu.cn
Website: http://www.tjuci.edu.cn/

President: Zhong Xian

Faculty

Science (Natural Sciences)

Unit
Sports (Sports)

College
Adult Education (Adult Education); **Arts**; **Foreign Languages** (English; Modern Languages)

School
Architecture (Architecture); **Civil Engineering** (Civil Engineering); **Computer and Information Engineering** (Computer Engineering; Information Technology); **Economics and Management** (Economics; Management); **Energy and Safety Engineering** (Energy Engineering; Safety Engineering); **Environmental and Municipal Engineering** (Environmental Engineering); **Materials Science and Engineering** (Materials Engineering); **Mechanical Engineering** (Mechanical Engineering)

Department
Social Sciences (Social Sciences)

Institute
Geology, Surveying and Mapping (Geology; Surveying and Mapping)

History: Founded 1978. Acquired present status and title 1987.

Main Language(s) of Instruction: Chinese

Degrees and Diplomas: *Xueshi Xuewei*; *Shuoshi Xuewei*

Academic Staff *2011-2012*: Total 862

STAFF WITH DOCTORATE: Total 208

Student Numbers *2011-2012*: Total 14,142

Last Updated: 30/11/12

TIANJIN MEDICAL UNIVERSITY (TMU)

22 Qixiangtai Road, Heping District,
Tianjin, Tianjin Province 300070
Tel: +86(22) 83336577
Fax: +86(22) 23542584
EMail: jwc@tijmu.edu.cn
Website: http://www.tijmu.edu.cn

President: Yongfeng Shang
Tel: +86(22) 23542688 EMail: hxs@tijmu.edu.cn

Vice-President: Wenging Zhang
Tel: +86(22) 23542588 EMail: zllf@tijmu.edu.cn

International Relations: Fenglin Guo, +86(22) 23542584
EMail: fenglin417@hotmail.com

Unit
Laboratory Animal Science (Laboratory Techniques; Zoology)

College
Basic Medical Studies (Medicine); **First Clinical Medical Studies** (Medicine); **Humanities** *(Medical)* (Arts and Humanities; English); **Integrative Medicine** *(International)* (Medicine); **Medical Laboratory** (Laboratory Techniques; Medical Technology); **Nursing** (Nursing); **Pharmacy** (Pharmacy); **Second Clinical Medical Studies** (Medicine)

School
Biomedical Engineering (Biomedical Engineering); **Clinical Medicine** (Medicine); **Continuing Education**; **Medical Imaging** (Medical Technology); **Public Health** (Public Health); **Stomatology**

Department
Rehabilitation and Sports Medicine (Rehabilitation and Therapy; Sports Medicine)

Institute
Medical English and Health Institute of Media (English; Health Sciences; Media Studies)

Centre
Basic Medical Experimental Teaching (Medicine); **Preventive Medicine Experimental Teaching** (Health Education; Social and Preventive Medicine)

Further Information: Also university hospitals; 13 non-immediate Clinical Colleges; 1 non-affiliated hospital; 9 teaching hospitals with (more than 15,000 beds capacity).

History: Founded 1951 as Tianjin Medical College. Merged with Tianjin Second Medical College and acquired present title 1993.

Academic Year: September to July

Admission Requirements: Graduation from high School

Fees: (US Dollars): 2,500-4,000 per annum

Main Language(s) of Instruction: Chinese, English, Japanese

Accrediting Agency: Tianjin Educational Committee

Degrees and Diplomas: *Xueshi Xuewei*; *Shuoshi Xuewei*; *Boshi*

Student Services: Academic Counselling, Canteen, Careers Guidance, Cultural Activities, Foreign Studies Centre, Health Services, Language Laboratory, Nursery Care, Social Counselling, Sports Facilities

Publications: Chinese Journal of Clinical Oncology; Foreign Medicine-Endocrinology; Journal of Tianjin Medical College; Medical Education Research of Foreign Countries

Publishing House: Tianjin University Publishing House

Academic Staff *2011-2012*: Total 8,445

Student Numbers *2011-2012*: Total 9,868

Last Updated: 30/11/12

TIANJIN MUSIC CONSERVATORY (TCM)

57 Eleventh Longitude Road, Hedong District,
Tianjin, Tianjin Province 300171
Tel: +86-22-24160049 +86-22-24133176
Fax: +86-22-24319205
EMail: hny@tjcm.edu.cn
Website: http://www.tjcm.edu.cn

Dean: Xu Changjun

International Relations: Huina Yang

Department
Accordion (Musical Instruments); **Art Management** (Art Management); **Composer** (Music Theory and Composition); **Contemporary Music** (Music); **Dance** (Dance); **Film and Television** (Cinema and Television; Film); **Folk Music** (Jazz and Popular Music; Music); **Keyboard** (Musical Instruments); **Music Education** (Music Education); **Musicology** (Musicology); **Orchestral Music** (Music); **Piano** (Musical Instruments); **Theatre** (Theatre); **Vocal Music** (Singing)

History: Founded 1958 as Central Conservatory of Music.

Fees: (US Dollars): Tuition, 3,700-5,000 per annum; research and scholar, 600 per month

Main Language(s) of Instruction: Chinese

Degrees and Diplomas: *Xueshi Xuewei*; *Shuoshi Xuewei*

Student Services: Canteen, Health Services, Sports Facilities

Academic Staff *2011-2012*	**TOTAL**
FULL-TIME	**406**
Student Numbers *2011-2012*	
All (Foreign included)	**3,214**
FOREIGN ONLY	**15**

Last Updated: 30/11/12

TIANJIN NORMAL UNIVERSITY (TJNU)

393 Xiqing Binshui Road, Tianjin, Tianjin Province 300387
Tel: +86(22) 23766666
Fax: +86(22) 23514100
EMail: fatru@public.tpt.tj.cn
Website: http://www.tjnu.edu.cn

President: Gao Yubao (1996-)
Tel: +86(22) 23542443 EMail: tigao@mail.tjnu.edu.cn

International Relations: Zhongying Hua, Director, International Relations Office Tel: +86(22) 23540665

College
Chemistry (Analytical Chemistry; Astrophysics; Biology; Chemistry; Geography (Human); Inorganic Chemistry; Organic Chemistry; Physical Chemistry); **Computer and Information Engineering** (Computer Engineering; Computer Science; Information Technology; Surveying and Mapping); **Education and Science**

(Curriculum; Education; Educational Psychology; Foreign Languages Education; Humanities and Social Science Education; Pedagogy; Physical Education; Preschool Education; Primary Education; Science Education); **Elementary Education** (Primary Education); **Foreign Languages** (English; French; Japanese; Korean; Modern Languages; Russian; Translation and Interpretation); **Liberal Arts** (Applied Linguistics; Arts and Humanities; Chinese; Comparative Literature; Linguistics; Literature); **Physics and Electronic Information** (Applied Physics; Atomic and Molecular Physics; Electronic Engineering; Information Sciences; Information Technology; Optics; Physics); **Sports Science** (Physical Education; Sports); **Urban and Environmental Science** (Computer Science; Ecology; Environmental Studies; Geography; Information Sciences; Town Planning; Urban Studies)

School

Art and Design (Design; Fine Arts; Painting and Drawing); **Economics** (Economics; International Business; International Economics); **Journalism and Communication** (Advertising and Publicity; Journalism; Mass Communication; Photography; Radio and Television Broadcasting); **Law** (Administrative Law; Civil Law; Commercial Law; Constitutional Law; History of Law; Law); **Life Sciences** (Biological and Life Sciences; Biology; Biotechnology; Botany; Cell Biology; Genetics; Zoology); **Management** (Accountancy; Business Administration; Information Management; Information Sciences; Management; Transport Management); **Marxism** (Political Sciences); **Mathematical Sciences** (Applied Mathematics; Computer Science; Information Sciences; Mathematics; Mathematics and Computer Science; Operations Research; Statistics); **Music and Film** (Dance; Film; Literature; Music; Music Education; Musical Instruments; Musicology; Theatre); **Politics and Administration** (Administration; Political Sciences; Social Work); **Software Engineering** (Software Engineering)

Institute

History and Culture (Cultural Studies; History; Library Science; Museum Studies; Tourism)

Further Information: 5 post-doctoral research stations.

History: Founded 1958 as Tianjin Teachers' College, acquired present title 1982. Merged with Tianjin Teachers College 1999.

Academic Year: September to July (September-January; March-July)

Admission Requirements: Graduation from senior middle school and entrance examination

Fees: (US Dollars): Foreign students (language learning) c.1,400

Main Language(s) of Instruction: Chinese

Accrediting Agency: Education Commission of Tanjin Municipal City

Degrees and Diplomas: *Xueshi Xuewei*; *Shuoshi Xuewei*; *Boshi*

Publications: Journal of Tianjin Normal University; Juvenile Heart of the World; Mathematics Education; Political History of Ideas Journals; Psychological and Behavioral Research; School Mathematics; Youth Science and Technology Expo

Academic Staff *2011-2012*	**TOTAL**
FULL-TIME	**1,381**
PART-TIME	**948**
Student Numbers *2011-2012*	
All (Foreign included)	**28,545**
FOREIGN ONLY	**2780**

Last Updated: 30/11/12

TIANJIN OPEN UNIVERSITY (TJRTVU)

1, Yingshui Road, Nankai District, Tianjin,
Tianjin Province 300191
Tel: +86(22) 23679931 +86(22) 23679972
Fax: +86(22) 23679972
EMail: tjrtvuxb@tjrtvu.edu.cn; xiaozhang@tjrtvu.edu.cn
Website: http://www.tjrtvu.edu.cn

President: Feng Xue-fei

College

Agricultural Education (Agricultural Education); **Binhai**; **Life Sciences** *(Vocational)* (Biological and Life Sciences)

School

Economics and Management (Economics; Management)

Department

Arts and Law (Arts and Humanities; Law; Natural Sciences)

Institute

Foreign Languages; **Technology** (Technology); **Training**

Centre

Educational Technology (Educational Technology); **Remote Public Education Service** *(Educational Institute for Individuals with Disabilities)* (Special Education)

Further Information: An open and distance higher education institution. Also 62 Study Centres (18 in communities, 40 in enterprises and institutions, and 4 in forms of organizations).

History: Founded 1958 as the Tianjin Hongzhuan Broadcast Correspondence University. Acquired present title 1979. Formerly known as Tianjin Radio and Television University.

Academic Year: September to July

Admission Requirements: Graduation from senior middle school and entrance examination.

Main Language(s) of Instruction: Chinese, English

Degrees and Diplomas: *Zhuanke*; *Xueshi Xuewei*. Also non-certificate training.

Academic Staff *2011-2012*	**TOTAL**
FULL-TIME	**381**
PART-TIME	**c. 2,449**
Student Numbers *2011-2012*	
All (Foreign included)	**c. 60,000**

Distance students, 49000.

Last Updated: 30/11/12

TIANJIN POLYTECHNIC UNIVERSITY (TJPU)

No. 399, Binshui Road, Xiqing District,
Tianjin, Tianjin Province 300387
Tel: +86(22) 24528077
Fax: +86(22) 24528001
EMail: xwzx@tjpu.edu.cn
Website: http://www.tjpu.edu.cn

President: Yang Qing

Faculty

Science (Natural Sciences); **Textile** (Textile Technology)

College

Computer Science and Software Engineering (Automation and Control Engineering; Computer Engineering; Computer Science; Software Engineering); **Electrical Engineering and Automation** (Automation and Control Engineering; Electrical and Electronic Engineering); **Electronic and Information Engineering** (Electronic Engineering; Information Technology); **Environmental and Chemical Engineering** (Chemical Engineering; Environmental Engineering); **Foreign Languages** (English; Foreign Languages Education; Japanese); **Humanities and Law** (Journalism; Law; Radio and Television Broadcasting); **Materials Science and Engineering** (Engineering; Materials Engineering)

School

Economics (Economics; International Business; International Economics); **Management** (Industrial Engineering; Industrial Management; Information Sciences; Management; Public Administration); **Mechanical Engineering** (Mechanical Engineering)

Institute

Art and Clothing (Advertising and Publicity; Clothing and Sewing; Design; Fashion Design); **International Education**; **Technology** *(School of Continuing Education)* (Technology)

History: Founded 1952 as Hebei Textile Industrial School. Renamed Tianjin Institute of Textile Science and Technology 1958. Acquired present title 2000.

Main Language(s) of Instruction: Chinese

Degrees and Diplomas: *Xueshi Xuewei*; *Shuoshi Xuewei*; *Boshi*. Also Post-doctoral Programmes; Vocational Education Programmes; MBA.

Publications: Journal

Academic Staff *2011-2012*	**TOTAL**
FULL-TIME	c. **1,600**
Student Numbers *2011-2012*	
All (Foreign included)	c. **28,000**
FOREIGN ONLY	**300**

Last Updated: 30/11/12

TIANJIN TIANSHI COLLEGE

Yuanquan Road, Wuqing Development Area, Tianjin 301700
Tel: +86(22) 82112575 +86(22) 82136328
Fax: +86(22) 82136328
EMail: tsbgs@tianshi.edu.cn
Website: http://www.tianshi.edu.cn/

President: Zhu Shihe (2008-) Tel: +86(22) 82122014

College

Arts and Design (Design; Fine Arts); **Biological Engineering** (Bioengineering; Dairy; Food Science; Food Technology; Meat and Poultry; Nursing; Safety Engineering); **Business** (Business Administration; International Business; Marketing); **Economics and Management** (Business Administration; E-Business/Commerce; Economics; Finance; Human Resources; Insurance; Management; Marketing; Social Welfare); **Foreign Languages** (English; Foreign Languages Education; Modern Languages); **Information and Automation** (Automation and Control Engineering; Computer Engineering; Computer Science; Electronic Engineering; Information Sciences; Information Technology; Telecommunications Engineering)

Department

Continuing Education; **Public Basic Courses** (Engineering; Mathematics; Military Science; Physics; Political Sciences; Psychiatry and Mental Health); **Sports** (Sports)

History: Tiens Vocational and Technical College. Acquired present status and title 2008.

Main Language(s) of Instruction: Chinese

Degrees and Diplomas: *Xueshi Xuewei*

Last Updated: 25/10/13

TIANJIN UNIVERSITY (TU)

92 Weijin Road, Nankai District, Tianjin, Tianjin Province 300072
Tel: +86(22) 27405474 +86(22) 27406146
Fax: +86(22) 27401819
EMail: ies@tju.edu.cn
Website: http://www.tju.edu.cn

President: Li Jiajun (2011-) Tel: +86(22) 27403536

International Relations: Fuling Yang, Director, International Cooperation Tel: +86(22) 27405475 EMail: fuling_yang@tju.edu.cn

College

Management and Economics (Accountancy; Business Administration; Economics; Engineering Management; Finance; Health Administration; Industrial Engineering; Information Management; Information Sciences; Management; Public Administration; Real Estate; Statistics; Tourism; Welfare and Protective Services); **Qiushi**; **Renai**

School

Architecture (Architecture); **Chemical Engineering** (Chemical Engineering); **Civil Engineering** (Bridge Engineering; Civil Engineering; Construction Engineering; Hydraulic Engineering; Marine Engineering; Marine Transport; Naval Architecture; Power Engineering; Transport Management); **Computer Science and Technology** (Computer Science; Information Technology); **Computer Software** (Computer Engineering; Software Engineering); **Continuing Education**; **Distance Education**; **Education** (Education); **Electrical Engineering and Automation** (Automation and Control Engineering; Electrical Engineering); **Electronic Information Engineering** (Electronic Engineering; Information Technology; Telecommunications Engineering); **Environmental Science and Engineering** (Building Technologies; Environmental Engineering; Environmental Studies); **International Education** (Chinese; Foreign Languages Education; Native Language); **Liberal Arts and Law** (Applied Linguistics; Arts and Humanities; Chinese; English; Japanese; Law; Linguistics; Modern Languages; Translation and Interpretation); **Marxism** (Political Sciences); **Materials Science and Engineering** (Materials Engineering); **Mechanical Engineering** (Automation and Control Engineering; Energy Engineering; Industrial Design; Mechanical Engineering; Mechanics; Power Engineering; Thermal Engineering); **Pharmaceutical Science and Technology** (Cell Biology; Chemistry; Computer Science; Medical Technology; Molecular Biology; Pharmacology; Pharmacy; Traditional Eastern Medicine); **Precision Instrument and Optoelectronics Engineering** (Biomedical Engineering; Electronic Engineering; Information Technology; Measurement and Precision Engineering; Optical Technology); **Sciences** (Chemistry; Geography; Mathematics; Natural Sciences; Physics)

Centre

Industrialization of Crystallization Technology *(Municipal Engineering Center)* (Technology); **Integrated Circuit and Computing System** *(Municipal Engineering Center)* (Computer Science); **Micro-nano Manufacturing Technology** *(Municipal Engineering Center)* (Nanotechnology); **Rapid Prototyping Engineering** *(Municipal Engineering Center)* (Engineering)

Research Centre

Chemical Filling Tower and Tower Internal *(State Key Center for Research and Promotion of Scientific and Technology Achievement)* (Chemistry); **Composite and Functional Materials** *(Engineering Research Center of the Ministry of Education)* (Materials Engineering); **Fermentation Technology** *(State Engineering Research Center)* (Technology); **Green Refining Process** *(Engineering Research Center of the Ministry of Education)*; **Hydraulic Engineering Simulation and Safety Monitoring** *(Engineering Research Center of the Ministry of Education)* (Hydraulic Engineering; Safety Engineering); **Industrial Crystallization** *(State Key Center for Research and Promotion of Scientific and Technology Achievement)* (Industrial Engineering); **Industrialization of Crystallization Technology** *(State Engineering Technology Research Center)* (Technology); **Light-duty Power Machine** *(Engineering Research Center of the Ministry of Education)* (Power Engineering); **Micro-nano Manufacturing and Measuring Technology** *(Engineering Research Center of the Ministry of Education)* (Measurement and Precision Engineering; Nanotechnology); **Rectification Technology** *(State Engineering Research Center)* (Technology); **State Engineering Technology**

History: Founded 1895 as Peiyang University. Merged with Hebei Technical College and acquired present title 1951.

Academic Year: September to July (September-January; February-July)

Admission Requirements: Graduation from senior middle school and national entrance examination

Fees: (Yuan): 4,200

Main Language(s) of Instruction: Chinese

Accrediting Agency: Ministry of Education

Degrees and Diplomas: *Xueshi Xuewei*; *Shuoshi Xuewei*; *Boshi*. Also MBA; Executive MBA (EMBA); Post-doctoral Research Programmes.

Student Services: Academic Counselling, Canteen, Careers Guidance, Cultural Activities, Foreign Studies Centre, Health Services, Language Laboratory, Nursery Care, Social Counselling, Sports Facilities

Publications: Collection of Research Papers; Journal

Publishing House: Tianjin University Publishing House

Academic Staff *2012-2013*: Total 4,390

Student Numbers *2012-2013*: Total 28,710

Last Updated: 03/12/12

TIANJIN UNIVERSITY OF COMMERCE (TUC)

East Entrance of Jinba Road, Beichen District,
Tianjin, Tianjin Province 300134
Tel: +86(22) 26686228
Fax: +86(22) 26653169
EMail: wl@tjcu.edu.cn
Website: http://www.tjcu.edu.cn

President: Liu Shuhan

College
Business (Business Administration); **Marxism** (Political Sciences)
School
Adult Education; **Arts** (Art Management; Design; Fine Arts; Industrial Design; Painting and Drawing; Visual Arts); **Biochemistry and Food Technology** (Bioengineering; Food Science; Food Technology); **Economics and Trade** (Banking; Economics; Finance; Industrial and Production Economics; International Business; Laboratory Techniques; Political Sciences; Social Welfare; Taxation; Transport and Communications; Transport Management); **Foreign Languages** (Economics; English; International Business; Japanese; Linguistics; Modern Languages; Translation and Interpretation); **Information Engineering** (Engineering; Information Technology); **International Education** (Chinese; Cooking and Catering; Cultural Studies; Economics; History; International Business); **Law** (Law); **Mechanical Engineering** (Construction Engineering; Design; Heating and Refrigeration; Industrial Design; Mechanical Engineering; Packaging Technology); **Science** (Applied Mathematics; Mathematics; Multimedia; Natural Sciences)

History: Founded 1984.

Academic Year: September to July (September-January; February-July)

Admission Requirements: Graduation from high school and entrance examination

Main Language(s) of Instruction: Chinese

Accrediting Agency: Ministry of Commerce; Provincial Government

Degrees and Diplomas: *Zhuanke*; *Xueshi Xuewei*; *Shuoshi Xuewei*

Publications: Journal of Tianjin University of Commerce

Publishing House: Tianjin University of Commerce Printing House

Last Updated: 04/12/12

TIANJIN UNIVERSITY OF FINANCE AND ECONOMICS (TJUFE)

25 Zhujiang Road, Hexi District, Tianjin, Tianjin Province 300222
Tel: +86(22) 28178279
Fax: +86(22) 28340028
EMail: nic@tjufe.edu.cn; tjcjsyws@public.tpt.tj.cn; liuxue@tjufe.edu.cn; network@tjufe.edu.cn
Website: http://www.tjufe.edu.cn

Principal: Zhang Jiaxing

International Relations: Zhan Min

College
Adult Education; **Humanities** (Applied Linguistics; Arts and Humanities; Chinese; Comparative Literature; English; International Business; Japanese; Literature; Modern Languages; Translation and Interpretation)

School
Business (Accountancy; Business Administration; Engineering Management; Information Management; Information Sciences; Management; Marketing; Tourism); **Economics** (Economics; Finance; International Business; International Economics); **Graduate Studies** (Accountancy; Law; Public Administration); **Law** (Civil Law; Commercial Law; Law)

Department
Modern Finance (Finance); **Sports Training** (Physical Education; Sports)

Institute
International Education; **Modern Economics and Management** (Economics; Management; Real Estate); **Technology** (Information Sciences; Information Technology; Mathematics; Statistics; Technology)

Academy
Arts (Architectural and Environmental Design; Design; Fine Arts; Visual Arts)

Centre
Customs Training (Taxation); **MBA Education** (Business Administration; International Business)

History: Founded 1958 as Hebei College of Finance and Economics. Renamed Tianjin College of Finance and Economics 1971. Acquired present title 2004.

Main Language(s) of Instruction: Chinese

Degrees and Diplomas: *Xueshi Xuewei*; *Shuoshi Xuewei*; *Boshi*. Also MBA; Post-doctoral programmes.

Publications: International Economics and Management; Modern Finance and Economics

Academic Staff *2011-2012*	**TOTAL**
FULL-TIME	**800**
STAFF WITH DOCTORATE	
FULL-TIME	**c. 440**
Student Numbers *2011-2012*	
All (Foreign included)	**c. 17,000**
FOREIGN ONLY	**500**

Part-time students, 5,000.

Last Updated: 04/12/12

TIANJIN UNIVERSITY OF SCIENCE AND TECHNOLOGY (TUST)

1038 Dagu Nanlu, Hexi District, Tianjin, Tianjin Province 300222
Tel: +86(22) 60273318
Fax: +86(22) 60273235 +86(22) 60273051
EMail: gjch@tust.edu.cn
Website: http://www.tust.edu.cn

President: Cao Xiaohong

College
International Studies

School
Art Design *(SAD)* (Design; Fine Arts); **Biological Engineering** *(SBE)* (Bioengineering); **Computer Science and Information Engineering** *(SCSIE)* (Computer Engineering; Computer Science; Information Technology); **Economics and Management** *(SEM)* (Economics; International Business; Management); **Electronic Automation** *(SEA)* (Automation and Control Engineering; Electronic Engineering); **Food Engineering and Biological Technology** *(SFEBT)* (Biotechnology; Food Science); **Foreign Languages** *(SFL)* (Modern Languages); **Futher Education**; **Law and Politics** *(SLP)* (Law; Political Sciences); **Material Science and Chemical Engineering** *(SMSCE)* (Chemical Engineering; Materials Engineering); **Ocean Science and Engineering** *(SOSE)* (Marine Engineering; Marine Science and Oceanography); **Packaging and Printing Engineering** *(SPPE)* (Packaging Technology; Printing and Printmaking); **Science** (Natural Sciences)

Further Information: Also Tianjin Economic and Technological Development Area (TEDA) campus; 2 mobile post-doctoral centres.

History: Founded 1958 as Tianjin Institute of Light Industry, acquired present title 2002.

Main Language(s) of Instruction: Chinese

Degrees and Diplomas: *Xueshi Xuewei*; *Shuoshi Xuewei*; *Boshi*

Publications: China Light Industrial Education; Journal of Tianjin Institute of Light Industry

Academic Staff *2011-2012*: Total: c. 1,750

Student Numbers *2011-2012*: Total: c. 17,000

Last Updated: 04/12/12

TIANJIN UNIVERSITY OF SPORT (TJUS)

51 South Weijin Road, Hexi District, Tianjin, Tianjin Province 300381
Tel: +86(22) 23012186
Fax: +86(22) 23383503
EMail: office@tjus.edu.cn
Website: http://www.tjipe.edu.cn

Dean: Yao Jia-Xin
Tel: +86(22) 23012788 EMail: yaojiaxin1956@yahoo.com.cn

International Relations: Li Shunzhang

Division
Graduate Studies

College
Vocational and Technical Studies

School
Continuing Education

Department
Health and Exercise Science (Health Sciences; Physical Therapy; Rehabilitation and Therapy; Sports Medicine); **Ideological and Political Theory Teaching** (Political Sciences); **Martial Arts** (Sports); **Physical Education and Training** (Physical Education); **Physical Education and Training II** (Physical Education); **Physical Education and Training III** (Physical Education); **Social Sports Management** (Social Welfare; Sports Management); **Sports and Arts** (Sports); **Sports Culture and Media** (Cultural Studies; Media Studies)

History: Founded 1958 as Tianjin Institute of Physical Education.

Main Language(s) of Instruction: Chinese

Degrees and Diplomas: *Xueshi Xuewei*; *Shuoshi Xuewei*; *Boshi*

Student Services: Sports Facilities

Academic Staff *2011-2012*	TOTAL
FULL-TIME	287
PART-TIME	161
STAFF WITH DOCTORATE	
FULL-TIME	c. 60
Student Numbers *2011-2012*	
All (Foreign included)	c. 6,000

Last Updated: 04/12/12

TIANJIN UNIVERSITY OF TECHNOLOGY (TUT)

263 Hongqinan Road, Nankai District,
Tianjin, Tianjin Province 300191
Tel: +86(22) 23679459
Fax: +86(22) 23369449
EMail: cie@tjut.edu.cn; gjjyxy@eyou.com
Website: http://www.tjut.edu.cn

President: Jianbiao Ma
Tel: +86(22) 23679638 EMail: jbg@tjut.edu.cn

Dean: Jingmin Li Tel: +86(22) 23679472 EMail: cie@tjut.edu.cn

International Relations: Hongxiang Cui
Tel: +86(22) 23679458 EMail: jgj@tjut.edu.cn

College
International Business and Technology (Business Administration; International Business; Technology; Transport Engineering); **International Education** *(CIE)* (Arts and Humanities; Chinese; Engineering; Law; Literature; Management; Natural Sciences); **Science** (Applied Mathematics; Applied Physics; Mathematics; Natural Sciences; Optics; Physics); **Technical Education for the Deaf** *(Technical)* (Computer Science; Design; Technology)

School
Chemistry and Chemical Engineering (Applied Chemistry; Biology; Biotechnology; Chemical Engineering; Engineering; Pharmacy); **Computer Science and Technology** (Computer Engineering; Computer Graphics; Computer Networks; Computer Science; Data Processing; Information Sciences; Information Technology; Safety Engineering; Software Engineering; Technology); **Electrical Engineering** (Artificial Intelligence; Automation and Control Engineering; Computer Networks; Electrical and Electronic Engineering; Electrical Engineering; Energy Engineering; Measurement and Precision Engineering; Power Engineering; Thermal Engineering); **Electronic Information Engineering** (Electronic Engineering; Engineering; Information Sciences; Information Technology; Microelectronics; Optical Technology; Optics; Solid State Physics; Telecommunications Engineering); **Environmental Science and Safety Engineering** (Environmental Engineering; Environmental Studies; Natural Resources; Rural Planning; Safety Engineering; Town Planning); **Fine Arts** (Architectural and Environmental Design; Communication Arts; Design; Fine Arts; Industrial Design; Photography; Visual Arts); **Foreign Languages** (Applied Linguistics; English; Japanese; Linguistics; Literature; Modern Languages); **Law and Politics** (Chinese; Economics; Educational Administration; Law; Literature; Political Sciences; Social Work; Sociology); **Management** (Advertising and Publicity; Business Administration; Economics; Engineering Management; Industrial Design; Information Management; Information Sciences; Insurance; Management; Transport Management); **Material Science and Engineering** (Automation and Control Engineering; Chemistry; Materials Engineering; Nanotechnology; Physics); **Mechanical Engineering** (Automation and Control Engineering; Electronic Engineering; Industrial Design; Mechanical Engineering); **Transportation** (Marine Engineering; Transport Engineering; Transport Management)

Research Centre
Nanometer Technology (Materials Engineering; Nanotechnology)

Research Institute
Physical Material (Materials Engineering; Physics)

History: Founded 1981 as Branch School of Tianjin University.

Degrees and Diplomas: *Xueshi Xuewei*; *Shuoshi Xuewei*

Student Services: Sports Facilities

Publications: Academic Journal of Technology; VIP Scientific Journal

Academic Staff *2011-2012*: Total: c. 990

Student Numbers *2011-2012*: Total: c. 16,050

Last Updated: 04/12/12

TIANJIN UNIVERSITY OF TECHNOLOGY AND EDUCATION (TUTE)

No.1310, Dagu South Road, Hexi District, Tianjin 300222
Tel: +86(22) 88181500 +86(22) 88181558
Fax: +86(22) 28116956
EMail: tute28113787@gmail.com
Website: http://www.tute.edu.cn/

President: Meng Qiangguo

College
International Studies *(For International Students)* (Accountancy; Adult Education; Applied Mathematics; Applied Physics; Automation and Control Engineering; Automotive Engineering; Computer Engineering; Computer Networks; Computer Science; Curriculum; Design; E-Business/Commerce; Education; Educational Technology; Electrical Engineering; Electronic Engineering; English; Finance; Fine Arts; Higher Education; History; Human Resources; Industrial Design; Information Sciences; Information Technology; Instrument Making; Machine Building; Maintenance Technology; Management; Materials Engineering; Mathematics; Mathematics and Computer Science; Measurement and Precision Engineering; Mechanical Engineering; Media Studies; Microelectronics; Operations Research; Pedagogy; Preschool Education; Production Engineering; Psychology; Railway Engineering; Social Welfare; Software Engineering; Special Education; Statistics; Technology Education; Telecommunications Engineering; Transport and Communications; Transport Management; Visual Arts; Vocational Education)

School
Art (Design; Fine Arts; Visual Arts); **Automation and Electrical Engineering** (Automation and Control Engineering; Electrical Engineering; Measurement and Precision Engineering); **Automotive and Transportation** (Automotive Engineering; Maintenance Technology; Telecommunications Engineering; Transport Engineering); **Economics and Management** (Accountancy; E-Business/Commerce; Economics; Finance; Human Resources; Management; Social Welfare; Statistics; Transport Management); **Electronic Engineering** (Electronic Engineering; Information Technology; Microelectronics; Telecommunications Engineering); **Foreign Language** (English; Japanese; Modern Languages; Translation and Interpretation); **Information Technology Engineering** (Computer Engineering; Computer Networks; Computer Science; Educational Technology; Information Technology; Media Studies; Software Engineering); **Mechanical Engineering** (Automation and Control Engineering; Electrical Engineering; Industrial Design; Machine Building; Maintenance Technology; Materials Engineering; Mechanical Engineering; Production Engineering); **Science** (Applied Mathematics; Applied Physics; Computer Science; Information Sciences; Mathematics; Natural Sciences; Statistics); **Vocational Education** (Pedagogy; Psychology; Technology Education; Vocational Education)

History: Founded 1979 as Tianjin Normal Technical College. Approved by Ministry of Labor and Personnel and renamed as Tianjin College of Vocational Technology and Education 1993. Approved by the General Office of the State Council 2000. Approved by the Ministry of Education and renamed as Tianjin College of Technology and Education. Acquired present title 2010.

Fees: (Yuan): Tuition 15,500-16,300 per annum for Bachelor's degree; 20,400 per annum for Master's degree

Main Language(s) of Instruction: Chinese, English

Degrees and Diplomas: *Xueshi Xuewei*; *Shuoshi Xuewei*: **Automation and Control Engineering; Computer Engineering; Educational Technology; Electronic Engineering; Information Technology; Machine Building; Management; Mathematics; Mechanical Engineering; Pedagogy; Production Engineering; Statistics; Transport Engineering.** Also non-degree programmes

Publications: Journal of Tianjin University of Technology and Education and Vocational Education Research

Student Numbers *2012-2013*: Total: c. 17,000
Last Updated: 28/10/13

TIANJIN UNIVERSITY OF TRADITIONAL CHINESE MEDICINE (TUTCM)

88 Yuquan Road, Nankai District, Tianjin,
Tianjin Province 300193
Tel: +86(22) 59596555 +86(22) 23734931
Fax: +86(22) 27374931
EMail: tutcm@hotmail.com; wailianb@tjutcm.edu.cn
Website: http://www.tjutcm.edu.cn

President: Zhang Boli EMail: president@tjutcm.edu.cn

College

Humanities and Management (Arts and Humanities; Chinese; Foreign Languages Education; Labour and Industrial Relations; Management; Marketing; Psychology; Public Administration; Social Welfare); **Traditional Chinese Medicine** (Traditional Eastern Medicine)

School

Continuing Education; **Nursing** (Nursing)

Department

Public Teaching; **Acupuncture and Moxibustion** (Acupuncture); **Experimental Teaching**; **Social Sciences** (Social Sciences); **Sports** (Sports); **Traditional Chinese Medicine** (Traditional Eastern Medicine)

Institute

International Education

Graduate School

Traditional Chinese Medicine Engineering (Engineering; Medicine; Traditional Eastern Medicine)

Further Information: Also 3 affiliated hospitals (2,000 beds and 16 clinical teaching and research offices); 15 teaching hospitals.

History: Founded 1958. Merged with Hebei Medical College 1968.

Fees: (Yuan): Tuition fee per annum for Bachelor's Programme, 24,000 for Foreign Students in Chinese; 36,000 for Foreign Students in English; 4,000 for Students from H.K., Macao, Taiwan and overseas Chinese. Master's Programme, 30,000 for Foreign Students in Chinese; 40,000 for Foreign Students in English; 6,000 for Students from H.K., Macao or Taiwan. Doctoral Programme, 42,000 for Foreign Students in Chinese; 52,000 for Foreign Students in English; 10,000 for Students from H.K., Macao or Taiwan

Main Language(s) of Instruction: Chinese

Degrees and Diplomas: *Xueshi Xuewei*; *Shuoshi Xuewei*; *Boshi*. Also 1 post-doctoral fellowship

Publications: Journal of Tianjin College of TCM

Academic Staff *2011-2012*	**TOTAL**
FULL-TIME	c. 3,200
Student Numbers *2011-2012*	
All (Foreign included)	c. 9,000
FOREIGN ONLY	1100

Last Updated: 04/12/12

TIANSHUI NORMAL UNIVERSITY (TSNC)

Qinzhou District of Tianshui City, Gansu Province by the Henan Road, Tianshui, Gansu 741001
Tel: +86 938-8362599
Fax: +86 938-8362454
EMail: xb@mail.tsnc.edu.cn
Website: http://www.tsnc.edu.cn/

President: Yang Xinke

College

Education (Art Education; Education; Educational Psychology; Educational Technology; Psychology); **Foreign Languages** (English; Foreign Languages Education; Modern Languages; Translation and Interpretation); **Life Science and Chemistry** (Analytical Chemistry; Biochemistry; Botany; Chemistry; Microbiology; Plant Pathology); **Mathematics and Statistics** (Applied Mathematics; Computer Science; Information Sciences; Mathematics; Mathematics and Computer Science; Mathematics Education; Statistics); **Physics and Information Science** (Information Sciences; Physics)

School

Engineering (Civil Engineering; Constitutional Law; Engineering; Engineering Drawing and Design; Materials Engineering); **Music** (Music; Musical Instruments; Singing)

Institute

Economic and Social Management (Economics; Finance; History; Management; Marketing; Philosophy; Taxation); **Literature and History** (Arts and Humanities; Chinese; Film; Geography (Human); History; Literature; Native Language Education; Writing)

Academy

Fine Arts (Art History; Design; Fine Arts; Painting and Drawing)

Centre

Continuing Education

Course

Physical Education (Physical Education; Sports)

History: Founded as a school 1959. Acquired current status 2000.

Main Language(s) of Instruction: Chinese

Degrees and Diplomas: *Xueshi Xuewei*; *Shuoshi Xuewei*: **Foreign Languages Education; Mathematics Education; Native Language Education.**

Publications: Chinese Academic Journal Comprehensive Evaluation Database; Longyou Cultural Studies; National College of Social Science Journals; National Outstanding Social Science Journal

Academic Staff *2013-2014*: Total 682
Student Numbers *2013-2014*: Total 14,018
Last Updated: 23/09/13

TIBET INSTITUTE FOR NATIONALITIES

No.6 Wenhui Dong Lu, Xianyang, Shaanxi Province 712082
Tel: +86(29) 33755000
Fax: +86(29) 33763081
EMail: xzmyyb@xzmy.edu.cn
Website: http://www.xzmy.edu.cn/

President: Luosong De Qing

School

Foreign Language (Modern Languages); **Information Engineering** (Information Technology); **Management** (Economics; Management); **Medicine** (Medicine)

Institute

Arts (Arts and Humanities; Chinese; History; Literature); **Education** (Education; Physical Education); **Finance** (Finance); **Journalism and Communication** (Journalism; Mass Communication); **Law** (Law); **Marxism** (Philosophy)

History: Founded 1958 as Tibet Public School. Acquired present status and title 1965.

Main Language(s) of Instruction: Chinese

Degrees and Diplomas: *Xueshi Xuewei*; *Shuoshi Xuewei*: **Chinese; Ethnology; History; Literature; Medicine.**

Publications: Journal of Tibet Institute for Nationalities

Academic Staff *2011-2012*: Total 832
Student Numbers *2011-2012*: Total: c. 10,000
Last Updated: 23/09/13

TIBET TRADITIONAL MEDICAL COLLEGE

10 DangRe road, Lhasa, Tibet 850000
Tel: +86(891) 6372391 +86(891) 6387272
Fax: +86(891) 6387272
EMail: lsdjbm_2006@yahoo.com.cn
Website: http://www.ttmc.edu.cn/

Dean: Nyima Tsering

Department

Astronomy calendar (Esoteric Practices); **Tibetan Medicine** (Traditional Eastern Medicine); **Tibetan Pharmacy** (Alternative Medicine; Pharmacy)

History: Founded 1989 as Traditional Tibetan Medical College of Tibet University.

Main Language(s) of Instruction: Chinese

Degrees and Diplomas: *Xueshi Xuewei*; *Shuoshi Xuewei*; *Boshi*

Publications: Traditional Tibetan Medicine Studies

Academic Staff *2011-2012*	**TOTAL**
FULL-TIME	**150**
PART-TIME	c. **80**
Student Numbers *2011-2012*	
All (Foreign included)	**1,030**

Last Updated: 05/12/12

TIBET UNIVERSITY (UTIBET)

36 Jiangsu Road, Lhasa, Tibet 850000
Tel: +86(891) 6321247
Fax: +86(891) 6334489
EMail: xzxx@utibet.edu.cn; nic@utibet.edu.cn
Website: http://www.utibet.edu.cn

President: Kelsang Choephel

Faculty

Science (Agriculture; Applied Mathematics; Biological and Life Sciences; Chemistry; Geography; Mathematics; Physics)

College

Arts (Architecture; Design; Fine Arts; Music; Performing Arts); **Continuing Education** *(Central TVU Tibet)*; **Education** (Education; Teacher Training); **Liberal Arts** (Arts and Humanities; History; Literature)

School

Economics and Management (Business Administration; Economics; Management; Marketing); **Medicine** (Medicine; Social and Preventive Medicine); **Tourism and Foreign Languages** (English; Modern Languages; Tourism)

Department

Ideological and Political Theory Teaching (Modern Languages; Political Sciences)

Institute

Cosmic Rays (Astrophysics); **Finance and Economics** (Economics; Finance); **Politics and Law** (Law; Political Sciences); **Technology** (Civil Engineering; Computer Science; Electronic Engineering; Information Technology; Technology)

Centre

Modern Educational Technology (Educational Technology); **Tibetan Studies** (Asian Studies; Tibetan)

Group

Logistics (Transport and Communications; Transport Management)

Research Centre

Tibetan Information Technology *(Information Technology)* (Asian Studies)

Further Information: Also Nyingchi campus.

History: Founded 1951 as Tibetan Cadres Training School. Acquired university status and current title 1985. Merged with Art school of the Tibet Autonomous Region, Tibet Medical College and the Medical Department of the Tibet Institute for Nationalities, Tibet Institute of Agriculture and Animal Husbandry, Tibet Autonomous Region Finance School 1999.

Main Language(s) of Instruction: Chinese

Degrees and Diplomas: *Xueshi Xuewei*; *Shuoshi Xuewei*. The construction of a doctorate conferring unit was approved in 2010.

Publications: Tibet University Journal

Academic Staff *2011-2012*	**TOTAL**
FULL-TIME	**523**
PART-TIME	**340**
STAFF WITH DOCTORATE	
FULL-TIME	**33**
Student Numbers *2011-2012*	
All (Foreign included)	c. **11,948**
FOREIGN ONLY	**2628**

Last Updated: 05/12/12

TONGHUA NORMAL UNIVERSITY (THNU)

950, Yucai Road, Tonghua, Jilin Province 134002
Tel: +86(435) 3208080 +86(435) 3209898
Fax: +86(435) 3209850
EMail: cnalfa@yahoo.com.cn
Website: http://www.thnu.edu.cn/

President: Kang Xuewei

International Relations: Ji Jianye

College

Adult Education

Department

Biology (Biology; Microbiology; Zoology); **Chemistry** (Chemistry; Organic Chemistry); **Chinese** (Chinese; Literature); **Computer Science** (Computer Science; Data Processing); **Fine Arts** (Fine Arts; Painting and Drawing); **Foreign Language** (Arts and Humanities; English; Modern Languages); **History** (Contemporary History; History); **Marxism-Leninism** (Political Sciences); **Mathematics** (Mathematics; Mathematics Education); **Modern Languages** (English; Japanese; Modern Languages); **Political Sciences and Law** (Economics; Law; Political Sciences); **Sports** (Physical Education; Sports); **Teacher Training** (Pedagogy; Teacher Training)

Course

Botany (Botany); **China's Ancient History** (Ancient Civilizations; History); **China's GaoGouli History** (History); **Contemporary Chinese** (Chinese); **Higher Degree Algebra** (Mathematics); **History Teaching Method** *(Junior Middle School)* (Humanities and Social Science Education; Pedagogy); **Optics** (Optics)

History: Founded 1978.

Fees: (Yuan): 3,500-4,600 per annum

Main Language(s) of Instruction: Chinese, English

Degrees and Diplomas: *Xueshi Xuewei*

Academic Staff *2011-2012*: Total: c. 370
Student Numbers *2011-2012*: Total: c. 8,500
Last Updated: 05/12/12

TONGJI UNIVERSITY

1239 Siping Road, Shanghai, Shanghai 200092
Tel: +86(21) 65982200
Fax: +86(21) 65985216
EMail: wsbgs@mail.tongji.edu.cn
Website: http://www.tongji.edu.cn

President: Pei Gang (2007-) Tel: +86(21) 65983300

International Relations: Qi Dong Tel: +86(21) 65983057

College

Aerospace Engineering and Mechanic (Aeronautical and Aerospace Engineering; Mechanical Engineering; Mechanics); **Applied Sciences** *(Sino-German - International Joint Programme)*

(Automotive Engineering; Building Technologies; Electronic Engineering; Mechanical Engineering); **Architecture and Urban Planning** (Architecture; Design; Industrial Design; Interior Design; Landscape Architecture; Tourism; Town Planning); **Arts and Communications** (Advertising and Publicity; Communication Arts; Fine Arts; Journalism; Literature; Mass Communication; Music; Performing Arts; Photography; Radio and Television Broadcasting; Visual Arts); **Automotive Engineering** (Automotive Engineering; Electronic Engineering; Information Management; Marketing; Mechanical Engineering; Power Engineering; Transport Management); **Civil Engineering** (Bridge Engineering; Civil Engineering; Computer Science; Construction Engineering; Geological Engineering; Hydraulic Engineering; Information Technology; Natural Resources; Safety Engineering; Structural Architecture; Surveying and Mapping; Water Science); **Electronics and Information Engineering** (Automation and Control Engineering; Computer Engineering; Computer Science; Electrical and Electronic Engineering; Electrical Engineering; Electronic Engineering; Information Technology; Microelectronics; Software Engineering; Telecommunications Engineering); **Environmental Science and Engineering** (Environmental Engineering; Environmental Studies; Waste Management; Water Management); **Foreign Languages** (Applied Linguistics; English; German; Japanese; Linguistics; Literature; Modern Languages); **Graduate Study** *(Sino-German - International Joint Programme)* (Administrative Law; Automation and Control Engineering; Automotive Engineering; Business Administration; Constitutional Law; Information Technology; Machine Building; Management); **Law/Intellectual Property Institute** (Administrative Law; Civil Law; Commercial Law; Constitutional Law; Criminal Law; International Law; Law); **Life Science and Technology** (Biochemistry; Bioengineering; Biological and Life Sciences; Biology; Biotechnology; Botany; Computer Science; Environmental Studies; Medicine; Microbiology; Molecular Biology; Neurology; Physical Therapy; Rehabilitation and Therapy; Safety Engineering); **Material Science and Engineering** (Building Technologies; Chemistry; Inorganic Chemistry; Materials Engineering; Nanotechnology; Physics; Polymer and Plastics Technology); **Mechanical Engineering** (Automation and Control Engineering; Automotive Engineering; Electronic Engineering; Energy Engineering; Heating and Refrigeration; Industrial Engineering; Machine Building; Mechanical Engineering; Power Engineering; Production Engineering; Thermal Engineering; Thermal Physics); **Ocean and Earth Science** (Coastal Studies; Earth Sciences; Environmental Engineering; Geological Engineering; Geology; Geophysics; Information Management; Information Technology; Marine Science and Oceanography; Mineralogy; Seismology; Software Engineering); **Sciences** (Analytical Chemistry; Applied Chemistry; Chemistry; Educational Technology; Environmental Studies; Inorganic Chemistry; Mathematics; Mathematics and Computer Science; Mechanics; Operations Research; Optical Technology; Optics; Organic Chemistry; Physical Chemistry; Physics; Polymer and Plastics Technology; Solid State Physics; Sound Engineering (Acoustics); Statistics); **Software Engineering** (Computer Engineering; Software Engineering); **Traffic and Transportation Engineering** (Railway Engineering; Road Engineering; Transport and Communications; Transport Engineering; Transport Management); **Women's** (Computer Engineering; Computer Graphics; Computer Science; Design; Public Administration; Visual Arts)

Programme

Business Administration *(Tongji-Reims Undergraduate Programme - International Joint Programme)* (Business Administration; Management)

School

Economics and Management (Accountancy; Business Administration; E-Business/Commerce; Economics; Finance; Government; Human Resources; Information Management; Information Sciences; International Business; Management; Marketing; Real Estate; Transport Management); **Film** (Art Education; Cinema and Television; Dance; Film; Performing Arts); **Liberal Arts** (Adult Education; Aesthetics; Arts and Humanities; Chinese; Cinema and Television; Comparative Literature; Economics; Educational Technology; Ethics; Film; Higher Education; International Relations; Literature; Opera; Philosophy; Political Sciences; Social Work; Sociology; Theatre; Vocational Education); **Medicine** (Anatomy; Biology; Biomedical Engineering; Cardiology; Dermatology; Embryology and Reproduction Biology; Epidemiology; Food Science; Gynaecology and Obstetrics; Histology; Laboratory Techniques; Medical Technology; Medicine; Nutrition; Oncology; Ophthalmology; Otorhinolaryngology; Paediatrics; Pathology; Physiology; Psychiatry and Mental Health; Public Health; Radiology; Statistics; Stomatology; Surgery; Traditional Eastern Medicine; Venereology)

Institute

Engineering and Management *(Sino-French - International Joint Programme)* (Artificial Intelligence; Business Administration; Environmental Engineering; Information Technology; International Business); **Environment and Sustainable Development** *(UNEP-Tongji - International Joint Programme)* (Environmental Engineering; Environmental Studies); **Technology** *(Tongji-Australian - International Joint Programme)* (English; Technology); **Vocational and Technical Education** *(International Joint Programme)* (Automation and Control Engineering; Business Administration; Civil Engineering; Electronic Engineering; Information Technology; Mechanical Engineering; Teacher Training; Technology Education; Vocational Education)

Campus

Sino-Italian *(-International Joint Programme)* (Information Technology; Mechanical Engineering; Production Engineering)

Further Information: Also 6 university hospitals; a traditional and distance learning institution.

History: Founded 1907 as Tongji German Medical School. Renamed Tongji Medical and Engineering School 1912. Acquired university status 1923. Acquired current title 1927. Merged with Shanghai Institute of Urban Construction and Shanghai Institute of Building Materials 1996 and Shanghai Railway University 2000.

Academic Year: September to July (September-January; February-June; June-July)

Admission Requirements: Graduation from senior middle school and entrance examination

Main Language(s) of Instruction: Chinese

Accrediting Agency: Ministry of Education; Shanghai Municipality

Degrees and Diplomas: *Xueshi Xuewei*; *Shuoshi Xuewei*; *Boshi*. Also Certificates and Diplomas; Postdoctorate degrees; MBA and Executive MBA.

Student Services: Academic Counselling, Canteen, Careers Guidance, Cultural Activities, Health Services, Nursery Care, Social Counselling, Sports Facilities

Publications: Higher Education Studies; Journal of Radioimmunology; Journal of Structural Engineering; Shanghai Journal of Mechanics; Study of German; Technical Acoustics; Time and Architecture; Tongji Journal

Publishing House: Tongji University Press

Academic Staff *2011-2012*	**TOTAL**
FULL-TIME	c. 4,200
Student Numbers *2011-2012*	
All (Foreign included)	c. 50,000
FOREIGN ONLY	275

Last Updated: 06/12/12

TONGLING UNIVERSITY

1335 Ciuh Silu Dongduan, Tongling, Anhui 244061
Tel: +86(562) 5881000
Fax: +86(562) 5881000
EMail: tlxywsb@tlu.edu.cn
Website: http://www.tlc.edu.cn/

President: Ding Jiayun

International Relations: Xia Meiwu, Director

Department

Accounting (Accountancy); **Basic Education** (Education; Physical Education); **Civil Engineering** (Civil Engineering); **Economics and Management** (Economics; Management); **Economics and Trading** (Economics); **Electrical Engineering** (Electrical Engineering); **Finance** (Finance); **Foreign Languages** (Foreign Languages Education); **Law and Political Sciences** (Administrative Law; Political Sciences; Social Sciences); **Literature, Arts and Media** (Arts and Humanities; Literature; Media Studies); **Mathematics and Computer Sciences** (Computer Engineering); **Mechanical**

Engineering (Mechanical Engineering); **Public Administration** (Public Administration)

History: Founded 1978 as Tongling Finance and Economics College. Acquired present title 2002.

Degrees and Diplomas: *Xueshi Xuewei*

Academic Staff *2011-2012*: Total 788

Student Numbers *2011-2012*: Total 14,000

Last Updated: 17/07/13

TONGREN UNIVERSITY (GZTRC)

No.103 Qingshui Road, Tongren, Guizhou 554300
Tel: +86(856) 5222556
Fax: +86(856) 5222556
EMail: gztrc2013@126.com
Website: http://www.gztrc.edu.cn/

President: Hou Changlin

Department

Biological Sciences and Chemistry (Biological and Life Sciences; Chemistry; Horticulture; Pharmacology; Science Education); **Building**; **Chinese Language and Literature** (Chinese; Literature); **Education Sciences** (Education; Pedagogy; Psychology); **Fine Arts** (Design; Fine Arts; Painting and Drawing); **Foreign Languages and Literatures** (English; Foreign Languages Education; Hotel Management; Japanese; Literature; Modern Languages; Tourism); **Law, Politics and History** (Economics; Geography; History; Law; Management; Political Sciences; Social Work); **Mathematics and Computer Science** (Applied Mathematics; Computer Science; Mathematics; Mathematics and Computer Science; Mathematics Education); **Music** (Dance; Music; Music Theory and Composition; Musical Instruments; Singing); **Physical Education** (Humanities and Social Science Education; Physical Education; Sports); **Physics and Electronic Science** (Applied Physics; Electronic Engineering; Physics); **Preschool Education** (Art Education; Preschool Education; Science Education); **Primary Education** (Education; Primary Education; Science Education)

History: Founde as Tongren Mingde Middle School 1920. Acquired present status and title 2006.

Main Language(s) of Instruction: Chinese

Degrees and Diplomas: *Xueshi Xuewei*

Academic Staff *2011-2012*: Total 459

STAFF WITH DOCTORATE: Total 42

Student Numbers *2011-2012*: Total 3,821

Last Updated: 28/10/13

TSINGHUA UNIVERSITY

1 Qinqhuayuan, Beijing 100084
Tel: +86(10) 62783769
Fax: +86(10) 62789392
EMail: xinxiban@tsinghua.edu.cn; international@tsinghua.edu.cn
Website: http://www.tsinghua.edu.cn

President: Chen Jining (2012-)

International Relations: He Kebin

School

Aerospace (Aeronautical and Aerospace Engineering; Engineering; Mechanics); **Architecture** (Architecture; Building Technologies; Landscape Architecture; Town Planning); **Civil Engineering** (Civil Engineering; Construction Engineering; Hydraulic Engineering); **Continuing Education**; **Economics and Management** (Accountancy; Business Administration; Economics; Finance; Human Resources; Management; Marketing); **Environmental** (Environmental Engineering; Environmental Management; Environmental Studies); **Finance** *(PBC)* (Finance); **Graduate studies** *(Shenzhen)* (Automation and Control Engineering; Biological and Life Sciences; Biology; Biomedical Engineering; Chemistry; Computer Science; Electrical Engineering; Electronic Engineering; Energy Engineering; Environmental Engineering; Environmental Management; Environmental Studies; Health Sciences; Information Sciences; Information Technology; Instrument Making; Management; Marine Science and Oceanography; Materials Engineering; Mechanical Engineering; Philosophy; Physics; Social Sciences; Telecommunications Engineering; Transport and Communications; Transport Management); **Humanities** (Arts and Humanities; Chinese; History; Literature; Modern Languages; Philosophy); **Information Science and Technology** (Automation and Control Engineering; Computer Science; Electronic Engineering; Information Sciences; Information Technology; Microelectronics; Nanotechnology; Software Engineering); **Journalism and Communication** (Journalism; Mass Communication); **Law** (Law); **Life Sciences** (Biochemistry; Biological and Life Sciences; Biology; Biophysics; Cell Biology; Genetics; Marine Biology; Molecular Biology); **Marxism** (Political Sciences); **Mechanical Engineering** (Automotive Engineering; Industrial Engineering; Measurement and Precision Engineering; Mechanical Engineering; Thermal Engineering); **Medicine** (Biomedical Engineering; Medicine; Pharmacology; Pharmacy; Public Health); **Public Policy and Management** (Management; Public Administration); **Sciences** (Natural Sciences); **Social Sciences** (Economics; International Relations; Political Sciences; Psychology; Social Sciences; Sociology; Technology)

Department

Chemical Engineering (Chemical Engineering); **Electrical Engineering** (Electrical Engineering); **Engineering Physics** (Engineering; Physics); **Materials Science and Engineering** (Materials Engineering); **Physical Education** (Physical Education; Sports)

Institute

Advanced Study (Biology; Computer Science; Mathematics; Physics); **Education** (Education; Educational Administration; Educational Psychology; Educational Technology; Higher Education); **Interdisciplinary Information Sciences** (Information Sciences); **Nuclear and New Energy Technology** (Energy Engineering; Nuclear Engineering)

Academy

Arts and Design (Architectural and Environmental Design; Art History; Ceramic Art; Communication Arts; Design; Fashion Design; Fine Arts; Handicrafts; Industrial Design; Painting and Drawing; Sculpture; Textile Design)

Centre

Applied Mathematics *(Zhou Peiyuan)* (Applied Mathematics); **Art** (Fine Arts)

History: Founded 1911 as Tsinghua Xuetang. Renamed Tsinghua School 1912. University section founded 1925. Acquired current title 1928.

Academic Year: September to June (September-January; February-June)

Fees: (Yuan): Undergraduate tuition fee, 24,000-40,000 per annum; Postgraduate tuition fee for programmes taught in Chinese, 28,000-50,000 per annum (except Master in Finance, 128,000 for the whole programme); for programmes taught in English, 30,000-50,000 (120,000-158,000 for the whole programme in Architecture, Business, Law,...)

Main Language(s) of Instruction: Chinese

Degrees and Diplomas: *Xueshi Xuewei*; *Shuoshi Xuewei*; *Boshi*. Also MBA and International MBA (IMBA).

Student Services: Academic Counselling, Canteen, Careers Guidance, Cultural Activities, Foreign Studies Centre, Health Services, Social Counselling, Sports Facilities

Publications: China Mediatech (Chinese); Computer Education (Chinese); Decorative Arts (Chinese); Journal of Tsinghua University (Chinese); Journal of Tsinghua University (Chinese); Modern Education Technology (Chinese); Physics and Engineering (Chinese); Tsinghua Journal of Education (Chinese); Tsinghua Science and Technology (English); Word Architecture (Chinese)

Publishing House: Tsinghua University Press

Academic Staff *2011-2012*	**TOTAL**
FULL-TIME	**3,133**
Student Numbers *2011-2012*	
All (Foreign included)	c. **39,470**
FOREIGN ONLY	**2500**

Last Updated: 06/12/12

UNIVERSITY OF ELECTRONIC SCIENCE AND TECHNOLOGY OF CHINA (UESTC)

No.4, Section2, North Jianshe Road,
Chengdu, Sichuan Province 610054
Tel: +86(28) 83202316 +86(28) 83202354
Fax: +86(28) 83200131 +86(28) 61830601
EMail: oice@uestc.edu.cn
Website: http://www.uestc.edu.cn

President: Wang Jinsong Tel: +86(28) 83203010

Chairman of University Executive Committee: Shuxiang Hu Tel: +86(28) 83202203

International Relations: Bin Jiang Tel: +86(28) 83202353

School

Automation Engineering (Automation and Control Engineering; Environmental Engineering; Measurement and Precision Engineering; Surveying and Mapping); **Communication and Information Engineering** (Electronic Engineering; Information Technology; Optical Technology; Telecommunications Engineering); **Computer Science and Engineering** (Computer Engineering; Computer Science; Information Technology; Safety Engineering; Software Engineering); **Electronic Engineering** (Electronic Engineering; Information Technology; Telecommunications Engineering); **Energy Science and Engineering** (Automation and Control Engineering; Electrical and Electronic Engineering; Electrical Engineering; Electronic Engineering; Energy Engineering; Materials Engineering; Microelectronics; Solid State Physics); **Foreign Languages** (Applied Linguistics; English; Japanese; Linguistics; Literature; Modern Languages; Translation and Interpretation); **Information and Software Engineering** (Information Technology; Software Engineering); **Life Science and Technology** (Biochemistry; Biological and Life Sciences; Biomedical Engineering; Biophysics; Biotechnology; Molecular Biology); **Management and Economics** (Business Administration; E-Business/Commerce; Economics; Finance; Human Resources; Information Management; Management; Marketing); **Marxism Education** (Political Sciences); **Mathematical Sciences** (Applied Linguistics; Computer Science; Information Technology; Mathematics; Operations Research; Statistics); **Mechatronics Engineering** (Automation and Control Engineering; Electrical and Electronic Engineering; Electrical Engineering; Electronic Engineering; Industrial Engineering; Mechanical Engineering; Production Engineering); **Microelectronics and Solid-State Electronics** (Applied Chemistry; Chemistry; Materials Engineering; Microelectronics; Physics; Solid State Physics); **Optoelectronic Information** (Electronic Engineering; Information Sciences; Information Technology; Materials Engineering; Optical Technology; Optics); **Physical Electronics** (Applied Physics; Electronic Engineering; Nuclear Physics; Optics; Physics; Radiophysics); **Political Science and Public Administration** (Administrative Law; Applied Linguistics; Constitutional Law; Political Sciences; Public Administration)

Institute

Astronautics and Aeronautic Introduction (Aeronautical and Aerospace Engineering; Automation and Control Engineering; Electronic Engineering; Measurement and Precision Engineering; Mechanical Engineering; Optical Technology); **Electronic and Information Engineering** *(Dongguan)* (Electronic Engineering; Information Technology)

Research Institute

Electronic Science and Technology (Computer Science; Electronic Engineering; Information Technology; Microelectronics; Microwaves; Telecommunications Engineering)

History: Founded 1956 as Chengdu Institute of Radio Engineering (CIRE). Acquired present title 1988.

Academic Year: September to June (September-January; February-June)

Admission Requirements: Senior middle school education with decent grades

Fees: (Yuan): Tuition fees for international students: Undergraduate programmes, 14,000-20,000 per annum; Master programmes, 17,000-24,000 per annum; Doctoral programmes, 22,000-37,000 per annum

Main Language(s) of Instruction: Chinese

Degrees and Diplomas: *Xueshi Xuewei*; *Shuoshi Xuewei*; *Boshi*

Student Services: Academic Counselling, Canteen, Careers Guidance, Cultural Activities, Health Services, Language Laboratory, Nursery Care, Sports Facilities

Publications: Journal of Electronic Science and Technology of China; Journal of the University of Electronic Science and Technology of China; Journal of the University of Electronic Science and Technology of China (Social Science Additional)

Publishing House: UESTC Press

Last Updated: 07/12/12

UNIVERSITY OF INTERNATIONAL BUSINESS AND ECONOMICS (UIBE)

10 Huixin East Street, Chaoyang District, Beijing 100029
Tel: +86(10) 64492131
Fax: +86(10) 64493860
EMail: sie@uibe.edu.cn
Website: http://www.uibe.edu.cn

President: Shi Jianjun (2009-) Tel: +86(10) 64492101

Vice-President: Liu Ya EMail: liuya@uibe.edu.cn

International Relations: Liqun Jia Tel: +86(10) 64492132

School

Chinese Language and Literature (Chinese; Literature; Modern Languages); **Continuing Education**; **Foreign Languages and Studies** (Arabic; French; Italian; Japanese; Korean; Modern Languages; Russian; Spanish; Vietnamese); **Graduate Studies**; **Information Technology and Management** *(SITM)* (Information Management; Information Sciences; Information Technology); **Insurance and Risk Management** *(SIRM)* (Insurance); **International Business** (International Business); **International Studies** *(SIS)* (International Studies); **International Trade and Economics** *(SITE)* (Crafts and Trades; Finance; International Business; International Economics; Transport Management); **Law** *(UIBESOL)* (Law); **Public Administration** *(SPA)* (Public Administration)

Department

Sports (Sports)

Institute

Advanced Training; **Banking and Finance** (Banking; Finance); **Distance Education**; **English Language** (English); **Higher Vocational Education**; **International Business Administration** *(Sino-French)* (Business Administration; International Business); **International Economics** (International Economics); **International Relations** (International Relations)

Centre

International Business Chinese Teaching and Resource Development Base (Chinese; International Business); **International Business English Studies** (English; English Studies; International Business)

Research Centre

Beijing Corporate Research Base of International Operations (International Business); **Field Logistics** (Transport Management); **International Business Ethics** (Ethics; International Business); **Lease** (Business Administration); **Luxury** (Business Administration); **Technology Management** (Management; Technology); **WTO** (Business Administration; International Business)

Further Information: Also Chinese Institute for WTO Studies. A traditional and distance education institution.

History: Founded 1951 as Senior Business cadres school. Renamed the Beijing College of Foreign Trade 1953. Acquired present title 1984. Acquired present status 1984. Merged with the China Institute of Finance and Banking 2000.

Academic Year: September to July (September-January; March-July)

Admission Requirements: Graduation from senior middle school and entrance examination

Fees: (Yuan): 6,000 per annum

Main Language(s) of Instruction: Chinese, English

Accrediting Agency: Ministry of Foreign Trade and Economic Co-operation; Ministry of Education

Degrees and Diplomas: *Xueshi Xuewei*; *Shuoshi Xuewei*; *Boshi*. Also MBA; Executive MBA; post-doctoral programmes.

Student Services: Academic Counselling, Careers Guidance, Cultural Activities, Health Services, Social Counselling, Sports Facilities

Publications: Issues in Higher Education; Japanese Study, Translation of International Trade Articles; Journal of International Trade; Research on Multinationals; Research on Taiwan, Hong Kong and Macao Economy; UIBE Journal

Publishing House: International Business Educational Press

Academic Staff *2011-2012*: Total: c. 780

Student Numbers *2011-2012*: Total: c. 14,000

Last Updated: 07/12/12

UNIVERSITY OF INTERNATIONAL RELATIONS (UIR)

12 Poshangcun, Haidian District, Beijing 100091
Tel: +86(10) 62861317
Fax: +86(10) 62861660
EMail: yzxx@uir.cn
Website: http://www.uir.edu.cn

President: Liu Hui

Department

Culture and Communication (Chinese; Communication Studies; Cultural Studies; Grammar; Literature; Media Studies; Public Relations); **English** (English; International Relations; International Studies; Linguistics; Literature; Translation and Interpretation; Writing); **French** (Economics; French; Grammar; International Business; Literature; Writing); **Information Science and Technology** (Computer Networks; Data Processing; Information Management; Information Sciences; Information Technology; Mathematics; Multimedia; Operations Research; Physics; Safety Engineering; Software Engineering; Statistics); **International Communication** (Communication Studies); **International Economics and Trade** (Banking; E-Business/Commerce; Economics; Finance; International Business; International Economics; Mathematics; Statistics); **International Politics** (Political Sciences); **Japanese** (Cultural Studies; Grammar; Japanese; Literature; Translation and Interpretation; Writing); **Law** (Administrative Law; Civil Law; Commercial Law; Constitutional Law; Criminal Law; History of Law; International Law; Law; Private Law); **Public Management** (Finance; Government; Information Management; International Law; Management; Public Administration)

Institute

International Public Relations (International Business; Public Relations); **Public Market and Government Procurement** (Business Administration; Government)

Centre

International Strategy and Security Studies (International Studies)

Research Centre

China and International Relations (International Relations)

History: Founded 1949.

Main Language(s) of Instruction: Chinese

Degrees and Diplomas: *Xueshi Xuewei*; *Shuoshi Xuewei*; *Boshi*

Last Updated: 07/12/12

UNIVERSITY OF JINAN (UJN)

106 Jiwei Road, Jinan, Shandong Province 250022
Tel: +86(531) 2767683
Fax: +86(531) 7963127
EMail: fao@ujn.edu.cn
Website: http://www.ujn.edu.cn

President: Xin Cheng

College

International Education and Exchange (Asian Studies; Chinese)

School

Chemistry and Chemical Engineering (Applied Chemistry; Bioengineering; Chemical Engineering; Chemistry; Environmental Engineering; Materials Engineering; Physical Chemistry); **City Development** (Environmental Studies; Geography; Natural Resources; Public Administration; Town Planning; Urban Studies; Water Science); **Civil and Architectural Engineering** (Architecture; Civil Engineering; Engineering; Structural Architecture; Town Planning; Water Science); **Control Science and Engineering** (Automation and Control Engineering; Electrical Engineering); **Economics** (Economics; Finance; International Business; International Economics); **Fine Arts** (Administration; Art Management; Design; Fine Arts); **Foreign Languages** (English; French; German; Japanese; Korean; Modern Languages); **Information Sciences and Engineering** (Computer Engineering; Computer Networks; Computer Science; Electronic Engineering; Engineering; Information Sciences; Information Technology; Telecommunications Engineering); **Law** (Administrative Law; Civil Law; Commercial Law; Constitutional Law; Criminal Law; Human Resources; International Law; Labour and Industrial Relations; Labour Law; Law; Private Law; Social Problems; Social Welfare; Social Work; Sociology); **Literature** (Chinese; History; Literature); **Management** (Accountancy; Business Administration; Information Management; Information Sciences; Management); **Materials Science and Engineering** (Materials Engineering); **Mechanical Engineering** (Automation and Control Engineering; Industrial Design; Industrial Engineering; Machine Building; Mechanical Engineering); **Physical Education** (Physical Education); **Science** (Applied Mathematics; Information Sciences; Information Technology; Mathematics; Mathematics and Computer Science; Optical Technology; Optics; Physics); **Social Sciences** (Administration; Education; Educational Psychology; International Studies; Political Sciences; Psychology; Social Sciences); **Tourism** (Cooking and Catering; Hotel and Restaurant; Nutrition; Tourism)

Institute

The Quancheng (American Studies; Automation and Control Engineering; Biotechnology; Chinese; Computer Science; Economics; Electrical Engineering; English; Finance; Information Sciences; International Business; International Economics; Law; Literature; Machine Building; Modern Languages; Psychology; Tourism; Translation and Interpretation)

History: Founded 1948 as Jinan Union University. Combined with Jinan Normal College and Jinan Vocational College 1998. Acquired present title following incorporation of the Jinan School of Civil Affairs and the Shandong School of Materials and Supplies 2001.

Fees: (US Dollars): 1,800-2,200 per annum

Main Language(s) of Instruction: Chinese

Accrediting Agency: Ministry of Education

Degrees and Diplomas: *Xueshi Xuewei*; *Shuoshi Xuewei*; *Boshi*

Publications: China Powder Science and Technology; Chinese Journal of Cancer Prevention and Treatment; Journal of University of Jinan!

Academic Staff *2012-2013*: Total 1,940

STAFF WITH DOCTORATE: Total 509

Student Numbers *2012-2013*: Total: c. 32,000

Last Updated: 10/12/12

UNIVERSITY OF SCIENCE AND TECHNOLOGY BEIJING (USTB)

30 Xueyuan Road, Haidian District, Beijing 100083
Tel: +86(1) 62332541
Fax: +86(1) 62327878
EMail: dfa@ustb.edu.cn; io@ustb.edu.cn
Website: http://www.ustb.edu.cn

President: Luo Weidong Tel: +86(10) 62332318

School

Applied Science (Applied Chemistry; Applied Mathematics; Applied Physics; Biological and Life Sciences; Biotechnology; Information Sciences; Information Technology; Inorganic Chemistry; Mathematics; Mechanics; Molecular Biology; Operations Research; Organic Chemistry; Physical Chemistry; Polymer and Plastics Technology; Solid State Physics); **Civil and Environmental Engineering** (Automotive Engineering; Biochemistry; Civil Engineering; Environmental Engineering; Geological Engineering; Mechanics; Mining Engineering; Natural Resources; Petroleum and Gas Engineering; Safety Engineering); **Economics and Management** (Accountancy; Business Administration; Business and Commerce; E-Business/Commerce; Economics; Finance; International Business; International Economics; Management; Tourism); **Foreign Studies** (African Languages; Applied Linguistics; Arabic; English;

European Languages; German; Indic Languages; Japanese; Linguistics; Russian; South and Southeast Asian Languages; Spanish); **Humanities and Social Science** (Administration; Arts and Humanities; Civil Law; Commercial Law; Educational Administration; Health Administration; Higher Education; Law; Political Sciences; Public Administration; Social Sciences; Social Work; Sociology); **Information Engineering** (Artificial Intelligence; Automation and Control Engineering; Computer Engineering; Computer Science; Electronic Engineering; Information Sciences; Information Technology; Measurement and Precision Engineering; Microelectronics; Microwaves; Robotics; Software Engineering; Telecommunications Engineering); **Materials Science and Engineering** (Automation and Control Engineering; Chemistry; Materials Engineering; Metallurgical Engineering; Physics); **Mechanical Engineering** (Automation and Control Engineering; Electronic Engineering; Industrial Engineering; Mechanical Engineering; Power Engineering; Thermal Engineering; Transport Engineering); **Metallurgical and Ecological Engineering** (Ecology; Environmental Engineering; Environmental Studies; Metallurgical Engineering; Physical Chemistry)

Centre

Materials Service Safety *(National)* (Materials Engineering)

Laboratory

New Materials *(State Key Lab)* (Materials Engineering); **Solid Electrolyte Testing Technology** *(State Specialized Lab)* (Physics)

Research Centre

Advanced Equipment of Plate and Strip *(National Engineering and Technology Research Centre)*; **Efficient Steel Rolling** *(State Engineering and Research Center)* (Metal Techniques)

Research Unit

Materials National Environment Corrosion Experiment Network *(National Science and Technology Platform)* (Materials Engineering); **Materials Science Data Sharing Network** *(National Science and Technology Platform)* (Data Processing; Materials Engineering); **Materials Service Safety Assessment Facilities** (Materials Engineering; Safety Engineering)

Further Information: Also 22 courses for foreign students. University Hospital USTB

History: Founded 1952 as Beijing Institute of Iron and Steel Technology. Renamed Beijing University of Iron and Steel Technology 1960. Acquired present title 1988.

Academic Year: February to January (February-July; September-January)

Admission Requirements: Graduation from senior middle school and entrance examination

Fees: (Yuan): c. 3,200 per annum

Main Language(s) of Instruction: Chinese

Accrediting Agency: Ministry of Education

Degrees and Diplomas: *Xueshi Xuewei*; *Shuoshi Xuewei*; *Boshi*. Also Postdoctoral Research Programmes

Student Services: Academic Counselling, Careers Guidance, Cultural Activities, Health Services, Nursery Care, Social Counselling

Publications: Higher Education Research; Journal of USTB; Logistic and Material Handling; Metal World

Academic Staff *2011-2012*	**TOTAL**
FULL-TIME	c. **1,130**
Student Numbers *2011-2012*	
All (Foreign included)	**23,439**
FOREIGN ONLY	**500**

Last Updated: 10/12/12

UNIVERSITY OF SCIENCE AND TECHNOLOGY LIAONING (USTL)

185 Qianshan Zhong Road, Anshan, Liaoning Province 114051
Tel: +86(412) 5929088 +86(412) 5929086
Fax: +86(412) 5929085
EMail: International@ustl.edu.cn; study@ustl.edu.cn; gjjl@ustl.edu.cn
Website: http://www.ustl.edu.cn

President: Sun Qiubai

School

Architectural Engineering (Architecture; Industrial Design; Structural Architecture; Visual Arts); **Business Administration** (Accountancy; Business Administration; E-Business/Commerce; Economics; Engineering Management; Finance; Marketing; Tourism); **Computer Science and Engineering** (Computer Engineering; Computer Networks; Computer Science; Software Engineering); **Economics and Law** (Economics; Finance; International Business; International Economics; Law); **Electronic and Information Engineering** (Automation and Control Engineering; Electronic Engineering; Information Technology; Metallurgical Engineering; Power Engineering; Telecommunications Engineering); **Foreign Languages** (American Studies; English; Linguistics; Literature; Modern Languages; Translation and Interpretation; Western European Studies); **Further Education**; **Higher Vocational Education** (Automation and Control Engineering; Civil Engineering; Computer Engineering; Computer Networks; Economics; Electrical Engineering; Management; Mechanical Engineering; Metallurgical Engineering); **Materials Science and Engineering** (Automation and Control Engineering; Energy Engineering; Inorganic Chemistry; Materials Engineering; Metallurgical Engineering; Power Engineering; Thermal Engineering); **Mechanical Engineering and Automation** (Automation and Control Engineering; Electronic Engineering; Engineering; Machine Building; Mechanical Engineering); **Resources and Civil Engineering** (Building Technologies; Civil Engineering; Geological Engineering; Mineralogy; Mining Engineering; Natural Resources; Surveying and Mapping; Transport Engineering); **Science** (Applied Mathematics; Applied Physics; Computer Networks; Computer Science; Mathematics; Nanotechnology; Operations Research; Physics)

Department

Arts (Music; Performing Arts; Singing); **Humanity and Social Sciences** (Arts and Humanities; Contemporary History; Educational Psychology; Health Education; History; Law; Modern History; Political Sciences; Psychology; Social Sciences)

Institute

Applied Mathematics (Applied Mathematics); **Design and Investigation on Refractory** (Physics); **Mapping Engineering** (Surveying and Mapping)

Centre

Advanced Ceramics R&D *(USTL & ASOG)* (Ceramics and Glass Technology); **Environmental Metallurgy** *(Technical)* (Environmental Engineering; Metallurgical Engineering); **Inorganic Material Engineering** (Inorganic Chemistry; Materials Engineering); **Organic Luminescence Material** *(R&D Centre)* (Materials Engineering; Physics); **Separation Technology** (Technology)

Research Centre

Electrical and Hydraulic Engineering *(Research and Test Centre)* (Electrical Engineering; Hydraulic Engineering); **Engineering Financial Facilities** (Engineering; Finance); **Magnetic Separator** (Physics)

History: Founded 1948 as the Anshan Institute of Iron and Steel. Transformed into Anshan Institute of Iron and Steel Technology (AIIST) 1958. Incorporated Anshan Advanced Vocational College 1994. Merged with Liaoning College of Food Industry, Liaoning College of Metallurgical Industry and Liaoning College of Construction Material Industry and their campuses 1999. Renamed Anshan University of Science and Technology (ASUST) 2002. Acquired present title 2006.

Main Language(s) of Instruction: Chinese

Degrees and Diplomas: *Xueshi Xuewei*; *Shuoshi Xuewei*; *Boshi*

Student Services: Canteen, Health Services, Sports Facilities

Academic Staff *2011-2012*: Total: c. 1,900
Student Numbers *2011-2012*: Total: c. 16,600
Last Updated: 10/12/12

UNIVERSITY OF SCIENCE AND TECHNOLOGY OF CHINA (USTC)

N°96, JinZhai Road, Baohe District, Hefei, Anhui Province 230026
Tel: +86(551) 360-2847 +86(551) 360-2695
Fax: +86(551) 363-2579
EMail: englishnews@ustc.edu.cn; iao@ustc.edu.cn
Website: http://www.ustc.edu.cn

President: Jianguo Hou
Tel: +86(551) 3602184 EMail: gszhu@ustc.edu.cn

Vice-Chancellor: Li Jiangang

International Relations: Jie Yang
Tel: +86(551) 3603301 EMail: jieyang@ustc.edu.cn

School

Chemistry and Materials (Chemistry; Materials Engineering; Physics; Polymer and Plastics Technology); **Computer Science and Technology** (Computer Engineering; Computer Networks; Computer Science); **Earth and Space Science** (Astronomy and Space Science; Earth Sciences; Environmental Studies; Geochemistry; Geophysics); **Engineering** (Energy Engineering; Engineering; Machine Building; Measurement and Precision Engineering; Mechanical Engineering; Mechanics; Safety Engineering; Thermal Engineering); **Gifted Young** (Computer Science; English; Mathematics; Natural Sciences; Physics); **Humanities and Social Sciences** (Applied Linguistics; Archaeology; Art Education; Arts and Humanities; Communication Studies; English; History; Humanities and Social Science Education; Linguistics; Modern Languages; Philosophy; Physical Education; Political Sciences; Russian; Social Sciences; Translation and Interpretation); **Information Science and Technology** (Automation and Control Engineering; Biomedical Engineering; Computer Science; Electronic Engineering; Information Sciences; Information Technology; Microwaves; Telecommunications Engineering); **Life Science** (Biological and Life Sciences; Biology; Biomedicine; Biophysics; Biotechnology; Cell Biology; Molecular Biology; Neurosciences); **Management** (Business Education; Finance; Management; Statistics); **Mathematical Science** (Mathematics); **Nuclear Science and Technology** (Nuclear Engineering; Nuclear Physics); **Physical Sciences** (Astronomy and Space Science; Optical Technology; Optics; Physics); **Public Affairs** (Law; Transport Economics; Transport Management); **Software Engineering** (Software Engineering)

Centre

National High Performance Computing *(NHPCC - Hefei)* (Computer Science)

Laboratory

Fire Science *(SKLFS - State Key Laboratory)* (Fire Science); **National Synchrotron Radiation** *(NSRL)* (Biological and Life Sciences; Chemistry; Materials Engineering; Medicine; Physics); **Physical Sciences at the Microscale** *(HFNL-Microscal - Hefei National)* (Physics)

History: Founded 1958. Incorporated Hefei Economic and Technological Institute and acquired present title 1999.

Admission Requirements: Graduation from senior middle school and entrance examination

Fees: (Yuan): Tuition fee for Undergraduate programmes, 25,000 per annum; Master's degree programmes, 30,000 per annum; Doctoral degree programmes, 35,000 per annum

Main Language(s) of Instruction: Chinese

Degrees and Diplomas: *Xueshi Xuewei*; *Shuoshi Xuewei*; *Boshi*. Alos MBA and Executive MBA

Student Services: Academic Counselling, Canteen, Careers Guidance, Cultural Activities, Health Services, Language Laboratory, Nursery Care, Social Counselling, Sports Facilities

Publications: USTC Academic Journal

Publishing House: USTC Publishing House

Academic Staff *2011-2012*: Total 1,162
Student Numbers *2011-2012*: Total: c. 15,500
Last Updated: 11/12/12

UNIVERSITY OF SHANGHAI FOR SCIENCE AND TECHNOLOGY (USST)

516 Jungong Road, Shanghai, Shanghai 200093
Tel: +86(21) 55277040
Fax: +86(21) 65681967
EMail: usstie@online.sh.cn
Website: http://www.usst.edu.cn

President: Shuang Yan

International Relations: Wu Fengyu, Director, International Exchange Office

Faculty

Science (Applied Chemistry; Applied Mathematics; Applied Physics; Chemistry; Mathematics; Operations Research; Physics; Solid State Physics; Statistics); **Social Sciences** (Social Sciences)

Deanery

Engineering Science and Technology (Engineering; Technology)

College

Art and Design (Advertising and Publicity; Design; Fine Arts; Industrial Design; Mass Communication; Packaging Technology; Publishing and Book Trade; Visual Arts); **Energy and Power Engineering** (Energy Engineering; Power Engineering); **Medical Devices and Food Sciences** (Biomedical Engineering; Food Science; Medical Technology; Pharmacology; Safety Engineering); **Optical-electrical Information and Computer Engineering** (Automation and Control Engineering; Biomedical Engineering; Computer Engineering; Computer Networks; Computer Science; Electrical Engineering; Information Technology; Optical Technology; Telecommunications Engineering); **Shanghai**; **Shanghai Medical Instrumentation** (Medical Technology); **Shanghai Publishing and Printing** (Design; Fine Arts; Mass Communication; Printing and Printmaking; Publishing and Book Trade)

School

British Studies *(International)* (English); **Continuing Education** (Business Administration; Engineering; International Business; Management; Public Administration; Translation and Interpretation); **Environmental Studies and Architecture** (Architecture; Building Technologies; Civil Engineering; Energy Engineering; Environmental Engineering; Environmental Studies; Safety Engineering); **Management** (Accountancy; Business Administration; E-Business/Commerce; Engineering Management; Finance; Human Resources; Industrial Engineering; Information Management; Information Sciences; International Business; International Economics; Management; Marketing; Public Administration; Transport Management); **Materials Science and Engineering** (Materials Engineering); **Mechanical Engineering** (Automation and Control Engineering; Automotive Engineering; Electronic Engineering; Mechanical Engineering)

Department

Physical Education (Physical Education)

Institute

Foreign Languages (English; German; Japanese; Literature; Modern Languages); **Foundation** (Accountancy; Automation and Control Engineering; Civil Engineering; E-Business/Commerce; Electrical Engineering; Electronic Engineering; Environmental Engineering; Finance; Information Technology; International Economics; Management; Marketing; Mechanical Engineering; Power Engineering; Transport Engineering); **International Engineering** *(Shanghai - Hamburg - CDHK)* (Engineering)

History: Founded 1907 as Tongji German Medical School. Merged with Shanghai Institute of Mechanical Engineering 1972, and acquired present status and title 1979.

Main Language(s) of Instruction: Chinese

Degrees and Diplomas: *Xueshi Xuewei*; *Shuoshi Xuewei*; *Boshi*. Also MBA; Postdoctoral programmes.

Publications: Journal of Shanghai University of Science and Technology

Last Updated: 11/12/12

UNIVERSITY OF SOUTH CHINA (USC)

28 Changsheng Road, Hengyang, Hunan Province 421001
Tel: +86(734) 8282553 +86(734) 8280805 +86(734) 8282718
Fax: +86(734) 8280805 +86(734) 8282718
EMail: web@mail.usc.edu.cn

President: Wen Gebo

International Relations: Zhang Zhiying

School

Arts and Design (Architecture; Industrial Design); **Chemistry and Chemical Engineering** (Chemical Engineering; Chemistry); **Computer Science and Technology** (Computer Science); **Economics and Management** (Economics; Management); **Electrical Engineering** (Automation and Control Engineering; Electronic Engineering; Information Sciences); **Foreign Languages** (English; Modern Languages); **Life Science and Technology** (Medicine; Pharmacy); **Literature and Law** (Law; Literature); **Mathematics and Physics** (Mathematics; Physics); **Mechanical Engineering** (Mechanical Engineering); **Medicine** (Medicine); **National Defense Technology** (Military Science); **Nuclear Engineering Resources and Safety** (Nuclear Engineering; Safety Engineering); **Nuclear Science and Technology** (Nuclear Engineering); **Nursing** (Nursing); **Public Health** (Public Health); **Urban Construction**

Institute

Chuanshan

Further Information: Also 4 direct affiliated hospitals, 9 cooperative affiliated hospitals, 178 students' practice bases and 3 clinical institutes, 3 first-level postdoctoral research exchange centers for Nuclear Science and Technology, Mining Industry Engineering and Preclinical Medicine.

History: Founded 1958 as Hengyang Medical College. Merged with Central South Institute of Technology 2000. Acquired present status and title 2002.

Main Language(s) of Instruction: Chinese

Degrees and Diplomas: *Xueshi Xuewei*; *Shuoshi Xuewei*; *Boshi*. Also MBA.

Academic Staff *2011-2012*: Total: c. 2,250

Student Numbers *2011-2012*: Total: c. 32,000

Last Updated: 11/12/12

UNIVERSITY OF THE CHINESE ACADEMY OF SCIENCES (UCAS)

No.19A Yuquan Road, Beijing 100049
Tel: +86-10-8825-6206
Fax: +86-10-8825-6207
EMail: faiso@ucas.ac.cn
Website: http://www.ucas.ac.cn

President: Chunli Bai

College

Earth Sciences (Earth Sciences); **Engineering and Information Technology** (Information Technology); **Humanities and Social Sciences** (Arts and Humanities; Social Sciences); **Life Sciences** (Biological and Life Sciences); **Materials Science and Opto-Electronic Technology** (Electronic Engineering; Materials Engineering); **Resources and Environment** (Environmental Studies; Natural Resources); **Technology Management** (Technology)

School

Chemistry and Chemical Engineering (Chemical Engineering; Chemistry); **Computer and Control Engineering** (Computer Engineering); **Electronic, Electric and Communication Engineering** (Electrical and Electronic Engineering); **Management** (Management); **Mathematical Sciences** (Mathematics); **Physics** (Physics)

Department

Foreign Languages (Modern Languages)

Centre

Education and Research (Sino-Danish) (Educational Research)

Laboratory

Beijing National Laboratory for Condensed Matter Physics; **Beijing National Laboratory for Molecular Sciences (BNLMS)**; **Computional Geodynamics** (Geological Engineering); **Shenyang National Laboratory for Materials Science (SYNL)**

Research Centre

Fictitious Economy and Data Science (Data Processing)

Further Information: Branches in Shenyang, Changchun, Shangai, Nanjing, Wuhan, Guangzhou, Chengdu, Kunming, Xi'an, Lanzhou, Xinjiang, and Hefei (Institutes of Physical Science)

History: Founded 1978 as Graduate School of Chinese Academy of Sciences (GSCAS).

Main Language(s) of Instruction: Chinese, English

Accrediting Agency: Ministry of Education

Degrees and Diplomas: *Shuoshi Xuewei*: **Aeronautical and Aerospace Engineering; Agricultural Management; Agriculture; Animal Husbandry; Astronomy and Space Science; Automation and Control Engineering; Biology; Biomedical Engineering; Business Administration; Chemical Engineering; Chemistry; Civil Engineering; Computer Engineering; Crop Production; Economics; Electrical Engineering; Electronic Engineering; Engineering; Environmental Studies; Fishery; Forestry; Geography; Geological Engineering; Geology; Geophysics; History; Information Sciences; Instrument Making; Journalism; Law; Library Science; Literature; Management; Management Systems; Marine Science and Oceanography; Materials Engineering; Mathematics; Mechanical Engineering; Mechanics; Medicine; Meteorology; Modern Languages; Nuclear Engineering; Optical Technology; Pharmacy; Philosophy; Physics; Power Engineering; Psychology; Public Administration; Statistics; Surveying and Mapping; Traditional Eastern Medicine; Translation and Interpretation.** *Boshi*: **Agricultural Management; Astronomy and Space Science; Automation and Control Engineering; Biology; Chemical Engineering; Chemistry; Civil Engineering; Computer Science; Electrical Engineering; Electronic Engineering; Environmental Studies; Fishery; Forest Management; Geography; Geological Engineering; Geology; Geophysics; History; Instrument Making; Library Science; Management; Management Systems; Marine Science and Oceanography; Materials Engineering; Mathematics; Mechanical Engineering; Mechanics; Meteorology; Nuclear Engineering; Optical Technology; Pharmacy; Physics; Power Engineering; Psychology; Surveying and Mapping; Telecommunications Engineering; Thermal Engineering.**

Student Services: Library

Last Updated: 14/04/14

WANNAN MEDICAL COLLEGE (WNMC)

Weiliu Road, University Park, Wuhu, Anhui Province 241002
Tel: +86(553) 3832468 Ext. 6306
Fax: +86(553) 3811994
EMail: webmaster@wnmc.edu.cn
Website: http://www.wnmc.edu.cn

President: Zhang Yao (2009-)

International Relations: Wu Jinyue

Unit

Cell Electroporation Chamber (Cell Biology); **Dental Clinic** (Dentistry)

Division

Graduate Studies

School

Nursing (Nursing)

Department

Anatomy (Anatomy); **Basic Medicine** (Medicine); **Biochemistry** (Biochemistry); **Biology** (Biology); **Chemistry** (Chemistry); **Clinical Teaching** (Health Education; Medicine); **Computer Education and Research** (Computer Education; Computer Science); **Diagnostic** (Medicine); **Disease Health** (Health Sciences); **Extra Oral Studies** (Medicine); **Foreign Language Teaching and Research** (English; Modern Languages); **Forensic Medicine and Dentistry** (Forensic Medicine and Dentistry); **Histology and Embryology** (Embryology and Reproduction Biology; Histology); **Humanities and Management** (Arts and Humanities; Management); **Ideological and Political Theory Teaching and Research** (Political Sciences); **Intra Oral Studies** (Medicine); **Medicine I** (Medicine); **Medicine II** (Medicine); **Medicine III** (Medicine); **Microbiology** (Microbiology); **Parasitology** (Parasitology); **Pathology** (Pathology); **Pharmacology** (Pharmacology); **Pharmacy** (Pharmacy); **Physics** (Physics); **Physiology** (Physiology); **Preventive Medicine** (Social and Preventive Medicine); **Psychological** (Psychology); **Rehabilitation and Therapy** (Rehabilitation and Therapy); **Sports** (Sports)

Institute
Adult Education

Centre
Forensic Identification (Forensic Medicine and Dentistry); **Function**; **Morphology**

Laboratory
Anatomy (Anatomy)

Research Institute
Venom (Toxicology)

Further Information: Also 58 teaching hospitals, among which are 8 affiliated hospitals (one under the leadership of the college), 7clinical hospitals, and 46 hospitals as bases for medical teaching and practice; 10 experimental centers

History: Founded 1958 as Wuhu Medical Vocational School. Merged with Anhui Medical College 1970 and functionned as its South Anhui branch in 1971. Acquired present title 1974.

Main Language(s) of Instruction: Chinese

Degrees and Diplomas: *Xueshi Xuewei*; *Shuoshi Xuewei*

Student Services: Sports Facilities

Publications: The Journal of Clinical Pharmacology and Therapeutics of China; The Journal of Wannan Medical College

Academic Staff *2011-2012*: Total: c. 2,600

Student Numbers *2011-2012*: Total: c. 23,083

Last Updated: 11/12/12

WEIFANG MEDICAL UNIVERSITY (WFMC)

Baotong West Street 7166, Weifang, Shandong Province 261053
Tel: +86(536) 8238243
Fax: +86(536) 8238243
EMail: nic@wfmc.edu.cn; office@wfmc.edu.cn
Website: http://www.wfmc.edu.cn

President: Lui Yurui

International Relations: Liu Dianen

College
Basic Medical Studies (Medicine); **Nursing** (Nursing)

School
Continuing Education; **Management** (Management); **Oral Medicine** *(Stomatology Hospital)* (Medicine; Oral Pathology; Stomatology); **Pharmaceutical and Biological Sciences** (Biological and Life Sciences; Pharmacy); **Public Health** (Public Health)

Department
Anaesthesiology (Anaesthesiology); **Foreign Languages** (English; Modern Languages); **Humanities and Social Sciences** (Arts and Humanities; Social Sciences); **Medical Imaging** (Medical Technology); **Medical Laboratory Science** (Laboratory Techniques); **Physical Education** (Physical Education); **Psychology** (Psychology)

Institute
Ophthalmology *(Eye Hospital)* (Ophthalmology); **Plastic Surgery** *(Plastic Surgery Hospital)* (Plastic Surgery)

Centre
Reproductive Medicine (Embryology and Reproduction Biology; Medicine)

Further Information: Also Cravens Campus; 17 affiliated hospitals.

History: Founded 1951 as Changwei Medical School, acquired present title 1987.

Fees: (Yuan): Undergraduate tuition fee, 18,000 per annum

Main Language(s) of Instruction: Chinese, English MBBS (Bachelor degrees in Medicine and Surgery)

Degrees and Diplomas: *Xueshi Xuewei*; *Shuoshi Xuewei*; *Boshi*

Publications: Journal of Weifang Medical College

Academic Staff *2012-2013*	**TOTAL**
FULL-TIME	c. **1,500**
Student Numbers *2012-2013*	
All (Foreign included)	**16,000**
FOREIGN ONLY	**500**

Last Updated: 20/12/12

WEIFANG UNIVERSITY (WFU)

149 East Dongfeng Street, Weifang, Shandong Province 261061
Tel: +86(536) 8785119 +86(536) 8785219
Fax: +86(536) 8785256 +86(536) 8785219
EMail: wsb@wfu.edu.cn; wfu@wfu.edu.cn
Website: http://www.wfu.edu.cn/

Dean: Wang Shoulun (2005-)

College
Architecture and Civil Engineering (Architecture; Civil Engineering); **Beihai** *(International)* (Automotive Engineering; Business Administration; Business Computing; Computer Science; English; Maintenance Technology; Marketing); **Biological and Agricultural Engineering** (Agricultural Engineering; Bioengineering); **Chemistry, Chemical and Environmental Engineering** (Chemical Engineering; Chemistry; Environmental Engineering); **Electromechanical and Vehicle Engineering** (Automotive Engineering; Electronic Engineering; Mechanical Engineering); **Historical Culture and Tourism** (Cultural Studies; Tourism); **Information and Control Engineering** (Automation and Control Engineering; Information Technology); **Mathematics and Information Science** (Information Sciences; Mathematics; Mathematics and Computer Science); **Physics and Optoelectronic Technology** (Electronic Engineering; Optical Technology; Physics); **Preschool and Special Education Teacher Training** (Preschool Education; Special Education; Teacher Training)

School
Computer Engineering (Computer Engineering); **Economics and Management** (Economics; Management); **Foreign Languages** (English; French; Japanese; Korean; Modern Languages); **Law** (Law); **Literature, Journalism and Communication** (Journalism; Literature; Mass Communication); **Teacher Training** (Teacher Training)

Department
Ideological and Political Theory Teaching (Political Sciences)

Institute
Physical Education (Physical Education); **Technology** *(GoerTek)* (Automation and Control Engineering; Electronic Engineering; Technology; Telecommunications Engineering)

Academy
Fine Arts (Fine Arts); **Music** (Music)

History: Created 1960 as Changwei Teachers Training College. Acquired current status and title 2003.

Main Language(s) of Instruction: Chinese

Degrees and Diplomas: *Xueshi Xuewei*

Publications: Academic Journal of Weifang University

Academic Staff *2011-2012*	**TOTAL**
FULL-TIME	**1,400**
PART-TIME	c. **700**
Student Numbers *2011-2012*	
All (Foreign included)	c. **22,000**

Last Updated: 20/12/12

WEIFANG UNIVERSITY OF SCIENCE AND TECHNOLOGY (WUST)

166 Xueyuan Road, Shouguang, Shandong 262700
Tel: +86(536) 5101992
EMail: info@wfkjxy.com.cn; xueyuanwaishichu@yahoo.cn
Website: http://www.wfkjxy.com.cn/

President: Yin Weilun

Department

Agriculture (Agricultural Engineering; Agriculture; Biotechnology; Horticulture; Landscape Architecture; Marketing; Plant and Crop Protection; Vegetable Production); **Architecture and Civil Engineering** (Architecture; Civil Engineering; Management; Real Estate; Structural Architecture); **Automotive Engineering** (Automotive Engineering); **Business Administration** (Business Administration; Commercial Law; Human Resources; International Business; Marketing; Transport Management); **Chemical and Environmental Engineering** (Applied Chemistry; Biotechnology; Chemical Engineering; Chemistry; Environmental Engineering; Industrial Chemistry); **Economics and Management** (Economics; Management); **Fine Arts** (Advertising and Publicity; Computer Graphics; Computer Science; Fine Arts; Painting and Drawing; Printing and Printmaking; Sculpture; Visual Arts); **Foreign Language** (English; Japanese; Korean; Modern Languages; Tourism); **Mechanical Engineering** (Automation and Control Engineering; Machine Building; Mechanical Engineering; Production Engineering)

Institute

Sino-India Software (Computer Engineering; Computer Science; Information Sciences; Information Technology; Software Engineering)

Main Language(s) of Instruction: Chinese

Degrees and Diplomas: *Xueshi Xuewei*

Academic Staff *2012-2013*: Total: c. 1,600

Student Numbers *2012-2013*: Total: c. 27,000

Last Updated: 29/10/13

WEINAN TEACHERS UNIVERSITY (WNTC)

24 Zhannan Road, Weinan, Shaanxi Province 714000
Tel: +86(913) 2133998
Fax: +86(913) 2136900
Website: http://www.wntc.edu.cn/index_4/

Dean: Ding Deke

College

Chemical and Life Sciences (Biological and Life Sciences; Chemistry); **Continuing Education**; **Economics and Management** (Economics; Management); **Educational Sciences** (Education; Educational Sciences; Physical Education; Police Studies); **Foreign Languages** (English; Modern Languages); **Humanities** (Arts and Humanities); **Mathematics and Information Science** (Information Sciences; Mathematics); **Music** (Music); **Physics and Electrical Engineering** (Electrical Engineering; Physics)

Department

Social Science and Technology (Social Sciences; Technology)

Institute

Media Studies (Media Studies)

Academy

Fine Arts (Fine Arts)

History: Founded 1978 as Weinan Teachers Training College. Merged with Weinan Educational College. Acquired present title 2000.

Main Language(s) of Instruction: Chinese

Degrees and Diplomas: *Xueshi Xuewei*; *Shuoshi Xuewei*; *Boshi*. Master's and Doctor's degrees are offered in cooperation with other famous universities.

Academic Staff *2011-2012*	**TOTAL**
FULL-TIME	**902**
PART-TIME	**353**
Student Numbers *2011-2012*	
All (Foreign included)	c. **17,000**

Last Updated: 21/12/12

WENSHAN UNIVERSITY (WSU)

66 Xuefu Road, Wenshan, Yunnan 663000
Tel: +86(876) 8886234
Fax: +86(876) 8886234
EMail: wenshanxueyuan@yahoo.cn
Website: http://www.wsu.edu.cn/

President: Hao Nan Ming (2004-)

College

Chemical and Engineering (Chemical Engineering; Chemistry; Food Science; Food Technology; Metallurgical Engineering; Mining Engineering; Nutrition); **Education and Science** (Education; Natural Resources; Preschool Education; Primary Education; Teacher Training); **Environmental and Resource Sciences** (Biological and Life Sciences; Biology; Botany; Environmental Studies; Geography; Measurement and Precision Engineering; Natural Resources; Pharmacology); **Foreign Languages** (English; French; Modern Languages; Vietnamese); **Humanities** (Arts and Humanities; Chinese; History; Journalism; Literature; Modern Languages; Political Sciences); **Information Science** (Computer Engineering; Computer Science; Information Sciences; Information Technology); **Mathematics** (Applied Mathematics; Mathematics; Mathematics Education); **Physical Education** (Physical Education; Sports)

School

Economics and Political Sciences (Economics; Finance; History; Management; Political Sciences; Tourism; Transport Management)

Institute

Arts (Architectural and Environmental Design; Art Education; Clothing and Sewing; Communication Arts; Dance; Design; Fine Arts; Music Education; Musicology; Visual Arts)

History: Approved by the Yunnan Provincial Government and accredited by the Ministry of Education of the People's Republic of China in 1984.

Fees: (Yuan): Tuition, 18,000 per annum for degree programmes; 14,000 per annum for non-degree programmes; 3,000 per month for Short term programmes

Main Language(s) of Instruction: Chinese

Degrees and Diplomas: *Zhuanke*; *Xueshi Xuewei*

Academic Staff *2012-2013*: Total: c. 400

Student Numbers *2012-2013*: Total: c. 8,000

Last Updated: 24/09/13

WENZHOU MEDICAL COLLEGE (WZMC)

University-town, Wenzhou, Zhejiang Province 325035
Tel: +86(577) 86689731 +86(577) 86689732
Fax: +86(577) 86689700
EMail: io@wzmc.net
Website: http://www.wzmc.edu.cn/en

President: Jia Qui

School

1st Clinical Medical Sciences (Gynaecology and Obstetrics; Medical Technology; Medicine; Neurology; Surgery); **2nd Clinical Medical Sciences** (Medicine); **Basic Medical Sciences** (Medicine); **Continual Education**; **Foreign Language Studies** (English; Modern Languages); **Humanities and Management** (Arts and Humanities; Management; Marketing; Public Administration; Social Welfare); **Information and Engineering** (Engineering; Information Sciences); **International Studies** (Dentistry; Medicine; Surgery); **Life Sciences** (Biological and Life Sciences); **Medical Lab Science** (Laboratory Techniques); **Nursing** (Nursing); **Ophthalmology and Optometry** (Ophthalmology; Optics; Optometry); **Pharmaceutical Sciences** (Pharmacy); **Postgraduate Studies**; **Public Health** (Public Health); **Renji**; **Sports Science** (Physical Education; Sports); **Stomatology** (Dental Technology; Dentistry; Oral Pathology; Orthodontics; Stomatology; Surgery)

Department

Social Sciences Education (Humanities and Social Science Education)

Centre

Laboratory Animals (Laboratory Techniques)

Further Information: 3 Campuses: Chashan Campus, Xueyuan road Campus and Xiushan Campus. Also 10 affiliated hospitals with a total of nearly 7,000 beds.

History: Founded 1958 after part of the Zhejiang Medical College (founded 1952) was moved to Wenzhou and named Zhejiang 2nd Medical College. Acquired present title later the same year. A key university in Zhejiang.

Main Language(s) of Instruction: Chinese, English (Programmes taught at the School of International Studies)

Degrees and Diplomas: *Xueshi Xuewei*; *Shuoshi Xuewei*; *Boshi*

Publications: Chinese Journal of Optometry and Ophthalmology; Journal of Hepatopancreatobiliary Surgery; Journal of Wenzhou Medical College; Zhejiang Traumatic Surgery and Laboratory Medical Education

Academic Staff *2011-2012*	**TOTAL**
FULL-TIME	c. **800**
Student Numbers *2011-2012*	
All (Foreign included)	c. **12,500**
FOREIGN ONLY	**500**

Last Updated: 21/12/12

WENZHOU UNIVERSITY (WZU)

Chashan University Town, Wenzhou, Zhejiang Province 325035
Tel: +86(577) 8659-6061 +86(577) 8659-6062
Fax: +86(577) 8659-6063
EMail: wzdx@wzu.edu.cn
Website: http://www.wzu.edu.cn

President: Cai Yuanqiang Tel: +86(577) 8659-8000

College

Adult and Further Education; **Architecture and Civil Engineering** (Architecture; Civil Engineering); **Art and Design** (Design; Engineering Drawing and Design; Fine Arts); **Chemistry and Materials Science** (Applied Chemistry; Chemistry; Materials Engineering; Organic Chemistry; Physical Chemistry); **City**; **Computer Science and Engineering** (Computer Engineering; Computer Networks; Computer Science); **Education** (Curriculum; Education; Pedagogy; Preschool Education; Primary Education); **Foreign Languages** (English; Modern Languages); **Humanities** (Advertising and Publicity; Arts and Humanities; Chinese; History; Literature); **International Cooperation** (International Business; International Economics); **Law and Politics** (Administration; Law; Political Sciences; Social Work); **Life and Environmental Science** (Bioengineering; Biological and Life Sciences; Environmental Studies); **Mathematics and Information Science** (Applied Mathematics; Computer Science; Information Sciences; Mathematics and Computer Science; Statistics); **Mechanical and Electrical Engineering** (Automation and Control Engineering; Electrical Engineering; Industrial Engineering; Mechanical Engineering); **Music** (Music; Musicology); **Ou Jiang**; **Physical Education** (Physical Chemistry; Sports); **Physics and Electronic Information** (Educational Sciences; Electronic Engineering; Information Sciences; Information Technology; Physics; Telecommunications Engineering)

School

Business (Business Administration; Economics; Information Management; Information Sciences; International Business; International Economics; Marketing)

Institute

Art and Design (Design; Fine Arts); **Fashion** (Fashion Design)

History: Founded in 1984 when merged with Wenzhou Normal College.

Fees: (Yuan): Bachelor's degree, 20,000 per academic year; Master's degree, 22,000 per annum

Main Language(s) of Instruction: Chinese

Degrees and Diplomas: *Xueshi Xuewei*; *Shuoshi Xuewei*

Last Updated: 02/01/13

WEST ANHUI UNIVERSITY (WXC)

Lu'an City, Anhui 273012
Tel: +86(564) 3305011
Website: http://www.wxc.edu.cn/

President: Zhang Wenbing

Faculty

Biological and Pharmaceutical Engineering (Bioengineering; Pharmacology); **Economics and Management** (Economics; Management); **Finance and Mathematics** (Applied Mathematics; Finance; Information Sciences; Mathematics; Mathematics and Computer Science); **Information Engineering** (Computer Engineering; Computer Networks; Computer Science; Electronic Engineering; Information Technology; Telecommunications Engineering); **Materials and Chemical Engineering** (Applied Chemistry; Chemical Engineering; Chemistry; Information Sciences; Information Technology; Materials Engineering; Optical Technology; Physics; Polymer and Plastics Technology); **Mechanical and Electronic Engineering** (Electrical Engineering; Electronic Engineering; Mechanical Engineering); **Physical Education** (Physical Education; Sports; Sports Management); **Resources, Environment and Tourism Management** (Environmental Engineering; Environmental Studies; Management; Rural Planning; Tourism; Town Planning)

College

Arts (Art Education; Communication Arts; Design; Fashion Design; Fine Arts; Musicology; Visual Arts); **Foreign Languages** (English; Modern Languages)

School

Applied Science and Technology (Accountancy; Computer Networks; Natural Sciences; Preschool Education; Technology); **Architecture and Civil Engineering** (Architecture; Civil Engineering; Waste Management; Water Management); **Culture and Media** (Advertising and Publicity; Cultural Studies; Journalism; Linguistics; Literature; Media Studies)

Institute

Politics and Law (Economics; Law; Management; Philosophy; Political Sciences; Public Administration)

History: Founded 2000. Acquired present status 2004.

Main Language(s) of Instruction: Chinese

Degrees and Diplomas: *Xueshi Xuewei*

Publications: Journal of West Anhui University

Academic Staff *2012-2013*: Total 771

Student Numbers *2012-2013*: Total: c. 18,000

Last Updated: 29/10/13

WUCHANG INSTITUTE OF TECHNOLOGY (WIT)

110 Baisazhou Avenue, Hongshan District, Wuhan 430065
Tel: +86(27) 88156938
Website: http://wpuic.net.cn/

President: Zhao Zuobin

School

Art and Design (Design; Fine Arts); **Civil Engineering** (Civil Engineering); **Economic Management** (Economics; Management); **Food Engineering** (Food Technology); **Information Engineering** (Computer Engineering; Information Technology); **Language and Literature** (Literature; Modern Languages); **Mechanical Engineering** (Mechanical Engineering)

Department

Ideology and Politics (Political Sciences); **Physical Education** (Physical Education)

Main Language(s) of Instruction: Chinese

Degrees and Diplomas: *Xueshi Xuewei*

Academic Staff *2013-2014*: Total: c. 650

Student Numbers *2013-2014*: Total: c. 12,000

Last Updated: 30/10/13

WUHAN CONSERVATORY OF MUSIC (WHCM)

255 Jiefang Road, Wuhan, Hubei Province 430060
Tel: +86(27) 88066354
Fax: +86(27) 88069436
EMail: whmusicc@public.wh.hb.cn
Website: http://www.whcm.com.cn

President: Peng Zhimin (2009-)

International Relations: Yang Danna

School

The Affiliated Middle Studies (Chinese; Dance; English; Geography; History; Information Technology; Mathematics; Music; Music Theory and Composition; Musical Instruments; Physical Education; Political Sciences)

Department

Chinese Traditional Instruments (Musical Instruments); **Composition** (Music Theory and Composition); **Dance** (Dance); **Music Education** (Music Education); **Musicology** (Musicology); **Orchestral Instruments** (Musical Instruments); **Piano** (Musical Instruments); **Postgraduate Studies** (Jazz and Popular Music; Law; Literature; Music; Music Theory and Composition; Musical Instruments; Musicology; Singing); **Vocal Music** (Singing)

Academy

Performing Arts (Performing Arts)

History: Founded 1920 as Wuchang Art School, acquired present status and title 1985.

Main Language(s) of Instruction: Chinese

Degrees and Diplomas: *Xueshi Xuewei*; *Shuoshi Xuewei*

Last Updated: 02/01/13

WUHAN DONGHU UNIVERSITY (WDU)

Wenhua Road, Jiangxia Zhifang Street Special No. 1,
Wuhan, Hubei 430212
Tel: +86(27) 81931555
Fax: +86(27) 81931333
EMail: wdu_nppc@163.com
Website: http://en.wdu.edu.cn

College

Communication and Artistic Design (Advertising and Publicity; Architectural and Environmental Design; Communication Arts; Communication Studies; Design; Fine Arts; Graphic Arts; Graphic Design; Journalism; Media Studies); **Computer Science** (Computer Engineering; Computer Networks; Computer Science; Media Studies; Software Engineering); **Continuing Education** (Accountancy; Administration; Adult Education; Computer Engineering; Computer Science; Construction Engineering; Continuing Education; Distance Education; Economics; Electronic Engineering; English; Finance; Graphic Design; Information Technology; International Business; Management; Mechanical Engineering; Technology Education; Vocational Education); **Economics** (Economics); **Electronics and Information Engineering** (Electronic Engineering; Information Technology; Telecommunications Engineering); **Foreign Languages and Literature** (Chinese; Cultural Studies; English; French; Literature; Modern Languages; Translation and Interpretation); **Life Sciences and Chemistry** (Applied Chemistry; Biological and Life Sciences; Biotechnology; Chemistry); **Management Science** (Accountancy; Business Administration; E-Business/Commerce; Hotel Management; Human Resources; Information Management; Management; Tourism; Transport Management); **Mechanical and Electronic Engineering** (Automation and Control Engineering; Electronic Engineering; Mechanical Engineering); **Political Science and Law** (Law; Political Sciences)

History: Founded 2000. Previously known as Donghu College, Wuhan University.

Fees: UK, Syracuse University, the US, Waiariki Institute of Technology, New Zealand, University of Victoria, Canada, and OKI, Japan

Main Language(s) of Instruction: Chinese

Degrees and Diplomas: *Xueshi Xuewei*

Student Services: Sports Facilities

Academic Staff *2013-2014*: Total 134

Student Numbers *2013-2014*: Total: c. 15,000

Last Updated: 30/10/13

WUHAN INSTITUTE OF BIOLOGICAL ENGINEERING (WHSW)

Economic Development Zone, Wuhan Yangluo Han Shi Road,
Wuhan, Hubei 430415
Tel: +86(27) 89645567
EMail: wsyxcb@163.com
Website: http://www.whsw.net/

College

Foreign Languages (Applied Linguistics; English; Linguistics; Literature; Modern Languages; Translation and Interpretation)

Department

Architecture (Architecture; Construction Engineering; Interior Design; Structural Architecture); **Art** (Architectural and Environmental Design; Design; Fine Arts; Graphic Arts; Visual Arts); **Biological Science and Technology** (Biological and Life Sciences); **Chemistry and Environmental Engineering** (Chemical Engineering; Environmental Engineering); **Computer and Information Engineering** (Computer Engineering; Information Technology); **Continuing Education** (Adult Education; Higher Education; Secondary Education); **Electrical Engineering** (Automation and Control Engineering; Automotive Engineering; Electrical Engineering; Electronic Engineering; Maintenance Technology; Mechanical Engineering); **Food Engineering** (Food Science; Food Technology; Nutrition; Safety Engineering); **Ideological and Political Theory** (Political Sciences); **Landscape Architecture** (Landscape Architecture); **Management Engineering** (Engineering Management; Management); **Pharmaceutical Engineering** (Biological and Life Sciences; Chemistry; Pharmacology; Pharmacy; Toxicology); **Physical Education** (Physical Education; Sports)

Academy

Entrepreneurship (Management)

Centre

Cultural Education (Cultural Studies)

History: Founded 1993.

Main Language(s) of Instruction: Chinese

Degrees and Diplomas: *Xueshi Xuewei*

Student Services: Canteen

Academic Staff *2012-2013*: Total 1,124

Student Numbers *2012-2013*: Total: c. 20,000

Last Updated: 24/09/13

WUHAN INSTITUTE OF PHYSICAL EDUCATION (WIPE)

461 Luoyu Road, Wuhan, Hubei Province 430079
Tel: +86(27) 87190851
Fax: +86(27) 87192007
EMail: WIPE_FAO@yahoo.com.cn
Website: http://www.wipe.edu.cn/international/english/index.html

President: Sun Yiliang (2006-)

School

Adult Education (Sports); **Chinese Martial Arts** (Sports); **Competitive Sports** (Sports); **Physical Education** (Physical Education); **Sports Art** (Arts and Humanities; Dance; Sociology; Sports); **Sports Economy and Management** (Management; Sports); **Sports Health and Science** (Health Sciences; Psychology; Sports; Sports Medicine); **Sports Physical Science** (Physics; Sports); **Sports Training** (Sports)

Department

Sports Information and Technology (Information Sciences; Information Technology; Sports); **Sports Journalism and Foreign Language** (English; Journalism; Modern Languages; Sports)

Further Information: Two Campuses: Majiazhuang Campus and Canglong Campus.

History: Founded 1953 as Zhongnan Institute of Physical Education, acquired present name 1956.

Admission Requirements: Senior middle School graduation certificate

Main Language(s) of Instruction: Chinese

Degrees and Diplomas: *Xueshi Xuewei*; *Shuoshi Xuewei*; *Boshi*

Student Services: Sports Facilities

Academic Staff *2010-2011*: Total: c. 400

Student Numbers *2010-2011*: Total: c. 11,000

Last Updated: 02/01/13

WUHAN INSTITUTE OF TECHNOLOGY (WIT)

693 Xiongchu Avenue, Wuhan, Hubei Province 430073
Tel: +86(27) 87195660
Fax: +86(27) 87801351
EMail: fao@mail.wit.edu.cn
Website: http://www.wit.edu.cn/english/

President: Li Jie

College

Electrical and Electronic Engineering (Automation and Control Engineering; Electrical and Electronic Engineering; Information Technology; Telecommunications Engineering)

School

Adult Education; **Arts** (Advertising and Publicity; Industrial Design; Visual Arts); **Chemical Engineering and Pharmacy** (Applied Chemistry; Bioengineering; Biotechnology; Chemical Engineering; Pharmacy); **Computer Science and Engineering** (Computer Engineering; Computer Networks; Computer Science); **Economic Management** (Accountancy; Business Administration; E-Business/Commerce; Information Management; Information Sciences; International Business; International Economics; Marketing; Public Administration); **Environment and Civil Engineering** (Civil Engineering; Environmental Engineering; Safety Engineering; Town Planning); **Foreign Languages** (English; Modern Languages); **International Education** (International Studies); **Law and Business** (Law); **Material Science and Engineering** (Materials Engineering; Physics; Polymer and Plastics Technology); **Mechanical and Electrical Engineering** (Automation and Control Engineering; Electrical Engineering; Engineering Drawing and Design; Mechanical Engineering; Production Engineering); **Science** (Computer Science; Energy Engineering; Information Sciences; Information Technology); **Telecommunication and Information Engineering** (Information Technology; Telecommunications Engineering)

Department

Physical Education (Physical Education; Sports)

History: Founded 1972 as Hubei Petrochemical Institute. Renamed Wuhan Institute of Chemical Technology (WICT) and put under the administration of the former Ministry of Chemical Industry of the Central Government 1980. Put under the joint administration of central and local authorities 1998. Acquired present title 2006.

Main Language(s) of Instruction: Chinese

Degrees and Diplomas: *Xueshi Xuewei*; *Shuoshi Xuewei*; *Boshi*. The doctorate degree programmes are co-offered with other research institutes and universities.

Student Services: Sports Facilities

Publications: Journal of Chemistry and Chemical Engineering; Journal of Wuhan Institute of Technology

Academic Staff *2011-2012*: Total 964

STAFF WITH DOCTORATE: Total 167

Student Numbers *2011-2012*: Total 18,318

Last Updated: 02/01/13

WUHAN POLYTECHNIC UNIVERSITY (WHPU)

68 Xuefu South Road, Changqing Garden,
Wuhan, Hubei Province 430023
Tel: +86(27) 8391-2601 +86(27) 8391-2602
Fax: +86(27) 8391-2601
EMail: wsb@whpu.edu.cn
Website: http://www.whpu.edu.cn/

President: Zeng Qilin

Vice President: Xiangyang Sun

International Relations: Shifeng Li, Director, International Office

School

Animal Science and Nutritional Engineering (Animal Husbandry; Aquaculture; Biotechnology; Food Science; Nutrition); **Arts and Media** (Administration; Communication Arts; Design; Industrial Design; Industrial Management; Literature; Mass Communication; Media Studies; Visual Arts); **Biology and Pharmaceutical Engineering** (Bioengineering; Biological and Life Sciences; Biology; Biotechnology; Pharmacy); **Chemical and Environmental Engineering** (Applied Chemistry; Chemical Engineering; Environmental Engineering; Environmental Studies; Materials Engineering); **Civil Engineering and Architecture** (Architecture; Civil Engineering; Engineering Management; Geological Engineering; Transport Engineering; Water Management); **Economics and Management** (Accountancy; Business Administration; Economics; Finance; International Business; International Economics; Management; Marketing; Tourism; Transport Management); **Electrical and Electronic Engineering** (Automation and Control Engineering; Electrical and Electronic Engineering; Electrical Engineering; Electronic Engineering; Information Sciences; Information Technology; Microelectronics; Telecommunications Engineering); **Food Science and Engineering** (Agricultural Engineering; Food Science; Food Technology; Safety Engineering); **Foreign Languages** (English; German; Modern Languages); **International Education** (Food Science; Food Technology; International Business; International Economics; Mechanical Engineering; Production Engineering); **Mathematics and Computer Science** (Computer Science; Information Management; Information Sciences; Mathematics; Mathematics and Computer Science; Software Engineering); **Mechanical Engineering** (Automation and Control Engineering; Industrial Design; Materials Engineering; Mechanical Engineering; Packaging Technology; Production Engineering); **Medical Technology and Nursing** (Child Care and Development; Community Health; Health Administration; Marketing; Medical Technology; Midwifery; Nursing; Pharmacology; Rehabilitation and Therapy)

Department

Teaching and Research of Ideological and Political Theory (Political Sciences); **Teaching and Research of Physical Education** (Physical Education; Sports)

History: Founded 1951 as Wuhan Food Industry College, acquired present title 1999.

Academic Year: September to July (September-January; February-July)

Admission Requirements: Entrance exam

Fees: (Yuan): 4,000-18,000 per annum

Main Language(s) of Instruction: Chinese

Degrees and Diplomas: *Xueshi Xuewei*; *Shuoshi Xuewei*

Student Services: Academic Counselling, Canteen, Cultural Activities, Health Services, Language Laboratory, Nursery Care, Social Counselling, Sports Facilities

Publications: Journal of Wuhan Polytechnic University

Academic Staff *2011-2012*: Total: c. 800

Student Numbers *2011-2012*: Total: c. 13,400

Last Updated: 02/01/13

WUHAN TEXTILE UNIVERSITY (WTU)

1 FangZhi Road, Wuhan, Hubei Province 430073
Tel: +86(27) 87611607 +86(27) 87611623
EMail: master@wuse.edu.cn
Website: http://www.wuse.edu.cn

President: Wei Yiliang

College

Adult Education; **Apparel Engineering** (Machine Building; Textile Technology); **Art and Design** (Design; Fine Arts); **Chemical Engineering** (Chemical Engineering); **Computer Science** (Computer Science); **Economics and Management** (Economics; Management); **Electromechanical Engineering** (Electronic Engineering; Mechanical Engineering); **Electronic Information Engineering** (Electronic Engineering; Information Technology); **Environment and Urban Construction** (Construction Engineering; Environmental Engineering; Town Planning); **High Vocational Technology** (Technology); **Humanistic and Social Sciences** (Arts and Humanities; Social Sciences); **Textile and Material Engineering** (Materials Engineering; Textile Technology)

Department

Foreign Languages (English; Modern Languages); **Mathematics and Physics** (Mathematics; Physics)

History: Founded 1958. Formerly known as Wuhan Institute of Textile Engineering (WIST). Renamed Wuhan University of Science and Engineering (WUSE) 1999. Acquired present title 2010.

Main Language(s) of Instruction: Chinese

Degrees and Diplomas: *Xueshi Xuewei*; *Shuoshi Xuewei*

Academic Staff *2011-2012*: Total: c. 1,000

Student Numbers *2011-2012*: Total: c. 30,000

Last Updated: 02/01/13

WUHAN UNIVERSITY (WHU)

Luo-jia-shan, Wuchang, Wuhan, Hubei Province 430072
Tel: +86(27) 68752810 +86(27) 68753912
Fax: +86(27) 87874669 +86(27) 87863154
EMail: fao@whu.edu.cn; fses@whu.edu.cn
Website: http://www.whu.edu.cn/

President: Li Xiaohong (2010-)

College

Basic Medicine (Medicine); **Chemistry and Molecular Science** (Analytical Chemistry; Chemistry; Inorganic Chemistry; Molecular Biology; Organic Chemistry; Physical Chemistry; Polymer and Plastics Technology); **Civil Engineering** (Architecture; Civil Engineering; Town Planning); **Computer Science** (Computer Science; Software Engineering); **Dynamics and Machinery** (Machine Building); **Education** (Education); **Electronic Information** (Electronic Engineering; Information Sciences); **History** (Ancient Civilizations; Archaeology; Contemporary History; Documentation Techniques; History; Modern History; Museum Studies); **Information Management** (Archiving; Information Management; Information Sciences; Information Technology; Library Science; Telecommunications Engineering); **Journalism and Mass Medium** (Journalism; Mass Communication; Media Studies; Radio and Television Broadcasting); **Liberal Studies** (Arts and Humanities; Chinese; Ethics; French; Literature; Logic; Philosophy; Religion); **Life Sciences** (Aquaculture; Biochemistry; Biological and Life Sciences; Biology; Biophysics; Botany; Cell Biology; Ecology; Genetics; Microbiology; Molecular Biology; Neurology; Physiology; Zoology); **Materials Science and Engineering** (Materials Engineering; Packaging Technology); **Mathematics and Statistics** (Applied Mathematics; Mathematics; Operations Research; Statistics); **Pharmacy** (Pharmacy); **Physics and Technology** (Atomic and Molecular Physics; Nuclear Physics; Optics; Physics; Radiophysics; Sound Engineering (Acoustics); Technology); **Remote Sensing Information Engineering** (Information Technology; Surveying and Mapping); **Resources and Environmental Science** (Environmental Studies; Natural Resources); **Stomatology** (Stomatology); **Water Resources and Hydroelectric Engineering** (Electrical Engineering; Hydraulic Engineering; Power Engineering; Water Management; Water Science); **WTO**

School

Business (Business Administration; Economics; Finance; Human Resources; Industrial Management; Insurance; International Business; International Economics; Management; Marketing; Public Administration; Social Welfare; Tourism); **Electrical Engineering** (Automation and Control Engineering; Electrical Engineering; Power Engineering; Thermal Engineering); **Foreign Languages and Literature** (Chinese; English; French; German; Japanese; Literature; Modern Languages; Russian); **Geodesy and Geomatics** (Geography; Geology; Geophysics); **International Software** (Software Engineering); **Law** (Administrative Law; Civil Law; Commercial Law; Constitutional Law; Criminal Law; Environmental Studies; International Law; Law; Private Law; Public Law); **Medicine** (Medicine; Nursing; Stomatology; Surgery); **Politics and Public Administration** (Political Sciences; Public Administration); **Public Hygiene** (Hygiene; Public Health); **Urban Studies** (Urban Studies)

Department

Art

History: Founded 1893 as Ziqiang Institute. Acquired present title 1949. Acquired present title 2000, following merger with Wuhan University, Wuhan University of Hydraulic and Electric Engineering, Wuhan Technical University of Surveying and Mapping, and Hubei Medical University.

Main Language(s) of Instruction: Chinese

Degrees and Diplomas: *Xueshi Xuewei*; *Shuoshi Xuewei*; *Boshi*. Also Post-Doctoral Research Programmes.

Publications: Journal of Wuhan University; Mathematics Journal

Academic Staff *2011-2012*	**TOTAL**
FULL-TIME	**3,639**
Student Numbers *2011-2012*	
All (Foreign included)	c. **54,000**
FOREIGN ONLY	**1433**

Last Updated: 02/01/13

WUHAN UNIVERSITY OF SCIENCE AND TECHNOLOGY (WUST)

947 Heping Road, Wuhan, Hubei Province 430081
Tel: +86(27) 68862470
Fax: +86(27) 68862860
EMail: webmaster@wust.edu.cn
Website: http://www.wust.edu.cn/wust_en/index.html

President: Kong Jianyi Tel: +86(27) 86841915

International Relations: Ma Jihua, Vice President, International Affairs

College

Art and Design (Architecture; Design; Fine Arts; Industrial Design); **Chemical Engineering and Technology** (Chemical Engineering; Chemistry); **Clinical Medicine** *(Affiliated Hospital)* (Medicine); **Computer Science and Technology** (Computer Engineering; Computer Science; Software Engineering); **Foreign Language** (Cinema and Television; English; Modern Languages); **Information Science and Engineering** (Automation and Control Engineering; Electrical and Electronic Engineering; Information Sciences; Information Technology); **International Education** (Business Administration; English; German); **Literature, Law and Economics** (Economics; International Business; International Economics; Law; Literature; Political Sciences; Public Administration); **Machinery and Automation** (Automation and Control Engineering; Automotive Engineering; Electronic Engineering; Industrial Engineering; Mechanical Engineering); **Management** (Accountancy; Business Administration; Information Management; Management; Marketing); **Material and Metallurgy** (Automation and Control Engineering; Materials Engineering; Metallurgical Engineering); **Medicine** (Medicine; Nursing; Pharmacy; Social and Preventive Medicine); **Natural Resource and Environment Engineering** (Environmental Engineering; Mineralogy; Mining Engineering; Natural Resources; Safety Engineering); **Science** (Applied Physics; Computer Science; Information Sciences; Mechanical Engineering); **Urban Construction** (Architecture; Civil Engineering; Construction Engineering; Transport and Communications)

Department

Physical Education (Physical Education; Sports)

History: Founded 1898 as Craftwork School. Renamed Wuhan Institute of Iron and Steel 1958. Wuhan Institute of Iron and Steel, Wuhan Junior College of Construction and Wuhan Junior Medical College of Metallurgical Industry, were then incorporated into Wuhan University of Metallurgic Science and Technology 1995. Acquired present title 1999.

Admission Requirements: Graduation from high school and entrance examination

Fees: (Yuan): 5,000 per annum

Main Language(s) of Instruction: Chinese, English

Accrediting Agency: Hubei Provincial Government

Degrees and Diplomas: *Xueshi Xuewei*; *Shuoshi Xuewei*; *Boshi*. Also postdoctoral research programmes

Student Services: Academic Counselling, Canteen, Careers Guidance, Cultural Activities, Foreign Studies Centre, Health Services, Language Laboratory, Nursery Care, Social Counselling, Sports Facilities

Publications: Higher Education Study; Journal of Wuhan University of Science and Technology

Academic Staff *2011-2012*: Total 1,510

Student Numbers *2011-2012*: Total 24,764

Last Updated: 03/01/13

WUHAN UNIVERSITY OF TECHNOLOGY (WHUT)

122 Luoshi Road, Wuhan, Hubei Province 430070
Tel: +86(27) 87658253 +86(27) 87651525
Fax: +86(27) 87163146
EMail: randygh@whut.edu.cn; rcb@whut.edu.cn
Website: http://www.whut.edu.cn

President: Zhang Qingjie EMail: zhangqj@whut.edu.cn

School

Art and Design (Design; Fine Arts; Industrial Design; Visual Arts); **Automation** (Automation and Control Engineering; Electrical Engineering); **Automotive Engineering** (Automotive Engineering; Mechanical Engineering; Power Engineering; Thermal Engineering); **Chemical Engineering** (Chemical Engineering; Chemistry; Pharmacology); **Civil Engineering and Architecture** (Architectural and Environmental Design; Architecture; Art History; Bridge Engineering; Civil Engineering; Heating and Refrigeration; Safety Engineering; Structural Architecture; Town Planning; Water Management); **Computer Science and Technology** (Computer Education; Computer Science; Software Engineering); **Economics** (E-Business/Commerce; Economics; Finance; Industrial and Production Economics; International Business; International Economics; Statistics); **Energy and Power Engineering** (Automation and Control Engineering; Energy Engineering; Marine Engineering; Mechanical Engineering; Petroleum and Gas Engineering; Power Engineering; Transport Engineering); **Foreign Languages** (Applied Linguistics; English; French; Japanese; Linguistics; Literature; Modern Languages); **Information Engineering** (Automation and Control Engineering; Electronic Engineering; Information Technology; Telecommunications Engineering); **International Education**; **Logistics Engineering** (Automation and Control Engineering; Electronic Engineering; Mechanical Engineering; Transport Engineering; Transport Management); **Management** (Accountancy; Business Administration; Finance; Human Resources; Information Management; Information Sciences; Management; Marketing; Social Welfare); **Materials Science and Engineering** (Biomedical Engineering; Biomedicine; Chemistry; Inorganic Chemistry; Materials Engineering; Physics); **Mechanical and Electronic Engineering** (Automation and Control Engineering; Electronic Engineering; Industrial Engineering; Measurement and Precision Engineering; Mechanical Engineering; Packaging Technology); **Media and Law** (Advertising and Publicity; Civil Law; Commercial Law; Contemporary History; Educational Technology; Ethics; Law; Mass Communication; Media Studies; Modern History; Political Sciences; Publishing and Book Trade); **Navigation** (Environmental Management; Information Technology; Marine Science and Oceanography; Marine Transport; Transport and Communications; Transport Engineering); **On-line and Continuing Education**; **Politics and Administration** (Administration; Political Sciences; Social Work); **Resources and Environmental Engineering** (Environmental Engineering; Environmental Studies; Information Technology; Mineralogy; Mining Engineering; Rural Planning; Safety Engineering; Town Planning); **Sciences** (Applied Chemistry; Applied Mathematics; Biotechnology; Computer Science; Electronic Engineering; Engineering; Information Sciences; Inorganic Chemistry; Mathematics and Computer Science; Mechanics; Optical Technology; Optics; Physical Chemistry; Physics; Statistics); **Transportation** (Bridge Engineering; Marine Engineering; Mechanics; Railway Engineering; Road Engineering; Sound Engineering (Acoustics); Structural Architecture; Transport and Communications; Transport Management); **Vocational Technology** (Automotive Engineering; English; International Business; International Economics; Telecommunications Engineering)

Institute

Higher Education (Educational Administration; Higher Education; Physical Education)

Further Information: 3 main campuses: the Mafanshan Campus, the Yujiatou Campus and the South Lake new Campus.

History: Founded 2000 on the basis of former Wuhan University of Technology (WUT, founded in 1948) under the Ministry of Education, Wuhan Transportation University (WTU, founded in 1945) under the Ministry of Communications and Wuhan Automotive Polytechnic University (WAPU, founded in 1958) under the China National Automotive Industry Corporation.

Academic Year: September to July (September-January; February-July)

Admission Requirements: Graduation from senior middle school and entrance examination

Fees: (Yuan): c. 3,000 per annum

Main Language(s) of Instruction: Chinese

Degrees and Diplomas: *Xueshi Xuewei*; *Shuoshi Xuewei*; *Boshi*. Also MBA.

Student Services: Academic Counselling, Careers Guidance, Health Services, Nursery Care, Social Counselling, Sports Facilities

Publications: Higher Education Development and Evaluation; International Journal of Nonlinear Sciences and Numerical Simulation; Journal of Blasting; Journal of Building Materials; Journal of Technology College Education; Journal of Transportation Information and Safety; Journal of Wuhan University of Technology; Journal of Wuhan University of Technology (Information & Management Engineering); Journal of Wuhan University of Technology (Materials Science Edition); Journal of Wuhan University of Technology (Social Sciences Edition); Journal of Wuhan University of Technology (Transportation Science and Engineering); Port Operation; Ship & Ocean Engineering; Transportation Enterprise Management; Transportation Science & Technology

Publishing House: Wuhan University of Technology Press

Academic Staff *2011-2012*	**TOTAL**
FULL-TIME	c. 5,500
Student Numbers *2011-2012*	
All (Foreign included)	c. 52,700
FOREIGN ONLY	570

Part-time students, 51,200.

Last Updated: 03/01/13

WUHAN YANGTZE BUSINESS UNIVERSITY (WYBU)

No.8 Huangjiahuxilu, Hongshan District, Wuhan, Hubei 430065
Tel: +86(27) 88147160
Fax: +86(27) 88147110
EMail: karenma96@hotmail.com
Website: http://www.wybu.cn/

President: Zhang Jinlong

College

Communication and Design (Advertising and Publicity; Architectural and Environmental Design; Communication Arts; Design; Fine Arts; Industrial Design; Journalism; Law; Mass Communication; Multimedia; Visual Arts); **Electronic Commerce** (E-Business/Commerce; Information Management; Information Sciences; Information Technology; Marketing); **Engineering** (Bioengineering; Biological and Life Sciences; Computer Engineering; Computer Science; Electronic Engineering; Engineering; Environmental Engineering; Environmental Studies; Information Technology; Telecommunications Engineering); **Finance and Business English** (Economics; English; Finance; International Business; International Economics; Literature; Management; Modern Languages); **Management** (Accountancy; Business Administration; Human Resources; Industrial Management; Management; Tourism); **Politics and Law** (Administrative Law; Chinese; Civil Law; Commercial Law; Constitutional Law; Criminal Law; English; History of Law; International Law; Labour and Industrial Relations; Law; Mathematics; Political Sciences; Private Law; Statistics)

School

International Education

History: Founded 2002 as Hongbo College of South-central University for Nationalities. Renamed as International Engineering and Commerce College of South-central University for Nationalities 2003. Renamed as Engineering and Commerce College of South-central University for Nationalities 2004. Acquired present status and title 2011.

Main Language(s) of Instruction: Chinese

Degrees and Diplomas: *Xueshi Xuewei*. Also Sino-Canadian 2+1 Double Diploma Programme; Sino-Canadian 2+2 Double Degrees Programme; Sino-Irish 2+2 Double Degrees Programme.

Student Services: Language Laboratory, Sports Facilities

Academic Staff *2013-2014*: Total 653

Student Numbers *2013-2014*: Total 12,783

Last Updated: 30/10/13

WUYI UNIVERSITY (WYU)

N°22, Dong Cheng Cun, Jiangmen, Guangdong Province 529020
Tel: +86(750) 3296120
Fax: +86(750) 3296126
EMail: wuyifao@yahoo.com.cn
Website: http://www.wyu.edu.cn

President: Zhang Kun Tel: +86(750) 3296111

Administrative Officer: Qiuying Ji
Tel: +86(750) 3296110 EMail: op@wyu.cn

International Relations: Changchun Zheng

School

Applied Physics and Material (Applied Mathematics; Applied Physics; Mathematics); **Chemical and Environmental Engineering** (Chemical Engineering; Environmental Engineering); **Civil Engineering and Architecture** (Architecture; Civil Engineering); **Computer Science** (Computer Engineering; Computer Networks; Computer Science; Software Engineering); **Economics and Management** (Economics; Management); **Foreign Languages** (English; Modern Languages); **Information Engineering** (Automation and Control Engineering; Computer Engineering; Electronic Engineering; Information Technology; Telecommunications Engineering; Transport Engineering); **Liberal Arts** *(School of Chinese Language and Literature)* (Arts and Humanities; Asian Studies; Chinese; Literature); **Mathematics and Computing Science** (Computer Science; Information Sciences; Mathematics and Computer Science); **Mechanical and Electrical Engineering** (Electrical Engineering; Mechanical Engineering); **Political Science and Law** (Law; Political Sciences); **Textiles and Clothing** (Textile Design; Textile Technology)

Department

Art Design (Architectural and Environmental Design; Architecture; Design; Fashion Design; Fine Arts; Graphic Design; Industrial Design); **Ideological and Political Theory Course Teaching** (Political Sciences); **Physical Education** (Physical Education; Sports)

Centre

Analysis and Testing

Research Centre

Guangdong Qiaoxiang Culture (Cultural Studies)

Further Information: Also courses in Chinese Language and Culture; English Language and Literature; Modern China (in English) for foreign students

History: Founded 1985.

Admission Requirements: High School Certificate or Bachelor Degree; Meeting requirements set for the relevant major; and sufficient Chinese language level (HSK level 4 at least)

Fees: (Yuan): Chinese Language Programme, 6,500 per semester and 13,000 per annum; Undergraduate Programmes, 13,000-15,000 per annum; Postgraduate Programmes, 16,000-18,000 per annum; HSK Intensive Training Programme, (minimum) 800 per week and 3,000 for four weeks; Short-term Chinese Social and Cultural Immersion Programme, (minimum) 2,000 per week (including tuition, sightseeing and accommodations)

Main Language(s) of Instruction: Chinese and English

Degrees and Diplomas: *Xueshi Xuewei*; *Shuoshi Xuewei*

Student Services: Academic Counselling, Canteen, Careers Guidance, Cultural Activities, Facilities for disabled people, Foreign Studies Centre, Health Services, Language Laboratory, Nursery Care, Social Counselling, Sports Facilities

Publications: Natural Sciences, Journal of Wuyi University; Social Sciences, Journal of Wuyi University; Wuyi University Newsletter

Academic Staff *2011-2012*	**TOTAL**
FULL-TIME	c. **740**

Student Numbers *2011-2012*	
All (Foreign included)	c. **17,000**
FOREIGN ONLY	**700**

Last Updated: 03/01/13

WUZHOU UNIVERSITY

No. 82 Fumin Road, Wuzhou, GuangXi
Tel: +86(774) 5820972 +86(774) 5827979
EMail: wzxyxcb@163.com; exchangeofficewz@163.com
Website: http://www.gxuwz.edu.cn/

President: Lifeng Sheng (2009-)

Department

Art (Advertising and Publicity; Design; Fashion Design; Fine Arts; Industrial Design; Jewellery Art; Music; Music Education; Visual Arts); **Business Administration** (Business Administration; Finance; Management; Marketing; Tourism); **Chinese** (Chinese); **Computer Science** (Computer Engineering; Computer Networks; Computer Science; Information Technology; Software Engineering); **Economics** (E-Business/Commerce; Economics; Finance; Information Sciences; Insurance; International Business; International Economics); **Education** (Education; Teacher Training); **Electronic and Information Engineering** (Automation and Control Engineering; Electrical Engineering; Electronic Engineering; Industrial Design; Information Technology; Mechanical Engineering; Telecommunications Engineering); **International Studies** (English; International Studies; Modern Languages); **Law and Public Administration** (Administration; Administrative Law; Communication Studies; Government; Law; Management; Political Sciences; Public Administration); **Mathematics and Physics** (Applied Physics; Chemistry; Computer Science; Information Sciences; Mathematics; Pharmacology; Physics); **Public Infrastructure** (Physical Education; Safety Engineering; Sports); **Social Sciences** (History; Philosophy; Political Sciences; Social Sciences)

Centre

Modern Education Technology (Educational Technology)

History: Founded 1985 as the Wuzhou Branch of Guangxi University. Acquired present status and title 2006.

Main Language(s) of Instruction: Chinese

Degrees and Diplomas: *Xueshi Xuewei*. Also 3-years degree programmes

Academic Staff *2012-2013*	**TOTAL**
FULL-TIME	**500**
PART-TIME	**620**

Student Numbers *2012-2013*	
All (Foreign included)	c. **15,000**
FOREIGN ONLY	**550**

Last Updated: 25/09/13

XI'AN ACADEMY OF FINE ARTS (XAFA)

100 Hanguang South Road, Xi'an, Shaanxi Province 710065
Tel: +86(29) 88216733
Fax: +86(29) 88216989
Website: http://www.xafa.edu.cn/

President: Wang Shengli

International Relations: Wu Shunong, Director, International Cooperation Office EMail: lavender.jasmine@yahoo.com.cn

Division

Graduate Studies

College

Fuzhong (Fine Arts)

Department

Adult Education; **Art Education** (Art Education); **Art History** (Art History); **Basic Studies** (Chinese; English; International Economics; Japanese; Literature; Political Sciences; Sports; Writing); **Chinese Painting** (Painting and Drawing); **Clothing** (Clothing and

Sewing); **Decorative Arts** (Painting and Drawing); **Design** (Design); **Fine Arts** (Fine Arts); **Oil Painting** (Painting and Drawing); **Printmaking** (Printing and Printmaking); **Sculpture** (Sculpture)

Centre

Primary Education Training (Primary Education); **Training** (Fine Arts)

History: Founded 1948 as Kangri Junzheng Northwest University, acquired present status 1960 and name 1980.

Admission Requirements: Entrance exam and HSK test (Chinese language test)

Main Language(s) of Instruction: Chinese

Degrees and Diplomas: *Xueshi Xuewei*; *Shuoshi Xuewei*; *Boshi*: **Arts and Humanities; Design; Fine Arts.**

Student Services: Academic Counselling, Foreign Studies Centre, Health Services, Language Laboratory, Nursery Care, Social Counselling, Sports Facilities

Academic Staff *2012-2013*: Total 768

Student Numbers *2012-2013*: Total: c. 7,500

Last Updated: 03/01/13

XI'AN CONSERVATORY OF MUSIC (XACOM)

108 Chang'an Road, Xi'an, Shaanxi Province 710061
Tel: +86(29) 5239738
Website: http://www.xacom.edu.cn

President: Zhao Jiping

International Relations: Sun Weiguo

School

Secondary Music Education *(Attached to the Conservatory)* (Music; Music Education; Secondary Education)

Department

Basic Studies; **Composition and Theory** (Music Theory and Composition); **Dance** (Dance); **Folk** (Jazz and Popular Music; Music); **Music** (Music); **Music Education** (Music Education); **Music Engineering** (Music; Sound Engineering (Acoustics)); **Orchestral** (Musical Instruments); **Piano** (Musical Instruments); **Postgraduate Studies** (Dance; Music; Music Education; Musical Instruments); **Solfeggio** (Music); **Vocal** (Singing)

History: Founded 1949 as Northwest Fine Arts School. Converted into Xi'an Music College 1956 before being upgraded to Xi'an Conservatory of Music in 1960.

Main Language(s) of Instruction: Chinese

Degrees and Diplomas: *Xueshi Xuewei*; *Shuoshi Xuewei*

Academic Staff *2011-2012*: Total: c. 380

Student Numbers *2011-2012*: Total: c. 4,000

Last Updated: 03/01/13

XI'AN EURASIA UNIVERSITY

No.1 Eurasia Road, Electronic Town, Xi 'an, Shaanxi 710065
Tel: +86(29) 88298754
Fax: +86(29) 88298629 +86(29) 88298771
EMail: zhaosheng@eurasia.edu
Website: http://www.eurasia.edu/

President: Hu Jianbo

School

Architectural Engineering (Architecture; Civil Engineering; Management; Structural Architecture); **Art and Design** (Advertising and Publicity; Architectural and Environmental Design; Design; Fine Arts; Graphic Design; Photography); **Business Administration** (Accountancy; Business Administration; Commercial Law; Finance; Management; Marketing; Secretarial Studies; Transport Management); **Finance and Trade** (Business Administration; Finance; Insurance; International Business; International Economics; Management; Real Estate); **Foreign Languages** (Applied Linguistics; English; Hotel and Restaurant; Modern Languages; Tourism; Translation and Interpretation); **Information and Engineering** (Computer Engineering; Computer Networks; E-Business/Commerce; Electronic Engineering; Information Technology; Measurement and Precision Engineering; Software Engineering; Telecommunications Engineering); **International** (Accountancy; Business Administration; Business Computing; Management); **Journalism and Mass Communication** (Journalism; Marketing; Mass Communication; Publishing and Book Trade); **Science and Technology** (Design; E-Business/Commerce; Fine Arts; Software Engineering; Structural Architecture)

History: Founded 1995.

Main Language(s) of Instruction: Chinese

Degrees and Diplomas: *Xueshi Xuewei*. Also 3-years degree programmes

Student Services: Canteen, Sports Facilities

Student Numbers *2012-2013*: Total: c. 22,000

Last Updated: 25/09/13

XI'AN FANYI UNIVERSITY (XFU)

Xi'an Chang'an Tai Gong 710105
Tel: +86(29) 85891139
Website: http://www.xfuedu.org/

President: Ding Jing Tel: Foreign Language

Department

Continuing Education Network; **Economics and Management** (Accountancy; Advertising and Publicity; Banking; Business Administration; Commercial Law; Documentation Techniques; E-Business/Commerce; Econometrics; Economics; Finance; Human Resources; Information Sciences; Information Technology; International Business; International Economics; International Law; Labour and Industrial Relations; Law; Management; Marketing; Statistics; Tourism; Transport Management); **Engineering and Technology** (Computer Engineering; Computer Science; E-Business/Commerce; Electronic Engineering; Engineering; Engineering Management; Information Sciences; Information Technology; Management; Software Engineering; Technology); **Humanities and Arts** (Advertising and Publicity; Arts and Humanities; Chinese; Design; English; Fine Arts; Industrial Design; Journalism; Linguistics; Literature; Modern Languages; Multimedia; Painting and Drawing; Radio and Television Broadcasting)

Institute

Foreign Languages (Business Administration; English; Foreign Languages Education; French; German; Japanese; Modern Languages; Tourism; Translation and Interpretation); **International Relations** (Computer Science; English; International Relations); **Translation Training** (Arts and Humanities; Business and Commerce; Chinese; Cultural Studies; English; Finance; French; German; International Business; Japanese; Journalism; Tourism; Translation and Interpretation; Writing)

Academy

Yi Chinese (Arts and Humanities; Chinese; Economics; Education; Engineering; English; Foreign Languages Education; Management; Modern Languages; Tourism)

Course

Sports (Sports)

History: Founded 1987. Authorized to grant Bachelor's degrees 2009.

Main Language(s) of Instruction: Chinese

Degrees and Diplomas: *Xueshi Xuewei*

Student Services: Canteen

Last Updated: 26/09/13

XI'AN INSTITUTE OF PHYSICAL EDUCATION (XAIPE)

65 Hanguang North Road, Xi'an, Shaanxi Province 710068
Tel: +86(29) 88409348
Fax: +86(29) 88409791
EMail: iecsport@yahoo.com.cn; iec04@xaipe.edu.cn
Website: http://www.xaipe.edu.cn/

President: Dang Qun

International Relations: Liu Guoyong

Department

Art (Dance; Musicology; Performing Arts; Radio and Television Broadcasting); **Graduate Study** (Physical Education; Psychology; Sociology; Sports); **Humanities** (Arts and Humanities; Economics; English Studies; Journalism; Marketing; Psychology; Sports Management); **Martial Arts** (Sports); **Physical Education** (Physical Education); **Physical Sociology** (Sociology); **Sports Human Body Science** (Health Sciences; Rehabilitation and Therapy; Sports); **Sports Training** (Sports)

History: Founded 1954 as Northwest Institute of Physical Education, acquired present name 1956.

Main Language(s) of Instruction: Chinese

Degrees and Diplomas: *Xueshi Xuewei*; *Shuoshi Xuewei*

Student Numbers *2011-2012*: Total: c. 7,000

Last Updated: 03/01/13

XI'AN INTERNATIONAL STUDIES UNIVERSITY (XISU)

No.1 Wenyuan Nanlu, Guodu Educational Sci-tech Industrial Zone, Xi'an, Shaanxi Province 710128

Tel: +86(29) 85319247 +86(29) 8531974

Fax: +86(29) 8531900 +86(29) 85319100

EMail: jyzxb@xisu.edu.cn; sss@xius.edu.cn

Website: http://www.xisu.edu.cn

President: Sishe Hu

Tel: +86(29) 85319002 EMail: hushishe@xisu.edu.cn

Chairman of the CCP Committee: Xiwen Yang

International Relations: Rong Bin, Director of International Affairs

Tel: +86(29) 85319417 EMail: guojichu@xisu.edu.cn

School

Chinese Studies (Asian Studies; Chinese); **Continuing Education**; **English Studies** *(SES)* (English; English Studies); **General Studies** (Computer Science; English; French; German; Japanese; Translation and Interpretation); **German Studies** (German; Germanic Studies); **International Programs** (International Studies); **International Relations** (International Relations); **Journalism and Communication** (Journalism; Mass Communication); **Oriental Languages and Cultures** (Cultural Studies; Oriental Languages); **Postgraduate Studies** (Applied Linguistics; Comparative Literature; Curriculum; English; French; Geography (Human); German; Japanese; Linguistics; Literature; Modern Languages; Native Language Education; Russian; Tourism; Translation and Interpretation); **Pre-Departure Training Programs and Services** (International Studies); **Russian Studies** (Cultural Studies; Russian); **Tourism and Research Institute of Human Geography** (Geography (Human); Tourism); **Translation Studies** *(STS)* (Translation and Interpretation); **Vocational Education** (Vocational Education); **Western Languages and Cultures** (English; European Studies; Modern Languages)

Research Centre

Foreign Language and Literature (Literature; Modern Languages); **Human Geography** (Geography (Human)); **Media Ethics** (Media Studies)

History: Founded 1952 as Northwest Institute of Russian. Renamed Xi'an Foreign Languages University 1958. Acquired present title 2006.

Academic Year: September to July

Admission Requirements: National Matriculation Examination

Main Language(s) of Instruction: Chinese

Accrediting Agency: Ministry of Education; Education Department of Shaanxi Province

Degrees and Diplomas: *Xueshi Xuewei*; *Shuoshi Xuewei*; *Boshi*

Student Services: Academic Counselling, Canteen, Careers Guidance, Cultural Activities, Facilities for disabled people, Foreign Studies Centre, Health Services, Language Laboratory, Nursery Care, Social Counselling, Sports Facilities

Publications: Foreign Language Education; Human Geography; Journal of Xi'an International Studies University

Publishing House: XISU Audio-visual Publishing House

Student Numbers *2011-2012*: Total: c. 24,000

Last Updated: 04/01/13

XI'AN JIAOTONG UNIVERSITY (XJTU)

28, Xianning West Road, Xi'an, Shaanxi Province 710049

Tel: +86(29) 2668830

Fax: +86(29) 3234716

EMail: xinxigl@mail.xjtu.edu.cn

Website: http://www.xjtu.edu.cn

President: Zheng Nanning (2003-)

Tel: +86(29) 2668234 EMail: office@mail.xjtu.edu.cn

International Relations: Yu Bingfeng

College

Chongshi; **ChungYing** (Management); **Lizhi**; **Nanyang**; **Pengkang** (Educational and Student Counselling; Leadership; Management); **Qide** (Ethics; Management); **Songlian** (Education; Educational Psychology); **Wenzhi**

School

Aerospace (Aeronautical and Aerospace Engineering; Automotive Engineering; Computer Science; Engineering; Environmental Engineering; Mechanics; Systems Analysis); **Continuing Education**; **Economics and Finance** (Banking; E-Business/Commerce; Economics; Finance; International Business; International Economics; Statistics); **Electrical Engineering** (Automation and Control Engineering; Electrical and Electronic Engineering; Electrical Engineering; Industrial Engineering; Power Engineering); **Electronic and Information Engineering** (Automation and Control Engineering; Computer Science; Electronic Engineering; Information Technology; Microelectronics; Telecommunications Engineering); **Energy and Power Engineering** (Energy Engineering; Power Engineering); **Foreign Studies**; **Human Settlement and Civil Engineering** (Architectural and Environmental Design; Architecture; Civil Engineering; Environmental Engineering; Environmental Studies; Structural Architecture); **Humanities and Social Sciences** (Arts and Humanities; Chinese; Cultural Studies; Design; Educational Technology; Fine Arts; History; Journalism; Mass Communication; Music Education; Philosophy; Political Sciences; Social Sciences; Sociology; Technology Education; Vocational Education); **International Education** (Chinese); **Law** (Constitutional Law; Government; International Economics; Law; Public Law); **Life Science and Technology** (Bioengineering; Biological and Life Sciences; Biomedical Engineering; Computer Science; Information Technology); **Management** (Accountancy; E-Business/Commerce; Engineering Management; Finance; Industrial Engineering; Information Management; Management; Marketing); **Materials Science and Engineering** (Materials Engineering); **Mathematics and Statistics** (Mathematics; Statistics); **Mechanical Engineering** (Automation and Control Engineering; Automotive Engineering; Industrial Design; Machine Building; Measurement and Precision Engineering; Mechanical Engineering); **Medicine** *(Former Xi'an Medical University)* (Dentistry; Medical Technology; Medicine; Nursing; Pharmacology; Social and Preventive Medicine); **Public Policy and Management** (Asian Studies; Demography and Population; European Studies; Health Administration; Higher Education; Management; Public Administration; Social and Community Services; Social and Preventive Medicine); **Science** (Analytical Chemistry; Applied Chemistry; Applied Mathematics; Applied Physics; Chemistry; Computer Science; Information Sciences; Mathematics; Mathematics and Computer Science; Nuclear Physics; Operations Research; Optical Technology; Optics; Physics; Polymer and Plastics Technology; Solid State Physics; Statistics); **Software Engineering** (Computer Engineering; Mathematics; Software Engineering)

Centre

Economic Research *(Jinhe)* (Economics); **Physical Education** (Physical Education)

Further Information: 3 campuses: the Xingqing campus, the Yanta campus and the Qujiang campus. Also 8 affiliated teaching hospitals. A traditional and distance learning institution.

History: Founded 1896 as Nanyang Public in South Ocean College. Renamed Jiaotong University 1921. Moved to Xi'an and renamed Xi'an Jiaotong University 1956. Merged with the Xi'an Medical University and the Shaanxi Institute of Finance and Economics 2000. One of the only two universities in China with a "class for gifted young people".

Academic Year: September to July (September-January; February-July)

Admission Requirements: Graduation from high school and entrance examination

Main Language(s) of Instruction: Chinese

Degrees and Diplomas: *Xueshi Xuewei*; *Shuoshi Xuewei*; *Boshi*. Also MBA and Executive MBA

Student Services: Academic Counselling, Canteen, Careers Guidance, Cultural Activities, Foreign Studies Centre, Health Services, Language Laboratory, Nursery Care, Social Counselling, Sports Facilities

Publications: Journal of Applied Mechanics; Journal of Engineering Mathematics; Journal of Xi'an Jiaotong University

Publishing House: Publishing House of Xi'an Jiaotong University

Academic Staff *2011-2012*: Total: c. 2,416

Student Numbers *2011-2012*: Total: c. 30,000

Distance students, 6700.

Last Updated: 04/01/13

XI'AN JIAOTONG-LIVERPOOL UNIVERSITY

111 Ren'ai Road, Dushu Lake Higher Education Town, Suzhou Industrial Park, Suzhou, Jiangsu 215123
Tel: +86(512) 88161000
Fax: +86(512) 88161899
EMail: Sam.Penney@xjtlu.edu.cn; external-collaboration@xjtlu.edu.cn
Website: http://www.xjtlu.edu.cn/en/

President: Youmin Xi (2008-)
Tel: +86(512) 88161004 EMail: Youmin.Xi@xjtlu.edu.cn

Vice President: Yimin Ding
Tel: +86(512) 88161021 EMail: Yimin.ding@xjtlu.edu.cn

International Relations: Fang Gui, Team Leader of External Liaison Office
Tel: +86(512) 88161894 EMail: fang.gui@xjtlu.edu.cn

School

Business (Accountancy; Business and Commerce; Economics; Finance; Management)

Department

Architecture (Architecture); **Biological Sciences** (Biochemistry; Biological and Life Sciences; Biology; Genetics; Microbiology; Molecular Biology); **Chemistry** (Chemistry); **Civil Engineering** (Civil Engineering); **Computer Science and Software Engineering** (Computer Science; Information Sciences; Software Engineering); **Electrical and Electronic Engineering** (Electrical and Electronic Engineering); **English, Culture and Communication** (Communication Studies; Cultural Studies; English); **Environmental Science** (Environmental Studies); **Mathematical Sciences** (Mathematics); **Urban Planning and Design** (Town Planning; Urban Studies)

History: Founded 2006. An international university jointly founded by Xi'an Jiaotong University China and the University of Liverpool UK.

Academic Year: Sep to Jan; Feb to June

Admission Requirements: Undergraduate course, Chinese mainland: High School Diploma, scores above Tier 1 line in National College Entrance Examination (Gaokao); Overseas: high school diploma or leaving certificate or equivalent qualifications with core modules 75% or above, and IELTS 5.5 or TOEFL (iBT) 75.

Fees: 60,000 per annum (Yuan Renminbi)

Main Language(s) of Instruction: English

Accrediting Agency: Ministry of Education

Degrees and Diplomas: *Xueshi Xuewei*: **Accountancy; Applied Chemistry; Applied Mathematics; Architecture; Automation and Control Engineering; Biological and Life Sciences; Business Administration; Civil Engineering; Communication Studies; Computer Science; Design; Economics; Electrical Engineering; Electronic Engineering; English; English Studies; Environmental Studies; Finance; Human Resources; Industrial Design; Information Management; Information Technology; International Business; Marketing; Mathematics; Media Studies; Telecommunications Engineering; Town Planning.** *Shuoshi Xuewei*: **Computer Engineering; Energy Engineering; Finance; Foreign Languages Education; Multimedia; Telecommunications Engineering.** *Boshi*: **Architectural and Environmental Design; Biological and Life Sciences; Business and Commerce; Civil Engineering; Communication Studies; Computer Science; Electrical and Electronic Engineering; Mathematics; Town Planning.**

Student Services: Academic Counselling, Canteen, Careers Guidance, Cultural Activities, Facilities for disabled people, Foreign Studies Centre, Health Services, Language Laboratory, Nursery Care, Social Counselling, Sports Facilities

Academic Staff *2012-2013*	MEN	WOMEN	TOTAL
FULL-TIME	252	258	**510**
PART-TIME	53	49	**102**
STAFF WITH DOCTORATE			
FULL-TIME	118	60	**178**
Student Numbers *2012-213*			
All (Foreign included)	3,541	3,826	**7,367**
FOREIGN ONLY	64	22	**86**

Last Updated: 15/03/13

XI'AN PEIHUA UNIVERSITY

Xi'an Chang'an South Road, Pui, Shaanxi 710125
Tel: +86(29) 85680000
Fax: +86(29) 85680001
EMail: phxc@peihua.cn
Website: http://www.peihua.cn/

President: Jiang Bo

College

Accounting (Accountancy; Finance; Management); **Adult Education** (Accountancy; Advertising and Publicity; Business Administration; Business and Commerce; Chinese; Civil Engineering; Clothing and Sewing; Computer Science; Construction Engineering; Design; Engineering Management; English; Finance; Human Resources; Industrial Management; Information Technology; International Business; Laboratory Techniques; Law; Literature; Marketing; Medical Technology; Medicine; Nursing; Real Estate; Secretarial Studies; Stomatology; Telecommunications Engineering; Tourism; Transport Management; Visual Arts); **Architectural Engineering** (Architectural and Environmental Design; Architecture; Civil Engineering; Construction Engineering; Design; Engineering Management; Structural Architecture); **Arts and Humanities** (Advertising and Publicity; Architectural and Environmental Design; Arts and Humanities; Communication Arts; Graphic Design; Journalism; Law; Literature; Native Language Education; Radio and Television Broadcasting; Visual Arts); **Business** (Administration; Business Administration; Business and Commerce; E-Business/Commerce; Hotel Management; Human Resources; International Business; International Economics; Management; Marketing; Real Estate; Secretarial Studies; Tourism; Transport Management); **Electrical and Information Engineering** (Computer Engineering; Computer Networks; Computer Science; Electrical Engineering; Information Management; Information Technology; Media Studies; Software Engineering; Telecommunications Engineering); **International Linguistic and Culture** (Applied Linguistics; Cultural Studies; English; International Business; Japanese; Linguistics; Tourism; Translation and Interpretation); **Medicine** (Marketing; Medicine; Nursing; Pharmacy); **Vocational Educational Studies** (Accountancy; Business Administration; Business Computing; Chinese; Construction Engineering; E-Business/Commerce; Education; English; Finance; International Business; Journalism; Literature; Management; Real Estate; Telecommunications Engineering; Tourism; Transport Management); **Women's** (Gender Studies; Women's Studies)

Department

Basic Education

History: Founded 1984 as West Peihua Women's University. Acquired present status and title 2003.

Main Language(s) of Instruction: Chinese

Degrees and Diplomas: *Xueshi Xuewei*. Also 3 yr Associate degree programmes

Last Updated: 27/09/13

XI'AN POLYTECHNIC UNIVERSITY (XPU)

19 South Jinhua Road, Xi'an, Shaanxi Province 710048
Tel: +86(29) 82330567 +86(29) 82330049
Fax: +86(29) 82330320
EMail: interoffi@xpu.edu.cn
Website: http://www.xpu.edu.cn

President: Gao Yong

International Relations: Hu Weihua, Director, International Office Tel: +86(29) 82330049 EMail: hwhfld@yahoo.com.cn

College

Apparel and Art Design (Advertising and Publicity; Architectural and Environmental Design; Clothing and Sewing; Design; Fashion Design; Fine Arts; Marketing; Photography; Visual Arts); **Art Engineering** (Architectural and Environmental Design; Cinema and Television; Design; Fashion Design; Radio and Television Broadcasting; Visual Arts); **Computer Science** (Computer Engineering; Computer Networks; Computer Science; Educational Technology; Electronic Engineering; Information Sciences; Information Technology; Software Engineering); **Electronics and Information** (Automation and Control Engineering; Electrical and Electronic Engineering; Electrical Engineering; Electronic Engineering; Information Sciences; Measurement and Precision Engineering; Power Engineering; Production Engineering; Telecommunications Engineering); **Environmental and Chemical Engineering** (Applied Chemistry; Architecture; Bioengineering; Biological and Life Sciences; Building Technologies; Chemical Engineering; Chemistry; Civil Engineering; Environmental Engineering; Environmental Studies; Heating and Refrigeration; Water Management; Water Science); **Humanities and Social Science** (Applied Linguistics; Arts and Humanities; Chinese; English; Law; Linguistics; Literature; Modern Languages; Social Sciences); **Management** (Accountancy; Automation and Control Engineering; Business Administration; Economics; Engineering Management; Human Resources; Industrial Engineering; Information Management; Information Sciences; International Business; Management; Marketing; Public Administration); **Mechanical and Electrical Engineering** (Automation and Control Engineering; Design; Electrical Engineering; Electronic Engineering; Engineering Management; Industrial Design; Industrial Engineering; Machine Building; Materials Engineering; Mechanical Engineering; Packaging Technology; Transport Engineering; Transport Management); **Science** (Applied Mathematics; Applied Physics; Computer Science; Electronic Engineering; Information Sciences; Mathematics; Microelectronics; Statistics); **Textiles and Materials** (Industrial Chemistry; Industrial Engineering; Materials Engineering; Polymer and Plastics Technology; Textile Design; Textile Technology)

Department

Ideological and Political Theory Teaching Research (Political Sciences); **Physical Education** (Physical Education; Sports)

Further Information: 2 campuses: Jinhua and Lintong

History: Founded 1912 as the Weaving Division of the Beijing Higher Industrial School. Upgraded to Northwest Institute of Textile Technology 1978. Acquired present title 2001.

Fees: (Yuan): Undergraduate tuition, 18,000-22,000 per annum; 20,000-24,000 per annum; Language training programme, 14,000 per annum; Short-term training programme, 250 per month

Main Language(s) of Instruction: Chinese

Accrediting Agency: Ministry of Education

Degrees and Diplomas: *Xueshi Xuewei*; *Shuoshi Xuewei*

Academic Staff *2011-2012*	**TOTAL**
FULL-TIME	c. **1,200**
Student Numbers *2011-2012*	
All (Foreign included)	c. **24,000**
FOREIGN ONLY	**150**

Last Updated: 04/01/13

XI'AN SHIYOU UNIVERSITY (XSYU)

2 Dianzi Road, Xi'an, Shaanxi Province 710065
Tel: +86(29) 8234449
Fax: +86(29) 8234449
EMail: waiban@xsyu.edu.cn
Website: http://www.xapi.edu.cn

President: Qu Zhan (2011-)

College

Chemistry and Chemical Engineering (Applied Chemistry; Chemical Engineering; Chemistry; Environmental Engineering); **Computer Science** (Artificial Intelligence; Computer Networks; Computer Science; Educational Technology; Information Sciences; Media Studies; Software Engineering; Telecommunications Engineering); **Economics and Business Management** (Accountancy; Business Administration; E-Business/Commerce; Economics; Finance; Human Resources; Information Management; Information Sciences; International Business; International Economics; Management; Marketing; Tourism); **Electronic Engineering** (Automation and Control Engineering; Electrical and Electronic Engineering; Electronic Engineering; Information Sciences; Information Technology; Instrument Making; Measurement and Precision Engineering; Power Engineering; Safety Engineering); **Humanities** (Administrative Law; Advertising and Publicity; Arts and Humanities; Chinese; Civil Law; Commercial Law; Criminal Law; Design; International Law; Journalism; Law; Literature; Marketing; Mass Communication; Modern Languages; Private Law; Psychology; Public Relations; Radio and Television Broadcasting; Secretarial Studies); **Material Science and Engineering** (Chemistry; Materials Engineering; Metal Techniques; Metallurgical Engineering; Physics; Solid State Physics); **Mechanical Engineering** (Automation and Control Engineering; Automotive Engineering; Chemical Engineering; Civil Engineering; Electronic Engineering; Industrial Design; Machine Building; Mechanical Engineering; Power Engineering; Production Engineering; Thermal Engineering); **Oil and Gas Resources** (Geological Engineering; Geology; Geophysics; Information Technology; Mineralogy; Mining Engineering; Natural Resources; Petroleum and Gas Engineering; Surveying and Mapping); **Petroleum Engineering** (Petroleum and Gas Engineering; Transport Engineering); **Science** (Applied Mathematics; Computer Science; Electronic Engineering; Information Sciences; Information Technology; Mathematics; Mathematics and Computer Science; Optical Technology; Optics; Physics); **Vocational and Technical Education** (Accountancy; Automation and Control Engineering; Business Computing; Computer Engineering; Computer Networks; Electrical Engineering; Geological Engineering; Industrial Engineering; Mechanical Engineering; Metal Techniques; Mining Engineering; Petroleum and Gas Engineering; Power Engineering; Safety Engineering; Thermal Engineering; Transport Engineering; Transport Management)

Department

Foreign Languages (English; Grammar; Linguistics; Literature; Modern Languages; Russian; Translation and Interpretation; Writing); **Music** (Dance; Music; Music Education; Music Theory and Composition; Musical Instruments; Singing); **Physical Education** (Human Resources; Management; Marketing; Physical Education; Sports; Sports Management)

History: Founded 1951 as Northwest Oil Industry Secondary School. Transformed into Xian Petroleum College 1958. Transformed into a factory 1969 and during the Great Cultural Revolution. Resumed educational activity 1980. Acquired present status and title 2003.

Main Language(s) of Instruction: Chinese

Degrees and Diplomas: *Xueshi Xuewei*; *Shuoshi Xuewei*; *Boshi*: **Petroleum and Gas Engineering.** The Doctor's Degree is a joint-training programme. Also MBA.

Academic Staff *2011-2012*	**TOTAL**
FULL-TIME	c. **1,000**
Student Numbers *2011-2012*	
All (Foreign included)	c. **21,000**
FOREIGN ONLY	**300**

Last Updated: 07/01/13

XI'AN SIYUAN UNIVERSITY (XASYU)

28 Shui An Rd., Dongjiao, Xian, Shaanxi 710038
Tel: +86(29) 82601888
Fax: +86(29) 82616888
EMail: wangzh@xasyu.cn; zb@xasyu.cn
Website: http://www.xasyu.cn/

President: Zhai Hong

Faculty
Arts (Information Technology); **Automobile and Transportation** (Automation and Control Engineering; Automotive Engineering; Industrial Engineering; Production Engineering; Telecommunications Engineering; Transport Engineering); **Economics and Trade** (Business Administration; Economics; Finance; Human Resources; International Business; International Economics; Management); **Electronic Information Engineering** (Electronic Engineering; Information Technology); **Energy and Electric Engineering** (Electrical Engineering; Energy Engineering); **Humanities** (Arts and Humanities; Chinese; Literature; Preschool Education; Publishing and Book Trade; Secretarial Studies); **International Education** (English; International Studies); **Management** (Management); **Mechanical and Electrical Engineering** (Electrical Engineering; Mechanical Engineering); **Science and Technology** (Computer Science; Information Technology; Natural Sciences; Technology); **Urban Construction** (Architecture; Civil Engineering; Construction Engineering; Interior Design; Town Planning); **Vocational Training** (Advertising and Publicity; Automation and Control Engineering; Computer Engineering; Computer Networks; Construction Engineering; Design; E-Business/Commerce; Electronic Engineering; English; Finance; Human Resources; Information Technology; International Business; Journalism; Maintenance Technology; Management; Marketing; Mechanical Engineering; Multimedia; Publishing and Book Trade; Real Estate; Software Engineering; Tourism; Transport and Communications; Transport Management)

School
Technicians (Technology)

Department
Sports (Sports)

History: Founded 1998 on the basis of the School of Mechanical Engineering, Xi'an Jiaotong University training center (founded 1994).

Main Language(s) of Instruction: Chinese

Degrees and Diplomas: *Xueshi Xuewei*. Also Sino-Canadian Joint Diploma Programme in Business Administration, Computer Engineering and Industrial Engineering; 3-year and 5-year Vocational Programmes

Student Services: Canteen, Sports Facilities

Student Numbers *2011-2012*: Total: c. 10,000

Last Updated: 30/09/13

XI'AN TECHNOLOGICAL UNIVERSITY (XATU)

4 Jinhua North Road, Xi'an, Shaanxi Province 710032
Tel: +86(29) 83208114
Fax: +86(29) 83244764
EMail: xait@mail.xait.edu.cn; sb2006@mail.xait.edu.cn
Website: http://www.xatu.cn/

President: Lian Zhenmin (2011-)

Faculty
Science (Applied Chemistry; Applied Mathematics; Chemistry; Computer Science; English; Information Sciences; Mathematics; Mechanics; Physics; Political Sciences; Sports; Surveying and Mapping)

College
Architecture and Civil Engineering (Architecture; Civil Engineering; Construction Engineering; Transport Engineering; Water Management); **Arts and Media** (Design; Fine Arts; Industrial Design; Media Studies; Visual Arts); **Computer Science and Engineering** (Computer Engineering; Computer Networks; Computer Science; Information Technology; Software Engineering); **Electronic and Information Engineering** (Automation and Control Engineering; Biomedical Engineering; Electrical and Electronic Engineering; Electrical Engineering; Electronic Engineering; Information Technology; Telecommunications Engineering); **Foreign Languages** (Applied Linguistics; English; German; Japanese; Linguistics; Modern Languages; Russian); **Humanities** (Arts and Humanities; Chinese; Communication Studies; Cultural Studies; Law; Literature); **Materials Science and Chemical Engineering** (Chemistry; Engineering; Environmental Engineering; Materials Engineering; Physics; Polymer and Plastics Technology); **Mechanical and Electrical Engineering** (Automation and Control Engineering; Electrical Engineering; Electronic Engineering; Industrial Design; Industrial Engineering; Mechanical Engineering; Packaging Technology; Production Engineering); **Optoelectronic Engineering** (Electronic Engineering; Engineering; Measurement and Precision Engineering; Microelectronics; Optical Technology; Optics; Solid State Physics)

School
Continuing Education; **Economics and Management** (Accountancy; Business Administration; Economics; Human Resources; Information Sciences; Management)

Department
Ideology and Political Sciences (History; Political Sciences)

Institute
Physical Education (Physical Education; Sports)

Centre
Industrial (Electronic Engineering; Industrial Engineering; Machine Building)

History: Founded 1955 as Xi'an Industrial School. Upgraded to Xi'an Instrument Professional School 1960 and then Xi'an Institute of Technology 1965. Acquired present title 2006.

Fees: (Yuan): Tuition fee, 3,500-9,000 per annum

Main Language(s) of Instruction: Chinese

Degrees and Diplomas: *Xueshi Xuewei*; *Shuoshi Xuewei*. Also MBA

Academic Staff *2011-2012*: Total: c. 1,400

Student Numbers *2011-2012*: Total: c. 19,000

Last Updated: 04/01/13

XI'AN UNIVERSITY OF ARCHITECTURE AND TECHNOLOGY (XAUAT)

13 Yanta Road, Xi'an, Shaanxi Province 710055
Tel: +86(29) 82202169
Fax: +86(29) 82224571
EMail: intlexchange@xauat.edu.cn
Website: http://www.xauat.edu.cn

President: Xu Delong

International Relations: Li Zheng

College
Architecture (Architecture; Landscape Architecture; Town Planning); **Arts** (Architectural and Environmental Design; Cinema and Television; Design; Film; Fine Arts; Graphic Design; Industrial Chemistry; Landscape Architecture; Multimedia; Museum Studies; Performing Arts; Photography; Sculpture); **Materials and Mineral Resources** (Materials Engineering; Mineralogy; Safety Engineering); **Vocational Technology** (Technology Education; Vocational Education)

School
Civil Engineering (Civil Engineering; Transport Engineering); **Environmental and Municipal Engineering** (Environmental Engineering; Environmental Studies; Waste Management; Water Management); **Information and Control Engineering** (Architecture; Automation and Control Engineering; Computer Science; Information Management; Information Technology); **Language, Literature and Law** *(SLLL)* (Chinese; English; French; German; Japanese; Law; Literature; Russian); **Management** (Business Administration; Engineering Management; Management); **Mechanical Engineering** (Mechanical Engineering); **Metallurgical Engineering** (Applied Chemistry; Chemical Engineering; Materials Engineering; Metallurgical Engineering; Physical Chemistry); **Science** (Applied Chemistry; Applied Mathematics; Applied Physics; Chemical Engineering; Civil Engineering; Engineering; Information Sciences; Information Technology; Mathematics; Mechanics; Physics); **Teaching and Research of Ideological and Political Theories** (Economics; History; Law; Philosophy; Political Sciences)

Department
Physical Education (Architecture; Architecture and Planning; Human Resources; Physical Education; Sports; Sports Management)

History: Founded 1956 as Xian Institute of Construction Engineering, became Xian Institute of Metallurgy and Construction Engineering 1963. Acquired present status and title 1994.
Academic Year: September to July (September-January; February-July)
Admission Requirements: Graduation from senior middle school and entrance examination
Fees: (Yuan): Tuition fee for overseas students, 25,000 per annum for Master's degree programmes; 35,000 per annum for Doctor's degree programmes; 2,500-3,500 per month for General and Advanced trainee programmes
Main Language(s) of Instruction: Chinese
Accrediting Agency: Ministry of Metallurgy
Degrees and Diplomas: *Xueshi Xuewei*; *Shuoshi Xuewei*; *Boshi*. Also post-doctoral studies programmes.
Publications: Architecture and Technology; Journal of Xi'an University of Architecture and Technology; Study of Higher Education
Publishing House: University Press

Academic Staff *2011-2012*: Total: c. 2,500
Student Numbers *2011-2012*: Total: c. 40,000
Last Updated: 07/01/13

XI'AN UNIVERSITY OF ARTS AND SCIENCE (XAWL)

168, South Taibai Road, Xi'an, Shaanxi Province 710065
Tel: +86(29) 88258556
EMail: xawlxyws@163.com
Website: http://www.xawl.org

President: Xu Kewei (2011-)

College

Arts (Communication Arts; Design; Fine Arts; Music; Performing Arts; Visual Arts); **Chemistry and Chemical Engineering** (Applied Chemistry; Chemical Engineering; Chemistry); **Education** (Applied Physics; Education; Physical Education; Primary Education); **Foreign Languages** (English; Literature; Modern Languages); **Kindergarten Teachers** (Preschool Education); **Liberal Arts** (Advertising and Publicity; Arts and Humanities; Chinese; Cinema and Television; Film; Literature; Modern Languages; Secretarial Studies; Theatre); **Mathematics and Computer Engineering** (Applied Mathematics; Computer Engineering; Computer Science; Information Sciences; Information Technology; Mathematics; Mathematics and Computer Science); **Physics and Mechanical and Electronic Engineering** (Applied Physics; Automation and Control Engineering; Electronic Engineering; Mechanical Engineering; Physics; Production Engineering)

School

Business *(Theory of Marxism Teaching and Research Department)* (Accountancy; Business Administration; Marketing; Political Sciences; Public Administration); **Continuing Education** (Accountancy; Applied Mathematics; Automation and Control Engineering; Business Administration; Business Computing; Chinese; Computer Science; Design; E-Business/Commerce; Education; Electrical Engineering; Electronic Engineering; English; Fine Arts; Foreign Languages Education; History; Information Management; Information Technology; Literature; Management; Marketing; Mathematics; Music; Physical Education; Political Sciences; Preschool Education; Production Engineering; Public Administration; Radio and Television Broadcasting; Secretarial Studies; Software Engineering; Tourism); **Culture and Tourism** (Cultural Studies; Tourism)

Institute

Biotechnology (Biological and Life Sciences; Biotechnology; Horticulture); **Software** (Software Engineering)
History: Created 2003 after merger between Xi'an United University and Xi'an College of Education.
Main Language(s) of Instruction: Chinese
Degrees and Diplomas: *Xueshi Xuewei*; *Shuoshi Xuewei*; *Boshi*. Also MBA and Postdoctoral programmes

Academic Staff *2011-2012*: Total: c. 1,100
Student Numbers *2011-2012*: Total: c. 13,000
Last Updated: 07/01/13

XI'AN UNIVERSITY OF FINANCE AND ECONOMICS (XAUFE)

81 Xiaozhai East Road, Xi'an, Shaanxi Province 710100
Tel: +86(29) 81556139
Fax: +86(29) 81556139
EMail: xkb@mail.xaufe.edu.cn; yuanzhang@mail.xaufe.edu.cn
Website: http://www.xaufe.edu.cn/English/survey.html

President: Hu Jian (2006-)
International Relations: Liu Zongzhao

College

Foreign Languages (English)

School

Business (Accountancy; Business Administration; Finance; Human Resources; Marketing; Tourism); **Continuing Education** *(Higher Vocational)*; **Economics** (Economics; Finance; International Business; Taxation); **Information Sciences** (Information Sciences); **Liberal Arts and Law** (Advertising and Publicity; Arts and Humanities; Chinese; Design; English; Journalism; Law; Literature; Mass Communication; Modern Languages; Radio and Television Broadcasting); **Management** (Agricultural Economics; Agricultural Management; Business Administration; Finance; Human Resources; Management; Marketing; Tourism); **Public Administration** (Public Administration); **Statistics** (Statistics)

Department

Graduate Studies; **Ideological and Political Theory Teaching and Research** (Political Sciences); **Physical Education** (Physical Education)
History: Founded 1978 as Shaanxi Business Management Institute. Merged with Shaanxi Institute of Economics and Trade, Xi' an Institute of Statistics and Xi' an Junior College of Finance 2002. Acquired present title the same year. Formerly known as Shaanxi Institute of Economics and Trade.
Main Language(s) of Instruction: Chinese
Degrees and Diplomas: *Xueshi Xuewei*; *Shuoshi Xuewei*

Academic Staff *2012-2013*: Total: c. 1,011
Student Numbers *2012-2013*: Total: c. 16,000
Last Updated: 07/01/13

XI'AN UNIVERSITY OF POSTS AND TELECOMMUNICATIONS (XUPT)

563 Chang'an Road, Xi'an, Shaanxi Province 710121
Tel: +86(29) 88166107
Fax: +86(29) 88166107
EMail: fao@xupt.edu.cn
Website: http://www.xupt.edu.cn/

President: Jian-Jun Lu (2009-)
International Relations: Jia Mingyuan

Faculty

Science (Applied Mathematics; Applied Physics; Computer Science; Information Sciences)

College

Communication and Information Engineering (Electronic Engineering; Information Management; Information Sciences; Information Technology; Radio and Television Broadcasting; Telecommunications Engineering); **Electronic Engineering** (Electrical and Electronic Engineering; Electronic Engineering; Information Technology; Microelectronics; Optical Technology); **Foreign Languages** (Applied Linguistics; English; Modern Languages); **Humanities and Social Sciences** (Administration; Arts and Humanities; Public Administration; Social Sciences; Social Work); **Management Engineering** (E-Business/Commerce; Industrial Engineering; Information Management; Information Sciences; Information Technology; Management; Transport Management); **National Defense Education** (Military Science)

School

Automation (Artificial Intelligence; Automation and Control Engineering; Electrical Engineering; Instrument Making; Measurement and Precision Engineering); **Computer Science** (Computer Engineering; Computer Networks; Computer Science; Software

Engineering); **Continuing Education, Vocational and Technical College**; **Economics and Management** (Accountancy; Business Administration; Economics; Finance; Human Resources; International Business; International Economics; Management; Marketing)

Department

Sports (Physical Education; Sports)

Institute

Digital Art (Communication Arts; Computer Networks; Computer Science; Fine Arts; Graphic Design; Media Studies; Multimedia; Painting and Drawing); **International Education**; **Internet** (Computer Science; Telecommunications Engineering)

Graduate School

Marxism Education (Contemporary History; Modern History; Philosophy; Political Sciences; Social Sciences)

Research Centre

Computational Financial and Risk Management (Finance; Insurance)

History: Founded 1950 as Northwest School of Post and Telecommunications, acquired present status and name 1959. Formerly known as Xi'an Institute of Posts and Telecommunications.

Main Language(s) of Instruction: Chinese

Degrees and Diplomas: *Xueshi Xuewei*; *Shuoshi Xuewei*. Also MBA

Student Services: Health Services

Academic Staff *2011-2012*: Total: c. 960

Student Numbers *2011-2012*: Total: c. 16,000

Last Updated: 08/01/13

XI'AN UNIVERSITY OF SCIENCE AND TECHNOLOGY (XUST)

14 Yanta Road, Xi'an, Shaanxi Province 710054
Tel: +86(29) 85583114
Fax: +86(29) 85583719
Website: http://www.xust.edu.cn

President: Su Sanqing Tel: +86(29) 85583031

International Relations: Xu Xingye

School

Architecture and Civil Engineering (Architecture; Civil Engineering); **Communication Engineering** (E-Business/Commerce; Electronic Engineering; Information Sciences; Information Technology; Telecommunications Engineering); **Electrical and Control Engineering** (Automation and Control Engineering; Electrical Engineering; Power Engineering); **Energy and Resource** (Construction Engineering; Energy Engineering; Mining Engineering; Safety Engineering); **Management** (Accountancy; Business Administration; Business Computing; Engineering Management; Information Management; Information Sciences; Management; Tourism); **Mechanical Engineering** (Automation and Control Engineering; Electronic Engineering; Industrial Design; Industrial Engineering; Mechanical Engineering)

Department

Basic Courses (Chemistry; Electronic Engineering; Mechanics; Mining Engineering; Physical Education; Technology); **Computer Science** (Computer Engineering; Computer Science; Information Technology); **Geology and Environmental Engineering** (Computer Science; Environmental Engineering; Geography; Geology); **Survey Engineering** (Surveying and Mapping)

History: Founded 1958 as Xi'an Mining institute. Renamed Xi'an College of Science and Technology 1999. Acquired present title 2003.

Main Language(s) of Instruction: Chinese

Degrees and Diplomas: *Xueshi Xuewei*; *Shuoshi Xuewei*; *Boshi*. Also MBA

Publications: Journal of Xi'an University of Science and Technology

Academic Staff *2012-2013*: Total: c. 1,100

Student Numbers *2011-2012*: Total: c. 23,740

Last Updated: 09/01/13

XI'AN UNIVERSITY OF TECHNOLOGY (XUT)

5 South Jinhua Road, Xi'an, Shaanxi Province 710048
Tel: +86(29) 82312558 +86(29) 82312541
Fax: +86(29) 82312558 +86(29) 83230026
EMail: waiban@xaut.edu.cn; xzb@mail.xaut.edu.cn
Website: http://www.xaut.edu.cn

President: Liu Ding

International Relations: Tian Jianing Tel: +86(29) 823-12545

Faculty

Automation and Information Engineering (Automation and Control Engineering; Chemistry; Electrical Engineering; Electronic Engineering; Information Sciences; Measurement and Precision Engineering; Microelectronics; Physics; Power Engineering; Telecommunications Engineering); **Computer Science and Engineering** (Computer Engineering; Computer Networks; Computer Science; Software Engineering); **Continuous Education** (Computer Engineering; Computer Science; Electronic Engineering; English; Information Technology; International Business; International Economics; Law; Mechanical Engineering); **Economics and Management** (Accountancy; Business Administration; E-Business/Commerce; Economics; Engineering; Finance; Industrial Engineering; Information Management; Information Sciences; International Business; International Economics; Management; Marketing); **High Vocational Education** (Automation and Control Engineering; Computer Engineering; Computer Science; E-Business/Commerce; Electrical Engineering; Electronic Engineering; Industrial Design; Information Technology; Measurement and Precision Engineering; Mechanical Engineering; Production Engineering; Secretarial Studies); **Humanities and Foreign Languages** (Applied Linguistics; Arts and Humanities; Chinese; Economics; English; Japanese; Law; Linguistics; Literature; Modern Languages; Political Sciences; Public Administration; Social Sciences); **Material Science and Engineering** (Automation and Control Engineering; Chemistry; Materials Engineering; Physics); **Mechanical and Precision Instrument Engineering** (Automation and Control Engineering; Automotive Engineering; Electronic Engineering; Industrial Design; Industrial Engineering; Information Sciences; Information Technology; Instrument Making; Measurement and Precision Engineering; Mechanical Engineering; Optical Technology; Packaging Technology); **Printing and Packaging Engineering** (Design; Electronic Engineering; Fine Arts; Food Science; Industrial Engineering; Information Management; Information Technology; Packaging Technology; Paper Technology; Photography); **Sciences** (Applied Chemistry; Applied Mathematics; Applied Physics; Computer Science; Engineering; Information Sciences; Mathematics and Computer Science; Mechanics; Pharmacology); **Water Resources and Hydraulic Power** (Agricultural Engineering; Automation and Control Engineering; Civil Engineering; Ecology; Electrical Engineering; Energy Engineering; Engineering; Environmental Engineering; Geological Engineering; Hydraulic Engineering; Power Engineering; Soil Management; Thermal Engineering; Town Planning; Water Management; Water Science)

School

Art and Design (Communication Arts; Design; Fine Arts; Packaging Technology; Photography; Visual Arts); **Civil Engineering** (Architecture; Bridge Engineering; Civil Engineering; Geological Engineering; Mechanical Engineering; Mechanics; Safety Engineering; Structural Architecture; Town Planning; Water Management); **Graduate Studies**; **National Defense Students Education (Navy)** (Military Science)

Further Information: 3 campuses: Jinhua, Qujiang and Lianhu.

History: Founded 1972 as Shaanxi Institute of Mechanical Engineering through the merger of Beijing Institute of Mechanical Engineering and Shaanxi Polytechnic University. Acquired present title 1994 and merged with Xi'an Instrument Technology School.

Main Language(s) of Instruction: Chinese and English

Degrees and Diplomas: *Xueshi Xuewei*; *Shuoshi Xuewei*; *Boshi*. Also MBA

Publications: Journal of Xi'an University of Technology

Academic Staff *2011-2012*	**TOTAL**
FULL-TIME	c. **1,300**
Student Numbers *2011-2012*	
All (Foreign Included)	c. **20,900**

Part-time students, 5,000.

Last Updated: 09/01/13

XIAMEN UNIVERSITY (XMU)

422 Siming South Road, Xiamen, Fujian Province 361005
Tel: +86(592) 2186237
Fax: +86(592) 2180240
EMail: ws@jingxian.xmu.edu.cn
Website: http://www.xmu.edu.cn

President: Zhu Chongshi (2003-)

College

Arts (Art Management; Design; Fine Arts; Music; Music Education; Painting and Drawing); **Chemistry and Chemical Engineering** (Biochemistry; Bioengineering; Biology; Chemical Engineering; Chemistry); **Continuing Education and Vacational Education** (Adult Education; Computer Education; Technology Education); **Foreign Languages and Cultures** (Cultural Studies; English; European Languages; French; German; Japanese; Literature; Modern Languages; Russian); **International Studies** (International Studies); **Materials Science** (Biological and Life Sciences; Materials Engineering); **Medical Studies** (Medicine; Nursing; Pharmacology; Social and Preventive Medicine; Traditional Eastern Medicine); **Oceanography and Environmental Science** (Automation and Control Engineering; Earth Sciences; Ecology; Electronic Engineering; Environmental Engineering; Environmental Studies; Marine Science and Oceanography; Telecommunications Engineering)

School

Architecture and Civil Engineering (Architecture; Civil Engineering; Town Planning); **Economics** (Banking; Economics; Finance; International Business; International Economics; Statistics); **Energy** (Energy Engineering); **Humanities** (Anthropology; Arts and Humanities; Chinese; Ethnology; History; Literature; Philosophy); **Information Science and Technology** (Automation and Control Engineering; Cognitive Sciences; Computer Science; Information Sciences; Information Technology; Telecommunications Engineering); **Journalism and Communication** (Advertising and Publicity; Journalism; Mass Communication); **Law** (Law); **Life Sciences** (Biochemistry; Biological and Life Sciences; Biology; Biomedicine; Biotechnology); **Management** (Accountancy; Business Administration; E-Business/Commerce; Hotel Management; Management; Tourism; Transport Management); **Marxist-Leninist Theories** (Energy Engineering); **Mathematical Sciences** (Applied Mathematics; Information Sciences; Mathematics; Mathematics and Computer Science); **Overseas Education** (Chinese; Foreign Languages Education); **Physics and Mechanical and Electrical Engineering** (Aeronautical and Aerospace Engineering; Automation and Control Engineering; Electrical and Electronic Engineering; Electrical Engineering; Measurement and Precision Engineering; Mechanical Engineering; Physics); **Public Affairs** (Political Sciences; Public Administration; Sociology); **Software Engineering** (Software Engineering)

Institute

Biomedical Research (Biomedicine); **Coastal and Ocean Management** (Coastal Studies; Environmental Management; Marine Science and Oceanography); **Cross-Strait Development Research** (Development Studies; Marine Science and Oceanography); **Education** (Education); **Financial and Accounting Studies** (Accountancy; Finance); **Studies in Economics** *(Wang Yanan - WISE)* (Economics)

Academy

International Law *(Xiamen)* (International Law)

Centre

Southeast Asian Studies (Southeast Asian Studies)

Research Centre

Taiwan (Southeast Asian Studies)

Research Institute

China (Asian Studies)

Further Information: Also 15 Post doctoral research centres.

History: Founded 1921, acquired present status 1937.

Academic Year: September to July (September-January; March-July)

Admission Requirements: Graduation from senior middle school and entrance examination

Fees: (Yuan): Undergraduate programmes, 18,000-20,000 for chinese-taught programmes and 24,000-26,000 for english-taught programmes; Master's programmes, 20,000-24,000 for chinese-taught programmes and 30,000-36,000 for english-taught programmes; MBA, 55,000; Doctoral programmes, 24,000-32,000 for chinese-taught programmes and 32,000-42,000 for english-taught programmes; Junior research programmes, 16,000-18,000. Senior research programmes, 20,000-24,000

Main Language(s) of Instruction: Chinese and English

Degrees and Diplomas: *Xueshi Xuewei*; *Shuoshi Xuewei*; *Boshi*. Also MBA

Student Services: Academic Counselling, Canteen, Careers Guidance, Cultural Activities, Foreign Studies Centre, Health Services, Language Laboratory, Nursery Care, Social Counselling, Sports Facilities

Publications: China Economy; Higher Education in Foreign Countries; Mathematics Studies; Natural Sciences Journal; Overseas Chinese Education; Social Sciences Journal; South-East Asian Studies

Publishing House: Xiamen University Press

Academic Staff *2011-2012*	**TOTAL**
FULL-TIME	**2,475**
Student Numbers *2011-2012*	
All (Foreign included)	c. **38,000**
FOREIGN ONLY	**2500**

Last Updated: 21/01/13

XIAMEN UNIVERSITY OF TECHNOLOGY (XMUT)

394, South Siming Rd, Xiamen 361005
Tel: +86(592) 6291536
EMail: xmlg@xmut.edu.cn
Website: http://www.xmut.edu.cn/

President: Huang Hongwu

Faculty

Computer Science and Technology (Automation and Control Engineering; Computer Engineering; Computer Networks; Computer Science; Information Technology; Software Engineering); **Cultural Communication** (Air Transport; Business Administration; Hotel and Restaurant; Industrial Management; Management; Marketing; Public Relations; Tourism); **Design Arts** (Design; Fashion Design; Fine Arts); **Electronic and Electric Engineering** (Electrical and Electronic Engineering; Electrical Engineering; Electronic Engineering; Information Technology; Telecommunications Engineering); **Environmental Engineering** (Environmental Engineering); **Humanities and Social Science** (Arts and Humanities; Real Estate; Social Sciences); **International Languages** (Business Administration; Chinese; English; Foreign Languages Education; Japanese; Korean; Literature; Modern Languages; Native Language Education; Special Education); **Management Science** (Information Management; Information Sciences; Management; Transport Management); **Mechanical Engineering** (Automation and Control Engineering; Automotive Engineering; Materials Engineering; Mechanical Engineering; Metal Techniques; Production Engineering)

History: Founded 2009.

Main Language(s) of Instruction: Chinese

Degrees and Diplomas: *Xueshi Xuewei*

Academic Staff *2012-2013*: Total: c. 1,200

Student Numbers *2012-2013*: Total: c. 20,000

Last Updated: 31/10/13

XIANGFAN UNIVERSITY (XFU)

7 Longzhong Road, Xiangfang, Hubei Province 441053
Tel: +86(710) 3591876
Fax: +86(710) 3591876
EMail: fao@xfu.edu.cn

President: Shu Bangxin

International Relations: Wang Weiyi

Department
Administration (Administration); **Art** (Fine Arts); **Chemistry and Chemical Engineering** (Chemical Engineering; Chemistry); **Chinese Language and Culture** (Asian Studies; Chinese); **Construction Engineering** (Construction Engineering); **Electrical and Information Engineering** (Electrical Engineering; Information Technology); **Foreign Languages and Culture** (Cultural Studies; English; Modern Languages); **Geography** (Geography); **Mathematics** (Mathematics); **Mechanical Engineering** (Mechanical Engineering); **Physical Education** (Physical Education); **Physics** (Physics)

Centre
Modern Education and Technology (Education; Educational Technology)

Main Language(s) of Instruction: Chinese

Degrees and Diplomas: *Xueshi Xuewei*

Publications: Journal of Xiangfan University; Research and Administration of Higher Education

XIANGNAN UNIVERSITY (XNU)

Eastern Wangxian Park, Chenzhou City, Hunan Province 423000
Tel: +86(735) 2653000 +86(735) 2653223
Fax: +86(735) 2653013
EMail: xnu2010@gmail.com; xnu2009@hotmail.com
Website: http://www.xnu.edu.cn

Department
Art and Design (Design; Fine Arts); **Arts and Humanities** (Arts and Humanities; Chinese); **Chemistry and Life Science** (Applied Chemistry; Biological and Life Sciences; Biotechnology; Chemistry); **Chinese Language and Literature** (Chinese; Literature); **Clinical Medicine** (Medicine; Nanotechnology; Rehabilitation and Therapy); **Common Curricula** (Curriculum); **Computer Science** (Automation and Control Engineering; Computer Networks; Computer Science; Electronic Engineering; Information Management; Information Technology); **English Teaching** (English; Foreign Languages Education); **Foreign Languages** (English; Modern Languages); **Mathematics** (Applied Mathematics; Mathematics); **Medical Image** (Medical Technology); **Medical Test** (Laboratory Techniques; Medical Technology); **Music** (Music; Musicology); **Nursing** (Nursing); **Physical Education** (Physical Education); **Physics** (Applied Physics; Electrical Engineering; Physics); **Preclinical Medicine** (Social and Preventive Medicine); **Public Administration** (Public Administration); **Social Sciences** (Human Resources; International Business; International Economics; Law; Social Sciences; Tourism)

Further Information: 3 affiliated Hospitals

History: Founded 2003.

Main Language(s) of Instruction: Chinese

Degrees and Diplomas: *Xueshi Xuewei*

Student Services: Sports Facilities

Academic Staff *2012-2013*: Total 780

Student Numbers *2012-2013*: Total 17,084

Last Updated: 30/09/13

XIANGTAN UNIVERSITY (XTU)

Xiangtan, Hunan Province 411105
Tel: +86(732) 8292130
Fax: +86(732) 8292282
EMail: webmaster@xtu.edu.cn
Website: http://www.xtu.edu.cn

Head: Luo He'an

School
Art (Fine Arts); **Business** (Business Administration); **Chemical Engineering** (Bioengineering; Chemical Engineering; Environmental Engineering; Environmental Studies; Food Science; Food Technology; Pharmacology); **Chemistry** (Chemistry); **Civil Engineering and Mechanics** (Civil Engineering; Mechanics); **Foreign Languages** (English; Modern Languages); **Information Engineering** (Information Technology); **International Exchanges** (International Studies); **Law** (Administrative Law; Civil Law; Commercial Law; Constitutional Law; Criminal Law; History of Law; International Law; Law); **Literature and Journalism** (Journalism; Literature); **Management** (Administration; Archiving; Information Management; Information Sciences; Library Science; Management; Public Administration); **Material and Phoelectronic Physics** (Materials Engineering); **Mathematics and Computational Science** (Applied Chemistry; Information Technology; Mathematics and Computer Science; Software Engineering; Statistics); **Mechanical Engineering** (Mechanical Engineering); **Philosophy and History** (History; Philosophy); **Tourism Management** (Hotel Management; Human Resources; Tourism); **Vocation and Technology**; **Xinxiang**

Department
College English Teaching (English; Foreign Languages Education); **Physical Education** (Physical Education)

Further Information: Also 5 postdoctoral stations

History: Founded 1958.

Main Language(s) of Instruction: Chinese

Degrees and Diplomas: *Xueshi Xuewei*; *Shuoshi Xuewei*; *Boshi*

Publications: Journal of Xiangtan University; Research in Higher Education

Publishing House: Xiangtan University Press

Academic Staff *2011-2012*: Total 1,475

Student Numbers *2011-2012*: Total 22,810

Last Updated: 21/01/13

XIANYANG NORMAL UNIVERSITY

Wenlin Road, Xianyang, Shaanxi 712000
Tel: +86(29) 3372-0011
Fax: +86(29) 3372-0011
EMail: hollywellhou@126.com

Programme
Administration of Land Resource (Natural Resources); **Advertisement Science** (Advertising and Publicity); **Applied Chemistry** (Applied Chemistry); **Artistic Design** (Graphic Design); **Chemistry** (Chemistry); **Chinese Language and Culture** *(For Foreign Undergraduate Students)* (Chinese; Cultural Studies; Fine Arts; Grammar; History; Music; Music Theory and Composition; Musical Instruments; Painting and Drawing; Writing); **Chinese Language and Literature** (Chinese; Literature); **Clerical and Secretarial Education** (Secretarial Studies); **Computer Science and Technology** (Computer Engineering; Computer Science); **Cultural Property Administration** (Art Management; Cultural Studies); **Dance** (Dance); **Education** (Education); **Educational Technology Science** (Educational Technology); **Electronic Information Engineering** (Electronic Engineering; Information Technology); **Electronic Information Engineering** (Electronic Engineering; Information Technology); **Elementary Education** (Primary Education); **Fine Arts** (Fine Arts); **Geographical Information Systems** (Geography; Information Technology); **Geography** (Geography); **History** (History); **Information and Numerical Science** (Information Sciences; Information Technology); **Information Control and Information Systems** (Information Management; Information Technology); **Journalism** (Journalism); **Material Chemistry** (Applied Chemistry); **Mathematics and Applied Mathematics** (Applied Mathematics; Mathematics); **Music** (Music); **Physical Education** (Physical Education); **Physics** (Physics); **Public Affairs Administration** (Public Administration); **Software Engineering** (Software Engineering); **Travel Administration** (Transport and Communications)

History: Founded 1978 as Xianyang Special Training Department of Shaanxi Normal University. Renamed Xianyang Teachers' College 1978. Authorized by the Ministry of Education to merge with Xianyang Education Institute and upgraded into Xianyang Normal University 2011.

Main Language(s) of Instruction: Chinese

Degrees and Diplomas: *Xueshi Xuewei*

Publications: Journal of Xianyang Normal University

Academic Staff *2011-2012*: Total 668

Student Numbers *2010-2011*: Total: c. 12,000

Last Updated: 30/09/13

XIAOGAN UNIVERSITY (XGU)

272 Jiaotong Road, Xiaogan, Hubei Province 432000
Tel: +86(712) 2345678
EMail: info@xgu.cn
Website: http://www.hbeu.cn/english/

President: Ding Yaoming

Programme

Advertising *(4-yr)* (Advertising and Publicity); **Agronomy** *(4-yr)* (Agronomy); **Applied Biotechnology** *(3-yr)* (Biotechnology); **Applied Chemistry, Architectural Designing and Technology** *(3-yr)* (Applied Chemistry; Architectural and Environmental Design; Structural Architecture); **Applied Computer Science and Technology** *(3-yr)* (Computer Engineering; Computer Science); **Applied Electronic, Information Science and Technology** *(3-yr)* (Electronic Engineering; Information Sciences; Information Technology); **Architectural Engineering and Technology** *(3-yr)* (Structural Architecture); **Architecture** *(4-yr)* (Architecture); **Artistic Designing** *(4-yr)* (Design); **Bioengineering** *(4-yr)* (Bioengineering); **Biological Science** *(4-yr)* (Biological and Life Sciences); **Chemistry** *(4-yr)* (Chemistry); **Chinese Language and Literature** *(4-yr)* (Chinese; Literature); **Civil Engineering** *(4-yr)* (Civil Engineering); **Computer Science and Technology** *(4-yr)* (Computer Engineering; Computer Science); **Economics** *(4-yr)* (Economics); **Education Technology** *(4-yr)* (Educational Technology); **Electronic Information Science and Technology** *(4-yr)* (Electronic Engineering; Information Sciences; Information Technology); **Engineering Budget** *(3-yr)* (Engineering Management); **English** *(4-yr)* (English); **English Education** *(3-yr)* (Foreign Languages Education); **Environmental Science** *(4-yr)* (Environmental Studies); **Fine ARTs** *(4-yr)* (Fine Arts); **Horticulture** *(4-yr)* (Horticulture); **Ideological and Political** *(4-yr)* (Political Sciences); **International Trade and Business** *(3-yr)* (International Business); **Law** *(4-yr)* (Law); **Macromolecule Materials and Engineering** *(4-yr)* (Materials Engineering); **Material Chemistry** *(4-yr)* (Applied Chemistry); **Mathematics and Applied Mathematics** *(4-yr)* (Applied Mathematics; Mathematics); **Maths Education** *(3-yr)* (Mathematics Education); **Musicology** *(4-yr)* (Musicology); **Physical Education** *(4-yr)* (Physical Education); **Physics** *(4-yr)* (Physics); **Primary-school-teacher Education** *(4-yr)* (Primary Education); **Public Affairs Management** *(3-yr)* (Public Administration); **Science Education** *(4-yr)* (Science Education); **Secretarial Studies** *(3-yr)* (Secretarial Studies); **Urban Planning** *(3-yr)* (Town Planning); **Urban Planning** *(4-yr)* (Town Planning); **Water Supply and Sewerage Engineering** *(4-yr)* (Water Management)

History: Founded 2000.

Main Language(s) of Instruction: Chinese

Degrees and Diplomas: *Xueshi Xuewei*. Also 3-yr undergraduate diploma

Academic Staff *2012-2013*: Total: c. 640
Student Numbers *2012-2013*: Total: c. 13,000
Last Updated: 01/10/13

XICHANG COLLEGE (XCC)

City North Industrial Park, Xichang, Sichuan Province 615000
Tel: +86(834) 2580001
Website: http://www.xcc.sc.cn/

President: Xiaming Zhong

College

Agricultural Sciences (Agriculture); **Animal Sciences** (Zoology); **Arts** (Fine Arts); **Automotive and Electronic Engineering** (Automotive Engineering; Electronic Engineering); **Continuing Education**; **Culture Media and Education Sciences** (Cultural Studies; Education; Media Studies); **Economics and Management** (Economics; Management); **Engineering and Technology** (Engineering; Technology); **Foreign Languages** (English; Modern Languages); **Minority Preparatory Education**; **Physical Education** (Physical Education)

Department

Ideological and Political Theory Course (Political Sciences)

Institute

Light Chemical Engineering (Chemical Engineering); **Yi Language and Culture** (Chinese; Cultural Studies; Modern Languages)

History: Founded 2003.

Main Language(s) of Instruction: Chinese

Degrees and Diplomas: *Xueshi Xuewei*

Academic Staff *2012-2013*: Total: c. 700
Student Numbers *2012-2013*: Total: c. 15,500
Last Updated: 01/10/13

XIDIAN UNIVERSITY

2 Taibai Road South, Xi'an, Shaanxi Province 710071
Tel: +86(29) 88202212
Fax: +86(29) 8201620
EMail: master@xidian.edu.cn
Website: http://www.xidian.edu.cn

President: Zheng Xiaojing (2012-) EMail: Xiaojing@xidian.edu.cn

College

Chang'an; Network and Continuing Education

School

Computer Science and Technology (Computer Engineering; Computer Graphics; Computer Science; Educational Technology; Software Engineering); **Economics and Management** (Accountancy; E-Business/Commerce; Economics; Finance; Industrial Engineering; Industrial Management; Information Management; Information Sciences; Library Science; Management); **Electronic Engineering** (Automation and Control Engineering; Biomedical Engineering; Electronic Engineering; Information Technology; Surveying and Mapping); **Humanities and Arts** (Aesthetics; Applied Linguistics; Art Education; Arts and Humanities; Business Administration; Economics; English; Higher Education; Human Resources; Japanese; Labour and Industrial Relations; Linguistics; Literature; Management; Marketing; Modern Languages; Physical Education; Political Sciences; Religious Studies; Social Sciences; Social Welfare; Sports); **International Education** (English); **Life Science and Technology** (Biological and Life Sciences; Biomedical Engineering; Biotechnology); **Mechano-electronic Engineering** (Automation and Control Engineering; Electronic Engineering; Industrial Design; Mechanical Engineering); **Microelectronics** (Microelectronics); **Science** (Applied Chemistry; Applied Mathematics; Applied Physics; Computer Science; Information Sciences; Information Technology; Optics; Radiophysics); **Software Engineering** (Software Engineering); **Technical Physics** (Chemistry; Materials Engineering; Optical Technology; Physics); **Telecommunications Engineering** (Electronic Engineering; Information Sciences; Information Technology; Telecommunications Engineering)

Further Information: Also South Campus; 7 mobile centers for post-doctoral research.

History: Founded 1931 as Radio School of the Military Commission of the CPC Central Committee in Ruijin. Moved to Xi'an 1958 and became a civilian institution 1966. Acquired present title 1988.

Main Language(s) of Instruction: Chinese

Degrees and Diplomas: *Xueshi Xuewei*; *Shuoshi Xuewei*; *Boshi*. Also postdoctoral research programme.

Publications: China Electronics Education; Journal of Xidian University

Academic Staff *2011-2012*: Total: c. 1,900
Student Numbers *2011-2012*: Total: c. 30,000
Last Updated: 21/01/13

XIHUA UNIVERSITY (XHU)

999, Jin Zhou Road, Jin Niu District,
Chengdu, Sichuan Province 610039
Tel: +86(28) 87720037 +86(28) 87720114
Fax: +86(28) 87720200 +86(28) 87725032
EMail: oice@mail.xhu.edu.cn
Website: http://www.xhu.edu.cn

President: Weiguo Sun
Tel: +86(28) 87720037 EMail: xiaoban@mail.xhu.edu.cn

International Relations: Jiachuan Zhang
Tel: +86(28) 87720114 EMail: oice@mail.xhu.edu.cn

School

Applied Technology *(Pengzhou branch campus)* (Automation and Control Engineering; Automotive Engineering; Electrical Engineering; Tourism); **Architecture and Civil Engineering** (Architecture; Civil Engineering; Engineering Management; Landscape Architecture; Real Estate; Town Planning); **Art** (Dance; Design; Fine Arts; Industrial Design; Musicology; Performing Arts; Visual Arts); **Bioengineering** (Bioengineering; Food Science; Food Technology; Pharmacology; Safety Engineering); **Economics and Trade** (Business Administration; E-Business/Commerce; Economics; Finance; Insurance; Tourism); **Electrical and Information Engineering** (Automation and Control Engineering; Electrical Engineering; Information Technology; Measurement and Precision Engineering); **Energy and Environment** (Chemical Engineering; Civil Engineering; Energy Engineering; Environmental Engineering; Heating and Refrigeration; Hydraulic Engineering; Power Engineering; Thermal Engineering; Water Science); **Foreign Languages** (English; Japanese; Modern Languages); **Graduate Studies** (Applied Linguistics; Automation and Control Engineering; Chemistry; Computer Engineering; Electrical Engineering; Electronic Engineering; English; Food Science; Heating and Refrigeration; Hydraulic Engineering; Linguistics; Management; Materials Engineering; Measurement and Precision Engineering; Mechanical Engineering; Physics; Political Sciences; Power Engineering; Software Engineering); **Humanities** (Arts and Humanities; Chinese; Contemporary History; Cultural Studies; Educational Sciences; History; Law; Linguistics; Literature; Modern History; Modern Languages; Pedagogy); **Management** (Accountancy; Business Administration; Engineering Management; Finance; Human Resources; Management; Marketing); **Materials Science and Engineering** (Materials Engineering; Metal Techniques); **Mathematics and Computer** (Applied Mathematics; Computer Education; Computer Engineering; Computer Science; Mathematics; Mathematics and Computer Science; Software Engineering); **Mechanical Engineering and Automation** (Automation and Control Engineering; Measurement and Precision Engineering; Mechanical Engineering); **Phoenix** (Media Studies; Radio and Television Broadcasting); **Physical Education** (Physical Education); **Physics and Chemistry** (Applied Physics; Chemistry; Microelectronics; Physics; Safety Engineering); **Politics** (History; Law; Modern History; Political Sciences); **Reserve Military Officer** (Military Science); **Transportation and Automotive Engineering** (Automotive Engineering; Power Engineering; Thermal Engineering; Transport Engineering; Transport Management); **Xihua**

Campus

Rennan Branch

History: Founded 1960 as Sichuan Institute of Agricutural Machinery. Renamed as Sichuan Institute of Technology 1983. Merged with Chengdu Teachers' College and acquired present title 2003. Merged with Sichuan Economic Management Institute 2008.

Admission Requirements: Senior high school graduation diploma and entrance examination

Fees: (Yuan): Tuition fee for degree programme general scholar 12,000 per annum; For undergraduate programmes, 16,000 per annum; For graduate programmes, 19,000 per annum; For Chinese (Mandarin) language and culture programmes, 6,500 per semester

Main Language(s) of Instruction: Chinese

Accrediting Agency: Ministry of Education

Degrees and Diplomas: *Xueshi Xuewei*; *Shuoshi Xuewei*. Also Dual Certificates; Dual-Bachelor Degree Programme

Student Services: Academic Counselling, Canteen, Careers Guidance, Cultural Activities, Foreign Studies Centre, Health Services, Language Laboratory, Nursery Care, Social Counselling, Sports Facilities

Publications: Higher Education Research; The Journal of Xihua University

Academic Staff *2011-2012*: Total: c. 2,340
Student Numbers *2011-2012*: Total: c. 41,000
Last Updated: 22/01/13

XIJING UNIVERSITY (XJU)

1 Xijing Road, Xi'an, Shaanxi 710123
Tel: +86(29) 85628111 +86(29) 85628112
Website: http://www.xijing.com.cn/

President: Ren Fang

Faculty

Basic Education; **Economics and Management** *(2)* (Economics; Management); **Economics and Management** (Business Administration; Economics; Management; Marketing; Tourism; Transport Management); **Electrical Engineering** (Automation and Control Engineering; Automotive Engineering; Electrical Engineering; Industrial Design; Mechanical Engineering); **Engineering Technology** (Engineering; Technology); **Humanities** (Arts and Humanities; English); **Medical Care** (Chemistry; Electrical Engineering; Health Sciences; Nursing)

Institute

Art and Science (Accountancy; Chinese; Computer Science; English; French; Graphic Design; Human Resources; Information Management; Japanese; Marketing; Nursing; Spanish); **Arts** (Design; Fine Arts; Visual Arts)

Graduate School

Graduate Studies (Automation and Control Engineering; Engineering; Mechanical Engineering)

History: Founded 1994.

Main Language(s) of Instruction: Chinese

Degrees and Diplomas: *Xueshi Xuewei*; *Shuoshi Xuewei*: **Automation and Control Engineering; Engineering; Mechanical Engineering.**

Student Services: Language Laboratory

Academic Staff *2012-2013*: Total: c. 2,000
Student Numbers *2012-2013*: Total: c. 28,000
Last Updated: 02/10/13

XINGHAI CONSERVATORY OF MUSIC (XHCOM)

Outer Ring Road No. 398, Guangzhou, Guangdong 510500
EMail: xinghaiyuanban@163.com
Website: http://www.xhcom.edu.cn/

President: Tang Yongbao

Department

Arts Management (Art Management); **Basic Music** (Music); **Composition Department** (Music Theory and Composition); **Continuing Education**; **Dance** (Dance); **Folk Music** (Folklore; Music); **Graduate Studies** (Art Management; Music; Music Education; Music Theory and Composition; Musicology; Singing); **Humanities and Social Sciences** (Arts and Humanities; Social Sciences); **Instrument Technology** (Instrument Making); **Modern Music** (Music); **Music** (Music); **Music Education** (Music Education); **National Vocal Music** (Singing); **Orchestral** (Conducting); **Piano** (Musical Instruments); **Pop Music** (Jazz and Popular Music; Music); **Vocal Studies** (Singing)

History: Founded 1957 as Guangzhou Academy of Music. Renamed the Guangzhou Music Institute 1958. Merged with the Guangdong Dance School to become the Guangdong College of Art 1965. Merged with the Guangzhou Academy of Fine Arts for the Guangdong People 1969. Transformed into Guangzhou Music Institute 1978. Upgraded into the Guangzhou Academy of Music 1981. Acquired present title 1985.

Main Language(s) of Instruction: Chinese

Degrees and Diplomas: *Xueshi Xuewei*; *Shuoshi Xuewei*: **Music.**

Student Numbers *2012-2013*: Total: c. 4,500
Last Updated: 02/10/13

XINGTAI UNIVERSITY

3 Shizhuan Street, Xingtai, Hebei Province 054001
Tel: +86(319) 3650111
Fax: +86(319) 3896566
EMail: kickball@sina.com
Website: http://www.xttc.edu.cn

President: Wang Jianxun (2005-) EMail: xtxywjx@126.com

Department

Accountancy (Accountancy; Finance); **Biochemistry** (Biochemistry); **Business Administration** (Business Administration); **Chinese** (Chinese; Literature); **Education and Science Teaching** (Education; Educational Psychology; Science Education); **Elementary Education** (Primary Education); **Fine Arts** (Art Education; Design; Fine Arts; Painting and Drawing; Sculpture); **Foreign Languages** (English; Modern Languages); **Geography** (Environmental Studies; Geography; Natural Resources; Rural Planning; Surveying and Mapping; Town Planning); **History** (History; Law; Political Sciences; Religious Studies); **Information Sciences and Technology** (Computer Engineering; Computer Networks; Computer Science; Information Sciences; Information Technology); **International Education Exchange** (Accountancy; English; Law; Management; Marketing); **Mathematics** (Applied Mathematics; Mathematics; Mathematics Education; Operations Research); **Music** (Dance; Music; Music Education; Musical Instruments); **Physical Education** (Physical Education; Sports); **Physics** (Physics); **Social Sciences** (Political Sciences; Social Sciences; Sociology); **Trade and Economics** (Economics; Hotel Management; International Business; International Economics; Marketing; Tourism)

History: Founded 1910 as Zhili primary Normal School. Renamed Zhili Fourth Normal School 1984. Transformed into Xingtai Teachers College following merger of Xingtai Institute of Education and Xingtai Economic Management Cadre School 1996. Acquired university status and present title 2002.

Main Language(s) of Instruction: Chinese

Degrees and Diplomas: *Xueshi Xuewei*

Publications: Journal of Xingtai University

Academic Staff *2011-2012*: Total 865
Student Numbers *2011-2012*: Total: c. 18,000
Last Updated: 22/01/13

XINGYI NORMAL UNIVERSITY FOR NATIONALITIES (XYNUN)

32 Hunan Road, Xingyi, Guizhou Province 562400
Tel: + 86(859) 3236966
Fax: + 86(859) 3236966
Website: http://xynun.edu.cn/

President: Wei Panshi

Department

Arts (Fine Arts); **Basic Education** (Education); **Chemistry and Biology** (Applied Chemistry; Biochemistry; Biological and Life Sciences; Biology; Biotechnology; Chemistry; Science Education); **Computer Science** (Computer Science; E-Business/Commerce; Information Sciences; Information Technology); **Economics and Trade** (Business Administration; Economics; Hotel Management; International Business; Marketing; Tourism); **Education Science** (Child Care and Development; Chinese; Dance; Developmental Psychology; Education; Educational Psychology; Experimental Psychology; History; Hygiene; Literature; Music; Painting and Drawing; Preschool Education; Primary Education; Psychiatry and Mental Health; Psychology; Singing; Statistics; Writing); **Foreign Languages and Literatures** (English; Foreign Languages Education; French; Grammar; Japanese; Linguistics; Literature; Modern Languages; Phonetics; Russian; Translation and Interpretation; Writing); **Literature and Communication** (Aesthetics; Chinese; Communication Studies; Folklore; Journalism; Literature; Media Studies; Photography; Radio and Television Broadcasting); **Marxism Teaching and Research** (Administration; Education; History; Law; Philosophy; Political Sciences); **Mathematics** (Applied Mathematics; Mathematics; Mathematics and Computer Science); **Physical Education** (Health Sciences; Physical Education; Sports); **Physics** (Electronic Engineering; Physics; Safety Engineering); **Political Science and History** (History; Political Sciences); **Public Administration** (Human Resources; Information Management; Information Technology; Natural Resources; Public Administration; Rural Planning; Social and Community Services; Social Welfare; Town Planning)

History: Founded 1813 as Bishan Academy.

Main Language(s) of Instruction: Chinese

Degrees and Diplomas: *Xueshi Xuewei*. 3-yr degree programmes

Publishing house: Academic Journal Editing Department

Academic Staff *2011-2012*: Total: c. 566
Student Numbers *2011-2012*: Total: c. 8,000
Last Updated: 03/10/13

XINJIANG AGRICULTURAL UNIVERSITY (XJAU)

42 Nanchang Road, Urumqi, Xinjiang Uygur Province 830052
Tel: +86(991) 8763920
Fax: +86(991) 4520159
EMail: WEBMASTER@xjau.edu.cn
Website: http://www.xjau.edu.cn

President: Luo Qiujiang

Faculty

Science and Technology

College

Agronomy (Agronomy; Biotechnology; Crop Production; Entomology; Genetics; Plant Pathology); **Animal Sciences** (Animal Husbandry; Aquaculture; Veterinary Science); **Chemical Engineering** (Applied Chemistry; Chemical Engineering; Chemistry); **Computer and Information Engineering** (Computer Engineering; Computer Science; Electronic Engineering; Information Management); **Economics and Trade** (Accountancy; Agricultural Economics; Business Administration; Economics; Statistics); **Food Science and Pharmacy** (Food Science; Pharmacy); **Foreign Languages** (English; Modern Languages); **Forestry and Horticulture** (Forestry; Horticulture); **Grassland and Environmental Sciences** (Botany; Ecology; Environmental Studies; Soil Science); **Mathematics and Physics** (Applied Physics; Laboratory Techniques; Mathematics; Physics; Statistics); **Veterinary Medicine** (Veterinary Science); **Water Conservancy and Civil** (Civil Engineering; Water Management)

School

Chinese Language (Chinese); **Continuing Education**; **Management** (Law; Management; Public Administration; Real Estate; Rural Planning; Social Welfare; Town Planning); **Mechanical and Transport Studies** (Mechanical Engineering; Transport and Communications)

Department

Sports (Physical Education; Sports)

Institute

Arid Desert Zone (Arid Land Studies); **International Education** (Agriculture; Agronomy; Chinese; Environmental Studies; International Business; Management)

Research Centre

Rural Development of the Arid Zone (Arid Land Studies; Rural Planning)

Research Department

Ideological and Political Education (Political Sciences)

Further Information: Also Post-doctorate Science and Research Mobility Stations.

History: Founded 1952 as Xinjiang August 1st Agricultural College, acquired present title 1995.

Main Language(s) of Instruction: Chinese

Degrees and Diplomas: *Xueshi Xuewei*; *Shuoshi Xuewei*; *Boshi*

Publications: Journal of Xinjiang Agricultural University

Academic Staff *2011-2012*: Total 892
Student Numbers *2011-2012*: Total 18,517
Last Updated: 22/01/13

XINJIANG ARTS UNIVERSITY (XJART)

734 Unity Road, Urumqi, Xinjiang Province 830001
Tel: +86(991) 2568202
Fax: +86(991) 2555429
Website: http://www.xjart.edu.cn

President: Abudureyimu Aierken

School

Art *(Affiliated Secondary)* (Fine Arts)

Department

Adult and Continuing Education; **Basic Education** (Arts and Humanities); **Culture and Tourism Management** (Cultural Studies; Tourism); **Dance** (Dance); **Fine Arts** (Fine Arts); **Ideological and Political Theory Teaching and Research** (Political Sciences); **Music** (Music); **Preparatory** (Theatre); **Sports Teaching and Research** (Sports); **Television Drama** (Radio and Television Broadcasting)

History: Founded 1958 as Xinjiang Art School. Tranformed into Xinjiang Institute of the Arts 1987.

Main Language(s) of Instruction: Chinese

Degrees and Diplomas: *Xueshi Xuewei*

Academic Staff *2012-2013*	**TOTAL**
FULL-TIME	c. **245**

Student Numbers *2012-2013*	
All (Foreign included)	c. **4,000**
FOREIGN ONLY	**30**

Last Updated: 03/10/13

XINJIANG INSTITUTE OF FINANCE AND ECONOMICS (XJIFE)

15 North Beijing Road, Urumqi, Xinjiang Uygur Province 830012
Tel: +86(991) 7842017
Fax: +86(991) 3740942
Website: http://www.xjife.edu.cn

President: Cui Guanglian Han

International Relations: Luan Xinrong

College

Business Administration (Business Administration; E-Business/Commerce; Human Resources; Marketing; Transport Management); **Foreign Languages** (English; Modern Languages); **Public Economics and Management** (Economics; Public Administration)

School

Accountancy (Accountancy); **Chinese Language** (Chinese); **Computer Science and Engineering** (Computer Engineering; Computer Science); **Continuing Education**; **Economics** (Economics); **Journalism and Media Studies** (Journalism; Mass Communication; Media Studies); **Law** (Law); **MBA** (Business Administration); **Statistics and Information** (Information Management; Statistics); **Tourism Studies** (Tourism)

Department

Marxism-Leninism Teaching and Research (Political Sciences); **Sports Teaching and Research** (Sports)

Institute

Applied Mathematics (Applied Mathematics); **Finance** (Accountancy); **International Education** (Chinese; International Studies); **International Trade** (International Business)

History: Founded 1950 as Xinjiang Province Cadre School. Became Xinjiang Institute of Finance and Economics following merger of Xinjiang Institute of Finance and Xinjiang Economic Management College and Xinjiang Finance, Taxation schools 2000. Acquired present title 2007.

Fees: (US Dollars): Short-term students, 300 for 4 weeks, 50 per additional week); further study students,1,500 per annum (750 per semester); undergraduate, 1,800; postgraduate, 2,400

Main Language(s) of Instruction: Chinese

Degrees and Diplomas: *Xueshi Xuewei*; *Shuoshi Xuewei*. Also MBA and Executive MBA.

Academic Staff *2011-2012*: Total: c. 830

Student Numbers *2011-2012*: Total: c. 20,000

Last Updated: 23/01/13

XINJIANG MEDICAL UNIVERSITY (XJMU)

393 Xinyi Road, Urumqi, Xinjiang Uygur Province 830054
Tel: +86(991) 4365721
Fax: +86(991) 4361881
EMail: muxj2002@hotmail.com; iec@xjmu.edu.cn
Website: http://www.xjmu.edu.cn

President: Maimaiti Yasin

International Relations: Zhou Hongxia

College

Basic Medical Sciences (Anatomy; Cell Biology; Immunology; Inorganic Chemistry; Mathematics; Medicine; Microbiology; Organic Chemistry; Physics); **Continuing Education**; **International Education**; **Language and Culture** (Asian Studies; Chinese); **Medicine** (Anaesthesiology; Anatomy; Dermatology; Embryology and Reproduction Biology; Gastroenterology; Genetics; Gynaecology and Obstetrics; Health Sciences; Histology; Medical Technology; Medicine; Molecular Biology; Neurology; Occupational Health; Oncology; Ophthalmology; Otorhinolaryngology; Paediatrics; Pathology; Physiology; Stomatology; Surgery); **Nurses Training** (Nursing); **Pharmacy** (Pharmacology; Pharmacy); **Public Health** (Epidemiology; Hygiene; Nutrition; Public Health; Statistics; Toxicology); **Traditional Medicine** (Acupuncture; Traditional Eastern Medicine); **Vocational Studies** (Laboratory Techniques)

Further Information: Also 6 directly-affiliated hospitals and 3 indirectly-affiliated hospitals; 3 mobile postdoctoral centers.

History: Founded 1956 as Xinjiang Medical College. Merged with Xinjiang Traditional Chinese Medicine College and acquired present title 1998.

Main Language(s) of Instruction: Chinese

Degrees and Diplomas: *Xueshi Xuewei*; *Shuoshi Xuewei*; *Boshi*

Publications: Acta Academia Medicine Xinjiang

Academic Staff *2011-2012*	**TOTAL**
FULL-TIME	**4,701**

Student Numbers *2011-2012*	
All (Foreign included)	c. **18,000**
FOREIGN ONLY	**832**

Last Updated: 23/01/13

XINJIANG NORMAL UNIVERSITY (XJNU)

102, New Medical Road, Urumqi, Xinjiang Uygur Province 830054
Tel: +86(991) 4841601 Ext. 2535
Fax: +86(991) 4812513
EMail: xsdxbm@mail.wl.xj.cn
Website: http://www.xjnu.edu.cn

President: David Leigh Paraty

College

Elementary Education (Primary Education); **Adult Education**; **Chemistry and Chemical Engineering** (Applied Chemistry; Chemical Engineering; Chemistry; Environmental Engineering; Environmental Studies); **Education and Science** (Education; Information Technology; Psychology); **Foreign Languages** (English; Japanese; Linguistics; Literature; Modern Languages; Russian; Translation and Interpretation); **Geographic Science and Tourism** (Demography and Population; Environmental Studies; Geography; Geography (Human); Human Resources; Tourism); **History and Ethnology** (Ancient Civilizations; Contemporary History; Ethnology; History; Modern History; Religious Studies; Sociology); **Liberal Arts** (Arts and Humanities; Chinese; Literature); **Network Education**; **Physical and Electronic Engineering** (Electronic Engineering; Information Sciences; Information Technology; Physics); **Youth Political**

School

Computer Science and Technology (Computer Science; Information Technology); **Continuing Education**; **International Cultural Exchange** (Applied Linguistics; Chinese; Linguistics); **Law and Economics** (Economics; Human Resources; Law; Political Sciences); **Life Sciences** (Biochemistry; Biological and Life

Sciences; Biology; Biotechnology; Cell Biology; Genetics; Microbiology; Molecular Biology; Zoology); **Marxism** (Civil Law; English; Ethnology; History; Political Sciences; Religion; Sociology); **Mathematical Sciences** (Applied Mathematics; Computer Science; Information Sciences; Mathematics)

Institute
Chinese (Chinese; Literature); **Language** (Chinese; Literature; Modern Languages; Native Language Education); **Physical Education** (Physical Education; Sports)

Academy
Fine Arts (Fine Arts); **Music** (Dance; Music; Music Education; Musicology; Performing Arts)

History: Founded 1978.

Academic Year: September to July

Admission Requirements: Graduation from senior middle school and entrance examination

Main Language(s) of Instruction: Uygur, Chinese, Mongolian

Degrees and Diplomas: *Xueshi Xuewei*; *Shuoshi Xuewei*

Publications: Journal of Xinjiang Normal University

Academic Staff *2011-2012*	**TOTAL**
FULL-TIME	**983**

Student Numbers *2011-2012*	
All (Foreign included)	c. **28,000**
FOREIGN ONLY	**889**

Last Updated: 23/01/13

XINJIANG UNIVERSITY (XJU)

14 Shengli Road, Urumqi, Xinjiang Uygur Province 830046
Tel: +86(991) 286753
Fax: +86(991) 286006
EMail: dice@xju.edu.cn
Website: http://www.xju.edu.cn

President: Taxifulati Teyibai

International Relations: Jiao Jian

College
Architecture and Civil Engineering (Architecture; Civil Engineering; Surveying and Mapping; Town Planning; Transport Engineering); **Chemistry and Chemical Engineering** (Chemical Engineering; Chemistry); **Chinese Language** (Chinese); **Economics and Management** (Economics; Management); **Electrical Engineering** (Electrical Engineering); **Electrical Engineering** (Automation and Control Engineering; Electrical Engineering; Electronic Engineering; Power Engineering; Thermal Engineering); **Foreign Languages** (English; Modern Languages); **Geological and Mining Engineering** (Geological Engineering; Mining Engineering); **Humanities** (Applied Linguistics; Arts and Humanities; Asian Studies; Chinese; Cinema and Television; Ethnology; History; Linguistics; Literature; Modern Languages; Turkish); **Information Sciences and Engineering** (Engineering; Information Sciences; Information Technology); **International Cultural Exchange** (Asian Studies; Chinese; Foreign Languages Education); **Journalism and Communication** (Journalism; Mass Communication); **Life Science and Technology** (Biological and Life Sciences); **Marxism** (Political Sciences; Psychology); **Mathematics and Systems Science** (Mathematics); **Mechanical Engineering** (Automation and Control Engineering; Electronic Engineering; Materials Engineering; Mechanical Engineering); **Physical Science and Technology**; **Politics and Public Administration** (Political Sciences; Public Administration; Sociology); **Resource and Environmental Science** (Ecology; Environmental Studies; Geography; Geological Engineering; Geology; Mining Engineering; Natural Resources; Surveying and Mapping); **Software Design** (Software Engineering); **Textiles and Clothing** (Design; Fashion Design; Fine Arts; Textile Design; Textile Technology); **Tourism Studies** (Tourism)

School
Law (Administrative Law; Civil Law; Commercial Law; Constitutional Law; Criminal Law; History of Law; International Law; Law)

Department
Sports Teaching and Research (Physical Education; Sports)

Further Information: Also North and South Campuses.

History: Founded 1924 as Xinjiang Russian Political and Law School. Converted into Xinjiang College 1935. Acquired present title 1960. Merged with Xinjiang Engineering Institute 2000.

Main Language(s) of Instruction: Chinese

Degrees and Diplomas: *Xueshi Xuewei*; *Shuoshi Xuewei*; *Boshi*

Student Services: Canteen, Health Services, Sports Facilities

Publications: Journal of Xinjiang University

Academic Staff *2011-2012*	**TOTAL**
FULL-TIME	**1,659**
STAFF WITH DOCTORATE	
FULL-TIME	**310**

Student Numbers *2011-2012*	
All (Foreign included)	**30,000**
FOREIGN ONLY	**400**

Last Updated: 24/01/13

XINXIANG MEDICAL UNIVERSITY (XXMU)

Jinsui Avenue 601, Hongqi District,
Xinxiang, Henan Province 453003
Tel: +86(373) 3029022
Fax: +86(373) 3029919
EMail: wzbjben@xxmu.edu.cn; fao@xxmu.edu.cn
Website: http://www.xxmu.edu.cn/

President: Duan Guangcai

College
Adult Education (Medical Technology; Medicine; Nursing)

School
Management (Management)

Department
First Teaching Hospital (Cardiology; Medical Technology; Medicine; Neurological Therapy; Paediatrics; Pathology); **Foreign Language** (English; Modern Languages); **Life Sciences and Technology** (Biological and Life Sciences; Biomedical Engineering; Cell Biology); **Medical Tests** (Biochemistry; Haematology; Immunology; Laboratory Techniques; Medical Technology; Medicine; Microbiology); **Physical Education** (Physical Education; Sports); **Psychology** (Clinical Psychology; Experimental Psychology; Psychology); **Public Health** (Epidemiology; Health Sciences; Hygiene; Nutrition; Occupational Health; Public Health; Social and Preventive Medicine; Statistics); **Second Teaching Hospital** (Medicine; Neurology; Physiology; Psychiatry and Mental Health); **Social Science** *(SSD)* (Political Sciences; Social Sciences); **Third Teaching Hospital** (Medicine; Nursing; Ophthalmology; Paediatrics; Rehabilitation and Therapy)

Institute
International Education (Chinese; International Studies); **Medical Teaching** (Anatomy; Biology; Chemistry; Embryology and Reproduction Biology; Immunology; Medicine; Neurology; Physiology); **Nursing** (Health Education; Nursing; Psychology); **Pharmacology** (Chemistry; Pharmacology)

Further Information: Also Xinxiang Central Hospital, Jiaozuo City People's Hospital, 12 non-affiliated hospitals, more than 120 teaching hospitals and practice base

History: Founded 1950 as school of administration. Changed its name to the Northern Henan Medical College 1962. Acquired present status title and name 1982.

Main Language(s) of Instruction: Chinese

Degrees and Diplomas: *Xueshi Xuewei*; *Shuoshi Xuewei*

Publications: Journal of Applied Clinical Pediatrics; Journal of Clinical Psychosomatic Diseases; Journal of Ophthalmic Recent Advances; Journal of Xinxiang Medical University

Academic Staff *2011-2012*: Total 4,018

Student Numbers *2011-2012*: Total 38,614

Last Updated: 24/01/13

XINXIANG UNIVERSITY (XXU)

East Road, Henan Golden Harvest, Xinxiang, Henan 453003
Tel: +86(373) 3683015
Website: http://www.xxu.edu.cn/

President: Yang Hongzhi

Faculty

Civil Engineering and Architecture (Architecture; Civil Engineering); **History** (History); **Liberal Arts** (Arts and Humanities); **Physical Education** (Health Sciences; Physical Education; Physiology; Psychology; Sports); **Physics and Electronic Engineering** (Electronic Engineering; Information Technology; Physics)

College

Arts (Architectural and Environmental Design; Communication Arts; Design; Fine Arts; Visual Arts); **Chemistry and Chemical Engineering** (Chemical Engineering; Chemistry; Pharmacology); **Computer and Information Engineering** (Computer Engineering; Computer Networks; Data Processing; Information Management; Information Technology; Software Engineering); **English Teaching and Researching** (English; Foreign Languages Education); **Foreign Languages** (Applied Linguistics; English; Foreign Languages Education; Japanese; Linguistics; Literature; Modern Languages; Translation and Interpretation); **Mathematics and Information Science** (Information Sciences; Mathematics; Mathematics and Computer Science); **Mechanical and Electrical Engineering** (Electrical Engineering; Mechanical Engineering); **Music** (Acting; Music; Music Theory and Composition; Musical Instruments; Singing); **Social Sciences** (History; Political Sciences; Social Sciences)

School

Business (Accountancy; Business Administration; Business Computing; E-Business/Commerce; Economics; International Economics; Marketing); **Journalism and Communication** (Communication Studies; Journalism; Radio and Television Broadcasting); **Management** (Management)

Department

Life Science and Technology (Biological and Life Sciences; Biotechnology); **Politics and Law** (Law; Political Sciences)

Institute

Education Sciences (Education; Educational Sciences; Preschool Education; Primary Education; Psychology; Teacher Training)

Main Language(s) of Instruction: Chinese

Degrees and Diplomas: *Xueshi Xuewei*

Academic Staff *2013-2014*: Total: c. 1,100

Student Numbers *2013-2014*: Total: c. 7,630

Last Updated: 04/10/13

XINYANG NORMAL UNIVERSITY (XYNU)

237 Chang'an Road, Xinyang, Henan Province 464000
Tel: +86(376) 6391166 +86(376) 6391165
Fax: +86(376) 6391165
EMail: gjc1166@sohu.com; gjc@mail2.xytc.edu.cn
Website: http://210.43.24.4/english/index.htm

President: Lu Keping

International Relations: Zhou Ziliang

College

Huarui (Applied Mathematics; Bioengineering; Chemistry; Chinese; Civil Engineering; Computer Engineering; Computer Science; Electronic Engineering; English; Fine Arts; Law; Literature; Marketing; Mathematics; Music; Physics)

School

Chemistry and Chemical Engineering (Applied Chemistry; Chemical Engineering; Chemistry); **Continuing Education** (Economics; Education; Engineering; History; Law; Literature; Management; Modern Languages; Natural Sciences); **Economics and Management** (Accountancy; Business Administration; Economics; Industrial Management; Management; Marketing; Tourism); **Educational Sciences** (Curriculum; Educational Psychology; Educational Sciences; Educational Technology); **Life Sciences** (Biological and Life Sciences; Biotechnology); **Literature** (Chinese; Literature; Secretarial Studies); **Mathematics and Information Science** (Applied Mathematics; Information Sciences; Mathematics); **Physics and Electronic Engineering** (Applied Physics; Automation and Control Engineering; Electrical Engineering; Electronic Engineering; Physics; Thermal Engineering); **Politics and Law** (Law; Political Sciences; Social Work)

Department

Architectural Engineering (Civil Engineering; Construction Engineering; Structural Architecture); **Computer Science and Technology** (Computer Science; Information Technology); **English Teaching and Research** (English); **Fine Arts** (Design; Fine Arts); **Foreign Languages** (English; French; Japanese; Literature; Modern Languages; Translation and Interpretation); **History** (History); **Marxism Teaching and Research** (Political Sciences); **Music** (Dance; Music; Music Theory and Composition; Musical Instruments; Performing Arts; Singing); **Physical Education** (Physical Education; Sports); **Urban and Environmental Science** (Environmental Studies; Geography; Rural Planning; Surveying and Mapping; Town Planning; Urban Studies)

History: Founded 1975 as a sub-college in Xinyang City affiliated to the then Kaifeng Teachers' College (now called Henan University in Kaifeng City). Acquired present status and title 1978.

Main Language(s) of Instruction: Chinese

Degrees and Diplomas: *Xueshi Xuewei*; *Shuoshi Xuewei*

Academic Staff *2011-2012*: Total: c. 1,300

Student Numbers *2011-2012*: Total: c. 30,000

Last Updated: 24/01/13

XINYU UNIVERSITY (XYU)

2666 Sunshine Avenue, Xinyu, Jiangxi 338004
Tel: +86(790) 6665099
Fax: +86(790) 6666098
EMail: xygzxcb@tom.com; yxybgs@163.com
Website: http://www.xyc.edu.cn/

President: Luo Yufeng

College

Architecture and Planning (Architecture and Planning); **Foreign Languages** (English; Foreign Languages Education; Japanese; Modern Languages); **Literature and Journalism and Communication** (Arts and Humanities; Journalism; Literature; Mass Communication); **Mechanical Engineering** (Mechanical Engineering); **Medicine and Life Sciences** (Biological and Life Sciences; Medicine); **New Energy Science and Engineering** (Energy Engineering; Materials Engineering); **Vocational and Technical Studies**

School

Economics and Management (Accountancy; Economics; Finance; Hotel Management; Management; Marketing; Tourism); **Golf** (Sports)

Department

Continuing Education; **Ideological and Political Theory Teaching and Research** (Political Sciences); **Physical Education** (Physical Education; Sports)

Institute

Mathematics and Computer Science (Applied Mathematics; Computer Engineering; Computer Networks; Computer Science; Information Management; Information Technology; Mathematics; Mathematics and Computer Science; Mathematics Education; Multimedia; Software Engineering)

Academy

Fine Arts *(Bouldering)* (Architectural and Environmental Design; Communication Arts; Design; Fine Arts; Visual Arts); **Music and Dance Academy** (Music; Musical Instruments; Musicology; Singing)

History: Founded 1986.

Main Language(s) of Instruction: Chinese

Degrees and Diplomas: *Xueshi Xuewei*

Academic Staff *2012-2013*: Total: c. 700

Student Numbers *2012-2013*: Total: c. 14,000

Last Updated: 31/10/13

XINZHOU TEACHERS UNIVERSITY (XZTC)

10 Heping Xijie, Xinzhou, Shanxi Province 034000
Tel: +86(350) 3048275
Fax: +86(350) 3031845
EMail: wlzx@xztc.edu.cn
Website: http://www.xztc.edu.cn

President: Wang Lian

Department

Basic Adult Education (Adult Education); **Chemical Biology** (Biochemistry; Chemistry); **Chinese** (Chinese); **Church and State** (Religion); **Computer Science** (Computer Science); **Dance** (Dance); **Education** (Education); **Fine Arts** (Fine Arts); **Foreign Languages** (English; Modern Languages); **Geography** (Geography); **Law** (Law); **Mathematics** (Mathematics); **Music** (Music); **Physical Education** (Physical Education); **Physical Electronics** (Electronic Engineering); **Political Sciences and History** (History; Political Sciences); **Radio and Television Broadcasting** (Radio and Television Broadcasting)

History: Founded 1958 as Xin Counties Teachers College. Merged with Datong Teachers College to form Shanxi Teachers College 1959. Merged with Xin County Normal seven district schools and changed name to Xin County fifty-seven School 1969. Changed name to Xin County Teachers College 1974. Changed name to Xinzhou Teachers College 1984. Merged with Xinzhou Staff University 1998. Acquired present status and title 2000 following merger with Xinzhou Normal School.

Main Language(s) of Instruction: Chinese

Degrees and Diplomas: *Xueshi Xuewei*

Student Services: Sports Facilities

Student Numbers *2011-2012*: Total 15,200

Last Updated: 25/01/13

XI'AN INTERNATIONAL UNIVERSITY (XAIU)

408 Zhangba North Road, Xi'an, Shaanxi 710077
Tel: +86(29) 88751484 +86(29) 88751314
Fax: +86(29) 88751030
EMail: intercenter_xaiu@yahoo.com.cn
Website: http://www.xaiu.edu.cn/

President: Teng Huang

College

Business (Accountancy; Administration; Business Administration; Business Computing; E-Business/Commerce; Finance; Food Technology; Hotel Management; Human Resources; Insurance; International Business; International Economics; Management; Marketing; Tourism; Transport Management); **Engineering** (Automation and Control Engineering; Building Technologies; Computer Engineering; Computer Science; Construction Engineering; Electronic Engineering; Engineering; Information Management; Maintenance Technology; Mechanical Engineering; Telecommunications Engineering); **Foreign Languages** (English; French; Japanese; Modern Languages); **Humanities** (Advertising and Publicity; Architectural and Environmental Design; Arts and Humanities; Chinese; Communication Arts; Design; Film; Foreign Languages Education; Journalism; Landscape Architecture; Law; Literature; Radio and Television Broadcasting; Secretarial Studies; Visual Arts); **International Cooperation** (Business Administration; Chinese; Cultural Studies); **Medical Studies** (Health Sciences; Medical Technology; Nursing; Pharmacy; Stomatology)

History: Founded 1992.

Admission Requirements: Applicants should be 18 years old or above provide certificates of high school graduation and good health

Fees: (Yuan): Tuition, 14,500 per annum

Main Language(s) of Instruction: Chinese

Degrees and Diplomas: *Xueshi Xuewei*. Also 3-year vocational programmes

Student Services: Canteen, Sports Facilities

Academic Staff *2012-2013*: Total 2,200

Student Numbers *2012-2013*: Total 36,000

Last Updated: 26/09/13

XUCHANG UNIVERSITY (XCU)

88 of Bayi road, Xuchang, Henan 461000
Tel: +86(374) 2968866
Website: http://www.xcu.edu.cn/

President: Chen Jianguo (2007-)

College

Chemistry and Chemical Engineering (Chemical Engineering); **Civil Engineering** (Civil Engineering); **Electrical Engineering** (Electrical Engineering); **Five-year junior**; **Food and Biological Engineering** (Bioengineering; Food Science); **Foreign Languages** (English; Modern Languages); **Information Engineering** (Information Technology); **Mathematics and Statistics** (Mathematics; Statistics); **New Materials and Energy** (Energy Engineering; Materials Engineering); **Urban Planning and Landscape Architecture** (Landscape Architecture; Town Planning)

School

Economics (Management); **Management** (Management)

Department

Continuing Education; **Foreign Language Teaching** (Foreign Languages Education); **Physical Education** (Physical Education); **Public Physical Education** (Physical Education); **Social Sciences Teaching** (Humanities and Social Science Education; Social Sciences)

Institute

Applied Mathematics (Applied Mathematics); **Culture** *(Wei)* (Cultural Studies); **Education and Science** (Education); **Higher Education** (Higher Education); **International Education** (International Studies); **Law and Politics** (Law; Political Sciences); **Literature and Media** (Literature; Media Studies); **Software** (Software Engineering); **Tourism Studies, History and Culture** (Cultural Studies; History; Tourism)

Academy

Fine Arts (Fine Arts); **Music and Dance** (Dance; Music)

Centre

Public Experiment

Research Centre

Central Rural Development (Development Studies; Rural Studies); **Meticulous Research Institute**; **Surface Micro and Nano Materials** (Nanotechnology)

History: Founded 1907 as Xuchang Teachers' learning House. Transformed into Xuchang Teachers' School 1911. Successively renamed Henan Provincial Xuchang Teachers' School, Xuchang Teachers' School, Secondary Teachers' School and Xuchang Teachers' College. Acquired present status 2002.

Main Language(s) of Instruction: Chinese

Degrees and Diplomas: *Xueshi Xuewei*

Academic Staff *2012-2013*: Total 753

Student Numbers *2012-2013*: Total: c. 16,000

Distance students, 5000.

Last Updated: 04/10/13

XUZHOU INSTITUTE OF TECHNOLOGY (XZIT)

No.2 Lishui Road Xincheng District, Xuzhou, Jiangsu 221000
Tel: +86(516) 83105286
Fax: +86(516) 83105000
EMail: wsb@xzit.edu.cn
Website: http://www.xzit.edu.cn

President: Han Baoping

Department

Adult Education (Accountancy; Adult Education; Automation and Control Engineering; Chinese; Civil Engineering; Computer Engineering; Computer Science; Finance; Food Science; Food Technology; Information Management; Information Sciences; Literature; Mechanical Engineering); **Art and Design** (Architectural and Environmental Design; Design; Fashion Design; Fine Arts; Interior Design; Visual Arts); **Civil Engineering** (Civil Engineering; Construction Engineering; Management; Structural Architecture; Water Management); **Computing Science** (Computer Science;

Information Sciences; Mathematics; Operations Research; Software Engineering); **Economics and Trade** (Business Administration; E-Business/Commerce; Economics; Finance; Information Management; Information Technology; International Business; International Economics; Marketing; Taxation); **Electronic Engineering** (Automation and Control Engineering; Computer Engineering; Computer Networks; Computer Science; Data Processing; Electronic Engineering; Industrial Engineering; Information Management; Information Sciences; Information Technology; Multimedia); **Financial Accounting** (Accountancy; Business Computing; Finance; International Business; Management); **Food Engineering** (Agricultural Engineering; Bioengineering; Cooking and Catering; Food Science; Food Technology); **Foreign Language** (American Studies; Business Administration; English; International Business; Modern Languages; Tourism; Writing); **Law, Politics and Literature** (Administrative Law; Chinese; Civil Law; Commercial Law; Constitutional Law; Criminal Law; English; International Business; Law; Literature; Political Sciences; Public Relations; Secretarial Studies; Translation and Interpretation; Writing); **Management Science** (Business Administration; Economics; Human Resources; Management; Marketing; Real Estate; Sales Techniques; Transport Management); **Mechanical and Electronic Engineering** (Automation and Control Engineering; Electronic Engineering; Maintenance Technology; Mechanical Engineering); **Physical Education** (Physical Education)

History: 2005.

Main Language(s) of Instruction: Chinese

Degrees and Diplomas: *Xueshi Xuewei*

Academic Staff *2012-2013*	**TOTAL**
FULL-TIME	**1,269**
Student Numbers *2012-2013*	
All (Foreign included)	**20,338**
FOREIGN ONLY	**40**

Last Updated: 04/11/13

XUZHOU MEDICAL UNIVERSITY

84 Huaihai West Road, Xuzhou, Jiangsu Province 221002
Tel: +86(516) 5748415
Fax: +86(516) 5748429
EMail: dice@xzmc.edu.cn
Website: http://www.xzmc.edu.cn

President: Wu Yongping
Tel: +86(516) 5748429 EMail: wyp@xzmc.edu.cn

International Relations: Liu Song

School

Anaesthesiology (Anaesthesiology); **Basic Medical Sciences** (Medicine); **Continuing Education**; **Graduate Studies** (Medicine); **Huafang**; **Medical Imagery** (Medical Technology); **Nursing** (Nursing); **Pharmacy** (Pharmacy); **Public Health** (Public Health)

Department

Clinical Medicine I (Medicine); **Clinical Medicine II** (Medicine); **Clinical Medicine III** (Medicine); **Social Sciences** (Social Sciences); **Stomatology** (Stomatology)

Further Information: Also 13 affiliated hospitals.

History: Founded 1958 as Xuzhou Branch of Nanjing Medical College, acquired present title 1960.

Main Language(s) of Instruction: Chinese, English

Degrees and Diplomas: *Xueshi Xuewei*; *Shuoshi Xuewei*

Student Numbers *2011-2012*: Total: c. 20,000

Last Updated: 25/01/13

YAN'AN UNIVERSITY (YAU)

Yan'an, Shaanxi Province 716000
Tel: +86(911) 2332015
Fax: +86(911) 2333677
EMail: chunhou2@163.com
Website: http://english.yau.edu.cn/aboutyau/ydgk/ydgk.jsp

President: Lian Zhengmin Tel: +86(911) 2332007

College

Arts *(Lu Xun)* (Fine Arts; Literature; Music); **Chemistry and Chemical Engineering** (Analytical Chemistry; Applied Chemistry; Chemical Engineering; Chemistry; Industrial Chemistry); **Continuing Education and Applied Technology** (Accountancy; Analytical Chemistry; Applied Mathematics; Art Education; Biological and Life Sciences; Business Administration; Chemistry; Chinese; Civil Engineering; Computer Engineering; Computer Science; Continuing Education; Educational Technology; Electronic Engineering; English; Environmental Management; Finance; Foreign Languages Education; Humanities and Social Science Education; Industrial Management; Information Management; Information Technology; Journalism; Landscape Architecture; Law; Library Science; Literature; Mathematics; Medicine; Nursing; Oral Pathology; Physical Education; Primary Education; Secretarial Studies; Technology; Water Management); **Economic Administration** (Accountancy; Business Administration; Economics; Finance; Human Resources; Tourism); **Educational Sciences** (Curriculum; Educational Psychology; Educational Sciences; Pedagogy; Primary Education); **Humanities and Social Sciences** (Arts and Humanities; History; Public Administration; Social Sciences; Social Work); **Life Sciences** (Anatomy; Biochemistry; Biological and Life Sciences; Biology; Biotechnology; Botany; Cell Biology; Genetics; Landscape Architecture; Microbiology; Molecular Biology; Pedagogy; Physiology; Science Education; Secondary Education; Zoology); **Literature and Journalism** (Chinese; Journalism; Literature; Radio and Television Broadcasting; Secretarial Studies); **Mathematics and Computer Science** (Applied Mathematics; Computer Science; E-Business/Commerce; Information Technology; Mathematics; Mathematics and Computer Science; Mathematics Education); **Medicine** (Genetics; Laboratory Techniques; Medicine; Nursing; Radiology; Surgery); **Physical Education** (Physical Education; Sports); **Physics and Electronic Information** (Chemistry; Civil Engineering; Electronic Engineering; Information Technology; Physics; Telecommunications Engineering); **Political Science and Law** (Law; Political Sciences)

School

Foreign Languages (Applied Linguistics; English; Japanese; Linguistics; Modern Languages)

Centre

Computer (Computer Science)

History: Founded 1941 through merger of Shanbei Public School with the Woman's University of China, the Zedong School of Young Cadres, the Yanan School of Natural Sciences, the School of Nationalities, the Shanganning Border Region School of Administration and the Xinwenzi Cadre School.

Academic Year: March to January (March-July; September-January)

Admission Requirements: Graduation from senior middle school and entrance examination

Degrees and Diplomas: *Xueshi Xuewei*; *Shuoshi Xuewei*. Also MBA

Student Services: Academic Counselling, Careers Guidance, Cultural Activities, Facilities for disabled people, Health Services, Nursery Care, Social Counselling, Sports Facilities

Publications: Journal of Higher Education; Journal of Yanan University

Last Updated: 25/01/13

YANBIAN UNIVERSITY (YBU)

977 Gongyuan Road, Yanji, Jilin Province 133002
Tel: +86(433) 2732052 +86(433) 2732350
Fax: +86(433) 2719618 +86(433) 2756759
EMail: xcb@ybu.edu.cn; liuxue@ybu.edu.cn
Website: http://www.ybu.edu.cn

President: Yonghao Pu
Tel: +86(433) 2732011 EMail: president@ybu.edu.cn

International Relations: Yongri Cui EMail: yrcui@ybu.edu.cn

College

Agriculture (Agriculture; Animal Husbandry; Biotechnology; Environmental Studies; Farm Management; Food Science; Food Technology; Forestry; Genetics; Horticulture; Landscape Architecture; Social and Preventive Medicine; Veterinary Science; Zoology); **Arts**

(Dance; Museum Studies; Music; Music Theory and Composition; Musicology; Performing Arts); **Basic Medicine** (Medicine; Oral Pathology; Toxicology); **Chinese Language and Culture** (Chinese; Cultural Studies; Foreign Languages Education); **Chinese Medicine** (Traditional Eastern Medicine); **Economics and Management** (Accountancy; Business Administration; Economics; Information Management; Information Sciences; International Business; International Economics; Management; Marketing; Tourism); **Engineering** (Agricultural Equipment; Architecture; Automation and Control Engineering; Chemical Engineering; Civil Engineering; Computer Science; Electronic Engineering; Engineering; Industrial Design; Information Technology; Machine Building; Media Studies; Structural Architecture; Telecommunications Engineering); **Fine Arts** (Design; Fine Arts; Painting and Drawing); **Foreign Languages** (Applied Linguistics; English; Japanese; Linguistics; Modern Languages; Russian); **Humanities and Social Science** (Arts and Humanities; Chinese; History; International Studies; Literature; Philosophy; Political Sciences; Public Administration; Social Sciences); **Korean Studies** (African Languages; Comparative Literature; Journalism; Korean; Literature; Modern Languages; South and Southeast Asian Languages); **Law** (Administrative Law; Civil Law; Commercial Law; Constitutional Law; Law); **Medicine** (Anatomy; Biochemistry; Biology; Chemistry; Embryology and Reproduction Biology; Gynaecology and Obstetrics; Hygiene; Immunology; Medicine; Molecular Biology; Nursing; Ophthalmology; Paediatrics; Pharmacology; Pharmacy; Physiology; Surgery; Toxicology; Traditional Eastern Medicine); **Nomal** (Educational Psychology; Educational Technology); **Nursing** (Nursing); **Pharmacy** (Medicine; Pharmacology; Pharmacy); **Physical Education** (Physical Education; Sports); **Science** (Analytical Chemistry; Applied Chemistry; Applied Mathematics; Chemistry; Geography; Geography (Human); Inorganic Chemistry; Mathematics; Optics; Organic Chemistry; Physical Chemistry; Physics; Statistics)

Department

Fundamental Social Science (Political Sciences; Social Sciences)

Centre

Bohai Culture Studies (Cultural Studies); **Inter-Korean Studies** (Asian Studies; Korean)

Laboratory

Natural Resources of Changbai Mountain and Functional Molecules *(Key Laboratory)* (Natural Resources)

Research Institute

Ethnology (Ethnology; History; Political Sciences)

Further Information: Also 2 post-doctoral research stations

History: Founded 1949. Separated into Yanbian University, Yanbian University, Yanbian Medical College, Yanbian Agricultural College, Yanbian Institute of Technology 1958. Merged with Yanbian Medical College, Yanbian Agricultural College, Yanbian Teachers College, Jilin College of the Arts the Yanbian Branch of and Sino-foreign cooperative education institution - the Yanbian University of Science and Technology 1996.

Admission Requirements: Senior high school certificate

Fees: (Yuan): Bachelor's degree, 18,000-27,000 per annum; Master's degree, 22,000-29,000 per annum; Doctor's degree, 29,000 per annum

Main Language(s) of Instruction: Chinese, Korean

Accrediting Agency: Ministry of Education; Jilin Province Education Commission

Degrees and Diplomas: *Xueshi Xuewei*; *Shuoshi Xuewei*; *Boshi*

Student Services: Academic Counselling, Canteen, Careers Guidance, Cultural Activities, Foreign Studies Centre, Health Services, Language Laboratory, Nursery Care, Social Counselling, Sports Facilities

Publications: Collection of Papers on Korean Issues; Collection of Papers on Korean Nationality; Collection of Papers on North and South Korean Study; Dongjiang; Research on Oriental Philosophy; Study Chinese; Yanbian University Journal of Agricultural Sciences; Yanbian University Journal of Medical Sciences; Yanbian University Journal of Sciences and Engineering; Yanbian University Journal of Social Sciences

Publishing House: Yanbian University Press

Academic Staff *2011-2012*	**TOTAL**
FULL-TIME	**1,900**
STAFF WITH DOCTORATE	
FULL-TIME	**c. 70**
Student Numbers *2011-2012*	
All (Foreign included)	**c. 24,000**
FOREIGN ONLY	**620**

Last Updated: 28/01/13

YANCHENG INSTITUTE OF TECHNOLOGY (YCIT)

No. 9 Yingbin Avenue, Yangcheng, Jiangsu Province 224003
Tel: +86(515) 88168666
Fax: +86(515) 88316719
EMail: ycmaster@tom.com
Website: http://www.ycit.edu.cn

President: Wang Baolin

School

Automotive Engineering (Automotive Engineering); **Boya Non-governmental** (Automation and Control Engineering; Automotive Engineering; Civil Engineering; Design; Electrical Engineering; English; Finance; International Business; International Economics; Machine Building); **Chemical and Biological Engineering** (Applied Chemistry; Bioengineering; Chemical Engineering; Food Science; Food Technology; Marine Engineering; Pharmacology); **Civil Engineering** (Architecture; Bridge Engineering; Civil Engineering; Construction Engineering; Irrigation; Road Engineering; Water Management); **Design and Art** (Design; Fashion Design; Fine Arts; Industrial Design; Industrial Engineering; Landscape Architecture); **Economics and Management** (Accountancy; Business Administration; E-Business/Commerce; Economics; Finance; Information Management; Information Sciences; International Business; International Economics; Management; Marketing; Transport Management); **Electrical Engineering** (Automation and Control Engineering; Electrical Engineering; Energy Engineering); **Environmental Engineering** (Environmental Engineering; Environmental Management; Environmental Studies); **Further and Open Education** (Accountancy; Administration; Building Technologies; Business Administration; Chemical Engineering; Civil Engineering; Computer Science; Design; Electrical Engineering; Electronic Engineering; English; Finance; Law; Machine Building; Materials Engineering; Public Administration; Textile Technology); **Humanities** (Arts and Humanities; Chinese; English; Japanese; Literature; Secretarial Studies; Tourism); **Information Engineering** (Computer Engineering; Computer Networks; Computer Science; Electronic Engineering; Information Technology; Materials Engineering; Metallurgical Engineering; Polymer and Plastics Technology; Software Engineering; Transport Engineering); **Mechanical Engineering** (Automation and Control Engineering; Industrial Engineering; Mechanical Engineering; Production Engineering); **Textile Engineering** (Chemical Engineering; Fashion Design; Textile Technology); **UGS** (Automation and Control Engineering; Business Computing; Computer Science; Mechanical Engineering; Production Engineering)

History: Founded 1958 as Yancheng College of Technology. Merged with Yancheng Vocational College and acquired present status and title 1996.

Main Language(s) of Instruction: Chinese

Degrees and Diplomas: *Xueshi Xuewei*. Also joint Master programmes: University of Moncton (Canada), University of Portsmouth (England), University of New England (Australia), University of Gangneung Wonju (South Korea).

Academic Staff *2011-2012*: Total 1,099

Student Numbers *2011-2012*: Total: c. 20,000

Last Updated: 25/01/13

YANCHENG TEACHERS UNIVERSITY (YCTC)

50 Kaifang Avenue, Yancheng, Jiangsu Province 224002
Tel: +86(515) 88334240 +86(515) 88233990
Fax: +86(515) 88221990
EMail: karenyu1983@yahoo.com; warwickwang@163.com
Website: http://www.yctc.edu.cn

President: Xue Jiabao EMail: xuejb@yctc.edu.cn

College

Chemistry and Chemical Engineering (Chemical Engineering; Chemistry); **Economic Law and Politics** (Economics; Law; Political Sciences); **Educational Sciences** (Education; Educational Sciences); **Foreign Languages** (English; Korean; Modern Languages; Russian; Translation and Interpretation); **Information Science and Technology** (Information Sciences; Information Technology); **Liberal Arts** (Arts and Humanities); **Life Science and Technology** (Biological and Life Sciences; Biotechnology); **Social Sciences** (Social Sciences); **Urban Studies, Natural Resources and the Environment** (Environmental Management; Environmental Studies; Geography; Natural Resources; Town Planning; Urban Studies)

School

Business (Business Administration); **Marxism** (Political Sciences); **Mathematical Sciences** (Applied Mathematics; Mathematics; Mathematics and Computer Science)

Department

Logistics Management (Transport Management)

Institute

Physical Education (Physical Education; Sports); **Physical Sciences and Electronic Technology** (Electronic Engineering; Physics); **Yellow Sea** (Accountancy; Administration; Applied Chemistry; Arts and Humanities; Biotechnology; Chinese; Computer Science; Design; Electronic Engineering; Engineering; English; Fine Arts; Information Sciences; Information Technology; Law; Literature; Marketing; Natural Sciences; Pharmacology; Psychology; Tourism; Transport Management)

Academy

Coastal Development *(Jiangsu)* (Coastal Studies; Development Studies); **Fine Arts** (Fine Arts); **Music** (Music)

Centre

Modern Educational Technology (Educational Technology)

Research Centre

Rural Education *(Jiangsu Rural Education Research Center)* (Agricultural Education; Rural Studies)

History: Founded 1958. Merged with Yancheng Institute of Education 1999.

Main Language(s) of Instruction: Chinese

Degrees and Diplomas: *Xueshi Xuewei*

Academic Staff *2011-2012*: Total: c. 950

Student Numbers *2011-2012*: Total: c. 20,000

Last Updated: 28/01/13

YANG-EN UNIVERSITY (YEU)

Majia Town, Quanzhou, Fujian Province 362014
Tel: +86(591) 2082001 Ext. 118
Fax: +86(591) 2082017
EMail: yeubgs@yeu.edu.cn; yeufao@mail.yeu.cn
Website: http://www.yeu.edu.cn

President: Hu Quanjun EMail: xiaozhang@yeu.edu.cn

College

Economics (Accountancy; Banking; Economics; English; Finance; Insurance; International Business; International Economics; Management; Statistics); **Foreign Languages** (English; Modern Languages); **Humanities** (Arts and Humanities; Literature; Social Sciences; Writing); **Information and Computer Science** (Computer Science; Information Sciences; Information Technology); **Management** (Management)

Department

Literary Teaching and Research (Literature); **Mathematics** (Mathematics); **Military Science** (Military Science); **Sports Teaching and Research** (Physical Education; Sports)

Institute

Political Sciences and Law (Law; Political Sciences)

History: Founded 1988 as School part of Huaqiao University. Gained independence and named Yang En College 1989. Privatised and acquired present title 1994.

Main Language(s) of Instruction: Chinese

Degrees and Diplomas: *Xueshi Xuewei*

Student Services: Sports Facilities

Publications: Learned Journal of Yang'en University

Student Numbers *2011-2012*: Total: c. 14,000

Last Updated: 28/01/13

YANGTZE NORMAL UNIVERSITY (YZNU)

98 Julong Rd., Lidu Fuling District, Chongqing 408000
EMail: yangtzenu@gmail.com
Website: http://www.yznu.edu.cn/

President: Li Lin

College

Minorities (Applied Mathematics; Chinese; English; Literature; Mathematics)

Department

Biological Science (Bioengineering; Biological and Life Sciences; Biotechnology; Food Technology; Science Education); **Chemistry and Environmental Science** (Analytical Chemistry; Chemistry; Environmental Studies; Inorganic Chemistry; Organic Chemistry; Physical Chemistry); **Chinese Language and Literature** (Chinese; Literature; Native Language Education; Secretarial Studies); **Computer Science** (Computer Engineering; Computer Science); **Economics and Law** (Economics; Law); **Fine Arts** (Fine Arts); **Foreign Language Teaching** (English; Foreign Languages Education); **Foreign Languages** (English; Japanese; Modern Languages); **History and Tourism Culture** (History; Tourism); **Management** (Management; Marketing; Public Administration); **Mathematics** (Applied Mathematics; Mathematics; Mathematics Education; Primary Education; Science Education); **Music** (Dance; Music; Music Education; Musical Instruments; Musicology); **Physical Education** (Physical Education); **Physics and Electronic and Information Engineering** (Educational Technology; Electronic Engineering; Information Technology; Physics); **Teachers Education** (Teacher Training)

Further Information: Also Jianfu and Jiangdong campuses; University Hospital (Health and Epidemic Prevention and Centers for Disease Control)

History: Founded as a college 1982. Renamed Fuling Teachers College 1993. Acquired university status 2001, following merger with Fuling Education Institute. Acquired present title 2006.

Fees: (US Dollar): Tuition fee for foreign students, 1,700-1,800 per annum

Main Language(s) of Instruction: Chinese

Degrees and Diplomas: *Xueshi Xuewei*

Student Services: Sports Facilities

Academic Staff *2012-2013*	**TOTAL**
FULL-TIME	**775**
Student Numbers *2012-2013*	
All (Foreign included)	**13,827**
FOREIGN ONLY	**30**

Last Updated: 07/10/13

YANGTZE UNIVERSITY (YU)

1 Nanhuan Road Jingzhou, Jingzhou, Hubei Province 434023
Tel: +86(716) 8060236
Fax: +86(716) 8060514
EMail: fao@yangtzeu.edu.cn
Website: http://www.yangtzeu.edu.cn

President: Zhang Changmin

School

Agriculture (Agriculture; Environmental Management; Natural Resources; Plant and Crop Protection); **Animal Science** (Animal Husbandry; Aquaculture; Zoology); **Arts** (Dance; Design; Fine Arts; Music; Musicology); **Chemistry and Environmental Engineering** (Applied Chemistry; Chemistry; Environmental Engineering; Materials Engineering); **City Construction** (Architecture; Architecture and Planning; Civil Engineering; Construction Engineering; Engineering Management; Town Planning; Water Management);

Computer Science (Computer Networks; Computer Science; Educational Technology); **Economics** (Agricultural Economics; Economics; Farm Management; Forest Economics; International Business; International Economics); **Educational Sciences** (Education; Educational Psychology; Educational Sciences); **Electronic Information** (Automation and Control Engineering; Electrical and Electronic Equipment and Maintenance; Electronic Engineering; Information Technology; Measurement and Precision Engineering; Telecommunications Engineering); **Foreign Languages** (Applied Linguistics; English; Japanese; Linguistics); **Gardening and Horticulture** (Forest Management; Horticulture); **Geophysics and Oil Resources** (Geophysics; Petroleum and Gas Engineering); **Geosciences** (Geology; Paleontology; Surveying and Mapping); **Information and Mathematics** (Applied Mathematics; Computer Science; Information Sciences; Mathematics); **International Studies** (Acupuncture; Chinese; Economics; Fine Arts; International Studies; Management; Medicine; Nursing); **Life Sciences** (Bioengineering; Biological and Life Sciences; Biotechnology; Food Science; Food Technology; Genetics); **Literature** (Chinese; History; Literature; Radio and Television Broadcasting); **Management** (Accountancy; Business Administration; Human Resources; Information Management; Marketing; Public Administration; Transport Management); **Mechanical Engineering** (Automation and Control Engineering; Industrial Design; Machine Building; Mechanical Engineering); **Medicine** (Medical Technology; Medicine; Nursing; Surgery); **Petroleum Engineering** (Petroleum and Gas Engineering); **Physical Education** (Physical Education; Sports); **Physics Science** (Applied Physics; Optics; Physics); **Politics and Law** (Law; Political Sciences; Social Work)

Department

Geochemistry (Geochemistry; Geological Engineering; Hydraulic Engineering)

History: Founded 2003, following merger of Jianghan Petroleum University, Hubei Agricultural University, Jingzhou Teacher's University and Hubei Medical Staff College.

Academic Year: September to July

Admission Requirements: Graduation from senior middle school and entrance examination

Fees: (Yuan): Undergraduate tuition, 3,000-3,500 per annum; Postgraduate tuition, 4,000-4,500 per annum

Main Language(s) of Instruction: Chinese, English, Japanese

Accrediting Agency: China National Petroleum Corporation

Degrees and Diplomas: *Xueshi Xuewei*; *Shuoshi Xuewei*; *Boshi*

Student Services: Academic Counselling, Canteen, Careers Guidance, Cultural Activities, Facilities for disabled people, Foreign Studies Centre, Health Services, Language Laboratory, Nursery Care, Social Counselling, Sports Facilities

Publications: Journal of Natural Sciences; Journal of Social Sciences

Academic Staff *2011-2012*: Total 2,149

STAFF WITH DOCTORATE: Total 241

Student Numbers *2011-2012*: Total: c. 34,000

Last Updated: 28/01/13

YANGZHOU UNIVERSITY (YZU)

88 South University Ave, Yangzhou, Jiangsu Province 225009
Tel: +86(514) 87971870
Fax: +86(514) 87352262
EMail: fao@yzu.edu.cn
Website: http://www.yzu.edu.cn

President: Xin'an Jiao

International Relations: Yongming Tang
EMail: ymtang@yzu.edu.cn

College

Agriculture (Agriculture; Agronomy; Biochemistry; Crop Production; Development Studies; Food Technology; Genetics; Information Technology; Regional Planning; Rural Planning; Safety Engineering); **Animal Science and Technology** (Animal Husbandry; Aquaculture; Biology; Food Science; Genetics; Nutrition; Sports); **Art** (Art Management; Design; Fashion Design; Fine Arts; Music; Musicology); **Bio-science and Bio-Technology** (Bioengineering; Biological and Life Sciences; Biotechnology; Cell Biology; Microbiology); **Business** (Accountancy; Administration; Agricultural Economics; Agricultural Management; Business Administration; E-Business/Commerce; Economics; Finance; Human Resources; International Business; International Economics; Marketing; Public Administration); **Chemistry and Chemical Engineering** (Analytical Chemistry; Applied Chemistry; Chemical Engineering; Chemistry; Inorganic Chemistry; Medical Technology; Organic Chemistry; Pharmacology; Physical Chemistry; Polymer and Plastics Technology); **Chinese Language and Literature** (Chinese; Literature); **Civil Science and Engineering** (Architecture; Architecture and Planning; Bridge Engineering; Civil Engineering; Engineering Management; Road Engineering; Safety Engineering; Structural Architecture; Transport Engineering); **Educational Science (Teachers' Education)** (Curriculum; Educational Administration; Educational Psychology; Educational Sciences; Pedagogy; Primary Education; Teacher Training); **Energy and Power Engineering** (Automation and Control Engineering; Building Technologies; Electrical and Electronic Engineering; Electrical Engineering; Energy Engineering; Measurement and Precision Engineering; Power Engineering; Thermal Engineering); **Environmental Science and Engineering** (Environmental Engineering; Environmental Studies; Natural Resources; Water Management); **Foreign Languages Studies** (Arabic; English; French; Japanese; Korean; Modern Languages); **Guangling** (Agriculture; Chemical Engineering; Economics; Electrical Engineering; Electronic Engineering; Engineering; Fine Arts; Law; Literature; Management; Mechanical Engineering; Medicine; Tourism); **Horticulture and Plant Protection** (Ecology; Entomology; Horticulture; Pest Management; Plant and Crop Protection); **Hydraulic Science and Engineering** (Hydraulic Engineering; Water Science); **Information Engineering** (Automation and Control Engineering; Computer Engineering; Computer Networks; Computer Science; Electronic Engineering; Information Management; Information Sciences; Information Technology; Software Engineering; Telecommunications Engineering); **Journalism and Communication** (Educational Technology; Journalism; Mass Communication; Photography; Radio and Television Broadcasting); **Law** (Law); **Mathematical Science** (Applied Mathematics; Computer Science; Mathematics; Mathematics and Computer Science); **Mechanical Engineering** (Agricultural Equipment; Automotive Engineering; Electronic Engineering; Industrial Chemistry; Industrial Engineering; Mechanical Engineering; Production Engineering); **Medicine** (Dermatology; Gynaecology and Obstetrics; Medicine; Nursing; Pharmacy; Venereology); **Physical Education** (Physical Education; Sports); **Physical Science and Technology** (Biophysics; Electronic Engineering; Information Sciences; Information Technology; Optical Technology; Optics; Physics; Science Education); **Social Science** (Archiving; History; Library Science; Philosophy; Political Sciences; Social Sciences; Social Welfare); **Tourism and Cuisine (Food Science and Engineering)** (Cooking and Catering; Dairy; Food Science; Food Technology; Nutrition; Safety Engineering); **Veterinary Medicine** (Dietetics; Immunology; Microbiology; Social and Preventive Medicine; Veterinary Science; Zoology)

School

Wen (Chinese; Foreign Languages Education; Literature)

Institute

Marxism (Political Sciences)

Further Information: 9 campuses: Yangzijin Campus, The Lotus Pond Campus, Slender West Lake Campus, Wenhui Road Campus, Huaihai Road Campus, North Jiangyang Road Campus, South Jiangyang Road Campus, Yanfu Road Campus, Guangling Campus. Also Teaching Hospital. Affiliated Animal Hospital, and Experimental Farm; 13 Postdoctoral Research Stations

History: Founded 1992 as a merger of 6 colleges: Teachers College of Yangzhou, Agricultural College of Jiangsu, Engineering College of Yangzhou, Medical College of Yangzhou, Water Conservancy Engineering College of Jiangsu and Business School of Jiangsu.

Academic Year: September to July (September-January; February-July)

Admission Requirements: Graduation from senior middle school and entrance examination

Fees: (US Dollars): 1,600-4,500 per annum

Main Language(s) of Instruction: Chinese

Accrediting Agency: Jiangsu Education Department

Degrees and Diplomas: *Xueshi Xuewei*; *Shuoshi Xuewei*; *Boshi*

Student Services: Academic Counselling, Canteen, Careers Guidance, Cultural Activities, Facilities for disabled people, Foreign Studies Centre, Health Services, Language Laboratory, Nursery Care, Social Counselling, Sports Facilities

Publications: Research Journal of Yangzhou University

Academic Staff *2011-2012*: Total: c. 2,000

Student Numbers *2011-2012*: Total: c. 54,100

Last Updated: 29/01/13

YANSHAN UNIVERSITY (YSU)

438 Hebei Ave. W., Qinhuangdao,
Hebei Province 066004
Tel: +86(335) 8057100
Fax: +86(335) 8061449
EMail: waiban@ysu.edu.cn
Website: http://www.ysu.edu.cn

President: Hongmin Liu Tel: +86(335) 8051260

College

Art and Design Academy (Design; Fine Arts; Industrial Design; Music; Sculpture); **Civil Engineering and Mechanics** (Architectural and Environmental Design; Architecture; Building Technologies; Civil Engineering; Mechanics); **Continuing Education**; **Economics and Management** (Accountancy; Business Administration; E-Business/Commerce; Economics; Engineering Management; Industrial Engineering; International Business; International Economics; Management; Operations Research; Public Administration; Tourism; Transport Engineering); **Electrical Engineering** (Automation and Control Engineering; Biomedical Engineering; Electrical and Electronic Engineering; Electrical Engineering; Instrument Making); **Environmental and Chemical Engineering** (Applied Chemistry; Automation and Control Engineering; Bioengineering; Chemical Engineering; Environmental Engineering); **Foreign Languages** (Applied Linguistics; English; French; German; Japanese; Linguistics; Modern Languages; Russian); **Humanities and Law** (Administration; Arts and Humanities; Chinese; Economics; International Relations; Journalism; Law; Literature; Philosophy; Political Sciences; Public Administration; Radio and Television Broadcasting); **Information Science and Engineering** (Computer Engineering; Computer Science; Educational Technology; Electronic Engineering; Information Sciences; Optical Technology; Telecommunications Engineering); **Liren**; **Materials Science and Engineering** (Chemistry; Materials Engineering; Physics; Polymer and Plastics Technology); **Mechanical Engineering** (Automation and Control Engineering; Electronic Engineering; Industrial Design; Materials Engineering; Mechanical Engineering; Production Engineering); **Science** (Applied Mathematics; Applied Physics; Computer Science; Electronic Engineering; Information Sciences; Mathematics and Computer Science; Operations Research; Optical Technology; Physics; Statistics); **Software Engineering** (Software Engineering); **Vehicle and Energy** (Automotive Engineering; Energy Engineering; Petroleum and Gas Engineering; Power Engineering; Thermal Engineering; Thermal Physics); **Vocational and Technical Studies**

School

Marxism (Arts and Humanities; Law; Political Sciences; Social Sciences)

Institute

International Education; **National Defence Science and Technology** (Military Science); **Physical Education** (Physical Education; Sports)

History: Founded as Harbin Institute of Technology 1920. Department of Heavy Machinery moved to Qiqihar, Heilongjan Province, to establish the Harbin Institute of Technology School of heavy machinery, then renamed Heavy Machinery Institute 1958. Completely separated from HIT and renamed Northeast Heavy Machinery Institute 1960. Moved to Hebei Province and acquired present title and status 1997.

Academic Year: September to July

Admission Requirements: Graduation from senior middle school and national college entrance examination

Main Language(s) of Instruction: Chinese

Accrediting Agency: Educational Department of Hebei Province

Degrees and Diplomas: *Xueshi Xuewei*; *Shuoshi Xuewei*; *Boshi*. Also post-doctoral programmes; MBA

Student Services: Academic Counselling, Canteen, Careers Guidance, Health Services, Language Laboratory, Nursery Care, Social Counselling, Sports Facilities

Publications: Journal of Yanshan University; Research in Teaching

Publishing House: Yanshan University Press

Academic Staff *2012-2013*: Total: c. 2,000

Student Numbers *2012-2013*: Total: c. 40,000

Last Updated: 29/01/13

YANTAI NANSHAN UNIVERSITY

Donghai Tourist Resort Zone, Longkou,
Yantai City, Shangdong 265713
Tel: +86(535) 8590703 +86(535) 8609306
Fax: +86(535) 8590701 +86(535) 8609926
EMail: nanshan@nanshan.edu.cn; nsiad@nanshan.edu.cn
Website: http://www.nanshan.edu.cn/

President: Hao Xianxiao

College

Accountancy and Finance (Accountancy; Finance); **Business Administration** (Business Administration); **Property Management** (Real Estate)

School

Arts (Fine Arts); **Automation Engineering** (Automation and Control Engineering); **Automobile Engineering** (Automotive Engineering); **Business** (Business Administration); **Continuing Education**; **Education** (Education); **Electromechanical Engineering** (Electronic Engineering; Mechanical Engineering); **Electronic Engineering** (Electronic Engineering); **Foreign Languages** (English; Modern Languages); **Information Science and Technology** (Information Sciences; Information Technology); **International Economy and Trade** (International Business; International Economics); **International Golf** (Sports); **Logistics Management** (Transport Management); **Materials and Metallurgical Engineering** (Materials Engineering; Metallurgical Engineering); **Mechanical Engineering** (Mechanical Engineering); **Nutritious Food and Health** (Food Science; Health Sciences); **Software Engineering** (Software Engineering); **Textile and Garment** (Textile Technology); **Tourism Management** (Tourism)

Department

Basic Courses; **Public Foreign Language Teaching** (Foreign Languages Education); **Teaching of Computer Application** (Computer Education); **Teaching of Public Physical Education** (Physical Education); **Teaching of Social Sciences Education** (Humanities and Social Science Education)

History: Founded 1991.

Main Language(s) of Instruction: Chinese

Degrees and Diplomas: *Xueshi Xuewei*

Academic Staff *2012-2013*: Total 2,262

Student Numbers *2012-2013*: Total: c. 30,000

Last Updated: 04/11/13

YANTAI UNIVERSITY (YTU)

32, Qingquan Road, Laishan District,
Yantai, Shandong Province 264005
Tel: +86(535) 6902143
Fax: +86(535) 6901858
EMail: ngelhanchengguo@163.com
Website: http://www.ytu.edu.cn

President: Fang Shaokun Tel: +86(535) 6902060

Secretary-General: Xiangli Han Tel: +86(535) 6902010

International Relations: Jie You, Director, International Office Tel: +86(535) 6903238 EMail: iaoyu2@ytu.edu.cn

College
EIE; **International Education Exchange**; **Life Sciences** (Biological and Life Sciences); **Reserve Officers** (Military Science)

School
Architecture (Architectural and Environmental Design; Architecture; Engineering Drawing and Design); **Arts** (Music; Theatre); **Chemical and Biological Science and Engineering** (Bioengineering; Biology; Chemical Engineering; Chemistry); **Civil Engineering** (Civil Engineering); **Computer Science** (Computer Science); **Continuing Education**; **Economics and Business Administration** (Business Administration; Economics); **Electromechanical Automobile Engineering** (Automotive Engineering; Electronic Engineering; Mechanical Engineering); **Environment and Material Engineering** (Environmental Engineering; Materials Engineering); **Foreign Languages** (English; Modern Languages); **Humanities** (Arts and Humanities; Chinese; Journalism; Literature; Social Sciences); **Law** (Law); **Mathematics and Information Science** (Information Sciences; Mathematics and Computer Science); **Oceanography** (Marine Science and Oceanography); **Opto-electronics** (Electrical and Electronic Engineering; Optical Technology); **Pharmacy** (Pharmacy); **Wenjing** (Economics)

Department
Marxist Theory (Political Sciences); **Physical Education Teaching** (Physical Education; Teacher Training)

Institute
Physical Education (Physical Education; Sports)

Research Centre
Intellectual Property *(Shandong Province)* (Civil Law; Private Law)

Further Information: Also 46 research institutes

History: Founded 1984.

Academic Year: September to July

Admission Requirements: Entrance Examination

Fees: (Yuan): 6,000 per annum

Main Language(s) of Instruction: Chinese

Accrediting Agency: Shandong Provincial Education Committee

Degrees and Diplomas: *Xueshi Xuewei*; *Shuoshi Xuewei*

Student Services: Academic Counselling, Canteen, Careers Guidance, Cultural Activities, Foreign Studies Centre, Health Services, Language Laboratory, Nursery Care, Social Counselling, Sports Facilities

Publications: Journal of Yantai University, Natural, Science and Engineering Edition; Journal of Yantai University, Philosophy and Social Sciences Edition

Publishing House: Yantai University Press

Academic Staff *2011-2012*	**TOTAL**
FULL-TIME	**1,183**
STAFF WITH DOCTORATE	
FULL-TIME	**375**
FOREIGN ONLY	**600**

Last Updated: 29/01/13

YI LI NORMAL UNIVERSITY

298 Jiefang Road, Yining, Xinjiang Uygur Province 835000
Tel: +86(999) 8120648
Fax: +86(999) 8124245
EMail: yuanzhang@ylsy.edu.cn
Website: http://www.ylsy.edu.cn

President: Wu Xiaocheng

International Relations: Liu Jianchang

College
Arts (Art Education; Design; Fine Arts); **Chemistry and Biological Sciences** (Biological and Life Sciences; Chemistry); **Educational Science** (Educational Sciences); **Electronic and Information Engineering** (Electronic Engineering; Information Technology); **Humanities** (Arts and Humanities; Chemistry; History; Literature); **Law and Politics** (Law; Political Sciences); **Physics and Technology** (Applied Physics; Physics; Technology)

School
Chinese Language (Chinese); **Mathematics and Statistics** (Mathematics; Statistics)

Department
Foreign Languages (English; Modern Languages)

Institute
Physical Education (Physical Education)

Research Centre
Aida Walters Art (Fine Arts); **Yili Studies** (Asian Studies; Cultural Studies)

Research Institute
Applied Math (Applied Mathematics); **Applied Mathematics** (Applied Mathematics); **Central Asia** (Asian Religious Studies); **Condensed Matter Physics and Materials Design** (Materials Engineering; Physics); **Educational Sciences** (Educational Sciences); **Kazakh Culture** (Asian Studies); **Landscape Gardening** (Horticulture; Landscape Architecture); **Natural Resources and Ecology** (Ecology; Natural Resources)

Research Unit
Tangjia Luck

History: Founded 1948 as Xinjiang province Yili College, then renamed Ahe Amat River College, Yili Normal School. Acquired College status and title 1980.

Main Language(s) of Instruction: Chinese

Degrees and Diplomas: *Xueshi Xuewei*; *Shuoshi Xuewei*

Academic Staff *2012-2013*: Total 803

Student Numbers *2012-2013*: Total 11,654

Last Updated: 29/01/13

YIBIN UNIVERSITY

8 Jiusheng Road, Wuliangye Avenue, Yibin, Sichuan 644000
Tel: +86(831) 3545086 +86(831) 3531186
Fax: +86(831) 3531186
EMail: shujimail@163.com; yuanzhangmail@163.com
Website: http://www.yibinu.cn/

President: Wang Mingyi (2009-) EMail: ybxywmy@163.com

College
Art and Design (Advertising and Publicity; Art History; Communication Arts; Design; Film; Fine Arts; Graphic Design; Media Studies; Packaging Technology; Painting and Drawing; Visual Arts); **Chemistry and Chemical Engineering** (Applied Chemistry; Chemical Engineering; Chemistry; Environmental Engineering; Pharmacology); **Chinese Wine Culture** *(Includes China Wine Culture Research Center)* (Viticulture); **Computer and Information Engineering** (Computer Engineering; Information Technology); **Economics and Management** (Economics; Management); **Foreign Languages** (English; Foreign Languages Education; Japanese; Tourism; Translation and Interpretation); **Government** (Government); **Law** (Law); **Life Science and Food Engineering** (Biological and Life Sciences; Food Technology); **Marxism** (Political Sciences); **Mathematics** (Applied Mathematics; Computer Science; Information Sciences; Mathematics); **Mining and Safety Engineering** (Mining Engineering; Safety Engineering); **Music and Performing Arts** (Dance; Music; Music Theory and Composition; Musical Instruments; Singing); **Physical and Electronic Engineering** (Electronic Engineering; Information Sciences; Information Technology; Mechanical Engineering; Physical Engineering; Physics; Telecommunications Engineering); **Physical Education** (Physical Education); **Teacher Education** (Education; Educational Psychology; Literature; Native Language Education; Pedagogy; Preschool Education; Primary Education; Teacher Training)

Institute
Literature and Media (Literature; Media Studies)

History: Founded 2001 through merger of Yibin Teachers College and the Yibin Teachers College Yibin and Yibin Sichuan College of Education Branch. Acquired present status 2006.

Main Language(s) of Instruction: Chinese

Degrees and Diplomas: *Xueshi Xuewei*

Student Services: Sports Facilities

Academic Staff *2013-2014*: Total 716

Student Numbers *2013-2014*: Total: c. 14,000

Last Updated: 07/10/13

YICHUN UNIVERSITY (YU)

Xuefu Road 16, Yichun, Jiangxi 336000
Tel: +86(135) 23494515
EMail: info@yichununiversity.com
Website: http://www.yichununiversity.com/

School

Adult Education (Adult Education); **Agriculture** (Agriculture; Agronomy; Animal Husbandry; Aquaculture; Biotechnology; Horticulture; Management; Town Planning; Zoology); **Art** (Fine Arts); **Business and Law** (Business Administration; Law); **Engineering** (Architecture; Automation and Control Engineering; Automotive Engineering; Bioengineering; Biological and Life Sciences; Biology; Biomedicine; Civil Engineering; Computer Engineering; Computer Science; Electrical Engineering; Electronic Engineering; Engineering; Environmental Studies; Food Technology; Information Management; Mechanical Engineering; Telecommunications Engineering); **Foreign Languages Studies** (English; Modern Languages); **Humanities** (Advertising and Publicity; Arts and Humanities; Chinese; English; Geography; History; Humanities and Social Science Education; Journalism; Literature; Modern Languages; Native Language Education; Political Sciences; Public Administration; Radio and Television Broadcasting; Secretarial Studies); **Medicine** (Cosmetology; Medical Technology; Medicine; Nursing; Social and Preventive Medicine); **Physical Education** (Physical Education); **Science** (Applied Mathematics; Chemistry; Computer Education; Computer Science; Electronic Engineering; Environmental Studies; Information Sciences; Information Technology; Mathematics; Mathematics Education; Medicine; Natural Sciences; Physics; Science Education; Telecommunications Engineering); **Vocational and Technical Education** (Technology Education; Vocational Education)

History: Founded 1958.

Main Language(s) of Instruction: Chinese

Degrees and Diplomas: *Xueshi Xuewei*

Academic Staff *2012-2013*: Total 633

Student Numbers *2012-2013*: Total 19,779

Last Updated: 04/11/13

YOUJIANG MEDICAL UNIVERSITY FOR NATIONALITIES (YMUN)

98 Chengxiang Road, Baise, Guangxi Autonomous Region 533000
Tel: +86(776) 2823054
Fax: +86(776) 2823054 +86(776) 2846565
EMail: http://www.ymcn.gx.cn/Index.html; youyiwai@163.com
Website: http://www.ymcn.gx.cn/Index.html

President: Li Peichun

International Relations: Lu Xianjie

Programme

Chinese Language Training *(Short-term)* (Chinese; Foreign Languages Education); **Clinical Medicine** (Gynaecology and Obstetrics; Health Administration; Medicine; Pharmacology; Psychology); **Medical Imaging** (Computer Graphics; Medical Technology; Radiology); **Medical Laboratory** (Laboratory Techniques); **Nursing** (Nursing); **Stomatology** (Stomatology); **Traditional Chinese Medicine** *(Short-term)* (Traditional Eastern Medicine)

History: Founded 1958 as Baise Medical School, acquired present status and name 1978. One of the unviersities under the administration of Education Department of Guangxi Zhuang Autonomous Region

Fees: (Yuan): Bachelor's degree, 16,000-18,000 per annum. Short-term programmes: Traditional Chinese Medicine, per week; Chinese Language Training Programme, varies accordingly to the programme's length (from 2,000 per month to 12,000 per annum)

Main Language(s) of Instruction: Chinese

Degrees and Diplomas: *Xueshi Xuewei*

Student Services: Sports Facilities

Academic Staff *2011-2012*: Total: c. 300

Student Numbers *2012-2013*: Total: c. 15,577

Last Updated: 29/01/13

YULIN NORMAL UNIVERSITY (YLU)

Guangxi Yulin Education Road No. 299, Yulin, Guangxi 537000
Website: http://www.ylu.edu.cn/

President: Liangwei Jiang

College

Chemistry and Materials Science (Applied Chemistry; Chemical Engineering; Chemistry; Materials Engineering); **Computer Science and Engineering** (Computer Engineering; Computer Science; Software Engineering); **Educational Sciences** (Education; Educational Sciences; Pedagogy; Preschool Education; Primary Education; Psychology); **Electronics and Communication Technology** (Electronic Engineering; Telecommunications Engineering); **Fine Arts and Design** (Design; Fine Arts); **Foreign Languages** (English; Japanese; Modern Languages); **Life Science and Technology** (Biological and Life Sciences); **Mathematics and Information Science** (E-Business/Commerce; Information Management; Information Sciences; Information Technology; Mathematics and Computer Science); **Physical Sciences and Engineering Technology** (Physical Engineering; Physics); **Political History** (Administration; Cultural Studies; History; Political Sciences; Tourism); **Vocational and Technical Studies** (Accountancy; Advertising and Publicity; Computer Engineering; Computer Networks; Computer Science; Cooking and Catering; E-Business/Commerce; English; Horticulture; Hotel Management; Landscape Architecture; Marketing; Nutrition; Secretarial Studies; Tourism; Veterinary Science)

School

French Business (Business Administration; Economics; Law; Marketing); **Literature and Media** (Advertising and Publicity; Chinese; International Studies; Literature; Media Studies; Radio and Television Broadcasting; Secretarial Studies)

Department

Ideological and Political Teaching (Political Sciences)

Institute

Physical Education (Physical Education; Sports)

Academy

Music and Dance (Dance; Music)

History: Founded 1945.

Main Language(s) of Instruction: Chinese

Degrees and Diplomas: *Xueshi Xuewei*

Student Services: Sports Facilities

Academic Staff *2013-2014*: Total 831

Student Numbers *2013-2014*: Total 15,383

Last Updated: 08/10/13

YULIN UNIVERSITY (YLU)

Yulin City, Shaanxi 719000
Tel: +86(912) 3896329
Fax: +86(912) 3896329
Website: http://www.yulinu.edu.cn/

President: Zhao Hongxing

College

Chemistry and Chemical Engineering (Chemical Engineering; Chemistry; Inorganic Chemistry; Maintenance Technology; Organic Chemistry; Petroleum and Gas Engineering); **Energy Engineering** (Automation and Control Engineering; Electrical Engineering; Energy Engineering; Instrument Making; Measurement and Precision Engineering; Mechanical Engineering; Petroleum and Gas Engineering; Physics; Power Engineering; Production Engineering; Safety Engineering; Thermal Engineering); **Information Engineering** (Computer Engineering; Computer Networks; Computer Science; Information Management; Information Sciences; Information Technology); **Life Sciences** (Agronomy; Animal Husbandry; Biological and Life Sciences; Biology; Botany; Forestry; Horticulture; Zoology); **Management** (Accountancy; Finance; Management;

Marketing; Tourism); **Political Sciences and Law** (History; Law; Political Sciences; Social Sciences)

Department

Architecture Engineering (Civil Engineering; Hydraulic Engineering; Water Management); **Arts** (Dance; Design; Fine Arts; Music); **Chinese Language and Literature** (Chinese; Journalism; Literature; Native Language Education); **Five-year Higher Vocational Education** (Accountancy; Automotive Engineering; Chemical Engineering; Electronic Engineering; Environmental Management; Hotel Management; Maintenance Technology; Mining Engineering; Nursing; Power Engineering; Safety Engineering); **Foreign Language** (English; Modern Languages; Translation and Interpretation); **Mathematics** (Applied Mathematics; Mathematics; Mathematics Education; Statistics); **Physical Education and Sports** (Physical Education; Sports)

Research Centre

Life Science (Biological and Life Sciences); **Northern Shaanxi Culture** (Cultural Studies; Folklore; History); **Shaanxi Provincial Engineering and Technology Research Center for Shaanbei Cashmere Goats** (Agricultural Engineering; Animal Husbandry; Technology)

Research Institute

Desert Plant (Botany); **Northern Shaanxi Sheep-breeding** (Animal Husbandry); **Photo Electricity** (Electrical Engineering; Physics); **Regional Economy** (International Economics)

History: Founded 1958 as Suide Teachers' College. Renamed Yulin College after merging with Yulin College of Agriculture and Forestry 1991. Acquired present status and title 2003.

Main Language(s) of Instruction: Chinese

Degrees and Diplomas: *Xueshi Xuewei*. Also undergraduate diplomas and non-degree programmes.

Academic Staff *2012-2013*	**TOTAL**
FULL-TIME	**668**
STAFF WITH DOCTORATE	
FULL-TIME	**63**
Student Numbers *2012-2013*	
All (Foreign included)	**12,276**
FOREIGN ONLY	**19**

Last Updated: 08/10/13

YUNCHENG UNIVERSITY (YCU)

1155 West Street, Fudan University, Yuncheng, Shanxi 044000
Tel: +86(359) 2090418
Fax: +86(359) 2090378
EMail: admin@ycu.edu.cn
Website: http://www.ycu.edu.cn/

President: Yao Jihuan

College

Adult Education

Department

Applied Chemistry (Applied Chemistry; Chemical Engineering; Chemistry; Primary Education; Science Education); **Applied Mathematics** (Applied Mathematics); **Art and Crafts Design** (Advertising and Publicity; Architectural and Environmental Design; Art History; Communication Arts; Design; Fine Arts; Industrial Design; Painting and Drawing; Photography; Sculpture; Visual Arts); **Chinese Language and Literature** (Chinese; Literature; Secretarial Studies); **College English Teaching** (English; Foreign Languages Education); **Computer Science and Technology** (Computer Education; Computer Engineering; Computer Science; Information Management; Information Sciences; Information Technology); **Economy and Management** (E-Business/Commerce; Economics; Finance; Hotel and Restaurant; Human Resources; Management; Public Administration; Tourism); **Education and Psychology Science** (Education; Psychology); **Foreign Languages** (Applied Linguistics; English; Foreign Languages Education; Japanese; Modern Languages; Russian); **Life Sciences** (Biological and Life Sciences; Biology; Food Science; Food Technology; Horticulture; Science Education); **Mechanical and Electronic** (Electronic Engineering; Mechanical Engineering); **Music** (Dance; Music; Music Education; Musical Instruments; Performing Arts; Singing); **Physical Education** (Physical Education); **Physics and Electronics** (Electronic Engineering; Information Technology; Physics); **Political Science and Law** (Arts and Humanities; Economics; Law; Political Sciences; Primary Education); **Public Computer Teaching** (Computer Education; Computer Science); **Social Science** (Social Sciences)

History: Founded 1983 as Yuncheng College of Education. Acquired present status and title 2002.

Main Language(s) of Instruction: Chinese

Degrees and Diplomas: *Xueshi Xuewei*

Academic Staff *2012-2013*: Total 583

Student Numbers *2012-2013*: Total 10,358

Last Updated: 05/11/13

YUNNAN AGRICULTURAL UNIVERSITY (YNAU)

Heilongtan, Kunming, Yunnan Province 650201
Tel: +86(871) 5211168 Ext. 2735
Fax: +86(871) 5150303
Website: http://www.ynau.edu.cn

President: Zhu Yong

College

Animal Science and Technology (Animal Husbandry; Veterinary Science; Zoology); **Architecture and Civil Engineering** (Architecture; Civil Engineering); **Basic and Information Engineering** (Applied Chemistry; Applied Mathematics; Computer Engineering; Computer Networks; Computer Science; Electronic Engineering; Information Technology); **Economics and Management** (Agricultural Economics; Agricultural Management; Development Studies; E-Business/Commerce; Economics; Forestry; Information Management; Information Sciences; Management); **Engineering** (Agricultural Engineering; Engineering); **Food Science and Technology** (Food Science; Food Technology); **Foreign Languages** (English; French; Japanese; Modern Languages; Vietnamese); **Humanities and Social Sciences** (Arts and Humanities; Social Sciences); **Landscape and Horticulture** (Horticulture; Landscape Architecture); **Plant Protection** (Plant and Crop Protection)

School

Agronomy and Biotechnology (Agriculture; Agronomy; Biotechnology; Botany; Entomology; Pest Management; Plant and Crop Protection; Plant Pathology; Traditional Eastern Medicine); **Continuing and Vocational Education** (Agriculture); **Physical Education** (Physical Education; Sports); **Resources and Environmental Sciences** (Environmental Studies; Natural Resources); **Water Resources, Hydraulics and Architecture** (Architecture; Hydraulic Engineering; Water Management; Water Science)

Department

Ideological and Political Theory Teaching and Research (History; Political Sciences)

Institute

Tobacco Science (Agriculture)

Academy

The Pu'er Tea *(Longrun)* (Agriculture)

Further Information: Also 18 university-level research institutes; postdoctoral research center.

History: Founded 1938 as the School of Agricultural at Yunnan University. Separated from Yunnan University and renamed Kunming Agriculture and Forestry College (KAFC) 1958. The formal title, Yunnan Agricultural University was adopted in 1971 following the merger between KAFC and Yunnan Agriculture Working University (YAWU).

Main Language(s) of Instruction: Chinese

Degrees and Diplomas: *Xueshi Xuewei*; *Shuoshi Xuewei*; *Boshi*

Publications: Journal of Yunnan Agricultural University

Academic Staff *2011-2012*	**TOTAL**
FULL-TIME	**547**
Student Numbers *2011-2012*	
All (Foreign included)	**16,137**
FOREIGN ONLY	**46**

Last Updated: 29/01/13

YUNNAN ARTS INSTITUTE (YNAI)

No.1577, Yu Hua Road, Chenggong County,
Kunming, Yunnan Province 650500
Tel: +86(871) 5937345
Fax: +86(871) 5937345
EMail: faoyau@gmail.com; faoyai_yn@yahoo.com.cn
Website: http://www.admissions.cn/ynart/index01.htm

President: Zhang Jiangzhong

International Relations: Cheng Chunyun

School
Art and Culture (Art Management; Cultural Studies; Fine Arts; History; Literature); **Art and Design** (Architectural and Environmental Design; Ceramic Art; Design; Fashion Design; Fine Arts; Interior Design; Packaging Technology); **Drama** (Acting; Sports; Theatre); **Music** (Music; Music Theory and Composition; Musical Instruments; Musicology; Opera; Singing)

Department
Continuing Education and Vocational Art Education

Institute
Film and Television (Cinema and Television; Film); **Wenhua**

Academy
Dance (Dance); **Fine Arts** (Fine Arts; Painting and Drawing; Photography; Printing and Printmaking; Sculpture)

Research Institute
Folk Art (Fine Arts; Folklore)

History: Founded 1959 as department of Kunming Teachers College.

Main Language(s) of Instruction: Chinese

Degrees and Diplomas: *Xueshi Xuewei*; *Shuoshi Xuewei*

Academic Staff *2011-2012*: Total: c. 600

Student Numbers *2011-2012*: Total: c. 7,000

Last Updated: 31/01/13

YUNNAN INDUSTRY AND COMMERCE COLLEGE

Kunming, Yunnan

Programme
Business and Commerce (Business and Commerce)

Main Language(s) of Instruction: Chinese

Degrees and Diplomas: *Xueshi Xuewei*

Last Updated: 05/11/13

YUNNAN NORMAL UNIVERSITY (YNNU)

121 Street in Kunming 298, Kunming, Yunnan Province 650092
Tel: +86(871) 55162515
Fax: +86(871) 5516804
EMail: admissionynnu@yahoo.com.cn
Website: http://www.ynnu.edu.cn

President: Yang Lin

College
Adult Continuing Education (Adult Education); **Arts** (Archaeology; Art Education; Communication Arts; Dance; Design; Fine Arts; Industrial Design; Music; Music Theory and Composition; Musicology; Painting and Drawing; Textile Design; Visual Arts); **Arts and Sciences** (Arts and Humanities; Natural Sciences); **Chemistry and Chemical Engineering** (Chemical Engineering; Chemistry); **Economics and Management** (Economics; Management); **Physics and Electronic Information** (Applied Physics; Astronomy and Space Science; Astrophysics; Electronic Engineering; Information Sciences; Information Technology; Optical Technology; Physics; Radiophysics; Science Education; Teacher Training); **Tourism and Geographical Sciences** (Economics; Geography; Geography (Human); Information Technology; Surveying and Mapping; Tourism); **Vocational and Technical Education** (Applied Chemistry; Art Education; Mathematics Education; Organic Chemistry; Preschool Education; Primary Education; Service Trades; Tourism)

School
Life Sciences (Biological and Life Sciences); **Business** (Business Administration); **Chinese Language and Literature** (Aesthetics; Applied Linguistics; Chinese; Comparative Literature; Curriculum; Linguistics; Literature; Native Language Education; Pedagogy; Philology; Secretarial Studies; Teacher Training); **Education Science and Management** (Curriculum; Education; Educational Administration; Educational Psychology; Educational Sciences; Pedagogy; Preschool Education; Public Administration); **Foreign Languages** (Applied Linguistics; English; Japanese; Linguistics; Literature; Modern Languages; Translation and Interpretation); **History and Administration** (Administration; History); **Information** (Information Sciences); **Mathematics** (Mathematics); **Philosophy and Law** (Law; Philosophy; Political Sciences)

Department
Marxism-Leninism Teaching *(Social Development College)* (History; Journalism; Philosophy; Political Sciences; Sociology)

Institute
Energy and Environmental Sciences *(Solar Energy Research Institute)* (Agricultural Engineering; Biotechnology; Building Technologies; Energy Engineering; Environmental Engineering; Environmental Studies); **Media** (Media Studies); **Physical Education/ Golf Academy** (Physical Education; Sports)

Academy
Chinese/International College for Chinese Language *(Yunnan)*

Further Information: Also courses for foreign students. Study Abroad programmes; Over 40 research institutions

History: Founded 1938 as Teachers' College of the State Southwest Associated University through the merger of Peking University, Tsinghua University and Nankai University. Renamed National Kunming Normal College 1946. Acquired present status and title 1984. Merged with Yunnan Education College and Yunnan Sports College. Under the jurisdiction of the Yunnan Provincial Government.

Academic Year: September to July (September-January; March-July)

Admission Requirements: Graduation from senior middle school and entrance examination

Fees: (Yuan): 2,000-3,000 per annum

Main Language(s) of Instruction: Chinese, English

Degrees and Diplomas: *Xueshi Xuewei*; *Shuoshi Xuewei*; *Boshi*. Also MBA; post-doctoral programme

Publications: The Journal of Yunnan Normal University (natural sciences); The Journal of Yunnan Normal University (social sciences); The Journal of Yunnan Normal University (Teaching and Research on Chinese as a Foreign Language)

Academic Staff *2011-2012*: Total: c. 1,600

Student Numbers *2011-2012*: Total: c. 28,000

Last Updated: 31/01/13

YUNNAN POLICE OFFICER ACADEMY

Kunming, Yunnan

President: Guo Baoyun

Department
Anti-drug (Law; Social Work); **Computer Science and Technology** (Computer Science; Information Management; Information Technology); **Criminal Investigation** (Criminal Law; Criminology; Law; Police Studies); **Law** (Administrative Law; Civil Law; Commercial Law; Criminal Law; International Law; Law; Private Law); **Marxism-Leninism** (Political Sciences); **Physical Education** (Physical Education); **Security Management** (Criminal Law; Management; Protective Services; Public Administration; Transport Engineering)

Institute
Information Security (Computer Engineering; Computer Networks; Criminology; Technology)

History: Founded 1950. Acquired present status and title 2003.

Main Language(s) of Instruction: Chinese

Degrees and Diplomas: *Xueshi Xuewei*; *Shuoshi Xuewei*: **Police Studies.** The Master's Degree in Police Studies in a pilot phase, to be launched 2014.

Publications: Yunnan Police College; Yunnan Yunnan Police Officer Academy Police College News

Academic Staff *2012-2013*: Total 303

Student Numbers *2012-2013*: Total: c. 4,000

Last Updated: 08/10/13

YUNNAN UNIVERSITY (YUN)

Kunming Green Lake Road No. 2,
Kunming, Yunnan Province 650091
Tel: +86(871) 5034248
Fax: +86(871) 5183424
EMail: cisynu@ynu.edu.cn
Website: http://www.ynu.edu.cn

President: He Tianchun (2007-)

College

Agronomy (Agronomy); **Business Administration and Tourism Management** (Business Administration; Management; Public Relations; Tourism); **Humanities and Social Sciences** (Archaeology; Arts and Humanities; Demography and Population; Ethnology; History; Literature; Museum Studies; Philosophy; Sociology); **International Studies** (International Studies); **Urban Construction and Management** (Construction Engineering; Town Planning)

School

Art and Design (Design; Fine Arts); **Chemical Science and Engineering** (Chemical Engineering; Chemistry; Organic Chemistry); **Economics** (Economics); **Information Science and Technology** (Information Sciences; Information Technology); **Law** (Law); **Life Sciences** (Biological and Life Sciences; Biology; Botany; Zoology); **Mathematics and Statistics** (Applied Mathematics; Mathematics; Statistics); **Physical Science and Technology** (Physical Engineering; Physics); **Public Administration** (Public Administration); **Resources, Environmental and Earth Sciences** (Biochemistry; Biophysics; Botany; Cell Biology; Earth Sciences; Ecology; Environmental Studies; Genetics; Meteorology; Microbiology; Molecular Biology; Natural Resources; Physiology); **Software Engineering** (Software Engineering); **Vocational and Continuing Education** (Technology)

Institute

Foreign Languages (Modern Languages); **Marxism** (Philosophy; Political Sciences); **Physical Education** (Education; Physical Education)

Further Information: 11 post-doctoral research stations; 8 Research Institutes.

History: Founded 1922. Renamed Yunnan Provincial University 1938 and Yunnan National University 1938. Acquired present title 1950.

Main Language(s) of Instruction: Chinese

Degrees and Diplomas: *Xueshi Xuewei*; *Shuoshi Xuewei*; *Boshi*. Also MBA and Executive MBA

Student Services: Canteen, Health Services, Sports Facilities

Publications: Journal of Yunnan University; Yunnan Higher Education; Yunnan Jurisprudence

Publishing House: Yunnan University Press

Academic Staff *2011-2012*: Total 1,669

Student Numbers *2011-2012*: Total 29,067

Last Updated: 01/02/13

YUNNAN UNIVERSITY OF FINANCE AND ECONOMICS (YUFE)

Longquan Road, Kunming, Yunnan Province 650221
Tel: +86(871) 5151723
Fax: +86(871) 5163384
EMail: YUFE@public.km.yn.cn
Website: http://www.ynufe.edu.cn/english/english.asp

President: Wang Rong

International Relations: Ge Changmin

School

Accountancy (Accountancy); **Business** (Business Administration); **Business Administration** (Business Administration); **Finance** (Finance); **Law** (Law); **Public Administration** (Public Administration); **Statistics and Information Sciences** (Information Sciences; Statistics)

Department

Computer Science (Computer Science); **Economics** (Economics; International Economics); **Foreign I** (English; Modern Languages); **Journalism and Communication** (Journalism; Mass Communication); **Tourism Management** (Tourism)

History: Founded 1951 as Yunan Finance, Trade and Management School, acquires present status 1999.

Main Language(s) of Instruction: Chinese

Degrees and Diplomas: *Xueshi Xuewei*; *Shuoshi Xuewei*. Also MBA

Academic Staff *2011-2012*: Total 1,300

STAFF WITH DOCTORATE: Total 70

Student Numbers *2011-2012*: Total: c. 24,000

Last Updated: 01/02/13

YUNNAN UNIVERSITY OF NATIONALITIES (YUN)

134 Yi Er Yi Avenue, Kunming, Yunnan Province 650031
Tel: +86(871) 5137826 +86(871) 5195141
Fax: +86(871) 5154308 +86(871) 5122139
EMail: feiyuan85@126.com; li494849@hotmail.com; tongchai1979@hotmail.com
Website: http://www.ynni.edu.cn/

President: Zhang Yingjie (2009-)

International Relations: Yang Hong

School

Arts (Dance; Design; Fine Arts; Musicology; Performing Arts); **Chemical and Biological Technology** (Analytical Chemistry; Applied Chemistry; Bioengineering; Chemical Engineering; Chemistry; Environmental Studies; Organic Chemistry); **Economics** (Economics; International Business; International Economics; Statistics); **Education** (Education; Educational Psychology; Educational Technology); **Ethnic Languages and Cultures** (Anthropology; Cultural Studies; Literature; Native Language; Printing and Printmaking; Publishing and Book Trade); **Foreign Languages** (Applied Linguistics; English; Japanese; Linguistics; Modern Languages); **Humanities** (Advertising and Publicity; Archaeology; Arts and Humanities; Chinese; Ethnology; Foreign Languages Education; History; Journalism; Literature; Museum Studies; Radio and Television Broadcasting; Religious Studies; Social Work; Sociology); **Law** (Civil Law; Commercial Law; International Relations; Law; Political Sciences; Public Administration); **Management** (Accountancy; Administration; Business Administration; Finance; Human Resources; Management; Public Administration; Tourism); **Mathematics and Computer Science** (Applied Mathematics; Computer Science; Information Sciences; Information Technology; Mathematics; Mathematics and Computer Science); **People's Forces** (Military Science); **Philosophy** (Philosophy); **Physical Education** (Physical Education; Sports); **Physics and Electronic/Electrical Information Engineering** (Automation and Control Engineering; Computer Networks; Electrical and Electronic Engineering; Electrical Engineering; Electronic Engineering; Information Technology; Physics; Telecommunications Engineering); **Pre-University Education**; **Southeast and South Asian Languages and Cultures** (South and Southeast Asian Languages; South Asian Studies; Southeast Asian Studies; Thai Languages; Vietnamese); **Vocational and Technical Education** (Accountancy; Business Computing; Business Education; Computer Engineering; Computer Graphics; Computer Networks; Cooking and Catering; Dance; Design; Display and Stage Design; English; Finance; Graphic Design; Information Management; Information Sciences; Interior Design; Marketing; Nutrition; Secretarial Studies; Software Engineering; Tourism)

Further Information: Also Yu Hua Campus.

History: Founded 1951.

Fees: (Yuan): Bachelor's degree, 14,000-20,000 per annum; Master's degree, 16,000-22,000 per annum

Main Language(s) of Instruction: Chinese

Degrees and Diplomas: *Xueshi Xuewei*; *Shuoshi Xuewei*; *Boshi*

Publications: Journal of Yunnan Nationalities University (natural sciences edition); Journal of Yunnan Nationalities University (philosophical and social sciences edition); The Ethnic Studies

Academic Staff *2011-2012*	**TOTAL**
FULL-TIME	c. **1,300**
Student Numbers *2011-2012*	
All (Foreign included)	c. **22,000**
FOREIGN ONLY	**500**

Part-time students, 12,000.

Last Updated: 31/01/13

YUNNAN UNIVERSITY OF TRADITIONAL CHINESE MEDICINE (YUTCM)

201 Shuangqiao Road, Guanshang District,
Kunming, Yunnan Province 650500
Tel: +86(871) 7150983
Fax: +86(871) 7150983
EMail: ynxcb@ynutcm.edu.cn; yutcmwu@sina.com; zsqamethyst@163.com
Website: http://www.ynutcm.edu.cn

President: Qingsheng Li (1999-)

International Relations: Ming Li EMail: kmlmlm@sina.com

College

Basic Medical Studies (Medicine); **Nursing** (Nursing); **Pharmacy** (Pharmacy); **Traditional Chinese Medicine** (Traditional Eastern Medicine)

School

Chinese Medicine *(National)* (Medicine; Traditional Eastern Medicine); **Clinical Medicine** (Medicine); **Continuing Education, Vocational and Technical Education**; **Humanities and Management** (Arts and Humanities; Management)

Department

Ideological and Political Teaching and Research (Political Sciences); **International Cooperation and Exchange** *(Hong Kong, Macao and Taiwan Office, the Institute of International Education)*; **Sports** (Sports)

Institute

Acupuncture and Massage Rehabilitation (Acupuncture; Physical Therapy; Rehabilitation and Therapy)

Centre

Modern Educational Technology *(Institute of Information Technology)* (Educational Technology; Information Technology)

Further Information: 2 campuses: Bai Ta and Guan Shang. Also hospital (6,000 beds; 66 teaching and training stations for medicinal units)

History: Founded 1960 as Yunnan College of Traditional Chinese Medicine.

Admission Requirements: Graduation from senior middle school. Knowledge of Chinese compulsory

Fees: (Yuan): Bachelor's Degree, 20,000; Master's Degree, 30,000

Main Language(s) of Instruction: Chinese

Accrediting Agency: Ministry of Education; Yunnan Provincial Education Bureau

Degrees and Diplomas: *Xueshi Xuewei*; *Shuoshi Xuewei*; *Boshi*. Also Certificate (short time training); The 2 doctor's degree programmes are jointly offered with Guangzhou University of Traditional Chinese Medicine.

Student Services: Cultural Activities, Social Counselling

Academic Staff *2011-2012*	**TOTAL**
FULL-TIME	c. **150**
Student Numbers *2011-2012*	
All (Foreign included)	c. **8,000**
FOREIGN ONLY	**200**

Last Updated: 01/02/13

YUXI NORMAL UNIVERSITY (XYNU)

134 Fenhuang Rd., Yuxi, Yunnan 653100
Tel: +86(877) 205-7488
Fax: +86(877) 205-3625
EMail: faffairs@yxtc.net
Website: http://www.yxnu.net/

President: Wang Libin

College

Adult Education (Adult Education); **Arts** (Dance; Fine Arts; Music); **Chinese Literacy** (Chinese; Foreign Languages Education; Literature); **Commerce** (Business Administration; Management; Marketing; Tourism); **Education** (Education; Preschool Education; Primary Education); **Foreign Language** (English; Modern Languages; Thai Languages); **Information and Technology** (Computer Science; Information Management; Information Sciences; Information Technology); **Law** (Law); **Physical Education** (Physical Education); **Resources and Environment** (Agriculture; Biology; Chemistry; Environmental Studies; Geography; Natural Resources; Science Education; Soil Management; Town Planning); **Science** (Mathematics; Physics)

History: Founded 2000.

Fees: (Yuan): Application fee, 500; Tuition fee, 14,000 per annum

Main Language(s) of Instruction: Chinese

Degrees and Diplomas: *Xueshi Xuewei*

Academic Staff *2012-2013*	**TOTAL**
FULL-TIME	**563**
PART-TIME	**34**
Student Numbers *2012-2013*	
All (Foreign included)	c. **11,000**

Last Updated: 09/10/13

ZAOZHUANG UNIVERSITY (UZZ)

Zaozhuang, Shandong 277160
Website: http://www.uzz.edu.cn/

President: Caosheng Jiang (2013-)

College

Art and Design (Design; Fine Arts); **Chemical Engineering and Materials Science** (Applied Chemistry; Chemical Engineering; Chemistry; Industrial Chemistry; Materials Engineering); **Economics and Management** (Economics; Management); **Foreign Languages** (English; Japanese; Modern Languages); **Information Science and Engineering** (Computer Engineering; Computer Networks; Computer Science; Information Sciences; Information Technology; Software Engineering); **Liberal Arts** (Arts and Humanities; Chinese; Foreign Languages Education); **Life Sciences** (Biological and Life Sciences; Biotechnology; Food Science; Pharmacology); **Mathematics and Statistics** (Applied Mathematics; Mathematics; Mathematics Education; Statistics); **Mechanical and Electrical Engineering** (Automation and Control Engineering; Electrical Engineering; Industrial Engineering; Mechanical Engineering); **Optoelectronic Engineering** (Electronic Engineering; Information Sciences; Information Technology; Optical Technology; Physics); **Physical Education** (Dance; Physical Education; Sports); **Political and Social Development** (Political Sciences; Social Sciences); **Psychology and Education Sciences** (Education; Psychology); **Tourism and Environmental Sciences** (Civil Engineering; Environmental Studies; Geography; Surveying and Mapping; Tourism)

Department

English Teaching (English); **Ideological and Political Theory Course** (History; Political Sciences; Social Sciences)

Institute

Media (Film; Media Studies; Photography; Radio and Television Broadcasting; Video; Visual Arts)

Academy

Music and Dance (Dance; Music; Musical Instruments)

History: Founded 1984 as Zaozhuang Teachers College. Merged with Radio and Television University in Zaozhuang 1999. Acquired present status 2004.

Main Language(s) of Instruction: Chinese

Degrees and Diplomas: *Xueshi Xuewei*

Academic Staff *2012-2013*	**TOTAL**
FULL-TIME	**645**
PART-TIME	**25**
Student Numbers *2012-2013*	
All (Foreign included)	**13,352**

Last Updated: 06/11/13

ZHANGZHOU NORMAL UNIVERSITY (FJZS)

Xianzhi Street, Xiangcheng District,
Zhangzhou, Fujian Province 363000
Tel: +86(596) 2023850
Fax: +86(596) 2026037
EMail: zzsyxz@fjzs.edu.cn
Website: http://www.fjzs.edu.cn

President: Fu-Xing Wang

Faculty

Political Science and Law (Law; Political Sciences)

College

Marxism (Political Sciences); **Overseas Education**

Department

Adult Education (Adult Education); **Biological Science and Technology** (Biological and Life Sciences; Technology); **Chemistry and Environmental Sciences** (Chemistry; Environmental Studies); **Chinese** (Chinese); **Computer Science and Engineering** (Computer Engineering; Computer Science); **Economics** (Economics); **Education Science and Technology** (Educational Sciences; Educational Technology); **Fine Arts** (Fine Arts); **Foreign Languages** (English; Modern Languages); **History and Sociology** (History; Sociology); **Journalism and Communication** (Journalism; Mass Communication); **Management Science** (Management); **Mathematics and Information Science** (Information Sciences; Mathematics); **Physical Education** (Physical Education; Sports); **Physics and Electronic Information Engineering** (Electronic Engineering; Information Technology; Physics); **Teacher Education** (Teacher Training)

Research Institute

Minnan Culture (Cultural Studies)

History: Founded 1963 as Fujian Second Teachers College, acquired present name 1986.

Main Language(s) of Instruction: Chinese

Degrees and Diplomas: *Xueshi Xuewei*; *Shuoshi Xuewei*; *Boshi*

Academic Staff *2011-2012*: Total 1,248
STAFF WITH DOCTORATE: Total 309
Student Numbers *2011-2012*: Total: c. 18,000
Last Updated: 01/02/13

ZHANJIANG NORMAL UNIVERSITY (ZHJNC)

29 Cunjin Road, Chikan, Zhanjiang, Guangdong Province 524048
Tel: +86(759) 3183075
Fax: +86(759) 3341440
EMail: waishi@zhjinc.edu.cn
Website: http://www.zhjnc.edu.cn

President: Luo Haiou

International Relations: Lee Ming

School

Arts (Design; Fine Arts; Music; Performing Arts; Visual Arts); **Business** (Accountancy; Business Administration; Business Education; E-Business/Commerce; Finance; Information Management; Information Sciences; International Business; International Economics); **Education Science** (Education; Educational Psychology; Mathematics Education; Native Language Education; Primary Education); **Foreign Language** (English; Modern Languages); **Humanities** (Arts and Humanities; Chinese; Journalism; Literature); **Information and Technology Science** (Computer Education; Computer Engineering; Computer Networks; Computer Science; Educational Technology; Industrial Design; Information Sciences; Information Technology; Physics; Science Education; Software Engineering); **Law and Political Sciences** (Administration; History; Law; Political Sciences; Public Administration); **Life Science and Chemistry Science** (Biological and Life Sciences; Biology; Biotechnology; Chemistry; Cooking and Catering; Food Science; Natural Sciences; Science Education); **Mathematics and Computer Science** (Computer Science; Information Sciences; Mathematics and Computer Science); **Physical Traning Science** (Physical Education; Sociology; Sports)

History: Founded as Leiyang College 1636. Renamed Leizhou Teachers School 1978. Acquired present title 1991.

Main Language(s) of Instruction: Chinese

Degrees and Diplomas: *Xueshi Xuewei*

Academic Staff *2012-2013*: Total 927
Student Numbers *2012-2013*: Total 26,534
Last Updated: 04/02/13

ZHAOQING UNIVERSITY (ZQU)

Donggang, Zhaoqing, Guangdong Province 526061
Tel: +86(758) 2716233 +86(758) 2752985
Fax: +86(758) 2716586 +86(758) 2716969
EMail: zqxyzsb@zqu.edu.cn; faozqu@yahoo.cn; zquwsc@yahoo.com.cn
Website: http://www.zqu.edu.cn

President: He Fei

International Relations: Xu Zhen Hui

Faculty

Chemistry and Chemical Engineering (Chemical Engineering; Chemistry; Food Science; Food Technology); **Chinese** (Chinese; Foreign Languages Education; Linguistics; Literature; Radio and Television Broadcasting); **Computer Science and Software** (Computer Networks; Computer Science; Information Technology; Software Engineering); **Economics and Management** (Accountancy; Economics; Human Resources; International Business; International Economics; Management; Marketing); **Education** (Education; Educational Psychology; Educational Sciences; Educational Technology; Preschool Education; Primary Education); **Electronics and Information Engineering** (Automation and Control Engineering; Electronic Engineering; Information Sciences; Information Technology; Mechanical Engineering; Physics; Science Education); **Fine Arts** (Design; Fine Arts; Industrial Design; Visual Arts); **Foreign Languages** (English; Japanese; Modern Languages); **Life Sciences** (Biological and Life Sciences; Landscape Architecture); **Mathematics and Information Science** (Applied Mathematics; Computer Engineering; Computer Science; Information Technology; Mathematics); **Music** (Art Education; Music; Performing Arts); **Physical Education and Health** (Physical Education; Sports); **Political Science and Law** (Administration; Law; Political Sciences); **Tourism** (History; Tourism)

Department

Ideological and Political Theory (Political Sciences)

History: Founded 1970 as Zhaoqing Teachers College, acquired present status and title 1999 through amalgamation.

Academic Year: September to July

Fees: (Yuan): 15,000 per annum

Main Language(s) of Instruction: Chinese

Degrees and Diplomas: *Xueshi Xuewei*

Student Services: Academic Counselling, Canteen, Sports Facilities

Academic Staff *2011-2012*: Total 881
Student Numbers *2011-2012*: Total 21,764
Last Updated: 04/02/13

ZHEJIANG A & F UNIVERSITY (ZAFU)

Lin'an, Zhejiang Province 311300
Tel: +86(571) 63740030
Fax: +86(571) 63740030
EMail: international@zjfc.edu.cn
Website: http://www.zjfc.edu.cn/

President: Zhou Guo
Tel: +86(571) 63732700 +86(571) 63732699

Division

Physical Education and Military Training (Military Science; Physical Education; Sports)

College

Continuing Education; **International** (Chinese; English); **Jixian**

School

Agriculture and Food Science (Agriculture; Food Science); **Art Design** (Design; Fine Arts); **Economics and Management** (Economics; Management); **Engineering** (Engineering); **Environment and Resources** (Environmental Studies; Natural Resources); **Foreign Languages** (English; Japanese; Modern Languages); **Forestry and Biotechnology** (Biotechnology; Forestry); **Humanities and Tea Culture** (Arts and Humanities; Horticulture); **Information Engineering** (Information Technology); **Landscape Architecture** (Landscape Architecture); **Law and Politics** (Law; Political Sciences); **Marxism** (Political Sciences); **Sciences** (Applied Mathematics; Chemistry; Natural Sciences; Physics; Statistics); **Tourism and Health** (Health Sciences; Tourism)

Further Information: East Lake and Yijin campuses

History: Founded 1958 as Zhejiang Tianmu Forestry College, acquired present status and name 1996. Formely known as Zhejiang Forestry University.

Main Language(s) of Instruction: Chinese

Degrees and Diplomas: *Xueshi Xuewei*; *Shuoshi Xuewei*

Publications: Journal of Zhejiang A & F University

Academic Staff *2011-2012*	**TOTAL**
FULL-TIME	c. **1,000**
Student Numbers *2011-2012*	
All (Foreign included)	c. **24,000**
FOREIGN ONLY	**3500**

Last Updated: 04/02/13

ZHEJIANG CHINESE MEDICAL UNIVERSITY (ZCMU)

548 Bin Wen Road, Bin Jiang District,
Hangzhou, Zhejiang Province 310053
Tel: +86(571) 86633077 +86(571) 86633177
Fax: +86(571) 86613500
EMail: zjtcmfao@mail.hz.zj.cn
Website: http://www.zjtcm.net

President: Xiao Luwei

International Relations: Chai Kefu

College

Audiology and Speech Science (Speech Therapy and Audiology); **Basic Medical Science** (Medicine); **Binjiang**; **Biological Engineering** (Bioengineering; Food Science; Food Technology); **Clinical Medical Studies** *(III)*; **Clinical Medical Studies** *(I)* (Acupuncture; Alternative Medicine; Medicine; Nursing; Orthopaedics; Paediatrics; Pharmacology; Rehabilitation and Therapy; Stomatology; Surgery; Traditional Eastern Medicine); **Clinical Medical Studies** *(II)* (Medicine); **Continous Education**; **Foreign Languages** (English; Literature; Modern Languages); **Information Technology** (Computer Engineering; Computer Science; Information Technology); **International Education** (English; Medicine); **Life Science** (Biological and Life Sciences); **Management** (Health Administration; Management; Marketing; Public Administration); **Nursing** (Nursing); **Pharmacological** (Pharmacology)

Department

Social Sciences (Social Sciences); **Sports** (Sports)

Further Information: 3 directly affiliated hospitals and 13 indirectly affiliated hospitals; 2 post-doctor stations, 5 doctor stations, 23 post-graduate stations

History: Founded 1953 as Zhejiang Training School of Traditional Chinese Medicine. Relocated to current site 2000. Acquired present status and title 2006.

Main Language(s) of Instruction: Chinese

Degrees and Diplomas: *Xueshi Xuewei*; *Shuoshi Xuewei*; *Boshi*

Publications: Journal of Zhejiang University of TCM

Academic Staff *2011-2012*	**TOTAL**
FULL-TIME	c. **3,600**
Student Numbers *2011-2012*	
All (Foreign included)	c. **10,300**
FOREIGN ONLY	**400**

Last Updated: 04/02/13

ZHEJIANG GONGSHANG UNIVERSITY (ZJSU)

No.18, Xuezheng Str., Xiasha University Town,
Hangzhou, Zhejiang Province 310018
Tel: +86(571) 28877315 +86(571) 28877318
Fax: +86(571) 88846798
EMail: international@mail.zjgsu.edu.cn
Website: http://www.hzic.edu.cn

President: Zhang Renshou

College

Commerce *(Hangzhou - HCC)* (Accountancy; Administration; Advertising and Publicity; Business Administration; Business and Commerce; Computer Science; Design; Economics; Electronic Engineering; Engineering Management; English; Environmental Management; Finance; Human Resources; Information Management; Information Technology; International Business; International Economics; Japanese; Law; Marketing; Public Administration; Publishing and Book Trade; Rural Planning; Soil Management; Statistics; Telecommunications Engineering; Tourism; Town Planning; Transport Management); **Further Education** *(CFE)* (Accountancy; Administration; Business Administration; E-Business/Commerce; English; English Studies; International Business; Marketing; Transport Management); **Zhang Naiqi Honors** *(ZHC)* (Business Administration; Economics)

School

Accounting *(SA)* (Accountancy; Finance); **Art and Design** *(SAD)* (Design; Fine Arts; Visual Arts); **Business Administration** *(SBA)* (Business Administration; Economics; Human Resources; Management; Marketing); **Computer Science and Information Engineering** *(SCIE)* (Computer Engineering; Computer Science; Electronic Engineering; Information Management; Information Sciences; Information Technology; Management; Software Engineering; Transport Engineering); **Economics** *(SE)* (Economics; Finance; International Business; International Economics; Social Welfare); **Environmental Science and Engineering** (Environmental Engineering; Environmental Studies; Water Management); **Finance** (Finance; Insurance); **Food Science and Biotechnology** *(SFSB)* (Agriculture; Aquaculture; Biotechnology; Chemistry; Crop Production; Engineering; Food Science; Food Technology; Safety Engineering); **Foreign Languages** *(SFL)* (Applied Linguistics; English; French; Linguistics; Literature; Modern Languages); **Humanities** *(SH)* (Advertising and Publicity; Arts and Humanities; Chinese; History; Journalism; Literature; Philosophy; Publishing and Book Trade); **Information and Electronic Engineering** *(SIEE)* (Computer Networks; Electronic Engineering; Information Sciences; Measurement and Precision Engineering; Telecommunications Engineering); **Japanese Language and Culture** *(SJLC)* (African Studies; Asian Religious Studies; Japanese; Literature); **Law** *(SL)* (Administrative Law; Civil Law; Constitutional Law; Criminal Law; International Law; Law); **Marxism Studies** *(SMS)* (Political Sciences); **Public Administration** *(SPA)* (Administration; Public Administration; Social Work); **Statistics and Mathematics** *(SSM)* (Applied Mathematics; Economics; Information Sciences; Information Technology; Mathematics; Mathematics and Computer Science; Statistics); **Tourism and City Administration** *(STCA)* (Environmental Management; History; Rural Planning; Tourism; Town Planning)

History: Founded 1911 as Hangzhou Business School. Renamed Hangzhou Institute of Commerce 1980. Acquired present title 2004. Under the jurisdiction of the Zhejiang Provincial Government.

Academic Year: September to June (September-January; February-June)

Admission Requirements: Graduation from senior middle school and entrance examination

Fees: (Yuan): 5,000-16,000 per annum

Main Language(s) of Instruction: Chinese, English

Accrediting Agency: Ministry of Education

Degrees and Diplomas: *Xueshi Xuewei*; *Shuoshi Xuewei*; *Boshi*. Also Post-doctoral Station

Student Services: Academic Counselling, Canteen, Careers Guidance, Cultural Activities, Facilities for disabled people, Foreign Studies Centre, Health Services, Language Laboratory, Nursery Care, Social Counselling, Sports Facilities

Publications: Business Economics and Administration; Journal of Zhejiang Gongshang University

Academic Staff *2011-2012*	**TOTAL**
FULL-TIME	**1,472**
Student Numbers *2011-2012*	
All (Foreign included)	**33,400**
FOREIGN ONLY	**400**

Last Updated: 04/02/13

ZHEJIANG INTERNATIONAL STUDIES UNIVERSITY (ZISU)

No 140, Wensan Road, Hangzhou, Zhejiang 310012
Tel: +86(571) 88833520
Website: http://www.zisu.edu.cn/

School

Adult Education and Lifelong Learning; **Applied Foreign Languages** (Applied Linguistics; Modern Languages); **Arts** (Arts and Humanities); **Chinese Language and Culture** (Chinese; Cultural Studies); **Educational Science** (Education); **English Language and Culture** (English; English Studies); **European and Asian Languages and Culture** (Asian Studies; European Languages; European Studies; South and Southeast Asian Languages); **International Business Administration** (Business Administration; International Business); **International Education** (International Studies); **Science and Technology** (Natural Sciences; Technology)

Department

Physical Education (Physical Education); **Social Sciences** (Social Sciences)

History: Founded 1955 as Zhejiang Education Institute. Acquired present status 1994 and present title 2010.

Main Language(s) of Instruction: Chinese

Degrees and Diplomas: *Xueshi Xuewei*

Publications: Children's World; Journal of ZISU; Teaching Monthly; Writing in a New Perspective

Academic Staff *2012-2013*: Total 333
Student Numbers *2012-2013*: Total 5,100
Last Updated: 06/11/13

ZHEJIANG NORMAL UNIVERSITY (ZNU)

688 Yingbin Road, Jinhua, Zhejiang Province 321004
Tel: +86(579) 82282380 +86(579) 82283146
Fax: +86(579) 82280337 +86(579) 82298797
EMail: wsc@zjnu.cn; lxs@zjnu.cn
Website: http://www.zjnu.edu.cn

President: Wu Fengmin Tel: +86(579) 2282358

Secretary-General: Lu Li
Tel: +86(579) 2283887 EMail: lilu@mail.zjnu.net.cn

International Relations: Jianxin Gu Tel: +86(579) 2282125

College

Chemistry and Life Sciences (Analytical Chemistry; Applied Chemistry; Biological and Life Sciences; Biology; Biotechnology; Botany; Chemistry; Ecology; Geography; Organic Chemistry; Physical Chemistry; Science Education; Zoology); **Chuyang Honors** (Arts and Humanities; English; Natural Sciences); **Communication and Creative Culture** (Administration; Advertising and Publicity; Arts and Humanities; Cinema and Television; Communication Studies; Cultural Studies; Film; Folklore; Heritage Preservation; Information Management; Information Technology; Media Studies; Theatre); **Economics and Management** (Accountancy; Business Administration; E-Business/Commerce; Economics; Finance; International Business; International Economics; Management; Marketing); **Engineering** (Automation and Control Engineering; Electronic Engineering; Engineering; Engineering Management; Mechanical Engineering; Production Engineering; Transport Engineering); **Fine Arts** (Art Education; Design; Fine Arts); **Foreign Languages** (Applied Linguistics; English; Japanese; Linguistics; Modern Languages; Translation and Interpretation); **Geography and Environmental Sciences** (Environmental Studies; Geography; Town Planning); **Humanities** (Applied Linguistics; Arts and Humanities; Chinese; History; Humanities and Social Science Education; Linguistics; Literature; Philology); **International Culture and Education** (Applied Linguistics; Chinese; Linguistics); **Law and Political Science** (Administration; Law; Political Sciences; Social Work); **Mathematics Physics and Information Technology** (Applied Mathematics; Computer Networks; Computer Science; Electronic Engineering; Information Sciences; Information Technology; Mathematics; Optical Technology; Optics; Software Engineering; Telecommunications Engineering); **Music** (Aesthetics; Music; Music Education; Music Theory and Composition; Musical Instruments; Musicology; Performing Arts); **Physical Education and Health Sciences** (Health Sciences; Physical Education; Sports); **Preschool Teacher Education** (Art Education; Preschool Education; Visual Arts); **Teacher Education** (Curriculum; Education; Educational Administration; Educational Technology; Health Education; Pedagogy; Primary Education; Psychology; Public Administration; Science Education); **Vocational and Technical Education** (Accountancy; Automation and Control Engineering; Automotive Engineering; Business Education; Electronic Engineering; Finance; Maintenance Technology; Mechanical Engineering; Service Trades; Tourism); **Xingzhi** (Administration; Applied Chemistry; Economics; Engineering; Law; Literature; Natural Sciences; Pedagogy)

Department

Postgraduate Teaching and Student Affairs

History: Founded 1956 as Hangzhou Junior Teacher's College. Evolved into Hangzhou Teacher's College 1958. Zhejiang Teacher's College formed 1965 through the merger of Zhejiang Education College and Zhejiang Physical Education College, that was then moved to Jinhua. Acquired university status and present title Zhejiang Normal University 1985. Merged with Zhejiang Financial School, Zhejiang School of Preschool-Teacher Education and Jinhua Railway Engineering School respectively in 2000, 2001, and 2004.

Academic Year: September to June (September-January; February-June)

Admission Requirements: Graduation from senior middle school and entrance examination

Fees: (Yuan): 14,600-22,000 per annum

Main Language(s) of Instruction: Chinese, English

Accrediting Agency: Provincial Educational Committee

Degrees and Diplomas: *Xueshi Xuewei*; *Shuoshi Xuewei*. Also MBA; Part-Time Vocational Education programmes.

Student Services: Academic Counselling, Canteen, Careers Guidance, Health Services, Language Laboratory, Nursery Care, Social Counselling, Sports Facilities

Publications: Adult Higher Education; College Teacher Education; Education of Higher Pedagogical Colleges; Higher Pedagogical Education by Correspondence; Teaching and Research of Secondary School Education; ZNU Journal

Academic Staff *2011-2012*: Total: c. 1,460
Student Numbers *2011-2012*: Total: c. 30,000
Last Updated: 05/02/13

ZHEJIANG OCEAN UNIVERSITY (ZJOU)

105 Wenhua Road, Dinghai District,
Zhoushan, Zhejiang Province 316004
Tel: +86(580) 2550008 +86(580) 2550009
Fax: +86(580) 2551319
EMail: xxbgs@zjou.edu.cn; zjhyxy@zjou.edu.cn
Website: http://61.153.216.111/zjouenglish

President: Changwen Wu
Tel: +86 (580) 255 0004 EMail: mzq@zjou.net.cn

Secretary-General: Dajun Zhou Tel: +86 (580) 818 1000

International Relations: Huaqing Lu, Director, International Office Tel: +86 (580) 255 0088 EMail: luwashington@126.com

School
Business Administration (Business Administration; Marketing; Tourism); **Continuing Education**; **Electrical and Mechanical Engineering** (Electrical Engineering; Mechanical Engineering); **Food and Pharmacy and Medical Studies** (Food Science; Medicine; Nursing; Pharmacy); **Foreign Languages** (English; Modern Languages); **Humanities** (Arts and Humanities); **Marine Fisheries and Maritime Studies** (Aquaculture; Fishery; Marine Science and Oceanography); **Marine Science** (Biological and Life Sciences; Environmental Studies; Marine Biology; Marine Engineering; Marine Science and Oceanography); **Mathematics, Physics and Information Science** (Applied Mathematics; Computer Science; Educational Technology; Information Sciences; Mathematics; Physics); **Naval Architecture and Civil Engineering** (Building Technologies; Civil Engineering; Energy Engineering; Heating and Refrigeration; Marine Engineering; Naval Architecture; Structural Architecture); **Petroleum and Chemical Engineering** (Chemical Engineering; Petroleum and Gas Engineering); **Public Administration** *(Department of Social Science)* (Public Administration); **Science and Technology** *(Donghai (Private College))* (Natural Sciences; Technology); **Science and Technology** *(Putuo)* (Natural Sciences; Technology); **Science and Technology** *(Xiaoshan)* (Natural Sciences; Technology)

Department
Physical Education and Art Teaching (Art Education; Physical Education)

Centre
Public Experiment and Computer Network (Computer Networks); **Teacher Development** (Teacher Training)

Research Institute
Marine Aquatic Products *(Zhejiang)*

Further Information: Also 24 research institutes and Centres

History: Founded 1998 after merger between Zhejiang Fishery University (founded 1958) and Zhoushan Junior Teachers College (founded 1978)

Academic Year: September to July

Admission Requirements: Senior Higher School Graduation Diploma, National Matriculation Test

Fees: (Yuan): 3,000 - 6,000 per annum

Main Language(s) of Instruction: Chinese, English

Accrediting Agency: Ministry of Education

Degrees and Diplomas: *Xueshi Xuewei*; *Shuoshi Xuewei*. Also Associated Degree Programme of 3 yrs duration

Student Services: Academic Counselling, Canteen, Careers Guidance, Cultural Activities, Foreign Studies Centre, Health Services, Language Laboratory, Nursery Care, Social Counselling, Sports Facilities

Publications: Journal of Zhejiang Ocean University

Student Numbers *2011-2012*: Total: c. 14,800
Last Updated: 05/02/13

ZHEJIANG POLICE COLLEGE (ZJPC)

Binwen Road, Binjiang District, Hangzhou, Zhejiang 310053
Tel: +86(571) 87787007
Fax: +86(571) 86615786
Website: http://www.zjjcxy.cn/zjpc/index.html

Course
Computer Science and Technology (Computer Engineering; Computer Science); **Law Science** (Law); **Traffic Management** (Transport Management)

History: Founded 1985.

Main Language(s) of Instruction: Chinese

Degrees and Diplomas: *Xueshi Xuewei*
Last Updated: 07/11/13

ZHEJIANG SCI-TECH UNIVERSITY (ZSTU)

5 Second Avenue, Xiasha Higher Education Zone, Hangzhou, Zhejiang 310018
Tel: +86(571) 86843114
EMail: zstu@zstu.edu.cn
Website: http://www.zstu.edu.cn/

President: Qiu Songliang

Faculty
Informatics and Electronics (Computer Engineering; Electronic Engineering; Information Technology; Telecommunications Engineering); **Materials and Textiles** (Applied Chemistry; Applied Physics; Materials Engineering; Textile Technology); **Mechanical Engineering and Automation** (Automation and Control Engineering; Automotive Engineering; Electronic Engineering; Measurement and Precision Engineering; Mechanical Engineering)

Division
Computer Technology *(Instructional)* (Computer Engineering)

College
Continuing Education; **Science and Art** (Applied Chemistry; Applied Physics; Arts and Humanities; Chinese; Mathematics; Natural Sciences; Organic Chemistry; Polymer and Plastics Technology; Psychology)

School
Art and Design (Design; Fine Arts; Packaging Technology; Visual Arts); **Civil Engineering and Architecture** (Architecture; Civil Engineering); **Culture Communication** (Communication Studies; Cultural Studies); **Economics and Management** (Accountancy; Advertising and Publicity; Business Administration; E-Business/Commerce; Economics; Human Resources; Industrial and Production Economics; International Economics; Management; Marketing; Social Work); **Fashion Design and Engineering** (Fashion Design; Textile Design; Textile Technology); **Foreign Languages Studies** (English; Literature; Modern Languages); **Law and Politics** (Law; Political Sciences); **Life Science** (Biochemistry; Biological and Life Sciences; Molecular Biology); **Marxism Studies** (Political Sciences); **Qixin**; **Sciences** (Natural Sciences)

Department
Physical Education (Physical Education)

Research Institute
Moral and Politician Education (Education; Political Sciences)

History: Founded as Silkworm School 1897. Acquired present status 1979. Renamed Zhejiang Silk Industrial College 1999. Acquired present title 2004.

Fees: (Yuan): Tuition for undergraduate programmes, 15,000-22,00; For Master's degree programmes, 25,000; For Doctor's degree, 30,000

Main Language(s) of Instruction: Chinese

Degrees and Diplomas: *Xueshi Xuewei*; *Shuoshi Xuewei*: **Applied Chemistry; Applied Physics; Automation and Control Engineering; Automotive Engineering; Biochemistry; Business Administration; Computer Engineering; Design; Education; Electronic Engineering; Fashion Design; Fine Arts; Industrial and Production Economics; Information Technology; International Economics; Management; Materials Engineering; Mathematics; Mechanical Engineering; Molecular Biology; Organic Chemistry; Production Engineering; Psychology; Textile Technology.** *Boshi*: **Mechanical Engineering.**

Student Services: Sports Facilities

Academic Staff *2012-2013*: Total: c. 1,700
Student Numbers *2012-2013*: Total: c. 18,600
Last Updated: 07/11/13

ZHEJIANG SHUREN UNIVERSITY (ZJSRU)

8 Shuren Street, Hangzhou, Zhejiang 310015
Tel: +86(571) 88297011
Website: http://www.zjsru.cn/

President: Xu Xu Qing

College
Arts (Architectural and Environmental Design; Communication Arts; Design; Fine Arts; Industrial Engineering; Visual Arts); **Biology and Environmental Engineering** (Applied Chemistry; Bioengineering; Biological and Life Sciences; Biology; Chemical Engineering; Environmental Engineering; Food Science; Food Technology); **Humanities** (Arts and Humanities; Chinese; Journalism; Literature; Secretarial Studies; Social Work)

School
Continuing Education; **Foreign Languages** (English; German; Japanese; Korean; Modern Languages); **Management** (Accountancy; Business Administration; Business Computing; Finance; Management; Marketing); **Modern Service Industry** (Art Management; E-Business/Commerce; Finance; International Business; International Economics; Tourism; Transport Management); **Urban Construction** (Architecture; Civil Engineering; Landscape Architecture; Town Planning)

Department
Continuing Education

Institute
Information Technology (Computer Engineering; Computer Science; E-Business/Commerce; Electronic Engineering; Information Technology; Media Studies; Telecommunications Engineering)

History: Founded 1984.

Main Language(s) of Instruction: Chinese

Degrees and Diplomas: *Xueshi Xuewei*

Academic Staff *2012-2013*: Total: c. 800

Student Numbers *2012-2013*: Total: c. 16,000

Last Updated: 08/11/13

ZHEJIANG UNIVERSITY (ZJU)

866 Yuhangtang Road, Hangzhou, Zhejiang Province 310058
Tel: +86(571) 88981109
Fax: +86(571) 87951315
EMail: zupo@zju.edu.cn
Website: http://www.zju.edu.cn

President: Zhaohui Wu (2015-) EMail: wscwsc@zju.edu.cn

International Relations: Wang Li, Dean of International College and Deputy Director of International Relation
Tel: +86(571) 87951398
EMail: li_wang@zju.edu.cn; opl_wl@zju.edu.cn

Faculty
Agriculture, Life and Environment (Agriculture; Agronomy; Animal Husbandry; Apiculture; Aquaculture; Bioengineering; Biological and Life Sciences; Biotechnology; Environmental Engineering; Environmental Studies; Food Science; Horticulture; Natural Resources; Nutrition; Plant and Crop Protection; Veterinary Science); **Engineering** (Aeronautical and Aerospace Engineering; Architecture; Bioengineering; Chemical Engineering; Civil Engineering; Electrical Engineering; Electronic Engineering; Energy Engineering; Engineering; Marine Engineering; Marine Science and Oceanography; Materials Engineering; Mechanical Engineering; Natural Resources; Polymer and Plastics Technology; Regional Planning; Town Planning; Water Management); **Humanities** (Arts and Humanities; Chinese; Cinema and Television; Communication Studies; Cultural Studies; English; European Languages; Film; Heritage Preservation; History; International Studies; Journalism; Linguistics; Literature; Media Studies; Museum Studies; Philosophy); **Information Technology** (Automation and Control Engineering; Biomedical Engineering; Computer Engineering; Computer Networks; Computer Science; Electronic Engineering; Engineering; Industrial Design; Information Sciences; Information Technology; Instrument Making; Media Studies; Optical Technology; Software Engineering); **Medicine** (Medicine; Nursing; Pharmacology; Public Health; Stomatology; Traditional Eastern Medicine); **Science** (Behavioural Sciences; Chemistry; Earth Sciences; Mathematics; Physics; Psychology); **Social Sciences** (Accountancy; Agricultural Economics; Agricultural Management; Economics; Education; Engineering Management; Finance; Government; Information Management; Information Sciences; International Economics; Law; Management; Physical Education; Physics; Political Sciences; Public Administration; Social Sciences; Social Welfare; Sociology; Tourism)

School
Graduate Studies (Agricultural Economics; Agricultural Engineering; Agricultural Management; Agriculture; Animal Husbandry; Architecture; Automation and Control Engineering; Biology; Biomedical Engineering; Business Administration; Chemical Engineering; Chemistry; Chinese; Civil Engineering; Computer Science; Crop Production; Economic History; Educational Sciences; Electrical Engineering; Electronic Engineering; Engineering Management; Environmental Engineering; Environmental Studies; Food Science; Food Technology; Forest Economics; Forest Management; Geological Engineering; Geology; History; Horticulture; Hydraulic Engineering; Information Sciences; Information Technology; Instrument Making; Journalism; Law; Literature; Management; Mass Communication; Materials Engineering; Mathematics; Mechanical Engineering; Mechanics; Medicine; Modern Languages; Optical Technology; Pharmacy; Philosophy; Physical Education; Physics; Plant and Crop Protection; Power Engineering; Psychology; Public Health; Social and Community Services; Sports; Stomatology; Telecommunications Engineering; Thermal Engineering; Thermal Physics; Veterinary Science)

Department
Continuing Education

History: Founded 1897 as Qiushi Academy. Established as Third National Sun Yat-sen University 1927. Acquired present status and title 1928. Move to Guizhou during the sino-japanese war. Moved back to 1946. Merged with Hangzhou University, Zhejiang Agricultural University and Zhejang Medical University to form the new Zhejiang University 1998.

Academic Year: September to June (September-January, February-June)

Admission Requirements: Graduation from senior middle school with satisfactory marks in special entrance examination

Fees: (Yuan): Chinese Language and Culture programme, 18,000 per annum; Undergraduate Programmes, 19,800-42,800 per annum; Master's Degree Programmes, 22,800-32,800 per annum; Doctoral Programmes, 29,800-39,800 per annum

Main Language(s) of Instruction: Chinese, English

Accrediting Agency: Ministry of Education

Degrees and Diplomas: *Xueshi Xuewei*; *Shuoshi Xuewei*; *Boshi*. Also MBA, executive MBA and MPA

Student Services: Academic Counselling, Canteen, Careers Guidance, Cultural Activities, Foreign Studies Centre, Health Services, Language Laboratory, Nursery Care, Social Counselling, Sports Facilities

Publications: Applied Psychology; China Higher Medical Education; Engineering Design; Journals of Zhejiang University; Management Engineering; Materials Science and Engineering; Population and Eugenics; Practical Oncology; Spatial Structures

Publishing House: Zhejiang University Press

Academic Staff *2011-2012*	**TOTAL**
FULL-TIME	c. **3,150**

Student Numbers *2011-2012*	
All (Foreign included)	c. **44,000**
FOREIGN ONLY	**2700**

Last Updated: 18/07/13

ZHEJIANG UNIVERSITY OF FINANCE AND ECONOMICS (ZUFE)

269 Wenhua Road, Hangzhou, Zhejiang Province 310018
Tel: +86(571) 86735880
Fax: +86(571) 8851146
EMail: wsb@zufe.edu.cn
Website: http://www.zufe.edu.cn/

President: Wong Chun Ho

International Relations: Jin Minxian

Faculty
Humanities *(School of Marxism)* (Arts and Humanities; Political Sciences)

College

Art (Design; Fine Arts; Graphic Design; Interior Design; Photography); **Business Administration** (Business Administration; Management); **Economics and International Trade** (Economics; International Business; International Economics); **Foreign Languages** (English; Japanese; Literature; Modern Languages); **Public Finance and Public Administration** (Finance; Labour and Industrial Relations; Public Administration; Social Studies; Taxation)

School

Accountancy (Accountancy); **Information Technology** (Computer Science; E-Business/Commerce; Engineering Management; Information Management; Information Technology; Management; Software Engineering); **Law** (Administrative Law; Civil Law; Commercial Law; Constitutional Law; Law); **Mathematics and Statistics** (Applied Mathematics; Mathematics; Statistics)

Department

Adult Education *(Continuing Education)*; **Physical Education and Military Science** (Military Science; Physical Education; Sports)

Institute

Finance (Finance); **Oriental Studies** (Oriental Studies)

History: Founded 1974 as Zhejiang Finance and Banking School. Previously known as Zhejian Institute of Finance and Economics. Acquired present status and name 1987.

Main Language(s) of Instruction: Chinese

Degrees and Diplomas: *Xueshi Xuewei*; *Shuoshi Xuewei*. Also MBA

Academic Staff *2011-2012*: Total 868

STAFF WITH DOCTORATE: Total 11

Student Numbers *2011-2012*: Total: c. 13,500

Last Updated: 05/02/13

ZHEJIANG UNIVERSITY OF MEDIA AND COMMUNICATIONS (ZJCM)

NO.998 Xueyuan Street, Xiasha Higher Education Zone, Hangzhou, Zhejiang 310018
Tel: +86(571) 86832066
Fax: +86(571) 86832084
EMail: wsb@zjicm.edu.cn
Website: http://www.zjicm.edu.cn/

President: Peng Pengshao

College

Film and TV Arts (Cinema and Television; Film; Music; Performing Arts; Photography; Radio and Television Broadcasting)

School

Animation (Media Studies; Visual Arts); **Broadcasting Arts** (Radio and Television Broadcasting); **Cultural Creativity** (Advertising and Publicity; Cinema and Television; Film; Media Studies; Public Relations); **Cultures and Communications** (Chinese; English; French; Radio and Television Broadcasting); **Design** (Cinema and Television; Design; Filipino; Fine Arts; Photography; Theatre); **Electronics and Information Engineering** (Electronic Engineering; Information Technology; Radio and Television Broadcasting); **Journalism and Communications** (Communication Studies; Journalism; Publishing and Book Trade; Radio and Television Broadcasting); **Literature** (Chinese; Cinema and Television; Film; Foreign Languages Education; Literature; Modern Languages; Secretarial Studies); **Management** (Art Management; Business Administration; Economics; Film; Management; Media Studies); **Music** (Dance; Music; Performing Arts); **New Media** (Computer Networks; Electronic Engineering; Information Management; Information Technology; Media Studies; Software Engineering)

History: Founded 1984 as Zhejiang Higher Vocational Training School of Radio and Television. Acquired present status and title 2004.

Fees: (Yuan): Tuition, 15,000-20,000 per annum

Main Language(s) of Instruction: Chinese

Degrees and Diplomas: *Xueshi Xuewei*. A Master's Degree in Journalism and Mass Communication was launched in 2012; No students were graduated yey (2013).

Academic Staff *2012-2013*: Total 1,086

Student Numbers *2012-2013*: Total: c. 10,000

Last Updated: 08/11/13

ZHEJIANG UNIVERSITY OF SCIENCE AND TECHNOLOGY (ZUST)

85 Xueyuan Road, Hangzhou, Zhejiang Province 310023
Tel: +86(571) 5124576
Fax: +86(571) 5121890
EMail: hiat@public.hz.zj.cn
Website: http://www.zust.edu.cn

President: Du Wei EMail: xb@zust.edu.cn

International Relations: Xu Liqin, Director, International Office

School

Humanities (Arts and Humanities; Chinese; Literature); **Automation and Electric Engineering** (Automation and Control Engineering; Electrical Engineering; Measurement and Precision Engineering); **Biological and Chemical Engineering** (Bioengineering; Chemical Engineering; Food Science; Food Technology; Materials Engineering; Pharmacology); **Civil Engineering and Architectures** (Architecture; Civil Engineering; Town Planning; Water Management); **Economics and Management** (Economics; Information Management; Information Sciences; International Business; International Economics; Management; Marketing; Transport Engineering); **Fashion Design** *(School of Arts Design)* (Design; Fashion Design; Industrial Design; Visual Arts); **Foreign Languages** (English; Modern Languages); **Information and Electronic Engineering** (Computer Science; Educational Technology; Electronic Engineering; Information Sciences; Information Technology; Media Studies; Telecommunications Engineering); **Light Industry** (Chemical Engineering; Packaging Technology; Printing and Printmaking); **Mechanical and Automotive Engineering** (Automation and Control Engineering; Automotive Engineering; Materials Engineering; Mechanical Engineering; Production Engineering); **Sciences** (Applied Physics; Computer Science; Information Sciences)

Institute

Chinese-German (German; Germanic Studies; Translation and Interpretation)

History: Founded 1980, acquired present title 1992. Acquired present title 2001, formerly known as Hanghzou Institute of Applied Engineering.

Main Language(s) of Instruction: Chinese, English for some programmes

Degrees and Diplomas: *Xueshi Xuewei*

Academic Staff *2011-2012*	**TOTAL**
FULL-TIME	c. **1,200**
Student Numbers *2011-2012*	
All (Foreign included)	c. **21,000**
FOREIGN ONLY	**600**

Last Updated: 06/02/13

ZHEJIANG UNIVERSITY OF TECHNOLOGY (ZUT)

18, Chao Wang Road, Hangzhou, Zhejiang Province 310014
Tel: +86(571) 88320114
Fax: +86(571) 88320272 +86(571) 88320667
EMail: wb@zjut.edu.cn
Website: http://www.zjut.edu.cn

President: Zhang Libin (2005-) EMail: lbz@zjut.edu.cn

International Relations: Zheng Huajun, Director, International Office
Tel: +86(571) 88320272
EMail: zhenghj@zjut.edu.cn; wb@zjut.edu.cn

College

Adult Education; **Art** (Architectural and Environmental Design; Dance; Design; Fine Arts; Industrial Design; Music; Visual Arts); **Biological and Environmental Engineering** (Biochemistry; Bioengineering; Chemical Engineering; Engineering; Environmental Engineering; Environmental Studies; Food Science; Food Technology; Microbiology; Molecular Biology); **Business and**

Administration (Administration; Business Administration; Business and Commerce; Engineering Management; Finance; Industrial and Production Economics; Industrial Engineering; Information Management; Information Sciences; International Business; International Economics; Management; Marketing; Tourism; Transport Management); **Chemical Engineering and Materials Science** (Analytical Chemistry; Applied Chemistry; Chemical Engineering; Chemistry; Industrial Chemistry; Marine Engineering; Materials Engineering; Organic Chemistry; Physical Chemistry); **Civil Engineering and Architecture** (Architecture; Bridge Engineering; Geological Engineering; Hydraulic Engineering; Power Engineering; Structural Architecture; Town Planning; Water Management); **Educational Science and Technology** (Economics; Educational Administration; Educational Sciences; Educational Technology); **Electro-Mechanical Engineering** (Automation and Control Engineering; Electronic Engineering; Industrial Engineering; Mechanical Engineering; Mechanics; Power Engineering; Production Engineering; Thermal Engineering; Transport Engineering); **Foreign Languages** (Applied Linguistics; English; Japanese; Linguistics; Literature; Modern Languages); **Information Engineering** (Automation and Control Engineering; Computer Engineering; Computer Science; Electrical Engineering; Electronic Engineering; Information Technology; Telecommunications Engineering); **International; Jianxing** (Architecture; Arts and Humanities; Biological and Life Sciences; Business Administration; Chemical Engineering; Civil Engineering; Environmental Engineering; Information Technology; Law; Materials Engineering; Mechanical Engineering; Natural Sciences; Pharmacy; Political Sciences; Public Administration; Software Engineering); **Pharmaceutical Science** (Biochemistry; Chemistry; Engineering; Pharmacy); **Politics and Public Administration** (Administration; Economics; Educational Administration; Management; Philosophy; Political Sciences; Public Administration); **Science** (Applied Mathematics; Applied Physics; Mathematics; Optical Technology; Optics); **Software Engineering and Software Vocational** (Computer Engineering; Computer Science; Multimedia; Software Engineering); **Vocational and Technical Education** (Technology Education; Vocational Education); **Zhijiang** (Administration; Architecture; Arts and Humanities; Business Administration; Civil Engineering; Economics; English; Fine Arts; Information Technology; Law; Literature; Management; Mechanical Engineering; Military Science; Modern Languages; Natural Sciences; Physical Education; Technology)

School

Humanities (Advertising and Publicity; Arts and Humanities; Chinese; Communication Studies; Comparative Literature; Journalism; Literature; Philology; Radio and Television Broadcasting); **Law** (Civil Law; Commercial Law; Criminal Law; International Law; Law)

Department

Physical Education and Military Training (Military Science; Physical Education)

History: Founded as Hangzhou Chemical School 1953. Changed name to Zhejiang Chemical College 1958. Renamed Zhejiang Institute of Chemical Technology following merger with Quzhou Chemical College 1960. Renamed Zhejiang Institute of Technology 1978. Acquired present title 1993. Merged with Economic and Management Institute of Zhejiang Province, Hangzhou Shipbuilding Industry School, Zhejiang Building Material Industry School respectively 1994, 1999 and 2001.

Academic Year: September to July (September-January; March-July)

Admission Requirements: High School certificate with minimum NMET score

Fees: (Yuan): General studies, 4,400; attached colleges, 15,000

Main Language(s) of Instruction: Chinese, English

Accrediting Agency: Ministry of Education; Zhejiang Provincial Education Department

Degrees and Diplomas: *Xueshi Xuewei*; *Shuoshi Xuewei*; *Boshi*. Also MBA; post-doctoral programmes

Student Services: Academic Counselling, Canteen, Careers Guidance, Cultural Activities, Facilities for disabled people, Foreign Studies Centre, Health Services, Language Laboratory, Nursery Care, Social Counselling, Sports Facilities

Publications: Journal of Zhejiang University of Technology; Journal of Zhejiang University of Technology

Publishing House: Campus News

Academic Staff *2011-2012*: Total 2,088

STAFF WITH DOCTORATE: Total 940

Student Numbers *2011-2012*: Total: c. 21,300

Last Updated: 06/02/13

ZHEJIANG WANLI UNIVERSITY (ZWU)

No.8, South Qian Hu Road, Ningbo, Zhejiang Province 315100

Tel: +86(574) 88222017 +86(574) 88222047 +86(574) 88222222

Fax: +86(574) 88222264

EMail: ftr@zwu.edu.cn; fso@zwu.edu.cn

Website: http://gjjl.zwu.edu.cn/english

President: Shi Zhongci

Faculty

Art and Design (Architecture; Design; Fine Arts; Landscape Architecture; Visual Arts); **Biological and Environmental Sciences** (Bioengineering; Biological and Life Sciences; Biotechnology; Environmental Studies; Food Science; Food Technology; Safety Engineering); **Computer Science and Information Technology** (Computer Science; Information Sciences; Information Technology); **Culture and Media Studies** (Advertising and Publicity; Chinese; Cultural Studies; Journalism; Literature; Mass Communication; Media Studies); **Electronic and Information Engineering** (Automation and Control Engineering; Electrical Engineering; Electronic Engineering; Information Technology; Telecommunications Engineering); **Foreign Languages** (English; Japanese; Modern Languages)

College

International (Asian Studies; Chinese; Painting and Drawing; Sports); **Junior** (Computer Science; English; Parks and Recreation; Social Sciences; Sports)

School

Business (Business Administration); **Law** (Administrative Law; Civil Law; Commercial Law; Comparative Law; Criminal Law; Fiscal Law; International Law; Law; Maritime Law; Public Administration); **Modern Logistics** (E-Business/Commerce; Information Management; Information Sciences; Management; Transport Engineering)

Further Information: Also Huilong Campus and Zhashan Base.

History: Founded 1950 as Ningbo Agricultural College, acquired present status and title 1999.

Fees: (Yuna): Language training programme, 16,000 per annumr Undergraduate programme, 16,000 per annum; Short- term programmes, 615 per week

Main Language(s) of Instruction: Chinese

Degrees and Diplomas: *Xueshi Xuewei*

Academic Staff *2011-2012*: Total: c. 1,000

Student Numbers *2011-2012*: Total: c. 20,000

Last Updated: 06/02/13

ZHEJIANG YUEXIU UNIVERSITY OF FOREIGN LANGUAGES (ZYUFL)

No.428 Kuaiji Road, Yue Cheng District, Shaoxing, Zhejiang 312000

Tel: +86(575) 88343188 +86(575) 88365125

Fax: +86(575) 88365125

Website: http://www.zyufl.edu.cn/

President: Yang Yinqian

College

Adult Education (Administration; Arabic; Banking; Business Administration; Education; English; French; German; International Business; Japanese; Korean; Management; Russian; Spanish; Tourism); **English** (Applied Linguistics; English; Foreign Languages Education; Tourism); **Euro-Languages** (Applied Linguistics; European Languages; French; German; Italian; Russian; Spanish); **International Business** (Business Administration; E-Business/Commerce; Finance; Information Management; International Business; International Economics; Marketing; Operations Research; Tourism; Transport Management); **International Education** (Chinese; International Studies; Linguistics; Literature; Secretarial

Studies); **Oriental Languages** (Arabic; Japanese; Korean; Oriental Languages)

Main Language(s) of Instruction: Chinese

Degrees and Diplomas: *Xueshi Xuewei*

Academic Staff *2011-2012*: Total: c. 518

Student Numbers *2011-2012*: Total: c. 10,790

Last Updated: 08/11/13

ZHENGZHOU HUAXIN UNIVERSITY (ZZHXXY)

Xinzheng, Henan 451150

Website: http://www.zzhxxy.com/

President: Zhao Guo

School

Art (Advertising and Publicity; Child Care and Development; Dance; Design; Fine Arts; Interior Design; Landscape Architecture; Music; Musical Instruments; Photography; Preschool Education; Primary Education; Secretarial Studies; Singing); **Construction Engineering** (Architecture; Civil Engineering; Construction Engineering; Engineering Management); **Management** (Business Administration; Hotel Management; Human Resources; Management; Tourism; Transport Management); **Mechatronic Engineering** (Automation and Control Engineering; Automotive Engineering; Electrical Engineering; Electronic Engineering; Industrial Engineering; Maintenance Technology; Mechanical Engineering; Power Engineering; Production Engineering; Transport Engineering); **Medicine** (Applied Chemistry; Cosmetology; Medical Technology; Medicine; Midwifery; Nursing; Pharmacology; Rehabilitation and Therapy; Treatment Techniques)

Department

Economics and Trade (Accountancy; Business Administration; Business and Commerce; Economics; Finance; Insurance; Management; Marketing); **Foreign Language** (Applied Linguistics; Child Care and Development; English; Foreign Languages Education; Modern Languages; Tourism); **Information Engineering** (Computer Engineering; Computer Networks; Computer Science; E-Business/Commerce; Information Management; Information Technology; Software Engineering; Telecommunications Engineering; Visual Arts)

Further Information: West campus and East campus

Main Language(s) of Instruction: Chinese

Degrees and Diplomas: *Xueshi Xuewei*. Also undergraduate diploma

Student Services: Sports Facilities

Academic Staff *2012-2013*	**TOTAL**
FULL-TIME	**1,256**
PART-TIME	**1,027**
Student Numbers *2012-2013*	
All (Foreign included)	**26,000**

Last Updated: 09/10/13

ZHENGZHOU INSTITUTE OF AERONAUTICAL INDUSTRY MANAGEMENT

2 Jinhai Road, Zhengzhou, Henan Province 450015

Tel: +86(371) 8986633 Ext. 5602

Fax: +86(371) 8889638

EMail: yanban@zia.whnet.edu.cn

Website: http://www.zzia.edu.cn/2008/

President: Shi Jinfa

College

Business Administration (Business Administration; Human Resources; Management); **Management Science and Engineering** (Engineering; Industrial Engineering; Transport Engineering; Transport Management)

School

Accountancy (Accountancy; Finance); **Art and Design** (Advertising and Publicity; Communication Arts; Design; Fine Arts; Industrial Design; Visual Arts); **Civil Engineering** (Architecture and Planning; Bridge Engineering; Building Technologies; Civil Engineering; Construction Engineering; Environmental Engineering; Road Engineering; Town Planning); **Continuing Education**; **Law** (Civil Law; Commercial Law; Criminal Law; International Law); **Mechatronics Engineering** (Electrical Engineering; Mechanical Engineering)

Department

Aerospace Engineering (Aeronautical and Aerospace Engineering); **Computer Science and Applications** (Computer Science); **Electronic and Communication Engineering** (Computer Networks; Electrical Engineering; Electronic Engineering; Information Technology; Telecommunications Engineering); **Foreign Languages** (English; French; Modern Languages); **Humanities and Social Sciences** (Administration; Arts and Humanities; Literature; Public Administration; Social Sciences); **Ideological and Political Theory** (History; Political Sciences); **Mathematics and Physics** (Applied Linguistics; Mathematics; Physics; Statistics); **Physical Education** (Health Sciences; Physical Education; Sports)

Institute

Economics and Trade (Business and Commerce; Economics; Finance; Insurance; International Business; Statistics); **International Education** (Engineering Management; Modern Languages; Western European Studies); **Software** (Computer Engineering; Computer Networks; Information Technology; Software Engineering)

History: Founded 1949 as Zhengzhou School of Aeronautical Industry; Changed name to Zhengzhou Aviation Technical School 1964. Upgraded to College of Zhengzhou Institute of Aeronautical Industry Management 1978. Acquired present status and title 1984.

Main Language(s) of Instruction: Chinese

Degrees and Diplomas: *Xueshi Xuewei*

Academic Staff *2012-2013*: Total: c. 900

Student Numbers *2012-2013*: Total: c. 26,000

Last Updated: 10/10/13

ZHENGZHOU INSTITUTE OF SCIENCE AND TECHNOLOGY (ZZIST)

Mazhai Industrial Park, Zhengzhou, Henan 450064

Tel: +86(371) 67862666 +86(371) 67862777

EMail: zkywg@163.com

Website: http://www.zzist.net/

President: Qing Xiaogang

Department

Adult Education (Adult Education); **Art** (Fine Arts); **Business Administration** (Business Administration); **Civil Construction** (Civil Engineering; Construction Engineering); **Economy and Trade** (Business Administration; Economics); **Electric Engineering** (Electrical Engineering); **Information Science and Engineering** (Information Sciences; Information Technology); **Mechanical Engineering** (Mechanical Engineering); **Traffic and Transportation** (Transport and Communications)

History: Founded 1988 as Zhengzhou Zhongyuan Vocational University. Renamed Zhengzhou Technology Training Institute 1996. Acquired present status 2008.

Main Language(s) of Instruction: Chinese

Degrees and Diplomas: *Xueshi Xuewei*

Academic Staff *2012-2013*: Total: c. 1,100

Student Numbers *2012-2013*: Total: c. 18,000

Last Updated: 08/11/13

ZHENGZHOU NORMAL UNIVERSITY (ZZNU)

6, Yingcai Street, Zhengzhou, Henan 450044

Tel: +86(371) 66501002

EMail: jesting@zznu.edu.cn

Website: http://www.zznu.edu.cn/

President: Zhao Jian

College

Foreign Languages (English; Hotel Management; Linguistics; Modern Languages; Russian; Tourism; Translation and Interpretation); **Information Science and Technology** (Information Sciences; Information Technology); **International Education**

(International Studies); **Liberal Arts** (Arts and Humanities; Chinese; Foreign Languages Education; Journalism; Linguistics; Literature; Modern Languages; Radio and Television Broadcasting; Writing); **Mathematics and Statistics** (Applied Mathematics; Mathematics; Statistics); **Music** (Music; Musical Instruments); **Physics and Electronic Science** (Electronic Engineering; Physics); **Primary Education** (Primary Education); **Software** (Software Engineering); **Special Education** (Computer Science; Fine Arts; Musicology; Rehabilitation and Therapy; Special Education)

School

Economics and Management (Economics; Management); **Education** (Curriculum; Education; Experimental Psychology; Pedagogy; Preschool Education; Primary Education; Psychology; Teacher Training)

Department

Chemistry (Chemistry); **Political Science and Public Management** (Political Sciences; Public Administration)

Academy

Fine Arts (Fine Arts)

History: Founded 1952 as Zhengzhou Teachers College. Acquired present status and title 2010.

Main Language(s) of Instruction: Chinese

Degrees and Diplomas: *Xueshi Xuewei*

Academic Staff *2012-2013*: Total: c. 590

Last Updated: 11/10/13

ZHENGZHOU UNIVERSITY (ZZU)

No.100 Science Road, Zhengzhou, Henan Province 450001
Tel: +86(371) 67783111 +86(371) 67780020 +86(371) 67780665
Fax: +86(371) 67783222 +86(371) 67781569
EMail: fao@zzu.edu.cn; sie@zzu.edu.cn
Website: http://www.zzu.edu.cn/

President: Shen Changyu Tel: +86(371) 7763025

College

Physical Education *(Joint-Education)* (Physical Education); **Shengda Business Management** *(Joint-Education)* (Business Administration; Management); **SIAS International Business Management** *(Joint-Education)* (Business Administration; International Business)

School

Adult Education; **Applied Science and Technology** (Educational Technology; Electronic Engineering; Human Resources; Information Technology; Medicine; Pedagogy); **Architecture** (Architectural and Environmental Design; Architecture; Design; Finance; Town Planning); **Basic Medicine** (Medicine); **Business** (Accountancy; Business Administration; Economics; Finance; International Business; International Economics; Statistics); **Chemical Engineering** (Automation and Control Engineering; Chemical Engineering; Environmental Engineering; Medical Technology; Power Engineering; Safety Engineering; Thermal Engineering); **City Planning and Designing** (Architectural and Environmental Design; Town Planning); **Civil Engineering** (Civil Engineering; Construction Engineering); **Clinical Medicine** *(I)* (Medicine); **Clinical Medicine** *(III)* (Medicine); **Clinical Medicine** *(II)* (Medicine); **Distance Learning**; **Education** (Education; Educational Psychology; Pedagogy; Political Sciences); **Electric Engineering** (Automation and Control Engineering; Biomedical Engineering; Electrical Engineering); **Environment and Water Conservancy Engineering** (Environmental Engineering; Geological Engineering; Hydraulic Engineering; Information Technology; Power Engineering; Surgery; Water Management); **Foreign Languages** (English; German; Japanese; Modern Languages; Russian); **History** (Archaeology; Arts and Humanities; History); **Information Engineering** (Computer Science; Electronic Engineering; Information Technology; Telecommunications Engineering); **International Education** (Chinese; Literature; Medicine); **Journalism and Communication** (Advertising and Publicity; Journalism; Mass Communication; Radio and Television Broadcasting); **Law** (Law); **Liberal Arts** (Arts and Humanities; Chinese; Literature); **Material Science and Engineering** (Automation and Control Engineering; Materials Engineering; Packaging Technology; Polymer and Plastics Technology); **Mechanical Engineering** (Automation and Control Engineering; Industrial Design; Mechanical Engineering; Production Engineering); **Nursing** (Nursing); **Physical Engineering** (Applied Physics; Automation and Control Engineering; Electronic Engineering; Information Sciences; Information Technology; Physics); **Public Health** (Public Health; Social and Preventive Medicine); **Public Management** (Administration; Management; Philosophy; Public Administration; Social Work); **Software Technology** (Software Engineering); **Stomatology** (Stomatology); **Tourist Management** (Tourism)

Department

Bio-engineering (Bioengineering); **Chemistry** (Applied Chemistry; Chemistry); **Clinical Medicine** (Anaesthesiology; Medical Technology; Medicine); **Engineering Mechanics** (Engineering; Mechanics; Safety Engineering); **Fine Arts** (Design; Fine Arts; Painting and Drawing; Sculpture); **Information Management** (Architecture and Planning; Information Management; Information Sciences; Library Science); **Management Engineering** (E-Business/Commerce; Engineering Management; Industrial Engineering; Transport Management); **Mathematics** (Applied Mathematics; Computer Science; Information Sciences; Mathematics); **Medicine Laboratory Science** *(Clinical)* (Laboratory Techniques); **Music** (Music; Musicology; Performing Arts); **Pharmacy** (Pharmacology; Pharmacy); **Physical Education** (Physical Education)

Further Information: 5 affiliated hospitals; 7 post-doctoral research stations

History: Founded 2000 through merger of Zhengzhou University, Zhengzhou University of Technology and Henan Medical University.

Admission Requirements: Graduation from high school and entrance examination

Fees: (Yuan): 3,000 per annum

Main Language(s) of Instruction: Chinese

Accrediting Agency: Ministry of Education; Henan Provincial Government

Degrees and Diplomas: *Xueshi Xuewei*; *Shuoshi Xuewei*; *Boshi*

Student Services: Academic Counselling, Canteen, Careers Guidance, Cultural Activities, Foreign Studies Centre, Health Services, Language Laboratory, Sports Facilities

Publications: Journal of Zhengzhou University

Academic Staff *2011-2012*	**TOTAL**
FULL-TIME	**3,056**
STAFF WITH DOCTORATE FULL-TIME	c. **960**
Student Numbers *2011-2012*	
All (Foreign included)	c. **36,000**
FOREIGN ONLY	**342**

Last Updated: 06/02/13

ZHENGZHOU UNIVERSITY OF LIGHT INDUSTRY (ZZULI)

5 Dongfeng Road, Zhengzhou, Henan Province 450002
Tel: +86(371) 63556926 +86(371) 63920143
Fax: +86(371) 63556927 +86(371) 63920143
EMail: fao@zzuli.edu.cn
Website: http://www.zzuli.edu.cn/

President: Ju Yiwen

International Relations: Yang Dongyou

College

Arts and Design (Architectural and Environmental Design; Design; Fine Arts; Industrial Design; Visual Arts); **Computer and Communication Engineering** (Computer Engineering; Computer Science; Information Management; Information Sciences; Information Technology; Telecommunications Engineering); **Continuing Education**; **Economy and Management** (Accountancy; Business Administration; E-Business/Commerce; Economics; Hotel Management; Information Management; Information Sciences; International Business; Management; Tourism); **Electrical and Information Engineering** (Automation and Control Engineering; Electrical Engineering; Electronic Engineering; Engineering; Information Sciences; Information Technology; Measurement and Precision Engineering; Surveying and Mapping); **Electromechanical Science**

and Engineering (Automation and Control Engineering; Electronic Engineering; Heating and Refrigeration; Maintenance Technology; Mechanical Engineering; Power Engineering; Production Engineering); **Food and Biological Engineering** (Bioengineering; Food Technology); **Material and Chemical Engineering** (Chemical Engineering; Materials Engineering)

Department

Foreign Languages *(DFL)* (English; Foreign Languages Education; Korean; Modern Languages); **Law and Administration** (Administration; Law); **Technology and Physics** (Physics; Technology)

History: Founded 1977.

Main Language(s) of Instruction: Chinese

Degrees and Diplomas: *Xueshi Xuewei*; *Shuoshi Xuewei*

Academic Staff *2011-2012*: Total: c. 400

Student Numbers *2011-2012*: Total: c. 15,000

Last Updated: 06/02/13

ZHONGKAI UNIVERSITY OF AGRICULTURE AND ENGINEERING (ZHKU)

24 Dongsha Street, Fangzhilu,
Guangzhou, Guangdong Province 510225
Tel: +86(20) 89003114
Fax: +86(20) 84429414
Website: http://www.zhku.edu.cn/

President: Luo Shaoming (2012-)

International Relations: He Bin

College

Art and Design (Design; Fine Arts); **Arts and Humanities** *(Keji)* (Arts and Humanities; Chinese; Literature); **Business and Economics** (Business Administration; Economics); **Chemistry and Chemical Engineering** (Chemical Engineering; Chemistry); **Computer Science and Engineering** (Computer Engineering; Computer Science); **Continuing Education**; **Environmental Science and Engineering** (Environmental Engineering; Environmental Studies); **Foreign Languages** (English; Modern Languages); **Horticulture and Landscape Architecture** (Horticulture; Landscape Architecture); **Light Industry and Food Science** (Food Science); **Mechanical and Electrical Engineering** (Agricultural Equipment; Automation and Control Engineering; Electrical Engineering; Energy Engineering; Mechanical Engineering; Power Engineering)

School

Information Sciences (Information Sciences); **Life Sciences** (Biological and Life Sciences; Biotechnology); **Management** (Management)

Department

Agronomy (Agriculture; Agronomy; Plant and Crop Protection; Plant Pathology); **Computer Science** (Computer Science); **Ideological and Political Theory Teaching** (Political Sciences); **Sports** (Sports)

Institute

Higher Education (Higher Education); **Urban Construction Engineering** (Construction Engineering; Town Planning)

Centre

International Exchange and Training; **Modern Educational Technology** (Educational Technology)

Further Information: Also post-doctoral research station

History: Founded 1927 as Zhongkai Worker and Farmer School, acquired present status and name 2008.

Main Language(s) of Instruction: Chinese

Degrees and Diplomas: *Xueshi Xuewei*; *Shuoshi Xuewei*

Academic Staff *2011-2012*: Total 931

Student Numbers *2011-2012*: Total: c. 15,000

Last Updated: 06/02/13

ZHONGNAN UNIVERSITY OF ECONOMICS AND LAW (ZUEL)

1 South Nanhu Road, Wuhan, Hubei Province 430073
Tel: +86(27) 88386557
Fax: +86(27) 88386557
EMail: ies@znufe.edu.cn
Website: http://www.znufe.edu.cn

President: Wu Handong

International Relations: Xiao Chongming

School

Accounting (Accountancy; Finance); **Business Administration** (Administration; Business Administration; Marketing; Tourism); **Criminal Justice** (Criminal Law; Criminology; Police Studies); **Economics** (Economics; International Economics); **Finance and Insurance** *(Xinhua)* (Banking; Finance; Insurance); **Finance and Taxation** (Finance; Taxation); **Foreign Languages** (English; Japanese; Modern Languages); **Humanities** (Arts and Humanities; History; Philosophy; Political Sciences); **Journalism and Mass Media** (Journalism; Mass Communication; Media Studies); **Law** (Civil Law; Commercial Law; Constitutional Law; Criminal Law; International Law; Law); **Public Administration** (Public Administration; Social Welfare); **Safety Science and Administration** (Safety Engineering); **Statistics and Mathematics** (Computer Science; Information Technology; Mathematics; Statistics)

Further Information: Also 74 research institutes

History: Founded 1948 as Zhongyuan University. Hubei University 1958. Renamed Hubei Training School of Finance and Economics 1971. Renamed Hubei Institute of School of Finance and Economics 1978. Renamed Zhongnan University of Finance and Economics 1985. Acquired present status and title 2000, following merger with South Central University of Political Science and Law.

Fees: (Yuan): Bachelor's Degree, 16,000 per annum; Master's Degree, 20,000 per annum; Doctor's Degree, 24,000 per annum; General Advanced Study, 16,000 per annum; Senior Advanced Study, 20,000 per annum

Main Language(s) of Instruction: Chinese

Degrees and Diplomas: *Xueshi Xuewei*; *Shuoshi Xuewei*; *Boshi*. Also MBA; Executive MBA; Post-doctoral programmes.

Student Services: Sports Facilities

Publications: Journal of Studies in Law and Business; Journal of Zhongnan University of Economics and Law

Academic Staff *2011-2012*: Total: c. 1,173

Student Numbers *2011-2012*: Total: c. 34,000

Last Updated: 07/02/13

ZHONGYUAN UNIVERSITY OF TECHNOLOGY (ZUT)

41 Zhongyuan Road, Zhengzhou, Henan Province 450007
Tel: +86(371) 62506983 +86(371) 62506888
Fax: +86(371) 62506859 +86(371) 62506095
EMail: zutco@hotmail.com; ieo@zut.edu.cn
Website: http://www.zzti.edu.cn

President: Cui Shizhong

College

Asia-Pacific International *(APII)* (Design; Fashion Design; Management; Marketing); **Information and Business** *(Independent Institute)* (Business Administration; Computer Science; Design; Economics; Fine Arts; Information Sciences; Information Technology; Law; Management; Mass Communication; Mechanical Engineering; Media Studies; Modern Languages; Political Sciences); **International Education** (Accountancy; Architectural and Environmental Design; Automotive Engineering; Construction Engineering; Design; Fashion Design; Marketing; Photography; Production Engineering; Technology; Textile Design; Video); **Software** (Computer Engineering; Computer Networks; Information Management; Information Technology; Software Engineering)

School

Art and Design (Architectural and Environmental Design; Communication Arts; Design; Fine Arts; Visual Arts); **Civil Engineering and Architecture** (Architecture; Building Technologies; Civil

Engineering; Construction Engineering; Mechanics; Structural Architecture); **Computer Science** (Computer Engineering; Computer Networks; Computer Science; Software Engineering); **Economics and Management** (Accountancy; Air and Space Law; Business Administration; Economics; Information Management; Information Sciences; Management; Marketing; Public Administration); **Electronic and Information Engineering** (Automation and Control Engineering; Electrical Engineering; Electronic Engineering; Measurement and Precision Engineering; Telecommunications Engineering); **Energy and Environmental Engineering** (Building Technologies; Energy Engineering; Environmental Engineering; Power Engineering; Safety Engineering; Thermal Engineering; Water Management); **Fashion Technology** (Clothing and Sewing; Design; Fashion Design; Textile Design; Textile Technology); **Foreign Languages** (Chinese; English; Japanese; Modern Languages); **Journalism and Communication** (Cinema and Television; Film; Journalism; Mass Communication; Media Studies; Radio and Television Broadcasting; Writing); **Materials and Chemical Engineering** (Applied Chemistry; Chemical Engineering; Materials Engineering); **Mechanical and Electronic Engineering** (Automation and Control Engineering; Automotive Engineering; Electronic Engineering; Industrial Design; Industrial Engineering; Mechanical Engineering; Production Engineering); **Political Science and Law** (History; Law; Philosophy; Political Sciences; Social Work); **Science** (Applied Mathematics; Applied Physics; Computer Science; Information Sciences; Mathematics; Optical Technology; Optics); **Textiles** (Chemical Engineering; Materials Engineering; Textile Design; Textile Technology)

Department

Continuing Education (Arts and Humanities; Building Technologies; Computer Graphics; Design; Economics; Engineering; Fashion Design; Law; Management; Natural Sciences; Textile Technology); **Ideological and Political Education** (Military Science; Modern History; Political Sciences); **Physical Education** (Physical Education; Sports)

Centre

Industrial Training (Automation and Control Engineering; Electrical Engineering; Electronic Engineering; Engineering; Metal Techniques; Production Engineering)

History: Founded 1955 as Zhengzhou Institute of Textile Technology (ZITT). Acquired present status and name 2000.

Main Language(s) of Instruction: Chinese

Degrees and Diplomas: *Xueshi Xuewei*; *Shuoshi Xuewei*

Academic Staff *2011-2012*	**TOTAL**
FULL-TIME	**926**
STAFF WITH DOCTORATE FULL-TIME	**181**

Student Numbers *2011-2012*	
All (Foreign included)	**30,000**
FOREIGN ONLY	**25**

Last Updated: 07/02/13

ZHOUKOU NORMAL UNIVERSITY (ZKNU)

East Wenchang Street, Chuanhui District, Zhoukou, Henan 466001
Tel: +86(394) 8178000
Fax: +86(394) 8178099
EMail: zhaoban@zknu.edu.cn
Website: http://www.zknu.edu.cn/

President: Liu Xiangyu

College

Computer Science and Technology (Computer Science; Information Technology); **Foreign Languages** (English; Foreign Languages Education; Japanese; Literature; Modern Languages); **Physical Education** (Physical Education; Sports; Sports Management)

Department

Chemistry (Chemistry); **Chinese Language and Literature** (Chinese; Literature); **Continuing Education**; **Economics and Management** (Economics; Management); **Education Science** (Education; Educational Technology; Preschool Education; Primary Education; Psychology); **Journalism** (Journalism); **Life Science** (Bioengineering; Biological and Life Sciences; Biotechnology); **Mathematics and Information Science** (Applied Mathematics; Computer Science; Information Sciences; Mathematics; Statistics); **Physics and Electronic Engineering** (Automation and Control Engineering; Electronic Engineering; Information Technology; Optical Technology; Physics); **Politics and Law** (Law; Political Sciences); **Public Fine Arts Education and Occupational Skills Education** (Art Education; Fine Arts; Painting and Drawing; Vocational Education); **Public Theoretical Research** (Education; History; Political Sciences); **Software Engineering** (Software Engineering)

Academy

Fine Arts (Design; Fine Arts; Graphic Design; Interior Design; Landscape Architecture; Painting and Drawing; Photography; Visual Arts); **Music and Dance** (Dance; Music; Music Education; Musicology; Opera)

History: Founded in 1973. Acquired present status 2002.

Main Language(s) of Instruction: Chinese

Degrees and Diplomas: *Xueshi Xuewei*

Publications: The Journal of Zhoukou Normal University

Academic Staff *2012-2013*: Total: c. 1,300
Student Numbers *2012-2013*: Total: c. 19,400
Last Updated: 11/10/13

ZUNYI MEDICAL COLLEGE (ZMC)

No.201 Dalian Road, Huichuan District,
Zunyi, Guizhou Province 563003
Tel: +86(852) 8609388
Fax: +86(852) 8609575
EMail: admin@zmc.edu.cn
Website: http://www.zmc.gd.cn/

President: Shi Jingshan (2005-)
Tel: +86(852) 8609788 EMail: shijs@zmc.edu.cn

School

Adult Continuing Education (Medicine); **Basic Medicine** (Medicine); **Clinical Medicine** *(I)* (Anaesthesiology; Dermatology; Gynaecology and Obstetrics; Medicine; Neurology; Oncology; Paediatrics; Pathology; Pharmacology; Psychiatry and Mental Health; Surgery); **Foreign Languages** (English; Modern Languages); **Nursing** (Nursing); **Pharmaceutical Sciences** (Biochemistry; Chemical Engineering; Engineering; Microbiology; Pharmacy); **Physical Education** (Physical Education); **Public Administration** (Public Administration); **Public Health** (Public Health); **Stomatology** (Stomatology)

Department

Anaesthesiology (Anaesthesiology); **Laboratory Medicine** (Analytical Chemistry; Anatomy; Biochemistry; Computer Science; Embryology and Reproduction Biology; Gynaecology and Obstetrics; Haematology; Histology; Immunology; Inorganic Chemistry; Laboratory Techniques; Medical Technology; Medicine; Microbiology; Molecular Biology; Organic Chemistry; Paediatrics; Parasitology; Pathology; Physiology; Statistics; Surgery); **Medical Cosmetology** *(ZMC)* (Cosmetology); **Medical Imaging** (Medical Technology); **Medical Information Technology** (Information Technology; Medical Technology); **Social Sciences** *(SSS)* (History; Law; Political Sciences; Social Sciences)

Research Centre

Medicine and Biology (Biology; Medicine)

Campus

Zuhai (Medicine)

Further Information: 3 affiliated hospitals; 58 non-affiliated hospitals.

History: Founded 1947 as Dalian Medical College. Moved to Zunyi and acquired present title 1969.

Main Language(s) of Instruction: Chinese

Degrees and Diplomas: *Xueshi Xuewei*; *Shuoshi Xuewei*; *Boshi*. The doctor's degree offered is joint programme (offered jointly with another university)

Academic Staff *2011-2012*: Total 701
Student Numbers *2011-2012*: Total: c. 14,000
Last Updated: 04/02/13

ZUNYI NORMAL COLLEGE (ZYNC)

Shanghai Road No.830, Zunyi, Guizhou 563002
Tel: +86(852) 8922406
EMail: ybgs@zync.edu.cn; webmaster@zync.edu.cn
Website: http://www.zync.edu.cn/

President: Wang Dazhong

School

Arts (Fine Arts; Industrial Design; Painting and Drawing); **Chemistry and Chemical Engineering** (Analytical Chemistry; Applied Chemistry; Chemical Engineering; Chemistry; Inorganic Chemistry; Organic Chemistry; Physical Chemistry; Science Education); **Education Science** (Curriculum; Education; Educational Administration; Educational Psychology; Human Resources; Pedagogy; Psychology); **Elementary Education** (Preschool Education; Primary Education); **Foreign Languages and Literature** (English; Literature; Modern Languages; Translation and Interpretation); **Historical Culture and Tourism** (Cultural Studies; Tourism); **Humanities and Media** (Arts and Humanities; Chinese; Literature; Media Studies; Native Language Education; Philology); **Life Sciences** (Biological and Life Sciences; Biotechnology); **Mathematics and Computing Science** (Applied Mathematics; Computer Science; Mathematics; Statistics); **Music and Dance** (Dance; Music; Music Education); **Physical Education** (Physical Education); **Physics and Mechanical-Electrical Engineering** (Automation and Control Engineering; Electrical Engineering; Electronic Engineering; Information Technology; Mechanical Engineering; Physics; Science Education); **Politics and Economic Management** (Economics; Law; Management; Philosophy; Political Sciences)

Department

Computer and Information Science (Computer Networks; Computer Science; Information Sciences; Software Engineering; Telecommunications Engineering)

Research Centre

Computing (Computer Science); **Education and Demonstration Bases for the Communist classics** (Education; Political Sciences); **Fundamental Education** (Education); **Higher Education** (Higher Education); **Ideological and Political Education** (Political Sciences); **Red Culture** (Cultural Studies); **Regional Economy** (International Economics); **Zunyi Culture** (Cultural Studies)

History: Founded 1958 as Zunyi Normal Specialized School. Acquired present status and title 2001.

Main Language(s) of Instruction: Chinese

Degrees and Diplomas: *Xueshi Xuewei*

Academic Staff *2012-2013*: Total 678

Student Numbers *2012-2013*: Total: c. 12,000

Last Updated: 14/10/13

China - Hong Kong SAR

STRUCTURE OF HIGHER EDUCATION SYSTEM

Description:

Higher education is provided by universities and other types of tertiary institutions. The University Grants Committee (UGC) is the advisory body which makes recommendations to the Government about the development of the tertiary education sector, the financing of UGC-funded tertiary institutions and the administration of government grants to higher education. Currently, there are eight UGC-funded institutions offering publicly-funded programmes at sub-degree, degree, taught-postgraduate and research-postgraduate levels. Among the eight institutions, seven are universities with self-accrediting status. The remaining is the Hong Kong Institute of Education (HKIEd) which has self-accrediting status in respect of its teacher education programmes at degree and above levels. Each of these institutions is an autonomous body with its own Ordinance and governing Council. They are free to manage their internal affairs within the restraints of the laws of Hong Kong.

Stages of studies:

University level first stage: *Associate degree, Higher Diploma, Bachelor's degree and Honours degree*
Associate degrees and Higher Diploma programmes normally last for two to three years. The first stage of higher education leads to a Bachelor's degree normally after three years os study. Some of the Bachelor's degree programmes may take up to six years depending on the subject areas.

University level second stage: *Postgraduate Certificate, Postgraduate Diploma, Master's degree and Master of Philosophy*
Postgraduate Diplomas and Certificates are offered after one year of full-time postgraduate studies. Master's degrees without research training are conferred after one to two years of full-time study following the Bachelor's degree, in general. Masters of Philosophy are conferred usually after two years of research training and on submission of a thesis following upon the Bachelor's degree.

University level third stage: *Doctorate*
The third stage leads to the award of a Doctor of Philosophy after a period of research work and on submission of a thesis. Studies generally last for three years.

ADMISSION TO HIGHER EDUCATION

Admission to university-level studies:

Name of secondary school credential required: Hong Kong Advanced Level Examination

Foreign students admission:

Quotas: Starting from the academic year 2005/2006, the quota for admission of non-local students is relaxed to 10% of the aggregate number of the approved publicly-funded student number targets of full-time programmes at the sub-degree, undergraduate and taught postgraduate levels. For part-time locally accredited and publicly-funded taught postgraduate programmes, in brief, the quota for non-local students is 10% of the approved student number target. There is no restriction for the number of non-local students at the research postgraduate level and for part-time self-financing taught programmes. In addition, for full-time self-financing undergraduate and sub-degree programmes, there is no restriction for the number of non-local students coming from places other than Mainland China, Taiwan and Macau. For students from these three places, they can be admitted to the full-time self-financing undergraduate and sub-degree programmes only up to 10% of the actual local student enrolment of the same programmes offered by individual institutions in the preceding year.

Admission requirements: Foreign students must satisfy the entrance requirements of the institution they wish to attend. There may be additional requirements for certain programmes. Application for exemption or credit transfer should be made to individual institutions.

Entry regulations: Foreign students entering Hong Kong for the purpose of education must hold a student visa/ entry permit issued by the Director of Immigration.

Language proficiency: Students should have a good knowledge of English. Depending on the discipline pursued, proficiency in Chinese may also be required.

NATIONAL BODIES

Education Bureau

Secretary for Education: Eddie Ng Hak-kim
Deputy Secretary, Further and Higher Education Branch: Brian Sal-hung Lo
15/F, Wu Chung House
213 Queen's Road East
Wan Chai
Hong Kong, Hong Kong SAR
Tel: +852 2891 0088
Fax: +852 2893 0858
EMail: edbinfo@edb.gov.hk
WWW: http://www.edb.gov.hk

Role of national body: The Bureau is responsible for formulating, developing and reviewing policies, programmes and legislation in respect of education from pre-primary to tertiary level; and overseeing the effective implementation of educational programmes.The Bureau monitors the services provided by: the University Grants Committee, the Student Financial Assistance Agency, the Hong Kong Examinations and Assessment Authority, the Hong Kong Council for Accreditation of Academic and Vocational Qualifications and the Vocational Training Council.

University Grants Committee - UGC

Chairman: Carlson Tong
Secretary-General: Richard Armour
7/F, Shui On Centre
6-8 Harbour Road
Wan Chai, Hong Kong SAR
Tel: +852 2524 3987
Fax: +852 2845 1596
EMail: ugc@ugc.edu.hk
WWW: http://www.ugc.edu.hk

Role of national body: The UGC seeks to promote responsible understanding between the institutions, the Government and the community at large. It allocates funding to its funded institutions, advises both institutions and the Government on campus development plans and proposals made by institutions, and promotes and supports institutions in quality assurance and enhancement initiatives and processes.

Hong Kong Examinations and Assessment Authority - HKEAA

Chair: Chen Chung-nin
Secretary-General: Tong Chong-sze
General Manager, International and Professional Examinations: Margaret Lo
13/F Southorn Centre
120 Hennesy Road
Wan Chai, Hong Kong SAR
EMail: international@hkeaa.edu.hk; info@hkeaa.edu.hk
WWW: http://www.hkeaa.edu.hk

Role of national body: The Hong Kong Examinations and Assessment Authority (HKEAA), established in 1977, is an independent, self-financing statutory body. Since its establishment it has been planning and conducting examinations and assessments for primary and secondary school levels to university admission.

Data for academic year: 2011-2012

Source: IAU from the Information and Public Relations Section, Education Bureau, Hong Kong, China, 2011. Bodies 2016.

INSTITUTIONS

PUBLIC INSTITUTIONS

CITY UNIVERSITY OF HONG KONG (CITYU)

83 Tat Chee Avenue, Kowloon, Hong Kong, Hong Kong SAR
Tel: +852 3442-7654
Fax: +852 2788-1167
EMail: webmaster@cityu.edu.hk
Website: http://www.cityu.edu.hk

President: Way Kuo (2008-)
Tel: +852 3442-8282 EMail: way@cityu.edu.hk

Division
Building Science and Technology (Architecture; Building Technologies; Construction Engineering; Engineering Management; Surveying and Mapping)

College
Business (Accountancy; Economics; Finance; Information Technology; Management; Marketing); **Liberal Arts and Social Sciences** (Chinese; Communication Studies; East Asian Studies; English; Linguistics; Media Studies; Psychology; Public Administration; Social Policy; Social Studies; Social Work; Southeast Asian Studies; Translation and Interpretation); **Science and Engineering** (Biology; Biomedical Engineering; Building Technologies; Chemistry; Civil Engineering; Computer Engineering; Computer Science; Electronic Engineering; Engineering Management; Materials Engineering; Mathematics; Mechanical Engineering; Physics; Structural Architecture)

School
Continuing and Professional Education (SCOPE); **Creative Media** (Cinema and Television; Media Studies; Photography; Writing); **Energy and Environment** (Energy Engineering; Environmental Engineering; Environmental Studies); **Graduate Studies** (Architecture; Business Administration; Engineering Management; Law); **Law** (Comparative Law; International Law; Law; Maritime Law)

Department
Accountancy (Accountancy; Commercial Law; Information Management); **Applied Social Studies** (Criminology; Educational and Student Counselling; Psychology; Social Work; Sociology); **Asian and International Studies** (East Asian Studies; International Studies; South and Southeast Asian Languages); **Biology and Chemistry** (Applied Chemistry; Biology; Environmental Management; Environmental Studies); **Chinese, Translation and Linguistics** (Chinese; Cultural Studies; Heritage Preservation; Linguistics; Modern Languages; Translation and Interpretation); **Civil and Architectural Engineering** (Architecture; Building Technologies; Civil Engineering; Construction Engineering; Management; Real Estate; Structural Architecture; Surveying and Mapping); **Computer Science** (Computer Education; Computer Science); **Economics and Finance** (Economics; Finance; Insurance); **Electronic Engineering** (Computer Engineering; Electronic Engineering; Information Technology; Telecommunications Engineering); **English** (English); **Information Systems** (Business Computing; E- Business/Commerce; Information Management; Marketing); **Management** (Business Administration; Human Resources; International Business; Management); **Management Sciences** (Business Administration; Management; Statistics); **Marketing** (Business and Commerce; Marketing); **Mathematics** (Actuarial Science; Applied Mathematics; Finance; Mathematics and Computer Science); **Mechanical and Biomedical Engineering** (Biomedical Engineering; Mechanical Engineering); **Media and Communication** (Communication Studies; English; Media Studies); **Physics and Materials Science** (Applied Physics; Materials Engineering; Nanotechnology; Physics); **Public Policy** (Administration; Environmental Management; Environmental Studies; Management; Public Administration; Social Policy; Social Studies; Town Planning); **Systems Engineering and Engineering Management** (Electronic Engineering; Engineering Drawing and Design; Engineering Management; Industrial Engineering; Production Engineering; Safety Engineering)

Centre
Chinese Civilisation (Architecture; Chinese; Literature; Music; Painting and Drawing; Philosophy; Sculpture; South Asian Studies); **Electronic Packaging & Assemblies, Failure Analysis & Reliability Engineering (EPA Centre)** (Electronic Engineering); **English Language** (English); **Innovative Applications of Internet and Multimedia Technologies (AIMtech Centre)** (Computer Networks; Multimedia); **Maritime and Transportation Law (HKCMT)** (Maritime Law); **Smart Energy Conversion and Utilization Research (CSCR)** (Energy Engineering)

Research Centre
Ability R&D Energy (AERC) (Energy Engineering); **Advanced Structural Materials (CASM)** (Materials Engineering); **Applied Computing and Interactive Studies (ACIM)** (Computer Science; Media Studies; Multimedia); **Asia-Pacific Climate Impact Centre (GCCC)** (Environmental Studies; Meteorology); **Biosystems, Neuroscience, and Nanotechnology (CBNN)** (Biotechnology; Nanotechnology); **Chaos and Complex Networks (CCCN)** (Engineering; Mathematics; Physics); **Chinese and Comparative Law (RCCL)** (Comparative Law); **Communication Research (CCR)** (Communication Studies); **East Asian and Comparative Philosophy (CEACOP)** (Philosophy); **Functional Photonics (CFP)**; **Governance in Asia (GARC)** (Asian Studies; Government); **Intelligent Applications of Language Studies (HCLS)** *(The Halliday Centre)* (Communication Studies; Linguistics); **Mathematical Sciences (LBJ)** *(Liu Bie Ju)* (Applied Mathematics; Computer Science; Mathematics); **Multimedia Software Engineering Research Centre (MERC)** (Software Engineering); **Prognostics and System Health Management**; **Robotics and Automation (CRA)** (Automation and Control Engineering); **Social Media Marketing and Business Intelligence (CSMR)** (Business Administration; Marketing); **Southeast Asia (SEARC)** (Southeast Asian Studies); **State Key Laboratory in Marine Pollution (SKLMP)** (Environmental Management; Marine Science and Oceanography); **State Key Laboratory of Millimeter Waves (SKLMW)** (Physics); **Super-Diamond and Advanced Films (COSDAF)** (Nanotechnology); **System Informatics Engineering (CSIE)** (Computer Engineering); **Transport, Trade and Financial Studies (CTFS)** (Business and Commerce; Finance; Transport and Communications)

Research Institute
Hong Kong Advanced Institute for Cross-Disciplinary Studies

History: Founded 1984 as City Polytechnic of Hong Kong. Acquired present status and title 1994.

Academic Year: September to May (September-December; January-May), Summer term, June-August

Admission Requirements: Meet general requirement, English and/or Chinese proficiency. Individual programmes may have additional entrance requirements. Consult university for details.

Main Language(s) of Instruction: English

Degrees and Diplomas: *Bachelor's Degree Honours*: **Arts and Humanities; Business Administration; Engineering; Law; Social Sciences.** *Postgraduate Certificate/Diploma*: **Accountancy; Building Technologies; Computer Networks; Engineering; Environmental Studies; Information Management; Law.** *Master's Degree*: **Arts and Humanities; Business Administration; Fine Arts; Law.** *Master of Philosophy*: **Accountancy; Applied Mathematics; Computer Science; E-Business/Commerce; Electronic Engineering; Environmental Studies; Finance; International Business; International Economics; Law; Linguistics; Management; Materials Engineering; Technology.** *Doctor's Degree*: **Accountancy; Business Administration; Construction Engineering; Economics; Engineering; Engineering Management; Law; Management; Mass Communication; Materials Engineering.**

Student Services: Academic Counselling, Canteen, Careers Guidance, Cultural Activities, Facilities for disabled people, Foreign Studies Centre, Health Services, Language Laboratory, Social Counselling, Sports Facilities

Publications: Research Report
Publishing House: City University of Hong Kong Press

Academic Staff *2010-2011*	MEN	WOMEN	TOTAL
FULL-TIME	859	297	**1,156**
PART-TIME	140	124	**264**
STAFF WITH DOCTORATE			
FULL-TIME	621	161	**782**
Student Numbers *2010-2011*			
All (Foreign included)	9,562	8,480	**18,042**
FOREIGN ONLY	–	–	**2,853**

Part-time students, 5,803.
Last Updated: 11/09/13

HONG KONG BAPTIST UNIVERSITY (HKBU)

Baptist University Road Campus, Kowloon Tong, Hong Kong
Tel: +852 3411 7400
Fax: +852 2338 7644
EMail: ar@hkbu.edu.hk
Website: http://www.hkbu.edu.hk

President and Vice-Chancellor: Albert Chan (2010-)
Tel: +852(3) 411-7500 EMail: pdo@hkbu.edu.hk
International Relations: Peter Li, Director, International Office
Tel: +852(3) 411-2187
EMail: intl@hkbu.edu.hk; peterli@hkbu.edu.hk

Faculty
Arts (Arts and Humanities; Chinese; English; Music; Philosophy; Religion; Translation and Interpretation); **Science** (Applied Mathematics; Applied Physics; Biology; Biotechnology; Chemistry; Computer Science; Environmental Studies; Information Technology; Mathematics; Operations Research; Physics; Statistics); **Social Sciences** (Economics; Education; European Studies; Geography; Geography (Human); Government; History; International Studies; Leisure Studies; Parks and Recreation; Physical Education; Social Sciences; Social Work; Sociology; South Asian Studies)

Division
Research and Development Division - School of Chinese Medicine (Traditional Eastern Medicine)

School
Business (Accountancy; Business and Commerce; E- Business/ Commerce; Economics; Finance; Human Resources; Information Technology; Marketing); **Chinese Medicine** (Biomedicine; Medicine; Pharmacy; Traditional Eastern Medicine); **Communication** (Advertising and Publicity; Cinema and Television; Communication Arts; Journalism; Public Relations; Radio and Television Broadcasting); **Continuing Education** (Business and Commerce; Information Technology; International and Comparative Education; Preschool Education; Teacher Training); **Graduate**

Institute
Advancement of Chinese Medicine (Traditional Eastern Medicine); **Advancing Translational Medicine in Bone & Joint Diseases** (Rheumatology); **Business Development (Wing Lung Bank Institute)** (Business and Commerce); **Computational Mathematics** (Mathematics and Computer Science); **Contemporary China Studies** *(Advanced Institute)* (Asian Studies); **Creativity**; **East-West Studies (David C. Lam)** (Cultural Studies); **Enterprise Development**; **Environmental Sciences (Croucher Institute)** (Environmental Studies); **Environmental Sciences (HKBU - RCEES Joint Institute)** (Environmental Studies); **Journalism and Society** (Journalism; Social Studies); **Sino-Humanitas (Mr. Simon Suen and Mrs. Mary Suen)** (Asian Studies)

Academy
Sinology (Jao Tsung-I) (Asian Studies); **Visual Arts** (Visual Arts)

Centre
Advanced Luminescence Materials (Materials Engineering); **Advancement of English for Professionals** *(Jockey Club Centre)* (English); **Advancement of Social Sciences Research** (Social Sciences); **Applied Ethics** (Ethics); **Child Development** (Child Care and Development); **China Urban and Regional Studies** (Regional Studies; Urban Studies); **Chinese Cultural Heritage**; **CIE Wellness Promotion**; **Corporate Governance and Finance Policy**; **European Documentation** (European Studies); **Geo-Computation Studies** (Geophysics); **High Performance Cluster Computing Centre** *(Supported by Dell and Intel (HPCCC))* (Computer Engineering); **Hong Kong Chinese Medicine Authentication** (Traditional Eastern Medicine); **Hong Kong Energy Studies** (Energy Engineering); **Hong Kong Organic Resource**; **Human Resources Strategy and Development** (Human Resources); **Liberal Studies in Schools** *(Resource Centre)*; **Mathematical Imaging and Vision** (Mathematics and Computer Science); **Nonlinear Studies** (Physics); **Nonlinear and Complex Systems (Beijing-Hong Kong-Singapore Joint Centre)** (Biology; Chemistry; Computer Science; Mathematics; Physics); **Olympic Studies** (Sports Management); **Quantitative Systems Biology** (Biology); **Science Consultancy Services** (Computer Science; Mathematics; Natural Sciences); **Sino-Christian Studies** (Chinese; Christian Religious Studies); **Translation** (Translation and Interpretation)

Laboratory
Chemical Testing Services/Advanced Instrumentation Laboratory (Chemistry); **Dioxin Analysis**; **Surface Analysis and Material Characterization** (Materials Engineering)

Research Centre
Advancement of Social Sciences Research (Social Sciences); **Cancer and Inflammation Research (Shum Yiu Foon Shum Bik Chuen Memorial Centre)** (Oncology); **Chinese Businesses Case Research** (Business Administration); **Comparative Governance and Policy Research** (Government); **e-Transformation Technology Research**; **Media and Communication Research** (Communication Studies; Media Studies); **Modern History Research** (History; Modern History); **Pearl River Delta Environment (Sino-Forest Applied Research Centre)** (Environmental Studies); **Physical Recreation and Wellness Research (Dr Stephen Hui)** (Parks and Recreation); **Statistics Research and Consultancy** (Statistics); **Surface Analysis and Research** (Materials Engineering); **Ubiquitous Computing** (Computer Science); **Youth Research and Practice**

Research Institute
Applied Mathematics (Peking University-HKBU Joint Research Institute) (Applied Mathematics); **Changshu**; **HKBU-UIC Joint Institute of Research Studies**

History: Founded 1956 as Hong Kong Baptist College, became autonomous 1983, and acquired present status and title 1994.

Academic Year: September to June (September-January; January-June). MBA programme: September to May

Admission Requirements: Either Hong Kong Certificate of Education Examination (HKCEE), with Grade E/Level 2 or above in 6 subjects including Chinese Language (or French or German) and English Language with at least 5 subjects in a single sitting; and Hong Kong Advanced Level Examination (HKALE), with Grade E or above in Advanced Supplementary ('AS') subjects of Chinese Language and Culture, and use of English and either 2 advanced Level (AL) subjects or 1 AL subject plus 2 AS subjects obtainable in any two sittings or an acceptable equivalent qualification. Under the new 4-year education system from 2012, the general entrance requirements for applicants with Hong Kong Diploma of Secondary Education (HKDSE) would be: Level 3 for English Language and Chinese Language, and Level 2 for Mathematics, Liberal Studies and One Elective subject. Some programmes have specific minimum entrance requirements, or additions to the above General Entrance Requirements.

Main Language(s) of Instruction: English, Chinese

Degrees and Diplomas: *Bachelor's Degree*; *Master's Degree*; *Doctor's Degree*: **Accountancy; Biology; Biomedical Engineering; Chemistry; Chinese; Communication Arts; Computer Science; Economics; English; Film; Finance; Journalism; Literature; Management; Marketing; Mathematics; Philosophy; Physics; Religious Studies; Translation and Interpretation.**

Student Services: Academic Counselling, Canteen, Careers Guidance, Cultural Activities, Facilities for disabled people, Foreign Studies Centre, Health Services, Language Laboratory, Social Counselling, Sports Facilities

Publications: Research Report

Academic Staff *2011-2012*	TOTAL
FULL-TIME	**721**
PART-TIME	**969**
Student Numbers *2012-2013*	
All (Foreign included)	**13,477**

Last Updated: 26/09/13

LINGNAN UNIVERSITY (LU)

8 Castle Peak Road, Tuen Mun, Hong Kong
Tel: +852 2616-8888
Fax: +852 2463-8363
EMail: registry@ln.edu.hk
Website: http://www.ln.edu.hk

President: Leonard K Cheng (2013-)
Tel: +852 2616-8004 EMail: po@ln.edu.hk

Vice-President: Jesús Seade (2008-)

International Relations: Joanne Wing-han Lai
Tel: +852 2616-8970 EMail: joannelai@ln.edu.hk

Faculty

Arts (Chinese; Cultural Studies; English; History; Modern Languages; Philosophy; Translation and Interpretation; Visual Arts); **Business** (Accountancy; Computer Science; Finance; Insurance; International Business; Management; Marketing); **Social Sciences** (Economics; Political Sciences; Psychology; Social Policy; Sociology)

College

Community College and Further Education

Programme

Hong Kong and South China Historical Research (History; South Asian Studies); **Kwan Fong Cultural Research and Development** (Cultural Studies); **Public Governance** (Government)

Institute

Asia-Pacific Institute of Ageing Studies; **Hong Kong Institute of Business Studies**; **Lingan Institute of Further Education**

Centre

Asian Pacific Studies (Asian Studies; Pacific Area Studies); **Public Policy Studies**

Research Centre

Humanities Research (Arts and Humanities)

History: Founded 1967. A degree-conferring tertiary institution fully funded by Hong Kong Government through the University Grants Committee. Acquired present status and title 1999.

Academic Year: September to May (September-December; January-May)

Fees: Tuition: 42,100 per annum for local students; 100,000 per annum for non-local students (Hong Kong Dollar)

Main Language(s) of Instruction: English

Degrees and Diplomas: *Bachelor's Degree Honours*: **Business Administration; Chinese; Cultural Studies; English Studies; History; Philosophy; Social Sciences; Translation and Interpretation; Visual Arts.** *Master of Philosophy*: **Business Administration; Chinese; Cultural Studies; Economics; English; History; Philosophy; Social Sciences; Translation and Interpretation; Visual Arts.** *Doctor's Degree*: **Business Administration; Chinese; Cultural Studies; Economics; English; History; Philosophy; Social Sciences; Translation and Interpretation; Visual Arts.**

Student Services: Academic Counselling, Canteen, Careers Guidance, Facilities for disabled people, Health Services, Language Laboratory, Social Counselling, Sports Facilities

Academic Staff *2012-2013*	MEN	WOMEN	**TOTAL**
FULL-TIME	–	–	**188**
Student Numbers *2012-2013*			
All (Foreign included)	845	1,856	**2,701**

Last Updated: 27/09/13

THE CHINESE UNIVERSITY OF HONG KONG (CUHK)

Shatin, New Territories
Tel: +852 3943-6000
Fax: +852 2603-5544
EMail: oal@cuhk.edu.hk
Website: http://www.cuhk.edu.hk

Vice-Chancellor and President: Joseph J.Y. Sung (2010-)
Tel: +852 3943-8600 EMail: js_vcoffice@cuhk.edu.hk

Director of Communications and Public Relations: Amy Y.M Tsui Tel: +852 2609-8894 EMail: amytsui@cuhk.edu.hk

International Relations: Shally Fan, Director, Office of Academic Links Tel: +852 3943-7778 EMail: shallyfan@cuhk.edu.hk

Faculty

Arts (Anthropology; Chinese; Cultural Studies; English; Fine Arts; History; Japanese; Linguistics; Literature; Modern Languages; Music; Philosophy; Religious Studies; Theology; Translation and Interpretation); **Business Administration** (Accountancy; Economics; Finance; Hotel Management; Management; Marketing; Tourism); **Education** (Curriculum; Educational Administration; Educational Psychology; Physical Education; Sports); **Engineering** (Automation and Control Engineering; Computer Engineering; Computer Science; Electronic Engineering; Engineering Management; Information Technology; Mechanical Engineering); **Law** (Law); **Medicine** (Anaesthesiology; Anatomy; Biomedicine; Cell Biology; Gynaecology and Obstetrics; Medicine; Microbiology; Nursing; Oncology; Ophthalmology; Orthopaedics; Otorhinolaryngology; Paediatrics; Pathology; Pharmacy; Psychiatry and Mental Health; Public Health; Radiology; Surgery); **Science** (Biological and Life Sciences; Chemistry; Mathematics; Physics; Statistics; Traditional Eastern Medicine); **Social Science** (Architecture; Communication Studies; Economics; Geography (Human); Government; Journalism; Psychology; Public Administration; Social Work; Sociology)

Unit

English Language Teaching (English; Foreign Languages Education); **Office of University General Education** (Higher Education)

Programme

International Asian Studies (Asian Studies; International Studies); **Postgraduate - Arts** (Anthropology; Art History; Chinese; Christian Religious Studies; Cultural Studies; English; Fine Arts; History; Japanese; Linguistics; Literacy Education; Literature; Music; Native Language; Native Language Education; Philosophy; Religion; Religious Studies; Theology; Translation and Interpretation; Visual Arts); **Postgraduate - Business Administration** (Accountancy; Business Administration; Finance; Hotel Management; Leadership; Management; Management Systems; Marketing; Tourism); **Postgraduate - Education** (Chinese; Curriculum; Educational Administration; Educational and Student Counselling; English; Ethics; Foreign Languages Education; Humanities and Social Science Education; Mathematics Education; Native Language; Native Language Education; Physical Education; Preschool Education; Primary Education; Secondary Education; Sports); **Postgraduate - Engineering** (Automation and Control Engineering; Biomedical Engineering; Computer Engineering; Computer Science; E- Business/Commerce; Electronic Engineering; Engineering Management; Information Technology; Mechanical Engineering; Transport Management); **Postgraduate - Law** (Commercial Law; International Law; Law); **Postgraduate - Medicine** (Anaesthesiology; Anatomy; Biochemistry; Biomedical Engineering; Gynaecology and Obstetrics; Microbiology; Nursing; Ophthalmology; Orthopaedics; Otorhinolaryngology; Pathology; Pharmacology; Pharmacy; Physiology; Public Health; Radiology; Surgery); **Postgraduate - Science** (Biochemistry; Biology; Chemistry; Environmental Studies; Food Science; Insurance; Materials Engineering; Mathematics; Molecular Biology; Nutrition; Physics; Statistics; Traditional Eastern Medicine); **Postgraduate - Social Sciences** (Advertising and Publicity; Architecture; Clinical Psychology; Communication Studies; Earth Sciences; Ecology; Economics; Environmental Studies; Family Studies; Gender Studies; Geography; Geology; Government; Industrial and Organizational Psychology; Journalism; Media Studies; Natural Resources; Political Sciences; Psychology; Public Administration; Social and Community Services; Social Policy; Social Sciences; Social Welfare; Social Work; Sociology; Tourism); **Summer Studies**; **Undergraduate - Art** (Anthropology; Chinese; Cultural Studies; English; Fine Arts; History; Japanese; Linguistics; Literature; Music; Native Language; Philosophy; Religious Studies; Theology; Translation and Interpretation); **Undergraduate - Business Administration** (Accountancy; Actuarial Science; Business Administration; Commercial Law; Finance; Hotel Management; Insurance; International Business; Tourism); **Undergraduate - Education** (Chinese; English; Foreign Languages Education; Humanities and Social Science Education; Native Language Education; Physical Education; Preschool Education; Sports);

Undergraduate - Engineering (Automation and Control Engineering; Biomedical Engineering; Computer Engineering; Computer Science; Electronic Engineering; Engineering Management; Information Technology; Mathematics; Mechanical Engineering); **Undergraduate - Law** (Law); **Undergraduate - Medicine** (Medicine; Nursing; Pharmacy; Public Health); **Undergraduate - Science** (Biochemistry; Biology; Biotechnology; Cell Biology; Chemistry; Environmental Studies; Food Science; Information Technology; Mathematics; Molecular Biology; Nutrition; Physics; Statistics; Traditional Eastern Medicine); **Undergraduate - Social Sciences** (Architecture; Communication Studies; Economics; Geography (Human); Government; Human Resources; Journalism; Law; Psychology; Public Administration; Social Work; Sociology)

School

Continuing and Professional Studies *(School)* (Continuing Education)

Centre

China Studies (Chinese); **Chinese Language (Yale-in-China)** *(Centre)* (Chinese; Linguistics); **East Asian Studies** (East Asian Studies); **Learning Enhancement and Research** *(Centre)* (Educational Research)

Research Institute

Advanced Engineering (Shun Hing) (Bioengineering; Biomedical Engineering; Computer Science; Multimedia); **Advanced Integration Technology (Shenzhen Institute, Chinese Academy of Sciences)** (Technology); **Asia-Pacific Institute Business (APIB)** (Air Transport; Asian Studies; Business and Commerce; Finance; Government; Institutional Administration; Management; Marketing; Pacific Area Studies; Real Estate; Tourism); **Asia-Pacific Studies** (Asian Studies; Pacific Area Studies; South Asian Studies); **Biotechnology** *(Hong Kong)* (Biotechnology); **Cancer** (Oncology); **Chinese Medicine (ICM)** (Traditional Eastern Medicine); **Chinese Studies** (Ancient Civilizations; Archaeology; Chinese; Cultural Studies; Fine Arts; Museum Studies; Translation and Interpretation); **Diabetes and Obesity (HKIDO)** (Diabetology); **Digestive Disease** (Gastroenterology); **Economics and Finance** (Economics; Finance); **Educational Research (HKIER)** (Education; Educational Administration; Educational Research; Educational Technology; Educational Testing and Evaluation; Information Technology); **Global Economics and Finance** (Economics; Finance); **Health Sciences (Li Ka Shing)** (Health Sciences); **Human Communicative Research** (Speech Therapy and Audiology); **Humanities** (Arts and Humanities; Asian Religious Studies; Comparative Sociology; Cultural Studies; Social Sciences; Urban Studies); **Mathematical Sciences** *(Cooperative Centre)* (Mathematics); **Network Coding** (Computer Networks); **Optical Science and Technology** (Optical Technology); **Plant Molecular Biology and Agricultural Biothechnology** (Agriculture; Biotechnology; Molecular Biology); **Precision Engineering** (Measurement and Precision Engineering); **Science and Technology** (Bioengineering; Materials Engineering; Sports; Sports Medicine; Technology); **Space and Earth Information Sciences (ISEIS)** (Earth Sciences; Environmental Studies; Information Sciences; Surveying and Mapping; Telecommunications Engineering); **Supply Chains and Logistics** (Store Management; Transport Management); **Theoretical Computer Science and Communications** (Communication Studies; Computer Science); **Theoretical Physics** (Physics); **Vascular Medicine** (Medicine)

Further Information: Teaching Hospital at Prince of Wales Hospital. Teaching and Learning Resource Centre in Central Hong Kong.

History: Founded in 1963. A bilingual, bicultural (Chinese, English) institution of higher learning, consisting of nine Constituent Colleges: New Asia College (founded 1949), Chung Chi College (founded 1951), United College (founded 1956), Shaw College (founded 1986), Morningside College (2006), S.H. College (2006), C.W. Chu College (founded 2007), Wu Yee Sun College (founded 2007) and Lee Woo Sing College (founded 2007). A self-governing corporation financed from grants made by the HKSAR Government, and fees and donations from private sources.

Academic Year: August to July

Admission Requirements: Local students, Hong Kong Certificate of Education Examination (HKCEE) and Hong Kong Advanced Level Examination (HKALE) or General Certificate of Education Examination (Advanced Level) or other equivalent qualifications. Non-local students, possess a qualification obtained outside Hong Kong which qualifies them for university admission in the country/region where such qualification is obtained.

Fees: 120,000 per annum (for non-local students) (Hong Kong Dollar)

Main Language(s) of Instruction: Chinese, English

Degrees and Diplomas: *Bachelor's Degree*: **Business Administration; Education; Engineering; Law; Medicine; Nursing; Pharmacy; Traditional Eastern Medicine.** *Postgraduate Certificate/Diploma*; *Master's Degree*: **Accountancy; Architecture; Business Administration; Education; Fine Arts; Law; Medicine; Music; Nursing; Occupational Health; Pharmacology; Public Health; Religious Studies; Social Work; Traditional Eastern Medicine.** *Master of Philosophy*; *Doctor's Degree*: **Education; Law; Music; Nursing; Philosophy; Psychology.**

Student Services: Academic Counselling, Canteen, Careers Guidance, Cultural Activities, Facilities for disabled people, Health Services, Language Laboratory, Social Counselling, Sports Facilities

Publishing house: The Chinese University Press

Academic Staff *2011-2012*	MEN	WOMEN	**TOTAL**
FULL-TIME	743	233	**976**
PART-TIME	263	114	**377**
STAFF WITH DOCTORATE			
FULL-TIME	717	225	**942**

Student Numbers *2011-2012*			
All (Foreign included)	–	–	**14,817**
FOREIGN ONLY	–	–	**4,122**

Part-time students, 910.

Last Updated: 30/09/13

THE HONG KONG ACADEMY FOR PERFORMING ARTS (HKAPA)

1 Gloucester Road, Wan Chai, Hong Kong
Tel: +852 2584-8500
Fax: +852 2802-4372
EMail: aso@hkapa.edu
Website: http://www.hkapa.edu

Director: Adrian Walter (2004-)
Tel: +852 2584-8598 EMail: director@hkapa.edu

Deputy Director (Administration) and Registrar: Herbert Huey
Tel: +852 2584-8587 EMail: herberthuey.dir@hkapa.edu

Programme

Liberal Arts

School

Dance (Dance); **Drama** (Acting; Theatre); **Film and Television** (Film; Radio and Television Broadcasting; Video); **Music** (Music; Musical Instruments); **Theatre and Entertainment Arts** (Performing Arts; Theatre)

Department

Languages (Chinese; English; French; German; Italian; Japanese; Korean; Spanish)

Centre

Chinese Traditional Theatre Programme (Theatre)

History: Founded 1984. Provides professional education, training and research, reflecting the cultural diversity of Hong Kong.

Academic Year: September to June

Admission Requirements: Undergraduate: 5 subject passes, including English and Chinese, in the Hong Kong Certificate of Education Examination (HKCEE), and a Diploma awarded by the Academy. Equivalent certificates are also considered. Master's programmes: Bachelor's Degree in relevant discipline with requisite marks.

Main Language(s) of Instruction: Chinese, English

Accrediting Agency: Hong Kong Council for Accreditation of Academic and Vocational Qualifications

Degrees and Diplomas: *Diploma*: **Dance; Music; Opera.** *Bachelor's Degree Honours*: **Cinema and Television; Dance; Music; Theatre.** *Master's Degree*: **Cinema and Television; Dance;**

Music; Theatre. Also: Advance Diploma (2 yrs); Professional Diploma (1-2 yrs); and Foundation Certificate (1 yr).

Student Services: Academic Counselling, Canteen, Health Services, Language Laboratory

Last Updated: 12/11/13

THE HONG KONG INSTITUTE OF EDUCATION (HKIED)

10, Lo Ping Road, Tai Po, New Territories,
Hong Kong
Tel: +852 2948-8888
Fax: +852 2948-6000
EMail: info@ied.edu.hk
Website: http://www.ied.edu.hk

President: Stephen Cheung Yan-leung

International Relations: Fiona Wong, Head, International Office
Tel: +852 2948-7654
EMail: Fiona@ied.edu.hk

Faculty

Education and Human Development (FEHD) (Continuing Education; Curriculum; Education; Educational Administration; Educational and Student Counselling; Educational Psychology; Educational Sciences; International and Comparative Education; Preschool Education; Psychology; Special Education); **Humanities (FHM)** (Chinese; Cultural Studies; English; Linguistics; Literature; Native Language); **Liberal Arts and Social Sciences (FLASS)** (Cultural Studies; Environmental Studies; Health Education; Information Technology; Mathematics; Natural Sciences; Physical Education; Social Sciences)

School

Graduate School (GS) (Chinese; Communication Studies; Education; Educational Administration; Educational Psychology; English; English Studies; Foreign Languages Education; Linguistics; Mathematics; Mathematics Education; Music Education; Native Language; Native Language Education; Pedagogy; Psychology; Science Education; Visual Arts)

Research Centre

Asia Pacific Centre for Leadership and Change (APCLC) *(The Joseph Lau Luen Hung Charitable Trust Asia Pacific Centre)*; **Assessment (ARC); Childhood Research and Innovation (CCRI)** *(Faculty of Education Studies R&D Centre)*; **Chinese Literature and Literacy Culture (RCCLC)** (Literacy Education; South Asian Studies); **Education in Environmental Sustainability (CEES)** *(Faculty of Liberal Arts and Social Sciences)*; **Governance and Citizenship CGC); Greater China Studies (CGCS)** *(Faculty of Arts and Sciences R&D Centre)* (South Asian Studies); **Learning Study CLS)** *(Faculty of Education Studies R&D Centre)*; **Lifelong Learning Research and Development (CLLRD)** *(Faculty of Education Studies R&D Centre)* (Continuing Education; Educational Research); **Popular Culture in the Humanities (CPCH)** *(Faculty of Languages R&D Centre)* (Educational Research; Folklore); **Psychosocial Health and Aging (CPHA)** *(Faculty of Education and Human Development)*; **Religious and Spirituality Education (CRSE)** *(Faculty of Education Studies R&D Centre)* (Religious Education); **Small Class Teaching (CSCT); Special Educational Needs and Inclusive Education (CSENIE)** *(Faculty of Education Studies R&D Centre)* (Special Education)

History: Established in 1994. A self-accrediting publicly-funded institution.

Main Language(s) of Instruction: Chinese, English

Degrees and Diplomas: *Bachelor's Degree*; *Bachelor's Degree Honours*: **Arts and Humanities; Chinese; English; Environmental Studies; Handicrafts; Health Education; Mathematics; Modern Languages; Music; Nursing; Physical Education; Preschool Education; Visual Arts.** *Postgraduate Certificate/Diploma*: **Education; Psychology.** *Master's Degree*: **Chinese; Communication Arts; Education; English; Linguistics; Mathematics; Pedagogy.** *Master of Philosophy*; *Doctor's Degree*: **Education; Philosophy.**

Student Services: Academic Counselling, Careers Guidance, Facilities for disabled people, Social Counselling

Last Updated: 12/11/13

THE HONG KONG POLYTECHNIC UNIVERSITY (POLYU)

Hung Hom, Kowloon, Hong Kong
Tel: +852 2766-5111
Fax: +852 2764-3374
EMail: polyu@polyu.edu.hk
Website: http://www.polyu.edu.hk

President: Timothy W. Tong Tel: +852 2766-5211

Academic Secretary: Nancy Tong EMail: asdept@polyu.edu.hk

International Relations: Winnie Eley
Tel: +852 2766-5118 EMail: polyu.international@polyu.edu.hk

Faculty

Applied Science and Textiles (Applied Mathematics; Applied Physics; Biology; Chemical Engineering; Clothing and Sewing; Textile Technology); **Business** (Accountancy; Finance; International Business; Management; Marine Transport; Marketing; Transport Management); **Construction and Environment** (Building Technologies; Civil Engineering; Construction Engineering; Environmental Management; Environmental Studies; Real Estate; Regional Planning; Structural Architecture; Surveying and Mapping); **Engineering** (Computer Engineering; Electrical Engineering; Electronic Engineering; Industrial Engineering; Information Technology; Mechanical Engineering); **Health and Social Sciences** (Health Sciences; Medical Technology; Nursing; Optometry; Rehabilitation and Therapy; Social Sciences; Social Studies); **Humanities** (Asian Studies; Bilingual and Bicultural Education; Chinese; Education; English)

School

Design (Design); **Hotel and Tourism Management** (Hotel Management; Tourism)

History: Founded 1937. Became Hong Kong Technical College 1947 and then Hong Kong Polytechnic 1972. Acquired present status and title 1994.

Academic Year: September to June (September-January; January-June). Also Summer Term, June to August

Admission Requirements: Local Student, Hong Kong Diploma of Secondary Education (HKDSE); Non local student, an academic level equivalent to GCE A level standard, or International Baccalaureate (IB) Diploma

Fees: Local student, 42,100 per annum (1,405 per credit); non-local student, 100,000 per annum (3,335 per credit) (Hong Kong Dollar)

Main Language(s) of Instruction: Chinese, English

Degrees and Diplomas: *Sub-degree*; *Bachelor's Degree*; *Bachelor's Degree Honours*; *Postgraduate Certificate/Diploma*: **Accountancy.** *Master's Degree*: **Accountancy; Business Administration; Finance; Management; Transport Management.** *Doctor's Degree*: **Business Administration; Computer Engineering; Engineering; Health Sciences; Hotel Management; Textile Technology; Tourism.** Also Higher Diplomas (2 yrs)

Student Services: Academic Counselling, Canteen, Careers Guidance, Cultural Activities, Facilities for disabled people, Foreign Studies Centre, Health Services, Language Laboratory, Nursery Care, Social Counselling, Sports Facilities

Academic Staff *2012-2013*	**TOTAL**
FULL-TIME	**3,618**
Student Numbers *2012-2013*	
All (Foreign included)	**32,676**

Part-time students, 11,415.

Last Updated: 12/11/13

THE HONG KONG UNIVERSITY OF SCIENCE AND TECHNOLOGY (HKUST)

Clear Water Bay, Kowloon, Hong Kong
Tel: +852(2) 358-6000
Fax: +852(2) 358-0537
EMail: pao@ust.hk
Website: http://www.ust.hk

President: Tony F. Chan (2009-)
Tel: +852(2) 358-6101 EMail: ophkust@ust.hk

International Relations: Yvonne Lee, Head of International Affairs and Marketing Tel: +852(2) 358-6304 EMail: yvon@ust.hk

Unit

Advanced Engineering Materials Facility (Materials Engineering); **Animal and Plant Care Facility** (Animal Husbandry; Horticulture); **Biosciences Central Research Facility** (Biological and Life Sciences); **CLP Power Wind/Wave Tunnel Facility**; **Design and Manufacturing Services Facility** (Maintenance Technology); **Environmental Central Facility** (Environmental Studies); **Geotechnical Centrifuge Facility** (Geological Engineering); **Materials Characterization and Preparation Facilty** (Materials Engineering); **Nanoelectronics Fabrication Facility** (Microelectronics; Nanotechnology)

Division

Biomedical Engineering; **Environment** (Environmental Engineering)

School

Business and Management (Accountancy; Business and Commerce; Economics; Finance; Information Management; Management; Marketing); **Engineering** (Aeronautical and Aerospace Engineering; Chemical Engineering; Civil Engineering; Computer Engineering; Computer Science; Electrical and Electronic Engineering; Environmental Engineering; Industrial Engineering; Mechanical Engineering); **Humanities and Social Sciences** (Arts and Humanities; Modern Languages; Social Sciences); **Science** (Biological and Life Sciences; Chemistry; Mathematics; Physics)

Centre

Advanced Computing and Communication Technologies *(International Centre)* (Communication Studies; Computer Engineering); **Advanced Microsystem Packaging (CAMP)** (Electronic Engineering); **Applied Social and Economic Research (CASER)** (Economics; Social Studies); **Asian Family Business and Entrepreneurship Studies (Tanoto)** (Small Business); **Asian Financial Markets** (Banking; Finance); **Atmospheric Research (Nansha)** (Meteorology); **Building Energy Research (BERC) [Nansha]** (Energy Engineering); **Business Case Studies** (Business and Commerce); **Business Data Analysis** (Business and Commerce; Data Processing); **Business Strategy and Innovation** (Business and Commerce); **Cancer Research** (Oncology); **Chinese Linguistics** (Chinese; Linguistics); **Chinese Medicine R&D** (Traditional Eastern Medicine); **Cyberspace** (Computer Engineering); **Digital Life Research (Nansha)** (Computer Engineering); **Display Research** (Electronic Engineering); **Economic Development** (Economic and Finance Policy; Economics); **Electronic Commerce (Tongyi Industrial Group)** (E- Business/Commerce); **Engineering Materials and Reliability (CEMAR) [Nansha]** (Engineering); **Environment, Energy and Resource Policy (CEERP)** (Environmental Management); **Experimental Business Research (cEBR)** (Administration; Business Education); **FINETEX R&D**; **Fundamental Physics** (Physics); **Green Products and Processing Technologies (Nansha)** (Environmental Engineering); **HKUST LED-FPD Technology R&D** *(Foshan)* (Electrical and Electronic Engineering); **Hong Kong-Beijing UST Joint Research (Nansha)**; **Huawei-HKUST Innovation Laboratory**; **Investing (Value Partners)** (Finance); **Marketing and Supply Chain Management** (Marketing; Transport Management); **Metamaterials Research** (Materials Engineering); **Molecular Neuroscience** (Neurosciences); **New Element - HKUST Digital Healthcare Joint Research**; **Organizational Research (Hang Lung)**; **Photonics Technology**; **Polymer Processing and Systems (Nansha)** (Polymer and Plastics Technology); **RFID**; **Scientific Computation** (Applied Mathematics; Computer Science); **Semiconductor Product Analysis and Design Enhancement** (Electronic Engineering); **Smart and Sustainable Infrastructure Research** (Architecture); **South China Research**; **Space Science Research** (Astronomy and Space Science); **Statistical Sciences** (Statistics); **Stem Cell Research** (Cell Biology); **Survey Research**; **Sustainable Energy Technology (CSET)** (Energy Engineering); **Systems Biology and Human Health** (Biological and Life Sciences); **Technology Transfer**; **Visual Computing and Imaging Science at HKUST** (Computer Graphics); **Wireless Information Technology (CenWIT)** (Information Technology)

Laboratory

Advanced Displays and Optoelectronics Technologies (Partner SKL) (Optical Technology); **Molecular Neuroscience (SKL)** *(State Key Laboratory)* (Neurosciences)

Research Institute

Advanced Manufacturing (AMI) (Production Engineering); **Advanced Study (IAS)**; **Biotechnology Research (BRI)** (Biotechnology); **Emerging Markets Studies (IEMS)** *(HKUST)* (Business and Commerce); **Energy (HKUST)** (Energy Engineering); **Environment (IENV)**; **Europe**; **Glassblowing Facility**; **Hongkong Telecom Information Technology (HKTIIT)** (Information Technology; Telecommunications Engineering); **Integrated Microsystems (I2MS)** (Microelectronics); **Logistics and Supply Chain Management (LSCMI)** (Transport Management); **Nano Science and Technology (WMINST)** *(William Mong)* (Nanotechnology; Physical Engineering); **Shenzhen**; **Sino Software Research (SSRI)** (Software Engineering)

History: Founded 1988, and opened October 1991 as a technological university devoted to the advancement of learning and scholarship, with special emphasis on research, postgraduate education, and close collaboration with business and industry.

Academic Year: September to May (September-December; February-May)

Admission Requirements: Hong Kong Certificate of Education (HKCEE) and Hong Kong Advanced Level Examination (HKALE), or equivalent

Fees: 42,100 per annum (National); 120,000 per annum (International) (Hong Kong Dollar)

Main Language(s) of Instruction: English

Degrees and Diplomas: *Bachelor's Degree*; *Postgraduate Certificate/Diploma*; *Master's Degree*; *Master of Philosophy*; *Doctor's Degree*. Also Executive Master of Business Administration (EMBA)

Student Services: Academic Counselling, Canteen, Careers Guidance, Cultural Activities, Facilities for disabled people, Health Services, Language Laboratory, Social Counselling, Sports Facilities

Academic Staff *2012-2013*	**TOTAL**
FULL-TIME	**538**
Student Numbers *2012-2013*	
All (Foreign included)	**8,958**
FOREIGN ONLY	**3626**

Last Updated: 27/11/13

THE OPEN UNIVERSITY OF HONG KONG (OUHK)

30, Good Shepherd Street, Homantin, Kowloon, Hong Kong
Tel: +852 2711-2100
Fax: +852 2715-0760
EMail: info@ouhk.edu.hk
Website: http://www.ouhk.edu.hk

President: John Chi-Yan Leong
Tel: +852 2768-6089 EMail: jcyleong@ouhk.edu.hk

Registrar: Sylvia Hui Wan-ling Tel: +852 2768-6651

International Relations: Stephen Ng Chin-ming, Director, Public Affairs Unit Tel: +852 2768-6350 EMail: jmfcheng@ouhk.edu.hk

School

Arts and Social Sciences (Arts and Humanities; Chinese; Economics; Film; Law; Literature; Performing Arts; Psychology; Public Administration; Regional Studies; Social Sciences; Translation and Interpretation; Writing); **Business and Administration (Lee Shau Kee)** (Accountancy; Business Administration; E- Business/Commerce; Finance; International Business; Law; Management; Management Systems; Marketing); **Education and Languages** (Education; Foreign Languages Education; Preschool Education); **Science and Technology** (Applied Chemistry; Computer Engineering; Computer Science; Electronic Engineering; Engineering; Environmental Studies; Industrial Design; Information Technology; Mathematics; Nursing)

Institute

Professional and Continuing Education (Li Ka Shing) (Arts and Humanities; Business Administration; Communication Arts; Educational Psychology; Finance; Health Sciences; Law; Management; Marketing; Modern Languages; Tourism)

History: Founded 1989 as Open Learning Institute of Hong Kong, acquired present self-accrediting status 1997. Its role is to make higher education available to all, principally through open and flexible learning.

Academic Year: Distance-learning programmes: April to March, (April-September; October-March); Full-time face-to-face programmes: September to August

Admission Requirements: Distance-learning programmes: Anyone aged 17 or above. No academic entry requirements, except for postgraduate and professional programmes. Full-time face-to-face programmes: Requirements vary according to different degree programmes: Form-6 school leavers, Associate Degree holders, Hong-Kong Advanced Level Examination (HKALE) and its equivalents

Fees: Undergraduate programmes: 52,000-156,000; Master's programme: 96,600 (Hong Kong Dollar)

Main Language(s) of Instruction: English, Chinese

Degrees and Diplomas: *Diploma*; *Bachelor's Degree*; *Master's Degree*; *Master of Philosophy*; *Doctor's Degree*: **Business Administration.**

Student Services: Academic Counselling, Careers Guidance, Facilities for disabled people

Publishing house: The OUHK Press

Academic Staff *2012-2013*	**TOTAL**
FULL-TIME	**735**
PART-TIME	**609**
STAFF WITH DOCTORATE	
FULL-TIME	**90**
Student Numbers *2012-2013*	
All (Foreign included)	**18,712**

Distance students, 11705.

Last Updated: 28/11/13

THE UNIVERSITY OF HONG KONG (HKU)

Pokfulam Road, Hong Kong
Tel: +852 2859-2111
Fax: +852 2858-2549
EMail: cpao@hku.hk; admissions@hku.hk
Website: http://www.hku.hk

Vice-Chancellor and President: Peter Mathieson (2014-) EMail: vcoffice@hku.hk

Director of Communications: Katherine Ma (2006-) Tel: +852 2859-2601 EMail: katherine.ma@hku.hk

International Relations: Henry W.K. Wai, Registrar, International Officer (2002-) Tel: +852 2859-2222 EMail: henrywai@hku.hk

Faculty

Architecture (Architecture); **Arts** (Arts and Humanities; Modern Languages); **Business and Economics** (Business and Commerce; Economics); **Dentistry** (Dentistry); **Education** (Education); **Engineering** (Engineering); **Law** (Law); **Medicine (Li Ka Shing)** (Medicine); **Science** (Natural Sciences); **Social Sciences** (Social Sciences)

School

Chinese Medicine (Traditional Eastern Medicine); **Graduate**; **Professional and Continuing Education (HKU SPACE)** (Continuing Education)

Institute

Advanced IT Training (Information Technology); **AIDS**; **Cardiovascular Science and Medicine** (Cardiology); **China and Global Development** (East Asian Studies); **Cyberport**; **Economics and Business Strategy** (Economics); **Emerging Technologies** (Technology); **Family (HKU)** (Family Studies); **Human Reproduction** (Genetics); **Humanities and Social Sciences** (Asian Studies); **Kadoorie** (Environmental Studies); **Management (Poon Kam Kai)** (Management); **Marine Science (Swire)** (Marine Science and Oceanography); **Mathematical Research** (Mathematics); **Medical and Health Sciences Education** (Science Education); **Transport Studies** (Transport Management)

Centre

Advancement in Special Education (Special Education); **Advancement of Chinese Language Education and Research** (Chinese); **Ageing (Sau Po)** (Gerontology); **Alimentary Research and Education** (Food Science); **American Studies** (American Studies); **Anthropological Research** (Anthropology); **Applied English Studies** (English Studies); **Applied Spectroscopy and Analytical Sciences** (Chemistry); **Architecture and Urban Design for China and Hong Kong** (Architecture and Planning); **Asian Entrepreneurship and Business Values** (Small Business); **Asian Studies** (Asian Studies); **Behavioural Health** (Health Sciences); **Biomedical Engineering** (Bioengineering); **Buddhist Studies** (Asian Religious Studies); **Cancer Research** (Oncology); **Cellular Biology** (Cell Biology); **China Development Studies** *(International Centre)* (East Asian Studies); **China Financial Research** (Finance); **Chinese Law** (Law); **Chinese Management** (Management); **Chong Yuet Ming Amenities**; **Civil Society and Governance** (Social Sciences); **Cleft Lip and Palate** (Surgery); **Clinical Trials** (Health Sciences); **Cognitive Science** (Cognitive Sciences); **Communication Disorders** (Communication Disorders); **Comparative and Public Law** (Comparative Law; Public Law); **Construct I.T.** (Building Technologies); **Criminology** (Criminology); **Cultural Policy Research** (Cultural Studies); **Development and Resources for Students**; **E-Commerce Infrastructure Development** (E- Business/Commerce); **Educational Leadership** (Educational Administration); **Electrical Energy Systems** (Electrical Engineering); **Endocrinology and Diabetes** (Diabetology; Endocrinology); **Enhancement of Teaching and Learning** (Pedagogy); **Environmental Engineering Research** (Environmental Engineering); **European Studies** (European Studies); **Financial Innovation and Risk Management** (Finance); **Fong Shu Chuen Amenities**; **Genomic Sciences** (Genetics); **Globalization and Cultures** (International Studies); **Hong Kong Prehistory** (Archaeology); **Hong Kong Putonghua Education and Assessment** (Educational Testing and Evaluation); **Human Development and Birth Defects**; **Human Reproduction** (Genetics); **Humanities and Medicine** (Arts and Humanities; Medicine); **Infection (Carol Yu)** (Virology); **Influenza Research** (Virology); **Information Security and Cryptography** (Information Technology); **Information Technology in Education** (Information Technology); **Infrastructure and Construction Industry Development** (Building Technologies); **Journalism and Media Studies** (Journalism; Media Studies); **Language** (Modern Languages); **Law and Technology** (Law; Technology); **Lung Fu Shan Environmental Education** (Environmental Studies); **Materials Science** (Materials Engineering); **Navigational Dentistry** (Dentistry); **Neuroscience** (Neurosciences); **Nonlinear Mechanics** (Mechanical Engineering); **Pokfulam Amenities**; **Real Estate and Urban Economics** (Real Estate); **Renewable Energy in Architecture** (Architectural and Environmental Design); **Research in Plant Drugs Development** (Pharmacology); **Social Sciences Research** (Social Sciences); **Study of Liver Disease** (Hepatology); **Teachers of English Language Education** (Foreign Languages Education); **Technology Support** (Technology); **Theoretical and Computational Physics** (Physics); **Urban Studies and Urban Planning** (Town Planning)

Research Centre

Advanced Mechanical Systems (Fong) (Mechanical Engineering); **Asia Case** (Asian Studies); **Chinese Language Cognitive Science** (Chinese); **Comparative Education** (Education); **Electric Vehicles** (Automotive Engineering); **Geographical/Land Information System** (Geography); **Heart, Brain, Hormone & Healthy Aging** (Gerontology); **HKU-Pasteur** (Virology); **Rock Engineering** (Geological Engineering); **Social Sciences** (Social Sciences); **Women's Studies** (Women's Studies)

Further Information: Also Teaching Hospitals

History: Founded 1911. A self-governing body financed mainly by the HKSAR government.

Academic Year: September to June

Admission Requirements: Hong Kong Certificate of Education (HKCEE) or equivalent, and Hong Kong Advanced Level Examination (HKALE) or equivalent, or other qualifications as equivalent

Fees: Local students, 42,100 per annum, overseas students, 135,000 (Hong Kong Dollar)

Main Language(s) of Instruction: English, Chinese

Degrees and Diplomas: *Bachelor's Degree*; *Postgraduate Certificate/Diploma*; *Master's Degree*; *Master of Philosophy*; *Doctor's Degree*

Student Services: Academic Counselling, Canteen, Careers Guidance, Health Services, Language Laboratory, Social Counselling, Sports Facilities

Publications: Current Research

Publishing House: University Press

Academic Staff *2010-2011*	MEN	WOMEN	TOTAL
FULL-TIME	721	287	**1,008**
Student Numbers *2010-2011*			
All (Foreign included)	10,554	11,523	**22,077**
FOREIGN ONLY	2,157	2,525	**4,682**

Last Updated: 28/11/13

PRIVATE INSTITUTION

HONG KONG SHUE YAN UNIVERSITY

10 Wai Tsui Crescent, Braemar Hill Road, North Point, Hong Kong
Tel: + 852 2570-7110
Fax: + 852 2806-8044
EMail: info@hksyu.edu
Website: http://www.hksyu.edu/

President: Henry H.L. Hu

Vice President, Administration: Fai-chung Hu

Department

Accounting (Accountancy); **Business Administration** (Business Administration); **Chinese Language and Literature** (Chinese; Literature); **Counselling and Psychology** (Educational and Student Counselling; Educational Psychology; Psychology); **Economics and Finance** (Economics; Finance); **English Language and Literature** (English; Literature); **History** (History); **Journalism and Communication** (Communication Studies; Journalism; Mass Communication); **Law and Business** (Commercial Law; Law); **Social Work** (Social Work); **Sociology** (Social Sciences; Sociology)

Institute

Conflict Engagement and Resolution (IICER) (Political Sciences)

Laboratory

Cognitive Psychology (Cognitive Sciences; Psychology); **Neuropsychology** (Neurological Therapy; Psychology)

Research Centre

Advanced Study in Dynamic Cooperative Games (SRS Consortium) (Business Administration; Economics; Management; Mathematics; Political Sciences; Statistics); **Business, Economic and Public Policy** (Public Administration); **Contemporary China** (Asian Studies); **Counselling and Research Centre; Enterprise and Social Development** (Small Business; Social Studies); **Online Communication** (Computer Networks); **Qualitative Social Research** (Social Studies); **Survey and Research Centre** (Journalism; Mass Communication; Statistics)

History: Founded in 1971 as Hong Kong Shue Yan College. Acquired current title and status 2006. Hong Kong's first private university.

Admission Requirements: Hong Kong Diploma of Secondary Education (or equivalent) in at least six subjects, including English and Chinese.

Fees: 55,000 per annum (Degree Programme); 45,000 per annum (Cooperative Degree Programme) (Hong Kong Dollar)

Main Language(s) of Instruction: English, Chinese

Degrees and Diplomas: *Bachelor's Degree Honours*; *Master's Degree*: **Business Administration; Social Work.** Split-degree Undergraduate programmes also offered with overseas institutions. Cooperative Master's degree programmes with overseas institutions.

Last Updated: 27/09/13

China - Macao SAR

STRUCTURE OF HIGHER EDUCATION SYSTEM

Description:

Higher education is offered by public and private institutions. Some of the institutions offer a wide variety of programmes, while others specialize in specific areas.

Stages of studies:

University level first stage: *Bacharelato/Licenciatura*

The minimum time needed to complete a Bacharelato is three years. Generally, students with Form five or equivalent qualifications can take this degree programme after passing the entrance examinations offered individually by institutions. The programmes are offered by universities, university level institutions, and polytechnic/professional institutes.

The minimum time needed to complete a Licenciatura is four years. Students with Form six or equivalent qualifications can take this degree programme after passing the entrance examinations offered individually by institutions. The programmes are offered by universities, university level institutions, and polytechnic/professional institutes.

University level second stage: *Mestrado*

Mestrado programmes involve both course work and the writing (and defence) of a dissertation/thesis. The period of course work is between one and two years. Generally, students with a Licenciatura are qualified to apply for the programme which is offered by universities and university-level institutions.

University level third stage: *Doutoramento*

Generally, students with a Mestrado or equivalent qualification can apply for Doutoramento programme. The duration of the programmes is between three and five years. The programmes are offered by universities and university-level institutions.

ADMISSION TO HIGHER EDUCATION

Admission to university-level studies:

Name of secondary school credential required: Certificate of Secondary (Form 5) Education

For entry to: Bacharelato programmes

Name of secondary school credential required: Certificate of Senior Secondary Education

For entry to: Associate degrees; Licenciatura programmes

Foreign students admission:

Definition of foreign student: Non-Resident of Macao.

Admission requirements: Depends on requirements imposed by individual institutions.

Entry regulations: Visa.

RECOGNITION OF STUDIES

Quality assurance system:

The main decree governing the establishment of higher education institutions and tertiary courses launched in Macao is Decree-Law n° 11/91/M.

NATIONAL BODIES

Gabinete de Apoio ao Ensino Superior (Tertiary Education Services Office)

Director: Sou Chio Fai

Avenida do Dr. Rodrigo Rodrigues, n°s 614A-640

Edificio Long Cheng, 5° a 7° andares

Macau

Tel: +853 2834 5403
Fax: +853 2831 8401
EMail: info@gaes.gov.mo; aeees@gaes.gov.mo
WWW: http://www.gaes.gov.mo
Role of national body: Government department responsible for higher education affairs in Macao.

Data for academic year: 2012-2013
Source: IAU from Tertiary Education Services Office, Macao SAR, 2013. Bodies 2016.

INSTITUTIONS

PUBLIC INSTITUTIONS

INSTITUTE FOR TOURISM STUDIES

Instituto de Formação Turística (IFT)
Colina de Mong-Há, Macao
Tel: +853 2856-1252
Fax: +853 2851-9058
EMail: iftpr@ift.edu.mo
Website: http://www.ift.edu.mo

President: Fanny Vong (2001-)
Tel: +853 8598-3084 EMail: fanny@ift.edu.mo

Administrative Officer: Louisa Lam
Tel: +853 8598-3126 EMail: louisa@ift.edu.mo

International Relations: Louisa Lam
Tel: +853 8598-3126 EMail: louisa@ift.edu.mo

College
Tourism (Tourism)

School
Professional and Continuing Education (Tourism)

Centre
Advanced Tourism Studies *(Macao-Europe)* (Tourism)

History: Founded 1995.

Main Language(s) of Instruction: English

Degrees and Diplomas: *Diploma/Certificate*: **Cooking and Catering.** *Licenciatura*: **Tourism.**

Student Services: Library
Last Updated: 27/02/14

MACAO POLYTECHNIC INSTITUTE

Instituto Politécnico de Macau (IPM)
Rua Luís Gonzaga Gomes, Macao
Tel: +853 2857-8722
Fax: +853 2830-8801
EMail: registry@ipm.edu.mo
Website: http://www.ipm.edu.mo

President: Heong-Iok Lei (1999-)
Tel: +853 599-6288 EMail: hilei@ipm.edu.mo

Secretary-General: Wai Cheong Chan
Tel: +853 557-275 EMail: waichan@ipm.edu.mo

School
Arts (Fine Arts); **Business** (Business Administration; Business and Commerce); **Continuing Education and Special Projects** (Continuing Education); **Health Sciences** (Health Sciences); **Language and Translation** (Modern Languages; Translation and Interpretation); **Physical Education and Sports** (Physical Education; Sports); **Public Administration** (Public Administration)

Academy
Seniors (Adult Education)

Centre
MPI-Bell Centre of English (English)

Research Centre
Gaming Teaching (Business and Commerce); **One Country Two Systems** (Administration); **Portuguese Language Teaching** (Portuguese); **Social, Economic and Public Policy** (Social Sciences)

History: Founded 1991.

Main Language(s) of Instruction: Chinese, English

Degrees and Diplomas: *Bacharelato*; *Licenciatura*. Also joint Master Degree Programme with Hong Kong Polytechnic University and Monash University.
Last Updated: 27/02/14

IAU UNIVERSITY OF MACAU

Universidade de Macau (UM)
Avenida Padre Tomás Pereira, Taipa, Macao
Tel: +853 2883-1622
Fax: +853 2883-1694
EMail: webmaster@umac.mo
Website: http://www.umac.mo

Rector: Wei Zhao (2008)
Tel: +853 8397-4301 EMail: UMRector_Zhao@umac.mo

Head of Information and Public Relations Office: Katrina Wai Kam Cheong Tel: +853 8397-4336 EMail: katrinac@umac.mo

Vice-Rector Administration: Alex LAI Iat Long
Tel: +853 3974-303 EMail: alexlai@umac.mo

International Relations: Annie Chan, Functional Head of International Relations Tel: +853 8397-4301 EMail: anniec@umac.mo

Faculty
Arts and Humanities (Chinese; English Studies; Portuguese); **Business Administration** (Accountancy; Business Administration; Business and Commerce; Finance; Information Management; Management; Marketing); **Education** (Chinese; Curriculum; Education; Educational Administration; Educational and Student Counselling; Educational Psychology; English; Physical Education; Preschool Education; Primary Education; Sports); **Health Sciences** (Biomedicine; Molecular Biology); **Law** (Comparative Law; European Union Law; International Business; International Law; Law; Political Sciences); **Science and Technology** (Civil Engineering; Computer Engineering; Computer Science; Electrical and Electronic Engineering; Electronic Engineering; Engineering; Environmental Engineering; Information Sciences; Mathematics; Mechanical Engineering); **Social Sciences** (Communication Arts; Economics; Government; History; Psychology; Public Administration; Sociology)

Institute
Chinese Medical Sciences (ICMS) (Biomedicine; Traditional Eastern Medicine)

Academy
Asia-Pacific Academy of Economics and Management (Economics; Management)

Centre
Continuing Education (Continuing Education); **English Language** (English); **Pre-University Studies** (Secondary Education); **Teaching and Learning Enhancement (CTLE)** (Teacher Training)

Research Centre
Business Research Training *(Faculty of Business Administration)* (Business and Commerce); **Educational** (Education); **Humanities in South China** (South Asian Studies); **Information and Communication Technology in Education** (Communication Studies; Education; Information Technology); **Japanese Studies** (Japanese); **Luso-Asian Studies** (Asian Studies); **Macau Studies** (Asian Studies); **Scientific and Technological Research**; **Social Science Research Centre on Contemporary China** (Social Sciences)

Research Institute
Advanced Legal Studies (IALS) (Law); **Study of Commercial Gaming** *(Faculty of Business Administration)* (Business and Commerce)

History: Founded 1981 as University of East Asia, a private institution. Became public institution 1988. Acquired present status and title 1991. Financially supported by the government, tuition fees and donations.

Academic Year: September to June

Admission Requirements: Completion of secondary school education (Form 6, Grade 12) and UM entrance examination

Fees: For foreign students only, Bacharelato's Degree 28,100, Bachelor's Degree 34,600 per annum, Master's Degree (whole programme): MBA, 85,000 and non-MBA: 76,800, Ph.D (whole programme), 94,500 (Pataca)

Main Language(s) of Instruction: Portuguese, English, Chinese

Degrees and Diplomas: *Bacharelato*: **Business Administration; Education; Engineering; Fine Arts; Law; Social Sciences.** *Postgraduate Diploma/Certificate*: **Education; Law.** *Mestrado*: **Business Administration; Education; Engineering; Fine Arts; Law; Social Sciences.** *Doutoramento*: **Biomedicine; Business Administration; Education; Fine Arts; Law; Molecular Biology; Social Sciences.**

Student Services: Academic Counselling, Canteen, Careers Guidance, Cultural Activities, Facilities for disabled people, Health Services, Language Laboratory, Social Counselling, Sports Facilities

Publications: Journal of Macau Studies

Last Updated: 27/02/14

PRIVATE INSTITUTIONS

CITY UNIVERSITY OF MACAU

Universidade da Cidade de Macau (CUM)

3° Andar, Edificio Royal Centre, Avenida do Dr. Rodrigo Rodrigues, Macao
Tel: +853 2878-1698
Fax: +853 2878-1691
EMail: info@cityu.edu.mo
Website: http://www.cityu.edu.mo

Rector: Yan Zexian

Executive Director: Chan Chon Pat

Faculty
Humanities and Social Science (Humanities and Social Science Education); **International Tourism and Management** (Tourism); **Management** (Management); **Portuguese Programs** (Portuguese)

School
Continuing Studies (Continuing Education)

Institute
Economic Research (Economics); **International Open**; **Macau Development** (Development Studies); **Tourism and Gaming** (Tourism)

Research Centre
Linguistic Studies (Linguistics); **Macau Social and Economic Development** (Development Studies; Economics; Social Studies)

Research Institute
Official Portuguese-speaking Countries (Portuguese)

History: Founded 1981 as the University of East Asia (UEA), restructured 1988 to become the public University of Macau, Macao Polytechnic Institute and the privately-owned East Asia Open Institute (Macau). Renamed 1992 Asia International Open University (Macau) by collaboration of East Asia Open Institute (Macau) and the Portuguese National Open University, and 2011 Universidade da Cidade de Macau (City University of Macau).

Main Language(s) of Instruction: Chinese, English, Portuguese

Degrees and Diplomas: *Bacharelato*; *Mestrado*; *Doutoramento*

Last Updated: 03/04/13

KIANG WU NURSING COLLEGE OF MACAU

Instituto de Enfermagem Kiang Wu de Macau (KWNC)

Est. Repouso No.35, Macao
Tel: +853 8295-6200
Fax: +853 2836-5204
EMail: admin@kwnc.edu.mo
Website: http://www.kwnc.edu.mo/

President: Iat-Kio Van (1999-)
Tel: +853 295-6202 EMail: van@kwnc.edu.mo

International Relations: Hoi Ieng Cheong, Deputy Executive Officer EMail: yoki@kwnc.edu.mo

Programme
Nursing (Nursing)

History: Founded 1923 as Kiang Wu Nursing School. Acquired present status and title 2002.

Main Language(s) of Instruction: Chinese, English

Degrees and Diplomas: *Diploma/Certificate*; *Bacharelato*: **Nursing.** *Postgraduate Diploma/Certificate*: **Nursing.** *Mestrado*: **Nursing.**

Student Services: IT Centre, Language Laboratory, Library

Academic Staff *2014-2015*	**TOTAL**
FULL-TIME	**55**
PART-TIME	**5**
STAFF WITH DOCTORATE	
FULL-TIME	**11**
Student Numbers *2014-2015*	
All (Foreign included)	**279**

Last Updated: 27/02/14

MACAU INSTITUTE OF MANAGEMENT

Instituto de Gestão de Macau (MIM)

Rua de Xangai No. 175, Edif. ACM, 9° Andar, Macao
Tel: +853 2832-3233
Fax: +853 2832-3267
EMail: registry@mim.edu.mo
Website: http://www.mim.edu.mo

Director: Kwing Chiu Oscar Chan

Programme
Accountancy (Accountancy); **Business Administration** (Business Administration)

History: Founded 1988, acquired present status and title 2000.

Main Language(s) of Instruction: Chinese, English

Degrees and Diplomas: *Bacharelato*; *Mestrado*. Also Higher Diploma.

Last Updated: 03/04/13

MACAU MILLENNIUM COLLEGE

Instituto Milénio de Macau (MMC)
Alameda Dr. Carlos d'Assumpção No. 255 China Civil Plaza 8/F, Macao
Tel: +853 2878-8186
Fax: +853 2878-8246
EMail: info@mmc.edu.mo
Website: http://www.mmc.edu.mo

President: Leung Chuen Chau

Vice-President: Kai-Cheong Fok

Chancellor: Ambrose So

International Relations: Kai-Cheong Fok, Vice-President

Department

Business Studies (Business and Commerce); **Literature** (Asian Studies)

History: Founded 2001.

Main Language(s) of Instruction: Chinese

Degrees and Diplomas: *Associate Degree*: **Cultural Studies; Hotel Management; Management.** *Licenciatura*: **Hotel Management; Management.**

Student Services: IT Centre, Language Laboratory, Library

Last Updated: 28/02/14

MACAU UNIVERSITY OF SCIENCE AND TECHNOLOGY

Universidade de Ciência e Tecnologia de Macau (MUST)
Avenida Wai Long, Taipa, Macao
Tel: +853 2888-1122
Fax: +853 2888-0022
EMail: aaxu@must.edu.mo
Website: http://www.must.edu.mo

Rector: Liang Liu

International Relations: Xi Chen, Vice Rector
Tel: +853 8897-2238 EMail: xichen@must.edu.mo

Faculty

Chinese Medicine (Traditional Eastern Medicine); **Health Sciences** (Health Sciences); **Hospitality and Tourism Management** (Hotel Management; Tourism); **Humanities and Arts** (Arts and Humanities); **Information Technology** (Information Technology); **Law** (Law)

School

Business (Administration; Management); **Continuing Education**; **Graduate Studies**

Department

General Education

Institute

Social and Cultural Research (Social Sciences); **Space Science** (Aeronautical and Aerospace Engineering); **Sustainable Development** (Development Studies)

Research Institute

Applied Research in Medicine and Health (Health Sciences)

History: Founded 2000.

Main Language(s) of Instruction: Chinese, English

Degrees and Diplomas: *Bacharelato*; *Mestrado*: **Accountancy; Business Administration; Communication Arts; Finance; Information Technology; Management; Nursing; Public Administration; Public Health; Tourism; Traditional Eastern Medicine.** *Doutoramento*: **Business Administration; Communication Arts; Information Technology; Management; Public Health; Tourism; Traditional Eastern Medicine.**

Student Services: Canteen, Cultural Activities, Health Services, IT Centre, Library, Residential Facilities, Sports Facilities

Last Updated: 27/02/14

UNIVERSITY OF SAINT JOSEPH

Universidade de São José (USJ)
Rua de Londres, N. 16, Nape, Macao
Tel: +853 8796-4400
Fax: +853 2872-5517
EMail: international@usj.edu.mo
Website: http://www.usj.edu.mo

Rector: Peter Stilwell (2012-)
Tel: +853 8796-4440 EMail: rector@usj.edu.mo

Director of Rector's Office: Lavena Cheong
Tel: +853 8796-4444 EMail: lavenacheong@usj.edu.mo

International Relations: Ana Paula Mota, Manager, International Relations Tel: +853 8796-4440 EMail: paulamota@usj.edu.mo

School

Arts, Letters and Sciences (Arts and Humanities; Education; Philosophy; Psychology; Social Studies); **Christian Studies** (Christian Religious Studies; Religion; Religious Studies); **Intelligent Systems and Technology** (Computer Science; Design; Information Technology; Technology); **Management, Leadership and Government** (Business Administration; Government; International Business; Leadership; Management; Marketing)

Centre

Language (English; French; Japanese; Portuguese; Russian; Spanish); **Russian** (Russian)

Research Centre

African Research and Development Studies (African Studies; Development Studies); **Arts Research for Human Expression** (Fine Arts); **Economic and Cultural Relations between China and Portuguese-speaking Countries**; **Environmental Sciences** (Environmental Studies); **Global and Strategic Studies** (Political Sciences; Social Sciences); **History and Heritage Studies** (Heritage Preservation; History; Southeast Asian Studies); **Psychological Research and Practice** (Psychology)

Further Information: Also Graduate School, which overseas all postgraduate programmes.

History: Founded 1996. Formerly known as Instituto Inter-Universitário de Macau (Macao Inter-University Institute). Acquired current status and title 2009.

Academic Year: September to July

Admission Requirements: Successful completion of Year 12 of secondary studies

Fees: 45,000 per annum, Undergraduate; 62,000-80,000 per programme, Master's degree; 50,000 per annum, PhD (Pataca)

Main Language(s) of Instruction: English

Degrees and Diplomas: *Bacharelato*; *Licenciatura*; *Mestrado*; *Doutoramento*

Student Services: Academic Counselling, Canteen, Careers Guidance, Cultural Activities, Facilities for disabled people, Foreign Studies Centre, Language Laboratory, Social Counselling, Sports Facilities

Publications: Compass

Academic Staff *2010-2011*	MEN	WOMEN	**TOTAL**
FULL-TIME	45	26	**71**
PART-TIME	57	32	**89**
STAFF WITH DOCTORATE			
FULL-TIME	20	7	**27**
Student Numbers *2012-2013*			
All (Foreign included)	–	–	**1,839**

Last Updated: 11/03/13

China - Taiwan

STRUCTURE OF HIGHER EDUCATION SYSTEM

Description:

Higher education is provided by junior colleges, colleges, and universities, both public and private.

Stages of studies:

University level first stage: *Bachelor's degree*

Admission to this first stage is based on the results obtained in the Universities and Colleges Joint Entrance Examination. A total of 128 credits is required for a Bachelor's degree. In most disciplines Bachelor's degree programs are four years in length. The exceptions are architecture (five years), veterinary medicine (five years), dentistry (six years), and medicine (seven years). Bachelor's degree programs undertaken at the Open University and at the Open University of Kaohsiung are seven to eight years in length.

University level second stage: *Master's degree*

Further specialization leads to a Master's degree which requires two to four years of study, and completion of a shorter thesis or related project. A Master's degree is commenced following completion of a Bachelor's degree. Some Master's degrees may be undertaken at an open university.

University level third stage: *Doctorate*

The third stage leads to the highest level university degree, the Doctorate. This requires a minimum of a further two years' study and research, and completion of a major thesis/dissertation.

ADMISSION TO HIGHER EDUCATION

Admission to university-level studies:

Name of secondary school credential required: Senior High School Leaving Certificate

Name of secondary school credential required: Senior Vocational School Leaving Certificate

Alternatives to credentials: Equivalent education level giving eligibility to enter university.

Admission requirements: There is no longer a common unified entrance exam. Individual institutions may require applicants to pass an entrance examination or special screening tests which they themselves determine. Individual institutions' entrance examinations and tests are subject to approval by the Ministry of Education.

Other requirements: Taiwan higher education institutions have multi-channel admission. Individual institutions and departments determine any additional entrance requirements. These may be specific to particular disciplines, courses, and/or the degree stage. Other basic requirements include completing the registration process.

Foreign students admission:

Definition of foreign student: 1. An individual of foreign nationality who has never held nationality of the Republic of China (R.O.C.) status and who does not possess an overseas Chinese student status at the time of their application.

2. An individual of foreign nationality who has resided overseas continuously for no less than 6 years is qualified to apply for admission.

3. An individual of foreign nationality who plans to apply to study in a department of medicine, dentistry, or Chinese medicine must have resided overseas continuously for no less than 8 years.

Admission requirements: Foreign students must have completed their senior secondary education. Individual institutions and departments determine any additional entrance requirements. These may be specific to particular disciplines, courses, and/or the degree stage.

Health requirements: Foreign students must undertake a health check as part of the student visa requirements.

Language proficiency: Students must have a reasonable command of the Chinese language. This is the only medium of instruction at undergraduate level.

RECOGNITION OF STUDIES

Quality assurance system:

Higher Education Evaluation and Accreditation Council of Taiwan is responsible for accrediting programs and educational institutions.

Bodies dealing with recognition:

Higher Education Evaluation and Accreditation Council of Taiwan - HEEACT

7F., No.179, Section 1, Heping E. Road
Da-an District
Taipei City 106
Tel: +886(2) 3343-1200
Fax: +886(2) 3343-1211
EMail: service@heeact.edu.tw
WWW: http://www.heeact.edu.tw

NATIONAL BODIES

Ministry of Education

Minister: Se-Hwa Wu
No.5, Zhongshan S. Rd., Zhongzheng District
Taipei City 10051
Tel: +886(2) 7736-6666
WWW: http://www.moe.gov.tw
Role of national body: Formulates policy and standards for all types of education at all levels in both the public and private sectors.

Department of Higher Education - DHE

Director-General: Wen-Ling Hunag
Ministry of Education
No.5, Zhongshan S. Rd., Zhongzheng District
Taipei City 10051
Tel: +886(2) 7736-6666
Fax: +886(2) 2397-6942
EMail: wenling@mail.moe.gov.tw
WWW: http://english.moe.gov.tw/content.asp?CuItem=15155
Role of national body: The Department of Higher Education assists and guides higher education institutions to carry out their respective missions and mandates, maintain quality, and undertake further development.

Higher Education Evaluation and Accreditation Council of Taiwan - HEEACT

Executive Director: Tung-liang Chiang
7F., No.179, Section 1, Heping E. Road
Da-an District
Taipei City 106
Tel: +886(2) 3343-1200
Fax: +886(2) 3343-1211
EMail: service@heeact.edu.tw
WWW: http://www.heeact.edu.tw
Role of national body: Responsible for the evaluation and accreditation of universities and colleges.

Foundation for International Cooperation in Higher Education of Taiwan - FICHET

CEO: Sam Sy-Sand Liaw
Room 202, No. 5, Lane 199, Kinghua Street
Taipei City 10650
Tel: +886(2) 2322-2280
Fax: +886(2) 2322-2528
EMail: fichet@fichet.org.tw
WWW: http://www.fichet.org.tw

Role of national body: FICHET facillitates international cooperation between Taiwanese and foreign universities. Its main operations are the planning of international educator assemblies in Europe, America, and Asia, and fostering human resources in the field of international education administration.

FICHET currently represents 114 member universities as an umbrella body for 4 national associations:

1. the Association of National Universities of Taiwan (ANUT);
2. the Association of Private Universities and Colleges of Taiwan (APUC);
3. the Association of National Universities and Colleges of Technology of Taiwan (ANUCT); and
4. the Association of Private Universities and Colleges of Technology of Taiwan (APUCT).

Data for academic year: 2014-2015

Source: IAU from Service Education du Bureau de Représentation de Taipei en France, from Ministry of Education, 2014. Bodies 2016.

INSTITUTIONS

PUBLIC INSTITUTIONS

NATIONAL CENTRAL UNIVERSITY (NCU)

300, Jhong-da Road, Jhongli, Taoyuan 320
Tel: +886(3) 422-7151
Fax: +886(3) 422-6062
EMail: ncu7010@ncu.edu.tw
Website: http://www.ncu.edu.tw

President: Jing-Yang Jou
Tel: +886(3) 425-4822 EMail: ncu7010@ncu.edu.tw

Secretary-General: Kuo-Kai Shyu
Tel: +886(3) 422-7151, Ext. 57010 EMail: kkshyu@ee.ncu.edu.tw

International Relations: Ping-Yu Hsu, Dean, Office of Office of International Affairs
Tel: +886(3) 420-7094 EMail: ncu57080@ncu.edu.tw

College

Earth Sciences (Astronomy and Space Science; Earth Sciences; Geology; Health Sciences; Marine Science and Oceanography; Meteorology; Organic Chemistry; Physics; Seismology; Water Science); **Electrical Engineering and Computer Science** (Computer Engineering; Computer Networks; Computer Science; Educational Technology; Electrical Engineering; Information Technology; Software Engineering; Telecommunications Engineering); **Engineering** (Biomedical Engineering; Chemical Engineering; Civil Engineering; Construction Engineering; Energy Engineering; Engineering; Environmental Engineering; Materials Engineering; Mechanical Engineering); **Hakka Studies** (Cultural Studies; Government; Law; Native Language; Social Sciences); **Liberal Arts** (Art History; Arts and Humanities; Asian Studies; Chinese; Cultural Studies; English; Fine Arts; French; History; Literature; Opera; Philosophy; Teacher Training; Visual Arts); **Management** (Accountancy; Business Administration; Economics; Finance; Human Resources; Industrial and Production Economics; Industrial Management; Information Management; Management); **Science** (Astronomy and Space Science; Biological and Life Sciences; Biology; Chemistry; Cognitive Sciences; Computer Science; Mathematics; Natural Sciences; Neurosciences; Optics; Physics; Statistics)

History: Founded 1962 incorporating Institute of Geophysics founded 1962, as re-establishment of National Central University, founded in Nanking 1915 and closed 1949. A State institution financed by the government.

Academic Year: August to June (August-January; February-June)

Admission Requirements: Graduation from high school and entrance examination or equivalent

Fees: 25,000-30,000 per semester (New Taiwan Dollar)

Main Language(s) of Instruction: Chinese, English

Degrees and Diplomas: *Bachelor's Degree*; *Master's Degree*: **Accountancy; Astronomy and Space Science; Biological and Life Sciences; Biology; Biomedical Engineering; Biophysics; Business Administration; Chemical Engineering; Chemistry; Chinese; Civil Engineering; Cognitive Sciences; Computer Engineering; Computer Networks; Construction Engineering; Cultural Studies; Development Studies; Earth Sciences; Economics; Electrical Engineering; Energy Engineering; English; Environmental Engineering; Finance; Fine Arts; French; Geology; Geophysics; Human Resources; Industrial and Production Economics; Industrial Management; Information Management; International Studies; Literature; Management; Marine Science and Oceanography; Materials Engineering; Mathematics; Native Language; Neurosciences; Optical Technology; Optics; Philosophy; Physics; Software Engineering; Statistics; Teacher Training; Telecommunications Engineering; Water Science.** *Doctorate*: **Astronomy and Space Science; Biological and Life Sciences; Biology; Biomedical Engineering; Biophysics; Business Administration; Chemical Engineering; Chemistry; Chinese; Civil Engineering; Cognitive Sciences; Computer Engineering; Construction Engineering; Cultural Studies; Earth Sciences; Economics; Educational Technology; Electrical Engineering; Energy Engineering; Environmental Engineering; Finance; Geology; Geophysics; Human Resources; Industrial and Production Economics; Industrial Management; Information Management; Literature; Marine Science and Oceanography; Materials Engineering; Mathematics; Meteorology; Native Language; Neurosciences; Optical Technology; Optics; Philosophy; Statistics; Teacher Training; Telecommunications Engineering; Water Science.**

Student Services: Academic Counselling, Canteen, Careers Guidance, Cultural Activities, Facilities for disabled people, Health Services, IT Centre, Language Laboratory, Library, Nursery Care, Sports Facilities

Publications: Research Summaries

Last Updated: 06/03/14

NATIONAL CHANGHUA UNIVERSITY OF EDUCATION (NCUE)

1, Jin-de Rd., Changhua 50007
Tel: +886(4) 723-2105
Fax: +886(4) 724-3074
EMail: en@cc2.ncue.edu.tw; prdnt@cc.ncue.edu.tw
Website: http://www.ncue.edu.tw

President: Yanguang Guo
Tel: +886(4) 723-2105, Ext. 1030
EMail: prdnt@cc.ncue.edu.tw; ykuo@cc.ncue.edu.tw

Secretary-General: Shih-Chi Chang
Tel: +886(4) 721-1010 EMail: shihchi@cc.ncue.edu.tw

International Relations: Hon Man Lee, Dean, Office of International and Cross-strait Affairs
Tel: +886(4) 723-2105, Ext. 1801 EMail: leehm@cc.ncue.edu.tw

Faculty
Science (Biology; Biotechnology; Chemistry; Educational Sciences; Electronic Engineering; Mathematics; Natural Sciences; Optical Technology; Physics; Statistics)

College
Education (Education; Psychology; Rehabilitation and Therapy; Social Work; Special Education); **Liberal Arts** (Art Education; Arts and Humanities; English; Environmental Studies; Fine Arts; Foreign Languages Education; Geography; History; Literature; Parks and Recreation; Tourism; Translation and Interpretation)

School
Management (Accountancy; Business Administration; Information Management; Information Sciences; Information Technology; Management; Marketing; Transport Management)

Institute
Engineering (Computer Engineering; Electrical Engineering; Electronic Engineering; Engineering; Information Technology; Mechanical Engineering; Telecommunications Engineering); **Social and Sports Science** (Civics; Physical Education; Public Administration; Social Sciences; Sports; Sports Management; Sports Medicine); **Technical and Vocational Education** (Automotive Engineering; Business Education; Education; Finance; Human Resources; Industrial Arts Education; Technology Education)

Centre
General Education

History: Founded 1971 as Taiwan Provincial College of Education. Renamed National Taiwan College of Education 1980. Acquired present status and title 1989.

Academic Year: August to July (September-January; February-July)

Admission Requirements: Graduation from high school and entrance examination

Main Language(s) of Instruction: Chinese

Degrees and Diplomas: *Bachelor's Degree*; *Master's Degree*: **Art Education; Arts and Humanities; Biology; Biotechnology; Business Administration; Business Education; Chemistry; Civics; Computer Engineering; Computer Science; Education; Electrical Engineering; Electronic Engineering; Environmental Studies; Finance; Fine Arts; Foreign Languages Education; Geography; History; Human Resources; Industrial Arts Education; Information Management; International Business; Linguistics; Literature; Marketing; Mathematics; Mathematics Education; Optical Technology; Parks and Recreation; Physical Education; Physics; Psychology; Science Education; Special Education; Sports; Sports Management; Sports Medicine; Statistics; Technology Education; Telecommunications Engineering; Tourism; Translation and Interpretation; Transport Management.** *Doctorate*: **Education; Geography; History; Human Resources; Industrial Arts Education; Mathematics Education; Psychology; Science Education; Special Education; Technology Education.**

Student Services: Canteen, IT Centre, Library, Residential Facilities, Sports Facilities

Publications: Business Education; Journal; Journal of Industrial Education; Journal of Special Education; Studies in Language Education

Academic Staff *2013-2014*: Total 397

Student Numbers *2013-2014*: Total: c. 7,702

Last Updated: 07/03/14

NATIONAL CHENG KUNG UNIVERSITY (NCKU)

No.1, University Road, Tainan 70101
Tel: +886(6) 275-7575
Fax: +886(6) 236-8660
EMail: em50100@email.ncku.edu.tw
Website: http://www.ncku.edu.tw

President: Huey-Jen Su EMail: em50000@email.ncku.edu.tw

Secretary-General: Chin-Cheng Chen
Tel: +886(6) 275-7575, Ext. 50030
EMail: em50030@email.ncku.edu.tw

International Relations: Hung Huang Cheng, Vice President for International Affairs
Tel: +886(6) 275-7575, Ext. 50951
EMail: em50950@email.ncku.edu.tw

College
Bioscience and Biotechnology (Biological and Life Sciences; Biology; Biotechnology; Botany; Computer Science; Tropical Agriculture); **Electrical Engineering and Computer Science** (Artificial Intelligence; Computer Engineering; Computer Science; Electrical Engineering; Information Technology; Microelectronics; Telecommunications Engineering); **Engineering** (Aeronautical and Aerospace Engineering; Air Transport; Biomedical Engineering; Chemical Engineering; Civil Engineering; Electronic Engineering; Energy Engineering; Engineering; Engineering Management; Environmental Engineering; Geography; Hydraulic Engineering; Marine Engineering; Marine Science and Oceanography; Materials Engineering; Mechanical Engineering; Surveying and Mapping); **Liberal Arts** (Arts and Humanities; Chinese; English; Fine Arts; History; Literature; Modern Languages; Native Language); **Management** (Accountancy; Banking; Business Administration; Finance; Health Sciences; Industrial Management; Information Management; International Business; Management; Parks and Recreation; Physical Education; Statistics; Telecommunications Services; Transport and Communications; Transport Management); **Medicine** (Anaesthesiology; Anatomy; Behavioural Sciences; Biochemistry; Biotechnology; Cell Biology; Dentistry; Dermatology; Forensic Medicine and Dentistry; Gerontology; Gynaecology and Obstetrics; Health Sciences; Immunology; Laboratory Techniques; Medical Technology; Medicine; Microbiology; Molecular Biology; Neurology; Nursing; Occupational Health; Occupational Therapy; Ophthalmology; Oral Pathology; Orthopaedics; Otorhinolaryngology; Paediatrics; Parasitology; Pathology; Pharmacology; Pharmacy; Physical Therapy; Physiology; Psychiatry and Mental Health; Public Health; Radiology; Rehabilitation and Therapy; Surgery; Urology); **Planning and Design** (Architecture; Design; Industrial Design; Town Planning); **Sciences** (Applied Mathematics; Astronomy and Space Science; Astrophysics; Chemistry; Earth Sciences; Mathematics; Natural Sciences; Optical Technology; Optics; Physics); **Social Sciences** (Economics; Education; Law; Political Sciences; Psychology; Social Sciences)

Programme
Cross-College Elite Programme

Further Information: Also Affiliated Hospital

History: Founded 1931 as Tainan Higher Technical School. Acquired present status and title 1971.

Academic Year: September to June (September-January; February-June)

Admission Requirements: Applicants must be graduates or under-graduates of accredited universities or college or senior high school graduates

Fees: 25,000-45,000 per semester (New Taiwan Dollar)

Main Language(s) of Instruction: Chinese, English

Degrees and Diplomas: *Bachelor's Degree*; *Master's Degree*: **Accountancy; Aeronautical and Aerospace Engineering; Air Transport; Anatomy; Architecture; Astronomy and Space Science; Astrophysics; Banking; Behavioural Sciences; Biology; Biomedical Engineering; Biotechnology; Botany; Business Administration; Cell Biology; Chemical Engineering; Chemistry; Chinese; Civil Engineering; Computer Engineering; Computer Science; Dentistry; Design; Earth Sciences; Economics; Education; Electrical Engineering; Electronic Engineering; Engineering; English; Environmental Engineering; Finance; Fine Arts; Gerontology; Health Sciences; History; Hydraulic Engineering; Immunology; Industrial Design; Industrial Management; Information Management; Information Technology; International Business; Laboratory Techniques; Law; Leisure Studies; Literature; Management; Marine Engineering; Materials Engineering; Mathematics; Mechanical Engineering; Medicine; Microbiology; Microelectronics; Molecular Biology; Nanotechnology; Natural Resources; Nursing; Occupational Health; Occupational Therapy; Optics; Pharmacology; Pharmacy; Physical Education; Physical Therapy; Physics; Physiology; Political Sciences; Psychology; Public Health; Statistics; Surveying and Mapping; Telecommunications Engineering; Telecommunications Services; Town**

Planning; Transport Management. *Doctorate*: **Accountancy; Aeronautical and Aerospace Engineering; Applied Mathematics; Architecture; Astronomy and Space Science; Astrophysics; Banking; Biological and Life Sciences; Biology; Biomedical Engineering; Biotechnology; Business Administration; Chemical Engineering; Chemistry; Chinese; Civil Engineering; Computer Engineering; Computer Science; Design; Earth Sciences; Education; Electrical Engineering; Engineering; English; Environmental Engineering; Finance; Health Sciences; History; Hydraulic Engineering; Industrial Design; Industrial Management; Information Management; Information Technology; International Business; Law; Literature; Management; Marine Engineering; Materials Engineering; Mechanical Engineering; Medicine; Microelectronics; Nanotechnology; Natural Resources; Occupational Health; Optical Technology; Pharmacology; Pharmacy; Physics; Political Sciences; Public Health; Statistics; Surveying and Mapping; Telecommunications Engineering; Town Planning; Transport and Communications.**

Student Services: Academic Counselling, Canteen, Careers Guidance, Cultural Activities, Facilities for disabled people, Health Services, IT Centre, Language Laboratory, Library, Nursery Care, Social Counselling, Sports Facilities

Last Updated: 07/03/14

NATIONAL CHENGCHI UNIVERSITY (NCCU)

64,Sec.2, Zhi-Nan Rd., Wenshan District, Taipei 11605
Tel: +886(2) 293-93091
Fax: +886(2) 293-79611
EMail: www@nccu.edu.tw
Website: http://www.nccu.edu.tw

President: Se Hwa Wu
Tel: +886(2) 936-8068 EMail: president@nccu.edu.tw

Secretary-General: Cai-Yan Li
Tel: +886(2) 939-0169 EMail: secrt@nccu.edu.tw

International Relations: Shu-Heng Chen, Dean, Office of International Cooperation
Tel: +886(2) 293-87279 EMail: research@nccu.edu.tw

College

Commerce (Accountancy; Banking; Business Administration; Business and Commerce; Finance; Information Technology; Insurance; International Business; Statistics); **Communication** (Advertising and Publicity; Journalism; Mass Communication; Radio and Television Broadcasting); **Education** (Education; Educational Administration; Preschool Education; Teacher Training); **Foreign Languages** (Arabic; English; European Languages; French; German; Japanese; Korean; Linguistics; Literature; Modern Languages; Slavic Languages; Spanish; Turkish); **International Affairs** (Eastern European Studies; International Relations; International Studies); **Law** (Administrative Law; Civil Law; Constitutional Law; Criminal Law; Law); **Liberal Arts** (Archiving; Arts and Humanities; Chinese; Foreign Languages Education; History; Information Sciences; Library Science; Literature; Philosophy; Religious Studies); **Science** (Applied Physics; Computer Science; Mathematics; Neurosciences; Psychology); **Social Sciences** (Asian Studies; Development Studies; Economics; Ethnology; Finance; Labour and Industrial Relations; Pacific Area Studies; Political Sciences; Public Administration; Social Policy; Social Sciences; Social Work; Sociology)

Research Centre

Aboriginal Studies (Social Sciences); **China Studies** (Asian Studies); **Creativity and Innovation Studies**; **Election Study** (Political Sciences); **Humanities** (Arts and Humanities); **Mind, Brain and Learning** (Neurosciences); **Study of Chinese Religions** (Asian Religious Studies); **Taiwan Studies** (Asian Studies); **Third Sector**

Research Institute

International Relations (International Relations)

History: Founded 1927 as Special School for the Training of Administrative Personnel, became Central Institute of Political Science 1929 and University 1946. Closed 1949 and re-established in Taiwan 1954 by the Ministry of Education. A State institution.

Academic Year: August to July (August-January; February-July)

Admission Requirements: Graduation from high school, or recognized foreign equivalent, and entrance examination

Main Language(s) of Instruction: Chinese

Degrees and Diplomas: *Bachelor's Degree*; *Master's Degree*: **Accountancy; Architectural and Environmental Design; Archiving; Asian Studies; Banking; Business Administration; Computer Science; Development Studies; Economics; Educational Administration; English; Ethnology; European Languages; Finance; Foreign Languages Education; History; Information Sciences; Information Technology; Insurance; International Business; International Relations; International Studies; Japanese; Journalism; Korean; Law; Library Science; Linguistics; Literature; Mass Communication; Mathematics; Modern Languages; Neurosciences; Pacific Area Studies; Philosophy; Political Sciences; Preschool Education; Psychology; Public Administration; Radio and Television Broadcasting; Real Estate; Religious Studies; Slavic Languages; Social Work; Sociology; Statistics; Surveying and Mapping; Teacher Training.** *Doctorate*: **Accountancy; Asian Studies; Banking; Computer Science; Development Studies; Education; English; Ethnology; Finance; Foreign Languages Education; History; Information Technology; Insurance; International Business; International Relations; Journalism; Literature; Pacific Area Studies; Philosophy; Political Sciences; Psychology; Public Administration; Real Estate; Religious Studies; Social Work; Statistics; Teacher Training.**

Student Services: Academic Counselling, Careers Guidance, Cultural Activities, Facilities for disabled people, Foreign Studies Centre, Health Services, IT Centre, Language Laboratory, Library, Sports Facilities

Publications: America and Europe Monthly; Bulletin of Library and Information Science; Chinese Accounting Review; East Asia Quarterly; Issues and Studies (in Spanish, Chinese, Japanese, English, and French); Journalistic Studies; Mainland China Studies; Management Review; National Chengchi University Legal Essays

Last Updated: 20/03/14

NATIONAL CHI NAN UNIVERSITY (NCNU)

1, University Road, Puli, Nantou Hsien 545
Tel: +886(49) 291-0960
Fax: +886(49) 291-0413
EMail: julianne@ncnu.edu.tw; yssung@ncnu.edu.tw
Website: http://www.ncnu.edu.tw

President: Oliver Yu-Long Su
Tel: +886(49) 291-0960, Ext. 2000
EMail: president@ncnu.edu.tw; yosu@ncnu.edu.tw

Secretary-General: Tung-Wen Sun
Tel: +886(49) 291-0960, Ext. 2100
EMail: sec@ncnu.edu.tw; twsun@ncnu.edu.tw

International Relations: Jen-Shin Hong, Dean of International Affairs
Tel: +886(49) 291-0960, Ext. 3650
EMail: oiancnu@gmail.com; jshong@ncnu.edu.tw

College

Education (Adult Education; Continuing Education; Education; Educational Administration; Educational and Student Counselling; Educational Technology; International and Comparative Education); **Humanities** (Anthropology; Arts and Humanities; Chinese; English; Foreign Languages Education; History; Literature; Management; Public Administration; Social Policy; Social Work; Southeast Asian Studies); **Management** (Banking; Business Administration; Economics; Finance; Hotel and Restaurant; Industrial Management; Information Management; International Business; Leisure Studies; Management; Tourism); **Science and Technology** (Applied Chemistry; Civil Engineering; Computer Engineering; Computer Science; Electrical Engineering; Electronic Engineering; Information Technology; Materials Engineering; Optical Technology; Seismology)

Section

Professional and Continuing Studies; **Research and Development**

Centre

Culture, Education and Economic Development of Indigenous Peoples (Cultural Studies; Economics; Education); **General**

Education; **Language Teaching and Research**; **Southeast Asian Studies** (Administration; Economics; Political Sciences; Sociology); **Teacher Education** (Teacher Training)

Research Centre

Family Education (Family Studies)

History: Founded 1995.

Fees: Tuition, 27,639-32,745 (New Taiwan Dollar)

Main Language(s) of Instruction: Chinese

Degrees and Diplomas: *Bachelor's Degree*; *Master's Degree*: **Adult Education; Anthropology; Applied Chemistry; Banking; Biomedicine; Business Administration; Chinese; Civil Engineering; Computer Engineering; Computer Science; Continuing Education; Curriculum; Educational Administration; Educational and Student Counselling; Educational Technology; Electrical Engineering; Electronic Engineering; English; Finance; Foreign Languages Education; History; Hotel and Restaurant; Information Management; Information Technology; International and Comparative Education; International Business; Leisure Studies; Literature; Management; Materials Engineering; Optical Technology; Physical Education; Political Sciences; Public Administration; Social Studies; Social Welfare; Social Work; Southeast Asian Studies; Telecommunications Engineering; Thai Languages; Tourism; Vietnamese.** *Doctorate*: **Adult Education; Applied Chemistry; Banking; Chinese; Civil Engineering; Computer Engineering; Computer Science; Continuing Education; Economics; Educational Administration; Educational and Student Counselling; Electrical Engineering; Finance; History; Information Management; Information Technology; International and Comparative Education; International Business; Literature; Malay; Social and Community Services; Social Policy; Social Studies; Social Welfare; Social Work; Southeast Asian Studies; Telecommunications Engineering; Thai Languages; Vietnamese.**

Student Services: Academic Counselling, Facilities for disabled people, Health Services, IT Centre, Library, Nursery Care, Residential Facilities, Sports Facilities

Publications: The National Chi Nan University Journal; The National Chi Nan University News

Academic Staff *2013-2014*: Total: c. 550

Student Numbers *2013-2014*: Total: c. 6,000

Last Updated: 07/03/14

NATIONAL CHIAO TUNG UNIVERSITY (NCTU)

1001 University Road, Hsinchu 30010
Tel: +886(3) 571-2121
Fax: +886(3) 572-1500
EMail: nctuwww@cc.nctu.edu.tw
Website: http://www.nctu.edu.tw/english/index.php

President: Yan-Hwa Wu Lee
Tel: +886(3) 571-8083 EMail: president@mail.nctu.edu.tw

Dean of General Affairs: Shyh-Chang Huang
Tel: +886(3) 571-2121, Ext. 51501
EMail: schuang@mail.nctu.edu.tw

International Relations: Shyh-Jye Jou, Vice President, Office of International Affairs
Tel: +886(3) 513-1250 EMail: vp_ia@nctu.edu.tw

College

Biological Science and Technology (Bioengineering; Biological and Life Sciences; Biology; Biotechnology; Chemical Engineering; Computer Science; Microbiology); **Computer Science** (Biomedical Engineering; Computer Engineering; Computer Networks; Computer Science; Multimedia); **Electrical and Computer Engineering** (Biomedical Engineering; Computer Engineering; Electrical Engineering; Electronic Engineering; Industrial Engineering; Optics); **Engineering** (Civil Engineering; Engineering; Environmental Engineering; Materials Engineering; Mechanical Engineering; Nanotechnology); **Hakka Studies** (Anthropology; Arts and Humanities; Communication Studies; Cultural Studies; Ethnology; History; Information Technology; Literature; Mass Communication; Social Sciences; Sociology); **Humanities and Social Sciences** (Aesthetics; Architecture; Art Therapy; Arts and Humanities; Communication Studies; Computer Graphics; Cultural Studies; Design; East Asian Studies; Education; English; Foreign Languages Education; Industrial Design; Linguistics; Literature; Mass Communication; Media Studies; Modern Languages; Multimedia; Music; Music Theory and Composition; Musical Instruments; Musicology; Phonetics; Political Sciences; Singing; Social Sciences; Translation and Interpretation); **Management** (Business Administration; Data Processing; Engineering Management; Human Resources; Industrial Engineering; Industrial Management; Information Management; Information Technology; Management; Marketing; Transport Engineering; Transport Management); **Photonics** (Biomedical Engineering; Medical Technology; Optical Technology; Optics; Physics; Solid State Physics); **Science** (Applied Chemistry; Applied Mathematics; Mathematics; Mathematics and Computer Science; Molecular Biology; Physics; Statistics)

Department

Chalmers International Taiwan Office

Centre

General Education (Arts and Humanities; Biotechnology; Business Administration; Communication Studies; Cultural Studies; Economics; Electronic Engineering; Engineering; Gender Studies; History; Information Sciences; International Studies; Literature; Management; Modern Languages; Natural Sciences; Philosophy; Political Sciences; Psychology; Social Sciences; Sociology; Writing)

Group

Advancement of Fundamental Science Teaching (Science Education)

History: Founded 1958 as Institute of Electronics. Undergraduate departments opened 1964. Became College of Engineering 1967. A State institution.

Academic Year: August to July (August-January; February-July)

Admission Requirements: Graduation from high school and entrance examination

Main Language(s) of Instruction: Chinese, English

Degrees and Diplomas: *Bachelor's Degree*; *Master's Degree*: **Applied Chemistry; Applied Mathematics; Applied Physics; Architecture; Automation and Control Engineering; Bioengineering; Biological and Life Sciences; Biology; Biomedical Engineering; Biomedicine; Biotechnology; Computer Engineering; Computer Graphics; Computer Networks; Computer Science; Construction Engineering; Cultural Studies; Education; Electrical Engineering; Electronic Engineering; Environmental Engineering; Ethnology; Foreign Languages Education; Industrial Management; Information Technology; Linguistics; Literature; Management; Mass Communication; Materials Engineering; Measurement and Precision Engineering; Media Studies; Microwaves; Molecular Biology; Multimedia; Music Theory and Composition; Musical Instruments; Musicology; Nanotechnology; Optical Technology; Optics; Physics; Robotics; Safety Engineering; Singing; Social Studies; Sound Engineering (Acoustics); Statistics; Telecommunications Engineering.** *Doctorate*: **Applied Chemistry; Applied Mathematics; Applied Physics; Architecture; Bioengineering; Biological and Life Sciences; Biology; Biomedicine; Biotechnology; Business Administration; Chemical Engineering; Computer Engineering; Computer Networks; Computer Science; Cultural Studies; Design; Education; Electrical Engineering; Engineering Management; Finance; Industrial Design; Industrial Engineering; Industrial Management; Information Management; Management; Mathematics and Computer Science; Molecular Biology; Optical Technology; Optics; Physics; Social Studies; Statistics; Transport Engineering; Transport Management; Visual Arts.**

Student Services: IT Centre, Library, Residential Facilities, Social Counselling

Last Updated: 10/03/14

NATIONAL CHIAYI UNIVERSITY (NCYU)

No. 300 Syuefu Rd., Chiayi 60004
Tel: +886(5) 271-7000
Fax: +886(5) 271-7095 +886(5) 271-7006
EMail: secretary@mail.ncyu.edu.tw; oia@mail.ncyu.edu.tw
Website: http://www.ncyu.edu.tw

President: Robin Y.-Y. Chiou
Tel: +886(5) 271-7100
EMail: presidentlet@mail.ncyu.edu.tw; rychiou@mail.ncyu.edu.tw

Vice President for Administrative Affairs: Huan-Hung Wu
Tel: +886(5) 226-3411, Ext. 1000
EMail: vicepresidenta@mail.ncyu.edu.tw; whh@mail.ncyu.edu.tw

International Relations: Yu-Jang Li, Dean, Office of International Affairs Tel: +886(5) 271-7299 EMail: yjli@mail.ncyu.edu.tw

College

Agriculture (Agriculture; Agronomy; Animal Husbandry; Biological and Life Sciences; Biotechnology; Cell Biology; Forest Products; Forestry; Genetics; Horticulture; Landscape Architecture; Molecular Biology; Plant Pathology; Veterinary Science; Zoology); **Humanities and Arts** (Applied Linguistics; Arts and Humanities; Chinese; Cultural Studies; English; Fine Arts; Foreign Languages Education; Geography; History; Literature; Modern Languages; Music; Performing Arts; Visual Arts); **Life Sciences** (Aquaculture; Biochemistry; Biological and Life Sciences; Biotechnology; Ecology; Food Science; Immunology; Microbiology; Molecular Biology; Natural Resources; Pharmacology; Zoology); **Management** (Agricultural Business; Banking; Business Administration; E-Business/Commerce; Economics; Finance; Hotel and Restaurant; Information Technology; Management; Marketing; Parks and Recreation; Tourism; Transport Management); **Science and Engineering** (Applied Chemistry; Applied Mathematics; Applied Physics; Bioengineering; Civil Engineering; Computer Engineering; Computer Science; Electrical Engineering; Electronic Engineering; Energy Engineering; Engineering; Hydraulic Engineering; Mechanical Engineering; Natural Sciences; Water Science); **Teachers** (Education; Educational Administration; Educational and Student Counselling; Educational Technology; Mathematics Education; Physical Education; Preschool Education; Science Education; Special Education; Teacher Training)

Graduate Institute

Public Policy (Administration; Constitutional Law; Political Sciences; Public Administration; Public Law)

History: Founded 1919 as Chiayi Agriculture and Forestry Public School. Reorganized and renamed Taiwan Provincial Chiayi Agri-Vocational School 1945. Upgraded into Taiwan Provincial Chiayi Junior College of AgricultureNational Chiayi Institute of Technology 1965 and then into National Chiayi Institute of Technology 1997. Acquired present status and title 2000, following merger with National Chiayi Teachers College (founded 1957).

Admission Requirements: Graduation from high school

Fees: National: c. 44,000 per semester (New Taiwan Dollar), International: Tuition, c. 3,300 per annum (US Dollar)

Main Language(s) of Instruction: Chinese

Degrees and Diplomas: *Bachelor's Degree*; *Master's Degree*: **Agricultural Business; Agriculture; Agronomy; Animal Husbandry; Applied Chemistry; Applied Mathematics; Applied Physics; Biochemistry; Bioengineering; Biotechnology; Business Administration; Chinese; Civil Engineering; Computer Engineering; Computer Science; Economics; Education; Educational Administration; Educational and Student Counselling; Educational Technology; Electrical Engineering; Electronic Engineering; English; Food Science; Foreign Languages Education; Forest Products; Forestry; Geography; History; Horticulture; Immunology; Information Technology; Leisure Studies; Literature; Management; Marketing; Mathematics Education; Mechanical Engineering; Microbiology; Modern Languages; Molecular Biology; Music; Parks and Recreation; Pharmacology; Physical Education; Preschool Education; Public Administration; Science Education; Sports; Teacher Training; Tourism; Transport Management; Veterinary Science; Visual Arts; Zoology.** *Doctorate*: **Agriculture; Biotechnology; Computer Engineering; Computer Science; Education; Food Science; Leisure Studies; Tourism.**

Student Services: Academic Counselling, Careers Guidance, Facilities for disabled people, Health Services, IT Centre, Library, Residential Facilities, Social Counselling, Sports Facilities

Academic Staff *2013-2014*: Total: c. 500

Student Numbers *2013-2014*: Total: c. 10,000

Last Updated: 20/03/14

NATIONAL CHIN-YI UNIVERSITY OF TECHNOLOGY (NCUT)

No.57, Sec. 2, Zhongshan Rd., Taiping Dist, Taichung 41170
Tel: +886(4) 239-24505
Fax: +886(4) 239-30681
EMail: htl@chinyi.ncit.edu.tw
Website: http://web2.ncut.edu.tw/bin/home.php

President: Min-Shiun Chao EMail: president@ncut.edu.tw

Chief-Secretary: Jun-Ho Chen
Tel: +886(4) 239-24505, Ext. 2111
EMail: chenjh@ncut.edu.tw; sec@ncut.edu.tw

International Relations: Dengmei Zhen, Director, Office of International Affairs
Tel: +886(4) 2392-4505, Ext. 2190 EMail: tengmj@ncut.edu.tw

College

Continuing Education (Arts and Humanities; Education); **Electrlcal Engineering and Computer Science** (Computer Engineering; Computer Science; Electrical Engineering; Electronic Engineering; Information Technology); **Engineering** (Chemical Engineering; Energy Engineering; Engineering; Heating and Refrigeration; Materials Engineering; Mechanical Engineering); **Humanities and Creativity** (Aesthetics; Art History; English; Landscape Architecture); **Management** (Industrial Engineering; Industrial Management; Information Management; Leisure Studies; Management; Transport Management)

History: Founded 1971 as Private Chin-yi Junior College of Industry and Technology. Renamed into Private Chin-yi Junior College of Industry 1973. Acquired public status 1987. Renamed as National Chin-yi Junior College of Industry and Commercestatus and title 1992. Upgraded into National Chin-yi Institute of Technology 1999. Acquired current status and title 2007.

Fees: Tuition for undergraduate programmes, 46,082-52,202 per semester; For Master's degree programmes, 46,606-52,055 per semester; For Ph.D. programmes, 53,877 per semester (New Taiwan Dollar)

Main Language(s) of Instruction: Chinese

Degrees and Diplomas: *Bachelor's Degree*; *Master's Degree*: **Business Administration; Computer Engineering; Computer Science; Electrical Engineering; Electronic Engineering; Heating and Refrigeration; Industrial Engineering; Information Management; Landscape Architecture; Leisure Studies; Management; Materials Engineering; Mechanical Engineering; Transport Management.** *Doctorate*: **Measurement and Precision Engineering; Production Engineering.**

Student Services: Academic Counselling, Canteen, Health Services, IT Centre, Library, Residential Facilities, Social Counselling, Sports Facilities

Last Updated: 10/03/14

NATIONAL CHUNG CHENG UNIVERSITY (CCU)

No.168, Sec. 1, University Rd., Min-Hsiung Township, Chiayi 62102
Tel: +886(5) 272-0411
Fax: +886(5) 272-0408
EMail: secretor@ccu.edu.tw
Website: http://www.ccu.edu.tw

President: Jyh-Yang Wu (2008-)
Tel: +886(5) 272-0400 EMail: president@ccu.edu.tw

Secretary-General: Chau-Huei Chen
Tel: +886(5) 272-0402
EMail: secretar@ccu.edu.tw; seichen@eq.ccu.edu.tw

International Relations: Amy Huey-Ling Shee, Director, Office of International Affairs
Tel: +886(5) 272-0411 EMail: lawamy@ccu.edu.tw

College

Education (Adult Education; Continuing Education; Criminology; Curriculum; Education; Leisure Studies; Physical Education; Sports; Teacher Training); **Engineering** (Chemical Engineering; Computer Engineering; Computer Science; Electrical Engineering; Electronic Engineering; Engineering; Information Technology; Mechanical Engineering; Optical Technology; Telecommunications Engineering); **Humanities** (Arts and Humanities; Chinese; English; Foreign Languages Education; History; Linguistics; Literature; Modern

Languages; Philosophy); **Law** (Commercial Law; Fiscal Law; Law); **Management** (Accountancy; Business Administration; Economics; Finance; Information Management; Information Technology; International Economics; Management; Marketing); **Science** (Applied Mathematics; Biochemistry; Biology; Chemistry; Earth Sciences; Environmental Studies; Geophysics; Mathematics; Molecular Biology; Natural Sciences; Physics; Seismology; Statistics); **Social Sciences** (Clinical Psychology; Communication Studies; International Relations; Labour and Industrial Relations; Political Sciences; Psychology; Social Sciences; Social Welfare; Telecommunications Services)

Centre

Ching-Jiang Learning (Distance Education; Educational Technology); **General Education** (Arts and Humanities); **Language Studies** (Chinese; English); **Teacher Education** (Teacher Training)

History: Founded 1989. A public research-oriented university.

Academic Year: September to June (September-January; February-June)

Admission Requirements: Graduation from high school and entrance examination

Main Language(s) of Instruction: Chinese, English

Degrees and Diplomas: *Bachelor's Degree*; *Master's Degree*: **Adult Education; Applied Mathematics; Biochemistry; Biology; Business Administration; Chemical Engineering; Chemistry; Chinese; Clinical Psychology; Commercial Law; Computer Engineering; Computer Science; Continuing Education; Criminology; Curriculum; Education; Electrical Engineering; Electronic Engineering; English; Finance; Fiscal Law; Foreign Languages Education; Geophysics; History; Information Management; Information Technology; International Economics; International Relations; Labour and Industrial Relations; Law; Leisure Studies; Linguistics; Literature; Management; Marketing; Mathematics; Mechanical Engineering; Molecular Biology; Optical Technology; Philosophy; Physics; Political Sciences; Psychology; Seismology; Social Welfare; Sports; Statistics; Telecommunications Engineering; Telecommunications Services.** *Doctorate*: **Accountancy; Adult Education; Applied Mathematics; Biochemistry; Business Administration; Chemical Engineering; Chemistry; Chinese; Computer Engineering; Computer Science; Continuing Education; Curriculum; Education; Electrical Engineering; English; Finance; History; Information Management; Information Technology; International Economics; Law; Linguistics; Literature; Mathematics; Mechanical Engineering; Molecular Biology; Philosophy; Physics; Political Sciences; Psychology; Seismology; Social Welfare; Telecommunications Engineering.**

Student Services: IT Centre, Library

Publications: Journal of National Chung-Cheng University

Student Numbers *2013-2014*: Total 12,000
Last Updated: 21/03/14

NATIONAL CHUNG HSING UNIVERSITY (NCHU)

250, Guo Kuang Road, Taichung 402
Tel: +886(4) 228-73181
Fax: +886(4) 228-70925
EMail: oia@nchu.edu.tw
Website: http://www.nchu.edu.tw/

President: Der-Tsai Lee
Tel: +886(04) 228-40201
EMail: presid@nchu.edu.tw; alice.ho@nchu.edu.tw

Secretary-General: Chi-Chung Chen
Tel: +886(04) 228-40202 EMail: mayjune@nchu.edu.tw

International Relations: Sy-Sang Liaw, Dean, Office of International Affairs
Tel: +886(4) 228-40206, Ext. 11
EMail: oia@nchu.edu.tw; liaw@phys.nchu.edu.tw

College

Agriculture and Natural Resources (Agricultural Business; Agricultural Management; Agriculture; Agronomy; Animal Husbandry; Biotechnology; Electronic Engineering; Entomology; Environmental Studies; Food Science; Forestry; Horticulture; Industrial Engineering; Industrial Management; Mechanical Engineering; Natural Resources; Plant Pathology; Rural Planning; Soil Conservation; Soil Science; Water Management); **Engineering** (Biomedical Engineering; Chemical Engineering; Civil Engineering; Electrical Engineering; Electronic Engineering; Engineering; Environmental Engineering; Materials Engineering; Measurement and Precision Engineering; Mechanical Engineering; Optical Technology; Telecommunications Engineering); **Law and Politics** (International Economics; International Studies; Law; Political Sciences; Public Administration); **Liberal Arts** (Arts and Humanities; Chinese; English; History; Information Sciences; Library Science; Literature; Modern Languages); **Life Sciences** (Biochemistry; Biological and Life Sciences; Computer Science; Genetics; Medical Technology; Molecular Biology); **Management** (Accountancy; Business Administration; Engineering Management; Finance; Health Administration; Management; Marketing; Sports Management); **Science** (Applied Mathematics; Chemistry; Computer Science; Multimedia; Nanotechnology; Natural Sciences; Physics; Statistics); **Veterinary Medicine** (Biology; Microbiology; Pathology; Public Health; Veterinary Science)

Centre

Biotechnology (Biotechnology); **General Education** (Arts and Humanities)

Research Centre

Humanities and Social Sciences (Arts and Humanities; Social Sciences); **Nano Centre** (Biochemistry; Biological and Life Sciences; Chemistry; Engineering; Nanotechnology; Physics)

History: Founded 1919 as Academy of Agriculture and Forestry, became part of Japanese Taihoku Imperial University 1928, transferred to Taichung as independent institution 1942, re-established as State institution 1945 and became Provincial College of Agriculture 1946 and university 1961. Acquired present title 1971.

Academic Year: August to July (August-January; February-July)

Admission Requirements: Graduation from secondary school or recognized foreign equivalent, and entrance examination

Main Language(s) of Instruction: Chinese, English

Degrees and Diplomas: *Bachelor's Degree*; *Master's Degree*: **Agricultural Business; Agricultural Economics; Agricultural Management; Agriculture; Agronomy; Animal Husbandry; Applied Mathematics; Biochemistry; Biological and Life Sciences; Biology; Biomedical Engineering; Biotechnology; Chemical Engineering; Chemistry; Chinese; Civil Engineering; Computer Science; Electrical Engineering; Electronic Engineering; English; Entomology; Environmental Engineering; Environmental Studies; Food Science; Forestry; History; Horticulture; Industrial Engineering; Industrial Management; Information Sciences; Law; Library Science; Literature; Management; Materials Engineering; Measurement and Precision Engineering; Mechanical Engineering; Medical Technology; Microbiology; Molecular Biology; Multimedia; Nanotechnology; Optical Technology; Pathology; Physics; Plant Pathology; Political Sciences; Public Health; Rural Planning; Soil Management; Soil Science; Statistics; Telecommunications Engineering; Veterinary Science; Water Management.** *Doctorate*: **Agricultural Economics; Agronomy; Animal Husbandry; Applied Mathematics; Biochemistry; Biological and Life Sciences; Biology; Biotechnology; Chemical Engineering; Chemistry; Civil Engineering; Computer Science; Electronic Engineering; Entomology; Environmental Engineering; Environmental Studies; Food Science; Forestry; History; Horticulture; Industrial Engineering; Management; Materials Engineering; Mechanical Engineering; Microbiology; Molecular Biology; Multimedia; Nanotechnology; Pathology; Physics; Plant Pathology; Political Sciences; Public Health; Soil Conservation; Soil Science; Statistics; Veterinary Science; Water Management.**

Student Services: Health Services, IT Centre, Library, Sports Facilities

Publications: Bulletin of Botanical Research; Bulletin of the Experimental Forest; Economics Studies; Journal of Agriculture and Forestry; Journal of Law and Commerce; Journal of Literature and History; Journal of Science and Engineering

Publishing House: Chung Hsing University Press Division; Taipei College of Law and Commerce Press Division

Academic Staff *2013-2014*	TOTAL
FULL-TIME	774
PART-TIME	279
STAFF WITH DOCTORATE	
FULL-TIME	734

Last Updated: 21/03/14

NATIONAL DONG HWA UNIVERSITY (NDHU)

No. 1, Sec. 2, Da Hsueh Rd., Shoufeng, Hualien 97401
Tel: +886(3) 863-5000
Fax: +886(3) 863-2010
EMail: admission@mail.ndhu.edu.tw
Website: http://www.ndhu.edu.tw

President: Maw-Kuen WU (2012-)
Tel: +886(3) 863-2001
EMail: president@mail.ndhu.edu.tw; clsun@mail.ndhu.edu.tw

Secretary-General: Ying-San Liou
Tel: +886(3) 863-2002 EMail: yingsan@mail.ndhu.edu.tw

International Relations: Chih-Peng Chu, Dean, Office of International Affairs Tel: +886(3) 863-4101 EMail: oia@mail.ndhu.edu.tw

College

Arts (Design; Fine Arts; Music; Visual Arts); **Education** *(Hua-Shih)* (Child Care and Development; Curriculum; Education; Educational Administration; Management; Pedagogy; Physical Education; Preschool Education; Special Education); **Environmental Studies** (Environmental Studies; Natural Resources); **Humanities and Social Sciences** (Arts and Humanities; Chinese; Clinical Psychology; Commercial Law; Economics; English; Finance; History; Law; Literature; Native Language; Psychology; Public Administration; Regional Studies; Social Sciences; Sociology); **Indigenous Studies** (Communication Studies; Cultural Studies; Development Studies; Ethnology; Indigenous Studies; Native Language; Social Work); **Management** (Accountancy; Business Administration; Environmental Management; Finance; Information Management; International Business; Leisure Studies; Management; Parks and Recreation; Tourism; Transport Management); **Marine Sciences** (Biological and Life Sciences; Biology; Biotechnology; Marine Science and Oceanography); **Science and Engineering** (Applied Mathematics; Applied Physics; Biological and Life Sciences; Chemistry; Computer Engineering; Computer Science; Electrical Engineering; Electronic Engineering; Engineering; Information Technology; Materials Engineering; Natural Sciences; Optical Technology; Physics)

Centre

General Education (Arts and Humanities; Chinese; Modern Languages; Physical Education); **Teacher Education** (Teacher Training)

History: Founded 1994. Merged with National Hualien University of Education 2008.

Academic Year: August to July

Admission Requirements: High school diploma

Fees: c. 23,000 per semester (New Taiwan Dollar)

Main Language(s) of Instruction: Chinese

Degrees and Diplomas: *Bachelor's Degree*; *Master's Degree*: **Accountancy; Applied Mathematics; Biological and Life Sciences; Biology; Biotechnology; Business Administration; Chemistry; Chinese; Clinical Psychology; Commercial Law; Computer Engineering; Computer Science; Cultural Studies; Curriculum; Design; Development Studies; Economics; Educational Administration; Electrical Engineering; Electronic Engineering; English; Environmental Studies; Ethnology; Finance; Fine Arts; History; Indigenous Studies; Information Management; International Business; Leisure Studies; Literature; Marine Science and Oceanography; Materials Engineering; Music; Natural Resources; Optical Technology; Parks and Recreation; Physical Education; Physics; Preschool Education; Psychology; Public Administration; Regional Studies; Social Work; Sociology; Special Education; Tourism; Visual Arts.** *Doctorate*: **Applied Mathematics; Biological and Life Sciences; Business Administration; Chemistry; Chinese; Computer Engineering; Computer Science; Cultural Studies; Curriculum; Economics; Electrical Engineering; English; Environmental Studies; Ethnology; Literature; Materials Engineering; Natural Resources; Physics.**

Student Services: Academic Counselling, Canteen, Facilities for disabled people, Health Services, Language Laboratory, Library, Nursery Care, Residential Facilities, Social Counselling, Sports Facilities

Last Updated: 21/03/14

NATIONAL FORMOSA UNIVERSITY (NFU)

No.64, Wunhua Rd., Huwei Township, Yunlin 63208
Tel: +886(5) 632-5000
Fax: +886(5) 631-5999
EMail: network@nfu.edu.tw
Website: http://www.nfu.edu.tw

President: Wen-Yu Jywe (2013-)
Tel: +886(5) 631-5000, Ext. 5001 EMail: president@nfu.edu.tw

Dean of Academic Affairs: Shinn-Liang Chang
Tel: +886(5) 631-5100 EMail: changsl@nfu.edu.tw

International Relations: Frank Lin, Director, Division of International Academic Affairs
Tel: +886(5) 631-5023
EMail: Frank.Lin@nfu.edu.tw; Chungyan_lin@hotmail.com

College

Applied Arts and Sciences (Biotechnology; Design; Leisure Studies; Multimedia; Natural Sciences; Parks and Recreation); **Electrical and Computer Engineering** (Computer Engineering; Computer Science; Electrical Engineering; Electronic Engineering; Information Technology; Materials Engineering; Optical Technology); **Engineering** (Aeronautical and Aerospace Engineering; Automation and Control Engineering; Automotive Engineering; Computer Engineering; Electronic Engineering; Energy Engineering; Engineering; Industrial Design; Materials Engineering; Measurement and Precision Engineering; Mechanical Engineering; Power Engineering); **Management** (Business Administration; Finance; Industrial Management; Information Management; Management)

Centre

General Education (Arts and Humanities; Chinese; Literature; Physics); **Language Teaching** (Arts and Humanities; Business Administration; Cultural Studies; English; Information Technology; Linguistics; Literature; Translation and Interpretation)

History: Founded 1980 as as Provincial Yunlin Institute of Technology. Renamed National Yunlin Institute of Technology 1981. Acquired present name and status 2004.

Main Language(s) of Instruction: Chinese

Degrees and Diplomas: *Associate Degree*; *Bachelor's Degree*; *Master's Degree*: **Aeronautical and Aerospace Engineering; Biotechnology; Business Administration; Computer Science; Electrical Engineering; Electronic Engineering; Energy Engineering; Industrial Management; Information Management; Information Technology; Leisure Studies; Management; Materials Engineering; Measurement and Precision Engineering; Mechanical Engineering; Optical Technology; Parks and Recreation.** *Doctorate*: **Electronic Engineering; Materials Engineering; Mechanical Engineering; Optical Technology.**

Student Services: Health Services, IT Centre, Library, Sports Facilities

Student Numbers *2013-2014*: Total: c. 10,000

Last Updated: 24/03/14

NATIONAL HSINCHU UNIVERSITY OF EDUCATION (NHUE)

No.521, Nanda Rd., Hsinchu 30014
Tel: +886(3) 521-3132, Ext. 1130
Fax: +886(3) 523-1380
EMail: yuing120@mail.nhcue.edu.tw; dora@mail.nhcue.edu.tw
Website: http://www.nhcue.edu.tw/

President: Hwei-Pang Chen
Tel: +886(3) 522-3132, Ext. 1100
EMail: chenhp@mail.nhcue.edu.tw

Secretary-General: Wen-Chi Zeng
Tel: +886(3) 521-3132, Ext. 1120
EMail: wenchih@mail.nhcue.edu.tw

College

Education (Distance Education; Education; Educational Psychology; Educational Technology; Human Resources; Physical Education; Preschool Education; Special Education); **Liberal Arts** (Art Education; Art History; Arts and Humanities; Chinese; Classical Languages; Crafts and Trades; Cultural Studies; Design; English; English Studies; Environmental Management; Environmental Studies; Fine Arts; Foreign Languages Education; Linguistics; Literature; Modern Languages; Music; Music Education; Musical Instruments; Native Language; Native Language Education; Parks and Recreation; Performing Arts; Phonetics; Primary Education; Social and Community Services; Social Studies; Writing); **Science** (Applied Chemistry; Applied Mathematics; Applied Physics; Biological and Life Sciences; Biology; Computer Science; Mathematics Education; Nanotechnology; Science Education)

Centre

Education (Arts and Humanities)

History: Founded 1940 as a three-year normal School. Acquired present status and title 2005.

Academic Year: September to June (September-January; February-June)

Admission Requirements: Graduation from high school and National Joint Examination for the Entrance to Universities and Colleges. Special requirements are subject to the demand of different departments

Fees: National: Tuition, 21,780-25,280 per semester (New Taiwan Dollar), International: Tuition, 39,460-41,280 per semester (New Taiwan Dollar)

Main Language(s) of Instruction: Chinese, English, Taiwanese, Hakka

Accrediting Agency: Ministry of Education

Degrees and Diplomas: *Bachelor's Degree*; *Master's Degree*: **Applied Mathematics; Art Education; Biological and Life Sciences; Chinese; Computer Networks; Data Processing; Design; Distance Education; Education; Educational Psychology; Educational Technology; Fine Arts; Human Resources; Literature; Mathematics; Mathematics Education; Multimedia; Music; Nanotechnology; Native Language; Native Language Education; Physical Education; Preschool Education; Science Education; Social Studies; Special Education.** *Doctorate*: **Education; Educational Technology; Native Language; Native Language Education.**

Student Services: Academic Counselling, Canteen, Careers Guidance, Cultural Activities, Facilities for disabled people, Health Services, IT Centre, Library, Residential Facilities, Sports Facilities

Publications: Educational Journal of NHCUE; Journal of Humanities and Social Sciences of NHCUE

Publishing House: Publication Section, Department of Academic Affairs

Last Updated: 24/03/14

NATIONAL ILAN UNIVERSITY (NIU)

1, Sec 1, Shen-Lung Road, Ilan 26041
Tel: +886(3) 935-7400
Fax: +886(3) 933-4290
EMail: sec@niu.edu.tw
Website: http://www.niu.edu.tw

President: Han-Chieh Chao (2010-)
Tel: +886(3) 931-7000 EMail: president@niu.edu.tw

Dean, Academic Affairs: Kai-Lih Chen
Tel: +886(3) 931-7085
EMail: acade@niu.edu.tw; klchen@niu.edu.tw

Secretary-General: Chi-Hsiang Lo
Tel: +886(3) 935-7010 EMail: sec@niu.edu.tw; chlo@niu.edu.tw

International Relations: Chung-Hsin Juan, Director, Center of International Affairs
Tel: +886(3) 935-7049 EMail: cia-1@niu.edu.tw

College

Bioresources (Agriculture; Animal Husbandry; Bioengineering; Biotechnology; Food Science; Forestry; Horticulture; Mechanical Engineering; Natural Resources; Zoology); **Electrical Engineering and Computer Science** (Computer Engineering; Computer Science; Electrical Engineering; Electronic Engineering; Information Technology); **Engineering** (Architecture and Planning; Chemical Engineering; Civil Engineering; Electronic Engineering; Engineering; Environmental Engineering; Materials Engineering; Mechanical Engineering); **Humanities and Management** (Arts and Humanities; Economics; English; European Languages; French; German; Health Sciences; Humanities and Social Science Education; Japanese; Leisure Studies; Linguistics; Literature; Management; Modern Languages; Science Education; Spanish)

Centre

General Education (Arts and Humanities; Chinese; English; Environmental Studies; Information Technology; Modern Languages; Sports)

History: Founded 1926 as Ilan School of Agriculture and Forestry. Formerly known as National Ilan Institute of Technology. Acquired present title and status 2003.

Academic Year: August to July

Fees: Undergraduate Tuition, 38,600-48,500 per semester; Graduate Tuition, 37,300-44,500 per semester

Main Language(s) of Instruction: Chinese

Accrediting Agency: Higher Education and Accreditation Council of Taiwan; Institute of Engineering Education Taiwan Accreditation Council

Degrees and Diplomas: *Bachelor's Degree*; *Master's Degree*: **Arts and Humanities; Bioengineering; Business Administration; Chemical Engineering; Civil Engineering; Computer Networks; Computer Science; Economics; Electrical Engineering; Electronic Engineering; English; Environmental Engineering; Environmental Studies; Food Science; Forestry; Horticulture; Information Technology; Leisure Studies; Literature; Management; Materials Engineering; Mechanical Engineering; Multimedia; Nanotechnology; Natural Resources; Safety Engineering; Zoology.** *Doctorate*: **Biotechnology; Zoology.**

Student Services: Health Services, Library, Sports Facilities

Publications: Bulletin of the College of Engineering; Ilan University Journal of Bioresources; Journal of Liberal Arts and Management

Academic Staff *2013-2014*: Total: c. 240
Student Numbers *2013-2014*: Total: c. 5,000
Last Updated: 25/03/14

NATIONAL KAOHSIUNG FIRST UNIVERSITY OF SCIENCE AND TECHNOLOGY (NKFUST)

No.1, University Rd., Yanchao Dist., Kaohsiung 824
Tel: +886(7) 601-1000
Fax: +886(7) 601-1069
EMail: cass@ccms.nkfust.edu.tw
Website: http://www.nkfust.edu.tw

President: Roger C.Y. Chen (2010-) EMail: roger@nkfust.edu.tw

Secretary-General: Kuo-Kuang Chu
Tel: +886(7) 601-1000, Ext. 1010 EMail: kkchu@nkfust.edu.tw

International Relations: Jeng Yih Hsu, Director of Center for International Affairs and Language Learning
Tel: +886(7) 601-1000, Ext. 5117 EMail: justice@nkfust.edu.tw

College

Electrical Engineering and Computer Science (Computer Science; Electrical Engineering; Electronic Engineering; Engineering; Telecommunications Engineering); **Engineering** (Automation and Control Engineering; Construction Engineering; Engineering; Engineering Drawing and Design; Environmental Engineering; Health Sciences; Industrial Design; Mechanical Engineering; Safety Engineering; Technology); **Finance and Banking** (Accountancy; Banking; Finance; Information Technology; Insurance); **Foreign Languages** (Applied Linguistics; English; Foreign Languages Education; German; Japanese; Modern Languages; Translation and Interpretation); **Management** (Business Administration; E-Business/Commerce; Finance; Information Management; Law; Management; Marketing; Transport Management)

Centre

General Education (Arts and Humanities; Business Administration; Chinese; Computer Science; Cultural Studies; Engineering; English; Fine Arts; German; Health Sciences; International Studies; Japanese; Management; Modern Languages; Natural Sciences; Social Sciences; Technology); **International Affairs and Language** (Chinese; English; German; Japanese; Modern Languages)

History: Founded 1995 as National Institute of Technology at Kaohsiung. Acquired present title and status 1998.

Academic Year: September to June

Main Language(s) of Instruction: Chinese

Degrees and Diplomas: *Bachelor's Degree*; *Master's Degree*: **Accountancy; Applied Linguistics; Automation and Control Engineering; Banking; Business Administration; Computer Engineering; Construction Engineering; E-Business/Commerce; Electrical Engineering; Electronic Engineering; Environmental Engineering; Finance; Foreign Languages Education; German; Health Sciences; Industrial Design; Information Management; Information Technology; Insurance; Japanese; Law; Management; Marketing; Mechanical Engineering; Optical Technology; Safety Engineering; Telecommunications Engineering; Translation and Interpretation; Transport Management.** *Doctorate*: **Banking; Engineering; Finance; Management; Technology.**

Student Services: Academic Counselling, Canteen, Careers Guidance, Facilities for disabled people, Health Services, IT Centre, Language Laboratory, Library, Nursery Care, Social Counselling, Sports Facilities

Publications: Journal of Industry Management

Academic Staff *2013-2014*: Total 248

Student Numbers *2013-2014*: Total: c. 7,600

Last Updated: 25/03/14

NATIONAL KAOHSIUNG MARINE UNIVERSITY (NKMU)

No.142, Haijhuan Rd., Nanzih Dist., Kaohsiung 81157
Tel: +886(7) 361-7141
Fax: +886(7) 362-8844
EMail: president@mail.nkmu.edu.tw; international@webmail.nkmu.edu.tw
Website: http://www.nkmu.edu.tw

President: Chao-Jen Chou EMail: president@mail.nkmu.edu.tw

Secretary-General: Yuan-Jen Yang
Tel: +886(7) 363-7141, Ext. 2002 EMail: secre@mail.nkmu.edu.tw

International Relations: Kelly Hsieh, Dean, Research and Development Division
Tel: +886(7) 361-7141, Ext. 2345
EMail: international@webmail.nkmu.edu.tw

College

Hydrosphere Science (Agricultural Management; Aquaculture; Biotechnology; Fishery; Food Science; Marine Science and Oceanography; Production Engineering); **Management** (Business Administration; Information Management; Leisure Studies; Marine Transport; Nautical Science; Transport Management); **Maritime Affairs** (Information Technology; Marine Engineering; Nautical Science; Transport Engineering); **Ocean Engineering** (Electronic Engineering; Environmental Engineering; Marine Engineering; Microelectronics; Naval Architecture; Telecommunications Engineering)

Centre

General Education (Arts and Humanities; Chinese; Mathematics; Military Science; Modern Languages; Natural Sciences; Physical Education; Physics; Social Sciences)

Further Information: Also Cijing Campus

History: Founded 1946 as Kaohsiung branch of the Provincial Keelung Marine and Fishery Senior Vocational school. Became the independent Kaohsiung Marine and Fishery Senior Vocational School 1948. Upgraded into a junior college 1967 and then into an institute of technology 1997. Acquired present title and status 2004.

Fees: National: Undergraduate tuition, 15,883-16,026 per annum; Graduate tuition, 12,000-13,000 per annum (New Taiwan Dollar), International: Undergraduate tuition, 31,766-32,052 per annum; Graduate tuition, 22,000-24,000 per annum (New Taiwan Dollar)

Main Language(s) of Instruction: Chinese

Degrees and Diplomas: *Bachelor's Degree*; *Master's Degree*: **Agricultural Management; Aquaculture; Biotechnology; Business Administration; Electrical Engineering; Electronic Engineering; Environmental Engineering; Fishery; Food Science; Information Technology; Marine Engineering; Marine Transport; Microelectronics; Naval Architecture; Telecommunications Engineering; Transport Engineering; Transport Management.**

Student Services: Academic Counselling, Canteen, Careers Guidance, Facilities for disabled people, Health Services, IT Centre, Language Laboratory, Library, Nursery Care, Residential Facilities, Social Counselling, Sports Facilities

Last Updated: 25/03/14

NATIONAL KAOHSIUNG NORMAL UNIVERSITY (NKNU)

No.116, Heping 1st Rd., Lingya District, Kaohsiung 80201
Tel: +886(7) 717-2930
Fax: +886(7) 711-0315
EMail: wwwadm@ccmail.nknu.edu.tw; r@nknucc.nknu.edu.tw
Website: http://www.nknu.edu.tw

President: Pei-Tsun Tsai EMail: tsai@nknucc.nknu.edu.tw

College

Education (Adult Education; Business Administration; Computer Education; Education; Educational and Student Counselling; Gender Studies; Human Resources; Information Sciences; Management; Physical Education; Psychology; Rehabilitation and Therapy; Special Education; Speech Therapy and Audiology); **Fine Arts** (Aesthetics; Art Criticism; Communication Arts; Computer Graphics; Design; Fine Arts; Media Studies; Music; Performing Arts; Visual Arts; Writing); **Humanities** (Arts and Humanities; Chinese; Cultural Studies; English; Foreign Languages Education; Geography; History; Native Language; Philosophy); **Science** (Biotechnology; Chemistry; Environmental Studies; Mathematics; Natural Sciences; Physics; Science Education); **Technology** (Electronic Engineering; Industrial Arts Education; Industrial Design; Industrial Engineering; Optical Technology; Software Engineering; Technology)

Centre

Education (Curriculum; Education); **Language Teaching** (Chinese; English; German; Japanese; Modern Languages); **Teacher Education** (Primary Education; Secondary Education; Teacher Training)

Further Information: Also Yanchao Campus

History: Founded 1954 as Provincial Kaohsiung Female Teachers College. Renamed the Taiwan Provincial Kaohsiung Teachers College 1967, National Kaohsiung Teachers College 1980. Acquired present status and title 1989.

Academic Year: August to July (August-January; February-July)

Admission Requirements: Graduation from high school and entrance examination or references

Fees: Undergraduates c. 19,800-23,150 per semester (New Taiwan Dollar)

Main Language(s) of Instruction: Chinese

Degrees and Diplomas: *Bachelor's Degree*; *Master's Degree*: **Adult Education; Biotechnology; Business Administration; Chemistry; Chinese; Cultural Studies; Design; Education; Educational and Student Counselling; Electronic Engineering; English; Environmental Studies; Fine Arts; Foreign Languages Education; Gender Studies; Geography; History; Human Resources; Industrial Design; Industrial Engineering; Mathematics; Music; Native Language; Optical Technology; Philosophy; Physical Education; Physics; Psychology; Rehabilitation and Therapy; Special Education; Speech Therapy and Audiology; Telecommunications Engineering; Visual Arts.** *Doctorate*: **Adult Education; Education; Educational and Student Counselling; English; Geography; Industrial Engineering; Physics; Psychology; Special Education.**

Student Services: Academic Counselling, Canteen, Careers Guidance, Cultural Activities, Facilities for disabled people, Health

Services, Language Laboratory, Library, Residential Facilities, Social Counselling, Sports Facilities

Publications: University Research Journal

Last Updated: 26/03/14

NATIONAL KAOHSIUNG UNIVERSITY OF APPLIED SCIENCES (KUAS)

415 Chien Kung Road, Sanmin District, Kaohsiung 80778
Tel: +886(7) 381-4526-30
Fax: +886(7) 383-8435
EMail: pboffice01@cc.kuas.edu.tw; yukiyen1021@kuas.edu.tw
Website: http://www.kuas.edu.tw

President: Cheng-Hong Yang EMail: chy@cc.kuas.edu.tw

Secretary-General: Hsiou-Hsiang Liu
Tel: +886(7) 381-4526, Ext. 2203 EMail: bachair@cc.kuas.edu.tw

College

Electrical Engineering and Computer Science (Computer Engineering; Computer Science; Electrical Engineering; Electronic Engineering; Information Technology; Optical Technology; Telecommunications Engineering); **Engineering** (Chemical Engineering; Civil Engineering; Engineering; Industrial Engineering; Industrial Management; Materials Engineering; Mechanical Engineering; Metallurgical Engineering); **Humanities and Social Sciences** (Arts and Humanities; Cultural Studies; Education; Human Resources; Modern Languages; Teacher Training); **Management** (Accountancy; Banking; Business Administration; Business and Commerce; Data Processing; Finance; Information Management; Information Sciences; International Business; Management; Taxation; Tourism)

Centre

General Education (Arts and Humanities; Natural Sciences; Social Sciences)

Further Information: Also Yanchao Campus

History: Founded 1963 as the Provincial Kaohsiung Institute of Technology, acquired present status and title 2000.

Main Language(s) of Instruction: Chinese

Degrees and Diplomas: *Bachelor's Degree*; *Master's Degree*: **Business Administration; Business and Commerce; Chemical Engineering; Civil Engineering; Computer Engineering; Computer Science; Electrical Engineering; Electronic Engineering; Finance; Human Resources; Industrial Engineering; Industrial Management; Information Management; Information Sciences; International Business; Materials Engineering; Mechanical Engineering; Metallurgical Engineering; Optical Technology; Telecommunications Engineering; Tourism.** *Doctorate*: **Business Administration; Chemical Engineering; Civil Engineering; Electrical Engineering; Materials Engineering; Mechanical Engineering; Metallurgical Engineering; Optical Technology; Telecommunications Engineering.**

Student Services: Academic Counselling, Careers Guidance, Cultural Activities, Facilities for disabled people, Foreign Studies Centre, Health Services, IT Centre, Library, Residential Facilities, Social Counselling, Sports Facilities

Publications: K.U.A.S Journal of College of Humanities and Social Sciences; Research Papers of the Faculty

Academic Staff *2013-2014*	**TOTAL**
FULL-TIME	**520**
Student Numbers *2013-2014*	
All (Foreign included)	c. **12,700**
FOREIGN ONLY	**170**

Last Updated: 26/03/14

NATIONAL KAOHSIUNG UNIVERSITY OF HOSPITALITY AND TOURISM (NKUHT)

No.1, Songhe Rd., Xiaogang Dist., Kaohsiung 81271
Tel: +886(7) 806-0505
Fax: +886(7) 806-1473
Website: http://www.nkuht.edu.tw/

President: Chi-Yeh Yung

Associate Professor and Secretary General: Jui-Chi Shen
Tel: +886(7) 806-0505, Ext. 1100
EMail: secretary@live.nkuht.edu.tw

International Relations: Sharon Hsing, Administrative Assistant, International Affairs Office
Tel: +886(7) 806-0505, Ext. 1701 EMail: hwl21@mail.nkuht.edu.tw

School

Culinary Arts (Cooking and Catering; Food Science); **Hospitality Management** (Food Technology; Hotel and Restaurant; Hotel Management; Marketing); **International Studies** (Applied Linguistics; Cooking and Catering; English; Japanese; Tourism); **Tourism** (Air Transport; Leisure Studies; Parks and Recreation; Tourism; Transport and Communications; Transport Management)

Centre

General Education (Arts and Humanities; Cultural Studies; Natural Sciences; Physical Education; Social Sciences); **Teacher Education** (Education; Educational Administration; Educational Psychology; Special Education; Teacher Training; Vocational Education)

History: Founded 1995 as National Kaohsiung Hospitality Management Academy. Transformed into National Kaohsiung Hospitality College 2000. Acquired present status and titlte 2008.

Fees: Undergraduate tuition, 31,253 per semester; Graduate tuition, 38,124 per semester (New Taiwan Dollar)

Main Language(s) of Instruction: Chinese, English

Degrees and Diplomas: *Associate Degree*; *Bachelor's Degree*; *Master's Degree*: **Cooking and Catering; Food Technology; Hotel and Restaurant; Leisure Studies; Teacher Training; Tourism; Transport and Communications; Vocational Education.** *Doctorate*: **Tourism; Transport and Communications.**

Student Services: Library, Sports Facilities

Last Updated: 25/03/14

NATIONAL OPEN UNIVERSITY (NOU)

No.172, Zhongzheng Rd., Luzhou Dist., Xinbei 247
Tel: +886(2) 228-29355 +886(2) 228-53555
Fax: +886(2) 228-86061
EMail: nouwww@mail.nou.edu.tw; nou@nou.edu.tw
Website: http://www.nou.edu.tw

President: Chi-Hao Chang

Department

Business (Accountancy; Business Administration; Economics; Finance; Information Sciences; Management; Statistics); **General Studies** (Arts and Humanities; Chinese; Civil Law; English; Literature; Modern Languages); **Liberal Arts** (Arts and Humanities; History; Information Sciences; Library Science; Literature; Mass Communication; Philosophy; Religion); **Life Sciences** (Environmental Management; Health Sciences; Home Economics; Nursing; Psychology; Tourism); **Management and Information** (Business Administration; Finance; Information Sciences; Information Technology; Management); **Public Administration** (Administration; Cultural Studies; Economics; Human Resources; Labour and Industrial Relations; Political Sciences; Public Administration); **Social Sciences** (Civil Law; Economics; Education; Law; Political Sciences; Psychology; Social and Community Services; Social Sciences; Sociology)

Further Information: Also Learning Centres in: Kee Lung, Taipei, Lu Chow, Hsin Chu, Tai Chung, Chia Yi, Tai Nan, Kao Hsiun, Ilan, Hua Lien, Tai Tung Peng Hu, Kin Men

History: Founded 1986, acquired present status 1994.

Academic Year: September to June (September-January; February-June)

Admission Requirements: Application process required for people over the age of 20. Non-Diploma students must be over the age of 18

Main Language(s) of Instruction: Chinese

Degrees and Diplomas: *Bachelor's Degree*

Student Services: IT Centre, Library

Last Updated: 26/03/14

NATIONAL PENGHU UNIVERSITY (NPIT)

300, Liu-He Road, Makung, Penghu 880
Tel: +886(6) 926-4115
Fax: +886(6) 927-8912
EMail: office9@npu.edu.tw; office1@npu.edu.tw
Website: http://www.npu.edu.tw

President: Ying-Wei Wang (2013-)
Tel: +886(6) 926-4115, Ext. 5513 EMail: ywwang@gms.npu.edu.tw

Unit

Ocean Engineering (Aquaculture; Computer Engineering; Electrical Engineering; Fishery; Food Science; Information Technology; Marine Engineering; Natural Resources; Telecommunications Engineering)

School

Humanities and Management (Arts and Humanities; English; Information Management; Information Technology; Management; Marine Transport; Modern Languages; Service Trades; Transport and Communications; Transport Management); **Tourism and Leisure** (Hotel and Restaurant; Hotel Management; Leisure Studies; Parks and Recreation; Sports; Sports Management; Tourism)

History: Founded 1995. Acquired present status 2000 and title 2005. Formerly known as National Penghu Institute of Technology.

Fees: Undergraduate tuition, 45,961-52,117 per semester; Graduate tuition, 46,524-52,013 per semester (New Taiwan Dollar)

Main Language(s) of Instruction: Chinese

Degrees and Diplomas: *Associate Degree*; *Bachelor's Degree*; *Master's Degree*: **Aquaculture; Computer Science; Electrical Engineering; Food Science; Leisure Studies; Natural Resources; Service Trades; Tourism.**

Student Services: IT Centre, Library, Residential Facilities

Academic Staff *2013-2014*	**TOTAL**
FULL-TIME	**125**
STAFF WITH DOCTORATE FULL-TIME	**94**
Student Numbers *2013-2014*	
All (Foreign included)	c. **3,100**
FOREIGN ONLY	**90**

Last Updated: 26/03/14

NATIONAL PINGTUNG INSTITUTE OF COMMERCE (NPIC)

51 Min Sheng E. Road, Pingtung 900
Tel: +886(8) 723-8700
Fax: +886(8) 723-8720
EMail: bcchiou@.npic.edu.tw
Website: http://www.npic.edu.tw

President: Jeun-Sheng Lin EMail: secretar@npic.edu.tw

Secretary-General: Tsair-Yuan Huang
Tel: +886(8) 723-8700, Ext 10200 EMail: huang@npic.edu.tw

International Relations: Ching-Ying Lin, Director, International Cooperation Section, Research and Development Division
Tel: +886(8) 723-8700, Ext. 15100
EMail: cylin66@npic.edu.tw; ics@npic.edu.tw

Centre

General Education (Arts and Humanities; Chinese; Constitutional Law; English; History; Law; Modern Languages; Natural Sciences; Political Sciences); **Physical Education** (Physical Education; Sports; Sports Management)

Group

Business (Accountancy; Banking; Finance; International Business); **Information Management** (Computer Engineering; Computer Science; Information Management; Information Technology; Telecommunications Engineering); **Language** (English; Japanese; Modern Languages; Translation and Interpretation); **Management** (Business Administration; Business and Commerce; E-Business/Commerce; Leisure Studies; Management; Marketing; Parks and Recreation; Real Estate; Transport Management)

History: Founded 1991, acquired present status 1998.

Fees: Undergraduate tuition, 46,727-52,672 per semester; Graduate tuition, 49,770-56,394 per semester (New Taiwan Dollar)

Main Language(s) of Instruction: Chinese

Degrees and Diplomas: *Bachelor's Degree*; *Master's Degree*: **Banking; Business Administration; Business and Commerce; Computer Engineering; Computer Science; English; Finance; Information Management; International Business; Leisure Studies; Marketing; Transport Management.**

Student Services: Academic Counselling, Health Services, IT Centre, Library, Sports Facilities

Last Updated: 27/03/14

NATIONAL PINGTUNG UNIVERSITY OF EDUCATION (NPUE)

No.4-18 Minsheng Rd., Pingtung 90003
Tel: +886(8) 722-6141
Fax: +886(8) 723-4406
Website: http://www.npue.edu.tw

President: Shyan-Jer Lee
Tel: +886(8) 722-6141, Ext.10001 EMail: lyu@mail.npue.edu.tw

Secretary-General: Chien-Huang Chen
Tel: +886(8) 722-6141, Ext.10200
EMail: chchen.academic@gmail.com

College

Education (Education; Educational Administration; Educational and Student Counselling; Educational Psychology; Preschool Education; Special Education); **Liberal Arts and Social Sciences** (Arts and Humanities; Chinese; Cultural Studies; English; Foreign Languages Education; Literature; Modern Languages; Music; Music Education; Music Theory and Composition; Musical Instruments; Singing; Social Policy; Visual Arts); **Lifelong Learning and Research** (Chinese; Continuing Education; Distance Education; Ecology; Educational Administration; Educational Technology; Educational Testing and Evaluation; Foreign Languages Education; Parks and Recreation; Social and Community Services; Teacher Training); **Sciences** (Applied Mathematics; Applied Physics; Biochemistry; Chemistry; Computer Science; Mathematics Education; Natural Sciences; Physical Education; Robotics; Science Education); **Teacher Education** (Preschool Education; Primary Education; Teacher Training)

Centre

General Education (Arts and Humanities; Chinese; Computer Science; Education; English; Physical Education)

History: Founded 1940. Acquired present status 2005.

Main Language(s) of Instruction: Mandarin, Chinese

Degrees and Diplomas: *Bachelor's Degree*; *Master's Degree*: **Applied Mathematics; Biochemistry; Chemistry; Chinese; Computer Science; Distance Education; Ecology; Education; Educational Administration; Educational Testing and Evaluation; Electronic Engineering; English; Foreign Languages Education; Literature; Materials Engineering; Mathematics Education; Music; Music Education; Optical Technology; Parks and Recreation; Physical Education; Preschool Education; Science Education; Social Policy; Special Education; Sports; Visual Arts.** *Doctorate*: **Educational Administration.**

Student Services: Academic Counselling, Facilities for disabled people, IT Centre, Language Laboratory, Library, Sports Facilities

Publications: Journal of Pingtung Teachers College

Last Updated: 27/03/14

NATIONAL PINGTUNG UNIVERSITY OF SCIENCE AND TECHNOLOGY (NPUST)

1, Shueh-Fu Road, Nei-Pu, Pingtung 912
Tel: +886(8) 770-3660
Fax: +886(8) 770-2226
EMail: mslin@mail.npust.edu.tw
Website: http://www.npust.edu.tw

President: Yuan-Kuang Guu
Tel: +886(8) 770-3660 EMail: president@mail.npust.edu.tw

Secretary-General: Ine-Wei Liu
Tel: +886(8) 774-0100
EMail: secretary@mail.npust.edu.tw; iwliu@mail.npust.edu.tw

International Relations: Henry H. H. Chen, Dean, Office of International Affairs Tel: +886(8) 774-0561, Ext. 6215 EMail: oia@mail.npust.edu.tw; international@mail.npust.edu.tw

College

Agriculture (Agriculture; Animal Husbandry; Aquaculture; Biological and Life Sciences; Biotechnology; Botany; Food Science; Forestry; Horticulture; Natural Resources; Plant and Crop Protection; Plant Pathology; Tropical Agriculture; Veterinary Science; Wildlife; Wood Technology); **Engineering** *(Graduate)* (Automotive Engineering; Bioengineering; Civil Engineering; Engineering; Environmental Engineering; Environmental Studies; Materials Engineering; Mechanical Engineering; Soil Conservation; Water Science); **Humanities and Social Sciences** (Arts and Humanities; Child Care and Development; Cultural Studies; Education; Health Sciences; Modern Languages; Parks and Recreation; Social Sciences; Social Work; Sports; Teacher Training; Technology Education; Vocational Education); **International Studies** (Agricultural Engineering; Food Science; Soil Conservation; Soil Science; Tropical Agriculture; Water Management; Water Science); **Management** *(Graduate)* (Agricultural Business; Business Administration; Engineering Management; Fashion Design; Finance; Hotel and Restaurant; Industrial Management; Information Management; Landscape Architecture; Management; Parks and Recreation); **Veterinary Medicine** (Veterinary Science; Wildlife)

History: Founded 1954 as Taiwan Provincial Institute of Agriculture. Acquired present status and title 1997.

Academic Year: September to June (September-December; February-June)

Admission Requirements: Graduation from high school for 4-year Bachelor programmes and Graduation from Junior College for 2-year Bachelor programmes

Fees: c. 30,000 per semester (New Taiwan Dollar)

Main Language(s) of Instruction: Chinese, English

Degrees and Diplomas: *Bachelor's Degree*; *Master's Degree*: **Agricultural Business; Animal Husbandry; Aquaculture; Automotive Engineering; Bioengineering; Biological and Life Sciences; Biotechnology; Business Administration; Child Care and Development; Civil Engineering; Cultural Studies; Engineering Management; Environmental Engineering; Environmental Studies; Fashion Design; Finance; Food Science; Forestry; Health Sciences; Industrial Management; Information Management; Information Technology; Landscape Architecture; Management; Materials Engineering; Mechanical Engineering; Parks and Recreation; Plant and Crop Protection; Plant Pathology; Social Work; Soil Conservation; Sports; Technology Education; Tropical Agriculture; Veterinary Science; Vocational Education; Water Management; Wildlife; Wood Technology.** *Doctorate*: **Civil Engineering; Environmental Engineering; Environmental Studies; Food Science; Horticulture; Natural Resources; Tropical Agriculture; Veterinary Science.**

Student Services: Academic Counselling, Canteen, Careers Guidance, Cultural Activities, Facilities for disabled people, Foreign Studies Centre, Health Services, IT Centre, Library, Nursery Care, Social Counselling, Sports Facilities

Publications: University Journal

Publishing House: NPUST Publishing division affiliated to the Office of Academic Affairs

Last Updated: 28/03/14

NATIONAL QUEMOY UNIVERSITY (NQU)

1, University Road, Kinmen
Tel: +886(82) 373-233
Fax: +886(82) 313-304 +886(82) 371-771
EMail: msg@nqu.edu.tw
Website: http://www.km.kuas.edu.tw

President: Chin-Cheng Lee (2010-)
Tel: +886(82) 313-302 EMail: chinchenglee@nqu.edu.tw

Secretary-General: Ko-Wei Weng
Tel: +886(82) 313-303 EMail: kowei@nqu.edu.tw

Faculty

Arts and Humanities (Architecture; Arts and Humanities; Chinese; Cultural Studies; English; Landscape Architecture; Literature; Modern Languages; Town Planning); **Social Sciences** (Architecture; Business Administration; Coastal Studies; International Business; Marine Science and Oceanography; Social Sciences)

School

Management (Business Administration; Industrial Engineering; Industrial Management; Leisure Studies; Management; Sports; Tourism)

Institute

Health Care (Health Sciences; Nursing; Social Work); **Technology** (Civil Engineering; Computer Engineering; Electronic Engineering; Engineering Management; Food Science; Information Technology; Technology)

Centre

Education (Education)

History: Formerly known as National Kinmen Institute of Technology.

Main Language(s) of Instruction: Chinese

Degrees and Diplomas: *Bachelor's Degree*; *Master's Degree*: **Architecture; Business Administration; Civil Engineering; Cultural Studies; Electronic Engineering; Engineering Management; English; Food Science; Foreign Languages Education; Information Sciences; International Business; Leisure Studies; Management; Sports; Tourism.**

Student Services: Health Services, IT Centre, Library, Residential Facilities, Sports Facilities

Last Updated: 27/03/14

NATIONAL SUN YAT-SEN UNIVERSITY (NSYSU)

70, Lienhai Road, Gushan Chiu, Kaohsiung 80424
Tel: +886(7) 525-2000
Fax: +886(7) 525-2039
EMail: academic@mail.nsysu.edu.tw; oia@mail.nsysu.edu.tw
Website: http://www.nsysu.edu.tw

President: Hung-Duen Yang (2008-)
Tel: +886(7) 525-2001 EMail: yang@mail.nsysu.edu.tw

Secretary-General: Yu-Chen Yang
Tel: +886(7) 525-2020 EMail: youngman@mail.nsysu.edu.tw

International Relations: Chih-Wen Kuo, Dean, Office of International Affairs
Tel: +886(7) 525-2000, Ext. 2630
EMail: iaozaa@mail.nsysu.edu.tw; cwkuo@mail.nsysu.edu.tw

College

Engineering (Computer Engineering; Computer Science; Electrical Engineering; Electronic Engineering; Engineering; Environmental Engineering; Materials Engineering; Mechanical Engineering; Optical Technology; Optics; Telecommunications Engineering); **Liberal Arts** (Arts and Humanities; Chinese; English; Literature; Modern Languages; Music; Philosophy; Theatre); **Management** (Business Administration; Finance; Health Administration; Human Resources; Information Management; Management; Telecommunications Services); **Marine Sciences** (Applied Physics; Biology; Biotechnology; Business Administration; Chemistry; Environmental Management; Geology; Marine Engineering; Marine Science and Oceanography; Natural Resources; Technology); **Science** (Applied Mathematics; Biological and Life Sciences; Biomedicine; Chemistry; Natural Sciences; Physics); **Social Sciences** (Asian Studies; Economics; Education; Pacific Area Studies; Political Sciences; Social Sciences; Sociology)

Centre

General Education (Applied Chemistry; Applied Mathematics; Applied Physics; Arts and Humanities; Health Sciences; Natural Sciences; Physical Education; Service Trades; Social Sciences)

Further Information: Also 49 research centres/units

History: Founded 1980.

Academic Year: September to June (September-January; February-June)

Admission Requirements: Graduation from high school and entrance examination

Main Language(s) of Instruction: Chinese

Degrees and Diplomas: *Bachelor's Degree*; *Master's Degree*: **Applied Mathematics; Applied Physics; Asian Studies; Biological and Life Sciences; Biology; Biomedicine; Biotechnology; Business Administration; Chemistry; Chinese; Computer Engineering; Computer Science; Economics; Education; Electrical Engineering; Electronic Engineering; English; Environmental Engineering; Finance; Geology; Health Administration; Human Resources; Information Management; Literature; Marine Engineering; Materials Engineering; Mechanical Engineering; Music; Natural Resources; Optical Technology; Optics; Pacific Area Studies; Physics; Political Sciences; Sociology; Technology; Telecommunications Engineering; Telecommunications Services; Theatre.** *Doctorate*: **Applied Mathematics; Asian Studies; Biological and Life Sciences; Biology; Biomedicine; Biotechnology; Business Administration; Chemistry; Chinese; Computer Engineering; Computer Science; Education; Electrical Engineering; Electronic Engineering; English; Environmental Engineering; Finance; Geology; Human Resources; Information Management; Literature; Marine Engineering; Marine Science and Oceanography; Materials Engineering; Mechanical Engineering; Natural Resources; Optical Technology; Optics; Pacific Area Studies; Physics; Political Sciences; Telecommunications Engineering.**

Student Services: Library, Sports Facilities

Last Updated: 28/03/14

NATIONAL TAICHUNG UNIVERSITY OF EDUCATION (NTCU)

No.140, Minsheng Rd., West Dist., Taichung 40306
Tel: +886(4) 221-83199
Fax: +886(4) 222-43450
EMail: ntcup@mail.ntcu.edu.tw; sec111@mail.ntcu.edu.tw
Website: http://www.ntcu.edu.tw

President: Szu-Wei Yang (2006-)
EMail: swyang@mail.ntcu.edu.tw

Secretary-General: Yu-Mao Yang
EMail: yum@mail.ntcu.edu.tw

College

Education (Business Administration; Cultural Studies; Curriculum; Education; Educational Testing and Evaluation; Environmental Studies; International Business; Parks and Recreation; Pedagogy; Physical Education; Preschool Education; Special Education; Tourism); **Humanities** (Arts and Humanities; Development Studies; English; Fine Arts; Literature; Modern Languages; Music; Native Language; Psychology; Social Studies); **Science** (Computer Science; Information Sciences; Marketing; Mathematics Education; Media Studies; Multimedia; Natural Sciences; Science Education)

School

Management (Art Management; Educational Administration; International Business; Management; Parks and Recreation; Tourism)

History: Founded as school 1923. Upgraded into Taiwan Provincial Taichung Teachers College 1987. Acquired present status and title 2005.

Fees: Undergraduate tuition, 30,400-32,830 per semester; Graduate tuition, 20,380-23,560 per semester (New Taiwan Dollar)

Main Language(s) of Instruction: Chinese

Degrees and Diplomas: *Bachelor's Degree*; *Master's Degree*: **Business Administration; Computer Science; Curriculum; Development Studies; Education; Educational Testing and Evaluation; Environmental Studies; Fine Arts; Information Sciences; Mathematics Education; Multimedia; Music; Native Language Education; Natural Sciences; Parks and Recreation; Pedagogy; Physical Education; Preschool Education; Psychology; Regional Studies; Special Education; Tourism.** *Doctorate*: **Education; Educational Testing and Evaluation; Native Language Education.**

Student Services: Library, Residential Facilities, Sports Facilities

Last Updated: 31/03/14

NATIONAL TAICHUNG UNIVERSITY OF SCIENCE AND TECHNOLOGY (NTCUST)

No.129,Sec.3, Sanmin Rd, North Dist., Taichung City 404
Tel: +886(4) 221-95678
Fax: +886(4) 222-32522
EMail: academic51@nutc.edu.tw
Website: http://www.ntit.edu.tw

President: Chung-Bo Lee
EMail: president@nutc.edu.tw; g9222713@nutc.edu.tw

Dean of Academic Affairs: William W. Sheng
Tel: +886(4) 222-11181, Ext. 2203
EMail: wwsheng@nutc.edu.tw; g9222713@nutc.edu.tw

College

Business (Accountancy; Business Administration; Finance; Information Sciences; Insurance; International Business; Leisure Studies; Statistics; Taxation); **Design** (Design; Interior Design; Multimedia); **Health** (Cosmetology; Gerontology; Health Sciences; Nursing; Service Trades); **Information and Distribution Science** (Computer Engineering; Computer Science; Information Management; Information Sciences; Information Technology; Transport Management); **Language** (Chinese; English Studies; Japanese; Modern Languages)

Centre

Hollistic Education (Arts and Humanities; English; Japanese; Modern Languages; Physical Education)

Further Information: Also Min-Sheng Campus

History: Founded 1919 as Taiwan Natinal Taichung Commercial School. Renamed Taichung State Taichung Business School 1921 and then Taiwan Provincial Taichung Commercial Vocational School 1945. Merged with Taiwan Provincial Taichung Tutorial School and changed as Commercial Professional Tutorial School 1949. Restructured as Taiwan Provincial Taichung College of Business 1963. Renamed as "National Taichung College of Business 1982. Renamed as "National Taichung Institute of Technology 1999. Acquired present status and title 2011 following merger with National Taichung Nursing College.

Main Language(s) of Instruction: Chinese

Degrees and Diplomas: *Bachelor's Degree*; *Master's Degree*: **Accountancy; Business Administration; Computer Engineering; Computer Science; Design; Finance; Information Management; Information Sciences; Interior Design; Japanese; Multimedia; Taxation; Transport Management.**

Student Services: Academic Counselling, IT Centre, Library

Last Updated: 31/03/14

NATIONAL TAIPEI COLLEGE OF BUSINESS (NTCB)

No.321, Sec. 1, Jinan Rd., Zhongzheng District, Taipei 100
Tel: +886(2) 239-35263
Fax: +886(2) 232-26219
EMail: beatrice@mail.ntcb.edu.tw
Website: http://www.ntcb.edu.tw

President (Acting): Chi-Chih Chiu (2014-)
Tel: +886(2) 2322-6000 EMail: preside@mail.ntcb.edu.tw

Secretary-General: Guey-Feng Lee
Tel: +886(2) 232-26002 EMail: gflee@webmail.ntcb.edu.tw

Department

Accounting Information (Accountancy); **Applied Foreign Languages** (English; Modern Languages); **Business Administration** (Business Administration); **Finance** (Finance); **General Education**; **Information Management** (Information Management); **International Business** (International Business); **Public Finance and Tax Administration** (Finance; Taxation)

Graduate Institute

Accounting Information (Accountancy); **Business Administration** (Business Administration); **Finance** (Finance); **information and Decision Science** (Information Sciences); **International Business** (International Business)

History: Founded 1917 as Taiwan Commercial School of the Governor's Office. Renamed Taipei County Commercial School 1921 and Taipei County Second Commercial School 1945. Merged with First Commercial Schools and renamed Taiwan Provincial Taipei Commercial School 1949. Renamed Taipei Municipal Commercial and Vocational school 1967. Reorganized into a junior college and renamed Taipei Municipal Junior College of Business 1968. Renamed National Taipei Junior College of Business 1982. Acquired present status and title 2001.

Fees: National: Tuition fee, 21,150-58,500 per semester (New Taiwan Dollar), International: Tuition fee, 43,040-58,500 per semester (New Taiwan Dollar)

Main Language(s) of Instruction: Chinese

Degrees and Diplomas: *Associate Degree*; *Bachelor's Degree*; *Master's Degree*: **Accountancy; Business Administration; Finance; Information Management; Information Sciences; International Business; Taxation.**

Student Services: IT Centre, Library, Sports Facilities

Publications: North quotient Journal; BBA innovative teaching Symposium; NTCB e-Paper

Last Updated: 20/03/14

NATIONAL TAIPEI UNIVERSITY (NTPU)

151, University Rd., Sanhsia District,
New Taipei City, Taiwan 23741
Tel: +886(2) 8674-1111
Fax: +886(2) 8671-8019
EMail: oia@gm.ntpu.edu.tw
Website: http://english.ntpu.edu.tw/bin/home.php

President: Fujiing Shiue (2011-)
Tel: +886(2) 8674-1111 Ext. 66027
EMail: president@mail.ntpu.edu.tw

Chief Secretary: Mong-Fong Lee
Tel: +886(2) 8674-1111 Ext. 66045
EMail: edmund@mail.ntpu.edu.tw

International Relations: Victor R.L. Shen, Dean of International Affairs Office
Tel: +886(2) 8674-1111 Ext. 68011
EMail: rlshen@mail.ntpu.edu.tw

College

Business (Accountancy; Business Administration; Finance; Information Management; International Business; Leisure Studies; Management; Sports Management; Statistics); **Electrical Engineering and Computer Science** (Computer Engineering; Computer Science; Electrical Engineering; Information Technology; Telecommunications Engineering); **Humanities** (Applied Linguistics; Arts and Humanities; Documentation Techniques; Folklore; History; Literature; Modern Languages); **Law** (Commercial Law; Comparative Law; European Union Law; International Law; Law; Public Law); **Public Affairs** (Environmental Management; Finance; Natural Resources; Public Administration; Real Estate; Town Planning); **Social Sciences** (Criminology; Economics; Social Sciences; Social Work; Sociology)

Centre

Comparative Law Documentation (Comparative Law; Documentation Techniques; Law); **Cooperative Economics and Non-Profit Organizations** (Economics); **General Education** (Education); **Global Change and Sustainability Science** (Natural Sciences); **International Negotiation and Interpretation** (International Business; Modern Languages; Translation and Interpretation); **Land and Environmental Planning** (Environmental Engineering; Soil Management); **Teacher Education** (Teacher Training)

Research Centre

Electronic Business (E-Business/Commerce); **Public Opinion and Election Studies**; **Taiwan Development** (Development Studies)

Further Information: Also Taipei Campus

History: Founded 1949 as Taiwan Provincial College of Law and Business. Transformed into National Chung Hsing University, College of Business and Law before it acquired present status and title 2000. Relocated its six colleges from the downtown campus in the Taipei City, to the present San-Shia main campus in the New Taipei City 2010.

Admission Requirements: Applicants must be graduated from a high school, college or university or hold equivalent qualifications

Fees: Tuition Fees (year 2011-2012), 45,691-52,668 per semester for Bachelor's degree programmes; 45,033-52,994 per semester for Master's degree programmes; 46,206-53,278 per semester for Ph. D programmes (New Taiwan Dollar)

Main Language(s) of Instruction: Chinese (Mandarin)

Accrediting Agency: Higher Education Evaluation and Accreditation Council of Taiwan; Institute of Engineering Education Taiwan (IEET) Accreditation

Degrees and Diplomas: *Bachelor's Degree*; *Master's Degree*; *Doctorate*: **Accountancy; Business Administration; Economics; Environmental Management; Law; Natural Resources; Town Planning.** Also Executive MBA

Student Services: Academic Counselling, Canteen, Careers Guidance, Cultural Activities, Facilities for disabled people, Foreign Studies Centre, Health Services, Language Laboratory, Nursery Care, Social Counselling, Sports Facilities

Publications: Crime and Criminal Justice International; Electronic Commerce Studies; Journal of Business Administration; Journal of Chinese Language and Literature; Journal of Humanities; Journal of Statistics and Computing; Journal of Taiwan Land Research; Journal of Taiwan Studies; NTPU Law Review; Public Administration & Policy; Taipei Economic Inquiry; The Historical Journal of National Taipei University

Publishing House: National Taipei University News

Academic Staff *2012-2013*	MEN	WOMEN	**TOTAL**
FULL-TIME	228	125	**353**
PART-TIME	172	77	**249**
STAFF WITH DOCTORATE			
FULL-TIME	219	114	**333**
Student Numbers *2012-2013*			
All (Foreign included)	4,360	5,513	**9,873**
FOREIGN ONLY	24	19	**43**

Last Updated: 24/05/13

NATIONAL TAIPEI UNIVERSITY OF EDUCATION (NTUE)

No.134, Sec. 2, Heping E. Rd., Da-an District, Taipei 106
Tel: +886(2) 2732-1104 +886(2) 6639-6688
Fax: +886(2) 273-30473
EMail: opinion@tea.ntue.edu.tw; study@tea.ntue.edu.tw
Website: http://www.ntue.edu.tw/

President: Shin-Jen Chang

College

Education (Communication Studies; Curriculum; Development Studies; Education; Educational Administration; Educational and Student Counselling; Educational Sciences; Educational Technology; Educational Testing and Evaluation; Information Technology; Law; Pedagogy; Preschool Education; Psychology; Social Policy; Special Education; Telecommunications Services); **Humanities and Arts** (Art Management; Arts and Humanities; Cultural Studies; Design; Fine Arts; Foreign Languages Education; Modern Languages; Music; Writing); **Science** (Computer Education; Computer Engineering; Computer Science; Information Sciences; Mathematics; Natural Sciences; Physical Education; Science Education; Software Engineering)

History: Founded 1896. Renamed Taiwan Provincial Normal School 1945 and then Taiwan Provincial Junior Teachers College 1961. Upgraded into Taiwan Provincial Taipei Normal College 1987. Renamed National Taipei Teachers College 1991. Acquired present status and title 2005.

Academic Year: September to July (September-January; February-July)

Admission Requirements: Graduation from high school and entrance examination

Fees: 19,800-32,230 per semester; Graduate, 8,960-10,380 per semester, 1,280 per credit hour (New Taiwan Dollar)

Main Language(s) of Instruction: Chinese

Degrees and Diplomas: *Bachelor's Degree*; *Master's Degree*: **Computer Engineering; Computer Science; Cultural Studies;**

Design; Development Studies; Education; Educational Administration; Educational and Student Counselling; Educational Testing and Evaluation; Fine Arts; Law; Mathematics Education; Modern Languages; Music; Physical Education; Preschool Education; Psychology; Science Education; Social Policy; Special Education; Writing. *Doctorate*: **Curriculum; Educational Administration; Educational Technology; Pedagogy; Science Education.**

Student Services: Academic Counselling, Canteen, Careers Guidance, Health Services, IT Centre, Library, Social Counselling, Sports Facilities

Publications: Elementary Education; Journal of National Taipei Teachers College

Last Updated: 01/04/14

NATIONAL TAIPEI UNIVERSITY OF NURSING AND HEALTH SCIENCES (NTUNHS)

365 Mingte Road, Beitou, Taipei 11257
Tel: +886(2) 282-27101
Fax: +886(2) 282-05680
EMail: kuji@ntcn.edu.tw
Website: http://www.ntcn.edu.tw

President: Nan-Chen Hsieh (2013-)
Tel: +886(2) 282-27101, Ext. 2000
EMail: president@ntunhs.edu.tw

Administrative Vice-President: Jin-Bao Yang
Tel: +886(2) 282-27101, Ext. 2007 EMail: kinbao@ntunhs.edu.tw

International Relations: Mei-Ling Gau
Tel: +886(2) 282-27101, Ext. 2730 EMail: meeiling@ntunhs.edu.tw

College

Healthcare Administration and Management (Health Administration; Health Sciences; Information Management; Tourism); **Human Development and Health** (Biological and Life Sciences; Child Care and Development; Health Sciences; Psychology; Speech Therapy and Audiology; Sports); **Nursing** (Health Education; Health Sciences; Midwifery; Nursing; Traditional Eastern Medicine)

Further Information: Also Teaching Hospital

History: Founded 1954 as as Taiwan Provincial Junior College of Nursing. Merged with Taipei Senior Vocational School of Medicine and renamed Taiwan Provincial Vocational School of Nursing and Midwifery 1963. Renamed National Taipei College of Nursing 1994. Acquired present title 2010.

Academic Year: September to July (September-February; March-July)

Admission Requirements: Graduation from high school and entrance examination

Main Language(s) of Instruction: Chinese, English

Degrees and Diplomas: *Bachelor's Degree*; *Master's Degree*: **Biological and Life Sciences; Child Care and Development; Health Administration; Health Sciences; Information Management; Midwifery; Nursing; Psychology; Speech Therapy and Audiology; Sports; Tourism; Traditional Eastern Medicine.** *Doctorate*: **Nursing.**

Student Services: Academic Counselling, Canteen, Careers Guidance, Cultural Activities, Facilities for disabled people, Health Services, IT Centre, Library, Social Counselling, Sports Facilities

Publications: Journal of National Taipei College of Nursing; News of National Taipei College of Nursing

Last Updated: 01/04/14

NATIONAL TAIPEI UNIVERSITY OF TECHNOLOGY (NTUT)

1, Sec. 3, Zhongxiao East. Road, Taipei 10608
Tel: +886(2) 2771-2171
Fax: +886(2) 275-13892 +886(2) 8773-1879
EMail: viola@ntut.edu.tw; oia@ntut.edu.tw; intstudy@ntut.edu.tw
Website: http://www.ntut.edu.tw

President: Leehter Yao
Tel: +886(2) 2771-2171, Ext. 1001
EMail: president@ntut.edu.tw; ltyao@ntut.edu.tw

Secretary-General: Chung-Kuang Yang
Tel: +886(2) 2771-2171, Ext. 1002
EMail: ckyang@ntut.edu.tw; hmlo@ntut.edu.tw

International Relations: Sheng-Tung Huang, Dean, Office of International Affairs
Tel: +886(2) 2771-2171, Ext. 6501
EMail: hd6501@ntut.edu.tw; intstudy@ntut.edu.tw

College

Design (Architectural and Environmental Design; Architecture; Communication Arts; Design; Industrial Design; Multimedia; Town Planning); **Electrical Engineering and Computer Science** (Computer Engineering; Computer Networks; Computer Science; Electrical Engineering; Electronic Engineering; Multimedia; Optical Technology; Software Engineering; Telecommunications Engineering); **Engineering** (Biochemistry; Bioengineering; Biomedical Engineering; Biotechnology; Chemical Engineering; Civil Engineering; Engineering; Environmental Engineering; Environmental Management; Materials Engineering; Mineralogy; Mining Engineering; Molecular Biology; Polymer and Plastics Technology; Safety Engineering; Textile Technology); **Humanities and Science** (Business Administration; Cultural Studies; English; International Business; Modern Languages; Optics; Physical Education; Private Law; Teacher Training; Technology Education; Vocational Education); **Management** (Business Administration; Finance; Industrial Engineering; Industrial Management; Information Management; Information Sciences; Management; Service Trades); **Mechanical and Electrical Engineering** (Automation and Control Engineering; Automotive Engineering; Electrical Engineering; Electronic Engineering; Energy Engineering; Heating and Refrigeration; Mechanical Engineering; Production Engineering)

History: Founded 1994, acquired present status 1997.

Fees: Master's degree programmes, 50,475-58,725 per semester; Doctorate programmes, 54,225-62,525 per semester (New Taiwan Dollar)

Main Language(s) of Instruction: Chinese, English

Degrees and Diplomas: *Bachelor's Degree*; *Master's Degree*: **Architecture; Automation and Control Engineering; Automotive Engineering; Biochemistry; Bioengineering; Biomedical Engineering; Business Administration; Chemical Engineering; Civil Engineering; Computer Engineering; Design; Electrical Engineering; Electronic Engineering; Energy Engineering; Engineering; Engineering Management; English; Environmental Engineering; Heating and Refrigeration; Industrial Engineering; Information Management; Management; Mechanical Engineering; Mineralogy; Mining Engineering; Optical Technology; Polymer and Plastics Technology; Private Law; Production Engineering; Safety Engineering; Technology Education; Telecommunications Engineering; Town Planning; Vocational Education.** *Doctorate*: **Business Administration; Chemical Engineering; Civil Engineering; Computer Engineering; Design; Electrical Engineering; Electronic Engineering; Energy Engineering; Engineering; Environmental Engineering; Environmental Management; Heating and Refrigeration; Industrial Engineering; Industrial Management; Mechanical Engineering; Mineralogy; Mining Engineering; Optical Technology; Polymer and Plastics Technology; Production Engineering; Safety Engineering; Technology Education; Telecommunications Engineering; Vocational Education.**

Student Services: IT Centre, Library, Residential Facilities, Sports Facilities

Student Numbers *2013-2014*: Total: c. 9,200

Last Updated: 07/04/14

NATIONAL TAITUNG UNIVERSITY (NTTU)

684, Section 1, Chung-Hua Road, Taitung 950
Tel: +886(89) 318-855
Fax: +886(89) 517-316
EMail: admin@nttu.edu.tw; coia@nttu.edu.tw
Website: http://www.nttu.edu.tw

President: Jinyuan Liu
Tel: +886(89) 353-100 EMail: president@nttu.edu.tw

Secretary-General: Zhuo-Mou Wen
Tel: +886(89) 318-855, Ext. 1003 EMail: chou@nttu.edu.tw

International Relations: Yao-Chung Chang
Tel: +886(89) 318-855, Ext. 1303 EMail: ycc@nttu.edu.tw

College

Humanities (Arts and Humanities; Chinese; Computer Graphics; Cultural Studies; English; Fine Arts; Leisure Studies; Literature; Multimedia; Music; Southeast Asian Studies; Sports); **Science and Engineering** (Applied Physics; Biological and Life Sciences; Biotechnology; Chemistry; Computer Engineering; Computer Science; Ecology; Information Management; Information Sciences; Information Technology; Marine Science and Oceanography; Mathematics; Mathematics Education; Microbiology; Nanotechnology; Natural Resources; Statistics; Traditional Eastern Medicine); **Teachers** (Education; Foreign Languages Education; Humanities and Social Science Education; Native Language Education; Physical Education; Preschool Education; Special Education; Teacher Training)

Centre

Education (Arts and Humanities; Mathematics; Modern Languages; Natural Sciences; Social Sciences; Technology)

Further Information: Also Jhihben Campus

History: Founded 1948 as National Taitung Teachers College. Acquired present status 2003.

Academic Year: September to June (September-January; February-June)

Admission Requirements: Graduation from high school or equivalent, and entrance examination

Fees: National: 610-710 per semester; graduate, 350-868 per semester (US Dollar), International: Undergraduate tuition, 10,300-15,550 per semester; Graduate tuition, 9,970-11,550 per semester (New Taiwan Dollar)

Main Language(s) of Instruction: Chinese, English

Degrees and Diplomas: *Bachelor's Degree*; *Master's Degree*: **Biological and Life Sciences; Education; Humanities and Social Science Education; Information Management; Leisure Studies; Literature; Physical Education; Preschool Education; Regional Studies; Southeast Asian Studies; Special Education.** *Doctorate*: **Education.**

Student Services: Academic Counselling, Canteen, Careers Guidance, Cultural Activities, Facilities for disabled people, Health Services, IT Centre, Library, Residential Facilities, Social Counselling, Sports Facilities

Publications: Journal of NTTU; NTTU Journal of Literature; NTTU Journal of Physical Education; NTTU Journal of Social Studies Education; NTTU Research Journal of Aboriginal Education; NTTU Research Report

Student Numbers *2010-2011*: Total: c. 4,500

Last Updated: 07/04/14

NATIONAL TAIWAN NORMAL UNIVERSITY (NTNU)

162, Heping East Road Section 1, Taipei 10610
Tel: +886(2) 7734-1111 +886(2) 7734-1088
Fax: +886(2) 239-22607 +886(2) 2366-0511
EMail: academic@deps.ntnu.edu.tw
Website: http://www.ntnu.edu.tw

President: Kuo-En Chang
Tel: +886(2) 7734-1014 EMail: president@deps.ntnu.edu.tw

Secretary-General: An-Pan Lin
Tel: +886(2) 7734-1021 EMail: anpanlin@ntnu.edu.tw

International Relations: Frank Ying, Dean, Office of International Affairs Tel: 886(2) 7734-1262 EMail: oia@deps.ntnu.edu.tw

College

Arts (Art History; Design; Fine Arts; Visual Arts); **Education** (Adult Education; Civics; Computer Education; Continuing Education; Curriculum; Development Studies; Education; Educational Administration; Educational and Student Counselling; Educational Psychology; Family Studies; Health Education; Health Sciences; Information Sciences; Leadership; Library Science; Pedagogy; Rehabilitation and Therapy; Special Education); **International Studies and Education for Overseas Chinese** (Arts and Humanities; Chinese; Cultural Studies; East Asian Studies; European Studies; Foreign Languages Education; Human Resources; Mathematics; Modern Languages; Natural Sciences; Social Sciences; Tourism); **Liberal Arts** (Arts and Humanities; Chinese; Cultural Studies; English; Geography; History; Translation and Interpretation); **Management** (Business Administration; International Business; Management); **Music** (Music; Musicology; Performing Arts); **Science** (Biological and Life Sciences; Chemistry; Computer Engineering; Computer Science; Earth Sciences; Electronic Engineering; Environmental Studies; Marine Engineering; Marine Science and Oceanography; Mathematics; Natural Sciences; Optical Technology; Physics; Science Education); **Social Sciences** (Mass Communication; Political Sciences; Social Sciences; Social Work); **Sports and Recreation** (Hotel and Restaurant; Leisure Studies; Physical Education; Sports); **Technology** (Communication Arts; Electrical Engineering; Electronic Engineering; Graphic Arts; Human Resources; Mechanical Engineering; Technology)

Further Information: National University Preparatory School for Overseas Chinese Students (see separate Division entry)

History: Founded 1946 as Taiwan Provincial Teachers' College. Acquired University status 1967 as the first University in Taiwan devoted to the training of secondary school teachers. A State institution responsible to the Ministry of Education.

Academic Year: September to June (September-January; February-June)

Admission Requirements: Graduation from senior high school or recognized foreign equivalent, and entrance examination

Fees: Tuition for Bachelor Programmes, 47,180-55,200 per semester; Tuition for graduate programmes, NTD 50,726-56,264 per semester (New Taiwan Dollar)

Main Language(s) of Instruction: Chinese, English

Degrees and Diplomas: *Bachelor's Degree*: **Arts and Humanities; Cultural Studies; Education; Educational Psychology; Engineering; Fine Arts; Management; Music; Natural Sciences; Physical Education; Psychology; Social Sciences; Sports.** *Master's Degree*: **Adult Education; Asian Studies; Biological and Life Sciences; Chemistry; Chinese; Civics; Communication Arts; Computer Science; Continuing Education; Development Studies; East Asian Studies; Education; Educational Administration; Educational and Student Counselling; Educational Psychology; Electronic Engineering; English; European Studies; Family Studies; Fine Arts; Geography; Graphic Arts; Health Education; History; Hotel and Restaurant; Human Resources; Industrial Engineering; Information Sciences; Leisure Studies; Library Science; Literature; Mathematics; Mechanical Engineering; Music; Physical Education; Psychology; Rehabilitation and Therapy; Science Education; Special Education; Sports; Tourism; Vocational Education.** *Doctorate*: **Adult Education; Biological and Life Sciences; Chemistry; Chinese; Civics; Computer Engineering; Continuing Education; Development Studies; Earth Sciences; Education; Educational and Student Counselling; Educational Psychology; Electronic Engineering; English; Environmental Studies; Family Studies; Fine Arts; Geography; Health Education; Health Sciences; History; Hotel and Restaurant; Human Resources; Industrial Engineering; Leisure Studies; Literature; Mathematics; Music; Native Language Education; Optical Technology; Physical Education; Physics; Political Sciences; Science Education; Special Education; Sports.**

Student Services: Canteen, Health Services, IT Centre, Library, Residential Facilities, Sports Facilities

Publications: Abstract of Chinese Educational Literature; Bulletin of Institute of Educational Research; Bulletin of National Taiwan Normal University; Bulletin of Research Institute of Chinese Literature

Academic Staff *2012-2013*	**TOTAL**
FULL-TIME	**853**
PART-TIME	**491**
Student Numbers *2012-2013*	
All (Foreign included)	**10,893**

Last Updated: 04/04/14

NATIONAL TAIWAN OCEAN UNIVERSITY (NTOU)

2 Pei-Ning Road, Keelung 20224
Tel: +886(2) 2462-2192
Fax: +886(2) 2462-0724
EMail: admission@mail.ntou.edu.tw; se@mail.ntou.edu.tw
Website: http://www.ntou.edu.tw

President: Ching-Fong Chang
Tel: +886(2) 246-22192, Ext. 1000-1004
EMail: po@ntou.edu.tw; B0044@mail.ntou.edu.tw

Secretary-General: Jih-Gau Juang
Tel: +886(2) 246-22192, Ext. 1001-1004
EMail: se@ntou.edu.tw; jgjuang@mail.ntou.edu.tw

International Relations: Yew-Hu Chien, Dean of Office of International Student Affairs
Tel: +886(2) 2462-2192, Ext. 1220/5204
EMail: yhchien@mail.ntou.edu.tw; oia@mail.ntou.edu.tw

College

Electrical Engineering and Computer Science (Automation and Control Engineering; Computer Engineering; Computer Science; Electrical Engineering; Electronic Engineering; Optical Technology; Telecommunications Engineering); **Engineering** (Civil Engineering; Computer Engineering; Electronic Engineering; Engineering; Materials Engineering; Mechanical Engineering; Naval Architecture); **Humanities and Social Sciences** (Cultural Studies; Economics; Education; English; Law; Teacher Training); **Life Sciences** (Aquaculture; Biological and Life Sciences; Biotechnology; Food Science; Marine Biology); **Maritime Science and Management** (Marine Engineering; Marine Science and Oceanography; Marine Transport; Transport and Communications; Transport Management); **Ocean Science and Resource** (Applied Chemistry; Biology; Chemistry; Computer Science; Earth Sciences; Ecology; Environmental Studies; Fishery; Marine Biology; Marine Science and Oceanography)

Further Information: Also Research and Extension Centres

History: Founded 1953 as Junior College, became Senior College 1964, and acquired present status and title 1989. Financed by and under the jurisdiction of the Ministry of Education.

Academic Year: August to July (August-January; February-July)

Admission Requirements: Senior high school certificate or recognized equivalent, and entrance examination

Main Language(s) of Instruction: Chinese

Degrees and Diplomas: *Bachelor's Degree*; *Master's Degree*: **Applied Chemistry; Aquaculture; Automation and Control Engineering; Biological and Life Sciences; Biotechnology; Business Administration; Civil Engineering; Computer Engineering; Computer Science; Cultural Studies; Earth Sciences; Ecology; Economics; Education; Electrical Engineering; Electronic Engineering; Energy Engineering; English; Environmental Studies; Fishery; Food Science; Human Resources; Law; Marine Biology; Marine Engineering; Marine Transport; Materials Engineering; Mechanical Engineering; Naval Architecture; Optical Technology; Power Engineering; Telecommunications Engineering; Transport and Communications; Transport Engineering; Transport Management.** *Doctorate*: **Aquaculture; Biological and Life Sciences; Biotechnology; Civil Engineering; Computer Engineering; Computer Science; Earth Sciences; Electrical Engineering; Electronic Engineering; Energy Engineering; Environmental Studies; Fishery; Food Science; Marine Biology; Marine Engineering; Marine Transport; Materials Engineering; Mechanical Engineering; Naval Architecture; Optical Technology; Transport Management.**

Student Services: Academic Counselling, Canteen, Careers Guidance, Cultural Activities, Facilities for disabled people, Health Services, IT Centre, Language Laboratory, Library, Social Counselling, Sports Facilities

Publications: Journal of Marine Science and Technology

Last Updated: 07/04/14

NATIONAL TAIWAN SPORT UNIVERSITY (NTSU)

No. 250, Wenhua 1st Rd., Guishan Township, Taoyuan 33301
Tel: +886(3) 328-3201
Fax: +886(3) 328-4047
EMail: ntsu@ntsu.edu.tw
Website: http://www.ntsu.edu.tw

President: Chin-Hsung Kao (2010-)
Tel: +886(3) 328-3201, Ext. 1608 EMail: president@ntsu.edu.tw

Dean of Academic Affairs: Zong-Wen Yang
Tel: +886(3) 328-0630 EMail: yangtw@mail.ntsu.edu.tw

International Relations: James Shih-Chung Cheng, Director, Centre for International Affairs
Tel: +886(3) 328-3201, Ext. 1288/2416
EMail: shihchung@ntsu.edu.tw

Division

General Courses (Arts and Humanities; Chinese; Computer Science; English; Information Sciences; Information Technology; Modern Languages)

College

Athletics (Sports; Sports Management); **Exercise and Health Sciences** (Health Sciences; Sports); **Management** (Business Administration; International Business; Leisure Studies; Parks and Recreation; Sports Management); **Physical Education** (Physical Education)

History: Founded 1987 as National College of Physical Education and Sports. Acquired present status and title 2008.

Main Language(s) of Instruction: Chinese

Degrees and Diplomas: *Bachelor's Degree*; *Master's Degree*: **Business Administration; Health Sciences; Leisure Studies; Parks and Recreation; Physical Education; Sports; Sports Management.** *Doctorate*: **Physical Education.**

Student Services: IT Centre, Library, Residential Facilities, Sports Facilities

Student Numbers *2013-2014*: Total: c. 2,300

Last Updated: 03/04/14

NATIONAL TAIWAN UNIVERSITY (NTU)

No.1, Sec. 4, Roosevelt Road, Taipei 10617
Tel: +886(2) 3366-3366
Fax: +886(2) 2362-7651
EMail: secretor@ntu.edu.tw
Website: http://www.ntu.edu.tw

President: Pan-Chyr Yang
Tel: +886(2) 3366-2000
EMail: pcyang@ntu.edu.tw; president@ntu.edu.tw

Secretary-General: Ta-Te Lin
Tel: +886(2) 2362-0619 +886(2) 3366-2030
EMail: secretariat@ntu.edu.tw

International Relations: Tung Shen, Dean, International Programmes
Tel: +886(2) 3366-2007 EMail: cfia@ntu.edu.tw; oia@ntu.edu.tw

Division

Continuing Education and Professional Development; Physical Education

College

Bio-Resources and Agriculture (Agricultural Business; Agricultural Economics; Agricultural Education; Agricultural Engineering; Agricultural Equipment; Agriculture; Agronomy; Animal Husbandry; Applied Chemistry; Automation and Control Engineering; Bioengineering; Biology; Biotechnology; Communication Studies; Electronic Engineering; Entomology; Environmental Engineering; Environmental Management; Farm Management; Food Science; Food Technology; Forestry; Genetics; Horticulture; Industrial Engineering; Landscape Architecture; Mechanical Engineering; Microbiology; Molecular Biology; Natural Resources; Plant and Crop Protection; Plant Pathology; Veterinary Science; Water Science); **Electrical Engineering and Computer Science** (Applied Physics; Computer Engineering; Computer Networks; Computer Science; Electrical Engineering; Electronic Engineering; Information Technology; Mechanical Engineering; Medical Technology; Multimedia; Nanotechnology; Optical Technology; Telecommunications Engineering); **Engineering** (Automation and Control Engineering; Biomedical Engineering; Building Technologies; Chemical Engineering; Civil Engineering; Engineering; Environmental Engineering; Hydraulic Engineering; Industrial Engineering; Marine Engineering; Materials Engineering; Mechanical Engineering; Mechanics; Nanotechnology; Petroleum and Gas Engineering; Polymer and Plastics

Technology; Seismology; Town Planning); **Law** (European Union Law; International Law; Law); **Liberal Arts** (Anthropology; Art History; Arts and Humanities; Asian Religious Studies; Chinese; English; European Languages; Foreign Languages Education; History; Information Sciences; Japanese; Library Science; Linguistics; Literature; Modern Languages; Musicology; Philosophy; Theatre; Translation and Interpretation); **Life Science** (Biochemistry; Biological and Life Sciences; Biology; Biotechnology; Botany; Cell Biology; Ecology; Fishery; Microbiology; Molecular Biology; Zoology); **Management** (Accountancy; Business Administration; Finance; Information Management; International Business; Management); **Medicine** (Anatomy; Biochemistry; Biomedical Engineering; Cell Biology; Forensic Medicine and Dentistry; Genetics; Immunology; Laboratory Techniques; Medical Parasitology; Medical Technology; Medicine; Microbiology; Molecular Biology; Neurosciences; Nursing; Occupational Therapy; Oncology; Pathology; Pharmacology; Physical Therapy; Physiology; Psychiatry and Mental Health; Social and Preventive Medicine; Toxicology); **Pharmacy** (Pharmacy); **Public Health** (Environmental Studies; Epidemiology; Health Administration; Hygiene; Management; Occupational Health; Public Health; Social and Preventive Medicine; Welfare and Protective Services); **Science** *(Also Instrumentation Centre)* (Applied Mathematics; Applied Physics; Astrophysics; Chemistry; Geography; Geology; Instrument Making; Marine Science and Oceanography; Mathematics; Meteorology; Physics; Psychology); **Social Sciences** (Asian Studies; Development Studies; East Asian Studies; Economics; Journalism; Law; Political Sciences; Social Policy; Social Sciences; Social Work; Sociology)

School

Dentistry (Biology; Dentistry; Oral Pathology); **Veterinary Medicine** (Biology; Molecular Biology; Pathology; Veterinary Science; Zoology)

Centre

Biodiversity (Biological and Life Sciences); **Biotechnology** (Biotechnology); **Condensed Matter Sciences** (Physics); **Cosmology and Particle Astrophysics** *(Leung)* (Astrophysics); **General Education** (Arts and Humanities; Biological and Life Sciences; Chinese; English; History; Literature; Mathematics; Modern Languages; Natural Sciences; Philosophy; Social Sciences); **Indigenous Studies** (Indigenous Studies); **Information and Electronics Technologies** (Electronic Engineering; Information Technology); **Neurobiology and Cognitive Science** (Instrument Making); **NTU-ITRI Nano** (Nanotechnology); **Ocean** (Marine Engineering; Technology); **Population and Gender Studies** (Demography and Population; Gender Studies)

Research Centre

Developmental Biology and Regenerative Medicine (Biology; Medicine); **Digital Humanities** (Arts and Humanities); **Weather Climate and Disaster** (Meteorology)

Further Information: Also University Hospital and Veterinary Hospital; 5 International Research Centres; National-Level Research Centres; 20 additional University-Level Research Centres

History: Founded 1928 as Taihoku Imperial University by the Japanese. Acquired present status and title 1945 following Taiwan's retrocession to Chinese sovereignty. The oldest University in Taiwan.

Academic Year: August to June (September-January; February-June)

Admission Requirements: Graduation from senior high school or foreign equivalent, and entrance examination for local students, direct application for foreign students

Fees: Undergraduate Programmes, 25,230-39,560; Graduate Programmes, 25,640-88,000 (New Taiwan Dollar)

Main Language(s) of Instruction: Chinese

Accrediting Agency: Higher Education Evaluation and Accreditation Council of Taiwan (HEEACT); Institute of Engineering Education Taiwan (IEET)

Degrees and Diplomas: *Bachelor's Degree*; *Master's Degree*: **Accountancy; Agricultural Business; Agricultural Economics; Agronomy; Anatomy; Animal Husbandry; Anthropology; Applied Chemistry; Applied Physics; Architecture and Planning; Art History; Astrophysics; Biochemistry; Bioengineering; Biomedical Engineering; Biotechnology; Botany; Building Technologies; Business Administration; Cell Biology; Chemical Engineering; Chemistry; Chinese; Civil Engineering; Computer Engineering; Computer Networks; Computer Science; Dentistry; Development Studies; Ecology; Economics; Electrical Engineering; Electronic Engineering; Entomology; Environmental Engineering; Environmental Studies; Finance; Fishery; Food Science; Food Technology; Forestry; Geography; Geology; Health Sciences; History; Horticulture; Hygiene; Immunology; Industrial Engineering; Information Management; Information Sciences; International Business; Japanese; Journalism; Laboratory Techniques; Landscape Architecture; Law; Library Science; Linguistics; Literature; Marine Engineering; Marine Science and Oceanography; Materials Engineering; Mathematics; Mechanical Engineering; Mechanics; Medical Technology; Medicine; Meteorology; Microbiology; Modern Languages; Molecular Biology; Multimedia; Musicology; Natural Resources; Nursing; Occupational Therapy; Optical Technology; Oral Pathology; Pathology; Pharmacology; Pharmacy; Philosophy; Physical Therapy; Physics; Physiology; Plant Pathology; Political Sciences; Polymer and Plastics Technology; Psychology; Social Work; Sociology; Theatre; Toxicology; Veterinary Science; Zoology.** *Doctorate*: **Accountancy; Agricultural Business; Agricultural Economics; Agronomy; Anatomy; Animal Husbandry; Anthropology; Applied Chemistry; Applied Physics; Architecture and Planning; Art History; Astrophysics; Biochemistry; Bioengineering; Biology; Biomedical Engineering; Biomedicine; Biotechnology; Botany; Building Technologies; Business Administration; Cell Biology; Chemical Engineering; Chemistry; Chinese; Civil Engineering; Computer Engineering; Computer Networks; Computer Science; Dentistry; Development Studies; Ecology; Economics; Electrical Engineering; Electronic Engineering; Entomology; Environmental Engineering; Environmental Studies; Finance; Fishery; Food Science; Food Technology; Forestry; Geography; Geology; Health Sciences; History; Horticulture; Hygiene; Immunology; Industrial Engineering; Information Management; Information Sciences; International Business; Laboratory Techniques; Landscape Architecture; Law; Library Science; Linguistics; Literature; Marine Engineering; Marine Science and Oceanography; Materials Engineering; Mathematics; Mechanical Engineering; Mechanics; Medical Technology; Medicine; Meteorology; Microbiology; Modern Languages; Molecular Biology; Multimedia; Natural Resources; Nursing; Occupational Health; Occupational Therapy; Optical Technology; Pathology; Pharmacology; Pharmacy; Philosophy; Physical Therapy; Physics; Physiology; Plant Pathology; Political Sciences; Polymer and Plastics Technology; Psychology; Social Work; Sociology; Telecommunications Engineering; Toxicology; Veterinary Science; Zoology.**

Student Services: Academic Counselling, Canteen, Careers Guidance, Cultural Activities, Facilities for disabled people, Health Services, IT Centre, Language Laboratory, Library, Nursery Care, Social Counselling, Sports Facilities

Publications: Acta Botanica Taiwanica; Acta Geologica Taiwanica; Acta Oceanographica Taiwanica; Acta Zoologica Taiwanica; Chinese Paleography; Chungwai Literary Monthly; Civil Engineering Studies; Forum of Women's and Gender Studies; History and Chinese Literature Series; Humanitas Taiwanica; Journal of Art History; Journal of Geographical Science; Journal of Population Studies; Journal of Women's and Gender Studies; Monographs of the College of Agriculture; National Taiwan University Journal of Sociology; National Taiwan University Journalist Forum Journal; National Taiwan University Law Journal; National Taiwan University Library and Information Science Journal; National Taiwan University Philosophical Review; NTU Management Review; NTU Social Work Review; NTU Studies in Japanese Language and Literature; NTU Studies in Language and Literature; Political Science Review; Studies in Chinese Literature; Taiwan Economic Review; Taiwanese Sociology; TAIWANIA; University Library Journal

Publishing House: National Taiwan University Press

Academic Staff *2012-2013*	**TOTAL**
FULL-TIME	1,993
PART-TIME	1,889
Student Numbers *2013-2014*	
All (Foreign included)	c. 33,000

Last Updated: 10/04/14

NATIONAL TAIWAN UNIVERSITY OF ARTS (NTUA)

59, Sec. 1, Daguan Rd., Banqiao Dist., Taipei 22058
Tel: +886(2) 2272-2181
Fax: +886(2) 296-87563
EMail: d01@mail.ntua.edu.tw
Website: http://www.ntua.edu.tw

President: Yung-cheng Hsieh
Tel: +886(2) 296-76414 EMail: pre@ntua.edu.tw; ych@ntua.edu.tw

Chief Secretary: Ming-yin Tsai
Tel: +886(2) 296-94416 EMail: susana9988@ntua.edu.tw

International Relations: Mei-Ling Chu, Dean, Office of International Affairs
Tel: +886(2) 227-22181, Ext. 1750 EMail: michu@ntua.edu.tw

College
Communication (Communication Arts; Film; Graphic Arts; Media Studies; Radio and Television Broadcasting); **Humanities** (Art Management; Arts and Humanities; Chinese; Education; Humanities and Social Science Education; Oriental Studies; Physical Education; Teacher Training); **Performing Arts** (Dance; Music; Performing Arts; Theatre)

School
Design (Communication Arts; Design; Earth Sciences; Industrial Design; Multimedia; Visual Arts)

Academy
Fine Arts (Architectural Restoration; Fine Arts; Painting and Drawing; Printing and Printmaking; Sculpture)

History: Founded 1955, acquired present status 2001.

Main Language(s) of Instruction: Chinese

Degrees and Diplomas: *Bachelor's Degree*; *Master's Degree*: **Architectural Restoration; Art Management; Chinese; Communication Arts; Dance; Design; Fine Arts; Graphic Arts; Humanities and Social Science Education; Music; Painting and Drawing; Performing Arts; Radio and Television Broadcasting; Sculpture; Theatre; Visual Arts.** *Doctorate*: **Art Management; Industrial Design; Painting and Drawing; Performing Arts.**

Student Services: IT Centre, Library

Academic Staff *2013-2014*	**TOTAL**
FULL-TIME	**190**
PART-TIME	c. **700**
Student Numbers *2013-2014*	
All (Foreign included)	c. **5,400**

Last Updated: 06/04/14

NATIONAL TAIWAN UNIVERSITY OF PHYSICAL EDUCATION AND SPORT (NTUPES)

16, Sec. 1, Shuan-shih Rd., Taichung 404
Tel: +886(4) 222-13108
Fax: +886(4) 222-32463
EMail: ntcpe@ntupes.edu.tw
Website: http://www.ntupes.edu.tw/

President: Wen-Ren Su
Tel: +886(4) 222-13108 EMail: wjsu@ntcpe.edu.tw

Department
Athletics *(Also Graduate School)* (Arts and Humanities; Sports; Sports Management; Sports Medicine); **Dance** *(Also Graduate School)* (Dance); **Physical Education** *(Also Graduate School)* (Physical Education); **Recreational Sport** *(Also Graduate School)* (Parks and Recreation; Sports); **Sport Management** *(Also Graduate School)* (Sports Management); **Sports and Health Science** (Health Sciences; Sports)

History: Founded 1961 as Taiwan Provincial College of Physical Education. Renamed Taiwan Junior College of Physical Education 1992 and National Taiwan College of Physical Education (NTCPE) 1996. Acquired present status and title 2011.

Academic Year: September to June (September-January; February-June)

Admission Requirements: Graduation from high school and entrance examination

Main Language(s) of Instruction: Chinese

Degrees and Diplomas: *Bachelor's Degree*; *Master's Degree*: **Dance; Health Sciences; Parks and Recreation; Physical Education; Sports; Sports Management.**

Student Services: IT Centre, Library, Sports Facilities

Last Updated: 03/04/14

NATIONAL TAIWAN UNIVERSITY OF SCIENCE AND TECHNOLOGY (NTUST)

No.43, Sec. 4, Keelung Rd., Da'an Dist., Taipei 10607
Tel: +886(2) 273-33141
Fax: +886(2) 273-31044
EMail: admission@mail.ntust.edu.tw
Website: http://www.ntust.edu.tw

President: Ching-Jong Liao (2013-)
Tel: +886(2) 2737-6101 EMail: president@mail.ntust.edu.tw

Secretary-General: Tzu-Chuan Chou
Tel: +886(2) 273-76102 EMail: tcchou@mail.ntust.edu.tw

International Relations: Cheng-Kang Lee, Dean of International Affairs
Tel: +886(2) 273-01130
EMail: oia@mail.ntust.edu.tw; cklee@mail.ntust.edu.tw

College
Design (Architecture; Design; Industrial Design); **Electrical and Computer Engineering** (Computer Engineering; Computer Science; Electrical Engineering; Electronic Engineering; Information Technology; Optical Technology); **Engineering** (Automation and Control Engineering; Chemical Engineering; Civil Engineering; Construction Engineering; Materials Engineering; Mechanical Engineering); **Honors** (Biomedical Engineering; Chemistry; Electronic Engineering; Materials Engineering; Natural Sciences; Psychology; Science Education; Technology); **Intellectual Property Studies** (Engineering Management; Private Law); **Liberal Arts and Social Sciences** (Arts and Humanities; Education; Educational Technology; Modern Languages; Social Sciences; Teacher Training; Technology Education; Vocational Education); **Management** (Business Administration; Finance; Industrial Management; Information Management; Management)

Centre
Business Incubation *(BIC)*; **Concern for Life**; **Continuing Education**; **General Affairs**; **General Education** (Arts and Humanities; Modern Languages; Social Sciences); **General Education**; **Humanities and the Arts** (Arts and Humanities); **Industry-University Cooperation** *(IUCC)*; **Intellectual Property and Business** (Business Administration; Private Law); **Taiwan Aborigine** (Indigenous Studies); **Technology Transfer** *(TTC)*; **Ventilation Technology**

Research Centre
Automation and Control (Automation and Control Engineering); **Chemical Mechanical Planarization Innovation** (Chemical Engineering; Mechanical Engineering); **Color Technology** (Physics); **Commatrix**; **Communication and Electromagnetic Technology** (Physical Engineering; Telecommunications Engineering); **Construction Safety and Health** (Safety Engineering); **E-Learning**; **Ecological and Hazard Mitigation Engineering** (Ecology); **Intelligent Robot** (Robotics); **IoT Inovation**; **Material Science and Technology** (Materials Engineering; Technology); **Nanotechnology** (Nanotechnology); **Occupational Health and Safety** (Occupational Health); **Opto-Mechatronics Technology** (Electronic Engineering; Optical Technology); **Power Electronics Technology** (Electronic Engineering; Power Engineering); **Study of Lottery and Commercial Gaming** (Social Studies); **Sustainable Energy Development** (Energy Engineering); **Taiwan Building Technology** (Building Technologies); **Taiwan Information Security** (Information Management)

History: Founded 1974 as National Taiwan Institute of Technology (NTIT). Acquired present status 1997.

Academic Year: September to June (September-January; February-June)

Admission Requirements: Graduation from senior high school (4-year new undergraduate programme), junior technical college (2-year programme), or vocational senior high school (4-year new undergraduate programme)

Fees: Undergraduate tuition, 47,000-53,000 per semester; Graduate tuition, 47,000-54,000 (New Taiwan Dollar)

Main Language(s) of Instruction: Chinese, English

Degrees and Diplomas: *Bachelor's Degree*; *Master's Degree*: **Architecture; Automation and Control Engineering; Biological and Life Sciences; Biomedical Engineering; Business Administration; Chemical Engineering; Chemistry; Computer Engineering; Computer Science; Construction Engineering; Design; Electrical Engineering; Electronic Engineering; Engineering Management; English; Foreign Languages Education; Industrial Design; Industrial Management; Information Technology; Materials Engineering; Mechanical Engineering; Optical Technology; Physics; Science Education.** *Doctorate*: **Architecture; Automation and Control Engineering; Biomedical Engineering; Chemical Engineering; Chemistry; Computer Science; Construction Engineering; Design; Electrical Engineering; Electronic Engineering; Engineering; Industrial Design; Industrial Management; Information Technology; Materials Engineering; Optical Technology; Physics; Science Education.** Also one-year Postbachelor programme in Color, Imaging and Illumination

Student Services: Academic Counselling, Careers Guidance, Facilities for disabled people, Health Services, IT Centre, Library, Residential Facilities, Sports Facilities

Academic Staff *2012-2013*	**TOTAL**
FULL-TIME	**522**
PART-TIME	**682**
STAFF WITH DOCTORATE	
FULL-TIME	**172**
Student Numbers *2012-2013*	
All (Foreign included)	**10,398**
FOREIGN ONLY	**521**

Last Updated: 11/04/14

NATIONAL TSING HUA UNIVERSITY (NTHU)

101, Sec. 2, Kuang-Fu Road, Hsinchu 30013
Tel: +886(3) 571-5131
Fax: +886(3) 572-2467
EMail: web@cc.nthu.edu.tw
Website: http://www.nthu.edu.tw

President: Lih J. Chen (2010-)
Tel: +886(3) 516-2001 EMail: presid@my.nthu.edu.tw

Chief of Staff: Chen-Fu Chien
Tel: +886(3) 573-1001 EMail: cfchien@mx.nthu.edu.tw

International Relations: Wei-Chung Wang, Vice President for Global Affairs
Tel: +886(3) 516-2456 EMail: wcwang@pme.nthu.edu.tw

College

Electrical Engineering and Computer Science (Computer Engineering; Computer Science; Electrical Engineering; Electronic Engineering; Information Sciences; Optical Technology; Telecommunications Engineering); **Engineering** (Biomedical Engineering; Chemical Engineering; Engineering Management; Industrial Engineering; Materials Engineering; Mechanical Engineering; Microelectronics; Nanotechnology; Power Engineering); **Humanities and Social Sciences** (Anthropology; Arts and Humanities; Chinese; History; Linguistics; Literature; Modern Languages; Philosophy; Social Sciences; Sociology); **Life Sciences** (Biological and Life Sciences; Biology; Biotechnology; Cell Biology; Computer Science; Medicine; Molecular Biology; Neurosciences); **Nuclear Science** (Biomedical Engineering; Engineering; Environmental Studies; Nuclear Engineering; Nuclear Physics); **Science** (Biological and Life Sciences; Biotechnology; Medicine); **Technology Management** (Business Administration; Economics; Engineering Management; Finance; Law; Service Trades)

History: Founded 1911 in Peking as Tsing Hua Academy. Acquired current title and university status 1928. Re-established in Hsinchu, Taiwan, 1956. A State institution.

Academic Year: August to July (August-January; February-July)

Admission Requirements: High school graduation certificate and national university entrance examination

Fees: c. 41,890-48,470 per semester (year 2012-2013) (New Taiwan Dollar)

Main Language(s) of Instruction: Mandarin Chinese

Accrediting Agency: Ministry of Education

Degrees and Diplomas: *Bachelor's Degree*; *Master's Degree*: **Arts and Humanities; Biological and Life Sciences; Computer Science; Electrical Engineering; Engineering; Nuclear Physics.** *Doctorate*: **Biological and Life Sciences; Computer Science; Electrical Engineering; Engineering; Nuclear Physics.** Also MBA, Executive MBA (MBA), International MBA (IMBA).

Student Services: Academic Counselling, Canteen, Careers Guidance, Cultural Activities, Facilities for disabled people, Foreign Studies Centre, Health Services, Language Laboratory, Nursery Care, Social Counselling, Sports Facilities

Publications: Alumni Newspaper; Inter-Asia Cultural Studies; NTHU Cover Story; NTHU Journal for General Education; NTHU Journal for History Education; NTHU Journal of Chinese Studies; Tsing Hua Newsletters

Publishing House: Tsing Hua University Press

Academic Staff *2012-2013*	MEN	WOMEN	**TOTAL**
FULL-TIME	483	824	**1,307**
PART-TIME	195	56	**251**
STAFF WITH DOCTORATE			
FULL-TIME	196	61	**257**
Student Numbers *2012-2013*			
All (Foreign included)	8,499	3,949	**12,448**
FOREIGN ONLY	304	226	**530**

Part-time students, 816. **Distance students,** 318.

Last Updated: 22/05/13

NATIONAL UNITED UNIVERSITY (NUU)

1, Lienda, Miaoli 36003
Tel: +886(37) 381-000
Fax: +886(37) 331-165
EMail: admission@nuu.edu.tw
Website: http://www.nuu.edu.tw

President: Ming-Hsi Hsu
Tel: +886(37) 381-871 EMail: president@nuu.edu.tw

Secretary-General: Justin Hung
Tel: +886(37) 381-188 EMail: hungjs@nuu.edu.tw

College

Design (Architecture; Design; Fine Arts; Industrial Design); **Electrical Engineering and Computer Science** (Computer Engineering; Computer Science; Electrical and Electronic Engineering; Electrical Engineering; Electronic Engineering; Optical Technology); **Engineering and Science** (Chemical Engineering; Civil Engineering; Energy Engineering; Engineering; Environmental Engineering; Health Sciences; Materials Engineering; Mechanical Engineering; Safety Engineering); **Hakka Studies** (Communication Studies; Economics; Information Sciences; Native Language; Social Studies; Sociology); **Humanities and Social Sciences** (Arts and Humanities; Chinese; Communication Studies; English; Literature; Modern Languages; Native Language; Native Language Education; Social Sciences); **Management** (Business Administration; Finance; Information Sciences)

Centre

General Education (Arts and Humanities; Education; Modern Languages)

Research Centre

Creative and Interdisciplinary Design; **Energy**; **Glass and Optic Fiber Materials**; **Glassfiber**; **Global Hakka**; **Hazards Mitigation and Recovery**; **MiaoLi**; **Optoelectronics**

History: Founded 1969, started operating 1972 as Lien Ho Industrial and Technological Junior College. Successively renamed Lien Ho Junior College of Technology (1973), Lien Ho College of Technology and Commerce (1992) National Lien Ho College of Technology and Commerce (1995), National Lien Ho Institute of Technology (1999). Acquired present status and title 2003.

Fees: c. 40,000 per semester (New Taiwan Dollar)

Main Language(s) of Instruction: Chinese

Degrees and Diplomas: *Bachelor's Degree*; *Master's Degree*: **Architecture; Business Administration; Chemical Engineering; Civil Engineering; Electrical Engineering; Electronic**

Engineering; Energy Engineering; Environmental Engineering; Health Sciences; Industrial Design; Information Management; Information Sciences; Materials Engineering; Mechanical Engineering; Optical Technology; Safety Engineering; Sociology. *Doctorate*: **Chemical Engineering; Materials Engineering.**

Student Services: Health Services, Library, Residential Facilities, Sports Facilities

Last Updated: 07/04/14

NATIONAL UNIVERSITY OF KAOHSIUNG (NUK)

700, Kaohsiung University Road, Nan-Tzu, Kaohsiung 811
Tel: +886(7) 591-9000
Fax: +886(7) 591-9083
EMail: admission@nuk.edu.tw
Website: http://www.nuk.edu.tw

President: Zhaorui Huang
Tel: +886(7) 591-9021
EMail: president@nuk.edu.tw; a1498@nuk.edu.tw

Secretary-General: Zhenhua Chen
Tel: +886(7) 591-9226
EMail: chchen@nuk.edu.tw; sec@nuk.edu.tw

International Relations: Yuan Jing, International Affairs Officer
Tel: +886(7) 591-9000, Ext. 8850 EMail: caroline@nuk.edu.tw

College

Engineering (Architecture; Chemical Engineering; Civil Engineering; Computer Engineering; Computer Science; Electrical Engineering; Engineering; Environmental Engineering; Information Technology; Materials Engineering; Town Planning); **Humanities and Social Sciences** (Arts and Humanities; Ceramic Art; Design; English; European Languages; Fine Arts; Foreign Languages Education; Handicrafts; Health Sciences; Japanese; Korean; Leisure Studies; Linguistics; Literature; Modern Languages; Social Sciences; South and Southeast Asian Languages; Sports; Vietnamese); **Law** (Administrative Law; Civil Law; Commercial Law; Constitutional Law; Criminal Law; Government; Justice Administration; Law; Political Sciences; Public Administration; Public Law); **Management** (Business Administration; Economics; Finance; Information Management; International Business; Law; Leadership; Management); **Science** (Applied Chemistry; Applied Mathematics; Applied Physics; Biological and Life Sciences; Biotechnology; Natural Sciences; Statistics)

Centre

Chinese Language (Chinese; Foreign Languages Education); **Language** (Chinese; English; Modern Languages; Translation and Interpretation)

History: Founded 2000.

Fees: Undergraduate tuition fees, 32,200-37,800 per semester; Graduate tuition fees, 46,000-54,000 per semester (New Taiwan Dollar)

Main Language(s) of Instruction: Chinese

Accrediting Agency: Higher Education Evaluation and Accreditation Council of Taiwan (HEEACT)

Degrees and Diplomas: *Associate Degree*; *Bachelor's Degree*; *Master's Degree*: **Applied Chemistry; Applied Mathematics; Applied Physics; Architecture; Biotechnology; Business Administration; Chemical Engineering; Civil Engineering; Commercial Law; Computer Engineering; Computer Science; Economics; Electrical Engineering; Environmental Engineering; Finance; Health Sciences; Information Management; International Business; Law; Leisure Studies; Management; Materials Engineering; Political Sciences; Sports; Statistics; Town Planning.** *Doctorate*: **Applied Mathematics; Electrical Engineering; Statistics.**

Student Services: Library, Residential Facilities, Sports Facilities

Last Updated: 11/04/14

NATIONAL UNIVERSITY OF TAINAN (NUTN)

33, Section 2, Shulin Street, Tainan 70010
Tel: +886(6) 213-3111
Fax: +886(6) 214-4409
EMail: yuan@mail.nutn.edu.tw
Website: http://www.nutn.edu.tw

President: Hsiu-Shuang Huang (2007-)
Tel: +886(6) +213-3111, Ext. 110-116
EMail: hshu@mail.nutn.edu.tw; president@mail.nutn.edu.tw

Secretary-General: Li-Chuan Chiang
Tel: +886(6) 213-3111, Ext. 110 EMail: lcchiang@mail.nutn.edu.tw

International Relations: Yeou-Xin Wu, Director, Division of International Affairs
Tel: +886(6) 2133-111, Ext. 143
EMail: randd-1@pubmail.nutn.edu.tw

College

Education (Education; Educational and Student Counselling; Physical Education; Preschool Education; Special Education); **Environmental Sciences and Ecology** (Biological and Life Sciences; Biotechnology; Ecology; Energy Engineering; Environmental Engineering; Environmental Studies); **Humanities** (Arts and Humanities; Chinese; Cultural Studies; East Asian Studies; English; Literature; Modern Languages; Natural Resources; Public Administration); **Performance and Visual Arts** (Computer Graphics; Fine Arts; Graphic Design; Multimedia; Music; Performing Arts; Theatre; Visual Arts); **Science and Engineering** (Applied Mathematics; Business Administration; Computer Science; Educational Technology; Electrical Engineering; Electronic Engineering; Information Technology; Management; Materials Engineering; Mechanical Engineering)

History: Founded 1898 as Tainan Normal School. Renamed Taiwan Provincial Tainan Normal School 1946. Succesively upgraded and renamed into Taiwan Provincial Tainan Junior Teachers College 1962, Taiwan Provincial Tainan Teachers College 1987, National Tainan Teachers College 1991. Acquired present status 2004.

Academic Year: September to June

Admission Requirements: Graduation from senior high school

Fees: Udergraduate tuition, 32,891-33,663 per semester; Graduate tuition, 45,033-52,679 per semester (New Taiwan Dollar)

Main Language(s) of Instruction: Chinese

Degrees and Diplomas: *Bachelor's Degree*; *Master's Degree*: **Administration; Applied Mathematics; Biotechnology; Chinese; Cultural Studies; East Asian Studies; Ecology; Education; Educational and Student Counselling; Educational Technology; Electrical Engineering; Energy Engineering; Fine Arts; Information Technology; Literature; Management; Materials Engineering; Mechanical Engineering; Multimedia; Music; Natural Resources; Physical Education; Preschool Education; Special Education; Theatre; Tourism; Visual Arts.** *Doctorate*: **Education; Educational Technology; Electrical Engineering; Special Education.**

Student Services: Academic Counselling, IT Centre, Library, Social Counselling, Sports Facilities

Last Updated: 11/04/14

NATIONAL YANG-MING UNIVERSITY (NYMU)

No.155, Sec.2, Linong Street, Taipei 112
Tel: +886(2) 2827-5657 +886(2) 2826-7000
Fax: +886(2) 282-64051
EMail: aca@ym.edu.tw; sec@ym.edu.tw
Website: http://www.ym.edu.tw

President: Kung-Yee Liang
Tel: +886(2) 282-67001 EMail: president@ym.edu.tw

Secretary-General: Ray-Yau Wang
Tel: +886(2) 282-67290 EMail: rywang@ym.edu.tw

International Relations: Yen-Jen Sung, Dean, Office of International Affairs
Tel: +886(2) 282-67000, Ext. 7160
EMail: yjsung@ym.edu.tw; oia@ym.edu.tw

School

Biomedical Science and Engineering (Applied Physics; Biomedical Engineering; Biomedicine; Biotechnology; Laboratory Techniques; Medical Technology; Physical Therapy; Radiology; Rehabilitation and Therapy); **Dentistry** (Biology; Dentistry; Oral Pathology); **Humanities and Social Sciences** (Arts and Humanities; English; German; Japanese; Modern Languages; Philosophy; Social Sciences; Social Studies; Sociology; Technology; Visual Arts); **Life Sciences** (Biochemistry; Biological and Life Sciences;

Biomedicine; Computer Science; Genetics; Immunology; Medicine; Microbiology; Molecular Biology; Neurosciences; Pharmacology); **Medicine** (Anatomy; Biomedicine; Cell Biology; Computer Science; Environmental Studies; Health Administration; Health Sciences; Medicine; Neurology; Occupational Health; Pharmacology; Physiology; Public Health; Traditional Eastern Medicine; Tropical Medicine; Welfare and Protective Services); **Nursing** (Community Health; Nursing; Psychiatry and Mental Health)

Centre

Biostatistical Consultation *(BCC)* (Statistics); **General Education** (Arts and Humanities); **Taiwan Joanna Briggs Institute Collaborating Centre** *(TJBCC)*

Research Centre

Biotechnology, and NanoTechnology Biophotonics *(Interdisciplinary)* (Applied Physics; Biological and Life Sciences; Biotechnology; Nanotechnology); **Brain** (Neurology); **Cancer** (Oncology); **Drug Discovery** (Pharmacology); **Genomic Medicine** (Genetics); **Infectious Disease and Immunology** (Epidemiology; Immunology; Microbiology; Social and Preventive Medicine); **International Classification of Functioning, Disability and Health (ICF) and Assistive Technology** *(RICFAT)* (Health Sciences; Medical Technology); **Neurology** (Cognitive Sciences; Neurology; Neurosciences)

Further Information: Also University Hospital

History: Founded 1974 as National Yang-Ming College of Medicine, acquired present status 1994.

Academic Year: August to July (August-January; February-July)

Admission Requirements: Graduation from high school and entrance examination

Main Language(s) of Instruction: Chinese, English

Degrees and Diplomas: *Bachelor's Degree*; *Master's Degree*: **Anatomy; Applied Physics; Biochemistry; Biological and Life Sciences; Biomedical Engineering; Biomedicine; Biotechnology; Cell Biology; Community Health; Computer Science; Dentistry; Environmental Studies; Genetics; Health Administration; Health Sciences; Immunology; Laboratory Techniques; Medical Technology; Medicine; Microbiology; Molecular Biology; Neurology; Neurosciences; Nursing; Occupational Health; Oral Pathology; Pharmacology; Philosophy; Physical Therapy; Physiology; Public Health; Radiology; Social Studies; Traditional Eastern Medicine; Welfare and Protective Services.** *Doctorate*: **Applied Physics; Biochemistry; Biological and Life Sciences; Biomedical Engineering; Biomedicine; Biotechnology; Dentistry; Environmental Studies; Genetics; Health Administration; Health Sciences; Immunology; Laboratory Techniques; Medical Technology; Medicine; Microbiology; Molecular Biology; Neurology; Neurosciences; Nursing; Occupational Health; Oral Pathology; Pharmacology; Physical Therapy; Physiology; Public Health; Radiology; Traditional Eastern Medicine.**

Student Services: Academic Counselling, Canteen, IT Centre, Library, Residential Facilities, Social Counselling, Sports Facilities

Publications: Scientific Papers

Academic Staff *2012-2013*	**TOTAL**
FULL-TIME	**401**
PART-TIME	**1,322**
Student Numbers *2012-2013*	
All (Foreign included)	**4,579**

Last Updated: 11/04/14

NATIONAL YUNLIN UNIVERSITY OF SCIENCE AND TECHNOLOGY (NYUST)

123 University Road, Section 3, Douliou, Yunlin 64002
Tel: +886(5) 534-2601
Fax: +886(5) 532-1719
EMail: lbsjack@yuntech.edu.tw; linshrry@yuntech.edu.tw
Website: http://www.yuntech.edu.tw

President: Chun-Kan Hou (2013-)
Tel: +886(5) 534-2601, Ext. 2100
EMail: president@yuntech.edu.tw

Secretary-General: Jung-Chuan Chou
Tel: +886(5) 534-2601, Ext. 2101 EMail: choujc@yuntech.edu.tw

International Relations: Dau-Chung Wang
Tel: +886(5) 534-2601, Ext. 2505 EMail: wangdc@yuntech.edu.tw

College

Design (Architecture; Communication Arts; Design; Industrial Design; Interior Design; Multimedia; Visual Arts); **Engineering** (Chemical Engineering; Computer Engineering; Computer Science; Construction Engineering; Electrical and Electronic Engineering; Electrical Engineering; Electronic Engineering; Engineering; Environmental Engineering; Health Sciences; Information Technology; Materials Engineering; Mechanical Engineering; Microelectronics; Optical Technology; Real Estate; Safety Engineering; Technology; Telecommunications Engineering); **Humanities and Applied Sciences** (Arts and Humanities; Chinese; English; Heritage Preservation; Law; Leisure Studies; Materials Engineering; Modern Languages; Natural Sciences; Sports; Technology Education; Vocational Education); **Management** (Accountancy; Business Administration; Finance; Industrial Engineering; Industrial Management; International Business; Management; Transport Management)

Further Information: 12 Research Centres

History: Founded 1991 as National Yunlin Institute of Technology. Acquired present status and title 1997.

Academic Year: August to July (August-January; February-July)

Admission Requirements: Graduation from high school and entrance examination

Fees: 60,000 per annum (New Taiwan Dollar)

Main Language(s) of Instruction: Chinese, English

Degrees and Diplomas: *Bachelor's Degree*; *Master's Degree*: **Accountancy; Architecture; Business Administration; Chemical Engineering; Communication Arts; Computer Engineering; Computer Science; Construction Engineering; Design; Electrical and Electronic Engineering; Electronic Engineering; English; Environmental Engineering; Finance; Health Sciences; Heritage Preservation; Industrial Design; Industrial Engineering; Industrial Management; Information Management; Interior Design; International Business; Law; Leisure Studies; Management; Materials Engineering; Mechanical Engineering; Microelectronics; Optical Technology; Real Estate; Safety Engineering; Sports; Technology Education; Telecommunications Engineering; Transport Management; Visual Arts; Vocational Education.** *Doctorate*: **Accountancy; Business Administration; Chemical Engineering; Design; Electronic Engineering; Engineering; Environmental Engineering; Finance; Health Sciences; Information Management; Materials Engineering; Mechanical Engineering; Safety Engineering; Technology; Technology Education; Vocational Education.**

Student Services: Academic Counselling, Canteen, Careers Guidance, Facilities for disabled people, Health Services, Language Laboratory, Library, Nursery Care, Residential Facilities, Social Counselling, Sports Facilities

Publications: Journal of Commerce and Management; Journal of Humanities and Sociology; Journal of Science and Technology

Academic Staff *2013-2014*: Total 344
STAFF WITH DOCTORATE: Total 294
Student Numbers *2013-2014*: Total 9,710
Last Updated: 11/04/14

OPEN UNIVERSITY OF KAOHSIUNG (OUK)

No. 436, Daye North Rd., Siaogang Dist., Kaohsiung 812
Tel: +886(7) 801-2008
Fax: +886(7) 806-6720
Website: http://www.ouk.edu.tw

President: Huey-Por Chang
Tel: +886(7) 806-6725
EMail: president@ouk.edu.tw; changhp@ouk.edu.tw

Administrative Officer: Chien-Hsiung Lin
Tel: +886(7) 803-4211 EMail: axel@ms1.ouk.edu.tw

International Relations: Tzung-Je Tsai, Chief-Secretary
Tel: +886(7) 801-2008, Ext. 1203
EMail: caijerryy@yahoo.com.tw

Department
Culture and Arts (Aesthetics; Art Criticism; Art History; Fine Arts; History; Literature; Music; Music Theory and Composition; Performing Arts; Visual Arts); **Foreign Languages and Literature** (Business Administration; Cultural Studies; English; Foreign Languages Education; Japanese; Linguistics; Literature; Modern Languages; Native Language Education; Preschool Education; Primary Education; Psychology); **Industrial and Business Management** (Business Administration; E-Business/Commerce; Finance; Industrial Management; Information Management; Information Technology; Management; Marketing; Transport Management); **Law and Political Science** (Administrative Law; Constitutional Law; Law; Political Sciences; Public Law); **Mass Communication** (Information Sciences; Mass Communication; Radio and Television Broadcasting); **Technology Management** (Biotechnology; Engineering Management; Environmental Studies; Human Resources; Law; Management; Marketing; Nanotechnology; Production Engineering)

Centre
General Education (Arts and Humanities; Education; History; Information Sciences; Literature; Natural Sciences; Philosophy; Psychology; Social Sciences)

History: Founded 1997. Acquired present status and title 2008.

Fees: c. 800 per credit (New Taiwan Dollar)

Main Language(s) of Instruction: Chinese

Degrees and Diplomas: *Bachelor's Degree*: **Aesthetics; Art History; Business Administration; Cultural Studies; E-Business/ Commerce; Engineering Management; English; Industrial Management; Japanese; Law; Literature; Marketing; Mass Communication; Performing Arts; Political Sciences; Transport Management; Visual Arts.**

Student Services: IT Centre, Library

Publications: Campus News of OUK

Academic Staff *2013-2014*: Total 20
STAFF WITH DOCTORATE: Total 1
Student Numbers *2013-2014*: Total 16,000
Last Updated: 04/04/14

TAINAN NATIONAL UNIVERSITY OF THE ARTS (TNUA)

66, Ta-Chi Tsun, Kuan Tien, Tainan 72045
Tel: +886(6) 693-0100
Fax: +886(6) 693-0251
EMail: em1102@mail.tnnua.edu.tw
Website: http://www.tnnua.edu.tw

President: Li Zhaoxiu Tel: +886(6) 693-0111

College
Letters and Cultural Heritage (Art Criticism; Art History; Arts and Humanities); **Music** (Music); **Sound and Image Arts** (Archiving; Cinema and Television; Film; Multimedia; Music; Performing Arts); **Visual Arts** (Art Criticism; Design; Fine Arts; History; Museum Studies; Visual Arts)

Department
Applied Music (Music)

Centre
Multimedia (Multimedia)

Graduate Institute
Animation and Film Art (Film); **Applied Arts** (Ceramic Art; Graphic Arts); **Architecture** (Architecture); **Art History and Art Criticism** (Art Criticism; Art History); **Collaborative Piano** (Musical Instruments); **Conservation of Cultural Relics and Museology** (Museum Studies; Restoration of Works of Art); **Documentary and Film Archiving** (Archiving; Film); **Ethnomusicology** (Cultural Studies; Musicology); **Museology** (Cultural Studies; Museum Studies); **Plastic Arts** (Fine Arts; Painting and Drawing; Sculpture)

Graduate School
Chinese Music (Music)

History: Founded 1996 as Tainan National College of the Art. Acquired present name 2004.

Degrees and Diplomas: *Bachelor's Degree*; *Master's Degree*: **Art Criticism; Art History.** *Doctorate*: **Visual Arts.**

Student Services: Cultural Activities, Library, Nursery Care, Sports Facilities

Publications: Artop

Last Updated: 08/04/14

TAIPEI NATIONAL UNIVERSITY OF THE ARTS (TNUA)

1, Shiueyuan Road, Beitou, Taipei 112
Tel: +886(2) 2896-1000
Fax: +886(2) 2893-8835
EMail: www@www.tnua.edu.tw
Website: http://www.tnua.edu.tw

President: Chyi Wen Yang (2013-)
Tel: +886(2) 2893-8701 EMail: president@www.tnua.edu.tw

Dean of Academic Affairs: Hsi-Chuan Liu
Tel: +886(2) 2896-1000, Ext. 1203
EMail: master-a@academic.tnua.edu.tw

International Relations: Hung-Hui Lu, Chief Director of International Exchange Tel: +886(2) 2896-1000, Ext. 2601

School
Culture Resources (Architecture; Art Management; Cultural Studies; Heritage Preservation; Museum Studies); **Dance** (Dance); **Film and New Media** (Cinema and Television; Film); **Fine Arts** (Fine Arts; Technology); **Music** (Music; Musical Instruments); **Theatre Arts** (Theatre)

Graduate Institute
Architecture and Cultural Heritage (Architectural Restoration; Architecture; Art History); **Arts Administration and Management** (Art Management); **Arts and Humanities Education** (Art Education; Arts and Humanities); **Dance** (Dance); **Museum Studies** (Museum Studies); **Musicology** (Musicology); **Orchestral Instruments** (Musical Instruments); **Plastic Arts** (Sculpture; Visual Arts); **Theatre Design and Technology** (Performing Arts; Theatre); **Theatre Performance and Playwriting** (Performing Arts; Theatre); **Traditional Music** (Music); **Trans-disciplinary Arts** (Fine Arts)

History: Founded 1982. Acquired present status and title 2008.

Academic Year: September to June (September-January; February-June)

Admission Requirements: Graduation from high school and entrance examination

Main Language(s) of Instruction: Chinese

Degrees and Diplomas: *Bachelor's Degree*: **Fine Arts.** *Master's Degree*: **Architecture; Art Management; Dance; Fine Arts; Music; Performing Arts; Theatre.** *Doctorate*: **Dance; Fine Arts; Heritage Preservation.**

Student Services: Academic Counselling, Canteen, Careers Guidance, Cultural Activities, Facilities for disabled people, Foreign Studies Centre, Health Services, IT Centre, Library, Social Counselling, Sports Facilities

Publications: Arts Review

Last Updated: 09/04/14

UNIVERSITY OF TAIPEI (UT)

West Road, Zhongzheng District, Taipei 10048
Tel: +886(2) 231-13040
Fax: +886(2) 238-14067
EMail: center@utaipei.edu.tw
Website: http://www.utaipei.edu.tw

President: Xialing Dai
Tel: +886(2) 231-15585 EMail: prexy@uTaipei.edu.tw

International Relations: Xianzong Chen, Chief Secretary
EMail: secretariat@uTaipei.edu.tw

Faculty
Science (Chemistry; Computer Science; Mathematics; Physical Education; Physics; Science Education; Teacher Trainers Education)

College
Education (Child Care and Development; Educational Administration; Educational Testing and Evaluation; Media Studies; Pedagogy; Preschool Education; Psychology; Special Education; Speech Therapy and Audiology)

School
Humanities and Arts (Art Therapy; Chinese; Dance; English; Foreign Languages Education; Geography; History; Literature; Music; Public Administration; Social Studies; Visual Arts)

Institute
Sports (Education of the Handicapped; Leisure Studies; Physical Education; Sports; Sports Management)

Centre
Arts (Performing Arts); **Chinese Language** (Chinese); **Confucianism** (Ethics; Philosophy); **Science Education** (Science Education)

History: Founded 1895 as Academy of Language. Acquired present status 2005. Formerly known Taipei Municipal University of Education. Merged with Taipei Physical Education College 2013.

Main Language(s) of Instruction: Chinese

Degrees and Diplomas: *Bachelor's Degree*; *Master's Degree*: **Art Therapy; Chemistry; Child Care and Development; Chinese; Computer Science; Education; English; Geography; History; Leisure Studies; Mathematics; Music; Physical Education; Physics; Psychology; Science Education; Social Studies; Speech Therapy and Audiology; Sports; Teacher Trainers Education; Visual Arts.** *Doctorate*: **Educational Administration; Educational Testing and Evaluation.**

Student Services: Academic Counselling, Library, Sports Facilities
Last Updated: 07/04/14

PRIVATE INSTITUTIONS

ALETHEIA UNIVERSITY (AU)

32, Chen-Li Street, Tamsui, Taipei 25103
Tel: +886(2) 262-12121
Fax: +886(2) 262-05236
EMail: cocoliu@email.au.edu.tw
Website: http://www.au.edu.tw

President: Wenchang Lin
Tel: +886(2) 262-12121
EMail: president@mail.au.edu.tw; au1626@mail.au.edu.tw

College
Arts and Humanities (Applied Linguistics; Computer Science; English; Japanese; Literature; Modern Languages; Music; Religion); **Finance and Economics** (Accountancy; Banking; Commercial Law; Economics; Finance; International Business; Law; Taxation); **Management** (Business Administration; Industrial Management; Information Management; Information Sciences; Management); **Mathematical Sciences** (Actuarial Science; Computer Science; Information Sciences; Information Technology; Mathematics; Mathematics and Computer Science; Statistics); **Tourism** (Air Transport; Health Sciences; Hotel and Restaurant; Hotel Management; Information Sciences; Leisure Studies; Parks and Recreation; Sports; Sports Management; Tourism)

School
Graduate (Actuarial Science; Business Administration; Computer Engineering; Computer Science; Economics; Finance; Information Technology; Leisure Studies; Parks and Recreation; Religion; Statistics; Tourism)

History: Founded 1882 as Oxford College. Became Tamsui Oxford College 1965, and Tamsui Oxford University College 1994. Acquired present title and status 1999.

Admission Requirements: Graduation from high school and entrance examination

Fees: Tuition, 90,000-100,000 per annum (New Taiwan Dollar)

Main Language(s) of Instruction: Chinese, English

Accrediting Agency: Ministry of Education

Degrees and Diplomas: *Bachelor's Degree*: **Arts and Humanities; Business Administration; Economics; Finance; Leisure Studies; Management; Mathematics and Computer Science; Tourism.** *Master's Degree*: **Actuarial Science; Business Administration; Computer Engineering; Economics; Finance; Information Technology; Leisure Studies; Parks and Recreation; Religion; Statistics.**

Student Services: Academic Counselling, Canteen, Careers Guidance, Facilities for disabled people, Foreign Studies Centre, Health Services, Language Laboratory, Nursery Care, Social Counselling, Sports Facilities

Publishing house: Aletheia University Press
Last Updated: 05/02/14

ASIA-PACIFIC INSTITUTE OF CREATIVITY (APIC)

110, XueFu Rd., Toufen, Miaoli 351
Tel: +886(37) 605-500
Fax: +886(37) 605-556
Website: http://www.apic.edu.tw/

President: Shao-Wen Liu
Tel: +886(37) 605-520 EMail: srcd@ms.apic.edu.tw

Dean of Academic Affairs: Wen-Ben Wu
Tel: +886(37) 605-530 EMail: wenbenwu@ms.apic.edu.tw

Division
Creative Design (Aesthetics; Ceramic Art; Communication Arts; Computer Graphics; Cultural Studies; Design; Display and Stage Design; Fashion Design; Furniture Design; Glass Art; Graphic Design; Handicrafts; Industrial Design; Jewellery Art; Multimedia; Packaging Technology; Visual Arts); **Digital Entertainment** (Computer Engineering; Multimedia; Robotics; Software Engineering); **Fashion and Life technology** (Agriculture; Biotechnology; Child Care and Development; Computer Engineering; Cosmetology; Dietetics; Family Studies; Fashion Design; Food Science; Health Sciences; Information Management; Multimedia; Nutrition; Parks and Recreation; Physical Therapy; Rehabilitation and Therapy; Software Engineering; Sports; Transport Management); **Tourism and Hospitality** (Cooking and Catering; Hotel and Restaurant; Hotel Management; Leisure Studies; Management; Marketing; Service Trades; Tourism)

History: Founded 1985, became Chin-Min Institute of Technology 1992. Acquired present title 2010.

Main Language(s) of Instruction: Chinese

Degrees and Diplomas: *Bachelor's Degree*. Also Professional Certificates

Student Services: IT Centre, Library
Last Updated: 04/02/14

ASIA UNIVERSITY (AU)

500, Lioufeng Rd., Wufeng, Taichung 41354
Tel: +886(4) 233-23456, Ext. 1012
Fax: +886(4) 233-16699
EMail: ciae@asia.edu.tw
Website: http://www.asia.edu.tw

President: Jing-Pha Tsai
Tel: +886(4) 233-23456, Ext 1007 EMail: president@asia.edu.tw

Chief Secretary: Neng-Yih Shih
Tel: +886(4) 233-23456, Ext. 1090 EMail: shih@asia.edu.tw

International Relations: C.W. Hsiao, Director, Center for International Academic Exchange
Tel: +886(4) 233-23456, Ext. 6277 EMail: hwhsiao@asia.edu.tw

College
Computer Science (Biomedical Engineering; Computer Engineering; Computer Science; Information Technology; Mass Communication; Multimedia; Optics; Telecommunications Engineering); **Creative Design** (Communication Arts; Design; Fashion Design; Graphic Design; Interior Design; Mass Communication; Media Studies; Multimedia; Visual Arts); **Humanities and Social Sciences** (Child Care and Development; English; French; German; Japanese; Literature; Malay; Modern Languages; Preschool Education; Social Work; South and Southeast Asian Languages; Spanish; Vietnamese); **International Studies** *(Some programmes*

offered (Master's and Doctorate courses Programmes) are taught in English) (Biomedical Engineering; Biotechnology; Business Administration; Chinese; Computer Engineering; Computer Science; Cultural Studies; English; Health Administration; Psychology); **Management** (Accountancy; Business Administration; Business Computing; Commercial Law; Finance; International Business; Leisure Studies; Management; Parks and Recreation; Taxation); **Medical and Health Science** (Biotechnology; Health Administration; Health Sciences; Nursing; Nutrition; Psychology)

History: Founded 2001 as Taichung Healthcare and Management University. Renamed Asia University 2005.

Fees: Tuition, 47,170-57,160 (New Taiwan Dollar)

Main Language(s) of Instruction: Chinese, English

Degrees and Diplomas: *Bachelor's Degree*: **Accountancy; Biomedical Engineering; Biotechnology; Business Administration; Child Care and Development; Commercial Law; Communication Arts; Computer Science; Design; Fashion Design; Finance; Health Administration; Health Sciences; Industrial Design; Information Technology; Interior Design; International Business; Leisure Studies; Modern Languages; Multimedia; Nutrition; Optics; Parks and Recreation; Preschool Education; Psychology; Social Work; Telecommunications Engineering; Visual Arts.** *Master's Degree*: **Accountancy; Biomedical Engineering; Biotechnology; Business Administration; Commercial Law; Communication Arts; Computer Engineering; Computer Science; Design; Finance; Graphic Design; Health Administration; Health Sciences; Industrial Design; Information Sciences; Information Technology; International Business; Leisure Studies; Literature; Media Studies; Modern Languages; Multimedia; Nutrition; Optics; Parks and Recreation; Psychology; Social Work; Telecommunications Engineering.** *Doctorate*: **Biomedical Engineering; Business Administration; Computer Engineering; Computer Science; Design; Health Administration; Media Studies.**

Student Services: Academic Counselling, Canteen, IT Centre, Library, Residential Facilities, Sports Facilities

Last Updated: 05/02/14

CENTRAL TAIWAN UNIVERSITY OF SCIENCE AND TECHNOLOGY (CTUST)

666, Buzih Road, Beitun District, Taichung 40601
Tel: +886(4) 223-91647, Ext. 8404
Fax: +886(4) 223-93305
EMail: f0104@ctust.edu.tw
Website: http://www.ctust.edu.tw

President: Li Mo
Tel: +886(4) 223-91647, Ext. 2000 EMail: B0100@ctust.edu.tw

Secretary-General: Cheng Yijia
Tel: +886(4) 2239-5111 EMail: yjcherng@ctust.edu.tw

International Relations: Yi-yueh Angela Li, Director, International Cooperation Section, R&D Office
Tel: +886(4) 223-91647, Ext. 8404, 7210 EMail: yhli@ctust.edu.tw

College

Health Sciences (Biotechnology; Dental Technology; Dentistry; Environmental Engineering; Food Science; Food Technology; Health Sciences; Laboratory Techniques; Medical Technology; Optometry; Pharmacology; Radiology; Safety Engineering); **Management** (Applied Linguistics; Health Administration; Information Management; International Business; Management; Marketing; Modern Languages); **Nursing** (Art Management; Child Care and Development; Educational Administration; Gerontology; Nursing)

History: Founded 1996 as Chungtai Junior College. Upgrade into a Medical Technology College 1998. Acquired present status and title 2005.

Fees: Tuition, 36,240-37,910 (New Taiwan Dollar)

Main Language(s) of Instruction: Chinese, English

Degrees and Diplomas: *Bachelor's Degree*: **Health Sciences; Management; Nursing.** *Master's Degree*: **Art Management; Biomedical Engineering; Biotechnology; Dental Technology; Educational Administration; Environmental Engineering; Food Science; Food Technology; Health Administration; Health Sciences; Laboratory Techniques; Medical Technology; Nursing; Pharmacology; Radiology; Safety Engineering.** *Doctorate*: **Medical Technology; Radiology.** Also 5 year diploma offered; Master's and PhD degrees in Radiology and Master's Degree in Nursing offered in English language

Student Services: Health Services, IT Centre, Library, Sports Facilities

Academic Staff *2013-2014*: Total 305

Last Updated: 05/02/14

CHANG GUNG UNIVERSITY (CGU)

259, Wen-Hwa 1st Road, Kwei-Shan, Tao-Yuan 333
Tel: +886(3) 211-8800
Fax: +886(3) 211-8700
EMail: acade@mail.cgu.edu.tw
Website: http://www.cgu.edu.tw

President: Chia-Chu Pao
Tel: +886(3) 211-8800, Ext. 5098
EMail: president@mail.cgu.edu.tw

Secretary-General: Yih-Ho Chen
Tel: +886(3) 211-8800, Ext. 5012 EMail: yoga@mail.cgu.edu.tw

International Relations: Prasan Kumar Sahoo, Director, Centre for International Academic Cooperation
Tel: +886(3) 211-8800, Ext. 3536
EMail: directoriac@mail.cgu.edu.tw

College

Engineering (Biochemistry; Bioengineering; Biomedical Engineering; Chemical Engineering; Computer Engineering; Computer Networks; Computer Science; Electrical and Electronic Engineering; Electrical Engineering; Electronic Engineering; Materials Engineering; Mechanical Engineering; Medical Technology; Optical Technology; Software Engineering); **Management** (Business Administration; Health Administration; Industrial Design; Industrial Management; Information Management; Management); **Medicine** (Anatomy; Arts and Humanities; Biochemistry; Biomedicine; Biotechnology; Dentistry; Immunology; Laboratory Techniques; Medical Technology; Medicine; Microbiology; Molecular Biology; Nursing; Occupational Therapy; Pharmacology; Physical Therapy; Physiology; Radiology; Respiratory Therapy; Social Sciences; Traditional Eastern Medicine)

Further Information: Also Graduate institutions, Teaching Hospital; Chang Gung Memorial Hospital

History: Founded 1987, acquired present status and title 1997. A private institution under the jurisdiction of the Ministry of Education.

Academic Year: September to June (September-January; February-June)

Admission Requirements: Graduation from high school or recognized equivalent, and entrance examination

Fees: Tuition fee for College of Medicine, 31,743-59,487 per semester; For College of Engineering, 44,477 per semester; For College of Management, 38,698-44,477 per semester (New Taiwan Dollar)

Main Language(s) of Instruction: Chinese

Degrees and Diplomas: *Bachelor's Degree*: **Biomedicine; Biotechnology; Business Administration; Chemical Engineering; Computer Engineering; Computer Science; Electrical Engineering; Electronic Engineering; Health Administration; Industrial Design; Industrial Management; Information Management; Laboratory Techniques; Management; Materials Engineering; Mechanical Engineering; Medical Technology; Medicine; Nursing; Occupational Therapy; Physical Therapy; Radiology; Respiratory Therapy; Traditional Eastern Medicine.** *Master's Degree*: **Behavioural Sciences; Bioengineering; Biomedical Engineering; Biomedicine; Biotechnology; Business Administration; Chemical Engineering; Computer Engineering; Computer Science; Electrical Engineering; Electronic Engineering; Industrial Design; Industrial Management; Information Management; Laboratory Techniques; Management; Materials Engineering; Mechanical Engineering; Medical Technology; Medicine; Nursing; Optical Technology; Radiology; Rehabilitation and Therapy; Traditional Eastern Medicine.** *Doctorate*: **Biomedical Engineering; Biomedicine; Business Administration; Chemical Engineering; Computer Engineering; Computer Science; Electrical Engineering; Electronic Engineering; Management; Materials Engineering; Mechanical Engineering; Medical Technology; Medicine; Radiology; Rehabilitation and Therapy; Traditional Eastern Medicine.**

Student Services: Academic Counselling, Health Services, Language Laboratory, Library, Residential Facilities, Sports Facilities

Academic Staff *2012-2013*: Total: c. 640

Student Numbers *2012-2013*: Total: c. 7,500

Last Updated: 05/02/14

CHANG GUNG UNIVERSITY OF SCIENCE AND TECHNOLOGY (CGUT)

261,Wen-hwa 1st Rd, Kwei-shan, Taoyuan 33303
Tel: +886(3) 211-8999
Fax: +886(3) 211-8866
EMail: president@mail.cgit.edu.tw
Website: http://www.cgit.edu.tw

President: Ying-Tung Lau
Tel: +886(3) 211-8999, Ext. 5502
EMail: president@gw.cgust.edu.tw

Dean of Academic Affairs: Lee-Ing Tsao
Tel: +886(3) 211-8999, Ext. 5530 EMail: litsao@mail.cgit.edu.tw

International Relations: Chou Chuan-Chiang Yao
Tel: +886(3) 211-8999, Ext. 5585 EMail: cyao@mail.cgit.edu.tw

College

Human Ecology (Child Care and Development; Cosmetology; Health Sciences; Information Management; Nutrition); **Nursing** (Community Health; Gerontology; Nursing; Respiratory Therapy)

Department

Information Management (Information Management)

Centre

General Education (Arts and Humanities; English; Fine Arts; Music; Natural Sciences; Physical Education; Social Sciences)

Further Information: Also Chiayi Campus

History: Founded 1988 as junior college named Chang Gung Institute of Nursing (CGIN). Upgraded into Chang Gung Institute of Technology (CGIT) 1991. Acquired present status and title 2011.

Main Language(s) of Instruction: Chinese

Degrees and Diplomas: *Associate Degree*: **Nursing.** *Bachelor's Degree*: **Cosmetology; Health Sciences; Nursing; Nutrition.** Also Professional Postgraduate Degree in Health Sciences and Nursing

Student Services: Academic Counselling, Health Services, Library, Residential Facilities, Sports Facilities

Last Updated: 05/02/14

CHANG JUNG CHRISTIAN UNIVERSITY (CJCU)

1, Changda Rd., Gueiren District, Tainan 71101
Tel: +886(6) 2785-123
Fax: +886(6) 2785-123
EMail: cweny@mail.cjcu.edu.tw
Website: http://www.cjcu.edu.tw

President: Yung-Lung Lee
Tel: +886(6) 2785-123, Ext. 1010 EMail: alexlee@mail.cjcu.edu.tw

College

Continuing Education (Chinese; Design; Fine Arts; Management); **Health Sciences** (Biotechnology; Health Administration; Health Sciences; Medicine; Nursing; Nutrition; Occupational Health; Psychology); **Humanities and Social Science** (Applied Linguistics; Fine Arts; Information Technology; Japanese; Mass Communication; Media Studies; Modern Languages; Painting and Drawing; Philosophy; Religious Studies; Social Work; Translation and Interpretation); **Information and Engineering** (Computer Engineering; Computer Science; Engineering; Engineering Management; Information Management; Information Sciences); **Management** (Accountancy; Air Transport; Business Administration; Finance; Information Sciences; International Business; Leisure Studies; Management; Marine Transport; Real Estate; Sports; Sports Management; Transport Management); **Theology** (Theology)

School

Liberal Arts Education (Arts and Humanities; Biological and Life Sciences; Chinese; Christian Religious Studies; English; French; German; History; Japanese; Literature; Military Science; Modern Languages; Music; Natural Sciences; Nursing; Physical Education; Russian; Service Trades; Social Sciences; Spanish)

History: Founded 1885 as Middle School by the English Presbyterian Missionaries, acquired present status and title 1993.

Academic Year: September to June (September-January; February-June)

Admission Requirements: Graduation from high school and entrance examination

Main Language(s) of Instruction: Chinese, English

Degrees and Diplomas: *Bachelor's Degree*; *Master's Degree*: **Air Transport; Applied Linguistics; Asian Studies; Biotechnology; Business Administration; Computer Graphics; Finance; Fine Arts; Health Administration; Information Management; International Business; Japanese; Leisure Studies; Management; Marine Transport; Nursing; Occupational Health; Real Estate; Social Work; Sports; Sports Management; Theology; Translation and Interpretation.** *Doctorate*: **Business Administration; Management.**

Student Services: IT Centre, Library, Residential Facilities, Sports Facilities

Publications: Chang Jung Hsue Yuan

Academic Staff *2013-2014*: Total 360

Student Numbers *2013-2014*: Total: c. 10,000

Last Updated: 05/02/14

CHAOYANG UNIVERSITY OF TECHNOLOGY (CYUT)

168, Jifeng E. Rd., Wufeng District, Taichung 41349
Tel: +886(4) 233-23000
Fax: +886(4) 233-29898
EMail: info@cyut.edu.tw
Website: http://www.cyut.edu.tw

President: Chung-Jen Chin
Tel: +886(4) 2332-3000, Ext. 3001
EMail: pres@cyut.edu.tw; sfsung@cyut.edu.tw

Secretary-general: Kuang-Hua Hsu (+886(4) 233-23000, Ext. 3011) EMail: slun0102@cyut.edu.tw

International Relations: Shiaofang Sung, Head, Division of Academic Exchange and Cooperation
Tel: +886(4) 233-23000, Ext. 3121 EMail: sfsung@mail.cyut.edu.tw

College

Design (Architecture; Communication Arts; Design; Industrial Design; Landscape Architecture; Town Planning; Visual Arts); **Humanities and Social Sciences** (Applied Linguistics; Child Care and Development; Communication Arts; Education; English; Modern Languages; Preschool Education; Social Work; Teacher Training); **Informatics** (Computer Engineering; Computer Science; Information Management; Information Technology; Telecommunications Engineering); **Management** (Accountancy; Business Administration; Finance; Industrial Management; Insurance; Leisure Studies; Management; Marketing; Transport Management); **Science and Engineering** (Applied Chemistry; Biotechnology; Construction Engineering; Engineering; Environmental Engineering; Environmental Management; Industrial Engineering; Industrial Management)

Centre

Foreign Language *(FLC)* (Chinese; English; French; German; Japanese; Modern Languages; Spanish); **General Education** (Arts and Humanities; Chinese; Cultural Studies; English; History; Law; Military Science; Natural Sciences; Philosophy; Physical Education; Political Sciences; Social Sciences); **Teacher Education** (Preschool Education; Secondary Education; Teacher Training)

History: Founded 1994. Acquired present status and title 1997.

Academic Year: August to July

Admission Requirements: Graduation from high school and entrance examination

Fees: Tuition, c. 47,639-54,874 per semester (New Taiwan Dollar)

Main Language(s) of Instruction: Chinese

Accrediting Agency: Ministry of Education

Degrees and Diplomas: *Bachelor's Degree*; *Master's Degree*: **Accountancy; Applied Chemistry; Architecture; Biotechnology; Business Administration; Construction Engineering; Environmental Engineering; Environmental Management; Finance; Industrial Engineering; Industrial Management; Insurance; Leisure Studies; Marketing; Preschool Education; Social Work.** *Doctorate*: **Applied Chemistry; Architecture; Biotechnology; Construction Engineering; Industrial Management; Information Management.** Also Executive MBA; Teacher Training Certification and Foreign Languages Certificates

Student Services: Academic Counselling, Canteen, Careers Guidance, Facilities for disabled people, Health Services, Language Laboratory, Library, Nursery Care, Residential Facilities, Sports Facilities

Publications: Chaoyang Business and Management Review; Chaoyang Journal of Design; Chaoyang Journal of Humanities and Social Sciences; International Journal of Applied Science and Engineering; The Journal of Chaoyang University of Technology

Academic Staff *2012-2013*	**TOTAL**
FULL-TIME	**394**
Student Numbers *2013-2014*	
All (Foreign included)	**1,732**
FOREIGN ONLY	**200**

Last Updated: 06/02/14

CHENG SHIU UNIVERSITY (CSU)

No.840, Chengcing Rd., Niaosong Dist., Kaohsiung 83347
Tel: +886(7) 735-8800 +886(7) 731-0606
Fax: +886(7) 731-5367
EMail: oia@csu.edu.tw; academic@csu.edu.tw
Website: http://www.csu.edu.tw

President: Jui-Chang Kung
Tel: +886(7) 732-1156 EMail: president@csu.edu.tw

Secretary: Wilson Lee Tel: +886(7) 731-3945

International Relations: Tommy Cheng, Director, Office of International Affairs EMail: tommy@csu.edu.tw

College

Engineering (Architecture; Automation and Control Engineering; Biotechnology; Chemical Engineering; Civil Engineering; Computer Engineering; Computer Science; Cosmetology; Electrical Engineering; Electronic Engineering; Energy Engineering; Engineering; Fashion Design; Industrial Engineering; Industrial Management; Information Technology; Interior Design; Materials Engineering; Measurement and Precision Engineering; Mechanical Engineering); **Life and Creativity** (Applied Linguistics; Child Care and Development; Design; Education; English; Leisure Studies; Modern Languages; Multimedia; Parks and Recreation; Preschool Education; Sports Management; Tourism); **Management** (Banking; Business Administration; Finance; Industrial Management; Information Management; International Business; Management)

Centre

General Education *(CGE)* (Arts and Humanities; Biological and Life Sciences; Chinese; English; Natural Sciences; Social Sciences); **Teacher Education** *(CTE)* (Secondary Education; Teacher Training)

History: Founded 1956 as Cheng-Shiu Junior College of Technology. Renamed Cheng Shiu Institute of Technology 1980. Upgraded into Cheng Shiu Institute of Technology 1999. Acquired present status and title 2003.

Fees: Tuition, 46,436-53,400 per semester

Main Language(s) of Instruction: Chinese

Degrees and Diplomas: *Bachelor's Degree*; *Master's Degree*: **Business Administration; Electronic Engineering; Industrial Engineering; Industrial Management; Information Management; Mechanical Engineering.** *Doctorate*: **Electrical Engineering; Mechanical Engineering.** Also Executive MBA

Student Services: Library, Residential Facilities, Sports Facilities

Last Updated: 06/02/14

CHIA NAN UNIVERSITY OF PHARMACY AND SCIENCE (CNU)

No.60, Sec. 1, Erren Rd., Rende Dist, Tainan, Taiwan 71710
Tel: +886(6) 266-4911
Fax: +886(6) 266-2774
EMail: box101@mail.chna.edu.tw
Website: http://www.chna.edu.tw

President: Suen-Zone Lee (2012-)
Tel: +886(6) 266-4911 Ext. 1001 EMail: box101@mail.chna.edu.tw

Vice-President: Tong-Po Ho
Tel:: +(886)6 266-4911 Ext. 1021
EMail: box1022@mail.chna.edu.tw

International Relations: Pin-Der Duh, Chief Officer, Research and Development Office
Tel: +(886)6 266-4911 Ext. 1401 EMail: ipdduh@mail.chna.edu.tw

College

Health and Information (Computer Science; Health Administration; Health Sciences; Information Management; Information Sciences; Multimedia); **Human Ecology** (Biological and Life Sciences; Child Care and Development; Food Science; Food Technology; Health Sciences; Hotel and Restaurant; Nursing; Nutrition); **Humanities and Social Sciences** (Arts and Humanities; Asian Studies; Cultural Studies; English; Gerontology; Modern Languages; Philosophy; Social Sciences; Social Work; Tourism); **Leisure and Recreation Management** (Health Sciences; Leisure Studies; Parks and Recreation; Sports Management; Tourism); **Pharmacy and Science** (Applied Chemistry; Biotechnology; Cosmetology; Pharmacy); **Sustainable Environment** (Environmental Engineering; Environmental Management; Health Sciences; Industrial Engineering; Natural Resources; Occupational Health; Safety Engineering; Surveying and Mapping; Tourism)

Centre

Arts and Culture (Cultural Studies; Fine Arts); **Environmental Safety and Hygiene** (Environmental Management; Hygiene); **General Education** (Education); **Green Industry Development** (Environmental Engineering; Industrial Engineering); **Human Ecology and Health Promotion** (Ecology)

Research Centre

Research and Development of Biopharmaceuticals and Technology (Bioengineering; Biological and Life Sciences; Biotechnology; Pharmacy); **Research and Development of Ecological Engineering and Technology** (Ecology; Environmental Engineering); **Taiwan Hot Spring** *(THSRC)* (Water Science)

History: Founded 1964 as Chia Nan Junior College of Pharmacy and approved by Ministry of Education 1966. Upgraded into Chia Nan College of Pharmacy and Science 1996. Acquired present status and title 2000.

Admission Requirements: For Master's Degree Programmes, Bachelor's degree from and accredited college or university or equivalent; entrance examination; each applicant can only apply to one program at this university. For 4-year Bachelor's Degree Programmes, a diploma from an accredited vocational high school or senior high school, or an equivalent qualification; entrance examination. For 2-year Bachelor's Degree Programmes, a diploma from an accredited junior college, or an equivalent qualification; entrance examination.

Fees: For programmes from the Department of Pharmacy, Department of Biotechnology or the Institute of Pharmaceutical Science, 120,000-150,000 per annum; For other programmes, 110,000-130,000 per annum (New Taiwan Dollar)

Main Language(s) of Instruction: Chinese (Mandarin)

Accrediting Agency: Ministry of Education

Degrees and Diplomas: *Bachelor's Degree*; *Master's Degree*: **Biotechnology; Business Administration; Cosmetology; Environmental Engineering; Environmental Studies; Health Administration; Health Sciences; Nutrition; Parks and Recreation; Pharmacy; Philosophy; Safety Engineering.** A 2 yr Bachelor's Degree is also offered in Cosmetic Science, Hotel and Restaurant Management, Senior Citizen Service Management

Student Services: Academic Counselling, Canteen, Careers Guidance, Cultural Activities, Facilities for disabled people, Health Services, Language Laboratory, Nursery Care, Social Counselling, Sports Facilities

Publications: Chia Nan Annual Bulletin

Publishing House: None

Academic Staff *2012-2013*	MEN	WOMEN	TOTAL
FULL-TIME	294	207	**501**
PART-TIME	260	197	**457**
STAFF WITH DOCTORATE			
FULL-TIME	208	119	**327**
Student Numbers *2012-2013*			
All (Foreign included)	5,102	7,988	**13,090**
FOREIGN ONLY	18	13	**31**

Part-time students, 54. **Distance students,** 0.
Last Updated: 24/05/13

CHIEN HSIN UNIVERSITY OF SCIENCE AND TECHNOLOGY (UCH)

229, Jianxing Road, Taoyuan County, Zhongli City 32097
Tel: +886(3) 458-1196
Fax: +886(3) 459-5684
Website: http://www.uch.edu.tw/

President: Ta-Wei Lee
Tel: +886(3) 458-1196, Ext. 2200 EMail: president@uch.edu.tw

Secretary General: Rong-Moo Hong
Tel: +886(3) 458-1196 Ext. 2500 EMail: hongrm@uch.edu.tw

International Relations: Anita Liu
Tel: +886(3) 458-1196 Ext. 5806 EMail: anita.liu@uch.edu.tw

College

Commerce (Banking; Business Administration; Business and Commerce; Cultural Studies; English; Finance; Foreign Languages Education; International Business; Japanese; Literature; Modern Languages; Translation and Interpretation); **Electronic Engineering and Computer Science** (Computer Science; Electrical Engineering; Electronic Engineering; Information Sciences; Information Technology; Optical Technology; Telecommunications Engineering); **Engineering** (Civil Engineering; Construction Engineering; Law; Measurement and Precision Engineering; Mechanical Engineering); **Graduate Institutes** (Asian Studies; Business Administration; Civil Engineering; Computer Science; Earth Sciences; Electrical Engineering; Electronic Engineering; English; International Business; Japanese; Management; Mechanical Engineering; Modern Languages; Russian; Safety Engineering; Surveying and Mapping); **Management** (Advertising and Publicity; Business Administration; E-Business/Commerce; Industrial Engineering; Industrial Management; Information Management; International Business; Management; Marketing; Transport Management)

Centre

General Education *(GEC)* (Arts and Humanities); **Green Energy** (Energy Engineering)

Research Centre

Digital Earth and Disaster Reduction *(DEDRRC)* (Earth Sciences; Safety Engineering); **Enhanced Global Positioning System** *(e-GPS)* (Surveying and Mapping); **Euro-Asian** (Asian Studies; European Studies); **Logistic Management** (Transport Management)

History: Founded 1996, renamed Ching-Yun Institute of Technology. Acquired present status and renamed Ching-Yun University 2003. Acquired present title 2012.

Main Language(s) of Instruction: Chinese

Degrees and Diplomas: *Bachelor's Degree*; *Master's Degree*: **Asian Studies; Business Administration; Electrical Engineering; Electronic Engineering; Management; Mechanical Engineering; Safety Engineering; Surveying and Mapping.** Also Language Specialised Programmes and Professional-Technical Programmes

Student Services: Canteen, Health Services, Library, Residential Facilities

Last Updated: 27/02/14

CHIEN KUO TECHNOLOGY UNIVERSITY (CTU)

1,Chiehshou North Road, Changhua 500
Tel: +886(4) 711-1111
Fax: +886(4) 711-1170
Website: http://www.ctu.edu.tw

President: Farn-Shing Chen
Tel: +886(4) 711-1111, Ext:1210 EMail: dialog@ctu.edu.tw

Director, Secretariat: Kuo-Hsing Lin
Tel: +886(4) 722-4676 Ext. 1213 EMail: jefflin@ctu.edu.tw

International Relations: Wilfred Lam, Director, International Cooperation and Exchange
Tel: +886(4) 711-1111, Ext. 1213 EMail: jefflin@ctu.edu.tw

College

Design (Architectural and Environmental Design; Design; Industrial Engineering; Interior Design; Software Engineering); **Engineering** (Automation and Control Engineering; Civil Engineering; Computer Engineering; Electrical Engineering; Electronic Engineering; Engineering; Information Technology; Mechanical Engineering; Production Engineering; Telecommunications Engineering); **Living Technology** (Applied Linguistics; Cosmetology; Health Sciences; Leisure Studies; Modern Languages; Physical Therapy; Tourism); **Management** (Industrial Engineering; Industrial Management; International Business; Management; Marketing)

Centre

General Education (Arts and Humanities; Natural Sciences; Social Sciences); **Physical Education** (Physical Education; Sports)

History: Founded 1965 as Chienkuo Commercial Junior College. Successively renamed Chienkuo Industrial Junior College (1974) and Chienkuo Industrial-and-Commercial Junior College (1992). Upgraded into Chienkuo Institute of Technology 1999. Acquired present status and title 2004.

Academic Year: August to July

Admission Requirements: Senior high school certificate with at least 12 years of school education

Fees: Tuition, 1,600-1,900 per semester (New Taiwan Dollar)

Main Language(s) of Instruction: Chinese

Accrediting Agency: Ministry of Education

Degrees and Diplomas: *Associate Degree*; *Bachelor's Degree*; *Master's Degree*: **Automation and Control Engineering; Civil Engineering; Electrical Engineering; Electronic Engineering; Mechanical Engineering.**

Student Services: Academic Counselling, Canteen, Careers Guidance, Cultural Activities, Facilities for disabled people, Foreign Studies Centre, Health Services, Language Laboratory, Library, Nursery Care, Social Counselling, Sports Facilities

Publications: Chienkuo Monthly; Journal of Chienkuo Technology University

Publishing House: Publishing Section, Office of Academic Affairs

Last Updated: 06/02/14

CHIHLEE INSTITUTE OF TECHNOLOGY (CIOT)

313, Sec. 1, Wunhua Rd., Banciao District, New Taipei City 220
Tel: +886(2) 2257-6167 +886(2) 2257-6168
Fax: +886(2) 2255-9674 +886(2) 2258-8518
EMail: i206@mail.chihlee.edu.tw
Website: http://portal.chihlee.edu.tw/bin/home.php

President: Shang Shichang
Tel: +886(2) 2257-6167, Ext. 1381
EMail: simon@mail.chihlee.edu.tw; a100@mail.chihlee.edu.tw

Administrative Officer: Zhang Li
Tel: +886(2) 225-89016, Ext. 1202
EMail: lchang@mail.chihlee.edu.tw

International Relations: Zhengxu Wang, Director, International Cooperation EMail: s100@mail.chihlee.edu.tw

School

Business and Management (Accountancy; Business Administration; Finance; Insurance; International Business; Management; Marketing; Transport Management); **Humanities and Human Services** (Applied Linguistics; English; Health Sciences; Japanese; Leisure Studies; Sports); **Information Management** (Design; E-Business/Commerce; Information Management; Information Technology; Management; Multimedia)

Further Information: Traditional and Open Learning Institution

History: Founded 1964. Acquired present status 2002.

Fees: Tuition, 46,800-47,1000 per semester (New Taiwan Dollar)

Main Language(s) of Instruction: Chinese

Degrees and Diplomas: *Associate Degree*: **Accountancy; Business Administration; English; Finance; International Business.** *Bachelor's Degree*: **Accountancy; Business Administration;**

Design; E-Business/Commerce; English; Finance; Health Sciences; Information Management; Information Technology; Insurance; International Business; Japanese; Leisure Studies; Management; Marketing; Multimedia; Sports; Transport Management.** *Master's Degree*: **Management.**
Student Services: Academic Counselling, Health Services, Library

Student Numbers *2013-2014*: Total: c. 10,000
Last Updated: 06/02/14

CHINA MEDICAL UNIVERSITY (CMU)

91, Hsueh-Shih Road, Taichung 40402
Tel: +886(4) 2205-3366
Fax: +886(4) 220-57895
EMail: cc@mail.cmu.edu.tw
Website: http://www.cmu.edu.tw

President: Jong-Tsun Huang (2005-)
Tel: +886(4) 220-57153 EMail: master@mail.cmu.edu.tw

Vice President and Provost: Walter Chen
Tel: +886(4) 220-57153
EMail: chenwalt@yahoo.com; chenwalt@mail.cmu.edu.tw

College

Chinese Medicine *(Post-Baccalaureate)* (Acupuncture; Medicine; Traditional Eastern Medicine); **Health Care** (Biotechnology; Dental Hygiene; Health Sciences; Laboratory Techniques; Medical Technology; Nursing; Nutrition; Physical Therapy; Radiology; Rehabilitation and Therapy; Respiratory Therapy; Sports Medicine); **Life Sciences** (Biological and Life Sciences; Biology; Biotechnology; Cognitive Sciences; Ecology); **Management** (Health Administration; Health Sciences; Insurance; Statistics); **Medicine** (Biology; Dentistry; Immunology; Medicine; Molecular Biology; Oncology); **Pharmacy** (Applied Chemistry; Cosmetology; Pharmacology; Pharmacy; Safety Engineering; Toxicology; Traditional Eastern Medicine); **Public Health** (Occupational Health; Public Health)
Further Information: Also Campus at Peikang Town. Two Teaching Hospitals
History: Founded 1958 as China Medical College. Acquired present title 2003. A private institution under the jurisdiction of the Ministry of Education.
Academic Year: August to June (August-January; February-June)
Admission Requirements: Graduation from high school or recognized equivalent, and entrance examination
Fees: Undergraduate tuition, 48,374-61,389; Graduate tuition, 56,936-72,299
Main Language(s) of Instruction: Chinese, English
Degrees and Diplomas: *Bachelor's Degree*; *Master's Degree*: **Acupuncture; Biological and Life Sciences; Biology; Biomedicine; Biotechnology; Cognitive Sciences; Cosmetology; Dentistry; Health Administration; Immunology; Laboratory Techniques; Medical Technology; Medicine; Neurology; Nursing; Nutrition; Occupational Health; Oncology; Pharmacology; Pharmacy; Public Health; Radiology; Rehabilitation and Therapy; Statistics; Traditional Eastern Medicine.** *Doctorate*: **Biological and Life Sciences; Biotechnology; Medicine; Nutrition; Pharmacy; Public Health; Traditional Eastern Medicine.**
Student Services: Library
Publications: Chinese Medicine and Pharmacy Magazine

Academic Staff *2012-2013*	**TOTAL**
FULL-TIME	525
PART-TIME	531
Student Numbers *2012-2013*	
All (Foreign included)	7,940
FOREIGN ONLY	274

Last Updated: 06/02/14

CHINA UNIVERSITY OF SCIENCE AND TECHNOLOGY (CUST)

245, Section 3, Yen-Chiu Yuan Road, Nan-Kang, Taipei
Tel: +886(2) 2782-1862
Fax: +886(2) 278-82607
EMail: www@www.chit.edu.tw
Website: http://www.cust.edu.tw/

President: Chen-Jung Tien
Tel: +886(2) 278-21683 EMail: president@www.cust.edu.tw

Secretary-General: Ching-Chun Fu
Tel: +886(2) 2782-1862, Ext. 290 EMail: ccfu@cc.cust.edu.tw

International Relations: Kent Sun
Tel: +886(2) 278-56180 EMail: kentsun@cc.chit.edu.tw

College

Aviation (Aeronautical and Aerospace Engineering; Air Transport; Electrical and Electronic Equipment and Maintenance; Electronic Engineering; Hotel and Restaurant; Mechanical Engineering; Mechanical Equipment and Maintenance; Tourism); **Commerce and Management** (Business Administration; Business and Commerce; Finance; Industrial Engineering; Industrial Management; Information Management; International Business; Management; Multimedia); **Engineering** (Architecture; Civil Engineering; Computer Engineering; Computer Science; Electrical Engineering; Electronic Engineering; Engineering; Mechanical Engineering; Optical Technology; Safety Engineering; Software Engineering); **Health Science and Technology** (Biological and Life Sciences; Biotechnology; Food Science; Health Sciences; Hotel and Restaurant; Medical Technology)
Further Information: Also Hsin Chu Campus
History: Founded 1968 as China Junior College of Technology. Renamed China Junior College of Technology and Commerce 1994. Acquired College status and renamed China Institute of Technology 1999. Acquired present title 2009.
Fees: Application fee, 1,000 (US Dollar)
Main Language(s) of Instruction: Chinese
Degrees and Diplomas: *Bachelor's Degree*; *Master's Degree*: **Aeronautical and Aerospace Engineering; Air Transport; Architecture; Civil Engineering; Electrical Engineering; Electronic Engineering; Management; Mechanical Engineering; Medical Technology.**
Student Services: Academic Counselling, Health Services, IT Centre, Library
Last Updated: 06/02/14

CHINA UNIVERSITY OF TECHNOLOGY (CUTE)

56, Sec. 3, Xinglong Rd., Wunshan District, Taipei 116
Tel: +886(2) 293-13416
Fax: +886(2) 293-13992
EMail: secr@mail.ckitc.edu.tw
Website: http://www.cute.edu.tw/eng/

President: Chia-hung Ku
Tel: +886(2)2931-3416, Ext. 2111 EMail: pres@cute.edu.tw

Dean of Academic Affairs: Ming-Te Liu
Tel: +886(2) 293-03362 EMail: acad@mail.ckitc.edu.tw

International Relations: Hsueh-Cherng Chang
Tel: +886(2) 293-42980 EMail: carr@mail.ckitc.edu.tw

College

Business (Accountancy; Business Administration; Finance; Taxation); **Computer Science** (Computer Engineering; Computer Science; Electrical Engineering; Information Management; Software Engineering; Telecommunications Engineering); **General Education** (Arts and Humanities; Cultural Studies; Fine Arts; Modern Languages; Natural Sciences; Social Sciences); **Management** (Applied Linguistics; Business Administration; English; Leisure Studies; Management; Marketing; Parks and Recreation; Transport Management); **Planning and Design** (Architecture; Civil Engineering; Communication Arts; Design; Interior Design; Multimedia; Safety Engineering)
Further Information: Also Hsin-chu Campus
History: Founded 1965 as Chinese Municipal Vocational School. Renamed China Junior College of Industrial and Commercial Management 1983 and Chung Kuo Institute of Technology 2003. Acquired present status and title 2005.
Main Language(s) of Instruction: Chinese
Degrees and Diplomas: *Bachelor's Degree*; *Master's Degree*: **Architecture; Business Administration; Civil Engineering; Communication Arts; Design; Information Technology; Interior Design; Safety Engineering; Transport Management.** Twin MBA degrees with Metropolitan State University (USA)

Student Services: Health Services, Library, Residential Facilities, Social Counselling
Last Updated: 06/02/14

CHINESE CULTURE UNIVERSITY (CCU)

55, Hwa-Kang Road, Yang-Ming-Shan, Taipei 111
Tel: +886(2) 2861-0511
Fax: +886(2) 286-15031
Website: http://www.pccu.edu.tw

President: Wann-Yih Wu
Tel: +886(2) 286-10511, Ext. 10101
EMail: president@staff.pccu.edu.tw

Secretary-General: Chenhu Sheng
Tel: +886(2) 286-10511, Ext. 10201
EMail: husheng@faculty.pccu.edu.tw

International Relations: Kung-chi Li, Director, Office of International Affairs
Tel: +886(2) 286-10511, Ext. 18001
EMail: LKZ2@ulive.pccu.edu.tw

College

Agriculture (Biological and Life Sciences; Biotechnology; Environmental Management; Food Science; Forestry; Horticulture; Natural Resources; Nutrition; Zoology); **Arts** (Dance; Fine Arts; Music; Theatre); **Business Administration** (Accountancy; Banking; Business Administration; Finance; Information Management; International Business; Tourism); **Education** (Education; Physical Education; Psychology; Sports); **Engineering** (Chemical Engineering; Computer Science; Electrical Engineering; Electronic Engineering; Materials Engineering; Mechanical Engineering; Nanotechnology; Textile Technology); **Environmental Design** (Architectural and Environmental Design; Environmental Management; Landscape Architecture; Town Planning); **Foreign Languages** (English; French; German; Japanese; Korean; Literature; Modern Languages; Russian); **Journalism and Mass Communication** (Advertising and Publicity; Communication Studies; Information Sciences; Journalism; Mass Communication); **Law** (Law); **Liberal Arts** (History; Literature; Philosophy; Writing); **Science** (Applied Chemistry; Applied Mathematics; Biological and Life Sciences; Chemistry; Earth Sciences; Geography; Geology; Mathematics and Computer Science; Meteorology; Natural Sciences; Physics); **Social Sciences** (American Studies; Asian Studies; Economics; Human Resources; Political Sciences; Public Administration; Social Welfare)

School

Continuing Education

Further Information: Also Extension Education Centre

History: Founded 1962 as a private College, became University 1980.

Academic Year: September to June (September-January; February-June)

Admission Requirements: Graduation from high school or foreign equivalent, and entrance examination

Fees: 40,000 per semester (New Taiwan Dollar)

Main Language(s) of Instruction: Chinese

Degrees and Diplomas: *Bachelor's Degree*; *Master's Degree*: **Accountancy; Applied Chemistry; Architectural and Environmental Design; Architecture and Planning; Asian Studies; Biological and Life Sciences; Business Administration; Chemical Engineering; Chinese; Computer Engineering; Dance; Earth Sciences; Economics; Electronic Engineering; English; Finance; Fine Arts; French; Geography; Geology; German; History; Information Management; Information Sciences; International Business; Japanese; Journalism; Korean; Landscape Architecture; Law; Literature; Marketing; Materials Engineering; Mechanical Engineering; Meteorology; Music; Philosophy; Physical Education; Political Sciences; Psychology; Russian; Theatre; Tourism; Town Planning.** *Doctorate*: **Architecture and Planning; Asian Studies; Chinese; Earth Sciences; History; International Business; Law; Literature; Philosophy; Physical Education; Political Sciences; Town Planning.**

Student Services: Academic Counselling, Foreign Studies Centre, Health Services, IT Centre, Social Counselling, Sports Facilities

Publications: Hwa Kang Journal (in Chinese); Hwa Kang Journal of English Languages and Literature; Hwa Kang Journal of Foreign Languages and Literature (in English); Hwa Kang Journal of TEFL; Sino-American Relations (in English)

Publishing House: Chinese Culture University Press

Academic Staff *2013-2014*: Total: c. 720
Student Numbers *2013-2014*: Total 30,000
Last Updated: 07/02/14

CHING KUO INSTITUTE OF MANAGEMENT AND HEALTH (CKU)

336, Fu-Hsin Road, Keelung 203
Tel: +886(2) 243-72093, Ext. 603
Fax: +886(2) 243-76209
EMail: ysliou@ems.cku.edu.tw
Website: http://www.cku.edu.tw

President: Ming-Yuan Chiu
Tel: +886(2) 243-72093, Ext. 111 EMail: sec@ems.cku.edu.tw

Vice-President: Chun-Pin Cheng
Tel: +886(2) 243-72093, Ext. 268
EMail: cpcheng@ems.cku.edu.tw

International Relations: Yi-Shin Liou
Tel: +886(2) 243-72093, Ext. 603 EMail: ysliou@ems.cku.edu.tw

Department

Applied Cosmetic Science (Cosmetology); **Applied Information and Mutlimedia** (Information Management; Multimedia); **Child Educare** (Child Care and Development); **Culinary Arts** (Food Science); **Food and Health Science** (Cooking and Catering; Food Science; Food Technology; Health Sciences); **Hotel and Restaurant Management** (Hotel and Restaurant); **Nursing** (Nursing); **Senior Citizen Service Management** (Service Trades); **Sports, Health and Leisure** (Health Sciences; Leisure Studies; Sports); **Style Design and Fashion Performance** (Fashion Design)

Centre

General Education (Arts and Humanities; Chinese; English; Modern Languages; Natural Sciences; Physical Education; Social Sciences)

Graduate Institute

Health Industry Management (Alternative Medicine; Analytical Chemistry; Chemistry)

History: Founded 1957 as Deh-Yu College of Nursing and Management. Acquired present title 2002.

Main Language(s) of Instruction: Chinese

Degrees and Diplomas: *Associate Degree*; *Bachelor's Degree*; *Master's Degree*: **Health Administration; Management.**

Student Services: Academic Counselling, IT Centre, Library, Sports Facilities

Last Updated: 24/02/14

CHRIST'S COLLEGE

51 Tze-Chiang Road, Tamsui Dist., New Taipei City 25162
Tel: +886(2) 2809-7661
Fax: +886(2) 2809-6631
EMail: admissions@cct.edu.tw
Website: http://www.cct.edu.tw/

President: Quentin Nantz

Department

Christian Liberal Arts (Communication Studies; English; Music)

History: Founded 1959. Ministerial accreditation granted 2012.

Main Language(s) of Instruction: Chinese

Degrees and Diplomas: *Bachelor's Degree*. Master's Degree with foreign univesities issuing the degree in the field of: Music with Regent University (USA); Business Administration with Dallas Baptist University (USA); Foreign Languages Teaching with Azusa Pacific University (USA)

Student Services: Library
Last Updated: 09/02/14

CHUNG-CHOU UNIVERSITY OF TECHNOLOGY

Chung-Chou Institute of Technology (CCUT)
No. 6, Lane 2, Sec. 3, Shanjiao Rd., Yuanlin Township, Changhua 510
Tel: +886(4) 831-1498
Fax: +886(4) 831-4515
EMail: comp208@dragon.ccut.edu.tw
Website: http://www.ccut.edu.tw

President: Chin-Yin Tseng (2012-)
Tel: +886(4) 835-9000, Ext. 1100
EMail: president@dragon.ccut.edu.tw

Chief Secretary: Shin-Kuan Chen
Tel: +886(4) 835-9000, Ext. 1103
EMail: chunhaoch02@dragon.ccut.edu.tw

College
Engineering (Automation and Control Engineering; Electrical Engineering; Electronic Engineering; Energy Engineering; Engineering; Mechanical Engineering; Multimedia; Robotics; Software Engineering); **Health** (Biotechnology; Child Care and Development; Cooking and Catering; Food Science; Food Technology; Health Sciences; Landscape Architecture; Nutrition; Sports); **Management** (Design; Fashion Design; Film; Hotel and Restaurant; Information Management; Leisure Studies; Management; Marketing; Tourism; Transport Management; Video)

Centre
General Education (Arts and Humanities; Cultural Studies; Modern Languages; Natural Sciences; Physical Education)

History: Founded 1969 as Chung Chou Vocational Institute of Engineering. Renamed Chung Chou Institute of Technology 2000. Acquired present title 2011.

Fees: 44,220-50,853 per semester (New Taiwan Dollar)

Main Language(s) of Instruction: Chinese

Degrees and Diplomas: *Bachelor's Degree*; *Master's Degree*: **Automation and Control Engineering; Biotechnology; Food Technology; Mechanical Engineering.**

Student Services: Academic Counselling, Health Services, Residential Facilities, Social Counselling, Sports Facilities

Last Updated: 24/02/14

CHUNG-HUA UNIVERSITY (CHU)

707, Sec.2, WuFu Rd., Hsinchu 30012
Tel: +886(3) 537-4281
Fax: +886(3) 518-2111
EMail: international@chu.edu.tw
Website: http://www.chu.edu.tw

President: Victor W. Liu
Tel: +886(3) 518-6100 EMail: vwliu@chu.edu.tw

Secretary-General: Yeong-Pei Tasi
Tel: +886(3) 518-6121, Ext. 818 EMail: yptsai@chu.edu.tw

International Relations: Hung-Nien Hsieh, Dean, International and Cross-Strait Affairs
Tel: +886(3) 351-86694 EMail: planner@chu.edu.tw

College
Architecture and Planning (Architecture; Civil Engineering; Construction Engineering; Design; Landscape Architecture; Town Planning); **Computer Science and Informatics** (Computer Engineering; Computer Science; Information Management; Information Technology); **Engineering** (Architecture and Planning; Civil Engineering; Computer Engineering; Electrical Engineering; Electronic Engineering; Engineering; Industrial Management; Information Technology; Mechanical Engineering; Optical Technology; Telecommunications Engineering); **Humanities and Social Sciences** (Applied Linguistics; Arts and Humanities; English; French; Japanese; Literature; Modern Languages; Public Administration; Spanish); **Management** (Business Administration; Engineering Management; Finance; Industrial Engineering; Industrial Management; Information Management; International Business; Management; Statistics; Transport Engineering; Transport Management); **Tourism** (Hotel and Restaurant; Leisure Studies; Parks and Recreation; Tourism)

History: Founded 1990 as Chung Hua Polytechnic Institute. Acquired present status and title 1997.

Main Language(s) of Instruction: Chinese

Degrees and Diplomas: *Bachelor's Degree*: **Engineering Management; Industrial Engineering; Industrial Management.** *Master's Degree*: **Business Administration; Computer Engineering; Computer Networks; Computer Science; Engineering Management; Industrial Engineering; Industrial Management; Information Management; Public Administration; Statistics; Telecommunications Engineering; Tourism; Transport Engineering; Transport Management.** *Doctorate*: **Engineering; Engineering Management; Industrial Engineering; Industrial Management; Information Management; Transport Management.**

Student Services: IT Centre, Library

Last Updated: 07/02/14

CHUNG-HWA UNIVERSITY OF MEDICAL TECHNOLOGY (CUMT)

No.89, Wenhwa 1st St., Rende Shiang, Tainan Hsien 717
Tel: +886(6) 267-1214 +886(6) 267-4567
Fax: +886(6) 290-2464
EMail: lin@mail.hwai.edu.tw
Website: http://www.hwai.edu.tw/

President: Jin-peng Lin
Tel: +886(6) 267-3388, Ext. 200
EMail: president@mail.hwai.edu.tw

Dean of Academic Affairs: Yu-Lin Yang
Tel: +886(6) 267-4567, Ext. 220
EMail: call0955443221@gmail.com

College
Health Care and Management (Cosmetology; Health Administration; Health Sciences; Information Management; Leisure Studies; Sports); **Human Science and Technology** (Biotechnology; Child Care and Development; Environmental Engineering; Health Sciences; Hotel and Restaurant; Nutrition; Occupational Health; Preschool Education; Safety Engineering); **Medicine and Life Science** (Biological and Life Sciences; Biomedicine; Biotechnology; Health Sciences; Laboratory Techniques; Medical Technology; Nursing; Optometry)

Centre
General Education (Arts and Humanities; English; Natural Sciences; Technology)

History: Founded 1968 as China Junior College of Medical Technology. Upgraded into Chung-Hwa College of Medical Technology 1999. Acquire present status and title 2007.

Main Language(s) of Instruction: Chinese

Degrees and Diplomas: *Certificate*; *Associate Degree*; *Bachelor's Degree*; *Master's Degree*: **Biological and Life Sciences; Biomedicine; Biotechnology; Information Management; Laboratory Techniques; Medical Technology; Safety Engineering.** *Doctorate*: **Information Management.**

Student Services: IT Centre, Library, Sports Facilities

Last Updated: 25/02/14

CHUNG SHAN MEDICAL UNIVERSITY (CSMU)

No.110,Sec.1, Jianguo N.Rd., Taichung 40201
Tel: +886(4) 247-30022
Fax: +886(4) 247-39030
EMail: cs1021@csmu.edu.tw
Website: http://www.csmu.edu.tw

President: Te-Jen Lai
Tel: +886(4) 2473-0022, Ext 11010
EMail: president@csmu.edu.tw; tejenlai@hotmail.com; ltj3123@ms2.hinet.net

Dean of Academic Affairs: Thomas Chang-Yao Tsao
Tel: +886(4) 247-30022, Ext. 1160 EMail: tcyt@csmu.edu.tw

International Relations: Jeng-Dong Hsu
Tel: +886(4) 247-09318 EMail: dongdong@csmu.edu.tw

College
Health Care and Management (Applied Chemistry; Dietetics; Health Administration; Health Sciences; Information Sciences; Nutrition; Occupational Health; Public Health); **Medical Humanities**

and Social Sciences (Applied Linguistics; English; Japanese; Modern Languages; Native Language; Social Work; Sociology); **Medical Science and Technology** (Biomedicine; Biotechnology; Clinical Psychology; Medical Technology; Medicine; Occupational Therapy; Optometry; Physical Therapy; Psychology; Radiology; Speech Therapy and Audiology); **Medicine** (Biochemistry; Biotechnology; Hygiene; Immunology; Medicine; Microbiology; Molecular Biology; Toxicology); **Nursing** (Nursing); **Oral Medicine** (Biology; Dentistry; Oral Pathology)

Further Information: Also Chung Shan Medical University Hospital; Rehabilitation Hospital; Chung Shan Affiliated Clinic, Miao-Li

History: Founded 1960 as Chung Shan Dental Junior College. Upgraded into Chung Shan Medical and Dental College 1977. Acquired present status and title 2001. A private institution under the jurisdiction of the Ministry of Education.

Academic Year: September to June (September-January; February-June)

Admission Requirements: Graduation from high school and entrance examination

Fees: Tuition fee for Graduate Programmes, 2,120-1,560; Graduate Programmes, 2,550-2,005 per semester (US Dollar)

Main Language(s) of Instruction: Chinese

Degrees and Diplomas: *Bachelor's Degree*: **Applied Chemistry; Applied Linguistics; Biomedicine; Biotechnology; Dentistry; Dietetics; English; Health Administration; Health Sciences; Information Sciences; Japanese; Laboratory Techniques; Medical Technology; Native Language; Nursing; Nutrition; Occupational Health; Optometry; Physical Therapy; Psychology; Public Health; Radiology; Social Work; Sociology; Speech Therapy and Audiology.** *Master's Degree*: **Applied Chemistry; Biochemistry; Biology; Biomedicine; Biotechnology; Dentistry; Health Administration; Immunology; Information Sciences; Laboratory Techniques; Medical Technology; Medicine; Microbiology; Molecular Biology; Nursing; Nutrition; Occupational Health; Oral Pathology; Psychology; Social Work; Sociology; Toxicology.** *Doctorate*: **Biochemistry; Biology; Biotechnology; Dentistry; Immunology; Medicine; Microbiology; Molecular Biology; Nutrition; Oral Pathology; Toxicology.**

Student Services: Academic Counselling, Facilities for disabled people, Health Services, IT Centre, Library, Residential Facilities, Sports Facilities

Publications: Journal; The Chung Shan Medical Journal

Academic Staff *2013-2014*	**TOTAL**
FULL-TIME	**400**
PART-TIME	c. **350**
Student Numbers *2013-2014*	
All (Foreign included)	c. **8,500**

Last Updated: 07/02/14

CHUNG YUAN CHRISTIAN UNIVERSITY (CYCU)

No. 200 Chung Pei Rd., Chung Li City, Taiwan 32023
Tel: +886(3) 265-9999
Fax: +886(3) 265-8888
EMail: cycubox@cycu.edu.tw
Website: http://www.cycu.edu.tw

President: Kwang-Cheng Chang (2012-)
Tel: +886(3) 265-1000 EMail: skcchang@cycu.edu.tw

Secretary-General: Ying-Yi Hong
Tel: +886(3) 265-1200 EMail: yyhong@dec.ee.cycu.edu.tw

International Relations: Johui Chen, Dean
Tel: +886(3) 265-1700 EMail: johui@cycu.edu.tw

College

Business (Accountancy; Business Administration; Finance; Information Management; International Business; Management); **Design** (Architecture; Design; Interior Design; Landscape Architecture); **Electrical Engineering and Computer Science** (Computer Engineering; Computer Science; Electrical Engineering; Electronic Engineering; Engineering; Industrial Engineering; Information Technology; Telecommunications Engineering); **Engineering** (Bioengineering; Biomedical Engineering; Chemical Engineering; Civil Engineering; Engineering; Environmental Engineering; Mechanical Engineering); **Humanities and Education** (Applied Linguistics; Arts and Humanities; Education; Modern Languages; Native Language Education; Religion; Special Education); **Science** (Applied Mathematics; Biotechnology; Chemistry; Nanotechnology; Physics; Psychology)

School

Law (Economics; Finance; Law)

Centre

CYCU Mandarin (Chinese)

History: Founded 1955 as a private Christian College of Science and Engineering recognized by the Ministry of Education. Acquired present status and title 1980.

Academic Year: August to July (August-January; February-July)

Admission Requirements: International Graduate Programme, TOEFL IBT with a minimum score of 61; Undergraduate Programmes, Test of Chinese as a Foreign Language (TOCFL) with basic/TOP 3 as a minimum level

Fees: 47,000-55,000 per semester (New Taiwan Dollar)

Main Language(s) of Instruction: Chinese

Accrediting Agency: Institute of Engineering Education Taiwan (IEET); Association to Advance Collegiate Schools of Business (AACSB),

Degrees and Diplomas: *Bachelor's Degree*; *Master's Degree*: **Architecture; Business Administration; Design; Engineering; Heritage Preservation; Interior Design; Management; Modern Languages; Religion; Special Education.** *Doctorate*: **Business Administration; Design; Engineering; Landscape Architecture.**

Student Services: Academic Counselling, Canteen, Careers Guidance, Facilities for disabled people, Foreign Studies Centre, Health Services, Language Laboratory, Social Counselling, Sports Facilities

Publications: An International Journal of Bible, Theology & Philosophy; Chung Yuan Financial & Economic Law Review; Chung Yuan Journal of Teaching Chinese as a Second Language; Chung Yuan Management Review; Chung Yuan Physical Education Journal; Journal of Advanced Engineering; Journal of Design Science

Publishing House: Holistic CYCU

Academic Staff *2012-2013*	MEN	WOMEN	**TOTAL**
FULL-TIME	374	142	**516**
PART-TIME	388	205	**593**
STAFF WITH DOCTORATE			
FULL-TIME	331	119	**450**
Student Numbers *2012-2013*			
All (Foreign included)	9,789	6,474	**16,263**
FOREIGN ONLY	100	92	**192**

Last Updated: 23/05/13

CHUNGYU INSTITUTE OF TECHNOLOGY (CIT)

40, Yi 7th Rd., Keelung
Tel: +886(2) 2423-7785
Fax: +886(2) 2429-3639
EMail: cwchiu@cit.edu.tw; entrance@cit.edu.tw; service@cit.edu.tw
Website: http://www.cit.edu.tw

President: Liangrong Hui
Tel: +886(2) 2423-7785, Ext. 201 EMail: jhliang@cit.edu.tw

Department

Accounting Information (Accountancy; Statistics); **Applied Foreign Languages** (Applied Linguistics; English; Modern Languages); **Business Administration** (Business Administration); **Finance** (Finance); **Financial and Economic Law** (Commercial Law; Finance; Law); **Information Law** (Information Sciences; Law); **Information Management** (Information Management); **International Business** (International Business); **Leisure, Recreation and Tourism Management** (Leisure Studies; Parks and Recreation; Tourism); **Multimedia and Game Science** (Multimedia; Software Engineering); **Visual Communication Design** (Communication Arts; Design; Visual Arts)

History: Founded 1967 as Chungyu Junior College of Business Administration. Acquired present status and title 2003.

Fees: Tuition, 38,055 per semester (New Taiwan Dollar)
Main Language(s) of Instruction: Chinese
Degrees and Diplomas: *Associate Degree*; *Bachelor's Degree*; *Master's Degree*: **Management.**
Student Services: Residential Facilities
Last Updated: 25/02/14

DAHAN INSTITUTE OF TECHNOLOGY

No.1, Shuren St., Dahan Village, Sincheng Township, Hualien 971
Tel: +886(3) 8210-888
Fax: +886(3) 8266-588
EMail: fu@ms01.dahan.edu.tw; web_master@ms01.dahan.edu.tw
Website: http://www.dahan.edu.tw

President: Peixuan Song (2009-)
Tel: +886(3) 826-7461, Ext. 1113

Secretary-General: Changlong Cai
Tel: +886(3) 8210-801, Ext. 1112
EMail: s214299@ms01.dahan.edu.tw

College

Industry (Civil Engineering; Computer Engineering; Computer Science; Construction Engineering; Environmental Management; Geological Engineering; Mechanical Engineering); **Management** (Banking; Business Administration; E-Business/Commerce; Finance; Information Management; International Business; Management; Taxation; Transport Management); **Tourism** (Hotel Management; Jewellery Art; Leisure Studies; Parks and Recreation; Sports Management; Tourism)

Centre

General Education (Arts and Humanities; Chinese; Cultural Studies; English; Environmental Studies; Information Technology; Modern Languages)

History: Founded 1977 as Dahan Junior College of Engineering and Business. Acquired present title and status 1999.
Main Language(s) of Instruction: Chinese
Degrees and Diplomas: *Bachelor's Degree*
Student Services: IT Centre, Library, Sports Facilities
Last Updated: 26/02/14

DA-YEH UNIVERSITY (DYU)

168, University Rd., Dacun, Changhua 51591
Tel: +886(4) 851-1888
Fax: +886(4) 851-1666
EMail: cc2600@mail.dyu.edu.tw
Website: http://www.dyu.edu.tw

President: Dong-Sing Wuu
Tel: +886(4) 851-1888 EMail: dsw@mail.dyu.edu.tw

Secretary-General: Tsai-Hsi Wu
Tel: +886(4) 851-1888, Ext. 1005 EMail: taiwu@mail.dyu.edu.tw

College

Biotechnology and Bioresources (Biotechnology; Botany; Health Sciences; Molecular Biology; Natural Resources; Traditional Eastern Medicine); **Design and Arts** (Architecture; Communication Arts; Design; Fine Arts; Graphic Design; Industrial Design; Interior Design; Visual Arts); **Engineering** (Automation and Control Engineering; Computer Engineering; Computer Science; Design; Electrical Engineering; Engineering; Environmental Engineering; Industrial Engineering; Industrial Management; Machine Building; Materials Engineering; Mechanical Engineering; Medical Technology; Multimedia; Packaging Technology); **Foreign Languages** (Applied Linguistics; Cultural Studies; English; European Languages; European Studies; Japanese; Modern Languages; Transport Management); **Management** (Accountancy; Business Administration; Finance; Human Resources; Information Management; International Business; Management; Private Law; Public Relations); **Nursing and Health Sciences** (Health Sciences; Nursing); **Tourism and Hospitality** (Business Administration; Hotel and Restaurant; Leisure Studies; Parks and Recreation; Sports Management; Tourism)

History: Founded 1990, acquired present status and title 1997.
Academic Year: September to June (September-January; February-June)
Admission Requirements: Graduation from high school and/or College entrance examination
Fees: Tuition, c. 41,250-47,500 (New Taiwan Dollar)
Main Language(s) of Instruction: Chinese, English
Accrediting Agency: Ministry of Education
Degrees and Diplomas: *Bachelor's Degree*; *Master's Degree*: **Accountancy; Agricultural Engineering; Applied Linguistics; Architecture; Automation and Control Engineering; Automotive Engineering; Biotechnology; Botany; Business Administration; Communication Arts; Computer Engineering; Computer Science; Electrical Engineering; English; Fine Arts; Food Technology; Graphic Design; Human Resources; Industrial Design; Industrial Engineering; Information Management; Interior Design; International Business; Japanese; Leisure Studies; Mechanical Engineering; Molecular Biology; Multimedia; Parks and Recreation; Private Law; Public Relations; Sports Management; Telecommunications Engineering; Tourism; Traditional Eastern Medicine; Visual Arts.** *Doctorate*: **Automation and Control Engineering; Electrical Engineering; Food Technology; Management; Mechanical Engineering.** Also College Degree Certificate, 2 yrs
Student Services: Academic Counselling, Canteen, Careers Guidance, Health Services, Language Laboratory, Nursery Care, Sports Facilities
Publications: Da-Yeh Communication; Journal of Da-Yeh University
Publishing House: Da-Yeh University Press

Student Numbers *2013-2014*: Total: c. 10,000
Last Updated: 07/02/14

DE LIN INSTITUTE OF TECHNOLOGY (DLIT)

No.1, Ln. 380, Qingyun Rd., Tucheng Dist., New Taipei City 236
Tel: +886(2) 227-33567
Fax: +886(2) 227-11492
EMail: ccadm@dlit.edu.tw
Website: http://www.dlit.edu.tw

President: Ship-Peng Lo (2009-)
Tel: +886(2) 227-33567, Ext. 788 EMail: president@dlit.edu.tw

Dean, Academic Affairs: Ching-Fang Lin
Tel: +886(2) 227-33567, Ext. 699 EMail: academic@dlit.edu.tw

School

Business and Management (Applied Linguistics; Business Administration; English; Finance; International Business; Management; Modern Languages); **Engineering** (Computer Engineering; Computer Science; Electronic Engineering; Engineering; Industrial Design; Information Technology; Mechanical Engineering; Optical Technology; Telecommunications Engineering); **Hospitality** (Cooking and Catering; Hotel and Restaurant; Leisure Studies); **Real Estate** (Architecture; Civil Engineering; Construction Engineering; Interior Design; Real Estate)

Centre

Foreign Language (English; Modern Languages); **General Education** (Arts and Humanities; Chinese; English)

History: Founded 1972. Acquired present status and title 2001.
Main Language(s) of Instruction: Chinese
Degrees and Diplomas: *Associate Degree*; *Bachelor's Degree*
Student Services: Library, Residential Facilities, Sports Facilities
Last Updated: 26/02/14

FAR EAST UNIVERSITY (FEU)

49, Zhonghua Rd., Xinshi Dist., Tainan 74448
Tel: +886(6) 597-9566
Fax: +886(6) 597-7050
EMail: feucc@cc.feu.edu.tw
Website: http://www.feu.edu.tw/feu-english/all.htm

President: Nai-Chang Wang Tel: +886(6) 597-7057

College

Commerce and Management (Business Administration; Business and Commerce; Computer Graphics; Design; Industrial Design;

Information Management; Management; Marketing; Multimedia; Transport Management); **Electrical and Computer Engineering** (Computer Engineering; Computer Science; Electrical Engineering; Electronic Engineering; Information Technology; Optical Technology); **Engineering** (Automation and Control Engineering; Computer Engineering; Energy Engineering; Engineering; Materials Engineering; Mechanical Engineering); **Hospitality and Leisure** (Cooking and Catering; Cosmetology; English; Hotel and Restaurant; Leisure Studies; Parks and Recreation; Sports Management; Tourism; Transport Management)

Centre

General Education (Arts and Humanities)

History: Founded 1968 as Far East Junior College of Technology. Acquired present status and title 2006.

Main Language(s) of Instruction: Chinese

Degrees and Diplomas: *Bachelor's Degree*; *Master's Degree*: **Computer Engineering; Electrical Engineering; Information Management; Management; Marketing; Materials Engineering; Mechanical Engineering.**

Student Services: Library

Last Updated: 07/02/14

FENG CHIA UNIVERSITY (FCU)

100, Wenhwa Rd., Seatwen, Taichung 40724
Tel: +886(4) 245-17250, Ext. 2075
Fax: +886(4) 245-10129
EMail: webadmin@fcu.edu.tw
Website: http://www.fcu.edu.tw

President: Bing-Jean Lee
Tel: +886(4) 2451-7250, Ext. 2013 EMail: president@fcu.edu.tw

Secretary-General: Hai-Ping Hsieh
Tel: +886(4) 245-17250, Ext. 2020 EMail: adm-pr@fcu.edu.tw

International Relations: Pei Liu, Dean of International Affairs
Tel: +886(4) 24517250, Ext. 2500 EMail: peiliu@fcu.edu.tw

College

Business (Accountancy; Business Administration; Commercial Law; Economics; Engineering Management; Finance; Fiscal Law; International Business; Marketing; Statistics); **Construction and Development** (Architecture; Civil Engineering; Hydraulic Engineering; Information Sciences; Landscape Architecture; Parks and Recreation; Real Estate; Surveying and Mapping; Town Planning; Transport Engineering; Transport Management; Water Management); **Engineering** (Aeronautical and Aerospace Engineering; Chemical Engineering; Electronic Engineering; Energy Engineering; Engineering; Industrial Engineering; Mechanical Engineering; Sound Engineering (Acoustics)); **Finance** (Finance; Insurance); **Humanities and Social Studies** (Ancient Civilizations; Arts and Humanities; Chinese; English; History; Literature; Modern Languages); **Information and Electrical Engineering** (Automation and Control Engineering; Biomedicine; Computer Engineering; Computer Science; Electrical Engineering; Electronic Engineering; Information Technology; Medical Technology; Telecommunications Services); **Science** (Applied Mathematics; Environmental Engineering; Materials Engineering; Mathematics and Computer Science; Optical Technology)

School

Management (Business Administration; Management)

Course

General Education (Arts and Humanities); **Physical Education** (Physical Education)

Further Information: Also Technical Training Division for overseas Chinese students

History: Founded 1961 as Feng Chia College of Engineering and Business. Acquired present status and title 1980.

Academic Year: September to June (September-January; February-June)

Admission Requirements: Graduation from high school and entrance examination

Fees: Tuition, 39,190-41,000 per semester (New Taiwan Dollar)

Main Language(s) of Instruction: Chinese, English

Degrees and Diplomas: *Bachelor's Degree*; *Master's Degree*: **Accountancy; Aeronautical and Aerospace Engineering; Ancient Civilizations; Applied Mathematics; Architecture; Automation and Control Engineering; Biomedical Engineering; Business Administration; Chemical Engineering; Civil Engineering; Commercial Law; Computer Engineering; Computer Science; Design; Economics; Electrical Engineering; Electronic Engineering; Energy Engineering; Engineering Management; Environmental Engineering; Environmental Studies; Finance; Fiscal Law; History; Hydraulic Engineering; Industrial Engineering; Information Technology; Insurance; International Business; Landscape Architecture; Literature; Materials Engineering; Mechanical Engineering; Optical Technology; Parks and Recreation; Real Estate; Sound Engineering (Acoustics); Statistics; Telecommunications Engineering; Town Planning; Transport Engineering; Transport Management.** *Doctorate*: **Accountancy; Aeronautical and Aerospace Engineering; Business Administration; Chemical Engineering; Civil Engineering; Computer Engineering; Computer Science; Electrical Engineering; Environmental Engineering; Environmental Studies; Finance; Hydraulic Engineering; Industrial Engineering; Literature; Materials Engineering; Mechanical Engineering; Taxation; Telecommunications Engineering.**

Student Services: Academic Counselling, Careers Guidance, Cultural Activities, Facilities for disabled people, Health Services, Library, Social Counselling, Sports Facilities, eLibrary

Publications: Feng Chia Journal

Academic Staff *2013-2014*	**TOTAL**
FULL-TIME	**1,245**
Student Numbers *2013-2014*	
All (Foreign included)	**20,214**
FOREIGN ONLY	**659**

Last Updated: 07/02/14

FO GUANG UNIVERSITY (FGU)

No.160, Linwei Rd., Jiaosi, Yilan 26247
Tel: +886(3) 987-1000
Fax: +886(3) 987-4806
EMail: secretary@mail.fgu.edu.tw
Website: http://www.fgu.edu.tw

President: Chaur-Shin Yung
Tel: +886(3) 987-4828
EMail: president@mail.fgu.edu.tw; kirbyyung@mail.fgu.edu.tw

College

Buddhist Studies (Asian Studies); **Humanities** (Arts and Humanities; Cultural Studies; Fine Arts; History; Literature; Modern Languages; Philosophy; Religion); **Science and Engineering** (Computer Engineering; Computer Science; Design; Educational Technology; Engineering; Industrial Design; Information Technology; Media Studies; Psychology); **Social Sciences and Management** (Communication Studies; Economics; Futurology; Management; Political Sciences; Public Administration; Social Sciences; Sociology)

History: Founded 2000 as Fo Guang College of Humanities and Social Sciences. Acquired present title 2006.

Main Language(s) of Instruction: Chinese

Degrees and Diplomas: *Bachelor's Degree*; *Master's Degree*: **Asian Religious Studies; Communication Studies; Computer Engineering; Computer Science; Cultural Studies; Economics; Educational Technology; English; Fine Arts; Futurology; History; Industrial Design; Information Technology; Literature; Management; Media Studies; Philosophy; Political Sciences; Psychology; Public Administration; Religion; Sociology.** *Doctorate*: **Literature.**

Student Services: Canteen, Library, Residential Facilities, Sports Facilities, eLibrary

Last Updated: 26/02/14

FOOYIN UNIVERSITY

151 Jinxue Rd., Daliao Dist., Kaohsiung 83102
Tel: +886(7) 781-1151, Ext.1600
Fax: +886(7) 782-6146
EMail: so@mail.fy.edu.tw; pr@fy.edu.tw
Website: http://www.fy.edu.tw

President: Sheila Sheu
Tel: +886(7) 781-1151, Ext. 1600 EMail: slsheu@mail.fy.edu.tw

School

Environmental and Life Sciences (Applied Chemistry; Biological and Life Sciences; Biotechnology; Environmental Engineering; Environmental Studies; Materials Engineering; Occupational Health; Safety Engineering); **Humanities and Social Sciences** (Applied Linguistics; Arts and Humanities; Child Care and Development; Educational Administration; English; Information Management; Information Technology; Leisure Studies; Modern Languages; Parks and Recreation; Social Sciences; Teacher Training; Tourism); **Medical and Health Sciences** (Biotechnology; Cosmetology; Health Sciences; Laboratory Techniques; Medical Technology; Medicine; Nutrition; Physical Therapy); **Nursing** (Business Administration; Gerontology; Health Sciences; Midwifery; Nursing)

Centre

Business Development and Incubation (Business Administration); **General Education** (Arts and Humanities; Modern Languages)

Further Information: Affiliated Hospital and Nursery School

History: Founded 1958 as a vocational high school. Successively upgraded into a junior college 1968, and into an institute of technology 1997. Acquired present title and status 2002.

Academic Year: August to July

Admission Requirements: Graduation from high school and entrance examination

Fees: c. 55,000 per semester (New Taiwan Dollar)

Main Language(s) of Instruction: Chinese

Degrees and Diplomas: *Associate Degree*; *Bachelor's Degree*; *Master's Degree*: **Biotechnology; Environmental Engineering; Environmental Studies; Health Sciences; Laboratory Techniques; Medical Technology; Nursing; Nutrition.**

Student Services: Academic Counselling, Canteen, Careers Guidance, Facilities for disabled people, Health Services, Language Laboratory, Library, Nursery Care, Social Counselling, Sports Facilities

Last Updated: 26/02/14

FORTUNE INSTITUTE OF TECHNOLOGY (FIT)

125-8, Chi-Wen Road, Chi-Shan, Kaohsiung 83160
Tel: +886(7) 788-9888
Fax: +886(7) 788-9777
EMail: webadvise@fotech.edu.tw
Website: http://www.fjtc.edu.tw

President: Ying-Fang Huang
Tel: +886(7) 788-9888, Ext. 2200 EMail: winner@fotech.edu.tw

Dean of Academic Affairs: Huang-Che Huang
Tel: +886(7) 788-9888, Ext. 2300
EMail: hchuang@fotech.edu.tw

College

Business and Management (Applied Linguistics; Business Administration; English; Finance; Information Management; Japanese; Management; Marketing; Modern Languages; Transport Management); **Design** (Advertising and Publicity; Communication Arts; Design; Fashion Design; Industrial Design; Multimedia); **Electrical and Computer Engineering** (Business Administration; Computer Engineering; Computer Science; E-Business/Commerce; Electrical Engineering; Electronic Engineering; Industrial Engineering; Management); **Food and Beverage Management** (Food Technology; Hotel and Restaurant; Leisure Studies; Real Estate; Tourism)

History: Founded 1989 as Fortune Junior College. Renamed Fortune Junior College of Technology and Commerce 1991. Acquired present status and title 1999.

Main Language(s) of Instruction: Chinese

Degrees and Diplomas: *Associate Degree*; *Bachelor's Degree*; *Master's Degree*: **Electrical Engineering.**

Student Services: Canteen, IT Centre, Library, Residential Facilities

Last Updated: 26/02/14

FU JEN CATHOLIC UNIVERSITY (FJCU)

No.510, Zhongzheng Rd., Xinzhuang Dist., New Taipei City 24205
Tel: +886(2) 2905-2000
Fax: +886(2) 2902-6201
EMail: pubwww@mail.fju.edu.tw
Website: http://www.fju.edu.tw

President: Vincent Han-Sun Chiang
Tel: +886(2) 2905-3016 EMail: president@mail.fju.edu.tw

Secretary-General: Chung-Jen Wey
Tel: +886(2) 2905-2203
EMail: secret@mail.fju.edu.tw; ph1004@mail.fju.edu.tw

International Relations: Yongqi Hou, Director, International Education Office
Tel: +886(2) 2905-2061 EMail: 035440@mail.fju.edu.tw

College

Arts (Communication Arts; Computer Graphics; Fine Arts; Handicrafts; Interior Design; Landscape Architecture; Music; Visual Arts); **Communication** (Advertising and Publicity; Communication Arts; Communication Studies; Journalism; Mass Communication; Public Relations); **Continuing Education** (Accountancy; Business Administration; Chinese; Economics; English; Finance; History; Hotel and Restaurant; Information Sciences; International Business; Japanese; Law; Library Science; Literature; Mass Communication; Mathematics; Philosophy; Statistics); **Education** (Education; Educational Administration; Information Sciences; Library Science; Physical Education); **Foreign Languages** (Comparative Literature; English; French; German; Italian; Japanese; Linguistics; Literature; Modern Languages; Spanish; Translation and Interpretation); **Human Ecology** (Child Care and Development; Clothing and Sewing; Family Studies; Food Science; Hotel and Restaurant; Management; Museum Studies; Nutrition); **Liberal Arts** (Arts and Humanities; Chinese; History; Literature; Philosophy); **Management** (Business Administration; Engineering Management; Finance; Information Management; Information Sciences; International Business; Management; Statistics); **Medicine** (Clinical Psychology; Gerontology; Medicine; Nursing; Occupational Therapy; Public Health; Respiratory Therapy); **Science and Engineering** (Biological and Life Sciences; Chemistry; Computer Engineering; Computer Science; Electrical Engineering; Engineering; Mathematics; Natural Sciences; Physics; Psychology); **Social Sciences** (Economics; Religious Studies; Social Sciences; Social Work; Sociology)

School

Law (Commercial Law; Finance; Law; Private Law)

Academy

Fu Jen Academia Catholica (Aesthetics; Asian Studies; Christian Religious Studies; Ethics; History; Literature; Peace and Disarmament; Philosophy; Religion)

Centre

Holistic Education

Further Information: Also Clininc, Catholic University Hospital; Study Abroad Programmes for Language Courses in Japan, Germany, France, Spain and Italy. Exchange Programmes for foreign students (courses in Chinese Culture, Chinese Society, and Chinese Economics)

History: Founded 1919 as Fu Jen Academy, became University 1926, and acquired present status 1963.

Academic Year: September to June (September-January; February-June)

Admission Requirements: Graduation from high school and entrance examination

Main Language(s) of Instruction: Chinese, English

Degrees and Diplomas: *Bachelor's Degree*; *Master's Degree*: **Biological and Life Sciences; Business Administration; Chemistry; Commercial Law; Computer Engineering; Computer Science; Economics; Education; Educational Administration; Electrical Engineering; Engineering Management; Food Science; International Business; Landscape Architecture; Law; Linguistics; Management; Mass Communication; Mathematics; Medicine; Museum Studies; Music; Natural Sciences; Nursing; Nutrition; Physical Education; Physics; Public Health; Religious Studies; Social Work; Sociology; Translation and Interpretation.** *Doctorate*: **Biochemistry; Biomedicine;**

Biotechnology; Business Administration; Chemistry; Comparative Literature; Computer Engineering; Computer Science; Electronic Engineering; Engineering; Food Science; Law; Music; Nutrition; Optical Technology; Religious Studies. Also Executive MBA, some Master's degree in Science and Engineering also offered in part-time mode.

Student Services: Academic Counselling, Canteen, Careers Guidance, Cultural Activities, Facilities for disabled people, Foreign Studies Centre, Health Services, IT Centre, Library, Nursery Care, Social Counselling, Sports Facilities

Publications: Economic Journal; Fu Jen Studies; Law Journal; Philosophy Journal; Social Prospective; Theologica Collectanea

Publishing House: Fu Jen Press

Last Updated: 27/02/14

HSING KUO UNIVERSITY (HKU)

89, Yu Ying Street, Annan, Tainan 709
Tel: +886(6) 287-3335 +886(6) 287-0026
Fax: +886(6) 287-3536
EMail: academic@mail.hku.edu.tw
Website: http://www.hku.edu.tw

President: Kuo-Qin Yan
Tel: +886(6) 287-3328 EMail: president@mail.hku.edu.tw

Secretary-General: Li Zhao EMail: secretariat@ms.hku.edu.tw

College

Digital Information (Information Management); **Fashion Creativity** (Applied Linguistics; Design; English; Fashion Design; Japanese; Jewellery Art; Management; Multimedia; Parks and Recreation; Tourism); **Management** (Business Administration; Commercial Law; Engineering Management; Finance; Law; Management; Marketing; Real Estate; Taxation; Transport Management)

Centre

General Education (Arts and Humanities)

History: Founded 2000.

Fees: Tuition fee, 35,634 per semester (Yuan Renminbi)

Main Language(s) of Instruction: Chinese, English

Degrees and Diplomas: *Bachelor's Degree*: **Business Administration; Commercial Law; Design; Fashion Design; Finance; Information Management; Japanese; Jewellery Art; Management; Marketing; Multimedia; Tourism; Transport Management.**

Student Services: Health Services, IT Centre, Library, Residential Facilities

Last Updated: 27/02/14

HSING WU UNIVERSITY (HWU)

No. 101, Sec.1, Fenliao Rd., LinKou District,
New Taipei City 24452
Tel: +886(2) 2601-5310
Fax: +886(2) 2601-0748
EMail: h040@mail.hwc.edu.tw
Website: http://www.hwu.edu.tw/

President: Tein-Chen Chou Tel: +886(2) 260-15310, Ext.1101
EMail: h001@mail.hwu.edu.tw

Vice-President: Yiwen Chen
Tel: +886(2) 260-15310, Ext. 1111
EMail: 082002@mail.hwu.edu.tw

College

Information (Communication Studies; Information Management; Information Sciences; Information Technology)

School

Business and Management (Business Administration; Finance; International Business; Management; Marketing; Transport Management); **Design** (Computer Graphics; Design; Fashion Design; Industrial Design); **Tourism and Hospitality** (Computer Science; English; Hotel and Restaurant; Leisure Studies; Tourism; Transport Management)

Centre

Education (Arts and Humanities; Chinese; Cultural Studies; English; Fine Arts; History; Leisure Studies; Natural Sciences; Philosophy; Religion; Social Sciences; Sports)

History: Founded 1965. Upgraded into Hsing-Wu College 2000. Acquired present status and title 2012.

Main Language(s) of Instruction: Chinese

Degrees and Diplomas: *Associate Degree*; *Bachelor's Degree*; *Master's Degree*: **Information Technology; Leisure Studies; Marketing; Tourism; Transport Management.**

Last Updated: 27/02/14

HSIUPING UNIVERSITY OF SCIENCE AND TECHNOLOGY (HUST)

No.11 Gongye Rd, Dali Dist., Taichung 412-80
Tel: +886(4) 2496-1100
Fax: +886(4) 2496-1187
EMail: service@mail.hust.edu.tw
Website: http://www.hust.edu.tw/

President: Ruey-gwo Chung
Tel: +886(4) 2496-1172 EMail: service@mail.hust.edu.tw

Vice-President: Pei-Chung Chen
Tel: +886(4) 2496-1523 EMail: service@mail.hust.edu.tw

College

Engineering (Computer Networks; Electrical Engineering; Electronic Engineering; Energy Engineering; Engineering; Industrial Engineering; Industrial Management; Information Technology; Materials Engineering; Measurement and Precision Engineering; Mechanical Engineering; Production Engineering); **Humanities and Creativity** (Applied Linguistics; Arts and Humanities; Chinese; English; Information Sciences; Information Technology; Japanese; Media Studies; Multimedia); **Management** (Applied Mathematics; Business Administration; Finance; Human Resources; Information Management; International Business; Management; Marketing; Parks and Recreation; Software Engineering; Tourism; Transport Management)

School

General Education (Aesthetics; Arts and Humanities; Asian Studies)

History: Founded 1965 as Shu-Teh Junior College. Renamed Shu-Teh Junior College of Technology 1970 and then Shu-Teh Junior College of Technology and Commerce 1994. Upgraded Hsiuping Institute of Technology 2000. Acquired present status and title 2011.

Main Language(s) of Instruction: Chinese

Degrees and Diplomas: *Associate Degree*; *Bachelor's Degree*; *Master's Degree*: **Electronic Engineering; Finance; Human Resources; Industrial Engineering; Mechanical Engineering; Production Engineering.**

Student Services: IT Centre, Library, Residential Facilities

Last Updated: 28/02/14

HSUAN CHUANG UNIVERSITY (HCU)

48, Hsuan Chuang Road, Hsinchu 300
Tel: +886(3) 530-2255
Fax: +886(3) 539-7400
EMail: hcu@wmail.hcu.edu.tw
Website: http://www.hcu.edu.tw

President: Deren Liu
Tel: +886(3) 539-1206 EMail: president@hcu.edu.tw

Secretary-General: Yaohong Cai
Tel: +886(3) 539-2120 EMail: tyh@hcu.edu.tw

International Relations: Ding-Ming Wang, Vice-President
Tel: +886(3) 530-2255, Ext. 2195 EMail: dmwang@hcu.edu.tw

College

Arts and Sciences (Applied Mathematics; Arts and Humanities; Chinese; English; History; Literature; Modern Languages; Religious Studies); **Information and Communication** (Communication Arts; Communication Studies; Computer Graphics; Graphic Design; Information Sciences; Journalism; Library Science; Mass Communication; Media Studies); **Management** (Banking; E-Business/Commerce; Finance; Information Management; International

Business; Management; Public Administration); **Social Sciences** (Adult Education; Education; Psychology; Social Sciences; Social Welfare; Teacher Training)

School

Design (Communication Arts; Design; Fashion Design; Fine Arts; Visual Arts)

Centre

General Education (Arts and Humanities)

History: Founded 1997 as Hsuan Chuang College of Humanities and Social Sciences. Acquired present status and title 2004.

Academic Year: August to July

Admission Requirements: Secondary school certificate

Fees: National: Tuition fee: Undergraduate, 1,460-1,665; Graduate, 1,470-1,635 (US Dollar), International: Tuition fee: Undergraduate, 44,825-50,200 per semester; Graduate, 5,250 per semester (New Taiwan Dollar)

Main Language(s) of Instruction: Chinese

Accrediting Agency: Higher Education Evaluation and Accreditation Council of Taiwan

Degrees and Diplomas: *Bachelor's Degree*; *Master's Degree*: **Adult Education; Banking; Finance; Information Management; International Business; Law; Literature; Mass Communication; Modern Languages; Psychology; Public Administration; Religious Studies; Social Welfare.** *Doctorate*: **Literature.**

Student Services: Academic Counselling, Canteen, Careers Guidance, Cultural Activities, Facilities for disabled people, Health Services, IT Centre, Language Laboratory, Library, Nursery Care, Residential Facilities, Social Counselling, Sports Facilities

Publications: Hsuan Chuang - General

Last Updated: 28/02/14

HUAFAN UNIVERSITY

1, Huafan Road, Shihtin Hsiang, Taipei 223
Tel: +886(2) 266-32102
Fax: +886(2) 266-33173
EMail: pr@cc.hfu.edu.tw
Website: http://www.hfu.edu.tw

President: Jien-Ming Jue
Tel: +886(2) 266-32102, Ext.2001 EMail: president@cc.hfu.edu.tw

Secretary-General: Zhang-Xi Zhuang
Tel: +886(2) 266-32102, Ext. 2111 EMail: csline@cc.hfu.edu.tw

College

Art and Design (Architectural and Environmental Design; Architecture; Art Management; Computer Graphics; Design; Fine Arts; Industrial Design; Multimedia; Painting and Drawing); **Buddhism** (Asian Religious Studies); **Engineering and Management** (Electrical Engineering; Electronic Engineering; Industrial Engineering; Industrial Management; Information Management; Mechanical Engineering); **Liberal Arts** (American Studies; Arts and Humanities; Asian Studies; Chinese; English; English Studies; French; German; Japanese; Literature; Philosophy; Sanskrit; Tibetan)

Research Centre

Advanced Manufacturing *(AMRC)* (Production Engineering); **Calligraphy** (Painting and Drawing); **Cultural Heritage** (Heritage Preservation); **Humanities** (Arts and Humanities); **Sustainable Development of Slope Land** (Environmental Studies); **Ven. Hiu Wan Studies** (Asian Religious Studies)

History: Founded 1990 to promote the humanistic spirit of Confucian and Buddhist concepts. Acquired present status and title 1997.

Academic Year: September to June (September-January; February-June)

Admission Requirements: Secondary school certificate and entrance examination

Fees: 50,000 per semester (New Taiwan Dollar)

Main Language(s) of Instruction: Chinese

Degrees and Diplomas: *Bachelor's Degree*; *Master's Degree*: **Architectural and Environmental Design; Architecture; Arts and Humanities; Asian Studies; Chinese; Electrical Engineering; Electronic Engineering; English; Fine Arts; Industrial Design; Industrial Engineering; Industrial Management; Information Management; Information Sciences; Literature; Mechanical Engineering; Philosophy.** *Doctorate*: **Arts and Humanities; Asian Studies; Electrical Engineering; Mechanical Engineering.**

Student Services: Academic Counselling, Canteen, Cultural Activities, Health Services, IT Centre, Library, Sports Facilities

Publications: Huafan Journal of Design; Huafan Journal of Humanities

Last Updated: 28/02/14

HUNG KUANG UNIVERSITY (HKU)

No. 1018, Sec. 6, Taiwan Boulevard, Shalu District, Taichung 43302
Tel: +886(4) 2631-8652, Ext. 1130
Fax: +886(4) 263-10744
EMail: sec@web.hk.edu.tw
Website: http://www.hk.edu.tw

President: Guor-Cheng Fang (2001-)
Tel: +886(4) 2631-9153
EMail: president@web.hk.edu.tw; gcfang@sunrise.hk.edu.tw

Chief Secretary: Vicky Wang
Tel: +886(4) 263-18652, Ext. 1130 EMail: vicky@sunrise.hk.edu.tw

International Relations: Ting-Chen Hu, Dean, Office of International and Cross-Straight Affairs
Tel: +886(4) 263-18652, Ext. 2232
EMail: htc@sunrise.hk.edu.tw; csc@web.hk.edu.tw

College

Human Ecology (Biotechnology; Child Care and Development; Cosmetology; Food Science; Food Technology); **Humanities and Social Sciences** (Applied Linguistics; Arts and Humanities; Business Administration; English; Leisure Studies; Physical Education; Sports; Welfare and Protective Services); **Management** (Business Administration; Computer Science; Health Administration; Hotel and Restaurant; Information Management; Management); **Medicine and Nursing** (Biomedicine; Biotechnology; Nursing; Nutrition; Physical Therapy)

Centre

General Education (Aesthetics; Biological and Life Sciences; Civics; Modern Languages; Natural Sciences; Social Sciences)

Campus

Engineering (Biomedical Engineering; Computer Engineering; Computer Science; Environmental Engineering; Health Sciences; Occupational Health; Safety Engineering)

History: Founded 1967 as Hung Kuang Junior College of Nursing. Acquired present title and status 2003.

Main Language(s) of Instruction: Chinese

Degrees and Diplomas: *Bachelor's Degree*; *Master's Degree*: **Cosmetology; Nursing; Nutrition.**

Student Services: Academic Counselling, Health Services, IT Centre, Library, Social Counselling, Sports Facilities

Student Numbers *2013-2014*: Total 12,704

Last Updated: 28/02/14

HWA HSIA INSTITUTE OF TECHNOLOGY (HWH)

No.111, Gongzhuan Rd., Zhonghe Dist., New Taipei City 235
Tel: +886(2) 8941-5100
Fax: +886(2) 984-15730
EMail: maolhu@cc.hwh.edu.tw
Website: http://www.hwh.edu.tw

President: Wenfang Yen
Tel: +886(2) 894-15166 EMail: wfyen@cc.hwh.edu.tw

Dean of Academic Affairs: Jeng-Hsiang Lin
Tel: +886(2) 8941-5150 EMail: hsiang@cc.hwh.edu.tw

International Relations: Fu-Ming Liu, Dean, General Affairs
Tel: +886(2) 8941-5155 EMail: fuming@cc.hwh.edu.tw

Department

Applied Cosmetology (Cosmetology); **Architecture** (Architecture); **Assets and Property Management** *(Graduate Institute*

included) (Management; Real Estate); **Business Administration** (Business Administration); **Chemical Engineering** (Chemical Engineering); **Computer Science and Information Engineering** (Computer Engineering; Computer Science; Information Technology; Software Engineering); **Digital Media Design** (Computer Graphics; Design; Multimedia); **Electrical Engineering** (Electrical Engineering); **Electronic Engineering** (Electronic Engineering); **Interior Design** (Interior Design); **Management Information Systems** (Information Technology; Management Systems); **Mechanical Engineering** (Mechanical Engineering)

Centre

General Education (Arts and Humanities; Fine Arts; Natural Sciences; Social Sciences)

History: Founded 1966, acquired present status and title 1994.

Main Language(s) of Instruction: Chinese

Degrees and Diplomas: *Associate Degree*; *Bachelor's Degree*; *Master's Degree*: **Management; Real Estate.**

Student Services: Library, Sports Facilities

Last Updated: 27/02/14

I-SHOU UNIVERSITY (ISU)

No.1, Sec. 1, Syuecheng Rd., Dashu District, Kaohsiung 84008
Tel: +886(7) 657-7711
Fax: +886(7) 657-7056
Website: http://www.isu.edu.tw

President: Jei-Fu Shaw (1990-)
Tel: +886(7) 657-7001 EMail: shawjf@isu.edu.tw

Secretary-General: Shao-Hua Li
Tel: +886(7) 657-7711, Ext. 2031 EMail: shli@isu.edu.tw

International Relations: Michael Wei, Dean of International Affairs
Tel: +886(7) 657-7711, Ext. 2081 EMail: wei3504D@isu.edu.tw

College

Communication and Design (Cinema and Television; Communication Arts; Design; Film; Mass Communication; Media Studies); **Electrical and Information Engineering** (Computer Engineering; Electrical Engineering; Electronic Engineering; Information Management; Information Technology; Telecommunications Engineering); **International Studies** (Finance; Hotel and Restaurant; International Business; Parks and Recreation; Tourism); **Language Arts** (Applied Linguistics; English; Japanese; Modern Languages); **Management** (Accountancy; Business Administration; Finance; Industrial Management; International Business; Management; Public Administration); **Medicine** (Biological and Life Sciences; Biomedical Engineering; Biotechnology; Health Administration; Health Sciences; Medical Technology; Nutrition; Occupational Therapy; Physical Therapy; Radiology; Traditional Eastern Medicine); **Science and Engineering** (Applied Mathematics; Automation and Control Engineering; Biotechnology; Chemical Engineering; Civil Engineering; Environmental Engineering; Materials Engineering; Mechanical Engineering); **Tourism and Hospitality** (Cooking and Catering; Hotel and Restaurant; Leisure Studies; Tourism)

History: Founded 1986 as Kaohsiung Polytechnic Institute, acquired present status and title 1997.

Admission Requirements: Graduation from high school and entrance examination

Main Language(s) of Instruction: Chinese, English

Degrees and Diplomas: *Bachelor's Degree*; *Master's Degree*: **Automation and Control Engineering; Biological and Life Sciences; Biomedical Engineering; Biotechnology; Business Administration; Chemical Engineering; Civil Engineering; Electrical Engineering; Electronic Engineering; English; Environmental Engineering; Finance; Health Administration; Industrial Management; Information Management; Information Technology; Japanese; Materials Engineering; Mechanical Engineering; Public Administration.** *Doctorate*: **Biotechnology; Chemical Engineering; Electrical Engineering; Electronic Engineering; Industrial Management; Information Technology; Management; Materials Engineering.**

Student Services: Academic Counselling, Canteen, Careers Guidance, Facilities for disabled people, Health Services, IT Centre, Language Laboratory, Library, Nursery Care, Residential Facilities, Social Counselling, Sports Facilities

Publications: Journal of I-Shou University; Pan Pacific Management Review

Academic Staff *2012-2013*: Total 563
STAFF WITH DOCTORATE: Total 490
Student Numbers *2012-2013*: Total 15,614
Last Updated: 03/03/14

JINWEN UNIVERSITY OF SCIENCE AND TECHNOLOGY (JUST)

No.99, Anzhong Rd., Xindian Dist., Taipei 23154
Tel: +886(2) 821-22000
Fax: +886(2) 821-22873
EMail: secret@just.edu.tw
Website: http://www.just.edu.tw/

President: Yung-Fu Cheng
Tel: +886(2) 8212-2887 EMail: president@just.edu.tw

Secretary-General: Shih-shion Liu
Tel: +886(2) 8212-2000, Ext. 2880
EMail: secret@just.edu.tw; liushsh@just.edu.tw

College

Business Management (Accountancy; Business Administration; Environmental Management; Finance; Information Management; International Business; Management; Marketing; Real Estate; Taxation; Transport Management); **Electrical, Information and Resources Engineering** (Computer Engineering; Computer Science; Electrical Engineering; Electronic Engineering; Information Technology; Telecommunications Engineering); **Hospitality and Tourism Management** (Food Science; Hotel Management; Tourism; Transport Management); **Humanities and Design** (Applied Linguistics; Architectural and Environmental Design; Arts and Humanities; Communication Arts; Design; English; Graphic Design; Japanese; Multimedia)

Centre

General Education

History: Founded 1980 as Jin-Wen College. Upgraded into Jin-Wen Institute of Technology 1998. Acquired present status and title 2007.

Main Language(s) of Instruction: Chinese

Degrees and Diplomas: *Associate Degree*; *Bachelor's Degree*; *Master's Degree*: **Computer Engineering; Design; Environmental Management; Hotel and Restaurant; Real Estate; Telecommunications Engineering; Tourism.**

Student Services: IT Centre, Library, Residential Facilities, Sports Facilities

Last Updated: 28/02/14

KAINAN UNIVERSITY (KNU)

1, Kainan Rd., Shinshing, Luchu, Taoyuan 33857
Tel: +886(3) 341-2500
Fax: +886(3) 341-2430
EMail: itc@mail.knu.edu.tw
Website: http://www.knu.edu.tw

President: An-Pang Kao Tel: +886(3) 341-2500, Ext. 1122

Secretary-General: Ai-An LI
Tel: +886(3) 341-2430, Ext. 1201 EMail: laa1202@mail.knu.edu.tw

School

Commerce (Accountancy; Banking; Business and Commerce; Finance; International Business; Management); **Health Care** (Business Administration; Health Administration; Health Sciences; Marketing; Nutrition); **Humanities and Social Sciences** (Applied Linguistics; Arts and Humanities; Chinese; English; Foreign Languages Education; Japanese; Law; Public Administration; Social Sciences); **Informatics** (Computer Science; E-Business/Commerce; Information Management; Information Technology); **Transportation and Tourism** (Air Transport; Hotel and Restaurant; Leisure Studies; Marine Transport; Parks and Recreation; Tourism; Transport and Communications; Transport Engineering; Transport Management)

Department

Lifetime Learning; **Physical Education**

Centre
Chinese Learning *(Taoyuan, Taipei campus)* (Chinese); **E-learning; General Education**

Further Information: Traditional and Open Learning Institution

History: Founded 1917 as Kainan Commercial andTechnical High School. Acquired present status and title 2000. Full accreditation received 2006.

Main Language(s) of Instruction: Chinese

Degrees and Diplomas: *Master's Degree*: **Accountancy; Air Transport; Banking; Business Administration; E-Business/ Commerce; English; Finance; Foreign Languages Education; Information Technology; International Business; Japanese; Law; Management; Marine Transport; Public Administration; Tourism; Transport Management.**

Student Services: IT Centre, Library

Last Updated: 03/03/14

KAO FONG COLLEGE OF DIGITAL CONTENTS (KFC)

38, Hsinhsing Rd., Fushing Village, Changchi, Pintung
Tel: +886(8) 762-6365
Fax: +886(8) 762-7882
EMail: admission@kfut.edu.tw
Website: http://www.kfcdc.edu.tw/

President (Acting): Chieh-Huang Hsieh

Department
Digital Animation Design (Design; Multimedia; Visual Arts); **Game Creation System** (Multimedia; Software Engineering); **Hospitality and Tourism Management** (Food Science; Hotel and Restaurant; Leisure Studies; Sports; Tourism); **Marketing and Distribution Management** (Advertising and Publicity; Business Administration; Management; Marketing; Public Relations; Transport Management); **Multimedia and Sound Design** (Multimedia; Sound Engineering (Acoustics)); **Popular Design Process** (Design; Fashion Design; Fine Arts; Industrial Design)

History: Founded 2004. Formerly known as Kao Fong Institute of Technology.

Main Language(s) of Instruction: Chinese

Degrees and Diplomas: *Bachelor's Degree*: **Design; E-Business/ Commerce; English; Fine Arts; Leisure Studies; Parks and Recreation; Sound Engineering (Acoustics); Transport Management.**

Last Updated: 03/03/14

KAO YUAN UNIVERSITY (KYU)

1821, Chung-Shan Road, Lu Chu Hsiang, Kaohsiung 821
Tel: +886(7) 607-7777
Fax: +886(7) 607-7788
EMail: query@cc.kyit.edu.tw
Website: http://www.kyu.edu.tw/

President: Tsahn-Deng Tseng
Tel: +886(7) 607-7777, Ext. 1020 EMail: presid@cc.kyit.edu.tw

Secretary-General: Tsung-Han Chang
Tel: +886(7) 607-7773 +886(7) 607-7787
EMail: secre@cc.kyu.edu.tw; t90082@cc.kyu.edu.tw

International Relations: Wen-Lung Wang, Director, International Cooperation Centre
Tel: +886(7) 607-7225, Ext. 1901 EMail: t10037@cc.kyu.edu.tw

College
Business and Management (Applied Linguistics; Business Administration; English; International Business; Japanese; Management; Marketing; Modern Languages; Parks and Recreation; Sports Management; Tourism; Transport Management); **Engineering** (Architecture; Biochemistry; Chemical Engineering; Civil Engineering; Cosmetology; Design; Environmental Engineering; Environmental Studies; Health Sciences; Information Technology; Multimedia); **Informatics** (Computer Graphics; Computer Science; Information Management; Information Technology; Mass Communication; Media Studies; Multimedia; Software Engineering; Visual Arts); **Mechatronic Engineering** (Automation and Control Engineering; Electrical and Electronic Engineering; Electrical Engineering; Electronic Engineering; Mechanical Engineering; Optical Technology; Optics)

Centre
Africanism (Automotive Engineering; Computer Engineering; Cultural Studies; Electrical Engineering; Environmental Engineering; Safety Engineering); **General Education** (Arts and Humanities; Modern Languages; Natural Sciences; Social Sciences; Technology)

History: Founded 1986 as Private Kao Yuan Junior College of Technology. Renamed Kao Yuan Junior College of Technology and Commerce 1991 and then Kao Yuan Institute of Technology 1998. Acquired present status and title 2005.

Main Language(s) of Instruction: Chinese

Degrees and Diplomas: *Associate Degree*; *Bachelor's Degree*; *Master's Degree*: **Architecture; Automation and Control Engineering; Biochemistry; Chemical Engineering; Civil Engineering; Electrical Engineering; Electronic Engineering; Information Technology; Management; Mechanical Engineering.**

Student Services: Canteen, IT Centre, Library, Residential Facilities

Publications: Discourses of Kao Yuan University; Journal of Kao Yuan University

Academic Staff *2013-2014*: Total: c. 310

Student Numbers *2013-2014*: Total: c. 9,000

Last Updated: 26/02/14

KAOHSIUNG MEDICAL UNIVERSITY (KMU)

100, Shih-Chuan 1st Road, Kaohsiung 80780
Tel: +886(7) 312-1101
Fax: +886(7) 321-2062
EMail: service@kmu.edu.tw
Website: http://www.kmu.edu.tw

President: Ching-Kuan Liu
EMail: president@kmu.edu.tw; ckliu@kmu.edu.tw

Dean, General Affairs: Chun-Cheng Hung
Tel: +886(7) 312-1101, Ext.2124 EMail: chuchh@kmu.edu.tw

International Relations: Cheng-Jie Jheng, Dean, Office of Global Affairs Tel: +886(7) 312-1101, Ext. 2383 EMail: jengcj@gmail.com

College
Dental Medicine (Dental Hygiene; Dentistry); **Health Sciences** (Biotechnology; Computer Science; Health Administration; Laboratory Techniques; Medical Technology; Occupational Therapy; Physical Therapy; Public Health; Radiology); **Humanities and Social Sciences** (Arts and Humanities; Gender Studies; Psychology; Social Sciences; Social Work; Sociology); **Life Sciences** (Applied Chemistry; Biological and Life Sciences; Biology; Biomedicine; Biotechnology); **Medicine** (Biochemistry; Genetics; Medicine; Pharmacology; Physiology; Respiratory Therapy; Sports Medicine; Urology); **Nursing** (Nursing); **Pharmacy** (Cosmetology; Pharmacology; Pharmacy; Toxicology)

Centre
General Education

Further Information: Also Chung-Ho Memorial Hospital, Hsiao-Kang Municipal Hospital, Kaohsiung Municipal Ta-Tung Hospital

History: Founded 1954 as Kaohsiung Medical College. Acquired present status and title 1999. A private institution under the jurisdiction of the Ministry of Education.

Academic Year: September to June (September-January; February-June)

Admission Requirements: Graduation from high school or equivalent, and entrance examination

Fees: 50,000-70,000 per semester (New Taiwan Dollar)

Main Language(s) of Instruction: Chinese, English

Accrediting Agency: Higher Education and Accreditation Council, Ministry of Education

Degrees and Diplomas: *Bachelor's Degree*: **Biotechnology; Computer Science; Dentistry; Health Administration; Laboratory Techniques; Medicine; Respiratory Therapy.** *Master's*

Degree: **Applied Chemistry; Cosmetology; Dentistry; Genetics; Health Sciences; Medicine; Nursing; Pharmacology; Pharmacy; Sports Medicine; Tropical Medicine.** *Doctorate*: **Applied Chemistry; Dentistry; Health Sciences; Medicine; Pharmacology; Tropical Medicine.**

Student Services: Academic Counselling, Canteen, Careers Guidance, Health Services, Language Laboratory, Library, Nursery Care, Social Counselling, Sports Facilities

Publications: Abstracts of Theses; Kaohsiung Journal of Medical Sciences

Academic Staff *2013-2014*: Total 537

Student Numbers *2013-2014*: Total 7,001

Last Updated: 03/03/14

KUNG SHAN UNIVERSITY (KSU)

949, Da Wan Road, Yung Kang, Tainan Hsien 71003
Tel: +886(6) 272-7175 +886(6) 205-0000
Fax: +886(6) 272-8944
Website: http://www.ksu.edu.tw

President: Yan-Kuin Su
Tel: +886(6) 272-7175, Ext. 201 EMail: rector@mail.ksu.edu.tw

International Relations: Ho-Wen Yang
Tel: +886(6) 205-0659 EMail: rndio@mail.ksu.edu.tw

College

Applied Human Ecology (Applied Linguistics; Child Care and Development; Cooking and Catering; Ecology; English; Fashion Design; Food Science; Health Sciences; Leisure Studies; Modern Languages; Preschool Education; Sports; Tourism); **Business and Management** (Accountancy; Banking; Business Administration; Finance; International Business; Management; Real Estate); **Creative Media** (Advertising and Publicity; Architectural and Environmental Design; Communication Arts; Design; Film; Mass Communication; Media Studies; Public Relations; Video; Visual Arts); **Engineering** (Electrical Engineering; Electronic Engineering; Energy Engineering; Engineering; Environmental Engineering; Materials Engineering; Mechanical Engineering; Optical Technology); **Information Technology** (Computer Engineering; Computer Science; Information Management; Information Technology; Telecommunications Engineering); **International Studies** (Chinese; International Studies)

Centre

General Education

History: Founded 1965 as Kun Shan Institute of Technology. Acquired present status 2000.

Main Language(s) of Instruction: Chinese

Degrees and Diplomas: *Bachelor's Degree*; *Master's Degree*: **Architectural and Environmental Design; Business Administration; Communication Arts; Computer Science; Design; Electrical Engineering; Electronic Engineering; Environmental Engineering; Information Management; Information Technology; Materials Engineering; Mechanical Engineering; Optical Technology; Real Estate; Visual Arts.** *Doctorate*: **Energy Engineering; Mechanical Engineering.**

Student Services: IT Centre, Library

Last Updated: 03/03/14

LANYANG INSTITUTE OF TECHNOLOGY (LYIT)

No.79, Fushin Rd., Yilan County, Tou-Chen, I-Lan 261
Tel: +886(3) 977-1997
Fax: +886(3) 977-1071
EMail: service@mail.fit.edu.tw
Website: http://www.fit.edu.tw/

President: Jianglong Lin
Tel: +886(3) 977-1997, Ext.112 EMail: president@mail.fit.edu.tw

Department

Applied Foreign Languages (English; Japanese); **Architecture** (Architecture; Structural Architecture); **Computer Application Engineering** (Computer Engineering; Computer Graphics); **Cosmetic Science and Application** (Cosmetology); **Creative Product and Technological Application** (Computer Engineering; Computer Graphics; Information Technology); **Finance and Insurance Management** (Banking; Commercial Law; Finance; Insurance); **Health and Leisure Management** (Health Administration; Leisure Studies; Marketing; Tourism); **Information Management** (Information Management); **Innovations in Digital Living** (Electronic Engineering; Energy Engineering; Optical Technology); **Marketing and Distribution Management** (Business Administration; Marketing)

History: Founded 1966 as Fushin Junior College of Technology. Renamed Fushin Institute of Technology 1983. Acquired present status and title 2001.

Fees: Tuition, 20,170-37,960 per annum (New Taiwan Dollar)

Main Language(s) of Instruction: Chinese, English

Degrees and Diplomas: *Associate Degree*; *Bachelor's Degree*

Student Services: IT Centre, Library, Residential Facilities

Last Updated: 04/03/14

LEE-MING INSTITUTE OF TECHNOLOGY (LIT)

2-2, Lizhuan Rd., Taishan, Taipei County 243
Tel: +886(2) 290-97811
Fax: +886(2) 229-95888
EMail: president@mail.lit.edu.tw
Website: http://www.lit.edu.tw

President: Jing-Dong Chow
Tel: +886(2) 229-97811, Ext. 1001
EMail: president@mail.lit.edu.tw

Secretary-General: Hongliang Chen
Tel: +886(2) 290-97811, Ext. 1002 EMail: hlchen@mail.lit.edu.tw

International Relations: Jui-Chih Chou
Tel: +886(2) 290-97811, Ext. 1521 EMail: job@mail.lit.edu.tw

Department

Applied Cosmetology (Cosmetology); **Business Administration** (Business Administration; Finance; Information Sciences; Management; Transport Management); **Chemical and Materials Engineering** (Chemical Engineering; Materials Engineering); **Digital Multimedia Technology** (Information Technology; Multimedia; Software Engineering); **Electrical Engineering** (Automation and Control Engineering; Electrical Engineering; Electronic Engineering; Energy Engineering; Heating and Refrigeration; Power Engineering); **Information Management** (Information Management); **Information Technology** (Computer Science; Information Technology); **Innovative Product Design** (Industrial Design); **Mechanical Engineering** (Mechanical Engineering); **Tourism and Hospitality Management** (Hotel and Restaurant; Parks and Recreation; Tourism)

Centre

General Education (Chinese; English; Mathematics; Military Science; Physical Education; Physics)

History: Founded 1969.

Main Language(s) of Instruction: Chinese

Degrees and Diplomas: *Associate Degree*; *Bachelor's Degree*

Student Services: Academic Counselling, Canteen, IT Centre, Library, Residential Facilities, Social Counselling, Sports Facilities

Student Numbers *2012-2013*: Total: c. 4,000

Last Updated: 04/03/14

LING TUNG UNIVERSITY (LTU)

1, Ling tung Rd., Taichung 408
Tel: +886(4) 2389-2088
Fax: +886(4) 238-95293
EMail: ltc226@teamail.ltu.edu.tw; ltu1211@teamail.ltu.edu.tw
Website: http://www.ltc.edu.tw

President: Zhiyang Zhao (2002-)
Tel: +886(4) 238-92088, Ext.1101
EMail: ltu1101@teamail.ltu.edu.tw

Vice-President: Jinlian Wu
Tel: +886(4) 238-92088, Ext. 1201
EMail: amberwu@teamail.ltu.edu.tw

College
Design (Communication Arts; Computer Graphics; Design; Fashion Design; Industrial Design; Multimedia; Visual Arts); **Finance and Economics** (Accountancy; Commercial Law; Economics; Finance; Information Technology; Insurance; Taxation); **Information Science** (Computer Networks; Information Management; Information Sciences; Information Technology); **Management** (Business Administration; English; International Business; Leisure Studies; Management; Marketing; Tourism; Transport Management)

History: Founded 1963 as Ling Tung Junior College of Accounting. Acquired present status and title 2005.

Fees: Tuition, 2,700 per annum (US Dollar)

Main Language(s) of Instruction: Chinese

Degrees and Diplomas: *Bachelor's Degree*; *Master's Degree*: **Accountancy; Business Administration; Commercial Law; Design; Fashion Design; Finance; Graphic Design; Industrial Design; Information Management; Information Technology; International Business; Leisure Studies; Marketing; Tourism; Transport Management.**

Last Updated: 04/03/14

LUNGHWA UNIVERSITY OF SCIENCE AND TECHNOLOGY

No.300, Sec.1, Wanshou Rd., Guishan, Taoyuan 33306
Tel: +886(2) 820-93211
Fax: +886(2) 820-94650
EMail: se@mail.lhu.edu.tw
Website: http://www.lhu.edu.tw

President: Tzu-Hsiang Ko
Tel: +886(2) 820-93211, Ext. 2001 EMail: thko@mail.lhu.edu.tw

Secretary-General: Sun Yi
Tel: +886(2) 820-93211
EMail: se@mail.lhu.edu.tw; lsun@mail.lhu.edu.tw

College
Engineering (Chemical Engineering; Computer Engineering; Computer Networks; Electrical Engineering; Electronic Engineering; Information Technology; Materials Engineering; Mechanical Engineering; Safety Engineering); **Humanities and Design** (Applied Linguistics; Arts and Humanities; Chinese; Cultural Studies; English; Leisure Studies; Media Studies; Modern Languages; Multimedia; Software Engineering; Tourism); **Management** (Business Administration; Business and Commerce; E-Business/Commerce; Finance; Industrial Management; Information Management; Information Technology; International Business)

History: Founded 1969 as Lunghwa Polytechnic. Renamed Lunghwa Junior College of Technology 1973 and then Lunghwa Junior College of Technology and Commerce 1983. Acquired present status 2001.

Fees: Undergraduate tuition, 1,380-1,585; Graduate tuition, 1,280-1,470 (US Dollar)

Main Language(s) of Instruction: Chinese

Degrees and Diplomas: *Bachelor's Degree*; *Master's Degree*: **Business Administration; Electrical Engineering; Electronic Engineering; Information Management; Mechanical Engineering.** Master's program in Chemical and Materials Engineering to be set up in 2013.

Student Services: Academic Counselling, Canteen, Careers Guidance, Cultural Activities, Facilities for disabled people, Health Services, Language Laboratory, Nursery Care, Residential Facilities, Social Counselling, Sports Facilities

Last Updated: 04/03/14

MACKAY MEDICAL COLLEGE (MMC)

No.46, Sec. 3, Zhongzheng Rd., Sanzhi Dist., New Taipei City 252
Tel: +886(2) 2636-0303
EMail: mmc@mmc.edu.tw
Website: http://www.mmc.edu.tw

President: Yau-Huei Wei

Department
Audiology and Speech Language Pathology (Speech Therapy and Audiology); **Biomedicine** (Biomedicine); **Medicine** (Medicine); **Nursing** (Nursing)

Centre
Holistic Education (Arts and Humanities)

Further Information: Also University Hospital

History: Founded 2009.

Main Language(s) of Instruction: Chinese

Degrees and Diplomas: *Associate Degree*; *Bachelor's Degree*: **Medicine.** *Master's Degree*: **Biomedicine.**

Last Updated: 12/02/14

MEIHO UNIVERSITY

Meiho Institute of Technology (MU)
23, Pingguang Rd., Neipu, Pingtung 912
Tel: +886(8) 779-9821
Fax: +886(8) 778-9837
EMail: iec@meiho.edu.tw
Website: http://www.meiho.edu.tw

President: Shean-Huei Lin
Tel: +886(8) 778-3428
EMail: president@meiho.edu.tw; shlin@newmail.meiho.edu.tw

Administrative Vice-President: Shun-Hsiang Weng
Tel: +886(8) 779-9821, Ext. 8138
EMail: x00009520@meiho.edu.tw

International Relations: Ming-Hsiu (David) Liu, Director, International Education and Collaborations Office
Tel: +886(8) 779-9821, Ext. 8739
EMail: meihoiec@gmail.com; akinai88@gmail.com

College
Business and Management (Art Management; Business Administration; Cultural Studies; Finance; Information Management; Management; Marketing); **Health and Nursing** (Biotechnology; Business Administration; Cosmetology; Food Science; Health Sciences; Information Technology; Nursing; Nutrition); **Human Ecology** (Child Care and Development; English; Health Sciences; Hotel and Restaurant; Jewellery Art; Modern Languages; Service Trades; Social Work; Sports; Tourism)

History: Founded 1964. Upgraded into Meiho Institute of Technology 2001. Acquired present status and title 2010.

Main Language(s) of Instruction: Chinese

Degrees and Diplomas: *Bachelor's Degree*; *Master's Degree*: **Biotechnology; Business Administration; Health Sciences; Management; Social Work; Sports.**

Student Services: IT Centre, Library, Residential Facilities, Sports Facilities

Academic Staff *2013-2014*: Total: c. 430
Student Numbers *2013-2014*: Total: c. 8,500
Last Updated: 05/03/14

MING CHI UNIVERSITY OF TECHNOLOGY (MIT)

84 Gungjuan Rd., Taishan Dist., Taipei 24301
Tel: +886(2) 2908-9899
Fax: +886(2) 2904-1914
EMail: mcut@mail.mcut.edu.tw
Website: http://www.mit.edu.tw

President: Thu-Hua Liu (2002-)
Tel: +886(2) 2901-4490, Ext. 4011 EMail: thliu@mail.mcut.edu.tw

Secretary-General: Ming-Hsong Shen
Tel: +886(2) 290-89899, Ext. 4012 EMail: peter@mail.mcut.edu.tw

College
Engineering (Electrical Engineering; Electronic Engineering; Engineering; Mechanical Engineering); **Environment and Resources** (Biochemistry; Chemical Engineering; Environmental Engineering; Health Sciences; Materials Engineering; Safety Engineering); **Management and Design** (Business Administration; Communication Arts; Design; Industrial Design; Industrial Engineering; Industrial Management; Management; Visual Arts)

Centre
General Education (Arts and Humanities; Chinese; English; History; Military Science; Modern Languages; Natural Sciences;

Physical Education; Service Trades; Social Sciences); **Thin Film Technologies and Applications**

Research Centre

Battery Research Center of Green Energy (Chemical Engineering; Electrical Engineering; Materials Engineering; Mechanical Engineering); **Biochemical Technology R&D Centre** (Biochemistry; Chemical Engineering)

History: Founded 1964.

Main Language(s) of Instruction: Chinese

Degrees and Diplomas: *Bachelor's Degree*; *Master's Degree*: **Bioengineering; Business Administration; Chemical Engineering; Communication Arts; Design; Electrical Engineering; Electronic Engineering; Environmental Engineering; Industrial Design; Industrial Management; Management; Materials Engineering; Mechanical Engineering; Optical Technology; Visual Arts.**

Student Services: Canteen, Library, Residential Facilities, Sports Facilities

Academic Staff *2012-2013*: Total 186

Student Numbers *2012-2013*: Total 4,109

Last Updated: 05/03/14

MING CHUAN UNIVERSITY (MCU)

250 Chung Shan N. Rd. Sec. 5, Taipei 111
Tel: +886(2) 2882-4564 Ext. 2537
Fax: +886(2) 8861-3491
EMail: laeyer@mail.mcu.edu.tw
Website: http://www.mcu.edu.tw

President: Chuan Lee (1998-) Tel: +886(2) 2882-4564 Ext. 2752

General Secretary: Chung-Yuan Fan
Tel: +886(2) 2882-4564 Ext. 2214

International Relations: Max Liu
Tel: +886(2) 2882-4564 Ext. 2606 EMail: ihp@mail.mcu.edu.tw

College

International *(Gweishan District, Taoyuan; including Graduate School of International Affairs)* (Business Computing; International Business; International Relations; Journalism; Mass Communication; Service Trades; Tourism)

School

Applied Languages *(Gweishan District, Taoyuan; including Graduate Schools of Applied Chinese, Applied Japanese and Applied English)* (Chinese; English; Foreign Languages Education; Japanese; Modern Languages; Teacher Training); **Communication** *(Including Graduate School of Communication Management)* (Advertising and Publicity; Communication Arts; Journalism; Management; Mass Communication; Radio and Television Broadcasting); **Design** *(Gweishan, Taoyuan; including Graduate Schools of Creative Design, Design Management, Media and Space Design)* (Architecture; Design; Graphic Design; Management; Safety Engineering; Town Planning); **Health** *(Gweishan District, Taoyuan)* (Biomedical Engineering; Biotechnology; Health Administration); **Information Technology** *(Gweishan District; Taoyuan; including Graduate Schools of Information Management, Computer and Communications Engineering, Information Engineering)* (Computer Engineering; Electronic Engineering; Information Management; Telecommunications Engineering); **Law** *(Including Graduate School of Law)* (Law); **Management** *(Some programmes at Gweishan District, Taoyuan; including Graduate Schools of Management, Finance, Economics, Accounting, Risk Management, International Business, Applied Statistics and Information Science)* (Accountancy; Business Administration; Economics; Finance; Insurance; International Business; Management; Statistics); **Social Sciences** *(Some programmes at Gweishan District, Taoyuan; including Graduate Schools of Education and Public Administration)* (Comparative Politics; Education; Educational Psychology; Public Administration; Regional Studies); **Tourism** *(Gweishan District, Taoyuan; including Graduate School of Tourism)* (Hotel and Restaurant; Leisure Studies; Management; Parks and Recreation; Tourism)

History: Founded 1957 as Ming Chuan (Commercial Junior Women's) College. Acquired present status and title 1997.

Academic Year: September to August (September-January; February-June; July-August)

Admission Requirements: Graduation from high school and entrance examination

Fees: c. 45,000-55,000 per semester (New Taiwan Dollar)

Main Language(s) of Instruction: Mandarin Chinese, English, Japanese

Accrediting Agency: Ministry of Education

Degrees and Diplomas: *Bachelor's Degree*; *Master's Degree*; *Doctorate*

Student Services: Academic Counselling, Canteen, Careers Guidance, Cultural Activities, Health Services, Language Laboratory, Social Counselling, Sports Facilities

Publications: Ming Chuan Journal

Publishing House: Ming Chuan Publishing Centre

Student Numbers *2012-2013*: Total: c. 20,000

Last Updated: 23/05/13

MINGDAO UNIVERSITY (MDU)

369, Wen-hua Road, Pettow, Changhua 52345
Tel: +886(4) 887-6660
Fax: +886(4) 887-6659
EMail: jdcheng@mdu.edu.tw
Website: http://www.mdu.edu.tw

President: Shixiong Chen
Tel: +886(4) 8778-0026 EMail: organic@mdu.edu.tw

Secretary-General: Xieqing Xiong
Tel: +886(4) 887-6660, Ext. 1600 EMail: hsiehch@mdu.edu.tw

International Relations: Nai-Chien Shih, Dean, Department of International Affairs
Tel: +886(4) 887-6660, Ext. 2000 EMail: naichien@mdu.edu.tw

College

Applied Sciences (Agriculture; Biotechnology; Computer Science; Electronic Engineering; Energy Engineering; Information Technology; Materials Engineering; Optical Technology; Telecommunications Engineering); **Design** (Architectural and Environmental Design; Computer Graphics; Design; Environmental Management; Fashion Design; Landscape Architecture; Multimedia); **Humanities** (Arts and Humanities; Asian Studies; Chinese; Curriculum; Education; Educational Testing and Evaluation; English; Foreign Languages Education; Japanese; Literature); **Management** (Business Administration; Cooking and Catering; Finance; Health Sciences; Hotel and Restaurant; Management; Marketing; Tourism; Transport Management)

History: Founded 1998 and acquired present status and title 2001.

Academic Year: August to July

Admission Requirements: Graduation from high school

Main Language(s) of Instruction: Chinese

Accrediting Agency: Ministry of Education

Degrees and Diplomas: *Bachelor's Degree*; *Master's Degree*: **Architectural and Environmental Design; Business Administration; Design; Electronic Engineering; Energy Engineering; Information Technology; Literature; Materials Engineering; Optical Technology; Telecommunications Engineering.**

Student Services: Academic Counselling, Canteen, Careers Guidance, Cultural Activities, Facilities for disabled people, Foreign Studies Centre, Health Services, Language Laboratory, Library, Nursery Care, Residential Facilities, Social Counselling, Sports Facilities, eLibrary

Publications: MingDao Journal

Last Updated: 05/03/14

MINGHSIN UNIVERSITY OF SCIENCE AND TECHNOLOGY (MUST)

No.1, Xinxing Rd., Hsin Feng, Hsinchu 30401
Tel: +886(3) 559-3142
Fax: +886(3) 559-5142
Website: http://www.must.edu.tw

President: Yuan Pao Hsin
Tel: +886(3) 559-3142, Ext. 2115 EMail: pre@must.edu.tw

Secretary-General: Jung-Tai Lee
Tel: +886(3) 559-3142, Ext. 2121
EMail: ljt@must.edu.tw; secretariat.must@must.edu.tw

International Relations: Chih-Hung Li, Director, Office of International Affairs
Tel: +886(3) 559-3142, Ext. 2143
EMail: oia@must.edu.tw; cl4e@must.edu.tw

College
Engineering (Chemical Engineering; Civil Engineering; Computer Engineering; Computer Science; Cosmetology; Electrical Engineering; Electronic Engineering; Engineering; Environmental Engineering; Industrial Engineering; Information Technology; Materials Engineering; Mechanical Engineering; Optical Technology); **Humanities, Social and Natural Sciences** (Arts and Humanities; Cultural Studies; English; Fine Arts; French; German; Japanese; Modern Languages; Natural Sciences; Social Sciences; Sports Management; Tourism; Translation and Interpretation); **Management** (Business Administration; Finance; Industrial Engineering; Industrial Management; Information Management; Marketing; Transport Management); **Service Industries** (Child Care and Development; Education; Hotel Management; Leisure Studies; Service Trades; Teacher Training)

Programme
Cross-cutting programs - Ministry of Education

Department
MUST Teacher Association

Centre
Baby Center Of Hsin-Chu County; **General Education** (Arts and Humanities; Chemistry; Fine Arts; History; Law; Literature; Mathematics; Modern Languages; Natural Sciences; Physics; Social Sciences)

History: Founded 1966 as Ming Hsin Junior College of Technology. Renamed Ming Hsin Institute of Technology and Commerce 1993. Acquired present status 2002.

Academic Year: September to June (September-January; February-June)

Admission Requirements: Graduation from high school or equivalent, and entrance examination

Fees: c. 200,000 per annum (New Taiwan Dollar)

Main Language(s) of Instruction: Chinese

Accrediting Agency: Ministry of Education

Degrees and Diplomas: *Bachelor's Degree*; *Master's Degree*: **Business Administration; Chemical Engineering; Construction Engineering; Electrical Engineering; Electronic Engineering; Industrial Engineering; Industrial Management; Information Management; Mechanical Engineering; Service Trades.** Diplomas 2-5 yrs

Student Services: Academic Counselling, Canteen, Careers Guidance, Facilities for disabled people, Health Services, IT Centre, Library, Social Counselling, Sports Facilities

Publications: Collected Research Papers; Journal of Ming Hsin Institute of Technology

Last Updated: 05/03/14

NAN JEON UNIVERSITY OF SCIENCE AND TECHNOLOGY (NJU)

178, Chauchin Road, Yanshuei, Tainan 73746
Tel: +886(6) 652-3111
Fax: +886(6) 652-9641
EMail: njtc@mail.nju.edu.tw
Website: http://www.njtc.edu.tw

President: Tsong-Liang Huang

Centre
General Education (Arts and Humanities; Chinese)

Group
Business and Management (Business Administration; Information Management; Management; Marketing); **Engineering** (Computer Science; Construction Engineering; Electrical and Electronic Engineering; Electrical Engineering; Electronic Engineering; Engineering; Information Technology; Mechanical Engineering; Technology); **Humanities and Social Science** (Arts and Humanities; Cosmetology; Hotel and Restaurant; Interior Design; Japanese; Social Sciences; Tourism)

History: Founded 1967 as Nan Jeon Junior College of Technology. Upgraded into Nan Jeon Junior college of Technology and Commerce (1993) and then into Nan Jeon Institute of Technology (2001). Acquired present status and title 2013.

Main Language(s) of Instruction: Chinese

Degrees and Diplomas: *Bachelor's Degree*; *Master's Degree*: **Engineering; Technology.**

Student Services: Health Services, IT Centre, Library, Sports Facilities

Student Numbers *2012-2013*: Total: c. 5,000

Last Updated: 05/03/14

NAN KAI UNIVERSITY OF TECHNOLOGY (NKUT)

No.568, Zhongzheng Rd., Caotun Township, Nantou County, Tsao Tuen, Nan Tou 542
Tel: +886(4) 925-63489
EMail: wwwadm@nkut.edu.tw; xxx@nkut.edu.tw
Website: http://www.nkut.edu.tw/

President: Tai -Ping Sun
Tel: +886(49) 256-3489, Ext. 1201
EMail: president.sun@nkut.edu.tw

Vice-President, Academic Affairs: Tsong-Shin Sheu
Tel: +886(49) 256-3489, Ext. 1212 EMail: tsheu@nkut.edu.tw

College
Electrical and Computer Engineering (Computer Engineering; Electrical Engineering); **Engineering** (Automation and Control Engineering; Engineering; Industrial Management; Mechanical Engineering); **Extension Education**; **Human Ecology** (Computer Graphics; Design; English; Foreign Languages Education; Graphic Design; Industrial Design; Information Technology; Modern Languages; Multimedia; Service Trades; Welfare and Protective Services); **Management** (Business Administration; Finance; Information Management; Leisure Studies; Management; Marketing; Transport Management)

Centre
Foreign Language (English); **General Education** (Arts and Humanities; Chinese; Civics; Health Sciences; Social Sciences)

History: Founded 1971 as Nan Kai Junior College. Renamed Nan Kai Junior College of Technology and Commerce 1993. Upgraded into Nan-Kai Institute of Technology (NKIT) 2001. Acquired present status and title 2008.

Main Language(s) of Instruction: Chinese

Degrees and Diplomas: *Bachelor's Degree*; *Master's Degree*: **Computer Science; Electrical Engineering; Gerontology; Service Trades; Welfare and Protective Services.**

Student Services: Library, Residential Facilities

Last Updated: 06/03/14

NANHUA UNIVERSITY (NHU)

No. 55, Sec. 1, Nanhua Rd., Dalin Township, Chiayi 62249
Tel: +886(5) 272-1001
Fax: +886(5) 272-0170
EMail: wclu@mail.nhu.edu.tw; oge@mail.nhu.edu.tw
Website: http://www2.nhu.edu.tw/

President: Tsong-Ming Lin
Tel: +886(5) 272-1001, Ext. 1041 EMail: tmlin@mail.nhu.edu.tw

Director of the Office of International and Cross-Strait Affairs: Ping Chou
Tel: +886(5) 272-1001, Ext. 1700
EMail: chouping@mail.nhu.edu.tw

Secretary-General: Tzong-Ho Yeh
Tel: +886(5) 272-1001, Ext. 1020 EMail: thyeh@mail.nhu.edu.tw

College
Arts (Architectural and Environmental Design; Architecture; Communication Arts; Ethnology; Fine Arts; Industrial Design; Landscape Architecture; Musicology; Visual Arts); **Humanities** (Arts and Humanities; English; Foreign Languages Education; Literature; Modern Languages; Philosophy; Religious Studies); **Management** (Accountancy; Art Management; Business Administration; Economics; Environmental Management; Finance; Information Sciences; Leisure Studies; Management; Tourism); **Science and Technology** (Biotechnology; Computer Engineering; Computer Science; E-Business/Commerce; Health Sciences; Information Management; Information Technology; Natural Sciences); **Social Sciences** (Asian Studies; Communication Studies; European Studies; International Studies; Pacific Area Studies; Public Administration; Sociology)

Centre
General Education (Asian Religious Studies; Asian Studies; Chinese; Environmental Studies; Gender Studies; Political Sciences; Psychiatry and Mental Health; Social Sciences; Western European Studies)

History: Founded 1996 as Nanhua Management College, acquired present title 1999.

Admission Requirements: Graduation from high school

Fees: Undergraduate tuition, 47,000-53,000; Graduate tuition, 48,000-50,000 (New Taiwan Dollar)

Main Language(s) of Instruction: Chinese

Accrediting Agency: Minstry of Education

Degrees and Diplomas: *Bachelor's Degree*; *Master's Degree*: **Alternative Medicine; Architectural and Environmental Design; Art Management; Asian Studies; Business Administration; Communication Arts; Communication Studies; Economics; Environmental Management; European Studies; Finance; Industrial Design; Landscape Architecture; Leisure Studies; Literature; Management; Musicology; Pacific Area Studies; Philosophy; Political Sciences; Preschool Education; Public Administration; Religious Studies; Social Policy; Sociology; Tourism; Visual Arts.** *Doctorate*: **Management.**

Student Services: Academic Counselling, Canteen, Careers Guidance, Cultural Activities, Facilities for disabled people, Health Services, IT Centre, Language Laboratory, Library, Residential Facilities, Social Counselling, Sports Facilities

Publications: Fu Guang Journal

Academic Staff *2012-2013*: Total 220

Student Numbers *2012-2013*: Total: c. 5,200

Last Updated: 06/03/14

ORIENTAL INSTITUTE OF TECHNOLOGY (OIT)

58, Sze-Chuan Road, Pan-Chiao, Taipei 220
Tel: +886(2) 7738-8000 +886(2) 7738-0145
Fax: +886(2) 295-92524
EMail: mjl@mail.oit.edu.tw
Website: http://www.oit.edu.tw

President: Daqin Rao (2012-) Tel: +886(2) 773-80145, Ext. 1112

Secretary-General: Guohong Xi

International Relations: Lai-Ling Chan, Head, International Relations
Tel: +886(2) 773-80145, Ext. 1616/2224
EMail: lilin@mail.oit.edu.tw

Group
Dentsu School (Electrical and Electronic Engineering; Electrical Engineering; Electronic Engineering; Information Technology; Telecommunications Engineering); **Engineering** (Engineering; Industrial Design; Materials Engineering; Mechanical Engineering; Telecommunications Engineering); **General Education** (Arts and Humanities; Education; English; Military Science; Physical Education; Sports); **Management and Health Science** (Health Administration; Health Sciences; Industrial Management; Information Management; Management; Marketing; Nursing; Operations Research; Transport Management)

History: Founded 1968. Renamed the Oriental Academy of Industry 1973. Acquired present status and title 2000.

Main Language(s) of Instruction: Chinese

Degrees and Diplomas: *Bachelor's Degree*; *Master's Degree*: **Marketing; Materials Engineering; Telecommunications Engineering; Transport Management.**

Student Services: Academic Counselling, Health Services, Library, Social Counselling

Last Updated: 04/04/14

OVERSEAS CHINESE UNIVERSITY (OCU)

100, Chiao Kwang Rd., Taichung 40721
Tel: +886(4) 270-16855
Fax: +886(4) 270-75420
EMail: cc@ocu.edu.tw
Website: http://www.ocu.edu.tw

President: Michael M. Wei
Tel: +886(4) 270-76855, Ext. 1101 EMail: president@ocu.edu.tw

Chief-Secretary: Kuo-Ping Kao
Tel: +886(4) 270-16855, Ext. 1103
EMail: Kuo@ocu.edu.tw; secretary@ocu.edu.tw

International Relations: Shu-Ting Jhuang, Dean, Office of Research and Development
Tel: +886(4) 27016855, Ext. 1501 EMail: kathy@ocu.edu.tw

School
Business and Management (Accountancy; Banking; Business Administration; Economics; Finance; Information Sciences; Insurance; International Business; Law; Management; Transport Management); **Information Technology and Design** (Chinese; Design; Industrial Engineering; Industrial Management; Information Management; Information Technology; Multimedia; Software Engineering; Visual Arts); **Tourism and Hospitality** (English; Food Science; Hotel and Restaurant; Hotel Management; Modern Languages; Parks and Recreation; Tourism)

Centre
General Education (Arts and Humanities; Natural Sciences)

History: Founded 1964. Previously known as the Overseas Chinese Institute of Technology.

Main Language(s) of Instruction: Chinese

Degrees and Diplomas: *Associate Degree*; *Bachelor's Degree*; *Master's Degree*: **Business Administration; Finance; Information Technology; International Business; Transport Management.**

Student Services: Health Services, IT Centre, Library, Residential Facilities, Sports Facilities

Academic Staff *2012-2013*	**TOTAL**
FULL-TIME	**240**
PART-TIME	c. **210**
Student Numbers *2012-2013*	
All (Foreign included)	c. **10,000**

Last Updated: 09/04/14

PROVIDENCE UNIVERSITY (PU)

200, Sec. 7, Taiwan Boulevard, Shalu Dist., Taichung 43301
Tel: +886(4) 2632-8001, Ext. 11560-11563
Fax: +886(4) 2652-6602
EMail: pu11600@pu.edu.tw
Website: http://www.pu.edu.tw

President: Chuan Yi Tang (2010-)
Tel: +886(4) 2632-8001, Ext. 11004 EMail: president@pu.edu.tw

Secretary-General: Qin Xie Xiu
Tel: +886(4) 2632-8001, Ext. 11001 EMail: chin@pu.edu.tw

International Relations: Victor Lin
Tel: +886(4) 2632-8001, Ext. 11560-11563 EMail: vic@pu.edu.tw

College
Computing and Informatics (Computer Engineering; Computer Science; Information Management; Information Technology; Telecommunications Engineering); **Foreign Languages and Literature** (English; Japanese; Linguistics; Literature; Modern Languages; Spanish); **Humanities and Social Sciences** (Child Care and Development; Chinese; Ecology; Education; Law; Literature; Mass Communication; Social Work; Teacher Training; Welfare and

Protective Services); **Management** (Accountancy; Business Administration; Finance; International Business; Tourism); **Science** (Applied Chemistry; Applied Mathematics; Cosmetology; Food Science; Information Sciences; Nutrition; Statistics)

Programme
Business Administration *(MBA - Graduate International Programs)* (Business Administration); **Master of Science** *(MS - Graduate International Programme)* (Computer Science; Information Technology)

Centre
Chinese Language Education (Chinese); **Foreign Language** (English; Modern Languages); **General Education** (Arts and Humanities; Cultural Studies; History; Literature; Philosophy; Religion; Social Sciences); **Service Learning Development** (Service Trades); **Teacher Education** (Teacher Training)

History: Founded 1956 as Women's College, acquired present status 1989, present title 1993. A private Catholic University.

Academic Year: August to July (August-January; February-July)

Admission Requirements: Graduation from high school and entrance examination

Fees: c. 50,000 per semester (New Taiwan Dollar)

Main Language(s) of Instruction: English, Chinese

Degrees and Diplomas: *Bachelor's Degree*; *Master's Degree*: **Accountancy; Applied Chemistry; Arts and Humanities; Business Administration; Child Care and Development; Chinese; Computer Engineering; Computer Science; Cosmetology; Ecology; Education; English; Finance; Food Science; Information Management; International Business; Law; Linguistics; Literature; Nutrition; Social Work; Spanish; Telecommunications Engineering; Tourism.** *Doctorate*: **Applied Chemistry; Food Science; Nutrition.**

Student Services: Academic Counselling, Canteen, Careers Guidance, Cultural Activities, Facilities for disabled people, Foreign Studies Centre, Health Services, IT Centre, Language Laboratory, Library, Nursery Care, Residential Facilities, Social Counselling, Sports Facilities

Last Updated: 11/04/14

SHIH CHIEN UNIVERSITY (SCU)

No.70, Dazhi St., Zhongshan Dist., Taipei 10462
Tel: +886(2) 253-81111
Fax: +886(2) 253-36293
EMail: register@mail.usc.edu.tw; presi@mail.usc.edu.tw
Website: http://www.usc.edu.tw

President: Michael J. K. Chen (2011-)
Tel: +886(2) 253-38411
EMail: president@mail.usc.edu.tw; presi@mail.usc.edu.tw

Secretary-General: Baolin Hu
Tel: +886(2) 253-81111, Ext. 1110
EMail: blhwu@mail.usc.edu.tw

International Relations: Tony Kuo, Dean, Office of International Affairs
Tel: +886(2) 253-81111, Ext. 1150
EMail: tonyskuo@mail.usc.edu.tw; oia@mail.usc.edu.tw

College
Business and Information *(Kaohsiung Campus)* (Accountancy; Business Administration; Computer Science; Design; Finance; Information Management; Information Technology; International Business; Management; Marketing; Multimedia; Taxation; Telecommunications Engineering; Telecommunications Services); **Culture and Creativity** *(Kaohsiung Campus)* (English; Fashion Design; Japanese; Leisure Studies; Literature; Management; Tourism); **Design** (Architecture; Design; Fashion Design; Industrial Design; Mass Communication); **Human Ecology** (Biotechnology; Child Care and Development; Cooking and Catering; Family Studies; Food Science; Gerontology; Hotel and Restaurant; Music; Nutrition; Social Work); **Management** (Accountancy; Banking; Business Administration; English; Finance; Information Management; Information Technology; Insurance; International Business; Management; Modern Languages)

School
Lliberal Education (Arts and Humanities; Chinese; Sports); **Lliberal Education** *(Kaohsiung Campus)* (Arts and Humanities; Natural Sciences; Social Sciences; Sports)

Further Information: Kaohsiung Campus

History: Founded 1958 as Home Economics College. Upgraded into Shih Chien College of Design and Management 1991. Acquired present status and title 1997.

Academic Year: September to June (September-January; February-June)

Admission Requirements: Graduation from senior high school

Fees: Tuition, 30,680-40,870 per semester (New Taiwan Dollar)

Main Language(s) of Instruction: Chinese

Degrees and Diplomas: *Bachelor's Degree*; *Master's Degree*: **Architecture; Biotechnology; Business Administration; Child Care and Development; Family Studies; Fashion Design; Finance; Food Science; Industrial Design; Information Management; Information Technology; Insurance; Management; Mass Communication; Music; Nutrition; Social Work.** *Doctorate*: **Management.**

Student Services: Library, Residential Facilities

Student Numbers *2012-2013*: Total: c. 15,000

Last Updated: 10/04/14

SHIH HSIN UNIVERSITY (SHU)

1, Lane 17, Sec. 1, Mu-Cha Rd, Taipei 116
Tel: +886(2) 223-68225
Fax: +886(2) 223-65133
EMail: sec@cc.shu.edu.tw; c15@cc.shu.edu.tw
Website: http://www.shu.edu.tw

President: Ting-Ming Lai (2008-)
Tel: +886(2) 223-69113, Ext. 2003 EMail: pres@cc.shu.edu.tw

Secretary-General: K. C. Lee
Tel: +886(2) 2236-8225, Ext. 2003-2014
EMail: sec@cc.shu.edu.tw

International Relations: Karen Huiping Lin, International Exchange Group Public Affairs Officer
Tel: +886(2) 223-68225, Ext. 2322 EMail: karenlin@cc.shu.edu.tw

College
Humanities and Social Sciences (Chinese; English; Gender Studies; Japanese; Literature; Social Psychology; Social Studies); **Journalism and Communications** (Advertising and Publicity; Communication Arts; Communication Studies; Film; Graphic Arts; Information Sciences; Journalism; Mass Communication; Multimedia; Public Relations; Radio and Television Broadcasting); **Law** (Law; Private Law); **Management** (Business Administration; Economics; Finance; Information Management; Management; Public Administration; Tourism)

Centre
General Education (Arts and Humanities; Military Science; Modern Languages; Physical Education)

History: Founded 1956. Renamed World College of Journalism 1960 and then World College of Journalism and Communications 1991. Acquired present status and title 1997.

Fees: Undergraduate tuition, 1,628.98-1,920.18 per semester; Graduate tuition, 1,628.98-1,920.18 per semester (US Dollar)

Main Language(s) of Instruction: Chinese, English

Accrediting Agency: Higher Education Evaluation and Accreditation Council of Taiwan (HEEACT)

Degrees and Diplomas: *Bachelor's Degree*; *Master's Degree*: **Advertising and Publicity; Business Administration; Chinese; Communication Arts; Communication Studies; Economics; English; Film; Finance; Gender Studies; Graphic Design; Information Management; Information Technology; Journalism; Law; Management; Mass Communication; Private Law; Public Administration; Public Relations; Radio and Television Broadcasting; Social Psychology; Social Studies; Telecommunications Engineering; Tourism.** *Doctorate*: **Chinese; Communication Studies; Public Administration.**

Student Services: IT Centre, Library

Last Updated: 10/04/14

SHU-TE UNIVERSITY (STU)

59, Hengshan Road, Yanchao, Kaohsiung 82445
Tel: +886(7) 615-8000
Fax: +886(7) 615-8001
EMail: iad@mail.stu.edu.tw
Website: http://www.stu.edu.tw

President: Ining Yuan-Hsiang Chu
Tel: +886(7) 615-8000, Ext. 1100 EMail: ining@mail.stu.edu.tw

Vice-President: Wen-Shyong Hsieh
Tel: +886(7) 615-8000, Ext. 1200 EMail: wshsieh@mail.stu.edu.tw

International Relations: Teresa Ju
Tel: +886(7) 615-8000, Ext. 1700 EMail: tju@mail.stu.edu.tw

College

Design (Architectural and Environmental Design; Architecture; Art Management; Design; Fashion Design; Graphic Design; Industrial Design; Interior Design; Performing Arts); **Information Technology** (Computer Engineering; Computer Science; Information Technology); **Liberal Education** (Arts and Humanities); **Management** (Business Administration; Finance; Hotel Management; Insurance; International Business; Leisure Studies; Management; Marketing; Parks and Recreation; Sports Management; Tourism; Transport Management); **Social Sciences** (Child Care and Development; Chinese; English; Social Sciences)

Centre

Teacher Education (Education; Teacher Training)

Further Information: Also Research Centres

History: Founded 1997. Acquired present status 2006.

Degrees and Diplomas: *Bachelor's Degree*; *Master's Degree*: **Architectural and Environmental Design; Architecture; Business Administration; Computer Science; Design; Finance; Information Management; Information Technology; Insurance; Sociology.**

Student Services: IT Centre, Library, Residential Facilities, Sports Facilities

Last Updated: 10/04/14

SOOCHOW UNIVERSITY (SU)

70 Linshi Road, Shihlin, Taipei 111
Tel: +886(2) 288-19471
Fax: +886(2) 288-29310
EMail: president@scu.edu.tw
Website: http://www.scu.edu.tw

President: Wei Ta Pan Tel: +886(2) 288-19471, Ext.5022
EMail: president@scu.edu.tw

Vice President: Wei-Liang Chao
Tel: +886(2) 288-19471, Ext. 5016
EMail: vicepresident@scu.edu.tw

International Relations: Chiung-Feng Ko
Tel: +886(2) 288-19471, Ext 5231 EMail: rae@scu.edu.tw

School

Arts and Social Sciences (Chinese; Education; History; Human Rights; Music; Philosophy; Political Sciences; Social Work; Sociology; Teacher Training); **Business** (Accountancy; Business Administration; Business and Commerce; Computer Science; Economics; Finance; Information Management; Information Sciences; International Business); **Foreign Languages and Cultures** (English; English Studies; German; Germanic Studies; Japanese); **Law** (Law); **Science** (Chemistry; Mathematics; Microbiology; Physics; Psychology)

History: Founded 1900 in Soochow and received Charter from State of Tennessee. Supported by the Methodist Episcopal Church, South. Closed 1949 and re-established in Taipei 1950. Acquired present status and title 1954. A private institution under the supervision of the Ministry of Education.

Academic Year: August to July (August-January; February-July)

Admission Requirements: Graduation from high school and entrance examination

Fees: 50,000-64,000 per semester (New Taiwan Dollar)

Main Language(s) of Instruction: Chinese, English

Degrees and Diplomas: *Bachelor's Degree*: **Accountancy; Administration; Business and Commerce; Chemistry; Chinese; Computer Science; Economics; Education; English; Germanic Studies; History; International Business; Japanese; Law; Literature; Mathematics; Microbiology; Music; Philosophy; Physics; Psychology; Social Work; Sociology.** *Master's Degree*: **Accountancy; Business Administration; Business and Commerce; Chemistry; Chinese; Computer Science; Economics; English; German; Germanic Studies; History; International Business; Japanese; Law; Literature; Mathematics; Microbiology; Music; Philosophy; Political Sciences; Psychology; Social Work; Sociology.** *Doctorate*: **Chinese; Economics; Japanese; Law; Microbiology; Political Sciences.**

Student Services: Academic Counselling, Canteen, Facilities for disabled people, Health Services, Language Laboratory, Library, Sports Facilities

Publications: Soochow Journal of Chinese Studies; Soochow Journal of Economics and Business; Soochow Journal of Foreign Languages and Cultures; Soochow Journal of History; Soochow Journal of Japanese Language Teaching; Soochow Journal of Mathematics; Soochow Journal of Philosophical Studies; Soochow Journal of Political Science; Soochow Journal of Social Work; Soochow Journal of Sociology; Soochow Law Journal; Soochow Law Review

Academic Staff *2012-2013*	**TOTAL**
FULL-TIME	**426**
PART-TIME	**728**
Student Numbers *2012-2013*	
All (Foreign included)	**15,024**

Last Updated: 10/04/14

SOUTHERN TAIWAN UNIVERSITY OF SCIENCE AND TECHNOLOGY (STUST)

No. 1, Nan-Tai Street, Yungkang Dist.,
Yung Kang, Tainan Hsien 710
Tel: +886(6) 253-3131
Fax: +886(6) 254-3031
EMail: darby56@mail.stust.edu.tw
Website: http://www.stust.edu.tw/

President: Tai Chein (2007-)
Tel: +886(6) 253-3920
EMail: chang@mail.stut.edu.tw; sec@mail.stust.edu.tw

Secretary-General: Sheng-Tsair Sheu
Tel: +886(6) 253-3131, Ext. 1100
EMail: sheust@mail.stust.edu.tw; secpublic@mail.stust.edu.tw

International Relations: Yung-Peng Wang, Dean, Office of International Affairs
Tel: +886(6) 253-1841 +886(6) 253-3131, Ext. 1601
EMail: darby56@mail.stust.edu.tw

College

Business (Accountancy; Business Administration; E-Business/ Commerce; Economics; Engineering Management; Finance; Hotel and Restaurant; Human Resources; Industrial Management; Information Management; Information Technology; International Business; Law; Leisure Studies; Management; Marketing; Parks and Recreation; Tourism; Transport Management); **Digital Design** (Communication Arts; Computer Graphics; Design; Graphic Design; Industrial Design; Information Sciences; Information Technology; Mass Communication; Multimedia; Software Engineering; Visual Arts); **Engineering** (Bioengineering; Biotechnology; Chemical Engineering; Computer Engineering; Computer Science; Electrical and Electronic Engineering; Electrical Engineering; Electronic Engineering; Energy Engineering; Information Technology; Materials Engineering; Mechanical Engineering; Nanotechnology; Optical Technology; Telecommunications Engineering); **Humanities and Social Sciences** (Arts and Humanities; Child Care and Development; Education; Educational Administration; Educational Testing and Evaluation; English; Japanese; Social Sciences)

Centre

Chinese Language (Chinese); **General Education** (Arts and Humanities; Chinese; English; Natural Sciences; Physical Education)

Further Information: Also 14 Research Centres

History: Founded 1969 as Nan-Tai Junior College of Engineering. Successively renamed Nan-Tai Junior College of Engineering and Business (1990), Nan-Tai Institute of Technology (NTIT) (1996), Southern Taiwan University of Technology (STUT) 1999, Southern Taiwan University (STUT) (2007). Acquired present title 2012.

Academic Year: August to July (August-January; February-July)

Fees: Tuition, 1,430-1,650 per semester (US Dollar)

Main Language(s) of Instruction: Chinese, English

Degrees and Diplomas: *Bachelor's Degree*; *Master's Degree*: **Accountancy; Bioengineering; Biotechnology; Business Administration; Chemical Engineering; Computer Engineering; Computer Science; Economics; Educational Administration; Educational Testing and Evaluation; Electrical Engineering; Electronic Engineering; Energy Engineering; Engineering Management; English; Finance; Hotel and Restaurant; Human Resources; Industrial Management; Information Management; Information Sciences; Information Technology; International Business; Japanese; Law; Leisure Studies; Marketing; Materials Engineering; Mechanical Engineering; Multimedia; Nanotechnology; Optical Technology; Parks and Recreation; Software Engineering; Telecommunications Engineering; Tourism; Transport Management.** *Doctorate*: **Business Administration; Electrical Engineering; Electronic Engineering; Management; Mechanical Engineering.**

Student Services: Facilities for disabled people, Foreign Studies Centre, Health Services, IT Centre, Library, Nursery Care, Residential Facilities, Social Counselling, Sports Facilities

Last Updated: 09/04/14

ST. JOHN'S UNIVERSITY (SJU)

499, Sec. 4, Tam King Road, Tamsui District, Taipei 25135
Tel: +886(2) 280-13131
Fax: +886(2) 280-13128
Website: http://sju.edu.tw/

President: Jinlian Chen

Secretary-General: Jianhang Wang
Tel: +886(2) 280-13131, Ext. 6105
EMail: wang6860@mail.sju.edu.tw

International Relations: Dengyou Guang, Director, Office of International Affairs
Tel: +886(2) 280-13131, Ext. 6820
EMail: lawrence@mail.sju.edu.tw

College

Business and Management (Business Administration; Finance; Information Management; International Business; Management; Marketing; Transport Management); **Electrical, Electronic and Computer Engineering** (Computer Engineering; Computer Science; Electrical and Electronic Engineering; Electrical Engineering; Electronic Engineering; Information Technology; Telecommunications Engineering); **Engineering** (Automation and Control Engineering; Electronic Engineering; Engineering; Industrial Engineering; Industrial Management; Mechanical Engineering); **Humanities and Social Sciences** (Arts and Humanities; English; Health Administration; Health Sciences; Leisure Studies; Literature; Social Sciences; Sports)

History: Founded 1967 as St. John's and St. Mary's Institute of Technology. Accredited as an Institute of Business and Industry 1963. Upgraded into an Institute of Technology 1999. Acquired present status and title 2005.

Fees: Undergraduate tuition, 1,466-1,686 per semester; Graduate tuition, 1,686 per semester (US Dollar)

Main Language(s) of Instruction: Chinese

Degrees and Diplomas: *Bachelor's Degree*; *Master's Degree*: **Automation and Control Engineering; Business Administration; Computer Engineering; Electrical Engineering; Electronic Engineering; Industrial Engineering; Industrial Management; Mechanical Engineering; Telecommunications Engineering.**

Student Services: IT Centre, Library, Residential Facilities

Last Updated: 04/04/14

TA HWA UNIVERSITY OF SCIENCE AND TECHNOLOGY (TUST)

No.1, Dahua Rd., Qionglin Shiang, Hsinchu 307
Tel: +886(3) 592-7700
Fax: +886(3) 592-4656
Website: http://www.tust.edu.tw/

President: Ching-Der Shih (2012-)
Tel: +886(3) 592-7700, Ext. 2100 EMail: president@tust.edu.tw

Secretary-General: Cheng-Hsiung Tseng
Tel: +886(3) 592-7700, Ext. 2105 EMail: chtseng@tust.edu.tw

College

Business and Management (Business Administration; E-Business/Commerce; English; Food Technology; Information Management; Management; Marketing; Tourism); **Engineering and Design** (Design; Electrical and Electronic Engineering; Electrical Engineering; Electronic Engineering; Engineering; Information Technology; Mechanical Engineering); **Living and Health Technology** (Biological and Life Sciences; Health Sciences; Industrial Engineering; Industrial Management; Sports)

Centre

General Education (Arts and Humanities; Education; Physical Education); **Physical Education** (Physical Education; Sports)

History: Founded 1967 as Ta Hwa College of Technology. Upgraded into Ta-Hwa Institute of Technology 1997. Acquired present status and title 2012.

Main Language(s) of Instruction: Chinese

Degrees and Diplomas: *Associate Degree*; *Bachelor's Degree*; *Master's Degree*: **Electronic Engineering.**

Student Services: Canteen, Residential Facilities, Sports Facilities

Last Updated: 06/04/14

TAINAN UNIVERSITY OF TECHNOLOGY (TUT)

529, Chung Cheng Road, Yung Kang, Tainan 71002
Tel: +886(6) 242-7595
Fax: +886(6) 254-1309
EMail: emoiss@mail.tut.edu.tw
Website: http://www.tut.edu.tw/

President: Pin-Chang Lin
Tel: +886(6) 253-5641 EMail: empred@mail.tut.edu.tw

Dean of Academic Affairs: Chia-Jui Weng
Tel: +886(6) 253-2106 EMail: emacad@mail.tut.edu.tw

College

Art (Dance; Fine Arts; Music); **Design** (Design; Handicrafts; Interior Design; Multimedia; Visual Arts); **Living Technology** (Child Care and Development; Cooking and Catering; Cosmetology; Fashion Design; Health Administration; Home Economics); **Management** (Accountancy; Business Administration; English; Finance; Hotel Management; Information Management; International Business; Management; Modern Languages)

History: Founded 1964 as Tainan Junior College of Home Economics. Acquired present status 1997 and title 2006, with an attached Junior College. The institution is the only Women's University in Taiwan. Formerly known as Tainan Woman's College of Arts and Technology.

Academic Year: September to June (September-January; February-June)

Admission Requirements: Graduation from junior college or high school and college entrance examination

Fees: c. 40,000-50,000 (New Taiwan Dollar)

Main Language(s) of Instruction: Chinese

Degrees and Diplomas: *Bachelor's Degree*

Student Services: Academic Counselling, Careers Guidance, Health Services, Library, Social Counselling, Sports Facilities

Publications: Han-Chia Magazine; Journal of Tainan Women's University; Youth Magazine of Junior College

Last Updated: 08/04/14

TAIPEI CHENGSHIH UNIVERSITY OF SCIENCE AND TECHNOLOGY (TPCU)

No. 2, Xueyuan Rd., Beitou, Taipei 112
Tel: +886(2) 2892-7154
Fax: +886(2) 2896-5951
EMail: q5000@tpcu.edu.tw
Website: http://www.tpcu.edu.tw/

President: Hsin-Chung Lien
Tel: +886(2) 2892-7154, Ext. 5000 EMail: q5000@tpcu.edu.tw

Secretary-General: Lishang Yi
Tel: +886(2) 289-27154, Ext. 5300
EMail: sylee@tpcu.edu.tw; jshuang@tpcu.edu.tw

College

Business and Management (Business Administration; Commercial Law; E-Business/Commerce; Economics; English; Finance; French; German; Information Management; International Business; Japanese; Law; Management; Modern Languages; Multimedia; Spanish); **Engineering** (Chemical Engineering; Computer Engineering; Electrical Engineering; Electronic Engineering; Engineering; Materials Engineering; Mechanical Engineering; Telecommunications Engineering); **Human Ecology** (Business Administration; Cooking and Catering; Cosmetology; Food Technology; Health Sciences; Hotel and Restaurant; Hotel Management; Leisure Studies; Performing Arts; Sports; Tourism)

Centre

General Education (Arts and Humanities; Chemistry; Chinese; Geography; History; Information Sciences; Law; Natural Sciences; Physics; Psychology; Social Sciences; Sports)

History: Founded 1971. Renamed Technology and Science Institute of Northern Taiwan 2006. Acquired present status and title 2012.

Main Language(s) of Instruction: Chinese

Degrees and Diplomas: *Associate Degree*; *Bachelor's Degree*

Student Services: Library, Sports Facilities

Academic Staff *2012-2013*: Total 271

STAFF WITH DOCTORATE: Total 146

Last Updated: 06/04/14

TAIPEI COLLEGE OF MARITIME TECHNOLOGY

No. 212, Sec. 9, Yen Ping N. Rd., Shihlin Dist., Taipei 111
Tel: +886(2) 2810-2292
Fax: +886(2) 2810-6688
EMail: computer@mail.tcmt.edu.tw; secretary@mail.tcmt.edu.tw
Website: http://www.tcmt.edu.tw/

President: Yen-Po Tang (+886(2) 2810-2292)
Tel: +886(2) 2810-1069 EMail: president@mail.tcmt.edu.tw

Programme

Cruise Management *(Bachelor)* (Marine Transport)

Department

Air and Sea Marketing and Logistics (Air Transport; Marine Transport; Marketing; Transport Management); **Aquatic Sport and Recreation** (Parks and Recreation; Sports); **Computer and Communication Engineering** (Computer Engineering; Telecommunications Engineering); **Digital Games and Animation** (Computer Graphics; Multimedia; Software Engineering; Visual Arts); **Fashion Styling Design and Management** (Fashion Design; Management); **Food and Beverage Management** (Cooking and Catering); **Food Technology and Marketing** (Food Technology; Marketing); **General Education** (Arts and Humanities); **Health Care and Social Work** (Health Sciences; Social Work); **International Trade and Business Management** (Business Administration; International Business); **Marine Leisure and Tourism** (Leisure Studies; Tourism); **Navigation** (Marine Transport); **Visual Communication Design** (Communication Arts; Design; Visual Arts)

Further Information: Also Tamsui Campus

History: Founded 1966.

Main Language(s) of Instruction: Indonesian

Degrees and Diplomas: *Associate Degree*; *Bachelor's Degree*: **Computer Engineering; Food Science; Food Technology; International Business; Marine Engineering; Marine Transport; Parks and Recreation; Social Work; Sports; Telecommunications Engineering.**

Last Updated: 12/02/14

TAIPEI MEDICAL UNIVERSITY

250, Wushing Street, Taipei 110
Tel: +886(2) 2736-1661
Fax: +886(2) 2738-7795
EMail: tmu@tmu.edu.tw
Website: http://www.tmu.edu.tw

President: Yen Yun (2011-)

College

Humanities and Social Sciences (Arts and Humanities; Biotechnology; Ethics; Modern Languages; Social Sciences); **Medical Science and Technology** (Medical Technology; Medicine); **Medicine** (Biotechnology; Health Administration; Laboratory Techniques; Medical Technology; Medicine; Respiratory Therapy); **Nursing** (Gerontology; Management; Nursing); **Oral Medicine** (Dental Hygiene; Dental Technology; Dentistry); **Pharmacy** (Pharmacology; Pharmacy); **Public Health and Nutrition** (Health Sciences; Nutrition; Public Health)

Graduate Institute

Biomedical Informatics (Biomedical Engineering; Medical Technology); **Biomedical Technology** (Biomedical Engineering; Medical Technology); **Cell and Molecular Biology** (Cell Biology; Molecular Biology); **Clinical Medicine** (Public Health); **Health Care Administration** (Social and Preventive Medicine); **Humanities in Medicine**; **Medical Laboratory Science and Biothecnlology** (Nursing); **Medical Sciences** (Medical Technology); **Neuroscience** (Neurosciences); **Pharmacology** (Pharmacology)

Further Information: Also Teaching Hospital: Taipei Medical University Hospital (TMUH); TMU-Taipei Municipal Wan Fang Hospital; TMU-Shuangho Hospital, DOH

History: Founded 1960 as Taipei Medical College by Dr. Shui-Wang Hu, Dr Cheng-Tien Hsu and other medical specialists. Acquired present status and title 2000.

Academic Year: August to July (August-January; February-July)

Admission Requirements: Graduation from senior high school or equivalent, or above. Foreign applicants need to submit diploma transcripts and pass basic Chinese language test. For graduate: transcripts, diploma, study plan and might vary for different institutes.

Fees: Undergraduate: 56,110-142,960 depending on programmes. Master: 53,450-68,080. PhD: 53,450

Main Language(s) of Instruction: Chinese, English

Degrees and Diplomas: *Bachelor's Degree*; *Master's Degree*: **Biomedical Engineering; Biotechnology; Dentistry; Health Sciences; Medicine; Nutrition; Public Health.** *Doctorate*: **Dentistry; Health Sciences; Medical Technology; Medicine; Nutrition; Oncology; Public Health.**

Student Services: Library

Publications: TMU Today

Last Updated: 08/04/14

TAIWAN HOSPITALITY AND TOURISM COLLEGE (THTC)

268 Chung-Hsing ST., Feng-Shan Village, Shou-Feng County, Hualien
Tel: +886(3) 865-3906
Fax: +886(3) 865-3910
EMail: core3333@mail.tht.edu.tw
Website: http://www.tht.edu.tw/

President: Ming-Huei Lee (2004-)

Department

Continuing Education; **Culinary Arts** (Cooking and Catering); **Food and Beverage Management** (Cooking and Catering); **General Education** (Arts and Humanities); **Hotel Management** (Hotel

Management); **Leisure Management** (Leisure Studies); **Tourism** (Tourism); **Travel Management** (Transport Management)

History: Founded 1989.

Main Language(s) of Instruction: Chinese

Degrees and Diplomas: *Associate Degree*; *Bachelor's Degree*

Student Services: Library

Student Numbers *2010-2011*: Total 2,392

Last Updated: 21/02/14

TAIWAN SHOUFU UNIVERSITY

168, Nanshis Li, Madou, Tainan
Tel: +886(6) 571-8888
Fax: +886(6) 572-2858
EMail: computer@mail.dwu.edu.tw
Website: http://www.tsu.edu.tw/

President (Acting): Xiong Daiwen (2013-)
EMail: president@tsu.edu.tw

College

Design (Computer Science; Design; Industrial Design; Industrial Engineering; Industrial Management; Multimedia); **Humanity and Education** (Education; English; Japanese; Preschool Education); **Leisure and Tourism** (Business Administration; Cooking and Catering; Cosmetology; Finance; Health Administration; Hotel and Restaurant; Hotel Management; Leisure Studies; Tourism)

Graduate Institute

Education

History: Founded 2000. Formerly known as Diwan College of Management.

Fees: 45,000˜55,000 per semester (New Taiwan Dollar)

Degrees and Diplomas: *Bachelor's Degree*; *Master's Degree*: **Education.**

Student Services: Language Laboratory, Library

Last Updated: 09/04/14

TAJEN UNIVERSITY (TU)

20, Weixin Road, Yanpu Shiang, Pingtung 90741
Tel: +886(8) 762-4002˜5
Fax: +886(8) 762-3924
EMail: admission@mail.tajen.edu.tw
Website: http://www.tajen.edu.tw

President: Jhing-Fa Wang Tel: +886(8) 762-4002, Ext. 102

College

Humantites and Social Sciences (Child Care and Development; English; Japanese; Modern Languages; Preschool Education; Primary Education; Social Work); **Informatics and management** (Computer Science; Health Administration; Information Sciences; Information Technology; Management; Management Systems; Multimedia); **Leisure and Hospitality** (Hotel and Restaurant; Hotel Management; Leisure Studies; Management; Parks and Recreation; Sports Management); **Pharmacy and Health care** (Biotechnology; Environmental Management; Environmental Studies; Food Science; Food Technology; Health Administration; Health Sciences; Hygiene; Nursing; Occupational Health; Pharmacy; Safety Engineering)

Graduate Institute

Biotechnology (Biotechnology); **Environmental Management** (Environmental Management); **Leisure Studies** (Health Administration; Leisure Studies); **Pharmaceutical Technology** (Pharmacy)

History: Founded 1966. Acquired present status and title 2005.

Fees: Undergraduate and graduate students pay approximately US$1,540 to US$ 1,710 per semester for tuition and fees

Degrees and Diplomas: *Bachelor's Degree*: **Biotechnology; Food Science; Hotel and Restaurant; Pharmacy.** *Master's Degree*: **Biotechnology; Environmental Management; Health Administration; Leisure Studies; Pharmacology; Pharmacy.**

Student Services: Library

Last Updated: 09/04/14

TAKMING UNIVERSITY OF SCIENCE AND TECHNOLOGY (TMUST)

No.56, Sec.1, Huanshan Rd., Neihu District, Taipei 11451
Tel: +886(2) 2658-5801
Fax: +886(2) 265-88448
Website: http://www.takming.edu.tw/

President: David So-De Shyu
Tel: +886(2) 2658-5801, Ext. 2000 EMail: dshyu@takming.edu.tw

Secretary-General: Neng-Ching Lo
Tel: +886(2) 2658-5801, Ext. 2010
EMail: Secretary@takming.edu.tw; nc4933@takming.edu.tw

International Relations: Qiuxiang Lin, Head, International Centre
Tel: +886(2) 2658-5801, Ext. 2420 EMail: chlin@takming.edu.tw

College

Finance (Accountancy; Banking; Finance; Information Sciences; Insurance; Real Estate; Taxation); **Informatics** (Computer Science; Data Processing; E-Business/Commerce; Information Management; Information Technology; Multimedia); **Management** (Business Administration; English; International Business; Japanese; Management; Marketing; Transport Management)

History: Founded 1962 as Takming College. Became Takming Business College, 1974 and Takming Institute of Technology, 2000. Acquired present status and title 2007.

Main Language(s) of Instruction: Chinese

Degrees and Diplomas: *Bachelor's Degree*; *Master's Degree*: **Finance; Management; Marketing; Taxation.**

Student Services: Canteen, Library, Residential Facilities, Sports Facilities

Academic Staff *2013-2014*	**TOTAL**
FULL-TIME	**243**
PART-TIME	**185**

Last Updated: 08/04/14

TAMKANG UNIVERSITY (TKU)

151, Yingzhuan Road, Tamsui District, New Taipei City 25137
Tel: +886(2) 2621-5656
Fax: +886(2) 2623-7384
EMail: olr@mail.tku.edu.tw
Website: http://foreign.tku.edu.tw/TKUEnglish/

President: Flora Chia I. Chang (2004-)
Tel: +886(2) 2621-6320 EMail: fcic@mail.tku.edu.tw

Vice-President for Academic Affairs: Kan-nan Chen
Tel: +886(2) 2623-5895 EMail: knchen@mail.tku.edu.tw

Vice-President for Administrative Affairs: Po-yuan Kao
Tel: +886(2) 2623-5965 EMail: vivid@mail.tku.edu.tw

International Relations: Pei-Wha Chi Lee, Director, Office of Exchange and International Education
Tel: +886(2) 2629-6579 EMail: pcwl@mail.tku.edu.tw

Division

Continuing Education (Chinese; Japanese; Teacher Training)

College

Business (Banking; Business and Commerce; Economics; Finance; Industrial and Production Economics; Insurance; International Business); **Community Development**; **Education** (Curriculum; Education; Educational Administration; Educational and Student Counselling; Educational Psychology; Educational Research; Educational Technology; Higher Education; Teacher Training); **Engineering** (Aeronautical and Aerospace Engineering; Architecture; Chemical Engineering; Civil Engineering; Computer Science; Electrical Engineering; Electronic Engineering; Environmental Engineering; Information Technology; Materials Engineering; Mechanical Engineering; Structural Architecture; Water Science); **Entrepreneurial Development**; **Foreign Languages and Literature** (English; French; German; Japanese; Literature; Modern Languages; Russian; Spanish); **Global Research and Development** (Cultural Studies; Development Studies; Economics; Linguistics; Political Sciences); **International Studies** (American Studies; Chinese; Eastern European Studies; European Studies; International Relations; International Studies; Japanese; Latin American Studies; Slavic Languages; Southeast Asian Studies); **Liberal Arts** (Arts and Humanities; Chinese; Communication

Studies; History; Information Sciences; Library Science; Linguistics; Mass Communication); **Management** (Accountancy; Business Administration; Information Management; Leadership; Management; Management Systems; Public Administration; Statistics; Transport Management); **Science** (Biological and Life Sciences; Chemistry; Mathematics; Physics)

Centre

Chinese Language (Chinese); **Data Processing** (Information Technology); **Extension Education** (Arts and Humanities; Business and Commerce; Continuing Education; Engineering; Natural Sciences); **Fine Arts** *(Carrie Chang)* (Fine Arts); **In-service Education**; **Japanese Language** (Japanese); **Teacher Education** (Teacher Training)

Graduate Institute

American Studies (American Studies); **China Studies** (Chinese; East Asian Studies); **Chinese Linguistics and Documentation** (Chinese; Linguistics); **Curriculum and Instruction** (Curriculum; Education); **Educational Policy and Leadership** (Educational Administration; Educational Sciences); **Educational Psychology and Counselling**; **European Studies** (European Studies); **Future Studies**; **Higher Education**; **International Affairs and Strategic Studies** (International Relations; Military Science); **Japanese Studies** (Japanese); **Latin American Studies** (Latin American Studies); **Life Sciences**; **Slavic Studies** (Eastern European Studies; Slavic Languages); **Southeast Asian Studies** (Southeast Asian Studies)

Research Centre

Champion Incubator; **China Studies**; **Cross-Strait Financial Research** (Finance); **Energy and Optoelectric Materials Research** (Energy Engineering); **European Union Studies** (European Studies); **Industrial and Financial Research**; **Information Application**; **Life Science Development** (Biological and Life Sciences); **Statistical Survey Research** *(SSRC)* (Statistics); **Study of Globalization and Cultural Differences**; **Tamkang Times**; **Tibetan Studies** (Tibetan); **Water Resources Management and Policy Research** (Water Management; Water Science); **Wind Engineering** *(WERC)* (Engineering)

Further Information: Tamkang University has four campuses: Tamsui, Taipei, Lanyang and Cyber campuses. Also student programmes with Japan, Russia, France, Germany, Spain, USA, Canada, and Belgium

History: Founded 1950 as Junior College of English, became College of Arts and Sciences 1958, and acquired present status and title 1980.

Academic Year: August to July (August-January; February-July)

Admission Requirements: Graduation from high school and entrance examination

Fees: 46,880-54,720 per semester (New Taiwan Dollar)

Main Language(s) of Instruction: Chinese, English

Degrees and Diplomas: *Bachelor's Degree*; *Master's Degree*; *Doctorate*

Student Services: Academic Counselling, Careers Guidance, Cultural Activities, Facilities for disabled people, Health Services, Social Counselling, Sports Facilities

Publications: International Journal of Information and Management Sciences; Journal of Educational Media and Library Sciences; Journal of Future Studies; Tamkang Journal of Humanities and Social Sciences; Tamkang Journal of International Affairs; Tamkang Journal of Mathematics; Tamkang Journal of Science and Engineering; Tamkang Review

Publishing House: Tamkang University Press

Student Numbers *2012-2013*: Total 27,153

Last Updated: 08/04/13

TAOYUAN INNOVATION INSTITUTE OF TECHNOLOGY (TIIT)

No. 414, Sec.3, Jhongshan E. Rd.,
Jhongli City, Taoyuan County 32091
Tel: +886(3) 436-1070
Fax: +886(3) 465-8965
EMail: NanyaService@tiit.edu.tw
Website: http://www.tiit.edu.tw/

President: Kao Wen-shiow
Tel: +886(3) 4361070 ext: 1401 EMail: president@tiit.edu.tw

Dean of Studies: Chang Wang
Tel: +886(3) 436-1070, Ext. 123 EMail: cwang@nanya.edu.tw

International Relations: Chuan-Shao Wu
Tel: +886(3) 436-1070, Ext. 502 EMail: transhow@nanya.edu.tw

College

Business and Management (Applied Linguistics; Business Administration; English; Finance; Information Management; Management; Marketing); **Design** (Architecture; Communication Arts; Cosmetology; Design; Fashion Design; Interior Design; Visual Arts); **Engineering** *(Includes a Graduate School of Materials Applied Technology)* (Automotive Engineering; Chemical Engineering; Civil Engineering; Computer Engineering; Computer Science; Electronic Engineering; Environmental Engineering; Environmental Management; Information Technology; Materials Engineering; Measurement and Precision Engineering; Mechanical Engineering); **Human Ecology** (Child Care and Development; Cooking and Catering; Hotel and Restaurant; Leisure Studies; Tourism)

Centre

Language (Chinese; English)

History: Founded 1969 as Nanya Polytechnic. Formerly know as Nanya Institute of Technology.

Main Language(s) of Instruction: Chinese

Degrees and Diplomas: *Bachelor's Degree*: **Business Administration; Design; Engineering; Home Economics; Service Trades.** *Master's Degree*: **Electronic Engineering; Materials Engineering; Mechanical Engineering.**

Student Services: IT Centre, Library, Sports Facilities

Last Updated: 09/04/14

TATUNG INSTITUTE OF COMMERCE AND TECHNOLOGY (ALSO CPIC CAMPUS)

600 Amitabha Road, Chiayi 253
Tel: +886(5) 222-3124
Fax: +886(5) 225-2393 +886(5) 222-6269
EMail: dog@sunipc.ttc.edu.tw
Website: http://www.ttc.edu.tw

President: Xuan Bo Kan
Tel: +886(5) 222-3124 EMail: hpchien@ms2.ttc.edu.tw

Secretary-General: Yi Yu Zeng
Tel: +886(5) 222-3124, Ext. 613 EMail: tyc123@ms2.ttc.edu.tw

Programme

Hotel Management Degree (Hotel Management); **Japanese Culinary Journey** (Cooking and Catering); **Popular Creative Product Design Degree** (Industrial Design); **Tea Culture and Career Degree** (Food Science; Management; Tourism)

Department

Baking Management (Cooking and Catering); **Business Administration** (Business Administration); **Business Management and Design** (Business Administration; Design); **Child Care** (Child Care and Development); **Digital Content Design** (Information Technology); **Digital Media Design** (Multimedia); **Fashion Design** (Fashion Design); **Information Management** (Information Management); **Restaurant Management** (Hotel and Restaurant); **Social Work and Service Management** (Social Work; Welfare and Protective Services); **Sports, Health and Leisure** (Health Sciences; Leisure Studies; Sports); **Tourism and Leisure Management** (Leisure Studies; Tourism); **Visual Communication Design** (Advertising and Publicity; Communication Arts; Graphic Design; Visual Arts); **Wedding Planning and Design** (Home Economics)

Centre

Education (Education)

History: Founded 1963 as TaTung Junior College of Commerce. Acquired present status and title 2003.

Main Language(s) of Instruction: Chinese

Degrees and Diplomas: *Associate Degree*; *Bachelor's Degree*

Student Services: Academic Counselling, Health Services, Library, Residential Facilities, Social Counselling, Sports Facilities

Last Updated: 08/04/14

TATUNG UNIVERSITY (TTU)

40, Zhongshan North Road, Section 3, Taipei 104
Tel: +886(2) 2182-2928
Fax: +886(2) 2592-5252
EMail: webmaster@ttu.edu.tw
Website: http://www.ttu.edu.tw

President (Acting): Her Ming-Guo (2013-)
EMail: mgher@ttu.edu.tw

College

Design (Design; Industrial Design); **Electrical and Information Engineering** (Applied Mathematics; Computer Engineering; Computer Science; Electrical Engineering; Information Technology; Optical Technology; Telecommunications Engineering); **Engineering** (Bioengineering; Chemical Engineering; Materials Engineering; Mechanical Engineering); **Management** (Business Administration; English; Information Management; Japanese)

History: Founded 1943 as private Vocational School of Industry. Junior college added 1956. Reorganized 1963 as Tatung Institute of Technology, and acquired present status and title 1999.

Academic Year: August to July (August-January; February-July)

Admission Requirements: Graduation from high school and entrance examination

Main Language(s) of Instruction: Chinese, English

Degrees and Diplomas: *Bachelor's Degree*; *Master's Degree*: **Design; Energy Engineering; Engineering Management; Telecommunications Engineering.** *Doctorate*

Student Services: Academic Counselling, Careers Guidance, Cultural Activities, Health Services, IT Centre, Library, Residential Facilities, Sports Facilities

Publications: Tatung Journal

Publishing House: Sun-chih Publishing Company

Last Updated: 09/04/14

TOKO UNIVERSITY

No.51, Sec. 2, Xuefu Rd., Pu-Tzu, Chia-Yi 61363
Tel: +886(5) 362-2889
Fax: +886(5) 362-2899
EMail: TZILIL@mail.toko.edu.tw
Website: http://www.toko.edu.tw

President: Steve Kuang-Husn Shih
Tel: +886(5) 362-2889, Ext. 115
EMail: president@office.toko.edu.tw; shihsteve33@gmail.com

Secretary-General: Cheng-chih Fang
Tel: +886(5) 3622889, Ext. 111 EMail: sec_dir@office.toko.edu.tw

College

Economy and Management (Business Administration; Economics; Finance; Hotel and Restaurant; Law; Leisure Studies; Marketing; Parks and Recreation; Transport and Communications; Transport Management); **Human Ecology** (Cosmetology; Nutrition; Preschool Education; Psychology; Social Work; Welfare and Protective Services); **Technology and Design** (Communication Arts; Computer Graphics; Computer Networks; Design; Fashion Design; Information Management; Information Technology; Multimedia; Performing Arts; Software Engineering; Visual Arts)

Centre

Genral Education (Arts and Humanities; Education; Sports)

History: Toko College of Technology and Management

Main Language(s) of Instruction: Chinese

Degrees and Diplomas: *Bachelor's Degree*; *Master's Degree*: **Business Administration; Information Technology; Leisure Studies; Transport Management.**

Last Updated: 08/04/14

TRANSWORLD UNIVERSITY (TWU)

No.1221, Zhennan Rd., Toulin City, Yunlin County 640
Tel: +886(5) 537-0988, Ext. 2230-2236
Fax: +886(5) 537-0989
EMail: cia@twu.edu.tw
Website: http://www.twu.edu.tw/

President: Shu-Hsiang Hsu
Tel: +886(5) 537-0988, Ext. 2112 EMail: president@twu.edu.tw

Secretary-General: Sanli Lin
Tel: +886(5) 557-0866, Ext. 2110 EMail: sunny@twu.edu.tw

International Relations: Winnie Chen, Dean, Office of International and Cross-Straight Affairs
Tel: +886(5) 537-0988, Ext. 2230 EMail: winnie@twu.edu.tw

College

Design (Communication Arts; Cosmetology; Design; Display and Stage Design; Fashion Design; Graphic Design; Industrial Design; Mass Communication; Multimedia; Visual Arts); **Health Sciences** (Biotechnology; Health Sciences; Preschool Education); **Management** (Business Administration; Finance; Information Management; Management; Marketing; Public Administration; Small Business)

School

Management (Business Administration; Information Management; Management; Management Systems)

Further Information: Also Chia-Tong Campus

History: Founded 1992 as Transworld Junior College of Commerce. Upgraded into Transworld Institute of Technology 2000. Acquired present status and title 2010.

Main Language(s) of Instruction: Chinese

Degrees and Diplomas: *Associate Degree*; *Bachelor's Degree*; *Master's Degree*: **Biotechnology; Business Administration; Communication Arts; Display and Stage Design; Environmental Management; Graphic Design; Multimedia; Public Administration; Small Business.**

Student Numbers *2013-2014*: Total: c. 8,000

Last Updated: 09/04/14

TUNG FANG DESIGN INSTITUTE (TF)

No. 110, Dongfang Rd., Hunei Township,
Kaohsiung 82941
Tel: +886(7) 693-2011
Fax: +886(7) 693-1611
EMail: chief@mail.tf.edu.tw
Website: http://www.tf.edu.tw

President: Shu-Ming Wu (2011-)
Tel: +886(7) 693-9503 EMail: chief@mail.tf.edu.tw

Secretary-General: Yiqun Wu Tel: +886(7) 693-9503
EMail: hyc416@mail.tf.edu.tw

Programme

Applied Life Esthetics Degree (Biology; Child Care and Development; Cosmetology; Education; Food Technology; Health Sciences; Management; Marketing); **Food and Beverage Management Degree** (Food Technology)

School

Arts and Design (Communication Arts; Design; Fine Arts; Handicrafts; Industrial Design; Interior Design); **Business and Management** (Business Administration; Cosmetology; English; Leisure Studies; Management; Marketing; Modern Languages; Transport Management); **Engineering** (Chemical Engineering; Computer Science; Electrical Engineering; Electronic Engineering; Engineering; Food Science; Food Technology; Materials Engineering)

Centre

Southern Regional Education Resource (Teacher Training)

History: Founded 1966 as Private Tung Fang Junior College of Industry and Arts. Approved by the Ministry and renamed Tung Fang Junior College of Industry 1969. Renamed Tung Fang Junior College of Industry and Commerce 1990. Upgraded as Tung Fang Institute of Technology 2002.

Main Language(s) of Instruction: Chinese

Degrees and Diplomas: *Associate Degree*; *Bachelor's Degree*; *Master's Degree*: **Design.**

Student Services: Library

Student Numbers *2013-2014*: Total: c. 4,600

Last Updated: 09/04/14

TUNGHAI UNIVERSITY (THU)

No.1727, Sec.4, Taiwan Boulevard, Xitun District, Taichung 40704
Tel: +886(4) 2359-0121
Fax: +886(4) 2359-0361
EMail: admission@thu.edu.tw
Website: http://www.thu.edu.tw

President: Tang Ming-Jer (2013-)
Tel: +886(4) 2359-0200 EMail: president@thu.edu.tw

Vice President: Jen-Teng Tsai
Tel: +886(4) 2359-2559 EMail: tsaijt@thu.edu.tw

Vice President: C. Chao Chih
Tel: +886(4) 2359-7126 EMail: ccchao@thu.edu.tw

International Relations: Y.F. Liu Evonne
Tel: +886(4) 23590121 Ext. 28509 EMail: iruka@thu.edu.tw

College

Agriculture (Agriculture; Biotechnology; Food Science; Hotel Management; Zoology); **Arts** (Chinese; Foreign Languages Education; History; Japanese; Literature; Modern Languages; Philosophy; Religious Studies); **Engineering** (Chemical Engineering; Computer Science; Electrical Engineering; Environmental Engineering; Industrial Engineering; Information Technology; Materials Engineering); **Fine Arts and Creative Design** (Design; Fine Arts); **Law** (Law); **Management** (Accountancy; Business Administration; Finance; Information Management; International Business; Statistics); **Science** (Biological and Life Sciences; Chemistry; Physics); **Social Sciences** (Economics; Political Sciences; Public Administration; Social Work; Sociology)

School

Extension Education School (Education); **Liberal Arts Education** (Communication Studies; Development Studies; Modern Languages; Regional Studies)

Centre

Chinese Language (Chinese); **English Language** (English)

Research Centre

Chinese Social and Management Studies (Social Sciences); **Life Science** (Biological and Life Sciences); **Microbiology** (Microbiology); **Nanotechnology** (Nanotechnology); **Software Engineering and Technology** (Software Engineering); **Tropical Ecology and Biodiversity** (Ecology; Tropical Agriculture)

History: Founded 1955 through the efforts of Christian leaders at home and abroad and the active support of the United Board for Christian Higher Education in Asia. The first private university in Taiwan.

Academic Year: September to June (September-January; February-June)

Admission Requirements: Graduation from recognized senior high school or school of equivalent standing, and entrance examination

Fees: 48,217-56,289 per semester (New Taiwan Dollar)

Main Language(s) of Instruction: Chinese, English

Accrediting Agency: Ministry of Education

Degrees and Diplomas: *Bachelor's Degree*; *Master's Degree*; *Doctorate*: **Agriculture; Biological and Life Sciences; Law; Management; Physics.**

Student Services: Academic Counselling, Canteen, Careers Guidance, Cultural Activities, Facilities for disabled people, Foreign Studies Centre, Health Services, Language Laboratory, Nursery Care, Social Counselling, Sports Facilities

Publications: Tunghai Journal

Publishing House: Tunghai University Press

Last Updated: 07/04/14

TUNGNAN UNIVERSITY (TNU)

N° 152, Section 3, Pei Shen Road, Shenkeng District, Taipei 22202
Tel: +886(2) 866-25900
Fax: +886(2) 266-43648
EMail: pschao@mail.tnu.edu.tw
Website: http://www.tnu.edu.tw/

President: Ching-Yin Lee
Tel: +886(2) 866-25888 EMail: cylee@mail.tnu.edu.tw

College

Administration (Business Administration; Industrial Management; Information Management; Management; Marketing; Tourism); **Applied Life** (English; Graphic Design; Hotel and Restaurant; Interior Design; Leisure Studies); **Electrical and Computer Engineering** (Computer Engineering; Electrical Engineering; Electronic Engineering; Information Technology); **Engineering** (Aeronautical and Aerospace Engineering; Automation and Control Engineering; Construction Engineering; Environmental Engineering; Mechanical Engineering; Thermal Engineering)

Institute

Construction Technology and Hazards Mitigation (Construction Engineering); **Electrical Engineering** (Electrical Engineering); **Industrial Management** (Industrial Management); **Mechanical Engineering** (Mechanical Engineering)

History: Founded 1970 as Tungnan Junior College of Technology.Became Tungnan Institute of Technology 2000. Acquired present status 2007.

Main Language(s) of Instruction: Chinese, English

Degrees and Diplomas: *Bachelor's Degree*: **Automation and Control Engineering; Business and Commerce; Civil Engineering; Computer Engineering; Construction Engineering; Electrical Engineering; Electronic Engineering; Environmental Engineering; Industrial Management; Information Management; Management; Mechanical Engineering; Modern Languages; Safety Engineering.**

Student Services: Library, Residential Facilities, Sports Facilities

Student Numbers *2013-2014*: Total: c. 7,500

Last Updated: 07/04/14

TZU CHI COLLEGE OF TECHNOLOGY (TCCT)

880, Sec.2, Chien-kuo Rd., Hualien 970
Tel: +886(3) 857-2158
Fax: +886(3) 857-7261
EMail: wwwadm@tccn.edu.tw
Website: http://www.tccn.edu.tw

President: Wen-Jui Lo (2011-) EMail: wjl@tccn.edu.tw

Secretary-General: Wei-Lin Hsu
Tel: +886(3) 857-2158, Ext. 319 EMail: wlhsu@tccn.edu.tw

International Relations: Chun-Tien Yang, Section Chief, International Academia and Industrial - Academia Cooperation
Tel: +886(3) 857-2158, Ext. 480 EMail: ctyang@tccn.edu.tw

Department

Accounting Information (Accountancy; Computer Engineering; Information Technology); **Health Administration** (Health Administration); **Information Engineering and Informatics** (Computer Engineering; Computer Graphics; Computer Science; E-Business/Commerce; Information Management; Information Technology; Multimedia); **Nursing** (Community Health; Health Sciences; Nursing; Psychiatry and Mental Health); **Radiological Technology** (Medical Technology; Radiology; Treatment Techniques)

Centre

General Education (Arts and Humanities)

History: Founded 1989. Acquired present status and title 1999.

Main Language(s) of Instruction: Chinese

Accrediting Agency: Higher Education Evaluation and Accreditation Council of Taiwan (HEEACT); Taiwan Nursing Accreditation Council (TNAC)

Degrees and Diplomas: *Associate Degree*; *Bachelor's Degree*; *Master's Degree*: **Radiology.**

Student Services: IT Centre, Library

Last Updated: 09/04/14

TZU CHI UNIVERSITY (TCU)

701, Section 3, Chung Yan Road, Hualien 97004
Tel: +886(3) 857-2677
Fax: +886(3) 856-2500
EMail: feedback@mail.tcu.edu.tw
Website: http://www.tcu.edu.tw

President: Pen-Jung Wang
Tel: +886(3) 856-5301, Ext.1002 EMail: president@mail.tcu.edu.tw

College
Education and Communication (Communication Studies; Education); **Life Sciences** (Biological and Life Sciences; Genetics; Molecular Biology); **Medicine** (Medicine)

School
Nursing (Nursing); **Public Health** (Public Health)

Department
Child Development and Family Learning (Child Care and Development; Family Studies); **Communication Studies** (Communication Studies); **Human Resources** (English; Human Resources; Philology; Social Work); **Laboratory Medicine and Biotechnology** (Biotechnology; Laboratory Techniques); **Medical Information Technologies** (Medical Technology); **Medicine** (Medicine); **Oriental Literature** (Literature); **Physical Therapy** (Physical Therapy); **Social Work** (Social Work)

Institute
Medical Science (Medicine)

Graduate Institute
Education (Education); **Pharmacology and Toxicology** (Pharmacology; Toxicology); **Public Health** (Public Health); **Religion and Culture** (Cultural Studies; Religious Studies); **Social Work** (Social Work)

History: Founded 1994 as Tzu Chi College of Medicine, expanded to Tzu Chi College of Medicine and Humanities 1998. Acquired present title 2000.

Academic Year: August to July (August-January; February-July)

Admission Requirements: Senior high school certificate and entrance examination. Selection through either a new version of the Joint University Entrance Examinations or by application and general (SAT II like) examination

Fees: 47,000-59,000 per semester (New Taiwan Dollar)

Main Language(s) of Instruction: Chinese

Accrediting Agency: Ministry of Education

Degrees and Diplomas: *Bachelor's Degree*: **Biological and Life Sciences; Child Care and Development; Communication Studies; Development Studies; Family Studies; Literature; Medical Technology; Nursing; Oriental Studies; Public Health; Social Work.** *Master's Degree*: **Anthropology; Cell Biology; Cultural Studies; Education; Genetics; Health Sciences; Medicine; Molecular Biology; Neurosciences; Nursing; Pharmacology; Religious Studies; Social Work; Toxicology.** *Doctorate*: **Medicine; Pharmacy.**

Student Services: Academic Counselling, Canteen, Careers Guidance, Cultural Activities, Facilities for disabled people, Health Services, Language Laboratory, Nursery Care, Social Counselling, Sports Facilities

Last Updated: 07/04/14

UNIVERSITY OF KANG NING (UKN)

188, Sec. 5, An Chung Rd., Annan District, Tainan 70970
Tel: +886(6) 255-2500
Website: http://www.ukn.edu.tw/ukn/index.html

President: Rong-Yung King

College
Health and Leisure (Construction Engineering; Cooking and Catering; Food Technology; Health Administration; Health Sciences; Hotel Management; Leisure Studies; Tourism; Town Planning); **Humanities and Information** (Applied Linguistics; Arts and Humanities; Asian Studies; Cultural Studies; English; Information Sciences; Information Technology; Japanese; Modern Languages); **Management** (Banking; Business Administration; Cosmetology; Engineering Management; Fashion Design; Finance; Health Sciences; Industrial Management; International Business; Management; Transport Management)

Centre
General Education (Arts and Humanities; Biological and Life Sciences; Civics; History; Literature; Natural Sciences; Philosophy; Psychology)

Research Centre
MICE

Main Language(s) of Instruction: Chinese

Degrees and Diplomas: *Bachelor's Degree*; *Master's Degree*: **Business Administration; Communication Studies; Cooking and Catering; English; Information Technology; Leisure Studies; Management; Town Planning.** Also Executive MBA

Student Services: Canteen, Health Services, Library, Residential Facilities, Sports Facilities

Last Updated: 08/02/14

VANUNG UNIVERSITY (VNU)

1 Van-Nung Rd., Chung-Li, Taoyuan 32061
Tel: +886(3) 451-5811
Fax: +886(3) 451-3786
EMail: koli1230@mail.vnu.edu.tw
Website: http://www.vnu.edu.tw

President: Shin-Shing Shyu Tel: +886(3) 451-5811, Ext 327

International Relations: Chien-Seng Wang
Tel: +886(3) 453-1279

College
Design (Cosmetology; Design; Industrial Design; Service Trades); **Engineering and Electronic Information** (Biotechnology; Civil Engineering; Computer Engineering; Computer Science; Electronic Engineering; Engineering; Environmental Engineering; Information Technology; Materials Engineering; Multimedia; Optical Technology; Telecommunications Engineering); **Management** (Business Administration; Finance; Industrial Management; Information Management; Management; Marketing; Transport Management); **Tourism and Hospitality** (Air Transport; Food Technology; Hotel and Restaurant; Hotel Management; Leisure Studies; Service Trades; Tourism; Transport and Communications)

History: Founded 1972. Renamed Van Nung Institute of Industry 1973 and then Van Nung Institute of Industry and Commerce 1990. Upgraded into Van Nung Institute of Technology 1999. Acquired present status and title 2004.

Fees: Tuition, 38,053-39,809 (New Taiwan Dollar)

Main Language(s) of Instruction: Chinese

Degrees and Diplomas: *Bachelor's Degree*; *Master's Degree*: **Business Administration; Civil Engineering; Environmental Engineering; Information Management; Materials Engineering.**

Last Updated: 04/04/14

WENZAO URSULINE UNIVERSITY OF LANGUAGES

Wenzao Ursuline College of Languages (WZU)
900 Mintsu 1st Road Kaohsiung, Kaoshiung 807
Tel: +886(7) 342-6031, Ext. 2611-2615
Fax: +886(7) 342-7942
EMail: oip@mail.wzu.edu.tw
Website: http://www.wtuc.edu.tw/

President: Lucia S. Lin
Tel: +886(7) 342-6031, Ext. 201 EMail: president@mail.wzu.edu.tw

Secretary-General: Zhenya Du
Tel: +886(7) 342-6031, Ext. 1111 EMail: 96004@mail.wzu.edu.tw

International Relations: Kit Lam, Dean, Office of International and Cross-Strait Cooperation
Tel: +886(7) 342-6031, Ext. 2601 EMail: kitlam@mail.wzu.edu.tw

College
Cultural and Educational Innovation (Chinese; Communication Arts; Foreign Languages Education; International Business; International Studies; Multimedia; Teacher Training); **English and International Studies** (English; Foreign Languages Education; International Business; International Relations; International Studies; Translation and Interpretation); **European and Asian Languages** (European Studies; French; German; Japanese; Spanish); **Holistic Education** (Arts and Humanities; Education; Physical Education)

History: Founded 1966. Upgraded into Wenzao Ursuline College of Languages 1999. Acquired present status and title 2013.

Fees: Tuition, 51,559 per semester (New Taiwan Dollar)

Main Language(s) of Instruction: Chinese, English

Degrees and Diplomas: *Associate Degree*; *Bachelor's Degree*; *Master's Degree*: **Chinese; Communication Arts; Foreign Languages Education; International Business; Translation and Interpretation.**

Student Services: Health Services, Library, Residential Facilities

Last Updated: 06/04/14

WUFENG UNIVERSITY (WFU)

117, Section 2, Chian-Kuo Road, Ming-Hsiung, Chiayi 62153
Tel: +886(5) 226-7125
Fax: +886(5) 226-4224
EMail: pr@wfu.edu.tw
Website: http://www.wfu.edu.tw

President: M.H. Su EMail: president@wfu.edu.tw

Vice-Chancellor: Wei Xin Lu
Tel: +886(5) 226-7125 Ext. 21213
EMail: vicepresident@wfu.edu.tw

Department

Applied Digital Media (Computer Engineering); **Applied Game Technology** (Computer Engineering); **Applied Japanese** (Japanese); **Computer Science and Information Engineering** (Computer Science; Information Technology); **Early Childhood Care and Education** (Child Care and Development; Preschool Education); **Electrical Engineering** (Electrical Engineering); **Finance** (Finance); **Fire Science** (Fire Science); **Hospitality Management** (Hotel and Restaurant); **Marketing and Distribution Management** (Marketing); **Mechanical Engineering** (Mechanical Engineering); **Recreation and Sports Management** (Parks and Recreation; Sports Management); **Science and Information Engineering** (Computer Engineering; Computer Science); **Security Technology and Management** (Protective Services); **Tourism and Leisure Management** (Tourism); **Tourism English** (English)

Graduate Institute

Electrical and Mechanical Materials (Electrical Engineering; Mechanical Engineering)

History: Founded 1963 as Wu Feng College of Business. Became Wu Feng Industrial College 1969, Wu Feng Industrial and Commercial College 1992, Wu Feng Institute of Technology 2000. Acquired present status and title 2012.

Main Language(s) of Instruction: Chinese

Degrees and Diplomas: *Bachelor's Degree*: **Accountancy; Chemical Engineering; Computer Science; Electrical Engineering; Electronic Engineering; English; Fire Science; Information Management; International Business; Japanese; Mechanical Engineering; Preschool Education.**

Student Services: Academic Counselling, Health Services, Library, Sports Facilities

Last Updated: 08/04/14

YUANPEI INSTITUTE OF SCIENCE AND TECHNOLOGY

No.306, Yuanpei Street, Hsinchu 30015
Tel: +886(3) 538-1183
Fax: +886(3) 538-5353
EMail: ctlin@mail.yust.edu.tw
Website: http://www.yust.edu.tw

President: Chih-Cheng Lin
Tel: +886(3) 538-1183, Ext. 2201 +886(3) 610-2201
EMail: sec2201@mail.ypu.edu.tw; sophia@mail.ypu.edu.tw

Secretary-General: Jiezhong Liu
Tel: +886(3) 538-1183, Ext. 2468
EMail: liujc@mail.ypu.edu.tw; sec2201@mail.ypu.edu.tw

International Relations: Hsiao-Ling Huang, Head, Office of International Affairs
Tel: +886(3) 538-1183, Ext. 8260 EMail: hlhuang@mail.ypu.edu.tw

College

Health Sciences (Biotechnology; Environmental Engineering; Food Science; Health Sciences; Hotel and Restaurant; Leisure Studies); **Industry and Management** (Business Administration; English; Finance; Information Management; Information Technology; Leisure Studies; Management; Tourism); **Medical Technology, Nursing and Wellbeing** (Biomedical Engineering; Biotechnology; Health Administration; Health Sciences; Laboratory Techniques; Medical Technology; Nursing; Optometry; Radiology; Welfare and Protective Services)

Centre

General Education (Arts and Humanities; Education; English; Sports)

History: Founded as a medical school 1964. Renamed Yuanpei College of Medical Technology 1968 and then upgraded into Yuanpei Institute of Science and Technology 1999. Acquired present status and title 2006.

Main Language(s) of Instruction: Chinese

Degrees and Diplomas: *Bachelor's Degree*; *Master's Degree*: **Biomedical Engineering; Biotechnology; Business Administration; Environmental Engineering; Food Science; Health Administration; Laboratory Techniques; Radiology.**

Student Services: Health Services, IT Centre, Library, Sports Facilities

Last Updated: 08/04/14

YUAN-ZE UNIVERSITY (YZU)

135, Yuan-Tung Road, Chung-Li, Taoyuan 32003
Tel: +886(3) 463-8800
Fax: +886(3) 455-8900
EMail: proffice@saturn.yzu.edu.tw
Website: http://www.yzu.edu.tw

President: Zhang Jinfu
Tel: +886(3) 463-8800 Ext. 2211 EMail: ptdept@saturn.yzu.edu.tw

Secretary-General: Yeh Liang Hsu
Tel: +886(3) 463-8800 Ext. 2206
EMail: metchsu@saturn.yzu.edu.tw

International Relations: James Wang
Tel: +886(3) 463-8800 Ext. 3280 EMail: iadept@saturn.yzu.edu.tw

College

Electrical and Communication Engineering (Communication Studies; Electronic Engineering; Optical Technology); **Engineering** (Chemical Engineering; Electrical Engineering; Electronic Engineering; Environmental Engineering; Industrial Engineering; Management; Mechanical Engineering; Natural Resources; Production Engineering); **General Studies** (International Studies); **Humanities and Social Sciences** (Applied Linguistics; Chinese; Literature; Modern Languages; Sociology); **Informatics** (Computer Engineering; Computer Networks; Computer Science; Information Management; Information Sciences); **Management** (Accountancy; Business Administration; Finance; International Business; Management)

Centre

Arts (Performing Arts); **Management Studies** (Management)

History: Founded 1989. Acquired present status and title 1997.

Academic Year: September to June (September- January; February- June)

Admission Requirements: High school certificate

Fees: 55,000 per semester (New Taiwan Dollar)

Main Language(s) of Instruction: Chinese, English

Degrees and Diplomas: *Bachelor's Degree*; *Master's Degree*: **Accountancy; Bioengineering; Chemical Engineering; Chinese; Communication Arts; Computer Science; Design; Electrical Engineering; Energy Engineering; Finance; Industrial Engineering; Information Management; International Business; Laser Engineering; Leadership; Linguistics; Management; Materials Engineering; Mechanical Engineering; Medical Technology; Modern Languages; Social Sciences; Telecommunications Engineering.** *Doctorate*: **Chemical Engineering; Computer Engineering; Electrical Engineering; Information Management; Laser Engineering; Materials Engineering; Mechanical Engineering; Telecommunications Engineering.**

Student Services: Academic Counselling, Facilities for disabled people, Health Services, Language Laboratory, Residential Facilities, Sports Facilities

Last Updated: 08/04/14

YU DA UNIVERSITY OF SCIENCE AND TECHNOLOGY (YDU)

168, Hsue-Fu Road, Tai-wen Tsun, Chao-Chiao Hsiang, Miao-Li Hsien 36143
Tel: +886(37) 651-188
Fax: +886(37) 620-525
EMail: ydu@ydu.edu.tw
Website: http://www.ydu.edu.tw

President: Jian-Shen Chen
Tel: +886(37) 651-168 EMail: prin@ydu.edu.tw

International Relations: Chuan-mei Chen
Tel: +886(37) 651-188, Ext. 8910 EMail: chuanmel@ydu.edu.tw

College

Business Management (Business Administration; Information Management; Marketing); **Finance and Economics** (Accountancy; Commercial Law; Finance; International Business); **Humanities and Social Sciences** (Child Care and Development; Chinese; English; Japanese; Social and Preventive Medicine; Social Work; Transport Management); **Leisure and Creativity** (Fashion Design; Hotel and Restaurant; Leisure Studies; Multimedia; Sports Management)

Department

Continuing Education (Continuing Education)

Centre

General Education

History: Founded 1999 as Yu Da College of Business. Acquired present title 2009.

Main Language(s) of Instruction: Chinese

Degrees and Diplomas: *Bachelor's Degree*

Student Services: Canteen, Library, Residential Facilities

Last Updated: 08/04/14

YUNG-TA INSTITUTE OF TECHNOLOGY AND COMMERCE (YT)

316, Chung Shan Rd., Linti, Linlo, Pingtung 909
Tel: +886(8) 723-3733
Fax: +886(8) 722-9603
EMail: cysu@mail.ytit.eud.tw
Website: http://www.ytit.edu.tw

President: Chen Liandong
Tel: +886(8) 723-3733, Ext. 201
EMail: president@mail.ytit.edu.tw; chenld@mail.ytit.edu.tw

Secretary-General: Zhenxing Chen

Department

Comprehensive Teaching (Arts and Humanities; Chinese; English; Natural Sciences; Social Sciences; Technology; Writing)

Group

Engineering (Architecture; Automotive Engineering; Electronic Engineering; Energy Engineering; Information Technology; Mechanical Engineering; Structural Architecture); **Llife Science Applications** (Biotechnology; Cosmetology; Health Sciences; Leisure Studies; Sports); **Management** (Business Administration; Health Sciences; Information Management; Leisure Studies; Management; Marketing; Sports; Tourism)

History: Founded 1967, acquired present status and title 1999.

Fees: c.800-1,000 per semester (US Dollar)

Main Language(s) of Instruction: Chinese, English

Degrees and Diplomas: *Bachelor's Degree*; *Master's Degree*: **Measurement and Precision Engineering; Production Engineering.**

Student Services: Library, Residential Facilities

Last Updated: 04/04/14

Colombia

STRUCTURE OF HIGHER EDUCATION SYSTEM

Description:

Higher education is provided by universities, university faculties, technological institutions, and professional technical institutions. These four types of institutions comprise both public and private institutions. The higher education sector comes under the responsibility of the Ministry of Education.

Stages of studies:

University level first stage: Pregrado

Undergraduate studies are offered at three levels:

1. Professional technological education is offered at technical, technological institutions, and universities, studies usually last for two years and lead to the title of Técnico Profesional;
2. Technical education is offered at technological institutions and universities, studies usually last for three years and lead to the title of Técnologo;
3. Professional education is offered at technological institutions and universities, studies usually last between 4 and 5 years and lead to a professional title.

University level second stage: Posgrado

All three undergraduate diplomas allow students to enter Specialist (Especialista) studies. Only the professional title allows students to enter Master's (Maestria) or Doctorate (Doctorado) programmes. Specialist programmes are usually offered in practical or applied disciplines and vary in length from one to two years. A Master is conferred after two years of study. The Doctorate is awarded after two to five years' postgraduate specialization study and the defence of a thesis.

ADMISSION TO HIGHER EDUCATION

Admission to university-level studies:

Name of secondary school credential required: Bachillerato

Minimum score/requirement: 50

Admission requirements: IFCES

Foreign students admission:

Admission requirements: Students must hold a secondary school leaving certificate equivalent to the Diploma de Bachiller and must sit for a state examination.

Entry regulations: Foreign students must hold a visa, a health certificate and warrant financial guarantees.

Language proficiency: Students must have a good knowledge of Spanish.

RECOGNITION OF STUDIES

Quality assurance system:

The quality assurance system of higher education comprises 3 interrelated elements: information (SNIES, ECAES, Labor Observatory for Education, SPADIES), evaluation (CNA), and promotion.

Bodies dealing with recognition:

Consejo Nacional de Acreditación - CNA (National Accreditation Council)

Calle 19 No 6-68 Piso 17
Bogotá
Tel: +57 (1) 341 1050
Fax: +57 (1) 341 1052
EMail: cna@cna.gov.co
WWW: http://www.cna.gov.co

NATIONAL BODIES

Ministerio de Educación Nacional (Ministry of Education)

Minister: Gina Parody
Calle 43 No. 57 - 14
Bogotá D.C.
Tel: +57 (1) 222 0206
Fax: +57 (1) 222 4953
EMail: SecrGeneral@mineducacion.gov.co
WWW: http://www.mineducacion.gov.co

Asociación Colombiana de Universidades - ASCUN (Association of Colombian Universities)

President: Jorge Humberto Pelaez Piedrahita
Executive Director: Carlos Hernando Forero Robayo
Calle 93 No 16 - 43
Bogota
Tel: +57 (1) 218 5127
Fax: +57 (1) 218 5098
EMail: secretaria@ascun.org.co
WWW: http://www.ascun.org.co

Consejo Nacional de Acreditación - CNA (National Accreditation Council)

Coordinator: Franco Alirio Vallejo Cabrera
Academic Coordinator: Luis Enrique Silva
Technical Secretary: Luz Amanda Viviescas
Calle 19 No 6-68 Piso 17
Bogotá
Tel: +57 (1) 341 1050
Fax: +57 (1) 341 1052
EMail: cna@cna.gov.co
WWW: http://www.cna.gov.co

Instituto Colombiano para la Evaluación de la Educación - ICFES (Colombian Institute for the Evaluation of Higher Education)

Director-General: Ximena Dueñas Herrera
Secretary-General: María Sofía Arango Arango
Calle 17 No. 3-40
Bogotá, D.C.
Tel: +57 (1) 489 7939
Fax: +57 (1) 338 7338
EMail: faxciudadano@icfes.gov.co
WWW: http://www.icfes.gov.co
Role of national body: A specialized body which is in charge of educational assessment at all educational levels and of the state exam for admission to higher education.

Data for academic year: 2015-2016
Source: IAU from the website of the Ministry of Education of Colombia, 2015.

INSTITUTIONS

PUBLIC INSTITUTIONS

ADMIRAL PADILLA NAVAL ACADEMY OF CADETS

Escuela Naval de Cadetes Almirante Padilla
Barrio Bosque, Sector Manzanillo, Cartagena
Tel: +57(5) 672-4610
EMail: atencionalciudadano@enap.edu.co
Website: http://www.escuelanaval.edu.co

Director: Antonio Jose Martinez Olmos

Programme
Administration (Administration); **Merchant Navy** (Marine Transport); **Nautical Science** (Nautical Science); **Postgraduate Studies** (International Relations; Marine Science and Oceanography; Naval Architecture; Political Sciences; Transport Management)

History: Founded 1907.
Main Language(s) of Instruction: Spanish
Degrees and Diplomas: *Profesional Universitario*: **Administration; Marine Transport; Nautical Science.** *Especialización*:

International Relations; Political Sciences. *Maestría*: **Marine Science and Oceanography; Naval Architecture; Transport Management.**

Student Services: Library
Last Updated: 10/11/15

ANTONIO JOSÉ CAMACHO UNIVERSITY INSTITUTION

Institución Universitaria Antonio José Camacho (UNIAJC)

Avenida 6N No 28N-102 A.A. 25663, Cali
Valle del Cauca
Tel: +57(2) 665-2828
Fax: +57(2) 556-9475
EMail: comunicaciones@admon.uniajc.edu.co; mercadeo@admon.uniajc.edu.co
Website: http://www.uniajc.edu.co

Rector: Hugo Alberto Gonzalez Lopez
Tel: +57(2) 665-2828 Ext. 4003 EMail: rectoria@itmajc.edu.co

Faculty
Administrative Sciences (Accountancy; Business Administration; International Business; Management; Marketing; Transport Management); **Distance and Virtual Education** (Health Administration; Occupational Health; Preschool Education); **Engineering** (Computer Engineering; Electronic Engineering; Industrial Engineering; Information Technology; Mechanical Engineering; Production Engineering; Telecommunications Engineering); **Social and Human Sciences** (Anthropology; Graphic Design; Social Work; Visual Arts)

Programme
Postgraduate Studies (Electronic Engineering; Energy Engineering; Telecommunications Engineering; Telecommunications Services)

Centre
Language (English; Foreign Languages Education; French)

History: Founded 1993 as Instituto Tecnológico Municipal Antonio José Camacho. Acquired present title and status 2007.

Main Language(s) of Instruction: Spanish

Degrees and Diplomas: *Tecnólogo*; *Profesional Universitario*; *Especialización*: **Electronic Engineering; Energy Engineering; Telecommunications Engineering; Telecommunications Services.** Also Licenciatura in Preschool Education
Last Updated: 07/10/15

CAPITAIN JOSÉ EDMUNDO SANDOVAL POSTGRADUATE SCHOOL OF THE COLOMBIAN AIRFORCE

Escuela Postgrados de la Fuerza Aerea Colombiana Capitan Jose Edmundo Sandoval (EPFAC)

Carrera 11, 102-50, Edificio ESDEGUE, Of. 412, Bogotá
Tel: +57(1) 620-4066
EMail: loqisticaaeronautica@epfac.edu.co
Website: https://www.epfac.edu.co

Director: Gerber Johan Alzate Gutiérrez

Programme
Aeronautical Logistics (Aeronautical and Aerospace Engineering; Transport Management); **Military Aeronautics** (Aeronautical and Aerospace Engineering; Military Science); **Operational Safety** (Safety Engineering)

History: Founded 2002.

Main Language(s) of Instruction: Spanish

Degrees and Diplomas: *Especialización*: **Aeronautical and Aerospace Engineering; Safety Engineering; Transport Management.** *Maestría*: **Aeronautical and Aerospace Engineering; Safety Engineering; Transport Management.** Also Diplomas and Postgraduate Programme in Military Aeronautics
Last Updated: 29/09/15

CARO Y CUERVO INSTITUTE

Instituto Caro y Cuervo (ICC)

Calle 10, 4-69, Bogotá
Tel: +57(1) 342-2121
Fax: +57(1) 284-1248
EMail: casacuervo@caroycuervo.gov.co; contactenos@caroycuervo.gov.co
Website: http://www.caroycuervo.gov.co

Directora: Carmen Millán de Benavides
Tel: +57(1) 342-2121 Ext. 101
EMail: direcciongeneral@caroycuervo.gov.co; ecretariadireccion@caroycuervo.gov.co

Subdirectora administrativa y financiera: Margarita Lucía Castañeda Vargas
Tel: +57(1) 342-2121
EMail: margarita.castaneda@caroycuervo.gov.co

Programme
Ancient Greek (Greek (Classical)); **Classical Latin** (Latin); **Computational Language Analysis** (Linguistics); **Creative Writing** (Writing); **Linguistics** *(Postgraduate)* (Linguistics); **Linguistics** (Linguistics); **Literature and Culture** (Cultural Studies; Literature); **Publishing** (Publishing and Book Trade); **Spanish as a Foreign Language (ELE Diploma)** (Foreign Languages Education)

History: Founded 1942.

Main Language(s) of Instruction: Spanish

Degrees and Diplomas: *Maestría*: **Cultural Studies; Linguistics; Literature.** Also Diplomados

Student Services: eLibrary
Last Updated: 28/09/15

CENTRAL TECHNICAL INSTITUTE

Escuela Technológica Instituto Técnico Central (ETITIC)

Calle 13 No. 16-74, Bogotá
Tel: +57(1) 344-3000
Fax: +57(1) 344-3029
EMail: atencionalciudadano@itc.edu.co
Website: http://www.itc.edu.co

Rector: José Gregorio Contreras Fernández
Tel: +57(1) 344-3029 Ext. 109 EMail: rectoria@itc.edu.co

Secretario General: Heyde del Carmen Rodríguez Pérez
Tel: +57(1) 344-3029 Ext. 123 EMail: sgeneral@itc.edu.co

Programme
Computing Systems (Computer Engineering); **Electro-Mechanics** (Electronic Engineering; Mechanical Engineering); **Industrial Processes** (Industrial Engineering); **Machine Design** (Industrial Design); **Mechatronics** (Electronic Engineering); **Postgraduate Studies** (Computer Networks; Industrial Maintenance; Instrument Making)

History: Founded 1905. Acquired current status 2006.

Main Language(s) of Instruction: Spanish

Degrees and Diplomas: *Técnico Profesional*; *Tecnólogo*; *Profesional Universitario*; *Especialización*: **Computer Networks; Industrial Maintenance; Instrument Making.**

Student Services: Library
Last Updated: 01/10/15

CENTRAL UNIT OF THE VALLEY OF THE CAUCA REGION

Unidad Central del Valle del Cauca (UCEVA)

Ciudadela Universitaria, Carrera 27 A No. 48-144, Kilómetro 1 salida Sur, Tuluá, Valle del Cauca
Tel: +57(926) 224-2202
Fax: +57(926) 225-9051
EMail: info@uceva.edu.co
Website: http://www.uceva.edu.co

Rector: Jairo Gutiérrez Obando
Tel: +57(2) 224-2202 Ext. 147 EMail: rectoria@uceva.edu.co

Vicerrectora Administrativa y Financiera: Luz Mireya González
EMail: vicerrectoriadm@uceva.edu.co

Faculty
Administrative Sciences, Economics and Accountancy (Accountancy; Business Administration; International Business); **Educational Sciences** (Education; Foreign Languages Education; Parks and Recreation; Physical Education; Sports); **Engineering** (Agriculture; Computer Engineering; Electronic Engineering; Environmental Engineering; Environmental Studies; Industrial Engineering; Transport Management); **Health Sciences** (Medicine; Nursing); **Law and Humanities** (Law)

Programme
Postgraduate Studies (Constitutional Law; Safety Engineering); **Virtual and Distance Education** (Administration; Business and Commerce; Civil Engineering; Education; Electrical Engineering; Finance; Health Administration; Humanities and Social Science Education; Mathematics Education; Native Language Education)

History: Founded 1971.

Main Language(s) of Instruction: Spanish

Degrees and Diplomas: *Técnico Profesional*; *Tecnólogo*; *Profesional Universitario*; *Especialización*: **Constitutional Law.** Also Especialización in Safety Engineering offered through Universidad Tecnológica de Pereira (UTP); Licenciatura

Student Services: Library

Last Updated: 21/10/15

DEPARTMENTAL INSTITUTE OF FINE ARTS

Instituto Departamental de Bellas Artes (BELLAS ARTES-CALI)

Avenida 2 Norte 7N -38, Cali, Valle del Cauca
Tel: +57(923) 688-3333
Fax: +57(923) 668-5583
EMail: bellasartes@bellasartes.edu.co
Website: http://www.bellasartes.edu.co

Rector: Ramón Daniel Espinosa Rodriguez
Tel: +57(923) 688-3333 Ext. 113
EMail: rector.bellasartescali@bellasartes.edu.co

Vicerrector Administrativo y Financiero: Gustavo Adolfo Díaz
Tel: +57(923) 620-3333 Ext. 312
EMail: vice.administrativo@bellasartes.edu.co

Vicerrectora Académica y de Investigaciones: Dora Inés Restrepo Patiño
Tel: +57(923) 688-3333 Ext. 200
EMail: vice.academica@bellasartes.edu.co

Faculty
Theatre (Acting; Theatre); **Visual and Applied Arts** (Fine Arts; Graphic Design; Painting and Drawing; Visual Arts)

Conservatory
Music *(Antonio María Valencia)* (Music; Musical Instruments; Singing)

History: Founded 1936, acquired present status 1992.

Academic Year: February to December (February-June; August-December)

Admission Requirements: Secondary school certificate (Bachillerato) and entrance examination (ICFES test)

Fees: 258.000-451.000 per annum (Colombian Peso)

Main Language(s) of Instruction: Spanish

Accrediting Agency: Consejo Nacional de Acreditación; Ministry of Education

Degrees and Diplomas: *Profesional Universitario*: **Fine Arts; Graphic Design; Visual Arts.** Also Licenciatura in Theatre

Student Services: Academic Counselling, Canteen, Library, Sports Facilities

Publications: Neocomics Magazine; Papel Escena Mazagine

Last Updated: 08/10/15

DIEGO LUIS CÓRDOBA TECHNOLOGICAL UNIVERSITY OF CHOCÓ

Universidad Tecnológica del Chocó Diego Luis Córdoba (UTCH)

A.A. 292, Cra. 22 No 18B-10 B/ Nicolás Medrano, Ciudadela Universitaria, Quibdó, Chocó
Tel: +57(4) 672-6565
Fax: +57(4) 710-274
EMail: utch@utch.edu.co; contactenos@utch.edu.co
Website: http://www.utch.edu.co

Rector: Eduardo Antonio García Vega
Tel: +57(4) 672-6565 Ext. 300/3001
EMail: rectoria@utch.edu.co; eduardo.garcia@utch.edu.co

Secretario General: Edwin Ethiel Aragon Lozano
EMail: a-edwin.aragon@utch.edu.co

Vicerrector Administrativo: Elkin Moisès Chaverra
EMail: a-elkin.chaverra@utch.edu.co

International Relations: Rebecca Gindele
Tel: +57) 3016451125 EMail: rebecca.gindele@utch.edu.co

Faculty
Arts and Affiliated Discipline (Architecture); **Economics, Administrative Sciences and Accountancy** (Accountancy; Business Administration; Hotel Management; Management; Tourism); **Educational Sciences** (Art Education; English; Foreign Languages Education; French; Humanities and Social Science Education; Linguistics; Literature; Mathematics; Parks and Recreation; Physical Education; Physics; Science Education; Sports); **Engineering** (Agricultural Engineering; Civil Engineering; Computer Engineering; Environmental Engineering; Environmental Management; Mining Engineering; Telecommunications Engineering); **Health Sciences** (Nursing); **Law and Political Sciences** (Law); **Natural and Exact Sciences** (Biology); **Social Sciences and Humanities** (Social Work)

Research Group
Biotechnology and Plant Genetic Resources; Foreign Languages Education; Natural Resources for Territorial Development (Natural Resources)

History: Founded 1975

Academic Year: February to December (February-July; August-December)

Admission Requirements: Secondary school certificate (bachillerato) and entrance examination

Main Language(s) of Instruction: Spanish

Degrees and Diplomas: *Profesional Universitario*; *Especialización*: **Educational Technology; Family Studies; Humanities and Social Science Education.** *Maestría*: **Education; Foreign Languages Education.** Also Licenciatura; Especialización in Law, Administrative Law and Maestría in Linguitics and Business Administration offered through agreements with other institutions.

Student Services: Library

Last Updated: 30/10/15

FRANCISCO DE PAULA SANTANDER UNIVERSITY

Universidad Francisco de Paula Santander (UFPS)

Edificio Torre Administrativa, Avenida Gran Colombia No. 12E-96, Barrio Colsag, Cúcuta, Norte de Santander
Tel: +57(7) 577-6655
Fax: +57(975) 753-893
EMail: oficinadeprensa@ufps.edu.co
Website: http://www.ufps.edu.co

Rectora: Claudia Elizabeth Toloza Martínez
Tel: +57(7) 577-6655 Ext. 317-318 EMail: rectoria@ufps.edu.co

Vicerrectora Administrativa: Jorge Sánchez Molina
Tel: +57(7) 577-6655 Ext.315
EMail: viceadministrativa@ufps.edu.co

Secretaria General: Adriana Rodriguez Lizcano
Tel: +57(7) 575-2920 Ext. 217
EMail: adrianarodriguez@ufps.edu.co

Faculty

Agricultural and Environmental Sciences (Agricultural Engineering; Agriculture; Agronomy; Animal Husbandry; Biotechnology; Environmental Engineering; Food Technology); **Basic Sciences** (Natural Sciences); **Business Administration** (Accountancy; Business Administration; International Business); **Education, Arts and Humanities** (Architecture; Law; Mass Communication; Mathematics Education; Social Work); **Engineering** (Civil Engineering; Computer Engineering; Electronic Engineering; Industrial Engineering; Mechanical Engineering; Mining Engineering); **Health Sciences** (Nursing)

Division

Distance Education (Business and Commerce; Computer Science; Finance; Pharmacy); **Postgraduate Studies** (Business Administration; Development Studies; Economics; Educational and Student Counselling; Educational Technology; Higher Education Teacher Training; Management; Materials Engineering; Occupational Health; Safety Engineering; Vocational Counselling)

Further Information: Branches in Ocaña and Chinácota

History: Founded 1962 as a private institution, recognized by the State 1970. Financed by the national, provincial, and local governments.

Academic Year: February to December (February-June; August-December)

Admission Requirements: Secondary school certificate (bachillerato) and entrance examination

Main Language(s) of Instruction: Spanish

Degrees and Diplomas: *Técnico Profesional*; *Tecnólogo*; *Profesional Universitario*: **Accountancy; Agricultural Engineering; Agriculture; Agronomy; Animal Husbandry; Architecture; Biotechnology; Business Administration; Civil Engineering; Computer Engineering; Electronic Engineering; Environmental Engineering; Industrial Engineering; International Business; Law; Mass Communication; Mechanical Engineering; Mining Engineering; Natural Sciences; Nursing; Social Work.** *Especialización*: **Business Administration; Economics; Educational and Student Counselling; Educational Technology; Higher Education Teacher Training; Management; Occupational Health; Safety Engineering; Vocational Counselling.** *Maestría*: **Business Administration; Development Studies; Materials Engineering.** Also Licenciatura

Student Services: Cultural Activities, Health Services, Sports Facilities

Publications: Oriente Universitario

Last Updated: 02/11/15

OCAÑA BRANCH
SECCIONAL OCAÑA (UFPSO)

Vía Acolsure, Sede el Algodonal,
Ocaña, Norte de Santander 546552
Tel: +57(7) 569-0088
EMail: info@ufpso.edu.co
Website: https://ufpso.edu.co

Director: Edgar Antonio Sánchez Ortiz
Tel: +57(97) 561-0066 EMail: dirección@ufpso.edu.co

Secretario General: Edwin Edgardo Espinel Blanco
Tel: +57(97) 569-0088
EMail: secretariageneral@ufpso.edu.co; eeespinelb@ufpso.edu.co

International Relations: Olga Yurith Carrascal Salazar, Jefe, Oficina de Relaciones Internacionales
EMail: oycarrascals@ufpso.edu.co

Faculty

Administrative Sciences and Economics (Accountancy; Business Administration; Business and Commerce; Finance); **Agricultural and Environmental Sciences** (Agricultural Engineering; Agriculture; Animal Husbandry; Environmental Studies); **Education, Arts and Humanities** (Arts and Humanities; Law; Mass Communication; Mathematics; Physics); **Engineering** (Civil Engineering; Computer Engineering; Mechanical Engineering)

School

Fine Arts *(Jorge Pacheco Quintero)* (Cinema and Television; Dance; Fine Arts; Musical Instruments)

History: Founded 1974.

Main Language(s) of Instruction: Spanish

Degrees and Diplomas: *Técnico Profesional*; *Tecnólogo*; *Profesional Universitario*; *Especialización*: **Civil Engineering; Educational Technology; Systems Analysis.** Also Diplomados; Licenciatura

Student Services: Library

FRANCISCO JOSÉ DE CALDAS DISTRICT UNIVERSITY

Universidad Distrital Francisco José de Caldas (UDISTRITAL)

Carrera 7 No. 40B-53, Bogotá
Tel: +57(1) 323-9300 57(1) 323-8400
Fax: +57(1) 310-5235
EMail: admisiones@udistrital.edu.co
Website: http://www.udistrital.edu.co

Rector: Carlos Javier Mosquera Suárez
Tel: +57(1) 288-1960 Ext. 1001 EMail: rectoria@udistrital.edu.co

Secretario General: Jose David Rivera Escobar
Tel: +57(1) 323-8333
EMail: sgral@udistrital.edu.co; websgral@udistrital.edu.co

Vicerrector Administrativo y Financiero: Vladimir Salazar Arévalo
Tel: +57(1) 323-9300 Ext.1804
EMail: vicerrecadmin@udistrital.edu.co

International Relations: Ivet Marli Castañeda Rodriguez
Tel: +57(1) 323-9300 Ext. 1010
EMail: convenios-ceri@udistrital.edu.co

Faculty

Arts (Dance; Fine Arts; Music; Theatre; Visual Arts); **Engineering** (Automation and Control Engineering; Bioengineering; Computer Engineering; Electrical Engineering; Electronic Engineering; Engineering; Geological Engineering; Hygiene; Industrial Engineering; Occupational Health; Production Engineering; Road Engineering; Safety Engineering; Surveying and Mapping; Telecommunications Engineering; Transport Management); **Environmental Sciences and Natural Resources** (Agricultural Engineering; Development Studies; Environmental Engineering; Environmental Studies; Forestry; Natural Resources; Sanitary Engineering; Sports Management; Transport and Communications); **Sciences and Education** (Applied Linguistics; Art Education; Child Care and Development; Communication Studies; Cultural Studies; Education; Environmental Management; Foreign Languages Education; Humanities and Social Science Education; Mathematics; Mathematics Education; Native Language Education; Pedagogy; Primary Education; Science Education; Technology Education); **Technology** (Technology)

History: Founded 1948 under the authority of the municipality of Bogotá. Nationally recognized as an official University 1963.

Academic Year: February to December (February-June; August-December)

Admission Requirements: Secondary school certificate (bachillerato) and entrance examination

Main Language(s) of Instruction: Spanish

Degrees and Diplomas: *Tecnólogo*; *Profesional Universitario*: **Agricultural Engineering; Automation and Control Engineering; Civil Engineering; Computer Engineering; Dance; Electrical Engineering; Environmental Engineering; Environmental Management; Fine Arts; Industrial Engineering; Mathematics; Mechanical Engineering; Music; Performing Arts; Power Engineering; Production Engineering; Sanitary Engineering; Sports Management; Surveying and Mapping; Telecommunications Engineering; Visual Arts.** *Especialización*: **Automation and Control Engineering; Bioengineering; Child Care and Development; Computer Science; Cultural Studies; Development Studies; Education; Engineering Management; Environmental Management; Environmental Studies; Hygiene; Industrial Engineering; Mass Communication; Mathematics Education; Media Studies; Modern Languages; Natural Resources; Occupational Health; Pedagogy; Production Engineering; Road Engineering; Safety Engineering; Software Engineering; Surveying and Mapping; Technology Education; Telecommunications Engineering;**

Transport and Communications; Transport Management. *Maestría*: **Applied Linguistics; Communication Studies; Development Studies; Education; Environmental Management; Fine Arts; Foreign Languages Education; Forestry; Industrial Engineering; Information Technology; Native Language Education; Social Studies; Technology Education; Telecommunications Engineering.** *Doctorado*: **Education; Engineering.** Also Licenciatura

Student Services: Library
Last Updated: 24/11/15

HIGHER COLLEGE OF ANTIOQUIA

Colegio Mayor de Antioquia
Carrera 78, No 65-46, Medellín, Antioquia
Tel: +57(4) 444-5611 Ext. 101
Fax: +57(4) 421-9947
EMail: colmayor@colmayor.edu.co
Website: http://www.colmayor.edu.co

Rector: Bernardo Arteaga Velásquez
Tel: +57(4) 444-5611 Ext. 181 EMail: rectoria@colmayor.edu.co

Faculty
Administration (Business Administration; Cooking and Catering; Tourism); **Architecture and Engineering** (Architecture; Architecture and Planning; Civil Engineering; Construction Engineering; Environmental Engineering); **Health Sciences** (Biochemistry; Biotechnology; Laboratory Techniques; Microbiology); **Social Sciences** (Social and Community Services; Social Work)

History: Founded 1945 as Colegio Mayor de Cultura Feminina de Antioquia. Acquired present status 1980.

Fees: Undergraduate programmes, 523,100-3,179,200 per semester; Postgraduate programmes, 3,325,150 per semester (Colombian Peso)

Main Language(s) of Instruction: Spanish

Degrees and Diplomas: *Técnico Profesional*; *Profesional Universitario*; *Especialización*: **Construction Engineering.** *Maestría*: **Biochemistry.**

Student Services: Library
Last Updated: 24/09/15

HIGHER COLLEGE OF CAUCA

Colegio Mayor del Cauca (COLMAYOR)
Carrera 5, No 5-40, Claustro de la Encarnación, Popayán, Cauca
Tel: +57(2) 824-0562
Fax: +57(2) 822-0022
EMail: institucional@unimayor.edu.co; admision@unimayor.edu.co
Website: http://www.colmayorcauca.edu.co

Rectora: Paola Andrea Umaña Aedo
EMail: rectoria@colmayor.edu.co

Vicerector Académico: Ricardo Riomalo Rivera
Tel: +57(5) 824-1109 Ext. 104
EMail: academica@unimayor.edu.co

Secretario General: Víctor Andrés Rodríguez Parra

Faculty
Art and Design (Architecture; Design; Visual Arts); **Engineering** (Engineering; Software Engineering); **Social Sciences and Administration** (Business Administration; Business and Commerce; Finance; Management; Marketing)

History: Founded 1967. Acquired present status 2008.

Main Language(s) of Instruction: Spanish

Degrees and Diplomas: *Técnico Profesional*; *Profesional Universitario*; *Especialización*: **Data Processing; Information Management; Management.**

Last Updated: 24/09/15

HIGHER COLLEGE OF MUSIC OF TOLIMA

Conservatorio del Tolima
Calle 9, No 1-18, Ibagué, Tolima
Tel: +57(8) 261-8526 +57(8) 263-9139
Fax: +57(8) 261-5378 +57(8) 262-5355
EMail: info@conservatoriodeltolima.edu.co
Website: http://www.conservatoriodeltolima.edu.co

Rector: James Enrique Fernández Córdoba
EMail: rectoria@conservatoriodeltolima.edu.co

Secretaría General: Hilda Carolina Giraldo Rubio
EMail: sec.general@conservatoriodeltolima.edu.co

Faculty
Education and Arts (Arts and Humanities; Music Education)

School
Music (Dance; Jazz and Popular Music; Music; Musical Instruments)

History: Founded 1909 as Escuela de Música. Acquired present title 1987.

Fees: 242,000-410,000 per semester (Colombian Peso)

Main Language(s) of Instruction: Spanish

Degrees and Diplomas: *Profesional Universitario*. Also Licenciatura (Teacher Training Degree) in Music Education

Student Services: Cultural Activities, Health Services, Library, Sports Facilities

Last Updated: 24/09/15

INDUSTRIAL UNIVERSITY OF SANTANDER

Universidad Industrial de Santander (UIS)
Carrera 27 Calle 9, Ciudad Universitaria, Bucaramanga, Santander
Tel: +57(7) 634-4000
EMail: rectoria@uis.edu.co
Website: http://www.uis.edu.co

Rector: Alvaro Ramírez García
Tel: +57(7) 634-3655 Ext. 2425
EMail: rectoria@uis.edu.co; argarcia@uis.edu.co

Secretaria General: Olga Cecilia González Noriega
EMail: sgeneral@uis.edu.co

Vicerrector Administrativo: Luis Carlos Gómez Flórez
Tel: +57(7) 645-7046
EMail: lcgomezf@uis.edu.co; lbecerra@uis.edu.co

International Relations: Viatcheslav Kafarov, Director, Relaciones Exteriores
Tel: +57(7) 632-0615 Ext. 2121
EMail: relext1@uis.edu.co; direlext@uis.edu.co

Faculty
Health Sciences (Dietetics; Gynaecology and Obstetrics; Health Sciences; Laboratory Techniques; Medicine; Microbiology; Natural Sciences; Nursing; Nutrition; Paediatrics; Pathology; Physical Therapy; Psychiatry and Mental Health; Public Health; Surgery; Virology); **Human Sciences** (Administration; Economics; Education; Fine Arts; History; Law; Modern Languages; Music; Philosophy; Physical Education; Political Sciences; Social Work; Sports); **Physicochemical Engineering** (Chemical Engineering; Engineering; Geology; Materials Engineering; Metallurgical Engineering; Petroleum and Gas Engineering); **Physicomechanical Engineering** (Business Administration; Civil Engineering; Computer Engineering; Computer Science; Electrical Engineering; Electronic Engineering; Engineering; Industrial Design; Industrial Engineering; Industrial Management; Mechanical Engineering; Telecommunications Engineering); **Sciences** (Biology; Chemistry; Mathematics; Physics)

Institute
Distance Education (Agricultural Business; Business Administration; Criminology; Justice Administration; Management; Pharmacy; Visual Arts)

Campus
Barbosa (Chemical Engineering; Civil Engineering; Electrical Engineering; Electronic Engineering; Industrial Engineering; Mechanical Engineering; Petroleum and Gas Engineering); **Barrancabermeja** (Chemical Engineering; Civil Engineering; Electrical Engineering; Electronic Engineering; Industrial Engineering; Mechanical Engineering; Petroleum and Gas Engineering); **Málaga** (Agricultural Engineering; Animal Husbandry; Chemical Engineering; Civil Engineering; Electrical Engineering; Electronic Engineering; Forestry; Industrial Engineering; Mechanical Engineering;

Petroleum and Gas Engineering); **Socorro** (Chemical Engineering; Civil Engineering; Electrical Engineering; Electronic Engineering; Industrial Engineering; Mechanical Engineering; Petroleum and Gas Engineering; Tourism)
History: Founded 1948.
Academic Year: February to December (February-June; August-December)
Admission Requirements: Secondary school certificace (bachillerato) and entrance examination
Main Language(s) of Instruction: Spanish
Accrediting Agency: Consejo Nacional de Acreditación
Degrees and Diplomas: *Tecnólogo*; *Profesional Universitario*: **Agricultural Engineering; Animal Husbandry; Archiving; Art Education; Biology; Chemical Engineering; Chemistry; Civil Engineering; Computer Engineering; Dietetics; Economics; Electrical Engineering; Electronic Engineering; Foreign Languages Education; Forestry; Geology; History; Humanities and Social Science Education; Industrial Design; Industrial Engineering; Law; Mathematics; Mechanical Engineering; Medicine; Metallurgical Engineering; Microbiology; Music Education; Native Language Education; Nursing; Nutrition; Petroleum and Gas Engineering; Philosophy; Physical Therapy; Physics; Science Education; Social Work; Tourism.** *Especialización*: **Anaesthesiology; Chemistry; Development Studies; Electrical Engineering; Environmental Engineering; Food Science; Forestry; Gynaecology and Obstetrics; Health Administration; Heating and Refrigeration; Higher Education Teacher Training; Industrial Management; Maintenance Technology; Management; Marketing; Medicine; Nursing; Nutrition; Ophthalmology; Orthopaedics; Paediatrics; Pathology; Petroleum and Gas Engineering; Plastic Surgery; Public Administration; Safety Engineering; Statistics; Surgery; Telecommunications Engineering; Transport Management.** *Maestría*: **Biology; Biomedicine; Chemical Engineering; Chemistry; Civil Engineering; Communication Studies; Computer Engineering; Development Studies; Economics; Education; Electrical Engineering; Electronic Engineering; Engineering Management; Environmental Engineering; Epidemiology; Geological Engineering; Geology; Geophysics; History; Human Rights; Industrial Engineering; Law; Maintenance Technology; Management; Materials Engineering; Mathematics; Mathematics Education; Mechanical Engineering; Native Language Education; Petroleum and Gas Engineering; Philosophy; Physical Therapy; Physics; Power Engineering; Public Administration; Public Health; Telecommunications Engineering.** *Doctorado*: **Biomedicine; Chemical Engineering; Chemistry; Electrical Engineering; Electronic Engineering; Engineering Management; History; Materials Engineering; Natural Sciences.** Also MBA; Licenciatura; Technological degrees are offered through distance mode
Student Services: Academic Counselling, Cultural Activities, Health Services, Language Laboratory, Library, Social Counselling, Sports Facilities
Publications: Boletín de Geología; Medical UIS; Revista de Humanidades; Revista de Investigaciones; Revista de Medicina; Revista ION
Publishing House: Centro de Publicaciones, UIS
Last Updated: 04/11/15

INSTITUTE OF PROFESSIONAL TECHNICAL EDUCATION OF ROLDANILLO

Instituto de Educación Técnica Profesional de Roldanillo (INTEP)

Carrera 7 No 10-20, Roldanillo, Valle del Cauca
Tel: +57(92) 229-8586
Fax: +57(92) 229-7226
EMail: secregeneral@intep.edu.co
Website: http://www.intep.edu.co

Rector: Germán Colonia Alcalde
Tel: +57() 229-8586 Ext. 105 EMail: rectoria@intep.edu.co

Secretaría General: Amparo Sanchez Gutierrez

Unit
Administration and Accounting (Accountancy; Business Administration); **Agricultural and Environmental Sciences** (Agricultural Business; Agricultural Management; Agriculture; Environmental Management; Environmental Studies); **Systems and Electrical Engineering** (Computer Graphics; Computer Science; Graphic Design; Information Technology)

Centre
Languages (English)

Fees: 455.555-650.794 per annum (Colombian Peso)
Main Language(s) of Instruction: Spanish
Degrees and Diplomas: *Técnico Profesional*; *Tecnólogo*; *Profesional Universitario*
Student Services: Health Services, Library, Sports Facilities
Last Updated: 08/10/15

JAIME ISAZA CADAVID COLOMBIAN POLYTECHNIC

Politécnico Colombiano Jaime Isaza Cadavid

Apartado aéro 4932,
Carrera 48 No 7-151 El Poblado, Medellin, Antioquia
Tel: +57(94) 319-7900
Fax: +57(94) 266-3635
EMail: admisiones@elpoli.edu.co
Website: http://www.politecnicojic.edu.co

Rector: John Fernando Escobar Martínez
EMail: rectoria@elpoli.edu.co
Vicerrectora Administrativa: Martha Cecila Lasso Peña
EMail: vadministrativa@elpoli.edu.co
Secretario General: Luquegi Gil Neira
International Relations: Catalina Maria Restrepo Gutierrez, Directora de Cooperación Nacional e Internacional
Tel: +57(94) 319-7959 EMail: cooperación@elpoli.edu.co

Faculty
Administration (Accountancy; Administration; Air Transport; Business Administration; Industrial Management; Information Sciences; Public Administration; Tourism; Transport Management); **Agricultural Sciences** (Agriculture; Farm Management); **Audiovisual Communication** (Radio and Television Broadcasting); **Engineering** (Accountancy; Agricultural Engineering; Automation and Control Engineering; Civil Engineering; Computer Engineering; Engineering; Information Technology; Occupational Health; Production Engineering; Safety Engineering; Sanitary Engineering); **Physical Education, Recreation and Sport** (Education; Parks and Recreation; Physical Education; Physical Therapy; Sports); **Social, Basic and Human Sciences** (Industrial Chemistry)
Further Information: Also Seccional Oriente (Rionegro), Urabá (Apartadó) and Convenio Bajo Cauca (Caucasia)
History: Founded 1964.
Main Language(s) of Instruction: Spanish
Degrees and Diplomas: *Técnico Profesional*; *Tecnólogo*; *Profesional Universitario*; *Especialización*: **Finance; Management; Occupational Health; Safety Engineering; Sanitary Engineering.** *Maestría*: **Animal Husbandry; Educational Sciences; Occupational Health; Physiology.** Also Licenciatura
Student Services: Library
Last Updated: 24/11/15

LA PAZ UNIVERSITY INSTITUTE

Instituto Universitario de La Paz (UNIPAZ)

Avenida Santander, Calle 9 No. 10-22,
Barrancabermeja, Santander
Tel: +57(976) 621-4049
Fax: +57(976) 621-5042
EMail: informacion@unipaz.edu.co; atencionalciudadano@unipaz.edu.co
Website: http://www.unipaz.edu.co

Rector: Oscar Orlando Porras Atencia
Tel: +57(310) 806-9280
EMail: rectoria@unipaz.edu.co
Vicerrectora: Kelly Cristina Torres Angulo
Tel: +57(311) 599-7869
EMail: vicerrectoria@unipaz.edu.co
Secretaria General: Jemnys Beltran Bacca
Tel: +57(300) 681-4314
EMail: secretaria.general@unipaz.edu.co

School
Agricultural Engineering (Agricultural Engineering); **Agro-Industrial Engineering** (Agricultural Business; Agricultural Engineering; Engineering; Industrial Engineering; Safety Engineering); **Environmental Engineering and Hygiene** (Civil Engineering; Environmental Engineering; Sanitary Engineering); **Production Engineering** (Electronic Engineering; Industrial Chemistry; Industrial Maintenance; Mechanical Engineering; Occupational Health; Packaging Technology; Production Engineering; Safety Engineering; Sanitary Engineering; Transport and Communications); **Sciences** (Art Education; Business Administration; Chemistry; Computer Engineering; International Business; Mass Communication; Social Work); **Veterinary Medicine and Zootechnics** (Animal Husbandry; Veterinary Science)

History: Founded 1987.

Main Language(s) of Instruction: Spanish

Accrediting Agency: ICFES

Degrees and Diplomas: *Técnico Profesional*; *Tecnólogo*; *Profesional Universitario*; *Especialización*: **Agricultural Business; Engineering; Food Technology; Industrial Maintenance; Packaging Technology; Safety Engineering; Transport Management.** Also Master in Innovation offered through an agreement with EAN University

Student Services: Academic Counselling, Cultural Activities, Health Services, IT Centre, Library, Social Counselling, Sports Facilities

Publications: Educación en Ciencia e Ingenieria

Last Updated: 09/11/15

METROPOLITAN TECHNOLOGICAL INSTITUTE

Instituto Tecnológico Metropolitano (ITM)

Campus Robledo, Calle 73, No 76A-354 Vía al Volador, Medellín, Antioquia
Tel: +57(4) 440-5100
Fax: +57(4) 440-5103
EMail: itm@itm.edu.co
Website: http://www.itm.edu.co

Rectora: Maria Victoria Mejia Orozco
Tel: +57(4) 440-5107
EMail: rector@itm.edu.co; marimejia@itm.edu.co

Secretaria General: Luz Patricia Tobón Rodríguez
Tel: +57(4) 440-5111 EMail: luztobon@itm.edu.co

International Relations: Sandra Julieth Muñoz Mejía, Directora Operativa - Cooperación y Relaciones Internacionales
Tel: +57(4) 440-5113 EMail: sandramuñoz@itm.edu.co

Faculty
Arts and Humanities (Industrial Design; Music Theory and Composition; Visual Arts); **Economics and Administrative Sciences** (Accountancy; Business Administration; Business and Commerce; Engineering Management; Finance; Industrial Management; Production Engineering; Safety Engineering); **Engineering** (Electronic Engineering; Information Technology; Mechanical Engineering; Systems Analysis; Telecommunications Engineering); **Exact and Applied Science** (Architecture; Biomedical Engineering; Medical Technology)

Programme
Postgraduate Studies (Automation and Control Engineering; Computer Engineering; Energy Engineering; Industrial Engineering; Natural Sciences; Social Studies; Technology)

History: Founded 1944 as Instituo Obrero Municipal. Became Universidad Obrera Municipal in the late 1940's and then Instituto de Cultura Popular in the 1960's. Acquired present title in the 1990's. Acquired present status 2005.

Academic Year: January to December

Admission Requirements: High school leaving certificate (Diploma de Bachiller), State Higher Education Entrance Examination (ICFES) and Institute's Entrance examination

Fees: 350,000 (Colombian Peso)

Main Language(s) of Instruction: Spanish

Accrediting Agency: Consejo Nacional de Acreditación (CNA), attached to the Ministry of Education

Degrees and Diplomas: *Tecnólogo*; *Especialización*: **Finance; Management.** *Maestría*: **Automation and Control Engineering; Computer Engineering; Energy Engineering; Industrial Engineering; Natural Sciences; Social Studies; Technology.**

Student Services: Academic Counselling, Careers Guidance, Cultural Activities, Facilities for disabled people, Foreign Studies Centre, Health Services, Language Laboratory, Library, Social Counselling, Sports Facilities

Publications: TechnoLógicas

Publishing House: Fondo Editorial ITM

Last Updated: 08/10/15

MILITARY EDUCATION CENTRE

Centro de Educacion Militar (CEMIL)

Calle 102 7-80, Usaquén "Cantón Norte", Bogota, Bogota D.C.
Tel: +57(1) 620-4985
Website: http://www.cemil.mil.co

Rector: Juvenal Diaz Mateus

School
Army Aviation (Military Science); **Artillery** (Military Science); **Cavalry** (Military Science); **Communications** (Communication Studies); **Human Rights and International Law** (Human Rights; International Law); **Infantry** (Military Science); **Integral International Mission Action** (Military Science); **Intelligence and Counterintelligence** (Protective Services); **Legal Affairs** (Law); **Logistics** (Transport Management); **Military Engineering** (Engineering); **Military Police** (Police Studies); **Riding** (Sports); **Support Service for Education** (Education); **Weapons and Services** (Military Science)

History: Founded 1999.

Main Language(s) of Instruction: Spanish

Degrees and Diplomas: *Técnico Profesional*; *Especialización*: **Environmental Management; Higher Education Teacher Training; Human Rights; International Law; Leadership; Military Science; Social and Community Services.**

Last Updated: 20/10/15

MILITARY ENGINEERING SCHOOL

Escuela de Ingenieros Militares (ESING)

Carrera 50, No. 18-06, Puente Aranda, Bogotá
Tel: +57(1) 446-9060 Ext.103
EMail: esing@ejercito.mil.co
Website: http://www.esing.mil.co

Rector: Ricardo Heriberto Roque Salcedo

Programme
Civil and Military Engineering *(Postgraduate)* (Civil Engineering; Military Science); **Civil Engineering** (Civil Engineering); **Construction Management** *(Postgraduate)* (Civil Engineering); **Explosive Technology** *(Postgraduate)* (Technology); **Risk Management and Development** *(Postgraduate)* (Safety Engineering); **Road and Airport Runway Engineering** *(Postgraduate)* (Civil Engineering; Road Engineering)

History: Founded 1983.

Main Language(s) of Instruction: Spanish

Degrees and Diplomas: *Profesional Universitario*; *Especialización*: **Civil Engineering; Construction Engineering; Military Science; Road Engineering; Technology.** *Maestría*: **Safety Engineering.**

Last Updated: 29/09/15

NATIONAL OPEN AND DISTANCE UNIVERSITY

Universidad Nacional Abierta y a Distancia (UNAD)

Calle 14 sur No.14-23, Bogotá, Cundinamarca 111511
Tel: +57(1) 344-3700
Fax: +57(1) 344-3700
EMail: atencionalusuario@unad.edu.co
Website: http://www.unad.edu.co

Rector: Jaime Alberto Leal Afanadro (2004-)
EMail: rectoria@unad.edu.co

Secretario General: Leonardo Sanchez
Tel: +57(1) 344-3700 Ext. 1502 EMail: sgeneral@unad.edu.co

International Relations: Patricia Illera Pacheco, Gerente de Relaciones Interinstitucionales
Tel: +57(1) 347-2523 +57(1) 346-0088
EMail: grelaciones@unad.edu.co; convenios@unad.edu.co

International Relations: Luigi Humberto López López Guzmán, Vicerrector de Relaciones Internacionales
Tel: +57(1) 334-3700 Ext. 1660 EMail: virel@unad.edu.co

International Relations: Adriana Lorena Bernal Fonseca, Gerente de Proyecto EMail: adriana.bernal@unad.edu.co

College

Agricultural and Environmental Sciences (Agronomy; Animal Husbandry; Environmental Engineering; Harvest Technology); **Basic Sciences, Technology and Engineering** (Computer Engineering; Electronic Engineering; Environmental Engineering; Food Technology; Industrial Engineering; Systems Analysis; Technology; Telecommunications Engineering); **Educational Sciences** (Bilingual and Bicultural Education; Foreign Languages Education; Mathematics Education; Natives Education; Pedagogy; Philosophy; Preschool Education; Teacher Trainers Education); **Management, Accountancy and Business Sciences** (Administration; Business and Commerce; Economics; Small Business; Transport Management); **Social Sciences, Art and Humanities** (Educational Sciences; Philosophy; Psychology; Sociology)

History: Founded 1981 as Unidad Universitaria del Sur de Bogotá. Acquired status of State institution 1997. Became an autonomous University 2006.

Academic Year: February to December (February-June; July-December)

Admission Requirements: Secondary school certificate (bachillerato) and entrance examination.

Main Language(s) of Instruction: Spanish

Accrediting Agency: Consejo Nacional de Acreditación (CNA)

Degrees and Diplomas: *Bachillerato*; *Tecnólogo*: **Agricultural Management; Agronomy; Animal Husbandry; Business and Commerce; Civil Engineering; Computer Networks; Electronic Engineering; Environmental Engineering; Food Technology; Horticulture; Industrial Engineering; Pharmacy; Software Engineering.** *Profesional Universitario*: **Administration; Agronomy; Child Care and Development; Classical Languages; Computer Engineering; Economics; Electronic Engineering; Environmental Engineering; Food Science; Industrial Engineering; Mathematics; Native Language; Pharmacy; Philosophy; Telecommunications Engineering; Veterinary Science.** *Especialización*: **Agricultural Management; Distance Education; Food Science; Humanities and Social Science Education; Information Management; Management; Marketing; Pedagogy; Public Administration; Veterinary Science.** *Maestría*: **Communication Studies; Development Studies; Information Management; Institutional Administration.** *Doctorado*. Also Licenciatura

Student Services: Academic Counselling, Cultural Activities, Facilities for disabled people, Foreign Studies Centre, IT Centre, Language Laboratory, Library, Social Counselling, Sports Facilities, eLibrary

Student Numbers *2015*: Total: c. 67
Last Updated: 24/11/15

NATIONAL PEDAGOGICAL UNIVERSITY

Universidad Pedagógica Nacional

Calle 72 No. 11-86, Bogotá
Tel: +57(1) 594-1894 +57(1) 347-1190
Fax: +57(1) 347-3535
EMail: informacion_upn@pedagogica.edu.co
Website: http://www.pedagogica.edu.co

Rector: Adolfo León Atehortua Cruz
Tel: +57(1) 594-1894 Ext.101 EMail: rector@pedagogica.edu.co

Vicerrector Académico: Luis Alberto Higuera Malaver
Tel: +57(1) 347-1190 Ext. 125/118
EMail: vad@pedagogica.edu.co; lahigueram@pedagogica.edu.co

Secretario General: Helberth Augusto Choachi González
Tel: +57(1) 594-1894 Ext. 116
EMail: hchoachi@pedagogica.edu.co; secretaria.general@uni.pedagogica.edu.co

International Relations: Lola Constanza Melo Salcedo, Jefe, Oficina de Relaciones Interinstitucionales
Tel: +57(1) 594-1720 +57(1) 594-1894 Ext. 105
EMail: oriupn@pedagogica.edu.co; lmelo@pedagogica.edu.co

Faculty

Education (Education; Educational Psychology); **Fine Arts** (Music Education); **Humanities** (Modern Languages; Social Sciences); **Physical Education** (Physical Education); **Science and Technology** (Biology; Chemistry; Mathematics; Physics; Technology)

History: Founded as School of Education 1936, became university for women 1955 and co-educational 1962. A State institution.

Academic Year: January to December (January-May; August-December)

Admission Requirements: Secondary school certificate (bachillerato) and entrance examination

Fees: According to parents' income

Main Language(s) of Instruction: Spanish, English, French

Degrees and Diplomas: *Especialización*: **Educational Sciences; Educational Technology; Mathematics Education; Pedagogy; Science Education; Special Education.** *Maestría*: **Education; Educational Sciences; Educational Technology; Foreign Languages Education; Mathematics Education; Primary Education; Science Education; Social Studies.** *Doctorado*: **Education.** Also Licenciatura

Student Services: Academic Counselling, Canteen, Careers Guidance, Health Services, Library, Social Counselling, Sports Facilities

Publications: Revista Colombiana de Educación
Last Updated: 05/11/15

NATIONAL SCHOOL OF SPORTS

Escuela Nacional del Deporte

esq. Carrera 32A, Cl. 9 #84-5, Cali, Valle del Cauca
Tel: +57(2) 554-0404
Fax: +57(2) 554-0404 Ext. 117
EMail: edeporte@emcali.net.co; atencionalusuario@endeporte.edu.co
Website: http://www.endeporte.edu.co

Rector: José Fernando Arroyo Valencia
Tel: +57(2) 554-0404 Ext. 107 EMail: rectoria@endeporte.edu.co

Programme

Business Administration (Business Administration); **Nutrition and Dietetics** (Dietetics; Nutrition); **Occupational Therapy** (Occupational Therapy); **Physiotherapy** (Physical Therapy); **Postgraduate Studies** (Sports; Sports Management); **Professional Sports** (Sports); **Sports** *(Technological Studies)* (Sports)

History: Founded 1984.

Main Language(s) of Instruction: Spanish

Degrees and Diplomas: *Tecnólogo*; *Profesional Universitario*; *Especialización*: **Sports; Sports Management.**

Student Services: Library
Last Updated: 30/09/15

NATIONAL UNIVERSITY OF COLOMBIA

Universidad Nacional de Colombia (UNAL)

Carrera 45 No 26-85 - Edificio Uriel Gutiérrez, Bogotá
Tel: +57(1) 316-5000, Ext.18220
Fax: +57(1) 316-5000, Ext.18220
EMail: dirori@unal.edu.co
Website: http://www.bogota.unal.edu.co

Rector: Ignacio Mantilla Prada (2012-)
Tel: +57(1) 316-5387
EMail: rectoriaun@unal.edu.co; rectoria@unal.edu.co

Secretaria General: Catalina Ramírez Gómez
Tel: +57(1) 316-5280 EMail: secgener@unal.edu.co

Vicerrector Sede Bogotá: Diego Fernando Hernández Losada
Tel: +57(1) 316-5000 Ext. 13552 EMail: dfhernandezl@unal.edu.co

International Relations: Catalina Arévalo Ferro, Directora, Relaciones Exteriores
Tel: +57(1) 316-5000 Ext. 18291 EMail: dirori@unal.edu.co

Faculty

Agricultural Sciences (Agriculture; Agronomy; Rural Planning); **Arts** (Architecture; Cinema and Television; Graphic Design; Industrial Design; Music; Town Planning; Visual Arts); **Economics** (Accountancy; Administration; Economics); **Engineering** (Agricultural Engineering; Chemical Engineering; Civil Engineering; Computer Engineering; Electrical and Electronic Engineering; Electronic Engineering; Engineering; Industrial Engineering; Mechanical Engineering; Systems Analysis); **Humanities** (Anthropology; Arts and Humanities; English; French; Geography (Human); German; History; Linguistics; Literature; Modern Languages; Philology; Philosophy; Psychology; Social Work; Sociology; Spanish); **Law and Political and Social Sciences** (Law; Political Sciences; Social Sciences); **Medicine** (Biochemistry; Communication Studies; Gynaecology and Obstetrics; Medical Technology; Medicine; Molecular Biology; Nutrition; Occupational Health; Physical Therapy; Physiology; Psychiatry and Mental Health; Public Health; Rehabilitation and Therapy; Surgery; Toxicology; Treatment Techniques); **Nursing** (Nursing; Public Health); **Odontology** (Dentistry; Health Sciences; Natural Sciences; Public Health); **Sciences** (Biology; Chemistry; Earth Sciences; Mathematics; Natural Sciences; Pharmacy; Physics; Statistics); **Veterinary Medicine and Animal Husbandry** (Animal Husbandry; Veterinary Science)

Institute

Biotechnology (Biotechnology; Mathematics; Natural Sciences); **Communication and Cultural Studies** *(IECO)* (Communication Studies; Cultural Studies); **Environmental Studies** *(IDEA)* (Environmental Management); **Food Science and Technology** *(ICTA)* (Food Technology; Health Sciences; Mathematics; Natural Sciences); **Genetics** (Genetics; Mathematics; Natural Sciences); **Political Studies** *(IEPRI)* (International Relations; Law; Political Sciences); **Urban Studies** (Architecture; Town Planning; Urban Studies)

Centre

Agriculture *(Marengo)* (Agriculture)

History: Founded 1867 as Universidad Nacional de los Estados Unidos de Colombia, the university was granted autonomy by the government 1935.

Academic Year: February to December (February-June; August-December)

Admission Requirements: Secondary school certificate (bachillerato) and entrance examination

Main Language(s) of Instruction: Spanish

Accrediting Agency: Consejo Nacional de Acreditación

Degrees and Diplomas: *Profesional Universitario*: **Agriculture; Architecture; Arts and Humanities; Business Administration; Education; Engineering; Fine Arts; Health Sciences; Law; Mathematics; Natural Sciences; Performing Arts; Social Sciences.** *Especialización*: **Administrative Law; Anaesthesiology; Art Education; Computer Engineering; Criminal Law; Dentistry; Dermatology; Electrical Engineering; Endocrinology; Epidemiology; Food Science; Food Technology; Gastroenterology; Gerontology; Gynaecology and Obstetrics; Haematology; Medicine; Neurology; Nursing; Occupational Health; Oncology; Ophthalmology; Orthodontics; Orthopaedics; Otorhinolaryngology; Paediatrics; Pathology; Peace and Disarmament; Periodontics; Physical Therapy; Plastic Surgery; Pneumology; Political Sciences; Private Law; Psychiatry and Mental Health; Public Administration; Radiology; Rehabilitation and Therapy; Rheumatology; Statistics; Stomatology; Surgery; Urology; Veterinary Science.** *Maestría*: **Accountancy; Administration; Agricultural Business; Agricultural Engineering; Agriculture; Animal Husbandry; Anthropology; Applied Mathematics; Archaeology; Architecture; Art History; Art Therapy; Astronomy and Space Science; Automation and Control Engineering; Biochemistry; Bioengineering; Biology; Biomedical Engineering; Botany; Chemical Engineering; Chemistry; Computer Engineering; Computer Science; Conducting; Construction Engineering; Criminal Law; Design; Economics; Education; Entomology; Environmental Studies; Epidemiology; Finance; Food Science; Food Technology; Genetics; Geology; Geophysics; Industrial Engineering; Law; Literature; Materials Engineering; Mathematics; Mechanical Engineering; Medical Technology; Meteorology; Modern Languages; Museum Studies; Music Education; Neurosciences; Nursing; Occupational Health; Pharmacology; Pharmacy; Philosophy; Physics; Physiology; Plant Pathology; Political Sciences; Psychology; Public Administration; Public Health; Regional Planning; Science Education; Social and Preventive Medicine; Sociology; Statistics; Surveying and Mapping; Telecommunications Engineering; Town Planning; Toxicology; Tropical Medicine; Urban Studies; Veterinary Science; Writing.** *Doctorado*: **Aesthetics; Agriculture; Animal Husbandry; Anthropology; Archaeology; Art Criticism; Art History; Arts and Humanities; Biochemistry; Biology; Biotechnology; Botany; Chemical Engineering; Chemistry; Civil Engineering; Computer Engineering; Earth Sciences; Ecology; Economics; Electrical Engineering; Electronic Engineering; Entomology; Genetics; Horticulture; Industrial Engineering; Materials Engineering; Mathematics; Mechanical Engineering; Nursing; Pharmacy; Philosophy; Physics; Physiology; Plant Pathology; Psychology; Public Health; Social Sciences; Vegetable Production; Veterinary Science.**

Student Services: Academic Counselling, Careers Guidance, Cultural Activities, Foreign Studies Centre, Health Services, Language Laboratory, Library, Nursery Care, Social Counselling, Sports Facilities

Publications: Acta Bibliográfica; Agronomía Colombiana; Alimentos (ICTA); Anuario Colombiano de Historia; Anuario del Observatorio Astronómico Nacional; Boletín de Matemáticas; Caldasia (Natural Science); Cuadernos de Economía; Forma y Función (Philology and Languages); Geografía; Geología Colombiana; Ideas y Valores; Ingeniería e Investigación; Lozania (Natural Sciences); Maguaré (Anthropology); Mutisia (Natural Sciences); Revistas (Faculty publications)

Publishing House: Unibiblos

Last Updated: 04/11/15

LETICIA BRANCH

SEDE LETICIA

Kilometro 2 Via Tarapacá, Leticia, Amazonas
Tel: +57(8) 592-7996
Fax: +57(1) 316-5284
EMail: diramazonia_let@unal.edu.co
Website: http://www.imani.unal.edu.co

Director de Sede: Pablo Alberto Palacios
Tel: +57(8) 592-7996 Ext. 29802
EMail: Diramazonia_let@unal.edu.co

Jefe Administrativa: Maria del Rosario Ortiz
Tel: +57(8) 592-7996 Ext. 29803 EMail: mdrortizm@unal.edu.co

Secretaria: Myriam Daza
Tel: +57(8) 592-7996 Ext. 29805 EMail: mdazan@unal.edu.co

Programme

Amazon Studies (Latin American Studies)

History: Founded 1989. Acquired current status 1995.

Academic Year: February-June; August-December

Main Language(s) of Instruction: Spanish

Accrediting Agency: Consejo Nacional de Acreditación

Degrees and Diplomas: *Especialización*: **Latin American Studies.** *Maestría*: **Latin American Studies.** *Doctorado*: **Latin American Studies.**

Student Services: Academic Counselling, Careers Guidance, Cultural Activities, Foreign Studies Centre, Health Services, IT Centre, Language Laboratory, Library, Nursery Care, Social Counselling, Sports Facilities

MANIZALES BRANCH

SEDE MANIZALES

Cra 27 # 64-60 Manizales, Manizales, Caldas
Tel: +57(6) 887-9300
Fax: +57(6) 886-3990
EMail: sisqueresu_man@unal.edu.co
Website: http://www.manizales.unal.edu.co

Vicerrector de Sede: Germán Albeiro Castaño Duque
Tel: +57(6) 887-9300 Ext. 50100-50101
EMail: vicsede_man@unal.edu.co

Secretaria de Sede: Amparo Zapata Gómez
Tel: +57(6) 887-9300 Ext. 50107-50313
EMail: secsede_man@unal.edu.co

International Relations: Natalia Jaramillo García, Coordinadora, Relaciones Interinstitucionales
Tel: +57(6) 887-9300 Ext. 50333-50336
EMail: ori_man@unal.edu.co

Faculty
Administration (Arts and Humanities; Business Administration; Computer Science; Information Technology); **Engineerig and Architecture** (Architecture; Chemical Engineering; Civil Engineering; Construction Engineering; Electrical and Electronic Engineering; Industrial Engineering; Town Planning; Urban Studies); **Exact and Natural Sciences** (Mathematics; Natural Sciences; Physics)

Institute
Biotechnology and Agricultural Business (Agricultural Business; Biotechnology); **Environmental Studies** *(IDEA)* (Automation and Control Engineering; Business Administration; Chemical Engineering; Civil Engineering; Environmental Engineering; Environmental Studies; Hydraulic Engineering; Industrial Engineering; Sanitary Engineering)

Centre
Languages (Modern Languages)

History: Founded 1948.

Academic Year: February-June; August-December

Admission Requirements: Secondary school certificate and entrance examination

Main Language(s) of Instruction: Spanish

Degrees and Diplomas: *Profesional Universitario*: **Architecture; Art Management; Business Administration; Chemical Engineering; Civil Engineering; Electrical Engineering; Electronic Engineering; Engineering; Industrial Engineering; Information Technology; Mathematics; Physics.** *Especialización*: **Art Management; Business Administration; Computer Networks; Data Processing; Environmental Engineering; Finance; Hydraulic Engineering; Industrial Management; Management; Road Engineering; Sanitary Engineering; Structural Architecture; Transport Engineering.** *Maestría*: **Applied Mathematics; Automation and Control Engineering; Business Computing; Chemical Engineering; Civil Engineering; Electrical Engineering; Environmental Engineering; Hydraulic Engineering; Industrial Engineering; Physics; Science Education; Transport Engineering.** *Doctorado*: **Automation and Control Engineering; Chemical Engineering; Industrial Engineering.**

Student Services: Academic Counselling, Careers Guidance, Cultural Activities, Foreign Studies Centre, Health Services, Language Laboratory, Nursery Care, Social Counselling, Sports Facilities

MEDELLÍN BRANCH
SEDE MEDELLÍN
Calle 59 A N 63-20 Edif. 24, Medellín
Tel: +57(94) 430-6435
Fax: +57(94) 430-9502
EMail: comunicarq_med@unal.edu.co
Website: http://www.unalmed.edu.co

Vicerrector: John Willian Branch Bedoya
Tel: +57(4) 430-9502 +57(4) 430-9503
EMail: vicmedel@unal.edu.co; jwbranch@unal.edu.co

Secretario de Sede: Jorge Eliécer Córdoba Maquilón
Tel: +57(4) 430-9508 +57(4) 430-9509
EMail: secresed_med@unal.edu.co

International Relations: Paula Marcela Arias P.
Tel: +57(1) 316-5650 EMail: ori_bog@unal.edu.co

Faculty
Agricultural Sciences (Agricultural Engineering; Agriculture; Agronomy; Animal Husbandry; Forestry); **Architecture** (Architecture; Construction Engineering; Fine Arts; Regional Planning; Town Planning; Visual Arts); **Humanities and Economics** (Aesthetics; Arts and Humanities; Economics; History; Political Sciences; Social Sciences); **Mining** (Automation and Control Engineering; Chemical Engineering; Civil Engineering; Computer Engineering; Electrical Engineering; Energy Engineering; Engineering; Environmental Engineering; Geological Engineering; Materials Engineering; Mining Engineering; Production Engineering); **Sciences** (Bioengineering; Biological and Life Sciences; Chemistry; Earth Sciences; Mathematics; Natural Sciences; Physics; Science Education; Statistics)

Institute
Environmental Studies *(IDEA)* (Environmental Studies)

Centre
Applied Statistics and Socioeconomic Studies *(CEAES)* (Economics; Social Sciences; Statistics); **Innovation and Development**; **Language** (Modern Languages)

Research Institute
Agriculture (Agriculture)

History: Founded 1936.

Academic Year: February-June; August-December

Admission Requirements: Secondary school certificate and entrance examination

Main Language(s) of Instruction: Spanish

Accrediting Agency: Consejo Nacional de Acreditacion

Degrees and Diplomas: *Tecnólogo*; *Profesional Universitario*; *Especialización*: **Aesthetics; Agricultural Management; Animal Husbandry; Architecture; Biotechnology; Business and Commerce; Civil Engineering; Computer Engineering; Energy Engineering; Engineering; Environmental Management; Finance; Food Science; Food Technology; Geological Engineering; Industrial Engineering; International Economics; Maintenance Technology; Materials Engineering; Mining Engineering; Political Sciences; Real Estate; Regional Planning; Road Engineering; Software Engineering; Statistics; Systems Analysis; Town Planning; Transport Engineering; Water Management.** *Maestría*: **Aesthetics; Agricultural Business; Agricultural Engineering; Agriculture; Architecture; Automation and Control Engineering; Biotechnology; Chemical Engineering; Chemistry; Computer Engineering; Construction Engineering; Economics; Electrical Engineering; Energy Engineering; Engineering Management; Entomology; Environmental Management; Fine Arts; Food Science; Food Technology; Forestry; Geological Engineering; Geology; History; Hydraulic Engineering; Industrial Engineering; Materials Engineering; Mathematics; Mechanical Engineering; Mining Engineering; Petroleum and Gas Engineering; Physics; Political Sciences; Production Engineering; Regional Planning; Science Education; Soil Science; Statistics; Town Planning; Transport Engineering; Visual Arts; Water Management.** *Doctorado*: **Agriculture; Arts and Humanities; Biotechnology; Civil Engineering; Computer Engineering; Ecology; Electronic Engineering; Energy Engineering; History; Hydraulic Engineering; Industrial Engineering; Marine Engineering; Materials Engineering; Mathematics; Mechanical Engineering; Physics; Social Sciences; Statistics.**

Student Services: Academic Counselling, Careers Guidance, Cultural Activities, Foreign Studies Centre, Health Services, Language Laboratory, Library, Nursery Care, Social Counselling, Sports Facilities

ORINOQUIA BRANCH
SEDE ORINOQUIA
Kilómetro 9 vía a Caño Limón, Arauca
Tel: +57(1) 316-5438
Fax: +57(1) 316-5284
EMail: correo_dependencia@unal.edu.co
Website: http://www.orinoquia.unal.edu.co

Director de Sede: Rodrigo Cardenas Acevedo
Tel: +57(1) 316-5000 Ext. 29710
EMail: direccion_ara@unal.edu.co

Secretaria General: Yalvy Esperanza Marta
Tel: +57(1) 316-5000 Ext. 29719
EMail: sec_orinoquia@unal.edu.co

Programme
Agricultural Management (Agricultural Management); **Environmental Management** (Environmental Management); **Occupational Health** (Occupational Health); **Political Science** (Peace and

Disarmament; Political Sciences); **Public Law** (Administrative Law; Public Law)

History: Founded 1996 as Sede Arauca. Acquired present title 2005.

Academic Year: February-June; August-December

Admission Requirements: Secondary school certificate and entrance examination

Main Language(s) of Instruction: Spanish

Accrediting Agency: Consejo Nacional de Acreditacíon

Degrees and Diplomas: *Especialización*: **Administrative Law; Agricultural Management; Environmental Management; Occupational Health; Peace and Disarmament; Political Sciences; Public Law.**

Student Services: Academic Counselling, Canteen, Careers Guidance, Foreign Studies Centre, Health Services, IT Centre, Language Laboratory, Library, Nursery Care, Social Counselling, Sports Facilities

PALMIRA BRANCH

SEDE PALMIRA

Carrera 32 No 12 - 00 Chapinero, Vía Candelaria, Palmira
Tel: +57(2) 286-8888
Fax: +57(2) 271-7004
EMail: idea_pal@unal.edu.co
Website: http://www.palmira.unal.edu.co

Vicerrector: Carlos Ivan Cardozo Conde (2006-)
EMail: vicerrector@palmira.unal.edu.co

Secretario General: Jorge Ernesto Durán P.
Tel: +57(1) 316-5280 EMail: secgener@unal.edu.co

International Relations: Catherine Domínguez von Rosen, Coordinadora Enlace Oficina de Relaciones Internacionales e Interinstitucionales
Tel: +57(2) 286-8888 Ext.35680 EMail: ori_pal@unal.edu.co

Faculty

Agricultural Sciences (Agricultural Engineering; Agronomy; Animal Husbandry); **Engineering and Administration** (Administration; Agricultural Engineering; Engineering; Environmental Engineering; Industrial Design)

History: Founded 1946.

Academic Year: February-June; August-December

Admission Requirements: Secondary school certificate and entrance examination

Main Language(s) of Instruction: Spanish

Accrediting Agency: Consejo Nacional de Acreditación

Degrees and Diplomas: *Profesional Universitario*: **Agricultural Engineering; Animal Husbandry; Business Administration; Environmental Engineering; Industrial Design; Industrial Engineering.** *Maestría*: **Administration; Agricultural Engineering; Agriculture; Biological and Life Sciences; Environmental Engineering; Science Education.** *Doctorado*: **Agriculture; Ecology.**

Student Services: Academic Counselling, Careers Guidance, Cultural Activities, Foreign Studies Centre, Health Services, Language Laboratory, Nursery Care, Social Counselling, Sports Facilities

SAN ANDRÉS ISLA BRANCH

SEDE SAN ANDRÉS ISLA

Carretera Circunvalar, San Luis Free Town, 52-44, San Andrés Isla
Tel: +57(8) 513-3310 Ext. 29615
EMail: sec_caribe@unal.edu.co
Website: http://www.caribe.unal.edu.co

Director de Sede: José Ernesto Mancera Pineda (2006-)
Tel: +57(1) 316-5438 EMail: vicgen_nal@unal.edu.co

Secretario General: Jorge Ernesto Durán Pinzón
Tel: +57(1) 316-5280 EMail: secgener@unal.edu.co

International Relations: Paula Marcela Arias P.
Tel: +57(1) 316-5650 EMail: ori_bog@unal.edu.co

Institute

Caribbean Studies (Caribbean Studies)

History: Founded 1997.

Academic Year: February-June; August-December

Admission Requirements: Secondary school certificate and entrance examination

Main Language(s) of Instruction: Spanish

Accrediting Agency: Consejo Nacional de Acreditacíon

Degrees and Diplomas: *Maestría*: **Caribbean Studies.**

Student Services: Academic Counselling, Careers Guidance, Cultural Activities, Foreign Studies Centre, Health Services, Language Laboratory, Nursery Care, Social Counselling, Sports Facilities

TUMACO BRANCH

SEDE TUMACO (UNA)

Carrera 44 No 45-67, Unidad Camilo Torres Bloque B Modulo 10 Oficina 702, Tumaco, Narinio
Tel: +57(1) 316-5000 Ext. 10547
Fax: +57(1) 316-5000 Ext. 10548
EMail: sedetumaco@unal.edu.co; secretaca_tum@unal.edu.co
Website: http://www.tumaco-pacifico.unal.edu.co

Director de Sede: Luis Enrique Gil Torres
Tel: +57(1) 316-5000 Ext. 10547 EMail: sedetumaco@unal.edu.co

International Relations: Monica Patricia Aldana Cifuentes, Directora, Relaciones Internacionales e Interinstitucionales y Convenios
EMail: mpaldanac@unal.edu.co

Programme

Architecture (Architecture); **Economics** (Economics); **Engineering** (Engineering); **Industrial Design** (Industrial Design); **Postgraduate Studies** (Science Education); **Sciences** (Natural Sciences)

History: Founded 1997.

Main Language(s) of Instruction: Spanish

Degrees and Diplomas: *Maestría*: **Science Education.**

NUEVA GRANADA MILITARY UNIVERSITY

Universidad Militar Nueva Granada (UMNG)

Carrera 11 No. 101-80, Bogotá
Tel: +57(1) 650-0000 +57(1) 634-3200
Fax: +57(1) 214-7280
EMail: umng@unimilitar.edu.co
Website: http://www.umng.edu.co

Rector: Hugo Rodríguez Durán
Tel: +57(1) 6500-000 +57(1) 634-3200 Ext. 1002-1003
EMail: rectoria@unimilitar.edu.co

Vicerrector Administrativo: Rafael Antonio Tovar Mondragón
Tel: +57(1) 650-0000 +57(1) 634-3200 Ext. 1551
EMail: vicadm@unimilitar.edu.co

Vicerrector General: Jairo Alfonso Aponte Prieto
Tel: +57(1) 6500-000 +57(1) 634-3200 Ext. 1051
EMail: vicegen@unimilitar.edu.co

International Relations: Ana Maria Novoa Garzón, Jefe de la Oficina Asesora de Relaciones Internacionales
Tel: +57(1) 6500-000 Ext. 1029 EMail: relinter@unimilitar.edu.co

Faculty

Basic and Applied Sciences (Biology; Horticulture); **Distance Studies** (Accountancy; Business Administration; Civil Engineering; Distance Education; International Relations; Political Sciences); **Economics** (Accountancy; Business Administration; Economics); **Education and Humanities** (Arts and Humanities; Education; Teacher Training); **Engineering** (Civil Engineering; Electronic Engineering; Engineering; Environmental Engineering; Industrial Engineering; Mechanical Engineering; Multimedia; Telecommunications Engineering); **International Relations, Strategies and Security** (International Relations; Occupational Health; Political Sciences); **Law** (Law); **Medicine and Health Sciences** (Health Sciences; Medicine)

Centre

Languages (Modern Languages)

History: Founded 1982.

Admission Requirements: Titulo de Bachiller; Examen ICFES (State Exam or equivalent)

Fees: 1.91m.-6.53m (Colombian Peso)

Main Language(s) of Instruction: Spanish

Accrediting Agency: Consejo Nacional de Accreditación

Degrees and Diplomas: *Tecnólogo*; *Profesional Universitario*: **Accountancy; Biology; Business Administration; Chemistry; Civil Engineering; Economics; Electronic Engineering; Industrial Engineering; International Relations; Law; Mathematics; Medicine; Multimedia; Occupational Health; Physics; Political Sciences; Protective Services; Telecommunications Engineering.** *Especialización*: **Administration; Administrative Law; Aeronautical and Aerospace Engineering; Anaesthesiology; Business Administration; Cardiology; Constitutional Law; Criminal Law; Dermatology; Endocrinology; Environmental Management; Finance; Gastroenterology; Geological Engineering; Gynaecology and Obstetrics; Haematology; Higher Education Teacher Training; Human Rights; International Business; Law; Management; Marketing; Medicine; Military Science; Natural Resources; Nephrology; Neurology; Oncology; Ophthalmology; Orthopaedics; Otorhinolaryngology; Paediatrics; Pathology; Plastic Surgery; Pneumology; Protective Services; Psychiatry and Mental Health; Public Administration; Radiology; Rehabilitation and Therapy; Rheumatology; Road Engineering; Safety Engineering; Surgery; Taxation; Urology.** *Maestría*: **Administrative Law; Biology; Civil Engineering; Criminal Law; Education; Electronic Engineering; International Business; International Relations; Management; Mechanical Engineering; Public Law; Transport Management.** *Doctorado*: **Biological and Life Sciences; Ethics.** Also Diplomados

Student Services: Academic Counselling, Careers Guidance, Facilities for disabled people, Health Services, Language Laboratory, Library, Social Counselling, Sports Facilities

Publications: Revista de la Facultad de Ciencias Básicas - Revista Latinoamericana de Bioética; Revista de la Facultad de Ciencias Economicas; Revista de la Facultad de Derecho; Revista de la Facultad de Ingenería; Revista de la Facultad de Medicina; Revista de la Facultad de Relaciones Internacionales, Estrategia y Seguridad; Revista Latinoamericana de Bioética

Last Updated: 10/11/15

PASCUAL BRAVO UNIVERSITY INSTITUTE

Institución Universitaria Pascual Bravo

Calle 73 No. 73A-226, Apartado aéreo: 6564, Medellín, Antioquia
Tel: +57(4) 448-0520 +57(4) 448-0520
Fax: +57(4) 264-7577
EMail: cis@pascualbravo.edu.co
Website: http://www.pascualbravo.edu.co

Rector: Mauricio Morales Saldarriaga
Tel: +57(4) 448-0520 Ext. 1050
EMail: rectoria@pascualbravo.edu.co

Secretario General: Juan Pablo Arboleda Gaviria
Tel: +57(4) 448-0520 Ext. 1066
EMail: secretaria@pascualbravo.edu.co

Vicerrectora Administrativa: Liliana Patricia Restrepo Villa
Tel: +57(4) 448-0520 Ext. 1095
EMail: diradmon@pascualbravo.edu.co

Vicerrector Académico: Juan Guillermo Rivera Berrío
Tel: +57(4) 448-0520 Ext. 1097
EMail: vicerrec@pascualbravo.edu.co

International Relations: Juan Guillermo Mazo González, Director de Internacionalización
Tel: +57(4) 448-0520 Ext. 1057
EMail: international@pascualbravo.edu.co

Deanery

Engineering (Electrical Engineering; Electronic Engineering; Mechanical Engineering; Natural Sciences); **Production and Design** (Industrial Engineering; Management)

Programme

English (English)

Further Information: Also Belén Campus

History: Founded 1938. Acquired present status 1982. Formerly known as Instituto Tecnológico Pascual Bravo.

Main Language(s) of Instruction: Spanish

Degrees and Diplomas: *Técnico Profesional*; *Tecnólogo*; *Profesional Universitario*; *Especialización*: **Management.**

Student Services: Library

Last Updated: 08/10/15

PEDAGOGICAL AND TECHNOLOGICAL UNIVERSITY OF COLOMBIA

Universidad Pedagógica y Tecnológica de Colombia (UPTC)

Avenida Central del Norte 39-115, Tunja, Boyacá 711
Tel: +57(8) 740-5626
Fax: +57(87) 436-205
EMail: portalweb@uptc.edu.co
Website: http://www.uptc.edu.co

Rector: Gustavo Orlando Alvarez Alvarez
Tel: +57(87) 436-236
EMail: rectoria@uptc.edu.co; alfonso.reyes@unibague.edu.co

Director Administrativo y Financiero: John William Rosso Murillo
Tel: +57(87) 436-217 EMail: administrativa@uptc.edu.co

International Relations: Miguel Baretto Sánchez, Asesor, Unidad de Relaciones Externas y Convenios
Tel: +57(87) 422-176 Ext. 1880 EMail: relinter@uptc.edu.co

Faculty

Agricultural Sciences (Agricultural Engineering; Agronomy; Animal Husbandry; Veterinary Science); **Distance Education** *(FESAD)* (Agricultural Business; Agricultural Engineering; Business and Commerce; Civil Engineering; Computer Networks; Electrical Engineering; Finance; Handicrafts; Health Administration; Humanities and Social Science Education; Information Technology; Machine Building; Marketing; Mathematics Education; Metallurgical Engineering; Mineralogy; Native Language Education; Primary Education; Telecommunications Engineering); **Economic and Administrative Sciences** (Accountancy; Business Administration; Economics); **Educational Sciences** (Art Education; Education; Educational Psychology; Educational Technology; Environmental Studies; Foreign Languages Education; Humanities and Social Science Education; Mathematics Education; Music Education; Native Language Education; Physical Education; Preschool Education; Science Education); **Engineering** (Civil Engineering; Computer Engineering; Computer Science; Electronic Engineering; Engineering; Metallurgical Engineering; Road Engineering; Transport Engineering); **Health Sciences** (Health Sciences; Medicine; Nursing; Psychology); **Law and Social Sciences** (Law; Political Sciences); **Sciences** (Biology; Chemistry; Food Science; Natural Sciences; Physics)

History: Founded 1827 as Escuela Normal de Tunja, became Facultad de Pedagogía 1933, Universidad 1953, and acquired present title 1968. A State institution.

Academic Year: February to December (February-July; August-December)

Admission Requirements: Secondary school certificate (bachillerato) and entrance examination

Fees: According to parents' income

Main Language(s) of Instruction: Spanish

Degrees and Diplomas: *Técnico Profesional*; *Tecnólogo*; *Profesional Universitario*; *Especialización*: **Archiving; Chemistry; Civil Engineering; Constitutional Law; Data Processing; Educational Administration; Engineering; Environmental Engineering; Finance; Food Technology; Humanities and Social Science Education; Labour Law; Literacy Education; Management; Marketing; Mathematics Education; Occupational Health; Regional Studies; Road Engineering; Science Education; Small Business; Taxation; Transport Engineering.** *Maestría*: **Agriculture; Biological and Life Sciences; Business Administration; Chemistry; Computer Science; Cultural Studies; Economics; Educational Technology; Electronic Engineering; Environmental Engineering; Foreign Languages Education; Geography; Geology; History; Human Rights; Industrial Engineering; Linguistics; Literature; Materials**

Engineering; Mathematics; Mathematics Education; Metallurgical Engineering; Modern Languages; Physical Education; Physics; Physiology; Road Engineering; Rural Planning; Transport Engineering; Veterinary Science. *Doctorado*: **Chemistry; Cultural Studies; Geography; History; Materials Engineering; Modern Languages; Science Education.** Also Licenciatura; Postdoctoral Programme in Educational Sciences

Student Services: Academic Counselling, Careers Guidance, Cultural Activities, Facilities for disabled people, Health Services, Language Laboratory, Nursery Care, Social Counselling, Sports Facilities

Publications: Pensamiento y Acción

Last Updated: 05/11/15

CHIQUINQUIRÁ BRANCH

SECCIONAL CHIQUINQUIRÁ

Calle 14 A No. 2-37, Chiquinquirá, Boyacá
Tel: +57(8) 726-2003 +57(8) 726-2598
Fax: +57(987) 262-003
EMail: decanatura.chiquinquira@uptc.edu.co; epostgradoch@latinmail.com
Website: http://www.uptc.edu.co/universidad/sedes/chiquinquira/index.html

Dean: Oscar Orlando Reina Vera
EMail: decanatura.chiquinquira@uptc.edu.co

Programme

Business Administration (Business Administration); **Gemology** (Mineralogy); **Physical Education, Recreation and Sports** (Parks and Recreation; Physical Education; Sports); **Postgraduate Studies** (Human Rights); **Public Accounting** (Accountancy)

History: Founded 1973.

Main Language(s) of Instruction: Spanish

Degrees and Diplomas: *Profesional Universitario*; *Maestría*: **Human Rights.** Also Licenciatura

DUITAMA BRANCH

SECCIONAL DUITAMA (UPTC)

Calle 23 No. 21-55, Duitama, Boyacá
Tel: +57(8) 760-4100 +57(8) 760-5306 +57(8) 7624-429
Fax: +57(987) 600-076
EMail: decanatura.duitama@uptc.edu.co
Website: http://www.uptc.edu.co/universidad/sedes/duitama/index.html

Director: Nelson Eduardo Castillo Ayala
EMail: nelson.castillo@uptc.edu.co

Programme

Basic Education with emphasis on Mathematics, Humanities and Spanish Language (Humanities and Social Science Education; Mathematics Education; Native Language Education; Teacher Training); **Commercial Administration and Finance** (Business and Commerce; Finance); **Electromechanical Engineering** (Electrical Engineering; Mechanical Engineering); **Farm Management** (Farm Management); **Health Administration** (Health Administration); **Industrial Design** (Industrial Design); **Industrial Education** (Industrial Arts Education); **Industrial Management** (Industrial Management); **Mathematics and Statistics Education** (Mathematics Education); **Postgraduate Studies** (Computer Science; Educational Technology; Floriculture; Fruit Production; Human Rights; Statistics; Tourism; Vegetable Production); **Technical Studies** (Business and Commerce; Finance; Health Administration); **Technological Studies** (Agricultural Business; Civil Engineering; Computer Engineering; Electrical Engineering; Pharmacy); **Technology Education** (Technology Education); **Tourism and Hotel Management** (Hotel Management; Tourism)

History: Founded 1971.

Main Language(s) of Instruction: Spanish

Degrees and Diplomas: *Técnico Profesional*; *Tecnólogo*; *Profesional Universitario*; *Especialización*: **Computer Science; Floriculture; Fruit Production; Human Rights; Statistics; Tourism; Vegetable Production.** *Maestría*: **Educational Technology.** Also Licenciatura (Teacher Training Degree), 5 yrs

Student Services: Library

SOGAMOSO BRANCH

SECCIONAL SOGAMOSO (UPTC)

Calle 4 Sur No.15-134, Sogamoso, Boyacá
Tel: +57(8) 772-3517 +57(8) 772-3518 +57(8) 770-5450
Fax: +57(987) 770-1693
EMail: decanatura.sogamoso@uptc.edu.co
Website: http://www.uptc.edu.co/universidad/sedes/sogamoso/index.html

Dean: Orlando Vergel Portillo (2007-)

Programme

Basic Education with emphasis on Mathematics, Humanities and Spanish Language (Humanities and Social Science Education; Mathematics Education; Native Language Education; Teacher Training); **Business Administration** (Business Administration); **Commercial and Financial Administration** (Business and Commerce; Finance); **Computer and Systems Engineering** (Computer Engineering); **Electronic Engineering** (Electronic Engineering); **Geological Engineering** (Geological Engineering); **Health Administration** (Health Administration); **Industrial Engineering** (Industrial Engineering); **Mining Engineering** (Mining Engineering); **Public Accounting** (Accountancy); **Technical Studies** (Business and Commerce; Finance; Health Administration; Metal Techniques); **Technological Studies** (Agricultural Business; Civil Engineering; Computer Engineering; Metal Techniques; Pharmacy)

History: Founded 1972.

Main Language(s) of Instruction: Spanish

Degrees and Diplomas: *Técnico Profesional*; *Tecnólogo*; *Profesional Universitario*; *Especialización*: **Automation and Control Engineering; Environmental Management; Geological Engineering; Human Resources; Occupational Health; Production Engineering; Safety Engineering; Taxation; Telecommunications Engineering.** *Maestría*: **Education; Electronic Engineering; Industrial Engineering.**

POPULAR UNIVERSITY OF CÉSAR

Universidad Popular del César (UPC)

Balneario Hurtado Vía a Patillal, Valledupar, César
Tel: +57(5) 584-2472
Fax: +57(5) 573-4943
EMail: contacto@unicesar.edu.co; secretariageneral@unicesar.edu.co
Website: http://www.unicesar.edu.co

Rector: Carlos Emiliano Oñate Gómez
Tel: +57(5) 584-2986 +57(5) 584-4355 Ext. 1020
EMail: rectoria@unicesar.edu.co

Vicerrector Administrativo: Ricardo Adolfo Suárez Belmonte
Tel: +57(5) 584-2406 Ext. 1038
EMail: viceadministrativa@unicesar.edu.co

International Relations: Ana Pumarejo Quintero, Jefe Oficina Relaciones Publicas e Internacionales
Tel: +57(5) 584-3488 Ext. 1040
EMail: relacionespublicas@unicesar.edu.co

Faculty

Administrative Sciences, Accountancy and Economics (Accountancy; Business Administration; Economics; International Business); **Basic Sciences and Education** (Environmental Studies; Foreign Languages Education; Humanities and Social Science Education; Mathematics Education; Native Language Education; Science Education; Teacher Training); **Engineering and Technology** (Agricultural Engineering; Computer Engineering; Electronic Engineering; Environmental Engineering; Sanitary Engineering); **Health Sciences** (Health Sciences; Medical Technology; Microbiology; Nursing); **Law, Political and Social Sciences** (Law; Psychology; Sociology)

Further Information: Also branch in Valledupar

History: Founded 1973 as school of technology, acquired present status 1976.

Academic Year: February to December (February-July; August-December)

Admission Requirements: Secondary school certificate (bachillerato) and national placement test

Fees: 450,000 per semester (Colombian Peso)

Main Language(s) of Instruction: Spanish

Degrees and Diplomas: *Tecnólogo*; *Profesional Universitario*; *Especialización*: **Civil Law; Criminal Law; Epidemiology; Government; Health Administration; Management; Marketing; Public Law; Safety Engineering; Transport Management.** Also Licenciatura

Student Services: Academic Counselling, Canteen, Cultural Activities, Health Services, Language Laboratory, Library, Social Counselling, Sports Facilities

Publications: Perspective

Student Numbers *2015-2016*: Total: c. 14,300

Last Updated: 05/11/15

AGUACHICA BRANCH

SECCIONAL AGUACHICA

Cra. 40 via al Mar, Aguachica, César

Tel: +57(5) 565-4900

EMail: egresados.aguachica@unicesar.edu.co

Website: http://aguachica.unicesar.edu.co

Rector: Carlos Emiliano Oñate Gómez

Programme

Agriculture (Agriculture); **Agroindustrial Engineering** (Agricultural Engineering; Industrial Engineering); **Business Administration** (Business Administration); **Public Accountancy** (Accountancy); **Systems Engineering** (Computer Engineering)

History: Founded 1996.

Main Language(s) of Instruction: Spanish

Degrees and Diplomas: *Tecnólogo*; *Profesional Universitario*

SCHOOL OF COMMUNICATIONS

Escuela de Comunicaciones (ESCOM)

Calle 5 con carrera 15 dos caminos, Facatativa, Cundinamarca

Tel: +57(1) 842-2020

EMail: lizethma@ejercito.mil.co; fabios@ejercito.mil.co

Website: http://www.escom.mil.co

Director: Julián Andrés Velásquez Mejía

Programme

Communications Integrated Management *(Postgraduate)* (Telecommunications Engineering); **Electronic and Telecommunications Engineering** (Electronic Engineering; Telecommunications Engineering); **Physical and Computer Security** *(Postgraduate)* (Computer Science; Protective Services); **Telecommunications Business Administration** (Business Administration; Telecommunications Engineering)

History: Founded 1992.

Main Language(s) of Instruction: Spanish

Degrees and Diplomas: *Profesional Universitario*; *Especialización*: **Computer Science; Protective Services; Telecommunications Engineering.**

Last Updated: 29/09/15

SCHOOL OF LOGISTICS

Escuela de Logistica (ESLOG)

Calle 11 SUR, No 12-95 Este, San Cristóbal Sur, Bogotá

Tel: +57(1) 280-3486 +57(1) 337-0207

EMail: admisiones@escueladelogistica.edu.co; secretariageneral@escueladelogistica.edu.co

Website: http://www.escueladelogistica.edu.co

Rector: Juan Vargas Barreto

Programme

Health Administration (Health Administration); **Logistics** (Transport Management); **Logistics** *(Graduate)* (Transport Management)

History: Founded 1995.

Main Language(s) of Instruction: Spanish

Degrees and Diplomas: *Profesional Universitario*: **Transport Management.** *Especialización*: **Health Administration; Transport Management.**

Last Updated: 29/09/15

SCHOOL OF PUBLIC ADMINISTRATION

Escuela Superior de Administración Pública (ESAP)

Sede Principal Calle 44, # 53-37 CAN, Bogotá

Tel: +57(1) 220-2790

Fax: +57(1) 222-4356

Website: http://www.esap.edu.co

Director General: Alejandro Larreamendy Joerns (2015-)
Tel: +57(1) 222-4315 Ext. 7344-7301
EMail: direccion.nacional@esap.edu.co; alejandro.larreamendy@esap.edu.co

Secretario General: César Norberto Barrera Ávila
Tel: +57(1) 220-2790 Ext. 7034 EMail: cesar.barrera@esap.edu.co

Subdirectora Administrativa y Financiera: Claudia Marcela Franco Domínguez
Tel: +57(1) 220-2790 Ext. 7336 EMail: claufran@esap.edu.co

International Relations: Mauricio Ballesteros
EMail: Mauricio.Ballesteros@esap.edu.co

Faculty

Postgraduate Studies (Environmental Management; Finance; Health Administration; Human Rights; Management; Public Administration; Social Work); **Research** (Public Administration); **Undergraduate Studies** (Administration; Public Administration)

Further Information: ESAP sedes: Cundinamarca (Fusagasuga), Atlántico (Baranquilla), Bolivar (Cartagena), Caldas (Manizales), Huila (Neiva), Risaralda (Dosquebradas), Boyacá (Tunja), Santander (Bucaramanga), Antioquia (Medellin), Valle (Cali), Cauca (Popayan), Nariño (Pasto), Norte de Santander (San José de Cúcuta), Tolima (Ibague) and Meta (Villavicencio)

History: Founded 1958, reorganized 2004.

Academic Year: January to December

Admission Requirements: Secondary school certificate (bachillerato) and entrance examination (ICFES test)

Fees: Postgraduate Studies, 2.577.400-5.799.150 per annum (Colombian Peso)

Main Language(s) of Instruction: Spanish

Degrees and Diplomas: *Profesional Universitario*; *Especialización*: **Environmental Management; Finance; Health Administration; Human Rights; Management; Public Administration; Social Work.** *Maestría*: **Public Administration.**

Student Services: Academic Counselling, Canteen, Cultural Activities, Health Services, IT Centre, Language Laboratory, Nursery Care, Social Counselling, Sports Facilities, eLibrary

Publications: Administración y Desarollo; Astrolabio; Nuevo Municipio; Revista Administracion & Desarollo; Revista Polémica; Revista Politica & Administracion

Last Updated: 01/10/15

SOUTH COLOMBIAN UNIVERSITY

Universidad Surcolombiana (USCO)

Avenida Pastrana Borrero - Carrera 1a./Carrera 5 No. 23 - 40, Neiva, Huila

Tel: +57(98) 875-4753 +57(98) 875-3686

Fax: +57(98) 875-8890 +57(98) 875-9124

EMail: rectoria@usco.edu.co

Website: http://www.usco.edu.co

Rector: Pedro Reyes Gaspar EMail: rectoria@usco.edu.co

Secretario General: Edwin Alirio Trujillo Cerquera
Tel: +57(8) 875-8963 EMail: secretariageneral@usco.edu.co

International Relations: Gloria Cotrino Trujillo, Jefe de Oficina de Relaciones Nacionales e Internacionales
Tel: +57(8) 875-4716 EMail: orni@usco.edu.co

Faculty
Economics and Administration (Accountancy; Business Administration; Economics; Finance); **Education** (Art Education; Education; Foreign Languages Education; Humanities and Social Science Education; Mathematics Education; Parks and Recreation; Physical Education; Preschool Education; Science Education; Sports); **Engineering** (Agricultural Engineering; Electronic Engineering; Forestry; Industrial Engineering; Petroleum and Gas Engineering; Software Engineering); **Exact and Natural Sciences** (Applied Mathematics; Aquaculture; Physics); **Health Sciences** (Medicine; Nursing); **Law** (Law; Political Sciences); **Social Sciences and Humanities** (Journalism; Mass Communication; Psychology)

Further Information: Also 15 branches

History: Founded 1968 as Instituto Técnico Universitario Surcolombiano, acquired present status and title 1976.

Academic Year: January to December (January-May; August-December)

Admission Requirements: Secondary school certificate (bachillerato) and entrance examination (ICFES test)

Fees: 300,000-1,200,000 per programme (Colombian Peso)

Main Language(s) of Instruction: Spanish

Degrees and Diplomas: *Tecnólogo*; *Profesional Universitario*; *Especialización*: **Anaesthesiology; Educational Sciences; Environmental Engineering; Epidemiology; Finance; Gynaecology and Obstetrics; Health Administration; International Business; Management; Marketing; Medicine; Nephrology; Nursing; Paediatrics; Pedagogy; Surgery; Taxation; Urology.** *Maestría*: **Cultural Studies; Educational Research; Environmental Management; Environmental Studies; Epidemiology; Foreign Languages Education; Geography (Human); Higher Education; Humanities and Social Science Education; Management; Peace and Disarmament; Public Law; Special Education.** Also Licenciatura (Teacher Training Degree), 5 yrs

Publications: Crear Empresarial; Cuardernos Surcolombiano; Revista

Academic Staff *2015-2016*	**TOTAL**
FULL-TIME	**309**
PART-TIME	**503**
Student Numbers *2015-2016*	
All (Foreign included)	**9,962**
FOREIGN ONLY	**29**

Distance students, 252.

Last Updated: 22/09/15

TECHNICAL AGRICULTURAL INSTITUTE

Instituto Técnico Agrícola (ITA)
Carrera 13 calle 26C, Guadalajara de Buga, Valle
Tel: +57(92) 228-7544
Fax: +57(92) 228-8080
EMail: info@ita.edu.co; instepa@uniweb.net.co
Website: http://www.ita.edu.co

Rector: Héctor Martínez Luna
EMail: hectorluna@uniweb.net.co; rectoria@ita.edu.co

Programme
Environmental Management of Mining and Energy *(Postgraduate)* (Environmental Management); **Evaluation of Mining and Energy Production** (Energy Engineering; Mining Engineering); **Health, Safety, Environmental and Quality (HSEQ)** *(Postgraduate)* (Environmental Engineering; Health Sciences; Safety Engineering); **Measurements Analysis** (Measurement and Precision Engineering); **Mining and Energy Goods and Services Supply** (Business Administration); **Mining and Energy Planning** (Energy Engineering; Mining Engineering)

History: Founded 1966.

Main Language(s) of Instruction: Spanish

Degrees and Diplomas: *Técnico Profesional*; *Tecnólogo*; *Especialización*: **Environmental Engineering; Environmental Management; Health Sciences; Safety Engineering.**

Last Updated: 08/10/15

TECHNOLOGICAL INSTITUTE OF PUTUMAYO

Instituto Tecnológico del Putumayo (ITP)
"Aire Libre", Barrio la Esmeralda, Mocoa, Putumayo
Tel: +57(98) 420-1206 +57(98) 429-6639
Fax: +57(98) 420-1205
EMail: itputumayo@itp.edu.co
Website: http://www.itp.edu.co

Rectora: Marisol Gonzalez Ossa EMail: mgonzalez@itp.edu.co

Vicerrector Académico: Wilson Juvenal Vallejo Fuenmayor

Programme
Business Administration (Business Administration); **Computer Engineering** (Computer Engineering); **Environmental Engineering** (Environmental Engineering); **Forestry** (Forestry); **Technical/ Professional Studies** (Agriculture; Business and Commerce; Ecology); **Technological Studies** (Agricultural Business; Agriculture; Biological and Life Sciences; Business Administration; Business and Commerce; Computer Engineering; Ecology; Environmental Management; Forestry)

Further Information: Also Sibundoy Campus

History: Founded 1989.

Main Language(s) of Instruction: Spanish

Degrees and Diplomas: *Técnico Profesional*; *Tecnólogo*; *Profesional Universitario*: **Agricultural Engineering; Business Administration; Computer Engineering; Environmental Engineering; Forestry.**

Student Services: Library

Last Updated: 08/10/15

TECHNOLOGICAL INSTITUTE OF SOLEDAD ATLANTICO

Instituto Tecnológico de Soledad Atlántico (ITSA)
Calle 18, No. 39-100, Soledad, Atlántico
Tel: +57(5) 311-2370
Fax: +57(5) 311-2379
EMail: comunicaciones@itsa.edu.co; admisiones@itsa.edu.co
Website: http://www.itsa.edu.co

Rector: Emilio Armando Zapata EMail: em_zapata@itsa.edu.co

Programme
Graphic Design (Graphic Design); **Industrial Maintenance** *(Postgraduate)* (Industrial Maintenance); **International Business** (International Business); **Maintenance Welding Processes** *(Postgraduate)* (Maintenance Technology; Metal Techniques); **Mechatronics Engineering** (Electronic Engineering); **Process Engineering** (Production Engineering); **Supply Chain Management** *(Postgraduate)* (Management); **Technical/Professional Studies** (Business Administration; Computer Science; Electrical and Electronic Equipment and Maintenance; Food Technology; Graphic Design; Industrial Maintenance; Industrial Management; International Business; Maintenance Technology; Mechanical Equipment and Maintenance; Metal Techniques; Multimedia; Occupational Health; Telecommunications Services; Tourism; Transport Management); **Technological Studies** (Agricultural Business; Automation and Control Engineering; Business Administration; Electrical and Electronic Equipment and Maintenance; Electronic Engineering; Graphic Design; Industrial Management; Information Technology; International Business; Maintenance Technology; Mechanical Engineering; Metal Techniques; Telecommunications Services; Tourism; Transport Management; Visual Arts); **Telecommunications Engineering** (Telecommunications Engineering); **Virtual Mode Studies** (Computer Science; Maintenance Technology)

Further Information: Also Barranquilla Campus

History: Founded 1997.

Main Language(s) of Instruction: Spanish

Degrees and Diplomas: *Técnico Profesional*; *Tecnólogo*; *Profesional Universitario*: **Electronic Engineering; Graphic Design; International Business; Production Engineering; Telecommunications Engineering.** *Especialización*: **Industrial Maintenance; Maintenance Technology; Management; Metal Techniques.**

Student Services: Library, Sports Facilities

Last Updated: 10/11/15

TECHNOLOGICAL UNITS OF SANTANDER

Unidades Tecnológicas de Santander (UTS)
Calle de los Estudiantes N° 9-82, Ciudadela Real de Minas, Bucaramanga, Santander
Tel: +57(7) 691-7700 Ext.2008
Fax: +57(7) 691-7691
EMail: cinv@correo.uts.edu.co; contactenos@uts.edu.co
Website: http://www.uts.edu.co

Rector: Omar Lengerke Pérez (2015-)
Tel: +57(7) 691-7700 Ext.1301 EMail: rectoria@uts.edu.co

Director Administrativo y Financiero: Jaime Alberto Pinzón de Moya Tel: +57(7) 691-7700 Ext.1312 EMail: financiera@uts.edu.co

Vicerrector: Alberto Serrano Acevedo
Tel: +57(7) 691-7700 Ext.1303

International Relations: Bernardo Patiño Mancilla, Jefe de Relaciones Interinstitucionales
Tel: +57(7) 691-7700 Ext.1322
EMail: relacionesinterinstitucionales@uts.edu.co

Faculty

Natural Sciences and Engineering (Computer Engineering; Computer Science; Electrical and Electronic Equipment and Maintenance; Electrical Engineering; Electronic Engineering; Environmental Engineering; Geological Engineering; Mechanical Engineering; Mechanical Equipment and Maintenance; Natural Resources; Petroleum and Gas Engineering; Surveying and Mapping; Telecommunications Engineering); **Socio-Economic and Managerial Sciences** (Accountancy; Agricultural Management; Banking; Business Administration; Business and Commerce; Finance; International Business; Management; Marketing; Sports; Tourism)

Programme

Education for Work and Human Development

Department

Languages (English; French; Linguistics; Modern Languages)

History: Founded 1963. Acquired present title 1986.

Admission Requirements: Secondary school certificate

Main Language(s) of Instruction: Spanish, English

Accrediting Agency: Ministry of Education

Degrees and Diplomas: *Técnico Profesional*; *Tecnólogo*; *Profesional Universitario*: **Accountancy; Business Administration; Computer Engineering; Electronic Engineering; Environmental Engineering; International Business; Marketing; Mechanical Engineering; Sports; Telecommunications Engineering.**

Student Services: Academic Counselling, Canteen, Careers Guidance, Cultural Activities, Health Services, Language Laboratory, Library, Social Counselling

Publications: Specialized Magazine about Electronics and Informatics Systems

Last Updated: 01/09/15

TECHNOLOGICAL UNIVERSITY INSTITUTE OF ANTIOQUIA

Tecnológico de Antioquia (TDEA)
Calle 78B 72A 220 Robledo, Medellín, Antioquia 011421
Tel: +57(4) 454-7000
Fax: +57(4) 442-2929
EMail: tecnologico@tdea.edu.co
Website: http://www.tdea.edu.co

Rector: Lorenzo Portocarrero Sierra
Tel: +57(4) 454-7001 EMail: rectoria@tdea.edu.co

Secretary General: Leonardo Garcia Botero
Tel: +57(4) 442-4444, Ext.711
EMail: secretariageneral@tdea.edu.co

Directora Administrativa: Beatriz Eugenia Muñoz Caicedo

Faculty

Administrative Sciences and Economics (Accountancy; Business and Commerce; Finance; International Business; Transport Management); **Education and Social Sciences** (Development Studies; Education; Gerontology; Native Language Education; Preschool Education; Psychology; Social Work); **Engineering** (Computer Science; Environmental Engineering; Environmental Studies; Information Management; Information Technology; Safety Engineering; Software Engineering; Waste Management); **Judicial Investigation, Forensic and Health Sciences** (Criminology; Forensic Medicine and Dentistry; Histology; Human Rights; International Law; Law)

Academic Year: February to November (February-June; July-November)

Admission Requirements: Secondary school certificate, ICFES examination

Fees: 300 (US Dollar)

Main Language(s) of Instruction: English, Spanish

Accrediting Agency: Consejo Nacional de Acreditación (CNA)

Degrees and Diplomas: *Técnico Profesional*; *Tecnólogo*: **Agriculture; Business and Commerce; Computer Science; Development Studies; Environmental Studies; Finance; Gerontology; Information Technology; International Business; Law; Transport Management.** *Profesional Universitario*: **Accountancy; Business and Commerce; Criminology; Environmental Engineering; Finance; International Business; Psychology; Social Work; Software Engineering.** *Especialización*: **Human Rights; Information Management; International Law; Safety Engineering; Transport Management; Waste Management.** *Maestría*: **Education.** Also Licenciatura

Student Services: Academic Counselling, Careers Guidance, Facilities for disabled people, Health Services, Social Counselling, Sports Facilities

Last Updated: 21/10/15

TECHNOLOGICAL UNIVERSITY OF PEREIRA

Universidad Tecnológica de Pereira (UTP)
Carrera 27 No. 10-02. Los Alamos, Pereira, Risaralda 660003
Tel: +57(6) 313-7300
Fax: +57(6) 321-3206
EMail: rector@utp.edu.co
Website: http://www.utp.edu.co

Rector: Luis Fernando Gaviria Trujillo
Tel: +57 (6) 3137350 EMail: rector@utp.edu.co

Vicerrector Académico: Jhoniers Guerrero Erazo
Tel: +57 (6) 313 7111 EMail: viceac@utp.edu.co

Secretaria General: Liliana Ardila Gómez
Tel: +57 (6) 313 7133 EMail: liliana.ardila@utp.edu.co

Jefe Oficina de Planeación: Francisco Antonio Uribe Gómez
Tel: +57 (6) 313 7102 EMail: planea@utp.edu.co

Vicerrector Administrativo y Financiero: Fernando Noreña Jaramillo Tel: +57 (6) 313 7210 EMail: vicead@utp.edu.co

Vicerrectora de Investigaciones, Innovación y Extensión: Martha Marulanda Ángel
Tel: +57 (6) 313 7114 EMail: viceiie@utp.edu.co

Vicerrectora de Responsabilidad Social y Bienestar Universitario: Diana Patricia Gómez Botero
Tel: +57 (6) 313 7184 EMail: responsabilidadsocial@utp.edu.co

International Relations: María Cristina Valderrama, Directora Oficina de Relaciones Internacionales
Tel: +57(6) 313 7131 EMail: relint@utp.edu.co

Faculty

Arts and Humanities (Arts and Humanities; Fine Arts; Graphic Arts; Music; Philosophy); **Basic sciences** (Applied Mathematics); **Education** (Education; Pedagogy; Preschool Education); **Engineering** (Computer Science; Electrical Engineering; Electronic Engineering; Physical Engineering); **Environmental Studies** (Environmental Management; Environmental Studies); **Health Sciences** (Medicine; Sports); **Industrial Engineering** (Industrial Engineering); **Mechanical Engineering** (Mechanical Engineering); **Technology** (Technology)

History: Founded 1958 as a State institution, supported by the central government and the federal and municipal authorities.

Academic Year: January to December (January-May; June-July; August-December)

Admission Requirements: Secondary school certificate (bachillerato) and entrance examination or ICFES (governmental)

Main Language(s) of Instruction: Spanish

Accrediting Agency: Consejo Nacional de Acreditación

Degrees and Diplomas: *Técnico Profesional*; *Tecnólogo*; *Profesional Universitario*; *Especialización*: **Agronomy; Biotechnology; Computer Networks; Data Processing; Electronic Engineering; Environmental Management; Health Administration; Medicine; Metal Techniques; Molecular Biology; Music; Parks and Recreation; Protective Services; Psychiatry and Mental Health; Radiology; Safety Engineering; Sports Management; Transport Management.** *Maestría*: **Aesthetics; Agricultural Business; Automation and Control Engineering; Biology; Business Administration; Communication Studies; Computer Engineering; Demography and Population; Ecology; Education; Electrical Engineering; Environmental Studies; Finance; Health Administration; History; Human Resources; Instrument Making; Linguistics; Literature; Mathematics; Mathematics Education; Mechanical Engineering; Molecular Biology; Music; Operations Research; Philosophy; Safety Engineering; Statistics.** *Doctorado*: **Biomedicine; Communication Studies; Educational Sciences; Engineering; Environmental Studies; Literature.** Also Licenciaturas (Teacher Training Degree Programmes), 5 yrs.

Student Services: Academic Counselling, Canteen, Cultural Activities, Facilities for disabled people, Health Services, IT Centre, Language Laboratory, Library, Sports Facilities, eLibrary

Publications: Miradas; Revista Medica de Risaralda; Scientia et Technica

Academic Staff *2015-2016*	MEN	WOMEN	TOTAL
FULL-TIME	312	89	**401**
PART-TIME	75	29	**104**
STAFF WITH DOCTORATE			
FULL-TIME	69	26	**95**
Student Numbers *2015-2016*			
All (Foreign included)	10,529	7,903	**18,432**

Part-time students, –

Last Updated: 10/09/15

TOLIMA INSTITUTE OF TECHNICAL TRAINING PROFESSIONAL

Instituto Tolimense de Formación Técnica Profesional (ITFIP)

Calle 18 Carrera 1ª, Barrio/Arkabal, Espinal, Tolima
Tel: +57(8) 248-3501 +57(8) 24-3503 +57(8) 248-0014
Fax: +57(8) 248-3502
EMail: info@itfip.edu.co
Website: http://www.itfip.edu.co

Rector: Aquileo Medina Arteaga
Tel: +57(8) 248-3501 Ext. 2201
EMail: amedina@itfip.edu.co

Vicerrector Administrativo: Gelber Gómez
Tel: +57(8) 248-3501 Ext. 2203
EMail: ggomez@itfip.edu.co

International Relations: Irma Rubiela Calderón
Tel: +57(8) 248-3501 Ext. 2225
EMail: icalderon@itfip.edu.co

Faculty

Economics (Accountancy; Administration; Business Administration; Transport Management); **Education** (Social Work); **Engineering** (Automation and Control Engineering; Civil Engineering; Computer Engineering; Computer Science; Construction Engineering; Electrical and Electronic Equipment and Maintenance; Electronic Engineering)

History: Founded 1980.

Main Language(s) of Instruction: Spanish

Degrees and Diplomas: *Técnico Profesional*; *Tecnólogo*; *Profesional Universitario*

Student Services: Library, eLibrary

Last Updated: 20/10/15

UNICOC UNIVERSITY COLLEGES OF COLOMBIA

Institución Universitaria Colegios de Colombia (UNICOC)

Cl. 12B No. 9-54, Bogotá
Tel: +57(1) 341-5141
Fax: +57(1) 676-0072
EMail: admisiones@unicoc.edu.co
Website: http://www.unicoc.edu.co

Rector: Alberto Carvajalino Slaghekke
Tel: +57(1) 668-3535 Ext. 1504 EMail: rector@unicoc.edu.co

Secretario General: Javier Barragán
Tel: +57(1) 668-3535 Ext. 1506 EMail: jbarragan@unicoc.edu.co

International Relations: Adriana Arango Rueda, Directora, Proyección Social e Internacionalización
Tel: +57(1) 668-3535 Ext. 1502 EMail: aarango@unicoc.edu.co

College

Administrative Sciences and Economics (Business Administration; Health Administration; International Business; Management; Marketing; Public Administration); **Law and Political Sciences** (Law); **Odontology** (Dental Technology; Dentistry; Health Administration; Oral Pathology; Orthopaedics; Surgery)

Further Information: Also Bogotá, Norte and Cali, Norte Campuses

History: Founded 1975 as Colegio Odontológico Colombiano. Renamed Colegio Universitario Colombiano 1997. Acquired present title 2007.

Main Language(s) of Instruction: Spanish

Degrees and Diplomas: *Profesional Universitario*; *Especialización*: **Dental Technology; Dentistry; Health Administration; Orthodontics; Orthopaedics; Periodontics.** *Maestría*: **Health Administration.** Also Maestría in Pathology offered with Universidad Andrés Bello (UNAB); Diplomados offered in continuing education mode

Student Services: Library

Last Updated: 07/10/15

UNIVERSITY COLLEGE OF CUNDINAMARCA

Universidad Colegio Mayor de Cundinamarca

Calle 28 No. 5B-02, Bogotá, Cundinamarca
Tel: +57(1) 284-1717 +57(1) 241-8800 Ext. 114,115 or 102
Fax: +57(1) 284-1717
EMail: info@unicolmayor.edu.co
Website: http://www.unicolmayor.edu.co

Rector: Carlos Alberto Corrales Medina
Tel: +57(1) 241-8800 Ext. 114-115
EMail: rectoria@unicolmayor.edu.co; carlos.corrales@unicolmayor.edu.co

Vicerrectoría Administrativa: Jaime de Jesus Mendez Henríquez
Tel: +57(1) 241-8800 Ext. 106-105
EMail: viceadmin@unicolmayor.edu.co

Secretaria General: Ana Patricia Ángel Moreno
Tel: +57(1) 241-8800 Ext. 104
EMail: secretariageneral@unicolmayor.edu.co

International Relations: José Mauricio Benavides Sandoval, Jefe División de Promoción y Relaciones Interinstitucionales
Tel: +57(1) 645-8980 EMail: promocion@unicolmayor.edu.co

Faculty

Administration and Economics (Administration; Business Administration; Economics); **Engineering and Architecture** (Architecture; Construction Engineering; Engineering); **Health Sciences** (Health Administration; Health Sciences; Laboratory Techniques); **Law** (Law); **Social Sciences** (Occupational Health; Social Sciences; Social Work; Tourism)

History: Founded 1945.

Main Language(s) of Instruction: Spanish

Accrediting Agency: Consejo Nacional de Acreditación (CNA)

Degrees and Diplomas: *Tecnólogo*; *Profesional Universitario*; *Especialización*: **Construction Engineering; Development Studies; Health Administration; Health Sciences; Laboratory Techniques; Occupational Health.**

Student Services: Academic Counselling, Canteen, Careers Guidance, Language Laboratory, Social Counselling, Sports Facilities

Publications: Boletín Institucional Pensamiento Universitario; Nova; Tabula Rasa

Publishing House: Universidad Colegio Mayor de Cundinamarca

Last Updated: 24/11/15

UNIVERSITY INSTITUTE OF FINE ARTS AND SCIENCE OF BOLIVAR

Institución Universitaria Bellas Artes y Ciencias de Bolívar (UNIBAC)

Barrio San Diego, Cr 9 No. 39-12, Cartagena de Indias, Bolivar

Tel: +57(5) 672-4603

Fax: +57(5) 660-1336

EMail: info@unibac.edu.co

Website: http://online.unibac.edu.co

Rectora: Sacra Norma Nader David
EMail: rectoria@esba.edu.co

Secretaria General: Elzie Torres Anaya
EMail: secgral@esba.edu.co

International Relations: Roben Gonzalez
EMail: info@esba.edu.co

Faculty

Audiovisual Communication (Radio and Television Broadcasting); **Graphic Design** (Graphic Design); **Industrial Design** (Industrial Design); **Music** (Music); **Plastic Arts** (Fine Arts); **Scenic Arts** (Theatre)

History: Founded 1899. Acquired present title 2008.

Academic Year: February to November

Admission Requirements: Secondary school certificate and ICFES test

Fees: 433-700 per semester (US Dollar)

Main Language(s) of Instruction: Spanish

Degrees and Diplomas: *Profesional Universitario*. Also Maestría in Art History through la Universidad de Antioquia

Student Services: Academic Counselling, Canteen, Careers Guidance, Cultural Activities, Facilities for disabled people, Health Services, Library, Nursery Care, Social Counselling, Sports Facilities

Publications: Ojo Al Arte

Publishing House: Grafikoral

Last Updated: 07/10/15

UNIVERSITY INSTITUTE OF KNOWLEDGE AND INNOVATION FOR JUSTICE

Institución Universitaria Conocimiento e Innovación para la Justicia (CIJ)

Kilómetro 4 via Suba, Cota, Cundinamarca

Tel: +57(1) 683-1062 Ext.122-138

EMail: info@cij.edu.co

Website: http://www.cij.edu.co

Rector: César Augusto Solanilla Chavarro
EMail: cesar.solanilla@cij.edu.co

Faculty

Justice (Arts and Humanities; Criminology; Law)

History: Founded 2013.

Main Language(s) of Instruction: Spanish

Degrees and Diplomas: *Tecnólogo*: **Criminology.** *Especialización*: **Arts and Humanities; Criminology; Law.**

Student Services: Library

Last Updated: 09/11/15

UNIVERSITY OF ANTIOQUÍA

Universidad de Antioquía

Apartado aéreo 1226, Calle 67 No. 53-108, Ciudad Universitaria, Medellín, Antioquía

Tel: +57(4) 219-8332

Fax: +57(4) 263-8282

EMail: comunicaciones@udea.edu.co; relacionespublicas@udea.edu.co

Website: http://www.udea.edu.co

Rector: Mauricio Alviar Ramírez (2015-)
Tel: +57(4) 219-5000 EMail: rectoria@udea.edu.co

Vicerrector Administrativo: Fernando Tobón Bernal
Tel: +57(4) 219-5200 EMail: viceadministrativo@udea.edu.co

Secretario General: Roberth Augusto Uribe Álvarez
Tel: +57(4) 219-5020 EMail: secretariogeneral@udea.edu.co

International Relations: Adriana González Moncada, Directora de Relaciones Internacionales
Tel: +57(4) 219-5210 +57(4) 219-5211
EMail: dirinternacionales@udea.edu.co

Faculty

Agricultural Sciences (Agriculture); **Arts** (Music; Theatre; Visual Arts); **Communication** (Journalism; Mass Communication); **Dentistry** (Dentistry); **Economics** (Accountancy; Business Administration; Economics); **Education** (Education; Pedagogy; Teacher Training); **Engineering** (Bioengineering; Chemical Engineering; Civil Engineering; Computer Engineering; Electrical Engineering; Electronic Engineering; Engineering; Environmental Engineering; Industrial Engineering; Materials Engineering; Mechanical Engineering; Telecommunications Engineering); **Exact and Natural Sciences** (Astronomy and Space Science; Biology; Chemistry; Mathematics; Physics); **Humanities and Social Sciences** (Anthropology; History; Psychoanalysis; Psychology; Social Work; Sociology); **Law and Political Sciences** (Law; Political Sciences); **Medicine** (Medicine); **Nursing** (Nursing); **Pharmaceutical and Food sciences** (Food Science; Pharmacy); **Public Health** (Health Administration; Public Health)

School

Languages (English; French; German; Italian; Modern Languages); **Library Science** *(Interamerican)* (Information Sciences; Library Science); **Microbiology** (Microbiology); **Nutrition and Dietetics** (Dietetics; Natural Sciences; Nutrition)

Institute

Philosophy (Philosophy); **Physical Education and Sports** (Physical Education; Sports); **Political Sciences** (Political Sciences); **Regional Studies** (Regional Studies)

Research Group

Agricultural Sciences (Agriculture); **Biological Sciences** (Biological and Life Sciences); **Chemical Engineering** (Chemical Engineering); **Chemical Sciences** (Chemistry); **Clinical Medicine** (Medicine); **Computer and Information Sciences** (Computer Science; Information Sciences); **Earth and Environmental Sciences** (Earth Sciences; Environmental Studies); **Economics and Commerce** (Business and Commerce; Economics); **Electrical, Electronic and Computer Engineering** (Computer Engineering; Electrical Engineering; Electronic Engineering); **Environmental Engineering** (Environmental Engineering); **Health Sciences** (Health Sciences); **History and Archaeology** (Archaeology; History); **Journalism and Communication** (Journalism; Mass Communication); **Languages and Literature** (Literature; Modern Languages); **Law** (Law); **Materials Engineering** (Materials Engineering); **Mathematics** (Mathematics); **Mechanical Engineering** (Mechanical Engineering); **Medicine** (Medicine); **Other Engineering and Technology** (Engineering; Technology); **Other Health Sciences** (Health Sciences); **Other Humanities** (Arts and Humanities); **Other Social Sciences** (Social Sciences); **Physical Sciences** (Physics); **Political Studies** (Political Sciences); **Psychology** (Psychology); **Social Sciences** (Social Sciences); **Sociology** (Sociology)

Further Information: Also Teaching Hospital: Hospital Universitario San Vicente de Paúl. Research Groups. Branches: Bajo Cauca, Magdalena Medio, Urabá, Suroeste, Oriente, Occidente, Nordeste, Norte, Envigado and Estación Piscícola

History: Founded 1803 as school by King Charles IV of Spain, became State university 1822.

Academic Year: February to December (February-June; July-December)

Admission Requirements: Secondary school certificate (bachillerato) and entrance examination

Fees: According to parents'/student's income

Main Language(s) of Instruction: Spanish

Accrediting Agency: Ministry of Education (Institutional Education Certification for a period of 9 years as from 2003)

Degrees and Diplomas: *Técnico Profesional*; *Tecnólogo*; *Profesional Universitario*; *Especialización*: **Administrative Law; Anaesthesiology; Banking; Cardiology; Child Care and Development; Clinical Psychology; Constitutional Law; Criminal Law; Cultural Studies; Dentistry; Dermatology; Development Studies; Education; Endocrinology; Environmental Management; Environmental Studies; Family Studies; Finance; Fine Arts; Forensic Medicine and Dentistry; Gynaecology and Obstetrics; Health Administration; Health Education; Health Sciences; Hepatology; Human Rights; Industrial and Organizational Psychology; International Law; International Studies; Labour Law; Law; Maintenance Technology; Management; Medicine; Nephrology; Neurology; Nursing; Occupational Health; Ophthalmology; Orthodontics; Orthopaedics; Otorhinolaryngology; Paediatrics; Pathology; Peace and Disarmament; Pedagogy; Performing Arts; Pharmacy; Photography; Physical Education; Physical Therapy; Plastic Surgery; Private Law; Psychiatry and Mental Health; Psychology; Publishing and Book Trade; Radiology; Rehabilitation and Therapy; Rheumatology; Safety Engineering; Social Sciences; Social Studies; Sports Management; Structural Architecture; Surgery; Surveying and Mapping; Taxation; Theatre; Toxicology; Urology; Veterinary Science.** *Maestría*: **Accountancy; Administration; Agricultural Business; Agriculture; Anthropology; Art History; Biology; Biomedicine; Biotechnology; Chemical Engineering; Chemistry; Child Care and Development; Cultural Studies; Dentistry; Development Studies; Economics; Education; Engineering; Engineering Management; Environmental Engineering; Environmental Management; Environmental Studies; Epidemiology; Finance; Fine Arts; Food Science; Foreign Languages Education; Health Education; History; Law; Linguistics; Literature; Management; Mass Communication; Materials Engineering; Mathematics; Mathematics Education; Mechanical Engineering; Microbiology; Natural Sciences; Nursing; Nutrition; Occupational Health; Pharmacy; Philosophy; Physics; Political Sciences; Psychiatry and Mental Health; Psychoanalysis; Psychology; Public Administration; Public Health; Rehabilitation and Therapy; Science Education; Social Work; Sociology; Telecommunications Engineering; Theatre; Translation and Interpretation; Transport Management; Veterinary Science; Zoology.** *Doctorado*: **Agriculture; Animal Husbandry; Biology; Biomedicine; Biotechnology; Chemical Engineering; Chemistry; Computer Engineering; Dentistry; Ecology; Education; Electronic Engineering; Engineering; Environmental Engineering; Epidemiology; Fine Arts; Linguistics; Literature; Marine Science and Oceanography; Materials Engineering; Mathematics; Nursing; Pharmacy; Physics; Public Health; Social Sciences; Veterinary Science.**

Student Services: Academic Counselling, Cultural Activities, Facilities for disabled people, Health Services, Language Laboratory, Library, Social Counselling, Sports Facilities

Publications: Actualidades Biológicas; Boletín de Antropología; Contaduría; Estudios de Derecho; Estudios de Filosofía; Estudios de Literatura Colombiana; Folios; Iatreia; Investigación y Educación en Enfermería; Lecturas de Economía; Perspectivas en Nutrición Humana; Revista de Contaduría; Revista de la Escuela Interamericana de Bibliotecología; Revista de Linguistica y Literatura; Revista Educación y Pedagogía; Revista Facultad de Ingeniería; Revista Facultad de Odontología; Revista Interamericana de Bibliotecología, Linguística y Literatura; Tecnológica Administrativa; Temas Microbiológicos; Utopía Siglo XXI; Vitae Revista de Química Farmacéutica

Publishing House: Editorial Universidad de Antioquia

Student Numbers *2015-2016*: Total: c. 39,900

Last Updated: 23/11/15

UNIVERSITY OF CALDAS

Universidad de Caldas

Calle 65 No. 26-10, Manizales, Caldas 170004
Tel: +57(6) 878-1500
Fax: +57(6) 878-1505
EMail: ucaldas@ucaldas.edu.co
Website: http://www.ucaldas.edu.co

Rector: Felipe César Londoño López
Tel: +57(6) 878-1505 EMail: rector@ucaldas.edu.co

Secretaria General: Diana Carolina Zuluaga Varon
Tel: +57(6) 878-1595 EMail: sgeneral@ucaldas.edu.co

International Relations: Paula Andrea Henao Ruiz, Internationalization Advisor
Tel: +57(6) 878-1500 Ext. 12169
EMail: paula.henao@ucaldas.edu.co

Faculty

Agriculture (Agricultural Business; Agriculture; Agronomy; Animal Husbandry; Botany; Crop Production; Ecology; Rural Planning; Veterinary Science); **Arts and Humanities** (Arts and Humanities; English; Literature; Modern Languages; Music; Painting and Drawing; Philosophy; Sculpture; Visual Arts); **Engineering** (Computer Engineering; Engineering; Food Technology); **Exact and Natural Sciences** (Biology; Chemistry; Geology; Natural Sciences; Physics); **Health Sciences** (Anaesthesiology; Dermatology; Gynaecology and Obstetrics; Health Sciences; Medicine; Nursing; Ophthalmology; Paediatrics; Physical Education; Psychiatry and Mental Health; Surgery); **Law and Social Sciences** (Anthropology; Family Studies; Law; Social Sciences; Social Work; Sociology)

History: Founded 1937 as Instituto Politécnico de Caldas, became Universidad Popular 1943, and national university 1967. Acquired present status in 1993.

Academic Year: February to December (February-June; July-December)

Admission Requirements: Secondary school certificate (bachillerato) and national entrance examination (Saber PRO)

Main Language(s) of Instruction: Spanish

Accrediting Agency: Consejo Nacional de Acreditación (CNA); Institutional High Quality Accreditation by the National Council of Accreditation of the Ministry of Education

Degrees and Diplomas: *Tecnólogo*; *Profesional Universitario*; *Especialización*; *Maestría*; *Doctorado*

Student Services: Canteen, Cultural Activities, Health Services, Language Laboratory, Nursery Care, Sports Facilities

Publications: Lumina-Spargo; Revista Cultural Hipsipila; Revista Universidad de Caldas; Universidad al Día

Publishing House: Centro Editorial

Last Updated: 24/11/15

UNIVERSITY OF CARTAGENA

Universidad de Cartagena

Apartado aéreo 1382, Centro Carrera 6 No. 36-100 Calle de la Universidad, Cartagena de Indias, Bolívar
Tel: +57(5) 660-0676
Fax: +57(5) 660-0380
EMail: admisiones@unicartagena.edu.co
Website: http://www.unicartagena.edu.co

Rector: Edgar Parra Chacón
Tel: +57(5) 6600-380 EMail: rectoria@unicartagena.edu.co

Secretaria General: Marly Mardini Llamas
Tel: +57(5) 6641-585 EMail: secretariagral@unicartagena.edu.co

International Relations: Josefina Quintero Lyons, Vicerrectora de Relaciones y Cooperación Internacional
EMail: rinternacionales@unicartagena.edu.co

Faculty

Dentistry (Dentistry); **Economics** (Accountancy; Business Administration; Economics; Industrial Management); **Engineering** (Chemical Engineering; Civil Engineering; Computer Engineering; Food Technology); **Exact and Natural Sciences** (Biology; Chemistry; Mathematics; Measurement and Precision Engineering); **Humanities** (English; French; History; Linguistics; Literature; Philosophy); **Law and Political Science** (Law); **Medicine** (Medicine); **Nursing**

(Nursing); **Pharmaceutical Sciences** (Chemistry; Pharmacology); **Social Sciences and Education** (Computer Science; Mass Communication; Primary Education; Social Work)

School

Health (Dental Hygiene; Health Sciences; Medical Auxiliaries); **Languages** (English; French)

Institute

Applied Mathematics (Applied Mathematics); **Caribbean Studies** *(IIECARIBE)* (Caribbean Studies); **Regional Public Policy and Government** *(IPREG)* (Government; Political Sciences; Regional Studies)

Centre

Information Technology and Communications *(CETIC)* (Information Technology; Telecommunications Engineering); **Virtual Technology and Distance Education** *(CTEV)* (Distance Education; Educational Technology; Higher Education Teacher Training)

Research Institute

Immunology (Immunology)

Further Information: Also Cartagena University Hospital

History: Founded 1774, became university 1827. A State institution.

Academic Year: February to December (February-June; July-December)

Admission Requirements: Secondary school certificate (Bachillerato) and entrance examination

Fees: According to parents' income

Main Language(s) of Instruction: Spanish

Degrees and Diplomas: *Técnico Profesional*; *Tecnólogo*; *Profesional Universitario*: **Biology; Chemical Engineering; Chemistry; Civil Engineering; Computer Engineering; Dentistry; English; Food Technology; French; History; Law; Linguistics; Literature; Mass Communication; Mathematics; Medicine; Nursing; Pharmacology; Philosophy; Social Work.** *Especialización*: **Anaesthesiology; Community Health; Construction Engineering; Criminal Law; Criminology; Dentistry; Finance; Gynaecology and Obstetrics; Health Administration; Hydraulic Engineering; Management; Mathematics; Medicine; Neurology; Nursing; Orthodontics; Orthopaedics; Otorhinolaryngology; Paediatrics; Pathology; Psychiatry and Mental Health; Public Health; Radiology; Road Engineering; Safety Engineering; Sanitary Engineering; Stomatology; Structural Architecture; Surgery; Taxation; Urology.** *Maestría*: **Biochemistry; Chemistry; Education; Environmental Engineering; Environmental Studies; Finance; Immunology; Law; Linguistics; Management; Mathematics; Microbiology; Nursing; Peace and Disarmament; Pharmacology; Pharmacy; Philosophy; Physics; Toxicology.** *Doctorado*: **Biomedicine; Educational Sciences; Engineering; Environmental Studies; Natural Sciences; Physics; Toxicology; Tropical Medicine.** Also Licenciatura through Distance Mode; Profesional Universitario through Distance Mode

Student Services: Careers Guidance, Cultural Activities, Health Services, Library, Sports Facilities

Publications: History and Culture; Revista de Ciencias Económicas; Revista Jurídica

Last Updated: 24/11/15

UNIVERSITY OF CAUCA

Universidad del Cauca (UNICAUCA)

Apartado Aéreo 1384, Calle 5, No. 4-70, Popayán, Cauca
Tel: +57(2) 820-9900
EMail: digital@unicauca.edu.co
Website: http://www.unicauca.edu.co

Rector: Juan Diego Castrillón Orrego
Tel: +57(2) 820-9910 Ext. 1100
EMail: rectoria@unicauca.edu.co

Secretaria General: Laura Ismenia Castellanos Vivas
Tel: +57(2) 824-3020, Ext. 1107
EMail: secgral@unicauca.edu.co

Vicerrector Administrativo: Yaneth Noguera Ramos
Tel: +57(2) 820-9900 Ext.1122 EMail: viceadm@unicauca.edu.co

International Relations: Henry Francois Tarlin, Jefe, Oficina de Relaciones Interinstitucionales e Internacionales
Tel: +57(2) 820-9900 Ext. 1163
EMail: henryfrancois1969@hotmail.com

Faculty

Accountancy, Economics and Administration (Accountancy; Administration; Economics; Tourism); **Agricultural Sciences** (Agricultural Business; Agricultural Engineering; Animal Husbandry; Forestry; Industrial Engineering); **Arts** (Design; Fine Arts; Graphic Design; Music; Music Education; Musical Instruments; Visual Arts); **Civil Engineering** (Civil Engineering; Construction Engineering; Environmental Engineering; Geological Engineering; Hydraulic Engineering; Natural Sciences; Road Engineering; Structural Architecture; Transport Engineering); **Electronics and Telecommunications** (Automation and Control Engineering; Computer Engineering; Electronic Engineering; Industrial Engineering; Telecommunications Engineering); **Health Sciences** (Anaesthesiology; Community Health; Gynaecology and Obstetrics; Health Sciences; Medicine; Nursing; Paediatrics; Pathology; Physical Therapy; Physiology; Speech Therapy and Audiology; Surgery); **Human and Social Sciences** (Anthropology; Cultural Studies; Geography; History; Linguistics; Literature; Modern Languages; Philosophy; Spanish); **Law and Political Science** (Criminal Law; Labour Law; Law; Mass Communication; Philosophy; Political Sciences; Private Law; Public Law; Social Sciences); **Natural, Exact and Educational Sciences** (Biology; Chemistry; Education; Mathematics; Mathematics Education; Parks and Recreation; Pedagogy; Physical Education; Physics; Science Education; Sports)

Centre

Distance Education

History: Founded 1827 by decree of General Santander. Title changed to Colegio provincial 1850. Reorganized and became Colegio mayor in 1857. Re-established as university in 1883, became a public autonomous institution 1964.

Academic Year: January to December (January-June; August-December)

Admission Requirements: Secondary school certificate (bachillerato) and entrance examination

Fees: According to parents' income

Main Language(s) of Instruction: Spanish

Degrees and Diplomas: *Tecnólogo*; *Profesional Universitario*: **Accountancy; Agricultural Engineering; Anthropology; Art Education; Automation and Control Engineering; Biology; Business Administration; Chemistry; Civil Engineering; Computer Engineering; Economics; Electronic Engineering; Engineering; Environmental Engineering; Environmental Studies; Foreign Languages Education; Forestry; Geography; Geological Engineering; Graphic Design; History; Industrial Engineering; Law; Linguistics; Literature; Mass Communication; Mathematics; Medicine; Modern Languages; Music; Musical Instruments; Native Language Education; Nursing; Parks and Recreation; Philosophy; Physical Education; Physical Therapy; Physics; Political Sciences; Primary Education; Science Education; Spanish; Speech Therapy and Audiology; Sports; Teacher Training; Telecommunications Engineering; Tourism; Visual Arts.** *Especialización*: **Accountancy; Administrative Law; Agricultural Business; Anatomy; Bilingual and Bicultural Education; Civil Law; Community Health; Computer Science; Construction Engineering; Criminal Law; Epidemiology; Government; Gynaecology and Obstetrics; Health Administration; Health Sciences; Literacy Education; Management; Marketing; Mathematics Education; Medicine; Paediatrics; Pathology; Private Law; Road Engineering; Sports; Structural Architecture; Surgery; Taxation; Teacher Training; Telecommunications Engineering.** *Maestría*: **Accountancy; Administrative Law; Agriculture; Agronomy; Anthropology; Arts and Humanities; Automation and Control Engineering; Biology; Chemistry; Computer Science; Construction Engineering; Cultural Studies; Education; Electronic Engineering; Ethics; Finance; History; Human Rights; Law; Management; Mathematics; Music; Native Language Education; Natural Resources; Philosophy; Road Engineering; Telecommunications Engineering; Transport Engineering; Visual Arts.** *Doctorado*: **Agricultural Business; Agriculture; Anthropology; Electronic Engineering; Environmental Studies; Science Education; Telecommunications**

Engineering. Also Licenciatura; Especialización in Telecommunications Engineering with Universidad Mariana - Pasto and Universidad de San Buenaventura - Cali; Especialización in Safety Engineering with Icontec; MBA in Health Administration; Maestría in International Relations with Fundación Norte Sur-Universidad del Cauca; Maestría in Electrical Engineering with Escuela Naval Almirante Padilla - Cartagena.

Student Services: Cultural Activities, IT Centre, Library, Sports Facilities

Publications: Faculty publications

Publishing House: Editorial de la Universidad del Cauca

Last Updated: 28/10/15

UNIVERSITY OF CÓRDOBA

Universidad de Córdoba (UNICOR)
Carrera 6 No. 76-103, Montería, Córdoba 230002
Tel: +57(4) 786-0151
Fax: +57(4) 786-0054
EMail: contacto@unicordoba.edu.co
Website: http://www.unicordoba.edu.co

Rectora: Alba Manuela Durango Villadiego (2012-)
EMail: rectoria@unicordoba.edu.co; durangoalba@yahoo.com

Secretario General: Rafael Pacheco Mizger
Tel: +57(4) 786-0567 EMail: secretariageneral@unicordoba.edu.co

International Relations: Manuel Antonio Anniciarico, Director Departamento de Relaciones Internacionales
Tel: +57(4) 781-8020 EMail: rinternacionales@unicordoba.edu.co

Faculty

Agriculture (Agricultural Engineering; Agronomy); **Basic Science** (Biology; Chemistry; Geography; Mathematics; Physics; Statistics); **Economics, Law and Administrative Sciences** (Business and Commerce; Finance; International Business; Law); **Education and Human Sciences** (Art Education; Education; Environmental Studies; Foreign Languages Education; Humanities and Social Science Education; Information Sciences; Media Studies; Music Education; Native Language Education; Parks and Recreation; Physical Education; Primary Education; Science Education; Sports); **Engineering** (Computer Engineering; Environmental Engineering; Food Technology; Industrial Engineering; Mechanical Engineering); **Health Sciences** (Health Administration; Health Sciences; Microbiology; Nursing; Pharmacy); **Veterinary Medicine and Animal Husbandry** *(Berástegui)* (Animal Husbandry; Aquaculture; Veterinary Science)

History: Founded 1966 by the provincial government, incorporating faculties of agriculture and veterinary medicine (founded 1962). The University is autonomous in administrative and academic matters. Financed by the national and provincial governments.

Academic Year: February to November (February-June; July-November)

Admission Requirements: Secondary school certificate (Bachillerato) and entrance examination

Fees: 109,400-237,000 (Colombian Peso)

Main Language(s) of Instruction: Spanish

Degrees and Diplomas: *Técnico Profesional*; *Tecnólogo*; *Profesional Universitario*: **Agricultural Engineering; Animal Husbandry; Aquaculture; Biology; Business and Commerce; Chemistry; Computer Engineering; Environmental Engineering; Food Technology; Geography; Health Administration; Industrial Engineering; International Business; Law; Mathematics; Mechanical Engineering; Microbiology; Nursing; Physics; Statistics; Veterinary Science.** *Especialización*: **Business Administration; Health Administration; Hygiene; Safety Engineering; Transport Management; Tropical Agriculture.** *Maestría*: **Agriculture; Agronomy; Biotechnology; Chemistry; Education; Environmental Studies; Geography; Microbiology; Physics; Public Health; Tropical Agriculture; Veterinary Science.** *Doctorado*: **Physics; Tropical Medicine.** Also Diplomados; Licenciatura

Student Services: Canteen, Cultural Activities, Health Services, Language Laboratory, Library, Social Counselling, Sports Facilities

Publications: Avance; Proyección Investigativa

Last Updated: 26/10/15

UNIVERSITY OF CUNDINAMARCA

Universidad de Cundinamarca (UDEC)
Diagonal 18 No. 20-29, Fusagasuga
Tel: +57(1) 873-2512
Fax: +57(1) 873-2554
EMail: unicundi@mail.unicundi.edu.co
Website: http://www.unicundi.edu.co

Rector: Adolfo Miguel Polo Solano
Tel: +57(1) 873-2512 Ext. 139/104
EMail: rectoria@unicundi.edu.co

Secretario General: Adriano Muñoz Barrera
Tel: +57(1) 873-2512 Ext. 136/137

Vicerrector Administrativo y Financiero: Fabio Alfonso Rodríguez Gil Tel: +57(1) 873-2512 Ext. 184/124

Faculty

Administration, Economics and Accountancy (Accountancy; Business Administration); **Agriculture** (Agricultural Engineering; Animal Husbandry; Environmental Engineering; Surveying and Mapping); **Education** (Foreign Languages Education; Humanities and Social Science Education; Mathematics Education; Native Language Education; Primary Education); **Engineering** (Computer Engineering; Electronic Engineering; Engineering; Industrial Engineering; Software Engineering); **Health Sciences** (Health Sciences; Nursing); **Social Sciences, Humanities and Political Sciences** (Music; Psychology); **Sports and Physical Education** (Parks and Recreation; Physical Education; Primary Education; Sports)

Further Information: Branches in Girardot, Ubaté, Chia, Chocontá, Soacha, Facatativá and Zipaquirá

History: Founded 1969. Acquired present status 1992.

Main Language(s) of Instruction: Spanish

Degrees and Diplomas: *Profesional Universitario*; *Especialización*: **Animal Husbandry; Development Studies; E- Business/Commerce; Education; Environmental Studies; Management; Nutrition; Pedagogy; Sports.** *Maestría*: **Education.** Also Licenciatura

Student Services: Library

Last Updated: 26/10/15

UNIVERSITY OF ENVIGADO

Institución Universitaria de Envigado
Carrera 27B No. 39 A Sur 57, Envigado, Antioquia
Tel: +57(574) 339-1010
Fax: +57(574) 333-0148
EMail: info@iue.edu.co
Website: http://www.iue.edu.co

Rectora: Blanca Libia Echeverri Londoño
EMail: rectoria@iue.edu.co

Secretario General: Carlos Andrés Echeverri Valencia
Tel: +57(4) 339-1010 Ext.311

International Relations: Natalia Marín Tabares, Jefe de Relaciones Interinstitucionales
Tel: +57(4) 339-1010 Ext. 115 EMail: natalia.marin@iue.edu.co

Faculty

Business Administration (Accountancy; International Business); **Engineering** (Computer Engineering; Computer Networks; Electronic Engineering; Information Technology; Telecommunications Engineering); **Law and Political Science** (Law); **Social Sciences** (Psychology)

Programme

Postgraduate Studies (Administrative Law; Business Administration; Finance; Government; Management; Psychology; Public Administration; Sports)

History: Founded 1993. Acquired present status 1996.

Main Language(s) of Instruction: Spanish

Degrees and Diplomas: *Técnico Profesional*; *Tecnólogo*; *Profesional Universitario*; *Especialización*: **Administrative Law; Business Administration; Finance; Government; Psychology; Public Administration; Sports.**

Student Services: Language Laboratory, Library, Sports Facilities

Last Updated: 07/10/15

UNIVERSITY OF LA GUAJIRA

Universidad de La Guajira (UNIGUAJIRA)
Apartado aéro 172, Km 5 Vía Maicao, Riohacha, La Guajira
Tel: +57(954) 728-2729
Fax: +57(954) 727-1991
Website: http://www.uniguajira.edu.co

Rector: Carlos Arturo Robles Julio (2009-)
EMail: rectoria@uniguajira.edu.co

Faculty

Basic and Applied Sciences (Agriculture; Biology; Physics); **Economics and Administrative Sciences** (Accountancy; Business Administration; Economics; Hotel Management; International Business; Tourism); **Education** (Education; Parks and Recreation; Physical Education; Primary Education; Sports); **Engineering** (Civil Engineering; Computer Engineering; Environmental Engineering; Industrial Engineering; Mechanical Engineering); **Social and Human Sciences** (Law; Social Work)

History: Founded 1976. A State institution.

Academic Year: January to December (January-July; August-December)

Admission Requirements: Secondary school certificate (bachillerato) and entrance examination

Main Language(s) of Instruction: Spanish

Degrees and Diplomas: *Técnico Profesional*; *Tecnólogo*; *Profesional Universitario*; *Especialización*: **Construction Engineering; Finance; Health Administration.** *Maestría*: **Education; Educational Administration; Environmental Studies; Physics; Technology Education.** Also Licenciatura; Maestria in Educational Sciences through Universidad de Matanzas (Cuba)

Student Services: Library

Publishing house: Centro de Publicaciones Uniguajira

Last Updated: 26/10/15

UNIVERSITY OF MAGDALENA

Universidad del Magdalena (UNIMAGDALENA)
Carrera 32 No. 22-08, Santa Marta, Magdalena 470004
Tel: +57(5) 421-7940 Ext. 3211
Fax: +57(5) 430-6237
EMail: admin@unimagdalena.edu.co
Website: http://www.unimagdalena.edu.co

Rector: Ruthber Antonio Escorcia Caballero
EMail: rectoria@unimagdalena.edu.co

International Relations: Carlos Coronado Vargas, Jefe, Oficina de Relaciones Internacionales
Tel: +57(5) 421-7940 Ext. 2278
EMail: relinternacional@unimagdalena.edu.co

International Relations: Brian Hernández Obregón, Gerente de Proyecto
Tel: +57(5) 421-7940 Ext. 2279
EMail: bhernandez@unimagdalena.edu.co

Faculty

Basic Science (Biology; Physics); **Business Administration and Economic Sciences** (Accountancy; Business Administration; Economics; Hotel Management; International Business; Tourism); **Education** (Computer Education; Education; Preschool Education); **Engineering** (Agricultural Engineering; Civil Engineering; Computer Engineering; Electronic Engineering; Environmental Engineering; Industrial Engineering); **Health Sciences** (Dentistry; Medicine; Nursing; Psychology); **Humanities** (Anthropology; Cinema and Television; Law; Visual Arts)

Institute

Distance Education (Distance Education); **Graduate Studies**; **Tropical Research** (Environmental Studies; Tropical Medicine)

Research Centre

Peace and Conflict Resolution (Peace and Disarmament)

History: Founded 1958. A State institution.

Academic Year: February to December (February-July; August-December)

Admission Requirements: Secondary school certificate (bachillerato) and entrance examination

Fees: 179,000-1,930,000 per semester (Colombian Peso)

Main Language(s) of Instruction: Spanish

Degrees and Diplomas: *Tecnólogo*: **Agriculture; Animal Husbandry.** *Profesional Universitario*: **Accountancy; Agricultural Economics; Agricultural Engineering; Agronomy; Anthropology; Biology; Cinema and Television; Civil Engineering; Computer Engineering; Dentistry; Economics; Education; Electronic Engineering; Environmental Engineering; Hotel Management; Industrial Engineering; International Business; Law; Medicine; Nursing; Preschool Education; Psychology; Tourism.** *Especialización*: **Aquaculture; Biology; Business Administration; Education; Environmental Studies; Finance; Food Science; Food Technology; Fruit Production; Higher Education; Rural Planning; Social Studies; Teacher Training; Town Planning; Transport Management; Tropical Agriculture; Water Management.** *Maestría*: **Agriculture; Chemistry; Coastal Studies; Education; Mathematics; Nursing; Philosophy; Physics; Public Health; Statistics.** *Doctorado*

Student Services: Academic Counselling, Careers Guidance, Cultural Activities, Facilities for disabled people, Health Services, IT Centre, Language Laboratory, Library, Nursery Care, Social Counselling, Sports Facilities, eLibrary

Publications: Clio America; Duazari; Gace; Jangwa Panwa; Praxis; Revista Intropica

Academic Staff *2015-2016*	MEN	WOMEN	TOTAL
FULL-TIME	116	152	**268**
PART-TIME	298	430	**728**
STAFF WITH DOCTORATE			
FULL-TIME	24	16	**40**
Student Numbers *2015-2016*			
All (Foreign included)	6,786	6,885	**13,671**
FOREIGN ONLY	4	8	**12**

Distance students, 298.

Last Updated: 24/11/15

UNIVERSITY OF NARIÑO

Universidad de Nariño (UDENAR)
Ciudad Universitaria Torobajo, Clle 18 Cr 50, Pasto, Nariño
Tel: +57(2) 731-1449
Fax: +57(927) 235-175
EMail: judiciales@udenar.edu.co; pobando@udenar.edu.co
Website: http://www.udenar.edu.co

Rector: Carlos Eugenio Solarte Portilla (2014-)
EMail: rectoria@udenar.edu.co

Secretaria General: Paola Cristina de los Ríos Gutiérrez
EMail: secgeneral@udenar.edu.co

Vicerrector Administrativo: Carlos Omar Ojeda
Tel: +57(2) 731-3303
EMail: v.administrativa@udenar.edu.co; v.adm.udenar@gmail.com

International Relations: Edith Del Carmen Castro
Tel: +57(2) 736-0088 EMail: internacionales.udenar@gmail.com

School

Agricultural Sciences (Agricultural Engineering; Fruit Production; Industrial Engineering; Vegetable Production); **Agro-industrial Engineering** (Agricultural Engineering; Industrial Engineering); **Arts** (Architecture; Fine Arts; Graphic Design; Industrial Design; Music; Visual Arts); **Economics and Administrative Sciences** (Accountancy; Business Administration; Economics; International Business; Marketing); **Education** (Education; Environmental Studies; Literature; Science Education; Spanish); **Engineering** (Civil Engineering; Computer Engineering; Computer Science; Electronic Engineering); **Exact and Natural Sciences** (Biology; Chemistry; Computer Science; Mathematics; Natural Sciences; Physics); **Health Sciences** (Health Sciences; Medicine); **Human Sciences** (Arts and Humanities; Education; English; French; Geography (Human); Literature; Philosophy; Psychology; Social Sciences; Sociology; Spanish); **Law** (Law); **Livestock Sciences** (Animal Husbandry; Aquaculture; Production Engineering; Veterinary Science)

History: Founded 1712 as college, became university 1904.

Academic Year: February to December (February-June; August-December)

Admission Requirements: Secondary school certificate (bachillerato) and entrance examination
Main Language(s) of Instruction: Spanish
Degrees and Diplomas: *Tecnólogo*; *Profesional Universitario*: **Accountancy; Agricultural Engineering; Animal Husbandry; Aquaculture; Architecture; Biology; Business Administration; Chemistry; Civil Engineering; Computer Engineering; Computer Science; Economics; Electronic Engineering; English; Environmental Engineering; Environmental Studies; Foreign Languages Education; French; Geography (Human); Graphic Design; Health Sciences; Humanities and Social Science Education; Industrial Design; Industrial Engineering; International Business; Law; Literature; Management; Marketing; Mathematics; Medicine; Music; Native Language Education; Philosophy; Physics; Primary Education; Psychology; Science Education; Sociology; Spanish; Veterinary Science; Visual Arts.** *Especialización*: **Administrative Law; Commercial Law; Finance; Government; Labour Law; Latin American Studies; Management; Occupational Health; Operations Research; Pedagogy; Social Welfare; Social Work; Software Engineering.** *Maestría*: **Agriculture; Biological and Life Sciences; Education; Ethnology; Forestry; Higher Education Teacher Training; Humanities and Social Science Education; Literature; Marketing; Native Language Education; Public Health; Tropical Agriculture.** *Doctorado*: **Educational Sciences.**
Student Services: Library
Publications: History of the Colombian Education; Journal of Agricultural Sciences; Latinamerican Journal of Ethno-mathematics; Trends; University and Health
Publishing House: Centro de Publicaciones Universidad de Nariño
Last Updated: 28/10/15

UNIVERSITY OF PAMPLONA

Universidad de Pamplona (UDEP)

Ciudad Universitaria 'El Buque', Pamplona, Norte de Santander
Tel: +57(7) 568-5303
Fax: +57(7) 562-2750
EMail: administrador@unipamplona.edu.co; admisiones@unipamplona.edu.co; quejas.reclamos.sugerencias@unipamplon
Website: http://www.unipamplona.edu.co

Rector: Elio Daniel Serrano Velasco
Tel: +57(7) 568-5303 Ext. 900
EMail: rectoria@unipamplona.edu.co

Secretaria General: Clara Liliana Parra Zabala
Tel: +57(7) 568-5303 Ext. 124
EMail: secregene@unipamplona.edu.co

Vicerrector Administrativo y Financiero: Freddy Solano Ortega
Tel: +57(7) 568-5303 Ext. 118
EMail: viceadmi@unipamplona.edu.co

Faculty
Agrarian Sciences (Agricultural Engineering; Agronomy; Animal Husbandry; Rural Planning; Veterinary Science); **Arts and Humanities** (Art Education; Law; Mass Communication; Music; Peace and Disarmament; Philosophy; Visual Arts); **Basic Sciences** (Biology; Biotechnology; Chemistry; Geology; Mathematics; Microbiology; Molecular Biology; Physics; Waste Management); **Economic and Business Sciences** (Business Administration; Economics; Management); **Educational Sciences** *(Includes undergraduate distant and graduate students)* (Communication Studies; Education; Foreign Languages Education; Higher Education Teacher Training; Humanities and Social Science Education; Native Language Education; Pedagogy; Primary Education; Spanish); **Engineering and Architecture** (Architecture; Chemical Engineering; Civil Engineering; Computer Engineering; Electrical Engineering; Electronic Engineering; Environmental Engineering; Food Technology; Industrial Design; Industrial Engineering; Mechanical Engineering; Telecommunications Engineering); **Health Sciences** (Dietetics; Health Sciences; Laboratory Techniques; Medicine; Microbiology; Nursing; Nutrition; Occupational Therapy; Parks and Recreation; Physical Education; Physical Therapy; Psychology; Speech Therapy and Audiology; Sports)
Further Information: Also Cúcuta and Villa del Rosario Campuses

History: Founded as a private school 1960. Acquired present status and title 1970. A State institution.
Academic Year: February to November (February-June; July-November)
Admission Requirements: Secondary school certificate (bachiller) and Certificate of the National Test Service. Entrance examination in some cases (Engineering, Food Science and Microbiology)
Main Language(s) of Instruction: Spanish
Accrediting Agency: Consejo Nacional de Acreditación
Degrees and Diplomas: *Tecnólogo*; *Profesional Universitario*: **Accountancy; Agricultural Engineering; Animal Husbandry; Architecture; Biology; Business Administration; Chemical Engineering; Chemistry; Civil Engineering; Computer Engineering; Economics; Electrical Engineering; Electronic Engineering; Engineering; Environmental Engineering; Fine Arts; Food Technology; Foreign Languages Education; Geology; Health Sciences; Industrial Design; Industrial Engineering; Law; Mass Communication; Mathematics; Mechanical Engineering; Medicine; Microbiology; Nursing; Performing Arts; Physics; Rehabilitation and Therapy; Teacher Training; Telecommunications Engineering; Veterinary Science; Visual Arts.** *Especialización*: **Art Education; Higher Education Teacher Training; Humanities and Social Science Education; Management; Parks and Recreation; Sports; Waste Management.** *Maestría*: **Biotechnology; Chemistry; Communication Studies; Economics; Education; Environmental Engineering; Food Technology; Industrial Engineering; Molecular Biology; Parks and Recreation; Peace and Disarmament; Physics; Rural Studies; Sports.** Also Licenciatura
Student Services: Academic Counselling, Canteen, Cultural Activities, Health Services, Language Laboratory, Library, Nursery Care, Sports Facilities
Last Updated: 29/10/15

UNIVERSITY OF QUINDÍO

Universidad del Quindío

Carrera 15 Calle 12 Norte, Armenia, Quindio 7359300
Tel: +57(6) 735-9300 +57(6) 746-0100
Fax: +57(6) 746-0223
EMail: uq@uniquindio.edu.co; admisiones@uniquindio.edu.co
Website: http://www.uniquindio.edu.co

Rector: José Fernando Echeverry Murillo
Tel: +57(6) 746-0112 EMail: rector@uniquindio.edu.co

Faculty
Agro-industrial Sciences (Agricultural Business; Animal Husbandry; Food Technology); **Basic Sciences and Technologies** (Biology; Chemistry; Electronic Engineering; Materials Engineering; Mathematics; Physics; Plant Pathology); **Economics and Administration** (Accountancy; Business Administration; Economics; Finance; International Business; Management; Taxation; Transport Management); **Education** (Educational Sciences; Environmental Studies; Humanities and Social Science Education; Mathematics Education; Native Language Education; Parks and Recreation; Pedagogy; Physical Education; Primary Education; Science Education; Sports); **Engineering** (Civil Engineering; Computer Engineering; Electronic Engineering; Engineering; Surveying and Mapping; Systems Analysis); **Health Sciences** (Biomedicine; Health Sciences; Medicine; Nursing; Occupational Health; Safety Engineering); **Humanities and Fine Arts** (Archiving; Documentation Techniques; Gerontology; Information Sciences; Journalism; Library Science; Mass Communication; Philosophy; Social Work)
History: Founded 1960 by the Municipality of Armenia with the assistance of the Universidad Nacional de Colombia and with the authorization of the Asociación Colombiana de Universidades. Receives financial support from national and provincial governments.
Academic Year: February to December
Admission Requirements: Secondary school certificate (bachillerato) and entrance examination
Fees: 365,000 per semester (Colombian Peso)
Main Language(s) of Instruction: Spanish
Accrediting Agency: Consejo Nacional de Acreditación (CNA)

Degrees and Diplomas: *Tecnólogo*; *Profesional Universitario*; *Maestría*: **Biomedicine; Business Administration; Chemistry; Engineering; Materials Engineering; Mathematics; Occupational Health; Plant Pathology; Safety Engineering; Science Education.** *Doctorado*: **Biomedicine; Science Education.** Also Licenciatura; Especialización in International Business, Finance, Transport Management with EAN Bogota; in Taxation with UNAB Bucaramanga.

Student Services: Academic Counselling, Canteen, Cultural Activities, Health Services, Language Laboratory, Social Counselling, Sports Facilities

Publications: Revista de Investigaciones; Revista del Quindiio; Revista Facultad de Educación

Last Updated: 29/10/15

UNIVERSITY OF SUCRE

Universidad de Sucre

Carrera 28, 5-267, Barrio Puerta Roja, Sincelejo, Sucre
Tel: +57(5) 282-1240
Fax: atencionalciudadano@unisucre.edu.co
EMail: rectoria@unisucre.edu.co
Website: http://www.unisucre.edu.co

Rector: Vicente de Paul Periñán Petro
Tel: +57 (5) 282-1240 ext 220
EMail: rectoria@unisucre.edu.co

Secretario General: Jeiny Emiliani Ruiz
Tel: +57(5) 282-1240 Ext. 139
EMail: secretaria.general@unisucre.edu.co

Vicerrector Administrativo: Antonio José Herrera Succar
Tel: +57(5) 282-1240 Ext. 138
EMail: vice.administrativa@unisucre.edu.co

International Relations: Luis Causado Mendoza, Luis Causado Mendoza
Tel: +57(322) 620-6444
EMail: internacionalizacion@unisucre.edu.co; causado95@hotmail.com

Faculty

Agriculture *(Located in El Perico)* (Animal Husbandry); **Economics and Administration** (Accountancy; Business Administration; Economics; Management); **Education and Science** (Biology; Foreign Languages Education; Law; Mathematics Education; Science Education); **Engineering** (Agricultural Engineering; Civil Engineering; Electronic Engineering; Industrial Engineering); **Medicine** (Medicine; Nursing; Pharmacy; Speech Therapy and Audiology)

History: Founded 1978 by State Assembly in order to develop the Sucre State. A State institution.

Academic Year: January to December (January-July; August-December)

Admission Requirements: National Test of Proficiency (ICFES)

Fees: (Pesos): c. 400,000

Main Language(s) of Instruction: Spanish

Accrediting Agency: Consejo Nacional de Acreditación (CNA)

Degrees and Diplomas: *Tecnólogo*: **Business Administration; Civil Engineering; Electronic Engineering; Management; Pharmacy.** *Profesional Universitario*: **Accountancy; Agricultural Engineering; Animal Husbandry; Biology; Business Administration; Civil Engineering; Economics; Foreign Languages Education; Industrial Engineering; Law; Mathematics Education; Medicine; Nursing; Science Education; Speech Therapy and Audiology.** *Maestría*: **Biology; Education; Public Health; Taxation.** *Doctorado*: **Physics.** Also Diplomados; Licenciatura; MBA and Maestria in Taxation with Universidad de Medellín; Maestría in Environmental Studies with SUE CARIBE; Especialización in Health Administration and Law with Universidad Nacional; Especialización in Bible Studies with Fundación Universitaria Claretiana - FUCLA; Especialización in Marketing with Universidad EAN

Student Services: Academic Counselling, Canteen, Cultural Activities, Health Services, Language Laboratory, Nursery Care, Social Counselling, Sports Facilities

Publications: Boletin Divulgativo Division de Investigacion

Last Updated: 27/10/15

UNIVERSITY OF THE AMAZON

Universidad de La Amazonia (UNIAMAZONIA)

Calle 17 Diagonal 17 con Carrera 3F, Barrio Porvenir, Florencia, Caquetá
Tel: +57(98) 435-8786 +57(98) 435-2905
Fax: +57(98) 435-8231 +57(98) 435-2434
EMail: atencionalciudadano@uniamazonia.edu.co; relinter@uniamazonia.edu.co
Website: http://www.uniamazonia.edu.co

Rector: Leonidas Rico Martinez
Tel: +57(98) 434-0594 Ext. 148
EMail: rectoria@uniamazonia.edu.co; l.rico@udla.edu.co

Secretario General: Juan Carlos Galindo Alvarado
Tel: +57(98) 435-8786 Ext. 103
EMail: sgeneral@uniamazonia.edu.co; jua.galindo@udla.edu.co

Faculty

Accountancy, Economics and Administration (Accountancy; Business Administration; Finance; Human Resources; Management; Marketing; Taxation); **Agriculture** (Agricultural Engineering; Agriculture; Animal Husbandry; Computer Engineering; Computer Science; Educational Technology; Environmental Studies; Forestry; Information Technology; Natural Sciences; Veterinary Science); **Basic Science** (Biological and Life Sciences; Biology; Chemistry; Natural Sciences); **Educational Sciences** (Education; Foreign Languages Education; Humanities and Social Science Education; Mathematics Education; Native Language Education; Occupational Health; Pedagogy; Science Education); **Engineering** (Agricultural Engineering; Computer Engineering; Engineering; Environmental Engineering; Food Technology); **Law** (Criminology; Law; Political Sciences)

History: Founded as the Instituto Tecnológico Universidad Surcolombiana (ITUSCO) in 1971. Acquired present status 1982.

Admission Requirements: Secondary school leaving certificate and ICFES entrance examination

Fees: c.150,000 per semester (Colombian Peso)

Main Language(s) of Instruction: Spanish, English

Accrediting Agency: Consejo Nacional de Acreditación

Degrees and Diplomas: *Tecnólogo*; *Profesional Universitario*; *Especialización*: **Education; Human Resources; Information Technology; Management; Taxation.** *Maestría*: **Biological and Life Sciences; Business Administration; Educational Sciences; Forestry; Industrial Management; Taxation.** *Doctorado*: **Development Studies; Education; Environmental Studies; Natural Sciences.** Also Diplomado; Licenciatura

Student Services: Academic Counselling, Canteen, Cultural Activities, Health Services, Language Laboratory, Social Counselling, Sports Facilities

Publications: Teachers and Pedagogy Magazine

Last Updated: 27/10/15

UNIVERSITY OF THE ATLANTIC

Universidad del Atlántico

Dirección Km 7 Antigua via Puerto Colombia, Barranquilla, Atlántico
Tel: +57(5) 319-7010
EMail: internacionales@uniatlantico.edu.co
Website: http://www.uniatlantico.edu.co

Rectora: Rafaela Vos Obeso
Tel: +57(5) 319-7010 EMail: rector@uniatlantico.edu.co

Vicerrector Administrativo y Financiero: Gaspar Hernandez Caamaño
Tel: +57(5) 319-7010 Ext. 1001
EMail: viceadministrativa@mail.uniatlantico.edu.co; gasparhernandez@mail.uniatlantico.edu.co

International Relations: Maralex Martinez Oléa, Jefe de la Oficina de Relaciones Interinstitucionales e Internacionale
EMail: internacionales@mail.uniatlantico.edu.co

Faculty

Architecture (Architecture); **Basic Sciences** (Biology; Chemistry; Mathematics; Physics); **Chemistry and Pharmacy** (Pharmacy); **Dietetics and Nutrition** (Dietetics; Nutrition); **Economics** (Accountancy; Business Administration; Economics; Tourism); **Education** (Art Education; Education; Education of the Gifted;

Education of the Handicapped; Foreign Languages Education; Humanities and Social Science Education; Mathematics Education; Native Language Education; Parks and Recreation; Physical Education; Preschool Education; Science Education; Sports); **Engineering** (Agricultural Engineering; Chemical Engineering; Industrial Engineering; Mechanical Engineering); **Fine Arts** (Dance; Music; Music Education; Theatre; Visual Arts); **Humanities** (History; Philosophy; Sociology); **Law** (Law)

History: Founded 1941 as Museo del Atlántico, acquired present structure and status 1946. A State institution.

Academic Year: January to December (January-June; July-December)

Admission Requirements: Secondary school certificate (bachillerato) and entrance examination

Main Language(s) of Instruction: Spanish

Degrees and Diplomas: *Técnico Profesional*; *Tecnólogo*; *Profesional Universitario*: **Accountancy; Agricultural Engineering; Architecture; Business Administration; Chemical Engineering; Dance; Dietetics; Economics; History; Industrial Engineering; Law; Mathematics; Mechanical Engineering; Music; Nutrition; Pharmacy; Philosophy; Physics; Sociology; Theatre; Visual Arts.** *Especialización*: **Construction Engineering; Energy Engineering; Environmental Studies; Finance; Labour Law; Mathematics Education; Organic Chemistry; Pharmacy; Physics; Safety Engineering; Science Education; Social Welfare; Statistics.** *Maestría*: **Biology; Education; Energy Engineering; Environmental Studies; Family Studies; Food Technology; Gender Studies; Linguistics; Literature; Mathematics; Nutrition; Physics.** *Doctorado*: **Educational Sciences; Physics; Tropical Medicine.**

Student Services: Canteen, Cultural Activities, Health Services, Nursery Care, Social Counselling, Sports Facilities

Publishing house: Fondo de Publicaciones Universidad del Atlántico

Last Updated: 28/10/15

UNIVERSITY OF THE PACIFIC

Universidad del Pacífico (UNIPACIFICO)

Ciudadela Colpuertos Etapa 3, Antiguo Intenalco, Buenaventura
Tel: +57(2) 244-7670 +57(2) 244-5133
Fax: +57(2) 243-1461
EMail: info@unipacifico.edu.co
Website: http://www.unipacifico.edu.co

Rector: José Félix Riascos Benavides
Tel: +57(2) 244-7670 Ext. 3004 EMail: rectoria@unipacifico.edu.co

Secretario General: Jose Herlin Colorado Cuero
Tel: +57(2) 240-5555 Ext. 3007
EMail: secregeneral@unipacifico.edu.co

Programme

Architecture (Architecture); **Agronomy of the Humid Tropics** (Tropical Agriculture); **Aquaculture** (Aquaculture); **Civil Engineering** (Civil Engineering); **Computer Science** (Computer Science); **Hotel Management and Tourism** (Hotel Management; Tourism); **Sociology** (Sociology); **Systems Engineering** (Computer Engineering)

Further Information: Also branches in Tumaco, Guapi and Bahia Solano

History: Founded 1988.

Main Language(s) of Instruction: Spanish

Degrees and Diplomas: *Tecnólogo*; *Profesional Universitario*

Last Updated: 27/10/15

UNIVERSITY OF THE PLAINS

Universidad de Los Llanos (UNILLANOS)

Sede Barcelona Km. 12 Vía Puerto López, Villavicencio, Meta
Tel: +57(8) 661-6800
Fax: +57(8) 669-8602
EMail: contacto@unillanos.edu.co; servicios.generales@unillanos.edu.co
Website: http://www.unillanos.edu.co

Rector: Oscar Domínguez González
Tel: +57(8) 661-6800 Ext. 105 EMail: rectoria@unillanos.edu.co

Secretario General: Giovanny Quintero Reyes
Tel: +57(8) 661-6800 Ext. 103 EMail: sgeneral@unillanos.edu.co

International Relations: Shirley Marcela Alfonso Ortiz, Jefe de Relaciones Interinstitucionales
Tel: +(57) 866-16800 Ext. 159
EMail: oiri@unillanos.edu.co; oiriunillanos@gmail.com

Faculty

Agricultural Science and Natural Resources *(Two schools: veterinary and Agronomy)* (Agricultural Engineering; Animal Husbandry; Aquaculture; Natural Resources; Veterinary Science); **Basic Sciences and Engineering** (Computer Engineering; Electronic Engineering); **Economics** (Economics); **Health Sciences** (Health Sciences; Nursing); **Humanities and Education** (Arts and Humanities; Education)

Institute

Distance Education

History: Founded 1974. Acquired present status 1992. A State institution.

Academic Year: February to December (February-June; July-December)

Admission Requirements: Secondary school certificate (bachillerato) and state examination

Fees: Vary according to family income

Main Language(s) of Instruction: Spanish

Accrediting Agency: Consejo Nacional de Acreditación (CNA)

Degrees and Diplomas: *Técnico Profesional*; *Tecnólogo*; *Profesional Universitario*: **Accountancy; Agricultural Engineering; Biology; Business Administration; Computer Engineering; Economics; Electronic Engineering; Industrial Engineering; Marketing; Nursing; Veterinary Science.** *Especialización*: **Aquaculture; Automation and Control Engineering; Automotive Engineering; Business Administration; Community Health; Environmental Management; Epidemiology; Finance; Health Administration; Marketing; Occupational Health; Safety Engineering; Software Engineering; Tropical Agriculture.** *Maestría*: **Animal Husbandry; Aquaculture; Development Studies; Environmental Studies; Epidemiology; Tropical Agriculture.** *Doctorado*: **Agriculture.** Also Diplomados; Licenciatura; Especialización in Law, Nursing offered through Universidad Nacional; Maestría in Administration through Universidad Nacional (sede Manizales); Maestría in Marketing, Economics through Universidad de Manizales.

Student Services: Academic Counselling, Cultural Activities, Health Services, Language Laboratory, Library, Nursery Care, Social Counselling, Sports Facilities

Publications: Cuaderno Pedagogia; Medicina Veterinaria y Zootécnica Juvenil

Last Updated: 26/10/15

UNIVERSITY OF THE VALLEY

Universidad del Valle (UNIVALLE)

Apartado aéreo 25360, Ciudad Universitaria Meléndez, Carrera 100 N°13-00, Cali, Valle del Cauca
Tel: +57(2) 321-2100 +57(2) 321-2257
Fax: +57(2) 331-5111
EMail: ori@univalle.edu.co
Website: http://www.univalle.edu.co

Rector: Iván Enrique Ramos Calderón (2007-)
Tel: +57(2) 321-2240 EMail: rector@univalle.edu.co

Vicerrector Administrativo: Javier Fong Lozano
Tel: +57(2) 321-2250 EMail: vrad@correounivalle.edu.co

Secretario General: Luis Alberto Herrera Ramírez
Tel: +57(2) 321-2221
EMail: secretariageneral@correounivalle.edu.co

International Relations: Julien Wist, Director de Relaciones Internacionales
Tel: +57(2) 321-2100 Ext. 2709
EMail: ori+director@correounivalle.edu.co

Faculty

Administrative Sciences (Accountancy; Administration; Business Administration; Finance; Hotel Management; International

Business; Marine Transport; Marketing; Tourism); **Engineering** (Agricultural Engineering; Automation and Control Engineering; Chemical Engineering; Civil Engineering; Computer Engineering; Ecology; Electrical Engineering; Electronic Engineering; Engineering; Environmental Engineering; Environmental Management; Food Technology; Geological Engineering; Industrial Engineering; Information Management; Materials Engineering; Mechanical Engineering; Sanitary Engineering; Statistics; Surveying and Mapping); **Health** (Biomedicine; Dentistry; Laboratory Techniques; Medicine; Nursing; Occupational Therapy; Physical Therapy; Speech Therapy and Audiology; Surgery); **Humanities** (Arts and Humanities; Development Studies; Family Studies; Foreign Languages Education; History; Humanities and Social Science Education; Latin American Studies; Linguistics; Literature; Modern Languages; Philosophy; Social Sciences; Social Work; Spanish; Translation and Interpretation); **Integrated Arts** (Architecture; Art Education; Dance; Graphic Design; Industrial Design; Journalism; Landscape Architecture; Mass Communication; Music; Music Education; Theatre); **Natural and Exact Sciences** (Biology; Chemistry; Mathematics; Natural Sciences; Physics); **Social and Economic Sciences** (Economics; Social Sciences; Sociology)

Institute

Education and Pedagogy (Education; Environmental Studies; Mathematics Education; Parks and Recreation; Physical Education; Science Education; Sports); **Psychology** (Clinical Psychology; Industrial and Organizational Psychology; Psychology; Social Psychology)

History: Founded 1945 as Industrial University of the Cauca Valley. Acquired present title in 1954. A State institution.

Academic Year: August to June (August-December; February-June)

Admission Requirements: Secondary school certificate (bachillerato) and entrance examination (ICFES test)

Fees: According to parents' income

Main Language(s) of Instruction: Spanish

Degrees and Diplomas: *Tecnólogo*; *Profesional Universitario*: **Accountancy; Agricultural Engineering; Architecture; Biology; Business Administration; Chemical Engineering; Chemistry; Civil Engineering; Computer Engineering; Dentistry; Economics; Electrical Engineering; Electronic Engineering; Environmental Engineering; Food Technology; Foreign Languages Education; Geography (Human); Graphic Design; History; Humanities and Social Science Education; Industrial Design; Industrial Engineering; International Business; Laboratory Techniques; Mass Communication; Materials Engineering; Mathematics; Mechanical Engineering; Medicine; Music; Nursing; Occupational Therapy; Philosophy; Physical Therapy; Physics; Psychology; Public Health; Social Work; Sociology; Speech Therapy and Audiology; Statistics; Surgery; Surveying and Mapping; Teacher Training; Tourism.** *Especialización*: **Anaesthesiology; Anatomy; Automation and Control Engineering; Biology; Business Administration; Cardiology; Chemical Engineering; Civil Engineering; Community Health; Dentistry; Dermatology; Electrical Engineering; Environmental Engineering; Ethnology; Family Studies; Finance; Geological Engineering; Gynaecology and Obstetrics; Health Administration; Industrial Engineering; Industrial Management; Landscape Architecture; Marketing; Medicine; Midwifery; Music Education; Nephrology; Neurology; Nursing; Ophthalmology; Orthodontics; Orthopaedics; Otorhinolaryngology; Paediatrics; Pathology; Periodontics; Plastic Surgery; Pneumology; Psychiatry and Mental Health; Public Administration; Radiology; Rehabilitation and Therapy; Safety Engineering; Sanitary Engineering; Social Studies; Social Work; Sociology; Statistics; Surgery; Telecommunications Engineering; Urology.** *Maestría*: **Accountancy; Administration; Aeronautical and Aerospace Engineering; Architecture; Automation and Control Engineering; Biology; Biomedicine; Business Administration; Chemical Engineering; Chemistry; Civil Engineering; Computer Engineering; Cultural Studies; Development Studies; Economics; Education; Electrical Engineering; Electronic Engineering; Engineering; Environmental Engineering; Epidemiology; Food Technology; Health Administration; History; Industrial Engineering; Linguistics; Literature; Materials Engineering; Mathematics; Mechanical Engineering; Natural Sciences; Nursing; Occupational Health; Philosophy; Physics; Psychology; Public Administration; Sanitary Engineering; Social Work; Sociology; Spanish; Statistics; Town Planning.** *Doctorado*: **Administration; Arts and Humanities; Biology; Biomedicine; Chemical Engineering; Chemistry; Computer Engineering; Education; Electrical Engineering; Electronic Engineering; Environmental Engineering; Environmental Studies; Food Technology; Industrial Engineering; Marine Science and Oceanography; Mathematics; Mechanical Engineering; Philosophy; Physics; Psychology; Sanitary Engineering.** Also Diplomados; Licenciatura

Student Services: Academic Counselling, Canteen, Careers Guidance, Cultural Activities, Language Laboratory, Social Counselling, Sports Facilities

Publications: Acta Medica del Valle; Boletín Coyuntura Socio-Económica; Colombia Médica Categoria A2; Cuardernos de Psicología; Diálogos Tecnología apropiada; Estomatologia; Historia y Espacio; Language; Neusítica; Poligramas; Praxis Filosofa; Reflexiones Pedagógicas; Revista de la Universidad del Valle

Publishing House: Centro Editorial Universidad del Valle

Last Updated: 03/11/15

BUGA BRANCH

SEDE BUGA

Carrera 13 5-21, Buga 763041

Tel: +57(2) 237-0000

Fax: +57(2) 228-1077

EMail: calidad.buga@correounivalle.edu.co

Website: http://buga.univalle.edu.co

Director: Gonzalo Ruiz Martinez

EMail: rector@correounivalle.edu.co; directorio@correounivalle.edu.co

Secretaria Académica: Ana Milena Vélez Vélez

Tel: +57(1) 237-0000 Ext. 115-120

EMail: academica.buga@correounivalle.edu.co

Programme

Business Administration (Business Administration); **Electronics** (Electronic Engineering); **History** (History); **Industrial Engineering** (Industrial Engineering); **Information Systems** (Computer Education; Systems Analysis); **Literature** (Literature); **Music** (Music); **Postgraduate Studies** (Social Work; Transport Management); **Public Accounting** (Accountancy); **Tourism and Hotel Administration** (Hotel Management; Tourism)

History: Founded 1986.

Main Language(s) of Instruction: Spanish

Degrees and Diplomas: *Tecnólogo*; *Profesional Universitario*; *Especialización*: **Social Work; Transport Management.** Also Licenciatura; Diplomados

Student Services: Cultural Activities, Library, Sports Facilities

PACIFIC BRANCH

SEDE PACÍFICO

Av. Simón Bolivar Km 9, Contiguo al Colegio ITI, GVC, Buenaventura

Tel: +57(2) 240-3669 +57(2) 240-1290

EMail: edwin.gallego@correo.univalle.edu.co

Website: http://pacifico.univalle.edu.co

Director: Luis Augusto Quiñonez Rodriguez

Tel: +57(2) 240-3669 Ext. 102

Faculty

Administrative Sciences (Accountancy; Business Administration; International Business; Marine Transport); **Education** (Mathematics Education; Primary Education; Science Education); **Engineering** (Electronic Engineering; Information Technology; Maintenance Technology; Marine Transport; Transport Management); **Humanities** (Social Work); **Integrated Arts** (Theatre)

History: Founded 1986.

Main Language(s) of Instruction: Spanish

Degrees and Diplomas: *Tecnólogo*; *Profesional Universitario*: **Accountancy; Business Administration; International Business; Social Work.** Also Licenciatura

Student Services: Health Services, Library

PALMIRA BRANCH
SEDE PALMIRA

Carrera 31 Av. La Carbonera, Palmira
Tel: +57(2) 271-4760 +57(2) 272-8755
Fax: +57(2) 270-4760 Ext. 114
Website: http://palmira.univalle.edu.co

Director: Carlos Augusto Osorio Marulanda
EMail: carlos.osorio@correounivalle.edu.co

Secretario Académico: Omar Julián Flórez Morales
EMail: academica.palmira@correounivalle.edu.co

Faculty
Administrative Sciences (Accountancy; Business Administration); **Engineering** (Agricultural Engineering; Electronic Engineering; Environmental Engineering; Food Technology; Industrial Engineering; Information Technology)

Programme
Psychology (Psychology)

Institute
Education and Pedagogy (Physical Education; Sports); **Literary Studies** (Literature)

Main Language(s) of Instruction: Spanish

Degrees and Diplomas: *Tecnólogo*; *Profesional Universitario*: **Accountancy; Business Administration; Industrial Engineering; Psychology.** Also Licenciatura

Student Services: Cultural Activities, Library, Sports Facilities

ZARZAL BRANCH
SEDE ZARZAL

Calle 14 N° 7-134, Barrio Bolivar, Zarzal
Tel: +57(2) 220-9193 212100 ext 8130
Fax: +57(2) 220-6971
EMail: zarzal@correounivalle.edu.co; zarzal@univalle.edu.co
Website: http://zarzal.univalle.edu.co/WebNueva/index.html

Directora: Cecilia Madriñan Polo EMail: cecmadri@univalle.edu.co

Faculty
Administration (Accountancy; Business Administration); **Engineering** (Electronic Engineering; Food Technology; Industrial Engineering; Information Technology); **Humanities** (Social Work)

Institute
Education and Pedagogy (Education; Mathematics Education)

History: Founded 1986.

Main Language(s) of Instruction: Spanish

Degrees and Diplomas: *Tecnólogo*; *Profesional Universitario*: **Accountancy; Business Administration; Industrial Engineering; Social Work.** Also Licenciatura

Student Services: Library

UNIVERSITY OF TOLIMA

Universidad del Tolima (UTOLIMA)
Apartado aéreo 546, Barrio Santa Helena, Ibagué, Tolima
Tel: +57(8) 264-4219
Fax: +57(8) 266-9166
EMail: info@ut.edu.co
Website: http://www.ut.edu.co

Rector: José Herman Muñoz Ñungo
Tel: +57(8) 277-2021
EMail: rectoria@ut.edu.co; jhmunoz@ut.edu.co

Secretario General: Omar A. Mejía Patiño
Tel: +57(8) 277-2022 EMail: sg@ut.edu.co; omejia@ut.edu.co

International Relations: José Alexander Arciniegas Torres, Coordinador General, Oficina de Relaciones Internacionales
Tel: +57(8) 277-1212 Ext. 9117 EMail: oriut@ut.edu.co

Faculty
Agricultural Engineering (Agricultural Business; Agricultural Engineering; Agricultural Equipment; Agricultural Management; Agriculture); **Economics and Administrative Sciences** (Business Administration; Economics; International Business); **Educational Sciences** (Environmental Studies; Foreign Languages Education; Mathematics Education; Native Language Education; Parks and Recreation; Physical Education; Science Education; Sports); **Forestry Engineering** (Agricultural Engineering; Forestry); **Health Sciences** (Medicine; Nursing); **Human Sciences and Art** (Fine Arts; History; Journalism; Law; Mass Communication; Political Sciences; Visual Arts); **Sciences** (Biology; Mathematics; Statistics); **Technologies** (Architecture; Surveying and Mapping; Technology); **Veterinary Medicine and Animal Husbandry** (Animal Husbandry; Veterinary Science)

Institute
Distance Education *(IDEAD)* (Art Education; Computer Engineering; Data Processing; Environmental Studies; Finance; Forest Management; Hotel Management; Management; Pharmacy; Primary Education; Science Education; Spanish; Tourism)

History: Founded 1945, opened 1954. A State institution.

Academic Year: January to December (January-June; July-December)

Admission Requirements: Secondary school certificate (Bachillerato) and entrance examination

Main Language(s) of Instruction: Spanish

Degrees and Diplomas: *Tecnólogo*; *Profesional Universitario*: **Administration; Agricultural Engineering; Agronomy; Architecture and Planning; Arts and Humanities; Biological and Life Sciences; Economics; Education; Fine Arts; Forestry; Health Sciences; Mathematics; Veterinary Science; Zoology.** *Especialización*: **Administration; Agricultural Business; Educational Administration; Environmental Management; Environmental Studies; Epidemiology; Finance; Forest Products; Health Administration; Human Resources; Human Rights; Humanities and Social Science Education; Management; Marketing; Nursing; Occupational Health; Pedagogy; Wood Technology.** *Maestría*: **Administration; Agronomy; Animal Husbandry; Biological and Life Sciences; Cultural Studies; Economics; Education; Environmental Management; Foreign Languages Education; Health Administration; Literature; Mathematics; Peace and Disarmament; Physics; Rural Planning; Water Management.** *Doctorado*: **Agriculture; Biomedicine; Educational Sciences; Environmental Management; Water Management.** Also Licenciatura

Student Services: Academic Counselling, Canteen, Cultural Activities, Facilities for disabled people, Foreign Studies Centre, Health Services, Library, Nursery Care, Social Counselling

Publications: Revista de Ciencias de la Universidad del Tolima

Publishing House: University Press

Last Updated: 03/11/15

PRIVATE INSTITUTIONS

ABRAHAM ESCUDERO MONTOYA UNIVERSITY FOUNDATION

Fundación de Estudios Superiores Monseñor Abraham Escudero Montoya (FUNDES)
Carrera 7 No. 10-37 B, Centro, Espinal, Tolima
Tel: +57(982) 248-8787 +57(982) 248-5862
Fax: +57(982) 248-5443
EMail: fundes@fundes.edu.co
Website: http://www.fundes.edu.co

Rector: Roberto José Guzmán Villanueva
EMail: rectoria@fundes.edu.co

Programme
Education (Education; Parks and Recreation; Physical Education; Primary Education; Sports); **Postgraduate Studies** (Marketing; Tourism); **Psychology** (Psychology)

Centre
Language (English); **Virtual Education** (Educational Administration; Educational Technology; Software Engineering)

History: Founded 1997. Acquired present status 2004.

Main Language(s) of Instruction: Spanish

Degrees and Diplomas: *Profesional Universitario*; *Especialización*: **Marketing; Tourism.** Also Licenciatura (Teacher Training Degree) in Primary Education, Arts Education, Physical Educacion, Parks and Recreation, Sports

Student Services: Library

Last Updated: 01/10/15

ADVANCED CENTRE UNIVERSITY CORPORATION

Corporación Universitaria Centro Superior (CUCES UNICUCES)

Apartado aéreo 5386, Calle 14 Norte No. 8N-35, Barrio Granada, Cali, Valle del Cauca

Tel: +57(2) 661-3142 +57(315) 565-2262

Fax: +57(2) 667-1140

EMail: info@unicuces.edu.co; secregeneral@unicuces.edu.co

Website: http://unicucesvirtual.co/unicuces

Rector: Augusto Narvaez Reyes EMail: rectoria@unicuces.edu.co

Secretaria General: Edilia Diaz de Narvaez

Faculty
Economics and Administration (Accountancy; Business Administration; Marketing; Transport Management); **Engineering** (Computer Engineering; Industrial Engineering)

History: Founded 1964.

Fees: 40,000 per annum (Colombian Peso)

Main Language(s) of Instruction: Spanish

Degrees and Diplomas: *Tecnólogo*; *Profesional Universitario*

Student Services: Library

Last Updated: 29/09/15

ADVENTIST UNIVERSITY CORPORATION

Corporación Universitaria Adventista (UNAC)

Apartado aéreo 877, Carrera 84 No. 33AA-01, Medellín, Antioquia

Tel: +57(4) 250-8328

Fax: +57(4) 250-7948

EMail: comunicaciones@unac.edu.co; admisiones@unac.edu.co

Website: http://www.unac.edu.co

Rector: Abraham A. Acosta EMail: rectoria@unac.edu.co

Secretario General: Uriel Barrero Sáenz
Tel: +57(4) 250-8328 Ext. 152
EMail: secretariageneral@unac.edu.co

Vicerrector Académico: Luis Enrique Ribero
EMail: viceacademica@unac.edu.co

International Relations: Enoc Iglesias, International Relations Director EMail: eiglesias@unac.edu.co

Faculty
Administration (Accountancy; Business Administration; Management; Marketing); **Education** (Music; Preschool Education; Primary Education; Teacher Training); **Engineering** (Computer Engineering); **Health Sciences** (Health Sciences; Nursing); **Theology** (Theology)

History: Founded 1937, acquired present status 1983.

Academic Year: February to November (February-June; July-November)

Admission Requirements: Secondary school certificate (bachillerato), Grade certificate and State examination (ICFES)

Fees: 1.75m. per semester (Colombian Peso)

Main Language(s) of Instruction: Spanish

Accrediting Agency: Adventist Accrediting Association, Consejo Nacional de Acreditación

Degrees and Diplomas: *Tecnólogo*; *Profesional Universitario*; *Especialización*: **Management; Teacher Training.** Also Licenciatura in Teacher Training (Preschool Education, Primary Education, Music Education) and Theology

Student Services: Academic Counselling, Canteen, Careers Guidance, Foreign Studies Centre, Health Services, Language Laboratory, Nursery Care, Social Counselling, Sports Facilities

Publications: Review Faculty of Business Adminsitration; Review Faculty of Theology

Last Updated: 28/09/15

AGRARIAN UNIVERSITY FOUNDATION OF COLOMBIA

Fundación Universitaria Agraria de Colombia (UNIAGRARIA)

Calle 170 No 54A-10, Bogotá

Tel: +57(1) 677-1515

Fax: +57(1) 672-3773

EMail: informes@uniagraria.edu.co

Website: http://www.uniagraria.edu.co

Rector: Jorge Orlando Gaitán Arciniegas
Tel: +57(1) 667-1515 Ext. 103 EMail: rector@uniagraria.edu.co

Secretario General: John Jairo Guarín Rivera
Tel: +57(1) 667-1515 Ext. 108/148

Faculty
Administration and Accountancy (Accountancy; Business Administration; Finance); **Agronomy** (Agronomy; Animal Husbandry; Food Technology; Hygiene; Occupational Health; Veterinary Science); **Education** (Education); **Engineering** (Agricultural Engineering; Civil Engineering; Electronic Engineering; Industrial Engineering; Safety Engineering); **Juridical and Social Sciences** (Law)

History: Founded 1985.

Admission Requirements: Secondary school certificate; ICFES examination

Fees: Depending on programmes

Main Language(s) of Instruction: Spanish

Degrees and Diplomas: *Profesional Universitario*; *Especialización*: **Environmental Studies; Hygiene; Occupational Health; Safety Engineering.**

Student Services: Academic Counselling, Canteen, Careers Guidance, Cultural Activities, Facilities for disabled people, Foreign Studies Centre, Health Services, IT Centre, Language Laboratory, Library, Nursery Care, Social Counselling, Sports Facilities

Last Updated: 02/10/15

ALEXANDER VON HUMBOLDT BUSINESS UNIVERSITY CORPORATION

Corporación Universitaria Empresarial Alexander von Humboldt (CUE)

Avenida Bolívar 1-189, Armenia, Quindio

Tel: +57(6) 745-0025

Fax: +57(6) 741-0173

EMail: info@cue.edu.co

Website: http://www.cue.edu.co

Rector: Diego Fernando Jaramillo Lopez
EMail: uempresarial@cue.edu.co; rector@uniempresarial.edu.co

Faculty
Administrative Sciences (Business Administration); **Engineering** (Industrial Engineering); **Health Sciences** (Medicine; Nursing); **Humanities** (Psychology); **Social and Legal Sciences** (Law)

Institute
Uniempresarial

History: Founded 2001.

Main Language(s) of Instruction: Spanish

Degrees and Diplomas: *Profesional Universitario*. Also Especializaciones in Constitutional Law, Commercial Law, Labour Law and Social Welfare, Criminal Law, Civil Law, Administrative Law offered through Universidad del Rosario; Especializaciones in Finance and MBA offered through Universidad EAFIT; Diplomados

Student Services: Cultural Activities, IT Centre, Library, Sports Facilities

Last Updated: 29/09/15

AMERICAN UNIVERSITY CORPORATION

Corporación Universitaria Americana (CORUNIAMERICANA)

Carrera 53, No 64-142, Barranquilla, Atlántico
Tel: +57(5) 385-1027
Fax: +57(5) 360-8372
EMail: info@coruniamericana.edu.co
Website: http://americana.edu.co/portal

Rectora: Alba Lucia Corredor Gómez
Tel: +57(5) 385-1027
EMail: acorredor@coruniamericana.edu.co; albasunrise@hotmail.fr

Vicerrectora Académica: Láster Gutiérrez

International Relations: Oscar Mauricio Caro Madero, International Relations Officer
EMail: ocaro@coruniamericana.edu.co; ijcvalledupar@gmail.com

Faculty

Economics, Administration and Accountancy (Accountancy; Business Administration; International Business; Marketing); **Engineering** (Computer Engineering; Industrial Engineering; Information Management; Systems Analysis); **Law** (Law)

Further Information: Also Campus in Medellín

History: Founded 2006.

Admission Requirements: Secondary school certificate and Secondary school certificate (bachillerato) and National test for higher school graduates (ICFES)

Fees: 1,438,500 (Colombian Peso)

Main Language(s) of Instruction: Spanish

Degrees and Diplomas: *Profesional Universitario*; *Especialización*: **Business Administration; Information Management; Marketing.**

Student Services: Academic Counselling, Canteen, Health Services, Language Laboratory, Social Counselling, Sports Facilities

Publications: Magazine "Pensiamento Americano"

Last Updated: 25/09/15

ANTONIO DE AREVALO TECHNOLOGICAL FOUNDATION

Fundación Tecnológica Antonio de Arevalo (TECNAR)

Avenida Pedro de Heredia #31-41, Sector TESCA, Cartagena de Indias, Bolívar
Tel: +57(5) 660-0671
Fax: +57(5) 664-0253
EMail: tecnar@tecnar.edu.co
Website: http://www.tecnar.edu.co

Rector: Dionisio Vélez White
Tel: +57(5) 660-0671 Ext. 1116 EMail: dioniso@tecnar.edu.co

Vicerrector Académico: Alejandro Jaramillo Velez
Tel: +57(5) 660-0645 Ext. 1408
EMail: alejandro.jaramillo@tecnar.edu.co

International Relations: Sandra Trofilllo, Director of National and International Relations
Tel: +57(5) 660-0645 EMail: sandra.trofillo@tecnar.edu.co

Faculty

Design and Engineering (Civil Engineering; Computer Engineering; Computer Networks; Computer Science; Construction Engineering; Distance Education; Educational Technology; Electrical and Electronic Equipment and Maintenance; Electrical Engineering; Electronic Engineering; Industrial Engineering; Information Technology; Mechanical Engineering; Petroleum and Gas Engineering; Telecommunications Engineering); **Economics** (Accountancy; Agricultural Business; Business Administration; Environmental Management; Finance; Human Resources; Industrial Management; International Business; Management; Management Systems; Marine Transport; Occupational Health; Safety Engineering; Transport Management); **Social Sciences** (Criminal Law; Criminology; Law; Management; Media Studies; Town Planning)

School

Tourism and Gastronomy (Cooking and Catering; Hotel and Restaurant; Marketing; Tourism)

History: Founded 1984.

Admission Requirements: Secondary school certificate, entrance examination (ICFES)

Fees: 1,000 (Colombian Peso)

Main Language(s) of Instruction: Spanish

Degrees and Diplomas: *Técnico Profesional*; *Tecnólogo*; *Profesional Universitario*; *Especialización*: **Distance Education; Educational Technology; Environmental Management; Management; Marine Transport.**

Student Services: Academic Counselling, Careers Guidance, Cultural Activities, Foreign Studies Centre, Health Services, Language Laboratory, Library, Nursery Care, Social Counselling, Sports Facilities

Publications: Saberes

Publishing House: Editora Bolivar

Last Updated: 02/10/15

ANTONIO NARIÑO UNIVERSITY

Universidad Antonio Nariño (UAN)

Calle 58 A No. 37, Bogotá
Tel: +57(1) 315-2980/7648
EMail: soporte@uan.edu.co
Website: http://www.uan.edu.co

Rectora: Marta Alicia Losada Falk
EMail: mariadel@uan.edu.co; rectoria@uan.edu.co; rector@uan.edu.co; asistente.rectoria@uan.edu.co

Secretaria General: Martha Carvalho Quigua
EMail: martha.carvalho@uan.edu.co

Vicerrector Administrativo: Victor Manuel Sierra Naranjo
EMail: asistente.vicerrectoria.administrativa@uan.edu.co

International Relations: Javier Cañon Pinto, Director Oficina de Relaciones Internacionales
Tel: +57(1) 338-4960 Ext. 130-140 EMail: relinter@uan.edu.co

Faculty

Arts (Architecture; Fine Arts; Graphic Design; Industrial Design; Music; Visual Arts); **Business Administration** (Accountancy; Business Administration; Finance; Hotel Management; Human Resources; International Business; International Economics; Public Administration; Service Trades; Tourism); **Civil Engineering** (Civil Engineering); **Economics and International Business** (Economics; International Business); **Education** (Art Education; Computer Education; Education; Foreign Languages Education; Humanities and Social Science Education; Mathematics Education; Native Language Education; Preschool Education; Science Education; Technology Education); **Electronic and Biomedical Engineering** (Biomedical Engineering; Electronic Engineering; Telecommunications Engineering); **Environmental Engineering** (Environmental Engineering); **Industrial Engineering** (Industrial Engineering; Industrial Management); **Law** (Law); **Mechanical Engineering** (Mechanical Engineering); **Medicine** (Medicine); **Nursing** (Nursing); **Odontology** (Dentistry); **Optometry** (Optometry); **Psychology** (Psychology); **Psychosocial Therapies** (Psychotherapy; Social Psychology); **Public Accountancy** (Accountancy); **Sciences** (Biology; Chemistry; Mathematics; Physics); **Systems Engineering** (Computer Engineering; Software Engineering); **Veterinary Medicine** (Animal Husbandry; Veterinary Science)

Further Information: 36 campuses

History: Founded 1976. Acquired present status 1993.

Admission Requirements: Secondary school certificate. State examination and interview

Main Language(s) of Instruction: Spanish

Accrediting Agency: Biomédica-Mexico; Consejo Nacional de Acreditación

Degrees and Diplomas: *Técnico Profesional*; *Tecnólogo*; *Profesional Universitario*; *Especialización*: **Accountancy; Administration; Administrative Law; Biomedical Engineering; Civil Law; Criminal Law; Educational Technology; Electronic Engineering; Finance; Human Resources; Industrial Design; International Business; Orthodontics; Periodontics; Public Administration;**

Software Engineering; Surveying and Mapping; Taxation. *Maestría*: **Automation and Control Engineering; Bioengineering; Computer Engineering; Computer Science; Education; Finance; Health Administration; Instrument Making; International Economics; Mathematics Education; Physical Engineering; Private Law; Social Work; Taxation.** *Doctorado*: **Health Sciences; Mathematics Education; Natural Sciences.**

Student Services: Academic Counselling, Careers Guidance, Health Services, Social Counselling, Sports Facilities

Academic Staff *2015*: Total 1,277
Student Numbers *2016*: Total 16,205
Last Updated: 21/10/15

ASTURIAS UNIVERSITY CORPORATION

Corporación Universitaria de Asturias (UNIASTURIAS)
Calle 106, 14-30, Bogotá
Tel: +57(1) 795-6999
EMail: diplomados@asturias.edu.co; admisiones.af@uniasturias.edu.co
Website: http://uniasturias.edu.co

Rectora: Ximena Serrano Quiroga

Programme
Business Administration (Business Administration); **Economics** (Economics); **International Business** (International Business)

History: Founded 2012.

Main Language(s) of Instruction: Spanish

Degrees and Diplomas: *Profesional Universitario*. Also Diplomas
Last Updated: 29/09/15

AUGUSTINIAN UNIVERSITY

Universitaria Agustiniana (UNIAGUSTINIANA)
Campus Tagaste, Avenida Ciudad de Cali No. 11b-95, Bogotá
Tel: +57(1) 419-3200 Ext.1030
Fax: +57(1) 346-5514
EMail: comunicaciones@uniagustiniana.edu.co
Website: http://www.uniagustiniana.edu.co

Rector: Carlos Alberto Villabona Vargas
EMail: rectoria@uniagustiniana.edu.co

Secretario General: Ricardo Rojas Lopez

International Relations: Nathaly González Villegas, Nathaly González Villegas Tel: +57(1) 419-3200 Ext. 1078

Faculty
Communication, Arts and Culture (Architecture; Cinema and Television; Cooking and Catering; Hotel Management; Media Studies; Tourism); **Economics and Administrative Sciences** (Accountancy; Business Administration; Environmental Management; International Business; Management; Marketing); **Engineering** (Industrial Engineering; Safety Engineering; Social Welfare; Software Engineering; Telecommunications Engineering); **Humanities, Social Sciences and Education** (Arts and Humanities; Pedagogy; Philosophy; Theology)

Further Information: Also Suba Campus

History: Founded 1996 as Corporación Universitaria Nueva Colombia. Acquired present title 2007.

Admission Requirements: Secondary school certificate, ICFES examination

Fees: Undergraduate, 2,049,000-3,800,000 per annum; Postgraduate, 7,550,000 per annum (Colombian Peso)

Main Language(s) of Instruction: Spanish

Degrees and Diplomas: *Tecnólogo*; *Profesional Universitario*: **Accountancy; Architecture; Business Administration; Cinema and Television; Hotel Management; Industrial Engineering; International Business; Marketing; Telecommunications Engineering; Tourism.** *Especialización*: **Business Administration; Environmental Management; Pedagogy; Safety Engineering; Social Welfare.** Also Licenciatura in Philosophy and Theology

Student Services: Academic Counselling, Careers Guidance, Cultural Activities, Health Services, IT Centre, Language Laboratory, Library, Social Counselling, Sports Facilities

Publications: Academic Magazine
Last Updated: 08/10/15

AUTONOMOUS UNIVERSITY CORPORATION OF NARIÑO

Corporación Universitaria Autónoma de Nariño (AUNAR)
Alle 19 No. 27-80, Pasto, Nariño
Tel: +57(27) 232-452 +57(27) 291-789
Fax: +57(27) 291-758
EMail: comunicaciones@aunar.edu.co
Website: http://www.aunar.edu.co

Rector: Tito Jaime Colunge Benavides
EMail: tj_cb74@hotmail.com; rectoria@aunar.edu.co

Course
Business Administration (Business Administration); **Computer Sciences** (Computer Science); **Dental Prosthesics** (Dental Technology); **Electronic Engineering** (Electronic Engineering); **English** (International Business); **Fashion Design** (Fashion Design); **Integrated Materials** (Materials Engineering); **Mechanical Engineering** (Mechanical Engineering); **Public Accounting** (Accountancy)

History: Founded 1982.

Main Language(s) of Instruction: Spanish

Degrees and Diplomas: *Tecnólogo*; *Profesional Universitario*

Student Services: IT Centre, Library, Sports Facilities
Last Updated: 28/09/15

AUTONOMOUS UNIVERSITY CORPORATION OF THE CAUCA REGION

Corporación Universitaria Autónoma del Cauca
Calle 5, No. 3-85, Popayán, Cauca
Tel: +57(2) 821-3000
Fax: +57(2) 821-4000
EMail: uniautonoma@uniautonoma.edu.co
Website: http://www.uniautonoma.edu.co

Rectora: Martha Elena Segura Sandoval
Tel: +57(2) 821-3000 Ext. 106
EMail: rectoria@uniautonoma.edu.co

Secretaria General: Lady Mabel Jimenez Rodriguez
Tel: +57(2) 821-3000 Ext. 106
EMail: secretoria@uniautonoma.edu.co

Faculty
Administration, Accounting and Economics (Accountancy; Business Administration; Criminal Law; Finance; International Business; Management); **Education** (Education; Educational Technology; Preschool Education; Sports); **Engineering** (Computer Engineering; Electronic Engineering); **Environmental Science and Sustainable Development** (Environmental Engineering); **Law, Social and Political Sciences** (Law)

History: Founded 1979.

Main Language(s) of Instruction: Spanish

Degrees and Diplomas: *Profesional Universitario*; *Especialización*: **Commercial Law; Education; Educational Technology; Finance; Management.**

Student Services: Library
Last Updated: 28/09/15

AUTONOMOUS UNIVERSITY FOUNDATION OF COLOMBIA

Fundación Universidad Autónoma de Colombia (FUAC)
Calle 12 No. 4 - 30 y Calle 13 No. 4 - 31, Bogotá
Tel: +57(1) 334-3696
Fax: +57(1) 334-3696
EMail: viceacad@fuac.edu.co
Website: http://www.fuac.edu.co

Rector: Ricardo Mosquera Meza EMail: rectoria@fuac.edu.co

Secretaria General: Liliana Bernal EMail: secgral@fuac.edu.co

Vicerrectoria Administrativa: Arturo Carrillo Suárez
EMail: viceadmi@fuac.edu.co

International Relations: Ernesto Rico, Vicepresidente
Tel: +57(1) 286-7407
EMail: vicepres@fuac.edu.co; ori@fuac.edu.co

Faculty

Economics, Administration and Accountancy (Accountancy; Administration; Economics; International Business); **Engineering** (Automation and Control Engineering; Business Computing; Computer Engineering; Electronic Engineering; Energy Engineering; Engineering Management; Environmental Engineering; Hydraulic Engineering; Industrial Design; Industrial Engineering; Mechanical Engineering; Operations Research; Safety Engineering; Statistics; Water Management); **Human Sciences** (History; Literature); **Law** (Arts and Humanities; Civil Law; Criminal Law; Labour Law; Law; Private Law; Public Law)

Higher Institute

Pedagogy (Pedagogy)

History: Founded 1971 as Fundación Universitaria Autónoma de Colombia.

Academic Year: January to December (January-June; July-December)

Admission Requirements: Secondary school certificate (bachillerato) and entrance examination

Main Language(s) of Instruction: Spanish

Degrees and Diplomas: *Profesional Universitario*; *Especialización*: **Automation and Control Engineering; Business Computing; Computer Engineering; Energy Engineering; Engineering Management; Hydraulic Engineering; Safety Engineering; Water Management.** *Maestría*: **Operations Research; Statistics.**

Student Services: Library
Last Updated: 02/10/15

AUTONOMOUS UNIVERSITY FOUNDATION OF THE AMERICAS

Fundación Universitaria Autónoma de las Américas (UAM)
Calle 34 A No 76-35, Medellín, Antioquia
Tel: +57(4) 411-4444
Fax: +57(4) 412-0595
EMail: info@uam.edu.co
Website: http://www.uam.edu.co

Rector: Alvaro Enrique Maestre Rocha EMail: rector@uam.edu.co

Faculty

Economics and Administrative Sciences (Administration; Advertising and Publicity; Business Administration; International Business; Marketing; Tourism); **Engineering** (Engineering); **Law** (Law); **Medicine** (Medicine); **Odontology** (Dental Technology; Dentistry); **Respiratory Therapy** (Respiratory Therapy); **Veterinary Medicine and Zootechnics** (Animal Husbandry; Veterinary Science)

Further Information: Also branch in Pereira

History: Founded 1983 as Fundación Tecnológica Politécnico Nacional. Acquired present status and title 2003.

Fees: 1,488,636-7,829,241 per annum (Colombian Peso)

Main Language(s) of Instruction: Spanish

Degrees and Diplomas: *Técnico Profesional*; *Profesional Universitario*

Student Services: Library

Publications: Libro de Investigación; Memorias Foro Bucal
Last Updated: 05/10/15

AUTONOMOUS UNIVERSITY OF BUCARAMANGA

Universidad Autónoma de Bucaramanga (UNAB)
Avenida 42 No. 48-11, Bucaramanga, Santander
Tel: +57(7) 643-6111 +57(7) 643-6261
Fax: +57(7) 643-3958
EMail: admisiones@unab.edu.co
Website: http://www.unab.edu.co

Rector: Alberto de Jesús Montoya Puyana
Tel: +57(7) 643-6111, Ext. 102
EMail: rectoria@unab.edu.co; amontoya2@unab.edu.co

Vicerrector administrativo y Financiero: Gilberto Ramírez Valbuena
Tel: +57(7) 643-6111, Ext 104 EMail: gramirez5@unab.edu.co

Vicerrectora académica: Eulalia García Beltrán
Tel: +57(7) 643-6111, Ext. 105 EMail: egarcia@unab.edu.co

International Relations: Maria Teresa Camargo Abello
Tel: +57(7) 647-4488 EMail: mcamargoa@unab.edu.co

Faculty

Administration (Business Administration; Hotel Management; International Business; Tourism); **Administrative Engineering** (Engineering; Finance; Marketing); **Communication and Audiovisual Arts** (Communication Studies; Radio and Television Broadcasting); **Economic Sciences and Accountancy** (Accountancy; Economics); **Education** (Education; Preschool Education); **Health Sciences** (Health Sciences; Medicine; Nursing; Psychology); **Law** (Law); **Music** (Music); **Physical and Mechanical Engineering** (Biomedical Engineering; Electronic Engineering; Energy Engineering; Mechanical Engineering); **System Engineering** (Computer Engineering; Systems Analysis); **Technical and Technological Studies** (Cooking and Catering; Criminology; Marketing; Occupational Health; Pharmacy; Protective Services; Transport Management)

Unit

Psychosocial Programmes and Projects *(UPPSI)* (Psychology; Social Sciences)

Institute

Languages (English; French; German; Italian; Modern Languages; Portuguese; Spanish); **Political Sciences** *(IEP)* (Political Sciences)

Research Centre

Biotechnology, Bioethics and Environment *(CINBBYA)* (Biotechnology; Environmental Studies; Ethics); **Economics, Management and Accounting** *(DYNAMICS)* (Accountancy; Economics; Management); **Engineering and Organizations** *(CIIO)* (Engineering); **Health and and Psychosocial Sciences** (Health Education; Health Sciences; Nursing; Psychology); **Social Sciences, Humanities and Arts** (Arts and Humanities; Social Sciences); **Socio-juridical Studies** (Law; Social Sciences)

History: Founded 1952 as Instituto Caldas.

Academic Year: January to November (January-May; July-November)

Admission Requirements: Secondary school certificate (bachillerato), and State examination (ICFES)

Fees: Undergraduate, 30,000-1,017,000 per credit; Postgraduate, per 220,000-626,000 credit (5,500,000-31,926,000 per programme) (Colombian Peso)

Main Language(s) of Instruction: Spanish

Accrediting Agency: CAN; GTZ; CLAEP; SGS

Degrees and Diplomas: *Técnico Profesional*; *Tecnólogo*; *Profesional Universitario*: **Accountancy; Biomedical Engineering; Business Administration; Computer Engineering; Cooking and Catering; Economics; Education; Electronic Engineering; Energy Engineering; Engineering; Finance; Hotel Management; International Business; Law; Literature; Marketing; Music; Nursing; Preschool Education; Psychology; Radio and Television Broadcasting; Tourism.** *Especialización*: **Administrative Law; Anaesthesiology; Business Administration; Child Care and Development; Civil Law; Clinical Psychology; Commercial Law; Constitutional Law; Criminal Law; Dermatology; Educational Technology; Engineering Management; Environmental Engineering; Epidemiology; Finance; Health Administration; Human Resources; Management; Marketing; Mechanical Engineering; Medical Technology; Medicine; Ophthalmology; Psychology; Public Law; Radiology; Social Problems; Social Welfare; Software Engineering; Surgery; Taxation; Telecommunications Engineering; Tourism; Transport Management; Urology.** *Maestría*: **Business Administration; Computer Engineering; Development Studies; Education; Political Sciences; Public Administration; Software Engineering; Telecommunications Engineering.** Also Licenciatura; Especializaciónes offered through agreement with UPC (in Taxation, Public Law, Criminal Law, Civil Law), Universidad del Rosario (in Administrative Law and

Constitutional Law), Unisangil (in Clinical Psychology, Civil Law, Public Law), Universidad del Quindío (Taxation), Universidad del Atlántico (Civil Law and Commercial Law); Maestria in Distance Education offered with the Universitat Oberta de Cataluña and in Engineering Management offered with EAN.

Student Services: Academic Counselling, Canteen, Careers Guidance, Cultural Activities, Health Services, Language Laboratory, Library, Social Counselling, Sports Facilities

Publications: Cuestiones; Medunab; Reflexion Politica; Revista Colombiana de Computación; Revista Colombiana de Marketing

Last Updated: 09/11/15

AUTONOMOUS UNIVERSITY OF MANIZALES

Universidad Autónoma de Manizales (UAM)
Apartado aéreo 441, Antigua Estación del Ferrocarril, Manizales, Caldas A.A. 441
Tel: +57(6) 872-7272
Fax: +57(6) 881-0290
EMail: uam@manizales.autonoma.edu.co
Website: http://www.autonoma.edu.co

Rector: Gabriel Cadena Gómez
Tel: +57(6) 872-7272 Ext. 127 EMail: rector@autonoma.edu.co

Secretario General: Lorenzo Octavio Calderón Jaramillo
Tel: +57(6) 872-7272 Ext. 119 EMail: lcalderon@autonoma.edu.co

Vicerrector Académico: Iván Escobar Escobar
Tel: +57(6) 872-7272 Ext. 185 EMail: ivesco@autonoma.edu.co

International Relations: Viviana Fernanda Nieto Padilla, Coordinadora Oficina de Relaciones Internacionales ORI
Tel: +57(6) 872-7272 Ext.181 EMail: ri@autonoma.edu.co

Faculty

Engineering (Automation and Control Engineering; Computer Science; Electronic Engineering; Engineering; Industrial Engineering; Mechanical Engineering); **Health Sciences** (Biology; Dentistry; Health Sciences; Natural Sciences); **Social and Business Studies** (Business Administration; Design; Economics; Education; Fine Arts; Government; Law; Peace and Disarmament; Physical Education; Political Sciences; Social Sciences; Sports)

Institute

Languages (Chinese; English; Modern Languages; Portuguese; Spanish)

History: Founded 1979, acquired present status and title 1993.

Academic Year: January to December (January-May; June-July; August-December)

Admission Requirements: Secondary school certificate (bachillerato) and State examination (ICFES)

Main Language(s) of Instruction: Spanish

Accrediting Agency: Consejo Nacional de Acreditación (CNA)

Degrees and Diplomas: *Técnico Profesional*; *Tecnólogo*: **Agricultural Management; Automation and Control Engineering; Business and Commerce; Health Sciences; Information Technology; Mechanical Equipment and Maintenance; Systems Analysis.** *Profesional Universitario*: **Biomedical Engineering; Business Administration; Computer Engineering; Cooking and Catering; Dentistry; Economics; Electronic Engineering; Fashion Design; Government; Industrial Design; Industrial Engineering; International Business; International Relations; Mechanical Engineering; Physical Therapy; Political Sciences.** *Especialización*: **Business Administration; Dentistry; Finance; Health Administration; Management; Marketing; Neurological Therapy; Orthodontics; Orthopaedics; Periodontics; Physical Therapy; Rehabilitation and Therapy; Software Engineering.** *Maestria*: **Biology; Computer Science; Engineering; Management; Neurology; Physical Education; Public Health; Regional Planning; Rehabilitation and Therapy; Science Education; Software Engineering; Sports; Translation and Interpretation.** *Doctorado*: **Cognitive Sciences.** Also MBA

Student Services: Academic Counselling, Canteen, Careers Guidance, Cultural Activities, Foreign Studies Centre, Health Services, Language Laboratory, Library, Nursery Care, Social Counselling, Sports Facilities

Publications: Salud UAM Magazine

Last Updated: 22/10/15

AUTONOMOUS UNIVERSITY OF THE CARIBBEAN

Universidad Autónoma del Caribe (UAC)
Calle 90 No. 46-112, Barranquilla, Atlántico
Tel: +57(5) 367-1000
Fax: +57(5) 357-5944
EMail: uautonom@3.telecom.com.co
Website: http://www.uac.edu.co

Rector: Ramsés Vargas Lamadrid
Tel: +57(958) 357-3835 EMail: rectoria@uac.edu.co

Vicer-rectori Administrativo: Pedro Sierra
Tel: +57(958) 357-5944 EMail: psierra@uac.edu.co

Faculty

Administrative Sciences, Economics and Accountancy (Accountancy; Finance; Fiscal Law; Health Administration; Hotel Management; Human Resources; Management; Marketing; Taxation; Tourism; Transport Management); **Architecture, Arts and Design** (Architecture; Fashion Design; Graphic Design; Interior Design; Marketing; Multimedia); **Engineering** (Business Computing; Computer Engineering; Electronic Engineering; Industrial Engineering; Industrial Management; Mechanical Engineering; Mining Engineering; Systems Analysis; Telecommunications Engineering; Transport Management); **Jurisprudence** (Law; Political Sciences); **Social Sciences and Humanities** (Communication Studies; Education; Journalism; Mass Communication; Psychology; Radio and Television Broadcasting)

Programme

Virtual Mode Studies (Finance; International Business; Occupational Health; Safety Engineering)

Further Information: Also Campuses in: Ocaña Campus, Norte de Santander; Miami, Florida (USA)

History: Founded 1967, formally recognized by the State as a University 1974. A private institution.

Academic Year: January to December (January-June; July-December)

Admission Requirements: Secondary school certificate (bachillerato) and entrance examination

Fees: Undergraduate, 1,527,000-4,208,000; Graduate, 3735.000-6,716,000 (Colombian Peso)

Main Language(s) of Instruction: Spanish

Degrees and Diplomas: *Tecnólogo*; *Profesional Universitario*: **Accountancy; Architecture; Business Administration; Business and Commerce; Computer Engineering; Electronic Engineering; Fashion Design; Finance; Graphic Design; Hotel Management; Industrial Engineering; Interior Design; International Business; Journalism; Law; Marine Transport; Mass Communication; Mechanical Engineering; Political Sciences; Psychology; Radio and Television Broadcasting; Sports; Systems Analysis; Telecommunications Engineering; Tourism.** *Especialización*: **Communication Studies; Finance; Human Resources; Industrial Management; Management; Marketing; Mining Engineering; Occupational Health; Safety Engineering; Taxation; Telecommunications Engineering; Transport Management.** *Maestría*: **Business Administration; Business Computing; Education; Electronic Engineering; Finance; Health Administration; Management; Marketing; Mechanical Engineering; Transport Management.**

Student Services: Academic Counselling, Canteen, Careers Guidance, Cultural Activities, Health Services, IT Centre, Library, Nursery Care, Social Counselling, Sports Facilities

Publishing house: Taller Litográfico Uniautónoma

Last Updated: 22/10/15

AUTONOMOUS UNIVERSITY OF THE WEST

Universidad Autónoma de Occidente (UAO)
Apartado aéreo 3119, Calle 25 No. 115-85 km.2 vía Cali- Jamundi, Cali, Valle del Cauca 760030
Tel: +57(2) 318-8000
Fax: +57(2) 555-3757
EMail: buzon@uao.edu.co
Website: http://www.uao.edu.co

Rector: Luís Hernán Pérez Páez (1973-)
Tel: +57(2) 555-3749 +57(2) 555-000, Ext. 11770
EMail: rector@uao.edu.co; lhperez@uao.edu.co

Secretario General: Roberto Navarro Sánchez
Tel: +57(2) 318-8000, Ext. 11590
EMail: sedecuao@uao.edu.co; navarro@uao.edu.co

International Relations: Sandra Toro
Tel: +57(2) 318-8000, Ext. 11210 EMail: sjtoro@uao.edu.co

Faculty

Basic Sciences (Environmental Studies; Mathematics; Physics); **Economics and Business Management** (Administration; Economics); **Engineering** (Automation and Control Engineering; Electronic Engineering; Energy Engineering; Industrial Management; Mechanical Engineering); **Humanities** (Social Sciences); **Social Communication** (Advertising and Publicity; Communication Studies; Modern Languages)

History: Founded 1969. Acquired present status 1969.

Academic Year: January to November

Admission Requirements: Secondary school certificate and National Government examination ICFES

Fees: 1,000 per semester (US Dollar)

Main Language(s) of Instruction: Spanish

Accrediting Agency: Consejo Nacional de Acreditación (CNA)

Degrees and Diplomas: *Tecnólogo*; *Profesional Universitario*: **Accountancy; Advertising and Publicity; Biomedical Engineering; Business Administration; Computer Engineering; Economics; Electrical Engineering; Electronic Engineering; Environmental Engineering; Environmental Management; Film; Graphic Design; Industrial Engineering; Industrial Management; International Business; Journalism; Marketing; Mass Communication; Mechanical Engineering; Multimedia; Tourism.** *Especialización*: **Automation and Control Engineering; Communication Studies; Energy Engineering; Environmental Management; Finance; Hygiene; Marketing; Medical Technology; Safety Engineering.** *Maestría*: **Business Administration; Engineering; Environmental Studies; Hygiene; Safety Engineering; Transport Management.** Also Especialización Telecommunications Engineering offered jointly with Universidad del Cauca; Maestría in Economics offered with Universidad de Sevilla, Spain and Maestría in Law offered in collaboration with the Institute of Human Rights "Bartolomé de las Casas of the Universidad Carlos III from Madrid, Spain.

Student Services: Academic Counselling, Canteen, Careers Guidance, Cultural Activities, Foreign Studies Centre, Health Services, Language Laboratory, Library, Nursery Care, Social Counselling, Sports Facilities
Last Updated: 04/09/15

BUSINESS UNIVERSITY CORPORATION OF SALAMANCA

Corporación Universitaria Empresarial de Salamanca (CUES)
Carrera 50 No 79-155, Barranquilla, Atlantico
Tel: +57(5) 360-6585 +57(5) 360-6585 Ext. 235-236-237
Fax: +57(954) 368-1013
EMail: admisiones@cues.edu.co; mercadeo@cues.edu.co
Website: http://cues.edu.co

Rectora: Maria Carolina Arango Esquivia
EMail: rectoria@cues.edu.co

Programme

Business Administration (Business Administration); **Finance and International Business** (Finance; International Business); **Public Accountancy** (Accountancy); **Technological Studies** (Banking; Business Administration; Business and Commerce; Finance; International Business; Software Engineering)

History: Founded 1999.

Main Language(s) of Instruction: Spanish

Degrees and Diplomas: *Tecnólogo*; *Profesional Universitario*: **Accountancy; Business Administration; Finance; International Business.**

Student Services: Cultural Activities, Health Services, Library, Sports Facilities
Last Updated: 29/09/15

BUSINESS UNIVERSITY FOUNDATION OF THE CHAMBER OF COMMERCE OF BOGOTÁ

Fundación Universitaria Empresarial de la Camara de Comercio de Bogotá (UNIEMPRESARIAL)
Carrera 33A No. 30-20, Bogotá, Bogotá DC
Tel: +57(1) 508-2244
EMail: rector@uniempresarial.edu.co
Website: http://www.uniempresarial.edu.co

Rector: José Alejandro Cheyne García
EMail: rector@uniempresarial.edu.co

Programme

Accounting (Accountancy); **Business Administration** (Business Administration; Business and Commerce; Industrial Management); **Environmental Administration** (Environmental Management); **Finance and International Commerce** (Finance; International Business); **Marketing and Logistics** (Marketing; Transport Management); **Tourism** (Tourism)

History: Founded 2001.

Main Language(s) of Instruction: Spanish

Accrediting Agency: ACBSP

Degrees and Diplomas: *Profesional Universitario*; *Especialización*
Last Updated: 24/11/15

CAFAM UNIVERSITY FOUNDATION

Fundación Universitaria Cafam (UNICAFAM)
Avenida Carrera 68, No 90-88, Bloque 1 Piso 1, Bogotá
Tel: +57(1) 652-8600
EMail: admisiones@unicafam.edu.co
Website: http://www.unicafam.edu.co

Rector: Francisco Cajiao Restrepo

Faculty

Administrative Sciences (Business Administration; Management); **Engineering** (Industrial Engineering; Information Technology; Occupational Health; Safety Engineering)

School

Pedagogy (Pedagogy); **Tourism and Gastronomy** (Cooking and Catering; Hotel and Restaurant; Tourism)

History: Founded 2008.

Main Language(s) of Instruction: Spanish

Degrees and Diplomas: *Técnico Profesional*; *Tecnólogo*; *Profesional Universitario*: **Hotel and Restaurant; Industrial Engineering; Telecommunications Engineering; Tourism.** *Especialización*: **Occupational Health; Safety Engineering.** Also Diplomas

Student Services: Library
Last Updated: 29/09/15

CATHOLIC UNIVERSITY FOUNDATION OF THE NORTH

Fundación Universitaria Católica del Norte (UCN)
Carrera 21 No. 34 B-07, Santa Rosa de Osos, Antioquia
Tel: +57(4) 605-1535
Fax: +57(4) 605-4220
EMail: info@ucn.edu.co; Infoinstitucional@ucn.edu.co
Website: http://www.ucn.edu.co

Rector: Francisco Luis Angel Franco (2009-)
EMail: rectoria@ucn.edu.co

Secretary General: Orlando Ramirez Serna
EMail: qecgeneral@ucn.edu.co

Director Académico: Juan Mauricio Árias Giraldo

International Relations: Germán Gallego, Coordinador Internacionalización EMail: internacionalizacion@ucn.edu.co

Programme

Business Administration (Business Administration); **Computer Engineering** (Computer Engineering); **Criminal Investigation** (Criminology); **Philosophy and Religious Education** (Philosophy; Religious Education); **Postgraduate Studies** (Agricultural Management; Computer Engineering; Criminal Law; Education; Educational Technology; Industrial and Organizational Psychology;

Information Technology); **Psychology** (Psychology); **Social Communication** (Mass Communication); **Spanish Language Teaching** (Native Language Education); **Technical/Professional Studies** (Administration; Computer Science); **Technological Studies** (Agricultural Business; Finance; Forestry; Information Technology); **Theology** (Theology)

Further Information: Also Campuses in Medellín

History: Founded 1996. Acquired present status 1997.

Admission Requirements: Secondary school leaving (Diploma de Bachiller), Higher Education National Entrance Examination (ICFES)

Fees: 1.56m. per semester (Colombian Peso)

Main Language(s) of Instruction: Spanish

Accrediting Agency: Ministerio Educación Nacional

Degrees and Diplomas: *Técnico Profesional*; *Tecnólogo*; *Profesional Universitario*; *Especialización*: **Agricultural Management; Criminal Law; Educational Administration; Educational Technology; Industrial and Organizational Psychology; Information Management; Information Technology.** *Maestría*: **Education.** Also Licenciatura in Philosophy, Religious Education, Native Language Teaching; Diplomados

Student Services: Academic Counselling, Cultural Activities, Language Laboratory, Social Counselling

Publications: Revista Fundación Universitaria Catolica Norte

Last Updated: 05/10/15

CATHOLIC UNIVERSITY OF COLOMBIA

Universidad Católica de Colombia (UCATOLICA)

Avenida Caracas No. 46-72, Bogotá, Cundinamarca

Tel: +57(1) 327-7300 +57(1) 327-7333

Fax: +57(1) 288-3737

EMail: rectoria@ucatolica.edu.co; admisiones@ucatolica.edu.co

Website: http://www.ucatolica.edu.co

Rector: Francisco José Gómez Ortiz
Tel: +57(1) 327-7300 Ext. 5151 EMail: rectoria@ucatolica.edu.co

Secretario General: Sergio Martínez Londoño
Tel: +57(1) 327-7300 Ext. 3270-3272
EMail: secregeneral@ucatolica.edu.co

International Relations: Maria Elvira Prieto Martinez, Director, International Relations EMail: meprietom@ucatolica.edu.co

Faculty

Design (Architecture; Design); **Economics and Administrative Sciences** (Business Administration; Economics); **Engineering** (Civil Engineering; Computer Engineering; Electronic Engineering; Industrial Engineering; Telecommunications Engineering); **Law** (Law); **Psychology** (Psychology)

Department

Basic Sciences (Natural Sciences); **Humanities** (Arts and Humanities)

Institute

Languages (English; Modern Languages; Spanish)

Further Information: Also branches in Ibagué and Neiva

History: Founded 1970. Acquired present status 1974.

Academic Year: January to December (January-May; July-December)

Admission Requirements: Secondary school certificate (bachillerato) or equivalent, and entrance examination

Fees: Undergraduate, 2,417,000-4,256,000; Graduate, 3,145,000-6,427,000 (Colombian Peso)

Main Language(s) of Instruction: Spanish

Degrees and Diplomas: *Profesional Universitario*; *Especialización*: **Administrative Law; Clinical Psychology; Constitutional Law; Criminal Law; Criminology; Educational Psychology; Finance; Fiscal Law; Government; Industrial and Organizational Psychology; Information Management; Information Technology; Labour Law; Law; Management; Psychology; Regional Planning; Road Engineering; Social Welfare; Taxation; Water Science.** *Maestría*: **Design; Human Rights; International Law; Political Sciences; Psychology.**

Student Services: IT Centre, Library, eLibrary

Academic Staff *2014-2015*	**TOTAL**
FULL-TIME	**678**
PART-TIME	**56**
STAFF WITH DOCTORATE	
FULL-TIME	**57**

Student Numbers *2014-2015*	
All (Foreign included)	**11,005**

Last Updated: 22/10/15

CATHOLIC UNIVERSITY OF MANIZALES

Universidad Católica de Manizales (UCM)

Carrera 23 No. 60-63 Avenida Santander, Manizales, Caldas

Tel: +57(6) 893-3050 +57(6) 878-2900

Fax: +57(6) 878-2950 +57(6) 878-2937

EMail: direxco@ucm.edu.co

Website: http://www.ucm.edu.co

Rectora: Gloria del Carmen Torres Bustamante
Tel: +57(6) 878-2901 EMail: rec@ucm.edu.co

Secretary-General: Julieta Henao Muñoz
Tel: +57(6) 878-2902 EMail: jhenao@ucm.edu.co

Vicerectora Administrativa y Financiera: Maria Offir Jaramillo López
Tel: +5(6) 893-3050 Ext. 4000-4001
EMail: mjaramillo@ucm.edu.co

Faculty

Administration (Safety Engineering; Service Trades; Tourism); **Education** (Computer Education; Education; Educational Administration; Educational Sciences; Educational Testing and Evaluation; Environmental Studies; Mathematics Education; Religious Education; Science Education; Special Education; Technology Education); **Engineering and Architecture** (Architecture; Environmental Engineering; Industrial Engineering; Real Estate; Safety Engineering; Telecommunications Engineering); **Social Sciences, Humanities and Theology** (Advertising and Publicity)

Programme

Health Sciences (Health Administration; Health Sciences; Microbiology; Nursing; Virology)

Research Institute

Microbiology and Agroindustrial Biotechnology (Agricultural Business; Microbiology)

History: Founded 1954 as Colegio Mayor by the Hermanas de la Caridad Dominicanas de la Presentación, became University 1978 and acquired present status and title 1993.

Academic Year: February to December (February-June; July-December)

Admission Requirements: Secondary school certificate and State examination (ICFES)

Fees: National: $3.500.000 (Colombian Peso), International: U$1095 (US Dollar)

Main Language(s) of Instruction: Spanish, English

Accrediting Agency: CNA Consejo Nacional de Acreditacion

Degrees and Diplomas: *Técnico Profesional*: **Tourism.** *Profesional Universitario*: **Administration; Advertising and Publicity; Architecture; Environmental Engineering; Industrial Engineering; Nursing; Telecommunications Engineering; Tourism; Virology.** *Especialización*: **Educational Administration; Educational Testing and Evaluation; Health Administration; Microbiology; Real Estate; Safety Engineering; Special Education; Telecommunications Engineering.** *Maestría*: **Education; Educational Sciences; Microbiology; Pedagogy; Surveying and Mapping.** *Doctorado*: **Education.** Also Preuniversitario in Health Sciences; Teacher Training degrees (Licenciatura) offered through distance mode in Sciences Education, Environmental Studies, Religious Education, Mathematics Education, Technology Education and Computer Education.

Student Services: Academic Counselling, Canteen, Careers Guidance, Cultural Activities, Health Services, Library, Nursery Care, Social Counselling, Sports Facilities

Publications: Newspaper "El Obelisco"; Revista de Investigación

Publishing House: Centro Editorial Universidad Católica

Last Updated: 31/08/15

CATHOLIC UNIVERSITY OF PEREIRA

Universidad Católica de Pereira (UCP)
Carrera 21 No. 49-95, Av. de las Américas, Pereira, Risaralda
Tel: +57(96) 312-4000
Fax: +57(96) 312-7613
Website: http://www.ucp.edu.co

Rector: Diego Augusto Arcila Vélez
Tel: +57(6) 312-4000 Ext. 1001 EMail: rectoria@ucp.edu.co

Vicerrector Académico: Luis Eduardo Peláez Valencia
Tel: +57(6) 312-4000 Ext. 1004

Secretaria General: José Fredy Aristizabal
Tel: +57(6) 312-4000 Ext. 2010

International Relations: Paula Andrea Velez Tinoco, Coordinadora oficina de Internacionalización y Relaciones Interinstitucionales
Tel: +57(6) 312-4000 Ext. 2011

Faculty

Architecture and Design (Architecture; Industrial Design); **Basic Sciences and Engineering** (Computer Engineering; Computer Science; Industrial Engineering; Software Engineering; Telecommunications Engineering); **Economics and Administrative Sciences** (Agricultural Business; Business Administration; Economics; Finance; International Business; Marketing; Regional Planning; Transport Management); **Humanities, Social Sciences and Education** (Communication Studies; Development Studies; Mass Communication; Psychology; Religious Studies)

History: Founded 1975.

Main Language(s) of Instruction: Spanish

Degrees and Diplomas: *Técnico Profesional*; *Tecnólogo*; *Profesional Universitario*; *Especialización*: **Architecture; Clinical Psychology; Communication Studies; Design; Development Studies; Economics; Educational Technology; Finance; Human Resources; Management; Pedagogy; Social Psychology; Social Work; Software Engineering; Town Planning.** *Maestría*: **Development Studies; Pedagogy; Regional Planning.** Also Licenciatura

Student Services: Canteen, Library

Last Updated: 23/10/15

CATHOLIC UNIVERSITY OF THE EAST

Universidad Católica de Oriente (UCO)
Sector 3, Carrera 46 No. 40B-50, Rionegro, Antioquia
Tel: +57(94) 531-6666
Fax: +57(94) 531-3972
EMail: uco@uco.edu.co
Website: http://www.uco.edu.co

Rector: Darío Gómez Zuluaga
Tel: +57(4) 569-9090 Ext. 231-232 EMail: rectoria@uco.edu.co

Directora Administrativa: Ana Maria Giraldo Sánchez
Tel: +57(4) 569-9090 Ext. 257-240
EMail: administrativa.dir@uco.edu.co

International Relations: Daniel Pérez Valencia, Oficina Relaciones Internacionales
Tel: +57(4) 569-9090 Ext. 335
EMail: internacional.jefe@uco.edu.co; internacional@uco.net.co

Faculty

Agriculture (Agriculture; Agronomy; Animal Husbandry; Biotechnology; Botany); **Economics and Administrative Sciences** (Accountancy; Business Administration; Finance; International Business; Marketing; Taxation; Transport Management); **Education** (Education; Foreign Languages Education; Humanities and Social Science Education; Mathematics Education; Parks and Recreation; Physical Education; Religious Studies; Sports); **Engineering** (Computer Engineering; Electronic Engineering; Environmental Engineering; Industrial Engineering; Software Engineering; Systems Analysis); **Health Sciences** (Community Health; Dietetics; Health Sciences; Nutrition); **Law** (Law; Social Sciences); **Social Sciences** (Gerontology; Mass Communication; Psychology); **Theology and Humaniries** (Arts and Humanities; Theology)

Further Information: Also five experimental farm centres. Regional distance education centres (CREAD)

History: Founded 1983. Acquired present status 1993.

Academic Year: February to November (February-June; July-November)

Admission Requirements: Secondary school certificate (bachillerato) and State examination (ICFES)

Main Language(s) of Instruction: Spanish

Degrees and Diplomas: *Técnico Profesional*; *Tecnólogo*; *Profesional Universitario*; *Especialización*: **Education; Finance; Marketing; Software Engineering; Taxation; Transport Management.** *Maestría*: **Arts and Humanities; Biotechnology; Community Health; Criminal Law; Education; Plant Pathology.** *Doctorado*: **Biotechnology; Theology.** Also Licenciatura

Student Services: Academic Counselling, Careers Guidance, Cultural Activities, Foreign Studies Centre, Library, Social Counselling, Sports Facilities

Publications: Revista Universidad Católica de Oriente

Publishing House: Publicaciones UCO

Last Updated: 22/10/15

CEIPA UNIVERSITY FOUNDATION

Fundación Universitaria CEIPA
Calle 77 Sur No. 40-165 Via Principal a Sabaneta, Sabaneta, Antioquia
Tel: +57(4) 305-6100
Fax: +57(4) 301-1736
EMail: comunicaciones@ceipa.edu.co
Website: http://www.ceipa.edu.co

Rector: Diego Mauricio Mazo Cuervo
EMail: diego.mazo@ceipa.edu.co; rectoria@ceipa.edu.co

Vicerrector: Diego Mauricio Mazo Cuervo

Programme

Business Administration (Business Administration); **Finance** (Finance); **Human Resources** (Human Resources); **International Business** (International Business); **Marketing** (Marketing); **Postgraduate Studies** (Finance; Human Resources; International Business; Management; Marketing; Transport Management); **Public Accountancy** (Accountancy)

Further Information: Also Barranquilla, Bogotá, Lima (Perú) Campuses

History: Founded 1972. Acquired present status 1992.

Main Language(s) of Instruction: Spanish

Degrees and Diplomas: *Profesional Universitario*; *Especialización*: **Finance; Human Resources; International Business; Management; Marketing; Transport Management.**

Last Updated: 02/10/15

CENDA UNIVERSITY CORPORATION

Corporación Universitaria CENDA (CENDA)
Av. Caracas, No 35-18/02, Bogotá
Tel: +57(1) 245-9170 +57(1) 310-7779 +57(1) 2351420
Fax: +57(1) 242-3216
EMail: cenda@cenda.edu.co; extensionydivulgacion@cenda.edu.co
Website: http://www.cenda.edu.co

Rector: Luis Hernando Ballestas Rincón
Tel: +57(1) 245-3216 Ext. 109 EMail: rectoria@cenda.edu.co

Vicerrector Académico: Yesid Manuel Hernández Riaño
Tel: +57(1) 245-3216 Ext. 119

Directora Administrativa y Financiera: Mónica Catalina Carreño Díaz Tel: +57(1) 245-3216 Ext. 118

Programme

Art Education and Performing Arts (Art Education; Performing Arts); **Dance** (Dance); **Pedagogy** (Pedagogy); **Physical Education, Recreation and Sports** (Parks and Recreation; Physical Education; Sports); **Postgraduate Studies**; **Preschool Education** (Preschool Education); **Software Development** (Software Engineering); **Sports** (Sports)

History: Founded 2011.

Main Language(s) of Instruction: Spanish

Degrees and Diplomas: *Técnico Profesional*; *Tecnólogo*; *Profesional Universitario*; *Especialización*: **Literacy Education;**

Mathematics Education; Physical Education. Also Diplomados and Licenciatura in Physical Education, Art Education and Performin Arts, Preschool Education

Student Services: Library

Last Updated: 29/09/15

CENTRAL UNIVERSITY

Universidad Central

Calle 21 No. 4-40, Bogotá

Tel: +57(1) 336-2607

EMail: admision@ucentral.edu.co

Website: http://www.ucentral.edu.co

Rector: Rafael Santos Calderón
Tel: +57(1) 323-9868 Ext. 1101-1104
EMail: rectoria@ucentral.edu.co

Vicerrector Administrativo y Financiero: Nelson Gnecco Iglesias
Tel: +57(1) 323-9868 +57(1) 326-68204 Ext. 2110/2106
EMail: viceadministrativa@ucentral.edu.co

Secretario General: Fabio Raúl Trompa Ayala
Tel: +57(1) 323-9868-3501 Ext. 2201/2202
EMail: secretariageneral@ucentral.edu.co

Faculty

Administrative Sciences, Economics and Accountancy (Accountancy; Business Administration; Economics; Marketing); **Engineering** (Computer Engineering; Electronic Engineering; Environmental Engineering; Industrial Engineering; Mathematics; Mechanical Engineering; Natural Sciences; Systems Analysis); **Social Sciences, Humanities and Arts** (Advertising and Publicity; Arts and Humanities; Cinema and Television; Journalism; Law; Literature; Mass Communication; Modern Languages; Music; Political Sciences; Social Sciences; Social Studies; Theatre)

History: Founded 1966, formerly Universidad Central de la Nueva Granada (1826).

Academic Year: February to December (February-June; July-December)

Admission Requirements: Secondary school certificate (bachillerato) and State examination (ICFES test)

Main Language(s) of Instruction: Spanish

Degrees and Diplomas: *Profesional Universitario*: **Accountancy; Advertising and Publicity; Biology; Business Administration; Cinema and Television; Computer Engineering; Economics; Electronic Engineering; Environmental Engineering; Industrial Engineering; Journalism; Law; Marketing; Mass Communication; Mathematics; Mechanical Engineering; Music; Theatre; Writing.** *Especialización*: **Accountancy; Electronic Engineering; Industrial Engineering; Management; Mechanical Engineering; Taxation; Telecommunications Services; Writing.** *Maestría*: **Computer Science; Management; Music; Social Sciences; Social Studies; Taxation; Writing.**

Student Services: Cultural Activities, Health Services, Language Laboratory, Library, Nursery Care, Sports Facilities

Publications: Colección de publicaciones del Instituto Colombiano de Estudios Latinoamericanos y del Caribe - ICELAC; Nomadas; Temas Humanísticos

Last Updated: 23/10/15

CES UNIVERSITY

Universidad CES

Calle 10 A No. 22-04, Medellín, Antioquia

Tel: +57(4) 444-0555

Fax: +57(4) 266-6046

EMail: osaldarriaga@ces.edu.co

Website: http://www.ces.edu.co

Rector: José María Maya Mejía (2000-)
Tel: +57(4) 268-3711 Ext. 151 EMail: jmayam@ces.edu.co

Secretaria General: Patricia Chejne EMail: pchejne@ces.edu.co

International Relations: Oscar Javier Saldarriaga, Head, International Relations EMail: osaldarriaga@ces.edu.co

Faculty

Administrative Sciences (Business Administration); **Law** (Law); **Medicine** (Medicine; Surgery); **Odontology** (Dentistry); **Physiotherapy** (Physical Therapy); **Psychology** (Psychology); **Sciences and Biotechnology** (Biotechnology; Natural Sciences); **Veterinary Medicine and Zootechnics** (Animal Husbandry; Veterinary Science)

Further Information: Also Bogotá Campuses

History: Founded 1977. Previously known as Instituto de Ciencias de la Salud.

Academic Year: January to November

Admission Requirements: Admission Examination, Colombian State Examination (ICFES), Interview

Fees: 1,500-2,500 per semester (US Dollar)

Main Language(s) of Instruction: Spanish

Degrees and Diplomas: *Profesional Universitario*; *Especialización*: **Business Administration; Dentistry; Law; Medicine; Physical Therapy; Psychology.** *Maestría*: **Biology; Biomedical Engineering; Business Administration; Dentistry; Medicine; Physical Therapy; Psychology; Veterinary Science.** *Doctorado*: **Medicine.**

Student Services: Academic Counselling, Cultural Activities, Foreign Studies Centre, Language Laboratory, Library, Sports Facilities

Publications: Faculties' Journals

Last Updated: 23/10/15

CIEO UNIVERSITY FOUNDATION

Fundación Universitaria CIEO (UNICIEO)

Dirección: Carrera 5, No. 118-10, Bogotá

Tel: +57(1) 743-7919

Fax: +57(1) 214-3297

EMail: contacto@unicieo.edu.co

Website: http://www.unicieo.edu.co

Rector: Alvaro Martinez Ocampo
Tel: +57(1) 743-7919 Ext.119 EMail: rectoria@unicieo.edu.co

Secretario General: Andres Ivan Toledo Bernal
Tel: +57(1) 743-7919 Ext.118
EMail: secretariageneral@unicieo.edu.co

Vicerrectora Académica: Amparo Varón de Gaitán
Tel: +57(1) 7437-919 Ext.115
EMail: viceacademica@unlcieo.edu.co

Programme

Dental Laboratory Technology (Medical Technology); **Endodontics** (Dentistry); **Oral Implantology and Reconstructive Dentistry** (Dental Technology); **Oral Rehabilitation** (Dentistry; Rehabilitation and Therapy); **Orthodontics and Dentofacial Orthopedics** (Orthodontics; Orthopaedics)

History: Founded 2010.

Main Language(s) of Instruction: Spanish

Degrees and Diplomas: *Tecnólogo*: **Medical Technology.** *Especialización*: **Dental Technology; Dentistry; Orthodontics; Orthopaedics; Rehabilitation and Therapy.**

Last Updated: 29/09/15

CLARETIAN UNIVERSITY FOUNDATION

Fundación Universitaria Claretiana (UNICLARETIANA)

14 Dirección Calle 20, No. 5-66, Barrio la Yesquita, Quibdó, Chocó

Tel: +57(4) 671-1217

Fax: +57(4) 670-9814

Website: https://uniclaretiana.edu.co

Rector: José Agustín Monroy Palacio

Faculty

Engineering (Computer Engineering; Industrial Engineering); **Religious Studies and Humanities** (Computer Engineering; Industrial Engineering; Psychology; Social Work; Theology)

Programme

Postgraduate Studies (Bible; Social and Community Services; Social Psychology; Social Studies)

History: Founded 2006.

Main Language(s) of Instruction: Spanish

Degrees and Diplomas: *Profesional Universitario*: **Computer Engineering; Industrial Engineering; Psychology; Social Work.**

Especialización: **Bible; Social and Community Services; Social Psychology; Social Studies.** Also Licenciatura in Religious Studies and Bible Studies; Diploma in Continuing Education
Last Updated: 10/09/15

COLEGIATURA COLOMBIANA UNIVERSITY INSTITUTION

Institución Universitaria Colegiatura Colombiana

Km 7 Vía Las Palmas, Medellín, Antioquia 05001000
Tel: +57(4) 354-7120
Fax: +57(4) 354-7120 Ext. 104
EMail: subdireccioncomunicaciones@colegiatura.edu.co
Website: http://www.colegiatura.edu.co

Rector: Julio Salleg (2013 - present)
Tel: 3547120 ext. 129 EMail: rectoria@colegiatura.edu.co

Director of Systemic Knowledge: Liliana Díaz Santamaría
Tel: 3547120 ext. 225
EMail: direccionsabersistemico@colegiatura.edu.co

Director of Sustainable Knowledge: Alcira Cano
Tel: 3547120 ext. 132
EMail: direccionsabersostenible@colegiatura.edu.co

Director of Transformer Knowledge: Gloria Patricia Díez Ruiz
Tel: 3547120 ext. 112
EMail: direccionsabertransformador@colegiatura.edu.co

General Secretary: María Eugenia Puerta Restrepo
Tel: 3547120 ext. 228 EMail: sgeneral@colegiatura.educ.o

Faculty

Comunication (Advertising and Publicity; Communication Studies; Mass Communication); **Design** (Display and Stage Design; Fashion Design; Graphic Design); **Gastronomy and Cooking** (Cooking and Catering)

History: Founded 1989. Acquired present status 2000.

Academic Year: February to November

Admission Requirements: High School certificate and National Examination from the Ministry of Education (SABER).

Fees: 6,500,000 per semester (Colombian Peso)

Main Language(s) of Instruction: Spanish

Accrediting Agency: Colombian Education Ministery

Degrees and Diplomas: *Bachillerato*; *Profesional Universitario*: **Advertising and Publicity; Communication Studies; Cooking and Catering; Display and Stage Design; Fashion Design; Graphic Design; International Relations.** *Especialización*: **Communication Studies; Cooking and Catering; Design.**

Student Services: Academic Counselling, Canteen, Careers Guidance, Cultural Activities, Health Services, Library, Social Counselling

Publications: (Currently untitled publication)
Last Updated: 09/11/15

COLLEGE OF ADVANCED ADMINISTRATION STUDIES

Colegio de Estudios Superiores de Administración (CESA)

Carrera 6 No. 34-51, Bogotá
Tel: +57(1) 339-5300
Fax: +57(1) 565-7737
EMail: info.formacionejecutiva@cesa.edu.co
Website: http://www.cesa.edu.co

Rector: Henry Bradford Sicard
Tel: +57(1) 339-5300 Ext. 2122
EMail: angelica.gonzalez@cesa.edu.co

Vicerrector Administrativo y Financiero: Xavier Malo Puig
Tel: +57(1) 339-5300 Ext. 2156 EMail: janneth.diaz@cesa.edu.co

Secretario General: Juan Santiago Correa Restrepo
Tel: +57(1) 339-5300 Ext. 1154

Programme

Business Administration (Business Administration); **ELITE Leadership and Entrepreneurship** (Leadership; Management); **Postgraduate Studies** (Business Administration; Finance; Marketing)

Centre

Business English *(CESA CBE)* (English)

History: Founded 1975 with support of INCOLDA (Colombian Business Institute) and ANDI (National Association of Industrials). A private, non-profit oriented institution.

Admission Requirements: Secondary school cerificate (Bachillerato) or recognized equivalent, entrance examination

Fees: 3,100 per semester (US Dollar)

Main Language(s) of Instruction: Spanish

Accrediting Agency: Consejo Nacional de Acreditación (CNA)

Degrees and Diplomas: *Profesional Universitario*: **Business Administration.** *Especialización*: **Finance; Marketing.** *Maestría*: **Finance; Marketing.** Also International MBA in Administration

Student Services: Academic Counselling, Careers Guidance, Cultural Activities, Health Services, Language Laboratory, Library, Social Counselling, Sports Facilities
Last Updated: 23/09/15

COLOMBIAN-AMERICAN UNIVERSITY INSTITUTION UNICA

Institución Universitaria Colombo Americana ÚNICA (UNICA)

19th Street, 2 A-49, Bogotá, Cundinamarca
Tel: +57(1) 281-1777
Fax: +57(1) 342-3442
EMail: info@unica.edu.co; rectoria@unica.edu.co
Website: http://www.unica.edu.co

Presidente: María Lucía Casas EMail: rectoria@unica.edu.co

Admissions and Walfare Department Director: Carolina Mendoza EMail: dir.admisiones@unica.edu.co

Programme

Bilingual Education (Bilingual and Bicultural Education; Education)

History: Founded 2004. Acquired present status 2011.

Admission Requirements: Internal admission process

Main Language(s) of Instruction: Spanish, English

Degrees and Diplomas: *Profesional Universitario*: **Bilingual and Bicultural Education.** *Especialización*: **Bilingual and Bicultural Education.**

Student Services: Academic Counselling, Cultural Activities, Foreign Studies Centre, Health Services, IT Centre, Language Laboratory, Library, Nursery Care, Residential Facilities, Social Counselling, Sports Facilities, eLibrary
Last Updated: 01/09/15

COLOMBIAN SCHOOL OF MARKETING FOUNDATION

Fundación Escuela Colombiana de Mercadotecnia (ESCOLME)

Apartado aéreo 4983, Calle 50 No. 40-39, Medellín, Antioquia
Tel: +57(4) 216-1700
Fax: +57(4) 239-4854
EMail: info@escolme.edu.co
Website: http://www.escolme.edu.co

Rector: Juan Carlos Cadavid Botero EMail: rector@escolme.edu.co

Programme

Business Administration *(Professional Cycle)* (Business Administration); **Business Administration** (Business Administration); **Finance** (Finance); **Information Systems Administration** (Information Technology); **International Business** (International Business); **Marketing** (Marketing); **Postgraduate Studies** (Finance); **Public Accountancy** *(Professional Cycle)* (Accountancy); **Public Accountancy** (Accountancy); **Technological Studies** (Computer Engineering; Computer Networks; Finance; Health Administration; Marketing)

History: Founded 1970.

Fees: Undergraduate, 982,262-2,059,778 per annum; Postgraduate, 3,615,150 per annum (Colombian Peso)

Main Language(s) of Instruction: Spanish

Degrees and Diplomas: *Tecnólogo*; *Profesional Universitario*; *Especialización*: **Finance.** Also DIploma
Last Updated: 01/10/15

COLOMBIAN SCHOOL OF REHABILITATION

Fundación Escuela Colombiana de Rehabilitación (ECR)

Av Carrera 15 No. 151-68, Bogotá
Tel: +57(1) 627-0366
Fax: +57(1) 614-1390
EMail: ecr@ecr.edu.co
Website: http://www.ecr.edu.co

Rectora: Martha Isabel Botero Álvarez EMail: rectoria@ecr.edu.co

International Relations: Luz Juanita Ruiz de Prada

Faculty
Occupational Therapy (Occupational Therapy); **Phonology and Audiology** (Speech Therapy and Audiology); **Physiotherapy** (Physical Therapy); **Postgraduate Studies** (Ergotherapy; Occupational Therapy; Physical Therapy; Safety Engineering; Speech Therapy and Audiology)

History: Founded 1952. Acquired present status 1995.

Fees: 2.77m (Colombian Peso)

Main Language(s) of Instruction: Spanish

Degrees and Diplomas: *Profesional Universitario*; *Especialización*: **Ergotherapy; Neurological Therapy; Physical Therapy; Speech Therapy and Audiology.**

Student Services: Academic Counselling, Canteen, Cultural Activities, Facilities for disabled people, Health Services, Library, Social Counselling, Sports Facilities
Last Updated: 01/10/15

COLOMBIAN TECHNOLOGICAL-INDUSTRIAL CORPORATION

Corporación Tecnológica Industrial Colombiana (TEINCO)

Calle 42, No. 16-86, Bogotá
Tel: +57(1) 485-6565
Fax: +57(1) 285-3458
EMail: oportunidades@teinco.edu.co
Website: http://www.teinco.edu.co

Rectora: Diana Patricia Camargo Ramírez
EMail: rectoria@teinco.edu.co

Programme
Accountancy (Accountancy; Finance; Taxation); **Business Administration** (Administration; Business Administration; Management; Social Welfare); **Graphic Design** (Communication Arts; Computer Graphics); **Mechatronics Engineering** (Automation and Control Engineering; Electronic Engineering; Mechanical Engineering); **Systems Engineering** (Computer Engineering; Computer Networks; Multimedia; Software Engineering)

History: Founded 1987.

Main Language(s) of Instruction: Spanish

Degrees and Diplomas: *Técnico Profesional*; *Tecnólogo*; *Profesional Universitario*

Student Services: Library
Last Updated: 25/09/15

COMFACAUCA UNIVERSITY CORPORATION

Corporación Universitaria Comfacauca (UNICOMFACAUCA)

Calle 4 N° 8-30, Popayán
Tel: +57(1) 822-0517
EMail: contacto@unicomfacauca.edu.co
Website: http://www.unicomfacauca.edu.co

Rectora: Isabel Ramírez Mejía

Vicerrectora General: Victoria Eugenia Patiño Arenas

Programme
Gastronomy and Professional Cooking (Cooking and Catering); **Industrial Engineering** (Industrial Engineering); **Mechatronics Engineering** (Electronic Engineering); **Professional/Technical Studies** (Engineering); **Public Accountancy** (Accountancy); **Social communication and Journalism** (Journalism; Mass Communication); **Systems Engineering** (Computer Engineering); **Technological Studies** (Engineering; Environmental Studies; Food Science)

History: Founded 2001.

Fees: 1,287,800-3,990,000 per semester (Colombian Peso)

Main Language(s) of Instruction: Spanish

Degrees and Diplomas: *Técnico Profesional*; *Tecnólogo*; *Profesional Universitario*: **Accountancy; Computer Engineering; Cooking and Catering; Electronic Engineering; Industrial Engineering; Journalism; Law; Mass Communication.** Also Maestria and Especializacion offered by Universidad de Manizales and Universidad Católica de Manizales.

Student Services: Canteen, Cultural Activities, Health Services, Library, Sports Facilities, eLibrary
Last Updated: 29/09/15

COMFANORTE FOUNDATION OF ADVANCED STUDIES

Fundación de Estudios Superiores Comfanorte

Av 4 # 15-14, La Playa, San Jóse de Cúcuta, Norte de Santander
Tel: +57(75) 582-9292 Ext. 111-222
Fax: +57(75) 583-3966
EMail: admisiones@fesc.edu.co
Website: http://www.fesc.edu.co

Rectora: Carmen Cecilia Quero de González
EMail: rectoria@fesc.edu.co

Secretaria General: Marlene Cecilia Duque Eugenio

Programme
Fashion Design and Business Administration (Business Administration; Fashion Design); **Financial Administration** (Finance); **Graphic Design** (Graphic Design); **International Business** *(Distance Mode)* (International Business); **International Business** (International Business); **Technical Studies** (Accountancy; Administration; Computer Networks; Fashion Design; Graphic Design; Marketing; Taxation; Tourism; Transport Management); **Technological/Professional Studies** (Advertising and Publicity; Business Administration; Fashion Design; Graphic Design; Hotel Management; International Business; Management; Marketing; Tourism; Transport Management; Welfare and Protective Services); **Tourism and Hotel Administration** (Hotel Management; Tourism); **Virtual Studies** (Business Administration; Hotel Management; Tourism; Transport Management; Welfare and Protective Services)

Campus
Ocaña (Advertising and Publicity; Finance; Graphic Design; International Business)

Further Information: Also Ocaña Campus

History: Founded 1993.

Main Language(s) of Instruction: Spanish

Degrees and Diplomas: *Técnico Profesional*; *Tecnólogo*; *Profesional Universitario*. Also Especialización in Esthetics and Cosmetology offered with FECS EDES; Especialización in Health Administration offered with Universidad Católica de Manizales

Student Services: Library
Last Updated: 01/10/15

COMFENALCO SANTANDER UNIVERSITY FOUNDATION

Fundación Universitaria Comfenalco Santander (UNC)

Avenida González Valencia, 52-69, Bucaramanga Santander
Tel: +57(7) 657-7000 Ext.4101
EMail: administracion@unc.edu.co; bienestaru@unc.edu.co
Website: http://www.unc.edu.co

Rectora: Carmen Cecilia Quintero Lozano
EMail: Rectoria@unc.edu.co

Programme
Logistics and Organizational Marketing (Marketing; Transport Management); **Tourism and Local Development** (Development Studies; Tourism); **Visual Communication Design** (Communication Arts)

History: Founded 2010.

Main Language(s) of Instruction: Spanish

Degrees and Diplomas: *Tecnólogo*; *Profesional Universitario*: **Marketing; Transport Management.**

Student Services: Sports Facilities

Last Updated: 29/09/15

COMFENALCO TECHNOLOGICAL UNIVERSITY FOUNDATION

Fundación Universitaria Tecnológico Comfenalco (TECNOLOGICO COMFENALCO)

Sede A Barrio España, Cr 44 D No 30A-91, Cartagena de Indias, Bolívar
Tel: +57(5) 669-0754
EMail: tecno@tecnologicocomfenalco.edu.co
Website: http://www.tecnologicocomfenalco.edu.co

Rector: Mauricio Ricardo Ruiz
Tel: +57(5) 669-0754 Ext. 2000
EMail: rropain@tecnologicocomfenalco.edu.co

Faculty
Administrative Sciences, Economics and Accounting (Accountancy; Business Administration; Finance; Human Resources; International Business; Management; Marketing; Sales Techniques; Taxation; Tourism; Transport Management); **Engineering** (Computer Engineering; Computer Networks; Electronic Engineering; Engineering Management; Environmental Engineering; Environmental Management; Industrial Engineering; Industrial Management; Occupational Health; Safety Engineering; Software Engineering); **Social and Human Sciences** (Administrative Law; Law; Psychology)

Further Information: Also Campuses B and C in Barrio Zaragocilla

History: Founded 1984.

Main Language(s) of Instruction: Spanish

Degrees and Diplomas: *Tecnólogo*; *Profesional Universitario*; *Especialización*: **Computer Engineering; Computer Networks; Environmental Management; Finance; Human Resources; International Business; Management; Marketing; Safety Engineering; Taxation; Transport Management.** Also Especialización and Maestria (and all degrees) in Law and Psychology are offered through University of Medellin; Diplomados

Student Services: IT Centre, Library

Student Numbers *2015-2016*: Total 11,478

Last Updated: 06/10/15

CO-OPERATIVE UNIVERSITY OF COLOMBIA

Universidad Cooperativa de Colombia (UCC)

Cra 42 No. 49-95, Bloque 8, Medellín
Tel: +57(4) 444-6065
Fax: +57(1) 232-0316
EMail: uccbogota@ucc.edu.co; tuttyk@hotmail.com
Website: http://www.ucc.edu.co

Rectora: Maritza Rondón Rangel
EMail: maritza.rondon@ucc.edu.co

Area
Agronomy, Veterinary and Related Sciences (Animal Husbandry; Veterinary Science); **Economics, Administration and Accountancy** (Accountancy; Administrative Law; Business Administration; Criminal Law; Environmental Engineering; Finance; Health Administration; Industrial Engineering; International Business; Management; Marketing; Mechanical Engineering; Occupational Health; Social Psychology; Taxation); **Educational Sciences** (Computer Education; Education; Educational Technology; Foreign Languages Education; Higher Education Teacher Training; Mathematics Education; Native Language Education; Parks and Recreation; Physical Education; Sports; Technology Education; Water Science); **Engineering, Architecture, Town Planning** (Civil Engineering; Computer Engineering; Computer Networks; Computer Science; Construction Engineering; Educational Technology; Electronic Engineering; Finance; Health Administration; Human Resources; Industrial Engineering; Information Technology; Peace and Disarmament; Pedagogy; Social Psychology; Software Engineering; Telecommunications Engineering; Transport Management); **Fine Arts** (Graphic Design); **Health Sciences** (Animal Husbandry; Dentistry; Electronic Engineering; Epidemiology; Health Administration; Hotel Management; Industrial Engineering; Medicine; Nursing; Orthodontics; Psychiatry and Mental Health; Veterinary Science); **Social Sciences, Law and Political Science** (Child Care and Development; Criminal Law; Educational Psychology; Environmental Studies; Law; Mass Communication; Occupational Health; Private Law; Psychology; Public Administration; Religious Education; Safety Engineering; Social and Community Services; Software Engineering)

Further Information: Also branches in Apartadó, Araucaã, Barrancabermeja, Bogotáã, Bucaramanga, Cali, Cartago, El Esã*pinal*, Ibagué, Medellín y Envigado, Montería, Neiva, Pasto, Pereira, Popayán, Quibdóã, Santa Marta, Villavicencio

History: Founded 1958. A private institution.

Admission Requirements: Secondary school certificate (bachillerato) and entrance examination

Main Language(s) of Instruction: Spanish

Degrees and Diplomas: *Técnico Profesional*; *Tecnólogo*; *Profesional Universitario*; *Especialización*: **Criminal Law; Educational Administration; Educational Technology; Epidemiology; Finance; Health Administration; Humanities and Social Science Education; Law; Marketing; Orthodontics; Parks and Recreation; Physical Education; Public Administration; Road Engineering; Safety Engineering; Social and Community Services; Software Engineering; Sports; Taxation; Telecommunications Engineering.** *Maestría*: **Child Care and Development; Development Studies; Education; Educational Psychology; Educational Technology; Information Technology; Management.** Also Licenciatura; Diplomados

Student Services: Library

Last Updated: 23/10/15

CORPORATE SCHOOL OF ARTS AND LETTERS

Corporación Escuela de Artes y Letras

Calle 70, No 13-29, Bogotá
Tel: +57(1) 704-2907 +57(1) 543-7601 +57(1) 544-7130
Fax: +57(1) 543-7601
EMail: Artesyltras@hotmail.com
Website: http://www.artesyletras.com.co

Rector: Edgar Ignacio Díaz Santos

Programme
Architectural Works Administration (Architecture); **Business Administration** (Business Administration); **Cinema and Television** (Cinema and Television); **Digital Arts Engineering** (Computer Graphics); **Dramatic Art** (Theatre); **Fashion Design** (Fashion Design); **Interior Design** (Interior Design); **Technical/Professional Studies** (Graphic Design; Painting and Drawing; Sculpture)

History: Founded 1969.

Main Language(s) of Instruction: Spanish

Degrees and Diplomas: *Técnico Profesional*; *Profesional Universitario*

Student Services: Library

Last Updated: 24/09/15

CORPORATE TECHNOLOGICAL SCHOOL OF THE EAST

Corporación Escuela Tecnológica del Oriente

Cl. 32, No 26-44, Bucaramanga, Santander
Tel: +57(7) 634-9810
Fax: +57(7) 645-4144
EMail: info@tecnologicadeloriente.edu.co
Website: http://tecnologicadeloriente.edu.co

Rector: Wilson Jaimes Martínez
EMail: rector@tecnologicadeloriente.edu.co

Communication and Journalism (Journalism; Mass Communication); **Social Sciences and Humanities** (Social Work)

Institute

Interdisciplinary Studies (Law; Peace and Disarmament)

Centre

Research and Special Projects *(CIPE)*

History: Founded 1886 as Faculty of Law, became university 1958. Privately financed but receives some support from the State.

Academic Year: February to December (February-July; July-December)

Admission Requirements: Secondary school certificate (bachillerato) and entrance examination

Main Language(s) of Instruction: Spanish

Degrees and Diplomas: *Profesional Universitario*; *Especialización*: **Accountancy; Administrative Law; Business Administration; Business and Commerce; Civil Law; Commercial Law; Constitutional Law; Demography and Population; Development Studies; Economics; Environmental Management; Environmental Studies; Finance; Geography (Human); Government; Human Resources; Human Rights; Information Technology; Insurance; International Business; International Law; Labour Law; Law; Management; Maritime Law; Marketing; Notary Studies; Peace and Disarmament; Political Sciences; Private Law; Public Administration; Public Law; Regional Studies; Social and Community Services; Social Welfare; Taxation; Telecommunications Services; Transport and Communications; Transport Management; Urban Studies.** *Maestría*: **Administrative Law; Business Administration; Civil Law; Commercial Law; Constitutional Law; Criminal Law; Criminology; Demography and Population; Development Studies; Econometrics; Economics; Education; Educational Administration; Educational Sciences; Family Studies; Finance; Fiscal Law; Geography (Human); Government; Human Resources; Human Rights; Information Technology; Insurance; International Law; International Relations; International Studies; Labour Law; Law; Management; Marketing; Mass Communication; Political Sciences; Private Law; Public Law; Social and Community Services; Taxation.** *Doctorado*: **Administration; Law; Political Sciences.** Also Diplomados

Student Services: Library

Publications: Boletín Bibliográfico

Publishing House: Editorial Universidad Externado de Colombia

Last Updated: 04/11/15

FINE ARTS UNIVERSITY FOUNDATION

Fundación Universitaria Bellas Artes

Palacio de Bellas Artes, Calle 52 # 42-08, Medellín, Antioquia

Tel: +57(4) 444-7787

Fax: +57(4) 239-4820

EMail: informacion@bellasartesmed.edu.co

Website: http://www.bellasartesmed.edu.co

Rectora: Egda Rubi García Valencia
Tel: +57(4) 444-7787 Ext. 3139
EMail: rectoria@bellasartesmed.edu.co

Secretaria General: Juliana Cadavid Arboleda
Tel: +57(4) 444-7787 Ext. 3149
EMail: secretariageneral@bellasartesmed.edu.co

Directora Administrativa y Financiera: Luz Estela Holguín Carmona
Tel: +57(4) 444-7787 Ext. 1125
EMail: luz.holguin@smp-medellin.org

International Relations: Carlos Alberto Vélez Escobar, Comunicaciones Internas
Tel: +57(4) 444-7787 Ext. 3141
EMail: bellasartes@bellasartesmed.edu.co; carlos.velez@bellasartesmed.edu.co

Programme

Fine Arts (Fine Arts); **Graphic Design** (Graphic Arts; Graphic Design); **Music** (Music)

Further Information: Also Ayacucho Campus

History: Founded 1910 as Escuela de Música, Pintura y Escultura. Acquired present status and title 2006.

Fees: 146.553-234.829 per credit

Main Language(s) of Instruction: Spanish

Degrees and Diplomas: *Profesional Universitario*

Student Services: Library

Last Updated: 02/10/15

FITEC FOUNDATION OF TECHNOLOGY

Fundación Tecnológica FITEC (FITEC)

Carrera 36, N. 48-99, Bucaramanga, Santander

Tel: +57(7) 643-1301

EMail: secretaria.general@fitec.edu.co

Website: http://fitec.com.co

Rector: Orlando Josué Calero Chacón EMail: rectoria@fitec.edu.co

Vicerrectoría Académica: Rosalba Montero Ojeda
EMail: vicerrectoria.academica@fitec.edu

Vicerrectoria Administrativa y Financiera: Cecilia Garcia Padilla
EMail: vicerrectoria.administrativa@fitec.edu.co

Programme

Occupational Studies (Medical Auxiliaries); **Specialization Studies** (Telecommunications Engineering); **Technical Studies** (Accountancy; Agricultural Business; Computer Science; Environmental Studies; Food Science; Food Technology; Management; Software Engineering; Transport Management); **Technological Studies** (Business Administration; Computer Science; Finance; Forestry; Tourism)

History: Founded 1990.

Main Language(s) of Instruction: Spanish

Degrees and Diplomas: *Técnico Profesional*; *Tecnólogo*; *Especialización*: **Telecommunications Engineering.**

Last Updated: 29/09/15

FOUNDATION FOR HIGHER EDUCATION SAN MATEO

Fundación para la Educación Superior San Mateo

Transversal 17, 25-25, Bogotá

Tel: +57(1) 330-9999

Fax: +57(1) 330-9999

EMail: secretariageneral@funsanmateo.edu.co

Website: http://www.sanmateo.edu.co

Rector: Rodrigo Ferreira Pinzon
EMail: rectoria@funsanmateo.edu.co

Vicerrectora Academica: Maria Luisa Acota Triviño
EMail: vice_academica@funsanmateo.edu.co

Gerencia Administrativa: Pedro Nel Sanchez Arciniega
EMail: admin@funsanmateo.edu.co

International Relations: Camilo Jose Meza Ferreira, Coordinador de Relaciones Internacionales
EMail: relacionesinternacionales@funsanmateo.edu.co

Faculty

Administrative Sciences (Accountancy; Administration; Business Administration; Cooking and Catering; Finance; Industrial Management; International Business; Labour Law; Management; Occupational Health); **Engineering** (Computer Engineering; Industrial Engineering; Safety Engineering; Software Engineering; Telecommunications Engineering); **Information and Communication Technologies** (Advertising and Publicity; Graphic Design; Information Sciences; Information Technology; Media Studies; Multimedia)

History: Founded 1987.

Main Language(s) of Instruction: Spanish

Degrees and Diplomas: *Técnico Profesional*; *Tecnólogo*; *Profesional Universitario*: **Accountancy; Business Administration; Computer Science; Cooking and Catering; Industrial Engineering; International Business; Multimedia; Occupational Health; Safety Engineering; Telecommunications Engineering.**

Last Updated: 29/09/15

GRANCOLOMBIANO POLYTECHNIC

Politécnico Grancolombiano

Apartado aéreo 90853, Calle 57 N° 3-00 Este, Bogotá
Tel: +57(1) 744-0740
Fax: +57(1) 745-5555
EMail: webmast@poligran.edu.co
Website: http://www.poligran.edu.co

Rector: Jurgen Chiari Escobar (2014-)
EMail: jchiarie@poligran.edu.co; rectoria@poligran.edu.co

Gerente Administrativo: Alejandro Otálora Galvis Director
Tel: +57(1) 745-5555 Ext.2221

International Relations: Raquel Bretón de Schultze-Kraft, Directora, Oficina de Relaciones Internacionales
EMail: rbreton@poligran.edu.co

Faculty

Administration Sciences, Economics and Accountancy (Accountancy; Banking; Business Administration; Economics; English; Environmental Management; Finance; Hotel Management; Human Resources; Insurance; International Business; Leadership; Management; Marketing; Public Administration; Public Health; Sales Techniques; Service Trades; Taxation; Tourism); **Engineering and Basic Sciences** (Applied Mathematics; Business Administration; Computer Engineering; Computer Networks; Industrial Engineering; Information Management; Management; Mathematics; Software Engineering; Telecommunications Engineering; Transport Management); **Marketing, Communication and Arts** (Accountancy; Advertising and Publicity; Business and Commerce; Communication Studies; Computer Engineering; Fashion Design; Finance; Graphic Design; Industrial Design; Journalism; Marketing; Mass Communication; Media Studies; Performing Arts; Radio and Television Broadcasting); **Social Sciences** (Business Administration; Commercial Law; Computer Education; Criminal Law; Educational Administration; Educational Technology; Law; Mathematics Education; Occupational Health; Political Sciences; Preschool Education; Private Administration; Psychology; Public Administration; Social Psychology; Social Sciences)

Further Information: Also Campus in Medellín

History: Founded 1981.

Main Language(s) of Instruction: Spanish

Degrees and Diplomas: *Técnico Profesional*; *Tecnólogo*; *Profesional Universitario*; *Especialización*: **Administrative Law; Business Administration; Commercial Law; Communication Studies; Computer Engineering; Computer Networks; Criminal Law; Educational Technology; Finance; Information Management; Insurance; International Business; Management; Marketing; Mass Communication; Private Administration; Psychology; Public Administration; Social Psychology; Taxation; Telecommunications Engineering; Tourism.** *Maestría*: **Computer Engineering; Marketing.** Also Licenciatura; Diplomados

Student Services: Library, eLibrary
Last Updated: 20/10/15

HORIZONTE UNIVERSITY FOUNDATION

Fundación Universitaria Horizonte (UNIHORIZONTE)

Calle 69, 14-30, Bogotá
Tel: +57(1) 743-7270
EMail: contactenos@unihorizonte.edu.co
Website: http://www.unihorizonte.edu.co

Rectora: Cecilia Garzon Daza
Tel: +57(1) 743-7270 Ext.124 EMail: rectoria@unihorizonte.edu.co

Vicerrectora Administrativa y Financiera: Esperanza Mariño Camacho
Tel: +57(1) 743-7270 Ext.132
EMail: vice.administrativa@unihorizonte.edu.co

Faculty

Administrative Sciences (Administration; Banking; Finance; Hotel and Restaurant; International Business; Marketing; Tourism); **Engineering** (Environmental Engineering; Industrial Engineering; Information Technology; Occupational Health); **Humanities, Arts and Letters** (Construction Engineering; Graphic Design)

History: Founded 1983.

Main Language(s) of Instruction: Spanish

Degrees and Diplomas: *Técnico Profesional*; *Profesional Universitario*: **Industrial Engineering; Occupational Health.**

Student Services: Library
Last Updated: 29/09/15

IBERO-AMERICAN UNIVERSITY CORPORATION

Corporación Universitaria Iberoamericana (IA)

Calle 67, No 5-27, Bogotá
Tel: +57(1) 348-9292
Fax: +57(1) 210-3553
EMail: contacto@iberoamericana.edu.co
Website: http://www.iberoamericana.edu.co

Rector: Javier Alfredo Barrera Pardo
Tel: +57(1) 348-9292 Ext. 106
EMail: rectoria@iberoamericana.edu.co; javier.barrera@iberoamericana.edu.co

Vicerrectora Académica: Marisol Acevedo Zuluaga
Tel: +57(1) 348-9292 Ext. 525
EMail: marisol.acevedo@iberoamericana.edu.co

Secretaria General: Tatiana Ruiz Farah
Tel: +57(1) 348-9292 Ext. 125
EMail: tatiana.ruiz@iberoamericana.edu.co

Vicerrector Administrativo: Raúl Mauricio Acosta Lema
Tel: +57(1) 348-9292 Ext. 336
EMail: raul.acosta@iberoamericana.edu.co

International Relations: Jorge Alexander Cortés Cortés, Director Administración y Finanzas/ Marketing y Negocios Internacionales
Tel: +57(1) 348-9292 Ext. 521
EMail: jorge.cortes@iberoamericana.edu.co

Faculty

Business Administration (Accountancy; Administration; Finance; Human Resources; International Business; Marketing; Transport Management); **Education, Human and Social Sciences** (Child Care and Development; Pedagogy; Preschool Education; Psychology; Special Education); **Health Sciences** (Physical Therapy; Speech Therapy and Audiology)

Further Information: Also Neiva Campus

History: Founded 1979 as Instituto de Pedagogía Infantil (INPI). Acquired current status 1985.

Admission Requirements: Secondary school certificate. ICFES examination

Main Language(s) of Instruction: Spanish

Degrees and Diplomas: *Profesional Universitario*; *Especialización*: **Child Care and Development; Physical Therapy; Speech Therapy and Audiology.** Also Diplomados

Student Services: Academic Counselling, Careers Guidance, Cultural Activities, Facilities for disabled people, Health Services, Language Laboratory, Library, Nursery Care, Social Counselling, Sports Facilities
Last Updated: 29/09/15

ICESI UNIVERSITY

Universidad ICESI

Calle 18 No. 122-135, Pance, Cali, Valle del Cauca
Tel: +57(2) 555-2334
Fax: +57(2) 555-1441
Website: http://www.icesi.edu.co

Rector: Francisco Piedrahita Plata (1996-)
Tel: +57(2) 321-2022
EMail: frapie@icesi.edu.co; rectoria@icesi.edu.co

Director: Carlos Gerarado Chaparro EMail: chaparro@icesi.edu.co

International Relations: Piedad Gómez Franco, Directora de la Oficina de Relaciones
Tel: +57(2) 555-2334. Ext. 8399 EMail: pgomez@icesi.edu.co

Faculty

Administrative Sciences and Economics (Accountancy; Business Administration; Economics; Finance; International Business; Marketing); **Engineering** (Design; Industrial Engineering;

Information Technology; Mathematics; Physics; Statistics; Telecommunications Engineering); **Health Sciences** (Health Sciences; Natural Sciences); **Law and Social Sciences** (Arts and Humanities; Law; Political Sciences; Psychology; Social Studies); **Natural Sciences** (Biological and Life Sciences; Chemistry; Pharmacology)

History: Founded 1979.

Academic Year: January to December (January-June; August-December)

Admission Requirements: School certificate, test of proficiency in Spanish, national admission test

Fees: 1,674-3,670 per semester according to field of study (US Dollar)

Main Language(s) of Instruction: Spanish

Degrees and Diplomas: *Profesional Universitario*; *Especialización*: **Cardiology; Commercial Law; Criminal Law; Dentistry; Dermatology; Environmental Management; Gynaecology and Obstetrics; Haematology; Law; Medicine; Nephrology; Oncology; Paediatrics; Psychiatry and Mental Health; Public Law; Radiology; Rheumatology; Safety Engineering; Social Welfare; Surgery.** *Maestría*: **Biotechnology; Chemistry; Economics; Education; Engineering Management; Finance; Foreign Languages Education; Government; Health Administration; Industrial Engineering; Information Technology; Journalism; Law; Marketing; Political Sciences; Social Psychology; Social Studies; Telecommunications Services.** Also Licenciatura; MBA

Student Services: Academic Counselling, Canteen, Careers Guidance, Cultural Activities, Facilities for disabled people, Health Services, Language Laboratory, Library, Nursery Care, Social Counselling, Sports Facilities, eLibrary

Publications: Estudios Gerenciales; Precedente; Sistemas y Telemática

Last Updated: 03/11/15

IDEAS UNIVERSITY CORPORATION OF COLOMBIA

Corporación Universitaria de Colombia IDEAS (IDEAS)

Calle 70, No. 10A-39, Bogotá
Tel: +57(1) 606-1102 +57(1) 702-3940
Fax: +57(1) 217-9073
EMail: info@ideas.edu.co; ideas@ideas.edu.co
Website: http://www.ideas.edu.co

Rectora: Ana Cristina Pedraza Alvarado
EMail: rectoria@ideas.edu.co

Faculty

Accountancy (Accountancy); **Administration** (Business Administration); **Law** (Law)

History: Founded 1984.

Fees: 3,274,000 per annum (Colombian Peso)

Main Language(s) of Instruction: Spanish

Degrees and Diplomas: *Profesional Universitario*

Student Services: Library

Last Updated: 06/11/15

INCCA UNIVERSITY OF COLOMBIA

Universidad INCCA de Colombia (UNINCCA)

Carrera 13 No. 24-15, Bogotá
Tel: +57(1) 444-2000
EMail: ofinter@unincca.edu.co
Website: http://www.unincca.edu.co

Rectora: María Carolina Villamizar Bonilla
Tel: +57(1) 444-2000 Ext. 233 EMail: rectoria@unincca.edu.co

Secretaria General: Julia Marina Villareal González
Tel: +57(1) 444-2000 Ext. 202-287
EMail: secretar@unincca.edu.co

International Relations: Alfredo Garcia Molsalve
EMail: vicered1@unincca.edu.co

International Relations: Maritza Ibarra Bravo
Tel: +57(1) 282-3120 EMail: ofinter@unincca.edu.co

Faculty

Engineering, Administration and Basic Sciences (Accountancy; Biology; Business Administration; Computer Engineering; Electronic Engineering; Food Technology; Industrial Engineering; Mechanical Engineering); **Law and Political Science** (Law); **Pedagogy, Humanities and Social Sciences** (Arts and Humanities; English; Foreign Languages Education; Humanities and Social Science Education; Music; Native Language Education; Physical Education; Preschool Education; Psychology; Spanish)

Unit

Postgraduate Studies (Computer Networks; Human Rights; Public Administration; Software Engineering)

Institute

Technological Studies (Administration; Agricultural Business; Data Processing; Software Engineering)

Further Information: Also Cartagena, Sopo, Fusagasuga Campuses

History: Founded 1955 as Institute of Administrative Sciences, recognized as a university by government decree 1970. A private institution.

Academic Year: January to November (January-May; July-November)

Admission Requirements: Secondary school certificate (bachillerato) and entrance examination

Main Language(s) of Instruction: Spanish

Degrees and Diplomas: *Tecnólogo*; *Profesional Universitario*; *Especialización*: **Computer Networks; Human Rights; Public Administration; Software Engineering; Taxation.** Also Licenciatura

Student Services: Library

Publications: Revista Cientifica

Publishing House: Unincca Publishing Unit

Last Updated: 30/10/15

INPAHU UNIVERSITY FOUNDATION

Fundación Universitaria INPAHU (UNINPAHU)

Diagonal 40A No. 15-58, Bogotá
Tel: +57(1) 332-0500
Fax: +57(1) 340-0341
EMail: uninpahu@uninpahu.edu.co
Website: http://www.inpahu.edu.co

Rectora: Myriam Velásquez Bustos
Tel: +57(1) 332-3534 EMail: mvelasquez@inpahu.edu.co

Secretaria General: Maria Angélica Cortés

Vicerrector Administrativo: Jorge Humberto Rodríguez Martínez

Faculty

Communication, Information and Language (Journalism; Mass Communication; Multimedia; Photography; Radio and Television Broadcasting); **Economics and Administrative Sciences** (Business and Commerce; Hotel Management; Human Resources; International Business; Occupational Health; Tourism); **Engineering and Information Technology** (Computer Engineering; Computer Science; Documentation Techniques; Industrial Engineering; Information Sciences; Library Science; Software Engineering)

History: Founded 1974.

Admission Requirements: Secondary school certificate. Entrance examination (ICFES)

Fees: 1.4m (Colombian Peso)

Main Language(s) of Instruction: Spanish

Degrees and Diplomas: *Técnico Profesional*; *Tecnólogo*; *Profesional Universitario*

Student Services: Academic Counselling, Canteen, Careers Guidance, Cultural Activities, Facilities for disabled people, Foreign Studies Centre, Health Services, IT Centre, Language Laboratory, Library, Nursery Care, Social Counselling, Sports Facilities

Publications: Coloquio; NOTISALUD; Tahu

Last Updated: 05/10/15

INTERNATIONAL COLOMBO UNIVERSITY FOUNDATION

Fundación Universitaria Colombo Internacional (UNICOLOMBO)

Av. Pedro de Heredia, Sector Cuatro Vientos, Cartagena de Indias, Bolívar
Tel: +57(5) 672-5800 +57(5) 672-6080
Fax: +57(5) 660-0415
EMail: info@unicolombo.edu.co
Website: http://www.unicolombo.edu.co

Rector: Mario Ramos Vélez

Programme

Business Administration (Business Administration); **Computer Engineering** (Computer Engineering); **Foreign Languages Education (English)** (Foreign Languages Education); **Industrial Engineering** (Industrial Engineering); **Information Systems Development** (Information Technology); **Law** (Law); **Postgraduate Studies** (Foreign Languages Education); **Public Accountancy** (Accountancy); **Quality Management Systems** *(Technological Studies)* (Management Systems); **Tourism and Hotel Administration** (Hotel Management; Tourism); **Tourism and Hotel Management** *(Technological Studies)* (Hotel Management; Tourism)

History: Founded 1961 as Centro Colombo Americano de Cartagena. Acquired present status and title 2006.

Main Language(s) of Instruction: Spanish

Degrees and Diplomas: *Tecnólogo*; *Profesional Universitario*; *Especialización*: **Foreign Languages Education.** Also Licenciatura (Teacher Training Degree) in Foreign Languages Education (English)

Student Services: Canteen, IT Centre, Language Laboratory

Last Updated: 02/10/15

INTERNATIONAL UNIVERSITY FOUNDATION OF THE AMERICAN TROPIC

Fundación Universitaria Internacional del Tropico Américano (UNITROPICO)

Carrera 19 No. 39-40, Yopal, Casanare
Tel: +57(987) 632-0700
Fax: +57(987) 632-0700
EMail: unitropico@unitropico.edu.co; admisiones@unitropico.edu.co
Website: http://www.unitropico.edu.co

Rector: Oriol Jiménez Silva EMail: rectoria@unitropico.edu.co

Secretario General: Cesar Rolando Castro Pineda

Faculty

Architecture and Arts (Architecture); **Economics and Administrative Sciences** (Accountancy; Administration; Business Administration; Economics; International Business; Tourism); **Education and Transdisciplnary Studies** (Arts and Humanities; Modern Languages; Natural Sciences); **Engineering** (Civil Engineering; Computer Engineering; Petroleum and Gas Engineering); **Natural and Agricultural Sciences** (Animal Husbandry; Biology; Environmental Studies; Veterinary Science)

History: Founded 2000.

Fees: 1,432,000 (Colombian Peso)

Main Language(s) of Instruction: Spanish

Accrediting Agency: ICFES

Degrees and Diplomas: *Tecnólogo*; *Profesional Universitario*; *Especialización*: **Environmental Management.**

Student Services: Academic Counselling, Cultural Activities, Library, Social Counselling, Sports Facilities

Last Updated: 05/10/15

INTERNATIONAL VIRTUAL UNIVERSITY

Universitaria Virtual Internacional (UVIRTUAL)

Carrera 19 No. 71A-23, Bogotá D.C, Bogotá D.C
Tel: +57(1) 7561-154
EMail: contactenos@uvirtual.edu.co; natalia.canon@uvirtual.edu.co
Website: http://www.uvirtual.edu.co

Rector: Alvaro Cano Aguillón
EMail: rectoria.uvirtual@uvirtual.edu.co

Programme

Advertising (Advertising and Publicity); **Business Administration** (Business Administration); **Courses and Diplomas** (Arts and Humanities; Business Administration; Economics; Fine Arts; Information Technology; Mass Communication); **Digital Graphic Design** (Computer Graphics; Graphic Design); **Public Accountancy** (Accountancy)

Centre

Virtual Language Studies (Chinese; English; French; German; Italian; Spanish)

History: Founded 2010. Acquired present status 2012.

Academic Year: Quarterly

Admission Requirements: High School Diploma

Fees: National: 1,914,800 (Colombian Peso), International: 613.91 (US Dollar)

Main Language(s) of Instruction: Spanish

Accrediting Agency: Ministerio de Educación Nacional

Degrees and Diplomas: *Técnico Profesional*: **Fine Arts; Technology.** *Profesional Universitario*: **Business Administration; Fine Arts; Technology.**

Student Services: Cultural Activities, Health Services, Social Counselling, Sports Facilities, eLibrary

Academic Staff *2015-2016*	MEN	WOMEN	TOTAL
FULL-TIME	19	11	**30**
PART-TIME	3	5	**8**

Last Updated: 10/09/15

J. EMILIO VALDERRAMA UNIVERSITY CORPORATION OF SABANETA

Corporación Universitaria de Sabaneta J. Emilio Valderrama (UNISABANETA)

Calle 75 Sur No. 34- 120, Vía La Doctora, Sabaneta, Sabaneta
Tel: +57(4) 301-1818
Fax: +57(4) 288-3018 Ext.102
EMail: unisabaneta@unisabaneta.edu.co
Website: http://www.unisabaneta.edu.co

Rector: Juan Carlos Trujillo Barrera

Secretario General: Luis Yesid Villaraga
EMail: secretaria.general@unisabaneta.edu.co

International Relations: Carlos Augusto Giraldo, Vicerrector de Internacionalización

Faculty

Business and Commerce (Accountancy; Business Administration; International Business); **Engineering** (Computer Engineering); **Law** (Law)

History: Founded 2008.

Main Language(s) of Instruction: Spanish

Degrees and Diplomas: *Profesional Universitario*; *Especialización*: **Human Rights; International Law; Law; Management.**

Student Services: Library

Last Updated: 29/09/15

JESUS PEREZ OVIEDO TECHNOLOGICAL SCHOOL OF NEIVA

Fundación Escuela Tecnológica de Neiva Jesus Oviedo Perez (FET)

Campus Universitario, Kilómetro 11 Via al Sur, Rivera
Tel: +57(8) 870-3107 +57(8) 860-0117
EMail: secretaria@fet.edu.co
Website: http://www.fet.edu.co

Rectora: Maria Amelia Monroy Ortegón (2015-)
EMail: rectoria@fet.edu.co

Vicerrector Académico: José del Carmen Yepes Casanova

Programme

Occupational Health Administration (Health Administration; Occupational Health); **Software Engineering** (Software Engineering)

Department

Natural and Environmental Sciences (Agricultural Business; Agricultural Management; Agronomy; Environmental Management; Environmental Studies); **Tourism Management** (Marketing; Tourism)

History: Founded 2011.

Main Language(s) of Instruction: Spanish

Degrees and Diplomas: *Técnico Profesional*; *Tecnólogo*; *Profesional Universitario*: **Environmental Management; Health Administration; Occupational Health; Software Engineering.**

Student Services: Library

Last Updated: 29/09/15

JORGE TADEO LOZANO UNIVERSITY FOUNDATION OF BOGOTA

Fundación Universidad de Bogotá Jorge Tadeo Lozano

Carrera 4 No. 22-61, Bogotá
Tel: +57(1) 242-7030
Fax: +57(1) 561-2107
EMail: centro.informacion@utadeo.edu.co
Website: http://www.utadeo.edu.co

Rectora: Cecilia María Vélez White EMail: rectoria@utadeo.edu.co

Vicerrectora Administrativa: Nohemy Arias Otero

Secretario General: Carlos Sánchez Gaitán

Faculty

Arts and Design (Advertising and Publicity; Cinema and Television; Design; Fashion Design; Fine Arts; Graphic Design; Industrial Design; Interior Design; Multimedia; Photography; Regional Planning; Town Planning); **Economics and Administration** (Accountancy; Business Administration; Economics; Farm Management; Finance; Health Administration; Human Resources; Information Management; International Business; Management; Marketing; Occupational Health; Safety Engineering; Taxation; Transport Management); **Natural Sciences and Engineering** (Automation and Control Engineering; Biology; Chemical Engineering; Computer Engineering; Data Processing; Energy Engineering; Environmental Management; Environmental Studies; Food Technology; Industrial Engineering; Marine Biology; Marine Science and Oceanography; Public Administration; Robotics); **Social Sciences** (Aesthetics; Art History; Cinema and Television; Communication Studies; Government; History of Law; Human Rights; International Relations; Journalism; Law; Mass Communication; Political Sciences; Speech Studies)

Department

Basic Sciences (Chemistry; Mathematics; Natural Sciences; Physics; Statistics); **Humanities** (Aesthetics; Art History; Communication Studies); **Languages** (English; French; Portuguese)

History: Founded 1954, a private institution partly financed by the State.

Academic Year: January to November (January-May; August-November)

Admission Requirements: Secondary school certificate (bachillerato) and State examination (ICFES test)

Main Language(s) of Instruction: Spanish

Degrees and Diplomas: *Tecnólogo*; *Profesional Universitario*; *Especialización*: **Accountancy; Advertising and Publicity; Business Administration; Data Processing; Design; Economics; Environmental Studies; Finance; Government; Health Administration; Human Resources; International Business; Journalism; Management; Marketing; Occupational Health; Public Administration; Safety Engineering; Taxation; Town Planning; Transport Management.** *Maestría*: **Advertising and Publicity; Aesthetics; Architecture; Art History; Communication Studies; Energy Engineering; Environmental Studies; Fine Arts; Human Rights; Industrial Engineering; International Business; International Relations; Marine Science and Oceanography; Regional Planning; Speech Studies; Town Planning.** *Doctorado*: **Marine Science and Oceanography; Public Administration.**

Student Services: Library

Last Updated: 02/10/15

CARIBBEAN BRANCH - CARTAGENA

SECCIONAL DEL CARIBE - CARTAGENA

Campus Internacional del Caribe, Anillo Vial Km 13, Cartagena
Tel: +57(5) 655-4000
EMail: cgn.admisiones@utadeo.edu.co; postgrados@utadeo.edu.co
Website: http://www.utadeo.edu.co/es/tadeo-caribe

Rectora: Cecilia María Vélez White EMail: rectoria@utadeo.edu.co

Department

Administrative Economic Sciences (Health Administration; Human Resources; International Business; Occupational Health; Transport Management); **Humanities, Arts and Design** (Advertising and Publicity; Architecture; Civil Law; Graphic Design; Human Rights; Journalism; Mass Communication; Radio and Television Broadcasting)

History: Founded 1959.

Main Language(s) of Instruction: Spanish

Degrees and Diplomas: *Tecnólogo*; *Profesional Universitario*: **Advertising and Publicity; Architecture; Graphic Design; Journalism; Mass Communication.** *Especialización*: **Advertising and Publicity; Health Administration; Human Resources; International Business; Occupational Health; Transport Management.** *Maestría*: **Civil Law; Human Rights.**

Student Services: Library

JUAN DE CASTELLANOS UNIVERSITY FOUNDATION

Fundación Universitaria Juan de Castellanos (JDC)

Carrera 11 # 11-44, Tunja, Boyocá
Tel: +57(98) 742-2944 +57(98) 742-8378
Fax: +57(98) 740-1541
EMail: info@jdc.edu.co; comunicaciones@jdc.edu.co
Website: http://www.jdc.edu.co

Rector: Luis Enrique Pérez Ojeda (2014-2018)
Tel: +57 (315) 316-5325 EMail: rector@jdc.edu.co

Secretaria General: Rosa P. Ayala Becerra
Tel: +57 (98) 744-7115 EMail: sgeneral@jdc.edu.co

Vicerrectora Administrativa: María del Carmen Rodríguez Mesa

International Relations: Luis Alfredo Cristancho Morales, Director de la Oficina de Relaciones Internacionales
Tel: +57(317) 369-9911 EMail: relaciones.inter@jdc.edu.co

Faculty

Agricultural Sciences (Agricultural Engineering; Animal Husbandry; Veterinary Science); **Educational Sciences** (Educational Administration; Educational Sciences; Educational Technology; Ethics; Parks and Recreation; Pedagogy; Physical Education; Preschool Education; Religious Education; Sports); **Engineering** (Civil Engineering; Computer Engineering; Electronic Engineering; Information Management; Telecommunications Engineering); **International Law and Political Sciences** (Law); **Social Sciences and Economics** (Accountancy; Hotel Management; Social Work; Tourism)

Further Information: Also Crisanto Luque Campus; Francisco de Asis Veterinary Clinic

History: Founded 1967 as Instituto Catequístico Juan de Castellanos. Acquired present status and title 2002.

Main Language(s) of Instruction: Spanish

Degrees and Diplomas: *Profesional Universitario*; *Especialización*: **Animal Husbandry; Educational Administration; Educational Sciences; Educational Technology; Ethics; Information Management; Pedagogy; Preschool Education.** Also Licenciatura in Physical Education, Sports, Parks and Recreation, Ethics, Religious Education

Student Services: Academic Counselling, Language Laboratory, Library, Social Counselling, Sports Facilities

Publications: Journal Cientific; Noticien

Last Updated: 06/10/15

JUAN N. CORPAS UNIVERSITY FOUNDATION

Fundación Universitaria Juan N. Corpas
Carrera 111 No. 159 A 61 (Av. Corpas Km. 3 Suba), Bogotá
Tel: +57(1) 662-2222
Fax: +57(1) 681-5612
EMail: info@juanncorpas.edu.co
Website: http://www.juanncorpas.edu.co

Rectora: Ana María Piñeros Ricardo
EMail: ana.pineros@juancorpas.edu.co

Programme

Medicine (Community Health; Epidemiology; Health Administration; Human Resources; Medicine; Neurology; Plastic Surgery); **Music** (Music; Music Theory and Composition; Musical Instruments; Musicology; Singing); **Premedical Studies** (Anthropology; Biochemistry; Cell Biology; English; Mathematics; Physical Education; Vocational Counselling)

History: Founded 1971 as Escuela de Medicina Juan N. Corpas. Acquired present status and title 1974.

Main Language(s) of Instruction: Spanish

Degrees and Diplomas: *Profesional Universitario*; *Especialización*: **Alternative Medicine; Community Health; Conducting; Epidemiology; Health Administration; Human Resources; Medicine; Neurology; Plastic Surgery; Psychiatry and Mental Health.** Also Diplomados

Student Services: Library

Last Updated: 06/10/15

JULIO GARAVITO COLOMBIAN SCHOOL OF ENGINEERING

Escuela Colombiana de Ingeniería Julio Garavito
Apartado aéreo 14520, Avenida 13 No. 205-59 Autopista Norte Km 13, Bogotá
Tel: +57(1) 676-0236
Fax: +57(1) 676-0479
EMail: info@escuelaing.edu.co; admisiones@escuelaing.edu.co
Website: http://www.escuelaing.edu.co

Rector: Germán Eduardo Acero Riveros
Tel: +57(1) 668-3600/210 EMail: rector@escuelaing.edu.co

Secretary-General: Ricardo Alfredo López Cualla
Tel: +57(1) 668-3600/211 EMail: secreci@escuelaing.edu.co

Vicerrector Administrativo: Mauricio Vela Prieto

International Relations: Santiago Restrepo
Tel: +57(1) 668-3600/328 EMail: srestrepo@escuelaing.edu.co

Programme

Biomedical Engineering (Biomedical Engineering); **Business Administration** (Business Administration); **Civil Engineering** (Civil Engineering); **Economics** (Economics); **Electrical Engineering** (Electrical Engineering); **Electronic Engineering** (Electronic Engineering); **Industrial Engineering** (Industrial Engineering); **Mathematics** (Mathematics); **Mechanical Engineering** (Mechanical Engineering); **Postgraduate Studies** (Civil Engineering; Electronic Engineering; Engineering Management; Environmental Management; Industrial Engineering; Industrial Management; Information Management; Management; Occupational Health; Road Engineering; Safety Engineering; Structural Architecture; Water Management)

Department

Humanities (Arts and Humanities); **Mathematics** (Mathematics); **Natural Sciences** (Natural Sciences)

Academic Year: January to December (January-June; August-December)

Admission Requirements: Bachillerato and State Examination (ICFES)

Fees: 800-1,600 per semester (US Dollar)

Main Language(s) of Instruction: Spanish

Degrees and Diplomas: *Tecnólogo*; *Profesional Universitario*; *Especialización*: **Civil Engineering; Engineering Management; Environmental Management; Industrial Management; Management; Occupational Health; Road Engineering; Safety Engineering; Structural Architecture; Water Management.** *Maestría*: **Civil Engineering; Electronic Engineering; Industrial Engineering; Information Management; Management.**

Student Services: Canteen, Careers Guidance, Health Services, Language Laboratory, Nursery Care, Social Counselling, Sports Facilities

Publications: Revista de la Escuela Colombiana de Ingeniería

Publishing House: Editorial Escuela Colombiana de Ingenería

Last Updated: 30/09/15

KONRAD LORENZ UNIVERSITY FOUNDATION

Fundación Universitaria Konrad Lorenz
Carrera 9bis No. 62-43, Bogotá
Tel: +57(1) 347-2311
Fax: +57(1) 347-2311 Ext. 131
EMail: info@konradlorenz.edu.co
Website: http://www.fukl.edu

Rectora: Lina Uribe Correa
Tel: +57(1) 347-2311 Ext. 116
EMail: comunicacionesrectoria@konradlorenz.edu.co

Director, Dirección Administrativa y Financiera: José Antonio Jaime Escobar

Department

Postgraduate Studies (Clinical Psychology; Consumer Studies; Human Resources; Psychology); **Undergraduate Studies** (Computer Engineering; Industrial Engineering; International Business; Marketing; Mathematics; Psychology)

History: Founded 1981.

Fees: Undergraduate, 2,694,000-4,295,000 per annum; Postgraduate, 5,063,000-6,694,000 per annum (Colombian Peso)

Main Language(s) of Instruction: Spanish

Degrees and Diplomas: *Profesional Universitario*; *Especialización*: **Clinical Psychology; Consumer Studies; Human Resources; Psychology; Rehabilitation and Therapy.** *Maestría*: **Clinical Psychology; Consumer Studies.**

Student Services: Library, Social Counselling

Publications: Revista Latinoamericana de Psicología; Suma de Negocios; Suma Psicológica

Last Updated: 06/10/15

LA GRAN COLOMBIA UNIVERSITY

Universidad La Gran Colombia (UGC)
Carrera 6 No. 12 B 40, Bogotá
Tel: +57(1) 243-8047 +57(1) 327-6999
EMail: admisiones@ugc.edu.co
Website: http://www.ugc.edu.co

Rector: José Galat Noumer EMail: rectorjg@ugc.edu.co

International Relations: Maria Angélica Lesmez Azuero, Directora, Relaciones Internacionales
Tel: +57 3103059438 EMail: maria.lesmez@ugc.edu.co; relaciones.internacionales@ugc.edu.co

Faculty

Accountancy (Accountancy); **Architecture** (Architecture); **Civil Engineering** (Civil Engineering); **Economics and Administrative Sciences** (Business Administration; Economics); **Educational Sciences** (English; Foreign Languages Education; History; Humanities and Social Science Education; Information Technology; Linguistics; Literature; Mathematics Education; Philosophy); **Law** (Law; Political Sciences); **Postgraduate Studies** (Criminal Law; Criminology; Economics; Education; Law; Management; Marketing; Regional Planning)

Further Information: Also branch in Armenia

History: Founded 1953.

Academic Year: February to December

Admission Requirements: Secondary school certificate (bachillerato) and entrance examination

Fees: 2,397,000-3,340,000 per annum (Colombian Peso)

Main Language(s) of Instruction: Spanish

Degrees and Diplomas: *Tecnólogo*; *Profesional Universitario*; *Especialización*: **Criminal Law; Criminology; Management; Marketing.**

Maestría: **Economics; Education; Law; Regional Planning.** Also Diplomados; Licenciatura

Student Services: Library

Publications: Revistas

Last Updated: 30/10/15

ARMENIA BRANCH

SECCIONAL ARMENIA (UGCA)

Avenida Bolívar No 7-46, Armenia, Quindío
Tel: +57(6) 746-0400
EMail: comunicaciones@ugca.edu.co
Website: http://www.ugca.edu.co

Rector Delegatario: Jaime Bejarano Alzate
EMail: rectorugc@ugca.edu.co

Asesora, Oficina de Relaciones Internacionales: Gloria Helena López Echeverri
Tel: +57(6) 746-0462 EMail: asisrectoria@ugca.edu.co; relaciones.internacionales@ugca.edu.co

Secretaria General: Ana Milena Londoño Palacio
Tel: +57(6) 746-0402 EMail: secgen@ugca.edu.co

Vicerrector Administrativo y Financiero: Jorge Alberto Quintero Pinilla Tel: +57(6) 746-0429 EMail: vicefinanciero@ugca.edu.co

Faculty

Architecture (Architecture); **Economics, Administrative Sciences and Accountancy** (Accountancy; Business Administration; Economics); **Engineering** (Agricultural Engineering; Computer Graphics; Computer Science; Environmental Engineering; Geography; Industrial Engineering; Multimedia); **Law** (Law)

History: Founded 1971.

Main Language(s) of Instruction: Spanish

Degrees and Diplomas: *Técnico Profesional*; *Tecnólogo*; *Profesional Universitario*; *Especialización*: **Administrative Law; Constitutional Law; Criminal Law; Criminology; Finance; Food Technology; Labour Law; Management; Marketing; Private Law; Safety Engineering; Social Welfare; Taxation.** *Maestría*: **Public Law.**

Student Services: IT Centre, Library

LA SALLE UNIVERSITY

Universidad de La Salle (UNISALLE)
Carrera 5 No. 59A-44, Bogotá, Cundinamarca 12032
Tel: +57(1) 348-8000
Fax: +57(1) 217-0881
EMail: rectoria@lasalle.edu.co; relainter@lasalle.edu.co
Website: http://www.lasalle.edu.co

Rector: Carlos Gabriel Gómez Restrepo
EMail: rectoria@lasalle.edu.co; carlosgomez@lasalle.edu.co

Vicerrector Administrativo: Eduardo Ángel

International Relations: Giovanni Anzola Pardo, Jefe de Relaciones Internacionales EMail: ganzola@lasalle.edu.co

Division

Administration and Accounting (Accountancy; Administration); **Agricultural Sciences** (Agriculture); **Economic and Social Sciences** (Economics; Social Sciences); **Education** (Education); **Engineering** (Engineering); **Habitat Sciences** (Environmental Studies); **Health Sciences** (Health Sciences); **Philosophy and Humanities** (Arts and Humanities; Philosophy)

History: Founded 1964 as a private institution, recognized by the State in 1975.

Academic Year: February to November (February-June; August-November)

Admission Requirements: Secondary school certificate (bachillerato) and entrance examination (Certificado de Pruebas de Estado del ICFES)

Fees: National: Undergraduate, 1,200,000-6,200,000 per semester; Graduate, 5,000,000-10,000,000 per semester (Colombian Peso); International: Undergraduate, up to 3,000; Graduate, up to 5,000 (US Dollar)

Main Language(s) of Instruction: Spanish

Accrediting Agency: National Accreditation Council

Degrees and Diplomas: *Maestría*: **Administration; Agricultural Business; Animal Husbandry; Business Administration; Education; Engineering; Environmental Studies; Information Management; Library Science; Ophthalmology; Optometry; Philosophy; Veterinary Science.** *Doctorado*: **Agriculture; Education.**

Student Services: Academic Counselling, Canteen, Cultural Activities, Foreign Studies Centre, Health Services, Language Laboratory, Social Counselling, Sports Facilities

Publications: Actualidades Pedagógicas; Códice; Diógenes; Epsilon; Equidad y Desarrollo; Journal of Social Work; Journal of Veterinary Medicine; Revista Universidad De La Salle

Last Updated: 24/11/15

LASALLIAN UNIVERSITY CORPORATION

Corporación Universitaria Lasallista (UL)
Carrera 51 118 Sur 57, Caldas, Antioquia
Tel: +57(4) 320-1999
Fax: +57(4) 300-0270 Ext. 184
EMail: comunicaciones@lasallista.edu.co; admisiones@lasallista.edu.co
Website: http://www.lasallista.edu.co

Rector: J. Eduardo Murillo Bocanegra
Tel: +57(4) 300-0200 Ext. 103
EMail: rector@lasallista.edu.co

Vicerrector Administrativo: José Alberto Montoya Cano
EMail: administrador@lasallista.edu.co

Vicerrectora Académica: Lucía Mercedes De La Torre Urán

International Relations: Mónica Alexandra Ríos, Head of International Relations
Tel: +57(4) 3000-200 Ext. 134
EMail: relinter@lasallista.edu.co

Faculty

Administrative and Agricultural Sciences (Agricultural Management; Animal Husbandry; Veterinary Science); **Engineering** (Computer Engineering; Environmental Engineering; Food Technology; Industrial Engineering); **Social Sciences and Education** (Education; Journalism; Law; Mass Communication; Psychology)

Further Information: Also Veterinary Clinic

History: Founded 1982 by ALDEA (Lasallian Association of Ex-alumni) and the "Brothers'Congregation of Christian Schools of Medellín". Acquired present status 1983.

Academic Year: January to December (January-June; August-December)

Admission Requirements: High school certificate, State examination (ICFES) or equivalent and interview

Fees: 500-1,500 per semester (US Dollar)

Main Language(s) of Instruction: Spanish

Accrediting Agency: Consejo Nacional de Acreditación (CNA)

Degrees and Diplomas: *Profesional Universitario*: **Agricultural Business; Animal Husbandry; Computer Engineering; Environmental Engineering; Food Technology; Foreign Languages Education; Industrial Engineering; Journalism; Law; Mass Communication; Preschool Education; Primary Education; Psychology; Religious Education; Veterinary Science.** *Especialización*: **Agricultural Management; Educational Psychology; Food Science; Nutrition; Waste Management.** *Maestría*: **Food Science; Nutrition.** Also Licenciatura in Primary Education, Religious Education, Preschool Education

Student Services: Academic Counselling, Canteen, Cultural Activities, Facilities for disabled people, Health Services, Language Laboratory, Library, Nursery Care, Social Counselling, Sports Facilities

Publications: Revista Lasallista de Investigación; Revista Producción + Limpia

Publishing House: Boletín Soy Lasallista

Last Updated: 29/09/15

LATIN AMERICAN AUTONOMOUS UNIVERSITY

Universidad Autónoma Latinoamericana (UNAULA)
Apartado aéreo 3455, Carrera 55 No. 49-51, Medellín, Antioquia
Tel: +57(4) 511-2199
Fax: +57(4) 512-3418
EMail: info@unaula.edu.co; secretariageneral@unaula.edu.co
Website: http://www.unaula.edu.co

Rector: José Rodrigo Flórez Ruiz EMail: rectoria@unaula.edu.co

Vicerrector Académico: Aníbal Vélez Muñoz
Tel: +57(4) 511-2199 Ext. 108-416
EMail: vicerectoria@unaula.edu.co

Secretario General: Alfonso Tito Mejía Restrepo
EMail: secretariageneral@unaula.edu.co

International Relations: Luis Felipe Tobón Ríos, Director
Oficina de Relaciones Internacionales e Institucionales - O.R.I.I
Tel: +57(4) 511-2199 Ext. 206
EMail: ori.director@unaula.edu.co

Faculty

Business Administration (Business Administration); **Economics** (Economics); **Educational Sciences** (Education; Humanities and Social Science Education); **Engineering** (Computer Engineering; Engineering; Industrial Engineering); **Law** (Law); **Postgraduate Studies** (Administrative Law; Commercial Law; Criminal Law; Economics; Education; Finance; Fiscal Law; Human Rights; Management; Marketing; Political Sciences; Private Law; Public Law; Social Welfare; Sports Management; Transport Management); **Public Accountancy** (Accountancy)

History: Founded 1966 as a private institution. Privately financed but receives some support from the State.

Academic Year: February to December

Admission Requirements: Secondary school certificate (bachillerato) and entrance examination

Fees: 1,370 per annum (US Dollar)

Main Language(s) of Instruction: Spanish

Degrees and Diplomas: *Profesional Universitario*; *Especialización*: **Administrative Law; Commercial Law; Criminal Law; Economics; Finance; Fiscal Law; Human Rights; Management; Marketing; Political Sciences; Private Law; Public Law; Social Welfare; Sports Management; Transport Management.** *Maestría*: **Administrative Law; Education; Human Rights.**

Student Services: Academic Counselling, Canteen, Careers Guidance, Facilities for disabled people, Health Services, Language Laboratory, Library, Social Counselling, Sports Facilities

Publications: Ratio Juris; UNAULA

Last Updated: 22/10/15

LATIN AMERICAN SCHOOL OF ENGINEERS,TECHNOLOGISTS AND ENTREPRENEURS

Escuela Latinoamericana de Ingenieros Tecnólogos y Empresarios (ELITE)
Cl. 140, 18-23, Bogotá
Tel: +57(1) 8000-186435
EMail: contacto@elite.edu.co
Website: http://elite.edu.co

Rector: Carlos Felipe Escobar Roa

Programme

Business Administration (Business Administration); **Business Processes** (Business Administration); **Commercial Engineering** (Business and Commerce; Engineering); **Industrial Engineering** (Industrial Engineering); **Industrial Processes** (Industrial Engineering); **Petroleum and Gas Engineering** (Petroleum and Gas Engineering)

History: Founded 2012.

Main Language(s) of Instruction: Spanish

Degrees and Diplomas: *Tecnólogo*; *Profesional Universitario*

Last Updated: 29/09/15

LATIN AMERICAN UNIVERSITY CORPORATION

Corporación Universitaria Latinoamericana (CUL)
Calle 58, 55-24A, Barranquilla
Tel: +57(5) 344-2272 +57(5) 344-1545
Fax: +57(5) 344-4720 +57(5) 360-6272
EMail: info@ul.edu.co; promocion@ul.edu.co
Website: http://www.ul.edu.co

Rector: José Eduardo Crissien Orellano

Vicerrector Administrativo: Javier Orellano
Tel: +57(5) 360-6272 Ext.104

Faculty

Economic Sciences (Accountancy; Finance); **Education** (Physical Education; Preschool Education); **Engineering** (Computer Engineering; Safety Engineering); **Health Sciences** (Medical Technology)

History: Founded 1971.

Main Language(s) of Instruction: Spanish

Degrees and Diplomas: *Técnico Profesional*; *Profesional Universitario*

Student Services: IT Centre, Library

Last Updated: 29/09/15

LATINA UNIVERSITY INSTITUTION

Institucion Universitaria Latina (UNILATINA)
Calle 46 No. 3-05, Chapinero Alto, Bogotá
Tel: +57(1) 287-9421 +57(1) 573-7488
Fax: +57(1) 573-7488
EMail: admisiones@unilatina.edu.co
Website: http://www.unilatina.edu.co

Rectora: Nelly Teresa Bautista Moller
Tel: +57(1) 573-7488 Ext. 117
EMail: nelly.bautista@unilatina.edu.co

Secretario General: Fabian Segura Leguizamón
Tel: +57(1) 573-7488 Ext. 126
EMail: secretariageneral@unilatina.edu.co

Faculty

Business Administration (Business Administration; Finance; International Business; Marketing; Sales Techniques); **Communication Sciences** (Advertising and Publicity; Radio and Television Broadcasting)

History: Founded 1978 as Escuela de Ciencias Económicas y Administrativas. Renamed Fundación Unión Latina 1994. Acquired present status and title 2008.

Fees: 2.100.000-3.242.000 per annum (Colombian Peso)

Main Language(s) of Instruction: Spanish

Degrees and Diplomas: *Técnico Profesional*; *Tecnólogo*; *Profesional Universitario*

Student Services: Health Services, Library, Sports Facilities

Last Updated: 07/10/15

LOS LIBERTADORES UNIVERSITY FOUNDATION

Fundación Universitaria Los Libertadores
Carrera 16 No. 63A-68, Bogotá
Tel: +57(1) 254-4750
Fax: +57(1) 314-5965
EMail: admisio@cit.ulibertadores.edu.co
Website: http://www.ulibertadores.edu.co

Rectora: Sonia Arciniegas Betancourt
EMail: rectoria@libertadores.edu.co

Faculty

Administrative Sciences (Administration; Business Administration; Business and Commerce; Finance; Hotel Management; Tourism); **Communication Sciences** (Advertising and Publicity; Graphic Design; Journalism; Marketing; Mass Communication); **Economics and Accountancy** (Accountancy; Economics); **Education** (Primary Education; Special Education); **Engineering** (Aeronautical and Aerospace Engineering; Automation and Control Engineering; Computer Engineering; Electronic Engineering; Industrial Engineering;

Mechanical Engineering); **Law, Political Science and International Relations** (Law); **Psychology** (Psychology)

School
Postgraduate Studies

Further Information: Aslo Cartagena Campus

History: Founded 1982.

Main Language(s) of Instruction: Spanish

Degrees and Diplomas: *Tecnólogo*; *Profesional Universitario*; *Especialización*: **Educational Sciences; Educational Technology; Environmental Studies; Pedagogy; Statistics; Transport Management.** Also Licenciatura in Primary Education and Special Education

Last Updated: 06/10/15

LUIS AMIGO UNIVERSITY FOUNDATION

Fundación Universitaria Luis Amigó (FUNLAM)
Transversal Fundación Universitaria, Luis Amigó 51A No. 67B-90, Medellín, Antioquia
Tel: +57(4) 448-7666
Fax: +57(4) 384-9797
Website: http://www.funlam.edu.co

Rector: José Wílmar Sánchez Duque (2012-)
Tel: +57(4) 260-5092 EMail: jwsanchez@funlam.edu.co

Secretary General: Francisco Acosta Gómez
Tel: +57(4) 260-6666 Ext.167 EMail: facosta@funlam.edu.co

International Relations: Andrés Muñoz Diazgranados
Tel: +57(4) 260-6666 Ext.211 EMail: ocri@funlam.edu.co

Faculty
Business Administration (Accountancy; Business Administration; Economics; International Business); **Computer Engineering**; **Education** (Education; Pedagogy; Preschool Education; Primary Education); **Family Studies** (Family Studies); **Law and Humanities** (Civil Law; Law); **Philosophy and Theology** (Philosophy; Theology); **Psychology** (Psychology; Social Psychology); **Social Communication**

Programme
Drug Addiction *(Postgraduate programme)*

Department
Modern Languages (Modern Languages)

Centre
Community Service; **Research Development** (Accountancy; Administration; Economics; Education; Information Technology; Social Sciences)

History: Founded 1984.

Academic Year: January to November (January-May; July-November)

Admission Requirements: Secondary school certificate and ICFES examination

Fees: National: 1,700,000 per semester for distance programmes; 2,200,000 for full attendance programmes (Colombian Peso), International: 566 per semester for distance programmes; 733 for full attendance programmes (US Dollar)

Main Language(s) of Instruction: Spanish

Accrediting Agency: Instituto Colombiano para el Fomento de la Educación Superior (ICFES); Consejo Nacional de Acreditación (CNA); Ministry of Education

Degrees and Diplomas: *Profesional Universitario*: **Accountancy; Business Administration; International Business; Law; Pedagogy; Philosophy; Preschool Education; Primary Education; Psychology; Social Sciences; Theology.** *Especialización*: **Economics; Finance; Law; Social Studies; Taxation; Toxicology.** *Maestría*: **Social Studies; Toxicology.**

Student Services: Canteen, Foreign Studies Centre, Health Services, Language Laboratory, Nursery Care, Social Counselling, Sports Facilities

Publications: Análisis; Theology and Philosophy Faculty Magazine; Vida Consagrada

Last Updated: 24/11/15

LUIS G. PAEZ COLOMBIAN SCHOOL OF HOMEOPATHIC MEDICINE UNIVERSITY FOUNDATION

Fundación Universitaria Escuela Colombiana de Medicina Homeopática Luis G. Páez (UNILUISGPAEZ)
Carrera 5, No. 65-50, Bogotá
Tel: +57(1) 310-5272
EMail: informacion@uniluisgpaez.edu.co; informacion.uniluisgpaez@gmail.com
Website: http://www.uniluisgpaez.edu.co

Rector: Iván Guillermo Torres Ruiz
EMail: rectoria@uniluisgpaez.edu.co

Programme
Homeopathic Medicine (Homeopathy); **Homeopathic Veterinary Medicine** (Homeopathy; Veterinary Science)

History: Founded 2011.

Main Language(s) of Instruction: Spanish

Degrees and Diplomas: *Especialización*: **Homeopathy; Veterinary Science.** Also Diplomas

Last Updated: 27/08/15

LUMEN GENTIUM CATHOLIC UNIVERSITY FOUNDATION

Fundación Universitaria Católica Lumen Gentium (UNICATOLICA)
Carrera 122 No. 12-459, Cali, Valle del Cauca
Tel: +57(2) 555-2767 Ext. 127-128-201
Fax: +57(2) 555-8767
Website: http://www.unicatolica.edu.co

Rector: Carlos Alfonso López Antolinez
EMail: rectoria@unicatolica.edu.co; asistenterectoria@unicatolica.edu.co

Secretario General: Jaime Posso
Tel: +57(2) 555-2767 Ext. 118-142
EMail: secretariageneral@unicatolica.edu.co

International Relations: María Elena Martínez Salazar, Directora Relaciones Interinstitucionales
Tel: +57(2) 555-2767 Ext. 145
EMail: direccionrelaciones@unicatolica.edu.co; coordinacionrelaciones@unicatolica.edu.co

Faculty
Business Studies (Accountancy; Business Administration); **Education** (Art Education; Computer Education; Education; Humanities and Social Science Education; Philosophy; Primary Education; Religious Studies); **Engineering** (Computer Engineering; Electronic Engineering; Industrial Engineering; Telecommunications Engineering; Transport Management); **Humanities and Social Sciences** (Graphic Design; Journalism; Mass Communication; Psychology; Social Work; Theology)

Programme
Postgraduate Studies (Educational Technology; Human Resources; Human Rights; International Business; Literacy Education; Management; Marketing)

Department
Basic Sciences (Engineering; Management; Natural Sciences); **Communication and Language** (Mass Communication); **Humanities** (Arts and Humanities; Social Sciences)

Further Information: Also Meléndez Campus

History: Founded 1996.

Main Language(s) of Instruction: Spanish

Degrees and Diplomas: *Profesional Universitario*; *Especialización*: **Educational Technology; Human Resources; Human Rights; International Business; Literacy Education; Management; Marketing.**

Student Services: Library

Last Updated: 05/10/15

MANUELA BELTRÁN UNIVERSITY

Universidad Manuela Beltrán (UMB)
Apartado aéreo 251046, Avenida Circunvalar No. 60-00, Bogotá
Tel: +57(1) 546-0600
Fax: +57(1) 546-0638 +57(1) 546-0622
Website: http://www.umb.edu.co

Rector: Guido Echeverry Piedrahita EMail: rector@umb.edu.co

Faculty

Arts (Cinema and Television); **Education, Humanities and Social Sciences** (Psychology; Sports); **Engineering** (Biomedical Engineering; Electronic Engineering; Environmental Engineering; Industrial Engineering; Software Engineering); **Health Studies** (Nursing; Occupational Health; Physical Therapy; Rehabilitation and Therapy; Speech Therapy and Audiology); **Law** (Law)

School

Postgraduate Studies (Criminal Law; Criminology; Educational Psychology; Environmental Management; Environmental Studies; Health Administration; Occupational Health; Peace and Disarmament; Rehabilitation and Therapy; Respiratory Therapy; Sports; Water Science)

Further Information: Also branch in Bucaramanga

History: Founded 1975. Acquired present status 1992.

Main Language(s) of Instruction: Spanish

Degrees and Diplomas: *Tecnólogo*; *Profesional Universitario*; *Especialización*: **Alternative Medicine; Criminal Law; Criminology; Educational Psychology; Environmental Management; Environmental Studies; Health Administration; Occupational Health; Peace and Disarmament; Rehabilitation and Therapy; Respiratory Therapy; Water Science.** *Maestría*: **Health Administration; Medical Technology; Sports.** Also Licenciatura in Sports; Diplomados

Student Services: Library

Last Updated: 08/10/15

MARÍA CAÑO UNIVERSITY FOUNDATION

Fundación Universitaria María Caño
Calle 56 No.41-90, Medellín, Antioquia
Tel: +57(4) 402-5500
Fax: +57(4) 254-5957
EMail: admisiones@fumc.edu.co
Website: http://www.fumc.edu.co

Rector: Prospero José Posada Mier EMail: rectoria@fumc.edu.co

Vicerrector Administrativo: Óscar Alberto Gaviria Palacio
Tel: +57(4) 402-5500 Ext. 115 EMail: viceadtiva@fumc.edu.co

Faculty

Business Administration (Accountancy; Business Administration); **Engineering** (Automation and Control Engineering; Medical Technology; Robotics; Software Engineering); **Health Sciences** (Physical Therapy; Psychology; Speech Therapy and Audiology)

History: Founded 1987.

Fees: Undergraduate, 1.270.000-4.450.000 per annum; Postgraduate, 7.300.000-9.660.000 per annum (Colombian Peso)

Main Language(s) of Instruction: Spanish

Degrees and Diplomas: *Tecnólogo*; *Profesional Universitario*; *Especialización*: **Health Administration; Health Sciences; Management; Occupational Health; Speech Therapy and Audiology.** Also Diplomados

Student Services: eLibrary

Last Updated: 06/10/15

MARÍA GORETTI UNIVERSITY INSTITUTE - CENTRE OF HIGHER STUDIES

Institución Universitaria Centro de Estudios Superiores María Goretti (CESMAG)
Carrera 20A No. 14-54, San Juan de Pasto, Nariño
Tel: +57(2) 721-6535 +57(2) 733-3600
Fax: +57(2) 721-2314
EMail: goreti@iucesmag.edu.co; recepcion@iucesmag.edu.co
Website: http://www.iucesmag.edu.co

Rector: Hugo Ariel Osorio Osorio
Tel: +57(2) 721-6535 Ext. 201
EMail: rectoria@iucesmag.edu.co

Vicerrector Administrativo Financiero: Juan Carlos Nandar López
Tel: +57(2) 721-6535 Ext. 200/241
EMail: viceadm@iucesmag.edu.co

Secretaria General: Garzón Mera Leonor
EMail: secregen@iucesmag.edu.co

Faculty

Administrative Sciences and Accountancy (Accountancy; Business Administration; Finance); **Architecture and Fine Arts** (Architecture; Graphic Design); **Education** (Physical Education; Preschool Education); **Engineering** (Computer Engineering; Electronic Engineering); **Human and Social Sciences** (Law; Psychology)

History: Founded 1982. Acquired present status and title 2000.

Academic Year: August to June (August-December; January-June)

Main Language(s) of Instruction: Spanish

Degrees and Diplomas: *Tecnólogo*; *Profesional Universitario*; *Maestría*: **Civil Law; Education; Environmental Management; Marketing; Taxation.** Also Licenciatura in Physical Education and Preschool Education

Student Services: Library, Sports Facilities

Last Updated: 07/10/15

MARIANA UNIVERSITY

Universidad Mariana
Apartado aéreo 811, Calle 18 No. 34-104,
San Juan de Pasto, Nariño 7314923
Tel: +57(927) 313-616
Fax: +57(927) 313-874
EMail: umariana@umariana.edu.co;
informacionunimar@gmail.com
Website: http://www.umariana.edu.co

Rectora: Amanda Lucero Vallejo
EMail: rectoria@umariana.edu.co

Secretaria General: Dora Lucy Arce Hidalgo

Vicerrectora Administrativa y Financiera: Dora Nancy Arcila Giraldo

Faculty

Accountancy, Economics and Administrative Sciences (Accountancy; International Business; Marketing); **Distance Education** (Education; Humanities and Social Science Education; Preschool Education; Primary Education; Religious Education); **Engineering** (Automation and Control Engineering; Civil Engineering; Electronic Engineering; Production Engineering); **Health Sciences** (Dietetics; Nursing; Nutrition; Occupational Therapy; Pharmacy; Physical Therapy; Radiology); **Humanities and Social Sciences** (Law; Mass Communication; Psychology; Social and Community Services; Social Work)

Programme

Education for Unlicensed Professional (Pedagogy)

History: Founded 1965.

Main Language(s) of Instruction: Spanish

Degrees and Diplomas: *Técnico Profesional*; *Tecnólogo*; *Profesional Universitario*; *Especialización*: **Accountancy; Engineering Management; Health Administration; Health Sciences; Literacy Education; Management; Nursing; Occupational Health; Pedagogy; Public Health; Safety Engineering; Software Engineering; Taxation; Teacher Training.** *Maestría*: **Administration; Business Administration; Environmental Engineering; Epidemiology; Finance; Health Administration; Law; Management; Pedagogy; Psychiatry and Mental Health; Taxation.** Also Licenciatura

Student Services: Academic Counselling, Cultural Activities, Health Services, Language Laboratory, Library, Social Counselling, Sports Facilities

Last Updated: 04/11/15

METROPOLITAN UNIVERSITY

Universidad Metropolitana (UNIMETRO)

Apartado aéreo 50-576, Calle 76 No. 42-78, Barranquilla, Atlántico
Tel: +57(95) 358-7995
Fax: +57(95) 358-3378
EMail: unimetro@unimetro.edu.co; admisiones@unimetro.edu.co
Website: http://www.unimetro.edu.co

Rector: Carlos Jorge Jaller Raad
Tel: +57(95) 368-6572 EMail: rectoria@unimetro.edu.co

Administrative Officer: Sara Silva
Tel: +57(95) 368-6571 EMail: veba13@hotmail.com

International Relations: Olga Lucía Acosta, Treasurer
Tel: +57(95) 360-5738 EMail: olgaacosta@hotmail.com

Programme

Bacteriology (Biological and Life Sciences); **Medicine** (Medicine); **Nursing** (Nursing); **Nutrition and Dietetics** (Dietetics; Nutrition); **Occupational Therapy** (Occupational Therapy); **Odontology** (Dentistry); **Optometry** (Optometry); **Phonology and Audiology** (Speech Therapy and Audiology); **Physiotherapy** (Physical Therapy); **Psychology** (Psychology); **Social Work** (Social Work)

History: Founded 1973.

Academic Year: January to December (January-June; July-December)

Admission Requirements: Secondary school certificate and state entrance examination

Fees: Undergraduate, 2,000,000-8,820,000 per semester; Postgraduate, 3,150,000-20,160,000 per semester (Colombian Peso)

Main Language(s) of Instruction: Spanish

Degrees and Diplomas: *Profesional Universitario*; *Especialización*: **Anaesthesiology; Clinical Psychology; Gynaecology and Obstetrics; Medicine; Paediatrics; Surgery.** *Maestría*: **Education; Microbiology; Neurological Therapy; Psychiatry and Mental Health.**

Student Services: Academic Counselling, Canteen, Cultural Activities, Health Services, Library

Last Updated: 04/11/15

MINUTO DE DIOS UNIVERSITY CORPORATION

Corporación Universitaria Minuto de Dios (UNIMINUTO)

Calle 81B, No.72 B-70, Barrio Minuto de Dios, Bogotá
Tel: +57(1) 291-6520
EMail: admisiones@uniminuto.edu
Website: http://www.uniminuto.edu

Rector: Leonidas López Herrán
EMail: rectorgeneral@uniminuto.edu

International Relations: Mauricio Izquierdo A., Director General de Internacionalización Académica
Tel: +57(1) 291-6520 Ext. 6496-6498-6587
EMail: mizquierdo@uniminuto.edu; internacionalizacion@uniminuto.edu

Area

Agronomy and Veterinary Science (Agricultural Management; Agriculture; Animal Husbandry; Business and Commerce; Crop Production; Dairy; Ecology; Environmental Management; Horticulture; Meat and Poultry; Pest Management; Soil Management; Water Management); **Architecture, Urbanism and Town Planning** (Automation and Control Engineering; Civil Engineering; Computer Engineering; Computer Networks; Computer Science; Construction Engineering; Data Processing; Hydraulic Engineering; Industrial Engineering; Telecommunications Engineering; Transport Management); **Economics, Administration and Accountancy** (Accountancy; Administration; Business Administration; Communication Studies; Economics; Engineering Management; Finance; International Business; Management; Marketing; Occupational Therapy; Safety Engineering; Transport Management); **Educational Sciences** (Art Education; Computer Education; Curriculum; Education; Educational Administration; Educational Sciences; Educational Testing and Evaluation; Foreign Languages Education; Literacy Education; Mathematics Education; Native Language Education; Parks and Recreation; Pedagogy; Physical Education; Primary Education; Special Education; Sports); **Fine Arts** (Cinema and Television; Communication Arts; Graphic Design; Marketing); **Health Sciences** (Nursing; Occupational Health); **Humanities and Social Sciences** (Bible; Communication Studies; Development Studies; Ethics; Journalism; Mass Communication; Psychology; Social Work); **Mathematics** (Electronic Engineering)

History: Founded 1988.

Main Language(s) of Instruction: Spanish

Degrees and Diplomas: *Técnico Profesional*; *Tecnólogo*; *Profesional Universitario*; *Especialización*: **Communication Studies; Development Studies; Educational Administration; Educational Sciences; Ethics; Finance; Literacy Education; Management; Occupational Health; Safety Engineering; Social Work.** *Maestría*: **Communication Studies; Development Studies; Education; Engineering Management; Social Work.** Also Licenciatura (Teacher Training Degree) in Education, Primary Education, Art Education, Foreign Language Education, Native Language Education, Humanities and Social Sciences Education, Computer Education, Physical Education and Sports; Diplomados

Student Services: Library

Last Updated: 30/09/15

BELLO BRANCH

SECCIONAL BELLO

Carrera 45, 22 D-25, Bello
Tel: +57(4) 466-9200 Ext. 4053
EMail: comunicacionesbello@uniminuto.edu; mercadeouniminutobello@uniminuto.edu
Website: http://www.uniminuto.edu/web/seccionalbello

Branch's Rector: Huberto Obando Gil

Programme

Business Administration *(Distance Mode)* (Business Administration); **Business Administration** (Business Administration); **Child Education** *(Distance Mode)* (Primary Education); **Financial Management** *(Distance Mode)* (Finance); **Occupational Health Administration** *(Distance Mode)* (Health Administration; Occupational Health); **Postgraduate Studies** (Education; Educational Administration; Management); **Psychology** *(Distance Mode)* (Psychology); **Psychology** (Psychology); **Public Accounting** *(Distance Mode)* (Accountancy); **Social Communication** *(Distance Mode)* (Mass Communication); **Social Communication - Journalism** (Journalism; Mass Communication); **Social Work** (Social Work); **Technical/Professional Studies** (Continuing Education); **Technological Studies** (Computer Science; International Business; Marketing; Telecommunications Services; Transport Management)

History: Founded 2002.

Main Language(s) of Instruction: Spanish

Degrees and Diplomas: *Técnico Profesional*; *Tecnólogo*; *Profesional Universitario*: **Business Administration; Journalism; Mass Communication; Psychology; Social Work.** *Especialización*: **Educational Administration; Management.** *Maestría*: **Education.** Also Profesional Universitario offered through distance mode in Business Administration, Finance, Health Administration, Mass Communication, Public Accountancy, Pedagogy and Psychology.

Student Services: Library

MONSERRATE UNIVERSITY FOUNDATION

Fundación Universitaria Monserrate (UNIMONSERRATE)

Campus Unión Social, Av. Calle 68, 62-11, Bogotá
Tel: +57(1) 390-2202
Fax: +57(1) 217-4912
EMail: info@fum.edu.co
Website: http://www.fum.edu.co

Rector: Ricardo Alonso Pulido Aguilar
Tel: +57(1) 249-4959 Ext. 121 EMail: rectoria@fum.edu.co

Vicerrector Administrativo y Financiero: Carlos Iván Martínez Urrea

Secretario General: Carlos Hipólito García Reina

International Relations: Claudia Patricia Rivera Morato, Directora, Relaciones Interinstitucionales
Tel: +57(1) 390-2202 Ext. 1406
EMail: direccionori@unimonserrate.edu.co

Faculty
Social Sciences and Economics (Social Work; Theology)

School
Economics and Administrative Sciences (Business Administration; Environmental Management; Finance; International Business); **Education** (Bilingual and Bicultural Education; Education; Native Language Education; Preschool Education; Primary Education); **Engineering** (Transport Management); **Postgraduate Studies** (Development Studies; Education; Family Studies; Hotel and Restaurant; Pedagogy)

Further Information: Also San Antonio, San José, San Pablo, Universitario, Jerusalén, Potosí, Zona Franca Occidente, Zona Franca Bogotá Campuses

History: Founded 1983.

Academic Year: February to November

Admission Requirements: Secondary school certificate (Bachillerato); entrance examination (ICFES)

Main Language(s) of Instruction: Spanish

Degrees and Diplomas: *Profesional Universitario*; *Especialización*: **Education; Family Studies; Hotel and Restaurant; Pedagogy.** *Maestría*: **Development Studies; Education; Family Studies.**

Student Services: Academic Counselling, Careers Guidance, IT Centre, Language Laboratory, Library, Nursery Care, Social Counselling, Sports Facilities

Publications: Nuevas Búsquedas; Revista Hojas y Hablas; Revista Perspectivas Universitarias

Last Updated: 05/10/15

NAVARRA UNIVERSITY FOUNDATION

Fundación Universitaria Navarra (UNINAVARRA)
Calle 10, 6-41, Neiva, Huila
Tel: +57(8) 874-0089 +57(8) 872-2049 +57(8) 871-1199
EMail: uninavarra@navarra.edu.co
Website: http://www.uninavarra.edu.co

Rectora: Sandra Liliana Navarro Parra

Programme
Environmental Engineering (Environmental Engineering); **Health Administration** (Health Administration); **Industrial Engineering** (Industrial Engineering); **Law** (Law); **Medicine** (Medicine); **Nursing** (Nursing)

History: Founded 2011.

Main Language(s) of Instruction: Spanish

Degrees and Diplomas: *Tecnólogo*: **Health Administration.** *Profesional Universitario*: **Environmental Engineering; Industrial Engineering; Law; Medicine; Nursing.**

Student Services: Library

Last Updated: 29/09/15

PILOT UNIVERSITY CORPORATION OF COLOMBIA

Corporación Universidad Piloto de Colombia
Carrera 9 No. 45 A-44, 1er Piso, Bogotá
Tel: +57(1) 332-2900
EMail: info@unipiloto.edu.co; inscripcion@unipiloto.edu.co
Website: http://www.unipiloto.edu.co

Rectora: Patricia Piedrahita Castillo
EMail: gppiedrahita@unipiloto.edu.co

Secretaria General: Francina Hernández Tascón
EMail: sgeneral@unipiloto.edu.co; fhernandez@unipiloto.edu.co

International Relations: Maria Isabel Cifuentes Martin, Directora Departamento de Relaciones
Tel: +57(1) 332-2900 Ext. 512 EMail: micifuentes@unipiloto.edu.co

Programme
Accountancy (Accountancy); **Architecture** (Architecture); **Business Administration** (Administration; Business Administration); **Civil Engineering** (Civil Engineering); **Display and Stage Design** (Display and Stage Design); **Economics** (Economics); **Environmental Management** (Environmental Management); **Finance Engineering** (Finance); **Graphic Design** (Graphic Design); **International Business** (International Business); **Marketing Engineering** (Marketing); **Mechatronics Engineering** (Electronic Engineering); **Postgraduate Studies** (Architecture; Computer Engineering; Environmental Management; Finance; Higher Education Teacher Training; Human Resources; Management; Marketing; Taxation; Telecommunications Engineering; Transport Management; Urban Studies); **Psychology** (Psychology); **Systems Engineering** (Computer Engineering); **Telecommunications Engineering** (Telecommunications Engineering)

Further Information: Also Seccional del Alto Magdalena, Girardot

History: Founded 1962.

Academic Year: January to December (January-July; August-December)

Admission Requirements: Secondary school certificate (bachillerato) and entrance examination

Main Language(s) of Instruction: Spanish

Degrees and Diplomas: *Profesional Universitario*; *Especialización*: **Architecture; Computer Engineering; Environmental Management; Finance; Human Resources; Management; Marketing; Taxation; Telecommunications Engineering; Transport Management.** *Maestría*: **Architecture; Transport Management; Urban Studies.**

Student Services: Academic Counselling, Canteen, Careers Guidance, Cultural Activities, Health Services, Library, Nursery Care, Social Counselling, Sports Facilities

Last Updated: 28/09/15

GIRARDOT BRANCH

SECCIONAL GIRARDOT
Carrera 19 No. 17-33, Barrio Las Quintas, Girardot, Cundinamarca
Tel: +57(1) 836-0600 +57(320) 454-4348
Fax: +57(183) 32-873
EMail: supilo1@col1.telecom.com.co
Website: http://girardot.unipiloto.edu.co

Rectora: Gloria Patricia Piedrahita Castillo
Tel: +57(1) 332-2900 Ext. 262
EMail: gppiedrahita@unipiloto.edu.co

Vicerector Administrativo y Financiero: Jose Ernesto Bermudez Rojas
Tel: +57(1) 836-0600 Ext. 102
EMail: g-jebermudez@unipiloto.edu.co

Programme
Civil Engineering (Civil Engineering); **Computer Networks** (Computer Networks); **Environmental Management** (Environmental Management); **Financial Engineering** (Finance); **Information Systems Development** (Information Technology); **Logistics Administration** (Transport Management); **Postgraduate Studies** *(Continuing Education)* (Management; Marketing); **Public Accountancy** (Accountancy); **Systems Engineering** (Computer Engineering); **Tourism and Hotel Management** (Hotel Management; Tourism)

History: Founded 1986.

Main Language(s) of Instruction: Spanish

Degrees and Diplomas: *Tecnólogo*; *Profesional Universitario*; *Especialización*: **Management; Marketing.** Also Diplomado

Student Services: Cultural Activities, Health Services, Library, Sports Facilities

POLYTECHNIC CORPORATION OF THE ATLANTIC COAST

Corporación Politécnico de la Costa Atlántica (PCA)
Avenida de los estudiantes, Carrera 38 No. 79A-67, Barranquilla, Atlántico
Tel: +57(5) 336-1800 Ext. 103-128-123-110 +57(5) 336-1803
Fax: +57(5) 358-7200
EMail: admisiones@pca.edu.co
Website: http://www.pca.edu.co

Rector: Hugo César Santander García EMail: husanta@pca.edu.co

Secretario: Antonio Valejo Morales

Programme
Business Administration (Business Administration); **Electronic Engineering** (Electronic Engineering); **Industrial Engineering** (Industrial Engineering); **International Business** (International Business); **Marketing** (Marketing); **Public Accountancy** (Accountancy); **Systems Engineering** (Computer Engineering); **Technological/Professional Studies** (Accountancy; Advertising and Publicity; Computer Graphics; Electronic Engineering; Finance; Human Resources; Industrial Engineering; Industrial Management; International Business; Marketing; Software Engineering; Transport Management)

Main Language(s) of Instruction: Spanish

Degrees and Diplomas: *Tecnólogo*; *Profesional Universitario*

Last Updated: 25/09/15

PONTIFICAL BOLIVARIAN UNIVERSITY

Universidad Pontificia Bolivariana (UPB)

Apartado Aéreo 56006, Cir. 1a No. 70-01, Medellín, Antioquia
Tel: +57(4) 415-9015
Fax: +57(4) 250-2080
EMail: relinter@logos.upb.edu.co
Website: http://www.upb.edu.co

Rector: Julio Jairo Ceballos Sepúlveda (2013-)
Tel: +57(4) 415-9000 EMail: rectoria@upb.edu.co

Secretaria General: Maria Clemencia Restrepo Posada
Tel: +57(4) 354-4594 Ext.10802

International Relations: Miguel Angel Betancur Betancur, Director Relaciones Internacionales e Interinstitucionales
Tel: +57(4) 354-4546
EMail: relaciones.internacionales@upb.edu.co

School
Architecture and Design (Architecture; Fashion Design; Graphic Design; Industrial Design); **Economics, Administration and Commerce** (Business Administration; Economics; International Business); **Education and Pedagogy** (Art Education; Education; Foreign Languages Education; Native Language Education); **Engineering** (Administration; Aeronautical and Aerospace Engineering; Agricultural Engineering; Chemical Engineering; Computer Engineering; Electrical Engineering; Electronic Engineering; Engineering; Industrial Engineering; Mechanical Engineering; Nanotechnology; Safety Engineering; Telecommunications Engineering; Textile Technology); **Health Sciences** (Medicine; Nursing); **Law and Political Science** (Law; Political Sciences); **Social Sciences** (Advertising and Publicity; Journalism; Mass Communication; Psychology; Social Work); **Theology, Philosophy and Humanities** (History; Humanities and Social Science Education; Literature; Philosophy; Religious Education; Theology)

History: Founded 1936 by the Archbishop of Medellín, acquired present status and title 1945.

Academic Year: January to November (January-June; July-November)

Admission Requirements: Secondary school certificate (bachillerato) and state entrance examination. Entrance examination for Graphic and Industrial Design

Main Language(s) of Instruction: Spanish

Degrees and Diplomas: *Profesional Universitario*; *Especialización*: **Administrative Law; Agricultural Business; Anaesthesiology; Automation and Control Engineering; Biomedical Engineering; Business Administration; Cardiology; Civil Law; Clinical Psychology; Commercial Law; Computer Engineering; Computer Science; Dermatology; Electrical Engineering; Engineering Management; Environmental Engineering; Environmental Management; Environmental Studies; Family Studies; Fiscal Law; Foreign Languages Education; Furniture Design; Gynaecology and Obstetrics; Haematology; Health Sciences; Human Resources; Insurance; Interior Design; International Business; Journalism; Labour Law; Law; Literature; Management; Marketing; Mass Communication; Mathematics Education; Medicine; Nephrology; Nursing; Ophthalmology; Orthopaedics; Packaging Technology; Paediatrics; Power Engineering; Private Law; Psychiatry and Mental Health; Public Administration; Radiology; Safety Engineering; Science Education; Social Psychology; Sports; Sports Medicine; Surgery; Taxation.** *Maestría*: **Architecture; Biotechnology; Civil Law; Communication Studies; Consumer Studies; Design; Development Studies; Education; Engineering; Engineering Management; Ethics; Foreign Languages Education; Human Resources; Industrial Design; Information Technology; Landscape Architecture; Law; Literature; Management; Marketing; Mathematics; Medicine; Multimedia; Natural Sciences; Philosophy; Political Sciences; Psychiatry and Mental Health; Psychology; Psychotherapy; Radio and Television Broadcasting; Rehabilitation and Therapy; Social Psychology; Telecommunications Engineering; Textile Technology; Theology.** *Doctorado*: **Canon Law; Civil Law; Engineering; Engineering Management; Medicine; Philosophy; Social Sciences; Theology.** Also Licenciatura; MBA; Especialización in Protective Services offered with Universidad Militar Nueva Granada

Student Services: Academic Counselling, Careers Guidance, Cultural Activities, Health Services, Social Counselling, Sports Facilities

Publications: Administración de Empresas; Cuestiones Teológicas y Filosóficas; Escritos; Integral Industrial; Pensamiento Humanista; Revista Comunicación Social UPB; Revista Facultad de Derecho y Ciencias Políticas; Revista Facultad de Trabajo Social

Publishing House: Bolivariana

Last Updated: 06/11/15

BUCARAMANGA BRANCH
SECCIONAL BUCARAMANGA

Autopista Piedecuesta Kilometro 7, Bucaramanga, Santander
Tel: +57(7) 679-6220
Fax: +57(76) 679-7080
Website: http://www.upb.edu.co/bucaramanga

Rector: Primitivo Sierra Cano
EMail: nnavarro@upbbga.edu.co; rectoria@upbbga.edu.co

Vicerrectora de Asuntos Administrativos y Financieros: Victoria Helena Pérez Goelkel

Secretario General: Carlos Augusto Mora González

International Relations: Mireya Otero Rodríguez, Directora Relaciones Internacionales e Interinstitucionales
Tel: +57(7) 679-6220 Ext. 576 EMail: mireya.otero@upb.edu.co

School
Engineering (Civil Engineering; Computer Engineering; Electronic Engineering; Environmental Engineering; Industrial Engineering; Mechanical Engineering); **Law and Political Sciences** (Law); **Social Sciences** (Journalism; Mass Communication; Psychology); **Strategic Sciences** (Business Administration; International Business)

History: Founded 1990.

Main Language(s) of Instruction: Spanish

Degrees and Diplomas: *Profesional Universitario*; *Especialización*: **Automation and Control Engineering; Civil Engineering; Clinical Psychology; Communication Studies; Computer Engineering; Environmental Management; Family Studies; Foreign Languages Education; Industrial Engineering; Information Technology; International Business; Management; Marketing; Natural Resources; Road Transport.** *Maestría*: **Civil Engineering; Electronic Engineering; Psychology.**

Student Services: Library

MONTERÍA BRANCH
SECCIONAL MONTERÍA

Carrera 6 # 97 A - 99, Montería, Córdoba
Tel: +57(4) 786-0146 +57(4) 786-0661 Ext. 121-163-227
Fax: +57(4) 786-0912
EMail: registro.monteria@upb.edu.co; crelinter@upb.edu.co
Website: http://www.upb.edu.co/monteria

Rector seccional: Jorge Alonso Bedoya Vásquez
Tel: +57(4) 782-3622 EMail: rectoria@upbmonteria.edu.co

Secretario General: Darío Peinado Babilonia
Tel: +57(4) 782-3622 Ext. 173

Vicerrector de Asuntos Administrativos y Económicos: Victor Jaime Valle Quiroz

International Relations: Carlos Enrique Ramos Cabrales, Director Relaciones Internacionales
Tel: +57(4) 786-0146 EMail: ori.monteria@upb.edu.co

Faculty

Agroindustrial Engineering (Agricultural Engineering; Industrial Engineering); **Architecture** (Architecture); **Business Administration** (Business Administration); **Civil Engineering** (Civil Engineering); **Economics** (Economics); **Electronic Engineering** (Electronic Engineering); **Industrial Engineering** (Industrial Engineering); **Law** (Law); **Mechanical Engineering** (Mechanical Engineering); **Psychology** (Psychology); **Sanitary and Environmental Engineering** (Environmental Engineering; Sanitary Engineering); **Social Communications and Journalism** (Journalism; Mass Communication)

History: Founded 1995.

Fees: Undergraduate, 2,942,954-5,397,720 per semester; Postgraduate, 4,268,553-6,122,909 per semester (Colombian Peso)

Main Language(s) of Instruction: Spanish

Degrees and Diplomas: *Profesional Universitario*; *Especialización*: **Criminal Law; Finance; Foreign Languages Education; Human Resources; Marketing.** Also MBA

Student Services: Library

PALMIRA BRANCH

SECCIONAL PALMIRA

Kilometro 1 Via Tienda Nueva, Palmira, Valle
Tel: +57(2) 270-2545
Fax: +57(2) 272-3121
Website: http://www.upb.edu.co/palmira

Rector: Luis Carlos González Gómez
EMail: upbpalmira@teleset.com.co; luiscarlos.gonzalez@upb.edu.co

Vicerrector académico: Oscar Alirio Millán González
EMail: upbviceacademico@telesat.com.co

Secretaria Rectoría y Secretaría General: Andrea Ximena Cobo Martínez
Tel: +57(2) 270-2545 Ext. 101 EMail: andrea.cobo@upb.edu.co

Programme

Advertising (Advertising and Publicity); **Business Administration** (Business Administration); **Industrial Engineering** (Industrial Engineering); **Law** (Law); **Psychology** (Psychology)

History: Founded 1997.

Main Language(s) of Instruction: Spanish

Degrees and Diplomas: *Profesional Universitario*; *Especialización*: **Finance; Human Resources; Management; Marketing; Public Administration.**

PONTIFICAL XAVIERIAN UNIVERSITY

Pontificia Universidad Javeriana

Apartado aéreo 56710, Carrera 7 a No. 40-62, Bogotá
Tel: +57(1) 320-8320
Fax: +57(1) 285-3348
EMail: contacto@javeriana.edu.co
Website: http://www.javeriana.edu.co

Rector: Jorge Humberto Peláez Piedrahita
Tel: +57(1) 320-8320 Ext.2009
EMail: rectoria@javeriana.edu.co; aldana.adriana@javeriana.edu.co

Vicerrectora Administrativa: Catalina Martínez de Rozo
Tel: +57(1) 320-8320 Ext. 2280
EMail: catalina.martinez@javeriana.edu.co

International Relations: Luis Fernando Álvarez Londoño, Vicerrector de Extensión y Relaciones Interinstitucionales
Tel: +57(1) 320-8320 Ext. 3484-3486 EMail: veri@javeriana.edu.co

Faculty

Economics and Administration (Accountancy; Business Administration; Economics; Finance; Health Administration; Human Resources; Insurance; Management; Marketing); **Architecture and Design** (Architecture; Industrial Design; Regional Planning; Town Planning); **Arts** (Music; Performing Arts; Visual Arts); **Canon Law** (Canon Law); **Communication and Languages** (Arts and Humanities; Communication Studies; Information Sciences; Library Science; Mass Communication; Modern Languages; Social Sciences); **Education** (Education; Foreign Languages Education; Pedagogy); **Engineering** (Civil Engineering; Computer Engineering; Construction Engineering; Electronic Engineering; Engineering Management; Industrial Engineering; Road Engineering; Software Engineering); **Environmental and Rural Studies** (Ecology; Environmental Management; Environmental Studies; Rural Studies); **Law** (Administrative Law; Commercial Law; Constitutional Law; Fiscal Law; Labour Law; Law; Private Law); **Medicine** (Epidemiology; Medicine; Statistics); **Nursing** (Gerontology; Health Sciences; Nursing); **Odontology** (Dentistry; Oral Pathology; Orthodontics; Periodontics; Rehabilitation and Therapy; Surgery); **Philosophy** (Philosophy); **Political Science and International Relations** (Government; International Relations; Marketing; Peace and Disarmament; Political Sciences; Public Administration; Social Policy); **Psychology** (Clinical Psychology; Psychology); **Science** (Analytical Chemistry; Biological and Life Sciences; Biology; Dietetics; Haematology; Laboratory Techniques; Mathematics; Microbiology; Nutrition); **Social Sciences** (Anthropology; Cultural Studies; History; Literature; Sociology); **Theology** (Religious Studies; Theology)

Institute

Ageing (Gerontology); **Architectural and Urban Heritage** *(Carlos Arbelaez Camacho)* (Architecture; Heritage Preservation); **Bioethics** (Ethics); **Development Policies** *(IPD)* (Development Studies); **Environmental Studies for Development** *(IDEADE)* (Environmental Studies); **Geophysics** (Geophysics); **Health Promotion** (Health Sciences); **Housing and Urbanism** *(INJAVIU)* (Town Planning); **Human Development** (Development Studies); **Human Genetics** (Genetics); **Human Rights and International Relations** *('Alfredo Vasquez Carrizosa')* (Human Rights; International Relations); **Inborn Errors of Metabolism** (Biological and Life Sciences); **Rural Studies** *(IER)* (Rural Studies); **Social and Cultural Studies** *(PENSAR)* (Cultural Studies; Social Studies)

Further Information: Also Teaching Hospital

History: Founded 1623 as Academia Javeriana by the Society of Jesus. Became university 1704. Formally inaugurated as Pontifical University 1937.

Academic Year: February to November (February-May; August-November)

Admission Requirements: Secondary school certificate (bachillerato), entrance examination and interview

Fees: 3,500-6,000 (US Dollar)

Main Language(s) of Instruction: Spanish

Accrediting Agency: Comité Nacional de Acreditación (CNA); Ministry of Education

Degrees and Diplomas: *Profesional Universitario*; *Especialización*: **Accountancy; Administrative Law; Anaesthesiology; Analytical Chemistry; Biochemistry; Cardiology; Commercial Law; Communication Studies; Computer Engineering; Construction Engineering; Dentistry; Design; Economics; Endocrinology; Engineering Management; Finance; Gastroenterology; Genetics; Geological Engineering; Gerontology; Government; Gynaecology and Obstetrics; Haematology; Health Administration; Human Resources; Industrial Management; Insurance; International Business; Laboratory Techniques; Labour Law; Law; Management; Marketing; Medicine; Nephrology; Neurology; Nursing; Occupational Health; Ophthalmology; Oral Pathology; Orthodontics; Orthopaedics; Otorhinolaryngology; Paediatrics; Pathology; Peace and Disarmament; Plastic Surgery; Pneumology; Private Law; Public Administration; Radio and Television Broadcasting; Road Engineering; Singing; Software Engineering; Surgery; Taxation; Urology.** *Maestría*: **Administration; Applied Linguistics; Archiving; Biological and Life Sciences; Canon Law; Civil Engineering; Civil Law; Clinical Psychology; Commercial Law; Computer Engineering; Cultural Studies; Economics; Education; Electronic Engineering; Environmental Management; Epidemiology; Ethics; Health Administration; History; Industrial Engineering; International Relations; Latin American Studies; Literature; Mass Communication; Medical Technology; Music; Nursing; Peace and Disarmament; Philosophy; Political Sciences; Public Health; Regional Planning; Rural Planning; Social Policy; Statistics; Theology; Town Planning; Water Science.** *Doctorado*: **Arts and Humanities; Biology; Canon Law; Engineering; Environmental**

Studies; Epidemiology; Law; Philosophy; Rural Studies; Social Sciences; Theology. Also Licenciatura

Student Services: Academic Counselling, Canteen, Cultural Activities, Health Services, Language Laboratory, Library, Social Counselling, Sports Facilities

Publications: Editorial Pontificia Universidad Javeriana; Revista Alternativa; Revista Cuadernos de Administración; Revista Cuadernos de Desarrollo Rural; Revista Cuadernos de Literatura; Revista Cuadernos de Música, Artes Visuales y Artes Escénicas; Revista Cuadrantephi; Revista Digitario; Revista Directo Bogotá; Revista Fractales; Revista Ingeniera y Universidad; Revista Interlenguajes; Revista Javeriana; Revista Memoria y Sociedad; Revista Nuevas Tecnologías de la Información; Revista Signo y Pensamiento; Revista Theologica Javeriana; Revista Universitas Humanistica; Revista Universitas Médica; Revista Universitas Psychologica; Revista Universitas Scientarum

Publishing House: Javegraf. Centro Editorial Javeriano (CEJA)

Last Updated: 20/10/15

CALI BRANCH

SECCIONAL CALI

Calle 18 No. 118-250, Vía Pance, Cali, Valle del Cauca
Tel: +57(2) 321-8200
Fax: +57(2) 555-2180
EMail: dircom@javerianacali.edu.co
Website: http://www.javerianacali.edu.co

Rector Seccional: Luis Felipe Gómez

International Relations: Claudia María Castaño Rodas, Directora Oficina de Relaciones Internacionales
Tel: +57(2) 321-8200 Ext. 8365
EMail: claudia.castano@javerianacali.edu.co

Faculty

Economics and Business Administration (Accountancy; Administration; Business Administration; Economics; Finance; International Business; Marketing); **Engineering** (Applied Mathematics; Biology; Civil Engineering; Computer Engineering; Electronic Engineering; Engineering; Industrial Engineering); **Health Sciences** (Medicine; Public Health); **Humanities and Social Sciences** (Architecture; Graphic Design; Law; Mass Communication; Political Sciences; Psychology; Visual Arts)

Institute

Intercultural Studies (Cultural Studies)

Research Group

Automation and Robotics (Automation and Control Engineering); **Mathematics and Applied Statistics** (Mathematics; Statistics); **Regional Development** (Development Studies)

Further Information: Special programme of Spanish as a Foreign Language

History: Founded 1970.

Academic Year: February to November (February-May; August-November)

Admission Requirements: Secondary school certificate (bachillerato) and entrance examination

Fees: 2,000-3,000 (US Dollar)

Main Language(s) of Instruction: Spanish

Accrediting Agency: Comité Nacional de Acreditación (CAN); Colombian Ministry of Education

Degrees and Diplomas: *Profesional Universitario*; *Especialización*: **Accountancy; Commercial Law; Construction Engineering; Engineering Management; Finance; Health Administration; International Business; Management; Marketing; Peace and Disarmament; Psychology; Safety Engineering; Social Work; Taxation; Transport Management.** *Maestría*: **Administration; Business Administration; Civil Engineering; Commercial Law; Engineering; Family Studies; Finance; Human Rights; Marketing; Peace and Disarmament; Psychology; Public Health.** *Doctorado*: **Engineering.**

Student Services: Academic Counselling, Canteen, Cultural Activities, Health Services, Language Laboratory, Library, Social Counselling, Sports Facilities

Publications: Del Lago al Samán; Periódico Estudiantil El Clavo; Revista Científica Epiciclos; Revista Criterio Jurídico; Revista Economía, Gestión y Desarrollo; Revista Nuestro Compromiso Social; Revista Pensamiento Psicológico; Revista Perspectivas Internacionales; Revista Universitas Xaveriana; Sello Editorial Javeriano

POPAYÁN UNIVERSITY FOUNDATION

Fundación Universitaria de Popayán (FUP)

Los Robles Km 8 vía al Sur, Popayán, Cauca
Tel: +57(2) 832-0225
EMail: rectoria@fup.edu.co; admisiones@fup.edu.co
Website: http://www.fup.edu.co

Rector: Mario Alfredo Polo Castellanos EMail: rectoria@fup.edu.co

Administrative Officer: Wilmer Urrea
Tel: +57(312) 257-3121 EMail: wurrea@fup.edu.co

Secretario General: Cristina isdith EMail: secretariag@fup.edu.co

International Relations: Sonia Gaviria Armero, Directora de Relaciones Internacionales
Tel: +57(2) 832-0225 Ext. 1030 EMail: ori@fup.edu.co

Programme

Architecture (Architecture); **Business Administration** (Business Administration); **Ecology** (Ecology); **Education** (Teacher Training); **Farm Management** (Farm Management); **Industrial Engineering** (Industrial Engineering); **Law** (Law); **Psychology** (Psychology); **Public Accounting** (Business Administration); **Social Communication** (Mass Communication); **Social Work** (Social Sciences); **Systems Engineering** (Computer Engineering; Systems Analysis); **Virtual Undergraduate Studies** (Agricultural Management)

School

Languages Studies (English; French); **Music** *(INFORMUS)* (Music)

Campus

Santander de Qilichao (Accountancy; Architecture; Computer Engineering; Industrial Engineering; Law; Psychology)

History: Founded 1980.

Fees: 785,650-2,474,850 per programme (Colombian Peso)

Main Language(s) of Instruction: Spanish

Degrees and Diplomas: *Técnico Profesional*; *Tecnólogo*; *Profesional Universitario*. Also Licenciatura

Student Services: Academic Counselling, Careers Guidance, Cultural Activities, Facilities for disabled people, Health Services, IT Centre, Language Laboratory, Library, Nursery Care, Social Counselling, Sports Facilities, eLibrary

Publications: biannual

Student Numbers *2015-2016*: Total: c. 6,500

Last Updated: 09/11/15

PRIVATE UNIVERSITY

Universidad Libre

Calle 8a No. 5-80, Bogotá
Tel: +57(1) 382-1000
Fax: +57(1) 382-1073
EMail: escueladocente@unilibre.edu.co
Website: http://www.unilibre.edu.co/Bogota

Rector: Nicolás Enrique Zuleta Hincapié
Tel: +57(1) 382-1000 Ext. 1004/1024
EMail: nzuleta_rectoria@unilibre.edu.co

Secretario General: Pablo Emilio Cruz Samboni
EMail: secgeneral@unilibre.edu.co

Faculty

Economics (Accountancy; Business Administration); **Educational Sciences** (Foreign Languages Education; Humanities and Social Science Education; Parks and Recreation; Physical Education; Primary Education; Sports); **Engineering** (Computer Engineering; Environmental Engineering; Industrial Engineering; Mechanical Engineering); **Law** (Criminal Law; Labour Law; Law; Private Law; Public Law; Social Welfare); **Philosophy** (Philosophy)

History: Founded 1923. Financed by the student fees.

Academic Year: February to December (February-June; July-December)

Admission Requirements: Secondary school certificate (bachillerato) and entrance examination

Main Language(s) of Instruction: Spanish

Degrees and Diplomas: *Profesional Universitario*; *Especialización*: **Administrative Law; Civil Law; Commercial Law; Constitutional Law; Criminal Law; Educational Administration; Environmental Management; Fiscal Law; Higher Education Teacher Training; Labour Law; Law; Marketing; Philosophy; Private Law; Safety Engineering; Sales Techniques; Social Welfare.** *Maestría*: **Accountancy; Administrative Law; Criminal Law; Educational Administration; Educational and Student Counselling; Educational Psychology; Educational Technology; Energy Engineering; Finance; Foreign Languages Education; Insurance; International Business; Native Language Education; Philosophy; Taxation.** *Doctorado*: **Law.** Also Licenciatura

Student Services: Library

Publications: Diálogo de Saberes

Last Updated: 03/11/15

BARRANQUILLA BRANCH

SECCIONAL BARRANQUILLA

Km. 7 Antigua Via a Puerto Colombia, Barranquilla, Atlántico
Tel: +57(5) 367-3800
Fax: +57(958) 415-110
EMail: admisionesyregistros@unilibrebaq.edu.co
Website: http://www.unilibrebaq.edu.co

Rector Seccional: Rachid Nader Orfale
EMail: rnader@unilibrebaq.edu.co

Faculty
Economics, Administrative Sciences and Accountancy (Accountancy; International Business; Marketing); **Engineering** (Computer Engineering; Industrial Engineering); **Exact and Natural Sciences** (Microbiology); **Health Sciences** (Medical Technology; Medicine; Microbiology; Physical Therapy); **Law and Political Sciences** (Law; Social Sciences)

History: Founded 1956.

Main Language(s) of Instruction: Spanish

Degrees and Diplomas: *Tecnólogo*; *Profesional Universitario*; *Especialización*: **Administrative Law; Commercial Law; Constitutional Law; Criminal Law; Criminology; Environmental Management; Finance; Fiscal Law; Gynaecology and Obstetrics; Health Administration; Health Sciences; Labour Law; Management; Medicine; Occupational Health; Paediatrics; Private Law; Safety Engineering; Social Welfare; Surgery; Taxation; Transport Management.** *Maestría*: **Administrative Law; Biotechnology; Computer Engineering; Criminal Law; Criminology; Industrial Engineering; Labour Law; Microbiology; Molecular Biology; Occupational Health; Private Law; Safety Engineering; Social Welfare; Taxation.**

Student Services: Library

CALI BRANCH

SECCIONAL CALI

Diagonal 37A No. 3-29, Santa Isabel,
Santiago de Cali, Valle del Cauca
Tel: +57(2) 524-0007
EMail: unilibre@unilibrecali.edu.co
Website: http://www.unilibrecali.edu.co

Rector seccional: Luis Fernando Parra Villanueva
EMail: luis.parra@unilibrecali.edu.co; contaduriadir@unilibrecali.edu.co

Secretario Seccional: Omar Bedoya Loaiza

Faculty
Economics, Administrative Sciences and Accountancy (Accountancy; Business Administration; Economics; Marketing); **Health Sciences** (Medicine; Nursing; Psychology); **Law, Political and Social Sciences** (Law)

Programme
Education (Education); **Engineering** (Computer Engineering; Industrial Engineering)

History: Founded 1946.

Main Language(s) of Instruction: Spanish

Degrees and Diplomas: *Profesional Universitario*; *Especialización*: **Administrative Law; Business Administration; Constitutional Law; Criminal Law; Finance; Haematology; Health Administration; Human Resources; International Business; Labour Law; Management; Marketing; Medicine; Occupational Health; Oncology; Psychiatry and Mental Health; Psychology; Taxation; Transport Management.** *Maestría*: **Administrative Law; Computer Education; Constitutional Law; Criminal Law; Criminology; Educational Technology; Epidemiology; Health Administration; Marketing; Occupational Health.** Also Diplomado

Student Services: Library

CÚCUTA BRANCH

SECCIONAL CÚCUTA

Urbanizacion El Bosque, Cúcuta, Norte de Santander
Tel: +57(97) 582-9810 Ext. 216
Fax: +57(97) 582-9810 Ext. 143
EMail: admisionesyregistro@unilibrecucuta.edu.co
Website: http://www.unilibrecucuta.edu.co

Rector seccional: Holger Cáceres Medina (2014-)
Tel: +57(97) 582-9810 Ext. 132
EMail: rectoria@unilibrecucuta.edu.co

Secretaria Seccional, Directora Gestión Humana: Nora Consuelo Ibarra
Tel: +57(97) 582-9810 Ext. 205
EMail: secgeneral@unilibrecucuta.edu.co; talentohumano@unilibrecucuta.edu.co

Faculty
Economics, Administration and Accountancy (Accountancy; Business Administration); **Engineering** (Industrial Engineering); **Law, Political and Social Sciences** (Communication Studies; Criminology; Law; Public Relations)

Programme
Postgraduate Studies (Accountancy; Business Administration; Law; Taxation)

Main Language(s) of Instruction: Spanish

Degrees and Diplomas: *Profesional Universitario*; *Especialización*: **Administrative Law; Civil Law; Criminal Law; Finance; Human Rights; International Business; Labour Law; Notary Studies; Private Law; Public Law; Social Welfare; Taxation.** *Maestría*: **Civil Law; Taxation.** Also MBA in Administration

Student Services: Library

PEREIRA BRANCH

SECCIONAL PEREIRA

Calle 40 No 7-30, Pereira, Risaralda
Tel: +57(6) 315-5600
Fax: +57(6) 314-7503
EMail: admisiones@unilibrepereira.edu.co
Website: http://www.unilibrepereira.edu.co/portal

Rector seccional: Jaime Alonso Arias Bermúdez
EMail: seacademicacentro@unilibrepereira.edu.co

Secretario seccional: Giovani Arias
EMail: secretariageneral@unilibrepereira.edu.co

International Relations: Angélica Viviana Morales Cortés, Coordinadora Oficina Relaciones Interinstitucionales
Tel: +57(6) 314-7519 EMail: ori@unilibreper

Faculty
Economics, Administrative Sciences and Accountancy (Accountancy; Business Administration; Economics); **Engineering** (Business and Commerce; Civil Engineering; Computer Engineering; Engineering; Finance); **Health Sciences** (Microbiology; Nursing); **Law** (Criminology; Law; Social Work)

History: Founded 1971.

Main Language(s) of Instruction: Spanish

Degrees and Diplomas: *Tecnólogo*; *Profesional Universitario*; *Especialización*: **Accountancy; Administrative Law; Agriculture; Business Administration; Business and Commerce; Constitutional Law; Criminal Law; Finance; International Business; Management; Occupational Health; Safety Engineering; Software Engineering; Taxation; Transport Management.** *Maestría*: **Administrative Law; Business Administration; Criminal Law; Marketing; Occupational Health; Safety Engineering.**

Student Services: Library

SOCORRO BRANCH

SECCIONAL SOCORRO (UNILIBRESOC)

Campus Universitario Majavita, Calle 16 No 14-08, Socorro, Santander
Tel: +57(97) 727-2639
Fax: +57(97) 727-6262
EMail: registro@mail.unilibresoc.edu.co
Website: http://www.unilibresoc.edu.co

Presidente-Rector Seccional: Nelson Omar Mancilla Medina
EMail: nelson.mancilla@mail.unilibresoc.edu.co

Faculty

Economics, Administration and Accountancy (Accountancy; Business Administration); **Educational Sciences** (Environmental Studies; Foreign Languages Education; Humanities and Social Science Education; Mathematics Education; Science Education; Teacher Training); **Engineering** (Environmental Engineering); **Law** (Law)

Programme

Postgraduate Studies (Accountancy; Business Administration; Economics; Engineering; Law); **Zootechnics** (Animal Husbandry)

Main Language(s) of Instruction: Spanish

Degrees and Diplomas: *Profesional Universitario*; *Especialización*: **Administrative Law; Business Administration; Civil Law; Constitutional Law; Criminal Law; Environmental Management; Labour Law; Social Welfare; Taxation.** *Maestría*: **Administrative Law.** Also Licenciatura (Teacher Training Degree), 5 yrs

RAFAEL NÚÑEZ UNIVERSITY CORPORATION

Corporación Universitaria Rafael Núñez (CURN)
Centro Calle de la Soledad No 5-70, Cartagena de Indias, Bolívar
Tel: +57(5) 660-7777
Fax: +57(5) 600-134
EMail: rafaelnunez@curn.edu.co
Website: http://www.curn.edu.co

Rector: Miguel Ángel Henriquez López
EMail: miguelhenriquez@curn.edu.co

Secretaria General: Viviana Henríquez López
EMail: secretariageneral@curn.edu.co

Vicerrector General: Miguel Henríquez Emiliani

Vicerrectora Académica: Patricia de Moya Carazo

International Relations: Vanessa Henriquez, Directora Depto Relaciones Nacionales e Internacionales
Tel: +57(5) 664-1208 Ext. 114

Faculty

Accountancy and Administration (Accountancy; Business Administration); **Engineering** (Computer Engineering; Information Technology; Software Engineering); **Health Sciences** (Cosmetology; Dental Technology; Dentistry; Medical Technology; Medicine; Microbiology; Nursing; Plastic Surgery; Surgery); **Social and Human Sciences** (Law; Preschool Education; Social Work)

Further Information: Also Barranquilla Campus

History: Founded 1984.

Fees: 56,400 per annum (US Dollar)

Main Language(s) of Instruction: Spanish

Degrees and Diplomas: *Tecnólogo*; *Profesional Universitario*. Also Diplomados

Student Services: Library

Last Updated: 30/09/15

REFORMED UNIVERSITY CORPORATION

Corporación Universitaria Reformada (CUR)
Carrera 38, 74-179, Barranquilla, Atlantico
Tel: +57(5) 361-0432
Fax: +57(5) 361-0432
EMail: rector@unireformada.edu.co
Website: http://www.unireformada.edu.co

Rector: James Harley Schutmaat Loew (2004-)
EMail: rector@unireformada.edu.co

Vice-Rector for Administration: Helis Barraza (2004-)

International Relations: Alice Winters, International Relations Officer (2004-)

Programme

International Business (International Business); **Music** (Music; Music Education; Music Theory and Composition); **Psychology** (Psychology); **Theology** (Theology)

History: Founded 2001. Acquired present status 2002

Admission Requirements: Diploma de Bachiller, National Examination for Higher Education Entrance (ICFES)

Fees: National: 1,900,000-3,200,000 (Colombian Peso), International: 650-1,200 (US Dollar)

Main Language(s) of Instruction: Spanish

Degrees and Diplomas: *Profesional Universitario*: **International Business; Music; Psychology; Theology.**

Student Services: Academic Counselling, Careers Guidance, Cultural Activities, Facilities for disabled people, Health Services

Publications: La Iguan; Noticias Virtual Pag. Web

Last Updated: 24/11/15

REGIONAL UNIVERSITY CORPORATION OF THE CARIBBEAN

Corporación Universitaria Regional del Caribe (CURC IAFIC)
Av. Pedro de Heredia, Sector Pie del Cerro, Calle 31 N° 18B-17, Cartagena de Indias, Bolívar
Tel: +57(5) 666-6470 +57(5) 666-5832 +57(5) 666-4479
Fax: +57(5) 666-6470
EMail: admiafic@iafic.edu.co
Website: http://www.iafic.edu.co

Rector: Luis Gustavo Fierro Maya EMail: rectoria@iafic.edu.co

Programme

Accountancy and Finance (Accountancy; Finance); **Children's Pedagogy** (Pedagogy); **Customs and Logistics** (Taxation; Transport Management); **Entrepreneurship** (Management); **Hotel Management** (Hotel Management); **International Business and Logistics** (International Business; Transport Management); **Maritime and Customs Law** (Maritime Law; Taxation); **Public Accountancy** (Accountancy); **Tourism Management** (Tourism); **Tourism Operation** (Tourism)

History: Founded 1985. Formerly known as Corporación de Educación Superior Instituto de Administración y Finanzas de Cartagena.

Main Language(s) of Instruction: Spanish

Degrees and Diplomas: *Técnico Profesional*; *Profesional Universitario*. Also Licenciatura (Teacher Training Degree) in Pedagogy

Student Services: Library

Last Updated: 30/09/15

REMINGTON UNIVERSITY CORPORATION

Corporación Universitaria Remington (UNIREMINGTON)
Ed. Coltabaco, Torre 1, Calle 51-27, Medellín, Antioquia
Tel: +57(4) 511-1000
EMail: info@remington.edu.co
Website: http://www.remington.edu.co

Rector: Jorge Vásquez Posada EMail: rectoria@remington.edu.co

Vicerrectora Administrativa y Financiera: María Elena Villegas Isaza

Faculty
Accountancy (Accountancy; Taxation); **Arts and Design** (Design; Graphic Design; Visual Arts); **Basic Sciences and Engineering** (Civil Engineering; Computer Engineering; Computer Science; Industrial Engineering; Information Management; Software Engineering); **Business Administration** (Business Administration; Business and Commerce; Engineering Management; International Business; Public Administration; Transport Management); **Juridical and Political Science** (Administrative Law; Civil Law; Law; Private Law); **Veterinary Medicine** (Veterinary Science)

School
Health Sciences (Gynaecology and Obstetrics; Health Administration; Health Sciences; Medicine; Nursing; Paediatrics; Pharmacy)

History: Founded 1915. Acquired present status 1996.

Main Language(s) of Instruction: Spanish

Degrees and Diplomas: *Tecnólogo*; *Profesional Universitario*; *Especialización*: **Administrative Law; Civil Law; Gynaecology and Obstetrics; Health Administration; Information Management; Management; Paediatrics; Private Law.**

Student Services: IT Centre, Library

Last Updated: 30/09/15

REPUBLICAN UNIVERSITY CORPORATION

Corporación Universitaria Republicana
Carrera 7 No. 19-38, Bogotá
Tel: +57(1) 286-2384
Fax: +57(1) 342-2771
EMail: informes@urepublicana.edu.co
Website: http://www.urepublicana.edu.co

Rector: Gustavo A. Tellez
EMail: secretariaacademica@urepublicana.edu.co

International Relations: María Lucelly Castro Hernández, Directora de Relaciones Internacionales
Tel: +57(1) 286-2384 Ext 131
EMail: relacionesinternacionales@urepublicana.edu.co

Programme
Finance and International Trade (Finance; International Business); **Industrial Engineering** (Industrial Engineering); **Law** (Law; Political Sciences); **Mathematics** (Mathematics); **Postgraduate Studies** (Administrative Law; Commercial Law; Criminal Law; Labour Law; Notary Studies; Private Law; Public Law; Social Work; Taxation); **Public Accountancy** (Accountancy); **Social Work** (Social Work); **Systems Engineering** (Computer Engineering)

History: Founded 1999.

Main Language(s) of Instruction: Spanish

Degrees and Diplomas: *Profesional Universitario*: **Accountancy; Computer Engineering; Finance; Industrial Engineering; International Business; Law; Mathematics; Social Work.** *Especialización*: **Administrative Law; Commercial Law; Criminal Law; Labour Law; Notary Studies; Private Law; Public Law; Social Work; Taxation.**

Student Services: Library, Sports Facilities

Last Updated: 10/11/15

ROSARY UNIVERSITY

Universidad del Rosario
Calle 12C, No. 6-25, Bogotá
Tel: +57(1) 297-0200 +57(1) 243-1716
Fax: +57(1) 281-8583
Website: http://www.urosario.edu.co

Rector: José Manuel Restrepo Abondano (2014-)
Tel: +57(1) 297-0200 Ext. 2362 EMail: jrestrepo@urosario.edu.co

Secretaria General: Catalina Lleras Figueroa
Tel: +57(1) 297-0200 Ext. 2431
EMail: catalina.llerasf@urosario.edu.co

International Relations: Jeannette Vélez Ramirez, Chancellor
Tel: +57(1) 297-0200 Ext.174
EMail: cancilleria@urosario.edu.co; jeannette.velez@urosario.edu.co

Faculty
Economics (Economics; Finance; International Business); **International Relations** (International Relations); **Law** (Law); **Medicine and Health Sciences** (Biomedical Engineering; Medicine; Occupational Therapy; Physical Therapy; Psychology; Speech Therapy and Audiology); **Natural Sciences and Mathematics** (Biology; Health Sciences); **Political Science and Government** (Government; International Relations; Political Sciences; Urban Studies)

School
Administration (Business Administration; International Business; Transport Management); **Humanities** (Anthropology; Arts and Humanities; History; Journalism; Philosophy; Social Sciences; Sociology)

Further Information: Also Teaching Hospital 'San José'

History: Founded 1653 by the Archbishop of Santafé on the model of the Fonseca's Colegio Mayor de Salamanca. Acquired present status 1658.

Academic Year: February to December (February-June; July-December)

Admission Requirements: Secondary school certificate (bachillerato), or equivalent, entrance examination, State examination (ICFES), and interview

Fees: 2,000-3,000 per semester (US Dollar)

Main Language(s) of Instruction: Spanish

Accrediting Agency: Consejo Nacional de Acreditación; EUA

Degrees and Diplomas: *Profesional Universitario*; *Especialización*: **Administrative Law; Anaesthesiology; Business Administration; Cardiology; Civil Law; Commercial Law; Constitutional Law; Criminal Law; Cultural Studies; Endocrinology; Epidemiology; Finance; Fiscal Law; Gastroenterology; Health Administration; Health Sciences; Human Resources; Human Rights; Information Technology; Insurance; International Business; International Law; Labour Law; Law; Management; Marketing; Medical Technology; Medicine; Nephrology; Neurology; Occupational Health; Ophthalmology; Orthopaedics; Otorhinolaryngology; Paediatrics; Physical Therapy; Physiology; Private Law; Psychiatry and Mental Health; Public Administration; Public Health; Radiology; Rehabilitation and Therapy; Respiratory Therapy; Social Welfare; Social Work; Sports; Surgery; Taxation; Telecommunications Services; Toxicology; Translation and Interpretation; Urology.** *Maestría*: **Administrative Law; Economic and Finance Policy; Economics; Epidemiology; Finance; Genetics; Health Administration; Health Sciences; International Studies; Journalism; Law; Leadership; Occupational Health; Philosophy; Political Sciences; Social Sciences; Sports.** *Doctorado*: **Biomedicine; Economics; International Studies; Law; Leadership; Political Sciences.**

Student Services: Academic Counselling, Canteen, Careers Guidance, Cultural Activities, Foreign Studies Centre, Health Services, Language Laboratory, Library, Social Counselling, Sports Facilities

Publications: Law Collection; Revista Colegio Mayor de Nuestra Señora del Rosario

Publishing House: Ediciones Rosaristas

Student Numbers *2015-2016*: Total: c. 11,450

Last Updated: 24/09/15

SALAZAR AND HERRERA UNIVERSITY INSTITUTION

Institución Universitaria Salazar y Herrera (IUSH)
Carrera 70 No 52-49, Barrio los Colores, Medellín, Antioquia
Tel: +57(4) 430-1600
Fax: +57(4) 496-6201
EMail: admisiones@iush.edu.co
Website: http://www.iush.edu.co

Rector: Gustavo Calle Giraldo EMail: rectoria@iush.edu.co

Secretario General: Hernán Rendón Valencia

School
Administration (Accountancy; Advertising and Publicity; Business Administration; Finance; Human Resources; International Business; Management; Marketing; Sales Techniques); **Arts** (Fashion Design;

Graphic Design); **Engineering** (Computer Engineering; Computer Science; Electronic Engineering; Industrial Engineering; Mechanical Engineering; Telecommunications Engineering); **Social and Human Sciences** (Communication Studies)

History: Founded 1991.

Main Language(s) of Instruction: Spanish

Degrees and Diplomas: *Tecnólogo*; *Profesional Universitario*; *Especialización*: **Management; Marketing.** *Maestría*: **International Business.**

Student Services: Library

Last Updated: 25/09/15

SAN AGUSTIN CERVANTINE UNIVERSITY FOUNDATION

Fundación Universitaria Cervantina San Agustín (UNICERVANTINA)
Calle 77, No. 11 - 63, Bogotá Colombia,, Bogotá
Tel: +57(1) 321-3381
EMail: admisiones@unicervantina.edu.co
Website: http://www.unicervantina.edu.co

Rector: Gregorio Tomás Román

Faculty

Psychology (Psychology)

Programme

Business Administration (Business Administration); **Finance and International Business** (Finance; International Business); **Industrial Engineering** (Industrial Engineering); **Law** (Law); **Marketing and Advertising** (Advertising and Publicity; Marketing); **Political Sciences** (Political Sciences); **Public Accounting** (Accountancy); **Social Work** (Social Work); **Telecommunications Engineering** (Telecommunications Engineering); **Theology** (Theology); **Visual Communication and Multimedia** (Communication Arts; Multimedia)

History: Founded 2009.

Main Language(s) of Instruction: Spanish

Degrees and Diplomas: *Profesional Universitario*: **Accountancy; Advertising and Publicity; Business Administration; Communication Arts; Finance; Industrial Engineering; International Business; Law; Multimedia; Political Sciences; Psychology; Social Work; Telecommunications Engineering; Theology.**

Student Services: Library

Last Updated: 29/09/15

SAN ALFONSO UNIVERSITY FOUNDATION

Fundación Universitaria San Alfonso (FUSA)
Calle 37 No. 24-47, (Barrio La Soledad), Bogotá
Tel: +57(91) 244-5053
Fax: +57(91) 268-3863
EMail: admisiones@fusa.edu.co; contacto@fusa.edu.co
Website: http://www.fusa.edu.co

Rector: Jerónimo Peñaloza Basto
Tel: +57(1) 244-5053 Ext. 115 EMail: rectoria@fusa.edu.co

Vicerrector Administrativo: Julio Roballo Lozano

Faculty

Administrative Sciences (Accountancy; Business Administration; Marketing); **Human Sciences and Religious Studies** (Philosophy; Theology); **Social Sciences** (Law; Mass Communication; Psychology; Social Work)

Programme

Postgraduate Studies (Ethics; Missionary Studies; Theology)

History: Founded 2000.

Main Language(s) of Instruction: Spanish

Degrees and Diplomas: *Profesional Universitario*; *Especialización*: **Ethics; Theology.** Also Licenciatura in Theology and Philosophy

Student Services: Library

Last Updated: 06/10/15

SAN GIL UNIVERSITY FOUNDATION

Fundación Universitaria de San Gil (UNISANGIL)
Km 2 via San Gil - Charalá, San Gil, Santander
Tel: +57(7) 724-5757 +57(7) 724-6565
EMail: admisiones@mail.unisangil.edu.co
Website: http://www.unisangil.edu.co

Rector: Luis Gustavo Álvarez Rueda
Tel: +57(7) 724-5757 Ext. 218 EMail: rectoria@unisangil.edu.co

Vicerrector Administrativo: Leonardo Porras Martínez
Tel: +57(7) 724-5757 Ext. 117
EMail: viceadministrativa@unisangil.edu.co

International Relations: Carlos Alfonso Angel Muñoz, Director Gestión e Internacionalización del Conocimiento
Tel: +57(91) 724-5757 Ext. 118

Faculty

Economics and Administrative Sciences (Accountancy; Administration; Business Administration; Economics; Finance; Hotel Management; Management; Marketing; Tourism); **Education and Health Sciences** (Bilingual and Bicultural Education; Education; Nursing); **Law and Political Science** (Civil Law; Law); **Natural Sciences and Engineering** (Agricultural Engineering; Computer Engineering; Electronic Engineering; Environmental Engineering; Maintenance Technology; Systems Analysis)

Further Information: Also Chiquinquirá and Yopal Campuses

History: Founded 1988. Acquired present status 1991.

Admission Requirements: High school diploma

Main Language(s) of Instruction: Spanish

Degrees and Diplomas: *Técnico Profesional*; *Tecnólogo*; *Profesional Universitario*; *Especialización*: **Educational Sciences; Finance; Marketing; Pedagogy; Tourism.** Also Especialización in Industrial Maintenance offered through agreement with Universidad Industrial de Santander (UIS) and in Public Law offered through agreement with UNAB

Student Services: Academic Counselling, Canteen, Cultural Activities, Health Services, Language Laboratory, Nursery Care, Social Counselling, Sports Facilities

Publications: Al Derecho y al Revés; Unisangil La Revista

Last Updated: 05/10/15

SAN JOSE FOUNDATION FOR HIGHER EDUCATION

Fundación de Educación Superior San José (FESSANJOSE)
Calle 67, 14A-29, Bogotá
Tel: +57(1) 347-0000
EMail: rectoria@fessanjose.edu.co
Website: http://www.usanjose.edu.co

Rector: Guillermo Hoyos Gomez
EMail: rectoria@fessanjose.edu.co

Faculty

Arts (Advertising and Publicity; Fashion Design; Fine Arts; Industrial Design; Interior Design); **Engineering** (Computer Engineering; Production Engineering; Telecommunications Engineering); **Management and Accounting** (Accountancy; Business Administration; International Business; Marketing); **Sports** (Sports)

History: Founded 1984.

Admission Requirements: Bachiller

Main Language(s) of Instruction: Spanish

Degrees and Diplomas: *Técnico Profesional*; *Tecnólogo*; *Profesional Universitario*: **Accountancy; Business Administration; Computer Engineering.** Also Diplomas

Last Updated: 24/11/15

SAN MARTÍN UNIVERSITY FOUNDATION

Fundación Universitaria San Martín
Carrera 18, No 80-45, Bogotá
Tel: +57(1) 530-1001 +57(1) 622-6422
Fax: +57(1) 235-8356
EMail: admisiones@sanmartin.edu.co
Website: http://www.sanmartin.edu.co

Rectora: Mayra Lucia Vieira Cano

Secretaria General: Lucía Bohórquez
EMail: sgeneral@sanmartin.edu.co

Programme

Advertising and Marketing (Advertising and Publicity; Marketing); **Business Administration** (Business Administration); **Engineering** (Computer Engineering; Industrial Engineering; Telecommunications Engineering); **Finance and International Studies** (Finance; International Business; International Relations); **Law** (Law); **Medicine** (Medicine); **Odontology** (Dentistry); **Open and Distance Education** (Accountancy; Business Administration; Computer Engineering); **Optometry** (Optometry); **Psychology** (Psychology); **Public Accountancy** (Accountancy); **Veterinary Science and Zootechnology** (Animal Husbandry; Veterinary Science)

History: Founded 1980.

Main Language(s) of Instruction: Spanish

Degrees and Diplomas: *Profesional Universitario*; *Especialización*: **Anaesthesiology; Gastroenterology; Gynaecology and Obstetrics; Medicine; Ophthalmology; Orthopaedics; Otorhinolaryngology; Paediatrics; Plastic Surgery; Radiology; Surgery.**

Student Services: Library

Last Updated: 06/10/15

SANITAS UNIVERSITY FOUNDATION

Fundación Universitaria Sanitas (UNISANITAS)
Calle 23 No. 66-46, Bogotá
Tel: +57(1) 222-1500 +57(1) 589-5377
EMail: unisanitas@unisanitas.edu.co
Website: http://www.unisanitas.edu.co

Rector: Mario Isaza Ruget EMail: misaza@unisanitas.edu.co

Vicerrectora: Sonia H. Roa Trujillo
EMail: shroa@unisanitas.edu.co

International Relations: Wimber Ortíz Martínez, Director Unidad de Vinculacion con el Sector Externo
EMail: wortiz@unisanitas.edu.co

Faculty

Business Administration (Business Administration); **Medicine** (Medicine); **Nursing** (Nursing); **Psychology** (Psychology)

Programme

Postgraduate Studies (Anaesthesiology; Dermatology; Gastroenterology; Gynaecology and Obstetrics; Health Administration; Medical Technology; Medicine; Ophthalmology; Orthopaedics; Paediatrics; Psychiatry and Mental Health; Public Health; Radiology; Surgery; Urology)

History: Founded 2001.

Academic Year: January to December (January-June; July-December)

Admission Requirements: National Examinstion Score (ICFES) and Interview

Fees: Medicine, 7.9m. per semester; Nursing, 2.9m. per semester (Colombian Peso)

Main Language(s) of Instruction: Spanish

Accrediting Agency: Ministry of Education

Degrees and Diplomas: *Profesional Universitario*; *Especialización*: **Anaesthesiology; Dermatology; Embryology and Reproduction Biology; Gastroenterology; Gynaecology and Obstetrics; Health Administration; Medical Technology; Medicine; Ophthalmology; Orthopaedics; Paediatrics; Psychiatry and Mental Health; Public Health; Radiology; Surgery; Urology.**

Student Services: Academic Counselling, Canteen, Careers Guidance, Cultural Activities, Facilities for disabled people, Health Services, Language Laboratory, Library, Nursery Care, Social Counselling, Sports Facilities

Publications: Revista Bienestar Sanitas; Revista Médica Sanitas

Publishing House: Editorial Bienestar

Last Updated: 06/10/15

SANTO TOMÁS UNIVERSITY

Universidad Santo Tomás (USTA)
Carrera 9 No. 51-11, Bogotá
Tel: +57(1) 587-8797
Fax: +57(1) 217-7749
EMail: usantotomas@correo.usta.edu.co
Website: http://www.usta.edu.co

Rector: Juan Ubaldo López Salamanca
EMail: rector@usantotomas.edu.co

Secretario General: Héctor Fabio Jaramillo Santamaria
Tel: +57(1) 587-8713 Ext. 1031
EMail: hectorjaramillo@usantotomas.edu.co

Vicerrector Administrativo - Financiero General: Diego Orlando Serna Salazar EMail: viceadmon@usantotomas.edu.co

International Relations: Ana Maria Arango Murcia, Director, Oficina de Relaciones Internacionales e Interinstitucionales
Tel: +57(1) 348-3815 Ext. 1930
EMail: anaarango@usantotomas.edu.co; ori@usantotomas.edu.co

Division

Economics and Administrative Sciences (Accountancy; Business Administration; Economics; International Business; Marketing; Statistics); **Engineering** (Civil Engineering; Electronic Engineering; Environmental Engineering; Industrial Engineering; Mechanical Engineering; Telecommunications Engineering); **Health Sciences** (Parks and Recreation; Physical Education; Psychology; Sports); **Law and Political Sciences** (Government; International Relations; Law); **Philosophy and Theology** (Humanities and Social Science Education; Native Language Education; Theology); **Social Sciences** (Graphic Design; Mass Communication; Sociology)

History: Founded 1580 by Pope Gregorio XIII. Closed 1861 by General Tomás Cipriano de Mosquera. Re-established 1965 and approved by government decree 1966.

Academic Year: February to December (February-June; August-December)

Admission Requirements: Secondary school certificate (bachillerato) and entrance examination

Main Language(s) of Instruction: Spanish

Degrees and Diplomas: *Profesional Universitario*; *Especialización*: **Administrative Law; Business Administration; Criminal Law; Data Processing; Electronic Engineering; Engineering Management; Finance; Health Administration; Human Rights; International Business; Multimedia; Psychology; Real Estate; Safety Engineering; Social Welfare; Systems Analysis; Taxation; Telecommunications Engineering.** *Maestría*: **Clinical Psychology; Communication Studies; Criminal Law; Development Studies; Economics; Electronic Engineering; Government; Health Sciences; Human Rights; Law; Literature; Philosophy; Political Sciences; Private Law; Psychology; Public Health; Public Law; Road Engineering; Safety Engineering; Social Sciences; Social Welfare; Sports; Telecommunications Engineering.** *Doctorado*: **Law; Philosophy.** Also MBA; Postdoctoral Degree Programme in Constitutional Law; Licenciatura

Student Services: Careers Guidance, Foreign Studies Centre, Health Services, Language Laboratory, Library, Nursery Care, Sports Facilities

Publications: Cuaderno de Filosofía; Cuaderno de Sociología; IUSTA; Módulos; Revista Análisis; Revista Económica 'Veritatem'

Publishing House: University Press

Last Updated: 06/11/15

BUCARAMANGA BRANCH

SECCIONAL BUCARAMANGA

Carrera 18 No. 9-27, Bucaramanga, Santander
Tel: +57() 6 800 801
EMail: admisiones@ustabuca.edu.co
Website: http://www.ustabuca.edu.co

Rector seccional: Samuel E. Forero Buitrago
Tel: +57() 671-2970
EMail: secrec@mail.ustabuca.edu.co;
secrec2@mail.ustabuca.edu.co

Vicerrector Administrativo y Financiero: Rubén Darío López García EMail: secvad@mail.ustabuca.edu.co

International Relations: fffff ddddd
EMail: profesionalorii2@mail.ustabuca.edu.co

Division

Economics and Administrative Sciences (Accountancy; Agricultural Business; Business Administration; Economics; International Business); **Engineering and Architecture** (Architecture; Chemical Engineering; Civil Engineering; Electronic Engineering; Environmental Engineering; Industrial Engineering; Mechanical Engineering; Telecommunications Engineering); **Health Sciences** (Dental Technology; Dentistry; Optometry; Parks and Recreation; Physical Education; Sports); **Law and Political Sciences** (Law)

History: Founded 1973.

Fees: Postgraduate, 3,300,000-8,560,000 per semester (Colombian Peso)

Main Language(s) of Instruction: Spanish

Degrees and Diplomas: *Profesional Universitario*; *Especialización*: **Accountancy; Administrative Law; Agricultural Management; Automation and Control Engineering; Constitutional Law; Criminal Law; Dentistry; Finance; Industrial Engineering; International Business; Labour Law; Optometry; Orthodontics; Periodontics; Rehabilitation and Therapy; Social Welfare; Sports Management; Taxation; Telecommunications Services.** *Maestría*: **Computer Engineering; Computer Networks; Dentistry; Education; Environmental Engineering; Environmental Management; Environmental Studies; Industrial Engineering; Law; Regional Planning; Safety Engineering; Telecommunications Engineering.** Also MBA

Student Services: Library

Student Numbers *2015-2016*: Total 5,761

TUNJA BRANCH

SECCIONAL TUNJA

Sede Centro Cll. 19 N° 11-64, Tunja, Boyaca
Tel: +57(8) 744-0404
Fax: +57(8) 744-0404
EMail: comunicaciones@ustatunja.edu.co
Website: http://www.ustatunja.edu.co/ustatunja

Rector seccional: Aldemar Valencia Hernández
EMail: rectoria@ustatunja.edu.co

Vicerrector Administrativo y Financiero: José Bernardo Vallejo Molina

Faculty

Architecture (Architecture); **Business Administration** (Business Administration); **Civil Engineering** (Civil Engineering); **Electronic Engineering** (Electronic Engineering); **Environmental Engineering** (Environmental Engineering); **International Business** (International Business); **Law** (Law); **Mechanical Engineering** (Mechanical Engineering); **Public Accounting** (Accountancy); **Systems Engineering** (Computer Engineering)

History: Founded 1996.

Main Language(s) of Instruction: Spanish

Degrees and Diplomas: *Profesional Universitario*; *Especialización*: **Administrative Law; Construction Engineering; Criminal Law; Geological Engineering; Government; Health Administration; Psychology; Public Law; Regional Planning; Safety Engineering; Social Welfare.** *Maestría*: **Administrative Law; Civil Engineering; Criminal Law; Heritage Preservation; Human Rights; Law; Pedagogy; Private Law.** *Doctorado*: **Administrative Law; Public Law.**

Student Services: Library

SCHOOL OF ADMINISTRATION AND MARKETING OF QUINDIO

Escuela de Administración y Mercadotecnia del Quindio (EAM)

Avenida Bolivar N. 3-11, Armenia, Quindio
Tel: +57(6) 745-1101
Fax: +57(6) 745-1101 Ext. 159
EMail: quindioeam@eam.edu.co
Website: http://www.eam.edu.co

Rector: Francisco Jairo Ramírez Concha
Tel: +57(6) 745-1101 Ext. 103 EMail: cvela@eam.edu.co

Vicerrector Administrativo: José Einer Gómez Arismendi
EMail: jheiner@eam.edu.co; mvillareal@eam.edu.co

Secretario General: William Humberto Martínez Morales
EMail: secgeneral@eam.edu.co;
Auxiliarsecretariageneral@eam.edu.co

Vicerrector Académico: Jorge Iván Quintero Salazar
EMail: jiqs@eam.edu.co; secreviceacademica@eam.edu.co

Faculty

Administration and Finance (Accountancy; Business Administration; Hotel Management; International Business; Tourism); **Design and Communication** (Advertising and Publicity; Graphic Design); **Engineering** (Electronic Engineering; Industrial Engineering; Software Engineering)

History: Founded 1971.

Fees: 1,400,000-2,000,000 per annum (Colombian Peso)

Main Language(s) of Instruction: Spanish

Degrees and Diplomas: *Técnico Profesional*; *Tecnólogo*; *Profesional Universitario*

Student Services: Library

Last Updated: 30/09/15

SCHOOL OF ENGINEERING OF ANTIOQUIA

Escuela de Ingeniería de Antioquia (EIA)

Sede de Las Palmas: Km 2 + 200 Via al Aeropuerto José María Córdova, Envigado, Antioquia 055428
Tel: +57(4) 354-9090
Fax: +57(4) 386-1160
EMail: relinter@eia.edu.co
Website: http://www.eia.edu.co

Rector: Carlos Felipe Londoño Alvarez (1996-)
EMail: secrerec@eia.edu.co

secrerec@eia.edu.co: Olga Lucía Ocampo Toro
EMail: secrerec@eia.edu.co

International Relations: Eloise Dumas, Director of International Relations EMail: relinter@eia.edu.co

Department

Administration, Finance and Computer Systems Engineering (Business Administration; Computer Engineering; Finance; Industrial Management; Management; Marketing; Service Trades; Statistics); **Biomedical, Mechatronic and Mechanical Engineering** (Biology; Biomedical Engineering; Electronic Engineering; Mechanical Engineering); **Civil, Environmental, Geological and Industrial Engineering** (Civil Engineering; Environmental Engineering; Geological Engineering; Industrial Engineering)

Further Information: Also Zúñiga

History: Founded 1978.

Admission Requirements: Bachillerato and ICFES examination

Main Language(s) of Instruction: Spanish

Accrediting Agency: National Council for Accreditation

Degrees and Diplomas: *Profesional Universitario*; *Especialización*: **Business Administration; Energy Engineering; Environmental Studies; Finance; Industrial Management; Management; Service Trades; Statistics; Town Planning.** *Maestría*: **Biological and Life Sciences; Biomedical Engineering; Communication Studies; Industrial Engineering; Information Technology; Marketing.**

Student Services: Academic Counselling, Canteen, Library, Social Counselling, Sports Facilities

Last Updated: 01/10/15

SCHOOL OF OPHTHALMOLOGY, BARRAQUER INSTITUTE OF AMERICA

Escuela Superior de Oftalmología, Instituto Barraquer de América

Avenida Calle 100 No. 18A-51, Bogotá
Tel: +57(1) 644-9540 Ext. 306 +57(1) 644-9552
Fax: +57(1) 644-9556
EMail: citas@barraquer.com.co
Website: http://www.institutobarraquer.com/eso/index.html

Rectora: Angela Maria Gutierrez Marin

Programme

Ophthalmology (Ophthalmology)

History: Founded 2005.

Main Language(s) of Instruction: Spanish

Degrees and Diplomas: *Especialización*: **Ophthalmology.**

Student Services: Library

Last Updated: 09/11/15

SERGIO ARBOLEDA UNIVERSITY

Universidad Sergio Arboleda (USA)

Calle 74 No. 14-14, Bogotá, 3257500

Tel: +57(1) 325-8181

Fax: +57(1) 347-1059

EMail: info@usa.edu.co

Website: http://www.usergioarboleda.edu.co

Rector: Rodrigo Francisco Noguera Calderón
EMail: rodrigo.noguera@usa.edu.co; rectoria@usa.edu.co

Vicerrector Académico: Germán Quintero Andrade

Secretario General: Leonardo Espinosa Quintero

School

Administration and Marketing *(International)* (Accountancy; Business Administration; Business and Commerce; Environmental Management; Finance; International Business; Marketing; Transport Management); **Advertising** (Advertising and Publicity); **Arts and Music** (Music); **Communication Sciences** (Journalism; Mass Communication; Psychology); **Economics** (Economics); **Exact Sciences and Engineering** (Computer Engineering; Electronic Engineering; Environmental Engineering; Industrial Engineering; Mathematics; Telecommunications Engineering); **Law** (Criminology; Law); **Philosophy and Humanities** (Arts and Humanities; Humanities and Social Science Education; Philosophy); **Political Science and International Relations** (International Relations; Political Sciences)

History: Founded 1984.

Main Language(s) of Instruction: Spanish

Degrees and Diplomas: *Profesional Universitario*; *Especialización*: **Administrative Law; Business and Commerce; Civil Law; Commercial Law; Constitutional Law; Criminal Law; Educational Research; Environmental Management; Finance; Health Administration; Higher Education Teacher Training; Human Resources; Human Rights; Industrial Management; Insurance; International Business; Journalism; Labour Law; Law; Management; Marketing; Mass Communication; Multimedia; Political Sciences; Private Law; Safety Engineering; Transport Management.** *Maestría*: **Educational Research; Environmental Management; Environmental Studies; Higher Education Teacher Training; Industrial Management; International Business; Law.** *Doctorado*: **Law.** Also Licenciatura; MBA; Executive MBA

Student Services: Library

Last Updated: 06/11/15

SANTA MARTA BRANCH
SECCIONAL SANTA MARTA

Campus Centro, Calle 18, 14 A-18, Santa Marta, Magdalena

Tel: +57(5) 434-6444

EMail: admisiones.sm@usa.edu.co

Website: http://www.usergioarboleda.edu.co/santamarta

Rector seccional: Alfredo Méndez Alzamora

Secretario General: Camilo Andres Noguera Abello

International Relations: Gina Lindo Montañéz, Directora, Oficina de Relaciones Internacionales
Tel: +57(5) 434-6444 Ext. 125
EMail: margarita.carrasquilla@usa.edu.co

Programme

Business Administration (Business Administration); **Finance and International Business** (Finance; International Business); **Law** (Law); **Marketing and International Business** (International Business; Marketing); **Postgraduate Studies** (Administration; Education; Law; Mass Communication); **Public Accounting** (Accountancy); **Social Communication and Journalism** (Communication Studies; Journalism; Mass Communication)

History: Founded 1994.

Main Language(s) of Instruction: Spanish

Degrees and Diplomas: *Profesional Universitario*; *Especialización*: **Administrative Law; Agricultural Business; Business and Commerce; Commercial Law; Communication Studies; Constitutional Law; Criminal Law; Finance; Health Administration; Higher Education Teacher Training; Human Resources; Industrial Management; Labour Law; Law; Maritime Law; Social Welfare; Transport Management.** *Maestría*: **Law.**

Student Services: Cultural Activities, Health Services, Library, Sports Facilities

SIMÓN BOLÍVAR UNIVERSITY

Universidad Simón Bolívar (USB)

Apartado aéreo 50595, Carrera 54 N° 59-102, Barranquilla, Atlántico

Tel: +57(5) 368-7759

Fax: +57(5) 368-2892

EMail: rectoria@unisimonbolivar.edu.co

Website: http://www.unisimon.edu.co

Rector: José Eusebio Consuegra Bolivar
EMail: rectoria@unisimonbolivar.edu.co; ebolivar@unisimonbolivar.edu.co

Secretario General: Rafael Bolaño Tel: +57(58) 344-4333

International Relations: Sonia Andrea Falla Barrontes
Tel: +57(58) 368-0593 EMail: soniafalla@hotmail.com

Faculty

Basic Education (Education); **Business Administration** (Business Administration); **Commercial Engineering** (Business and Commerce; Engineering); **Economics** (Economics); **Engineering** (Engineering); **Industrial Engineering** (Industrial Engineering); **Law** (Law); **Nursing** (Nursing); **Physiotherapy** (Physical Therapy); **Psychology** (Psychology); **Public Accountancy** (Accountancy); **Social Studies** (Social Studies); **Social Work** (Anthropology; Social and Community Services; Social Welfare; Social Work)

History: Founded 1972. Formerly known as Corporación Educativa Mayor del Desarrollo Simón Bolívar.

Academic Year: January to December (January-June; August-December)

Admission Requirements: Secondary school certificate (bachillerato) and entrance examination

Fees: 600-964 per semester (US Dollar)

Main Language(s) of Instruction: Spanish

Accrediting Agency: Consejo Nacional de Acreditación, CNA

Degrees and Diplomas: *Profesional Universitario*; *Especialización*; *Doctorado*: **Law.**

Student Services: Cultural Activities, Health Services, Social Counselling

Publications: Desarrollo Indoamericano; Educación y Humanismo; Encuentro Bolivariano; Gestión Bolivariána; Justicia; Perspectiva Social; Psicogente; Salud en Movimiento

Last Updated: 24/11/15

TECHNOLOGICAL UNIVERSITY OF BOLIVAR

Universidad Tecnológica de Bolívar (UTB)

Parque Industrial y Tecnológico Carlos Vélez Pombo, Km 1 vía Turbaco, Cartagena de Indias, Bolívar

Tel: +57(5) 653-5200

Fax: +57(5) 661-9240

Website: http://www.unitecnologica.edu.co

Rector: Jaime Eduardo Bernal Villegas
Tel: +57(5) 653-5200 Ext. 201
EMail: rectorutb@unitecnologica.edu.co

Vicerrectora Administrativa y Financiera: María del Rosario Gutiérrez de Piñeres Perdomo
EMail: mrpineres@unitecnologica.edu.co

Secretaria General: Irina Garcia Cáliz
Tel: +57(5) 653-5211 EMail: lgarcia@unitecnologica.edu.co

International Relations: Ericka Duncan Ortega, Directora Oficina de Internacionalización International
Tel: +57(5) 653-5351 Ext. 152
EMail: eduncan@unitecnologica.edu.co

Faculty
Basic Sciences (Statistics); **Business and Economics** (Accountancy; Business Administration; Economics; Finance; International Business); **Engineering** (Civil Engineering; Computer Engineering; Electrical Engineering; Electronic Engineering; Environmental Engineering; Industrial Engineering; Mechanical Engineering); **Social Sciences and Humanities** (International Relations; Law; Mass Communication; Political Sciences; Psychology)

Programme
UTB Convention - Edupol Education Convergence (Accountancy; Finance; Software Engineering)

School
Technical and Technological Studies (Accountancy; Computer Science; Finance; Industrial Maintenance; Transport Management)

Further Information: Also Casa Lemaitre Campus

History: Founded 1970. Acquired present status 2003.

Academic Year: January to November (January-May; June- July; August-November)

Admission Requirements: State examination (ICFES test) and interview

Fees: Undergraduate, 1,545,000-5,100,000 per programme; Graduate, 10,000,000-29,000,000 per programme (Colombian Peso)

Main Language(s) of Instruction: Spanish

Accrediting Agency: Instituto Colombiano para el Fomento de la Educación Superior (ICFES)

Degrees and Diplomas: *Técnico Profesional*; *Tecnólogo*; *Profesional Universitario*; *Especialización*: **Automation and Control Engineering; Business Administration; Data Processing; Educational Administration; Environmental Management; Health Administration; Human Resources; Industrial Management; Information Technology; International Business; Maintenance Technology; Management; Marketing; Mathematics Education; Science Education; Small Business; Statistics; Taxation; Telecommunications Engineering; Transport Management.** *Maestría*: **Business Administration; Development Studies; Education; Engineering; Engineering Management; Environmental Studies; International Business; Management; Marine Engineering; Naval Architecture; Production Engineering; Tourism; Transport Management.** Also MBA

Student Services: Academic Counselling, Careers Guidance, Language Laboratory, Library, Social Counselling, Sports Facilities

Publications: Contraste; Economía y Región; Investigación & Desarrollo

Last Updated: 29/10/15

UNIFIED NATIONAL CORPORATION OF HIGHER EDUCATION

Corporación Unificada Nacional de Educación Superior (CUN)

Calle 12B, No 4-79, Bogotá
Tel: +57(1) 307-8180 +57(1) 381-3222
Fax: +57(1) 334-3884
EMail: contactenos@cun.edu.co
Website: http://www.cun.edu.co

Rector: Jaime Alberto Rincón Prado
EMail: rectoria@cun.edu.co

Programme
Continuing Education (Advertising and Publicity; Agriculture; Apiculture; Computer Engineering; Cooking and Catering; Fashion Design; Graphic Design; Parks and Recreation)

School
Administrative Sciences (Accountancy; Business Administration; Cooking and Catering; Health Administration; Hotel Management; International Business; Tourism); **Communications and Fine Arts** (Fashion Design; Graphic Design; Mass Communication; Radio and Television Broadcasting); **Engineering** (Computer Engineering; Electronic Engineering)

Centre
GEO Languages (Modern Languages)

History: Founded 1983.

Main Language(s) of Instruction: Spanish

Degrees and Diplomas: *Técnico Profesional*; *Tecnólogo*; *Profesional Universitario*. Also Diplomas (Continuing Education)

Student Services: Cultural Activities, Library, Sports Facilities

Last Updated: 25/09/15

UNIPANAMERICANA PANAMERICANA UNIVERSITY FOUNDATION

Unipanamericana Fundación Universitaria Panamericana (UNIPANAMERICANA)

Avenida (Calle) 32 No. 17-62, Bogotá
Tel: +57(1) 423-5777
Fax: +57(91) 338-0666
EMail: unipanamericana@unipanamericana.edu.co
Website: http://www.unipanamericana.edu.co

Rector: Camilo Gaitán García
EMail: rectoria@unipanamericana.edu.co

Vicerrector Académico: César Augusto Corredor Velandia
EMail: cacorredorv@unipanamericana.edu.co

Faculty
Business Administration (Accountancy; Administration; Banking; Business Administration; Finance; Health Administration; International Business; Safety Engineering; Transport Management); **Communication** (Advertising and Publicity; Graphic Design; Marketing; Mass Communication); **Education** (Bilingual and Bicultural Education; Education; Foreign Languages Education; Pedagogy; Preschool Education); **Engineering** (Computer Engineering; Software Engineering; Systems Analysis; Telecommunications Engineering)

Programme
Virtual Education (Advertising and Publicity; Banking; Business Administration; Computer Engineering; Finance; Graphic Design; International Business; Marketing; Telecommunications Engineering)

History: Founded 1981.

Fees: 117,000-194,000 per credit (Colombian Peso)

Main Language(s) of Instruction: Spanish

Degrees and Diplomas: *Técnico Profesional*; *Tecnólogo*; *Profesional Universitario*. Also Licenciatura

Student Services: Careers Guidance, Cultural Activities, IT Centre, Library

Last Updated: 10/11/15

UNITEC UNIVERSITY CORPORATION

Corporación universitaria UNITEC (UNITEC)

Calle 76, No. 12-58, Bogotá
Tel: +57(1) 743-4343
Fax: +57(1) 235-1541
EMail: fparra@unitec.edu.co
Website: http://www.unitec.edu.co

Rector: Carlos Eduardo Rodriguez Pulido
EMail: rectoria@unitec.edu.co

Secretario General: Gonzalo Murcia Rios
Tel: +57(1) 248-5789 EMail: gmurcia@unitec.edu.co

Vicerrector Académico: José Ignacio Duarte

International Relations: Alcides Muñoz Medina
Tel: +57(1) 248-5789 EMail: almunoz@unitec.edu.co

School
Arts and Communication Sciences (Advertising and Publicity; Cinema and Television; Computer Graphics; Graphic Design; Music; Photography; Sound Engineering (Acoustics)); **Economics**

and Administration (Advertising and Publicity; Air Transport; Business Administration; Cooking and Catering; Finance; Hotel Management; Human Resources; International Business; Marketing; Occupational Health; Tourism; Transport Management); **Engineering** (Computer Engineering; Industrial Engineering; Telecommunications Engineering)

History: Founded 1977.

Main Language(s) of Instruction: Spanish

Degrees and Diplomas: *Tecnólogo*; *Profesional Universitario*; *Especialización*: **Human Resources; Occupational Health.**

Student Services: Cultural Activities, IT Centre, Library, Social Counselling, Sports Facilities

Last Updated: 30/09/15

UNIVERSITY CENTRE OF RURAL WELFARE

Centro Universitario de Bienestar Rural (CUBR)

Vereda Perico Negro, Puerto Tejada, Cauca

Tel: +57(2) 828-2412 +57(2) 828-2413 +57(2) 550-4142

Fax: +57(2) 550-4142

EMail: cubr@cubr.edu.co

Website: http://www.cubr.edu.co

Rector: Taraneh Rezvani
EMail: rectoria@cubr.edu.co

Secretaria Académica: Gloria Mina
EMail: secretariadministrativa@cubr.edu.co

Decana: Carmen Eugenia Pedraza
EMail: decanatura@cubr.edu.co

Programme

Administration of Local Economies *(Technical/Professional Studies)* (Administration; Economics); **Education and Social Development** *(Postgraduate)* (Development Studies; Education; Social and Community Services); **Rural Education** (Agricultural Education)

History: Founded 1988.

Academic Year: January to November (January-June; July-November)

Main Language(s) of Instruction: Spanish

Degrees and Diplomas: *Técnico Profesional*; *Especialización*: **Development Studies; Education; Social and Community Services.** Also Licenciatura (Teacher Training Degree) in Agricutlural Education

Student Services: Careers Guidance, Health Services, Social Counselling, Sports Facilities

Last Updated: 23/09/15

UNIVERSITY CORPORATION FOR BUSINESS AND SOCIAL DEVELOPMENT

Corporacion Universitaria para el Desarrollo Empresarial y Social (CUDES)

Av. 6N, 47-197, Las Vallas, Cali

Tel: +57(2) 651-8200

EMail: directormercadeo@cudes.edu.co; comercial@cudes.edu.co

Website: http://www.cudes.edu.co

Rector: Jose Ricardo Llano Valencia

Programme

International Business (International Business); **Logistics** (Transport Management)

History: Founded 2011.

Main Language(s) of Instruction: Spanish

Degrees and Diplomas: *Tecnólogo*; *Profesional Universitario*: **International Business.**

Student Services: eLibrary

Last Updated: 29/09/15

UNIVERSITY CORPORATION OF BUSINESS STUDIES, EDUCATION AND HEALTH

Corporación Universitaria de Ciencias Empresariales, Educación y Salud (CORSALUD)

Carrera 53 No.59-70, Barranquilla, Atlántico

Tel: +57(5) 318-7498 +57(5) 368-2896 +57(5) 368-2894

Fax: +57(5) 368-2895

EMail: info@corsalud.edu.co; direccion@corsalud.edu.co

Website: http://www.corsalud.edu.co

Rectora: Luz Stella Gómez Lima
Tel: +57(35) 368-2896 EMail: rectoria@corsalud.edu.co

Secretaria General: Mónica Orozco González
Tel: +57(35) 368-2896 Ext. 111
EMail: secretariageneral@corsalud.edu.co

International Relations: Katherine Paola Bermúdez Gómez, Directora, Oficina de Cooperación y Relaciones Internacionales
Tel: +57(35) 368-2896 Ext: 105
EMail: katherine.bermudez@corsalud.edu.co

Faculty

Business Sciences, Economics and Affiliated Disicplines (Accountancy; Business Administration; Finance); **Engineering** (Civil Engineering); **Health Sciences** (Cosmetology; Occupational Health; Radiology)

History: Founded 1993.

Main Language(s) of Instruction: Spanish

Degrees and Diplomas: *Técnico Profesional*; *Tecnólogo*; *Profesional Universitario*; *Especialización*: **Occupational Health.**

Student Services: Library

Last Updated: 09/11/15

U UNIVERSITY CORPORATION OF COLOMBIA

Corporacion Universitaria U de Colombia (UDECOLOMBIA)

Calle 56, N° 41-147 (Bolivia con Girardot), Medellín, Antioquia

Tel: +57(4) 239-8080

EMail: rector@udecolombia.edu.co

Website: http://www.udecolombia.edu.co

Rector: Giovani Orozco Arbeláez
EMail: rector@udecolombia.edu.co

Programme

Financial Administration (Finance); **Law** (Law); **Public Accounting** (Accountancy)

History: Founded and recognized by the Ministry of National Education of Colombia 2010. Formerly known as Corporación Universitaria de Ciencia y Tecnología de Colombia.

Academic Year: Februrary to December (February-June; August-December)

Admission Requirements: For undergraduate programmes: secondary education completion; "Saber-11" test submitted; and an interview with the Dean of the programme selected.

Fees: Law programme, 1,770,000; Accounting and Financial Management programmes, 1,432,000 (US Dollar)

Main Language(s) of Instruction: Spanish

Accrediting Agency: Ministry of National Education of Colombia

Degrees and Diplomas: *Profesional Universitario*

Student Services: Cultural Activities, Library, Sports Facilities

Last Updated: 04/09/15

UNIVERSITY CORPORATION OF RESEARCH AND DEVELOPMENT

Corporación Universitaria de Investigación y Desarrollo UDI

Calle 9 No. 23-55, Barrio la Universidad, Bucaramanga, Santander

Tel: +57(7) 632-8811 +57(7) 635-2525

Fax: +57(7) 634-5775

Website: http://www.udi.edu.co

Rector: Jairo Castro Castro EMail: rector@udi.edu.co

Vicerrector Administrativo: Julio Enrique Anaya Rincón
EMail: vice.administrativa@udi.edu.co

International Relations: Martha Cecilia Guarnizo García, Directora, Oficina Relaciones Internacionales e Interinstitucionales
Tel: +57(7) 690-9638
EMail: secre.ori@udi.edu.co

Faculty
Administrative Sciences, Economics and Accountancy (Accountancy; Business Administration; International Business; Taxation); **Communication, Arts and Design** (Advertising and Publicity; Communication Arts; Design; Graphic Design; Industrial Design; Mass Communication); **Engineering** (Computer Engineering; Electronic Engineering; Industrial Engineering; Software Engineering); **Postgraduate Studies** (Advertising and Publicity; Graphic Design; Information Management; Information Technology; Management; Occupational Health; Teacher Training; Telecommunications Engineering); **Social Sciences and Humanities** (Criminology; Law; Psychology)

Department
Basic Sciences and Humanities (Arts and Humanities; Natural Sciences)

Institute
Languages (English; French; Modern Languages)

History: Founded 1982 as Centro Superior de Sistemas - CENTROSISTEMAS. Acquired present status and title 2003.

Main Language(s) of Instruction: Spanish

Degrees and Diplomas: *Técnico Profesional*; *Tecnólogo*; *Profesional Universitario*; *Especialización*: **Advertising and Publicity; Graphic Design; Information Management; Management; Occupational Health; Teacher Training; Telecommunications Engineering.** *Maestría*: **Information Technology.**

Student Services: Library
Last Updated: 10/11/15

UNIVERSITY CORPORATION OF SANTA ROSA DE CABAL

Corporación Universitaria de Santa Rosa de Cabal (UNISARC)

Apartado aéreo 1371, Km 4 vía Santa Rosa de Cabal - Chinchina, Vereda el Jazmín, Santa Rosa de Cabal, Risaralda
Tel: +57(63) 633-548 +57(63) 363-3874
Fax: +57(63) 633-700
EMail: unisarc@unisarc.edu.co
Website: http://www.unisarc.edu.co

Rectora: Elizabeth Villamil Castañeda
Tel: +57(63) 633-634
EMail: rectoria@unisarc.edu.co

Secretario General: Carlos Eduardo Castro García
EMail: secgeneral@unisarc.edu.co

International Relations: Isabel Cristina Muñoz Alzate
EMail: viceadministrativa@unisarc.edu.co

Faculty
Administration and Rural Development (Agricultural Business; Agricultural Management; Animal Husbandry; Heritage Preservation; Rural Planning; Tourism; Tropical Agriculture); **Agricultural Sciences** (Agriculture; Agronomy; Biology; Ecology); **Animal Sciences** (Animal Husbandry; Cattle Breeding; Veterinary Science; Zoology); **Basic Sciences** (Biology; Biotechnology; Pedagogy); **Information and Communication Sciences and Technology** (Computer Engineering; Computer Science)

History: Founded 1982.

Admission Requirements: High school certificate

Main Language(s) of Instruction: Spanish

Degrees and Diplomas: *Tecnólogo*; *Profesional Universitario*; *Especialización*: **Agricultural Management; Biology; Ecology; Pedagogy; Tropical Agriculture.**

Student Services: Academic Counselling, Cultural Activities, Facilities for disabled people, Health Services, Language Laboratory, Nursery Care, Social Counselling, Sports Facilities
Last Updated: 29/09/15

UNIVERSITY CORPORATION OF SCIENCE AND DEVELOPMENT

Corporación Universitaria de Ciencia y Desarrollo (UNICIENCIA)

Calle 74, No. 15-73, Bogotá
Tel: +57(1) 542-9874
Fax: +57(1) 317-0988
EMail: uniciencia@uniciencia.edu.co; admisiones@uniciencia.edu.co
Website: http://www.uniciencia.edu.co

Rector: Reynaldo Ríos Pérez
EMail: rectoriabogota@uniciencia.edu.co

Vicerrector Academico: Gonzalo Tellez
EMail: academica@uniciencia.edu.co

Programme
Advertising (Advertising and Publicity); **Fashion Design** (Fashion Design); **Law** (Law)

Further Information: Also branches in Cali, Medellín, Montería, Sabaneta and Restrepo

History: Founded 1993. Acquired present status 1996.

Main Language(s) of Instruction: Spanish

Degrees and Diplomas: *Profesional Universitario*

Student Services: Library
Last Updated: 29/09/15

UNIVERSITY CORPORATION OF THE CARIBBEAN

Corporación Universitaria del Caribe (CECAR)

Apartado aéreo 248, Carretera Troncal Occidente Via Corozal, Sincelejo, Sucre
Tel: +57(5) 280-1060
Fax: +57(5) 280-1554
EMail: jorge.ganem@cecar.edu.co
Website: http://www.cecar.edu.co

Rectora: Piedad Martinez Carazo (2013-)
EMail: rectoria@cecar.edu.co

Vicerrector Administrativo y Financiero: Camilo Guerrero Buelvas

International Relations: Liliana Alvarez Ruíz, Directora, Internacionalización
Tel: +57(5) 280-4017 +57(5) 280-4018
EMail: liliana.alvarez@cecar.edu.co

Faculty
Basic Sciences, Engineering and Architecture (Architecture; Computer Engineering; Industrial Engineering); **Economics and Administrative Sciences** (Accountancy; Business Administration; Economics); **Humanities and Education** (Art Education; Foreign Languages Education; Native Language Education; Primary Education; Psychology; Social Work; Sports); **Law and Political Science** (Law)

Programme
Virtual Mode Studies (Administration; Foreign Languages Education; Information Management; International Business; Tourism)

History: Founded 1978.

Main Language(s) of Instruction: Spanish

Degrees and Diplomas: *Profesional Universitario*; *Especialización*: **Administrative Law; Construction Engineering; Engineering; Environmental Management; Finance; Information Technology; Public Administration; Town Planning.** Also Especialización in Safety Engineering and Occupational Health offered through Universidad del Norte; Licenciatura in Art Education, Foreign Languages Education and Native Language Education; Profesional Universitario in Business Administration, Public Administration and Licenciatura in Science Education, Computer Education, Technology Education, Humanities and Socila Sciences Education, Foreign Languages Education, Native Language Education offered through distance mode.

Student Services: Health Services, Library

Publications: Revista Institucional
Last Updated: 29/09/15

UNIVERSITY CORPORATION OF THE COAST

Corporación Universidad de la Costa (CUC)
Calle 58, No. 55-66, Barranquilla, Atlántico
Tel: +57(5) 511-974 +57(5) 511-974
Fax: +57(5) 417-678
EMail: info@cuc.edu.co
Website: http://www.cuc.edu.co

Rector: Tito José Crissien Borrero
Tel: +57(5) 336-2203 EMail: rectoria@cuc.edu.co

Vicerrector Administrativo: Jaime Diaz Arenas
Tel: +57(5) 336-2227 EMail: vadministrativa@cuc.edu.co

Faculty

Architecture (Architecture); **Economics** (Accountancy; Advertising and Publicity; Banking; Business Administration; E- Business/ Commerce; Finance; Health Administration; International Business; International Relations; Marketing); **Engineering** (Civil Engineering; Computer Engineering; Electrical Engineering; Electronic Engineering; Industrial Engineering); **Environmental Sciences** (Agricultural Engineering; Environmental Engineering; Environmental Management); **Humanities** (Mass Communication; Media Studies; Primary Education); **Law** (Law); **Psychology** (Psychology)

Programme

Postgraduate Studies (Accountancy; Automation and Control Engineering; Business Administration; Civil Engineering; Computer Networks; Construction Engineering; Education; Educational Administration; Educational Psychology; Energy Engineering; Engineering; Environmental Engineering; Environmental Management; Finance; Health Administration; Information Technology; International Business; Management; Pedagogy; Psychology; Psychotherapy; Safety Engineering; Social Psychology; Social Welfare; Software Engineering; Taxation; Telecommunications Engineering; Transport Management)

History: Founded 1970.

Admission Requirements: Secondary school certificate (bachillerato) and entrance examination

Main Language(s) of Instruction: Spanish

Degrees and Diplomas: *Profesional Universitario*; *Especialización*: **Accountancy; Automation and Control Engineering; Business Administration; Civil Engineering; Computer Networks; Construction Engineering; Educational Administration; Educational Psychology; Energy Engineering; Environmental Management; Finance; Health Administration; Information Technology; International Business; Management; Pedagogy; Psychotherapy; Safety Engineering; Social Psychology; Social Welfare; Software Engineering; Taxation; Telecommunications Engineering; Transport Management.** *Maestría*: **Business Administration; Education; Engineering; Psychology.** Also Licenciatura (Teacher Training Degree), in Primary Education

Last Updated: 25/09/15

UNIVERSITY CORPORATION OF THE HUILA REGION

Corporación Universitaria del Huila (CORHUILA)
Calle 21, No. 6-01, Neiva, Huila
Tel: +57(988) 753-046
Fax: +57(988) 754-289
EMail: contacto@corhuila.edu.co
Website: http://www.corhuila.edu.co

Rector: Roque González Garzón
Tel: +57(988) 875-4220 Ext. 112 EMail: rectoria@corhuila.edu.co

Vicerrector Administrativo: Luis Eduardo Cabezas Montes
Tel: +57(988) 875-4220 Ext. 115
EMail: viceacademica@corhuila.edu.co

Vicerrector Académico: Fabio Lozada Pérez
Tel: +57(988) 875-4220 Ext. 115
EMail: viceacademica@corhuila.edu.co

Faculty

Economics and Administration (Advertising and Publicity; Banking; Business Administration; Farm Management; Finance; International Business; Marketing; Sales Techniques; Tourism); **Engineering** (Computer Engineering; Environmental Engineering; Industrial Engineering); **Veterinary Medicine and Allied Sciences** (Animal Husbandry; Veterinary Science)

History: Founded 1989.

Fees: 46,000 per annum (US Dollar)

Main Language(s) of Instruction: Spanish

Accrediting Agency: Ministerio de Educación Nacional

Degrees and Diplomas: *Profesional Universitario*

Student Services: Academic Counselling, Canteen, Cultural Activities, Facilities for disabled people, Health Services, Library, Nursery Care, Sports Facilities

Publications: Nueva Clase; Nueva Clase

Last Updated: 29/09/15

UNIVERSITY CORPORATION OF THE META REGION

Corporación Universitaria del Meta (UNIMETA)
Apartado aéreo 3244, Carrera 32 No. 34B-26, Barrio San Fernando, Villavicencio, Meta
Tel: +57(6) 662-1825 Ext. 101
Fax: +57(6) 6621827
EMail: rectoria@unimeta.edu.co
Website: http://www.unimeta.edu.co

Rector: Rafael Maria Mojica Garcia
Tel: +57(6) 662-1825 Ext. 101 EMail: rectoria@unimeta.edu.co

Secretario General: Álvaro Augusto Arévalo Navarro
Tel: +57(6) 662-1825 Ext. 111
EMail: secretariageneral@unimeta.edu.co

School

Administrative Sciences (Accountancy; Advertising and Publicity; Business Administration; Marketing); **Engineering and Architecture** (Agricultural Engineering; Architecture; Civil Engineering; Computer Engineering; Electronic Engineering; Environmental Engineering; Food Technology; Graphic Design; Industrial Engineering); **Law and Social Sciences** (Journalism; Law; Mass Communication; Social Work)

Department

Basic Sciences (Soil Science; Water Science); **Postgraduate Studies; University Corporation of the Region of Meta Educational Method (MEUM)** (Teacher Training)

History: Founded 1982. Acquired present status 1985.

Admission Requirements: Secondary school certificate and Prueba del ICFES

Fees: 1,285,000-1,705,000 (Colombian Peso)

Main Language(s) of Instruction: Spanish

Accrediting Agency: ICFES; Consejo Nacional de Acreditación (CNA)

Degrees and Diplomas: *Profesional Universitario*; *Especialización*: **Accountancy; Finance; Health Administration; Management; Marketing; Occupational Health; Safety Engineering; Taxation.**

Student Services: Academic Counselling, Canteen, Careers Guidance, Cultural Activities, Health Services, Language Laboratory, Library, Sports Facilities

Publications: Revista Cientifica

Publishing House: Meta Universitaria

Academic Staff *2014-2015*	**TOTAL**
FULL-TIME	**96**
PART-TIME	**63**
Student Numbers *2014-2015*	
All (Foreign included)	**3,680**

Last Updated: 29/09/15

UNIVERSITY FOUNDATION OF AMERICA

Fundación Universidad de América (FUA)
Campus de Los Cerros, Avda Circunvalar No. 20-53, Bogotá
Tel: +57(1) 337-6680
Fax: +57(1) 336-2941
EMail: payalam@uamerica.edu.co
Website: http://www.uamerica.edu.co

Rector: Jaime Posada Díaz EMail: rectoria@uamerica.edu.co

Vicerrectora Académica de Posgrados: Ana Josefa Herrera Vargas EMail: jherrera@uamerica.edu.co

Secretario General: Juan Carlos Posada García-Peña EMail: juancarlosposada@uamerica.edu.co

Faculty

Architecture (Architecture; Construction Engineering; Regional Planning; Town Planning); **Continuing and Advance Education** (Accountancy; Construction Engineering; Educational Technology; Finance; Food Technology; Industrial Chemistry; Information Management; Management Systems; Occupational Health; Petroleum and Gas Engineering; Safety Engineering; Small Business; Urban Studies; Water Management); **Economics** (Business Administration; Economics; Human Resources; International Business); **Engineering** (Chemical Engineering; Industrial Engineering; Mechanical Engineering; Petroleum and Gas Engineering; Production Engineering)

History: Founded 1952, reorganized several times, acquired present status 1973.

Academic Year: January to November (January-June; July-November)

Admission Requirements: Secondary school certificate (bachillerato) and entrance examination

Main Language(s) of Instruction: Spanish

Degrees and Diplomas: *Profesional Universitario*; *Especialización*: **Business Administration; Construction Engineering; Economics; Environmental Management; Human Resources; International Business; Regional Planning; Safety Engineering.** Also Diplomados (Continuing Education)

Student Services: Academic Counselling, Canteen, Careers Guidance, Cultural Activities, Health Services, Library, Social Counselling, Sports Facilities

Last Updated: 02/10/15

UNIVERSITY FOUNDATION OF HEALTH SCIENCES

Fundación Universitaria de Ciencias de la Salud (FUCS)

Cra 19 No. 8A-32, Hospital San José, Bogotá
Tel: +57(1) 353-8008
EMail: informacion@fucsalud.edu.co
Website: http://www.fucsalud.edu.co

Rector: Sergio Augusto Parra Duarte
EMail: rectoria@fucsalud.edu.co

Vicerrector: Darío Cadena Rey

Programme

Business Administration (Business Administration); **Postgraduate Studies** (Anaesthesiology; Epidemiology; Health Administration; Health Education; Medicine; Nephrology; Nursing; Surgery); **Psychology** (Psychology); **Surgical Instruments** (Instrument Making; Surgery); **Technological Studies** (Cell Biology; Health Sciences; Histology)

History: Founded 1976.

Main Language(s) of Instruction: Spanish

Degrees and Diplomas: *Tecnólogo*; *Profesional Universitario*; *Especialización*: **Anaesthesiology; Epidemiology; Health Administration; Health Education; Medicine; Nephrology; Nursing.**

Student Services: Library

Last Updated: 05/10/15

UNIVERSITY FOUNDATION OF THE ANDEAN REGION

Fundación Universitaria del Area Andina

Cra 14A No.70A-34, Bogotá 7449191
Tel: +57(1) 744-9191
Fax: +57(1) 211-5477
EMail: areandina@areandina.edu.co
Website: http://www.areandina.edu.co

Rector Nacional: Fernando Laverde Morales
EMail: rector@areandina.edu.co

Secretaria General: María Jetzabel Herrán Duarte

Programme

Business Administration (Business Administration); **Culinary Arts and Gastronomy** (Cooking and Catering); **Fashion Design** (Fashion Design); **Graphic Design** (Graphic Design); **International Business** (International Business); **Marketing and Advertising** (Advertising and Publicity; Marketing); **Mining Engineering** (Mining Engineering); **Nursing** (Nursing); **Optometry** (Optometry); **Postgraduate Studies** (Environmental Management; Epidemiology; Health Administration; Occupational Health; Optometry; Rehabilitation and Therapy; Social and Community Services); **Psychology** (Psychology); **Public Accounting** (Accountancy); **Respiratory Therapy** (Respiratory Therapy); **Sports Training** (Sports); **Surgical Instrumentation** (Medical Technology); **Systems Engineering** (Computer Engineering); **Technical/Professional Studies** (Cooking and Catering; Cosmetology; Medical Auxiliaries; Nursing; Sports); **Technological Studies** (Cinema and Television; Food Technology; Radiology)

Campus

Medellín (Fashion Design; Graphic Design); **Pereira** (Administrative Law; Advertising and Publicity; Cardiology; Constitutional Law; Cooking and Catering; Cosmetology; Dentistry; Epidemiology; Fashion Design; Finance; Food Technology; Government; Graphic Design; Health Administration; Human Rights; International Business; Law; Marketing; Medical Auxiliaries; Medical Technology; Multimedia; Nursing; Occupational Health; Optometry; Physical Therapy; Pneumology; Psychology; Public Administration; Radio and Television Broadcasting; Radiology; Rehabilitation and Therapy; Respiratory Therapy; Safety Engineering; Software Engineering); **Valledupar** (Civil Engineering; Cooking and Catering; Geological Engineering; Graphic Design; Law; Mining Engineering; Psychology)

Further Information: Also Campuses in Pereira, Medellín and Valledupar

Main Language(s) of Instruction: Spanish

Degrees and Diplomas: *Técnico Profesional*; *Tecnólogo*; *Profesional Universitario*; *Especialización*: **Administrative Law; Cardiology; Constitutional Law; Environmental Management; Epidemiology; Government; Health Administration; Human Rights; Marketing; Occupational Health; Optometry; Pneumology; Public Administration; Rehabilitation and Therapy; Safety Engineering; Software Engineering.** *Maestría*: **Social and Community Services.**

Last Updated: 05/10/15

PEREIRA BRANCH

SECCIONAL PEREIRA

Calle 24 No. 8-55, Pereira, Risaralda
Tel: +57(6) 340-2282 Ext.2062
EMail: funandi@funandi.edu.co
Website: http://www.funandi.edu.co/pereira

Branch's Rector: Edgar Orlando Cote Rojas
EMail: rectoria@funandi.edu.co

Programme

Audiovisual and Mutlimedia (Multimedia; Radio and Television Broadcasting); **Dentistry** (Dentistry); **Distance Postgraduate Studies** (Epidemiology); **Fashion Design** (Fashion Design); **Finance** (Finance); **Graphic Design** (Graphic Design); **International Business** (International Business); **Law** (Law); **Marketing, Advertising and Publicity** (Advertising and Publicity; Marketing); **Nursing** (Nursing); **Optometry** (Optometry); **Physical Therapy** (Physical Therapy); **Political Sciences** (Political Sciences); **Posgraduate Studies** (Administrative Law; Epidemiology; Government; Health Administration; Human Rights; Marketing; Occupational Health; Political Sciences; Respiratory Therapy; Software Engineering); **Psychology** (Psychology); **Respiratory Therapy** (Respiratory Therapy); **Surgical Instruments** (Medical Technology); **Technical/Professional Studies** (Cooking and Catering; Cosmetology); **Technological Studies** (Cooking and Catering; Radiology)

History: Founded 1983.

Main Language(s) of Instruction: Spanish

Degrees and Diplomas: *Técnico Profesional*; *Tecnólogo*; *Profesional Universitario*: **Advertising and Publicity; Dentistry; Fashion Design; Finance; Graphic Design; International Business; Law; Marketing; Medical Technology; Multimedia; Nursing;**

Optometry; Physical Therapy; Political Sciences; Psychology; Radio and Television Broadcasting; Respiratory Therapy. *Especialización*: **Administrative Law; Epidemiology; Government; Health Administration; Health Sciences; Human Rights; Marketing; Occupational Health; Political Sciences; Respiratory Therapy; Software Engineering.** Especialización in Epidemiology also offered through distance mode.

Student Services: IT Centre, Library

UNIVERSITY OF APPLIED AND ENVIRONMENTAL SCIENCES

Universidad de Ciencias Aplicadas y Ambientales (UDCA)

Calle 222 No. 55-37, Bogotá
Tel: +57(1) 668-4700
Fax: +57(1) 676-0096
EMail: campus@udca.edu.co
Website: http://www.udca.edu.co

Rector: Germán Anzola Montero (1986-)
Tel: +57(1) 668-4700 Ext. 124 EMail: ganzola@udca.edu.co

Secretaria General: Gladys Eliana Sánchez Saldarriaga
Tel: +57(1) 668-4700 Ext. 155 EMail: glasanchez@udca.edu.co

Vicerrector Administrativo y Financiero: Jaime Andrés Arboleda Oviedo
Tel: +57(1) 668-4700 Ext. 132 EMail: jaarboleda@udca.edu.co

International Relations: Ximena Cardoso Arango, Directora Departamento de Relaciones Internacionales
Tel: +57(1) 668-4700 Ext. 233 EMail: relint@udca.edu.co

Faculty

Agricultural Sciences (Agriculture; Animal Husbandry; Veterinary Science); **Economics, Administrative Sciences, Accountancy and Affiliated Disciplines** (Accountancy; Business Administration; Economics; Finance; International Business; Marketing); **Educational Sciences** (Education; Environmental Studies; Science Education); **Engineering** (Agricultural Engineering; Business and Commerce; Engineering; Environmental Engineering; Environmental Management; Forestry; Geography; Social Work; Soil Management; Surveying and Mapping; Tropical Agriculture); **Environmental Studies** (Environmental Studies); **Health Sciences** (Medicine; Nursing; Pharmacy; Sports); **Law, Social and Human Sciences** (Law); **Sciences** (Chemistry)

Further Information: Also Campus in Cartagena

History: Founded 1983 as Corporación Universitaria de Ciencias Agropecuarias.

Academic Year: January-May, August-December

Admission Requirements: High school certificate and ICFES National examination

Main Language(s) of Instruction: Spanish

Degrees and Diplomas: *Técnico Profesional*; *Tecnólogo*; *Profesional Universitario*; *Especialización*: **Animal Husbandry; Environmental Management; Higher Education Teacher Training; Laboratory Techniques; Nursing; Nutrition; Social Work; Soil Management; Sports; Veterinary Science.** *Maestría*: **Education; Environmental Management; Environmental Studies; Forestry; Sports; Tropical Agriculture.** Also Licenciatura

Student Services: Academic Counselling, Canteen, Cultural Activities, Health Services, Language Laboratory, Library, Social Counselling, Sports Facilities

Publications: Actualidad y Divulgación Científica

Last Updated: 26/10/15

UNIVERSITY OF BOYACÁ

Universidad de Boyacá (UNIBOYACA)

Apartado aéreo 1118, Carrera 2a Este No. 64-169, Tunja, Boyacá
Tel: +57(8) 745-0000
Fax: +57(8) 745-0044
EMail: informa@uniboyaca.edu.co; comunicaciones@uniboyaca.edu.co
Website: http://www.uniboyaca.edu.co

Rectora: Rosa Amalia Cuervo Payeras
EMail: racuervo@uniboyaca.edu.co; rectoria@uniboyaca.edu.co

Assistant Rectory: Lillia Maria Alaroon Abella
EMail: lmalarcon@miboyaca.edu.co

International Relations: Diana Plata Alarcón, Directora División de Relaciones Interinstitucionales e Internacionales
Tel: +57(8) 745-1910
EMail: dcplata@uniboyaca.edu.co; diri@uniboyaca.edu.co

Faculty

Administration and Accountancy (Accountancy; Administration; Business Administration; Finance; International Business; Management; Marketing; Taxation); **Architecture and Fine Arts** (Architecture; Fashion Design; Graphic Design; Town Planning; Urban Studies); **Health Sciences** (Epidemiology; Health Administration; Health Sciences; Laboratory Techniques; Medical Technology; Medicine; Nursing; Rehabilitation and Therapy); **Human Sciences and Education** (Child Care and Development; Education; Humanities and Social Science Education; Psychology); **Law and Social Sciences** (Law; Mass Communication; Media Studies; Political Sciences; Social Sciences); **Postgraduate Studies** (Architecture and Planning; Business Computing; Child Care and Development; Computer Engineering; Epidemiology; Finance; Health Administration; Higher Education Teacher Training; Information Technology; International Business; Laboratory Techniques; Law; Management; Marketing; Mass Communication; Media Studies; Taxation; Town Planning); **Science and Engineering** (Business Computing; Civil Engineering; Computer Engineering; Electronic Engineering; Engineering; Environmental Engineering; Industrial Engineering; Information Technology; Mechanical Engineering; Natural Sciences; Safety Engineering)

Further Information: Campuses in Sogamoso, Chiquinquirá, Yopal, Bogotá

History: Founded 1979, as a private and non-profit foundation approved by the Colombian Government. Acquired present university status 2004.

Academic Year: January to December (January-June; July-December)

Admission Requirements: Secondary school certificate (bachillerato) and entrance examination

Fees: 450-1,600 per semester (US Dollar)

Main Language(s) of Instruction: Spanish

Degrees and Diplomas: *Tecnólogo*; *Profesional Universitario*; *Especialización*: **Business Computing; Environmental Engineering; Epidemiology; Finance; Health Administration; Information Technology; International Business; Laboratory Techniques; Law; Management; Marketing; Mass Communication; Media Studies; Taxation; Town Planning.** *Maestría*: **Town Planning.** Also Diplomados; Postgraduate Diploma Programmes in Architecture and Planning, Higher Education Teacher Training, Child Care and Development

Student Services: Academic Counselling, Canteen, Cultural Activities, Health Services, Language Laboratory, Social Counselling, Sports Facilities

Publications: Proyección Universitaria

Last Updated: 23/10/15

UNIVERSITY OF COLOMBIA

Universitaria de Colombia

Carrera 7 No. 35-85, Bogotá
Tel: +57(1) 288-0871 +57(1) 232-4070
Website: http://www.universitariadecolombia.edu.co

Rector: Carlos Abraham Moreno de Caro (2014-)
EMail: cmorenodecaro@yahoo.com

Programme

Business Administration (Business Administration); **Graphic Design** (Graphic Design); **Industrial Engineering** (Industrial Engineering); **Law** (Law); **Psychology** (Psychology); **Public Accounting** (Accountancy); **Social Communication** (Mass Communication); **Systems Engineering** (Computer Engineering)

History: Founded 2010.

Main Language(s) of Instruction: Spanish

Degrees and Diplomas: *Profesional Universitario*: **Accountancy; Business Administration; Computer Engineering; Graphic Design; Industrial Engineering; Law; Mass Communication; Psychology.**

Last Updated: 29/09/15

UNIVERSITY OF IBAGUÉ

Universidad de Ibagué (UDI)

Apartado aéreo 487, Carrera 22, Calle 67, Barrio Ambalá, Ibagué, Tolima

Tel: +57(8) 270-9444

Fax: +57(8) 270-9443

EMail: informacion@unibague.edu.co

Website: http://www.unibague.edu.co

Rector: Alfonso Reyes Alvarado
Tel: +57(8) 275-3834
EMail: alfonso.reyes@unibague.edu.co; areyes@unibague.edu.co

Secretaria General: Eleonora Rios González

Vicerrectora Académica: Gloria Piedad Barreto Bonilla

Faculty

Economics (Accountancy; Business Administration; Economics; Finance; International Business; Marketing); **Engineering** (Civil Engineering; Computer Engineering; Electronic Engineering; Industrial Engineering; Mechanical Engineering); **Humanities, Arts and Social Sciences** (Architecture; Design; Journalism; Mass Communication; Psychology); **Law and Political Science** (Law; Political Sciences); **Natural Sciences and Mathematics** (Environmental Management)

Programme

Technological Studies (Criminology; Hygiene; Industrial Maintenance; Protective Services; Safety Engineering; Telecommunications Engineering)

History: Founded 1980. Previously known as Corporación Universitaria de Ibagué. Acquired present status 2003.

Academic Year: January to November (January-May; July-November)

Admission Requirements: Secondary school certificate

Fees: 1,9-2,6m. per semester (Colombian Peso)

Main Language(s) of Instruction: Spanish

Accrediting Agency: Consejo Nacional de Acreditación

Degrees and Diplomas: *Tecnólogo*; *Profesional Universitario*: **Accountancy; Architecture; Civil Engineering; Computer Engineering; Design; Economics; Electronic Engineering; Environmental Management; Finance; Industrial Engineering; International Business; Journalism; Law; Marketing; Mass Communication; Mechanical Engineering; Political Sciences; Psychology.** *Especialización*: **Safety Engineering.** *Maestria*: **Industrial Engineering; Industrial Management; Safety Engineering.** Also Maestria in Regional Planning and Town Planning offered through Universidad Autónoma de Manizales; MBA offered though University ICESI Cali; Especialización in Commercial Law offered through Universidad de la Sabana; Especialización in Finance, Marketing and Management through Universidad del Rosario; Especialización in Environmental Studies with Universidad Jorge Tadeo Lozano.

Student Services: Academic Counselling, Canteen, Cultural Activities, Foreign Studies Centre, Health Services, Language Laboratory, Nursery Care, Social Counselling, Sports Facilities

Publications: Actas Pedagógicas; Temas y Reflexiones

Last Updated: 26/10/15

UNIVERSITY OF LA SABANA

Universidad de La Sabana

Campus del Puente del Común, Km. 7, Autopista Norte de Bogotá, Chia, Cundinamarca

Tel: +57(1) 861-5555 +57(1) 861-6666

Fax: +57(1) 861-6010

EMail: admisiones@unisabana.edu.co

Website: http://www.unisabana.edu.co

Rector: Obdulio Velásquez Posada
EMail: obdulio.velasquez@unisabana.edu.co; rector@unisabana.edu.co

Vicerrectora de Profesores y Estudiantes: Liliana Eugenia Ospina Gómez EMail: liliana.ospina@unisabana.edu.co

Direcotra de Comunicación Institucional: Maria del Pilar Velez EMail: Pilar.velez@unisabana.edu.co

Vicerrector de Proyección y Desarrollo: Mauricio Rojas Perez EMail: mauricio.rojas@unisabana.edu.co

Vicerrector de Procesos Académicos: Rolando Andres Roncancio Rachid EMail: rolando.roncancio@unisabana.edu.co

Secretaria General: Angela Maria De Valdenebro Campo EMail: angela.valdenebro@unisabana.edu.co

Secretario del Consejo Fundacional: Alfonso Aza Jacome EMail: Alfonso.Aza@unisabana.edu.co

Director General Administrativo: Carlos Alberto Aponte Gomez EMail: carlos.aponte@unisabana.edu.co

International Relations: María Carolina Serrano Ramírez, Directora de Relaciones Internacionales
EMail: maria.serrano@unisabana.edu.co

Faculty

Communication (Journalism; Multimedia); **Education** (Pedagogy); **Engineering** (Chemical Engineering; Civil Engineering; Computer Engineering; Industrial Engineering; Mechanical Engineering; Production Engineering); **Law** (Law; Political Sciences); **Medicine** (Medicine); **Nursing and Rehabilitation** (Nursing; Rehabilitation and Therapy); **Philosophy** (Philosophy); **Psychology** (Psychology); **School of Economics and Administrative Sciences** *(International)* (Administration; Cooking and Catering; Economics; International Business; Marketing; Service Trades)

School

INALDE Business School (Administration)

Department

Foreign Languages and Cultures (Modern Languages)

Institute

Family Studies (Family Studies); **Postgraduate Studies** (Administration)

Centre

Technology *(For the Academy)* (Education)

History: Founded 1971 as Institute for Higher Education. Acquired present status and title 1979.

Academic Year: February to November

Admission Requirements: Secondary school certificate (bachillerato), National Secondary Examination (ICFES) and entrance examination

Fees: National: 5,000,000-14,000,000 per semester, according to parents' income (Colombian Peso), International: 1,650-4,700 per semester, according to parents' income

Main Language(s) of Instruction: Spanish

Accrediting Agency: Consejo Nacional de Acreditación de Colombia (CNA)

Degrees and Diplomas: *Profesional Universitario*: **Business Administration; Education; Engineering; Law; Mass Communication; Medicine; Nursing; Philosophy; Psychology; Rehabilitation and Therapy.** *Especialización*: **Administration; Education; Family Studies; Law; Mass Communication; Medicine; Nursing; Psychology.** *Maestria*: **Business Administration; Education; Engineering; Journalism; Law; Medicine; Nursing; Philosophy; Psychology.** *Doctorado*: **Biomedicine; Education; Engineering.**

Student Services: Academic Counselling, Canteen, Careers Guidance, Cultural Activities, Facilities for disabled people, Foreign Studies Centre, Health Services, IT Centre, Language Laboratory, Library, Nursery Care, Residential Facilities, Sports Facilities, eLibrary

Publications: Aquichan; Díkaion; Educación y Educadores; Latin American Journal of Content & Language Integrated Learning; Palabra Clave; Pensamiento y Cultura; Persona y Bioética

Publishing House: Revistas Universidad de La Sabana (http://revistas.unisabana.edu.co)

Academic Staff *2014-2015*	MEN	WOMEN	TOTAL
FULL-TIME	458	788	**1,246**
PART-TIME	459	329	**788**
STAFF WITH DOCTORATE			
FULL-TIME	54	36	**90**
Student Numbers *2014-2015*			
All (Foreign included)	4,300	6,681	**10,981**
FOREIGN ONLY	160	161	**321**

Distance students, 837.

Last Updated: 24/11/15

UNIVERSITY OF MANIZALES

Universidad de Manizales
Carrera 9 No. 19-03, Manizales, Caldas 868
Tel: +57(6) 884-1450
Fax: +57(6) 884-1443
EMail: um@um.umanizales.edu.co
Website: http://www.umanizales.edu.co

Rector: Guillermo Orlando Sierra Sierra
Tel: +57(68) 883-3211 EMail: rectoria@umanizales.edu.co

Vicerrector Académico y Administrativo: Jorge Iván Jurado Salgado (rectoria@umanizales.edu.co)
Tel: +57(6) 887-9680 Ext. 1205
EMail: vicacad@um.umanizales.edu.co

Secretario General: César Augusto Sepulveda Ortiz
Tel: +57(6) 887-9680 Ext. 1209
EMail: casepulveda@umanizales.edu.co

International Relations: Gabriel Fernando Lotero Arias, Coordinador Oficina de Relaciones Internacionales -ORI
Tel: +57(6) 872-1021
EMail: ori@umanizales.edu.co; gflotero@umanizales.edu.co

Faculty

Accountancy, Economics and Administrative Sciences (Accountancy; Business Administration; Health Administration; International Business; Marketing); **Health Sciences** (Medicine); **Juridical Sciences** (Law); **Sciences and Engineering** (Computer Engineering; Computer Science; Telecommunications Engineering); **Social and Human Sciences** (Journalism; Mass Communication; Primary Education; Psychology)

History: Founded 1972, acquired present status 1992.

Main Language(s) of Instruction: Spanish

Degrees and Diplomas: *Técnico Profesional*; *Tecnólogo*; *Profesional Universitario*; *Especialización*: **Computer Networks; Finance; Human Resources; International Business; Marketing; Psychology; Psychotherapy; Sales Techniques; Social Welfare; Surveying and Mapping; Telecommunications Engineering.** *Maestría*: **Economics; Education; Environmental Management; Human Resources; Law; Marketing; Surveying and Mapping; Taxation; Teacher Training.** *Doctorado*: **Child Care and Development; Environmental Studies; Social Sciences.**

Student Services: Health Services, Library, Social Counselling, Sports Facilities

Last Updated: 22/10/15

UNIVERSITY OF MEDELLIN

Universidad de Medellín (UDEM)
Carrera 87 No. 30-65, Belén Los Alpes, Medellín, Antioquia
Tel: +57(4) 340-5555
EMail: udem@guayacan.udem.edu.co
Website: http://www.udem.edu.co

Rector: Néstor Hincapié Vargas (2000-)
Tel: +57(4) 238-3906 EMail: nhincapie@guayacan.udem.edu.co

Secretaria General: Esperanza Restrepo de Isaza
Tel: +57(4) 238-1252

International Relations: Milena Mejía Vásquez, Jefe, División de Relaciones Internacionales
Tel: +57(4) 340-5172
EMail: lhbotero@udem.edu.co; relinternacionales@udem.edu.co

Faculty

Communication (Advertising and Publicity; Communication Studies; Graphic Design; Information Management; Information Sciences; Marketing; Mass Communication; Multimedia; Public Relations; Radio and Television Broadcasting); **Economics and Administration** (Accountancy; Agricultural Business; Business Administration; Cooking and Catering; Economics; Human Resources; International Business; Marketing; Political Sciences; Private Administration; Public Administration; Service Trades; Taxation; Transport Management); **Engineering** (Business Administration; Civil Engineering; Computer Engineering; Construction Engineering; Energy Engineering; Environmental Engineering; Finance; Geological Engineering; Industrial Engineering; Information Technology; Law; Marketing; Materials Engineering; Software Engineering; Telecommunications Engineering; Transport Engineering); **Law** (Administrative Law; Civil Law; Commercial Law; Criminal Law; Criminology; International Law; Labour Law; Law; Notary Studies; Private Law; Public Law)

Department

Basic Sciences (Business Administration; Computer Science; Engineering); **Human and Social Sciences** (Government; Human Rights; Political Sciences; Social Sciences)

Campus

Bogotá (Finance; Law; Management; Marketing; Notary Studies)

History: Founded 1950 as a private institution.

Academic Year: February to December (February-June; August-December)

Admission Requirements: Secondary school certificate (bachillerato) and entrance examination

Fees: c. 1,097,000-3,698,000 (Colombian Peso)

Main Language(s) of Instruction: Spanish, English

Accrediting Agency: Consejo Nacional de Acreditación

Degrees and Diplomas: *Profesional Universitario*; *Especialización*: **Administrative Law; Civil Engineering; Civil Law; Commercial Law; Construction Engineering; Criminal Law; Environmental Engineering; Environmental Studies; Finance; Fiscal Law; Food Technology; Gender Studies; Government; Human Resources; Human Rights; Information Management; Information Technology; Insurance; International Business; International Law; Labour Law; Law; Management; Marketing; Mass Communication; Private Administration; Private Law; Public Administration; Public Law; Public Relations; Radio and Television Broadcasting; Road Engineering; Service Trades; Software Engineering; Taxation; Town Planning; Transport Engineering; Transport Management.** *Maestría*: **Accountancy; Business Administration; Civil Engineering; Computer Science; Criminal Law; Criminology; Education; Finance; Government; Human Rights; Information Management; International Law; International Relations; Law; Literature; Marketing; Mass Communication; Mathematics Education; Peace and Disarmament; Software Engineering; Taxation; Transport Management.** *Doctorado*: **Business Administration; Computer Science; Engineering; Law.** Also Diplomado; MBA

Student Services: Academic Counselling, Canteen, Careers Guidance, Cultural Activities, Health Services, Language Laboratory, Library, Nursery Care, Social Counselling, Sports Facilities

Publications: Revista Avanzada

Publishing House: Sello Editorial Universidad de Medellín

Last Updated: 27/10/15

UNIVERSITY OF SAN BUENAVENTURA

Universidad de San Buenaventura (USB)
Carrera 8H # 172 -20, Bogotá 75010
Tel: +57(1) 677-1090
Fax: +57(1) 677-3003
EMail: informacion@usbbog.edu.co
Website: http://www.usbbog.edu.co

Rector: José Arturo Rojas
Tel: +57(1) 667-1090 Ext. 1101-1104
EMail: rector@usbbog.edu.co

Senior Administrative Officer: Miguel Roberto Hernández-Saavedra EMail: mhernand@usbbog.edu.co

International Relations: Irma Liliana Vásquez, Jefe de Oficina de Relaciones Interinstitucionales - ORI
Tel: +57(1) 667-1090 Ext. 4181
EMail: jefe.ori@usbbog.edu.co

Faculty

Basic Sciences and Engineering (Aeronautical and Aerospace Engineering; Computer Engineering; Electronic Engineering; Engineering; Mechanical Engineering; Multimedia; Software Engineering; Sound Engineering (Acoustics); Telecommunications Engineering; Telecommunications Services); **Human and Social Sciences** (Arts and Humanities; Clinical Psychology; Education; English; Higher Education Teacher Training; Neurological Therapy; Philosophy; Preschool Education; Psychology; Technology Education; Theology); **Legal and Political Sciences** (Accountancy; Business Administration; Business and Commerce; Economics;

International Business; International Relations; Law; Management; Political Sciences)

History: Founded 1708 by Royal decree. Closed 1861; officially reopened 1961 and recognized by the Ministry of Education 1964. A private institution under the supervision of the Franciscan Order.

Academic Year: February to November

Admission Requirements: Secondary school certificate (bachillerato) and ICFES entrance examination

Fees: 2,272,000-3.5m. per semester (Colombian Peso)

Main Language(s) of Instruction: Spanish

Degrees and Diplomas: *Tecnólogo*: **Electronic Engineering; Software Engineering; Telecommunications Engineering.** *Profesional Universitario*: **Accountancy; Aeronautical and Aerospace Engineering; Business Administration; Computer Engineering; Economics; Electronic Engineering; Engineering; International Relations; Law; Mechanical Engineering; Multimedia; Political Sciences; Psychology; Sound Engineering (Acoustics).** *Especialización*: **Aeronautical and Aerospace Engineering; Higher Education Teacher Training; International Business; Management; Neurological Therapy; Pedagogy; Philosophy; Psychology; Sound Engineering (Acoustics); Technology Education; Telecommunications Services.** *Maestría*: **Bible; Education; Philosophy; Psychology.** *Doctorado*: **Arts and Humanities.** Also Licenciatura in Theology, Preschool Education, English (virtual mode)

Student Services: Academic Counselling, Careers Guidance, Facilities for disabled people, Foreign Studies Centre, Library, Social Counselling, Sports Facilities

Publications: Breviloquio; Franciscanum; Ingenium; Itinerario Educativo; Management

Last Updated: 27/10/15

CALI BRANCH

SECCIONAL CALI (USBCALI)

Avenida 10 de Mayo, La Umbría, Vía a Pance,
Cali, Valle del Cauca
Tel: +57(2) 488-2222
Fax: +57(2) 488-2231
EMail: informacion@usbcali.edu.co
Website: http://www.usbcali.edu.co

Rector: Ernesto Londoño Orozco
Tel: +57(2) 488-2222 Ext. 201 EMail: rectoria@usbcali.edu.co

Secretario General: Jorge Botero Pineda
Tel: +57(2) 488-2222 Ext. 298
EMail: secretariacali@usbcali.edu.co

Vicerrector Administrativo y Financiero: Félix Rodríguez Ballesteros
Tel: + +57(2) 318-2255/48/20
EMail: vicerrectoriaadmin@usbcali.edu.co

Faculty

Architecture, Art and Design (Architecture; Fashion Design); **Economics** (Accountancy; Business Administration; Economics); **Education** (Native Language Education; Preschool Education); **Engineering** (Agricultural Engineering; Computer Engineering; Electronic Engineering; Engineering; Industrial Engineering; Multimedia); **Law and Political Sciences** (Government; International Relations; Law); **Psychology** (Psychology)

Centre

Continuing Education; **Languages** (Modern Languages)

Research Group

Architecture and Fashion Design; **Economics**; **Education**; **Engineering**; **Law**; **Psychology**

History: Founded 1708 by Royal decree. Closed 1861; officially reopened 1961 and recognized by the Ministry of Education 1964. A private institution under the supervision of the Franciscan Order.

Academic Year: February to November

Admission Requirements: Secondary school certificate (bachillerato) and ICFES entrance examination

Main Language(s) of Instruction: Spanish

Degrees and Diplomas: *Profesional Universitario*: **Accountancy; Agricultural Engineering; Architecture; Business Administration; Computer Engineering; Economics; Electronic Engineering; Fashion Design; Government; Industrial Engineering; International Relations; Law; Multimedia; Psychology.** *Especialización*: **Business and Commerce; Clinical Psychology; Criminal Law; Criminology; Environmental Management; Environmental Studies; Finance; Industrial Management; Insurance; Labour Law; Management; Marine Transport; Marketing; Occupational Health; Psychoanalysis; Psychology; Religious Education; Social Welfare; Software Engineering; Telecommunications Engineering.** *Maestría*: **Architecture; Bioengineering; Education; Educational Administration; Finance; Psychology; Software Engineering.** Also Diplomados; Licenciatura

Student Services: Academic Counselling, Careers Guidance, Facilities for disabled people, Foreign Studies Centre, Health Services, Library, Social Counselling, Sports Facilities

Publications: Breviloquio; Guillermo de Ockham

CARTAGENA BRANCH

SECCIONAL CARTAGENA (USBCTG)

Calle Real de Ternera, Diag. 32 No. 30-966, Cartagena, Bolivar
Tel: +57(956) 653-5555
Fax: +57(956) 653-9590
EMail: usabuctg@ctgred.net.co
Website: http://www.usbctg.edu.co

Rector: Alvaro de Jesús Cepeda Van Houten
Tel: +57(956) 653-5555 Ext. 132
EMail: rectoria@usbcartagena.edu.co

Vicerrector Administrativo y Financiero: Christian Ayola Escallón
Tel: +57(956) 653-5555 Ext. 124
EMail: cayola@usbcartagena.edu.co

International Relations: Mercedes Posada Meola, Director ELACID (Cooperación Internacional)
Tel: +57(956) 653-5555 Ext. 206
EMail: mercedes.posada@usbcartagena.edu.co

Faculty

Administrative Sciences and Accountancy (Accountancy; Business Administration; Business and Commerce; Finance; Insurance; International Business); **Education, Human and Social Sciences** (Clinical Psychology; Educational Sciences; English; Foreign Languages Education; French; Parks and Recreation; Physical Education; Preschool Education; Psychology; Sports); **Engineering, Architecture, Arts and Design** (Architecture; Chemical Engineering; Engineering; Multimedia; Petroleum and Gas Engineering; Regional Planning; Town Planning); **Health Sciences** (Biochemistry; Health Sciences; Microbiology; Physical Therapy; Speech Therapy and Audiology); **Law and Political Sciences** (International Law; Law; Maritime Law; Natural Resources; Public Law)

School

International Cooperation for Development *(Latinamerican)* (English; Foreign Languages Education; French; Parks and Recreation; Physical Education; Preschool Education; Psychology; Sports)

History: Founded 1992.

Academic Year: February-June; July-December

Fees: 1.012.000-3.652.000 per annum (Colombian Peso)

Main Language(s) of Instruction: Spanish

Degrees and Diplomas: *Profesional Universitario*; *Especialización*: **Business and Commerce; Finance; Health Administration; Human Resources; Information Management; Insurance; Law; Maritime Law; Natural Resources; Occupational Health; Psychology; Regional Planning; Safety Engineering; Sports; Town Planning; Transport Management.** *Maestría*: **Biochemistry; Education; English; Foreign Languages Education; French.** Also Licenciatura; Maestría in Biochemistry with Institución Universitaria Colegio Mayor de Antioquia; Especialización in Microbiology with Universitaria Colegio Mayor de Antioquia; Especialización in Insurance with Universidad Militar Nueva Granada; Maestría and Especialización in Development Studies with Universidad de Pavía, Italy.

MEDELLÍN BRANCH

SECCIONAL MEDELLÍN (USBMED)

Calle 45 N° 61-40, Barrio Salento, Bello, Medellín, Antioquia

Tel: +57(4) 514-5600

EMail: comunicaciones.usb@usbmed.edu.co

Website: http://www.usbmed.edu.co

Rector: José Alirio Urbina Rodriguez (rectoria@usbmed.edu.co) Tel: +57(4) 4500-300 EMail: rectoria@usbmed.edu.co

Secretario General: Juan de la Cruz Castellanos Alarcón EMail: asistente.secretaria@usbmed.edu.co

Vicerrector Administrativo y Financiero: Jorge Albeiro Herrera Builes EMail: vice.administrativa@usbmed.edu.co

International Relations: Manuela Vélez Restrepo, Jefe de Relaciones Internacionales
Tel: +57(4) 514-5600 Ext. 4474
EMail: jefe.relaciones@usbmed.edu.co

Faculty

Business Administration (Accountancy; Business Administration; International Business; Tourism); **Education** (Art Education; Educational Administration; Native Language Education; Physical Education; Preschool Education; Sports); **Engineering** (Computer Engineering; Electronic Engineering; Environmental Engineering; Industrial Engineering; Multimedia; Sound Engineering (Acoustics)); **Integrated Arts** (Architecture; Industrial Design); **Law** (Law); **Psychology** (Psychology)

History: Founded 1967. Acquired present status 1975.

Academic Year: February to May and July to November

Admission Requirements: High school Diploma

Main Language(s) of Instruction: Spanish

Accrediting Agency: National Secretary of Education

Degrees and Diplomas: *Tecnólogo*; *Profesional Universitario*; *Especialización*: **Criminal Law; Data Processing; Educational Administration; Higher Education Teacher Training; Industrial and Organizational Psychology; Information Management; Psychology; Religious Education; Social and Community Services; Sound Engineering (Acoustics); Surveying and Mapping.** *Maestría*: **Biological and Life Sciences; Clinical Psychology; Educational Sciences; Industrial and Organizational Psychology; Meteorology; Neurosciences; Psychology; Surveying and Mapping.** *Doctorado*: **Psychology.** Also Diplomados; Licenciatura; Maestría in Psychology with Universidad Autónoma de Bucaramanga; Maestría in Education offered with Universidad de San Buenaventura Cali

Student Services: Careers Guidance, Cultural Activities, Facilities for disabled people, Health Services, Language Laboratory, Library, Nursery Care, Social Counselling, Sports Facilities

UNIVERSITY OF SANTANDER

Universidad de Santander (UDES)

Campus Universitario Lagos del Cacique Calle 70 No. 55-210, Bucaramanga, Santander

Tel: +57(7) 651-6500

Fax: +57(7) 651-6492

EMail: sbenavides@udes.edu.co

Website: http://www.udes.edu.co

Rector: Jaime de Jesús Restrepo Cuartas
EMail: rectoria@udes.edu.co; jrestrepo@udes.edu.co

Secretario General: José Asthul Rangel Chacón
Tel: +57(97) 651-6500 Ext. 228
EMail: jrangel@udes.edu.co

Vicerrectora Administrativa y Financiera: Omaira Nelly Buitrago Bohórquez
Tel: +57(7) 651-6500 Ext. 1920
EMail: omairabuitrago@udes.edu.co

International Relations: Susan Benavides Trujillo, Directora de Relaciones Internacionales
Tel: +57(7) 651-6500 Ext. 1170-1171-1041
EMail: relacionesinternacionales@udes.edu.co; sbenavides@udes.edu.co

Faculty

Agricultural Sciences (Animal Husbandry; Veterinary Science); **Communication, Art and Design** (Advertising and Publicity; Marketing); **Economics, Management and Accountancy** (Accountancy; Finance; International Business); **Engineering** (Agricultural Engineering; Civil Engineering; Electronic Engineering; Environmental Engineering; Industrial Engineering; Software Engineering); **Exact, Physical and Natural Sciences** (Microbiology); **Health Sciences** (Health Sciences; Laboratory Techniques; Medical Technology; Medicine; Microbiology; Nursing; Occupational Therapy; Physical Therapy; Speech Therapy and Audiology; Surgery); **Humanities, Social and Educational Sciences** (Psychology); **Law and Political Sciences** (Law)

History: Founded 1985 as Corporación Universitaria de Santander offering technical programmes in Administration and Health. Became as a University institution in 1996.

Academic Year: February to November (February-May; August-November)

Admission Requirements: High school diploma and National Government Examination (ICFES)

Fees: c. 3,000,000 (Colombian Peso)

Main Language(s) of Instruction: Spanish

Accrediting Agency: National Council for Accreditation - CNA

Degrees and Diplomas: *Tecnólogo*; *Profesional Universitario*; *Especialización*: **Construction Engineering; Environmental Engineering; Finance; Geological Engineering; Health Administration; Health Sciences; Law; Medicine; Occupational Health; Paediatrics; Safety Engineering.** *Maestría*: **Educational Technology; Energy Engineering; Finance; Government; Health Administration; Law; Nursing; Public Administration.**

Student Services: Academic Counselling, Health Services, IT Centre, Language Laboratory, Library, Sports Facilities

Last Updated: 24/11/15

UNIVERSITY OF SANTIAGO DE CALI

Universidad Santiago de Cali (USACA)

Calle 5, No. 62-00, Barrio Pampalinda, Cali, Valle del Cauca 4102

Tel: +57(2) 518-3000

Fax: +57(2) 555-1656 +57(2) 552-5250

EMail: secretaria@usc.edu.co

Website: http://www.usc.edu.co

Rector: Carlos Andrés Pérez Galindo (2011-)
Tel: +57(2) 551-6567
EMail: rectoria@usc.edu.co

Secretario General: Fortunato García Wallis
EMail: secgeneral@usc.edu.co; fortunatogarcia@usc.edu.co

Vicerrector: Arturo Hernán Arenas Fernández

Faculty

Basic Sciences (Chemistry; Microbiology); **Economics and Business Administration** (Accountancy; Business Administration; Economics; Finance; International Business; Marketing); **Education** (Computer Education; Environmental Studies; Foreign Languages Education; Humanities and Social Science Education; Mathematics Education; Native Language Education; Preschool Education; Primary Education); **Engineering** (Bioengineering; Business and Commerce; Computer Engineering; Electronic Engineering; Engineering; Industrial Engineering; Industrial Management; Information Technology); **Health Sciences** (Dentistry; Health Sciences; Medical Technology; Medicine; Nursing; Pharmacy; Physical Therapy; Psychology; Respiratory Therapy; Speech Therapy and Audiology); **Law** (Law); **Mass Communication and Advertising** (Advertising and Publicity; Mass Communication; Social Work)

Institute

Languages (English; French; German; Italian; Portuguese; Spanish)

Further Information: Also branch in Palmira

History: Founded 1958. Acquired present status 1964.

Fees: Undergraduate, 1,463,235-8,346,052 per programme; Postgraduate, 3,068,828-6,157,575 per programme (Colombian Peso)

Main Language(s) of Instruction: Spanish

Degrees and Diplomas: *Técnico Profesional*; *Tecnólogo*; *Profesional Universitario*; *Especialización*: **Business Administration; Constitutional Law; Criminal Law; Education; Environmental**

Management; Environmental Studies; Finance; Foreign Languages Education; Health Administration; Human Resources; Information Technology; International Business; Management; Marketing; Occupational Health; Primary Education; Private Law; Taxation; Transport Management. *Maestría*: **Business Administration; Computer Science; Criminal Law; Education; Environmental Studies; Industrial Engineering; Law; Private Law; Public Administration.** Also Licenciatura

Student Services: Library

Last Updated: 02/11/15

PALMIRA BRANCH

SECCIONAL PALMIRA

Carrera 30 con Calle 38 esquina, Barrio Alfonso López, Palmira
Tel: +57(2) 518-3000 Ext. 528
EMail: cindycortes@usc.edu.co
Website: http://palmira.usc.edu.co

Director: Julio Cesar Escobar

Faculty

Economics and Business Administration (Service Trades; Tourism; Transport Management); **Education** (Preschool Education); **Health Sciences** (Medicine; Nursing; Physical Therapy); **Law** (Law)

History: Founded 1996.

Main Language(s) of Instruction: Spanish

Degrees and Diplomas: *Técnico Profesional*; *Tecnólogo*; *Profesional Universitario*. Also Licenciatura

UNIVERSITY OF THE ANDES

Universidad de Los Andes

Apartado aéreo 4976, Carrera 1a No. 18 A 10, Bogotá
Tel: +57(1) 339-4999
Fax: +57(1) 332-4448
EMail: rectoria@uniandes.edu.co
Website: http://www.uniandes.edu.co

Rector: Pablo del Carmen Navas Sanz de Santamaría
Tel: +57(1) 332-4370 EMail: rectoria@uniandes.edu.co

Secretaria General: María Teresa Tobón
Tel: +57(1) 332-4376 EMail: secgal@uniandes.edu.co

International Relations: Catalina Rizo
Tel: +57(1) 339-4949, Ext. 3288 EMail: crizo@uniandes.edu.co

Faculty

Administration (Administration); **Architecture and Design** (Architecture; Industrial Design; Textile Design); **Arts and Humanities** (Arts and Humanities; Literature; Music; Painting and Drawing; Sculpture); **Economics** (Economics); **Engineering** (Chemical Engineering; Civil Engineering; Computer Engineering; Electrical Engineering; Electronic Engineering; Engineering; Environmental Engineering; Industrial Engineering; Mechanical Engineering); **Law** (Law); **Medicine** (Medicine); **Science** (Biology; Chemistry; Mathematics; Microbiology; Physics); **Social Sciences** (Anthropology; Cultural Studies; History; Modern Languages; Philosophy; Political Sciences; Psychology; Social Sciences; Social Studies)

Institute

Genetics

Centre

Advanced Computation *(MOX)*; **Bioengineering** *(GIP)*; **Economic Development** *(CEDE)*; **Engineering Research** *(CIFI)*; **Environmental Engineering** *(CIIA)*; **Ethnolinguistic Studies** *(CCELA)* (Ethnology; Indigenous Studies; Linguistics); **Innovation and Technological Development** *(CITEC)*; **Interdisciplinary Regional Studies** *(CIDER)* (Regional Studies); **Journalism** *(CEPER)* (Journalism); **Material and Civil Construction** *(CIMOC)*; **Mechanic Properties and Material Structures** *(CIPEM)*; **Microbiology** *(CIMIC)*; **Microbiology and Tropical Parasitology** *(CIMPAT)*; **Microelectronics** *(CMUA)*; **Polymer Processing** *(CIPP)*; **Research and Development of Informatics in Education** *(LIDIE)*; **Social and International Affairs Studies** *(CESO)*; **Socio-juridical Studies** *(CIJUS)*; **Telecommunications** *(CTUA)*; **Water and Sewage** *(CIACUA)*

History: Founded 1948 as an independent private institution. Acquired present status 1949.

Academic Year: January to December (January-May; August-December)

Admission Requirements: Secondary school certificate (bachillerato) and University or State examination (ICFES)

Main Language(s) of Instruction: Spanish

Accrediting Agency: EQUIS/AMBA/AACSB/ABET/Consejo Nacional de Acreditación (CNA)

Degrees and Diplomas: *Profesional Universitario*: **Accountancy; Administration; Anthropology; Architecture; Art History; Biology; Biomedical Engineering; Chemical Engineering; Chemistry; Civil Engineering; Computer Engineering; Cultural Studies; Design; Economics; Electrical and Electronic Engineering; Environmental Engineering; Fine Arts; Geophysics; History; Industrial Engineering; Law; Literature; Mathematics; Mechanical Engineering; Medicine; Microbiology; Music; Philosophy; Physics; Political Sciences; Psychology.** *Especialización*; *Maestría*: **Administration; Anthropology; Architecture; Biological and Life Sciences; Biomedical Engineering; Chemical Engineering; Chemistry; Civil Engineering; Computer Engineering; Design; Development Studies; Economics; Education; Electrical Engineering; Electronic Engineering; Environmental Engineering; Finance; Geography (Human); History; Industrial Engineering; Law; Literature; Management; Mathematics; Mechanical Engineering; Petroleum and Gas Engineering; Philosophy; Physics; Psychology; Software Engineering.** *Doctorado*: **Administration; Anthropology; Biological and Life Sciences; Chemistry; Economics; Education; Engineering; History; Law; Literature; Mathematics; Philosophy; Physics; Political Sciences; Psychology.**

Student Services: Academic Counselling, Careers Guidance, Cultural Activities, Facilities for disabled people, Health Services, Language Laboratory, Nursery Care, Sports Facilities

Publications: Actualidad y Discusiones; Antípoda: Revista de Antropología y Arqueología; Catedra Corona; Colombia Internacional; Conversaciones de Arquitectura; Cuadernos Azules; Cuadernos Grises; Desarrollo y Sociedad; Documentos CEDE; Documentos CESO; Estudios Ocasionales; Galeras de Administración; Hipotetis: Apuntes Científicos; Historia Critica; Mejores Proyectos de Grado; Monografias Meritorias en Literatura; Monografiías de Administración; Nuevos Estudios Sociojurídicos; Revista de Derecho Privado; Revista de Derecho, Comunicaciones y Nuevas Tecnologías; Revista de Ingenieria; Revista Derecho Público; Revista Estudios Sociales; Revista Territorios; Serie Investigaciones Sociojurídicas

Publishing House: Ediciones Uniandes

Academic Staff *2014-2015*	MEN	WOMEN	**TOTAL**
FULL-TIME	1,020	925	**1,945**
PART-TIME	582	311	**893**
STAFF WITH DOCTORATE			
FULL-TIME	474	217	**691**
Student Numbers *2014-2015*			
All (Foreign included)	10,139	7,669	**17,808**
FOREIGN ONLY	320	284	**604**

Part-time students, 5,790. **Distance students,** 0.

Last Updated: 24/11/15

UNIVERSITY OF THE NORTH

Universidad del Norte (UNINORTE)

Kilometro 5 Vía Puerto Colombia, Barranquilla, Atlántico
Tel: +57(5) 350-9509
Fax: +57(5) 350-9548
Website: http://www.uninorte.edu.co

Rector: Jesús Ferro Bayona (1980-)
Tel: +57(5) 350-9388 EMail: jferro@uninorte.edu.co

Vicerrectora Administrativa y Financiera: Alma Lucía Díaz Granados Meléndez
Tel: +57(5) 350-9419 +57(5) 350-9000
EMail: adiazgra@uninorte.edu.co; vadmin@uninorte.edu.co

International Relations: Jeannie Caicedo Torres, Directora de Cooperación y Desarrollo Internacional (jcaicedo@uninorte.edu.co Tel: 3509509 Ext. 42)

Tel: +57(5) 350-9230 Ext. 4230
EMail: jcaicedo@uninorte.edu.co; internacional@uninorte.edu.co

Division

Basic Sciences (Biology; Chemistry; Mathematics; Physics; Statistics); **Engineering** (Civil Engineering; Computer Engineering; Electrical Engineering; Electronic Engineering; Environmental Engineering; Industrial Engineering; Mechanical Engineering); **Health Sciences** (Health Sciences; Medicine; Nursing); **Humanities and Social Sciences** (Arts and Humanities; Economics; History; Mass Communication; Philosophy; Psychology; Social Sciences); **Law, Political Science and International Relations** (International Relations; Law; Political Sciences)

School

Architecture, Urbanism and Design (Architecture; Design; Town Planning); **Commerce** (Finance; International Business; Marketing)

Institute

Education (Education); **Languages** (Chinese; English; French; German; Italian; Portuguese; Spanish); **Latin American and Caribbean Studies** (Caribbean Studies; Economics); **Music** (Music); **Sustainable Development** (Development Studies)

Centre

Urban and Regional Studies *(URBANUM)* (Regional Studies; Urban Studies)

Research Group

Human Development (Child Care and Development; Development Studies)

Further Information: Also Teaching Hospital and 54 laboratories

History: Founded 1966. A private institution, recognized by the State as a degree granting institution 1973.

Academic Year: January to December (January-May; July-December)

Admission Requirements: Secondary school certificate (bachillerato) or equivalent, State examination (ICFES), admission test and entrance examination

Fees: 4m. per semester (Colombian Peso)

Main Language(s) of Instruction: Spanish

Accrediting Agency: Consejo Nacional de Acreditación; Accreditation Board of Engineering and Technology (ABET) for Industrial and Mechanical undergraduate programmes; SACS; EQUIS

Degrees and Diplomas: *Profesional Universitario*: **Accountancy; Architecture; Arts and Humanities; Business Administration; Civil Engineering; Computer Engineering; Dentistry; Electrical Engineering; Electronic Engineering; Geology; Government; Graphic Design; Industrial Design; Industrial Engineering; International Business; International Relations; Journalism; Law; Mass Communication; Mathematics; Mechanical Engineering; Medicine; Music; Nursing; Philosophy; Political Sciences; Psychology.** *Especialización*: **Administrative Law; Automation and Control Engineering; Business Administration; Business and Commerce; Civil Law; Commercial Law; Communication Studies; Computer Networks; Constitutional Law; Construction Engineering; Development Studies; Educational Administration; Educational Technology; Electrical Engineering; Engineering Management; Environmental Engineering; Environmental Management; European Studies; Family Studies; Finance; Foreign Languages Education; Health Administration; Higher Education Teacher Training; Human Resources; Industrial Engineering; Industrial Management; Information Technology; Insurance; International Business; Labour Law; Law; Management; Marketing; Mathematics; Medicine; Nursing; Occupational Health; Ophthalmology; Paediatrics; Pedagogy; Political Sciences; Psychiatry and Mental Health; Psychology; Public Administration; Public Law; Radiology; Road Engineering; Safety Engineering; Social Welfare; Social Work; Software Engineering; Structural Architecture; Taxation; Telecommunications Engineering; Transport Engineering; Transport Management.** *Maestría*: **Applied Physics; Biomedicine; Business Administration; Civil Engineering; Clinical Psychology; Cognitive Sciences; Commercial Law; Communication Studies; Computer Engineering; Development Studies; Economics; Education; Electrical Engineering; Electronic Engineering; Engineering Management; Environmental Engineering; Epidemiology; Finance; Foreign Languages Education; Government; History; Industrial Engineering; Information Technology; International Business; International Relations; International Studies; Law; Marketing; Mathematics; Mechanical Engineering; Occupational Health; Philosophy; Political Sciences; Psychology; Public Health; Public Law; Regional Planning; Social and Community Services; Statistics; Telecommunications Engineering; Town Planning.** *Doctorado*: **Business Administration; Civil Engineering; Communication Studies; Computer Engineering; Economics; Education; Electrical and Electronic Engineering; Industrial Engineering; Law; Marine Science and Oceanography; Mechanical Engineering; Natural Sciences; Psychology; Social Sciences.** Also Licenciatura

Student Services: Academic Counselling, Canteen, Careers Guidance, Cultural Activities, Facilities for disabled people, Foreign Studies Centre, Health Services, Language Laboratory, Library, Social Counselling, Sports Facilities

Publications: Anuario Científico; CERES Documentos y Monografías; EIDOS; Ensayo en Desarrollo Humano; Huellas; Investigación y Desarrollo; Pensamiento y Gestión; Psicología desde el Caribe; Revista de Derecho; Revista Ingeniería y Desarrollo; Salud Uninorte

Publishing House: Ediciones Uninorte (Uninorte Editions)
Last Updated: 30/10/15

UNIVERSITY OF THE SINU RIVER

Universidad del Sinú (UNISINU)

Campus Elías Bechara Zainúm, Cra. 1w No. 38-153,
Barrio Juan XXIII, Montería, Córdoba 4536534
Tel: +57(4) 784-0340 +57(4) 781-1717
Fax: +57(401) 841-954
EMail: admisiones@unisinu.edu.co
Website: http://www.unisinu.edu.co

Rectora General: Mara Bechara de Zuleta
Tel: +57(4) 781-1688 EMail: marabechara@unisinu

Vicerrectora General: María Fátima Bechara
Tel: +57(4) 781-1688
EMail: mfbechara@unisin

Secretario General: Jorge Escobar Aviléz
Tel: +57(4) 784-0340
EMail: jescobar@unisinu.edu.co

Faculty

Economics, Administration and Accountancy (Accountancy; Business Administration; Economics; International Business; Management; Tourism); **Health Sciences** (Dentistry; Medical Technology; Medicine; Nursing; Orthopaedics; Paediatrics; Physical Therapy; Psychology); **Human Sciences, Art and Design** (Architecture; Mass Communication); **Law, Social Sciences and Education** (Labour Law; Law; Private Law; Public Law; Social Welfare; Social Work); **Science and Engineering** (Civil Engineering; Computer Engineering; Electrical Engineering; Industrial Engineering; Information Technology; Road Engineering; Telecommunications Engineering; Transport Engineering)

Centre

Languages (English; Modern Languages)

History: Founded 1975 as Corporación Universitaria del Sinú.

Main Language(s) of Instruction: Spanish

Degrees and Diplomas: *Técnico Profesional*; *Tecnólogo*; *Profesional Universitario*; *Especialización*: **Administrative Law; Civil Engineering; Constitutional Law; Dentistry; Labour Law; Law; Management; Orthopaedics; Paediatrics; Public Law; Road Engineering; Social Welfare; Telecommunications Engineering; Transport Engineering.** *Maestría*: **Criminal Law; Criminology; Management; Psychology.**

Student Services: IT Centre, Library
Last Updated: 30/10/15

CARTAGENA BRANCH

SECCIONAL CARTAGENA

Pie de la popa, Cll 30 N° 20-88, Cartagena
Tel: +57(5) 681-0800
EMail: info@unisinucartagena.edu.co
Website: http://www.unisinucartagena.edu.co

Rectora: Rolando Bechara Castilla
Tel: +57(5) 681-0800 +57(5) 658-1688
EMail: rector@unisinucartagena.edu.co

International Relations: Natalia Navarro, Jefe de Relaciones Internacionales
Tel: +57(5) 681-0801 Ext. 204-221
EMail: jeferelinternacionales@unisinucartagena.edu.co; relinternacionales@unisinucartagena.edu.co

Faculty

Economics, Administrative Sciences and Accountancy (Accountancy; International Business); **Engineering** (Computer Engineering; Computer Networks; Industrial Engineering; Industrial Management; Software Engineering; Transport Management); **Health Sciences** (Dentistry; Dietetics; Health Administration; Medicine; Nursing; Nutrition; Optometry; Surgery); **Natural Sciences** (Biotechnology; Marine Biology); **Social Sciences and Humanities** (Law; Psychology; Social Sciences)

History: Founded 1999.

Main Language(s) of Instruction: Spanish

Degrees and Diplomas: *Técnico Profesional*; *Tecnólogo*; *Profesional Universitario*; *Especialización*: **Administrative Law; Anaesthesiology; Gynaecology and Obstetrics; Health Administration; Medicine; Neurology; Ophthalmology; Paediatrics; Plastic Surgery; Social Sciences; Surgery.**

Student Services: Library

URABÁ ANTONIO ROLDÁN BETANCUR FOUNDATION OF ADVANCED UNIVERSITY STUDIES

Fundación de Estudios Superiores Universitarios de Urabá Antonio Roldán Betancur (FESU)

Carrera 111 No 101-64, Barrio los Pinos, Apartado, Antioquia
Tel: +57(94) 829-0100
Fax: +57(94) 829-0100
EMail: admisionesyregistros@fesu.edu.co
Website: www.fesu.edu.co

Rectora: Edna Margarita Martinez Acosta
EMail: rectoria@fesu.edu.co

Programme

Finance (Finance); **International Business** (International Business); **Technical/Professional Studies** (Administration; English; Environmental Management; Finance; Management; Marketing; Safety Engineering; Sales Techniques); **Technological Studies** (Business Administration; Finance; International Business)

History: Founded 2001.

Main Language(s) of Instruction: Spanish

Degrees and Diplomas: *Técnico Profesional*; *Tecnólogo*; *Profesional Universitario*

Last Updated: 01/10/15

Congo

STRUCTURE OF HIGHER EDUCATION SYSTEM

Description:

Higher education is provided by one public university, one private university and several private institutes and schools.

Stages of studies:

University level first stage: *Premier cycle*

The first stage of studies leads to the Licence in three years.

University level second stage: *Deuxième cycle*

The second cycle leads to the Master in two years. In Medicine, the State degree of Doctorat en Médecine is awarded after six years of study.

University level third stage: *Troisième cycle*

The third cycle leads to the Doctorat in three years following upon a Master.

ADMISSION TO HIGHER EDUCATION

Admission to university-level studies:

Name of secondary school credential required: Baccalauréat

Name of secondary school credential required: Baccalauréat technique

Other requirements: Competitive entrance examination for access to university institutes and portfolio for access to university faculties.

Foreign students admission:

Quotas: 10% of study places are reserved for foreign students.

NATIONAL BODIES

Ministère de l'Enseignement supérieur (Ministry of Higher Education)

Minister: Georges Moyen
BP 2682
Brazzaville
Tel: +242 810 359
Fax: +242 810 815
Role of national body: Supervises the higher education system and the institutions.

Data for academic year: 2012-2013

Source: IAU from World Data on Education 2010/2011, UNESCO-IBE and documentation, 2012. Bodies 2016.

INSTITUTION

PUBLIC INSTITUTION

MARIEN NGOUABI UNIVERSITY

Université Marien Ngouabi (UMNG)
BP 69, Brazzaville
Tel: +242(81) 01-41 +242(81) 18-28
Fax: +242(81) 01-41
EMail: unimariengouabi@yahoo.fr
Website: http://www.univ-mngb.net/

Recteur: Armand Moyikoua (2009-) EMail: amoyikoua@yahoo.fr

Vice-Rector: Paul Louzolo-Kimbembe EMail: louzkim@yahoo.fr

Secrétaire général: Joseph Asselam

International Relations: Scholastique Dianzinga
EMail: dianzinga_s@yahoo.fr

Faculty

Arts and Humanities *(FLSH)* (African Studies; Arts and Humanities; Communication Studies; English; Geography; History;

Linguistics; Literature; Philosophy; Social Sciences; Sociology); **Economics** *(FSE)* (Econometrics; Economics; Finance); **Health Sciences** *(FSSA)* (Embryology and Reproduction Biology; Haematology; Health Sciences; Histology; Medicine; Microbiology; Midwifery; Physiology; Surgery); **Law** *(FD)* (Law; Private Law; Public Law); **Science** *(FS)* (Biology; Chemistry; Earth Sciences; Mathematics; Natural Sciences; Physics; Statistics)

School

Administration and Magistracy *(ENAM)* (Administration; Finance; International Relations; Law; Taxation); **Education** *(ENS)* (Educational Sciences; Teacher Training); **Engineering** *(ENSP)* (Civil Engineering; Electrical and Electronic Engineering; Electrical Engineering; Food Technology; Mechanical Engineering; Petroleum and Gas Engineering)

Institute

Agriculture *(IDR)* (Agricultural Management; Agronomy; Forestry); **Business Administration** *(ISG)* (Accountancy; Administration; Business and Commerce; Human Resources; Management; Secretarial Studies); **Physical Education and Sport** *(ISEPS)* (Physical Education; Sports)

Further Information: Also Campus universitaire francophone in Brazzaville, in collaboration with the Agence Universitaire Francophone (AUF)

History: Founded 1959 as Centre d'Etudes administratives et techniques supérieures. Previously formed part of the Fondation de l'Enseignement supérieur en Afrique centrale. Became Université de Brazzaville 1971, acquired present title 1977.

Academic Year: October to July (October-February; March-July)

Admission Requirements: Secondary school certificate (baccalauréat) or equivalent. Competitive entrance examination for schools and institutes and the faculty of health sciences

Fees: (CFA Francs): Licence (Bachelor): 7750; Master: 28,500; Doctorate: 50,000; Foreign students: Bachelor: 149,500; Master: 175,000; Doctorate 200,000

Main Language(s) of Instruction: French

Accrediting Agency: Conseil Africain et Malgache pour l'enseignement Supérieur (CAMES)

Degrees and Diplomas: *Licence*; *Master*; *Doctorat*: **Medicine.**

Student Services: Health Services, Sports Facilities

Publications: Revue médicale du Congo

Academic Staff *2011-2012*	MEN	WOMEN	**TOTAL**
FULL-TIME	511	58	**569**
PART-TIME	1,080	109	**1,189**
STAFF WITH DOCTORATE			
FULL-TIME	471	50	**521**
Student Numbers *2011-2012*			
All (Foreign included)	–	–	**26,166**

Last Updated: 31/05/12

Congo (Democratic Republic)

STRUCTURE OF HIGHER EDUCATION SYSTEM

Description:

Higher education is provided by both public and private institutions. Higher education is composed of universities, higher teacher training institutes and higher technological institutes. It comes under the authority of the Ministry of Higher Education. Each institution has a University or Institute Council, an Administrative Committee, faculties (or sections) and departments.

Stages of studies:

University level first stage: *Premier cycle*
The first stage of higher education lasts for three years and leads to the Graduat.

University level second stage: *Deuxième cycle*
The second cycle lasts for two years and grants the Licence, except in Medicine and Veterinary Medicine where this stage lasts for three years and leads to the title of Docteur en Médecine and Docteur en Médecine vétérinaire.

University level third stage: *Troisième cycle*
The third cycle mainly consists in a programme of higher studies leading to the Diplôme d'Etudes supérieures (DES). This programme lasts for two years and includes a certain number of courses and seminars, as well as the presentation of a dissertation. After obtaining the DES, the candidate can register in a doctoral programme and prepare the thesis. The next stage leads to the Doctorate which is conferred after a further four to seven years' further study.

ADMISSION TO HIGHER EDUCATION

Admission to university-level studies:

Name of secondary school credential required: Diplôme d'Etat d'Etudes secondaires du Cycle long
Admission requirements: Entrance examination.

Foreign students admission:

Admission requirements: Students must hold a diploma giving access to higher education in their country of origin.
Entry regulations: Students must ask for a visa at the Embassy of their country.
Language proficiency: Students must have a good knowledge of French. Those who wish to improve their knowledge of French may follow courses in learning centres.

NATIONAL BODIES

Ministère de l'Enseignement supérieur (Ministry of Higher Education)

Minister: Theophile Mbemba Fundu
PO Box 5429
Av. des Forces Armées N.10
Kinshasa/Gombe

Présidence des Universités du Congo (Presidence of the Universities of the Congo)

PO Box 13399
Kinshasa 1
Tel: +243(99) 18198
EMail: caurdcg@hotmail.com

Réseau UNESCO de Bibliothèques Associées (UNESCO Network of Associated Libraries)
Bibliothécaire en chef, l'Université Pédagogique Nationale: Bongangi Bo-Louka M.B.
Chargé des rélations internationales: Kabongo Celestin
Université Pédagogique Nationale (UPN), Kinshasa-Binza
BP 8 815
Kinshasa
Tel: +243(81) 3536369
EMail: bbongangi@yahoo.fr

Data for academic year: 2012-2013
Source: IAU from World Data on Education 2010-2011, UNESCO-IBE, 2012. Bodies 2016.

INSTITUTIONS

PUBLIC INSTITUTIONS

ACADEMY OF FINE ARTS

Académie des Beaux-Arts (ABA)
Avenue du 24 novembre, Gombe, Kinshasa 8249
Tel: +243 8989 20686
EMail: ademieba@yahoo.fr

Directeur Général: Patrick Missassi (2012-)
EMail: patrickmissassi@yahoo.fr

Department
Ceramics (Ceramic Art); **Interior Architecture** (Architecture; Interior Design); **Metal Work** (Interior Design); **Painting** (Painting and Drawing); **Sculpture** (Sculpture); **Visual Communication** (Communication Disorders)

History: Founded 1943 as Ecole Saint Luc. Acquired present status and title 1957.

Main Language(s) of Instruction: French

Degrees and Diplomas: *Graduat*. Also 2nd cycle studies

Student Numbers *2010-2011*: Total 1,543
Last Updated: 02/10/12

INFORMATION AND COMMUNICATION SCIENCES UNIVERSITY COLLEGE

Institut Facultaire des Sciences de l'Information et de la Communication (IFASIC)
B.P. 14 998, Kinshasa I
Tel: +243(12) 25117 +243 810-305-975
EMail: ifasicongo@yahoo.fr

Recteur: Jean Lucien Kitima Kasendwe
Tel: +234(99) 959-934 EMail: jeanlucienkit@yahoo.fr

Secrétaire Académique: Emmanuel Mwangaliwa

International Relations: Vivien Nzikani Tel: +243(99) 8265-845

Faculty
Communication Studies (Communication Studies); **Information and Multimedia** (Information Technology; Multimedia)

Research Centre
Communication Studies *(CECOM)* (Communication Studies)

History: Founded 1973 as Institut supérieur des Techniques de l'Information. Acquired present status and title 1997.

Main Language(s) of Instruction: French

Accrediting Agency: Ministère de l'Enseignement Supérieur et Universitaire

Degrees and Diplomas: *Graduat*; *Licence*; *Diplôme d'Etudes supérieures*; *Doctorat*

Student Services: Academic Counselling, Canteen, Sports Facilities

Publications: Cahier Congolais de Communication

Student Numbers *2010-2011*: Total 3,761
Last Updated: 10/10/12

INSTITUTE OF AGRONOMY OF YANGAMBI

Institut Facultaire des Sciences Agronomiques de Yangambi (IFA/YANGAMBI)
BP 28, Yangambi, Province Orientale
Tel: +243(99) 8539-647

Recteur: Richard Risasi Etutu EMail: ifarectorat@yahoo.fr

Faculty
Agronomy (Agronomy)

Further Information: Campus temporarily in Kisangani.

History: Founded 1976.

Main Language(s) of Instruction: French

Degrees and Diplomas: *Graduat*; *Licence*; *Diplôme d'Etudes supérieures*; *Doctorat*

Student Numbers *2010-2011*: Total 625
Last Updated: 09/10/12

INSTITUTE OF APPLIED TECHNIQUES

Institut Supérieur des Techniques Appliquées (ISTA/KIN)
BP 6593, Kinshasa 31
Tel: +243 810836280
EMail: ista-kin@yahoo.fr
Website: http://www.ista.ac.cd/

Directeur général: Pierre Motumbe Kasengedia

Programme
Civil Aviation (Aeronautical and Aerospace Engineering); **Computer Engineering** (Computer Engineering); **Electronic Engineering** (Electronic Engineering); **Industrial Electrical Engineering** (Electrical Engineering; Industrial Engineering); **Mechanical Engineering** (Mechanical Engineering); **Meteorology** (Meteorology); **Telecommunications** (Telecommunications Engineering)

Further Information: Branches in Kolwezi; Goma; Ebonda

History: Founded 1971 as Institut Météorologique, d'Aviation Civile et de Télécommunications (IMAT). Acquired present status and title 1973.

Main Language(s) of Instruction: French

Accrediting Agency: Ministère de l'Enseignement Supérieur et Universitaire

Degrees and Diplomas: *Graduat*; *Licence*

Student Numbers *2010-2011*: Total 10,440
Last Updated: 05/11/12

INSTITUTE OF ARCHITECTURE AND URBANISM

Institut Supérieur d'Architecture et d'Urbanisme (ISAU)

Gombe, Kinshasa
EMail: isaugombe@yahoo.fr

Principal: Martin Tshisuaka
Tel: +243(99) 992-6821 EMail: tnkza@yahoo.fr

Secrétaire Général: René Bias Mpuru Tel: +243(99) 8173-334

International Relations: Christopher Mbolela Ngoie
Tel: +243(99) 0167-992

Department
Architecture (Architecture); **Urbanism** (Town Planning; Urban Studies)

History: Created 2010 further to the split with Institut du Bâtiment et des Travaux Publics.

Admission Requirements: Diplôme d'Etat or equivalent

Main Language(s) of Instruction: French

Accrediting Agency: Ministère de l'Enseignement Supérieur et Universitaire

Degrees and Diplomas: *Licence*: **Architecture; Urban Studies.**

Student Services: Academic Counselling, Careers Guidance, Language Laboratory, Sports Facilities

Publications: First Semester; Second Semester

Publishing House: University Press of Congo (P.U.C.)

Academic Staff *2011-2012*	MEN	WOMEN	TOTAL
FULL-TIME	61	2	**63**
PART-TIME	5	–	**5**
Student Numbers *2011-2012*			
All (Foreign included)	1,676	89	**1,765**
FOREIGN ONLY	21	–	**21**

Last Updated: 30/07/12

INSTITUTE OF COMMERCE OF KINSHASA

Institut Supérieur de Commerce de Kinshasa (ISC)

BP 16596, Kinshasa-Gombe I
Tel: +243(898) 109-143 +243(899) 438-957
Fax: +243(99) 13771
Website: http://iscetudiants.com

Directeur général: Albert Kabamba Mueu

Programme
Business Computing (Computer Engineering); **Commerce and Finance** (Accountancy; Business and Commerce; Finance; Marketing); **Management** (Management); **Secretarial Studies** (Secretarial Studies)

Research Centre
Interdisciplinary Research in Management and Development *(Interdisciplinary)*

History: Founded 1964. Acquired present status and title 1981.

Main Language(s) of Instruction: French

Accrediting Agency: Ministère de l'Enseignement Supérieur et Universitaire

Degrees and Diplomas: *Graduat*; *Licence*

Student Numbers *2010-2011*: Total 19,600
Last Updated: 10/10/12

INSTITUTE OF RURAL DEVELOPMENT OF TSHIBASHI

Institut Supérieur de Développement rural de Tshibashi (ISDR/TSHIBASHI)

BP 70, Kananga, Kasaï Occidental
Tel: +243 81 604 12 98

Directeur général: Abbé Modeste Bukasa Tubadikubub
Tel: +243(81) 604-1298 EMail: bukamul@yahoo.fr

Programme
Regional Planning (Regional Planning); **Rural Management** (Rural Planning); **Social Organizations** (Social Sciences)

History: Founded 1982.

Main Language(s) of Instruction: French

Accrediting Agency: Ministère de l'Enseignement Supérieur et Universitaire

Degrees and Diplomas: *Graduat*: **Architecture and Planning.** *Licence*: **Architecture and Planning.**

Last Updated: 10/10/12

INSTITUTE OF SOCIAL STUDIES OF LUBUMBASHI

Institut Supérieur d'Etudes sociales de Lubumbashi (ISES)

BP 1575, Lubumbashi, Katanga

Directeur général: Médard Kayamba Badye

Programme
Community Development (Development Studies); **Human Resources Management** (Human Resources); **Industrial Sociology** (Sociology); **Social Studies** (Social Studies)

History: Founded 1971. Acquired present status and title 1981.

Main Language(s) of Instruction: French

Accrediting Agency: Ministère de l'Enseignement Supérieur et Universitaire

Degrees and Diplomas: *Graduat*; *Licence*

Last Updated: 10/10/12

INSTITUTE OF STATISTICS OF KINSHASA

Institut Supérieur de Statistique de Kinshasa (ISS)

BP 1757 No 1, 6105 bd Sendwe - Commune de Kalamu, Kinshasa I
EMail: isskin@yahoo.fr

Directeur général: Rugishi Muhindo Gyenano

Programme
Business Computing (Business Computing); **Commerce and Finance** (Business and Commerce; Finance); **Documentation** (Documentation Techniques); **Statistics** (Statistics)

History: Founded 1965 as Institut d'études du développement économique et social (I.E.D.E.S.). Acquired present status and title 1974.

Main Language(s) of Instruction: French

Accrediting Agency: Ministère de l'Enseignement Supérieur et Universitaire

Degrees and Diplomas: *Graduat*; *Licence*

Student Numbers *2010-2011*: Total 2,280
Last Updated: 10/10/12

INSTITUTE OF STATISTICS OF LUBUMBASHI

Institut Supérieur de Statistique de Lubumbashi (ISS/LUBUMBASHI)

BP 2471, Lubumbashi
Website: http://www.iss-lubumbashi.org/issl/

Directeur général: Lunda-wa-Ngoyi Mutonkole

Secrétaire général académique: Saïdi Mpungu Mulenda

Department
Applied Demography (Demography and Population); **Business and Finance** (Accountancy; Marketing); **Business Computing** (Business Computing); **Statistics** (Statistics)

History: Founded 1971. Acquired present status and title 1981.

Main Language(s) of Instruction: French

Degrees and Diplomas: *Graduat*; *Licence*. Also Diplôme d'Etudes Approfondies (DEA).

Last Updated: 05/11/12

NATIONAL INSTITUTE OF ARTS

Institut National des Arts (INA)
BP 8332, Kinshasa

Directeur général: André Yoka Iye Mudaba (2012-)

Programme

Leisure Activities; **Music** (Music); **Theatre** (Theatre)

History: Founded 1971. Acquired present status and title 1981.

Accrediting Agency: Ministère de l'Enseignement Supérieur et Universitaire

Degrees and Diplomas: *Graduat*; *Licence*

Student Numbers *2010-2011*: Total 764
Last Updated: 10/10/12

NATIONAL INSTITUTE OF CIVIL AND CONSTRUCTION ENGINEERING

Institut National du Bâtiment et des Travaux publics (INBTP)
Avenue de la Montagne n°21, Q. Joli Parc, Ngaliema, Kinshasa
Tel: +243(99) 824 5073
EMail: info@inbtp.cd
Website: http://inbtp.cd/v22/

Directeur général: Lutimba Hubert Makengo (2012-)
Tel: +243(99) 99 26 821
EMail: dg@inbtp.cd; makengo238@yahoo.fr

Section

Architecture (Architecture); **Building Engineering** (Building Technologies; Engineering); **Topography** (Surveying and Mapping); **Town Planning** (Town Planning)

History: Founded 1971 following the merger of the Institut National du Bâtiment et des Travaux Publics, the Institut Supérieur des Géomètres Experts Immobiliers and the Institut Supérieur d'Architecture. Formerly Institut du Bâtiment et des Travaux Publics (IBTP) further to the split with the Institut Supérieur d'Architecture et d'Urbanisme (ISAU). Acquired present status 2010.

Main Language(s) of Instruction: French

Degrees and Diplomas: *Licence*: **Architecture; Civil Engineering; Surveying and Mapping; Town Planning.**

Student Services: Academic Counselling, Careers Guidance, Cultural Activities, Health Services, Social Counselling, Sports Facilities

Student Numbers *2010-2011*: Total 3,539
Last Updated: 05/10/12

NATIONAL PEDAGOGICAL UNIVERSITY

Université pédagogique nationale (UPN)
BP 8815, Quartier Binza, Kinshasa I
Tel: +243(1) 513-1815
EMail: rectorat_upn@upn.ac.cd
Website: http://www.upn.ac.cd/upn/

Recteur: Edouard Tshisungu
Tel: +243(8) 1607-3641
EMail: edouard.tshisungu_upn@upn.ac.cd

Administrative Officer: Clement Kasinga
Tel: +243(9) 9998-3070
EMail: clemence.kasinga_upn@upn.ac.cd

International Relations: Frederic Kasongo - Amunda, Directeur Chef de Service de la Coopération interuniversitaire
Tel: +243(8) 9771-5563
EMail: Frederic.kasongo_upn@upn.ac.cd

Faculty

Agronomy (Agricultural Education; Agronomy); **Arts and Humanities** (African Studies; Communication Studies; English; Foreign Languages Education; French; History; Humanities and Social Science Education; Information Sciences; Latin; Philosophy; Romance Languages; Translation and Interpretation); **Economics and Management** (Business Administration; Business and Commerce; Economics; Management); **Psychology and Education Sciences** (Educational Administration; Educational and Student Counselling; Educational Psychology; Educational Sciences); **Science** (Applied Physics; Biological and Life Sciences; Chemistry; Dietetics; Environmental Management; Geography; Health Sciences; Hotel and Restaurant; Laboratory Techniques; Mathematical Physics; Mathematics; Mathematics and Computer Science; Medical Technology; Nursing; Nutrition; Physical Education; Physical Therapy; Science Education; Sports Management; Technology; Tourism); **Social, Political, and Administrative Sciences** (Administration; Anthropology; International Relations; Political Sciences; Sociology); **Veterinary Medicine** (Veterinary Science)

Bureau

Doctoral Studies

Chair

Education Sciences for Central Africa - Kinshasa Branch *(UNESCO)* (Educational Sciences)

History: Founded 1961 as Institut pédagogique national de Kinshasa. Acquired present title and status 2005.

Admission Requirements: High school diploma

Fees: (CDF): 211,600.00 per annum (US$ 230.00)

Main Language(s) of Instruction: French

Accrediting Agency: Ministère de l'Enseignement Supérieur et Universitaire

Degrees and Diplomas: *Graduat*; *Licence*; *Diplôme d'Etudes supérieures*; *Doctorat*

Student Services: Academic Counselling, Canteen, Careers Guidance, Cultural Activities, Health Services, Language Laboratory, Social Counselling, Sports Facilities

Publications: CERUPN Review

Academic Staff *2011-2012*	MEN	WOMEN	**TOTAL**
FULL-TIME	222	15	**237**
STAFF WITH DOCTORATE			
FULL-TIME	21	13	**34**
Student Numbers *2011-2012*			
All (Foreign included)	7,672	5,078	**12,750**
FOREIGN ONLY	391	187	**578**

Last Updated: 24/05/12

OFFICIAL UNIVERSITY OF BUKAVU

Université Officielle de Bukavu (UOB)
B.P. 570, Bukavu, Sud-Kivu
Tel: +243 99 70 30 648
EMail: univoffbukavu@yahoo.fr
Website: http://www.univoffbukavu.ac.cd/

Recteur: Jean de Dieu Byamungu Bin-Rusangiza

Faculty

Economics and Management (Economics; Finance; Management); **Law** (Private Law; Public Law); **Letters and Humanities** (English Studies; French Studies; Philosophy); **Medicine and Pharmacy** (Biomedicine; Pharmacy; Public Health); **Science and Applied Sciences** (Biology; Geology); **Social, Political and Administrative Sciences** (Administration; International Studies; Political Sciences; Sociology)

School

Mining (Mining Engineering)

History: Founded 1993 as Centre universitaire de Bukavu. Acquired present status 1997.

Admission Requirements: Secondary school credential (Diplôme de fin d'études secondaires) or equivalent

Main Language(s) of Instruction: French

Accrediting Agency: Ministère de l'Enseignement Supérieur et Universitaire

Degrees and Diplomas: *Graduat*; *Licence*; *Diplôme d'Etudes supérieures*

Student Services: Academic Counselling, Social Counselling
Last Updated: 10/10/12

PEDAGOGICAL AND TECHNICAL INSTITUTE OF KINSHASA

Institut Supérieur Pédagogique et Technique de Kinshasa (ISPT/KIN)
BP 3287, Kinshasa

Directeur général: Désiré-Didier Tengeneza Baguma

Programme
Electrical and Mechanical Engineering (Electrical Engineering; Mechanical Engineering); **Electrical and Technical Studies** (Electrical Engineering; Technology); **Electrical Engineering** (Electrical Engineering); **Electronic Engineering** (Electronic Engineering); **Mechanical Engineering**

History: Founded 1976.

Main Language(s) of Instruction: French

Accrediting Agency: Ministère de l'Enseignement Supérieur et Universitaire

Degrees and Diplomas: *Graduat*; *Licence*

Student Numbers *2010-2011*: Total 652
Last Updated: 05/11/12

PEDAGOGICAL INSTITUTE OF BUKAVU

Institut Supérieur Pédagogique de Bukavu (ISP/BUKAVU)
BP 854, Bukavu, Sud-Kivu
EMail: ispcg_ceruki@yahoo.fr
Website: http://www.ispbukavu.net/

Directeur général: Boniface Kaningini Mwenyimali
EMail: dg@ispbukavu.net

Section
Arts and Humanities (African Languages; African Studies; English; French; History; Pedagogy; Social Sciences); **Business, Administrative and Computer Sciences** (Business and Commerce; Computer Engineering); **Exact Sciences** (Biology; Chemistry; Geography; Geology; Health Sciences; Mathematics; Natural Sciences; Physics)

Further Information: Branches in Rutshuru and Kindu

History: Founded 1961. Acquired present status and title 1981.

Main Language(s) of Instruction: French

Accrediting Agency: Ministère de l'Enseignement Supérieur et Universitaire

Degrees and Diplomas: *Graduat*; *Licence*

Student Services: Sports Facilities

Last Updated: 05/11/12

PEDAGOGICAL INSTITUTE OF KANANGA

Institut Supérieur Pédagogique de Kananga (ISP/KANANGA)
BP 282, Kananga, Kasaï-Occidental

Directeur général: Pierre Tshimbombo Mudiba

School
Arts and Social Sciences (Administration; African Studies; Business and Commerce; English; French; History; Latin; Linguistics; Social Sciences); **Exact Sciences** (Agronomy; Biology; Chemistry; Geography; Mathematics; Natural Sciences; Physics; Technology; Veterinary Science)

History: Founded 1958 as Ecole Normale. Acquired present status and title 1981.

Main Language(s) of Instruction: French

Accrediting Agency: Ministère de l'Enseignement Supérieur et Universitaire

Degrees and Diplomas: *Graduat*; *Licence*

Last Updated: 05/11/12

PEDAGOGICAL INSTITUTE OF LA GOMBE

Institut Supérieur Pédagogique de La Gombe (ISP/GOMBE)
BP 3580, Croisement des Avenues Père Boka et Kisangani/Gombe, Kinshasa
Tel: +243(15) 125-331
EMail: contact@ispgombe.net
Website: http://ispgombe.com/accueil.html

Directeur général: Valentin Matumele Maliya
Tel: +243 999-953-935

Secrétaire Général Académique: Emilienne Akonga Edumbe
Tel: +243 815-170-299

Section
Arts and Humanities (African Languages; Arts and Humanities; English; French; History; Pedagogy; Psychology); **Business and Computer Sciences** (Business and Commerce; Computer Science; Hotel Management; Tourism); **Exact Sciences** (Biology; Geography)

History: Founded 1961 by Catholic Sisters to promote women's level of education. Acquired present status and title 1981.

Admission Requirements: Secondary school certificate (state diploma)

Main Language(s) of Instruction: French, English

Accrediting Agency: Ministère de l'Enseignement Supérieur et Universitaire

Degrees and Diplomas: *Graduat*; *Licence*

Student Services: Academic Counselling, Careers Guidance, Cultural Activities, Health Services, Sports Facilities

Publications: Les cahiers de l'ISP/Gombe

Student Numbers *2010-2011*: Total 6,123
Last Updated: 05/11/12

PEDAGOGICAL INSTITUTE OF LUBUMBASHI

Institut Supérieur Pédagogique de Lubumbashi (ISP/LUBUMBASHI)
BP 1796/L'Shi, Lubumbashi
Website: http://isplubum.wordpress.com/

Directeur général: Lukoba Chabala

Section
Arts and Humanities (African Studies; English; French; History; Latin; Social Sciences); **Exact Sciences** (Agronomy; Biology; Chemistry; Computer Science; Geography; Mathematics; Natural Sciences; Physical Education; Physics; Veterinary Science)

Research Centre
Teacher Training (*C.R.A.P.*) (Teacher Training)

History: Founded 1959. Acquired present status and title 1981.

Main Language(s) of Instruction: French

Accrediting Agency: Ministère de l'Enseignement Supérieur et Universitaire

Degrees and Diplomas: *Graduat*; *Licence*

Student Numbers *2010-2011*: Total 309
Last Updated: 05/11/12

PEDAGOGICAL INSTITUTE OF MBANZA-NGUNGU

Institut Supérieur Pédagogique de Mbanza-Ngungu (ISP/MBANZA-NGUNGU)
BP 127, Mbanza-Ngungu, Bas Congo
EMail: ispmbngu@yahoo.fr

Directeur général: Pierre Ntiama Nsiku
Tel: +243(81) 5253-609 EMail: ispmbngu@yahoo.fr

Secrétaire général administratif: Pambu Ntima
Tel: +243(81) 5097-956

Secrétaire général académique: Wamuini Nkayilakio
Tel: +243(81) 1726-665

Section
Arts and Social Sciences (African Studies; English; French; History; Latin; Social Sciences); **Exact Sciences** (Biology; Chemistry; Computer Science; Electronic Engineering; Mathematics; Physics; Technology); **Technical Sciences** (Agriculture; Business and Commerce; Veterinary Science)

History: Founded 1981.

Admission Requirements: Secondary school certificate (state diploma)

Fees: (US Dollars): 500 per annum

Main Language(s) of Instruction: French

Accrediting Agency: Ministère de l'Enseignement Supérieur et Universitaire

Degrees and Diplomas: *Graduat*; *Licence*

Student Services: Academic Counselling, Health Services, Sports Facilities

Publications: Scientia - Revue de Sciences, Lettres et Pédagogie appliquée

Student Numbers *2010-2011*: Total 950

PEDAGOGICAL INSTITUTE OF MBUJI-MAYI

Institut Supérieur Pédagogique de Mbuji-Mayi (ISP/MBUJI-MAYI)

BP 682, Mbuji-Mayi, Kasaï-Oriental
EMail: sgacispmjm@yahoo.fr

Directeur général: wa Badinga Astrid Nseya (2009-)
Tel: +243(99) 7684 238 EMail: musampanseya@yahoo.fr

Secrétaire général académique: Nzeji Jean Willy Biayi
Tel: +243(81) 5074 575 EMail: jeanwillybiayi@yahoo.fr

Section
Arts and Humanities (African Studies; Arts and Humanities; Business and Commerce; English; French; History; Latin; Linguistics; Pedagogy; Psychology); **Exact Sciences** (Biology; Chemistry; Geography; Mathematics; Natural Sciences; Physics)

History: Founded 1968. Acquired present status and title 1981.

Academic Year: October to July

Admission Requirements: High or Secondary School certificate (Diplôme d'Etat)

Main Language(s) of Instruction: French

Accrediting Agency: Ministère de l'Enseignement Supérieur et Universitaire

Degrees and Diplomas: *Graduat*; *Licence*

Student Services: Academic Counselling, Language Laboratory, Nursery Care, Social Counselling

Publications: Annales de l'ISP de Mbujimayi; Collection Travaux et Recherche

Publishing House: Candip/ISP

Student Numbers *2010-2011*: Total 1,100
Last Updated: 05/11/12

PEDAGOGICAL INSTITUTE OF MUHANGI AT BUTEMBO

Institut Supérieur Pédagogique de Muhangi à Butembo (ISP/MUHANGI)

BP 380, Butembo, Nord-Kivu
Tel: +243(99) 7623-482
EMail: ispmuhangi@yahoo.fr

Directeur général: Alphonsine Kakuhi Kaswera
Tel: +243(99) 7235-239

Section
Arts and Humanities (African Languages; African Studies; Arts and Humanities; Educational Psychology; English; French; History; Latin; Linguistics); **Business Administration** (Business and Commerce; Business Computing; Information Technology; Management); **Exact Sciences** (Biology; Chemistry; Environmental Studies; Geography; Mathematics; Physics)

History: Founded 1993. Acquired public status 2004.

Main Language(s) of Instruction: French, English

Accrediting Agency: Ministère de l'Enseignement Supérieur et Universitaire

Degrees and Diplomas: *Graduat*; *Licence*

Student Services: Sports Facilities

Student Numbers *2010-2011*: Total 649
Last Updated: 05/11/12

UNIVERSITY OF KINSHASA

Université de Kinshasa (UNIKIN)

B.P. 190, Kinshasa 11
Tel: +243(12) 27793
Fax: +243(12) 21360
EMail: centreinfo@ic.cd
Website: http://www.unikin.cd/

Recteur: Jean Berchmans Labana Lasay' abar
Tel: +243(15) 11 61 85
EMail: rectorat@unikin.cd; labanafr@yahoo.fr

Faculty
Agronomy (Agronomy); **Economics** (Economics); **Law** (Law); **Literature and Humanities** (Humanities and Social Science Education; Literature); **Medicine** (Dentistry; Medicine); **Pharmacy** (Pharmacy); **Polytechnic** (Civil Engineering; Engineering; Technology); **Psychology** (Psychology); **Science** (Mathematics and Computer Science; Natural Sciences); **Social, Political Sciences and Administration** *(SSPA)* (Administration; Political Sciences; Social Sciences)

School
Public Health *(ESP)* (Public Health); **Tropical Forest Management** *(ERAIFT)* (Forest Management; Tropical Agriculture)

History: Founded 1954 as Université Lovanium, became a campus of the Université nationale du Zaïre 1971. Acquired present status and title 1981. A State institution.

Academic Year: October to June (October-February; February-June)

Admission Requirements: Secondary school certificate and entrance examination

Main Language(s) of Instruction: French

Accrediting Agency: Ministère de l'Enseignement Supérieur et Universitaire

Degrees and Diplomas: *Graduat*; *Docteur en Médecine*; *Licence*: **Civil Engineering; Economics; Law.** *Diplôme d'Etudes supérieures*: **Law.** *Doctorat*: **Economics; Pharmacy.**

Publications: Annales of the Faculties of Science, Polytechnic and Pharmacy; Cahiers économiques et sociaux des Religions africaines

Publishing House: Presses universitaires de l'Université de Kinshasa

Student Numbers *2010-2011*: Total 26,000
Last Updated: 10/10/12

UNIVERSITY OF KISANGANI

Université de Kisangani (UNIKIS)

B.P. 2012, Kisangani, Province Orientale
Tel: +243(21) 1335
EMail: unikis2005@yahoo.fr
Website: http://www.unikis.ac.cd/index.php

Recteur: Faustin Toengaho Lokundo
EMail: faustintoengaho@yahoo.fr

Faculty
Agronomy (Forest Management; Water Science); **Economics and Management** (Economics; Management); **Law** (Law; Private Law; Public Law); **Literature and Humanities** (African Studies; Communication Studies; English Studies; French Studies; History; Information Sciences; Philosophy); **Medicine** (Biomedical Engineering; Dermatology; Gynaecology and Obstetrics; Medicine; Nutrition; Paediatrics; Public Health; Stomatology); **Psychology and Education Sciences** (Educational Sciences; Psychology);

Science (Biochemistry; Biology; Ecology; Natural Sciences); **Social Sciences, Administration, and Political Science** (Administration; International Relations; Political Sciences; Social Sciences; Sociology)

History: Founded 1963 as Université libre du Congo, became a campus of the Université nationale du Zaïre 1971. Acquired present status and title 1981. A State institution.

Academic Year: October to July (October-February; February-July)

Admission Requirements: Secondary school certificate and entrance examination

Main Language(s) of Instruction: French

Accrediting Agency: Ministère de l'Enseignement Supérieur et Universitaire

Degrees and Diplomas: *Graduat*; *Docteur en Médecine*; *Licence*: **Administration; Education; Psychology; Sociology.** *Diplôme d'Etudes supérieures*: **Pedagogy; Psychology.** *Doctorat*: **Pedagogy; Psychology; Sociology.**

Student Numbers *2010-2011*: Total 8,333

Last Updated: 10/10/12

UNIVERSITY OF LUBUMBASHI

Université de Lubumbashi (UNILU)

BP 1825, Lubumbashi, Shaba

Tel: +243 9970 33047 +243 9930 08316

Fax: +243(22) 8099

EMail: secretariat.rectorat@unilu.ac.cd

Website: http://www.unilu.ac.cd

Recteur: Chabu Mumba (2008-)
Tel: +243 9970 26956 EMail: chabu.mumba@unilu.ac.cd

Secretary-General: Nkiko Munya Rugero
Tel: +243 8105 12043 EMail: nkikodismas@yahoo.fr

International Relations: Lubala Toto, Directeur à la Coopération
Tel: +243 9970 23164 EMail: lubala.toto@unilu.ac.cd

Faculty

Agronomy (Agronomy); **Arts and Humanities** (Advertising and Publicity; African Languages; African Studies; Ancient Civilizations; English; English Studies; French; French Studies; History; Information Sciences; Journalism; Latin; Linguistics; Literature; Performing Arts; Philosophy; Translation and Interpretation); **Economics and Management** (Demography and Population; Economics; Management); **Law** (Commercial Law; Law; Private Law; Public Law); **Medicine** (Biomedicine; Gynaecology and Obstetrics; Medicine; Paediatrics; Pharmacy; Public Health; Surgery); **Polytechnic** (Electronic Engineering; Industrial Chemistry; Mechanical Engineering; Metallurgical Engineering; Mining Engineering); **Psychology and Educational Sciences** (Educational Sciences; Psychology); **Science** (Chemistry; Geography; Geology; Mathematics); **Social, Political, and Administrative Sciences** (Administration; Anthropology; International Relations; Political Sciences; Sociology); **Veterinary Medicine** (Veterinary Science)

School

Criminology (Criminology); **Industrial Engineering** *(ESI)* (Chemical Engineering; Construction Engineering; Electrical Engineering; Electronic Engineering; Inorganic Chemistry; Laboratory Techniques; Mechanical Engineering; Mining Engineering; Organic Chemistry); **Tourism** (Hotel and Restaurant; Hotel Management; Tourism)

Further Information: Campuses in Kamina, Likasi, Kolwesi and Kasumbalesa

History: Founded 1955 as Université officielle du Congo-Belge et du Ruanda-Urundi, became a campus of the Université nationale du Zaïre 1971, and acquired present status and title 1981. A State institution.

Academic Year: October to July

Admission Requirements: Diplôme d'Etat d'études secondaires (secondary school certificate); applicants with less than 60% in the secondary school certificate are admitted by cometetive exam.

Fees: (CDF): 297,000.00 per annum, first year; 207,000.00 other years

Main Language(s) of Instruction: French

Accrediting Agency: Ministère de l'Enseignement Supérieur et Universitaire

Degrees and Diplomas: *Graduat*; *Licence*; *Doctorat*. Also Diplôme d'Etudes Approfondies (DEA).

Student Services: Academic Counselling, Cultural Activities, Health Services, Language Laboratory, Nursery Care, Social Counselling, Sports Facilities

Academic Staff *2011-2012*	MEN	WOMEN	**TOTAL**
FULL-TIME	838	85	**923**
STAFF WITH DOCTORATE			
FULL-TIME	213	58	**271**
Student Numbers *2011-2012*			
All (Foreign included)	20,054	6,362	**26,416**
FOREIGN ONLY	19	14	**33**

Last Updated: 10/06/13

UNIVERSITY OF MBANDAKA

Université de Mbandaka (UNIMBA)

B.P. 10, Avenue Revolution - Quartier Mbandaka 2, Mbandaka, Equateur

EMail: unimba.2009@yahoo.fr

Recteur: Bernard Ilinga Lopaka

Faculty

Economic and Social Sciences (Economics; Social Sciences); **Law** (Law); **Medicine** (Medicine); **Social, Political and Administrative Sciences** (Administration; Political Sciences; Social Sciences)

History: Founded 2004. Acquired present status and title 2010.

Main Language(s) of Instruction: French

Accrediting Agency: Ministère de l'Enseignement Supérieur et Universitaire

Degrees and Diplomas: *Graduat*; *Licence*; *Diplôme d'Etudes supérieures*

Student Numbers *2010-2011*: Total 1,824

Last Updated: 06/11/12

UNIVERSITY OF UÉLÉ

Université de l'Uélé (UNIUELE)

Avenue de Langues 45, B.P. 670, Isiro, Province Orientale

Tel: +243 81 81 40 679

Website: http://uniuele.net/

Recteur: Roger Gaise
Tel: +243 818140679 EMail: gaiseroger@yahoo.fr

Faculty

Agronomy (Agronomy); **Economics** (Economics); **Law** (Law); **Social, Political and Administrative Sciences** (Administration; Political Sciences; Social Sciences)

History: Founded 1998.

Main Language(s) of Instruction: French

Accrediting Agency: Ministère de l'Enseignement Supérieur et Universitaire

Degrees and Diplomas: *Graduat*: **Agronomy; Economics.** *Licence*: **Economics.** Also Diplôme d'Etudes Approfondies (DEA).

Student Numbers *2010-2011*: Total 720

Last Updated: 10/10/12

PRIVATE INSTITUTIONS

ADVENTIST UNIVERSITY OF LUKANGA

Université Adventiste de Lukanga (UNILUK)

BP 180 Butembo Territoire de Lubero, (à 40 km de Butembo), Lukanga, Nord-Kivu

Tel: +243 998 606 216; +243 998 384 565

EMail: amirgulzar2000@hotmail.com

Website: http://www.uniluk.org

Recteur: Paul Kakule Mithimbo EMail: kakmithimbo@yahoo.fr

Faculty
Arts (Literature); **Economics and Management** (Economics; Management); **Medicine** (Medicine); **Psychology and Educational Sciences** (Educational Sciences; Psychology); **Theology** (Theology)

History: Founded 1996.

Main Language(s) of Instruction: French

Accrediting Agency: Ministère de l'Enseignement Supérieur et Universitaire

Degrees and Diplomas: *Graduat*; *Licence*
Last Updated: 29/10/12

BEL CAMPUS TECHNOLOGICAL UNIVERSITY

Université Technologique Bel Campus (UTBC)
8ème Rue Limete, Quartier Industriel, Kinshasa
Tel: +243 9982 19098
EMail: belcampus@yahoo.fr

Recteur: Albert Essanga Tolongo (2008-)

Faculty
Computer Management (Computer Networks; Information Management; Information Sciences); **Economics and Management** (Business Administration; Economics; International Economics; Management); **Law** (Law; Private Law; Public Law); **Medicine** (Medicine); **Social, Political and Administrative Sciences** (Administration; Information Sciences; International Relations; Political Sciences; Social Sciences)

Research Centre
Recherche Interdisciplinaire pour le Développement Economique et Sociale *(CRDES)*

History: Founded 1996.

Admission Requirements: State Diploma with at least 60% mark

Main Language(s) of Instruction: French

Accrediting Agency: Ministère de l'Enseignement Supérieur et Universitaire

Degrees and Diplomas: *Graduat*; *Docteur en Médecine*; *Licence*

Student Services: Academic Counselling, Cultural Activities, Sports Facilities
Last Updated: 31/10/12

CARDINAL MALULA CHRISTIAN UNIVERSITY

Université chrétienne Cardinal Malula (UCCM)
BP 10.883, Saio no 2317/bis Q/IEM, Commune de Kasa-Vubu, Kinshasa
Tel: +243(81) 9905-188
Fax: +243(89) 5127-659
EMail: lspluc@yahoo.fr

Recteur: Alexis-Bruno Tshibalabala Kankolongo (2011-)

Faculty
Arts (Arts and Humanities); **Economics and Management** (Economics; Management); **International Relations** (International Relations); **Law** (Law); **Philosophy and Humanities** (Arts and Humanities; Philosophy); **Social Sciences** (Social Sciences)

History: Founded 1984 by Biangany Emmanuel. Acquired present status 2006. Formerly known as University Institute of Economics, Philosophy and Humanities (Institut universitaire des Sciences économiques, Philosophie et Lettres - ISPL).

Main Language(s) of Instruction: French, English

Accrediting Agency: Ministère de l'Enseignement Supérieur et Universitaire

Degrees and Diplomas: *Graduat*; *Licence*

Student Services: Academic Counselling, Careers Guidance, Cultural Activities, Facilities for disabled people, Health Services, Language Laboratory, Nursery Care, Social Counselling, Sports Facilities

Publications: Logos

Publishing House: ISPL Press
Last Updated: 30/10/12

CARDINAL MALULA UNIVERSITY

Université Cardinal Malula (UCM)
B.P. 14464, 2973 avenue Kingabwa - Limete, Kinshasa I

Recteur: Charles Mazinga
Secrétaire général: Anastase Nzeza

Faculty
Economics (Economics); **Environmental Sciences** (Environmental Studies); **Law** (Law); **Social Sciences** (Social Sciences)

History: Founded 1989. Acquired present status 1996.

Admission Requirements: State diploma

Main Language(s) of Instruction: French

Accrediting Agency: Ministère de l'Enseignement Supérieur et Universitaire

Degrees and Diplomas: *Graduat*; *Licence*

Student Services: Cultural Activities, Language Laboratory, Sports Facilities
Last Updated: 29/10/12

CATHOLIC UNIVERSITY OF BUKAVU

Université Catholique de Bukavu (UCB)
BP 285, Bukavu, Sud-Kivu
Tel: +243 997086603; +243 853720655
EMail: recteurucb@ucbukavu.cd
Website: http://www.ucbukavu.cd

Recteur: Paul Kadundu Karhamikire (2002-)
EMail: pkadundu@yahoo.fr

Administrateur Général: Guillaume Bidubula Juwa
EMail: bidubula.juwa@ucbukavu.cd; gbidjuwa@hotmail.com

Vice-Recteur aux Affaires académiques: Wenceslas Busane Ruhanamirindi
EMail: vraucb@ucbukavu.cd; busanewenceslas@yahoo.fr

Faculty
Agronomy (Agronomy); **Economics and Management** (Economics; Management); **Law** (Law); **Medicine** (Medicine); **Science**

History: Founded 1989 by the archbishop of Bukavu.

Academic Year: October to July (October-December; January-March; April-July)

Admission Requirements: Secondary school certificate and entrance examination

Main Language(s) of Instruction: French

Accrediting Agency: Ministère de l'Enseignement Supérieur et Universitaire

Degrees and Diplomas: *Graduat*; *Licence*: **Agronomy; Computer Science; Economics; Law.** *Doctorat*: **Medicine; Midwifery; Surgery.**

Student Services: Academic Counselling, Health Services, Nursery Care, Social Counselling, Sports Facilities

Publications: Annales de l'U.C.B.
Last Updated: 29/10/12

CATHOLIC UNIVERSITY OF CONGO

Université Catholique du Congo (UCC)
BP 1534, 2, Avenue de l'Université, Limete, Kinshasa
Tel: +243(99) 930 62 26
EMail: rectorat.ucc@gmail.com
Website: http://www.ucc.ac.cd/index.php

Recteur: Jean-Bosco Matand Bulembat (2007-)

Faculty
Canon Law (Canon Law); **Economics and Development** (Development Studies; Economics); **Law and Political Sciences** (Law; Political Sciences); **Philosophy** (Philosophy); **Social Communication** (Communication Studies; Social Studies); **Theology** (Christian Religious Studies; Theology)

Centre
African Religions *(CERA)* (African Studies; Religious Studies); **Ecclesiastical Archives** *(Abbé Stephano (CAEK))* (Religious Studies)

History: Founded 1957 as Facultés catholiques de Kinshasa. Acquired present status and title 2008.

Admission Requirements: State Diploma (+60%), and recommendation by a member of the Clergy

Main Language(s) of Instruction: French

Accrediting Agency: Ministère de l'Enseignement Supérieur et Universitaire

Degrees and Diplomas: *Graduat*; *Licence*: **Development Studies; Journalism; Philosophy; Theology.** *Diplôme d'Etudes supérieures*; *Doctorat*: **Philosophy; Theology.**

Publications: Journal of African Religions; Journal of African Theology; Kinshasa Journal of Philosophy

Last Updated: 29/10/12

CATHOLIC UNIVERSITY OF THE GRABEN

Université Catholique du Graben (UCG)

BP 29, Butembo, Nord-Kivu
Tel: +243(81) 3052-753
Fax: +243(99) 8232-754
EMail: contact@ucg-rdc.org

Recteur: Angelus Mafikiri Tsongo EMail: tsongoa@yahoo.fr

Faculty

Agronomy (Agronomy); **Economics** (Economics); **Law** (Law); **Medicine** (Medicine); **Pharmacy** (Pharmacy); **Social and Political Sciences and Administration** (Administration; Political Sciences; Social Sciences); **Veterinary Medicine** (Veterinary Science)

History: Founded 1989.

Main Language(s) of Instruction: French

Accrediting Agency: Ministère de l'Enseignement Supérieur et Universitaire

Degrees and Diplomas: *Graduat*; *Docteur en Médecine*: **Animal Husbandry; Medicine; Veterinary Science.** *Licence*

Student Services: Health Services, Language Laboratory

Last Updated: 30/10/12

CEPROMAD UNIVERSITY (MASINA)

Université du CEPROMAD (Masina) (UNIC)

BP 768 KIN XI, Avenue Petro-Congo, Masina, Kinshasa I
Tel: +243 89 832 07 48
EMail: cepromad@yahoo.fr

Recteur: Oscar Nsaman-O-Lutu (1982-)
Tel: +243(89) 7976-686 EMail: oscarlutu@yahoo.fr

Secrétaire général académique: Payanzo Nsomo
Tel: +243(89) 9924-6871 EMail: ppayanzo@yahoo.fr

International Relations: Maseke Raph, Chargé du Partenariat et de la Coopération internationale Tel: +243(81) 699-402

Faculty

Economics (Economics); **International Relations** (International Relations; Peace and Disarmament); **Law I** (Human Rights; Law; Public Law); **Law II** *(Bukavu; Goma; Lubumbashi; Kolwezi; Butembo; Boma; Matadi; Mbandaka; Kalemi; Isiro; Bunia; Kikwit)* (Human Rights; Law; Public Law); **Social, Political and Administrative Sciences** *(Bukavu; Goma; Lubumbashi; Beni; Buytembo; Matadi; Kananga; Mbandaka; Likasi; Kolwezi; Mweka; Isiro; Goma; Bunia)* (Administration; Political Sciences; Social Sciences); **Technology and Development Studies** (Development Studies; Nursing; Technology)

Institute

Health Sciences *(Institut Facultaire)* (Health Sciences)

Further Information: Other campuses in Lubumbashi, Kinshasa and Bukavu.

History: Founded 1982 as Institut supérieur de Gestion des Affaires. Acquired present status 2006.

Admission Requirements: Secondary school certificate

Main Language(s) of Instruction: French

Accrediting Agency: Ministère de l'Enseignement Supérieur et Universitaire

Degrees and Diplomas: *Graduat*; *Licence*; *Diplôme d'Etudes supérieures*; *Doctorat*

Student Services: Academic Counselling, Cultural Activities, Language Laboratory, Nursery Care, Social Counselling, Sports Facilities

Last Updated: 30/10/12

CHRISTIAN UNIVERSITY OF KINSHASA

Université chrétienne de Kinshasa (UCKIN)

BP 4742, Av. de l'Université no 1 bis, Binza/Ozone-Ngaliema, Kinshasa II

Recteur: Joseph Mbelolo

Faculty

Economics (Economics); **Theology** (Theology)

History: Founded 1967.

Admission Requirements: Secondary school certificate

Main Language(s) of Instruction: French

Accrediting Agency: Ministère de l'Enseignement Supérieur et Universitaire

Degrees and Diplomas: *Graduat*: **Economics; Theology.** *Licence*: **Economics; Theology.**

Student Services: Health Services, Language Laboratory, Social Counselling, Sports Facilities

Last Updated: 30/10/12

DIVINE GLORY UNIVERSITY

Université Divina Gloria (UDG)

BP 327, Butembo, Nord-Kivu
Tel: +243(99) 8548-850
Fax: +243(871) 76252-3410
EMail: universitedivinagl@yahoo.fr

Recteur: Pierre Kalala Nkudi (2000-)

Vice-Recteur: Kakule Mumbere Kasindi
Tel: +243(99) 8548-820 EMail: kasindiv@yahoo.fr

International Relations: Wasingya Kalwaghe, Chancelier
Tel: +243(99) 8386-663 EMail: wasingya@yahoo.fr

Faculty

Arts and Humanities (English; French; History); **Management and Computer Science** (Computer Science; Management); **Pharmacy** (Pharmacy); **Psychology and Educational Sciences** (Educational Sciences; Psychology); **Science** (Biology; Geology); **Social Sciences, Politics and Administration** (Administration; Political Sciences; Social Sciences); **Theology** (Theology)

History: Founded 2000.

Academic Year: October to June (October-February; March-June)

Admission Requirements: Diplôme d'Etat (Secondary school certificate)

Main Language(s) of Instruction: French

Accrediting Agency: Ministère de l'Enseignement Supérieur et Universitaire

Degrees and Diplomas: *Graduat*; *Licence*

Student Services: Academic Counselling, Careers Guidance, Cultural Activities, Facilities for disabled people, Health Services, Language Laboratory, Social Counselling, Sports Facilities

Last Updated: 30/10/12

EVANGELICAL UNIVERSITY IN AFRICA

Université Evangélique en Afrique (UEA)

BP 3323, Bukavu, Sud-Kivu
Tel: +243(98) 665-052
EMail: ueabukavu@yahoo.fr
Website: http://www.ueafrique.org/

Recteur: Gustave Mushagalusa Nachigera (2009-)
Tel: +243(99) 308-4623

Faculty

Agronomy and Environmental Sciences (Agronomy; Environmental Studies); **Economics Applied to Business** (Economics); **Medicine and Community Health** (Community Health; Medicine); **Protestant Theology** (Protestant Theology)

History: Founded 1991.

Main Language(s) of Instruction: French

Accrediting Agency: Ministère de l'Enseignement Supérieur et Universitaire

Degrees and Diplomas: *Graduat*; *Docteur en Médecine*; *Licence*

Publications: The Annals of the U.E.A.

Last Updated: 30/10/12

HIGHER INSTITUTE OF ECONOMIC, LEGAL AND COOPERATIVE SCIENCES

Institut Supérieur des Sciences Economiques, Juridiques et Coopératives (ISSEC)

BP 825, no 99 bis av. de l'Université, Quartier Mombele, Kinshasa-Limete
Tel: +243(89) 8914 747
EMail: issecfr@yahoo.fr
Website: http://www.issec-rdc.org/index.php

Directeur général: Gaston Kuyu Lubaku
EMail: kuyu_gaston@yahoo.fr

Programme

Computer Science and Information Technology Secretariat (Computer Science; Secretarial Studies); **Cooperative Sciences and Techniques and Micro-finance** (Finance); **Economics and Management** (Economics; Management); **Journalism and Audiovisual Production** (Journalism); **Law** (Law)

History: Founded 1988. Formerly known as Institut Supérieur Technique d'Etudes Economiques et Coopératives. Acquired present status and title 2006.

Main Language(s) of Instruction: French

Accrediting Agency: Ministère de l'Enseignement Supérieur et Universitaire

Degrees and Diplomas: *Graduat*; *Licence*

INSTITUTE OF COMPUTER SCIENCE, PROGRAMMING AND ANALYSIS

Institut Supérieur d'Informatique, Programmation et Analyse (ISIPA)

BP 1895, Avenue Kitega no 238, C/Lingwala, Kinshasa I
Tel: +243 898948919
EMail: contact@isipa.cd
Website: http://www.isipa.cd/

Président Directeur Général: Martin Ekanda Onyangunga (1975-)

Section

Commerce and Finance (Business Administration; Business and Commerce; Finance; International Business; Taxation); **Computer Science** (Artificial Intelligence; Computer Engineering; Computer Science; Telecommunications Engineering)

History: Founded 1975. Acquired present status 1993.

Academic Year: October-June (October/February; March/June)

Main Language(s) of Instruction: French

Accrediting Agency: Ministère de l'Enseignement Supérieur et Universitaire

Degrees and Diplomas: *Graduat*; *Licence*

Last Updated: 05/11/12

INSTITUTE OF DEVELOPMENT

Institut Facultaire de Développement (IFAD)

BP 1800, Avenue Saio no 2317, Commune de Kasa-Vubu, Kinshasa KIN I
Tel: +243(99) 9939-536

Recteur: Emmanuel Eyenga Liongo On'Asi
Tel: +243(99) 9939-536 EMail: emmanueleyenga@yahoo.fr

Secrétaire général académique: Bonolo Ngilima
Tel: +243(99) 9970-832

International Relations: Itoko Lian'dja, Secrétaire général administratif Tel: +243(99) 8122-503 EMail: itoko_gilles@yahoo.fr

Faculty

Development Science and Techniques; Health Sciences and Techniques (Health Administration; Health Sciences; Laboratory Techniques; Medical Technology; Nursing)

History: Founded 1993 as Institut supérieur de Formation des Agents de Développement.

Academic Year: October to July

Main Language(s) of Instruction: French

Degrees and Diplomas: *Graduat*: **Development Studies; Health Sciences.** *Licence*

Student Services: Language Laboratory

Publications: Revue "IFAD"

Last Updated: 05/10/12

INSTITUTE OF MANAGEMENT AND COMMUNICATION

Institut Facultaire de Gestion et de Communication (IFGC)

17ème rue Limete, Kinshasa

Recteur Honoraire: Malembe Tamandiak

Faculty

Advertising and Business Administration (Advertising and Publicity; Business Administration); **Commerce and Finance** (Finance); **Computer Science and Humanities** (Computer Science); **Documentation Techniques** (Documentation Techniques); **Economics** (Economics); **Journalism-Communication** (Communication Studies; Journalism)

History: Founded 1994. Formerly Institut facultaire de Gestion. Present status acquired 2006.

Main Language(s) of Instruction: French

Degrees and Diplomas: *Graduat*; *Licence*

Last Updated: 05/10/12

INTER-UNIVERSITY INSTITUTE OF KINSHASA

Institut Inter-universitaire de Kinshasa (INTERKIN)

BP 14.130, Av. Irebu n°6/C, Commune de Kasa-Vubu, Kinshasa I
Tel: +243(89) 5090-548
EMail: interkin@yahoo.fr

Faculty

Business Computing (Business Computing); **Economics** (Economics); **Social, Political and Administrative Sciences** (Administration; Political Sciences; Social Sciences)

History: Founded 1981.

Admission Requirements: State Diploma

Main Language(s) of Instruction: French

Accrediting Agency: Ministère de l'Enseignement Supérieur et Universitaire

Degrees and Diplomas: *Graduat*; *Licence*

Last Updated: 30/10/12

KONGO UNIVERSITY

Université Kongo (UK)

BP 202, Avenue Kolo, 23, Mbanza-Ngungu, Bas-Congo
Tel: +243 9999-39405
EMail: info@universitekongo.org
Website: http://www.universitekongo.org

Recteur: Oscar Kambu Kabangu (2008-)
EMail: oscar.kambu@universitekong.org

Secrétaire Général Administratif: Flavien Makiese Ndoma
EMail: flavien.makiese@universitekongo.org

Secrétaire Général Académique: Guillaume Kiyombo Mbela
EMail: guillaume.kiyombo@universitekongo.org

Faculty

Agronomy *(Kisantu)* (Agronomy); **Arts and Social Communication** *(Kisantu)* (Arts and Humanities; Communication Studies); **Economics and Management** (Economics; Management); **Law** (Law); **Medicine** *(Kisantu)* (Medicine); **Polytechnic** (Electrical and Electronic Engineering; Mechanical Engineering)

History: Founded 1990.

Admission Requirements: Diplôme d'Etat

Main Language(s) of Instruction: French

Accrediting Agency: Ministère de l'Enseignement Supérieur et Universitaire

Degrees and Diplomas: *Graduat*; *Docteur en Médecine*: **Medicine.** *Licence*

Student Services: Health Services, Social Counselling

Publications: Racines et Croissance

Last Updated: 30/10/12

METHODIST UNIVERSITY IN KATANGA

Université méthodiste au Katanga (UMK)
BP 521, Mulungwishi-Likasi

Recteur: Kasap Owan Tshibang

Faculty
Computer Science (Computer Science); **Educational Sciences** (Educational Sciences); **Theology** (Theology)

History: Founded 1951 as Faculté Méthodiste de Théologie de Mulungwishi. Acquired present status and title 2000.

Main Language(s) of Instruction: French

Accrediting Agency: Ministère de l'Enseignement Supérieur et Universitaire

Degrees and Diplomas: *Graduat*; *Licence*; *Diplôme d'Etudes supérieures*

Last Updated: 31/10/12

NOTRE DAME OF THE KASAYI UNIVERSITY

Université Notre Dame du Kasayi (UKA)
BP 70, Collège Saint Louis, Kananga II
Website: http://uka-rdc.org/

Recteur: André Kabasele Mukenge
Tel: +243(99) 99 03 161 EMail: kamuke@yahoo.com

Faculty
Computer Science (Computer Science); **Law** *(Kananga and Kabinda)* (Law); **Medicine** *(Kananga and Tshumbe)* (Medicine)

History: Founded 1996 by the Episcopal Conference of the province of Kananga. Acquired present status 2004.

Main Language(s) of Instruction: French

Accrediting Agency: Ministère de l'Enseignement Supérieur et Universitaire

Degrees and Diplomas: *Graduat*; *Licence*; *Doctorat*: **Medicine.**

Last Updated: 31/10/12

PATRICE EMERY LUMUMBA UNIVERSITY OF WEMBO-NYAMA

Université Patrice Emery Lumumba de Wembo-Nyama (UPEL/WN)
BP 560, Wembo-Nyama, Kananga, Kasaï Oriental

Président: Djundu Lunge

Faculty
Arts (Arts and Humanities); **Economics** (Economics); **Law** (Law); **Medicine** (Medicine); **Science** (Natural Sciences); **Social Sciences** (Social Sciences); **Theology** (Theology)

Further Information: Also branch in Kinshasa

History: Founded 1992.

Main Language(s) of Instruction: French

Accrediting Agency: Ministère de l'Enseignement Supérieur et Universitaire

Degrees and Diplomas: *Graduat*; *Licence*

Last Updated: 31/10/12

PRESIDENT JOSEPH KASA-VUBU UNIVERSITY

Université Président Joseph Kasa-Vubu (UKV)
BP 314, Boma, Bas-Congo
Tel: +243(98) 179-706
EMail: ukvboma@yahoo.fr
Website: http://www.congovision.com/ukv/index.html

Recteur: Joseph Ntedika Konde EMail: josntedika@yahoo.fr

Secrétaire Général Administratif: Eddy Maphasi Nuimba

Faculty
Agronomy (Agronomy); **Economics and Management** (Economics; Management); **Law** (Law); **Medicine** (Medicine); **Polytechnic** (Engineering)

History: Founded 1999.

Main Language(s) of Instruction: French

Accrediting Agency: Ministère de l'Enseignement Supérieur et Universitaire

Degrees and Diplomas: *Graduat*; *Docteur en Médecine*; *Licence*

Last Updated: 31/10/12

PRIVATE UNIVERSITY OF KINSHASA

Université Libre de Kinshasa (ULK)
BP 1333, 15ème Rue no 36, Commune de Limete, Kinshasa
Tel: +243(99) 821 0630
EMail: directeuracademique@ulk-rdc.org
Website: http://ulk-rdc.org/

Recteur: André Bola Ntotele

Faculty
Economics and Management (Computer Engineering; Economics; Management); **Law** (Commercial Law; Law; Private Law; Public Law); **Social, Political and Administrative Sciences** (Administration; International Relations; Political Sciences; Social Sciences; Sociology)

History: Founded 1988.

Main Language(s) of Instruction: French

Accrediting Agency: Ministère de l'Enseignement Supérieur et Universitaire

Degrees and Diplomas: *Graduat*; *Licence*

Last Updated: 31/10/12

PRIVATE UNIVERSITY OF LUOZI

Université libre de Luozi (ULL)
BP 14, Luozi
Tel: +243(98) 127-885
EMail: univ_lluozi@yahoo.fr
Website: http://www.ne-kongo.net/uni_luozi/

Recteur: Matukanga Mbalu

Secrétaire Général: Kiana Ndeke

Faculty
Agronomy (Agronomy); **Business Administration and Computer Science** (Business Administration; Computer Science); **Development and Environmental Studies** (Development Studies; Environmental Studies); **Health Sciences** (Health Sciences); **Polytechnic** (Civil Engineering; Electrical Engineering; Mechanical Engineering)

History: Founded 1967 as Fonds de l'Institut Tombouctou de Luozi (FITL). Formerly known as Centre de Vulgarisation Agricole (CVA), Institut Supérieur de Développement/CEDEAC and Institut Supérieur Technique et Universitaire du Manianga (ISTUM). Acquired present title and status 1997.

Main Language(s) of Instruction: French

Accrediting Agency: Ministère de l'Enseignement Supérieur et Universitaire

Degrees and Diplomas: *Graduat*; *Licence*

Last Updated: 31/10/12

PRIVATE UNIVERSITY OF THE GREAT LAKES REGION

Université libre des Pays des Grands Lacs (ULPGL)
BP 368, Goma, Nord-Kivu
Tel: +243(99) 409 5179
EMail: dbakenga@yahoo.fr
Website: http://www.ulpgl.net/

Recteur: Léopold Kambale Karafuli

Faculty

Economics and Management (Business Administration; Economics; Finance; Management); **Health and Community Development** (Community Health; Health Administration); **Law** (Commercial Law; Private Law; Public Law); **Protestant Theology** (Missionary Studies; Protestant Theology); **Psychology and Educational Sciences** (Educational Administration; Educational Sciences; Psychology); **Science and Applied Technology** (Civil Engineering; Computer Engineering; Electrical and Electronic Engineering; Mechanical Engineering)

History: Founded 1990 on the basis of the Institut Supérieur de Théologie Protestante (founded 1985). Acquired present status and title 1996.

Admission Requirements: National Degree; Admission Test; Financial Support

Main Language(s) of Instruction: French

Accrediting Agency: Minsitère de l'Enseignement Supérieur et Universitaire

Degrees and Diplomas: *Graduat*; *Licence*

Student Services: Academic Counselling, Canteen, Careers Guidance, Health Services, Language Laboratory, Nursery Care, Social Counselling, Sports Facilities

Publications: Annales de la Faculté de Droit; Bulletin de recherches théologiques et sociologiques; L'Analyste Topique; Revue de la Faculté de Droit; Revue de la Faculté de Théologie Protestante

Last Updated: 31/10/12

PROTESTANT UNIVERSITY OF CONGO

Université Protestante au Congo (UPC)
BP 4745, Croisement des avenues de la Victoire et de libération, Kinshasa/Lingwala, Kinshasa II
Tel: +243(81) 5087-561
EMail: univprocongo@kin.maf.net
Website: http://www.upc-rdc.cd/

Recteur: Daniel Ngoy Boliya (1992-)
EMail: recteur@upc-rdc.cd; ngoyboliya@yahoo.fr

Secrétaire général académique: Mampunza Ma Miezi
EMail: sgacad@upc-rdc.cd

Secrétaire général administratif: Léon Nondo Manenga
EMail: sgadm@upc-rdc.cd

Faculty

Business and Economics (Accountancy; Administrative Law; African Studies; Agricultural Economics; Business Administration; Commercial Law; Computer Science; Economics; English; Environmental Studies; Finance; Geography (Human); Industrial Management; Insurance; International Economics; Law; Management; Marketing; Philosophy; Psychology; Small Business; Sociology; Staff Development); **Law** (Commercial Law; Private Law; Public Law); **Medicine** (African Studies; Anatomy; Biochemistry; Biology; Biophysics; Botany; Chemistry; Community Health; Embryology and Reproduction Biology; English; Entomology; Epidemiology; Ethics; French; Histology; Immunology; Logic; Mathematics; Medicine; Molecular Biology; Nutrition; Organic Chemistry; Parasitology; Pathology; Pharmacology; Philosophy; Physics; Physiology; Public Health; Radiology; Surgery; Urology; Virology; Zoology); **Theology** (Protestant Theology)

History: Founded 1959 in Lubumbashi as a Theology Department. Became Free University of the Congo 1963, Protestant University of Zaire 1990. Acquired present status and title 1994.

Academic Year: October to July

Admission Requirements: State diploma or equivalent

Main Language(s) of Instruction: French

Accrediting Agency: Ministère de l'Enseignement Supérieur et Universitaire

Degrees and Diplomas: *Graduat*; *Docteur en Médecine*; *Licence*

Student Services: Academic Counselling, Canteen, Careers Guidance, Facilities for disabled people, Health Services, Language Laboratory, Social Counselling, Sports Facilities

Publications: Revue Congolaise de Théologie Protestante; Revue de la Faculté d'Administration des Affaires et Sciences Economiques; Revue de la Faculté de Droit

Publishing House: Editions de l'Université Protestante au Congo

Last Updated: 31/10/12

PROTESTANT UNIVERSITY OF KIMPESE

Université Protestante de Kimpese (UPK)
BP 67, Kimpese
Tel: +243(81) 017 0480
Fax: +243(99) 162 7590
EMail: upk_kimpese@yahoo.fr

Recteur: Luyindula Ndiku

Faculty

Agronomy (Agronomy); **Health Sciences** (Health Sciences); **Theology** (Theology)

Centre

Pastoral Studies

History: Founded 1994.

Main Language(s) of Instruction: French

Accrediting Agency: Ministère de l'Enseignement Supérieur et Universitaire

Degrees and Diplomas: *Graduat*; *Licence*

Last Updated: 31/10/12

SAINT-AUGUSTIN UNIVERSITY OF KINSHASA

Université Saint-Augustin de Kinshasa (USAKIN)
BP 241 A, Kindele Monastère, (Près du Prieuré des Chanoines Prémontrés à Kinshasa/Mont-Ngafula), Kinshasa
Tel: +243 015 1640 12
EMail: usakin@usakin.com
Website: http://usakin.com/

Recteur: Willy Okey

Secrétaire Général Académique: Denis Bosomi

Vice-Recteur: Valentin Ntumba

Faculty

Philosophy (Philosophy); **Psychology** (Psychology); **Theology** (Theology)

History: Founded 1993. Formerly known as Institut Supérieur de Théologie et de Philosophie - Saint-Augustin and Philosophat Saint-Augustin.

Main Language(s) of Instruction: French

Accrediting Agency: Ministère de l'Enseignement Supérieur et Universitaire

Degrees and Diplomas: *Graduat*; *Licence*

Last Updated: 05/11/12

SHEPPARD AND LAPSLEY PRESBYTERIAN UNIVERSITY OF THE CONGO

Université presbytérienne Sheppard et Lapsley du Congo (UPRECO)
BP 159, Q. Kamupongo, C/de Ndesha, Kananga
Website: http://upreco.org

Recteur: Mulumba Musumbu Mukundi

Faculty

Law (Law); **Theology** (History of Religion; Missionary Studies; Theology)

History: Founded 1976. Acquired university status in 1998.

Main Language(s) of Instruction: French

Accrediting Agency: Ministère de l'Enseignement Supérieur et Universitaire

Degrees and Diplomas: *Graduat*; *Licence*

Last Updated: 31/10/12

SIMON KIMBANGU UNIVERSITY

Université Simon Kimbangu (USK)

BP 1441, 44 avenue Bongolo, Q/ Kauka, Commune de Kalamu, Kinshasa I

Tel: +243(99) 8183-862

EMail: contact@universitesk.net; universitsimonkimbangu@yahoo.fr

Website: http://www.universitesk.net/

Recteur: Simon Masamba N'Kazi Angani (2003-)
EMail: simon.masamba@gmail.com; masamba@universitesk.net

Assistant du Recteur: Dilenga Munyanga
EMail: munyangadilenga@yahoo.fr

International Relations: Jean Akakiwa Bayago, Secrétaire général administratif EMail: bayagoa@gmail.com

Faculty

Agronomy (Agronomy); **Computer Science** (Computer Science); **Law and Economics** (Econometrics; Economics; Law); **Medicine** (Medicine); **Theology** (Theology); **Veterinary Science** (Veterinary Science)

Further Information: Also campus in Lutendele.

History: Founded 1990. Acquired present status 2006.

Academic Year: November to August (November-March; Exams in April; May-August)

Admission Requirements: Diplôme d'Etat or equivalent

Fees: (US Dollars): 500,00 per annum

Main Language(s) of Instruction: French

Degrees and Diplomas: *Graduat*; *Docteur en Médecine*: **Animal Husbandry; Medicine; Veterinary Science.** *Licence*

Student Services: Academic Counselling, Canteen, Careers Guidance, Cultural Activities, Foreign Studies Centre, Health Services, Language Laboratory, Social Counselling, Sports Facilities

Last Updated: 20/07/12

UNIVERSITY INSTITUTE OF CONGO, LUBUMBASHI

Institut Universitaire du Congo de Lubumbashi (IUC/LUBUMBASHI)

BP 4869, Avenue Likasi no 491, Lubumbashi

Recteur: Jean Kandé

Faculty

Business Administration (Business Administration); **Business Computing** (Business Computing); **Economics** (Economics); **Law** (Law); **Social, Political and Administrative Science** (Administration; Political Sciences; Social Sciences); **Theology** (Theology)

History: Founded 1989.

Main Language(s) of Instruction: French

Accrediting Agency: Ministère de l'Enseignement Supérieur et Universitaire

Degrees and Diplomas: *Graduat*; *Licence*

Last Updated: 05/11/12

UNIVERSITY OF MBUJI-MAYI

Université de Mbuji-Mayi (UM)

BP 225, 80, Avenue de l'Université, Campus de Tshikama, Dibindi, Mbuji-Mayi, Kasaï Oriental

Tel: +243(99) 713 112

EMail: univmayi@yahoo.fr

Website: http://um-rdc.org/

Recteur: Ghislain Disashi Ntumba

Secrétaire général: Charles Tshula

Faculty

Applied Sciences (Polytechnic) (Computer Engineering; Mechanical Engineering; Mining Engineering); **Economics** (Economics); **Law** (Law; Notary Studies; Private Law; Public Law); **Medicine** (Biomedicine; Medicine)

History: Founded 1990. Acquired present status 1992.

Academic Year: November to July

Admission Requirements: State diploma (secondary school certificate) or equivalent

Main Language(s) of Instruction: French

Accrediting Agency: Ministère de l'Enseignement Supérieur et Universitaire

Degrees and Diplomas: *Graduat*; *Licence*; *Doctorat*: **Medicine.**

Student Services: Academic Counselling, Canteen, Cultural Activities, Health Services, Nursery Care, Social Counselling, Sports Facilities

Publications: Actes des Journées Scientifiques de l'U.M.

Last Updated: 30/10/12

WILLIAM BOOTH UNIVERSITY

Université William Booth (UWB)

12 Avenue du Kasai, Kinshasa-Gombe I

Website: http://uwbcongo.org/

Recteur: Gaston Mpuitu ne Mbodi

Vice Recteur: Roger Bimwala

Secrétaire Général Administratif: Bernard Nzingua Luzi

Faculty

Business Science and Computer Management (Business and Commerce; Computer Engineering); **Economics and Administration** (Administration; Economics); **Law** (Law); **Science and Medical Technology** (Medical Technology)

School

Accountancy (Accountancy)

Institute

Public Management (Public Administration)

History: Founded 1996.

Main Language(s) of Instruction: French

Accrediting Agency: Ministère de l'Enseignement Supérieur et Universitaire

Degrees and Diplomas: *Graduat*; *Licence*

Student Services: Language Laboratory, Sports Facilities

Last Updated: 31/10/12

Costa Rica

STRUCTURE OF HIGHER EDUCATION SYSTEM

Description:

Higher education is composed of both public and private parauniversity (short courses) and university (graduate education) systems. Public university education is coordinated by the Consejo Nacional de Rectores (CONARE). Private universities are supervised by the Consejo Nacional de Enseñanza Superior Universitaria Privada (CONESUP).

Stages of studies:

University level first stage: *Pregrado: Diplomado*

The first stage of higher education leads, after two or three years of short-term study, to the award of the title of Diplomado. Holders of this diploma are called diplomados. This diploma does not give the holders professional status. Students may choose whether or not they wish to continue their studies.

University level second stage: *Grado: Bachillerato universitario, Licenciatura*

The second stage of higher education leads to the award of the Bachiller or Bachillerato universitario after four years, and to the Licentiatura after five years. The Licenciatura may be awarded after a minimum of one year after the Bachillerato universitario or as a first degree.

University level third stage: *Posgrado: Maestría, Especialidad profesional, Doctorado académico*

A Maestría degree requires two years' study after a first degree (Bachiller). The Especialidad Profesional forms part of postgraduate studies centred on specialized practical training in a given professional field. Candidates should hold the Licenciatura. The Doctorado académico is the highest degree.

ADMISSION TO HIGHER EDUCATION

Admission to university-level studies:

Name of secondary school credential required: Bachillerato

Admission requirements: Entrance examinations at some institutions.

Foreign students admission:

Admission requirements: Students must hold a Bachillerato or a recognized equivalent diploma. They must sit for an entrance examination or have their studies recognized.

Entry regulations: Foreign students must obtain a residence permit and give a financial guarantee.

Language proficiency: Students must have good knowledge of Spanish.

RECOGNITION OF STUDIES

Quality assurance system:

Higher education institutions are authorized by an organic act for public universities, an agreement adopted by the CONESUP for private universities, an act of approval by the Legislative Assembly for international universities.

NATIONAL BODIES

Ministerio de Educación Pública (Ministry of Public Education)

Minister: Sonia Marta Mora Escalante
VI piso, edificio Rofas
San José
Tel: +506 2256 8132 Ext.1100
Fax: +506 2256 8093
WWW: http://www.mep.go.cr

Consejo Nacional de Enseñanza Superior Universitaria Privada - CONESUP (National Council of Private Higher Education)

Executive Director: Mario Sanabria Ramírez
San José, VII piso, edificio Raventós, Avenida 0 y 2, calle 6, costado sur del Mercado Central
San José
Tel: +506 2233 6118 Ext. 2081
Fax: +506 2258 3101
EMail: CONESUP@mep.go.cr; inspeccion.conesup@mep.go.cr
WWW: http://www.mep.go.cr/conesup

Consejo Nacional de Rectores - CONARE (National Council of Rectors)

President: Alberto Salom Echeverría
Apdo. 1174-1200
San José
Tel: +506 2519 5700
Fax: +506 2296 5626
EMail: conare@conare.ac.cr
WWW: http://www.conare.ac.cr
Role of national body: Sets the guidelines for the National Plan for Public Higher Education (PLANES); approves PLANES; distributes the lump sum allocated to Public Higher Education among the four public universities; establishes the instruments and coordination procedures for Public Higher Education; designates representatives of Public Higher Education to other public boards; evaluates, creates and closes degree programmes and formulates policy recommendations for public universities.

Consejo Superior de Education - CSE (National Education Council)

Secretary-General: Ingrid Bustos Rojas
San José
Tel: +506 2256 8230
EMail: consejosuperior@mep.go.cr
WWW: http://cse.go.cr/
Role of national body: In charge of all education levels except university.

Sistema Nacional de Acreditación de la Educación Superior - SINAES (National Higher Education Accreditation System)

Executive Director: Gilberto Alfaro Varela
Apartado Postal 1174-1200
San José
Tel: +506 2519 5813
Fax: +506 2290 8653
EMail: sinaes@sinaes.ac.cr
WWW: http://www.sinaes.ac.cr/

Data for academic year: 2015-2016
Source: IAU from MEP and SINAES websites, 2015.

INSTITUTIONS

PUBLIC INSTITUTIONS

COSTA RICA INSTITUTE OF TECHNOLOGY

Instituto Tecnológico de Costa Rica (ITCR)
Apartado 159-7050, Cártago 159-7050
Tel: +506 2552-5333
Website: http://www.tec.ac.cr
Rector: Julio Calvo Alvarado EMail: Rector. jucalvo@tec.ac.cr

School
Agricultural Engineering (Agricultural Engineering); **Agrobusiness** (Agricultural Business); **Biology** (Biology; Biotechnology); **Business Administration** (Business Administration); **Chemistry** (Chemistry); **Computer Engineering** (Computer Engineering; Computer Science); **Construction Engineering** (Construction Engineering); **Culture and Sport** (Cultural Studies; Sports); **Electrical and Mechanical Engineering** (Electrical Engineering; Mechanical Engineering); **Electronic Engineering** (Electronic Engineering); **Forestry Engineering** (Forestry); **Industrial Design**

(Industrial Design); **Language** (Communication Studies; English); **Material Science and Engineering** (Materials Engineering); **Mathematics** (Mathematics); **Occupational Safety and Environmental Health** (Environmental Engineering; Occupational Health; Safety Engineering); **Physics** (Physics); **Production Engineering** (Production Engineering); **Social Sciences** (Law; Philosophy; Social Sciences); **Technology Education** (Technology Education)

Campus

Alajuela (Computer Engineering); **Limón** (Business Administration; Computer Engineering; Production Engineering); **San Carlos** (Agricultural Engineering; Business Administration; Computer Engineering; Production Engineering; Tourism); **San José** (Architecture; Business Administration; Computer Engineering; Rural Planning; Technology Education)

Further Information: Campuses in San José, San Carlos, Limón, and Alajuela.

History: Founded 1971. A State institution financed by the government.

Academic Year: February to November (February-May; August-November)

Admission Requirements: Secondary school certificate (bachillerato) or equivalent, and entrance examination

Main Language(s) of Instruction: Spanish

Accrediting Agency: Canadian Engineering Accreditation Board; Sistema Nacional de Acreditación de la Educación Superior (SINAES).

Degrees and Diplomas: *Bachillerato Universitario*; *Licenciatura*; *Maestría*: **Business Administration; Computer Science; Electronic Engineering; Engineering Management; Forestry; Production Engineering; Technology Education.** *Doctorado Académico*: **Business Administration; Engineering; Natural Sciences.**

Student Services: Academic Counselling, Canteen, Careers Guidance, Facilities for disabled people, Health Services, Language Laboratory, Nursery Care, Social Counselling, Sports Facilities

Last Updated: 28/08/15

NATIONAL UNIVERSITY

Universidad Nacional (UNA)
Avenida 1, Calle 1, Heredia, Heredia 86-3000
Tel: +506 2277-3000
EMail: rectoria@una.ac.cr
Website: http://www.una.ac.cr

Rector: Alberto Salom Echeverría

Faculty

Exact and Natural Sciences (Biology; Computer Science; Earth Sciences; Industrial Chemistry; Information Technology; Mathematics; Natural Sciences; Science Education; Surveying and Mapping); **Health Sciences** (Health Sciences; Parks and Recreation; Physical Education; Sports; Sports Medicine; Veterinary Science); **Land and Sea Sciences** (Agricultural Engineering; Earth Sciences; Environmental Management; Forestry; Geography; Marine Science and Oceanography; Surveying and Mapping); **Philosophy and Letters** (English; French; Gender Studies; Information Sciences; Latin American Studies; Library Science; Philosophy; Publishing and Book Trade; Spanish; Theology); **Social Sciences** (Business Education; Economics; History; International Business; International Relations; Leadership; Management; Psychology; Social Policy; Social Sciences; Social Studies; Sociology)

Further Information: Campuses in Nicoya, Liberia, Coto, Pérez Zeledón, Sarapiquí and Benjamín Núñez.

History: Founded 1973.

Academic Year: February to November (Two semesters divided into: February-June and August-November)

Admission Requirements: Secondary school certificate (bachillerato) and entrance examination

Main Language(s) of Instruction: Spanish

Accrediting Agency: SINAES

Degrees and Diplomas: *Bachillerato Universitario*; *Licenciatura*; *Maestría*; *Doctorado Académico*: **Arts and Humanities; Latin American Studies; Natural Sciences; Social Sciences.**

Student Services: Academic Counselling, Canteen, Careers Guidance, Cultural Activities, Facilities for disabled people, Health Services, IT Centre, Language Laboratory, Library, Nursery Care, Social Counselling, Sports Facilities, eLibrary

Publications: Revista ABRA; Revista Ambien-TICO; Revista Educare; Revista Geográfia de Costa Rica; Revista Ístmica; Revista Letras; Revista Perspectivas; Revista Relaciones Internacionales; Revista Uniciencia

Academic Staff *2015-2016*	**TOTAL**
FULL-TIME	**650**
PART-TIME	c. **1,240**

Student Numbers *2015-2016*	
All (Foreign included)	**19,415**

Last Updated: 17/12/15

STATE UNIVERSITY OF DISTANCE EDUCATION

Universidad Estatal a Distancia (UNED)
Apartado 474-2050, De la Rotonda La Betania 500m al este, Carretera a Sabanilla, Mercedes de Montes de Oca, San José
Tel: +506 2527-2000
EMail: webmaster1@uned.ac.cr
Website: http://www.uned.ac.cr

Rector: Luis Guillermo Carpio Malavassi
EMail: rectoria@uned.ac.cr

School

Administrative Sciences (Administration; Business Administration); **Education** (Civics; Education; Educational Psychology; Educational Technology; English; French; Mathematics Education; Preschool Education; Primary Education; Science Education; Secondary Education; Special Education; Teacher Training; Technology Education); **Exact and Natural Sciences** (Agricultural Engineering; Computer Science; Health Administration; Industrial Engineering; Mathematics; Natural Resources; Natural Sciences); **Social Sciences** (Commercial Law; Constitutional Law; Criminology; Family Studies; Human Rights; International Law; Labour Law; Social Work)

History: Founded 1977 to give access to higher education to those who are unable to attend university, particularly those living in rural areas. An autonomous institution financed by the State.

Academic Year: January to November (January-April; May-August; September-November)

Admission Requirements: Secondary school certificate (bachillerato) or equivalent

Main Language(s) of Instruction: Spanish

Accrediting Agency: SINAES

Degrees and Diplomas: *Diplomado*: **Secretarial Studies.** *Bachillerato Universitario*: **Accountancy; Agricultural Engineering; Agricultural Management; Business Administration; Computer Engineering; Criminology; Distance Education; Education; Environmental Management; Finance; Foreign Languages Education; Health Administration; Human Resources; Industrial Engineering; International Business; Library Science; Marketing; Mathematics Education; Music; Police Studies; Religious Education; Science Education; Special Education; Teacher Training; Theology; Tourism.** *Licenciatura*: **Accountancy; Agricultural Engineering; Business Administration; Computer Engineering; Criminology; Educational Administration; Environmental Management; Finance; Foreign Languages Education; Human Resources; Industrial Engineering; International Business; Library Science; Marketing; Mathematics Education; Music; Police Studies; Religious Education; Science Education; Special Education; Teacher Training; Theology; Tourism.** *Maestría*: **Agriculture; Business Administration; Commercial Law; Constitutional Law; Criminology; Distance Education; Educational Administration; Educational Psychology; Educational Technology; Health Administration; International Business; Labour Law; Mass Communication; Natural Resources; Social Welfare.** *Doctorado Académico*: **Administration; Education; Law; Natural Sciences.**

Last Updated: 14/09/15

UNIVERSITY OF COSTA RICA

Universidad de Costa Rica (UCR)

Apartado 2060, Ciudad Universitaria Rodrigo Facio,
San José 11501 2060 UCR
Tel: +506 2511-1250
Fax: +506 2234-0452
EMail: consultas.odi@ucr.ac.cr
Website: http://www.ucr.ac.cr

Rector: Henning Jensen Pennington (2012-)
Tel: +506 2511-1212
EMail: henning.jensen@ucr.ac.cr

International Relations: Julieta Carranza Velásquez, Director, International Relations
Tel: +506 2511-5080
EMail: oaice@ucr.ac.cr

Faculty

Agronomy (Agricultural Economics; Agronomy; Animal Husbandry; Food Technology; Zoology); **Dentistry** (Dentistry); **Economics** (Accountancy; Business Administration; Economics; Health Administration; Public Administration; Taxation); **Education** (Arts and Humanities; Curriculum; Education; Educational Administration; Educational and Student Counselling; Educational Testing and Evaluation; English; French; Higher Education; Information Sciences; Library Science; Literature; Management; Mathematics Education; Music Education; Physical Education; Primary Education; Science Education; Secondary Education; Social Studies; Spanish; Special Education; Sports; Teacher Training); **Engineering** (Agricultural Engineering; Architecture; Chemical Engineering; Civil Engineering; Computer Engineering; Computer Science; Electrical Engineering; Engineering; Industrial Engineering; Mechanical Engineering; Surveying and Mapping); **Fine Arts** (Advertising and Publicity; Fine Arts; Graphic Arts; Music; Painting and Drawing; Sculpture; Theatre); **Humanities** (Arts and Humanities; Literature; Modern Languages; Philology; Philosophy); **Law** (Law); **Medicine** (Anaesthesiology; Biochemistry; Biomedicine; Cardiology; Chemistry; Community Health; Dentistry; Dermatology; Endocrinology; Gastroenterology; Gerontology; Gynaecology and Obstetrics; Haematology; Medicine; Microbiology; Neurological Therapy; Neurology; Nursing; Nutrition; Oncology; Ophthalmology; Paediatrics; Pharmacology; Pharmacy; Physical Therapy; Plastic Surgery; Pneumology; Psychiatry and Mental Health; Public Health; Radiology; Rehabilitation and Therapy; Respiratory Therapy; Surgery; Urology); **Microbiology** (Haematology; Microbiology; Parasitology); **Pharmacy** (Pharmacy); **Science** (Biology; Chemistry; Computer Science; Geology; Mathematics; Meteorology; Natural Sciences; Physics; Statistics); **Social Sciences** (Anthropology; Communication Studies; Geography; History; Mass Communication; Political Sciences; Psychology; Social Sciences; Social Work; Sociology)

Research Centre

Abnormal Haemoglobin and Related Disorders *(CIHATA)* (Pathology); **Agricultural Economics and Agribusiness** *(CIEDA)* (Agricultural Business); **Agronomy** *(CIA)* (Agronomy); **Animal Nutrition** *(CINA)* (Animal Husbandry); **Atomic, Molecular and Nuclear Sciences** *(CICANUM)* (Atomic and Molecular Physics; Nuclear Physics); **Cellular and Molecular Biology** *(CIBCM)* (Cell Biology; Molecular Biology); **Central American History** *(CIHAC)* (History; Latin American Studies); **Crop Protection** *(CIPROC)* (Crop Production); **Electro-Chemistry and Chemical Energy** *(CELEQ)* (Chemistry); **Environmental Pollution** *(CICA)* (Environmental Studies); **Food Science and Technology** *(CITA)* (Food Science; Food Technology); **Geology** *(CICG)* (Geology); **Geophysics** *(CIGEFI)* (Geophysics; Seismology); **Grains and Seeds** *(CIGRAS)* (Plant Pathology); **Latin American Identity and Culture** *(CIICLA)* (Cultural Studies; Latin American Studies); **Materials Engineering** *(CICIMA)* (Materials Engineering); **Mathematics and Applied Mathematics** *(CIMPA)* (Applied Mathematics; Mathematics); **Mathematics and Meta-Mathematics** *(CIMM)* (Mathematics); **Microstructures** *(CIEMIC)* (Microelectronics); **Natural Products** *(CIPRONA)* (Natural Resources); **Population Studies** *(Central American, CCP)* (Demography and Population); **Public Administration** *(CICAP)* (Public Administration); **Sea Sciences and Limnology** *(CIMAR)* (Limnology; Marine Science and Oceanography); **Space Studies** *(CINESPA)*; **Tropical Diseases** *(CIET)* (Tropical Medicine); **Women's Studies** *(CIEM)* (Women's Studies)

Research Institute

Agriculture *(IIA)* (Agriculture); **Clodomiro Picado** *(ICP)*; **Economics** *(IICE)* (Economics); **Education** *(INIE)* (Education); **Engineering** *(INII)* (Engineering); **Health Sciences** *(INISA)* (Health Sciences); **Law** *(IIJ)* (Law); **Linguistics** *(INIL)* (Linguistics); **Pharmacy** *(INIFAR)* (Pharmacy); **Philosophy** *(IIF)* (Philosophy); **Psychology** *(IIP)* (Psychology); **Social Studies** *(IIS)* (Social Studies)

History: Founded 1940, incorporating former schools of the Universidad de Santo Tomás. An autonomous institution.

Academic Year: February to December (February-July; August-December)

Admission Requirements: Secondary school certificate (bachillerato) or foreign equivalent, and entrance examination

Fees: 3,250 per credit (Costa Rican Colon)

Main Language(s) of Instruction: Spanish

Degrees and Diplomas: *Diplomado*; *Bachillerato Universitario*: **Agriculture; Arts and Humanities; Education; Engineering; Health Sciences; Natural Sciences; Social Sciences.** *Licenciatura*: **Agriculture; Arts and Humanities; Education; Engineering; Health Sciences; Natural Sciences; Social Sciences.** *Especialidad Profesional*: **Forensic Medicine and Dentistry; Meteorology.** *Maestría*: **Agricultural Business; Agriculture; Anthropology; Applied Mathematics; Architecture; Astrophysics; Biology; Biomedicine; Business Administration; Chemical Engineering; Chemistry; Civil Engineering; Communication Arts; Computer Science; Construction Engineering; Curriculum; Dentistry; Economics; Educational Sciences; Electrical Engineering; Environmental Management; Film; Food Science; Foreign Languages Education; Geography; Geological Engineering; Gerontology; Higher Education; History; Hotel Management; Hydraulic Engineering; Immunology; Industrial Chemistry; Industrial Engineering; Law; Library Science; Linguistics; Literature; Mathematics; Mathematics Education; Mechanical Engineering; Medicine; Meteorology; Microbiology; Music; Native Language Education; Nursing; Nutrition; Parasitology; Parks and Recreation; Pharmacy; Physics; Political Sciences; Psychology; Public Administration; Public Health; Social Work; Sociology; Sports; Statistics; Surgery; Tourism; Transport Engineering; Visual Arts; Women's Studies.** *Doctorado Académico*: **Agriculture; Computer Science; Cultural Studies; Education; Engineering; Government; Natural Sciences; Philosophy; Political Sciences.**

Student Services: Academic Counselling, Cultural Activities, Facilities for disabled people, Health Services, Nursery Care, Sports Facilities

Last Updated: 12/10/15

PRIVATE INSTITUTIONS

ADVENTIST UNIVERSITY OF CENTRAL AMERICA

Universidad Adventista de Centroamérica (UNADECA)

1.5 Km. al Norte de los Tribunales de Justicia, La Ceiba, Apartado 138-4050, Alajuela 4050
Tel: +506 2436-3300
EMail: admisiones@unadeca.net
Website: http://unadeca.ac.cr

Rector: Rosa Herminia Perla Perla
EMail: herminiaperla@hotmail.com

School

Business Administration (Business Administration); **Education** (Education); **Nursing** (Nursing); **Psychology** (Psychology); **Systems Engineering** (Engineering); **Theology** (Theology)

History: Founded 1986.

Academic Year: January to November

Admission Requirements: Secondary school certificate (bachillerato)

Main Language(s) of Instruction: Spanish

Accrediting Agency: Consejo Nacional de Enseñanza Universitaria Privada (CONESUP); Ministerio de Educación Pública

Degrees and Diplomas: *Bachillerato Universitario*: **Business Administration; Education; Engineering; Secretarial Studies; Theology.** *Licenciatura*: **Business Administration; Business Education; Computer Education; Humanities and Social Science Education; Mathematics Education; Native Language Education; Nursing; Preschool Education; Primary Education; Psychology; Religion; Theology.** *Maestría*: **Business Administration; Educational Administration; Pastoral Studies.**

Student Services: Academic Counselling, Facilities for disabled people, Health Services, Language Laboratory, Sports Facilities

Last Updated: 11/09/15

ALMA MATER UNIVERSITY

Universidad Fundepos Alma Mater

Frente al Puente Juan Pablo II, Edificio San José 2000, tercer piso., San José
Tel: +506 2290-2916
EMail: matricula@fundepos.ac.cr
Website: http://www.fundepos.ac.cr

Programme

Accountancy (Accountancy); **Business Administration** (Business Administration); **Marketing** (Marketing); **Preschool Education** (Preschool Education); **Primary Education** (Primary Education)

History: Founded 2003.

Main Language(s) of Instruction: Spanish

Accrediting Agency: CONESUP

Degrees and Diplomas: *Bachillerato Universitario*: **Accountancy; Business Administration; Management; Marketing; Preschool Education; Primary Education.** *Licenciatura*: **Accountancy; Management; Marketing; Preschool Education; Primary Education.** *Maestria*: **Finance; Hotel Management; Human Resources; Management; Marketing.**

Last Updated: 14/09/15

AMERICAN UNIVERSITY

Universidad Americana

Apartado 1901-1002, Barrio Los Yoses, frente a Pollos Kentucky, Calle 21, San José
Tel: +506 2207-7000
Fax: +506 2224-6842
EMail: matricula@uam.ac.cr
Website: http://www.uam.ac.cr

Rector: Rosa María Monge Monge

School

Administration and Accounting (Accountancy; Administration); **Communication and Design** (Advertising and Publicity; Graphic Design); **Education** (Education); **Englsh Languages Education** (English; Foreign Languages Education); **Industrial Engineering** (Industrial Engineering); **Law** (Law); **Mathematics Education** (Mathematics Education); **Physical Therapy** (Physical Therapy); **Psychology** (Industrial and Organizational Psychology; Psychology); **Systems Engineering** (Engineering)

Further Information: Branches in Cartago and Heredia

History: Founded 1997.

Main Language(s) of Instruction: Spanish

Accrediting Agency: CONESUP

Degrees and Diplomas: *Bachillerato Universitario*: **Accountancy; Advertising and Publicity; Business Administration; Business Education; Computer Education; Design; Education; Foreign Languages Education; Human Resources; Humanities and Social Science Education; Industrial Engineering; Law; Marketing; Mathematics Education; Native Language Education; Physical Therapy; Preschool Education; Primary Education; Psychology; Science Education; Secondary Education.** *Licenciatura*: **Accountancy; Advertising and Publicity; Business Administration; Design; Foreign Languages Education; Human Resources; Humanities and Social Science Education; Industrial and Organizational Psychology; Industrial Engineering; Marketing; Mathematics Education; Native Language Education; Notary Studies; Physical Therapy; Preschool Education; Primary Education; Science Education; Secondary Education.** *Maestría*: **Business Administration; Educational Administration; Physical Therapy; Special Education; Teacher Training.**

Last Updated: 11/09/15

AUTONOMOUS UNIVERSITY OF CENTRAL AMERICA

Universidad Autónoma de Centro América (UACA)

Apartado 7637, San José 1000
Tel: +506 2272-9100
Fax: +506 2271-2046
EMail: info@uaca.ac.cr
Website: http://www.uaca.ac.cr

Rector: Guillermo Malavassi Vargas (1997-)
EMail: gmalavassi@uaca.ac.cr

Faculty

Architecture (Architecture); **Engineering** (Civil Engineering; Electrical Engineering; Industrial Engineering; Mechanical Engineering; Surveying and Mapping); **Health Sciences** (Medicine; Nursing; Physical Therapy); **Humanities** (History; Library Science; Philology; Philosophy; Physical Education; Psychology; Theology); **Social Sciences** (Administration; Economics; International Relations; Journalism; Law; Tourism)

Further Information: Campuses in Nicoya, Ciudad Neilly, San Ramón de Alajuela, and Guápiles.

History: Founded 1976 as an independent institution authorized by the government. Includes eight independent self-governing Colleges.

Academic Year: January to December (January-April; May-August; September-December)

Admission Requirements: Secondary school certificate (bachillerato) or foreign equivalent, and entrance examination

Main Language(s) of Instruction: Spanish

Accrediting Agency: Consejo Nacional de Enseñanza Universitaria Privada (CONESUP)

Degrees and Diplomas: *Bachillerato Universitario*: **Architecture; Business Administration; Education; Engineering; Health Sciences; Law.** *Licenciatura*: **Architecture; Business Administration; Civil Engineering; Computer Engineering; Economics; Education; Engineering; Industrial Engineering; International Relations; Journalism; Law; Mechanical Engineering; Medicine; Music; Nursing; Philology; Philosophy; Physical Therapy; Psychology; Public Relations; Tourism.** *Especialidad Profesional*: **Notary Studies.** *Maestría*: **Advertising and Publicity; Business Administration; Education; Environmental Management; Industrial Engineering; Law; Psychology; Psychotherapy; Public Relations.** *Doctorado Académico*: **Arts and Humanities; Business Administration; Engineering; Health Sciences; Law.**

Student Services: Academic Counselling, Canteen, Cultural Activities, Health Services, Sports Facilities

Last Updated: 10/09/15

AUTONOMOUS UNIVERSITY OF MONTERREY

Universidad Autónoma de Monterrey

Apartado 3510-1000, San José
Tel: +506 2283-7853
Fax: +506 2253-4395
EMail: info@unam.ac.cr
Website: http://www.unam.ac.cr

Rector: Oscar Sáenz Vargas EMail: rectoria@unam.ac.cr

Programme

Accountancy (Accountancy); **Banking** (Banking); **Business Administration** (Business Administration); **Finance** (Finance); **Human Resources** (Human Resources); **Psychology** (Psychology)

History: Founded 1994.

Main Language(s) of Instruction: Spanish

Accrediting Agency: CONESUP

Degrees and Diplomas: *Bachillerato Universitario*: **Accountancy; Administration; Business Administration; Finance; Human Resources; Psychology.** *Licenciatura*: **Accountancy; Business**

Administration; Finance; Human Resources; Psychology; Public Administration. *Maestría*: **Accountancy; Environmental Management; Human Resources; Industrial and Organizational Psychology; Psychology.**
Last Updated: 11/09/15

BRAULIO CARRILLO UNIVERSITY

Universidad Braulio Carrillo
Apartado 1184-2050, Avenida 1, Calle 28/38, San José
Tel: +506 222-6780
Fax: +506 222-6775
EMail: carrillo@racsa.co.cr
Website: http://www.ubrauliocarrillo.com

Rector: Juan Manuel Gómez Solera

Division

Administration (Administration); **Foreign Trade** (International Business)

History: Founded 1994.

Main Language(s) of Instruction: Spanish

Accrediting Agency: CONESUP

Degrees and Diplomas: *Bachillerato Universitario*: **International Business; Taxation.** *Licenciatura*: **Taxation.** *Maestría*: **International Business.**
Last Updated: 10/09/15

BUSINESS UNIVERSITY OF COSTA RICA

Universidad Empresarial de Costa Rica (UNEM)
San José 62-2050
Tel: +506 2217-8931
Fax: +506 2219-4544

Rector: William Zamora González

Programme

Business Administration (Accountancy; Business Administration; Finance; Human Resources; International Business; Management; Marketing)

History: Founded 1992 as International Postgraduate School. Acquired present status and title 1997.

Academic Year: January to December

Admission Requirements: Secondary school certificate for all undergraduate programmes.

Main Language(s) of Instruction: English, Spanish

Accrediting Agency: Consejo Nacional de Enseñanza Universitaria Privada (CONESUP)

Degrees and Diplomas: *Bachillerato Universitario*: **Accountancy; Business Administration.** *Maestría*: **Business Administration.**

Student Services: Academic Counselling, Canteen, Careers Guidance, Cultural Activities, Foreign Studies Centre, Language Laboratory, Social Counselling, Sports Facilities
Last Updated: 05/01/16

CASTRO CARAZO METROPOLITAN UNIVERSITY

Universidad Metropolitana Castro Carazo (UMCA)
Apartado 325-1005, San José
Tel: +506 2542-0300
Fax: +506 2248-1553
EMail: info@umca.net
Website: http://www.umca.net

Rector: Estrella Porras Z.

Faculty

Accountancy (Accountancy); **Administration** (Business Administration); **Computer Science** (Computer Science); **Education** (Education); **Law** (Law)

Further Information: Campuses also in Limón, Puntarenas, Palmares, Pérez Zeledón, Puriscal, Paso Canoas.

History: Founded 1996.

Accrediting Agency: CONESUP

Degrees and Diplomas: *Bachillerato Universitario*: **Business Administration; Computer Science; Education; Engineering; Law.** *Licenciatura*: **Business Administration; Computer Science; Education; Educational Administration; Law.** *Maestría*: **Business Administration; Educational Administration.** *Doctorado Académico*: **Educational Sciences.**
Last Updated: 27/10/15

CATHOLIC UNIVERSITY OF COSTA RICA

Universidad Católica de Costa Rica
Apartado postal 519-2100, San José
Tel: +506 2240-7272
Fax: +506 2240-2121
EMail: info@ucatolica.ac.cr
Website: http://www.ucatolica.ac.cr

Rector: Fernando A. Muñoz (2010-)
EMail: rectoria@ucatolica.ac.cr

Faculty

Business Administration (Business Administration); **Education** (Education); **Law** (Law); **Philosophy** (Philosophy); **Psychology** (Psychology); **Systems Engineering** (Engineering); **Theology** (Theology)

Further Information: Campuses in San Carlos, Nicoya, and Ciudad Neilly.

History: Founded 1993 by the Conferencia Episcopal de Costa Rica. Also known as Universidad Católica de Costa Rica Anselmo Llorente y Lafuente.

Academic Year: January to December (January-April; May-August; September-December)

Admission Requirements: Secondary school certificate (bachillerato)

Main Language(s) of Instruction: Spanish

Accrediting Agency: CONESUP; SINAES

Degrees and Diplomas: *Bachillerato Universitario*: **Business Administration; Educational Sciences; Industrial Engineering; Law; Philosophy; Psychology; Teacher Training; Theology.** *Licenciatura*: **Business Administration; Educational Administration; Educational Sciences; Engineering; Law; Psychology; Teacher Training; Theology.** *Maestría*: **Business Administration; Educational Psychology; Educational Sciences; Engineering; Finance; Industrial and Organizational Psychology; International Business; Management; Marketing; Psychology; Theology.** *Doctorado Académico*: **Educational Sciences.**

Student Services: Academic Counselling, Canteen, Careers Guidance, Cultural Activities, Health Services, Sports Facilities
Last Updated: 11/09/15

CENFOTEC UNIVERSITY

Universidad CENFOTEC
Santa Marta – San Pedro de Montes Oca, del Cruce de la Escuela de Santa Marta 400 metros noreste carretera al Cristo de Sabanilla, San José 11501
Tel: +506 2281-1555
EMail: info@ucenfotec.ac.cr
Website: https://www.ucenfotec.ac.cr

Rector: Ignacio Trejos Zelaya

Programme

Engineering (Computer Engineering; Information Technology; Software Engineering)

History: Created 2000 as a specialised institution awarding degrees of Universidad Latina de Costa Rica. Acquired own degree-awarding powers in 2011

Accrediting Agency: CONESUP

Degrees and Diplomas: *Bachillerato Universitario*: **Information Technology; Software Engineering.** *Maestría*: **Computer Engineering.**
Last Updated: 27/10/15

CENTRAL AMERICAN BUSINESS UNIVERSITY

Universidad Centroamericana de Ciencias Empresariales (UCEM)

110 metros norte de la Catedral, Alajuela
Tel: +506 2430 6553 +506 2440-2090
EMail: info@ucem.ac.cr
Website: http://universidaducem.cr

Rector: Chester J. Zelaya-Goodman (1998-)

Division

Accountancy (Accountancy); **Bilingual Preschool Education** (Preschool Education); **Bilingual Primary and Secondary Education** (Primary Education; Secondary Education); **Business Administration** (Business Administration); **Industrial Engineering** (Industrial Engineering); **Systems Engineering** (Computer Engineering); **Tourism and Hotel Management** (Hotel Management; Tourism)

History: Founded 1997.

Academic Year: 3 periods starting January, May and September

Admission Requirements: High school diploma

Main Language(s) of Instruction: Spanish

Accrediting Agency: CONESUP

Degrees and Diplomas: *Bachillerato Universitario*: **Business Administration; Education; Engineering; Hotel Management; Tourism.** *Licenciatura*: **Accountancy.**

Student Services: Academic Counselling, Careers Guidance, Language Laboratory, Social Counselling

Last Updated: 11/09/15

CENTRAL AMERICAN UNIVERSITY OF SOCIAL SCIENCES

Universidad Centroamericana de Ciencias Sociales (UCACIS)

Banco Nacional de San Pedro, 2 cuadras al sur, 5 cuadras al este y 4 cuadras al Sur, San José
Tel: +506 2280-5310
Fax: +506 2280-1607
EMail: info@ucacis.ac.cr
Website: http://ucacis.ac.cr

Rector: Maribel Soto Arguedas

Programme

Education (Preschool Education); **Psychology** (Psychology)

Accrediting Agency: CONESUP

Degrees and Diplomas: *Bachillerato Universitario*: **Preschool Education; Psychology.** *Licenciatura*: **Preschool Education; Psychology.** *Maestria*: **Psychoanalysis; Psychology.**

Last Updated: 11/09/15

CENTRAL UNIVERSITY

Universidad Central

Apartado 1788-1002, De la Iglesia Sta. Teresita, 200 Norte y 225 Este, Diagonal Rotonda el Farolito, San José
Tel: +506 2212-0400
Fax: +506 2212-0422
EMail: mercadeo@universidadcentral.com
Website: http://www.universidadcentral.com

Rector: Sergio Mata Navarro
EMail: Rector@universidadcentral.com

Faculty

Economic Sciences (Accountancy; Banking; Business Administration; Business and Commerce; Finance; Human Resources; International Business; Management); **Education** (Curriculum; Education; Educational Administration; Educational and Student Counselling; Mathematics Education; Preschool Education; Science Education; Teacher Training); **Engineering Sciences** (Architecture; Civil Engineering; Computer Engineering; Electrical and Electronic Engineering; Electronic Engineering; Industrial Engineering); **Postgraduate Studies**; **Social Sciences** (Journalism; Law; Psychology)

Programme

Medicine (Medicine; Surgery)

Further Information: Campuses in Los Santos, Alajuela, Heredia, Desamparados, Cartago, and Puriscal.

History: Founded 1990.

Main Language(s) of Instruction: Spanish

Accrediting Agency: CONESUP

Degrees and Diplomas: *Bachillerato Universitario*: **Accountancy; Business Administration; Educational Sciences; Engineering; International Business; International Relations; Journalism; Law; Psychology; Teacher Training; Tourism.** *Licenciatura*: **Accountancy; Advertising and Publicity; Architecture; Business Administration; Civil Engineering; Computer Engineering; Educational Sciences; Electrical and Electronic Engineering; Industrial Engineering; International Relations; Journalism; Medicine; Surgery; Teacher Training; Tourism.** *Maestría*: **Educational Administration; Teacher Training.**

Student Services: Language Laboratory, Social Counselling

Last Updated: 11/09/15

CONTINENTAL UNIVERSITY OF ARTS AND SCIENCE

Universidad Continental de las Ciencias y el Arte

300 mts este del Museo Nacional, San José, Diagonal a INTACO, San José
Tel: +506 2256-7944
EMail: info@uccart.com
Website: http://www.uccart.com

Rector: Leonardo Villegas Gómez EMail: rectoria@uccart.com

Programme

Art Education (Art Education); **Graphic Design** (Graphic Design); **Higher Education** (Higher Education); **Music** (Music); **Music Education** (Music Education); **Preschool Education** (Preschool Education)

History: Created 1999.

Accrediting Agency: CONESUP

Degrees and Diplomas: *Bachillerato Universitario*: **Art Education; Design; Fine Arts; Music; Music Education; Preschool Education.** *Maestria*: **Higher Education Teacher Training; Preschool Education.**

Last Updated: 11/09/15

COSTA RICAN TECHNOLOGICAL UNIVERSITY

Universidad Tecnológica Costarricense (UTEC)

50 metros del Banco de Costa Rica, Edificio Paz, San José
Tel: +506 2223-1124
Fax: +506 2222-3722
EMail: info@utccr.com
Website: http://www.utccr.com

Rector: Carlos Castro Quesada

Programme

Business Administration (Business Administration); **Computer Science** (Computer Science)

Further Information: Campuses also in Grecia, Barrio El Socorro, Pérez Zeledón, and Guápiles

Accrediting Agency: CONESUP

Degrees and Diplomas: *Bachillerato Universitario*: **Accountancy; Business Administration; Computer Engineering.** *Licenciatura*: **Accountancy; Business Administration; Computer Engineering; Information Management.** *Maestria*: **Finance; Human Resources.**

Last Updated: 10/09/15

CREATIVE UNIVERSITY

Universidad Creativa

San Pedro Montes de Oca, frente al Servicentro El Higuerón, edificio esquinero, segundo piso., San José, San José
Tel: +506 2528-5095
Fax: +506 2234-5594
EMail: info@ucreativa.com
Website: http://www.ucreativa.com

Rector: Luis Montoya Salas

Coordinadora de Mercadeo: Ana Vallejo
Tel: (506) 2528-5095 ext1200 EMail: ana.vallejo@ucreativa.com

General Director: Oscar Romero
EMail: oscar.romero@ucreativa.com

International Relations: Giselle Melendez, Marketing Manager
EMail: giselle.melendez@ucreativa.com

Programme
3D Digital Modeling; **Architectural Design** (Architectural and Environmental Design); **Architecture** (Architecture); **Cultural Management** (Art Management); **Development and Web Design** (Software Engineering); **Digital Animation**; **Digital Audio Visual Production**; **Digital Communications**; **Digital Marketing**; **Digital Photography** (Photography); **Fashion Design** (Fashion Design); **Graphic Design** (Graphic Design); **Interior Design** (Interior Design); **Ilustrations and Concept Art** (Painting and Drawing); **Music Education** (Music Education); **Publicity** (Advertising and Publicity); **Video Game Programming and Design** (Computer Graphics)

History: Founded 1995, and began opeating as a university in 2000.

Fees: 75,000 per annum (Costa Rican Colon)

Main Language(s) of Instruction: Spanish

Accrediting Agency: Tecnical Degree: Universidad Creativa; Undergratuate: Ministerio de Educación Pública; Bachelor Degree: CONESUP

Degrees and Diplomas: *Diplomado*: **Architecture and Planning; Arts and Humanities; Mathematics and Computer Science.** *Bachillerato Universitario*: **Architecture and Planning; Fine Arts; Graphic Design; Interior Design.** *Licenciatura*: **Architecture and Planning; Graphic Design; Interior Design.**

Student Services: Academic Counselling, Careers Guidance, Cultural Activities, Facilities for disabled people, IT Centre, Library, Social Counselling, eLibrary

Academic Staff *2015-2016*	MEN	WOMEN	TOTAL
FULL-TIME	31	22	**53**
PART-TIME	4	4	**8**
Student Numbers *2015-2016*			
All (Foreign included)	875	1,087	**1,962**
FOREIGN ONLY	11	9	**20**

Last Updated: 07/07/15

EARTH UNIVERSITY

Universidad EARTH (EARTH)
Apartado 4442-1000, San José
Tel: +506 2713-0000
Fax: +506 2713-0001
EMail: jzaglul@earth.ac.cr
Website: http://www.earth.ac.cr

Rector: José A. Zaglul (1989-) EMail: jzaglul@earth.ac.cr

Programme
Agricultural Sciences (Agriculture)

History: Founded 1990.

Academic Year: January to December (3 trimesters)

Admission Requirements: Secondary school certificate

Main Language(s) of Instruction: Spanish

Accrediting Agency: Sistema Nacional de Acreditatión de la Educatión Superior (SINAES)

Degrees and Diplomas: *Licenciatura*: **Agriculture.**

Last Updated: 11/09/15

EVANGELICAL UNIVERSITY OF THE AMERICAS

Universidad Evangélica de las Américas (UNELA)
Costado Oeste de la Clínica Bíblica, Torre Omega 9 piso, San José
Tel: +506 2221-7870
Fax: +506 2255-0257
EMail: info@unela.ac.cr
Website: http://unela.ac.cr

Rector: Enrique Guang Tapia

School
Applied Sciences and Interdisciplinary Studies (Cultural Studies; Missionary Studies); **Education** (Education); **Theology** (Theology)

History: Founded 1992 by the Church of Nazarene. Acquired present status and title 1999.

Academic Year: March to November

Admission Requirements: Secondary school certificate (bachillerato)

Main Language(s) of Instruction: Spanish

Accrediting Agency: Consejo Nacional de Enseñanza Universitaria Privada (CONESUP)

Degrees and Diplomas: *Bachillerato Universitario*: **Theology.** *Licenciatura*: **Religious Education; Theology.** *Maestría*: **Religion; Religious Education; Theology.** *Doctorado Académico*: **Theology.**

Last Updated: 14/09/15

FEDERATED UNIVERSITY OF COSTA RICA

Universidad Federada de Costa Rica (UNIFE)
Apartado 250-2120, frente Principal del Museo Nacional, San José
Tel: +506 2223-2767
Fax: +506 2257-0104
EMail: info@ufederada.ac.cr
Website: http://www.ufederada.ac.cr/

Rector: Helia Betancourt Plasencia

College
San Judas *(University College)* (Education; Journalism; Medicine; Surgery); **Santo Tomás** *(University College)* (Business Administration; Law)

History: Founded 1995.

Academic Year: January to December (January-May; May-August; September-December)

Admission Requirements: Secondary school certificate (bachillerato)

Fees: (Colones): 14,000-35,000 per annum

Main Language(s) of Instruction: Spanish, English

Degrees and Diplomas: *Bachillerato Universitario*: **Administration; Education; Health Sciences; Journalism; Law; Medicine; Surgery.** *Licenciatura*: **Business Administration; Law; Mass Communication; Medicine; Multimedia; Preschool Education; Primary Education; Surgery.** *Especialidad Profesional*: **Notary Studies.** *Maestría*: **Communication Studies; Fiscal Law.**

Student Services: Academic Counselling, Canteen, Careers Guidance, Sports Facilities

Publishing house: Editorial San Judas Tadeo

Last Updated: 10/09/15

FIDELITAS UNIVERSITY

Universidad Fidélitas
Apartado 8063-1000, Escuela Santa Marta de Montes de Oca, San José
Tel: +506 2206-8600
EMail: info@ufidelitas.ac.cr
Website: http://www.ufidelitas.ac.cr

Rector: Ana Isabel Solano Brenes

Faculty
Economic and Social Sciences (Accountancy; Advertising and Publicity; Business Administration; Design; Law; Psychology); **Engineering** (Civil Engineering; Computer Engineering; Electrical Engineering; Industrial Engineering; Mechanical Engineering)

Programme
Education (Educational Sciences; Teacher Training)

History: Founded 1980 as Collegium Fidelitas, acquired present status and title 1995.

Academic Year: January to December (January-April; May-August; September-December)

Admission Requirements: Secondary school certificate (bachillerato) or foreign equivalent

Main Language(s) of Instruction: Spanish

Accrediting Agency: CONESUP

Degrees and Diplomas: *Bachillerato Universitario*: **Business Administration; Design; Education; Engineering; Law; Psychology.** *Licenciatura*: **Accountancy; Business Administration; Civil Engineering; Computer Engineering; Educational Administration; Electrical Engineering; Finance; Industrial Engineering; Law; Marketing; Mechanical Engineering; Preschool Education; Primary Education; Psychology.** *Especialidad Profesional*: **Notary Studies.** *Maestría*: **Accountancy; Business Administration; Clinical Psychology; Finance; Human Resources; Industrial Management; Management; Marketing; Preschool Education; Primary Education.** *Doctorado Académico*: **Business Administration.**

Last Updated: 14/09/15

FLORENCIO DEL CASTILLO UNIVERSITY

Universidad Florencio del Castillo

Apartado 653-7050, 100 Metros Sur de la Esquina Sureste de los Tribunales, Cártago

Tel: +506 2591-4562

Fax: +506 2552-2200

EMail: info@uca.ac.cr

Website: http://www.uca.ac.cr

Rector: Christian Chinchilla Monge

Division

Accountancy (Accountancy); **Administration** (Administration); **Business Administration** (Business Administration); **Education** (Education); **Human Resource Management** (Human Resources); **Law** (Law); **Tourism** (Tourism)

Further Information: Campuses at Heredia, Desamparados, Turrialba, and Siquirres

History: Founded 1980 and acquired status 1995.

Main Language(s) of Instruction: Spanish

Degrees and Diplomas: *Bachillerato Universitario*: **Business Administration; Education; Tourism.** *Licenciatura*: **Accountancy; Business Administration; Education; Law; Tourism.** *Maestría*: **Educational Administration; Educational Psychology; Preschool Education; Primary Education.**

Last Updated: 10/09/15

FREE SCHOOL OF LAW UNIVERSITY

Universidad Escuela Libre de Derecho

Zapote, 75 metros al oeste del Registro Nacional, San José

Tel: +506 2283-5533

Fax: +506 2283-8061

EMail: info@uescuelalibre.ac.cr

Website: http://www.uescuelalibre.ac.cr

Rector: Ricardo Guerrero Portilla

Programme

Administration and Business Law (Administration; Commercial Law); **International Relations** (International Relations); **Law** (Law)

History: Founded 1996.

Main Language(s) of Instruction: Spanish

Degrees and Diplomas: *Bachillerato Universitario*: **Law.** *Licenciatura*: **International Relations; Law.** *Especialidad Profesional*: **Notary Studies.** *Maestría*: **Administrative Law; Commercial Law.** *Doctorado Académico*: **Law.**

Publications: Revistas

Last Updated: 11/09/15

FREE UNIVERSITY OF COSTA RICA

Universidad Libre de Costa Rica (ULICORI)

Apartado 1053-1000, Av. Central y 2, Calle 25, 100 Este de Bomba La Primavera en Barrio La California, San José

Tel: +506 2258-0033

Fax: +506 2222-5507

EMail: info@ulicori.ac.cr

Website: http://www.ulicori.com

Rector: Carlos Paniagua Vargas EMail: rectoria@ulicori.ac.cr

Faculty

Administrative Sciences (Business Administration); **Economics** (Economics); **Educational Sciences** (Education); **Health Sciences** (Health Sciences); **Social Sciences** (Social Sciences)

History: Founded 1993.

Academic Year: January to December

Admission Requirements: Secondary school certficate (bachillerato)

Main Language(s) of Instruction: Spanish

Accrediting Agency: CONESUP

Degrees and Diplomas: *Bachillerato Universitario*: **Business Administration; Criminology; Education; Health Administration; Physical Therapy; Political Sciences; Social Work.** *Licenciatura*: **Business Administration; Criminology; Education; Health Administration; Physical Therapy; Political Sciences; Social Work.** *Maestría*: **Education; International Business.** *Doctorado Académico*: **Education.**

Last Updated: 26/10/15

HISPANO-AMERICAN UNIVERSITY

Universidad Hispanoamericana

Apartado 408-1002, 100 Oeste y 100 Norte Santa Teresita, Barrio Aranjuez, San José

Tel: +506 2256-8197

Fax: +506 2223-2349

EMail: info@uh.ac.cr

Website: https://uh.ac.cr

Rector: Ángel Marín Espinoza

Faculty

Architecture and Engineering (Architecture; Computer Engineering; Electronic Engineering; Industrial Engineering); **Economic Sciences** (Business Administration); **Education** (Bilingual and Bicultural Education; Education; Educational Administration; Preschool Education; Primary Education); **Health Sciences** (Medicine; Nursing; Nutrition; Psychology; Surgery); **Social Sciences** (Advertising and Publicity; Design; Law; Tourism)

School

Postgraduate Studies

Further Information: Campuses in Llorente de Tibás, Heredia, and Puntarenas.

History: Founded 1992. A private institution authorized by the government.

Academic Year: January to December (January-May; May-September; September-December)

Admission Requirements: Secondary school certificate (bachillerato)

Main Language(s) of Instruction: Spanish

Accrediting Agency: Consejo Nacional de Enseñanza Universitaria Privada (CONESUP)

Degrees and Diplomas: *Bachillerato Universitario*: **Architecture; Business Administration; Design; Education; Engineering; Law; Nursing; Nutrition; Psychology; Tourism.** *Licenciatura*: **Accountancy; Advertising and Publicity; Architecture; Business Administration; Design; Education; Engineering; Law; Medicine; Nursing; Nutrition; Psychology; Surgery; Tourism.** *Maestría*: **Accountancy; Business Administration; Education; Educational Administration; Educational Psychology; Health Administration; Nursing.** *Doctorado Académico*: **Medicine; Rehabilitation and Therapy.**

Last Updated: 14/09/15

INDEPENDENT UNIVERSITY OF COSTA RICA

Universidad Independiente de Costa Rica (UNICOR)

Apartado 414-2400, Desamparados 50 E. Esquina Noreste del Cementerio, San José

Tel: +506 2562-7330

EMail: info@uindependiente.ac.cr

Website: http://www.uindependiente.ac.cr

Rector: Sonia Abarca Mora

Faculty
Education and Human Sciences (Education); **Social Sciences and Administration** (Administration; Business Administration; Psychology)

History: Founded 1996.

Admission Requirements: Secondary school certificate (Bachillerato)

Main Language(s) of Instruction: Spanish

Accrediting Agency: CONESUP

Degrees and Diplomas: *Bachillerato Universitario*: **Administration; Education; Psychology; Secretarial Studies.** *Licenciatura*: **Administration; Business Education; Education; Psychology.** *Maestría*: **Clinical Psychology; Computer Education; Educational Psychology; Industrial and Organizational Psychology; Preschool Education; Primary Education; Psychology.**

Last Updated: 14/09/15

INTERNATIONAL CHRISTIAN UNIVERSITY

Universidad Cristiana Internacional
200 metros este del WalMart en San Sebastián
(calle paralela a la pista), San José
Tel: +506 2227-1958
EMail: comunicacion@esepa.org
Website: http://www.esepa.org

Director: Sadrac Meza Pérez

Programme
Business Administration (Business Administration); **Education** (Education); **Law** (Law)

Accrediting Agency: CONESUP

Degrees and Diplomas: *Bachillerato Universitario*: **Accountancy; Business Administration; Education; Law.** *Licenciatura*: **Accountancy; Business Administration; Education; Law.**

Last Updated: 11/09/15

INTERNATIONAL UNIVERSITY OF THE AMERICAS

Universidad Internacional de las Américas (UIA)
Apartado 1447-1002, San José
Tel: +506 2212-5500
EMail: info@uia.ac.cr; registro@uia.ac.cr
Website: http://www.uia.ac.cr

Rector: Máximo Sequeira Alemán

Faculty
Economic Sciences (Accountancy; Business Administration; Economics; International Business; International Economics); **Engineering and Architecture** (Architecture; Computer Engineering; Electrical Engineering; Engineering; Industrial Engineering; Mechanical Engineering); **Health Sciences** (Medicine; Pharmacy); **Languages** (English; Modern Languages); **Law** (Law); **Social Sciences** (Advertising and Publicity; International Relations; Social Sciences; Tourism)

Further Information: Campus also in San Francisco de Heredia.

History: Founded 1986 by the International Foundation of the Americas. Acquired present status 1987.

Academic Year: January to December (January-April; May-August; September-December)

Admission Requirements: Secondary school certificate (bachillerato) or foreign equivalent, and entrance examination

Main Language(s) of Instruction: Spanish

Accrediting Agency: CONESUP

Degrees and Diplomas: *Bachillerato Universitario*: **Business Administration; Education; Engineering; International Relations; Journalism; Modern Languages; Tourism.** *Licenciatura*: **Accountancy; Architecture; Business Administration; Dentistry; Economics; Finance; Foreign Languages Education; Industrial Engineering; International Business; Journalism; Management; Marketing; Medicine; Pharmacy; Preschool Education; Software Engineering; Surgery; Tourism.** *Especialidad Profesional*: **Notary Studies.** *Maestría*: **Business Administration; Commercial Law; Computer Engineering; Educational Administration; Finance; Human Resources; Industrial Engineering; International Business; Management; Marketing; Oncology; Radiology.** *Doctorado Académico*: **Business Administration; Medicine; Surgery.**

Last Updated: 15/09/15

ISAAC NEWTON UNIVERSITY

Universidad Isaac Newton
125 m este de la rotonda de Betania Sabanilla, San José
Tel: +506 2225-9081
Fax: +506 2234-1893
Website: http://www.unin.ac.cr

Rector: Luis Alberto Valverde Obando

Programme
Advertising (Advertising and Publicity); **Business Administration** (Administration; Advertising and Publicity; Business Administration; Public Relations); **Civil Engineering** (Civil Engineering); **Environmental Engineering** (Environmental Engineering); **Industrial Engineering** (Industrial Engineering); **Public Relations** (Public Relations)

History: Founded 1995.

Main Language(s) of Instruction: Spanish

Accrediting Agency: CONESUP

Degrees and Diplomas: *Bachillerato Universitario*: **Business Administration; Engineering.** *Licenciatura*: **Business Administration; Civil Engineering; Industrial Engineering; Public Relations.** *Maestría*: **Environmental Engineering.**

Last Updated: 24/09/15

JOHN PAUL II UNIVERSITY

Universidad Juan Pablo II
Apartado 11161 Esquina Norteste Iglesia de Curridabat, San José
Tel: +506 2272-5901
Fax: +506 2272-5923
EMail: admision@ujpii.ac.cr
Website: http://www.ujpii.ac.cr

Rector: Emilio Garreaud Indacochea

Programme
Family Studies (Family Studies); **Religion** (Religion)

History: Founded 1996.

Main Language(s) of Instruction: Spanish

Accrediting Agency: CONESUP

Degrees and Diplomas: *Bachillerato Universitario*: **Business Administration; Industrial Engineering; Psychology; Religion.** *Licenciatura*: **Business Administration; Industrial Engineering.** *Maestría*: **Business Administration; Pedagogy; Religious Education.**

Last Updated: 06/11/15

LATIN AMERICAN BIBLICAL UNIVERSITY

Universidad Bíblica Latinoamericana (UBL)
Cedros de Montes de Oca, 375 Este del Perimercado, Apartado Postal 901-1000, San José
Tel: +506 2283-8848
Fax: +506 2283-6826
EMail: registro@ubila.net
Website: http://www.ubila.net

Rector: Edwin Mora

School
Bible (Bible); **Theology** (Theology)

History: Founded 1997.

Main Language(s) of Instruction: Spanish

Accrediting Agency: CONESUP

Degrees and Diplomas: *Bachillerato Universitario*: **Bible; Theology.** *Licenciatura*: **Bible; Theology.** *Maestría*: **Bible; Pastoral Studies; Theology.**

Last Updated: 11/09/15

LATIN AMERICAN UNIVERSITY OF SCIENCE AND TECHNOLOGY

Universidad Latinoamericana de Ciencia y Tecnología (ULACIT)

Apartado 10235, San José 1000
Tel: +506 2523-4000
Fax: +506 2223-9739
EMail: info@ulacit.ac.cr
Website: http://www.ulacit.ac.cr

Rector: Silvia Castro

Faculty

Engineering (Computer Engineering; Electronic Engineering; Industrial Engineering; Occupational Health); **Health Sciences** (Dentistry); **Social Sciences** (Educational Administration; English; Foreign Languages Education; Law; Preschool Education; Psychology; Special Education)

Graduate School

Graduate Studies *(Masters Degrees)* (Business Administration; Curriculum; Educational Psychology; English; Foreign Languages Education; Higher Education Teacher Training; Information Technology; Law; Orthodontics)

History: Founded 1988.

Academic Year: January to December

Admission Requirements: Secondary school certficate (bachillerato)

Main Language(s) of Instruction: Spanish

Accrediting Agency: CONESUP; SINAES

Degrees and Diplomas: *Bachillerato Universitario*: **Business Administration; Economics; Education; Engineering; English; Hotel and Restaurant; Law; Psychology; Special Education.** *Licenciatura*: **Accountancy; Behavioural Sciences; Business Administration; Chemical Engineering; Computer Engineering; Education; Finance; Industrial Engineering; International Business; Law; Marketing; Occupational Health; Orthodontics; Psychology; Tourism.** *Especialidad Profesional*: **Notary Studies; Orthodontics.** *Maestría*: **Business Administration; Commercial Law; Curriculum; Educational Psychology; Fiscal Law; Tourism.** *Doctorado Académico*: **Economics; Law.**

Student Services: Canteen, Cultural Activities

Last Updated: 26/10/15

LATIN UNIVERSITY - HEREDIA

Universidad Latina Campus Heredia

Apartado 6495-1000, Contiguo a Pricesmart carretera a Heredia, Heredia
Tel: +506 2277-8000
EMail: regresa.heredia@ulatina.cr
Website: http://www.ulatina.ac.cr

Rector: Henry Rodríguez Serrano

Faculty

Business Administration (Business Administration); **Engineering and Architecture** (Architecture; Engineering); **Health Sciences** (Health Sciences); **Information Technology** (Information Sciences); **Social Sciences** (Administration; Education; Social Sciences)

School

Hospitality Management (Cooking and Catering; Hotel Management)

History: Founded 1986 as Universidad Interamericana de Costa Rica (Interamerican University of Costa Rica). Acquired current title 2010. Recognized in its own right.

Academic Year: January to December (January-April; May-August; September-December)

Admission Requirements: Secondary school certificate (bachillerato)

Main Language(s) of Instruction: Spanish

Accrediting Agency: CONESUP

Degrees and Diplomas: *Bachillerato Universitario*: **Architecture; Business Administration; Cooking and Catering; Education; Engineering; Hotel and Restaurant; Interior Design; Journalism; Psychology; Public Relations; Religion; Special Education; Tourism.** *Licenciatura*: **Accountancy; Architecture; Business Administration; Civil Engineering; Computer Engineering; Educational Administration; Educational Technology; Electrical Engineering; Electronic Engineering; Engineering; Industrial Engineering; Law; Mass Communication; Mechanical Engineering; Media Studies; Psychology; Special Education.** *Especialidad Profesional*: **Notary Studies.** *Maestría*: **Accountancy; Business Administration; Commercial Law; Criminal Law; Educational Administration; Environmental Management; Finance; Homeopathy; Hotel Management; Human Resources; Industrial Engineering; Industrial Management; Insurance; International Law; Labour Law; Law; Management; Marketing; Rehabilitation and Therapy; Software Engineering; Special Education; Transport Management.** *Doctorado Académico*: **Educational Sciences.**

Last Updated: 15/09/15

LATIN UNIVERSITY OF COSTA RICA

Universidad Latina de Costa Rica (ULATINA)

Apartado 1561-2050, 300 Norte y 150 Este de Muñoz y Nanne, Lourdes, San Pedro de Montes de Oca
Tel: +506 283-2611
Fax: +506 225-2801
EMail: mercadeo@ulatina.ac.cr
Website: http://www.ulatina.ac.cr

Rector: Clotilde Fonseca Quesada

Faculty

Economics (Accountancy; Administration; Business Administration; Economics; Human Resources; International Relations); **Education** (Education; English; History; Philosophy; Special Education); **Engineering and Architecture** (Architecture; Civil Engineering; Computer Engineering; Engineering; Software Engineering; Telecommunications Engineering); **Health Sciences** (Dentistry; Health Sciences; Nursing; Optometry; Pharmacy; Psychology); **Social Sciences** (Advertising and Publicity; Journalism; Law; Public Relations; Social Sciences); **Tourism and Environmental Management** (Biological and Life Sciences; Hotel and Restaurant; Hotel Management; Tourism)

Further Information: Campuses also in Puntarenas, Limón, Palmares, Paso Canoas, Cañas, Santa Cruz de Guanacaste, Ciudad Neilly, Pérez Zeledón, Grecia.

History: Founded as college 1979, acquired present status 1989. Branches in major cities in Costa Rica and Panama.

Academic Year: January to December (January-April; May-August; September-December)

Admission Requirements: Secondary school certificate (bachillerato) or foreign equivalent

Main Language(s) of Instruction: Spanish

Accrediting Agency: CONESUP

Degrees and Diplomas: *Bachillerato Universitario*: **Accountancy; Architecture; Biological and Life Sciences; Business Administration; Economics; Education; Engineering; Environmental Management; Environmental Studies; Fine Arts; Health Sciences; Journalism; Law; Mass Communication; Nursing; Psychotherapy; Social Work; Tourism.** *Licenciatura*: **Accountancy; Architecture; Biological and Life Sciences; Business Administration; Dentistry; Economics; Education; Educational Technology; Engineering; International Relations; Journalism; Law; Medicine; Nursing; Pharmacy; Physical Therapy; Psychology; Social Work; Surgery; Tourism.** *Especialidad Profesional*: **Dentistry.** *Maestría*: **Agricultural Business; Business Administration; Economics; Educational Sciences; Educational Technology; Educational Testing and Evaluation; History; International Relations; Philosophy; Psychology; Teacher Training; Tourism.** *Doctorado Académico*: **Economics; Education; Educational Administration.**

Student Services: Academic Counselling, Canteen, Careers Guidance, Cultural Activities, Health Services, Social Counselling, Sports Facilities

Last Updated: 20/10/15

MAGISTER UNIVERSITY

Universidad Magister

Apartado 988-1000, Barrio Dent de la Facultad de Derecho de la U.C.R., 200 metros oeste, San José

Tel: +506 2234-0435

Fax: +506 2283-0324

EMail: info@umagister.com

Website: http://www.umagister.com

Rectora: Vivian González Trejos EMail: rectoria@umagister.com

Programme

Business Administration (Administration; Business Administration); **Computer Science** (Computer Science); **Education** (Education); **English** (English)

History: Founded 1996.

Main Language(s) of Instruction: Spanish

Degrees and Diplomas: *Bachillerato Universitario*: **Business Administration; Computer Science; Engineering; English; Foreign Languages Education; Preschool Education.** *Licenciatura*: **Business Administration; Education; Engineering; Human Resources.** *Maestría*: **Business Administration; Education.**

Last Updated: 13/10/15

MEDICAL SCIENCES UNIVERSITY

Universidad de Ciencias Médicas (UCIMED)

Apartado 638-1007, Sabana Oeste, 400 Oeste del Ministerio de Agricultura, San José

Tel: +506 2549-0000

Fax: +506 2290-6116

EMail: info@ucimed.com

Website: http://www.ucimed.com

Rector: Pablo Guzmán Stein

Division

Medicine (Medicine); **Nutrition** (Nutrition); **Pharmacy** (Pharmacy); **Physiotherapy** (Physical Therapy)

History: Founded 1976.

Academic Year: January to December (January-June; July-December)

Admission Requirements: Secondary school certificate

Main Language(s) of Instruction: Spanish

Accrediting Agency: SINAES; CONESUP

Degrees and Diplomas: *Bachillerato Universitario*: **Dietetics; Health Sciences; Medicine; Microbiology; Nutrition; Pharmacy; Physical Therapy; Surgery.** *Licenciatura*: **Dietetics; Medicine; Microbiology; Nutrition; Pharmacy; Physical Therapy; Surgery.** *Especialidad Profesional*: **Dermatology.** *Maestría*: **Anatomy; Health Administration; Medicine.**

Student Services: Academic Counselling, Facilities for disabled people, Health Services, Language Laboratory, Nursery Care, Social Counselling

Last Updated: 11/09/15

METHODIST UNIVERSITY OF COSTA RICA

Universidad Metodista de Costa Rica (UNIMET)

Apartado 2148-2050 San Pedro Montes de Oca, San José

Tel: +506 2280-1230

Fax: +506 2280-1240

EMail: unimet@metodista.ed.cr

Rector: Oscar Aguilar Marín

School

Business (Business Administration); **Educational Sciences** (Education); **Law** (Law); **Theology** (Theology)

History: Founded 2000. Acquired present status 2001.

Admission Requirements: Diploma de Conclusión de Estudios Secundarios

Main Language(s) of Instruction: Spanish

Degrees and Diplomas: *Bachillerato Universitario*: **Business Administration; Education; Law; Psychology; Theology.** *Licenciatura*: **Business Administration; Educational Psychology; Law.** *Maestría*: **Education.**

Last Updated: 10/09/15

PANAMERICAN UNIVERSITY OF SAN JOSÉ

Universidad Panamericana de San José

Del Costado sur del Museo Nacional 50 metros al sur, mano izquierda, San José

Tel: +506 2233-5382

Rectora: Gina Brilla Ramírez

Programme

Administration (Administration); **Architecture** (Architecture); **Graphic Design, Advertising and Publicity** (Advertising and Publicity; Graphic Design); **Nursing** (Nursing)

Further Information: Campus also in Santiago de Puriscal

History: Founded 1988.

Academic Year: January to December (January-April; May-August; September-December)

Admission Requirements: Secondary school certificate (bachillerato) or foreign equivalent, and entrance examination

Main Language(s) of Instruction: Spanish

Accrediting Agency: CONESUP

Degrees and Diplomas: *Bachillerato Universitario*: **Agricultural Business; Architecture; Business Administration; Computer Science; Education; Engineering; Law; Nursing; Tourism.** *Licenciatura*: **Agricultural Business; Architecture; Business Administration; Civil Engineering; Law; Nursing.** *Maestría*: **Administration; Advertising and Publicity; Agricultural Business; Finance; International Business; Management; Marketing.**

Last Updated: 10/09/15

SAINT LUCY UNIVERSITY

Universidad Santa Lucía

100 mts este del Cine Omni, San José

Tel: +506 2257-4552

EMail: recepcion@usl.ac.cr

Website: http://usl.ac.cr

Rectora: Ligia Meneses Sanabria

Programme

Business Administration (Accountancy; Administration; Business Administration); **Education** (Education); **Health Sciences** (Health Administration; Public Health); **Law** (Law); **Nursing** (Nursing)

Further Information: Campuses also in Alajuela, San Carlos, Puntarenas, Limón, Guápiles, Cartago.

History: Founded 1996.

Main Language(s) of Instruction: Spanish

Accrediting Agency: CONESUP

Degrees and Diplomas: *Bachillerato Universitario*: **Business Administration; Education; Law; Nursing.** *Licenciatura*: **Business Administration; Education; Health Administration; Law; Nursing.** *Maestría*: **Business Administration; Gynaecology and Obstetrics; Health Administration; Psychiatry and Mental Health; Public Health.**

Last Updated: 27/10/15

SAINT MARK UNIVERSITY FOR ADMINISTRATIVE SCIENCES

Universidad en Ciencias Administrativas San Marcos (USAM)

Avenida 3, Calle 11, San José

Tel: +506 2257-87

Fax: +506 2221-9024

EMail: info@usam.ac.cr

Website: http://www.usam.ac.cr

Rector: Joaquín Brizuela Rojas

Programme

Accountancy (Accountancy); **Business Administration** (Business Administration); **Education** (Education); **Marketing** (Marketing)

History: Founded 1996.

Admission Requirements: Secondary school certificate (bachillerato)

Main Language(s) of Instruction: Spanish

Degrees and Diplomas: *Bachillerato Universitario*: **Accountancy; Business Administration; Marketing.** *Licenciatura*: **Accountancy; Banking; Business Administration; Education; Finance; Human Resources; International Business; Management; Marketing.** *Maestría*: **Accountancy; Finance; Human Resources; Marketing.**
Last Updated: 11/09/15

SAN ISIDRO LABRADOR INTERNATIONAL UNIVERSITY

Universidad Internacional San Isidro Labrador
300 mts sur de la Escuela Morazán, Barrio Morazán, San Isidro de El General, Pérez Zeledón, Pérez Zeledón
Tel: +506 2771-6767
Fax: +506 2771-6173
EMail: info@uisil.com
Website: http://www.uisil.com

Rector: Olga Montero Ceciliano

Programme
Business Administration (Accountancy; Business Administration; Finance); **Education** (Education); **Engineering** (Systems Analysis); **Law** (Law); **Tourism** (Tourism)

Further Information: Campuses also in Heredia, San Vito de Coto Brus, Quepos, San Carlos, Grecia, Buenos Aires, Río Claro.

History: Founded 1997.

Main Language(s) of Instruction: Spanish

Accrediting Agency: CONESUP

Degrees and Diplomas: *Bachillerato Universitario*: **Business Administration; Education; Hotel Management; Tourism.** *Licenciatura*: **Business Administration; Education; Hotel Management; Tourism.** *Especialidad Profesional*: **Notary Studies.** *Maestría*: **Educational Administration; Educational Sciences; Marketing; Preschool Education.**
Last Updated: 24/09/15

SAN JUAN DE LA CRUZ UNIVERSITY

Universidad San Juan de la Cruz
100 metros al Norte Palacio Municipal, San Pablo Heredia
EMail: info@universidadsanjuan.com
Website: http://www.universidadsanjuan.com

Rector: Guillermo Eladio Quirós Álvarez
EMail: rectoria@univeridadsanjuan.com

School
Accounting (Accountancy); **Business** (Business Administration); **Law** (Law)
History: Founded 1996.
Main Language(s) of Instruction: Spanish

Accrediting Agency: CONESUP

Degrees and Diplomas: *Bachillerato Universitario*: **Accountancy; Business Administration; Human Resources; Law; Management; Transport Management.** *Licenciatura*: **Accountancy; Business Administration; Human Resources; Law; Management; Transport Management.** *Maestría*: **Business Administration; Human Resources; Labour and Industrial Relations; Marketing.**
Last Updated: 28/08/15

SCIENCE AND ARTS UNIVERSITY OF COSTA RICA

Universidad de las Ciencias y el Arte de Costa Rica (UNICA)
250 m Sur de la Corte Suprema de Justicia, Barrio Luján, San José
Tel: +506 4031-0700
EMail: info@udelascienciasyelarte.ac.cr
Website: http://www.udelascienciasyelarte.ac.cr

Rector: Francisco Jiménez Villalobos (1997-)

School
Administrative Science (Administration); **Architecture** (Architecture); **Art, Communication and Design** (Communication Arts; Fine Arts); **Education** (Education); **Law** (Law); **Nursing** (Nursing)

Further Information: Campuses: Naranjo, Esparza, Cartago, Heredia, Alajuela, Desamparados, Tibás.

History: Founded 1981 as San Agustín College. Acquired present status 1997.

Academic Year: January to December

Admission Requirements: Secondary School Certificate or equivalent recognized by the Ministry of Education

Main Language(s) of Instruction: Spanish

Accrediting Agency: Consejo Nacional de Enseñanza Superior Privada (CONESUP)

Degrees and Diplomas: *Bachillerato Universitario*: **Advertising and Publicity; Agricultural Business; Architecture; Business Administration; Education; Fine Arts; Law; Nursing.** *Licenciatura*: **Advertising and Publicity; Agricultural Business; Architecture; Business Administration; Design; Education; Educational Sciences; Fine Arts; Law; Special Education.** *Maestría*: **Advertising and Publicity; Agricultural Business; Architecture; Banking; Business Administration; Curriculum; Educational Administration; Finance; Fine Arts; International Business; Law.** *Doctorado Académico*: **Administration.**

Student Services: Academic Counselling, Canteen, Careers Guidance, Facilities for disabled people, Health Services, Language Laboratory
Last Updated: 10/09/15

SOUTHERN CHRISTIAN UNIVERSITY

Universidad Cristiana del Sur
50 mts sur de Pizza Hut, Paseo Colón, Oficentro Grano de Oro Oficina #1000, San José
Tel: +506 2222-5302
Fax: +506 2222-5303
EMail: info@educacion.ac.cr
Website: http://www.educacion.ac.cr

Rector: Sonia Romero Mora

School
Business (Business Administration); **Law** (Law); **Theology** (Bible; Theology)

History: Founded 1998.

Fees: (US dollars): 150-175 per credit

Main Language(s) of Instruction: Spanish

Accrediting Agency: Consejo Nacional de Enseñanza Superior Privada (CONESUP)

Degrees and Diplomas: *Bachillerato Universitario*: **Business Administration; Law; Theology.** *Licenciatura*: **Accountancy; Business Administration; Law; Management; Theology.**
Last Updated: 11/09/15

TECHNOLOGICAL UNIVERSITY OF CENTRAL AMERICA MONSEÑOR OSCAR ARNULFO ROMERO

Universidad Teológica de América Central Monseñor Oscar Arnulfo Romero (UTAC)
200 metros al norte del Más por Menos, San Pedro de Montes de Oca
Tel: +506 2224-8238
EMail: info@utac.ac.cr
Website: http://www.utac.ac.cr

Rector: Carlos A. Villalobos EMail: rectoria@utac.ac.cr

Programme
Philosophy (Philosophy); **Religion** (Religion); **Theology** (Theology)

History: Created 2010.

Accrediting Agency: CONESUP

Degrees and Diplomas: *Bachillerato Universitario*: **Philosophy; Religion; Theology.** *Licenciatura*: **Philosophy; Religion; Theology.**
Last Updated: 27/10/15

UNIVERSITY FOR INTERNATIONAL COOPERATION

Universidad para la Cooperación Internacional
Apartado 504-2050, San José
Tel: +506 2283-6464
EMail: info@uci.ac.cr
Website: http://www.uci.ac.cr

Rector: Eduard Müller Castro EMail: emuller@uci.ac.cr

Faculty
Economics, Business and Technology (Economics); **Environmental Studies and Development** (Environmental Studies); **Health and Education** (Food Science); **Law and Social Sciences** (Law; Social Sciences)

School
Project Management (Management)

Campus Abroad
Mexico (Economics); **Panama** (Economics)

History: Founded 1994.

Academic Year: January to December

Admission Requirements: Bachelorate Degree for Graduate Programmes

Main Language(s) of Instruction: Spanish

Accrediting Agency: CONESUP

Degrees and Diplomas: *Bachillerato Universitario*: **Administration; Economics; Law.** *Licenciatura*: **Law.** *Maestría*: **Administration; Agricultural Business; Clinical Psychology; Criminology; Environmental Management; Finance; Information Management; Law; Tourism.**

Last Updated: 27/10/15

UNIVERSITY FOR PEACE

Universidad para la Paz (UPEACE)
Apartado 138-6100, Ciudad Colón, San José
Tel: +506 2205-9000
Fax: +506 2249-1929
EMail: info@upeace.org
Website: http://www.upeace.org

Rector: Francisco Rojas Aravena

Department
Environment and Development (Development Studies; Economics; Environmental Studies; International Relations; Peace and Disarmament; Political Sciences); **International Law** (Human Rights; Peace and Disarmament; Religion); **Peace and Conflict Studies** (Economics; Government; Human Rights; International Relations; Peace and Disarmament)

History: Founded 1980 by the General Assembly of the United Nations.

Academic Year: September to June

Admission Requirements: Bachelor's degree with sufficient average grade, TOEFL and entrance examination (essay)

Main Language(s) of Instruction: English

Accrediting Agency: United Nations; SINAES

Degrees and Diplomas: *Maestría*: **Environmental Studies; Gender Studies; Human Rights; International Law; Peace and Disarmament.**

Student Services: Academic Counselling, Canteen, Facilities for disabled people, Language Laboratory, Social Counselling, Sports Facilities

Last Updated: 27/10/15

UNIVERSITY INVENIO

Universidad INVENIO
7km carretera hacia Los Ángeles, Tilarán
Tel: +506 2695-1300
EMail: info@invenio.org
Website: http://invenio.org

Rector: Adrián Lachner Castro

Programme
Engineering (Industrial Engineering; Information Technology; Mechanical Engineering)

Accrediting Agency: CONESUP

Degrees and Diplomas: *Licenciatura*: **Industrial Engineering; Information Technology; Mechanical Engineering.**

Last Updated: 27/10/15

UNIVERSITY OF DESIGN

Universidad del Diseño (INIDIS)
Apartado 1775-2050, Montes de Oca, San José
Tel: +506 2258-6290
Fax: +506 2258-7632
EMail: info@unidis.ac.cr
Website: http://unidis.ac.cr

Rector: Adolfo Enrique Bonilla Leiva

Division
Architecture (Architecture; Town Planning); **Interior Design** (Design; Interior Design)

History: Founded 1993.

Academic Year: February to December (February-June; August-December)

Admission Requirements: Secondary school certificate, interview and aptitude test

Main Language(s) of Instruction: Spanish

Accrediting Agency: CONESUP

Degrees and Diplomas: *Bachillerato Universitario*: **Interior Design.** *Licenciatura*: **Architecture.**

Last Updated: 11/09/15

UNIVERSITY OF IBERO-AMERICA

Universidad de Iberoamérica (UNIBE)
Apartado 11870-1000, 200 mts. este del ICE de Tibás, San José
Tel: +506 2297-2242
Fax: +506 2236-0426
EMail: info@unibe.ac.cr
Website: http://www.unibe.ac.cr

Rector: Israel Hernández Morales (1995-)

Faculty
Health Administration (Health Administration); **Medicine** (Medicine); **Nursing** (Nursing); **Pharmacy** (Pharmacy); **Psychology** (Psychology)

History: Founded 1995.

Academic Year: January to December

Admission Requirements: Secondary school certificate (bachillerato)

Main Language(s) of Instruction: Spanish

Accrediting Agency: CONESUP

Degrees and Diplomas: *Bachillerato Universitario*: **Medicine; Nursing; Pharmacy; Psychology.** *Licenciatura*: **Medicine; Nursing; Pharmacy; Psychology; Surgery.** *Maestría*: **Clinical Psychology; Educational Psychology; Health Administration; Nursing.** *Doctorado Académico*: **Medicine; Surgery.**

Student Services: Academic Counselling

Last Updated: 10/09/15

UNIVERSITY OF LA SALLE

Universidad de La Salle (ULASALLE)
Apartado 536-1007, Centro Colón, San José
Tel: +506 2290-1010
Fax: +506 2231-7898
EMail: info@ulasalle.ac.cr
Website: http://www.ulasalle.ac.cr

Rector: Oscar Guillermo Azmistia Barranco

School
Administration (Accountancy; Administration; Business Administration; Finance; Marketing); **Education** (Education; Education of the Handicapped; Educational Administration; Educational Psychology; Educational Sciences; English; French; Pedagogy; Preschool Education; Primary Education; Psychology; Secondary

Education; Social Studies; Spanish); **Law** (Law); **Psychology** (Psychology)
History: Founded 1994.
Academic Year: January to December (January-April, May-August, September-December)
Admission Requirements: Secondary school certificate
Main Language(s) of Instruction: Spanish
Accrediting Agency: CONESUP
Degrees and Diplomas: *Bachillerato Universitario*: **Business Administration; Civil Engineering; Education; Educational Administration; Foreign Languages Education; Law; Psychology; Teacher Training.** *Licenciatura*: **Accountancy; Business Administration; Civil Engineering; Education; Finance; Foreign Languages Education; Law; Management; Marketing; Preschool Education; Psychology; Religion; Special Education.** *Especialidad Profesional*: **Notary Studies.** *Maestría*: **Education; Educational Administration; Educational Psychology; Environmental Management; Preschool Education; Public Administration; Special Education; Sports Management.** *Doctorado Académico*: **Education.**
Student Services: Careers Guidance, Social Counselling, Sports Facilities
Last Updated: 11/09/15

UNIVERSITY OF SAN JOSÉ

Universidad de San José (USJ)

Apartado 7446-1000, San José
Tel: +506 2218-0747
EMail: info@usanjose.net
Website: http://www.usanjose.net

Rector: Manuel Sandí Murillo

Programme
Aquaculture (Aquaculture); **Business Administration** (Accountancy; Banking; Business Administration; Finance; Human Resources; International Business); **Education** (Education; Primary Education; Secondary Education); **Food Technology**; **Law** (Law); **Nutrition** (Nutrition)
Further Information: Also campuses in Alajuela, San Ramón, San José, Guápiles, Nicoya, and Liberia.
History: Founded 1978 as Colegio Académico, acquired present title 1992. A private institution authorized by the Government.
Academic Year: January to December (January-April; May-August; September-December)
Admission Requirements: Secondary school certificate or foreign equivalent, and entrance examination
Main Language(s) of Instruction: Spanish
Accrediting Agency: CONESUP
Degrees and Diplomas: *Bachillerato Universitario*: **Aquaculture; Business Administration; Education; Food Technology; Law; Nutrition.** *Licenciatura*: **Accountancy; Aquaculture; Business Computing; Finance; Human Resources; Insurance; International Business; Law; Management; Marketing; Nutrition; Teacher Training.** *Especialidad Profesional*: **Notary Studies.** *Maestría*: **Business Administration; Educational Administration; Educational Psychology.**
Student Services: Academic Counselling, Canteen, Sports Facilities
Last Updated: 11/09/15

UNIVERSITY OF THE VALLEY

Universidad del Valle

Apartado 1994-1002, Costado Norte Apartotel, San José
Tel: +506 2280-8311
Fax: +506 2280-8448
EMail: info@udelvalle.com
Website: http://www.udelvalle.com

Rector: Miguel Ángel Alfaro Rodríguez

Faculty
Business Administration (Business Administration); **Education** (Education); **Engineering** (Engineering); **Law** (Law); **Social Sciences** (Psychology)
History: Founded 1998.
Main Language(s) of Instruction: Spanish
Accrediting Agency: CONESUP
Degrees and Diplomas: *Bachillerato Universitario*: **Accountancy; Business Administration; Computer Engineering; Finance; Human Resources; Industrial Engineering; Law; Marketing; Psychology.** *Licenciatura*: **Accountancy; Business Administration; Computer Engineering; Education; Finance; Human Resources; Industrial Engineering; Law; Marketing; Psychology.** *Especialidad Profesional*: **Notary Studies.**
Last Updated: 11/09/15

UNIVERSITY SAINT PAULA

Universidad Santa Paula (USP)

Apartado Postal 627-2050, Sanchéz de Curridabat, Curridabat, San José 2050
Tel: +506 2216-4400
Fax: +506 2272-7123
EMail: info@uspsantapaula.com
Website: http://www.uspsantapaula.com

Rectora: Rocío Valverde Gallegos

School
Audiology (Speech Therapy and Audiology); **Occupational Therapy** (Occupational Therapy); **Physical Therapy** (Physical Therapy); **Respiratory Therapy** (Respiratory Therapy); **Speech Therapy** (Speech Therapy and Audiology)
History: Founded 1994.
Admission Requirements: High school diploma, psychological interview, interview with the programme director
Main Language(s) of Instruction: Spanish
Accrediting Agency: SINAES; CONESUP
Degrees and Diplomas: *Bachillerato Universitario*: **Occupational Therapy; Physical Therapy; Respiratory Therapy; Speech Therapy and Audiology.** *Licenciatura*: **Occupational Therapy; Physical Therapy; Respiratory Therapy; Speech Therapy and Audiology.** *Maestría*: **Neurological Therapy; Physical Therapy; Speech Therapy and Audiology.**
Student Services: Academic Counselling, Careers Guidance, Cultural Activities, Facilities for disabled people, Foreign Studies Centre, Health Services, Language Laboratory, Sports Facilities
Last Updated: 27/10/15

VERITAS UNIVERSITY

Universidad Veritas (UVERITAS)

Apartado postal 1380-1000, San José
Tel: +506 2246-4600
Fax: +506 2225-2907
EMail: info@veritas.cr
Website: http://www.veritas.cr

Rector: José Joaquín Seco Aguilar (1994-)
EMail: rectoria@veritas.cr

Executive President: Ronald Sasso EMail: rsasso@uveritas.ac.cr

Faculty
Dental Sciences *(Facultad Autónoma de Ciencias Odontológicas)* (Dentistry)

School
Architecture (Architecture); **Cinema and TV** (Cinema and Television); **Fashion Design** (Fashion Design); **Interior Design** (Interior Design); **Photography** (Photography); **Product Design** (Design)
History: Founded 1994 as a non-profit private university.
Academic Year: January to December
Main Language(s) of Instruction: Spanish
Accrediting Agency: SINAES; CONESUP
Degrees and Diplomas: *Bachillerato Universitario*: **Architecture; Business Administration; Design; Electronic Engineering; Fine Arts.** *Licenciatura*: **Architecture; Business Administration; Cinema and Television; Electrical Engineering; Fashion Design; Industrial Design; Interior Design; Orthodontics; Photography.** *Especialidad Profesional*: **Orthodontics.** *Maestría*: **Design.**
Student Services: Academic Counselling, Careers Guidance, Foreign Studies Centre, Health Services, Language Laboratory, Social Counselling
Last Updated: 27/10/15

Côte d'Ivoire

STRUCTURE OF HIGHER EDUCATION SYSTEM

Description:

Higher education is offered at universities as well as at centres universitaires and at institutions providing higher professional training. There are also some private institutions. The higher education system is undergoing a reform that includes the implementation of the LMD (three-tier) system for credentials.

Stages of studies:

University level first stage: *Premier cycle*

As from 2012, three years of university study lead to the Licence. A Diplôme universitaire de Technologie is awarded after three years' study.

University level second stage: *Deuxième cycle*

The Maîtrise in Arts and Science subjects requires one year's study after the Licence and includes a mini-thesis. In Engineering schools, studies last for five years and lead to the professional qualification of Ingénieur and the Diplôme d'Ingénieur des Travaux publics. In Agriculture, a Diplôme d'Agronomie générale is conferred after four years and a Diplôme d'Ingénieur agronome is awarded after five years' study with a further year's specialization. In Medicine, a professional Doctorate is awarded after seven years and in Dentistry and Pharmacy after five years. The Master is in the process of being implemented.

University level third stage: *Troisième cycle*

The Diplôme d'Etudes supérieures spécialisées (DESS) and the Diplôme d'Etudes approfondies (DEA) are conferred after one year's further study beyond the Maîtrise. After three more years candidates may be awarded the Doctorat. The qualification of Docteur-Ingénieur is conferred after three years' study and the submission of a thesis to holders of a diploma in Engineering. The three-year Doctorate following upon a Master is in the process of being implemented.

ADMISSION TO HIGHER EDUCATION

Admission to university-level studies:

Name of secondary school credential required: Baccalauréat

Foreign students admission:

Admission requirements: Foreign students must hold a qualification that is equivalent to the Baccalauréat.

Entry regulations: Foreign students must have a valid passport, a visa and scholarship from their government or an international organization.

Health requirements: Students must be vaccinated against yellow fever.

Language proficiency: Knowledge of French is necessary.

NATIONAL BODIES

Ministère de l'Enseignement supérieur et de la Recherche scientifique (Ministry of Higher Education and Research)

Minister: Bakayoko Ly Ramata
Cité Administrative, Tour C 20e étage
Abidjan
Tel: +225 2033-5464
Fax: +225 2021-2225
WWW: http://www.enseignement.gouv.ci

Data for academic year: 2012-2013

Source: IAU from the website of the Ministère de l'Enseignement supérieur, Côte d'Ivoire, 2012. Bodies 2016.

INSTITUTIONS

PUBLIC INSTITUTIONS

AFRICAN CENTRE FOR MANAGEMENT AND PROFESSIONAL UPGRADING

Centre Africain de Management et de Perfectionnement des Cadres (CAMPC)

08 BP 878, Abidjan 08
Tel: +225(22) 44-49-46 +225(22) 44-43-22 +225(22) 44-49-94
Fax: +225(22) 44-03-78
EMail: info@campc.net; campc_ci@yahoo.fr
Website: http://www.campc.net

Directeur général: Jean-Emmanuel Somda
Tel: +225(22) 44-49-46 EMail: jesomda@campc.net

Programme

Health Management (Health Administration); **Human Resources** (Human Resources); **Management** (Management); **Management and Business Computing** (Business Computing; Management); **Organisational Management** (Industrial Management)

Further Information: A traditional and distance education institution.

History: Founded 1970.

Accrediting Agency: Conseil Africain et Malgache pour l'Enseignement Supérieur (CAMES)

Degrees and Diplomas: *Diplôme d'Etudes supérieures spécialisées*: **Human Resources.** Also Diplôme de formation et de Perfectionnement (equivalent to Licence) in Management, Organisational Management, Health Management, 3-4 yrs; Master in Management, 5yrs; Diplôme supérieur spécialisé (equivalent to Licence) in Human Resources, 3 yrs; Diplôme supérieur de Perfectionnement in Organisations Management (DPMO), Management (DSPMI) with a specialisation in Business Computing (equivalent to DESS).

Last Updated: 24/04/12

FÉLIX HOUPHOUËT-BOIGNY NATIONAL POLYTECHNIC INSTITUTE

Institut national polytechnique Félix Houphouët-Boigny (INP-HB)

BP 1093, Yamoussoukro
Tel: +225(30) 64-67-00 +225(30) 64-66-66
Fax: +225(30) 64-04-06 +225(22) 44-32-93
EMail: info@inphb.edu.ci; serviceconcours@inphb.edu.ci
Website: http://www.inphb.edu.ci

Directeur général: Koffi N'Guessan (2011-)

Secrétaire général: Adama Sylla Tel: +225(30) 64-11-36

International Relations: Koffi Kra EMail: karandre@yahoo.fr

School

Preparatory Studies (Biology; Business and Commerce; Technology)

Higher School

Agriculture (Agriculture); **Agronomy** *(ESA)* (Agricultural Business; Agricultural Economics; Agricultural Equipment; Agriculture; Agronomy; Animal Husbandry; Crop Production; Forestry); **Commerce and Business Administration** *(ESCAE)* (Accountancy; Business Administration; Business and Commerce; Communication Studies; Cultural Studies; English; Finance; Human Resources; Insurance; International Relations; Law; Management; Modern Languages; Transport Management); **Industrial Engineering** *(ESI)* (Automotive Engineering; Chemical Engineering; Computer Engineering; Computer Science; Electronic Engineering; Energy Engineering; Food Technology; Industrial Engineering; Maintenance Technology; Mechanical Engineering; Petroleum and Gas Engineering; Production Engineering; Telecommunications Engineering); **Lifelong Education and Executive Proficiency** *(EFCPC)* (Administration; Agronomy; Civil Engineering; Computer Science; Industrial Engineering; Mining Engineering); **Mining and Geology** *(ESMG)* (Geology; Mining Engineering; Petroleum and Gas Engineering)

Department

Administrative Techniques and Sciences *(TSA)* (Administration); **Agriculture and Animal Ressources** *(ARA)* (Agriculture; Animal Husbandry); **Building and Urbanism** *(BU)* (Building Technologies; Urban Studies); **Chemical Engineering and Agricultural Business** *(GCAA)* (Agricultural Business; Chemical Engineering); **Chemistry and Agricultural Business** *(CEA)* (Agricultural Business); **Electrical and Electronic Engineering** *(GEE)* (Electrical and Electronic Engineering; Electrical Engineering; Electronic Engineering); **Finance, Accountancy and Law** *(FCD)* (Accountancy; Finance; Law); **Geology and Mining Engineering** *(STERMI)* (Biological and Life Sciences; Geology; Mining Engineering); **Langues et Sciences Humaines (LSH)** *(LSH)* (Arts and Humanities; Modern Languages); **Management, Commerce and Applied Economics** *(GCEA)* (Economics; Management); **Mathematics and Computer Science** *(MI)* (Computer Science; Mathematics); **Mechanical and Energy Engineering** *(GME)* (Energy Engineering; Mechanical Engineering); **Rural Planning and Geography** *(GRSG)* (Geography; Rural Planning); **Transport and Communications** *(IT)* (Transport and Communications); **Water Science, Forestry and Environmental Studies** *(FOREN)* (Environmental Studies; Forestry; Water Science)

History: Founded 1996, incorporating previously existing institutions, including Ecole nationale supérieure d'Agronomie (ENSA), Ecole nationale supérieure des Travaux Publics (ENSTP), Institut national supérieur de l'Enseignement technique (INSET) and Institut agricole de Bouaké (IAB).

Academic Year: September to June

Admission Requirements: Baccalauréat

Fees: (CFA Francs): c. 3m. per annum

Main Language(s) of Instruction: French

Degrees and Diplomas: *Diplôme universitaire de Technologie*; *Diplôme d'Ingénieur*, *Diplôme d'Etudes supérieures spécialisées*

Student Services: Academic Counselling, Canteen, Cultural Activities, Health Services, Nursery Care, Social Counselling, Sports Facilities

Last Updated: 02/07/12

INSTITUTE OF COMMUNICATION SCIENCES AND TECHNOLOGIES

Institut des Sciences et Techniques de la Communication (ISTC)

BP V 205, Boulevard de l'Université, Abidjan
Tel: +225(22) 44-88-58
Fax: +225(22) 44-84-33
EMail: infos@istc.ci
Website: http://istc-ci.net/

Directeur: Alfred Dan Moussa (2011-) Tel: +225(22) 44-88-58

Department

Advertising, Publicity and Marketing (Advertising and Publicity; Marketing); **Audiovisual Production** (Film; Video); **Digital Arts and Images** (Multimedia; Video; Visual Arts); **Journalism** (Journalism; Radio and Television Broadcasting); **Telecommunications** (Telecommunications Engineering)

History: Founded 1992.

Main Language(s) of Instruction: French

Degrees and Diplomas: *Licence*; *Maîtrise*; *Doctorat*

Last Updated: 02/07/12

NATIONAL INSTITUTE FOR HEALTH WORKERS TRAINING

Institut national de Formation des Agents de la Santé (INFAS)

18 BP 720, CHU de Treichville, Abidjan 18
Tel: +225(21) 24-29-00 +225(21) 24-29-89
Fax: +225(21) 24-28-87
EMail: info@infas-ci.com
Website: http://infas-ci.net

Directeur Général: Daniel Sess

Programme

Midwifery *(SF)* (Midwifery); **Nursing** *(IDE)* (Nursing); **Technical Studies** *(TSS)* (Biology; Hygiene; Laboratory Techniques; Medical Technology; Pharmacy; Physical Therapy)

Section

Specialists Training (Anaesthesiology; Biology; Cardiology; Chemistry; Dermatology; Health Sciences; Hygiene; Medical Technology; Neurology; Ophthalmology; Otorhinolaryngology; Pharmacy; Physiology; Psychiatry and Mental Health; Public Health)

History: Founded 1991. An institution under the authority of the Ministry of Public Health.

Admission Requirements: Candidates must: be of Ivorian nationality; Aged 18-30; Hold a secondary school leaving certificate (Baccalauréat) or equivalent; Attend an entrance examination

Main Language(s) of Instruction: French

Accrediting Agency: Minister of Health

Degrees and Diplomas: *Diplôme d'Ingénieur*, *Diplôme d'Etudes supérieures spécialisées*. Also National Diploma in Nursing and Midwifery, 3 yrs; Undergraduate vocational diploma in Heath Sciences (Diplôme de technicien supérieur de santé), 2 yrs

Last Updated: 03/07/12

NATIONAL INSTITUTE FOR HEALTH WORKERS TRAINING (ABOISSO)

INSTITUT NATIONAL DE FORMATION DES AGENTS DE LA SANTÉ (ABOISSO) (INFAS)

B.P. 1056, Aboisso
Tel: +225(21) 30-60-43 +225(21) 30-67-05
Fax: +225(21) 30-60-43
EMail: aboisso@infas-ci.com

Directeur général: Daniel Sess

Programme

Midwifery (Midwifery); **Nursing** (Nursing)

History: Founded 2007.

Main Language(s) of Instruction: French

Degrees and Diplomas: National Diploma, 3 yrs

NATIONAL INSTITUTE FOR HEALTH WORKERS TRAINING (BOUAKÉ)

INSTITUT NATIONAL DE FORMATION DES AGENTS DE LA SANTÉ (BOUAKÉ)

BP V 20, Bouaké
Tel: +225(31) 63-10-26
Fax: +225(31) 63-10-28

Directeur Général: Daniel Sass

Programme

Midwifery (Midwifery); **Nursing** (Nursing)

History: Founded 1987.

Main Language(s) of Instruction: French

Degrees and Diplomas: National Diploma, 3 yrs

Student Numbers *2010-2011*: Total: c. 620

NATIONAL INSTITUTE FOR HEALTH WORKERS TRAINING (DALOA)

INSTITUT NATIONAL DE FORMATION DES AGENTS DE LA SANTÉ (DALOA) (INFAS)

Daloa

Directeur général: Daniel Sess

Programme

Midwifery (Midwifery); **Nursing** (Nursing)

Main Language(s) of Instruction: French

Degrees and Diplomas: National Diploma, 3 yrs

NATIONAL INSTITUTE FOR HEALTH WORKERS TRAINING (KORHOGO)

INSTITUT NATIONAL DE FORMATION DES AGENTS DE LA SANTÉ (KORHOGO)

BP 426, Korhogo
Tel: +225(36) 86-11-85
Fax: +225(36) 86-08-58

Programme

Midwifery (Midwifery); **Nursing** (Nursing)

History: Founded 1993.

Main Language(s) of Instruction: French

Degrees and Diplomas: National Diploma, 3 yrs

NATIONAL SCHOOL OF ADMINISTRATION

Ecole nationale d'Administration (ENA)

BP V 20, Abidjan
Tel: +225(22) 41-40-33
EMail: ena@globeaccess.net

Directrice: Evelyne Yapo (2010-) Tel: +225(22) 44-52-25

Secrétaire général: Mameri Diaby Tel: +225(22) 41-52-31

School

Administrative and Diplomatic Management *(EGAD)* (Administration; International Relations; Management Systems; Political Sciences); **Economics and Financial Management** *(EGEF)* (Economics; Finance; Management); **Magisterial and Judicial Studies** (Justice Administration; Law)

Centre

Lifelong Education and Executive Retraining (Management)

History: Founded 1960.

Last Updated: 24/04/12

NATIONAL SCHOOL OF FINE ARTS

Ecole nationale des Beaux-Arts (ENBA)

Cocody boulevard de l'Université, 08 BP 49, Abidjan 08
Tel: 225(22) 44-26-73
EMail: padec@ci.refer.org

Directeur: Tiburce Koffi

School

Cultural Action Training *(EFAC)* (Cultural Studies; Documentation Techniques; Museum Studies); **Fine Arts** *(ENBA)* (Fine Arts); **Music** *(ENM)* (Music; Musicology); **Theatre and Dance** *(ENTD)* (Dance; Theatre)

Centre

Pedagogical Training for Arts and Culture *(CFPAC)* (Art Education; Educational Sciences)

Research Centre

Arts and Culture *(CRAC)* (Fine Arts)

History: Founded as Institut National des Arts (INA). Acquired present title 1991.

Admission Requirements: Applicants for first cycle programmes must not be older than 23, hold a secondary leaving certificate (Baccalauréat) and attend an entrance examination. For second cycle programmes, they must not be older than 25 and hold a first degree (licence, diplôme d'aptitude à l'action culturelle (DAAC), diplôme d'Etudes Artistiques générales (DEAG), brevet de Technicien Supérieur (BTS)). For 3rd cycle programmes, they must not be older than 27 and hold a 2nd cycle diploma (maitrise, diplôme d'Etudes Supérieures Artistiques (DESA), Diplôme Supérieur d'Action Culturelle (DSAC) or equivalent. Applicants to the Centre for Pedagogical Training for Arts and Culture must be holding one of the following diplomas or its equivalent: diplôme d'Etudes artistique Générale (DEAG), DEUG II, Licence, Master in Art.

Main Language(s) of Instruction: French

Degrees and Diplomas: *Diplôme d'Etudes supérieures spécialisées*. Also Diplôme d'études artistiques générales (DEAG), 2 yrs; Diplôme d'études supérieures artistiques (DESA), 3 yrs; Professional Master in Cultural Development, 2 yrs

Last Updated: 03/07/12

NATIONAL SCHOOL OF STATISTICS AND APPLIED ECONOMICS

Ecole nationale supérieure de Statistique et d'Economie appliquée (ENSEA)
08 BP 3, Abidjan 08
Tel: +225(22) 48-32-32 +225(22) 48-32-00
Fax: +225(22) 44-39-88
EMail: ensea@ensea.ed.ci
Website: http://www.ensea.ci

Directeur: Koffi N'Guessan (1994-) EMail: nguessan@ensea.ed.ci

Programme

Statistics and Applied Economics (Economics; Statistics)

History: Founded 1961.

Academic Year: October to July

Admission Requirements: Entrance examination

Fees: (CFA Francs): 850,000 per annum

Main Language(s) of Instruction: French

Accrediting Agency: Ministère de l'Enseignement supérieur et de la Recherche scientifique

Degrees and Diplomas: *Diplôme d'Ingénieur*: **Economics; Statistics.** *Diplôme d'Etudes supérieures spécialisées*. Also Diplomas of Agent Technique (1 yr) and Adjoint Technique (2 yrs)

Student Services: Canteen, Health Services, Sports Facilities

Publications: Etude et Recherche (sur la population et le développement)

Publishing House: ENSEA Press

Last Updated: 24/04/12

TEACHER TRAINING SCHOOL OF ABIDJAN

Ecole normale supérieure d'Abidjan (ENS)
08 BP 10, Abidjan 08
Tel: +225(22) 44-31-10
Fax: +225(22) 44-42-32
Website: http://ensabidjan.ci/

Directeur Général: Sidibe Valy (2012-)
Tel: +225(22) 44-42-32 EMail: valy_sidibey@yahoo.fr

Directrice, Affaires Administratives et Financières: Agnes Epse Soumahoro Toh
Tel: +225(22) 44-18-82 EMail: agnestoh21@yahoo.com

Department

Arts and Humanities (Arts and Humanities; Humanities and Social Science Education; Linguistics); **Educational Sciences** (Educational and Student Counselling; Educational Sciences; Primary Education; Teacher Training); **History and Geography** (Geography; History; Humanities and Social Science Education); **Languages** (English; Foreign Languages Education; German; Modern Languages; Spanish); **Science and Technology** (Biological and Life Sciences; Mathematics Education; Natural Sciences; Physics; Science Education; Technology; Technology Education)

Section

Mathematics (Mathematics)

Further Information: Also traditional and distance education institution. Also distance education programme - "Tele-education" - offered in cooperation with Indian Universities in the field of: Finance and control; Business Administration; Finance, Audit and Control; Information Technology; Management; Early child care education; Tourism; Nutrition.

History: Founded 1964.

Accrediting Agency: Ministry of Higher Education

Degrees and Diplomas: *Licence*; *Maîtrise*. Also Bachelor and Master's degrees offered through the "Télé-éducation" distance programme with Indian universities (University of Madras, Amity University et Indira Ghandi Open University).

Student Services: Sports Facilities

Academic Staff *2011-2012*: Total 159
STAFF WITH DOCTORATE: Total 6

Student Numbers *2011-2012*: Total 1,365

Last Updated: 02/07/12

UNIVERSITY FÉLIX HOUPHOUËT-BOIGNY

Université Félix Houphouët-Boigny
01 BP V34, Abidjan 01
Tel: +225(22) 44-08-95 +225(22) 44-90-00
Fax: +225(22) 44-17-07
EMail: courrier@univ-fhb.edu.ci
Website: http://www.univ-fhb.edu.ci

Président: Bakayoko Ly Ramata (2012-)
EMail: presidence@univ-fhb.edu.ci

Unit

Biosciences (Biological and Life Sciences); **Criminology** (Criminology); **Earth Sciences and Mining Resources** (Earth Sciences; Mining Engineering); **Economics and Management** (Economics; Management); **Information, Communication and Art** (Arts and Humanities; Communication Studies; Information Sciences); **Languages, Literature and Civilizations** (Cultural Studies; Literature; Modern Languages); **Law, Administration and Political Science** (Administration; Law; Political Sciences); **Mankind and Society** (Social Studies); **Mathematics and Computer Science** (Computer Science; Mathematics); **Medical Sciences** (Medicine); **Odonto-Stomatology** (Dentistry; Stomatology); **Pharmacy and Biological Sciences** (Biological and Life Sciences; Pharmacy); **Structure of Matter and Technology** (Technology)

Institute

African History, Arts and Archaeology *(IHAAA)* (African Studies; Archaeology; Fine Arts); **Anthropology and Development Studies** *(ISAD)* (Anthropology; Development Studies); **Applied Linguitics** *(ILA)* (Applied Linguistics); **Ethno-Sociology** *(IES)* (Ethnology; Sociology); **Floristics** *(CNF - National)* (Botany); **Pedagogical Research, Experimentation and Teaching** *(IREEP)* (Pedagogy); **Tropical Geography** *(IGT)* (Geography)

Centre

Applied Psychology Teaching and Research *(CIERPA)* (Psychology); **Economic and Social Research** *(CIRES)* (Economics; Social Sciences); **Lifelong Education** *(CUFOP)*

Research Centre

Architecture and Town Planning *(CRAU)* (Architecture; Architecture and Planning; Town Planning); **Distance Education** *(CURAT)* (Distance Education)

Research Institute

Mathematics *(IRMA)* (Mathematics)

History: Founded 1958 as University Centre. Acquired status of autonomous university 1964. Closed in March 2011 and reopened in 2012 with current name. Previously known as Université de Cocody.

Admission Requirements: Baccalauréat or equivalent

Fees: (CFA Francs): c. 6,000-25,000; foreign students, c. 200,000-500,000 (if agreements, foreign students may pay same fees as nationals)

Main Language(s) of Instruction: French

Degrees and Diplomas: *Licence*: **Arts and Humanities; Economics; Fine Arts; Law; Modern Languages.** *Diplôme de Docteur*: **Medicine.** *Diplôme d'Etudes supérieures spécialisées*: **Dentistry; Pharmacy.** *Maîtrise*; *Diplôme d'Etudes approfondies*; *Doctorat*

Student Services: Academic Counselling, Canteen, Facilities for disabled people, Health Services, Language Laboratory, Nursery Care, Social Counselling, Sports Facilities

Publications: En-Quête; Repères; Revues médicales; Revues sociales

Publishing House: EDUCI

Academic Staff *2011-2012*: Total: c. 1,350

Student Numbers *2011-2012*: Total: c. 53,700

Last Updated: 04/02/14

UNIVERSITY OF ABOBO-ADJAMÉ

Université d'Abobo-Adjamé (UAA)

02 BP 801, Abidjan 02
Tel: +225(20) 30-42-00 +225(20) 37-74-48 +225(20) 37-81-21
Fax: +225(20) 30-43-00 +225(20) 37-81-18
EMail: info@uabobo.ci
Website: http://www.uabobo.ci

Président: Yao Tano (2012-)
Tel: +225(20) 30-42-10 EMail: tanoy@ci.refer.org

Secrétaire général: Inza Doumbia
Tel: +225(20) 30-42-27

International Relations: Jocelyne Bosson, Head Manager
Tel: +225(20) 30-42-47 EMail: mamaketci@yahoo.fr

Unit

Basic and Applied Sciences *(SFA)* (Chemistry; Computer Science; Mathematics; Natural Sciences); **Environmental Science and Management** *(SGE)* (Environmental Management; Environmental Studies); **Food Science and Technology** *(STA)* (Food Science; Food Technology); **Higher Education** *(URES Daloa)* (Higher Education); **Natural Sciences** *(SN)* (Animal Husbandry; Mathematics and Computer Science; Natural Sciences; Plant and Crop Protection)

School

Health Sciences *(Preparatory - EPSS)* (Dentistry; Health Sciences; Medicine; Pharmacy; Stomatology)

Institute

Research; **Research in Renewable Energy** (Energy Engineering)

Centre

Continuing Education *(CFCAA)*; **Ecology Research** *(CRE)* (Ecology; Energy Engineering; Environmental Studies)

History: Founded 1996 as University Centre. Closed since March 2011. Reopening scheduled for October 2012

Main Language(s) of Instruction: French

Degrees and Diplomas: *Licence*; *Maîtrise*; *Diplôme d'Etudes approfondies*; *Doctorat*

UNIVERSITY OF BOUAKÉ

Université de Bouaké

27 BP 529, Abidjan 27
Tel: +225(31) 63-32-42 +225(22) 42-58-74
Fax: +225(31) 63-25-13 +225(22) 42-59-80
Website: http://www.ubouake.ci/

Président: Lazare Marcellin Poamé
Tel: +225(31) 63-48-57

Vice-Président: G. Emmanuel Crezoit
Tel: +225(22) 42-47-78 EMail: crezoit@yahoo.fr

Secrétaire général: Germain Adja-Diby

Unit

Communication, Environment and Society *(CMS)* (Communication Studies; Environmental Studies); **Economics and Development Studies** *(SED)* (Development Studies; Economics); **Higher Education** *(URES, Korhogo)* (Higher Education); **Law, Administration and Management** *(SJAG)* (Administration; Law; Management); **Medicine** *(SM)* (Medicine)

Institute

"Indicametry" Study, Research and Training *(MERFI - Multipolar)* (Development Studies)

Centre

Development Research *(CRD)* (Development Studies); **Lifelong Education** *(CFC)*; **Medical and Veterinary Entomology** *(CEMV)* (Entomology; Medicine; Veterinary Science)

History: Founded in Bouaké 1992 as University Centre. Acquired status of autonomous university 1995. Relocated to Abidjan 2002 following political turmoil.

Main Language(s) of Instruction: French

Degrees and Diplomas: *Licence*; *Maîtrise*

Student Numbers *2010-2011*: Total: c. 18,000

PRIVATE INSTITUTIONS

AGITEL - TRAINING INSTITUTE

Agitel - Formation

03 BP 882, Abidjan 03
Tel: +225(20) 22-26-37 +225(22) 47-83-03
Fax: +255(22) 47-20-07
EMail: agitelformation@aviso.ci
Website: http://www.agitel.ci

Directeur Général: Mamadou Sanogo
Tel: +225(20) 21-80-16 EMail: mhsanogo@yahoo.fr

General Secretary: Sory Bamba
Tel: +225(07) 99-90-48 EMail: colbams@yahoo.fr

Higher Institute

Communication and Human Resources Management *(HICHR)* (Advertising and Publicity; Communication Arts; Communication Studies; Computer Science; Economics; Human Resources; Law; Management; Marketing; Media Studies; Public Relations; Statistics); **Computer Science and New Information and Communication Technologies** *(HICS-NICT)* (Advertising and Publicity; Computer Engineering; Computer Science; Criminal Law; Economics; English; Finance; Information Technology; International Business; International Studies; Management; Marketing; Telecommunications Engineering); **Finance and Accounting** *(HIFA)* (Accountancy; Banking; Computer Science; English; Finance; Fiscal Law; Industrial and Organizational Psychology; Insurance; Management; Operations Research; Taxation); **Management and International Trade Presentation** *(HIMIT)* (Advertising and Publicity; Business Administration; Computer Science; Criminal Law; Economics; English; Finance; International Business; International Studies; Management; Marketing; Transport Management)

History: Founded 1989.

Accrediting Agency: African and madagascan Council for High Education (CAMES); Association to Advance Collegiate Schools of Business (AACSB)

Degrees and Diplomas: *Brevet de Technicien supérieur*; *Diplôme d'Ingénieur*; *Diplôme d'Etudes supérieures spécialisées*. Also Licence professionnelle, 3 yrs; Diplôme de Technicien Supérieur Spécialisé, 1-4 yrs; MBA and Masters in Commerce, Finance and Communication, 6 yrs.

Student Services: Canteen, Cultural Activities, Sports Facilities
Last Updated: 23/04/12

CANADIAN UNIVERSITY OF ARTS, SCIENCES AND MANAGEMENT

Université Canadienne des Arts, des Sciences et du Management (UC-ASM)

06 BP 2875, Abidjan 06
Tel: +225(22) 47-63-16
Fax: +225(22) 47-72-66
EMail: accueil@pucao.org
Website: http://www.pucao.org

Recteur: Hugues Albert EMail: alberthughes@yahoo.ca

Vice-Rectrice à l'Enseignement et à la Recherche: Nicole Laverdure EMail: nicolelaverdure@yahoo.ca

Programme

Business Administration *(Bachelor)* (Business Administration); **Business Administration** *(Executive MBA)* (Business Administration); **Computer Science** (Computer Science); **Human Resources** *(Certificate)* (Human Resources); **Law** (Commercial Law; International Law; Labour Law; Law); **Marketing** *(Certificate)* (Marketing); **Mining Engineering** (Mining Engineering); **Project Management** *(Postgraduate)* (Information Technology; Management; Marketing)

History: Founded 1998 as Université Ivoiro-Canadienne/Ivory-Canadian University (UICA). Acquired present title 2003.

Academic Year: September to July

Admission Requirements: Baccalauréat, Secondary school certificate, Entrance examination

Fees: (CFA Francs): 400,000-4,400,000 per annum (including tuition, textbooks, uniform)

Main Language(s) of Instruction: French

Degrees and Diplomas: *Diplôme d'Etudes supérieures spécialisées*; *Maîtrise*: **Business Administration; Computer Science; Law.** Also Bachelor's degree in Business Administration, Computer Science (4 yrs), Law (4,5 yrs), Mining Engineering (5 yrs); Executive MBA (evening courses), 3 yrs; Certificates in Administration, Human Resources Management and Marketing, 1yr

Student Services: Academic Counselling, Canteen, Careers Guidance, Language Laboratory, Social Counselling, Sports Facilities

Last Updated: 03/07/12

CATHOLIC UNIVERSITY OF WEST AFRICA/ UNIVERSITY OF ABIDJAN UNIT

Université Catholique de l'Afrique de l'Ouest/Unité universitaire d'Abidjan (UCAO/UUA)

08 BP 22, Abidjan 08, Cocody
Tel: +225(22) 40-06-50 +225(22) 40-06-52
Fax: +225(22) 44-15-98 +225(22) 44-15-93
EMail: info@ucao-uua.org; ucao@aviso.ci

Président: Raphaël Tossou

Secrétaire général: Roger Afan

International Relations: Célestin Gnako
EMail: aviso@ucao.ci

Faculty
Law (Law); **Theology** (Theology)

School
Theological Training for the Lay (Theology)

Institute
Communication Studies *(Institut Supérieur de Communication)* (Communication Studies)

Higher Institute
Christian Religious Studies *(Institut Supérieur de Catéchèse (ISC))* (Christian Religious Studies); **Pastoral Studies** *(Institut Supérieur de Pastorale (ISP))* (Pastoral Studies)

Research Unit
Philosophy (Philosophy)

History: Founded 1969 as Institute (ICAO). Acquired present status and title 2000.

Admission Requirements: Baccalauréat or equivalent

Fees: (CFA Francs): 500,000-700,000 per annum

Main Language(s) of Instruction: French

Degrees and Diplomas: *Licence*: **Christian Religious Studies; Communication Studies; Philosophy.** *Diplôme d'Etudes supérieures spécialisées*; *Maîtrise*: **Philosophy; Theology.** *Diplôme d'Etudes approfondies*: **Philosophy; Theology.** *Doctorat*: **Philosophy; Theology.**

Student Services: Academic Counselling, Canteen, Careers Guidance, Health Services, Nursery Care, Sports Facilities

Student Numbers *2011-2012*: Total: c. 250

Last Updated: 03/07/12

HIGHER INTERNATIONAL SCHOOL OF LAW

Ecole supérieure internationale de Droit (ESID)

BP 825, Abidjan 03
Tel: +225(22) 42-88-10
Fax: +225(22) 42-88-10
EMail: esid@aviso.ci

Directrice: Anne-Marie Hortense Assi Esso

Department
Law (Law)

History: Founded 1999.

Degrees and Diplomas: *Licence*; *Maîtrise*; *Doctorat*

NEW SCHOOL OF ADVANCED ENGINEERING AND TECHNOLOGY STUDIES

Ecole nouvelle supérieure d'Ingénieurs et de Technologies (ENSIT)

Bld des Martyrs (Latrille), Rue Farandole K22, Cocody 2 Plateaux, 01 BP 3427, Abidjan 01
Tel: +225(22) 41-65-63
Fax: +225(22) 41-87-24
EMail: scolarite@ensit.ci
Website: http://www.ensit.ci

Directeur: N'Guessan Alain Ahouzi

Department
Engineering (Computer Engineering; Computer Networks; Computer Science; Data Processing; Engineering Management; Information Management; Information Technology; Mathematics; Safety Engineering; Software Engineering; Statistics; Telecommunications Engineering); **Management and Entrepreneurship** (Accountancy; Banking; Business Administration; Finance; Insurance; International Business; Management; Marketing)

Main Language(s) of Instruction: Français

Accrediting Agency: Conseil Africain et Malgache de l'Enseignement Supérieur (CAMES)

Degrees and Diplomas: *Diplôme d'Ingénieur*; *Diplôme d'Etudes supérieures spécialisées*. Also Bachelor's Degree and Master's Degree

Last Updated: 02/07/12

PIGIER CÔTE D'IVOIRE

01 BP 1585, 23 Boulevard de la République, Abidjan 01
Tel: +225(20) 30-35-00
Fax: +255(20) 22-67-64
EMail: abidjan@pigier.com
Website: http://www.pigierci.com/

Director: Jeremie N'gouan EMail: pigierci@aviso.com

Programme
Audit and Cost Controlling *(2nd Cycle)* (Accountancy); **Audit, Accountancy and Cost Controlling** *(1st Cycle)* (Accountancy); **Bilingual Assistant Manager** *(1st Cycle)* (Communication Studies; English; Management; Public Relations; Secretarial Studies); **Bilingual Management Assistant** *(1st Cycle - Day only)* (Communication Studies; English; Management; Public Relations; Secretarial Studies); **Business Administration** *(2nd Cycle)* (Advertising and Publicity; Business Administration; Communication Studies; International Business; Marketing); **Business Computing** *(1st Cycle - Day only)* (Business Computing; Computer Engineering; Computer Networks; Computer Science; Software Engineering); **Commercial Management** *(1st Cycle - Day only)* (Business Administration; Business and Commerce; Management; Marketing; Sales Techniques); **Computer Science** *(2nd Cycle)* (Computer Engineering; Computer Networks; Computer Science; Data Processing; Telecommunications Engineering); **Corporate Communication** *(1st Cycle - Day only)* (Communication Studies; Marketing; Sales Techniques); **Finance and Accountancy** *(1st Cycle - Day only)* (Accountancy; Finance); **Finance and Accountancy** *(2nd Cycle)* (Accountancy; Finance); **Management Assistant/ Small and Mid-sized Business** *(1st Cycle - Day only)* (Administration; Business Administration; Communication Studies; Management; Marketing); **Marketing** *(2nd Cycle)* (Advertising and Publicity; Business Administration; Communication Studies; International Business; Marketing); **Negotiation and Multimedia Communication** *(1st Cycle)* (Communication Studies; Multimedia); **Software Engineering** *(1st Cycle)* (Computer Engineering; Software Engineering); **Taxation and Commercial Law** *(2nd Cycle)* (Commercial Law; Taxation)

Further Information: Also Seminars and Continuing Education programmes

History: Founded 1956.

Accrediting Agency: Conseil Africain et Malgache pour l' Enseignement Supérieur (CAMES)

Degrees and Diplomas: *Brevet de Technicien supérieur*; *Licence*: **Business Computing.** *Diplôme d'Ingénieur*; *Diplôme d'Etudes supérieures spécialisées*: **Accountancy; Finance.** Also Professional Licence (Software Engineering; Audit, Accountancy and Cost

Controlling; Negociation and Multimedia Communication; Bilingual Assistant Manager) and Master (Business Administration, Accountancy, Marketing, Fiscal and Commercial Law)

Student Numbers *2011-2012*: Total: c. 7,000
Last Updated: 02/07/12

REGIONAL ACADEMY OF MARINE SCIENCE AND TECHNOLOGY

Académie régionale des Sciences et Techniques de la Mer (ARSTM)

BP V 158, Abidjan
Tel: +225(23) 46-08-08 +225(23) 46-08-09
Fax: +225(23) 46-08-11
EMail: info@arstm.org
Website: http://www.arstm.org

Directeur général: Karim Coulibaly (2004-)
EMail: coulakar@yahoo.fr

International Relations: Chantal Diarrassouba, Head of Marketing and Communication EMail: cocha333@yahoo.fr

Higher School

Marine Transport (International Business; Marine Transport; Transport Management); **Navigation** (Maintenance Technology; Marine Engineering; Marine Transport; Telecommunications Engineering)

Centre

Maritime Education and Training (Marine Engineering; Marine Transport)

History: Founded 1987. The regional institution of maritime and industrial training of fifteen French speaking countries of West and Central Africa (Benin, Burkina Faso, Cameroun, Central African Republic, Chad, Congo, Côte d'Ivoire, Gabon, Guinea, Mali, Mauritania, Niger, Senegal, and Democratic Republic of Congo).

Main Language(s) of Instruction: French

Accrediting Agency: International Maritime Organisation (IMO)

Degrees and Diplomas: *Diplôme d'Ingénieur*. Diplôme d'Etudes supérieures in Industrial Maintenance (DESMI), 3 yrs; Diplôme d'Etudes Techniques in Maritime Transport and Logistics (DETTML), 2 yrs; Fully-licensed Captain training, 7 yrs.

Student Services: Academic Counselling, Canteen, Careers Guidance, Health Services, Language Laboratory, Sports Facilities

Academic Staff *2010-2011*	MEN	WOMEN	**TOTAL**
FULL-TIME	17	1	**18**
PART-TIME	–	–	**65**
Student Numbers *2010-2011*			
All (Foreign included)	526	66	**592**

Distance students, 592.
Last Updated: 23/04/12

UNIVERSITY OF THE ATLANTIC

Université de l'Atlantique (UA)

06 PO Box 6631, Cocody Boulevard Mitterand, Cité EECI, Abidjan 06
Tel: +225(22) 48-72-55
Fax: +225(22) 44-21-72
EMail: atlantiqueuniversite@ymail.com
Website: http://www.uatlantique.info/

Recteur: Antoine Asseypo Hauhouot
Tel: +225(22) 41-08-44 EMail: asseypo@yahoo.fr

Intendante générale: Isabelle Amani

International Relations: Enok Okomien Dadié EMail: uatl@aviso.ci

Faculty

Arts and Humanities (Arts and Humanities; Social Sciences); **Economic Sciences and Business Administration** (Business Administration; Economics); **Law and Political Sciences** (Law; Political Sciences; Private Law; Public Law); **Social sciences** (Development Studies; Economics; Law; Social Sciences)

Institute

Health Agents Training *(IPFAS - Private Institute)* (Midwifery; Nursing); **High Professional Studies** (Accountancy; Administration; Business Administration; Finance; Fiscal Law; International Relations; Management; Marine Transport; Transport and Communications); **Journalism and Mass Communication** (Advertising and Publicity; Business Administration; Journalism; Marketing; Mass Communication; Radio and Television Broadcasting); **Political Sciences and International Relations** (International Relations; Political Sciences); **Research and Development** *(IURD)* (Arabic; Communication Studies; Cultural Studies; Gender Studies; International Relations; Mass Communication; Pedagogy; Political Sciences; Women's Studies); **Women and Gender Studies** (Advertising and Publicity; Gender Studies; Marketing; Women's Studies)

Centre

Arts and Research on Theatre and Aesthetics *(CARTE)* (Aesthetics; Fine Arts; Performing Arts; Theatre; Writing)

History: Founded 2000.

Admission Requirements: Baccalauréat

Fees: (CFA Francs): Undergraduate programmes, 500,000-1,900,000; Postgraduate programmes, 950,000-1,900,000

Main Language(s) of Instruction: French

Degrees and Diplomas: *Diplôme universitaire de Technologie*: **Journalism; Mass Communication.** *Licence*; *Diplôme d'Etudes supérieures spécialisées*: **Accountancy; Business Administration; Finance.** *Maîtrise*; *Diplôme d'Etudes approfondies*; *Doctorat*. Also Certificate in International Relations, Professional Diploma in Accountancy and Finance (DUPCF), Diplomas in Nursing, MBA.

Student Services: Health Services, Sports Facilities

Last Updated: 29/06/12

Croatia

STRUCTURE OF HIGHER EDUCATION SYSTEM

Description:

Croatian higher education is regulated by the Scientific Activity and Higher Education Act which came into force in August of 2003. The Act established a binary system composed of professional education offered at polytechnics (veleučilišta), independent schools of professional higher education (visoke škole) and universities (sveučilišta), and academic education solely conducted in universities. Only universities can offer third-cycle education (postgraduate studies). Private and public higher education institutions are treated equally. Public higher education institutions are those established by the state. Private universities, polytechnics and schools of professional higher education can be established as prescribed in the law and regulations relating to the establishment of institutions. The Act on Academic and Professional Titles and Academic Degrees was passed in September 2007. It established an overarching system of titles for students graduating from Bologna study programmes, as well as a framework for comparison of pre-Bologna and Bologna titles. Higher education is organized according to the system of transferable credits (ECTS) and has three levels: undergraduate, graduate and postgraduate. At the end of each level, a final qualification (certificate or diploma) is awarded together with the Diploma supplement. In 2010, Croatia counts 120 recognized higher education institutions, of which 10 are universities (sveučilišta), 15 are polytechnics (veleučilišta) and 27 are schools of professional higher education/ colleges (visoke škole) and 67 are faculties and academies which are part of universities, but legally recognized as separate entities. While most higher education institutions are publicly owned, 3 universities, 2 polytechnics and 24 schools of professional higher education are private. In 2004, the Agency for Science and Higher Education (ASHE) was created to be in charge of quality assurance and quality improvement in the fields of science and higher education. With the enactment of the Act on Quality Assurance in Science and Higher Education in April 2009, ASHE became an independent public institution responsible for external quality assurance and development in the fields of science and higher education and in charge of carrying out procedures of initial accreditation, re-accreditation, thematic evaluation and audit. The Act on Quality Assurance in Science and Higher Education stipulates that all public and private higher education institutions are subject to re-accreditation in five-year cycles.

With the introduction of the state graduation examination, the Central Applications Office (CAO) was established as a part of ASHE to serve as the national centre for processing applications at higher education institutions and consolidating the related procedures.

Stages of studies:

University level first stage: *Baccalaureaus*

Universities offer 3-4-year courses at undergraduate level leading to a degree of university baccalaureaus after accumulating 180 - 240 ECTS credits. This qualifies students for specialized, artistic or scientific work. They can continue their studies at graduate level studies or enter the labour market.

University level second stage: *Magistar/Magistra*

Universities offer 1-2-year graduate courses leading to the degree of Magistar/Magistra after accumulating a minimum of 300 ECTS credit points. In some fields, integrated 5- or 6-year courses are offered (medical studies, law, pharmacy...) and specific titles are awarded (e.g.Doctor in (Dental) Medicine). Graduates can continue their studies at postgraduate level or enter the labour market.

University level third stage: *University Specialist Degree; Doctor of Sciences/Arts.*

The University Specialist Degree is awarded after one to two years of postgraduate university studies and 60-120 ECTS credit points. The title of Doctor of Sciences (Dr.Sc.) or the Doctor of Arts (in Arts field) are awarded after three years of doctoral study and upon defence of a doctoral thesis. It is equivalent to a PhD degree.

ADMISSION TO HIGHER EDUCATION

Admission to university-level studies:

Name of secondary school credential required: Svjedodzba o drzavnoj maturi

For entry to: All programmes

Alternatives to credentials: All programmes. Minimum marks: Decided after processing all results of State Graduation Examination. It can differ each year. For certain study programmes (e.g. in Arts, ...) additional requirements can be required.

Admission requirements: No admission test. Some higher education institutions may, however, require mandatory additional tests as part of their admission procedure.

Numerus clausus: Yes

Other requirements: Mandatory requirements for some higher education institutions: additional test of knowledge, skills and competences (i.e. art academies, dentistry), medical certificate (i.e. medicine, veterinary medicine), passing certain subjects during secondary education, motivational interview, etc.

Foreign students admission:

Definition of foreign student: A student with citizenship other than Croatian.

Quotas: Foreign students with EU citizenship are in the same quota with Croatian students. Other foreign students are in the separate quota for foreigners.

Admission requirements: Foreign students need a certified copy of their school-leaving certificate and any required secondary education documents submitted in their English translation. The certificate must be validated by the Ministry of Science, Education and Sports.

Entry regulations: A student visa is required

Health requirements: Health insurance is required.

Language proficiency: Foreign students who do not speak Croatian or do not have a certificate of Croatian language proficiency are requested to complete a 2-semester course in the Croatian language and sit for a final examination.

RECOGNITION OF STUDIES

Quality assurance system:

Recognition is a formal acknowledgment of the value of a foreign education qualification or period of study, issued by the competent authority, for the purpose of the continuation of education or employment.
Recognition is carried out by the Agency for Science and Higher Education (for general employment purpose) or by the competent authorities (ministries or professional organizations) for employment in certain regulated profession. Recognition is regulated by the Act on Regulated Professions and Recognition of Foreign Professional Qualifications (Official Gazette, 124/2009, 45/2011) which regulate questions of recognition of foreign professional qualifications in the Republic of Croatia for the purpose of establishment and free provision of services on a temporary and occasional basis in the Republic of Croatia on the basis of foreign professional qualifications and the Act on Recognition of Foreign Educational Qualifications (Official Gazette, no. 158/2003, 198/2003, 138/2006 and 045/2011).
Croatian citizens, foreign citizens and persons without citizenship are entitled to the recognition of foreign education qualifications.
Competent authorities responsible for the recognition of different types of qualifications:
Recognition of primary and secondary school qualifications:
a) Recognition of qualifications attesting to the completion of primary education and general, gymnasium and secondary art education programmes (for the purpose of employment or continuing education) – falls under the authority of Education and Teacher Training Agency;
b) Recognition of qualifications attesting to the completion of vocational secondary education programmes (for the purpose of employment or continuing education) – falls under the authority of Agency for Vocational Education and Training and Adult Education;
c) Recognition for the purpose of continuing primary or secondary education – falls under the authority of the school where the applicant wishes to pursue his/her education;
d) Recognition of primary education for the purpose of access to secondary education – falls under the authority of the secondary school where the applicant wishes to pursue his/her education.
Recognition of higher education qualifications and a period of study:
a) for the purpose of continuing education in Croatia (academic recognition and recognition of periods of study) – falls under the authority of Croatian universities, polytechnics and colleges;

b) for the purpose of employment in Croatia (professional recognition) – falls under the authority of the Agency for Science and Higher Education, Croatian ENIC/NARIC Office.
Recognition of specializations and professional examinations – falls under the authority of a relevant ministry and professional organizations.

Bodies dealing with recognition:

Agencija za znanost i visoko obrazovanje, Croatian ENIC/NARIC office (Agency for Science and Higher Education)

Donje Svetice 38/V
Zagreb 10 000
Tel: + 385(1) 6274-800
Fax: + 385(1) 6274-801
EMail: enic@azvo.hr
WWW: www.azvo.hr

Agencija za odgoj i obrazovanje (Education and Teacher Training Agency.)

Donje Svetice 38
Zagreb 10 000
Tel: + 385(1) 2785-000
Fax: + 385(1) 2785-001
EMail: agencija@azoo.hr
WWW: www.azoo.hr

Agencija za strukovno obrazovanje i obrazovanje odraslih (Agency for Vocational Education and Training and Adult Education)

Radnička cesta 37b
Zagreb 10 000
Tel: +385 1 62 74 666
Fax: +385 1 62 74 606
EMail: ured@asoo.hr
WWW: www.asoo.hr

Special provisions for recognition:

Recognition for university level studies: Academic recognition (with continuation of education in the Republic of Croatia as its purpose) is under the authority of Croatian higher education institutions (Croatian universities, polytechnics and colleges) and is based on the.Act on Recognition of Foreign Educational Qualifications (Official Gazette, no. 158/2003, 198/2003, 138/2006 and 045/2011)

For exercising a profession: Recognition is done by Agency for Science and Higher Education (for employment for general purpose) or by the competent authorities (ministries or professional organizations) for employment in certain regulated profession. Act on Regulated Professions and Recognition of Foreign Professional Qualifications (Official Gazette, 124/2009, 45/2011) regulates the question of recognition of foreign professional qualifications in the Republic of Croatia for the purpose of establishment and free provision of services on a temporary and occasional basis in the Republic of Croatia on the basis of foreign professional qualifications.

NATIONAL BODIES

Ministarstvo znanosti, obrazovanja i sporta (Ministry of Science, Education and Sport)

Minister: Predrag Šustar
Donje Svetice 38
Zagreb 10000
Tel: +385(1) 456-9000
Fax: +385(1) 459-4301
EMail: office@mzos.hr; uzoj@mzos.hr
WWW: http://www.mzos.hr

Agencija za znanost i visoko obrazovanj (Agency for Science and Higher Education)

President: Mile Dželalija
Director: Jasmina Havranek
Donje Svetice 38/5
Zagreb 10000

Tel: +385(1) 627-4800
Fax: +385(1) 627-4801
EMail: enic@azvo.hr; ured@azvo.hr
WWW: http://www.azvo.hr
Role of national body: Specialized institution that carries out professional tasks related to the assessment of scientific activity in higher education, and the recognition of foreign qualifications through the ENIC/NARIC (established within the Agency).

Hrvatska zaklada za znanost (Croatian Science Foundation)
President of the Board: Dario Vretenar
Executive Director: Hrvoje Mataković
Ilica 24
Zagreb 10000
WWW: http://www.hrzz.hr
Role of national body: Promotion of science, higher education and technological development in the Republic of Croatia with the basic aims of ensuring economic development and stimulate employment.

Rektorski zbor Republike Hrvatske (Croatian Rectors' Conference)
President: Damir Boras
Secretary: Paula Pavletić
Sveučilište u Zagrebu
Krlaja Zvonimirova 8
Zagreb 10000
Tel: +385(1) 469-8109
Fax: +385(1) 469-8141
EMail: paula.pavletic@unizg.hr
WWW: http://www.rektorski-zbor.hr
Role of national body: Coordinates the activities and participates in the development of higher education.

Data for academic year: 2014-2015
Source: IAU from Croatian ENIC/NARIC Office, 2014. Bodies 2016.

INSTITUTIONS

PUBLIC INSTITUTIONS

COLLEGE OF AGRICULTURE IN KRIŽEVCI

Visoko gospodarsko učilište u Križevcima
Milislava Demerca 1, 48260 Križevci
Tel: +385(48) 279-180 +385(48) 279-199
Fax: +385(48) 682-790 +385(48) 279-189
EMail: uprava@vguk.hr
Website: http://www.vguk.hr

Dean: Vinko Pintić

Programme
Agriculture (Agriculture; Animal Husbandry; Crop Production)

Degrees and Diplomas: *Diploma diplomskog studija*
Last Updated: 10/02/15

COLLEGE OF SLAVONSKI BROD

Veleučilište u Slavonskom Brodu
Dr. Mile Budaka 1, 35000 Slavonski Brod
Tel: +385(35) 492-800
EMail: uprava@vusb.hr
Website: http://www.vusb.hr/hr/

Department
Agriculture (Farm Management; Horticulture); **Social** (Management); **Technical** (Production Engineering)

History: Founded 2006.

Degrees and Diplomas: *Diploma stručnog studija - stručni prvostupnik (baccalaureus)*; *Diploma specijalističkog diplomskog stručnog studija - stručni specijalist*
Last Updated: 09/02/15

JOSIP JURAJ STROSSMAYER UNIVERSITY OF OSIJEK

Sveučilište Josipa Jurja Strossmayera u Osijeku
Trg. Sv. Trojstva 3, 31 000 Osijek
Tel: +385(31) 224-102
Fax: +385(31) 207-015
EMail: rektorat@unios.hr
Website: http://www.unios.hr

Rektor: Željko Turkalj

Faculty
Agriculture (Agricultural Economics; Agricultural Equipment; Agriculture; Animal Husbandry; Biology; Chemistry; Crop Production; Fishery; Horticulture; Soil Science); **Civil Engineering** (Civil Engineering); **Economics** (Business Computing; Economics; Finance; Management; Marketing); **Education** (Education); **Electrical**

Engineering (Electrical Engineering); **Food Technology** (Food Technology); **Law** (Law); **Mechanical Engineering** *(Slavonski Brod)* (Mechanical Engineering); **Medicine** (Medicine); **Philosophy** (Philosophy); **Theology** (Theology)

College
Teacher Training (Teacher Training)

Department
Biology (Biology); **Chemistry** (Chemistry); **Cultural Studies** (Cultural Studies); **Mathematics** (Mathematics); **Physics** (Physics)

Academy
Arts (Arts and Humanities)

Further Information: Also Branch in Slavonski Brod

History: Founded 1975, incorporating Faculty of Economics formerly attached to University of Zagreb. Acquired present title 1990. An independent self-governing institution.

Academic Year: October to September (October-February; March-September)

Admission Requirements: Secondary school certificate (Svjedodžba o završenoj srednjoj skoli), or foreign equivalent and Croatian Language examination

Fees: Foreign students, c. 1,000-1,800 per annum (US Dollar)

Main Language(s) of Instruction: Croatian

Degrees and Diplomas: *Diploma preddiplomskog sveucilisnog studija - sveučilišni prvostupnik (baccalaureus)*; *Diploma poslijediplomskog specijalističkog studija - sveučilišni specijalist*; *Diploma poslijediplomskog sveučilišnog studija - doktor znanosti/doktor umjetnosti*: **Agriculture; Electrical Engineering; Food Technology; Law; Management; Medicine; Philosophy.**

Student Services: Canteen

Publications: Ekonomski vjesnik (Economic Courier); Medical Courier; Pravni vjesnik (Law Courier); Research and Practice in Agriculture and Food Technology

Last Updated: 04/02/15

JURAJ DOBRILA UNIVERSITY OF PULA

Sveučilište Jurja Dobrile u Puli
Zagrebačka 30, 52100 Pula
Tel: +385(52) 377-000
EMail: ured@unipu.hr
Website: http://www.unipu.hr/

Rektor: Alfio Barbieri EMail: abarbieri@unipu.hr

Department
Economics and Tourism (Economics; Tourism); **Education** (Education; Teacher Training); **Humanities** (Arts and Humanities; Classical Languages; History; Native Language; Philology; Romance Languages); **Italian Studies** (Italian); **Music** (Music)

History: Founded 2006.

Main Language(s) of Instruction: Croatian

Degrees and Diplomas: *Diploma diplomskog studija*; *Diploma poslijediplomskog specijalističkog studija - sveučilišni specijalist*; *Diploma poslijediplomskog sveučilišnog studija - doktor znanosti/doktor umjetnosti*: **Economics.**

Last Updated: 04/02/15

MARKO MARULIĆ POLYTECHNIC, KNIN

Marko Marulić Polytechnic in Knin
Petra Krešimira IV 30, 22300 Knin
Fax: +385(22) 661-374
EMail: info@veleknin.hr
Website: http://www.veleknin.hr

Rektor: Marko Jelić

Department
Agriculture (Agriculture); **Commercial Business and Entrepreneurship** (Business Administration; Business and Commerce); **Food Technology** (Food Science; Food Technology)

History: Founded 2005.

Last Updated: 04/02/15

MEĐIMURJE POLYTECHNIC IN ČAKOVEC

Međimursko veleučilište u Čakovcu
Bana Josipa Jelačića 22a, 40 000 Čakovec
Tel: +385(4) 039-6990
EMail: veleuciliste@mev.hr
Website: http://www.mev.hr/

Dean: Nevenka Breslauer

Department
Computer Engineering (Computer Engineering); **Management of Tourism and Sports** (Management; Sports; Tourism); **Sustainable Development** (Environmental Engineering; Mechanical Engineering; Thermal Engineering)

Degrees and Diplomas: *Diploma stručnog studija - stručni prvostupnik (baccalaureus)*; *Diploma poslijediplomskog specijalističkog studija - sveučilišni specijalist*

Last Updated: 04/02/15

POLICE COLLEGE

Visoka policijska škola u Zagrebu
Avenija Gojka Šuška 1, 10000 Zagreb
Tel: +385(1) 2426-311
EMail: policijska.akademija@mup.hr
Website: http://www.policija.hr/

Programme
Police Studies (Civil Security; Police Studies)

POLYTECHNIC OF APPLIED HEALTH STUDIES IN ZAGREB

Zdravstveno veleučilište u Zagrebu
Mlinarska cesta 38, HR-10000 Zagreb
Tel: +385(1) 5495 805
Fax: +355(1) 5495 900
Website: http://www.zvu.hr/

Dean: Aleksandar Racz EMail: aleksandar.racz@zvu.hr

General Secretary: Nenad Mojsović
EMail: nenad.mojsovic@zvu.hr

Programme
Ergotherapy (Ergotherapy); **Laboratory Techniques** (Medical Technology); **Nursing** (Nursing); **Physiotherapy** (Physical Therapy); **Radiology** (Radiology)

Degrees and Diplomas: *Diploma diplomskog studija*; *Diploma poslijediplomskog specijalističkog studija - sveučilišni specijalist*

Last Updated: 16/12/15

POLYTECHNIC OF KARLOVAC

Veleučilište u Karlovcu
Ivana Meštrovića 10, 47000 Karlovac
Tel: +385(47) 415-455
Fax: +385(47) 415-450
EMail: dekanat@vuka.hr
Website: http://www.vuka.hr

Dean: Branko Wasserbauer

Department
Business (Economics; Management; Marketing); **Food Technology** (Food Technology); **Gamekeeping and Environmental Protection** (Wildlife); **Mechanical Engineering** (Mechanical Engineering); **Safety and Protection** (Safety Engineering); **Textile Technology** (Textile Technology)

History: Founded 1997.

Degrees and Diplomas: *Diploma diplomskog studija*; *Diploma diplomskog sveučilišnog studija - magistar*

Last Updated: 06/02/15

POLYTECHNIC OF POŽEGA

Veleučilište u Požegi
Ul. Pape Ivana Pavla II br.6, 34000 Požega
Tel: +385(34) 271-018
Fax: +385(34) 271-008
EMail: ured@vup.hr
Website: http://www.vup.hr

Rektor: Stjepan Madjar

Department
Agriculture (Agriculture; Food Technology; Viticulture); **Social Sciences** (Accountancy; Administration; Business and Commerce; Social Sciences)

History: Founded 1998.
Last Updated: 06/02/15

POLYTECHNIC OF RIJEKA

Veleučilište u Rijeci
Trpimirova 2/V, 51000 Rijeka
Tel: +385(51) 321-300
Fax: +385(51) 211-270
EMail: ured@veleri.hr
Website: http://www.veleri.hr

Rector: Marčelo Dujanić

Department
Administration *(Otočac)* (Administration); **Agriculture** (Agriculture); **Business** (Business and Commerce); **Traffic** (Transport Management)

History: Founded 1998.
Last Updated: 09/02/15

POLYTECHNIC OF ŠIBENIK

Veleučilište u Šibeniku
Trg Andrije Hebranga 11, Šibenik
EMail: dekanat@vus.hr
Website: http://www.vus.hr/

Department
Management (Management; Tourism); **Public Administration** (Public Administration); **Transport and Traffic** (Transport and Communications)

History: Founded 2006.

Degrees and Diplomas: *Diploma stručnog studija - stručni prvostupnik (baccalaureus)*; *Diploma poslijediplomskog specijalističkog studija - sveučilišni specijalist*
Last Updated: 06/02/15

POLYTECHNIC OF ZAGREB

Tehničko veleučilište u Zagrebu
Ivana Lučića 5, 10000 Zagreb
Tel: +385(1) 6168-580
Fax: +385(1) 6157-107
Website: http://www.tvz.hr

Rector: Dragutin Ščap

Department
Civil Engineering (Civil Engineering); **Electrical Engineering** (Electrical Engineering); **Information Technology** (Information Technology); **Mechanical Engineering** (Mechanical Engineering); **Textile Technology** (Textile Technology); **Traffic Engineering** (Transport Management)

Degrees and Diplomas: *Diploma stručnog studija - stručni prvostupnik (baccalaureus)*; *Diploma diplomskog sveučilišnog studija - magistar*
Last Updated: 09/02/15

UNIVERSITY OF DUBROVNIK

Sveučilište u Dubrovniku
Ćire Carića 4, 20000 Dubrovnik
Tel: +385(20) 445-700
Fax: +385(20) 435-590
EMail: rektorat@unidu.hr
Website: http://www.unidu.hr

Rektor: Mateo Milković

Programme
Nursing (Nursing)

Department
Aquaculture (Aquaculture); **Art and Restoration** (Art History; Fine Arts; Heritage Preservation; Restoration of Works of Art); **Economics and Business Economics** (Accountancy; Business Administration; Business Computing; E-Business/Commerce; Economics; Finance; Hotel Management; Human Resources; Marketing); **Electrical Engineering and Computing** (Business Computing; Computer Science); **Marine Engineering** (Engineering; Marine Engineering; Nautical Science); **Maritime** (Marine Engineering); **Mass Communication** (Cultural Studies; Mass Communication; Media Studies); **Tourism** (Tourism)

History: Founded 2003. Formerly known as Dubrovnik Polytechnic.

Main Language(s) of Instruction: Croatian

Degrees and Diplomas: *Diploma diplomskog studija*; *Diploma poslijediplomskog sveučilišnog studija - doktor znanosti/doktor umjetnosti*
Last Updated: 04/02/15

UNIVERSITY OF RIJEKA

Sveučilište u Rijeci
Trg braće Mažuranića 10, HR 51000 Rijeka
Tel: +385(51) 406-500
Fax: +385(51) 216-671 +385(51) 216-091
EMail: ured@uniri.hr
Website: http://www.uniri.hr

Rektor: Pero Lučin EMail: pero.lucin@uniri.hr

Generalen Sekretar: Roberta Hlača-Mlinar

International Relations: Darko Štefan
EMail: darko@uniri.hr

Faculty
Civil Engineering (Building Technologies; Civil Engineering; Construction Engineering; Geological Engineering; Hydraulic Engineering); **Economics** (Accountancy; Banking; Economics; Finance; Information Technology; International Business; Leadership; Management; Marketing); **Engineering** (Electrical Engineering; Engineering; Mechanical Engineering; Naval Architecture); **Humanities and Social Sciences** *(Pula)* (Art History; Comparative Literature; Computer Science; Cultural Studies; English; German; History; Italian; Latin; Literature; Music; Musical Instruments; Pedagogy; Philosophy; Psychology; Serbocroatian; Slavic Languages); **Law** (Administrative Law; Law); **Maritime Studies** (Electronic Engineering; Information Sciences; Marine Engineering; Marine Science and Oceanography; Marine Transport; Nautical Science; Transport and Communications; Transport Management); **Medicine** (Dentistry; Family Studies; Medicine; Nursing; Psychiatry and Mental Health; Public Health; Radiology; Sanitary Engineering); **Teacher Education** *(Teacher's School, Gospić)* (Primary Education); **Tourism and Hospitality Management** *(Opatija)* (Business and Commerce; Hotel Management; Tourism)

Academy
Applied Arts (Fine Arts)

History: Founded 1973, incorporating various institutions of higher education which were established during the 17th and 18th centuries.

Academic Year: October to June

Admission Requirements: Secondary school certificate (Svjedodžba o završnom ispitu) or recognized equivalent

Fees: Foreign students, c. 55 per annum (Croatian Kuna)

Main Language(s) of Instruction: Croatian. Some courses in Italian, English

Degrees and Diplomas: *Svjedodžba stručnog studija - stručni pristupnik*; *Diploma diplomskog sveučilišnog studija - magistar*, *Diploma poslijediplomskog sveučilišnog studija - doktor znanosti/ doktor umjetnosti*: **Computer Science; Economics; Engineering; Law; Medicine; Nautical Science; Philosophy.**

Student Services: Canteen, Careers Guidance, Cultural Activities, Health Services, Social Counselling
Last Updated: 04/02/15

UNIVERSITY OF SPLIT

Sveučilište u Splitu
Livanjska 5, 21 000 Split
Tel: +385(21) 558-200 +385(21) 348-966
Fax: +385(21) 355-163
EMail: rektorat.office@unist.hr
Website: http://www.unist.hr

Rektor: Šimun Anđelinović

Generalen Sekretar: Paula Vučemilović Šimunović EMail: paula@unist.hr

Faculty

Catholic Theology (Catholic Theology; Religious Studies; Theology); **Chemistry and Technology** (Chemistry; Technology); **Civil Engineering, Architecture and Geodesy** (Architecture; Civil Engineering; Geology); **Economics** (Economics; Finance; Marketing); **Electrical Engineering, Mechanical Engineering and Naval Architecture** (Computer Science; Electrical Engineering; Industrial Engineering; Mechanical Engineering; Naval Architecture); **Kinesiology** (Physical Therapy); **Law** (Law); **Maritime Studies** (Electronic Engineering; Management; Marine Engineering; Marine Transport; Nautical Science); **Philosophy** (Education; English; History; Italian; Philosophy; Preschool Education; Primary Education; Slavic Languages; Teacher Training); **Science** (Biology; Chemistry; Computer Science; Mathematics; Mathematics and Computer Science; Physical Education; Physics; Technology; Technology Education)

School

Medicine (Medicine)

Department

Marine Studies (Biology; Ecology; Fishery; Marine Science and Oceanography); **Professional Studies**

Academy

Arts (Art Education; Communication Arts; Design; Fine Arts; Music; Music Education; Musical Instruments; Musicology; Painting and Drawing; Restoration of Works of Art; Sculpture; Singing)

Further Information: Also Branches in Zadar, Šibenik and Dubrovnik

History: Founded 1974. Formerly College of Philosophy and Theology in Zadar established 1396 by the Dominican Order, incorporating existing faculties in the region and some departments formerly attached to University of Zagreb. An independent self-governing institution financed by the Republic.

Academic Year: October to September (October-February; March-September)

Admission Requirements: Secondary school certificate (Svjedodžba o završnom ispitu) or recognized equivalent, and entrance examination

Fees: None for Croatian citizens. Foreign students: dependent on decision of Ministry of Science and Technology

Main Language(s) of Instruction: Croatian

Degrees and Diplomas: *Svjedodžba stručnog studija - stručni pristupnik*; *Diploma preddiplomskog sveucilisnog studija - sveučilišni prvostupnik (baccalaureus)*; *Diploma diplomskog studija*; *Diploma poslijediplomskog sveučilišnog studija - doktor znanosti/doktor umjetnosti*: **Arts and Humanities; Chemical Engineering; Civil Engineering; Economics; Electrical Engineering; Information Technology; Marine Science and Oceanography; Mechanical Engineering; Medicine; Physical Therapy; Theology.**

Student Services: Academic Counselling, Canteen, Facilities for disabled people, Health Services, Language Laboratory

Last Updated: 06/02/15

UNIVERSITY OF ZADAR

Sveučilište u Zadru (UNIZD)
Ulica Mihovila Pavlinovića bb, 23000 Zadar
Tel: +385(23) 200-555
Fax: +385(23) 316-882
EMail: rektorat@unizd.hr
Website: http://www.unizd.hr

Rector: Ante Uglešic EMail: ante.uglesic@unizd.hr

Secretary-General: Antonella Lovric EMail: alovric@unizd.hr

International Relations: Maja Kolega EMail: mkolega@unizd.hr

Department

Archaeology (Archaeology); **Art History** (Art History); **Classical Philology** (Philology); **Croatian and Slavic Studies** (Slavic Languages); **Ecology, Agronomy and Aquaculture** (Agriculture; Aquaculture; Crop Production; Ecology); **English Language and Literature** (English; Literature); **Ethnology and Cultural Anthropology** (Anthropology; Ethnology); **French and Iberoromance Studies** (French; Literature; Philology; Spanish); **Geography** (Geography); **German Studies** (German); **Health Studies** (Dietetics; Epidemiology; Health Sciences; Nursing; Radiology); **History** (History); **Italian Studies** (Italian); **Library and Information Science** (Information Sciences; Library Science); **Linguistics** (Linguistics); **Maritime Studies** (Marine Transport; Nautical Science); **Pedagogy** (Pedagogy); **Philosophy** (Philosophy); **Psychology** (Psychology); **Sociology** (Sociology); **Tourism and Communication Studies** (Communication Studies; Tourism)

History: Founded 2002, incorporating former Faculty of Philosophy of the University of Split.

Academic Year: October to June

Admission Requirements: High School Certificate

Main Language(s) of Instruction: Croatian

Degrees and Diplomas: *Svjedodžba stručnog studija - stručni pristupnik*; *Diploma diplomskog studija*; *Diploma poslijediplomskog sveučilišnog studija - doktor znanosti/doktor umjetnosti*: **Archaeology; Arts and Humanities; Information Sciences; Sociology.**

Student Services: Canteen

Publications: Radovi Sveučilišta u Zadru

Publishing House: University Publishing House

Last Updated: 06/02/15

IAU UNIVERSITY OF ZAGREB

Sveučilište u Zagrebu
Trg Maršala Tita 14, HR-10000 Zagreb
Tel: +385(1) 4564-255
Fax: +385(1) 4564-008
EMail: office@unizg.hr
Website: http://www.unizg.hr

Rector: Damir Boras EMail: rector@unizg.hr

International Relations: Ana Ružička
Tel: +385(1) 4698-101 EMail: aruzicka@unizg.hr

Faculty

Agriculture (Agricultural Economics; Agricultural Engineering; Agriculture; Animal Husbandry; Horticulture; Landscape Architecture; Plant Pathology); **Architecture** (Architectural and Environmental Design; Architecture; Town Planning); **Catholic Theology** (Catholic Theology); **Chemical Engineering and Technology** (Chemical Engineering; Technology); **Civil Engineering** (Civil Engineering); **Education and Rehabilitation** (Art Therapy; Behavioural Sciences; Criminal Law; Rehabilitation and Therapy; Speech Therapy and Audiology); **Electrical Engineering and Computer Science** (Computer Science; Electrical Engineering); **Food Technology and Biotechnology** (Biotechnology; Food Technology); **Forestry** (Forestry); **Geodesy** (Earth Sciences; Surveying and Mapping); **Geotechnical Engineering** (Earth Sciences; Geophysics); **Graphic Arts** (Graphic Arts); **Humanities and Social Sciences** (Arts and Humanities; Social Sciences); **Kinesiology** (Physical Education; Sports; Sports Medicine); **Law** (Law); **Mechanical Engineering and Naval Architecture** (Mechanical Engineering; Naval Architecture); **Metallurgy** (Metallurgical Engineering); **Mining, Geology, and Petroleum Engineering** (Geological Engineering; Mining Engineering; Petroleum and Gas Engineering); **Organization and Information Studies** (Business Administration; Information Management; Information Sciences); **Pharmacy and Biochemistry** (Biochemistry; Pharmacy); **Philosophy** (Archaeology; Art History; Comparative Literature; English; Ethnology; French; German; Greek; History; Humanities and Social Science Education; Hungarian; Information Sciences; Italian; Latin; Linguistics; Modern Languages; Philosophy; Phonetics; Polish; Psychology; Scandinavian Languages; Serbocroatian; Slavic Languages; Sociology; Spanish); **Political Science** (Political Sciences); **Science** (Biology; Chemistry; Geography; Geology; Geophysics; Mathematics; Natural Sciences; Physics); **Teacher Education**

(Education; Teacher Trainers Education; Teacher Training); **Textile Technology** (Textile Technology); **Transport and Traffic Engineering** (Road Transport; Transport Engineering; Transport Management); **Veterinary Science** (Veterinary Science)

School

Dental Medicine (Dentistry); **Medicine** *(Also Graduate School)* (Medicine)

Academy

Dramatic Arts (Film; Theatre); **Fine Arts** (Fine Arts); **Music** (Music)

Centre

Croatian Studies *(Studia Croatica)* (Cultural Studies; Philology; Religious Studies; Serbocroatian; Social Studies)

Further Information: Also Centre for Advanced Academic Studies (CAAS) in Dubrovnik; International Centres of Croatian Universities (ICCU) in Istria and Motovun

History: Founded 1669 as Royal Academy of Sciences by edict of Emperor Leopold I granting University status to the existing Jesuit Academy of the Royal Free City of Zagreb. Reorganized 1874 as University of Zagreb, the largest and oldest Croatian university.

Academic Year: October to June (October-January; February-June)

Admission Requirements: Secondary school certificate (Svjedodžba završene srednje škole) or recognized equivalent, and entrance examination (Razredbeni ispit)

Main Language(s) of Instruction: Croatian

Degrees and Diplomas: *Svjedodžba stručnog studija - stručni pristupnik*; *Diploma diplomskog studija*; *Diploma diplomskog sveučilišnog studija - magistar*; *Diploma poslijediplomskog specijalističkog studija - sveučilišni specijalist*; *Diploma poslijediplomskog sveučilišnog studija - doktor znanosti/doktor umjetnosti*: **Architecture; Biochemistry; Biomedicine; Chemical Engineering; Civil Engineering; Dentistry; Electrical Engineering; Fashion Design; Geology; Graphic Design; Health Sciences; Metallurgical Engineering; Mining Engineering; Naval Architecture; Petroleum and Gas Engineering; Pharmacy; Textile Technology; Veterinary Science.** Also Postgraduate Professional/Vocational studies in Arts

Student Services: Canteen, Cultural Activities, Health Services, Language Laboratory, Sports Facilities

Publishing house: Sveučiliána tiskara; Hrvatska sveučilišna naklada

Last Updated: 06/02/15

PRIVATE INSTITUTIONS

BALTAZAR ADAM KRČELIĆ COLLEGE OF BUSINESS ADMINISTRATION

Visoka škola za poslovanje i upravljanje "Baltazar Adam Krčelić"

Vladimira Novaka 23, 10290 Zaprešić

Tel: +385(1) 3310-321

Fax: +385(1) 3310-264

EMail: info@vspu.hr

Website: http://www.vspu.hr

Dean: Milan Jurina

Programme

Business and Finance (Business and Commerce; Finance); **Cultural Management** (Management); **Office Management** (Business and Commerce; Management)

History: Founded 2001.

Degrees and Diplomas: *Diploma stručnog studija - stručni prvostupnik (baccalaureus)*; *Diploma specijalističkog diplomskog stručnog studija - stručni specijalist*

Last Updated: 11/02/15

BUSINESS COLLEGE LIBERTAS

Visoka poslovna škola "Libertas"

Trg. J.F. Kennedya 6b, 10000 Zagreb

Tel: +385(1) 2323-377

Fax: +385(1) 2315-851

EMail: poslovna.skola@libertas.hr

Website: http://www.vps-libertas.hr

Dean: Davor Žmegač

Programme

Business Economics (Banking; Economics; Finance); **Sports Management** (Sports Management); **Toursim and Hotel Management** (Hotel Management; Management; Tourism)

History: Founded 2004.

Main Language(s) of Instruction: Croatian

Degrees and Diplomas: *Diploma diplomskog studija*; *Diploma poslijediplomskog specijalističkog studija - sveučilišni specijalist*

Last Updated: 06/02/15

BUSINESS COLLEGE WITH PUBLIC RIGHTS, VIŠNJAN

Visoka poslovna škola s pravom javnosti, Višnjan

Ul. Istarska 23/I, 52463 Višnjan, Poreč

Tel: +385(52) 449-464

Fax: +385(52) 449-500

Website: http://www.manero.hr

Dean: Robin B. Paulović

Programme

Tourism Management (Management; Tourism)

History: Founded 2000.

Degrees and Diplomas: *Diploma stručnog studija - stručni prvostupnik (baccalaureus)*; *Diploma poslijediplomskog specijalističkog studija - sveučilišni specijalist*

Last Updated: 09/02/15

COLLEGE FOR FINANCE AND LAW EFFECTUS

Effectus Visoko učilište - visoka škola za financije i pravo

Trg J.F.Kennedy 2, Zagreb

EMail: referada@vsfp.eu

Website: http://www.effectus-uciliste.eu/

Dean: Mira Lenardić

Programme

Financial Management (Finance; Management); **Law and Finance** (Finance; Law); **Taxation** (Taxation)

Degrees and Diplomas: *Diploma stručnog studija - stručni prvostupnik (baccalaureus)*; *Diploma specijalističkog diplomskog stručnog studija - stručni specijalist*

Last Updated: 11/02/15

COLLEGE FOR SAFETY

Visoka škola za sigurnost

Zagreb

Website: http://www.vss.hr

Dean: Liljana Dolšak

Course

Safety (Civil Security)

Degrees and Diplomas: *Diploma preddiplomskog sveucilisnog studija - sveučilišni prvostupnik (baccalaureus)*; *Diploma specijalističkog diplomskog stručnog studija - stručni specijalist*

Last Updated: 10/04/15

COLLEGE OF AGORA

Visoka škola tržišnih komunikacija Agora

Trnjanska cesta 114, Zagreb

Tel: +385(1) 222- 5 700

EMail: agora@vsa.hr

Website: http://www.vsa.hr/hr/naslovna

Programme

Design (Design); **Management** (Management)

COLLEGE OF ECONOMICS, ENTREPRENEURSHIP AND MANAGEMENT ZRINSKI

Visoka škola za ekonomiju, poduzetništvo i upravljanje "Nikola Šubić Zrinski"
Selska cesta 119, 10100 Zagreb
Tel: +385(1) 36 47 099
Website: http://www.zrinski.org/nikola/

Dean (Acting): Vitomir Tafra EMail: marina.gregoric@zrinski.org

Programme
Economics of Entrepreneurship (Business Administration; Economics)

Degrees and Diplomas: *Diploma stručnog studija - stručni prvostupnik (baccalaureus); Diploma poslijediplomskog specijalističkog studija - sveučilišni specijalist*
Last Updated: 11/02/15

COLLEGE OF MANAGEMENT AND DESIGN ASPIRA

Visoka škola za menadžment i dizajn "Aspira"
Domovinskog rata 65, 21000 Split
Tel: +385(21) 382-802
EMail: info@aspira.hr
Website: http://www.aspira.hr/

Dean: Slobodan Dragičević

Programme
Sports Management (Sports Management); **Tourism Management** (Hotel Management; Management; Tourism)

History: Founded 2009.

Degrees and Diplomas: *Diploma stručnog studija - stručni prvostupnik (baccalaureus); Diploma diplomskog sveučilišnog studija - magistar.* **Sports Management.**
Last Updated: 10/02/15

CROATIAN CATHOLIC UNIVERSITY

Hrvatsko katoličko sveučilište
Ilica 242 (ulaz iz Domobranske ulice), 10000 Zagreb
Tel: +385(1) 370-6600
Fax: + 385 (1) 370-6601
EMail: info@unicath.hr
Website: http://www.unicath.hr

Rector: Željko Tanjić

Department
Communication Sciences (Communication Studies); **History** (History); **Psychology** (Psychology); **Sociology** (Sociology)

History: Founded 2006.

Main Language(s) of Instruction: Croatian

Accrediting Agency: Ministry of Science, Education and Sports

Degrees and Diplomas: *Diploma stručnog studija - stručni prvostupnik (baccalaureus); Diploma diplomskog sveučilišnog studija - magistar*
Last Updated: 04/02/15

DAG HAMMARSKJÖLD UNIVERSITY COLLEGE OF INTERNATIONAL RELATIONS AND DIPLOMACY

Visoka škola međunarodnih odnosa i diplomacije Dag Hammarskjöld
Ilica 242, Zagreb
Tel: +385(1) 3700-826
EMail: tajnistvo@diplomacija.hr
Website: http://www.diplomacija.hr/

Dean: Ivo Šlaus

Programme
International Relations and Diplomacy (International Relations)

Degrees and Diplomas: *Diploma stručnog studija - stručni prvostupnik (baccalaureus); Diploma poslijediplomskog specijalističkog studija - sveučilišni specijalist*
Last Updated: 09/02/15

DIU LIBERTAS INTERNATIONAL UNIVERSITY

DIU Libertas Medunarodno sveučilište
Sv. Dominika 4, Dubrovnik
Tel: +385(20) 414 111
EMail: diu@diu.hr
Website: http://www.diu.hr

Rector: Božidar Jelčić

School
Diplomacy (International Relations); **Health Science** (Embryology and Reproduction Biology; Gynaecology and Obstetrics; Health Sciences); **International Business and Economics** (Commercial Law; Economics; Finance; International Business; International Economics; Management; Marketing); **Theatre** (Theatre)

History: Founded 2008.

Fees: 3500 per semester (Euro)

Accrediting Agency: Ministry of Science, Education and Sports

Degrees and Diplomas: *Diploma stručnog studija - stručni prvostupnik (baccalaureus); Diploma diplomskog sveučilišnog studija - magistar*
Last Updated: 04/02/15

POLYTECHNIC PULA - COLLEGE OF APPLIED SCIENCES

Politehnika Pula - Visoka tehničko-poslovna škola s pravom javnosti
Riva 6, 52100 Pula
Tel: +385(5) 2381-412
Fax: +385(5) 2381-412
EMail: marilena.radolovic@politehnika-pula.hr
Website: http://www.politehnika-pula.hr/

Dean (Acting): Davor Mišković

Programme
Engineering

History: Founded 2009.

Degrees and Diplomas: *Diploma preddiplomskog sveucilisnog studija - sveučilišni prvostupnik (baccalaureus); Diploma diplomskog sveučilišnog studija - magistar*
Last Updated: 04/02/15

RIT CROATIA

Don Frana Bulića 6, Dubrovnik
Tel: + 385(20) 433-000
EMail: admissions@croatia.rit.edu
Website: http://www.croatia.rit.edu/

Dean: Don Hudspeth

Programme
Information Technology (Information Technology); **International Business** *(Zagreb)* (International Business); **International Hospitality and Service Management** (Hotel and Restaurant; Management)

Further Information: Also campus in Zagreb

History: Founded 1995. Acquired present status 2013.

Degrees and Diplomas: *Diploma preddiplomskog sveucilisnog studija - sveučilišni prvostupnik (baccalaureus); Diploma diplomskog sveučilišnog studija - magistar*
Last Updated: 04/02/15

RRIF COLLEGE OF FINANCIAL MANAGEMENT

RRiF Visoka škola za financijski menadžment
Martićeva 29, 10000 Zagreb
Tel: +385(1) 4699-735
EMail: visoka-skola@rrif.hr
Website: http://www.visoka-skola-rrif.hr/

Dean: Đurđica Jurić

Programme
Accounting and Finance (Accountancy; Finance)

History: Founded 2006.

Degrees and Diplomas: *Diploma preddiplomskog sveucilisnog studija - sveučilišni prvostupnik (baccalaureus)*; *Diploma diplomskog sveučilišnog studija - magistar*
Last Updated: 04/02/15

UNIVERSITY OF APPLIED SCIENCES VELIKA GORICA

Veleučilište Velika Gorica
Zagrebačka cesta 5, 10410 Velika Gorica
Tel: +385(1) 622-2501
EMail: info@vvg.hr
Website: http://www.vvg.hr/

Dean: Ivan Toth

Programme
Aircraft Maintenance (Maintenance Technology); **Computer Systems Maintenance** (Maintenance Technology); **Crisis Management** (Peace and Disarmament); **Information Systems** (Information Sciences); **Motor Vehicle Maintenance** (Maintenance Technology); **Optometry** (Optometry)

Degrees and Diplomas: *Diploma stručnog studija - stručni prvostupnik (baccalaureus)*; *Diploma specijalističkog diplomskog stručnog studija - stručni specijalist*
Last Updated: 09/02/15

VERN POLYTECHNIC

Veleučilište VERN
Ban Jelačić Square, 3, Fax:, 10000 Zagreb
Tel: +385(1) 48-25-927
Fax: +385(1) 48-25-910
EMail: kristijan.paksec@vern.hr
Website: http://www.vern.hr/

Dean: Vlatko Cvrtila

Department
Applied Mathematics and Information Technology (Applied Mathematics; Computer Science; Information Technology); **Economics and Marketing** (Economics; Marketing); **Entrepreneurship and Management** (Business Administration); **Finance, Accountancy and Law** (Accountancy; Finance; Law); **Languages and Culture** (Cultural Studies; Modern Languages); **Psychology and Communications** (Communication Studies; Psychology); **Tourism** (Tourism)

Degrees and Diplomas: *Diploma stručnog studija - stručni prvostupnik (baccalaureus)*; *Diploma diplomskog sveučilišnog studija - magistar*
Last Updated: 10/02/15

ZAGREB SCHOOL OF ECONOMICS AND MANAGEMENT

Zagrabačka škola ekonomije i managementa
Jordanovac 110, 10000 Zagreb
Tel: +385(1) 2354-242
Fax: +385(1) 2354-243
EMail: dekan@zsem.hr
Website: http://www.zsem.hr

Dean: Djuro Njavro

Department
Accountancy (Accountancy); **Economics** (Economics); **Finance** (Finance); **Foreign Languages** (Modern Languages); **Information and Communication Technology** (Information Technology); **Law** (Law); **Management** (Management); **Marketing** (Marketing); **Mathematics and Statistics** (Mathematics; Statistics)

Degrees and Diplomas: *Diploma diplomskog studija*; *Diploma diplomskog sveučilišnog studija - magistar*
Last Updated: 10/04/15

Cuba

STRUCTURE OF HIGHER EDUCATION SYSTEM

Description:

Higher education is provided by universities, higher institutes, and university centres. All higher education institutions are public and free of charge. The Ministerio de Educación Superior (MES) is responsible for policy in matters of undergraduate and postgraduate education. It controls teaching, methodology, courses and programmes and the allocation of student places, even though some specialized higher education institutions come under the control of other ministries such as the Ministry of Education for teachers' training institutions and the Ministry of Health for medical faculties.

Stages of studies:

University level first stage: *Pregrado*

The first and main stage of higher education usually lasts for five years. In Medicine, studies last for six years. At the end of the first stage, students are awarded a Licenciatura or a Título profesional (professional diploma) as follows: Ingeniero in technical and agricultural sciences, Arquitecto in Architecture, and Doctor in Medicine and Veterinary Medicine.

University level second stage: *Posgrado*

Diplomado courses have three levels, each requiring some 200 hours of theoretical instruction, practical work, industrial internship and a final project. Students can gain academic credit towards completion of a Master's degree and are allowed to work on a Master's thesis as they progress through Diplomado studies. The second stage corresponds to a period of in-depth study and research which leads to the Maestria after two years. Especialista programmes last two years.Three to four years' studies and research with a supervisor lead to the Doctor degree. The research results must have been defended before a jury and published in academic journals.

ADMISSION TO HIGHER EDUCATION

Admission to university-level studies:

Name of secondary school credential required: Bachillerato

Admission requirements: For access to degree courses, students must sit for the Examen de Ingreso. It is taken in two or three subjects.

Foreign students admission:

Admission requirements: Foreign students must hold a Bachiller or an equivalent degree.

Entry regulations: Students must have a visa.

Health requirements: Students must have a health certificate.

Language proficiency: Foreign students arriving from countries whose official language is not Spanish will take an examination to establish the level of the Spanish course they must follow. Spanish and Cuban culture courses are offered in several universities throughout the year.

RECOGNITION OF STUDIES

Quality assurance system:

The National Accreditation Committee was created to promote, organize, implement and control the policy of accreditation for higher education in the country. In addition, the Committee grants the different categories of accreditation to evaluated programmes and institutions.

Bodies dealing with recognition:

Junta de Acreditación Nacional - JAN (National Accreditation Committee)

Calle 23 esquina F El Vedado
La Havana 10400

NATIONAL BODIES

Ministerio de Educación Superior (Ministry of Higher Education)
Minister: Rodolfo Alarcon Ortiz
Calle 23 esq. F # 565. Plaza de la Revolución
La Habana
Tel: +53 838 2314
EMail: contacto@mes.gob.cu
WWW: http://www.mes.gob.cu/

Junta de Acreditación Nacional - JAN (National Accreditation Committee)
Secretary-General: Marcia Noda Hersnández
Calle 23 esquina F El Vedado
La Havana 10400

Data for academic year: 2015-2016
Source: IAU from the website of the Ministerio de Educación Superior, Cuba, 2015.

INSTITUTIONS

PUBLIC INSTITUTIONS

AGRARIAN UNIVERSITY OF HAVANA FRUCTUOSO RODRÍGUEZ PÉREZ

Universidad Agraria de la Habana Fructuoso Rodríguez Pérez (UNAH)
Autopista Nacional Km. 23 1/2 y Carretera de Tapaste, San José de las Lajas, La Habana 32700
Tel: +53(47) 863013 +53(47) 861752
EMail: rcta@unah.edu.cu
Website: https://www.unah.edu.cu

Rector: Maria Irene Balbin Tel: +53(47) 864176
Vicerrectora: Adianez Taboada Zamora

Faculty
Agricultural Engineering (Agricultural Engineering); **Agriculure** (Agricultural Business; Agronomy; Biology; Chemistry; Soil Science); **Computer Science** (Computer Engineering); **Economics** (Economics); **Pedagogical Science** (Education; Pedagogy); **Physical Education** (Physical Education); **Social Sciences and Humanities** (Arts and Humanities; Social Sciences); **Stockraising** (Animal Husbandry; Cattle Breeding; Mathematics); **Veterinary Science** (Veterinary Science)

Further Information: Traditional and Open Learning Institution

History: Founded 1976.

Main Language(s) of Instruction: Spanish

Degrees and Diplomas: *Licenciatura*; *Maestría*: **Veterinary Science.**
Last Updated: 20/10/15

CAMILO CIENFUEGOS UNIVERSITY OF MATANZAS

Universidad de Matanzas Camilo Cienfuegos (UMCC)
Km 3 Carretera a Varadero, Matanzas 44740
Tel: +53(45) 256714
Fax: +53(45) 253501
EMail: rector@umcc.cu
Website: http://www.umcc.cu

Rector: Leyda Finlé de la Cruz
Tel: +53(45) 261950 EMail: rector@umcc.cu

Vicerrectora: Benita Nancy García Gutiérez
EMail: benita.garcia@umcc.cu

International Relations: Alberto Medina León, Director
EMail: alberto.medina@umcc.cu

Faculty
Agronomy (Agriculture; Agronomy; Biology; Chemistry); **Economics and Computer Science** (Accountancy; Computer Engineering; Computer Science; Economics; Industrial Engineering; Management); **Education** *(Juan Marinello Vidaurreta)* (Education; Educational Sciences); **Engineering** (Chemical Engineering; Industrial Engineering; Mathematics; Mechanical Engineering; Physics); **Physical Education** (Physical Education; Sports); **Social Sciences and Humanities** (Arts and Humanities; English; Law; Modern Languages; Psychology; Social Sciences; Spanish)

Further Information: Also campus in Panamá.

History: Founded 1972. Merged with Universidad de Ciencias Pedagógicas "Juan Marinello Vidaurreta" and Facultad de Ciencias Pedagógicas "Juan Marinello Vidaurreta".

Main Language(s) of Instruction: Spanish

Degrees and Diplomas: *Licenciatura*; *Especialista*: **Animal Husbandry; Business Administration; Hotel Management; Tourism.** *Maestría*: **Agriculture; Environmental Studies; Higher Education; Mathematics Education; Tourism.** *Doctor en Ciencias*: **Agriculture; Arts and Humanities; Biotechnology; Business Administration; Chemical Engineering; Computer Science; Economics; Education; Educational Sciences; Energy Engineering; Industrial Engineering; Mechanical Engineering; Physical Education; Social Sciences; Tourism.**

Academic Staff *2014-2015*: Total 300
Student Numbers *2014-2015*: Total 32,000
Last Updated: 19/11/15

ENRIQUE JOSÉ VARONA PEDAGOGICAL UNIVERSITY

Universidad de Ciencias Pedagógicas Enrique José Varona (UCPEJV)
Calle 108 No 29, Ciudad Escolar Liberdad, Marianao, La Habana 11400
Tel: +53(7) 260450 +53(7) 2671083
Fax: +53(7) 2671083
EMail: mripes@ucpejv.rimed.cu
Website: http://www.ucpejv.rimed.cu

Rectora: Deisy Fraga Cedré

Secretaria General: Maritza Rippes Aller

International Relations: Mercedes Mora Carnet
Tel: +53(7) 260-0353

Faculty

Educational Sciences (Art Education; Education; Special Education); **Foreign Languages** (Foreign Languages Education); **Humanities** (Arts and Humanities); **Primary Education** (Preschool Education; Primary Education); **Science** (Biology; Chemistry; Natural Sciences; Physics)

History: Founded 1977 as Instituto Superior Pedagógico Enrique José Varona de La Habana. Acquired present title and status 2009.

Main Language(s) of Instruction: Spanish

Degrees and Diplomas: *Diplomado*; *Maestría*: **Education; Educational Sciences.** *Doctor en Ciencias*

Last Updated: 18/11/15

FÉLIX VARELA MOALES PEDAGÒGICAL UNIVERSITY OF VILLA CLARA

Universidad de Ciencias Pedagógicas Félix Varela Morales

Carretera de Circunvalacíon y Maleza, Apartado 288, Santa Clara, Villa Clara 50100
Tel: +53(42) 201077

Rectora: C. Noris B. Cárdenas Martínez
Tel: +53(422) 26139

Department

Biology (Biology; Natural Sciences); **Educational Sciences** (Education); **Foreign Languages** (English; French); **Humanities** (Arts and Humanities); **Primary Education** (Preschool Education; Primary Education); **Technical Sciences** (Technology)

Centre

Environmental Sciences (Environmental Studies)

Further Information: Traditional and Open Learning Institution

History: Founded in 1964 as a School of the Central University of Las Villas, became Instituto Superior Pedagógico Félix Varela de Villa Clara, 1976. Acquired present title and status 2009.

Main Language(s) of Instruction: Spanish

Accrediting Agency: Ministry of Higher Education

Degrees and Diplomas: *Licenciatura*: **Primary Education.** *Maestría*: **Educational Sciences.**

Last Updated: 13/11/15

FRANK PAÍS GARCÍA PEDAGOGICAL UNIVERSITY

Universidad Ciencias Pedagógica Frank País García

Carretera de la Autopista, Km 3 1/2, Santiago de Cuba 90100
Tel: +53(226) 41298
Fax: +53(226) 43113
EMail: rector@ucp.sc.rimed.cu
Website: http://www.ucp.sc.rimed.cu

Rectora: Maribel Ferrer Vincente (2008-)

Faculty

Education (Preschool Education; Primary Education); **Humanities** (Arts and Humanities); **Science** (Natural Sciences); **Technical Sciences** (Technology)

Centre

Educational Sciences (Education)

History: Founded 1964 as Instituto Pedagógico "Frank País García". Acquired present status 2009.

Main Language(s) of Instruction: Spanish

Degrees and Diplomas: *Diplomado*; *Maestría*: **Education.** *Doctor en Ciencias*: **Education.**

Last Updated: 17/11/15

GUANTÁNAMO UNIVERSITY

Universidad de Guantánamo

Avenida Ché Guevara, Carretera a Jamaica, Km 1 1/2, Sabatena, Guantánamo 95100
Tel: +53(21) 325558 +53(21) 325375
Fax: +53(21) 324756
EMail: comunicacion@cug.co.cu
Website: http://www.cug.co.cu

Rector: Alberto Turro Breff
Tel: +53(21) 325-925 EMail: rector@cug.co.cu

Vicerrector: Victor M. Álvarez Villar

Faculty

Agro-Forestry (Agriculture; Forest Products); **Economics and Business Administration** (Business Administration; Economics); **Law** (Law); **Social Sciences** (Social Sciences)

History: Founded 1992.

Main Language(s) of Instruction: Spanish

Degrees and Diplomas: *Licenciatura*; *Maestría*; *Doctor en Ciencias*

Last Updated: 03/12/15

HIGHER INSTITUTE OF INTERNATIONAL RELATIONS RAUL ROA GARCÍA

Instituto Superior de Relaciones Internacionales Raúl Roa García

Calle Calzada No.308 esq. H, Vedado, Plaza. C., La Habana 10400
Tel: +53(7) 8319495
Fax: +53(7) 8381359
EMail: isri@isri.minrex.gov.cu
Website: http://www.isri.cu

Rectora: Isabel Allende Karam
EMail: isabelallende@isri.minrex.gov.cu; rectoria@isri.minrex.gov.cu

Vicerrector de Investigaciones: Jorge Casals Llano
EMail: casalsj@isri.minrex.gov.cu

Course

International Relations (International Relations)

History: Founded 1960.

Main Language(s) of Instruction: Spanish

Degrees and Diplomas: *Diplomado*: **International Relations.** *Maestría*: **International Relations.** Joint PhD programmes in Political Sciences with Universidad de la Habana

Student Services: Library

Last Updated: 26/11/15

INSTITUTE OF ANIMAL SCIENCE

Instituto de Ciencia Animal (ICA)

Carretera Central, Km 47 1/2, San José de las Lajas, Mayabeque
Tel: +53(5) 99180 ext:223
EMail: diazuntoria@ica.co.cu
Website: http://www.ciencia-animal.org

Director General: José Andrés Diaz Untoria

Programme

Animal Science (Animal Husbandry)

History: Founded 1965.

Main Language(s) of Instruction: Spanish

Degrees and Diplomas: *Diplomado*; *Maestría*: **Animal Husbandry; Dairy; Meat and Poultry.** *Doctor en Ciencias*: **Animal Husbandry.** Also joint PhD program in Animal Production for the Tropical Zone with Universidad Agraria de la Habana

Last Updated: 12/11/15

INSTITUTE OF CARDIOLOGY AND CARDIOVASCULAR SURGERY

Instituto de Cardiología y Cirugía Cardiovascular

Calle 17, 702, A y Paseo, Plaza de la Revolución, La Habana 10400
Tel: +53(7) 8386003
EMail: dircardio@infomed.sld.cu
Website: http://instituciones.sld.cu/iccc/contactenos

Director: Lorenzo D. LLerena Rojas Tel: +53(7) 838-6004

Coordinator: Nurys Armas EMail: nurysarmas@infomed.sld.cu

Department

Cardiovascular Surgery (Cardiology)

History: Founded 1966.

Main Language(s) of Instruction: Spanish

Degrees and Diplomas: *Especialista*: **Cardiology.**

Last Updated: 12/11/15

INSTITUTE OF INDUSTRIAL DESIGN

Instituto Superior de Diseño Industrial (ISDI)

Belascoaín, 710 Padre Varela, La Habana

Tel: +53(7) 8745148

EMail: isdi.universidad@gmail.com

Website: http://www.isdi.co.cu

Rector: Sergio Luis Peña Martínez EMail: sergio@isdi.co.cu

Vicerrector de Formación Básica: Antonio Berazaín

Department

Fashion Design (Fashion Design); **Industrial Design** (Industrial Design); **Theory and Methodology** (Design); **Visual Communication** (Communication Arts; Communication Studies)

History: Founded 1984.

Main Language(s) of Instruction: Spanish

Degrees and Diplomas: *Licenciatura*; *Maestría*: **Design.**

Last Updated: 13/11/15

INSTITUTE OF MINING AND METALLURGY OF MOA DR. ANTONIO NÚÑEZ JIMÉNEZ

Instituto Superior Minero Metalúrgico de Moa Dr. Antonio Núñez Jiménez (ISMMM)

Las Coloradas s/n, Moa, Holguín 82329

Tel: +53(24) 606502

EMail: jmestre@ismm.edu.cu

Website: http://www.ismm.edu.cu

Rector: Ángel Columbié Navarro

Faculty

Geology and Mining (Geology; Mining Engineering); **Humanities** (Accountancy; Arts and Humanities; Cultural Studies; Finance; Library Science; Social Sciences); **Metallurgy and Electromechanics** (Computer Engineering; Electrical Engineering; Mechanical Engineering; Metallurgical Engineering)

Further Information: Also Research Centers

History: Founded 1976.

Main Language(s) of Instruction: Spanish

Degrees and Diplomas: *Licenciatura*; *Especialista*: **Electrical Engineering; Mining Engineering.**

Last Updated: 26/11/15

JESÚS MONTANÉ OROPESA UNIVERSITY OF ISLA DE LA JUVENTUD

Universidad de la Isla de la Juventud Jesús Montané Oropesa (UIJ)

Carretera Aeroporto Km 3 1/2., Reparto Aluras De Nueva Gerona, Isla de la Juventud 25100

Tel: +53(46) 324819

EMail: uij@cuij.edu.cu

Website: http://www.cuij.edu.cu

Rector: Leonardo Cruz Cabrera

Faculty

Education (Art Education; Biology; Chemistry; Computer Education; Education; Educational Psychology; Foreign Languages Education; History; Mathematics Education; Preschool Education; Primary Education; Science Education; Spanish; Special Education; Teacher Training); **Social Sciences and Humanities** (Accountancy; Arts and Humanities; Communication Studies; Economics; Finance; Law; Library Science; Psychology; Social Sciences; Tourism); **Technical Sciences** (Agricultural Engineering; Civil Engineering; Computer Education; Computer Engineering; Electrical Engineering; Industrial Engineering; Veterinary Science)

Foundation

Physical Education (Physical Education)

History: Founded 1973. Acquired present title from merging of Instituto Superior Pedagógico Carlos Manuel de Céspedes de la Isla de la Juventud and Universidad Jesús Montané Oropesa, 2012.

Main Language(s) of Instruction: Spanish

Degrees and Diplomas: *Licenciatura*

Last Updated: 19/11/15

JOSÉ ANTONIO ECHEVERRÍA POLYTECHNIC INSTITUTE

Instituto Superior Politécnico José Antonio Echeverría (CUJAE)

Calle 114, No. 11901. e/ Ciclovía y Rotonda, Marianao, La Habana, 19390

Tel: +53(7) 8791313

EMail: rectorado@tesla.cujae.edu.cu

Website: http://cujae.edu.cu

Rector: Alicia Alonso Becerra
Tel: +53(7) 260-8030 EMail: alonso@tesla.cujae.edu.cu

Secretary-General: Esther Rosalina Ansola Hazday
EMail: esther@ind.cujae.edu.cu

Faculty

Architecture (Architecture; Design; Technology; Urban Studies); **Chemical Engineering** (Chemical Engineering); **Civil Engineering** (Civil Engineering; Hydraulic Engineering); **Computer Engineering** (Computer Engineering); **Electrical Engineering** (Automation and Control Engineering; Biomedical Engineering; Electrical Engineering; Telecommunications Engineering); **Industrial Engineering** (Industrial Engineering); **Mechanical Engineering** (Mechanical Engineering; Metallurgical Engineering)

Further Information: Also Research Centers

History: Founded 1964.

Fees: PhD: 7 200 (Cuban Peso)

Main Language(s) of Instruction: Spanish

Degrees and Diplomas: *Licenciatura*; *Diplomado*: **Architecture; Automation and Control Engineering; Civil Engineering; Mechanical Engineering; Social Sciences.** *Especialista*: **Industrial Engineering.** *Maestría*: **Applied Mathematics; Architecture; Biotechnology; Civil Engineering; Computer Engineering; Electrical Engineering; Engineering; Environmental Engineering; Food Technology; Higher Education; Human Resources; Hydraulic Engineering; Industrial Engineering; Mechanical Engineering; Social Sciences; Telecommunications Engineering.** *Doctor en Ciencias*: **Architecture; Chemical Engineering; Hydraulic Engineering; Transport Management.**

Student Services: Library

Last Updated: 19/11/15

JOSÉ DE LA LUZ Y CABALLERO PEDAGOGICAL UNIVERSITY

Universidad de Cienciais Pedagógica José de la Luz y Caballero (UCP)

Avenida de los Libertadores, 287, Holguín 80100

Tel: +53(24) 481217

Fax: +53(24) 481168

Website: http://www.ucp.ho.rimed.cu

Rectora: Graciela Florencia Góngora Suárez

Secretaria General: Cristina Virgen Aldana Zayas

International Relations: Luis Ernesto Ruiz Martínez, Director de Relaciones Internacionales Tel: +53(24) 482653

Faculty

Educational Sciences (Educational Sciences); **Humanities** (Arts and Humanities; Foreign Languages Education; Spanish); **Primary Education** (Preschool Education; Primary Education); **Science** (Art Education; Biology; Chemistry; History; Natural Sciences; Physics); **Technical Sciences** (Agriculture; Computer Education; Computer

Science; Construction Engineering; Economics; Electrical Engineering; Mechanical Engineering; Technology)

History: Founded 1968. Acquired present status and title 2009..

Main Language(s) of Instruction: Spanish

Degrees and Diplomas: *Licenciatura*; *Diplomado*; *Doctor en Ciencias*: **Pedagogy.**

Student Services: Library

Last Updated: 17/11/15

LAS TUNAS UNIVERSITY VLADIMIR ILICH LENIN

Universidad Vladimir Ilich Lenin de las Tunas (ULT)

Avenida Carlos J. Finlay s/n, Reparto: Santos, Buenavista, Las Tunas 75200

Tel: +53(31) 346501

Fax: +53(31) 48158

EMail: correoinstitucional@ult.edu.cu

Website: http://www.ult.edu.cu

Rectora: Marlene del Toro Borrego

Faculty

Agricultural Sciences (Agricultural Engineering; Agronomy); **Basic Education** (Preschool Education; Primary Education; Special Education); **Economics** (Accountancy; Economics; Finance; Political Sciences); **Physical Education** (Physical Education); **Secondary Education** (Educational Sciences; Science Education; Secondary Education); **Social Sciences and Humanities** (Arts and Humanities; Cultural Studies; Economics; Law; Psychology; Social Sciences); **Technology** (Agricultural Engineering; Computer Engineering; Computer Science; Industrial Engineering; Mathematics; Technology)

History: Founded 1976. Acquired present title 2009. Merged with Universidades de Ciencias Pedagogicas Pepito, 2015.

Degrees and Diplomas: *Licenciatura*; *Diplomado*: **Communication Studies; Economics; Gender Studies; History; Human Resources; Journalism; Management; Public Administration; Public Health.** *Especialista*: **Agricultural Engineering; Computer Engineering; Industrial Engineering.** *Maestría*

Student Services: Library

Last Updated: 03/12/15

LATIN AMERICAN REFERENCE CENTER FOR SPECIAL EDUCATION

Centro de Referencia Latinoamericano para la Educación Especial (CELAEE)

108 e/ 29e y 29f, Ciudad Libertad, La Habana

Tel: +53(7) 2741484

EMail: celaee@cubaeduca.cu; infocelaee@cubaeduca.cu

Website: http://www.celaee.rimed.cu

Director: Santiago Borges Rodríguez

Asesor Técnico Docente: Caridad Rosario Zurita Cruz
EMail: cachizuri26@celaee.rimed.cu

Programme

Special Education (Special Education)

Main Language(s) of Instruction: Spanish

Degrees and Diplomas: *Especialista*: **Special Education.** *Maestría*: **Special Education.** *Doctor en Ciencias*: **Pedagogy.**

Student Services: Library

Last Updated: 10/11/15

LATIN AMERICAN SCHOOL OF MEDICINE

Escuela Latinoamericana de Medicina (ELAM)

Km 3 1/2 de la Carretera Panamericana, Santa Fe, La Habana 19108

Tel: +53(7) 2014130

EMail: atamayo@elacm.sld.cu

Website: http://instituciones.sld.cu/elam

Rector: Rafael González Ponce de León

Vicerrectora Académica: Heidi Soca González

Programme

Dentistry (Dentistry); **Medicine** (Medicine); **Nursing** (Nursing)

History: Founded 1998 as Escuela Latinoamericana de Ciencias Médicas.

Main Language(s) of Instruction: Spanish

Degrees and Diplomas: *Licenciatura*; *Especialista*: **Anaesthesiology; Cardiology; Dentistry; Dermatology; Endocrinology; Gastroenterology; Genetics; Gynaecology and Obstetrics; Haematology; Immunology; Medicine; Neurosciences; Nursing; Oncology; Ophthalmology; Orthodontics; Paediatrics; Pharmacology; Psychology; Rehabilitation and Therapy; Stomatology; Surgery; Urology.**

Last Updated: 12/11/15

MANUEL ASCUNCE DOMENECH PEDAGOGICAL UNIVERSITY

Universidad de Ciencias Pedagógicas Manuel Ascunce Domenech (UCPCA)

Carretera Ceballos, Km 1 1/2, Ciego de Avila 65100

Tel: +53(33) 227196 +53(33) 228952

Fax: +53(33) 227196 +53(33) 227713

Website: http://www.ucp.ca.rimed.cu

Rectora: Anisia Ruíz Gutiérrez

Faculty

Humanities (Arts and Humanities; English; History; Spanish); **Pre-School Teacher Training** (Preschool Education; Primary Education); **Sciences** (Natural Sciences); **Secondary Teacher Training** *(PGISB)* (Secondary Education); **Technical Sciences** (Computer Education; Technology; Technology Education)

History: Founded 1996 as Instituto Superior Pedagógico Manuel Ascunce Domenech de Ciego de Avila.

Main Language(s) of Instruction: Spanish

Degrees and Diplomas: *Licenciatura*

Last Updated: 18/11/15

MEDICAL UNIVERSITY DR. JUAN GUITERAS GENER OF MATANZAS

Universidad de Ciencias Médicas Juan Guiteras Gener de Matanzas (UCMM)

Carretera Central Km 102, Matanzas 40100

Tel: +53(45) 525060

EMail: edgar@ucm.vcl.sdl.cu

Website: http://www.mtz.sld.cu/

Dean: Víctor Junco

Director Centro Provincial de Información: Lázaro de León Rosales Tel: +53 (045) 243757

Programme

Medicine (Medicine; Nursing; Pharmacology; Stomatology)

History: Founded as Facultad de Ciencias Médicas de Matanzas, 1969.

Main Language(s) of Instruction: Spanish

Degrees and Diplomas: *Licenciatura*; *Especialista*: **Dentistry; Medicine.**

Last Updated: 02/12/15

NATIONAL CENTER FOR AGRICULTURAL HEALTH

Centro Nacional de Sanidad Agropecuaria (CENSA)

Carretera de Jamaica y Autopista Nacional, Apdo Postal 10, San José de las Lajas, Mayabeque

Tel: +53(47) 863206

Fax: +53(47) 861104

Website: http://www.censa.edu.cu

Coordinator Postgraduate Courses: C. Sandra Cuello Porta
EMail: sandra@censa.edu.cu

Department

Animal Health and Production (Animal Husbandry); **Biopharmaceutical Productions** (Biology; Pharmacology); **Engineering and Services** (Engineering); **Human Resources**

Management (Human Resources); **Microbiology** (Microbiology); **Plant Protection** (Plant Pathology); **Quality Assurance** (Safety Engineering); **Technological Innovation** (Technology)

History: Fonded 1969.

Fees: 7000 for PhD (Cuban Peso)

Main Language(s) of Instruction: Spanish

Degrees and Diplomas: *Diplomado*: **Information Technology.** *Maestría*: **Veterinary Science.** *Doctor en Ciencias*: **Animal Husbandry; Plant Pathology.**

Student Services: Library

Last Updated: 10/11/15

NATIONAL COORDINATION CENTER FOR CLINICAL TRIALS

Centro nacional coordinator de essayos clínicos
5ta A e/ 60 y 62 Miramar, Habana, Playa 11300
Tel: +53(7) 2164100
EMail: cencec@cencec.sld.cu
Website: http://www.cencec.sld.cu

Director: Alberto Hernández Rodríguez
EMail: alberto@cencec.sld.cu

Vicerrectora: Ania Torres Pombert EMail: ania@cencec.sld.cu

Department

Clinical Trials (Medicine)

History: Founded 1991.

Main Language(s) of Instruction: Spanish

Degrees and Diplomas: *Diplomado*: **Medicine.** *Maestría*: **Medicine.**

Last Updated: 10/11/15

NATIONAL INSTITUTE OF AGRICULTURAL SCIENCES

Instituto Nacional de Ciencias Agrícolas (INCA)
Gaveta postal 1, San josé de las lajas, Mayabeque 32700
Tel: +53 (7) 240942
Fax: +53 (47) 863867
EMail: direccion@inca.edu.cu
Website: http://www.inca.edu.cu

Directora General: C. María del Carmen Pérez Hernández
EMail: direccion@inca.edu.cu

Director de Desarrollo: Walfredo Torres de la Noval Telefax
EMail: posgrado@inca.edu.cu

Division

Applied Mathematics (Applied Mathematics); **Genetics** (Genetics); **Nutrition** (Nutrition); **Physiology and Vegetal Biochemistry** (Biochemistry; Physiology); **Phytotechnics** (Agriculture)

History: Founded 1970.

Main Language(s) of Instruction: Spanish

Degrees and Diplomas: *Diplomado*; *Especialista*; *Maestría*; *Doctor en Ciencias*

Publications: Cultivos Tropicales

Last Updated: 24/11/15

NATIONAL INSTITUTE OF HEALTH WORKERS

Instituto Nacional de Salud de los Trabajadores (INSAT)
Calzada de Bejucal km 7 1/2. Arroyo Naranjo, AP 9064, La Habana 10900
Tel: +53(7) 6442211
EMail: insatdoc@infomed.sld.cu
Website: http://www.sld.cu/sitios/insat

Directora: Tomasa María Esther Linares Fernández
Tel: +53(7) 6438343 EMail: insatdir@infomed.sld.cu

Department

Chemistry and Biology (Biology; Chemistry); **Health Sciences** (Health Sciences); **Physiology** (Physiology); **Psychology** (Psychology)

History: Founded 1978.

Main Language(s) of Instruction: Spanish

Degrees and Diplomas: *Maestría*: **Health Sciences; Occupational Health.**

Student Services: Library

Last Updated: 26/11/15

NATIONAL INSTITUTE OF HYGIENE, EPIDEMIOLOGY AND MICROBIOLOGY

Instituto Nacional de Higiene Epidemiología y Microbiología (INHEM)
Infanta No. 1158 e/ Llinas y Clavel, Centro Habana, La Habana 10300
EMail: adolfo@inhem.sld.cu
Website: http://instituciones.sld.cu/inhem/

Director General: Disnardo Raúl Pérez González

Director de Docencia e Investigaciones: Adolfo Alvarez Pérez

Programme

Biochemistry and Physiology (Biochemistry; Physiology); **Epidemiology** (Epidemiology); **Food Science** (Food Science); **Hygiene** (Hygiene); **Microbiology** (Microbiology); **Nutrition** (Nutrition); **Public Health** (Public Health)

History: Founded 1902.

Main Language(s) of Instruction: Spanish

Degrees and Diplomas: *Diplomado*: **Nutrition.** *Especialista*: **Epidemiology; Hygiene.** *Maestría*: **Epidemiology; Health Sciences; Nutrition; Public Health.**

Last Updated: 25/11/15

PEDAGOGICAL UNIVERSITY HECTOR PINEDA ALFREDO ZALDIVAR

Universidad de Ciencias Pedagógicas Héctor Alfredo Pineda Zaldívar (UCPETP)
Calle Arday e/1ra y Santa Ana. Rpto. El Trigal. Mcpio, Boyeros, La Habana 19220
Tel: +53(7) 578052
Fax: +53(7) 578508
EMail: abel@ucpetp.rimed.cu
Website: http://www.ucpetp.rimed.cu

Rectora: Odelaisis Deliz de los Santos Tel: +53(7) 442571

Faculty

Computer Science and General Studies (Computer Science; Industrial Chemistry); **Technical Sciences** (Accountancy; Agriculture; Construction Engineering; Economics; Mechanical Engineering; Technology)

History: Founded 1976 as Instituto Superior Pedagógico para la Enseñanza Técnica y Profesional Héctor Pineda Zaldivar (ISPETP). Acquired present title and status 2009.

Main Language(s) of Instruction: Spanish

Degrees and Diplomas: *Licenciatura*; *Maestría*; *Doctor en Ciencias*: **Pedagogy.**

Last Updated: 16/11/15

PEDRO KOURÍ TROPICAL MEDICINE INSTITUTE

Instituto de Medicina Tropical Pedro Kourí (IPK)
Apdo. Postal 601, Marianao 13, La Habana
Tel: +53(7) 2020430
EMail: ciipk@ipk.sld.cu
Website: http://instituciones.sld.cu/ipk

Vicedirectora Docente: Nereyda Cantelar de Francisco
EMail: nereyda@ipk.sld.cu

Course

Tropical Mecicine (Epidemiology; Medicine; Microbiology; Parasitology; Tropical Medicine; Virology)

History: Founded 1937.

Fees: PhD Full Time: 20 000 (Cuban Peso)

Main Language(s) of Instruction: Spanish

Degrees and Diplomas: *Especialista*; *Maestría*: **Epidemiology; Medicine; Tropical Medicine; Virology.** *Doctor en Ciencias*: **Medicine; Tropical Medicine.**

Last Updated: 12/11/15

PROF. DR RAFAEL ESTRADA GONZÁLEZ INSTITUTE OF NEUROLOGY AND NEUROSURGERY

Instituto de Neurología y Neurocirugía Prof. Dr Rafael Estrada González (INN)

Calle 29, esquina D, Vedado, Plaza de la Revolución, La Habana

EMail: amineuro@inn.sld.cu

Website: http://www.ineuro.sld.cu

Director: Enrique Michel Esteban

Course

Neurology (Neurology)

History: Founded 1966.

Main Language(s) of Instruction: Spanish

Degrees and Diplomas: *Especialista*: **Neurology.** *Maestría*: **Neurology.**

Last Updated: 16/11/15

RAFAEL MARÍA DE MENDIVE PEDAGOGICAL UNIVERSITY OF PINAR DEL RÍO

Universidad Pedagógica de Pinar del Río Rafael María de Mendive

Calle Los Pinos final. Esquina Avenida Borrego, Reparto Hermanos Cruz, Pinar del Río, Pinar del Río 20200

Tel: +53(48) 762443

EMail: vrip@ucp.pr.rimen.cu

Website: http://www.ucp.pr.rimed.cu

Rector: Mario Luis Gómez Ivizate
Tel: +53(48) 763902
EMail: rector@ucp.pr.rimed.cu, mariol@ucp.pr.rimed.cu

Faculty

Education (Computer Science; Mathematics; Preschool Education; Primary Education; Special Education); **Humanities** (Arts and Humanities); **Science** (Biology; Chemistry; Natural Sciences; Physics)

History: Founded 1976 as Instituto Superior Pedagogico "Rafael María de Mendive". Acquired present title and status 2009.

Main Language(s) of Instruction: Spanish

Degrees and Diplomas: *Licenciatura*

Student Services: Library

Last Updated: 17/11/15

SERAFÍN RUIZ DE ZÁRATE UNIVERSITY OF MEDICAL SCIENCES OF VILLA CLARA

Universidad de Ciencias Médicas Serafín Ruiz de Zárate de Villa Clara (UCMVC)

Carretera del Acueducto Km 2 1/2 y Circunvalación Santa Clara, Villa Clara 50200

Tel: +53(42) 271367

EMail: relint@ucm.vcl.sld.cu

Website: http://ucmvc.org

Rector: Frank Quintana Gómez
Tel: +53(42) 272667 EMail: rector@ucm.vcl.sld.cu

Vicerrectora General: Nancy Rodríguez Fernández
Tel: +53(42) 271480 EMail: vrprim@ucm.vcl.sld.cu

International Relations: Julio González Rodriguez, Director
Tel: +53(42) 271947

Faculty

Health Technology (Medical Technology); **Medical Sciences** (Gynaecology and Obstetrics; Health Sciences; Medicine; Paediatrics; Psychotherapy; Public Health; Surgery); **Nursing** (Nursing); **Stomatology** (Stomatology)

History: Founded 1976 as Instituto Superior de Ciencias Médicas de Villa Clara Dr. Serafín Ruiz de Zárate Ruiz.

Main Language(s) of Instruction: Spanish

Degrees and Diplomas: *Licenciatura*; *Especialista*: **Anaesthesiology; Anatomy; Cardiology; Dentistry; Dermatology; Epidemiology; Gastroenterology; Gerontology; Gynaecology and Obstetrics; Haematology; Medicine; Microbiology; Oncology; Ophthalmology; Orthodontics; Orthopaedics; Otorhinolaryngology; Paediatrics; Psychiatry and Mental Health; Public Health; Radiology; Stomatology; Surgery; Urology.** *Maestría*; *Doctor en Ciencias*

Last Updated: 30/11/15

UNIVERSITY JOSÉ MARTÍ PÉREZ OF SANCTI SPIRITUS

Universidad de Sancti Spiritus José Marti Pérez (UNISS)

Avenida de los Martines, 360 Esquina Bartolomé Masó Carretera Central, Sancti Spíritu 60100

Tel: +53(41) 328357

EMail: yanderfc@uniss.edu.cu

Website: http://www.uniss.edu.cu

Rectora: Naima Trujillo Barretto

Vicerrector: Martín Santana

Faculty

Accountancy and Finance (Accountancy; Finance); **Engineering** (Computer Engineering; Energy Engineering; Industrial Engineering; Mathematics); **Humanities** (Arts and Humanities); **Pedagogy** (Education; Pedagogy; Preschool Education; Primary Education; Secondary Education); **Stockbreeding** *(Montaña del Escambray)* (Animal Husbandry)

History: Founded 1976. Merged with Universidad de Ciencias Pedagógicas Capitán Silverio Blanco Nuñez, 2014.

Main Language(s) of Instruction: Spanish

Degrees and Diplomas: *Licenciatura*; *Maestría*

Student Services: Library

Publications: Márgenes; Pedagogía y Sociedad

Last Updated: 16/11/15

UNIVERSITY MARTA ABREU OF LAS VILLAS

Universidad Central Marta Abreu de Las Villas (UCLV)

Carretera de Camajuaní Km 5.5, Santa Clara, Villa Clara

Tel: +53(42) 281178

Fax: +53(42) 281608

EMail: mas@uclv.edu.cu

Website: http://www.uclv.edu.cu

Rector: Andrés Castro Alegria EMail: castroalegria@uclv.edu.cu

International Relations: Luis Antonio Barranco Olivera, Vicerrector de Investigación, Internacionalización y Postgrado
Tel: +53(42) 281-415 EMail: luisbo@uclv.edu.cu

Faculty

Agriculture (Agricultural Engineering; Agricultural Equipment; Agriculture; Agronomy; Biology; Veterinary Science); **Business Administration** (Accountancy; Economics; Finance; Tourism); **Chemistry and Pharmacy** (Chemical Engineering; Chemistry; Pharmacy); **Construction Engineering** (Architecture; Civil Engineering; Construction Engineering; Hydraulic Engineering); **Electrical Engineering** (Automation and Control Engineering; Biomedical Engineering; Electrical Engineering; Telecommunications Engineering); **Humanities** (Arts and Humanities; Communication Studies; English; Journalism; Literature; Modern Languages); **Industrial and Mechanical Engineering** (Industrial Engineering; Mechanical Engineering); **Information Science and Education** (Education; Information Sciences); **Law** (Law); **Mathematics, Physics and Computer Science** (Computer Science; Information Sciences; Library Science; Mathematics; Physics); **Mechanical Engineering** (Mechanical Engineering); **Social Sciences** (Cultural Studies; Philosophy; Psychology; Social Sciences; Sociology)

Institute

Plant Biotechnology *(IBP)* (Biotechnology; Botany)

Centre

Agricultural Research *(CIAP)* (Agriculture; Animal Husbandry); **Applied Chemistry Studies** (Applied Chemistry; Chemistry); **Bioactive Chemistry** *(CBQ)* (Biochemistry; Chemistry); **Botanical Garden Studies** *(CEJB)* (Botany); **Business Administration** *(CED)* (Business Administration; Business and Commerce; Management); **Community Studies** *(CEC)* (Social Sciences); **Computational Mechanics and Numerical Methods in Engineering** *(CIMCNI)* (Mathematics and Computer Science; Mechanical Engineering); **Educational Sciences** *(CEEd)* (Education; Educational

Sciences; Higher Education); **Electrical Energy Studies** *(CEE)* (Electronic Engineering); **Energy and Environmental Technologies** *(CETA)* (Energy Engineering; Environmental Engineering); **Informatics Studies** *(CEI)* (Computer Science); **Information Technology and Electronic Studies** *(CEETI)* (Electronic Engineering; Information Technology); **Physical Education and Sport** (Physical Education; Sports); **Research and Development of Structures and Materials** *(CIDEM)* (Civil Engineering); **Welding Studies** *(CIS)* (Metal Techniques)

History: Founded 1952 and reorganized 1959. Faculty of Medicine and Institute of Education detached 1976 as independent institutions. A State institution financed by the government and under the jurisdiction of the Ministry of Education.

Academic Year: September to July (September-January; February-July)

Admission Requirements: Secondary school certificate or Technical school certificate

Main Language(s) of Instruction: Spanish

Degrees and Diplomas: *Licenciatura*; *Diplomado*: **Agriculture; Biology; Botany; Ecology; Economics; Entomology; Environmental Studies; Genetics; Microbiology; Rural Studies; Sociology; Soil Science.** *Maestría*: **Accountancy; Agricultural Engineering; Agriculture; Animal Husbandry; Computer Science; Industrial Engineering.** *Doctor en Ciencias*: **Agricultural Engineering; Animal Husbandry; Tropical Agriculture; Veterinary Science.**

Student Services: Academic Counselling, Canteen, Cultural Activities, Health Services, Language Laboratory, Library, Nursery Care, Social Counselling, Sports Facilities

Publications: Biotecnología Vegetal; Centro Agrícola; Centro Azúcar; Islas

Last Updated: 27/11/15

UNIVERSITY OF ARTS

Universidad de las Artes (ISA)

Calle 120 No. 1110 e/ 9na y 13 Cubanacán, Municipio Playa, La Habana 11600

Tel: +53(7) 2089771

EMail: dircom@isa.cult.cu

Website: http://www.isa.cult.cu

Rector: Rolando González Patricio

International Relations: Sonia Ortega Bravo, Director Tel: +53(7) 208-8075 EMail: vrri@isa.cult.cu

Faculty

Audiovisual Media Communications (Cinema and Television; Media Studies); **Dance** (Dance); **Music** (Music); **Plastic Arts** (Fine Arts; Painting and Drawing; Sculpture); **Theatre** (Display and Stage Design; Theatre)

History: Founded 1976 as Art Institute.

Admission Requirements: High School Diploma and entrance examination.

Fees: PhD: 6000. Masters: 4000. Undergraduate: 3000. Postgraduate: between 10.00 and 15.00 (per hour). Graduates: between 900 and 1200 (depending on the specialization and the Professors) (US Dollar)

Main Language(s) of Instruction: Spanish

Degrees and Diplomas: *Licenciatura*; *Diplomado*; *Maestría*; *Doctor en Ciencias*

Last Updated: 25/11/15

UNIVERSITY OF CAMAGÜEY IGNACIO AGRAMONTE LOYNAZ

Universidad de Camagüey Ignacio Agramonte Loynaz (UC)

Carretera de Circunvalación, Norte Km 5, Camagüey 74650

Tel: +53(32) 262451

EMail: vrd@reduc.edu.cu

Website: http://www.reduc.edu.cu

Rector: Santiago Lajes Choy Tel: +53(322) 621-29 EMail: rector@rec.reduc.edu.cu

Faculty

Agriculture (Agriculture; Agronomy; Animal Husbandry; Veterinary Science); **Construction Engineering** (Applied Mathematics; Architecture; Civil Engineering; Construction Engineering); **Economics** (Accountancy; Economics; Finance; Management); **Electromechanics** (Computer Science; Electrical Engineering; Machine Building; Mechanical Engineering; Physics); **Humanity** (Arts and Humanities; Communication Studies; English; History; Psychology; Sociology); **Law and Economics** (Accountancy; Economics; Finance; Law; Tourism); **Physical Education** (Physical Education); **Primary Education** (Preschool Education; Primary Education); **Science Applied to Industry** (Chemical Engineering; Chemistry; Food Technology; Industrial Engineering); **Teachers Training** (Art Education; Biology; Chemistry; Computer Education; English; Geography; Health Education; History; Literature; Mathematics; Mathematics Education; Natural Sciences; Spanish)

Further Information: Also Research Center

History: Founded 1967 as Centro Universitario de Camagüey, incorporating institutions previously forming part of the Universidad de Las Villas. Acquired present title 1974. A state institution financed by the government and under the jurisdiction of the Ministry of Education.

Main Language(s) of Instruction: Spanish

Degrees and Diplomas: *Licenciatura*; *Especialista*; *Doctor en Ciencias*

Publications: Revista de Producción Animal

Last Updated: 23/11/15

UNIVERSITY OF CIEGO DE AVILA

Universidad de Ciego de Avila (UNICA)

Carretera de Morón Km 9 1/2, Ciego de Avila 69450

Tel: +53(33) 24544 +53(33) 5702

Fax: +53(33) 266365

EMail: rector@rect.unica.cu

Website: http://www.unica.cu

Rector: Mario Ares Sánchez

International Relations: Oscar Fernández Tel: +53(33) 266211

Faculty

Agronomy (Agricultural Equipment; Agronomy; Animal Husbandry; Biology; Cattle Breeding); **Computer Science** (Computer Science); **Economics** (Accountancy; Economics; Tourism); **Engineering** (Civil Engineering; Computer Engineering; Hydraulic Engineering); **Law** (Law); **Social Sciences and Humanities** (Arts and Humanities; English; Social Sciences)

Further Information: Also Distance Education

History: Founded 1978.

Main Language(s) of Instruction: Spanish

Degrees and Diplomas: *Licenciatura*; *Especialista*

Last Updated: 20/11/15

UNIVERSITY OF CIENFUEGOS

Universidad de Cienfuegos

Carretera a Rodas Km 4, Cuatro Caminos, Cienfuegos 59430

Tel: +53(432) 521521

Fax: +53(432) 522762

EMail: reducf@ucf.edu.cu

Website: http://www.ucf.edu.cu

Rector: Juan B. Cogollos Martínez EMail: rector@ucf.edu.cu

Vicerrector Administrativo: Frank Hernandez Gonzalez Tel: +53(43) 522-167 EMail: fkherdez@ucf.edu.cu

Vicerrector de Investigación y Postgrado: Nereida E. Moya Padilla EMail: asocorro@ucf.edu.cu

Vicerrector de Formación: Victor Millo Carmenate EMail: vmillo@ucf.edu.cu

International Relations: Lourdes Pomares Castellon, Directora Tel: +53(43) 523-345 EMail: lpomares@ucf.edu.cu

Faculty

Agronomy (Agricultural Engineering; Agronomy; Veterinary Science); **Economics and Business** (Accountancy; Economics; Industrial Engineering; Management); **Engineering** (Chemical Engineering; Computer Engineering; Industrial Engineering;

Mechanical Engineering); **Humanities** (English; History; Spanish); **Pedagogic Sciences** (Education; Pedagogy; Psychology); **Physical Education** (Physical Education; Sports); **Social Sciences** (Anthropology; Archaeology; Communication Studies; Cultural Studies; Gender Studies; Law; Regional Studies; Rural Studies)

Centre

Environmental and Energy Studies *(CEEMA)* (Energy Engineering; Environmental Management; Environmental Studies); **Hydraulic Oil and Pneumatic Studies** *(CEDON)* (Hydraulic Engineering); **Pedagogical Studies and Higher Education** *(CEDDES)* (Curriculum; Educational Technology; Higher Education; Pedagogy; Teacher Training); **Sociocultural** (Cultural Studies; Religious Studies; Social Studies); **Sustainable Agriculture** *(CETAS)* (Agriculture)

History: Founded 1979. Acquired present title 1998.

Academic Year: September to July

Admission Requirements: Entrance examination

Main Language(s) of Instruction: Spanish

Degrees and Diplomas: *Licenciatura*: **Accountancy; Agricultural Engineering; Chemical Engineering; Communication Studies; Computer Engineering; Economics; Education; English; History; Industrial Engineering; Law; Psychology; Sociology.** *Maestría*: **Accountancy; Agriculture; Education; Engineering; History; Mathematics.** *Doctor en Ciencias*: **Education; Engineering; Finance.**

Student Services: Academic Counselling, Canteen, Careers Guidance, Cultural Activities, Facilities for disabled people, Foreign Studies Centre, Health Services, IT Centre, Language Laboratory, Library, Nursery Care, Residential Facilities, Social Counselling, Sports Facilities, eLibrary

Publications: Revista Conrado; Universidad y Sociedad

Publishing House: Universo Sur

Academic Staff *2014-2015*	MEN	WOMEN	**TOTAL**
FULL-TIME	572	829	**1,401**
PART-TIME	132	113	**245**
STAFF WITH DOCTORATE			
FULL-TIME	85	32	c. **117**
Student Numbers *2014-2015*			
All (Foreign included)	1,377	1,697	c. **3,074**
FOREIGN ONLY	32	86	**118**

Part-time students, 1,346. **Distance students,** 147.

Last Updated: 17/11/15

UNIVERSITY OF COMPUTER SCIENCE

Universidad de las Ciencias Informáticas (UCI)

Carretera a San Antonio de los Baños, Km. 2 1/2., Torrens, La Habana

Tel: +53(7) 8372548

EMail: uci@uci.cu

Website: http://www.uci.cu

Rectora: Miriam Nicado García EMail: nicado@uci.cu

Vicerrectora de Formación: Natalia Martínez Sánchez EMail: natalia@uci.cu

Programme

Computer Science (Computer Engineering; Computer Science; Software Engineering)

History: Founded 2002.

Main Language(s) of Instruction: Spanish

Degrees and Diplomas: *Licenciatura*; *Especialista*: **Computer Science.** *Maestría*: **Computer Science; Information Technology; Software Engineering.** *Doctor en Ciencias*: **Computer Science.**

Student Services: Canteen, Residential Facilities, Sports Facilities

Publications: Revista Cubana de Ciencias Informáticas; UCI Scientific Series

Last Updated: 27/11/15

UNIVERSITY OF GRANMA

Universidad de Granma

Apartado 21, Carretera de Manzanillo Km. 17 1/2, Bayamo, Granma, 85100

Tel: +53(23) 92130

Fax: +53(23) 92131

EMail: root@udg.granma.inf.cu

Website: http://www.udg.co.cu/

Rector: Quirino Arias Cedeño (2007-)

Faculty

Agriculture (Agriculture; Animal Husbandry; Biology; Physics; Surveying and Mapping); **Computer Science** (Applied Mathematics; Computer Science; Engineering); **Economics and Business Administration** (Accountancy; Business Administration; Computer Science; Economics; Political Sciences); **Engineering** (Agricultural Engineering; Computer Engineering; Engineering; Mechanical Engineering; Natural Sciences); **Social Sciences and Humanities** (Arts and Humanities; Communication Studies; Law; Psychology; Social Sciences); **Veterinary Science** (Veterinary Science)

Centre

Animal Production (Animal Husbandry); **Applied Chemistry** (Applied Chemistry); **Higher Education** (Higher Education); **Management and Local Developpment Studies** (Development Studies; Management); **Vegetal Biotechnology** (Biotechnology; Botany)

History: Founded 1967.

Main Language(s) of Instruction: Spanish

Degrees and Diplomas: *Diplomado*; *Especialista*; *Maestría*: **Accountancy; Agricultural Equipment; Agriculture; Animal Husbandry; Chemistry; Development Studies; Environmental Studies; Higher Education; Management; Nutrition; Veterinary Science.**

Student Services: Library

Last Updated: 02/12/15

UNIVERSITY OF HAVANA

Universidad de la Habana (UH)

San Lázaro y L. Municipio Plaza de la Revolución, La Habana 10400

Tel: +53(7) 8783231

Fax: +53(7) 8735774

EMail: rector@rect.uh.cu

Website: http://www.uh.cu

Rector: Gustavo Cobreiro Suárez
Tel: +53(7) 8791313 EMail: gcobreiro@rect.uh.cu

International Relations: Magda Luisa Arias Rivera, Directora de Relaciones Internacionales
Tel: +53(7) 8786200 EMail: relacionesinternacionales@rect.uh.cu

Faculty

Accountancy and Finance (Accountancy; Finance; Tourism); **Biology** (Biochemistry; Biology; Microbiology); **Chemistry** (Chemistry); **Communication Studies** (Communication Studies; Industrial Management; Information Sciences; Journalism; Library Science); **Distance Education** (Accountancy; Cultural Studies; Economics; Finance; History; Information Sciences; Law; Library Science; Social Studies); **Economics** (Economics); **Fine Arts and Modern Languages** (Fine Arts; Literature; Modern Languages); **Foreign Languages** (Chinese; English; French; German; Italian; Modern Languages; Portuguese; Russian; Spanish; Speech Therapy and Audiology); **Geography** (Geography); **Latino American Social Sciences** *(FLACSO)* (Latin American Studies; Social Sciences); **Law** (Law); **Mathematics and Computer Science** (Computer Science; Mathematics); **Philosophy and History** (History; Philosophy; Political Sciences; Sociology); **Physics** (Physical Engineering; Physics); **Psychology** (Psychology); **Tourism** (Tourism)

College

Preservation and Management of the Cultural Historical Patrimony *(San Gerónimo)* (Heritage Preservation)

Institute
Pharmacy and Food Technology *(IFAL)* (Food Technology; Pharmacy); **Science and Technology of Materials** *(IMRE)* (Materials Engineering; Technology)

Centre
Biotechnology and Biomedicine (Biomedicine; Biotechnology); **Cuban Economics** *(CEEC)* (Economics); **Demographic Studies** *(CEDEM)* (Demography and Population); **Environmental Studies** *(CEMA)* (Environmental Studies); **Health and Well-being** *(CESBH)* (Health Sciences; Welfare and Protective Services); **Higher Education Development** *(CEPES)* (Education; Higher Education); **International Economics Research** *(CIEI)* (International Economics); **International Migration** *(CEMI)* (Political Sciences); **Marine Biology** *(CIM)* (Marine Science and Oceanography); **National Botanical Garden** (Biology); **Public Administration** *(CEAP)* (Political Sciences; Public Administration); **Social Sciences** *(Latin American Faculty (FLACSO))* (Social Sciences)

History: Founded 1728 by the monks of Santa Cruz of the Dominican Order of Preaching Friars following Papal Bull 1721. Approved by the Spanish Royal Council of the Indies 1722. Secularized 1842 and granted autonomy 1933. Reorganized 1959 and university reform law promulgated 1962.

Academic Year: September to July (September-January; February-July)

Admission Requirements: Secondary school certificate

Main Language(s) of Instruction: Spanish

Degrees and Diplomas: *Licenciatura*: **Engineering.** *Diplomado*; *Especialista*: **Accountancy; Communication Studies; Cooking and Catering; Criminal Law; Finance; Mass Communication; Public Relations; Tourism.** *Maestría*: **Administrative Law; Aquaculture; Art History; Biochemistry; Biology; Chemistry; Coastal Studies; Commercial Law; Constitutional Law; Contemporary History; Demography and Population; Development Studies; Distance Education; Environmental Studies; Ethics; Geography; Higher Education; Information Management; Labour Law; Latin American Studies; Linguistics; Materials Engineering; Mathematics; Medical Technology; Microbiology; Pharmacology; Pharmacy; Physiology; Social Sciences; Sociology; Spanish; Tourism; Toxicology; Zoology.** *Doctor en Ciencias*: **Accountancy; Communication Studies; Demography and Population; Economics; Education; Educational Sciences; Finance; Fine Arts; Food Science; Geography; History; Information Sciences; Law; Linguistics; Literature; Mathematics; Modern Languages; Pharmacy; Philosophy; Physics; Political Sciences; Psychology; Sociology.**

Student Services: Library

Publications: Journals of the Faculties and Institutes

Last Updated: 03/12/15

UNIVERSITY OF HOLGUÍN

Universidad de Holguín
Gaveta Postal 57, Avenida XX Aniversario, Carretera Vía Guardalavaca, Piedra Blanca, Holguín 80100
Tel: +53(244) 481851
Fax: +53(244) 481843
Website: http://www.uho.edu.cu

Rector: Reynaldo Velazquez Zaldivar

International Relations: David Almaguer la Rosa, Director
Tel: +53(24) 481-690 EMail: dri@ict.uho.edu.cu

Faculty
Agricultural Engineering (Agricultural Engineering; Chemistry; Physics; Veterinary Science); **Economics** (Accountancy; Business Administration; Economics); **Education** (Education); **Engineering** (Civil Engineering; Industrial Maintenance; Mechanical Engineering); **Humanities** (Arts and Humanities; Cultural Studies; English; History; Modern Languages; Spanish); **Industrial Engineering and Tourism** (Industrial Engineering; Tourism); **Law** (Law); **Mathematics and Computer Science** (Mathematics and Computer Science); **Physical Education** (Physical Education); **Social Sciences** (Journalism; Psychology; Social Sciences; Sociology)

Further Information: Also Research Centers

History: Founded 1973. Merged with Facultad de Cultura Física and Universidad de Ciencias Pedagógicas, 2015.

Main Language(s) of Instruction: Spanish

Degrees and Diplomas: *Especialista*: **Criminal Law; Development Studies; Hotel Management; Social Work.** *Maestría*: **Accountancy; Agricultural Equipment; Business Administration; Computer Graphics; Finance; Graphic Design; Higher Education; History; Industrial Engineering; Information Sciences; Mathematics; Mathematics and Computer Science; Spanish; Tourism.** *Doctor en Ciencias*: **Educational Sciences; Industrial Engineering; Mechanical Engineering; Social Sciences.**

Student Services: Residential Facilities

Last Updated: 30/11/15

UNIVERSITY OF MEDICAL SCIENCES OF CAMAGUEY CARLOS J. FINLAY

Universidad de Ciencias Médicas de Camagüey Carlos J. Finlay
Carretera Central Oeste e/ Madame Curie y 9, Camagüey 70100
Tel: +53(32) 295241
Fax: +53(32) 292100
EMail: boris@finlay.cmw.sld.cu

Rectora: María del Carmen Romero

Director: Eloy Ortiz Hernández EMail: eoh@finlay.cmw.sld.cu

Faculty
Medical Sciences (Health Sciences; Medical Technology; Medicine; Nursing; Psychology); **Stomatology** (Stomatology)

History: Founded as Instituto Superior de Ciencias Médicas de Camagüey, 1981.

Main Language(s) of Instruction: Spanish

Degrees and Diplomas: *Licenciatura*; *Especialista*: **Medicine.** *Maestría*: **Medicine.** *Doctor en Ciencias*: **Medicine.**

Last Updated: 27/11/15

UNIVERSITY OF MEDICAL SCIENCES OF CIEGO DE AVILA

Universidad de Ciencias Médicas de Ciego de Avila (UCMCA)
Circunvalación y carretera de Morón, Ciego de Avila 65100
Tel: +53(33) 225589
EMail: mverano@centro.cav.sld.cu

Rector: Venerando Sevilla Pérez Tel: +53(33) 25589

Directora: Magaly Rita Gómez Verano

Faculty
Medicine (Medicine; Nursing)

History: Founded as Facultad de Ciencias Médicas de Ciego de Avila, 1978.

Degrees and Diplomas: *Licenciatura*: **Nursing.** *Especialista*: **Medicine.**

Last Updated: 27/11/15

UNIVERSITY OF MEDICAL SCIENCES OF CIENFUEGOS

Universidad de Ciencias Médicas de Cienfuegos (UCMCF)
Calle 51 A y Ave. 5 de Septiembre, Cienfuegos 55100
Tel: +53(43) 500600
Website: http://www.ucm.cfg.sld.cu

Rector: Roberto Baños
Tel: +53(432) 3832 EMail: rector@ucm.cfg.sld.cu

Directora: Elinor Dulzaides Iglesias
Tel: +53(43) 516602 EMail: elinor@jagua.cfg.sld.cu

Programme
Medicine (Medicine; Nursing)

History: Founded as Facultad de Ciencias Médicas de Cienfuegos, 1979.

Main Language(s) of Instruction: Spanish

Degrees and Diplomas: *Licenciatura*: **Nursing.** *Especialista*: **Medicine.**

Last Updated: 27/11/15

UNIVERSITY OF MEDICAL SCIENCES OF GRANMA

Universidad de Ciencias Médicas de Granma (UCMG)
Avenida Camilo Cienfuegos esq. Carretera de Campechuela Km. 1., Manzanillo 87600
Tel: +53(23) 424464
EMail: hcastillo@ucm.grm.sld.cu

Rector: Adrián Fonseca Botello Tel: +53(23) 53359
Diectora: Magdalena Sánchez Fernández
EMail: nelka.grm@infomed.sld.cu

Programme
Medicine (Medicine; Nursing; Stomatology)
History: Founded as Facultad de Ciencias Médicas de Granma, 1978.
Main Language(s) of Instruction: Spanish
Degrees and Diplomas: *Licenciatura*; *Especialista*: **Medicine.**
Last Updated: 27/11/15

UNIVERSITY OF MEDICAL SCIENCES OF GUANTANAMO

Universidad de Ciencias Médicas de Guantánamo (UCMGT)
Calle 5 Oeste entre 6 y 9 Norte, Guantánamo, Guantánamo 95200
Tel: +53(21) 381004
EMail: rector@infosol.gtm.sld.cu
Website: http://www.gtm.sld.cu/

Rector: María del Rosario Parra Tel: +53(21) 326-119

Programme
Medicine (Medicine; Nursing; Stomatology)
History: Founded as Facultad de Ciencias Médicas de Guantánamo, 1979.
Main Language(s) of Instruction: Spanish
Degrees and Diplomas: *Licenciatura*; *Especialista*: **Medicine.**
Last Updated: 27/11/15

UNIVERSITY OF MEDICAL SCIENCES OF HAVANA

Universidad de Ciencias Médicas de la Habana (UCMH)
Calle 146 Número 2504 entre 25 y 31, Cubanacán. Playa, La Habana 11600
Tel: +53(7) 202-0981
Fax: +53(7) 33-6257
EMail: vrdocch@infomed.sld.cu
Website: http://instituciones.sld.cu/ucmh

Rector: Jorge González Pérez. EMail: rectorch@infomed.sld.cu
Vicerrector académico: Mayrim Lago
International Relations: Celia Ojeda, Directora
EMail: ojeda@infomed.sld.cu

Faculty
Dentistry - Raúl González Sánchez (Dentistry; Stomatology); **Heath Technoligy** (Medical Technology); **Medical Sciences - 10 de octubre** (Medicine); **Medical Sciences - Calixto García Iñiguez** (Medicine); **Medical Sciences - Dr. Miguel Enriquez** (Medicine); **Medical Sciences - Dr. Salvador Allende** (Medicine; Nursing); **Medical Sciences - Enrique Cabrera** (Medicine); **Medical Sciences - Finlay- Albarrán** (Medicine); **Medical Sciences - Julio Trigo** (Medicine); **Medical Sciences - Manuel Fajardo Rivero** (Medicine); **Nursing - Lidia Doce** (Nursing)

Institute
Biomedical Sciences - Victoria de Girón *(ICBP)* (Medicine)
Further Information: Also Centers of Graduate Studies
History: Founded 1728.
Main Language(s) of Instruction: Spanish
Degrees and Diplomas: *Licenciatura*: **Epidemiology; Hygiene; Medical Technology; Nursing; Nutrition; Psychology.** *Especialista*: **Anaesthesiology; Cardiology; Epidemiology; Gastroenterology; Gerontology; Gynaecology and Obstetrics; Hygiene; Medicine; Nursing; Oncology; Ophthalmology; Paediatrics; Stomatology; Surgery; Traditional Eastern Medicine; Urology.** *Maestría*: **Medicine; Public Health.** *Doctor en Ciencias*: **Health Sciences; Medicine; Nursing; Stomatology.**

Student Services: Residential Facilities
Last Updated: 30/11/15

UNIVERSITY OF MEDICAL SCIENCES OF PINAR DEL RIO

Universidad de Ciencias Médicas de Pinar del Río (UCMPR)
Carretera Central Km 89, Pinar del Rio, Pinar del Rio 20100
Tel: +53(82) 62889
EMail: taimara@princesa.pri.sld.cu

Rector: Blas Nivaldo Porras Pérez
Tel: +53(82) 63754 +53(82) 62722
EMail: rectorprucm@princesa.pri.sld.cu
Director: Taimara Ramírez Acosta

Programme
Medicine (Medical Technology; Medicine; Nursing; Psychology; Stomatology)
History: Founded as Facultad de Ciencias Médicas de Pinar del Rio Dr. Ernesto Ché Guevara de la Serna, 1968.
Main Language(s) of Instruction: Spanish
Degrees and Diplomas: *Licenciatura*; *Especialista*: **Dentistry; Medical Technology; Medicine; Nursing; Psychology.**
Last Updated: 02/12/15

UNIVERSITY OF MEDICAL SCIENCES OF SANCTI SPIRITU

Universidad de Ciencias Médicas de Sancti Spíritus (UCMSS)
Carretera Circunvalación Norte, Placetas, Sancti Spíritu 60100
Tel: +53(41) 324019
EMail: director@centromed.ssp.sld.cu

Rector: Alexis Lorente Jiménez Tel: +53(41) 23776
Directora: Carmen Fidelina Sánchez Sánchez
EMail: carmen@centromed.ssp.sld.cu

Programme
Medicine (Medicine)
History: Founded as Facultad de Ciencias Médicas de Sancti Spíritu, 1978. Affiliated with Latin American School Of Medicine in Havana (ELAM).
Main Language(s) of Instruction: Spanish
Accrediting Agency: Ministry of Public Health
Degrees and Diplomas: *Licenciatura*; *Especialista*: **Medicine.**
Last Updated: 02/12/15

UNIVERSITY OF MEDICAL SCIENCES OF SANTIAGO DE CUBA

Universidad de Ciencias Médicas Santiago de Cuba (UCM - SANTIAGO DE CUBA)
Avenida de las Américas e/calle E y calle I Reparto Sueño, Santiago de Cuba 90100
Tel: +53(226) 26679
Fax: +53(226) 96200
EMail: silvia.reynoso@medired.scu.sld.cu
Website: http://instituciones.sld.cu/ucmscu

Rector: Antonio López (2009-) Tel: +53(226) 626679
Secretary-General: Lilliam Leyva Rosales Tel: +53(226) 53011
International Relations: José Suárez Lorens

Faculty
Dentistry (Dentistry; Stomatology); **Health Technology** (Medical Technology); **Medical Sciences I** *(Facimed I)* (Health Sciences; Medicine); **Medical Sciences II** *(Dr Salvado Allende)* (Medicine)

School
Nursing (Nursing)
History: Founded 1976, as Instituto Superior de Ciencias Médicas de Santiago de Cuba.
Main Language(s) of Instruction: Spanish
Degrees and Diplomas: *Licenciatura*; *Diplomado*; *Especialista*: **Medicine.** *Maestría*: **Child Care and Development; Nursing.**
Last Updated: 02/12/15

UNIVERSITY OF ORIENTE

Universidad de Oriente (UO)
Avenida Patricio Lumumba s/n, Santiago de Cuba 90500
Tel: +53(22) 633011 +53 (22) 631860
Fax: +53(22) 632689
EMail: dri@ri.uo.edu.cu
Website: http://www.uo.edu.cu

Rectora: Martha del Carmen Mesa Valenciano
EMail: rectororiente@consejo.uo.edu.cu

Secretaria Genera: Josefina Fonseca Ramis
EMail: sg@consejo.uo.edu.cu

International Relations: Luisa Villafruela Loperena, Directora
Tel: +53(22) 641-701

Faculty

Agriculture (Agricultural Engineering; Agriculture); **Chemical Engineering** (Chemical Engineering); **Construction** (Architecture; Construction Engineering; Hydraulic Engineering; Structural Architecture; Urban Studies); **Distance Education** (Accountancy; Economics; Finance; History; Information Sciences; Law; Library Science); **Economics and Business Administration** (Accountancy; Business Administration; Economics; Finance; Marketing); **Electrical Engineering** (Automation and Control Engineering; Biomedical Engineering; Computer Science; Electrical Engineering; Electronic Engineering; Telecommunications Engineering); **Humanities** (Art History; Arts and Humanities; Communication Studies; History; Modern Languages; Philosophy; Physiology; Political Sciences; Psychology; Sociology); **Law** (Civil Law; Constitutional Law; Criminal Law; Labour Law; Law); **Mathematics and Computer Science** (Mathematics and Computer Science); **Mechanical Engineering** (Architecture; Engineering Drawing and Design; Machine Building; Mechanical Engineering; Thermal Engineering; Transport Engineering); **Natural Sciences** (Biology; Chemistry; Natural Sciences; Pharmacy; Physics); **Social Sciences** (Communication Studies; History; Philosophy; Psychology; Social Sciences; Sociology)

Centre

Applied Electromagnetics *(CNEA)* (Electronic Engineering); **Cuba - Caribbean Studies** *(CECUCA)* (Caribbean Studies); **Energetics** *(CEEFE)* (Energy Engineering); **Higher Education Studies** *(CEES)* (Curriculum; Educational Sciences; Higher Education); **Industrial Biotechnology** *(CEBI)* (Biotechnology); **Integral Development of Culture** *(CEDIC)* (Cultural Studies); **Medical Biophysics** *(CBM)* (Biophysics); **Multidisciplinary Studies of Coastal Zones** *(CEMZOC)* (Coastal Studies); **Neurosciences** *(CENPIS)* (Medical Technology; Neurosciences); **Pattern Recognition and Data Mining** *(CERPAMID)* (Data Processing; Mathematics and Computer Science); **Refrigeration Studies** *(CER)* (Heating and Refrigeration); **Sugar Research** *(CEIA)* (Agriculture; Food Science); **Tourism Studies** *(CETUR)* (Tourism)

Further Information: Also Antonio Maceo and Julio Antonio Mella campuses

History: Founded 1947. Recognized by the State and reorganized 1948. Became an official institution 1949 and reorganized 1959. Under the responsibility of the Ministry of Higher Education.

Academic Year: September to July

Admission Requirements: Secondary school certificate or entrance examination

Fees: Masters: 3500.00. PhD: 6000.00 (Cuban Peso)

Main Language(s) of Instruction: Spanish

Degrees and Diplomas: *Licenciatura*: **Architecture; Education; Engineering; Law; Medicine.** *Maestría*: **Biotechnology; Business Administration; Caribbean Studies; Chemical Engineering; Chemistry; Civil Engineering; Coastal Studies; Computer Science; Construction Engineering; Cultural Studies; Economics; Electrical Engineering; English; Higher Education; Mechanical Engineering; Natural Sciences; Pharmacology; Social Sciences; Social Studies; Spanish.** *Doctor en Ciencias*: **Architecture; Art Education; Biochemistry; Biology; Biomedical Engineering; Business Administration; Chemistry; Construction Engineering; Economics; Electrical Engineering; Engineering; Higher Education; Hydraulic Engineering; Linguistics; Literature; Mechanical Engineering; Microbiology; Physics; Social Sciences; Town Planning.**

Student Services: Academic Counselling, Careers Guidance, Cultural Activities, Foreign Studies Centre, Health Services, Language Laboratory, Library, Nursery Care, Social Counselling, Sports Facilities

Publications: Revista Cubana de Química; Revista Santiago; Revista Tecnologia Química; Taller Literario de la Escuela de Letras

Last Updated: 03/12/15

UNIVERSITY OF PINAR DEL RÍO HERMANOS SAIZ MONTES DE OCA (UPR)

Martí 300 final, Pinar del Río, Pinar del Río 20100
Tel: +53(48) 777-923
Fax: +53(48) 772-245
EMail: mfdez@vrect.upr.edu.cu
Website: http://www.upr.edu.cu

Rector: Andrés Erasmo Ares Rojas
Tel: +53(48) 779-348 EMail: erasmoar@rectoria.upr.edu.cu

Vicerrectora: Teresa de la Caridad Díaz Domínguez
Tel: +53(48) 779-351

Faculty

Agronomía *(Montaña de San Andrés (FAMSA))* (Agronomy; Development Studies; Forestry; Regional Studies; Rural Studies; Social Studies); **Economics** (Economics); **Engineering** (Computer Engineering; Electrical Engineering; Engineering; Geological Engineering; Mechanical Engineering; Telecommunications Engineering); **Forestry and Agronomy** *(FFA)* (Agronomy; Biochemistry; Biotechnology; Forestry); **Social Science and Humanity**

Centre

Environmental and Natural Resources *(CEMARNA)* (Ecology; Environmental Management; Environmental Studies; Natural Resources); **Higher Education Sciences** *(CECES)* (Educational Research; Higher Education Teacher Training; Pedagogy); **Management, Development Studies and Tourism** *(GEDELTUR)* (Development Studies; Ecology; Management; Tourism)

History: Founded 1972, acquired present status 1994.

Academic Year: September to July

Admission Requirements: Secondary school certificate

Fees: First and Second yrs, 4,000; Third yr, 4,500; Fourth yr, 5,000; Fifth yr, 6,000 (US Dollar)

Main Language(s) of Instruction: Spanish

Degrees and Diplomas: *Licenciatura*; *Maestría*: **Economics; Forestry.** *Doctor en Ciencias*: **Agricultural Business; Economics; Education; Educational Sciences; Forestry; Geology; Pedagogy.** Also Diplomas in Spanish as a foreign language, Natural Resources, Business Administration, Tourism, Pedagogy, Cooperativism and Community Work, Agroecology, Forestry, Local Development

Student Services: Canteen, Cultural Activities, Health Services, Language Laboratory, Nursery Care, Sports Facilities

Publications: Educational Sciences Review; Mining and Geology; Scientific Year Book

Last Updated: 19/11/15

ZOILO MARINELLO UNIVERSITY OF MEDICAL SCIENCES OF LAS TUNAS

Universidad de Ciencias Médicas Zoilo Marinello de Las Tunas (UCMLT)
Avenida de la Juventud s/n, Tunas 75100
Tel: +53(31) 48015
Fax: +53(31) 43325
EMail: kiss@ltu.sld.cu

Rector: Luis Manuel Pérez Tel: +53(31) 43325

Programme

Dentistry (Dentistry); **Medical Technology** (Medical Technology); **Medicine** (Gynaecology and Obstetrics; Medicine; Paediatrics; Surgery); **Nursing** (Nursing)

History: Founded as Facultad de Ciencias Médicas Dr. Zoilo E. Marinello Vidaurreta de Las Tunas, 1984.

Main Language(s) of Instruction: Spanish

Degrees and Diplomas: *Licenciatura*; *Especialista*: **Medicine.**

Last Updated: 01/12/15

Curaçao

STRUCTURE OF HIGHER EDUCATION SYSTEM

Description:

Higher education is provided by the University of Curaçao (previously the Universiteit van de Nederlandse Antillen). It is an autonomous institution and its governing bodies are the Board of Trustees and the University Council.

Stages of studies:

University level first stage: *Bachelor's degree*

Studies last for four years (or two years after Propedeuse in Law).

University level second stage: *Master's degree*

A Master's degree is offered two years after the Bachelor's degree in such fields as Business Administration and Accounting.

ADMISSION TO HIGHER EDUCATION

Admission to university-level studies:

Name of secondary school credential required: Voorbereidend Wetenschappelijk Onderwijs Certificate

NATIONAL BODIES

Ministerio di Enseñansa, Siensia, Kultura i Deporte (Ministry of Education, Science, Culture and Sports)

Minister: Irene Dick
Schouwburgweg 24-26
Schottegatweg Oost 10
Willemstad
Tel: +599(9) 434 3700
EMail: OWCS.Communicatie@gobiernu.cw
WWW: http://www.gobiernu.cw/web/site.nsf/web/D89CE2767CF135850425782B0073CBE8?opendocument

Data for academic year: 2013-2014
Source: IAU from documentation, 2014. Bodies 2016.

INSTITUTION

PUBLIC INSTITUTION

UNIVERSITY OF CURAÇAO

Jan Noorduynweg 111, Willemstad
Tel: +599(9) 744-2222
Fax: +599(9) 744-2100
EMail: uoc@uoc.cw
Website: http://www.uoc.cw

Rector Magnificus: F.B.G. de Lanoy

Faculty

Arts (Dutch; English; Foreign Languages Education; Native Language; Spanish; Teacher Training); **Engineering** (Architecture; Civil Engineering; Electrical Engineering; Engineering; Engineering Drawing and Design; Industrial Engineering; Information Technology; Mechanical Engineering); **Law** (Law); **Social and Behavioral Sciences** (Social Work); **Social Sciences and Economics** (Accountancy; Business Administration)

History: Founded 1970 as Law School, became Institute of Higher Studies 1973 and became Universiteit van de Nederlandse Antillen (University of the Netherlands Antilles) in 1979, incorporating the School of Engineering, which was founded in 1972. Acquired current title 2013. The University is responsible to the Ministry of Education.

Academic Year: September to June (September-December; January-April)

Admission Requirements: Secondary school certificate or equivalent

Degrees and Diplomas: *Bachelor's Degree*: **Accountancy; Business Administration; Education; Engineering; Law; Social Work.** *Master's Degree*: **Accountancy; Education; Finance.**

Last Updated: 18/03/16

Cyprus

STRUCTURE OF HIGHER EDUCATION SYSTEM

Description:

The higher education system of Cyprus comprises both public and private institutions. Studies are organized in semesters, and subjects taught are counted in credits.
The Turkish Cypriot education system in the occupied area of the Republic of Cyprus is not recognized by the Republic of Cyprus.

Stages of studies:

University level first stage: *Ptychio*
The first stage of university level education lasts for 4 years and leads to the award of a Ptychio (240 ECTS).

University level second stage: *Magister Artium/Scientae (Masters)*
After completion of the first stage, graduates may follow three to four semesters of full time study (90 to 120 ECTS) leading to a Magister Artium or Magister Scientae degree.

University level third stage: *Doctorate*
The third cycle lasts between 4 to 8 years and leads to the Didactoriko Diploma. It consists of at least 60 ECTS, a comprehensive examination, the presentation of a research proposal and the defense of an original research thesis.

ADMISSION TO HIGHER EDUCATION

Admission to university-level studies:

Name of secondary school credential required: Apolytirion

For entry to: University of Cyprus. Also access to university in Greece.

Alternatives to credentials: General Certificate of Education Advanced Level

Admission requirements: Admission to State universities is granted upon success in the competitive entrance examinations (Pancyprian Examinations) which are used to rank students. Admission to private universities is granted upon submission of a relevant application and the fulfilment of criteria set by each institution.

Foreign students admission:

Admission requirements: Foreign students should hold a secondary school leaving certificate awarded after six years of secondary education. Entrance examinations are held for the University of Cyprus and all post-secondary non-university institutions. Entrance to private post-secondary non-university institutions requires 12 years of schooling or a secondary school certificate obtained after 6 years of secondary education or its equivalent.

Entry regulations: A visa may be required depending on the country.

Language proficiency: Students should have a good knowledge of Greek to study at the University of Cyprus and some public institutions, and English for other institutions.

RECOGNITION OF STUDIES

Quality assurance system:

The competent authority in the Republic of Cyprus for carrying out programmatic evaluation and accreditation of the private institutions of higher education is the Council of Educational Evaluation–Accreditation (C.E.E.A). The Evaluation Committee of Private Universities is the competent authority in the Republic of Cyprus for the examination of the applications submitted for the establishment and operation of a private university.

Bodies dealing with recognition:

Cyprus Council for the Recognition of Higher Education Qualifications - KY.S.A.T.S.

Chairperson: Nikos Vafeas
Ministry of Education and Culture, Kimonos and Thoukidydou Corner, Akropoli
Lefkosia 1434

Tel: +357(22) 806357
Fax: +357(22) 800866
EMail: info@kysats.ac.cy
WWW: http://www.kysats.ac.cy

NATIONAL BODIES

Ministry of Education and Culture
Minister: Costas Kadis
Thoukides and Kimonos Corner, Akropoli
Lefkosia 1434
Tel: +357(22) 800600
Fax: +357(22) 800700
EMail: moec@moec.gov.cy
WWW: http://www.moec.gov.cy

Evaluation Committee of Private Universities - ECPU
Chairperson: George Philokyprou
Ministry of Education and Culture, Kimonos and Thoukidydou Corner, Akropoli
Lefkosia 1434
Tel: +357(22) 800986
Fax: +357(22) 800645
EMail: administration@ecpu.ac.cy
WWW: http://www.ecpu.ac.cy

SEKAP (Council of Educational Evaluation Accreditation)
President: George Philokyprou
Ministry of Education and Culture, Kimonos and Thoukidydou Corner, Akropoli
Lefkosia 1434
Tel: +357(22) 806304
Fax: +357(22) 800645
EMail: sekap@cytanet.com.cy
WWW: http://www.moec.gov.cy/sekap
Role of national body: Independent expert body, appointed by the Council of Ministers upon the recommendation of the Minister of Education and Culture, competent for carrying out the evaluation and accreditation of the private institutions of higher education.

Data for academic year: 2014-2015
Source: Ministry of Education and Culture, Department of Higher and Tertiary Education, 2014. Bodies 2016.

INSTITUTIONS

PUBLIC INSTITUTIONS

CYPRUS UNIVERSITY OF TECHNOLOGY
P.O. Box 50329, Archbishop Kyprianos 30, 3036 Limassol
Tel: +357(25) 00-2500
Fax: +357(25) 00-2750
EMail: administration@cut.ac.cy
Website: http://www.cut.ac.cy

Rector: Elpida Keravnou Papailiou (2012-) EMail: rector@cut.ac.cy
Vice Rector for Academic Affairs: Toula Onoufriou

Department
Agricultural Sciences, Biotechnology and Food Science (Agriculture; Animal Husbandry; Biotechnology; Crop Production; Fishery; Food Science); **Civil Engineering and Geomatics** (Civil Engineering; Surveying and Mapping); **Commerce, Finance and Shipping** (Business and Commerce; Economics; Finance; Marine Transport; Transport Management); **Communication and Internet Studies** (Communication Studies; Information Management; Information Technology; Media Studies); **Electrical Engineering, Computer Engineering and Informatics** (Computer Engineering; Electrical Engineering); **Environmental Science and Technology** (Environmental Management; Environmental Studies); **Hotel and Tourism Management** (Hotel Management; Tourism); **Mechanical Engineering and Material Science and Engineering** (Materials Engineering; Mechanical Engineering); **Multimedia and Graphic Arts** (Communication Studies; Fine Arts; Graphic Arts; Multimedia); **Nursing** (Nursing; Public Health); **Rehabilitation Sciences** (Rehabilitation and Therapy)

Institute

Environmental and Public Health *(International)* (Public Health)

Centre

Language (French; German; Greek; Italian; Russian; Spanish)

History: Founded 2003. Admitted its first students 2007.

Accrediting Agency: Ministry of Education and Culture

Degrees and Diplomas: *Ptychio*; *Magister Artium/Magister Scientae*: **Banking; Design; Energy Engineering; Epidemiology; Finance; Graphic Design; Hotel Management; Information Technology; Journalism; Mechanical Engineering; Multimedia; Public Health; Tourism; Transport Management.** *Didactoriko*: **Computer Engineering; Mechanical Engineering; Public Health.**

Last Updated: 23/01/15

MEDITERRANEAN INSTITUTE OF MANAGEMENT (MIM)

77 Kallipoleos Avenue, 2100 Nicosia
Tel: +357(22) 80-61-17
Fax: +357(22) 37-68-72
EMail: mim@kepa.mlsi.gov.cy
Website: http://www.mim.ac.cy

MIM Manager: Akis Nicolaides
Tel: +(357) 22 806117 EMail: knicolaides@kepa.mlsi.gov.cy

Department

Management (Management; Marketing; Public Administration)

Further Information: http://www.mlsi.gov.cy/kepa

History: Founded 1976. A State institution.

Admission Requirements: •University degree or equivalent qualification in any subject. •Very good command of the english language (for the Full-Time Postgraduate Programme) •Success in the entrance examination (aptitude tests) conducted by the MIM.

Fees: 3.426 (Euro)

Main Language(s) of Instruction: English, Modern Greek

Accrediting Agency: Ministry of Education and Culture KYSATS (Cyprus Council for the Recognition of Higher Education Qualifications)

Degrees and Diplomas: Postgraduate Diploma in 'Management' and 'Management and Public Administration'.

Student Services: Canteen, Careers Guidance, Cultural Activities, Facilities for disabled people, IT Centre, Library, Sports Facilities, eLibrary

Academic Staff *2015*	MEN	WOMEN	**TOTAL**
FULL-TIME	10	10	**20**
PART-TIME	5	5	**10**
STAFF WITH DOCTORATE			
FULL-TIME	3	–	**3**
Student Numbers *2015*			
All (Foreign included)	30	35	**65**

Part-time students, 35.

Last Updated: 09/01/15

OPEN UNIVERSITY OF CYPRUS (OUC)

P.O. Box 12794, 2252 Nicosia, Latsia
Tel: +357(22) 41-16-00
Fax: +357(22) 41-16-01
EMail: info@ouc.ac.cy
Website: http://www.ouc.ac.cy

President: Christos Christou

International Relations: Erato-Ioanna Sarri, Coordinating Officer
Tel: (+357) 22411659 EMail: sarri@ouc.ac.cy

Faculty

Economics and Management *(Banking and Finance)* (Banking; Business Administration; Educational Administration; Educational Sciences; European Union Law; Health Administration; Management Systems; Police Studies); **Humanities and Social Sciences** (Arts and Humanities; Continuing Education; Cultural Studies; Development Studies; Greek; Information Management; Journalism; Performing Arts; Social Sciences; Theatre); **Pure and Applied Sciences** (Computer Science; Environmental Management; Information Technology; Medical Technology)

History: Founded in 2002 as the second public University of Cyprus and the only University devoted entirely to open and distance learning education at all levels (undergraduate, postgraduate and doctoral).

Admission Requirements: For a Bachelor degree, a secondary education degree is the basic prerequisite. For a Master's degree, applicants must hold a Bachelor degree or other relevant documentation from an accredited university. Master programmes may have other additional requirements (e.g. good knowledge of a foreign language) depending on the specific programme. Doctorate programmes candidates requires a Master's degree from an accredited university. Applicants who meet the admission criteria will be randomly selected for enrollment to the respective study programmes.

Main Language(s) of Instruction: Modern Greek, English

Accrediting Agency: Ministry of Education and Culture

Degrees and Diplomas: *Certificate*; *Ptychio*; *Magister Artium/Magister Scientae*: **Banking; Business Administration; Communication Studies; Computer Engineering; Computer Science; Cultural Studies; Development Studies; Education; Educational Administration; Environmental Studies; Finance; Greek; Health Sciences; Information Sciences; Information Technology; Journalism; Law; Literature; Management; Social Sciences; Theatre.** *Didactoriko*: **Communication Studies; Education; Environmental Studies; Greek; Health Sciences; Information Sciences; Journalism; Theatre.**

Student Services: Academic Counselling, Facilities for disabled people, IT Centre, Library, eLibrary

Academic Staff *2015*	MEN	WOMEN	**TOTAL**
FULL-TIME	34	61	**95**
PART-TIME	180	112	**292**
STAFF WITH DOCTORATE			
FULL-TIME	12	6	**18**
Student Numbers *2014-2015*			
All (Foreign included)	1,856	2,628	**4,484**

Distance students, 4,484.

Last Updated: 09/01/15

UNIVERSITY OF CYPRUS (UCY)

University House "Anastasios G. Leventis", P.O. Box 20537, 1678 Nicosia
Tel: +357(22) 89-40-00
Fax: +357(22) 89-21-00
EMail: admin@ucy.ac.cy
Website: http://www.ucy.ac.cy

Rector: Constantinos Christofides (2010-)
Tel: +357(22) 89-40-08 EMail: ccc@ucy.ac.cy; rector@ucy.ac.cy

Vice-Rector, Academic Affairs: Athanasios Gagatsis
Tel: +357(22) 89-40-03 EMail: gagatsis@ucy.ac.cy

International Relations: Constantinos Constantinou, Vice-Rector, International Affairs, Administration and Finance
Tel: +357(22) 89-94-06

Faculty

Economics and Management (Business Administration; Economics; Management; Public Administration); **Engineering** (Architecture; Civil Engineering; Computer Engineering; Electrical Engineering; Engineering; English; Environmental Engineering; French; Mechanical Engineering; Production Engineering); **Humanities** (Arts and Humanities; English Studies; French Studies; Middle Eastern Studies; Modern Languages; Turkish); **Letters** (Ancient Civilizations; Archaeology; Arts and Humanities; Classical Languages; Greek; History; Philosophy); **Pure and Applied Sciences** (Biological and Life Sciences; Chemistry; Computer Science; Mathematics; Physics; Statistics); **Social Sciences and Education** (Curriculum; Education; Educational Administration; Law; Mathematics Education; Preschool Education; Primary Education; Psychology)

School

Medicine (Medicine)

Centre
Banking and Financial Research (Banking; Finance); **Economics Research** (Economics); **Intelligent Systems and Networks Research** *(KIOS Research Center)* (Artificial Intelligence; Computer Networks); **Language** (Modern Languages); **Nanotechnology Research** (Nanotechnology); **Oceanography** (Marine Science and Oceanography)

History: Founded 1989. Acquired present status 1992.

Academic Year: September to May (September-December; January-May)

Admission Requirements: Undergraduate students: General Certificate of Education (GCE) with Ordinary ('O') level in Greek and 3 Advanced ('A') levels, with minimum grades of B or C, or High School Diploma (Apolitirio) and entrance examinations.

Fees: National: Undergraduate: 3,417 per annum for Cypriots and other EU students. Master Programmes: 4,100- 10,250 per annum depending on field of studies (Euro), International: Undergraduate: 6,834 per annum for non-European students (Euro)

Main Language(s) of Instruction: Turkish, Modern Greek

Accrediting Agency: Ministry of Education and Culture

Degrees and Diplomas: *Ptychio*: **Accountancy; Archaeology; Architecture; Biology; Chemistry; Civil Engineering; Classical Languages; Computer Engineering; Computer Science; Economics; Electrical Engineering; English; Environmental Engineering; European Studies; Finance; French; Greek (Classical); History; International Studies; Literature; Marketing; Mathematics; Mechanical Engineering; Oriental Studies; Philosophy; Physics; Political Sciences; Preschool Education; Primary Education; Production Engineering; Psychology; Sociology; Statistics; Turkish.** *Magister Artium/Magister Scientae*: **Agriculture; Ancient Civilizations; Applied Linguistics; Banking; Business Administration; Chemistry; Civil Engineering; Classical Languages; Cognitive Sciences; Computer Engineering; Cultural Studies; Curriculum; Developmental Psychology; Economics; Educational Administration; Educational Psychology; English; Finance; Greek; Information Technology; Literature; Mathematics; Mathematics Education; Mechanical Engineering; Mediterranean Studies; Molecular Biology; Natural Sciences; Oriental Studies; Pedagogy; Philology; Physics; Production Engineering; Statistics; Translation and Interpretation; Turkish.** *Didactoriko*: **Accountancy; Ancient Civilizations; Applied Linguistics; Applied Mathematics; Archaeology; Architecture; Biological and Life Sciences; Chemistry; Civil Engineering; Classical Languages; Clinical Psychology; Computer Engineering; Computer Science; Contemporary History; Cultural Studies; Curriculum; Developmental Psychology; Economics; Education; Educational Administration; Educational Psychology; Electrical Engineering; English; Environmental Engineering; Finance; French; Gender Studies; Greek (Classical); History; Literature; Mathematics; Mathematics Education; Mechanical Engineering; Mediterranean Studies; Middle Eastern Studies; Molecular Biology; Natural Sciences; Oriental Studies; Philology; Philosophy; Physics; Political Sciences; Production Engineering; Social Sciences; Sociology; Special Education; Statistics; Turkish.**

Student Services: Academic Counselling, Canteen, Careers Guidance, Cultural Activities, Foreign Studies Centre, Health Services, Library, Sports Facilities

Student Numbers *2013-2014*: Total 7,048
Last Updated: 26/01/15

PRIVATE INSTITUTIONS

AIGAIA SCHOOL OF ART AND DESIGN

Aigaia Sxoli Kalon ke Efarmosmenon
81, Ayion Omoloyiton, 1080 Nicosia
Tel: +(357) 22445757
Fax: +(357) 22028342
EMail: info@aigaia.com.cy
Website: http://www.aigaia.com.cy

Director: Alexia Eliadou Hadjistefanou

Programme
Fine Arts (Ceramic Art; Design; Fine Arts; Painting and Drawing; Photography; Sculpture; Visual Arts)

History: Founded 2005.

Accrediting Agency: Ministry of Education and Culture

Degrees and Diplomas: *Diploma*; *Ptychio*: **Fine Arts.**

Last Updated: 23/01/15

ALEXANDER COLLEGE (ACC)

P.O. Box 45081, 2 Artas Street, 7110 Aradhippou, Larnaca
Tel: +357(24) 53-23-73
Fax: +357(24) 53-23-65
EMail: info@alexander.ac.cy
Website: http://www.alexander.ac.cy

Director: Andy Loppas EMail: loppas@alexander.ac.cy

Faculty
Arts and Creative Industries (Law); **Business and Law** (Fine Arts)

History: Founded 1991.

Fees: National: 7000 (Euro), International: 7000 (Euro)

Main Language(s) of Instruction: English

Degrees and Diplomas: *Ptychio*: **Business Administration; Criminology; Fashion Design; Finance; Fine Arts; Graphic Design; Interior Design; Law; Photography.** Also Bachelor's and Master's degree (Business Administration, Design, Education) delivered in cooperation with University of West England.

Student Services: Academic Counselling, Canteen, Careers Guidance, Cultural Activities, Facilities for disabled people, Foreign Studies Centre, Health Services, IT Centre, Language Laboratory, Library, Residential Facilities, Social Counselling, Sports Facilities, eLibrary

Publications: Av proyectos; British Journal of Photography; Computer Arts; Criminal Justice Matters; Elephant; EVolo; Frame; Harvard Business Review; Icon; International Journal of leadership in education: Theory and practice; Landscape architecture magazine; Mark: Another achitecture; National Geographic; New Law Journal; Professional Photographer; Scape: the international magazine for landscape architecture and Urbanism; The economist; Topos: the international review of landscape architecture and Urban design; Turning Pro; Vogue

Academic Staff *2014-2015*	MEN	WOMEN	TOTAL
FULL-TIME	9	7	**16**
PART-TIME	14	14	**28**
STAFF WITH DOCTORATE			
FULL-TIME	5	3	**8**
Student Numbers *2014-2015*			
All (Foreign included)	172	195	**367**
FOREIGN ONLY	32	28	**60**

Last Updated: 05/12/14

AMERICAN COLLEGE

P.O. Box 22425, 2 & 3 Omirou Avenue, 1521 Nicosia
Tel: +357(22) 66-11-22
Fax: +357(22) 66-41-18
EMail: college@ac.ac.cy
Website: http://www.ac.ac.cy

Director: Marios Americanos

International Relations: Tasos Anastasiou
EMail: tasos.anastasiou@ac.ac.cy

Programme
Business Administration (Accountancy; Business Administration; Commercial Law; Finance); **Computer Science** (Computer Science); **Culinary Arts** (Cooking and Catering); **Hotel Management** (Hotel Management); **Human Resource Management** (Human Resources); **International Business** (International Business); **Management Information Systems** (Business Computing; Management Systems); **Marketing** (Marketing); **Travel and Tourism Management** (Tourism)

History: Founded 1975. Previously known as Americanos College.

Admission Requirements: Secondary School Leaving Certificate

Accrediting Agency: Ministry of Education and Culture

Degrees and Diplomas: *Diploma*; *Ptychio*: **Business Administration; Computer Science; Hotel Management; Human Resources; International Business; Marketing; Tourism; Transport Management.** *Magister Artium/Magister Scientae*: **Business Administration.**

Student Services: Canteen, IT Centre, Library, Sports Facilities

Last Updated: 26/01/15

ARTE MUSIC ACADEMY

P.O. Box 21207, 34 - 36 Leonidou Street, 1504 Nicosia
Tel: +357(22) 67-68-23
Fax: +357(22) 66-56-95
EMail: academy@artemusic.org

Principal: Pitsa Spyridaki

Programme

Music (Music)

History: Founded 2002.

Degrees and Diplomas: *Diploma*; *Ptychio*: **Music.**

Last Updated: 26/01/15

CASA COLLEGE

18. Theophani Theodotou Str., ZENA PALACE, 1160 Nicosia
Tel: +357(22) 66-18-82
Fax: +357(22) 66-24-14
EMail: info@casacollege.com; casacollegeadmissions@gmail.com
Website: http://www.casacollege.com

Director: Yiannis Saveriades Tel: +357(22) 681882 Ext.6 EMail: yiannis@casacollege.com

Programme

Business Studies (Business and Commerce); **Hotel Administration** (Hotel Management; Tourism)

Course

Secretarial Studies (English; Secretarial Studies)

History: Founded 1961.

Fees: (Bachelor's degree): 4000 per annum (Euro)

Main Language(s) of Instruction: English, Modern Greek

Accrediting Agency: Ministry of Education and Culture

Degrees and Diplomas: *Ptychio*: **Business Administration; Hotel Management.**

Student Services: Library

Last Updated: 26/01/15

C.D.A. COLLEGE

P.O. Box 21972, 2, Evagorou Aveenue, Eleftherias Square, 1515 Nicosia
Tel: +357(22) 37-64-38
Fax: +357(22) 67-13-87
EMail: cdaadm@spidernet.com.cy; cdacoll@spidernet.com.cy
Website: http://www.cdacollege.ac.cy/

Director: D. A. Christoforou

Programme

Accounting and Finance (Accountancy; Finance); **Beauty Therapy** (Cosmetology); **Business Administration** (Business Administration); **Police Studies and Criminology** (Criminology; Police Studies); **Travel and Tourism Management** (Tourism)

Further Information: Larnaka, Lemosos, Lefkosia, and Paphos

History: Founded 1976.

Accrediting Agency: Department of Higher and Tertiary Education, Ministry of Education and Culture.

Degrees and Diplomas: *Diploma*; *Ptychio*: **Accountancy; Business Administration; Cosmetology; Criminology; Finance; Hotel Management; Police Studies; Tourism.** *Magister Artium/Magister Scientae*: **Business Administration; Cosmetology.**

Last Updated: 23/01/15

CITY UNITY COLLEGE

79, Aglantzias Avenue, 2107 Nicosia
Tel: +(357) 22-33-2333
Fax: +(357) 22-33-2313
EMail: info@cityu.ac.cy
Website: http://cityu.ac.cy

Department

Business and Finance (Business Administration; Finance; Management); **Computer Science** (Computer Science); **Hospitality and Tourism Management** (Hotel Management; Tourism); **Psychology** (Psychology)

History: Founded as White City College 2012. Acquired present title 2014.

Accrediting Agency: Ministry of Education and Culture

Degrees and Diplomas: *Ptychio*: **Accountancy; Economics; Finance; Management; Psychology.** *Magister Artium/Magister Scientae*: **Business Administration; Finance; Hotel Management; Law; Psychology; Tourism.** City Unity College in cooperation with Cardiff Metropolitan University offers Bachelor's and Master's programmes in the areas of Business, Computing, Psychology, Law, Tourism and Hospitality.

Last Updated: 23/01/15

COLLEGE OF TOURISM AND HOTEL MANAGEMENT

P.O. Box 21115, 29 Onasagorou Street, 1502 Nicosia
Tel: +357(22) 46-28-46
Fax: +357(22) 33-62-95
EMail: info@cothm.ac.cy
Website: http://www.cothm.ac.cy

Director: Savvas Adamides EMail: adamides@cothm.ac.cy

Programme

Accounting and Finance (Accountancy; Finance); **Business Administration** (Business Administration); **Events Management** (Management); **Hospitality Management** (Hotel Management; Tourism); **Hotel Administration** (Hotel Management); **Information Technology** (Information Technology); **International Business Studies** (International Business); **Leisure Management** (Leisure Studies); **Travel and Tourism Administration** (Tourism)

History: Founded 1987.

Fees: Undergraduate Programs (for one year): 6.100; Masters Programs (for 18 months): 10.550 (Euro)

Accrediting Agency: Ministry of Education and Culture

Degrees and Diplomas: *Ptychio*: **Business Administration; Tourism.** *Magister Artium/Magister Scientae*: **Business Administration.** Also Postgraduate Diplomas

Last Updated: 23/01/15

CYPRUS INTERNATIONAL INSTITUTE OF MANAGEMENT (CIIM MANAGEMENT SCHOOL)

P.O. Box 20378, 21 Akademias Avenue, Aglandjia, 2151 Nicosia
Tel: +357(22) 46-22-46
Fax: +357(22) 33-11-21
EMail: ciim@ciim.ac.cy; gaurav@ciim.ac.cy
Website: http://www.ciim.ac.cy

Director: Theodore Panayotou (2000-)

International Office: Mario Siathas
Tel: +357(22) 46-22-46 EMail: marios.siathas@ciim.ac.cy

International Relations: Gaurav Dubey, Marketing Manager
Tel: +357 22462246 EMail: gaurav@ciim.ac.cy

Programme

Business Administration (Accountancy; Business Administration; Business and Commerce; Commercial Law; Economics; Environmental Management; Finance; Human Resources; Management; Marketing); **Educational Leadership and Management** (Educational Administration; Leadership); **Human Resource Management and Organisational Behaviour** (Human Resources; Management); **Management** (Management); **Public Service Management** (Accountancy; Commercial Law; Economics; Environmental

Management; Finance; Human Resources; Management; Marketing; Public Administration)

Campus

Limassol (Business Administration)

Further Information: Also Limassol Campus

History: Founded 1990.

Academic Year: September to June, however there are rolling admissions

Admission Requirements: BBA: To be considered for admission into the program the candidate must have the following: Documented proficiency in the English language through one of the following: IELTS with at least 6.0+; TOEFL with a score of at least 550+ (213+ for computerized test); GCE O level in the English language with at least C Graduation from an English-language speaking high-school. Documented educational achievement through at least one of the following: High-school leaving certificate with a minimum grade of 18/20 (for public schools) or 85 (for private schools) or Pancyprian or Panhellenic Entrance Examinations with a minimum average grade of 85 (17/20) or Three GSE A Level with grades ABB International Baccalaureate with a minimum of 32 points. Successful personal interview, an integral part of the selection process. MBA/MPSM: Bachelor degree from an accredited programme. A minimum of three years postgraduate work experience. Proficiency in English (graduation from an English speaking institution, TOEFL, IELTS or similar standardised test). Success in a personal interview. MSc admission requirements: Bachelor's degree from an accredited programme or an equivalent professional qualification. Working knowledge of the English language evidenced by having graduated from an English speaking institution or satisfactory score in TOEFL, IELTS or other standardised test. Success in a personal interview.

Fees: National: BBA: 9000. MBA/MPSM: 15000. MSc: 8500 (Euro), International: BBA: 9000. MBA/MPSM: 15000. MSc: 8500 (Euro)

Main Language(s) of Instruction: English

Accrediting Agency: Ministry of Education and Culture (SEKAP)

Degrees and Diplomas: *Ptychio*; *Magister Artium/Magister Scientae*: **Business Administration; Finance; Human Resources; Management.**

Student Services: Academic Counselling, Canteen, Careers Guidance, Facilities for disabled people, IT Centre, Library, Residential Facilities, eLibrary

Academic Staff *2014*	MEN	WOMEN	TOTAL
FULL-TIME	18	13	**31**
STAFF WITH DOCTORATE			
FULL-TIME	5	3	**8**
Student Numbers *2014*			
All (Foreign included)	91	146	**237**
FOREIGN ONLY	11	18	**29**

Part-time students, 159.

Last Updated: 23/01/15

CYPRUS SCHOOL OF MOLECULAR MEDICINE - THE CYPRUS INSTITUTE OF NEUROLOGY AND GENETICS (CSMM)

P.O. Box 23462, 1683 Nicosia
Tel: +(357) 22 358600
Fax: +(357) 22 392845
EMail: csmm@cing.ac.cy
Website: http://www.cing.ac.cy/csmm/

Dean: Kyriacos Kyriacou

Chief Executive Medical Director - Provost: Leonidas Phylactou

Administartive Services Officer: Operations and Admissions: Maria Lagou Tel: +(357) 22 392841 EMail: marial@cing.ac.cy

Administrative Services Officer: Marketing and Promotions: Andria Ioakem Tel: +(357) 22 392843 EMail: andriai@cing.ac.cy

Department

Biochemical Genetics (Biochemistry); **Cardiovascular Genetics and Laboratory of Forensic Genetics** (Genetics); **Cytogenetics and Genomics** (Genetics); **Electron Microscopy and Molecular Pathology** (Molecular Biology); **Molecular Genetics Thalassaemia** (Genetics); **Molecular Genetics, Function & Therapy** (Genetics); **Molecular Virology** (Virology); **Neurogenetics** (Genetics; Neurology)

Section

Clinical Genetics Clinic (Genetics); **Neurology Clinic A,B, C, D, & E** (Neurology)

Research Unit

Translational Genetics (Genetics)

Further Information: http://www.cing.ac.cy

History: Founded 2011. The Cyprus Institute of Neurology and Genetics has established a postgraduate school, named the Cyprus School of Molecular Medicine (CSMM) open to students with research interests applicable to the Institute's activities. The postgraduate school is organized as a distinct entity within CING.

Academic Year: September to September

Admission Requirements: To be admitted to an MSc or a PhD program, a student must meet at least the minimum requirements listed below: A Bachelors degree from a recognized accredited institution, in a related field- English Language Certification or other accepted International Standard, if graduated from a school where English is not the teaching language. Required Documents: A Completed Application Form; Two Academic References; Academic Transcripts. English Language Certificate (if not graduated from an English speaking University).

Main Language(s) of Instruction: English

Accrediting Agency: The Council of Educational Evaluation Accreditations (CEEA)

Degrees and Diplomas: *Magister Artium/Magister Scientae*: **Biomedicine; Genetics; Neurosciences.** *Didactoriko*: **Genetics; Molecular Biology; Neurosciences.** MSc in Molecular Medicine PhD in Molecular Medicine

Student Services: Academic Counselling, Canteen, Careers Guidance, Cultural Activities, Facilities for disabled people, Foreign Studies Centre, Health Services, IT Centre, Library, eLibrary

Last Updated: 09/01/15

EUROPEAN UNIVERSITY CYPRUS (EUC)

P.O. Box 22006, 6, Diogenes Street, Engomi, 22006 Nicosia
Tel: +357(22) 71-30-00
Fax: +357(22) 66-20-51
EMail: Rector@euc.ac.cy
Website: http://www.euc.ac.cy

President: Kostas Gouliamos EMail: K.Gouliamos@euc.ac.cy

Vice-Rector, Academic Affairs: Andreas Makris

School

Arts and Education Sciences (Advertising and Publicity; Educational Administration; Educational Psychology; Educational Sciences; Graphic Design; Mathematics Education; Music; Music Education; Preschool Education; Primary Education; Special Education); **Business Administration** *(Ioannis Gregoriou)* (Accountancy; Advertising and Publicity; Banking; Business Administration; Business and Commerce; Economics; Finance; Graphic Design; Hotel Management; Human Resources; International Business; Management; Marketing; Public Relations; Sports Management; Tourism); **Humanities and Social Sciences** (Arts and Humanities; Behavioural Sciences; Communication Studies; Comparative Literature; English; European Languages; European Studies; Journalism; Law; Linguistics; Literature; Psychology; Public Relations; Social Sciences; Social Work; Sociology); **Medicine** (Medicine); **Science** (Computer Engineering; Computer Science; Nursing; Physical Therapy)

History: Founded 1961 as Cyprus College. Acquired present status and title 2007.

Academic Year: From October to July (October-January, January-May, June-July)

Accrediting Agency: Ministry of Education and Culture

Degrees and Diplomas: *Ptychio*: **Biology; Medicine; Nursing.** *Magister Artium/Magister Scientae*: **Computer Science; Information Technology; Nursing; Nutrition; Public Health; Sports.** Also Doctorate degrees in Computer Science; Physiotherapy and Public Health

Student Services: IT Centre, Library, Sports Facilities

Last Updated: 23/01/15

CYPRUS COLLEGE

P.O. Box 22006, 6, Genouillés Str. Engomi, 1516 Nicosia
Tel: +(357) 22-713000
Fax: +(357) 22-662051
EMail: reg@cycollege.ac.cy
Website: http://www.cycollege.ac.cy

School

Computer Science (Computer Science)

Campus

Limassol (Arts and Humanities; Social Sciences)

Further Information: Also a campus in Limassol

History: Founded 1961.

Admission Requirements: High School Leaving Certificate

Accrediting Agency: Ministry of Education Cyprus

Degrees and Diplomas: *Ptychio*; *Magister Artium/Magister Scientae*: **Business Administration.**

FREDERICK INSTITUTE OF TECHNOLOGY (FIT)

7, Y. Frederickou Street, Palouriotissa, 1036 Nicosia
Tel: +357(22) 431355
Fax: +357(22) 438234
EMail: internationalOffice@fit.ac.cy
Website: http://www.fit.ac.cy

Director: Michael Frederickou

Programme

Business Administration (Business Administration); **Design** (Design)

Campus

Limassol

Further Information: Also a campus in Limassol

History: Founded 1965.

Admission Requirements: School leaving certificate from a recognised six-form secondary school (high school) with an average grade of 75% (Greek Cypriot secondary schools) or a grade of "C" or its equivalent.

Accrediting Agency: Ministry of Education and Culture

Degrees and Diplomas: *Diploma*; *Ptychio*: **Radio and Television Broadcasting.** *Magister Artium/Magister Scientae*: **Business Administration.**

Student Services: IT Centre, Library

Last Updated: 23/01/15

FREDERICK UNIVERSITY

7, Yiannis Frederickou Street, Pallouriotissa, 1036 Nicosia
Tel: +357(22) 39-43-94
Fax: +357(22) 43-82-34
EMail: info@frederick.ac.cy
Website: http://www.frederick.ac.cy

President: Michalis Frederickou

Rector: George Demosthenous

School

Architecture, Fine and Applied Arts (Architecture; Fine Arts; Graphic Design; Interior Design); **Economics and Administration** (Accountancy; Business Administration; Economics; Finance; Marine Transport); **Education** (Preschool Education; Primary Education); **Engineering and Applied Sciences** (Automotive Engineering; Civil Engineering; Computer Engineering; Computer Science; Electrical Engineering; Engineering; Mechanical Engineering); **Health Sciences** (Health Administration; Nursing); **Humanities and Social Sciences** (Arts and Humanities; Journalism; Social Sciences; Social Work)

Further Information: Also campus in Limassol

History: Founded 1965 as Frederick Institute of Technology. Acquired present status and title 2007.

Accrediting Agency: Ministry of Education and Culture

Degrees and Diplomas: *Ptychio*: **Accountancy; Business Administration; Civil Engineering; Computer Engineering; Computer Science; Education; Finance; Journalism; Law; Mechanical Engineering; Pharmacy; Social Work.** *Magister Artium/Magister Scientae*: **Business Administration; Design; Education; Electrical Engineering; Energy Engineering; Engineering Management; Health Administration; Petroleum and Gas Engineering; Social Work.** *Didactoriko*: **Civil Engineering; Computer Engineering; Computer Science; Education; Electrical Engineering; Engineering; Fine Arts; Health Administration; Management; Mechanical Engineering; Social Work.** Also Postgraduate Diploma

Student Services: Sports Facilities

Last Updated: 23/01/15

INTERCOLLEGE

8 Markou Drakou Street, Engomi, 2409 Nicosia
Tel: +357(22) 842500
Fax: +357(22) 842555
EMail: info@intercollege.ac.cy
Website: http://www.intercollege.ac.cy/

Executive Director: Stylianos Mavromoustakos

Administrative Officer, Academic Affairs: Andrianna Adamantou
EMail: adamantou.a@intercollege.ac.cy

Programme

Business Administration (Business Administration; Economics; Finance; Marketing); **Business Information Technology** (Business Computing); **Business Studies** (Business and Commerce); **Computer Engineering** (Computer Engineering); **Computing** (Computer Science; Information Technology); **Graphic and Digital Design** (Graphic Design); **Hotel Management** (Hotel Management); **Pre-Primary Education** (Preschool Education); **Sports Science** (Sports; Sports Management)

Campus

Larnaka (Business Administration; Computer Science); **Limassol** (Business Administration; Hotel Management)

Further Information: Also campuses in Larnaka and Limassol

History: Founded 1980.

Main Language(s) of Instruction: Modern Greek

Accrediting Agency: Ministry of Education and Culture. Council for Educational Evaluation - Accreditation (SEKAP)

Degrees and Diplomas: *Diploma*; *Ptychio*: **Aesthetics; Cooking and Catering.**

Last Updated: 26/01/15

INTERNAPA COLLEGE

P.O. Box 35004, 5390 Sotira
Tel: +357(23) 829840
Fax: +357(23) 826831
EMail: admin@internapa.ac.cy
Website: http://www.internapa.ac.cy/

Managing Director: George Takkas

Programme

Business Administration (Business Administration); **Chinese** (Chinese); **Education** (Education); **Food and Agribusiness Management** (Agricultural Business; Food Science); **Hospitality and Tourism Management** (Hotel and Restaurant; Tourism)

History: Founded 2003.

Degrees and Diplomas: *Diploma*; *Higher Diploma*; *Ptychio*: **Agricultural Business; Business Administration; Food Science; Hotel Management; Tourism.**

Student Services: Library

Last Updated: 26/01/15

LARNACA COLLEGE

Mehmet Ali 75, 6026 Larnaca
Tel: +357(24) 828899
Fax: +357(24) 622299
EMail: info@larnacacollege.ac.cy
Website: http://www.larnacacollege.ac.cy

School

Business Administration (Business Administration); **Health and Medicine** (Cosmetology; Health Administration; Health Sciences;

Medicine); **Tourism and Hospitality** (Hotel and Restaurant; Tourism)

Accrediting Agency: Ministry of Education and Culture

Degrees and Diplomas: *Diploma*; *Higher Diploma*; *Ptychio*: **Business Administration; Hotel Management; Tourism.**

Last Updated: 26/01/15

LEDRA COLLEGE

13, Lagkada Street, Strovolos, 2023 Nicosia
Tel: +357(22) 514044
Fax: +357(22) 879250
EMail: info@ledra.ac.cy
Website: http://www.ledra.ac.cy/

Principal: George Kakouris

Course

Digital Marketing (Marketing); **Finance** (Finance); **Mobile and Web Applications Development** (Computer Engineering; Computer Science)

History: Founded 2007.

Fees: Bachelor: 5250 per annum (Euro)

Degrees and Diplomas: *Ptychio*: **Finance.**

Student Services: IT Centre, Library

Last Updated: 28/01/15

MESOYIOS COLLEGE

2 Ayiou Filona Street, 8049 Paphos
Tel: +357(26) 937-300
Fax: +357(26) 936-200
EMail: info@mesoyios.ac.cy
Website: http://www.mesoyios.ac.cy/

President: Theodoros Antoniou

Accountant: Evgenia Evgeniou Tel: +357(26) 937-391

International Relations: Gordana Banduka, International Admissions Manager
Tel: +357(26) 937-385 EMail: gbanduka@mesoyios.ac.cy

School

Business Administration (Accountancy; Administration; Business Administration; Economics; Educational Sciences; Human Resources; Management; Public Relations; Secretarial Studies); **Fine Arts** (Music); **Hospitality and Culinary Arts** (Cooking and Catering; Hotel and Restaurant; Hotel Management); **Science and Technology** (Civil Engineering; Computer Networks; Computer Science; Information Technology; Mass Communication; Petroleum and Gas Engineering; Production Engineering; Robotics)

History: Created 1998 as the Mesoyios Institute of Career Advancement.

Admission Requirements: Application Form (with €50 application fee), Original or certified/attested copies (plus official or certified/attested English translations, where necessary) of: a) Secondary (High) school Leaving Certificate and Grade Report/Mark Sheet, or equivalent qualification. b) Previous studies' Degree and Transcript and Evidence of English or Greek Language Proficiency.

Fees: Postgraduate Diploma: 6,300/year, Master's Degree: 5,600/year, Bachelor's Degree: 5,250/year, Higher Diploma: 4,450/year, Diploma: 3,850/year and Certificate: 2.100/year. Stand-alone foundation: 1,400/semester and Academic Foundation: 1,050/semester (Euro)

Main Language(s) of Instruction: English, Modern Greek

Accrediting Agency: Polish Ministry of Education (for franchised programs) and Cyprus Ministry of Education (for own programs)

Degrees and Diplomas: *Certificate*: **Hotel and Restaurant.** *Diploma*: **Administration; Cooking and Catering; Hotel and Restaurant.** *Higher Diploma*: **Hotel Management.** *Postgraduate Diploma*: **Administration; Computer Networks; Education; Human Resources; Management; Public Relations.** *Ptychio*: **Accountancy; Business Administration; Civil Engineering; Computer Science; Hotel and Restaurant; Information Technology; International Relations; Mass Communication; Music; Petroleum and Gas Engineering; Production Engineering.** *Magister Artium/Magister Scientae*: **Business Administration; Civil Engineering; Economics; International Relations; Mass Communication; Petroleum and Gas Engineering.**

Student Services: Academic Counselling, Careers Guidance, Cultural Activities, Foreign Studies Centre, IT Centre, Library, Residential Facilities, Social Counselling, Sports Facilities, eLibrary

Academic Staff *2014*	MEN	WOMEN	TOTAL
FULL-TIME	8	6	**14**
PART-TIME	1	4	**5**
STAFF WITH DOCTORATE			
FULL-TIME	2	–	**2**
Student Numbers *2014*			
All (Foreign included)	7	7	**14**
FOREIGN ONLY	3	1	**4**

Part-time students, 1.

Last Updated: 07/01/15

M.K.C.CITY COLLEGE

M.K.C. City College

P.O. Box 40830, 25 Arch. Makariou III Avenue, 6308 Larnaca
Tel: +357(24) 818571
Fax: +357(24) 818572
EMail: info@citycollege.ac.cy
Website: http://www.citycollege.ac.cy/

Course

Business Administration (Business Administration); **Computer Studies** (Computer Science); **Hotel Management** (Hotel Management); **Retail Management** (Management; Retailing and Wholesaling)

Fees: Bachelor: 3700 per annum (Euro)

Degrees and Diplomas: *Diploma*; *Ptychio*: **Business Administration.**

Student Services: Academic Counselling, Library, eLibrary

Last Updated: 28/01/15

NEAPOLIS UNIVERSITY PAPHOS (NUP)

2 Danais Avenue, 8042 Paphos
Tel: +357(26) 84-33-00
Fax: +357(26) 93-19-44
EMail: info@nup.ac.cy
Website: http://www.nup.ac.cy/

Rector: Elias Dinenis

Programme

Accountancy, Banking, and Finance (Accountancy; Banking; Finance); **Architecture and Environmental Design** *(Undergraduate)* (Architecture; Environmental Studies); **Business Administration** (Business Administration); **Construction Management** *(Postgraduate)* (Construction Engineering; Management); **Educational Psychology** (Educational Psychology); **Psychology** *(Postgraduate)* (Psychology); **Real Estate** (Real Estate); **Real Estate, Valuation and Development** *(Undergraduate)* (Real Estate)

History: Created 2007. Programmes commenced 2010-2011.

Fees: 6,400 per annum (US Dollar)

Main Language(s) of Instruction: English

Accrediting Agency: Ministry of Education and Culture

Degrees and Diplomas: *Ptychio*: **Architectural and Environmental Design; Business Administration; Economic and Finance Policy; Psychology; Real Estate.** *Magister Artium/Magister Scientae*: **Banking; Business Administration; Construction Engineering; Educational Psychology; Finance; Real Estate.**

Last Updated: 04/12/14

P.A. COLLEGE

P.O. Box 40763, 6307 Larnaca
Tel: +357(24) 62-49-75
Fax: +357(24) 62-88-60
EMail: prgmdean@pacollege.ac.cy; information@pacollege.ac.cy
Website: http://www.pacollege.ac.cy

Director: Andreas Z. Patsalides

Course
Business Administration (Business Administration); **Business Computing** (Business Computing)

History: Founded 1983.

Accrediting Agency: Ministry of Education and Culture.

Degrees and Diplomas: *Ptychio*: **Accountancy; Banking; Business Administration; Business Computing.**

Student Services: Library

Last Updated: 28/01/15

SUSINI COLLEGE

P.O. Box 51147, 10 Tagmatarchou Pouliou str, 3502 Limassol
Tel: +357(25) 36-61-96
Fax: +357(25) 36-97-02
EMail: susini@spidernet.com.cy
Website: http://www.susini.ac.cy/

Director-General: Kyriacos J. Poupoutsis

Director of Studies: Phanie Antoniadou-Poupoutsi

Programme
Aesthetics and Beauty Therapy

Further Information: Also campus in Nicosia

History: Founded 1982.

Accrediting Agency: Ministry of Education and Culture

Degrees and Diplomas: *Diploma*; *Ptychio*: **Cosmetology.**

Last Updated: 28/01/15

THE C.T.L EUROCOLLEGE

P.O. Box 51938, 3509 Limassol
Tel: +357(25) 73-65-01
Fax: +357(25) 73-66-29
EMail: college@ctleuro.ac.cy
Website: http://www.ctleuro.ac.cy

Executive Director: Andreas Papathomas

Programme
Accounting (Accountancy); **Business** (Business Administration; E-Business/Commerce); **Computing** (Computer Science; Information Technology); **Hospitality and Tourism** (Hotel Management; Tourism); **Law** (Law); **Office Administration** (Administration)

Further Information: Also a branch in Nicosia and in Hyderabad (India)

History: Created 1966 as CTL Academy. Acquired status and current name 1991.

Fees: Undergraduate Programmes: 143; Postgraduate Programmes: 194; MBA: 5500 (Euro)

Accrediting Agency: Ministry of Education and Culture

Degrees and Diplomas: *Ptychio*: **Accountancy; Business Administration; Computer Science; Hotel Management.** *Magister Artium/Magister Scientae*: **Business Administration.**

Student Services: Library

Last Updated: 23/01/15

THE CYPRUS INSTITUTE (CYI)

20 Konstantinou Kavafi St., 2121 Nicosia, Aglantzia
Tel: +357(22) 20-87-00
Fax: +357(22) 44-78-00
EMail: info@cyi.ac.cy
Website: http://www.cyi.ac.cy/

President: Costas N. Papanicolas

Programme
Computational Sciences (Computer Science; Mathematics and Computer Science); **Digital Cultural Heritage** (Cultural Studies); **Environment and Atmospheric Sciences** (Environmental Management; Environmental Studies)

Research Centre
Computation-based Science and Technology (Computer Science); **Science and Technology in Archaeology** (Archaeology)

History: Founded 2005. Programmes commenced 2010-2011. A research institute offering Doctoral programmes.

Main Language(s) of Instruction: Modern Greek

Accrediting Agency: Ministry of Education and Culture

Degrees and Diplomas: *Didactoriko*: **Computer Engineering; Environmental Studies; Heritage Preservation; Meteorology; Physics.**

Last Updated: 02/12/14

THE CYPRUS INSTITUTE OF MARKETING (CIM)

P.O. Box 25288, 1308 Nicosia
Tel: +357(22) 77-84-75
Fax: +357(22) 77-93-31
EMail: info@cima.ac.cy
Website: http://www.cima.ac.cy/

Director-General: Theophanis Hadjiyiannis (1978-) EMail: theo@cima.ac.cy

Deputy Director: Yangos Hadjiyannis EMail: yangos@cima.com.cy

International Relations: Christia Koursarou, International Relations Officer EMail: christia@cima.ac.cy

Programme
Banking (Banking); **Business Administration** (Accountancy; Administration; Finance; Human Resources; Insurance; International Business; Marketing); **European Studies** (European Studies); **Financial and Computers Studies** (Business Computing; Finance; Information Sciences); **Insurance** (Insurance); **Shipping** (Marine Transport; Maritime Law); **Tourism Management** (Tourism)

Further Information: Also Campuses in Limassol (1984 and British Virgin Islands

History: Founded 1978.

Academic Year: January to September; October to June

Admission Requirements: Secondary School Certificate.

Fees: 4290-7000 per annum depending on programs (Euro)

Main Language(s) of Instruction: English

Accrediting Agency: Ministry of Education and Culture

Degrees and Diplomas: *Ptychio*: **Banking; Business Administration; Computer Science; European Studies; Insurance; Management; Marine Transport.** *Magister Artium/Magister Scientae*: **Business Administration.** Also Postgraduate Diploma in Corporate Management and Strategic Planning.

Student Services: Academic Counselling, Canteen, Careers Guidance, Facilities for disabled people, Foreign Studies Centre, Health Services, Language Laboratory, Library, Social Counselling

Publications: The Global Market

Academic Staff *2012-2013*	**TOTAL**
FULL-TIME	**6**
PART-TIME	**43**
Student Numbers *2012-2013*	
All (Foreign included)	**230**

Last Updated: 02/12/14

THE LIMASSOL COLLEGE - T.L.C.

2-4 Pasikratous Stree, 3085 Limassol
Tel: +357(25) 381095
Fax: +357(25) 383360
EMail: info@thelimassolcollege.ac.cy
Website: http://www.thelimassolcollege.ac.cy

Course
Aesthetics and Cosmetology (Cosmetology); **Dietetics and Nutrition** (Dietetics; Nutrition)

Degrees and Diplomas: *Diploma*; *Ptychio*: **Cosmetology; Dietetics; Nutrition.**

Last Updated: 28/01/15

THE PHILIPS COLLEGE

P.O. Box 28008, Strovolos, 2090 Nicosia
Tel: +357(22) 441860
Fax: +357(22) 441863
EMail: info@philips.ac.cy; admissions@philips.ac.cy
Website: http://www.thephilipscollege.com/

President: Philippos Constantinou

International Relations: Constantina Shiakallis

Faculty

Economics and Management (Accountancy; Business Administration; Business and Commerce; Economics; Finance; Real Estate); **Informatics and Telecommunications** (Computer Engineering; Information Technology; Multimedia); **Languages and Communication** (European Languages; Journalism; Public Relations); **Law and Social Studies** (Education; Law; Nursing; Psychology)

History: Created 1978. Acquired status 2000.

Accrediting Agency: Accreditation Council of the Republic of Cyprus. Ministry of Education and Culture

Degrees and Diplomas: *Ptychio*: **Business Administration; Business and Commerce; European Languages; Information Technology; Journalism; Nursing; Public Relations.** *Magister Artium/Magister Scientae*: **Business Administration; Education; Finance; Management.**

Student Services: Library

Last Updated: 26/01/15

UNIVERSITY OF NICOSIA (UNIC)

PO Box 24005, 46 Makedonitissas Avenue, 1700 Nicosia
Tel: +357 22 841500
Fax: +357 22 357481
EMail: admissions@unic.ac.cy
Website: http://www.unic.ac.cy

Director of Admissions Department: Tasos Demetriou
Tel: +357 22841528 EMail: demetriou.t@unic.ac.cy

Rector: Michalis Attalides EMail: attalides.m@unic.ac.cy

Vice Rector: Philippos Pouyioutas
Tel: +357 99697330 EMail: pouyioutas.p@unic.ac.cy

Vice President for Enrollment and Development: Pavlos Pavlou
Tel: +357 22841734 EMail: pavlou.p@unic.ac.cy

School

Business (Accountancy; Administration; Advertising and Publicity; Agricultural Business; Agricultural Management; Business Administration; Business and Commerce; Business Computing; E- Business/ Commerce; Economics; Finance; Hotel and Restaurant; Hotel Management; Human Resources; Information Management; Institutional Administration; International Business; Leadership; Leisure Studies; Management; Management Systems; Marketing; Public Administration; Public Relations; Real Estate; Sports Management; Tourism); **Education** (Dance; Distance Education; Education; Education of the Handicapped; Educational Administration; Educational and Student Counselling; Educational Research; Educational Sciences; Educational Technology; Educational Testing and Evaluation; English; Humanities and Social Science Education; Jazz and Popular Music; Literature; Mathematics Education; Music; Music Education; Music Theory and Composition; Pedagogy; Preschool Education; Primary Education; Special Education; Teacher Trainers Education; Teacher Training; Vocational Education; Writing); **Humanities, Social Sciences and Law** (Architecture; Architecture and Planning; Arts and Humanities; Civil Law; Clinical Psychology; Communication Arts; Communication Studies; Comparative Politics; Criminology; English; European Studies; European Union Law; Fine Arts; Graphic Arts; Graphic Design; History of Law; International Law; International Relations; International Studies; Labour Law; Law; Linguistics; Literature; Marketing; Modern Languages; Multimedia; Political Sciences; Psychology; Public Administration; Public Law; Public Relations; Social and Community Services; Social Problems; Social Psychology; Social Sciences; Social Studies; Social Work; Speech Studies; Vocational Counselling); **Medical** (Biomedicine; Health Sciences; Medicine); **Sciences and Engineering** (Applied Mathematics; Artificial Intelligence; Biology; Civil Engineering; Computer Education; Computer Engineering; Computer Science; Dietetics; Electrical and Electronic Engineering; Electrical Engineering; Electronic Engineering; Engineering; Environmental Engineering; Environmental Management; Environmental Studies; Health Education; Limnology; Mathematics; Nursing; Orthopaedics; Petroleum and Gas Engineering; Pharmacy; Physical Education; Sports; Sports Management; Sports Medicine; Statistics)

Further Information: Also campuses in Limassol and Larnaca

History: University of Nicosia was founded in 1980 as Intercollege. In 2007, following changes in the relevant local legislation and a comprehensive accreditation; the University of Nicosia emerged. Through its five schools, the University offers a diverse range of academic programmes of study, at both the undergraduate and postgraduate levels (Bachelor, Master and PhD degrees). Intercollege remains an associate institution, complementing the University's study offerings through its vocational and shorter duration programmes, and through a variety of joint programmes in partnership with UK universities.

Admission Requirements: Undergraduate Admission: The general admission requirement for entry to an undergraduate programme of study is a High School Leaving Certificate or equivalent qualification. Post-Graduate Admission:The minimum requirement for admission into a post-graduate degree programme is a Bachelor's Degree. The University of Nicosia welcomes transfer students from other accredited colleges and universities and accepts courses which are of the same quality and equivalency as courses offered on its campus.

Main Language(s) of Instruction: English

Accrediting Agency: Ministry of Education and Culture, Evaluation Committee for Private Universities

Degrees and Diplomas: *Ptychio*: **Accountancy; Administration; Advertising and Publicity; Architecture; Art Education; Business Administration; Business and Commerce; Computer Graphics; Computer Science; Dance; Dietetics; Economics; Education; Educational Administration; Educational Sciences; Electrical and Electronic Engineering; Electrical Engineering; Engineering Management; English; Environmental Engineering; Finance; Fine Arts; Hotel Management; Human Resources; Information Technology; Interior Design; International Business; International Relations; Law; Literature; Management; Management Systems; Marketing; Mathematics; Mathematics and Computer Science; Media Studies; Multimedia; Music; Music Education; Nursing; Orthopaedics; Physical Therapy; Power Engineering; Preschool Education; Primary Education; Psychology; Public Administration; Public Relations; Real Estate; Science Education; Social Work; Software Engineering; Special Education; Sports; Sports Management; Statistics; Technology Education; Tourism.** *Magister Artium/Magister Scientae*: **Administration; Architecture; Biomedicine; Business Administration; Clinical Psychology; Communication Arts; Communication Studies; Computer Science; Criminology; Dance; Design; Economics; Education; Educational Administration; Educational Psychology; Educational Sciences; Engineering; Engineering Management; English; Foreign Languages Education; International Relations; Law; Literature; Management; Media Studies; Medicine; Music; Music Education; Orthopaedics; Psychology; Public Administration; Rehabilitation and Therapy; Social Studies; Social Work; Special Education; Sports.** *Didactoriko*: **Administration; Architecture; Business Administration; Clinical Psychology; Communication Arts; Computer Science; Criminology; Education; Educational Administration; Educational Sciences; Electrical and Electronic Engineering; Electrical Engineering; Engineering; Finance; Health Sciences; Human Resources; Law; Literature; Management; Marketing; Media Studies; Medicine; Psychology; Public Administration; Sports; Sports Management.** 6B: Ptychio - Bachelor Degree 7C: Magister Artium/Magister Scientae - Master Degree 7D: Didactoriko - Doctorate

Student Services: Academic Counselling, Canteen, Careers Guidance, Cultural Activities, Facilities for disabled people, Foreign Studies Centre, Health Services, IT Centre, Language Laboratory, Library, Nursery Care, Residential Facilities, Social Counselling, Sports Facilities, eLibrary

Publications: Euromed Journal of Business; The Cyprus Review

Publishing House: University of Nicosia Press

Academic Staff *2014*	MEN	WOMEN	**TOTAL**
FULL-TIME	29	44	**73**
PART-TIME	58	75	**133**
STAFF WITH DOCTORATE			
FULL-TIME	136	145	**281**
Student Numbers *2014*			
All (Foreign included)	2,864	4,401	**7,265**
FOREIGN ONLY	1,523	2,813	**4,336**

Part-time students, 2,967. **Distance students,** 2,678.

Last Updated: 15/12/14

Czech Republic

STRUCTURE OF HIGHER EDUCATION SYSTEM

Description:

Higher professional schools (vyšší odborná škola) provide ISCED 65 (655) level education. These are considered tertiary education institutions but not part of the higher education system. Higher professional schools offer namely practically oriented programmes in economics and health care. There are two types of higher education institutions: universities and non-university HEIs. However, there are not many differences between these two categories since both of them issue completely equal qualifications on ISCED 64 and 74 level but only universities are allowed to provide ISCED 8 level education (PhD) and set faculties as their organizational units. Despite a high number of private institutions, most students are enrolled at one of the public institutions. The Police Academy and the University of Defence have special statuses and are governed directly by the Ministry of the Interior and Ministry of Defence respectively.

Stages of studies:

University level first stage: *Bachelor studies*

The Bachelor study programme usually takes three to four years and covers all the main disciplines, except Medicine, Dentistry, Veterinary Medicine, Pharmacy, Law and some other fields. The programme aims at providing a qualification to both practice a profession and continue studying at the Master level. This cycle leads to the academic degree of "bakalář" (Bc.) or "bakalář umění" (BcA) in the field of Arts. Students must sit for a state final examination, part of which is usually the defence of a Bachelor thesis.

University level second stage: *Master studies (magisterské studium)*

The Master programme lasts for one to three years after the Bachelor. In Medicine, Dentistry, Veterinary Medicine, Pharmacy and Law, where there are no Bachelor studies, the Master programme lasts between 4 and 6 years (Medicine, Veterinary Medicine: 6 years; Dentistry, Law, Teacher Training for secondary schools: 5 years; Teacher Training for the first stage of basic school: 4 years). Graduates in the Humanities, Education and Social Sciences, Natural Sciences, Pharmacy, Theology and Law are awarded the academic degree of "magistr" (Mgr.), "magistr umění" (MgA.) in Arts, "inženýr" (Ing.) in Engineering, Economics, Agriculture and Chemistry and Military fields, "inženýr architekt" (Ing.arch.) in Architecture, "doktor medicíny" (MUDr.) in Medicine, "doktor zubního lékařství" (MDDr.) in Dentistry, "doktor veterinární medicíny" (MVDr.) in Veterinary Medicine. At the end of this stage, students must sit for a final State examination, part of which is composed of the defence of a diploma thesis. In Medicine, Dentistry and Veterinary Medicine, they must sit for the "státní rigorózní zkouška (State Rigorosum examination). The holders of the degree of "magistr" can sit for a State Rigorosum examination in the same field and defend a thesis to acquire the academic degree of "doktor práv" (JUDr.) in Law, "doktor filosofie" (PhDr.) in the Humanities, Education and Social Sciences, "doktor přírodních věd" (RNDr.) in Natural Sciences, "doktor farmacie" (PharmDr.) in Pharmacy, "doktor teologie" (ThDr.) or "licenciát teologie" (ThLic.) in Theology. The abbreviations of all the academic degrees mentioned above are written in front of the name.

University level third stage: *Doctoral studies (doktorské studium)*

The third and highest level of higher education consists of studies for the Doctorate under the guidance of a tutor. The programme comprises scientific research and independent study. It usually lasts between three and four years. Holders of a Master's Degree (Mgr., MgA., Ing., Ing.arch., MUDr., MDDr., MVDr.) may apply. Studies lead to the academic degree of "doktor" (Ph.D.) or "doktor teologie" (Th.D.) in the field of Theology. The abbreviations are written after the name. Studies end with the State Doctoral examination and the defence of a dissertation.

ADMISSION TO HIGHER EDUCATION

Admission to university-level studies:

Name of secondary school credential required: Maturitní zkouška

For entry to: all higher education institutions

Other requirements: Further admission criteria (besides the high school leaving exam) are subject to the autonomy of individual education institutions.

Foreign students admission:

Definition of foreign student: A foreign student is a person enrolled at a Czech higher education institution and who is not a permanent resident of the Czech Republic.

Quotas: None

Admission requirements: The Secondary School Leaving Certificate must be validated by the Regional School Authorities (školská oddělení krajských úřadů).

Health requirements: A health certificate might be required.

Language proficiency: Foreign students who want to study in the Czech language and who do not have sufficient command of it can enroll in a one-year course. Information is available at http://ujop.cuni.cz/. A significant proportion of programmes are offered in foreign languages (namely English) in which case language proficiency requirements are set by individual institutions.

RECOGNITION OF STUDIES

Quality assurance system:

The study programmes of all higher education institutions are subject to accreditation. Accreditation is conferred by the Ministry of Education, Youth and Sports which decides on the basis of the Accreditation Commission statement.

Bodies dealing with recognition:

Středisko pro ekvivalenci dokladů o vzdělání ENIC/NARIC (Centre for Equivalence of Documents on Education - Czech ENIC/NARIC)

Head:Lucie Trojanová
Ministerstvo školství, mládeže a tělovýchovy
Karmelitská 7
Praha 1 118 12
Tel: +420(2) 3481-2152
Fax: +420(2) 3481-1727
EMail: enic-naric@msmt.cz
WWW: http://www.msmt.cz/vzdelavani/vysoke-skolstvi/strediska-enic-naric

Special provisions for recognition:

Recognition for university level studies: Recognition of higher education diplomas obtained abroad is the responsibility of public higher education institutions with similar or equal study programmes. In special cases, recognition is provided by the Ministry of Education, Youth and Sports.

For access to advanced studies and research: Recognition of higher education diplomas obtained abroad is the responsibility of public higher education institutions with similar or equal study programmes. In special cases, recognition is provided by the Ministry of Education, Youth and Sports.

For exercising a profession: Recognition of higher education diplomas obtained abroad is the responsibility of public higher education institutions with similar or equal study programmes. In special cases, recognition is provided by the Ministry of Education, Youth and Sports. The recognition of regulated professions is provided by the competent recognition authority (http://www.msmt.cz/international-cooperation-1/recognition-of-qualifications-and-education).

NATIONAL BODIES

Ministerstvo školství, mládeže a tělovýchovy (Ministry of Education, Youth and Sports)

Minister: Kateřina Valachová
Deputy Minister, Research and Higher Education: Robert Plaga
Karmelitská 7
Praha 1 118 12
Tel: +420(2) 3481-1111
Fax: +420(2) 3481-1753
EMail: info@msmt.cz
WWW: http://www.msmt.cz

Role of national body: Responsible for public administration in education, for developing educational, youth and sport policies and international cooperation in these fields.

Akreditační komise Česka Republika (Accreditation Commission of the Czech Republic)

Secretary-General: Vladimíra Dvořáková
Ministerstvo školství, mládeže a tělovýchovy
Karmelitská 7
Praha 1 118 12
EMail: akreditacnikomise@msmt.cz
WWW: http://www.akreditacnikomise.cz/

Centrum pro studium vysokého školství (Centre for Higher Education Studies)

Director: Helena Šebková
U Dvou srpu 2024/2
Praha 5 150 00
Tel: +420(2) 5701-1311
Fax: +420(2) 5753-2409
EMail: csvs@csvs.cz
WWW: http://www.csvs.cz

Česká konference rektorů (Czech Rectors' Conference)

President: Tomáš Zima
Secretary-General: Marie Fojtíková
Masarykova univerzita
Žerotínovo nám. 9
Brno 601 77
Tel: +420(54) 949-1121
Fax: +420(54) 949-1122
EMail: crc@muni.cz
WWW: http://crc.muni.cz
Role of national body: Represents the universities in their dealings with the Ministry.

Rada vysokých škol (Council of Higher Education Institutions)

President: Jakub Fischer
José Martího 31
Praha 6 - Veleslavín 162 52
Tel: +420(2) 2056-0221
Fax: +420(2) 2056-0221
EMail: arvs@ftvs.cuni.cz
WWW: http://www.radavs.cz

Data for academic year: 2014-2015

Source: Data provided by the Ministry of Education, Youth and Sports, Czech Republic, 2014. Bodies 2016.

INSTITUTIONS

PUBLIC INSTITUTIONS

ACADEMY OF ARTS, ARCHITECTURE AND DESIGN IN PRAGUE

Vysoká škola umělecko-průmyslová v Praze (VŠUP)
Náměstí Jana Palacha 80, 116 93 Praha 1
Tel: +420 251 098 111
Fax: +420 251 098 289
EMail: pr@vsup.cz
Website: http://www.vsup.cz

Rektor: Jindřich Smetana
Tel: +420 251 098 274 EMail: zippeova@vsup.cz

Secretariate of Vice-presidents and Bursar: Jana Dobřichovská
EMail: dobrichovska@vsup.cz

Department
Applied Arts (Ceramic Art; Fashion Design; Glass Art; Graphic Arts; Textile Design); **Architecture** (Architecture); **Design** (Design; Furniture Design; Industrial Design; Interior Design); **Fine Arts** (Fine Arts; Painting and Drawing; Photography; Sculpture); **Graphic Arts** (Cinema and Television; Design; Film; Graphic Arts; Multimedia; Video); **Theory and History of Art** (Art History)

Further Information: Branch in Zlín

History: Founded 1885 as School of Decorative Arts. Acquired present title 2005.

Academic Year: October to June (October-January; February-June)

Admission Requirements: Secondary school certificate (Maturita) and artistic entrance examination

Fees: None

Main Language(s) of Instruction: Czech

Accrediting Agency: Ministry of Education, Youth and Sports

Degrees and Diplomas: *Bakalář*; *Magistr*: **Design; Fine Arts; Visual Arts.** *Doktor*: **Art History; Fine Arts.** Also Postgraduate studies, a further 3 yrs

Student Services: Academic Counselling, Library, Residential Facilities

Last Updated: 03/02/15

ACADEMY OF FINE ARTS IN PRAGUE

Akademie výtvarných umění v Praze (AVU)
U Akademie 4, 170 22 Praha 7
Tel: +420 220 408 200
Fax: +420 233 381 662
EMail: a.kratka@avu.cz
Website: http://www.avu.cz

Rector: Jiří T. Kotalík Tel: +420 220 408 211

International Relations: Diana David, International Department and LLP Erasmus co-ordinator
Tel: +420 220 408 214 EMail: avuinternational@avu.cz

School

Fine Arts (Architecture; Fine Arts; Media Studies; Painting and Drawing; Printing and Printmaking; Restoration of Works of Art; Sculpture)

History: Founded 1799, nationalized 1896, and reorganized 1990 as a postgraduate State institution.

Academic Year: October to June (October-February; February-June)

Admission Requirements: Entrance examination

Main Language(s) of Instruction: Czech

Degrees and Diplomas: *Magistr umění*: **Fine Arts.** *Doktor*: **Architectural Restoration; Architecture; Fine Arts.**

Student Services: Canteen, Language Laboratory, Library, Sports Facilities

Last Updated: 28/01/15

ACADEMY OF PERFORMING ARTS IN PRAGUE

Akademie múzických umění v Praze (AMU)
Nám. Malostranské 12, 118 00 Praha 1
Tel: +420 257 534 205
Fax: +420 234 244 515
EMail: info@amu.cz
Website: http://www.amu.cz

Rektor: Jan Hančil
Tel: +420 234 244 501 EMail: jan.hancil@amu.cz

Vice-Rector for Studies and Art: Noemi Zárubová-Pfeffermannová
Tel: +420 234 244 505 EMail: noemi.zarubova@hamu.cz

International Relations: Daniela Jobertová, Vice-Rector for international activities
Tel: +420 234 244 506 EMail: daniela.jobertova@damu.cz

Faculty

Film and Television *(FAMU)* (Cinema and Television; Film; Photography); **Music and Dance** *(HAMU)* (Dance; Music; Music Theory and Composition); **Theatre** *(DAMU)* (Theatre)

History: Founded 1945, acquired present status 1946.

Academic Year: October to September

Admission Requirements: Secondary school certificate (Maturitní vysvědčeni) and entrance examination

Main Language(s) of Instruction: Czech

Degrees and Diplomas: *Bakalář umění*; *Magistr umění*; *Doktor*

Student Services: Academic Counselling, Canteen, Health Services, IT Centre, Language Laboratory, Library, Sports Facilities

Last Updated: 28/01/15

BRNO UNIVERSITY OF TECHNOLOGY

Vysoké učení technické v Brně (VUT V BRNĚ)
Antonínská 548/1, 601 90 Brno
Tel: +420 541 141 111
Fax: +420 541 211 309
EMail: international@vutbr.cz
Website: http://www.vutbr.cz

Rector: Petr Štěpánek (2014-)
Tel: +420 541 145 201 EMail: rektor@ro.vutbr.cz

Kvestor: Ladislav Janíček
Tel: +420 541 145 555 EMail: kvestor@ro.vutbr.cz

International Relations: Marcela Karmazínová, Prorektor
Tel: +420 54114 5218 EMail: vicerector-international@ro.vutbr.cz

Faculty

Architecture (Architecture; Town Planning); **Business and Management** (Business and Commerce; Computer Science; Economics; Finance; Management); **Chemistry** (Biotechnology; Chemical Engineering; Chemistry; Consumer Studies; Environmental Studies; Food Science); **Civil Engineering** (Architecture; Building Technologies; Chemistry; Civil Engineering; Computer Engineering; Computer Science; Construction Engineering; Geophysics; Landscape Architecture; Mathematics; Mechanical Engineering; Metal Techniques; Physics; Railway Engineering; Road Engineering; Social Sciences; Structural Architecture; Water Management; Water Science; Wood Technology); **Electrical Engineering and Communication** (Automation and Control Engineering; Biomedical Engineering; Electrical and Electronic Engineering; Electrical Engineering; English; German; Mathematics; Microelectronics; Modern Languages; Physics; Power Engineering; Russian; Spanish; Telecommunications Engineering); **Fine Arts** (Design; Environmental Studies; Fashion Design; Fine Arts; Graphic Arts; Graphic Design; Media Studies; Multimedia; Painting and Drawing; Performing Arts; Publishing and Book Trade; Sculpture; Video); **Information Technology** (Applied Mathematics; Artificial Intelligence; Computer Engineering; Computer Graphics; Information Technology; Multimedia); **Mechanical Engineering** (Aeronautical and Aerospace Engineering; Automation and Control Engineering; Automotive Engineering; Computer Science; Electronic Engineering; Energy Engineering; Engineering Management; Environmental Engineering; Heating and Refrigeration; Industrial Design; Materials Engineering; Mathematics; Modern Languages; Physical Engineering; Production Engineering; Robotics; Solid State Physics)

Institute

Forensic Engineering (Forensic Medicine and Dentistry); **Technology** *(Central European)* (Nanotechnology)

Further Information: Also Branch in Zlín

History: Founded 1849 as Technical School in Brno, a bilingual German-Czech institute. Reorganized 1899 as Czech Technical University of Franz Joseph in Brno. Became the Czech Technical University of Brno 1918 and Technical University of Dr. E. Beneš in Brno 1937. Closed during the German occupation, reopened 1945, and acquired present title 1956. An institution financed by the State. Also derives income from research undertaken for industry.

Academic Year: September to August

Admission Requirements: Secondary school certificate (Maturitní vysvědčeni) and entrance examination

Fees: None for studies taught in Czech

Main Language(s) of Instruction: English, Czech

Degrees and Diplomas: *Bakalář*; *Magistr*: **Nanotechnology.** *Doktor*: **Architecture; Biomedical Engineering; Chemistry; Civil Engineering; Economics; Electrical Engineering; Finance; Fine Arts; Forensic Medicine and Dentistry; Information Technology; Management; Mechanical Engineering; Nanotechnology.**

Student Services: Academic Counselling, Canteen, Health Services, Language Laboratory, Library, Sports Facilities

Publications: Události na VUT v Brně

Publishing House: Publishing Centre of TU Brno

Last Updated: 02/02/15

IAU CHARLES UNIVERSITY IN PRAGUE

Univerzita Karlova v Praze (UK)
Ovocny trh 3/5, 116 36 Praha 1
Tel: +420 224 491-301
Fax: +420 224 229-487
EMail: sekretariat@ruk.cuni.cz; oas@ruk.cuni.cz; zahran@ruk.cuni.cz
Website: http://www.cuni.cz

Rector: Tomas Zima Tel: +420 224 491 312 EMail: rektor@cuni.cz

International Relations: Jan Skrha, Vice-Rector for International Affairs Tel: +420 224 491 650 EMail: zahran@prorektor.cuni.cz

Faculty

Catholic Theological Faculty *(http://www.ktf.cuni.cz/KTFENG-1.html)* (Bible; Catholic Theology; Ethics; History of Religion; Pastoral Studies; Philosophy; Religion; Religious Art); **Faculty of Arts** *(http://www.ff.cuni.cz/home/)* (Adult Education; Aesthetics; African Studies; Albanian; Ancient Civilizations; Arabic; Archaeology; Archiving; Art History; Arts and Humanities; Asian Studies; Bulgarian; Central European Studies; Chinese; Cinema and Television; Communication Studies; Cultural Studies; Czech; Danish; Dutch; East Asian Studies; Eastern European Studies; Economic History; Education; English; English Studies; Ethnology; European Studies; Finnish; Foreign Languages Education; French Studies; Gender Studies; German; Germanic Languages; Germanic Studies; Greek; Greek (Classical); Hebrew; Hispanic American Studies; History; Hungarian; Information Sciences; Islamic Studies; Italian; Japanese; Korean; Latin; Latin American Studies; Library Science; Linguistics; Literature; Logic; Media Studies; Medieval Studies; Middle Eastern Studies; Modern History; Modern Languages; Mongolian; Musicology; Native Language; Native Language Education; Oriental Studies; Philology; Philosophy; Phonetics; Physical Education; Political Sciences; Portuguese; Prehistory; Psychology; Religious Studies; Romance Languages; Romanian; Russian; Scandinavian Languages; Secondary Education; Serbocroatian; Slavic Languages; Social Psychology; Social Sciences; Social Work; Sociology; South Asian Studies; Spanish; Theatre; Tibetan; Translation and Interpretation; Turkish; Vietnamese; Visual Arts); **Faculty of Education** *(http://www.pedf.cuni.cz/?lang=en)* (Art Education; Computer Education; Continuing Education; Education; Education of the Handicapped; Education of the Socially Disadvantaged; Educational Administration; Educational Psychology; Educational Research; Educational Sciences; Foreign Languages Education; Humanities and Social Science Education; Mathematics Education; Music Education; Native Language Education; Pedagogy; Philosophy of Education; Physical Education; Preschool Education; Primary Education; Psychology; Science Education; Secondary Education; Social Sciences; Special Education; Staff Development; Teacher Training; Technology Education); **Faculty of Humanities** *(http://fhs.cuni.cz/FHSENG-1.html)* (Anthropology; Arts and Humanities; Cultural Studies; Environmental Studies; Ethics; Ethnology; Gender Studies; History; Media Studies; Philosophy; Social Sciences; Social Work; Sociology; Welfare and Protective Services); **Faculty of Law** *(http://www.prf.cuni.cz/en/)* (Administrative Law; Civil Law; Commercial Law; Constitutional Law; Criminal Law; European Union Law; History of Law; Human Rights; International Law; Labour Law; Law; Private Law; Public Law); **Faculty of Mathematics and Physics** *(http://www.mff.cuni.cz/to.en/)* (Actuarial Science; Applied Mathematics; Applied Physics; Artificial Intelligence; Astronomy and Space Science; Astrophysics; Atomic and Molecular Physics; Biophysics; Computer Education; Computer Graphics; Computer Networks; Computer Science; Geophysics; Mathematical Physics; Mathematics; Mathematics and Computer Science; Mathematics Education; Meteorology; Natural Sciences; Nuclear Physics; Optics; Physics; Secondary Education; Statistics); **Faculty of Medicine in Hradec Kralove** *(https://www.lfhk.cuni.cz/default.aspx/?lang=en-GB)* (Anaesthesiology; Anatomy; Biochemistry; Biology; Biophysics; Cardiology; Dentistry; Dermatology; Embryology and Reproduction Biology; Epidemiology; Forensic Medicine and Dentistry; Genetics; Gerontology; Gynaecology and Obstetrics; Health Sciences; Histology; Hygiene; Immunology; Medicine; Microbiology; Neurology; Occupational Health; Oncology; Ophthalmology; Orthopaedics; Otorhinolaryngology; Paediatrics; Pathology; Pharmacology; Physiology; Pneumology; Psychiatry and Mental Health; Radiology; Social and Preventive Medicine; Surgery; Urology; Venereology); **Faculty of Medicine in Plzen** *(http://www.lfp.cuni.cz/?lang=en)* (Anaesthesiology; Anatomy; Applied Chemistry; Biochemistry; Biology; Biophysics; Dentistry; Dermatology; Embryology and Reproduction Biology; Epidemiology; Forensic Medicine and Dentistry; Genetics; Gynaecology and Obstetrics; Haematology; Health Sciences; Histology; Hygiene; Immunology; Medicine; Microbiology; Neurology; Neurosciences; Occupational Health; Oncology; Ophthalmology; Orthopaedics; Otorhinolaryngology; Paediatrics; Pathology; Pharmacology; Physiology; Psychiatry and Mental Health; Public Health; Radiology; Respiratory Therapy; Social and Preventive Medicine; Surgery; Toxicology; Urology; Venereology); **Faculty of Pharmacy in Hradec Kralove** *(http://www.faf.cuni.cz/en/)* (Analytical Chemistry; Biochemistry; Inorganic Chemistry; Natural Sciences; Organic Chemistry; Pharmacology; Pharmacy; Physical Chemistry; Toxicology); **Faculty of Physical Education and Sport** *(http://www.ftvs.cuni.cz/eng/)* (Biomedicine; Education; Leisure Studies; Physical Education; Physical Therapy; Public Health; Rehabilitation and Therapy; Social Sciences; Sports; Sports Management; Sports Medicine; Welfare and Protective Services); **Faculty of Science** *(https://www.natur.cuni.cz/eng)* (Analytical Chemistry; Anatomy; Anthropology; Biochemistry; Biological and Life Sciences; Biology; Botany; Cell Biology; Chemistry; Demography and Population; Earth Sciences; Ecology; Epidemiology; Genetics; Geography; Geography (Human); Geology; Immunology; Inorganic Chemistry; Microbiology; Molecular Biology; Natural Resources; Natural Sciences; Organic Chemistry; Parasitology; Physical Chemistry; Physiology; Secondary Education; Social Sciences; Teacher Training; Toxicology; Zoology); **Faculty of Social Sciences** *(http://fsveng.fsv.cuni.cz/)* (American Studies; Arts and Humanities; Central European Studies; Contemporary History; Eastern European Studies; Econometrics; Economic and Finance Policy; Economic History; Economics; European Studies; Germanic Studies; International Economics; International Relations; International Studies; Journalism; Media Studies; Political Sciences; Social Policy; Social Problems; Social Sciences; Sociology; Western European Studies); **First Faculty of Medicine** *(http://www.lf1.cuni.cz/en)* (Anaesthesiology; Anatomy; Biochemistry; Biology; Biomedical Engineering; Biophysics; Cardiology; Cell Biology; Dentistry; Dermatology; Embryology and Reproduction Biology; Endocrinology; Epidemiology; Forensic Medicine and Dentistry; Gastroenterology; Genetics; Gerontology; Gynaecology and Obstetrics; Haematology; Health Sciences; Hepatology; Histology; Hygiene; Immunology; Medical Parasitology; Medicine; Microbiology; Nephrology; Neurology; Nursing; Occupational Health; Occupational Therapy; Oncology; Ophthalmology; Orthopaedics; Otorhinolaryngology; Paediatrics; Pathology; Pharmacology; Physical Therapy; Physiology; Plastic Surgery; Pneumology; Psychiatry and Mental Health; Public Health; Radiology; Rehabilitation and Therapy; Rheumatology; Social and Preventive Medicine; Speech Therapy and Audiology; Sports Medicine; Stomatology; Surgery; Toxicology; Urology; Venereology); **Hussite Theological Faculty** *(http://www.htf.cuni.cz/HTFN-1.html)* (Bible; Ethics; History of Religion; Humanities and Social Science Education; Judaic Religious Studies; Orthodox Theology; Philosophy; Protestant Theology; Religion; Religious Studies; Secondary Education; Social Work; Theology); **Protestant Theological Faculty** *(http://web.etf.cuni.cz/ETFENG-1.html)* (Bible; Comparative Religion; Ethics; History of Religion; New Testament; Philosophy; Protestant Theology; Religion; Social Work; Theology); **Second Faculty of Medicine** *(http://www.lf2.cuni.cz/en)* (Anaesthesiology; Anatomy; Applied Chemistry; Biochemistry; Biology; Biomedical Engineering; Cardiology; Cell Biology; Dermatology; Embryology and Reproduction Biology; Endocrinology; Epidemiology; Genetics; Gerontology; Gynaecology and Obstetrics; Haematology; Health Sciences; Histology; Immunology; Medicine; Microbiology; Neurology; Neurosciences; Nursing; Oncology; Ophthalmology; Orthopaedics; Otorhinolaryngology; Paediatrics; Pathology; Pharmacology; Physical Therapy; Physiology; Pneumology; Psychiatry and Mental Health; Public Health; Radiology; Rehabilitation and Therapy; Social and Preventive Medicine; Stomatology; Surgery; Toxicology; Urology; Venereology); **Third Faculty of Medicine** *(http://www.lf3.cuni.cz/en/index.html)* (Anaesthesiology; Anatomy; Applied Chemistry; Biochemistry; Biology; Biomedicine; Biophysics; Cardiology; Cell Biology; Dental Hygiene; Embryology and Reproduction Biology; Epidemiology; Forensic Medicine and Dentistry; Genetics; Gynaecology and Obstetrics; Haematology; Health Sciences; Histology; Hygiene; Immunology; Medicine; Microbiology; Molecular Biology; Neurology; Nursing; Occupational Health; Oncology; Orthopaedics; Otorhinolaryngology; Pathology; Pharmacology; Physical Therapy; Physiology; Plastic Surgery; Pneumology; Psychiatry and Mental Health; Public Health; Radiology; Social and Preventive Medicine; Sports Medicine; Surgery; Toxicology; Urology)

Institute

Computer Science Centre *(http://uvt.cuni.cz/UVTENG-1.html)* (Computer Science; Mathematics and Computer Science); **History of Charles University and Archive of Charles University** *(http://www.udauk.cuni.cz/ARCHIVENG-1.html)* (Archiving; Arts and Humanities; History); **Language and Preparatory Studies**

(http://ujop.cuni.cz/en/) (Arts and Humanities; English; German; Modern Languages; Russian; Spanish)

Centre

Center for Economic Research and Graduate Education *(https://www.cerge-ei.cz/)* (Economics; Social Sciences); **Center for Theoretical Study** *(CTS performstheoretical research in diverse fields, ranging from the humanities through various social science disciplines to the exact sciences. CTS stimulates transdisciplinary approaches to science.)* (Arts and Humanities; Natural Sciences; Social Sciences); **Environment Center** *(http://www.czp.cuni.cz/czp/index.php/en/)* (Ecology; Environmental Management; Environmental Studies; Welfare and Protective Services)

Further Information: Campus of Charles University is located in three cities of the Czech Republic: Prague, Hradec Kralove, Plzen

History: Founded 1348 by King Charles IV. Became a State institution 1773 when the Society of Jesus was dissolved. Divided in 1882 into separate Czech and German universities each bearing the title Charles-Ferdinand. Present title adopted 1918. Closed in November 1939 during the German occupation; reopened 1945 at which time the German university was abolished. Acquired present status 1999.

Academic Year: October to September (July – August = summer vacations). Winter Semester = October – mid-February. Summer Semester = Mid-February – September (July – August = summer vacations). For more information see: http://www.cuni.cz/UKEN-26.html.

Admission Requirements: Secondary school certificate (Maturitní vysvědčeni) and entrance examination

Fees: National: 0 € (In the Czech Republic it is not nationality that is decisive for tuition fees but the language of instruction, i.e. there are no tuition fees for foreign/international students who study in the Czech language (except when they exceed the standard duration of the degree programme plus one year, but the same holds for "domestic" students). All students pay modest admission fees (Euro), International: From 1800 to 13600 € (depending on study programme and EU or non-EU citizenship) (Euro)

Main Language(s) of Instruction: Czech, English, German, French

Accrediting Agency: Programme accreditation (not institutional accreditation, since it does not exist in the Czech Republic) provided by the Accreditation Commission of the Czech Republic.

Degrees and Diplomas: *Bakalář*: **Actuarial Science; Anthropology; Art History; Arts and Humanities; Biological and Life Sciences; Chemistry; Classical Languages; Computer Science; Cultural Studies; Demography and Population; Earth Sciences; Economics; Education; Educational Sciences; Environmental Studies; Fine Arts; Gender Studies; Geography (Human); Health Sciences; History; History of Religion; Holy Writings; Information Sciences; International Studies; Library Science; Linguistics; Literature; Mass Communication; Mathematics; Mathematics and Computer Science; Midwifery; Modern Languages; Natural Sciences; Nursing; Pastoral Studies; Philosophy; Physics; Political Sciences; Psychology; Public Health; Rehabilitation and Therapy; Religion; Religious Studies; Social Sciences; Social Work; Sociology; Special Education; Sports; Teacher Training; Theology; Translation and Interpretation; Visual Arts; Welfare and Protective Services.** *Doktor medicíny*: **Medicine.** *Doktor zubního lékařství*: **Dentistry.** *Magistr*: **Actuarial Science; Anthropology; Archaeology; Art History; Arts and Humanities; Astronomy and Space Science; Biological and Life Sciences; Chemistry; Classical Languages; Computer Science; Cultural Studies; Demography and Population; Earth Sciences; Economics; Education; Educational Sciences; Environmental Studies; Fine Arts; Gender Studies; Geography (Human); Health Sciences; History; History of Religion; Holy Writings; Information Sciences; International Studies; Law; Library Science; Linguistics; Literature; Mass Communication; Mathematics; Mathematics and Computer Science; Midwifery; Modern Languages; Natural Sciences; Nursing; Pastoral Studies; Philosophy; Physics; Political Sciences; Psychology; Public Health; Rehabilitation and Therapy; Religion; Religious Studies; Social Sciences; Social Work; Sociology; Special Education; Sports; Statistics; Teacher Training; Theology; Translation and Interpretation; Visual Arts; Welfare and Protective Services.** *Doktor*: **Actuarial Science; Anthropology; Archaeology; Art History; Arts and Humanities; Astronomy and Space Science; Biological and Life Sciences; Biomedicine; Chemistry; Computer Science; Criminal Law; Cultural Studies; Demography and Population; Dentistry; Earth Sciences; Economics; Education; Educational Sciences; Environmental Studies; European Union Law; Fine Arts; Health Sciences; History; History of Law; History of Religion; Holy Writings; Human Rights; Information Sciences; International Law; International Studies; Labour Law; Law; Library Science; Linguistics; Literature; Mass Communication; Mathematics; Mathematics and Computer Science; Medicine; Meteorology; Modern Languages; Music; Natural Sciences; Optometry; Pastoral Studies; Pharmacy; Philosophy; Physics; Political Sciences; Private Law; Psychology; Public Health; Public Law; Religion; Religious Studies; Social Sciences; Sociology; Special Education; Sports; Statistics; Surgery; Theology; Translation and Interpretation; Treatment Techniques; Visual Arts; Welfare and Protective Services.** Holders of the academic degree of "Magistr" are entitled to take an advanced Master's ("rigorózní") state examination in the same area of study and defend an advanced Master's ("rigorózní") thesis. They are awarded the following academic degrees: a) "Doktor práv" ("Doctor of Law", abbreviated as "JUDr.", used in front of the name) in the field of law; b) "Doktor filozofie" ("Doctor of Philosophy", abbreviated as "PhDr.", used in front of the name) in the area of the humanities, teacher education and the social sciences; c) "Doktor přírodních věd" ("Doctor of Natural Sciences", abbreviated as "RNDr.", used in front of the name) in the area of the natural sciences; d) "Doktor farmacie" ("Doctor of Pharmacy", abbreviated as "PharmDr.", used in front of the name) in the field of pharmacy; e) "Licenciát teologie" ("Licentiate of Theology", abbreviated as "ThLic.", used in front of the name) or "Doktor theologie" ("Doctor of Theology", abbreviated as "ThDr.", used in front of the name) in the field of theology; for the field of Catholic theology "Licenciát teologie". It is the same degree level as "Doktor medicíny" ("Doctor of Medicine", abbreviated as "MUDr.", used in front of the name - see above) and "Zubní lékař" ("Doctor of Dental Medicine", abbreviated as "MDDr." used in front of the name-see above). Both these studies are directly finished by the advanced Master's ("rigorózní") state examination. All these degrees are Master level (i.e. level 7 of the ISCED 2011). Sometimes they are called "small doctorate" - please do not confuse with "doctor" at the level of 8 of ISCED 2011 Source of information: Act No. 111/1998 on Higher Education Institutions including amendments to some other acts (the Higher Education Act)

Student Services: Academic Counselling, Canteen, Careers Guidance, Cultural Activities, Facilities for disabled people, Foreign Studies Centre, Health Services, IT Centre, Language Laboratory, Library, Nursery Care, Residential Facilities, Social Counselling, Sports Facilities, eLibrary

Publications: Acta medica (Hradec Kralove); Acta politologica; Acta Universitatis Carolinae theologica; Acta Universitatis Carolinae. Geographica; Acta Universitatis Carolinae. Historia Universitatis Carolinae Pragensis; Acta Universitatis Carolinae. Iuridica; Acta Universitatis Carolinae. Kinanthropologica; Acta Universitatis Carolinae. Mathematica et physica; Acta Universitatis Carolinae. Oeconomica. Czech Economic Review; Acta Universitatis Carolinae. Philologica; Acta Universitatis Carolinae. Philologica. Monografia; Acta Universitatis Carolinae. Studia philosophica Europeanea. Interpretationes; Acta Universitatis Carolinae. Studia territorialia; Acta Universitatis Carolinae. Studia territorialia. Supplementum; Aktuality v prevenci detskych urazu; Ceska kinantropologie: casopis Vedecke spolecnosti kinantropologie; Clovek: casopis pro humanitni vedy; Commentationes Mathematicae Universitatis Carolinae; Communio viatorum: a theological journal; Cornova: revue Ceske spolecnosti pro vyzkum 18. stoleti a FF UK; Dejiny-teorie-kritika = History-Theory-Criticism; Didakticke studie; Dvacate stoleti = the twentieth century; Envigogika; Estetika: casopis pro estetiku a teorii umeni; European Journal of Environmental Sciences; Finance a uver = Czech journal of economics and finance.; Folia Biologica; Forum; Forum socialni prace; Forum socialni prace; HOP: Historie - Otazky - Problemy; Hudebni vychova: casopis pro hudebni a obecne estetickou vychovu skolni a mimoskolni; Ibero-Americana Pragensia. Supplementum; iForum; Komunikace, media, spolecnost = Studia Nuntios Communicandi; Lide mesta: revue pro etnologii, antropologii a etnologii komunikace; Litteraria Pragensia: Studies in Literature and Culture; Marginalia historica: casopis pro dejiny vzdelanosti a kultury; Medialni studia: odborny casopis pro kritickou reflexi medii; Orbis scholae; Paideia;

Pandanus; Pedagogika; Plzensky lekarsky sbornik = Plzen medical report; Plzensky lekarsky sbornik. Supplementum; Prager wirtschafts- und sozialhistoriche Mitteilungen = Prague economic and social history papers; Prague Medical Report; Prague papers on the history of international relations; Pravnehistoricke studie; Prazske egyptologicke studie (PES); Psychologie pro praxi; Scientia in educatione; Slovo a smysl: casopis pro mezioborova bohemisticka studia; Specialni pedagogika; Studia ethnologica Pragensia; Studia Hercynia; Studia mediaevalia Pragensia; Studia praehistorica; Studie a texty Evangelicke teologicke fakulty; Studie z aplikovane lingvistiky = Studies in applied linguistics; Telesna vychova a sport mladeze: odborny casopis pro ucitele, trenery a cvicitele; Teologicka reflexe: casopis pro teologii; The Annual of Language and Politics and Politics of Identity; The Central European Journal of Public Policy; The Prague Bulletin of Mathematical Linguistics; Vlak: contemporary poetics and the arts; Vytvarna vychova: casopis pro vytvarnou a obecne estetickou vychovu skolni a mimoskolni

Publishing House: Carolinum (The Charles University Press)

Academic Staff *2013*	MEN	WOMEN	**TOTAL**
FULL-TIME	–	–	**3,100**
PART-TIME	–	–	**4,200**
Student Numbers *2014*			
All (Foreign included)	19,603	31,234	**50,837**
FOREIGN ONLY	3,301	4,489	**7,790**

Part-time students, 9,885.

Last Updated: 12/01/15

CZECH TECHNICAL UNIVERSITY IN PRAGUE

České vysoké učení technické v Praze (ČVUT)

Ul. Zikova 4, 16636 Praha
Tel: +420(2) 2434-1111
Fax: +420(2) 2431-1042
EMail: jiri.nozicka@fs.cvut.cz
Website: http://www.cvut.cz

Rector: Petr Konvalinka (2014-) EMail: rector@cvut.cz

Kvestor-Bursar: Jan Gazda EMail: gazda@fsv.cvut.cz

Faculty

Architecture (Architecture; Civil Engineering; Town Planning; Urban Studies); **Biomedical Engineering** (Anatomy; Biochemistry; Biomedical Engineering; Physiology); **Civil Engineering** (Building Technologies; Civil Engineering; Construction Engineering; Engineering Management; Environmental Engineering; Surveying and Mapping; Transport Engineering); **Electrical Engineering** (Applied Mathematics; Applied Physics; Artificial Intelligence; Automation and Control Engineering; Biomedical Engineering; Computer Engineering; Electrical and Electronic Equipment and Maintenance; Electrical Engineering; Electronic Engineering; Engineering Management; Mathematics and Computer Science; Power Engineering; Software Engineering; Systems Analysis; Technology; Telecommunications Engineering); **Information Technology** (Computer Engineering; Computer Science; Information Technology; Multimedia; Software Engineering); **Mechanical Engineering** (Aeronautical and Aerospace Engineering; Automation and Control Engineering; Automotive Engineering; Energy Engineering; Engineering; Engineering Drawing and Design; Engineering Management; Hydraulic Engineering; Machine Building; Materials Engineering; Mechanical Engineering; Metallurgical Engineering; Nuclear Engineering; Production Engineering); **Nuclear Sciences and Physical Engineering** (Mathematics; Nuclear Engineering; Nuclear Physics; Physical Engineering; Physics; Solid State Physics); **Transport Sciences** (Air Transport; Railway Transport; Road Transport; Transport and Communications; Transport Economics; Transport Management)

Institute

Advanced Studies *(Masaryk)* (Business Administration); **Physical Education and Sport** (Physical Education; Sports)

Further Information: Also Klokner Institute

History: Founded 1707 as Czech State Engineering School, became Polytechnic 1803. Granted university status 1864. Closed 1939 during the German occupation, reopened 1945. A State institution. Acquired present status 1999.

Academic Year: September to June (September-February; February-June)

Admission Requirements: Secondary school certificate (Maturitní vysvědčeni) and entrance examination

Fees: None for Czech students

Main Language(s) of Instruction: Czech, English

Degrees and Diplomas: *Bakalář*; *Inženýr*: **Engineering.** *Doktor*

Student Services: Canteen, Foreign Studies Centre, Health Services, Language Laboratory, Sports Facilities

Publications: Acta Polytechnica; Pražská Technika

Publishing House: Edični středisko ČVUT

Academic Staff *2014*	MEN	WOMEN	**TOTAL**
FULL-TIME	1,726	1,000	**2,726**
PART-TIME	1,216	475	**1,691**
STAFF WITH DOCTORATE			
FULL-TIME	858	151	**1,009**
Student Numbers *2013-2014*			
All (Foreign included)	16,991	5,601	**22,592**
FOREIGN ONLY	1,982	994	**2,976**

Part-time students, 2,409. **Distance students,** 0.

Last Updated: 09/01/15

CZECH UNIVERSITY OF LIFE SCIENCES IN PRAGUE

Česká zemědělská univerzita v Praze (ČZU/CUA)

Ul. Kamýcká 129, 165 21 Praha, 6-Suchdol
Tel: +420 224 381 076
Fax: +420 220 920 431
EMail: stichova@rektorat.czu.cz
Website: http://www.czu.cz

Rector: Jiří Balík Tel: +420 224 384 081 EMail: balik@af.czu.cz

Vice-rector for education: Petr Zasadil
Tel: +420 224 382 856 EMail: zasadil@fzp.czu.cz

International Relations: Michal Lošťák, Vice-rector for international relations
Tel: +420 22 4382 311 EMail: iro@czu.cz; lostak@pef.czu.cz

Faculty

Agrobiology, Food and Natural Resources (Agronomy; Animal Husbandry; Applied Chemistry; Aquaculture; Cattle Breeding; Crop Production; Fishery; Food Science; Fruit Production; Harvest Technology; Horticulture; Natural Resources; Organic Chemistry; Soil Conservation; Soil Management; Soil Science; Vegetable Production; Veterinary Science; Viticulture); **Economics and Management** (Accountancy; Administration; Agricultural Business; Agricultural Economics; Agricultural Equipment; Banking; Business and Commerce; Economics; Finance; Human Resources; Information Technology; Management; Marketing; Statistics; Taxation); **Engineering** (Automation and Control Engineering; Electrical Engineering; Materials Engineering; Mathematics; Mechanical Engineering; Physics); **Environmental Science** (Ecology; Irrigation; Water Management; Water Science); **Forestry and Wood Sciences** (Forest Management; Forestry; Wildlife; Wood Technology); **Tropical and AgriSciences** (Agricultural Economics; Animal Husbandry; Crop Production; Forestry; Tropical Agriculture)

Institute

Education and Communication (Agricultural Education; Agriculture; Communication Studies; Education; Educational Psychology; Forestry; Pedagogy; Science Education; Secondary Education; Veterinary Science)

History: The origins go back to 1786 when the Department of Agriculture was established at Charles Ferdinand University. Founded 1906 as Faculty of Agriculture at Prague Polytechnic (now CTU). Independent University established 1952. Acquired present status 1995. Formerly known as Czech University of Agriculture in Prague.

Academic Year: October to September (October-February; March-September)

Admission Requirements: Secondary school certificate (Maturitní vysvědčeni) and entrance examination

Fees: None

Main Language(s) of Instruction: Czech
Accrediting Agency: Ministry of Education, Youth and Sports
Degrees and Diplomas: *Bakalář*: **Agricultural Engineering; Economics; Forestry.** *Magistr*: **Agricultural Engineering; Forestry.** *Doktor*: **Agriculture; Economics; Forestry; Management; Natural Resources; Tropical Agriculture.**
Student Services: Academic Counselling, Canteen, Foreign Studies Centre, Health Services, Language Laboratory, Library, Sports Facilities
Publications: Scientia Agriculturae Bohemica
Last Updated: 29/01/15

JANÁČEK ACADEMY OF MUSIC AND PERFORMING ARTS IN BRNO

Janáčkova akademie múzických umění v Brně (JAMU)

Ul. Beethovenova 2, 662 15 Brno
Tel: +420 542 591 111
Fax: +420 542 591 140
EMail: jamu@jamu.cz; rektor@jamu.cz
Website: http://www.jamu.cz

Rektor: Ivo Medek (2010-)
Tel: +420 542 591 101 EMail: rektor@jamu.cz; medek@jamu.cz

Kvestor-Bursar: Lenka Valová
Tel: +420 542 591 115 EMail: valova@jamu.cz

International Relations: Leoš Faltus, Prorektor
EMail: faltus@jamu.cz

Faculty

Music (Music; Music Theory and Composition; Musical Instruments; Musicology; Theatre); **Theatre** (Acting; Performing Arts; Theatre)
History: Founded 1881 as Conservatoire of Dramatic Arts, Brno, acquired present status 1945 and title 1947, named after Leoš Janáček. A State institution.
Admission Requirements: Secondary school leaving certificate
Main Language(s) of Instruction: Czech, German, English
Accrediting Agency: Ministry of Education, Youth and Sports
Degrees and Diplomas: *Bakalář*: **Art Management; French; Music; Music Theory and Composition; Musical Instruments; Opera; Performing Arts; Religious Music; Singing; Theatre.** *Magistr*: **Acting; Art Management; Conducting; Dance; Music; Music Theory and Composition; Musical Instruments; Singing; Theatre.** *Doktor*: **Art Education; Art Management; Music Theory and Composition; Theatre; Translation and Interpretation; Writing.**
Student Services: Academic Counselling, Canteen, Foreign Studies Centre, Health Services, Language Laboratory
Publications: Obcăsník
Last Updated: 29/01/15

JAN EVANGELISTA PURKYNĚ UNIVERSITY IN ÚSTÍ NAD LABEM

Univerzita Jana Evangelisty Purkyně v Ústí nad Labem (UJEP)

Pasteurova Street 1, 400 96 Ústí nad Labem
Tel: +420 475 282 111
Fax: +420 472 772 982
EMail: alena.chvatalova@ujep.cz
Website: http://www.ujep.cz

Rector: René Wokoun
Tel: +420 475 286 211
EMail: rektor@ujep.cz; rene.wokoun@ujep.cz

Kvestor: Jana Janáková
Tel: +420 475 282 116 EMail: jana.janakova@ujep.cz

International Relations: Zdeněk Radvanovský, Vice-Rector for External Relations EMail: zdenek.radvanovsky@ujep.cz

Faculty

Art and Design (Art History; Ceramic Art; Fashion Design; Glass Art; Graphic Design; Interior Design; Media Studies; Painting and Drawing; Photography; Textile Design); **Education** (Education); **Environment** (Ecology; Environmental Management; Environmental Studies; Waste Management; Water Management); **Health Studies** (Ergotherapy; Midwifery; Physical Therapy); **Philosophy** (Germanic Studies; Philosophy; Slavic Languages); **Production Technology and Management** (Design; Economics; Industrial Management; Management; Materials Engineering; Mechanical Engineering; Production Engineering; Technology); **Science** (Biology; Chemistry; Geography; Natural Sciences; Physics); **Social and Economics Studies** (Accountancy; Business Administration; Development Studies; Economics; Finance; Information Technology; Law; Mathematics; Modern Languages; Political Sciences; Regional Planning; Social Work; Statistics; Town Planning)
History: Founded 1954 as Higher Teacher Training College. Acquired present status and title 1991.
Academic Year: September to August (September-January; February-August)
Admission Requirements: Secondary school certificate (Maturitní vysvědčeni ze střední školy)
Main Language(s) of Instruction: Czech, English
Degrees and Diplomas: *Bakalář*: **Economics; Environmental Studies; Management; Production Engineering; Social Sciences.** *Bakalář umění*: **Graphic Design.** *Inženýr*: **Economics; Environmental Studies; Social Sciences.** *Magistr*: **Secondary Education; Teacher Training.** *Magistr umění*: **Graphic Design.** *Doktor*: **Arts and Humanities; Music Theory and Composition; Physics.**
Student Services: Academic Counselling, Canteen, Careers Guidance, Cultural Activities, Foreign Studies Centre, Health Services, Language Laboratory, Social Counselling, Sports Facilities
Publications: Acta Universitatis Purkyniana

Student Numbers *2014-2015*: Total: c. 10,000
Last Updated: 02/02/15

MASARYK UNIVERSITY

Masarykova univerzita (MU)

Žerotínovo nám 9, 601 77 Brno
Tel: +420(549) 491-111
Fax: +420(549) 491-070
EMail: info@muni.cz; studijni@rect.muni.cz
Website: http://www.muni.cz

Rector: Mikuláš Bek (2011-)
Tel: +420(549) 491-001 EMail: rektor@muni.cz

Rector's Secretariat: Iva Zlatušková
Tel: +420(549) 491-1000 EMail: secretary@rect.muni.cz

International Relations: Jan Pavlík, Director, Centre for International Cooperation
Tel: +420(549) 491-106 EMail: director@czs.muni.cz

Faculty

Arts (Aesthetics; American Studies; Archaeology; Art History; Baltic Languages; Classical Languages; Czech; Dutch; Education; English; Ethnology; Film; German; History; Japanese; Linguistics; Museum Studies; Musicology; Philosophy; Psychology; Religion; Romance Languages; Scandinavian Languages; Slavic Languages; Theatre; Visual Arts); **Economics and Administration** (Administration; Applied Mathematics; Business Administration; Communication Studies; Computer Science; Economics; Finance; Information Technology; Law; Public Administration; Regional Studies); **Education** (Art Education; Biology; Chemistry; Civics; Czech; Education; English; Family Studies; French; Geography; German; Health Education; History; Information Sciences; Literature; Mathematics; Modern Languages; Music Education; Native Language; Native Language Education; Physical Education; Physics; Primary Education; Psychology; Russian; Special Education; Technology Education); **Informatics** (Computer Engineering; Computer Graphics; Computer Science; Design; Information Technology); **Law** (Administrative Law; Civil Law; Commercial Law; Constitutional Law; Criminal Law; Economic and Finance Policy; Economics; Environmental Studies; European Union Law; History of Law; International Law; Labour Law; Law; Political Sciences); **Medicine** (Anaesthesiology; Anatomy; Biochemistry; Biology; Biophysics; Cardiology; Dentistry; Dermatology; Embryology and Reproduction Biology; Ethics; Forensic Medicine and Dentistry; Gastroenterology; Gerontology; Gynaecology and Obstetrics; Haematology; Health Administration; Histology; Immunology; Laboratory Techniques; Medicine; Microbiology; Midwifery; Neurology; Nursing; Nutrition; Occupational Health; Oncology; Ophthalmology; Optometry; Orthopaedics; Otorhinolaryngology; Paediatrics;

Pathology; Pharmacology; Physiology; Plastic Surgery; Pneumology; Psychiatry and Mental Health; Radiology; Rehabilitation and Therapy; Social and Preventive Medicine; Stomatology; Surgery; Urology; Venereology); **Science** (Anthropology; Astrophysics; Biochemistry; Biology; Biomedical Engineering; Biophysics; Botany; Chemistry; Earth Sciences; Environmental Studies; Geography; Geology; Mathematics; Molecular Biology; Natural Sciences; Physics; Statistics; Toxicology; Zoology); **Social Studies** (Anthropology; Environmental Studies; European Studies; Gender Studies; International Studies; Journalism; Media Studies; Political Sciences; Psychology; Social Work; Sociology); **Sports Studies** (Physical Therapy; Social Sciences; Sports; Sports Management; Sports Medicine)

Further Information: Also Summer School of Slavonic Studies, University of the Third Age, Central European Studies Programme, TESOL TE programme and Faculty Hospital BRNO.

History: Founded in 1919 with Faculties of Law, Medecine, Science and Arts; Faculty of Education established in 1947, Economics and Administration in 1990, Informatics in 1994, Social Studies in 1998 and Sports Studies in 2002. Closed 1939-1945 during the German occupation. Became Jan Evangelista Purkyně University in 1960; Renamed Masaryk University again since 1989.

Academic Year: September to June (fall term: September-January; spring term: February-June)

Admission Requirements: Secondary school certificate (Maturitní vysvědčeni) and entrance examination; also working knowledge of the Czech language except for courses in English.

Fees: National: No fees for programmes accredited and taught in Czech, International: c. 3,000-9,000 per annum. (Programmes accredited and taught in foreign languages) (US Dollar)

Main Language(s) of Instruction: Czech, English

Degrees and Diplomas: *Bakalář*: **Archaeology; Art History; Art Management; Baltic Languages; Biological and Life Sciences; Business Administration; Chemistry; Chinese; Computer Science; Czech; Dutch; Earth Sciences; Educational Sciences; English; French; German; Germanic Languages; Greek; Greek (Classical); History; Information Sciences; Italian; Japanese; Latin; Library Science; Linguistics; Mathematics; Museum Studies; Norwegian; Philosophy; Physics; Polish; Portuguese; Religious Studies; Romance Languages; Russian; Scandinavian Languages; Serbocroatian; Social Sciences; Spanish; Special Education; Swedish.** *Doktor medicíny*: **Medicine.** *Inženýr*: **Business Administration; Economics.** *Magistr*: **Aesthetics; Ancient Languages; Archaeology; Art History; Art Management; Baltic Languages; Biological and Life Sciences; Chemistry; Czech; Dutch; Earth Sciences; Economics; Educational Sciences; English; French; German; Germanic Languages; Greek; Greek (Classical); History; International Studies; Italian; Latin; Law; Linguistics; Mathematics and Computer Science; Norwegian; Philosophy; Physics; Polish; Political Sciences; Portuguese; Psychology; Religious Studies; Romance Languages; Russian; Scandinavian Languages; Serbocroatian; Slavic Languages; Social Sciences; Sociology; Spanish; Special Education; Swedish; Translation and Interpretation.** *Doktor*

Student Services: Academic Counselling, Canteen, Careers Guidance, Cultural Activities, Facilities for disabled people, Foreign Studies Centre, Health Services, IT Centre, Language Laboratory, Library, Residential Facilities, Social Counselling, Sports Facilities, eLibrary

Publications: Special Periodical Publications of the Faculties; Universitas

Publishing House: University Press

Academic Staff *2013-2014*	MEN	WOMEN	TOTAL
FULL-TIME	1,515	1,662	**3,177**
PART-TIME	898	1,097	**1,995**
STAFF WITH DOCTORATE			
FULL-TIME	912	588	**1,500**
Student Numbers *2013-2014*			
All (Foreign included)	15,644	25,200	**40,844**
FOREIGN ONLY	3,714	3,307	**7,021**

Part-time students, 8,978. **Distance students,** 0.

Last Updated: 19/12/14

MENDEL UNIVERSITY IN BRNO

Mendelova univerzita v Brně (MENDELU)

Zemědělská 1, 613 00 Brno
Tel: +420 545 131-111
Fax: +420 545 211-128
EMail: info@mendelu.cz
Website: http://www.mendelu.cz

Rektor: Ladislav Havel (2014-)
Tel: +420 545 135-004 EMail: ladilslav.havel@mendelu.cz

Chancellor: Markéta Vejrostová
Tel: +420 545 135-291 EMail: marketa.vejrostova@mendelu.cz

Bursar: Lujza Oravcová
Tel: +420 545 135-009 EMail: lujza.oravcova@mendelu.cz

Faculty

Agronomy (Agriculture; Agronomy; Apiculture; Applied Chemistry; Automotive Engineering; Biochemistry; Biology; Cattle Breeding; Chemistry; Crop Production; Ecology; Engineering; Environmental Engineering; Fishery; Food Technology; Meteorology; Microbiology; Molecular Biology; Physical Education; Plant and Crop Protection; Soil Science; Zoology); **Business and Economics** (Accountancy; Business Administration; Business and Commerce; Computer Science; Economics; Finance; Law; Management; Marketing; Operations Research; Social Sciences; Statistics; Taxation); **Forestry and Wood Technology** (Forest Economics; Forest Management; Forest Products; Forestry; Furniture Design; Landscape Architecture; Natural Resources; Tropical Agriculture; Wood Technology); **Horticulture** *(Lednice na Moravě)* (Fruit Production; Horticulture; Landscape Architecture; Vegetable Production; Viticulture); **Regional Development and International Studies** (Development Studies; International Studies; Regional Studies)

Institute

Lifelong Education (Educational Sciences; Teacher Training)

History: Founded 1919, acquired present status and title 1995. Formerly known as Mendel University of Agriculture and Forestry in Brno (Mendelova zemědělská a lesnická univerzita v Brně).

Academic Year: September 1 to August 31 (winter semester: September-February; summer semester: February-July)

Admission Requirements: Secondary school certificate and entrance examination

Fees: None

Main Language(s) of Instruction: Czech

Degrees and Diplomas: *Bakalář*: **Agriculture; Architecture and Planning; Business Administration; Natural Sciences.** *Magistr*: **Agronomy; Business Administration; Forestry; Natural Sciences.** *Doktor*: **Agriculture; Business Administration; Natural Sciences.**

Student Services: Academic Counselling, Canteen, Careers Guidance, Cultural Activities, Facilities for disabled people, Foreign Studies Centre, Health Services, IT Centre, Language Laboratory, Library, Nursery Care, Residential Facilities, Sports Facilities

Publications: Acta Universitatis Agriculturae; Silviculturae Mendelianae Brunensis

Publishing House: University Publishing Centre

Academic Staff *2012-2013*	TOTAL
FULL-TIME	c. **1,982**
Student Numbers *2012-2013*	
All (Foreign included)	**9,600**

Part-time students, 4,344.

Last Updated: 09/01/15

PALACKÝ UNIVERSITY IN OLOMOUC

Univerzita Palackého v Olomouci (UP)

Křížkovského 8, 771 47 Olomouc
Tel: +420 585 631 111
Fax: +420 585 232 012
EMail: kancler@upol.cz
Website: http://www.upol.cz

Rector: Jaroslav Miller (2014-2018)
Tel: +420 585 631 001 EMail: rektor@upol.cz

Bursar: Jiří Přidal (2014-2018)
Tel: +420 585 631 008 EMail: jiri.pridal@upol.cz

Vice-Rector for Education: Vít Zouhar (2014 - 2018)
Tel: 00420 585 631 004 EMail: prorektor.studium@upol.cz

Vice-Rector for Research: Jitka Ulrichová (2014 - 2018)
Tel: 00420 585 631 002 EMail: jitka.ulrichova@upol.cz

Vice-Rector for External Affairs and Communication: Petr Bilík (2014 - 2018) Tel: 00420 585 631 007 EMail: petr.bilik@upol.cz

International Relations: Ivana Oborná, Vice-Rector for International Relations (2014-2018)
Tel: +420 585 631 005 EMail: ivana.oborna@upol.cz

Faculty

Education (Anthropology; Art Education; Biology; Czech; Education; English; German; Health Education; Information Technology; Literature; Mathematics; Mathematics Education; Music; Music Education; Native Language; Pathology; Primary Education; Psychology; Social Sciences; Special Education; Technology Education); **Law** (Administrative Law; Civil Law; Comparative Law; Constitutional Law; Criminal Law; Economics; European Union Law; Finance; Fiscal Law; History of Law; International Law; Labour Law; Law; Modern Languages; Political Sciences; Private Law; Public Law; Social Sciences; Taxation); **Medicine and Dentistry** (Anaesthesiology; Anatomy; Applied Chemistry; Biochemistry; Biology; Biophysics; Cardiology; Cell Biology; Czech; Dental Technology; Dentistry; Dermatology; Embryology and Reproduction Biology; English; Ethics; Forensic Medicine and Dentistry; Genetics; German; Gynaecology and Obstetrics; Haematology; Health Administration; Histology; Hygiene; Immunology; Laboratory Techniques; Latin; Medicine; Microbiology; Midwifery; Modern Languages; Molecular Biology; Native Language; Neurology; Nursing; Occupational Health; Oncology; Ophthalmology; Oral Pathology; Orthopaedics; Otorhinolaryngology; Paediatrics; Pathology; Pharmacology; Physical Therapy; Physiology; Pneumology; Psychiatry and Mental Health; Radiology; Rehabilitation and Therapy; Social and Preventive Medicine; Sports; Stomatology; Surgery; Urology; Venereology); **Philosophy** (Adult Education; American Studies; Art History; Arts and Humanities; Asian Studies; Chinese; Classical Languages; Czech; Dutch; Economics; English Studies; European Studies; Film; French; German; History; Italian; Japanese; Jewish Studies; Journalism; Linguistics; Literature; Media Studies; Modern Languages; Musicology; Native Language; Philology; Philosophy; Polish; Political Sciences; Portuguese; Psychology; Romance Languages; Russian; Slavic Languages; Social Sciences; Sociology; Spanish; Theatre); **Physical Education** (Anthropology; Leisure Studies; Parks and Recreation; Physical Education; Physical Therapy; Physiology; Social Sciences; Sports); **Science** (Analytical Chemistry; Anthropology; Applied Physics; Biochemistry; Biology; Botany; Cell Biology; Chemistry; Development Studies; Earth Sciences; Ecology; Genetics; Geography; Geology; Inorganic Chemistry; Mathematics and Computer Science; Modern Languages; Optics; Organic Chemistry; Physical Chemistry; Physics; Zoology); **Theology** *(St. Cyril and Methodius Faculty of Theology)* (Religious Education; Religious Studies; Theology)

Centre

Advanced Technologies and Materials *(Regional (RCPTM))*; **Lifelong Learning programmes**

Research Centre

Biotechnical and Agricultural Research *(Haná Region)* (Agriculture)

History: Founded 1566 as Jesuit College, granted University rights 1573 and closed 1860. Re-established and acquired present status 1946.

Academic Year: September to June (September-December; February- end June)

Admission Requirements: Secondary school certificate (Maturitní vysvědčeni) and entrance examination

Fees: National: None for those who study in Czech, International: Undergraduate students: c. 4 600. Graduate/postgraduate students: c. 2 600, only students who are not able to attend courses in the Czech language pay tuition fees. Tution fees vary by study programme and faculty (Euro)

Main Language(s) of Instruction: Czech, English

Accrediting Agency: Ministry of Education, Youth and Sports; Accreditation Commission, Czech Republic

Degrees and Diplomas: *Bakalář*; *Doktor medicíny*: **Dentistry; Medicine.** *Magistr*; *Doktor*

Student Services: Academic Counselling, Canteen, Cultural Activities, Facilities for disabled people, Foreign Studies Centre, Health Services, IT Centre, Language Laboratory, Library, Nursery Care, Residential Facilities, Social Counselling, Sports Facilities, eLibrary

Publications: Acta Iuridica Olomucensis; Acta Universitatis Palaskianae; Biomedical Papers; Bohemica Olomuncensia; Civilia; Contemporary European Studies; Czech and Slovak Journal of Humanities; Czech and Slovak Linguistic Review; e-Pedagogium; Gnosis Medica; Historica Olomucensia; International and Comparative Law Review; Journal of Exceptional People; Journal of Technology and Information Education; Moravian Journal of Literature and Film; Profese online; Romanica Olomucensia; Rossica Olomuncensia; Studia Thelogica

Publishing House: Palacký University Journal: Žurnál UP

Academic Staff *2013*	MEN	WOMEN	TOTAL
FULL-TIME	682	499	**1,181**
PART-TIME	647	475	**1,122**
STAFF WITH DOCTORATE			
FULL-TIME	522	341	**863**
Student Numbers *2013*			
All (Foreign included)	6,628	15,205	**21,833**
FOREIGN ONLY	527	993	**1,520**

Part-time students, 4,941.
Last Updated: 16/03/15

POLICE ACADEMY OF THE CZECH REPUBLIC IN PRAGUE

Policejní akademie České republicky v Praze (PAČR)
P.O. Box 54, Ul. Lhotecká 559/7, 143 01 Praha 4
Tel: +420 974 828 140 +420 241 714 809
Fax: +420 974 827 273
EMail: polac@polac.cz
Website: http://www.polac.cz

Rector: Josef Salač
Tel: +420 974 828 501 EMail: veliskova@polac.cz

Kvestor: Karel Vokurka
Tel: +420 974 828 508 EMail: kvestor@polac.cz

Faculty

Security and Law (Criminology; Police Studies); **Security Management** (Administrative Law; Information Sciences; Public Administration)

History: Founded 1992. The Police Academy of the Czech Republic is an institution of higher education responsible to the Ministry of Interior. A State institution.

Academic Year: September to June

Admission Requirements: Secondary school certificate (Maturitní vysvědčeni) and entrance examination

Main Language(s) of Instruction: Czech

Degrees and Diplomas: *Bakalář*: **Law; Protective Services.** *Magistr*: **Criminology; Management; Police Studies; Public Administration.** *Doktor*: **Criminology; Management; Police Studies.**

Student Services: Academic Counselling, Canteen, Careers Guidance, Cultural Activities, Health Services, Nursery Care, Social Counselling, Sports Facilities

Last Updated: 29/01/15

SILESIAN UNIVERSITY IN OPAVA

Slezská univerzita v Opavě (SU)
Na Rybníčku 626/1, 746 01 Opava
Tel: +420 553 684 621
Fax: +420 553 718 019
EMail: rektorat@slu.cz
Website: http://www.slu.cz

Rector: Rudolf Žáček
Tel: +420 553 684 620 EMail: rudolf.zacek@slu.cz

Kvestor: Jaroslav Kania
Tel: +420 55368 4630 EMail: kvestor@slu.cz

Faculty
Philosophy and Science (Natural Sciences; Philosophy; Photography); **Public Policies** (Social and Community Services)

School
Business Administration *(Karviná)* (Business Administration)

Institute
Mathematics (Mathematics)

History: Founded 1991, incorporating faculties of Masaryk University, Brno.

Academic Year: September to August (September-February; February-August)

Admission Requirements: Secondary school certificate (Maturitní vysvědčeni) or recognized foreign equivalent, and entrance examination

Fees: None for Czech students

Main Language(s) of Instruction: Czech, English

Accrediting Agency: Ministry of Education, Youth and Sports

Degrees and Diplomas: *Bakalář*: **Administration; Central European Studies; Computer Engineering; Computer Science; Economics; History; Hotel and Restaurant; Law; Library Science; Linguistics; Literature; Management; Mathematics; Photography; Physics; Public Administration; Tourism.** *Inženýr*: **Administration; Economics; Law; Management.** *Magistr*: **Computer Science; History; Linguistics; Mathematics; Photography; Physics.** *Doktor*: **Astrophysics; Business and Commerce; Economics; History; Management; Mathematics; Photography; Physics.**

Student Services: Canteen, Cultural Activities, Language Laboratory, Sports Facilities

Publications: Differential Geometry and its Applications
Last Updated: 29/01/15

TECHNICAL UNIVERSITY OF LIBEREC

Technická univerzita v Liberci (TUL)
Studentská 1402/2, 461 17 Liberec 1
Tel: +420 485 351 111
Fax: +420 485 105 882
EMail: info@tul.cz
Website: http://www.tul.cz

Rector: Zdeněk Kůs Tel: +420 485 353 597 EMail: rektor@tul.cz

Kvestor-Bursar: Vladimír Stach
Tel: +420 485 105 617
EMail: vladimir.stach@tul.cz; kvestor@tul.cz

Faculty
Architecture (Architecture); **Economics** (Accountancy; Business Administration; Communication Studies; Computer Science; Economics; Finance; Information Management; Insurance; Law; Modern Languages; Statistics); **Education** (Economics; Education; Geography; Geography (Human); History; Management; Mathematics; Pedagogy; Philology; Philosophy; Physical Education; Physics; Special Education; Sports); **Mechanical Engineering** (Automation and Control Engineering; Engineering; Industrial Engineering; Materials Engineering; Mechanical Engineering; Production Engineering); **Mechatronics and Interdisciplinary Engineering Studies** (Computer Engineering; Computer Science; Electronic Engineering; Engineering; Information Technology); **Textile Engineering** (Textile Design; Textile Technology)

Institute
Health Studies (Biomedical Engineering; Nursing)

History: Founded 1953 as College, acquired present status and title 1995.

Academic Year: September to June (September-January; February-June)

Admission Requirements: Secondary school certificate (Maturitní vysvědčeni)

Main Language(s) of Instruction: Czech

Accrediting Agency: Ministry of Education, Youth and Sports

Degrees and Diplomas: *Bakalář*: **Biomedical Engineering; Nursing.** *Inženýr*: **Administration; Architecture; Computer Engineering; Economics; Industrial Engineering; Management; Mechanical Engineering.** *Magistr*: **Textile Technology.** *Doktor*: **Applied Mathematics; Materials Engineering; Mechanical Engineering; Physical Engineering; Textile Technology.**

Student Services: Academic Counselling, Canteen, Facilities for disabled people, Health Services, Library, Sports Facilities

Publications: Annals of the University
Last Updated: 30/01/15

TOMAS BATA UNIVERSITY IN ZLÍN

Univerzita Tomáše Bati ve Zlíně (UTB)
nám. T. G. Masaryka 5555, 760 01 Zlín
Tel: +420 57 603 8120
Fax: +420 57 603 2121
EMail: kancler@utb.cz
Website: http://www.utb.cz

Rektor: Petr Sáha Tel: +420 57 603 2222 EMail: rektor@utb.cz

Bursar: Alexander Cerný
Tel: +420 57 603 2777 EMail: kvestor@utb.cz

International Relations: Pavel Krutil, Vice-Rector for International Relations EMail: krutil@fmk.utb.cz; international@utb.cz

Faculty
Applied Informatics (Automation and Control Engineering; Chemical Engineering; Computer Engineering; Electronic Engineering; Engineering Management; Mathematics; Measurement and Precision Engineering); **Humanities** (American Studies; Business Administration; English Studies; German; Modern Languages; Pedagogy; Philology; Public Health); **Logistics and Crisis Management** (Management); **Management and Economics** (Economics; Management); **Multimedia Communications** (Communication Studies; Fashion Design; Graphic Design; Multimedia; Visual Arts); **Technology** (Chemistry; Food Technology; Materials Engineering; Polymer and Plastics Technology; Production Engineering; Technology)

History: Founded 2000. Acquired present status 2001.

Academic Year: September to June

Admission Requirements: High school diploma, entrance examination

Main Language(s) of Instruction: Czech, English

Accrediting Agency: Ministry of Education, Youth and Sports

Degrees and Diplomas: *Bakalář*, *Magistr*, *Doktor*. Also Postdoctoral studies (Postdoktorské)

Student Services: Academic Counselling, Canteen, Careers Guidance, Cultural Activities, Facilities for disabled people, Foreign Studies Centre, Language Laboratory, Library, Social Counselling, Sports Facilities

Publications: Universalia
Last Updated: 16/03/15

UNIVERSITY OF CHEMISTRY AND TECHNOLOGY, PRAGUE

Vysoká škola chemicko-technologická v Praze (VŠCHT PRAHA)
Technická 5, 166 28 Praha 6
Tel: +420 220 444 144
Fax: +420 220 445 018
EMail: rektor@vscht.cz
Website: http://www.vscht.cz

Rector: Karel Melzoch
Tel: +420 222 044 3824 EMail: Karel.Melzoch@vscht.cz

Registrar: Ivana Chválná
Tel: +420 220 443 162 EMail: Ivana.Chvalna@vscht.cz

International Relations: Pavel Hasal, Vice-Rector for International Relations Tel: +420 220 443 167 EMail: pavel.hasal@vscht.cz

Faculty
Chemical Engineering (Ceramics and Glass Technology; Chemical Engineering; Inorganic Chemistry; Metallurgical Engineering; Organic Chemistry; Physical Chemistry; Polymer and Plastics

Technology; Solid State Physics); **Chemical Technology** (Analytical Chemistry; Automation and Control Engineering; Chemical Engineering; Food Science; Food Technology; Mathematics; Physical Chemistry; Physics; Robotics); **Environmental Technology** (Applied Chemistry; Environmental Engineering; Environmental Management; Natural Resources; Petroleum and Gas Engineering; Power Engineering); **Food and Biochemical Technology** (Applied Chemistry; Biochemistry; Biotechnology; Chemistry; Dairy; Food Science; Food Technology; Microbiology)

History: Founded 1952 as Institute of Chemical Technology in Prague. Acquired present title 2015. A State institution.

Admission Requirements: Secondary school certificate (Maturitní vysvědčeni)

Fees: (Koruna): 125,000 per annum

Main Language(s) of Instruction: Czech, English

Degrees and Diplomas: *Bakalář*, *Magistr*: **Applied Chemistry; Biotechnology; Chemical Engineering; Chemistry; Engineering.** *Doktor*: **Chemical Engineering; Chemistry; Microbiology.**

Student Services: Academic Counselling, Canteen, Health Services, IT Centre, Language Laboratory, Library, Sports Facilities

Publishing house: ICT Press

Academic Staff *2014-2015*: Total 420

Student Numbers *2014-2015*: Total 3,100

Last Updated: 02/02/15

UNIVERSITY OF DEFENCE

Univerzita Obrany
Kounicova 65, 662 10 Brno
Tel: +420 973 201 111
Fax: +420 973 401 111
EMail: so@unob.cz; vladimir.sidla@unob.cz
Website: www.unob.cz/en

Rector: Bohuslav Přikryl (2012-) EMail: bohuslav.prikryl@unob.cz

Faculty

Military Health Sciences (Health Sciences); **Military Leadership** (Military Science); **Military Technology** (Military Science)

History: Founded 2004 by the merger of Military University of the Ground Forces Vyškov, Military Academy Brno and Military Medical Academy Hradec Králové.

Main Language(s) of Instruction: Czech

Degrees and Diplomas: *Bakalář*, *Magistr*: **Health Sciences; Management; Military Science.** *Doktor*: **Health Sciences.**

Last Updated: 02/02/15

UNIVERSITY OF ECONOMICS, PRAGUE

Vysoká škola ekonomická v Praze (VŠE)
Nám. Winstona Churchilla 4, 130 67 Praha 3
Tel: +420 224 095 111
Fax: +420 224 095 673
EMail: ozs@vse.cz
Website: http://www.vse.cz

President: Hana Machková (2014-)
Tel: +420 224 095 720 EMail: machkova@vse.cz

Vice-Rector for Academic Affairs: Petr Dvořák
Tel: +420 224 09 5724 EMail: ptackova@vse.cz

International Relations: Jiří Hnilica, Vice-Rector
Tel: +420 224 095 799 EMail: jiri.hnilica@vse.cz

Faculty

Business Administration (Art Management; Business Administration; Human Resources; Management; Marketing; Psychology; Sociology; Transport Management); **Economics** (Development Studies; Economic History; Economics; Environmental Management; Law; Philosophy; Public Administration; Regional Studies; Social Policy); **Finance and Accounting** (Accountancy; Banking; Economics; Finance; Human Resources; Insurance; Management); **Informatics and Statistics** (Demography and Population; Econometrics; Information Management; Information Technology; Mathematics and Computer Science; Operations Research; Statistics); **International Relations** (Business and Commerce; Commercial Law; English; European Studies; European Union Law; German; International Business; International Economics; International Relations; Political Sciences; Romance Languages; Russian; Tourism); **Management** *(Jindřichův Hradec)* (Business Administration; Health Administration; Information Management; Management; Public Administration; Public Health)

Centre

European Studies (Cultural Studies; Economics; European Languages; European Studies; European Union Law; History; Law; Modern Languages; Political Sciences)

History: Founded 1949 as Prague College of Economic Sciences. Acquired present status and title 1953. A State institution.

Academic Year: September to June (September-January; February-June)

Admission Requirements: Secondary school certificate (Maturitní vysvědčeni) and entrance examination

Main Language(s) of Instruction: Czech

Degrees and Diplomas: *Bakalář*, *Inženýr*: **Economics.** *Doktor*: **Accountancy; Business Computing; Commercial Law; Computer Science; Economics; European Studies; Finance; International Business; International Relations; Management; Political Sciences; Statistics.**

Student Services: Academic Counselling, Canteen, Facilities for disabled people, Foreign Studies Centre, Language Laboratory, Library, Residential Facilities, Social Counselling, Sports Facilities

Publications: Acta Economica Pragensia; Politická Ekonomie; Prague Economic Papers

Publishing House: Zpravodaj Uše

Last Updated: 02/02/15

UNIVERSITY OF HRADEC KRÁLOVÉ

Univerzita Hradec Králové (UHK)
Rokitanského 62, 500 03 Hradec Králové 3
Tel: +420 493 332 508
Fax: +420 495 545 911
EMail: rektor@uhk.cz
Website: http://www.uhk.cz

Rektor: Josef Hynek (2012-)
Tel: +420 493-332-286 EMail: josef.hynek@uhk.cz

Kvestor-Bursar: Stanislav Klik
Tel: +420 493 331 511 EMail: stanislav.klik@uhk.cz

International Relations: Antonín Slabý, Prorektor
Tel: +420 493 331 512 EMail: antonin.slaby@uhk.cz

Faculty

Arts (African Studies; Archaeology; Archiving; Arts and Humanities; Czech; History; Latin American Studies; Modern Languages; Philosophy; Political Sciences; Social Sciences; Sociology); **Education** (Art Education; Biology; Chemistry; Computer Science; Cultural Studies; Czech; Education; Educational Psychology; English; German; Literature; Mathematics; Multimedia; Music; Music Education; Native Language; Pedagogy; Physical Education; Physics; Preschool Education; Primary Education; Psychology; Religious Education; Slavic Languages; Social Studies; Social Work; Sociology; Special Education; Sports; Textile Design); **Informatics and Management** (Computer Science; Economics; English; German; Information Technology; Leisure Studies; Management; Tourism); **Science** (Biology; Chemistry; Computer Science; Mathematics; Physics)

Institute

Social Work (Social Work)

History: Founded 1959 as Institute of Education, reorganized 1992 as University College of Education and acquired present status and title 2000.

Academic Year: September to June

Admission Requirements: Secondary school certificate (Maturitní vysvědčeni)

Main Language(s) of Instruction: Czech, English

Accrediting Agency: Accreditation Commission

Degrees and Diplomas: *Bakalář*, *Magistr*, *Doktor*

Student Services: Academic Counselling, Careers Guidance, Facilities for disabled people, Health Services, Language Laboratory, Library, Sports Facilities

Publishing house: GAUDEAMUS

Student Numbers *2013-2014*: Total: c. 8,500

Last Updated: 30/01/15

UNIVERSITY OF OSTRAVA

Ostravská univerzita v Ostravě (OU)

Dvořákova 7, 701 03 Ostrava

Tel: +420 596 160 151

Fax: +420 596 118 219

EMail: info@osu.cz

Website: http://www.osu.cz

Rektor: Jiří Močkoř
Tel: +420 597 091 001 EMail: Jiri.Mockor@osu.cz

Bursar: Jana Poloková
Tel: +420 597 091 004 EMail: Jana.Polokova@osu.cz

International Relations: Igor Fojtík, Vice-Rector for Coordination of Research and External Relations
Tel: +420 597 091 013 EMail: Igor.Fojtik@osu.cz

Faculty

Arts (American Studies; Art History; Czech; English Studies; Germanic Studies; History; Linguistics; Literature; Native Language; Philosophy; Psychology; Regional Studies; Romance Languages; Slavic Languages; Social and Community Services; Social Work); **Fine Arts** (Art History; Graphic Arts; Media Studies; Musical Instruments; Painting and Drawing; Sculpture; Singing); **Health Studies** (Anatomy; Biomedicine; Epidemiology; Forensic Medicine and Dentistry; Midwifery; Nursing; Pathology; Pharmacology; Physiology; Psychiatry and Mental Health; Public Health; Rehabilitation and Therapy; Surgery); **Pedagogical Studies** (Adult Education; Art Education; Communication Studies; Czech; Education; Educational Psychology; Foreign Languages Education; Information Technology; Literature; Mathematics Education; Music Education; Native Language; Native Language Education; Pedagogy; Physical Education; Primary Education; Religious Education; Social Sciences; Special Education; Technology Education); **Science** (Applied Mathematics; Biology; Biophysics; Chemistry; Computer Science; Development Studies; Ecology; Economics; Geography; Geology; Management; Mathematics; Modern Languages; Natural Sciences; Physics; Regional Studies; Technology); **Social Studies** (Social Studies; Social Work)

Institute

Research and Application of Fuzzy Modelling (Applied Mathematics); **Social Work** *(European Research Institute)* (Social Work)

History: Founded 1953 as Pedagogical School of Higher Learning at Opava. Became Pedagogical Institute 1959 and moved to Ostrava. Acquired present status and title 1991. A State institution.

Academic Year: October to September (October-February; February-July)

Admission Requirements: Secondary school certificate (Maturitní vysvědčeni)

Fees: None

Main Language(s) of Instruction: Czech

Accrediting Agency: Accreditation Agency of the Czech Republic

Degrees and Diplomas: *Bakalář*; *Magistr*: **Czech; Education; English; German; Mathematics; Medicine; Music Education; Natural Sciences; Nursing; Physics; Social Work.** *Doktor*: **Czech; Education; English; Mathematics; Music Education; Natural Sciences; Nursing; Physics; Social Policy; Social Work.**

Student Services: Canteen, Library, Sports Facilities

Publications: Acta Facultatis Paedagogicae Universitatis Ostraviensis; Acta Facultatis Philosophicae Universitatis Ostraviensis (Studia Slavica, Historica, Psychologia Series); Acta Facultatis Rerum Naturalium Universitatis Ostraviensis (Biologia-Ecologia, Geographia-Geologia, Physica-Chemia Series); Acta Mathematica et Informatica Universitatis Ostraviensis

Publishing House: University Publishing House

Last Updated: 05/01/15

UNIVERSITY OF PARDUBICE

Univerzita Pardubice (UPA)

Studentská 95, 532 10 Pardubice

Tel: +420 466 036 111

Fax: +420 466 036 361

EMail: promotion@upce.cz

Website: http://www.upce.cz

Rektor: Miroslav Ludwig (2010 -)
Tel: +420 466 036 553 EMail: rektor@upce.cz

Kvestor - Bursar: Petr Gabriel (2013 -)
Tel: +420 466 036 556 EMail: kvestor@upce.cz

International Relations: Monika Vejchodová, Head of Office of International Affairs and Development (2002 -)
Tel: + +420 466 036 417 EMail: monika.vejchodova@upce.cz

Faculty

Faculty of Arts and Philosophy (American Studies; Arts and Humanities; Cultural Studies; English Studies; German; History; Modern Languages; Philosophy; Religious Studies; Social Sciences); **Faculty of Chemical Technology** (Analytical Chemistry; Applied Mathematics; Applied Physics; Biochemistry; Biological and Life Sciences; Chemical Engineering; Chemistry; Environmental Engineering; Food Technology; Graphic Arts; Inorganic Chemistry; Materials Engineering; Nanotechnology; Organic Chemistry; Physical Chemistry; Solid State Physics); **Faculty of Economics and Administration** (Administration; Computer Engineering; Economics; Law; Management; Management Systems; Marketing; Mathematics and Computer Science; Public Administration; Public Law); **Faculty of Electrical Engineering and Informatics** (Automation and Control Engineering; Computer Engineering; Electrical Engineering; Information Technology; Software Engineering; Systems Analysis); **Faculty of Health Studies** (Health Sciences; Midwifery; Nursing; Public Health); **Faculty of Restoration** (Art History; Chemistry; Fine Arts; Heritage Preservation; Restoration of Works of Art; Visual Arts); **Jan Perner Transport Faculty** (Building Technologies; Civil Engineering; Electrical and Electronic Engineering; Maintenance Technology; Materials Engineering; Mechanical Engineering; Safety Engineering; Transport and Communications; Transport Economics; Transport Engineering; Transport Management)

Department

Department of Physical Education and Sports (Physical Education; Sports)

Centre

Language Centre (English; German; Linguistics; Translation and Interpretation)

History: Founded 1950 as the Institute of Chemical Technology, in Pardubice. After the year 1990, the character of the Institute changed, new faculties were founded offering a wide range of study programmes not only chemistry-related. Acquired present status and title 1994.

Academic Year: October to September (October - February; March - September)

Admission Requirements: Secondary school certificate (Maturitní vysvědčeni), recognition of previous study and entrance examination

Fees: 2.000 - 3.500 for study programmes accredited in English (Euro)

Main Language(s) of Instruction: Czech, English

Degrees and Diplomas: *Bakalář*: **Anthropology; Archiving; Biochemistry; Biomedical Engineering; Business Administration; Computer Engineering; Computer Science; Economics; Environmental Engineering; Environmental Studies; Food Technology; German; History; Information Technology; Linguistics; Literature; Materials Engineering; Midwifery; Nursing; Philosophy; Radiology; Religious Studies; Restoration of Works of Art; Sociology; Transport and Communications; Transport Economics; Transport Engineering; Transport Management; Visual Arts.** *Inženýr*: **Analytical Chemistry; Applied Physics; Automation and Control Engineering; Business Administration; Chemical Engineering; Chemistry; Civil Engineering; Computer Engineering; Electrical and Electronic Engineering; Environmental Engineering; Food Technology; Information Sciences; Inorganic Chemistry; Materials**

Engineering; Mathematics and Computer Science; Mechanical Engineering; Nanotechnology; Organic Chemistry; Physical Chemistry; Railway Transport; Road Engineering; Road Transport; Solid State Physics; Telecommunications Services; Transport Economics; Transport Engineering; Transport Management. *Magistr.* **Anthropology; Biochemistry; English; History; Literature; Midwifery; Nursing; Painting and Drawing; Pedagogy; Philosophy; Radiology; Religious Studies; Sociology.** *Doktor.* **Analytical Chemistry; Applied Physics; Automation and Control Engineering; Biological and Life Sciences; Biomedical Engineering; Chemical Engineering; Civil Engineering; Computer Engineering; Economics; Electrical and Electronic Engineering; Environmental Engineering; Explosive Engineering; History; Industrial Management; Information Sciences; Inorganic Chemistry; Nanotechnology; Nursing; Organic Chemistry; Philosophy; Physical Chemistry; Polymer and Plastics Technology; Public Administration; Religious Studies; Social and Preventive Medicine; Solid State Physics; Transport and Communications.**

Student Services: Academic Counselling, Canteen, Careers Guidance, Cultural Activities, Facilities for disabled people, Foreign Studies Centre, IT Centre, Language Laboratory, Library, Residential Facilities, Social Counselling, Sports Facilities, eLibrary

Publications: Scientific Papers

Academic Staff *2013*	TOTAL
FULL-TIME	1,000
PART-TIME	c. 200
Student Numbers *2013*	
All (Foreign included)	c. 10,450
FOREIGN ONLY	526

Last Updated: 17/12/14

UNIVERSITY OF SOUTH BOHEMIA IN ČESKÉ BUDĚJOVICE

Jihočeská univerzita v Českých Budějovicích (JU)

Branišovská 1645/31a, 37005 České Budějovice
Tel: +420 389 032-191
EMail: info@jcu.cz
Website: http://www.jcu.cz

Rector: Libor Grubhoffer
Tel: +420 389 032-001 EMail: rektor@jcu.cz

Kvestor-Bursar: Hana Kropáčková
Tel: +420 389 032-002 EMail: hkropack@jcu.cz

International Relations: Dagmar Škodová Parmová
Tel: +420 389 032-007 EMail: prorektor-zahranici@jcu.cz

Faculty

Agriculture *(ZF)* (Agricultural Equipment; Agriculture; Anatomy; Animal Husbandry; Applied Chemistry; Biological and Life Sciences; Cattle Breeding; Crop Production; Ecology; Fishery; Genetics; Nutrition; Physical Education; Physiology; Veterinary Science); **Economics** (Accountancy; Applied Mathematics; Computer Science; Crafts and Trades; Development Studies; Economics; European Studies; Finance; Law; Management; Rural Planning; Rural Studies; Tourism); **Fisheries and Protection of Waters** (Fishery; Water Management; Water Science); **Health and Social Studies** *(ZSF)* (Economics; Ethics; Health Education; Information Technology; Laboratory Techniques; Law; Management; Medical Technology; Medicine; Nursing; Philosophy; Psychiatry and Mental Health; Psychology; Public Health; Radiology; Social and Preventive Medicine; Social Studies; Social Work; Toxicology); **Pedagogy** *(PF)* (Art Therapy; Biology; Chemistry; Czech; Education; English; Fine Arts; Geography; Geography (Human); Germanic Studies; Health Education; History; Information Sciences; Mathematics; Music; Pedagogy; Physics; Primary Education; Psychology; Romance Languages; Russian; Social Sciences; Sports); **Philosophy** *(FF)* (Philosophy); **Science** *(BF)* (Biological and Life Sciences; Biology; Chemistry; Mathematics; Physics); **Theology** *(TF)* (Bible; Canon Law; Civil Law; Education; Ethics; History of Religion; Philosophy; Psychology; Religion; Religious Studies; Sociology; Theology)

Institute

Physical Biology (Biology)

Research Institute

Fish Farming and Hydrobiology *(VURH, Vodňany)* (Fishery; Marine Biology)

Further Information: Also Branches in Vodňany and Český Krumlov

History: Founded 1991, incorporating the Faculty of Agronomy (detached part of Prague Agricultural University) with independent Faculty of Education, and recruiting additional staff from several research institutes of the Czech Academy of Sciences located in the area (Botany, Entomology, Hydrobiology, Landscape Ecology, Microbiology, Molecular Biology of Plants, Parasitology, Soil Science), and from local hospitals and religious institutions. Close extramural collaboration and a high proportion of part-time teachers remain a typical feature of the University, financed by the State.

Academic Year: October to June (October-January, February-June)

Admission Requirements: Secondary school certificate (Maturitní vysvědčeni) with leaving examination, and entrance examinations

Fees: National: free tuition (programmes in Czech), International: 50 - 2 500 EUR per annum (programmes in English) - depending on the faculty

Main Language(s) of Instruction: Czech, English

Degrees and Diplomas: *Bakalář, Inženýr, Magistr, Doktor*

Student Services: Canteen, Careers Guidance, Cultural Activities, Facilities for disabled people, Health Services, Library, Residential Facilities, Sports Facilities, eLibrary

Publications: Bulletin of Agricultural Faculty; Effective (Faculty of Economics); JU - Magazine (students)

Publishing House: JU Journal

Last Updated: 09/01/15

UNIVERSITY OF VETERINARY AND PHARMACEUTICAL SCIENCES BRNO

Veterinární a farmaceutická univerzita Brno (VFU BRNO (UVPS BRNO))

Palackého 1/3, 612 42 Brno
Tel: +420 541 561-111
Fax: +420 549 250-478
EMail: vfu@vfu.cz
Website: http://www.vfu.cz

Rektor: Pavel Suchý (2014)
Tel: +420 541 562 000 +420 541 562 002 EMail: rektor@vfu.cz

Kvestor: Daniela Němcová
Tel: +420 541 562 025 EMail: nemcovad@vfu.cz

Vice-Rector for Education: Radka Opatřilová (2014)
Tel: 420 54156 2015 EMail: opatrilovar@vfu.cz

Vice-Rector for Strategy and Development: Vladimír Večerek (2014-) Tel: 420 54156 2012 EMail: vecerekv@vfu.cz

International Relations: Alfred Hera, Vice-Rector, Science, reserch and foreign relations (2014)
Tel: +420 541 562 020 EMail: prorektorvvz@vfu.cz

Faculty

Faculty of Pharmacy (Pharmacy); **Faculty of Veterinary Hygiene and Ecology** (Food Science; Veterinary Science; Welfare and Protective Services); **Faculty of Veterinary Medicine** (Veterinary Science)

Institute

Foreign Languages and History of Veterinary Medicine (History; Latin; Modern Languages); **Information Technology** (Information Technology); **Lifelong Education and Informatics** (Animal Husbandry; Food Science; Pharmacy; Veterinary Science); **Sports** (Sports); **Wildlife Ecology** (Wildlife)

History: Founded 1918 as Czechoslovak College of Veterinary Medicine, reorganized as University 1969. A State institution.

Academic Year: September to June (September-December; February-June)

Admission Requirements: Secondary school certificate (Maturitní vysvědčení) and entrance examination in Biology, Chemistry and Physics (for Faculty of Pharmacy)

Fees: National: None for education in Czech study programmes (Euro), International: Faculty of Veterinary Medicine - 7.600 EUR (Master's study programme) Faculty of Veterinary Hygiene and Ecology - 7.600 EUR (Master's study programme); 4.000 EUR (Bachelor's study programme Veterinary Hygiene and Ecology in the field of Food Safety and Quality - in English language); 4.000 EUR (Continuing master's study programme Veterinary Hygiene and Ecology in the field of Food Safety and Quality - in English language) Faculty of Pharmacy - 6.700 EUR (Master's study programme) (Euro)

Main Language(s) of Instruction: Czech, English

Degrees and Diplomas: *Bakalář*: **Food Science; Welfare and Protective Services.** *Doktor veterinární medicíny*: **Animal Husbandry; Food Science; Veterinary Science; Welfare and Protective Services.** *Magistr*: **Food Science; Pharmacy; Welfare and Protective Services.** *Doktor*: **Animal Husbandry; Food Science; Pharmacy; Veterinary Science; Welfare and Protective Services.**

Student Services: Academic Counselling, Canteen, Careers Guidance, Cultural Activities, Health Services, IT Centre, Library, Sports Facilities, eLibrary

Publications: Acta Veterinaria Brno; Vita Universitatis; Výfuk

Academic Staff *2014*	**TOTAL**
FULL-TIME	**750**
STAFF WITH DOCTORATE FULL-TIME	c. **220**
Student Numbers *2014*	
All (Foreign included)	c. **3,035**
FOREIGN ONLY	**300**

Last Updated: 07/01/15

UNIVERSITY OF WEST BOHEMIA

Západočeská univerzita v Plzni (ZČU/UWB)

Univerzitní 8, 306 14 Plzeň
Tel: +420 377 631 111
Fax: +420 377 631 112
EMail: info@rek.zcu.cz
Website: http://www.zcu.cz

Rektor: Ilona Mauritzová
Tel: +420 377 631 000 EMail: rektor@rek.zcu.cz

Registrar: Hynek Gloser

Faculty

Applied Sciences (Automation and Control Engineering; Business Computing; Computer Engineering; Computer Graphics; Computer Networks; Computer Science; Engineering; Information Technology; Mathematics; Mechanics; Natural Sciences; Physical Engineering; Physics; Software Engineering; Statistics); **Art and Design** *(Ladislav Sutnar)* (Ceramic Art; Design; Fashion Design; Fine Arts; Graphic Arts; Industrial Design; Jewellery Art; Metal Techniques; Multimedia; Painting and Drawing; Printing and Printmaking; Sculpture); **Economics** *(Plzeň Cheb)* (Accountancy; Administration; Economic and Finance Policy; Economics; English; Finance; French; German; Information Sciences; Management; Management Systems; Marketing; Modern Languages; Operations Research; Russian; Spanish; Statistics); **Education** (Biology; Chemistry; Computer Science; Cultural Studies; Czech; Education; Educational Technology; English; Fine Arts; French; Geography; Geography (Human); German; History; Literature; Mathematics; Mathematics Education; Music; Music Education; Native Language; Native Language Education; Physical Education; Physics; Psychology; Russian; Sports; Technology Education); **Electrical Engineering** (Computer Science; Ecology; Electrical and Electronic Equipment and Maintenance; Electrical Engineering; Electronic Engineering; Energy Engineering; Multimedia; Power Engineering; Telecommunications Engineering; Transport Engineering); **Health Care Studies** (Nursing; Physical Therapy; Public Health); **Law** (Law; Public Administration); **Mechanical Engineering** (Electrical and Electronic Equipment and Maintenance; Industrial Design; Industrial Engineering; Industrial Management; Maintenance Technology; Materials Engineering; Mechanical Engineering; Metal Techniques; Metallurgical Engineering; Physical Education; Power Engineering; Production Engineering; Sports; Transport Engineering); **Philosophy and Arts** (Anthropology; Archaeology; English; German; Germanic Studies; History; International Relations; Literature; Philosophy; Political Sciences; Romance Languages; Sociology)

Institute

Applied Language Studies (Dutch; English; Foreign Languages Education; French; German; Portuguese; Russian; Spanish)

Centre

Information Technology (Information Technology)

Further Information: Also Parallel study programmes in English are offered to foreign students. International Summer Language School

History: Founded 1991, incorporating Institute of Technology (founded 1949) and Faculty of Education (founded 1948).

Academic Year: September to June (September-December; February-May)

Admission Requirements: Secondary school certificate (maturitní vysvědčeni) and entrance examination (Přijímací zkoušky)

Fees: None

Main Language(s) of Instruction: Czech

Degrees and Diplomas: *Bakalář*; *Magistr*: **Business and Commerce; Design; Electrical Engineering; Fine Arts; Law; Management; Mechanical Engineering; Nursing; Pedagogy; Power Engineering; Teacher Training.** *Doktor*: **Archaeology; Economics; Electrical Engineering; Ethnology; History; Management; Mechanical Engineering; Pedagogy; Political Sciences; Power Engineering; Science Education; Teacher Training.**

Student Services: Academic Counselling, Canteen, Careers Guidance, Cultural Activities, Foreign Studies Centre, Health Services, Language Laboratory, Sports Facilities

Publications: Sborník ZČU; Výroční zpráva o činnosti Západočeské univerzity v Plzni

Publishing House: University Publishing Centre (Vydavatelství ZČU)

Student Numbers *2014*: Total: c. 14,000

Last Updated: 03/02/15

VŠB - TECHNICAL UNIVERSITY OF OSTRAVA

Vysoká škola báňská - Technická univerzita Ostrava (VŠB-TUO)

17 listopadu 15, Poruba, 70833 Ostrava
Tel: +420(59) 7321 111
Fax: +420(59) 6918 507
EMail: university@vsb.cz
Website: http://www.vsb.cz

Rektor: Ivo Vondrák (2010-)
Tel: +420(59) 7325-279 EMail: rektor@vsb.cz; ivo.vondrak@vsb.cz

Kvestor: Zdeněk Hodula
Tel: +420(59) 7325-276 +420(59) 7325-279
EMail: kvestor@vsb.cz; zdenek.hodula@vsb.cz

Faculty

Civil Engineering *(Architecture and Construction)* (Architecture and Planning; Civil Engineering); **Economics** (Accountancy; Applied Mathematics; Business Administration; Business Computing; Computer Engineering; Econometrics; Economics; Finance; Information Technology; Law; Management; Marketing; Public Administration); **Electrical Engineering and Computer Science** (Applied Mathematics; Computer Science; Electrical and Electronic Equipment and Maintenance; Electrical Engineering; Measurement and Precision Engineering; Power Engineering; Telecommunications Engineering); **Mechanical Engineering** (Automation and Control Engineering; Energy Engineering; Hydraulic Engineering; Machine Building; Materials Engineering; Mechanical Engineering; Mechanical Equipment and Maintenance; Mechanics; Robotics; Technology; Transport and Communications); **Metallurgy and Materials Engineering** (Analytical Chemistry; Automation and Control Engineering; Chemical Engineering; Chemistry; Environmental Management; Materials Engineering; Metal Techniques; Metallurgical Engineering; Physical Chemistry; Safety Engineering; Thermal Engineering); **Mining and Geology** (Astronomy and Space Science; Environmental Engineering; Geological Engineering; Geology; Mathematics; Mining Engineering; Physics; Safety

Engineering; Surveying and Mapping); **Safety Engineering** (Safety Engineering)

Programme

Civil Engineering *(Bachelor, Master, Doctoral)*; **Faculty** *(Architecture and Construction)*

Higher Institute

Analytical Chemistry and Material Testing (Analytical Chemistry; Physics); **European Studies** (European Studies)

Research Centre

Energy (Energy Engineering; Environmental Engineering; Natural Resources); **Nanotechnology** (Nanotechnology)

History: Founded 1716 as School of Mining and Metallurgy at Jáchymov in Bohemia, became part of the Charles University of Prague 1763. Moved to Slovakia 1770 as Mining Academy, Banská Štiavnica, and Příbram, Bohemia 1849. Acquired university status 1904 and moved to present location in Ostrava 1945.

Academic Year: September to May (September-December; February-May)

Admission Requirements: Secondary school certificate (Maturitní vysvědčeni) for Bachelor study programmes; Bachelor degree for Master study programmes; Master degree for Doctoral Study Programmes. Entrance examination.

Fees: National: Study in Czech: none (Czech Koruna), International: Programme in English: 3,500 EUR/per annum for Bachelor and Doctoral study programmes; 4,000 EUR - Master study programmes (Euro)

Main Language(s) of Instruction: Czech, English

Accrediting Agency: Ministry of Education, Youth and Sports

Degrees and Diplomas: *Bakalář*, *Inženýr*, *Doktor*

Student Services: Canteen, Careers Guidance, Cultural Activities, Facilities for disabled people, Foreign Studies Centre, Health Services, IT Centre, Language Laboratory, Library, Residential Facilities, Sports Facilities, eLibrary

Publications: Proceedings of Scientific Papers

Last Updated: 09/01/15

PRIVATE INSTITUTIONS

BANKING INSTITUTE/COLLEGE OF BANKING, INC.

Bankovní institut vysoká škola, a. s. (BIVŠ)

Nárožní 2600/9, 158 00 Praha 5

Tel: +420(2) 3307-4536

Fax: +420(2) 3307-2083

EMail: info@bivs.cz

Website: http://www.bivs.cz

Rektor: Pavel Mertlík

Tel: +420 251 114 501 EMail: pmertlik@bivs.cz

Assistant of General Manager, Rector and Vice-Rectors: Jana Haunerová EMail: jhaunerova@bivs.cz

Department

Banking and Insurance (Banking; Economics; Finance; Information Technology; Insurance; Management)

History: Founded 1999.

Main Language(s) of Instruction: Czech, Russian, English

Degrees and Diplomas: *Bakalář*, *Magistr*. **Finance; Information Technology; Management.**

Student Services: Canteen, Library

Last Updated: 28/01/15

BRNO INTERNATIONAL BUSINESS SCHOOL (BIBS)

Lidická 81, 602 00 Brno

Tel: +420 545 210 792

Fax: +420 545 570 115

EMail: info@bibs.cz

Website: http://www.bibs.cz

Rektor: Miloslav Keřkovský EMail: kerkovsky@bibs.cz

Vice-Rector for Academic Development: Lenka Cimbálníková EMail: Cimbálníková@bibs.cz

Programme

Business (Business Administration; Commercial Law; Economics; Law; Management)

Further Information: Also a branch in Prague

History: Founded 1998. Acquired present status 2005.

Accrediting Agency: Ministry of Education, Youth and Sports

Degrees and Diplomas: *Bakalář*, *Magistr*. **Business Administration; Economics; Law; Management.** *Doktor*. **Business Administration.** Also International Doctorate (PhD) in Business and Administration

Student Services: Library

Last Updated: 28/01/15

BUSINESS SCHOOL OSTRAVA, PLC.

Vysoká škola podnikání, a.s. (VŠP)

Michálkovická 1810/181, 710 00 Ostrava

Tel: +420 595 228 111

Fax: +420 595 228 199

EMail: info@vsp.cz

Website: http://www.vsp.cz

Rektor: Jiří Cienciala

Tel: +420 595 228 100 EMail: jiri.cienciala@vsp.cz

Prorektor: Renáta Nešporková

Tel: +420 737 207 966 EMail: renata.nesporkova@vsp.cz

International Relations: Růžena Dvořáčková, Director

Tel: +420 595 228 127 EMail: ruzena.dvorackova@vsp.cz

Department

Business Administration (Business Administration); **Economics, Law and Social Science** (Economics; Law; Social Sciences); **Information Technology and Computer Science** (Computer Science; Information Technology); **Marketing** (Management; Marketing)

History: Founded 2000.

Degrees and Diplomas: *Bakalář*, *Magistr*. **Business Administration.**

Last Updated: 02/02/15

CEVRO INSTITUTE

CEVRO Institut

Jungmannova 17, 11000 Prague

Tel: +420 (221) 506-00

EMail: info@vsci.cz

Website: http://www.vsci.cz/

President: Josef Šíma

Tel: +420 221 506-777 EMail: josef.sima@vsci.cz

International Relations: Miloš Brunclík

Tel: +420 221 506-701 EMail: milos.brunclik@vsci.cz

Programme

Economic Policy and Administration (Business Administration); **Legal Specializations** (Law); **Politics** (Political Sciences); **Private study** (Business and Commerce); **Public Administration** (Public Administration)

History: Founded 2005.

Academic Year: Fall: October-January Spring: February-June

Admission Requirements: Interview

Fees: National: 50.000 per annum (Czech Koruna), International: 2000/year (Euro)

Main Language(s) of Instruction: Czech, English

Accrediting Agency: Accreditation Commission, Czech Republic

Degrees and Diplomas: *Bakalář*, *Magistr*. **Business and Commerce; Political Sciences; Protective Services; Public Administration.**

Last Updated: 09/01/15

COLLEGE OF POLITICAL AND SOCIAL SCIENCES

Academia Rerum Civilium - Vysoká škola politických a společenských věd, s.r.o. (VŠPSV)
Ovčárecká 312, 280 02 Kolín V
Tel: +420(32) 173-4711
Fax: +420(32) 173-4720
EMail: arc@vspsv.cz
Website: http://www.vspsv.cz

Rector: Ján Liďák EMail: lidak@vspsv.cz

Prorektor: Vladimír Srb EMail: srb@vspsv.cz

Programme
Political Sciences (Political Sciences)

History: Founded 2001. Acquired present status 2003.

Fees: National: 19900 per semester (Czech Koruna), International: 19900 per semester (Czech Koruna)

Main Language(s) of Instruction: Czech

Accrediting Agency: Ministry of Education, Youth and Sport, Czech Republic

Degrees and Diplomas: *Bakalář*: **Political Sciences.** *Magistr*: **Political Sciences.** *Doktor*: **Political Sciences.**

Student Services: Academic Counselling, IT Centre, Library

Last Updated: 15/12/14

EUROPEAN POLYTECHNIC INSTITUTE, LTD.

Evropský politechnický institut, s.r.o. (EPI)
Osvobození 699, 686 04 Kunovice
Tel: +420(57) 254-8035
Fax: +420(57) 254-9018
EMail: epi@edukomplex.cz
Website: http://edukomplex.cz/

Rektor: Oldřich Kratochvíl EMail: epi@vos.cz

Vice-Rector for Education: Ladislav Obdržálek

Programme
Business

History: Founded 1999.

Degrees and Diplomas: *Bakalář*, *Magistr*: **Computer Science; Economics.**

Last Updated: 03/02/15

FILM ACADEMY OF MIROSLAVA ONDŘÍČEK IN PÍSEK, P.B.C.

Filmová Akademie Miroslava Ondříčka v Písku, o.p.s. (FAMO)
Lipová alej 2068, 397 01 Písek
Tel: +420 382 264 212
Fax: +420 380 602 080
EMail: famo@filmovka.cz
Website: http://www.filmovka.cz/

Rektor: Jindřich Goetz (2011-2015)

International Relations: Veronika Lederová, Head of International Film Studies, Erasmus coordinator (2014-)
EMail: ifs@filmovka.cz; veronika.lederova filmovka.cz

Department
Animated Film (Film); **Cinematography** (Cinema and Television); **Directing and Screenwriting** (Film); **Film and Television Production** (Cinema and Television; Film); **Film Editing** (Film); **Film Sound** (Film; Sound Engineering (Acoustics))

History: Founded 2003 as Film Academy in Písek. Acquired present title 2005.

Main Language(s) of Instruction: Czech

Accrediting Agency: Czech Ministry of Education.

Degrees and Diplomas: *Bakalář*, *Magistr*: **Cinema and Television; Film.**

Last Updated: 29/01/15

INSTITUTE OF HOSPITALITY MANAGEMENT, LTD

Vysoká škola hotelová, s.r.o. (VŠH)
Svídnická 506, 181 00 Praha 8
Tel: +420(283) 101-121
Fax: +420(233) 541-905
EMail: info@vsh.cz
Website: http://www.vsh.cz

Rektor: Václav Vinš Tel: +420(2) 8310-1122 EMail: rektor@vsh.cz

Vice-Rector for Academic Affairs: Jan Máče
Tel: +420(2) 8310-1120 EMail: han@vsh.cz

International Relations: Zuzana Roldánová, Prorektor
Tel: +420(2) 8310-1139 EMail: roldanova@vsh.cz

Department
Economy and Economics (Economics); **Hotel Management** (Cooking and Catering; Hotel Management); **Language Studies** (Modern Languages); **Management** (Management); **Marketing** (Marketing; Media Studies); **Travel and Tourism** (Tourism)

History: Founded 1999. It was one of the first three private universities accredited in 1999 under the new laws regarding tertiary education.

Fees: National: For the 2014/2015 academic year: 32,500/ semester – full-time study – bachelor's program, all major fields of study (except for Management of Transportation Services). 20,000/ semester – part-time study – bachelor's program, all major fields of study. 32,500/ semester – full and part-time study – all major fields of study for the integrated master's program (Czech Koruna), International: For the 2014/2015 academic year: 39,500/ semester – full-time study – bachelor's program for Hospitality Management in English (approximately 1,600 Euros/semester depending on actual exchange rates) (Czech Koruna)

Main Language(s) of Instruction: Czech, English

Accrediting Agency: National accrediting agency

Degrees and Diplomas: *Bakalář*, *Magistr*

Student Services: Academic Counselling, Canteen, Cultural Activities, Foreign Studies Centre, IT Centre, Language Laboratory, Library, Residential Facilities, eLibrary

Publications: Czech Hospitality and Tourism Papers; VŠH News

Academic Staff *2014-2015*	**TOTAL**
FULL-TIME	**1,586**
Student Numbers *2014-2015*	
All (Foreign included)	**91**

Part-time students, 522.

Last Updated: 07/01/15

INSTITUTE OF TECHNOLOGY AND ECONOMICS IN ČESKÉ BUDEJOVICE

Vysoká škola technická a ekonomická v Českých Budějovicích (VŠTE)
Okružní 517/10, 370 01 České Budějovice
Tel: +420 387 842 111
EMail: vstecb@vstecb.cz
Website: http://www.vstecb.cz

Rector: Marek Vochozka
Tel: +420 725 007 337 EMail: vochozka@mail.vstecb.cz

International Relations: Štefan Husár, Vice-Rector of Internal Relations Tel: +420 387 842 192 EMail: husar@mail.vstecb.cz

Department
Civil Engineering (Building Technologies); **Economics and Management** (Business and Commerce); **Foreign Languages**; **Mechanical Engineering** (Mechanical Engineering); **Natural Sciences** (Natural Sciences); **Tourism and Marketing** (Marketing; Tourism); **Transport and Logistics** (Transport Management)

History: Founded 2006.

Admission Requirements: Secondary school certificate

Fees: Bachelor's degree courses and Master's degree courses: 40.000 per semester (Czech Koruna)

Main Language(s) of Instruction: Czech

Degrees and Diplomas: *Bakalář*; *Magistr*: **Transport Management.**

Student Services: Canteen, Library, Residential Facilities

Last Updated: 03/02/15

INTERNATIONAL ART CAMPUS PRAGUE, S.R.O.

Literární akademie

Na Pankráci 420/54, 140 00 Prague, 4

Tel: +420 226 539 741

EMail: studijni@art-campus.cz

Website: http://www.art-campus.cz/la/

Rector: Petr Kanka (2013-)

Tel: +420 724 118 422 EMail: petr.kanka@art-campus.cz

Institute

Health and Social Services (Health Administration; Health Sciences; Social and Community Services)

Academy

Literary (Literature; Media Studies; Writing)

History: Founded 2000. Merger of Josef Škvorecký Writers' Academy (Literární akademie - Soukromá vysoká škola J. Škvoreckého, s.r.o.) 2013.

Main Language(s) of Instruction: Czech

Degrees and Diplomas: *Bakalář*: **Literature.** *Magistr*: **Media Studies; Printing and Printmaking; Writing.**

Last Updated: 29/01/15

JAN AMOS KOMENSKÝ UNIVERSITY PRAGUE

Univerzita Jana Amose Komenského Praha, s.r.o. (VŠJAK)

Roháčova 63, 130 00 Praha 3

Tel: +420(2) 6719-9015

Fax: +420(2) 6719-9001

EMail: international@ujak.cz

Website: http://www.ujak.cz

Rektor: Luboš Chaloupka (2001-)

Tel: +420(2) 6719-9001 EMail: rektor@ujak.cz

International Relations: Marcela Křížová

Tel: +420(2) 6719-9033 EMail: krizova.marcela@ujak.cz

Department

Adult Education (Adult Education); **Andragogy** (Education; Human Resources); **European Economic and Public Administration Studies** (Economics; Public Administration); **Human Resources Development and the European Union** (European Studies; Human Resources); **Social and Mass Communication** (Communication Studies; Mass Communication); **Special Education** (Special Education)

History: Founded 2001 as Vysoká škola Jana Amose Komenského, s.r.o.

Fees: 4,800 per annum (Euro)

Main Language(s) of Instruction: Czech, English

Degrees and Diplomas: *Bakalář*; *Magistr*: **Business Administration.** *Doktor*

Last Updated: 30/01/15

METROPOLITAN UNIVERSITY PRAGUE, O.P.S

Metropolitni Univerzita Praha, o.p.s (VŠVSMV)

Dubečská 900/10, 100 31 Praha 10, Strašnice

Tel: +420 274 815 044

Fax: +420 274 817 190

EMail: info@mup.cz

Website: http://www.mup.cz

Rektor: Michal Klíma (2005-)

Tel: +420(2) 7418-8133 EMail: klima@mup.cz

Prorektor: Jan Bureš EMail: bures@mup.cz

Department

Anglophone Studies (English); **Asian Studies** (Asian Studies); **Economics** (Economics); **Foreign Languages** (Modern Languages); **Humanities** (Arts and Humanities); **Industrial Property** (Industrial Arts Education); **Information Technologies** (Information Technology); **International Relations and European Studies** (European Studies; International Relations); **International Trade** (International Business); **Law and Public Administration** (Law; Public Administration)

History: Founded 2001 as University of Public Administration and International Relations.

Fees: Bachelor's Degree and Master's Degree Programmes: 5000 per annum (2039 euro) (Czech Koruna)

Main Language(s) of Instruction: Czech, English

Degrees and Diplomas: *Bakalář*, *Magistr*, *Doktor*: **European Studies; International Business; International Relations; International Studies.** Metropolitan University Prague has launched 5 Double Degree programmes in cooperation with its international partners on the Bachelor's Degree as well as on the Master's Degree level, namely with Nottingham Trent University, Matej Bel University, SRH Hochschule Berlin, University of Trento, and Manipal University. Upon due completion of the Bachelor's or Master's Degree study programmes at MUP, students shall receive a diploma from both partner universities.

Student Services: Library

Publications: Journal of International and Security Studies

Last Updated: 29/01/15

PRAGUE COLLEGE OF PSYCHOSOCIAL STUDIES

Pražská vysoká škola psychosociálních studií, s.r.o. (PVŠPS)

Hekrova 805, 149 00 Praha, 4

Tel: +420(267) 913-634

Fax: +420(267) 913-634

EMail: info@pvsps.cz

Website: http://www.pvsps.cz/

Rektor: Jiří Ružička Tel: +420(2) 6791-0424

Registrar: Milena Balá

Tel: +420 272 937 713 EMail: tajemnice@pvsps.cz

International Relations: Michaela Klabanová

Tel: +420(2) 6791-3634 EMail: mobility@pvsps.cz

Programme

Psychological and Social Studies (Psychology; Social Policy; Social Studies; Social Work)

History: Founded 2001.

Fees: 25 000- 28 500 depending on programmes (Czech Koruna)

Main Language(s) of Instruction: Czech

Accrediting Agency: Ministry of Education, Youth and Sport

Degrees and Diplomas: *Bakalář*; *Magistr*: **Psychology; Social Work.**

Last Updated: 16/03/15

PRIVATE COLLEGE OF ECONOMIC STUDIES, LTD.

Soukromá vysoká škola ekonomických studií, s.r.o. (SVŠES)

Lindnerova 575/1, 180 00 Praha 8

Tel: +420(2) 8484-1027

Fax: +420(2) 8484-1196

EMail: info@svses.cz

Website: http://www.svses.cz

Rector: Lucie Marková (2011-)

Tel: +420 284 840 027

EMail: rektor@svses.cz; lucie.markova@svses.cz

Programme

Economics and Management (Accountancy; Commercial Law; Economics; International Economics; International Law; Management); **Protection and Safety of Organizations** (Protective Services)

History: Founded 1996. Acquired present status 2001.

Fees: 53,000 per academic year (Czech Koruna)

Degrees and Diplomas: *Bakalář*; *Magistr*: **Finance; International Business; Management.**

Last Updated: 30/01/15

RAŠÍN COLLEGE, LTD.

Rašínova vysoká škola, s.r.o. (RVŠ)
Šámalova 60, 615 00 Brno
Tel: +420 516 116 180
Fax: +420 516 116 616
EMail: info@ravys.cz
Website: http://www.ravys.cz

Rektor: Vladimír Klaban

Kvestor: Miroslav Boršek

Programme

Law and Economics (Accountancy; Administrative Law; Banking; Civil Law; Commercial Law; Constitutional Law; Criminal Law; Economics; English; Finance; German; Human Resources; Information Technology; Labour Law; Law; Management; Marketing; Psychology; Sociology; Taxation)

History: Founded 2003.

Main Language(s) of Instruction: Czech

Degrees and Diplomas: *Bakalář*: **Economics; Management.** *Magistr*: **Economics.**
Last Updated: 29/01/15

ŠKODA AUTO UNIVERSITY

ŠKODA AUTO Vysoká Škola, a.s. (ŠAVŠ)
Na Karmeli 1457, 293 01 Mladá Boleslav
Tel: +420(3) 2682-3029
Fax: +420(3) 2682-3113
EMail: info@is.savs.cz
Website: http://www.savs.cz

Rektor: Petr Šulc EMail: Petr.Sulc@savs.cz

International Relations: Lenka Stejskalová, Vice-Rector for International Relations
Tel: +420 823 029 EMail: Lenka.Stejskalova@savs.cz

Programme

Economics and Management (Economics; Management; Marketing)

History: Founded 2000.

Fees: Bachelor's degree programme: CZK 56,000 per academic year (specialisations in Czech). EUR 7,000 per academic year (Specialisations in English). Master's degree programme: CZK 64,000 per academic year (specialisations in Czech). EUR 9,000 per academic year. (Specialisations in English)

Main Language(s) of Instruction: Czech, English, German

Degrees and Diplomas: *Bakalář*, *Magistr*: **Business Administration; Commercial Law; Finance; Management; Marketing.**
Last Updated: 29/01/15

STING ACADEMY, P.B.C

Akademie Sting, o.p.s (AS)
Stromovka 1, 637 00 Brno
Tel: +420 541 221-801-2
Fax: +420 541 220-334
EMail: info@akademiesting.cz
Website: http://www.sting.cz

Rektor: Zdeněk Sadovský

Vice-Rector for Education: David Král

International Relations: Zdeněk Karpišek, Vice-Rector for International Relations and development activitie

Department

Accounting and Taxes (Accountancy; Taxation); **Applied Disciplines; Economics and Management** (Administration; Economics; Management)

History: Founded 2000.

Fees: Bachelor: 40.000 per annum; Master: 50 000 per annum (Czech Koruna)

Main Language(s) of Instruction: Czech

Degrees and Diplomas: *Bakalář*, *Magistr*: **Business Administration; Management.**
Last Updated: 28/01/15

THE ANGLO-AMERICAN UNIVERSITY, P.B.C.

Anglo-Americká vysoká škola, o.p.s. (AAVŠ)
Letenska 5, 118 00 Praha 1
Tel: +420 257 530 202
Fax: +420 257 532 911
EMail: info@aauni.edu
Website: http://www.aauni.edu

Rektor: Alan Krautstengl EMail: alan.krautstengl@aauni.edu

Provost: Milada Polišenská
EMail: milada.polisenska@aauni.edu

International Relations: Cyril Simsa, Director of International Cooperation EMail: cyril.simsa@aauni.edu

School

Business Administration (Business Administration; Finance; International Business; Law); **Humanities and Social Sciences** (Arts and Humanities; Cultural Studies; Economics; Gender Studies; Political Sciences; Social Sciences); **International Relations and Diplomacy** (Central European Studies; Eastern European Studies; International Relations); **Journalism** (Journalism); **Law** *(John H. Carey II)* (Comparative Law; Law)

History: Founded 1990 as Anglo-American College. Renamed Anglo-American Institute for Liberal Studies 1999. Acquired present status 2001 and title 2003.

Admission Requirements: Secondary School Certificate. for nonnative English speakers: TOEFL (min 525 paper-based, 197 computer-based, 71 Internet-based test; DI-CODE of Anglo-americká vysoká škola: 9734), or FCE (mark A or B), or CAE (mark A or B or C) or Všeobecná státní zkouška, or IELTS (min. 6), or International Baccalaureaute (IB)

Fees: Bachelor's program: 2000 per credit; Master's program: 2.300 per credit (Czech Koruna)

Main Language(s) of Instruction: English

Degrees and Diplomas: *Bakalář*: **Arts and Humanities; Business Administration; Comparative Law; Cultural Studies; International Relations; Social Sciences; Social Studies.** *Magistr*: **Arts and Humanities; Business Administration; International Relations; Law; Social and Community Services.**

Student Services: Academic Counselling, Facilities for disabled people
Last Updated: 28/01/15

THE COLLEGE OF LOGISTICS, P.B.C

Vysoká škola logistiky, o.p.s. (VŠL)
Palackého 1381/25, 750 02 Přerov 1, Město
Tel: +420(58) 125-9120
Fax: +420(58) 125-9131
EMail: vslg@vslg.cz
Website: http://www.vslg.cz

Rector: Ivan Barančík
Tel: +420(58) 125-9126 EMail: ivan.barancik@vslg.cz

Vice-Rector for Education: Kamil Peterek
Tel: +420(58) 125-9127 EMail: Peterek

Department

Economics, Law and Social Studies (Economics; Law; Social Studies); **Humanities and Natural Sciences** (Arts and Humanities; Geography; Natural Sciences; Tourism); **Logistics and Technical Disciplines** (Information Management; Transport Management)

History: Founded 2004.

Fees: Undergraduate: 38,000 per annum (Czech Koruna)

Main Language(s) of Instruction: Czech

Degrees and Diplomas: *Bakalář*, *Magistr*: **Transport Management.**
Last Updated: 02/02/15

UNIVERSITY COLLEGE OF INTERNATIONAL AND PUBLIC RELATIONS PRAGUE, P.B.C.

Vysoká škola mezinárodních a veřejných vztahů Praha, o.p.s. (VŠMVVP)

U Santošky 17, 150 00 Praha 5
Tel: +420(2) 5156-3158 +420(2) 5156-2124
Fax: +420(2) 5156-1557
EMail: info@vip-vs.cz
Website: http://www.vip-vs.cz

Rektor: Judita Štouračová (2005-) EMail: stouracova@vip-vs.cz

International Relations: Felix Černoch, Prorektor
EMail: cernoch@vip-vs.cz

Department

European Studies, Public Administration and Law (European Studies; Law; Public Administration); **Foreign Languages** (English; French; German; Italian; Russian); **International Relations and Diplomacy** (International Relations); **Political and Social Sciences** (Political Sciences; Social Sciences); **Public Relations and Communication Studies** (Communication Studies; Management; Philosophy; Psychology; Public Relations; Sociology)

Further Information: Also has several branches in Bratislava, Olomouc and České Budějovice

History: Founded 2001.

Fees: Bachelor's degree program: 64.000 per annum. Master's degree program: 56.000 per annum (Czech Koruna)

Main Language(s) of Instruction: Czech

Degrees and Diplomas: *Bakalář*; *Magistr*: **European Studies; International Relations; International Studies; Political Sciences; Public Administration.**

Last Updated: 02/02/15

UNIVERSITY OF BUSINESS IN PRAGUE

Vysoká škola obchodní v Praze, o.p.s. (VŠO)

Spálená 76/14, 110 00 Praha, 1
Tel: +420(2) 2405-6011
Fax: +420(2) 2405-6336
EMail: info@vso-praha.eu
Website: http://www.vso.cz

Rektor: Jaroslava Durčáková EMail: studijni@vso-praha.eu

Department

Air Transport (Air Transport); **Computer Science** (Computer Science); **Economics and Finance** (Economics; Finance); **Foreign Languages** (Foreign Languages Education); **Law** (Law); **Management and Marketing** (Management; Marketing); **Mathematics and Statistics** (Mathematics; Statistics); **Social Sciences** (Social Sciences); **Tourism** (Tourism)

History: Founded 2000. Formerly known as College of Business Studies in Prague, p.b.c.

Main Language(s) of Instruction: Czech

Degrees and Diplomas: *Bakalář*; *Magistr*: **Air Transport; Tourism.**

Last Updated: 16/03/15

UNIVERSITY OF ECONOMICS AND MANAGEMENT, LTD

Vysoká škola ekonomie a managementu, s.r.o. (VŠEM)

Nárožni 2600/9a, 15800 Praha 5
Tel: +420 841-133-166
Fax: +420 475-600-135
EMail: info@vsem.cz
Website: http://www.vsem.cz

Rector: Milan Žák EMail: rektor@vsem.cz

International Relations: Julie Šmejkalová, Vice-President for Development and Foreign Relations

Department

Applied Methods (Computer Engineering; Mathematics and Computer Science); **Business Economics** (Advertising and Publicity; Business Administration; Economics; Marketing); **Economics** (Economics); **Human Resources** (Human Resources; Psychology; Public Administration; Sociology); **Management** (Management)

Further Information: Also online professional courses

History: Founded 2001.

Academic Year: January-April-October

Admission Requirements: "Maturitni zkouška" and "Potvrzeni o praxi"

Fees: Bachelor level, 40,000 per annum; for Master level, 40,000 per annum. MBA: 60,000 (Czech Koruna)

Main Language(s) of Instruction: Czech

Accrediting Agency: Ministry of Education, Youth and Sports; European Council for Business Administration(ECBE)

Degrees and Diplomas: *Bakalář*: **Business Administration; Economics; Management.** *Magistr*: **Business Administration; Finance; Human Resources; International Business; Management.**

Student Services: Academic Counselling, IT Centre, Library, Residential Facilities, Sports Facilities

Publications: Aktualizace dlouhodobého zóměru

Publishing House: Zpravodaj VŠEM

Last Updated: 02/02/15

UNIVERSITY OF FINANCE AND ADMINISTRATION, P.B.C.

Vysoká škola finanční a správní, o. p. s. (VŠFS)

Estonská 500, 101 00 Praha 10
Tel: +420(2) 1008-8800
Fax: +420(2) 7174-1597
EMail: info@vsfs.cz; sekretariat@vsfs.cz
Website: http://www.vsfs.cz

Rektor: Bohuslava Šenkýřová
Tel: +420(210) 088 849 EMail: bohuslava.senkyrova@vsfs.cz

International Relations: Petr Budinský, Vice-Rector for Education and External Relations
Tel: +420(2) 1008-8818 EMail: petr.budinsky@vsfs.cz

Department

Computer Science and Mathematics (Computer Science; Mathematics; Statistics); **Finance** (Finance; Management); **Foreign Languages**; **Law** (Law); **Macroeconomics and International Relations** (Economic and Finance Policy; Economics; International Relations); **Marketing Communication** (Communication Studies; Management; Marketing); **Public Administration** (Public Administration); **Sociology** (Sociology)

History: Founded 1999 by the Bank Academy and Czech Coal Group, in accordance with the state approval to act as a private institution of higher education. In 2001 its study centers in Most and Kladno were opened. A year later MBA study programs were launched in cooperation with City University Seattle (USA). Another year later the school set up Eupress, a publishing house producing study materials and books. In March 2003 VSFS acquired accreditation for the follow-up Master study. In the course of its first 5 years of existence the school became the biggest private institution of higher education in the CR in terms of the number of both students and teachers. In 2009, the University of Finance and Administration has received state approval for Doctoral study program and became the first private University of Economics in the Czech Republic.

Admission Requirements: The basic conditions for admission to university study are stipulated in the Act No. 111/1998 Coll. on Higher Education Institutions and on Amendments and Supplements to Other Acts (the Higher Education Act) as follows: Admission to study in Bachelor's degree programmes is conditional upon the completion of full secondary education or full secondary specialized education. Admission to a Master's degree programme following a Bachelor's degree programme is conditional upon the completion of a Bachelor's degree programme. Admission to a Doctoral degree programme is conditional upon the completion of study in a Master's degree programme.

Fees: Programs taught in English, Bachelor Studies: Full-time: 66,000 - Part-time: 64,000 Master Studies: Full-time: 69,000 - Part-time: 67,000. Joint Degree B (BSBA + Bc. in Business Management and Corporate Finance): Full-time: CZK 258,000 - Part-time: 252,000. Joint Degree B (BSBA + Bc. in Marketing Communication): Full-time: CZK 264,000 - Part-time: 258,000. MBA: Full time course: 240,000. Joint Degree M (MBA + Ing. in Business

Management and Corporate Finance): Full-time: CZK 282,000 - Part-time: CZK 278,000. Joint Degree M (MBA + Ing. in Marketing Communication): Full-time: 282,000 - Part-time: 278,000. MPA: Full time course: 250,000 Programs taught in Czech, Bachelor Studies: Full-time: CZK 51,000 - Part-time: CZK 50,000. Master Studies: Full-time: CZK 55,000 - Part-time: CZK 53,000. Doctoral Studies: Full-time: CZK 55,000 - Part-time: CZK 55,000 (Czech Koruna)

Main Language(s) of Instruction: Czech, English

Degrees and Diplomas: *Bakalář*; *Magistr*. **Business Administration; Marketing.**

Last Updated: 16/03/15

UNIVERSITY OF NEW YORK IN PRAGUE, S.R.O

Londýnská 41, 120 00 Praha

Tel: +420(224) 221-261 +420(224) 221-281

Fax: +420(224) 221-247

EMail: unyp@unyp.cz

Website: http://www.unyp.cz/

President: Elias Foutsis

International Relations: William Barnard, Dean of Academic Development EMail: wbarnard@unyp.cz

Department

Business Administration (Business Administration; Finance; Marketing); **Communications and Mass Media** (Communication Studies; Information Technology; Journalism; Mass Communication; Media Studies); **English Language and Literature** (English; Literature); **International and Commercial Law** (Commercial Law; International Law); **International Economic Relations** (International Economics; International Relations); **Psychology** (Psychology)

Further Information: Also a secondary Campus at: Legerova 72, Praha

History: Created 1998. Acquired status 2001.

Fees: PhD Program: 250,000 per annum (Czech Koruna)

Main Language(s) of Instruction: English

Accrediting Agency: Ministry of Education, Youth and Sports

Degrees and Diplomas: *Bakalář*; *Magistr*. **Business Administration; English; International Business; Law; Management; Transport Management.** *Doktor*. Both European- and American-style degrees.

Student Services: Academic Counselling, Careers Guidance, Sports Facilities

Last Updated: 30/01/15

Denmark

STRUCTURE OF HIGHER EDUCATION SYSTEM

Description:

Higher education is offered by five types of higher education institutions:
1. Academies of Professional Higher Education (Erhvervsakademi) offering professionally oriented short cycle and first cycle degree programmes;
2. University Colleges (Professionshøjskole) offering professionally oriented first cycle degree programmes;
3. Maritime Education Institutions offering professionally oriented short cycle and first cycle degree programmes;
4. Research universities (Universitet) offering first, second and third cycle degree programmes in all academic disciplines;
5. University-level institutions offering first, second and third cycle degree programmes in subject fields such as architecture, design, music and fine and performing arts.
Most of the higher education institutions are regulated by the Ministry of Higher Education and Science (type 1-5). The Ministry of Culture regulates a small number of higher education institutions offering first, second and third cycle degree programmes in fine and performing arts (type 5).

Stages of studies:

University level first stage: *Bachelor's degree*
Degrees at bachelor's level, i.e. first cycle degrees (EQF level 6), include:
1) Bachelor's degree from a university, awarded after 3 years of study (180 ECTS);
2) Bachelor's degree within the arts, also awarded after 3 years of study (180 ECTS);
3) Professional Bachelor's degree, awarded after 180-270 ECTS (usually 180-240 ECTS), including a period of work placement of at least 30 ECTS.

University level second stage: *Master's degree*
Degrees at master's level, i.e. second cycle degrees (EQF level 7), include:
1) The Master's degree from a university (candidatus/candidata, Danish: kandidatgrad), awarded after 2 years of study (120 ECTS points). A few Master's programmes are longer: Medicine (3 years, 180 ECTS points) and Veterinary Medicine ($2\frac{1}{2}$ years, 150 ECTS points);
2) The Master's degree within fine arts, awarded after 120-180 ECTS.

University level third stage: *PhD degree*
The PhD degree, i.e. third cycle degree (EQF Level 8) is awarded after a total of normally 8 years of higher education and research. The PhD programme itself normally lasts 3 years (180 ECTS points).

University level fourth stage: *Doctoral degree*
This traditional higher doctoral degree (doktorgrad) may be obtained by mature researchers, usually after a minimum of 5-8 years of individual and original research and public defence of a dissertation. There is no formal study programme for this award.

ADMISSION TO HIGHER EDUCATION

Admission to university-level studies:

Name of secondary school credential required: Højere Forberedelseseksamen (Higher Preparatory Examination)

Minimum score/requirement: Depending on institution and programme

Name of secondary school credential required: Højere Handelseksamen (Higher Commercial Examination)

Minimum score/requirement: Depending on institution and programme

Name of secondary school credential required: Højere Teknisk Eksamen (Higher Technical Examination)

Minimum score/requirement: Depending on institution and programme

Name of secondary school credential required: Studentereksamen (Upper Secondary School Leaving Examination)

Minimum score/requirement: Depending on institution and programme

Name of secondary school credential required: Special upper secondary programme for non-Danish speaking students

Alternatives to credentials: Individual assessment.

Numerus clausus: The Minister for Higher of Education and Science may fix a maximum number of student admissions within certain fields of study. Apart from that, individual institutions may have restricted admission for certain fields of study.

Other requirements: Depending on which studies the applicant wishes to follow, there may be other requirements concerning the entrance qualification, e.g. subject combinations, levels and minimum marks.

Foreign students admission:

Definition of foreign student: A non-Danish citizen with a foreign entrance qualification.

Quotas: Three quotas are fixed annually for applications for first-cycle programmes. Quota 1 is for applicants with a Danish upper secondary qualification and for applicants with an EU/EEA upper secondary qualification which the Danish Agency for Higher Education has assessed as being comparable to a Danish upper secondary qualification. Applicants in quota 1 are assessed solely on the basis of the grade point average in the upper secondary qualification. This means that applicants with the highest grade point averages are admitted until all the seats are taken.

Quota 2 is for applicants with the abovementioned upper secondary qualifications who do not have a sufficiently high grade point average to be admitted in quota 1 and who also wish to be assessed on other qualifications such as work experience, extra-curricular activities, living abroad, etc. Each educational institution sets the criteria for admission through quota 2 for each programme. The application is automatically assessed in quota 1 simultaneously in case the applicant meets the required grade point average. Furthermore, quota 2 is for applicants holding non-EU/EEA upper secondary qualifications and residing in Denmark as well as for applicants who do not have an upper secondary qualification, but who have obtained qualifications comparable to an upper secondary qualification (exemptees).

Quota 3 is for non-EU/EEA nationals applying for an English study programme on the basis of a non-Danish upper secondary qualification and need a student residence permit to study in Denmark.

Admission requirements: The general admission requirement is a qualification that gives access to higher education in the country of origin and which is assessed and found comparable to the Danish entrance qualifications. For many programmes, there are also specific requirements which must be fulfilled. Further information about admission requirements and foreign qualifications accepted for entry to higher education programmes taught in English is available at the Study in Denmark website: http://studyindenmark.dk/study-options/admission-requirements

Entry regulations: The procedures vary according to nationality. For information on visas, permits, etc., please visit the Study in Denmark website: http://studyindenmark.dk/live-in-denmark/permits-visas-red-tape

Students from outside the EU/EEA should be aware that the residence permit must be applied for from your home country and that there are certain financial requirements. If you need help when applying for a Danish residence permit, contact the International Office at the institution you have been accepted to.

Health requirements: Generally speaking, international students have access to the Danish healthcare system. Please refer to the Study in Denmark website for details on healthcare coverage: http://studyindenmark.dk/live-in-denmark/health-safety/healthcare

Language proficiency: Applicants to English-taught programmes have to prove English proficiency comparable to a specified level in the Danish upper secondary school, depending on the programme in question.

If the programme is taught in Danish you have to prove proficiency in Danish, both oral and in writing.

For details about language requirements and tests, please visit the website of the higher education institution or Study in Denmark: http://studyindenmark.dk/study-options/admission-requirements.

RECOGNITION OF STUDIES

Quality assurance system:

1) Accreditation:
Accreditation is mandatory for higher education institutions and a precondition for attaining public funding. The accreditation system is based on the 2013 Accreditation of Higher Education Institutions Act. The act is being phased in until 2017, changing the system of accreditation from programme accreditation to institution accreditation with focus on the ongoing systematic work of the educational institution to safeguard and develop the quality and relevance of its study programmes. Institutions with a positive institution accreditation are entitled to establish new study programmes and new offerings of study programmes after these have been pre-qualified and approved and to make adjustments to existing study programmes. Institutions that have not yet obtained a positive institution accreditation must have their study programmes accredited.
The Danish Accreditation Agency prepares accreditation reports for the purpose of the Accreditation Council's decisions concerning the accreditation of educational institutions and study programmes. Accreditation takes place on the basis of centrally laid down criteria including learning outcomes as defined by the Danish Qualifications Framework.
Institutions are required to set up their own internal quality assurance procedures. The Universities Act specifies the role of deans, heads of department and study boards, respectively, in assuring and developing the quality of education and teaching. Self-evaluation, in which students normally participate, is an integral mandatory part of any evaluation.
For more information, please visit the website of the Danish Accreditation Instituiton: http://en.akkr.dk/

2) Foreign qualifications recognition:
The Danish Agency for Higher Education (Danish ENIC/NARIC office) provides assessments of foreign qualifications at all levels for academic as well as professional purpose. Decisions on admission of applicants with foreign qualifications are made by the educational institutions themselves, taking into consideration any assessment by the Danish Agency for Higher Education as far as the level of the foreign qualification is concerned. Decisions on credit transfer of foreign qualifications to replace parts of a Danish study programme are made by the higher education institutions, but foreign qualification holders may appeal the decision to a special complaints board. Decisions on access to regulated professions are made by the competent public authorities.
For more information, please visit the website of the Ministry of Higher Education and Science: http://ufm.dk/recognition

Bodies dealing with recognition:

Danmarks Akkrediteringsinstitution (The Danish Accreditation Institution)

Executive Director: Anette Dørge
Bredgade 38
København K 1260
Tel: +45 33-92-69-00
EMail: akkr@akkr.dk
WWW: http://akkr.dk

Styrelsen for Videregående Uddannelser (Danish Agency for Higher Education)

Head of Division: Mikkel Buchter
Bredgade 43
København K 1260
Tel: +45 72-31-78-00
Fax: +45 72-31-78-01
EMail: uds@uds.dk
WWW: http://ufm.dk/recognition

Special provisions for recognition:

Recognition for university level studies: For admission to undergraduate studies, applicants with foreign credentials should apply through www.optagelse.dk before March 15. However, there may be different deadlines for applicants who are seeking admission to an English-language programme and need a residence

permit for that – in that case please ask the educational institution for information about the deadline.
To learn more about admission requirements and applications, please visit the Study in Denmark website: http://studyindenmark.dk/study-options/admission-requirements
Information about foreign qualifications satisfying the level requirement for entry to undergraduate studies is available on the website of Ministry of Higher Education and Science: http://ufm.dk/recognition/entry

For access to advanced studies and research: Applications should be sent to the relevant institution of higher education.

For exercising a profession: Approval of foreign qualifications with a view to practising regulated professions is given by the authority administering the regulated profession in question. Applications should be sent directly to the relevant competent authority. More information about access to the regulated professions is available at the website of the Ministry for Higher Education and Science: http://ufm.dk/recognition/rp
For non-regulated professions, the Danish Agency for Higher Education offers assessment of foreign qualifications: http://ufm.dk/recognition

NATIONAL BODIES

Uddannelses-og Forskningsministeriet (Ministry of Higher Education and Science)

Minister: Ulla Tørnæs
PO Box 2135
København K 1015
Tel: +45 33-92-97-00
Fax: +45 33-32-35-01
EMail: ufm@ufm.dk
WWW: http://ufm.dk
Role of national body: Responsible for science, innovation and higher education

Kulturministeriet (Danish Ministry of Culture)

Minister: Bertel Haarder
Nybrogade 2
København K 1203
Tel: +45 33-92-33-70
EMail: kum@kum.dk
WWW: http://kum.dk
Role of national body: Responsible for parts of higher education in fine and performing arts.

Data for academic year: 2014-2015
Source: IAU from the Danish Agency for Higher Education, 2015. Bodies 2016.

INSTITUTIONS

PUBLIC INSTITUTIONS

AALBORG UNIVERSITY

Aalborg Universitet (AAU)
Postboks 159, Fredrik Bajers vej 5, 9100 Aalborg
Tel: +45 99-40-95-00
Fax: +45 98-15-22-01
EMail: aau@aau.dk
Website: http://www.aau.dk

Rector: Per Michael Johansen (2014-) EMail: rektor@aau.dk
University Director: Peter Plenge EMail: director@adm.aau.dk
International Relations: Louise Bredgard EMail: lb@adm.aau.dk

Faculty
Engineering and Science *(Copenhagen Institute of Technology; Esberg Institute of Technology)* (Architecture; Biotechnology; Building Technologies; Chemistry; Civil Engineering; Computer Science; Design; Development Studies; Education; Electrical and Electronic Engineering; Electrical Engineering; Energy Engineering; Engineering; Environmental Engineering; Health Sciences; Industrial Engineering; Mathematics; Mechanical Engineering; Nanotechnology; Natural Sciences; Pedagogy; Physics; Production Engineering; Surveying and Mapping; Technology); **Humanities** (Arts and Humanities; Communication Studies; Cultural Studies; Education; History; International Studies; Modern Languages; Pedagogy; Philosophy; Philosophy of Education; Psychology); **Social Sciences** (Business Administration; Cultural Studies; Education; International Studies; Law; Management; Pedagogy; Philosophy of Education; Political Sciences; Social Sciences; Social Studies; Social Work; Sociology)

Research Institute
Building *(Danish)* (Administration; Building Technologies; Communication Studies; Energy Engineering; Environmental Engineering; Management)

History: Founded 1974. A State Institution incorporating previously established Centres of Education in Aalborg and employing new teaching and learning methods based on an 'integrated' approach to higher education, with emphasis on project work in groups. Financed by the State. The University has Departments in Esbjerg and Copenhagen

Academic Year: September to June (September-January; February-June)

Admission Requirements: Secondary school certificate (studentereksamen) or Højere-Forberedelseseksamen (HF), Højere, Handelseksamen, (HHX) or Højere Teknisk eksamen (HTX), or recognized equivalent

Main Language(s) of Instruction: Danish

Degrees and Diplomas: *Bachelorgrad (Bachelor's degree)*; *Professionsbachelorgrad (Professional Bachelor's degree)*; *Kandidatgrad (Master's degree)*; *Ph.d.-grad (PhD degree)*: **Arts and Humanities; Biomedicine; Engineering; Medicine; Natural Sciences; Social Sciences.**

Student Services: Academic Counselling, Canteen, Careers Guidance

Publications: Årsberetning; Uglen

Publishing House: Aalborg Universitetsforlag

Student Numbers *2011-2012*: Total: c. 15,000

Last Updated: 07/02/15

AARHUS SCHOOL OF ARCHITECTURE

Arkitektskolen i Aarhus
Nørreport 20, 8000 Aarhus, C
Tel: +45 89-36-00-00
Fax: +45 86-13-06-45
EMail: a@aarch.dk
Website: http://aarch.dk

Rector: Torben Nielsen EMail: torben.nielsen@aarch.dk

Department

Architectural Heritage (Architecture); **Architecture** (Architecture); **Design** (Design); **Urbanism and Landscape** (Architecture; Landscape Architecture; Town Planning; Urban Studies)

History: Founded 1965.

Academic Year: September to June (September-January; February-June)

Admission Requirements: Secondary school certificate (Studentereksamen) or recognized equivalent

Main Language(s) of Instruction: Danish

Degrees and Diplomas: *Bachelorgrad (Bachelor's degree)*: **Architecture.** *Kandidatgrad (Master's degree)*: **Architecture.** *Ph.d.-grad (PhD degree)*: **Architecture.**

Last Updated: 11/02/15

AARHUS UNIVERSITY

Århus Universitet
Nordre Ringgade 1, 8000 Aarhus, C
Tel: +45 87-15 00-00
Fax: +45 87-15-00-01
EMail: au@au.dk
Website: http://www.au.dk/en

Rector: Brian Bech Nielsen (2013-) EMail: rektor@au.dk

University Director: Jane Kraglund
EMail: direktor@au.dk; jak@au.dk

School

Engineering *(Previously independant school - merged with the university in 2012.)* (Chemical Engineering; Civil Engineering; Electrical Engineering; Electronic Engineering; Engineering; Mechanical Engineering; Power Engineering)

Department

Aesthetics and Communication (Anthropology; Arts and Humanities; Cultural Studies; Fine Arts; Mass Communication; Modern Languages; Musicology); **Agroecology** (Agriculture; Ecology; Environmental Management; Natural Resources); **Animal Science** (Veterinary Science; Zoology); **Biomedicine** (Biomedicine); **Bioscience** (Biological and Life Sciences); **Business Administration** (Business Administration); **Business Communication** (Business and Commerce; Management; Marketing); **Chemistry** (Chemistry); **Clinical Medicine** (Medicine); **Computer Science** (Computer Science); **Culture and Society** (Anthropology; Arabic; Archaeology; Chinese; Eastern European Studies; History; Japanese; Philosophy; Religion; South Asian Studies); **Dentistry** (Dentistry); **Economics and Business** (Business Administration; Economics); **Education** (Education); **Engineering** (Engineering); **Environmental Science** (Environmental Management; Environmental Studies; Natural Resources); **Food Science** (Food Science); **Forensic Medicine** (Forensic Medicine and Dentistry); **Geoscience** (Earth Sciences; Geology); **Law** (Law); **Mathematics** (Mathematics); **Molecular Biology and Genetics** (Genetics; Molecular Biology); **Physics and Astronomy** (Astronomy and Space Science; Physics); **Political Science and Government** (Government; Political Sciences); **Psychology and Behavioural Sciences** (Behavioural Sciences; Psychology); **Public Health** (Public Health)

Further Information: Also University Hospital and Interdisciplinary Research Centres

History: Founded 1928 by municipal authorities, recognized by Parliament 1931, and awarded Government grant. Achieved full University status 1934. Became State Institution 1970 under the supervision of the Ministry of Education.

Academic Year: September to June (September-December; February-June)

Admission Requirements: Secondary school certificate (studentereksamen) or equivalent

Main Language(s) of Instruction: Danish

Degrees and Diplomas: *Bachelorgrad (Bachelor's degree)*; *Kandidatgrad (Master's degree)*; *Ph.d.-grad (PhD degree)*

Student Services: Academic Counselling, Canteen, Foreign Studies Centre, Sports Facilities

Publications: Acta Jutlandica

Publishing House: Aarhus Universitetsforlag

Last Updated: 07/02/15

COPENHAGEN BUSINESS SCHOOL

Handelshøjskolen i København
Solbjerg Plads 3, 2000 Frederiksberg
Tel: +45 38-15-38-15
Fax: +45 38-15-20-15
EMail: cbs@cbs.dk
Website: http://www.cbs.dk

President: Per Holten-Andersen EMail: rektor@cbs.dk

Faculty

Economics and Business Administration (Business Administration; Economics); **Languages, Communication and Cultural Studies** *(Frederiksberg)* (Communication Studies; Cultural Studies; Modern Languages)

Department

Accounting and Auditing *(Frederiksberg)* (Accountancy; Finance; Management); **Business and Politics** (Business Administration; International Economics; Political Sciences); **Computer Assisted Linguistics** *(Frederiksberg)* (Computer Science; Linguistics); **Economics** (Economics); **English** *(Frederiksberg)* (English; Linguistics; Modern Languages; Translation and Interpretation); **Finance** *(Frederiksberg)* (Finance; Insurance); **French, German, Italian, Russian and Spanish** *(Frederiksberg)* (French; German; Italian; Linguistics; Russian; Spanish; Translation and Interpretation); **Innovation and Organizational Economics** (Economics; Industrial Management); **Intercultural Communication and Management** *(Frederiksberg)* (Communication Studies; Cultural Studies; Management); **International Culture and Communication Studies** (Communication Studies; Cultural Studies; Modern Languages; Social Sciences); **International Economics and Management** *(Frederiksberg)* (International Economics; Management); **International Languages Studies and Computational Linguistics** (Arts and Humanities; Modern Languages; Translation and Interpretation); **IT Management** (Computer Science; E-Business/Commerce; Information Sciences; Information Technology; Mathematics); **Law** *(International Law related to Business with* *focus on Law as a Management Tool, Frederiksberg)* (Commercial Law; European Union Law; International Law; Labour Law; Law); **Management, Politics and Philosophy** *(Copenhagen)* (Management; Philosophy; Political Sciences); **Marketing** *(Frederiksberg)* (Marketing); **Operations Management** *(Frederiksberg)* (Industrial Management; Management); **Organization** *(Frederiksberg)* (Human Resources; Industrial Management; Management; Sociology); **Strategic Management and Globalisation** *(Frederiksberg)* (International Business; Management)

Centre
Applied Management Studies (Management; Small Business); **Art and Leadership** (Leadership); **Asian Research** (Asian Studies); **Biotech Business** (Management); **Business Development and Management Technology** (Management); **Business History** (Economic History; Sociology); **Corporate Communication** (Communication Studies); **Corporate Values and Responsibility** (Management; Sociology); **East European Studies** *(Frederiksberg)* (Eastern European Studies); **Electronic Commerce** (E- Business/Commerce); **Financial Law** (Commercial Law; Finance; Law); **Hospital Management and Organization** (Institutional Administration; Management); **Industrial Dynamics** (Business and Commerce); **Innovation and Entrepreneurship** (Small Business); **IT in Policy Organizations** (Information Technology; Public Administration); **Knowledge Governance** (Management); **Law, Economics and Finance** (Economics; Finance; Law); **Management, Organization and Competence** (Management; Small Business); **Market Economics** (Business and Commerce; Economics); **Marketing Communication** (Marketing); **Study of the Americas** (American Studies)

History: Founded 1917 as a private Institution, integrated into the national system, thus becoming self-governing 1965. Acquired present status 2003.

Academic Year: September to June (September-January; February-June)

Admission Requirements: Secondary school leaving certificate (studentereksamen) or Højere Forberedelseseksamen, Højere Handelseksamen, Højere Teknisk eksamen or recognized equivalent

Main Language(s) of Instruction: Danish, English

Degrees and Diplomas: *Bachelorgrad (Bachelor's degree)*: **Business Administration; Economics; European Studies; Mathematics.** *Kandidatgrad (Master's degree)*: **Accountancy; Business Administration; Business Computing; Commercial Law; Economics; Finance; Human Resources; International Business; Management; Marketing.** *Ph.d.-grad (PhD degree)*: **Econometrics; Management.**
Last Updated: 11/02/15

FUNEN ART ACADEMY

Det Fynske Kunstakademi
Brandts Torv 1, 4. sal, 5000 Odense, C
Tel: +45 66-11-12-88
Fax: +45 66-19-26-88
EMail: info@detfynskekunstakademi.dk
Website: http://www.detfynskekunstakademi.dk

Pro-Rector: Kristine Kemp EMail: kk@detfynskekunstakademi.dk

Programme
Fine Arts (Fine Arts)

Main Language(s) of Instruction: Danish

Degrees and Diplomas: *Kunstnerisk bachelorgrad (Bachelor's degree within the arts)*: **Fine Arts.** *Kunstnerisk kandidatgrad (Master's degree within the arts)*: **Fine Arts.**
Last Updated: 11/02/15

IT UNIVERSITY OF COPENHAGEN

IT-Universitetet i København (ITU)
Rued Langgaards Vej 7, 2300 København S
Tel: +45 72-18-50-00
Fax: +45 72-18-50-01
EMail: itu@itu.dk
Website: http://www.itu.dk

Rector: Mads Tofte EMail: tofte@itu.dk; rektor@itu.dk

Programme
Information Technology (Communication Arts; Computer Graphics; Design; E- Business/Commerce; Information Technology; Media Studies; Software Engineering; Technology)

History: Founded 1999 as faculty hosted by the Copenhagen Business School. Acquired present status 2003.

Academic Year: September to June

Admission Requirements: Bachelor Degree

Main Language(s) of Instruction: Danish, English

Degrees and Diplomas: *Bachelorgrad (Bachelor's degree)*: **Information Technology.** *Kandidatgrad (Master's degree)*: **Information Technology; Software Engineering.** *Ph.d.-grad (PhD degree)*: **Information Technology.**
Last Updated: 11/02/15

JUTLAND ART ACADEMY

Det Jyske Kunstakademi
Mejlgade 32-34, 8000 Aarhus, C
Tel: +45 86-13-69-19
Fax: +45 86-13-69-71
EMail: djk@djk.nu
Website: http://www.djk.nu

Rector: Jesper Rasmussen

Programme
Fine Arts (Art History; Fine Arts)

History: Created 1959.

Degrees and Diplomas: *Kunstnerisk bachelorgrad (Bachelor's degree within the arts)*: **Fine Arts.** *Kunstnerisk kandidatgrad (Master's degree within the arts)*: **Fine Arts.**
Last Updated: 11/02/15

KOLDING SCHOOL OF DESIGN

Designskolen Kolding
Ågade 10, 6000 Kolding
Tel: +45 76-30-11-00
Fax: +45 76-30-11-12
EMail: dk@designskolenkolding.dk
Website: http://www.designskolenkolding.dk

Rector: Elsebeth Gerner Nielsen EMail: egn@dskd.dk

Programme
Accessory Design (Handicrafts; Jewellery Art); **Communication Design** (Design; Graphic Design); **Fashion and Textile Design** (Fashion Design; Textile Design); **Industrial Design** (Industrial Design)

History: Founded 1967 as Kunsthåndværkerskole (Arts and Crafts School). In 1998, the school changed its name to Kolding School of Design. Acquired present status 2010.

Main Language(s) of Instruction: Danish

Degrees and Diplomas: *Kunstnerisk bachelorgrad (Bachelor's degree within the arts)*: **Design.** *Kunstnerisk kandidatgrad (Master's degree within the arts)*: **Fashion Design; Graphic Design; Industrial Design; Interior Design; Textile Design.** *Ph.d.-grad (PhD degree)*: **Design.**
Last Updated: 11/02/15

RHYTHMIC MUSIC CONSERVATORY

Rytmisk Musikkonservatorium
Leo Mathisens Vej 1, 1437 København, K
Tel: +45 41-88-25-00
EMail: rmc@rmc.dk
Website: http://www.rmc.dk

Principal: Henrik Sveidahl EMail: hs@rmc.dk

Programme
Music (Music; Music Education; Music Theory and Composition)

Degrees and Diplomas: *Kunstnerisk bachelorgrad (Bachelor's degree within the arts)*: **Music.** *Kunstnerisk kandidatgrad (Master's degree within the arts)*: **Music.**
Last Updated: 11/02/15

ROSKILDE UNIVERSITY

Roskilde Universitet (RUC)
Postbox 260, Universitetsvej 1, 4000 Roskilde
Tel: +45 46-74-20-00
Fax: +45 46-74-30-00
EMail: ruc@ruc.dk
Website: http://www.ruc.dk

Rector: Hanne Leth Andersen (2014-) EMail: rektor@ruc.dk

Department

Communication, Business and Information Technologies (Business Administration; Communication Studies; Computer Science; Design; Information Technology; Journalism); **Culture and Identity** (Cultural Studies; Danish; English; French; German; History; Philosophy); **Environmental, Social and Spatial Change** (Environmental Studies); **Psychology and Educational Studies** (Educational Sciences; Psychology); **Science, Systems and Models** (Biology; Chemistry; Mathematics; Molecular Biology; Physics); **Society and Globalisation** (Administration; European Studies; Political Sciences; Social Sciences)

History: Founded 1972 by Government decree. A State Institution employing new teaching and learning methods based on an 'integrated' approach to higher education and placing emphasis on group work.

Academic Year: September to June (September-January; February-June)

Admission Requirements: Secondary school certificate (studentereksamen), or appropriate educational level reached through formal or non-formal education

Main Language(s) of Instruction: Danish, English

Degrees and Diplomas: *Bachelorgrad (Bachelor's degree)*: **Arts and Humanities; Health Sciences; Social Sciences.** *Kandidatgrad (Master's degree)*: **Arts and Humanities; Natural Sciences; Social Sciences.** *Ph.d.-grad (PhD degree)*: **Business Administration; Cultural Studies; Environmental Studies; Natural Sciences; Philosophy; Technology.**

Last Updated: 11/02/15

ROYAL ACADEMY OF MUSIC

Det Jyske Musikkonservatorium
Skovgaardsgade 2C, 8000 Aarhus, C
Tel: +45 72-26-74-00
Fax: +45 51-17-64-69
EMail: mail@musikkons.dk
Website: http://www.musikkons.dk/

Rector: Claus Olesen

Programme

Music (Music; Music Education; Music Theory and Composition; Musical Instruments; Religious Music)

History: Founded 1927. The Academy of Music, Aalborg, and The Royal Academy of Music, Aarhus merged in 2010.

Main Language(s) of Instruction: Danish

Degrees and Diplomas: *Kunstnerisk bachelorgrad (Bachelor's degree within the arts)*: **Music.** *Kunstnerisk kandidatgrad (Master's degree within the arts)*: **Music.**

Last Updated: 11/02/15

ROYAL DANISH ACADEMY OF FINE ARTS, SCHOOLS OF ARCHITECTURE, DESIGN AND CONSERVATION

Det Kongelige Danske Kunstakademis Skoler for Arkitektur, Design og Konservering
Philip De Langes Allé 10, 1435 København, K
Tel: +45 3268 6000
EMail: info@kadk.dk
Website: http://www.kadk.dk

Rector: Lene Dammand Lund (2012-) EMail: rl@kons.dk

School

Fine Arts and Conservation (Architecture; Design; Fine Arts; Graphic Arts; Heritage Preservation; Sculpture)

History: Founded 1973. Acquired present status following merger between the Royal Danish Academy of Fine Arts, School of Architecture and the Danish Design School.

Academic Year: September to June

Admission Requirements: Upper secondary school leaving certificate (Studentereksamen), Higher preparatory examination (Højere Forberedelseseksamen, HF) or equivalent

Main Language(s) of Instruction: Danish

Degrees and Diplomas: *Kunstnerisk bachelorgrad (Bachelor's degree within the arts)*: **Architecture; Art Management; Design.** *Kunstnerisk kandidatgrad (Master's degree within the arts)*: **Architecture; Art Management; Design.** *Ph.d.-grad (PhD degree)*: **Heritage Preservation.**

Last Updated: 11/02/15

ROYAL DANISH ACADEMY OF MUSIC

Det Kongelige Danske Musikkonservatorium (DKDM)
Rosenørns Allé 22, 1970 Frederiksberg C
Tel: +45 72-26-72-26
Fax: +45 72-26-72-72
EMail: dkdm@dkdm.dk
Website: http://www.dkdm.dk

President: Bertel Krarup EMail: rektor@dkdm.dk

Department

Brass, Percussion and Orchestra Conducting (Conducting; Musical Instruments); **Church Music** (Religious Music); **Composition/Theory** (Music Theory and Composition); **Educational Theory** (Music Education); **Piano, Guitar and Accordion** (Musical Instruments); **Recording** (Sound Engineering (Acoustics)); **Singing** (Singing); **Strings** (Musical Instruments); **Woodwind and Harp** (Musical Instruments)

History: Founded 1867 as a private institution. Became a State institution under the jurisdiction of the Ministry of Cultural Affairs 1949.

Academic Year: September to June (September-December; January-June)

Admission Requirements: Entrance examination

Main Language(s) of Instruction: Danish, English

Degrees and Diplomas: *Kunstnerisk bachelorgrad (Bachelor's degree within the arts)*: **Music.** *Kunstnerisk kandidatgrad (Master's degree within the arts)*: **Music.**

Last Updated: 11/02/15

TECHNICAL UNIVERSITY OF DENMARK

Danmarks Tekniske Universitet
Anker Engelundsvej 1, Bygning 101A, 2800 Kgs. Lyngby
Tel: +45 45-25-25-25
Fax: +45 45-88-17-99
EMail: dtu@dtu.dk
Website: http://www.dtu.dk

Rector: Anders Overgaard Bjarklev (2011-)
EMail: dtu-rektor@adm.dtu.dk

Department

Applied Mathematics and Computer Science (Applied Mathematics; Computer Science); **Chemical Engineering** (Biotechnology; Chemical Engineering); **Chemistry** (Chemistry); **Civil Engineering** (Architecture; Civil Engineering); **Electrical Engineering** (Electrical Engineering; Sound Engineering (Acoustics)); **Energy Conversion and Storage** (Energy Engineering; Environmental Management); **Environmental Engineering** (Environmental Engineering); **Management Engineering** (Engineering Management; Industrial Management); **Mechanical Engineering** (Mechanical Engineering); **Micro- and Nanotechnology** (Physics); **Photonics Engineering** (Computer Networks; Information Technology; Physical Engineering; Telecommunications Engineering); **Physics** (Physics); **Systems Biology** (Bioengineering; Biological and Life Sciences; Biotechnology); **Transport** (Bridge Engineering; Railway Engineering; Road Engineering; Transport Engineering; Transport Management); **Wind Energy** (Energy Engineering)

Institute

Aquatic Resources (Aquaculture; Marine Science and Oceanography; Water Science); **Food Technology** (Brewing; Food Technology); **National Space Institute** (Aeronautical and Aerospace Engineering; Astronomy and Space Science); **National Veterinary Institute** (Veterinary Science)

History: Founded 1829 as a State Institution under the supervision of the Ministry of Education. Departments restructured 1996. Acquired present status 2001. Merged with Copenhagen University College of Engineering (IHK) in 2013.

Academic Year: September to July (September-January; February-July)

Admission Requirements: Secondary school certificate (studentereksamen) or foreign equivalent with defined levels of education in mathematics, physics and chemistry

Main Language(s) of Instruction: Danish, English

Degrees and Diplomas: *Bachelorgrad (Bachelor's degree)*: **Agriculture; Engineering; Mathematics and Computer Science; Natural Sciences; Technology.** *Professionsbachelorgrad (Professional Bachelor's degree)*: **Agriculture; Engineering; Mathematics and Computer Science; Natural Sciences; Technology.** *Kandidatgrad (Master's degree)*: **Aeronautical and Aerospace Engineering; Applied Chemistry; Aquaculture; Architecture; Biological and Life Sciences; Biotechnology; Chemical Engineering; Chemistry; Civil Engineering; Computer Engineering; Computer Science; Design; Electrical Engineering; Energy Engineering; Engineering Management; Environmental Engineering; Food Technology; Industrial Design; Petroleum and Gas Engineering; Physics; Production Engineering; Sound Engineering (Acoustics); Telecommunications Engineering; Transport Management.** *Ph.d.-grad (PhD degree)*: **Agriculture; Engineering; Food Technology; Mathematics and Computer Science; Natural Sciences.** Bachelor's degrees taught in Danish. Master's courses taught in English.

Last Updated: 11/02/15

THE ACADEMY OF MUSIC AND DRAMATIC ARTS, SOUTHERN DENMARK

Syddansk Musikkonservatorium og Skuespillerskole (SMKS)

Islandsgade 2, 5000 Odense C
Tel: +45 63-11-99-00
Fax: +45 63-11-99 20
EMail: info@sdmk.dk
Website: http://www.sdmk.dk/

Rector: Claus Skjold Larsen (2012-) EMail: csl@sdmk.dk

Programme

Music (Jazz and Popular Music; Music; Music Theory and Composition; Religious Music)

Further Information: Branch in Esberg.

History: Founded 1929 as a private institution,Det Fynske Musikkonservatorium became a government institution under the supervision of the Ministry of Cultural Affairs 1972. Reoganised and merged with the Academic of Music and Music Communication in Esberg, and the Acting school in Odense, 2010.

Academic Year: September to June

Admission Requirements: Audition in the respective major instrument/academic area, plus minors (eartraining, piano, music theory)

Main Language(s) of Instruction: Danish

Degrees and Diplomas: *Kunstnerisk bachelorgrad (Bachelor's degree within the arts)*: **Music.** *Kunstnerisk kandidatgrad (Master's degree within the arts)*: **Music.**

Last Updated: 11/02/15

THE ROYAL DANISH ACADEMY OF FINE ARTS, SCHOOL OF VISUAL ARTS

Det Kongelige Danske Kunstakademi, Billedkunstskolerne

Kongens Nytorv 1, 1050 København
Tel: +45 33-74-46-00
Fax: +45 33-74-46-66
EMail: bks@kunstakademiet.dk
Website: http://www.kunstakademiet.dk

Rector: Sanne Kofod Olsen
EMail: sanne.kofod@kunstakademiet.dk

Department

Art Theory (Art Education); **Graphic Arts** (Graphic Arts; Printing and Printmaking; Visual Arts); **Media Arts** (Computer Science; Media Studies; Video); **Painting** (Painting and Drawing); **Sculpture** (Sculpture; Visual Arts); **Visual Arts** (Visual Arts)

History: Founded 1754 on the same lines as the Académie des Beaux Arts in France, and later acquired the status of a modern School of Art.

Academic Year: October to June (October-December; January-June)

Admission Requirements: Entrance competition

Main Language(s) of Instruction: Danish

Degrees and Diplomas: *Kunstnerisk bachelorgrad (Bachelor's degree within the arts)*: **Fine Arts.** *Kunstnerisk kandidatgrad (Master's degree within the arts)*: **Fine Arts.**

Last Updated: 11/02/15

UNIVERSITY OF COPENHAGEN

Københavns Universitet

Postboks 2177, Nørregade 10, 1017 København K
Tel: +45 35-32-26-26
Fax: +45 35-32-26-28
EMail: ku@ku.dk
Website: http://www.ku.dk

Rector: Ralf Hemmingsen (2005-)
Tel: +45 35-32-26-12 EMail: rektor@adm.ku.dk

International Relations: Trine Sand, Interim Director, International Relations Tel: +45 35-32-39-27 EMail: tsm@adm.ku.dk

Faculty

Health and Medical Sciences (Dentistry; Medicine; Pharmacy; Veterinary Science); **Humanities** (Arts and Humanities; Cultural Studies; English; Germanic Languages; Information Sciences; Library Science; Linguistics; Media Studies; Nordic Studies; Regional Studies; Romance Languages); **Law** (Law); **Science** (Biology; Chemistry; Computer Science; Environmental Studies; Food Science; Mathematics; Natural Resources; Natural Sciences; Nutrition; Science Education; Sports); **Social Sciences** (Anthropology; Economics; Political Sciences; Psychology; Social Sciences; Sociology); **Theology** (African Studies; Theology)

History: Founded 1479. Acquired present status 2007 following the merger between the former Den Kgl. Veterinær- og Landbohøjskole (The Royal Veterinary and Agricultural University) and the Danmarks Farmaceutiske Universitet (The Danish University of Pharmaceutical Sciences). Financed by the State.

Academic Year: September to July (September-January; February-July)

Admission Requirements: Secondary school certificate (studentereksamen), or foreign equivalent, and entrance examination in Danish language. Foreign exchange and guest students should be enrolled at a University in their home country or elsewhere abroad during their proposed stay at the University of Copenhagen

Main Language(s) of Instruction: Danish, English

Degrees and Diplomas: *Bachelorgrad (Bachelor's degree)*: **Arts and Humanities; Health Sciences; Law; Natural Sciences; Social Sciences; Theology; Veterinary Science.** *Kandidatgrad (Master's degree)*: **Architecture; Arts and Humanities; Biology; Biotechnology; Chemistry; Communication Arts; Cultural Studies; Economics; Environmental Studies; Fine Arts; Food Science; Health Sciences; History; Information Technology; Law; Mathematics; Media Studies; Medicine; Natural Resources; Natural Sciences; Philosophy; Physics; Political**

Sciences; Psychology; Social Sciences; Theology. Bachelor programmes taught in Danish. Many Master programmes taught in English.

Student Numbers *2012-2013*: Total 32,820
Last Updated: 11/02/15

UNIVERSITY OF SOUTHERN DENMARK

Syddansk Universitet
Campusvej 55, 5230 Odense M
Tel: +45 65-50-10-00
Fax: +45 66-50-10-90
EMail: sdu@sdu.dk
Website: http://www.sdu.dk

Rector: Henrik Dam (2014-) EMail: rektor@sdu.dk

International Relations: Lisbeth Pinholt, Director of International Relations Tel: +45 65-50-31-81 EMail: lp@sdu.dk

Faculty

Business and Social Sciences (Business and Commerce; Economics; European Studies; Journalism; Law; Political Sciences); **Engineering** (Biotechnology; Engineering; Mechanics; Robotics); **Health Sciences** (Chiropractic; Health Sciences; Medicine; Sports); **Humanities** (American Studies; Arts and Humanities; Classical Languages; Comparative Literature; Danish; English; French; German; History; Hotel and Restaurant; Marine Science and Oceanography; Mass Communication; Middle Eastern Studies; Nordic Studies; Philosophy; Religion; Spanish; Tourism); **Science** (Biology; Chemistry; Computer Science; Marine Science and Oceanography; Mathematics; Natural Sciences; Physics)

History: Founded in 1966 through a merger involving Odense University, the Southern Denmark School of Business and Engineering and South Jutland University Centre.

Academic Year: September to June (September-January; February-June)

Admission Requirements: Secondary school certificate (studentereksamen) or Højere-Forberedelseseksamen or Handelseksamen, or recognized foreign equivalent

Main Language(s) of Instruction: Danish, English

Degrees and Diplomas: *Bachelorgrad (Bachelor's degree)*: **Arts and Humanities; Business Administration; Engineering; Health Sciences; Natural Sciences; Social Sciences.** *Kandidatgrad (Master's degree)*: **Arts and Humanities; Business Administration; Engineering; Health Sciences; Mathematics; Natural Sciences; Social Sciences.** *Ph.d.-grad (PhD degree)*: **Arts and Humanities; Business Administration; Education; Health Sciences; Natural Sciences; Social Sciences.**

Last Updated: 11/02/15

Djibouti

STRUCTURE OF HIGHER EDUCATION SYSTEM

Description:

Higher education is mainly offered at the University of Djibouti, created in 2006, and the School of Medicine.

Stages of studies:

University level first stage: Licence
A Licence is awarded after three years' study.

University level second stage: Master
A Master is awarded after two years' study following upon the Licence.

NATIONAL BODIES

Ministère de l'Enseignement supérieur et de la Recherche
Minister: Nabil Mohamed Ahmed
Djibouti

Data for academic year: 2012-2013
Source: IAU from World Data on Education 2010/2011, rev. 2012, UNESCO-IBE, Base Curie, Ministère des Affaires Etrangères et Européennes, France, and Documentation, 2012. Bodies, 2015.

INSTITUTIONS

PUBLIC INSTITUTIONS

MEDICINE SCHOOL OF DJIBOUTI

Ecole de Médecine de Djibouti (EMD)
rue Abdoulkader Waberi, Djibouti
Tel: +253 32 21 70
Fax: +253 35 21 73
Website: http://www.emd-edu.sante.dj

Doyen: Ali Barre Matan
Secrétaire Général: Chehem Mahomed Watta

Programme
Medicine (Medicine)
History: Founded 2007.
Admission Requirements: Baccalaureate (scientific section)
Main Language(s) of Instruction: French
Accrediting Agency: Ministère de la Santé
Degrees and Diplomas: *Docteur en Médecine*
Last Updated: 09/10/12

UNIVERSITY OF DJIBOUTI

Université de Djibouti (U.D.)
BP 1904, Djibouti
Tel: +253 25 04 59
Fax: +253 25 04 74
EMail: ud@univ.edu.dj
Website: http://www.univ.edu.dj

President: Djama Mohamed Hassan (2012-)

Faculty
Law, Economics and Management *(FDEG)* (Administration; Administrative Law; African Studies; Civil Law; Commercial Law; Constitutional Law; Criminal Law; Development Studies; Economic and Finance Policy; Economics; European Studies; European Union Law; Finance; International Law; International Relations; Labour Law; Law; Management; Maritime Law; Modern Languages; Political Sciences; Public Law); **Literature, Languages and Humanities** *(FLLSH)* (Business Administration; Communication Studies; Economics; English; Geography (Human); History; Information Management; Journalism; Literature; Modern Languages); **Science** *(FS)* (Biological and Life Sciences; Chemistry; Computer Science; Geology; Mathematics; Natural Sciences; Physics; Sports)

Institute
Technology *(IUT)* (Administration; Business Administration; Civil Engineering; Computer Engineering; Industrial Engineering; Industrial Maintenance; Statistics; Transport Management)

Centre
Continuing Education *(CFC)* (Accountancy; Arabic; Business Administration; Business Computing; Computer Science; English; Industrial Engineering; Maintenance Technology; Modern Languages); **Research** *(CRUD)* (African Languages; Cultural Studies; Development Studies; Economics; Energy Engineering; Environmental Studies; Modern Languages; Transport Management)

History: Founded 2006 on the basis of the Pôle universitaire de Djibouti.
Academic Year: October-May (October/January; February/May)
Main Language(s) of Instruction: French
Degrees and Diplomas: *Licence*; *Master*
Student Services: Academic Counselling, Sports Facilities
Publications: Revue Universitaire de Djibouti
Publishing House: CRUD
Last Updated: 09/10/12

Dominican Republic

STRUCTURE OF HIGHER EDUCATION SYSTEM

Description:

Higher education is provided by one public and several private universities and higher institutes.

Stages of studies:

University level first stage: Grado

Courses usually last for four years and lead to the Licenciatura. Courses in fields such as Engineering, Architecture, Veterinary Science, Dentistry, Medicine, etc. take between four to six years and lead to a professional title.

University level second stage: Postgrado

Studies last between one and three years following the Licenciatura and lead to the title and/or degree of Especialista or Maestría. The only Doctorados conferred are professional qualifications in Law, Medicine, Veterinary Medicine and Dentistry. Studies last for approximately six years and lead to the title of Doctor.

ADMISSION TO HIGHER EDUCATION

Admission to university-level studies:

Name of secondary school credential required: Bachillerato

Foreign students admission:

Quotas: 33%

Admission requirements: Students must hold the Bachillerato, pass an Examen de Admisión, and hold a copy of their academic record, together with a certification by their home university.

Entry regulations: Foreign students must possess a student visa or a residence permit, depending on their nationality.

Health requirements: Foreign students must hold a health certificate.

Language proficiency: Students must have a good command of Spanish.

RECOGNITION OF STUDIES

Quality assurance system:

The MESCYT authorizes the opening of higher education institutions.

Bodies dealing with recognition:

Ministerio de Educación Superior, Ciencia y Tecnología - MESCyT (Ministry of Higher Education, Science and Technology)

Av. Máximo Gómez No. 31, esq Pedro Henriquez Ureña
Santo Domingo
Tel: +1(809) 731-1100
Fax: +1(809) 731-1101
EMail: info@mescyt.gob.do
WWW: http://www.mescyt.gob.do

NATIONAL BODIES

Ministerio de Educación Superior, Ciencia y Tecnología - MESCyT (Ministry of Higher Education, Science and Technology)

Minister: Ligia Amada Melo de Cardona
Av. Máximo Gómez No. 31, esq Pedro Henriquez Ureña
Santo Domingo

Tel: +1(809) 731-1100
Fax: +1(809) 731-1101
EMail: info@mescyt.gob.do
WWW: http://www.mescyt.gob.do
Role of national body: Responsible for the formulation of higher education policies, planning, promotion, and evaluation.

Asociación Dominicana de Rectores de Universidades - ADRU (Dominican University Rectors' Conference)
President: José Armando Tavárez
Executive Director: Lorenzo Cuevas Mercedes
Calle Juan Paradas Bonilla No. 5, Apto. 3, tercer Nivel, Ensanche Naco - Apartado Postal No.2465 Santo Domingo
Tel: +1(809) 683-0003
Fax: +1(809) 565-4933
EMail: adru@claro.net.do
WWW: http://www.adru.org
Role of national body: Encourages inter-university relations to promote academic activities, research and lifelong education and exchanges with national and international bodies. Funded in 1980.

Data for academic year: 2015-2016
Source: IAU from the website of the Ministry of Higher Education, Science and Technology, 2015.

INSTITUTIONS

PUBLIC INSTITUTIONS

AUTONOMOUS UNIVERSITY OF SANTO DOMINGO

Universidad Autónoma de Santo Domingo (UASD)
Apartado postal 1355, Ave. Alma Mater, Ciudad Universitaria, Santo Domingo
Tel: +1 809 533-8273
Fax: +1 809 508-7374 +1 809 508-7375
EMail: info@uasd.edu.do
Website: http://www.uasd.edu.do

Rector: Iván Grullón Fernández (2014-)
EMail: rectoria@uasd.edu.do
Vicerrector Docente: Jorge Asjana
EMail: Jasjana59@uasd.edu.do

Faculty
Agronomy and Veterinary Science (Agronomy; Animal Husbandry; Dairy; Veterinary Science); **Arts** (Advertising and Publicity; Cinema and Television; Design; Fine Arts; Music; Theatre); **Economics and Social Sciences** (Accountancy; Administration; Economics; Marketing; Public Administration; Social Work; Sociology; Statistics); **Engineering and Architecture** (Agricultural Engineering; Architecture; Chemical Engineering; Civil Engineering; Electrical Engineering; Engineering; Industrial Engineering; Mechanical Engineering); **Health Sciences** (Medicine; Nursing; Orthodontics; Pharmacology; Pharmacy; Radiology); **Humanities** (Arts and Humanities; Communication Studies; History; Modern Languages; Pedagogy; Philosophy; Psychology; Social Sciences); **Law** (Law; Political Sciences); **Science** (Biology; Chemistry; Computer Science; Mathematics; Microbiology; Natural Sciences; Parasitology; Physics)

College
Basic Studies *(for 1st yr students)*

History: Founded 1538 by Bull of Pope Paul III. Directed by Dominican Order of Preachers until 1802. Closed during the French occupation. Became a lay institution in 1815 but again closed 1822-1844 during Haitian occupation. Again reopened and reorganized 1865, 1914, and 1937. Following Law on University autonomy 1961 adopted new status 1966. Financially supported by the State.

Academic Year: January to December (January-May; July-December)

Admission Requirements: Secondary school certificate (bachillerato) or recognized foreign equivalent

Fees: (US Dollars): 300 per semester; foreign students, 900

Main Language(s) of Instruction: Spanish

Degrees and Diplomas: *Doctorado en Medicina*: **Dentistry; Medicine; Veterinary Science.** *Ingeniero, Arquitecto*: **Architecture; Electrical Engineering; Mechanical Engineering.** *Licenciatura*: **Accountancy; Arts and Humanities; Biology; Business Administration; Chemistry; Computer Science; Economics; Education; History; Law; Marketing; Modern Languages; Pharmacy; Philosophy; Physics; Political Sciences; Psychology; Public Administration; Sociology.** *Especialidad; Maestría*: **Accountancy; Agronomy; Business Administration; Dentistry; Educational Administration; Educational and Student Counselling; Educational Psychology; International Business; Law; Marketing; Medical Technology; Pedagogy; Physics; Public Health; Visual Arts.**

Student Services: Academic Counselling, Canteen, Cultural Activities, Facilities for disabled people, Health Services, Language Laboratory, Social Counselling, Sports Facilities

Last Updated: 19/01/16

BARNA BUSINESS SCHOOL

Av. John F. Kennedy no. 34, Ensanche Naco, Santo Domingo
Tel: +1(809) 683-4461
Fax: +1(809) 683-4873
EMail: info@barna.edu.do
Website: http://www.barna.edu.do

Rector: Ryan Larrauri EMail: r.larrauri@barna.edu.do

Programme
Business Administration

History: Founded 2005.

Main Language(s) of Instruction: Spanish

Degrees and Diplomas: *Maestría*: **Business Administration.**

Last Updated: 15/01/16

DR. EDUARDO LATORRE RODRÍGUEZ HIGHER EDUCATION INSTITUTE IN DIPLOMATIC AND CONSULAR TRAINING

Instituto de Educación Superior en Formación Diplomatica y Consular Dr. Eduardo Latorre Rodríguez

Av. Independencia No. 752, Estancia San Gerónimo, Santo Domingo

Tel: +1 809 987-7616

EMail: info@inesdyc.edu.do

Website: http://www.inesdyc.edu.do

Rector: Reynaldo Espinal

Programme

Diplomacy and Consular Services

History: Founded 1939 as Escuela Diplomática y Consular. Acquired present status and title 2012.

Main Language(s) of Instruction: Spanish

Degrees and Diplomas: *Especialidad*; *Maestría*: **International Relations.**

Last Updated: 21/01/16

SALOMÉ UREÑA TEACHER TRAINING INSTITUTE

Instituto Superior de Formacion Docente Salomé Ureña

Calle Caonabo esq. C/ Leonardo Da Vinci, Urbanización Renacimiento, Sector Mirador Sur, Santo Domingo

Tel: +1(809) 482-3797

Fax: +1(809) 482-5119

EMail: informacion@isfodosu.edu.do

Website: http://www.isfodosu.edu.do

Rectora: Ana Dolores Guzmán De Camacho

Programme

Education (Education; Physical Education)

History: Founded 2003.

Main Language(s) of Instruction: Spanish

Degrees and Diplomas: *Licenciatura*; *Especialidad*; *Maestria*: **Educational Administration; Linguistics; Mathematics Education; Teacher Training.**

Last Updated: 15/01/16

PRIVATE INSTITUTIONS

APEC UNIVERSITY

Universidad APEC (UNAPEC)

Avenida Máximo Gómez 72, Santo Domingo

Tel: +1 809 686-0021

Fax: +1 809 685-5581

EMail: apec@apec.edu.do

Website: http://www.unapec.edu.do

Rector: Radhamés Mejía

Division

Post-Baccalaureate and Master's Degrees (Administration; Finance; Industrial and Production Economics; International Law; Management; Marketing)

School

Accountancy (Accountancy); **Administration** (Administration); **Arts** (Advertising and Publicity; Architectural and Environmental Design; Arts and Humanities; Graphic Design; Interior Design); **Computer Science** (Computer Science; Systems Analysis); **Engineering and Technology** (Electrical Engineering; Electronic Engineering; Industrial Engineering; Technology); **Languages** (Modern Languages); **Law** (Law); **Marketing** (Marketing); **Tourism** (Hotel Management; Tourism)

History: Founded 1965 as Instituto de Estudios Superiores by the Acción Pro-Educación y Cultura, Inc. (APEC). Acquired present status 1983. A private Institution authorized by the Government to award degrees in 1968.

Academic Year: January to December (January-April; May-August; September-December)

Admission Requirements: Secondary school certificate (bachillerato) and entrance examination

Main Language(s) of Instruction: Spanish

Accrediting Agency: Secretariat for Higher Education, Science and Technology of the Dominican Republic

Degrees and Diplomas: *Técnico*; *Ingeniero, Arquitecto*: **Architecture; Electronic Engineering; Engineering; Industrial Engineering; Interior Design.** *Licenciatura*: **Accountancy; Advertising and Publicity; Business Administration; Hotel Management; Law; Marketing; Tourism.** *Especialidad*; *Maestría*: **Business Administration; E-Business/Commerce; Law; Management; Mathematics.**

Student Services: Academic Counselling, Canteen, Careers Guidance, Health Services, Language Laboratory, Sports Facilities

Publications: Coloquios Jurídicos; Investigación y Ciencia; Revista Científica

Publishing House: Imprenta Cenapec

Last Updated: 19/01/16

CATHOLIC TECHNOLOGICAL UNIVERSITY OF BARAHONA

Universidad Católica Tecnológica de Barahona

Calle Primera, #01, Sector Juan Pablo Duarte, Villa Central, Barahona 006

Tel: +1(809) 524-4025

EMail: universidaducateba@ucateba.edu.do

Website: http://www.ucateba.edu.do/

Rector: Secilio Espinal

School

Business Studies (Accountancy; Business Administration; Hotel Management; Marketing; Tourism); **Computer Science** (Computer Science); **Education** (Education); **Law** (Law); **Nursing** (Nursing)

History: Founded 1995 as Instituto Católico Tecnológico de Barahona. Acquired present status 2004.

Main Language(s) of Instruction: Spanish

Degrees and Diplomas: *Licenciatura*; *Especialidad*; *Maestría*: **Educational Administration; Management.**

Last Updated: 19/01/16

CATHOLIC UNIVERSITY OF SANTO DOMINGO

Universidad Católica de Santo Domingo (UCSD)

Avenida Bolívar #902, Ens. La Julia, Santo Domingo

Tel: +1 809 544-2812

Fax: +1 809 540-2351

EMail: ucsd@verizon.net.do

Website: http://www.ucsd.edu.do

Rector: Jesús Castro Marte

Vicerrectora Académica: Zeneyda de Jesús Contreras

Faculty

Architecture and Fine Arts (Architecture; Design; Fine Arts; Graphic Design; Interior Design); **Economics and Administration** (Accountancy; Banking; Business Administration; Economics; Finance; Hotel Management; Marketing; Tourism); **Health Sciences** (Dentistry; Health Sciences; Nursing; Occupational Therapy; Physical Therapy; Psychology); **Humanities and Education** (Education); **Law and Political Science** (Law; Political Sciences); **Religious Sciences** (Religious Studies; Theology); **Science and Technology** (Computer Engineering; Computer Science; Information Sciences); **Social Sciences and Communication** (Advertising and Publicity; Communication Studies; Social Sciences)

Research Centre

Family Studies and Research (Family Studies)

History: Founded 1982.

Academic Year: January to December (January-May; August-December)

Admission Requirements: Secondary school certificate (bachillerato)

Main Language(s) of Instruction: Spanish

Degrees and Diplomas: *Técnico*; *Licenciatura*; *Especialidad*; *Maestría*: **Educational Administration; Health Administration; Pedagogy; Political Sciences; Religious Studies.**

Publishing house: Catholic University Press

Last Updated: 19/01/16

CENTRAL UNIVERSITY OF THE EAST

Universidad Central del Este (UCE)

Apartado postal 512, Avenida Francisco Alberto Caamaño Deño,
San Pedro de Macorís
Tel: +1 809 520-3562
Fax: +1 809 246-2266
EMail: info@uce.edu.do
Website: http://www.uce.edu.do

Rector: José E. Hazim-Frappier EMail: jhazim@uce.edu.do

Vicerrector Ejecutivo: Richard Peguero
Tel: +1 809 529-3562, Ext. 241 EMail: rpeguero@uce.edu.do

International Relations: Kamel Hazim, International Affairs Director
Tel: +1 809 529-3562, Ext. 280 EMail: khazim@uce.edu.do

Faculty

Architecture (Architecture); **Dentistry** (Dentistry); **Economics and Social Sciences** (Accountancy; Business Administration; Hotel Management; Information Sciences; Marketing; Pedagogy; Tourism); **Engineering** (Civil Engineering; Electrical and Electronic Engineering; Industrial Engineering; Mechanical Engineering); **Law** (Law); **Medicine** (Medicine; Nursing; Pharmacy)

Further Information: Also Teaching Hospitals, Spanish course for foreign students, teaching hotel

History: Founded 1970. A private Institution recognized by the State 1971.

Academic Year: January to December (January-April; May-August; September-December)

Admission Requirements: Secondary school certificate (bachillerato) or equivalent, or recognized foreign equivalent

Main Language(s) of Instruction: Spanish

Accrediting Agency: Secretariado de Estado de Educación Superior, Ciencia y Tecnología

Degrees and Diplomas: *Doctorado en Medicina*: **Dentistry; Medicine.** *Ingeniero, Arquitecto*: **Architecture; Engineering.** *Licenciatura*: **Accountancy; Biology; Business Administration; Education; Law; Pharmacy.** *Maestría*: **Administration; Environmental Engineering; Higher Education; Hotel Management; Human Resources; Industrial Management; Public Health.** Also Doctorado in Education

Student Services: Academic Counselling, Social Counselling, Sports Facilities

Publications: Medical Journal

Last Updated: 19/01/16

DOMINICAN ADVENTIST UNIVERSITY

Universidad Adventista Dominicana (UNAD)

Aut. Duarte, Km 74 1/2, Sonador, Bonao, Monseñor Nouel
Tel: +1 809 525-7533
Fax: +1 809 525-4048
EMail: info@unad.edu.do
Website: http://www.unad.edu.do

Rector: Feliberto Martínez

Faculty

Administration (Accountancy; Business Administration; Marketing); **Engineering and Technology** (Computer Engineering; Computer Science; Engineering; Systems Analysis); **Health Sciences** (Nursing); **Humanities** (Education; English; French; Psychology); **Theology** (Theology)

Further Information: Also branch in Santo Domingo

History: Founded 1982.

Academic Year: September to May (September-December; January-May)

Admission Requirements: Secondary school certificate (bachillerato)

Main Language(s) of Instruction: Spanish

Accrediting Agency: Adventista Acrediting Association (AAA), Secretaria Educacíon Superior

Degrees and Diplomas: *Licenciatura*; *Maestría*: **Education; Educational Administration; Higher Education; Theology.**

Student Services: Academic Counselling, Canteen, Careers Guidance, Cultural Activities, Foreign Studies Centre, Health Services, Language Laboratory, Nursery Care, Social Counselling, Sports Facilities

Publications: Ciencia y Humanismo

Last Updated: 19/01/16

DOMINICAN-AMERICAN UNIVERSITY

Universidad Dominico-Americana (ICDA)

Avenida Abraham Lincoln 21, Santo Domingo
Tel: +1 809 535-0665
Fax: +1 809 533-8809
EMail: dir.dominicana@codetel.net.do
Website: http://www.icda.edu.do

Rector: Rafael Marion-Landais

Area

Business Administration (Accountancy; Business Administration; Marketing); **Education** (Education); **Engineering** (Computer Engineering); **Tourism and Hotel Management** (Hotel Management; Tourism)

History: Founded 2001.

Main Language(s) of Instruction: Spanish

Degrees and Diplomas: *Licenciatura*; *Especialidad*; *Maestría*: **Business Administration.**

Last Updated: 20/01/16

DOMINICAN O&M UNIVERSITY

Universidad Dominicana O&M

Ave. 27 de Febrero, 589, Edificio Profesional O&M, Suite 304,
Santo Domingo
Tel: +1 809 533-7733
Website: http://www.udoym.edu.do

Rector: José Rafael Abinader
EMail: rectoria@udoym.edu.do

Faculty

Economics and Administration (Accountancy; Advertising and Publicity; Banking; Business Administration; Hotel Management; Marketing; Modern Languages; Tourism); **Engineering and Technology** (Architecture; Civil Engineering; Computer Science; Electronic Engineering; Engineering Drawing and Design; Industrial Engineering; Systems Analysis); **Health Sciences** (Medicine); **Humanities and Science** (Arts and Humanities; Communication Studies; Natural Sciences; Psychology); **Juridical Sciences** (Law)

Unit

Continuing Education (Continuing Education)

Centre

Postgraduate and Maestría Studies

Further Information: Branches in Moca, Puerto Plata, Romana, San José de Ocoa and Santiago

History: Founded 1966.

Main Language(s) of Instruction: Spanish

Degrees and Diplomas: *Licenciatura*; *Especialidad*; *Maestría*: **Accountancy; Computer Engineering; Computer Science.**

Last Updated: 10/04/16

DOMINICAN UNIVERSITY OF DENTISTRY

Universidad Odontológica Dominicana (UOD)

Avenida 27 de Febrero, esq. Las Palmas,
Santo Domingo
Tel: +1 809 560-7477
Fax: +1 809 560-7524
EMail: adm@uod.edu.do
Website: http://www.uod.edu.do

Rectora: Vilma Deschamps De Baez

School

Dentistry (Dentistry)

History: Founded 1985.

Main Language(s) of Instruction: Spanish

Degrees and Diplomas: *Doctorado en Medicina*: **Dentistry.**

Last Updated: 10/04/16

DOMINICAN UNIVERSITY OF INDUSTRIAL PSYCHOLOGY

Universidad Psicología Industrial Dominicana (UPID)

Apartado postal 2327, Calle 1ra. 27Urb. KG Carr. Sánchez Km. 6 1/2, Santo Domingo

Tel: +1 809 533-7141

Fax: +1 809 533-4544

EMail: psicologiadom@codetel.net.do

Website: http://www.upid.edu.do

Rector: Ricardo Winter

Programme

Administration (Accountancy; Human Resources; Industrial and Organizational Psychology; Management; Marketing)

History: Founded 1996 as Instituto Superior de Psicología Industrial Dominicana, acquired present title 2001.

Degrees and Diplomas: *Licenciatura*; *Maestría*: **Human Resources; Management.**

Last Updated: 20/01/16

EUGENIO MARÍA DE HOSTOS UNIVERSITY

Universidad Eugenio María de Hostos (UNIREMHOS)

Avenida Abraham Lincoln 126, Santo Domingo

Tel: +1 809 532-2495

Fax: +1 809 535-4636

EMail: uni.eugenio@codetel.net.do

Website: http://www.uniremhos.edu.do/

Rector: José Díaz Vargas

Faculty

Economics and Administration (Administration; Business Administration; Economics; Marketing); **Health Sciences** (Dentistry; Health Sciences; Medicine; Nursing); **Humanities and Social Sciences** (Arts and Humanities; Education; Social Sciences); **Law** (Law)

History: Founded 1980.

Main Language(s) of Instruction: Spanish

Degrees and Diplomas: *Licenciatura*; *Maestría*: **Public Health.**

Last Updated: 20/01/16

FEDERICO HENRÍQUEZ Y CARVAJAL UNIVERSITY

Universidad Federico Henríquez y Carvajal (UFHEC)

Avenida Isabel Aguiar 100 casi esq. Guarocuya, Santo Domingo

Tel: +1 809 531-1000

Fax: +1 809 531-5288

EMail: info@ufhec.edu.do

Website: http://www.ufhec.edu.do

Rector: Alberto Ramírez Cabral EMail: rectoria@ufhec.edu.do

Programme

Accountancy (Accountancy); **Business Administration** (Business Administration); **Computer Science** (Computer Science); **Dentistry** (Dentistry); **Education** (Primary Education); **Engineering** (Electrical Engineering); **Law** (Law); **Nursing** (Nursing)

Further Information: Also branches in La Romana, Bani, and Moca

History: Founded 1991.

Main Language(s) of Instruction: Spanish

Degrees and Diplomas: *Ingeniero, Arquitecto*; *Licenciatura*

Last Updated: 22/01/16

FELIX ADAM EXPERIMENTAL UNIVERSITY

Universidad Experimental Felix Adam (UNEFA)

Calle Salvador Espinal Miranda #6, Mirador Norte, Santo Domingo

Tel: +1 809 530-0224

EMail: info@unefa.edu.do

Website: http://www.unefa.edu.do

Rector: Andrés Matos Sena

School

Business Administration (Business Administration); **Law** (Law); **Marketing**

History: Founded 1996.

Main Language(s) of Instruction: Spanish

Degrees and Diplomas: *Licenciatura*

Last Updated: 20/01/16

FERNANDO ARTURO DE MERIÑO UNIVERSITY OF AGRICULTURE AND FORESTRY

Universidad Agroforestal Fernando Arturo de Meriño (UAFAM)

Avenida La Confluencia, Jarabacoa

Tel: +1 809 574-6234 +1 809 574-2136

Fax: +1 809 574-6405

EMail: info@uafam.edu.do

Website: http://uafam.edu.do

Rector: Rolando Reyes

Faculty

Agronomy and Forestry (Agronomy; Forestry); **Economics and Social Sciences** (Accountancy; Tourism); **Humanities** (Education); **Science and Technology** (Computer Science)

History: Founded 1996.

Main Language(s) of Instruction: Spanish

Degrees and Diplomas: *Ingeniero, Arquitecto*; *Licenciatura*

Last Updated: 19/01/16

GLOBAL INSTITUTE OF ADVANCED STUDIES IN SOCIAL SCIENCES

Instituto Global de Altos Estudios en Ciencias Sociales

C/ César Nicolás Penson, 127, La Esperilla, Santo Domingo

Tel: +1 809 685-9966

EMail: admisiones@iglobal.edu.do

Website: http://www.iglobal.edu.do/

Rector: Marcos Villamán

Programme

Business Administration (Business Administration); **Constitutional Law and Fundamental Liberties** (Constitutional Law); **Economic Regulation of the Electrical Industry** (Economics); **International Business** (International Business); **International Relations** (International Relations); **Law of State Administration** (Administrative Law); **Political Science for Democratic Development** (Political Sciences); **Public Administration** (Public Administration); **Security, Crisis and Emergency Management** (Civil Security); **Technology of Learning and Education** (Education); **Urban Development** (Urban Studies)

History: Founded 2006.

Main Language(s) of Instruction: Spanish

Degrees and Diplomas: *Especialidad*; *Maestría*: **Administration; Business Administration; Education; International Business; International Relations; Law; Political Sciences; Urban Studies.**

Last Updated: 19/01/16

IBERO-AMERICAN UNIVERSITY

Universidad Iberoamericana (UNIBE)

Av. Francia No. 129, Gazcue, Santo Domingo

Tel: +1(809) 689-4111

Fax: +1(809) 687-9384

EMail: info@unibe.edu.do

Website: http://www.unibe.edu.do

Rector: Julio Castaños Guzmán EMail: rectoria@unibe.edu.do

School
Advertising and Communication (Advertising and Publicity; Communication Arts); **Architecture** (Architecture); **Business Administration** (Business Administration); **Civil Engineering** (Civil Engineering); **Dentistry** (Dentistry); **Early Chilhood Education** (Preschool Education); **Industrial Engineering** (Industrial Engineering); **Information and Communication Technology** (Information Technology); **Interior Design** (Interior Design); **Law** (Law); **Marketing** (Marketing); **Medicine** (Medicine); **Psychology** (Clinical Psychology; Educational Psychology; Psychology); **Religion** (Bible; Religion; Theology); **Tourism and Hotel Management** (Hotel Management; Tourism)

Further Information: Also Teaching Hospital (INDEN); National Centre for Diabetes

History: Founded 1982 as the result of joint efforts of Dominican and Spanish institutions and private citizens interested in the advancement of higher education.

Academic Year: September to August (September-December; January-May; June-August)

Admission Requirements: Secondary school certificate (bachillerato) and entrance exam

Main Language(s) of Instruction: Spanish

Degrees and Diplomas: *Doctorado en Medicina*: **Medicine.** *Licenciatura*: **Fine Arts.** *Especialidad*; *Maestría*: **Constitutional Law; Economics; Educational Administration; Human Resources; Management; Marketing.**

Student Services: Academic Counselling, Canteen, Facilities for disabled people, Social Counselling, Sports Facilities

Publications: Revista de Ciencia y Cultura

Last Updated: 20/01/16

INTERAMERICAN UNIVERSITY

Universidad Interamericana (UNICA)
Calle Dr. Báez 2, Gazcue, Santo Domingo
Tel: +1 809 685-6562 +1 809 687-2529
Fax: +1 809 689-8581
EMail: unica@codetel.net.do
Website: http://www.unica.edu.do

Rector: Gabriel Read

Vice-Rector Académico: Raúl Parmenio Díaz

Faculty
Law and Political Science (Law; Political Sciences); **Science and Technology** (Computer Science; Dental Technology); **Social Sciences and Humanities** (Accountancy; Advertising and Publicity; Arts and Humanities; Biology; Business Administration; Chemistry; Communication Studies; Economics; Education; Educational Administration; Educational Psychology; English; French; Human Resources; International Business; Pedagogy; Philosophy; Physical Education; Preschool Education; Primary Education; Psychology; Public Relations; Social Sciences; Sociology; Tourism)

History: Founded 1982.

Degrees and Diplomas: *Ingeniero, Arquitecto*; *Licenciatura*; *Especialidad*; *Maestría*: **Administration; Business Administration; Educational Administration; Health Administration; Higher Education; Marketing; Political Sciences.** Also Doctorado

Last Updated: 20/01/16

ISA UNIVERSITY

Universidad ISA
Apartado postal 166, Avenida Antonio. Guzmán, Km. 51/2, la Herradura, Santiago de los Caballeros
Tel: +1 809 247-2000
Fax: +1 809 247-2626
EMail: info@isa.edu.do
Website: http://www.isa.edu.do/

Rector: Benito Ferreiras

Faculty
Agriculture, Food Technology and Environment (Agronomy; Animal Husbandry; Ecology; Environmental Management; Food Technology; Forestry; Veterinary Science); **Social Sciences and Administration** (Accountancy; Business Administration; Education; Marketing)

History: Founded 1962 as Instituto Superior de Agricultura. Acquired present status and title 1986.

Main Language(s) of Instruction: Spanish

Degrees and Diplomas: *Licenciatura*; *Especialidad*; *Maestría*: **Animal Husbandry; Biotechnology; Food Technology; Veterinary Science.**

Last Updated: 15/01/16

NATIONAL EVANGELICAL UNIVERSITY, SANTIAGO

Universidad Nacional Evangélica, Santiago
Av. Salvador Estrella Sadhalá #202, Urbanización La Terraza., Santiago de los Caballeros
Tel: +1 809 575-3535/5211
EMail: info@unev.edu.do
Website: http://www.unev.edu.do

Rector: Wilfredo Mañón Rossi

Faculty
Business Studies (Accountancy; Business Administration; Marketing); **Health Sciences** (Nursing)

School
Education (Education); **Psychology** (Clinical Psychology; Educational Psychology; Industrial and Organizational Psychology); **Theology** (Theology)

Further Information: Also branches in Santo Domingo and Villa Altagracia

History: Founded 1986 to bring an Evangelical Christian perspective to higher education in the Dominican Republic.

Academic Year: January to December

Admission Requirements: High School Diploma and Transcripts (legalized by the Dominican Consulate in country of origin for foreign students)

Main Language(s) of Instruction: Spanish

Degrees and Diplomas: *Licenciatura*; *Maestría*: **Educational Administration; Family Studies; Theology.**

Student Services: Academic Counselling, Canteen, Careers Guidance, Health Services, Language Laboratory, Sports Facilities

Publications: Homo Novus

Publishing House: EDUNEV

Last Updated: 20/01/16

NATIONAL TECHNOLOGICAL UNIVERSITY

Universidad Nacional Tecnológica
Dr. Delgado esq. Bolívar, Gazcue
EMail: info@unnatec.edu.do
Website: http://www.insutec.edu.do/portal/index.html

Rector: William Capellan Ferreira

School
Business Administration (Accountancy; Business Administration; Marketing; Systems Analysis); **Technology** (Computer Science)

Degrees and Diplomas: *Licenciatura*

Last Updated: 19/01/16

NATIONAL UNIVERSITY-INSTITUTE OF EXACT SCIENCES

Universidad-Instituto Nacional de Ciencias Exactas (INCE)
Apartado postal 1796, Avenida Gustavo Mejía Ricart 211 esq. Dr. Defilló, Ens. Quisqueya, Santo Domingo
Tel: +1 809 540-7300
Fax: +1 809 567-7424
EMail: ince@tricom.net
Website: http://www.ince.edu.do/

Rector: Manuel Bergés

Faculty
Economics and Social Sciences (Economics; Social Sciences); **Engineering, Architecture and Technology** (Architecture; Engineering; Technology); **Law and Political Science** (Law; Political Sciences)

Department
Lifelong Education (Accountancy; Architecture; Business Administration; Computer Science; Economics; Engineering; Finance; Fine Arts; Human Resources; Law; Marketing)

History: Founded 1974 as Instituto Nacional de Ciencias Exactas Inc

Main Language(s) of Instruction: Spanish

Degrees and Diplomas: *Licenciatura*

Last Updated: 19/01/16

NORDESTANA CATHOLIC UNIVERSITY

Universidad Católica Nordestana (UCNE)

Apartado postal 239, Calle 27 de Febrero, Esqo Restauración, San Francisco de Macorís, Duarte 239

Tel: +1 809 588-3505

Fax: +1 809 244-1647

Website: http://www.ucne.edu

Rector: Fausto Mejía Vallejo EMail: rectoria@ucne.edu

Faculty
Economics and Social Sciences (Accountancy; Business Administration; Economics; Education; Marketing; Social Sciences); **Engineering** (Architecture; Civil Engineering; Computer Engineering; Engineering); **Health Sciences** (Dentistry; Health Sciences; Medicine); **Law** (Law)

History: Founded 1978. A private non-profit institution recognized by the State.

Academic Year: January to December (January-April; May-August; September-December)

Admission Requirements: High school degree or official transcript recognised by the University

Main Language(s) of Instruction: Spanish

Accrediting Agency: ADAAC

Degrees and Diplomas: *Ingeniero, Arquitecto*: **Architecture; Computer Engineering; Engineering.** *Licenciatura*; *Especialidad*; *Maestría*: **Administration; Human Resources; Law; Marketing; Pedagogy.**

Student Services: Academic Counselling, Canteen, Careers Guidance, Cultural Activities, Health Services, Language Laboratory, Library, Social Counselling, Sports Facilities

Publications: Ciencia Humanismo

Last Updated: 19/01/16

OPEN UNIVERSITY FOR ADULTS

Universidad Abierta para Adultos (UAPA)

Avenida Hispanoamérica #100, Urb. Thomén, Santiago de los Caballeros, Santiago 51000

Tel: +1 809 724-0266

Fax: +1 809 724-0329

EMail: angel.hernandez.c@gmail.com

Website: http://www.uapa.edu.do

Rector: Ángel Hernández

Vicerrectora Administrativa y Financera: Mirian Acosta EMail: mirianacostap@yahoo.com

International Relations: Luz Rosa Estrella, Vicerrectora de Relaciones Internacionales y Cooperacíon

School
Business (Business Administration; Industrial and Organizational Psychology; Marketing); **Education** (Education; Foreign Languages Education; Mathematics Education; Modern Languages; Physical Education; Science Education; Social Sciences; Spanish; Technology); **Engineering and Technology** (Computer Science; Technology); **Languages** (Modern Languages; Tourism); **Law and Political Science** (Law; Political Sciences); **Psychology** (Clinical Psychology; Psychology); **Tourism** (Tourism)

History: Founded 1995.

Academic Year: January to December

Admission Requirements: Secondary school certificate (bachillerato)

Main Language(s) of Instruction: Spanish

Accrediting Agency: Asociación Dominicana de Auto-estudio y Acreditación

Degrees and Diplomas: *Licenciatura*; *Especialidad*; *Maestría*: **Clinical Psychology; Education; Finance; Law; Marketing.**

Student Services: Academic Counselling, Careers Guidance, Cultural Activities, Facilities for disabled people, Language Laboratory, Nursery Care, Sports Facilities

Publications: Revista Científica Educación Superior

Last Updated: 19/01/16

PEDRO HENRÍQUEZ UREÑA NATIONAL UNIVERSITY

Universidad Nacional Pedro Henríquez Ureña (UNPHU)

Apartado postal 1423, Avenida John F. Kennedy, Km. 5 1/2, Santo Domingo

Tel: +1 809 562-6601

EMail: info@unphu.edu.do

Website: http://www.unphu.edu.do

Rector: Miguel R. Fiallo Calderón

Faculty
Agriculture and Veterinary Science (Agricultural Economics; Agricultural Equipment; Agriculture; Agronomy; Animal Husbandry; Forestry; Natural Resources; Veterinary Science); **Architecture and Arts** (Advertising and Publicity; Architecture; Arts and Humanities; Graphic Design; Heritage Preservation; Interior Design); **Economics and Social Sciences** (Accountancy; Banking; Business Administration; Economics; Hotel Management); **Health Sciences** (Dentistry; Health Sciences; Medicine; Pharmacy); **Humanities and Education** (Arts and Humanities; Education; Educational Sciences; Philosophy; Primary Education; Psychology); **Law and Political Science** (International Relations; Law; Political Sciences; Public Administration); **Science and Technology** (Chemical Engineering; Civil Engineering; Computer Engineering; Industrial Engineering)

Institute
Biomedical Sciences (Biomedicine)

History: Founded 1966.

Academic Year: August to May (August-December; January-May)

Admission Requirements: Secondary school certificate (bachillerato) and entrance examination

Main Language(s) of Instruction: Spanish

Degrees and Diplomas: *Doctorado en Medicina*; *Licenciatura*; *Especialidad*; *Maestría*: **Accountancy; Administration; Architecture; Business and Commerce; Environmental Management; Heritage Preservation; Natural Resources; Political Sciences.**

Publications: Cuadernos de Filosofía; Cuadernos Jurídicos

Publishing House: Imprenta UNPHU

Last Updated: 20/01/16

PONTIFICAL CATHOLIC UNIVERSITY MADRE Y MAESTRA

Pontificia Universidad Católica Madre y Maestra (PUCMM)

Autopista Duarte Km 11/2, Santiago de los Caballeros

Tel: +1 809 580-1962

Fax: +1 809 582-4549

EMail: info@pucmm.edu.do

Website: http://www.pucmm.edu.do

Rector: Ramón Alfredo de la Cruz Baldera

Academic Vice-Rector: Rafaela Carrasco Ramos

Faculty
Engineering (Civil Engineering; Computer Engineering; Electronic Engineering; Industrial Engineering; Systems Analysis; Telecommunications Engineering); **Health Sciences** (Anaesthesiology; Cardiology; Gastroenterology; Gynaecology and Obstetrics; Health Sciences; Medicine; Nephrology; Nursing; Ophthalmology; Orthopaedics; Paediatrics; Pathology; Physical Therapy; Radiology; Stomatology; Surgery; Urology); **Humanities and Sciences** (Architecture; Communication Studies; Design; Ecology;

Educational Administration; Environmental Management; Interior Design; Philosophy; Primary Education; Psychology; Spanish); **Social Sciences and Administration** (Business Administration; Economics; Finance; Hotel Management; Law; Marketing)

History: Founded 1962.

Academic Year: August to July

Admission Requirements: Secondary school certificate

Main Language(s) of Instruction: Spanish

Degrees and Diplomas: *Ingeniero, Arquitecto*: **Engineering.** *Licenciatura*; *Especialidad*; *Maestría*: **Administration; Business Administration; Economics; Law.**

Student Services: Academic Counselling, Canteen, Careers Guidance, Cultural Activities, Foreign Studies Centre, Health Services, Language Laboratory, Social Counselling, Sports Facilities

Publications: Eme y Eme

Publishing House: PUCMM Editorial

Last Updated: 19/01/16

SANTO TOMÁS DE AQUINO BRANCH

CAMPUS RECINTO SANTO TOMÁS DE AQUINO (RSTA)

Avenida Abraham Lincoln Esquina Rómulo Betancourt, Santo Domingo
Tel: +1 809 535-0111
Fax: +1 809 535-0053
EMail: info@pucmm.edu.do
Website: http://www.pucmm.edu.do/somos/campus-santo-tomas-aquino

Faculty

Engineering; **Humanities and Social Sciences** (Accountancy; Business Administration; Development Studies; Economics; Educational Administration; Finance; Hotel Management; Human Resources; Law; Marketing; Mathematics; Philosophy; Primary Education; Public Administration)

Further Information: Also Laboratories

History: Founded 1981.

Main Language(s) of Instruction: Spanish

Degrees and Diplomas: *Licenciatura*; *Maestría*: **Business Administration; Economics; Law.**

SPECIALIZED INSTITUTE IN LAW STUDIES

Instituto Especializado de Estudios Superiores de Derecho

Apartado 425, Calle El Recodo, 2, Edificio Monte Mirador, 3er Piso, Santo Domingo
Tel: +1 809 535-9511
Fax: +1 809 535-6649
EMail: info@idempresa.edu.do
Website: http://idempresa.edu.do

Presidente: Luis Heredia Bonetti
EMail: lheredia@idempresa.edu.do

Programme

Industrial Law (Commercial Law)

History: Founded 2012.

Main Language(s) of Instruction: Spanish

Degrees and Diplomas: *Especialidad*; *Maestría*: **Commercial Law.**

Last Updated: 20/01/16

SPECIALIZED INSTITUTE IN RESEARCH AND TRAINING IN LEGAL SCIENCES OMG INSTITUTE

Instituto Especializado de Investigación y Formación en Ciencias Jurídicas OMG (IOMG)

Pedro Henríquez Ureña 150, Torre Diandy XIX, Piso 2, Santo Domingo
Tel: +1 809 533-8826
Fax: +1 809 535-4556
EMail: info@iomg.edu.do
Website: http://www.iomg.edu.do

Rectora: Belkis Guerrero Villalona

Programme

Legal Strategies (Law); **Public Economic Law** (Law)

History: Founded 2008.

Main Language(s) of Instruction: Spanish

Degrees and Diplomas: *Maestría*: **Law.**

Last Updated: 21/01/16

TECHNOLOGICAL INSTITUTE OF EASTERN CIBAO

Instituto Tecnológico del Cibao Oriental (ITECO)

Avenida Universitaria, Km 1, Cotuí
Tel: +1 809 585-2291
Fax: +1 809 240-0603
EMail: iteco@codetel.net.do
Website: http://www.iteco.edu.do

Rector: Esteban Tiburcio Gómez

Faculty

Engineering and Natural Resources (Agriculture; Computer Science; Engineering; Geological Engineering; Mining Engineering; Natural Resources; Zoology); **Humanities** (Accountancy; Administration; Arts and Humanities; Biology; Education; Law; Marketing; Natural Sciences)

History: Founded 1982.

Main Language(s) of Instruction: Spanish

Degrees and Diplomas: *Ingeniero, Arquitecto*; *Licenciatura*; *Especialidad*

Last Updated: 22/01/16

TECHNOLOGICAL INSTITUTE OF SANTO DOMINGO

Instituto Tecnológico de Santo Domingo (INTEC)

Apartado postal 342-9, Avenida de Los Próceres, 49, Los Jardines del Norte 10602, Santo Domingo
Tel: +1(809) 567-9271
Fax: +1(809) 566-3200
EMail: informacion@intec.edu.do
Website: http://www.intec.edu.do

Rector: Rolando M. Guzmán EMail: rectoria@intec.edu.do

Area

Basic and Environmental Sciences (Biotechnology; Mathematics; Statistics); **Business Administration** (Accountancy; Business Administration; Economics; International Business; Marketing); **Engineering** (Civil Engineering; Computer Engineering; Electrical and Electronic Engineering; Engineering; Industrial Design; Mechanical Engineering; Software Engineering); **Health Sciences** (Health Sciences; Medicine); **Social Sciences and Humanities** (Arts and Humanities; Philosophy; Psychology)

History: Founded 1972.

Academic Year: August to July

Admission Requirements: Secondary school certificate

Main Language(s) of Instruction: Spanish

Accrediting Agency: Asociacion Dominicana para el Autoestudio y Acreditacion (ADAAC)

Degrees and Diplomas: *Doctorado en Medicina*: **Medicine.** *Ingeniero, Arquitecto*: **Civil Engineering; Electrical and Electronic Engineering; Industrial Engineering; Mechanical Engineering.** *Licenciatura*: **Business Administration; Economics; Industrial Design; Marketing; Psychology.** *Especialidad*; *Maestría*: **Construction Engineering; Development Studies; Education; Educational Administration; Environmental Studies; Gender Studies; Health Sciences; Management.**

Student Services: Academic Counselling, Careers Guidance, Health Services, Language Laboratory, Sports Facilities

Publications: Ciencia Y Sociedad; Genero y Sociedad

Last Updated: 19/01/16

TECHNOLOGICAL UNIVERSITY OF SANTIAGO

Universidad Tecnológica de Santiago (UTESA)
Av. Estrella Sadhalá, Esq. Av. Circunvalación,
Santiago de los Caballeros
Tel: +1 809 241-7156
Fax: +1 809 582-7644
EMail: utesa.santiago@verizon.net.do
Website: http://www.utesa.edu

Rector: Priamo Rodríguez Castillo (2000-)
EMail: rectoria@utesa.edu

Vice-Rector Académico: Arnaldo R. Peña V.
EMail: arnaldop@utesa.edu

Faculty

Architecture and Engineering (Architecture; Civil Engineering; Computer Science; Construction Engineering; Electrical Engineering; Electronic Engineering; Interior Design; Mechanical Engineering; Painting and Drawing); **Economics and Social Sciences** (Accountancy; Business Administration; Marketing; Tourism); **Health Sciences** (Biochemistry; Medicine; Nursing; Pharmacology; Veterinary Science; Zoology); **Science and Humanities** (Administration; Education; Law; Modern Languages; Psychology; Social Work); **Secretarial Studies** (Secretarial Studies)

Research Centre

Agriculture, Animal Husbandry and Development (Agriculture; Animal Husbandry; Development Studies); **Bird Study and Development** (Development Studies; Zoology); **Meat Processing and Development** (Development Studies; Food Technology)

Further Information: Also branches in Santo Domingo de Guzmán, Puerto Plata, Mao and Moca and two teaching hospitals

History: Founded 1974.

Academic Year: January to December (January-April; May-August; September-December)

Admission Requirements: Secondary school certificate and entrance examination

Main Language(s) of Instruction: Spanish, English for Medicine Students

Degrees and Diplomas: *Ingeniero, Arquitecto*; *Licenciatura*; *Maestria*

Publications: Aves de mi Pais; Codigo Penal Anotado Dominicano; Curso de Trigonometria Plana y Esférica; Desarrollo y Proyección de UTESA; Diálogo Utesiano; Educación para el Medio Ambiente; Epigramas o Voces Folklóricas; Hábitos, Métodos y Técnicas de Estudio; Historia Económica Dominicana; Introduccion a la Medicina Geriátrica; La Educación Superior y sus Aspectos Organizativos; Metodología de la Investigación Aplicada; Neoliberalismo y Globalización; Reflexiones sobre el Sistema Educativo Dominicano; Reflexiones sobre: Educación y Desarrollo; Revistas Universitarias; Una Vida Dedicada a la Ciencia; Versos Escolares; Visión Educativa

Publishing House: Editora Teófilo y Nueva Editora La Información

Last Updated: 19/01/16

TECHNOLOGICAL UNIVERSITY OF THE CIBAO

Universidad Católica Tecnológica del Cibao (UTECI)
Apartado postal 401, Avenida Universitaria esq. Pedro A. Rivera, La Vega
Tel: +1 809 573-1020
Fax: +1 809 573-6194
EMail: info@ucateci.edu.do
Website: http://www.ucateci.edu.do

Rector: Hector Rafael Rodriguez Rodriguez

Faculty

Administration (Accountancy; Administration; Marketing); **Health Sciences** (Dentistry; Medicine; Nursing; Psychology); **Humanities** (Architecture; Arts and Humanities; Education; Law)

School

Science and Technology (Agronomy; Civil Engineering; Computer Science; Industrial Engineering; Technology)

History: Founded 1983 as Instituto Tecnológico del Cibao Acquired present title and status 2002..

Academic Year: January to December (January-May; August-December)

Admission Requirements: Secondary school certificate (bachillerato)

Main Language(s) of Instruction: Spanish

Degrees and Diplomas: *Técnico*; *Doctorado en Medicina*: **Dentistry; Medicine; Veterinary Science.** *Ingeniero, Arquitecto*: **Agricultural Engineering; Architecture; Civil Engineering; Engineering.** *Licenciatura*: **Accountancy; Business Administration; Education; Law; Nursing.** *Maestría*: **Educational Administration; Finance; Management; Marketing.**

Student Services: Library
Last Updated: 19/01/16

TECHNOLOGICAL UNIVERSITY OF THE SOUTH

Universidad Tecnológica del Sur
Calle Enriquillo 1, Azua 71000
Tel: +1 809-521-3785
Website: http://www.utesur.edu.do

Rector: Virgilio López Azuán EMail: rectoria@utesur.edu.do

School

Accountancy (Accountancy); **Agronomy** (Agronomy); **Bioanalysis** (Biomedicine); **Business Administration** (Business Administration); **Computer Science** (Computer Science); **Education** (Education); **Law** (Law); **Marketing** (Marketing); **Nursing** (Nursing)

History: Founded 1974.

Main Language(s) of Instruction: Spanish

Degrees and Diplomas: *Licenciatura*
Last Updated: 20/01/16

UNIVERSITY OF THE CARIBBEAN

Universidad del Caribe (UNICARIBE)
Autopista 30 de Mayo, Km 7 1/2, P.O. Box 67-2,
Santo Domingo
Tel: +1 809 616-1616
Fax: +1 809 535-0489
EMail: info@unicaribe.edu.do
Website: http://www.unicaribe.edu.do

Rector: José Andrés Aybar Sánchez
EMail: jose.aybar@codetel.net.do;
jaybar@unicaribe.edu.do

Vicerrectora Ejecutiva: Ariadna Aybar Martin
EMail: protocolo.uni@hotmail.com;
ariadna.aybar@unicaribe.edu.do

International Relations: Rosa Anna Oviedo, International Relations Officer
EMail: roviedo@unicaribe.edu.do

Programme

Accountancy (Accountancy); **Advertising** (Advertising and Publicity); **Computer Science** (Computer Science); **Education** (Education); **Hotel Management** (Hotel Management); **International Relations** (International Relations); **Law** (Law); **Marketing** (Marketing); **Social Communication** (Communication Studies)

History: Founded 1995.

Admission Requirements: Bachiller

Main Language(s) of Instruction: Spanish

Degrees and Diplomas: *Licenciatura*

Academic Staff *2012-2013*	**TOTAL**
FULL-TIME	**50**
PART-TIME	**12**
STAFF WITH DOCTORATE	
FULL-TIME	**9**
Student Numbers *2012-2013*	
All (Foreign included)	**21,338**

Last Updated: 19/01/16

UNIVERSITY OF THE THIRD AGE

Universidad de la Tercera Edad (UTE)

Calle Camila Henríquez Ureña, Esq. Jesús Maestro, Miarador Norte, Santo Domingo, Distrito Nacional
Tel: +1 809 482-7093
Fax: +1 809 482-0109
EMail: ute@ute.edu.do
Website: http://www.ute.edu.do

Rector: José Nicolás Almanzar García
EMail: nalmanzar@codetel.net.do

International Relations: Fanny Victoria Polanco Jorge

Department

Economics and Administration (Accountancy; Business Administration; Marketing); **Health Sciences** (Health Sciences; Optometry); **Humanities** (Arts and Humanities; Design; Education; Journalism; Literature; Psychology; Public Relations); **Law and Political Science** (Law; Political Sciences)

History: Founded 1989. Acquired present status 1992.

Admission Requirements: Secondary school certificate

Main Language(s) of Instruction: Spanish

Degrees and Diplomas: *Licenciatura*: **Administration; Education; Law; Marketing; Psychology; Public Relations.** *Especialidad*; *Maestría*: **International Law; International Relations; Management.**

Student Services: Academic Counselling, Canteen, Careers Guidance, Cultural Activities, Facilities for disabled people, Health Services, Language Laboratory, Social Counselling, Sports Facilities

Publications: Scientific Magazine

Last Updated: 20/01/16

Ecuador

STRUCTURE OF HIGHER EDUCATION SYSTEM

Description:

Higher education is provided by universities, polytechnics and, at non-university level, institutos técnicos superiores and tecnologicos. All universities, whether public or private, are autonomous.

Stages of studies:

University level first stage: *Tercer nivel - Grado*

The first stage of long-cycle higher education lasts for a period of four and a half to six years. Depending on the subject and the type of institution. It leads to the award of the Licenciatura after four and 1/2 years, or to a professional qualification after five to six years (Arquitecto, Ingeniero, Doctor, etc..).

University level second stage: *Cuarto nivel - Postgrado*

Some institutions offer postgraduate specialized courses leading to the qualification of Maestría after one and a half to two years' further study. Especialista programmes are mainly offered in Health and Medicine and require a minimum of 9 months' study. Some universities offer the Doctorado.

ADMISSION TO HIGHER EDUCATION

Admission to university-level studies:

Name of secondary school credential required: Bachillerato

Alternatives to credentials: Cursos pre-universitarios and entrance examination.

Admission requirements: Some private institutions require an entrance examination.

Foreign students admission:

Admission requirements: Foreign students must hold the Bachiller or an equivalent title recognized by the Secretariat for Higher Education. Candidates applying to some universities must sit for an entrance examination and, in most cases, follow a Curso de Nivelación or a Curso Preuniversitario.

Entry regulations: Foreign students must be in possession of a visa and residence permit.

Language proficiency: Foreign students must have a perfect command of Spanish. Some universities offer courses for foreign students to improve their knowledge of Spanish.

RECOGNITION OF STUDIES

Bodies dealing with recognition:

Secretaría de Educación Superior, Ciencia, Tecnología e Innovación - SENESCYT (State Secretariat for Higher Education, Science, Technology and Innovation)

Whymper E7-37 y Alpallana
Quito 170516
Tel: +593(2) 250 5660
WWW: http://www.educacionsuperior.gob.ec

Special provisions for recognition:

For access to advanced studies and research: For access to post-graduate studies and research, a review of studies completed and qualifications awarded by the foreign country will be undertaken. Recognition will be granted according to the provisions of each one of the universities and polytechnics in accordance with the international agreements and treaties in force. All documents must be provided in Spanish.

For exercising a profession: Those who wish to exercise a profession should apply to the Consejo de Educacion Superior. They must add the original or the professional qualification recognized by an Ecuadorian university or polytechnic.

NATIONAL BODIES

Secretaría de Educación Superior, Ciencia, Tecnología e Innovación - SENESCYT (State Secretariat for Higher Education, Science, Technology and Innovation)

Minister: René Ramírez Gallegos
Under Secretary for Higher Education: María del Pilar Troya
Whymper E7-37 y Alpallana
Quito 170516
Tel: +593(2) 250 5660
WWW: http://www.educacionsuperior.gob.ec

Consejo de Educación Superior - CES (Council for Higher Education)

President: René Ramírez Gallegos
Secretary-General: Marcelo Calderón Vintimilla
Av. República E7-226 y Diego de Almagro
Quito
Tel: +593(2) 394 7820
EMail: comunicacion@ces.gob.ec
WWW: http://www.ces.gob.ec
Role of national body: To define the higher education policy and to structure, plan, lead, regulate, coordinate, control, and evaluate the national higher education system.

Consejo de Evaluación, Acreditación y Aseguramiento de la Calidad de la Educación Superior- CEAACES (Higher Education Quality Evaluation and Accreditation Council)

President: Francisco Cadena Villota
Germán Alemán E11-32 y Javier Arauz
Quito
Tel: +593(2) 292 0098
EMail: info@ceaaces.gob.ec
WWW: http://www.ceaaces.gob.ec/

Data for academic year: 2015-2016
Source: IAU from the websites of the SENESCYT and CES, 2015

INSTITUTIONS

PUBLIC INSTITUTIONS

AGRARIAN UNIVERSITY OF ECUADOR

Universidad Agraria del Ecuador (UAE)
Avenida 25 de Julio y Pio Jaramillo, 09-01-1248 Guayaquil, Guyagas
Tel: +593(4) 243-9995
EMail: info@uagraria.edu.ec
Website: http://www.uagraria.edu.ec

Rectora: Martha Bucaram Leverone De Jorgge (2012-)
EMail: mbucaram@uagraria.edu.ec

Vicerrector: Ricardo Márquez Ramirez
EMail: rialmara@hotmail.com

International Relations: Carlos Campos Valverde
EMail: convenios@uagraria.edu.ec

Faculty
Agrarian Sciences *(Guayaquil and Milagro Campuses)* (Agriculture; Agronomy; Computer Engineering; Environmental Engineering; Food Science; Food Technology); **Agricultural Economics** *(Guayaquil and Milagro Campuses)* (Agricultural Economics); **Veterinary Science and Zootechnology** (Veterinary Science; Zoology)

Graduate School
SIPUAE *(Guayaquil Campus)* (Agricultural Economics; Agriculture; Higher Education Teacher Training; Irrigation; Natural Resources; Plant and Crop Protection)

History: Founded 1992.

Academic Year: April to January

Admission Requirements: Pre-university course, entrance examination; Bachelor's degree for postgraduate courses

Main Language(s) of Instruction: Spanish

Degrees and Diplomas: *Tecnólogo*: **Aquaculture; Computer Engineering; Food Technology.** *Professional Title*: **Agronomy; Computer Engineering; Economics; Environmental Engineering; Food Science; Veterinary Science.** *Maestria*

Student Services: Academic Counselling, Careers Guidance, Cultural Activities, Facilities for disabled people, Foreign Studies Centre, Health Services, Language Laboratory, Nursery Care, Social Counselling, Sports Facilities

Publications: Labour Activities

Last Updated: 02/10/15

ARMED FORCES UNIVERSIDAD

Universidad de las Fuerzas Armadas (ESPE)

Av. General Rumiñahui S/N, Sector Santa Clara - Valle de los Chillos, Sangolquí

Tel: +593(2) 239-89400

Fax: +593(2) 233-4952

Website: http://www.espe.edu.ec

Rector: Roque Apolinar Moreira Cedeño (2013-)
EMail: rector@espe.edu.ec

Vicerrector Académico: Francisco Armendáriz Sáenz
EMail: vag@espe.edu.ec

School

Escuela de Ciencias Tecnológicas Héroes del Cenepa (Distance Education)

Institute

Modern Languages (Modern Languages)

Campus

Campus Sangolquí *(Av. General Rumiñahui S/N, Sector Santa Clara - Valle de los Chillos Sangolquí - Ecuador)* (Animal Husbandry; Applied Linguistics; Automation and Control Engineering; Biotechnology; Chemistry; Civil Engineering; Computer Science; Educational Administration; Electronic Engineering; Environmental Engineering; Environmental Studies; Mathematics; Mechanical Engineering; Physical Education; Physics; Preschool Education; Sports; Telecommunications Engineering); **Latacunga** *(Quijano Ordoñez y Marquéz de Maenza, Latacunga - Ecuador)* (Administration; Automation and Control Engineering; Biotechnology; Business Administration; Civil Engineering; Computer Engineering; Computer Science; Earth Sciences; Education; Educational Sciences; Electrical Engineering; Electronic Engineering; Engineering; Environmental Studies; Geography; Mathematics and Computer Science; Mechanical Engineering; Military Science; Modern Languages; Physical Education; Systems Analysis); **Santo Domingo de los Colorados** *(Hda. Zoila Luz, Vía Santo Domingo - Quevedo Km. 24)* (Agriculture; Animal Husbandry)

History: Founded 1922 by Government Act as Military School; 1937 is changed to Engineering Technical School, and acquires present title 1977.

Academic Year: March to February (March-August; September-February)

Admission Requirements: Secondary school certificate (bachillerato) and entrance examination

Main Language(s) of Instruction: Spanish

Degrees and Diplomas: *Tecnólogo*; *Licenciatura*: **Education; Finance; Hotel and Restaurant; Physical Education.** *Professional Title*: **Engineering.** *Maestría*: **Information Technology.**

Student Services: Academic Counselling, Careers Guidance, Cultural Activities, Facilities for disabled people, Health Services, Language Laboratory, Social Counselling, Sports Facilities

Publications: Ciencia; Ingenieria de Estructuras

Last Updated: 05/11/15

CENTRAL UNIVERSITY OF ECUADOR

Universidad Central del Ecuador

Ciudadela Universitaria, Avenida América entre Gilberto Gatto Sobral y Bolivia, Quito, Pichincha

Tel: +593(2) 223-4722

Fax: +593(2) 223-6367

EMail: direccion.academica@uce.edu.ec

Website: http://www.uce.edu.ec

Rector: Jorge Daniel Ortiz Herrera EMail: rectorado@uce.edu.ec.

Faculty

Administration (Accountancy; Business Administration; Public Administration); **Agriculture** (Agricultural Engineering; Agriculture; Agronomy); **Architecture and Town Planning** (Architecture; Town Planning); **Arts** (Aesthetics; Art History; Ceramic Art; Fine Arts; Painting and Drawing; Photography; Sculpture; Theatre); **Chemistry** (Chemistry); **Dentistry** (Dentistry); **Economics** (Economics; Finance; Statistics); **Engineering, Physics and Mathematics** (Civil Engineering; Computer Engineering; Industrial Design; Mathematics; Physics); **Geology, Mining, Petroleum and Environmental Engineering** (Environmental Engineering; Geology; Mining Engineering; Petroleum and Gas Engineering); **Law, Political and Social Sciences** (Law; Political Sciences; Social Work; Sociology); **Medicine** (Gynaecology and Obstetrics; Medical Technology; Medicine; Nursing; Occupational Therapy; Physical Therapy; Radiology; Speech Therapy and Audiology; Statistics); **Philosophy, Letters and Education** (Biology; Business Administration; Chemistry; Linguistics; Literature; Mathematics; Modern Languages; Philosophy; Physical Education; Psychology; Social Sciences; Teacher Training); **Psychology** (Clinical Psychology; Psychology); **Social Communication** (Communication Studies); **Veterinary Science** (Veterinary Science; Zoology)

History: Founded 1586 as Universidad de San Fulgencio and 1622 as Universidad de San Gregorio Magno. Replaced 1786 under Don Carlos III by Real y Pontificia Universidad de Santo Tomás de Aquino. Title changed to Universidad Central 1897. Granted autonomy 1925. Financed by the State.

Academic Year: October to June (October-December; January-March; April-June)

Admission Requirements: Secondary school certificate (bachillerato) or equivalent

Fees: According to parents' income

Main Language(s) of Instruction: Spanish

Degrees and Diplomas: *Licenciatura*: **Administration; Banking; Economics; Education; Fine Arts; International Law; Journalism; Nursing; Political Sciences; Psychology; Social Sciences; Statistics.** *Professional Title*: **Accountancy; Agricultural Engineering; Architecture; Biochemistry; Business Administration; Chemical Engineering; Civil Engineering; Design; Earth Sciences; Economics; Educational Administration; Geology; Law; Midwifery; Mining Engineering; Nursing; Occupational Therapy; Painting and Drawing; Sculpture; Statistics; Veterinary Science.** *Especialista*; *Maestría*. Also posgrados

Student Services: Canteen, Cultural Activities, Health Services, Language Laboratory, Nursery Care, Social Counselling, Sports Facilities

Publications: Anales; Revistas de: Economía, Derecho, Derecho Internacional, Derecho Comparado, Medicina, Odontología, Bioquímica

Last Updated: 20/10/15

ECOTEC TECHNOLOGICAL UNIVERSITY

Universidad Tecnológica ECOTEC

Av Juan Tanca Marengo Km 2 entre La Llave y Automotores y Anexos, Guayaquil

Tel: +593(04) 268-1740

EMail: adminsiones@universidadecotec.edu.ec

Website: http://www.ecotec.edu.ec

Rector: Fidel Márquez Sánchez (2014-)
EMail: fmarquez@ecotec.edu.ec

Vicerrectora Académica: Gilda Alcívar de Gilbert
EMail: galcivar@ecotec.edu.ec

Faculty

Computer Systems and Telecommunications (Computer Science; Telecommunications Engineering); **Economics and Business Administration** (Business Administration; Economics); **Law and Governance** (Law); **Marketing and Communication** (Communication Studies; Marketing); **Tourism and Hotel Management** (Hotel Management; Tourism)

Degrees and Diplomas: *Licenciatura*; *Professional Title*

Last Updated: 30/10/15

INSTITUTE OF ADVANCED NATIONAL STUDIES

Instituto de Altos Estudios Nacionales

Av. Rio Amazonas N37-271 y Villalengua (esq.), Quito

Tel: +593(2) 382-9900

Fax: +593(2) 423-6338

EMail: infoiaen@iaen.edu.ec

Website: http://www.iaen.edu.ec

Rectora: Analía Minteguiaga
EMail: analia.minteguiaga@iaen.edu.ec

Centre
Government and Administration (Administration; Management); **International Relations** (International Relations); **Law and Justice** (Law; Public Administration; Public Law); **Public Economics** (Economics)

History: Founded 1972. Acquired present status 2008.

Main Language(s) of Instruction: Spanish

Degrees and Diplomas: *Especialista*; *Maestría*
Last Updated: 01/10/15

INSTITUTE OF TECHNOLOGY OF CHIMBORAZO

Escuela Superior Politécnica de Chimborazo (ESPOCH)

Apartado 06-01-4703, Panamericana Sur Km. 11/2, Riobamba
Tel: +593(3) 296-5269
Fax: +593(3) 961977 +593(3) 961-977
EMail: info@espoch.edu.ec; info@live.espoch.edu.ec
Website: http://www.espoch.edu.ec

Rectora: Rosa Elena Pinos (2013-)
EMail: rpinos@live.espoch.edu.ec

Vicerrector Académico: Geovanny Novillo Andrade
EMail: gnovillo@espoch.edu.ec

Faculty
Animal Husbandry (Animal Husbandry; Fishery; Zoology); **Business Administration** (Accountancy; Administration; Business Administration; Finance; International Business; Marketing); **Computer Science and Electronics** (Computer Engineering; Computer Networks; Electronic Engineering; Graphic Design; Systems Analysis; Telecommunications Engineering); **Mechanical Engineering** (Industrial Engineering; Maintenance Technology; Mechanical Engineering); **Natural Resources** (Agricultural Engineering; Forestry; Natural Resources; Tourism); **Public Health** (Cooking and Catering; Dietetics; Food Technology; Health Education; Medicine; Nutrition; Public Health); **Science** (Biochemistry; Biophysics; Chemical Engineering; Chemistry; Industrial Chemistry; Mathematics; Natural Sciences; Pharmacy; Physics)

History: Founded 1969 as a State institution under the jurisdiction of the Ministry of Education, enjoying some autonomy. Acquired present status as Polytechnic 1973.

Academic Year: October to July (October-February; March-July)

Admission Requirements: Secondary school certificate (bachillerato)

Main Language(s) of Instruction: Spanish

Degrees and Diplomas: *Tecnólogo*; *Licenciatura*: **Engineering; Nutrition.** *Especialista*; *Maestría*

Publishing house: Departamento de Publicaciones
Last Updated: 01/10/15

IAU INSTITUTE OF TECHNOLOGY OF THE COAST

Escuela Superior Politécnica del Litoral (ESPOL)

Apartado 09-01-5863, Campus Gustavo Galindo V Km 30.5, Via Perimetral, Guayaquil
Tel: +593(4) 226-9101
Fax: +593(4) 285-4629
EMail: httpd@espol.edu.ec
Website: http://www.espol.edu.ec

Rector: Sergio Flores Macías (2012-)
EMail: rector@espol.edu.ec; sergio.flores@gmail.com

Vicerrectora Académica: Cecilia Paredes
EMail: cparedes@espol.edu.ec

Faculty
Earth Sciences (Archaeology; Civil Engineering; Earth Sciences; Geology; Mining Engineering; Petroleum and Gas Engineering); **Electrical Engineering and Computer Science** (Automation and Control Engineering; Computer Science; Electrical Engineering; Electronic Engineering; Telecommunications Engineering); **Marine Science, Biological Sciences, Oceanography and Natural Resources** (Aquaculture; Environmental Studies; Marine Biology; Marine Science and Oceanography; Tourism); **Mechanical Engineering and Production Engineering** (Agricultural Engineering; Bioengineering; Food Technology; Mechanical Engineering; Production Engineering); **Natural Sciences and Mathematics** (Accountancy; Chemistry; Environmental Studies; Mathematics; Physics; Statistics; Transport Management); **Social Sciences and Humanities** (Business Administration; Business and Commerce; Economics; Finance; International Business; Marketing)

School
Design and Visual Communication (Computer Science; Graphic Design)

Research Centre
Biotechnology (Biotechnology); **Environmental Studies** (Environmental Studies; Welfare and Protective Services); **Marine Sciences** (Marine Science and Oceanography); **Statistics**

History: Founded 1958 as a State institution under the jurisdiction of the Ministry of Education, but enjoys some autonomy.

Academic Year: May to February (May-September; October-February)

Admission Requirements: Secondary school certificate (bachillerato) and entrance examination

Main Language(s) of Instruction: Spanish

Degrees and Diplomas: *Tecnólogo*; *Licenciatura*; *Professional Title*; *Maestría*

Student Services: Academic Counselling, Careers Guidance, Cultural Activities, Health Services, Language Laboratory, Social Counselling, Sports Facilities
Last Updated: 01/10/15

LATIN AMERICAN FACULTY OF SOCIAL SCIENCES

Facultad Latinoamericana de Ciencias Sociales sede Ecuador

La Pradera E7-174 y Av. Diego de Almagro, Quito, Pichincha
Tel: +593(2) 294 6800
Fax: +593(2) 294 6803
EMail: flacso@flacso.edu.ec
Website: http://www.flacso.edu.ec

Director: Juan Ponce EMail: jponce@flacso.edu.ec

Subdirectora Académica: Gioconda Herrerra
EMail: gherrera@flacso.edu.ec

Coordinador de Investigación: Carlos Espinosa
EMail: cespinosa@flacso.edu.ec

Coordinadora Docente: Belén Albornoz
EMail: balbornoz@flacso.edu.ec

Department
Anthropology, History and Humanities (Anthropology; Arts and Humanities; History); **Development, Environment and Territory** (Development Studies; Economics; Rural Studies); **International Studies and Communication** (Communication Studies; International Studies); **Political Studies** (Political Sciences; Social Policy); **Public Affairs** (Political Sciences; Urban Studies); **Sociology and Gender Studies** (Gender Studies; Sociology)

History: Founded 1975. Acquired present status 2000.

Main Language(s) of Instruction: Spanish

Degrees and Diplomas: *Especialista*: **Social Sciences.** *Maestría*: **Social Sciences.** *Doctorado*: **Cultural Studies; Economics; History; International Studies; Latin American Studies; Political Sciences; Social Sciences.**

Student Services: Academic Counselling, Careers Guidance, Cultural Activities, Facilities for disabled people, Health Services, IT Centre, Library, Nursery Care, Social Counselling, Sports Facilities, eLibrary

Academic Staff *2014-2015*	MEN	WOMEN	**TOTAL**
FULL-TIME	39	31	**70**
STAFF WITH DOCTORATE			
FULL-TIME	31	28	**59**
Student Numbers *2014-2015*			
All (Foreign included)	441	509	**950**
FOREIGN ONLY	149	195	**344**

Last Updated: 09/09/15

LUIS VARGAS TORRES DE ESMERALDAS TECHNICAL UNIVERSITY

Universidad Técnica Luis Vargas Torres de Esmeraldas (UTELVT)

Apartado 179-619, Avenida Kennedy y Las Palmas, Esmeraldas
Tel: +593 (6) 272-3702
EMail: utelvt@utelvt.edu.ec
Website: http://www.utelvt.edu.ec

Rector: Diógenes Alberto Díaz Segarra (2014-)
EMail: rector@utelvt.edu.ec

Vicerrector Académico: Félix Preciado Quiñones

Faculty

Administration and Economics (Administration; Economics); **Animal Husbandry and Environmental Sciences** (Agriculture; Animal Husbandry; Environmental Studies; Forestry); **Engineering and Technology** (Chemical Engineering; Electrical Engineering; Mechanical Engineering); **Social Sciences and Development Studies** (Hotel Management; Political Sciences; Social Work; Sociology; Tourism)

History: Founded 1970. An autonomous State institution.

Main Language(s) of Instruction: Spanish

Degrees and Diplomas: *Licenciatura*: **Biology; Chemistry; Economics; Geography; History; Industrial Engineering; Mathematics; Physical Education; Physics; Psychology; Social Work; Sociology; Vocational Education.** *Professional Title*: **Animal Husbandry; Business Administration; Forestry.** *Especialista*; *Maestría*

Last Updated: 29/10/15

MANUEL FÉLIX LÓPEZ INSTITUTE OF AGRICULTURAL TECHNOLOGY OF MANABI

Escuela Superior Politécnica Agropecuaria de Manabí Manuel Félix López (ESPAM MFL)

10 de Agosto 82 y Granda Centeno, Calceta
Tel: +593(5) 268-5676
Fax: +593(5) 268-5156
EMail: espam@espam.edu.ec
Website: http://www.espam.edu.ec

Rectora: Miryam Elizabeth Félix López
EMail: rectorado@espam.edu.ec

Vicerrectora Académica: Ángela Lorena Carreño Mendoza

Programme

Agricultural Industry (Agricultural Business); **Agriculture** (Agriculture; Cattle Breeding); **Business Administration** (Business Administration; Public Administration); **Computer Engineering** (Computer Engineering); **Environmental Studies** (Environmental Studies); **Fishery** (Fishery); **Tourism** (Tourism)

History: Founded 1999.

Main Language(s) of Instruction: Spanish

Degrees and Diplomas: *Professional Title*

Last Updated: 01/10/15

MILAGRO STATE UNIVERSITY

Universidad Estatal de Milagro (UNEMI)

Km 1, via Milagro km. 26, Milagro, Guayas
Tel: +593 (4) 297-0881
Fax: +593 (5) 297-4317
Website: http://www.unemi.edu.ec

Rector: Fabricio Guevara Viejó (2014-)
EMail: rectorado@unemi.edu.ec

Vicerrectora Académica y de Investigación: Jesennia Cárdenas Cobo EMail: jcardenasc@unemi.edu.ec

Faculty

Administration and Commercial Sciences (Accountancy; Administration; Business Administration; Business and Commerce; Economics; Marketing; Tourism); **Education and Communication Science** (Communication Studies; Education; Graphic Design; Physical Education; Preschool Education; Psychology); **Engineering** (Computer Engineering; Computer Science; Industrial Maintenance; Systems Analysis); **Health Sciences** (Nursing; Nutrition; Respiratory Therapy)

History: Founded 2001. Former branch of Guayaquil State University.

Academic Year: May to September; October to March

Admission Requirements: Secondary school certificate (bachillerato) or equivalent

Main Language(s) of Instruction: Spanish

Degrees and Diplomas: *Tecnólogo*: **Advertising and Publicity; Business Administration; Computer Science; Graphic Design; Industrial Maintenance; Marketing; Systems Analysis; Tourism.** *Licenciatura*: **Accountancy; Business Administration; Business and Commerce; Computer Science; Economics; Education; Industrial Management; Nursing; Physical Education; Tourism.** *Maestría*

Student Services: Academic Counselling, Canteen, Cultural Activities, Facilities for disabled people, Health Services, Language Laboratory, Library, Nursery Care, Social Counselling, Sports Facilities

Publications: Agora

Last Updated: 22/10/15

NATIONAL POLYTECHNIC SCHOOL

Escuela Politécnica Nacional (EPN)

Apartado 17-12-866, Ladrón de Guevara E11-253, José Rubén Orellana Ricaurte Campus, Quito, Pichincha
Tel: +593(2) 250-7144
Fax: +593(2) 256-7848
EMail: info@epn.edu.ec
Website: http://www.epn.edu.ec

Rector: Jaime Alfonso Calderon Segovia (2013-)
EMail: rector@epn.edu.ec

Vicerrector: Tarquino Sánchez EMail: vrector@epn.edu.ec

Faculty

Business Sciences (Business Administration; Finance; Health Administration; Higher Education; Human Resources; Management; Marketing); **Chemical Engineering and Agroindustry** (Agricultural Business; Agricultural Engineering; Biotechnology; Chemical Engineering; Food Science; Industrial Engineering; Metallurgical Engineering; Nuclear Engineering); **Civil and Environmental Engineering** (Civil Engineering; Engineering; Environmental Engineering; Water Management; Water Science); **Electrical and Electronic Engineering** (Automation and Control Engineering; Electrical and Electronic Engineering; Electrical Engineering; Electronic Engineering; Energy Engineering; Telecommunications Engineering); **Geology and Petroleum** (Geology; Petroleum and Gas Engineering); **Mechanical Engineering** (Materials Engineering; Mechanical Engineering); **Science** (Mathematics; Natural Sciences; Physics); **Systems Engineering** (Computer Science; Information Technology)

School

Technology (Construction Engineering; Electronic Engineering; Industrial Maintenance; Information Technology; Mechanical Engineering; Production Engineering; Systems Analysis; Technology)

History: Founded 1869 as Esceula Politécnica by President Gabriel García Moreno. Acquired present title 1946.

Academic Year: October to September (October-March; April-September)

Admission Requirements: Secondary school certificate (bachillerato) and entrance examination

Fees: (US Dollars): pregraduate, 50-600 per semester; postgraduate, 700-1500 per semester

Main Language(s) of Instruction: Spanish

Degrees and Diplomas: *Tecnólogo*: **Construction Engineering; Electrical Engineering; Electronic Engineering; Industrial Maintenance; Mechanical Engineering; Systems Analysis; Telecommunications Engineering.** *Professional Title*: **Administration; Agricultural Engineering; Chemical Engineering; Civil Engineering; Economics; Electrical Engineering; Electronic Engineering; Environmental Engineering; Finance; Geological Engineering; Mathematics; Mechanical Engineering; Petroleum and Gas Engineering; Physical Engineering.** *Maestría*:

Administration; Engineering. *Doctorado*: **Civil Engineering; Electrical Engineering; Environmental Engineering; Food Technology; Mathematics; Mechanical Engineering.** Also Diplomado Superior in Engineering (Postgraduate), 1 sem.

Student Services: Academic Counselling, Canteen, Cultural Activities, Health Services, Language Laboratory, Social Counselling, Sports Facilities

Publications: Revista Politécnica
Last Updated: 01/10/15

NATIONAL UNIVERSITY OF CHIMBORAZO

Universidad Nacional de Chimborazo (UNACH)
Avenida Eloy Alfaro y 10 de Agosto, Riobamba
Tel: +593(3) 294-1999
Fax: +593(3) 296-0345
EMail: contactos@unach.edu.ec
Website: http://www.unach.edu.ec

Rectora: María Angélica Barba Maggi (2013-)
EMail: rector@unach.edu.ec

Vicerrectora Académica: Anita Cecilia Rios
EMail: arios@unach.edu.ec

Faculty

Education, Humanities and Technology (Art Education; Bilingual and Bicultural Education; Biology; Business and Commerce; Chemistry; Educational Sciences; Gerontology; Laboratory Techniques; Literature; Modern Languages; Natural Sciences; Physical Education; Primary Education; Psychology; Social Sciences; Spanish; Special Education); **Engineering** (Agricultural Engineering; Civil Engineering; Electrical Engineering; Engineering; Environmental Engineering; Industrial Engineering); **Health Sciences** (Clinical Psychology; Medical Technology; Medicine; Nursing; Physical Education); **Political Science and Administration** (Accountancy; Administration; Communication Studies; Economics; Law)

History: Founded 1995.

Main Language(s) of Instruction: Spanish

Degrees and Diplomas: *Licenciatura*; *Maestría*
Last Updated: 23/10/15

NATIONAL UNIVERSITY OF LOJA

Universidad Nacional de Loja (UNL)
Ciudadela Universitaria 'Guillermo Falconí Espinosa' La Argelia, 11012636 Loja, Loja
Tel: +593(7) 254-7200
Fax: +593(7) 254-6075
EMail: dgb@unl.edu.ec
Website: http://www.unl.edu.ec

Rector: Gustavo Enrique Villacís Rivas (2011-)
EMail: rector@unl.edu.ec

Vicerrectora: Martha Esther Reyes Coronel
EMail: vrector@unl.edu.ec

Area

Agriculture and Renewable Natural Resources (Agricultural Equipment; Agricultural Management; Agriculture; Agronomy; Animal Husbandry; Aquaculture; Environmental Management; Forestry; Irrigation; Rural Studies; Tropical Agriculture; Veterinary Science); **Education, Arts and Communication Studies** (Aesthetics; Biology; Chemistry; Child Care and Development; Clothing and Sewing; Communication Disorders; Computer Education; Education; Educational Administration; Educational and Student Counselling; Educational Psychology; Educational Research; Educational Technology; English; Higher Education Teacher Training; Information Sciences; Library Science; Literature; Mathematics; Mathematics Education; Music; Physical Education; Physics; Preschool Education; Science Education; Social Sciences; Spanish; Special Education; Teacher Trainers Education; Visual Arts); **Energy, Industry and non-Renewable Natural Resources** (Automotive Engineering; Computer Science; Construction Engineering; Electrical Engineering; Electronic Engineering; Energy Engineering; Engineering; Environmental Management; Geological Engineering; Geology; Information Technology; Mechanical Engineering; Telecommunications Engineering); **Health Sciences** (Anaesthesiology; Clinical Psychology; Community Health; Dentistry; Gynaecology and Obstetrics; Health Administration; Laboratory Techniques; Medical Technology; Medicine; Nursing; Orthopaedics; Paediatrics; Public Health; Radiology; Surgery); **Law, Social Sciences and Administration** (Accountancy; Banking; Business Administration; Development Studies; Economics; Finance; Law; Public Administration; Social Work; Tourism)

History: Founded 1859 as School of Law, acquired present status 1943. An autonomous institution, largely financed by the State.

Academic Year: October to July

Admission Requirements: Secondary school certificate (bachillerato)

Fees: First module (Presence Modality): 56-229; (Distance Modality): 200-373 (US Dollar)

Main Language(s) of Instruction: Spanish

Accrediting Agency: Consejo Nacional de Educación Superior (CONESUP); Consejo Nacional de Evaluación y Acreditación (CONEA)

Degrees and Diplomas: *Técnico Superior*; *Tecnólogo*: **Electrical Engineering; Electronic Engineering; Interior Design; Music; Protective Services; Radiology.** *Licenciatura*: **Accountancy; Agricultural Engineering; Agricultural Management; Agronomy; Aquaculture; Banking; Business Administration; Civil Engineering; Clinical Psychology; Communication Studies; Computer Education; Computer Engineering; Crop Production; Dentistry; Economics; Education; Educational Technology; Engineering; English; Environmental Engineering; Environmental Management; Finance; Forestry; Information Sciences; Laboratory Techniques; Literature; Mechanical Engineering; Medicine; Music; Native Language Education; Nursing; Philosophy; Political Sciences; Psychology; Public Administration; Social Sciences; Social Work; Special Education; Tourism; Veterinary Science.** *Especialista*: **Anaesthesiology; Environmental Management; Gynaecology and Obstetrics; Irrigation; Law; Medicine; Orthopaedics; Paediatrics; Radiology; Surgery; Tourism.** *Maestría*: **Accountancy; Agricultural Engineering; Animal Husbandry; Business Administration; Development Studies; Electrical Engineering; Environmental Management; Forestry; Irrigation; Law; Mechanical Engineering; Rural Studies; Tropical Agriculture.**

Student Services: Academic Counselling, Canteen, Careers Guidance, Cultural Activities, Facilities for disabled people, Health Services, Language Laboratory, Nursery Care, Social Counselling, Sports Facilities

Publications: Cigüeña de Papel; El Canto del Llangache; Estudios Universitarios; Mar de Tinta; Revistas Universitaria

Publishing House: Editorial Universitaria
Last Updated: 23/10/15

PENINSULA OF SANTA ELENA STATE UNIVERSITY

Universidad Estatal Península de Santa Elena (UPSE)
Casilla Postal No. 09 - 11 - 16459, Vía La Libertad-Santa Elena, EC240350 La Libertad, Santa Elena
Tel: +593(4) 278-1732 2781738
Fax: +593(4) 278-4006
Website: http://www.upse.edu.ec

Rectora: Lilia Esther Valencia Cruzaty (2015-)
EMail: lvalencia@upse.edu.ec; rectorado@upse.edu.ec

Vicerrector Académico: Jimmy Candell Soto
EMail: jcandell@upse.edu.ec

Faculty

Administration (Accountancy; Business Administration; Tourism); **Agriculture** (Agricultural Engineering; Agriculture); **Education and Languages** (Physical Education; Preschool Education; Sports); **Engineering** (Civil Engineering; Industrial Engineering; Petroleum and Gas Engineering); **Marine Sciences** (Marine Biology); **Social and Health Sciences** (Nursing); **Systems and Telecommunications** (Computer Science; Electronic Engineering; Telecommunications Engineering)

History: Founded on Wednesday, July 22nd., 1998. Location: La Libertad, Provincia de Santa Elena, Ecuador, South America Accredited

Academic Year: First semester: May - August Second Semester: October-February

Admission Requirements: ENES, National Exam for Higher Education

Fees: State Universities are free in Ecuador (US Dollar)

Main Language(s) of Instruction: Spanish

Accrediting Agency: CEAASES: Consejo de Evaluación, Acreditación y Aseguramiento de la Educación Superior

Degrees and Diplomas: *Licenciatura*; *Professional Title*

Last Updated: 22/10/15

POLYTECHNIC STATE UNIVERSITY OF CARCHI

Universidad Politécnica Estatal del Carchi

Calle Antisana y Av. Universitaria, Tulcán, Carchi

Tel: +593(6) 298-1009

EMail: info@upec.edu.ec

Website: http://upec.edu.ec

Rector: Hugo Milton Ruiz Enríquez (2015-)

Vicerectorra: Liliana Montenegro

Faculty

Agronomy and Environment (Agronomy; Environmental Studies; Tourism); **International Business, Integration, Business Administration and Economics** (Business Administration; Economics; International Business; Marketing); **Medicine** (Medicine; Nursing)

History: Founded 2008.

Main Language(s) of Instruction: Spanish

Degrees and Diplomas: *Professional Title*

Last Updated: 27/10/15

SIMÓN BOLÍVAR ANDEAN UNIVERSITY ECUADOR

Universidad Andina Simón Bolívar Ecuador (UASB)

Real Audiencia 73, Sucre

Tel: +591(4) 646-0265

Fax: +591(4) 646-0833

EMail: uasb@uasb.edu.ec

Website: http://www.uasb.edu.ec

Rector: Manuel Enrique Alejandro Ayala Mora (1997-)
EMail: rector@uasb.edu.ec; enrique.ayalamora@uasb.edu.ec

Vicerrector: Santiago Andrade
EMail: santiago.andrade@uasb.edu.ec

Area

Communication (Communication Studies); **Education** (Education; Educational Research); **Health Sciences** (Epidemiology; Health Sciences); **History** (Archiving; History; Museum Studies); **Law** (Human Rights; Law); **Letters and Cultural Studies** (Arts and Humanities; Literature); **Management** (Management); **Social and Global Studies** (Cultural Studies; International Studies; Latin American Studies)

Further Information: Also campuses in Quito, La Paz

History: Founded 1985 by the Parlamento Andino. An international Institution for Andean co-operation and integration, mostly oriented towards Postgraduate studies. Ecuador branch founded in 1992.

Academic Year: October to September (October-December; January-March; April-June; July-September)

Admission Requirements: Recognized University Degree

Main Language(s) of Instruction: Spanish

Degrees and Diplomas: *Professional Title*; *Especialista*; *Maestría*; *Doctorado*: **Administration; Community Health; Cultural Studies; History; Latin American Studies; Law; Literature.** Also Doctorado

Student Services: Academic Counselling, Cultural Activities

Publications: Kipus (Revista Andina de Letras); Procesos (Revista Ecuadoriana de Historia)

Last Updated: 20/10/15

STATE TECHNICAL UNIVERSITY OF QUEVEDO

Universidad Técnica Estatal de Quevedo (UTEQ)

Campus "Ingeniero Manuel Haz Álvarezrdquo;, Av. Quito km. 1 1/2 vía a Santo Domingo de los Tsachilas, Quevedo, Los Rios

Tel: +593(5) 275-7463

EMail: secretariageneral@uteq.edu.ec

Website: http://www.uteq.edu.ec

Rector: Eduardo Díaz Ocampo (2015-)
EMail: rector@uteq.edu.ec; ediaz@uteq.edu.ec

Vicerrectora Académica: Guadalupe del Pilar Murillo Campuzano
EMail: vicerrectoracademico@uteq.edu.ec

Faculty

Agriculture (Agricultural Economics; Agricultural Engineering; Agricultural Management; Business Administration); **Business Studies** (Accountancy; Business Administration; Economics; Finance; Marketing); **Environmental Science** (Environmental Management; Forestry; Tourism); **Law** (Law); **Stockbreeding** (Cattle Breeding; Food Technology; Zoology)

Further Information: Also 2 experimental farms

History: Founded 1976 as branch of University of Esmeraldas, acquired present status and title 1984.

Academic Year: May to March (May-September; October-March)

Admission Requirements: Secondary school certificate (bachillerato) and entrance examination (curso pre-universitario-tres meses)

Main Language(s) of Instruction: Spanish

Degrees and Diplomas: *Professional Title*: **Agronomy; Environmental Studies; Forestry; Zoology.** *Maestría*

Student Services: Cultural Activities, Health Services, Language Laboratory, Nursery Care, Sports Facilities

Publications: Magazine of Agronomy Research

Last Updated: 29/10/15

STATE UNIVERSITY OF BOLÍVAR

Universidad Estatal de Bolívar (UEB)

Campus Universitario: "Alpachaca" Av. Ernesto Che Guevara s/n y Av. Gabriel Secaira, Guaranda, Bolivar

Tel: +593(3) 3220-6010

Fax: +593(3) 298-0123

EMail: info@ueb.edu.ec

Website: http://www.ueb.edu.ec

Rector: Ulices Eduardo Barragan Vinueza (2015-)
EMail: rector@ueb.edu.ec

Vicerrectora Académica: Beatriz Lucio Quintana
EMail: vrector@ueb.edu.ec

Faculty

Administration, Business Administration and Computer Science (Administration; Business Administration; Communication Studies; Computer Science; Hotel Management; Secretarial Studies; Tourism); **Agriculture and Animal Husbandry** (Agricultural Engineering; Agriculture; Agronomy; Animal Husbandry; Ceramics and Glass Technology; Industrial Engineering; Veterinary Science; Zoology); **Educational Sciences** (Educational Administration; Educational Sciences; English; Fashion Design; Fine Arts; Musicology; Physical Education; Primary Education; Spanish; Sports); **Health Sciences** (Health Sciences; Nursing); **Law, Social Sciences and Political Science** (Law; Political Sciences; Sociology)

History: Founded 1977. Acquired present status and title 1989.

Main Language(s) of Instruction: Spanish

Degrees and Diplomas: *Tecnólogo*; *Licenciatura*; *Especialista*; *Maestría*

Last Updated: 21/10/15

STATE UNIVERSITY OF THE AMAZON

Universidad Estatal Amazónica (UEA)

Alvaro Valladares y Cristóbal Colón Puyo, Pastaza

Tel: +593(3) 288-7476

Fax: +593(3) 288-8118

EMail: info@uea.edu.ec

Website: http://www.uea.edu.ec

Rector: Julio César Vargas Burgos (2011-)
EMail: rectorado@uea.edu.ec

Vicerrectora Académica: Nelly Narcisa Manjarrez Fuentes

Programme

Agricultural and Industrial Engineering (Agricultural Engineering; Industrial Engineering); **Environmental Engineering** (Environmental Engineering); **Tourism** (Tourism)

School

Agricultural Engineering (Agricultural Engineering)

History: Founded 2002.

Main Language(s) of Instruction: Spanish

Degrees and Diplomas: *Professional Title*
Last Updated: 21/10/15

STATE UNIVERSITY OF THE SOUTH OF MANABI

Universidad Estatal del Sur de Manabi (UNESUM)
Calle Santiesteban entre Alejo Lascano y Mejia, Campus Universitario, m 1 vía a Noboa, Jipijapa
Tel: +593(5) 260-0229
EMail: unesum@hotmail.com
Website: http://www.unesum.edu.ec

Rector: Omelio Enrique Borroto Leal (2015-)
EMail: rector@unesum.edu.ec; omelio.borroto@unesum.edu.ec

Unit

Administration and Economics (Business Administration; Business and Commerce; International Business; Tourism); **Health Sciences** (Medical Technology; Nursing); **Technical Sciences** (Agricultural Engineering; Civil Engineering; Computer Engineering; Computer Networks; Environmental Engineering; Forestry)

History: Founded 2001.

Main Language(s) of Instruction: Spanish

Degrees and Diplomas: *Professional Title*

Student Services: Library
Last Updated: 22/10/15

TECHNICAL UNIVERSITY OF AMBATO

Universidad Técnica de Ambato (UTA)
Apartado 18-01-334, Avenida Colombia y Chile, Ambato, Tungurahua
Tel: +593(3) 284-3011
Fax: +593(3) 284-9164
EMail: uta@uta.edu.ec
Website: http://www.uta.edu.ec

Rector: Galo Oswaldo Naranjo López (2014-)
EMail: utarectorado@uta.edu.ec.

Vicerrector Administrativo: Jorge Leon
EMail: jleonm@uta.edu.ec.

Faculty

Accountancy and Auditing (Accountancy; Economics; Finance); **Administration** (Administration; Marketing; Private Administration; Public Administration); **Agricultural Engineering** (Agricultural Engineering; Agronomy; Veterinary Science; Zoology); **Civil and Mechanical Engineering** (Civil Engineering; Mechanical Engineering); **Design, Architecture and Arts** (Architecture; Fashion Design; Graphic Design); **Food Science and Engineering** (Biochemistry; Food Science; Food Technology); **Health Sciences** (Clinical Psychology; Health Sciences; Medical Technology; Medicine; Nursing; Physical Therapy); **Humanities and Educational Sciences** (Educational Psychology; Hotel Management; Industrial and Organizational Psychology; Physical Education; Preschool Education; Primary Education; Tourism); **Social Sciences and Law** (Law; Public Law; Social Sciences; Social Work); **Systems, Electrical and Industrial Engineering** (Automation and Control Engineering; Computer Engineering; Electronic Engineering; Industrial Engineering; Software Engineering; Systems Analysis)

History: Founded 1959 as an Institute of Accountancy, became an autonomous higher education institution 1963, and acquired University status 1969.

Academic Year: October to August

Admission Requirements: Secondary school certificate (bachillerato)

Fees: (US Dollars): c. 60-120, depending on field of study

Main Language(s) of Instruction: Spanish

Degrees and Diplomas: *Licenciatura*: **Accountancy; Education; Health Sciences.** *Professional Title*: **Administration; Agronomy; Civil Engineering; Computer Engineering; Electrical Engineering; Food Technology; Industrial Engineering; Management; Mechanical Engineering.** *Especialista*; *Maestría*. Also Diplomado

Student Services: Academic Counselling, Canteen, Careers Guidance, Cultural Activities, Social Counselling, Sports Facilities

Publications: Research Publications

Publishing House: Editorial Universitaria
Last Updated: 27/10/15

TECHNICAL UNIVERSITY OF BABAHOYO

Universidad Técnica de Babahoyo (UTB)
Av. Universitaria Km 21/2 Av. Montalvo, Babahoyo, Los Ríos
Tel: +593 (5) 257-0368
Fax: +593 (7) 273-0646
EMail: webutb@utb.edu.ec
Website: http://www.utb.edu.ec

Rector: Rafael Falconi Montalván (2013-)
EMail: rectorado@utb.edu.ec

Vicerrector Académico: Pedro Rodríguez Vargas
EMail: prodriguez@utb.edu.ec

Faculty

Administration, Finance and Computer Studies (Administration; Banking; Computer Science; Finance); **Agriculture** (Agricultural Engineering; Agriculture; Animal Husbandry; Veterinary Science); **Health Sciences** (Gynaecology and Obstetrics; Health Sciences; Medical Technology; Nursing; Nutrition; Optometry; Physical Therapy; Respiratory Therapy); **Social Sciences and Education** *(Quevedo)* (Education; Pedagogy; Social Sciences)

School

Agronomy (Agronomy); **Clinical Laboratory** (Laboratory Techniques); **Computer Science** (Computer Science); **Natural Sciences** (Natural Sciences); **Psychology** (Psychology); **Social Communication**; **Technology** (Technology)

Centre

Research

History: Founded 1971.

Degrees and Diplomas: *Licenciatura*: **Education.** *Professional Title*: **Agricultural Engineering.** *Especialista*; *Maestría*. Also Teaching qualifications, secondary level and Diplomado Superior
Last Updated: 31/12/15

TECHNICAL UNIVERSITY OF COTOPAXI

Universidad Técnica de Cotopaxi (UTC)
Campus Universitario, Av. Simón Rodríguez S/N, Barrio El Ejido, Sector San Felipe, Latacunga, Cotopaxi
Tel: +593(3) 281-0296 +593(3) 281-3157
Fax: +593(3) 281-0295
EMail: institucional@utc.edu.ec
Website: http://www.utc.edu.ec

Rector: Fabricio Tinajero EMail: rectorado@utc.edu.ec

Vicerrector: Idalia Pacheco EMail: vicerrectorado@utc.edu.ec

Faculty

Administration, Arts and Humanities (Accountancy; Business and Commerce; Communication Studies; Physical Education; Preschool Education; Primary Education; Secretarial Studies); **Animal Husbandry and Natural Resources** (Agricultural Engineering; Ecology; Environmental Engineering; Industrial Engineering; Tourism; Veterinary Science); **Engineering and Applied Sciences** (Computer Engineering; Electrical and Electronic Engineering; Graphic Design; Industrial Engineering; Mechanical Engineering)

History: Founded 1991, acquired present status 1995.

Academic Year: October to March

Admission Requirements: Secondary School Certificate (bachillerato) or equivalent

Main Language(s) of Instruction: Spanish

Accrediting Agency: CONESUP

Degrees and Diplomas: *Licenciatura*; *Professional Title*; *Maestría*: **Education; Engineering; Social Studies.** Also Diplomado

Student Services: Academic Counselling, Canteen, Careers Guidance, Health Services, Language Laboratory, Social Counselling, Sports Facilities

Publications: Alma Mater

Publishing House: Arcoiris

Last Updated: 27/10/15

TECHNICAL UNIVERSITY OF MACHALA

Universidad Técnica de Machala (UTMACH)

Ciudadela Universitaria, Av. Panamericana Km. 5 1/2 Via a Pasaje, Machala, El Oro

Tel: +593(7) 298-3362

Fax: +593(7) 298-3371

EMail: utmachala@utmachala.edu.ec

Website: http://www.utmachala.edu.ec

Rector: César Javier Quezada Abad (2012-)
EMail: cquezada@utmachala.edu.ec

Vicerrectora Académica: Laura Amarilis Borja Herrera
Tel: +593(7) 298-3365, Ext.103 EMail: lborja@utmachala.edu.ec

Unit

Agriculture (Agricultural Economics; Agronomy; Aquaculture; Veterinary Science); **Business Administration** (Accountancy; Administration; Advertising and Publicity; Banking; Business Administration; Economics; Finance; Hotel Management; International Business; Marketing; Secretarial Studies; Tourism); **Chemistry and Health Sciences** (Biochemistry; Chemical Engineering; Chemistry; Food Technology; Medicine; Nursing; Pharmacy); **Civil Engineering** (Civil Engineering; Systems Analysis); **Social Sciences** (Chemistry; Clinical Psychology; Communication Studies; Computer Science; Educational Psychology; Educational Sciences; English; Environmental Studies; Fine Arts; Law; Literature; Modern Languages; Physical Education; Preschool Education; Social Studies; Social Work; Sociology)

History: Founded 1969.

Admission Requirements: Bachillerato, curso preuniversitario, personal documents

Main Language(s) of Instruction: Spanish

Accrediting Agency: CONEA (Consejo Nacional de Evaluación y Acreditación) (en proceso)

Degrees and Diplomas: *Licenciatura*; *Professional Title*: **Accountancy; Administration; Agricultural Engineering; Animal Husbandry; Biochemistry; Business Administration; Civil Engineering; Industrial Engineering; Marine Engineering; Nursing; Pharmacy; Sociology; Veterinary Science.** Also diplomas in Food Engineering, Arts and English.

Student Services: Academic Counselling, Cultural Activities, Health Services, Language Laboratory, Nursery Care, Social Counselling, Sports Facilities

Publications: Cumbres Magazine

Last Updated: 28/10/15

TECHNICAL UNIVERSITY OF MANABÍ

Universidad Técnica de Manabí (UTM)

Avenida Universitaria Apdo 82, Portoviejo, Manabí

Tel: +593(5) 263-2677

Fax: +593(5) 265-1569

EMail: bc1@utm.edu.ec

Website: http://www.utm.edu.ec

Rector: Vicente Félix Véliz Briones (2012-)
EMail: rectorado@utm.edu.ec

Vicerrectora Académica: Mara Molina de Lozano
EMail: viceacademico@utm.edu.ec

Faculty

Administration and Economics (Accountancy; Administration; Business and Commerce; Economics); **Agricultural Engineering** (Agricultural Engineering); **Agronomy** (Agronomy); **Computer Science** (Computer Engineering); **Health Sciences** (Health Sciences; Medicine; Nursing; Nutrition; Optometry; Surgery); **Humanities and Social Sciences** (Arts and Humanities; Clinical Psychology; Information Sciences; Library Science; Secretarial Studies; Social Work); **Mathematics, Physics and Chemistry** (Chemical Engineering; Civil Engineering; Electrical Engineering; Industrial Engineering; Mathematics; Mechanical Engineering; Physics); **Philosophy, Literature and Education** (Biology; Chemistry; Education; Geography; History; Linguistics; Literature; Modern Languages; Philosophy; Physical Education; Physics; Spanish); **Veterinary Medicine** (Aquaculture; Veterinary Science); **Zoology** (Zoology)

Institute

Basic Sciences (Chemistry; Mathematics; Physics; Statistics)

History: Founded 1952 as a State Institution.

Academic Year: May to March

Admission Requirements: Secondary school certificate (bachillerato) or foreign equivalent

Main Language(s) of Instruction: Spanish

Degrees and Diplomas: *Licenciatura*: **Biology; Chemistry; Mathematics; Modern Languages; Nursing; Physics; Psychology.** *Professional Title*: **Agricultural Engineering; Agronomy; Animal Husbandry; Civil Engineering; Electrical and Electronic Engineering; Industrial Engineering; Mechanical Engineering; Veterinary Science; Vocational Counselling.** *Maestría*

Last Updated: 28/10/15

TECHNICAL UNIVERSITY OF THE NORTH

Universidad Técnica del Norte (UTN)

Ciudadela Universitaria, Avenida 17 de Julio 5-21 y General José María Cordova, Barrio el Olivo, 199 Ibarra, Imbabura

Tel: +593(6) 299-7800

EMail: info@utn.edu.ec

Website: http://www.utn.edu.ec

Rector: Edmund Naranjo Miguel Toro (2012-)
EMail: rectorado@utn.edu.ec

Vicerrectora Académica: Maria de la Portilla Vera
EMail: viceacademico@utn.edu.ec

Faculty

Administration and Economics (Accountancy; Business and Commerce; Finance; Marketing); **Animal Husbandry and Environment** (Agricultural Business; Agricultural Engineering; Animal Husbandry; Biotechnology; Energy Engineering; Forestry; Industrial Engineering); **Education, Science and Technology** (Advertising and Publicity; Automation and Control Engineering; Design; Education; Educational Psychology; Educational Sciences; Electrical Engineering; English; Graphic Design; Management; Mathematics; Physical Education; Physics; Psychology; Secretarial Studies); **Engineering in Applied Sciences** (Computer Engineering; Electronic Engineering; Industrial Engineering; Mechanical Engineering; Telecommunications Engineering; Textile Technology); **Health Sciences** (Community Health; Cooking and Catering; Nursing; Nutrition; Physical Therapy)

History: Founded 1986.

Main Language(s) of Instruction: Spanish

Degrees and Diplomas: *Licenciatura*; *Professional Title*; *Especialista*; *Maestría*. Also Diplomado Superior

Last Updated: 28/10/15

UNIVERSITY OF CUENCA

Universidad de Cuenca

Apartado 01-01-168, Avenida 12 de Abril s/n Ciudadela Universitaria, Cuenca

Tel: +593(7) 283-1688

Fax: +593(7) 283-5197

EMail: coordaca@ucuenca.edu.ec

Website: http://www.ucuenca.edu.ec

Rector: Fabian Carrasco Castro EMail: rector@ucuenca.edu.ec

Faculty

Agronomy (Agricultural Engineering; Animal Husbandry; Veterinary Science; Zoology); **Architecture and Town Planning** (Architecture); **Arts** (Art Education; Art History; Dance; Design; Graphic

Design; Interior Design; Music; Theatre; Visual Arts); **Chemistry** (Biochemistry; Chemical Engineering; Chemistry; Environmental Engineering; Industrial Engineering; Pharmacy); **Dentistry** (Dentistry); **Economics and Administration** (Accountancy; Business Administration; Economics; Marketing; Sociology); **Engineering** (Civil Engineering; Computer Engineering; Electrical Engineering; Electronic Engineering; Engineering; Telecommunications Engineering); **Hospitality** (Cooking and Catering; Hotel and Restaurant; Tourism); **Law, Political and Social Sciences** (Development Studies; Family Studies; Gender Studies; Law); **Medicine** (Medicine); **Philosophy, Letters and Education** (Arts and Humanities; Cinema and Television; Education; Film; Literature; Philosophy); **Psychology** (Psychology)

Centre

Postgraduate Studies *(CEP)*

History: Founded 1867, the University is an autonomous institution, but receives financial support from the State.

Academic Year: October to July (October-January; April-July)

Admission Requirements: Secondary school certificate (bachillerato) or recognized foreign equivalent

Main Language(s) of Instruction: Spanish

Degrees and Diplomas: *Licenciatura*; *Professional Title*: **Accountancy; Architecture; Business Administration; Civil Engineering; Economics; Electrical Engineering; Midwifery; Nursing.** *Especialista*; *Maestría*; *Doctorado*: **Hydraulic Engineering.** Also Diplomado Superior

Publications: Anales de la Universidad de Cuenca

Last Updated: 20/10/15

UNIVERSITY OF GUAYAQUIL

Universidad de Guayaquil

Apartado postal 471, Ciudadela Universitaria Salvador Allende y Malecón del Salado, Guayaquil

Tel: +593(4) 229-6580

Fax: +593(4) 228-1559

EMail: vgeneral@ug.edu.ec

Website: http://www.ug.edu.ec

Rector: Roberto Cassis Martínez EMail: ugrector@ug.edu.ec

Vicerrector Administrativo: Alfredo Govea Maridueña

EMail: vadminis@ug.edu.ec

Faculty

Administration (Accountancy; Administration; Business and Commerce; Finance; Marketing); **Agriculture** (Agricultural Economics; Agricultural Engineering; Agricultural Equipment; Biology; Botany; Chemistry; Entomology; Horticulture; Hydraulic Engineering; Meteorology; Microbiology; Plant Pathology; Rural Planning; Soil Conservation; Zoology); **Architecture and Town Planning** (Architecture; Town Planning); **Chemical Engineering** (Chemical Engineering); **Chemistry** (Chemistry); **Dentistry** (Dentistry); **Economics** (Economics); **Industrial Engineering** (Industrial Engineering); **Law, Political and Social Sciences** (Law; Political Sciences; Social Sciences; Sociology); **Mathematics and Physics** (Civil Engineering; Mathematics; Physics); **Medicine** (Gynaecology and Obstetrics; Medical Technology; Medicine; Nursing); **Natural Sciences** (Analytical Chemistry; Aquaculture; Biology; Botany; Chemistry; Embryology and Reproduction Biology; Entomology; Forestry; Geology; Hydraulic Engineering; Limnology; Marine Science and Oceanography; Mathematics; Mineralogy; Natural Sciences; Paleontology; Petroleum and Gas Engineering; Tropical Agriculture; Zoology); **Philosophy, Letters and Educational Sciences** (Arts and Humanities; Educational Sciences; Library Science; Linguistics; Philosophy); **Physical Education, Sports and Recreation** (Leisure Studies; Physical Education; Sports); **Psychology** (Clinical Psychology; Psychology); **Social Communication** (Communication Studies; Social Studies); **Systems Engineering** (Systems Analysis); **Veterinary Medicine and Zoology** (Medicine; Veterinary Science; Zoology)

Institute

International Studies and Diplomacy *(Postgraduate)*; **Research and Studies in Mathematics** *(Postgraduate)*

History: Founded 1867 as Junta Universitaria, became Universidad del Guayas, then Universidad de Guayaquil 1897. Became autonomous 1925. Financed mainly by the State, partly by student fees.

Academic Year: April to January

Admission Requirements: Secondary school certificate (bachillerato) or recognized foreign equivalent, and entrance examination

Main Language(s) of Instruction: Spanish

Degrees and Diplomas: *Tecnólogo*: **Medical Technology.** *Licenciatura*: **Education; Library Science; Nursing; Sociology.** *Professional Title*: **Accountancy; Architecture; Biology; Chemistry; Economics; Engineering; Geology; Library Science; Midwifery; Nursing; Psychology; Sociology.** *Especialista*; *Maestría*

Publishing house: Litografía e Imprenta de la Universidad Guayaquil

Last Updated: 21/10/15

UNIVERSITY OF THE ARTS

Universidad de las Artes

Guayaquil, Guayas

EMail: info@uartes.edu.ec

Website: http://www.uartes.edu.ec

Rector: Ramiro Fabricio Noriega Fernández (2015-)

EMail: ramiro.noriega@uartes.edu.ec

Vicerrectorada Académica: Alicia Del Rosario Ortega Caicedo

EMail: alicia.ortega@uartes.edu.ec

School

Cinema

Main Language(s) of Instruction: Spanish, English, Portuguese, French

Degrees and Diplomas: *Licenciatura*

Student Services: Careers Guidance, Cultural Activities, Library, Nursery Care, Sports Facilities

Last Updated: 21/10/15

YACHAY-TECH EXPERIMENTAL RESEARCH UNIVERSITY

Universidad de Investigacion Experimental Yachay-Tech

San Miguel de Urcuquí, Hacienda San José s/n y Proyecto Yachay, Urcuquí, Imbabura

EMail: info@yachay.gob.ec

Website: http://yachaytech.edu.ec

Chief Executive Officer: Héctor Rodríguez

EMail: hector@yachay.gob.ec

School

Geology and Geotechnical Sciences (Geology); **Life Sciences and Biomedical Engineering** (Biology; Biomedical Engineering); **Material and Petro-Chemical Sciences** (Chemistry; Petroleum and Gas Engineering; Polymer and Plastics Technology); **Mathematics and Computer Science** (Computer Science; Information Technology; Mathematics); **Physics and Nanotechnology** (Nanotechnology; Physics); **Social Sciences and Business Studies** (Business Administration; Economics)

History: Founded 2013.

Main Language(s) of Instruction: Spanish

Degrees and Diplomas: *Licenciatura*; *Professional Title*

Last Updated: 29/10/15

PRIVATE INSTITUTIONS

AUTONOMOUS REGIONAL UNIVERSITY OF THE ANDES

Universidad Regional Autónoma de los Andes (UNIANDES)

Km. 51/2 Via a Baños, Ambato

Tel: +593(2) 274-8098

Fax: +593(2) 285-1105

EMail: desarrollouniandes@uniandesonline.edu.ec

Website: http://www.uniandes.edu.ec

Rector: Corona Emperatriz Gómez Armijos

EMail: rectorado@uniandesmail.edu.ec

Faculty

Business Administration (Business Administration; Cooking and Catering; Hotel Management; Tourism); **Health Sciences** (Dentistry; Medicine; Nursing); **Law** (Law)

History: Founded 1997.

Main Language(s) of Instruction: Spanish

Degrees and Diplomas: *Licenciatura*; *Especialista*; *Maestría*

Last Updated: 27/10/15

CASA GRANDE UNIVERSITY

Universidad Casa Grande (UCG)
Frente a la puerta n°6 del C.C Albán Borja,
Guayaquil
Tel: +593(4) 220-2180
Fax: +593(4) 220-2180
Website: http://www.casagrande.edu.ec

Rectora: Audelia High
EMail: rectorado@casagrande.edu.ec

Vicerrectora: María Mercedes Zerega

Area

Administration and Political Science (Administration; Marketing); **Communication Studies** (Communication Studies; Journalism); **Political Science and International Relations** (International Relations; Political Sciences)

History: Founded 1999.

Main Language(s) of Instruction: Spanish

Accrediting Agency: International Advertising Association (IAA); CONESUP (Consejo Nacional Educacíon Superior)

Degrees and Diplomas: *Licenciatura*; *Maestría*. Also Técnico superior and Tecnólogos: Associate degrees

Student Services: Academic Counselling, Careers Guidance

Last Updated: 20/10/15

CATHOLIC UNIVERSITY OF CUENCA

Universidad Católica de Cuenca (UCACUE)
Av. de las Américas y Humbolt, Cuenca
Tel: +593(7) 283-4037
Fax: +593(7) 283-8011
EMail: info@ucacue.edu.ec
Website: http://www.ucacue.edu.ec

Rector: Enrique Eugenio Pozo Cabrera (2013-)
EMail: epozo@ucacue.edu.ec

Vicerrector Administrativo: Ana Luisa Guijarro Cordero

Faculty

Accountancy and Audit (Accountancy); **Architecture and Town Planning** (Architecture); **Biopharmacy** (Pharmacy); **Business Administration** (Business and Commerce); **Civil Engineering** (Civil Engineering); **Dentistry** (Dentistry); **Economics** (Economics; Finance); **Education** (Education); **Law** (Law); **Marketing** (Marketing); **Medicine** (Health Sciences; Medicine); **Nursing** (Nursing); **Psychology, Pedagogy and Education** (Education; Pedagogy; Psychology); **Social Communication** (Journalism; Radio and Television Broadcasting)

Further Information: Also branches in Azogues and Macas

History: Founded 1970. A private institution receiving some financial support from the State.

Academic Year: October to July (October-February; March-July)

Admission Requirements: Secondary school certificate (bachillerato) or recognized foreign equivalent

Main Language(s) of Instruction: Spanish

Degrees and Diplomas: *Licenciatura*: **Education; Law; Modern Languages; Physical Education; Psychology; Secretarial Studies; Social Sciences; Social Work.** *Professional Title*: **Agricultural Engineering; Animal Husbandry; Business Administration; Chemical Engineering; Economics; Industrial Engineering; Psychology; Veterinary Science.**

Last Updated: 28/10/15

CATHOLIC UNIVERSITY OF SANTIAGO DE GUAYAQUIL

Universidad Católica de Santiago de Guayaquil (UCSG)
Avenida C. J. Arosemena Km 11/2, Via Daule,
Guayaquil
Tel: +593(4) 220-9210
Fax: +593(4) 220-0071
EMail: alternativas@ucsg.edu.ec; aaguilar@ucsg.edu.ec
Website: http://www.ucsg.edu.ec

Rector: Lino Mauro Toscanini Segale (2011-)
EMail: lino.toscanini@cu.ucsg.edu.ec

Vicerrectora Académica: María Cecilia Loor Dueñas De Tamariz
Tel: +593(4) 220-2130

Faculty

Architecture and Design (Architecture; Graphic Design; Interior Design); **Arts and Humanities** (Arts and Humanities; Dance; English; Modern Languages; Multimedia; Music); **Economics and Administration** (Accountancy; Administration; Economics; International Business; Management); **Engineering** (Civil Engineering; Engineering; Systems Analysis); **Law** (Law; Political Sciences; Social Sciences); **Medicine** (Dentistry; Dietetics; Medicine; Nursing; Nutrition; Physical Therapy); **Philosophy, Literature and Education** (Educational Sciences; Literature; Philosophy; Preschool Education; Psychology); **Technology for Development** (Agricultural Economics; Electronic Engineering; Mechanical Engineering; Natural Resources; Rural Planning; Technology; Telecommunications Engineering; Veterinary Science; Zoology)

Institute

Tropical Molecular Biology (Molecular Biology)

Centre

Lifelong Education; **Research** *(SINDE)*

History: Founded 1962 by the Catholic Church in Ecuador. Legally recognized as an autonomous institution.

Academic Year: May to February (May-September; October-February)

Admission Requirements: Secondary school certificate (bachillerato), or recognized foreign equivalent, and entrance examination

Main Language(s) of Instruction: Spanish

Degrees and Diplomas: *Licenciatura*: **Arts and Humanities; Education; Law; Nursing; Philosophy; Psychology; Social Work.** *Professional Title*: **Animal Husbandry; Architecture; Business Administration; Computer Engineering; Design; Economics; Law; Nursing; Psychology; Social Work.** *Especialista*; *Maestría*. Also Diplomados superiores

Student Services: Library

Publications: Revista de Historia del Derecho; Revista de Investigación

Publishing House: Centro de Publicaciones

Last Updated: 20/10/15

COMANDANTE RAFAEL MORÁN VALVERDE NAVAL UNIVERSITY

Universidad Naval Comandante Rafael Morán Valverde
Malecón Sector Chipipe, Base Naval de Salinas,
Salinas
Tel: +593(4) 277-3383
EMail: aromerv@hotmail.com

Rector: Carlos Moncayo

Programme

Nautical Science (Nautical Science); **Naval Logistics** (Nautical Science)

History: Founded 2006.

Main Language(s) of Instruction: Spanish

Degrees and Diplomas: *Licenciatura*

Last Updated: 25/11/15

ELOY ALFARO LAY UNIVERSITY OF MANABÍ

Universidad Laica Eloy Alfaro de Manabí (ULEAM)
Casilla 13-05-2732, Ciudadela Universitaria Vía Circunvalación, Portoviejo, Manabí
Tel: +593(5) 262-5095
Fax: +593(5) 262-3009
EMail: uleam@uleam.edu.ec; uleam.secretaria@gmail.com
Website: http://www.uleam.edu.ec

Rectora: Alba Amalia Reyes Moreira (2015-)
EMail: uleamrectorado@yahoo.com

Vicerrector Académico: Ever Darío Morales

Faculty

Accountancy and Auditing (Accountancy); **Administration** (Administration; Business Administration; Marketing); **Animal Husbandry** (Agricultural Engineering; Animal Husbandry; Environmental Engineering); **Architecture** (Architecture); **Communication Studies** (Advertising and Publicity; Communication Studies; Journalism; Marketing); **Computer Science** (Computer Science); **Economics** (Economics; International Business); **Education** (Education; Preschool Education; Primary Education); **Engineering** (Civil Engineering; Electrical Engineering; Engineering; Naval Architecture); **Industrial Engineering** (Industrial Engineering); **Law** (Law); **Management, Development and Secretarial Studies** (Management; Secretarial Studies); **Marine Science and Oceanography** (Marine Science and Oceanography; Naval Architecture); **Medicine** (Medicine); **Nursing** (Nursing); **Physical Education, Sports and Recreation** (Parks and Recreation; Physical Education; Sports); **Psychology** (Psychology); **Social Work** (Social Work); **Tourism and Hotel Management** (Hotel Management; Tourism)

Further Information: Also Chone, Bahía de Caráquez, Pedernales and El Carmen branches

History: Founded 1985.

Academic Year: May to April

Admission Requirements: Secondary school certificate and entrance examination

Main Language(s) of Instruction: Spanish

Degrees and Diplomas: *Licenciatura*; *Professional Title*; *Especialista*; *Maestría*
Last Updated: 06/11/15

EQUINOX UNIVERSITY OF TECHNOLOGY

Universidad Tecnológica Equinoccial (UTE)
Apartado 17-01-2764, Burgeois N34-102 y Rumipamba, Quito
Tel: +593(2) 299-0800
Fax: +593(2) 244-2288
EMail: info@ute.edu.ec
Website: http://www.ute.edu.ec

Rector: José Julio Cevallos Gómez (2013-)
EMail: jcevallo@ute.edu.ec; vicerectorado@ute.edu.ec

Faculty

Architecture, Arts and Design (Architecture; Fashion Design; Fine Arts; Interior Design; Restoration of Works of Art); **Economics and Trade** (Business Administration; Business and Commerce; Economics; Finance; Marketing); **Engineering** (Computer Engineering; Computer Science; Engineering; Environmental Engineering; Food Technology; Industrial Engineering; Petroleum and Gas Engineering; Textile Technology); **Health Sciences** *(Eugenio Espejo)* (Dentistry; Health Sciences; Medicine); **Social Sciences and Communication** (Advertising and Publicity; Communication Studies; Education; Graphic Design; Public Relations; Social Sciences); **Tourism, Hotel Management and Gastronomy** (Environmental Studies; Hotel and Restaurant; Hotel Management; Tourism)

Department

Modern Languages (English; French; German; Modern Languages)

Further Information: Branches in Santo Domingo de los Colorados, Santa Elena

History: Founded 1986.

Academic Year: October to July

Admission Requirements: Secondary school certificate (bachillerato) and entrance examination

Main Language(s) of Instruction: Spanish

Degrees and Diplomas: *Tecnólogo*; *Licenciatura*; *Professional Title*: **Engineering.** *Especialista*; *Maestría*

Student Services: Cultural Activities, Library, Sports Facilities

Publishing house: Departamento de Publicaciones UTE
Last Updated: 30/10/15

ESPIRITU SANTO UNIVERSITY OF SPECIALIZATIONS

Universidad de Especialides Espíritu Santo (UEES)
Apartado 09-01-4842, Vía La Puntilla, Samborondón, Km 2.5, Guayaquil
Tel: +593(4) 283-5630
Fax: +593(4) 283-5483
EMail: uees@uees.edu.ec
Website: http://www.uees.edu.ec

Rector: Joaquín Enrique Hernández Alvarado (2014-)
EMail: jhernandez@uees.edu.ec; rector@uees.edu.ec

Vicerrectora Académica: Marlena León Mendoza
EMail: mleon@uees.edu.ec

Faculty

Architecture and Civil Engineering (Architectural and Environmental Design; Architecture; Construction Engineering; Industrial Design; Interior Design; Landscape Architecture); **Communication** (Communication Studies; Graphic Design; Journalism; Marketing); **Economics and Business Management** (Business Administration; Business and Commerce; Economics; Finance; Human Resources; International Business; Marketing); **Law, Political Science and Development** (Development Studies; Law; Political Sciences); **Liberal Arts and Education** *(Dr. Albert Eyde)* (Bilingual and Bicultural Education; Clinical Psychology; Dance; English; Environmental Studies; Industrial and Organizational Psychology; Music; Special Education); **Medicine** *(Enrique Ortega Moreira)* (Medicine; Nutrition); **Tourism and Hotel Management** (Environmental Management; Hotel Management; Tourism)

School

International Studies (Latin American Studies; Spanish)

History: Founded 1993.

Academic Year: April to December. (Full year study is also possible)

Admission Requirements: Secondary school certificate (bachillerato) or recognized foreign equivalent, and entrance examination, or satisfactory completion of a pre-university programme

Fees: (US Dollars): 1500 per semester

Main Language(s) of Instruction: Spanish, English

Accrediting Agency: CONESUP

Degrees and Diplomas: *Técnico Superior*: **Finance; Human Resources; Law; Management.** *Licenciatura*: **Arts and Humanities; Business and Commerce; Communication Arts; Education.** *Professional Title*: **Economics.** *Especialista*; *Maestría*: **Business Administration; Business and Commerce; Finance; Marketing.**

Student Services: Academic Counselling, Canteen, Careers Guidance, Cultural Activities, Facilities for disabled people, Foreign Studies Centre, Health Services, Language Laboratory, Nursery Care, Social Counselling, Sports Facilities

Publications: Cuadernos
Last Updated: 20/10/15

IBERO-AMERICAN UNIVERSITY OF ECUADOR

Universidad Iberoamericana del Ecuador (UNIBE)
9 de Octubre y Colón N25-12, Quito
Tel: +593(2) 254-3142
Fax: +593(2) 223-0377
EMail: info@unibe.edu.ec
Website: http://www.unibe.edu.ec

Rector: Diego Nsam Castro Mbwini (2015-)
EMail: dncastro@unibe.edu.ec

Director Académico: Fabián Terán EMail: fteran@unibe.edu.ec

Programme

Communication and Audiovisual Production (Multimedia; Radio and Television Broadcasting); **Cosmetology** (Cosmetology); **Gastronomy Management** (Business Administration; Cooking and Catering; Hotel and Restaurant); **Hotel Management** (Hotel Management); **Tourism Management** (Tourism)

History: Founded 2005.

Main Language(s) of Instruction: Spanish

Degrees and Diplomas: *Licenciatura*
Last Updated: 22/10/15

INDO-AMERICAN TECHNOLOGICAL UNIVERSITY

Universidad Tecnológica Indoamérica (UTI)

Ambato-Bolívar 2035 entre Guayaquil y Quito, Ambato, Tungurahua
Fax: +593(3) 242-1713
EMail: indoamerica@uti.edu.ec
Website: http://www.uti.edu.ec

Rector: Franklin Edmundo Tapia Défaz (2015-)

Faculty

Administration and Economics (Accountancy; Banking; Business Administration; Commercial Law; Economic and Finance Policy; International Business; Management; Marketing)

Programme

Architecture (Architecture); **Biodiversity and Genetic Resources** (Biological and Life Sciences); **Digital Design and Multimedia** (Design; Multimedia); **Education and Social Development** (Education; Educational Administration; Preschool Education; Primary Education); **Industrial Engineering** (Industrial Engineering); **Law** (Constitutional Law; Criminal Law; Ethics; History of Law; Justice Administration; Law; Private Law; Public Law); **Psychology** (Psychology); **Systems Engineering** (Artificial Intelligence; Computer Science; Electrical and Electronic Engineering; English; Mathematics; Systems Analysis)

Institute

Languages (English)

History: Founded 1998.

Academic Year: October to September (October-March; April-September)

Fees: (US Dollars): c. 120 per semester

Main Language(s) of Instruction: Spanish, English

Degrees and Diplomas: *Tecnólogo*; *Licenciatura*: **Law.** *Professional Title*; *Maestría*

Student Services: Careers Guidance, Sports Facilities
Last Updated: 24/11/15

INTERNATIONAL UNIVERSITY OF ECUADOR

Universidad Internacional del Ecuador (UIDE)

Km 3 Av. Simon Bolivar, Collacoto, Quito
Tel: +593(2) 2985-600
Fax: +593(2) 2985-666
EMail: informa@internacional.edu.ec
Website: http://uide.edu.ec

Rector: Xavier Fernandez Orrantia (2014-)

Vicerrectora Académica: Marisol Bermeo

Faculty

Administration (Business and Commerce; International Business; Marketing); **Architecture and Design** (Architecture; Interior Design); **Automotive Engineering** (Automotive Engineering); **Basic Sciences** (Business Administration; Computer Science; Cultural Studies; Ethics; Mathematics; Peace and Disarmament); **Law** (Law); **Medicine, Health and Life Sciences** (Dentistry; Health Sciences; Medicine; Nutrition; Psychology)); **Social Sciences and Communication Studies** (Communication Studies; International Relations; Social Sciences)

School

Applied Science and Technology (Computer Science; Electronic Engineering; Mechanical Engineering; Multimedia; Telecommunications Engineering); **Gastronomy** (Cooking and Catering); **Hotel Management** (Hotel Management); **Tourism and Environmental Studies** (Environmental Studies; Tourism)

Institute

Languages (Modern Languages)

Further Information: Also branches in Guayaquil and Loja
History: Founded 1996.

Admission Requirements: Secondary school certificate (bachillerato) and entrance examination

Main Language(s) of Instruction: Spanish

Accrediting Agency: Consejo Nacional de Evaluación y Acreditación

Degrees and Diplomas: *Licenciatura*; *Professional Title*; *Maestría*. Also Diplomado superior

Student Services: Academic Counselling, Cultural Activities, Foreign Studies Centre, Health Services, Language Laboratory, Sports Facilities
Last Updated: 22/10/15

ISRAEL TECHNOLOGICAL UNIVERSITY

Universidad Tecnológica Israel (UISRAEL)

Fco. Pizarro E4-142 y Av. Orellana (Diagonal al Colegio Militar), Quito, Pichincha
Tel: +593(2) 255-741
Fax: +593(2) 255-812
EMail: info@uisrael.edu.ec
Website: http://uisrael.edu.ec

Rector: René Ceferino Cortijo Jacomino (2012-)
EMail: rector@uisrael.edu.ec

Faculty

Administration and Commerce (Administration; Business and Commerce); **Computer Systems** (Computer Science; Systems Analysis); **Design and Multimedia** (Design; Multimedia); **Electronics and Robotics** (Electronic Engineering; Robotics)

School

Languages (English; French; German; Italian; Modern Languages)

History: Founded 1999 following merger of the Instituto Tecnológico Israel and the Instituto Tecnológico Italia,.

Main Language(s) of Instruction: Spanish

Degrees and Diplomas: *Licenciatura*; *Professional Title*
Last Updated: 24/11/15

METROPOLITAN UNIVERSITY

Universidad Metropolitana

Ciudadela Garzota 1era etapa Mz.23, Guayaquil, Guayas
Tel: +593(2) 227-8346
Fax: +593(2) 227-8344
EMail: info@umet.edu.ec
Website: http://umet.edu.ec

Rector: Carlos Espinoza Cordero (2015-)
EMail: cespinoza@umet.edu.ec

Vicerrectora Académica: Lucia Brito Vallina
EMail: lbrito@umet.edu.ec

Area

Administration and Management (Accountancy; Administration; Agricultural Business; Health Sciences; Human Resources; Leisure Studies; Management; Tourism); **Education** (Education); **Engineering** (Engineering); **Exact Sciences and Technology** (Business Computing; Computer Science; Marine Transport; Mathematics and Computer Science; Natural Sciences; Technology); **Health Sciences** (Health Sciences); **Political and Social Sciences** (International Relations; Law; Political Sciences; Social Sciences); **Service Trades** (Service Trades); **Transport and Communications** (Transport and Communications)

Further Information: Branches in Machala and Quito

History: Founded 2000.

Main Language(s) of Instruction: Spanish

Degrees and Diplomas: *Licenciatura*; *Professional Title*; *Especialista*

Student Services: Academic Counselling, Facilities for disabled people, Language Laboratory, Social Counselling
Last Updated: 23/10/15

PONTIFICAL CATHOLIC UNIVERSITY OF ECUADOR

Pontificia Universidad Católica del Ecuador (PUCE)
Avenida 12 de Octubre n°1076 entre Patria y Veintimilla, 17-01-2184 Quito, Pichincha
Tel: +593(2) 299-1608; +593(2) 299-1700
Fax: +593(2) 299-1609; +593(2) 256-7117
EMail: relint@puce.edu.ec
Website: http://www.puce.edu.ec

Prorectora: María Josefa Rubio Gómez

Faculty

Architecture, Design and Fine Arts (Architecture; Design; Fine Arts); **Business Administration and Accountancy** (Accountancy; Business Administration); **Communication, Linguistics and Literature** (Communication Studies; Journalism; Linguistics; Literature; Modern Languages); **Economics** (Economics); **Education** (Education); **Engineering** (Civil Engineering; Engineering; Systems Analysis); **Human Sciences** (Anthropology; Ecology; Geography; History; Political Sciences; Sociology; Tourism); **Law** (Law); **Medicine** (Medicine); **Natural and Exact Sciences** (Biology; Chemistry; Natural Sciences); **Nursing** (Nursing; Nutrition; Physical Therapy); **Philosophy and Theology** (Philosophy; Theology); **Psychology** (Clinical Psychology; Educational Psychology; Industrial and Organizational Psychology; Psychology)

School

Bioanalysis (Histology; Medical Technology; Microbiology); **Social Work** (Social Work)

History: Founded 1946 under the Cardinal Archbishop of Quito. Legally recognized as an autonomous Institution but partly supported by the State. Other income derived from student fees, from the University's own resources, and from gifts and donations.

Academic Year: September to July (September-February; March-July)

Admission Requirements: Secondary school certificate (bachillerato) or authenticated foreign equivalent, and entrance examination

Fees: (US Dollars): 2000-3500 per semester

Main Language(s) of Instruction: Spanish

Degrees and Diplomas: *Licenciatura*: **Accountancy; Applied Linguistics; Architecture; Biological and Life Sciences; Biology; Business Administration; Chemistry; Civil Engineering; Communication Arts; Design; Economics; Foreign Languages Education; Geography; Histology; History; Hotel Management; Law; Medical Technology; Microbiology; Nursing; Nutrition; Philosophy; Physical Therapy; Social Work; Sociology; Surgery; Theology; Tourism; Visual Arts.** *Especialista*; *Maestría*

Student Services: Academic Counselling, Canteen, Careers Guidance, Cultural Activities, Facilities for disabled people, Foreign Studies Centre, Health Services, Language Laboratory, Nursery Care, Social Counselling, Sports Facilities

Publications: Revista

Publishing House: Centro de Publicaciones
Last Updated: 01/10/15

AMBATO BRANCH

SEDE AMBATO (PUCESA)

2011 - Av. Manuelita Sáenz Sector El Tropezón, Ambato
Tel: +593(32) 586-016
Fax: +593(3) 241-1868
EMail: pucesa@puce.edu.ec
Website: http://www.pucesa.edu.ec

Pro-rector: César González Loor

School

Business Management *(PYMES)* (Business Administration); **Industrial Design** (Industrial Design); **Languages and Linguistics** (Linguistics; Modern Languages); **Law** (Law); **Psychology** (Psychology); **Systems Engineering** (Systems Analysis)

History: Founded 1986.

Main Language(s) of Instruction: Spanish

Degrees and Diplomas: *Licenciatura*; *Professional Title*; *Maestría*. Also Diplomado

ESMERALDAS BRANCH

SEDE ESMERALDAS

Apartado 08-01-0065 Calle Espejo y Santa Cruz s/n, Esmeraldas
EMail: pucese@pucese.net
Website: http://www.pucese.edu.ec

Pro-rector: Aitor Urbina García de Vicuña

School

Administration and Accountancy (Accountancy; Administration); **Clinical Laboratory** (Medical Technology); **Computer Science** (Computer Science; Systems Analysis); **Educational Sciences** (Education; Primary Education); **Environmental Engineering** (Environmental Engineering; Environmental Management); **Graphic Design** (Graphic Design); **Hotel Management and Tourism** (Hotel Management; Tourism); **International Business** (International Business); **Linguistics** (Linguistics); **Nursing** (Nursing)

History: Founded 1981.

Main Language(s) of Instruction: Spanish

Degrees and Diplomas: *Tecnólogo*; *Licenciatura*; *Professional Title*; *Maestría*

IBARRA BRANCH

SEDE IBARRA

Av. Jorge Guzmán Rueda y Av. Aurelio Espinosa Pólit. ciudadela, Ibarra
Tel: +593(6) 261-5500
Fax: +593(6) 264787
EMail: prorect@pucesi.edu.ec
Website: http://www.pucesi.edu.ec

Pro-rector: María José Rubio

School

Agriculture and Environmental Sciences (Agriculture; Animal Husbandry; Environmental Studies); **Architecture** (Architecture); **Business and International Trade** (Accountancy; Business Administration; International Business); **Law** (Law); **Social Communication** (Journalism; Radio and Television Broadcasting); **Systems Engineering** (Systems Analysis)

History: Founded

Degrees and Diplomas: *Licenciatura*, *Professional Title*

MANABÍ BRANCH

SEDE MANABÍ

Apartado 13-02-100 Ciudadela Primero de Mayo, Calle Eudoro Loor s/n, Portoviejo
Tel: +593(5) 244-0300
Fax: +593(5) 263-7305
EMail: pucema@interactive.net.ec
Website: http://www.puce.edu.ec/sinapuce/index.php?pagina=manabi

Prorrector: Homero César Fuentes Vera

Programme

Administration (Business Administration); **Agro-industry** *(Chone)* (Agricultural Business); **Hydrology** *(Bahía)* (Hydraulic Engineering); **Marine Biology** *(Bahía)* (Marine Biology); **Tourism** (Tourism)

History: Founded 1993.

Main Language(s) of Instruction: Spanish

Degrees and Diplomas: *Tecnólogo*; *Licenciatura*; *Professional Title*

SANTO DOMINGO BRANCH

SEDE SANTO DOMINGO

Apartado 17-24-377, Av. Chone Km 2 y San Cristóba, Santo Domingo de losTsáchilas
EMail: pucesd@pucesd.edu.ec
Website: http://www.pucesd.edu.ec

Porrectora: Margalida Font Roig

School

Administration and Accountancy (Accountancy; Administration; Business and Commerce); **Design** (Graphic Design); **Education** (Education; Educational Administration); **Hotel Management and Tourism** (Hotel Management; Tourism); **Nursing** (Nursing); **Social Communication** (Communication Studies); **Systems Engineering** (Computer Science)

History: Founded 1996.

Main Language(s) of Instruction: Spanish

Degrees and Diplomas: *Licenciatura*; *Professional Title*; *Maestría*. Also Diploma superior

PRIVATE TECHNICAL UNIVERSITY OF LOJA

Universidad Técnica Particular de Loja (UTPL)

Casilla Postal 11-01-608, Barrio San Cayetano Alto s/n, Loja
Tel: +593(7) 257-0275
Fax: +593(7) 256-3159
EMail: info@utpl.edu.ec
Website: http://www.utpl.edu.ec

Rector: José Barbosa Corbacho (2010-)
EMail: jbarbosa@utpl.edu.ec

Vicerrector: Santiago Acosta EMail: sacosta@utpl.edu.ec

Department

Administration (Administration); **Architecture and Fine Arts** (Architecture; Fine Arts); **Chemistry** (Chemistry); **Communication Studies** (Communication Studies); **Computer Science and Electronics** (Computer Science; Electronic Engineering); **Economics** (Economics); **Education** (Education); **Finance and Accountancy** (Accountancy; Finance); **Food Science** (Food Science); **Geology, Mining and Civil Engineering** (Civil Engineering; Geology; Mining Engineering); **Health Sciences** (Health Sciences); **Modern Languages and Literature** (Literature; Modern Languages); **Natural Sciences** (Natural Sciences); **Psychology** (Psychology); **Social Sciences and Law** (Law; Social Sciences)

Further Information: Also Campuses in Zamora, Cariamanga, San Cayetano Alto

History: Founded 1971 as School by the Marist Brothers. A private Institution under the jurisdiction of the Comunidad de Misioneros y Misioneras de Cristo Redentor, largely financed by the State.

Academic Year: October to August (October-March; April-August)

Admission Requirements: Secondary school certificate (bachillerato) or recognized foreign equivalent, and entrance examination

Main Language(s) of Instruction: Spanish

Degrees and Diplomas: *Licenciatura*: **Accountancy; Agricultural Engineering; Animal Husbandry; Architecture; Chemistry; Civil Engineering; Economics; Education; Painting and Drawing; Religion; Sculpture; Secretarial Studies; Systems Analysis; Tourism.** *Especialista*; *Maestría*: **Education; Engineering Management; Health Administration; Regional Planning.**

Student Services: Library

Publications: Reloj; Revista; Universidad

Publishing House: Editorial UTPL

Last Updated: 29/10/15

SALESIAN POLYTECHNIC UNIVERSITY

Universidad Politécnica Salesiana (UPS)

Calle Vieja 12-30 y Elia Liurt, 46 Sector 2 Cuenca, Azuay
Tel: +593(7) 286-2213
EMail: srector@ups.edu.ec
Website: http://www.ups.edu.ec

Rector: Javier Herrán Gómez (2014-) EMail: jherran@ups.edu.ec

Vicerrector: Luis Tobar Pesántez EMail: ltobar@ups.edu.ec

Programme

Accountancy (Accountancy); **Business Administration** (Business Administration); **Engineering** (Automation and Control Engineering; Computer Engineering; Electrical Engineering; Electronic Engineering; Environmental Engineering; Mechanical Engineering); **Labour Psychology** (Industrial and Organizational Psychology; Psychology); **Management** (Management; Regional Planning); **Pedagogy** (Pedagogy); **Physical Education** (Physical Education); **Veterinary Medicine and Zootechnology** (Veterinary Science; Zoology)

History: Founded 1994.

Academic Year: In Quito and Cuenca: September-July/October-February. In Guayaquil: May-September/October-March

Admission Requirements: Secondary school certificate

Fees: (US Dollars): c. 1200 per annum

Main Language(s) of Instruction: Spanish, English

Degrees and Diplomas: *Licenciatura*; *Professional Title*; *Maestría*: **Anthropology; Business Administration; Cultural Studies; Design; Development Studies; Education; Psychology; Social Studies.**

Student Services: Academic Counselling, Careers Guidance, Cultural Activities, Facilities for disabled people, Health Services, Language Laboratory, Nursery Care, Social Counselling, Sports Facilities

Publications: Alteridad; El Emprendedor; Ingenius; La Granja; Sophia; Universitas

Last Updated: 13/11/15

GUAYAQUIL BRANCH

SEDE GUAYAQUIL (UPS-G)

Gral Francisco Robles 107, Guayaquil
Tel: +593(4) 580447
Fax: +593(4) 583464
Website: http://www.ups.edu.ec/sede-guayaquil

Vicerrector: Andrés Bayolo Garay EMail: abayolo@ups.edu.ec

Programme

Administration and Economics (Accountancy; Administration; Business Administration; Economics); **Engineering** (Automation and Control Engineering; Electrical Engineering; Electronic Engineering; Mechanical Engineering; Systems Analysis)

History: Founded 1998

Main Language(s) of Instruction: Spanish

Degrees and Diplomas: *Tecnólogo*; *Licenciatura*; *Professional Title*

QUITO BRANCH

SEDE QUITO

Av. Isabel La Católica N. 23-52 y Madrid, Quito
Tel: +593(2) 396-2900
EMail: svicerrectoruio@ups.edu.ec
Website: http://www.ups.edu.ec/sede-quito

Vicerrector: José Juncosa Blasco EMail: jjuncosa@ups.edu.ec

Programme

Accountancy (Accountancy); **Applied Anthropology** (Anthropology); **Business Administration** (Accountancy; Administration; Business Administration; Economics); **Engineering** (Automation and Control Engineering; Computer Engineering; Electrical Engineering; Electronic Engineering; Environmental Engineering; Mechanical Engineering); **Intercultural Bilingual Education** (Bilingual and Bicultural Education); **Management and Leadership** (Leadership; Management); **Pedagogy** (Pedagogy); **Philosophy and Pedagogy** (Pedagogy; Philosophy); **Psychology** (Psychology); **Social Communication** (Communication Studies)

History: Founded 1994.

Main Language(s) of Instruction: Spanish

Degrees and Diplomas: *Licenciatura*; *Professional Title*; *Maestría*

SAN FRANCISCO UNIVERSITY OF QUITO

Universidad San Francisco de Quito (USFQ)

Diego de Robles y Vía Interoceánica, Circulo de Cumbayá, Quito, Pichincha
Tel: +593(2) 297-1700
Fax: +593(2) 289-0070
EMail: oasa@usfq.edu.ec
Website: http://www.usfq.edu.ec

Rector: Carlos Miguel Montúfar Barba Freile (2015-)
EMail: cmontufar@usfq.edu.ec; carlosm@usfq.edu.ec

Vicerrectora Académica: Ximena Córdova

International Relations: Gonzalo Mendieta, Vice President of Academic Affairs EMail: gonzalom@usfq.edu.ec

College

Administration and Economics (Administration; Economics; Finance; Marketing); **Architecture and Design** *(CARQ)* (Architectural and Environmental Design; Architecture; Interior Design); **Biology and Environmental Sciences** (Biology; Biotechnology; Ecology; Environmental Management; Environmental Studies; Marine Biology; Microbiology); **Communication and Contemporary Arts** *(COCOA)* (Advertising and Publicity; Communication Studies; Computer Graphics; Cultural Studies; Design; Film; Fine Arts; Journalism; Media Studies; Multimedia; Photography; Public Relations; Video); **Health Sciences** *(COSCA)* (Dentistry; Health Sciences; Medicine; Nutrition; Optometry; Public Health; Veterinary Science); **Law** *(JUR)* (Law); **Music** (Music); **Science and Engineering** (Aeronautical and Aerospace Engineering; Chemical Engineering; Chemistry; Civil Engineering; Electronic Engineering; Engineering; Environmental Engineering; Food Technology; Industrial Engineering; Mathematics; Mechanical Engineering; Physics; Systems Analysis); **Social Sciences and Humanities** (Arts and Humanities; Education; International Relations; Sociology); **Tourism, Hospitality Management and Culinary Arts** (Accountancy; Cooking and Catering; Hotel and Restaurant; Management; Tourism)

History: Founded 1988. Acquired present status 1995.

Academic Year: August to May

Admission Requirements: Secondary school certificate and entrance examination, or foreign equivalent

Fees: (US Dollars): Tuition: 3825; Books: 190; Studies Insurance: 185

Main Language(s) of Instruction: Spanish

Degrees and Diplomas: *Tecnólogo*; *Licenciatura*: **Architecture; Clinical Psychology; Dentistry; Engineering; Law; Medicine; Nutrition; Optometry; Veterinary Science.** *Especialista*; *Maestría*; *Doctorado*: **Microbiology.**

Student Services: Academic Counselling, Canteen, Careers Guidance, Facilities for disabled people, Foreign Studies Centre, Health Services, Language Laboratory, Social Counselling, Sports Facilities

Publications: El Periódico

Publishing House: San Francisco University Press
Last Updated: 27/10/15

SAN GREGORIO PRIVATE UNIVERSITY OF PORTOVIEJO

Universidad Particular San Gregorio de Portoviejo (USGP)

Av. Metropolitana Eloy Alfaro #2005 y Av. Olimpica, Portoviejo
Tel: +593(5) 2632927
EMail: rectorado@usgp.edu.ec
Website: http://www.sangregorio.edu.ec/index.php

Rector: Marcelo Iván Farfán Intriago (2015-)
EMail: mifarfan@sangregorio.edu.ec

Vicerrector Académico: Jaime Alarcón Zambrano
EMail: jaalarcon@sangregorio.edu.ec

Programme

Accountancy (Accountancy); **Architecture** (Architecture); **Business Administration** (Business Administration); **Communication Studies** (Communication Studies); **Dentistry** (Dentistry); **Economics** (Economics); **Education** (Accountancy; Computer Education; Education; Environmental Studies; Geography; History; Literature; Natural Sciences; Secretarial Studies; Spanish; Tourism); **Finance and Commercial Relations** (Business and Commerce; Finance); **Graphic Design** (Graphic Design); **International Business** (International Business); **Journalism** (Journalism); **Law** (Law); **Marketing** (Marketing); **Radio and Television Production** (Radio and Television Broadcasting)

History: Founded 2000.

Main Language(s) of Instruction: Spanish

Degrees and Diplomas: *Licenciatura*; *Professional Title*
Last Updated: 23/10/15

SEK INTERNATIONAL UNIVERSITY

Universidad Internacional SEK (UISEK)

Calle El Calvarion s/n y Francisco Compte, Guápulo, Quito
Tel: +593(2) 398-4800
EMail: uisek.jm@uisek.edu.ec
Website: http://www.uisek.edu.ec

Rector: Alfonso Algora Buenafé (2015-) EMail: rc@uisek.edu.ec

Vicerrector: José María Delgado M.

Faculty

Architecture and Town Planning (Architecture; Town Planning); **Environmental Studies** (Biotechnology; Environmental Engineering; Environmental Studies; Forestry); **Law and Social Sciences** (Comparative Law; International Law; International Relations; Law; Social Sciences); **Mechanical Engineering** (Mechanical Engineering); **Psychology** (Clinical Psychology; Psychology)

Programme

Occupational Health (Occupational Therapy)

History: Founded 1892 in Madrid, with 15 Schools in 11 countries and 3 Universities in Segovia, Santiago de Chile and Quito (1993).

Academic Year: October to June

Admission Requirements: Secondary school certificate (bachillerato)

Main Language(s) of Instruction: Spanish

Degrees and Diplomas: *Licenciatura*; *Professional Title*: **Architecture; Engineering.** *Maestría*

Student Services: Academic Counselling, Canteen, Careers Guidance, Cultural Activities, Social Counselling, Sports Facilities

Publishing house: Ediciones de Universidad International SEK
Last Updated: 06/11/15

TECHNICAL BUSINESS UNIVERSITY OF GUAYAQUIL

Universidad Tecnológica Empresarial de Guayaquil (UTEG)

Urdesa Central, Guayacanes 399 y la 5ta, Guayaquil, Guayas
Tel: +593(4) 288-6728
Fax: +593(4) 288-4833
EMail: admision@uteg.edu.ec
Website: http://www.uteg.edu.ec

Rector: Galo Cabanilla Guerra (2014-)
EMail: gcabanilla@uteg.edu.ec

Faculty

Business Administration and Economics (Business Administration; Economics); **Foreign Trade** (Business and Commerce; International Business; Taxation; Transport Management); **Information Technology** (Computer Networks; Information Technology; Telecommunications Engineering); **Tourism and Environment** (Environmental Studies; Tourism)

Division

Foreign Languages (English; French)

History: Founded 2000.

Academic Year: April to February (April-August; October-February)

Admission Requirements: Secondary school certificate (bachillerato)

Main Language(s) of Instruction: Spanish

Degrees and Diplomas: *Tecnólogo*; *Licenciatura*; *Professional Title*; *Maestría*
Student Services: Academic Counselling, Careers Guidance, Language Laboratory
Publications: Bitacora Economica
Last Updated: 30/10/15

TOURISM UNIVERSITY

Universidad de Especialidades Turísticas (UCT)
Avenida Patria E3-67 y 9 Octubre, Edificio UCT, 171292 Quito, Pichincha
Tel: +593(2) 254-4100
Fax: +593(2) 254-4104
EMail: info@uct.edu.ec
Website: http://www.uct.edu.ec

Rectora: María de Lourdes Jarrín (2000-)
EMail: mjarrin@uct.edu.ec

Vicerrector: Gustavo Freire EMail: ecabanilla@uct.edu.ec

School

Hotel Management (Cooking and Catering; Hotel Management); **Tourism** (Business Administration; Tourism)

History: Founded 2000.
Academic Year: October to March; April to September
Admission Requirements: Secondary school certificate (bachillerato) and English language examination
Fees: (US Dollars): 1650 per semester
Main Language(s) of Instruction: Spanish
Degrees and Diplomas: *Professional Title*; *Especialista*; *Maestría*. Also Diplomado superior
Student Services: Academic Counselling, Careers Guidance, Health Services, Language Laboratory, Social Counselling
Last Updated: 20/10/15

UNIVERSITY OF AZUAY

Universidad del Azuay (UDA)
Apartado 01-01-981, Avenida 24 de Mayo 7-77 y Hernán Malo, Cuenca, Azuay
Tel: +593(7) 409-1000
EMail: dge@uazuay.edu.ec
Website: http://www.uazuay.edu.ec

Rector: Carlos Iván Cordero Díaz (2012-)
EMail: rectorado@uazuay.edu.ec

Vicerrectora: Miriam Briones García
EMail: vicerrectorado@uazuay.edu.ec

Faculty

Administration (Accountancy; Business Administration; Computer Science; Economics; Marketing); **Design** (Fashion Design; Furniture Design; Graphic Design; Interior Design; Textile Design; Theatre); **Law** (International Studies; Law); **Medicine** (Medicine); **Philosophy, Letters and Educational Sciences** (Clinical Psychology; Communication Studies; Educational Psychology; Industrial and Organizational Psychology; Preschool Education; Special Education; Tourism); **Science and Technology** (Automation and Control Engineering; Civil Engineering; Electronic Engineering; Engineering; Food Science; Mechanical Engineering; Mining Engineering; Production Engineering)

History: Founded 1968. Acquired present status 1990.
Academic Year: September to July (September-January; March-July)
Admission Requirements: Secondary school certificate (bachillerato) and entrance examination
Main Language(s) of Instruction: Spanish
Degrees and Diplomas: *Tecnólogo*; *Licenciatura*; *Professional Title*: **Design; Engineering; Law.** *Especialista*; *Maestría*
Student Services: Academic Counselling, Careers Guidance, Cultural Activities, Health Services, Language Laboratory, Social Counselling, Sports Facilities
Publications: Coloquio
Last Updated: 21/10/15

UNIVERSITY OF OTAVALO

Universidad de Otavalo
Cdla. Imbaya, Av. De los Sarances s/n y Pendoneros, Otavalo
Tel: +593(6) 2952-0461
EMail: info@uotavalo.edu.ec
Website: http://www.uotavalo.edu.ec

Rectora: Nora Espí Lacomba (2015-)
Vicerrectora Académica: Mariana Guzmán Villena

Programme

Business Administration (Business Administration); **Computer Science** (Computer Science); **Graphic Design** (Graphic Design); **International Business and Finance** (Finance; International Business); **Law** (Law); **Social and Cultural Development** (Cultural Studies; Development Studies; Social Studies); **Tourism** (Management; Marketing; Tourism)

History: Founded 2002.
Academic Year: September to February
Admission Requirements: Secondary School Certificate (bachillerato)
Main Language(s) of Instruction: Spanish and English
Degrees and Diplomas: *Professional Title*
Student Services: Academic Counselling, Cultural Activities, Health Services, Language Laboratory, Library, Social Counselling, Sports Facilities
Publications: Revista Sarance
Last Updated: 05/11/15

UNIVERSITY OF THE AMERICAS

Universidad de Las Américas (UDLA)
Av. De los Granados, 170137 Quito
Tel: +593(2) 255-5735
Fax: +593(2) 256-3757
EMail: admisiones@udla.edu.ec
Website: http://www.udla.edu.ec

Rector: Carlos Larreátegui Nardi (2014-)
EMail: clarreategui@uamericas.edu.ec

Vicerrector: Simón Cueva
Tel: +593(2) 255-6263 EMail: scueva@uamericas.edu.ec

International Relations: Alegría Donosso
Tel: +593(2) 290-1200

Faculty

Architecture and Design (Architecture; Graphic Design; Industrial Design; Interior Design); **Communication and Visual Arts** (Advertising and Publicity; Communication Studies; Film; Journalism; Multimedia); **Economics and Administration** (Business Administration; Economics; Finance; International Business; Marketing); **Education** (Bilingual and Bicultural Education; Educational Psychology); **Engineering and Agronomy** (Agricultural Engineering; Biotechnology; Computer Engineering; Computer Networks; Electronic Engineering; Environmental Engineering; Food Technology; Industrial Engineering; Sound Engineering (Acoustics); Telecommunications Engineering); **Health Sciences** (Nursing; Physical Therapy; Veterinary Science); **Law and Social Sciences** (International Relations; Law; Political Sciences); **Medicine** (Biotechnology; Dentistry; Medicine; Nursing; Physical Therapy)

Programme

Business Administration (Business Administration)

School

Gastronomy (Cooking and Catering); **Music** (Music); **Psychology** (Clinical Psychology; Industrial and Organizational Psychology; Psychology); **Tourism and Hospitality** (Cooking and Catering; Hotel Management)

History: Founded 1994.
Main Language(s) of Instruction: Spanish
Degrees and Diplomas: *Tecnólogo*; *Licenciatura*; *Professional Title*; *Especialista*; *Maestria*
Last Updated: 28/10/15

UNIVERSITY OF THE HEMISPHERES

Universidad de los Hemisferios (UDLH)
Paseo de la Universidad N° 300 y Juan Díaz - Urb. Iñaquito Alto, Quito
Tel: +593(2) 401-4100
EMail: info@uhemisferios.edu.ec
Website: http://www.uhemisferios.edu.ec

Rector: Diego Alejandro Jaramillo Arango (2015-)

Vice-Rectora: Maria Graciela Crespo Ponce
Secretario General: Sebastián Borja Silva

Faculty
Arts and Humanities (Arts and Humanities; Cooking and Catering; Educational Psychology; Music); **Business Studies** (Business and Commerce); **Communication Studies** (Communication Studies); **Law and Political Science** (International Relations; Law; Political Sciences)

History: Founded 2004.

Main Language(s) of Instruction: Spanish

Degrees and Diplomas: *Licenciatura*; *Professional Title*. Also posgrados
Last Updated: 21/10/15

UNIVERSITY OF THE PACIFIC - BUSINESS SCHOOL

Universidad del Pacífico - Escuela de Negocios (UPACIFICO)
Apartado 17-08-8229, El Pinar Alto, Calle B N48-177, Quito
Tel: +593(2) 244-4509
Fax: +593(2) 245-9593
EMail: info@upacifico.edu.ec
Website: http://www.upacifico.edu.ec

Canciller: Sonia Roca EMail: sroca@upacifico.edu.ec

Secretario General: José Mario Borja

International Relations: Roberto Houser
EMail: intrel@upacifico.edu.ec

Faculty
Applied Sciences (Computer Science; Information Technology); **Business and Economics** (Accountancy; Banking; Business Administration; Business and Commerce; Economics; Finance; Human Resources; International Business; Marketing); **Liberal Arts** (Cooking and Catering; Law; Modern Languages; Political Sciences; Tourism); **Sea** (Environmental Studies; Marine Transport)

Institute
Modern Languages (Modern Languages)

Centre
Competitiveness Research; **Latin American Studies** (Latin American Studies)

Further Information: Also branch in Guayaquil

History: Founded 1994, legally recognized by the Government of Ecuador 1997.

Academic Year: October to August (Quito and Cuenca) and April to February (Guayaquil)

Admission Requirements: Secondary school certificate (bachillerato)

Main Language(s) of Instruction: Spanish, English

Degrees and Diplomas: *Licenciatura*; *Maestría*: **Banking; Business Administration; Economics; Finance; Human Resources; Information Technology; International Business; Management; Political Sciences.**

Student Services: Academic Counselling, Careers Guidance, Cultural Activities, Language Laboratory
Last Updated: 21/10/15

VICENTE ROCAFUERTE LAY UNIVERSITY OF GUAYAQUIL

Universidad Laica Vicente Rocafuerte de Guayaquil (ULVR)
Avenida de las Américas frente al Cuartel Modelo, Apdo.1133, Guayaquil
Tel: +593(4) 228-7200
EMail: admisiones@ulvr.edu.ec
Website: http://www.ulvr.edu.ec

Rector: Jorge Bernardino Torres Prieto (2012-)

Vicerrector: Otto Cevallos Mieles

Faculty
Administration (Accountancy; Administration; Advertising and Publicity; International Business; Marketing); **Education** (Education; Educational Psychology); **Engineering, Industry and Construction** (Architecture; Civil Engineering); **Social Sciences and Law** (Economics; Journalism; Law)

History: Founded 1966.

Academic Year: April to January (April-August; August-January)

Main Language(s) of Instruction: Spanish

Degrees and Diplomas: *Licenciatura*: **Administration; Education; Journalism; Political Sciences; Social and Community Services.** *Professional Title*: **Accountancy; Architecture; Civil Engineering; Design; Economics; Law; Social Work.** *Maestría*: **Accountancy; Education.** Also teaching qualifications, secondary level

Student Services: Library
Last Updated: 23/10/15

Egypt

STRUCTURE OF HIGHER EDUCATION SYSTEM

Description:

Higher education is provided by universities and higher institutes of technical and professional training, both public and private. Responsibility for higher education lies mainly with the Ministry of Higher Education. Universities have full academic and administrative autonomy. They also carry out scientific research. The higher institutes of professional and technical training award qualifications that are equivalent to the first qualification conferred by the universities. Private universities are entitled to implement their own admission criteria and to set fees without intervention from the Ministry.

Stages of studies:

University level first stage:
The first stage of higher education consists of four to six years of multidisciplinary study in basic subjects leading to the award of the Bachelor's or Licence degree. In Medicine, studies last for six years.

University level second stage:
The second stage is more specialized and comprises two years of training. The degree awarded is that of Master.

University level third stage:
The third stage leads to the Doctorate after at least three years' study following the Master's degree. It is awarded for advanced research work culminating in a thesis.

ADMISSION TO HIGHER EDUCATION

Admission to university-level studies:

Name of secondary school credential required: Diploma of Advanced Technical Studies

Name of secondary school credential required: General Secondary Education Certificate

For entry to: Universities and higher specialized institutes

Name of secondary school credential required: Secondary School Technical Diploma

Numerus clausus: The Supreme Council of Universities at the Ministry of Higher Education determines the number of students to be admitted by the faculties of each university.

Foreign students admission:

Admission requirements: Foreign students should have qualifications equivalent to the GSSC.

Entry regulations: Foreign students must obtain a student visa.

Language proficiency: Knowledge of Arabic is essential for regular university studies. English is the language of instruction at the American University in Cairo, some faculties of Helwan University and at the Faculty of Agriculture of the University of Alexandria. French is the language of instruction at Senghor University.

NATIONAL BODIES

Ministry of Higher Education

Minister: Ashraf El-Sheehi
No. 101 Kasr El Ainy Street
Cairo
Tel: +20(2) 792 03 23
Fax: +20(2) 794 10 05
EMail: mohe.info@gmail.com
WWW: http://www.egy-mhe.gov.eg
Role of national body: Coordinates and supervises post-secondary education

Supreme Council of Universities
Cairo
Tel: +20(2) 3573 8583
Fax: +20(2) 3572 8877
EMail: scu@eun.eg
WWW: http://www.scu.eun.eg
Role of national body: Determines the overall policy of higher education and scientific research in the universities and determines the number of students admitted in each faculty.

Egyptian Universities Network
Acting Director: Ahmed Hassan
PO Box 268 Orman
Egypt Supreme Council of Universities Building
Cairo University Campus
Giza 12613
Tel: +20(2) 377 423 47
Fax: +20(2) 357 064 71
EMail: info@eun.eg
WWW: http://wcm.portal.eun.eg:10040/wps/portal

Data for academic year: 2012-2013
Source: IAU from World Data on Education 2010/2011, rev. 2012, UNESCO-IBE and documentation, 2012. Bodies 2015.

INSTITUTIONS

PUBLIC INSTITUTIONS

AIN SHAMS UNIVERSITY

Khalifa El-Maamon St, Abbasiya Square, Cairo 11566
Tel: +20(2) 683-1231 +20(2) 683-1417
Fax: +20(2) 684-7824
Website: http://www.asu.edu.eg

President: Hussein Moahmed Ahmed Eissa (2012-)
EMail: hussein_eissa@hotmail.com

Secretary-General: Hassan Abd Elazeez Ammar

Faculty
Agriculture (Agricultural Economics; Agricultural Equipment; Agriculture; Agronomy; Animal Husbandry; Botany; Food Science; Genetics; Horticulture; Meat and Poultry; Microbiology; Plant Pathology; Soil Science); **Arts** (Ancient Civilizations; Arabic; Arts and Humanities; English; French; Geography; Hebrew; History; Library Science; Literature; Mass Communication; Persian; Philosophy; Psychology; Sociology; Tourism; Turkish; Urdu); **Commerce** (Accountancy; Business Administration; Business and Commerce; Economics; Insurance; Mathematics; Statistics); **Computer and Information Science** (Computer Science); **Dentistry** (Dentistry; Oral Pathology; Orthodontics; Periodontics); **Education** (Arabic; Biology; Chemistry; Curriculum; Educational Psychology; Educational Sciences; English; French; Geography; Geology; German; History; Islamic Studies; Mathematics; Pedagogy; Philosophy; Physics; Psychiatry and Mental Health; Sociology); **Engineering** (Architecture; Automation and Control Engineering; Civil Engineering; Computer Engineering; Design; Electrical and Electronic Engineering; Engineering; Hydraulic Engineering; Irrigation; Mechanical Engineering; Power Engineering; Production Engineering; Structural Architecture; Systems Analysis; Town Planning); **Languages** *(Al-Alsun)* (African Languages; Arabic; Chinese; Czech; English; French; German; Italian; Japanese; Modern Languages; Persian; Russian; Spanish; Turkish; Urdu); **Law** (Civil Law; Commercial Law; Criminal Law; History of Law; International Law; Islamic Law; Law; Political Sciences; Private Law; Public Law); **Medicine** (Anaesthesiology; Anatomy; Biochemistry; Cardiology; Clinical Psychology; Community Health; Dermatology; Forensic Medicine and Dentistry; Gerontology; Gynaecology and Obstetrics; Histology; Immunology; Medicine; Microbiology; Occupational Health; Ophthalmology; Otorhinolaryngology; Paediatrics; Parasitology; Pathology; Pharmacology; Physiology; Psychiatry and Mental Health; Radiology; Surgery; Toxicology; Tropical Medicine); **Nursing** (Nursing); **Pharmacy** (Biochemistry; Immunology; Microbiology; Organic Chemistry; Pharmacology; Pharmacy; Toxicology); **Science** (Biochemistry; Botany; Chemistry; Entomology; Geology; Geophysics; Mathematics; Microbiology; Natural Sciences; Physics; Zoology); **Specific Education** (Education); **Women for Arts, Science and Education** (Arabic; Biochemistry; Botany; Chemistry; Curriculum; Education; English; French; Geography; History; Home Economics; Literature; Mathematics; Nutrition; Pedagogy; Philosophy; Physics; Psychology; Social Sciences; Zoology)

Institute
Environmental Studies and Research (Environmental Studies); **Postgraduate Childhood Studies** (Child Care and Development; Psychology; Sociology)

Centre
Genetic Engineering and Biotechnology; **University Education Development** (Higher Education); **Vectors of Diseases** (Epidemiology)

Research Centre
Middle East (Middle Eastern Studies); **Papyrus Studies** (Ancient Civilizations); **Public Service and Development** (Business Administration; English; French; German; Oriental Languages; Radio and Television Broadcasting; Social and Community Services; Video); **Science Education Development** (Science Education); **Scientific Computing** (Computer Science)

Further Information: Also University Hospitals and specialized Hospital

History: Founded 1950, incorporating Abbassia School of Medicine. Formerly known as Ibrahim Pasha University and also as

Economics; Insurance; Management; Statistics); **Computers and Informatics** (Computer Science; Information Technology); **Education** (Education; Educational Administration; Psychiatry and Mental Health; Psychology); **Engineering** (Architecture; Civil Engineering; Electrical Engineering; Industrial Engineering; Mechanical Engineering; Physical Engineering; Surveying and Mapping); **Law** (Civil Law; Commercial Law; Islamic Law; Law; Public Law); **Medicine** (Anatomy; Biochemistry; Cardiology; Dermatology; Forensic Medicine and Dentistry; Gastroenterology; Gynaecology and Obstetrics; Hepatology; Histology; Immunology; Medicine; Microbiology; Neurology; Ophthalmology; Otorhinolaryngology; Paediatrics; Parasitology; Pathology; Pharmacology; Physiology; Rheumatology; Surgery; Toxicology; Urology); **Nursing** (Child Care and Development; Nursing); **Physical Education** (Physical Education; Physical Therapy; Sports; Sports Management); **Science** (Biochemistry; Botany; Entomology; Geology; Mathematics; Physics; Zoology); **Veterinary Science** (Anatomy; Animal Husbandry; Biochemistry; Embryology and Reproduction Biology; Histology; Nutrition; Parasitology; Pathology; Pharmacology; Physiology; Surgery; Veterinary Science; Virology)

Institute

Technology *(Benha)* (Civil Engineering; Electrical Engineering; Mechanical Engineering; Natural Sciences)

History: Founded 2005 following separation from Zagazig University.

Degrees and Diplomas: *Lîsâns*; *Mâjistêr*, *Dukturâh*. Also postgraduate diploma

Last Updated: 19/06/12

BENI-SUEF UNIVERSITY (BSU)

Salah Salem Street, Beni-Suef
Tel: +20(82) 232-4879
Fax: +20(82) 232-4879
EMail: info@bsu.edu.eg
Website: http://www.bsu.edu.eg/default.aspx

President: Amin Lotfy EMail: president@bsu.edu.eg

Faculty

Arts (Arts and Humanities; English; European Studies; Geography; Journalism; Library Science; Mediterranean Studies; Psychology); **Commerce** (Business and Commerce); **Education** (Education); **Engineering** (Engineering); **Industrial Science** (Industrial Engineering); **Law** (Law); **Medicine** (Medicine); **Nursing** (Nursing); **Pharmacy** (Pharmacy); **Physical Education** (Physical Education); **Science**; **Veterinary Medicine** (Veterinary Science)

History: Founded 1983 as Beni-Suef Branch of Cairo University. Acquired present status and title 2005.

Academic Year: September to June (September to January, February to June

Admission Requirements: High School Certificate or equivalent

Main Language(s) of Instruction: Arabic, English

Degrees and Diplomas: *Lîsâns*: **Engineering; Industrial Engineering; Medicine; Nursing; Pharmacy; Physical Education; Veterinary Science.** Also Licentiate of Law, Arts, Education (4 yrs)

Student Services: Academic Counselling, Canteen, Careers Guidance, Cultural Activities, Facilities for disabled people, Health Services, Language Laboratory, Nursery Care, Social Counselling, Sports Facilities

Last Updated: 07/12/12

CAIRO UNIVERSITY

PO Box 12613, Nahdet Misr Street, Giza, Cairo
Tel: +20(2) 572-9584
Fax: +20(2) 568-8884
EMail: scc@cu.edu.eg
Website: http://www.cu.edu.eg

President: Gaber Nassar (2013-)

Faculty

Agriculture (Agriculture; Biological and Life Sciences); **Archaeology** (Ancient Civilizations; Archaeology; Art History; Museum Studies; Restoration of Works of Art; Tourism); **Arts** (Arabic; Arts and Humanities; English; French; Geography; German; Greek (Classical); History; Japanese; Latin; Library Science; Philosophy; Psychology; Sociology; Spanish); **Commerce** (Accountancy; Banking; Business Administration; Business and Commerce; Health Administration; Hotel Management; Insurance; Marketing; Mathematics; Public Administration; Taxation); **Computer Science and Informatics** (Computer Science; Information Sciences; Information Technology); **Dar el Ulum** *(Dar El-Ulum)* (Arabic; Comparative Literature; Grammar; History; Islamic Law; Islamic Studies; Linguistics; Literature; Oriental Studies; Philosophy); **Dentistry** (Dental Hygiene; Dentistry; Oral Pathology; Orthodontics; Surgery); **Economics and Political Science** (Economics; Political Sciences; Public Administration; Statistics); **Engineering** (Aeronautical and Aerospace Engineering; Architecture; Biomedical Engineering; Civil Engineering; Electrical Engineering; Engineering; Hydraulic Engineering; Irrigation; Mathematics; Mechanical Engineering; Metallurgical Engineering; Petroleum and Gas Engineering; Physics; Telecommunications Engineering); **Kindergarten** (Preschool Education); **Law** (Civil Law; Commercial Law; Criminal Law; Finance; History of Law; International Law; Islamic Law; Labour Law; Law; Public Law); **Mass Communication** (Advertising and Publicity; Journalism; Mass Communication; Radio and Television Broadcasting); **Medicine** (Anaesthesiology; Anatomy; Biochemistry; Cardiology; Dermatology; Forensic Medicine and Dentistry; Gynaecology and Obstetrics; Histology; Hygiene; Medicine; Neurology; Occupational Health; Ophthalmology; Orthopaedics; Paediatrics; Parasitology; Pathology; Physiology; Psychiatry and Mental Health; Radiology; Surgery; Tropical Medicine; Urology; Venereology); **Nursing** (Nursing); **Oral and Dental Medicine** (Dentistry); **Pharmacy** (Analytical Chemistry; Biochemistry; Microbiology; Organic Chemistry; Pharmacology; Pharmacy); **Physiotherapy** (Neurological Therapy; Orthopaedics; Physical Therapy; Plastic Surgery); **Regional and Town Planning** (Regional Planning; Town Planning); **Science** (Analytical Chemistry; Astronomy and Space Science; Botany; Chemistry; Computer Science; Entomology; Geology; Geophysics; Mathematics; Meteorology; Microbiology; Mineralogy; Natural Sciences; Physics; Statistics; Zoology); **Veterinary Medicine** (Anatomy; Animal Husbandry; Biochemistry; Fishery; Forensic Medicine and Dentistry; Histology; Microbiology; Nutrition; Parasitology; Pharmacology; Physiology; Toxicology; Veterinary Science)

Institute

Cancer *(National)* (Anaesthesiology; Biology; Epidemiology; Oncology; Pathology; Radiology; Surgery); **Educational Studies and Research** (Curriculum; Educational and Student Counselling; Educational Research; Educational Technology; Pedagogy; Preschool Education; Teacher Training); **Laser Science** *(National)* (Laser Engineering); **Statistical Studies and Research** (Statistics)

Centre

Development and Technology Planning (Development Studies); **Environmental Studies and Research**; **Future Studies and Research**; **Open University E-Learning** (Distance Education)

Further Information: Also Qars El Ainy Hospital; Tumour Hospital and Infants' Hospital

History: Founded 1908 as National University, became State University 1925. Known as Fouad I University between 1940 and 1953.

Academic Year: September to June (September-January; January-June)

Admission Requirements: Secondary school certificate or equivalent. University degree for Institutes of Statistical Studies and African Studies

Main Language(s) of Instruction: Arabic, English, French

Degrees and Diplomas: *Bachelor's Degree*: **African Studies; Statistics.** *Lîsâns*: **Business and Commerce; Dentistry; Economics; Engineering; Journalism; Pharmacology; Political Sciences; Statistics.** *Mâjistêr*: **Anaesthesiology; Dentistry; Medicine; Surgery.** *Dukturâh*: **Anaesthesiology; Dentistry; Medicine; Oncology; Paediatrics; Pathology; Pharmacy; Surgery; Veterinary Science.**

Student Services: Academic Counselling, Canteen, Careers Guidance, Cultural Activities, Facilities for disabled people, Health Services, Nursery Care, Social Counselling, Sports Facilities

Publications: Computer Magazine; Egyptian Journal of Genetics and Psychology; Medical Journal of Cairo University; Population and Family Planning Magazine; Publications of the Faculties; The Egyptian Statistical Magazine

Publishing House: Cairo University Press; Agriculture Faculty Press; Statistical Studies and Research Press; Law Faculty Press; Science Faculty Press
Last Updated: 24/07/13

DAMANHOUR UNIVERSITY

27 Galal Quretam Sq., Damanhour, Behira
Tel: +20(3) 591-2147 +20(4) 5336-8069
Fax: +20(3) 591-2147 +20(4) 5336-8069
Website: http://www.damanhour.edu.eg

President: Hatim Salah El-Din Abdel-Hamid

Faculty

Agriculture (Agriculture); **Arts** (Fine Arts); **Commerce** (Business and Commerce); **Education** (Education); **Kindergarten** (Preschool Education); **Nursing** (Nursing); **Pharmacy** (Pharmacy); **Science** (Animal Husbandry; Botany; Chemistry; Geology; Mathematics; Physics); **Veterinary Medicine** (Veterinary Science)

History: Founded 2010 following separation from Alexandria University..

Degrees and Diplomas: *Lîsâns*
Last Updated: 07/12/12

FAYOUM UNIVERSITY (FU)

Said Soliman Street, Fayoum 63514
Tel: +20(84) 633-3274
Fax: +20(84) 637-8666
EMail: sssg00@fayoum.edu.eg; admin@fayoum.edu.eg
Website: http://www.fayoum.edu.eg

President: Abdel Hammed Abdel Tawab
Tel: +20(84) 633-3278
EMail: aas02@fayoum.edu.eg

Vice-President for Postgraduate Studies and Research: Magdy Tawfik Hanna EMail: mth00@fayoum.edu.eg

Faculty

Agriculture (Agriculture; Agronomy; Animal Husbandry; Biochemistry; Botany; Crop Production; Dairy; Food Science; Food Technology; Genetics; Horticulture; Meat and Poultry; Microbiology; Plant and Crop Protection; Soil Science; Water Science); **Archaeology** (Archaeology; Islamic Studies; Restoration of Works of Art); **Arts** (Arabic; Documentation Techniques; English; French; Geography (Human); History; Information Sciences; Library Science; Philosophy; Psychology; Sociology); **Computer and Information Sciences** (Computer Science; Information Sciences); **Dar Al Oloom (Arabic and Islamic Studies)** (Arabic; Islamic Studies); **Early Childhood Education** (Educational Sciences; Preschool Education; Psychology); **Education** (Curriculum; Education; Educational Administration; Educational Psychology; International and Comparative Education); **Engineering** (Civil Engineering; Electrical Engineering; Engineering; Industrial Engineering; Structural Architecture); **Medicine** (Anaesthesiology; Anatomy; Biochemistry; Cardiology; Community Health; Dermatology; Epidemiology; Forensic Medicine and Dentistry; Gynaecology and Obstetrics; Histology; Immunology; Medicine; Microbiology; Neurology; Occupational Health; Oncology; Ophthalmology; Orthopaedics; Otorhinolaryngology; Paediatrics; Parasitology; Pathology; Pharmacology; Physiology; Psychiatry and Mental Health; Public Health; Radiology; Rheumatology; Surgery; Toxicology); **Science** (Botany; Chemistry; Geology; Mathematics; Physics; Zoology); **Social Work** (Social Sciences; Social Work); **Specific Education** (Art Education; Educational Technology; Home Economics Education); **Tourism and Hotels** (Hotel and Restaurant; Hotel Management; Tourism)

History: Founded 1976 as Al-Fayoum Branch of Cairo University. Declared independent and acquired present title 2005.

Academic Year: September to May (September-December; February-May)

Admission Requirements: Secondary education certificate or equivalent

Fees: (Egyptian Pounds): 209-229.5

Main Language(s) of Instruction: Arabic

Degrees and Diplomas: *Bachelor's Degree*: **Agriculture; Engineering; Fine Arts; Hotel Management; Social Work; Tourism.** *Lîsâns*: **Agriculture; Archaeology; Computer Science; Education; Engineering; Fine Arts; Hotel Management; Islamic Theology; Medicine; Preschool Education; Social Work; Tourism.** *Mâjistêr*: **Agriculture; Engineering; Fine Arts; Hotel Management; Islamic Theology; Social Work; Tourism.** *Dukturâh*: **Agriculture; Engineering; Fine Arts; Hotel Management; Islamic Theology; Social Work; Tourism.** Also General/Professional/Special Diploma in Education

Student Services: Academic Counselling, Canteen, Careers Guidance, Cultural Activities, Facilities for disabled people, Foreign Studies Centre, Health Services, Language Laboratory, Nursery Care, Social Counselling, Sports Facilities

Publications: Fayoum Journal of Agricultural Research and Development; Journal of Tourism and Hotels

Publishing House: Press and Print Unit
Last Updated: 19/06/12

HELWAN UNIVERSITY

Ein Helwan, Cairo 11795
Tel: +20(2) 556-9064
Fax: +20(2) 555-5023
EMail: helwan@helwan.edu.eg
Website: http://www.helwan.edu.eg

President: Yasser Sakr
Tel: +20(2) 556-9061 EMail: president@helwan.edu.eg

Faculty

Applied Arts (Fine Arts); **Art Education** (Art Education); **Arts** (Ancient Civilizations; Arabic; Arts and Humanities; English; French; Geography; German; Hebrew; History; Information Sciences; Italian; Library Science; Mass Communication; Modern Languages; Persian; Philosophy; Psychology; Sociology; Spanish; Theatre; Turkish); **Commerce and Business Administration** (Accountancy; Business Administration; Business and Commerce; Insurance; International Business; Political Sciences; Statistics); **Computer and Information Sciences** (Computer Science; Information Sciences); **Education** (Curriculum; Education; Educational Psychology; Educational Technology; Pedagogy); **Engineering** *(Mattaria)* (Architecture; Automation and Control Engineering; Civil Engineering; Engineering; Mechanical Engineering; Power Engineering); **Engineering** (Computer Engineering; Electrical and Electronic Engineering; Engineering; Production Engineering; Telecommunications Engineering); **Fine Arts** (Architecture; Fine Arts; Graphic Arts; Interior Design; Painting and Drawing; Sculpture); **Home Economics** (Food Science; Home Economics; Nutrition; Textile Technology); **Law** (Civil Law; Commercial Law; Criminal Law; History of Law; International Law; Law; Private Law; Public Law); **Music Education** (Music Education; Musical Instruments; Singing); **Pharmacy** (Analytical Chemistry; Biochemistry; Chemistry; Microbiology; Organic Chemistry; Pharmacology; Pharmacy); **Physical Education** *(for women)* (Physical Education); **Physical Education** *(for men)* (Health Sciences; Parks and Recreation; Physical Education; Physical Therapy; Sports Management); **Science** (Astronomy and Space Science; Botany; Chemistry; Geology; Natural Sciences; Physics; Zoology); **Social Work** (Social and Community Services; Social Work); **Tourism and Hotel Management** (Hotel Management; Tourism)

Centre

Foreign Trade Studies and Research (International Business); **Scientific Computing** (Computer Science); **Scientific Instrument Maintenance** (Instrument Making); **Small Projects Support**; **Social Service** (Social and Community Services); **Technology Development Studies and Research** (Technology); **University Education Development** (Pedagogy); **Youth Studies and Research** (Child Care and Development)

Further Information: Also 46 self-sponsored Research Centres and Units. Traditional and Open Learning Institution

History: Founded 1975, incorporating previously existing Faculties and Institutes of Higher Education. A state Institution under the supervision of the Ministry of Higher Education and financed by the State.

Academic Year: September to June

Admission Requirements: Secondary school certificate or equivalent

Main Language(s) of Instruction: Arabic, English

Degrees and Diplomas: *Bachelor's Degree*: **Education.** *Lîsâns*: **Fine Arts.** *Mâjistêr*. **Fine Arts.** *Dukturâh*: **Fine Arts.**

Student Services: Academic Counselling, Canteen, Careers Guidance, Cultural Activities, Facilities for disabled people, Foreign Studies Centre, Health Services, Language Laboratory, Nursery Care, Social Counselling, Sports Facilities

Publications: Helwan University Journal

Publishing House: University Press at the Faculty of Applied Arts
Last Updated: 07/12/12

KAFRELSHEIKH UNIVERSITY

El-Geish Street, Kafr Al-Sheikh 33516
Tel: +20(47) 322-4707
Fax: +20(47) 322-3419
EMail: aman485@yahoo.com
Website: http://www.kfs.edu.eg

President: Maged Abdeltawab El Kemary

Vice-President for Graduate Studies: Ibrahim Mohamed Aman

Secretary-General: Moharam Barakat

Faculty

Agriculture (Agricultural Economics; Agricultural Engineering; Agriculture; Agronomy; Animal Husbandry; Dairy; Entomology; Horticulture; Meat and Poultry; Soil Science); **Arts** (Arts and Humanities); **Commerce** (Business and Commerce); **Education** (Curriculum; Education; Educational Administration; Educational Psychology; Psychiatry and Mental Health; Special Education); **Engineering** (Civil Engineering; Electrical Engineering; Engineering; Mechanical Engineering); **Physical Education** (Physical Education; Sports); **Science** (Botany; Chemistry; Geology; Mathematics; Physics; Zoology); **Specific Education** (Art Education; Educational Sciences; Educational Technology; Home Economics; Mass Communication; Music Education; Psychology); **Veterinary Medicine** (Veterinary Science)

History: Founded 1982 as Kafr El-Sheikh Branch of Tanta University. Acquired present status and title 2006.

Academic Year: September to June (2 sems)

Fees: (Egyptian Pounds): Undergraduate, 190; postgraduate, 500-1,000

Main Language(s) of Instruction: English, Arabic

Accrediting Agency: Ministry of Higher Education

Degrees and Diplomas: *Lîsâns*; *Mâjistêr*, *Dukturâh*

Student Services: Canteen, Health Services, Sports Facilities

Publications: Journal of Agricultural Research; Journal of Education Faculty; Kafr El Sheikh Veterinary Medical
Last Updated: 20/06/12

MANSOURA UNIVERSITY

60, El Gomhoria Street, Mansoura, Dakahliya 35516
Tel: +20(50) 239-7054 +20(50) 239-7055 +20(50) 238-3781
Fax: +20(50) 239-7330 +20(50) 239-7900
EMail: mua@mans.edu.eg; hamzaaa@mum.mans.eun.eg
Website: http://www.mans.edu.eg

President: El-Sayed Abdel-Khalek
Tel: +20(50) 239-7387 +20(50) 224-7800
EMail: president@mans.edu.eg

Secretary-General: Amira Al-Sorongy Tel: +20(50) 247-330

International Relations: Yehia Hussein Ebeid
Tel: +20(50) 243-587

Faculty

Agriculture (Agricultural Economics; Agricultural Engineering; Agriculture; Agronomy; Animal Husbandry; Botany; Chemistry; Dairy; Floriculture; Food Science; Genetics; Microbiology; Plant Pathology; Soil Science; Vegetable Production; Zoology); **Arts** (Arabic; Archaeology; Arts and Humanities; Documentation Techniques; English Studies; French Studies; Geography; Greek; History; Journalism; Latin; Library Science; Oriental Languages; Philosophy; Psychology; Sociology); **Commerce** (Accountancy; Business Administration; Business and Commerce; Economics; Insurance; Statistics); **Computer and Information Science** (Computer Science; Information Management; Information Sciences); **Dentistry** (Dentistry; Oral Pathology; Orthodontics); **Education** (Arabic; Chemistry; Curriculum; Education; Educational Psychology; Educational Technology; Geography; Geology; History; Islamic Studies; Modern Languages; Primary Education; Teacher Training); **Education** *(Damietta)* (Arabic; Biology; Curriculum; Education; Educational Psychology; Educational Technology; English; French; Geography; Geology; History; Islamic Studies; Modern Languages; Philosophy); **Engineering** (Architectural and Environmental Design; Automation and Control Engineering; Civil Engineering; Computer Engineering; Construction Engineering; Electrical and Electronic Engineering; Engineering; Hydraulic Engineering; Industrial Engineering; Irrigation; Mathematics; Mechanical Engineering; Physics; Power Engineering; Textile Technology); **Law** (Civil Law; Commercial Law; Criminal Law; History of Law; International Law; Islamic Law; Law; Private Law; Public Law); **Medicine** (Anaesthesiology; Anatomy; Biochemistry; Cardiology; Community Health; Dermatology; Forensic Medicine and Dentistry; Gynaecology and Obstetrics; Histology; Medicine; Microbiology; Neurology; Ophthalmology; Orthodontics; Orthopaedics; Paediatrics; Parasitology; Pathology; Pharmacology; Physical Therapy; Physiology; Psychiatry and Mental Health; Radiology; Surgery; Urology); **Nursing** (Community Health; Gerontology; Gynaecology and Obstetrics; Hygiene; Nursing); **Pharmacy** (Analytical Chemistry; Microbiology; Pharmacy); **Science** *(Damietta)* (Botany; Chemistry; Environmental Studies; Geology; Mathematics; Physics; Science Education; Zoology); **Science** (Botany; Chemistry; Geology; Mathematics; Natural Sciences; Physics; Zoology); **Veterinary Science** (Anatomy; Animal Husbandry; Biochemistry; Embryology and Reproduction Biology; Food Science; Forensic Medicine and Dentistry; Histology; Hygiene; Immunology; Nutrition; Parasitology; Pathology; Pharmacology; Physiology; Surgery; Veterinary Science; Virology)

Centre

Urology and Nephrology (Nephrology; Urology)

Further Information: Also 2 Teaching Hospitals and 3 Laboratories. Traditional and Open Learning Institution

History: Founded 1972 as East Delta University, incorporating Faculties previously attached to the University of Cairo. Acquired present title 1973. A State Institution under the authority of the Ministry of Higher Education.

Academic Year: September to June (September-January; February-June)

Admission Requirements: Secondary school certificate or equivalent

Main Language(s) of Instruction: Arabic

Degrees and Diplomas: *Lîsâns*; *Mâjistêr*, *Dukturâh*

Student Services: Academic Counselling, Canteen, Careers Guidance, Cultural Activities, Health Services, Nursery Care, Social Counselling, Sports Facilities

Publications: Periodicals of the Community and Environmental Council and the Cultural Affairs and Research Branch; Scientific Journal

Publishing House: University Press
Last Updated: 20/06/12

MENOUFIA UNIVERSITY

PO Box 32511, Gamal Abdel Nasser Street,
Shebin Al-Kom, Menoufia
Tel: +20(48) 2222-170 +20(2) 2575-2777
Fax: +20(48) 2222-170 +20(2) 5752-7779
EMail: menofia@menofia.edu.eg
Website: http://www.menofia.edu.eg

President: Mohamed A. Izzularab Tel: +20(48) 225-298

Faculty

Agriculture (Agricultural Engineering; Agriculture; Agronomy; Animal Husbandry; Dairy; Food Technology; Genetics; Horticulture; Meat and Poultry; Soil Science); **Arts** (Arabic; Arts and Humanities; English; French; Geography; German; History; Library Science; Literature; Oriental Languages; Philosophy; Psychology; Sociology); **Commerce** *(Sadat City)* (Accountancy; Business Administration; Business and Commerce; Economics; Insurance; Statistics); **Commerce** (Accountancy; Business Administration; Business and Commerce; Economics; Insurance; Statistics); **Computer Science**

and Information Technology (Computer Science; Information Technology); **Education** (Curriculum; Education; Educational Psychology; Pedagogy); **Education** *(Sadat City)*; **Electronic Engineering** (Automation and Control Engineering; Computer Engineering; Computer Science; Electronic Engineering; Telecommunications Engineering); **Engineering** (Civil Engineering; Electrical Engineering; Engineering; Mechanical Engineering; Power Engineering); **Home Economics** (Clothing and Sewing; Food Science; Home Economics; Nutrition; Textile Design); **Law** (Civil Law; Commercial Law; Criminal Law; International Law; Islamic Law; Law; Public Law); **Medicine** (Anaesthesiology; Anatomy; Biochemistry; Cardiology; Forensic Medicine and Dentistry; Histology; Medicine; Microbiology; Oncology; Ophthalmology; Orthopaedics; Otorhinolaryngology; Paediatrics; Parasitology; Pathology; Pharmacology; Physiology; Radiology; Surgery; Toxicology; Tropical Medicine; Urology); **Nursing** (Health Administration; Nursing); **Physical Education** (Physical Education); **Science** (Botany; Chemistry; Geology; Mathematics; Mathematics and Computer Science; Natural Sciences; Physics; Zoology); **Specific Education** (Art Education; Economics; Educational Technology; Media Studies; Music Education; Psychology; Social Sciences); **Tourism and Hotels** *(Sadat City)* (Hotel and Restaurant; Hotel Management; Tourism); **Veterinary Medicine** *(Sadat City)* (Anatomy; Cell Biology; Embryology and Reproduction Biology; Pathology; Veterinary Science)

Institute

Biotechnology Engineering *(Sadat City)* (Biotechnology; Genetics; Molecular Biology); **Environmental Studies and Research** *(Sadat City)* (Arid Land Studies); **Hepatology Studies and Research** *(Shebin)* (Hepatology)

History: Founded 1976. A State institution under the authority of the Ministry of Higher Education.

Academic Year: September to May

Admission Requirements: Secondary school certificate or equivalent

Fees: (Egyptian Pounds): 85-100 per annum

Main Language(s) of Instruction: Arabic, English

Accrediting Agency: Ministry of Higher Education, Supreme Council of Universities

Degrees and Diplomas: *Lîsâns*; *Mâjistêr*; *Dukturâh*

Student Services: Academic Counselling, Canteen, Careers Guidance, Cultural Activities, Facilities for disabled people, Foreign Studies Centre, Health Services, Language Laboratory, Nursery Care, Social Counselling, Sports Facilities

Publications: Journal of Psychological and Educational Research; Minufiya Journal of Agricultural Research; Minufiya Journal of Electronic Engineering Research; Minufiya Veterinary Journal

Last Updated: 07/12/12

MINIA UNIVERSITY

PO Box 61519, El-Minia
Tel: +20(86) 321-443
Fax: +20(86) 342-601
EMail: minia@minia.edu.eg
Website: http://www.minia.edu.eg

President: Mohamed Ahmed Shrief
Tel: +20(86) 233-4646 EMail: drmsherif_aly@yahoo.com

Vice-President, Graduate Studies and Research: Gaber Zayed Abdulwanes Bresha
Tel: +20(86) 347-460 EMail: gaberbresha@yahoo.com

Faculty

Agriculture (Agriculture); **Arabic and Islamic Studies** *(Dar El-Uloom)* (Arabic; Islamic Studies); **Dentistry** (Dentistry); **Education** (Education); **Engineering** (Architecture; Automation and Control Engineering; Chemical Engineering; Civil Engineering; Electrical Engineering; Energy Engineering; Engineering; Mechanical Engineering; Production Engineering); **Fine Arts** (Architecture; Fine Arts; Graphic Arts; Interior Design; Painting and Drawing; Sculpture); **Languages** *(Al-Alsun)* (English; French; German; Spanish); **Medicine** (Anatomy; Biochemistry; Community Health; Embryology and Reproduction Biology; Forensic Medicine and Dentistry; Gynaecology and Obstetrics; Histology; Medicine; Ophthalmology; Otorhinolaryngology; Paediatrics; Physiology; Surgery); **Nursing** (Nursing); **Pharmacy** (Analytical Chemistry; Anatomy; Botany; Histology; Organic Chemistry; Pharmacy; Physics; Physiology); **Physical Education** (Physical Education; Sports); **Science** (Biology; Chemistry; Computer Science; Geology; Mathematics; Natural Sciences; Physics); **Special Education** (Special Education); **Tourism and Hotel Management** (Hotel Management; Tourism)

History: Founded 1976, incorporating Faculties of Agriculture, Education, Humanities, Science, and Engineering which were previously part of the University of Assiut. A State Institution enjoying administrative autonomy. Financed by the Government.

Academic Year: October to May (October-January; February-May)

Admission Requirements: Secondary school certificate or equivalent

Main Language(s) of Instruction: Arabic, English

Degrees and Diplomas: *Bachelor's Degree*; *Lîsâns*: **Agriculture; Education; Engineering; Physical Education; Surgery.** *Mâjistêr*: **Art Education.** *Dukturâh*

Publications: Educational and Psychological Research Magazine; History and Future Magazine; Journal of Agricultural Research; Minia Medical Magazine; Technical Scientific Magazine

Publishing House: University Press

NATIONAL TELECOMMUNICATIONS INSTITUTE (NTI)

5 Mahmoud El Miligui St., 6th district, Nasr City, Cairo
Tel: +20 240-23-154
Fax: +20 263-6802
EMail: activity@nti.sci.eg
Website: http://www.nti.sci.eg

Director: Magdy El-Soudani
Tel: +20 240-23-855 EMail: melsoudani@nti.sci.eg

Programme

Postgraduate (Computer Networks; Information Technology; Telecommunications Engineering)

Department

Computer and Systems (Computer Engineering; Computer Networks; Computer Science; Systems Analysis); **Electronics** (Electronic Engineering); **Networks Planning** (Computer Networks); **Switching anf Traffic** (Computer Engineering; Computer Networks); **Transmission** (Telecommunications Engineering)

Further Information: Smart Village: Bldg. B 147- 28th Km. Cairo Alex. Desert Road

History: Founded 1983.

Academic Year: October to June (October-January; Februry-June)

Admission Requirements: Bachelor of Science in Electronics or Communication Engineering or Computer Engineering

Fees: (Egyptian pounds): Egyptian students, 2,000 per annum; foreign students, (US Dollars, 2,000)

Main Language(s) of Instruction: English

Accrediting Agency: Ministry of Communications and Information Technology.

Degrees and Diplomas: *Mâjistêr*: **Computer Engineering.** post graduate diploma

Student Services: Academic Counselling, Canteen, Health Services, Sports Facilities

Last Updated: 07/12/12

PORT-SAID UNIVERSITY

Port-Said 42526
EMail: portal@psu.edu.eg
Website: http://www.psu.edu.eg/en

President: Emad Yahiya Abdul Galiel

Faculty

Arts (Arabic; History; Social Studies); **Commerce** (Accountancy; Business Administration; Business and Commerce; Economics; Finance; Insurance; Law; Mathematics and Computer Science; Political Sciences; Public Relations; Statistics); **Education** (Arabic; Chemistry; Education; Educational Psychology; Islamic Studies; Literature; Mathematics; Modern Languages; Physics; Social

Sciences); **Engineering** (Electrical Engineering; Engineering; Mechanical Engineering; Naval Architecture; Production Engineering); **Kindergarten** (Preschool Education); **Nursing** (Nursing; Paediatrics; Psychiatry and Mental Health; Public Health); **Physical Education** (Physical Education); **Science** (Botany; Chemistry; Geology; Marine Science and Oceanography; Mathematics and Computer Science; Natural Sciences; Toxicology; Zoology); **Specific Education** (Special Education)

Higher Institute

Management and Computer (Computer Engineering; Management)

History: Founded 1989. Acquired present status following separation from Suez Canal University.

Degrees and Diplomas: *Lîsâns*; *Mâjistêr*; *Duktûrâh*

Last Updated: 20/06/12

SOHAG UNIVERSITY

PO Box 82524, Sohag
Tel: +(20) 93457-0001
Fax: +(20) 93460-5745
EMail: president@sohag.edu.eg
Website: http://www.sohag-univ.edu.eg

President: Mohammad E. Ibrahim
Tel: +(20) 934611920
EMail: sohag_uni_president@sohag-univ.edu.eg

Vice-President for Post-Graduate Studies and Research: Lotfy H. Abo-Dahab
Tel: +(20) 93461-2589 EMail: lotfy_hamed@yahoo.com

International Relations: Lotfy H. Abo-Dahab
Tel: +(20) 93461-2589 EMail: lotfy_hamed@yahoo.com

Faculty

Agriculture (Agriculture); **Arts** (Arts and Humanities); **Commerce** (Business and Commerce); **Education** (Education); **Engineering** (Engineering); **Medicine** (Medicine); **Nursing** (Nursing); **Science** (Mathematics and Computer Science; Natural Sciences); **Veterinary Medicine** (Veterinary Science)

History: Founded 1979 as Sohag Branch of South Valley University. Acquired present status and title 2006.

Accrediting Agency: Supreme Council of Universities

Degrees and Diplomas: *Lîsâns*; *Mâjistêr*; *Duktûrâh*

Publications: Sohag Faculty of Arts Journal; Sohag Faculty of Medicine Journal

Last Updated: 20/06/12

SOUTH VALLEY UNIVERSITY

Qena 83523
Tel: +20(96) 521-1281
Fax: +20(96) 521-1279
EMail: info@svu.edu.eg
Website: http://www.svu.edu.eg

President: Abbas Mohamed Mansour (2006-)
Tel: +20(96) 521-1717 EMail: psvu@svu.edu.eg

International Relations: Mahmoud Khodari Maeila Hamed, Vice-President for Graduate Affairs EMail: vpstd@svu.edu.eg

Faculty

Agriculture (Agricultural Economics; Agriculture; Animal Husbandry; Dairy; Fruit Production; Horticulture; Meat and Poultry; Plant and Crop Protection; Plant Pathology; Soil Science; Water Science); **Archaeology** (Ancient Civilizations; Archaeology; Restoration of Works of Art); **Arts** (Arabic; Arts and Humanities; English; French; Geography; Greek; History; Islamic Studies; Latin; Library Science; Media Studies; Oriental Languages; Philosophy; Sociology); **Commerce** (Business Administration; Business and Commerce; Economics; Insurance); **Education** *(Qena)* (Education); **Education** *(Hurghada)* (Education); **Education** *(Aswan)* (Education); **Energy Engineering** *(Aswan)* (Energy Engineering); **Engineering** *(Aswan)* (Architecture; Civil Engineering; Electrical Engineering; Mechanical Engineering); **Engineering** *(Qena)* (Civil Engineering; Electrical Engineering; Engineering); **Fine Arts** *(Luxor)* (Fine Arts; Graphic Design; Interior Design; Painting and Drawing; Sculpture); **Hotels and Tourism** *(Luxor)* (Hotel and Restaurant; Tourism); **Law** (Islamic Law; Law; Private Law; Public Law); **Medicine** (Medicine); **Nursing** (Nursing); **Physical Education** (Education; Physical Education; Sports); **Science** *(Qena)* (Mathematics; Mathematics and Computer Science; Natural Sciences); **Science** *(Aswan)* (Computer Science; Mathematics; Mathematics and Computer Science; Natural Sciences); **Social Work** *(Aswan)* (Social Work); **Special Education** (Education; Special Education); **Veterinary Medicine** (Veterinary Science)

History: Founded as branch of Assiut University 1970. Separated from Assuit University 1995 to become South Valley University based in Qena, with campuses in Sohag, Luxor, Aswan and Red Sea. Sohag Campus separated to become Sohag University 2006.

Academic Year: September to June

Admission Requirements: General Secondary Certificate

Fees: (Egyptian Pounds): Free of charge for undergraduate programmes; c. 500 for postgraduate programmes

Main Language(s) of Instruction: Arabic and English

Accrediting Agency: Ministry of Higher Education and Scientific Research

Degrees and Diplomas: *Bachelor's Degree*: **Education; Natural Sciences.** *Lîsâns*: **Agriculture; Animal Husbandry; Business and Commerce; Education; Engineering; Medicine; Pharmacy; Social Work; Surgery; Veterinary Science.** *Mâjistêr*: **Agriculture; Animal Husbandry; Arts and Humanities; Business Administration; Business and Commerce; Computer Science; Economics; Education; Engineering; Law; Mathematics; Medicine; Natural Sciences; Physical Education; Social Sciences; Soil Science; Special Education; Veterinary Science.** *Duktûrâh*: **Agriculture; Animal Husbandry; Arts and Humanities; Business Administration; Business and Commerce; Computer Science; Economics; Education; Engineering; Fine Arts; Law; Mathematics; Medicine; Natural Sciences; Nursing; Physical Education; Social Sciences; Soil Science; Special Education; Veterinary Science.**

Student Services: Academic Counselling, Canteen, Health Services, Language Laboratory, Nursery Care, Social Counselling, Sports Facilities

Last Updated: 20/06/12

SUEZ CANAL UNIVERSITY

4,5 Km, New Building, Ismaïlia
Tel: +20(64) 3200-125 +20(64) 3223-007
Fax: +20(64) 320-508
EMail: infor@suez.eun.eg
Website: http://www.scuegypt.edu.eg

President: Mohamed Mohamaden
Tel: +20-127-962-994 EMail: mohamed.am54@gmail.com

Faculty

Agriculture (Agricultural Business; Agricultural Engineering; Agriculture; Agronomy; Animal Husbandry; Botany; Crop Production; Fishery; Food Science; Food Technology; Horticulture; Plant and Crop Protection; Soil Science); **Arts and Humanities**; **Commerce** (Accountancy; Advertising and Publicity; Business Administration; Business and Commerce; Economics; Insurance; Marketing; Political Sciences; Public Relations; Statistics; Taxation); **Computer and Information Science** (Computer Science; Information Sciences; Mathematics and Computer Science); **Dentistry** (Dentistry); **Education** (Curriculum; Education; Educational Psychology; Educational Sciences; Home Economics; Pedagogy; Social Psychology); **Medicine** (Anaesthesiology; Anatomy; Biochemistry; Cardiology; Community Health; Dermatology; Genetics; Gynaecology and Obstetrics; Histology; Medicine; Microbiology; Neurology; Occupational Health; Ophthalmology; Osteopathy; Paediatrics; Pathology; Physiology; Psychiatry and Mental Health; Public Health; Radiology; Speech Therapy and Audiology; Surgery; Tropical Medicine; Urology); **Nursing** (Nursing); **Pharmacy** (Analytical Chemistry; Biochemistry; Immunology; Microbiology; Organic Chemistry; Pharmacology; Pharmacy; Toxicology); **Science** (Botany; Chemistry; Geology; Marine Science and Oceanography; Mathematics and Computer Science; Natural Sciences; Toxicology; Zoology); **Tourism and Hotel Management** (Hotel Management; Tourism); **Veterinary Medicine** (Biochemistry; Forensic Medicine and Dentistry; Histology; Microbiology; Parasitology; Pathology; Pharmacology; Physiology; Veterinary Science; Wildlife; Zoology)

Centre
Education Development (Education)

Research Institute
Biotechnology (Biotechnology)

Further Information: Also Teaching Hospital

History: Founded 1976. A State institution under the supervision of the Ministry of Higher Education.

Academic Year: September to June (September-January; February-June)

Admission Requirements: Secondary school certificate or equivalent

Main Language(s) of Instruction: Arabic

Degrees and Diplomas: *Lîsâns*: **Business and Commerce; Dentistry; Education; Engineering; Medicine; Pharmacy; Surgery.** *Mâjistêr, Dukturâh.* Also postgraduate Diplomas

Publications: Scientific Bulletins (Human Sciences, Basic Sciences, Applied Sciences)

Publishing House: Suez Canal University Press

Last Updated: 07/12/12

NORTH SINAI BRANCH
El-Arish
EMail: webmaster@suez-foe.com

Faculty
Education (Education); **Environmental Agricultural Sciences** (Agriculture; Environmental Studies)

Degrees and Diplomas: *Lîsâns*; *Mâjistêr*, *Dukturâh*. Also Postgraduate Diploma

SUEZ BRANCH
Suez
EMail: Webmaster@Suez-foe.com

Faculty
Commerce (Business and Commerce); **Education** (Education); **Industrial Education** (Industrial Arts Education); **Petroleum Engineering and Mining** (Mining Engineering; Petroleum and Gas Engineering); **Science** (Botany; Chemistry; Geology; Marine Science and Oceanography; Mathematics and Computer Science; Natural Sciences; Toxicology; Zoology)

Degrees and Diplomas: *Lîsâns*; *Mâjistêr*, *Dukturâh*

TANTA UNIVERSITY

PO Box 31512, El-Geish Street, Tanta, Al-Gharbia
Tel: +20(40) 337-7929
Fax: +20(40) 331-3308
EMail: President@unv.tanta.edu.eg
Website: http://www.tanta.edu.eg

President: Abdel Hakim Abdel Khalek Khalil

Vice-President for Graduate Studies and Research: Ibrahim Abdel Wahab Salem EMail: vp_research@unv.tanta.edu.eg

Faculty
Agriculture (Agricultural Equipment; Agriculture; Agronomy; Animal Husbandry; Botany; Dairy; Economics; Food Science; Food Technology; Genetics; Horticulture; Soil Science); **Arts** (Arabic; Arts and Humanities; French; Geography; History; Philosophy; Psychology; Sociology); **Commerce** (Accountancy; Business Administration; Business and Commerce; Economics; Finance; Insurance; Mathematics; Public Administration; Statistics; Taxation); **Dentistry** (Dentistry); **Education** (Science Education); **Engineering** (Architecture; Design; Electrical Engineering; Electronic Engineering; Engineering; Hydraulic Engineering; Irrigation; Mathematics; Mechanical Engineering; Physical Engineering; Production Engineering; Town Planning); **Law** (Law); **Medicine** (Anaesthesiology; Gynaecology and Obstetrics; Medicine; Paediatrics); **Pharmacy** (Biochemistry; Microbiology; Pharmacy; Toxicology); **Physical Education** (Physical Education); **Science** (Botany; Chemistry; Geology; Mathematics; Natural Sciences; Physics; Zoology); **Specific Education** (Art Education; Educational Technology; Home Economics; Mass Communication; Music Education; Psychology)

Institute
Nursing (Gynaecology and Obstetrics; Nursing; Paediatrics)

Further Information: Also Teaching Hospital and Study Abroad Programmes

History: Founded 1972, incorporating Faculties attached to the University of Alexandria. In 2006, branch of Tanta University in Kafr El-Sheikh became Kafr El-Shiekh University.A State Institution under the supervision of the Ministry of Higher Education.

Academic Year: October to June

Admission Requirements: Secondary school certificate or equivalent

Fees: None

Main Language(s) of Instruction: Arabic, English

Degrees and Diplomas: *Lîsâns*: **Agriculture; Business and Commerce; Dentistry; Education; Fine Arts; Law; Medicine; Pharmacy; Surgery.** *Mâjistêr, Dukturâh*: **Agriculture; Animal Husbandry; Business and Commerce; Dentistry; Education; Engineering; Fine Arts; Law; Medicine; Nursing; Pharmacy; Philosophy; Physical Education; Veterinary Science.** Also postgraduate Diploma

Publications: Commerce and Finance

Last Updated: 21/06/12

TIBIN INSTITUTE FOR METALLURGICAL STUDIES

Tibin Iron and Steal St., Helwan, Cairo
Tel: +20(2) 501-1575 +20(2) 501-0176
Fax: +20(2) 501-0171 +20(2) 501-0170
EMail: tins@idsc.gov.eg

Programme
Chemical Industries (Chemical Engineering); **Metallurgical Engineering** (Metallurgical Engineering); **Mining Engineering** (Mining Engineering)

UNIVERSITY OF SADAT CITY (USC)

Sadat City, Menofia
Tel: +20(48) 260-3205
Fax: +20(48) 261-2139
Website: http://www.usc.edu.eg/

President: Salah Al Bellal EMail: president@usc.edu.eg

Secretary-General: Radwan Al-Kerm EMail: rakerm@usc.edu.eg

International Relations: Rifai Rifai, Vice President for Higher Studies and Researche EMail: ririfai@usc.edu.eg

Faculty
Commerce (Business Administration; Economics); **Education** (Education; Educational Psychology; Foreign Languages Education; Humanities and Social Science Education; Preschool Education; Science Education); **Law** (Law); **Physical Education** (Leisure Studies; Physical Education); **Tourism** (Hotel and Restaurant; Tourism); **Veterinary Medicine** (Animal Husbandry; Veterinary Science)

Institute
Environmental Studies and Research (Ecology; Environmental Studies; Natural Resources); **Genetic Engineering and Biotechnology** (Bioengineering; Biomedical Engineering; Biotechnology; Molecular Biology)

History: Created 1992 as a branch of Menoufia University. Acquired current title and status 2013.

Academic Year: October to July

Admission Requirements: High school certificate.

Fees: None

Main Language(s) of Instruction: Arabic, English

Accrediting Agency: National Authority for Quality Assurance and Accreditation

Degrees and Diplomas: *Bachelor's Degree*: **Business and Commerce; Education; Hotel Management; Law; Medicine; Physical Education; Veterinary Science.** *Lîsâns*; *Mâjistêr*.

Biotechnology; Education; Environmental Studies; Genetics; Hotel Management; Physical Education; Tourism; Veterinary Science. *Dukturâh*: **Biotechnology; Education; Environmental Studies; Genetics; Hotel Management; Physical Education; Tourism; Veterinary Science.**

Academic Staff *2014-2015*	**TOTAL**
FULL-TIME	**1,363**
PART-TIME	**98**
STAFF WITH DOCTORATE	
FULL-TIME	**691**
Student Numbers *2014-2015*	
All (Foreign included)	c. **29,702**
FOREIGN ONLY	**1136**

Last Updated: 28/01/14

ZAGAZIG UNIVERSITY

Zagazig, Sharkia 44519
Tel: +20(55) 238-470
Fax: +20(55) 238-470
EMail: info@zu.edu.eg
Website: http://www.zu.edu.eg

President: Ashraf El-Sheehi

Faculty

Agriculture (Agriculture; Agronomy; Animal Husbandry; Biochemistry; Fruit Production; Geophysics; Harvest Technology; Nutrition; Plant and Crop Protection); **Arts** (Arabic; Arts and Humanities; English; French; Geography; History; Media Studies; Philosophy; Physiology; Sociology); **Commerce** (Accountancy; Business Administration; Business and Commerce; Mathematics; Statistics); **Computer and Information Science** (Computer Science; Information Sciences; Information Technology); **Education** (Curriculum; Education; Educational Psychology; International and Comparative Education; Pedagogy; Psychiatry and Mental Health); **Engineering** (Civil Engineering; Computer Engineering; Construction Engineering; Electronic Engineering; Engineering; Industrial Engineering; Materials Engineering; Mathematics; Mechanical Engineering; Physical Engineering; Power Engineering; Production Engineering; Structural Architecture); **Law** (Civil Law; Commercial Law; Criminal Law; History of Law; International Law; Islamic Law; Law); **Medicine** (Anaesthesiology; Anatomy; Biochemistry; Cardiology; Community Health; Dermatology; Forensic Medicine and Dentistry; Gynaecology and Obstetrics; Histology; Medicine; Microbiology; Neurology; Ophthalmology; Orthopaedics; Paediatrics; Parasitology; Pathology; Pharmacology; Physiology; Psychiatry and Mental Health; Radiology; Rheumatology; Surgery; Tropical Medicine; Urology); **Nursing** (Gynaecology and Obstetrics; Health Education; Nursing; Surgery); **Pharmacy** (Analytical Chemistry; Biochemistry; Organic Chemistry; Pharmacology; Pharmacy); **Physical Education** *(for women)* (Physical Education); **Physical Education** (Physical Education); **Science** (Botany; Chemistry; Geology; Mathematics and Computer Science; Natural Sciences; Physics; Zoology); **Special Education** (Art Education; Educational Sciences; Educational Technology; English; Home Economics; Music Education; Preschool Education; Special Education); **Veterinary Medicine**

Higher Institute

Ancient Near Eastern Studies (Middle Eastern Studies); **Asian Studies and Research** (Asian Studies); **Production Efficiency** (Agriculture; Civil Engineering; Economics; Industrial and Production Economics; Management)

History: Founded 1969 as a branch of Ain-Shams University. Acquired present status 1974.

Academic Year: October to May (October-January; January-May)

Admission Requirements: Secondary school certificate or equivalent

Fees: None

Main Language(s) of Instruction: Arabic, English, French

Degrees and Diplomas: *Bachelor's Degree*; *Lîsâns*: **Fine Arts.** *Mâjistêr*: **Fine Arts.** *Dukturâh*

Student Services: Canteen, Cultural Activities, Facilities for disabled people, Health Services, Nursery Care, Social Counselling, Sports Facilities

Publications: Scientific Journals

Last Updated: 07/12/12

PRIVATE INSTITUTIONS

AKHBAR AL-YOM ACADEMY

4th Industrial Zone, beside Akhbar Print House,
6th of October City, Giza
Tel: +202 383 471 20
EMail: info@akhbaracademy.edu.eg
Website: http://www.akhbaracademy.edu.eg

Dean: Ahmad Zaki Badr (2000-)

Department

Business Administration (Accountancy; Business Administration); **Computer Science and Information Technology** (Computer Science; Information Technology); **Electrical Engineering** (Electrical Engineering; Engineering); **Journalism** (Journalism); **Mechanical Engineering** (Mechanical Engineering)

History: Founded 1999.

Accrediting Agency: Supreme Council of Universities

Degrees and Diplomas: *Lîsâns*: **Engineering.**

Last Updated: 19/06/12

AL-ABBASYA INSTITUTE FOR COMPUTER AND COMMERCIAL SCIENCES

Abdu Basha Square, Abbasya

Department

Computer Science (Computer Science); **Finance** (Finance)

History: Founded 1958 as "The Management and Secretarial Institute in Al-Abbasya". Acquired present title 1996.

Degrees and Diplomas: *Bachelor's Degree*: **Finance.** *Lîsâns*: **Computer Science.**

Last Updated: 10/12/12

AL-AHRAM CANADIAN UNIVERSITY

6th of October City, Giza
Tel: +20(2) 833-3078
Fax: +20(2) 833-4379
EMail: info@acu.edu.eg
Website: http://www.acu.edu.eg

President: Farouk Ismail

Faculty

Computer Science and Information Technology (Computer Networks; Computer Science; Information Technology; Software Engineering); **Mass Communication** (Advertising and Publicity; Communication Arts; Graphic Arts; Journalism; Mass Communication; Public Relations; Radio and Television Broadcasting); **Pharmacy** (Biochemistry; Microbiology; Pharmacology; Pharmacy; Toxicology)

School

Business (Accountancy; Economics; Finance; Hotel Management; Management; Public Health; Tourism)

History: Founded 2004.

Degrees and Diplomas: *Lîsâns*; *Diploma of Higher Studies*

Last Updated: 19/06/12

AL-ALSUN HIGHER INSTITUTE OF TOURISM AND HOTEL MANAGEMENT (AHITH)

Block n° 96, Makram Ebeid Ex., 8th District, Nasr City, Cairo
Tel: +20(2) 287-7522

Director: Nadia Refa'at Abdel-Rahman (2000-)

Department

Computer Science (Computer Science); **Hotel Management** (Hotel Management); **Tourism Studies** (Tourism); **Tourist Guidance** (Tourism)

History: Founded 1992.

Degrees and Diplomas: *Lîsâns*; *Mâjistêr*. Also Postgraduate Diploma.

ALEXANDRIA HIGHER INSTITUTE OF ENGINEERING AND TECHNOLOGY

Victor Emanuel Str., Sidi Gaber, Samouha, Alexandria
Tel: +20(3) 425-4942
EMail: info@ait.edu.eg
Website: http://www.aiet.edu.eg

Dean: Adel Ali Abou El-Ela

Department
Computer Engineering (Computer Engineering); **Electronics and Communications Engineering** (Electronic Engineering; Telecommunications Engineering); **Industrial Engineering** (Industrial Engineering); **Mechatronics Engineering** (Electronic Engineering; Mechanical Engineering)

History: Founded 1996. Acquired present status 1997.

Admission Requirements: Student must hold the Egyptian high school certificate, Mathematics Section, or an equivalent certificate and obtain a high grade in an entrance examination.

Degrees and Diplomas: *Lîsâns*
Last Updated: 19/06/12

AL-MA'AREF HIGHER INSTITUTE FOR LANGUAGES AND TRANSLATION

10, Nasouh Str., Al-Zaytoun
Tel: +20(2) 2257-1324
Fax: +20(2) 2258-005

Director: Mohamed R. Radwan (2005-)
EMail: prfradwan@hotmail.com

Chairman: Micheal Magdy

Institute
Languages and Translation (Modern Languages; Translation and Interpretation)

History: Founded 1994. Accredited 2006.

Admission Requirements: General Secondary Certificate

Accrediting Agency: Supreme Council for Universities

Degrees and Diplomas: *Lîsâns*

Student Services: Academic Counselling, Canteen, Language Laboratory, Nursery Care, Social Counselling, Sports Facilities
Last Updated: 10/12/12

AL-MADINA HIGHER INSTITUTE FOR INTERNATIONAL LANGUAGES

Shoubra Ment

Director: Ahmad Kamal Mohamed Safwat

Department
English (English); **French** (French); **German** (German)

Admission Requirements: Secondary school certificate (thanawya amma) or equivalent.

Degrees and Diplomas: *Lîsâns*

AL-OBOUR HIGHER INSTITUTE FOR ENGINEERING AND TECHNOLOGY

31 Km Ismailia Desert Road, Cairo
Tel: +20(2) 477-0037
Fax: +20(2) 241-3550

Director: Refa'at Rezq Baseli (2000-)

Programme
Architectural Engineering (Structural Architecture); **Computer and Control Technology Engineering** (Automation and Control Engineering; Computer Engineering); **Construction Engineering** (Construction Engineering); **Electronics and Communciation Technology Engineering** (Electronic Engineering; Telecommunications Engineering)

History: Founded 1996.

Main Language(s) of Instruction: English

Degrees and Diplomas: *Lîsâns*

AL-OBOUR HIGHER INSTITUTE FOR MANAGEMENT AND INFORMATICS

21, Belbais High Way, Sharquia
Tel: +20(2) 263-6882
Fax: +20(2) 403-0804
EMail: info@ahiedu.com

President: Abd Allah El-Dahshan

Programme
Business Administration (Accountancy; Business Administration; Management); **Computer Science** (Computer Science); **Management Information System** (Information Management; Information Sciences; Management)

History: Founded 1999.

Degrees and Diplomas: *Lîsâns*

ARAB ACADEMY FOR SCIENCE, TECHNOLOGY AND MARITIME TRANSPORT (AASTMT)

PO Box 1029, Gamal Abdel Nasser Street, Miami, Alexandria
Tel: +20(3) 556-1497 +20(3) 556-5429
Fax: +20(3) 548-7786 +20(3) 550-6042
EMail: admission@aast.edu; international.unit@aast.edu
Website: http://www.aast.edu

President: Ismail Abdel Ghafar (2011-)
EMail: ismail.ghafar@aast.edu

International Relations: Hanan Gouda, Director of Cooperation Unit EMail: hanan.gouda@aast.edu

College
Computing and Information Technology (Computer Science; Information Technology); **Engineering and Technology** (Architectural and Environmental Design; Automation and Control Engineering; Computer Engineering; Construction Engineering; Electrical and Electronic Engineering; Engineering; Industrial Engineering; Marine Engineering; Mechanical Engineering; Natural Sciences; Technology); **International Transport and Logistics** (Transport and Communications; Transport Management); **Management and Technology** (Accountancy; Arts and Humanities; Business Administration; Finance; Hotel Management; Management; Marketing; Modern Languages; Tourism); **Maritime Transport and Technology** (Marine Engineering; Marine Science and Oceanography; Marine Transport; Meteorology; Nautical Science; Safety Engineering)

Institute
Language Studies (English); **Marine Safety** (Safety Engineering); **Port Training** (Transport Management); **Productivity and Quality** (Management; Production Engineering); **Trade and Commodities Exchange** *(Arab)* (International Business; Retailing and Wholesaling)

Centre
Industrial Service Center; **Maritime Research and Consultation**

Graduate School
Business (Business Administration; Business and Commerce)

Further Information: Also campuses in Cairo, South Valley, Syria

History: Founded 1972. A specialized University in Maritime Transport and Building. The majority of national staff members and personnel provided by the Egyptian Government.

Academic Year: September to June

Admission Requirements: High school certificate and admission test

Main Language(s) of Instruction: English, Arabic

Degrees and Diplomas: *Lîsâns*: **Business and Commerce; Engineering; Transport Management.** *Diploma of Higher Studies*: **Computer Science; Engineering; Management.** *Mâjistêr*: **Computer Science; Engineering.** *Dukturâh*: **Business Administration.** Also Master's Degree in Computer Science from George Washington University, USA (off-campus degree)

Student Services: Academic Counselling, Canteen, Careers Guidance, Cultural Activities, Health Services, Language Laboratory, Social Counselling, Sports Facilities

Publications: Journal of Arab Maritime Academy; MRCC Research Magazine
Last Updated: 19/06/12

ARAB OPEN UNIVERSITY - EGYPT BRANCH

Intersection of Makram Ebeid Street and Abd Al-Razeq Al-Sanhoury Street, Nasr City, Cairo
Tel: +20(2) 671-1862 +20(2) 671-1865
Fax: +20(2) 671-1868
EMail: info@aou.edu.eg
Website: http://www.aou.edu.eg

Branch Director: Abdel Aziz Khamis

Faculty

Business Administration (Business Administration); **English Language and Literature** (English; Literature)

Programme

Information Technology and Computer Science (Computer Science; Information Technology)
Degrees and Diplomas: *Lîsâns*

CAIRO ACADEMY OF ARTS

Gamal El-Din Al-Afghani Str., Al-Haram Route, Giza
Tel: +20(2) 585-0727
Fax: +20(2) 561-1230
EMail: aoarts@idsc.gov.eg

Director: Awad Kamel Fahmi

Higher Institute

Arab Music (Music); **Art Criticism** (Art Criticism); **Ballet** (Dance); **Cinema** (Cinema and Television); **Folklore** (Folklore); **Theatre** (Theatre)

Conservatory

Music (Music)
History: Founded 1959. Acquired present status 1969.
Degrees and Diplomas: *Bachelor's Degree*; *Lîsâns*; *Mâjistêr*; *Dukturâh*
Last Updated: 19/06/12

CAIRO HIGHER INSTITUTE FOR COMPUTER, INFORMATION SYSTEMS AND ADMINISTRATION "AL-GOLF"

3, Samir Mokhtar Str., Nabil Al-Waqad Corner, Ard Al-Golf, Heliopolis
Tel: +20(2) 417-6550
Fax: +20(2) 417-6551

Director: Mohamed Abdul-Moneim Hashish (1995-)

Department

Business Administration and Information System (Business Administration; Information Sciences); **Computer Science** (Computer Science); **Engineering** (Electronic Engineering; Structural Architecture)
History: Founded 1995.
Degrees and Diplomas: *Lîsâns*: **Engineering.**

CAIRO HIGHER INSTITUTE FOR LANGUAGES, SIMULTANEOUS TRANSLATION AND ADMINISTRATIVE SCIENCES

Muqatam, Tugaryyan Station, 5 Str. N° 54, off Route 9, In front of Al-Quds Mosque, Cairo
Tel: +20(2) 508-1700
Fax: +20(2) 508-1613

Director: Mohamed Rehan Hussein (2002-)

Department

Administrative Sciences (Accountancy; Administration; Business Administration; International Business); **Computer Science** (Computer Science); **Languages and Simultaneous Translation** (Modern Languages; Translation and Interpretation)
History: Founded 1995.
Degrees and Diplomas: *Lîsâns*

CANADIAN INTERNATIONAL COLLEGE - CAIRO CAMPUS (CIC)

El Tagamoa El Khames, South of the Police Academy New Cairo City, New Cairo
Tel: +20(10) 288-0288
Fax: +20(2) 617-3110
EMail: admission@cic-cairo.com
Website: http://www.cic-cairo.com/cic/

President: Magdy El Kady
Tel: +20 16242 EMail: magdy_elkady@cic-cairo.com
Academic Vice-President: Roger Winn
Tel: +20 16242 EMail: roger_winn@cic-cairo.com
International Relations: Roger Winn

School

Business (Business Administration); **Engineering** (Electrical and Electronic Engineering; Engineering; Industrial Engineering; Technology); **Mass Communication** (Mass Communication)
History: Founded 2004.
Academic Year: September to May (September-January; February-May)
Fees: (Egyptian Pounds): 30,000
Main Language(s) of Instruction: English
Degrees and Diplomas: *Lîsâns*. Canadian Bachelor of Business Administration Degree, with concentrations (majors) available in Marketing, Finance, Accounting and Tourism Management; Canadian Bachelor of Technology in Manufacturing Engineering or Computer Systems Development.
Student Services: Academic Counselling, Canteen, Careers Guidance, Cultural Activities, Facilities for disabled people, Foreign Studies Centre, Health Services, Language Laboratory, Nursery Care, Social Counselling, Sports Facilities
Last Updated: 10/12/12

DELTA UNIVERSITY FOR SCIENCE AND TECHNOLOGY

Gamasa Coastal International Road, El Mansourah
EMail: info@deltauniv.edu.eg
Website: http://deltauniv.edu.eg

Rector: Abbas El-Hefnawy (2000-)
EMail: abbaselhefnawy@yahoo.com

Faculty

Business Administration (Business Administration); **Dentistry** (Dentistry); **Engineering** (Engineering); **Pharmacy** (Biochemistry; Biotechnology; Microbiology; Pharmacology; Pharmacy)
History: Acquired present status 2007. Formerly known as Delta Higher Institute for Computers.
Main Language(s) of Instruction: Arabic, English
Accrediting Agency: Ministry of Higher Education
Degrees and Diplomas: *Lîsâns*
Student Services: Academic Counselling, Canteen, Careers Guidance, Cultural Activities, Foreign Studies Centre, Health Services, Language Laboratory, Nursery Care, Social Counselling, Sports Facilities
Last Updated: 10/12/12

EGYPTIAN E-LEARNING UNIVERSITY

33, Elmesaha St., Dokki, Giza
Tel: +202 33318498
EMail: info@eelu.edu.eg
Website: http://www.eelu.edu.eg

President: Yasser Dakroury

Faculty

Business Administration (Accountancy; Banking; Business Administration; Management; Marketing); **Computer and Information Technology** (Information Technology); **Education** (Distance Education)
History: Founded 2008.
Accrediting Agency: Supreme Council of Universities
Degrees and Diplomas: *Lîsâns*; *Mâjistêr*
Last Updated: 20/06/12

EGYPTIAN HIGHER INSTITUTE FOR TOURISM AND HOTELS (EHITH)

6 Al-Obour St., Off Al-Tahrair St., behind Sheraton Airport Housing, Heliopolis
Tel: +20(2) 266-5951
Fax: +20(2) 266-5950

Director: Ahmad Abdul-Razek Mohamed (2001-)

Department
Hotel Management (Hotel Management); **Tourism Guidance** (Tourism); **Tourism Studies** (Tourism)

History: Founded 1992.

Main Language(s) of Instruction: Arabic and other Foreign Languages

Degrees and Diplomas: *Lîsâns*

EGYPTIAN HIGHER INSTITUTE OF THE ALEXANDRIA ACADEMY FOR ADMINISTRATION AND ACCOUNTING

Mosque Square, behind Al-Moursa Abu Al-Aabbas Mosque, Alexandria
Tel: +20(3) 484-3384

Director: Adel Abdel-Hamid Ez (2000-)

Department
Accountancy; **Auditing**; **Finance** (Finance); **Management** (Finance; Management)

History: Founded 1996.

Main Language(s) of Instruction: Arabic, English for programmes offered at the Management Department.

Degrees and Diplomas: *Lîsâns*

EGYPTIAN RUSSIAN UNIVERSITY (ERU)

Suez Road, Badr City
Tel: +20(2) 2864-3342
Fax: +20(2) 2864-3332
EMail: info@eruegypt.com
Website: http://eru.edu.eg

President: Sherif Helmy (2006-) EMail: president@eruegypt.com

Secretary-General: Ekram Agha

Faculty
Engineering (Aeronautical and Aerospace Engineering; Construction Engineering; Electronic Engineering; Energy Engineering; Engineering; Mechanical Engineering; Nuclear Engineering; Structural Architecture; Telecommunications Engineering); **Pharmacy** (Biochemistry; Chemistry; Microbiology; Pharmacy; Toxicology)

History: Founded 2006.

Admission Requirements: Thanaweya Amma (Secondary School Certificate) or equivalent

Main Language(s) of Instruction: English

Degrees and Diplomas: *Lîsâns*

Student Services: Academic Counselling, Canteen, Sports Facilities

Last Updated: 19/06/12

EL SHOROUK ACADEMY

El Abasya Square El Moltka Towers, Elnakheel Suburb, 6th of October City, Giza Al-Shorouk Academy
Tel: +20(2) 687-0881 +20(2) 687-0882 +20(2) 687-0883
Fax: +20(2) 687-0887
EMail: info@elshoroukacademy.edu.eg
Website: http://www.elshoroukacademy.edu.eg

President: Mohamed Farid Khamis

Higher Institute
Computer and Information Technology (Computer Engineering; Information Technology); **Engineering** (Biomedical Engineering; Computer Engineering; Construction Engineering; Electronic Engineering; Engineering; Industrial Engineering; Information Technology)

History: Founded 1995. Acquired present status 2002.

Admission Requirements: Secondary school certificate (Thanaweya Amma) or equivalent.

Degrees and Diplomas: *Lîsâns*

FRENCH UNIVERSITY IN EGYPT

Université française d'Egypte (UFE)

BP 21, Km 37 Cairo-Ismailia Highway, Shorouk City
Tel: +20(2) 687-34-00 +20(2) 687-52-52
Fax: +20(2) 687-53-53
EMail: info@ufe.eg.org
Website: http://www.ufe.edu.eg/

President: Hassan Nadir Kheirallah (2012-)

Faculty
Applied Languages (Arabic; English; French; Modern Languages; Translation and Interpretation); **Engineering** (Architecture; Automation and Control Engineering; Energy Engineering; Information Technology; Production Engineering; Telecommunications Engineering); **Management and Information Technology** (Cultural Studies; Information Management; Information Technology; Management)

Unit
Lifelong Education and Distance Education (Continuing Education; Distance Education)

History: Founded 2002.

Degrees and Diplomas: *Lîsâns*; *Mâjistêr*
Last Updated: 10/12/12

FUTURE ACADEMY

Cairo-Ismaïlia Road, Ismaïlia
Tel: +20(2) 477-22 48
Fax: +20(2) 477-1900
EMail: futureacademy@fa-hists.edu.eg
Website: http://futureacademyegypt.com/english/index.html

Dean: Saeed Tawfeek Ebid

Division
Business Administration and Accountancy (Accountancy; Business Administration); **Computer Science** (Computer Science); **Information Systems** (Information Technology)

History: Founded 1993.

Degrees and Diplomas: *Lîsâns*
Last Updated: 10/12/12

FUTURE UNIVERSITY

Al Tagamoa Al Khames, End of 90th Street, New Cairo
Tel: +20(2) 261-86100 +20(2) 261-86110
Fax: +20(2) 261-86111
EMail: info@fue.edu.eg
Website: http://www.futureuniversity.edu.eg

President: Ebada Sarhan

Faculty
Commerce and Business Administration (Business Administration; Business and Commerce); **Computers and Information Technology** (Computer Networks; Information Technology); **Economics and Political Science** (Economics; Political Sciences; Public Administration); **Engineering and Technology** (Architectural and Environmental Design; Biomedical Engineering; Computer Engineering; Electrical Engineering; Electronic Engineering; Engineering; Mechanical Engineering; Petroleum and Gas Engineering; Structural Architecture; Technology); **Oral and Dental Medicine** (Dentistry; Oral Pathology); **Pharmaceutical Sciences and Pharmaceutical Industries** (Pharmacy)

History: Founded 2006.

Accrediting Agency: Supreme Council of Universities

Degrees and Diplomas: *Lîsâns*; *Mâjistêr*
Last Updated: 10/12/12

HIGHER INSTITUTE FOR ADMINISTRATION AND COMPUTERS

Street 51, Next to the Labour University, Ras Al-Barr, Damietta

Department
Administration (Administration); **Computer Science** (Computer Science)

Degrees and Diplomas: *Lîsâns*

HIGHER INSTITUTE FOR ADMINISTRATION AND TECHNOLOGY

Sakkara Tourist Road, Shoubra Ment

Department
Business Administration (Business Administration; Finance; Industrial Management; Marketing); **Computer Sciences** (Computer Science; Information Sciences)

History: Founded 2000.

Degrees and Diplomas: *Lîsâns*

HIGHER INSTITUTE FOR ADMINISTRATION SCIENCES - 6TH OF OCTOBER CITY

Science and Culture City, Central area, Plot 1/1, Central Route, 6th of October City, Giza
Tel: +20(11) 354-271

Director: Mohamed Sayed Hamzawi

Department
Administration (Administration)

History: Founded 1994.

Degrees and Diplomas: *Lîsâns*

HIGHER INSTITUTE FOR ADMINISTRATION SCIENCES AND COMPUTERS

Seventh Neighbourhood, First Complex, New Cairo

Department
Administration (Administration); **Computer Science** (Computer Science)

Degrees and Diplomas: *Lîsâns*

HIGHER INSTITUTE FOR ADMINISTRATION SCIENCES AND FOREIGN TRADE

Fifth Urban Complex, third district, fourth zone, New Cairo

Programme
Administrative Information System (Administration; Information Sciences); **Business Administration** (Accountancy; Business Administration; Economics; International Business)

Degrees and Diplomas: *Lîsâns*

HIGHER INSTITUTE FOR ADMINISTRATION SCIENCES - NEW CAIRO

Qatamya, Mahmoudia - Housing Project, Third Complex, New Cairo

Department
Business Administration (Business Administration); **Information Administration System** (Computer Science; Information Sciences; Information Technology)

Degrees and Diplomas: *Lîsâns*

HIGHER INSTITUTE FOR APPLIED ARTS, 6TH OF OCTOBER CITY

First District, 6th of October City
Tel: +20(2) 835-2806
Fax: +20(2) 835-2807
EMail: info@appliedarts.org
Website: http://www.appliedarts.org

Chairman: Moustafa Kamal (1998-)
EMail: profkamal@appliedarts.org

Dean: Mahmoud Ahmad Abdel A'al

Department
Decoration and Interior Design (Furniture Design; Interior Design); **Fashion** (Fashion Design; Jewellery Art; Textile Design); **Graphics and Advertising** (Advertising and Publicity; Graphic Arts); **Industrial Design** (Industrial Design)

History: Founded 1994.

Admission Requirements: General secondary school certificate and Skills Test

Main Language(s) of Instruction: Arabic and English

Accrediting Agency: Supreme Council of Universities

Degrees and Diplomas: *Lîsâns*
Last Updated: 19/06/12

HIGHER INSTITUTE FOR CIVIL AND ARCHITECTURAL ENGINEERING

15th of May City, Third Neighbourhood, Helwan

Department
Architectural Engineering (Structural Architecture); **Civil Engineering** (Civil Engineering)

Degrees and Diplomas: *Lîsâns*

HIGHER INSTITUTE FOR COMMERCE AND ECOLOGY

Science and Culture City, Central Area, plot 1/1, 6th of October City, Giza

Department
Business and Commerce; **Ecology** (Ecology)

Degrees and Diplomas: *Lîsâns*

HIGHER INSTITUTE FOR COMMERCIAL SCIENCES AND COMPUTERS

Army Suburb, behind the Education Directorate, Al-Arish, North Sinai

Department
Business and Commerce (Business and Commerce); **Computer Science** (Computer Science)

Degrees and Diplomas: *Lîsâns*

HIGHER INSTITUTE FOR COMPUTER SCIENCES AND INFORMATION SYSTEMS - 6TH OF OCTOBER CITY

Science and Culture City, Central Area, plot 1/1, 6th of October City, Giza
Tel: +20(11) 231-041

Director: Hussein Magdy Zain Al-Din (2001-)

Department
Computer Science (Computer Science); **Information Systems** (Information Management)

History: Founded 1994.

Degrees and Diplomas: *Lîsâns*

HIGHER INSTITUTE FOR COMPUTER SCIENCES AND INFORMATION SYSTEMS - NEW CAIRO

Fifth Urban Complex, Third District, Fourth Zone, New Cairo

Department
Computer Science (Computer Science); **Information Systems** (Information Management)

Degrees and Diplomas: *Lîsâns*

HIGHER INSTITUTE FOR COMPUTER SCIENCES AND MANAGEMENT TECHNOLOGY

Al-Kouser district, Sohag
Tel: +20(93) 605-714

Director: Ahmad Abdel A'al Al-Darder (1999-)

Department
Computer Science (Computer Science); **Management Technology** (Management Systems)

History: Founded 1996.

Degrees and Diplomas: *Lîsâns*

HIGHER INSTITUTE FOR COMPUTER STUDIES

31 Km Al-Kafouri, Cairo Desert Road, King Mariot
Tel: +20(3) 448-3200
EMail: info_king@kinginstitutes.edu.eg; computer_king@kinginstitutes.edu.eg
Website: http://www.kma.edu.eg/en

Department
Computer Science (Computer Science)

History: Founded 1996.

Degrees and Diplomas: *Lîsâns*
Last Updated: 22/06/12

HIGHER INSTITUTE FOR COMPUTERS AND ADMINISTRATION INFORMATION SYSTEMS

Street 72 off Street 9, across from Al-Quds Mosque, Higher Elevation, Muqatam

Department
Computer Science (Computer Science); **Information Management** (Information Management)

Degrees and Diplomas: *Lîsâns*

HIGHER INSTITUTE FOR COMPUTERS AND BUSINESS ADMINISTRATION

High Way, Al-Zarqa City, Damietta
Tel: +20(57) 852-236

Director: Rashed Mokhtar (2002-)

Department
Business Administration (Business Administration); **Computer Science** (Computer Science)

History: Founded 1999.

Degrees and Diplomas: *Lîsâns*

HIGHER INSTITUTE FOR COMPUTERS AND INFORMATION SYSTEMS

Toson's Land, Abi Qier, Abi Qier

Department
Computer Science (Computer Science); **Information Systems**

Degrees and Diplomas: *Lîsâns*

HIGHER INSTITUTE FOR COOPERATIVE AND ADMINISTRATIVE STUDIES (HICAS)

Al-Mounira, Sayeda Zainab, Cairo
Tel: +20(2) 795-5135
Fax: +20(2) 795-5686

Programme
Administration (Administration); **Public Administration** (Public Administration); **Social Services** (Social and Community Services)

Degrees and Diplomas: *Lîsâns*

HIGHER INSTITUTE FOR DEVELOPED STUDIES

12 Sherif Str., off Al-Haram Str., besides Al-Farouq School, Haram, Giza
Tel: +20(2) 386-0008 +20(2) 384-4030
Fax: +20(2) 388-5405

Department
Computer Science; **Trade and Accountancy**

History: Founded 1995.

Degrees and Diplomas: *Lîsâns*

HIGHER INSTITUTE FOR ECONOMICS AND THE ENVIRONMENT

Division 1/1, Central Road, 6th of October City, Giza
Tel: +20(11) 231-161

Programme
Economics and Environmental Studies (Economics; Environmental Studies)

History: Founded 1994.

Degrees and Diplomas: *Lîsâns*

HIGHER INSTITUTE FOR ENGINEERING

Neighbourhood n°13, 10th of Ramadan City
Tel: +20(15) 365-667

Programme
Engineering (Engineering)

History: Founded 1995.

Degrees and Diplomas: *Lîsâns*

HIGHER INSTITUTE FOR HOTEL MANAGEMENT "EGOTH"

31, Mostafa Abou Hief Street, Saba Basha, Alexandria
Tel: +20(2) 583-3924 +20(2) 583-3706
Fax: +20(2) 584-2873
EMail: egoth@dataxprs.com.eg
Website: http://www.egoth.com.eg/en/alex.htm

Programme
Hotel Management (Hotel Management)

Degrees and Diplomas: *Lîsâns*

HIGHER INSTITUTE FOR HOTEL MANAGEMENT "EGOTH"

10 Ahmed Orabi st., Luxor
Tel: +20(95) 237-4821 +20(95) 236-5351
Fax: +20(95) 237-3357
Website: http://www.egoth.com.eg/en/luxor.htm

Programme
Hotel Management (Hotel Management)

Degrees and Diplomas: *Lîsâns*

HIGHER INSTITUTE FOR INDUSTRIAL ENGINEERING

Division 1/1, Central Route, 6th of October City, Giza
Tel: +20(11) 355-275

Head: Ali Mohamed Tal'at

Programme
Industrial Engineering (Industrial Engineering)

History: Founded 1994.

Main Language(s) of Instruction: English and Arabic

Degrees and Diplomas: *Lîsâns*

HIGHER INSTITUTE FOR LANGUAGES (HIL)

Terminal of Nozha Metro, Sheraton Housing Project, Heliopolis 17361
Tel: +20(2) 226-72689
Fax: +20(2) 226-72689

Head: Fawzia El Sadr EMail: prof.fawziasadr@yahoo.com

Administrative Officer: Mohamed Abdel Salam

International Relations: Ahmed Al-Kahby Tel: +20(0) 050-63531

Department
English Language and Literature (English; Literature); **French Language and Literature** (French; Literature); **German Language and Literature** (German; Literature); **Spanish Language and Literature** (Literature; Spanish)

Further Information: A Department of Italian Language and Literature is being established.

History: Founded 1993.

Academic Year: December to May (2 academic terms)

Admission Requirements: General Secondary Education Certificate or IGC

Fees: (Egyptian Pounds): 1st year, 1,970; 2nd year, 2,840; 3rd year, 2,985; 4th year, 2,850

Main Language(s) of Instruction: Arabic, English, German, Spanish, French, Italian

Accrediting Agency: The Supreme Council of Higher Education for B.A. and Ain-Shams University for Postgraduate Studies

Degrees and Diplomas: *Lîsâns*: **Foreign Languages Education; French; German; Literature; Spanish.**

Student Services: Academic Counselling, Canteen, Careers Guidance, Cultural Activities, Foreign Studies Centre, Health Services, Language Laboratory, Social Counselling, Sports Facilities

Publications: El Shabab in Arabic

Publishing House: University Printing House

HIGHER INSTITUTE FOR LANGUAGES

Division 1/1, Central Route, 6th of October City, Giza
Tel: +20(11) 231-161
Fax: +20(2) 231-560

Programme
Modern Languages (Modern Languages)

History: Founded 1994.

Degrees and Diplomas: *Lîsâns*

HIGHER INSTITUTE FOR LITERARY STUDIES

Km 31 Al-Kafouri, Cairo Desert Road, Al-Kafouri, King Mariott, Alexandria
Tel: +20(2) 484-6155
Website: http://www.kma.edu.eg/en

Programme
Literary Studies (Arts and Humanities; Literature)

Degrees and Diplomas: *Lîsâns*

Last Updated: 22/06/12

HIGHER INSTITUTE FOR MASS MEDIA AND COMMUNICATION

Science and Culture City, Central area, Plot 1/1, 6th of October City, Giza
Tel: +20(11) 355-281
Fax: +20(2) 266-4472

Department
Communication Studies (Communication Studies); **Media Studies** (Media Studies)

History: Founded 1994.

Degrees and Diplomas: *Lîsâns*

HIGHER INSTITUTE FOR OPTICS TECHNOLOGY

6 Al-Obour Str., off Al-Tahrair str., Al-Sheraton blocks, Heliopolis
Tel: +20(2) 2267-2688
Fax: +20(2) 2267-2688
EMail: kmshasan@link.net

Dean: Karam Mahmoud El-Shazly (2008-) Tel: +20(10) 560-2735

Department
Information Systems (Information Technology); **Optical Technology** (Optical Technology)

Academic Year: September to June (September-January; February-June)

Admission Requirements: Secondary School Certificate and Diploma from a Medium Institute for Optics

Main Language(s) of Instruction: English and Arabic

Degrees and Diplomas: *Lîsâns*

Student Services: Academic Counselling, Canteen, Careers Guidance, Cultural Activities, Foreign Studies Centre, Health Services, Language Laboratory, Nursery Care, Social Counselling, Sports Facilities

Last Updated: 10/12/12

HIGHER INSTITUTE FOR SOCIAL SERVICES - 6TH OF OCTOBER CITY

Science and Culture City, Central Area, Plot 1/1, 6th of October City, Giza
Tel: +20(11) 355-276

Programme
Social Services (Social and Community Services)

History: Founded 1994.

Degrees and Diplomas: *Lîsâns*

HIGHER INSTITUTE FOR SOCIAL SERVICES - ALEXANDRIA

72, Al-Resafa Street, Moharam Bey, Alexandria
Tel: +20(3) 494-8190
Fax: +20(3) 495-1560

Department
Community Order; **Community Service** (Social and Community Services); **Fundamental Sciences**; **Individual Services** (Social and Community Services; Social Work); **Social Planning** (Social Welfare)

History: Founded 1934.

Degrees and Diplomas: *Lîsâns*

HIGHER INSTITUTE FOR SOCIAL SERVICES - ASWAN

Qisar Al-Hagar Street, Aswan
Tel: +20(97) 314-995

Programme
Social Services (Social and Community Services)

History: Founded 1974.

Degrees and Diplomas: *Lîsâns*

HIGHER INSTITUTE FOR SOCIAL SERVICES - DAMANHOUR

Damanhour
Tel: +20(45) 315-386
Fax: +20(45) 318-420

Department
Social Services (Social and Community Services)

History: Founded 1980.

Degrees and Diplomas: *Lîsâns*

HIGHER INSTITUTE FOR SOCIAL SERVICES - KAFR AL-SHEIKH

Al-Gaish Street, Qisar Al-Malak, Kafr Al-Sheikh
Tel: +20(47) 227-835
Fax: +20(47) 223-184

Department
Social Services (Social and Community Services)

History: Founded 1971.

Degrees and Diplomas: *Lîsâns*

HIGHER INSTITUTE FOR SOCIAL SERVICES - MANSOURA

Abdel-Salam Aref Str., Talkha, Mansoura
Tel: +20(50) 367-077

Programme
Social Services (Social and Community Services)

History: Founded 1995.

Degrees and Diplomas: *Lîsâns*

HIGHER INSTITUTE FOR SOCIAL SERVICES - NEW BANHA

Al-Almal Hospital Str., New Banha
Tel: +20(13) 235-885
Fax: +20(13) 220-554

Programme
Social Services (Social and Community Services)

History: Founded 1993.

Degrees and Diplomas: *Lîsâns*

HIGHER INSTITUTE FOR SOCIAL SERVICES - PORT-SAID

Close to Al-Raswa Port, Port-Said
Tel: +20(66) 324-365

Department
Social Services (Social and Community Services)

History: Founded 1981.

Degrees and Diplomas: *Lîsâns*

HIGHER INSTITUTE FOR SOCIAL SERVICES - QENA

Qena
Tel: +20(96) 334-908

Programme
Social Services (Social and Community Services)

History: Founded 1997.

Degrees and Diplomas: *Lîsâns*

HIGHER INSTITUTE FOR SOCIAL SERVICES - SOHAG

Al Kosar district, Akhmem, Sohag
Tel: +20(93) 640-222

Programme
Social Services (Social and Community Services)

History: Founded 1993.

Degrees and Diplomas: *Lîsâns*

HIGHER INSTITUTE FOR SOCIAL WORK - CAIRO

Nasr City, Abdel Latif Hamza Str., Off Ahmed Fakhari str., Sixth area, Cairo
Tel: +20(2) 2272-0557
Fax: +20(2) 2272-0556
EMail: c.g.c@hisw-cairo.com; cgcp@hisw-cairo.com
Website: http://www.hisw-cairo.com

Dean: Ikbal El-Samaloty (1974-)

Senior Administrative Officer: Amin Gamil

Department
Community Organization (Social and Community Services); **Community Services and Social Planning**; **Fundamental Sciences**; **Group Work**; **Individual Services and Case Work** (Social and Community Services; Social Work); **Social Work**

History: Founded 1937 through the Egyptian Association of Social Studies.

Academic Year: September to May (September-January; February-May)

Admission Requirements: Secondary school certificate

Fees: (Egyptian Pounds): 1st year, 668; 2nd year, 632; 3rd year, 615; 4th year, 599 per annum

Main Language(s) of Instruction: Arabic

Accrediting Agency: Ministry of Higher Education and Scientific Research

Degrees and Diplomas: *Bachelor's Degree*: **Family Studies; Social Work.** *Lîsâns*

Student Services: Academic Counselling, Canteen, Careers Guidance, Cultural Activities, Facilities for disabled people, Health Services, Language Laboratory, Nursery Care, Social Counselling, Sports Facilities

Publications: Cairo Magazine for Social Work

Publishing House: Dar El-Mohandes Printing Press

Last Updated: 10/12/12

HIGHER INSTITUTE FOR SPECIFIC STUDIES (HISS)

General Moh Aly Fahmy street behind Siag Hotel, Haram, Giza, Pyramids
Tel: +20(2) 385-9104
Fax: +20(2) 384-5505 +20(2) 374-26552
EMail: info@tmaegypt.com

Chairman: Mohamed Elbatran
Tel: +202(358) 50660 EMail: mbatran@idsc.gov.eg

Dean: Mohse Elbatran Tel: +202(385) 9104

International Relations: May Elbatran Tel: +202(374) 26557-8

Department
Computer Science; **Economics and Business Administration**; **Languages** (English; French; German; Modern Languages); **TMA Development, Training and Consulting** (Computer Science; Environmental Studies; Industrial Management; Management); **Tourism and Hotel Management**

History: Founded 1994.

Academic Year: September to June

Admission Requirements: Thanaweya Amma, High school diploma

Fees: (Egyptian Pounds): 1,400-1,600 (for Egyptians); 1,000 (for non-Egyptian)

Main Language(s) of Instruction: Arabic, English for the Language Department and some Business Administration courses

Accrediting Agency: Ministry of Higher Education

Degrees and Diplomas: *Lîsâns*. Also Diplomas and certificates for short courses (2days to 9 months)

Student Services: Canteen, Health Services, Sports Facilities

Last Updated: 10/12/12

HIGHER INSTITUTE FOR SPECIFIC STUDIES (HISTSH)

154 Al-Hegaz Square, Heliopolis

Department
Hotel Management (Hotel Management); **Tourism Guidance** (Tourism); **Tourism Studies** (Tourism)

Degrees and Diplomas: *Lîsâns*

HIGHER INSTITUTE FOR TOURISM AND HOTELS (CHITH)

Sixth District, 6th of October City
Tel: +202-38334002
EMail: hith@must.edu.eg
Website: http://hith.must.edu.eg

Dean: Hassan El-Mansoury

Department
Hotel Management (Hotel Management); **Tour Guidance** (Tourism); **Tourism Studies** (Tourism)

History: Founded 1990.

Academic Year: September to December and from February to May

Admission Requirements: Secondary school certificate and admission test

Main Language(s) of Instruction: Arabic, English and French

Accrediting Agency: Supreme Council of Universities

Degrees and Diplomas: *Lîsâns*

Last Updated: 19/06/12

HIGHER INSTITUTE FOR TOURISM AND HOTELS - ALEXANDRIA (HITHK)

Km 31 Cairo Desert Road, Al-Kafouri, King Mariout, Alexandria
EMail: info_king@kinginstitutes.edu.eg; tourism_king@kinginstitutes.edu.eg
Website: http://www.kma.edu.eg/en

Department
Hotels Studies (Hotel Management); **Tourism Guidance** (Tourism); **Tourism Studies** (Tourism)

History: Founded 1996.

Degrees and Diplomas: *Lîsâns*

HIGHER INSTITUTE FOR TOURISM AND HOTELS - HURGHADA

Safaga road, Red Sea, Hurghada
Tel: +20(2) 290-1017 +20 65 3464-801
Fax: +20 65-3464-810
EMail: info@hihtm.com.eg
Website: http://www.hihtmhurghada.com

Dean: Abd-Elfatah El-Sabahy

Chairman: Kamel Hassan Abo Ali
Tel: +20 65-3464-802 EMail: kamel@pickalbotros.com

Vice-President: Khaled Abd-El-Salam
EMail: khaled@hihtm.com.eg

Programme
Hotel Management and Tourism (Hotel Management; Tourism)

History: Founded 2000.

Fees: (Egyptian Pounds): 4,200 per annum

Main Language(s) of Instruction: Arabic

Degrees and Diplomas: *Lîsâns*

Student Services: Foreign Studies Centre, Health Services, Language Laboratory, Sports Facilities

HIGHER INSTITUTE FOR TOURISM, HOTELS AND COMPUTERS (HITHC)

2, Adel Mostafa Chawki St., Seyouf, Alexandria
Tel: +20(3) 526-1505 +20(3) 526-0377
Fax: +20(3) 526-5254
Website: http://www.seyouf.org/en/main/home

Department
Business and information Systems Management (Business Administration; Information Sciences; Management); **Hotel Management** (Hotel Management); **Tourism** (Tourism)

History: Founded 1992. Acquired present status 1994.

Main Language(s) of Instruction: Arabic, English, French, German.

Accrediting Agency: Supreme Council of Universities

Degrees and Diplomas: *Lîsâns*

HIGHER INSTITUTE FOR TOURISM, HOTELS AND MONUMENTS RESTORATION

7 Mostafa Kamel St., Behind Faculty Of Physical Education For Boys, Abou Kir

Department
Hotel Management (Hotel Management); **Monuments Restoration** (Restoration of Works of Art); **Tourism Studies**

Degrees and Diplomas: *Lîsâns*

HIGHER INTERNATIONAL INSTITUTE FOR LANGUAGES AND SIMULTANEOUS INTERPRETATION

Fifth urban complex, New Cairo

Programme
Languages; **Simultaneous Interpretation** (Translation and Interpretation)

Degrees and Diplomas: *Lîsâns*

HIGHER TECHNOLOGICAL INSTITUTE (HTI)

PO Box 228, Industrial Area 2, Next to Small Industries Complex, 10th of Ramadan City
Tel: +20(15) 363-497
Fax: +20(15) 351-296
Website: http://www.hti.edu.eg

Dean: Amr m.A. Amin

Department
Computer Science (Computer Networks; Computer Science); **Engineering** (Biomedical Engineering; Chemical Engineering; Civil Engineering; Computer Engineering; Electrical Engineering; Engineering; Environmental Engineering; Mechanical Engineering; Structural Architecture; Textile Technology); **Technology Management and Information** (Accountancy; Economics; Finance; Insurance; Management; Marketing; Political Sciences)

Further Information: Also branches in Matrouh and 6th of October City.

History: Founded 1987.

Academic Year: September to July (3 semesters)

Admission Requirements: General Secondary School Certificate (Thanaweya Am'ma); International General Certificate of Secondary Education (IGCSE) or equivalent

Fees: (Egyptian Pounds): 10,000 per annum

Main Language(s) of Instruction: English, Arabic

Accrediting Agency: Supreme Council of Universities; Ministry of Higher Education

Degrees and Diplomas: *Lîsâns*: **Business Computing; Engineering.**

Student Services: Academic Counselling, Canteen, Careers Guidance, Cultural Activities, Language Laboratory, Social Counselling, Sports Facilities

Last Updated: 10/12/12

INSTITUTE FOR ADMINISTRATION AND SECRETARIAT

2 New Woman St., Misr Al-Qadima

Programme
Administration (Administration); **Secretarial Studies**

History: Founded 1960 as a vocational institute. Acquired present status 1998.

Degrees and Diplomas: *Bachelor's Degree*; *Lîsâns*

INSTITUTE OF ARAB STUDIES

1 Association of Arab Lawyers St., Garden City, Cairo
Tel: +20(2) 795-1648 +20(2) 792-2679
Fax: +20(2) 796-2543
Website: http://www.iars.net

Department

Economy (Economics); **Education** (Education); **Geography** (Geography); **Heritage Verification** (Heritage Preservation); **History** (History); **Law** (Law); **Literature and Language** (Literature; Modern Languages); **Mass Media** (Mass Communication; Media Studies); **Political Sciences** (Political Sciences); **Sociology** (Sociology)

History: Founded 1952.

Degrees and Diplomas: *Bachelor's Degree*; *Mâjistêr*; *Dukturâh*

INTERNATIONAL ACADEMY FOR ENGINEERING AND MEDIA SCIENCE (IAEMS)

Egyptian Media Production City, Oasis Rd., 6th of October City
Tel: +20(2) 855-5380
Fax: +20(2) 855-5489
EMail: info@iams.edu.eg
Website: http://www.iams.edu.eg

President: Mohamed Safwat El-Sherif

Department

Media Engineering (Engineering; Media Studies); **Media Science** (Media Studies)

History: Founded 2002.

Degrees and Diplomas: *Lîsâns*. Also offers specialized technical diplomas and advanced training courses

MISR INTERNATIONAL UNIVERSITY

Cairo-Ismalia Road, Km 28, Cairo
Tel: +20(2) 2477-2033
EMail: miu@miuegypt.edu.eg
Website: http://www.miuegypt.edu.eg/

President: Mohamed Shebl El Komy

Faculty

Al Alsun (English; Linguistics; Translation and Interpretation); **Business Administration and International Trade** (Accountancy; Business Administration; Economics; Finance; International Business; Marketing); **Computer Science** (Computer Science; Information Technology; Software Engineering; Systems Analysis); **Dentistry** (Anatomy; Biochemistry; Botany; Chemistry; Dentistry; Microbiology; Pathology; Pharmacology; Physics; Physiology; Surgery; Zoology); **Engineering** (Architecture; Electronic Engineering; Engineering; Telecommunications Engineering); **Mass Communication** (Advertising and Publicity; Journalism; Mass Communication; Public Relations; Radio and Television Broadcasting); **Pharmacy** (Pharmacy)

History: Founded 1996.

Accrediting Agency: Supreme Council of Universities

Degrees and Diplomas: *Lîsâns*

Last Updated: 20/06/12

IAU MISR UNIVERSITY FOR SCIENCE AND TECHNOLOGY (MUST)

P.O. Box 77, Al Motamayez District, 6th of October City, Giza
Tel: +20(11) 3835-468
Fax: +20(11) 3835-4699
EMail: must@must.edu.eg
Website: http://www.must.edu.eg

President: Muhammad H. El-Azzazi Tel: +20(11) 354-708

International Relations: Muhammad El-Saadani, Vice-President, International Relations Commissioner EMail: vp@must.edu.eg

Faculty

Archaeology and Tourism Guidance (Ancient Civilizations; Archaeology; Heritage Preservation; Tourism); **Biotechnology** (Biotechnology); **Engineering** (Biomedical Engineering; Computer Engineering; Construction Engineering; Electronic Engineering; Industrial Engineering; Software Engineering; Structural Architecture; Telecommunications Engineering); **Foreign Languages** (Arabic; Chinese; English; French; German; Greek; Italian; Japanese; Modern Languages; Spanish; Translation and Interpretation); **Information Technology** (Computer Science; Information Technology); **Mass Media** (Advertising and Publicity; Journalism; Public Relations; Radio and Television Broadcasting)

College

Applied Medical Science (Laboratory Techniques; Nursing; Radiology; Respiratory Therapy); **Business** (Accountancy; Business Administration; Business and Commerce; Computer Science; Economic and Finance Policy; Finance; Health Administration; Information Sciences; Political Sciences); **Dental Surgery** (Dentistry; Surgery); **Medicine** (Medicine); **Pharmacy** (Pharmacy); **Physical Therapy** (Physical Therapy)

History: Founded 1996.

Main Language(s) of Instruction: Arabic and English

Accrediting Agency: Supreme Council of Universities

Degrees and Diplomas: *Lîsâns*; *Mâjistêr*, *Dukturâh*

Student Services: Academic Counselling, Canteen, Careers Guidance, Cultural Activities, Foreign Studies Centre, Health Services, Language Laboratory, Nursery Care, Social Counselling, Sports Facilities

Last Updated: 20/06/12

MODERN ACADEMY

304 Saqr Qureish St, New Maadi
Tel: +20(2)) 72 70 518
EMail: infocs@modern-academy.edu.eg
Website: http://www.modern-academy.edu.eg

Dean: Nabil Deabes

Department

Computer Science and Management Technology (Accountancy; Computer Science; Economics; Management); **Engineering and Technology** (Architecture; Building Technologies; Computer Engineering; Electronic Engineering; Information Technology; Production Engineering)

History: Founded 1993. Acquired present status 2001.

Degrees and Diplomas: *Lîsâns*: **Accountancy; Administration; Business and Commerce; Business Computing; Computer Science; Engineering.** *Mâjistêr*: **Computer Engineering; Electrical Engineering; Electronic Engineering; Telecommunications Engineering.** *Dukturâh*: **Electronic Engineering.**

MODERN SCIENCES AND ARTS UNIVERSITY (MSA)

11/14 Amer Street, off Mesaha Square, Dokki, Giza
Tel: +20(2) 3837-1517
Fax: +20(2) 3837-1543
EMail: Info@msa.eun.eg; admission@msa.eun.eg
Website: http://www.msa.eun.eg

President: Khayri Abd El Hamied Tel: +20(2) 336-7844

Secretary-General: Omayma Ouf

Faculty

Arts and Design (Cinema and Television; Fashion Design; Graphic Arts; Interior Design; Landscape Architecture; Media Studies; Theatre); **Biotechnology** (Analytical Chemistry; Biochemistry; Biology; Biotechnology; Cell Biology; Molecular Biology; Organic Chemistry); **Computer Science** (Computer Science); **Dentistry** (Dentistry); **Engineering** (Computer Engineering; Engineering; Industrial Engineering); **Languages** (Arabic; English; Translation and Interpretation); **Management** (Accountancy; Economics; Management; Marketing); **Mass Communication** (Advertising and Publicity; Journalism; Mass Communication; Public Relations; Radio and Television Broadcasting); **Pharmacy** (Pharmacy)

History: Founded 1996.

Degrees and Diplomas: *Lîsâns*. A British Bachelor's Degree is also offered.

Last Updated: 10/12/12

MODERN UNIVERSITY FOR TECHNOLOGY AND INFORMATION

Elhadaba Elwosta, Mokatam, 5th District, Cairo
Tel: +20(2) 727-2145
Fax: +20(2) 727-2148
EMail: Info@mti.edu.eg
Website: http://www.mti.edu.eg

President: Olfat Kamel

Faculty

Computer Science (Computer Science; Information Technology); **Engineering** (Civil Engineering; Electrical Engineering; Engineering; Mechanical Engineering; Structural Architecture); **Management** (Accountancy; Economics; Finance; Information Management; Management; Marketing); **Mass Communication** (Advertising and Publicity; Journalism; Mass Communication; Media Studies; Public Relations; Radio and Television Broadcasting); **Nursing** (Nursing); **Pharmacy** (Pharmacy)

History: Founded 2004.

Accrediting Agency: Supreme Council of Universities

Degrees and Diplomas: *Lîsâns*; *Mâjistêr*; *Dukturâh*
Last Updated: 10/12/12

NAHDA UNIVERSITY

Nahda University Road, Beni-Suef
Tel: +20(82) 224-668-011
EMail: nub@nub.edu.eg
Website: http://www.nahdauniversity.org

President: Seddik Afifi

Faculty

Computer Science (Computer Science; Information Technology); **Marketing and Business Administration** (Accountancy; Business Administration; E- Business/Commerce; Management; Marketing); **Mass Communication** (Mass Communication; Media Studies; Printing and Printmaking); **Oral and Dental Medicine** (Dental Hygiene; Dentistry; Oral Pathology); **Pharmacy** (Analytical Chemistry; Biochemistry; Microbiology; Pharmacology; Pharmacy)

History: Founded 2006. Acquired present status 2007.

Accrediting Agency: Supreme Council of Universities

Degrees and Diplomas: *Lîsâns*
Last Updated: 20/06/12

NILE UNIVERSITY

Smart Village - B2 - Km 28, Cairo-Alex Desert Rd, Cairo 12677
Tel: +20(2) 3534 2072
EMail: info@nileuniversity.edu.eg
Website: http://www.nileu.edu.eg

President: Tarek Khalil

Secretary-General: Hani Keira

School

Business (Business Administration); **Communications and Information Technology** (Computer Engineering; Electronic Engineering; Information Technology; Radio and Television Broadcasting; Software Engineering); **Engineering and Applied Sciences** (Construction Engineering; Industrial Engineering; Industrial Management; Nanotechnology; Transport and Communications)

Graduate School

Management of Technology (Business Administration; Finance; Marketing; Technology)

History: Founded 2006.

Accrediting Agency: Ministry of Higher Education

Degrees and Diplomas: *Lîsâns*; *Mâjistêr*; *Dukturâh*
Last Updated: 20/06/12

OCTOBER 6 UNIVERSITY (O6U)

Giza-Governerate, Central Axis-Plot 1, 6th of October City, Giza
Tel: +20(2) 835-3942 +20(2) 835-3987
Fax: +20(2) 835-3867 +20(2) 835-3987
EMail: President-office@o6u.edu.eg
Website: http://www.o6u.edu.eg

President: Ahmed Attia Seida
EMail: ahmedseida@hotmail.com

Vice-President for Postgraduate Studies and Research: Talaat Rihan EMail: trihan@o6u.edu.eg

International Relations: Abdellatif Kheireldin
Tel: +20(2) 835-3987 EMail: kheiredin@o6u.edu.eg

Faculty

Applied Arts (Advertising and Publicity; Cinema and Television; Design; Furniture Design; Photography); **Applied Medical Sciences** (Laboratory Techniques; Nursing; Radiology); **Dentistry** (Dentistry); **Economics and Management** (Accountancy; Economics; Management; Political Sciences); **Education** (Arabic; Biology; Curriculum; Education; Educational Psychology; Mathematics and Computer Science; Modern Languages; Special Education); **Engineering** (Architecture; Building Technologies; Computer Engineering; Construction Engineering; Electrical Engineering; Electronic Engineering; Industrial Engineering; Mechanical Engineering); **Hotel Management and Tourism** (Hotel Management; Tourism); **Information Systems and Computer Science** (Computer Science; Information Sciences); **Languages and Translation** (English; French; German; Modern Languages; Spanish; Translation and Interpretation); **Media and Mass Communication** (Advertising and Publicity; Journalism; Mass Communication; Media Studies; Public Relations; Radio and Television Broadcasting); **Medicine** (Medicine); **Pharmacy** (Pharmacy); **Physiotherapy** (Physical Therapy); **Social Sciences** (Library Science; Political Sciences; Psychology; Theatre)

Further Information: University Hospital

History: Founded 1996.

Admission Requirements: High school certificate

Accrediting Agency: Supreme Council of Universities

Degrees and Diplomas: *Bachelor's Degree*; *Lîsâns*; *Mâjistêr*
Last Updated: 20/06/12

OCTOBER HIGH INSTITUTE FOR ENGINEERING AND TECHNOLOGY

Third District, 2nd Zone, 6th of October City, Giza
Tel: +20(23) 835-6496 +20(23) 606-9292
Fax: +20(23) 835-9464
EMail: hi4ab@hiinstitutearch.com
Website: http://www.hiinstitutearch.com

Chairman: Basma Sherin

International Relations: Basma Sherin Bayoumy, Head of International Relations EMail: basma_shr@hotmail.com

School

Business Administration (Banking; Business Administration; Computer Science; Marketing)

Department

Architectural Engineering (Architectural Restoration; Architecture; Building Technologies; Environmental Engineering; Heritage Preservation)

History: Founded 1993. Acquired status 1999.

Academic Year: Sept - July

Fees: (Egyptian Pounds): 6,995 per annum for home students; 3,000 first year, 1,500 subsequent years for overseas students (Architecture); 3,520 per annum for home students; 2,000 first year, 1,000 subsequent years for overseas students (Business Administration)

Main Language(s) of Instruction: Arabic, English

Degrees and Diplomas: *Lîsâns*: **Architecture; Business Administration; Engineering.**

Student Services: Canteen, Careers Guidance, Sports Facilities

Student Numbers *2012-2013*: Total 165
Last Updated: 19/06/12

PHARAOHS HIGHER INSTITUTE FOR COMPUTERS AND INFORMATION ADMINISTRATION

Sakkarra Road, Km 9, Marriott - Haram, Giza

Programme

Computer Science; **Information Management** (Information Management)

Degrees and Diplomas: *Lîsâns*

PHARAOHS HIGHER INSTITUTE FOR TOURISM AND HOTELS

Sakkarra Tourism Road, Km 9, Marriott - Haram, Giza

Programme

Hotel Management and Tourism (Hotel Management; Tourism)

History: Founded 2000.

Degrees and Diplomas: *Lîsâns*

PHAROS UNIVERSITY IN ALEXANDRIA (PUA)

Pharos University, Canal, El Mahmoudia Street, Beside Green Plaza Complex, Alexandria
Tel: +20(3) 387-7200
Fax: +20(3) 383-0249
EMail: info@pua.edu.eg
Website: http://www.pua.edu.eg

President: Abd Al Monem Mousa

Faculty

Allied Medical Sciences (Laboratory Techniques; Nursing; Radiology); **Arts and Design** (Fashion Design; Furniture Design; Graphic Design; Industrial Design; Interior Design); **Dentistry** (Dentistry; Oral Pathology; Orthodontics; Periodontics; Surgery); **Engineering** (Architectural and Environmental Design; Chemical Engineering; Computer Engineering; Construction Engineering; Electrical Engineering; Engineering; Mechanical Engineering; Petroleum and Gas Engineering); **Financial and Administrative Sciences** (Accountancy; Business Administration; Finance; International Business; Marketing); **Languages and Translation** (English; French; Modern Languages; Translation and Interpretation); **Legal Studies and International Relations** (Civil Law; Commercial Law; Criminal Law; History of Law; International Law; International Relations; Islamic Law; Law; Maritime Law; Private Law; Public Law); **Pharmacy and Drug Manufacturing** (Pharmacology; Pharmacy); **Physical Therapy** (Physical Therapy); **Tourism and Hotel Management** (Hotel Management; Tourism)

History: Founded 2006.

Fees: (Egyptian Pounds): Egyptian students, 7,875-15,750; (US Dollars): Foreign students, 1,730-3,455 per annum

Accrediting Agency: Supreme Council of Universities

Degrees and Diplomas: *Lîsâns*

Last Updated: 20/06/12

POSTGRADUATE HIGHER INSTITUTE FOR ISLAMIC STUDIES

26, Yolyo Str., Meet Oqba, Giza
Tel: +20(2) 346-8547

Director: Baghat Oteba

Programme

Islamic Studies (Islamic Studies)

POSTGRADUATE HIGHER INSTITUTE FOR SOCIAL DEFENCE STUDIES

1, Al-Shahed Ra'af Zaki, Polak Al-Dakrour, Giza
Tel: +20(2) 330-5352

Director: Mohamed Shehata Ali

Programme

Social Defence Studies (Social and Community Services; Social Policy; Social Problems; Social Welfare)

RA'AS AL-BAR HIGHER INSTITUTE FOR SPECIFIC STUDIES AND COMPUTER SCIENCE

Domitta Governate, Al-Ara'as City, Street 77, Ras Al-Barr
Website: http://www.rbi.edu.eg/ar/home.aspx

Director: Ahmad Diaa M. Mousa

Programme

Computer Science (Computer Science)

Degrees and Diplomas: *Lîsâns*

SADAT ACADEMY FOR MANAGEMENT SCIENCES (SAMS)

Cornish E-Nil Road, Maadi Entrance (1), Cairo 2222
Tel: +20(2) 378-7628 +20(2) 378-7629 +20(2) 378-7630
Fax: +20(2) 753-0043 +20(2) 02-3582901
EMail: info@sadatacademy.edu.eg
Website: http://www.sadatacademy.edu.eg

President: Alaa Eldin Mohamed El Ghazali
EMail: aelghazali@sadatacademy.edu.eg

Vice-President for Education and Research Affairs: Ibrahim Hassan Ibrahim EMail: d.ibrahim_h@sadatacademy.edu.eg

Faculty

Management (Accountancy; Behavioural Sciences; Business Administration; Computer Science; Economics; Insurance; Mathematics; Modern Languages; Public Administration; Staff Development; Statistics)

Further Information: Branches in Ramsis, Port Said, Dekernes, Tanta, Alexandria and Assuit

History: Founded 1954 as Public Administration Institute. Acquired present status and title 1981.

Degrees and Diplomas: *Lîsâns*; *Mâjistêr*; *Dukturâh*. Also Postgraduate Diploma

Last Updated: 20/06/12

SENGHOR UNIVERSITY

Université Senghor/Université internationale de Langue française au Service du Développement africain

BP 21111-415, El Mancheya, 1 Place Ahmed Orabi, Alexandria
Tel: +20(3) 4843-374 +20(3) 4843-504
Fax: +20(3) 4843-479
EMail: info@usenghor-francophonie.org
Website: http://www.usenghor-francophonie.org

Recteur: Albert Lourde
Tel: +20(3) 4843-504 EMail: rectorat@usenghor-francophonie.org

Department

Administration (Administration; Government; Management; Public Administration); **Cultural Studies** (Communication Studies; Cultural Studies; Heritage Preservation; Media Studies); **Environmental Management** (Environmental Management; Environmental Studies); **Health Studies** (Health Administration; Health Sciences; Nutrition)

Centre

Distance Education, Information and Communication Technologies *(FAD & TICE)* (Development Studies; Law)

History: Founded 1990 following a meeting of Heads of State of Francophone Countries. A private postgraduate institution whose objective is to train and assist professionals and higher level teachers.

Academic Year: September to May

Admission Requirements: University degree and professional experience

Main Language(s) of Instruction: French

Degrees and Diplomas: *Mâjistêr*. **Development Studies.**

Student Services: Canteen, Health Services, Sports Facilities

Publications: Actes des Conférences; Lettres d'Alexandrie; Patrimoine Culturel Francophone

Student Numbers *2011-2012*	MEN	WOMEN	**TOTAL**
All (Foreign included)	142	39	**181**

Last Updated: 12/03/12

SINAI HIGHER INSTITUTE FOR TOURISM AND HOTELS (SHITH)

14 Al Sadaka St., Ra'as Sedr, South Sinai
Tel: +20(69) 400-871
Fax: +20(2) 402-4977
EMail: sinai_institute@hotmail.com
Website: http://www.sinainstitute.org

Dean: Nervana Mokhtar Harraz (1999-)

Secretary-General: Ra'afat El-Nakhal

International Relations: Emad Eddin Abu El-Enain

Department
Hotel Management (Hotel Management); **Tourism** (Tourism)

History: Founded 1993.

Main Language(s) of Instruction: Arabic, English

Degrees and Diplomas: *Lîsâns*

Student Services: Academic Counselling, Careers Guidance, Health Services, Social Counselling, Sports Facilities

Publications: Egyptian Journal of Tourism and Hospitality
Last Updated: 20/06/12

SINAI UNIVERSITY

Katamia (Sama Tower) 5th Floor, Cairo
EMail: sinai@su.edu.eg
Website: http://www.su.edu.eg

President: Hatem Mostafa El-bolok EMail: hbolok@su.edu.eg

Faculty
Business Administration and International Marketing (Accountancy; Business Administration; Finance; International Business; Marketing); **Dentistry** (Dentistry; Oral Pathology; Surgery); **Engineering Sciences** (Biomedical Engineering; Chemical Engineering; Civil Engineering; Computer Engineering; Electrical Engineering; Electronic Engineering; Engineering; Materials Engineering; Mechanical Engineering; Structural Architecture; Telecommunications Engineering); **Humanities** (Arts and Humanities; English; Literature; Writing); **Information Technology and Computer Sciences** (Computer Science; Information Technology); **Mass Communication Technology** (Communication Studies; Marketing; Mass Communication; Media Studies; Radio and Television Broadcasting); **Pharmacy and Pharmaceutical Industries** (Biochemistry; Immunology; Microbiology; Pharmacology; Pharmacy; Toxicology)

History: Founded 2006.

Accrediting Agency: Supreme Council of Universities

Degrees and Diplomas: *Lîsâns*
Last Updated: 20/06/12

TECHNICAL COMMERCIAL INSTITUTE FOR COMPUTERS

Hodh Al-Dars, Port Tawfiq, Suez

Programme
Computer Science

Degrees and Diplomas: *Bachelor's Degree*; *Lîsâns*

IAU THE AMERICAN UNIVERSITY IN CAIRO (AUC)

PO Box 74, New Cairo 11835
Tel: +20(2) 2615-1000 +1(212) 7308800 (New York Office)
Fax: +20(2) 2795-7565 +1(212) 7301600 (New York Office)
EMail: ouc@aucegypt.edu
Website: http://www.aucegypt.edu

President: Lisa Anderson (2011-)
Tel: +20(2) 2615-1501/3 EMail: president@aucegypt.edu

Provost: Amr Shaarawi EMail: yvettefi@aucegypt.edu

International Relations: Ann Lesch, Associate Provost for International Programs
Tel: +20(2) 2615-3509 EMail: alesch@aucegypt.edu

School
Business, Economics and Communication (Accountancy; Administration; Business Administration; Business and Commerce; Communication Studies; Economics; Journalism; Management; Mass Communication); **Continuing Education** (Accountancy; Arabic; Computer Science; Education; Finance; Human Resources; Human Rights; Information Technology; International Law; Marketing; Tourism; Translation and Interpretation); **Humanities and Social Sciences** (Anthropology; Arts and Humanities; Comparative Law; Comparative Literature; Demography and Population; English; Film; History; International Relations; Islamic Studies; Middle Eastern Studies; Music; Performing Arts; Political Sciences; Psychology; Social Sciences; Sociology; Theatre; Visual Arts); **Science and Engineering** (Actuarial Science; Analytical Chemistry; Biology; Chemistry; Construction Engineering; Electronic Engineering; Engineering; Mathematics and Computer Science; Mechanical Engineering; Natural Sciences; Organic Chemistry; Physical Chemistry; Physics)

Institute
Arabic Language (Arabic); **English Language** (English); **Gender and Women's Studies** *(Cynthia Nelson)* (Gender Studies; Women's Studies)

Centre
American Studies and Research *(Prince Alwaleed Bin Talal Bin Abdulaziz Alsaud)* (American Studies); **Arabic Study Abroad** (Arabic); **Desert Development** (Arid Land Studies; Development Studies); **Journalism** *(Kamal Adham)* (Journalism); **Management** (Management); **Philanthropy and Civic Engagement** *(John Gerhart)* (Civics); **Social Research** (Social Studies)

Research Centre
Economics and Business History (Economic History); **Science and Technology** *(Youssef Jameel)* (Natural Sciences; Technology)

Further Information: Through the Centre of Adult and Continuing Education's Outreach Services programme in English, Computer Education, Arabic and Translation, and/or Business Studies are offered in: The United Arab Emirates (Abu Dhabi and Dubai), Saudi Arabia (Jeddah and Riyadh), and in other cities in Egypt (Alexandria, Damanhour, Ismailia, El Minia, Esna, Heliopolis, Hurgada, Kafr El Sheikh, Mansoura, Tabbin, and Tanta)

History: Founded 1919. A private non-profit Institution located in New Cairo. It operates as a private educational/cultural Institute within the framework of the 1962 Egyptian-American Cultural Cooperation Agreement and in accordance with a protocol with the Government of Egypt through which the University's degrees are recognized as those awarded by the Egyptian national universities. Accredited in the United States by the Middle States Commission on Higher Education, 3624 Market Street, Philadelphia, PA 19104, +1(267) 284-5000, and licensed to grant degrees and incorporated by the State of Delaware.

Academic Year: September to July (September-January; February-June); Winter Session in February and Summer Session in June-July

Admission Requirements: Secondary school certificate (Thanawiya 'Amma) or recognized equivalent

Main Language(s) of Instruction: English

Accrediting Agency: USA Council for Accreditation of Higher education, the Middle States Association of Colleges and Schools; Protocol with the Egyptian Government

Degrees and Diplomas: *Lîsâns*: **Accountancy; Actuarial Science; Ancient Civilizations; Anthropology; Biology; Business Administration; Chemistry; Computer Science; Construction Engineering; Cultural Studies; Economics; Electronic Engineering; English; Fine Arts; Journalism; Literature; Mass Communication; Mathematics; Mechanical Engineering; Middle Eastern Studies; Modern History; Philosophy; Physics; Psychology; Sociology; Theatre.** *Mâjistêr*: **Business Administration; Computer Science; Cultural Studies; Economics; Engineering; English; Gender Studies; Human Rights; International Business; International Law; Law; Literature; Mass Communication; Middle Eastern Studies; Physics; Public Administration; Women's Studies.** Also graduate Diplomas in Computer Science; Economic/International Development; Engineering, European Studies; Middle East Studies; Forced Migration and Refugee Studies; Islamic Studies; Physics; Political Science;

Teaching Arabic as a Foreign Language; Teaching English as a Foreign Language; Television Journal

Student Services: Academic Counselling, Canteen, Careers Guidance, Health Services, Language Laboratory, Nursery Care, Social Counselling, Sports Facilities

Publications: ALIF: Journal of Comparative Poetry; Cairo Papers in Social Science; Khamasin; Middle East Management Review

Publishing House: American University Press in Cairo

Student Numbers *2012-2013*: Total: c. 6,500
Last Updated: 14/03/13

THE BRITISH UNIVERSITY IN EGYPT

Suez Desert Road, El-Shourouk
Tel: +20(2) 689-0000
Fax: +20(2) 687-5889 +20(2) 687-5897
EMail: info@bue.edu.eg
Website: http://www.bue.edu.eg

President: Ahmed Amin Hamza

Faculty

Business Administration, Economics and Political Science (Business Administration; Economics; Political Sciences); **Engineering** (Automation and Control Engineering; Civil Engineering; Computer Engineering; Electrical and Electronic Engineering; Engineering; Mechanical Engineering; Petroleum and Gas Engineering; Structural Architecture; Technology; Telecommunications Engineering); **Informatics and Computer Science** (Computer Science; Information Technology; Software Engineering); **Nursing** *(Magrabi Mansour)* (Nursing)

Department

English (English)

History: Founded 2004.

Fees: (UK Pounds): 3,500 per annum for Business, Economics, Political Science, Informatics and Computer Science Programmes; 4,500 per annum for Engineering, Pharmacy, Dentistry

Degrees and Diplomas: Honours Degrees
Last Updated: 21/06/12

THE GERMAN UNIVERSITY IN CAIRO (GUC)

Main Entrance Al Tagamoa Al, Khames, New Cairo City
Tel: +20(2) 758-9990
Fax: +20(2)7581-041
EMail: contact@guc.edu.eg
Website: http://www.guc.edu.eg/

President: Mahmoud H. Abdel-Kader (2002-)

Faculty

Applied Science and Arts (Design); **Engineering and Materials Science** (Architecture; Civil Engineering; Design; Electronic Engineering; Materials Engineering; Mechanical Engineering; Production Engineering); **Information Engineering and Technology** (Computer Engineering; Information Technology); **Management Technology** (Business Computing; Management); **Media Engineering and Technology** (Information Technology; Management; Mass Communication; Materials Engineering; Media Studies); **Pharmacy and Biotechnology** (Biotechnology; Pharmacy)

Centre

Languages and Translation; **Lifelong Learning and Distance Education** (Continuing Education)

History: Founded 2002.

Degrees and Diplomas: *Lîsâns*; *Mâjistêr*; *Dukturâh*. Also German Diploma
Last Updated: 21/06/12

THEBES ACADEMY (ITA)

Maadi Corniche first - behind the Nile Badrawi Hospital, Maadi, Cairo 11 434
Tel: +20(2) 524-7980
Fax: +20(2) 524-7984
EMail: contact@thebesacademy.org
Website: http://www.thebesacademy.org

President: A.D. Seddik EMail: s.afifi@thebesacademy.org

Institute

Computer Sciences (Accountancy; Business Administration; Computer Science; Information Sciences; Management)

Higher Institute

Engineering (Architecture; Civil Engineering; Computer Engineering; Electronic Engineering; Telecommunications Engineering); **Institute of Management and Information Technology** (Accountancy; Administration; Banking; Information Technology; Management)

Further Information: The Academy is composed of two Centres in Maadi and Giza.

History: Founded 1995. Giza Centre established 1995. Maadi Centre established 1999. Received accreditation 2004.

Degrees and Diplomas: *Lîsâns*
Last Updated: 21/06/12

WORKERS' UNIVERSITY (WU)

6 Al-Nasr Rd., Abbas Al-Aquad, Nasr City, Cairo
Tel: +20(2) 275-4646
Fax: +20(2) 275-4604
EMail: info@workersuniversity.org

President: Hussein Magawer

Vice-President: Mostafa El Sayed

International Relations: Ahmed Abdel Salam, Secretary-General

Programme

Academic Studies (Labour and Industrial Relations; Safety Engineering; Technology); **Trade Union and Labour Economics Studies** (Labour and Industrial Relations; Management; Protective Services; Social Welfare)

Academy

Specialized Studies

Further Information: Also 11 branches in Egypt

History: Formerly known as Labour University.

Degrees and Diplomas: *Lîsâns*: **Business Administration.**

El Salvador

STRUCTURE OF HIGHER EDUCATION SYSTEM

Description:

Higher education is provided by universities, both public and private, and specialized institutions. The National University is autonomous and is financed by credits from the State, gifts and student fees. The governing bodies are the General Assembly, the Higher University Council and the Rector. The Ministerio de Educación, through the Dirección Nacional de Educación Superior, is responsible for higher education policy and study programmes. Private universities must submit their programmes to the approval of the Ministry of Education.

Stages of studies:

University level first stage: *Licenciatura, Ingeniero, Arquitecto*
The title of Ingeniero (Agricultural, Civil, Industrial, Mechanical and Electrical Engineering) requires five years' study, as does that of Arquitecto. The Licenciatura is generally awarded after five years' study in most fields.

University level second stage: *Maestria*
The Maestría is usually awarded two years after the Licenciatura. Candidates must prepare a short thesis (monograph).

University level third stage: *Doctorado (Doctor en Medicina and Ph.D.)*
There are two kinds of Doctorates in the country. The first one is the title of Doctor of Medicine (Doctor en Medicina), awarded after 7 years' study. The second is the title of Doctor of which can be obtained three years after having completed a Maestría/ Licenciatura degree course.

University level fourth stage: *Especialidad*
Post-graduate degree for Doctors en Medicina.

ADMISSION TO HIGHER EDUCATION

Admission to university-level studies:

Name of secondary school credential required: Bachillerato General

Minimum score/requirement: 5.00 (Scale from 0 to 10)

Name of secondary school credential required: Bachillerato Técnico Vocacional

Admission requirements: Entrance examination for some universities.

Foreign students admission:

Definition of foreign student: A person studying at a Salvadorean educational institution who does not have Salvadorean nationality.

Admission requirements: Foreign students must hold a Título de Bachiller and must sit for an entrance examination. In addition, academic documents must be authenticated by the Ministry of Education and by the Ministry of Foreign Affairs. Students wishing to study in higher education must enrol in the Sistema de Educación Media Salvadoreño before enrolling at university.

Entry regulations: Students must have a residence permit.

Language proficiency: Students must have a good knowledge of Spanish.

RECOGNITION OF STUDIES

Quality assurance system:

All higher education training must be recognized by the Ministry of Education of El Salvador.

Bodies dealing with recognition:
Ministerio de Educación (Ministry of Education)
Edificio A-1 Plan Maestro, Alameda Juan Pablo II y Calle Guadalupe, Centro de Goblerno
San Salvador 1175
Tel: +503 2592-2000
EMail: educacion@mined.gob.sv
WWW: http://www.mined.gob.sv

NATIONAL BODIES

Ministerio de Educación (Ministry of Education)
Minister: Carlos Mauricio Canjura Linares
Director, Higher Education: José Francisco Marroquin
Edificio A-1 Plan Maestro, Alameda Juan Pablo II y Calle Guadalupe, Centro de Goblerno
San Salvador 1175
Tel: +503 2592-2000
EMail: educacion@mined.gob.sv
WWW: http://www.mined.gob.sv

Consejo Nacional de Ciencia y Tecnologia - CONACYT (National Council for Science and Technology)
Col. Medica Av. Dr. Emilio Alvarez y Paje. Dr. Guillermo Rodriguez Pacas, Edif Espinoza, No. 51
San Salvador 3103
Tel: +503 2234-8400
Fax: +503 2225-6255
EMail: info@conacyt.gob.sv
WWW: http://www.conacyt.gob.sv/

Data for academic year: 2015-2016
Source: IAU from Higher Education Law, 2004 and documents, 2015

INSTITUTIONS

PUBLIC INSTITUTIONS

ITCA-FEPADE SPECIALIZED ENGINEERING SCHOOL

Escuela Especializada en Ingenieria ITCA-FEPADE (ITCA)
Km. 11 Carretera a Santa Tecla, Nueva San Salvador
Tel: +503 2132-7400
Fax: +503 2132-7406 +503 2241-7599
EMail: fep_itca@di.itca.edu.sv
Website: http://www.itca.edu.sv

Rectora: Elsy Escolar Santo Domingo

School
Automotive Engineering (Automotive Engineering); **Basic Sciences** (Natural Sciences); **Chemical Engineering** (Chemical Engineering); **Civil Engineering and Architecture** (Architecture; Civil Engineering); **Computer Engineering** (Computer Engineering); **Dual Education** (Electronic Engineering; Industrial Chemistry; Industrial Maintenance; Mechanical Engineering; Transport Engineering); **Electrical and Electronic Engineering** (Electrical and Electronic Engineering); **Food Technology** (Food Technology); **Mechatronic Engineering** (Electronic Engineering; Mechanical Engineering)

Further Information: Four regional centres in Zacatecoluca, San Miguel, Santa Ana, and La Unión.

History: Founded 1969 as Instituto Tecnológico Centroamericano (Central-American Technological Institute). Acquired current title 2008.

Main Language(s) of Instruction: Spanish

Accrediting Agency: Comisión de Acreditación de la Calidad Académica

Degrees and Diplomas: *Técnico*; *Licenciado, Ingeniero, Arquitecto*: **Electronic Engineering; Mechanical Engineering; Transport Engineering.**

Student Services: Library

Last Updated: 18/12/15

SPECIALIZED INSTITUTE OF HIGHER EDUCATION FOR THE DIPLOMATIC TRAINING

Instituto Especializado de Educación Superior para la Formación Diplomática (IEESFORD)
Edificio 2, 4a. planta, Calle El Pedregal, Blvd. Cancillería, Ministerio de Relaciones Exteriores de El Salvador, Antiguo Cuscatlán
Tel: +503 2231-1343
Fax: +503 2231-1344
EMail: iesford@rree.gob.sv
Website: http://www.iesford.edu.sv

Rectora: Claudia María Samayoa Herrera
Tel: +503 2231-1343 EMail: cmsamayoa@rree.gob.sv

Secretária General: Nelly Yohana Cuéllar de Yamagiwa
Tel: +503 2231-2987 EMail: nycuellar@rree.gob.sv

Programme
Diplomacy (International Relations)

Course
Consular Management (Management); **International Maritime Law** *(Universidad Internacional de Andalucía (UNIA, España))* (International Law; Maritime Law); **Languages** (Modern Languages)

History: Founded 2010.

Admission Requirements: Public competition for admission; Licenciado degree or equivalent; Advanced knowledge of English

Fees: Maestria, 600 per month; Especialista, 415 per month (US Dollar)

Main Language(s) of Instruction: Spanish

Degrees and Diplomas: *Maestro*: **International Relations.** *Especialista*: **Management.**
Last Updated: 17/12/15

UNIVERSITY OF EL SALVADOR

Universidad de El Salvador (UES)
Ciudad Universitaria, Final 25 Avenida Norte, San Salvador
Tel: +503 2511-2000
Fax: +503 2225-8826
EMail: csu@ues.edu.sv
Website: http://www.ues.edu.sv

Rector (Acting): Luis Argueta Antillon (2015-)
EMail: rectoria@ues.edu.sv

Secretaría General: Ana Leticia Zavaleta de Amaya

Faculty
Agronomy (Agricultural Engineering; Agriculture; Veterinary Science; Zoology); **Chemistry and Pharmacy** (Chemistry; Pharmacy); **Dentistry** (Dentistry; Stomatology); **Economics** (Accountancy; Business Administration; Economics; International Business; Marketing); **Engineering and Architecture** (Architecture; Chemical Engineering; Civil Engineering; Electrical Engineering; Engineering; Food Technology; Industrial Engineering; Mechanical Engineering; Systems Analysis); **Law and Social Sciences** (International Relations; Law; Social Sciences); **Medicine** (Anaesthesiology; Child Care and Development; Clinical Psychology; Medical Technology; Medicine; Nursing; Nutrition; Occupational Therapy; Physical Therapy; Radiology); **Multidisciplinary Studies of the East** (Agronomy; Architecture; Arts and Humanities; Biology; Chemistry; Dentistry; Economics; Engineering; Law; Mathematics; Medicine; Natural Sciences; Pharmacy); **Multidisciplinary Studies of the West** (Biology; Chemistry; Economics; Engineering; Law; Mathematics; Medicine; Modern Languages; Physics; Social Sciences); **Natural Sciences and Mathematics** (Biology; Chemistry; Mathematics; Natural Sciences; Physics); **Regional Multidisciplinary Studies** (Agronomy; Computer Science; Economics; Education); **Science and Humanities** (Arts and Humanities; Education; Fine Arts; Journalism; Literature; Modern Languages; Natural Sciences; Philosophy; Psychology; Social Sciences)

Further Information: Also regional centres in Santa Ana, San Miguel and San Vicente

History: Founded 1841, became University 1847. Acquired autonomous status 1950.

Academic Year: May to March (May-October; October-March)

Admission Requirements: Secondary school certificate (bachillerato) and entrance examination

Main Language(s) of Instruction: Spanish

Degrees and Diplomas: *Técnico*: **Interior Design; Laboratory Techniques; Library Science.** *Licenciado, Ingeniero, Arquitecto*: **Accountancy; Agricultural Business; Agriculture; Agronomy; Animal Husbandry; Architecture; Arts and Humanities; Biology; Business Administration; Chemistry; Economics; Education; Engineering; Health Sciences; International Relations; Journalism; Law; Marketing; Mathematics; Philosophy; Physics; Psychology; Veterinary Science.** *Maestro*: **Business and Commerce; Computer Engineering; Construction Engineering; Dentistry; Development Studies; Economics; Engineering Management; English; Environmental Engineering; Environmental Studies; Finance; Food Science; Health Administration; Higher Education Teacher Training; Human Rights; Latin American Studies; Law; Literature; Microbiology; Public Health; Software Engineering; Spanish; Teacher Training; Translation and Interpretation.** *Doctor*: **Education; Social Sciences.** *Doctor en Medicina*: **Dentistry; Medicine.** Also Diplomados

Student Services: Health Services, Language Laboratory, Nursery Care, Sports Facilities

Publications: Aquí Odontología; Búho Dilecto; Cuadernos Didácticos; El Quehacer Científico; El Salvador: Coyuntura Económica; El Universitario; Enfoque Tecnológico
Last Updated: 21/12/15

PRIVATE INSTITUTIONS

ALBERT EINSTEIN UNIVERSITY

Universidad Albert Einstein (UAE)
Final Avenida Albert Einstein y Calle Teotl, Urb. Lomas de San Francisco, Antiguo Cuscatlán, La Libertad
Tel: +503 2273-3700 +503 2273-3780 +503 2212-7600
Fax: +503 2273-3783 +503 2273-3784
EMail: infouae@uae.edu.sv
Website: http://www.uae.edu.sv

Rectora: Juana Salazar Alvarenga de Pacheco
Tel: +503 2212-7612 EMail: rectoria@einstein.edu.sv

Secretaría General: Flor de María Figueroa de Arriaza
Tel: +503 2212-7615
EMail: secretaria.general@einstein.edu.sv; flor.figueroa@einstein.edu.sv

Faculty
Architecture (Architectural and Environmental Design; Architecture); **Business Administration** (Business Administration; Marketing); **Engineering** (Civil Engineering; Computer Engineering; Electrical Engineering; Industrial Engineering; Mechanical Engineering)

History: Founded 1973, first students admitted 1977.

Admission Requirements: Secondary school certificate (bachillerato) and entrance examination

Fees: 55-200 per month (US Dollar)

Main Language(s) of Instruction: Spanish

Accrediting Agency: Asociación de Universidades Privadas de Centro América (AUPRICA)

Degrees and Diplomas: *Licenciado, Ingeniero, Arquitecto*: **Architectural and Environmental Design; Architecture; Business Administration; Civil Engineering; Computer Engineering; Electrical Engineering; Industrial Engineering; Marketing; Mechanical Engineering.**

Student Services: Academic Counselling, Canteen, Cultural Activities, Facilities for disabled people, Language Laboratory, Library, Social Counselling, Sports Facilities
Last Updated: 18/12/15

ALBERTO MASFERRER SALVADOREAN UNIVERSITY

Universidad Salvadoreña Alberto Masferrer (USAM)
19 Avenida Norte entre 3a. Calle Poniente y Alameda 'Juan Pablo II', San Salvador
Tel: +503 2231-9600
Fax: +503 2231-9601
EMail: informacion@usam.edu.sv
Website: http://www.usam.edu.sv

Rector: Cesar Augusto Calderón EMail: rectoria@usam.edu.sv

Faculty
Business Studies (Accountancy; Advertising and Publicity; Business Administration; Computer Science; Marketing); **Chemistry and Pharmacy** (Chemistry; Pharmacology; Pharmacy); **Dental Surgery** (Dentistry; Surgery); **Law and Social Sciences** (Law; Social Sciences); **Medicine** (Medicine; Nursing); **Veterinary Science and Zoology** (Veterinary Science; Zoology)

Institute
Science and Technological Research (Natural Sciences; Technology)
Further Information: Also 4 hospitals
History: Founded 1979. Received official authorization 1980.
Academic Year: February to December (February-June; July-December)
Admission Requirements: Secondary school certificate (bachillerato) and entrance examination
Main Language(s) of Instruction: Spanish
Accrediting Agency: Comisión de Acreditación de la Calidad Académica
Degrees and Diplomas: *Licenciado, Ingeniero, Arquitecto*; *Maestro*: **Forensic Medicine and Dentistry; Health Sciences.** *Doctor en Medicina*: **Dentistry; Medicine.**
Student Services: Library, eLibrary
Last Updated: 22/12/15

ANDRÉS BELLO UNIVERSITY

Universidad Andrés Bello (UDAB)
1a. Calle Poniente No. 2128, entre 39 y 41 Avenida Norte No 2128, Colonia Flor Blanca, San Salvador
Tel: +503 2510-7400 +503 2510-7413 +503 2260-8533
Fax: +503 2260-8541
EMail: informacion@unab.edu.sv
Website: http://unab.edu.sv

Rector: Marco Tulio Magaña Escalante EMail: rector@unab.edu.sv
Secretaria General: Sandra Concepción Ventura

Faculty
Economics (Accountancy; Business Administration; Computer Networks; Computer Science; Graphic Design; Marketing; Public Relations; Tourism); **Health Sciences** (Health Sciences; Laboratory Techniques; Nursing; Radiology); **Human Sciences** (Social Work)

Programme
Masters and Courses (Health Administration; Higher Education Teacher Training; Social Problems)
Further Information: Also branches in Sonsonate, Chalatenango and San Miguel
History: Founded 1991.
Main Language(s) of Instruction: Spanish
Degrees and Diplomas: *Técnico*; *Tecnólogo*; *Licenciado, Ingeniero, Arquitecto*; *Maestro*: **Health Administration; Higher Education Teacher Training; Social Problems.**
Student Services: IT Centre, Library
Last Updated: 18/12/15

AUTONOMOUS UNIVERSITY OF SANTA ANA

Universidad Autónoma de Santa Ana (UNASA)
Autopista Sur Pte. Km. 63 1/2, Santa Ana
Tel: +503 2440-0245
EMail: unasarec@sv.intercomnet.net; fisioterapia@unasa.edu.sv
Website: http://www.unasa.edu.sv

Rector: Sergio Ernesto Carranza Vega
Vice-Rector: Guillermo A. Martínez Mendoza
EMail: unasarec@sv.cciglobal.net
Secretario General: Sergio Amilcar Carranza
EMail: secretariaderectoria@unasa.edu.sv; secretariageneral@unasa.edu.sv

Faculty
Health Sciences (Dentistry; Laboratory Techniques; Medicine; Nursing; Physical Therapy); **Social Sciences** (Communication Studies; Graphic Design; Multimedia)
History: Founded 1982.
Academic Year: February to January (February-July; August-January)
Admission Requirements: Secondary school certificate (bachillerato) and entrance examination
Main Language(s) of Instruction: Spanish
Degrees and Diplomas: *Licenciado, Ingeniero, Arquitecto*: **Communication Studies; Graphic Design; Laboratory Techniques; Multimedia; Nursing; Physical Therapy.** *Doctor en Medicina*: **Dentistry; Medicine.**
Student Services: Library
Last Updated: 18/12/15

CAPTAIN GENERAL GERARDO BARRIOS UNIVERSITY

Universidad Capitán General Gerardo Barrios (UGB)
Calle Las Flores y Avenida Las Magnolias, Colonia Escolán, San Miguel
Tel: +503 2645-6500
Fax: +503 2669-7489
EMail: nuevoingreso@ugb.edu.sv
Website: http://www.ugb.edu.sv

Rector: Raúl Rivas Quintanilla EMail: rrivas@ugb.edu.sv
Vicer-Rector Académico: Sirhan Raúl Rivas
EMail: rrivas@ugb.edu.sv
International Relations: Eugenia Gomez
EMail: eugomez@ugb.edu.sv

Faculty
Business Administration (Accountancy; Business Administration; Marketing; Sales Techniques; Tourism); **Engineering and Architecture** (Architecture; Civil Engineering; Construction Engineering; Industrial Engineering); **Juridical Sciences** (Law); **Science and Technology** (Automation and Control Engineering; Computer Engineering; Computer Networks; Computer Science; Electronic Engineering; Systems Analysis; Telecommunications Engineering); **Sciences and Humanities** (English; Foreign Languages Education; Humanities and Social Science Education; Journalism; Mass Communication; Mathematics; Mathematics Education; Primary Education; Psychology; Science Education; Secondary Education; Spanish; Teacher Training)

Programme
Postgraduate Studies (Business Administration; Child Care and Development; Clinical Psychology; Computer Engineering; Construction Engineering; Criminal Law; Private Law)
Further Information: Also Usulután Campus
History: Founded 1980.
Academic Year: January to December (January-June; July-December)
Admission Requirements: Secondary school certificate
Main Language(s) of Instruction: Spanish
Degrees and Diplomas: *Técnico*; *Profesor*; *Licenciado, Ingeniero, Arquitecto*: **Architecture; Business Administration; Civil Engineering; Computer Engineering; Computer Science; English; Industrial Engineering; Journalism; Law; Marketing; Mass Communication; Psychology; Systems Analysis; Tourism.** *Maestro*: **Business Administration; Child Care and Development; Clinical Psychology; Computer Engineering; Construction Engineering; Criminal Law; Private Law.**
Student Services: Academic Counselling, Careers Guidance, Cultural Activities, Facilities for disabled people, Health Services, Language Laboratory, Library, Nursery Care, Social Counselling, Sports Facilities
Publications: Catarsis Magazine; Millenium Magazine
Last Updated: 18/12/15

CATHOLIC UNIVERSITY OF EL SALVADOR

Universidad Católica de El Salvador (UNICAES)
Bypass carretera a Metapán y carretera antigua a San Salvador, Santa Ana
Tel: +503 2484-0600
Fax: +503 2441-2655
EMail: catolica@catolica.edu.sv
Website: http://www.catolica.edu.sv
Rector: Romeo Tovar Astorga (2000-)
Tel: +503 2447-0602 EMail: rector@unico.edu.sv

Secretario General: Cástulo Afranio Hernández Robles
Tel: +503 2447-0606 EMail: secretaria@unico.edu.sv

International Relations: Claudia Velásquez de Figueroa, Director, Communication
Tel: +503 2447-0621
EMail: ucom@uinco.edu.sv; claudia.velasquez@catolica.edu.sv

Faculty

Architecture and Engineering (Agricultural Engineering; Architecture; Civil Engineering; Computer Science; Environmental Engineering; Industrial Engineering); **Business Administration** (Accountancy; Business Administration; Computer Science; International Business; Marketing; Tourism); **Health Sciences** (Medicine; Nursing); **Science and Humanities** (Educational Sciences; Educational Testing and Evaluation; Foreign Languages Education; Graphic Design; Humanities and Social Science Education; Law; Mass Communication; Mathematics Education; Native Language Education; Pedagogy; Physical Education; Preschool Education; Primary Education; Radio and Television Broadcasting; Religious Education; Secondary Education; Teacher Training)

Centre

Multidisciplinary Faculty of Ilobasco *(Ilobasco Regional Centre)* (Business Administration; Computer Engineering; Educational Administration; Educational and Student Counselling; Foreign Languages Education; International Business; Marketing; Mathematics Education; Nursing; Teacher Training)

History: Founded 1982 as Universidad Católica del Occidente following the Episcopal Conference of El Salvador agreement. Acquired present status and title 2008.

Academic Year: January to November (January-June; July-November)

Admission Requirements: Secondary school certificate (bachillerato)

Main Language(s) of Instruction: Spanish

Accrediting Agency: Comisión de Accreditación de la Calidad Académica

Degrees and Diplomas: *Técnico*; *Profesor*, *Licenciado, Ingeniero, Arquitecto*; *Maestro*: **Business Administration; Child Care and Development; Educational Testing and Evaluation; Tourism.** *Doctor en Medicina*: **Medicine.**

Student Services: Academic Counselling, IT Centre, Language Laboratory, Library, Sports Facilities

Last Updated: 18/12/15

CHRISTIAN UNIVERSITY OF THE ASSEMBLIES OF GOD

Universidad Cristiana de las Asambleas de Dios (UCAD)

27 Calle Oriente No 234, Barrio San Miguelito, San Salvador
Tel: +503 2225-5046 +503 2226-3155 +503 2226-4548
Fax: +503 2235-6264 +503 2235-3392
EMail: informacion@ucad.edu.sv
Website: http://www.ucad.edu.sv

Rector: Augusto Ferrufino Aguilar

Faculty

Economics (Accountancy; Business Administration; Computer Engineering); **Law and Social Sciences** (Law; Social Sciences); **Science and Humanities** (Communication Studies; Educational Sciences; English; Preschool Education); **Theology** (Missionary Studies; Theology)

History: Founded 1983.

Academic Year: February to November (February-June; August-November)

Admission Requirements: Secondary school certificate (bachillerato)

Main Language(s) of Instruction: Spanish

Degrees and Diplomas: *Profesor*: **Preschool Education.** *Licenciado, Ingeniero, Arquitecto*: **Accountancy; Business Administration; Computer Engineering; Educational Sciences; English; Law; Missionary Studies; Social Sciences; Theology.**

Last Updated: 18/12/15

DON BOSCO UNIVERSITY

Universidad Don Bosco (UDB)

Ciudadela Don Bosco, Cantón Venecia, Calle Plan del Pino Km 1 1/2, Soyapango 1874
Tel: +503 2251-8220
Fax: +503 2251-5080
EMail: huguet@udb.edu.sv
Website: http://www.udb.edu.sv

Rector: Oscar Rodríguez Blanco
Tel: +503 2251-5031 EMail: rectoria@udb.edu.sv

Vicerrectora Académica: Reina Durán de Alvarado
Tel: +503 2251-8200 Ext. 1805 EMail: reina.alvarado@udb.edu.sv

Faculty

Aeronautics (Aeronautical and Aerospace Engineering); **Economics** (Accountancy; Business Administration; Economics; Marketing); **Engineering** (Automation and Control Engineering; Biomedical Engineering; Computer Engineering; Computer Science; Electrical and Electronic Engineering; Electrical Engineering; Engineering; Industrial Engineering; Mechanical Engineering); **Rehabilitation** (Rehabilitation and Therapy); **Science and Humanities** (Communication Studies; Education; Educational Sciences; English; Graphic Design; Industrial Design; Modern Languages; Multimedia; Preschool Education; Primary Education; Secondary Education; Teacher Training; Theology; Tourism); **Technological Studies** (Biomedical Engineering; Computer Engineering; Electrical and Electronic Engineering; Mechanical Engineering; Technology)

Department

Basic Sciences (Applied Physics; Chemistry; Mathematics; Physics)

Institute

Pedagogical Training (Education; Teacher Training)

Centre

Research and Transfer (Biomedicine; Communication Studies; Computer Engineering; Electrical and Electronic Engineering; Measurement and Precision Engineering; Mechanical Engineering)

Further Information: Also Distance Education

History: Founded 1984. Follows the Salesian tradition and philosophy.

Academic Year: January to December (January-June; July-December)

Admission Requirements: Secondary school certificate (bachillerato) and entrance examination

Main Language(s) of Instruction: Spanish, English

Accrediting Agency: Comisión de Acreditación de la Calidad de la Educación Superior

Degrees and Diplomas: *Técnico*; *Profesor*, *Licenciado, Ingeniero, Arquitecto*; *Maestro*: **Computer Engineering; Curriculum; Education; Educational Testing and Evaluation; Energy Engineering; Safety Engineering; Social Sciences; Software Engineering.** *Doctor*: **Social Sciences; Theology.**

Student Services: Academic Counselling, Canteen, Careers Guidance, Cultural Activities, Health Services, Language Laboratory, Library, Nursery Care, Social Counselling, Sports Facilities

Publications: Engineering; Revista Científica; Revista Puntos; Teoría y Praxis

Last Updated: 21/12/15

DR. JOSÉ MATÍAS DELGADO UNIVERSITY

Universidad Dr. José Matías Delgado (UDJMD)

Apartado postal 1849, Km. 8 1/2 Carretera a Santa Tecla Cuidad Merliot, Antiguo Cuscatlán, La Libertad
Tel: +503 2212-9400
Fax: +203 2289-5314
EMail: vicerectoriaacademica@ujmd.edu.sv
Website: http://ujmd.edu.sv

Rector: David Escobar Galindo
Tel: +503 2278-1011 Ext. 138
EMail: rectoriacampus@ujmd.edu.sv

Vicerrector Académico: Jose Enrique Sorto Cambell
EMail: jesortoc@ujmd.edu.sv

Faculty
Agriculture and Agricultural Research (Agricultural Business; Agricultural Engineering; Agriculture; Environmental Engineering; Food Science); **Economics, Business and Commerce** (Accountancy; Business Administration; Business and Commerce; Economics; Finance; Information Technology; Marketing; Tourism); **Engineering** (Engineering; Industrial Engineering); **Health Sciences** (Health Sciences); **Law and Social Sciences** (Law; Social Sciences); **Science and Fine Arts** *(Francisco Gavidia)* (Communication Studies; Design; Fine Arts; Graphic Design; Natural Sciences; Psychology; Theatre)

History: Founded 1977. Financed by student fees and private and Government grants.

Academic Year: January to December (January-June; July-December)

Admission Requirements: Secondary school certificate (bachillerato) or foreign equivalent, and entrance examination. Presentation of original work for School of Applied Arts

Main Language(s) of Instruction: Spanish

Accrediting Agency: Comisión de Acreditación de la Calidad de la Educación Superior

Degrees and Diplomas: *Licenciado, Ingeniero, Arquitecto*; *Maestro*: **Administrative Law; Business Administration; Clinical Psychology; Constitutional Law; Finance; Human Resources; International Business; Law; Management.** *Doctor*: **Private Law.** Also Diplomado and Online International Masters

Student Services: Academic Counselling, Canteen, Careers Guidance, Facilities for disabled people, Health Services, Language Laboratory, Library, Sports Facilities

Last Updated: 21/12/15

EVANGELICAL UNIVERSITY OF EL SALVADOR

Universidad Evangélica de El Salvador (UEES)
Prolongación Alameda Juan Pablo II y Calle El Carmen,
San Antonio Abad, San Salvador
Tel: +503 2275-4000; +503 2275-4033
Fax: +503 2275-4040
EMail: uevange@uees.edu.sv
Website: http://www.uees.edu.sv

Rector: César Emilio Quinteros Martínez Tel: +503 2262-4000

Vicerrectora Academica: Cristina de Amaya

Faculty
Business Administration and Economics (Accountancy; Business Administration; Economics; Marketing; Public Relations; Tourism); **Dentistry** (Dentistry); **Engineering** (Computer Networks; Computer Science; Engineering); **Law** (International Business; International Relations; Law); **Medicine** (Food Science; Medicine; Nursing; Nutrition); **Social Sciences** (Preschool Education; Psychology; Social Sciences; Special Education; Theology; Translation and Interpretation)

Research Unit
Martin Eugenio Rodríguez (Development Studies; Service Trades)

History: Founded 1981.

Academic Year: February to November (February-June; August-November)

Admission Requirements: Secondary school certificate (bachillerato) and entrance examination

Main Language(s) of Instruction: Spanish

Accrediting Agency: Comisión de Acreditación de la Calidad de la Educación Superior

Degrees and Diplomas: *Técnico*; *Licenciado, Ingeniero, Arquitecto*: **Dietetics; Education; English; Nutrition; Psychology; Social Work; Translation and Interpretation.** *Maestro*: **Education; Health Sciences; Human Resources; Law; Medical Auxiliaries; Nursing; Public Health.** *Doctor en Medicina*: **Dentistry; Medicine.** Also Diplomado

Student Services: Academic Counselling, Careers Guidance, Cultural Activities, Library, Social Counselling, Sports Facilities

Publications: Revista Vision Odontológica

Last Updated: 21/12/15

FRANCISCO GAVIDIA UNIVERSITY

Universidad Francisco Gavidia (UFG)
Calle El Progreso 2748, Edificio de Rectoría, San Salvador
Tel: +503 2249-2700
Fax: +503 2209-2837
EMail: info@ufg.edu.sv
Website: http://www.ufg.edu.sv

Rector: Mario Antonio Ruiz Ramírez (1996-)
EMail: mruiz@ufg.edu.sv

Secretaria General: Teresa de Jesús Gonzáles de Mendoza
EMail: tmendoza@ufg.edu.sv

Faculty
Arts and Design (Architecture; Computer Graphics; Design; Fashion Design; Fine Arts; Graphic Design); **Economics** (Accountancy; Advertising and Publicity; Business Administration; Communication Studies; Computer Science; Economics; Hotel and Restaurant; International Business; Marketing; Public Relations; Tourism); **Engineering and Systems** (Computer Engineering; Electronic Engineering; Engineering; Industrial Engineering; Systems Analysis; Telecommunications Engineering); **Law** (International Relations; Law); **Social Sciences** (English; Psychology)

Further Information: Also Santa Ana Campus

History: Founded 1981.

Academic Year: January to December (January-June; July-December)

Admission Requirements: Secondary school certificate (bachillerato) and entrance examination

Main Language(s) of Instruction: Spanish

Accrediting Agency: Comisión de Acreditación de la Calidad de la Educación Superior

Degrees and Diplomas: *Profesor*, *Licenciado, Ingeniero, Arquitecto*: **Accountancy; Business Administration; Computer Engineering; Economics; Education; Educational Administration; Industrial Engineering; Law; Marketing; Psychology; Social Work.** *Maestro*: **Business Administration; Education.** Also Diplomado, and Phd in Public Management and Business in agreement with the Central American Institute of Public Administration (ICAP)

Student Services: Academic Counselling, Careers Guidance, Cultural Activities, Social Counselling, Sports Facilities

Publications: Realidad y Reflexión; Societatis; Theorethikos

Last Updated: 21/12/15

HOLY SPIRIT SPECIALIZED INSTITUTE OF HIGHER EDUCATION

Instituto Especializado de Educación Superior El Espíritu Santo
Urbanización Jardines de Merliot, Av. El Boquerón y Calle Chiltiupán. Lote No. 5, Polígono "O" Cuidad Merliot, La Libertad
Tel: +503 2278-6683
Fax: +503 2289-6265 +503 2278-6683
EMail: informacion@ieeses.edu.sv; info@ieeses.edu.sv
Website: http://www.ieeses.edu.sv/index.php

Rectora: Elsa América Mendoza Mejía

Programme
Educational Sciences (Educational Sciences; Primary Education; Secondary Education; Special Education); **Postgraduate Studies** (Educational Testing and Evaluation; Technology Education; Vocational Education); **Teacher Training** (Higher Education Teacher Training; Humanities and Social Science Education; Mathematics Education; Media Studies; Native Language Education; Physical Education; Primary Education; Special Education; Sports; Teacher Training)

History: Founded 1995 as Instituto Tecnológico "El Espíritu Santo". Acquired present title 1996 and present status status 1999.

Main Language(s) of Instruction: Spanish

Degrees and Diplomas: *Profesor*, *Licenciado, Ingeniero, Arquitecto*; *Maestro*: **Educational Testing and Evaluation.** Also Postgraduate Teacher Training Course for Professional, Technical and Technological Education

Student Services: Library

Last Updated: 18/12/15

INSTITUTE OF ECONOMICS AND BUSINESS ADMINISTRATION

Instituto Superior de Economía y Administración de Empresas (ISEADE)

Calle El Pedregal y Calle de Acceso a Escuela Militar, Antiguo Cuscatlán, La Libertad
Tel: +503 2212-1700
Fax: +503 2212-1736
EMail: contacto@iseade.edu.sv; maestria@iseade.edu.sv; iseade@telemovil.net
Website: http://www.iseade.edu.sv

Rector: Joaquín Samayoa

Programme

Business Administration (Business Administration); **Specialized Postgraduate Studies** (Business Administration; Commercial Law; Design; Finance; Human Resources; International Business; International Economics; International Law; Marketing; Transport Management)

History: Founded 1997.

Main Language(s) of Instruction: Spanish

Accrediting Agency: Comisión de Acreditación de la Calidad Académica

Degrees and Diplomas: *Maestro*: **Business Administration.** Also Postgrado Especializado (Postgraduate Specialized Degree)

Student Services: eLibrary

Last Updated: 18/12/15

JOSÉ SIMEÓN CAÑAS CENTRAL AMERICAN UNIVERSITY

Universidad Centroamericana José Simeón Cañas (UCA)

Dirección de Comunicaciones, Bulevar Los Próceres, Antiguo Cuscatlán, La Libertad
Tel: +503 2210-6600
Fax: +503 2210-6655 +503 2210-6648 +503 2210-6640
EMail: correo@www.uca.edu.sv; ofi-com@uca.edu.sv
Website: http://www.uca.edu.sv

Rector: Andreu Oliva de la Esperanza
Tel: +503 2210-6620 EMail: rectoria@uca.edu.sv

Secretaria General: Silvia Elinor Azucena de Fernández
Tel: +503 2210-6600 EMail: sazucena@uca.edu.sv

Faculty

Business and Economic Sciences (Accountancy; Business Administration; Economics; Marketing); **Engineering and Architecture** (Architecture; Chemical Engineering; Civil Engineering; Computer Science; Electrical Engineering; Industrial Engineering; Mechanical Engineering); **Social Sciences and Humanities** (Foreign Languages Education; Law; Mass Communication; Philosophy; Preschool Education; Primary Education; Psychology; Religious Education; Secondary Education; Theology)

Department

Postgraduate Studies (Business Administration; Commercial Law; Development Studies; Educational Administration; Educational Testing and Evaluation; Finance; Industrial Maintenance; Mass Communication; Philosophy; Political Sciences; Social Sciences; Social Work; Statistics; Theology)

History: Founded 1965, first students admitted 1966.

Academic Year: March to December (March-July; August-December)

Admission Requirements: Secondary school certificate (bachillerato) or equivalent, and entrance examination

Fees: 44-218 per month (US Dollar)

Main Language(s) of Instruction: Spanish

Accrediting Agency: Comisión de Acreditación de la Calidad Académica

Degrees and Diplomas: *Técnico*: **Accountancy; Marketing.** *Profesor*: **Foreign Languages Education; Preschool Education; Primary Education; Religious Education; Secondary Education.** *Licenciado, Ingeniero, Arquitecto*: **Accountancy; Architecture; Business Administration; Chemical Engineering; Civil Engineering; Computer Science; Economics; Electrical Engineering; Industrial Engineering; Law; Marketing; Mass Communication; Mechanical Engineering; Philosophy; Psychology; Theology.** *Maestro*: **Business Administration; Commercial Law; Development Studies; Educational Administration; Educational Testing and Evaluation; Finance; Industrial Maintenance; Mass Communication; Philosophy; Political Sciences; Social Sciences; Social Work; Statistics; Theology.** *Doctor*: **Philosophy; Social Sciences.**

Student Services: Academic Counselling, Careers Guidance, Cultural Activities, Language Laboratory, Library, Sports Facilities

Publications: Boletín de Ciencias Económicas y Sociales; Carta a las Iglesias; ECA Número reciente Ediciones anteriores; Letra Capciosa, número 4, junio 2012; Realidad; Revista Latinoamericana de Teología; UCA Editores

Last Updated: 18/12/15

LATIN AMERICAN TECHNICAL UNIVERSITY

Universidad Técnica Latinoamericana (UTLA)

5a Calle Poniente No. 3-8B, Santa Tecla, La Libertad
Tel: +503 2228-4775
EMail: registroacademico@utla.edu.sv
Website: http://www.utla.edu.sv

Rector: Mauricio Rosendo Sermeño Palacios
EMail: msermeno@yahoo.com

Vicerrector: Francisco Alfredo Carrillo Larreynaga

Faculty

Economics (Accountancy; Business Administration; Economics); **Engineering** (Agricultural Engineering; Civil Engineering; Electrical Engineering; Electronic Engineering; Engineering; Industrial Engineering; Mechanical Engineering)

History: Founded 1981.

Academic Year: February to November (February-June; July-November)

Admission Requirements: Secondary school certificate (bachillerato) and entrance examination

Main Language(s) of Instruction: Spanish

Accrediting Agency: Ministry of Education

Degrees and Diplomas: *Licenciado, Ingeniero, Arquitecto*

Student Services: Library

Last Updated: 22/12/15

LUTHERAN SALVADOREAN UNIVERSITY

Universidad Luterana Salvadoreña (ULS)

Apdo Postal 3039-3057, Km. 3 1/2 Carretera a los Planes de Renderos, Autopista a Comalapa, San Salvador
Tel: +503 2133-2600
Fax: +503 2133-2614
EMail: uls@uls.edu.sv
Website: http://www.uls.edu.sv

Rector: Fidel Nieto Láinez

Vicerrector: Dagoberto Gutiérrez

Faculty

Human and Natural Sciences (Accountancy; Agriculture; Business Administration; Computer Science; Ecology; Law); **Theology and Humanities** (Social Work; Theology)

History: Founded 1991.

Academic Year: February to June; August to September

Admission Requirements: Secondary school certificate

Main Language(s) of Instruction: Spanish

Accrediting Agency: Ministry of Education

Degrees and Diplomas: *Licenciado, Ingeniero, Arquitecto*

Student Services: Academic Counselling, Canteen, Careers Guidance, Health Services, Language Laboratory

Last Updated: 22/12/15

MÓNICA HERRERA SCHOOL OF COMMUNICATION STUDIES

Escuela de Comunicación Mónica Herrera (ECMH)
Avenida Manuel Gallardo 3-3, Nueva San Salvador (Santa Tecla), La Libertad 25076500
Tel: +503 2507-6500 +503 2228-1300 +513 2228-8813
Fax: +503 2229-9226 +513 2228-0148
EMail: info@monicaherrera.edu.sv
Website: http://monicaherrera.com

Directora: Teresa Palacios de Chávez
EMail: tdechavez@monicaherrera.edu.sv

Programme
Communication and Digital Strategy (Communication Studies; Multimedia); **Integrated Marketing Communications** (Communication Studies; Marketing); **Strategic Design** (Design)

History: Founded 1995.

Main Language(s) of Instruction: Spanish

Accrediting Agency: Comisión de Acreditación de la Calidad Académica

Degrees and Diplomas: *Licenciado, Ingeniero, Arquitecto*: **Communication Studies; Design; Multimedia.**

Student Services: Canteen, Cultural Activities, IT Centre, Library, Sports Facilities

Last Updated: 18/12/15

MONSEÑOR OSCAR ARNULFO ROMERO UNIVERSITY

Universidad Monseñor Oscar Arnulfo Romero (UMOAR)
Km. 53 Cantón Aldeita, Tejutla, Chalatenango
Tel: +503 2309-3914; +503 2309-3915
Fax: +503 2347-7912
EMail: nfo@umoar.edu.sv
Website: http://www.umoar.edu.sv

Rector: Juan José Solórzano Arriola
EMail: rectoria@umoar.edu.sv

Faculty
Agriculture and Forestry (Agricultural Engineering; Agriculture; Forestry); **Economics and Business Sciences** (Accountancy; Business Administration; Computer Science); **Law and Social Sciences** (Law; Social Sciences); **Science and Humanities** (Arts and Humanities; Computer Science; Education; Natural Sciences)

History: Founded 1993.

Admission Requirements: Secondary school certificate

Main Language(s) of Instruction: Spanish

Degrees and Diplomas: *Técnico; Licenciado, Ingeniero, Arquitecto*

Student Services: eLibrary

Last Updated: 22/12/15

NEW UNIVERSITY SAN SALVADOR

Universidad Nueva San Salvador (UNSSA)
Alameda Roosevelt y 41 Av. Sur, San Salvador
Tel: +503 2526-4500
Fax: +503 2261-2693
EMail: unssa@unssa.edu.sv
Website: http://www.unssa.edu.sv

Rector: Rafael Hernán Contreras Rodríguez

Vicerrector: Eric Roberto Salguero

Faculty
Economics (Accountancy; Business Administration; Economics); **Health Sciences** (Chemistry; Dentistry; Health Sciences; Medicine; Pharmacy); **Law and Social Sciences** (Advertising and Publicity; Law; Political Sciences; Public Relations; Social Sciences; Social Work)

History: Founded 1981.

Academic Year: January to October (January-May; June-October)

Admission Requirements: Secondary school certificate (bachillerato) and entrance examination

Main Language(s) of Instruction: Spanish

Degrees and Diplomas: *Técnico; Licenciado, Ingeniero, Arquitecto; Doctor en Medicina*: **Dentistry; Medicine.**

Student Services: IT Centre, Library

Publications: Revista Analisis

Last Updated: 22/12/15

OPEN UNIVERSITY OF SAN SALVADOR

Universidad Modular Abierta (UMA)
1a. Calle Poniente No. 2117, San Salvador
Tel: +503 2260-5320
EMail: informacion@uma.edu.sv
Website: http://www.uma.edu.sv

Rector: Judith Virginia Mendoza de Díaz

Vicerrector: Edgar Armando Jiménez Yánez

Faculty
Economics (Accountancy; Business Administration; Computer Science; Economics; Human Resources; Marketing; Software Engineering); **Law** (Law); **Science and Humanities** (Arts and Humanities; Education; English; Literature; Natural Sciences; Preschool Education; Primary Education; Psychology; Social Sciences)

Further Information: Also campuses in Santa Ana; San Miguel; Sonsonate.

History: Founded 1982.

Main Language(s) of Instruction: Spanish

Degrees and Diplomas: *Técnico; Licenciado, Ingeniero, Arquitecto; Maestro*: **Higher Education Teacher Training.** Also Diplomado

Student Services: IT Centre, Library, Social Counselling

Last Updated: 22/12/15

PANAMERICAN UNIVERSITY

Universidad Panamericana (UPAN)
Calle Progreso No. 234 a 60 Metros de Avenida Bernal, Colonia Miramonte Poniente, San Salvador
Tel: +503 2527-2000
Fax: +503 2260-1991, Ext.122
EMail: informacionss@upan.edu.sv
Website: http://www.upan.edu.sv

Rector: Oscar Armando Morán Fólgar (1996-)
Tel: +503 2260-1991, Ext.102
EMail: rectoria@upan.edu.sv

Vicerrectora Administrativa: Nubia A. Mendoza Figueroa
Tel: +503 2260-1991, Ext.103
EMail: nmendoza@upan.edu.sv

International Relations: Roberto Molina Castro, Secreterio General Tel: +503 2260-1991, Ext.106
EMail: rmolina@upan.edu.sv

Faculty
Economics (Accountancy; Business Administration; Economics; Marketing; Tourism); **Humanities and Science** (Arts and Humanities; Educational Sciences; English; Library Science; Social Work; Teacher Training); **Law** (Law)

Further Information: Also branches in Ahuachapán and San Vicente.

History: Founded 1990.

Academic Year: January to December (January-June; July-December)

Admission Requirements: Secondary school certificate

Main Language(s) of Instruction: Spanish

Accrediting Agency: Ministry of Education

Degrees and Diplomas: *Técnico*: **Marketing.** *Licenciado, Ingeniero, Arquitecto*

Student Services: Academic Counselling, Canteen, Careers Guidance, Language Laboratory, Library, Social Counselling, Sports Facilities

Last Updated: 22/12/15

PEDAGOGICAL UNIVERSITY OF EL SALVADOR

Universidad Pedagógica de El Salvador (UPED)
25 Avenida Norte, Diagonal Arturo Romero y Primera Diagonal, Colonia Médica
Tel: +503 2226-4065; +503 2226-4059
Fax: +503 2226-4486
EMail: info@pedagogica.edu.sv
Website: http://www.pedagogica.edu.sv

Rector: Luis Alonso Aparicio Guzmàn
EMail: luis.aparicio@salnet.net

International Relations: Carmen Aparicio
EMail: carmen.aparicio@salnet.net

Faculty
Economics (Accountancy; Business and Commerce; Communication Studies; Computer Science; Marketing); **Education** (Education; Educational Sciences; English; Literature; Mathematics Education; Physical Education; Preschool Education; Primary Education; Science Education; Secondary Education; Social Sciences; Social Work)

History: Founded 1982.

Academic Year: January to December (January-July; August-December)

Admission Requirements: Secondary school certificate (bachillerato) and entrance examination

Fees: (Colones): Registration, 275; tuition, 2,100 per semester

Main Language(s) of Instruction: Spanish

Accrediting Agency: Asociación de Universidades Privadas de Centroamérica (AUPRICA)

Degrees and Diplomas: *Licenciado, Ingeniero, Arquitecto*: **Accountancy; Business Administration; Education; Marketing; Social Work.** *Maestro*: **Educational Administration; Preschool Education.** Also Teaching Qualifications, 3 yrs;

Student Services: Academic Counselling, Health Services, IT Centre, Social Counselling

Last Updated: 22/12/15

POLYTECHNIC UNIVERSITY OF EL SALVADOR

Universidad Politécnica de El Salvador (UPES)
Boulevard Tutunichapa y 5ta Avenida Norte, Frente a redondel José Martí (Don Rúa), San Salvador
Tel: +503 2231-8800 +503 2231-8819
EMail: politecnica@upes.edu.sv
Website: http://www.upes.edu.sv

Rector: Roberto López Meyer
Tel: +503 2222-5193
EMail: roberto.meyer@politecnica.edu.sv

Vicerrector Académico: Roberto Antonio Argueta Quan
Tel: +503 2231-8803
EMail: rarguetaq@politecnica.edu.sv

Faculty
Economics and Business (Accountancy; Business Administration; Economics; Marketing); **Engineering and Architecture** (Architecture; Civil Engineering; Computer Engineering; Electrical Engineering; Engineering; Industrial Engineering; Systems Analysis); **Law and Social Sciences** (Law)

Further Information: Also a Research Institute

History: Founded 1979.

Academic Year: January to December (January-June; July-December)

Admission Requirements: Secondary school certificate (bachillerato)

Main Language(s) of Instruction: Spanish

Accrediting Agency: Associación de Universidades Privadas de Centro América (AUPRICA)

Degrees and Diplomas: *Técnico; Licenciado, Ingeniero, Arquitecto*

Student Services: Academic Counselling, IT Centre, Library

Last Updated: 22/12/15

SCHOOL OF ECONOMICS AND COMMERCE

Escuela Superior de Economía y Negocios (ESEN)
Km. 12 1/2 Carretera al Puerto de La Libertad, Nueva Calle a Comasagua, Santa Tecla, La Libertad
Tel: +503 2234-9292 +503 2234-9275
EMail: info@esen.edu.sv; admision@esen.edu.sv; contacto@esen.edu.sv
Website: http://www.esen.edu.sv

Rector: José Ricardo Poma Delgado

Director General: José Everardo Rivera Bonilla

Programme
Business Engineering (Business Administration; Engineering); **Economics and Business** (Business and Commerce; Economics); **Juridical Sciences** (Law)

History: Founded 1994.

Main Language(s) of Instruction: Spanish

Accrediting Agency: Comisión de Acreditación de la Calidad Académica

Degrees and Diplomas: *Licenciado, Ingeniero, Arquitecto*

Last Updated: 18/12/15

UNIVERSITY OF SONSONATE

Universidad de Sonsonate (USO)
29 Calle Oriente y Avenida Central Final Colonia 14 de Diciembre, Sonsonate
Tel: +503 2429-9500
Fax: +503 2429-9503
EMail: informacion@usonsonate.edu.sv
Website: http://www.usonsonate.edu.sv

Rector: Jesús Adalberto Díaz Pineda

Vicepresidente: Fernando Rodríguez Villalobos

Faculty
Economics and Social Sciences (Accountancy; Business Administration; Economics; Education; Social Sciences); **Engineering and Natural Sciences** (Agricultural Business; Computer Engineering; Electrical Engineering; Engineering; Industrial Engineering; Natural Sciences); **Law** (Law)

History: Founded 1982.

Academic Year: February to December (February-July; August-December)

Admission Requirements: Secondary school certificate (bachillerato)

Main Language(s) of Instruction: Spanish

Degrees and Diplomas: *Profesor, Licenciado, Ingeniero, Arquitecto*

Student Services: Academic Counselling, Careers Guidance, Library, Sports Facilities

Last Updated: 21/12/15

UNIVERSITY OF TECHNOLOGY OF EL SALVADOR

Universidad Tecnológica de El Salvador (UTEC)
Calle Arce No. 1120, San Salvador
Tel: +503 2275-8888
Fax: +503 2271-0765
EMail: infoutec@utec.edu.sv
Website: http://www.utec.edu.sv

Rector: Nelson Zárate Sánchez

Faculty
Business Administration (Accountancy; Administration; Business Administration; Finance; Marketing; Tourism); **Computer and Applied Sciences** (Computer Science; Engineering); **Law** (Law); **Postgraduate Studies** (Banking; Business Administration; Finance; Marketing); **Social Sciences** (Anthropology; Communication Studies; Modern Languages; Psychology)

History: Founded 1980.

Academic Year: January to December (January-June; August-December)

Admission Requirements: Secondary school certificate (bachillerato) and entrance examination

Main Language(s) of Instruction: Spanish

Accrediting Agency: Comisión de Acreditación de la Calidad Académica

Degrees and Diplomas: *Técnico*: **Computer Engineering; Computer Networks; Graphic Design; Journalism; Marketing; Public Relations; Sales Techniques; Software Engineering; Tourism.** *Licenciado, Ingeniero, Arquitecto*: **Accountancy; Anthropology; Archaeology; Architecture; Business Administration; Communication Studies; Computer Engineering; Computer Science; English; Graphic Design; Industrial Engineering; International Business; Marketing; Psychology; Tourism.** *Maestro*: **Banking; Business Administration; Finance; Marketing.**

Student Services: Academic Counselling, Cultural Activities, Health Services, Language Laboratory, Nursery Care, Social Counselling

Last Updated: 18/12/15

UNIVERSITY OF THE EAST

Universidad de Oriente (UNIVO)

4a. Calle Poniente No. 705, San Miguel
Tel: +503 2668-3700
Fax: +503 2661-8354
EMail: info@univo.edu.sv
Website: http://www.univo.edu.sv

Rector: Pedro Fausto Arieta Vega
Tel: +503 2668-3707 EMail: parieta@univo.edu.sv

Vicerrectora Academica: Maria Louisa Sevillano
Tel: +503 2668-3755 EMail: msevillano@univo.edu.sv

Faculty

Agronomy (Agronomy; Veterinary Science); **Economics** (Accountancy; Business Administration; Computer Science; Marketing); **Engineering and Architecture** (Architecture; Civil Engineering; Engineering; Industrial Engineering; Systems Analysis); **Health Siences** (Health Sciences; Nursing); **Humanities** (Art Education; Arts and Humanities; Communication Studies; English; Mathematics Education; Physical Education; Preschool Education; Psychology; Science Education); **Law** (Law)

History: Founded 1982.

Admission Requirements: Secondary school certificate.

Main Language(s) of Instruction: Spanish

Accrediting Agency: Ministerio de Educación

Degrees and Diplomas: *Licenciado, Ingeniero, Arquitecto*; *Maestro*: **Business Administration; Child Care and Development; Civil Law; Clinical Psychology; Criminal Law; Economics; Finance; Higher Education Teacher Training; Marketing; Preschool Education.**

Student Services: Library

Last Updated: 21/12/15

Equatorial Guinea

STRUCTURE OF HIGHER EDUCATION SYSTEM

Description:

Higher education is provided by the University of Equatorial Guinea and several graduate schools.

Stages of studies:

University level first stage: *First cycle*

The first cycle offers professional training in three years' study leading to the titles of Diplomado Universitario, Ingeniero Tecnico, or Arquitecto Tecnico.

University level second stage: *Second cycle*

The second cycle leads to the diploma of Licenciado in 4 to 6 years' study depending on the specialty.

NATIONAL BODIES

Ministerio de Educación y Ciencia (Ministry of Education and Science)

Minister: Maria Del Carmen Ekoro

Malabo

Data for academic year: 2012-2013

Source: IAU from Base Curie, Fiche Guinée Equatoriale, Ministère des Affaires étrangères et européennes, France, 2012. Bodies 2016.

INSTITUTION

PUBLIC INSTITUTION

UNIVERSITY OF EQUATORIAL GUINEA

Universidad Nacional de Guinea Ecuatorial (UNGE)

Avenida. Hassan II s/n, 661, Malabo
Tel: +240(333) 09-16-44
Fax: +240(333) 09-43-61
EMail: unge@orange.gq
Website: http://www.unge.gq/unge

Rector: Carlos Nsé Nsuga
Tel: +240(222) 27-50-44 EMail: nsuga52@yahoo.com

Vice-Rector, Malabo: Manuela Roka Botey
Tel: +240(333) 09-16-41

Vice-Recteur, Bata: Pedro Ndongo-Asumu
EMail: terealene@hotmail.com; ndongoasumu@yahoo.es

Secrétaire général: Diosdado Nguema Obono
Tel: +240(333) 09-16-44 +240(222) 51-41-81
EMail: dionguema5@yahoo.es

International Relations: Tito Mitogo, Director, Inter-University Cooperation

Faculty

Arts and Social Sciences *(FLCS)* (Administration; Arts and Humanities; Business Administration; Business Computing; Economics; Journalism; Law; Pedagogy; Philology; Political Sciences; Social Sciences; Sociology; Spanish); **Environmental Studies** *(FMA)* (Environmental Management; Environmental Studies; Human Resources); **Humanities** *(Founded 2011)* (Arts and Humanities); **Medicine** *(FM)* (Medicine; Nursing; Public Health; Surgery)

School

Administration *(EUA)* (Administration; Banking; Finance; Human Resources; Public Administration; Small Business); **Agriculture, Fishery and Forestry** *(EUEAPF)* (Agricultural Business; Agricultural Engineering; Agriculture; Fishery; Forestry; Geological Engineering; Mechanical Engineering; Metallurgical Engineering; Mining Engineering; Petroleum and Gas Engineering); **Health and Environment** *(EUSMA - Bata)* (Health Sciences; Nursing); **Teacher Training - Bata** *(EUFP - Bata)* (Education; Foreign Languages Education; Humanities and Social Science Education; Physical Education; Preschool Education; Primary Education; Sports; Teacher Training); **Teacher Training - Malabo** *(EUFP - Malabo)* (Education; Foreign Languages Education; Humanities and Social Science Education; Physical Education; Preschool Education; Primary Education; Secondary Education; Sports; Teacher Training); **Technical Engineering** *(EUIT - Bata)* (Architecture; Civil Engineering; Electrical Engineering; Electronic Engineering; Engineering; Industrial Engineering; Mechanical Engineering; Structural Architecture; Technology)

Further Information: Campuses in Malabo and Bata

History: Founded 1995.

Main Language(s) of Instruction: Spanish

Degrees and Diplomas: *Diploma Universitario*; *Licenciatura*: **Medicine.**

Academic Staff *2010-2011*: Total 431

STAFF WITH DOCTORATE: Total 23

Student Numbers *2010-2011*: Total: c. 6,500

Last Updated: 04/07/12

Eritrea

STRUCTURE OF HIGHER EDUCATION SYSTEM

Description:

Higher education is provided by several colleges and institutes, some of which are private. The University of Asmara was restructured to give rise to 7 institutions of higher education (IHE) in different parts of the country, in 2006.

Stages of studies:

University level first stage: *Bachelor's degree*

A Bachelor's Degree is obtained after four years of regular study for day students in a majority of the fields of study except Engineering, Law, Pharmacy, and Veterinary Science which take five years. Medicine and Dentistry require eight years of study. Extension students take seven years to finish their studies.

University level second stage: *Master's degree*

The postgraduate programme at Master's level is carried out after obtaining a BA or BSC degree and several years of work experience (preferably 5 years and above). Candidates with a Cumulative Grade Point Average (CGPA) of 2.5 and above (on a 4.00 scale) are selected. Studies require one year of intensive course work and one year of research work. Candidates will be required to write a thesis and defend it at the end of the period of study in the presence of internal and external examiners. Successful, candidates are awarded a Master of Science (MSc) or a Master of Arts (MA) degree.

ADMISSION TO HIGHER EDUCATION

Admission to university-level studies:

Name of secondary school credential required: Eritrean Secondary Education Certificate Examination (ESECE)

Minimum score/requirement: Five subject passes including English and Mathematics

For entry to: Colleges and all institutions of higher education.

Name of secondary school credential required: Orientation Examination

Other requirements: Advice by the University Placement Office

Foreign students admission:

Admission requirements: Foreign students must hold a certificate equivament to the Eritrean Secondary School Leaving Certificate Examination.

Entry regulations: A visa is required.

Health requirements: Overseas students must be free from HIV and Hepatitis.

Language proficiency: Good knowledge of English is essential.

RECOGNITION OF STUDIES

Quality assurance system:

The Bureau of Standards and Evaluation within the NBHE undertakes quality assurance of all tertiary institutions of higher education.

NATIONAL BODIES

Ministry of Education

Minister: Semere Russom
Harenet Avenue
PO Box 1056
Asmara

Tel: +291(1) 127-817 +291(1) 127-808
Fax: +291(1) 125-369
Role of national body: National body responsible for higher education.

National Board for Higher Education - NBHE
Executive Director: Mehari Tadesse
Director of Administration and Finance: Sebhatleab Tewolde
Director of HE Administration and International Linkages: Zemenfes Tsighe
PO Box 1220
Asmara
Tel: +291(1) 161-932
Fax: +291(1) 162-236
EMail: nbhe@nbhe.org.er
WWW: http://www.nbhe.org.er
Role of national body: To promote higher education and facilitate the advancement of all institutions to be centers of excellence in terms of education and research. Through this process, the NBHE intends to play an important role in spearheading the building up of a knowledge-based economy in the country.

Data for academic year: 2011-2012
Source: IAU from National Board for Higher Education, Asmara, 2012. Bodies 2016.

INSTITUTIONS

PUBLIC INSTITUTIONS

ASMARA COLLEGE OF HEALTH SCIENCES (ACHS)

PO Box 1220, Asmara

Dean: Azieb Ogabagebriel

Programme
Health Sciences (Dentistry; Health Education; Medical Auxiliaries; Medical Technology; Medicine; Nursing; Public Health)
History: Created 2006.
Accrediting Agency: National Board of Higher Education (NBHE)
Degrees and Diplomas: *Bachelor's Degree*; *Master's degree*
Last Updated: 23/07/12

COLLEGE OF ARTS AND SOCIAL SCIENCES (CASS)

Adi Keyh

Programme
Arts (Archaeology; Arts and Humanities; English; Fine Arts; Geography; History); **Social Sciences** (Anthropology; Journalism; Mass Communication; Social Sciences; Social Work; Sociology)
History: Created 2006.
Accrediting Agency: National Board of Higher Education (NBHE)
Degrees and Diplomas: *Bachelor's Degree*; *Master's degree*
Last Updated: 23/07/12

COLLEGE OF BUSINESS AND ECONOMICS (CBE)

Halhale

Programme
Business and Economics (Business Administration; Economics)
History: Created 2006.
Accrediting Agency: National Board of Higher Education (NBHE)
Degrees and Diplomas: *Bachelor's Degree*; *Master's degree*
Last Updated: 23/07/12

COLLEGE OF MARINE SCIENCES AND TECHNOLOGY (COMSAT)

Massawa

Programme
Marine Science (Marine Biology; Marine Science and Oceanography)
History: Created 2006.
Accrediting Agency: National Board of Higher Education (NBHE)
Degrees and Diplomas: *Bachelor's Degree*; *Master's degree*
Last Updated: 23/07/12

ERITREA INSTITUTE OF TECHNOLOGY (EIT)

P. O. Box 1056, Asmara 1276
Tel: +291(1) 837-1120
Fax: +291(1) 837-3092
Website: http://eit.edu.er/

Acting President: Haile Tesfamichael
EMail: ararat20042003@yahoo.com
Director of Administration and Finance: Alibekit Awelkier
Tel: +291(1) 837-1121
International Relations: Tekie Asehun, International Relations Officer EMail: tekieal@eit.edu.er

College
Education (Education; Educational Administration; Educational Psychology; Foreign Languages Education; Humanities and Social Science Education; Mathematics Education; Physical Education; Science Education); **Engineering and Technology** (Chemical Engineering; Civil Engineering; Computer Engineering; Electrical and Electronic Engineering; Mechanical Engineering; Mining Engineering); **Science** (Biology; Chemistry; Computer Science; Geology; Information Sciences; Library Science; Mathematics; Physics)

Programme
Postgraduate (Biology; Chemistry; Mathematics; Physics)

Centre
Information Technology (Information Technology)
History: Created 2004.

Academic Year: September to July

Admission Requirements: Eritrea Education Certificate Examination

Fees: Free

Main Language(s) of Instruction: English

Accrediting Agency: National Board of Higher Education (NBHE)

Degrees and Diplomas: *Bachelor's Degree*: **Biology; Chemistry; Computer Science; Education; Educational Administration; Educational Psychology; Engineering; Geology; Information Sciences; Library Science; Mathematics; Physics.** *Master's degree*: **Information Technology; Mathematics; Physics.** Also Diploma in 2-3 yrs.

Student Services: Academic Counselling, Canteen, Facilities for disabled people, Health Services, Nursery Care, Sports Facilities

Academic Staff *2012-2013*	MEN	WOMEN	TOTAL
FULL-TIME	243	35	**278**
PART-TIME	27	4	**31**
STAFF WITH DOCTORATE			
FULL-TIME	–	–	**64**
Student Numbers *2012-2013*			
All (Foreign included)	4,860	1,890	**6,750**
FOREIGN ONLY	–	–	**30**

Last Updated: 25/09/12

HAMELMALO AGRICULTURAL COLLEGE (HAC)

Hamelmalo, Anseba

Dean: Semere Amlesom

Programme

Agriculture (Agricultural Economics; Agricultural Engineering; Agriculture; Agronomy; Animal Husbandry; Crop Production; Environmental Management; Horticulture)

History: Created 2006.

Accrediting Agency: National Board of Higher Education (NBHE)

Degrees and Diplomas: *Bachelor's Degree*; *Master's degree*

Last Updated: 23/07/12

OROTTA SCHOOL OF MEDICINE AND DENTAL MEDICINE (OSM & DM)

Asmara

Programme

Dentistry (Dentistry); **Medicine** (Medical Technology)

History: Created 2004.

Accrediting Agency: National Board of Higher Education (NBHE)

Degrees and Diplomas: *Bachelor's Degree*; *Master's degree*

Last Updated: 23/07/12

Estonia

STRUCTURE OF HIGHER EDUCATION SYSTEM

Description:

The higher education system is binary and consists of universities (ülikool) and professional higher education institutions (rakenduskõrgkool). Since the academic year 2002/2003, the general structure of higher education is divided into two main cycles. The first cycle is the bachelor's level (3 to 4 years: 180 to 240 ECTS credits); the second cycle is the master's level (1 to 2 years: 60 to 120 ECTS credits). For some fields of study, the programmes have been integrated into a single long cycle, following the master's level qualification (5 to 6 years: 300-360 ECTS credits). The highest stage at universities is doctoral studies (3 to 4 years: 180 to 240 ECTS credits). Professional higher education programmes are first cycle programmes of higher education and correspond to the bachelor's degree programmes. The duration of studies is 3 to 4.5 years (180 to 270 ECTS credits). Higher education is regulated by Republic of Estonia Education Act, Universities Act, Institutions of Professional Higher Education Act, Private Schools Act, and Standard of Higher Education. The administration of higher education institutions or their study programmes are the responsibility of the Ministry of Education and Research, Estonian Ministry of the Interior, Estonian Ministry of Defence.

Stages of studies:

University level first stage: *Bachelor studies*
Bachelor's programmes are first-cycle higher education programmes. The purpose of bachelor studies is to broaden the scope of general education, to develop the basic knowledge and skills required for a certain field of study necessary for continuing at the master's level or for access to the labour market. The nominal duration of the programmes is generally 3 years (180 ECTS credits), as an exception, it may be up to 4 years (240 ECTS credits). The qualification awarded upon completion of the programme is Bakalaureus. The qualification gives access to master's programmes.
Professional higher education institutions also provide first-cycle higher education programmes. The nominal period of study is 3-4 years (180-240 ECTS credits). Midwifery and specialized nursing studies last 4 1/2 years (270 ECTS credits). The qualification awarded is Rakenduskõrghariduse diplom (Diploma of Professional Higher Education). The qualification gives access to master's programmes.

University level second stage: *Magister studies*
Master's programmes are second-cycle higher education programmes. The purpose of master's level studies is to develop the knowledge and skills required for a certain field of study and to acquire the necessary competences in order to enter the labour market or to continue studies at the doctoral level. The access requirement is a first-cycle higher education qualification. The nominal duration of the programmes is 1 to 2 years (60-120 ECTS credits), but together with the first-cycle studies it is at least 5 years (300 ECTS credits). The qualification awarded upon completion of a Master's degree programme is Magister. The qualification gives access to doctoral programmes. Integrated bachelor's and master's programmes comprise both basic and specialized studies. Such long-cycle programmes are offered in the fields of medicine, dentistry, pharmacy, veterinary medicine, architecture, civil engineering, and class-teacher training. The nominal duration of medical studies and of veterinary studies effective from the 2002/2003 academic year admissions, is 6 years (360 ECTS credits). The nominal duration of other integrated programmes is 5 years (300 ECTS credits). The qualification awarded upon completion of an integrated study programme in the fields of pharmacy, architecture, civil engineering, and class-teacher training is Magister, the other qualifications are Arstikraad (in medicine), Hambaarstikraad (in dentistry) and Loomaarstikraad (in veterinary medicine). The qualifications give access to doctoral programmes.

University level third stage: *Doktor studies*
Doctoral programmes represent higher education of the third cycle, the purpose of which is to acquire knowledge and skills necessary for independent research, development or professional creative work. The access requirement for doctoral studies is a degree of Magister or a corresponding qualification. The nominal period of study is 3 to 4 years (180-240 ECTS credits). The qualification awarded upon completion of doctoral studies is Doktor. The degree of Doktor is a research degree obtained after the completion and public defence of a dissertation (doktoritöö) based on independent scientific research or creative work.

ADMISSION TO HIGHER EDUCATION

Admission to university-level studies:

Name of secondary school credential required: Gümnaasiumi lõputunnistus

For entry to: Universities and professional higher education institutions.

Name of secondary school credential required: Kutsekeskhariduse lõputunnistus

For entry to: Universities and professional higher education institutions.

Alternatives to credentials: Lõputunnistus kutsekeskhariduse omandamise kohta or Lõputunnistus keskhariduse baasil kutseõppe omandamise kohta which are certificates conferred on completion of secondary vocational education.

Admission requirements: Since 1997, students must sit for the state examinations (riigieksamid) to have access to higher education institutions. Depending on the speciality, higher education institutions may require some additional entrance examinations.

Numerus clausus: In reasoned cases, a university may establish the upper limit for students to be matriculated in the terms for admission by filling student places based on the ranking of the applicants.

Other requirements: Riigieksamitunnistus (State Examination Certificate)

There is a selection procedure for most higher education institutions and programmes. In general, the results of state examinations passed in a general secondary school (gümnaasium) are accepted as the basis of admission, sometimes an interview or a professional aptitude test is required. It may also include a number of entrance examinations.

Entrance examinations are most commonly set by faculties and approved by the boards of higher education institutions. Prevalent subjects are usually those relevant to the course of study. The basis for the admission decision is usually a combination of state examination results of general subjects and entrance examination results in the subject relevant to the course of study.

Foreign students admission:

Definition of foreign student: A student who is studying at an Estonian university and who is the citizen of a foreign country and does not have a permanent residence permit.

Quotas: There are quotas established at the institution level.

Admission requirements: Applicants must be eligible for higher education in their own country and have a qualification corresponding to Estonian qualification giving access to higher education. Foreign students must usually apply for admission on the same terms as Estonian students. Specific requirements depend on the higher education institution requirements and on the chosen field of study. These can include entrance examinations, an interview, or minimum marks on the secondary-level school leaving certificate.

Entry regulations: Citizens of all third countries need a visa for visits that are 3 to 6 months long. A temporary residence permit for study is required if a third country student intends to stay in Estonia for more than three months (in some cases only one month).

Language proficiency: All applicants need to provide proof of proficiency in the language of a respective study programme. Most international students apply for programmes taught in English, but there are also those who prefer to study in Estonian or Russian. Documented proof is usually not required from native-speakers or from applicants who have completed their previous education in a respective language. In most cases, results of internationally accepted foreign language tests are accepted. Some institutions carry out their own language tests and/or interviews.

RECOGNITION OF STUDIES

Quality assurance system:

Since 2009, higher education quality has been assessed by an independent agency Eesti Kõrghariduse Kvaliteediagentuur (The Estonian Higher Education Quality Agency). The responsibility of the agency is to conduct institutional accreditation of higher education institutions and quality assessment of study programme groups. Within the assessment process of study programme groups it is assessed if the programmes correspond with the current legislation and with the national and international standards, including the quality of theoretical and practical training, the qualifications of the teaching and research staff, as well as the availability of the necessary resources. On the basis of external assessment, the Government of the Republic grants the higher education institution the right, for an indefinite or a fixed (1 to 3 years) period of time, to conduct studies according to the programme belonging to the respective study programme group. Until 01.01.2010, external assessment of study programmes resulted in adopting accreditation decisions. Full accreditation was granted for seven years, conditional accreditation is valid for three years.

Bodies dealing with recognition:

Eesti Kõrghariduse Kvaliteediagentuur - EKKA (EKKA Quality Assessment Council)

Toompuiestee 30
Tallinn 10149
Tel: +372 640 0455
EMail: ekka@archimedes.ee
WWW: http://ekka.archimedes.ee/

Akadeemilise Tunnustamise Infokeskus (Eesti ENIC/NARIC) (Academic Recognition Information Centre (Estonian ENIC/NARIC))

Head: Gunnar Vaht
Koidula 13a
Tallinn 10125
Tel: +372 697 9214
Fax: +372 697 9226
EMail: enic-naric@archimedes.ee
WWW: http://www2.archimedes.ee/enic/

Special provisions for recognition:

Recognition for university level studies: Starting from 2009, educational institutions may provide higher education programmes, award academic degrees and issue diplomas, if, as a result of the assessment of the respective study programme group, the Government of the Republic has granted them such a right. At the same time, until 31.12.2011, official recognition of qualifications is also based upon accreditation decisions. In addition to diplomas issued after accreditation was granted, diplomas issued up to two years before the accreditation decision was adopted, are also recognized. Besides, diplomas issued by public universities, certifying the completion of study programmes entered into the Estonian Education Information System (database) before 01.06.2002, and diplomas issued by state professional higher education institutions, certifying the completion of study programmes entered into the database before 30.06.2003, are officially recognized without accreditation.

For access to advanced studies and research: State recognised diploma is required which will be provided after accreditation.

For exercising a profession: State recognised diploma is required which will be provided after accreditation.

NATIONAL BODIES

Eesti Vabariigi Haridus-ja Teadusminsteerium (Ministry of Education and Research)

Minister: Jürgen Ligi
Deputy Secretary General for Higher Education and Research: Indrek Reimand
Munga 18
Tartu 50088
Tel: +372 735 0222
Fax: +372 730 1080
EMail: hm@hm.ee
WWW: http://www.hm.ee

Role of national body: The Ministry of Education and Research is responsible for the planning of education, research, youth and language related national policies and, in conjunction thereof, managing the fields of pre-primary, basic, general upper secondary, vocational secondary, higher, hobby and adult education, organising research and development activities, youth work and special youth work, and compiling drafts of corresponding legal acts.

Eesti Kõrghariduse Kvaliteediagentuur - EKKA (EKKA Quality Assessment Council)

Director: Heli Mattisen
Council Secretary: Hillar Bauman
Toompuiestee 30
Tallinn 10149
Tel: +372 640 0455
EMail: ekka@archimedes.ee
WWW: http://ekka.archimedes.ee/

Role of national body: The responsibility of the agency is to conduct institutional accreditation of higher education institutions and quality assessment of study programme groups. EKKA also provides accreditation of study programme groups in vocational education and training and analyses the evaluation results and makes recommendations for improvement to educational institutions and the Ministry of Education and Research.

Rektorite Nõukogu (Universities Estonia)

President: Tiit Land
Secretary-General: Hanna Kanep
Postal address: Ülikooli 18
Visiting address: Lossi 40
Tartu 50090
Tel: +372 737 6516
EMail: ern@ern.ee
WWW: http://www.ern.ee

Role of national body: The non-profit association Universities Estonia was established by six Estonian public universities on November 1, 2000. The aim of the association is to contribute to the promotion of the fields of education, research and culture in Estonia through the representation of its members and the opinion formation concerning the issues of common interest.

Data for academic year: 2014-2015
Source: IAU from the Estonian ENIC/NARIC, 2014. Bodies 2016.

INSTITUTIONS

PUBLIC INSTITUTIONS

ESTONIAN ACADEMY OF ARTS

Eesti Kunstiakadeemia (EKA)
Tartu mnt. 1, 10145 Tallinn
Tel: +372 6267-301
Fax: +372 6267-350
EMail: artun@artun.ee
Website: http://www.artun.ee

Rector: Signe Kivi
Tel: +372 6267-309 EMail: karolin.magi@artun.ee

Vice-Rector: Liina Siib EMail: liina.siib@artun.ee

International Relations: Maria Jürisson
Tel: +372 6267-369 EMail: maria.jurisson@artun.ee

Faculty
Architecture (Architecture; Interior Design; Landscape Architecture; Town Planning); **Art and Culture** (Art Education; Art History; Cultural Studies; Folklore; Heritage Preservation); **Design** (Ceramic Art; Fashion Design; Glass Art; Jewellery Art; Leather Techniques; Textile Design); **Fine Arts** (Graphic Arts; Media Studies; Painting and Drawing; Photography; Sculpture)

School
Restoration (Heritage Preservation)

Institute
Art History and Aesthetics (Aesthetics; Art History)

History: Founded 1914 as the Tallinn Industrial Art School of the Estonian Society of Art, became Art University 1989 and acquired present title 1996.

Academic Year: September to May (September-December; January-May)

Admission Requirements: Secondary school certificate (keskkooli lõputunnistus)

Main Language(s) of Instruction: Estonian, English

Degrees and Diplomas: *Bakalaureus*: **Fine Arts.** *Rakenduskõrghariduse diplom*; *Magister*: **Fine Arts.** *Doktor*: **Fine Arts.**

Student Services: Academic Counselling, Canteen, Social Counselling

Last Updated: 10/04/15

ESTONIAN ACADEMY OF MUSIC AND THEATRE

Eesti Muusika-ja Teatriakadeemia (EMTA/EAMT)
Rävala pst 16, 10143 Tallinn
Tel: +372 6675-700
Fax: +372 6675-800
EMail: ema@ema.edu.ee
Website: http://www.ema.edu.ee

Rector: Peep Lassmann (1992-) EMail: peep@ema.edu.ee

Vice-Rector: Margus Pärtlas EMail: margus@ema.edu.ee

International Relations: Marje Lohuaru EMail: marje@ema.edu.ee

School
Drama (Theatre)

Department
Brass and Woodwind (Musical Instruments); **Chamber Music** (Music); **Composition** (Music Theory and Composition); **Conducting** (Conducting); **Cultural Management and Humanities**; **Jazz Music** (Jazz and Popular Music; Musical Instruments); **Musicology** (Musicology); **Piano** (Musical Instruments; Religious Music); **Strings** (Musical Instruments); **Voice** (Singing)

Institute
Music Education (Music Education); **Musical Performance Teacher Training** (Music Education)

Centre
Continuing Education; **Humanities**

History: Founded 1919.

Academic Year: August to June

Admission Requirements: Secondary school certificate (keskkooli lõputunnistus)

Fees: 4,600 per annum. Citizens of the EU can compete for state-commissioned student places (Euro)

Main Language(s) of Instruction: Estonian

Degrees and Diplomas: *Bakalaureus*: **Fine Arts.** *Magister*: **Music; Music Education.** *Doktor*: **Music; Theatre.**

Student Services: Academic Counselling, Facilities for disabled people, Language Laboratory, Social Counselling, Sports Facilities

Last Updated: 10/04/15

ESTONIAN AVIATION ACADEMY

Eesti Lennuakadeemia (ELA)
Lennu 40, Reola, Tartu
Tel: +372(7) 448-100
Fax: +372(7) 448-101
EMail: eava@eava.ee
Website: http://www.eava.ee

Rector: Jaan Tamm (2009-)
Tel: +372(7) 448-100 EMail: jaan.tamm@eava.ee

Vice-Rector: Ants Aaver
Tel: +372(7) 309-227 EMail: ants.aaver@eava.ee

International Relations: Paul Lääne, Coordinator of Co-operation Programmes Tel: +372(7) 448-106 EMail: paul.laane@eava.ee

Programme
Air Traffic Management (Air Transport); **Aircraft Engineering** (Aeronautical and Aerospace Engineering); **Aircraft Piloting** (Air Transport); **Aviation Management** (Air Transport; Transport Management)

History: Founded 1993 as Tartu Lennukolledž. Acquired present status and title 2008. A State institution.

Accrediting Agency: Ministry of Education and Research

Degrees and Diplomas: *Rakenduskõrghariduse diplom*; *Magister*

Last Updated: 10/04/15

ESTONIAN UNIVERSITY OF LIFE SCIENCES

Eesti Maaülikool (EMÜ)
Kreutzwaldi 64, 51014 Tartu
Tel: +372(7) 313-001
Fax: +372(7) 313-068
EMail: info@emu.ee
Website: http://www.emu.ee

Rector: Mait Klaassen EMail: rektor@emu.ee

College
Technology (Technology)

Institute
Agricultural and Environmental Sciences (Agriculture; Environmental Studies); **Economics and Social Sciences** (Economics; Social Sciences); **Forestry and Rural Engineering** (Forestry; Rural Studies); **Technology** (Technology); **Veterinary Medicine and Animal Sciences** (Animal Husbandry; Veterinary Science)

Centre
Science Studies *(Karl Ernst von Baer House)* (Natural Sciences)

Further Information: Also Open Distance Learning courses

History: Founded 1951. Acquired present status and title 1991.

Academic Year: September to August (September-January; January-August)

Admission Requirements: Secondary school certificate (Keskkooli lõputunnistus)

Main Language(s) of Instruction: Estonian

Degrees and Diplomas: *Bakalaureus*; *Arstikraad; Hambaarstikraad; Loomaarstikraad*: **Animal Husbandry; Veterinary Science.** *Magister*, *Doktor*: **Biological and Life Sciences.**

Last Updated: 10/04/15

TALLINN UNIVERSITY

Tallinna Ülikool (TU (TLÜ))
Narva mnt. 25, 10120 Tallinn
Tel: +372 640-9101
Fax: +372 640-9116
EMail: tlu@tlu.ee
Website: http://www.tlu.ee

Rector: Tiit Land (2011-)
Tel: +372 6409-100 EMail: tiit.land@tlu.ee

International Relations: Tiina Mäe, International Relations Coordinator Tel: +372 6409-144 EMail: tiina.mae@tlu.ee

International Relations: Doris Altin, International Marketing Specialist EMail: altin@tlu.ee

College
Catherine's College *(Liberal Arts)* (Arts and Humanities; Social Sciences); **Haapsalu College** (Computer Science; Handicrafts; Management; Primary Education; Technology); **Pedagogical** (Continuing Education; Preschool Education; Social Work); **Rakvere College** (Preschool Education; Social Work)

School
Film and Media *(Baltic School)* (Cinema and Television; Film; Journalism; Mass Communication; Public Relations); **Law** *(Tallin University Law School formerly University Nord (Akadeemia Nord))* (Advertising and Publicity; Commercial Law; European Union Law; International Law; Law; Marketing; Public Law)

Institute
Communication (Advertising and Publicity; Communication Studies; Media Studies); **Confucius Institute** (Chinese); **Ecology** (Ecology); **Educational Sciences** (Adult Education; Educational Sciences; Preschool Education; Primary Education; Secondary Education; Special Education; Teacher Training; Vocational Education); **Estonian Institute for Future Studies**; **Estonian Institute for Humanities** (Anthropology; Arts and Humanities; Cultural Studies; Literature; Modern Languages); **Estonian Language and Culture** (Applied Linguistics; Baltic Languages; Finnish; Linguistics; Literature; Modern Languages; Native Language); **Fine Arts** (Art Therapy; Dance; Fine Arts; Music); **Germanic-Romance Languages and Cultures** (Cultural Studies; Germanic Languages; Romance Languages; Translation and Interpretation); **Health Sciences and Sport** (Leisure Studies; Physical Education; Sports); **History** (Archaeology; History; Medieval Studies); **Informatics** (Information Technology; Multimedia); **Information Studies** (Information Management; Information Sciences); **International and Social Studies** (Gender Studies; International Studies; Social Sciences; Sociology); **Mathematics and Natural Sciences** (Biology; Chemistry; Environmental Management; Geology; Mathematics; Physics); **Political Science and Governance** (Government; Political Sciences; Public Administration); **Population Studies** (Demography and Population); **Psychology** (Behavioural Sciences; Industrial and Organizational Psychology; Psychology); **Slavonic Languages and Culture** (Journalism; Russian; Slavic Languages); **Social Work** (Social Work)

Centre
Entrepreneurship and Business Studies

History: A parliamentary decision by the Republic of Estonia consolidated several Tallinn universities and institutes into a single institution that resulted in the founding of Tallinn University as a public university on 18 March 2005. Tallinn University is an innovative and academically enriching university. It is acknowledged both locally and internationally for its role as a centre for science and education. The mission of Tallinn University is to support the sustainable development of Estonia through research and its application to academic partnership, including the preparation of intellectuals as well as public dialogue in order to facilitate this partnership. Tallinn University incorporates six schools and two colleges. By focusing resources and activities we aim to develop five interdisciplinary research-based focus fields: Educational Innovation Digital and Media Culture Cultural Competencecs Healthy and Sustainable Lifestyle Society and Open Governance

Academic Year: September to June

Admission Requirements: Copy of a secondary education certificate/Bachelor's degree certificate or equivalent/Master's degree certificate or equivalent; Transcript of Records; Proof of English Proficiency

Fees: 830 to 2376 per semester (Euro)

Main Language(s) of Instruction: Estonian, Russian, English

Accrediting Agency: Estonian Higher Education Quality Agency

Degrees and Diplomas: *Bakalaureus*: **Arts and Humanities; Education; Fine Arts; Law; Natural Sciences; Social Sciences.** *Magister*: **Arts and Humanities; Education; Fine Arts; Law; Natural Sciences; Social Sciences.** *Doktor*: **Arts and Humanities; Education; Fine Arts; Natural Sciences; Social Sciences.**

Student Services: Academic Counselling, Canteen, Careers Guidance, Cultural Activities, Facilities for disabled people, Foreign Studies Centre, Language Laboratory, Nursery Care, Social Counselling, Sports Facilities

Academic Staff *2010-2011*	MEN	WOMEN	**TOTAL**
FULL-TIME	121	199	**320**
PART-TIME	104	166	**270**
STAFF WITH DOCTORATE			
FULL-TIME	68	85	**153**
Student Numbers *2012-2013*			
All (Foreign included)	–	–	**9,961**

Last Updated: 28/09/15

TALLINN UNIVERSITY OF TECHNOLOGY

Tallinna Tehnikaülikool
Ehitajate tee 5, 19086 Tallinn
Tel: +372 6202-002
Fax: +372 6202-020
EMail: ttu@ttu.ee
Website: http://www.ttu.ee

Rector: Andres Keevallik
Tel: +372 6202-003 EMail: peep.surje@ttu.ee

Vice-Rector for Academic Affairs: Kalle Tammemäe
EMail: kalle.tammemae@ttu.ee

Faculty

Chemicals and Materials Technology (Chemical Engineering; Environmental Engineering; Food Technology; Inorganic Chemistry; Materials Engineering; Polymer and Plastics Technology); **Civil Engineering** (Building Technologies; Civil Engineering; Construction Engineering; Environmental Engineering; Transport Engineering); **Information Technology** (Computer Engineering; Electronic Engineering; Information Technology; Telecommunications Engineering); **Mechanical Engineering** (Automotive Engineering; Mechanical Engineering; Metal Techniques; Power Engineering; Production Engineering; Thermal Engineering; Transport Engineering); **Power Engineering** (Electrical Engineering; Geological Engineering; Mining Engineering; Power Engineering); **Science** (Applied Physics; Genetics; Mathematics; Molecular Biology; Organic Chemistry; Physics); **Social Sciences** (Law; Psychology; Public Administration; Social Sciences)

School

Economics and Business Administration (Accountancy; Administration; Banking; Business and Commerce; Economics; International Relations; Law; Marketing)

History: Founded 1918 as Engineering College, acquired University status 1936. Name changed to Tallinn Polytechnical Institute 1989. Under the supervision of the Ministry of Education.

Academic Year: September to June

Admission Requirements: State examination and secondary school certificate (Keskkooli lõputunnistus)

Fees: (Kroons): For EU students: Bachelor, 18,800 per semester; Master, 21,000. For students outside of the EU: Bachelor, 23,500; Master, 27,000

Main Language(s) of Instruction: Estonian

Accrediting Agency: Estonian Higher Education Accreditation Centre

Degrees and Diplomas: *Bakalaureus*: **Arts and Humanities; Engineering; Natural Sciences; Social Sciences.** *Magister*: **Arts and Humanities; Business Administration; Engineering; Natural Sciences; Public Administration; Social Sciences.** *Doktor*: **Arts and Humanities; Business Administration; Engineering; Natural Sciences; Public Administration; Social Sciences.**

Student Services: Academic Counselling, Careers Guidance, Cultural Activities, Language Laboratory, Social Counselling, Sports Facilities

Publications: Proceedings of the Tallinn Technical University and the Estonian Academy of Sciences, Engineering

Publishing House: Tallinn Technical University Press

Last Updated: 10/04/15

UNIVERSITY OF TARTU

Tartu Ülikool (TÜ)
Ülikooli 18, 50090 Tartu
Tel: +372(7) 375-100
Fax: +372(7) 375-440
EMail: info@ut.ee
Website: http://www.ut.ee

Rector: Volii Kalm (2012-)
Tel: + 372 737 5600 EMail: rektor@ut.ee

Director of Administration: Andres Liinat (2009-)
Tel: +372 737 6500 EMail: andres.liinat@ut.ee

International Relations: Reesi Lepa, Head of International Cooperation (2012-) Tel: +372 737 6123 EMail: reesi.lepa@ut.ee

Faculty

Economics and Business Administration (Business Administration; Economics); **Exercise and Sport Sciences** (Physical Therapy; Sports); **Law** (Law); **Mathematics and Computer Science** (Computer Science; Mathematics); **Medicine** (Dentistry; Medicine; Nursing; Pharmacy); **Philosophy** (Educational Sciences; History; Modern Languages; Painting and Drawing; Philosophy); **Science and Technology**; **Social Sciences and Education** (Cultural Studies; Journalism; Linguistics; Political Sciences; Psychology; Public Administration; Public Relations; Social Sciences; Social Work; Sociology; Special Education; Teacher Training); **Theology** (Theology)

College

Eurocollege (European Studies); **Narva** (Modern Languages); **Pärnu** (Business Administration; Economics; Environmental Management; Hotel Management; Social Work; Tourism)

Institute

Law *(Tallinn)* (Law)

Academy

Culture *(Viljandi)* (Fine Arts; Performing Arts)

History: Founded 1802 as Universitas Dorpantensis by Alexander I, with German as the language of instruction but tracing its origins to the Academy founded by Gustav II Adolphus of Sweden in 1632. German was replaced by Russian in 1893, when the University was renamed Universitas Iurievensis. Acquired present title 1919. Has incorporated the Institute of Law, Tallinn, and Tartu Teacher Training College.

Academic Year: September to July (September-January; February-July)

Admission Requirements: Secondary school certificate (Keskkooli lõputunnistus) and entrance examination (Sisseastumiseksamid)

Fees: None

Main Language(s) of Instruction: Estonian, Russian, English, German

Accrediting Agency: Estonian Higher Education Quality Agency

Degrees and Diplomas: *Bakalaureus*: **Arts and Humanities; Business Administration; Education; Fine Arts; Health Sciences; Information Sciences; Law; Mathematics and Computer Science; Natural Sciences; Religion; Social Sciences; Welfare and Protective Services.** *Rakenduskõrghariduse diplom*: **Arts and Humanities; Business Administration; Fine Arts; Higher Education; Performing Arts; Service Trades; Welfare and Protective Services.** *Arstikraad; Hambaarstikraad; Loomaarstikraad*: **Health Sciences.** *Magister*: **Arts and Humanities; Business Administration; Education; Fine Arts; Health Sciences; Information Sciences; Law; Mathematics and Computer Science; Natural Sciences; Religion; Social Sciences; Welfare and Protective Services.** *Doktor*: **Arts and Humanities; Education; Health Sciences; Law; Mathematics and Computer Science; Natural Sciences; Religion; Social Sciences; Technology.**

Student Services: Academic Counselling, Canteen, Careers Guidance, Cultural Activities, Facilities for disabled people, Foreign Studies Centre, IT Centre, Language Laboratory, Library, Residential Facilities, Social Counselling, Sports Facilities, eLibrary

Publications: Acta et Commentationes Universitatis Tartuensis de Mathematica; Acta Kinesiologiae Universitatis Tartuensis; Ajalooline Ajakiri. The Estonian Historical Journal; Baltic Journal of Art History; Estonian Journal of Education; Folia Cryptogamica Estonica; Interlitteraria; Journal of Estonian and Finno-Ugrian Linguistics; Juridica International; Methis; Papers on Anthropology; Sign Systems Studies; Studia Metrica et Poetica; Studia Philosophica Estonica

Publishing House: University of Tartu Press

Academic Staff *2013-2014*	MEN	WOMEN	TOTAL
FULL-TIME	687	600	**1,287**
PART-TIME	248	281	**529**
STAFF WITH DOCTORATE			
FULL-TIME	578	376	**954**
Student Numbers *2013-2014*			
All (Foreign included)	5,391	10,634	**16,025**
FOREIGN ONLY	337	247	**584**

Last Updated: 24/09/15

PRIVATE INSTITUTIONS

ESTONIAN BUSINESS SCHOOL (EBS)

Lauteri 3, 10114 Tallinn
Tel: +372 6651-300
Fax: +372 6313-959
EMail: ebs@ebs.ee
Website: http://www.ebs.ee

Rector: Arno Almann EMail: arno.almann@ebs.ee

Programme

Business Administration *(Full-time and Master Studies)* (Business Administration; Information Technology; International Business; Leadership; Management; Modern Languages; Public Administration)

Higher School

EBS High School

Department

Accounting and Finance (Accountancy; Finance); **Behaviour Sciences** (Behavioural Sciences); **Economics** (Economics); **Entrepreneurship** (Business Administration); **Information Technology** (Information Technology); **Management** (Management); **Marketing** (Marketing)

Institute

Foreign Languages (Modern Languages); **Management** (Accountancy; Ethics; Finance; Leadership; Management); **Social Sciences** (Administrative Law; Behavioural Sciences; Economics; Information Technology; Public Administration)

Centre

EBS Executive Training; **Entrepreneurship** (Business Administration); **Ethics** (Ethics)

Further Information: Also an Open University Structure Unit

History: Founded 1988, acquired University status 1995, and accredited by the Estonian Government 1997.

Academic Year: September to June (September-December; January-June)

Admission Requirements: Secondary school certificate (Keskkooli lõputunnistus) or equivalent

Fees: For EU citizens: 3304 per annum (Bachelor's level), 3500 per annum (Master's level), 2700 per annum (Doctoral level) (Euro)

Main Language(s) of Instruction: Estonian, English, Russian

Accrediting Agency: Council of Higher Education in Estonia; Central and East European Management Development Association (CEEMAN)

Degrees and Diplomas: *Bakalaureus*: **Social Sciences.** *Magister*: **Business Administration; Social Sciences.** *Doktor*: **Management.**

Student Services: Academic Counselling, Sports Facilities

Publications: EBS Review; Publications of Estonian Business School

Last Updated: 10/04/15

ESTONIAN ENTREPRENEURSHIP UNIVERSITY OF APPLIED SCIENCES

Eesti Ettevõtluskõrgkool Mainor (EUAS)
Suur-Sõjamäe 10A, 11415 Tallinn
Tel: +372 6057-222
Fax: +372 6207-533
EMail: eek@eek.ee
Website: http://www.eek.ee/

Rector: Krista Tuulik (2010-) EMail: krista.tuulik@eek.ee

Administrative Officer: Tauno Õunapuu
EMail: tauno.ounapuu@eek.ee

Institute

Design (Graphic Design; Interior Design; Textile Design); **Entrepreneurship** (Business Administration); **Information Technology** (Information Technology); **Management** (Management)

History: Founded 1992 as Mainori Majanduskool. Acquired present title and status 2010

Degrees and Diplomas: *Bakalaureus*; *Magister*

Last Updated: 10/04/15

EUROACADEMY

Euroakadeemia
Mustamäe tee 4, 10621 Tallinn
Tel: +372 6115-801
Fax: +372 6115-811
EMail: euro@euroakadeemia.ee
Website: http://www.eurouniv.ee

Rector: Jüri Martin EMail: jmartin@euroakadeemia.ee

Vice-rector: Peeter Karing
EMail: peeter.karing@euroakadeemia.ee

International Relations: Toomas Alatalu
EMail: toomas.alatalu@euroakadeemia.ee

Faculty

Business Administration (Business Administration); **Design** (Design); **Environmental Protection** (Environmental Studies); **International Relations** (International Relations); **Translation and Interpretation** (Translation and Interpretation)

History: Founded as Euro University 1997. Acquired present title 2009.

Degrees and Diplomas: *Bakalaureus*; *Magister*

Last Updated: 10/04/15

Ethiopia

STRUCTURE OF HIGHER EDUCATION SYSTEM

Description:

Higher education is provided by universities, university colleges and specialized institutions. They are under the responsibility of the Ministry of Education. There are also Junior colleges and colleges offering diploma programmes that are under the responsibility of regional governments and private providers.

Stages of studies:

University level first stage: Bachelor's degree

The first stage of university level education leads to the Bachelor's degree after three to four years' study. Examinations are organized at the end of each semester. In Medicine and Veterinary Medicine, the professional qualification of Doctor is conferred after five years' study.

University level second stage: Master's degree; Specialization

The second stage leads to a Master's degree after a minimum of two years' further study. In Medicine and Veterinary Medicine the specialization degree is obtained after a minimum of three years' further study beyond the MD and DVM degrees.

University level third stage: Doctor of Philosophy

The Doctor of Philosophy is conferred after some three years' study beyond the Master's degree.

ADMISSION TO HIGHER EDUCATION

Admission to university-level studies:

Name of secondary school credential required: Ethiopian Higher Education Entrance Examination

Other requirements: Special privileges for female students and students from disadvantaged/remote regions.

Foreign students admission:

Definition of foreign student: A person enrolled at an institution of higher education in a country of which he/she is not permanently resident.

Admission requirements: Foreign students must provide the academic certificates required by the institution concerned. Foreign qualifications recognized as equivalent to the Ethiopian school-leaving certificate are: the General Certificate of Education of the University of London; the Cambridge Overseas Examination; the West African School Certificate and the Oxford Examination. The Higher Education Department may grant equivalence to other secondary school-leaving certificates in individual cases. All foreign students must cover their living expenses.

Entry regulations: Visas; financial guarantee. In addition, all foreign students, including ECOWAS citizens, are required to secure resident permits for the period of their stay.

Health requirements: Students must present a health certificate.

Language proficiency: Students must be proficient in English at TOEFL level.

RECOGNITION OF STUDIES

Quality assurance system:

The University Senate awards credentials which are recognized by the country. The Ministry of Education is mandated to accredit private and public higher education institutions according to whether they fulfil the required standards.

Bodies dealing with recognition:

Higher Education Sector, Ministry of Education

PO Box 1367
Addis Ababa

NATIONAL BODIES

Ministry of Education
Minister: Shiferaw Shigutie
PO Box 1367
Addis Ababa
Tel: +251 11 155 3133
Fax: +251 11 155 0877
EMail: moe.heducation@yahoo.com
WWW: http://www.moe.gov.et

Data for academic year: 2012-2013
Source: IAU from the website of the Ministry of Education and World Data on Education 2010/2011, UNESCO-IBE, 2012. Bodies 2016.

INSTITUTIONS

PUBLIC INSTITUTIONS

ADAMA SCIENCE AND TECHNOLOGY UNIVERSITY (ADU)

PO Box 1888, Nazareth, Oromia
Tel: +251(22) 111-0400
Fax: +251(22) 111-0480
Website: http://www.astu.edu.et/

President: Jang Gyu Lee
Tel: +251(22) 111-0494 EMail: president@astu.edu.et

Vice-President for Administration: Habtamu Kebu
Tel: +251(22) 111-0038

School
Agriculture (Agricultural Business; Agricultural Engineering; Agricultural Management; Animal Husbandry; Marketing; Plant and Crop Protection); **Business** (Accountancy; Business Computing; Economics; Finance; Management; Marketing; Tourism); **Educational Science and Technology Teachers' Education** (Adult Education; Distance Education; Educational Administration; Educational Sciences; Pedagogy; Technology Education); **Engineering and Information Technology** (Agricultural Engineering; Architecture; Chemical Engineering; Civil Engineering; Electrical Engineering; Energy Engineering; Information Technology; Mechanical Engineering; Wood Technology); **Health Sciences** (Biomedicine; Gynaecology and Obstetrics; Medicine; Midwifery; Nursing; Orthopaedics; Paediatrics; Pharmacy; Public Health; Radiology; Surgery); **Humanities and Law** (African Languages; Civics; English; Environmental Management; Ethics; Geography; History; Law; Social Work; Sociology); **Natural Sciences** (Biology; Chemistry; Mathematics; Physics; Statistics)

History: Founded 1993 as Nazareth Technical College (NTC). Became Nazareth College of Technical Teacher Education (NCTTE) 2000. Adama University 2005. Acquired present title 2011.

Main Language(s) of Instruction: Amharic

Degrees and Diplomas: *Bachelor's Degree*: **Agriculture.** *Master's Degree*.

Publications: The Ethiopian Journal of Sciences and Sustainable Development
Last Updated: 05/08/14

ADDIS ABABA UNIVERSITY (AAU)

PO Box 1176, Addis Ababa
Tel: +251(11) 123-9800
Fax: +251(11) 123-9768
EMail: commoffice@aau.edu.et
Website: http://www.aau.edu.et

President: Admasu Tsegaye
Tel: +251(11) 123-9752
EMail: poffice@aau.edu.et; commoffice@aau.edu.et

Vice-President for Business and Development: Estifanos G. Hawariat Tel: +251(11) 123-9783 EMail: hawariat7@yahoo.com

International Relations: Abye Tasse, Associate Vice-President for International Affairs
Tel: +251(11) 123-1084 EMail: abyetas@aau.edu.et

College
Business and Economics (Accountancy; Business Administration; Business and Commerce; Economics; Finance; Management; Marketing; Public Administration); **Development Studies** (Demography and Population; Environmental Studies; Gender Studies; Regional Studies; Rural Planning; Water Science); **Education and Behavioural Studies** (Curriculum; Education; Educational Administration; Educational and Student Counselling; Educational Psychology; Educational Research; Educational Sciences; Educational Testing and Evaluation; Higher Education; Social Psychology; Special Education); **Health Sciences** (Anaesthesiology; Anatomy; Biochemistry; Community Health; Dental Hygiene; Dermatology; Gynaecology and Obstetrics; Medical Technology; Medicine; Microbiology; Midwifery; Neurology; Nursing; Ophthalmology; Orthopaedics; Otorhinolaryngology; Paediatrics; Parasitology; Pathology; Pharmacology; Physiology; Plastic Surgery; Psychiatry and Mental Health; Radiology; Surgery; Venereology; Veterinary Science); **Humanities, Language Studies, Journalism and Communication** (African Languages; Communication Studies; Journalism; Linguistics; Literature; Modern Languages); **Law and Governance Studies** (Commercial Law; Constitutional Law; Government; Human Rights; International Law; Law; Public Law); **Natural Sciences** (Astronomy and Space Science; Biological and Life Sciences; Cell Biology; Chemistry; Computer Science; Earth Sciences; Environmental Studies; Food Science; Geophysics; Marine Science and Oceanography; Mathematics; Microbiology; Paleontology; Physics; Plant and Crop Protection; Seismology; Sports; Statistics; Zoology); **Performing and Visual Arts** *(Skunder Boghossian)* (Fine Arts; Music; Theatre); **Social Sciences** (Anthropology; Archaeology; European Languages; Geography; Heritage Preservation; History; International Relations; Linguistics; Philosophy; Political Sciences; Sociology); **Veterinary Medicine and Agriculture** (Agriculture; Animal Husbandry; Biomedicine; Epidemiology; Immunology; Microbiology; Pathology; Veterinary Science)

School
Social Work (Social Work)

Institute
African Studies (African Studies); **Ethiopian Studies** (African Studies); **Language Studies** (African Languages; Foreign

Languages Education; Linguistics; Literature; Modern Languages; Philology; Theatre); **Pathobiology** *(Aklilu Lemma)* (Biology; Pathology)

Academy
Ethiopian Languages and Cultures (African Languages; Cultural Studies)

History: Founded 1961 as Haile Sellassie I University, incorporating University College of Addis Ababa, founded 1950; Imperial College of Engineering, 1953; Ethio-Swedish Institute of Building Technology, 1954; Imperial Ethiopian College of Agricultural and Mechanical Arts, 1951; Public Health College, 1954; and Theological College of the Holy Trinity, 1960. Acquired present title 1975.

Academic Year: September to July (September-February; February-July). Also Summer programme (July-August)

Admission Requirements: Preparatory Programme certificate, or foreign equivalent

Main Language(s) of Instruction: English

Degrees and Diplomas: *Bachelor's Degree*: **Animal Husbandry; Arts and Humanities; Engineering; Medicine; Natural Sciences; Physics; Veterinary Science.** *Master's Degree*: **Arts and Humanities; Engineering; Natural Sciences; Physics.** *Doctorate*: **Biology; Chemistry; History; Modern Languages.**

Student Services: Academic Counselling, Canteen, Cultural Activities, Health Services, Social Counselling, Sports Facilities

Publications: The Ethiopian Journal of Business and Economics

Publishing House: Addis Ababa University Press

Last Updated: 11/12/12

ADDIS ABABA UNIVERSITY COLLEGE OF COMMERCE (AACC)

PO Box 3131, Addis Ababa, Addis Ababa
Tel: +251(11) 551-5786
EMail: aacomcollege@telecom.net.et
Website: http://www.aaucc.edu.et

Dean: Fesseha Afewerk (2003-)

Department
Accountancy (Accountancy); **Administrative Service Management** (Administration); **Audit Management** (Management); **Business Administration and Information Systems** (Business Administration; Information Sciences); **Finance and Development Economics** (Development Studies; Economics; Finance); **Marketing Management** (Management; Marketing); **Procurement and Supply Management** (Retailing and Wholesaling)

History: Founded in 1943 as a Commercial School.

Degrees and Diplomas: *Bachelor's Degree*; *Master's Degree*

Last Updated: 22/06/12

AMBO UNIVERSITY

PO Box 19, Ambo
EMail: info@ambou.edu.et
Website: http://www.ambou.edu.et

President: Mitiku Tesso

College
Agriculture and Veterinary Sciences (Agriculture; Animal Husbandry; Management; Natural Resources; Plant and Crop Protection; Veterinary Science); **Business and Economics** (Accountancy; Development Studies; Economics; Management; Marketing); **Medicine and Public Health** (Biomedicine; Medicine; Nursing; Pharmacy; Public Health); **Natural and Computer Sciences** (Biology; Chemistry; Health Education; Mathematics; Physical Education; Physics); **Social Sciences and Humanities** (African Languages; Civics; English; Ethics; Law; Literature; Sociology)

Institute
Development Studies (Development Studies; Rural Planning); **Education and Professional Studies** (Educational Administration; Pedagogy); **Technology** (Agricultural Engineering; Civil Engineering; Computer Science; Mechanical Engineering)

History: Founded 1939.

Main Language(s) of Instruction: English

Accrediting Agency: Ministry of Education

Degrees and Diplomas: *Bachelor's Degree*; *Master's Degree*

Last Updated: 22/06/12

ARBA-MINCH UNIVERSITY (AMU)

PO Box 21, Arba Minch, Debub
Tel: +251(46) 881-0097
Fax: +251(46) 881-0279
EMail: president@arbaminch-univ.com
Website: http://www.arbaminch-univ.com/

President: Tarekegn Tadesse
Tel: +251(46) 881-0071 EMail: Tarekegn.tadess@amu.edu.et

Vice-President for Administration and Development: Alemayehu Cufamo
EMail: AVP@arbaminch-univ.com; president@arbaminch-univ.com

International Relations: Getu Lema
Tel: +251(46) 881-4986 EMail: shewareged2000@yahoo.com

Faculty
Applied Sciences (Applied Chemistry; Applied Mathematics; Applied Physics; Biology); **Business and Economics** (Accountancy; Economics; Finance; Management); **Education** (Education); **Engineering** (Architecture; Civil Engineering; Computer Engineering; Electrical Engineering; Information Technology; Mechanical Engineering)

School
Postgraduate Studies (Analytical Chemistry; Biotechnology; Botany; Economics; Environmental Engineering; Hydraulic Engineering; Irrigation; Mathematics; Meteorology; Power Engineering; Water Management; Water Science)

Institute
Water Technology (Hydraulic Engineering; Irrigation; Meteorology; Water Management; Water Science)

History: Founded 1986 as Arba Minch Water Technology Institute. Acquired present status and title 2004.

Academic Year: September to June

Admission Requirements: High School certificate, National General School Leaving Certificate

Fees: (Ethiopian Birr): Engineering and Technology: 3011.80; Teacher Education and Social Sciences: 3011.76; Business and Economics: 2970.32; Applied Science: 2971.22 (per Annum)

Main Language(s) of Instruction: English

Accrediting Agency: Ministry of Education; Higher Education Relevance and Quality Agency of Ethiopia

Degrees and Diplomas: *Bachelor's Degree*: **Computer Science; Engineering; Natural Sciences; Technology.** *Master's Degree*: **Analytical Chemistry; Biotechnology; Botany; Economics; Environmental Engineering; Hydraulic Engineering; Irrigation; Mathematics; Meteorology; Power Engineering; Water Management.** Also advanced diploma programmes.

Student Services: Academic Counselling, Canteen, Facilities for disabled people, Health Services, Language Laboratory, Nursery Care, Social Counselling, Sports Facilities

Publications: Sustainable Water Resources Development in Ethiopia

Last Updated: 25/05/12

BAHIR DAR UNIVERSITY (BDU)

PO Box 1345, Bahir Dar, Amhara
Tel: +251(58) 220-0137
Fax: +251(58) 220-2025
EMail: infobdu@gmail.com
Website: http://www.bdu.edu.et

President: Baylie Damtie Yeshita EMail: bayliedamtie@yahoo.com

International Relations: Moges Abraha Arage, Director, External Relations and Partnership Directorate
EMail: mogbdu@gmail.com; mogesa@bdu.edu.et

Faculty
Educational and Behavioural Sciences (Adult Education; Curriculum; Educational Administration; Educational Psychology; Special Education; Teacher Training); **Humanities** (African Languages;

Communication Studies; English; Folklore; Journalism; Literature); **Social Sciences** (Anthropology; Civics; Environmental Studies; Ethics; Geography; History)

College
Agriculture and Environmental Sciences (Agricultural Management; Agriculture; Botany; Development Studies; Environmental Management; Fishery; Natural Resources; Rural Planning; Water Management; Water Science; Wildlife; Zoology); **Business and Economics** (Accountancy; Business Administration; Business and Commerce; Economics; Information Technology; Management; Marketing; Transport Management); **Health and Medical Sciences** (Health Sciences; Medicine; Nursing; Public Health); **Science** (Biology; Chemistry; Earth Sciences; Industrial Chemistry; Mathematics; Physics; Sports; Statistics)

School
Law (Law)

Institute
Disaster Risk Management and Food Security; **Land Administration** (Rural Planning); **Technology** (Civil Engineering; Computer Engineering; Computer Science; Electrical Engineering; Information Technology; Water Science); **Textile and Fashion Technologies** (Clothing and Sewing; Fashion Design; Textile Design; Textile Technology)

Academy
Maritime Academy (Marine Engineering); **Sport** (Sports)

History: Founded 2000 following merger of Bahir Dar Teachers College and Bahir Dar Polytechnic Institute (Bahir Dar Teachers College, initially known as College of Pedagogy founded 1972 following a tripartite agreement signed between the Ethiopian Government, UNESCO and UNDP; Bahir Dar Polytechnic Institute created 1963 based on an agreement between the former USSR and the Imperial Government of Ethiopia).

Academic Year: September to June (September-December; January-March; April-June)

Admission Requirements: Ethiopian School Leaving Certificate (ESLCE) or equivalent

Main Language(s) of Instruction: English

Accrediting Agency: Ministry of Education

Degrees and Diplomas: *Bachelor's Degree*: **Education; Engineering.** *Master's Degree*: **Engineering Management; Hydraulic Engineering; Sports.** *Doctorate*: **Water Management.**

Student Services: Academic Counselling, Canteen, Cultural Activities, Health Services, Sports Facilities

Academic Staff *2015-2016*: Total 1,631
STAFF WITH DOCTORATE: Total 172
Student Numbers *2015-2016*: Total 53,320
Last Updated: 30/03/16

DEBRE BERHAN UNIVERSITY

PO Box 445, Debre Berhan, Amhara
Tel: +251(11) 681-5440
Fax: +251(11) 681-3191
EMail: teferiadnew@yahoo.com
Website: http://www.dbu.edu.et

President: Getachew Tefera

College
Agriculture and Natural Resource Sciences (Agriculture; Animal Husbandry; Irrigation; Plant and Crop Protection; Water Management); **Business and Economics** (Accountancy; Economics; Management); **Natural and Computational Science** (Biology; Chemistry; Mathematics; Physics; Sports); **Social Science and Humanities** (African Languages; Civics; English; Environmental Studies; Ethics; Geography; Heritage Preservation; History; Psychology)

School
Computing (Computer Science; Information Technology); **Engineering** (Building Technologies; Chemical Engineering; Civil Engineering; Electrical Engineering; Mechanical Engineering); **Health Sciences** (Health Sciences; Nursing)

Institute
Education (Education)

History: Founded 1999.

Degrees and Diplomas: *Bachelor's Degree*; *Master's Degree*
Last Updated: 25/05/12

DILLA UNIVERSITY

P.O. Box 419, Dilla
Tel: +251(46) 331-2097
Fax: +251(46) 331-2674
EMail: Dillauniversity@yahoo.com
Website: http://www.dillauniversity.edu.et

President: Admasu Tsegaye

College
Health Sciences (Anaesthesiology; Medicine; Midwifery; Psychiatry and Mental Health)

School
Agricultural Sciences (Agricultural Economics; Agriculture; Animal Husbandry; Horticulture; Plant and Crop Protection); **Business and Economics** (Accountancy; Business Administration; Economics; Management; Public Administration); **Languages and Journalism** (African Languages; Communication Studies; English; Journalism; Literature); **Law** (Law); **Life and Sports Sciences** (Biological and Life Sciences; Sports); **Mathematics and Computer Science** (Computer Science; Mathematics; Statistics); **Natural Resources and Earth Sciences** (Earth Sciences; Environmental Studies; Geography; Geology; Natural Resources); **Pedagogical Science** (Curriculum; Educational Administration; Leadership; Psychology; Special Education; Teacher Training); **Physical Science** (Chemistry; Physics); **Social Sciences and Humanities** (Anthropology; Journalism; Law; Sociology); **Technology** (Building Technologies; Civil Engineering; Mechanical Engineering)

Institute
Indigenous Studies (African Studies)

History: Founded 1996 as Dilla College of Teachers' Education and Health Sciences. Acquired present status 2004.

Degrees and Diplomas: *Bachelor's Degree*; *Master's Degree*
Last Updated: 25/05/12

ETHIOPIAN CIVIL SERVICE UNIVERSITY

CMC Road, Addis Ababa
Tel: +251(11) 6463015
EMail: info@ecsu.edu.et
Website: http://www.ecsc.edu.et

President: Haile Michael Aberra (1996-)
EMail: hailemichael.aberra@ecsc.edu.et

Academic Vice-President: Samson Kassahun
EMail: samson.kassahun@ecsu.edu.et

Institute
Certification of Accountants and Auditors (Accountancy; Finance; Management); **Continuing and Distance Education** *(ICDE)* (Public Administration; Urban Studies); **Federalism and Legal Studies** (Comparative Law; Government; International Law; Public Law); **Leadership and Good Governance** (Government; Leadership); **Public Management and Development Studies** (Development Studies; Public Administration); **Tax and Customs Administration** (Finance; Management; Public Administration; Taxation); **Urban Development Studies** (Town Planning; Urban Studies)

Centre
Public Policy Studies (Public Administration)

History: Founded 1995.

Academic Year: September to August

Admission Requirements: Ethiopian School Leaving Certificate and pass in entrance examination

Fees: Cost sharing scheme adopted, students pay 25% of net salary to the College

Main Language(s) of Instruction: English

Accrediting Agency: Ministry of Education

Degrees and Diplomas: *Bachelor's Degree*: **Civil Engineering; Finance; Management; Surveying and Mapping; Taxation; Town Planning.** *Master's Degree*: **Administration; Ecology; Environmental Management; International Law; International Relations; Law; Leadership; Town Planning; Transport Management.** *Doctorate*: **Finance; Management; Public Administration; Town Planning.**

Student Services: Academic Counselling, Canteen, Health Services, Language Laboratory, Social Counselling, Sports Facilities

Publications: Ethiopian Journal of Public Management and Development (EJPMD); Journal of African Development Studies

Last Updated: 25/05/12

HARAMAYA UNIVERSITY (HU)

PO Box 138, Dire Dawa, Harrar
Tel: +251(25) 553-0319
Fax: +251(25) 553-0325
EMail: haramaya@haramaya.edu.et
Website: http://www.haramaya.edu.et

President: Belay Kassa
Tel: +251(25) 661-0707 EMail: belayk@hotmail.com

College

Agricultural and Environmental Sciences (Agricultural Economics; Agricultural Engineering; Agriculture; Animal Husbandry; Development Studies; Environmental Studies; Natural Resources; Plant and Crop Protection; Rural Planning); **Business and Economics** (Accountancy; Economics; Management; Public Administration); **Computing and Informatics** (Computer Science; Information Technology; Statistics); **Education and Behavioural Sciences** (Education; Educational Administration; Pedagogy; Special Education); **Health Sciences** (Health Sciences; Midwifery; Nursing; Public Health); **Law** (Law); **Medical Sciences** (Anatomy; Biochemistry; Medicine; Microbiology; Pathology; Pharmacology; Physiology); **Natural and Computer Sciences** (Biology; Chemistry; Mathematics; Physics; Sports); **Social Sciences and Humanities** (Arts and Humanities; English; Environmental Studies; Gender Studies; Geography; Heritage Preservation; History; Native Language; Social Sciences; Sociology); **Veterinary Science** (Veterinary Science)

Institute

Technology (Civil Engineering; Computer Engineering; Electrical Engineering; Environmental Engineering; Food Science; Harvest Technology; Natural Resources)

Further Information: Also international Research Centres

History: Founded 1954 as Alemaya University,. A State institution. Acquired present status 1985.

Academic Year: September to July (September-February; February-July)

Admission Requirements: Secondary school certificate or equivalent

Main Language(s) of Instruction: English

Degrees and Diplomas: *Diploma*: **Accountancy; Law; Management.** *Bachelor's Degree*: **Accountancy; African Languages; Agricultural Business; Agricultural Economics; Agricultural Management; Animal Husbandry; Biology; Botany; Business Administration; Chemistry; Civil Engineering; Computer Science; Crop Production; Economics; Electrical Engineering; English; Environmental Management; Environmental Studies; Food Science; Geography; Harvest Technology; Health Sciences; History; Law; Management; Mathematics; Medical Technology; Natural Resources; Nursing; Physics; Public Health; Small Business; Veterinary Science.** *Master's Degree*: **Agricultural Economics; Agricultural Equipment; Agriculture; Agronomy; Animal Husbandry; Biology; Botany; Chemistry; English; Entomology; Food Science; Food Technology; Harvest Technology; Horticulture; Irrigation; Pest Management; Physics; Plant Pathology; Soil Science; Technology.** *Doctorate*: **Agricultural Economics; Agriculture; Agronomy; Animal Husbandry; Crop Production; Entomology; Horticulture; Plant Pathology; Soil Science.** Also Certificate Programmes. Also summer and distance learning programmes.

Student Services: Academic Counselling, Cultural Activities, Health Services, Nursery Care, Social Counselling, Sports Facilities

Publications: East African Journal of Sciences; Harar Bulletin of Health Sciences

Last Updated: 25/05/12

HAWASSA UNIVERSITY (HU)

PO Box 05, Hawassa
Tel: +251(46) 220-9676 +251(46) 220-9677
Fax: +251(46) 220-5421
EMail: info@hu.edu.et
Website: http://www.hu.edu.et

President: Yosef Mamo Tel: +251(46) 220-4627

Vice-President for Administration and Development: Bekele Bulado Tel: +251(46) 220-4628 EMail: bekelebulado@yahoo.com

International Relations: Seyuom Hameso
Tel: +251(46) 220-5168 EMail: hameso@gmail.com

College

Agriculture *(Awassa)* (Agricultural Engineering; Agriculture; Animal Husbandry; Farm Management; Food Science; Home Economics; Nutrition; Plant and Crop Protection); **Business and Economics** (Accountancy; Business Administration; Economics; Hotel Management; Management; Tourism); **Forestry and Natural Resources** *(Wondo Genet)* (Fishery; Forest Products; Forestry; Heritage Preservation; Natural Resources; Soil Science; Tourism; Wildlife); **Health Sciences** (Health Sciences); **Law and Governance** (Development Studies; Government; Law); **Medicine and Health Sciences** (Environmental Studies; Laboratory Techniques; Medicine; Midwifery; Nursing; Public Health); **Natural and Computer Sciences** (Applied Chemistry; Applied Mathematics; Applied Physics; Biology; Computer Science; Sports; Statistics; Veterinary Science); **Social Sciences and Humanities** (Anthropology; Behavioural Sciences; Civics; Education; English; Ethics; Geography; Journalism; Literature; Mass Communication; Psychology; Social Sciences; Sociology)

Institute

Technology (Bioengineering; Building Technologies; Civil Engineering; Electrical Engineering; Irrigation; Mechanical Engineering; Soil Management; Technology; Urban Studies; Water Management)

History: Founded 2000 following merger of Awassa College of Agriculture (ACA), Dilla College of Teachers Education and Health Sciences (DCTEHS) and Wondo Genet College of Forestry (WGCF). Previously known as Debub University. Acquired present title 2006.

Academic Year: September to June

Admission Requirements: Secondary school leaving certificate

Fees: (US Dollars): 100 per credit hour for foreign students

Main Language(s) of Instruction: English

Accrediting Agency: Ministry of Education

Degrees and Diplomas: *Diploma*; *Bachelor's Degree*: **Agricultural Engineering; Education; Fine Arts.** *Master's Degree*: **Botany; Veterinary Science.**

Student Services: Academic Counselling, Canteen, Health Services, Language Laboratory, Social Counselling, Sports Facilities

Publications: Journal of Science and Development

Last Updated: 29/05/12

JIJIGA UNIVERSITY

P.O.Box 1020, Jijiga, Somali
Fax: +251(25) 775-2622
EMail: jju@ethionet.et
Website: http://www.jju.edu.et

President: Ahmed Abdinasir EMail: abdinasir@ethionet.et

Faculty

Business and Economics (Accountancy; Banking; Economics; Finance; Management; Marketing); **Education** (Education); **Engineering and Technology** (Computer Engineering; Computer Science; Electrical Engineering; Information Technology); **Health Sciences** (Health Administration; Midwifery; Nursing); **Natural Sciences** (Applied Chemistry; Biology; Mathematics; Physics)

History: Founded 2007.

Degrees and Diplomas: *Bachelor's Degree*

JIMMA UNIVERSITY (JU)

PO Box 378, Jimma, Oromia
Tel: +251(47) 111-2202 +251(47) 111-1458
Fax: +251(47) 111-1450 +251(47) 111-2040
EMail: main.registrar@ju.edu.et
Website: http://www.ju.edu.et

President: Fikre Lemessa
Tel: +251(47) 111-1457 EMail: Fikre.Lemessa@ju.edu.et

Vice-President for Administration and Development: Kora Tushune Godana
Tel: +251(47) 111-1095
EMail: korat@ju.edu.et; kora.tushune@ju.edu.et

International Relations: Melkamu Dumessa, Director for Public Relations and Communications
Tel: +251(47) 111-2202 EMail: ero@ju.edu.et

College

Agriculture and Veterinary Medicine (Agricultural Economics; Animal Husbandry; Aquaculture; Crop Production; Fishery; Forestry; Harvest Technology; Horticulture; Natural Resources; Plant and Crop Protection; Soil Science); **Business and Economics** (Accountancy; Banking; Business Administration; Economics; Finance; Management); **Natural Sciences** (Biology; Chemistry; Mathematics; Physical Education; Physics; Sports; Statistics); **Public Health and Medical Sciences** (Medicine; Public Health); **Social Sciences and Law** (African Languages; English; Environmental Studies; Folklore; Geography; Government; History; Law; Psychology; Sociology)

Programme

Continuing and Distance Education (Accountancy; African Languages; Banking; Biology; Chemistry; Civil Engineering; Economics; Electrical Engineering; English; Geography; History; Horticulture; Information Technology; Insurance; Law; Management; Marketing; Mathematics; Native Language; Nursing; Pharmacy; Physics; Secretarial Studies)

School

Graduate Studies (Entomology; Epidemiology; Gynaecology and Obstetrics; Horticulture; Medicine; Natural Resources; Paediatrics; Plant Pathology; Public Health; Surgery)

Institute

Technology (Biomedical Engineering; Chemical Engineering; Civil Engineering; Computer Engineering; Computer Science; Electrical Engineering; Information Technology; Mechanical Engineering; Water Science)

History: Founded 1999 through amalgamation of Jimma College of Agriculture (founded 1952) and Jimma Institute of Health Sciences (founded 1983).

Academic Year: September to June

Admission Requirements: Ethiopian General Secondary School examination

Fees: None

Main Language(s) of Instruction: English, (Afan)Oromo
Accrediting Agency: HERQA

Degrees and Diplomas: *Bachelor's Degree*: **Accountancy; Agricultural Economics; Biology; Biomedical Engineering; Chemical Engineering; Chemistry; Civil Engineering; Computer Engineering; Computer Science; Dentistry; Development Studies; Economics; Educational Administration; Electrical Engineering; Engineering; English; Environmental Engineering; Horticulture; Information Technology; Law; Literature; Management; Mathematics; Mechanical Engineering; Medicine; Native Language; Natural Resources; Nursing; Pharmacy; Physics; Plant Pathology; Sociology; Sports; Statistics; Veterinary Science; Zoology.** *Master's Degree*: **Accountancy; Adult Education; Agricultural Business; Agronomy; Analytical Chemistry; Animal Husbandry; Applied Linguistics; Astrophysics; Business Administration; Chemistry; Construction Engineering; Cultural Studies; Curriculum; Development Studies; Economics; Educational Administration; Educational Psychology; Electrical Engineering; Entomology; Environmental Engineering; Environmental Management; Environmental Studies; Epidemiology; Finance; Folklore; Geological Engineering; Gynaecology and Obstetrics; Health Administration; Health Education; History; Horticulture; Hydraulic Engineering; Information Management; Inorganic Chemistry; Literature; Mathematics; Microbiology; Natural Resources; Nursing; Ophthalmology; Organic Chemistry; Paediatrics; Parasitology; Pharmacy; Physical Chemistry; Physiology; Plant Pathology; Power Engineering; Psychiatry and Mental Health; Public Administration; Public Health; Sports Management; Structural Architecture; Surgery; Telecommunications Engineering; Zoology.** *Doctorate*: **Animal Husbandry; Ecology; Environmental Studies; Horticulture; Microbiology; Plant Pathology.**

Student Services: Academic Counselling, Canteen, Cultural Activities, Health Services, Sports Facilities

Publications: Ethiopian Journal of Applied Sciences and Technology; Ethiopian Journal of Health Science; Journal of applied sciences and education; Journal of law

Last Updated: 25/05/12

MEKELLE UNIVERSITY (MU)

PO Box 231, Mekelle, Tigrai
Tel: +251(344) 40-4005
Fax: +251(344) 40-9304
EMail: muccm@mu.edu.et
Website: http://www.mu.edu.et

President: Kindeya Gebrehiwot

International Relations: Fredu Nega, Director, Corporate Communication and Marketing
Tel: +251(34) 440-404005
EMail: fredu.nega@mu.edu.et; tfredu@yahoo.com

College

Business and Economics (Accountancy; Business and Commerce; Economics; Finance; Management); **Dry Land Agriculture and Natural Resources** *(FDAR)* (Agricultural Economics; Agricultural Management; Agriculture; Animal Husbandry; Arid Land Studies; Crop Production; Development Studies; Environmental Studies; Horticulture; Natural Resources; Pastoral Studies; Rural Planning; Soil Management; Tropical Agriculture; Wildlife); **Health Sciences** (Anaesthesiology; Biomedicine; Dentistry; Health Sciences; Medicine; Midwifery; Nursing; Pharmacy; Public Health); **Law and Governance** (Civics; Ethics; Law); **Natural and Computational Science** (Biology; Chemistry; Earth Sciences; Mathematics; Mathematics and Computer Science; Natural Sciences; Physics; Sports); **Social Sciences and Languages** (Communication Studies; Environmental Studies; Geography; History; Journalism; Modern Languages; Native Language; Psychology; Social Sciences); **Veterinary Medicine** (Veterinary Science)

Institute

Geo-information and Earth Observation Sciences (Earth Sciences; Natural Resources; Rural Planning; Town Planning); **Paleo Environment and Heritage Conservation** (Heritage Preservation; Paleontology); **Pedagogical Sciences** (Pedagogy); **Technology** (Architecture and Planning; Engineering; Information Technology)

History: Founded 2000 following merger of Mekelle Business College and Mekelle University College.

Academic Year: September to June (September-January; February-June)

Main Language(s) of Instruction: English

Degrees and Diplomas: *Bachelor's Degree*: **Accountancy; African Languages; Animal Husbandry; Biology; Business Administration; Chemistry; Communication Studies; Crop Production; Economics; Environmental Management; Ethics; Geography; Geology; History; Horticulture; Journalism; Law; Mathematics; Medicine; Natural Resources; Nursing; Petroleum and Gas Engineering; Pharmacy; Physics; Psychology; Public Health; Rural Planning; Veterinary Science.** *Master's Degree*: **Agronomy; Animal Husbandry; Arid Land Studies; Business Administration; Development Studies; Economics; Finance; Geological Engineering; Geology; Gynaecology and Obstetrics; Marketing; Natural Resources; Pastoral Studies; Physics; Public Health; Surgery; Tropical Agriculture; Water Science.**

Student Services: Academic Counselling, Canteen, Cultural Activities, Health Services, Sports Facilities

Publications: Momona Ethiopian Journal of Science; Profile of Research Projects
Last Updated: 25/05/12

UNIVERSITY OF GONDAR (UGR)

PO Box 196, Gondar, Amhara
Tel: +251(58) 111-0174
Fax: +251(58) 114-1240
EMail: uogmail@uog.edu.et
Website: http://www.uog.edu.et

President: Mengesha Admasu
Tel: +251(58) 114-1231 EMail: kal_meng@yahoo.com
International Relations: Ephrem Melaku Mamo
EMail: ephmelk@yahoo.com

Faculty
Business and Economics (Accountancy; Business Administration; Economics; Management; Marketing; Tourism); **Agriculture** (Agricultural Economics; Natural Resources; Plant and Crop Protection; Rural Planning; Water Management); **Natural and Computer Sciences** (Biology; Chemistry; Computer Science; Mathematics; Physics; Statistics); **Social Sciences and Humanities** (Anthropology; English; Environmental Management; Environmental Studies; Geography; History; Modern Languages; Psychology; Sociology; Zoology); **Veterinary Science** (Veterinary Science; Zoology)

College
Medicine and Health Sciences (Anaesthesiology; Health Sciences; Laboratory Techniques; Medicine; Midwifery; Nursing; Nutrition; Occupational Health; Ophthalmology; Optometry; Pharmacy; Public Health)

School
Education (Education); **Engineering** (Civil Engineering; Electrical Engineering; Mechanical Engineering); **Law** (Law)

Further Information: Campuses: Maraki, Science Amba, Tewodros

History: Founded 1954 as Gondar Public Health College and Training Centre. Acquired present status 2004.

Admission Requirements: Ministry of Education decides

Fees: (Ethiopian Birr): 2937.43-3829.15

Main Language(s) of Instruction: English

Degrees and Diplomas: *Bachelor's Degree*; *Master's Degree*; *Doctorate*. Also satellite Training Programmes (diploma level degrees offered in junior colleges outside Gondar); Semi-distance Training (students need to be present only 10-12 weeks per annum).

Student Services: Academic Counselling, Canteen, Health Services, Nursery Care, Social Counselling, Sports Facilities

Publications: Ethipian Journal of Health and Biomedical Sciences
Last Updated: 11/12/12

WOLLEGA UNIVERSITY (WU)

PO Box 395, Nekemte, Oromia
Tel: +251(57) 661-7981
Fax: +251(57) 661-7980
EMail: wu@ethionet.et
Website: http://www.wuni.edu.et

President: Fekadu Beyene
Tel: +257(57) 661-7979 EMail: fekadu.beyene@yahoo.com

Vice-President for Administration and Development: Abera Fite

International Relations: Getu Abebe, Public and External Relation Officer

Faculty
Education (Psychology); **Engineering and Technology** (Architecture; Civil Engineering; Computer Science; Electrical Engineering; Engineering; Information Technology; Mechanical Engineering); **Health and Medical Sciences** (Health Sciences; Laboratory Techniques; Midwifery; Nursing; Pharmacy; Public Health); **Language Studies and Journalism** (African Languages; Communication Studies; English; Journalism); **Natural Sciences** (Biology; Chemistry; Earth Sciences; Mathematics; Physics; Statistics); **Social Sciences** (Civics; Environmental Studies; Geography; International Relations; Political Sciences; Sociology)

College
Agriculture and Natural Resources (Agriculture; Animal Husbandry; Food Science; Food Technology; Irrigation; Natural Resources; Plant and Crop Protection; Rural Studies; Soil Management; Water Management)

School
Accountancy and Finance (Accountancy; Banking; Finance); **Cooperative and Management** (Business Administration; Management; Marketing; Public Administration; Sales Techniques); **Economics** (Economics); **Law** (Law); **Veterinary Science** (Veterinary Science)

Institute
Food Science and Biotechnology (Biotechnology; Food Science)

History: Founded 2007.

Academic Year: October to June: (October-January; March-June)

Admission Requirements: General Secondary School Completion Certificate Examination; Completion of Preparatory Program (10+2), pass mark in Entrance Examination

Main Language(s) of Instruction: English

Degrees and Diplomas: *Bachelor's Degree*: **Animal Husbandry; Law; Natural Sciences; Social Sciences; Technology; Veterinary Science.** *Master's Degree*

Student Services: Academic Counselling, Canteen, Careers Guidance, Cultural Activities, Health Services, Language Laboratory, Social Counselling, Sports Facilities

Publications: Research Report; WU Info Sciences
Last Updated: 29/05/12

PRIVATE INSTITUTIONS

GAMBY COLLEGE OF MEDICAL SCIENCES

209, 106 Code 1035, Bahir Dar
Tel: +251 5822 02636
Fax: +251(11) 647-7717
EMail: gcmsaddis@gmail.com; zewdie1984@gmail.com

Dean: Gebeyaw Tiruneh (2015-) EMail: gebeyawt@yahoo.com

International Relations: Zewdie Aderaw, International relations Officer EMail: zewdie1984@gmail.com

Department
Clinical Pharmacy (Pharmacy); **Medicine** (Medicine); **Midwifery** (Midwifery); **Nursing** (Nursing); **Public Health** (Public Health)

History: Created 1998

Accrediting Agency: HERQA

Degrees and Diplomas: *Bachelor's Degree*: **Medicine; Midwifery; Nursing; Pharmacy; Public Health.** *Master's Degree*: **Public Health.**

Academic Staff *2015-2016*	**TOTAL**
FULL-TIME	**45**
PART-TIME	**23**
STAFF WITH DOCTORATE	
FULL-TIME	**18**
Student Numbers *2015-2016*	
All (Foreign included)	**784**

Last Updated: 11/03/16

SAMARA UNIVERSITY (SU)

Samara, Afar
Tel: +251(33) 666-0591
Fax: +251(33) 666-0621
EMail: samarauniversity@su.edu.et
Website: http://www.su.edu.et

President: Mohammed Usman Darsa
EMail: mabuzikra@yahoo.com

International Relations: Dawud Mohammed Ali, Director, International Relations EMail: davegc2000@yahoo.com

Faculty

Business and Economics (Accountancy; Economics; Finance; Management); **Dry Land Agriculture** (Crop Production; Environmental Management; Natural Resources; Plant and Crop Protection); **Engineering and Technology** (Chemical Engineering; Computer Science); **Medical and Health Sciences** (Nursing); **Natural and Computational Sciences** (Biology; Chemistry; Mathematics; Physics; Sports); **Social Science and Humanities** (Anthropology; English; Ethics; Heritage Preservation; History; Literature; Native Language; Sociology); **Veterinary Medicine** (Veterinary Science)

Centre

Agricultural Technology Adaptation Trial and Training (Agriculture)

Research Centre

Agricultural Research and Demonstration (Agriculture)

History: Created 2007.

Degrees and Diplomas: *Diploma*; *Bachelor's Degree*; *Master's Degree*

Academic Staff *2012-2013*: Total 534

STAFF WITH DOCTORATE: Total 17

Student Numbers *2012-2013*: Total 6,331

Last Updated: 15/02/13

ST. MARY'S UNIVERSITY COLLEGE (SMUC)

Lideta Kifle Ketema, Wereda 9, Addis Ababa 18490 1211
Tel: +251(11) 553-8025
Fax: +251(11) 553-8000
EMail: smu@smuc.edu.et
Website: http://www.smuc.edu.et/

President: Wondwosen Tamrat Wolde
Tel: +251(11) 553-7994 EMail: preswond@smuc.edu.et

Executive Vice President: Tedla Haile Shilmat
Tel: +251(11) 553-8024 EMail: tedla_haile@smuc.edu.et

International Relations: Misganaw Solomon Mengistu, Associate Vice President for Academic Affairs
Tel: +251(11) 553-8025 EMail: misganaw_solomon@smuc.edu.et

Faculty

Business (Accountancy; Human Resources; Management; Marketing; Public Administration; Secretarial Studies); **Information Science** (Computer Science; Information Sciences; Library Science); **Law** (Law)

School

Graduate Studies (Business Administration; Information Sciences)

Institute

Agricultural and Development Studies (Agricultural Business; Agricultural Economics; Agriculture; Rural Studies)

History: Created 1998. Acquired current status 2000.

Academic Year: October-January; February-June; August-September

Main Language(s) of Instruction: English

Accrediting Agency: Higher Education Relevance and Quality Agency (HERQA)

Degrees and Diplomas: *Bachelor's Degree*: **Computer Science; Law; Management; Marketing.** *Master's Degree*: **Business Administration; Business and Commerce; Economics; Human Resources; Information Sciences; Library Science; Public Administration; Social Work; Sociology.**

Student Services: Academic Counselling, Canteen, Careers Guidance, Health Services, Language Laboratory, Nursery Care, Sports Facilities

Academic Staff *2012-2013*	MEN	WOMEN	TOTAL
FULL-TIME	96	8	**104**
PART-TIME	25	4	**29**
STAFF WITH DOCTORATE			
FULL-TIME	15	–	**15**
Student Numbers *2012-2013*			
All (Foreign included)	1,065	1,055	**2,120**
FOREIGN ONLY	2	7	**9**

Distance students, 13,078.

Last Updated: 17/06/13

UNITY UNIVERSITY

Gerji
Website: http://www.uu.edu.et

President: Arega Yirdaw

Faculty

Business and Economics (Business and Commerce; Economics); **Engineering and Architecture** (Architecture; Town Planning); **Humanities and Social Sciences** (Modern Languages; Philosophy; Psychology); **Information Technology and Computer Science** (Computer Science; Information Technology; Mathematics; Statistics)

School

Distance and Continuing Education (Continuing Education; Distance Education); **Health Sciences** (Health Sciences); **Journalism and Communication** (Communication Studies; Journalism); **Law and International Studies** (International Studies; Law)

History: Founded 1991 Unity Language School. Became Unity College 1998 and Unity University College 2002. Acquired present status 2008.

Degrees and Diplomas: *Bachelor's Degree*; *Master's Degree*

Last Updated: 18/07/11

Faroe Islands

STRUCTURE OF HIGHER EDUCATION SYSTEM

Description:

Higher education comprises a university sector and a college sector, i.e. the professionally-oriented higher education sector. The university sector includes 1 university. The university sector offers programmes at three levels: Bachelor's Degree (3 years of study), Master's Degree (normally 2 years following the Bachelor's Degree) and the PhD Degree (normally 3 years' study after the Masteŕs Degree). Study programmes of the university sector are research based. The college sector comprises specialized institutions of higher education offering professionally oriented programmes. The University of the Faroe Islands is publicly financed and state regulated. The University must follow national legislation concerning degree structures, teacher qualifications and examinations, including a system of external examiners. A nationally established – fully independent – evaluation panel assures the quality and the relevance of higher education programmes. The use of the European Credit Transfer System (ECTS) and the use of the Diploma Supplement is mandatory in all study programmes at the University.

Stages of studies:

University level first stage: *Bachelor's level studies*

Undergraduate study lasts for 3 or 4 years (180 or 240 ECTS) and leads to the award of a Bachelor's Degree. The degree is awarded by the universities/specialized higher education institutions upon completion of a research-based study programme concentrating from the first year on the major subject area chosen for the degree. The final year includes a major project. All Bachelor programmes must follow the same national standards and there are no classifications in honours/ordinary programmes. The Bachelor programmes prepare the students for occupational functions and for studies for the Master's degree.

University level second stage: *Master's level studies*

The Master's degree can be obtained at the University of the Faroe Islands. Admission requires a Bachelor's degree in the same field of study. The degree is normally awarded after a total of 5 years of study: the Bachelor's degree (3 years, 180 ECTS) and a Master programme, which is 2 years (120 ECTS). Independent research activities are an important part of the Master's programme. The Masteŕs thesis (serritgerð) is a major requirement and is normally scheduled for 6 months' full-time study (30 ECTS).

University level third stage: *Doctoral studies*

A PhD degree can be obtained at universities and other research-based institutions of higher education. The typical PhD programme is a 3-year programme following the Master's degree. The programme must include a scientific project, participation in research programmes and seminars corresponding to six months' work, experience in teaching or other kinds of communication of research results, mobility, and finally public defence of the PhD thesis.

ADMISSION TO HIGHER EDUCATION

Admission to university-level studies:

Name of secondary school credential required: Gymnasial miðnámsútbúgving

Other requirements: Home students to apply by 1 July.

Foreign students admission:

Quotas: None

Admission requirements: International students must apply by 15 April.

RECOGNITION OF STUDIES

Quality assurance system:

The Faroe Islands do not have an accreditation body. The University of the Faroe Islands is State regulated. The University must follow the national legislation concerning e.g. degree structures, teacher qualifications and examinations, including a system of external examiners. A nationally established – fully independent – evaluation panel appointed by the Ministry of education assures the quality and the relevance of higher education programmes.

Bodies dealing with recognition:

Mentamálaráðið (Ministry of Education, Resarch and Culture)

Hoyvíksvegur 72
Tórshavn 100
Tel: +298 35 60 00
Fax: +298 35 65 55
EMail: mmr@mmr.fo
WWW: http://www.mmr.fo

NATIONAL BODIES

Mentamálaráðið (Ministry of Education, Research and Culture)

Minister: Rigmor Dam
Permanent Secretary: Poul Geert Hansen
Hoyvíksvegur 72
Tórshavn 100
Tel: +298 35 60 00
Fax: +298 35 65 55
EMail: mmr@mmr.fo
WWW: http://www.mmr.fo
Role of national body: Responsible for education and research

Data for academic year: 2015-2016
Source: Ministry of Education, Research and Culture of the Faroe Islands, 2015. Bodies 2016.

INSTITUTION

UNIVERSITY OF THE FAROE ISLANDS

Fróðskaparsetur Føroya
J.C.Svabos gøta 14, Box 272, Tórshavn 100
Tel: +298 29 25 00
Fax: +298 35 25 01
EMail: setur@setur.fo
Website: http://setur.fo/

Rector: Sigurð í Jákupsstovu (2011-)
Tel: +298 29 25 03 EMail: sigurdj@setur.fo

International Relations: Holger Arnbjerg, Director of the International Office Tel: +298 29 25 13 EMail: holgera@setur.fo

Department

Education (Educational and Student Counselling; Pedagogy; Teacher Training); **History and Social Sciences** (History; Law; Management Systems; Political Sciences; Social Sciences; Theology); **Language and Literature** (Linguistics; Literature; Native Language); **Nursing** (Nursing); **Science and Technology** (Biology; Energy Engineering; Information Technology)

History: Created 1965 as an academy by the Faroese Parliament. Reorganised as a university in 1987.

Academic Year: August to July

Admission Requirements: Upper secondary school for Bachelor degrees; Bachelor-level education for Master degrees.

Fees: National: None, International: For NON-EU nationals: (eg. 40,000 Dkk at master level) (Danish Krone)

Main Language(s) of Instruction: Faroese

Degrees and Diplomas: *Bachelorútbúgvingar/Bachelor's degree*: **Biology; Educational and Student Counselling; Energy Engineering; History; Information Technology; Linguistics; Literature; Native Language; Nursing; Pedagogy; Political Sciences; Social Sciences; Teacher Training.** *Candidate/Master's degree*: **History; Law; Linguistics; Literature; Management Systems; Native Language; Political Sciences; Social Sciences.** *Doctorate degree*: **Biology; Energy Engineering; History; Information Technology; Law; Linguistics; Literature; Native Language; Political Sciences; Social Sciences.**

Student Services: Academic Counselling, Canteen, Careers Guidance, Cultural Activities, Facilities for disabled people, Library, Sports Facilities, eLibrary

Publications: Frøði

Publishing House: www.setur.fo

Academic Staff *2014-2015*	MEN	WOMEN	**TOTAL**
FULL-TIME	49	48	**97**
PART-TIME	–	5	**5**
STAFF WITH DOCTORATE			
FULL-TIME	5	2	**7**
Student Numbers *2014-2015*			
All (Foreign included)	263	394	**657**

Last Updated: 22/06/15

Fiji

STRUCTURE OF HIGHER EDUCATION SYSTEM

Description:

Higher education is provided by three universities - including a regional university - agencies of overseas higher education institutions, and many medium and small tertiary institutions offering a wide range of technical and vocational courses.

Stages of studies:

University level first stage: *Bachelor's degree*

The first stage of higher education leads, after three years' study, to the Bachelor's degree.

University level second stage: *Master's degree*

The Master's degree is conferred after one to three years' study beyond the Bachelor's degree. It is awarded either after the submission of a thesis following research in an approved topic or after course work, examination and thesis.

University level third stage: *Doctor of Philosophy*

The third stage leads to the award of a Doctor of Philosophy degree. Candidates must submit a thesis after research in an approved subject.

ADMISSION TO HIGHER EDUCATION

Admission to university-level studies:

Name of secondary school credential required: Fiji School Leaving Certificate

Alternatives to credentials: Seventh Form Certificate

Other requirements: One-year foundation course at the University.

Foreign students admission:

Admission requirements: Foreign students must hold qualifications equivalent to the university's foundation programme.

RECOGNITION OF STUDIES

Quality assurance system:

Registration and recognition of all tertiary and vocational institutes by the Higher Education Commission is compulsory to be able to operate.

NATIONAL BODIES

Ministry for Education, National Heritage, Culture and Arts

Minister: Mahendra Reddy

Acting Permanent Secretary: Kelera Taloga

Marela House, Thurston Street

Suva

Tel: +679 331-4477

Fax: +679 330-3511

WWW: http://www.education.gov.fj

Role of national body: The Ministry is concerned with broad policy issues on all aspects of education.

Fiji Higher Education Commission - FHEC
Executive Chairman: Richard Wah
Director: Salote Rabuka
Red Cross Building
22 Gorrie Street
Suva
Tel: +679 310-0031
Fax: +679 310-0302
EMail: SRabuka001@govnet.gov.fj
WWW: http://www.fhec.gov.fj/
Role of national body: Its role is to advise the Minister of Education on the steps to be undertaken in developing and promoting the higher education sector. It regulates the operation of higher education institutions.

Data for academic year: 2013-2014
Source: IAU from Fiji Higher Education Commission website, 2013. Bodies 2015.

INSTITUTIONS

PUBLIC INSTITUTIONS

FIJI NATIONAL UNIVERSITY (FNU)

P.O. Box 7222, Nasinu
Tel: +679 339-4000
Fax: +679 339-4003
EMail: enquiry-business@fnu.ac.fj; enquiry.academic@fnu.ac.fj
Website: http://www.fnu.ac.fj/new/

College
Agriculture, Fisheries and Forestry (Agriculture; Animal Husbandry; Fishery; Forestry; Veterinary Science; Zoology); **Business, Hospitality and Tourism** (Accountancy; Banking; Business Computing; Finance; Hotel Management; Management; Tourism); **Engineering, Science and Technology** (Automotive Engineering; Biology; Chemistry; Civil Engineering; Electrical and Electronic Engineering; Environmental Studies; Marine Science and Oceanography; Mathematics; Mechanical Engineering; Physics; Printing and Printmaking); **Humanities and Education** (Business Education; Education; Ethics; Film; Geography; Government; Graphic Design; History; Humanities and Social Science Education; Journalism; Music; Music Education; Physical Education; Primary Education; Radio and Television Broadcasting; Science Education; Secondary Education; Visual Arts); **Medicine, Nursing and Health Sciences** (Dental Hygiene; Dentistry; Dietetics; Epidemiology; Medical Technology; Medicine; Nursing; Nutrition; Pharmacy; Physical Therapy; Public Health)

Institute
The Pacific Eye Institute *(Postgraduate Diplomas)* (Ophthalmology)

History: Founded 1855. Acquired present status and title 2010 following merger of Suva Medical School, Fiji School of Nursing, Fiji Institute of Technology, Fiji College of Agriculture, and Fiji College of Advanced Education.
Main Language(s) of Instruction: English
Accrediting Agency: Fiji Higher Education Commission (FHEC)
Degrees and Diplomas: *Certificate/ Diploma*; *Bachelor's Degree*: **Dentistry; Medicine; Pharmacy.** *Postgraduate Diploma*; *Master's Degree*
Last Updated: 02/04/13

UNIVERSITY OF THE SOUTH PACIFIC (USP)

P.O. Box 1168, Suva
Tel: +679 323-1000 +679 323 2313
Fax: +679 323-1502
EMail: vcpa@usp.ac.fj
Website: http://www.usp.ac.fj

Vice-Chancellor, President: Rajesh Chandra
Tel: +679 323-2312 EMail: chandra_r@usp.ac.fj
Deputy Vice-Chancellor, Administration and Regional Campuses: Esther Williams
Tel: +679 323-2073 EMail: williams_e@usp.ac.fj
International Relations: John Bythell, Pro Vice-Chancellor, Research and International
Tel: +679 323-2247 EMail: john.bythell@usp.ac.fj

Faculty
Arts, Law, and Education (Chinese; Education; Journalism; Law; Linguistics; Literature; Media Studies; Modern Languages; Social Sciences); **Business and Economics** (Accountancy; Business Administration; Business and Commerce; Economics; Finance; Management; Public Administration; Tourism); **Science, Technology, and Environment** (Biology; Chemistry; Computer Science; Earth Sciences; Electrical Engineering; Engineering; Environmental Management; Environmental Studies; Food Science; Geography; Information Sciences; Information Technology; Marine Science and Oceanography; Mathematics; Mechanical Engineering; Nutrition; Physics; Statistics)

Institute
The Pacific Eye Institute *(Master's degrees)* (Ophthalmology)

Further Information: Campuses in Fiji (Laucala Campus), Samoa (Alafua Campus) and Vanuatu (Emalus Campus). Also Centres in Cook Islands, Fiji, Kiribati, Nauru, Niue, Marshall Islands, Samoa, Solomon Islands, Tokelau, Tonga, Tuvalu and Vanuatu. Also Analytical Laboratory. Courses in Pacific Culture and English bridging programmes for foreign students
History: Founded 1968. Acquired present status 1970. It is jointly owned by the governments of 12 member countries: Cook Islands, Fiji, Kiribati, Marshall Islands, Nauru, Niue, Solomon Islands, Tokelau, Tonga, Tuvalu, Vanuatu and Samoa.
Academic Year: February to November (February-June; July-November)
Admission Requirements: Secondary school certificate and successful completion of the Foundation programme
Main Language(s) of Instruction: English
Accrediting Agency: Fiji Higher Education Commission (FHEC)
Degrees and Diplomas: *Certificate/ Diploma*: **Accountancy; Austronesian and Oceanic Languages; Banking; Computer Engineering; Demography and Population; Development Studies; Economics; Educational Testing and Evaluation; Fishery; Geography; Hindi; Industrial Management; Information Sciences; Information Technology; Journalism; Library Science; Management; Marine Science and Oceanography; Modern**

Languages; Natural Resources; Police Studies; Preschool Education; Real Estate; Rural Planning; Social Work; Tropical Agriculture. *Bachelor's Degree*: **Agriculture; Education; Engineering; Fine Arts; Law.** *Postgraduate Diploma*: **Accountancy; Banking; Biology; Business Administration; Chemistry; Computer Science; Demography and Population; Development Studies; Earth Sciences; Economics; Education; Engineering; Environmental Management; Finance; Geography; History; Linguistics; Literature; Management; Media Studies; Physics; Psychology; Real Estate; Sociology; Tourism.** *Master's Degree*: **Education; Fine Arts; Law.** *Doctor of Philosophy*. Also 1 to 2 yr certificates

Student Services: Academic Counselling, Cultural Activities, Health Services, Nursery Care, Social Counselling, Sports Facilities

Publications: Report of the Higher Education Mission to the South Pacific (the Morris Report); USP Strategic Plan/Planning for the Fourth Decade

Student Numbers *2012-2013*: Total 23,720

Last Updated: 11/03/13

PRIVATE INSTITUTIONS

PACIFIC FLYING SCHOOL

P. O. Box 9452, Nadi International Airport, Nadi
Tel: +679 6727-666
Fax: +679 6727-330
EMail: pacificflying@connect.com.fj
Website: http://www.pfs.com.fj/

Chief Executive Officer: Ian Collingwood

Programme

Airline Transport (Aeronautical and Aerospace Engineering; Air Transport)

History: Created 1985.

Accrediting Agency: Fiji Higher Education Commission (FHEC); Civil Aviation Authority (CAA).

Degrees and Diplomas: *Bachelor's Degree*: **Air Transport.** *Postgraduate Diploma*: **Engineering.**

Last Updated: 05/07/13

SANGAM SCHOOL OF NURSING

Sangam Avenue, P.O. Box 2047, Labasa
Tel: +679 8818-691
Fax: +679 8818-693
EMail: sangam@connect.com.fj
Website: http://www.sangamfiji.com.fj/

Programme

Nursing (Midwifery; Nursing)

History: Created 2005. Part of the Sangam Institute of Technology.

Accrediting Agency: Fiji Higher Education Commission (FHEC)

Degrees and Diplomas: *Certificate/ Diploma*: **Nursing.** *Bachelor's Degree*: **Nursing.** *Postgraduate Diploma*: **Midwifery.**

Last Updated: 05/07/13

THE UNIVERSITY OF FIJI (UNIFIJI)

Private Mail Bag, Lautoka
Tel: +679 664-0600
Fax: +679 664-0700
EMail: info@unifiji.ac.fj; admissions@unifiji.ac.fj
Website: http://www.unifiji.ac.fj/

Acting Vice-Chancellor: Chandra Dulare

School

Business and Economics (Accountancy; Business Administration; Economics; Hotel Management; Human Resources; Management); **Humanities and Arts** (Education; Educational Administration; English; Hindi; Literature; Teacher Training); **Law** (Law); **Medicine** *(Umanand Prasad)* (Medicine; Surgery); **Science and Technology** (Biology; Business Computing; Chemistry; Computer Science; Information Technology; Mathematics; Physics)

Centre

Climate Change, Energy, Environment and Sustainable Development (Environmental Management; Environmental Studies); **Diasporic Studies**; **Gender Research** (Gender Studies); **International and Regional Affairs** (International Studies; Regional Studies); **Itaukei Studies** (Native Language)

History: Created 2005.

Accrediting Agency: Fiji Higher Education Commission (FHEC)

Degrees and Diplomas: *Certificate/ Diploma*; *Bachelor's Degree*; *Postgraduate Diploma*; *Master's Degree*; *Doctor of Philosophy*: **Education; Literature; Women's Studies.**

Last Updated: 05/07/13

Finland

STRUCTURE OF HIGHER EDUCATION SYSTEM

Description:

Finland has a binary system of higher education which is comprised of universities (yliopisto/universitet) and polytechnics (ammattikorkeakoulu, AMK/yrkeshögskola, YH). Some universities are multi-faculty universities and others are specialized institutions. All universities engage in both education and research and have the right to award doctorates. The polytechnics are multi-field institutions of professional higher education. They are specialized in applied research and development. Universities award first cycle university degrees (Kandidaatti/Kandidat), second cycle university degrees (Maisteri/Magister) and third cycle scientific post-graduate degrees (Lisensiaatti/Licentiat and Tohtori/Doktor). Polytechnics award first cycle polytechnic degrees (ammattikorkeakoulututkinto - AMK/yrkehögskoleexamen - YH) and second cycle polytechnic degrees (ylempi ammattikorkeakoulututkinto - ylempi AMK/högre yrkeshögskoleexamen - högre YH).

Stages of studies:

University level first stage: *Universities: kandidaatti/kandidat (first cycle)*
First-cycle university degrees consist of at least 180 credits (3 years of full-time study). They are called kandidaatti/kandidat in all fields except in Law (oikeusnotaari/rättsnotarie) and Pharmacy (farmaseutti/farmaceut). Studies leading to the degree provide the student with: (1) knowledge of the fundamentals of the major and minor subjects or corresponding study entities or studies included in the degree programme and the prerequisites for following developments in the field; (2) knowledge and skills needed for scientific thinking and the use of scientific methods or knowledge and skills needed for artistic work; 3) knowledge and skills needed for studies leading to a higher university degree and for continuous learning; (4) a capacity for applying the acquired knowledge and skills to work; and (5) adequate language and communication skills. Studies may include: basic and intermediate studies; language and communication studies; interdisciplinary programmes; other studies and work practice for professionnal development. The degree includes a Bachelor's thesis (6-10 credits).

University level second stage: *Universities: maisteri/magister (second cycle)*
The second-cycle university degree consists of at least 120 credits (two years of full-time study). The degree is usually called maisteri/magister. Other second-cycle degrees are diplomi-insinööri/diplomingenjör (Technology); arkkitehti/arkitekt (Architecture); and proviisori/provisor (Pharmacy). The admission requirement to second cycle university courses is a first cycle degree. The second cycle university degree title in the fields of medicine, dentistry and veterinary medicine is lisensiaatti/licentiate. In the field of medicine and dentistry, the university may arrange the education leading to the second cycle university degree without including a lower university degree. In medicine, the degrees consists of 360 credits (6 years of full-time study) and in dentistry the degree consists of 300 credits (5 years of full-time study). Studies leading to the second cycle university degree provide the student with: (1) good overall knowledge of the major subject or a corresponding entity and conversant with the fundamentals of the minor subject or good knowledge of the advanced studies included in the degree programme; (2) knowledge and skills needed to apply scientific knowledge and methods or knowledge and skills needed for independent and demanding artistic work; (3) knowledge and skills needed for operating independently as an expert and developer of the field; (4) knowledge and skills needed for scientific or artistic postgraduate education; and (5) good language and communication skills. Studies leading to the second cycle university degree may include: basic, intermediate and advanced studies, language and communication studies; interdisciplinary study programme; other studies; and internship improving expertise. The degree includes a Master's thesis (20-40 credits). The reformed university degree structure was adopted August 1, 2005. The reform created a two-tier degree structure with an obligatory first cycle degree in all fields except for medicine, dentistry and veterinary medicine. Before, students were able to pursue one-cycle Masters in five years. The degrees from the former structure are fully comparable to the new degrees and they give the same academic and professional rights.

University level third stage: *Universities: lisensiaati/licenciat; tohtori/doktor (third cycle)*
Students can apply for doctoral programmes after the completion of a relevant second-cycle degree. The aim of doctoral studies is to provide the student with in-depth knowledge of his/her field of research and capabilities to produce new scientific knowledge independently. A pre-doctoral degree (lisensiaati/licenciat) in two years may be

taken before the Doctor's Degree programme. Studies for the Doctor's degree take approximately four years of full-time study beyond a second-cycle degree or two years of full-time study beyond a pre-doctoral degree. Students admitted to doctoral studies must complete a certain number of courses, show independent and critical thinking in their field of research and write a doctoral dissertation to be defended in public.

ADMISSION TO HIGHER EDUCATION

Admission to university-level studies:

Name of secondary school credential required: Ammatillinen perustutkintotodistus/Betyg över yrkesinriktad grundexamen

For entry to: Universities

Name of secondary school credential required: Ylioppilastutkintotodistus/Studentexamensbetyg

For entry to: Universities

Alternatives to credentials: Lukion päättötodistus/Avgångsbetyg från gymnasiet; Certificate for the International Baccalaureate; European Baccalaureate, Reifeprüfung; Vocational (3 years) Qualification Certificate (Ammatillinen perustutkintotodistus/Betyg over yrkesinriktad grundexamen). Foreign equivalents.

Admission requirements: Various types of entrance examinations.

Numerus clausus: Restricted entry in all fields of study.

Foreign students admission:

Definition of foreign student: The term foreign student usually applies to students, regardless of nationality or native language, who have completed their secondary education in any country other than Finland.

Admission requirements: Students must have completed secondary education. Foreign qualifications equivalent to Finnish qualifications that give eligibility to apply for higher education in the country of origin can be accepted. Higher education institutions select their students independently. Entrance examinations are applied and there is a numerus clausus in all fields of study.

Entry regulations: Depending on the nationality and the length of stay in Finland, a visa or a residence permit may be required by the immigration authorities.

Language proficiency: In most cases, students must have good working knowledge of Finnish or Swedish. In international degree programmes, the teaching language can be English or some other foreign language in which case the applicants must show proof of their good knowledge of the foreign language.

RECOGNITION OF STUDIES

Quality assurance system:

The Finnish degrees of higher education are listed in the Decree on the structure of higher education degrees. The field-specific national decrees on university degrees define the objectives, length and overall structure of university degrees. The national decree on polytechnics defines the objectives, length and overall structure of polytechnic degrees. The Ministry of Education confirms the degree programmes of the polytechnics.

Universities and polytechnics are obliged by legislation to evaluate their activities systematically. The Finnish Higher Education Evaluation Council is an independent expert body assisting universities, polytechnics and the Ministry of Education in matters relating to evaluation. The Finnish Higher Education Evaluation Council (FINHEEC) has been conducting audits of the quality assurance (QA) systems of higher education institutes (HEIs) since autumn 2005, with the aim of auditing all Finnish HEIs by the end of 2011. Auditing assesses the comprehensiveness, performance and effectiveness of the QA system and focuses on two levels: the HEI's QA system as a whole and the quality assurance related to the HEI's basic mission (education, research/R&D, interaction with and impact on society and regional development).

In 2003, the five Nordic ENIC/NARIC offices (Denmark, Finland, Iceland, Norway and Sweden) established a regional network named Nordic National Recognition Information Centres (NORRIC) to initiate joint Nordic projects to learn from each other and reduce barriers to the recognition of foreign qualifications in the Nordic region (www.norric.org).

The academic recognition of qualifications is the responsibility of the higher education institution to which the holder of a foreign qualification is applying for admission. The institutions decide independently on matters related to student selection and the recognition of previous studies.

Bodies dealing with recognition:

Opetushallitus/Utbildningsstyrelsen - ENIC-NARIC Finland (Finnish National Board of Education)

PO Box 380
Helsinki 00531
Tel: +358 29 533 1000
Fax: +358 29 533 1035
EMail: recognition@oph.fi
WWW: http://www.oph.fi/english/services/recognition

Special provisions for recognition:

Recognition for university level studies: Universities make the decisions concerning admissions and credit transfer independently. The Finnish National Board of Education (ENIC/NARIC) supports the work of universities.

For access to advanced studies and research: Recognition decisions concerning studies and research for access into Finnish higher education are passed in the higher education institutions. The Finnish National Board of Education supports the work of the higher education institutions.
Further information from the National Board of Education, www.oph.fi/recognition - or directly from the higher education institution in question.

For exercising a profession: The National Board of Education decides on the competence for civil service posts conferred by qualifications taken abroad. Decisions on the right to practise a profession are made by the competent authority in the respective field. The right to practice a profession in Finland is required from, e.g. health-care professionals and seafarers.
The recognition of professional competence of citizens of EU/EEA countries, who have gained their professional competence in another EU/EEA country, is regulated by law (1093/2007). Recognition decisions concerning other foreign qualifications are made in accordance with law (531/1986) on the professional competence of foreign qualifications.
Further information from the National Board of Education, www.oph.fi/recognition.

NATIONAL BODIES

Opetus- ja kulttuuriministeriö (Ministry of Education and Culture)

Minister: Sanni Grahn-Laasonen
PO Box 29
Helsinki 00023
Tel: +358 2953 30004
Fax: +358(9) 135 9335
EMail: kirjaamo@minedu.fi
WWW: http://www.minedu.fi
Role of national body: Responsible for the development of educational, science, cultural, sport and youth policies as well as international cooperation in these fields.

Opetushallitus (Finnish National Board of Education)

Director General: Aulis Pitkälä
Hakaniemenranta 6
PO Box 380
Helsinki 00531
Tel: +358 29 533 1000
EMail: opetushallitus@oph.fi
WWW: http://www.oph.fi/english
Role of national body: Development, evaluation and information servives related to education; Finnish ENIC-NARIC; competent authority for the professional recognition of foreign higher education qualifications.

Korkeakoulujen arviointineuvosto - KKA (Finnish Higher Education Evaluation Council - FINHEEC)
PO Box 133
Helsinki 00171
Tel: +358 2953 30072
EMail: finheec@minedu.fi
Role of national body: Independent expert body assisting universities, polytechnics and the Ministry of Education in matters relating to evaluation.

Kansinvâlisen henkilövaihdon keskus (Centre for International Mobility - CIMO)
PO Box 343 (Hakaniemenkatu 6)
Helsinki 00531
Tel: +358 295 338 500
EMail: cimoinfo@cimo.fi
WWW: http://www.cimo.fi
Role of national body: Services and expertise in cross-cultural communication; promotion and administration of scholarship and exchange programmes; implementation of EU education, training, culture and youth programmes at national level.

Ammattikorkeakoulujen Rehtorineuvosto - ARENE (Rectors' Conference of Finnish Universities of Applied Sciences)
Pohjoinen Makasiinikatu 7 A 2
Helsinki 00130
WWW: http://www.arene.fi

Suomen yliopistot (Universities Finland - UNIFI)
Chair: Jouko Niinimäki
Pohjoinen Makasiinikatu 7 a 2
Helsinki 00130
Tel: +358 50 522 9421
EMail: rectors-council@helsinki.fi; unifi@unifi.fi
WWW: http://www.rectors-council.helsinki.fi/
Role of national body: Development of the university sector of higher education; a common forum for universities.

Data for academic year: 2014-2015
Source: The Finnish National Board of Education, Helsinki, 2014. Bodies 2016.

INSTITUTIONS

PUBLIC INSTITUTIONS

AALTO UNIVERSITY

Aalto-yliopisto
Lämpömiehenkuja 2- Otaniemi, 02015 Espoo
Tel: +358(9) 47001
EMail: reception@aaltouniversity.fi
Website: http://www.aalto.fi/fi/

President: Tuula Teeri
Tel: +358(50) 512-4194 EMail: president@aaltouniversity.fi

International Relations: Hannu Seristö, Vice-President, External Relations
Tel: +358(50) 383-2478 EMail: hannu.seristo@aaltouniversity.fi

School
Arts, Design and Architecture (Art Education; Art History; Business and Commerce; Ceramics and Glass Technology; Cinema and Television; Design; Display and Stage Design; Fashion Design; Film; Fine Arts; Furniture Design; Graphic Design; Industrial Design; Interior Design; Media Studies; Painting and Drawing; Photography; Sculpture; Textile Design); **Business** (Accountancy; Commercial Law; Communication Studies; Economics; English; Finance; Information Sciences; Information Technology; International Business; International Economics; Labour Law; Leadership; Management; Management Systems; Marketing; Small Business); **Chemical Technology** (Applied Physics; Biotechnology; Building Technologies; Chemical Engineering; Chemistry; Computer Science; Engineering; Forest Products; Geophysics; Industrial Management; Materials Engineering; Mathematics; Mechanics; Physics; Real Estate; Regional Studies; Systems Analysis; Technology; Urban Studies); **Electrical Engineering** (Automation and Control Engineering; Computer Networks; Electrical Engineering; Electronic Engineering; Nanotechnology; Radio and Television Broadcasting; Sound Engineering (Acoustics)); **Engineering** (Architecture; Civil Engineering; Construction Engineering; Energy Engineering; Engineering Drawing and Design; Environmental Engineering; Mechanical Engineering; Surveying and Mapping); **Science** (Applied Physics; Biomedical Engineering; Computer Engineering; Computer Science; Industrial Engineering; Industrial Management; Mathematics; Media Studies; Systems Analysis)

Institute
Information Technology *(Helsinki)* (Information Technology); **Physics** *(Helsinki)* (Physics)

History: Founded 2010 following the merger of Helsingin kauppakorkeakoulu (Helsinki School of Economics and Business Administration - HSE) founded 1911; Taideteollinen korkeakoulu - Konstindustriella högskolan (University of Art and Design, Helsinki - TaiK) founded 1871 and Teknillinen korkeakoulu-Tekniska högskolan (Helsinki University of Technology - TKK) founded 1849.

Admission Requirements: Secondary school certificate (ylioppilastutkinto) or equivalent and entrance examination

Main Language(s) of Instruction: Finnish, Swedish, English

Accrediting Agency: Ministry of Education and Culture

Degrees and Diplomas: *Kandidaatti/Kandidat*; *Arkkitehti/Arkitekt*; *Diplomi-insinööri/Diplomingenjör*; *Lisensiaatti/Licentiat*; *Maisteri/Magister*: **Accountancy; Applied Mathematics; Architecture; Chemical Engineering; Cinema and Television; Computer Science; Design; Display and Stage Design; Economics; Environmental Engineering; Environmental Studies; Fashion Design; Finance; Graphic Design; Industrial Design; Industrial Engineering; Management; Marketing; Mechanical Engineering; Media Studies; Natural Sciences; Physical Engineering; Real Estate; Small Business.** *Tohtori/Doktor*: **Business and Commerce; Design; Engineering; Technology.**

Student Services: Academic Counselling, IT Centre, Library

Last Updated: 03/02/15

ÅBO AKADEMI UNIVERSITY

Åbo Akademi
Tuomiokirkontori 3, 20500 Turku
Tel: +358(2) 215-31
Fax: +358(2) 251-7553
EMail: infowww@abo.fi
Website: http://www.abo.fi

Rector: Mikko Hupa (2015-)

Faculty

Arts, Psychology and Theology (Art History; Communication Disorders; Comparative Religion; English; Ethnology; Gender Studies; German; History; Nordic Studies; Psychology; Religion; Russian; Swedish; Theology); **Economics and Social Sciences** (Accountancy; Business Administration; Civil Law; Commercial Law; Economics; Information Sciences; International Business; International Economics; International Law; International Relations; Law; Management; Maritime Law; Political Sciences; Private Law; Public Administration; Social Policy; Social Sciences; Sociology; Statistics; Women's Studies); **Education and Welfare Studies** (Adult Education; Developmental Psychology; Education; Home Economics; Mathematics Education; Physical Education; Preschool Education; Science Education; Special Education); **Science and Engineering** (Biochemistry; Cell Biology; Chemistry; Computer Engineering; Computer Science; Geology; Marine Biology; Mathematics; Mineralogy; Molecular Biology; Paper Technology; Pharmacy; Physics; Software Engineering; Wood Technology); **Social Sciences, Business and Economics** (Accountancy; Business Computing; Commercial Law; Economics; International Law; Law; Maritime Law; Marketing; Mass Communication; Political Sciences; Public Administration; Public Law; Sociology)

Institute

Human Rights (Human Rights)

Centre

Biotechnology *(Turku/Åbo)* (Biotechnology)

Research Institute

Social Sciences (Social Sciences)

Further Information: Also Graduate Schools, Centres of Excellence and National Centres of Excellence. Branch in Vaasa

History: Founded 1918 as Centre of Research and Higher Education for the Swedish-speaking minority in Finland. First University established at Åbo 1640, and transferred to Helsingfors (Helsinki) 1828. Incorporated Swedish School of Economics, Åbo 1980. Under supervision of the Ministry of Education.

Academic Year: August to July

Admission Requirements: Secondary school certificate (ylioppi lastutkinto/studentexamen) or equivalent, and in some cases entrance examination

Fees: None

Main Language(s) of Instruction: Swedish, Finnish

Accrediting Agency: Ministry of Education and Culture

Degrees and Diplomas: *Farmaseutti/Farmaceut*: **Pharmacy.** *Kandidaatti/Kandidat*: **Economics; Education; Fine Arts; Law; Natural Sciences; Political Sciences; Religion.** *Maisteri/Magister*: **Economics; Education; Engineering; Fine Arts; Natural Sciences; Religion.** *Tohtori/Doktor*: **Business Administration; Education; Engineering; Natural Sciences.**

Student Services: Academic Counselling, Canteen, Careers Guidance, Cultural Activities, Health Services, Nursery Care, Social Counselling, Sports Facilities

Publications: Acta Academiae Aboensis; Meddelanden från Åbo Akademi

Publishing House: Åbo Akademi University Press

Last Updated: 16/02/15

ARCADA UNIVERSITY OF APPLIED SCIENCES

ARCADA
Jan-Magnus Janssonin aukio 1, 00560 Helsinki
Tel: +358(9) 207-699 699
Fax: +358(9) 0207-699-622
EMail: information@arcada.fi
Website: http://www.arcada.fi

Rector: Henrik Wolff EMail: henrik.wolff@arcada.fi

Department

Business Mangement and Analytics (Business Administration; Information Technology; International Business; Media Studies); **Culture and Communication** (Cultural Studies; Mass Communication); **Energy and Materials Technology** (Energy Engineering; Industrial Management; Polymer and Plastics Technology); **Health and Welfare** (Nursing; Physical Therapy; Public Health; Social and Community Services; Sports)

History: Founded 1996. Acquired present status 1998.

Main Language(s) of Instruction: Finnish

Accrediting Agency: Ministry of Education and Culture

Degrees and Diplomas: *Ammattikorkeakoulututkinto (AMK)/Yrkeshögskoleexamen (YH)*: **Business Administration; Cultural Studies; Energy Engineering; Environmental Engineering; Information Technology; International Business; Media Studies; Midwifery; Nursing; Occupational Therapy; Physical Therapy; Production Engineering; Public Health; Social Work; Sports.** *Ylempi ammattikorkeakoulututinto (ylempi AMK)/Högre yrkeshögskoleexamen (högre YH)*: **International Business; Management; Public Health.**

Last Updated: 16/02/15

CENTRIA UNIVERSITY OF APPLIED SCIENCES

Centria ammattikorkeakoulu
Talonpojankatu 2, 67100 Kokkola
Tel: +358(6) 825-0000
Fax: +358(6) 825-2000
EMail: info@centria.fi; admissions@centria.fi
Website: http://web.centria.fi/

Rector: Pekka Hulkko

Department

Culture (Cultural Studies); **Humanities and Education** (Arts and Humanities; Education); **Natural Resources and the Environment** (Environmental Studies; Natural Resources); **Natural sciences** (Natural Sciences); **Social Sciences, Business and Administration** (Business Administration; Social Sciences); **Social Services, Health and Sport** (Health Administration; Public Health; Social Welfare; Sports); **Technology, Communication and Transport** (Technology; Transport and Communications); **Tourism, Catering and Domestic Services** (Hotel and Restaurant; Tourism)

Further Information: Camuses also in Pietarsaari and Ylivieska.

History: Founded 1991, acquired present status and title 1998.

Main Language(s) of Instruction: English, Finnish, Swedish

Accrediting Agency: Ministry of Education and Culture

Degrees and Diplomas: *Ammattikorkeakoulututkinto (AMK)/Yrkeshögskoleexamen (YH)*: **Business Administration; Education; Engineering; Industrial Management; Information Technology;**

Nursing; Social Sciences. *Ylempi ammattikorkeakoulututinto (ylempi AMK)/Högre yrkeshögskoleexamen (högre YH)*: **Business Administration; Engineering; Health Administration.**
Last Updated: 16/02/15

DIACONIA UNIVERSITY OF APPLIED SCIENCES

Diakonia-ammattikorkeakoulu
Sturenkatu 2, 00510 Helsinki
Tel: +358(20) 690-431
EMail: admissions@diak.fi
Website: http://www.diak.fi

Rector: Jorma Niemelä EMail: jorma.niemela@diak.fi

International Relations: Riikka Hälikkä
EMail: riikka.halikka@diak.fi

Programme

Social Services *(Taught in English)* (Nursing; Public Health; Social and Community Services; Social Welfare); **Social Services** *(Taught in Finnish)* (Nursing; Social and Community Services; Social Welfare)

History: Founded 2000.

Main Language(s) of Instruction: English, Finnish

Accrediting Agency: Ministry of Education and Culture

Degrees and Diplomas: *Ammattikorkeakoulututkinto (AMK)/Yrkeshögskoleexamen (YH)*: **Midwifery; Nursing; Social and Community Services; Social Welfare.** *Ylempi ammattikorkeakoulututinto (ylempi AMK)/Högre yrkeshögskoleexamen (högre YH)*: **Social and Community Services; Social Welfare.**
Last Updated: 16/02/15

HAAGA-HELIA UNIVERSITY OF APPLIED SCIENCES

HAAGA-HELIA ammattikorkeakoulu - HAAGA-HELIA yrkeshögskolan (HAAGA-HELIA)
Ratapihantie 13, 00520 Helsinki
Tel: +358(9) 229-611
EMail: viestinta@haaga-helia.fi
Website: http://www.haaga-helia.fi

President: Teemu Kokko EMail: teemu.kokko@haaga-helia.fi

International Relations: Sirpa Holmström, Head, International Services EMail: sirpa.holmstrom@haaga-helia.fi

Department

Business (Business Administration; Business and Commerce; Finance; International Business); **Hotel, Restaurant and Tourism** (Cooking and Catering; Hotel Management; Leisure Studies; Tourism); **Information Technology** (Business Administration; Business Computing; Information Management; Information Sciences; Information Technology; Management Systems); **Management Assistant and Journalism** (Journalism; Modern Languages; Secretarial Studies); **Sports** *(Vierumäki)* (Leisure Studies; Sports; Sports Management); **Tourism** *(Porvoo)* (Business and Commerce; International Business; Tourism); **Vocational Teacher Education** (Teacher Training)

History: Founded 1992. Acquired present title 2007, following merger with Haaga ammattikorkeakoulu (Haaga Polytechnic). Formerly known as Helsingin liiketalouden ammattikorkeakoulu Helsingfors yrkeshögskola för företagsekonomi (Helsinki Business Polytechnic).

Academic Year: August to December; January to May

Admission Requirements: Bachelor level: lukion päättötodistus/ylioppilastutkintotodistus = Upper secondary education and Matriculation examination completed in Finland; opistoasteen/ammatillisen korkea-asteen tutkinto = a vocational college diploma or higher vocational diploma completed in Finland (ex. insinööri, merkonomi); ammatillinen perustutkinto = Vocational upper secondary diploma/higher vocational diploma/vocational qualification in adult education completed in Finland (ex. liiketalouden perustutkinto, tietojenkäsittelyn perustutkinto, matkailualan perustutkinto); ammattitutkinto = further vocational qualification completed in Finland; erikoisammattitutkinto = specialist vocational qualification completed in Finland; Foreign degree or qualification which gives eligibility for higher education in the awarding country. Entrance examination. In English-language programmes, applicants who are not a citizen of an EU/EEA country must provide proof of his/her English language skills (example IELTS, TOEFL). Master level: alempi ammattikorkeakoulututkinto = Bachelor's degree completed in Finland in University of Applied Sciences (ex. tradenomi, restonomi (AMK), medianomi (AMK)); kandidaatin tutkinto = Bachelor's degree completed in Finland in University; maisterin tutkinto = Master's degree completed in Finland in University; Foreign Bachelor or Master's degree; Minimum requirements: Entrance examination. Degree must be completed from the corresponding field. Three years of working experience after the degree from the same field.

Fees: None for EU/EEA students; Master students from outwith EU/EEA, 3,750 Euro per semester

Main Language(s) of Instruction: Finnish, English, Swedish

Accrediting Agency: Ministry of Education and Culture

Degrees and Diplomas: *Ammattikorkeakoulututkinto (AMK)/Yrkeshögskoleexamen (YH)*: **Business Administration; Computer Education; Cultural Studies; Hotel and Restaurant; Information Technology; Tourism.** *Ylempi ammattikorkeakoulututinto (ylempi AMK)/Högre yrkeshögskoleexamen (högre YH)*: **Business Administration; Computer Education; Physical Education; Sports Management; Tourism.** Also MBA

Student Services: Academic Counselling, Canteen, Careers Guidance, Facilities for disabled people, Foreign Studies Centre, Health Services, Language Laboratory, Nursery Care, Social Counselling, Sports Facilities
Last Updated: 16/02/15

HÄME UNIVERSITY OF APPLIED SCIENCES

Hämeen ammattikorkeakoulu HAMK (HAMK)
PO Box 230, 13100 Hämeenlinna
Tel: +358(3) 6461
EMail: hamk@hamk.fi
Website: http://www.hamk.fi

Rector: Pertti Puusaari
Tel: +358400469605 EMail: pertti.puusaari@hamk.fi

Administrative Officer: Mirja Pöhö
Tel: +358(3) 646-4810 EMail: mirja.poho@hamk.fi

Vice President, Education: Risto Salminen
Tel: +358 3 6464283 EMail: risto.salminen@hamk.fi

Vice President, RDI and System Developement: Janne Salminen
Tel: +358 3 6464282 EMail: janne.salminen@hamk.fi

International Relations: Marja Räikkönen, Head of international affairs Tel: +358 3 6464401 EMail: marja.raikkonen@hamk.fi

Programme

Culture (Cultural Studies); **Natural Resources and the Environment** (Natural Resources); **Natural Sciences** (Natural Sciences); **Social Sciences, Business and Administration** (Business Administration; Social Sciences); **Social Services, Health and Sports** (Social and Community Services; Sports); **Technology, Communication and Transport** (Technology; Transport and Communications)

Further Information: http://www.hamk.fi/english

History: Founded 1840 as School for agricultural studies. Unit for forestry studies created 1862, Handicraft school for girls 1885, Horticultural school 1910. Acquired present title and status 1996.

Academic Year: September-May

Admission Requirements: General upper secondary school syllabus or Matriculation Examination

Main Language(s) of Instruction: Finnish, English

Accrediting Agency: Ministry of Education and Culture

Degrees and Diplomas: *Ammattikorkeakoulututkinto (AMK)/Yrkeshögskoleexamen (YH); Ylempi ammattikorkeakoulututinto (ylempi AMK)/Högre yrkeshögskoleexamen (högre YH); Maisteri/Magister*: **Business Administration; Social and Preventive Medicine.**

Student Services: Academic Counselling, Canteen, Careers Guidance, Cultural Activities, Health Services, IT Centre, Library, Residential Facilities, Social Counselling, Sports Facilities, eLibrary

Academic Staff *2014*	**TOTAL**
FULL-TIME	**700**
STAFF WITH DOCTORATE	
FULL-TIME	c. **100**
Student Numbers *2014*	
All (Foreign included)	c. **7,000**
FOREIGN ONLY	**650**

Last Updated: 26/11/14

HANKEN SCHOOL OF ECONOMICS

Hanken Svenska handelhögskolan (HANKEN)
PO Box 479, Arkadiankatu 22, 00101 Helsinki
Tel: +358 (0)29 431 331
EMail: info@hanken.fi
Website: http://www.hanken.fi

Rector: Karen Spens (2015-) EMail: karen.spens@hanken.fi

Planning officer: Linnéa Kangas EMail: linnea.kangas@hanken.fi

Doctoral Studies Coordinator: Marianne Dingstad Cambier EMail: marianne.dingstad-cambier@hanken.fi; doctoral.studies@hanken.fi

International Relations: Maj-Britt Hedvall, Associate Dean of Research and Internationalisation
EMail: maj-britt.hedvall@hanken.fi; doctoral.studies@hanken.fi

Department

Accounting and Commercial Law (Accountancy; Commercial Law); **Economics** (Economics); **Finance** (Finance; Statistics); **Management and Organisation** (Information Technology; Leadership; Management; Political Sciences); **Marketing** (Geography (Human); Marketing)

Further Information: Also operations in Vaasa

History: Founded 1909. Authorised to grant Master of Science 1927, PhD 1944, and Licentiate 1953. Unit in Vaasa established 1980. Reports to the Ministry of Education and Culture. Accredited by EQUIS, AACSB and AMBA.

Academic Year: August to July

Admission Requirements: BSc: Secondary school certificate (studentexamen) or equivalent and entrance examination. MSc: BSc-degree, language proficiency, and documented ability to conduct MSc-level studies. Executive MBA: BSc-degree, language proficiency, and documented ability to conduct MBA-level studies. PhD: MSc-degree, language proficiency, and documented ability to conduct PhD-level studies.

Main Language(s) of Instruction: Swedish, English

Accrediting Agency: Ministry of Education and Culture

Degrees and Diplomas: *Kandidaatti/Kandidat*: **Business Administration; Economics.** *Lisensiaatti/Licentiat*: **Business Administration; Economics.** *Maisteri/Magister*: **Business Administration; Economics.** *Tohtori/Doktor*: **Business Administration; Economics.**

Student Services: Academic Counselling, Canteen, Careers Guidance, Facilities for disabled people, Foreign Studies Centre, Health Services, IT Centre, Language Laboratory, Library, Sports Facilities, eLibrary

Publications: Economics and Society

Last Updated: 07/12/15

HELSINKI METROPOLIA UNIVERSITY OF APPLIED SCIENCES

Metropolia Ammattikorkeakoulu
Bulevardi 31, 01800 Helsinki
Tel: +358(9)74245100
Fax: +358(9)74245500
EMail: hakijapalvelut@metropolia.fi
Website: http://www.metropolia.fi

President: Riitta Konkola EMail: riitta.konkola@metropolia.fi

Faculty

Culture and Creative Industries (Cinema and Television; Design; Fashion Design; Heritage Preservation; Jazz and Popular Music; Media Studies; Music; Performing Arts); **Health Care and Nursing** (Biomedicine; Nursing; Oral Pathology; Radiology; Social and Community Services); **Welfare and Human Functioning** (Dental Technology; Gerontology; Occupational Therapy; Optometry; Osteopathy; Physical Therapy; Rehabilitation and Therapy; Social and Community Services)

School

Business (Business Administration; Business Computing; International Business; Management); **Civil Engineering and Building Services** (Building Technologies; Civil Engineering; Construction Engineering; Real Estate; Surveying and Mapping); **ICT** (Industrial Management; Information Technology); **Industrial Engineering** (Automation and Control Engineering; Automotive Engineering; Biotechnology; Chemical Engineering; Electrical Engineering; Food Technology; Materials Engineering; Mechanical Engineering; Transport Engineering)

History: Founded 2008 following merger of EVTEK University of Applied Sciences and Helsinki Polytechnic Stadia.

Main Language(s) of Instruction: Finnish

Accrediting Agency: Ministry of Education and Culture

Degrees and Diplomas: *Ammattikorkeakoulututkinto (AMK)/Yrkeshögskoleexamen (YH)*; *Ylempi ammattikorkeakoulututinto (ylempi AMK)/Högre yrkeshögskoleexamen (högre YH)*: **Performing Arts; Social and Community Services; Technology.**

Last Updated: 01/12/14

HUMAK UNIVERSITY OF APPLIED SCIENCES

Humanistinen ammattikorkeakoulu (HUMAK)
Ilkantie 4, 00400 Helsinki
EMail: viestinta@humak.fi
Website: http://www.humak.edu

Rector: Tapio Huttula

Faculty

Cultural Management (Art Management; Cultural Studies); **NGO and Youth Work** (Social Work); **Sign Language Interpretation** (Special Education)

History: Founded 1998.

Main Language(s) of Instruction: Finnish

Accrediting Agency: Ministry of Education and Culture

Degrees and Diplomas: *Ammattikorkeakoulututkinto (AMK)/Yrkeshögskoleexamen (YH)*: **Art Management; Social and Community Services; Social Welfare.** *Ylempi ammattikorkeakoulututinto (ylempi AMK)/Högre yrkeshögskoleexamen (högre YH)*: **Art Management; Social Work.**

Last Updated: 16/02/15

JYVÄSKYLÄ UNIVERSITY OF APPLIED SCIENCES

Jyväskylän ammattikorkeakoulu
PO Box 207, 40101 Jyväskylä
Tel: +358(20) 743-8100
Fax: +358(14) 449-9700
EMail: jamk@jamk.fi
Website: http://www.jamk.fi

Rector: Jussi Halttunen EMail: Jussi.Halttunen@jamk.fi

College

Teacher Education *(Professional training)* (Teacher Training)

School

Business (Business Administration; Hotel Management; Management; Tourism); **Health and Social Studies** (Health Sciences; Music Education; Nursing; Social Studies); **Technology** (Civil Engineering; Information Technology; Mechanical Engineering; Natural Resources)

History: Founded 1992, acquired present status and title 1997.

Main Language(s) of Instruction: Finnish

Accrediting Agency: Ministry of Education and Culture

Degrees and Diplomas: *Ammattikorkeakoulututkinto (AMK)/Yrkeshögskoleexamen (YH)*: **Business Administration; Hotel Management; Nursing; Tourism; Transport Management.** *Ylempi ammattikorkeakoulututinto (ylempi AMK)/Högre yrkeshögskoleexamen (högre YH)*: **Hotel Management; Information Technology; International Business; Music Education; Public Health; Social and Community Services; Social Welfare.**

Last Updated: 16/02/15

KAJAANI UNIVERSITY OF APPLIED SCIENCES

Kajaanin ammattikorkeakoulu
PO Box 52, Ketunpolku 3, 87101 Kajaani
Tel: +358(8) 618-991
Fax: +358(8) 6189-9620
EMail: kajaanin.amk@kajak.fi; admissions@kamk.fi,
Website: http://www.kajak.fi

President: Turo Kilpeläinen

School

Business (Business Administration); **Engineering** (Construction Engineering; Information Technology; Mechanical Engineering; Production Engineering); **Health and Sports** (Leisure Studies; Nursing; Sports; Sports Management); **Tourism** (Tourism)

History: Founded 1992. Acquired present status 1996.

Main Language(s) of Instruction: English, Finnish

Accrediting Agency: Ministry of Education and Culture

Degrees and Diplomas: *Ammattikorkeakoulututkinto (AMK)/Yrkeshögskoleexamen (YH)*: **Business Administration; Business Computing; Construction Engineering; Electronic Engineering; Leisure Studies; Mechanical Engineering; Nursing; Sports Management; Telecommunications Engineering; Tourism.** *Ylempi ammattikorkeakoulututinto (ylempi AMK)/Högre yrkeshögskoleexamen (högre YH)*: **Health Administration; Information Technology.**

Last Updated: 16/02/15

KARELIA UNIVERSITY OF APPLIED SCIENCES

Karelia-ammattikorkeakoulu
Tikkarinne 9, 80200 Joensuu
Tel: +358(13) 260-600
EMail: info@karelia.fi
Website: http://www.karelia.fi

Rector: Petri Raivo EMail: petri.raivo@karelia.fi

Programme

Culture (Communication Studies; Design; Fine Arts; Media Studies; Music); **Natural Resources and the Environment** (Environmental Studies; Forest Products; Forestry; Natural Resources; Rural Studies); **Natural Sciences** (Natural Sciences); **Social Sciences, Business and Administration** (Administration; Business and Commerce; Economics; Information Technology; International Business); **Social services, Health and Sports** (Biomedicine; Nursing; Physical Therapy; Social Sciences; Social Welfare; Social Work); **Technology, Communication and Transport** (Civil Engineering; Environmental Engineering; Information Technology; Mechanical Engineering; Production Engineering; Wood Technology); **Tourism, Catering and Domestic Services** (Cooking and Catering; Tourism)

History: Founded 1992. Acquired present status and title 1996.

Main Language(s) of Instruction: Finnish, English

Accrediting Agency: Ministry of Education and Culture

Degrees and Diplomas: *Ammattikorkeakoulututkinto (AMK)/Yrkeshögskoleexamen (YH)*: **Business Administration; Construction Engineering; Economics; Electrical Engineering; Environmental Engineering; Forestry; Information Technology; International Business; Mass Communication; Mechanical Engineering; Music Education; Nursing; Physical Therapy; Production Engineering; Social Welfare; Tourism.** *Ylempi ammattikorkeakoulututinto (ylempi AMK)/Högre yrkeshögskoleexamen (högre YH)*: **Business Administration; Environmental Management; Health Administration; Industrial Management.**

Last Updated: 16/02/15

KYMENLAAKSO UNIVERSITY OF APPLIED SCIENCES

Kymenlaakson ammattikorkeakoulu
PO Box 9, 48401 Kotka
EMail: kirjaamo@kyamk.fi
Website: http://www.kyamk.fi

Rector: Petteri Ikonen

Programme

Culture (Design; Media Studies; Restoration of Works of Art); **Social Sciences, Business and Administration** (Administration; Business and Commerce; Social Sciences); **Social Services and Health Care** (Nursing; Public Health; Social and Community Services); **Technology, Communications and Transport** (Technology; Telecommunications Engineering; Transport Engineering; Transport Management)

History: Founded 1996.

Main Language(s) of Instruction: Finnish, English

Accrediting Agency: Ministry of Education and Culture

Degrees and Diplomas: *Ammattikorkeakoulututkinto (AMK)/Yrkeshögskoleexamen (YH)*: **Business Administration; Computer Graphics; Design; Engineering; Health Administration; Industrial Management; Marine Transport; Nursing; Restoration of Works of Art.** *Ylempi ammattikorkeakoulututinto (ylempi AMK)/Högre yrkeshögskoleexamen (högre YH)*: **Business Administration; Computer Graphics; Design; Health Administration.**

Last Updated: 16/02/15

LAHTI UNIVERSITY OF APPLIED SCIENCES

Lahden ammattikorkeakoulu
PO Box 214, 15101 Lahti
Tel: +358(44) 708-0983
EMail: intoffice@lamk.fi
Website: http://www.lamk.fi

President: Outi Kallioinen

Faculty

Business (Business Administration; Business and Commerce; Business Computing; Finance; Information Technology; International Business; Management; Marketing); **Social and Health Care** (Health Administration; Nursing); **Technology** (Biotechnology; Environmental Engineering; Environmental Management; Information Technology; Materials Engineering; Mechanical Engineering; Polymer and Plastics Technology; Production Engineering; Software Engineering; Telecommunications Engineering; Textile Technology; Wood Technology); **Tourism and Hospitality** *(Fellmanni Institute)* (Hotel and Restaurant; Hotel Management; Tourism)

Institute

Design and Fine Arts (Art Education; Design; Fashion Design; Furniture Design; Graphic Design; Industrial Design; Interior Design; Jewellery Art; Multimedia; Photography; Radio and Television Broadcasting); **Music and Drama** (Music; Music Education; Performing Arts; Theatre)

History: Founded 1991, acquired present status and title 1996.

Main Language(s) of Instruction: Finnish, English

Accrediting Agency: Ministry of Education and Culture

Degrees and Diplomas: *Ammattikorkeakoulututkinto (AMK)/Yrkeshögskoleexamen (YH)*: **Business Administration; Design; Environmental Engineering; Graphic Design; Health Administration; Information Technology; Materials Engineering; Mechanical Engineering; Music; Music Education; Nursing.** *Ylempi ammattikorkeakoulututinto (ylempi AMK)/Högre yrkeshögskoleexamen (högre YH)*: **Business Administration; Design; Engineering; Health Administration; Information Technology.**

Last Updated: 16/02/15

LAPLAND UNIVERSITY OF APPLIED SCIENCES

Lapin ammattikorkeakoulu (LAPIN AMK)
Jokiväylä 11C, 96300 Rovaniemi
Tel: +358(20) 798-6000
EMail: hakutoimisto@lapinamk.fi
Website: http://www.lapinamk.fi/fi

Rector: Martti Lampela

School

Business and Culture (Business Administration; Economics; Information Technology; International Business); **Hospitality and Tourism** (Cooking and Catering; Hotel and Restaurant; Hotel Management; Tourism); **Industry and Natural Resources** (Agricultural Engineering; Agricultural Equipment; Forestry); **Social Services, Health and Sport** (Health Administration; Nursing;

Physical Therapy; Public Health; Social and Community Services; Social Welfare; Sports)

History: Founded 1996, acquired present status and title 1998. Formed by the merger of Rovaniemi University of Applied Sciences (Rovaniemen ammattikorkeakoulu) and Kemi-Tornio University of Applied Sciences (Kemi-Tornion ammattikorkeakoulu) 2014.

Main Language(s) of Instruction: English, Finnish

Accrediting Agency: Ministry of Education and Culture

Degrees and Diplomas: *Ammattikorkeakoulututkinto (AMK)/Yrkeshögskoleexamen (YH)*: **Engineering; Humanities and Social Science Education; Information Technology; International Business; Nursing; Tourism.** *Ylempi ammattikorkeakoulututinto (ylempi AMK)/Högre yrkeshögskoleexamen (högre YH)*: **Business Administration; Hotel Management; Industrial Management; International Business; Nursing; Physical Therapy; Social and Community Services; Surveying and Mapping.**

Student Services: Library

Last Updated: 17/02/15

LAPPEENRANTA UNIVERSITY OF TECHNOLOGY

Lappeenrannan teknillinen yliopisto (LUT)
PO Box 20, Skinnarilankatu 34, 53851 Lappeenranta
Tel: +358(5) 621-11
Fax: +358(5) 621-2350
EMail: info@lut.fi
Website: http://www.lut.fi

President: Anneli Pauli (2014-)

Provost: Juha-Matti Saksa

International Relations: Janne Hokkanen, Director for international affairs

Faculty

Technology (Chemical Engineering; Electrical Engineering; Energy Engineering; Environmental Engineering; Mathematics; Mechanical Engineering; Physics); **Technology Management** (Industrial Management; Information Technology)

School

Business (Finance; Marketing)

Research Centre

Carelian Drives and Motor *(CDMC)* (Electrical Engineering); **Computational Engineering and Integrated Design** *(CEID)* (Computer Engineering); **Northern Dimension** *(NORDI)* (Central European Studies; Eastern European Studies; Russian); **Separation Technology** *(CST)* (Environmental Engineering; Environmental Management); **Technology Business Research** (Business and Commerce; Technology)

Research Institute

South Karelian (Arts and Humanities; Development Studies; Regional Studies; Social Sciences)

History: Founded 1969. A State institution under the supervision of the Ministry of Education.

Academic Year: September to May (September-December; January-May)

Admission Requirements: Secondary school certificate (ylioppilastutkinto) or equivalent at the bachelor level Minimum bachelor of engineering or business in the field admission at the master level

Fees: National: None, International: None (intake 2015-16)

Main Language(s) of Instruction: Finnish, English

Accrediting Agency: Ministry of Education and Culture

Degrees and Diplomas: *Kandidaatti/Kandidat*: **Natural Sciences.** *Diplomi-insinööri/Diplomingenjör*: **Engineering.** *Lisensiaatti/Licentiat*: **Business Administration; Economics; Technology.** *Maisteri/Magister*: **Business Administration; Economics.** *Tohtori/Doktor*: **Business Administration; Economics; Philosophy; Technology.**

Student Services: Academic Counselling, Canteen, Careers Guidance, Cultural Activities, Health Services, IT Centre, Language Laboratory, Library, Nursery Care, Social Counselling, Sports Facilities, eLibrary

Publications: Lappeenranta University of Technology Research Papers

Academic Staff *2014-2015*	MEN	WOMEN	**TOTAL**
FULL-TIME	–	–	**930**
Student Numbers *2014-2015*			
All (Foreign included)	3,850	1,650	**5,500**
FOREIGN ONLY	300	200	**500**

Last Updated: 17/02/15

LAUREA UNIVERSITY OF APPLIED SCIENCES

Laurea-ammattikorkeakoulu
Ratatie 22, 01300 Vantaa
EMail: intl.info@laurea.fi
Website: http://www.laurea.fi

Rector: Jouni Koski EMail: jouni.koski(at)laurea.fi

Programme

Postgraduate (Business Administration; Health Administration; Social Work); **Undergraduate** (Business Administration; Health Administration; Nursing; Service Trades; Welfare and Protective Services)

History: Founded 2001.

Main Language(s) of Instruction: English, Finnish

Accrediting Agency: Ministry of Education and Culture

Degrees and Diplomas: *Ammattikorkeakoulututkinto (AMK)/Yrkeshögskoleexamen (YH)*: **Business Administration; Civil Security; Hotel and Restaurant; Information Technology; Nursing; Social Work.** *Ylempi ammattikorkeakoulututinto (ylempi AMK)/Högre yrkeshögskoleexamen (högre YH)*: **Business Administration; Health Administration; Social Work.**

Last Updated: 16/02/15

MIKKELI UNIVERSITY OF APPLIED SCIENCES

Mikkelin ammattikorkeakoulu (MAMK)
Patteristonkatu 1 H, 50101 Mikkeli
Tel: +358(15) 355-61
Fax: +358(15) 355-6464
EMail: mamk@mamk.fi
Website: http://www.mamk.fi

President and CEO: Heikki Saastamoinen
Tel: +358(15) 355-6300 EMail: heikki.saastamoinen@mamk.fi

International Relations: Henrik Luikko Tel: +358(44) 702-8232

Programme

Business Operations in Forestry *(Master's degree)* (Forest Management; Forestry; Natural Resources); **Development and Management in Health Care and Social Services** *(Master's degree)* (Health Administration); **e-Services and Digital Archiving** *(Master's degree)* (Archiving); **Entrepreneurship and Business Operations** *(Master's degree)* (Business Administration; Management); **Environmental Technology** *(Master's degree)* (Environmental Engineering); **Hospitality Management** *(Master's degree)* (Tourism); **Humanities and Education - Civic Activities and Youth Work** (Civics; Social Work); **Natural Resources and the Environment - Forestry** (Environmental Management; Environmental Studies; Forestry; Natural Resources); **Natural Sciences - Business Information Technology** (Business Computing; Information Technology); **NGO and Youth Work** *(Master's degree)*; **Social Sciences, Business and Administration** (Business Administration; Social Sciences); **Social Services, Health and Sports** (Nursing; Physical Therapy; Public Health; Social and Community Services; Social Work; Sports); **Technology, Communication and Transport** (Electrical Engineering; Environmental Engineering; Information Technology; Materials Engineering; Transport and Communications); **Tourism, Catering and Domestic Services** (Cooking and Catering; Tourism)

Further Information: Savonniemi campus, Savonlinna, Finland

History: Founded 1997.

Academic Year: First year students: from last week of August to mid May. Other students: from first week of September to mid May. International summer term on selected topics.

Admission Requirements: Degree from a secondary level school (12 years of education).

Fees: 00

Main Language(s) of Instruction: Finnish, English

Accrediting Agency: Ministry of Education and Culture

Degrees and Diplomas: *Ammattikorkeakoulututkinto (AMK)/Yrkeshögskoleexamen (YH)*; *Ylempi ammattikorkeakoulututinto (ylempi AMK)/Högre yrkeshögskoleexamen (högre YH)*: **Archiving; Business Administration; Environmental Engineering; Forestry; Health Administration; Tourism.**

Student Services: Academic Counselling, Canteen, Careers Guidance, Cultural Activities, Facilities for disabled people, Foreign Studies Centre, Health Services, IT Centre, Language Laboratory, Library, Nursery Care, Social Counselling, Sports Facilities, eLibrary

Academic Staff *2013*	MEN	WOMEN	**TOTAL**
FULL-TIME	125	244	**369**
Student Numbers *2014*			
All (Foreign included)	2,000	2,500	c. **4,500**

Last Updated: 25/11/14

NOVIA UNIVERSITY OF APPLIED SCIENCES

Yrkeshögskolan Novia
PO Box 6, 65201 Vaasa
Tel: +358(6) 328-5000
Fax: +358(6) 328-5110
EMail: info@novia.fi; admissions@novia.fi
Website: http://www.novia.fi

Rector: Örjan Andersson (2007-) EMail: orjan.andersson@novia.fi

Programme

Postgraduate (Health Administration; Management; Natural Resources; Social and Community Services); **Undergraduate** (Business Administration; Education; Engineering; Hotel Management; Social and Community Services)

History: Founded 2008 following the merger of Yrkeshögskolan Sydväst (Sydväst University of Applied Sciences) and Svenska yrkeshögskolan (Swedish Polytechnic, Finland).

Main Language(s) of Instruction: English, Finnish, Swedish

Accrediting Agency: Ministry of Education and Culture

Degrees and Diplomas: *Ammattikorkeakoulututkinto (AMK)/Yrkeshögskoleexamen (YH)*: **Business Administration; Engineering; Environmental Engineering; Marine Engineering; Marine Transport; Natural Resources; Nursing; Social and Community Services.** *Ylempi ammattikorkeakoulututinto (ylempi AMK)/Högre yrkeshögskoleexamen (högre YH)*: **Art Management; Business Administration; Engineering; Environmental Management; Health Administration; Hotel Management; Natural Resources; Social and Community Services.**

Last Updated: 17/02/15

OULU UNIVERSITY OF APPLIED SCIENCES

Oulun ammattikorkeakoulu
PO Box 222, 90101 Oulu
Tel: +358(10) 6110-200
Fax: +358(8) 372-144
EMail: international@oamk.fi
Website: http://www.oamk.fi

Rector: Jouko Paaso (1996-) EMail: jouko.paaso@oamk.fi

School

Business and Information Management (Business and Commerce; Economics; Information Management; Information Technology; International Business; Library Science); **Engineering and Natural Resources** (Automation and Control Engineering; Civil Engineering; Electrical Engineering; Environmental Studies; Information Technology; Laboratory Techniques; Mechanical Engineering; Natural Resources; Production Engineering); **Health and Social Care** (Nursing; Occupational Therapy; Optometry; Physical Therapy; Public Health; Radiology; Social and Community Services); **Media and Performing Arts** (Dance; Media Studies; Music); **Vocational Teacher Education** (Teacher Training)

History: Founded 1992. Acquired present status and title 1996.

Main Language(s) of Instruction: Finnish, English

Accrediting Agency: Ministry of Education and Culture

Degrees and Diplomas: *Ammattikorkeakoulututkinto (AMK)/Yrkeshögskoleexamen (YH)*: **Architecture; Business Administration; Business Computing; Education; Engineering; Health Sciences; Information Technology; International Business; Performing Arts; Social Sciences.** *Ylempi ammattikorkeakoulututinto (ylempi AMK)/Högre yrkeshögskoleexamen (högre YH)*: **Business Administration; Engineering; Health Administration; Industrial Management; Information Technology; Rural Planning.**

Last Updated: 17/02/15

SAIMAA UNIVERSITY OF APPLIED SCIENCES

Saimaan ammattikorkeakoulu
Skinnarilankatu 36, 53850 Lappeenranta
Tel: +358(20) 496-6411
Fax: +358(20) 496-6505
EMail: info@saimia.fi
Website: http://www.saimia.fi/fi-FI/

Rector: Anneli Pirttilä EMail: anneli.pirttila@saimia.fi

Faculty

Business and Culture (Business Administration; Fine Arts; International Business); **Health Care and Social Services** (Nursing; Occupational Therapy; Physical Therapy; Public Health; Social and Community Services); **Technology** (Chemical Engineering; Civil Engineering; Construction Engineering; Electrical Engineering; Industrial Engineering; Industrial Management; Information Technology; Mechanical Engineering; Paper Technology; Technology; Transport Management)

Unit

Tourism and Hospitality (Cooking and Catering; Hotel and Restaurant; Tourism); **Visual Arts** (Design; Fine Arts; Visual Arts)

History: Founded 1992. Acquired present title 2009. Formerly known as Etelä-Karjalan ammattikorkeakoulu (South-Karelia University of Applied Sciences).

Main Language(s) of Instruction: Finnish, English

Accrediting Agency: Ministry of Education and Culture

Degrees and Diplomas: *Ammattikorkeakoulututkinto (AMK)/Yrkeshögskoleexamen (YH)*: **Business Administration; Engineering; Fine Arts; Hotel Management; Social and Community Services; Social Welfare; Technology.** *Ylempi ammattikorkeakoulututinto (ylempi AMK)/Högre yrkeshögskoleexamen (högre YH)*: **Business Administration.**

Last Updated: 17/02/15

SATAKUNTA UNIVERSITY OF APPLIED SCIENCES

Satakunnan ammattikorkeakoulu
Tiedepuisto 3, 28600 Pori
Tel: +358(2) 620-3000
EMail: info@samk.fi; int.office@samk.fi
Website: http://www.samk.fi

Rector: Juha Kämäri

Faculty

Energy and Construction (Engineering); **Health** (Nursing; Public Health); **Information Technology** (Information Technology); **Logistics and Maritime Technology** (Industrial Engineering; Marine Transport; Production Engineering; Transport Management); **Service Business** (Business Administration; Business and Commerce; International Business; Management; Marketing; Tourism); **Welfare** (Fine Arts; Rehabilitation and Therapy; Social Welfare)

Further Information: Also campuses in Rauma, Huittinen, Kankaanpää and Harjavalta

History: Founded 1997.

Main Language(s) of Instruction: English, Finnish

Accrediting Agency: Ministry of Education and Culture

Degrees and Diplomas: *Ammattikorkeakoulututkinto (AMK)/Yrkeshögskoleexamen (YH)*: **Business Administration; Engineering; Health Sciences; Information Technology; Marine Transport; Transport Management.** *Ylempi ammattikorkeakoulututinto (ylempi AMK)/Högre yrkeshögskoleexamen (högre YH)*: **Business Administration; Marine Transport; Medical Technology; Public Health; Rehabilitation and Therapy; Social and Community Services.**

Last Updated: 17/02/15

SAVONIA UNIVERSITY OF APPLIED SCIENCES

Savonia ammattikorkeakoulu
Microkatu 1, 70201 Kuopio
Tel: +358(17) 255-6000
EMail: savonia@savonia.fi
Website: http://www.savonia.fi

Rector: Mervi Vidgrén

Programme

Business and Administration *(Iisalmi, Kuopio and Varkaus)* (Administration; Business and Commerce; International Business); **Engineering and Technology** *(Kuopio and Varkaus)* (Engineering; Industrial Management); **Natural Resources** *(Peltosalmi)* (Agriculture; Natural Resources; Rural Planning; Rural Studies); **Social and Health Care** *(Kuopio and Iisalmi)* (Nursing; Public Health; Social and Community Services); **Tourism and Catering** *(Kuopio)* (Cooking and Catering; Hotel and Restaurant; Hotel Management; Tourism)

Academy

Design *(Kuopio)* (Ceramic Art; Fashion Design; Furniture Design; Glass Art; Graphic Design; Industrial Design; Interior Design; Jewellery Art; Textile Design); **Music and Dance** *(Kuopio)* (Dance; Music)

History: Founded 1992, acquired present status and title 1998.

Main Language(s) of Instruction: English, Finnish

Accrediting Agency: Ministry of Education and Culture

Degrees and Diplomas: *Ammattikorkeakoulututkinto (AMK)/Yrkeshögskoleexamen (YH)*: **Business Administration; Engineering; Fine Arts; Health Sciences.** *Ylempi ammattikorkeakoulututinto (ylempi AMK)/Högre yrkeshögskoleexamen (högre YH)*: **Hotel Management; Industrial Management; Rehabilitation and Therapy; Social and Community Services.**

Last Updated: 17/02/15

SEINÄJOKI UNIVERSITY OF APPLIED SCIENCES

Seinäjoen ammattikorkeakoulu
PO Box 412, Keskuskatu 34, 60101 Seinäjoki
Tel: +358(20) 124-3000
EMail: seamk@seamk.fi
Website: http://www.seamk.fi

Rector: Tapio Varmola EMail: tapio.varmola@seamk.fi

School

Business and Culture (Business Administration; Library Science; Tourism); **Food and Agriculture** (Agricultural Business; Food Science; Forestry; Hotel and Restaurant); **Health Care and Social Work** (Health Administration; Nursing; Rehabilitation and Therapy; Social and Community Services; Social Work); **Technology** (Engineering; Information Technology)

History: Founded 1996.

Academic Year: September to June (September-December; January-June)

Main Language(s) of Instruction: Finnish and English

Accrediting Agency: Ministry of Education and Culture

Degrees and Diplomas: *Ammattikorkeakoulututkinto (AMK)/Yrkeshögskoleexamen (YH)*: **Agriculture; Business Administration; Engineering; Public Health; Rehabilitation and Therapy.** *Ylempi ammattikorkeakoulututinto (ylempi AMK)/Högre yrkeshögskoleexamen (högre YH)*: **Agricultural Business; Construction Engineering; Health Administration; Industrial Management; International Business; Social Work.**

Last Updated: 17/02/15

TAMPERE UNIVERSITY OF APPLIED SCIENCES

Tampereen ammattikorkeakoulu (TAMK)
Kuntokatu 3, 33520 Tampere
Tel: +358(3) 245-2111
Fax: +358(3) 245-2222
EMail: international.office@tamk.fi
Website: http://www.tamk.fi

Rector: Markku Lahtinen (2010-) EMail: essi.kannelkoski@tamk.fi

Programme

Postgraduate, Master's Programmes in English *(Master's Programmes in English)* (Business Administration; Education; Engineering; Forestry; Media Studies); **Postgraduate, Master's Programmes in Finnish** *(Master's Programmes in Finnish)* (Business Administration; Engineering; Health Sciences; Hotel and Restaurant; Media Studies); **Undergraduate, Bachelor's Programmes in English** *(Bachelor's Programmes in English)* (Business Administration; Engineering; Media Studies); **Undergraduate, Bachelor's Programmes in Finnish** *(Bachelor's Programmes in Finnish)* (Business Administration; Engineering; Forestry; Health Sciences; Hotel and Restaurant; Media Studies; Social Work)

History: Founded 2010 following the merger of Pirkanmaan ammattikorkeakoulu (PIRAMK University of Applied Sciences) and Tampereen ammattikorkeakoulu (TAMK University of Applied Sciences).

Main Language(s) of Instruction: English, Finnish

Accrediting Agency: Ministry of Education and Culture

Degrees and Diplomas: *Ammattikorkeakoulututkinto (AMK)/Yrkeshögskoleexamen (YH)*: **Business Administration; Engineering; Fine Arts; Forestry; Health Sciences; Hotel Management; Media Studies; Social Sciences.** *Ylempi ammattikorkeakoulututinto (ylempi AMK)/Högre yrkeshögskoleexamen (högre YH)*: **Business Administration; Engineering; Fine Arts; Health Sciences; Hotel Management; Media Studies; Social Sciences.**

Last Updated: 30/03/15

TAMPERE UNIVERSITY OF TECHNOLOGY

Tampereen teknillinen yliopisto (TUT)
PO Box 527, Korkeakoulunkatu 10, 33101 Tampere
Tel: +358 3 311 511
EMail: interoff@tut.fi
Website: http://www.tut.fi

Rector: Markku Kivikoski Tel: +358 3 311 511

Director of Administration: Tiina Äijälä
Tel: +358 3 311 511 EMail: tiina.aijala@tut.fi

International Relations: Minna Haka-Risku, Head of International Office Tel: +358 3 311 511 EMail: minna.haka-risku@tut.fi

Faculty

Business and Built Environment *(The Faculty consists of seven departments)* (Architecture; Business Administration; Civil Engineering; Continuing Education; Industrial Management; Information Management; Modern Languages; Transport Management); **Computing and Electrical Engineering** *(The Faculty consists of four departments)* (Biomedical Engineering; Computer Engineering; Electrical Engineering; Information Technology; Software Engineering; Telecommunications Engineering); **Engineering Sciences** *(The Faculty consists of four departments)* (Automation and Control Engineering; Materials Engineering; Mechanical Engineering; Production Engineering); **Natural Sciences** *(The Faculty consists of three departments)* (Bioengineering; Chemical Engineering; Energy Engineering; Mathematics; Physics)

Further Information: Eight international Master's programmes in English with over 20 study options. Also courses for foreign exchange students in various fields.

History: Founded 1965 and attached to the Helsinki University of Technology. Acquired independent status 1972. An autonomous State institution under the supervision of the Ministry of Education.

Academic Year: September to May (September-January; February-May)

Admission Requirements: Secondary school certificate (lukion päästötodistus) or equivalent, and entrance examination for programmes at bachelor level (in Finnish). For master's programmes, a bachelor's degree or equivalent in a suitable field is required.

Fees: National: -, International: -

Main Language(s) of Instruction: Finnish, English

Accrediting Agency: Ministry of Education and Culture

Degrees and Diplomas: *Arkkitehti/Arkitekt*: **Architecture.** *Diplomi-insinööri/Diplomingenjör*: **Technology.** *Lisensiaatti/Licentiat*: **Technology.** *Maisteri/Magister*: **Technology.** *Tohtori/Doktor*: **Technology.** Also Tekniikan kandidaatti (Bachelor of Science in Technology, in Finnish), Master of Science in Technology, Licenciate of Science, Doctor of Science (Architecture/Technology), Doctor of Philosophy.

Student Services: Academic Counselling, Canteen, Careers Guidance, Cultural Activities, Foreign Studies Centre, Health Services, IT Centre, Language Laboratory, Library, Social Counselling, Sports Facilities, eLibrary

Academic Staff *2013-2014*	**TOTAL**
FULL-TIME	c. **2,000**
Student Numbers *2013-2014*	
All (Foreign included)	c. **10,500**
FOREIGN ONLY	**1400**

Last Updated: 01/12/14

TURKU UNIVERSITY OF APPLIED SCIENCES

Turun ammattikorkeakoulu - Åbo yrkeshögskola
Joukahaisenkatu 3 A, 20520 Turku
Tel: +358(2) 263-350
EMail: ammattikorkeakoulu@turkuamk.fi
Website: http://www.turkuamk.fi

Rector: Vesa Taatila EMail: vesa.taatila@turkuamk.fi

Faculty

Business, ICT and Chemical Engineering (Business Administration; Chemical Engineering; Information Technology); **Health and Well-being** (Health Administration; Nursing; Rehabilitation and Therapy; Social and Community Services); **Technology, Environment and Business** (Automotive Engineering; Civil Engineering; Engineering Drawing and Design; Environmental Engineering; Industrial Engineering; Transport Engineering)

Academy

Arts (Fine Arts; Media Studies; Music; Performing Arts)

Further Information: Campuses also in Salo and Loimaa.

History: Founded 1997.

Main Language(s) of Instruction: English, Finnish

Accrediting Agency: Ministry of Education and Culture

Degrees and Diplomas: *Ammattikorkeakoulututkinto (AMK)/Yrkeshögskoleexamen (YH)*: **Business Administration; Chemical Engineering; Design; Engineering; Health Administration; Information Sciences; Midwifery; Nursing; Rehabilitation and Therapy; Social and Community Services.** *Ylempi ammattikorkeakoulututinto (ylempi AMK)/Högre yrkeshögskoleexamen (högre YH)*: **Business Administration; Construction Engineering; Design; Industrial Management; Information Sciences; Library Science; Nursing; Rehabilitation and Therapy; Social and Community Services.**

Last Updated: 17/02/15

UNIVERSITY OF EASTERN FINLAND

Itä-Suomen yliopisto (UEF)
Yliopistonranta 1, PO Box 1627, 70211 Kuopio
Tel: +358 294 45 1111
EMail: kirjaamo@uef.fi
Website: http://www.uef.fi

Rector: Jukka Mönkkönen (2015-2019)
EMail: jukka.monkkonen@uef.fi

Research Development Manager: Anu Liikanen
EMail: anu.liikanen@uef.fi

Academic Rector: Jaakko Puhakka EMail: jaakko.puhakka@uef.fi

International Relations: Outi Savonlahti, Director of International Relations EMail: outi.savonlahti@uef.fi

Faculty

Health Sciences (Biomedicine; Biotechnology; Dentistry; Health Sciences; Medicine; Molecular Biology; Neurosciences; Nursing; Pharmacology; Pharmacy; Public Health; Toxicology); **Philosophy** (Arts and Humanities; Education; Psychology; Teacher Training; Theology); **Science and Forestry** (Applied Physics; Biology; Chemistry; Computer Science; Environmental Studies; Forestry; Information Technology; Mathematics and Computer Science; Natural Sciences; Physics); **Social Sciences and Business** (Business Administration; Geography; Health Administration; History; Law; Social Sciences; Social Work; Sociology; Tourism)

Institute

A. I. Virtanen (Biomedicine)

Centre

Language centre (Chinese; English; Finnish; French; German; Latin; Russian; Spanish; Swedish); **Training and Development, Aducate** *(Also Open University)* (Continuing Education)

Research Institute

Karelian (Eastern European Studies; Ethnology; History; Rural Studies; Social Sciences)

Research Unit

Mekrijärvi Research Station (Ecology; Forestry; Laboratory Techniques)

Further Information: Also campuses in Joensuu and Savonlinna, Mekrijärvi Research Station in Ilomantsi, and Kuopio University Hospital.

History: Founded 2010 following merger of Joensuun yliopisto (University of Joensuu, founded 1969) and Kuopion yliopisto (University of Kuopio, founded 1966).

Academic Year: August to July (September-December; January-May)

Admission Requirements: Secondary school certificate (ylioppilastutkinto) or equivalent, and entrance examination. Applicants not fluent in Finnish need to have good skills in English verified by an internationally recognised language proficiency test.

Fees: None

Main Language(s) of Instruction: Finnish, English

Accrediting Agency: Ministry of Education and Culture

Degrees and Diplomas: *Farmaseutti/Farmaceut*: **Pharmacy.** *Kandidaatti/Kandidat*: **Applied Physics; Biology; Biomedicine; Business Administration; Chemistry; Economics; Education; English; Environmental Studies; Finnish; Forestry; Geography; German; Health Administration; History; Linguistics; Mathematics and Computer Science; Nursing; Physics; Psychology; Public Health; Russian; Social Sciences; Social Work; Swedish; Theology.** *Oikeusnotaari/Rättsnotarie*: **Law.** *Hammaslääketieteen lisensiaatti/Odontologie licentiat*: **Dentistry.** *Lääketieteen lisensiaatti/Medicine licentiat*: **Medicine.** *Lisensiaatti/Licentiat*: **Arts and Humanities; Business Administration; Education; Environmental Studies; Forestry; Health Sciences; Law; Mathematics and Computer Science; Natural Sciences; Pharmacy; Social Sciences; Theology.** *Proviisori/Provisor*: **Pharmacy.** *Maisteri/Magister*: **Applied Physics; Biology; Biomedicine; Business Administration; Chemistry; Economics; Education; English; Environmental Studies; Finnish; Forestry; Geography; German; Health Administration; History; Linguistics; Mathematics and Computer Science; Nursing; Physics; Psychology; Public Health; Russian; Social Sciences; Social Work; Swedish; Theology.** *Tohtori/Doktor*: **Arts and Humanities; Business Administration; Dentistry; Education; Environmental Studies; Forestry; Health Sciences; Law; Mathematics and Computer Science; Medicine; Natural Sciences; Pharmacy; Social Sciences; Theology.**

Student Services: Academic Counselling, Canteen, Careers Guidance, Facilities for disabled people, Foreign Studies Centre, Health Services, IT Centre, Language Laboratory, Library, Sports Facilities, eLibrary

Publications: Saima - Itä-Suomen yliopistolehti; UEF Bulletin

Academic Staff *2014-2015*	**TOTAL**
FULL-TIME	c. **2,600**
Student Numbers *2014-2015*	
All (Foreign included)	c. **15,000**
FOREIGN ONLY	**650**

Last Updated: 09/12/14

UNIVERSITY OF HELSINKI

Helsingin yliopisto
PO Box 33, Yliopistonkatu 4, 00014 Helsinki
Tel: +358 2941 911
Fax: +358 2941 23008
Website: http://www.helsinki.fi/university

Rector: Jukka Kola (2013-) EMail: Jukka.Kola@helsinki.fi

Communications Director: Kirsti Lehumusto
Tel: +358(9) 191-23225 EMail: kirsti.lehmusto@helsinki.fi

International Relations: Markus Laitinen, Head of International affairs Tel: +358(9) 191-22605 EMail: matti.j.tikkanen@helsinki.fi

Faculty

Agriculture and Forestry (Agricultural Management; Agriculture; Arctic Studies; Environmental Studies; Food Science; Forestry); **Arts** (Aesthetics; African Studies; Archaeology; Art History; Asian Studies; Baltic Languages; Cinema and Television; Comparative Literature; Comparative Religion; Cultural Studies; English; Ethnology; Film; Finnish; Folklore; German; History; Hungarian; Linguistics; Literature; Marine Science and Oceanography; Museum Studies; Musicology; Philology; Philosophy; Romance Languages; Scandinavian Languages; Slavic Languages; Theatre; Translation and Interpretation; Women's Studies); **Behavioural Sciences** (Behavioural Sciences; Cognitive Sciences; Education; Educational Testing and Evaluation; Handicrafts; Higher Education; Home Economics; Psychology; Speech Studies); **Biological and Environmental Sciences** (Biochemistry; Biotechnology; Ecology; Genetics; Microbiology; Neurosciences; Physiology; Plant Pathology; Zoology); **Law** (Commercial Law; Criminal Law; Human Rights; International Economics; International Law; Justice Administration; Private Law; Public Law); **Medicine** (Biomedicine; Dentistry; Forensic Medicine and Dentistry; Medicine; Public Health); **Pharmacy** (Pharmacy); **Science** (Astronomy and Space Science; Chemistry; Computer Science; Geography; Geology; Mathematics; Physics; Statistics); **Social Sciences** (Anthropology; Economics; Political Sciences; Social Psychology; Social Studies; Social Work); **Theology** (Bible; Comparative Religion; History of Religion; Orthodox Theology; Theology); **Veterinary Medicine** (Veterinary Science)

College

Advanced Studies *(Helsinki Collegium)*

Institute

Biotechnology; **Information Technology** *(Helsinki Institute)*; **Molecular Medicine - Finland** *(FIMM)*; **Physics** *(HIP, Helsinki)*; **Ruralia** *(Mikkeli and Seinäjoki units)*; **Russian and East European Studies** *(Aleksanteri Institute)*; **Seismology**; **Verification of the Chemical Weapons Convention** *(VERIFIN)*

Centre

Continuing Education *(Palmenia Centre)*; **Economic Research** *(HECER, Helsinki)*; **Genome**; **Language**; **Neurosciences**

Further Information: Traditional and Open Higher Education Institution

History: Founded as Royal Academy of Turku 1640. Transferred to Helsinki 1828. The first and only university in the country until 1919.

Academic Year: September to May (September-December; January-May)

Admission Requirements: Secondary school certificate (ylioppilastutkinto/studentexamen) or foreign equivalent, BA/BSc for admission into Master's programmes.

Fees: National: None, International: None (subject to change for 2016)

Main Language(s) of Instruction: Finnish, Swedish, English

Accrediting Agency: Ministry of Education and Culture

Degrees and Diplomas: *Eläinlääketieteen lisensiaatti/Veterinärmedicine licentiat*; *Hammaslääketieteen lisensiaatti/Odontologie licentiat*: **Dentistry.** *Lääketieteen lisensiaatti/Medicine licentiat*; *Lisensiaatti/Licentiat*: **Animal Husbandry; Education; Fine Arts; Forestry; Law; Pharmacy; Psychology; Social Sciences; Theology; Veterinary Science.** *Maisteri/Magister*: **Education; Fine Arts; Forestry; Law; Pharmacy; Social Sciences; Theology.** *Tohtori/Doktor*: **Animal Husbandry; Education; Fine Arts; Forestry; Law; Pharmacy; Philosophy; Psychology; Social Sciences; Theology; Veterinary Science.**

Student Services: Academic Counselling, Canteen, Careers Guidance, Facilities for disabled people, Foreign Studies Centre, Health Services, Language Laboratory, Social Counselling, Sports Facilities

Publications: Universitas Helsingiensis

Publishing House: Helsinki University Press

Last Updated: 01/12/14

UNIVERSITY OF JYVÄSKYLÄ

Jyväskylän yliopisto (JY)
PO Box 35, Seminaarinmäki, 40014 Jyväskylä
Tel: +358(14) 260-1211
Fax: +358(14) 260-1021
EMail: tiedotus@jyu.fi
Website: http://www.jyu.fi

Rector: Matti Manninen (2012-) EMail: matti.manninen@jyu.fi

Vice-Rector: Kaisa Miettinen EMail: kaisa.miettinen@jyu.fi

Vice-Rector: Helena Rasku-Puttonen
EMail: helena.rasku-puttonen@jyu.fi

International Relations: Anna Grönlund, Head of the International Office Tel: +358(50) 313 0401 EMail: anna.gronlund@jyu.fi

Faculty

Education (Adult Education; Curriculum; Education; Educational Administration; Educational and Student Counselling; Preschool Education; Primary Education; Special Education; Teacher Training); **Humanities** (Applied Linguistics; Art Education; Art History; Arts and Humanities; Communication Studies; Cultural Studies; English; Ethnology; Finnish; French; German; History; Hungarian; Journalism; Linguistics; Literature; Modern Languages; Museum Studies; Music; Music Education; Musicology; Public Relations; Romance Languages; Russian; Speech Studies; Swedish; Teacher Training); **Information Technology** (Applied Mathematics; Cognitive Sciences; Information Technology; Mathematics and Computer Science); **Mathematics and Science** (Biological and Life Sciences; Biology; Cell Biology; Chemistry; Ecology; Environmental Management; Environmental Studies; Marine Science and Oceanography; Mathematics; Mathematics Education; Molecular Biology; Natural Resources; Natural Sciences; Nuclear Physics; Physics; Science Education; Statistics); **Social Sciences** (Philosophy; Political Sciences; Psychology; Social Policy; Social Sciences; Social Work; Sociology); **Sports and Health Sciences** (Biology; Gerontology; Health Education; Health Sciences; Physical Education; Physical Therapy; Physiology; Public Health; Social Sciences; Sociology; Sports Management; Sports Medicine)

School

Business and Economics (Jyväskylä) (Business and Commerce; Economics; Environmental Management)

Institute

Chydenius *(Kokkola)* (Education; Information Technology; Teacher Training); **Educational Research** (Educational Research); **Open University**

Centre

Computing (Computer Science); **Continuing Education** (Continuing Education); **Environmental Research** (Environmental Studies); **Human Technologies** *(Agora)* (Computer Science; Information Technology; Psychology); **Language** (Communication Studies; Linguistics; Modern Languages)

History: Founded 1863 as a Teacher Training College, became College of Education 1934 and acquired present status and title 1966. An autonomous State institution under the supervision of the Ministry of Education.

Academic Year: August to July (September-December; January-May; June-July)

Admission Requirements: Secondary school certificate (ylioppilastutkinto) or foreign equivalent, and entrance examination

Main Language(s) of Instruction: Finnish, English

Accrediting Agency: Ministry of Education and Culture

Degrees and Diplomas: *Kandidaatti/Kandidat*: **Business Administration; Economics; Education; Fine Arts; Health Sciences; Natural Sciences; Psychology; Social Sciences; Sports.** *Lisensiaatti/Licentiat*: **Business Administration; Economics; Education; Fine Arts; Health Sciences; Natural Sciences; Psychology; Social Sciences; Sports.** *Maisteri/Magister*: **Business Administration; Economics; Education; Fine Arts; Health Sciences; Natural Sciences; Psychology; Social Sciences; Sports.** *Tohtori/Doktor*: **Business Administration; Economics; Education; Fine Arts; Health Sciences; Psychology; Social Sciences; Sports.**

Student Services: Academic Counselling, Canteen, Careers Guidance, Cultural Activities, Facilities for disabled people, Health Services, Nursery Care, Social Counselling, Sports Facilities

Publications: Jyväskylä Studies in Arts; Jyväskylä Studies in Biological and Environmental Science; Jyväskylä Studies in Business and Economics; Jyväskylä Studies in Communication; Jyväskylä Studies in Computing; Jyväskylä Studies in Education, Psychology and Social Research; Jyväskylä Studies in Sport, Physical Education and Health; Kasvatus (Finnish Journal of Education); Studia Historica Jyväskyläensia; Studia Philologica Jyväskyläensia

Publishing House: University Printing House
Last Updated: 17/02/15

UNIVERSITY OF LAPLAND

Lapin yliopisto
Yliopistonkatu 8, 96300 Rovaniemi
Tel: +358(16) 341-341
Fax: +358(16) 362-936
EMail: international.relations@ulapland.fi
Website: http://www.ulapland.fi

Rector: Mauri Ylä-Kotola (2006-)
EMail: mauri.yla-kotola@ulapland.fi

Director of Communication and Pr: Olli Tiwaniemi
Tel: +358 400 695 418 EMail: olli.tiwaniemi@ulapland.fi

International Relations: Outi Snellman, Director of International Relations Tel: +358 40 201 0209 EMail: outi.snellman@ulapland.fi

Faculty

Art and Design (Art Education; Clothing and Sewing; Fashion Design; Graphic Design; Industrial Design; Interior Design; Media Studies; Textile Design); **Education** (Adult Education; Education; Gender Studies; Primary Education; Teacher Training; Technology Education); **Law** (Comparative Law; International Law; Law); **Social Sciences** (Administration; International Relations; Management; Political Sciences; Psychology; Public Law; Social Sciences; Social Welfare; Social Work; Sociology; Tourism)

Institute

Lapland Institute for Tourism Research and Education (Tourism)

Centre

Arctic (Arctic Studies; Environmental Studies); **Language** *(For basic language courses and Finnish courses for overseas students.)* (Modern Languages)

History: Founded 1979. A State institution.

Academic Year: August to May (August-December; January-May)

Admission Requirements: Secondary school certificate (ylioppilastutkinto) or equivalent

Main Language(s) of Instruction: Finnish, English

Accrediting Agency: Ministry of Education and Culture

Degrees and Diplomas: *Kandidaatti/Kandidat*: **Administration; Fine Arts; Law; Social Sciences.** *Lisensiaatti/Licentiat*: **Administration; Education; Law; Social Sciences.** *Maisteri/Magister*: **Administration; Design; Education; Fine Arts; Law; Social Sciences.** *Tohtori/Doktor*: **Administration; Education; Fine Arts; Law; Social Sciences.**

Student Services: Academic Counselling, Canteen, Careers Guidance, Cultural Activities, Foreign Studies Centre, Health Services, Language Laboratory, Nursery Care, Social Counselling, Sports Facilities

Publications: Acta Universitatis Lapponiensis
Last Updated: 17/02/15

UNIVERSITY OF OULU

Oulun yliopisto (OY)
PO Box 8000, 90014 Oulu
Tel: +358(8) 553-4011
Fax: +358(8) 554-4551
EMail: international.office@oulu.fi; oulun.yliopisto@oulu.fi
Website: http://www.oulu.fi/yliopisto
Rector: Jouko Niinimäki (2015-) EMail: jouko.niinimaki@oulu.fi

Faculty

Biochemistry and Molecular Medicine (Biochemistry; Molecular Biology); **Education** (Education; Educational Sciences; Teacher Training); **Humanities** (Anthropology; Archaeology; Communication Disorders; English; German; History; Literature; Philology); **Information Technology and Electrical Engineering** (Computer Engineering; Computer Science; Electrical Engineering; Information Technology; Telecommunications Engineering); **Medicine** (Biomedicine; Dentistry; Medicine); **Science** (Biology; Botany; Chemistry; Genetics; Mathematics; Zoology); **Technology** (Environmental Engineering; Industrial Engineering; Industrial Management; Materials Engineering; Mechanical Engineering)

School

Architecture (Architectural Restoration; Architecture; Town Planning); **Business** *(Oulu)* (Accountancy; Business Administration; Economics; Finance; International Business; Management; Marketing); **Mining** (Mining Engineering)

Centre

Arctic Medicine; **Biocentre**; **Environment and Energy**; **Excellence in Cell-Extracellular Matrix Research**; **Health and Technology**; **Internet Excellence**; **Life Course Epidemiology Research**; **Microcopy and Nanotechnology**; **Wireless Communications**

Research Centre

Bioeconomy; **Eudaimonia Research Center**; **Medical Research Centre**

Further Information: Also University Central Hospital and Teacher Training School

History: Founded 1958. An autonomous State institution financed by the Government.

Academic Year: September to July (September-December; January-May)

Admission Requirements: Secondary school certificate (ylioppilastutkinto), or equivalent, and selection according to entrance examination results

Main Language(s) of Instruction: Finnish, English

Accrediting Agency: Ministry of Education and Culture

Degrees and Diplomas: *Kandidaatti/Kandidat*: **Architecture; Arts and Humanities; Economics; Education; Fine Arts; Natural Sciences.** *Arkkitehti/Arkitekt*: **Architecture.** *Diplomi-insinööri/Diplomingenjör*: **Engineering; Technology.** *Hammaslääketieteen lisensiaatti/Odontologie licentiat*: **Dentistry.** *Lääketieteen lisensiaatti/Medicine licentiat*: **Medicine.** *Maisteri/Magister*: **Arts and Humanities; Economics; Education; Fine Arts; Natural Sciences; Public Health.** *Tohtori/Doktor*: **Business Administration; Dentistry; Economics; Education; Engineering; Medicine; Philosophy; Technology.**

Student Services: Academic Counselling, Canteen, Careers Guidance, Facilities for disabled people, Health Services, Language Laboratory, Sports Facilities

Publications: Acta Universitatis Ouluensis
Last Updated: 17/02/15

UNIVERSITY OF TAMPERE

Tampereen yliopisto
Kalevantie 4, 33100 Tampere
Tel: +358(3) 355-111
Fax: +358(3) 213-4473
EMail: registry@uta.fi
Website: http://www.uta.fi

Rector: Liisa Laakso EMail: rector@uta.fi

International Relations: Mikko Markkola, Head of Department Academic and International Affairs EMail: mikko.markkol@uta.fi

School

Communication, Media and Theatre (Journalism; Mass Communication; Media Studies; Speech Studies; Theatre); **Education** (Adult Education; Education; Preschool Education); **Health Sciences** (Nursing; Public Health); **Information Sciences** (Computer Science; Mathematics; Statistics); **Language, Translation and Literary Studies** (Cultural Studies; Finnish; Literature; Modern Languages; Swedish; Translation and Interpretation); **Management**

(Business Administration; Economics; European Studies); **Medicine** (Health Sciences; Medicine; Nursing; Public Health); **Social Sciences and Humanities** (Ethnology; History; Information Sciences; International Relations; Journalism; Mass Communication; Musicology; Pedagogy; Philosophy; Political Sciences; Psychology; Social Policy; Social Psychology; Social Sciences; Social Work; Sociology; Women's Studies)

Institute

Biomedical Technology (Biological and Life Sciences; Biomedical Engineering; Biomedicine; Biotechnology)

Centre

Computer (Computer Science)

Research Institute

Regenerative Medicine; **Social Sciences** (Social Sciences)

Further Information: Also Hämeenlinna and Seinäjoki Centres for Extension Studies; International School of Social Sciences; Hämeenlinna Teacher Training Department

History: Founded 1925 as private Civic College in Helsinki, became School of Social Sciences 1930 and transferred to Tampere 1960. Formerly known as Yhteiskunnallinen korkeakoulu. Acquired present status and title 1966. An autonomous institution until August 1974, financed by the State 75%, by the city of Tampere 20%, and by student fees 5%. Subsequently under the supervision of the Ministry of Education and entirely financed by the State.

Academic Year: September to May (September-December; January-May)

Admission Requirements: Secondary school certificate (ylioppilastutkinto) or foreign equivalent, and entrance examination

Fees: None

Main Language(s) of Instruction: Finnish, English

Accrediting Agency: Ministry of Education and Culture

Degrees and Diplomas: *Kandidaatti/Kandidat*: **Arts and Humanities; Education; Engineering; Mathematics and Computer Science; Social Sciences; Welfare and Protective Services.** *Lääketieteen lisensiaatti/Medicine licentiat*: **Medicine.** *Lisensiaatti/Licentiat*: **Business Administration; Education; Philosophy; Psychology; Public Health; Social Sciences; Theatre.** *Maisteri/Magister*: **Business Administration; Economics; Education; Fine Arts; Psychology; Social Sciences; Theatre.** *Tohtori/Doktor*: **Anthropology; Biomedicine; Biotechnology; Communication Disorders; Education; Gender Studies; History; Information Technology; Linguistics; Literature; Management; Media Studies; Medicine; Peace and Disarmament; Philosophy; Psychology; Social Psychology; Social Work; Sociology; Theatre.**

Student Services: Academic Counselling, Canteen, Careers Guidance, Facilities for disabled people, Foreign Studies Centre, Health Services, Language Laboratory, Nursery Care, Sports Facilities

Publications: Acta Universitatis Tamperensis (Tampereen yliopiston julkaisusarja)

Publishing House: Tampere University Press

Last Updated: 17/02/15

UNIVERSITY OF THE ARTS

Taideyliopisto
PO Box 1, 00097 Helsinki
Tel: +358 294 47 2000
EMail: rehtori@uniarts.fi
Website: http://www.uniarts.fi/fi

Rector: Tiina Rosenberg (2013-2017) EMail: rehtori@uniarts.fi

Academy

Fine Arts (Fine Arts); **Sibelius** (Music); **Theatre** (Theatre)

History: Founded 2013 by the merger of Finnish Academy of Fine Arts (Kuvataideakatemia - Bildkunstakademin), Sibelius Academy (Sibelius-Akatemia, Sibelius-Akademin) and Theatre Academy Helsinki (Teatterikorkeakoulu - Teaterhögskolan).

Main Language(s) of Instruction: Finnish

Accrediting Agency: Ministry of Education and Culture

Degrees and Diplomas: *Kandidaatti/Kandidat*: **Fine Arts.** *Maisteri/Magister*: **Dance; Fine Arts; Music; Theatre.** *Tohtori/Doktor*: **Fine Arts; Music; Theatre.**

Last Updated: 17/02/15

UNIVERSITY OF TURKU

Turun yliopisto
20014 Turku
Tel: +358(2) 333-51
EMail: international@utu.fi
Website: http://www.utu.fi

Rector: Kalervo Väänänen (2014-)
Tel: +358(2) 333-6101 EMail: rector@utu.fi

Director of Communications and Publics Affairs: Maija Palonheimo Tel: +(358) 2 333 6129

International Relations: Irinja Paakkanen, Head of International Affairs Tel: +358(2) 333-6142 EMail: international@utu.fi

Faculty

Education (Adult Education; Education; Educational Sciences; Preschool Education; Special Education; Teacher Training; Technology Education); **Humanities** (American Studies; Anthropology; Archaeology; Art History; Baltic Languages; Classical Languages; Comparative Literature; Comparative Religion; Cultural Studies; English; Ethnology; Finnish; Folklore; Foreign Languages Education; French; German; History; Hungarian; Italian; Linguistics; Literature; Media Studies; Museum Studies; Musicology; Phonetics; Romanian; Russian; Scandinavian Languages; Spanish; Swedish; Translation and Interpretation; Women's Studies; Writing); **Law** (Law); **Mathematics and Natural Sciences** (Mathematics; Natural Sciences); **Medicine** (Dentistry; Health Sciences; Medicine; Nursing); **Social Sciences** (Asian Studies; Contemporary History; Economics; Philosophy; Political Sciences; Psychology; Social Policy; Social Work; Sociology; Statistics)

School

Cultural Production and Landscape Studies *(Rauma and Pori)* (Cultural Studies; Landscape Architecture); **Economics** *(Turku)* (Economics)

Institute

Archipelago Research *(in Nauvo, Seili Island)*; **Kevo Subarctic Research** *(in Utsjoki)*; **Satakunta Environmental Research** *(in Pori)*

Centre

Biotechnology (Biotechnology); **Computer Science** (Computer Science); **Extension Studies**; **Functional Foods Forum**; **Language**; **Maritime Studies**; **Turku PET Centre**

Further Information: Also Turku University Central Hospital. Master programmes and non-degree programmes in English in various fields.

History: Founded 1920 as a private institution on the initiative of the Finnish University Society. Inaugurated 1922. Became State institution 1974 under the supervision of the Ministry of Education. Merged with Turku School of Economics 2010.

Academic Year: August to July (August-December; January-July)

Admission Requirements: Secondary school certificate (Ylioppilastutkinto) or foreign equivalent, and entrance examination. Applicants not fluent in Finnish are required to hold a lower university degree (BA, BSc) and TOEFL test

Fees: None

Main Language(s) of Instruction: Finnish, English

Accrediting Agency: Ministry of Education and Culture

Degrees and Diplomas: *Kandidaatti/Kandidat*: **Education; Fine Arts; Health Sciences; Psychology; Social Sciences.** *Diplomi-insinööri/Diplomingenjör*: **Information Technology.** *Hammaslääketieteen lisensiaatti/Odontologie licentiat*: **Dentistry.** *Lääketieteen lisensiaatti/Medicine licentiat*: **Medicine.** *Lisensiaatti/Licentiat*: **Education; Law; Philosophy; Psychology; Public Health; Social Sciences.** *Maisteri/Magister*: **Astronomy and Space Science; Biology; Computer Science; Ecology; Education; Fine Arts; Food Technology; Geography; Geology; Health Sciences; Information Technology; Law; Mathematics; Physics; Physiology; Psychology; Social Sciences.** *Tohtori/Doktor*:

Dentistry; Education; Law; Medicine; Philosophy; Psychology; Public Health; Social Sciences.

Student Services: Academic Counselling, Canteen, Careers Guidance, Cultural Activities, Facilities for disabled people, Health Services, Language Laboratory, Social Counselling, Sports Facilities

Publications: Turun yliopiston julkaisuja - Annales Universitatis Turkuensis

Last Updated: 17/02/15

UNIVERSITY OF VAASA

Vaasan yliopisto

PO Box 700, 65101 Vaasa

Tel: +358(29) 449-8000

EMail: information@uva.fi

Website: http://www.uva.fi/en

Rector: Suvi Ronkainen (2015-)

EMail: rehtori@uwasa.fi; suvi.ronkainen@uva.fi

Faculty

Business Studies (Accountancy; Commercial Law; Economics; Finance; Management; Marketing); **Philosophy** (Communication Studies; English; Finnish; German; Health Administration; Public Administration; Public Law; Regional Studies; Scandinavian Languages; Translation and Interpretation); **Technology** (Automation and Control Engineering; Computer Science; Electrical Engineering; Mathematics; Statistics)

History: Founded 1968 as private School of Economics and Business Administration. Became state institution 1977. Acquired present status and title 1991.

Academic Year: September to May (September-December; January-May)

Admission Requirements: Secondary school certificate or certificate of secondary vocational education or Bachelor degree for master-level courses.

Main Language(s) of Instruction: Finnish, English, Swedish

Accrediting Agency: Ministry of Education and Culture

Degrees and Diplomas: *Kandidaatti/Kandidat*: **Administration; Arts and Humanities; Business Administration; Economics.** *Diplomi-insinööri/Diplomingenjör*: **Engineering; Technology.** *Lisensiaatti/Licentiat*: **Administration; Arts and Humanities; Business Administration; Economics; Engineering.** *Maisteri/Magister*: **Administration; Business Administration; Economics; Fine Arts.** *Tohtori/Doktor*: **Administration; Arts and Humanities; Business Administration; Economics; Engineering.**

Student Services: Academic Counselling, Canteen, Careers Guidance, Cultural Activities, Facilities for disabled people, Health Services, Social Counselling, Sports Facilities

Publications: Acta Wasaensia; Proceedings of the University of Vaasa

Publishing House: University of Vaasa Publishing House

Last Updated: 17/02/15

VAASA UNIVERSITY OF APPLIED SCIENCES

Vaasan ammattikorkeakoulu - Vaasa yrkeshögskola (VAMK)

Wolffintie 30, 65200 Vaasa

Tel: +358(207) 663-300

Fax: +358(207) 663-628

EMail: info@vamk.fi

Website: http://www.puv.fi/fi/

Rector: Tauno Kekäle EMail: tauno.kekale@vamk.fi

School

Business (Business Administration; Economics); **Health Care and Social Services** (Nursing; Public Health; Social and Community Services; Social Work); **Technology** (Civil Engineering; Electrical Engineering; Environmental Engineering; Mechanical Engineering)

History: Founded 1996, acquired present status and title 2006.

Academic Year: August to July

Admission Requirements: Completed Finnish Matriculation Examination or Upper Secondary Examination, European or International Baccalaureate or Reifeprufung examination or vocational qualification of 3 years or more or other non-Finnish equivalents.

Fees: None

Main Language(s) of Instruction: Finnish, English, Swedish

Accrediting Agency: Ministry of Education and Culture

Degrees and Diplomas: *Ammattikorkeakoulututkinto (AMK)/Yrkeshögskoleexamen (YH)*: **Business Administration; Engineering; Nursing; Social Sciences.** *Ylempi ammattikorkeakoulututinto (ylempi AMK)/Högre yrkeshögskoleexamen (högre YH)*: **Business Administration; Engineering; Nursing.**

Student Services: Academic Counselling, Canteen, Careers Guidance, Foreign Studies Centre, Health Services, Language Laboratory, Nursery Care, Social Counselling

Last Updated: 17/02/15

France

STRUCTURE OF HIGHER EDUCATION SYSTEM

Description:

Higher education in France is characterized by a dual system : it is provided in universities (including Instituts nationaux polytechniques) opened to a large number of students, whose programmes are generally geared towards research and its applications and in "Grandes Ecoles" and other professional higher education institutions which have more selective admission policies. Lycées also offer non-university higher education courses leading to the Brevet de Technicien supérieur (BTS). Whereas most institutions come under the responsibility of the Ministry of National Education, Higher Education and Research, some "Grandes Ecoles" come under the responsibility of other Ministries. Universities are made up of units offering curricula in academic fields and of various institutes and schools, such as IUTs (Instituts universitaires de Technologie) which offer courses in Engineering and Technology and special programmes in Management, Political Science, Languages and Physical Education and IUPs (Instituts universitaires professionalisés) which offer technological courses and practical training with an introduction to research and foreign languages. The "Grandes Ecoles" offer a high standard of professional education in three or more years after two years of "classes préparatoires" and the passing of a very selective competitive entrance examination. They offer scientific training, teacher training or advanced business studies. Five Catholic higher education institutions (Etablissements d'Enseignement supérieur catholique) prepare for either national and professional diplomas or for church diplomas. National diplomas are awarded by universities.

Stages of studies:

University level first stage: *Premier Cycle*

Three years' study after the Baccalauréat leads to the Licence degree which confers 180 ECTS. Prior to the Bologna reform, the Diplôme d'Etudes universitaires générales (DEUG) was awarded after two years' study. It has been maintained in the new system as an intermediate diploma corresponding to 120 ECTS that can be awarded upon request. It gives access to the third and final year of the Licence. Two years in Classes préparatoires aux Grandes Ecoles (CPGE) are generally required to enter a Grande Ecole. No diploma is awarded but, since 2007, this carries 120 ECTS.

University level second stage: *Deuxième Cycle*

The second cycle leads to the Grade de Master which corresponds to 120 ECTS after the Licence and gives access to third cycle study. It replaced the former Diplôme d'Etudes approfondies (DEA) and Diplôme d'Etudes supérieures spécialisées (DESS) which also represented a total of five years higher education study. The Grade de Master has however also been awarded since 1999 to holders of DEA, DESS and Engineering degrees (titres d'ingénieur). Today it is also awarded to select Ecoles de Commerce degrees (diplômes visés). In the Grandes Ecoles, a Diploma is awarded in Engineering or Commerce, generally three years after two years at university or at CPGE. The Titre d'Ingénieur is conferred upon successful completion of five years of study beyond the Baccalauréat. Some Ecoles d'Ingénieur accept students on the basis of a competitive examination generally taken two years after the Baccalauréat (in this case, studies last three years at most) or according to the Baccalauréat results, followed by aptitude tests and an interview (in this case, studies last four or five years). In the old system, there was also the Maîtrise awarded one year after the Licence. The Maîtrise has been maintained as an intermediate diploma and can be awarded upon request of the student. There is a common first year of study to all medical fields. Medicine requires 9 years of study, Dentistry and Pharmacy 6 years of study, and Midwidery 5 years of study.

University level third stage: *Troisième Cycle*

In the post-Bologna system, the third cycle corresponds to Doctoral studies. A Doctorate is usually obtained after at least three years of extensive research under the supervision of a thesis director and the writing and successful defence of a thesis. In the pre-Bologna system, the Doctorat was obtained three or four years after the DEA and after extensive research, either individual or as part of a group, supervised by a Directeur de Thèses (thesis director) and the writing and successful defence of a thesis. In specialised Medicine, it takes two years' further study after the first degree in Medicine.

ADMISSION TO HIGHER EDUCATION

Admission to university-level studies:

Name of secondary school credential required: Baccalauréat

Minimum score/requirement: 10/20

Alternatives to credentials: Diplomas or titles accepted in place of Baccalauréat. Diplôme d'Accès aux Etudes universitaires (DAEU). Capacité en Droit for Law studies only.

Other requirements: Competitive entrance examination to some Grandes Ecoles and other institutions following two years of preparatory courses given in lycées or integrated in the institution itself.

Foreign students admission:

Definition of foreign student: Foreign student holding a foreign Secondary School-Leaving Certificate.

Admission requirements: Students must hold the Baccalauréat or a diploma giving access to higher education in their country. For more information, visit: http://www.enseignementsup-recherche.gouv.fr/cid24144/-dossier-blanc-demande-prealable-a-une-inscription-en-premier-cycle.html

Entry regulations: Student visa issued by French consulates abroad (long-stay visa: more than 3 months) except for EU, Andorra, Holy See, Liechtenstein, Monaco, San Marino and Swiss students who must present a valid passport. Students must ask for a "carte de séjour" (except for EU citizens). For other documents to be presented, see: http://www.cnous.fr

Language proficiency: Foreign students (except EEA students) must hold either the DELF (diplôme d'études en langue française), the DALF (diplôme approfondi de langue française), or pass the TCF DAP (test de connaissance du français pour une demande d'admission préalable) to register for a 1st university cycle, or another test of French as a foreign language for other higher education institutions or registration to higher university levels.

RECOGNITION OF STUDIES

Quality assurance system:

The Agence d'évaluation de la recherche et de l'enseignement supérieur (AERES), created in 2007, is the agency for the evaluation of higher education in France.

Bodies dealing with recognition:

Conférence des Directeurs des Ecoles françaises d'Ingénieurs - CDEFI

79 avenue Denfert-Rochereau
Paris 75014
Tel: +33(0) 1 5363 3501
Fax: +33(0) 1 5363 3525
EMail: contact@cdefi.fr
WWW: http://www.cdefi.fr

Conférence des Grandes Ecoles - CGE (Grandes Ecoles' Conference)

11 rue Carrier-Belleuse
Paris 75015
Tel: +33(0)1 4634 0842
EMail: info@cge.asso.fr
WWW: http://www.cge.asso.fr/

Conférence des Présidents d'Université - CPU (Conference of University Presidents)

103 boulevard Saint-Michel
Paris 75005
Tel: +33(0)1 4432 9000
Fax: +33(0)1 4432 9158
EMail: cpu@cpu.fr
WWW: http://www.cpu.fr

Union des Etablissements d'Enseignement supérieur catholique - UDESCA (Union of Catholic Higher Education Institutions)

WWW: http://www.udesca.fr/

Commission des Titres d'Ingénieur - CTI

President: Philippe Massé
27, rue Duret
Paris 75116
Tel: +33(1) 45 02 84 81
EMail: secretariat@cti-commission.fr
WWW: http://www.cti-commission.fr/

Centre International d'Etudes Pédagogiques - CIEP

Head of Diploma Recognition Department: Claudia Gelleni
1 avenue Léon Journault
Sèvres 92318
Tel: +33(1) 70 19 30 31
Fax: +33(1) 45 07 63 02
EMail: enic-naric@ciep.fr
WWW: http://www.ciep.fr/enic-naricfr/

Special provisions for recognition:

Recognition for university level studies: The applicant should first get in touch with the HEI as they are autonomous in their admission policies and decisions. Should the institution require a recognition document, the French ENIC-NARIC can issue a comparability statement ("attestation de comparabilité") for foreign qualifications upon request of the applicant.

For access to advanced studies and research: The applicant should first get in touch with the HEI as they are autonomous in their admission policies and decisions. Should the institution require a recognition document, the French ENIC-NARIC can issue a comparability statement ("attestation de comparabilité") for foreign qualifications upon request of the applicant.

For exercising a profession: For non-regulated professions, the applicant should directly ask the employer. The employer decides if the foreign diploma corresponds to the competencies required. The French ENIC-NARIC can award a comparability statement ("attestation de comparabilité") upon request of the applicant.
For each regulated profession, there is a designated competent authority responsible for the assessment of qualifications in order to give authorization to exercise the relevant profession.

NATIONAL BODIES

Ministère de l'Education nationale, de l'Enseignement supérieur et de la Recherche (Ministry of Education, Higher Education, and Research)

Minister: Najat Vallaud-Belkacem
Secrétaire d'Etat: Thierry Mandon
1 rue Descartes
Paris, Cedex 05 75231
Tel: +33(0)1 5555 9090
WWW: http://www.enseignementsup-recherche.gouv.fr
Role of national body: Prepares and implements the Government's policy relative to higher education development.

Haut Conseil de l'évaluation de la recherche et de l'enseignement supérieur - HCERES (Evaluation Agency for Research and Higher Education)

20 rue Vivienne
Paris 75002
Tel: +33(0)1 5555 6000
WWW: http://www.hceres.fr/

Conférence des Directeurs des Ecoles françaises d'Ingénieurs - CDEFI

President: Jean-Marie Chesniaux
Executive Director: Isabelle Schöninger
79 avenue Denfert-Rochereau
Paris 75014
Tel: +33(0) 1 5363 3501
Fax: +33(0) 1 5363 3525
EMail: contact@cdefi.fr
WWW: http://www.cdefi.fr

Role of national body: Public consultative body responsible for the study of the profession and training of engineers.

Conférence des Grandes Ecoles - CGE (Grandes Ecoles' Conference)

President: Anne-Lucie Wack
11 rue Carrier-Belleuse
Paris 75015
Tel: +33(0)1 4634 0842
EMail: info@cge.asso.fr
WWW: http://www.cge.asso.fr/

Role of national body: Non-profit association of Engineering schools, Management schools and other higher education institutions.

Conférence des Présidents d'Université - CPU (Conference of University Presidents)

President: Jean-Loup Salzmann
General Delegate (Acting): Denis Ehrsam
103 boulevard Saint-Michel
Paris 75005
Tel: +33(0)1 4432 9000
Fax: +33(0)1 4432 9158
EMail: cpu@cpu.fr
WWW: http://www.cpu.fr

Role of national body: Exchange and stopping place between the academic community and civil society

Union des Etablissements d'Enseignement supérieur catholique - UDESCA (Union of Catholic Higher Education Institutions)

President: Philippe Bordeyne
General Delegate: Jean-Louis Vichot
WWW: http://www.udesca.fr/

Role of national body: Regroups the five French Catholic universities.

Data for academic year: 2015-2016

Source: IAU from CIEP, ENIC-NARIC France, 2011, updated from the website of the Ministry, 2015.

INSTITUTIONS

PUBLIC INSTITUTIONS

AERONAUTICAL AND SPACE INSTITUTE

Institut supérieur de l'Aéronautique et de l'Espace (ISAE - SUPAERO)

BP 54032, 10 avenue Edouard Belin, 31055 Toulouse, Cedex 4
Tel: +33(5) 62-17-80-80
Fax: +33(5) 62-17-83-30
EMail: isae@isae.fr
Website: http://www.isae.fr

Director General: Olivier Lesbre (2014-)
Tel: +33(5) 62-17-80-01 EMail: Olivier.Lesbre@isae.fr

Secretaire Général: Jean-Sébastien Guyere
Tel: +33(5) 62-17-82-02 EMail: jean-sebastien.guyere@isae.fr

International Relations: Didier Delorme
Tel: +33(5) 61-33-80-15 EMail: d.delorme@isae.fr

School

Aeronautical and Space Engineering *(SUPAERO)* (Aeronautical and Aerospace Engineering); **Aeronautical Construction** *(ENSICA)* (Aeronautical and Aerospace Engineering; Applied Mathematics; Mechanical Engineering)

History: The Institute was created in 2007 through the merger of two "Grandes Ecoles": ENSICA and SUPAERO.

Academic Year: September to June

Admission Requirements: Competitive entrance examination (1st year); on application (2nd year)

Fees: Engineering programme: 2,300 (Euro)

Main Language(s) of Instruction: French, English

Accrediting Agency: Commission des titres d'ingénieur, Conférence des Grandes Ecoles

Degrees and Diplomas: *Diplôme d'Ingénieur*: **Applied Mathematics; Astronomy and Space Science; Astrophysics; Electrical and Electronic Engineering; Microelectronics; Physics; Telecommunications Engineering; Transport Economics.** *Mastère spécialisé*: **Aeronautical and Aerospace Engineering; Astronomy and Space Science; Engineering; Management.** *Master*: **Aeronautical and Aerospace Engineering.** *Doctorat*: **Aeronautical and Aerospace Engineering; Civil Engineering; Electrical and Electronic Engineering; Energy Engineering; Mechanics.** Also Research Masters

Student Services: Canteen, Careers Guidance, Health Services, Language Laboratory, Social Counselling, Sports Facilities

Publications: Reseach Reports and Publications

Last Updated: 31/03/15

AGROCAMPUS WEST

Agrocampus Ouest
65, rue de Saint-Brieuc, 35042 Rennes
Tel: +33(2) 23-48-50-00
Fax: +33(2) 23-48-55-10
EMail: direction.generale@agrocampus-ouest.fr
Website: http://www.agrocampus-ouest.fr

Director: Grégoire Thomas (2008-)
Tel: +33(2) 23 48 55 02
EMail: direction.generale@agrocampus-ouest.fr

Secretary General: Sylvain Bagarie
Tel: +33(02) 23-48-55-02
EMail: direction.generale@agrocampus-ouest.fr

International Relations: Joelle Chancerel, Head of International Relations
Tel: +33(02) 23-48-51-72
EMail: joelle.chancerel@agrocampus-ouest.fr

Department

Animal Science and Food Sciences *(P3AN)* (Animal Husbandry; Biochemistry; Food Science; Genetics; Microbiology; Nutrition); **Applied Mathematics and Computer Science** *(based in Rennes and Angers)* (Applied Mathematics; Mathematics and Computer Science; Statistics); **Ecology** (Botany; Ecology); **Economics, Management and Society** *(EGS - two units based in: Angers and Rennes)* (Agricultural Economics; Economics; Management; Marketing); **Physical Environment, Landscape Architecture and Territorial Development** *(MilPPaT)* (Earth Sciences; Geography; Geography (Human); Landscape Architecture; Physics; Social Sciences; Soil Science; Surveying and Mapping); **Plant Sciences applied to Agriculture and Horticulture** *(SVAH - based in Rennes and Angers)* (Agronomy; Horticulture; Plant and Crop Protection; Plant Pathology)

Further Information: also sites in: Angers, Fouesnant

History: Founded 1999. A merger between Ecole nationale supérieure agronomique de Rennes (ENSAR) and Institut national supérieur de Formation agro-alimentaire (INSFA). Acquired present title and status following merger in 2008 between Agrocampus Rennes and the Institut national d'Horticulture d'Angers.

Admission Requirements: Secondary school Certificate (Baccalauréat) or equivalent secondary school exam

Main Language(s) of Instruction: French

Degrees and Diplomas: *Licence professionnelle*; *Diplôme d'Ingénieur*: **Agronomy; Engineering; Food Science; Horticulture; Landscape Architecture.** *Master*: **Agronomy; Biology; Economics; Environmental Engineering; Environmental Studies; Fishery; Food Science; Landscape Architecture; Marine Science and Oceanography; Statistics.** *Doctorat*: **Agronomy; Applied Mathematics; Biochemistry; Biology; Ecology; Economics; Environmental Studies; Food Science; Management; Social Sciences.**

Student Services: Cultural Activities, Facilities for disabled people, Health Services, Social Counselling, Sports Facilities

Last Updated: 11/03/15

AIX-MARSEILLES UNIVERSITY

Aix-Marseilles Université
Jardin du Pharo, 58 bd Charles Livon, 13284 Marseille
Tel: +33(4) 91-39-65-00
Fax: +33(4) 91-31-31-36
EMail: suio-pharo@univmed.fr
Website: http://www.univ-amu.fr

President: Yvon Berland (2004-)
Tel: +33(4) 91-39-65-01 EMail: presidence@univ-amu.fr
International Relations: Ariane Bliek, Head of International Relations Tel: +33(4) 42-17-10-96 EMail: ariane.bliek@univ-amu.fr

Area

Arts, Literature, Languages and Human Sciences (Ancient Civilizations; Anthropology; Arts and Humanities; Behavioural Sciences; Cinema and Television; Cognitive Sciences; Cultural Studies; Education; English; Geography; German; Jewish Studies; Linguistics; Literature; Modern Languages; Mountain Studies; Music Education; Oriental Languages; Psychology; Regional Planning; Romance Languages; Slavic Languages; Social Sciences; Teacher Training; Theatre); **Economics and Management** (Accountancy; Administration; Banking; Communication Studies; Economics; Finance; Human Resources; International Business; Journalism; Management); **Health** (Biological and Life Sciences; Dentistry; Medicine; Midwifery; Nutrition; Oncology; Pharmacy; Physical Education; Physical Therapy; Sanitary Engineering); **Law and Political Science** (Commercial Law; Criminology; Fiscal Law; Law; Maritime Law; Political Sciences; Public Administration; Regional Planning); **Science and Technology** (Aeronautical and Aerospace Engineering; Applied Mathematics; Astronomy and Space Science; Atomic and Molecular Physics; Bioengineering; Chemistry; Civil Engineering; Earth Sciences; Ecology; Energy Engineering; Environmental Engineering; Hydraulic Engineering; Industrial Engineering; Information Technology; Marine Biology; Marine Science and Oceanography; Materials Engineering; Mathematics and Computer Science; Mechanical Engineering; Microbiology; Microelectronics; Multimedia; Neurosciences; Oenology; Physical Chemistry; Physics; Software Engineering; Sound Engineering (Acoustics); Sports; Technology; Thermal Engineering; Water Science)

Further Information: Also campuses in Aix-en-Provence, Arles, Aubagne, Avignon, Digne-les-Bains, Gap, La Ciotat, Lambesc and Salon de Provence

History: Founded 1409 as University of Provence. Re-organized into 3 institutions in 1968. Acquired present status 2012 following merger of Université de Provence, Université Paul Cézanne and Université de la Méditerranée.

Academic Year: September to June

Admission Requirements: Secondary school certificate (baccalauréat) or equivalent, or special entrance examination.

Main Language(s) of Instruction: French

Degrees and Diplomas: *Diplôme universitaire de Technologie*; *Licence*; *Licence professionnelle*; *Master*; *Doctorat*: **Arts and Humanities; Business and Commerce; Chemistry; Cognitive Sciences; Earth Sciences; Education; Environmental Studies; Law; Management; Mathematics and Computer Science; Mechanical Engineering; Modern Languages; Nanotechnology; Physical Engineering; Physics; Political Sciences.** Also Magistère ; Diplome d'Etat ; Diplômes d'ingénieur ; Diplômes d'état en Médecine ; Diplômes d'état en Pharmacie ; Diplômes d'état en Odontologie.

Student Services: Careers Guidance, Facilities for disabled people, Library, Sports Facilities

Academic Staff *2014*	**TOTAL**
FULL-TIME	**8,000**
Student Numbers *2014*	
All (Foreign included)	**72,000**
FOREIGN ONLY	**10000**

Last Updated: 30/03/15

CONSTRUCTION AND PUBLIC WORKS INSTITUTE

INSTITUT SUPÉRIEUR DU BÂTIMENT ET DES TRAVAUX PUBLICS (ISBA-TP)
5 rue Enrico Fermi, 13453 Marseille, cedex 13
Tel: +33(4) 91-10-68-65
EMail: isba@isba.fr
Website: http://www.isba.fr

Director: Bernard Le Tallec

Programme

Construction engineering (Civil Engineering; Construction Engineering; Engineering)

History: Founded 1952.

Admission Requirements: Engineering Diploma or five years of higher education or equivalent.

Fees: 5,800 (Euro)

Main Language(s) of Instruction: French

Accrediting Agency: Commission des Titres d'Ingénieur (CTI)

Degrees and Diplomas: *Diplôme d'Ingénieur*: **Civil Engineering; Construction Engineering; Engineering.**

AMIENS SCHOOL OF ART AND DESIGN

Ecole supérieure d'Art et de Design d'Amiens

40 rue des Teinturiers, 80080 Amiens

Tel: +33(3) 22-66-49-90

EMail: esad@amiens-metropole.com

Website: http://www.esad-amiens.fr

Director: Barbara Dennys
EMail: b.dennys@amiens-metropole.com

International Relations: Jean-François Danquin
EMail: jf.danquin@amiens-metropole.com

Programme

Graphic Design (Graphic Design; Painting and Drawing; Photography; Sculpture); **Visual Communication** (Multimedia)

Department

3D animation *(Department Waide Somme)* (Graphic Arts)

History: Founded 1990. Acquired present status 2011.

Admission Requirements: Secondary school certificate. Competitive entrance examination

Fees: 906 per annum (Euro)

Main Language(s) of Instruction: French

Accrediting Agency: Ministère de la culture et de la communication

Degrees and Diplomas: *Master*: **Design; Fine Arts; Graphic Design; Visual Arts.** Diplôme national d'arts plastiques (DNAP in Design,Graphic Design, Art and Animated) 3 years; Diplôme national d'expression plastique (DNSEP) a further 2 years

Last Updated: 17/03/15

ART COLLEGE OF NANTES MÉTROPOLE

Ecole supérieure des Beaux-Arts de Nantes Métropole (ESBA NANTES)

Place Dulcie September, 44001 Nantes

Tel: +33(2) 40-35-90-20

Fax: +33(2) 40-35-90-69

EMail: contact@esba-nantes.fr

Website: http://www.esba-nantes.fr/

Directeur: Pierre-Jean Galdin
EMail: pierre-jean.galdin@esba-nantes.fr

International Relations: Hubert Bernier
Tel: +33(2) 40-35-90-33 EMail: hubert.bernier@esba-nantes.fr

Programme

Art (Fine Arts)

Further Information: Engaged in a research project, Abstraction.

History: Founded 1904. Acquired present status 2010.

Admission Requirements: Baccalauréat or equivalent secondary school exam. Entrance exam with a selection jury.

Fees: 579 (Euro)

Main Language(s) of Instruction: French

Accrediting Agency: Ministry of Culture and Communication

Degrees and Diplomas: Diplôme national d'arts plastiques (DNAP) 3 years; Diplôme national supérieur d'expression plastique (DNSEP) a further 2 years equivalent to Master level

Last Updated: 18/03/15

ART SCHOOL OF AIX EN PROVENCE

Ecole supérieure d'Art d'Aix-en-Provence

1 rue Émile Tavan, 13100 Aix-en-Provence

Tel: +33(4) 42-91-88-70

Fax: +33(4) 42-91-88-69

EMail: secretariat@ecole-art-aix.fr

Website: http://www.ecole-art-aix.fr

Directeur: Jean-Paul Ponthot

International Relations: Julie Karsenty
EMail: karsenty@ecole-art-aix.fr

Programme

Visual Arts (Visual Arts); **Visual Arts and Design** (Design; Graphic Design; Visual Arts)

History: Founded 1765. Acquired present status 1972.

Admission Requirements: Baccalauréat or equivalent secondary school exam. Entrance exam with a selection jury.

Fees: National : 260 for local residents (Euro), International : 360 for EU citizens; 390 for other citizens (Euro)

Main Language(s) of Instruction: French

Accrediting Agency: Ministry of Culture and Communication

Degrees and Diplomas: Diplome national d'arts plastiques (DNAP) 3 yrs; Diplome national supérieur d'expression plastique (DNSEP) a further 2 yrs, Master's Degree in Fine Arts

Last Updated: 16/03/15

ART SCHOOL OF THE AGGLOMERATION OF ANNECY

Ecole supérieure d'Art de l'Agglomération d'Annecy (ESAAA)

52 bis, rue des Marquisats, 74000 Annecy

Tel: +33(4) 50-33-65-50

Fax: +33(4) 50-33-65-55

EMail: contact@esaaa.fr

Website: http://www.esaaa.fr

Director: Stéphane Sauzedde

Programme

Art (Fine Arts; Painting and Drawing; Photography; Video); **Design** (Design)

Admission Requirements: Secondary school certificate or equivalent and competitive entrance examination

Fees: 562 per annum (Euro)

Main Language(s) of Instruction: French

Accrediting Agency: Ministry of Culture and Communication

Degrees and Diplomas: *Master*. Diplôme national d'arts plastiques (DNAP) 3 yrs; Diplôme national d'arts et techniques (DNAT) 3 yrs; Diplôme national supérieur d'expression plastique (DNSEP) a further 2 yrs; Diplôme Supérieur de Recherche en Art (DSRA)

Last Updated: 17/03/15

ARTOIS UNIVERSITY

Université d'Artois

BP 10665, 9, rue du Temple, 62030 Arras, Cedex

Tel: +33(3) 21-60-37-00

Fax: +33(3) 21-60-37-37

EMail: sri@univ-artois.fr

Website: http://www.univ-artois.fr

President: Francis Marcoin (2012-)
Tel: +33(3) 21-60-37-16 EMail: francis.marcoin@univ-artois.fr

Administrative Director: Claire Galy
EMail: claire.galy@univ-artois.fr

International Relations: Stephen Rowley
Tel: +33(3) 21-60-38-96 EMail: sri@univ-artois.fr

Faculty

Applied Sciences *(Béthune campus - FSA)* (Civil Engineering; Construction Engineering; Electrical Engineering; Industrial Engineering; Industrial Maintenance); **Economics, Administration and Social Sciences** *(Arras campus - FEGASS)* (Administration; Banking; Economics; Finance; Health Administration; Human Resources; Management); **Foreign Languages and Civilizations**

(Arras campus) (English; German; Literature; Modern Languages; Spanish); **History and Geography** *(Arras campus)* (Geography; History); **Law** *(Alexis de Toqueville, Douai campus)* (Law); **Letters and Arts** *(Arras campus)* (Comparative Literature; Linguistics; Literature); **Science** *(Jean Perrin, Lens campus)* (Biology; Chemistry; Computer Science; Food Technology; Natural Sciences; Physics; Waste Management); **Sports and Physical Education** *(STAPS, Liévin campus)* (Physical Education; Sports)

Unit

Economic and Social Administration *(AES, Arras)* (Administration; Economics; Social Policy); **Social Economics, Regional Planning and Management** *(ED SESAM)* (Agricultural Management; Development Studies; Economics; Environmental Studies; Regional Planning; Regional Studies)

School

Teacher Training *(ESPE for Nord-Pas de Calais with seven sites)* (Teacher Trainers Education; Teacher Training)

Institute

Confucius (Chinese); **Study of Religious Facts** (Religious Studies); **Technology** *(IUT, Béthune)* (Chemistry; Civil Engineering; Computer Engineering; Electrical Engineering; Management; Mechanical Engineering; Production Engineering; Technology; Telecommunications Engineering); **Technology** *(IUT, Lens)* (Business Administration; Business and Commerce; Computer Science; Management; Technology)

Laboratory

Blood-Brain Barrier *(Lens, LBHE)* (Biochemistry; Cell Biology; Molecular Biology; Physiology); **Electronic Systems and Environment** *(Bethune, LSEE)* (Electronic Engineering; Energy Engineering)

Graduate School

Administration, Political Science and Law *(ED SJPG)* (Ethics; Heritage Preservation; Justice Administration; Law; Public Administration); **Engineering** *(ED SPI)* (Automation and Control Engineering; Civil Engineering; Computer Engineering; Environmental Engineering; Mathematics); **Human Sciences and Societies** *(ED SHS)* (Arts and Humanities; Comparative Literature; French; History; Linguistics; Translation and Interpretation); **Matter, Laser and Environment** *(ED SMRE)* (Chemistry)

Research Centre

Computer Science *(Lens, CRIL)* (Computer Science); **Economic Environment, Modernization, European Integration** *(Arras, CRHEC)* (Economics; European Studies); **Electronic Literary Texts** *(CERTEL, Arras)* (Comparative Literature; Computer Science; Linguistics); **Ethics and Procedures** *(Douai campus)* (Ethics; Law); **Grammar** *(Arras, GRAMATICA)* (Grammar; Linguistics); **History and Societies** *(CRHES)* (Ancient Civilizations; Education; History; Political Sciences; Religious Studies; Social Studies)

History: Founded 1991.

Academic Year: September to June (September-February; February-June)

Admission Requirements: Secondary school certificate (baccalauréat) or equivalent

Main Language(s) of Instruction: French

Degrees and Diplomas: *Diplôme universitaire de Technologie*: **Business Administration; Business and Commerce; Chemistry; Civil Engineering; Computer Science; Industrial Management; Telecommunications Services.** *Licence*: **Administration; Biological and Life Sciences; Economics; French; Geography; History; Law; Literature; Mathematics and Computer Science; Modern Languages; Physical Education; Sports.** *Licence professionnelle*: **Banking; Building Technologies; Business and Commerce; Electrical and Electronic Engineering; Food Technology; Human Resources; Insurance; Justice Administration; Mechanical Engineering; Robotics; Transport Management; Waste Management.** *Master*: **Arts and Humanities; Business and Commerce; Economics; Engineering; Food Technology; French; Heritage Preservation; History; Human Resources; Law; Management; Mathematics and Computer Science; Modern Languages; Physical Education; Public Administration; Sports.** *Doctorat*: **Administration; Arts and Humanities; Biological and Life Sciences; Biomedicine; Civil Engineering; Economics; Electrical Engineering; Engineering; Environmental Studies; Law; Mathematics and Computer Science; Mechanical Engineering; Organic Chemistry; Physics.** Master recherche, Master professionnel

Student Services: Academic Counselling, Canteen, Careers Guidance, Cultural Activities, Facilities for disabled people, Health Services, Residential Facilities, Social Counselling, Sports Facilities

Publishing house: Artois Presse Université (A.P.U.)

Academic Staff *2013*: Total 469

Student Numbers *2013-2015*: Total 9,959

Last Updated: 11/03/15

ARTS HIGH SCHOOL OF THE RHINE

Haute école des arts du Rhin (HEAR)

1, rue de l'Académie, CS 10032, 67082 Strasbourg, Cedex

Tel: +33(3) 69-06-37-77

EMail: strasbourg@hear.fr

Website: http://www.hear.fr/

Director: David Cascar

Tel: +33(3) 69-06-37-64 EMail: david.cascaro@hear.fr

International Relations: Julia Reth EMail: julia.reth@hear.fr

Programme

Communication *(Graphic communication in Strasbourg)* (Graphic Design; Media Studies); **Design** *(Mulhouse and Strasbourg - Textile Desing in Mulhouse)* (Design; Textile Design); **Music** (Music); **Visual Arts** *(Illustration and Art–object in Strasbourg; Art in both sites Mulhouse and Strasbourg)* (Ceramic Art; Glass Art; Jewellery Art; Painting and Drawing)

Further Information: site in Mulhouse

History: Founded in 2011 following the merger of the Ecole supérieure des arts décoratifs de Strasbourg (ESADS), the Ecole supérieure d'art de Mulhouse (Le Quai) and the higher education of music of Strasbourg Conservatory.

Admission Requirements: Fine Arts: Baccalauréat or equivalent secondary school exam, Entrance exam with a selection jury; Music: For admissions to the Bachelor DNSPM (performance or composition), the candidate must possess a DEM (a musical education diploma) or foreign equivalent. Admissions to the Masters programme are open to candidates with a Bachelor.

Fees: Art course: 657 (Euro)

Main Language(s) of Instruction: French

Accrediting Agency: Ministry of Culture and Communication

Degrees and Diplomas: *Licence*: **Music.** *Master*: **Communication Arts; Design; Fine Arts; Music; Textile Design.** Diplôme national d'arts plastiques (DNAP) 3 yrs; Diplôme national supérieur d'expression plastique (DNSEP-Master level) a further 2 yrs; Diplôme national supérieur professionnel de musicien (DNSPM)

Last Updated: 07/04/15

AVIGNON ART SCHOOL

Ecole supérieure d'Art d'Avignon

500 chemin de Baigne Pieds, 84000 Avignon

Tel: +33(4) 90-27-04-23

Fax: +33(4) 90-86-46-10

EMail: secretariat.ecole-beaux-arts@mairie-avignon.com

Website: http://www.esaavignon.fr/

Director: Dominique BOULARD

International Relations: Elodie Mollé

EMail: elodie.molle@esaavignon.fr

Programme

Fine Arts (Fine Arts; Restoration of Works of Art)

History: Founded 1801. Acquired present status 1979.

Admission Requirements: Baccalauréat or equivalent. Entrance examination.

Main Language(s) of Instruction: French

Degrees and Diplomas: *Master*: **Fine Arts; Restoration of Works of Art.** Diplôme national d'arts plastiques (DNAP) 3 yrs; Diplôme national supérieur d'expression plastique (DNESP) a further 2 yrs

Last Updated: 16/03/15

BLAISE PASCAL UNIVERSITY

Université Blaise Pascal (Clermont-II) (UBP)

BP 185, 34, avenue Carnot, 63006 Clermont-Ferrand, Cedex 01
Tel: +33(4) 73-40-63-63
Fax: +33(4) 73-40-64-31
EMail: Secretaire.General@univ-bpclermont.fr
Website: http://www.univ-bpclermont.fr

President: Mathias Bernard (2012-)
Tel: +33 4 73 40 61 06 EMail: mathias.bernard@univ-bpclermont.fr

Director of Services: Hervé Combaz Tel: +33(4) 73-40-63-03

International Relations: Lamaison Stéphanie, In charge of Internationale Relations
Tel: +33 4 73 40 63 18
EMail: stephanie.lamaison@univ-bpclermont.fr

Unit

Arts and Humanities (Art History; Arts and Humanities; Geography; History; Literature; Modern Languages; Philosophy; Tourism); **Languages, Commerce and Communication** *(LACC)* (Applied Linguistics; Business and Commerce; Modern Languages); **Physical Education and Sport** *(STAPS, Aubière)* (Physical Education; Sports); **Psychology, Social Sciences, and Education** (Education; Educational Sciences; Psychology; Social Sciences); **Science and Technology** (Biological and Life Sciences; Biology; Chemistry; Computer Science; Earth Sciences; Ecology; Engineering; Mathematics; Mathematics and Computer Science; Meteorology; Natural Sciences; Physics; Seismology)

Division

French for Foreign Students (French)

School

Teacher Training *(IUFM d'Auvergne)* (Teacher Training)

Institute

Industrial Systems Engineering *(IUP GSI)* (Industrial Engineering); **Information and Communication Studies** *(IUP Infocom)* (Communication Studies); **International Commerce** *(IUP CI)* (Business and Commerce; International Business); **Print and Electonic Publishing** *(IUP)* (Publishing and Book Trade); **Science and Technology** *(CUST, Aubière)* (Natural Sciences; Technology); **Teacher Training** *(IUFM has four sites in the Province of Auvergne)*; **Technology** *(IUT Montlucon with two additional sites at Moulins and Vichy-Lardy)* (Business and Commerce; Mechanics; Multimedia; Technology; Transport Management); **Tourism** *(IUP Tourisme)* (Tourism)

Higher Institute

Engineering and Computer Science *(ISIMA)* (Computer Science; Engineering); **Polytechnic** *(Polytech'Clermont-Ferrand)* (Bioengineering; Civil Engineering; Electrical Engineering; Engineering; Mathematics; Physical Engineering; Production Engineering)

Graduate School

Arts and Humanities (Arts and Humanities); **Engineering** *(EDSPI works with University of Clermint-Ferrand I)* (Automation and Control Engineering; Civil Engineering; Mechanical Engineering; Microelectronics); **Fundamental Sciences** (Astronomy and Space Science; Chemistry; Mathematics; Physics); **Life and Health Sciences** *(In cooperation with University of Clermont-Ferrand I)* (Biological and Life Sciences; Health Sciences)

History: Founded 1970 under the 1968 law reforming higher education and replacing former Université de Clermont-Ferrand, founded 1854 as Faculty of Letters and Faculty of Science. Became University 1896 and acquired present title 1987. The University, which until 1976 formed a single institution with the University of Clermont-Ferrand I, is a State Institution enjoying academic and financial autonomy, operating under the jurisdiction of the Minister of Education and financed by the State.

Academic Year: September to June (September-January; February-June)

Admission Requirements: Secondary school certificate (baccalauréat) or brevet supérieur, or recognized foreign equivalent, or special entrance examination

Fees: Registration,184-391 per annum (Euro)

Main Language(s) of Instruction: French

Degrees and Diplomas: *Diplôme universitaire de Technologie*: **Electrical Engineering; Industrial Engineering; Marketing; Mass Communication; Mechanical Engineering; Sports; Thermal Engineering; Transport Management.** *Licence*: **Arts and Humanities; Mathematics and Computer Science; Modern Languages; Natural Sciences; Physical Education; Social Sciences; Sports.** *Licence professionnelle*: **Agriculture; Documentation Techniques; Health Education; Industrial Maintenance; Journalism; Marketing; Mass Communication; Multimedia; Packaging Technology; Social Sciences; Sports; Technology; Tourism.** *Diplôme d'Ingénieur*: **Bioengineering; Civil Engineering; Electrical Engineering; Mathematics; Physical Engineering; Production Engineering.** *Master*: **Archaeology; Art History; Arts and Humanities; Automation and Control Engineering; Biology; Civil Engineering; Communication Studies; Computer Science; Earth Sciences; Electronic Engineering; Energy Engineering; English Studies; Environmental Studies; European Studies; Food Science; Genetics; German; Health Education; Health Sciences; History; Italian; Literature; Mathematics; Mathematics and Computer Science; Mechanical Engineering; Modern Languages; Musicology; Natural Sciences; Nutrition; Packaging Technology; Philosophy; Physical Education; Physiology; Portuguese; Psychology; Public Health; Rehabilitation and Therapy; Robotics; Rural Studies; Slavic Languages; Social Sciences; Spanish; Sports; Teacher Training.** *Doctorat*: **Agronomy; Arts and Humanities; Astronomy and Space Science; Chemistry; Ecology; Engineering; Environmental Studies; Food Science; Genetics; Health Sciences; Mathematics; Microbiology; Natural Sciences; Neurosciences; Nutrition; Physics; Physiology.** Diplome université; Diplomes nationaux

Student Services: Academic Counselling, Canteen, Cultural Activities, Facilities for disabled people, Foreign Studies Centre, Health Services, Social Counselling, Sports Facilities

Student Numbers *2013-2014*: Total 16,007

Last Updated: 03/04/15

CLERMONT-FERRAND'S SUPERIOR NATIONAL SCHOOL OF CHEMISTRY

ECOLE NATIONALE SUPÉRIEURE DE CHIMIE DE CLERMONT-FERRAND (ENSCCF)

24 Avenue des Landais - BP 187, 63174 Cedex, Aubière
Tel: +33(4) 73-40-71-46
Fax: +33(4) 73-40-70-95
EMail: scolarite@ensccf.fr
Website: http://www.ensccf.fr

Director: Sophie Commereuc

International Relations: Hélène Perriquet
Tel: +33(4) 73-40-71-47 EMail: relations.internationales@ensccf.fr

Programme

Chemistry (Chemical Engineering; Chemistry; Inorganic Chemistry; Organic Chemistry)

History: Founded 1908. Founding member of Clermont-Université PRES

Academic Year: September to June

Admission Requirements: Secondary school certificate (Baccalauréat) and competitive entrance examination or after 2-3 years further study after secondary school certificate (baccalauréat).

Main Language(s) of Instruction: French

Degrees and Diplomas: *Diplôme d'Ingénieur*: **Chemical Engineering.** *Master*: **Chemistry; Materials Engineering; Organic Chemistry.**

BORDEAUX I UNIVERSITY

Université Bordeaux I

351, cours de la Libération CS 10004, 33405 Talence, Cedex
Tel: +33(5) 56-84-60-00
Fax: +33(5) 56-80-08-37
EMail: communication@presidence-bx1.u-bordeaux.fr
Website: http://www.u-bordeaux1.fr/

President: Manuel Tunon de Lara (2014-)
EMail: manuel.tunondelara@u-bordeaux.fr

Director of Services: Eric Dutil
Tel: +33 (0)5 47 30 43 00 EMail: sgal@u-bordeaux1.fr

International Relations: Véronique Debord-Lazaro, Head of International Relations
Tel: +33(5) 47 30 42 37
EMail: veronique.debord-lazaro@u-bordeaux.fr

Faculty

Biology *(attached to the College of Health Sciences)* (Biochemistry; Biology; Cell Biology; Chemistry; Genetics; Immunology; Marine Biology; Microbiology; Molecular Biology; Natural Sciences; Physiology; Virology)

College

Health Sciences (Dentistry; Medicine; Midwifery; Pharmacy); **Human Sciences** (Anthropology; Educational Sciences; Ethnology; Psychology; Sociology; Sports); **Law, Political Science, Economics and Management** (Administration; Economics; Law; Management; Political Sciences); **Science and Technology** (Biology; Chemistry; Computer Science; Engineering; Mathematics; Modern Languages; Physics)

School

Education and Teaching Training (Primary Education; Secondary Education; Teacher Training)

Department

Sciences *(Based in Agen, the Science departement (DUSA) is born from the desire of a number of actors, eager to see development in this region, a range of scientific and technical training that might interest students such as ind)* (Biological and Life Sciences; Earth Sciences; Food Technology; Natural Sciences; Nuclear Engineering)

Institute

Balneology *(attached to the College of Health Sciences)* (Environmental Studies; Tourism); **Business Administration and Management** *(I.A.E)* (Business Administration; Finance; Management); **Business Administration and Transport** *(IUT Bordeaux-Montesquieu)* (Accountancy; Business Administration; Human Resources; Transport and Communications); **Business Administration Studies and Research Center** *(IRGO attached to IAE Bordeaux University School of Management)* (Accountancy; Business Administration; Finance; Human Resources; Management; Marketing); **Business Administration, Tourism, Engineering** *(IUT Périgueux)* (Bioengineering; Business Administration; Chemical Engineering; Engineering Management; Tourism); **Labour** *(attached to the College of Law, Political Science, Economics and Management)* (Labour and Industrial Relations; Labour Law); **Oenology** *(ISVV)* (Oenology); **Public Health, Epidemiology and Development Studies** *(ISPED attached to the College of Health Sciences.)* (Biological and Life Sciences; Public Health); **Technology** *(IUT Bordeaux)* (Business Administration; Civil Engineering; Computer Science; Electrical and Electronic Engineering; Environmental Studies)

Centre

Applied Social Sciences *(attached to the College of Human Sciences)* (Social Sciences); **Educational Psychology** *(attached to the College of Human sciences)* (Educational Psychology); **Sport Management** *(attache to the College of Human Sciences)* (Sports Management)

Graduate School

Chemical Sciences (Chemistry; Engineering Management); **Companies, Economics and Society** (Demography and Population; Economics; Management); **Environment Sciences** (Environmental Studies); **Law** (Criminal Law; History of Law; Political Sciences; Private Law; Public Law); **Life and Health Sciences** (Biochemistry; Biological and Life Sciences; Cell Biology; Genetics; Health Sciences; Immunology; Microbiology; Neurosciences; Oenology); **Mathematics and Information Technology** (Mathematics and Computer Science); **Physical Sciences and Engineering** (Astrophysics; Engineering; Laser Engineering; Physics); **Societies, Politics and Public Health** (Educational Sciences; English; Pharmacology; Political Sciences; Psychology; Social Sciences; Sports)

Research Department

Life and Health Sciences (Biochemistry; Biological and Life Sciences; Biophysics; Pharmacology; Physiology; Plant Pathology; Zoology); **Science and Technology** (Information Sciences; Laser Engineering; Optics); **Social and Human Sciences** (Demography and Population; Economics; Law; Management; Political Sciences; Psychology; Social Sciences; Sociology)

Further Information: Also campuses in Bordeaux and Pessac

History: Founded 1970 under the 1968 law reforming higher education as one of the four Universities replacing the former Université de Bordeaux - founded 1441 by Papal Bull with Faculties of Theology; Canon Law; Civil Law; Medicine; and Arts. The University was suppressed by the Revolution and replaced by Faculties of Theology; Letters; and Science of the Université de France. Reconstituted as university 1896. A State institution enjoying academic and financial autonomy, operating under the jurisdiction of the Minister of Education and financed by the State.

Academic Year: October to June (October-February; February-June)

Admission Requirements: Secondary school certificate (baccalauréat) or equivalent, or special entrance examination

Fees: The amount of this fee is determined every year by the Ministry of Higher Education and Research and varies according to the degree and the existence of specific complementary contributions. Depending on your situation, payment for the French student social security scheme and complementary health insurance (optional) is added to the registration fees (Euro)

Main Language(s) of Instruction: French

Degrees and Diplomas: *Capacité en Droit*: **Law.** *Diplôme universitaire de Technologie*: **Business Administration; Civil Engineering; Technology.** *Licence*: **Anthropology; Biological and Life Sciences; Business Administration; Chemistry; Earth Sciences; Educational Sciences; Ethnology; Food Technology; Law; Mathematics and Computer Science; Natural Sciences; Physical Chemistry; Physical Engineering; Political Sciences; Psychology; Social Work; Sociology; Sports; Sports Management.** *Licence professionnelle*: **Agrobiology; Energy Engineering; Environmental Engineering; Environmental Studies; Food Science; Food Technology; Industrial Engineering; Nuclear Engineering; Social Psychology; Sports Management; Tourism.** *Master*: **Accountancy; Aeronautical and Aerospace Engineering; Anthropology; Automation and Control Engineering; Banking; Biological and Life Sciences; Biology; Chemistry; Clinical Psychology; Cognitive Sciences; Developmental Psychology; Earth Sciences; Ecology; Economics; Educational Sciences; Electronic Engineering; Environmental Studies; Ethnology; European Union Law; Finance; Food Technology; Health Sciences; Industrial and Organizational Psychology; International Law; Management; Marketing; Mathematics; Mechanical Engineering; Physics; Private Law; Psychology; Public Law; Social Psychology; Sociology; Sports; Sports Management; Statistics.** *Doctorat*: **Astrophysics; Biological and Life Sciences; Chemistry; Cognitive Sciences; Criminal Law; Demography and Population; Economics; Educational Sciences; Electronic Engineering; English; Environmental Studies; Ethnology; History of Law; Law; Management; Mathematics and Computer Science; Mechanical Engineering; Oenology; Pharmacology; Political Sciences; Private Law; Psychology; Public Health; Public Law; Sociology; Sports.**

Student Services: Canteen, Careers Guidance, Facilities for disabled people, Health Services, Library, Residential Facilities, Sports Facilities

Publications: Bordeaux 1 recherche

Academic Staff *2015*: Total 5,600
Student Numbers *2015*: Total 52,000
Last Updated: 11/03/15

INSTITUTE OF ADVANCED INDUSTRIAL TECHNOLOGIES

ECOLE SUPÉRIEURE DES TECHNOLOGIES INDUSTRIELLES AVANCÉES (ESTIA)

Technopole Izarbel, 92, allée Théodore Monod, 64210 Bidart
Tel: +33(5) 59-43-84-00
Fax: +33(5) 59-43-84-01
EMail: estia@estia.fr
Website: http://www.estia.fr

Director: Jean-Roch Guiresse
Tel: +33(5) 59-43-84-00 EMail: j.guiresse@estia.fr

Programme
Information Technology (Information Technology)

History: Founded in 1985.

Admission Requirements: Preparatory classes degree, 2-3 years undergraduate studies in sciences or technology

Main Language(s) of Instruction: French

Accrediting Agency: Commission des Titres d'ingénieur (CTI); Conférence des Grandes Ecoles

Degrees and Diplomas: *Diplôme d'Ingénieur*: **Engineering.** *Mastère spécialisé*

BORDEAUX INSTITUTE OF TECHNOLOGY

Institut polytechnique de Bordeaux
1 avenue du Dr Albert Schweitzer, 33402 Talence, Cedex
Tel: +33(5) 56-84-61-00
Fax: +33(5) 56-84-60-99
EMail: direction@ipb.fr
Website: http://www.ipb.fr

Director General: François Cansell (2009-) EMail: direction@ipb.fr

Head of Administration: Catherine Hardouin
Tel: +33(5) 56-84-60-33 EMail: secretariat.general@ipb.fr

International Relations: Jean-Marc Heintz, International Relations Coordinator Tel: +33(5) 40-00-66-94 EMail: heintz@ipb.fr

School
Biomolecular Technology *(ENSTBB)* (Biotechnology; Microbiology); **Chemistry, Biology and Physics** *(ENSCBP)* (Biology; Chemical Engineering; Food Science; Food Technology; Physics); **Cognitive Sciences** *(National-ENSC)* (Artificial Intelligence; Computer Science; Neurosciences); **Electronics, Computer Science, Telecommunications, Mathematics and Mechanics** *(ENSEIRB-MATMECA)* (Computer Science; Electronic Engineering; Mathematics; Mechanical Engineering; Telecommunications Engineering); **Environment, Georesources, and Sustainable Development** *(ENSEGID)* (Environmental Management; Environmental Studies; Geology; Hydraulic Engineering; Natural Resources)

History: Founded 2009.

Admission Requirements: Competitive entrance examination following 2-3 years further study after secondary school certificate (Baccalauréat) or equivalent.

Main Language(s) of Instruction: French

Accrediting Agency: Commision des Titres d'Ingénieur (CTI)

Degrees and Diplomas: *Diplôme d'Ingénieur*: **Biotechnology; Engineering.** *Mastère spécialisé*: **Aeronautical and Aerospace Engineering; Microelectronics; Safety Engineering; Technology.**
Last Updated: 31/03/15

BORDEAUX MONTAIGNE UNIVERSITY

Université Bordeaux Montaigne (BORDEAUX 3 MICHEL DE MONTAIGNE)
Domaine Universitaire, 33607 Pessac, cedex
Tel: +33(5) 57-12-44-44
Fax: +33(5) 57-12-44-90
EMail: accueil@u-bordeaux-montaigne.fr
Website: http://www.u-bordeaux-montaigne.fr/

President: Jean-Paul Jourdan (2012-)
Tel: +33(5) 57-12-46-46 EMail: presidence@u-bordeaux3.fr

Head of Adminsitration: Thomas Rambaud
Tel: +33(5) 57-12-45-45 EMail: secretariat-dgs@u-bordeaux3.fr

International Relations: Patricia Budo, Head of International Relations
Tel: +33(5) 57-12-47-47
EMail: relations.internationales@u-bordeaux3.fr

Unit
Humanities (Art History; Arts and Humanities; Fine Arts; History; Linguistics; Literature; Philosophy); **Langages and Civilisations** (English; German; Germanic Studies; Latin American Studies; Mediterranean Studies; Modern Languages; Oriental Languages; Slavic Languages; Spanish); **Regional Studies and Communication** (Communication Studies; Geography; Regional Planning; Regional Studies; Tourism; Town Planning)

Department
French as Foreign Language *(DEFLE)* (French)

Institute
Journalism (Journalism; Mass Communication); **Technology** *(IUT Bordeaux Montaigne)* (Communication Studies; Documentation Techniques; Information Sciences; Library Science; Publishing and Book Trade; Technology)

History: Founded 1970 under the 1968 law reforming higher education as one of four Universities replacing the former Université de Bordeaux - founded 1441 by Papal Bull with Faculties of Theology; Canon Law; Civil Law; Medicine and Arts. The University was suppressed by the Revolution and replaced by Faculties of Theology; Letters and Science of the Université de France. Reconstituted as university in 1896. Becomes Université Bordeaux Montaigne in 2014. A state institution enjoying academic and financial autonomy, operating under the jurjdiction of the Minister of Education and financed by the State.

Academic Year: September to June (September toJanuary; January-June)

Admission Requirements: Secondary school certificate (baccalauréat) or equivalent

Fees: 189,10 - 261,10 (Euro)

Main Language(s) of Instruction: French

Degrees and Diplomas: *Diplôme universitaire de Technologie*; *Licence*: **Arts and Humanities; Social Sciences.** *Licence professionnelle*: **Arts and Humanities.** *Master*: **Arts and Humanities; Social Sciences.** *Doctorat*: **Art History; Arts and Humanities; Communication Studies; Geography; History; Information Sciences; Linguistics; Literature; Modern Languages; Philosophy; Urban Studies.** 'Certificat d'études françaises' (for foreign students), Masters recherche, Master professionnel

Student Services: Academic Counselling, Canteen, Cultural Activities, Facilities for disabled people, Social Counselling, Sports Facilities

Publications: Bulletin hispanique; Cahiers d'Outre-Mer; Les annales du Midi - REvue géographique des Pyrénées et du Sud Ouest; Revue des études anciennes
Last Updated: 02/04/15

BORDEAUX SCHOOL OF ARCHITECTURE AND LANDSCAPE

Ecole nationale supérieure d'Architecture et de Paysage de Bordeaux (ENSAPBX)
740 cours de la Libération - BP 70109, 33405 Talence, Cedex
Tel: +33(5) 57-35-11-00
Fax: +33(5) 56-37-03-23
Website: http://www.bordeaux.archi.fr

Director: Martin Chénot
Associate Director: Philippe Cougrand Tel: +33(5) 57-35-11-11

International Relations: Jeanne-France Ruan
Tel: +33(5) 57-35-11-54

Programme
Architecture (Architecture); **Landscape Architecture** (Landscape Architecture)

History: Founded 1968.

Admission Requirements: Competitive entrance examination for students at baccalauréat + 2 years level

Main Language(s) of Instruction: French

Degrees and Diplomas: *Licence*: **Architecture.** *Master*: **Architecture; Architecture and Planning.** *Doctorat*: **Architecture; Landscape Architecture.** Habilitation à l'exercice de la maîtrise d'oeuvre en son nom propre (HMONP).Diplôme de Paysagiste (DPLG)

Student Services: Residential Facilities
Last Updated: 12/03/15

BURGUNDY BUSINESS SCHOOL

Groupe ESC Dijon-Bourgogne (GROUPE ESC DIJON-BOURGOGNE)
29, rue Sambin, BP 50608, 21006 Dijon, Cedex
Tel: +33(3) 80-72-59-00
Fax: +33(3) 80-72-59-99
Website: http://www.escdijon.eu

Director: Stéphan Bourcieu

Director of studies: Alexandre Asselineau
EMail: alexandre.asselineau@escdijon.eu

International Relations: Sarah Chefirat
Tel: +33(3) 80-72-59-75 EMail: sarah.chefirat@escdijon.eu

School

Wine and Spirits Business (Business and Commerce; International Business; Management; Oenology)

Department

Finance and Law (Accountancy; Finance; Law); **Foreign Languages and Cultures** (Cultural Studies; Modern Languages); **Management and Human Organization** (Labour and Industrial Relations; Management); **Marketing** (Marketing)

Further Information: Also Study Abroad programmes and US Study programme

History: Founded 1900. A public 'Grande Ecole', now under the jurisdiction of the Chamber of Commerce.

Academic Year: September to May

Admission Requirements: Secondary school certificate (baccalauréat) and competitive entrance exam.

Fees: 7000 per annum (Euro)

Main Language(s) of Instruction: French, English

Accrediting Agency: Conférence des Grandes Ecoles

Degrees and Diplomas: *Licence professionnelle*: **Business and Commerce.** *Diplôme d'Etudes d'Ecole de Commerce et Gestion*: **Business Administration.** *Mastère spécialisé*: **International Business; Management; Oenology.** *Master*: **Business Administration; Business and Commerce; European Studies; International Business.**

Student Services: Academic Counselling, Canteen, Careers Guidance, Facilities for disabled people, Foreign Studies Centre, Language Laboratory, Social Counselling, Sports Facilities

Last Updated: 24/03/15

CAEN/CHERBOURG SCHOOL OF ARTS AND MEDIA

Ecole supérieure d'Arts et Médias de Caen/Cherbourg

17 cours Caffarelli, 14000 Caen
Tel: +33(2) 14-37-25-00
Fax: +33(2) 14-37-25-01
EMail: info@esam-c2.fr
Website: http://www.esam-c2.fr

Director: Eric Lengereau

International Relations: France Jacquel-Blanc
EMail: f.jacquel-blanc@esam-c2.fr

Programme

Art and Communication (Communication Arts; Design; Graphic Design; Visual Arts)

Further Information: also site in Cherbourg

History: Founded in 2011 following the merger of the Ecole supérieure d'arts et média de Caen and the Ecole supérieure des beaux-arts de Cherbourg-Octeville.

Academic Year: September to June

Admission Requirements: Baccalauréat or equivalent secondary school exam. Entrance exam with a selection jury.

Fees: 300 per annum (Euro)

Main Language(s) of Instruction: French

Accrediting Agency: Ministry of Culture and Communication

Degrees and Diplomas: Diplôme national des Arts et Techniques (DNAT in Graphic Design); Diplôme national d'arts plastiques (DNAP in Communication and Art) 3 yrs; Diplôme national supérieur d'expression plastique (DNSEP in Communication and Art) a further 2 yrs

Last Updated: 07/04/15

CAMBRAI REGIONAL ART SCHOOL

Ecole supérieure d'Art de Cambrai

7 rue du Paon, 59400 Cambrai
Tel: +33(3) 27-83-81-42
Fax: +33(3) 27-72-78-79
EMail: jmgeridan@esac-cambrai.net
Website: http://www.esac-cambrai.net/wordpress

Director: Jean-Michel Géridan

Programme

Communication and Design (Communication Arts; Design; Graphic Design; Multimedia)

History: Founded 1780.

Admission Requirements: Baccalauréat or equivalent secondary school exam. Entrance exam with a selection jury.

Fees: Non-grant students: 645 per annum

Main Language(s) of Instruction: French

Accrediting Agency: Ministry of Culture and Communication

Degrees and Diplomas: *Master*: **Communication Arts.** Diplôme national d'arts plastiques (DNAP) 3 yrs; Diplôme national supérieur d'expression plastique (DNSEP in Communication) a further 2 yrs

Last Updated: 16/03/15

CENTRAL SCHOOL OF LILLE

Ecole centrale de Lille (EC LILLE)

BP 48, Cité scientifique, 59651 Villeneuve d'Ascq, Cedex
Tel: +33(3) 20-33-53-53
Fax: +33(3) 20-33-54-99
EMail: renseignements@ec-lille.fr
Website: http://www.ec-lille.fr

Director: Emmanuel Duflos (2014-2019)
EMail: emmanuel.duflos@ec-lille.fr

International Relations: Zoubeir Lafhaj, Head of International Relations EMail: zoubeir.lafhaj@ec-lille.fr

Department

Automation and Industrial Engineering (Automation and Control Engineering; Computer Science); **Civil Engineering** (Civil Engineering); **Electronical and Electrical Engineering** (Electrical and Electronic Engineering; Power Engineering); **General Mathematics and Computer Engineering** (Computer Engineering; Mathematics); **Material Engineering** (Materials Engineering); **Mechanics** (Materials Engineering; Mechanical Engineering); **Systems Engineering** (Computer Engineering; Industrial Engineering; Systems Analysis)

Institute

Computer Technology and Industrial Engineering *(IG21)* (Computer Engineering; Engineering; Industrial Engineering; Technology)

History: Founded 1872. A public 'Grande Ecole'.

Academic Year: September to June (September-December; January-June)

Admission Requirements: Competitive entrance examination following 2-3 yrs further study after secondary school certificate (baccalauréat) or equivalent

Main Language(s) of Instruction: French, English

Degrees and Diplomas: *Diplôme d'Ingénieur*: **Computer Engineering; Industrial Engineering.** *Mastère spécialisé*: **Business Administration.** *Master*: **Civil Engineering; Electrical Engineering; Engineering; Environmental Engineering; Industrial Engineering; Mechanical Engineering; Nanotechnology; Robotics.** *Doctorat*: **Automation and Control Engineering; Civil Engineering; Computer Engineering; Electrical Engineering; Mechanics; Nanotechnology; Sound Engineering (Acoustics); Telecommunications Engineering.**

Student Services: Academic Counselling, Canteen, Careers Guidance, Cultural Activities, Library, Nursery Care, Residential Facilities, Sports Facilities

Last Updated: 30/03/15

SKEMA BUSINESS SCHOOL

60 Rue Dostoïevski, 06902 Sophia Antipolis
Tel: +33(4) 93-95-44-44
Fax: +33(4) 93-65-45-24
EMail: campus-sophia@skema.edu
Website: http://www.skema-bs.fr

Director General: Alice Guilhon

School

Commerce (Business Administration; Business and Commerce; Finance; Management; Marketing; Technology); **Management**

(Aeronautical and Aerospace Engineering; Law; Management; Marine Science and Oceanography)

Further Information: Also campuses in Paris, Lille, Suzhou (China), Raleigh (US)

History: Founded 1963 as CERAM Business School. Acquired present status following merger with ESC Lille in 2009.

Admission Requirements: Competitive entrance examination following secondary school certificate (baccalauréat) and 2 years preparatory class. Also admissions following first university qualification

Main Language(s) of Instruction: French, English

Degrees and Diplomas: *Mastère spécialisé*; *Master*; *Doctorat*: **Finance; Management.** Also Bachelor

Student Services: Academic Counselling, Canteen, Careers Guidance, Health Services, Language Laboratory, Social Counselling, Sports Facilities

CENTRAL SCHOOL OF LYON

Ecole centrale de Lyon (ECL)

BP 163, 36, avenue Guy de Collongue, 69131 Ecully
Tel: +33(4) 72-18-60-00
Fax: +33(4) 78-43-39-62
EMail: brigitte.pavone@ec-lyon.fr
Website: http://www.ec-lyon.fr

Director: Frank Debouck (2011-) EMail: frank.debouck@ec-lyon.fr

Secretary General: Françoise Taillebot
Tel: +33(4) 72-18-63-72 EMail: francoise.taillebot@ec-lyon.fr

International Relations: Magali Phaner-Goutorbe
Tel: +33(4) 72-18-63-95 EMail: magali.phaner@ec-lyon.fr

Department

Communication, Languages, Business, Sport (Arts and Humanities; Economics; Management; Modern Languages; Sports); **Electronics and Automation** (Automation and Control Engineering; Electrical Engineering; Electronic Engineering); **Fluid Mechanics, Acoustics and Energy** (Energy Engineering; Mechanical Engineering; Sound Engineering (Acoustics)); **Materials and Surfaces Science and Techniques** (Chemistry; Materials Engineering; Physical Engineering; Physics); **Mathematics and Computer Science** (Mathematics and Computer Science); **Solid Mechanics, Mechanical Engineering and Civil Engineering** (Civil Engineering; Mechanical Engineering)

Further Information: Has 6 research laboratories

History: Founded 1857, became public 1947, and acquired present status 1992. A public 'Grande Ecole'.

Academic Year: September to July

Admission Requirements: Competitive entrance examination following 2-3 yrs further study after secondary school certificate (baccalauréat) or equivalent

Main Language(s) of Instruction: French

Degrees and Diplomas: *Diplôme d'Ingénieur*: **Energy Engineering; Engineering.** *Master*: **Applied Mathematics; Automation and Control Engineering; Biomedical Engineering; Civil Engineering; Computer Science; Economics; Electrical and Electronic Engineering; Energy Engineering; Finance; History; Industrial Engineering; Insurance; Materials Engineering; Mathematics; Mechanics; Nanotechnology; Philosophy; Psychology; Public Health; Science Education; Sound Engineering (Acoustics); Telecommunications Engineering.** *Doctorat*: **Automation and Control Engineering; Civil Engineering; Computer Engineering; Electrical and Electronic Engineering; Energy Engineering; Materials Engineering; Mathematics; Mechanical Engineering.**

Student Services: Canteen, Health Services, Library, Residential Facilities, Sports Facilities

Last Updated: 30/03/15

CENTRAL SCHOOL OF MARSEILLES

Ecole centrale Marseille (EC-MARSEILLE)

38, rue Frédéric Joliot Curie, 13013 Marseille
Tel: +33 (4) 91-05-45-45
Fax: +33 (4) 91-05-43-80
Website: http://www.centrale-marseille.fr/

Director: Frédéric Fotiadu (2009-)
EMail: direction@centrale-marseille.fr

Director of Services: Laurent Barbieri
Tel: +33(4) 91-05-47-98 EMail: dgs@centrale-marseille.fr

International Relations: Christophe Pouet
EMail: christophe.pouet@centrale-marseille.fr

School

Applied Physics (Applied Physics; Engineering; Physics); **Engineering** (Engineering)

Research Institute

Optical Science and Technology *(Fresnel)* (Computer Graphics; Microwaves; Optics; Physics; Surveying and Mapping)

History: Founded 1891 as École Supérieure d'Ingénieurs de Marseille. Acquired present status 2004 following the merger of three engineering schools (ENSPM, ENSSPICAM and ESM2) and title 2006.

Academic Year: September to June (September-February; March-June)

Admission Requirements: 2 years study following secondary school certificate (baccalauréat)

Main Language(s) of Instruction: French

Degrees and Diplomas: *Diplôme d'Ingénieur*: **Engineering.** *Mastère spécialisé*: **Marine Engineering.** *Master*: **Applied Mathematics; Chemical Engineering; Chemistry; Computer Science; Economics; Electronic Engineering; Law; Management; Mathematics; Mechanics; Nuclear Engineering; Physics.** *Doctorat*: **Chemistry; Engineering; Natural Sciences; Physics.**

Student Services: Academic Counselling, Canteen, Careers Guidance, Language Laboratory, Social Counselling, Sports Facilities

Last Updated: 30/03/15

CENTRAL SCHOOL OF NANTES

Ecole centrale de Nantes (ECN)

BP 92101, 1, rue de la Noë, 44321 Nantes, Cedex 03
Tel: +33(2) 40-37-16-00
Fax: +33(2) 40-74-74-06
EMail: international@ec-nantes.fr
Website: http://www.ec-nantes.fr

Director: Arnaud Poitou (2012-)
Tel: +33(2) 40-37-25-15 EMail: arnaud.poitou@ec-nantes.fr

Director of Services: Annabelle Wajs (2014-)
EMail: direction@ec-nantes.fr

International Relations: Foaud Bennis
EMail: international@ec-nantes.fr

Department

Automation and Robotics (Automation and Control Engineering; Robotics); **Communication, Language and Business administration** (Business Administration; Business Education; English; German; Physical Education; Spanish); **Computer Engineering and Mathematics** (Computer Engineering; Mathematics); **Fluid Mechanics and Energy** (Energy Engineering; Marine Engineering; Mechanics); **Material, Mechanical and Civil Engineering** (Civil Engineering; Materials Engineering; Mechanical Engineering); **Production and Systems Engineering** (Mechanics; Production Engineering)

Further Information: Has 5 research laboratories

History: Founded 1919 as Institut polytechnique de l'Ouest by the Chambre de Commerce de Nantes, became Ecole nationale supérieure de Mécanique de Nantes 1947. Acquired present status and title 1991. A public 'Grande Ecole'.

Academic Year: September to June

Admission Requirements: National competitive entrance examination following 2-3 years further study after secondary school certificate (baccalauréat) or equivalent

Main Language(s) of Instruction: French

Degrees and Diplomas: *Diplôme d'Ingénieur*: **Architecture; Civil Engineering; Engineering; Engineering Management.** *Mastère spécialisé*: **Design; Marketing; Materials Engineering.** *Master*: **Automation and Control Engineering; Civil Engineering; Computer Science; Marine Engineering; Mechanics; Naval**

Architecture; Robotics; Urban Studies. *Doctorat*: **Architecture and Planning; Astrophysics; Automation and Control Engineering; Civil Engineering; Earth Sciences; Engineering; Geography; Geography (Human); Mathematics and Computer Science; Mechanical Engineering; Physics.**

Student Services: Canteen, Foreign Studies Centre, Health Services, Library, Residential Facilities

Publishing house: Éditions Central Nantes

Student Numbers *2015*: Total 2,150
Last Updated: 30/03/15

CENTRAL SCHOOL PARIS

Ecole centrale Paris (ECP)

Grande Voie des Vignes, 92295 Châtenay-Malabry, Cedex
Tel: +33(1) 41-13-10-00
Fax: +33(1) 41-13-10-10
EMail: communication@ecp.fr
Website: http://www.ecp.fr

Director: Hervé Biaussier (2003-)
Tel: +33(1) 41-13-10-00 EMail: direction@ecp.fr

Secretary General: Martine Beurton
Tel: +33(1) 41-13-14-45 EMail: martine.beurton@ecp.fr

International Relations: Christopher Cripps
Tel: +33(1) 41-13-11-60 EMail: contact.international@ecp.fr

Department

Business Studies (Business Administration; Business Education); **Energy Engineering** (Energy Engineering); **Humanities and Social Sciences** (Arts and Humanities; Social Sciences); **Information Technology** (Information Technology); **Languages and Cultures** (Cultural Studies; Modern Languages); **Leadership and Engineering Professions** (Engineering; Leadership); **Mathematics** (Mathematics); **Mechanical and Civil Engineering** (Civil Engineering; Mechanical Engineering); **Physics** (Physics); **Processes** (Production Engineering); **Sports** (Sports)

Further Information: Also 13 Research Laboratories. Institut Centralien des Technologies et du Management (ICTM)

History: Founded 1829 as the first 'Grande Ecole' to train engineers, became State Institution 1857. Transferred from Paris to Châtenay-Malabry 1969. Acquired present status 1991. Under the jurisdiction of the Ministry of Education. A public 'Grande Ecole'.

Academic Year: September to June

Admission Requirements: Competitive entrance examination following 2-3 yrs further study after secondary school certificate (baccalauréat scientifique) or equivalent

Fees: Diplôme d'ingénieur, 686 ; Mastère spécialisé, 12500 (Euro)

Main Language(s) of Instruction: French

Degrees and Diplomas: *Diplôme d'Ingénieur*: **Engineering.** *Mastère spécialisé*: **Applied Mathematics; Civil Engineering; Computer Science; Development Studies; Industrial Management; Information Management; International Business; Leadership; Management; Public Health; Technology.** *Master*: **Automation and Control Engineering; Civil Engineering; Economics; Electrical and Electronic Engineering; Energy Engineering; Industrial Engineering; Materials Engineering; Mathematics and Computer Science; Mechanical Engineering; Nuclear Engineering; Physical Engineering; Physics; Production Engineering.** *Doctorat*: **Applied Mathematics; Industrial Engineering; Materials Engineering; Mechanical Engineering; Nanotechnology; Production Engineering.**

Student Services: Academic Counselling, Canteen, Careers Guidance, Cultural Activities, Facilities for disabled people, Health Services, Social Counselling, Sports Facilities

Publications: Echos de Centrale Paris
Last Updated: 11/03/15

CERGY-PONTOISE UNIVERSITY

Université de Cergy-Pontoise (UCP)

33, boulevard du Port, 95011 Cergy-Pontoise, Cedex
Tel: +33(1) 34-25-60-00
EMail: communication@ml.u-cergy.fr
Website: http://www.u-cergy.fr

President: François Germinet (2012-)
Tel: +33(1) 34-25-61-25 EMail: francois.germinet@u-cergy.fr

Head of Administration: Véronique Balbo Bonneval
Tel: +33(1) 34-25-61-04 EMail: dgs@ml.u-cergy.fr

International Relations: The Hung DIEP, Vice-President in charge of International development
Tel: +33(1) 34-25-61-30/75-01 EMail: Hung-The.Diep @ u-cergy.fr

Unit

Arts and Humanities (Arts and Humanities; Geography; History; Literature); **Economics and Management** (Economics; Management); **Languages and international Studies** (Chinese; English; German; International Business; Japanese; Literature; Modern Languages; Spanish); **Law** (Law); **Science and Technology** (Biology; Chemistry; Civil Engineering; Computer Science; Earth Sciences; Electrical Engineering; Environmental Studies; Mathematics; Natural Sciences; Physics; Technology)

Institute

Advanced Studies *(IEA In cooperation with LabEX laboratories)* (Applied Mathematics; Computer Science; Cultural Studies; Heritage Preservation); **Political Sciences** *(Sciences Po Saint-Germain en Laye- Polytechnique -CPAG)* (Administration; Political Sciences); **Teacher Training** *(ESPE with 5 sites)* (Teacher Trainers Education; Teacher Training); **Technology** *(IUT Neuville-sur-Oise, Cergy-Saint-Christophe, Saint-Martin, Sarcelles and Argenteuil)* (Business and Commerce; Civil Engineering; Computer Engineering; Electrical Engineering; Marketing; Multimedia; Production Engineering; Transport Management)

Graduate School

Economics, Management and Mathematics (Economics; Management; Mathematics); **Law and Humanities** (Arts and Humanities; Law); **Science and Engineering** (Information Sciences; Physics)

History: Founded 1991.

Academic Year: September to June

Admission Requirements: Secondary school certificate (baccalauréat) or foreign equivalent, or special entrance examination

Main Language(s) of Instruction: French, English

Degrees and Diplomas: *Diplôme universitaire de Technologie*: **Business and Commerce; Civil Engineering; Communication Arts; Computer Engineering; Electrical Engineering; Industrial Management.** *Licence*: **English; Information Sciences; Literature; Modern Languages; Performing Arts; Spanish; Teacher Training.** *Licence professionnelle*: **Arts and Humanities; Business and Commerce; Economics; Law; Natural Sciences; Transport and Communications.** *Master*: **Applied Mathematics; Applied Physics; Biochemistry; Biological and Life Sciences; Business and Commerce; Civil Engineering; Economics; Electrical Engineering; Environmental Engineering; European Studies; European Union Law; Finance; Fiscal Law; Geography; International Business; International Law; International Relations; Law; Linguistics; Literature; Management; Marketing; Modern Languages; Primary Education; Private Law; Public Law; Publishing and Book Trade; Secondary Education; Social Sciences; Sports Management; Teacher Trainers Education; Teacher Training; Town Planning; Translation and Interpretation.** *Doctorat*: **Astronomy and Space Science; Biological and Life Sciences; Chemistry; Civil Engineering; Comparative Literature; Earth Sciences; Economics; Educational Sciences; Electrical and Electronic Engineering; English Studies; Geography; Germanic Studies; Health Sciences; History; Information Sciences; Information Technology; Law; Literature; Management; Mathematics; Physics; Political Sciences; Spanish.** Masters recherche, Masters professionnel, Preparation for CAPES, Agrégation, Judicial and Administrative exams

Student Services: Academic Counselling, Canteen, Careers Guidance, Facilities for disabled people, Health Services, Language Laboratory, Residential Facilities, Social Counselling, Sports Facilities

Academic Staff *2013*	**TOTAL**
FULL-TIME	**1,721**
Student Numbers *2012-2013*	
All (Foreign included)	**15,000**
FOREIGN ONLY	**1818**

Last Updated: 11/03/15

INSTITUTE OF POLITICAL STUDIES SAINT-GERMAIN-EN-LAYE -'SCIENCES PO SAINT-GERMAIN-EN-LAYE'

INSTITUT D'ETUDES POLITIQUES DE SAINT-GERMAIN-EN-LAYE - 'SCIENCES PO' SAINT-GERMAIN-EN-LAYE (IEP)

5 rue Pasteur, 78 100 Saint-Germain-en-Laye
Tel: +33(1) 30-87-47-83
EMail: contact@sciencespo-saintgermainenlaye.fr
Website: http://www.sciencespo-saintgermainenlaye.fr/

Director: Cecile Braconnier
EMail: celine.braconnier@sciencespo-saintgermainenlaye.fr

Secretary General: Francine Ahouangnimon
Tel: +33 (1) 30-87-47-88
EMail: francine.ahouangnimon@sciencespo-saintgermainenlaye.fr

International Relations: Catherine Marshall, Head of International Relations
EMail: catherine.marshall@sciencespo-saintgermainenlaye.fr

Programme
Political sciences (Economics; History; International Studies; Political Sciences; Public Administration; Public Law; Sociology)

Centre
Administration *(CPGA, opening in 2016)* (Administration)

History: Founded 2014

Academic Year: September to June

Admission Requirements: Competitive entrance examination and secondary school certificate (Baccalauréat)

Fees: 300-4,000 (Euro)

Main Language(s) of Instruction: French

Degrees and Diplomas: *Master*: **Business Administration; Communication Studies; International Studies; Mass Communication; Public Administration.** School Diploma in political sciences (Master Level)

CLERMONT-FERRAND SCHOOL OF ARCHITECTURE

Ecole nationale supérieure d'Architecture de Clermont-Ferrand (EACF)

71, boulevard Côte-Blatin, 63000 Clermont-Ferrand
Tel: +33(4) 73-34-71-50
Fax: +33(4) 73-34-71-69
EMail: eacf@clermont-fd.archi.fr
Website: http://www.clermont-fd.archi.fr

Director: Agnès Barbier (2014-)
EMail: abarbier@clermont-fd.archi.fr

Secretary General: Alain Fayard
EMail: afayard@clermont-fd.archi.fr

Programme
Architecture (Architecture)

History: Founded 1970.

Main Language(s) of Instruction: French

Degrees and Diplomas: *Licence*: **Architecture.** *Master*: **Architecture; Town Planning.** Also HEMONP - Habilitation d'Exercer la Maîtrise d'Oeuvre en son Nom Propre (HMONP)

Last Updated: 11/03/15

CLERMONT GRADUATE SCHOOL OF MANAGEMENT

Groupe ESC Clermont

4, boulevard Trudaine, 63000 Clermont-Ferrand
Tel: +33(4) 73-98-24-24
Fax: +33(4) 73-98-24-49
EMail: info@esc-clermont.fr
Website: http://www.esc-clermont.fr

Director: Françoise Roudier
EMail: françoise.roudier@france-bs.com

International Relations: Myriam Reveret, Head of International Office
Tel: +33(4) 73-98-24-08 EMail: myriam.reveret@france-bs.com

Programme
'Graduate School' *(Programme Grande Ecole)* (Business Administration; Engineering Management); **Bachelor Studies** (International Business; International Economics); **Graduate Studies** (Banking; International Business; International Economics; Management; Marketing)

History: Founded 1919. A public 'Grande Ecole'.

Academic Year: September to May (September-December; January-May)

Admission Requirements: Secondary school certificate (baccalauréat) and competitive entrance examination.

Main Language(s) of Instruction: French. English for international programmes

Accrediting Agency: AACSB, Ministry of Higher Education, Edufrance

Degrees and Diplomas: *Mastère spécialisé*: **Human Resources.** *Master*: **Finance; International Business; Management.** Bachelor, postgraduate degrees

Student Services: Academic Counselling, Language Laboratory, Sports Facilities

Last Updated: 10/04/15

CLERMONT METROPOLE GRADUATE SCHOOL OF ART

Ecole supérieure d'Art de Clermont Métropole (ESACM)

25, rue Kessler, 63000 Clermont-Ferrand
Tel: +33(4) 73-17-36-10
Fax: +33(4) 73-17-36-11
EMail: esa@esacm.fr
Website: http://www.esacm.fr

Director: Muriel Lepage (2010-)

Administrative Officer: Frédérique Rutyna

Programme
Visual Arts (Design; Graphic Arts; Visual Arts)

History: Founded 2005 as Ecole supérieure d'Art de Clermont-Communauté. Acquired present title and status 2010.

Admission Requirements: Baccalauréat or equivalent secondary school exam. Entrance exam with a selection jury.

Fees: 450-500 per annum (Euro)

Main Language(s) of Instruction: French

Accrediting Agency: Ministry of Culture and Communication

Degrees and Diplomas: *Master*: **Visual Arts.** Diplôme national d'arts plastiques (DNAP in visual arts) 3yrs; Diplôme national supérieur d'expression plastique (DNSEP in visual arts) a further 2 yrs. Also Certificates (CEAP) after 2 yrs and (CESAP) for 4th yr.

Last Updated: 17/03/15

CNAM - PARIS

Conservatoire National des Arts et Métiers (CNAM)

292, rue Saint-Martin, 75141 Paris, Cedex 03
Tel: +33(1) 40-27-20-00
Fax: +33(1) 42-71-93-29
EMail: secretariat.general@cnam.fr
Website: http://www.cnam.fr

General Administrator: Olivier Faron
Tel: +33(1) 40-27-20-00 EMail: administrateur.general @cnam.fr

Director of Services: Didier Bouquet
Tel: +33(1) 40-27-22-17 EMail: dgs@cnam.fr

International Relations: Solange Vernhes
EMail: solange.vernhes@cnam.fr; relations.internationales@cnam.fr

Division
Industrial Sciences and Communication Technology (Agricultural Engineering; Automation and Control Engineering; Biochemistry; Biological and Life Sciences; Biology; Chemistry; Civil Engineering; Computer Science; Construction Engineering; Economics; Electrical Engineering; Electronic Engineering; Energy Engineering; Engineering; Geological Engineering; Geology; Heating and Refrigeration; Hygiene; Industrial Engineering; Instrument Making; Laser Engineering; Law; Machine Building; Maintenance

Technology; Management; Marine Science and Oceanography; Materials Engineering; Measurement and Precision Engineering; Mechanical Engineering; Mechanics; Nuclear Engineering; Nuclear Physics; Organic Chemistry; Physics; Polymer and Plastics Technology; Real Estate; Safety Engineering; Sound Engineering (Acoustics); Technology; Telecommunications Services; Water Management); **Management and Society** (Accountancy; Banking; Commercial Law; Communication Studies; Cultural Studies; Economics; Fashion Design; Health Administration; Health Sciences; Insurance; International Business; International Relations; Management; Marketing; Real Estate; Sales Techniques; Social Work; Technology; Technology Education; Tourism; Town Planning; Transport and Communications; Transport Management)

School

Engineering School *(ElCnam)* (Surveying and Mapping)

Further Information: Has 28 regional institutes

History: Founded 1794 as an Institute of Adult Education, reorganized as College of Applied Sciences 1819. The Conservatoire offers Professional Training courses outside normal working hours in a wide variety of fields. Courses are also given in associated Centres in all parts of the country and some are offered through distance learning technology.

Academic Year: October to June

Admission Requirements: High school certificate (Baccalauréat). Open to people at any stage of their working life. Foreign students admitted in the third cycle only, except for those working in France

Fees: Basis, 125 per annum; plus 80 (1st and 2nd cycle)-100 (3rd cycle) per UV and 40 (1st and 2nd cycle)-50 per 1/2 UV (Euro)

Main Language(s) of Instruction: French, some MBA courses offered by the International Institute of Management are in English

Degrees and Diplomas: *Diplôme universitaire de Technologie*; *Licence*; *Licence professionnelle*; *Diplôme d'Ingénieur*: **Bioengineering; Biomedical Engineering; Chemical Engineering; Food Science; Nuclear Engineering; Sanitary Engineering.** *Mastère spécialisé*: **Engineering.** *Master*: **Accountancy; Chemical Engineering.** *Doctorat*: **Biology; Engineering Management; Management; Public Health; Technology.** Also IIM MBA in Economics and Management, 1 yr (full-time)-3 yrs (part-time); Certificate of Competence;

Student Services: Academic Counselling, Canteen, Careers Guidance, Language Laboratory, Social Counselling

Last Updated: 30/03/15

COLLÈGE DE FRANCE

11, place Marcelin Berthelot, 75231 Paris, Cedex 05
Tel: +33(1) 44-27-12-11
Fax: +33(1) 44-27-11-09
Website: http://www.college-de-france.fr

Administrator: Serge Haroche

Administrative Officer: Marylène Meston de Ren
Tel: +33(1) 44-27-11-02

International Relations: Guillaume Kasperski
EMail: international@college-de-france.fr; guillaume.kasperski@college-de-france.fr

Programme

History, Philology, Literature and Archaeology (Archaeology; History; Literature; Philology); **Mathematics and Digital Sciences** (Computer Science; Mathematics); **Natural Sciences** (Biology; Chemistry; Genetics; Immunology; Medicine; Meteorology; Microbiology; Natural Sciences; Paleontology; Physiology; Psychology); **Philosophy and Sociology** (Anthropology; Comparative Law; Contemporary History; Cultural Studies; Economics; European Studies; History; International Law; Law; Middle Eastern Studies; Modern History; North African Studies; Philosophy; Political Sciences; Social Sciences); **Physics and Chemistry** (Chemistry; Physics)

History: Founded 1530 by François I, a Centre of Adult Education and Research at the highest level. The institution has 52 professorial chairs, 33 in Human Sciences and 19 in Exact Sciences, each held by a scholar of exceptional distinction.

Academic Year: September to July

Admission Requirements: None. Courses are open to the public

Fees: None

Main Language(s) of Instruction: French

Degrees and Diplomas: No Degrees and Diplomas awarded

Student Services: Library

Publications: Annuaire du Collège de France - Recueil de travaux

Last Updated: 30/03/15

EBABX SCHOOL OF ART

École d'enseignement supérieur d'art de Bordeaux (EBABX)
7 rue des Beaux-Arts, 33800 Bordeaux
Tel: +33(5) 56-33-49-10?
Website: http://www.ebabx.fr/

Director: Sonia Criton EMail: sonia.criton@ebabx.fr

Programme

Arts and Design (Art History; Design; Multimedia; Painting and Drawing; Photography; Sculpture; Visual Arts)

Admission Requirements: Entrance examination. Secondary school certificate (Baccalauréat) or foreign equivalent

Fees: Non-grant students: 480 (Euro)

Main Language(s) of Instruction: French

Degrees and Diplomas: *Master*: **Design; Visual Arts.** Diplôme National d'Art (DNA); Diplôme national d'arts plastiques (DNAP) 3 years; Diplôme national supérieur d'expression plastique (DNSEP) a further 2 years

Last Updated: 07/04/15

EHESP SCHOOL OF PUBLIC HEALTH

Ecole des Hautes Etudes en Santé Publique (EHESP)
Avenue du Professeur Léon Bernard, CS 74312, 35043 Rennes, Cedex
Tel: +33(2) 99-02-22-00
Fax: +33(2) 99-02-26-25
EMail: scolarite@ehesp.fr
Website: http://www.ehesp.fr/

Director: Laurent Chambaud (2013-)
Tel: +33(2) 99-02-27-11
EMail: laurent.chambaud@ehesp.fr

Secretary General: Elisabeth De Larochelambert (2014-)
Tel: +33(2) 99-02-27-51

International Relations: Claudine Mauduit
Tel: +33(2) 99-02-26-92
EMail: claudine.mauduit@ehesp.fr

Department

Environmental and Occupational Health and Sanitary Engineering *(DSETGS)* (Health Sciences; Sanitary Engineering); **Epidemiology and Biostatistics** *(EPIBIOSTAT)* (Computer Science; Epidemiology; Statistics); **Human and Social Sciences and Health Behaviour** *(SHSC)* (Civil Law; Economics; Ethics; Health Administration; Health Education; Public Law; Sociology)

Institute

Management *(IdM)* (Health Administration; Management)

History: Founded 1945. Previously known as Ecole nationale de la Santé Publique. Acquired current title and status 2008.

Main Language(s) of Instruction: French

Degrees and Diplomas: *Diplôme d'Ingénieur*: **Public Health.** *Mastère spécialisé*: **Health Administration; Medical Technology; Public Health.** *Master*: **Health Administration; Health Education; Law; Nursing; Public Health; Social Sciences.** *Doctorat*: **Biological and Life Sciences; Epidemiology; Health Sciences; Public Health.** Preparation for national exams for Medical and Health Administrative Positions

Student Services: Canteen, Residential Facilities

Last Updated: 30/03/15

EIVP - PARIS

Ecole des Ingénieurs de la Ville de Paris (EIVP)

80, rue Rébeval, 75019 Paris
Tel: +33(1) 56-02-61-00
EMail: eivp@eivp-paris.fr
Website: http://www.eivp-paris.fr

Director: Régis Vallée (2008-) EMail: eivp@eivp-paris.fr

Secretary General: Laurence Berry
EMail: laurence.berry@eivp-paris.fr

International Relations: Eugénia Llamas, Head of International Relations EMail: eugenia.llamas@eivp-paris.fr

Department

Computer Science (Computer Science); **Construction and Environment** (Civil Engineering; Construction Engineering; Waste Management; Water Management); **Languages** (Chinese; English; German; Italian; Spanish); **Management** (Law; Management); **Public Space Management** (Town Planning; Transport and Communications; Transport Management)

History: Founded in 1959. become "Ecole des ingénieurs de la Ville de Paris - Ecole supérieure du génie urbain" in 2005

Admission Requirements: Entrance exam

Fees: 1036 per annum (Euro)

Main Language(s) of Instruction: French (English compulsory)

Accrediting Agency: Commission des Titres d'Ingénieur (CTI)

Degrees and Diplomas: *Licence professionnelle*: **Architecture and Planning.** *Diplôme d'Ingénieur*: **Architecture; Civil Engineering.** *Mastère spécialisé*: **Civil Engineering; Information Technology; Town Planning; Water Management.** also: Town Planning Diploma (DAUCEQ)

Student Services: Canteen

Publications: Les Carrefours du Génie urbain; Revue Générale des Routes et des Aérodromes

Last Updated: 02/04/15

ENPC - MARNE-LA-VALLÉE

Ecole des Ponts ParisTech (ENPC)

6 et 8, avenue Blaise Pascal, Cité Descartes, Champs sur Marne, 77455 Marne-la-Vallée, Cedex 2
Tel: +33(1) 64-15-30-00
Fax: +33(1) 64-15-34-09
Website: http://www.enpc.fr

Director: Armel de la Bourdonnaye (2012-)

Secretary General: Xavier Guérin Tel: +33(1) 64-15-34-29

International Relations: Pierre Michaux Tel: +33(1) 64-15-36-69

School

Business *(Ecole des Ponts-Business School)* (Management)

Department

Civil and Construction Engineering (Civil Engineering; Construction Engineering); **Economics, Management and Finance** (Economics; Finance; Management); **Humanities and Social Sciences** (Arts and Humanities; Philosophy; Social Sciences; Sociology); **Industrial Engineering** (Industrial Engineering); **Mathematics and Computer Science** (Mathematics and Computer Science); **Mechanical Engineering and Material Science** (Materials Engineering; Mechanical Engineering); **Town, Environment and Transport** (Environmental Engineering; Transport Engineering; Urban Studies)

History: Founded 1747, acquired present status 1994. A public 'Grande Ecole'.

Admission Requirements: Engineering courses: competitive entrance examination.

Main Language(s) of Instruction: French

Degrees and Diplomas: *Diplôme d'Etat*: **Architecture; Town Planning.** *Diplôme d'Ingénieur*: **Civil Engineering; Engineering; Industrial Engineering.** *Mastère spécialisé*: **Automotive Engineering; Civil Engineering; Construction Engineering; Engineering Management; Information Technology; Railway Engineering; Transport Engineering.** *Master*: **Applied Mathematics; Architecture and Planning; Automotive Engineering; Development Studies; Economics; Environmental Engineering; Finance; Information Technology; Materials Engineering; Mathematics; Mechanical Engineering; Nuclear Engineering; Social Policy; Transport and Communications; Transport Engineering.** *Doctorat*: **Civil Engineering; Development Studies; Economics; Engineering; Environmental Engineering; Materials Engineering.** Also: MBA; Two State Diplomas leading to careers in the public sphere: Ingénieurs des Ponts, des eaux et des forêts; Architectes et Urbanistes de l'Etat

Student Services: Academic Counselling, Canteen, Careers Guidance, Health Services, Language Laboratory, Residential Facilities, Social Counselling, Sports Facilities

Publishing house: Presses des Ponts

Academic Staff *2014*: Total 457

Student Numbers *2014*: Total 1,797

Last Updated: 30/03/15

ENS - CACHAN

Ecole normale supérieure de Cachan (ENS CACHAN)

61, avenue du Président-Wilson, 94235 Cachan
Tel: +33(1) 47-40-20-00
Fax: +33(1) 47-40-20-74
EMail: ri@ens-cachan.fr
Website: http://www.ens-cachan.fr

President: Pierre-Paul Zalio EMail: presidence@ens-cachan.fr

Head of Administration: Gwenaëlle Verscheure
EMail: dgs@ens-cachan.fr

International Relations: Bogdana Neuville
Tel: +33(1) 47-40-21-71 EMail: ri@ens-cachan.fr

Department

Biochemistry and Bioengineering (Biochemistry; Bioengineering); **Chemistry** (Chemistry); **Civil Engineering** (Civil Engineering); **Computer Science** (Computer Science); **Computer Science and Telecommunications** *(Ker Lann campus)* (Computer Science; Telecommunications Engineering); **Design** (Design); **Economics and Management** (Accountancy; Economics; Finance; Management; Marketing); **Economics, Law and Management** *(Ker Lann campus)* (Economics; Law; Management); **Electrical Engineering and Applied Physics** (Applied Physics; Electrical Engineering); **Electronics, Electronic Techniques and Automation** (Applied Physics; Automation and Control Engineering; Electronic Engineering; Nanotechnology; Systems Analysis; Telecommunications Engineering); **English** (English); **Mathematics** *(Ker Lann campus)* (Mathematics); **Mathematics** (Mathematics); **Mechanical Engineering** (Mechanical Engineering); **Mechatronics** *(Ker Lann campus)* (Electronic Engineering; Mechanical Engineering); **Physical and Sport Education** *(Ker Lann campus)* (Physical Education; Sports); **Physics** (Physics); **Social Sciences** (Social Sciences)

Laboratory

Automated Production Research (Automation and Control Engineering); **Biotechnology and Applied Genetic Pharmacology**; **Centre for Mathematical Studies and their Applications** (Mathematics); **Institutions and Historical Dynamics of Economics** (Economics); **Mathematical Research** *(Rennes)* (Mathematics); **Mechanics of Materials and Structures** (Materials Engineering; Mechanical Engineering); **Public Policy Analysis Group** (Political Sciences); **Quantum and Molecular Photonics** (Physics); **Science, Techniques, Education, Training**; **Specifications and Verification**; **Supramolecular and Macromolecular Photophysics and Photochemistry** (Chemistry; Physics); **Systems and Applications of Information Technology and Energy** (Energy Engineering; Information Technology)

History: Founded 1912. A public 'Grande Ecole'.

Admission Requirements: Competitive entrance examination or jury selection

Main Language(s) of Instruction: French

Degrees and Diplomas: *Master*, *Doctorat*: **Arts and Humanities; Automation and Control Engineering; Biological and Life Sciences; Chemistry; Civil Engineering; Computer Science; Economics; Electrical and Electronic Engineering; Health Sciences; History; Law; Management; Mathematics; Mechanical Engineering; Mechanics; Philosophy; Physics; Social**

Sciences. Preparation for Agrégation examination; Diplôme d'Université

Student Services: Academic Counselling, Canteen, Foreign Studies Centre, Health Services, Language Laboratory, Social Counselling, Sports Facilities

Last Updated: 30/03/15

ENS - LYON

Ecole normale supérieure de Lyon (ENS LYON)
15 Parvis René Descartes, 69364 Lyon, Cedex 07
Tel: +33(4) 72-72-60-00
EMail: communication@ens-lyon.fr
Website: http://www.ens-lyon.eu

President: Jean-François Pinton (2014-)
EMail: president@ens-lyon.fr

Head of Administration: Jean-Luc Argentier
Tel: +33(4) 37-37-60-16
EMail: directeur.general.services@ens-lyon.fr

International Relations: Mathilde Bégrand
EMail: international@ens-lyon.fr

Department

Arts (Arts and Humanities; Music; Musicology; Theatre); **Biology** (Biology); **Chemistry** (Chemistry); **Computer Science** (Computer Science); **Earth Sciences** (Earth Sciences); **Foreign Languages, Literature and Civilizations** (Cultural Studies; Literature; Modern Languages); **Humanities** (Arts and Humanities; Philosophy); **Letters** (French; Greek (Classical)); **Mathematics** (Computer Science; Mathematics); **Physics** (Physics); **Social Sciences** (Geography; History; Social Sciences); **Transversal Studies** (Documentation Techniques; English; Sports)

Institute

Education *(Français)* (Education)

History: Founded 1987. A public 'Grande Ecole'. Acquired present status following merge with Ecole normale supérieure Lettres et sciences humaines.

Academic Year: September to July

Admission Requirements: Competitive entrance examination following two years of studies after secondary school certificate (baccalauréat). Admission via application following undergraduate studies

Main Language(s) of Instruction: French (with some courses in English)

Accrediting Agency: Ministry of Higher Education and Research

Degrees and Diplomas: *Licence*; *Master*: **Arts and Humanities; Biology; Chemistry; Computer Science; Earth Sciences; Mathematics; Modern Languages; Physics; Social Sciences.** *Doctorat*: **Biology; Chemistry; Computer Science; Earth Sciences; Mathematics; Physics.** Preparation for Agrégation examination

Student Services: Academic Counselling, Canteen, Foreign Studies Centre, Health Services, Language Laboratory, Sports Facilities

Publishing house: ENS Editions

Last Updated: 30/03/15

ENS - PARIS

Ecole normale supérieure Paris (ENS)
45, rue d'Ulm, 75230 Paris, Cedex 05
Tel: +33(1) 44-32-30-00
Fax: +33(1) 44-32-20-99
EMail: com@ens.fr
Website: http://www.ens.fr

Director: Marc Mézard (2012-) EMail: direction@ens.fr

International Relations: Isabelle de Vendeuvre
Tel: +33(1) 44-32-31-36

Department

Ancient Civilizations (Archaeology; Greek (Classical); Latin; Oriental Languages); **Art History and Theories** (Aesthetics; Art History; Cinema and Television; Musicology; Theatre); **Biology** (Biology); **Chemistry** (Chemistry); **Cognitive Studies** (Cognitive Sciences; Neurosciences); **Computer sciences** (Computer Science); **Geography** (Geography); **Geosciences** (Geology; Marine Science and Oceanography; Meteorology); **History** (History); **Languages and Literature** (English; German; Literature; Modern Languages; Russian; Spanish); **Mathematics and Applications** (Applied Mathematics; Mathematics); **Philosophy** (Philosophy); **Physics** (Physics); **Social Sciences** (Anthropology; Economics; Law; Political Sciences; Social Sciences; Sociology)

History: Founded 1794. Acquired present status following merger of the Ecole normale supérieure de la rue d'Ulm and the Ecole normale supérieure de jeunes filles (Sèvres). A public 'Grande Ecole'.

Admission Requirements: Competitive entrance examination or jury selection

Main Language(s) of Instruction: French

Degrees and Diplomas: *Master*: **Ancient Civilizations; Applied Mathematics; Applied Physics; Astronomy and Space Science; Cell Biology; Chemical Engineering; Chemistry; Cinema and Television; Cognitive Sciences; Comparative Law; Computer Science; Earth Sciences; Economics; Environmental Studies; Genetics; Geography; Immunology; Literature; Mathematics; Medieval Studies; Microbiology; Molecular Biology; Neurosciences; Philosophy; Physics; Social Sciences; Sociology; Theatre.** *Doctorat*: **Arts and Humanities; Astronomy and Space Science; Chemistry; Cognitive Sciences; Earth Sciences; Environmental Studies; Mathematics; Physics; Social Sciences.** Preparation of Agrégation exam; Diplôme d'Université

Student Services: Cultural Activities, Library, Sports Facilities

Last Updated: 30/03/15

ENS - RENNES

Ecole normale supérieure de Rennes (ENS)
Campus de Ker Lann, Avenue Robert Schuman, 35170 Bruz
Tel: +33(2) 99 05 93 00
Fax: +33(2) 99 05 93 29
Website: http://www.ens-rennes.fr/

President: Patrice Quinton (2014-) Tel: +33 2 99 05 93 02

International Relations: Deborah France Piquet
Tel: +33(2) 99 05 94 20
EMail: deborah.france@bretagne.ens-cachan.fr

Department

Computer Science and Telecommunications (Computer Science; Telecommunications Engineering); **Economics Law Management** (Economics; Law; Management); **Mathematics** (Mathematics); **Mechatronics** (Automation and Control Engineering; Construction Engineering; Electrical Engineering; Mechanical Engineering); **Sport Sciences and Physical Education** (Physical Education; Sports)

History: Founded in 1994 as a satellite campus of the ENS Cachan. Acquired present title and status 2013.

Admission Requirements: Competitive entrance examination or jury selection.

Main Language(s) of Instruction: French

Accrediting Agency: Ministry of Higher Education and Research

Degrees and Diplomas: *Master*: **Computer Science; Engineering; Law; Mathematics; Mechanics; Sports; Teacher Training.**

Student Services: Canteen, Sports Facilities

Last Updated: 30/03/15

ENSA DIJON ART & DESIGN

Ecole nationale supérieure d'Art de Dijon (ENSA DIJON)
3, rue Michelet, BP 22566, 21025 Dijon, Cedex
Tel: +33(3) 80-30-21-27
EMail: contact@ensa-dijon.fr
Website: http://www.ensa-dijon.fr

Director: Sophie Claudel (2014-)

Secretary General: Jean-Louis Villemin
Tel: +33(3) 80-30-93-00 EMail: jeanlouis.villemin@ensa-dijon.fr

International Relations: François Geissmann, Manager of International Relations EMail: erasmus@ensa-dijon.fr

Programme
Fine Arts and Design (Design; Fine Arts)

History: Founded 1765.

Academic Year: September to June

Admission Requirements: Baccalauréat or equivalent secondary school exam. Exam and jury selection

Fees: 433 per annum (Euro)

Main Language(s) of Instruction: French

Accrediting Agency: Ministry of Culture

Degrees and Diplomas: *Licence*: **Design; Fine Arts.** *Master*: **Design; Fine Arts.** Diplôme national d'arts plastiques (DNAP Art and DNAP Design) 3 yrs equivalent to a Licence; Diplôme national supérieur d'expression plastique (DNSEP Art and DNSEP Design) a further 2 yrs equivalent to a Master's as from June 2012.

Academic Staff *2014-2015*	**TOTAL**
FULL-TIME	**55**
Student Numbers *2014-2015*	
All (Foreign included)	**209**
FOREIGN ONLY	**39**

Last Updated: 13/03/15

ENSAIT - ROUBAIX

Ecole nationale supérieure des Arts et Industries textiles (ENSAIT)

BP 30329, 2 Allée Louise et Victor Champier, 59 056 Roubaix, Cedex 1
Tel: +33(3) 20-25-64-64
Fax: +33(3) 20-24-84-06
EMail: contact@ensait.fr
Website: http://www.ensait.fr

Director: Jacques Hervé Levy (2013-)
Tel: +33(3) 20-25-64-51 EMail: direction@ensait.fr

Head of Administration: Gaël Monfrier
Tel: +33(3) 20-25-64-60 EMail: gael.monfrier@ensait.fr

International Relations: Marie-Pierre Delespierre, Head of International Relations
Tel: +33(3) 20-25-64-87 EMail: marie-pierre.delespierre@ensait.fr

Division
Economics and Social Sciences (Economics; Social Sciences); **Science for Engineering** (Applied Mathematics; Automation and Control Engineering; Computer Engineering; Electronic Engineering; Engineering; Mechanical Engineering); **Specialisation** (Textile Design; Textile Technology)

History: Founded 1889, acquired present status 1945. A public 'Grande Ecole'.

Admission Requirements: Competitive entrance examination following 2-3 years further study after secondary school certificate (baccalauréat) or following first university qualification (DEUG, DUT or BTS), or equivalent

Main Language(s) of Instruction: French

Degrees and Diplomas: *Diplôme d'Ingénieur*: **Business and Commerce; Engineering; Engineering Drawing and Design; Production Engineering; Safety Engineering.** *Mastère spécialisé*: **Business and Commerce; Textile Technology.** *Master*: **Materials Engineering; Textile Technology.**

Student Services: Academic Counselling, Facilities for disabled people, Health Services, Language Laboratory, Library, Sports Facilities

Publications: Fil d'Ariane

Last Updated: 30/03/15

ENSAM - PARIS

Ecole nationale supérieure d'Arts et Métiers - Paris Tech (ENSAM)

141, boulevard de l'Hôpital, 75013 Paris
Tel: +33(1) 44-24-62-76
Fax: +33(1) 45-24-63-26
EMail: direction.generale@ensam.fr
Website: http://www.ensam.fr

Directeur général: Laurent Carraro
EMail: directeur.general@ensam.eu

Directeur général adjoint: Alexandre Rigal

International Relations: Audrey Stewart, Directeur des Relations internationales
Tel: +33(1) 44-24-64-25 EMail: aurelie.dobremetz@ensam.eu

Institute
Image Processing *(Chalon-sur-Saône)*; **Mechanics and Environmental Sciences** *(Le Bourget-du-Lac/Chambéry)* (Environmental Studies; Mechanical Engineering)

Centre
Mechanical Engineering and Industrial Engineering *(Paris, Aix-en-Provence, Angers, Bordeaux-Talence, Châlons-en-Champagne, Cluny, Lille, Metz)* (Industrial Engineering; Management; Mechanical Engineering)

Laboratory
Advanced Instrumentation and Robotics *(Angers)* (Robotics); **Automatic Control** (Automation and Control Engineering); **Biomechanics** (Mechanical Engineering); **Design of New Products** (Design); **Energetics and Internal Fluid Mechanics** (Energy Engineering; Mechanics); **Energetics and Transfer Phenomena** *(Bordeaux)* (Energy Engineering); **Manufacturing Processes and Production Techniques** (Production Engineering); **Materials and Processes** *(Cluny)* (Materials Engineering); **Materials, Biomechanics, Solids Dynamics** *(MECASURF, Aix-en-Provence)* (Materials Engineering); **Materials, Damage, Reliability** *(Bordeaux)* (Materials Engineering); **Mechanics** *(Lille)* (Mechanical Engineering); **Microstructure and Mechanics of Materials** (Materials Engineering; Mechanical Engineering); **Numerical Simulation in Fluid Mechanics** (Mechanics); **Polymers Processing, Transformation and Ageing** (Polymer and Plastics Technology); **Production Engineering** *(Bordeaux)* (Production Engineering); **Structural Mechanics** (Mechanics); **Surface Physico-Chemistry** *(Angers)* (Chemistry; Physical Chemistry); **Systems and Machine Engineering** *(Aix-en-Provence)* (Machine Building)

Further Information: Also Teaching and Research Centres in Aix-en-Provence, Angers, Bordeaux, Châlons-en-Champagne, Chalon-sur-Saône, Chambéry, Cluny, Lille and Metz. ENSAM institutes in Bastia and Chambéry

History: Founded 1780, became Ecole nationale supérieure 1963, Grande Ecole 1966, reorganized 1990. Acquired present title 2007.

Academic Year: September to June (September-February; March-June)

Admission Requirements: Competitive entrance examination following 2 yrs further study after secondary school certificate (baccalauréat) or following first university qualification (DUT, BTS, Maîtrise), or equivalent

Main Language(s) of Instruction: French

Degrees and Diplomas: *Diplôme d'Ingénieur*: **Engineering.** *Mastère spécialisé*: **Aeronautical and Aerospace Engineering; Automotive Engineering; Building Technologies; Energy Engineering; Engineering; Environmental Management; Safety Engineering.** *Master*: **Energy Engineering; Engineering; Industrial Engineering; Materials Engineering; Mechanical Engineering; Mechanics.** *Doctorat*: **Engineering.** Masters recherche

Student Services: Academic Counselling, Canteen, Careers Guidance, Language Laboratory, Social Counselling, Sports Facilities

Last Updated: 20/03/15

ESTP - PARIS

ECOLE SPÉCIALE DES TRAVAUX PUBLICS, DU BÂTIMENT ET DE L'INDUSTRIE (ESTP)

28 avenue du Président Wilson, 94234 Cachan, Cedex
Tel: +33(1) 49-08-56-50
Fax: +33(1) 45-47-60-39
EMail: information@adm.estp.fr
Website: http://www.estp.fr

Director: Florence Darmon (2008-) EMail: cmauguin@adm.estp.fr

Secretary General: Annie Auvray
Tel: +33(1) 49-08-24-42 EMail: lzambeaux@adm.estp.fr

International Relations: Marie-Jo Goedert
Tel: +33(1) 44-41-11-26
EMail: information@adm.estp.fr; lzambeaux@adm.estp.fr

Programme

Engineering (Civil Engineering; Construction Engineering; Electrical Engineering; Mechanical Engineering; Surveying and Mapping)

Further Information: Has been annexed to National School of Applied Arts (ENSAM).

History: Founded 1891.

Academic Year: September to June, practical training periods in July and August

Admission Requirements: Baccalauréat, Bachelor degree, Master's degree

Main Language(s) of Instruction: French

Accrediting Agency: Commission des Titres d'Ingénieurs, Conférence des Grandes Ecoles

Degrees and Diplomas: *Licence professionnelle*; *Diplôme d'Ingénieur*: **Civil Engineering; Construction Engineering; Electronic Engineering; Mechanical Engineering; Surveying and Mapping.** *Mastère spécialisé*: **Building Technologies; Civil Engineering; Construction Engineering; Management; Real Estate.** *Master*: **Nuclear Engineering.** *Doctorat*: **Building Technologies; Nuclear Engineering.**

Student Services: Academic Counselling, Canteen, Careers Guidance, Foreign Studies Centre, Language Laboratory, Social Counselling, Sports Facilities

Publishing house: Editions Eyrolles

ENSBA - PARIS

Ecole nationale supérieure des Beaux-Arts (ENSBA)

14, rue Bonaparte, 75006 Paris
Tel: +33(1) 47-03-50-00
Fax: +33(1) 47-03-50-80
EMail: info@ensba.fr
Website: http://www.ensba.fr

Director: Nicolas Bourriaud (2011-)

International Relations: Laurence Nicod
Tel: +33(1) 47-03-50-75 EMail: re.internationales@ensba.fr

School

Fine Arts (Design; Fine Arts; Graphic Arts; Graphic Design; Printing and Printmaking)

History: Founded 1648 as Academy. Acquired present name 1816 and status 1984. A public 'Grande Ecole'.

Academic Year: October to June

Admission Requirements: School jury selection and entrance exam.

Main Language(s) of Instruction: French

Accrediting Agency: Ministry of Culture

Degrees and Diplomas: *Licence*: **Fine Arts.** *Master*: **Fine Arts.** Diplôme national supérieur d'arts plastiques (Dnsap)

Student Services: Careers Guidance, Foreign Studies Centre, Health Services, Language Laboratory, Social Counselling, Sports Facilities

Publications: Journal des Beaux-Arts

Last Updated: 13/03/15

ENSEA

Ecole nationale supérieure de l'Electronique et de ses Applications (ENSEA)

6, avenue du Ponceau, 95014 Cergy-Pontoise, Cedex
Tel: +33(1) 30-73-66-66
EMail: directeur@ensea.fr
Website: http://www.ensea.fr

Director: Laurence Hafemeister

International Relations: Thomas Tang, Head of International Relations Tel: +33(1) 30-73-66-06

Department

Automation (Automation and Control Engineering); **Computer Science and Digital Technology** (Computer Science); **Electronics and Physics** (Electronic Engineering; Physics); **Humanities** (Communication Studies; Economics; English; German; Spanish); **Signals and Telecommunications** (Mathematics; Telecommunications Engineering)

History: Founded 1952. Moved to Cergy-Pontoise 1977.

Academic Year: September to June

Admission Requirements: Competitive entrance examination following 2-3 yrs further study after secondary school certificate (baccalauréat) or following first university qualification (DUT or BTS), or equivalent

Fees: 596 per annum (Euro)

Main Language(s) of Instruction: French

Accrediting Agency: Ministère de l'enseignement Supérieur et de la recherche; Commission des Titres d'Ingénieur (CTI)

Degrees and Diplomas: *Diplôme d'Ingénieur*: **Computer Engineering; Electronic Engineering; Engineering.** *Mastère spécialisé*: **Telecommunications Engineering.** *Master*: **Computer Graphics; Electronic Engineering.**

Last Updated: 12/03/15

ENSTA - BRETAGNE

Ecole nationale supérieure de Techniques Avancées Bretagne

2, rue François Verny, 29806 Brest, Cedex 9
Tel: +33(2) 98-34-88-00
Fax: +33(2) 98-34-88-46
EMail: eliane.fonseca@ensta-bretagne.fr
Website: http://www.ensta-bretagne.fr

Director: Patrick Puyhabilier
Tel: +33(2) 98-34-88-14
EMail: directeur@ensta-bretagne.fr;
patrick.puyhabilier@ensta-bretagne.fr

Secretary General: Jean-Pierre Baudu
EMail: jean-pierre.baudu@ensta-bretagne.fr

International Relations: Éliane Fonseca
Tel: +33(2) 98-34-89-01 EMail: eliane.fonseca@ensta-bretagne.fr

Programme

Detection and Information Systems (Electronic Engineering; Information Technology; Marine Engineering; Nautical Science); **Energy Materials** (Energy Engineering); **Hydrographic and Cartographic Engineering**; **Mechanics, Automatics** (Mechanical Engineering); **Naval Architecture** (Naval Architecture)

Department

Electronics, Automatics, Computer Science (Automation and Control Engineering; Computer Engineering; Computer Science; Electronic Engineering; Power Engineering); **Mechanics** (Mechanical Engineering)

History: Founded 1971as ENSIETA. Acquired present status and title 2010. A public 'Grande Ecole'.

Academic Year: September to June

Admission Requirements: Competitive entrance examination following 2-3 yrs further study after secondary school certificate (baccalauréat) or equivalent

Fees: National : Engineer course 1100 per annum, master 1100-1850 per annum; Mastère spécialisé 6000-7500 per course (Euro), International : Master 4000-6000 per annum (Euro)

Main Language(s) of Instruction: French

Accrediting Agency: Commission des Titres d'Ingénieurs (Engineer Course); Conférence des Grandes Ecoles (Master Courses)

Degrees and Diplomas: *Diplôme d'Ingénieur*: **Engineering.** *Mastère spécialisé*: **Automotive Engineering; Marine Science and Oceanography; Naval Architecture; Surveying and Mapping.** *Master*: **Automotive Engineering; Marine Engineering; Marine Science and Oceanography.**

Student Services: Academic Counselling, Canteen, Careers Guidance, Language Laboratory, Library, Residential Facilities, Sports Facilities

Last Updated: 13/03/15

ENSTA - PARIS TECH

Ecole nationale supérieure de Techniques avancées (ENSTA PARIS TECH)
828, boulevard des Maréchaux, 91762 Palaiseau, Cedex
Tel: +33(1) 81-87-17-40
Fax: +33(1) 81-87-17-55
EMail: secretariat.direction@ensta-paristech.fr
Website: http://www.ensta-paristech.fr

Director: Elisabeth Crépon (2012-)
Tel: +33(1) 81-87-17-43
EMail: secretariat.direction@ensta-paristech.fr

Secretary General: Lise Guénot
Tel: +33(1) 81-87-17-51
EMail: secretariat-general@ensta-paristech.fr

International Relations: Cécile Vigouroux
Tel: +33(1) 81-87-17-61
EMail: International@ensta.fr; cecile.vigouroux@ensta-paristech.fr

Department
Applied Economics (Economics); **Applied Mathematics** *(UMA-Unité d'Enseignement et de Recherche en Mathématiques Appliquées)* (Applied Mathematics; Automation and Control Engineering; Mathematics); **Chemical Engineering** *(UCP- Unité d'Enseignement et de Recherche en Chimie et Procédés)* (Chemical Engineering; Organic Chemistry); **Electronics and Computer Science** *(UEI-Unité d'Enseignement et de Recherche en Electronique et Informatique)* (Computer Science; Electronic Engineering; Telecommunications Engineering); **Mechanics** *(UME- Unité d'Enseignement et de Recherche en Mécanique)* (Marine Science and Oceanography; Materials Engineering; Mechanical Engineering; Naval Architecture; Nuclear Engineering)

Laboratory
Applied Optics *(LOA)* (Optical Technology)

History: Founded 1741 as École du Génie Maritime. Changed name to ENSTA 1970.

Academic Year: September to June

Admission Requirements: Competitive entrance examination following 2 yrs further study after secondary school certificate (baccalauréat). Also Master 1 (4yrs higher education) or foreign equivalent

Fees: Diplôme d'Ingénieur, registration fees:1100, tuition fees: 450 per annum; Master, 12 000; Mastère spécialisé, 6000 (Euro)

Main Language(s) of Instruction: French

Degrees and Diplomas: *Diplôme d'Ingénieur*: **Engineering.** *Mastère spécialisé*: **Automotive Engineering; Information Technology; Naval Architecture; Surveying and Mapping.** *Master*: **Automotive Engineering; Computer Science; Energy Engineering; Environmental Studies; Marine Engineering; Materials Engineering; Nuclear Engineering; Waste Management.** *Doctorat*: **Applied Mathematics; Chemistry; Economics; Electronic Engineering; Information Technology; Mechanics; Optics.**

Student Services: Academic Counselling, Canteen, Careers Guidance, Facilities for disabled people, Foreign Studies Centre, Language Laboratory, Library, Social Counselling, Sports Facilities

Publishing house: les Presses de l'ENSTA
Last Updated: 12/03/15

ENTPE - VAULX-EN-VELIN

Ecole nationale des Travaux publics de l'Etat (ENTPE)
Rue Maurice Audin, BP 2, 69518 Vaulx-en-Velin
Tel: +33(4) 72-04-70-70
Fax: +33(4) 72-04-62-54
EMail: jean-pierre.rajot@entpe.fr
Website: http://www.entpe.fr

Director: Jean-Baptiste Lesort (2010-)
EMail: jean-baptiste.lesort@entpe.fr

Department
Civil and Construction Engineering (Civil Engineering; Construction Engineering; Materials Engineering); **Town and Environment** (Biological and Life Sciences; Ecology; Urban Studies); **Transport** (Transport Engineering; Transport Management)

History: Founded 1953.

Academic Year: September to June (September-December; January-March; April-June)

Admission Requirements: Competitive entrance examination following 3 yrs further study after secondary school certificate (baccalauréat). Direct entrance to second and third yr following appropriate university degree (Maîtrise)

Fees: 379 per annum (Euro)

Main Language(s) of Instruction: French

Accrediting Agency: Ministre de l'Ecologie, de l'Energie du Développement durable et de la Mer (MEEDDM), habilité depuis 1972 par la Commission du Titre d'Ingénieur (CTI)

Degrees and Diplomas: *Diplôme d'Ingénieur*: **Civil Engineering; Environmental Engineering; Transport Engineering.** *Master*: **Civil Engineering; Environmental Studies; Mechanical Engineering; Political Sciences; Sound Engineering (Acoustics); Transport and Communications; Transport Engineering; Urban Studies.** *Doctorat*: **Civil Engineering; Energy Engineering; Mechanical Engineering; Sound Engineering (Acoustics).** Masters recherche, Masters professionnel

Student Services: Academic Counselling, Canteen, Careers Guidance, Facilities for disabled people, Health Services, Nursery Care, Social Counselling, Sports Facilities
Last Updated: 11/03/15

EP - PALAISEAU

Ecole polytechnique (EP/X)
Route de Saclay, 91128 Palaiseau, Cedex
Tel: +33 (1) 69-33-33-33
Fax: +33 (1) 69-33-30-40
EMail: dre@polytechnique.edu
Website: http://www.polytechnique.edu

President: Jacques Nicolas Biot (2013-)

Secretary General: Marcel Belloc
Tel: +33 (1) 69-33-40-04 EMail: marcel.belloc@polytechnique.edu

Managing Director: Yves Demay (2012-)
Tel: +33 (1) 69-33-40-01 EMail: yves.demay@polytechnique.edu

International Relations: Elisabeth Crepon
Tel: +33(1) 69-33-39-40
EMail: Elisabeth.crepon@polytechnique.edu

Department
Applied Mathematics (Applied Mathematics); **Biology** (Biology; Cell Biology; Molecular Biology); **Chemistry** (Chemistry); **Computer Science** (Computer Science); **Economics** (Economics); **Foreign Languages, Cultures and Communication** (Communication Studies; Cultural Studies; Modern Languages); **Humanities and Social Sciences** (Anthropology; Arts and Humanities; Demography and Population; Economics; Law; Linguistics; Management; Social Sciences; Sociology); **Mathematics** (Mathematics); **Mechanical Engineering** (Mechanical Engineering); **Physics** (Physics)

Research Laboratory
Applied Epistemology (Philosophy); **Applied Mathematics** (Applied Mathematics); **Applied Optics** (Optics); **Biochemistry**; **Computer Science** (Computer Science); **Condensed Matter Physics** (Physics); **Economics and Management Research** (Economics; Management); **Hydrodynamics** (Hydraulic Engineering); **Irradiated Solids**; **Leprince-Ringuet** (Nuclear Physics); **Mathematics** *(Laurent Schwartz)* (Mathematics); **Meteorology** (Meteorology); **Optics and Biosciences** (Biology; Optics); **Organic Synthesis**; **Particle Physics and Astrophysics** (Astrophysics; Physics); **Physics of Interfaces and Thin Films** (Physics); **Plasma Physics** (Physics); **Solids Mechanics** (Physics); **Use of Intense Lasers** (Laser Engineering)

History: Founded 1794 during the French Revolution. Its main missions are: to prepare students to assume positions of responsibility and leadership in industry, business, government and research; and, to develop the most advanced research. It recruits prestigious and diverse faculty from the academic, research, government and industrial world.

Academic Year: September to July

Admission Requirements: Ingénieur Polytechnicien curriculum: Competitive entrance examination following 2-3 yrs university level studies in Sciences after secondary school certificate (baccalauréat), or equivalent. Master of Science: Students must hold a Bachelor's degree; PhD programme: students must hold a Master of Science by Research degree and obtain prior approval of a thesis director and of the director of host laboratory

Fees: Ph.D. programme, c. 220 per annum; Master programme, 440-11,000 depending on the duration of the programme; Ingénieur Polytechnicien, 22,000 per annum (Euro)

Main Language(s) of Instruction: French

Degrees and Diplomas: *Master*, *Doctorat*. Diplôme de l'Ecole Polytechnique: Engineering, 6 yrs (2 yrs of preparatory classes and 4 yrs at Ecole Polytechnique)

Student Services: Academic Counselling, Canteen, Careers Guidance, Cultural Activities, Facilities for disabled people, Foreign Studies Centre, Health Services, Language Laboratory, Social Counselling, Sports Facilities

Publications: La Jaune et la Rouge; X-Passion

Last Updated: 11/03/15

EPHE - PARIS

Ecole pratique des Hautes Etudes (EPHE)

4-14 rue Ferrus, 75014 Paris
Tel: +33(1) 53-63-61-20
Fax: +33(1) 53-63-61-94
EMail: presidence.ephe@ephe.sorbonne.fr
Website: http://www.ephe.sorbonne.fr

President: Hubert Bost (2013-)
Tel: +33(1) 53-63-61-63
EMail: presidence.ephe@ephe.sorbonne.fr

Head of Administration: Hélène Frimour
Tel: +33(1) 53-63-61-76 EMail: helene.frimour@ephe.sorbonne.fr

International Relations: Laurence Frabolot
Tel: +33(1) 53-63-61-80
EMail: laurence.frabolot@ephe.sorbonne.fr

Institute

Ageing *(Transdisciplinary - ITEV)* (Gerontology); **Pacific Coral Reefs** *(IRCP)* (Coastal Studies); **Religious Sciences** *(European, Institut Européen en Sciences des Religions (IESR))* (Religious Studies)

Section

History and Philology (Ancient Civilizations; Archaeology; Art History; Asian Studies; History; Linguistics; Middle Eastern Studies; Philology); **Life and Earth Sciences** (Biological and Life Sciences; Cell Biology; Earth Sciences; Ecology; Environmental Studies; Molecular Biology; Neurosciences); **Religious Sciences** (Asian Religious Studies; Christian Religious Studies; Islamic Theology; Judaic Religious Studies; Religious Studies)

History: Founded 1868 by Victor Duruy, a centre of postgraduate education and research at the highest level.

Academic Year: October to September

Admission Requirements: University degree

Fees: 474,10 - 609,10 per annum (Euro)

Main Language(s) of Instruction: French

Degrees and Diplomas: *Master*: **Asian Studies; Biological and Life Sciences; Cognitive Sciences; Ecology; European Studies; Health Sciences; Mediterranean Studies; Religion.** *Doctorat*: **Biological and Life Sciences; Environmental Studies; History; Religion.** *Habilitation à Diriger les Recherches*. Also Diplômes de l'EPHE

Student Services: Academic Counselling, Facilities for disabled people, Language Laboratory

Publications: Hautes Etudes du Monde Gréco-Romain; Hautes Etudes Médiévales et Modernes; Hautes Etudes Orientales; Histoire et Civilisation du Livre; Publications of the Sections

Last Updated: 17/03/15

ESIGETEL

Ecole supérieure d'Ingénieurs en Informatique et Génie des Télécommunications (ESIGETEL)

1, rue des Port de Valvins, 77215 Avon, Cedex
Tel: +33(1) 60-72-70-51
Fax: +33(1) 60-72-11-32
EMail: info@esigetel.fr
Website: http://www.esigetel.fr

Director: Roger Ceschi EMail: roger.ceschi@esigetel.fr

International Relations: Christiane Michel, Head of International Relations Tel: +33(1) 46-77-47-51 EMail: christiane.michel@efrei.fr

Programme

Engineering (Aeronautical and Aerospace Engineering; Automation and Control Engineering; Computer Engineering; Energy Engineering; Telecommunications Engineering)

History: Founded in 1988.

Admission Requirements: Competitive entrance examination, secondary school certificate (baccalauréat) in sciences or equivalent.

Fees: 5,990-7,390 (Euro)

Main Language(s) of Instruction: French

Accrediting Agency: Commission des Titres d'Ingénieur (CTI)

Degrees and Diplomas: *Brevet de Technicien supérieur*; *Licence*: **Mathematics and Computer Science.** *Diplôme d'Ingénieur*: **Engineering.** Also Master

Last Updated: 19/03/15

ESM-SAINT - CYR

Ecole spéciale militaire de St Cyr (ESM SAINT-CYR)

56381 Coëtquidan, Cedex
Tel: +33(2) 97-70-72-99
Fax: +33(2) 97-79-75-87
EMail: dircom@st-cyr.terre.defense.gouv.fr
Website: http://www.st-cyr.terre.defense.gouv.fr

General: Antoine Windeck (2012-)

Programme

Engineering (Engineering); **International Relations and Strategy** (International Relations); **Military Studies** (Military Science)

History: Founded 1802. Moved to Britanny 1945.

Admission Requirements: Competitive entrance examination following 2-3 yrs further study after secondary school certificate (baccalauréat) or following first university qualification, or equivalent

Main Language(s) of Instruction: French

Degrees and Diplomas: *Diplôme d'Etat*; *Master*

Last Updated: 17/03/15

ESPCI PARISTECH

Ecole supérieure de Physique et de Chimie industrielles de la Ville de Paris (ESPCI PARISTECH)

10, rue Vauquelin, 75231 Paris, Cedex 05
Tel: +33(1) 40-79-44-00
EMail: contact@espci.fr
Website: http://www.espci.fr

Director: Jean-François Joanny (2014-)
EMail: jean-francois.joanny@espci.fr; direction@espci.fr

Secretary General: Jean-Baptiste Hennequin
Tel: +33(1) 40-79-45-25 EMail: natasa.ilic@espci.fr

Laboratory

Applied Statistics (Statistics); **Biology** (Neurosciences); **Colloids and Divided Materials**; **Electromagnetism and General Electronics** (Electrical and Electronic Engineering); **Electronics** (Applied Mathematics; Electronic Engineering); **Environment and Analytical Chemistry** (Chemistry); **Hydrodynamics and Physical Mechanics** (Hydraulic Engineering; Physical Engineering); **Microfluids, MEMS and Nanostructures**; **Organic Chemistry** (Chemistry); **Physical Chemistry of Macromolecules** (Organic Chemistry; Physical Chemistry); **Physical Optics** (Optics; Physical Engineering); **Polymer Physical Chemistry and Spectroscopy** (Physical Chemistry); **Quantum Physics** (Mathematical Physics); **Soft Matter and Chemistry** (Chemistry); **Solid State Physics** (Solid State Physics); **Theoretical Chemical Physics** (Chemical Engineering); **Thermal Physics** (Thermal Physics); **Waves and Acoustics** (Microwaves; Sound Engineering (Acoustics))

History: Founded 1882. A 'Grande Ecole'.

Academic Year: September to June

Admission Requirements: Competitive entrance examination following 2 years preparatory classes

Fees: Registration fees: 150 per annum; Tuition fees : 700 per annum (Euro)

Main Language(s) of Instruction: French

Accrediting Agency: Commission des Titres de l'Ingénieur (CTI)

Degrees and Diplomas: *Diplôme d'Ingénieur*: **Biology; Chemistry; Physics.** *Master*: **Applied Physics; Bioengineering; Chemical Engineering; Chemistry; Environmental Engineering; Materials Engineering; Measurement and Precision Engineering; Nanotechnology; Nuclear Engineering; Physics.** *Doctorat*: **Biological and Life Sciences; Chemistry; Physics.** Masters professionnel

Student Services: Canteen, Language Laboratory, Library, Residential Facilities

Last Updated: 30/03/15

EUROPEAN ART SCHOOL OF BRITANNY

Ecole européenne supérieure d'art de Bretagne (EESAB)

34 rue Hoche, 35000 Rennes
Tel: +33(2) 23 62 22 64
Fax: +33(2) 23 62 22 69
EMail: contact@eesab.fr
Website: http://www.eesab.fr/

Managing Director: Philippe Hardy (2011-)
EMail: phardy@ville-rennes.fr

International Relations: Marie-Noëlle Haslé, In charge of Administration and International Relations EMail: mn.hasle@ville-rennes.fr

School

European Art School of Britanny - Lorient *(http://www.eesab.fr/lorient)* (Performing Arts; Visual Arts); **European Art School of Britanny - Rennes** *(http://www.eesab.fr/rennes)* (Design; Performing Arts; Visual Arts); **European Art School of Britany - Brest** *(http://www.eesab.fr/brest)* (Design; Visual Arts); **European Art School of Britany-Quimper** *(http://www.eesab.fr/quimper)* (Visual Arts)

Further Information: and also Brest, Lorient, Quimper

History: Founded 2011 following the merger of the art schools in Brest, Lorient, Quimper and Rennes.

Academic Year: September to June

Admission Requirements: Secondary school certificate (Baccalauréat) or equivalent secondary school exam, or foreign equivalent, or professional experience; Entrance Exam with a selection jury

Main Language(s) of Instruction: French

Degrees and Diplomas: *Diplôme d'Etat*: **Arts and Humanities; Technology; Visual Arts.** DNAP: National Diploma in Arts (equivalent of a Licence); DNSEP: Higher National Diploma in Arts (equivalent of a Master)

Student Services: Cultural Activities, Library

Student Numbers *2014-2015*: Total 900

Last Updated: 11/03/15

EUROPEAN ART SCHOOL OF BRITANNY - BREST

ECOLE EUROPÉENNE SUPÉRIEURE D'ART DE BRETAGNE - SITE DE BREST

18 rue du Château, 29200 Brest
Tel: +33(2) 98 00 87 20
EMail: courrier@esa-brest.fr
Website: http://www.eesab.fr/brest

Director: Yannick Lucéa (2010-)
EMail: yannick.lucea@mairie-brest.fr

International Relations: Morgane Pipolo, In charge of International Relations EMail: morgane.pipolo@esa-brest.fr

Programme

Arts (Visual Arts); **Design** (Design)

Course

Public courses (Visual Arts)

History: Merged with Ecole européenne supérieure d'art de Bretagne 2011.

Admission Requirements: Secondary school Certificate (Baccalauréat) or other secondary school Certificate, or foreign equivalent, or professional experience. Entrance exam with a selection jury.

Fees: 500 per annum (Euro)

Main Language(s) of Instruction: French

Degrees and Diplomas: Diplôme national d'arts plastiques (DNAP) 3 yrs; Diplôme national supérieur d'expression plastique (DNSEP) a further 2 yrs both in fields of Art and Design.

Student Services: Library

EUROPEAN ART SCHOOL OF BRITANNY - LORIENT

ECOLE EUROPÉENNE SUPÉRIEURE D'ART DE BRETAGNE - SITE DE LORIENT

1 avenue de Kergroise, 56100 Lorient
Tel: +33(2) 97 35 31 70
EMail: ecole.sup.art@mairie-lorient.fr
Website: http://www.eesab.fr/lorient

Director: Pierre Cochard (2003-) EMail: pcochard@mairie-lorient.fr

International Relations: Françoise Giquel, Head of International Relations EMail: fgiquel@mairie-lorient.fr

Programme

Visual Arts and Communication (Communication Arts; Visual Arts)

Course

Public courses (Visual Arts)

History: Merged with Ecole européenne supérieure d'art de Bretagne 2011.

Academic Year: September to June

Admission Requirements: Secondary school Certificate (Baccalauréat) or other secondary school Certificate, or foreign equivalent, or professional experience. Entrance exam with a selection jury.

Main Language(s) of Instruction: French

Degrees and Diplomas: Diplôme national d'arts plastiques (DNAP) 3 yrs; Diplôme national supérieur d'expression plastique (DNSEP) a further 2 yrs both in field of Art.

Student Services: Canteen

EUROPEAN ART SCHOOL OF BRITANNY - QUIMPER

ECOLE EUROPÉENNE SUPÉRIEURE D'ART DE BRETAGNE - SITE DE QUIMPER

8, esplanade François Mitterrand, 29000 Quimper
Tel: +33(2) 98-55-61-57
EMail: contact@esa-quimper.fr
Website: http://www.eesab.fr/quimper

Directrice: Danièle Yvergniaux (2007-)
Tel: +33(2) 98 55 61 57 EMail: daniele.yvergniaux@esa-quimper.fr

International Relations: Eimer Birkbeck, In charge of International Relations EMail: ebirkbeck@googlemail.com

Programme

Visual Arts and Design (Design; Painting and Drawing; Visual Arts)

Course

Public courses

History: Merged with Ecole européenne supérieure d'art de Bretagne 2011.

Academic Year: September-June

Admission Requirements: Baccalauréat or equivalent secondary school exam. Entrance exam with a selection jury.

Main Language(s) of Instruction: French

Accrediting Agency: Ministry of Culture and Communication

Degrees and Diplomas: Diplôme national d'arts plastiques (DNAP) 3 yrs; Diplôme national supérieur d'expression plastique (DNSEP) a further 2 yrs both in field of Art.

Student Services: Canteen, Library, Nursery Care, Social Counselling, Sports Facilities

EUROPEAN ART SCHOOL OF BRITANNY - RENNES
ECOLE EUROPÉENNE SUPÉRIEURE D'ART DE BRETAGNE - SITE DE RENNES

34 rue Hoche, 35000 Rennes
Tel: +33(2) 23 62 22 60
EMail: erba@ville-rennes.fr
Website: http://www.eesab.fr/rennes

Director: Philippe Hardy (2009-) EMail: phardy@ville-rennes.fr

International Relations: Amanda Auffray-Liddiart
EMail: erasmus@erba-rennes.fr

Programme
Visual Arts, Communication and Design (Communication Arts; Design; Painting and Drawing; Visual Arts)

History: Merged with Ecole européenne supérieure d'art de Bretagne 2011.

Academic Year: September to June

Admission Requirements: Secondary school Certificate (Baccalauréat) or other secondary school Certificate, or foreign equivalent, or professional experience. Entrance exam with a selection jury.

Main Language(s) of Instruction: French

Degrees and Diplomas: Diplôme national d'arts plastiques (DNAP) 3 yrs; Diplôme national supérieur d'expression plastique (DNSEP) a further 2 yrs both in fields of Art, Communication and Design.

Student Services: Library

Publications: Pratiques

EUROPEAN SCHOOL OF VISUAL ARTS

Ecole européenne supérieure de l'Image (EESI)
134 rue de Bordeaux, 16000 Angoulême
Tel: +33(5) 45-92-66-02
EMail: direction.generale@eesi.eu
Website: http://www.eesi.eu/site/index.php

Managing Director: Sabrina Grassi-Fossier (2005-)
EMail: direction.generale@eesi.eu; s.burel@eesi.eu

Executive and Financial Director: Catherine Beaudeau
Tel: +33(6) 32-69-46-18 EMail: c.beaudeau@eesi.eu

International Relations: Charlotte Martin, In charge of Development and International Relations
Tel: +33(5) 45-92-86-28 EMail: c.martin@eesi.eu

Programme
Design and Art (Design; Fine Arts; Visual Arts)

Further Information: Has a second site in Poitiers.

History: Founded 1995.

Admission Requirements: Baccalauréat or equivalent secondary school exam. Entrance exam with a selection jury.

Main Language(s) of Instruction: French

Accrediting Agency: Ministry of Culture and Communication

Degrees and Diplomas: *Master*: **Graphic Design; Visual Arts.** *Doctorat*: **Graphic Design.** Diplome national d'arts plastiques (DNAP) 3 yrs; Diplome national supérieur d'expression plastique (DNSEP, speciality in digital art) a further 2 yrs; Masters recherche (digital art)

Publications: Au Fil du Nil; De l'empreinte au numérique; L'Idiote; Pratiquer

Last Updated: 07/04/15

FRANÇOIS RABELAIS UNIVERSITY - TOURS

Université François-Rabelais de Tours
BP 4103, 3, rue des Tanneurs, 37041 Tours, Cedex 01
Tel: +33(2) 47-36-66-00
Fax: +33(2) 47-36-64-10
EMail: secretariat.general@univ-tours.fr
Website: http://www.univ-tours.fr

President: Loïc Vaillant (2008-)
Tel: +33(2) 47-36-64-00 EMail: president@univ-tours.fr

Secretary General: Pierre Gabette
Tel: +33(2) 47-36-64-01 EMail: pierre.gabette@univ-tours.fr

International Relations: Arnaud Giacometti
EMail: arnaud.giacometti@univ-tours.fr

Faculty
Arts and Humanities (Archaeology; Art History; Educational Sciences; History; Music; Musicology; Psychology; Sociology); **Law, Economics and Social Sciences** (Economics; Geography; Law; Management; Public Administration; Social Sciences); **Letters and Languages** (English; Linguistics; Literature; Modern Languages; Portuguese; Spanish); **Medicine** (Medicine); **Pharmacy** (Pharmacy); **Science and Technology** (Behavioural Sciences; Biochemistry; Biology; Chemistry; Computer Science; English; Environmental Studies; Geology; Mathematics; Microbiology; Natural Sciences; Physics; Physiology; Technology)

Programme
Environmental, Water and River Engineering *(IUP IMACOF, Chinon)* (Environmental Engineering; Water Management)

School
Engineering *(Polytech' Tours)* (Computer Engineering; Computer Science; Engineering; Industrial Engineering); **Engineering** *(ENIVL Blois)* (Engineering)

Institute
Lifelong Education (Continuing Education); **Technology** *(IUT Tours)* (Bioengineering; Business Administration; Communication Studies; Electrical Engineering; Sales Techniques; Social Work; Technology); **Technology** *(IUT Blois)* (Materials Engineering; Technology; Telecommunications Engineering)

Centre
Renaissance Studies *(CESR)* (Medieval Studies)

Graduate School
Health, Science, Technology; Social Sciences

Further Information: Also 'Antenne universitaire' at Blois (Law, Economics, Economic and Social Administration, Science and Techniques)

History: Founded 1970 under the 1968 law reforming higher education as one of two Universities replacing the Université d'Orléans-Tours, re-established 1962, but tracing its history to the original Université d'Orléans, 1306-1793. A State institution enjoying academic and financial autonomy, operating under the jurisdiction of the Minister of Education and financed by the State.

Academic Year: October to June (October-December; January-March; April-June)

Admission Requirements: Secondary school certificate (baccalauréat) or equivalent, or special entrance examination

Main Language(s) of Instruction: French

Degrees and Diplomas: *Capacité en Droit*: **Law.** *Diplôme universitaire de Technologie*; *Licence*: **Arts and Humanities; Biological and Life Sciences; Chemistry; Earth Sciences; Economics; Fine Arts; Health Sciences; Law; Management; Mathematics and Computer Science; Modern Languages; Physics; Social Sciences; Technology.** *Licence professionnelle*: **Biology; Economics; Engineering; Fine Arts; Health Sciences; Law; Management; Social Sciences; Technology.** *Diplôme d'Etat*: **Medicine; Midwifery; Pharmacy.** *Master*: **Arts and Humanities; Biological and Life Sciences; Business Administration; Computer Science; Fine Arts; Law; Management; Modern Languages; Natural Sciences; Social Sciences; Teacher Training; Technology.** *Doctorat*: **Art History; Biological and Life Sciences; Chemistry; Classical Languages; Earth Sciences; Economics; Engineering; Fine Arts; Health Sciences; Law; Literature; Management; Mathematics; Medicine; Modern Languages; Music; Natural Sciences; Pharmacy; Physics; Social Sciences.** *Certificat de Spécialité*: **Medicine.** Certificats and Diplômes d'Etudes françaises (for foreign students), Masters recherche, Masters professionnel

Student Services: Canteen, Cultural Activities, Foreign Studies Centre, Health Services, Social Counselling, Sports Facilities

Student Numbers *2013-2014*: Total 24,761

Last Updated: 12/03/15

FRENCH ARMY ENGINEERING SCHOOL

Ecole du Génie (ESAG)

BP 34125, 106, rue Eblé, 49041 Angers
Tel: +33(2) 41-24-82-99
Fax: +33(2) 41-24-83-39
EMail: oci@esag.terre.defense.gouv.fr
Website: http://www.esag.terre.defense.gouv.fr/index_esag.html

Général de division: Patrick Alabergère (2013-)

Division

Military Engineering (Engineering; Military Science)

History: Founded 1771 as Ecole royale du génie de Mézières. Acquired present status and title 2009.

Admission Requirements: 2 yrs university science studies plus service as army officer

Fees: None

Main Language(s) of Instruction: French

Accrediting Agency: C.T.I., Ministry of Defence

Degrees and Diplomas: *Diplôme d'Ingénieur*: **Engineering.** *Mastère spécialisé*: **Engineering.** also: Technical Certificates (C.T) and Technical Diplomas (D.T) in Construction engineering

Last Updated: 06/03/15

FRENCH INSTITUTE FOR ADVANCED MECHANICS

Institut français de Mécanique avancée (IFMA)

CS 20265, Campus de Clermont-Ferrand/Les Cézeaux, 63175 Aubière, Cedex
Tel: +33(4) 73-28-80-00
Fax: +33(4) 73-28-81-00
EMail: direction@ifma.fr
Website: http://www.ifma.fr

Director: Pascal Ray
Tel: +33(4) 73-28-80-01 EMail: Direction@ifma.fr

Secretary General: Frantz Hurtebise
Tel: +33(4) 73-28-80-09 EMail: Frantz.Hurtebise@ifma.fr

International Relations: David Turner, Head of International Relations
Tel: +33(4) 73-28-80-08
EMail: david.turner@ifma.fr; RelationsInternationales@ifma.fr

Division

Advanced Mechanical Engineering (Civil Engineering; Mechanical Engineering)

History: Founded 1993.

Admission Requirements: Competitive entrance examination following 2 years further study after secondary school certificate (baccalauréat) or equivalent

Main Language(s) of Instruction: French

Accrediting Agency: Ministry of Higher Education, Commission des Titres d'Ingénieur (CTI)

Degrees and Diplomas: *Diplôme d'Ingénieur*: **Mechanical Engineering.** *Master*: **Industrial Engineering; Mechanical Engineering; Robotics.**

Student Services: Academic Counselling, Canteen, Careers Guidance, Cultural Activities, Facilities for disabled people, Foreign Studies Centre, Health Services, Language Laboratory, Social Counselling, Sports Facilities

Student Numbers *2014*: Total 581

Last Updated: 30/03/15

FRENCH NAVAL ACADEMY

Ecole navale (EN)

BCRM Brest, École navale, CC 600, 29240 Brest, Cedex 9
Tel: +33(2) 98-23-36-84
Fax: +33(2) 98-23-37-59
EMail: dircom@ecole-navale.fr
Website: http://www.ecole-navale.fr

Commandant: Benoît Lugan (2015-) EMail: amiral@ecole-navale.fr

International Relations: Audrey Boutteville, Capitaine de corvette
Tel: +33(2) 98-23-42-62 EMail: dircom@ecole-navale.fr

Division

Humanities and Management (Arts and Humanities; Management); **Maritime Studies** (Marine Transport); **Naval Studies** (Nautical Science)

Further Information: Has a research laboratory, IRENav

History: Founded 1830.

Academic Year: September to July

Admission Requirements: Competitive entrance examination following 2-3 yrs further study after secondary school certificate (baccalauréat)

Main Language(s) of Instruction: French, English

Accrediting Agency: Commission des titres d'Ingénieurs

Degrees and Diplomas: *Diplôme d'Ingénieur*: **Marine Engineering; Military Science; Nautical Science.** *Mastère spécialisé*: **Marine Science and Oceanography.** *Master*: **Marine Engineering; Military Science; Nautical Science.** Masters professionnel; Brevet Chef de Quart

Student Services: Canteen, Sports Facilities

Last Updated: 16/03/15

GRENOBLE I UNIVERSITY

Université Joseph Fourier (Grenoble I) (UJF)

BP 53, Domaine universitaire St Martin d'Hères, 621, Avenue Centrale, 38041 Grenoble, Cedex 09
Tel: +33(4) 76-51-46-00
Fax: +33(4) 76-51-48-48
EMail: dgs@ujf-grenoble.fr
Website: http://www.ujf-grenoble.fr

President: Patrick Lévy (2012-)
Tel: +33(4) 76-51-47-01 EMail: presidence@ujf-grenoble.fr

Head of Administration: Joris Benelle
Tel: +33(4) 76-51-48-20; +33 (4) 76-51-48-20
EMail: dgs@ujf-grenoble.fr

International Relations: Sophie-Adelaide Magnier, Head or International Relations
Tel: +33(4) 76-51-45-13
EMail: relations.internationales@ujf-grenoble.fr; marie-Odile.-garcia@ujf-grenoble.fr

Unit

Chemistry-Biology (Analytical Chemistry; Biochemistry; Biology; Botany; Cell Biology; Chemistry; Ecology; Genetics; Inorganic Chemistry; Microbiology; Molecular Biology; Neurosciences; Organic Chemistry; Physical Chemistry; Physiology); **Computer Science, Mathematics and Applied Mathematics** *(IMAG)* (Applied Mathematics; Artificial Intelligence; Computer Science; Operations Research; Systems Analysis); **Geography** (Geography; Mountain Studies; Regional Planning); **Medicine** *(La Tronche)* (Medicine; Surgery); **Pharmacy** *(La Tronche)* (Pharmacology; Pharmacy); **Physical Education and Sport** *(APS)* (Physical Education; Sports; Sports Management); **Physics, Engineering, Earth and Environmental Sciences, Mechanics** *(PHITEM)* (Applied Physics; Astronomy and Space Science; Atomic and Molecular Physics; Civil Engineering; Earth Sciences; Geological Engineering; Geology; Geophysics; Mechanical Engineering; Nuclear Physics; Optics; Physics; Seismology; Solid State Physics)

School

Engineering *(Polytech' Grenoble)* (Computer Networks; Geological Engineering; Industrial Engineering; Information Technology; Materials Engineering; Multimedia); **Teacher Training** *(ESPE in partnership with Grenoble I)* (Teacher Trainers Education; Teacher Training)

Department

Science and Technology *(DLST Offers undergraduate degrees)* (Applied Mathematics; Biological and Life Sciences; Chemistry; Earth Sciences; Physics)

Institute

Engineering *(IUT Grenoble I with a second site at Isle d'Abeau - ENEPS)* (Chemical Engineering; Civil Engineering; Computer Engineering; Computer Networks; Electrical Engineering; Energy

Engineering; Mechanical Engineering; Physical Engineering; Production Engineering; Technology; Telecommunications Engineering); **Industrial, Materials, Mechanical and Process Engineering** *(I-MEP2 in collaboration with Institut National Polytechnique de Grenoble)* (Industrial Engineering; Materials Engineering; Mechanical Engineering; Production Engineering); **Technological** *(IUT Grenoble I)* (Chemical Engineering; Civil Engineering; Computer Engineering; Computer Networks; Electrical Engineering; Energy Engineering; Mechanical Engineering; Physical Engineering; Production Engineering; Technology; Telecommunications Engineering)

Centre

Drôme-Ardèche *(Valence)* (Natural Sciences; Physical Education; Tourism)

Graduate School

Chemistry and Life Sciences (Biological and Life Sciences; Chemistry; Microbiology); **Computer Science** *(MSTII in collaboration with Institut National Polytechnique de Grenoble)* (Mathematics and Computer Science); **Earth, Astronomy and Environment** *(In collaboration with Institut National Polytechnique de Grenoble)* (Earth Sciences; Geography; Marine Science and Oceanography; Meteorology); **Electrical and Electronic Engineering** *(EEATS In collaboration with Institut National Polytechnique de Grenoble)* (Automation and Control Engineering; Electrical and Electronic Engineering; Microelectronics; Telecommunications Engineering); **Health Engineering** *(EDISCE)* (Biomedicine; Cognitive Sciences; Health Sciences); **Humanities and Political Science** *(In collaboration with University Pierre Mendes-France)*; **Physics** *(In collaboration with Institut National Polytechnique de Grenoble)* (Astrophysics; Atomic and Molecular Physics; Physics)

Further Information: also campus in Valence

History: Founded 1970 under the 1968 law reforming higher education as one of three Universities replacing former Université de Grenoble. Founded 1339 and confirmed by Papal Bull. Suppressed by the Revolution, replaced by Faculties of Law; Letters; and Science. Reconstituted as University 1896. A State institution enjoying academic and financial autonomy, operated under the jurisdiction of the Minister of Education and financed by the State. Member of the COMUE Grenoble-Alpes University

Academic Year: September to June (September-December; January-June)

Admission Requirements: 1st year: Secondary school certificate (baccalauréat) or foreign equivalent, or special entrance examination. For later years by individual application examined by validation committee

Fees: Undergraduates, 195 per annum; graduates, 255 per annum; Engineering, 575 per annum (Euro)

Main Language(s) of Instruction: French

Degrees and Diplomas: *Diplôme universitaire de Technologie*: **Chemistry; Civil Engineering; Communication Arts; Computer Networks; Electrical Engineering; Energy Engineering; Mechanical Engineering; Physical Engineering; Production Engineering; Telecommunications Engineering; Thermal Engineering.** *Licence*: **Biology; Chemistry; Earth Sciences; Electrical Engineering; Geography; Mathematics and Computer Science; Mechanical Engineering; Natural Sciences; Physical Education; Physics; Sports; Technology.** *Licence professionnelle*: **Building Technologies; Computer Networks; Electrical and Electronic Engineering; Energy Engineering; Environmental Studies; Food Technology; Health Sciences; Industrial and Production Economics; Regional Planning; Telecommunications Engineering; Veterinary Science.** *Diplôme d'Etat*: **Medicine; Pharmacy.** *Diplôme d'Ingénieur*: **Civil Engineering; Electrical and Electronic Engineering; Materials Engineering; Safety Engineering; Telecommunications Engineering.** *Master*: **Automation and Control Engineering; Biology; Biomedical Engineering; Chemistry; Cognitive Sciences; Earth Sciences; Electrical and Electronic Engineering; Environmental Studies; Health Sciences; Mathematics and Computer Science; Nanotechnology; Natural Sciences; Physics; Sports; Technology; Urban Studies.** *Doctorat*: **Astronomy and Space Science; Biological and Life Sciences; Biomedical Engineering; Chemistry; Cognitive Sciences; Computer Science; Earth Sciences; Electronic Engineering; Environmental Studies; Geography; Materials Engineering; Mathematics; Mechanics; Physics; Telecommunications Engineering.** Numerous Certificates of Specialization in Medicine

Student Services: Academic Counselling, Canteen, Facilities for disabled people, Health Services, Library, Residential Facilities, Social Counselling, Sports Facilities

Publishing house: Edition Grenoble sciences

Last Updated: 10/04/15

GRENOBLE II UNIVERSITY

Université Pierre-Mendès-France (Grenoble II) (UPMF)

BP 47, 151, rue des Universités, 38040 Cédex 9 Grenoble
Tel: +33(4) 76-82-54-00
Fax: +33(4) 76-82-56-54
EMail: communication@upmf-grenoble.fr; accueil@upmf-grenoble.fr
Website: http://www.upmf-grenoble.fr

President: Sébastien Bernard (2012-)
Tel: +33(4) 76-82-55-74
EMail: presidence@upmf-grenoble.fr; Sebastien.Bernard@upmf-grenoble.fr

Head of Administration: Nicolas Mathey
EMail: Nicolas.Mathey@upmf-grenoble.fr

International Relations: Séverine Wozniak, Vice-President in charge of International Relations
Tel: +33(4) 76-82-81-25 EMail: vpri@upmf-grenoble.fr

Faculty

Economics *(Grenoble)* (Business and Commerce; Economics; International Business; Management; Regional Planning; Social Policy); **Law** *(Also in Valence)* (Commercial Law; European Union Law; Human Rights; International Law; Law; Private Law; Public Law)

Unit

Human and Social Sciences *(UFR SHS)* (Cognitive Sciences; Educational Sciences; Information Sciences; Psychology; Social Sciences; Sociology); **Humanities** *(UFR SH)* (Art History; Arts and Humanities; Geography (Human); History; Music; Philosophy)

Institute

Business Administration *(IAE also in Valence)* (Business Administration); **Juridical Studies** *(IEJ)* (Law); **Mediat Rhône-Alpes** (Library Science); **Technology** *(IUT Valence)* (Administration; Business Administration; Computer Networks; Computer Science; Technology; Telecommunications Engineering); **Technology** *(IUT de Grenoble 2: second site at Vienne)* (Business Administration; Computer Science; Information Management; Sales Techniques; Technology); **Town Planning** *(UFR IUG)* (Town Planning; Urban Studies)

Centre

Library, Documentation and Books *(Médiat is an interuniversity centre providing services to partner Universities Grenoble III, Lyon I, II and III)*

Graduate School

Economics (Economics); **Health, Cognitive and Environmental Engineering** *(In collaboration with Universities Grenoble I and Savoie and Institut National Polytechnique de Grenoble)* (Cognitive Sciences; Environmental Engineering; Health Sciences; Psychology); **Humanities and Political Science** *(In collaboration with University Grenoble I)* (Political Sciences; Social Sciences); **Industrial Organisation and System Production** *(In partnership with Institut National Polytechnique de Grenoble)*; **Juridical Studies** (Human Rights; Law; Public Administration); **Management** (Management); **Mathematics, Information Technology and Computer Science** *(ED MSTII in collaboration with Grenoble I and Savoie Universities and Institut National Polytechnique de Grenoble)* (Applied Mathematics; Mathematics; Mathematics and Computer Science); **Philosophy** *(In partnership with University Lyon I)*

History: Founded 1970 under the 1968 law reforming higher education as one of three Universities replacing former Université de Grenoble - founded 1339 and confirmed by Papal Bull. Suppressed by the Revolution, replaced by Faculties of Law; Letters; and Science. Reconstituted as University 1896. A State Institution enjoying academic and financial autonomy, operating under the jurisdiction of the Minister of Education and financed by the State. Member of the COMUE Grenoble-Alpes University

Academic Year: October to June (October-December; December-April; April-June)

Admission Requirements: Secondary school certificate (baccalauréat) or foreign equivalent, or special entrance examination

Main Language(s) of Instruction: French

Degrees and Diplomas: *Capacité en Droit*; *Diplôme universitaire de Technologie*: **Business Administration; Communication Arts; Computer Science; Statistics; Telecommunications Engineering.** *Licence*: **Applied Mathematics; Art History; Economics; Educational Sciences; History; Law; Management; Music; Psychology; Public Administration; Sociology.** *Licence professionnelle*: **Biological and Life Sciences; Communication Studies; Computer Engineering; Documentation Techniques; Economics; Human Resources; Management; Statistics; Tourism.** *Diplôme d'Etat*: **Accountancy; Educational and Student Counselling; Social Work.** *Master*: **Art History; Cognitive Sciences; Economics; Educational Sciences; European Union Law; Finance; History; Information Management; International Business; International Law; Management; Marketing; Private Law; Psychology; Public Law; Sociology; Town Planning.** *Doctorat*: **Applied Mathematics; Clinical Psychology; Cognitive Sciences; Computer Science; Criminal Law; Economics; Educational Sciences; European Union Law; History; Human Rights; Industrial Engineering; International Law; International Relations; Management; Military Science; Philosophy; Political Sciences; Private Law; Psychology; Public Administration; Public Law; Regional Planning; Sociology; Town Planning.** *Certificat de Spécialité*: **Economics; Energy Engineering; Psychology.** Masters de Recherche, Masters professionnel, Certificat d'université, Diplôme de l'IEP

Student Services: Academic Counselling, Canteen, Cultural Activities, Facilities for disabled people, Foreign Studies Centre, Health Services, Language Laboratory, Social Counselling, Sports Facilities

Publications: ARES-Sécurité Défense Internationale; Bulletin du Centre de Documentation départemental du Travail; Cahiers de l'Institut de Recherche Economique et de Planification; Cahiers de Philo; Cahiers de Sciences Economiques; Economie Appliquée; Les Cahiers de l'Espace Europe

Last Updated: 10/04/15

GRENOBLE III UNIVERSITY

Université Stendhal (Grenoble III)

BP 25, Domaine universitaire St. Martin d'Hyères, 38040 Grenoble, Cedex 09
Tel: +33(4) 76-82-43-00
Fax: +33(4) 76-82-41-85
EMail: presidence@u-grenoble3.fr
Website: http://www.u-grenoble3.fr

Presidente: Lise Dumasy (2008-2016)
Tel: +33(4) 76-82-43-01 EMail: lise.dumasy@u-grenoble3.fr

Head of Administration: Martine Pevet
Tel: +33(4) 76-82-43-46; +33(4) 76-82-43-02
EMail: martine.pevet@u-grenoble3.fr

International Relations: Nathalie Janin, International Relations Manager
Tel: +33(4) 76-82-43-10 EMail: nathalie.janin@u-grenoble3.fr

Unit

Foreign Languages *((LLCE-LEA))* (English; German; Italian; Literature; Modern Languages; Oriental Languages; Russian; Spanish); **Languages, Arts and Literature, Information and Communication Sciences** *(LLASIC)* (Communication Studies; Linguistics; Literature; Performing Arts)

School

Journalism *(EJDG)* (Journalism)

Department

Computer Science Teaching *(DIP)* (Computer Science); **Continuing Education** *(SCFC)* (Computer Science); **Language Studies for Specialists in Other Disciplines** *(LANSAD)* (Foreign Languages Education; Teacher Trainers Education)

Centre

French Studies *(CUEF)* (French); **Self-Study** *(CAA)* (Modern Languages); **Stendhal** (English; German; Library Science; Literature; Spanish; Theatre)

Graduate School

Cultural Studies and Letters (Arts and Humanities; Communication Studies; Education; Linguistics; Modern Languages)

History: Founded 1970 under the 1968 law reforming higher education as one of three Universities replacing former Université de Grenoble - founded 1339 and confirmed by Papal Bull. Suppressed by the Revolution, replaced by Faculties of Law; Letters; and Science. Reconstituted as University 1896. A State institution enjoying academic and financial autonomy, operating under the jurisdiction of the Minister of Education and financed by the State. Member of the COMUE Grenobles-Alpes University

Academic Year: October to June (October-February; February-June)

Admission Requirements: Secondary school certificate (baccalauréat) or equivalent, or special entrance examination

Main Language(s) of Instruction: French

Degrees and Diplomas: *Diplôme d'Accès aux Etudes universitaires*; *Licence*: **Art History; Classical Languages; Foreign Languages Education; Information Technology; Modern Languages.** *Licence professionnelle*: **Communication Arts; Information Technology.** *Master*: **Arts and Humanities; English; French; Germanic Studies; Information Technology; Journalism; Linguistics; Literature; Mediterranean Studies; Modern Languages; Slavic Languages.** *Doctorat*: **Arts and Humanities; Education; Information Technology; Linguistics; Modern Languages.** Masters recherche, Masters professionnel

Student Services: Canteen, Cultural Activities, Facilities for disabled people, Health Services, Library, Residential Facilities, Sports Facilities

Student Numbers *2014*: Total 11,245
Last Updated: 10/04/15

GRENOBLE INSTITUTE OF TECHNOLOGY

Institut polytechnique de Grenoble (INP GRENOBLE)

46 avenue Félix Viallet, 38031 Grenoble, Cedex 1
Tel: +33(4) 76-57-45-00
Fax: +33(4) 76-57-45-01
EMail: contact@grenoble-inp.fr
Website: http://www.grenoble-inp.fr

General Administrator: Brigitte Plateau (2012-)
Tel: +33(4) 76-57-45-05 EMail: presidence@grenoble-inp.fr

Head of Administration: Xavier Fauveau
EMail: Secretariat-General@grenoble-inp.fr

International Relations: Severine Giroud, International Relations Manager EMail: international.office@grenoble-inp.fr

College

Doctoral (Applied Mathematics; Automation and Control Engineering; Cognitive Sciences; Computer Science; Earth Sciences; Electronic Engineering; Engineering; Environmental Engineering; Environmental Studies; Health Sciences; Materials Engineering; Mathematics; Mechanical Engineering; Physics; Power Engineering)

Programme

Preparatory Class *(Prépa INP - CPP)* (Mathematics; Physics)

Department

Advanced Systems and Networks *(ESISAR)* (Computer Networks; Systems Analysis); **Applied Mathematics and Computer Science** *(ENSIMAG)* (Applied Mathematics; Computer Science); **Energy, Water and Environmental Science** *(Ense 3)* (Energy Engineering; Environmental Studies; Water Science); **Industrial Engineering** *(ENSGI)* (Industrial Engineering); **Lifelong Education** *(CUEFA, two sites)*; **Paper Science, Print Media and Biomaterials** *(Pagora)* (Materials Engineering; Media Studies; Paper Technology; Printing and Printmaking); **Physics, Applied Physics, Electronics and Materials Science** *(Phelma)* (Applied Physics; Electronic Engineering; Materials Engineering; Physics)

Further Information: 30 laboratories

History: Founded 1971 under the 1968 law reforming higher education and incorporating various Ecoles nationales supérieures, the first of which was founded in 1901. Acquired Grand Etablissement status 2007.

Academic Year: September to June

Admission Requirements: Competitive entrance examination following 2-3 years further study after secondary school certificate (baccalauréat) or equivalent

Fees: Bachelor and Engineering: 568,57; Master: 241,57 (Euro)

Main Language(s) of Instruction: French, English (10 international degrees)

Accrediting Agency: Commission des Titres d'Ingénieurs (CTI); EURACE

Degrees and Diplomas: *Licence professionnelle*; *Diplôme d'Ingénieur*: **Applied Mathematics; Automation and Control Engineering; Chemical Engineering; Chemistry; Computer Science; Electrical Engineering; Electronic Engineering; Energy Engineering; Engineering; Graphic Arts; Hydraulic Engineering; Industrial Engineering; Metallurgical Engineering; Multimedia; Nanotechnology; Nuclear Engineering; Paper Technology; Physical Engineering; Telecommunications Engineering.** *Master*: **Automation and Control Engineering; Business Administration; Chemistry; Cognitive Sciences; Earth Sciences; Electrical Engineering; Electronic Engineering; Energy Engineering; Environmental Studies; Information Sciences; Management; Materials Engineering; Mathematics and Computer Science; Mechanical Engineering; Paper Technology; Physical Engineering; Physics; Sanitary Engineering.** *Doctorat*: **Cognitive Sciences; Computer Science; Earth Sciences; Electrical Engineering; Electronic Engineering; Energy Engineering; Environmental Studies; Industrial Management; Information Sciences; Information Technology; Materials Engineering; Mathematics; Mechanical Engineering; Physics; Sanitary Engineering.** International Masters

Student Services: Academic Counselling, Canteen, Careers Guidance, Health Services, Language Laboratory, Social Counselling, Sports Facilities

Publications: Ingénieur INPG

Publishing House: Presses universitaires de Grenoble (PUG)

Academic Staff *2015*: Total 1,100

Student Numbers *2015*: Total 5,500

Last Updated: 31/03/15

GRENOBLE SCHOOL OF ARCHITECTURE

Ecole nationale supérieure d'Architecture de Grenoble (ENSAG)

CS12636, 60, avenue de Constantine, 38036 Grenoble, Cedex 02

Tel: +33(4) 76-69-83-00

Fax: +33(4) 76-69-83-38

EMail: lucie.scotet@grenoble.archi.fr

Website: http://www.grenoble.archi.fr

Director: Lucie Scotet
Tel: +33(4) 76-69-83-20
EMail: lucie.scotet@grenoble.archi.fr

International Relations: Hélène Casalta
Tel: +33(4) 76-69-83-22
EMail: helene.casalta@grenoble.archi.fr

Programme

Architecture (Architecture)

History: Founded 1927. Acquired present status 1968.

Admission Requirements: Competitive entrance examination. Baccalauréat or foreign equivalent.

Main Language(s) of Instruction: French

Degrees and Diplomas: *Licence*: **Architecture.** *Master*: **Architectural and Environmental Design; Architecture.** *Doctorat*: **Architecture.** Also DSA : diplôme de spécialisation et d'approfondissement; DPEA : diplôme propre aux écoles d'architecture

Last Updated: 11/03/15

GRENOBLE-VALENCE SCHOOL OF ART AND DESIGN

Ecole supérieure d'Art et Design Grenoble-Valence

Place des Beaux-Arts, CS 40ã074, 26000 Valence, Cedex 9

Tel: +33(4) 75-79-24-00

Fax: +33(4) 75-79-24-40

EMail: valence@esad-gv.fr

Website: http://www.esad-gv.fr/fr/

Director: Jacques Norigeon (2008-)
EMail: jacques.norigeon@esad-gv.fr

Programme

Visual Arts and Graphic Design

Further Information: also site in: Grenoble

History: Founded 2011 following merger of the l'École supérieure d'art de Grenoble and the École régionale des beaux-arts de Valence.

Academic Year: October to June (October-February; February-June)

Admission Requirements: Baccalauréat or equivalent secondary school exam. Entrance exam with a selection jury.

Main Language(s) of Instruction: French

Accrediting Agency: Ministry of Culture and Communication

Degrees and Diplomas: Diplome national d'arts plastiques (DNAP) 3 yrs; Diplome national d'arts et techniques (DNAT) 3 yrs; Diplome national supérieur d'expression plastique (DNSEP) a further 2 yrs

Last Updated: 07/04/15

HIGHER INSTITUTE OF FINE ARTS OF BESANÇON

Institut Supérieur des Beaux-Arts Besançon-Franche comté (ISBA BESANÇON)

12 rue Denis Papin, 25000 Besançon

Tel: +33(3) 81-87-81-30

EMail: christelle.botton@isba.besancon.fr

Website: http://www.isba-besancon.fr/

Director: Laurent Deveze

International Relations: Brigitte Chorvot
EMail: brigitte.chorvot@isba.besancon.fr

Programme

Visual Arts (Communication Arts; Design; Visual Arts)

History: Founded 1756. ex Besançon Regional School of Art.

Admission Requirements: Baccalauréat or equivalent secondary school exam. Entrance exam with a selection jury.

Fees: Non-grant students: 550 per annum (Euro)

Main Language(s) of Instruction: French

Accrediting Agency: Ministry of Culture and Communication

Degrees and Diplomas: *Master*: **Visual Arts.** Diplôme national d'arts plastiques (DNAP) 3 yrs; Diplôme national supérieur d'expression plastique (DNSEP in Design) a further 2 yrs

Student Services: Library

Last Updated: 10/04/15

IFP SCHOOL

228-232, Avenue Napoléon Bonaparte, 92852 Rueil-Malmaison, Cedex

Tel: +33(1) 47-52-64-57

Fax: +33(1) 47-52-67-65

Website: http://www.ifp-school.com

Dean: Philippe Pinchon EMail: catherine.charlier@ifpen.fr

Secretary General: Pierre Duclos
EMail: catherine.charlier@ifpen.fr

International Relations: Gilles Azencott, Internation Relations Manager EMail: gilles.azencott@ifpen.fr

Centre

Economics and Management (Economics; Finance; Management); **Exploration-Production** (Earth Sciences; Petroleum and Gas Engineering; Production Engineering); **Internal Combustion**

Engines and Hydrocarbon Utilizations (Automotive Engineering; Energy Engineering; Environmental Studies); **Refining, Petrochemicals, Gas** (Chemical Engineering; Construction Engineering; Engineering; Petroleum and Gas Engineering; Polymer and Plastics Technology; Technology)
History: Founded 1924, IFP School is an integral part of "Institut Français du Petrole".
Academic Year: September to July
Admission Requirements: University Degree or Diplôme d'Ingénieur or equivalent
Main Language(s) of Instruction: French, English
Accrediting Agency: Ministry of Education
Degrees and Diplomas: *Diplôme d'Ingénieur*: **Engineering.** *Master*: **Automotive Engineering; Ecology; Energy Engineering; Environmental Studies; Industrial Engineering; Transport Engineering.** Master recherche
Student Services: Academic Counselling, Canteen, Careers Guidance, Cultural Activities, Facilities for disabled people, Health Services, Language Laboratory, Social Counselling, Sports Facilities
Publications: Revue de l'Institut français du Pétrole
Publishing House: Editions TECHNIP
Last Updated: 25/03/15

INSA - LYON

Institut national des Sciences appliquées de Lyon (INSA LYON)

20 avenue Albert Einstein, 69621 Vileurbanne, Cedex
Tel: +33(4) 72-43-83-83
Fax: +33(4) 72-43-85-00
EMail: accueil@insa-lyon.fr
Website: http://www.insa-lyon.fr

Director: Eric Maurincomme (2011-) EMail: dir@insa-lyon.fr

International Relations: Marie-Pierre Favre, Head of International Relations Tel: +33(4) 72-43-83-91 EMail: dri@insa-lyon.fr

School
Applied Sciences (Bioengineering; Civil Engineering; Computer Engineering; Electrical Engineering; Energy Engineering; Engineering; Environmental Engineering; Industrial Engineering; Materials Engineering; Mechanical Engineering; Telecommunications Engineering; Town Planning)
Further Information: 20 research laboratories
History: Founded 1957.
Academic Year: September to June
Admission Requirements: Competitive entrance examination, secondary school certificate (baccalauréat) or equivalent
Fees: Engineering programme: 610; Master: 256; Doctorat: 391 (Euro)
Main Language(s) of Instruction: French
Degrees and Diplomas: *Diplôme d'Ingénieur*: **Engineering.** *Mastère spécialisé*: **Computer Engineering; Computer Science; Environmental Management; Industrial Engineering; Performing Arts.** *Master*: **Biochemistry; Computer Science; Environmental Studies; Materials Engineering; Mechanics; Microbiology; Nanotechnology; Physics; Public Health; Urban Studies.** *Doctorat*: **Arts and Humanities; Automation and Control Engineering; Biological and Life Sciences; Chemistry; Civil Engineering; Electronic Engineering; Materials Engineering; Mathematics and Computer Science; Mechanics; Social Sciences; Sound Engineering (Acoustics).** Masters recherche
Student Services: Academic Counselling, Canteen, Foreign Studies Centre, Health Services, Language Laboratory, Sports Facilities
Last Updated: 01/04/15

INSA - RENNES

Institut national des Sciences appliquées de Rennes (INSA RENNES)

20 avenue des Buttes de Coësmes, CS 70839, 35708 Rennes, Cedex 7
Tel: +33(2) 23-23-82-00
Fax: +33(2) 23-23-83-96
EMail: direction@insa-rennes.fr
Website: http://www.insa-rennes.fr

Directeur: M'Hamed Drissi
Tel: +33(2) 23-23-83-26 EMail: Mhamed.Drissi@insa-rennes.fr

International Relations: Stéphanie Prigent, International Relations Manager EMail: international@insa-rennes.fr

Department
Civil Engineering and Urban Planning (Architecture; Business Administration; Construction Engineering; Geology; Hydraulic Engineering; Labour Law; Materials Engineering; Mechanics; Statistics; Surveying and Mapping); **Computer Science** (Computer Science; Software Engineering; Systems Analysis); **Electronic and Computer Engineering** (Computer Engineering; Electronic Engineering; Mathematics); **Electronics and Communication Systems** (Computer Science; Electronic Engineering; Telecommunications Engineering); **Materials Science and Nanotechnology** (Materials Engineering; Nanotechnology); **Mechanical and Control System Engineering** (Automation and Control Engineering; Mechanical Engineering; Mechanics; Production Engineering); **Science and Technology for Engineers** (Engineering; Technology)
History: Founded 1966.
Academic Year: September to June
Admission Requirements: Secondary school certificate (Baccalauréat) and Selection Committee
Main Language(s) of Instruction: French
Accrediting Agency: Commission des Titres d'Ingénieurs (CTI)
Degrees and Diplomas: *Diplôme d'Ingénieur*: **Civil Engineering; Communication Arts; Computer Engineering; Electrical Engineering; Engineering; Materials Engineering; Mechanical Engineering; Nanotechnology; Town Planning.** *Master*: **Chemistry; Electronic Engineering; Mathematics and Computer Science; Mechanics; Physics.** *Doctorat*: **Astronomy and Space Science; Chemistry; Earth Sciences; Electronic Engineering; Engineering; Materials Engineering; Mathematics and Computer Science; Optical Technology; Physics; Telecommunications Engineering.**
Student Services: Academic Counselling, Canteen, Careers Guidance, Cultural Activities, Facilities for disabled people, Foreign Studies Centre, Health Services, Language Laboratory, Nursery Care, Social Counselling, Sports Facilities
Last Updated: 01/04/15

INSA - ROUEN

Institut national des Sciences appliquées de Rouen (INSA ROUEN)

Avenue de l'Université, 76801 Saint-Étienne-du-Rouvray, Cedex
Tel: +33(2) 32-95-97-00
Fax: +33(2) 32-95-98-60
EMail: insa@insa-rouen.fr
Website: http://www.insa-rouen.fr

Directeur: Jean-Louis Billoët (2007-)
Tel: +33(2) 32-95-97-07 EMail: jean-louis.billoet@insa-rouen.fr

Directrice générale des Services: Marie France Detalminil
Tel: +33(2) 32-95-65-12
EMail: marie-france.detalminil@insa-rouen.fr

International Relations: Morgan Jones, Head of International Relations
Tel: + 33(2) 32-95-66-93 EMail: morgan.jones@insa-rouen.fr

Department
Chemistry and Engineering (Chemical Engineering; Chemistry; Polymer and Plastics Technology); **Civil and Construction Engineering** (Civil Engineering; Construction Engineering); **Energy Engineering and Propulsion** (Energy Engineering); **Information Systems Design** (Computer Science; Data Processing; Electronic Engineering); **Mathematical and Software Engineering** (Mathematics and Computer Science; Software Engineering); **Mechanical Engineering** (Mechanical Engineering); **Risk Management** (Environmental Management)
History: Founded 1985. Moved to Saint-Étienne-du-Rouvray 2009.
Admission Requirements: According to baccalauréat results and academic record
Fees: Engineering programme: 610; Master: 256; PhD: 391 (Euro)
Main Language(s) of Instruction: French

Accrediting Agency: Commission des Titres d'Ingénieur (CTI)

Degrees and Diplomas: *Diplôme d'Ingénieur*: **Engineering.** *Master*: **Chemistry; Computer Engineering; Engineering; Mathematics; Mechanics; Physics.** *Doctorat*: **Chemistry; Civil Engineering; Ecology; Energy Engineering; Mathematics and Computer Science; Mechanical Engineering.**

Student Services: Academic Counselling, Canteen, Foreign Studies Centre, Health Services, Language Laboratory, Sports Facilities

Last Updated: 01/04/15

INSA - STRASBOURG

Institut national des Sciences appliquées de Strasbourg (INSA STRASBOURG)

24, boulevard de la Victoire, 67084 Strasbourg, Cedex
Tel: +33(3) 88-14-47-00
EMail: secretariat.direction@insa-strasbourg.fr
Website: http://www.insa-strasbourg.fr

Director: Marc Renner
Tel: +33(3) 88-14-47-01
EMail: secretariat.direction@insa-strasbourg.fr

Head of Administration: Roger Cervantès
Tel: +33(3) 88-14-47-08
EMail: secretariat.general@insa-strasbourg.fr

International Relations: Angelika Hammann
Tel: +33(3) 88-14-47-80 +33(3) 88-14-47-02
EMail: relations.internationales@insa-strasbourg.fr; angelika.hammann@insa-strasbourg.fr

Department

Architecture (Architecture); **Civil Engineering and Topography** (Civil Engineering; Surveying and Mapping); **Electrical Engineering and Climate** (Electrical Engineering); **Fluids and Solids Mechanics** (Physics); **Mechanical Engineering** (Mechanical Engineering); **Technology and Humanities** (Arts and Humanities; Technology)

History: Founded 1875.

Admission Requirements: Competitive entrance examination following 2-3 years further study after secondary school certificate (baccalauréat) or following first university qualification (DEUG, DUT or BTS) or equivalent.

Main Language(s) of Instruction: French

Accrediting Agency: Ministry of Higher Education and Research

Degrees and Diplomas: *Diplôme d'Ingénieur*: **Civil Engineering; Electrical and Electronic Engineering; Electronic Engineering; Energy Engineering; Mechanical Engineering; Polymer and Plastics Technology; Surveying and Mapping.** *Mastère spécialisé*; *Master*: **Materials Engineering; Nanotechnology; Urban Studies.**

Student Services: Careers Guidance, Health Services, Sports Facilities

Last Updated: 31/03/15

INSA - TOULOUSE

Institut national des Sciences appliquées de Toulouse (INSA TOULOUSE)

135, avenue de Rangueil, 31077 Toulouse, Cedex 4
Tel: +33(5) 61-55-95-13
Fax: +33(5) 61-55-95-00
EMail: servicecom@insa-toulouse.fr
Website: http://www.insa-toulouse.fr/

Director: Bertrand Raquet EMail: bertrand.raquet@insa-toulouse.fr

Head of Adminsitration: Pierre Stoecklin
EMail: pierre.stoecklin@insa-toulouse.fr

International Relations: Danièle Fournier, Head of International Relations EMail: daniele.fournier@insa-toulouse.fr

Department

Biochemical Engineering (Biochemistry; Bioengineering; Biological and Life Sciences; Biotechnology; Chemistry; Microbiology; Molecular Biology); **Civil Engineering** (Building Technologies; Civil Engineering); **Computer and Network Engineering** (Computer Engineering; Computer Networks); **Mathematical and modeling Engineering** (Engineering; Mathematics); **Mechanical Engineering** (Mechanical Engineering); **Physical Engineering** (Physical Engineering); **Process and Environmental Engineering** (Industrial Engineering); **Sciences and Technology** (Biochemistry; Chemical Engineering; Computer Engineering; Construction Engineering; Environmental Studies; Materials Engineering)

History: Founded 1963.

Academic Year: September to June

Admission Requirements: Competitive entrance examination following secondary school certificate (baccalauréat) or equivalent. Selection on grades

Main Language(s) of Instruction: French

Accrediting Agency: Conférence des Grandes Ecoles

Degrees and Diplomas: *Diplôme d'Ingénieur*: **Biology; Civil Engineering; Computer Engineering; Energy Engineering; Engineering; Nanotechnology; Safety Engineering.** *Mastère spécialisé*: **Industrial Engineering; Management; Safety Engineering.** *Master*: **Applied Mathematics; Biology; Civil Engineering; Computer Science; Environmental Engineering; Materials Engineering; Mechanical Engineering; Mechanics; Microbiology; Physical Engineering; Telecommunications Engineering.** *Doctorat*: **Applied Mathematics; Automation and Control Engineering; Chemical Engineering; Civil Engineering; Computer Engineering; Computer Graphics; Computer Networks; Electronic Engineering; Energy Engineering; Film; Industrial Engineering; Information Technology; Materials Engineering; Mechanical Engineering; Microbiology; Microwaves; Nanotechnology; Physics; Telecommunications Engineering.** Also Master of Science programmes for non-French speaking students.

Student Services: Academic Counselling, Canteen, Facilities for disabled people, Foreign Studies Centre, Health Services, Language Laboratory, Social Counselling, Sports Facilities

Last Updated: 31/03/15

INSA - VAL DE LOIRE CENTRE

Institut national des Sciences appliquées - Centre Val de Loire

88 boulevard Lahitolle, CS 60013, 18022 Bourges
Tel: +33(2) 48-48-40-00
EMail: communication@insa-cvl.fr
Website: http://www.insa-centrevaldeloire.fr/drupal/

Director: Jean-Marie Castelain (2014-)

International Relations: Alina Gruner
Tel: +33(2) 48-48-40-42
EMail: alina.gruner@insa-cvl.fr; relationsinternationales@insa-cvl.fr

Department

Energy, Risks and Environment *(ERE)* (Energy Engineering; Environmental Studies; Safety Engineering); **Industrial engineering** *(GSI)* (Engineering; Industrial Engineering); **Industrial risk** *(MRI)* (Engineering; Safety Engineering); **Security and Computer Technology** *(STI)* (Computer Engineering)

Further Information: also campuse in: Blois

History: Founded in 2013.

Admission Requirements: Competitive entrance examination, secondary school certificate in Science (Baccalauréat S)

Main Language(s) of Instruction: French

Accrediting Agency: Minsitry of higher education and research

Degrees and Diplomas: *Mastère spécialisé*: **Nuclear Engineering; Safety Engineering.** *Master*: **Automation and Control Engineering; Computer Engineering; Electronic Engineering; Energy Engineering; Environmental Studies; Mechanical Engineering; Robotics.**

Student Services: Library

Last Updated: 02/04/15

INS HEA - INSTITUTE OF DISABILITY AND SPECIAL EDUCATIONAL NEEDS

Institut d'enseignement supérieur et de recherche Handicap et besoins éducatifs particuliers (INS HEA)

58/60 avenue des Landes, 92150 Suresnes
Tel: +33(1) 41-44-31-00
EMail: contact@inshea.fr
Website: http://www.inshea.fr/

Director: José Puig EMail: jose.puig@inshea.fr

Secretary General: Rémy Auriat EMail: remy.auriat@inshea.fr

International Relations: Nel Saumont, International Relations Manager
Tel: +33(1) 41-44-31-21
EMail: nel.saumont@inshea.fr; international@inshea.fr

Programme

Disability and Special educational needs (Education; Rehabilitation and Therapy; Social Work)

History: Founded in 1954 as Centre national d'éducation de plein air (Cnepa). Become Institute of Disability and Special educational needs (INS HEA) in 2005

Main Language(s) of Instruction: French

Accrediting Agency: Ministry of Higher Education and Research; Ministry of Education

Degrees and Diplomas: *Licence professionnelle*; *Diplôme d'Etat*; *Master*: **Education; Social Work.**

Last Updated: 02/04/15

INSTITUTE MINES TELECOM

Institut Mines Télécom
46 rue Barrault, 75634 Paris, Cedex 13
Tel: +33(1) 45-81-80-80
Fax: +33(1) 45-88-66-68
EMail: international@mines-telecom.fr
Website: http://www.mines-telecom.fr/en/

Director General: Philippe Jamet Tel: +33(1) 45-81-72-20

Secretary General: Rachel Fracz-Vitani (2014-)

Programme

Engineering (Computer Engineering; Computer Science; Electronic Engineering; Energy Engineering; Engineering; Industrial Engineering; Nuclear Engineering; Polymer and Plastics Technology); **Management** (Management)

History: Founded 2012.

Admission Requirements: Competitive entrance examination following 2 years further study after secondary school certificate (baccalauréat)

Main Language(s) of Instruction: French

Accrediting Agency: Minisrty of Industry; Commission des Titres d'ingénieurs (CTI); Conférence des Grandes Écoles

Degrees and Diplomas: *Diplôme d'Etudes d'Ecole de Commerce et Gestion*; *Diplôme d'Ingénieur*: **Engineering.** *Mastère spécialisé*; *Master*: **Engineering; Management.** *Doctorat*: **Economics; Energy Engineering; Environmental Studies; Health Sciences; Materials Engineering; Multimedia; Natural Resources; Transport Engineering.** Also Bachelor

Last Updated: 02/04/15

EMA - ALES

ECOLE DES MINES D'ALÈS (EMA)
6, avenue de Clavières, 30319 Alès
Tel: +33(4) 66-78-50-00
Fax: +33(4) 66-78-50-34
EMail: contact@ema.fr
Website: http://www.ema.fr

Director: Bruno Goubet (2013-)

Secretary General: André Moulin EMail: Andre.Moulin@ema.fr

Programme

Mining Engineering (Mining Engineering)

Department

Civil Engineering (Civil Engineering); **Eco-Innovation Design and Advanced Materials Engineering** (Materials Engineering; Technology); **Engineering and Management of Complex Systems** (Engineering Management); **Management, Energy and Environmental Engineering** (Energy Engineering; Environmental Engineering; Management); **Risks and Crises** (Safety Engineering)

Institute

Mines Télécom

Research Centre

Computer Engineering and Automation (Artificial Intelligence; Automation and Control Engineering; Computer Engineering; Electrical Engineering; Electronic Engineering; Software Engineering; Telecommunications Engineering); **Industrial Environment and Risk Management** (Chemical Engineering; Environmental Engineering; Safety Engineering; Surveying and Mapping; Waste Management); **Mass Materials** (Automation and Control Engineering; Civil Engineering; Construction Engineering; Geological Engineering; Industrial Engineering; Materials Engineering; Mechanical Engineering; Mining Engineering; Production Engineering)

Further Information: Campuses in Nîmes and Pau.

History: Founded 1843.

Academic Year: September to June

Admission Requirements: Competitive entrance examination following 1 or 2 years university studies after secondary school certificate (baccalauréat)

Fees: For postgraduate diploma of 'Ingénieur diplômé' 450 per annum; 1 530-3 800 per annum for specialization courses (Euro)

Main Language(s) of Instruction: French, English

Accrediting Agency: Commission des Titres d'Ingénieur (CTI)

Degrees and Diplomas: *Diplôme d'Ingénieur*: **Engineering.** *Mastère spécialisé*: **Environmental Engineering; Industrial Engineering; Mining Engineering.** *Master*: **Bioengineering; Engineering Drawing and Design; Multimedia.** *Doctorat*. Also Ingénieur de spécialisation in Computer Science and Digital Communication

Student Services: Canteen, Cultural Activities, Foreign Studies Centre, Language Laboratory, Social Counselling, Sports Facilities

EMAC - ALBI

ECOLE DES MINES D'ALBI-CARMAUX (EMAC)
Campus Jarlard, 81013 Albi, Cedex 09
Tel: +33(5) 63-49-30-00
Fax: +33(5) 63-49-30-99
EMail: ecole@mines-albi.fr
Website: http://www.mines-albi.fr

Director: Alain-Louis Schmitt (2012-)
Tel: +33(5) 63-49-30-10 EMail: alain.schmitt@mines-albi.fr

Secretary General: Michel Monchal
Tel: +33(5) 63-49-30-90 EMail: michel.monchal@mines-albi.fr

International Relations: Radu Barna, Director for international relations
Tel: +33(5) 63-49-30-00 EMail: international@mines-albi.fr

Division

Chemical Engineering (Chemical Engineering); **Environmental and Energy Engineering** (Energy Engineering; Environmental Engineering); **Materials Engineering** (Materials Engineering); **Pharmacy and Engineering** (Engineering; Pharmacology); **Process Engineering** (Engineering)

History: Founded 1992 under the authority of the Ministry of Industry.

Academic Year: September to July (September-January; February-July)

Admission Requirements: Entrance examination

Main Language(s) of Instruction: French

Accrediting Agency: Commission des Titres d'Ingénieur (CTI)

Degrees and Diplomas: *Diplôme d'Ingénieur*: **Aeronautical and Aerospace Engineering; Biomedical Engineering; Building Technologies; Engineering; Industrial Engineering; Pharmacology.** *Mastère spécialisé*: **Aeronautical and Aerospace Engineering; Building Technologies; Engineering Management.** *Master*: **Aeronautical and Aerospace Engineering; Environmental Engineering; Materials Engineering; Mechanical Engineering; Mechanics; Microbiology; Natural Resources; Pharmacology.** *Doctorat*: **Civil Engineering; Energy Engineering; Industrial Engineering; Mechanical Engineering.**

Student Services: Canteen, Careers Guidance, Cultural Activities, Health Services, Residential Facilities, Social Counselling, Sports Facilities

EMD - DOUAI

ECOLE DES MINES DE DOUAI (EMD)

BP 838, 941, rue Charles Bourseul, 59508 Douai
Tel: +33(3) 27-71-22-22
Fax: +33(3) 27-71-25-25
EMail: mines@ensm-douai.fr
Website: http://www.ensm-douai.fr

Director: Daniel Boulnois (2012-)
Tel: +33(3) 27-71-24-63 EMail: daniel.boulnois@mines-douai.fr

Secretary General: Kader Amara
Tel: +33(3) 27-71-25-01 EMail: kader.amara@mines-douai.fr

International Relations: Emmanuel Dequeker
Tel: +33(3) 27-71-20-46
EMail: emmanuel.dequeker@mines-douai.fr

Department

Atmospheric Sciences and Environment (Chemistry; Environmental Management; Environmental Studies; Waste Management; Water Management); **Civil and Environmental Engineering** (Civil Engineering; Environmental Engineering); **Computer Science and Automation** (Automation and Control Engineering; Computer Science; Information Technology; Systems Analysis); **Industrial Energy** (Energy Engineering; Heating and Refrigeration; Industrial Engineering); **Polymer Technology and Mechanical Engineering** (Materials Engineering; Mechanical Engineering; Polymer and Plastics Technology)

History: Founded 1878. A public 'Grande Ecole'.

Admission Requirements: Competitive entrance examination following 2 years further study after secondary school certificate (baccalauréat) or following first university qualification (DEUG, DUT or BTS), or equivalent

Fees: 400 per annum (Euro)

Main Language(s) of Instruction: French and English

Accrediting Agency: Commission des Titres d'Ingénieurs (CTI)

Degrees and Diplomas: *Diplôme d'Ingénieur*: **Engineering.** *Mastère spécialisé*: **Building Technologies; Business Administration; Industrial Engineering; Measurement and Precision Engineering.** *Master*: **Automation and Control Engineering; Civil Engineering; Computer Science; Environmental Engineering; Industrial Engineering; Mechanical Engineering; Polymer and Plastics Technology.** *Doctorat*: **Automation and Control Engineering; Chemistry; Civil Engineering; Computer Science; Energy Engineering; Environmental Engineering; Mechanical Engineering; Polymer and Plastics Technology.**

Student Services: Academic Counselling, Canteen, Careers Guidance, Foreign Studies Centre, Language Laboratory, Social Counselling, Sports Facilities

Student Numbers *2013*: Total 900

EMNANTES SCHOOL OF ENGINEERING

ECOLE DES MINES DE NANTES (EMN)

BP 20722, La Chanterie 4, rue Alfred Kastler, 44307 Nantes, Cedex 03
Tel: +33(2) 51-85-81-00
Fax: +33(2) 51-85-81-99
EMail: concours@mines-nantes.fr
Website: http://www.mines-nantes.fr

Director: Anne Beauval (2012-)
Tel: +33(2) 51-85-81-10 EMail: anne.beauval@mines-nantes.fr

Secretary General: Serge Wattelier
EMail: serge.wattelier@mines-nantes.fr

Department

Automation and Industrial Engineering (Automation and Control Engineering; Industrial Engineering; Production Engineering; Robotics); **Computer Science** (Computer Science; Systems Analysis); **Energetics and Environment** (Energy Engineering; Environmental Engineering; Environmental Management); **Human and Social Sciences** (Development Studies; Industrial Design; Industrial Management; Social Sciences); **Subatomic Physics and Associated Technologies** (Nuclear Physics; Physics; Technology; Waste Management)

History: Founded 1990. A public 'Grande Ecole'.

Academic Year: September to July

Admission Requirements: Competitive entrance examination following 2 years higher education after secondary school certificate (baccalauréat) or equivalent

Fees: Engineer diploma (Master in Engineering), 800 per annum; master of science and technology 15 000 for the 2-year programme (Euro)

Main Language(s) of Instruction: French (Diplôle d'Ingénieur), English (Master of Science and Technology)

Accrediting Agency: Commission des Titres d'Ingénieur (CTI)

Degrees and Diplomas: *Diplôme d'Ingénieur*: **Automation and Control Engineering; Computer Engineering; Computer Science; Energy Engineering; Engineering; Environmental Engineering; Environmental Studies; Information Technology; Management; Nuclear Engineering; Transport Management.** *Master*: **Automation and Control Engineering; Computer Science; Energy Engineering; Engineering Management; Environmental Engineering; Industrial Engineering; Nuclear Engineering; Physics; Robotics; Social Sciences; Town Planning.** Master of Science and Technology in English

Student Services: Academic Counselling, Canteen, Careers Guidance, Facilities for disabled people, Health Services, Language Laboratory, Sports Facilities

Publications: Talents des Mines

ENGINEERING SCHOOL - EURECOM

ECOLE D'INGÉNIEURS - EURECOM (EURECOM)

Campus SophiaTech, 450 Route des Chappes, CS 50193, 06904 Biot Sophia Antipolis, Cedex
Tel: +33(4) 93-00-81-00
Fax: +33(4) 93-00-82-00
EMail: communication@eurecom.fr
Website: http://www.eurecom.fr/en

Director: Ulrich Finger
Tel: +33(4) 93-00-81-02 EMail: director@eurecom.fr

Secretary General: Catherine Betrancourt
Tel: +33(4) 93-00-81-05 EMail: seg@eurecom.fr

Programme

Engineering (Computer Engineering; Computer Networks; Engineering; Multimedia; Telecommunications Engineering)

Department

Mobile Communications (Telecommunications Engineering); **Multimedia Communications** (Multimedia); **Networking and Security** (Computer Engineering; Computer Networks)

History: Founded 1991.

Main Language(s) of Instruction: French

Accrediting Agency: Commission des Titres d'Ingénieur (CTI)

Degrees and Diplomas: *Diplôme d'Ingénieur*: **Computer Engineering; Telecommunications Engineering.** *Master*: **Computer Engineering; Information Technology; Transport and Communications.**

ENSM - SAINT ETIENNE

ECOLE NATIONALE SUPÉRIEURE DES MINES DE SAINT-ETIENNE (ENSM SAINT-ETIENNE)

158, cours Fauriel, 42023 Saint-Etienne, Cedex 02
Tel: +33(4) 77-42-01-23
Fax: +33(4) 77-42-00-00
EMail: inform@emse.fr
Website: http://www.mines-stetienne.fr

Directeur: Pascal Ray

International Relations: Michel Cournil
Tel: +33(4) 77-42-01-10 EMail: international@emse.fr

Programme
Electronical Engineering *(Georges Charpak Centre in Provence)* (Electronic Engineering; Microelectronics); **Engineering Sciences for Health** (Engineering); **Materials Science and Mechanical Engineering** (Materials Engineering; Mechanical Engineering)

School
Applied Microelectronics *(ISMEA)*; **Industrial Techniques** (Computer Science; Electronic Engineering; Industrial Engineering); **Microelectronics Engineering** (Microelectronics); **Software Engineering** (Software Engineering)

Institute
Henri Fayol (Computer Science; Environmental Engineering; Industrial Engineering)

Further Information: also campuse in Gardanne

History: Founded 1816. Acquired present status 1991.

Admission Requirements: Competitive entrance examination following 2 yrs further study after secondary school certificate (baccalauréat)

Fees: National : Civil Engineering course, Registration fees: 1850 per annum; Mastère spécialisé, 7000-7500 depending on course, International : Civil Engineering course, Registration fees: 3 850 per annum

Main Language(s) of Instruction: French

Degrees and Diplomas: *Diplôme d'Ingénieur*: **Civil Engineering; Computer Engineering; Electronic Engineering; Industrial Engineering; Nuclear Engineering.** *Mastère spécialisé*: **Building Technologies; Computer Engineering.** *Doctorat*: **Applied Mathematics; Computer Science; Earth Sciences; Engineering Management; Environmental Engineering; Industrial Engineering; Materials Engineering; Mechanical Engineering; Microelectronics.**

Student Services: Academic Counselling, Careers Guidance, Cultural Activities, Facilities for disabled people, Health Services, Language Laboratory, Social Counselling, Sports Facilities

GRADUATE ENGINEERING SCHOOL FOR INFORMATION AND COMMUNICATION TECHNOLOGIES - TELECOM PARIS TECH

TÉLÉCOM PARIS TECH

46, rue Barrault, 75634 Paris, Cedex 13
Tel: +33(1) 45-81-77-77
Fax: +33(1) 45-89-79-06
EMail: communication@telecom-paristech.fr
Website: http://www.telecom-paristech.fr

Director: Yves Poilane
Tel: +33(1) 45-81-73-99 EMail: yves.poilane@telecom-paristech.fr

International Relations: Catherine Vazza
Tel: +33(1) 45-81-81-49
EMail: catherine.vazza@telecom-paristech.fr

Programme
Engineering (Computer Engineering; Computer Networks; Economics; Electrical and Electronic Engineering; Electronic Engineering; Mathematics; Modern Languages; Physics; Social Sciences; Telecommunications Engineering)

History: Founded 1878. Acquired present status 2007.

Academic Year: September to July

Admission Requirements: Competitive entrance examination following 2-3 years further study after secondary school certificate (baccalauréat) or following first university qualification (Licence/ Master)

Fees: National : Diplôme d'Ingénieur, 2,300 per annum (Euro), International : Non-European union students: diplôme d'Ingénieur, 4,300 per annum (Euro)

Main Language(s) of Instruction: French or English (Sophia Antipolis)

Accrediting Agency: Commission des Titres d'Ingénieur (CTI)

Degrees and Diplomas: *Diplôme d'Ingénieur*: **Engineering.** *Mastère spécialisé*: **Computer Engineering; Computer Networks; Engineering Management; Software Engineering.** *Master*: **Computer Science; Information Technology; Telecommunications Engineering.** *Doctorat*: **Computer Networks; Computer Science; Economics; Electrical Engineering; Social Sciences; Telecommunications Engineering.**

Student Services: Academic Counselling, Canteen, Careers Guidance, Facilities for disabled people, Foreign Studies Centre, Language Laboratory, Social Counselling, Sports Facilities

MINES PARIS TECH GRADUATE SCHOOL

MINES PARIS TECH

60, boulevard Saint-Michel, 75272 Paris, Cedex 06
Tel: +33(1) 40-51-90-00
Fax: +33(1) 43-54-18-98
EMail: contact@mines-paristech.fr
Website: http://www.mines-paristech.fr

Director: Romain Soubeyran (2012-)
Tel: +33(1) 40-51-94-43
EMail: romain.soubeyran@mines-paristech.fr

Secretary General: Alain Girard
Tel: +33(1) 40-51-94-35 EMail: alain.girard@mines-paristech.fr

International Relations: Julien Bohdanowicz
Tel: +33(1) 40-51-91-46
EMail: julien.bohdanowicz@mines-paristech.fr

Programme
Economic Evaluation of Mining Projects *(CESPROMIN, Fontainebleau)*; **Environmental Engineering and Management** (Environmental Engineering; Environmental Management); **Environmental Management** (Environmental Management); **Gas Engineering and Management** (Engineering Management; Petroleum and Gas Engineering); **Geostatics** *(CSFG, Fontainebleau)*; **Industrial Management and Logistics Systems** (Production Engineering); **Information and Technology Systems Management** (Information Management; Systems Analysis); **Materials and Shaping** (Polymer and Plastics Technology); **Materials Behaviour and Structural Design** (Materials Engineering; Structural Architecture); **Multimedia Network Applications Engineering** (Computer Networks; Multimedia); **Numerical Mechanics** (Mechanical Engineering); **Opencast Mining Quarries** *(CESECO)* (Mining Engineering); **Production Engineering** (Production Engineering); **Public Administration of Mines** *(CESAM, Fontainebleau)* (Administration; Mining Engineering)

Department
Earth Sciences and Environment (Earth Sciences; Environmental Management; Geology; Geophysics); **Economics, Management and Society** (Economics; Management; Sociology); **Energy and Process Engineering** (Energy Engineering; Materials Engineering; Thermal Engineering); **Mathematics and Systems** (Applied Mathematics; Automation and Control Engineering; Computer Science; Mathematics; Robotics); **Mechanical and Material Engineering** (Materials Engineering; Mechanical Engineering); **Physical Sciences and Engineering** (Biotechnology; Energy Engineering; Materials Engineering; Mechanical Engineering; Physics)

Laboratory
Applied Mathematics *(Sophia Antipolis)* (Applied Mathematics); **Computational Biology** *(Fontainebleau)*; **Computer Science** *(Fontainebleau)* (Computer Science); **Energy and Processes** (Energy Engineering); **Geosciences** *(Fontainebleau)* (Geology; Geophysics; Mining Engineering); **Industrial Economics** (Industrial Management); **Materials Engineering** *(Evry)* (Materials Engineering); **Materials Forming** *(Sophia Antipolis)* (Materials Engineering); **Mathematical Morphology** *(Fontainebleau)* (Mathematics); **Robotics** (Automation and Control Engineering); **Scientific Management** (Management); **Sociology of Innovation** (Sociology); **Solids Mechanics** *(Palaiseau)* (Mechanics; Solid State Physics); **Systems and Control** *(Fontainebleau)* (Automation and Control Engineering)

History: Founded 1783, moved to its present location 1816, expanded to Fontainebleau and Evry 1969, and to Sophia Antipolis, near Nice, 1976.

Academic Year: September to June

Admission Requirements: Competitive entrance examination following 2-3 years further study after secondary school certificate (baccalauréat) or following first university qualification (maîtrise ès-science), Ecole Polytechnique alumni, or B.Sc level.

Main Language(s) of Instruction: French

Degrees and Diplomas: *Diplôme d'Ingénieur*; *Mastère spécialisé*; *Master*: **Engineering.** *Doctorat*

Student Services: Academic Counselling, Cultural Activities, Health Services

Publishing house: Presses de l'Ecole des Mines de Paris

TÉLÉCOM BRETAGNE

CS 83818, Technopôle de Brest Iroise, 29238 Brest, Cedex 03
Tel: +33(2) 29-00-11-11
Fax: +33(2) 29-00-10-00
Website: http://www.telecom-bretagne.eu

Director: Paul Friedel
Tel: +33(2) 29-00-11-00
EMail: directeur@telecom-bretagne.eu

Secretary General: Jean-Pierre Belleudy
Tel: +33(2) 29-00-12-00
EMail: jp.belleudy@telecom-bretagne.eu

International Relations: Anne Pierre-Duplexis, International Relations Manager
Tel: +33(2) 29-00-14-80
EMail: anne.pierre-duplessix@telecom-bretagne.eu

Department

Computer Engineering *(INFO)* (Computer Engineering; Computer Science); **Electronics** *(ELEC)* (Electronic Engineering); **Image and Data Processing** *(ITI)* (Computer Graphics; Data Processing); **Languages and International Culture** *(LCI)* (Cultural Studies; Linguistics; Modern Languages); **Logics in Uses, Social Science and Information Science** *(LUSSI)* (Artificial Intelligence; Arts and Humanities; Cognitive Sciences; Economics; Social Sciences); **Microwaves** *(MO)* (Microwaves); **Multimedia Networks and Systems** *(RSM)* (Computer Networks; Computer Science; Data Processing; Multimedia); **Optics** *(OPT)* (Optics); **Signal and Telecommunications Engineering** *(SC)* (Computer Engineering; Telecommunications Engineering)

Further Information: Also campuses in Rennes.

History: Founded 1977. Acquired present title 2008.

Academic Year: September to June

Admission Requirements: Competitive entrance examination following 2-3 years further study after secondary school certificate (baccalauréat) or following first university qualification in Science subjects (DEUG, DUT or BTS)

Fees: National : 2,300 per annum (Euro), International : Non-European Union students: 2,300-4,300 (Euro)

Main Language(s) of Instruction: French

Accrediting Agency: Commission des Titres d'Ingénieur (CTI)

Degrees and Diplomas: *Diplôme d'Ingénieur*: **Telecommunications Engineering.** *Mastère spécialisé*: **Computer Engineering; Marine Engineering; Mathematics.** *Master*: **Computer Networks; Telecommunications Engineering.** *Doctorat*: **Computer Science; Electronic Engineering; Information Technology; Microwaves; Modern Languages; Optics; Telecommunications Engineering.** alos MSc

Student Services: Academic Counselling, Canteen, Careers Guidance, Language Laboratory, Social Counselling, Sports Facilities

TÉLÉCOM LILLE

Cité scientifique , Rue Guglielmo Marconi, BP 20145, 59653 Villeneuve d'Ascq, Cedex
Tel: +33(3) 20-33-55-77
Fax: +33(3) 20-33-55-99
EMail: directeur@telecom-lille.fr
Website: http://www.telecom-lille.fr/en

Director: Narendra Jussien Tel: +33(3) 20-33-55-85

Secretary General: Brigitte Priem
Tel: +33(3) 20-33-55-85 EMail: brigitte.priem@telecom-lille.fr

International Relations: Dean Hipple, International Relations Manager
Tel: +33(3) 20-33-55-41 EMail: international@telecom-lille.fr

Programme

Engineering (Applied Physics; Communication Studies; Computer Engineering; Economics; Electronic Engineering; Management; Modern Languages; Physics)

History: Founded in 1990. Become Telecom Lille in 2013

Admission Requirements: Competitive entrance examination and secondary school certificate (baccalauréat) or 2 years further study after secondary school certificate.

Fees: 1,800-2,300 (Euro)

Main Language(s) of Instruction: French

Accrediting Agency: Commission des Titres d'Ingénieur (CTI); Conférence des Grandes Ecoles

Degrees and Diplomas: *Diplôme d'Ingénieur*: **Engineering.**

TELECOM SCHOOL OF MANAGEMENT

TÉLÉCOM ECOLE DE MANAGEMENT (IMT)

9 Rue Charles Fourier, 91000 Evry
Tel: +33(1) 60-76-40-40
EMail: communication@telecom-em.eu
Website: http://www.telecom-em.eu/

President: Denis Guibard (2014-)

Department

Foreign Languages and Humanities *(LSH)* (Arabic; Arts and Humanities; Chinese; English; French; German; Italian; Japanese; Modern Languages; Social Sciences; Spanish); **Information System** *(DSI)* (Computer Engineering; Information Management; Information Technology); **Law, Economics and Finance** *(DEFI)* (Accountancy; Business Administration; Economics; Finance; Law); **Marketing, Management and Strategy** *(MMS)* (Business Administration; E- Business/Commerce; Engineering Management; Information Technology; International Business; Management; Marketing)

History: Founded 1979.

Admission Requirements: Competitive entrance examination after secondary school certificate (Baccalauréat) or after following 2-3 years further study after secondary school certificate (baccalauréat)

Fees: Depends on the programme

Main Language(s) of Instruction: French, English

Accrediting Agency: Ministry of Economy and Finance; Conference des Grandes Ecoles; AACSB

Degrees and Diplomas: *Diplôme d'Etudes d'Ecole de Commerce et Gestion*; *Master*: **Business Administration.** *Doctorat*: **Accountancy; Business Administration; Economics; Finance; Human Resources; Information Sciences; Management; Marketing.** Also Bachelor

Student Services: Residential Facilities

TÉLÉCOM SUDPARIS

9 rue Charles Fourier, 91011 Evry, Cedex
Tel: +33(1) 60-76-40-40
Fax: +33(1) 60-76-43-37
EMail: infos@telecom-sudparis.eu
Website: http://www.telecom-sudparis.eu/

Director: Christophe Digne
Tel: +33160764204
EMail: christophe.digne@telecom-sudparis.eu

Secretary General: Maurice Daccord
Tel: +33(1) 60-76-42-43 EMail: maurice.daccord@tem-tsp.eu

International Relations: Roisin Donohoe
Tel: +33(1) 60-76-42-32
EMail: roisin.donohoe@telecom-sudparis.eu

Programme

Engineering (Computer Engineering; Economics; Electronic Engineering; Engineering; Information Technology; Marketing; Mathematics; Modern Languages; Multimedia; Physics; Social Sciences; Statistics; Telecommunications Engineering)

School
Continuing Education

Research Centre
Business Administration *(Telecom Ecole de Management)* (Business Administration; Economics; Human Resources; Law; Management; Marketing; Production Engineering)

Research Department
Advanced Research and Techniques for Multidimensional Imaging Systems *(ARTEMIS)* (Multimedia; Technology); **Computer Science** *(INF)* (Computer Science; Human Resources); **Electronics and Physics** *(EPH)* (Electronic Engineering; Optics; Physics); **Signal and Image Processing and Data processing** *(CITI)* (Computer Engineering; Electronic Engineering; Information Technology); **Software Networks** *(LOR)* (Computer Networks; Software Engineering); **Telecommunications Networks and Services** *(RST)* (Computer Networks; Telecommunications Engineering); **Wireless networks and multimedia services** *(RS2M)* (Telecommunications Engineering)

History: Founded 1979. Became Institut national des Télécommunications (INT) 1996. Acquired present title and status 2010.

Admission Requirements: Competitive entrance examination following 2 years further study after secondary school certificate (baccalauréat) or equivalent

Fees: National : Engineer diploma course 2,300 per annum (Euro), International : Non-European union students: 2,300-4,300 per annum (Euro)

Main Language(s) of Instruction: French, English

Accrediting Agency: Commission des Titres de d'Ingénieur (C.T.I.)

Degrees and Diplomas: *Diplôme d'Etudes d'Ecole de Commerce et Gestion*: **Business Administration; Management.** *Diplôme d'Ingénieur*: **Engineering; Engineering Management; Statistics.** *Mastère spécialisé*: **Computer Engineering; Computer Networks; Management; Telecommunications Engineering.** *Master*: **Computer Science; Electronic Engineering; Telecommunications Engineering.** also Master of Science

Student Services: Academic Counselling, Canteen, Careers Guidance, Cultural Activities, Facilities for disabled people, Foreign Studies Centre, Health Services, Language Laboratory, Nursery Care, Social Counselling, Sports Facilities

INSTITUTE OF EARTH PHYSICS OF PARIS

Institut de Physique du Globe de Paris

IPGP - 1, rue Jussieu, 75238 Paris, Cedex 05
Tel: +33(1) 83-95-74-00
EMail: accueil@ipgp.fr
Website: http://www.ipgp.fr

Directeur: Claude Jaupart (2010-)
Tel: +33(1) 83-95-74-09 EMail: jaupart@ipgp.fr

Directrice générale des Services: Lydia Zerbib
EMail: zerbib@ipgp.fr

International Relations: Sylvie Larousse
Tel: +33(1) 83-95-74-40 EMail: larousse@ipgp.fr

Programme
Physics of the Globe (Astronomy and Space Science; Biology; Earth Sciences; Environmental Studies; Geochemistry; Physics; Seismology)

History: Founded 1921; became a 'Grand Etablissement' 1991.

Admission Requirements: Licence: Secondary school certificate (Baccalauréat); Master: University degree

Main Language(s) of Instruction: French

Accrediting Agency: Centre national de la Recherche scientifique (CNRS)

Degrees and Diplomas: *Licence*; *Master*: **Astronomy and Space Science; Earth Sciences; Environmental Studies.** *Doctorat*: **Astronomy and Space Science; Earth Sciences; Environmental Studies.**

Publications: Rapport d'Activité scientifique

Last Updated: 26/03/15

INSTITUTE OF MECHANICAL ENGINEERING OF PARIS

Institut supérieur de Mécanique de Paris (SUPMECA)

3, rue Fernand Hainaut, 93407 Saint-Ouen, Cedex
Tel: +33(1) 49-45-29-00
Fax: +33(1) 49-45-29-91
EMail: informations@supmeca.fr
Website: http://www.supmeca.fr

Director: Alain Rivière
Tel: +33(1) 49-45-29-99 EMail: alain.riviere@supmeca.fr

International Relations: Ioana Herman, Manager of international relationships
Tel: +33(1) 49-45-25-39 EMail: ioana.herman@supmeca.fr

Division
Engineering (Automation and Control Engineering; Industrial Engineering; Materials Engineering; Production Engineering)

Department
Automated Systems and Industrial Processes (Automation and Control Engineering); **Materials Engineering and Processes** (Materials Engineering); **Mechatronics** *(St Ouen; Toulon)* (Mechanical Engineering; Systems Analysis)

Further Information: Branch in Toulon

History: Founded 1956. The ISMCM (Institut Supérieur des Matériaux et de la Construction Mécanique) was created 1948 jointly by the Federation of Mechanical Industries and by the Ministry of Education : it is an autonomous State Institution of Training and Research in Mechanical Engineering, placed under the Ministry of Education. Since 1956 in Paris and 1994 in Toulon, the Institute has launched the CESTI (Centre d'Etudes supérieures des Techniques Industrielles) Engineering curriculum. In 2004, ISMCM-CESTI changed its name to Supméca.

Academic Year: September to July

Admission Requirements: French students : Secondary school certificate (baccalauréat) and "Classes préparatoires" (intensive selective scientific curriculum preparing for the national competitive exam to Enginnering Schools), or selective entrance exam for holders of a French university degree. For foreign students : Bachelor's degree and proficiency in French and selection of the applicants.

Fees: Minimum, 606 per annum (Euro)

Main Language(s) of Instruction: French

Accrediting Agency: Commission des Titres d'Ingénieurs (CTI)

Degrees and Diplomas: *Diplôme d'Ingénieur*: **Mechanical Engineering.** *Master*

Student Services: Canteen, Residential Facilities, Sports Facilities

Last Updated: 27/03/15

EISTI - CERGY-PONTOISE

ECOLE INTERNATIONALE DES SCIENCES DU TRAITEMENT DE L'INFORMATION (EISTI)

Avenue du Parc, 95011 Cergy-Pontoise, Cedex
Tel: +33(1) 34-25-10-10
Fax: +33(1) 34-25-10-00
EMail: administration@eisti.fr
Website: http://www.eisti.fr

Director: Nesim Fintz (1983-) EMail: fintz@eisti.fr

International Relations: Marie-Josée Lamerre
Tel: +33(1) 34-25-10-03 EMail: mjl@eisti.eu

Programme
Engineering (Computer Science; Information Sciences; Mathematics)

Further Information: Also campus in Pau.

History: Founded 1983.

Academic Year: September to June

Admission Requirements: Secondary school Certificate (Baccalauréat)

Fees: 4580-7060 per annum (Euro)

Main Language(s) of Instruction: French

Degrees and Diplomas: *Diplôme d'Ingénieur*: **Computer Science; Mathematics.** *Mastère spécialisé*: **Computer Science; Economics; Environmental Management; Management; Safety Engineering.** *Master*: **Business and Commerce; Finance.**

Student Services: Academic Counselling, Canteen, Careers Guidance, Facilities for disabled people, Social Counselling, Sports Facilities

GRADUATE SCHOOL OF FOUNDRY AND FORGE

ECOLE SUPÉRIEURE DE FONDERIE ET DE FORGE (ESFF)

44 avenue de la Division Leclerc, 92310 Sèvres
Tel: +33(1) 55-64-04-40
Fax: +33(1) 55-64-04-45
EMail: contact@esff.fr
Website: http://www.esff.fr/

Director: Pierre-Yves Brazier

Programme

Metallurgical Engineering (Metallurgical Engineering)

History: Founded in 1924. Become 'Ecole Supérieure de Fonderie et de Forge' in 2005

Admission Requirements: Competitive entrance examination following 2 years further study after secondary school certificate (baccalauréat)

Fees: Depends on the programme

Main Language(s) of Instruction: French

Accrediting Agency: Ministry of Higher Education and Research; Commission des titres d'ingénieur (CTI)

Degrees and Diplomas: *Diplôme d'Ingénieur*: **Metallurgical Engineering.**

INSTITUTE OF POLITICAL STUDIES AIX-EN-PROVENCE - 'SCIENCES PO AIX'

Institut d'Etudes politiques d'Aix-en-Provence - 'Sciences Po Aix'

25 rue Gaston de Saporta, 13625 Aix-en-Provence, Cedex 1
Tel: +33(4) 42-17-01-60
Fax: +33(4) 42-96-36-99
EMail: sciencespo.aix@sciencespo-aix.fr
Website: http://www.sciencespo-aix.fr

Head of Administration: Patricia Rigaud
Tel: +33(4) 42-17-01-98 EMail: patricia.rigaud@sciencespo-aix.fr

International Relations: Guy Scoffoni, Head of International Relations EMail: guy.scoffoni@sciencespo-aix.fr

Programme

Political Science (Economic History; History; International Relations; International Studies; Law; Political Sciences; Public Administration)

Centre

Public administration *(Centre de Préparation à l'Administration Générale (CPAG))* (Administration; Public Administration)

History: Founded 1956.

Admission Requirements: Competitive entrance examination, secondary school certificate (Baccalauréat).

Main Language(s) of Instruction: French

Degrees and Diplomas: *Licence*: **Public Administration.** *Master*: **Political Sciences; Public Administration.**

Last Updated: 30/03/15

INSTITUTE OF POLITICAL STUDIES BORDEAUX -'SCIENCES PO BORDEAUX'

Institut d'Etudes politiques de Bordeaux - 'Sciences Po Bordeaux'

11 Allée ausone, Domaine Universitaire, 33607 Pessac, Cedex
Tel: +33(5) 56-84-42-52
Fax: +33(5) 56-84-44-00
EMail: j.petaux@sciencespobordeaux.fr
Website: http://www.sciencespobordeaux.fr

Directeur: Vincent Hoffmann-Martinot
EMail: l.pinchault@sciencespobordeaux.fr

Secretary General: Didier Chabault
EMail: d.chabault@sciencespobordeaux.fr

International Relations: Ludovic Renard, Head of Interanational Relations EMail: l.renard@sciencespobordeaux.fr

Programme

Political Science (Administration; Economics; Law; Management; Political Sciences)

History: Founded 1948.

Academic Year: September to April (September-December; January-April)

Admission Requirements: Secondary school certificate (Baccalauréat) or equivalent, entrance examination.

Main Language(s) of Instruction: French

Degrees and Diplomas: *Master*: **Political Sciences.** *Doctorat*: **Political Sciences; Public Health; Sociology.**

Last Updated: 30/03/15

INSTITUTE OF POLITICAL STUDIES GRENOBLE -'SCIENCES PO GRENOBLE'

Institut d'Etudes politiques de Grenoble - 'Sciences Po Grenoble'

1030 avenue centrale, Domaine Universitaire,
38400 Saint-Martin-d'Hères
Tel: +33(4) 76-82-60-00
Fax: +33(4) 76-82-60-70
Website: http://www.sciencespo-grenoble.fr/

Directeur: Jean-Charles Froment (2012-)

International Relations: Jean Marcou
EMail: jean.marcou@sciencespo-grenoble.fr

Programme

Economics and Finance (Economics; Finance; Management); **Political Sciences** (European Studies; History; International Relations; International Studies; Law; Political Sciences; Public Administration)

Centre

Public Administration *(CPAG)* (Administration; Public Administration)

History: Founded 1948.

Admission Requirements: Secondary school certificate (Baccalauréat) or equivalent, entrance examination.

Main Language(s) of Instruction: French

Degrees and Diplomas: *Licence*; *Master*: **Administration; Comparative Politics; Government; International Studies; Political Sciences; Public Administration; Public Health; Social Policy; Tourism.** Bachelor, Executive Master; Certificat d'études politiques

Student Numbers *2013*: Total 1,700

Last Updated: 30/03/15

INSTITUTE OF POLITICAL STUDIES LILLE - 'SCIENCES PO LILLE'

Institut d'Etudes politiques de Lille - 'Sciences Po Lille'

84 rue de Trévise, 59000 Lille
Tel: +33(3) 20-90-48-40
Fax: +33(3) 20-90-48-60
EMail: secretariat.direction@sciencespo-lille.eu
Website: http://iep.univ-lille2.fr/

Directeur: Pierre Mathiot (2007-)
Tel: +33(3) 20-90-48-63 EMail: directeur@sciencespo-lille.eu

Head of Administration: Frédérique Madeuf
Tel: +33(3) 20-90-48-63
EMail: frederique.madeuf@sciencespo-lille.eu

International Relations: Patrick Mardellat, Head of International Relations
Tel: +33(3) 59-57-64-15
EMail: patrick.mardellat@sciencespo-lille.eu

Programme
Political Science (Administration; International Studies; Law; Political Sciences)

History: Founded 1948.

Academic Year: September to June

Admission Requirements: Secondary school certificate (Baccalauréat) or equivalent, entrance examination.

Main Language(s) of Instruction: French

Degrees and Diplomas: *Master*: **Administration; Political Sciences; Public Administration.**
Last Updated: 30/03/15

INSTITUTE OF POLITICAL STUDIES LYON - 'SCIENCES PO LYON'

Institut d'Etudes politiques de Lyon - 'Sciences Po Lyon'

14 avenue Berthelot, 69365 Lyon, Cedex 07
Tel: +33(4) 37-28-38-00
Fax: +33(4) 37-28-38-01
EMail: info@sciencespo-lyon.fr
Website: http://www.sciencespo-lyon.fr/

Director: Vincent Michelot (2014-)
Tel: +33(4) 37-28-38-20
EMail: vincent.michelot@sciencespo-lyon.fr
Secretary General: Valérie Misery
Tel: +33(4) 37-28-38-22 EMail: valerie.misery@sciencespo-lyon.fr
International Relations: Thierry Fortin, Head of International Relations
Tel: +33(4) 37-28-38-03 EMail: thierry.fortin@sciencespo-lyon.fr

Programme
Political Science (Administration; International Studies; Law; Political Sciences); **Public Administration** (Public Administration)

Centre
Public Administration *(CPAG)* (Administration; Public Administration)

History: Founded 1948.

Academic Year: September to June

Admission Requirements: Secondary school certificate (Baccalauréat), entrance examination.

Main Language(s) of Instruction: French

Degrees and Diplomas: *Licence*; *Master*: **Asian Studies; Political Sciences.** *Doctorat*: **Political Sciences.**
Last Updated: 30/03/15

INSTITUTE OF POLITICAL STUDIES PARIS- 'SCIENCES PO'

Institut d'Etudes politiques de Paris - 'Sciences Po' (IEP PARIS)

27, rue Saint-Guillaume, 75337 Paris, Cedex 07
Tel: +33(1) 45-49-50-50
Fax: +33(1) 42-22-31-26
EMail: admission@sciences-po.fr
Website: http://www.sciences-po.fr

President: Frédéric Mion (2013-)

International Relations: Francis Vérillaud, Director of International Affairs Division
Tel: +33(1) 45-49-50-48 EMail: info@international.sciences-po.fr; nadia.nazet@sciences-po.fr

Division
Lifelong Education (Business and Commerce; Communication Studies; Finance; Human Resources; Law; Management)

Programme
Masters Programme (Administrative Law; Commercial Law; Communication Studies; Finance; Human Resources; International Business; International Economics; International Studies; Marketing; Public Administration; Regional Planning; Urban Studies)

Institute
Journalism (Journalism)

Section
Business and Finance (Business and Commerce; Economics; Finance); **Communication and Human Resources** (Communication Studies; Human Resources); **International Affairs** (European Studies; International Relations; International Studies; Political Sciences); **Public Administration** (Public Administration); **Sociology** (History; Sociology)

Research Centre
20th Century European History; **Administrative Research** (Administration); **Economic Activity** (Economics); **French Economic Conditions** (Economics); **French Politics** (Political Sciences); **Inter-regional Politics** (Political Sciences); **International Studies** (International Studies); **Sociological Change** (Sociology)

Further Information: Also branches in Aix, Lille, Lyon, Rennes, Strasbourg, Grenoble, Toulouse, Bordeaux and Menton. Special programmes for foreign students: one-year undergraduate programme; one year graduate programme (CIEP), postgraduate research project programme; European Union Summer Programme. A variety of Study Abroad programmes for 200 students

History: Founded 1871 as Ecole libre des Sciences politiques; became institute attached to the Université de Paris 1945, independent autonomous institution 1969 and 'Grand Etablissement' 1984. Under the supervision of and financially supported by the Fondation nationale des Sciences politiques.

Admission Requirements: Entrance by competition following 1 undergraduate programmes study after secondary school certificate (baccalauréat) or two university years (foreigners). Direct entrance to graduate programme (master degree) by competition following appropriate university degree

Main Language(s) of Instruction: French

Degrees and Diplomas: *Master*: **Business Administration; Economics; European Studies; Human Resources; Urban Studies.** *Doctorat*: **Economics; History; Law; Political Sciences; Sociology.** Certificat for foreign Students, Masters recherche

Student Services: Academic Counselling, Careers Guidance, Health Services, Library, Sports Facilities

Publishing house: Presses de Sciences Po
Last Updated: 26/03/15

INSTITUTE OF POLITICAL STUDIES RENNES - 'SCIENCES PO RENNES'

Institut d'Etudes politiques de Rennes - 'Sciences Po Rennes'

104 boulevard de la Duchesse Anne, 35700 Rennes
Tel: +33(2) 99-84-39-39
Fax: +33(2) 99-84-39-00
Website: http://www.sciencespo-rennes.fr/

Directeur: Patrick Le Floch EMail: +33(2) 99-84-39-11
International Relations: Rebecca Pinheiro-Croisel, Head of International Relations Tel: +33(2) 99-84-39-24

Programme
Political Science (Administration; Communication Studies; Economics; International Studies; Law; Media Studies; Political Sciences)

Centre
Public Administration *(Centre de prépartation à l'ENA)* (Administration)

History: Founded 1991.

Academic Year: September to July

Admission Requirements: Secondary school certificate (Baccalauréat), entrance examination.

Main Language(s) of Instruction: French

Degrees and Diplomas: *Master*: **Administration; International Studies; Management; Mass Communication; Natural Resources; Political Sciences.**
Last Updated: 30/03/15

INSTITUTE OF POLITICAL STUDIES TOULOUSE -'SCIENCES PO TOULOUSE'

Institut d'Etudes politiques de Toulouse - 'Sciences Po Toulouse'
CS 88526, 2 ter, rue des Puits-creusés, 31685 Toulouse, Cedex 6
Tel: +33(5) 61-11-02-60
Fax: +33(5) 61-22-94-80
EMail: contact@sciencespo-toulouse.fr
Website: http://www.sciencespo-toulouse.fr/

Directeur: Philippe Raimbault (2010-2015)
EMail: direction@sciencespo-toulouse.fr

Head of Administration: Julien Saint Laurent
Tel: +33(5) 61-11-17-91 EMail: dgs@sciencespo-toulouse.fr

International Relations: Nadia El Gharbi, International Relations Manager
Tel: +33(5) 61-11-17-97
EMail: international@sciencespo-toulouse.fr

Programme

Political Science (Administration; Economics; International Studies; Law; Political Sciences)

History: Founded 1948.

Admission Requirements: Secondary school certificate (Baccalauréat), entrance examination.

Main Language(s) of Instruction: French

Degrees and Diplomas: *Master*: **International Relations; Political Sciences.**

Student Numbers *2014*: Total 1,709
Last Updated: 30/03/15

ISMANS - LE MANS

Institut supérieur des Matériaux et Mécaniques avancées du Mans (ISMANS)
44, avenue Frédéric Auguste Bartholdi, 72000 Le Mans
Tel: +33(2) 43-21-40-00
Fax: +33(2) 43-21-40-39
EMail: ismans@ismans.fr
Website: http://www.ismans.fr

Director: André Quinquis (2014-) EMail: ismans@ismans.fr

Division

Engineering (Engineering; Engineering Management; Materials Engineering; Mechanical Engineering); **Management** (Business Administration; Economics; Management)

History: One of the youngest 'Grandes Ecoles', it is modelled after Quebec Universities, being created in 1987 by the Chamber of Commerce and Industry of Le Mans and Sarthe..

Admission Requirements: Entrance exam with 2 years undergraduate studies or preparatory classes.

Fees: 4,800 per annum (Euro)

Main Language(s) of Instruction: French, English

Accrediting Agency: Ministry of Economy, Finance and Industry, Commission des Titres d'Ingénieur (CTI), Conference des Grandes Ecole (CGE)

Degrees and Diplomas: *Diplôme d'Ingénieur*: **Engineering; Engineering Management; Materials Engineering; Mechanical Engineering.** *Mastère spécialisé*: **Fire Science.** Masters professional in Project Management;

Academic Staff *2012*: Total 23
Student Numbers *2012*: Total 200
Last Updated: 09/04/15

JEAN-FRANÇOIS CHAMPOLLION UNIVERSITY CENTRE FOR STUDY AND RESEARCH - ALBI

Centre universitaire de Formation et de Recherche Jean-François Champollion
Place de Verdun, 81012 Albi
Tel: +33(5) 63-48-17-17
Fax: +33(5) 63-48-17-19
EMail: contact.albi@univ-jfc.fr
Website: http://www.univ-jfc.fr

Director: Brigitte Pradin (2014-)
Tel: +33(5) 63-48-16-99 EMail: odile.deligne@univ-jfc.fr

Director of Services: Pascal Guerrin
Tel: +33(5) 63-48-16-99 EMail: pascal.guerrin@univ-jfc.fr

International Relations: Patricia Dumont
Tel: +33(5) 63-48-64-19 EMail: patricia.dumont@univ-jfc.fr

School

Engineering *(Castres campus)* (Engineering; Information Technology)

Department

Human and Social Sciences (Geography; History; Psychology; Rural Planning; Sociology; Town Planning); **Languages and Literature** *(Rodez campus)* (English; Literature; Modern Languages; Spanish); **Law and Social Sciences** *(Rodez campus)* (Administration; Economics; Law); **Physical Education and Sports** *(Rodez campus)* (Physical Education; Sports); **Science, Technology and Health** (Biology; Chemical Engineering; Chemistry; Computer Engineering; Mathematics; Physics)

Further Information: Also campuses in Castres, Figeac and Rodez

History: Founded 2002.

Academic Year: September to June (September-January; January-June)

Admission Requirements: secondary school certificate (baccalauréat) or equivalent

Main Language(s) of Instruction: French

Degrees and Diplomas: *Licence*: **Administration; Automation and Control Engineering; Biological and Life Sciences; Chemistry; Economics; Electrical and Electronic Engineering; English; Geography; History; Law; Literature; Mathematics and Computer Science; Modern Languages; Physical Education; Physics; Private Law; Psychology; Sociology; Spanish; Sports; Sports Management; Town Planning.** *Licence professionnelle*: **Agriculture; Animal Husbandry; Business Administration; Business and Commerce; Electrical and Electronic Equipment and Maintenance; Heritage Preservation; Industrial Maintenance; Management; Sports; Sports Management; Water Science.** *Diplôme d'Ingénieur*: **Computer Engineering.** *Master*: **Criminal Law; Ecology; European Studies; Geography; International Studies; Law; Management; Notary Studies; Private Law; Psychology; Public Law; Town Planning.**

Student Services: Canteen, Cultural Activities, Health Services, Sports Facilities

Publishing house: Presses Univesitaire

Student Numbers *2014*: Total 3,700
Last Updated: 30/03/15

JEAN MONNET UNIVERSITY - SAINT-ETIENNE

Université Jean Monnet Saint-Etienne (UJM)
Maison de l'Université, 10 rue Tréfilerie - CS 82301, 42023 Saint-Etienne, Cedex 02
Tel: +33(4) 77-42-17-00
Fax: +33(4) 77-42-17-99
EMail: secgen@univ-st-etienne.fr
Website: http://www.univ-st-etienne.fr

President: Khaled Bouabdalla (2007-)
Tel: +33(4) 77-42-17-04 EMail: president@univ-st-etienne.fr

Head of Administration: Paul Pouilhe
Tel: +33(4) 69-66-11-19 EMail: paul.pouilhe@univ-st-etienne.fr

International Relations: Serge Riffard
Tel: +33(4) 77-42-17-53 EMail: serge.riffard@univ-st-etienne.fr

Faculty

Arts, Letters and Languages *(ALL)* (Arts and Humanities; Modern Languages; Philology); **Human and Social Sciences** *(SHS)* (Arts and Humanities; Geography; History; Social Sciences; Sociology); **Law** (History of Law; Law; Political Sciences; Private Law; Public Law); **Medicine** (Medicine; Sports); **Science and Technology** (Biology; Chemistry; Computer Science; Geology; Mathematics; Natural Sciences; Physics; Technology)

Department

Physical Education and Sports *(STAPS)* (Physical Education; Sports)

Institute
Technology *(IUT Roanne)* (Industrial Management; Marketing; Technology); **Technology** *(IUT de Saint-Etienne)* (Biology; Computer Engineering; Electrical Engineering; Industrial Management; Marketing; Measurement and Precision Engineering; Mechanical Engineering; Production Engineering; Public Administration; Technology)

Higher Institute
Advanced Techniques - Engineering *(ISTASE - Telecom Saint Etienne)* (Electronic Engineering; Engineering; Optical Technology; Telecommunications Engineering); **Economics, Business Administration, Management** *(IAE)* (Business Administration; Economics; Management; Public Administration)

Centre
Language and Civilization *(CILEC, for foreign students)* (French); **Lifelong Education** *(SUFC)* (Continuing Education)

Graduate School
Interdisciplinary Studies *(ED SE in cooperation with ENSM and ENI of St. Etienne)* (Archaeology; Architecture and Planning; Arts and Humanities; Economics; Educational Sciences; Engineering; Geography; Health Sciences; Information Sciences; Law; Linguistics; Literature; Management; Modern Languages; Psychology; Social Sciences)

Further Information: Centre Universitaire Roannais (CUR-facultés) is a decentralised centre offering Licence, Masters and professional courses.

History: Founded 1970 under the 1968 law reforming higher education and incorporating Colleges previously attached to the former Université de Lyon. The University is a State institution enjoying academic and financial autonomy, operating under the jurisdiction of the Minister of Education and financed by the State.

Academic Year: September to June (September-January; February-June) and Summer University

Admission Requirements: Secondary school certificate (baccalauréat) or foreign equivalent, or special entrance examination

Fees: 220 per annum (Euro)

Main Language(s) of Instruction: French

Accrediting Agency: Ministère de l'Education/Conseil national d'Evaluation (CNE)

Degrees and Diplomas: *Capacité en Droit*; *Diplôme d'Accès aux Etudes universitaires*; *Diplôme universitaire de Technologie*: **Business Administration; Maintenance Technology.** *Licence*: **Applied Mathematics; Arts and Humanities; Biological and Life Sciences; Biology; Computer Science; Earth Sciences; Economics; Environmental Studies; Literature; Management; Mathematics; Mechanics; Medicine; Modern Languages; Physical Chemistry; Physical Engineering; Physics; Social Sciences; Technology.** *Licence professionnelle*: **Administration; Computer Education; Economics; Law; Management; Natural Sciences; Social Sciences; Social Work; Technology; Town Planning.** *Diplôme d'Etat*: **Medicine.** *Diplôme d'Ingénieur*: **Electronic Engineering; Optical Technology; Telecommunications Engineering.** *Master*: **Applied Mathematics; Architecture and Planning; Arts and Humanities; Banking; Biological and Life Sciences; Classical Languages; Computer Engineering; Ecology; Economics; English Studies; Finance; Fine Arts; German; Graphic Arts; Industrial Engineering; Information Sciences; International Business; Italian; Law; Literature; Management; Mechanical Engineering; Medicine; Music; Musicology; Optics; Physical Education; Social Policy; Social Sciences; Spanish; Sports; Sports Medicine; Teacher Training.** *Doctorat*: **Ancient Civilizations; Ancient Languages; Applied Mathematics; Architecture and Planning; Biological and Life Sciences; Biology; Chemistry; Classical Languages; Comparative Literature; Contemporary History; Design; Earth Sciences; Economics; Educational Sciences; Electronic Engineering; English Studies; Environmental Engineering; Fine Arts; Geography; German; History; Industrial Engineering; Italian; Law; Literature; Management; Materials Engineering; Mathematics and Computer Science; Mechanical Engineering; Medicine; Medieval Studies; Modern History; Modern Languages; Music; Musicology; Optics; Philosophy; Public Health; Sociology; Spanish.** *Certificat de Spécialité*: **Medicine.** *Habilitation à Diriger les Recherches*. Masters recherche, Masters professionnel, Preparation for CAPES and Agrégation exams

Student Services: Academic Counselling, Canteen, Careers Guidance, Cultural Activities, Facilities for disabled people, Foreign Studies Centre, Health Services, Library, Residential Facilities, Social Counselling, Sports Facilities

Publishing house: Presses Universitaires de Saint Etienne

Academic Staff *2013*	**TOTAL**
FULL-TIME	**1,500**
Student Numbers *2013*	
All (Foreign included)	**17,000**
FOREIGN ONLY	**2500**

Last Updated: 12/03/15

LE HAVRE-ROUEN SCHOOL OF ART AND DESIGN

Ecole supérieure d'Art et Design Le Havre-Rouen (ESADHAR)

65 rue Demidoff, 76600 Le Havre
Tel: +33(2) 35-53-30-31
Fax: +33(2) 35-24-04-38
EMail: esadhar@esadhar.fr
Website: http://www.esadhar.fr

Director: Thierry Heynen

Department
Art (Fine Arts); **Design** (Design; Graphic Design)

Further Information: also site in: Rouen

History: Founded 1800. Acquired present status and title following merger of the Ecole Régionale des Beaux-Arts de Rouen and the Ecole Supérieure d'Art du Havre.

Admission Requirements: Baccalauréat or equivalent secondary school exam. Entrance exam with a selection jury.

Main Language(s) of Instruction: French

Accrediting Agency: Ministry of Culture and Communication

Degrees and Diplomas: *Master*: **Design; Fine Arts; Literature.** Diplôme national d'arts plastiques (DNAP) 3 yrs; Diplôme national supérieur d'expression plastique (DNSEP) a further 2 yrs

Last Updated: 07/04/15

LES ATELIERS-PARIS DESIGN INSTITUTE

Ecole nationale supérieure de Création industrielle (ENSCI)

48, rue Saint-Sabin, 75011 Paris
Tel: +33(1) 49-23-12-12
EMail: davis@ensci.com
Website: http://www.ensci.com

Director: Bernard Kahane
Tel: +33(1) 49-23-12-01 EMail: directeur@ensci.com

Secretary General: Véronique Delahais
Tel: +33(1) 49-23-12-06 EMail: veronique.delahais@ensci.com

International Relations: Liz Davis
Tel: +33(1) 49-23-12-30 EMail: liz.davis@ensci.com

Programme
Industrial Design (Industrial Design); **New Media** (Media Studies); **Textile Design** (Textile Design)

History: Founded in 1982, ENSCI is the first French public institute specialising in advanced studies in design. In 1985 ENSCI extended its activities to include the ANAT, National Textile Art Studio.

Admission Requirements: Entrance examination

Main Language(s) of Instruction: French

Degrees and Diplomas: *Mastère spécialisé*: **Design; Technology.** *Master*: **Industrial Design.** 3-year Diploma in Textile Design

Last Updated: 12/03/15

LILLE 1 UNIVERSITY

Université des Sciences et Technologies de Lille (Lille I)

Cité scientifique, 59655 Villeneuve d'Ascq, Cedex
Tel: +33(3) 20-43-43-43
Fax: +33(3) 20-43-49-95
EMail: communication@univ-lille1.fr
Website: http://www.univ-lille1.fr

President: Philippe Rollet (2007-)
Tel: +33 (0)3 20 43 43 01
EMail: president@univ-lille1.fr; cabinet-president@univ-lille1.fr

Head of Administration: Patrice Serniclay
Tel: +33(0)3 20-33-61-45 EMail: dgs@univ-lille1.fr

International Relations: François-Olivier Seys, Vice-President in charge of International Relations
Tel: + 33(3) 20-43-66-51 EMail: international@univ-lille1.fr

Unit

Biology (Biochemistry; Biology; Cell Biology; Microbiology; Physiology); **Chemistry** (Chemistry); **Computer Science, Electronics and Automation** *(IEEA)* (Automation and Control Engineering; Computer Science; Electronic Engineering); **Earth Sciences** (Earth Sciences; Geology; Paleontology; Soil Science; Water Science); **Economics and Social Sciences** *(Groups two institutions: Economics and Management Institute and Sociology and Anthropology Institute)* (Anthropology; Banking; Business Administration; E-Business/Commerce; Economics; Ethnology; Finance; Insurance; Public Administration; Social Sciences; Sociology); **Geography and Regional Planning** (Geography; Regional Planning); **Mathematics** (Applied Mathematics); **Physics** (Physics)

School

Engineering *(Ecole Polytechnique Universitaire de Lille)* (Civil Engineering; Computer Engineering; Engineering; Food Technology; Materials Engineering; Mechanical Engineering; Microelectronics; Production Engineering; Statistics; Water Management)

Department

Educational Sciences (Educational Sciences); **Marine and Regional Biology** *(Wimereux)* (Coastal Studies; Marine Biology; Marine Science and Oceanography)

Institute

Business Administration *(IAE)* (Business Administration; Business and Commerce; Management; Marketing); **Technology** *(IUT 'A')* (Bioengineering; Business Administration; Chemistry; Computer Science; Electrical Engineering; Mechanical Engineering; Production Engineering; Technology); **Telecommunications Engineering** *(TELECOM Lille I)* (Telecommunications Engineering)

Centre

Educational Sciences *(CUEEP)* (Adult Education; Educational Sciences)

Graduate School

Biomedicine *(In cooperation with University Lille II)* (Biomedicine; Genetics; Neurosciences); **Economics and Social Sciences** (Economics; Social Sciences); **Matter, Laser and Environment** (Biochemistry; Ecology; Environmental Engineering; Environmental Studies; Microbiology); **Sciences for Engineers** *(In cooperation with Universities of Artois, Lille III, Littoral and Valenciennes)* (Automation and Control Engineering; Business Computing; Civil Engineering; Electrical and Electronic Engineering; Mathematics; Mechanical Engineering)

History: Founded 1970 under the 1968 law reforming higher education as one of three Universities replacing the former Université de Lille - founded 1560 at Douai and authorized by Papal Bull. The University was suppressed by the Revolution and replaced by Faculties in Lille and Douai, the latter being subsequently transferred to Lille in 1887. Reconstituted as University 1896. A State institution enjoying academic and financial autonomy, operating under the jurisdiction of the Ministry of Education and financed by the State.

Academic Year: October to June (October-February; February-June)

Admission Requirements: Secondary school certificate (baccalauréat) or recognized foreign equivalent, or special entrance examination

Main Language(s) of Instruction: French

Degrees and Diplomas: *Diplôme universitaire de Technologie*; *Licence*: **Applied Mathematics; Automation and Control Engineering; Biological and Life Sciences; Chemistry; Civil Engineering; Earth Sciences; Economics; Educational Sciences; Electrical and Electronic Engineering; Geography; Management; Mathematics and Computer Science; Mechanical Engineering; Physics; Sociology; Technology.** *Licence professionnelle*: **Banking; Business and Commerce; Human Resources; Industrial Engineering; Insurance; Management; Mass Communication; Natural Sciences; Social Work; Technology; Telecommunications Engineering.** *Diplôme d'Ingénieur*: **Engineering.** *Master*: **Applied Mathematics; Automation and Control Engineering; Biology; Biotechnology; Chemistry; Civil Engineering; Earth Sciences; Ecology; Economics; Educational Sciences; Electrical Engineering; Environmental Studies; Ethnology; Industrial Engineering; Management; Marketing; Mathematics and Computer Science; Mechanical Engineering; Nanotechnology; Natural Sciences; Nutrition; Physics; Sociology; Telecommunications Engineering; Town Planning.** *Doctorat*: **Biology; Chemistry; Earth Sciences; Engineering; Environmental Studies; Health Sciences; Physics.** Also Certificates and Diplomas, Masters recherche and Masters profesionnel

Student Services: Canteen, Careers Guidance, Cultural Activities, Facilities for disabled people, Health Services, Nursery Care, Residential Facilities, Sports Facilities

Publications: Espace, populations, sociétés; Hommes et Terres du Nord; Le Bulletin de l'Institut de Recherche dans l'Enseignement des Mathématiques; Les Cahiers de Géographie physique; Les Cahiers de l'Institut d'administration des entreprises; Les Cahiers de l'Institut de Recherches sur les mathématiques avancées; Les Cahiers lillois d'Economie et de Sociologie; Les Nouvelles d'Archimède; Sphères d'échanges

Academic Staff *2014*: Total 2,913
Student Numbers *2014*: Total 20,204
Last Updated: 03/04/15

NATIONAL GRADUATE SCHOOL OF ENGINEERING CHEMISTRY OF LILLE

ECOLE NATIONALE SUPÉRIEURE DE CHIMIE DE LILLE (ENSCL)

Cité Scientifique - Bât. C7, Avenue Mendeleïev, CS 90108,
59652 Villeneuve d'Ascq, Cedex
Tel: +33(3) 20-43-69-30
Fax: +33(3) 20-47-05-99
EMail: direnscl@ensc-lille.fr
Website: http://www.ensc-lille.fr/

Director: Bernard Fontaine
Tel: +33(3) 20-43-69-30 EMail: direnscl@ensc-lille.fr

Secretary General: Olivier Durreau
EMail: olivier.durreau@ensc-lille.fr

International Relations: Zahia Turpin, Head of International Relations
Tel: +33(3) 20-33-71-35
EMail: zahia.turpin@ensc-lille.fr international@ensc-lille.fr

Programme

Chemistry (Chemical Engineering)

History: Founded in 1894 as Institute of Chemistry .

Academic Year: September to May

Admission Requirements: Secondary school certificate (Baccalauréat) and jury selection and interview, or competitive entrance examination or jury selection and 2-3 years of further studies after secondary school certificate.

Main Language(s) of Instruction: French

Degrees and Diplomas: *Diplôme d'Ingénieur*: **Chemical Engineering.** *Master*: **Chemistry; Polymer and Plastics Technology.**

LILLE 2 UNIVERSITY OF LAW AND HEALTH

Université Lille 2 Droit et Santé
42, rue Paul Duez, 59000 Lille
Tel: +33(3) 20-96-43-43
Fax: +33(3) 20-88-24-32
EMail: sg@univ-lille2.fr; administration@univ-lille2.fr
Website: http://www.univ-lille2.fr

President: Xavier Vandendriessche (2012-)
Tel: +33(3) 20-96-43-01 EMail: presidence@univ-lille2.fr

Head of Administration: Pierre-Marie Robert
Tel: +33(3) 20-96-43-48 EMail: pierre-marie.robert@univ-lille2.fr

International Relations: Eric Boulanger
Tel: +33(3) 20-96-43-21 EMail: rilille@univ-lille2.fr

Faculty
Dentistry (Dentistry); **Finance, Banking and Accountancy** *(FFBC)* (Accountancy; Banking; Finance); **Health Engineering** *(ILIS)* (Public Health); **Law, Political and Social Sciences** (Law; Political Sciences; Social Sciences); **Medicine** (Medicine); **Pharmacy** (Pharmacy); **Physical Education and Sports Sciences** *(Ronchin)* (Physical Education; Sports)

Institute
Criminal Law *(IEJ)* (Criminal Law; Law); **Criminology** (Criminology); **Forensic and Social Medicine** *(IML)* (Forensic Medicine and Dentistry; Social and Preventive Medicine); **Labour Relations** *(IST)* (Labour and Industrial Relations); **Marketing Retail Management** *(IMMD)* (Management; Marketing; Retailing and Wholesaling); **Pharmaceutical Chemistry** *(ICPAL)* (Pharmacology); **Preparatory Administrative Studies** *(IPAG)* (Administration); **Speech Therapy** *(Institut d'Orthophonie Gabriel Decroix)* (Speech Therapy and Audiology); **Technology** *(IUT C, Roubaix)* (Business and Commerce; Justice Administration; Statistics; Technology)

Graduate School
Health and Biology *(Offered by Universities of Lille I and II)* (Biology; Health Sciences); **Law, Political Science and Administration** (Administration; Law; Political Sciences)

History: Founded 1970 under the 1968 law reforming higher education as one of three Universities replacing the former Université de Lille - founded 1559 at Douai and authorized by Papal Bull. The University was suppressed by the Revolution and replaced by Faculties in Lille and Douai, the latter being subsequently transferred to Lille in 1887. Reconstituted as university 1896. A State institution enjoying academic and financial autonomy, operating under the jurisdiction of the Minister of Education and financed by the State.

Academic Year: September to June

Admission Requirements: Secondary school certificate (baccalauréat) or recognized foreign equivalent, or special entrance examination

Fees: 184-549 per annum (Euro)

Main Language(s) of Instruction: French

Degrees and Diplomas: *Diplôme universitaire de Technologie*; *Licence*: **Administrative Law; Banking; Business and Commerce; Economics; Law; Public Administration; Sports.** *Licence professionnelle*: **Business Administration; Environmental Studies; Health Sciences; Real Estate.** *Diplôme d'Etat*: **Dentistry; Medicine; Midwifery; Pharmacy.** *Master*: **Accountancy; Biomedical Engineering; Business Administration; Commercial Law; Human Resources; International Business; Law; Medicine; Pharmacy; Public Law; Sanitary Engineering; Sports; Sports Management.** *Doctorat*: **Finance; Health Sciences; Law; Pharmacy; Political Sciences.** *Certificat de Spécialité*: **Medicine; Pharmacy.** Capacity of Speech Therapy, Masters recherche, Masters professionnel

Student Services: Academic Counselling, Canteen, Careers Guidance, Cultural Activities, Facilities for disabled people, Health Services, Language Laboratory, Social Counselling, Sports Facilities

Academic Staff *2011-2012*: Total 1,139

Student Numbers *2011-2012*: Total 27,760

Last Updated: 09/04/15

LILLE 3 UNIVERSITY

Université Charles de Gaulle (Lille 3)

BP 60149, Domaine universitaire du "Pont de Bois", rue du Barreau -, 59653 Villeneuve d'Ascq, Cedex
Tel: +33(3) 20-41-60-00
Fax: +33(3) 20-91-91-71
EMail: ri.direction@univ-lille3.fr
Website: http://www.univ-lille3.fr

President: Fabienne Blaise (2012-)
Tel: +33(3) 20-41-65-97
EMail: presidence@univ-lille3.fr; fabienne.blaise@univ-lille3.fr

Secretary General: Emmanuel Parisis
Tel: +33(3) 20-41-62-33 EMail: emmanuel.parisis@univ-lille3.fr

International Relations: Richard Davis
EMail: richard.davis@univ-lille3.fr

Unit
Ancient Languages and Cultures (Ancient Civilizations; Ancient Languages); **Applied Foreign Languages** *(UFR LEA)* (International Business; Modern Languages); **Arts and Culture** (Communication Studies; Cultural Studies; Dance; Fine Arts; Media Studies; Music; Theatre); **Educational Sciences** (Educational Sciences); **Germanic and Scandinavian Studies** (Danish; Dutch; German; Icelandic; Scandinavian Languages; Swedish); **History, Arts, and Political Science** (Arts and Humanities; History; Political Sciences); **Information and Communication Studies** *(Infocom, Roubaix)* (Communication Studies; Information Sciences; Mass Communication); **Language, Literatures and Civilizations of English-speaking Countries** *(UFR Angellier)* (English Studies; Linguistics; Literature; Modern Languages); **Mathematics, Economics, and Social Sciences** *(UFR MSES)* (Economics; Mathematics; Social Sciences); **Modern Literature** (Linguistics; Literature); **Philosophy** (Philosophy); **Psychology** (Psychology); **Romance, Slavonic and Oriental Studies** (Arabic; Chinese; Hebrew; Italian; Japanese; Oriental Languages; Oriental Studies; Polish; Portuguese; Romance Languages; Russian; Slavic Languages; Spanish); **Scientific and Information Techniques and Documentation** *(UFR IDIST)* (Documentation Techniques; Information Sciences; Information Technology); **Sociology and Scoial Development** *(SDS)* (Sociology)

Department
Books and Documentation *(DFMLD MédiaLille)* (Documentation Techniques; Library Science; Publishing and Book Trade)

Institute
Technology *(IUT B, Tourcoing)* (Information Technology; Technology; Transport Management)

Centre
Lifelong Education; **Music Teacher Training** *(CFMI)*

Graduate School
Human Sciences and Society *(Works in collaboration with the University of the Littoral Cote d'Opal (ULCO))* (Aesthetics; Archaeology; Arts and Humanities; Automation and Control Engineering; Cognitive Sciences; Computer Engineering; Cultural Studies; History; Information Sciences; Linguistics; Neurosciences; Psychology; Social Sciences)

Further Information: Also 29 Research Centres and Institutes

History: Founded 1970 under the 1968 law reforming higher education as one of three Universities replacing the former Université de Lille - founded 1560 at Douai and authorized by Papal Bull. The University was suppressed by the Revolution and replaced by Faculties in Lille and Douai, the latter being subsequently transferred to Lille in 1887. Reconstituted as university 1896. A State institution enjoying academic and Financial autonomy, operating under the jurisdiction of the Ministry of Education and financed by the State.

Academic Year: October to June (October-December; January-March; April-June)

Admission Requirements: Secondary school certificate (baccalauréat) or recognized foreign equivalent, or special entrance examination

Main Language(s) of Instruction: French

Degrees and Diplomas: *Diplôme universitaire de Technologie*: **Information Technology; Publishing and Book Trade; Social Work; Transport Management.** *Licence*: **Administration; Arts and Humanities; Information Technology; Modern Languages; Social Sciences.** *Licence professionnelle*: **Administration; Communication Arts; Documentation Techniques.** *Diplôme d'Etat*: **Educational and Student Counselling.** *Master*: **Administration; Applied Mathematics; Arts and Humanities; Behavioural Sciences; Computer Science; Cultural Studies; Documentation Techniques; Economics; Educational Sciences; History; Information Technology; Linguistics; Modern Languages; Philosophy; Psychology; Social Work.** *Doctorat*: **Arts and Humanities; Modern Languages; Social Sciences.** Masters Recherche, Masters professionnel, Diplôme Universitaire - Proficiency in Modern Languages, Preparation for CAPES, Agrégation and IEP

Student Services: Academic Counselling, Canteen, Careers Guidance, Cultural Activities, Facilities for disabled people, Health Services, Nursery Care, Social Counselling, Sports Facilities

Publications: Revue des Sciences humaines; Revue du Centre de Recherches sur l'Histoire de l'Europe du Nord-Ouest; Revue du Nord

Publishing House: Presses Universitaires du Septentrion

Student Numbers *2013-2014*: Total 19,837

Last Updated: 11/03/15

LILLE SCHOOL OF ARCHITECTURE AND LANDSCAPE

Ecole nationale supérieure d'Architecture et de Paysage de Lille (ENSAPL)

2 rue Verte, 59650 Villeneuve d'Ascq
Tel: +33(3) 20-61-95-50
Fax: +33(3) 20-61-95-51
EMail: ensap@lille.archi.fr
Website: http://www.lille.archi.fr

Director: Jean-Marc Zuretti (2006-)
Tel: +33(3) 20-61-95-52 EMail: jm-zuretti@info1.lille.archi.fr

Secretary General: Jean Pierre Houssier
Tel: +33(3) 20-61-95-72 EMail: jp-houssier@lille.archi.fr

International Relations: Sarah Aït Haddi
Tel: +33(3) 20-61-95-18 EMail: s-aïthaddi@lille.archi.fr

Programme

Architecture (Architecture); **Landscape Architecture** (Landscape Architecture)

History: Founded 1979.

Admission Requirements: Secondary school Certificate (Baccalauréat) or equivalent.

Main Language(s) of Instruction: French

Accrediting Agency: Ministère de la Culture

Degrees and Diplomas: *Licence*: **Architecture.** *Diplôme d'Etat*: **Landscape Architecture.** *Master*: **Architecture.** *Doctorat*: **Architecture.** Diplôme d'Architecte Diplômé d'Etat; Habilitation à exercer la maîtrise d'oeuvre en son nom propre (HMONP)

Student Services: Library

Last Updated: 12/03/15

LIMOGES-AUBUSSON NATIONAL ART SCHOOL

Ecole nationale supérieure d'Art de Limoges-Aubusson (ENSA LIMOGES)

19 avenue Martin Luther King, 87038 Limoges, Cedex 01
Tel: +33(5) 55-43-14-00
Fax: +33(5) 55-43-14-01
EMail: accueillimoges@ensa-l-a.fr
Website: http://www.ensa-limoges.fr

Director: Jeanne Gailhoustet

Secretary General: Yvon Brouillaud Tel: +33(5) 55-43-14-08

International Relations: Viviane Raffier Tel: +33(5) 55-43-14-06

Programme

Visual Arts (Ceramic Art; Design; Textile Design; Visual Arts)

Further Information: Has studio in Jingdezhen (China).

History: The school was formed by the merger of two Arts Schools: The National School of Decorative Art established in1881 and the Municipal Art School founded in 1868. Acquired present status in 2003.

Admission Requirements: Baccalauréat or equivalent secondary school exam. Entrance exam with a selection jury.

Main Language(s) of Instruction: French

Accrediting Agency: Ministry of Culture and Communication

Degrees and Diplomas: Diplome national d'arts plastiques (DNAP) 3 years; Diplome national supérieur d'expression plastique (DNSEP) a further 2 years

Student Services: Library

Last Updated: 12/03/15

LORRAINE SCHOOL OF ART

Ecole supérieure d'Art de Lorraine

1 rue de la Citadelle, 57000 Metz
Tel: +33(3) 87-39-61-30
EMail: metz@esalorraine.fr
Website: http://esam.metzmetropole.fr

Director: Nathalie Filser

Programme

Visual Arts (Communication Arts; Multimedia; Visual Arts)

Further Information: Also branch in Epinal

History: Founded 1950.

Academic Year: October-May

Admission Requirements: Baccalauréat or equivalent secondary school exam. Entrance exam with a selection jury.

Main Language(s) of Instruction: French

Accrediting Agency: Ministry of Culture and Communication

Degrees and Diplomas: *Master*. Diplôme national d'arts plastiques (DNAP) 3 years; Diplôme national supérieur d'expression plastique (DNSEP) a further 2 years; Certificat d'Études d'Arts Plastiques (CEAP)

Last Updated: 07/04/15

LOUVRE SCHOOL

Ecole du Louvre

Palais du Louvre, Place du Carroussel, porte Jaujard, 75038 Paris, Cedex 01
Tel: +33(1) 55-35-18-35
Fax: +33(1) 55-35-18-64
EMail: international@ecoledulouvre.fr
Website: http://www.ecoledulouvre.fr

Director: Philippe Durey (2002-)
EMail: philippe.durey@ecoledulouvre.fr

International Relations: Stefania Tullio Cataldo, Head of International Department
Tel: +33(1) 55-35-19-12 EMail: international@ecoledulouvre.fr

Programme

History of Art and Museum Studies (Anthropology; Archaeology; Art History; History; Museum Studies)

History: Established in 1882.

Academic Year: September-May

Admission Requirements: Baccalauréat or equivalent Secondary School Degree; competitive entrance exam

Fees: 360 per annum for undergraduate studies; 520 per annum for graduate studies (Euro)

Main Language(s) of Instruction: French, English, Italian, Greman

Accrediting Agency: Ministry of Culture

Degrees and Diplomas: Undergraduate Degree in History of Arts (3yrs); Diplôme de deuxième cycle de l'Ecole du Louvre (Masters-level Degree, a further 2 yrs); Diplôme de recherche approfondie de l'Ecole du Louvre

Last Updated: 04/03/15

LYON 1 UNIVERSITY

Université Claude Bernard (Lyon I) (ULB)

43, boulevard du 11 novembre 1918, 69622 Villeurbanne, Cedex
Tel: +33(4) 72-44-80-00
Fax: +33(4) 72-43-10-20
EMail: secretaire.general@adm.univ-lyon1.fr
Website: http://www.univ-lyon1.fr

President: François-Noël Gilly (2012-)
Tel: +33(4) 72-44-80-16
EMail: secretariat.presidence@univ-lyon1.fr

Director of Services: Alain Heulleu
Tel: +33(4) 72-44-80-28; +33(4) 72-44-80-28
EMail: secretaire.general@univ-lyon1.fr

International Relations: Denis Bourgeois, Vice-President in charge of International Relations

Tel: +33(4) 78-77-86-84
EMail: Denis.Bourgeois@univ-lyon1.fr; vpri@univ-lyon1.fr

Unit

Biology (Biology); **Dentistry** (Dentistry); **Earth Sciences** (Earth Sciences); **Medicine** *(Lyon Est)* (Medicine); **Medicine** *(Lyon Sud)* (Medicine); **Physical Education and Sports** *(STAPS)* (Physical Education; Sports); **Sciences and Technology** (Biochemistry; Chemistry; Computer Science; Electrical Engineering; Mathematics; Mechanical Engineering; Physics)

Department

Research in Human Biology (Biological and Life Sciences; Biology)

Institute

Applied Mathematics, Management and Economics (Applied Mathematics; Economics; Finance; Management); **Engineering Science and Techniques** *(EPUL)* (Engineering; Technology); **Finance and Insurance** *(ISFA)* (Finance; Insurance); **Pharmacy and Biology** *(ISPB)* (Biology; Pharmacy); **Readaptation Techniques** *(ISTR)* (Medical Technology; Rehabilitation and Therapy); **Teacher Training** *(IUFM Lyon with 5 centres: Bourg en Bresse, Lyon, Saint-Etienne, Venissieux and Villeurbanne)* (Teacher Trainers Education; Teacher Training); **Technology** *(IUT Lyon 1, two sites: Bourg en Bresse and Lyon-Villeurbanne)* (Biotechnology; Computer Engineering; Technology; Thermal Engineering)

Centre

Astronomy *(OAL)* (Astronomy and Space Science; Astrophysics)

Graduate School

Chemistry, Processes and Environment *(In collaboration with INSA Lyon, ENS Lyon, IFP School and partner with ENTPE)* (Chemistry; Environmental Studies); **Computer Science and Mathematics** *(ED InfoMaths in collaboration with INSA, ENS, ECL and University Lyon II)* (Computer Science; Mathematics); **Economics and Management Sciences** *(ED SEG in collaboration with University Lyon III, Lyon II and Jean Monnet University of Saint-Etienne)* (Economics; Management); **Education, Psychology, Information and Communication** *(ED EPIC in collaboration with University Lyon II, University Lyon III, Jean Monnet University of Saint-Etienne, IEP of Lyon, INSA of Lyon, ENS of Lyon)* (Communication Studies; Education; Information Sciences; Psychology); **Electronics, Electro Techniques and Automation of Lyon** *(ED EEA In collaboration with INSA and ECL of Lyon)* (Electrical Engineering; Electronic Engineering; Production Engineering); **Evolution, Ecosystems and Microbiology Modelling** *(E2MR In collaboration with INSA of Lyon and partner with VetAgro Sup of Lyon)* (Ecology; Microbiology); **Interdisplinary Basic and Health Sciences** *(EDISS in collaboration with INSA and partner with VetAgro Sup of Lyon)* (Biochemistry; Biotechnology); **Materials Sciences and Engineering** *(In collaboration with INSA, ECL and ENS)* (Materials Engineering; Mathematics; Nanotechnology); **Mechanics, Energy, Civil and Acoustics Engineering** *(ED MEGA in collaboration with INSA and ECL)* (Civil Engineering; Energy Engineering; Mechanical Engineering; Sound Engineering (Acoustics)); **Molecular, Integrative and Cellular Biology** *(ED BMIC in collaboration with ENS Lyon)* (Biology; Cell Biology; Molecular Biology); **Neurosciences and Cognition** *(ED NSCo in collaboration with University Lyon II)* (Cognitive Sciences; Neurosciences); **Physics and Astrophysics** *(ED PHAST in collaboration with ENS Lyon)* (Astrophysics; Physics); **Polytech Lyon** (Biomedical Engineering; Computer Engineering; Engineering; Industrial Engineering; Materials Engineering; Mathematics; Mechanical Engineering)

History: Founded 1970 under the 1968 law reforming higher education as one of two universities replacing the former Université de Lyon, founded 1809 as Faculties of Letters, Science, and Theology, although the origin of higher education in Lyon may be traced back to a Papal Bull of 1245. Constituted as university 1896. A State institution enjoying academic and financial autonomy, operating under the jurisdiction of the Minister of Education and financed by the State.

Academic Year: September to June (September-February; February-June)

Admission Requirements: Secondary school certificate (baccalauréat) or equivalent, or special entrance examination

Main Language(s) of Instruction: French

Degrees and Diplomas: *Diplôme universitaire de Technologie*: **Bioengineering; Business Administration; Business and Commerce; Chemical Engineering; Chemistry; Civil Engineering; Computer Science; Electrical Engineering; Energy Engineering; Engineering Management; Industrial Engineering; Mechanical Engineering; Thermal Engineering.** *Licence*: **Biochemistry; Biology; Chemistry; Computer Science; Earth Sciences; Engineering; Mathematics; Physical Education; Physics; Social Sciences; Sports.** *Licence professionnelle*; *Diplôme d'Etat*: **Dentistry; Engineering; Medicine; Pharmacy.** *Master*: **Applied Mathematics; Atomic and Molecular Physics; Automation and Control Engineering; Biochemistry; Biotechnology; Cell Biology; Civil Engineering; Computer Science; Documentation Techniques; Earth Sciences; Economics; Electronic Engineering; Environmental Studies; Finance; Genetics; Health Education; Health Sciences; Information Sciences; Library Science; Management; Mathematics; Mechanics; Medical Technology; Microbiology; Neurosciences; Pharmacology; Philosophy; Physical Chemistry; Physics; Physiology; Psychology; Public Health; Sports Medicine; Teacher Training.** *Doctorat*: **Anthropology; Astrophysics; Automation and Control Engineering; Biochemistry; Biology; Biomedical Engineering; Chemistry; Cognitive Sciences; Economics; Educational Sciences; Electronic Engineering; Endocrinology; Genetics; Immunology; Information Sciences; Management; Marketing; Materials Engineering; Mathematics and Computer Science; Microbiology; Molecular Biology; Neurosciences; Nutrition; Pharmacology; Pharmacy; Physics; Physiology; Social Psychology; Sociology; Sports.** *Certificat de Spécialité*: **Medicine.** Also various professional qualifications for health personnel

Student Services: Canteen, Cultural Activities, Facilities for disabled people, Foreign Studies Centre, Health Services, Library, Residential Facilities, Social Counselling, Sports Facilities

Publications: Isotopes

Academic Staff *2012-2013*: Total 5,000

Student Numbers *2012-2013*: Total: c. 35,000

Last Updated: 30/03/15

LYON SCHOOL OF CHEMISTRY, PHYSICS AND ELECTRONICS
ECOLE SUPÉRIEURE DE CHIMIE PHYSIQUE ELECTRONIQUE DE LYON (CPE LYON)

BP 82077, 43, boulevard du 11 Novembre 1918, 69616 Villeurbanne, Cedex
Tel: +33(4) 72-43-17-00
Fax: +33(4) 72-43-16-88
EMail: tizon@cpe.fr
Website: http://www.cpe.fr

Director: Gérard Pignault (2004-) EMail: pignault@cpe.fr

Secretary General: Thierry Tizon Tel: +33(4) 72-43-17-38

Department

Chemistry and Chemical Engineering (Chemical Engineering; Chemistry); **Computer Science and Telecommunications** *(IRC)* (Computer Science; Telecommunications Engineering); **Electronics, Telecommunications, Computer Science** (Computer Engineering; Computer Science; Electronic Engineering)

Further Information: Also 16 Research Laboratories

History: Founded 1994 incorporating Lyons School of Industrial Chemistry (1883) and Industrial Chemistry and Physics Institute (1919).

Academic Year: September to June

Admission Requirements: Competitive entrance examination following 2-3 years further study after secondary school certificate (baccalauréat) in Science; Preparatory class: secondary school certificate (baccalauréat) and entrance examination.

Fees: 2150-5700 per annum (Euro)

Main Language(s) of Instruction: French

Accrediting Agency: Commission des Titres d'Ingénieur

Degrees and Diplomas: *Diplôme d'Ingénieur*: **Chemical Engineering; Chemistry; Computer Science; Electronic Engineering; Telecommunications Engineering.** *Mastère spécialisé*:

Biotechnology. *Master*: **Automation and Control Engineering; Biomedical Engineering; Chemistry; Computer Science; Electrical and Electronic Engineering; Environmental Studies; Materials Engineering.**

Student Services: Academic Counselling, Canteen, Careers Guidance, Facilities for disabled people, Health Services, Language Laboratory, Nursery Care, Social Counselling, Sports Facilities

LYON 2 UNIVERSITY

Université Lumière (Lyon II)

86, rue Pasteur, 69365 Lyon, Cedex 07
Tel: +33(4) 78-69-70-00
Fax: +33(4) 78-69-56-01
EMail: dri@univ-lyon2.fr
Website: http://www.univ-lyon2.fr

President: Jean-Luc Mayaud (2012-)
Tel: +33(4) 78-69-71-52 EMail: president@univ-lyon2.fr

Secretary General: Pascal Misery
Tel: +33 (4) 78-69-56-01 EMail: pascal.misery@univ-lyon2.fr

International Relations: Emmanuelle Lop
Tel: +33(4) 78-69-76-56 EMail: emmanuelle.lop@univ-lyon2.fr

Faculty

Anthropology, Sociology and Political Sciences *(Bron campus - FASSP)* (Anthropology; Political Sciences; Sociology); **Economics and Management** *(Lyon - FSEG)* (Economics; Management); **Geography, History, Art History and Tourism** *(Bron - UFR Temps et Territoires)* (Ancient Civilizations; Archaeology; Art History; Geography; History; Rural Studies; Urban Studies); **Languages** (Arabic; English; German; Portuguese; Spanish; Translation and Interpretation); **Law and Political Science** *(Bron - FDSP)* (Administration; Economics; Law); **Letters, Language Sciences and Arts** *(LESLA Lyon)* (Arts and Humanities; Cinema and Television; Gender Studies; Linguistics; Literature; Music; Musicology; Theatre; Visual Arts)

Institute

Communication and Fashion University *(Bron -ICOM - Université de la Mode)* (Communication Studies; Fashion Design); **Educational Sciences** *(ISPEF)* (Educational Sciences); **Labour Studies** *(Lyon -IETL)* (Labour and Industrial Relations; Labour Law); **Psychology** *(Bron)* (Psychology); **Technology** *(IUT Bron)* (Business Administration; Hygiene; Safety Engineering; Technology; Transport Management); **Union Training** *(IFS Lyon)* (Labour and Industrial Relations)

Centre

French Studies *(CIEF for foreign students)* (French); **Lifelong Education**; **Modern Languages** *(Lyon)* (Modern Languages); **Preparatory Administrative Studies** *(CPAG)* (Public Administration); **Training of Music Teachers** *(CFMI)* (Music Education)

Graduate College

Arts and Humanities, Geography, Urbanism, Political Sciences ans Social sciences *(ED ScSO In cooperation with ENS)* (Anthropology; Architecture and Planning; Geography; History; Labour and Industrial Relations; Political Sciences; Sociology)

Graduate School

Arts and Humanities *(ED HSH In cooperation with ENS)* (Arabic; Arts and Humanities; English Studies; Germanic Studies; Hispanic American Studies; Information Sciences; Linguistics; Literature; Mediterranean Studies; Psychology; Translation and Interpretation); **Cognitive Sciences** *(ED CS In cooperation with ENS Lyon)* (Cognitive Sciences; Neurosciences; Psychology); **Computer Science and Information for Societies** *(ED ISS In partnership with INSA, ECL and University Lyon I)* (Computer Science); **Economics and Administration** *(ED ECOGEST In cooperation with ENS)* (Administration; Economics); **Law** *(ED SSD In cooperation with ENS)* (Administrative Law; Law; Private Law; Public Law)

Further Information: Two sites: Central campus located in Lyon and 2nd campus located at Bron

History: Founded 1970 under the 1968 law reforming higher education as one of three Universities replacing the former Université de Lyon, founded 1809 as Faculties of Letters; Science; and Theology, although the origin of higher education in Lyons may be traced back to a Papal Bull of 1245. Constituted as University 1896. A State institution enjoying academic and financial autonomy, operating under the jurisdiction of the Minister of Education and financed by the State.

Academic Year: October to June (October-February; February-June)

Admission Requirements: Secondary school certificate (baccalauréat) or equivalent, or special entrance examination

Fees: c. 181,57per annum (Euro)

Main Language(s) of Instruction: French

Degrees and Diplomas: *Capacité en Droit*: **Law.** *Diplôme d'Accès aux Etudes universitaires*; *Diplôme universitaire de Technologie*: **Industrial Management.** *Licence*: **Administration; Arts and Humanities; Classical Languages; Economics; French; Law; Modern Languages; Social Sciences.** *Licence professionnelle*: **Administration; Banking; Human Resources; Industrial Management; Textile Technology.** *Master*: **Administration; Ancient Civilizations; Archaeology; Architecture and Planning; Arts and Humanities; Classical Languages; Contemporary History; Economics; Fashion Design; French; Heritage Preservation; Law; Library Science; Medieval Studies; Modern History; Modern Languages; Publishing and Book Trade; Rural Planning; Social Sciences; Teacher Training; Tourism; Town Planning; Water Science.** *Doctorat*: **Administration; Administrative Law; Ancient Civilizations; Anthropology; Architecture; Cognitive Sciences; Computer Science; Demography and Population; Economics; Educational Sciences; English Studies; Geography; Germanic Studies; History; Information Sciences; Labour Law; Law; Linguistics; Literature; Management; Mediterranean Studies; Modern Languages; Neurosciences; Political Sciences; Private Law; Psychology; Public Law; Sociology; Translation and Interpretation.** Masters de recherche, Masters professionnel, Diplome de l'IEP

Student Services: Canteen, Careers Guidance, Cultural Activities, Facilities for disabled people, Health Services, Library, Residential Facilities, Social Counselling, Sports Facilities

Publications: Textes et documents

Publishing House: Presses universitaires de Lyon

Academic Staff *2012*: Total 828
STAFF WITH DOCTORATE: Total 631

Student Numbers *2015*: Total 28,497

Last Updated: 30/03/15

LYON 3 UNIVERSITY

Université Jean Moulin (Lyon III)

Manufacture des Tabacs, 6 cours Albert Thomas,
69008 Lyon
Tel: +33(4) 78-78-78-78
Fax: +33(4) 78-78-79-79
EMail: ri@univ-lyon3.fr
Website: http://www.univ-lyon3.fr

President: Jacques Comby (2012-2016)
Tel: +33(4) 26-31-85-12
EMail: presidence@univ-lyon3.fr; jacques.comby@univ-lyon3.fr

Secretary General: Bernard Pascal
Tel: +33(4) 78-78-70-05 EMail: dgs@univ-lyon3.fr; bernard.pascal@univ-lyon3.fr

International Relations: Robert Sherratt, Head of International Relations
Tel: +33(4) 78-78-73-93
EMail: ri@univ-lyon3.fr; robert.sherratt@univ-lyon3.fr

Faculty

Humanities (Arts and Humanities; Classical Languages; Communication Studies; Geography; Information Technology; Literature; Modern Languages); **Languages** (Cultural Studies; Linguistics; Modern Languages); **Law** (European Union Law; International Law; Law; Notary Studies; Political Sciences); **Philosophy** (Aesthetics; Ethics; Philosophy)

School

Business Studies *(IAE)* (Accountancy; Economics; Finance; Human Resources; Information Technology; Management)

Institute
Business Administration *(IAE)* (Business Administration; Management); **Health Services Management** *(IFROSS in collaboration with IAE)* (Health Administration); **Technology** *(IUT)* (Communication Studies; Information Sciences; Information Technology; Justice Administration; Management; Technology)
Centre
Law, Letters and Languages *(CEUBA, Antenne Bourg-en-Bresse)* (Arts and Humanities; Law; Modern Languages)
Graduate School
Law (Law); **Management, Information, Finance** *(ED MIF in cooperation with University Lyon I)* (Finance; Management; Mass Communication); **Systems, Images and Languages**
Further Information: also campus in Bourg-en-Bresse
History: Founded 1973, formerly part of Université de Lyon II and tracing its origins to the former Université de Lyon, founded 1809 as Faculties of Letters; Science and Theology, although the origin of higher education in Lyon may be traced back to a Papal Bull of 1245. Constituted as University 1896. A State institution enjoying academic and financial autonomy, operating under the jurisdiction of the Minister of Education and financed by the State.
Academic Year: September to May (September-December/January; January- April/May)
Admission Requirements: Secondary school certificate (baccalauréat) or equivalent, or special entrance examination
Main Language(s) of Instruction: French
Degrees and Diplomas: *Diplôme universitaire de Technologie*; *Licence*: **Arts and Humanities; Business Administration; Law; Modern Languages.** *Licence professionnelle*: **Business Administration; Human Resources; Management.** *Master*: **Ancient Civilizations; Archaeology; Architecture and Planning; Archiving; Business Administration; Chinese; Classical Languages; Comparative Law; Contemporary History; Criminal Law; Economics; Education; English Studies; European Union Law; Finance; Fiscal Law; French Studies; Geography; Germanic Studies; History; History of Law; Human Resources; Indic Languages; Information Management; Information Sciences; International Business; International Law; International Relations; International Studies; Italian; Japanese; Law; Linguistics; Literature; Management; Marketing; Medieval Studies; Middle Eastern Studies; Modern History; Notary Studies; Philosophy; Political Sciences; Private Law; Public Law; Public Relations; Regional Planning; Religious Studies; Russian; Slavic Languages; Translation and Interpretation.** *Doctorat*: **Ancient Civilizations; Asian Studies; Classical Languages; Communication Arts; Comparative Law; Comparative Literature; Computer Science; Eastern European Studies; Economics; English Studies; European Union Law; Finance; French Studies; Geography; Germanic Studies; History; History of Law; International Law; Islamic Studies; Law; Linguistics; Literature; Management; Middle Eastern Studies; Modern Languages; Oriental Studies; Philosophy; Political Sciences; Private Law; Public Law; Romance Languages; Slavic Languages; Sociology.** *Certificat de Spécialité*: **Accountancy; Modern Languages.**
Student Services: Canteen, Careers Guidance, Cultural Activities, Facilities for disabled people, Health Services, Language Laboratory, Library, Residential Facilities, Social Counselling, Sports Facilities
Publications: Annales de la Faculté de Droit; Revue d'Etudes indoeuropéennes

Academic Staff *2013-2014*	**TOTAL**
FULL-TIME	**627**
STAFF WITH DOCTORATE FULL-TIME	**651**
Student Numbers *2013-2014*	
All (Foreign included)	**26,640**
FOREIGN ONLY	**4400**

Last Updated: 13/03/15

LYON SCHOOL OF ARCHITECTURE

Ecole nationale supérieure d'Architecture de Lyon (ENSAL)

BP 170, 3, rue Maurice Audin, 69512 Vaulx-en-Velin
Tel: +33(4) 78-79-50-50
Fax: +33(4) 78-80-40-68
EMail: ensal@lyon.archi.fr
Website: http://www.lyon.archi.fr

Director: Nathalie Mezureux
Tel: +33(4) 78-79-50-69 EMail: nathalie.mezureux@lyon.archi.fr
Secretary General: Jean-François Agier
Tel: +33(4) 78-79-50-56 EMail: jean-francois.agier@lyon.archi.fr
International Relations: Olivier Chabert
Tel: +33(4) 78-79-50-67 EMail: olivier.chabert@lyon.archi.fr

Programme
Architecture (Architecture)
History: Founded 1906 as École d'Architecture de Lyon.
Admission Requirements: Baccalauréat or equivalent. Competitive entrance examination
Main Language(s) of Instruction: French
Degrees and Diplomas: *Licence*: **Architecture.** *Master*: **Architecture and Planning.** *Doctorat*: **Architecture.** Habilitation de l'architecte diplômé d'état à l'exercice de la Maîtrise d'Œuvre en son Nom Propre (HMONP)

Academic Staff *2013-2014*	**TOTAL**
FULL-TIME	**40**
Student Numbers *2013-2014*	
All (Foreign included)	**846**
FOREIGN ONLY	**42**

Last Updated: 11/03/15

MARSEILLES-MEDITERRANEAN SCHOOL OF ART AND DESIGN

Ecole supérieure d'Art et de Design Marseille-Méditerranée (ESADMM)

184 avenue de Luminy, 13288 Marseille, Cedex 9
Tel: +33(4) 91-82-83-10
Fax: +33(4) 91-82-83-11
EMail: contact@esadmm.fr
Website: http://www.esadmm.fr

Director General: Jean Mangion
International Relations: Claude Puig-Legros
EMail: cpuig@esadmm.fr

Programme
Design (Design); **Fine Arts** (Fine Arts)
History: Founded 1752 as École des beaux-arts de Marseille. Acquired present title 2011 and status 2012.
Academic Year: October to June
Admission Requirements: Baccalauréat or equivalent secondary school exam. Entrance exam with a selection jury.
Fees: 586 (Euro)
Main Language(s) of Instruction: French
Accrediting Agency: Ministry of Culture and Communication
Degrees and Diplomas: Diplôme national d'arts plastiques (DNAP in design) 3 yrs; Diplôme national supérieur d'expression plastique (DNSEP) a further 2 yrs
Last Updated: 17/03/15

MARSEILLES SCHOOL OF ARCHITECTURE

Ecole nationale supérieure d'Architecture de Marseille (ENSA-MARSEILLE)

184, avenue de Luminy - case 924, 13288 Marseille, Cedex 09
Tel: +33(4) 91-82-71-00
Fax: +33(4) 91-82-71-80
EMail: contact@marseille.archi.fr
Website: http://www.marseille.archi.fr

Director: Marielle Riche (2009-)
EMail: sophie.dauzet@marseille.archi.fr
Secretary General: Noël Fornari
Tel: +33(4) 91-82-71-10 EMail: noel.fornari@marseille.archi.fr
International Relations: Caroline Petre
Tel: +33(4) 91-82-71-58 EMail: caroline.petre@marseille.archi.fr

Programme
Architecture (Architecture)
History: Founded 1752.

Main Language(s) of Instruction: French

Degrees and Diplomas: *Licence*: **Architecture.** *Master*: **Architecture.** *Doctorat*: **Architecture.** Also master professionnel; Diplôme Propre aux Écoles d'Architecture; Habilitation de l'architecte diplômé d'État à exercer la Maîtrise d'Oeuvre en son Nom Propre

Student Services: Library

Publishing house: Éditions de l'ENSA-M

Academic Staff *2014-2015*	TOTAL
FULL-TIME	52
Student Numbers *2014-2015*	
All (Foreign included)	1,107
FOREIGN ONLY	156

Last Updated: 11/03/15

MEDIA ART SCHOOL - FRUCTIDOR

École media art Fructidor (EMAFRUCTIDOR)

34, rue Fructidor, 71100 Chalon-sur-Saône
Tel: +33(3) 85-48-14-11
Fax: +33(3) 85-94-75-93
EMail: secretariat.ema@chalonsursaone.fr
Website: http://emafructidor.com/

Director: Dominique Pasqualini

Programme

Media and Arts (Art History; Multimedia; Painting and Drawing; Visual Arts)

History: Founded 1999

Admission Requirements: Entrance examination. Secondary school certificate (Baccalauréat)

Main Language(s) of Instruction: French

Accrediting Agency: Ministry of Culture

Degrees and Diplomas: Diplôme national d'arts plastiques (DNAP) in Media 3 years ; Diplôme d'Enseignement Supérieur in Media and Art (DNEMA) a further 2 years

Last Updated: 07/04/15

MONTPELLIER 3 UNIVERSITY

Université Paul Valéry (Montpellier 3)

Route de Mende, 34199 Montpellier, Cedex 05
Tel: +33(4) 67-14-20-00
Fax: +33(4) 67-14-20-52
EMail: presidence@univ-montp3.fr
Website: http://www.univ-montp3.fr

President: Anne Fraïsse (2008-)
Tel: +33(4) 67-14-54-47 EMail: presidence@univ-montp3.fr

International Relations: Anne-Marie Mottard, Vice-President in charge of International Relations
EMail: thierry.mazerand@univ-montp3.fr

Unit

Economics, Management and Social Sciences (Administration; Applied Mathematics; Computer Science; Economics; Educational Sciences; Management; Sanitary Engineering; Social Policy; Social Sciences); **Education and Applied Sciences** *(LLASHS - in cooperation with ESPE)* (Education; Educational Sciences; Mathematics and Computer Science; Sports; Statistics; Teacher Training); **Foreign and Regional Languages** (Arabic; Catalan; Chinese; English; German; Greek; Hebrew; Italian; Polish; Portuguese; Regional Studies; Romanian; Russian; Slavic Languages; Spanish); **Human and Environmental Sciences** (Archaeology; Art History; Biology; Ecology; Environmental Studies; History; Regional Planning); **Letters, Arts, Philosophy, and Psychoanalysis** (Arts and Humanities; Cinema and Television; Classical Languages; Fine Arts; Linguistics; Literature; Music; Performing Arts; Philosophy; Psychoanalysis; Theatre); **Man and Society** (Ethnology; Information Sciences; Psychology; Social Sciences; Sociology)

Department

Applied Languages *(LEA)*; **Lifelong Education** *(SUFCO)*

Institute

French Studies for Foreign Students *(IEFE)* (French); **Information and Communication Technosciences** *(ITIC)* (Communication Studies; Documentation Techniques; Information Sciences; Linguistics)

History: Founded 1970 under the 1968 law reforming higher education as one of three Universities replacing the former Université de Montpellier, founded 1220 by promulgation of statutes by Cardinal Conrad and confirmed by Papal Bull 1242. The University was suppressed by the Revolution and replaced by Faculties of Medicine; Pharmacy; Science; and Letters of the Université de France. Reconstituted as University 1896. A State institution enjoying academic and financial autonomy, operating under the jurisdiction of the Minister of Education and financed by the State. Member of the COMUE Languedoc Roussillon Universities

Academic Year: October to June (October-December; January-March; April-June)

Admission Requirements: Secondary school certificate (baccalauréat) or equivalent, or special entrance examination

Main Language(s) of Instruction: French

Degrees and Diplomas: *Licence*: **Arts and Humanities; Literature; Modern Languages; Social Sciences.** *Licence professionnelle*: **Agronomy; Documentation Techniques; Environmental Studies; Social Work.** *Master*: **Arts and Humanities; Literature; Modern Languages; Performing Arts; Social Sciences.** *Doctorat*: **Classical Languages; Comparative Literature; Cultural Studies; English Studies; Germanic Studies; Greek; Literature; Mediterranean Studies; Oriental Studies; Performing Arts; Philosophy; Regional Studies; Romance Languages; Scandinavian Languages.** Masters recherche, Masters professionnel, Preparation for Agrégation exams

Student Services: Canteen, Careers Guidance, Cultural Activities, Facilities for disabled people, Health Services, Library, Residential Facilities, Sports Facilities

Academic Staff *2013-2014*: Total 484
STAFF WITH DOCTORATE: Total 694
Student Numbers *2013-2014*: Total 19,627

Last Updated: 10/04/15

MONTPELLIER ART SCHOOL

Ecole supérieure des Beaux-Arts Montpellier Agglomération (ESBAMA)

130 rue Yéhudi Menuhin, 34000 Montpellier
Tel: +33(4) 99-58-32-85
Fax: +33(4) 99-58-32-86
EMail: contact@esbama.fr
Website: http://www.esbama.fr/

Director: Philippe Reitz (2011-) EMail: p.reitz@esbama.fr

Programme

Visual Arts (Fine Arts)

Further Information: Branch in Nîmes

History: Founded in 1779.

Admission Requirements: Baccalauréat or equivalent secondary school exam. Entrance exam with a selection jury.

Main Language(s) of Instruction: French

Accrediting Agency: Ministry of Culture and Communication

Degrees and Diplomas: *Master*: **Fine Arts.** Diplôme national d'arts plastiques (DNAP) 3 years; Diplôme national supérieur d'expression plastique (DNSEP) a further 2 years; Certificat d'Études d'Arts Plastiques (CEAP); Certificat d'Études Supérieures d'Arts Plastiques (CESAP)

Last Updated: 20/03/15

MONTPELLIER SCHOOL OF ARCHITECTURE

Ecole nationale supérieure d'Architecture de Montpellier (ENSAM)

179, rue de l'Espérou, 34093 Montpellier, Cedex 05
Tel: +33(4) 67-91-89-89
Fax: +33(4) 67-41-35-07
EMail: christine.beauvallet@montpellier.archi.fr
Website: http://www.montpellier.archi.fr

Director: Alain DEREY (2014-)
Tel: +33(4) 67-91-89-50 EMail: alain.derey@montpellier.archi.fr

Secretary General: Ahmide Radi
Tel: +33(4) 67-91-89-83 EMail: ahmide.radi@montpellier.archi.fr

International Relations: Sandrine Chiaraviglio
Tel: +33(4) 67-91-89-68
EMail: sandrine.chiaraviglio@montpellier.archi.fr

Programme

Architecture (Architecture)

Further Information: Ecole d'architecture de l'île de la Réunion

History: Founded 1903 as Ecole Régionale d'Architecture.

Main Language(s) of Instruction: French

Degrees and Diplomas: *Licence*: **Architecture.** *Master*: **Architecture.** Habilitation de l'architecte diplômé d'Etat à l'exercice de la maîtrise d'oeuvre en son nom propre

Publishing house: les Editions de l'Espérou

Academic Staff *2013-2014*: Total 50
Student Numbers *2013-2014*: Total 900
Last Updated: 11/03/15

MONTPELLIER SUPAGRO (INRA)

2 place Pierre Viala, 34060 Montpellier, Cedex 02
Tel: +33(4) 99-61-22-00
Fax: +33(4) 99-61-29-00
EMail: dirdri@dupagro.inra.fr
Website: http://www.supagro.fr

Director General: Anne-Lucie Wack (2013)
EMail: dgmsa@supagro.inra.fr

Head of Administration: Philippe de Cornelissen
EMail: cornelis@supagro.inra.fr

International Relations: J.L. Bosio EMail: dirdri@dupagro.inra.fr

Department

Agro-Bio-Process Science (Biochemistry; Biotechnology; Computer Science; Mathematics; Microbiology; Physics; Production Engineering; Statistics); **Biology and Ecology** (Crop Production; Plant and Crop Protection); **Ecology and Plant Health** (Agronomy; Biology; Ecology; Genetics; Plant and Crop Protection); **Economics, Social Sciences and Management** (Agricultural Economics; Business Administration; Environmental Management; Food Science; Management; Natural Resources; Rural Planning; Water Management); **Environment, Crops, Resources and Systems** (Agriculture; Agronomy; Animal Husbandry; Crop Production; Irrigation; Soil Science; Water Science)

Institute

Agro-Environment *(Supagro Florac)* (Agriculture); **Tropical Agrofood Industries and Rural Development** *(IRC)* (Agriculture; Agronomy; Food Science; Rural Planning; Rural Studies; Tropical Agriculture); **Vine and Wine Advanced Studies** *(IHEV)* (Oenology; Viticulture)

History: Founded 1872. Acquired present status 2007 following merger of Montpellier National School of Agronomy, The National Centre for Tropical and Sub-tropical Environments, The National School of Agro-Food Industry.

Academic Year: Organized on a semester and modular basis

Admission Requirements: Competitive entrance examination following 2 years further study after secondary school certificate (baccalauréat) or specific examination after a Bachelor of Science in Agricultural Sciences for foreign students

Main Language(s) of Instruction: French

Accrediting Agency: Commission des Titres d'Ingenieurs (CTI); Conférence des Grandes Ecoles (CGE); Ministry of Agriculture; Ministry of Education

Degrees and Diplomas: *Licence professionnelle*; *Diplôme d'Ingénieur*: **Agriculture; Agronomy; Food Science.** *Mastère spécialisé*: **Food Science; Management.** *Master*: **Agricultural Economics; Agronomy; Animal Husbandry; Biological and Life Sciences; Biotechnology; Cattle Breeding; Crop Production; Ecology; Environmental Studies; Food Science; Food Technology; Fruit Production; Management; Microbiology; Molecular Biology; Oenology; Plant and Crop Protection; Plant Pathology; Soil Science; Tropical Agriculture; Viticulture.** *Doctorat*: **Agronomy; Biology; Economics; Food Science; Management; Soil Science; Water Science.**

Student Services: Academic Counselling, Canteen, Careers Guidance, Facilities for disabled people, Language Laboratory, Sports Facilities

Student Numbers *2015*: Total 1,600
Last Updated: 31/03/15

MONTPELLIER UNIVERSITY
Université de Montpellier

Université de Montpellier, 163 rue Auguste Broussonnet, 34 090 Montpellier
Tel: +33(4) 67-41-74-00
Fax: +33(4) 67-41-74-56
EMail: sri@univ-montp1.fr
Website: http://www.umontpellier.fr/

President: Philippe Augé (2014-)
EMail: presidence@sc.univ-montp1.fr

Head of Administration: Pascal Beauregard
Tel: +33(4) 34-43-33-36 EMail: christine.michel@univ-montp1.fr

International Relations: Françoise Aubujeault, Director
Tel: +33(4) 34-43-23-23 EMail: sri@univ-montp1.fr

Unit

Dentistry (Dentistry); **Economic and Social Administration** *(UFR AES)* (Business Administration; Marketing; Public Administration); **Economics** (Economics); **Education** *(also ESPE with 5 campuses: Carcassonne, Mende, Montpellier, Nîmes et Perpignan (former IUFM))* (Educational Sciences; Teacher Training); **Law and Political Science** (Law; Political Sciences); **Medicine** (Medicine); **Pharmaceutical and Biological Sciences** (Biological and Life Sciences; Pharmacy); **Physical Education and Sports** *(STAPS)* (Physical Education; Sports); **Sciences** (Biological and Life Sciences; Chemistry; Earth Sciences; Engineering; Mathematics and Computer Science; Mechanical Engineering; Natural Sciences; Physics; Technology)

School

Engineering *(Polytech Montpellier)* (Engineering)

Institute

Business *(ISEM)* (Business and Commerce); **Business Administration** *(IAE)* (Business Administration); **Preparatory Administrative Studies** *(IPAG)* (Administration); **Technology** *(IUT Béziers)* (Business and Commerce; Multimedia; Technology; Telecommunications Engineering); **Technology** *(IUT Nimes)* (Business Administration; Civil Engineering; Electrical Engineering; Materials Engineering; Mechanical Engineering); **Technology** *(IUT Montpellier-Sètes)* (Computer Science; Natural Sciences; Technology)

Centre

Lifelong Education *(DIDERIS)*

Graduate School

Mediterranean Environment *(OREME-Observatoire de recherche Méditerranéen de l'Environnement)* (Environmental Studies)

History: Founded 1970 under the1968 law reforming higher education as one of three Universities replacing the former Université de Montpellier, founded 1220 by promulgation of statutes by Cardinal Conrad and confirmed by Papal Bull 1289. The university was suppressed by the Revolution and replaced by Faculties of Medicine; Pharmacy; Science; and Letters of the Université de France. Reconstituted as University 1896. A State institution enjoying academic and financial autonomy, operating under the jurisdiction of the Minister of Education and financed by the State. in 2015, the Universities of Montpellier 1 and 2 merged and became Université de Montpellier. Member of the COMUE Languedoc Roussillon Universities.

Academic Year: October to June

Admission Requirements: Secondary school certificate (baccalauréat) or equivalent, or special entrance examination

Main Language(s) of Instruction: French

Degrees and Diplomas: *Capacité en Droit*: **Law.** *Diplôme universitaire de Technologie*; *Licence*: **Administration; Business Administration; Economics; Health Sciences; Law; Management; Mathematics and Computer Science; Natural Sciences; Political Sciences; Sports.** *Licence professionnelle*: **Administration; Biology; Law; Management; Pharmacy; Sports.** *Diplôme d'Etat*: **Dentistry; Medicine; Midwifery; Pharmacy.** *Diplôme d'Ingénieur*: **Engineering.** *Master*: **Automation and Control Engineering; Biological and Life Sciences; Biotechnology; Business Administration; Chemistry; Earth Sciences; Economics; Education; Electrical and Electronic Engineering; Energy Engineering; Engineering; Environmental Studies; Health Sciences; Law; Management; Marine Science and Oceanography; Mathematics and Computer Science; Mechanical Engineering; Medicine; Natural Sciences; Philosophy; Physics; Political Sciences; Sports; Teacher Training; Water Science.** *Doctorat*: **Agronomy; Biological and Life Sciences; Biology; Chemistry; Dentistry; Economics; Environmental Studies; Food Technology; Management; Physical Education; Physics; Social Sciences; Sports.** *Certificat de Spécialité*: **Medicine.** Masters recherche, Masters professionnel, Preparation for CAPES and Agrégation

Student Services: Canteen, Cultural Activities, Facilities for disabled people, Health Services, Library, Residential Facilities, Sports Facilities

Publications: La Revue de l'Economie méridionale; LUS : Littérature ultrasonore / Faculté de Médecine Nîmes

Last Updated: 10/04/15

NATIONAL GRADUATE SCHOOL OF CHEMISTRY OF MONTPELLIER

ECOLE NATIONALE SUPÉRIEURE DE CHIMIE DE MONTPELLIER (ENSCM)

8 Rue de l'Ecole Normale, 34296 Montpellier, Cedex 5
Tel: +33(4) 67-14-43-00
Fax: +33(4) 67-14-43-53
EMail: communication@enscm.fr
Website: http://www.enscm.fr/

Director: Pascal DUMY Tel: +33(4) 67-14-43-71
EMail: direction.enscm@enscm.fr

Programme

Chemistry (Biology; Chemical Engineering; Chemistry; Environmental Studies; Organic Chemistry)

History: Founded 1957.

Admission Requirements: Competitive entrance examination after 2 years of further studies after secondary school certificate (Baccalauréat)

Main Language(s) of Instruction: French

Accrediting Agency: Commission de Titres d'Ingénieur (CTI)

Degrees and Diplomas: *Diplôme d'Ingénieur*: **Chemical Engineering.** *Master*: **Biology; Chemistry.**

NANCY NATIONAL ART SCHOOL

Ecole nationale supérieure d'Arts de Nancy (ENSAN)

BP 13129, 1, avenue Boffrand, 54013 Nancy, Cedex
Tel: +33(3) 83-41-61-61
Fax: +33(3) 83-28-78-60
EMail: ecole.art@ensa-nancy.fr
Website: http://www.ensa-nancy.fr

Director: Christian Debize
Tel: +33(3) 83 41 61 62 EMail: direction@ensa-nancy.fr

International Relations: Susan Mollon
Tel: +33(3) 83-41-68-83 EMail: susan.mollon@ensa-nancy.fr

Department

Communication (Communication Arts; Communication Studies); **Design** (Design); **Fine Arts** (Fine Arts)

History: Founded 1702 as Académie de peinture et de sculpture. Acquired present status 2003.

Admission Requirements: Entrance exam.

Fees: 387 per annum (Euro)

Main Language(s) of Instruction: French

Accrediting Agency: Ministère de la culture et de la communication

Degrees and Diplomas: *Master*: **Design.** Diplome national d'arts plastiques (DNAP) 3 years, 180 Ects; Diplome national supérieur d'expression plastique (DNSEP) a further 2 years, 120 Ects

Student Services: Library, Sports Facilities

Last Updated: 12/03/15

NANCY SCHOOL OF ARCHITECTURE

Ecole nationale supérieure d'Architecture de Nancy (ENSA)

BP 40435, 2, rue Bastien Lépage, 54001 Nancy, Cedex
Tel: +33(3) 83-30-81-00
Fax: +33(3) 83-30-81-30
EMail: ensa@nancy.archi.fr
Website: http://www.nancy.archi.fr

Director: Lorenzo Diez
Tel: +33(3) 83-30-81-25
EMail: ensa@nancy.archi.fr

Secretary General: Bernadette Clavel
Tel: +33(3) 83-30-81-24 EMail: bernadette.clavel@nancy.archi.fr

International Relations: Fabrice Picquet
Tel: +33(3) 83-30-81-05 EMail: ri@nancy.archi.fr

School

Architecture (Architecture)

History: Founded 1970. Under the responsibility of the Ministry of Culture and Communication.

Academic Year: October to June

Admission Requirements: Secondary school certificate (baccalauréat)

Main Language(s) of Instruction: French

Degrees and Diplomas: *Licence*: **Architecture.** *Master*: **Architecture; Architecture and Planning.** *Doctorat*: **Architecture.** Habilitaton de l'architecte diplômé d'Etat à l'exercice de la maîtrise d'oeuvre en son nom propre (HMONP)

Student Services: Canteen

Last Updated: 11/03/15

NANTES-ATLANTIQUE NATIONAL SCHOOL OF VETERINARY SCIENCE, FOOD PROCESSING AND FOOD STUDIES

Ecole nationale vétérinaire, agroalimentaire et de l'alimentation, Nantes-Atlantique (ONIRIS)

BP 82225, Rue de la Géraudière, 44322 Nantes, Cedex 03
Tel: +33(2) 51-78-54-54
Fax: +33(2) 51-78-54-55
EMail: contact@oniris-nantes.fr
Website: http://www.oniris-nantes.fr

Director General: Pierre Saï EMail: direction@vet-nantes.fr

International Relations: Lionel Boillereaux, Head of International Relations EMail: iro@oniris-nantes.fr

Area

Engineering (Biotechnology; Engineering; Pharmacology); **Food and Food Processing** (Food Science; Food Technology); **Veterinary Science** (Veterinary Science)

History: Founded 2009 following merger of the École nationale d'ingénieurs des techniques des industries agricoles et agroalimentaires (ENITIAA) and the École nationale vétérinaire de Nantes (ENVN).

Academic Year: September to June

Admission Requirements: Competitive entrance examination following 2-3 years further study after secondary school certificate (Baccalauréat) or following first university qualification (DEUG, DUT, BTS), or equivalent

Main Language(s) of Instruction: French

Accrediting Agency: Ministry of Agriculture

Degrees and Diplomas: *Brevet de Technicien supérieur*; *Licence professionnelle*; *Diplôme d'Etat*: **Veterinary Science.** *Diplôme d'Ingénieur*: **Biotechnology; Food Science.** *Master*: **Biology; Biotechnology; Environmental Studies; Food Science; Food Technology; Marine Biology; Safety Engineering; Veterinary Science.** Diplôme d'étude fondamentales vétérinaire (DEFV); Masters recherche; Masters professionnel

Student Services: Academic Counselling, Canteen, Careers Guidance, Cultural Activities, Facilities for disabled people, Language Laboratory, Sports Facilities

Last Updated: 30/03/15

NANTES SCHOOL OF ARCHITECTURE

Ecole nationale supérieure d'Architecture de Nantes (ENSA-NANTES)

BP 16202, 6 quai François Mitterrand, BP 81931, 44262 Nantes, Cedex 2
Tel: +33(2) 40-16-01-21
Fax: +33(2) 40-59-16-70
EMail: ensa@nantes.archi.fr
Website: http://www.nantes.archi.fr

Director: Christian Dautel
EMail: martine.cornuaille@nantes.archi.fr

Secretary General: Nicolas Schmitt Tel: +33(2) 40-16-09-31

International Relations: Nathalie Aknin
Tel: +33(2) 40-16-02-41 EMail: nathalie.aknin@nantes.archi.fr

Programme
Architecture (Architecture)

History: Founded 1945.

Main Language(s) of Instruction: French

Degrees and Diplomas: *Licence*: **Architecture.** *Master*: **Architecture and Planning; Urban Studies.** Also DPEA Naval Architecture (13 mths), Scenography (3 yrs), Habilitation à exercer la maîtrise d'oeuvre en son nom propre for graduate architects (HMONP)

Last Updated: 11/03/15

NATIONAL ART SCHOOL OF BOURGES

Ecole nationale des Beaux-Arts de Bourges (ENSA BOURGES)

BP 297, 7, rue Edouard Branly, 18006 Bourges, Cedex
Tel: +33(2) 48-69-78-78
Fax: +33(2) 48-69-79-90
EMail: contact@ensa-bourges.fr
Website: http://www.ensa-bourges.fr

Director: Antoine Réguillon (2014-)
EMail: direction@ensa-bourges.fr

Administrative Officer: Patrice Ducher
EMail: patrice.ducher@ensa-bourges.fr

International Relations: Krystel Cosquéric
Tel: +33(2) 48-69-76-33
EMail: international@ensa-bourges.fr

Department
Fine Arts (Art History; Fine Arts; Sound Engineering (Acoustics); Video; Visual Arts)

History: Founded 1824.

Academic Year: September to June

Admission Requirements: Baccalauréat or equivalent secondary school exam. Entrance exam and selection jury.

Fees: National : Non-grant students : 433 per annum (Euro), International : Non-grant students: 433 per annum (Euro)

Main Language(s) of Instruction: French

Accrediting Agency: Ministry of Culture and Communication

Degrees and Diplomas: *Master*: **Art Education.** National Degree in Visual Arts (DNAP) 3 years, Bachelor equivalent; Postgraduate Degree in Visual Expression (DNSEP) a further 2 years, Master equivalent

Student Services: Library

Last Updated: 11/03/15

NATIONAL ART SCHOOL OF LYON

Ecole nationale des Beaux-Arts de Lyon (ENSBA LYON)

8 bis quai St Vincent, 69001 Lyon
Tel: +33(4) 72-00-11-71
Fax: +33(4) 72-00-11-70
EMail: infos@ensba-lyon.fr
Website: http://www.ensba-lyon.fr

Director: Emmanuel Tibloux (2011-)
EMail: emmanuel.tibloux@ensba-lyon.fr

International Relations: Anabelle Pigot
Tel: +33(4) 78-28-13-67 EMail: anabelle.pijot@ensba-lyon.fr

Department
Fine Arts (Design; Fine Arts; Industrial Design; Interior Design; Textile Design); **Urban Design** (Design; Graphic Design; Textile Design)

History: Founded 1756 as Ecole Royale Académique de Dessin et Géométrie. Became the Ecole Nationale des Beaux-Arts 1848.

Admission Requirements: Baccalauréat or equivalent secondary school exam. Entrance exam and selection jury.

Fees: 396 per annum (Euro)

Main Language(s) of Instruction: French

Accrediting Agency: Ministry of Culture and Communication

Degrees and Diplomas: National Degree in Visual Arts (DNAP) 3 years; National Arts and Techniques Diploma (DNAT) 3 yrs; Postgraduate Degree in Visual Expression (DNSEP), Master equivalent

Student Services: Library

Publications: Initiales

Publishing House: Édition ENSBA Lyon

Student Numbers *2014-2015*: Total 350
Last Updated: 11/03/15

NATIONAL FILM, PHOTOGRAPHY AND SOUND ENGINEERING SCHOOL

Ecole nationale supérieure Louis Lumière (ENS LOUIS LUMIÈRE)

La Cité du Cinéma, 20, rue Ampère - BP 12, 93213 La Plaine Saint-Denis, Cedex
Tel: +33(1) 84-67-00-01
EMail: direction@ens-louis-lumiere.fr
Website: http://www.ens-louis-lumiere.fr/

Director: Francine Lévy (2007-)
EMail: direction@ens-louis-lumiere.fr

Secretary General: Noëlle Blanc EMail: sg@ens-louis-lumiere.fr

Department
Cinema (Cinema and Television); **Photography** (Photography; Visual Arts); **Sound Engineering** (Sound Engineering (Acoustics))

History: Founded in 1926.

Admission Requirements: Baccalauréat or equivalent Secondary School Degree and two years of higher education. Competitive entrance exam

Main Language(s) of Instruction: French

Accrediting Agency: Ministry of Education

Degrees and Diplomas: *Master*. University Diploma in Cinema, Photography and Sound engineering

Last Updated: 30/03/15

NATIONAL INSTITUTE FOR NUCLEAR SCIENCE AND TECHNOLOGY

Institut national des Sciences et Techniques nucléaires (INSTN)

Point courrier n° 35 - Centre CEA de Saclay, 91191 Gif-sur-Yvette
Tel: +33(1) 69-08-60-00
Website: http://www-instn.cea.fr

Director: Xavier Vitart

Programme
Applied Physics (Applied Physics); **Nuclear Engineering** (Applied Physics; Nuclear Engineering); **Radiology** (Radiology)

Further Information: Also four branches set up in CEA's centres at Grenoble, Cadarache and Valrhô-Marcoule, and campus of Cherbourg-Octeville.

History: Founded in 1956.

Main Language(s) of Instruction: French

Accrediting Agency: French Atomic Energy Commission (CEA), both Ministries of Education and Industry

Degrees and Diplomas: *Brevet de Technicien supérieur*; *Diplôme d'Ingénieur*: **Nuclear Engineering.** *Master*; *Doctorat*. Masters with the University of Paris-Saclay and The Joseph Founier University (Grenoble)

Last Updated: 08/04/15

NATIONAL INSTITUTE OF ORIENTAL LANGUAGES AND CIVILIZATIONS - PARIS

Institut national des Langues et Civilisations orientales (INALCO)

65 rue des Grands Moulins, CS21351, 75013 Paris
Tel: +33(1) 81-70-10-14
Website: http://www.inalco.fr

President: Manuelle Franck (2013-) Tel: +33(1) 81-70-10-31

Head of Administration: Pascal Jorland Tel: +33(1) 81-70-10-40

International Relations: Martine Montoya
Tel: +33(1) 81-70-11-74 EMail: martine.montoya@inalco.fr

Department

African Studies (African Languages; African Studies; Anthropology; Art History; Development Studies; Economics; Geography; History; Literature; Political Sciences; Religion; Swahili); **Arab Studies** (Anthropology; Arabic; Art History; Arts and Humanities; Cultural Studies; Development Studies; Economics; Geography; History; Literature; Political Sciences; Religion); **Central and Eastern European Studies** (Albanian; Anthropology; Art History; Baltic Languages; Central European Studies; Czech; Development Studies; Eastern European Studies; Economics; Finnish; Geography; Greek; History; Hungarian; Literature; Polish; Political Sciences; Religion; Romance Languages; Romanian; Slavic Languages); **Chinese Studies** (Anthropology; Art History; Chinese; Development Studies; Economics; Geography; History; International Relations; Literature; Political Sciences; Religion; Translation and Interpretation); **Civilizations of the Americas** (American Studies; Amerindian Languages; Anthropology; Art History; Development Studies; Economics; Geography; History; Indigenous Studies; Political Sciences; Religion); **French as a Foreign Language** (French); **Hebrew and Jewish Languages and Civilizations** (Anthropology; Art History; Development Studies; Economics; Geography; Hebrew; History; Jewish Studies; Political Sciences; Religion); **International Business** (International Business; International Economics); **International Studies** *(HEI)* (International Relations; International Studies); **Japanese Studies** (Anthropology; Art History; Development Studies; Economics; Geography; History; International Relations; Literature; Political Sciences; Religion); **Russian Studies** (Anthropology; Armenian; Art History; Development Studies; Economics; Geography; History; Literature; Mongolian; Oriental Languages; Political Sciences; Religion; Russian; Slavic Languages); **South Asian Studies** (Anthropology; Art History; Development Studies; Economics; Geography; Hindi; History; Indic Languages; Literature; Political Sciences; Religion; South and Southeast Asian Languages; South Asian Studies; Urdu); **South East Asian, Upper Asian and Pacific Studies** (Anthropology; Art History; Development Studies; Economics; Filipino; Geography; History; Literature; Malay; Political Sciences; Religion; South and Southeast Asian Languages; Tibetan; Vietnamese)

Research Centre

ASIEs (Austronesian and Oceanic Languages; Chinese; Korean; Literature; South and Southeast Asian Languages); **Automatic Language Processing** (Linguistics; Modern Languages); **Central Europe-Eurasia** (Central European Studies; Russian); **History, Societies and World Territories** (History; Social Sciences); **Iranian and Indian Worlds** (Asian Studies; Middle Eastern Studies); **Japanese Studies** (History; Japanese; Literature; Southeast Asian Studies); **Languages and Cultures of Black Africa** (African Languages; Cultural Studies); **Languages and Cultures of North Africa and Diasporas** (Arabic; Cultural Studies; Jewish Studies; North African Studies); **Linguistic Research on East Asia** (East Asian Studies; Linguistics); **Middle Eastern and Mediterranean Studies** (Hebrew; Jewish Studies; Mediterranean Studies; Middle Eastern Studies); **Plurality of Languages and Identities in Teaching** (Applied Linguistics)

History: Founded 1699 as Royal School, reorganized 1795 and 1866. Became Ecole nationale 1870, Centre universitaire 1969, and acquired present status and title 1991. Since 1985, INALCO has been recognized as a 'Grand établissement à caractère scientifique, culturel et professionnel'.

Admission Requirements: Secondary school certificate (baccalauréat) or foreign equivalent, or entrance examination

Main Language(s) of Instruction: French

Degrees and Diplomas: *Licence*: **Modern Languages.** *Master*: **Cultural Studies; Foreign Languages Education; International Studies; Modern Languages; Teacher Training; Translation and Interpretation.** *Doctorat*. Degrees in Teaching French as a Foreign Language, Masters recherche, Masters professionnel

Publications: Cahiers Balkaniques; Cahiers de Littérature Orale; Cipango; Comptes rendus du Groupe Linguistique d'études chamito-sémitiques; Etudes de l'Océan Indien; Slovo; Yod

Last Updated: 01/04/15

NATIONAL INSTITUTE OF SPORTS, EXPERTISE AND PERFORMANCE

Institut national du Sport, de l'Expertise et de la Performance (INSEP)

11 avenue du Tremblay, 75012 Paris
Tel: +33(1) 41-74-41-00
Fax: +33(1) 41-74-45-30
EMail: communication@insep.fr
Website: http://www.insep.fr

Director: Jean-Pierre De Vincenzi (2007-) Tel: +33(1) 41-74-42-44

International Relations: Agathe Barbieux, Head of Communication and Interational Relations
Tel: +33(1) 41-74-42-00 EMail: agathe.barbieux@insep.fr

Programme

Sports and Physical Activity *(STAPS)* (Physical Education; Sports; Sports Medicine); **Sports Management** (Sports Management); **Sports Trainer** (Physical Education; Sports)

History: Founded in 2009 on the basis of the Institut National du Sport et de l'Éducation Physique (INSEP).

Main Language(s) of Instruction: French

Accrediting Agency: Ministry of Youth and Sports

Degrees and Diplomas: *Brevet de Technicien supérieur*: **Sports.** *Licence*: **Sports.** *Master*: **Sports; Sports Management.** Preparation for CAPEPS exam.

Last Updated: 31/03/15

NATIONAL MARITIME SCHOOL

Ecole nationale supérieure maritime (ENSM)

Antenne Voltaire - 1 place des Degrés, 92055 Paris la Défense
Tel: +33(1) 40-81-87-88
EMail: ensm@supmaritime.fr
Website: http://www.supmaritime.fr

Director General: François Marendet (2012-)
EMail: ensm@supmaritime.fr

School

Le Havre (Marine Engineering); **Marseille** (Marine Engineering); **Nantes** (Marine Engineering); **Saint-Malo** (Marine Engineering)

Further Information: Le Havre, Marseille, Nantes, Saint Malo

History: Founded 2010 following merger of the 4 Merchant Navy Schools of Le Havre, Marseilles, Nantes and St Malo.

Admission Requirements: Baccalauréat or equivalent and entrance exam and jury selection or Baccalauréat and 2 years of higher education, Entrance exam and jury selection.

Main Language(s) of Instruction: French

Accrediting Agency: Commission des titres d'ingénieur (CTI)

Degrees and Diplomas: *Diplôme d'Ingénieur*: **Engineering; Marine Transport.** Double degree in Marine Transport (DESMM) and

Engineering; Diplôme d'officier chef de quart machine; Diplôme de chef mécanicien 8000 kW;
Last Updated: 30/03/15

NATIONAL MARITIME SCHOOL - LE HAVRE CENTRE

ECOLE NATIONALE SUPÉRIEURE MARITIME - CENTRE DU HAVRE

Quai du Cameroun, 76600 Le Havre
Tel: +33(2) 35-54-78-00
EMail: ensm.le-havre@supmaritime.fr

Head: Christian Larrieu EMail: christian.larrieu@supmaritime.fr

Programme
Nautical Studies (Nautical Science)

History: Founded in 1665 as Ecole d'Hydrographie de Marseille. Became National Maritime School of Le Havre in 2010.

Main Language(s) of Instruction: French

Accrediting Agency: Commission des Titres d'Ingénieur (CTI)

Degrees and Diplomas: *Diplôme d'Ingénieur*: **Marine Transport.** Diplôme d'élève officier de 1ère classe de la marine marchande (DEO1MM); Diplôme d'études supérieures de la marine marchande (DESMM); Brevet de capitaine de 1ère classe de la navigation maritime

NATIONAL MARITIME SCHOOL - MARSEILLE CENTRE

ECOLE NATIONALE SUPÉRIEURE MARITIME - CENTRE DE MARSEILLE (ENMM)

39, avenue du Corail, 13285 Marseille, Cedex 08
Tel: +33(9) 70-00-03-00
Fax: +33(9) 70-00-04-79
EMail: marseille@supmaritime.fr

Director: Cyrille Le Camus EMail: cyrille.le-camus@supmaritime.fr

Department
Energy (Energy Engineering); **Naval Architecture** (Naval Architecture); **Navigation** (Marine Engineering; Marine Transport)

History: Founded 1761 as Ecole d'Hydrographie de Marseille. Acquired present status 2010.

Admission Requirements: Entrance examination. Baccalauréat or equivalent Secondary School degree

Main Language(s) of Instruction: French

Degrees and Diplomas: *Licence*: **Marine Transport.** Diplôme d'élève officier de 1ère classe de la marine marchande (Licence Level)

NATIONAL MARITIME SCHOOL - NANTES CENTRE

ECOLE NATIONALE SUPÉRIEURE MARITIME - CENTRE DE NANTES

rue Gabriel Peri, BP 90303, 44103 Nantes, Cedex 04
Tel: +33(2) 40-71-01-80
EMail: ensm.nantes@supmaritime.fr

Director: Yann Vachias EMail: yann.vachias@supmaritime.fr

Programme
Nautical Studies (Engineering; Nautical Science)

History: Founded 1672. Acquired present status 2010.

Main Language(s) of Instruction: French

Accrediting Agency: Commission des titres d'ingénieur (CTI)

Degrees and Diplomas: *Diplôme d'Ingénieur*: **Marine Transport.** Diplôme d'études supérieures de la marine marchande (DESMM)

NATIONAL MARITIME SCHOOL - ST MALO CENTRE

ECOLE NATIONALE SUPÉRIEURE MARITIME - CENTRE DE SAINT MALO (ENMM)

BP 109, 4, rue de la Victoire, 35412 Saint-Malo, Cedex
Tel: +33(2) 99-40-68-80
Fax: +33(9) 70-00-04-09
EMail: ensm.saint-malo@supmaritime.fr

Director: Pierre Leonard EMail: pierre.leonard@supmaritime.fr

Programme
Marine Transport (Marine Engineering)

History: Founded 1669. Acquired present status 2010.

Main Language(s) of Instruction: French

Degrees and Diplomas: Diplome d'Officier Chef de Quart Machine (OCQM)

Student Services: Canteen

NATIONAL SCHOOL OF ADVANCED AGRONOMY STUDIES - DIJON

AgroSup Dijon

26, boulevard Docteur Petitjean, BP 87999, 21079 Dijon, Cedex
Tel: +33(3) 80-77-25-25
Fax: +33(3) 80-77-25-00
EMail: international.agrosupdijon@agrosupdijon.fr
Website: http://www.agrosupdijon.fr

Interim Managing Director: Pierre-André Maréchal
EMail: direction@agrosupdijon.fr

Director of Services: Christine Le Noan
Tel: +33(3) 80-77-25-04 EMail: christine.lenoan@agrosupdijon.fr

International Relations: Gaëlle Roudaut
EMail: international@agrosupdijon.fr

Department
Agronomy, Agricultural Equipment, Animal Husbandry and Environment *(D2A2E)* (Agricultural Equipment; Agronomy; Animal Husbandry; Environmental Studies); **Engineering and Processing Sciences** *(DSIP)* (Engineering); **Food Sciences and Nutrition** *(DSAN)* (Food Science; Nutrition); **Human and Social Sciences** *(DSHS)* (Humanities and Social Science Education)

Institute
Eduter (Computer Engineering; Engineering; Rural Planning)

History: Founded 2009 following merger of the Établissement National d'Enseignement Supérieur Agronomique de Dijon (ENESAD - formation d'ingénieurs agronomes) and the École Nationale Supérieure de Biologie Appliquée à la Nutrition et à l'Alimentation (ENSBANA - formation d'ingénieurs en agroaliment)

Admission Requirements: Competitive entrance examination following 2 yrs further study after secondary school certificate (baccalauréat) or equivalent

Fees: 900 per annum (Euro)

Main Language(s) of Instruction: French

Accrediting Agency: Ministry of Agriculture

Degrees and Diplomas: *Licence professionnelle*: **Agricultural Equipment; Teacher Training.** *Diplôme d'Ingénieur*: **Agriculture.** *Master*: **Agricultural Economics; Agricultural Management; Arts and Humanities; Biological and Life Sciences; Economics; Education; Environmental Studies; Food Science; Health Sciences; Technology.** *Doctorat*: **Agriculture; Food Science; Information Technology; Social Sciences.** Also Mastère

Student Services: Canteen, Facilities for disabled people, Residential Facilities, Sports Facilities

Last Updated: 30/03/15

NATIONAL SCHOOL OF ADVANCED STUDIES IN NATURE AND LANDSCAPE ARCHITECTURE, BLOIS

Ecole nationale supérieure de la Nature et du Paysage (ENSNP)

9 rue de La Chocolaterie, cs 2902, 41029 Blois, cedex
Tel: +33(2) 54-78-37-00
Fax: +33(2) 54-78-40-70
EMail: ensnp@ensnp.fr
Website: http://www.ensnp.fr/

Director: Marc Claramunt EMail: claramunt@ensnp.fr

International Relations: Sabine Bouché-Pillon, in charge of International Relations EMail: s.bouche-pillon@ensnp.fr

Programme
Nature and Landscape Architecture (Biology; Botany; Ecology; English; Geography; Geology; Landscape Architecture; Mathematics and Computer Science; Painting and Drawing; Photography)
History: Founded 1993.
Academic Year: September-June
Admission Requirements: Entrance examination,Secondary School certificate (baccalauréat) or equivalent, entrance exam or professional experience
Main Language(s) of Instruction: French
Degrees and Diplomas: *Master*: **Landscape Architecture.**
Student Services: Library
Last Updated: 12/03/15

NATIONAL SCHOOL OF AGRICULTURAL ENGINEERING OF BORDEAUX AQUITAINE

Bordeaux Sciences Agro
1, cours du Général de Gaulle, CS40201, 33175 Gradignan
Tel: +33(5) 57-35-07-07
Fax: +33(5) 57-35-07-09
EMail: direction@agro-bordeaux.fr
Website: http://www.agro-bordeaux.fr

Director: Olivier Lavialle
Tel: +33(5) 57-35-07-01 EMail: direction@agro-bordeaux.fr
Secretary General: Frédéric Bousquet
Tel: +33(5) 57-35-07-01
EMail: frederic.bousquet@agro-bordeaux.fr
International Relations: Tanya Froute-Pardo, In charge of International Relations
Tel: +33(5) 57-35-07-18 EMail: tanya.pardo@agro-bordeaux.fr

Department
Agriculture and Biotechnology (Agriculture; Biological and Life Sciences; Crop Production; Environmental Engineering; Forestry; Oenology; Soil Science); **Continuing Education** (Agriculture; Fishery; Forestry); **Economics, Rural Development and Engineering** (Agricultural Economics; Business Administration; Computer Science; Engineering; Farm Management; Rural Planning)
History: Founded 1963 as École Nationale d'Ingénieurs des Travaux Agricoles. Acquired present title 2011.
Academic Year: September to June
Admission Requirements: Two years of preparatory studies after baccalauréat and competitive entrance examination
Main Language(s) of Instruction: French, English
Accrediting Agency: Commission des titres d'ingénieurs; Ministère de l'agriculture et de la pêche.
Degrees and Diplomas: *Licence professionnelle*: **Rural Studies.** *Diplôme d'Ingénieur*: **Agriculture.** *Mastère spécialisé*: **Viticulture.** *Master*: **Agricultural Management; Agronomy; Ecology; Forestry; Oenology; Viticulture.**
Student Services: Canteen, Facilities for disabled people, Health Services, Language Laboratory, Residential Facilities, Social Counselling, Sports Facilities

Academic Staff *2014*: Total 140
Student Numbers *2014*: Total 580
Last Updated: 11/03/15

NATIONAL SCHOOL OF AGRICULTURE STUDIES OF TOULOUSE-AUZEVILLE

Ecole nationale de Formation agronomique de Toulouse-Auzeville (ENFA)
BP 87, 2, route de Narbonne, 31326 Castanet Tolosan, Cedex
Tel: +33(5) 61-75-32-32
Fax: +33(5) 61-75-03-09
EMail: secretariat-direction.enfa@educagri.fr
Website: http://www.enfa.fr

Director: Emmanuel Delmotte (2014-2019)
Tel: +33(5) 61-75-32-16
EMail: secretariat-direction.enfa@educagri.fr
International Relations: Sophie Raynaud
Tel: +33(5) 61-75-34-63 EMail: coop-inter.enfa@educagri.fr

Programme
Agricultural Education (Agricultural Education; Agricultural Equipment; Management; Rural Planning)
History: Founded 1963.
Main Language(s) of Instruction: French
Degrees and Diplomas: *Licence*; *Licence professionnelle*; *Master*: **Agricultural Education; Engineering Management.** Masters recherche, Masters professionnel
Student Services: Canteen, Residential Facilities
Last Updated: 11/03/15

NATIONAL SCHOOL OF APPLIED ARTS

Ecole nationale supérieure des Arts appliqués et des Métiers d'Art (ENSAAMA)
63-65, rue Olivier-de-Serres, 75015 Paris
Tel: +33(1) 53-68-16-90
Fax: +33(1) 53-68-16-99
EMail: relations-internationales@ensaama.net
Website: http://www.ensaama.net

Director: Laurent Scordino
International Relations: Marie Ogée, Head of International Relations
Tel: +33(6) 89-94-57-91
EMail: relations-internationales@ensaama.net

Programme
Applied Arts (Ceramic Art; Design; Fine Arts; Industrial Design; Textile Design; Visual Arts)
History: Established in 1922, ENSAAMA was later created in 1969 through the merger of the École des Arts Appliqués à l'industrie and the École des Métiers d'Art
Academic Year: September – May
Admission Requirements: Baccalauréat STI arts appliqués or upgrade classes for applied arts (MAN). Entrance exam and selection jury.
Fees: None
Main Language(s) of Instruction: French
Accrediting Agency: Ministry of Culture and Communication
Degrees and Diplomas: *Brevet de Technicien supérieur*: **Ceramic Art; Design; Visual Arts.** Diplôme des métiers d'art (DMA) 3 yrs; Diplôme supérieur d'arts appliqués créateur-concepteur (DSAA) 4 yrs
Last Updated: 12/03/15

NATIONAL SCHOOL OF ARCHIVAL STUDIES PARIS

Ecole nationale des Chartes (EDC)
65, rue de Richelieu, 75002 Paris
Tel: +33(1) 55-42-75-00
Fax: +33(1) 55-42-75-09
EMail: secretariat@enc.sorbonne.fr
Website: http://www.enc.sorbonne.fr

Director: Jean-Michel Leniaud (2011-)
EMail: secretariat@enc.sorbonne.fr
Administrative Officer: Jocelyne Cazorla
EMail: dgs@enc.sorbonne.fr
International Relations: Amélie de Miribel
Tel: +33(1) 55-42-75-19 EMail: ri@enc.sorbonne.fr

Programme
Art History and Archaeology (Archaeology; Art History); **Books and Media** (Information Technology); **History of Books and Bibliography** (Ancient Books; Library Science); **History of Civil and Canon Law** (Canon Law; Civil Law; Law); **History of French Institutions, Archives and Diplomatic Studies** (Archiving; Documentation Techniques; History); **Mediaeval Literature and Codicology** (Literature; Medieval Studies); **Modern Languages** (English; German; Italian; Russian; Spanish); **Palaeography** (Ancient Civilizations; Ancient Languages); **Roman Philology** (Latin; Philology; Romance Languages)

History: Founded 1821, reorganized 1846. An autonomous institution.

Academic Year: October to June (October-February; February-June)

Admission Requirements: Competitive entrance examination following 2-3 yrs further study after secondary school certificate (baccalauréat) or equivalent

Main Language(s) of Instruction: French

Degrees and Diplomas: *Master*: **Information Technology; Medieval Studies; Multimedia; Video.** Diplôme d'archiviste paléographe; doctorats conjoints, avec les universités Paris I-Panthéon-Sorbonne et Paris-Sorbonne Paris-IV.

Student Services: Library

Publications: Livraisons d'histoire de l'architecture; Positions des thèses

Last Updated: 30/03/15

NATIONAL SCHOOL OF CIVIL AVIATION

Ecole nationale de l'Aviation civile (ENAC)

BP 4005, 7, avenue Edouard Belin, 31055 Toulouse
Tel: +33(5) 62-17-40-00
Fax: +33(5) 62-17-40-23
EMail: guy.lagarrigue@enac.fr
Website: http://www.enac.fr

Director: Marc Houalla (2008-) EMail: marc.houalla@enac.fr

Secretary General: Gildas Le Breton

International Relations: Guy Lagarrigue
Tel: +33(5) 62-17-40-05 EMail: guy.lagarrigue@enac.fr

School

Civil Aviation (Aeronautical and Aerospace Engineering; Air Transport; Transport Management)

Further Information: also campuses in: Melun, Saint Yan, Grenoble, Montpellier, Carcasonne, Castelnaudary, Muret, Biscarrosse

History: Founded 1948.

Academic Year: September to June (September-January; February-June)

Admission Requirements: Competitive entrance examination following 2 years further study after secondary school certificate (Baccalauréat) or following at least first university qualification (L2, DUT or BTS), or equivalent.

Main Language(s) of Instruction: French, English

Accrediting Agency: Ministry of Transport

Degrees and Diplomas: *Diplôme d'Ingénieur*: **Aeronautical and Aerospace Engineering; Air Transport.** *Mastère spécialisé*: **Aeronautical and Aerospace Engineering; Air Transport; Transport Management.** *Master*: **Air Transport; Transport Management.** also: TSA, Aviation Senior Technician training; ATCO, International Air Traffic Controller training; EPL, Air Transport Pilot training; TAE, Aircraft Dispatcher training;

Student Services: Canteen, Cultural Activities, Library, Residential Facilities, Sports Facilities

Academic Staff *2011-2012*: Total 930

Student Numbers *2011-2012*: Total 1,900

Last Updated: 11/03/15

NATIONAL SCHOOL OF DECORATIVE ARTS

Ecole nationale supérieure des Arts décoratifs (ENSAD)

31, rue d'Ulm, 75240 Paris, cedex 05
Tel: +33(1) 42-34-97-00
Fax: +33(1) 42-34-97-85
EMail: frederique.bruelle@ensad.fr
Website: http://www.ensad.fr

Director: Marc Partouche (2014-)

International Relations: Frédérique Bruelle, Head of International Relations
Tel: +33(1) 42-34-98-13 EMail: frederique.bruelle@ensad.fr

School

Fine Arts (Fine Arts; Furniture Design; Industrial Design; Photography; Video; Visual Arts)

History: ENSAD has its roots in the Royal Free School of 1766 to develop crafts relating to the arts in order to improve the quality of manufactured goods. After several name changes, in 1877 the school became the National School of Decorative Arts (l'Ecole nationale des arts décoratifs) before taking its present name of ENSAD (l'Ecole nationale supérieure des arts décoratifs) in 1927.

Academic Year: September-June

Admission Requirements: Entrance exam and Jury selection. Candidates can only apply up to three times.

Fees: 433 per annum (Euro)

Main Language(s) of Instruction: French

Accrediting Agency: Ministry of Culture.

Degrees and Diplomas: *Master*: **Cinema and Television; Design; Fashion Design; Graphic Design; Interior Design; Painting and Drawing; Photography; Textile Design; Video; Visual Arts.** Diplôme de l'ENSAD (5yrs)

Student Numbers *2014*: Total 700

Last Updated: 12/03/15

NATIONAL SCHOOL OF ENGINEERING - SAINT-ETIENNE

Ecole nationale d'Ingénieurs de Saint-Etienne (ENISE)

58, rue Jean Parot, 42023 Saint-Etienne, Cedex 2
Tel: +33(4) 77-43-84-84
EMail: direction@enise.fr
Website: http://www.enise.fr

Director: Roland Fortunier (2010-) EMail: fortunier@enise.fr

International Relations: Emilie Favier
Tel: +33(4) 77-43-84-35 EMail: international@enise.fr

Programme

Engineering (Civil Engineering; Engineering; Mechanical Engineering)

History: Founded 1961.

Admission Requirements: Competitive entrance examination following 2-3 years further study after secondary school certificate (baccalauréat) or following first university qualification (DEUG, DUT or BTS), or equivalent

Main Language(s) of Instruction: French

Accrediting Agency: Commission des Titres de l'Ingénieurs (CTI)

Degrees and Diplomas: *Diplôme d'Ingénieur*: **Civil Engineering; Mechanical Engineering.** *Mastère spécialisé*: **Energy Engineering.** *Master*: **Construction Engineering; Industrial Engineering; Materials Engineering.**

Student Services: Library, Nursery Care, Sports Facilities

Academic Staff *2012*	MEN	WOMEN	**TOTAL**
FULL-TIME	72	23	**95**
Student Numbers *2012*			
All (Foreign included)	719	119	**838**

Last Updated: 02/04/15

NATIONAL SCHOOL OF GEOGRAPHIC SCIENCES

Ecole nationale des Sciences géographiques (ENSG-GÉO)

6 et 8, avenue Blaise Pascal, Cité Descartes, Champs-sur-Marne, 77455 Marne-la-Vallée, Cedex 2
Tel: +33(1) 64-15-30-01
Fax: +33(1) 64-15-31-07
EMail: info@ensg.ign.fr
Website: http://www.ensg.ign.fr

Director: Denis Priou (2011-)
Tel: +33(1) 64-15-32-02 EMail: denis.priou@ensg.ign.fr

Division

Cartography (Arts and Humanities; Computer Science; Geography; Surveying and Mapping)

History: Founded 1941.

Admission Requirements: Entrance examination following 2 years of post-secondary study (scientific prep school courses) or L2 or associate degree (BTS) in ' Computer Science ', ' Statistics and Decisional Computer Science ', ' Electrical Engineering and Industrial Computer Science ' and ' Services and Network Communications ' or equivalent degree in Sciences. Undergraduate course of study: Baccalauréat in Sciences or foreign equivalent

Fees: 690 per annum for non salaried students not subsidized by an official institution (Euro)

Main Language(s) of Instruction: French

Accrediting Agency: Ministry of Ecology and Sustainable Development; Ministry of Higher Education, Commission des Titres d'Ingénieur (CTI)

Degrees and Diplomas: *Brevet de Technicien supérieur*: **Surveying and Mapping.** *Diplôme d'Ingénieur*: **Information Management; Information Technology; Surveying and Mapping.** *Mastère spécialisé*: **Geography; Surveying and Mapping.** Advanced Certificate in Geomatics

Student Services: Cultural Activities, Sports Facilities

Last Updated: 11/03/15

NATIONAL SCHOOL OF INSURANCE

Ecole nationale d'Assurances (ENASS)

Paris La Défense 8, 20 bis Jardins Boieldieu, 92071 la Défense cedex Paris
Tel: +33(1) 47-76-58-00
Fax: +33(1) 47-76-59-52
EMail: infoenass@enass.fr
Website: http://www.enass.fr

Director: Benoit Chapelotte (2014-)

Programme

Insurance (Insurance)

History: Founded 1946.

Admission Requirements: Licence professionnelle: 2 years further study after secondary school certificate (baccalauréat); Master: Entrance exam

Fees: Master, 5190 per annum (Euro)

Main Language(s) of Instruction: French

Degrees and Diplomas: *Brevet de Technicien supérieur*: **Insurance.** *Licence professionnelle*: **Insurance.** *Master*: **Insurance.** MBA; Certificat assurance des risques internationaux

Student Services: Cultural Activities, Sports Facilities

Last Updated: 09/03/15

NATIONAL SCHOOL OF LANDSCAPE ARCHITECTURE OF VERSAILLES-MARSEILLES

Ecole nationale supérieure du Paysage de Versailles-Marseille

10 rue Maréchal Joffre, 78000 Versailles
Tel: +33(1) 39-24-62-00
Fax: +33(1) 39-24-62-01
EMail: a.decastelnau@ecole-paysage.fr
Website: http://www.ecole-paysage.fr

Director: Vincent Piveteau EMail: v.piveteau@ecole-paysage.fr

Secretary General: Sylvie Benedetti
Tel: +33(1) 39-24-62-04 EMail: s.benedetti@ecole-paysage.fr

International Relations: Géraldine Lecanuet
Tel: +33(1) 39-24-62-66 EMail: international@ecole-paysage.fr

Programme

Landscape Architecture (Landscape Architecture)

Further Information: Branch in Marseilles

History: Founded 1976.

Admission Requirements: Competitive entrance examination for students following baccalauréat + 2 years' study

Main Language(s) of Instruction: French

Degrees and Diplomas: *Diplôme d'Etat*: **Landscape Architecture.** *Master*: **Landscape Architecture.** Certificat d'études supérieures paysagères (CESP); Masters recherche in Theory and Methods in Landscaping

Publications: Les Carnets du paysage

Last Updated: 13/03/15

NATIONAL SCHOOL OF LIBRARY AND INFORMATION SCIENCES

Ecole nationale supérieure des Sciences de l'Information et des Bibliothèques (ENSSIB)

17-21, boulevard du 11 Novembre 1918, 69623 Villeurbanne, Cedex
Tel: +33(4) 72-44-43-43
Fax: +33(4) 72-44-43-44
EMail: virginie.destez@enssib.fr
Website: http://www.enssib.fr

Director: Yves Alix (2015-)
Tel: +33(4) 72-44-43-08 EMail: direction@enssib.fr

Secretary General: Colette Gumez
Tel: +33(4) 72-44-43-10 EMail: colette.gumez@enssib.fr

International Relations: Raphaëlle Bats
Tel: +33(4) 44-75-98 EMail: raphaelle.bats@enssib.fr

Division

Information and Documentation Sciences Research (Documentation Techniques; Information Sciences); **Library Science** (Library Science)

History: Founded 1964. Acquired present status 1992.

Admission Requirements: Licence and competitive entrance examination for civil servants preparing the DCB, licence for students preparing the master degree

Main Language(s) of Instruction: French

Degrees and Diplomas: *Diplôme d'Etat*: **Library Science.** *Master*: **Archiving; Cultural Studies; Information Sciences; Library Science; Publishing and Book Trade.** *Doctorat*: **Information Technology.** School Diploma in Library Science and Documentation

Student Services: Canteen, Health Services, Library, Sports Facilities

Publications: Bulletin des Bibliothèques de France

Publishing House: Enssib

Last Updated: 30/03/15

NATIONAL SCHOOL OF MAGISTRACY STUDIES

Ecole nationale de la Magistrature

10, rue des Frères-Bonie, 33000 Bordeaux
Tel: +33(5) 56-00-10-10
Fax: +33(5) 56-00-10-99
EMail: enm-info-di@justice.fr
Website: http://www.enm.justice.fr

Director: Xavier Ronsin (2012-) EMail: xavier.ronsin@justice.fr

International Relations: Anthony Manwarning, Head of international Relations EMail: enm-info-di@justice.fr

Programme

Judicial Studies (Criminal Law; Justice Administration; Law)

Department

Languages and Civilizations (Cultural Studies; Modern Languages)

Further Information: Has a second site in Paris focusing on in-service and non-professional training and international relations.

History: Created in 1958 to train future judges and public prosecutors.

Admission Requirements: Entrance exam, 4 yrs of University studies or a degree from an Institute of Political Science. Also possible with a minimum of 4 yrs professional experience.

Main Language(s) of Instruction: French

Accrediting Agency: Ministry of Justice

Degrees and Diplomas: Studies cover a continuous 31-month period with internships. The third year is devoted to a specialisation in a field.

Publications: La revue des cahiers de la justice

Last Updated: 11/03/15

NATIONAL SCHOOL OF METEOROLOGICAL STUDIES - TOULOUSE

Ecole nationale de la Météorologie (ENM)
42 Avenue Gaspard Coriolis, BP 45712, 31057 Toulouse, Cedex 1
Tel: +33(5) 61-07-80-80
Fax: +33(5) 61-07-96-30
EMail: enm.fr@meteo.fr
Website: http://www.enm.meteo.fr

Director: Jean-Marc Bonnet EMail: jean-marc.bonnet@meteo.fr

Secretary General: Jean-Claude Camoin
EMail: jean-claude.camoin@meteo.fr

Programme

Meteorology (Meteorology)

History: Founded 1922, acquired present status 1969.

Academic Year: September to July

Admission Requirements: Competitive entrance examination following 2-3 yrs' further study after secondary school certificate (baccalauréat)

Main Language(s) of Instruction: French

Accrediting Agency: Ministry of Transport, Commission des Titres d'Ingénieur (CTI)

Degrees and Diplomas: *Diplôme d'Ingénieur*: **Meteorology.** also: Titre de Technicien des Métiers de la Météorologie (TMM)

Student Services: Academic Counselling, Canteen, Cultural Activities, Facilities for disabled people, Health Services, Nursery Care, Social Counselling, Sports Facilities

Last Updated: 09/03/15

NATIONAL SCHOOL OF PHOTOGRAPHY, ARLES

Ecole nationale supérieure de la Photographie (ENSP)
16, rue des Arènes, BP 10149, 13631 Arles, Cedex
Tel: +33(4) 90-99-33-33
Fax: +33(4) 90-99-33-59
EMail: communication@ensp-arles.com
Website: http://www.ensp-arles.com

Director: Rémy Fenzy (2010-)

International Relations: Laurence Canaux
EMail: laurence.canaux@ensp-arles.com

Board of Study

Photography (Photography)

History: Founded 1982.

Academic Year: October to June

Admission Requirements: Competitive examination two years after the Baccalauréat

Fees: 433 per annum (Euro)

Main Language(s) of Instruction: French

Accrediting Agency: Ministère de la Culture et de la Communication

Degrees and Diplomas: *Master*: **Photography.** Diplôme de l'École Nationale Supérieure de la Photographie

Publications: Infra-mince

Last Updated: 12/03/15

NATIONAL SCHOOL OF PUBLIC ADMINISTRATION

Ecole nationale d'Administration (ENA)
1, rue Sainte Marguerite, 67080 Strasbourg, Cedex
Tel: +33(3) 88-21-44-44
Fax: +33(3) 88-21-44-59
EMail: presentation@ena.fr
Website: http://www.ena.fr

Director: Nathalie Loiseau (2012-) EMail: nathalie.loiseau@ena.fr

Secretary General: Thierry Rogelet

International Relations: Pierre Thenard, Head of International Relations Tel: +33(1) 44-41-85-90

Programme

Administration (Administration; Public Administration); **European Studies** (European Studies); **Territorial Administration** (Public Administration)

Further Information: Also 2 branches in Paris

History: Founded 1945. Incorporated the Institut international d'Administration publique, Paris, 2002.

Admission Requirements: University or engineer school diploma or competitive entrance examination for active civil servants

Main Language(s) of Instruction: French

Degrees and Diplomas: *Diplôme d'Etat*; *Mastère spécialisé*: **Public Administration.** *Master*: **Administration; European Studies; Public Administration.**

Last Updated: 09/03/15

NATIONAL SCHOOL OF STATISTICS AND INFORMATION ANALYSIS

Ecole nationale de la Statistique et de l'Analyse de l'Information (ENSAI)
Campus de Ker-Lann, Rue Blaise Pascal, BP 37203, 35172 Bruz
Tel: +33(2) 99-05-32-32
Fax: +33(2) 99-05-32-05
EMail: communication@ensai.fr
Website: http://www.ensai.com

Director: Pascal Chevalier (2011-)
Tel: +33(2) 99-05-32-83 EMail: pascal.chevalier@ensai.fr

Secretary General: Jean-Michel Grignon
EMail: jean-michel.grignon@ensai.fr

International Relations: Esther Lalau Keraly
Tel: +33(2) 99-05-32-43 EMail: international@ensai.fr

School

Statistics (Arts and Humanities; Computer Science; Economics; Management; Marketing; Statistics)

History: Founded 1942 (see ENSAE).

Academic Year: September to June

Admission Requirements: Competitive entrance examination following 2-3 years study after secondary school certificate (baccalauréat) or transfer following first university qualification or equivalent

Fees: Engineering courses: 737 per annum; Master in Public Statistics: 270 per annum (Euro)

Main Language(s) of Instruction: French

Accrediting Agency: Ministry of Finance, Commission des Titres d'Ingénieur (CTI)

Degrees and Diplomas: *Diplôme d'Etat*: **Statistics.** *Diplôme d'Ingénieur*: **Statistics.** *Master*: **Data Processing; Statistics.**

Student Services: Academic Counselling, Canteen, Facilities for disabled people, Language Laboratory, Sports Facilities

Academic Staff *2013*	**TOTAL**
FULL-TIME	39
Student Numbers *2013*	
All (Foreign included)	414
FOREIGN ONLY	41

Last Updated: 30/03/15

NATIONAL SCHOOL OF THEATRE ARTS AND TECHNIQUES

Ecole nationale supérieure des Arts et Techniques du Théâtre (ENSATT)
4, rue Soeur Bouvier, 69322 Lyon, Cedex 05
Tel: +33(4) 78-15-05-05
Fax: +33(4) 78-15-05-39
EMail: administration@ensatt.fr
Website: http://www.ensatt.fr

Director: Thierry Pariente (2012-)

Head of Administration: Antonietta Mendez

International Relations: Manuele Debrinay-Rizos, In charge of International Relations EMail: manuele.debrinayrizos@ensatt.fr

Programme
Theatre Studies (Performing Arts; Theatre)
History: Founded 1941 in Paris. Moved to Lyon 1997.
Admission Requirements: Minimum age of 25 and must pass the Institute's own exam, specific for each department
Fees: Licence, 267; Master, 400 (Euro)
Main Language(s) of Instruction: French
Degrees and Diplomas: Diplôme d'Université; Diplôme Arts et Techniques du théâtre (Master Level)

Academic Staff *2014*: Total 39
Student Numbers *2014*: Total 167
Last Updated: 30/03/15

NATIONAL SCHOOL OF WATER AND ENVIRONMENTAL ENGINEERING - STRASBOURG

Ecole nationale du Génie de l'Eau et de l'Environnement de Strasbourg (ENGEES)
BP 61039, 1, quai Koch, 67070 Strasbourg, Cedex
Tel: +33(3) 88-24-82-82
Fax: +33(3) 88-37-04-97
EMail: contact@engees.unistra.fr
Website: http://engees.unistra.fr

Director: Jean-François Quéré (2011-)
EMail: jean-francois.quere@engees.unistra.fr
International Relations: Didier Bellefleur
Tel: +33(3) 88-24-82-16 EMail: cathie.hoerth@engees.unistra.fr

Unit
Continuing Education (Civil Engineering; Construction Engineering; Environmental Studies; Human Resources; Public Administration; Public Law; Waste Management); **Engineering** (Biotechnology; Environmental Engineering; Environmental Management; Hydraulic Engineering; Irrigation; Waste Management; Water Management); **Research** (Biotechnology; Environmental Engineering; Environmental Management; Hydraulic Engineering; Public Administration; Social and Community Services; Water Science)

Research Laboratory
Plant Ecology and Hydrology (Ecology; Hydraulic Engineering); **Public Utilities Management** *(GSP)* (Management; Social and Community Services); **Urban Hydraulic Systems** *(IMFS-HU)* (Water Science)
History: Founded 1952. Acquired present status and title 1992.
Academic Year: September to June
Admission Requirements: From 2 to 5 years following secondary school certificate (baccalauréat) in accordance with the degree
Fees: 6200 per annum (Euro)
Main Language(s) of Instruction: French
Accrediting Agency: Commission des Titres d'Ingénieur
Degrees and Diplomas: *Licence professionnelle*: **Environmental Studies.** *Diplôme d'Ingénieur*: **Environmental Engineering; Water Science.** *Master*: **Business Administration; Civil Engineering; Computer Engineering; Development Studies; Earth Sciences; Environmental Studies.**
Student Services: Academic Counselling, Canteen, Careers Guidance, Facilities for disabled people, Health Services, Social Counselling, Sports Facilities
Last Updated: 01/04/15

NATIONAL VETERINARY SCHOOL - MAISONS-ALFORT

Ecole nationale vétérinaire d'Alfort (ENVA)
7, avenue du Général de Gaulle, 94704 Maisons-Alfort, Cedex
Tel: +33(1) 43-96-71-00
Fax: +33(1) 43-96-71-25
EMail: communication@vet-alfort.fr
Website: http://www.vet-alfort.fr
Director: Marc Gogny (2012-) EMail: direction@vet-alfort.fr

Programme
Veterinary Science (Veterinary Science)
Further Information: Has 8 research laboratories
History: Founded 1765.
Academic Year: September to July
Admission Requirements: Competitive entrance examination following a preparatory class after secondary school certificate (baccalauréat) or (DEUG) or equivalent
Main Language(s) of Instruction: French
Accrediting Agency: Ministry of Agriculture
Degrees and Diplomas: *Diplôme d'Etat*: **Animal Husbandry; Veterinary Science.** *Master*. Masters professionnel, Masters recherche; Certificate of Advanced Veterinary Studies (CEAV); Diploma of Specialised Veterinary Studies (DESV)
Student Services: Canteen, Cultural Activities, Library, Residential Facilities, Sports Facilities
Publications: Recueil de Médecine vétérinaire
Last Updated: 30/03/15

NATIONAL VETERINARY SCHOOL - TOULOUSE

Ecole nationale vétérinaire de Toulouse (ENVT)
23, chemin des Capelles, BP 87614, 31100 Toulouse, cedex 3
Tel: +33(5) 61-19-38-00
EMail: direction@envt.fr
Website: http://www.envt.fr
Directeur: Alain Milon (2005-)
International Relations: Françoise Artero
Tel: +33(5) 61-19-32-09 EMail: f.artero@envt.fr

Programme
Veterinary Medicine (Veterinary Science)
History: Founded 1828. New campus 1964. Academic link to Institut National Polytechnique de Toulouse 2010.
Admission Requirements: Competitive entrance examination following 2-3 years further study after secondary school certificate (baccalauréat) or following first university qualification, or equivalent
Fees: 2150 per annum (Euro)
Main Language(s) of Instruction: French
Accrediting Agency: Ministry of Agriculture
Degrees and Diplomas: *Diplôme d'Etat*: **Veterinary Science.** *Master*: **Agrobiology; Biology; Food Science; Pharmacology; Toxicology; Zoology.** Diplôme d'Etudes Fondamentales Vétérinaires (DEFV-Master Level); Diplôme d'Ecole
Student Services: Canteen, Library, Residential Facilities, Sports Facilities

Student Numbers *2014-2014*: Total 675
Last Updated: 30/03/15

NICE NATIONAL ART SCHOOL - VILLA ARSON

Ecole nationale supérieure d'Art de Nice
20 avenue Stéphen Liégeard, 06105 Nice, Cedex 2
Tel: +33(4) 92-07-73-73
Fax: +33(4) 93-84-41-55
EMail: verchere@villa-arson.org
Website: http://www.villa-arson.org
Director: Jean-Pierre Simon EMail: direction@villa-arson.org
International Relations: Catherine Verchère
EMail: international@villa-arson.org

Programme
Design (Design; Graphic Arts; Multimedia; Photography; Sculpture; Video; Visual Arts)
History: Founded in 1973.
Academic Year: Ocotober to June
Admission Requirements: Baccalauréat or equivalent secondary school exam. Entrance exam with a selection jury.
Main Language(s) of Instruction: French
Accrediting Agency: Ministry of Culture and Communication

Degrees and Diplomas: Diplôme national d'arts plastiques (DNAP) 3 yrs; Diplôme national supérieur d'expression plastique (DNSEP) a further 2 yrs

Student Services: Library

Last Updated: 12/03/15

NÎMES ART SCHOOL

École supérieure des beaux-arts de Nîmes (ESBAN)

10, Grand Rue, 30000 Nîmes
Tel: +33(4) 66-76-70-22
EMail: ecole.beauxarts@ville-nimes.fr
Website: http://ecoleartnimes.tumblr.com/

President: Daniel-Jean Valade

International Relations: Lola Wolfhart
EMail: lola.wohlfahrt@ville-nimes.fr

Programme

Arts (Art History; Graphic Arts; Painting and Drawing; Photography; Video; Visual Arts)

Admission Requirements: Entrance examination

Main Language(s) of Instruction: French

Accrediting Agency: Ministry of Culture

Degrees and Diplomas: Diplôme national d'arts plastiques (DNAP) 3 years; Diplôme national supérieur d'expression plastique (DNSEP) a further 2 years

Last Updated: 07/04/15

NORD-PAS-DE-CALAIS ART SCHOOL

Ecole supérieure d'Art du Nord-Pas-de Calais, Dunkerque/Tourcoing

36 bis, rue des Ursulines, 59200 Tourcoing
Tel: +33(3) 59-63-43-20
EMail: contact@esa-n.info
Website: http://www.esa-n.info

Director General: Ronan Prigent EMail: ronan.prigent@esa-n.info

Programme

Fine Arts (Aesthetics; Art History; Painting and Drawing; Photography; Video)

Further Information: also site in Dunkerque

History: Founded 2010 following merger of the Ecole régionale des beaux arts de Dunkerque and the Ecole régionale supérieure d'expression plastique de Tourcoing.

Admission Requirements: Secondary school Certificate (Baccalauréat) or equivalent. Entrance exam with a selection jury.

Fees: Non-grant students: 650 (Euro)

Main Language(s) of Instruction: French

Degrees and Diplomas: *Master*. Diplôme National d'art plastique (DNAP) 3 years; Diplôme National Supérieur d'Expression Plastique (DNSEP) a further 2 years

Publishing house: Editions LUE

Last Updated: 07/04/15

NORMANDY NATIONAL SCHOOL OF ARCHITECTURE

Ecole nationale supérieure d'Architecture de Normandie

27 rue Lucien Fromage, BP 04, 76161 Darnétal
Tel: +33(2) 32-83-42-00
Fax: +33(2) 32-83-42-10
EMail: ecole@rouen.archi.fr
Website: http://www.rouen.archi.fr

Director: Fabienne Fendrich
Tel: +33(2) 32-83-42-01 EMail: fabienne.fendrich@rouen.archi.fr

Administrative and Financial Manager: Philippe Leporcher
Tel: +33(2) 32-83-42-22 EMail: philippe.leporcher@rouen.archi.fr

Programme

Architecture (Architecture; Urban Studies)

History: Founded 1904.

Main Language(s) of Instruction: French

Degrees and Diplomas: *Licence*: **Architecture.** *Master*: **Architectural Restoration; Architecture.** Habilitation à la maîtrise d'oeuvre en son nom propre (HMONP)

Student Services: Canteen

Last Updated: 11/03/15

ORLEANS SCHOOL OF HIGHER EDUCATION IN ART AND DESIGN

Ecole supérieure d'Art et de Design d'Orléans (ESAD)

14 rue Dupanloup, 45000 Orléans
Tel: +33(2) 38-79-24-67
EMail: esad@ville-orleans.fr
Website: http://www.esad-orleans.com

Director: Jacqueline Febvre

International Relations: Isabelle Pagot
EMail: ipagot@esad-orleans.fr

Programme

3D Design (Design; Furniture Design; Interior Design; Production Engineering); **Visual Design** (Design; Graphic Design; Multimedia; Photography; Video)

History: Originally known as the Ecole gratuite de dessin de la Ville d'Orléans, in 1991 it changed its focus to design and applied arts, becoming L'École supérieure d'Art et de Design d'Orléans in 2011.

Academic Year: September to June (September-January; February-June)

Admission Requirements: Baccalauréat or equivalent secondary school exam. Entrance exam with a selection jury.

Fees: Non-grant students: 635 (Euro)

Main Language(s) of Instruction: French

Accrediting Agency: Ministry of Culture and Communication

Degrees and Diplomas: Diplôme National d'Arts Plastiques (DNAP) 3 years; Diplome national supérieur d'expression plastique (DNSEP) a further 2 yrs (MA level)

Last Updated: 17/03/15

PARIS 1 PANTHÉON-SORBONNE UNIVERSITY

Université Paris 1 Panthéon Sorbonne

12, place du Panthéon, 75231 Paris, Cedex 05
Tel: +33(1) 44-07-80-00
Fax: +33(1) 46-34-20-56
EMail: secom@univ-paris1.fr
Website: http://www.univ-paris1.fr

President: Philippe Boutry (2012-)
Tel: +33(1) 44-07-77-03 EMail: cabpresi@univ-paris1.fr

Head of Administration: François Riou
Tel: +33(1) 47-07-77-05 EMail: secretg@univ-paris1.fr

International Relations: Christiane Prigent
Tel: +33(1) 44-07-76-71 EMail: relinter@univ-paris1.fr

School

Law *(Sorbonne-EDS)* (Law)

Department

Business Law *(UFR05)* (Commercial Law); **Economics** *(UFR02)* (Economics); **Economics and Social Administration, Labour and Social Studies** *(AES et Droit social, UFR12)* (Business Administration; Economics; Labour Law; Social Studies); **General Law** *(UFR26)* (Law); **Geography** *(UFR08)* (Environmental Studies; Geography; Rural Planning); **History** *(UFR09)* (Ancient Civilizations; History; Medieval Studies; Modern History); **History of Art and Archaeology** *(UFR03)* (Archaeology; Art History); **International and European Studies** *(UFR07)* (European Studies; International Studies); **Law, Administration and Public Sector Studies** *(UFR01)* (Administration; Law; Public Administration); **Management** *(Ecole de Management de la Sorbonne- UFR06)* (Management); **Mathematics and Computer Science** (Applied Mathematics; Mathematics and Computer Science); **Modern Languages** *(SGEL)*; **Philosophy** *(UFR10)* (Philosophy); **Plastic Arts and Arts Sciences** *(UFR04)* (Aesthetics; Cinema and Television; Design; Fine Arts; Media Studies; Multimedia; Painting and Drawing; Sculpture); **Political Science** *(UFR11)* (Political Sciences); **Sociology** *(UFR10)* (Sociology)

Technology *(IUT, Montreuil)* (Business Administration; Computer Engineering; Production Engineering; Technology); **Technology** *(IUT, Tremblay-en-France)* (Business Administration; Industrial Maintenance; Technology; Transport Management)

Graduate School

Aesthetics, Science and Technologies of the Arts *(EDESTA)* (Fine Arts; Performing Arts); **Applied and Theoritical Linguistics** (Applied Linguistics; Archaeology; Educational Sciences; History; Literature; Modern Languages; Philosophy; Political Sciences; Psychology); **Cognition, Language, Interaction** *(ED SIIC)* (Linguistics; Psycholinguistics; Psychology); **Humanities** (Arts and Humanities)

History: Founded as experimental academic centre 1969. Moved to Saint Denis 1980. Member of the COMUE Paris Lumières University

Academic Year: October to June (October-February; February-June)

Admission Requirements: Secondary school certificate (baccalauréat) or equivalent, or special entrance examination

Main Language(s) of Instruction: French

Degrees and Diplomas: *Diplôme universitaire de Technologie*: **Administration; Technology.** *Licence*: **Arts and Humanities; Fine Arts; Law; Mathematics and Computer Science; Modern Languages; Social Sciences; Technology.** *Licence professionnelle*: **Mathematics and Computer Science; Social Work; Technology.** *Master*: **Applied Mathematics; Archiving; Arts and Humanities; Cinema and Television; Cognitive Sciences; Communication Arts; Comparative Law; Computer Science; Cultural Studies; Economics; Education; European Studies; Fine Arts; Fiscal Law; Gender Studies; Geography; Hebrew; History; Information Sciences; International Studies; Law; Linguistics; Literature; Management; Mass Communication; Mathematics and Computer Science; Media Studies; Mediterranean Studies; Modern Languages; Museum Studies; Music; Performing Arts; Philosophy; Political Sciences; Psychoanalysis; Psychology; Social Sciences; Sociology; Technology.** *Doctorat*: **Aesthetics; Anthropology; Architecture and Planning; Cinema and Television; Comparative Literature; Computer Science; Contemporary History; Criminal Law; Dance; Documentation Techniques; Economics; Educational Sciences; European Studies; Fine Arts; French Studies; Gender Studies; Geography; Geography (Human); Germanic Languages; Hebrew; Hispanic American Studies; History; Industrial Chemistry; Information Sciences; Italian; Law; Linguistics; Management; Medieval Studies; Modern History; Music; North African Studies; Performing Arts; Philosophy; Photography; Political Sciences; Portuguese; Private Law; Psychoanalysis; Psychology; Public Law; Slavic Languages; Social Sciences; Sociology; Spanish; Theatre; Urban Studies; Women's Studies.** Masters recherche, Masters professionnel

Student Services: Academic Counselling, Canteen, Cultural Activities, Facilities for disabled people, Health Services, Library, Nursery Care, Residential Facilities, Social Counselling, Sports Facilities

Publications: 'Le fil d'Ariane' (IEE); Extrême-Orient/Extrême-Occident; Histoire, Epistémologie, Langage; Médiévales; Pratiques de Formation; Recherches linguistiques de Vincennes; Théorie Littérature Enseignement

Publishing House: Presses Universitaires de Vincennes (PUV)

Academic Staff *2012-2013*: Total 654

Student Numbers *2012-2013*: Total 21,974

Last Updated: 10/04/15

PARIS 13 UNIVERSITY

Université Paris 13 - Nord (UP13)

Avenue Jean-Baptiste Clément, 93430 Villetaneuse
Tel: +33(1) 49-40-30-00
Fax: +33(1) 49-40-33-33
EMail: secretaire.gen@univ-paris13.fr
Website: http://www.univ-paris13.fr

President: Jean-Loup Salzmann (2008-)
Tel: +33(1) 49-40-30-07 EMail: cab-pres@univ-paris13.fr

Head of Administration: François Lair
Tel: +33(1) 49-40-30-09 EMail: secretaire.general@univ-paris13.f

International Relations: Solange Montagne-Vilette, Vice-President in charge of International Relations
Tel: +33(1) 49-40-31-60 EMail: solange.villette@orange.fr

Unit

Arts, Human Sciences and Social Sciences (Arts and Humanities; Educational Sciences; English; Geography; History; History of Societies; Literature; Psychology; Spanish); **Communication Sciences** (Communication Studies); **Economics and Management** (Economics; Management); **Health, Medicine and Human Biology** *(Léonard de Vinci, Bobigny)* (Biology; Health Sciences; Medicine); **Law, Social and Political Science** (Law; Political Sciences; Social Sciences)

Institute

Galilée (Chemistry; Computer Science; Electrical Engineering; Laser Engineering; Materials Engineering; Mathematics; Physics; Statistics; Systems Analysis; Telecommunications Engineering); **Technology** *(IUT Villetaneuse)* (Accountancy; Banking; Business Administration; Computer Science; Electronic Engineering; Finance; Human Resources; Insurance; Law; Technology; Telecommunications Engineering); **Technology** *(IUT Bobigny)* (Bioengineering; Business Administration; Business Computing; Computer Networks; Computer Science; Social Work; Technology; Telecommunications Engineering); **Technology** *(IUT, Saint-Denis)* (Business Administration; Business and Commerce; Civil Security; Industrial Maintenance; Measurement and Precision Engineering; Mechanical Engineering; Production Engineering; Public Administration; Technology)

Graduate School

Life and Societies (Communication Studies; Linguistics; Psychology); **Science, Technology and Health** *(Institut Galilé)* (Engineering; Health Sciences; Information Sciences; Mathematics)

Further Information: Also 46 Research Laboratories and Centres and offers 4 higher education professional programmes (IUP).

History: Founded 1970 under the 1968 law reforming higher education as one of the Universities replacing the former Université de Paris - founded in 12th century, constituted as Universitas Magistrorum and confirmed by Papal Bull 1215; suppressed by the Revolution in 1793; replaced 1808 by an Academy of the Université impériale; reconstituted as University 1890. A State institution enjoying academic and financial autonomy, operating under the jurisdiction of the Minister of Education and financed by the State. Member of the COMUE Sorbonne-Paris-Cité University

Academic Year: October to June (October-January; February-June)

Admission Requirements: Secondary school certificate (baccalauréat) or equivalent, or special entrance examination

Main Language(s) of Instruction: French

Degrees and Diplomas: *Capacité en Droit*; *Diplôme universitaire de Technologie*; *Licence*: **Arts and Humanities; Communication Studies; Economics; Engineering; Health Administration; Law; Literature; Management; Mathematics and Computer Science; Modern Languages; Natural Sciences; Social Sciences; Technology.** *Licence professionnelle*: **Administration; Design; Documentation Techniques; Economics; Finance; Graphic Design; Human Resources; Industrial and Production Economics; Management; Mass Communication; Social and Community Services; Social Sciences; Technology; Telecommunications Services; Transport and Communications.** *Diplôme d'Etat*: **Medicine.** *Diplôme d'Ingénieur*: **Applied Mathematics; Computer Engineering; Energy Engineering; Telecommunications Engineering.** *Master*: **Accountancy; Banking; Biology; Clinical Psychology; Computer Science; Cultural Studies; Developmental Psychology; Economics; Engineering; English Studies; Ethnology; European Union Law; Finance; Geography; History; Information Sciences; International Law; Law; Linguistics; Literature; Management; Marketing; Mass Communication; Mathematics; Multimedia; Physics; Political Sciences; Psychology; Public Health; Public Law; Publishing and Book Trade; Sports; Technology.** *Doctorat*: **Biochemistry; Bioengineering; Biomedical Engineering; Chemistry; Comparative Literature; Computer Science; Economics; Educational Sciences; English Studies; Ethnology; Geography; Health Sciences; History; History of Law; Information Sciences; Literature; Management; Materials Engineering; Mathematics; Physics; Political Sciences; Private Law;**

Psychology; Public Health; Public Law; Sociology. Also Diplômes d'Université, Masters recherche, Masters professionnel, Preparation for CAPES, Agrégation and Administrative exams

Student Services: Academic Counselling, Canteen, Careers Guidance, Cultural Activities, Facilities for disabled people, Foreign Studies Centre, Health Services, Language Laboratory, Library, Residential Facilities, Social Counselling, Sports Facilities

Academic Staff *2013*: Total 1,077
Student Numbers *2012-2013*: Total 23,387
Last Updated: 10/04/15

PARIS-BELLEVILLE SCHOOL OF ARCHITECTURE

Ecole nationale supérieure d'Architecture de Paris-Belleville (ENSAPB)

60 bld de la Villette, 75019 Paris
Tel: +33(1) 53-38-50-00
Fax: +33(1) 53-38-50-01
EMail: ensa-pb@paris-belleville.archi.fr
Website: http://www.paris-belleville.archi.fr

Director: François Brouat
EMail: françois.brouat@paris-belleville.archi.fr

International Relations: Blandine Crestin-Billet
Tel: +33(1) 53-38-50-26
EMail: blandine.crestin-billet@paris-belleville.archi.fr

Programme

Architecture (Architecture)

History: Founded 1969. Acquired present status 1986.

Admission Requirements: secondary school certificate (baccalauréat) or equivalent. Competitive entrance examination

Main Language(s) of Instruction: French

Degrees and Diplomas: *Licence*: **Architecture.** *Master*: **Architecture.** *Doctorat*: **Architecture; Architecture and Planning; Town Planning.** Graduate degrees in Architecture: DSA and DPEA; Habilitation de l'architecte diplômé d'Etat à l'exercice de la maîtrise d'oeuvre en son nom propre (HMONP)

Last Updated: 11/03/15

PARIS-CERGY NATIONAL ART SCHOOL

Ecole nationale supérieure d'Arts Cergy-Pontoise (ENSAPC)

2 rue des Italiens, Parvis de la Préfecture, 95000 Cergy-Pontoise
Tel: +33(1) 30-30-54-44
Fax: +33(1) 30-38-38-09
EMail: accueil@ensapc.fr
Website: http://www.ensapc.fr/

Director: Sylvain Lizon EMail: sylvain.lizon@ensapc.fr

Secretary General: Chloé Samaniego
EMail: chloe.samaniego@ensapc.fr

International Relations: Thomas Bregeon
EMail: thomas.bregeon@ensapc.fr

Programme

Fine Arts (Fine Arts)

History: Founded in 1975.

Admission Requirements: Baccalauréat or equivalent secondary school exam. Entrance exam with a selection jury.

Main Language(s) of Instruction: French

Accrediting Agency: Ministry of Culture and Communication

Degrees and Diplomas: Diplome national d'arts plastiques (DNAP) 3 yrs; Diplome national supérieur d'expression plastique (DNSEP) a further 2 yrs

Last Updated: 12/03/15

PARIS-DAUPHINE UNIVERSITY

Université Paris Dauphine

Place du Maréchal de Lattre de Tassigny, 75775 Paris, Cedex 16
Tel: +33(1) 44-05-44-05
Fax: +33(1) 44-05-49-49
EMail: service.communication@dauphine.fr
Website: http://www.dauphine.fr

President: Laurent Batsch (2007-)
Tel: +33(1) 44-05-42-18 +33(1) 44-05-43-64
EMail: Laurent.Batsch@dauphine.fr

Secretary General: Gérard Broussois
Tel: +33(1) 44-05-40-15 +33(1) 44-05-43-11/12
EMail: gerard.broussois@dauphine.fr; secretariatgeneral@dauphine.fr

International Relations: Nadia Wajnapel, Director
Tel: +33 1 44 05 48 04 EMail: nadia.wajnapel@dauphine.fr

Unit

Applied Economics *(MSO 2nd cycle)* (Business Administration; Economics; Law; Management; Political Sciences); **Applied Economics** *(LSO 1st cycle)* (Business Administration; Economics; Management); **Mathematics and Computer Science of Decision-Making and Applied Economics** *(MIDO 1st, 2nd, 3d cycles)* (Computer Science; Economics; Management; Mathematics)

Institute

Finance *(IFD)* (Finance); **Research and Innovation Management** *(IMRI)* (Economics; Management)

Centre

Lifelong Education (Business Administration; Economics; Finance; Management)

Graduate School

Management *(EDOGEST)* (Economics; Management); **Science of Organisations** *(EDOCIF)*; **Sciences of Decision-Making** *(EDDIMO)* (Economic and Finance Policy; Mathematics and Computer Science); **Social Sciences** *(EDOSSOC)*

Research Centre

Business Management *(CEREG)* (Accountancy; Business Administration; Business and Commerce; Finance; Management); **Economics and Applied Economics** *(CREPA)* (Economics); **Economics and Management of Health Organizations** *(CERESA-LEGOS)* (Economics; Health Administration; Management); **Energy and Raw Materials Geopolitics** *(IRI-CGEMP)* (Comparative Politics); **European Finance and Management** *(CREFIGE)* (Accountancy; Finance; Management); **Finance and Management** *(IRI-GRES)* (Finance; Management; Media Studies); **Identities and Cultural Interactions on Applied Linguistics in Languages for Special Purpose** *(CICLaS)* (Applied Linguistics); **Institutional Management** *(EURISCO)* (Economics; Institutional Administration); **Law** *(I2D)* (Law); **Management and Sociology of Organizations** *(CERSO)* (Management; Sociology); **Mathematics of Decision-Making** *(CEREMADE)* (Mathematics); **Prospective Marketing Strategy** *(DMSP)* (Marketing); **Rationalization of Systems Design for Decision-Making** *(LAMSADE)*; **Sociology, Economics, Political Science** *(IRISES)* (Economics; Political Sciences; Sociology)

History: Founded 1970 under the 1968 Law reforming higher education as one of the Universities replacing the former Université de Paris founded in 12th century, constituted as Universitas Magistrorum and confirmed by Papal Bull 1215; suppressed by the Revolution in 1793; replaced 1808 by an Academy of the Université impériale; reconstituted as university 1890. A State institution enjoying academic and financial autonomy, operating under the jurisdiction of the Minister of Education and financed by the State. Its structure is based on a series of Unités d'enseignement et de recherche (teaching and research Units) with emphasis on studies in Management Sciences. Each Unit enjoys academic and administrative independence. Becomes grand établissement 2004.

Academic Year: September to July (September-February; February-June)

Admission Requirements: Secondary school certificate (baccalauréat) or equivalent, or special entrance examination

Main Language(s) of Instruction: French

Degrees and Diplomas: *Licence*: **Business Administration; Economics; Law; Management; Mathematics and Computer**

Science. *Licence professionnelle*: **Hotel Management; Tourism.** *Master*: **Banking; Economics; Finance; Human Resources; Information Technology; International Relations; Journalism; Law; Management; Management Systems; Marketing; Mathematics; Media Studies; Public Administration; Technology; Telecommunications Services.** *Doctorat*: **Applied Mathematics; Computer Science; Economics; Law; Management; Political Sciences; Social Sciences; Sociology.** Masters recherche, Masters professionnel

Student Services: Academic Counselling, Canteen, Careers Guidance, Cultural Activities, Facilities for disabled people, Health Services, Language Laboratory, Library, Nursery Care, Social Counselling, Sports Facilities

Academic Staff *2013*: Total 437

Student Numbers *2013*: Total 8,721

Last Updated: 10/04/15

PARIS DESCARTES UNIVERSITY

Université Paris Descartes (Paris 5)

12, rue de l'Ecole de Médecine, 75270 Paris, Cedex 06
Tel: +33(1) 76-53-16-16
Fax: +33(1) 76-53-16-15
EMail: dgs@parisdescartes.fr
Website: http://www.parisdescartes.fr

President: Frédéric Dardel (2011-)
Tel: +33(1) 76 53 16 58 EMail: president@parisdescartes.fr

Secretary General: François Paquis
Tel: +33(1) 76-53-16-98
EMail: secretariat.general@parisdescartes.fr

International Relations: Philippe Carlevan, Director of International Relations
Tel: +33(1) 76 53 16 58 EMail: dpi@parisdescartes.fr

Faculty

Biomedical Studies (Biomedicine); **Humanities and Social Sciences** (Arts and Humanities; Social Sciences); **Law** (Law); **Mathematics and Computer Science** (Mathematics and Computer Science); **Medicine** (Medicine); **Ondotology** (Dentistry); **Pharmacy** (Biology; Pharmacy); **Physical Education and Sports** *(STAPS)* (Physical Education; Sports)

College

Doctoral Schools Paris Descartes

Institute

Psychology (Psychology); **Technology** *(IUT Paris 5)* (Business Administration; Communication Studies; Computer Science; Information Sciences; Marketing; Social Work; Statistics; Technology)

Centre

Lifelong Education

Graduate School

Cultures, Citizens, Societies *(ED SHS)* (Cultural Studies; Social Sciences); **Frontiers in Life Sciences** (Biological and Life Sciences); **Genetic, Cell, Contagious Diseases Studies** *(GC2ID)* (Cell Biology; Genetics); **Human Behaviour** (Behavioural Sciences); **International Relations** (International Law; International Relations); **Molecular Biology** (Biochemistry; Molecular Biology)

History: Founded 1970 under the 1968 law reforming higher education as one of the Universities replacing the former Université de Paris - founded 12th century, constituted as Universitas Magistrorum and confirmed by Papal Bull 1215; suppressed by the Revolution in 1793; replaced 1808 by an Academy of the Université impériale; reconstituted as University 1890. A State institution enjoying academic and financial autonomy, operating under the jurisdiction of the Minister of Education and financed by the State. Member of the COMUE Sorbonne-Paris-Cité University

Academic Year: September to June (September-January; February-June)

Admission Requirements: Secondary school certificate (baccalauréat) or equivalent, or special entrance examination

Fees: c. 150-300 per annum (Euro)

Main Language(s) of Instruction: French

Degrees and Diplomas: *Diplôme universitaire de Technologie*; *Licence*; *Licence professionnelle*; *Diplôme d'Etat*: **Dentistry; Medicine; Pharmacy.** *Master*: **Accountancy; Applied Mathematics; Art Therapy; Banking; Biochemistry; Bioengineering; Biological and Life Sciences; Biology; Cognitive Sciences; Educational Sciences; Finance; Genetics; Health Sciences; History of Law; Law; Management; Microbiology; Neurosciences; Notary Studies; Nutrition; Pharmacy; Physiology; Psychology; Public Health; Social Sciences; Sports; Toxicology.** *Doctorat*: **Biological and Life Sciences; Biomedical Engineering; Chemical Engineering; Engineering; Social Sciences.** Two types for Masters recherche, Masters professionnel

Student Services: Academic Counselling, Canteen, Facilities for disabled people, Health Services, Library, Residential Facilities, Social Counselling, Sports Facilities

Publications: Dialogues de Descartes

Student Numbers *2015*: Total 38,900

Last Updated: 10/04/15

PARIS DIDEROT UNIVERSITY (PARIS 7)

Université Paris Diderot (Paris 7)

5 rue Thomas Mann, 75205 Paris, Paris Cedex 13
Tel: +33(1) 57-27-57-27
EMail: communic@univ-paris-diderot.fr
Website: http://www.univ-paris-diderot.fr/

President: Christine Clerici (2014-)
Tel: +33(1) 57 27 55 16
EMail: secretariat.president@univ-paris-diderot.fr

Permanent Secretary: Quentin Guillemain
EMail: dircab.president@univ-paris-diderot.fr

International Relations: Frédéric Ogée, Vice-President in charge of International Relations
Tel: +33(1) 57-27-55-08 +33(1) 57-27-58-80
EMail: vice.presidentbri@univ-paris-diderot.fr

Unit

Arts, Literatures, Languages (American Studies; Asian Studies; English Studies; Film; French Studies; Journalism; Linguistics; Literature; Performing Arts); **Humanities and Social Sciences** (Clinical Psychology; Educational Sciences; Gender Studies; Geography; History; Philosophy; Psychiatry and Mental Health; Psychoanalysis; Psychology; Social Sciences; Sociology); **Medecine and Odontology** (Dentistry; Medicine); **Sciences and Technology** (Astronomy and Space Science; Biochemistry; Biological and Life Sciences; Biology; Chemistry; Computer Science; Earth Sciences; Environmental Studies; Genetics; Geophysics; Mathematics; Physics)

School

Engineering *(Denis Diderot)* (Computer Engineering; Engineering; Nanotechnology)

Institute

Contemporary Thought *(IPC)* (Philosophy); **Haematology** *(IUH)* (Haematology); **Mathematics Education Research** *(IREM)* (Mathematics Education); **Technology** *(IUT Paris 7)* (Measurement and Precision Engineering; Safety Engineering; Technology)

Graduate School

Science, Health and Applications *(Houses 4 Doctoral Schools and offers several other graduate studies in partnership with other Paris institutes)* (Biological and Life Sciences; Earth Sciences; Health Sciences; Physics; Public Health); **Social Sciences, Languages, Arts and Humanities** *(Houses 5 Doctoral Schools and offers several other graduate studies in partnership with other Paris institutes)* (Arts and Humanities; English Studies; French Studies; Linguistics; Literature; Modern Languages; Psychoanalysis; Social Sciences; Town Planning)

History: Founded 1970 under the 1968 law reforming higher education as one of the Universities replacing the former Université de Paris, founded in 12th century, constituted as Universitas Magistrorum and confirmed by Papal Bull 1215; suppressed by the Revolution in 1793; replaced by an Academy of the Université impériale; reconstituted as University 1890. A State Institution enjoying academic and financial autonomy, operating under the jurisdiction of the Minister of Education and financed by the State. Member of the COMUE Sorbonne-Paris-Cité University

Academic Year: October to June (October-February; February-June)

Admission Requirements: Secondary school certificate (baccalauréat) or equivalent, or special entrance examination

Main Language(s) of Instruction: French

Degrees and Diplomas: *Diplôme d'Accès aux Etudes universitaires*; *Licence*: **Arts and Humanities; Modern Languages; Social Sciences.** *Diplôme d'Etat*: **Dentistry; Medicine.** *Diplôme d'Ingénieur*: **Biomedical Engineering; Engineering.** *Master*: **Anthropology; Applied Mathematics; Biochemistry; Chemistry; Cinema and Television; Computer Science; Cultural Studies; Earth Sciences; Ecology; Education; Educational Sciences; Energy Engineering; English Studies; Environmental Studies; Film; Genetics; Geography; Geophysics; History; Immunology; Linguistics; Literature; Nanotechnology; Performing Arts; Physical Engineering; Psychology; Public Health; Sociology; Toxicology.** *Doctorat*: **Analytical Chemistry; Arts and Humanities; Astronomy and Space Science; Astrophysics; Biochemistry; Earth Sciences; Environmental Studies; Genetics; Geography; Immunology; Linguistics; Materials Engineering; Mathematics; Physical Chemistry; Physiology; Psychoanalysis; Public Health; Social Sciences; Toxicology.** *Habilitation à Diriger les Recherches.* Masters recherche, Masters professionnel, Preparation for CAPES, Agrégation exams

Academic Staff *2013*: Total 3,766

Student Numbers *2012-2013*: Total 24,823

Last Updated: 10/04/15

PARIS EAST CRÉTEIL VAL DE MARNE UNIVERSITY

Université Paris-Est Créteil Val de Marne (UPVM)

61, avenue du Général de Gaulle, 94010 Créteil
Tel: +33(1) 45-17-10-00 +33(1) 45-17-12-61
Fax: +33(1) 42-07-70-12 +33(1) 45-17-12-52
EMail: communication@u-pec.fr
Website: http://www.u-pec.fr/

President: Luc Hittinger (2012-)
Tel: +33(1) 45-17-10-11
EMail: president@univ-paris12.fr; hittinger@u-pec.fr

Head of Administration: François Tavernier
Tel: +33(1) 45-17-10-15 EMail: sgp12@u-pec.fr

International Relations: Isabelle Alfandary, Vice Présidente relations internationales
Tel: +33(1) 45-17-10-11
EMail: alfandary@u-pec.fr

Faculty

Administration and International Exchanges (Administration; Business Administration; Human Resources; International Business; Public Administration); **Economics and Management** *(La Varenne-St. Hilaire)* (Business Administration; Economics; Management); **Law** *(La Varenne-St.-Hilaire)* (Civil Law; Constitutional Law; Criminal Law; Economic and Finance Policy; Economic History; European Union Law; Finance; History of Law; International Relations; Law; Political Sciences; Private Law); **Letters, Languages and Humanities** (Arts and Humanities; Communication Studies; Cultural Studies; English; Geography; German; History; Literature; Philosophy; Romance Languages); **Medicine** (Medicine); **Physical Education, Sports, Social and Educational Sciences** (Educational Sciences; Physical Education; Sports); **Science and Technology** (Biological and Life Sciences; Biology; Chemistry; Computer Science; Earth Sciences; Engineering; Mathematics; Physics)

Unit

Science and Technology (Biology; Ecology; Mathematics; Medicine; Natural Sciences; Technology)

Programme

French Language for Foreigners *(DELCIFE)* (French)

School

Health Administration *(Ecole Supérieure Montsouris)* (Health Administration; Sanitary Engineering)

Department

Lifelong Education

Institute

Data Processing for Management *(ESIAG-IUP MIAGE, Saint Simon Créteil)* (Data Processing); **Ergotherapy** (Rehabilitation and Therapy); **Preparatory Administrative Studies** *(IPAG)* (Administration); **Teacher Training** *(ESPE Académie de Créteil)* (Teacher Training); **Technology** *(IUT Sénart-Fontainebleau)* (Business Administration; Business and Commerce; Computer Engineering; Electrical Engineering; Industrial Maintenance; Sales Techniques; Technology); **Technology** *(IUT Créteil / Vitry)* (Bioengineering; Biology; Chemistry; Computer Engineering; Electrical Engineering; Marketing; Measurement and Precision Engineering; Technology; Telecommunications Engineering); **Town Planning** (Town Planning; Urban Studies)

Further Information: Also numerous research centres within the units

History: Founded 1970 under the 1968 law reforming higher education as one of the Universities replacing the former Université de Paris - founded in 12th century, constituted as Universitas Magistrorum and confirmed by Papal Bull 1215; suppressed by the Revolution in 1793; replaced 1808 by an Academy of the Université impériale; reconstituted as University 1890. A State institution enjoying academic and financial autonomy, operating under the jurisdiction of the Minister of Education and financed by the State. Previously known as Université Paris-Val-de-Marne (Paris 12) (University of Paris 12).

Academic Year: October to June (October-February; February-June)

Admission Requirements: Secondary school certificate (baccalauréat) or equivalent, or special entrance examination

Fees: c.170-400 per annum

Main Language(s) of Instruction: French

Degrees and Diplomas: *Capacité en Droit*; *Diplôme d'Accès aux Etudes universitaires*; *Diplôme universitaire de Technologie*; *Licence*: **Administration; Arts and Humanities; Chemistry; Economics; Engineering; Law; Mathematics and Computer Science; Physical Education; Physics; Sports.** *Licence professionnelle*: **Administration; Chemistry; Construction Engineering; Economics; Electrical and Electronic Equipment and Maintenance; Energy Engineering; Food Science; Modern Languages; Social Sciences; Technology; Telecommunications Services.** *Diplôme d'Etat*: **Ergotherapy; Medicine; Veterinary Science.** *Master*: **Administration; Arts and Humanities; Biology; Chemistry; Computer Science; Economics; Education; Engineering; Environmental Engineering; Health Sciences; Law; Modern Languages; Sports; Town Planning.** *Doctorat*: **Arts and Humanities; Economics; Law; Management; Natural Sciences.** Masters recherche, Masters professionnels, Préparation for CAPES, Agrégation, Judicial and Administrative exams

Student Services: Academic Counselling, Canteen, Careers Guidance, Cultural Activities, Facilities for disabled people, Health Services, Language Laboratory, Library, Social Counselling, Sports Facilities

Academic Staff *2013*: Total 2,629

Student Numbers *2013*: Total: c. 31,016

Last Updated: 10/04/15

PARIS EAST MARNE-LA-VALLÉE UNIVERSITY

Université Paris-Est Marne-la-Vallée (UMLV)

Cité Descartes, 5, boulevard Descartes, Champs-sur-Marne, 77454 Cedex 2 Marne-la-Vallée
Tel: +33(1) 60-95-75-00
Fax: +33(1) 60-95-75-75
EMail: presidence@u-pem.fr
Website: http://www.u-pem.fr

President: Gilles Roussel (2012-2016)
Tel: +33(1) 60-95-70-02 EMail: presidence@u-pem.fr

Head of Administration: Solange Bonneaud
Tel: +33(1) 60-95-70-03
EMail: direction.generale.services@u-pem.fr

International Relations: Thierry Berkover
Tel: +33(1) 60-95-70-24 +33(1) 60-95-70-19
EMail: Thierry.Berkover@u-pem.fr

Unit

Economics and Management (Economics; Management); **Human and Social Sciences** (Geography; History; Social Sciences);

Languages and Civilizations (American Studies; English Studies; Germanic Languages; Hispanic American Studies; Modern Languages; Spanish); **Literature, Arts, Communication and Technology** (Arts and Humanities; Communication Studies; Literature; Technology); **Mathematics** (Mathematics); **Physical Education and Sports** *(STAPS)* (Physical Education; Sports; Sports Management)

School

School of Engineering *(Ingénieurs 2000 (Esipe))* (Computer Engineering; Mechanical Engineering; Production Engineering)

Institute

Applied Sciences *(Institut Francilien (ISFA))* (Computer Science; Electronic Engineering; Engineering; Mechanical Engineering; Technology; Town Planning); **Electronics and Computer Science** *(Gaspard Monge (IGM))* (Electronic Engineering; Mathematics and Computer Science; Telecommunications Engineering); **Services Engineering** *(Institut Francilien d'Ingénierie des Services (IFSA))* (Engineering; Management; Real Estate; Service Trades; Technology; Tourism); **Technology** *(IUT Marne-la-Vallée)* (Business Administration; Civil Engineering; Energy Engineering; Industrial Engineering; Marketing; Public Administration; Technology); **Town Planning** *(IFU)* (Town Planning)

History: Founded 1991. Acquired present title 2007.

Academic Year: September to June (September-January; February-June)

Admission Requirements: Secondary school certificate (baccalauréat)

Main Language(s) of Instruction: French

Degrees and Diplomas: *Diplôme universitaire de Technologie*; *Licence*: **Economics; Fine Arts; Health Sciences; Law; Literature; Management; Modern Languages; Physical Education; Social Sciences; Sports; Technology.** *Licence professionnelle*: **Business and Commerce; Computer Graphics; Economics; Environmental Studies; Fine Arts; Health Education; Hotel and Restaurant; Law; Management; Publishing and Book Trade; Social Sciences; Technology; Tourism; Urban Studies.** *Diplôme d'Ingénieur*: **Civil Engineering; Computer Engineering; Electronic Engineering; Mechanical Engineering; Surveying and Mapping.** *Master*: **Applied Mathematics; Automation and Control Engineering; Chemistry; Civil Engineering; Computer Science; Economics; Electrical and Electronic Engineering; English Studies; Finance; Fine Arts; Geography; Health Sciences; History; Human Resources; Industrial Engineering; Law; Literature; Management; Marketing; Materials Engineering; Mechanics; Modern Languages; Music; Philosophy; Physical Education; Political Sciences; Public Administration; Public Health; Publishing and Book Trade; Social Sciences; Spanish; Sports; Technology; Tourism; Translation and Interpretation; Transport and Communications; Urban Studies.** *Doctorat*: **Economics; Management.** Preparation for CERPE and CAPES exams; Doctoral Schools: Cultures and Societies, City, Transport and Territories, Mathematics and ICST, Organizations, Markets, Institutions, Science, Engineering and Environment

Student Services: Canteen, Facilities for disabled people, Health Services, Language Laboratory, Library, Social Counselling, Sports Facilities

Student Numbers *2014*: Total 11,000
Last Updated: 10/04/15

PARIS INSTITUTE OF TECHNOLOGY FOR LIFE, FOOD AND ENVIRONMENTAL SCIENCES

AgroParisTech

16 rue Claude Bernard, 75231 Paris, Cedex 05
Tel: +33(1) 44-08-18-43
Fax: +33(1) 44-08-16-00
EMail: ri@agroparistech.fr
Website: http://www.agroparistech.fr

Managing Director: Gilles Trystram (2011-)
Tel: +33(1) 45-49-89-88 EMail: gilles.trystram@agroparistech.fr

International Relations: Christophe Sodore, Director of International Relations Tel: +33(1) 44-08-17-95 EMail: ri@agroparistech.fr

School

Rural Engineering, Water and Forest Sciences *(ENGREF)* (Agricultural Engineering; Forestry; Rural Planning; Water Science)

Department

Agronomy, Forestry, Water and Environmental Science and Technology (Agronomy; Environmental Studies; Forestry; Soil Science; Water Management; Water Science); **Economics, Social Sciences and Management** (Agricultural Business; Business Administration; Economics; Management; Rural Planning; Sociology); **Life Science and Health** (Biochemistry; Biological and Life Sciences; Biology; Demography and Population; Genetics; Microbiology; Nutrition; Plant and Crop Protection; Plant Pathology); **Modeling: Mathematics, Informatics and Physic** (Computer Science; Mathematics; Physical Engineering); **Science and Engineering for Food and Bioproducts** (Analytical Chemistry; Food Science; Food Technology; Wood Technology)

History: Founded 2007 following merger of the Ecole nationale du génie rural, des eaux et des forêts; ENSIA, Ecole nationale supérieure des industries agricoles et alimentaires and INA P-G, Institut national agronomique Paris-Grignon.

Academic Year: September to July

Admission Requirements: Competitive entrance examination following 2-3 years further study after secondary school certificate (baccalauréat) or following first university qualification (DEUG, DUT or BTS), or equivalent

Main Language(s) of Instruction: French

Degrees and Diplomas: *Diplôme d'Ingénieur*: **Engineering; Environmental Engineering.** *Master*: **Agriculture; Applied Mathematics; Biology; Ecology; Economics; Energy Engineering; Environmental Studies; Food Science; Food Technology; Forestry; Nutrition; Technology; Tropical Agriculture; Water Science.** *Doctorat*: **Agricultural Economics; Agricultural Engineering; Agricultural Management; Applied Mathematics; Biological and Life Sciences; Computer Science; Development Studies; Environmental Engineering; Environmental Studies; Food Science; Forestry; Water Science.** Masters recherche

Student Services: Academic Counselling, Canteen, Careers Guidance, Social Counselling, Sports Facilities

Publications: la Revue forestière française

Publishing House: Editions d'AgroParistech
Last Updated: 30/03/15

PARIS-LA-VILLETTE SCHOOL OF ARCHITECTURE

Ecole nationale supérieure d'Architecture de Paris-la-Villette (EAPLV)

144, avenue de Flandre, 75019 Paris
Tel: +33(1) 44-65-23-00
Fax: +33(1) 44-65-23-01
EMail: directeur@paris-lavillette.archi.fr
Website: http://www.paris-lavillette.archi.fr/

Director: Bruno Mengoli
Tel: +33(1) 44-65-23-26
EMail: bruno.mengoli@paris-lavillette.archi.fr

Secretary General: Paul Astruc
Tel: +33(1) 44-65-23-06 EMail: paul.astruc@paris-lavillette.archi.fr

International Relations: Danielle Hugues
Tel: +33(1) 44-65-23-19
EMail: danielle.hugues@paris-lavillette.archi.fr

Programme

Architecture (Architecture)

History: Founded 1969 as Unité Pédagogique d'Architecture n° 6 (UPA n°6).

Admission Requirements: Baccalauréat or equivalent

Main Language(s) of Instruction: French

Degrees and Diplomas: *Licence*: **Architecture.** *Master*: **Architecture.** *Doctorat*: **Architecture; Architecture and Planning.** Diplômes propres aux écoles d'architecture (DPEA), diplômes de spécialisation et d'approfondissement en architecture; Habilitation à exercer la maîtrise d'œuvre en son nom propre (HMONP)

Publishing house: Les Éditions de la Villette
Last Updated: 11/03/15

PARIS-MALAQUAIS SCHOOL OF ARCHITECTURE

Ecole nationale supérieure d'Architecture Paris-Malaquais (ENSA DE PARIS-MALAQUAIS)

14 rue Bonaparte, 75272 Paris, Cedex 06
Tel: +33(1) 55-04-56-50
Fax: +33(1) 55-04-56-97
EMail: info@paris-malaquais.archi.fr
Website: http://www.paris-malaquais.archi.fr

Director: Nasrine Seraji
EMail: secretariat.direction@paris-malaquais.archi.fr

International Relations: Caroline Kornig
Tel: +33(1) 55-04-51-69
EMail: caroline.kornig@paris-malaquais.archi.fr

Department

Architectures, Materials and Constructive Cultures *(AMC2)* (Architecture; Building Technologies); **Art, Architecture, Politics** *(AAP)* (Architecture); **Digital Knowledge** *(DK)* (Computer Science); **Pass** (Architecture; Town Planning); **Theory, History and Project** *(THP)* (Architecture and Planning); **Town, Architecture, Territories** *(VAT)* (Architecture; Landscape Architecture; Town Planning)

History: Founded in 2000. Acquired present status 2001

Admission Requirements: Secondary school Certificate (Baccalauréat) other secondary school Certificate. Entrance exam

Main Language(s) of Instruction: French

Degrees and Diplomas: *Licence*: **Architecture.** *Master*: **Architecture.** *Doctorat*: **Architecture.** Diplome d'Etat d'Architecte; Habilitation à l'exercice de la maitrise d'œuvre en son nom propre (HMONP)

Last Updated: 13/03/15

PARIS NATIONAL CONSERVATORY OF MUSIC AND DANCE

Conservatoire national supérieur de Musique et de Danse de Paris (CNSMDP)

Parc de la Villette, 209, avenue Jean Jaurès, 75019 Paris
Tel: +33(1) 40-40-45-45
Fax: +33(1) 40-40-45-00
EMail: cnsmdp@cnsmdp.fr
Website: http://www.cnsmdp.fr

Director: Bruno Mantovani (2010-)
Tel: +33(1) 40-40-45-00 EMail: direction@cnsmdp.fr

International Relations: Gretchen Amussen
Tel: +33(1) 40-40-45-79 EMail: international@cnsmdp.fr

Programme

Performing Arts (Dance; Jazz and Popular Music; Music; Music Education; Sound Engineering (Acoustics))

History: Founded in 1795.

Academic Year: September to July

Admission Requirements: Competitive entrance examination

Fees: 500 per annum (Euro)

Main Language(s) of Instruction: French

Degrees and Diplomas: *Licence*: **Musicology; Performing Arts.** *Diplôme d'Etat*: **Music Education.** *Master*: **Music; Music Education.** *Doctorat*: **Music; Music Theory and Composition.** Diplôme national supérieur professionnel de musicien (DNSPM), Diplôme d'Artiste Interprète, Diplôme de compositeur de Musique, Diplôme National Supérieur Professionnel de Danseur (DNSP), Certificats d'Aptitude.

Student Services: Canteen, Cultural Activities, Library, Residential Facilities, Social Counselling

Publishing house: CREC Editions

Academic Staff *2012*	**TOTAL**
FULL-TIME	**407**
Student Numbers *2012*	
All (Foreign included)	**1,160**
FOREIGN ONLY	**201**

Last Updated: 11/03/15

PARIS SORBONNE UNIVERSITY (PARIS 4)

Université Paris Sorbonne (Paris 4)

1, rue Victor Cousin, 75230 Paris, Cedex 05
Tel: +33(1) 40-46-22-11
Fax: +33(1) 40-46-25-12
EMail: president@paris-sorbonne.fr
Website: http://www.paris-sorbonne.fr

Président: Barthélémy Jobert (2012-)
Tel: +33(1) 40-46-33-79 EMail: president@paris-sorbonne.fr

Directrice générale des services: Sylvie Nguyen
EMail: direction-generale-des-services@paris-sorbonne.fr

International Relations: Araceli GUILLAUME-ALONSO, Professeur délégué aux relations internationales
Tel: +33(1) 40 46 33 76 EMail: contact.ri@paris-sorbonne.fr

Unit

Arts (Archaeology; Art History; Music; Musicology); **Communication** (Communication Studies); **Education** *(ESPE)* (Teacher Training); **French and Classics** (Comparative Literature; French; Greek (Classical); Latin); **Humans Sciences** (Geography; History; Philosophy; Sociology); **Languages** (Arabic; English Studies; Germanic Studies; Hebrew; Hispanic American Studies; Italian; Modern Languages; Nordic Studies; Slavic Languages; Spanish)

School

Information and Communication Sciences *(CELSA)* (Communication Studies; Human Resources; Information Sciences; Journalism; Marketing; Public Relations)

Institute

Applied Humanities *(ISHA)* (Arts and Humanities); **Modern Western Civilizations** *(IRCOM)* (Western European Studies); **Religious Studies** *(IREL)* (Anthropology; History of Religion; Jewish Studies; Religious Studies); **Teacher Training** *(IUFM 2 sites)* (Teacher Trainers Education; Teacher Training); **Town Planning** *(IUAS)* (Town Planning)

Graduate School

Ancient and Medieval Civilisations (Ancient Civilizations; Medieval Studies); **Art History and Archaeology** (Archaeology; Art History); **Civilization, Cultural and Literature Studies** (Cultural Studies; Literature); **Concepts and Languages** (Applied Linguistics; Applied Mathematics; Communication Studies; Social Sciences); **French Literature** (Comparative Literature; French Studies); **Geography** (Geography); **Modern and Contemporary History** (Contemporary History; Modern History)

History: Founded 1970 under the 1968 law reforming higher education as one of the new Universities replacing the former Université de Paris - founded in 12th century, constituted as Universitas Magistrorum and confirmed by Papal Bull 1215; suppressed by the Revolution in 1793; replaced 1808 by an Academy of the Université impériale; reconstituted as university 1890. A State institution enjoying academic and financial autonomy, operating under the jurisdiction of the Minister of Education and financed by the State.

Academic Year: October to June (October-February; February-June)

Admission Requirements: Secondary school certificate (baccalauréat) or equivalent, or special entrance examination

Fees: c. 150 per annum

Main Language(s) of Instruction: French

Degrees and Diplomas: *Licence*: **Arts and Humanities.** *Mastère spécialisé*: **Communication Studies; Media Studies.** *Master*: **Ancient Civilizations; Arabic; Archaeology; Art History; Arts and Humanities; Communication Studies; Contemporary History; Documentation Techniques; English; Geography (Human); Germanic Studies; Hebrew; Hispanic American Studies; History; History of Law; Human Resources; Information Management; Information Technology; International Business; International Relations; Islamic Studies; Italian; Journalism; Law; Library Science; Linguistics; Literature; Middle Eastern Studies; Multimedia; Musicology; North African Studies; Philosophy; Polish; Portuguese; Publishing and Book Trade; Russian; Slavic Languages; Sociology; Spanish; Teacher Training; Translation and Interpretation; Transport and Communications; Urban Studies.** *Doctorat*: **Ancient Civilizations; Arabic; Archaeology; Art History; Comparative Literature; Contemporary History; Cultural Studies; English Studies;**

European Studies; Germanic Studies; History; Information Sciences; International Business; Linguistics; Medieval Studies; Modern History; Musicology; Philosophy; Slavic Languages; Sociology. *Habilitation à Diriger les Recherches*. Masters recherche, Masters professionnel, National Diplomas for French and French Studies

Student Services: Academic Counselling, Canteen, Careers Guidance, Cultural Activities, Foreign Studies Centre, Language Laboratory, Library, Social Counselling, Sports Facilities

Publications: Actes des différents colloques publiés aux Presses de l'Université de Paris-Sorbonne

Publishing House: Presses de l'Université Paris-Sorbonne

Last Updated: 28/01/15

PARIS-SUD UNIVERSITY (PARIS 11)

Université Paris-Sud (Paris 11) (UPS)

Batiment 300, rue du chateau, 91405 Orsay, Cedex
Tel: +33(1) 69-15-74-06
Fax: +33(1) 69-15-61-03
EMail: president@u-psud.fr
Website: http://www.u-psud.fr

President: Jacques Bittoun (2012-)
Tel: +33(1) 69-15-74-06 EMail: president@u-psud.fr

Head of Administration: Christine Arnulf-Koechlin
Tel: +33(1) 69-15-70-41
EMail: direction.dgs@u-psud.fr; christine.Arnulf-Koechlin@u-psud.fr

International Relations: Severine Fogel, Head of International Relations Tel: +33(1) 69-15-30-86 EMail: severine.fogel@u-psud.fr

Faculty

Law, Economics and Management *(Jean Monnet)* (Accountancy; Business Administration; Economics; Law; Management); **Medicine** *(Kremlin-Bicêtre)* (Medicine); **Pharmacy** *(Châtenay-Malabry)* (Pharmacy); **Science** *(Orsay)* (Biology; Chemistry; Computer Science; Earth Sciences; Mathematics; Natural Sciences); **Sports** *(Orsay - STAPS)* (Sports; Sports Management)

School

Engineering *(Polytech Paris-Sud)* (Computer Engineering; Electronic Engineering; Engineering; Materials Engineering; Optical Technology); **Teacher training** *(ESPE académie Versailles)* (Higher Education Teacher Training; Primary Education; Secondary Education)

Institute

Technology *(IUT Cachan)* (Automation and Control Engineering; Computer Engineering; Electrical Engineering; Mechanical Engineering; Production Engineering; Robotics; Technology; Telecommunications Engineering); **Technology** *(IUT Orsay)* (Applied Physics; Chemistry; Computer Science); **Technology** *(IUT Sceaux)* (Business and Commerce)

Graduate School

Doctoral Schools (Ecology; Environmental Engineering; Genetics; Law; Mathematics; Medicine; Molecular Biology; Neurosciences; Physical Chemistry; Public Health; Sports; Telecommunications Engineering)

Further Information: also campuses in: Kremlin-Bicêtre, Cachan, Sceaux, Châtenay-Malabry.

History: Founded 1970 under the 1968 law reforming higher education as one of the Universities replacing the former Université de Paris - founded 12th century, constituted as Universitas Magistrorum and confirmed by Papal Bull 1215; suppressed by the Revolution in 1793; replaced 1808 by an Academy of the Université impériale; reconstituted as University 1890. A State institution enjoying academic and financial autonomy, operating under the jurisdiction of the Minister of Education and financed by the State. in 2014, Member of the COMUE Paris-Saclay University

Academic Year: September to June (September-January; February-June)

Admission Requirements: Secondary school certificate (baccalauréat) or equivalent, or special entrance examination. Admissions at various levels is possible, subject to recognition of previous degrees.

Degrees and Diplomas: *Diplôme universitaire de Technologie*; *Licence*: **Economics; Health Sciences; Law; Management; Mathematics and Computer Science; Natural Sciences; Technology.** *Licence professionnelle*: **Economics; Health Sciences; Law; Management; Natural Sciences; Sports; Technology.** *Diplôme d'Etat*: **Medicine; Pharmacy.** *Diplôme d'Ingénieur*: **Computer Engineering; Electrical and Electronic Engineering; Energy Engineering; Engineering; Materials Engineering.** *Master*: **Accountancy; Economics; Ethics; Health Sciences; History of Law; Law; Notary Studies; Optometry; Private Law; Sports.** *Doctorat*: **Agriculture; Astrophysics; Biological and Life Sciences; Biology; Cell Biology; Chemistry; Engineering; Environmental Studies; Food Science; Genetics; Health Sciences; Law; Mathematics and Computer Science; Medicine; Pharmacy; Physics; Plant Pathology; Public Health; Social Sciences; Sports.** *Certificat de Spécialité*: **Medicine.** Masters recherche, Masters professionnel

Student Services: Canteen, Cultural Activities, Facilities for disabled people, Health Services, Library, Residential Facilities, Sports Facilities

Academic Staff *2013*	**TOTAL**
FULL-TIME	**5,000**
Student Numbers *2013*	
All (Foreign included)	**27,603**
FOREIGN ONLY	**4700**

Last Updated: 10/04/15

INSTITUTE OF OPTICS GRADUATE SCHOOL

INSTITUT D'OPTIQUE GRADUATE SCHOOL (IOTA)

2 avenue Augustin Fresnel, 91127 Palaiseau, Cedex
Tel: +33(1) 64-53-31-00
Fax: +33(1) 64-53-31-01
EMail: accueil@institutoptique.fr
Website: http://www.institutoptique.fr/

Director General: Jean-Louis Martin
Tel: +33(1) 64-53-31-03
EMail: dg@institutoptique.fr; laurence.franchiset@institutoptique.fr

Secretary General: Annie Montagnac
Tel: +33(1) 64-53-32-03 EMail: daf@institutoptique.fr

International Relations: Alan Swan, International Coordinator
Tel: +33(1) 64-53-31-08 EMail: international@institutoptique.fr

School

Optical Science and Engineering *(Also Saint-Etienne Campus)* (Electrical Engineering; Laboratory Techniques; Optics; Physics; Technology; Telecommunications Engineering)

Graduate School

Optical Science *(Joint programme - Ecole Polytechnique)* (Optical Technology)

Research Laboratory

Charles Fabry (Optics)

Further Information: Also sites in Palaiseau, Saint-Etienne and Bordeaux

History: Founded 1920.

Academic Year: September to June

Admission Requirements: Competitive entrance examination following 2 years further study after secondary school certificate (baccalauréat) or equivalent

Main Language(s) of Instruction: French

Accrediting Agency: Ministry of Education, Commission des Titres d'Ingénieur (CTI)

Degrees and Diplomas: *Diplôme d'Ingénieur*: **Optical Technology; Optics.** *Mastère spécialisé*; *Master*: **Optical Technology; Optics.** Master Erasmus Mundus "Optics in Science and Technology"

Student Services: Academic Counselling, Canteen, Careers Guidance, Cultural Activities, Facilities for disabled people, Health Services, Language Laboratory, Sports Facilities

Publications: Fiat Lux; Opto

PARIS-VAL-DE-SEINE SCHOOL OF ARCHITECTURE

Ecole nationale supérieure d'Architecture Paris-Val-de-Seine (ENSAPVS)

3 quai Panhard et Levassor, 75013 Paris
Tel: +33(1) 72-69-63-00
Fax: +33(1) 72-69-63-81
Website: http://www.paris-valdeseine.archi.fr

Director: Philippe Bach EMail: direction@paris-valdeseine.archi.fr

Associate Director: Evelyne Berger
Tel: +33(1) 72-69-63-02
EMail: evelyne.berger@paris-valdeseine.archi.fr

International Relations: Cécile Mauras
Tel: +33(1) 72-69-63-36
EMail: cecile.mauras@paris-valdeseine.archi.fr; arnaud.miseriaux@paris-valdeseine.archi.fr

Programme

Architecture (Architecture)

History: Founded 2001.

Academic Year: September-February; February-July

Admission Requirements: Secondary school certificate (Baccalauréat)

Main Language(s) of Instruction: French

Degrees and Diplomas: *Licence*: **Architecture.** *Master*: **Architecture; Architecture and Planning; Heritage Preservation; Urban Studies.** Diplôme d'études en architecture (3 yrs); Diplôme d'Etat en architecture (5 yrs); Habilitation à exercer la maîtrise d'oeuvre en son nom propre (HMONP) (6 yrs)

Publications: Laboratoire Architecture Ville Urbanisme Environnement (LAVUE)

Academic Staff *2010-2011*: Total 220

Student Numbers *2010-2011*: Total 1,850

Last Updated: 12/03/15

PARIS WEST NANTERRE LA DÉFENSE UNIVERSITY

Université Paris Ouest Nanterre La Défense

200, avenue de la République, 92001 Nanterre, Cedex
Tel: +33(1) 40-97-72-00
Fax: +33(1) 40-97-75-71
EMail: presidence@u-paris10.fr
Website: http://www.u-paris10.fr

President: Jean-François Balaudé (2012-)
Tel: +33(1) 40 97 47 05
EMail: presidence@u-paris10.fr

Head of Administration: Didier Ramond
Tel: +33(1) 40-97-74-39
EMail: didier.ramond@u-paris10.fr

International Relations: Sylvianne Hughes, Vice-President in charge of International Relations
EMail: relations-internationales@u-paris10.fr; sylvaine.hughes@u-paris10.fr

Faculty

Economics, Management, Mathematics and Computer sciences *(SEGMI)* (Economics; Management; Mathematics and Computer Science); **Educational sciences and Psychology** *(SPSE)* (Educational Sciences; Psychology); **Industrial system and Communication techniques** *(SITEC)* (Aeronautical and Aerospace Engineering; Energy Engineering; Engineering; Industrial Engineering; Library Science; Materials Engineering; Publishing and Book Trade; Telecommunications Engineering); **Law and Political sciences** *(DSP)* (Law; Political Sciences); **Modern Languages** *(LCE)* (English Studies; German; Italian; Portuguese; Russian; Spanish); **Philosphy, Information-communication, Language, Literature and Performing Arts** *(PHILLIA)* (Classical Languages; Information Sciences; Linguistics; Literature; Mass Communication; Performing Arts; Philosophy); **Physical Education and Sport sciences** *(STAPS)* (Physical Education; Sports); **Social sciences and Administration** *(SSA)* (Administration; Art History; Ethnology; Geography; History; Social Sciences; Sociology)

School

Teacher Training *(ESPE Versailles with 5 sites)* (Teacher Trainers Education; Teacher Training)

Institute

Preparatory Administrative Studies *(IPAG)* (Administration); **Publishing** *(IUT Site Saint Cloud)* (Documentation Techniques; Information Technology; Library Science; Multimedia; Publishing and Book Trade); **Technology** *(IUT, Ville-d'Avray)* (Computer Engineering; Electrical Engineering; Electronic Engineering; Mechanical Engineering; Production Engineering; Technology; Thermal Engineering)

Centre

Lifelong Education (Computer Science; Labour Law; Social Psychology)

Research Institute

Archaeology and Ethnology *(René Ginouvès House, MAE)* (Archaeology; Ethnology); **Economics, Sociology, Political Science and Geography** *(Max Weber House)*; **International and Contemporary Documentation** *(BDIC, Member of IALHI Network)* (Library Science); **Law Studies** *(IEJ/Henri Motulsky)*

Further Information: also campuses in: Avray, Saint Cloud

History: Founded 1970 under the 1968 law reforming higher education as one of the Universities replacing the former Université de Paris - founded in 12th century, constituted as Universitas Magistrorum and confirmed by Papal Bull 1215; suppressed by the Revolution in 1793; replaced 1808 by an Academy of the Université impériale; reconstituted as university 1890. A State institution enjoying academic and financial autonomy, operated under the jurisdiction of the Minister of Education and financed by the State. Acquired present title 2010.Member of the COMUE Paris Lumières University

Academic Year: October to June (October-January; February-June)

Admission Requirements: Secondary school certificate (baccalauréat) or equivalent, or special entrance examination

Fees: c. 200 per annum (Euro)

Main Language(s) of Instruction: French

Degrees and Diplomas: *Capacité en Droit*; *Diplôme d'Accès aux Etudes universitaires*; *Diplôme universitaire de Technologie*; *Licence*: **Archaeology; Art History; Arts and Humanities; Comparative Literature; Economics; Engineering; Geography; History; Information Technology; Law; Linguistics; Literature; Management; Mathematics and Computer Science; Modern Languages; Performing Arts; Political Sciences; Publishing and Book Trade; Sociology.** *Licence professionnelle*: **Aeronautical and Aerospace Engineering; Banking; Business and Commerce; Documentation Techniques; Electrical and Electronic Engineering; Finance; Health Administration; Hotel and Restaurant; Human Resources; Industrial and Production Economics; Library Science; Management; Mass Communication; Service Trades; Sports; Technology; Town Planning.** *Master*: **Accountancy; Anthropology; Archaeology; Art History; Arts and Humanities; Cinema and Television; Classical Languages; Comparative Law; Comparative Literature; Criminal Law; Cultural Studies; Economics; Educational Sciences; European Union Law; Finance; Geography; History; Human Resources; Industrial and Production Economics; Industrial Engineering; Information Sciences; Information Technology; International Law; International Studies; Law; Literature; Management; Marketing; Notary Studies; Performing Arts; Philosophy; Physical Education; Political Sciences; Private Law; Psychology; Public Administration; Public Law; Publishing and Book Trade; Social Sciences; Sociology; Sports; Theatre; Translation and Interpretation; Urban Studies.** *Doctorat*: **Aesthetics; Anthropology; Applied Mathematics; Archaeology; Architecture and Planning; Comparative Literature; Computer Science; Demography and Population; Educational Sciences; Electronic Engineering; Energy Engineering; English Studies; Ethnology; Fine Arts; Geography; Geography (Human); Germanic Languages; History; Information Sciences; Italian; Linguistics; Literature; Mathematics; Mechanics; Musicology; Neurosciences; Nordic Studies; Performing Arts; Philosophy; Portuguese; Prehistory; Psychology; Sociology; Spanish; Sports; Translation and Interpretation.** Masters recherche, Masters professionnel

Student Services: Academic Counselling, Canteen, Careers Guidance, Cultural Activities, Facilities for disabled people, Foreign Studies Centre, Health Services, Language Laboratory, Library, Social Counselling, Sports Facilities

Publications: Cahiers de Recherche Freudienne; Cahiers de RITM; Cahiers de Sémiotique Textuelle; Cinéma et Sciences humaines; Confluences; CRISOL; Culture/Cultures; Droit et Cultures; Etudes Lawrenciennes; Ibériques; Italian Studies; Italie

Années 90; LINX; Litérales; Musique et Sciences Humaines; Narrativa; Parcours J.; Temps philosophique; Tropismes

Publishing House: Publidix

Student Numbers *2013*: Total 31,000

Last Updated: 10/04/15

PERPIGNAN ART SCHOOL

Haute Ecole d'Art de Perpignan (HEART)

3, rue du Maréchal Foch, BP 20931,
66931 Perpignan
Tel: +33(4) 68-66-31-84
Fax: +33(4) 68-35-68-52
Website: http://www.epcc-heart.eu/

Director: Jordi Vidal

Programme

Art (Fine Arts; Painting and Drawing; Photography)

Admission Requirements: Secondary school certificate (Baccalauréat) and competitive entrance examination

Main Language(s) of Instruction: French

Degrees and Diplomas: Diplôme National d'Art Plastique (3 years), Diplôme National Supérieur d'Expression Plastique (5 years)

Last Updated: 13/04/15

PIERRE AND MARIE CURIE UNIVERSITY (PARIS 6)

Université Pierre et Marie Curie (Paris 6) (UPMC)

4, place Jussieu, 75252 Paris,
Cedex 05
Tel: +33(1) 44-27-44-27
Fax: +33(1) 44-27-38-29
EMail: relations.internationales@upmc.fr
Website: http://www.upmc.fr

President: Jean Chambaz (2012-) Tel: +33(1) 44-27-33-49
EMail: presidence@upmc.fr;
jean.chambaz@upmc.fr

Head of Administration: Hervé Combaz
Tel: +33(1) 44-27-33-27 EMail: herve.combaz@upmc.fr;
directiongeneraledesservices@upmc.fr

International Relations: Sabine Lopez
Tel: +33(1) 44-27-26-74 +33(1) 44-27-32-06
EMail: sabine.lopez@upmc.fr;
relations.internationales@upmc.fr

Faculty

Chemistry (Chemistry); **Earth, Environment and Biodiversity** (Earth Sciences; Environmental Studies); **Engineering** (Engineering); **Life Sciences** (Biological and Life Sciences); **Mathematics** (Mathematics); **Medicine** *(Site Pierre and Marie Curie)* (Medicine); **Theoretical and Applied Physics** (Applied Physics; Physics)

School

Engineering *(Polytech' Paris-UPMC)* (Engineering); **Midwifery** *(Ecole de sage-femme de Saint Antoine, in cooperation with the Faculty of Medicine)* (Midwifery); **Teacher Training** *(ESPE 2 sites)* (Teacher Training)

Institute

Astrophysics *(Paris)* (Astrophysics); **Doctorate Studies**; **Mathematics** *(Henri Poincaré)* (Mathematics); **Statistics** *(Isup)* (Statistics)

Centre

Marine Station *(Villefranche-sur-Mer)* (Marine Science and Oceanography); **Marine Station** *(Roscoff)* (Marine Science and Oceanography); **Marine Station** *(Banyuls sur Mer)* (Marine Science and Oceanography)

Research Centre

Biomedicine *(CRC)* (Biomedicine)

Research Unit

Energy, Matter and the Universe (Energy Engineering; Physics); **Life and Health** (Health Sciences); **Living Earth and Environment** (Earth Sciences; Environmental Studies); **Modelling and Engineering** (Engineering)

History: Founded 1970 under the 1968 law reforming higher education as one of the Universities replacing the former Université de Paris - founded in the 12th century, constituted as Universitas Magistrorum and confirmed by Papal Bull 1215; suppressed by the Revolution in 1793; replaced 1808 by an Academy of the Université impériale; reconstituted as University 1890.

Academic Year: September to June (September-December; January-March; April-June)

Admission Requirements: Secondary school certificate (baccalauréat)or equivalent, or special entrance examination

Main Language(s) of Instruction: French

Degrees and Diplomas: *Licence*: **Automation and Control Engineering; Biological and Life Sciences; Chemistry; Earth Sciences; Electrical and Electronic Engineering; Health Sciences; Mathematics and Computer Science; Mechanics; Natural Sciences; Physics; Technology.** *Licence professionnelle*: **Architecture and Planning; Chemistry; Civil Engineering; Electrical and Electronic Engineering; Environmental Studies; Health Sciences; Mechanical Engineering; Nutrition; Physics; Publishing and Book Trade.** *Diplôme d'Etat*: **Medicine; Midwifery.** *Diplôme d'Ingénieur*: **Agricultural Business; Business Computing; Computer Engineering; Computer Science; Earth Sciences; Electronic Engineering; Engineering; Materials Engineering.** *Master*: **Applied Mathematics; Applied Physics; Astronomy and Space Science; Biological and Life Sciences; Biology; Cell Biology; Chemistry; Computer Science; Ecology; Environmental Studies; Health Sciences; Higher Education Teacher Training; Management; Mathematics and Computer Science; Medicine; Molecular Biology; Natural Sciences; Paramedical Sciences; Physics; Teacher Training.** *Doctorat*: **Astronomy and Space Science; Astrophysics; Biological and Life Sciences; Chemistry; Cognitive Sciences; Ecology; Engineering; Environmental Studies; Materials Engineering; Mathematics and Computer Science; Medicine; Natural Sciences; Paramedical Sciences; Physics; Physiology; Public Health.** Also Certificates and Diplomas in Statistics and Programming

Student Services: Academic Counselling, Canteen, Cultural Activities, Facilities for disabled people, Health Services, Library, Residential Facilities, Social Counselling, Sports Facilities

Publications: Futur(e)s

Academic Staff *2014*: Total 10,100

Student Numbers *2014*: Total 33,900

Last Updated: 03/04/15

NATIONAL GRADUATE SCHOOL OF CHEMISTRY OF PARIS - CHIMIE PARISTECH

ECOLE NATIONALE SUPÉRIEURE DE CHIMIE DE PARIS (ENSCP)

11, rue Pierre et Marie Curie, 75231 Paris, Cedex 05
Tel: +33(1) 44-27-66-72
Fax: +33(1) 43-29-20-59
EMail: communication@chimie-paristech.fr
Website: https://www.chimie-paristech.fr/

Secretary General: Hélène Gérard-Grabois
EMail: secretariat-general@chimie-paristech.fr

Administrator (acting): Christian Lerminiaux
EMail: directeur@chimie-paristech.fr

International Relations: Maud Girault
Tel: +33(1) 44-27-66-81 EMail: service-ri@chimie-paristech.fr

Programme

Chemistry (Chemical Engineering; Chemistry)

History: Founded 1896.

Admission Requirements: Competitive entrance examination or jury selection after 2-3 years of further studies after secondary school certificate (Baccalauréat)

Main Language(s) of Instruction: French

Degrees and Diplomas: *Diplôme d'Ingénieur*: **Chemical Engineering; Engineering.** *Master*: **Chemistry.**

PYRENEES - PAUTARBES ART SCHOOL

Ecole supérieure d'Art des Pyrénées - Pau Tarbes
25 rue René Cassin, 64000 Pau
Tel: +33(5) 59-02-20-06
EMail: administration-pau@esapyrenees.fr
Website: http://www.esapyrenees.fr

Director: Odile Biec

Head of Administration: Magali Chavagneux
EMail: administration-pau@esapyrenees.fr

International Relations: Johanna Peixoto
EMail: johanna.peixoto@esapyrenees.fr

Programme
Applied Arts *(Pau and Tarbes)* (Design; Furniture Design); **Ceramic Art** *(Tarbes)* (Ceramic Art); **Graphic Arts** *(Pau and Tarbes)* (Graphic Arts); **Plastic Arts** *(Pau and Tarbes)* (Engraving; Fine Arts; Painting and Drawing; Sculpture); **Visual Communication** *(Pau and Tarbes)* (Advertising and Publicity; Photography)

Further Information: also campus in: Tarbes

History: Founded 2011 following merger of the Ecole supérieure des Arts et de la Communication de Pau and the Ecole supérieure d'arts et céramique de Tarbes.

Academic Year: September to June

Admission Requirements: Baccalauréat or equivalent secondary school exam. Entrance exam with a selection jury.

Main Language(s) of Instruction: French

Accrediting Agency: Ministry of Culture and Communication and Ministère de l'Enseignement Supérieur et de la Recherche

Degrees and Diplomas: *Master*: **Ceramic Art; Fine Arts; Graphic Design; Multimedia.** Diplome national d'arts plastiques (DNAP in graphic design and multimedia, art) 3years; Diplôme National d'Arts et Techniques (DNAT in Object Design-ceramics) option in Tarbes;Diplome national supérieur d'expression plastique (DNSEP in graphic design and multimedia in Pau and Art and Ceramics in Tarbes) a further 2 years.
Last Updated: 07/04/15

REGIONAL INSTITUTE OF ADMINISTRATION - BASTIA

Institut régional d'Administration de Bastia (IRA)
BP 317, Quai des Martyrs de la Libération, 20297 Bastia, cedex
Tel: +33(4) 95-32-87-00
Fax: +33(4) 95-31-06-43
EMail: accueil@ira-bastia.gouv.fr
Website: http://www.ira-bastia.fr

Director: Yvon Alain
Tel: +33(4) 95-32-87-11 EMail: valerie.stadtler@ira-bastia.gouv.fr

Secretary General: Antoine Pizzorni
Tel: +33(4) 95-32-87-03 EMail: antoine.pizzorni@ira-bastia.gouv.fr

Programme
Administration (Administration; Public Administration)
History: Founded in 1979
Academic Year: September to July
Admission Requirements: External competitive examination: Licence or Master or equivalent
Main Language(s) of Instruction: French
Degrees and Diplomas: Training course in Public Administration (Cadres A)
Last Updated: 08/04/15

REGIONAL INSTITUTE OF ADMINISTRATION - LILLE

Institut régional d'Administration de Lille (IRA)
CS 80008, 49, rue Jean-Jaurès, 59040 Lille, Cedex
Tel: +33(3) 20-29-87-10
Fax: +33(3) 20-29-87-11
EMail: iradelille@ira-lille.gouv.fr
Website: http://www.ira-lille.gouv.fr

Director: Brigitte Mangeol EMail: iradelille@ira-lille.gouv.fr
Secretary General: Philippe Dantoing EMail: sg@ira-lille.gouv.fr

Programme
Administration (Administration)
History: Founded 1971
Admission Requirements: External competitive examination: Licence or Master or equivalent
Main Language(s) of Instruction: French
Degrees and Diplomas: Training course in Public Administration (Cadres A)
Last Updated: 08/04/15

REGIONAL INSTITUTE OF ADMINISTRATION - LYON

Institut régional d'Administration de Lyon
BP 72076, Parc de l'Europe Jean Monnet, 69616 Villeurbanne, Cedex
Tel: +33(4) 72-82-17-17
Fax: +33(4) 72-82-17-12
Website: http://www.ira-lyon.gouv.fr

Director: Pierre-Henri Vray Tel: +33(4) 72-82-17-17
Secretary General: Christian Mathais Tel: +33(4) 72-82-17-20

Programme
Administration (Administration; Public Administration)
History: Founded 1970
Admission Requirements: External competitive examination: Licence or Master or equivalent
Main Language(s) of Instruction: French
Degrees and Diplomas: Training course in Public Administration (Cadres A)
Last Updated: 08/04/15

REGIONAL INSTITUTE OF ADMINISTRATION - METZ

Institut régional d'Administration de Metz
15, avenue de Lyon, CS 85822, 57078 Metz, Cedex
Tel: +33(3) 87-75-44-11
Fax: +33(3) 87-75-60-13
EMail: ira@ira-metz.gouv.fr
Website: http://www.ira-metz.fr

Director: François Chambon (2009-)

Programme
Administration (Administration; Public Administration)
History: Founded 1973
Admission Requirements: External competitive examination: Licence or equivalent
Main Language(s) of Instruction: French
Degrees and Diplomas: Training course in Public Administration (Cadres A)
Last Updated: 08/04/15

REGIONAL INSTITUTE OF ADMINISTRATION - NANTES

Institut régional d'Administration de Nantes
BP 82234, 1, rue de la Bourgeonnière, 44322 Nantes, Cedex 3
Tel: +33(2) 40-74-34-77
Fax: +33(2) 40-74-22-07
Website: http://www.ira-nantes.gouv.fr

Director: Jean-Luc Guillemoto
Secretary General: Eliane Bouché

Programme
Administration (Administration; Public Administration)
History: Founded in 1972
Admission Requirements: External competitive examination: Licence or equivalent
Main Language(s) of Instruction: French
Degrees and Diplomas: Training course in Public Administration (Cadres A)
Last Updated: 08/04/15

REIMS SCHOOL OF ART AND DESIGN

Ecole supérieure d'Art et de Design de Reims
12 rue Libergier, 51100 Reims
Tel: +33(3) 26-89-42-70
Fax: +33(3) 26-89-42-78
EMail: contact@esad-reims.fr
Website: http://www.esad-reims.fr/

Director: Claire Peillod (2005-)

International Relations: Véronique Pintelon
EMail: veronique.pintelon@esad-reims.fr

Programme

Visual Arts and Design (Design; Fine Arts; Furniture Design; Graphic Design)

History: Created in 1748, acquiring its current status in 2000.

Admission Requirements: Baccalauréat or equivalent secondary school exam. Entrance exam with a selection jury.

Fees: 630-840 per annum (Euro)

Main Language(s) of Instruction: French

Accrediting Agency: Ministry of Culture and Communication

Degrees and Diplomas: *Master*: **Fine Arts.** Diplôme national d'arts plastiques (DNAP) 3 years; Diplôme national supérieur d'expression plastique (DNSEP in Design) a further 2 years. Prepares for the teaching exams: Visual Arts CAPES and Applied Arts CAPET.

Last Updated: 17/03/15

RENNES 1 UNIVERSITY

Université de Rennes I
2, rue du Thabor, CS 46510, 35065 Rennes, Cedex
Tel: +33(2) 23-23-35-35
Fax: +33(2) 23-23-36-00
EMail: webur1@listes.univ-rennes1.fr
Website: http://www.univ-rennes1.fr

President: Guy Cathelineau (2012-)
Tel: +33(2) 23-23-36-61 EMail: guy.cathelineau@univ-rennes1.fr

Head of Administration: Martine Ruaud
Tel: +33(2) 23-23-36-41 +33(2) 23-23-36-83
EMail: martine.ruaud@univ-rennes1.fr

International Relations: Pierre Van de Weghe, Vice-president in charge of International Relations
EMail: vp-relations-internationales@univ-rennes1.fr

Faculty

Dental Surgery (Dentistry); **Economics** (Banking; Business Administration; Economics; Finance; Public Administration; Public Health; Statistics); **Law and Political Science** (Law; Political Sciences); **Medicine** (Health Sciences; Medicine); **Pharmacy** (Biological and Life Sciences; Biology; Biomedicine; Pharmacology; Pharmacy)

Unit

Computer science and Electronic *(IFSIC)* (Computer Science; Electronic Engineering); **Life and Environmental Sciences** *(SVE)* (Biochemistry; Biological and Life Sciences; Biology; Ecology; Environmental Studies; Food Science; Genetics; Microbiology; Physiology); **Mathematics** *(IMR)* (Mathematics); **Philosophy** (Philosophy); **Structure and Properties of Matter** *(SPM)* (Archaeology; Chemistry; Earth Sciences; Materials Engineering; Mechanical Engineering; Physics)

School

Applied Sciences and Technology *(ENSSAT, Lannion)* (Computer Science; Electronic Engineering; Software Engineering; Telecommunications Engineering); **Engineering** *(ESIR, Rennes)* (Bioengineering; Computer Science; Materials Engineering; Telecommunications Engineering); **Teacher Training** *(ESPE Bretagne with 5 sites throughout region)* (Teacher Trainers Education; Teacher Training)

Institute

Management *(IGR)* (Management); **Preparatory Administrative Studies** *(IPAG)* (Administration); **Technology** *(IUT, St Brieuc)* (Bioengineering; Business Education; Civil Engineering; Materials Engineering; Polymer and Plastics Technology; Real Estate; Sales Techniques; Technology); **Technology** *(IUT, St Malo)* (Administration; Business Administration; Industrial Maintenance; Law; Telecommunications Engineering); **Technology** *(IUT, Lannion)* (Computer Engineering; Computer Science; Journalism; Measurement and Precision Engineering; Technology; Telecommunications Engineering); **Technology** *(IUT, Rennes)* (Administration; Chemistry; Civil Engineering; Computer Engineering; Electrical Engineering; Industrial Maintenance; Mechanical Engineering; Production Engineering; Technology)

History: Founded 1970 under the 1968 law reforming higher education as one of the Universities replacing the former Université de Rennes, established in 1461 as University of Nantes with Colleges and Faculties in Nantes and Rennes; suppressed by the Revolution, reconstituted 1896. A State institution enjoying academic and financial autonomy, operating under the jurisdiction of the Minister of Education and financed by the State.

Academic Year: September to June (September-January; February-June)

Admission Requirements: Secondary school certificate (baccalauréat) or equivalent, or special entrance examination

Fees: 189,10-396,10 per annum (Euro)

Main Language(s) of Instruction: French

Accrediting Agency: Ministère de l'Education Nationale

Degrees and Diplomas: *Capacité en Droit*: **Law.** *Diplôme d'Accès aux Etudes universitaires*; *Diplôme universitaire de Technologie*; *Licence*: **Arts and Humanities; Economics; Law.** *Licence professionnelle*: **Agriculture; Business Administration; Business and Commerce; Journalism; Law; Technology.** *Diplôme d'Etat*: **Dentistry; Medicine; Pharmacy.** *Diplôme d'Ingénieur*: **Engineering.** *Master*: **Arts and Humanities; Biological and Life Sciences; Chemistry; Earth Sciences; Economics; Engineering; Environmental Studies; Finance; Health Sciences; Human Resources; Information Sciences; Law; Marketing; Mathematics and Computer Science; Philosophy; Physics; Political Sciences; Public Health; Statistics; Teacher Training; Telecommunications Engineering.** *Doctorat*: **Archaeology; Arts and Humanities; Biological and Life Sciences; Biology; Biomedical Engineering; Chemistry; Earth Sciences; Economics; Educational Sciences; Electronic Engineering; Information Sciences; Law; Management; Mathematics and Computer Science; Mechanical Engineering; Pharmacy; Philosophy; Physics; Political Sciences; Telecommunications Engineering.** *Certificat de Spécialité*: **Medicine.** *Habilitation à Diriger les Recherches*. Masters recherche, Masters professionnel, Preparation for CAPES, CAPET and Administrative exams

Student Services: Academic Counselling, Canteen, Cultural Activities, Facilities for disabled people, Foreign Studies Centre, Health Services, Language Laboratory, Library, Residential Facilities, Social Counselling, Sports Facilities

Publications: Bulletin de la Société Scientifique de Bretagne

Publishing House: Université de Rennes I Publishing House

Student Numbers *2013*: Total 26,762
Last Updated: 03/04/15

NATIONAL GRADUATE SCHOOL OF CHEMISTRY OF RENNES

ECOLE NATIONALE SUPÉRIEURE DE CHIMIE DE RENNES (ENSCR)
11, allée de Beaulieu - CS 50837, 35708 Rennes, Cedex 7
Tel: +33(2) 23-23-80-00
Fax: +33(2) 23-23-81-99
EMail: contact@ensc-rennes.fr
Website: http://www.ensc-rennes.fr/

Director: Pierre Le Cloirec EMail: pierre.le-cloirec@ensc-rennes.fr

International Relations: Pierre Briend
Tel: +33(2) 23-23-80-47
EMail: relations-internationales@ensc-rennes.fr

Programme

Chemistry (Chemical Engineering)

History: Founded 1919.

Main Language(s) of Instruction: French

Accrediting Agency: Ministry of Higher Education and Research

Degrees and Diplomas: *Diplôme d'Ingénieur*: **Chemical Engineering.** *Master*: **Chemistry; Water Science.**

RENNES 2 UNIVERSITY

Université Rennes 2

Place du Recteur Henri le Moal CS 24307, 35043 Rennes, Cedex
Tel: +33(2) 99-14-10-00
Fax: +33(2) 99-14-10-17
EMail: presidence@univ-rennes2.fr
Website: http://www.univ-rennes2.fr

President: Jean-Emile Gombert (2011-)
Tel: +33(2) 99-14-10-12
EMail: president@univ-rennes2.fr

Head of Administration: Amine Amar
Tel: +33(2) 99-14-10-26
EMail: amine.amar@univ-rennes2.fr

International Relations: Thierry Goater, Vice-Pseident in charge of International Relations Tel: +33(2) 99-14-10-98
EMail: thierry.goater@univ-rennes2.fr

Unit

Arts, Letters and Communication (Art History; Fine Arts; Information Sciences; Literature; Music; Performing Arts); **Human Sciences** (Educational Sciences; Linguistics; Psychology; Sociology); **Languages** (Arabic; Celtic Languages and Studies; Chinese; English; German; Italian; Portuguese; Russian; Spanish); **Physical Education and Sports** *(STAPS)* (Physical Education; Sports); **Social Sciences** (Administration; Applied Mathematics; Business Administration; Geography; History; Regional Planning; Social Sciences)

Institute

Criminology *(ICSH)* (Criminology; Psychology); **Labour Studies in the West** *(ISSTO)* (Labour and Industrial Relations); **Teacher Training** *(IUFM Bretagne with 5 sites in the region)* (Teacher Trainers Education; Teacher Training)

Centre

Distance Education *(SUED)* (Distance Education); **French for Foreign Students** *(CIREFE)* (French); **Lifelong Education** (Continuing Education); **Modern Languages** (Modern Languages); **Music Teacher Training** *(CFMI)* (Music; Teacher Training)

Graduate School

Humanities (Applied Linguistics; Cultural Studies; Linguistics); **Social Sciences** (Social Sciences)

Further Information: Also campus in Saint-Brieuc and 19 research units

History: Founded 1970 under the 1968 law reforming higher education as one of the Universities replacing the former Université de Rennes, established in 1461 as University of Nantes with Colleges and Faculties in Nantes and Rennes; suppressed by the Revolution, reconstituted 1896. A State institution enjoying academic and financial autonomy, operating under the jurisdiction of the Minister of Education and financed by the State.

Academic Year: September to June

Admission Requirements: Secondary school certificate (baccalauréat) or equivalent, or special entrance examination

Main Language(s) of Instruction: French

Degrees and Diplomas: *Diplôme d'Accès aux Etudes universitaires*; *Licence*: **Applied Mathematics; Arts and Humanities; Business Administration; Educational Sciences; Geography; Information Sciences; Modern Languages; Musicology; Social Sciences; Sports.** *Licence professionnelle*: **Documentation Techniques; Graphic Arts; Multimedia; Social Sciences; Sports; Tourism.** *Master*: **Archaeology; Arts and Humanities; Business Administration; Educational Sciences; Fine Arts; Geography; History; Information Sciences; Linguistics; Literature; Modern Languages; Performing Arts; Psychology; Public Health; Regional Studies; Sociology; Sports; Statistics; Teacher Training; Urban Studies.** *Doctorat*: **Arts and Humanities; Modern Languages; Social Sciences.**

Student Services: Academic Counselling, Canteen, Careers Guidance, Cultural Activities, Facilities for disabled people, Health Services, Language Laboratory, Library, Nursery Care, Residential Facilities, Social Counselling, Sports Facilities

Publishing house: Presses Universitaires de Rennes

Academic Staff *2013-2014*	**TOTAL**
FULL-TIME	**1,305**
Student Numbers *2013-2014*	
All (Foreign included)	**21,445**
FOREIGN ONLY	**2580**

Last Updated: 03/04/15

SAINT-ETIENNE SCHOOL OF ARCHITECTURE

Ecole nationale supérieure d'Architecture de Saint-Etienne (EASE)

1, rue Buisson, BP 94, 42003 Saint-Etienne, Cedex 1
Tel: +33(4) 77-42-35-42
Fax: +33(4) 77-42-35-40
EMail: ensase@st-etienne.archi.fr
Website: http://www.st-etienne.archi.fr

Director: Jacques Porte

Secretary General: Catherine Skrzat Tel: +33(4) 77-42-35-41

International Relations: Morgane Bediee
Tel: +33(4) 77-42-35-49
EMail: morgane.bediee@st-etienne.archi.fr

Programme

Architecture (Architecture)

History: Founded 1971.

Main Language(s) of Instruction: French

Accrediting Agency: Ministère de la Culture et de la Communication

Degrees and Diplomas: *Licence*: **Architecture.** *Master*: **Architecture.** Habilitation à exercer la maîtrise d'œuvre en son nom propre (HMONP)

Last Updated: 11/03/15

SAINT-ETIENNE SCHOOL OF ART AND DESIGN

Ecole supérieure d'Art et Design de Saint Etienne (ESADSE)

3, rue Javelin Pagnon, 42048 Saint-Etienne, Cedex 1
Tel: +33(4) 77-47-88-00
Fax: +33(4) 77-47-88-01
EMail: infos@esadse.fr
Website: http://www.esadse.fr

Director: Yann Fabès

Programme

Art (Graphic Arts; Painting and Drawing; Photography; Video; Visual Arts); **Design** (Design)

History: Founded 1803 as École de dessin. Became École régionale des arts industriels in 1884, École régionale des beaux arts in 1923, and École supérieure d'art et design en 2006.

Academic Year: September to June

Admission Requirements: Baccalauréat or equivalent secondary school exam. Entrance exam with a selection jury.

Main Language(s) of Instruction: French

Accrediting Agency: Ministry of Culture and Communication

Degrees and Diplomas: Diplome national d'arts plastiques (DNAP) 3 years; Diplome national supérieur d'expression plastique (DNSEP) a further 2 years. Also has a Post-graduate Certificate in design and research: Certificat d'Études d'Arts Plastiques

Last Updated: 20/03/15

SCHOOL OF ADVANCED STUDIES IN SOCIAL SCIENCES (EHESS) - PARIS

Ecole des Hautes Etudes en Sciences Sociales (EHESS)

190-198 avenue de France, 75013 Paris
Tel: +33(1) 49-54-25-25
Fax: +33(1) 45-44-93-11
Website: http://www.ehess.fr

President: Pierre-Cyrille Hautcœur EMail: presidence@ehess.fr

Director of Services: Hélène Moulin-Rodarie

Department

Cultural Affairs (Cultural Studies); **Economics** (Economics); **History** (History); **Sociology, Social Anthropology and Psychology** (Anthropology; Psychology; Sociology)

Further Information: Has Centres in Marseilles, Lyon and Toulouse

History: Founded 1975, as the VIth Section of the Ecole pratique des hautes Etudes, founded 1868 by Victor Duruy. A centre of postgraduate education and research at the highest level. Financially supported by the Ministry of Education.

Admission Requirements: Master: University degree in sociology; Doctorat: Master degree

Fees: 256-391 (Euro)

Main Language(s) of Instruction: French

Degrees and Diplomas: *Master*: **Anthropology; Applied Mathematics; Arts and Humanities; Economics; Ethnology; History; Musicology; Philosophy; Social Policy; Social Sciences; Sociology; Urban Studies.** *Doctorat*: **Aesthetics; Anthropology; Applied Mathematics; Archaeology; Arts and Humanities; Cognitive Sciences; Economics; Ethnology; Geography; History; History of Societies; Information Sciences; Law; Musicology; Political Sciences; Psychology; Social Policy; Social Sciences; Sociology; Urban Studies.** *Habilitation à Diriger les Recherches*. Diplôme de l'EHESS

Student Services: Sports Facilities

Publications: Bulletins des centres de recherches; Revues

Publishing House: Editions de l'Ecole des Hautes Etudes en Sciences Sociales

Last Updated: 30/03/15

SCHOOL OF AERONAUTICS - SALON DE PROVENCE

Ecole de l'Air de Salon de Provence (EA)
Base Aérienne 701, 13661 Salon-de-Provence
Tel: +33(4) 90-17-80-00
Fax: +33(4) 90-17-61-77
EMail: cab.ea-ema@inet.air.defense.gouv.fr
Website: http://ecole-air.fr/

Général de brigade aérienne: Francis Pollet (2013-)
Tel: +33(4) 90-17-82-10
EMail: cab.ea-ema@inet.air.defense.gouv.fr

School

Aeronautical and Aerospace Engineering (Aeronautical and Aerospace Engineering)

Further Information: Has a research centre and several labs

History: Founded 1935.

Academic Year: September to July

Admission Requirements: Competitive entrance examination following 2 yrs further study after secondary school certificate (baccalauréat) or following first university qualification (Bachelor degree) or competitive political science examination

Main Language(s) of Instruction: French

Accrediting Agency: Ministry of Defence, Commission des Titres d'Ingénieur

Degrees and Diplomas: *Licence*: **Aeronautical and Aerospace Engineering; Computer Science; Management; Public Administration.** *Diplôme d'Ingénieur*: **Aeronautical and Aerospace Engineering.** *Master*: **Engineering; Political Sciences.** Also: Diplomas

Last Updated: 04/03/15

SCHOOL OF AGRICULTURAL ENGINEERING

Ecole d'Ingénieurs en Agriculture (ESITPA)
3 rue du Tronquet, CS 40118, 76134 Mont-Saint-Aignan, Cedex
Tel: +33(2) 32-82-91-99
Fax: +33(2) 35-05-27-40
EMail: contact@esitpa.fr
Website: http://www.esitpa.org/

Managing Director: Daniel Roche (2009-)
EMail: droche@esitpa.org

International Relations: Nathalie Roguez
EMail: international@esitpa.org

Department

Agronomy (Agronomy; Animal Husbandry; Biotechnology; Environmental Studies; Vegetable Production); **Biometrics and Computer Science** (Computer Science; Mathematics; Statistics); **Economics and Management** (Economics; Management); **Food Processing** (Agricultural Business; Biotechnology; Chemistry; Food Science); **Humanities** (Arts and Humanities; Communication Studies; English; German; Spanish)

History: Founded 1919 as Institut technique de pratique agricole. Becomes Ecole supérieure d'ingénieurs et de techniciens pour l'agriculture 1970. Acquired present title 2007. Becomes a Public Institution in 2013.

Admission Requirements: Baccalauréat, Equivalent Secondary School Degree

Fees: 3500 per year (Euro)

Main Language(s) of Instruction: French

Accrediting Agency: Commission des titres d'ingénieur (CTI). Ministry of Agriculture

Degrees and Diplomas: *Licence professionnelle*: **Agriculture; Animal Husbandry.** *Diplôme d'Ingénieur*: **Agriculture.** *Mastère spécialisé*: **Agriculture.** *Master*: **Agriculture; Plant and Crop Protection.**

Last Updated: 11/03/15

SCHOOL OF ARCHITECTURE OF THE CITY AND TERRITORIES OF MARNE-LA-VALLÉE

Ecole d'Architecture de la Ville et des Territoires à Marne-la-Vallée (EAVT)
10-12 avenue Blaise-Pascal,
77447 Champs-sur-Marne,
Cedex 02
Tel: +33(1) 60-95-84-00
Fax: +33(1) 60-95-84-47
EMail: vt@marnelavallee.archi.fr
Website: http://www.marnelavallee.archi.fr

Director: Amina Sellali
Tel: +33(1) 60-95-84-64
EMail: amina.sellali@marnelavallee.archi.fr

Executive Director: Sophie Perdrial
Tel: +33(1) 60-95-84-11
EMail: sophie.perdrial@marnelavallee.archi.fr

Programme

Architecture (Architecture and Planning)

History: Founded 1998.

Admission Requirements: After secondary school certificate (baccalauréat) or equivalent

Main Language(s) of Instruction: French

Degrees and Diplomas: *Licence*: **Architecture.** *Licence professionnelle*: **Architecture and Planning.** *Master*: **Architecture.** *Doctorat*: **Architecture.** Diploma of Architectural studies: the first cycle leads to a Bachelor's degree, the second cycle leads to a Master's degree. Diploma of specialisation in Architecture (DSA); Diploma in Architecture and Urbanism studies; Project Management Certificate.

Student Services: Canteen, Library

Publications: les cahiers du DPEA Architecture post-carbone; les cahiers du DSA d'architecte-urbaniste; Marnes, documents d'architecture

Student Numbers *2012-2013*: Total 604

Last Updated: 11/03/15

SCHOOL OF STATISTICS AND ECONOMIC ADMINISTRATION PARISTECH

Ecole nationale de la Statistique et de l'Administration économique (ENSAE ParisTech) (ENSAE)

3, avenue Pierre Larousse, 92245 Malakoff, Cedex
Tel: +33(1) 41-17-65-25
Fax: +33(1) 41-17-38-52
EMail: info@ensae.fr
Website: http://www.ensae.fr

Director: Julien Pouget (2011-) EMail: julien.pouget@ensae.fr

Secretary General: Pierre Bertiaux
EMail: pierre.bertiaux@ensae-paristech.fr

International Relations: Rodolphe Pauvert
EMail: rodolphe.pauvert@ensae-paristech.fr

Division
Finance, Insurance, Economics and Statistics (Economics; Finance; Insurance; Statistics)

History: Founded 1942. Founding member of the Paris Institute of Technology (ParisTech).

Academic Year: September to June

Admission Requirements: Competitive entrance examination following 2 years further study after secondary school certificate (baccalauréat) or equivalent. On the basis of their academic qualification. Graduates in economics and/or mathematics or graduates of Grandes Ecoles

Fees: Statistician course, 737 per annum; Mastère spécialisé 5000 (Euro)

Main Language(s) of Instruction: French

Degrees and Diplomas: *Diplôme d'Etat*; *Mastère spécialisé*: **Economics; Finance; Statistics.** *Certificat de Spécialité*

Student Services: Library, Sports Facilities

Student Numbers *2014-2015*: Total 423
Last Updated: 11/03/15

STRASBOURG CONSERVATORY

Conservatoire de Strasbourg

1 Place Dauphine, 67076 Strasbourg, Cedex
Tel: +33(3) 68 98 51 00
EMail: conservatoire@strasbourg.eu
Website: http://www.conservatoire.strasbourg.eu

Director: Vincent Dubois (2011-)
EMail: vincent.dubois@strasbourg.eu

Programme
Dance (Dance); **Music** (Music; Music Theory and Composition; Musical Instruments; Singing); **Theatre** (Acting; Theatre)

History: Founded 1855.

Main Language(s) of Instruction: French

Degrees and Diplomas: *Licence*; *Master*. Diplôme national supérieur professionnel de musicien, diplôme supérieur d'interprète ou de compositeur, certificat d'études théâtrales, Diplôme d'études chorégraphiques

Student Services: Library

Publishing house: Éditions du Conservatoire de Strasbourg
Last Updated: 11/03/15

STRASBOURG SCHOOL OF ARCHITECTURE

Ecole nationale supérieure d'Architecture de Strasbourg (ENSAS)

BP 10037, 8, boulevard Président Wilson, 67068 Strasbourg
Tel: +33(3) 88-32-25-35
Fax: +33(3) 88-32-25-41
EMail: ecole@strasbourg.archi.fr
Website: http://www.strasbourg.archi.fr

Director: Eric Gross EMail: direction@strasbourg.archi.fr

International Relations: Jill Ferrier
EMail: jill.ferrier@strasbourg.archi.fr

Programme
Architecture (Architecture)

History: Founded 1922 as École d'Architecture de Strasbourg. Acquired present title 2005.

Main Language(s) of Instruction: French

Accrediting Agency: Ministry of Culture

Degrees and Diplomas: *Licence*: **Architecture.** *Licence professionnelle*: **Building Technologies.** *Master*: **Archaeology; Architecture; Urban Studies.** Habilitation à l'exercice de la maîtrise d'œuvre en son nom propre (HMONP); Master de recherche EST; DPEA

Last Updated: 30/03/15

THE BRITANNY NATIONAL COLLEGE OF ARCHITECTURE

Ecole nationale supérieure d'Architecture de Bretagne (ENSA BRETAGNE)

44, boulevard de Chézy - CS 16427, 35064 Rennes, Cedex
Tel: +33(2) 99-29-68-00
Fax: +33(2) 99-30-42-49
EMail: ensab@rennes.archi.fr
Website: http://www.rennes.archi.fr

Director: Jean-François Roullin
Tel: +33(2) 99-29-68-03
EMail: jean-françois.roullin@rennes.archi.fr

Secretary General: Marie-Françoise Neveu
Tel: +33(2) 99-29-68-06
EMail: marie-françoise.neveu@rennes.archi.fr

International Relations: Catherine David
Tel: +33(2) 99-29-68-08 EMail: catherine.david@rennes.archi.fr

Programme
Architecture (Architecture; Real Estate; Urban Studies)

History: Founded 1905 as École Régionale d'Architecture de Rennes. Became Britanny School of Architecture 1984. Acquired present title 2005.

Admission Requirements: Baccalauréat (www.admission-postbac.fr)

Main Language(s) of Instruction: French

Degrees and Diplomas: *Licence*: **Architecture.** *Master*: **Architecture and Planning; Civil Engineering; Town Planning.** Diplôme d'études in architecture; Diplôme d'habilitation de l'architecte diplômé d'Etat à l'exercice de la Maîtrise d'Oeuvre (HMONP)

Academic Staff *2014-2015*: Total 39
Student Numbers *2014-2015*: Total 682
Last Updated: 11/03/15

TOULON PROVENCE MEDITERRANEAN ART AND DESIGN SCHOOL

Ecole supérieure d'Art et Design de Toulon Provence Méditerranée (ESADTPM)

168 boulevard du Commandant Nicolas, 83000 Toulon
Tel: +33(4) 94-62-01-48
EMail: infoesatpm@tpmed.org
Website: http://www.esadtpm.fr/

Director: Jean-Marc Avrilla

International Relations: Estelle Arnaud Tel: +33(4) 94-62-01-48

Programme
Art (Fine Arts); **Design** (Design)

History: Founded in 1899. Acquired present status 2010. Become Toulon Provence Mediterranean Art and Design School in 2014.

Academic Year: October to June

Admission Requirements: Baccalauréat or equivalent, entrance exam and jury selection

Fees: 150-300 per annum (Euro)

Main Language(s) of Instruction: French

Degrees and Diplomas: *Licence*: **Design; Fine Arts.** *Master*: **Design; Fine Arts.** Diplôme National d'Art Plastique (DNAP) 3 years; Diplôme National d'Art et Technique (DNAT) 3 years;

Diplôme National Supérieur d'Expression Plastique (DNSEP) a further 2 years.
Last Updated: 07/04/15

TOULOUSE ART SCHOOL

Institut supérieur des Arts de Toulouse (ISDAT)
5, quai de la Daurade, 31000 Toulouse
Tel: +33(5) 31-47-12-11
Fax: +33(5) 31-47-11-96
EMail: info@isdat.eu
Website: http://www.isdat.eu

Director: Anne Dallant (2014-) EMail: beatrix.puret@isdat.fr

Programme

Fine Arts (Cinema and Television; Communication Arts; Design; Engraving; Fine Arts; Painting and Drawing; Photography; Video)

History: Founded 2011 following merger of the Ecole supérieure des beaux-arts de Toulouse and the Centre d'enseignement supérieur de musique et danse (CESMD)

Admission Requirements: Entrance examination

Main Language(s) of Instruction: French

Accrediting Agency: Ministry of Culture and Communication

Degrees and Diplomas: DNAP - Diplôme national d'arts plastique (3 years) and DNESP - Diplôme national supérieur d'expression plastique (5 years) in Design and Arts
Last Updated: 08/04/15

TOULOUSE I CAPITOLE UNIVERSITY

Université Toulouse I Capitole (UT1)
2 rue du Doyen-Gabriel-Marty, 31042 Toulouse, Cedex 9
Tel: +33(5) 61-63-35-00
Fax: +33(5) 61-63-37-98
EMail: scolarite.generale@ut-capitole.fr
Website: http://www.ut-capitole.fr

President: Bruno Sire (2008-2016)
Tel: +33(5) 61-63-35-26 EMail: Bruno.Sire@ut-capitole.fr

Head of Administration: Cécile Chicoye
Tel: +33(5) 61-63-35-24 EMail: Cecile.Chicoye@ut-capitole.fr

International Relations: Claudine Chambert
Tel: +33(5) 61-63-39-14
EMail: Claudine.Chambert@ut-capitole.fr; relinter@ut-capitole.fr

Faculty

Computer Science (Computer Science); **Economic and Social Administration** (Economics; Public Administration); **Economics** (Economics); **Law** (Law)

Programme

Organizational Management and Development (Management); **Social Sciences, Computer Research and Studies** *(IUP)* (Data Processing; Social Sciences)

School

Economics *(TSE)* (Economics); **Teacher Training** *(ESPE Midi-Pyrénées with 9 sites throughout region)* (Teacher Training)

Department

History (History); **Languages and Civilizations** *(DLC)* (Catalan; Chinese; English; French; Modern Languages; Spanish); **Mathematics** (Mathematics); **Physical Education and Sports** *(DAPS)* (Physical Education; Sports; Sports Management); **Sociology and Political Sciences** (Political Sciences; Sociology)

Institute

Business Administration *(IAE)* (Business Administration; Management); **Confucius** *(ICT)* (Chinese); **Juridical Studies** *(IEJ)* (Law); **Technology** *(IUT, Rodez)* (Business Administration; Data Processing; Management; Mechanical Engineering; Production Engineering; Technology)

Centre

Preparatory Administrative Studies *(CPAG)* (Administration)

Laboratory

Economic, Political and Social Structures Research *(LEREPS)* (Economics; Political Sciences); **Environmental Economics and Natural Resources** *(LERNA)*; **Social Sciences of Policy-Making** *(LaSSP (IEP))* (European Union Law; Journalism; Political Sciences)

Graduate School

Economics (Economics); **Management** (Management); **Political Science and Law** (Law; Political Sciences)

Research Centre

Business Law *(CDA)* (Commercial Law); **Constitutional and Political Studies** *(CERCP)* (Constitutional Law; Political Sciences); **European Research on Economic Law** *(IRDEIC)* (Commercial Law); **History of Law of Institutions and Political Ideas** *(CTHDIP)* (History of Law; Political Sciences); **Human Resources and Employment** *(LIRHE)* (Human Resources; Law); **Management** *(CRG)* (Management); **Mathematical and Quantitative Economics** *(GREMAQ)* (Econometrics; Mathematics); **Mathematics** *(IMT-CEREMATH)* (Mathematics); **Military Studies** *(CMJ Morris Janowitz)* (Military Science); **Police Studies** *(CERP)* (Police Studies); **Private Law** *(CDA)* (Law; Private Law); **Quantitative Methods Applied for Economic Development** *(ARQADE)* (Econometrics); **Security and Governance** *(GRSG)* (Leadership; Military Science; Political Sciences); **Space, Territories and Communication Law** *(IDETCOM)* (Communication Studies; Law); **Theory of Public Institutions Control** *(TACIP)* (Law; Public Administration); **Town Planning and Construction Laws** *(IEJUC)* (Law; Town Planning)

History: Founded 1970 under the 1968 law reforming higher education as one of three Universities replacing the former Université de Toulouse, founded 1229. Suppressed by the Revolution and replaced by Faculties of Law; Theology; Science; Letters; and Medicine 1808. Reconstituted as University 1896. A State institution enjoying academic and financial autonomy, operating under the jurisdiction of the Minister of Education and financed by the State. Acquired present title 2010.

Academic Year: October to June (October-February; February-June)

Admission Requirements: Secondary school certificate (baccalauréat) or equivalent

Main Language(s) of Instruction: French

Degrees and Diplomas: *Capacité en Droit*: **Law.** *Licence*: **Administration; Applied Mathematics; Economics; Information Sciences; Law; Management; Mathematics and Computer Science; Political Sciences.** *Licence professionnelle*: **Accountancy; Agronomy; Business and Commerce; Computer Science; Finance; Human Resources; Insurance; Law; Management.** *Master*: **Accountancy; Administration; Banking; Economics; Finance; Human Resources; Information Sciences; Law; Management; Marketing; Mathematics and Computer Science; Political Sciences; Teacher Training.** *Doctorat*: **Economics; Law; Management.** Masters recherche, Masters professionnel

Student Services: Academic Counselling, Canteen, Cultural Activities, Facilities for disabled people, Foreign Studies Centre, Health Services, Language Laboratory, Residential Facilities, Social Counselling, Sports Facilities

Publications: Annales; Civilisations; Livret de la Recherche; Publications de Sciences Politiques; Working Papers (Cahier de Publications de l'U.E.R. Sciences économiques)

Student Numbers *2013-2014*: Total 21,300
Last Updated: 07/04/15

TOULOUSE III UNIVERSITY

Université Toulouse III Paul Sabatier
118, route de Narbonne, 31062 Toulouse, Cedex 09
Tel: +33(5) 61-55-66-11
Fax: +33(5) 61-55-64-70
EMail: contact-ups@adm.ups-tlse.fr
Website: http://www.ups-tlse.fr

Provisional Administrator: Amal Sayah (2015-)
Tel: +33(5) 61-55-60-28

Head of Administration: Claude Debat
Tel: +33(5) 61-55-66-13 EMail: secgen@adm.ups-tlse.fr

International Relations: Eric Crubézy, Vice-President in charge of International relations
Tel: +33(05) 61-55-66-24 EMail: eric.crubezy@univ-tlse3.fr

Faculty

Dentistry (Dentistry); **Medicine** *(Rangueil)* (Medicine); **Medicine** *(Purpan)* (Medicine); **Pharmacy** (Pharmacy)

Unit

Life Sciences and Earth Sciences *(STV)* (Biochemistry; Biological and Life Sciences; Biology; Biotechnology; Chemistry; Earth Sciences; Ecology; Health Sciences); **Mathematics, Computer Science and Management** (Health Administration; Management; Mathematics and Computer Science; Mechanical Engineering); **Modern Languages** (English; German; Modern Languages; Russian; Spanish); **Physical Education and Sports** *(STAPS)* (Physical Education; Sports); **Physics, Chemistry, and Automation** *(PCA)* (Automation and Control Engineering; Chemistry; Physics)

School

Engineering *(UPSSITECH)* (Civil Engineering; Energy Engineering; Environmental Engineering; Instrument Making; Systems Analysis; Telecommunications Engineering); **Midwifery** (Midwifery)

Department

Engineering (Engineering)

Institute

Observatory Midi-Pyrénées *(OMP)*; **Teacher Training** *(IUFM Midi-Pyreenes with 9 sites throughout region)*; **Technology** *(IUT, Site de Tarbes)* (Business Administration; Business and Commerce; Computer Engineering; Electrical Engineering; Management; Production Engineering; Sales Techniques; Technology; Telecommunications Engineering); **Technology** *(IUT Paul Sabatier: sites at Toulouse, Auch, Castres)* (Business Administration; Business and Commerce; Chemical Engineering; Civil Engineering; Computer Science; Management; Measurement and Precision Engineering; Mechanical Engineering; Production Engineering; Sales Techniques; Technology)

Centre

Lifelong Education

Graduate School

Doctoral Schools *(Houses 6 Doctoral Schools and works in partnership with other regional universities to offer other graduate programmes)* (Agronomy; Biology; Chemistry; Earth Sciences; Ecology; Health Sciences; Information Sciences; Medicine)

History: Founded 1970 under the 1968 law reforming higher education as one of three Universities replacing the former Université de Toulouse, founded 1229. Suppressed by the Revolution and replaced by Faculties of Law; Theology; Science; Letters; and Medicine 1808. Reconstituted as University 1896. A State Institution enjoying academic and financial autonomy, operating under the jurisdiction of the Minister of Education and financed by the State. Its structure is based on a series of Unités de formation et de recherche (training and research Units). Each Unit enjoys academic and administrative independence.

Academic Year: September to June (September-January; February-June)

Admission Requirements: Secondary school certificate (Baccalauréat) or equivalent, or special entrance examination

Main Language(s) of Instruction: French

Degrees and Diplomas: *Diplôme universitaire de Technologie*; *Licence*: **Economics; Engineering; Health Sciences; Information Sciences; Law; Management; Natural Sciences; Social Sciences; Sports; Technology.** *Licence professionnelle*: **Agronomy; Engineering; Health Sciences; Sports; Technology.** *Diplôme d'Etat*: **Dentistry; Medicine; Midwifery; Pharmacy; Veterinary Science.** *Diplôme d'Ingénieur*: **Civil Engineering; Engineering; Robotics; Telecommunications Engineering.** *Master*: **Aeronautical and Aerospace Engineering; Astrophysics; Automation and Control Engineering; Biological and Life Sciences; Biotechnology; Business Administration; Chemistry; Civil Engineering; Ecology; Electronic Engineering; Engineering; Environmental Studies; Health Sciences; Mathematics and Computer Science; Mechanical Engineering; Natural Sciences; Physics; Public Health; Social Sciences; Sports; Technology.** *Doctorat*: **Arts and Humanities; Engineering; Health Sciences; Mathematics and Computer Science; Natural Sciences; Pharmacy; Social Sciences; Technology.** *Certificat de Spécialité*: **Health Sciences; Medicine.** Masters recherche, Masters professionnel

Student Services: Academic Counselling, Canteen, Cultural Activities, Facilities for disabled people, Health Services, Residential Facilities, Social Counselling, Sports Facilities

Last Updated: 07/04/15

TOULOUSE INSTITUTE OF TECHNOLOGY

Institut national polytechnique de Toulouse (INP TOULOUSE)

BP 34038, 6, Allée Emile Monso, 31029 Toulouse, Cedex 4
Tel: +33(5) 34-32-30-00
Fax: +33(5) 34-32-31-00
EMail: inp@inp-toulouse.fr
Website: http://www.inp-toulouse.fr

President: Olivier Simonin (2012-)
Tel: +33(5) 34-32-30-03
EMail: president@inp-toulouse.fr; edith.gal@inp-toulouse.fr

Head of Administration: Odile Jankowiak-Gratton (2013-)
Tel: +33(5) 34-32-30-04 EMail: anne.angelino@inp-toulouse.fr

International Relations: Joëlle Courbières
Tel: +33(5) 34-32-31-80
EMail: courbieres@inp-toulouse.fr; sri@inp-toulouse.fr

School

Agriculture (INP-EI PURPAN) (Agriculture; Agronomy; Animal Husbandry; Arts and Humanities; Biological and Life Sciences; Computer Science; Cultural Studies; Engineering; Management); **Agronomy (INP-ENSAT)** (Agriculture; Agronomy; Crop Production; Food Science; Meat and Poultry; Oenology); **Chemical Engineering and Technology (INP-ENSIACET)** (Analytical Chemistry; Applied Chemistry; Bioengineering; Biomedical Engineering; Chemical Engineering; Chemistry; Industrial Chemistry; Inorganic Chemistry; Organic Chemistry; Physical Chemistry; Technology); **Electrical Engineering, Electronics, Computer Science and Hydraulics (INP-ENSEEIHT)** (Automation and Control Engineering; Automotive Engineering; Computer Science; Electrical Engineering; Electronic Engineering; Engineering Management; Hydraulic Engineering; Physical Engineering; Telecommunications Engineering); **Engineering School (INP-ENIT)** (Engineering); **Meteorology** *(ENM)* (Meteorology); **Veterinary Science** *(ENVT)* (Veterinary Science)

Department

Polytechnic Preparatory School *(()* (Engineering; Technology)

Centre

Continuing Education (Continuing Education)

Graduate School

Energy, Civil and Mechanical Engineering (ED MEGeP) (Civil Engineering; Energy Engineering; Hydraulic Engineering; Mechanical Engineering)

History: Founded 1970 under the 1968 law reforming higher education and incorporating various Ecoles nationales supérieures. Acquired present status and title 1984.

Academic Year: September to September

Admission Requirements: Competitive entrance examination following 2 years further study after secondary school certificate (baccalauréat)

Main Language(s) of Instruction: French, English

Accrediting Agency: Ministry of Higher Education and Research; Commission des Titres d'Ingénieurs (CTI)

Degrees and Diplomas: *Diplôme d'Ingénieur*: **Engineering.** *Master*: **Computer Science; Ecology; Engineering; Environmental Studies; Geography; Materials Engineering; Mechanical Engineering; Mechanics; Natural Sciences; Rural Planning.** *Doctorat*: **Aeronautical and Aerospace Engineering; Bioengineering; Civil Engineering; Earth Sciences; Ecology; Electrical and Electronic Engineering; Engineering; Environmental Studies; Materials Engineering; Mathematics and Computer Science; Veterinary Science.** Also Diplôme national d'Oenologue

Student Services: Academic Counselling, Canteen, Careers Guidance, Facilities for disabled people, Health Services, Language Laboratory, Social Counselling, Sports Facilities

Publications: Les Activités de Recherche; Polytech.

Last Updated: 07/04/15

NATIONAL ENGINEERING SCHOOL OF TARBES - ENIT

ÉCOLE NATIONALE D'INGÉNIEURS DE TARBES (ENIT)

47, avenue d'Azereix, BP 1629, 65016 Tarbes, Cedex
Tel: +33(5) 62-44-27-00
Fax: +33(5) 62-44-27-27
EMail: directeur@enit.fr
Website: http://www.enit.fr/fr/index.html

Director: Talal Masri
Tel: +33(5) 62-44-27-01 EMail: directeur@enit.fr

Head of Administration: Bernard Souflet
Tel: +33(5) 62-44-27-70 EMail: souflet@enit.fr

International Relations: Carmen Martin, Head of International Relations Office
Tel: +33(5) 62-44-27-36 /50 EMail: danielle.barthares@enit.fr

Programme
Engineering (Engineering; Materials Engineering; Mechanical Engineering)

History: Founded 1963

Admission Requirements: Entrance examination and interview, secondary school certificate (Baccalauréat)

Main Language(s) of Instruction: French

Accrediting Agency: Commission des Titres d'Ingénieurs (CTI)

Degrees and Diplomas: *Diplôme d'Ingénieur*: **Engineering; Industrial Engineering; Mechanical Engineering.** *Master*. also Masters in Mechanical engineering and Material engineering with the National Polytechnic Institute of Toulouse and a Master in Production engineering with the University of Pau and Pays de l'Adour

PURPAN ENGINEERING SCHOOL

ECOLE D'INGÉNIEURS DE PURPAN

75 voie du TOEC, BP57611, 31076 Toulouse, Cedex 3
Tel: +33(5) 61-15-30-30
Fax: +33(5) 61-15-30-60
EMail: iro@purpan.fr
Website: http://www.purpan.fr/fr

Director General: Michel Roux

International Relations: Marie Odile Bisch, Head of International Relations EMail: iro@purpan.fr

Department
Agronomic and food-processing science (Agriculture; Agronomy); **Economic sciences, administration, marketing and management** (Administration; Business Administration; Economics; Management; Marketing); **Social and environmental sciences and biodiversity** (Agriculture; Environmental Studies)

History: Founded in 1919

Admission Requirements: jury selection and interview. Secondary school certificate (Baccalauréat) or first university qualification (DEUG, DUT or BTS)

Main Language(s) of Instruction: French

Degrees and Diplomas: *Licence*; *Licence professionnelle*; *Diplôme d'Ingénieur*: **Agricultural Engineering; Agriculture; Engineering.** *Mastère spécialisé*: **Engineering.** *Master*: **Agriculture; Animal Husbandry; Food Science.**

TOULOUSE SCHOOL OF ARCHITECTURE

Ecole nationale supérieure d'Architecture de Toulouse (ENSA)

83 rue Aristide Maillol, BP 10629, 31106 Toulouse, Cedex 01
Tel: +33(5) 62-11-50-50
Fax: +33(5) 62-11-50-99
EMail: ensa@toulouse.archi.fr
Website: http://www.toulouse.archi.fr

Director: Monique Reyre EMail: direction@toulouse.archi.fr

International Relations: Sophie Vialle
EMail: relations-internationales@toulouse.archi.fr

Programme
Architecture (Architecture)

History: Founded 1969.

Main Language(s) of Instruction: French

Degrees and Diplomas: *Licence*: **Architecture.** *Master*: **Architecture.** Diplôme propre aux écoles d'architecture (DPEA); Habilitation de l'architecte diplômé d'Etat à l'exercice de la maîtrise d'oeuvre en son nom propre

Student Numbers *2013-2014*: Total 802

Last Updated: 11/03/15

TOURS - ANGERS - LE MANS ART SCHOOL

Ecole supérieure des Beaux-Arts Tours - Angers - Le Mans

Hôtel d'Ollone, 72 rue Bressigny, 49100 Angers
Tel: +33(2) 41-24-13-50
Fax: +33(2) 41-87-26-49
EMail: contact@esba-angers.eu
Website: http://www.esba-angers.eu

Director: Stéphane Doré

International Relations: Lucie Delefosse
Tel: +33(2) 41-24-14-37 EMail: lucie.delefosse@ville.angers.fr

Department
Art and Sculpture *(in Tours)* (Sculpture); **Conservation** *(in Tours)* (Restoration of Works of Art); **Design** *(in Le Mans)* (Architectural and Environmental Design; Design); **Visual Art** *(Arts Médias in Angers)* (Cinema and Television; Graphic Arts; Painting and Drawing; Photography; Video; Visual Arts)

Further Information: site in: Tours and Le Mans

History: Founded in 1760. Acquired present status 2010.

Admission Requirements: Baccalauréat or equivalent secondary school exam. Entrance exam with a selection jury.

Fees: 425 per annum (Euro)

Main Language(s) of Instruction: French

Accrediting Agency: Ministry of Culture and Communication

Degrees and Diplomas: Diplôme national d'arts plastiques (DNAP) 3 yrs; Diplôme national d'arts et techniques (DNAT) 3 yrs; Diplôme national supérieur d'expression plastique (DNSEP) a further 2 yrs; Diplôme de Conservateur-Restaurateur des oeuvres sculptées (Masters level).

Last Updated: 07/04/15

UNIVERSITY OF ANGERS

Université d'Angers

BP 73532, 40, rue de Rennes, 49035 Angers, Cedex 01
Tel: +33(2) 41-96-23-23
Fax: +33(2) 41-23-23-00
EMail: relations.internationales@univ-angers.fr
Website: http://www.univ-angers.fr

President: Jean-Paul Saint-André (2012-)
Tel: +33(2) 41-35-45-62; +33(2) 41-23-23-63
EMail: jean-paul.saint-andre@univ-angers.fr

Director of Services: Olivier Tacheau
Tel: +33(2) 41-96-23-05 EMail: olivier.tacheau@univ-angers.fr

International Relations: John Webb, Vice-President in charge of International Relations
Tel: +33(2) 41-22-64-96; +33(2) 41-96-23-01
EMail: john.webb@univ-angers.fr

Faculty
Languages, Humanities and Social Sciences (Arts and Humanities; Geography; History; Modern Languages; Psychology); **Law, Economics, and Business Studies** (Business Education; Economics; Law); **Medicine** (Medicine); **Pharmacology and Health Engineering** (Pharmacology; Sanitary Engineering); **Science** (Biology; Chemistry; Computer Science; Environmental Studies; Geology; Materials Engineering; Natural Sciences; Physics; Plant and Crop Protection)

Unit
Tourism and Hospitality Management *(ESTHUA)* (Cooking and Catering; Heritage Preservation; Hotel and Restaurant; Hotel Management; Protective Services; Service Trades; Tourism)

School

Engineering *(ISTIA)* (Automation and Control Engineering; Computer Engineering; Industrial Engineering)

Institute

Technology *(IUT Angers 2 sites: Angers, Cholet)* (Biotechnology; Business Computing; Electrical Engineering; Mechanical Engineering; Social Work; Technology)

Further Information: 3 campuses at Cholet Antenna and Saumur site

History: Founded 1971 as Centre universitaire d'Angers under the 1968 law reforming higher education and incorporating Institutions previously attached to the Ministry of Health and Université de Nantes and Université de Rennes. Acquired full University status 1972. A state Institution enjoying academic and financial autonomy operating under the jurisdiction of the Minister of Higher Education and Research and financed by the State.

Academic Year: October to June (October-December; January-March; April-June)

Admission Requirements: Secondary school certificate (baccalauréat) or equivalent, or special entrance examination

Main Language(s) of Instruction: French

Degrees and Diplomas: *Capacité en Droit*; *Diplôme universitaire de Technologie*; *Licence*: **Biological and Life Sciences; Chemistry; Civil Engineering; Economics; Geography; Health Administration; History; Law; Literature; Management; Mathematics and Computer Science; Modern Languages; Physics; Psychology; Public Administration; Social Sciences; Technology.** *Licence professionnelle*; *Diplôme d'Etat*: **Dentistry; Medicine; Pharmacy.** *Diplôme d'Ingénieur*; *Master*: **Applied Mathematics; Banking; Biological and Life Sciences; Biology; Chemistry; Computer Science; Ecology; Economics; Education; Environmental Studies; Finance; Geography (Human); Health Sciences; History; History of Societies; Law; Literature; Management; Modern Languages; Physics; Prehistory; Private Law; Psychology; Public Law; Publishing and Book Trade; Teacher Training; Translation and Interpretation; Treatment Techniques.** *Doctorat*: **Atomic and Molecular Physics; Biological and Life Sciences; Economics; English Studies; Environmental Studies; Geography (Human); Health Sciences; History; Law; Linguistics; Literature; Management; Mathematics and Computer Science; Neurosciences; Political Sciences; Psychology.** *Certificat de Spécialité*: **Medicine.**

Student Services: Canteen, Careers Guidance, Cultural Activities, Facilities for disabled people, Health Services, Library, Residential Facilities, Social Counselling, Sports Facilities

Academic Staff *2014*	**TOTAL**
FULL-TIME	**676**
Student Numbers *2014*	
All (Foreign included)	**21,132**
FOREIGN ONLY	**2392**

Last Updated: 11/03/15

UNIVERSITY OF AVIGNON AND THE VAUCLUSE

Université d'Avignon et des Pays de Vaucluse

74, rue Louis-Pasteur, 84029 Avignon, Cedex 01
Tel: +33(4) 90-16-25-00
Fax: +33(4) 90-16-25-10
EMail: uapv@univ-avignon.fr
Website: http://www.univ-avignon.fr

President: Emmanuel Ethis (2007-)
Tel: +33(4) 90-16-27-32
EMail: emmanuel.ethis@univ-avignon.fr

Administrative Director: Fathie Boubertekh
Tel: +33(4) 90-16-25-11
EMail: fathie.boubertekh@univ-avignon.fr

International Relations: Nathalie Hascoët
Tel: +33(0)4 90-16-25-58
EMail: sri@univ-avignon.fr

Faculty

Applied Sciences (Geography; Geology; Information Sciences); **Arts and Humanities** (English; French; History; Italian; Literature; Spanish); **Exact and Natural Sciences and Health** (Applied Mathematics; Biological and Life Sciences; Biology; Chemistry; Earth Sciences; Mathematics; Organic Chemistry; Physical Education; Physics; Sports); **Law, Political and Economic Sciences** (Business Administration; International Economics; Private Law; Public Law; Social Policy)

Institute

Technology *(IUT)* (Agrobiology; Business and Commerce; Molecular Biology)

Centre

Computer Science (Computer Science)

Research Centre

Christian and Muslim Mediaeval History and Archaeology (Archaeology; Medieval Studies)

Research Laboratory

Avignon Research Laboratory for Computer Science (Computer Science); **Bees and Environment** (Environmental Studies); **Cardiovascular Adaptations to Exercise** (Cardiology; Medicine); **Chemistry: Vectorial Molecular Systems and Bioorganic Chemistry, Chemistry Applied to Art and Archaeology** (Chemistry); **Cultural Identity, Texts and Theatricality** (Cultural Studies); **Culture and Communication: Cultural Institutions and Audiences** (Communication Studies; Cultural Studies); **Fruit and Vegetable Physiology** (Fruit Production; Vegetable Production); **Geography** (Geography); **History: Territories, Powers and Identities** (Cultural Studies; Political Sciences; Sociology); **Law: Possessions, Norms, Contracts** (Law); **Mediterranean Institute of Ecology and Paleoecology** (Biological and Life Sciences; Biology); **Modelling of Agricultural and Hydrological Systems** (Agricultural Equipment; Water Science); **Nonlinear Analysis and Geometry** (Mathematics); **Safety and Quality of Plant Products** (Agronomy)

Further Information: French Language Study Centre (CUEFA) offers French as a foreign language and French teacher training courses.

History: Founded in 1303 under the Pope. Closed during the French Revolution. Founded in 1972 as Centre universitaire. Formerly the Unit of Arts and Humanities of the Université de Provence. Acquired present status and title 1984. The Head of the Institution is its elected President. The Chancelier, who represents the Minister of Education, is the Recteur of the Académie d'Aix-Marseille.

Academic Year: September to June

Admission Requirements: Secondary school certificate (baccalauréat) or equivalent, or special entrance examination.

Main Language(s) of Instruction: French

Degrees and Diplomas: *Diplôme universitaire de Technologie*: **Bioengineering; Business and Commerce; Packaging Technology.** *Licence*: **Administration; Biological and Life Sciences; Business and Commerce; Chemistry; Communication Arts; Computer Science; Earth Sciences; Foreign Languages Education; French; Geography; History; Law; Management; Mathematics; Modern Languages; Physics; Public Administration; Sports.** *Licence professionnelle*: **Agricultural Engineering; Banking; Economics; Hotel Management; Human Resources; Information Management; International Business; Management; Medical Technology; Occupational Health; Safety Engineering; Tourism; Transport Management.** *Master*: **Agriculture; Arts and Humanities; Chemistry; Computer Science; Cultural Studies; Geography; History; International Business; Law; Management; Modern Languages; Social Policy; Sports.** *Doctorat*: **Agronomy; Biological and Life Sciences; Biology; Chemistry; Communication Arts; Comparative Literature; Computer Science; Earth Sciences; Foreign Languages Education; Geography; History; Law; Linguistics; Literature; Management; Mathematics; Mechanics; Sports.**

Student Services: Academic Counselling, Canteen, Facilities for disabled people, Health Services, Residential Facilities, Sports Facilities

Publications: Culture et Musées; Etudes vauclusiennes; Glossalalia; Mythes, Croyances et Religions; Théâtres du Monde

Last Updated: 01/04/15

UNIVERSITY OF BURGUNDY, DIJON

Université de Bourgogne

BP 27877, Maison de l'Université, Esplanade Erasme, 21078 Dijon, Cedex

Tel: +33(3) 80-39-50-00

Fax: +33(3) 80-39-50-69

EMail: president@u-bourgogne.fr

Website: http://www.u-bourgogne.fr

President: Alain Bonnin (2012-)
Tel: +33(3) 80-39-50-11
EMail: alain.bonnin@u-bourgogne.fr

Administrative Manager: Gilles Robin
Tel: +33(3) 80-39-50-13
EMail: direction.generale.des.services@u-bourgogne.fr

International Relations: Bénédicte Fortier
Tel: +33(3) 80-39-39-44 EMail: RI@u-bourgogne.fr; benedicte.fortier@u-bourgogne.fr

Unit

Human Sciences (Archaeology; Art History; Educational Sciences; English; Geography; History; Musicology; Psychology; Social Sciences; Sociology); **Law, Political Science and Economics** (Administration; Business Administration; Economics; Law; Management; Political Sciences); **Letters and Philosophy** (Arts and Humanities; Classical Languages; Literature; Philosophy); **Life Sciences, Earth Sciences and Environment** (Biological and Life Sciences; Earth Sciences; Environmental Studies); **Medicine, Pharmaceutical and Biological Sciences** (Biological and Life Sciences; Dentistry; Medicine; Midwifery; Pharmacology; Physical Therapy); **Modern Languages and Communication** (Communication Studies; Modern Languages); **Physical Education and Sports** (Physical Education; Sports); **Science and Technology** (Applied Linguistics; Chemistry; Computer Science; Mathematics; Natural Sciences; Physics; Technology)

School

Materials Research *(ESIREM)* (Materials Engineering); **Teacher Training** *(ESPE)* (Teacher Training)

Institute

Business Administration *(IAE)* (Accountancy; Agricultural Business; Business Administration; Finance; Management; Marketing); **Denis Diderot** (Cultural Studies; Education; Management); **Engineering in Business Documentation, Networks and Image** (Computer Networks; Documentation Techniques); **Management and Business Administration** *(IUP)* (Business Administration; Management); **Preparatory Administrative Studies** *(IPAG)* (Administration); **Technology** *(IUT Chalon-sur-Saône)* (Materials Engineering; Transport Management); **Technology** *(IUT Auxerre)* (Marketing; Production Engineering); **Technology** *(IUT Dijon-Auxerre)* (Archiving; Bioengineering; Biotechnology; Communication Studies; Computer Networks; Computer Science; Information Technology; Management); **Technology** *(IUT Le Creusot)* (Aeronautical and Aerospace Engineering; Automation and Control Engineering; Electrical Engineering; Electronic Engineering; Laser Engineering; Measurement and Precision Engineering; Mechanical Engineering; Production Engineering; Technology); **Wine Studies** *(IUVV Jules Guyot)* (Oenology)

Higher Institute

Automobile and Transport *(ISAT)* (Automotive Engineering; Transport and Communications)

Centre

University Centre *(Condorcet Centre)*

History: Founded 1970 under the 1968 law reforming higher education and replacing former Université de Dijon, founded 1722.The University was suppressed by the Revolution and replaced by Faculties of Law; Science; and Letters. Reconstituted as University 1896. A State Institution enjoying academic and financial autonomy, operating under the jurisdiction of the Minister of Education and financed by the State.

Academic Year: October to June (October-January; January-June)

Admission Requirements: Secondary school certificate (baccalauréat) or equivalent, or special entrance examination

Main Language(s) of Instruction: French

Degrees and Diplomas: *Diplôme universitaire de Technologie*; *Licence*: **Administration; Archaeology; Art History; Arts and Humanities; Biology; Business Administration; Chemistry; Earth Sciences; Economics; Education; Engineering; Environmental Studies; Geography; History; Information Sciences; Law; Literature; Management; Mathematics and Computer Science; Modern Languages; Music; Natural Sciences; Oenology; Performing Arts; Philosophy; Physics; Psychology; Sociology; Sports; Sports Management; Sports Medicine.** *Licence professionnelle*: **Agriculture; Business Administration; Business and Commerce; Computer Science; Documentation Techniques; Electrical and Electronic Engineering; Finance; Food Science; Hotel Management; Human Resources; Industrial Management; Landscape Architecture; Law; Mass Communication; Multimedia; Oenology; Performing Arts; Social and Community Services; Tourism; Water Science.** *Diplôme d'Ingénieur*: **Engineering; Industrial Engineering; Materials Engineering; Technology; Transport Engineering.** *Master*: **Administration; Applied Mathematics; Arts and Humanities; Biological and Life Sciences; Chemistry; Computer Engineering; Cultural Studies; Earth Sciences; Economics; Education; Educational Sciences; Electrical Engineering; Engineering; Environmental Studies; Food Science; Geography; Health Sciences; History; Information Sciences; Law; Literature; Management; Materials Engineering; Mathematics; Modern Languages; Musicology; Natural Sciences; Philosophy; Private Law; Psychology; Public Health; Public Law; Sociology; Sports; Teacher Training.** *Doctorat*: **Arts and Humanities; Chemistry; Economics; Environmental Studies; Geography; Health Sciences; Information Sciences; Law; Management; Mathematics; Mathematics and Computer Science; Modern Languages; Natural Sciences; Philosophy; Physics; Social Sciences; Sociology; Sports.**

Student Services: Academic Counselling, Canteen, Cultural Activities, Facilities for disabled people, Health Services, Nursery Care, Residential Facilities, Social Counselling, Sports Facilities

Publications: La Recherche à l'Université de Bourgogne

Academic Staff *2013-2014*: Total 2,900

Student Numbers *2013-2014*: Total 26,550

Last Updated: 11/03/15

UNIVERSITY OF CAEN-BASSE-NORMANDIE

Université de Caen Basse-Normandie (UNICAEN)

Esplanade de la Paix, B.P. 5186, 14032 Caen, Cedex

Tel: +33(2) 31-56-55-00

Fax: +33(2) 31-56-56-00

EMail: relations.internationales@unicaen.fr

Website: http://www.unicaen.fr

President: Pierre Sineux (2012-)
Tel: +33(2) 31-56-55-70 EMail: presidence@unicaen.fr

International Relations: Benoit Veron, Head of International Relations EMail: intl.direction@unicaen.fr

Unit

Economics and Management (Business Administration; Economics; Management); **Geography** (Development Studies; Environmental Studies; Geography; Regional Studies); **History** (History); **Human Sciences** (Ancient Civilizations; Comparative Literature; Educational Sciences; Linguistics; Literature; Performing Arts; Philosophy; Sociology); **Law and Political Science** (Administration; Law; Political Sciences); **Medicine** (Medicine; Speech Therapy and Audiology); **Modern Languages** *(LVE)* (English Studies; German; Italian; Latin American Studies; Modern Languages; Romance Languages; Scandinavian Languages; Slavic Languages; Spanish); **Pharmacy** (Pharmacy); **Physical Education and Sports** *(STAPS)* (Physical Education; Sports); **Psychology** (Psychology); **Sciences** (Automation and Control Engineering; Chemistry; Computer Science; Electronic Engineering; Environmental Studies; Mathematics; Mechanical Engineering; Natural Sciences; Physics)

School

Engineering *(ESIX-Cherbourg, Caen, St Lô)* (Cooking and Catering; Dairy; Engineering; Food Technology; Industrial Engineering)

Institute

Basic and Applied Biology *(IBFA)* (Biology); **Business Administration and Management** *(IAE)* (Banking; Business Administration; Insurance; Management); **Preparatory Administrative Studies** *(IMDA)* (Administration; Law); **Teacher Training and Education** *(ESPE)* (Teacher Training); **Technology** *(IUT, Alençon)* (Mechanical Engineering; Production Engineering; Social and Community Services; Technology; Transport Management); **Technology** *(IUT, Cherbourg Manche also included: IUT Cherbourg Manche-antenne de Saint lô)* (Business Administration; Energy Engineering; Human Resources; Industrial Maintenance; Management; Mass Communication; Multimedia; Technology; Thermal Engineering); **Technology** *(IUT Caen included IUT-Caen antenne d'IFs and IUT-antenne de Lisieux)* (Biology; Business Administration; Business and Commerce; Computer Science; Food Technology; Information Sciences; Library Science; Management; Physics; Statistics; Technology; Telecommunications Services)

Centre

French for Foreign Students *(CEUIE)* (French)

Graduate School

Chemistry (Medicine; Physical Chemistry); **Chemistry and Biology** *(In collaboration with Universities of Rouen and Havre; IBFA)* (Medical Technology; Sanitary Engineering); **Economics Management** *(In collaboration with Universities of Rouen and Havre; ED 242 Economie-gestion Normandie)* (Economics); **History, Culture and Language** *(MRSH)* (Ancient Civilizations; Archaeology; Cultural Studies; Linguistics; Medieval Studies); **Law** *(In collaboration with Universities of Rouen and Havre; ED 98 Droit Normandie)* (Law; Political Sciences); **Literature, Cultures and Social Sciences** *(MRSH)* (Arts and Humanities; Cultural Studies; Literature; Psychology; Social Sciences; Sports); **Materials Engineering** *(In collaboration with ENSICAEN)* (Materials Engineering)

Research Centre

Coastal Environment *(CREC)* (Coastal Studies)

Further Information: Six antenna sites: four IUT sites are located at Ifs, Lisieux, Vire, and Saint Lo. Cherbourg and Alencon have sites for Sciences, Law and LVE Units.

History: Founded 1970 under the 1968 law reforming higher education and replacing former Université de Caen, founded 1432 by Henry VI of England and granted Papal recognition 1437. The university was suppressed by the Revolution. Reconstituted 1896. A State institution enjoying academic and financial autonomy, operating under the jurisdiction of the Minister of Education and financed by the State. In 2014, Member of The COMUE Normandie University

Academic Year: October to June

Admission Requirements: Secondary school certificate (baccalauréat) or equivalent, or special entrance examination

Main Language(s) of Instruction: French

Degrees and Diplomas: *Capacité en Droit*; *Diplôme universitaire de Technologie*; *Licence*; *Licence professionnelle*; *Diplôme d'Etat*: **Medicine; Pharmacy.** *Diplôme d'Ingénieur*: **Industrial Engineering.** *Master*: **Arts and Humanities; Biological and Life Sciences; Chemistry; Cultural Studies; Economics; Educational Sciences; Epidemiology; Law; Library Science; Management; Mechanical Engineering; Medical Technology; Modern Languages; Natural Sciences; Physics; Social Sciences.** *Doctorat*: **Ancient Civilizations; Applied Mathematics; Archaeology; Arts and Humanities; Biological and Life Sciences; Biology; Biomedical Engineering; Biomedicine; Cell Biology; Chemistry; Civil Engineering; Computer Science; Criminal Law; Economics; Educational Sciences; Electrical and Electronic Engineering; English Studies; Fine Arts; Geology; History of Law; Linguistics; Literature; Mechanical Engineering; Modern History; Molecular Biology; Optics; Optometry; Pharmacy; Philosophy; Physiology; Political Sciences; Private Law; Production Engineering; Public Law; Sociology; Translation and Interpretation.** *Certificat de Spécialité*: **Medicine.** Certificat and Diplôme d'études françaises (for foreign students), Masters recherche, Masters professionnel

Student Services: Academic Counselling, Canteen, Facilities for disabled people, Foreign Studies Centre, Health Services, Language Laboratory, Social Counselling, Sports Facilities

Last Updated: 10/04/15

GRADUATE SCHOOL OF ENGINEER - ENSICAEN

ECOLE NATIONALE SUPÉRIEURE D'INGÉNIEURS DE CAEN (ENSICAEN)

6, boulevard Maréchal Juin, CS 45053, 14050 Caen, cedex 04
Tel: +33(2) 31-45-27-50
Fax: + 33(2) 31-45-27-60
EMail: contact@ensicaen.com
Website: http://www.ensicaen.fr/

Director General: Jean-François Hamet
EMail: jean-francois.hamet@ensicaen.fr

Head of Administration: Arnaud Mezieres
EMail: arnaud.mezieres@ensicaen.fr

International Relations: Chantal Gunther, Head of International Relations
Tel: +33(2) 31-45-27-72
EMail: chantal.gunther@ensicaen.fr; international@ensicaen.fr

Programme

Engineering (Applied Physics; Chemical Engineering; Computer Engineering; Electronic Engineering; Materials Engineering; Mechanical Engineering)

Department

Modern Languages and Humanities (Business Administration; Economics; Management; Modern Languages)

History: Founded in 1976 as 'Institut des Sciences de la Matière et du Rayonnement' (ISMRA). Become 'Ecole Nationale Supérieure d'Ingénieurs de Caen et Centre de Recherche' (Ensicaen) in 2002. in 2014, Member of the COMUE Normandie University

Admission Requirements: Entrance exam after 2 years further study after secondary school certificate (baccalauréat)

Main Language(s) of Instruction: French

Accrediting Agency: Commission des Titres d'ingénieur (CTI)

Degrees and Diplomas: *Diplôme d'Ingénieur*: **Applied Physics; Chemistry; Computer Engineering; Electronic Engineering; Engineering; Industrial Engineering; Materials Engineering; Mechanical Engineering.** *Mastère spécialisé*. also Research Masters with the University of Caen

UNIVERSITY OF CORSICA PASCAL PAOLI

Université de Corse Pascal Paoli

BP 52, Campus Caraman, 7, avenue Jean Nicoli, 20250 Corte, Cedex
Tel: +33(4) 95-45-00-00
EMail: presidence@univ-corse.fr
Website: http://www.univ-corse.fr

President: Paul-Marie Romani (2012-)
Tel: +33(4) 95-45-00-00 EMail: presidence@univ-corse.fr

Secretary General: Fabrice Bernardi
Tel: +33(4) 20-20-21-63 EMail: bernardi@univ-corse.fr

International Relations: Emilie Simon, International Relations Manager
Tel: +33(4) 95-45-02-23; +33(4) 95-45-06-46
EMail: simon@univ-corse.fr

Unit

Law, Economics and Management (Economics; Law; Management); **Letters, Languages, Humanities and Social Sciences** (Arts and Humanities; Literature; Modern Languages; Social Sciences); **Science and Techniques** *(FST)* (Natural Sciences; Technology)

School

Engineering *(Paoli Tech')* (Engineering); **Teacher Training** *(ESPE with two sites: Ajaccio and Bastia)* (Teacher Trainers Education; Teacher Training)

Institute

Business Administration *(IAE)* (Business Administration; Management); **Health Studies** (Health Sciences; Nursing); **Technology** *(IUT Corte)* (Biology; Management; Sales Techniques; Technology)

Graduate School

Environment and Society (Environmental Studies)

Further Information: Two Sites: Ajaccio and Bastia Centres

History: Founded 1765 as Université de Corte. Reopened 1981.

Academic Year: September to June

Admission Requirements: DAFL-DEFL

Main Language(s) of Instruction: French

Degrees and Diplomas: *Capacité en Droit*; *Diplôme universitaire de Technologie*; *Licence*: **Arts and Humanities; Biological and Life Sciences; Business Administration; Chemical Engineering; Computer Engineering; Health Sciences; Law; Management; Mathematics; Modern Languages; Natural Sciences; Physical Engineering; Social Sciences; Sports; Technology.** *Diplôme d'Ingénieur*: **Engineering.** *Master*: **Arts and Humanities; Business Administration; Computer Science; Economics; Environmental Engineering; Environmental Studies; History; Information Sciences; Information Technology; Law; Management; Modern Languages; Nutrition; Social Sciences; Teacher Training; Technology.** *Doctorat*: **Biological and Life Sciences; Environmental Studies; Law; Social Sciences.**

Student Services: Canteen, Cultural Activities, Facilities for disabled people, Health Services, Language Laboratory, Library, Residential Facilities, Social Counselling, Sports Facilities

Academic Staff *2013*: Total 200

Student Numbers *2013*: Total 4,300

Last Updated: 11/03/15

UNIVERSITY OF EVRY-VAL D'ESSONNE

Université d'Evry-Val d'Essonne

Boulevard François Mitterrand, Bât. Ile-de-France, 91025 Evry, Cedex

Tel: +33(1) 69-47-70-00

Fax: +33(1) 64-97-27-34

EMail: rel.int@univ-evry.fr

Website: http://www.univ-evry.fr

President: Patrick Curmi (2015-)
Tel: +33(1) 69-47-71-25 EMail: presidence@univ-evry.fr

Head of Administration: Foulo BASSE
Tel: +33(1) 69 47 90 26 EMail: direction-generale@univ-evry.fr

International Relations: Saïd MAMMAR, Vice-President in charge of International Relations
EMail: said.mammar@ibisc.univ-evry.fr; rel-int@univ-evry.fr

Unit

Basic and Applied Sciences *(DSP)* (Applied Mathematics; Biology; Biotechnology; Chemistry; Computer Science; Physical Education; Physics; Sports); **Languages, Arts and Music** *(LAM)* (Fine Arts; Modern Languages; Music; Performing Arts); **Law and Political sciences** *(DSP)* (Law; Political Sciences); **Science and Technology** *(ST)* (Automation and Control Engineering; Chemistry; Electrical Engineering; Engineering; Mechanical Engineering; Natural Sciences; Physics; Robotics; Technology; Telecommunications Engineering); **Social Sciences and Management** *(SHS)* (Economics; History; Management; Social Sciences; Sociology)

School

Teacher Training *(ESPE Versailles with 5 sites)*

Institute

Technology *(IUT Evry)* (Business and Commerce; Computer Engineering; E- Business/Commerce; Electrical Engineering; Information Technology; Mechanical Engineering; Production Engineering; Technology; Transport Management)

Graduate School

Genetics (Cell Biology; Genetics; Molecular Biology); **Sciences and Engineering** (Chemistry; Engineering; Information Sciences; Mathematics; Physics); **Social Sciences** (Economics; History; Law; Management; Performing Arts; Sociology)

History: Founded 1993, acquired present status 1997.

Academic Year: September to June (September-January; February-June)

Admission Requirements: Secondary school certificate (baccalauréat)

Main Language(s) of Instruction: French

Degrees and Diplomas: *Diplôme d'Accès aux Etudes universitaires*; *Diplôme universitaire de Technologie*: **Electrical Engineering; Mechanical Engineering.** *Licence*: **Arts and Humanities; Economics; Law; Management; Natural Sciences; Social Sciences; Technology.** *Licence professionnelle*: **Banking; Business and Commerce; Communication Studies; E- Business/Commerce; Insurance; Management; Performing Arts; Technology.** *Master*: **Accountancy; Applied Mathematics; Automation and Control Engineering; Biological and Life Sciences; Business Administration; Commercial Law; Economic History; Economics; Electrical Engineering; Engineering; Finance; Genetics; Industrial Engineering; Information Technology; Law; Management; Materials Engineering; Mathematics Education; Mechanical Engineering; Modern Languages; Music; Performing Arts; Public Law; Science Education; Sociology; Sports; Sports Medicine; Teacher Training; Technology Education.** *Doctorat*: **Applied Mathematics; Biochemistry; Biological and Life Sciences; Biology; Cell Biology; Economics; Engineering; Genetics; History; Information Sciences; Law; Management; Molecular Biology; Performing Arts; Social Sciences; Sociology.** Masters recherche, Masters professionnel, Preparation for CAPES and Law Administration exams

Student Services: Academic Counselling, Canteen, Careers Guidance, Cultural Activities, Facilities for disabled people, Health Services, Residential Facilities, Social Counselling, Sports Facilities

Publications: Les cahiers d'Evry

Academic Staff *2014*: Total 420

STAFF WITH DOCTORATE: Total 426

Student Numbers *2014*: Total 9,545

Last Updated: 03/04/15

COMPUTER SCIENCE FOR INDUSTRY AND BUSINESS SCHOOL - ENSIIE

ECOLE NATIONALE SUPÉRIEURE D'INFORMATIQUE POUR L'INDUSTRIE ET L'ENTREPRISE (ENSIIE)

1, Square de la Résistance, 91025 Évry, Cedex

Tel: +33(1) 69-36-73-50

Fax: +33(1) 69-36-73-05

EMail: info@ensiie.fr

Website: http://www.ensiie.fr/

Director: Ménad Sidahmed Tel: +33(1) 69-36-73-21

International Relations: Amélie Coince
Tel: +33(1) 69-36-73-15 EMail: rel-int@ensiie.fr

Programme

Engineering (Computer Engineering; Engineering Management; Management; Mathematics)

History: Founded 1968

Admission Requirements: competitive entrance exams or on qualifications

Main Language(s) of Instruction: French

Accrediting Agency: Ministry of Higher Education and Research; Conférence des Grandes Écoles (CGE); Commission des Titres d'Ingénieurs (CTI)

Degrees and Diplomas: *Diplôme d'Ingénieur*: **Computer Engineering; Engineering.** also Master in Mathematics and Computer Engineering

UNIVERSITY OF FRANCHE-COMTÉ

Université de Franche-Comté (UFC)

1, rue Claude Goudimel, 25030 Besançon

Tel: +33(3) 81-66-66-66

Fax: +33(3) 81-66-50-09

EMail: dri@univ-fcomte.fr

Website: http://www.univ-fcomte.fr

President: Jacques Bahi (2012-)
Tel: +33(3) 81 66 50 03 EMail: president@univ-fcomte.fr

Head of Administration: Christophe De Casteljau
Tel: +33(3) 81 66 50 02 EMail: dgs@univ-fcomte.fr

International Relations: Anne-Emmanuelle Grossi, Head of French-speaking communities and International Relations
Tel: +33(3) 81 66 52 03
EMail: anne-emmanuelle.grossi@univ-fcomte.fr

Unit

Languages, Human and Social Sciences (Archaeology; Art History; Arts and Humanities; Geography; History; Linguistics; Mass Communication; Modern Languages; Musicology; Performing Arts; Philosophy; Psychology; Social Sciences; Sociology; Theatre); **Law, Economics and Political Science, Management** *(SJEPG, Besançon)* (Administration; Economics; Law; Management; Political Sciences; Social Sciences); **Medicine and Pharmacy** *(SMP, Besançon)* (Medicine; Nursing; Pharmacy; Speech Therapy and Audiology); **Physical Education and Sports** *(STAPS, Besançon)* (Physical Education; Sports); **Science and Technology** (Biology; Chemistry; Computer Science; Earth Sciences; Engineering; Geology; Mathematics; Natural Sciences; Neurosciences; Physics; Technology; Waste Management); **Science, Technology and Industrial Administration** *(STGI Belfort)* (Administration; Economics; Electrical Engineering; Energy Engineering; Industrial Engineering; Industrial Management; Water Science)

School

Engineering *(ENSMM)*

Institute

Business Administration *(IAE)* (Private Administration); **Engineering** *(ISIFC Franche-Comté)* (Biological and Life Sciences; Biomedical Engineering; Engineering); **Preparatory Administrative Studies** *(IPAG)* (Administration); **Technology** *(IUT Belfort-Montbéliard)* (Business and Commerce; Computer Engineering; Electrical Engineering; Energy Engineering; Mechanical Engineering; Social Studies; Technology; Telecommunications Engineering; Thermal Engineering); **Technology** *(IUT Besançon-Vesoul)* (Business Administration; Chemistry; Hygiene; Industrial Engineering; Industrial Maintenance; Information Technology; Mechanical Engineering; Production Engineering; Technology; Transport and Communications)

Centre

Applied Linguistics *(CLA)* (Applied Linguistics); **Distance Education** *(CTU)* (Administration; Economics; History; Mathematics; Social Sciences)

Laboratory

Astronomy and Space Science (Astronomy and Space Science; Astrophysics)

Graduate School

Carnot-Pasteur (Astronomy and Space Science; Chemistry; Economic and Finance Policy; Mathematics; Nuclear Physics; Optics; Physics); **Engineering and Microtechnology** *(ED SPIM In collaboration with University of Technology - Belfort-Montbéliard and National School of Mechanics and Microelectronics)* (Automation and Control Engineering; Electronic Engineering; Materials Engineering; Mechanical Engineering; Microelectronics; Optical Technology); **Environment and Health** *(ED ES)* (Biology; Cell Biology; Environmental Studies; Health Sciences); **Language, Space, Time and Society** *(ED LETS)* (Arts and Humanities; Law; Linguistics; Literature; Management; Social Sciences); **Teaching training and Education** *(In 2013, the IUFM de Franche-Comté institute became: l'École Supérieure du Professorat et de l'Éducation (ESPE))* (Business Education; Secondary Education; Teacher Trainers Education; Teacher Training)

Further Information: The University is spread across 5 campuses, located in Belfort, Montbéliard, Lons le Saunier and Vesoul.

History: Established 1971 under the 1968 law reforming higher education as one of the new Universities and replacing the former Université de Besançon founded 1422 at Dôle and transferred to Besançon 1691. The University was suppressed by the Revolution and replaced by Faculties of Science and Letters and School of Medicine. Reconstituted as university 1896. A State institution enjoying academic and financial autonomy, operating under the jurisdiction of Minister of Education and financed by the State.

Academic Year: October to June (October-January; February-June)

Admission Requirements: Secondary school certificate (baccalauréat) or equivalent, or special entrance examination

Main Language(s) of Instruction: French

Degrees and Diplomas: *Capacité en Droit*: **Law.** *Diplôme universitaire de Technologie*; *Licence*: **Administration; Arts and Humanities; Biological and Life Sciences; Biology; Chemistry; Earth Sciences; Economics; Information Sciences; Law; Mathematics and Computer Science; Modern Languages; Natural Sciences; Physics; Sports.** *Licence professionnelle*: **Automation and Control Engineering; Banking; Environmental Studies; Law; Social Work.** *Diplôme d'Etat*: **Dentistry; Medicine; Pharmacy.** *Diplôme d'Ingénieur*: **Automation and Control Engineering; Electrical and Electronic Engineering; Materials Engineering; Mechanical Engineering; Microelectronics.** *Master*: **Administration; Arts and Humanities; Computer Science; Economics; Environmental Studies; Food Science; Geology; Health Administration; Information Sciences; Law; Management; Mathematics; Modern Languages; Natural Sciences; Public Law; Science Education; Sports; Statistics; Water Science.** *Doctorat*: **Arts and Humanities; Astronomy and Space Science; Biology; Cell Biology; Chemistry; Economic and Finance Policy; Economics; Environmental Studies; Health Sciences; History; Law; Pharmacy; Physics; Social Sciences; Sports; Welfare and Protective Services.** Masters recherche, Masters professionnel

Student Services: Canteen, Careers Guidance, Cultural Activities, Facilities for disabled people, Health Services, Library, Residential Facilities, Social Counselling, Sports Facilities

Publications: Combined Humanities

Publishing House: Presses Universitaires Franc-comtoises

Academic Staff *2013*	**TOTAL**
FULL-TIME	**2**
Student Numbers *2013-2014*	
All (Foreign included)	**21**
FOREIGN ONLY	**2585**

Last Updated: 11/03/15

NATIONAL HIGHER SCHOOL OF MECHANICS AND MICROTECHNOLOGY

ECOLE NATIONALE SUPÉRIEURE DE MÉCANIQUE ET DES MICROTECHNIQUES (ENSMM)

26, rue de l'Épitaphe, 25030 Besançon, cedex
Tel: +33(3) 81-40-27-00
Fax: +33(3) 81-80-98-70
EMail: relations.internationales@ens2m.fr
Website: http://www.ens2m.fr/

Director: Bernard Cretin
Tel: +33(3) 81-40-27-02 EMail: direction@ens2m.fr

Secretary General: Sabine Courbet
Tel: +33(3) 81-40-27-02 EMail: direction@ens2m.fr

Programme

Mechanics and Microtechnology (Energy Engineering; Industrial Engineering; Materials Engineering; Mechanical Engineering; Mechanics; Technology)

History: Founded in 1902 as Laboratoire de Chronométrie

Admission Requirements: Competitive entrance examination after 2-3 years of further studies after secondary school certificate(Baccalauréat)

Main Language(s) of Instruction: French

Accrediting Agency: Commission des Titres d'Ingénieurs (CTI)

Degrees and Diplomas: *Diplôme d'Ingénieur*: **Engineering.** *Master*: **Materials Engineering; Mechanical Engineering.**

UNIVERSITY OF HAUTE ALSACE

Université de Haute-Alsace

2, rue des Frères Lumière, 68093 Mulhouse, Cedex
Tel: +33(3) 89-33-60-00
Fax: +33(3) 89-33-63-19
EMail: international@uha.fr
Website: http://www.uha.fr

President: Christine Gangloff-Ziegler (2012-)
Tel: +33(3) 89-33-63-10 EMail: presidence@uha.fr

Head of Administration: Emilie Verany
Tel: +33(3) 89-33-63-09 EMail: emilie.verany(at)uha.fr

International Relations: Laurence Schacher, Vice-President in charge of the international relations
Tel: +33(3) 89-33-64-11 EMail: laurence.schacher@uha.fr

Faculty

Agricultural Production (Agriculture); **Arts and Humanities** *(FLSH)* (Arts and Humanities); **Commerce and Marketing** *(PEPS)* (Business and Commerce; Marketing); **Economics, Social Sciences and Law** *(FSEJ)* (Economics; Law; Social Sciences); **Science and Techniques** *(FST)* (Natural Sciences; Technology)

School

Applied Sciences for Engineering *(ESSAIM)* (Applied Chemistry; Applied Mathematics; Applied Physics; Computer Science; Engineering); **Chemistry** *(ENSCMu)* (Chemistry); **Textile Engineering** *(ENSITM)* (Textile Technology)

Institute

Technology *(IUT)* (Business Administration; Business and Commerce; Electrical Engineering; Mechanical Engineering; Technology; Transport Management); **Technology** *(IUT, Colmar)* (Biology; Business and Commerce; Hygiene; Law; Technology; Telecommunications Engineering)

Centre

Foreign Languages (Modern Languages); **Lifelong Education** *(SERFA)*; **Sports** (Sports)

History: Founded 1970 as Centre Universitaire under the 1968 law reforming higher education and incorporating Institutions previously attached to former Université de Strasbourg. Became Université du Haut-Rhin with full University status 1975. Acquired present title 1977. The Head of the Institution is its elected President. The Chancelier, who represents the Minister of Education, is the Recteur of the Académie de Strasbourg.

Academic Year: September to June (September-December; January-March; April-June)

Admission Requirements: Secondary school certificate (baccalauréat) or recognized equivalent, or special entrance examination

Main Language(s) of Instruction: French

Degrees and Diplomas: *Diplôme universitaire de Technologie*; *Licence*: **Agronomy; Arts and Humanities; Automation and Control Engineering; Business Administration; Chemistry; Education; Electrical and Electronic Engineering; Environmental Studies; Law; Mass Communication; Mathematics and Computer Science; Modern Languages; Physics; Technology.** *Licence professionnelle*: **Biotechnology; Business Administration; Business and Commerce; Development Studies; Education; Graphic Arts; Human Resources; Library Science; Mass Communication; Technology; Tourism.** *Diplôme d'Ingénieur*: **Engineering.** *Master*: **Archiving; Arts and Humanities; Automation and Control Engineering; Business Administration; Chemistry; Economics; Education; Environmental Studies; Information Sciences; Law; Mathematics and Computer Science; Mechanical Engineering; Modern Languages; Museum Studies; Publishing and Book Trade; Teacher Training.** *Doctorat*: **Archaeology; Automation and Control Engineering; Biological and Life Sciences; Chemical Engineering; Chemistry; Computer Science; Electronic Engineering; History; Law.**

Student Services: Academic Counselling, Canteen, Careers Guidance, Cultural Activities, Facilities for disabled people, Health Services, Social Counselling, Sports Facilities

Academic Staff *2014*: Total 446
Student Numbers *2014*: Total 7,464
Last Updated: 11/03/15

UNIVERSITY OF LA ROCHELLE

Université de La Rochelle

Technoforum, 23, avenue Albert Einstein, 17071 La Rochelle, Cedex 9
Tel: +33(5) 46-45-91-14
Fax: +33(5) 46-44-93-76
EMail: vp-ri@univ-lr.fr
Website: http://www.univ-larochelle.fr

President: Gérard Blanchard (2008-)
Tel: +33(5) 46-45-87-09 EMail: president.larochelle@univ-lr.fr

Head of Administration: Marlène Barbotin
Tel: +33(5) 46-45-87-45 EMail: sgu@univ-lr.fr

International Relations: Paco Bustamante, Vice-President of International Relations
Tel: +33(5) 46-50-76-25 EMail: vp-ri@univ-lr.fr

Unit

Exact Sciences and Engineering (Biochemistry; Biology; Chemistry; Civil Engineering; Computer Science; Earth Sciences; Mathematics; Natural Sciences; Physics); **Law, Political Science and Management** (Law; Management; Political Sciences; Private Law; Public Administration; Public Law); **Letters, Languages, Arts and Humanities** *(FLASH)* (Economics; Geography; History; International Relations; Literature; Modern Languages)

Institute

Technology *(IUT La Rochelle)* (Bioengineering; Business and Commerce; Civil Engineering; Data Processing; Sales Techniques; Technology; Telecommunications Engineering)

Centre

Preparatory Administrative Studies (Administration)

Graduate School

Doctoral School

History: Founded 1993.

Academic Year: September to June

Main Language(s) of Instruction: French

Degrees and Diplomas: *Diplôme universitaire de Technologie*; *Licence*: **Aquaculture; Arts and Humanities; Business Administration; Engineering; Environmental Studies; Food Science; Law; Mathematics and Computer Science; Modern Languages; Multimedia; Natural Sciences; Optometry; Technology.** *Licence professionnelle*: **Aquaculture; Arts and Humanities; Environmental Studies; Laboratory Techniques; Modern Languages; Technology.** *Master*: **Arts and Humanities; Biological and Life Sciences; Biotechnology; Business Administration; Engineering; Environmental Studies; Law; Literature; Mathematics and Computer Science; Modern Languages; Natural Sciences; Teacher Training; Technology.** *Doctorat*: **Arts and Humanities; Engineering; Environmental Studies; Fine Arts; Geography; Law; Mathematics; Political Sciences; Social Sciences; Urban Studies.** Masters recherche, Masters professionnel, Preparation for Teaching, Administrative and Judicial Exams

Student Services: Canteen, Facilities for disabled people, Health Services, Language Laboratory, Social Counselling, Sports Facilities

Academic Staff *2014*: Total 386
Student Numbers *2014*: Total 7,405
Last Updated: 11/03/15

UNIVERSITY OF LE HAVRE

Université du Havre

BP 1123, 25, rue Philippe Lebon, 76063 Le Havre, Cedex
Tel: +33(2) 32-74-40-00
Fax: +33(2) 35-21-49-59
EMail: sri@univ-lehavre.fr
Website: http://www.univ-lehavre.fr

President: Pascal Reghem (2012-)
Tel: +33(2) 32-74-40-54 EMail: presidence@univ-lehavre.fr

Secretaru General: Juliette Le Luyer
Tel: +33(2) 32-74-40-65 EMail: juliette.le-luyer@univ-lehavre.fr

International Relations: Sandrine Danger-Pujol
Tel: +33(2) 32-74-42-26
EMail: sri@univ-lehavre.fr; sandrine.danger@univ-lehavre.fr

Faculty

International Affairs (Cultural Studies; English; German; History; International Business; International Economics; Law; Management; Marketing; Modern Languages; Oriental Languages; Romance Languages)

Unit

Arts and Humanities (Geography; History; Literature; Sociology); **Science and Techniques** (Biology; Chemistry; Civil Engineering; Computer Science; Cosmetology; Electronic Engineering; Industrial Engineering; Mathematics; Mechanical Engineering; Physics; Technology)

Department

Commerce Engineering and Sales Techniques *(IUP)* (Sales Techniques)

Institute

Technology *(IUT Le Havre)* (Business Administration; Civil Engineering; Communication Studies; Computer Science; Electrical Engineering; Human Resources; Mechanical Engineering; Sales Techniques; Technology; Transport and Communications)

Higher Institute

Logistic Studies *(ISEL)* (Arts and Humanities; Engineering; Management; Natural Sciences; Technology)

Centre

Lifelong Education

History: Founded 1984.

Academic Year: October to June (October-December; January-March; April-June)

Admission Requirements: Secondary school certificate (baccalauréat) or brevet supérieur, or recognized foreign equivalent, or specialized entrance examination

Main Language(s) of Instruction: French

Degrees and Diplomas: *Diplôme d'Accès aux Etudes universitaires*; *Diplôme universitaire de Technologie*; *Licence*: **Arts and Humanities; Business Administration; Economics; Engineering; Law; Management; Mathematics and Computer Science; Natural Sciences; Social Sciences.** *Licence professionnelle*: **Business and Commerce; Maintenance Technology; Management; Social Work; Technology.** *Diplôme d'Ingénieur*: **Transport Engineering.** *Master*: **Arts and Humanities; Business and Commerce; Civil Engineering; Coastal Studies; Construction Engineering; Economics; Environmental Studies; Law; Management; Materials Engineering; Mathematics and Computer Science; Social Sciences; Teacher Training; Tourism.** *Doctorat*: **Biology; Chemistry; Engineering; Mathematics and Computer Science; Social Sciences.** Masters recherche, Masters professionnel

Student Services: Canteen, Cultural Activities, Facilities for disabled people, Health Services, Residential Facilities, Sports Facilities

Academic Staff *2013-2014*: Total 840

Student Numbers *2013-2014*: Total 7

Last Updated: 12/03/15

UNIVERSITY OF LIMOGES

Université de Limoges

BP 23204, 33, rue François-Mitterrand, 87032 Limoges, Cedex 1
Tel: +33(5) 55-14-91-00
Fax: +33(5) 55-14-91-01
EMail: ri@unilim.fr
Website: http://www.unilim.fr

President: Hélène Piaulat (2012-)
Tel: +33(5) 55-14-91-11
EMail: presidence@unilim.fr; jacques.fontanille@unilim.fr

Head of Administration: Vincent Jolys
Tel: +33(5) 55-14-91-13 EMail: vincent.jolys@unilim.fr

International Relations: Hélène Déjoux
Tel: +33(5) 55-14-90-96 +33(5) 55-45-73-25

Faculty

Arts and Humanities (Arts and Humanities; Comparative Literature; Educational Sciences; English; Geography; German; Greek; Heritage Preservation; Hispanic American Studies; History; Latin; Library Science; Linguistics; Literature; Sociology; Spanish); **Law and Economics** *(FDSE)* (Administration; Economics; Law); **Medicine** (Medicine); **Pharmacy** (Pharmacy); **Science and Technology** (Biological and Life Sciences; Chemistry; Civil Engineering; Computer Science; English; Information Technology; Mathematics; Natural Sciences; Physical Education; Physics; Sports)

School

Engineering *(ENSIL)* (Electronic Engineering; Engineering; Environmental Engineering; Materials Engineering; Mechanical Engineering; Telecommunications Engineering; Water Science); **Teacher Training** *(ESPE Limousin with 3 sites: Guéret, Tulle, Limoges)* (Teacher Trainers Education; Teacher Training)

Institute

Business Administration *(IUP, formerly known as IAE)* (Business Administration); **Preparatory Administrative Studies** *(IPAG)* (Administration; Public Administration); **Technology** *(IUT Limoges with 4 sites: Brive, Egletons, Limoges and Tulle)* (Biology; Civil Engineering; Computer Science; Electrical Engineering; Industrial Engineering; Maintenance Technology; Management; Marketing; Measurement and Precision Engineering; Mechanical Engineering; Production Engineering; Safety Engineering; Technology)

Centre

Lifelong Education *(CFASup)*

Graduate School

Man and Society (Economics; European Union Law; Finance; French Studies; Law; Linguistics; Modern Languages; Social Sciences); **Science, Technology and Health** (Applied Chemistry; Biomedicine; Ceramics and Glass Technology; Chemistry; Civil Engineering; Computer Engineering; Ecology; Mathematics)

Further Information: Also 4 research institutes

History: Founded 1970 under the 1968 law reforming higher education and incorporating former Université de Limoges with School of Law, founded 1909, and School of Medicine tracing its history to 1626. A State institution enjoying academic and financial autonomy, operating under the jurisdiction of the Minister of Education and financed by the State.

Academic Year: October to June

Admission Requirements: Secondary school certificate (baccalauréat) or equivalent or foreign equivalent, or special entrance examination

Main Language(s) of Instruction: French

Degrees and Diplomas: *Capacité en Droit*: **Law.** *Diplôme universitaire de Technologie*: **Technology.** *Licence*: **Administration; Biological and Life Sciences; Business Administration; Chemistry; Economics; Engineering; Health Sciences; Law; Management; Mathematics and Computer Science; Modern Languages; Natural Sciences; Physics; Technology.** *Licence professionnelle*: **Accountancy; Business and Commerce; Management; Real Estate.** *Diplôme d'Etat*: **Medicine; Pharmacy.** *Diplôme d'Ingénieur*: **Engineering.** *Master*: **Biological and Life Sciences; Biomedicine; Business Administration; Chemistry; Cultural Studies; Economics; Engineering; Environmental Studies; Finance; Health Sciences; Law; Linguistics; Mathematics and Computer Science; Medicine; Natural Sciences; Neurosciences; Regional Studies; Teacher Training; Technology.** *Doctorat*: **Arts and Humanities; Engineering; Health Sciences; Pharmacy; Social Sciences; Technology.**

Student Services: Canteen, Cultural Activities, Health Services, Sports Facilities

Publishing house: Pulin

Last Updated: 07/04/15

3IL ENGINEERING SCHOOL

INSTITUT D'INGÉNIERIE INFORMATIQUE DE LIMOGES (3IL)

BP 834, 43 rue Saint Anne, 87015 Limoges, Cedex 01
Tel: +33(5) 55-31-67-24
Website: http://www.3il-ingenieurs.fr/index.php/fr/

Director: Ali Mankar-Bennis Tel: +33(5) 55-31-67-27

International Relations: Annabelle Dumontheil
Tel: +33(5) 55-31-67-62

Programme

Computer Engineering (Computer Engineering)

Further Information: also campuses in: Rodez, Morocco (Rabat), Cameroon (Douala)

History: Founded in 1987, acquiring present status in 1995.

Admission Requirements: Competitive entrance exam, secondary school certificate (Baccalauréat) in Science or equivalent.
Fees: Engineering Programme: 5,900 per annum; Preparatory Studies: 3,000 (Euro)
Main Language(s) of Instruction: French
Accrediting Agency: Commission des Titres d'Ingénieur (CTI)
Degrees and Diplomas: *Diplôme d'Ingénieur*: **Computer Engineering.**

UNIVERSITY OF LORRAINE

Université de Lorraine

34 cours Léopold, CS 25233, 54052 Nancy
Tel: +33(3) 54-50-54-00
Fax: +33(3) 54-50-54-01
EMail: administrateur.provisoire@univ-lorraine.fr
Website: http://www.univ-lorraine.fr

President: Pierre Mutzenhardt (2012-2016)
Tel: +33(3) 83 68 20 10 EMail: president@uhp-nancy.fr; pierre.mutzenhardt@univ-lorraine.fr; cabinet-president@univ-lorraine.fr

Director of Services: Jean-François Molter
Tel: +33(3) 54-50-54-36
EMail: jean-francois.molter@univ-lorraine.fr

International Relations: Mariama Traoré
EMail: drie-info-contact@univ-lorraine.fr; mariama.traore@univ-lorraine.fr

Area

Arts, Letters and Languages (Arts and Humanities; Cinema and Television; English; European Studies; Fine Arts; Geography; German; History; Linguistics; Literature; Mathematics and Computer Science; Music; Musicology; Philosophy; Spanish; Teacher Training; Theology); **Humanities and Social Sciences** (Arts and Humanities; Psychology; Regional Planning; Social Sciences; Sociology); **Law, Economics and Management** (Banking; Business Administration; Economics; Finance; Hotel Management; Insurance; Labour and Industrial Relations; Labour Law; Law; Management; Marketing; Political Sciences); **Science, Technology and Health** (Agronomy; Applied Chemistry; Applied Mathematics; Applied Physics; Aquaculture; Automation and Control Engineering; Biological and Life Sciences; Chemical Engineering; Civil Engineering; Computer Engineering; Computer Science; Dentistry; Earth Sciences; Ecology; Electrical Engineering; Electronic Engineering; Energy Engineering; Engineering; Food Science; Geology; Industrial Engineering; Materials Engineering; Mathematics and Computer Science; Mechanical Engineering; Medical Technology; Medicine; Mining Engineering; Optics; Pharmacy; Physical Chemistry; Physical Education; Sports; Technology; Telecommunications Engineering)

History: Founded 2012 following merger of Université Henri Poincaré, Université Nancy 2, Institut national polytechnique de Lorraine and Université Paul Verlaine-Metz
Main Language(s) of Instruction: French
Degrees and Diplomas: *Diplôme universitaire de Technologie*; *Licence*: **Arts and Humanities; Business Administration; Engineering; Environmental Studies; Fine Arts; Law; Literature; Mathematics and Computer Science; Modern Languages; Performing Arts; Social Sciences.** *Licence professionnelle*: **Arts and Humanities; Business Administration; Engineering; Law; Mathematics and Computer Science; Natural Sciences; Performing Arts; Social Sciences; Technology.** *Diplôme d'Ingénieur*: **Engineering.** *Master*: **Arts and Humanities; Biological and Life Sciences; Business Administration; Chemistry; Cultural Studies; Design; Earth Sciences; Economics; Education; Engineering; Environmental Studies; Fine Arts; Law; Literature; Mathematics and Computer Science; Modern Languages; Natural Sciences; Performing Arts; Physics; Public Health; Social Sciences; Sports; Teacher Training; Theology.** *Doctorat*: **Engineering.**
Student Services: Canteen, Cultural Activities, Facilities for disabled people, Health Services, Library, Residential Facilities, Sports Facilities

Academic Staff *2013*	**TOTAL**
FULL-TIME	**3,700**
Student Numbers *2013*	
All (Foreign included)	**52,478**
FOREIGN ONLY	**7540**

Last Updated: 30/03/15

ICN BUSINESS SCHOOL

ICN BUSINESS SCHOOL (ICN)

13 rue Maréchal Ney, 54000 Nancy
Tel: +33(3) 54-50-25-00
Fax: +33(3) 54-50-25-01
EMail: direction@icn-groupe.fr
Website: http://www.icn-groupe.fr/fr

Director General: Jérôme Caby
Tel: +33(3) 54-50-25-68 EMail: direction@icn-groupe.fr

International Relations: Frédérique Boutin, International Relations Manager
Tel: +33(3) 54-50-25-25 EMail: international@icn-groupe.fr

Department

Business Environment (Business Administration); **Finance, Audit, Accounting and Control** (Accountancy; Finance); **Human Resources Management and Organizational Behavior** (Human Resources; Management); **Languages and Foreign Cultures** (Modern Languages); **Marketing** (Marketing); **Strategy and Entrepreneurship** (Business Administration); **Supply Chain Management and Information Systems** (Management)

Further Information: Metz

History: Founded in 1905 as 'Institut Commercial de Nancy'. Become 'ICN Business School' in 2003
Admission Requirements: Competitive entrance examination and secondary school certificate (baccalauréat) or after 2 years further study after secondary school certificate (baccalauréat)
Main Language(s) of Instruction: French
Accrediting Agency: Ministry of Higher Education and Research; AACSB
Degrees and Diplomas: *Diplôme d'Etudes d'Ecole de Commerce et Gestion*: **Business Administration.** *Master*. also Bachelor; MSc; Ecricome PhD Universa Programme

NATIONAL ENGINEERING SCHOOL OF METZ

ECOLE NATIONALE D'INGÉNIEURS DE METZ (ENIM)

1 route d'Ars Laquenexy, CS65820, 57078 Metz, Cedex 3
Tel: +33(3) 87-34-69-00
EMail: enim@enim.fr
Website: http://www.enim.fr/portail/lecole.php

Director: Pierre Chevrier (2011-)

International Relations: Kondo Adjallah, Head of International Relations EMail: adjallah@enim.fr; relinter@enim.fr

Department

Construction (Construction Engineering); **Electical and Electronics engineering, Automatism and computer engineering and Management** (Computer Engineering; Electrical and Electronic Engineering; Industrial Engineering; Management); **Material Engineering** (Materials Engineering); **Mechanics, Physics, Mathematics** (Mathematics; Mechanical Engineering; Physics); **Modern Languages and Communication** (Communication Studies; Modern Languages)

History: Founded 1961.
Main Language(s) of Instruction: French
Accrediting Agency: Ministry of Education
Degrees and Diplomas: *Diplôme d'Ingénieur*: **Engineering.** *Mastère spécialisé*: **Management; Transport Management.** *Master*: **Engineering; Management; Transport Management.** also Bachelor

UNIVERSITY OF MAINE

Université du Maine

Avenue Olivier Messiaen, 72085 Le Mans, Cedex 9
Tel: +33(2) 43-83-30-00
Fax: +33(2) 43-83-30-77
EMail: ri@univ-lemans.fr
Website: http://www.univ-lemans.fr

President: Rachid El Guerjouma (2012-)
Tel: +33(2) 43-83-30-01 EMail: president@univ-lemans.fr

Head of Administration: Anne-Marie Riou
Tel: +33(2) 43-83-30-02
EMail: dgs@univ-lemans.fr; Anne-Marie.Riou@univ-lemans.fr

International Relations: Eliane Elmaleh, Vice-President in charge of International Relations
Tel: +33(2) 43-83-30-05 +33(2) 43-83-37-34
EMail: vpri@univ-lemans.fr; ri@univ-lemans.fr

Faculty

Law *(Laval-Mayenne)* (Commercial Law; Law); **Law, Economics and Management** (Economics; Law; Management); **Letters, Languages and Humanities** (Arts and Humanities; English; French; Geography; German; History; Literature; Modern Languages; Spanish); **Science and Techniques** (Biology; Chemistry; Computer Science; Earth Sciences; Mathematics; Mechanical Engineering; Natural Sciences; Physical Education; Physics; Physiology; Sound Engineering (Acoustics); Sports; Technology)

School

Engineering *(ENSIM)* (Computer Engineering; Engineering; Sound Engineering (Acoustics))

Institute

Technology *(IUT Le Mans)* (Business and Commerce; Chemistry; Mechanical Engineering; Public Administration; Technology); **Technology** *(IUT Laval)* (Biology; Biotechnology; Business and Commerce; Computer Engineering; Multimedia; Technology)

Centre

Law and Economics *(CESDEML)* (Economics; Law); **Lifelong Education**

History: Founded 1969 as Centre Universitaire under the 1968 law reforming higher education and replacing Institutions attached to former Université de Caen. Acquired full University status 1976. The University is a State institution enjoying academic and financial autonomy, operating under the jurisdiction of the Minister of Education and financed by the State.

Academic Year: October to June (October-December; January-April; May-June)

Admission Requirements: Baccalauréat or foreign equivalent, or ESAEU (Examen spécial d'accès aux études universitaires)

Main Language(s) of Instruction: French

Degrees and Diplomas: *Capacité en Droit*: **Law.** *Diplôme universitaire de Technologie*: **Administration; Economics; Natural Sciences; Technology.** *Licence*: **Administration; Arts and Humanities; Biological and Life Sciences; Chemistry; Computer Science; Economics; Engineering; Environmental Studies; Law; Mathematics; Modern Languages; Physics; Social Sciences; Sports; Technology.** *Licence professionnelle*: **Administration; Arts and Humanities; Economics; Law; Modern Languages; Natural Sciences; Social Sciences; Sports; Technology.** *Diplôme d'Ingénieur*: **Computer Engineering.** *Master*: **Applied Mathematics; Arts and Humanities; Chemistry; Computer Science; Economics; Environmental Studies; Geography; History; Human Resources; Law; Modern Languages; Optics; Physics; Private Law; Public Law; Social Sciences; Sound Engineering (Acoustics); Sports; Sports Medicine; Teacher Training; Technology.** *Doctorat*: **Arts and Humanities; Biology; Chemistry; Economics; Educational Sciences; English Studies; Geography; Geology; Germanic Studies; History; Law; Literature; Management; Mathematics and Computer Science; Mechanical Engineering; Physics; Sound Engineering (Acoustics); Spanish; Sports.** Certificat and Diplômes d'Etudes françaises (for foreign students), Masters recherche, Masters professionnel

Student Services: Canteen, Cultural Activities, Facilities for disabled people, Health Services, Language Laboratory, Residential Facilities, Social Counselling, Sports Facilities

Academic Staff *2011*: Total 1,000
Student Numbers *2011*: Total 10,000
Last Updated: 12/03/15

UNIVERSITY OF NANTES

Université de Nantes

BP 13522, 1, quai de Tourville, 44035 Nantes, Cedex 01
Tel: +33(2) 40-99-83-83
Fax: +33(2) 40-99-83-00
EMail: international@univ-nantes.fr
Website: http://www.univ-nantes.fr

President: Olivier Laboux (2012-)
Tel: +33(2) 40-99-83-20
EMail: president@univ-nantes.fr; cabinet@univ-nantes.fr

Head of Administration: Thierry Biais
Tel: +33(2) 40-99-83-33
EMail: dsg@univ-nantes.fr; thierry.biais@univ-nantes.fr

International Relations: Nadège Souchereau, Head of International Relations
Tel: +33 (0)2 53 46 22 04
EMail: Nadege.Souchereau@univ-nantes.fr; international@univ-nantes.fr

Unit

Health sciences (Biological and Life Sciences; Dentistry; Medicine; Pharmacy); **Languages** (Arabic; Chinese; English; German; Italian; Japanese; Modern Languages; Portuguese; Russian; Slavic Languages; Spanish); **Law, Economics and Management** (Law; Political Sciences); **Literature and Humanities** (Archaeology; Art History; Classical Languages; Comparative Literature; Educational Sciences; History; Linguistics; Literature; Philosophy; Psychology; Sociology); **Sciences** (Astronomy and Space Science; Chemistry; Earth Sciences; Environmental Studies; Mathematics and Computer Science; Natural Sciences; Physical Education; Physics; Radiophysics; Seismology; Sports)

School

Engineering *(Polytech' Nantes)* (Computer Engineering; Electrical Engineering; Electronic Engineering; Energy Engineering; Materials Engineering; Thermal Engineering); **Teacher Training** *(ESPE)* (Teacher Trainers Education; Teacher Training)

Institute

Economics and Management *(IAE-IEMN)* (Accountancy; Banking; Business Administration; Economics; Finance; Insurance; Management); **French for Foreigners** *(IRRFLE)* (French; French Studies); **Geography and Regional Development** *(IGARUN - OSUNA - Sciences Unit)* (Geography; Regional Planning); **Juridical Studies** *(IEJ- in cooperation with the faculty of Law and Political sciences (Law, Economics and Management Unit))* (Law); **Preparatory Administrative Studies** *(IPAG)* (Administration); **Technology** *(IUT, La Roche-sur-Yon)* (Bioengineering; Business Administration; Information Technology; Mass Communication; Public Administration; Telecommunications Engineering); **Technology** *(IUT, Saint-Nazaire)* (Business and Commerce; Chemical Engineering; Civil Engineering; Industrial Engineering; Sales Techniques; Technology); **Technology** *(IUT Nantes)* (Business Administration; Data Processing; Electrical Engineering; Energy Engineering; Materials Engineering; Mechanical Engineering; Public Administration; Technology; Thermal Engineering)

Centre

Lifelong Education (Continuing Education)

Graduate School

Chemistry Biology (Agronomy; Biology; Chemistry; Ecology); **Information and Material Engineering** *(STIM in cooperation with Ecole Centrale Nantes)* (Applied Mathematics; Information Technology); **Knowledge, Language, Culture** (Cognitive Sciences; Cultural Studies; Modern Languages); **Law, Social Sciences** (Law; Social Sciences)

History: Founded 1970 under the 1968 law reforming higher education and replacing former Université de Nantes, founded 1962, incorporating previously existing faculties, but tracing its history to the original Universities of Nantes, founded by Papal Bull in 1460, and of Angers, recognized and authorized by Charles V in 1364. A State institution enjoying academic and financial autonomy, operating under the jurisdiction of the Minister of Education and financed by the State.

Academic Year: October to June (October-February; February-June)

Admission Requirements: Secondary school certificate (baccalauréat) or equivalent, or special entrance examination

Fees: 159,60 per annum (Euro)

Main Language(s) of Instruction: French

Degrees and Diplomas: *Capacité en Droit*: **Law.** *Diplôme d'Accès aux Etudes universitaires*; *Diplôme universitaire de Technologie*; *Licence*: **Arts and Humanities; Biological and Life Sciences; Chemistry; Earth Sciences; Economics; Engineering; Health Sciences; Law; Management; Mass Communication; Mathematics and Computer Science; Modern Languages; Natural Sciences; Physics; Social Sciences; Technology.** *Licence professionnelle*: **Agronomy; Arts and Humanities; Economics; Engineering; Environmental Studies; Health Sciences; Industrial and Production Economics; Industrial Design; Law; Management; Mass Communication; Social Sciences; Technology; Telecommunications Services.** *Diplôme d'Etat*: **Dentistry; Medicine; Pharmacy; Speech Therapy and Audiology.** *Diplôme d'Ingénieur*: **Civil Engineering; Computer Engineering; Electrical and Electronic Engineering; Energy Engineering; Engineering; Materials Engineering.** *Master*: **Accountancy; Applied Mathematics; Archaeology; Art History; Astronomy and Space Science; Automation and Control Engineering; Biological and Life Sciences; Biology; Chemistry; Civil Engineering; Classical Languages; Comparative Literature; Computer Science; Criminal Law; Earth Sciences; Economics; Education; Educational Sciences; Electronic Engineering; Environmental Studies; European Studies; European Union Law; Finance; Foreign Languages Education; Health Sciences; Heritage Preservation; History; Information Sciences; International Law; International Studies; Labour Law; Law; Linguistics; Literature; Management; Maritime Law; Mechanical Engineering; Modern Languages; Philosophy; Physics; Political Sciences; Private Law; Psychology; Public Law; Robotics; Social and Preventive Medicine; Sociology; Sports; Teacher Training; Urban Studies.** *Doctorat*: **Applied Mathematics; Astronomy and Space Science; Biotechnology; Civil Engineering; Classical Languages; Cognitive Sciences; Computer Science; Dentistry; Earth Sciences; Economics; Education; Electronic Engineering; Energy Engineering; Environmental Studies; Geography (Human); Health Sciences; History; Immunology; Information Sciences; Law; Linguistics; Literature; Management; Maritime Law; Materials Engineering; Mathematics; Mechanical Engineering; Molecular Biology; Neurosciences; Nuclear Physics; Nutrition; Philosophy; Plant Pathology; Private Law; Public Law; Sports; Telecommunications Engineering; Thermal Engineering.** *Certificat de Spécialité*: **Medicine.** Masters recherche, Masters professionnel

Student Services: Academic Counselling, Canteen, Cultural Activities, Facilities for disabled people, Health Services, Language Laboratory, Library, Residential Facilities, Social Counselling, Sports Facilities

Academic Staff *2014*	**TOTAL**
FULL-TIME	**1,069**
PART-TIME	**552**
STAFF WITH DOCTORATE	
FULL-TIME	**1,543**

Student Numbers *2013-2015*	
All (Foreign included)	**34,714**

Last Updated: 11/03/15

UNIVERSITY OF NICE-SOPHIA ANTIPOLIS

Université de Nice-Sophia Antipolis (UNSA)

BP 2135, Grand Château, 28 avenue de Valrose, 06103 Nice, Cedex 02

Tel: +33(4) 92-07-60-60

Fax: +33(4) 92-07-66-00

EMail: com@unice.fr

Website: http://unice.fr

President: Frédérique Vidal (2012-)

Tel: +33(4) 92-07-66-01 EMail: presidence@unice.fr

Head of Administration: Fabienne Palermo

Tel: +33(4) 92-07-66-10; +33(4) 92-07-60-60 EMail: dgs@unice.fr

International Relations: Magsud Safin, Director

Tel: +33(4) 92-07-61-28; +33(4) 92-07-61-28

EMail: Magsud.SAFIN@unice.fr; relint@unice.fr

Faculty

Arts and Humanities *(LASH)* (Arts and Humanities); **Dentistry** (Dentistry); **Geography and Culture** *(UFR Espaces et Cultures)* (Cultural Studies; Geography (Human)); **Law and Political Science** (Development Studies; Economics; Law; Management; Peace and Disarmament; Political Sciences); **Medicine** (Medicine); **Physical Education and Sports** *(STAPS)* (Physical Education; Sports); **Sciences** (Natural Sciences)

Programme

Business Administration *(IUP)* (Business Administration; Econometrics); **Data Processing for Management** *(IUP MIAGE)* (Data Processing); **Tourism and Hotel Management** *(IUP Tourisme)* (Hotel Management; Tourism)

School

Teacher Training *(ESPE with 4 sites throughout Nice)* (Teacher Trainers Education; Teacher Training)

Higher School

Computer Science *(PolyTech)* (Computer Engineering; Computer Science; Engineering; Software Engineering)

Institute

Business Administration *(IAE)* (Business Administration); **Law and Development** *(IDPD)* (Development Studies; Law); **Sustainable devolepment and Environmental studies** *(IMREDD)* (Environmental Studies); **Technology** *(IUT Nice with 4 sites: Nice, Menton, Cannes, Sophia-Antipolis)* (Business Administration; Business and Commerce; Business Computing; Data Processing; Electrical Engineering; Management; Technology; Telecommunications Engineering)

Higher Institute

Economics and Management *(ISEM)* (Economics; Management)

Centre

Juridical Studies *(IEJ)* (Law); **Lifelong Education** *(ASURE)* (Continuing Education)

Graduate School

Arts and Humanities (Arts and Humanities); **Basic and Applied Sciences** (Applied Physics; Physics); **Economies and Organisations** *(ED MODEG)*; **Information Sciences** *(EDSTIC)* (Information Sciences); **Medicine** (Medicine); **National, European and International Relations** *(ED INEI)* (International Law); **Physical Therapy** *(Works in cooperation with Universities of Aix-Marseiles II, Montpellier I, Toulon and Avignon)*

History: Founded 1971 under the 1968 law reforming higher education and replacing former Université de Nice, founded 1965. A State institution enjoying academic and financial autonomy, operating under the jurisdiction of the Minister of Education and financed by the State.

Academic Year: October to June (October-February; February-June)

Admission Requirements: Secondary school certificate (baccalauréat) or equivalent, or special entrance examination

Main Language(s) of Instruction: French

Degrees and Diplomas: *Capacité en Droit*: **Law.** *Diplôme universitaire de Technologie*; *Licence*: **Arts and Humanities; Business Administration; Economics; Health Sciences; Law; Management; Mathematics and Computer Science; Modern Languages; Natural Sciences; Performing Arts; Political Sciences; Social Sciences; Sports; Technology; Tourism.** *Licence professionnelle*: **Building Technologies; Business Administration; Computer Science; Engineering; Hotel and Restaurant; Information Sciences; Mass Communication; Social Work; Technology; Tourism.** *Diplôme d'Etat*: **Dentistry; Medicine; Pharmacy.** *Diplôme d'Ingénieur*: **Engineering.** *Master*: **Arts and Humanities; Business Administration; Communication Studies; Economics; Engineering; Environmental Studies; Health Sciences; Hotel Management; Information Sciences; Law; Management; Mathematics and Computer Science; Modern Languages; Natural Sciences; Performing Arts; Political Sciences; Protective Services; Social Sciences; Sports; Teacher Training; Technology; Tourism; Translation and Interpretation; Water Science.** *Doctorat*: **Arts and Humanities; Astronomy and Space Science; Astrophysics; Biological and Life Sciences; Chemistry; Comparative Literature; Economics; Educational**

Sciences; Engineering; Environmental Studies; Health Sciences; History; Law; Literature; Management; Mathematics and Computer Science; Mechanics; Modern Languages; Natural Sciences; Performing Arts; Philosophy; Physics; Political Sciences; Psychology; Social Sciences; Sports; Technology. *Certificat de Spécialité*: **Medicine.** Masters recherche, Masters professionnel

Student Services: Academic Counselling, Canteen, Cultural Activities, Facilities for disabled people, Foreign Studies Centre, Health Services, Language Laboratory, Social Counselling, Sports Facilities

Publications: Annales de la Faculté de Droit; Annales de la Faculté des Lettres; Revue d'Odonto-stomatologie tropicale; Specialized scientific reviews

Academic Staff *2013-2014*	**TOTAL**
FULL-TIME	**2,701**
Student Numbers *2013-2014*	
All (Foreign included)	**26,404**
FOREIGN ONLY	**4854**

Last Updated: 11/03/15

UNIVERSITY OF NÎMES

Université de Nîmes (UNÎMES)

Rue du Docteur Georges Salan, 30021 Nîmes, Cedex 01

Fax: 33(4) 66-36-45-87

EMail: contact@unimes.fr

Website: http://www.unimes.fr

President: Emmanuel ROUX
Tel: +33(4) 66-36-46-18 EMail: presidence@unimes.fr

Head of Administration: Agnès Begue
Tel: +33(4) 66-36-46-18 EMail: agnes.begue@unimes.fr

International Relations: Karine Weiss, Vice-President in charge of International Relations
Tel: +33(4) 66-36-46-22
EMail: karine.weiss@unimes.fr; international@unimes.fr

Unit

Arts (Fine Arts; Textile Design); **Law, Economy and Management** (Criminal Law; Economics; Law; Management; Private Law; Public Law); **Psychology, Literature, Languages and History** (Arts and Humanities; English; History; Linguistics; Literature; Psychology; Spanish)

Laboratory

Art creation *(SITE)* (Design; Fine Arts); **Bio-Organic Chemistry** *(LCBO)* (Biochemistry; Biological and Life Sciences); **Geochemistry (GIS)** (Geochemistry); **Mathematics, Computer sciences and Applied Physics** *(MIPA)* (Applied Physics; Mathematics and Computer Science)

Further Information: Also Carmes Site

History: Previously known as the University Centre for Study and Training, the University of Nimes was created in 2007. It becomes the first French University solely dedicated to professional training. 2014, Member of the COMUE Languedoc Roussillon Universities

Main Language(s) of Instruction: French

Degrees and Diplomas: *Licence*: **Biology; Business Administration; Chemistry; Design; English Studies; Environmental Studies; Fine Arts; History; Law; Literature; Mathematics; Physics; Psychology; Spanish.** *Licence professionnelle*: **Biotechnology; Design; Environmental Studies; Fashion Design; History; Insurance; Management; Notary Studies; Optics; Protective Services; Real Estate; Tourism; Waste Management.** *Master*: **Archaeology; Art Education; Biotechnology; Clinical Psychology; Design; Environmental Studies; History; Law; Psychology; Teacher Training; Town Planning.**

Student Services: Canteen, Cultural Activities, Facilities for disabled people, Health Services, Library, Residential Facilities, Sports Facilities

Academic Staff *2014*: Total 194

Student Numbers *2014*: Total 3,736

Last Updated: 10/04/15

UNIVERSITY OF ORLÉANS

Université d'Orléans

BP 6749, Château de la Source, 45067 Orléans, Cedex 02

Tel: +33(2) 38-41-71-71

Fax: +33(2) 38-41-70-69

EMail: international@univ-orleans.fr

Website: http://www.univ-orleans.fr

President: Youssoufi Touré (2009-)
Tel: +33(2) 38-49-47-48 EMail: president@univ-orleans.fr

Administrative Director: André Pillot
Tel: +33(2) 38-41-71-96 EMail: secretaire.general@univ-orleans.fr

Faculty

Law, Economics and Management (Business Administration; Economics; Law; Management); **Letters, Humanities, and Languages** (Arts and Humanities; English; Geography; History; Modern Languages; Spanish); **Science and Tecnology** (Biochemistry; Biology; Chemistry; Computer Science; Earth Sciences; Environmental Studies; Mathematics; Natural Sciences; Physics; Sports; Technology)

School

Engineering *(ENSI de Bourges)* (Engineering); **Engineering** *(Polytech' Orléans)* (Civil Engineering; Electronic Engineering; Energy Engineering; Environmental Engineering; Mechanical Engineering; Optics; Production Engineering); **Teacher Training** *(ESPE Orléans, Blois, Chartres, Tours, Bourges, Châteauroux)* (Teacher Trainers Education; Teacher Training)

Institute

Technology *(IUT, Bourges)* (Business Administration; Civil Engineering; Mechanical Engineering; Production Engineering; Technology); **Technology** *(IUT Indre)* (Business Administration; Chemistry; Computer Science; Mechanical Engineering; Production Engineering; Technology); **Technology** *(IUT, Chartres)* (Business Computing; Electrical Engineering; Maintenance Technology; Technology; Transport Engineering); **Technology** *(IUT, Châteauroux)* (Business Administration; Computer Engineering; Electrical Engineering; Management; Technology)

Graduate School

Science and Technology (Chemistry; Information Sciences; Mathematics; Physics); **Social Sciences**

Further Information: University Centres: Bourges, Châteauroux

History: Founded 1970 under the 1968 law reforming higher education as one of two Universities replacing the Université d'Orléans-Tours, re-established 1962, but tracing its history to the original Université d'Orléans, 1306-1793. A State Institution enjoying academic and financial autonomy, operating under the jurisdiction of the Minister of Education and financed by the State.

Academic Year: October-June (October-December; January-March; April-June)

Admission Requirements: Secondary school certificate (baccalauréat) or equivalent, or special entrance examination

Main Language(s) of Instruction: French

Degrees and Diplomas: *Diplôme universitaire de Technologie*; *Licence*: **Administration; Arts and Humanities; Business Administration; Chemistry; Earth Sciences; Economics; Health Sciences; Law; Literature; Management; Mathematics and Computer Science; Modern Languages; Natural Sciences; Physics; Social Sciences; Sports.** *Licence professionnelle*: **Administration; Arts and Humanities; Business Administration; Earth Sciences; Engineering; Health Sciences; Law; Natural Sciences; Social Sciences; Sports; Technology.** *Diplôme d'Ingénieur*: **Engineering.** *Master*: **Administration; Arts and Humanities; Automation and Control Engineering; Biological and Life Sciences; Business Administration; Earth Sciences; Economics; Environmental Studies; Health Sciences; Law; Mathematics and Computer Science; Modern Languages; Natural Sciences; Robotics; Social Sciences; Sports; Teacher Training.** *Doctorat*: **Administration; Arts and Humanities; Biological and Life Sciences; Business Administration; Earth Sciences; Economics; Energy Engineering; Health Sciences; Law; Materials Engineering; Mathematics and Computer Science; Modern Languages; Physics; Social Sciences; Sports.** Preparation for Agrégation exam

Student Services: Canteen, Cultural Activities, Facilities for disabled people, Health Services, Residential Facilities, Sports Facilities
Publications: Revue 'Symbioses' Biologie
Last Updated: 11/03/15

UNIVERSITY OF PAU AND THE ADOUR REGION

Université de Pau et des Pays de l'Adour (UPPA)
avenue de l'Université, BP 576, 64012 Pau, Cedex
Tel: +33(5) 59-40-70-00
Fax: +33(5) 59-40-70-01
EMail: communication@univ-pau.fr
Website: http://www.univ-pau.fr

President: Mohamed Amara (2012-)
Tel: +33(5) 59 40 70 21/22
EMail: president@univ-pau.fr; mohamed.amara@univ-pau.fr

International Relations: Marielle Peyret-Terpolilli, Head of International Relations
Tel: +33(5) 59-40-70-00
EMail: david.bessieres@univ-pau.fr; marielle.peyret@univ-pau.fr

Unit
Law, Economics and Management *(Pau)* (Economics; International Business; Law; Management; Marketing); **Letters, Sports, Languages and Humanities** *(Pau, Tarbes)* (Arts and Humanities; Modern Languages; Sports); **Multidisciplinary** *(Bayonne)* (Accountancy; Economics; International Law; Law; Modern Languages); **Research Unit** (Applied Mathematics; Arts and Humanities; Economics; Environmental Studies; Information Sciences; Law; Literature; Management; Mechanical Engineering; Modern Languages; Petroleum and Gas Engineering; Social Sciences; Sports); **Science and Technology** *(Anglet)* (Biology; Chemistry; Civil Engineering; Computer Science; Physics); **Science and Technology** *(Pau)* (Mathematics and Computer Science; Natural Sciences)

School
Education and Teacher Training *(ESPE has 5 training sites in the 5 departments of the Academy of Bordeaux: Gironde (Mérignac et Bordeaux-Caudéran), Dordogne (Périgueux), Landes (Mont-de-Marsan), Lot-et-Garonne (Agen) et Pyrénées-Atlantiques (Pau)* (Primary Education; Secondary Education; Teacher Training); **Industrial Technology Engineering** *(ENSGTI)* (Industrial Engineering)

Department
Lifelong Education *(FORCO)* (Education)

Institute
Building Technologies *(ISA-BTP)* (Building Technologies); **Business Administration** *(IAE)* (Business Administration); **French courses for foreigners students** *(IEFE)* (French); **Industrial Systems Engineering** *(IUT Pays de l'Ardour, Pau site)* (Bioengineering; Energy Engineering; Materials Engineering; Statistics; Transport and Communications); **Technology** *(IUT, Bayonne)* (Business Administration; Computer Science; Marketing; Technology); **Technology** *(IUT Pays de l'Ardour, Mont de Marsan site)* (Biology; Computer Science; Statistics; Technology; Telecommunications Engineering)

Centre
Languages training center *(CLEREMO)* (English; French; Spanish)

Graduate School
Applied Sciences (Applied Chemistry; Applied Physics; Biology); **Social Sciences** (Arts and Humanities)

Further Information: The University is spread across five sites: Pau (central institution), Bayonne, Anglet, Tarbes and Mont-de-Marsan
History: Founded 1970, The Université de Pau et des Pays de l'Ardour is a network of 4 campuses (Pau, Bayonne/Anglet, Mont de Marsan and Tarbes). It is supported by the state and regional authorities.
Academic Year: October to June
Admission Requirements: Secondary school certificate (baccalauréat) or equivalent, or special entrance examination
Main Language(s) of Instruction: French
Accrediting Agency: Ministry of National Education
Degrees and Diplomas: *Diplôme universitaire de Technologie*; *Licence*: **Arts and Humanities; Economics; Law; Management; Mathematics and Computer Science; Natural Sciences; Social Sciences; Sports; Technology.** *Licence professionnelle*: **Arts and Humanities; Economics; Law; Management; Natural Sciences; Social Sciences; Sports; Technology.** *Master*: **Arts and Humanities; Economics; Educational Sciences; European Union Law; Geography; Management; Private Law; Public Law.** *Doctorat*: **Analytical Chemistry; Applied Chemistry; Applied Mathematics; Archaeology; Art History; Arts and Humanities; Astronomy and Space Science; Biology; Cell Biology; Classical Languages; Economics; Educational Sciences; Electrical Engineering; Energy Engineering; Ethnology; Fine Arts; Geography; History; History of Law; Law; Linguistics; Management; Mathematics; Modern Languages; Philosophy; Physical Chemistry; Physics; Political Sciences; Private Law; Public Law; Regional Studies; Sociology; Sports.**
Student Services: Canteen, Cultural Activities, Facilities for disabled people, Foreign Studies Centre, Health Services, Language Laboratory, Library, Social Counselling, Sports Facilities
Publishing house: Presses Universitaires de Pau et des Pays de l'Adour (PUPPA)

Academic Staff *2013-2014*: Total 1,325
Student Numbers *2013-2014*: Total 11,581
Last Updated: 08/04/15

NATIONAL SCHOOL OF INDUSTRIAL CERAMICS

ECOLE NATIONALE SUPÉRIEURE
DE CÉRAMIQUE INDUSTRIELLE DE LIMOGES (ENSCI)
12, rue Atlantis, 87068 Limoges, Cedex
Tel: +33(5) 87-50-23-00
Website: http://www.ensci.fr/

Director: Claire Peyratout
Tel: +33(5) 87-50-25-00 EMail: claire.peyratout@unilim.fr

International Relations: David Smith, International Relations Officer EMail: david.smith@unilim.fr

Programme
Engineering (Aeronautical and Aerospace Engineering; Biomedical Engineering; Ceramics and Glass Technology; Civil Engineering; Design; Electronic Engineering; Energy Engineering; Environmental Engineering; Materials Engineering; Transport Engineering)
History: Founded in 1893
Admission Requirements: Competitive entrance examination following 2 years further study after secondary school certificate (Baccalauréat) or following first university qualification (L2, DUT or BTS or equivalent)
Fees: 610 (Euro)
Main Language(s) of Instruction: French
Accrediting Agency: Commission des Titres d'Ingénieur (CTI); Conférence des Grandes Ecoles (CGE)
Degrees and Diplomas: *Diplôme d'Ingénieur*: **Ceramics and Glass Technology.** also Master in materials sciences; Technological Research Diploma (DRT) in Industrial Ceramics and Surface Treatments

UNIVERSITY OF PERPIGNAN VIA DOMITIA

Université de Perpignan Via Domitia (UPVD)
52, avenue Paul Alduy, 66860 Perpignan, Cedex
Tel: +33(4) 68-66-20-00
Fax: +33(4) 68-66-20-19
EMail: sec-dir@univ-perp.fr
Website: http://www.univ-perp.fr

President: Fabrice Lorente (2012-)
Tel: +33(4) 68-66-20-02 +33(4) 68-66-21-67
EMail: president@univ-perp.fr; fabrice.lorente@univ-perp.fr

Secretary General: Paul Taverner
Tel: +33(4) 68-66-20-04 EMail: sec-gen@univ-perp.fr

International Relations: Jean-Louis Marty, Vice-President in charge of International Relations
Tel: +33(4) 68-66-22-54 +33(4) 68-66-24-31
EMail: jlmarty@univ-perp.fr

Faculty

Arts and Humanities *(LSH)* (Archaeology; Art History; Arts and Humanities; Catalan; Classical Languages; English; Geography; History; Literature; Modern Languages; Sociology; Spanish); **Exact and Experimental Sciences** *(SEE)* (Applied Mathematics; Biological and Life Sciences; Earth Sciences; Geology; Heating and Refrigeration; Marine Science and Oceanography; Mathematics; Mathematics and Computer Science; Physical Engineering; Physics; Social Sciences); **Law and Economics** *(SJE)* (Economics; Law); **Legal Systems in Francophone African Countries** *(FIDAF)* (Law); **Sports, International Hotel Management and Tourism** *(STHI)* (Hotel Management; International Business; Sports; Tourism; Transport and Communications)

Institute

Business Administration *(IAE)* (Business Administration; Management); **Franco-Catalan Studies** *(Trans Frontier Institute IFCT)* (Catalan; French); **Preparatory Administrative Studies** (Administration); **Technology** *(IUT Perpignan with 2 other sites at Carcassone and Narbonne)* (Administrative Law; Biotechnology; Business Administration; Data Processing; Industrial Maintenance; Technology; Transport Engineering); **Urban and Real Estate Law** (Law; Real Estate)

Centre

Lifelong Education *(CREUFOP)*

Graduate School

Energy and Environment (Environmental Studies)

History: Founded 1970 as Centre Universitaire de Perpignan under the 1968 law reforming higher education and incorporating institutions previously attached to the former Université de Montpellier. Acquired present status and title 1979. A State Institution enjoying academic and financial autonomy, operating under the jurisdiction of the Minister of Education and financed by the State. 2014, Member of the COMUE Languedoc Roussillon Universities

Academic Year: October to June

Admission Requirements: Secondary school certificate (baccalauréat) or foreign equivalent, or special entrance examination

Main Language(s) of Instruction: French

Degrees and Diplomas: *Diplôme d'Accès aux Etudes universitaires*; *Diplôme universitaire de Technologie*; *Licence*: **Arts and Humanities; Biological and Life Sciences; Business Administration; Chemistry; Earth Sciences; Economics; Engineering; Geography; Health Sciences; History; Law; Mathematics and Computer Science; Modern Languages; Physics; Social Sciences; Sociology; Sports; Teacher Training; Technology.** *Licence professionnelle*: **Business Administration; Computer Science; Heritage Preservation; Law; Social Work; Tourism; Translation and Interpretation; Urban Studies.** *Diplôme d'Ingénieur*: **Engineering.** *Master*: **Arts and Humanities; Biology; Chemistry; Economics; Geography; Health Sciences; History; Law; Marine Science and Oceanography; Modern Languages; Social Sciences; Teacher Training; Technology.** *Doctorat*: **Arts and Humanities; Business Administration; Earth Sciences; Energy Engineering; Environmental Studies; Fine Arts; History; Law; Modern Languages; Social Sciences; Sociology.** Also Master 2 recherche 1 yr following Master 1; Master 2 professionnel 1 yr following Master 1

Student Services: Canteen, Cultural Activities, Facilities for disabled people, Health Services, Residential Facilities, Sports Facilities

Student Numbers *2013*: Total 9,500
Last Updated: 10/04/15

UNIVERSITY OF PICARDIE JULES VERNE

Université de Picardie Jules Verne (UPJV)
Chemin du Thil, Campus, 80025 Amiens
Tel: +33(3) 22-82-72-72
Fax: +33(3) 22-82-75-00
Website: http://www.u-picardie.fr

President: Michel Brazier (2012-)
Tel: +33 (3)22-82-72-63 EMail: michel.brazier@u-picardie.fr

Head of Administration: Laurent Anne
Tel: +33(3) 22-82-72-65 EMail: laurent.anne@u-picardie.fr

International Relations: Sabler Wolfang
Tel: +33 3 22 82 73 91 EMail: wolfgang.sabler@u-picardie.fr

Faculty

Arts (Art History; Fine Arts; Performing Arts); **Economics and Management** *(Pôle Université Cathédrale)* (Economics; Management); **Foreign Languages and Cultures** *(Pôle Campus)* (Chinese; Communication Studies; English; German; Italian; Spanish); **History and Geography** *(Pôle Campus)* (Archaeology; Geography; History); **Law and Political Sciences** *(Pôle Université Cathédrale)* (Law; Political Sciences); **Letters** *(Pôle Campus)* (Arts and Humanities; Communication Studies; Library Science; Literature; Media Studies; Teacher Training); **Medicine** *(Pôle Santé)* (Medicine); **Pharmacy** *(Pôle Santé)* (Pharmacy); **Philosophy, Human and Social Sciences** *(Pôle Campus)* (Arts and Humanities; Educational Sciences; Philosophy; Psychology; Social Sciences; Sociology); **Science** *(Pôle Science)* (Automation and Control Engineering; Biological and Life Sciences; Biology; Chemistry; Computer Science; Earth Sciences; Electronic Engineering; Mathematics; Physics); **Sport Sciences** *(Pôle Campus)* (Sports)

Institute

Business Administration *(IAE de Picardie)* (Accountancy; Business Administration); **Preparatory Administration Studies** *(IPAG)* (Administration); **Science and Technology** *(INSSET, Saint Quentin)* (Education; Engineering; Management; Software Engineering; Technology); **Teacher Training** *(IUFM: Training is also provided at INSSET and the Technology University of Compiegne)* (Teacher Trainers Education; Teacher Training); **Technology** *(IUT, Amiens)* (Bioengineering; Business Administration; Civil Engineering; Computer Science; Mechanical Engineering; Sales Techniques; Technology)

Graduate School

Health Sciences (Neurosciences); **Social Sciences** (Social Sciences)

History: Founded 1970 under the 1968 law reforming higher education as one of the new Universities and replacing former Université d'Amiens founded 1964 as Centre Universitaire de Picardie and incorporating previously existing Institutions of higher education. A State institution enjoying academic and financial autonomy, operating under the jurisdiction of the Minister of Education and financed by the State.

Academic Year: October to June (October-February; February-June)

Admission Requirements: Secondary school certificate (baccalauréat) or equivalent

Main Language(s) of Instruction: French

Degrees and Diplomas: *Capacité en Droit*; *Diplôme universitaire de Technologie*: **Accountancy; Business Administration; Industrial Chemistry; Transport and Communications.** *Licence*; *Licence professionnelle*; *Diplôme d'Etat*: **Dentistry; Medicine; Pharmacy.** *Master*: **Accountancy; Applied Mathematics; Archaeology; Archiving; Art History; Cinema and Television; Clinical Psychology; Cultural Studies; E- Business/Commerce; Educational Sciences; European Union Law; Geography; History; Industrial and Organizational Psychology; Information Sciences; Law; Literature; Management; Mathematics; Medical Technology; Modern Languages; Music; Musicology; Performing Arts; Philosophy; Physical Engineering; Political Sciences; Psychology; Regional Studies; Rehabilitation and Therapy; Social and Preventive Medicine; Social Studies.** *Doctorat*: **Biology; Cell Biology; Chemistry; Immunology; Mathematics; Physics; Physiology; Social Sciences.** *Certificat de Spécialité*: **Medicine.**

Student Services: Canteen, Careers Guidance, Facilities for disabled people, Health Services, Library
Publications: Bouillon de Culture; Bulletin de l'Ecole doctorale en sciences humaines et sociales
Last Updated: 11/03/15

UNIVERSITY OF POITIERS

Université de Poitiers
15, rue de l'Hôtel-Dieu, 86034 Poitiers, Cedex
Tel: +33(5) 49-45-30-00
Fax: +33(5) 49-45-30-50
EMail: communication@univ-poitiers.fr
Website: http://www.univ-poitiers.fr

President: Yves Jean (2012-)
Tel: +33(5) 49-45-30-33 EMail: president@univ-poitiers.fr
Head of Administration: Nicole Gontier
Tel: +33(5) 49-45-30-43 EMail: sg@univ-poitiers.fr
International Relations: Christine Robuchon
Tel: +33(5) 49-45-30-49
EMail: ri@univ-poitiers.fr; christine.robuchon@univ-poitiers.fr

Unit

Basic and Applied Sciences *(SFA)* (Applied Chemistry; Applied Mathematics; Applied Physics; Biological and Life Sciences; Chemistry; Computer Science; Mathematics; Natural Sciences); **Economics** (Economics); **Humanities and Arts** (Arts and Humanities; Classical Languages; Cognitive Sciences; Geography; History; Medieval Studies; Music; Philosophy; Psychology; Sociology); **Languages and Literature** (Cinema and Television; Classical Languages; Latin American Studies; Linguistics; Literature; Medieval Studies; Modern Languages; Theatre); **Law and Social Sciences** (Criminal Law; Law; Private Law; Public Law; Social Sciences); **Medicine and Pharmacy** (Health Sciences; Medicine; Pharmacy); **Sports** (Physical Education; Sports)

School

Engineering *(ENSIP)* (Automation and Control Engineering; Chemistry; Civil Engineering; Electrical Engineering; Engineering; Environmental Engineering; Materials Engineering; Sound Engineering (Acoustics); Water Management); **Mechanical and Aeronautical Engineering** *(ENSMA)* (Aeronautical and Aerospace Engineering; Mechanical Engineering); **Teacher Training** *(ESPE with sites in Angoulême, La Rochelle, Niort)* (Teacher Trainers Education; Teacher Training)

Institute

Business Administration *(IAE)* (Business Administration); **Industrial, Insurance and Financial Risks Studies** *(IRIAF)* (Finance; Insurance); **Preparatory Administrative Studies** *(IPAG)* (Administration); **Technology** *(IUT, Angoulême)* (Business and Commerce; Computer Engineering; Electrical Engineering; Management; Mechanical Engineering; Production Engineering; Technology); **Technology** *(IUT Poitiers)* (Business Administration; Chemistry; Computer Engineering; Data Processing; Electrical Engineering; Energy Engineering; Mechanical Engineering; Production Engineering; Sanitary Engineering; Technology; Telecommunications Engineering)

Centre

French as a Foreign Language *(CFLE)* (Foreign Languages Education; French); **Training for Music Teachers** *(CFMI)* (Music Education)

Graduate School

Doctoral Studies (Aeronautical and Aerospace Engineering; Arts and Humanities; Bioengineering; Chemical Engineering; Geological Engineering; Law)

History: Founded 1970 under the 1968 law reforming higher education and replacing the former Université de Poitiers, founded 1431 by Bull of Pope Eugene IV, and confirmed by letters patent granted by Charles VII, 1432. The University was suppressed by the Revolution and replaced by Faculties of Law; Letters; and Science and a School of Medicine of the Université de France. Reconstituted as University 1896. A State institution enjoying academic and financial autonomy, operating under the jurisdiction of the Ministry of Education and financed by the State.

Academic Year: October to June (October-February; February-June)

Admission Requirements: Secondary school certificate (baccalauréat) or foreign equivalent, or special entrance examination

Main Language(s) of Instruction: French

Degrees and Diplomas: *Capacité en Droit*: **Law.** *Diplôme d'Accès aux Etudes universitaires*; *Diplôme universitaire de Technologie*: **Business Administration; Economics; Health Sciences; Natural Sciences; Technology.** *Licence*: **Arts and Humanities; Business Administration; Economics; Law; Literature; Mathematics and Computer Science; Modern Languages; Natural Sciences; Sports; Technology.** *Licence professionnelle*: **Business Administration; Economics; Health Sciences; Natural Sciences; Sports; Technology.** *Diplôme d'Etat*: **Medicine; Pharmacy.** *Diplôme d'Ingénieur*: **Civil Engineering; Energy Engineering; Engineering.** *Master*: **Arts and Humanities; Business Administration; Economics; Engineering; Environmental Studies; Health Sciences; Law; Literature; Mathematics and Computer Science; Modern Languages; Natural Sciences; Sports; Teacher Training; Technology.** *Doctorat*: **Aeronautical and Aerospace Engineering; Arts and Humanities; Cognitive Sciences; Engineering; Environmental Studies; Information Sciences; Law; Linguistics; Materials Engineering; Mechanical Engineering; Political Sciences; Social Sciences; Sports.** *Certificat de Spécialité*: **Medicine.** Masters recherche, Masters professionnel

Student Services: Canteen, Cultural Activities, Health Services, Language Laboratory, Social Counselling, Sports Facilities
Last Updated: 12/03/15

NATIONAL SCHOOL OF MECHANICAL AND AERONAUTICAL ENGINEERING

ÉCOLE NATIONALE SUPÉRIEURE DE MÉCANIQUE ET D'AÉROTECHNIQUE DE POITIERS (ENSMA)
Téléport 2, 1 avenue Clément Ader, BP 40109, 86961 Futuroscope Chasseneuil, Cedex
Tel: +33 (0)5 49 49 80 80
Fax: +33 (0)5 49 49 80 00
Website: http://www.ensma.fr/

Director: Francis Cottet EMail: francis.cottet@ensma.fr

International Relations: Aurélie Cotillon
Tel: +33(5) 49-49-80-05 EMail: international@ensma.fr

Programme

Engineering (Aeronautical and Aerospace Engineering; Arts and Humanities; Computer Engineering; Economics; Engineering; Materials Engineering; Mechanical Engineering; Mechanics; Social Sciences; Thermal Engineering)

History: Founded 1948. Become ISAE-ENSMA in 2011

Admission Requirements: Competitive entrance examination or academic qualifications for students who have: a bachelor's degree (mechanics, applied mathematics, physics, electronics) or a University Technological Diploma (specialities: Mechanical and Industrial Automation Engineering, Thermal and Energy Engineering, Industrial Engineering and Maintenance, Electrical Engineering and Industrial Computing, Science and Materials Engineering, Mathematics and Physics) or a Bachelor's degree in ' Sciences and Technologies ' from the University of Poitiers

Main Language(s) of Instruction: French

Accrediting Agency: Ministry of Higher Education and Research; Commission des Titres d'Ingénieur (CTI)

Degrees and Diplomas: *Diplôme d'Ingénieur*: **Engineering.** also 3 Masters in 'Air and Ground Transportation',' High Performance Materials', 'Computer Science' with the University of Poitier; 2 Masters of science in 'Aeronautical mechanics and Energetics', 'Turbulence'; ISAE-ENSMA is associated with the University of Poitiers in a joint Doctoral School

UNIVERSITY OF REIMS CHAMPAGNE-ARDENNE

Université de Reims Champagne-Ardenne (URCA)
Villa Douce, 9, boulevard de la Paix, 51097 Reims, Cedex
Tel: +33(3) 26-91-30-00
Fax: +33(3) 26-91-30-98
EMail: presidence@univ-reims.fr
Website: http://www.univ-reims.fr

President: Gilles Baillat (2012-)
Tel: +33(3) 26-91-39-55 EMail: presidence@univ-reims.fr

Head of Administration: Daouya Berka
EMail: dgs@univ-reims.fr; daouya.berka@univ-reims.fr

International Relations: Harald Schraeder, Head of International Relations
Tel: +33(3) 26-91-39-54
EMail: sri@univ-reims.fr; harald.schraeder@univ-reims.fr

Unit

Physical Education and Sports Science and Techniques *(STAPS)* (Physical Education; Sports); **Arts and Humanities** (Arts and Humanities; English; Geography; German; History; Literature; Musicology; Philosophy; Psychology; Romance Languages); **Dentistry** (Dentistry); **Economics, Social Sciences and Management** (Economics; Management; Social Work); **Exact and Natural Sciences** (Automation and Control Engineering; Biochemistry; Biology; Chemistry; Civil Engineering; Earth Sciences; Electronic Engineering; Energy Engineering; Environmental Studies; Mathematics and Computer Science; Mechanical Engineering; Natural Sciences; Physics; Thermal Engineering); **Law and Political Science** (Law; Political Sciences; Public Administration); **Medicine** (Medicine); **Pharmacy** (Pharmacy)

School

Engineering *(ESIReims)* (Energy Engineering; Packaging Technology; Thermal Engineering); **Teacher Training** *(ESPE Champagne Ardenne with 5 sites throughout region)* (Teacher Trainers Education; Teacher Training)

Institute

Juridical Studies *(IEJ)* (Law); **Preparatory Administrative Studies** *(IPAG)* (Administration); **Rural Planning, Environmental Studies and Town Planning** *(IATEUR)* (Environmental Studies; Rural Planning; Town Planning); **Technical Training** *(IFTS, Charleville-Mézières)* (Materials Engineering; Metallurgical Engineering; Polymer and Plastics Technology; Technology Education); **Technology** *(IUT, Troyes)* (Business Administration; Business and Commerce; Computer Engineering; Electrical Engineering; Mechanical Engineering; Production Engineering; Technology); **Technology** *(IUT Reims with sites: Châlonsand Charleville)* (Business Administration; Business and Commerce; Civil Engineering; Data Processing; Mechanical Engineering; Physics; Technology; Transport Management)

Centre

French Studies *(International)*; **Distance Education**; **Lifelong Education** (Continuing Education)

Graduate School

Human Sciences and Societies; **Science, Technology and Health** (Biology; Health Sciences; Medicine)

Research Centre

Decentralization *(C.R.D.T.)*

History: Founded 1970 under the 1968 law reforming higher education and replacing the former Université de Reims, founded 1967, which incorporated previously existing Faculties and re-established the original University created by Papal Bull in 1548 and suppressed by the Revolution. A State Institution enjoying academic and financial autonomy operating under the jurisdiction of the Minister of Education and financed by the State.

Academic Year: September to June (September-December; January-March; April-June)

Admission Requirements: Secondary school certificate (baccalauréat) or equivalent, or special entrance examination

Main Language(s) of Instruction: French

Degrees and Diplomas: *Capacité en Droit*: **Law.** *Diplôme universitaire de Technologie*: **Business Administration; Economics; Management; Natural Sciences; Technology.** *Licence*: **Arts and Humanities; Biological and Life Sciences; Chemistry; Computer Science; Earth Sciences; Economics; Law; Management; Natural Sciences; Physics; Political Sciences; Social Sciences; Sports; Technology.** *Licence professionnelle*: **Economics; Management; Natural Sciences; Technology.** *Diplôme d'Etat*: **Dentistry; Medicine; Oenology; Pharmacy.** *Diplôme d'Ingénieur*: **Engineering.** *Master*: **Agriculture; Arts and Humanities; Economics; Engineering; Law; Management; Mathematics and Computer Science; Modern Languages; Natural Sciences; Oenology; Political Sciences; Public Health; Social Sciences; Sports; Teacher Training; Technology; Urban Studies.** *Doctorat*: **Agriculture; Arts and Humanities; Economics; Engineering; Health Sciences; Law; Mathematics; Natural Sciences; Oenology; Pharmacy; Public Health; Social Sciences.** *Certificat de Spécialité*: **Medicine.** Masters recherche, Masters professionnel, Preparation for Teaching exams

Student Services: Canteen, Cultural Activities, Health Services, Residential Facilities, Sports Facilities

Publishing house: Presses Universitaires de Reims

Academic Staff *2013-2014*: Total 1,300
Student Numbers *2013-2014*: Total 22,903
Last Updated: 12/03/15

UNIVERSITY OF ROUEN

Université de Rouen

1, rue Thomas Becket, 76821 Mont-Saint-Aignan, Cedex
Tel: +33(2) 35-14-60-00
Fax: +33(2) 35-14-63-48
EMail: communication@univ-rouen.fr
Website: http://www.univ-rouen.fr

President: Cafer Ozkul (2007-)
Tel: +33(2) 35-14-63-32
EMail: presidence@univ-rouen.fr; Cafer.Ozkul@univ-rouen.fr

Head of Administration: Valérie Gibert
Tel: +33(2) 35-14-60-91; +33(2) 35-14-67-67
EMail: dgs@univ-rouen.fr

International Relations: Thi Anh-Dao TRAN, Head of International Relations EMail: service.international@univ-rouen.fr

Faculty

Law, Economics and Management (Economics; Law; Management); **Pharmacy and Medicine** (Medicine; Pharmacy)

Unit

Human and Social Sciences (Education; Psychology; Sociology); **Letters and Humanities** (Arts and Humanities; English; Geography; German; History; Literature; Musicology; Philosophy; Spanish); **Physical Education and Sports** (Physical Education; Sports); **Science and Technology** (Biology; Chemistry; Communication Studies; Computer Science; Geology; Mathematics; Natural Sciences; Physics; Technology)

School

Teacher Training *(ESPE-académie de Rouen)* (Teacher Training)

Higher School

Engineering and Technology *(ESITECH)* (Engineering; Technology)

Institute

Business Administration *(IAE)* (Business Administration); **Juridical Studies** *(IEJ)* (Administrative Law; Law); **Preparatory Administrative Studies** *(IPAG)* (Administration); **Technology** *(IUT, Evreux)* (Biology; Business Administration; Business and Commerce; Measurement and Precision Engineering; Packaging Technology; Sales Techniques; Technology); **Technology** *(IUT Rouen with sites at Elbeuf, Mont St. Aignan and Pasteur)* (Business and Commerce; Chemistry; Computer Networks; Electrical Engineering; Energy Engineering; Law; Measurement and Precision Engineering; Physical Engineering; Technology; Telecommunications Engineering; Telecommunications Services)

Centre

Lifelong Education *(CFC)*

Graduate School

Biology, Health and Environment (Biology; Environmental Studies; Health Sciences); **Chemistry** *(Normandy)* (Chemistry); **Knowledge, Critique, and Expertise** (Arts and Humanities); **Law** *(Normandy)* (Law)

History: Founded 1970 under the 1968 law reforming higher education and replacing the former Université de Rouen, founded 1966 and incorporating previously existing facilities. A State institution enjoying academic and financial autonomy, operating under the jurisdiction of the Minister of Education and financed by the State.

Academic Year: October to June (October-February; February-June)

Admission Requirements: Secondary school certificate (baccalauréat) or equivalent, or special entrance examination

Main Language(s) of Instruction: French

Degrees and Diplomas: *Capacité en Droit*: **Law.** *Diplôme universitaire de Technologie*; *Licence*: **Accountancy; Arts and Humanities; Automation and Control Engineering; Biological and Life Sciences; Chemistry; Cultural Studies; Economics; Education; Electronic Engineering; Finance; Foreign Languages Education; French; Geography; German; History; Law; Literature; Mathematics and Computer Science; Mechanics; Modern Languages; Musicology; Native Language Education; Philosophy; Physics; Psychology; Public Administration; Sociology; Sports; Sports Management.** *Licence professionnelle*: **Business and Commerce; Law; Management.** *Diplôme d'Etat*: **Dentistry; Medicine; Pharmacy.** *Master*: **Arts and Humanities; Automation and Control Engineering; Biological and Life Sciences; Chemistry; Cultural Studies; Education; Electronic Engineering; Foreign Languages Education; French; Geography; German; History; Literature; Mathematics and Computer Science; Mechanics; Modern Languages; Musicology; Native Language Education; Natural Sciences; Philosophy; Physics; Social Sciences; Sports.** *Doctorat*: **Arts and Humanities; Economics; Mathematics and Computer Science; Natural Sciences; Pharmacy; Social Sciences; Sports; Technology.**

Student Services: Canteen, Facilities for disabled people, Health Services, Library, Residential Facilities, Sports Facilities

Student Numbers *2013-2014*: Total 26,002

Last Updated: 12/03/15

UNIVERSITY OF SOUTHERN BRITTANY

Université de Bretagne Sud

BP 92116, Rue Armand Guillemot, 56321 Lorient, Cedex

Tel: +33(2) 97-87-66-66

Fax: +33(2) 97-87-66-00

EMail: arlette.eveno@univ-ubs.fr

Website: http://www.univ-ubs.fr

President: Jean Peeters (2012-)
Tel: +33(2) 97-87-66-10
EMail: president@univ-ubs.fr; Jean.Peeters@univ-ubs.fr

Secretary General: Jean-Michel Le Pimpec
Tel: +33(2) 97-01-70-89 EMail: dgs@listes.univ-ubs.fr

International Relations: Mariannick GUENNEC, Vice-President
International EMail: vp-ri@univ-ubs.fr

Faculty

Law, Economics and Management (Economics; Law; Management); **Letters, Languages, Humanities and Social Sciences** (Arts and Humanities; Documentation Techniques; English; Heritage Preservation; History; Literature; Publishing and Book Trade; Social Sciences; Social Work; Spanish); **Science and Engineering** (Biology; Biotechnology; Chemistry; Civil Engineering; Computer Science; Cosmetology; Electronic Engineering; Energy Engineering; Engineering; Environmental Studies; Health Sciences; Mathematics; Mechanical Engineering; Natural Sciences; Physics; Polymer and Plastics Technology; Statistics)

School

Engineering *(ENSIBS)* (Computer Engineering; Electrical Engineering; Engineering; Industrial Engineering; Mechanical Engineering)

Institute

Technology *(IUT, Vannes)* (Business Administration; Business and Commerce; Data Processing; Statistics; Technology); **Technology** *(IUT Lorient with antenna at Pontivy)* (Energy Engineering; Industrial Maintenance; Management; Safety Engineering; Technology)

Graduate School

Doctoral School

Further Information: Also branches in Vannes and Pontivy

History: Founded 1995.

Academic Year: October to June (October-February; February-June)

Admission Requirements: Secondary school certificate (baccalauréat) or equivalent, or special entrance examination

Main Language(s) of Instruction: French

Degrees and Diplomas: *Diplôme d'Accès aux Etudes universitaires*; *Diplôme universitaire de Technologie*; *Licence*: **Arts and Humanities; Biological and Life Sciences; Earth Sciences; Economics; Engineering; English; Geography; German; History; Law; Literature; Management; Mathematics and Computer Science; Modern Languages; Publishing and Book Trade; Social Sciences; Social Studies; Spanish; Statistics; Teacher Training.** *Licence professionnelle*: **Agricultural Management; Business Administration; Coastal Studies; Cosmetology; Modern Languages; Natural Sciences; Service Trades; Social Work; Technology.** *Diplôme d'Ingénieur*: **Engineering.** *Master*: **Documentation Techniques; Engineering; Geography; History; Law; Library Science; Management; Marine Science and Oceanography; Mathematics and Computer Science; Modern Languages; Private Law; Public Law; Publishing and Book Trade; Social Policy; Teacher Training; Technology.** *Doctorat*: **Astronomy and Space Science; Biological and Life Sciences; Chemistry; Economics; Engineering; English; Ethnology; History; Law; Literature; Management; Mathematics and Computer Science; Natural Sciences; Spanish.** Masters recherche, Masters professionnel, Preparation for CAPES, Agrégation exams

Student Services: Canteen, Cultural Activities, Facilities for disabled people, Health Services, Library, Nursery Care, Residential Facilities, Sports Facilities

Academic Staff *2013-2014*: Total 900

Student Numbers *2013-2014*: Total 9,000

Last Updated: 11/03/15

UNIVERSITY OF STRASBOURG

Université de Strasbourg

4, rue Blaise Pascal, 90032 Strasbourg, Cedex

Tel: +33(3) 68-85-00-00

Website: http://www.unistra.fr

President: Alain Beretz (2008-)
Tel: +33(3) 68-85-70-80 EMail: president@unistra.fr

Head of Administration: Frédéric Dehan
Tel: +33(3) 68-85-70-92; +33(3) 68-85-70-90
EMail: frederic.dehan@unistra.fr

International Relations: Roya Naddaf, Head of International Relations
Tel: +33(3) 68-85-65-36; +33(3) 68-85-65-25
EMail: dri-contact@unistra.fr; roya.naddaf@unistra.fr

Faculty

Catholic Theology (Catholic Theology); **Chemistry** (Chemistry); **Dental Surgery** (Dentistry; Surgery); **Economics and Management** (Economics; Management); **Geography and Regional Planning** (Geography; Regional Planning); **History** (History); **Languages and Applied Humanities** *(LSHA)* (Computer Science; Economics; European Studies; International Relations; International Studies; Law; Modern Languages); **Law, Political Science and Management** (Law; Management; Political Sciences); **Life Sciences** (Biological and Life Sciences); **Literature** (Literature; Teacher Training); **Medicine** (Medicine); **Modern Languages and Cultural studies** (Cultural Studies; Modern Languages); **Pharmacy** (Pharmacy); **Philosophy** (Philosophy); **Protestant Theology** (Protestant Theology); **Psychology** (Psychology); **Social sciences** (Demography and Population; Ethnology; Social Sciences; Social Work; Sociology; Urban Studies); **Sports** (Sports)

School

Biotechnology *(Strasbourg-ESBS)* (Biotechnology); **Chemistry, Polymers and Materials** *(European-ECPM)* (Chemistry; Materials Engineering; Polymer and Plastics Technology); **Management**

(EM-Strasbourg) (Management); **Observatory and Earth Sciences** *(EOST)* (Earth Sciences); **Physics and Engineering** *(National-Telecom Physique Strabourg)* (Biomedical Engineering; Engineering; Physics; Robotics; Telecommunications Engineering); **Teacher Training** *(ESPE)* (Teacher Training)

Institute

European Studies (European Studies); **Labour**; **Preparation for General Administration** (Administration); **Technology** *(Haguenau)* (Technology); **Technology** *(Robert Schuman)* (Technology); **Technology** *(Louis Pasteur)* (Bioengineering; Business Administration; Industrial Engineering)

Centre

Intellectual Proprerty *(International)*; **Journalism** (Journalism)

History: Founded 1970 under the 1968 law reforming higher education as one of three Universities replacing the former Université de Strasbourg, founded 1537 as School. Became Academy 1566 and University 1621, suppressed by the Revolution, replaced by German university 1872-1918, evacuated to Clermont-Ferrand 1939-1945. A state institution enjoying academic and financial autonomy, operating under the jurisdiction of the Minister of Education and financed by the State. Acquired present status 2009 following the merge of the Université Louis Pasteur, Marc Bloch and Robert Schuman.

Academic Year: September to June (September-February; February-June)

Admission Requirements: Secondary school certificate (baccalauréat) or recognized equivalent, or special entrance examination

Fees: 174 per annum for Bachelor's degree; 273 for Master's and 359 for a Doctorate (Euro)

Main Language(s) of Instruction: French

Degrees and Diplomas: *Capacité en Droit*: **Law.** *Diplôme d'Accès aux Etudes universitaires*; *Diplôme universitaire de Technologie*; *Licence*: **Arts and Humanities; Business Administration; Cultural Studies; Education; Fine Arts; Health Sciences; Information Sciences; Law; Mathematics and Computer Science; Modern Languages; Natural Sciences; Performing Arts; Religion; Social Sciences; Sports.** *Licence professionnelle*: **Business Administration; Engineering; Health Sciences; Information Sciences; Mathematics and Computer Science; Natural Sciences; Technology.** *Diplôme d'Ingénieur*: **Engineering.** *Master*: **Administration; Arts and Humanities; Business Administration; Cultural Studies; Economics; Engineering; European Studies; Fine Arts; Health Sciences; Information Sciences; International Studies; Law; Management; Mathematics and Computer Science; Modern Languages; Natural Sciences; Performing Arts; Political Sciences; Public Health; Social Sciences; Theology.** *Doctorat*: **Archaeology; Architecture and Planning; Arts and Humanities; Astronomy and Space Science; Astrophysics; Catholic Theology; Chemistry; Civil Engineering; Computer Science; Earth Sciences; Economics; Education; Electronic Engineering; Energy Engineering; Environmental Studies; Ethics; Fine Arts; Geography; Health Sciences; History; Industrial Engineering; Law; Linguistics; Literature; Management; Mathematics; Mechanical Engineering; Medicine; Modern Languages; Natural Sciences; Performing Arts; Pharmacy; Philosophy; Physics; Political Sciences; Protestant Theology; Psychology; Robotics; Theology.** *Habilitation à Diriger les Recherches*

Student Services: Academic Counselling, Canteen, Cultural Activities, Facilities for disabled people, Language Laboratory, Social Counselling, Sports Facilities

Publications: Bulletin Analytique d'Histoire Romaine; DESHIMA, revue d'histoire globale des pays du Nord; KTÈMA Civilisations de l'Orient, de la Grèce et de Rome antiques; Les Cahiers philosophiques de Strasbourg; RANAM Recherches anglaises et nord-américaines; Recherches Culture et Histoire dans l'Espace Roman; Recherches Germaniques; Revue des Sciences Sociales; SCOLIA, revue de linguistique

Academic Staff *2014*: Total 2,030

Student Numbers *2014*: Total 44,991

Last Updated: 12/03/15

INSTITUTE OF POLITICAL STUDIES STRASBOURG - 'SCIENCES PO STRASBOURG'

INSTITUT D'ETUDES POLITIQUES DE STRASBOURG - 'SCIENCES PO STRASBOURG'

47 avenue de la Forêt-Noire, 67082 Strasbourg, Cedex
Tel: +33(3) 68-85-84-00
Fax: +33(3) 68-85-86-15
EMail: scolarite.iep@unistra.fr
Website: http://www.iep-strasbourg.fr/

Directeur: Sylvain Schirmann EMail: s.schirmann@unistra.fr

Administrative Officer: Catherine Hmae
EMail: catherine.hmae@unistra.fr

International Relations: Michelle Benoit
Tel: +33(3) 68-85-81-05 EMail: michelle.benoit@unistra.fr

Programme

Political Science (Administration; Cultural Studies; Economics; European Studies; Finance; History; International Studies; Law; Management; Political Sciences; Social Sciences; Sociology)

History: Founded 1948.

Academic Year: September to July

Admission Requirements: Secondary school certificate (Baccalauréat) and entrance examination.

Main Language(s) of Instruction: French

Degrees and Diplomas: *Master*: **Business Administration; European Studies; International Studies; Political Sciences; Public Administration.**

Student Numbers *2013-2014*: Total 1,500

UNIVERSITY OF TECHNOLOGY - BELFORT-MONTBELIARD

Université de Technologie de Belfort-Montbéliard (UTBM)

90010 Belfort, Cedex
Tel: +33(3) 84-58-30-00
Fax: +33(3) 84-58-30-30
EMail: contact@utbm.fr
Website: http://www.utbm.fr

Director: Pascal Brochet (2011-2016)
EMail: pascal.brochet@utbm.fr

International Relations: Frédéric Holweck
Tel: +33(3) 84-58-32-92 EMail: relations.internationales@utbm.fr

Department

Computer Science (Computer Science); **Electrical Engineering** (Electrical Engineering); **Engineering and Processing** (Production Engineering); **Ergonomy, Design and Mechanical Engineering** (Industrial Design; Mechanical Engineering); **Mechanical Engineering** (Mechanical Engineering)

Graduate School

Engineering and Microtechnology *(ED SPIM In collaboration with University of France-Comté and National School of Mechanics and Microelectronics)* (Engineering); **Language, Space, Time and Society** *(In collaboration with University of France-Comté)* (Arts and Humanities; Law; Management)

Further Information: 2 other campuses at Severans and Montbéliard

History: Founded 1962 as Ecole nationale d'Ingénieurs de Belfort and 1985 as Polytechnic Institute of Sévenans. Acquired present status and title 1998 after merging with IPSé and Ecole nationale d'Ingénieurs de Belfort.

Main Language(s) of Instruction: French

Degrees and Diplomas: *Diplôme d'Ingénieur*: **Engineering.** *Master*: **Computer Engineering; Economic History; Electrical and Electronic Engineering; History of Societies; Industrial and Production Economics; Industrial Engineering; Technology; Transport Engineering.** *Doctorat*: **Electronic Engineering; Materials Engineering; Metallurgical Engineering; Technology; Transport and Communications.** Also Diplôme d'Etudes universitaires de Technologie (DEUTEC)

Student Services: Cultural Activities, Facilities for disabled people, Nursery Care, Residential Facilities, Sports Facilities
Last Updated: 12/03/15

UNIVERSITY OF TECHNOLOGY - COMPIEGNE

Université de Technologie de Compiègne (UTC)
Centre Pierre Guillaumat, rue du docteur Schweitzer,
60220 Compiègne
Tel: +33(3).44.23.49.99
Fax: +33(3).44.23.52.53
EMail: srp@utc.fr
Website: http://www.utc.fr

Director: Alain Storck (2012-2016)
Tel: +33(3) 44-23-43-39
EMail: presidence@utc.fr

International Relations: Schoefs Olivier
Tel: +33(3) 44 23 73 87
EMail: olivier.schoefs@utc.fr

Department

Biological Engineering (Biotechnology; Engineering); **Computer Science** (Computer Science); **Industrial Process Engineering** (Industrial Engineering); **Mechanical Engineering** (Mechanical Engineering); **Mechanical Systems Engineering** (Agricultural Engineering); **Technology and Humanities** (Cognitive Sciences; Information Sciences; Management; Technology); **Urban Systems Engineering** (Civil Engineering; Environmental Engineering)

Graduate School

Engineering Sciences (Engineering)

Further Information: Also: Benjamin Franklin Center; Research Center; Innovation Center

History: A public 'Grande Ecole', and University.

Academic Year: September to June (September-January; February-June)

Admission Requirements: Secondary school certificate (baccalauréat) or equivalent/or 2 years after the baccalauréat

Main Language(s) of Instruction: French

Accrediting Agency: Comité national d'Evaluation; Commission du Titre d'Ingénieur

Degrees and Diplomas: *Licence professionnelle*: **Maintenance Technology.** *Diplôme d'Ingénieur*: **Bioengineering; Chemical Engineering; Civil Engineering; Computer Engineering; Industrial Engineering; Mechanical Engineering.** *Mastère spécialisé*: **Medical Technology; Railway Transport; Road Transport.** *Master*: **Agronomy; Automation and Control Engineering; Bioengineering; Biomedical Engineering; Computer Science; Industrial Design; Mechanical Engineering; Robotics; Technology; Water Science.** *Doctorat*: **Applied Mathematics; Automation and Control Engineering; Bioengineering; Biomedical Engineering; Cell Biology; Electrical and Electronic Engineering; Mechanical Engineering; Molecular Biology; Sound Engineering (Acoustics).**

Student Services: Academic Counselling, Canteen, Cultural Activities, Foreign Studies Centre, Health Services, Language Laboratory, Residential Facilities, Sports Facilities

Academic Staff *2015*	**TOTAL**
PART-TIME	**400**
STAFF WITH DOCTORATE FULL-TIME	**450**
Student Numbers *2015*	
All (Foreign included)	**5,025**

Last Updated: 30/03/15

SCHOOL OF ORGANIC AND MINERAL CHEMISTRY
ECOLE SUPÉRIEURE DE CHIMIE ORGANIQUE ET MINÉRALE (ESCOM)
1 allée du réseau Jean-Marie Buckmaster, 60200 Compiègne
Tel: +33(3) 44-23-88-00
Fax: +33(3) 44-97-15-91
EMail: s.jourdain@escom.fr
Website: http://www.escom.fr

President: François Darrort

Programme

Chemistry (Analytical Chemistry; Chemical Engineering; Chemistry; Inorganic Chemistry; Organic Chemistry)

History: Founded 1957. Associate status with Institut catholique de Paris.

Admission Requirements: Competitive entrance examinnation, secondary school certificate (baccalauréat) in Sciences or first university qualification (DEUG, DUT, BTS).

Main Language(s) of Instruction: French

Degrees and Diplomas: *Diplôme d'Ingénieur*: **Chemical Engineering; Engineering.** *Mastère spécialisé*: **Cosmetology.** *Master*: **Biotechnology; Chemistry; Water Science.**

UNIVERSITY OF TECHNOLOGY - TROYES

Université de Technologie de Troyes (UTT)
BP 2060, 12, rue Marie Curie, 10010 Troyes, Cedex
Tel: +33(3) 25-71-76-00
Fax: +33(3) 25-71-76-76
EMail: infos.utt@utt.fr
Website: http://www.utt.fr

Director: Pierre Koch (2014-) EMail: president@utt.fr

International Relations: Michel Legault, Head of International Relations
Tel: +33(3) 25-71-58-14 EMail: international.center@utt.fr

Unit

Aleatory Systems and Decision Methods; Knowledge Management and Communication *(SIM2C)* (Communication Studies; Information Management); **Languages** (Modern Languages); **Logistics and Operational Research** *(LRO)*; **Mechanical and Materials Engineering** (Materials Engineering; Mechanical Engineering); **Networks and Telecommunications** *(RT)* (Computer Networks; Telecommunications Engineering); **Physics, Materials and Nanotechnology** *(PMN)* (Materials Engineering; Nanotechnology; Physics); **Sustainable Development** *(DD)* (Development Studies; Environmental Studies)

History: Founded 1994 as State University, cooperating with University of Technology of Compiègne and University of Belfort-Montbéliard.

Academic Year: September to June (September-January; March-June)

Admission Requirements: Competitive entrance examination after secondary school certificate (baccalauréat) or after 1st cycle (engineering degree), or after 2nd cycle (master's degree). Adequate knowledge of French required.

Main Language(s) of Instruction: French

Accrediting Agency: Ministry of Higher Education and Research. Commission des Titres d'Ingénieur

Degrees and Diplomas: *Licence professionnelle*: **Energy Engineering; Technology.** *Diplôme d'Ingénieur*: **Computer Engineering; Engineering; Industrial Engineering; Materials Engineering; Mechanical Engineering; Telecommunications Engineering.** *Master*: **Engineering; Information Technology; Management; Mechanical Engineering; Nanotechnology; Optics; Physics; Technology.** *Doctorat*: **Business Administration; Computer Networks; Materials Engineering; Mechanical Engineering; Nanotechnology; Optics.**

Student Services: Academic Counselling, Canteen, Careers Guidance, Cultural Activities, Facilities for disabled people, Foreign Studies Centre, Health Services, Language Laboratory, Social Counselling, Sports Facilities
Last Updated: 12/03/15

EPF SCHOOL OF ENGINEERING
EPF ECOLE D'INGÉNIEURS (EPF)
3 bis, rue Lakanal, 92330 Sceaux
Tel: +33(1) 41-13-01-51
Fax: +33(1) 46-60-39-94
EMail: communication@epf.fr
Website: http://www.epf.fr

Director: Jean-Michel Nicolle Tel: +33(1) 41-13-01-62

International Relations: Sophie Telliez EMail: sophie.telliez@epf.fr

Department

General Engineering (Energy Engineering; Engineering; Engineering Management; Environmental Engineering; Industrial Engineering; Mechanical Engineering); **Information Sciences** (Information Sciences); **Urbanism** (Construction Engineering)

Further Information: Also branch in Troyes and Montpellier

History: Founded 1925 as Institut électromécanique féminin, became École polytechnique féminine (EPF) 1933. Acquired present title 1994.

Academic Year: September to June

Admission Requirements: Secondary school certificate (baccalauréat 'S') or equivalent and competitive entrance examination

Fees: 5,750 - 7,270 (Euro)

Main Language(s) of Instruction: French

Degrees and Diplomas: *Diplôme d'Ingénieur*: **Engineering.** *Master*: **Engineering.** Also Master professionnel in Business Engineering

Student Services: Academic Counselling, Canteen, Careers Guidance, Facilities for disabled people, Foreign Studies Centre, Health Services, Language Laboratory, Social Counselling, Sports Facilities

Publications: Interfaces

Academic Staff *2014-2015*: Total 140
Student Numbers *2014-2015*: Total 1,700

UNIVERSITY OF THE AUVERGNE

Université d'Auvergne (UDA)

BP 32, 49, boulevard François Mitterrand, 63001 Clermont-Ferrand, Cedex 01
Tel: +33(4) 73-17-79-79
Fax: +33(4) 73-17-72-01
EMail: mathonnatj@wanadoo.fr
Website: http://www.u-clermont1.fr

President: Philippe Dulbecco (2007-)
Tel: +33(4)73177272 EMail: Philippe.dubecco@udamail.fr

International Relations: Christine Chevalliler, In charge of International Relations Tel: christine.chevallier@udamail.fr

Faculty

Dental Surgery (Dentistry; Surgery); **Medicine** (Medicine; Midwifery); **Pharmacy** (Pharmacy)

School

Economy (Administration; Economics; Law); **Law** (Business Administration; Law; Notary Studies; Political Sciences; Real Estate; Social and Community Services); **Management** (Accountancy; Administration; Banking; Business Administration; Economics; Finance; Human Resources; Industrial and Production Economics; Management; Marketing; Transport Management)

Institute

Preparatory Administrative Studies *(IRPAG attached to the school of Law)* (Administration); **Technology** *(IUT, Aurillac)* (Biotechnology; Business Administration; Food Science; Technology); **Technology** *(IUT Clermont-Ferrand)* (Biology; Business Administration; Computer Engineering; Industrial Engineering; Physics; Technology; Telecommunications Engineering); **Technology** *(IUT, Puy-en-Velay)* (Chemistry; Computer Science; Multimedia; Technology)

Centre

Longlife Education (Adult Education)

Graduate School

Economics, Law and Management (Economics; Law; Management); **Health and Life Sciences** *(In cooperation with University of Clermont-Ferrand II)* (Health Sciences)

History: Founded 1970 under the 1968 law reforming higher education and replacing former Université de Clermont-Ferrand, founded 1854 as Faculty of Letters and Faculty of Science. Became University 1896. The University, which until 1976 formed a single institution with the University of Clermont-Ferrand II, is a State institution enjoying academic and financial autonomy, operating under the jurisdiction of the Minister of Education and financed by the State.

Academic Year: October to June (October-December; January-March; April-June)

Admission Requirements: Secondary school certificate (baccalauréat) or brevet supérieur, or recognized foreign equivalent, or special entrance examination

Fees: The amount of this fee is determined every year by the Ministry of Higher Education and Research and varies according to the degree and the existence of specific complementary contributions. Depending on your situation, payment for the French student social security scheme and complementary health insurance (optional) is added to the registration fees

Main Language(s) of Instruction: French

Degrees and Diplomas: *Capacité en Droit*: **Law.** *Diplôme universitaire de Technologie*; *Licence*: **Administration; Dentistry; Economics; Law; Management; Medicine; Pharmacy; Technology.** *Licence professionnelle*: **Administration; Banking; Business Administration; Health Sciences; Management; Notary Studies; Public Administration.** *Master*: **Administration; Administrative Law; Banking; Civil Law; Dentistry; Economics; Finance; Human Resources; Law; Management; Marketing; Medicine; Pharmacy; Police Studies; Protective Services.** *Doctorat*: **Administration; Dentistry; Economics; Law; Management; Medicine; Pharmacy; Technology.** Diplome universitaire: 2 yrs

Student Services: Canteen, Cultural Activities, Facilities for disabled people, Health Services, Library, Residential Facilities, Sports Facilities

Last Updated: 11/03/15

UNIVERSITY OF THE LITTORAL CÔTE D'OPALE

Université du Littoral Côte d'Opale (ULCO)

BP 1022, 1, place de l'Yser, 59375 Dunkerque, Cedex 1
Tel: +33(3) 28-23-73-73
Fax: +33(3) 28-23-73-13
EMail: relinter@univ-littoral.fr
Website: http://www.univ-littoral.fr

President: Roger Durand (2009-2016)
Tel: +33(3) 28-23-73-00 EMail: president@univ-littoral.fr

Secretary General: Catherine Sion
Tel: +33(3) 28-23-73-18 EMail: catherine.sion@univ-littoral.fr

International Relations: Carl Vetters
Tel: +33(3) 28-23-73-28; +33(3) 21-99-43-31
EMail: relinter@univ-littoral.fr; carl.vetters@univ-littoral.fr

Division

Arts, Letters and Languages *(Boulogne and Dunkirk)* (Cultural Studies; English; German; Literature; Media Studies; Spanish); **Human and Social Sciences** *(Dunkirk, Boulogne)* (Geography; History); **Law, Economics and Management** *(Dunkirk, Boulogne, Saint Omer)* (Economics; Health Administration; Hotel Management; Human Resources; Law; Management; Marketing; Public Administration; Sales Techniques; Tourism; Transport Management); **Science, Technology and Health** *(Calais, Boulogne, Dunkirk, Saint-Omer)* (Biology; Chemistry; Computer Science; Electrical and Electronic Engineering; Food Technology; Industrial Engineering; Mathematics; Metallurgical Engineering; Physical Education; Physics; Sports; Telecommunications Engineering)

School

Business and Commerce *(ISCID-CO)* (Business and Commerce); **Engineering** *(Littoral-EILCO)* (Computer Engineering; Engineering; Industrial Engineering)

Institute

Technology *(IUT Saint Omer-Dunkerque: two sites)* (Technology); **Technology** *(IUT Calais-Boulogne: two sites)* (Biotechnology; Business Administration; Computer Engineering; Electrical Engineering)

Centre

Lifelong Education *(CUEEP)*

History: Founded 1991.

Admission Requirements: Secondary school certificate (baccalauréat) or equivalent

Fees: 150-300 per annum (Euro)

Main Language(s) of Instruction: French

Degrees and Diplomas: *Diplôme universitaire de Technologie*: **Biotechnology; Business Administration; Computer Science; Electrical Engineering; Energy Engineering; Industrial Engineering; Maintenance Technology; Thermal Engineering.** *Licence*: **Administration; Arts and Humanities; Economics; Law; Modern Languages; Natural Sciences; Social Sciences; Technology.** *Licence professionnelle*: **Administrative Law; Electrical and Electronic Engineering; Human Resources; Industrial Engineering; International Business; Management; Marketing; Safety Engineering; Telecommunications Engineering.** *Diplôme d'Etudes d'Ecole de Commerce et Gestion*: **Business and Commerce; Management.** *Master*: **Administration; Arts and Humanities; Economics; Environmental Management; Environmental Studies; Geography; History; Law; Management; Marine Science and Oceanography; Mathematics and Computer Science; Measurement and Precision Engineering; Modern Languages; Nutrition; Physics; Social Sciences; Sports; Teacher Training; Tourism; Transport Management; Urban Studies.** *Doctorat*: **Coastal Studies; Cultural Studies; Engineering; Environmental Studies; History; Literature; Mathematics; Modern Languages.** Preparation for CAPES and Agrégation, Masters professionnel, Masters recherche

Student Services: Academic Counselling, Canteen, Cultural Activities, Facilities for disabled people, Health Services, Social Counselling, Sports Facilities

Publications: L'Esprit de la Côte

Academic Staff *2014*	**TOTAL**
FULL-TIME	**519**

Student Numbers *2014*	
All (Foreign included)	**10,015**
FOREIGN ONLY	**1265**

Last Updated: 12/03/15

UNIVERSITY OF THE SAVOIE, CHAMBÉRY

Université de Savoie

BP 1104, 27, rue Marcoz, 73011 Chambéry, Cedex
Tel: +33(4) 79-75-85-85
Fax: +33(4) 79-75-84-44
EMail: dri@univ-savoie.fr
Website: http://www.univ-savoie.fr

President: Denis Varaschin (2012-)
Tel: +33(4) 79-75-84-22 EMail: Presidence@univ-savoie.fr

Head of Administration: Véronique Drogue
Tel: +33(4) 79-75-84-81 EMail: Veronique.Drogue@univ-savoie.fr

International Relations: Emilie Viret-Thasiniphone
Tel: +33(4) 79-75-83-50 EMail: international@univ-savoie.fr; Emilie.Viret-Thasiniphone@univ-savoie.fr

Faculty

Fundamental and Applied Sciences *(SFA, Le Bourget-du-Lac)* (Chemistry; Information Technology; Mathematics; Physics); **Law and Economics** *(FDE Chambéry)* (Economics; Law); **Literature, Languages and Human Sciences** *(LLSH)* (Arts and Humanities; Cultural Studies; History; Literature; Modern Languages; Philosophy; Psychology; Social Sciences; Sociology)

School

Engineering *(Polytech in partnership with ITII of Savoies. Second site at Annecy)* (Automation and Control Engineering; Civil Engineering; Energy Engineering; Environmental Engineering; Mechanical Engineering)

Institute

Business Administration *(IAE Savoie Mont-Blanc, Annecy-le-Vieux with a second site at Chambéry)* (Business Administration; Finance; Hotel Management; International Business; Management; Marketing; Tourism); **Environmental Engineering for Mountainous Regions** (Environmental Studies; Mountain Studies); **French Studies** *(for foreign students, AGISEFE)* (French; French Studies); **Technology** *(IUT, Chambéry)* (Administration; Business and Commerce; Materials Engineering; Packaging Technology; Technology); **Technology** *(IUT Annecy-le-Vieux)* (Administration; Computer Engineering; Electrical Engineering; Management; Marketing; Mechanical Engineering; Production Engineering; Technology; Telecommunications Engineering); **Transport Management, Tourism and Hotel Management** *(IUP THTL)* (Hotel Management; Tourism; Transport Management)

Centre

Mountain Research *(Interdisciplinary, CISM Le Bourget du Lac)* (Mountain Studies)

Further Information: Science Campus at Le Bourget du Lac site. Annecy-le-Vieux is the second site.

History: Founded 1970 as Centre Universitaire de Savoie under the 1968 law reforming higher education and replacing institutions attached to former Université de Grenoble. Acquired present status and title 1979. A State institution enjoying academic and financial autonomy, operating under the jurisdiction of the Minister of Education and financed by the State.

Academic Year: September to June

Admission Requirements: Secondary school certificate (baccalauréat) or foreign equivalent, or special entrance examination

Main Language(s) of Instruction: French

Degrees and Diplomas: *Diplôme universitaire de Technologie*; *Licence*: **Administration; Applied Mathematics; Arts and Humanities; Biological and Life Sciences; Business Administration; Chemistry; Earth Sciences; Economics; English; Geography; History; Information Sciences; Italian; Law; Literature; Management; Mathematics and Computer Science; Modern Languages; Physics; Psychology; Social Sciences; Sociology; Spanish; Sports.** *Licence professionnelle*: **Agronomy; Business and Commerce; Computer Science; Design; Engineering; Environmental Studies; Finance; Health Education; Industrial and Production Economics; Insurance; Maintenance Technology; Management; Sports; Telecommunications Services; Tourism.** *Diplôme d'Ingénieur*: **Engineering; Environmental Engineering; Materials Engineering; Mechanical Engineering.** *Master*: **Arts and Humanities; Chemistry; Computer Science; Economics; Electronic Engineering; Law; Literature; Management; Mathematics; Modern Languages; Mountain Studies; Optics; Physics; Psychology; Social Sciences; Sociology; Sports; Teacher Training; Telecommunications Engineering.** *Doctorat*: **Applied Mathematics; Applied Physics; Arts and Humanities; Astrophysics; Biology; Civil Engineering; Cognitive Sciences; Comparative Literature; Earth Sciences; Ecology; Economics; Engineering; Environmental Studies; Geography; History; Industrial Engineering; Law; Literature; Management; Mathematics and Computer Science; Mechanics; Modern Languages; Nanotechnology; Optics; Performing Arts; Physics; Psychology; Sociology.** Certificat and Diplômes d'études françaises (for foreign students), Masters recherche, Masters professionnel

Student Services: Canteen, Facilities for disabled people, Health Services, Library, Residential Facilities, Sports Facilities

Academic Staff *2013-2014*: Total 1,271

Student Numbers *2013-2014*: Total 12,806

Last Updated: 12/03/15

UNIVERSITY OF THE SOUTH TOULON-VAR

Université du Sud Toulon-Var

BP 132, Avenue de l'Université, 83957 La Garde, Cedex
Tel: +33(4) 94-14-20-00
Fax: +33(4) 94-14-21-57
EMail: sri@univ-tln.fr
Website: http://www.univ-tln.fr

President: Marc Saillard (2011-2015)
Tel: +33(4) 94-14-23-69 +33(4) 94-14-22-61
EMail: president@univ-tln.fr

Head of Administration: Olivier Chourrot
Tel: +33(4) 94-14-22-62 EMail: chourrot@univ-tln.fr

International Relations: Karine Benet-Cattin, Head of International Relations Tel: +33(4) 94-14-29-08 EMail: cattin@univ-tln.fr;

Faculty

Arts and Humanities (Arts and Humanities; Cultural Studies; English; Literature; Spanish; Tourism); **Economics and Management** (Economics; Management); **Information and Communication sciences** *(Ingémédia)* (Communication Studies; Information Sciences; Media Studies); **Law** (Law); **Physical Education and Sports** *(STAPS)* (Physical Education; Sports); **Science and Techniques** (Biology; Chemistry; Computer Science; Electronic Engineering; Marine Science and Oceanography; Mathematics; Physics; Telecommunications Engineering)

School

Teacher Training *(ESPE with 5 sites in Nice, Draguignan, La Seyne-sur-Mer, La Garde)* (Teacher Training)

Institute

Business Administration *(IAE)* (Business Administration; Management); **Engineering Sciences** *(SeaTech)* (Engineering; Marine Engineering; Materials Engineering; Telecommunications Engineering); **Technology** *(IUT Toulon)* (Bioengineering; Business Administration; Electrical Engineering; Industrial Engineering; Management; Sales Techniques; Technology; Telecommunications Engineering)

Centre

Lifelong Education

Graduate School

Euro-Mediterranean Comparative Civilizations and Societies (Mediterranean Studies); **Law and Political sciences** *(ED461 in cooperation with Montpellier 1)* (Law; Political Sciences); **Science and Sea** *(ED 548)* (Astronomy and Space Science; Biological and Life Sciences; Engineering; Health Sciences; Mathematics and Computer Science; Natural Sciences; Sports; Technology)

Further Information: also campuses in: Garde - La Valette-du-Var, Draguignan, Saint-Raphaël, La Seyne-sur-Mer.

History: Founded 1970 as Centre universitaire under the 1968 law reforming higher education. Acquired present status and title 1979. A State institution enjoying academic and financial autonomy, operating under the jurisdiction of the Minister of Education and financed by the State.

Academic Year: September to July (September-December; January-March; April-July)

Admission Requirements: Secondary school certificate (baccalauréat) or equivalent, or special entrance examination

Main Language(s) of Instruction: French

Degrees and Diplomas: *Capacité en Droit*: **Law.** *Diplôme d'Accès aux Etudes universitaires*; *Diplôme universitaire de Technologie*; *Licence*: **Arts and Humanities; Business Administration; Economics; Engineering; Health Sciences; Law; Mathematics and Computer Science; Natural Sciences; Sports; Technology.** *Licence professionnelle*: **Law; Multimedia; Sports; Technology; Tourism.** *Diplôme d'Ingénieur*: **Engineering; Environmental Engineering; Marine Engineering; Telecommunications Engineering.** *Master*: **Arts and Humanities; Business Administration; Comparative Literature; Economics; Engineering; Finance; Information Sciences; Law; Literature; Marine Science and Oceanography; Mathematics and Computer Science; Modern Languages; Multimedia; Natural Sciences; Sports; Teacher Training; Tourism.** *Doctorat*: **Applied Mathematics; Arts and Humanities; Astronomy and Space Science; Automation and Control Engineering; Biological and Life Sciences; Chemistry; Economics; Electrical and Electronic Engineering; Health Sciences; Industrial Engineering; Information Sciences; Law; Management; Mathematics and Computer Science; Mechanical Engineering; Mechanics; Physics; Political Sciences; Robotics; Sports; Technology.** Also Certificat d'Aptitude à la Profession d'Avocat, 5 yrs, Masters recherche, Masters professionnel

Student Services: Academic Counselling, Canteen, Careers Guidance, Cultural Activities, Facilities for disabled people, Health Services, Language Laboratory, Social Counselling, Sports Facilities

Academic Staff *2012-2013*: Total 400

Student Numbers *2012-2013*: Total 8,597

Last Updated: 12/03/15

UNIVERSITY OF TOULOUSE JEAN JAURÈS

Université Toulouse - Jean Jaurès

5, allée Antonio Machado, 31058 Toulouse, Cedex 9
Tel: +33(5) 61-50-42-50
Fax: +33(5) 61-50-42-09
EMail: presidence@univ-tlse2.fr
Website: http://www.univ-tlse2.fr

President: Jean-Michel Minovez
Tel: +33(5) 61-50-44-99/98
EMail: presidence@univ-tlse2.fr; minovez@univ-tlse2.fr

Head of Administration: Alain Miaoulis
Tel: +33(5) 61-50-43-65 EMail: secretariat.general@univ-tlse2.fr

International Relations: Mélanie Le Bihan, In charge of International Relations
Tel: +33(5) 61-50-45-99 ; +33(5) 61 50-36-46
EMail: rintutm@univ-tlse2.fr; melanie.le-bihan@univ-tlse2.fr

Unit

Foreign Languages, Literatures and Civilizations (Cultural Studies; Literature; Modern Languages); **History, Arts and Archaeology** (Archaeology; Arts and Humanities; History); **Letters, Philosophy and Music** (Arts and Humanities; Music; Philosophy); **Psychology** (Psychology); **Science, Geography and Civilisations** (Economics; Educational Sciences; Geography; Mathematics and Computer Science; Social Sciences; Sociology)

School

Audiovisual Studies *(ESAV)* (Media Studies); **Teacher Training** *(ESPE Midi-Pyrénées with 9 sites in the region)* (Teacher Trainers Education; Teacher Training)

Institute

Archival and Library Sciences *(IUP)* (Archiving; Library Science); **Arts and Culture, Applied Arts** (Cultural Studies; Fine Arts); **Latin American Studies** *(IPEALT)* (Latin American Studies); **Maintenance, Reliability, Quality Control, Ergonomy**; **Regional Development and Management** (Management; Regional Planning); **Regional Labour Institute** *(IRT)* (Labour and Industrial Relations); **Sociology, Management and Business Administration** (Business Administration; Management; Sociology); **Technology** *(IUT Blagnac)* (Technology); **Technology** *(IUT Figeac)* (Technology); **Tourism, Hotel Management and Transport** *(IUP, Site de Foix)* (Hotel Management; Tourism; Transport and Communications); **Tourism, Hotel Management and Transport** (Hotel Management; Tourism; Transport and Communications); **Training of Music Teachers** *(IFMI)* (Music Education)

Centre

University Centre *(Albi)*; **University Centre** *(Rodez)*

Graduate School

Doctoral Schools (Arts and Humanities; Behavioural Sciences; Cognitive Sciences; Education; Modern Languages; Social Sciences)

History: Founded 1970 under the 1968 law reforming higher education as one of three Universities replacing the former Université de Toulouse, founded 1229. Suppressed by the Revolution and replaced by Faculties of Law; Theology; Science; Letters; and Medicine 1808. Reconstituted as University 1896. A State institution enjoying academic and financial autonomy, operating under the jurisdiction of the Minister of Education and financed by the State. Known as University of Toulouse - Le Mirail and acquired current title 2014.

Academic Year: October to June (October-December; January-April; April-June)

Admission Requirements: Secondary school certificate (baccalauréat) or equivalent, or Diplôme d'Accès aux Etudes Universitaires (DAEU)

Main Language(s) of Instruction: French

Degrees and Diplomas: *Diplôme universitaire de Technologie*: **Business and Commerce; Social Work; Technology.** *Licence*: **Arts and Humanities; Health Sciences; Mathematics and Computer Science; Modern Languages; Performing Arts; Social Sciences; Technology.** *Licence professionnelle*: **Arts and Humanities; Computer Science; Health Sciences; Modern Languages; Social Sciences; Technology.** *Master*: **Applied Mathematics; Architecture and Planning; Computer Science;**

Educational Sciences; Health Sciences; Linguistics; Literature; Mathematics; Modern Languages; Performing Arts; Philosophy; Psychology; Social Sciences; Sociology; Teacher Training; Technology; Tourism; Translation and Interpretation. *Doctorat*: **Ancient Civilizations; Anthropology; Architecture; Art History; Arts and Humanities; Economics; Educational Sciences; Fine Arts; Geography; History; Information Sciences; Linguistics; Literature; Management; Modern Languages; Neurosciences; Performing Arts; Philosophy; Prehistory; Psychology; Rural Studies; Social Sciences; Sociology; Translation and Interpretation.** Diplomas for Languages, French, and Teaching French as a Foreign Language; Masters recherche, Masters professionnel

Student Services: Canteen, Cultural Activities, Facilities for disabled people, Health Services, Library, Residential Facilities, Sports Facilities

Publications: Correspondances

Publishing House: Presses universitaires du Mirail (PUM)
Last Updated: 12/03/15

UNIVERSITY OF VALENCIENNES AND HAINAUT-CAMBRÉSIS

Université de Valenciennes et du Hainaut-Cambrésis (UVHC)

Le Mont-Houy, 59313 Valenciennes, Cedex 9
Tel: +33(3) 27-51-12-34
Fax: +33(3) 27-51-11-00
EMail: uvhc@univ-valenciennes.fr
Website: http://www.univ-valenciennes.fr

President: Mohamed Ourak (2012-)
Tel: +33(3) 27-51-16-76 +33(3) 27-51-16-97
EMail: president@univ-valenciennes.fr

Secretary General: Pierre Chabasse
Tel: +33(3) 27-51-11-03
EMail: secretaire.general@univ-valenciennes.fr; manuel.varago@univ-valenciennes.fr

International Relations: Fabrice Guizard
Tel: +33(3) 27-51-77-36
EMail: int.relations@univ-valenciennes.fr; sylvie.merviel@univ-valenciennes.fr

Faculty

Law, Economics and Management *(FDEG)* (Economics; Law; Private Law; Public Law); **Letters, Languages, Arts and Humanities** *(FLLASH)* (Arts and Humanities; English; Fine Arts; French; German; History; Information Sciences; Literature; Modern Languages; Multimedia; Performing Arts; Spanish; Theatre; Visual Arts); **Sports Sciences** *(FSMS)* (Sports; Sports Management; Welfare and Protective Services)

School

Engineering *(ENSIAME)* (Automation and Control Engineering; Computer Engineering; Electronic Engineering; Energy Engineering; Mechanical Engineering)

Institute

Business Administration *(IAE)* (Accountancy; Administration; Business Administration; Finance; Human Resources; Management; Marketing; Real Estate); **Public Administration** *(IPAG)* (Administration; Institutional Administration; Public Administration); **Science and Technology** *(ISTV)* (Business Computing; Chemistry; Food Technology; Materials Engineering; Mathematics and Computer Science; Mechanics; Multimedia; Telecommunications Engineering); **Technology** *(IUT de Valenciennes with 3 sites: Valenciennes, Cambrai and Maubeuge)* (Computer Science; Electrical Engineering; Maintenance Technology; Management; Marketing; Physical Engineering; Production Engineering)

Higher Institute

Industrial Engineering *(ISIV)* (Electrical Engineering; Industrial Engineering; Mechanical Engineering)

Centre

Continuing Education

Further Information: Also courses of French as a foreign language for foreign students. Has 9 research labs. Campuses in Cambrai and Maubeuge

History: Founded 1970 as Centre Universitaire de Valenciennes under the 1968 law reforming higher education and incorporating institutions previously attached to the former Université de Lille. Acquired present status and title 1979. A State institution enjoying academic and financial autonomy, operating under the jurisdiction of the Minister of Education and financed by the State.

Academic Year: September to June (September-Januaryr; February-June)

Admission Requirements: Secondary school certificate (baccalauréat) or foreign equivalent

Main Language(s) of Instruction: French

Accrediting Agency: National Ministry of Education

Degrees and Diplomas: *Diplôme universitaire de Technologie*: **Computer Science; Electrical Engineering; Maintenance Technology; Management; Marketing; Physical Engineering; Production Engineering.** *Licence*: **Civil Engineering; Computer Science; Economics; Electrical Engineering; Fine Arts; Food Technology; French; History; Law; Literature; Management; Materials Engineering; Mathematics; Mechanical Engineering; Modern Languages; Physics; Public Administration.** *Licence professionnelle*: **Accountancy; Civil Engineering; Computer Science; Electronic Engineering; Industrial Engineering; Maintenance Technology; Management; Marketing; Production Engineering.** *Diplôme d'Ingénieur*: **Engineering.** *Master*: **Accountancy; Automation and Control Engineering; Civil Engineering; Computer Science; Electronic Engineering; Finance; Fine Arts; Food Technology; French; German; History; Information Technology; International Business; Law; Linguistics; Literature; Management; Materials Engineering; Mathematics; Measurement and Precision Engineering; Mechanical Engineering; Multimedia; Performing Arts; Radio and Television Broadcasting; Railway Transport; Real Estate; Sports.** *Doctorat*: **Civil Engineering; Economics; Electronic Engineering; Food Technology; Materials Engineering; Mathematics; Multimedia; Service Trades; Transport and Communications.**

Student Services: Academic Counselling, Canteen, Careers Guidance, Cultural Activities, Facilities for disabled people, Health Services, Language Laboratory, Residential Facilities, Social Counselling, Sports Facilities

Publishing house: Presses Universitaires de Valenciennes (PUV); Septentrion

Student Numbers *2013-2014*: Total 10,201
Last Updated: 07/04/15

UNIVERSITY OF VERSAILLES SAINT-QUENTIN-EN-YVELINES

Université de Versailles Saint-Quentin-en-Yvelines (UVSQ)

55 avenue de Paris, 78035 Versailles, Cedex
Tel: +33(1) 39-25-78-00
Fax: +33(1) 39-25-78-01
EMail: relations.internationales@uvsq.fr
Website: http://www.uvsq.fr

President: Jean-Luc Vayssière (2012-)
Tel: +33(1) 39-25-78-03 EMail: president@uvsq.fr

Head of Administration: Jean Narvaez
Tel: +33(1) 39-25-78-13 EMail: jean.narvaez@uvsq.fr

International Relations: Celine Delacourt-Gollain, Head of international Relations
Tel: +33(1) 39-25-79-81
EMail: celine.delacourt-gollain@uvsq.fr; relations.internationales@admin.uvsq.fr

Faculty

Law and Political Science *(DSP)* (Law; Political Sciences)

Unit

Health Sciences *(Simone Veil, Garches, Hopital Raymond Poincaré)* (Anatomy; Biochemistry; Biology; Biophysics; Biotechnology; Chemistry; Embryology and Reproduction Biology; Genetics; Haematology; Health Administration; Health Sciences; Histology; Immunology; Medicine; Midwifery; Oncology; Pathology; Physics; Physiology; Public Health; Radiology; Virology); **Science** (Applied Mathematics; Biology; Biotechnology; Chemistry; Computer Science; Earth

Sciences; Engineering; Environmental Studies; Industrial Chemistry; Mathematics; Molecular Biology; Natural Sciences; Optics; Physics; Robotics); **Social Sciences** *(Saint-Quentin-en-Yvelines)* (Banking; Business Administration; Demography and Population; Economics; Environmental Management; Finance; Geography (Human); Hotel and Restaurant; Human Resources; Insurance; Law; Management; Social Sciences; Sociology; Tourism)

School

Teacher Training *(ESPE Versailles with 5 sites)* (Education; Teacher Trainers Education; Teacher Training)

Institute

Cultural studies, Languages and International Studies *(IECI)* (Cultural Studies; History; International Studies; Literature; Modern Languages; Musicology); **Law** *(IEJ- Branch of the faculty of Law and Political Science)* (Justice Administration; Law); **Management** *(ISV-UVSQ)* (Management); **Techniques and Sciences** *(ISTY Ecole d'ingénieur)* (Computer Engineering; Engineering; Mechanical Engineering); **Technology** *(IUT Vélizy with Antenne de Rambouillet)* (Business Administration; Business and Commerce; Chemical Engineering; Communication Studies; Computer Engineering; Electrical Engineering; Technology; Telecommunications Engineering); **Technology** *(IUT Mantes-en-Yvelines)* (Business Administration; Business and Commerce; Civil Engineering; Hygiene; Industrial Engineering; Mechanical Engineering; Sales Techniques; Technology)

Graduate School

Astrophysics and Astronomy *(AA)* (Astronomy and Space Science; Astrophysics); **Cultures, Organisations, Legislation** *(CRIT)* (Cultural Studies; Public Law); **Environmental sciences** *(SEIF)* (Environmental Studies); **Genetics** *(GAO)* (Biological and Life Sciences; Genetics); **Public Health** *(SP)* (Public Health); **Sciences and Technology** *(STV-Versailles)* (Chemistry; Computer Science; Engineering; Physics)

History: Founded 1991, incorporating divisions of University Paris VI and University Paris X. in 2014, Member of the COMUE Paris-Saclay University

Fees: 180-400 per annum (Euro)

Main Language(s) of Instruction: French

Degrees and Diplomas: *Diplôme d'Accès aux Etudes universitaires*; *Diplôme universitaire de Technologie*; *Licence*: **Applied Mathematics; Arts and Humanities; Biological and Life Sciences; Chemistry; Cultural Studies; Earth Sciences; Economics; English Studies; European Studies; International Studies; Law; Management; Mathematics and Computer Science; Physics; Political Sciences; Spanish; Sports.** *Licence professionnelle*: **Banking; Building Technologies; Business and Commerce; Construction Engineering; Environmental Studies; Finance; Hotel Management; Human Resources; Insurance; Landscape Architecture; Management; Marketing; Natural Sciences; Social and Community Services; Social Work; Technology.** *Diplôme d'Etat*: **Medicine; Midwifery.** *Diplôme d'Ingénieur*: **Computer Engineering; Engineering; Mechanical Engineering.** *Master*: **Administrative Law; Agronomy; Applied Mathematics; Archiving; Automation and Control Engineering; Biological and Life Sciences; Business and Commerce; Chemistry; Communication Studies; Cultural Studies; Earth Sciences; Economics; Electrical and Electronic Engineering; Energy Engineering; English Studies; Environmental Studies; European Union Law; Health Sciences; History; Human Resources; International Law; Law; Management; Mathematics and Computer Science; Mechanical Engineering; Musicology; Nutrition; Pharmacy; Physics; Political Sciences; Public Health; Social Sciences; Sociology; Spanish; Sports Medicine; Teacher Training; Tourism; Transport and Communications.** *Doctorat*: **Anthropology; Architecture and Planning; Astronomy and Space Science; Astrophysics; Biological and Life Sciences; Chemistry; Economics; Engineering; Environmental Studies; Genetics; Geography; History; Law; Management; Mathematics and Computer Science; Modern Languages; Physics; Political Sciences; Public Health; Sociology.** Several Diplômes universitaires in Medicine. Preparation for CAPES, Agrégation, Administrative and Judicial exams

Student Services: Academic Counselling, Canteen, Cultural Activities, Facilities for disabled people, Health Services, Library, Residential Facilities, Social Counselling, Sports Facilities

Academic Staff *2014*	**TOTAL**
FULL-TIME	**744**
Student Numbers *2014*	
All (Foreign included)	c. **20,000**
FOREIGN ONLY	**2669**

Last Updated: 10/04/15

UNIVERSITY OF WESTERN BRITTANY, BREST

Université de Bretagne Occidentale (UBO)

CS 93837, 3, rue des Archives, 29238 Cedex 3 Brest
Tel: +33(2) 98-01-60-00
Fax: +33(2) 98-01-60-01
EMail: drh@univ-brest.fr
Website: http://www.univ-brest.fr

President: Pascal Olivard (2007-)
Tel: +33(2) 98-01 -60-03 EMail: president@univ-brest.fr

Administrative Manager: Stéphane Charpentier
Tel: +33(2) 98-01-60-04
EMail: Stephane.Charpentier@univ-brest.fr; dgs@univ-brest.fr

International Relations: Nathalie Sarradin, Director Europe and International
Tel: +33(2) 98-01-82-09 EMail: nathalie.sarradin@univ-brest.fr

Unit

Arts and Humanities (Archaeology; Art History; Arts and Humanities; Ethnology; Geography; Gerontology; History; Literature; Modern Languages; Philosophy; Psychology; Social Sciences; Tourism); **Dentistry** (Dentistry); **Law, Economics and Management** (Economics; Law; Management); **Medicine and Health Sciences** (Health Sciences; Medicine); **Physical Education and Sports** (Physical Education; Sports); **Science and Technology** (Biology; Chemistry; Computer Science; Earth Sciences; Electronic Engineering; Mathematics; Modern Languages; Natural Sciences; Physics; Technology; Town Planning)

School

Food Engineerring *(ESMISAB)* (Food Technology; Microbiology); **Midwifery** (Midwifery); **Teacher Training** *(ESPE Bretagne with campuses in Brest, Quimper, Rennes, Saint-Brieuc, Vanne)* (Teacher Trainers Education; Teacher Training)

Institute

Architecture *(Géoarchitecture)* (Architecture and Planning); **Art and Culture Professions** (Art Education; Cultural Studies; Heritage Preservation); **Business Administration** (Banking; Business Administration; Finance; Management); **Computer Engineering** *(Brest)* (Computer Engineering); **Euro Actuarial Studies** *(EURIA)* (Actuarial Science); **Food Industries** *(IUP IIA, Quimper)* (Food Science); **Marine Studies** *(IUEM)* (Marine Science and Oceanography); **Mechanical and Production Engineering** (Mechanical Engineering; Production Engineering); **Physical Therapy** *(IFMK)* (Physical Therapy; Rehabilitation and Therapy); **Preparatory Administrative Studies** *(IPAG)* (Administration); **Technology** *(IUT, Quimper)* (Biology; Business Administration; Business and Commerce; Technology; Transport Management); **Technology** *(IUT Brest with 2nd site at Morlaix)* (Biology; Business Administration; Civil Engineering; Computer Engineering; Electrical Engineering; Mechanical Engineering; Production Engineering; Technology); **Telecommunications and Networks** *(Brest)* (Computer Networks; Telecommunications Engineering)

Graduate School

Health, Information-Communication, Mathematics, Matter (Analytical Chemistry; Biology; Health Sciences; Mathematics; Physics); **Human and Social Sciences** *(EDSHS)* (Celtic Languages and Studies; Cognitive Sciences; Communication Studies; Education; Ethics; Psychology; Sociology); **Languages, Literature and Societies** (Arts and Humanities; Management; Modern Languages; Social Sciences); **Marine Studies** (Marine Science and Oceanography); **Social sciences** *(EDSHOS)* (Social Sciences)

Research Centre

Rural Food Science and Production Sciences *(ISAMOR, Brest)* (Food Science)

Research Institute

Mathematics Education *(IREM)* (Mathematics Education)

Further Information: Also campuses in: Quimper, Brest, Morlaix

History: Founded 1970 under the 1968 law reforming higher education as one of two Universities replacing the former Université de Rennes, established in 1461 as University of Nantes with Colleges and Faculties in Nantes and Rennes; suppressed by the Revolution, reconstituted 1896. A State Institution enjoying academic and financial autonomy, operating under the jurisdiction of the Minister of Education and financed by the State.

Academic Year: October to June (October-December; January-March; April-June)

Admission Requirements: Secondary school certificate (baccalauréat) or equivalent, or special entrance examination

Main Language(s) of Instruction: French

Degrees and Diplomas: *Capacité en Droit*: **Law.** *Diplôme universitaire de Technologie*; *Licence*: **Archaeology; Art History; Arts and Humanities; Business Administration; Classical Languages; Economics; Geography; History; Law; Literature; Modern Languages; Philosophy; Psychology; Regional Studies; Social Sciences; Sociology.** *Licence professionnelle*: **Agronomy; Business Administration; Food Science; Industrial and Production Economics; Law; Social Sciences; Sports; Technology.** *Diplôme d'Etat*: **Dentistry; Medicine; Midwifery; Pharmacy.** *Diplôme d'Ingénieur*: **Engineering.** *Master*: **Art Management; Arts and Humanities; Business Administration; Educational Sciences; Fine Arts; Law; Management; Modern Languages; Psychology; Public Health; Publishing and Book Trade; Social Sciences; Sports; Teacher Training; Translation and Interpretation.** *Doctorat*: **Arts and Humanities; Health Sciences; Marine Science and Oceanography; Social Sciences.** *Certificat de Spécialité*: **Medicine.** Masters recherche, Masters professionnel

Student Services: Canteen, Cultural Activities, Facilities for disabled people, Health Services, Library, Residential Facilities, Sports Facilities

Student Numbers *2014*: Total 18,002

Last Updated: 11/03/15

NATIONAL ENGINEERING SCHOOL OF BREST

ÉCOLE NATIONALE D'INGÉNIEURS DE BREST (ENIB)

Technopôle Brest-Iroise, CS 73862, 29238 Brest, Cedex 3
Tel: +33(2) 98-05-66-00
Fax: +33(2) 98-05-6-10
EMail: contact@enib.fr
Website: http://www.enib.fr/index.php/fr

Director: Romuald Boné EMail: international@enib.fr

Programme

Engineering (Computer Engineering; Electronic Engineering; Mechanical Engineering)

History: Founded 1961.

Admission Requirements: interview and secondary school examniation (Baccalauréat)

Main Language(s) of Instruction: French

Accrediting Agency: Ministry of Higher Education and Research; Commission des Titres d'ingénieur (CTI)

Degrees and Diplomas: *Diplôme d'Ingénieur*: **Engineering.** also: research masters

VALENCIENNES SCHOOL OF ART AND DESIGN

École Supérieure d'Art et de Design de Valenciennes (ESAD VALENCIENNES)

132 Avenue du Faubourg de Cambrai, 59300 Valenciennes
Tel: +33(3) 27-24-80-12
EMail: contact@esad-valenciennes.fr
Website: http://www.esad-valenciennes.fr/

Director: Alice Vergara EMail: alice.vergara@esad-valenciennes.fr

Secretary General: Marc Besancenot
EMail: marc.besancenot@esad-valenciennes.fr

Programme

Art (Engraving; Multimedia; Painting and Drawing; Photography; Sculpture; Video); **Design** (Design)

History: Founded 1782. Become Valenciennes School of Art and Design in 2011

Academic Year: September to June (September-February; February-June)

Admission Requirements: Secondary school certificate (baccalauréat) or equivalent. Entrance examination

Main Language(s) of Instruction: French

Degrees and Diplomas: Diplôme national d'arts plastique (DNAP) 3 years; Diplôme national supérieur d'expression plastique (DNSEP) a further 2 years

Last Updated: 18/03/15

VERSAILLES SCHOOL OF ARCHITECTURE

Ecole nationale supérieure d'Architecture de Versailles (ENSA-V)

5 avenue de Sceaux, BP 674, 78006 Versailles, Cedex
Tel: +33(1) 39-07-40-00
Fax: +33(1) 39-07-40-99
EMail: ensav@versailles.archi.fr
Website: http://www.versailles.archi.fr

Director: Vincent Michel EMail: vincent.michel@versailles.archi.fr

Associate Director: Amal Lahlou-Loubatières
Tel: +33(1) 39-07-40-35 EMail: amal.lahlou@versailles.archi.fr

International Relations: Pascal Hamon, In charge or International Relations
Tel: +33(1) 39-07-40-28 EMail: international@versailles.archi.fr

Programme

Architecture (Architecture)

History: Founded 1969.

Main Language(s) of Instruction: French

Accrediting Agency: Ministère de la Culture et de la Communication

Degrees and Diplomas: *Licence*: **Architecture.** *Master*: **Architecture.** *Doctorat*: **Architecture.** Habilitation à exercer la maîtrise d'oeuvre en son nom propre (HMONP)

Last Updated: 11/03/15

VETAGRO SUP SCHOOL

VetAgro Sup

1 avenue Bourgelat, 69280 Marcy l'Etoile
Tel: +33(4) 78-87-25-25
Fax: +33(4) 78-87-25-48
EMail: communication@vetagro-sup.fr
Website: http://www.vetagro-sup.fr

Director General: Stéphane Martinot (2009-2014)
Tel: +33(4) 78-87-25-00 EMail: direction@vetagro-sup.fr

International Relations: Gabriella Sonohat-Sinoquet
EMail: international@vetagro-sup.fr

School

Veterinary Services (Veterinary Science)

Campus

Agronomy *(Clermont)* (Agricultural Engineering; Biology; Environmental Studies; Food Science; Nutrition; Rural Planning); **Veterinary Medicine** (Animal Husbandry; Microbiology; Pathology; Physiology; Veterinary Science)

History: Founded 2010 following merger of the École nationale vétérinaire de Lyon, the École nationale d'ingénieurs des travaux agricoles de Clermont-Ferrand and the École nationale des services vétérinaires. Veterinary campus founded 1762.

Academic Year: September to June

Admission Requirements: Competitive entrance examination following 2-3 years further study after secondary school certificate (baccalauréat) or following first university qualification (DEUG, DUT or BTS), or equivalent

Main Language(s) of Instruction: French

Degrees and Diplomas: *Licence professionnelle*; *Diplôme d'Etat*: **Veterinary Science.** *Diplôme d'Ingénieur*, *Mastère spécialisé*: **Animal Husbandry.** *Master*, *Doctorat*

Student Services: Canteen, Cultural Activities, Health Services, Sports Facilities

Last Updated: 10/04/15

PRIVATE INSTITUTIONS

ACADEMY OF WOOD SCIENCE AND TECHNOLOGY

Ecole supérieure du Bois (ESB NANTES)
BP 10605, Atlanpole, Rue Christian Pauc, 44306 Nantes, Cedex 03
Tel: +33(2) 40-18-12-12
Fax: +33(2) 40-18-12-00
EMail: direction@ecoledubois.fr
Website: http://www.ecoledubois.fr

Directeur: Arnaud Godevin EMail: direction@ecoledubois.fr

International Relations: Antoine Lebeau
Tel: +33(2) 40-18-12-12
EMail: antoine.lebeau@ecoledubois.fr

Division
Forestry (Forestry); **Wood Technology** (Wood Technology)

Further Information: Also French language courses for foreign students

History: Founded 1934 in Paris. Moved to Nantes 1994.

Admission Requirements: Competitive entrance examination following 2 yrs further study after secondary school certificate (baccalauréat) or equivalent

Fees: 4,800 per annum (Euro)

Main Language(s) of Instruction: French, English

Accrediting Agency: Commission des Titres d'Ingénieurs (CTI)

Degrees and Diplomas: *Licence professionnelle*: **Forestry.** *Diplôme d'Ingénieur*: **Forestry; Wood Technology.** *Master*: **Teacher Training.**

Student Services: Academic Counselling, Canteen, Careers Guidance, Facilities for disabled people, Language Laboratory, Social Counselling

Publications: Research publications

Last Updated: 20/03/15

ANGERS SCHOOL OF COMPUTER AND PRODUCTION ENGINEERING

Ecole supérieure angevine d'Informatique et de Productique (ESAIP)
BP 80022, 18, rue du 8 Mai 1945, 49180 Saint Barthélémy d'Anjou, Cedex
Tel: +33(2) 41-96-65-10
Fax: +33(2) 41-96-65-11
EMail: info@esaip.org
Website: http://www.esaip.org/

Director: Christophe Rouvrais

Department
IT and Networks (Computer Science; Environmental Engineering; Safety Engineering); **Safety and Risk Management** (Safety Engineering)

Further Information: Other campuses in Grasse, Rennes, Nantes, Dijon, La Roche sur Yon, Lyon and Toulouse

History: Founded 1988.

Admission Requirements: Baccalauréat or 2 yrs of university studies in science and technology and entrance exam and jury selection.

Main Language(s) of Instruction: French, English, German, Spanish, Italian

Accrediting Agency: Commission des Titres d'Ingénieurs

Degrees and Diplomas: *Diplôme d'Ingénieur*: **Computer Networks; Environmental Engineering; Information Technology; Insurance.** International Master in Computer Science (5 yrs)

Student Services: Academic Counselling, Careers Guidance, Facilities for disabled people, Foreign Studies Centre, Language Laboratory, Sports Facilities

Student Numbers *2014*: Total 450

Last Updated: 17/03/15

AUDENCIA NANTES SCHOOL OF MANAGEMENT

Audencia Group (AUDENCIA-NANTES)
BP 31222, 8, route de la Jonelière, 44312 Nantes, Cedex 3
Tel: +33(2) 40-37-34-34
Fax: +33(2) 40-37-34-07
Website: http://www.audencia.com

Directeur général: Christophe Germain (2016-)
EMail: cgermain@audencia.com

International Relations: Desi Schmitt
Tel: +33(2) 40-37-46-37
EMail: dschmitt@audencia.com; international@audencia.com

School
Commerce *(Atlantique)* (Business and Commerce; Marketing); **Communication and Media** *(Sciences Com)* (Communication Studies; Journalism; Media Studies); **Management** (Business Administration; Business and Commerce; Management; Sales Techniques)

Further Information: Also Summer School for foreign students

History: Founded 1900 as l'École Supérieure de Commerce de Nantes. Acquired present title 2011 following merger of Audencia Nantes, the Ecole atlantique de Commerce and Sciences Com.

Academic Year: September to June (September-December; January-March; March-June)

Admission Requirements: Competitive entrance examination following 1-2 yrs further study after secondary school certificate (baccalauréat) or following first 3-yr university qualification (Licence or Maîtrise), or equivalent

Fees: Management diploma course, 5,183 per annum; Master 9,147 (Euro)

Main Language(s) of Instruction: French, English (Summer School)

Degrees and Diplomas: *Diplôme d'Etudes d'Ecole de Commerce et Gestion*: **Management.** *Master*: **Agricultural Business; Agricultural Management; Engineering Management; International Business; Management.** Also Mastères, MBA

Student Services: Academic Counselling, Canteen, Careers Guidance, Cultural Activities, Facilities for disabled people, Health Services, Social Counselling, Sports Facilities

Last Updated: 11/03/15

BUSINESS MANAGEMENT SCHOOL

Institut de Formation aux Affaires et à la Gestion (IFAG)
61 bis rue des Peupliers, 92 100 Boulogne Billancourt
Tel: +33(1) 46-59-20-76
EMail: paris@ifag.com
Website: http://www.ifag.com

Director: Dominique Lemaire

Programme
Management (Business Administration; International Business; Management; Marketing)

Further Information: Also schools in: Paris, Lyon, Toulouse, Montluçon, Auxerre, Angers, Nîmes and Caen

History: Founded in 1986.

Admission Requirements: Secondary school certificate (Baccalauréat) and entrance exam

Fees: Bachelor: 5700-7060; Master 7200-7690 (Euro)

Main Language(s) of Instruction: French, English

Degrees and Diplomas: *Master*: **Business Administration.** Also MSc International Business & Management

Last Updated: 26/03/15

BUSINESS SCHOOL - SUP DE CO COMPIÈGNE

Ecole supérieure de Commerce de Compiègne (ESC COMPIEGNE)
32 rue Hippolyte Bottier, 60200 Compiègne
Tel: +33(3) 44-38-55-00
EMail: contact@esc-compiegne.com
Website: http://www.esc-compiegne.com

Directrice: Odile Gonzalez de Peredo

Department

Economics (Economics); **Finance** (Finance); **Languages** (Modern Languages); **Law** (Law); **Management** (Human Resources; Management); **Marketing** (E- Business/Commerce; Marketing); **Sales Techniques** (Sales Techniques)

History: Founded 1985.

Admission Requirements: Baccalauréat or equivalent Secondary School Degree to enter Preparatory Classes (2 yr programme); National exam or ESCC entrance exam for the Second cycle programme

Main Language(s) of Instruction: French

Degrees and Diplomas: *Diplôme d'Etudes d'Ecole de Commerce et Gestion.* Licence in Business management, trade and international development in association with the CNAM Picardie

Last Updated: 19/03/15

CATHOLIC INSTITUTE OF ADVANCED STUDIES

Institut catholique d'Etudes supérieures (ICES)

17, boulevard des Belges, BP 691, 85000 La Roche-sur-Yon
Tel: +33(2) 51-46-12-13
Fax: +33(2) 51-46-15-17
Website: http://www.ices.fr

President: Éric de Labarre

International Relations: Émilie Daudin-Clavaud
EMail: edc@ices.fr

Department

Biology (Biological and Life Sciences; Biology; Biotechnology; Genetics; Molecular Biology; Pharmacology; Physiology); **History** (Ancient Civilizations; Contemporary History; History; Medieval Studies); **Languages** (Modern Languages); **Law** (Law); **Letters** (Arts and Humanities; Literature); **Mathematics** (Mathematics; Physics); **Physics and Chemistry** (Chemistry; Physics); **Political Science** (Economics; International Relations; Political Sciences)

History: Founded 1990.

Academic Year: September to June (September-December; January-June)

Admission Requirements: Secondary School Certificate (Baccalauréat) or equivalent Secondary School degree, entrance exams and interview.

Main Language(s) of Instruction: French, some courses in English

Degrees and Diplomas: *Licence*: **Arts and Humanities; Biology; History; Law; Mathematics; Modern Languages; Physics; Political Sciences.** *Master*: **History; International Relations; Law; Political Sciences.**

Student Services: Academic Counselling, Facilities for disabled people, Foreign Studies Centre, Language Laboratory, Social Counselling, Sports Facilities

Publishing house: Les Presses universitaires de l'ICES

Last Updated: 25/03/15

CATHOLIC INSTITUTE OF TOULOUSE

Institut catholique de Toulouse

BP 7012, 31, rue de la Fonderie, 31068 Toulouse, Cedex 7
Tel: +33(5) 61-36-81-00
EMail: dircabrectorat@ict-toulouse.fr
Website: http://www.ict-toulouse.fr

Rector: Luc-Thomas Somme (2004-) Tel: +33(5) 61-36-81-27

International Relations: Annie Despatureaux
EMail: ri@ict-toulouse.asso.fr

Faculty

Arts and Humanities (Arts and Humanities; Communication Studies; History; Literature; Modern Languages; Psychology); **Canon Law** (Canon Law); **Law** (Law); **Philosophy** (Philosophy); **Theology** (Theology)

College

Occitan Studies *(by correspondence)* (Regional Studies)

School

Agriculture *(ESAP, Purpan)* (Agriculture); **Journalism** *(EJT)* (Journalism)

Institute

Communication *(ISCAM)* (Communication Studies; Multimedia); **French Studies for Foreigners** *(IULCF)* (French; French Studies); **Preschool and Health Education** *(IFRASS)* (Health Education; Preschool Education; Special Education); **Religions and Pastoral Studies** *(IERP)* (Pastoral Studies; Religion); **Religious Art and Sacred Music** *(IAMS)* (Religious Art; Religious Music); **Religious Training** *(AFP)* (Religious Education; Religious Studies); **Sciences and Theology of Religions** *(ISTR)* (Religious Studies; Theology); **Teacher Training** *(ISFEC)* (Teacher Training)

Centre

African Studies *(CEA)* (African Studies); **Hygiene and Social Studies** *(CEPRESS)* (Social Sciences); **Religious Training** *(AFP)* (Religious Education); **Teacher Training** *(CFP)* (Teacher Training)

Further Information: Has sites in Bayonne, Bordeaux, Perpignan and Rodez.

History: Founded 1877 but traces its history to the original University of Toulouse founded 1229.

Admission Requirements: Secondary school certificate (baccalauréat) or equivalent; competitive examination for certain schools

Main Language(s) of Instruction: French

Degrees and Diplomas: *Licence*: **Theology.** *Master*; *Doctorat*: **Theology.** Under French law Catholic institutions are not entitled to award official degrees and diplomas. Students prepare for State degrees and diplomas at the same time. However, the Faculties of Theology, Canon Law, and Philosophy award a Baccalauréat canonique, Licence canonique and Doctorat canonique and the various schools award their own diplomas

Publications: Bulletin de Littérature Ecclésiastique; Les Cahiers de l'ISTR; Les Cahiers de la Faculté de Théologie; Recherches philosophiques

Last Updated: 01/04/15

CATHOLIC UNIVERSITY OF LILLE

Université catholique de Lille

CS 4019, 60, boulevard Vauban, 59016 Lille, Cedex
Tel: +33(3) 20-13-40-00
EMail: saio@univ-catholille.fr
Website: http://www.univ-catholille.fr/

President-Rector: Pierre Giorgini (2012-)

Head of Administration: Jean-Marc Assié

International Relations: Anne-Marie Michel
Tel: +33(3) 3-59-56-69-98
EMail: international@univ-catholille.fr;
anne-marie.michel@univ-catholille.fr

Faculty

Arts and Humanities (Arts and Humanities; Communication Studies; Cultural Studies; History; Literature; Marketing; Media Studies; Modern Languages; Psychology; Social Sciences); **Law** (Commercial Law; Criminal Law; Law; Private Law; Public Law); **Management, Economics, and Science** (Economics; Finance; Management; Natural Sciences); **Medicine** (Health Sciences; Medicine; Midwifery); **Theology** (Theology)

School

Applied Sciences *(ESPAS)* (Applied Chemistry; Applied Mathematics; Applied Physics; Natural Sciences); **Business Management** *(ESPEME Nice)* (Accountancy; Finance; Law; Management; Marketing); **Business Management** *(ESPEME Lille)* (Accountancy; Finance; Law; Marketing); **Commercial Studies** *(EDHEC)* (Business and Commerce); **Industrial Studies** *(HEI)* (Industrial Management); **International Business** *(ESTICE)* (Business Administration); **Management** *(IÉSEG (Lille and Paris La Défense))* (Accountancy; Finance; Management; Marketing); **Political and Social Sciences** *(ESPOL (European School of Political and Social Sciences))* (Political Sciences; Social Sciences)

Department

Ethics (Ethics)

Institute

Agricultural Studies *(ISA)* (Agriculture); **Catechism** *(IiFAC)* (Religious Education); **Civil and Mechanical Engineering** *(ICAM)* (Civil Engineering; Mechanical Engineering); **Electronics** *(ISEN)* (Electronic Engineering); **Medical Communication**; **Nursing and Child Welfare** *(IFSanté)* (Child Care and Development; Nursing); **Physiotherapy and Chiropody** (Chiropractic; Physical Therapy); **Scientific Economics and Management** *(IESEG)* (Economics; Management); **Social Work** *(ISL)* (Social Work); **Strategy and Communication Techniques** *(ISTC)* (Communication Studies); **Teacher Training** *(IFP Lille/Arras)* (Primary Education; Teacher Training)

Research Laboratory

Economics and Social Sciences *(LEM)* (Economics; Social Sciences); **Medicine** (Medicine); **Science** (Natural Sciences)

Further Information: Also French courses for foreign students

History: Founded 1875 as a Catholic Faculty of Law; Letters and Science added 1876; Medicine and Pharmacy, and Theology added 1877. Reorganised and acquired present title 1974. In civil matters the Institution is subject to the jurisdiction of the Ministry of Education.

Admission Requirements: Secondary school certificate (baccalauréat) or recognized foreign equivalent, and entrance examination

Main Language(s) of Instruction: French

Degrees and Diplomas: *Licence*; *Diplôme d'Etat*: **Medicine; Midwifery; Nursing; Physical Therapy; Podiatry; Social Work.** *Diplôme d'Etudes d'Ecole de Commerce et Gestion*: **Business Administration.** *Diplôme d'Ingénieur*: **Agricultural Engineering; Electronic Engineering; Engineering; Environmental Engineering; Landscape Architecture; Textile Technology.** *Master*, *Doctorat*: **Theology.**

Student Services: Academic Counselling, Canteen, Cultural Activities, Facilities for disabled people, Foreign Studies Centre, Health Services, Language Laboratory, Nursery Care, Social Counselling, Sports Facilities

Publications: Catho-International; Encyclopédie catholicisme; Journal des Sciences médicales; Mélanges de Science Religieuse; Mémoires et Travaux (63 vols); Vie et Foi

Last Updated: 07/04/15

CATHOLIC UNIVERSITY OF LYON

Université catholique de Lyon (UCLY)

25, rue du Plat, 69288 Lyon, Cedex 2

Tel: +33(4) 72-32-50-12

EMail: riucl@univ-catholyon.fr

Website: http://www.univ-catholyon.fr

Rector: Thierry Magnin (2011-)

Secretary General: Claudine Dargent

International Relations: Franck Violet, Head of International Relations Tel: +33(4) 72 -32-50-79 EMail: riucl@univ-catholyon.fr

Faculty

Law, Economics, and Social Sciences *(FDSES)* (Development Studies; Economics; Family Studies; Human Rights; Law; Management; Social Sciences); **Letters and Languages** (Arts and Humanities; French; Modern Languages; Regional Studies; Translation and Interpretation); **Philosophy and Human Sciences** (Educational and Student Counselling; Philosophy; Psychology); **Science** (Biochemistry; Biology; Biotechnology; Health Education; Laboratory Techniques; Natural Sciences); **Theology and Religious Studies** (Judaic Religious Studies; Pastoral Studies; Religious Studies; Theology)

History: Founded 1875.

Admission Requirements: Secondary school certificate (baccalauréat) or recognized foreign equivalent

Main Language(s) of Instruction: French

Degrees and Diplomas: *Licence*: **Fine Arts; Law; Philosophy; Psychology.** *Master*: **Canon Law; Philosophy; Theology.** *Doctorat*: **Philosophy; Theology.**

Student Services: Canteen, Language Laboratory, Sports Facilities

Publications: Cahiers

Last Updated: 01/04/15

CATHOLIC UNIVERSITY OF PARIS

Institut catholique de Paris

21, rue d'Assas, 75270 Paris, Cedex 06

Tel: +33(1) 44-39-52-00

Fax: +33(1) 42-39-52-90

Website: http://www.icp.fr

Rector: Philippe Bordeyne (2011-)

International Relations: Hugues Boiteau
Tel: +33(1) 70-64-14-42

Faculty

Canon Law (Canon Law); **Economics and Social Sciences** *(FASSE)* (Economics; Social Sciences); **Education** *(ISP)* (Education); **Letters** (Arts and Humanities); **Philosophy** (Philosophy); **Theology** *(FTSR)* (Religious Studies; Theology)

School

Library Science *(EBD)* (Library Science); **Psycho-pedagogical Training** *(EFPP)* (Education; Psychology); **Psychology** *(EPP)* (Psychology)

Institute

French Language and Culture *(ILCF, for foreign students)* (Cultural Studies; French); **Physical Education** *(ILEPS)* (Physical Education); **Religious Studies** *(IER)* (Religious Studies)

History: Founded 1875.

Academic Year: September to July (September-January; January-June)

Admission Requirements: Secondary school certificate (baccalauréat) or recognized equivalent

Main Language(s) of Instruction: French

Degrees and Diplomas: *Licence*: **Arts and Humanities; Educational Sciences; Modern Languages; Religion; Social Sciences.** *Master*: **Philology; Philosophy; Social Sciences; Theology.** *Doctorat*: **Educational Sciences; Philology; Philosophy; Theology.** Under French law, Catholic Institutions are not entitled to award official degrees and diplomas. Students prepare for State degrees and diplomas at the same time. The Faculties of Theology, Canon Law, and Philosophy award a Baccalauréat canonique, Licence canonique and Doctorat canonique recognized by the Holy See, and the various institutes and schools award their own specialised diplomas. The Faculty of Theology also awards an MBA.

Student Services: Cultural Activities, Health Services, Library, Social Counselling, Sports Facilities

Publications: Eduquer et Former; Transversalités. Revue de l'Institut Catholoique de Paris

Last Updated: 08/04/15

CATHOLIC UNIVERSITY OF THE WEST, ANGERS

Université catholique de l'Ouest (UCO)

3, place André Leroy, 49008 Angers

Tel: +33(2) 41-81-66-00

Fax: +33(2) 72-79-63-30

EMail: comm@uco.fr

Website: http://www.uco.fr

Rector: Dominique Vermersch (2012-) EMail: rectorat@uco.fr

Secretary General: Eric HOUIVET Houivet EMail: rectorat@uco.fr

International Relations: Pierrick Picot
Tel: +33(2) 41-81-67-24 EMail: pole.international@uco.fr

Faculty

Education *(Angers, Nantes)* (Education); **Human and Social Sciences** *(Angers, Guingamp and Papeete)* (Psychology; Social Sciences; Sociology); **Humanities** *(Angers)* (Arts and Humanities; Information Sciences); **Sciences** *(Angers, Guingamp, Laval, Vannes)* (Biology; Economics; Environmental Studies; Management; Mathematics and Computer Science; Natural Sciences; Sports); **Theology** (Theology)

Unit

Catholic Studies *(South Brittany)* (Christian Religious Studies); **Catholic Studies** *(North Brittany)* (Christian Religious Studies)

School
Chemistry *(ETSCO)* (Chemistry); **Commercial Sciences** *(ESSCA)* (Business and Commerce); **Computer Science and Production** *(ESAIP)*

Institute
Applied Mathematics *(IMA)* (Applied Mathematics; Computer Science); **Applied Psychology and Sociology** *(IPSA)* (Clinical Psychology; Psychology; Sociology); **Arts and Humanities** *(IALH)* (Arts and Humanities; Cultural Studies; Fine Arts; History; Literature; Music; Musicology); **Biology and Applied Ecology** *(IBEA)* (Biology; Ecology; Environmental Studies); **Communication and Educational Sciences** (Communication Studies; Education; Educational Sciences; Teacher Training); **Modern Languages** *(IPVL)* (Arabic; Chinese; Dutch; English; German; Hungarian; Italian; Japanese; Modern Languages; Portuguese; Russian; Spanish; Translation and Interpretation); **Physical Education and Sports** *(IFEPSA)* (Physical Education; Sports); **Pure Mathematics** *(DMP)* (Mathematics); **Teacher Training** *(IFUCOME)* (Teacher Training)

Centre
International French Studies (International Studies); **Lifelong Education**

Further Information: Campuses in Guingamp and Arradon

History: Founded between 1875 and 1879 when higher education institutions in France became fully secular. Reorganized 1970 following establishment of a State university in Angers.

Admission Requirements: Secondary school certificate (baccalauréat) or equivalent

Main Language(s) of Instruction: French

Degrees and Diplomas: *Licence*; *Master*; *Doctorat*: **Arts and Humanities; Education; Theology.** Under French law, Catholic faculties are not entitled to award official degrees and diplomas without State University agreement. Students prepare for State degrees and diplomas under convention with several French State Universities. Professional titles of Ingénieur are officially recognized. The University awards specific professional titles

Student Services: Careers Guidance, Cultural Activities, Facilities for disabled people, Foreign Studies Centre, Health Services, Language Laboratory, Social Counselling

Publications: Cahiers du C.R.E.O.; Impacts (revue de l'Université Catholique de l'Ouest); Les Cahiers de l'I.M.A.; Les Cahiers de l'I.P.S.A. (Institut de Psychologie); Moreana

Last Updated: 07/04/15

CENTRAL SCHOOL OF ELECTRONICS

Ecole centrale d'Electronique (ECE)

Immeuble POLLUX, 37, Quai de Grenelle, CS 71520, 75007 Paris
Tel: +33(1) 44-39-06-00
Fax: +33(1) 42-22-59-02
EMail: contact@ece.fr
Website: http://www.ece.fr

Director: Christophe Baujault (2013-) EMail: baujault@ece.fr

International Relations: Julie Pidell
Tel: +33(1) 82-53-98-90 EMail: pidell@ece.fr

Programme
Connected devices, Networks and Services (Computer Engineering; Engineering; Multimedia); **Embedded Systems** (Computer Engineering; Engineering); **Energy and Environment** (Energy Engineering; Environmental Engineering); **Financial Engineering** (Computer Engineering; Economics; Finance; Mathematics); **Health and Technology** (Biomedical Engineering; Medical Technology); **Information Systems** (Artificial Intelligence; Computer Engineering); **Transport and Mobility** (Engineering; Transport Engineering)

History: Founded 1919 as l'Ecole Centrale de TSF.

Admission Requirements: Examination Entrance

Main Language(s) of Instruction: French

Accrediting Agency: Commission des Titres d'Ingénieurs (CTI)

Degrees and Diplomas: *Diplôme d'Ingénieur*: **Engineering.** *Master*: **Engineering.**

Student Services: Canteen

Last Updated: 11/03/15

CENTRE FOR JOURNALISM STUDIES

Centre de Formation des Journalistes (CFJ)

35, rue du Louvre, 75002 Paris
Tel: +33(1) 44-82-20-00
Fax: +33(1) 44-82-20-09
Website: http://www.cfpj.com

Director: Julie Joly (2012-) EMail: jjoly@cfpj.com

Executive Assistant: Michèle Martin
EMail: mmartin@cfjparis.com

Programme
Journalism (Journalism; Modern Languages; Radio and Television Broadcasting)

Further Information: Is part of the CFPJ Groupe which also includes a Centre for Continuing Education in Journalism.

History: Founded 1946.

Academic Year: October-May

Admission Requirements: Entrance examination

Fees: 2-year Journalism course 3500 per annum. Students on special grants 1900 (Euro)

Main Language(s) of Instruction: French

Accrediting Agency: Commission Nationale Paritaire pour l'Emploi des Journalistes (CNPEJ); Ministère de l'Enseignement supérieur et de la Recherche

Degrees and Diplomas: CFJ diploma (2 yrs after degree course), Masters-level degree in Journalism (2 yrs with internship) in partnership with Université de Paris I Panthéon Sorbonne, Executive Master.

Last Updated: 11/03/15

CENTRE OF ADVANCED INDUSTRIAL STUDIES

Groupe CESI

30 rue Cambronne, 75015 Paris, Cedex
Tel: +33(1) 44-19-23-45
Fax: +33(1) 42-50-25-06
EMail: contact@cesi.fr
Website: http://www.cesi.fr/

Director General: Vincent Cohas Tel: +33(1) 44-19-23-45

Division
Continuing Education (Construction Engineering; Human Resources; Industrial Management; Information Technology; Management; Marketing; Real Estate)

School
Computer Science *(EXIA)* (Computer Science; Information Technology); **Engineering** *(EI CESI)* (Civil Engineering; Construction Engineering; Human Resources; Industrial Management; Management; Safety Engineering)

Centre
Apprenticeship Centre *(CESFA Nanterre)* (Construction Engineering); **Industrial Training in Alternance** *(CEFIPA Nanterre)* (Engineering)

Further Information: Branches in Lyon; Arras; Nantes; Toulouse; Strasbourg; Aix-en-Provence; Le Mans; Bordeaux; Grenoble; Rouen; Orléans; Nancy; CESI Iberia - Montpellier; Reims; Angoulême; Saint Nazaire; Pau; CESI Algérie; Rennes; Nice

History: Founded 1958.

Admission Requirements: Secondary school certificate and a 2 yr university diploma (DUT, BTS or equivalent), tests, interview and portfolio

Main Language(s) of Instruction: French

Accrediting Agency: Commission des Titres d'Ingénieur, Conférence des Grandes Ecoles

Degrees and Diplomas: *Diplôme d'Ingénieur*: **Construction Engineering; Electrical and Electronic Engineering; Engineering; Industrial Engineering.** *Mastère spécialisé*: **Human Resources; Industrial Management; Management.**

Last Updated: 24/03/15

CHAMPAGNE SCHOOL OF MANAGEMENT

Groupe ESC Troyes (ESC TROYES)
217, avenue Pierre Brossolette, CS 20710,
10002 Troyes, Cedex
Tel: +33(3) 25-71-22-22
EMail: infos@groupe-esc-troyes.com
Website: http://www.groupe-esc-troyes.com

Directeur: Francis Bécard
Tel: +33(3) 25-71-22-46
EMail: francis.becard@groupe-esc-troyes.com

International Relations: Jean-Louis Chaperon
Tel: +33(3) 25-71-22-39
EMail: jean.louis.chaperon@groupe-esc-troyes.com

Programme

ESC Troyes Grande Ecole (Business Administration; Finance; Human Resources; Management; Marketing)

School

Graphic Arts and Design *(ESAA)* (Design; Graphic Arts); **Management** *(International INBA)* (International Business; Management); **Tourism** *(International EMVOL)* (Management; Regional Planning; Tourism)

History: ESC Troyes founded in 1992, acquiring current title and status in 1999.

Admission Requirements: ESC Troyes 2 years undergraduate studies and entrance exam; INBA, EMVOL and ESAA high school certificate or equivalent and entrance examination

Main Language(s) of Instruction: French

Degrees and Diplomas: *Master*: **Management.** Also Bachelors, MBA and DBA

Last Updated: 08/04/15

ECAM GRADUATE SCHOOL OF ENGINEERING LYON

Ecole catholique d'Arts et Métiers (ECAM)
40, montée Saint-Barthélemy, 69321 Lyon,
Cedex 05
Tel: +33(4) 72-77-06-00
Fax: +33(4) 72-77-06-11
EMail: info@ecam.fr
Website: http://www.ecam.fr

Managing Director: Didier Desplanche (2009-)
Tel: +33(4) 72-77-06-70 EMail: gessica.paparozzi@ecam.fr

Director of Studies: Patrice Couvrat
Tel: +33(4) 72-77-06-42 EMail: direction.etudes@ecam.fr

International Relations: Edith Frey
Tel: +33(4) 72-77-06-54 EMail: edith.frey@ecam.fr

Department

Computer Engineering (Computer Engineering); **Electrical and Electronic Engineering and Automation** (Automation and Control Engineering; Electrical and Electronic Engineering); **Industrial Engineering** (Industrial Engineering); **Materials Science** (Materials Engineering); **Mechanical Engineering** (Mechanical Engineering)

Further Information: Forms the Groupe ECAM which includes ECAM Rennes- Louis de Broglie, ECAM Strasbourg and EPMI Cergy

History: Founded 1900.

Admission Requirements: Scientific high school certificate (baccalauréat S)

Fees: 1,316-2,054 per annum (1-2 yrs); 4750 (3-5 yrs) (Euro)

Main Language(s) of Instruction: French

Accrediting Agency: Commission des Titres d'Ingénieur (CTI)

Degrees and Diplomas: *Diplôme d'Ingénieur*: **Engineering.** *Mastère spécialisé*: **Management.** *Master*: **Engineering.**

Student Services: Academic Counselling, Careers Guidance, Language Laboratory, Social Counselling, Sports Facilities

Publications: Journal de l'Association des Ingénieurs ECAM; Revue des Ingénieurs ECAM/ICAM

Last Updated: 11/03/15

ECAM RENNES -LOUIS DE BROGLIE

ECAM Rennes- Louis de Broglie
Campus de Ker Lann-Bruz, 35091 Rennes, Cedex 9
Tel: +33(2) 99-05-84-00
Fax: +33(2) 99-05-84-19
EMail: contact@ecam-rennes.fr
Website: http://www.ecam-rennes.fr

Director: Jean Vimal du Monteil (2008-)
EMail: jean.vimal@ecam-rennes.fr

Department

Communications Engineering (Telecommunications Engineering); **Industrial Engineering** (Automation and Control Engineering; Energy Engineering; Industrial Engineering; Mechanical Engineering; Robotics); **Materials Engineering** (Materials Engineering); **Software Engineering and Information Technology** (Information Technology; Software Engineering)

History: Founded 1990.

Admission Requirements: Baccalauréat in Sciences or Baccalauréat and two years of higher education.

Fees: 2550-6660 per annum (Euro)

Main Language(s) of Instruction: French

Accrediting Agency: CTI (Commission des Titres d'ingénieur)

Degrees and Diplomas: *Diplôme d'Ingénieur*: **Engineering; Industrial Engineering.**

Student Services: Cultural Activities, Residential Facilities, Sports Facilities

Last Updated: 11/03/15

EDHEC BUSINESS SCHOOL

24, avenue Gustave Delory, CS 50411, 59057 Roubaix, Cedex 1
Tel: +33(3) 20-15-45-00
Fax: +33(3) 20-15-45-01
EMail: contact@edhec.edu
Website: http://www.edhec.com

Director General: Olivier Oger
Tel: +33(3) 20-15-45-07 EMail: oger.ol@edhec.edu

International Relations: Anne Zuccarelli Tel: +33(3) 20-15-44-54

Programme

Commerce (Business and Commerce; Finance; Management)

Further Information: Also campus in Nice, Paris, London, Singapore.

History: Founded 1906. A private 'Grande Ecole'.

Admission Requirements: Competitive entrance examination following 2 yrs further study after secondary school certificate (baccalauréat) or following first university qualification (DEUG, DUT), or equivalent

Main Language(s) of Instruction: French

Degrees and Diplomas: *Mastère spécialisé*; *Master*: **Accountancy; Business Administration; Finance; Management.** *Doctorat*: **Finance.** Also Bachelor

Student Services: Library, Residential Facilities, Sports Facilities

Student Numbers *2014*: Total 6,200

Last Updated: 23/03/15

EFAP, SCHOOL OF COMMUNICATION PROFESSIONALS

EFAP, Ecole des Métiers de la Communication
61, rue Pierre-Charron, 75008 Paris
Tel: +33(1) 53-76-88-00
EMail: paris@efap.com
Website: http://www.efap.com

Directeur général: Serge Le Strat

International Relations: Sophie-Caroline De Koning
Tel: +33(1) 53-76-88-37 EMail: international@groupe-edh.com

Programme

Public Relations (Communication Studies; Marketing; Media Studies; Public Relations)

Further Information: Has schools in Paris, Bordeaux, Lille and Lyon. Also in New York, Lisbon, Tokyo, Abidjan and Algiers

History: Founded in 1961, acquiring its present status in 1993.

Academic Year: September to following October for Masters

Admission Requirements: Baccalauréat or equivalent Secondary School Degree for Undergraduate Studies

Fees: 7 650 (Euro)

Main Language(s) of Instruction: French, English

Degrees and Diplomas: *Master*: **Communication Arts; Environmental Studies; Management; Marketing; Media Studies.** Diplôme d'Université

Student Numbers *2013*: Total 2,300

Last Updated: 20/03/15

EIGSI LA ROCHELLE ENGINEERING SCHOOL

Ecole d'Ingénieurs généralistes La Rochelle (EIGSI)

26, rue Vaux de Foletier, 17041 La Rochelle, Cedex 1
Tel: +33(5) 46-45-80-00
Fax: +33(5) 46-45-80-10
EMail: communication@eigsi.fr
Website: http://www.eigsi.fr

Managing Director: Sylvain Orsat (2002-)
Tel: +33(5) 46-45-80-01 EMail: direction-generale@eigsi.fr

International Relations: Hannelore Guerrand
Tel: +33(5) 46-45-80-09 EMail: international@eigsi.fr

Programme

General Engineering (Engineering); **Industrial Engineering** (Engineering Management; Industrial Engineering)

Further Information: Also branch in Casablanca

History: Founded 1901as École d'Électricité et de Mécanique Industrielle (EEMI). Acquired present status and title 1990.

Admission Requirements: Baccalauréat S or STI

Fees: 6290 per annum (Euro)

Main Language(s) of Instruction: French

Accrediting Agency: CTI (Ministry of Education)

Degrees and Diplomas: *Diplôme d'Ingénieur*: **Computer Engineering; Construction Engineering; Energy Engineering; Engineering; Engineering Management; Environmental Engineering; Industrial Engineering; Mechanical Engineering; Transport Engineering.** 3ème Cycle Management Industriel

Student Services: Canteen, Cultural Activities, Library, Residential Facilities, Sports Facilities

Last Updated: 11/03/15

EM LYON BUSINESS SCHOOL

Ecole de Management de Lyon (EM LYON)

23, avenue Guy de Collongue, CS 40203, 69134 Ecully, Cedex
Tel: +33(4) 78-33-78-00
Fax: +33(4) 78-33-61-69
Website: http://www.em-lyon.com

Director General: Bernard Belletante (2014-)
EMail: belletante@em-lyon.com

International Relations: Damien Roux
Tel: +33(4) 78-33-78-29 EMail: roux@em-lyon.com

Programme

Bachelor in Business Administration *(The first 2 years of the BBA program take place on the campus of Saint Etienne (ex ESC Saint-Etienne))* (Business Administration)

Department

Economics, Finance and Control (Accountancy; Economics; Finance; Management); **Management, Law and Human Resources** (Human Resources; Law; Leadership; Management); **Markets and Innovation** (Business Administration; Management; Marketing); **Strategy and Organisation** (Business Administration)

Graduate School

Business Administration and Management (Business Administration; Finance; International Business; Management; Marketing)

Research Centre

Management (Management)

Further Information: Campuses in Shanghai and Saint-Etienne

History: Founded 1872. Included ESC Saint-Etienne in 2014.

Academic Year: September to June

Admission Requirements: Competitive entrance examination. Secondary school certificate and 2 yrs preparatory classes in Business and Commerce or Literature, or first university degree

Main Language(s) of Instruction: French, English

Degrees and Diplomas: *Mastère spécialisé*: **Finance; International Business; Management; Marketing; Technology.** *Master*: **Business Administration; Management; Marketing; Sports Management.** *Doctorat*: **Business Administration; International Business; Management.** Also: Bachelor, MBA

Student Services: Academic Counselling, Canteen, Careers Guidance, Cultural Activities, Health Services, Social Counselling, Sports Facilities

Last Updated: 20/03/15

ESA GROUP - GRADUATE SCHOOL OF FOOD, AGRONOMY AND AGRIBUSINESS, ANGERS

Groupe Ecole supérieure d'Agriculture d'Angers (ESA)

55, rue Rabelais, BP 30748, 49007 Angers, Cedex 01
Tel: +33(2) 41-23-55-55
Fax: +33(2) 41-23-55-45
EMail: info-orientation@groupe-esa.com
Website: http://www.groupe-esa.com

Directeur général: Patrick Vincent

International Relations: Stéphane Brochier, Head of International Relations EMail: s.brochier@groupe-esa.com

Programme

Adult Continuing Education (Agriculture; Business and Commerce; Horticulture)

Department

Agronomy and Ecology (Agriculture; Agronomy; Biology; Crop Production; Ecology; Plant and Crop Protection); **Animal Production** (Animal Husbandry; Cattle Breeding; Meat and Poultry); **Basic Science and Methods** (Computer Science; Information Sciences; Statistics); **Business Management** (Agricultural Business; Business Administration; Business and Commerce; Management; Marketing); **Cultures, Languages and Communication** (Communication Studies; Information Sciences; Management; Modern Languages; Multimedia; Pedagogy); **Economics and Social Sciences** (Agricultural Business; Business and Commerce; Development Studies; Economics); **Environment, Plants and Landscape** (Biology; Ecology; Environmental Management; Environmental Studies; Geology; Landscape Architecture); **Food, Bioresources Science and Techniques** (Agricultural Business; Biochemistry; Chemistry; Food Science; Mechanics; Microbiology; Nutrition; Optics); **Viticulture and Oenology** (Oenology; Viticulture)

Laboratory

Plant Eco-physiology and Agro-ecology (Agriculture; Ecology; Plant and Crop Protection); **Social Sciences** *(LARESS)*

Graduate School

Graduate School

Research Group

Agro-industries specializing in Products and Processes (Agricultural Business)

Higher Vocational School

Agritec (Agricultural Business; Agriculture; Farm Management; Horticulture)

History: Founded 1898. Acquired present status 2004. Became a non-profit organization 1970.

Academic Year: September to June

Admission Requirements: Competitive entrance examination after secondary school certificate (baccalauréat). Foreign students integrate ESA with a Bachelor or Master of Science (or equivalent). Selection on C.V, university marks and referees' recommendation and interview. Good knowledge of English and French

Main Language(s) of Instruction: French, English

Accrediting Agency: Ministry of Agriculture; Ministry of Education

Degrees and Diplomas: *Brevet de Technicien supérieur*: **Agriculture; Business and Commerce; Horticulture.** *Licence professionnelle*: **Crop Production; Management.** *Diplôme d'Ingénieur*: **Agricultural Business; Agriculture; Economic and Finance Policy; Environmental Studies; Social Sciences.** *Mastère spécialisé*: **Environmental Studies.** *Master*: **Agriculture; Botany; Horticulture; Oenology.** Agricadre Diploma, Management and Trade 2 years (Diploma level: 4 years of higher education); BSc Honours -European Engineer Degree (EED) in Biotechnology, Seeds and Horticulture or Animal Husbandry or International Agribusiness, 1 1/2 year; Master of Science 2 years

Student Services: Academic Counselling, Canteen, Careers Guidance, Cultural Activities, Facilities for disabled people, Foreign Studies Centre, Health Services, Language Laboratory, Nursery Care, Social Counselling, Sports Facilities

Publications: Mag'ESA

Publishing House: None

Last Updated: 24/03/15

ESC PAU

Groupe ESC Pau

3, rue Saint John Perse, 64000 Pau
Tel: +33(5) 59-92-64-64
Fax: +33(5) 59-92-64-55
EMail: info@esc-pau.fr
Website: http://www.esc-pau.fr

Director: Stéphane Platt (2014-) EMail: stephen.platt@esc-pau.fr

International Relations: Véronique Boulloud, International Coordinator
Tel: +33(5) 59-92-64-43 EMail: veronique.boulloud@esc-pau.fr

Department

Finance and Economics (Accountancy; Economics; Finance); **Management** (Human Resources; Management); **Marketing** (Business and Commerce; Marketing)

History: Founded 1969.

Admission Requirements: Competitive entrance examination following 2 yrs further study after secondary school certificate (baccalauréat) or equivalent

Accrediting Agency: Ministry of Higher Education and Research

Degrees and Diplomas: *Diplôme d'Etudes d'Ecole de Commerce et Gestion*; *Mastère spécialisé*: **Accountancy.** *Master*: **Business Administration.**

Last Updated: 24/03/15

ESC RENNES BUSINESS SCHOOL

2, rue Robert d'Abrissel, CS 76522, 35065 Rennes
Tel: +33(2) 99-54-63-63
Fax: +33(2) 99-33-08-24
Website: http://www.esc-rennes.fr

Director Genral-Dean: Olivier Aptel (2001-)
EMail: olivier.aptel@esc-rennes.fr

International Relations: Cathy Racault, Head for International Development EMail: cathy.racault@esc-rennes.com

Division

Finance and Operations (Finance); **Management and Organization** (Management); **Strategy and Marketing** (Marketing; Sales Techniques)

Further Information: Also campus in Rabat

History: Founded 1990 by a group of company managers to train global managers.

Academic Year: September to June

Admission Requirements: Bachelor degree with or without work experience and good level of English (TOEFL: 213 and computer based).

Main Language(s) of Instruction: English

Accrediting Agency: Ministry of Higher Education (France); Open University (UK); European Foundation for Management Development (EFMD); EPAS

Degrees and Diplomas: *Master*: **Finance; Human Resources; International Business; Management.** *Doctorat*: **Management.** Bachelor Degree (IBPM) Master Programme Grande Ecole; Master of Arts in International Business; Executive MBA; PhD

Student Services: Academic Counselling, Canteen, Careers Guidance, Foreign Studies Centre, Health Services, Language Laboratory, Social Counselling, Sports Facilities

Last Updated: 23/03/15

ESCEM BUSINESS SCHOOL AND MANAGEMENT - POITIERS

Ecole supérieure de Commerce et de Management Paris-Tours-Poitiers (ESCEM)

11, rue de l'Ancienne Comédie, CS 20005, 86001 Poitiers
Tel: +33(5) 49-60-58-00
EMail: info@escem.fr
Website: http://www.escem.fr

President: David Cottereau

International Relations: Helena Ferreira, Head of International Office EMail: hferreira@escem.fr

Programme

Marketing and Management (International Business; Management; Marketing)

Further Information: Also campuses in Prague and Athens, Orleans and Tours

History: Founded 1961, merged 1998 with ESCEM Tours, acquired present status and title same year.

Academic Year: September to May

Admission Requirements: National competitive entrance examination, secondary school certificate (baccalauréat) or following first university qualification

Fees: 4,700 - 5,850 per annum (Euro)

Main Language(s) of Instruction: French, English

Degrees and Diplomas: *Diplôme d'Etudes d'Ecole de Commerce et Gestion*: **International Business; Management; Marketing.** *Mastère spécialisé*: **Management.** Also Bachelor

Student Services: Academic Counselling, Canteen, Careers Guidance, Facilities for disabled people, Language Laboratory, Sports Facilities

Last Updated: 19/03/15

ESCP-EUROPE - PARIS (ESCP-EAP)

79, avenue de la République, 75543 Paris, Cedex 11
Tel: +33(1) 49-23-20-00
Fax: +33(1) 43-55-99-63
EMail: info.fr@escpeurope.eu
Website: http://www.escp-eap.eu/campus/paris/

Director: Bruno Poirel EMail: bpoirel@escpeurope.eu

Secretary General: Hervé Dufoort (2014-)
Tel: +33(1) 49-23-21-75 EMail: hdufoort@escpeurope.eu

International Relations: Léon Laulusa, Head of International Relations Tel: +33(1) 49-23-22-36 EMail: llaulusa@escpeurope.eu

Programme

Business Administration *(MBA programmes)* (Finance; Management; Marketing); **Executive Education**; **Postgraduate Studies** (Management)

Further Information: Also branches in London, Madrid, Berlin and Turin

History: Founded 1819. Previously known as ESCP-EAP European School of Management. Acquired current name 2009.

Academic Year: September to July

Admission Requirements: First university degree or equivalent (BSc)

Main Language(s) of Instruction: French

Accrediting Agency: European Advisory Council

Degrees and Diplomas: *Diplôme d'Etudes d'Ecole de Commerce et Gestion*: **Business and Commerce; Management.** *Mastère spécialisé*; *Master*: **Business Administration; European Studies;**

Management. *Doctorat*: **Business Administration; Economics; Management; Marketing.**

Student Services: Academic Counselling, Canteen, Careers Guidance, Facilities for disabled people, Health Services, Social Counselling, Sports Facilities

Publications: ESCP-EAP News; ESCP-EAP Sector News; European Management Journal; International Journal of Cross-Cultural Management

Last Updated: 23/03/15

ESEO - ANGERS

Ecole supérieure d'Electronique de l'Ouest (ESEO)

10 Bd Jeanneteau - CS 90717, 49107 Angers, Cedex 2
Tel: +33(2) 41-86-67-67
Fax: +33(2) 41-87-99-27
EMail: information@eseo.fr
Website: http://www.eseo.fr

Director General: Olivier Paillet (2013-)
EMail: olivier.paillet@eseo.fr

International Relations: Pierre-Yves Paques
EMail: pierre-yves.paques@eseo.fr

Programme

Engineering and Mathematics (Automation and Control Engineering; Biomedical Engineering; Computer Engineering; Data Processing; Electronic Engineering; Mathematics; Telecommunications Engineering); **Management and Modern Languages** (Management; Modern Languages)

Further Information: Also campuses in Paris, Dijon and Shanghai.

History: Founded 1956.

Academic Year: September to June

Admission Requirements: Competitive entrance examination following 2-3 yrs further study after secondary school certificate (baccalauréat) or following first university qualification (DEUG, DUT or BTS), or equivalent

Fees: Engineering course: 7210 per annum (Euro)

Main Language(s) of Instruction: French

Accrediting Agency: Commission des Titres d'Ingénieur (CTI)

Degrees and Diplomas: *Diplôme d'Ingénieur*: **Engineering.** Also joint degrees

Student Services: Academic Counselling, Careers Guidance, Cultural Activities, Facilities for disabled people, Health Services, Social Counselling, Sports Facilities

Last Updated: 18/03/15

ESIEA

Ecole supérieure d'Informatique, Electronique et Automatique (ESIEA)

9, rue Vésale, 75005 Paris
Tel: +33(1) 55-43-23-23
EMail: accueil@esiea.fr; contact@esiea.fr
Website: http://www.esiea.fr

Director General: Philippe Volle

International Relations: Susan Loubet
Tel: +33(2) 43-59-46-11 EMail: loubet@esiea-ouest.fr

Division

Computer Engineering (Computer Engineering); **Control Engineering and Automation** (Automation and Control Engineering); **Electronic Engineering** *(ESIEA Ouest, Laval)* (Electronic Engineering); **Electronic Engineering** (Electronic Engineering)

Further Information: Also campus in Laval

History: Founded 1958 by Maurice Lafargue, became property of the Association des anciens Elèves et des Amis de l'ESIEA 1975; diplomas officially recognized 1985.

Academic Year: September to June

Admission Requirements: Competitive entrance examination after secondary school certificate (baccalauréat) or following 2-3 years further study after secondary school certifictae or first university qualification (DEUG, DUT or BTS), or equivalent

Fees: 5,600-6,760 (Euro)

Main Language(s) of Instruction: French

Accrediting Agency: Commission des Titres d'Ingénieur (CTI)

Degrees and Diplomas: *Diplôme d'Ingénieur*: **Engineering.** *Mastère spécialisé*: **Computer Networks; Information Management; Information Sciences.** *Master*

Student Services: Academic Counselling, Canteen, Careers Guidance, Language Laboratory

Last Updated: 30/03/15

ESIEE AMIENS

ESIEE-Amiens

14 Quai de la Somme, BP 10100, 80082 Amiens, Cedex 2
Tel: +33(3) 22-66-20-00
Fax: +33(3) 22-66-20-10
Website: http://www.esiee-amiens.fr

Director General: Jérôme Fortin EMail: fortin@esiee-amiens.fr

International Relations: Laurent Baroux
EMail: baroux@esiee-amiens.fr

Programme

Engineering (Electrical Engineering; Energy Engineering; Engineering; Production Engineering; Telecommunications Engineering)

Admission Requirements: Entrance exam after a secondary school degree in Science or 1st university studies in Science. Compettitve entrance exam or Jury selection

Main Language(s) of Instruction: French

Accrediting Agency: Commission des Titres d'Ingénieur, Ministry of Industry

Degrees and Diplomas: *Diplôme d'Ingénieur*: **Electronic Engineering; Engineering.**

Last Updated: 23/03/15

ESIEE PARIS

2 boulevard Blaise Pascal, Cité Descartes, BP 99, 93162 Noisy-le-Grand, Cedex
Tel: +33(1) 45-92-65-00
Fax: +33(1) 45-92-66-99
Website: http://www.esiee-paris.fr

Directeur Général: Dominique Perrin
EMail: dominique.perrin@esiee.fr

International Relations: Derek Mainwaring
Tel: +33(1) 45-92-66-14 EMail: derek.mainwaring@esiee.fr

Department

Health and environment (Biotechnology; Natural Resources); **Information Technology and telecommunications** (Computer Science; Information Technology; Telecommunications Services); **Systems engineering** (Electronic Engineering; Industrial Engineering); **Technology Management and Languages** (Communication Studies; English; Management; Modern Languages)

History: Founded 1904 as Ecole Breguet.

Admission Requirements: 2-3 yrs of University Studies in Science and Technology

Main Language(s) of Instruction: French

Accrediting Agency: Chambre de Commerce et d'Industrie de Paris

Degrees and Diplomas: *Diplôme d'Ingénieur*: **Electronic Engineering.** *Mastère spécialisé*: **Computer Science; Technology.** *Master*: **Computer Engineering; Computer Science; Electronic Engineering; Management.**

Student Services: Canteen, Library, Sports Facilities

Last Updated: 23/03/15

ESME-SUDRIA ENGINEERING SCHOOL

ESME SUDRIA

38 rue Molière, 94200 Ivry-sur-Seine
Tel: +33(1) 56-20-62-00
Fax: +33(1) 56-20-62-62
EMail: contact@esme.fr
Website: http://www.esme.fr

Director General: Eric Simon

International Relations: Catherine Coquan
Tel: + +33(1) 56-20-62-49 EMail: coquan@esme.fr

Programme

Computer Engineering and Information Sciences (Computer Engineering; Information Sciences); **Electrical Engineering** (Automation and Control Engineering; Electrical Engineering; Electronic Engineering; Energy Engineering); **Electronics, Telecommunications, Signal Processing and Networks** (Computer Networks; Electronic Engineering; Telecommunications Engineering); **Systems and Energy** (Computer Science; Energy Engineering; Industrial Engineering)

Further Information: also campuses in Paris, Lille, Lyon

History: Founded 1905. State-accredited since 1922. Under supervision of the Ministry of Education.

Admission Requirements: Secondary School degree (Baccalauréat) in Sciences or equivalent, entrance exam

Fees: 7,250 -8,850 per annum according to level (Euro)

Main Language(s) of Instruction: French

Accrediting Agency: Campus France, Commission des Titres d'Ingénieur, Conférence des Grandes Ecoles, N+I

Degrees and Diplomas: *Diplôme d'Ingénieur*: **Engineering.**

Student Services: Academic Counselling, Canteen, Language Laboratory, Sports Facilities

Last Updated: 23/03/15

ESSCA BUSINESS SCHOOL - ANGERS

Ecole supérieure des Sciences commerciales d'Anger (ESSCA)

BP 40348, 1, rue Lakanal, 49003 Angers, Cedex 01
Tel: +33(2) 41-73-47-47
Fax: +33(2) 41-73-47-48
Website: http://www.essca.fr

Directrice générale: Catherine Leblanc
International Relations: Carol Chaplais
Tel: +33(2) 41-73-47-02 EMail: carol.chaplais@essca.fr

Programme

Management (Management)

Further Information: Has schools in Paris, Shanghai and Budapest.

History: Founded 1909.

Admission Requirements: Competitive entrance examination following secondary school certificate (baccalauréat). Entrance in 3rd year following DEUG, DUT, BTS or equivalent

Fees: 9,190 (Euro)

Main Language(s) of Instruction: French

Accrediting Agency: EPAS

Degrees and Diplomas: *Diplôme d'Etudes d'Ecole de Commerce et Gestion*; *Master*: **Finance; International Business; Management.**

Last Updated: 20/03/15

ESSEC BUSINESS SCHOOL

Ecole supérieure des Sciences économiques et commerciales (ESSEC)

BP 50105, 1, avenue Bernard Hirsch, 95021 Cergy-Pontoise
Tel: +33(1) 34-43-30-00
Fax: +33(1) 34-43-30-01
Website: http://www.essec.fr

Directeur général: Jean-Michel Blanquet (2013-)
Tel: +33(1) 34-43-31-35

International Relations: Michèle Pekar Lempereur
Tel: +33(1) 34-43-31-43

Programme

International Management *(EPSCI)* (Economics; Finance; Management); **Luxury Brand Management** *(MBA Luxe)* (Consumer Studies; Management; Marketing); **Management** *(ESSEC MBA)* (Accountancy; Business and Commerce; Economics; Finance; Management)

Institute

Health Management (Economics; Health Administration; Management); **International Agro-Business Management** (Agricultural Business; Management); **International Hotel Management** *(IMHI)* (Hotel and Restaurant; Management; Tourism); **Research of Negotiation in Europe** *(IRENE)* (Business and Commerce); **Service Innovation and Strategy** *(ISIS)* (Business and Commerce; Management; Service Trades); **Urban and Regional Management** (Management; Real Estate; Regional Planning; Urban Studies)

Further Information: Also French Language courses for foreign students and a school in Singapore.

History: Founded 1907. Accredited by the International Association for Management Education 1997 for all the programmes. Associated with the Institut catholique de Paris.

Academic Year: September to June

Admission Requirements: Secondary school certificate (baccalauréat), or equivalent, preparatory courses for 'Grandes Ecoles', and entrance examination

Main Language(s) of Instruction: French, English

Accrediting Agency: International Association for Management Education

Degrees and Diplomas: *Diplôme d'Etudes d'Ecole de Commerce et Gestion*; *Mastère spécialisé*: **Agronomy; Finance; Human Resources; Insurance; International Business; Management; Public Administration; Sports Management.** *Doctorat*: **Business Administration.**

Student Services: Academic Counselling, Canteen, Careers Guidance, Cultural Activities, Facilities for disabled people, Residential Facilities, Social Counselling, Sports Facilities

Publications: Research Publications

Last Updated: 20/03/15

ESTA - BELFORT

Ecole supérieure des Technologies et des Affaires (ESTA)

3, rue du Docteur Fréry, 90000 Belfort
Tel: +33(3) 84-54-53-53
EMail: cbedeville@esta-belfort.fr
Website: http://www.esta-belfort.fr

Directeur: Jean Grenier Godard

Programme

Business and Commerce (Business and Commerce)

History: Founded 1986.

Admission Requirements: Baccalauréat or equivalent Secondary School degree. Competitive entrance examination

Fees: 4,300 per annum (Euro)

Main Language(s) of Instruction: French

Accrediting Agency: Ministry of Education

Degrees and Diplomas: *Diplôme d'Etudes d'Ecole de Commerce et Gestion*; *Master*: **Business and Commerce.**

Last Updated: 23/03/15

ESTACA - LEVALLOIS-PERRET

Ecole supérieure des Techniques aéronautiques et de Construction automobile (ESTACA)

34, rue Victor Hugo, 92532 Levallois-Perret, Cedex
Tel: +33(1) 41-27-37-00
Fax: +33(1) 47-37-50-83
EMail: infos@estaca.fr
Website: http://www.estaca.fr

Directrice: Pascale Ribon Tel: +33(1) 41-27-37-02

Programme

Engineering (Aeronautical and Aerospace Engineering; Automotive Engineering; Railway Engineering; Transport Engineering)

Further Information: Also campus in Laval

History: Founded 1925.

Academic Year: September to June

Admission Requirements: Competitive entrance examination following 2 yrs further study after secondary school certificate (baccalauréat) or equivalent

Fees: 7,200 (Euro)

Main Language(s) of Instruction: French

Accrediting Agency: Commission des Titres d'Ingénieur (CTI)

Degrees and Diplomas: *Diplôme d'Ingénieur*: **Aeronautical and Aerospace Engineering; Automotive Engineering.** *Master*. Also European Master in Design and Technology of Advanced Vehicle Systems; Aeronautical and Aerospace Engineering; Marine Engineering; Automotive Engineering 18 mths

Student Services: Academic Counselling, Careers Guidance

Last Updated: 20/03/15

EUROPEAN BUSINESS SCHOOL

Ecole européenne de Gestion (EBS)

10 rue Sextius Michel, 75015 Paris

Tel: +33(1) 84-14-02-13

Fax: +33(1) 40-71-37-04

EMail: contact@ebs-paris.com

Website: http://www.ebs-paris.com

Managing Director: Bruno Neil (2001-)

EMail: brunoneil@ebs-paris.com

Programme

Management (Finance; International Business; Management; Marketing)

Further Information: Has 8 centres in Europe, New York and Shanghai.

History: Founded in 1967.

Admission Requirements: Competitive entrance exam, fluent in two languages

Fees: 7400 per annum (Euro)

Main Language(s) of Instruction: French, English

Accrediting Agency: Ministry of Education

Degrees and Diplomas: *Licence*: **Business and Commerce; Management.** *Master*: **Finance; International Business; Management; Marketing.**

Student Services: Cultural Activities, Sports Facilities

Last Updated: 11/03/15

EUROPEAN INTERNATIONAL TRAINING CENTRE

Centre International de Formation Européenne (CIFE)

10 avenue des Fleurs, 06000 Nice

Tel: +33(4) 93-97-93-70

Fax: +33(4) 93-97-93-71

EMail: cife@cife.eu

Website: http://www.cife.eu

Managing Director: Matthias Waechter

Programme

European and International Organisations (International Studies); **Master in Advanced European and International Studies** (International Studies)

History: Founded 1954.

Main Language(s) of Instruction: French, English, German

Degrees and Diplomas: *Master*: **European Studies.**

Last Updated: 11/03/15

GRADUATE SCHOOL OF FASHION

Institut francais de la mode (IFM)

36 quai d'Austerlitz, 75013 Paris

Tel: +33(1) 70-38-89-89

Fax: +33(1) 70-38-89-00

EMail: ifm@ifm-paris.com

Website: http://www.ifm-paris.com

Directeur général: Dominique Jacomet

Tel: +33(1) 56-59-22-11 EMail: direction@ifm-paris.com

Programme

International Fashion Management Executive MBA (International Business); **Management** (Management); **Postgraduate Fashion Design** (Fashion Design)

History: Founded in 1986.

Admission Requirements: Design Programme: BA (Bachelor of Arts) with a master degree from an Art, Design, Style or Architecture school; Management Programme: a 4 or 5 year graduate level degree

Fees: Depends on the programme

Main Language(s) of Instruction: French, English

Accrediting Agency: Ministry of Industry

Degrees and Diplomas: Master of Science in International Luxury Management; Executive MBA in fashion and design management; Diploma of management in fashion and luxury; Diploma in Fashion Design

Last Updated: 23/03/15

GRENOBLE SCHOOL OF MANAGEMENT

Grenoble Ecole de Management

Grenoble Ecole de Management, 12, rue Pierre Sémard, BP 127, 38000 Grenoble, Cedex 01

Tel: +33(4) 76-70-60-60

Fax: +33(4) 76-70-60-99

EMail: info@grenoble-em.com

Website: http://www.grenoble-em.com

Directeur: Loïck Roche (2012-)

EMail: loick.roche@grenoble-em.com

Directeur adjoint: Jean-François Fiorina (2012-)

School

ESC Grenoble *(ESC Grenoble)* (Business Administration; Management); **Grenoble Graduate School of Business** *(GGSB)* (Business Administration; International Business; Marketing); **Information Systems Management** *(EMSI)* (Management; Systems Analysis)

History: Founded 1984. Previously known as Ecole supérieure de Commerce de Grenoble (Grenoble Graduate School of Business). Acquired current title 2003.

Admission Requirements: Competitive entrance examination following 2 yrs further study after secondary school certificate (baccalauréat) or equivalent

Fees: Depends on the programme

Main Language(s) of Instruction: French, English

Accrediting Agency: AACSB, EQUIS and AMBA

Degrees and Diplomas: *Diplôme d'Etudes d'Ecole de Commerce et Gestion*; *Mastère spécialisé*: **Business Computing; Industrial Management; Management.** *Master*: **Accountancy; Business and Commerce; E- Business/Commerce; Finance; International Business; Management.** *Doctorat*: **Business Administration.**

Student Services: Academic Counselling, Canteen, Careers Guidance, Cultural Activities, Facilities for disabled people, Foreign Studies Centre, Language Laboratory, Social Counselling, Sports Facilities

Publications: Les Cahiers du Management Technologique

Last Updated: 23/03/15

HEC SCHOOL OF MANAGEMENT

Ecole des Hautes Etudes Commerciales (GROUPE HEC)

1, rue de la Libération, 78351 Jouy-en-Josas, Cedex

Tel: +33(1) 39-67-70-00

Fax: +33(1) 39-67-74-40

EMail: hecinfo@hec.fr

Website: http://www.hec.fr

Director General: Bernard Ramanantsoa (1995-)

EMail: ramanantsoa@hec.fr

Secretary General: Olivier Moreau

International Relations: François Collin, Director

Faculty

Doctoral Studies (Management); **Executive Development**

Deanery

Operations Management and Information Technology (Business Administration; E- Business/Commerce; Management)

Department

Accounting and Management Control (Accountancy; Management); **Economics and Decision Sciences** (Economics); **Finance** (Finance); **Languages and Cultures** (Chinese; English; German; Hebrew; Italian; Japanese; Russian; Spanish); **Management and Human Resources** (Human Resources; Management); **Marketing** (Marketing); **Strategy and Business Policy** (Business Administration); **Tax and Law** (Business Administration; Law)

Graduate School

Higher Management (Management); **MBA Programme** (Management); **Specialized Studies in Higher Management** (Management)

History: Founded 1881. HEC became one of the academic partners in Europe with the American Association AIMR for the preparation of the CFA (Chartered Financial Analysts) diploma.

Academic Year: September to July (September-January; January-July)

Admission Requirements: Competitive entrance examination following further study after secondary school certificate (baccalauréat)

Fees: Diplôme 7500 per annum (6950-7500, varies according to year); mastère 13300; MBA, 38000 (Euro)

Main Language(s) of Instruction: French, English, 9 other languages

Degrees and Diplomas: *Mastère spécialisé*: **Business Administration; Finance; International Business; Management; Marketing.** *Master*: **Business Administration; Commercial Law; Management; Public Administration.** *Doctorat*: **Accountancy; Business Administration; Finance; Human Resources; Management; Marketing.**

Student Services: Academic Counselling, Canteen, Careers Guidance, Cultural Activities, Facilities for disabled people, Health Services, Language Laboratory, Social Counselling, Sports Facilities

Publications: Les Cahiers de recherche

Last Updated: 05/03/15

ICAM SCHOOL OF ENGINEERING

Groupe ICAM - Institut catholique d'Arts et Métiers (ICAM)

35, rue de la Bienfaisance, 75008 Paris
Tel: +33(1) 53-77-22-20
Fax: +33(1) 53-77-22-23
Website: http://www.icam.fr

Director General: Jean-Michel Viot

International Relations: Olivier du Bourblanc
Tel: +33(6) 07-25-83-73

Programme

Engineering (Engineering)

Further Information: The ICAM Group is composed of 3 main ICAM Campuses and 4 Technology Institutes (IST) in Lille, Vannes, La Roche-sur-Yon and Toulouse, 2 in Central Africa (Pointe Noire and Douala) and 1 in India (Chennai)

History: Founded 1898.

Academic Year: September-June

Admission Requirements: Competitive entrance examination following 2 yrs further study after secondary school certificate (baccalauréat) or equivalent.

Fees: Engineering programme: 2,950 per annum the first 2 years, 6,700 the third year (Euro)

Main Language(s) of Instruction: French

Accrediting Agency: Commission des Titres d'Ingénieur (CTI)

Degrees and Diplomas: *Diplôme d'Ingénieur*: **Engineering.** *Mastère spécialisé*: **Energy Engineering; Railway Engineering.** *Master*. Offers Preparatory Classes (2 years) to take entrance exam for the Engineering Schools.

Last Updated: 24/03/15

ICAM LILLE SCHOOL OF ENGINEERING

ICAM LILLE - INSTITUT CATHOLIQUE D'ARTS ET MÉTIERS (ICAM LILLE)

6, rue Auber, 59000 Lille
Tel: +33(3) 20-22-61-61
Fax: +33(3) 20-93-14-89
EMail: contact.lille@icam.fr
Website: http://www.icam.fr

Directeur: Bernard-Gilles Flipo EMail: bernard-gilles.flipo@icam.fr

Programme

Engineering (Engineering; Railway Engineering)

History: Founded in 1898.

Admission Requirements: Secondary school Certificate (Baccalauréat) in Science and jury selection

Main Language(s) of Instruction: French

Degrees and Diplomas: *Diplôme d'Ingénieur*: **Engineering.** *Mastère spécialisé*: **Railway Engineering.** *Master*

ICAM NANTES SCHOOL OF ENGINEERING

ICAM NANTES - INSTITUT CATHOLIQUE D'ARTS ET MÉTIERS (ICAM NANTES)

35, avenue du Champ de Manoeuvres, 44470 Carquefou
Tel: +33(2) 40-52-40-52
Fax: +33(2) 40-52-40-99
EMail: icam.nantes@groupe-icam.fr
Website: http://www.groupe-icam.fr

Directeur: Jean-Louis Bigotte (2000-)

International Relations: Geneviève Baines

Department

Automation and Electrical Engineering (Automation and Control Engineering; Electrical Engineering); **Computer Science** (Computer Science); **Engineering** (Engineering); **Human Sciences and Languages** (Arts and Humanities; Human Resources; Management; Modern Languages); **Materials Science** (Materials Engineering; Polymer and Plastics Technology); **Mechanics** (Mechanical Engineering)

Admission Requirements: Secondary school certificate (baccalauréat) in Science or equivalent and jury selection.

Main Language(s) of Instruction: French

Degrees and Diplomas: *Diplôme d'Ingénieur*: **Engineering.** *Mastère spécialisé*

Student Services: Academic Counselling, Canteen, Careers Guidance, Cultural Activities, Facilities for disabled people, Sports Facilities

ICAM TOULOUSE SCHOOL OF ENGINEERING

ICAM TOULOUSE - INSTITUT CATHOLIQUE D'ARTS ET MÉTIERS DE TOULOUSE (ICAM TOULOUSE)

75, avenue de Grande Bretagne, CS 97615, 31376 Toulouse, Cedex 3
Tel: +33(5) 34-50-50-50
Fax: +33(5) 34-50-50-51
EMail: toulouse@icam.fr
Website: http://www.groupe-icam.fr

Directeur: Louis de Montety (2011-)

Department

Computer Science (Computer Science); **Electrical Engineering** (Electrical Engineering); **Energy Engineering** (Energy Engineering); **Humanities** (Arts and Humanities); **Industrial Management** (Industrial Management); **Materials Engineering** (Materials Engineering); **Mechanical Engineering** (Mechanical Engineering)

History: Founded 1993.

Admission Requirements: secondary school certificate (baccalauréat) in Science or equivalent and jury selection

Main Language(s) of Instruction: French

Degrees and Diplomas: *Diplôme d'Ingénieur*: **Engineering.** *Mastère spécialisé*; *Master*

Student Services: Facilities for disabled people

ICD INTERNATIONAL BUSINESS SCHOOL

Institut international de Commerce et de Distribution (IDC PARIS)

12 rue Alexandre Parodi, 75010 Paris
Tel: +33(1) 40-03-15-52
Fax: +33(1) 40-03-15-45
EMail: sfranquet@groupe-igs.fr
Website: http://www.icd-ecoles.com

Director: Tawhid Chtioui

International Relations: Marjorie BRUN-PAN Brun-Pan
Tel: +33(1) 80-97-66-07 EMail: mbrun-pan@groupe-igs.fr

Programme

Management (Business Administration; Business and Commerce; E- Business/Commerce; International Business; Management; Marketing)

Further Information: Also campus in Toulouse, Dublin and Shangai

History: Founded 1980.

Admission Requirements: Entrance examination.

Fees: 8,330-9,800 (Euro)

Main Language(s) of Instruction: French, English

Accrediting Agency: Ministry of Education

Degrees and Diplomas: *Master*: **International Business.**
Last Updated: 27/03/15

IGS GROUP

Groupe IGS

1, rue Jacques Bingen, 75017 Paris
Tel: +33(1) 80-97-55-01
EMail: kgrivot@groupe-igs.fr
Website: http://www.groupe-igs.asso.fr

Directeur: Olivier Dusserre

School

American Business School *(ABS Paris)* (Business Administration); **Decision** (Economics; International Relations; Law; Marketing; Modern History; Political Sciences; Sales Techniques; Taxation)

Institute

Human Resources Management *(IGS Paris, Lyon and Toulouse)* (Human Resources; Management; Marketing; Service Trades); **International Commerce and Distribution** *(ICD Paris and Toulouse)* (Business and Commerce; International Business; Management; Marketing); **Marketing and Management of Health Services** *(IMIS Lyon)* (Health Administration; Management; Marketing); **Media** *(ISCPA Paris, Lyon)* (Journalism; Media Studies); **Operations Management** *(ESAM Paris, Lyon, Toulouse in partnership with Lille II)* (Business Administration; Finance; Management; Real Estate; Service Trades); **Real Estate** *(IMSI Paris)* (Real Estate)

Further Information: Has three sites: Paris, Lyon and Toulouse.

History: Founded in 1975 as the Ecole de Gestion Sociale, expanding to integrate new business schools and training centres over the last 30 years.

Main Language(s) of Instruction: French

Accrediting Agency: Ministry of Education

Degrees and Diplomas: *Brevet de Technicien supérieur*: **Management.** *Licence*: **Business and Commerce; Management.** Masters professionnel
Last Updated: 24/03/15

INSEAD

Boulevard de Constance, 77305 Fontainebleau
Tel: +33(1) 60-72-40-00
Fax: +33(1) 60-74-55-00
EMail: communications@insead.edu
Website: http://www.insead.edu

Dean: Ilian Mihov (2013-)
Tel: +33(1) 60-72-44-58 EMail: wendy.burwood@insead.edu

International Relations: Melissa Joelson
Tel: +33(1) 60-71-26-62 EMail: communications.fb@insead.edu

Programme

Accounting and Control (Accountancy); **Decision Sciences** (Leadership; Management; Statistics); **Economics and Political Science** (Economics; Political Sciences); **Entrepreneurship and Family Enterprise** (Management); **Finance** (Finance); **Marketing** (Marketing); **Organizational Behaviour** (Leadership; Management); **Strategy** (Management); **Technology and Operations Management** (Management)

Further Information: Also campuses in Singapore and Abu Dhabi

History: Founded 1957.

Academic Year: August to June (August-December; January-June)

Admission Requirements: Bachelor's degree or equivalent, entrance examination (TOEFL, Essay, Interview)

Main Language(s) of Instruction: English

Accrediting Agency: Association of Advanced Collegiate Schools of Business (AACSB); EQUIS

Degrees and Diplomas: *Master*: **Business Administration; Finance.** *Doctorat*: **Accountancy; Business Administration; Finance; Leadership; Management; Marketing.** Also Executive MBA, 14 months (EMBA)

Student Services: Academic Counselling, Canteen, Careers Guidance, Facilities for disabled people, Health Services, Language Laboratory, Social Counselling, Sports Facilities
Last Updated: 25/03/15

INSEEC BUSINESS SCHOOL

Institut des hautes Etudes économiques et commerciales (INSEEC)

Hangar 19 - Quai de Bacalan , CS 60083, 33070 Bordeaux, Cedex
Tel: +33(5) 56-00-73-73
EMail: clenier@inseec.com
Website: http://www.inseec.com/

Director: Dominique Didier

International Relations: Sylvie Hovine, Head of International Relations Tel: +33(5) 56-01-77-56 EMail: shovine@inseec.com

Programme

Digital (E- Business/Commerce; Multimedia); **Finance** (Banking; Finance; International Business; Real Estate); **International** (Finance; International Business; Management; Marketing; Real Estate); **Luxury and Hospitality** (Fashion Design; Management; Marketing; Service Trades); **Management** (Business Administration; Business and Commerce; Human Resources; International Business; Management; Marketing; Tourism); **Marketing and Communication** (Communication Studies; Management; Marketing); **Wine and Spirits** (Management; Marketing; Oenology)

Further Information: Campus in Paris, Lyon, London and Monaco, Chambéry, Chicago.

History: Founded in 1975.

Admission Requirements: Competitive entrance exam.

Fees: Depends on the programme

Main Language(s) of Instruction: French

Degrees and Diplomas: *Diplôme d'Etudes d'Ecole de Commerce et Gestion*: **Business Administration.** *Master*. MSc and MBA
Last Updated: 27/03/15

INSTITUTE OF INTERCULTURAL MANAGEMENT AND COMMUNICATION

Institut de Management et de Communication interculturels (ISIT)

12, rue Cassette, 75006 Paris
Tel: +33(1) 42-22-33-16
Fax: +33(1) 45-44-17-67
EMail: direction@isit-paris.fr
Website: http://www.isit-paris.fr

Directrice: Nathalie Gormezano (2012-)
EMail: direction@isit-paris.fr

Head of Administration and Finance: Anne Etienne
EMail: a.etienne@isit-paris.fr

International Relations: Catherine Jourdainne, Head of International relations EMail: c.jourdainne@isit-paris.fr

Programme

International Law (International Law); **Interpreting** (Translation and Interpretation); **Management, Communication and Translation** (Communication Studies; Management; Translation and Interpretation)

History: Founded 1957 as Institut Supérieur d'Interprétation et de Traduction within the Institut catholique de Paris. Acquired present title 2008. Became associate of the Institut catholique de Paris.

Admission Requirements: High school degree (Baccalauréat, all sections) or equivalent and entrance examination. Prerequisite: students must be fluent or have an excellent understanding in French and English.

Fees: 3,500-8,400 per annum (Euro)

Main Language(s) of Instruction: French

Degrees and Diplomas: *Master*: **Translation and Interpretation.**

Last Updated: 26/03/15

INTERNATIONAL BUSINESS SCHOOL

Ecole supérieure du Commerce extérieur (ESCE)

10 rue Sextius Michel, 75015 Paris, Cedex
Tel: +33(1) 84-14-02-98
Fax: +33(1) 81-51-15-04
EMail: esce@esce.fr
Website: http://www.esce.fr

Director: Paul-Jacques Lehmann

Deputy CEO: Yves Marmiesse EMail: yves.marmiesse@esce.fr

International Relations: Karine Gautier, Director of International Relations Tel: +33(1) 81-51-15-35 EMail: karine.gautier@esce.fr

Programme

International Business (Business Administration; Business and Commerce; International Business)

Further Information: Has schools in Lyon, Beijing, Mexico and Sao Paulo.

History: Founded in 1968.

Academic Year: September to June (September-December; Januaru- June)

Admission Requirements: SESAME national exam

Main Language(s) of Instruction: French, English

Accrediting Agency: Ministry of Education

Degrees and Diplomas: *Diplôme d'Etudes d'Ecole de Commerce et Gestion*: **International Business.** *Master*: **Human Resources; International Business; Management; Marketing.**

Last Updated: 23/03/15

INTERNATIONAL SPACE UNIVERSITY (ISU)

1 rue Jean-Dominique Cassini, 67400 Illkirch-Graffenstaden
Tel: +33(3) 88-65-54-30
Fax: +33(3) 88-65-54-47
EMail: info@isu.isunet.edu
Website: http://www.isunet.edu/

Président: Walter Peeters Tel: +33(3) 88-65-54-62

Programme

Master of Space Management (Aeronautical and Aerospace Engineering; Air and Space Law; Architecture; Astronomy and Space Science; Astrophysics; Biological and Life Sciences; Business Administration; Information Management; International Economics; International Studies; Telecommunications Services); **Master of Space Studies** (Aeronautical and Aerospace Engineering; Air and Space Law; Architecture; Astronomy and Space Science; Astrophysics; Biological and Life Sciences; Business Administration; Information Management; International Business; International Studies; Telecommunications Services); **Space Studies Programme** *(9-week certificate programme)* (Aeronautical and Aerospace Engineering; Air and Space Law; Architecture; Astronomy and Space Science; Astrophysics; Biological and Life Sciences; Business Administration; Information Management; International Economics; International Studies; Telecommunications Services)

History: Founded in 1987 and first Space Studies Programme held in MIT, Massachusetts, USA in 1988. Moved to Strasbourg in 1994. Acquired current title and status 2004.

Academic Year: September to August

Admission Requirements: Bachelor's degree or equivalent. (BAC + 4 in French system)

Fees: (Euros): 25,000

Main Language(s) of Instruction: English

Accrediting Agency: Ministry of Education and Research

Degrees and Diplomas: MSc: Space Studies; Space Management (1 yr). Also 9-week Space Studies Programme Certificate (held around the world every year)

Student Services: Academic Counselling, Careers Guidance, Facilities for disabled people, Foreign Studies Centre, Language Laboratory, Social Counselling

Publications: The Universe

Last Updated: 09/04/15

IPAG BUSINESS SCHOOL

Institut de Préparation à l'Administration et à la Gestion (GROUPE IPAG)

184, bd Saint-Germain, 75006 Paris
Tel: +33(1) 53-63-36-00
Fax: +33(1) 45-44-40-46
EMail: international@ipag.fr
Website: http://www.ipag.fr

Directeur général: Guillaume Bigot

International Relations: Bernard Terrany EMail: b.terrany@ipag.fr

Programme

'Graduate school' *(Prgoramme Grande Ecole)* (Business Administration); **Management** (Accountancy; Advertising and Publicity; Banking; E- Business/Commerce; Finance; International Business; Management; Marketing; Multimedia; Public Relations)

Further Information: Has a school in Nice.

History: Founded in 1965, having its origins in the Collège des sciences sociales et économiques.

Admission Requirements: Baccalauréat or equivalent Secondary School degree and entrance exam.

Main Language(s) of Instruction: French, English

Accrediting Agency: Ministry of Education

Degrees and Diplomas: *Master*: **Business Administration.** Also Bachelor and MBA

Last Updated: 26/03/15

ISARA LYON

Institut supérieur d'Agriculture et d'Agro-alimentaire Rhône-Alpes (ISARA)

23, rue Jean Baldassini, 69364 Lyon, Cedex 07
Tel: +33(4) 27-85-85-85
EMail: com@isara.fr
Website: http://www.isara.fr

Director: Pascal Désamais (2009-)
Tel: +33(4) 27-85-85-82 EMail: contact@isara.fr

International Relations: Sophie Rotteleur
Tel: +33(4) 27-85-85-51 EMail: relint@isara.fr

Department

Agriculture, Agrosystem and Territories *(ASTER)* (Agriculture; Food Science; Sociology); **Agroecology and Environment** *(AGE)* (Agriculture; Agronomy; Animal Husbandry; Aquaculture; Biology; Ecology; Farm Management; Fishery; Geography; Soil Science; Water Science); **Food Processing** (Food Science; Food Technology; Microbiology); **Methodology and Engineering** *(MINT)* (Applied Physics; Biochemistry; Biology; Chemistry; Computer Engineering; Engineering; Mathematics and Computer Science; Rural Studies; Statistics)

History: Founded 1968.

Admission Requirements: Secondary school certificate (Baccalauréat)

Fees: 4,850 per annum (Euro)

Main Language(s) of Instruction: French

Accrediting Agency: Commission des titres d'ingérieur (CTI); Ministry of Agriculture

Degrees and Diplomas: *Diplôme d'Ingénieur*: **Agriculture; Engineering; Food Technology; Management; Natural Resources; Viticulture.** *Mastère spécialisé*: **Agriculture; Ecology; Food Science; Food Technology; Management.** Also doubles diplômes: Pharmacist/Engineer; Engineer/ Master Entrepreneurship and Management of SMOs; Engineer/Master of Science

Student Services: Careers Guidance, Language Laboratory, Sports Facilities

Last Updated: 08/04/15

ISC PARIS SCHOOL OF MANAGEMENT

Institut supérieur du Commerce de Paris (ISC PARIS)

22 boulevard du Fort de Vaux, 75017 Paris
Tel: +33(1) 40-53-99-99
Fax: +33(1) 40-53-98-98
EMail: contact@groupeisc.com; kangeli@iscparis.com
Website: http://www.iscparis.com

Director General: Bruno Neil

International Relations: Michael J. Dolan, Dean of international Affairs Tel: +33(1) 40-53-99-99 EMail: mjdolan@iscparis.com

Programme

Management (E- Business/Commerce; Finance; International Business; Management; Marketing)

History: Founded 1963.

Admission Requirements: National entrance exam (CPGE) or 2 years undergraduate studies in Economics and Technology followed by an entrance exam

Fees: Master "Grande Ecole": 10,780 per annum (Euro)

Main Language(s) of Instruction: French, English

Accrediting Agency: Ministry of Education

Degrees and Diplomas: *Diplôme d'Etudes d'Ecole de Commerce et Gestion*: **Business Administration.** *Mastère spécialisé*: **International Business; Marketing.** *Master*: **Management.** Also Bachelor and MBA

Last Updated: 09/04/15

KEDGE BUSINESS SCHOOL

rue Antoine Bourdelle, Marseille
Tel: +33(4) 91.82.78.00
Fax: +33(4) 91.82.78.01
EMail: info@kedgebs.com; csr@kedgebs.com
Website: http://www.kedgebs.com/en

Dean and Director General: Thomas Froehlicher (2014-)
EMail: thomas.froehlicher@kedgebs.com

International Relations: Jacques Olivier Pesme, International Programmme Director
Tel: +33(5) 56.84.55.55 EMail: pesme@kedgebs.com

Programme

Commerce and Finance (Business and Commerce; Finance); **Commerce and Finance Bachelor Programme** *(SUP'TG)* (Business and Commerce; Finance); **Industrial Logistics** *(ISLI)* (Transport Management); **Industrial Purchasing Management** *(MAI)* (Management); **International Business** *(MACI)* (International Business; Management); **International Management** *(EBP International)* (International Business; Management); **International Purchasing** *(MAI)* (Management); **Management** *(ESC Bordeaux Grande Ecole)* (Business Administration; Management); **Quality Management** *(ISMQ)* (Management; Safety Engineering); **Real Estate and Asset Management** *(IMPI)* (Management; Notary Studies; Real Estate); **Risk Management** *(IMR)* (Insurance; Management); **Short Programmes** *(International Summer Schools in Marseille)* (Cultural Studies; Development Studies; Sports Management); **Supply Chain Management** *(ISLI)* (Management; Transport Management); **Wine and Spirits Management** (Management; Viticulture)

Department

Accounting, Management and Control Law (Accountancy; Law; Management); **Finance and Economics** (Economics; Finance); **Management** (Management); **Marketing** (Marketing); **Operations Management and Information System** (Business Administration; Management); **Strategy** (Business Administration; Economics)

Further Information: Also campuses in: Bayonne, Paris, Avignon, Toulon

History: Founded 1874 as Ecole Supérieure de Commerce . Acquired present title 2007. In July 2013, two Management Schools (BEM-Bordeaux Management School and Euromed Management) merged to create a new global Business School: KEDGE Business School.

Admission Requirements: After secondary school certificate (baccalauréat) or equivalent or following two years' further study after the Baccalauréat or Baccalauréat and five years of higher education

Fees: depending on the programme (Euro)

Main Language(s) of Instruction: French, English

Degrees and Diplomas: *Diplôme d'Etudes d'Ecole de Commerce et Gestion*; *Master*: **Art Management; Business Administration; Business and Commerce; Finance; Management; Marketing; Sports Management.** MSc, MBA and Master Grande Ecole,Certificates

Publications: Logistique & Management; Supply Chain Forum

Academic Staff *2014-2015*	**TOTAL**
FULL-TIME	**178**
PART-TIME	**478**
STAFF WITH DOCTORATE	
FULL-TIME	**329**
Student Numbers *2014-2015*	
All (Foreign included)	**12,290**

Last Updated: 02/03/15

LA ROCHELLE BUSINESS SCHOOL

Groupe Sup de Co La Rochelle (ESC LA ROCHELLE)

102, rue de Coureilles - Les Minimes, 17024 La Rochelle, Cedex 1
Tel: +33(5) 46-51-77-00
Fax: +33(5) 46-51-77-98
EMail: com@esc-larochelle.fr
Website: http://www.esc-larochelle.fr

Directeur général: Daniel Peyron EMail: peyrond@esc-larochelle.fr

International Relations: Bénédicte Julien
Tel: +33(5) 46-51-77-71 EMail: julienb@esc-larochelle.fr

Programme

Business administration (Business Administration; Business and Commerce; International Business; Marketing; Service Trades); **Management** (Management; Sports Management; Tourism)

School

Tourism (Tourism)

History: Founded in 1988.

Admission Requirements: Entrance exam

Fees: depends on the programme

Main Language(s) of Instruction: French and English

Degrees and Diplomas: *Diplôme d'Etudes d'Ecole de Commerce et Gestion*: **Business Administration; Management.**

Student Services: Academic Counselling, Canteen, Careers Guidance, Cultural Activities, Facilities for disabled people, Foreign Studies Centre, Health Services, Language Laboratory, Nursery Care, Social Counselling, Sports Facilities

Student Numbers *2014-2015*: Total 3,100

Last Updated: 25/03/15

LASALLE BEAUVAIS POLYTECHNIC INSTITUTE

Institut polytechnique LaSalle Beauvais

19, rue Pierre Waguet - BP 30313, 60026 Beauvais, Cedex
Tel: +33(3) 44-06-25-25
Fax: +33(3) 44-06-25-26
EMail: contact@lasalle-beauvais.fr
Website: http://www.lasalle-beauvais.fr

President: Gérard Friès

International Relations: Marie Lummerzheim, Head of International Relations
Tel: + 33 (3) 44-06-38-41
EMail: marie.lummerzheim@lasalle-beauvais.fr

Department

Agro-Industrial Science and Technology (Analytical Chemistry; Biochemistry; Biotechnology; Food Science; Industrial Management; Microbiology; Nanotechnology; Organic Chemistry; Physics; Production Engineering; Statistics); **Agronomy and Animal Science** (Agronomy; Analytical Chemistry; Animal Husbandry; Biotechnology; Cell Biology; Crop Production; Ecology; Forestry; Microbiology; Molecular Biology; Plant Pathology; Soil Science); **Geoscience** (Geology; Geophysics; Marine Science and Oceanography; Mining Engineering; Petroleum and Gas Engineering); **Nutrition and Health** (Analytical Chemistry; Biotechnology; Epidemiology; Immunology; Microbiology; Molecular Biology; Nutrition; Pharmacology; Physiology; Toxicology); **Transversal Engineering Science and Management** (Accountancy; Communication Studies; Economics; Engineering; Management; Marketing; Sociology)

History: Founded 1854 as Institut Normal Agricole. Acquired present title and status 2006 following merger of the Institut Géologique Albert-de-Lapparent and the Institut Supérieur d'Agriculture de Beauvais. Associated with the Institut catholique de Paris.

Admission Requirements: Secondary school certificate in Science (Baccalauréat S) or equivalent, entrance examination and jury selection

Fees: 4501 - 6208 (Euro)

Main Language(s) of Instruction: French

Degrees and Diplomas: *Brevet de Technicien supérieur*; *Diplôme d'Ingénieur*: **Agricultural Engineering; Food Science; Geology.** *Mastère spécialisé*; *Master*

Last Updated: 08/04/15

LILLE SCHOOL OF JOURNALISM

Ecole supérieure de Journalisme de Lille (ESJ)
50, rue Gauthier-de-Châtillon, 59046 Lille, Cedex
Tel: + 33(3) 20-30-44-00
Fax: + 33(3) 20-30-44-95
Website: http://esj-lille.fr/

President: Louis Dreyfus (2013-)

Head of Administration: Pierre Savary (2013-)

International Relations: Sylvie Larrière (2013-)
Tel: + 33(3) 20-30-44-32 EMail: sylvie.larriere@esj-lille.fr

Programme

Journalism (Journalism)

Campus

ESJ Lille *(Montpellier)* (Journalism); **ESJ PRO Lille** *(Paris)* (Journalism)

History: Created 1956.

Academic Year: September to May

Admission Requirements: Entrance examination following 3 years further study after secondary school certificate (baccalauréat).

Fees: Non-grant students: 4,500 (Euro)

Main Language(s) of Instruction: French

Degrees and Diplomas: School Diploma in Journalism (Master level); International Master in Media Management (Master Level)

Last Updated: 19/03/15

LYON TEXTILE AND CHEMICAL INSTITUTE

Institut textile et chimique de Lyon (ITECH LYON)
87, chemin des Mouilles, 69134 Ecully, Cedex
Tel: + 33(4) 72-18-04-80
Fax: + 33(4) 77-18-95-45
EMail: info@itech.fr
Website: http://www.itech.fr

Director: Jérôme Marcilloux (2012-)
EMail: jerome.marcilloux@itech.fr

Secretary General: Estelle Vlieghe EMail: e.vlieghe@itech.fr

International Relations: Nathalie Pinton EMail: n.pinton@itech.fr

Department

Textiles and Chemical Engineering (Chemical Engineering; Leather Techniques; Painting and Drawing; Polymer and Plastics Technology; Textile Technology)

Further Information: site in Roannes

History: Founded 1988 following merger of the Ecole supérieure des Industries Textiles de Lyon, founded in 1840 and the Ecole Française de Tannerie, founded in 1899.

Academic Year: September to June

Admission Requirements: Competitive entrance examination following 2 years further study after secondary school certificate (L2, DUT or BTS)

Fees: Engineering programme: 6,500 per annum; Mastère: 5 900 (Euro)

Main Language(s) of Instruction: French

Degrees and Diplomas: *Brevet de Technicien supérieur*: **Leather Techniques; Painting and Drawing.** *Licence professionnelle*; *Diplôme d'Ingénieur*: **Chemistry; Leather Techniques; Materials Engineering; Painting and Drawing; Polymer and Plastics Technology; Textile Technology.** *Mastère spécialisé*: **Management.** *Master*: **Polymer and Plastics Technology.** Licence professionnelle with Claude Bernard University (Lyon I); Masters of Engineering in Formulation Chemistry

Student Services: Academic Counselling, Careers Guidance, Social Counselling

Last Updated: 09/04/15

MANAGEMENT AND BUSINESS SCHOOL NETWORK

Ecole de Gestion et de Commerce (RÉSEAU EGC)
46 avenue de la Grande Armée, 75016 Paris
Tel: + 33(1) 40-69-38-61
Fax: + 33(1) 53-57-18-61
EMail: reseauegc@6tm.com
Website: http://www.bachelor-egc.fr

President: Bruno Bouniol
Tel: + 33(1) 40-69-38-61 EMail: reseauegc@6tm.com

Programme

Business and Commerce (Business Administration; Business and Commerce; Marketing)

Further Information: EGC consists of a network of 25 schools throughout France

History: Founded in 1975 by Les Chambres de Commerce et d'Industries (CCI).

Admission Requirements: Baccalauréat, Equivalent Secondary School Degree, and entrance exam

Fees: 3580 (Euro)

Main Language(s) of Instruction: French

Accrediting Agency: Association des Chambres Française de Commerce et d'Industrie (ACFCI), Répertoire Nationale des Certifications Professionnelles (RNCP), Ministry of Education

Degrees and Diplomas: *Licence*: **Marketing.** *Diplôme d'Etudes d'Ecole de Commerce et Gestion*. Business-Marketing and Sales Manager Diploma (Diplome EGC)

Last Updated: 11/03/15

MONTPELLIER BUSINESS SCHOOL

Groupe Sup de Co Montpellier (ESC MONTPELLIER)
2300, avenue des Moulins, 34185 Montpellier, Cedex 4
Tel: + 33(4) 67-10-25-00
Fax: + 33(4) 67-45-13-56
Website: http://www.montpellier-bs.com

Directeur: Didier Jourdan Tel: + 33(4) 67-10-25-33

International Relations: Carole Santos Magliozzi
Tel: + 33(4) 67-10-25-17 EMail: c.santos@montpellier-bs.com

Programme

Business Administration (Business Administration; International Business; Management; Tourism)

History: Founded 1897 by the Chambre de Commerce et d'Industrie de Montpellier. Become Montpellier Business School in 2014.

Academic Year: September to June

Admission Requirements: Competitive entrance examination following 2 yrs further study after secondary school certificate (baccalauréat) or equivalent

Fees: Depends on the programme

Main Language(s) of Instruction: French

Degrees and Diplomas: *Diplôme d'Etudes d'Ecole de Commerce et Gestion*: **Business Administration.** *Master*: **Business Administration.** Bachelor's degree in International Business

Student Services: Canteen, Sports Facilities

Last Updated: 25/03/15

NEW SCHOOL OF ECONOMIC AND SOCIAL ORGANISATION

Ecole nouvelle d'Organisation économique et sociale (ENOES)

62, rue de Miromesnil, 75008 Paris
Tel: +33(1) 45-62-80-59
Fax: +33(2) 53-75-33-80
EMail: contact@enoes.com
Website: http://www.enoes.com

President: Thierry Carlier

School

Human Resources *(ERH)* (Human Resources; Management); **Transport** *(EST)* (Transport Economics; Transport Management)

Centre

Accountancy *(CECS)* (Accountancy)

History: Founded in 1937 with the creation of the Accounting Centre, the Ecole Nationale d'Organisation Economique et Sociale was goverened directly by the Ministry of Economy until gaining its autonomy in 1949.

Fees: Depending on the programme

Main Language(s) of Instruction: French

Accrediting Agency: Ministry of Economy, Finance and Industry.

Degrees and Diplomas: *Diplôme d'Etat*: **Accountancy.** Masters 1 (2 yrs) in Transport and Logistics; Human Resources

Last Updated: 16/03/15

NORMANDY BUSINESS SCHOOL

Ecole de Management de Normandie

30, rue Richelieu, 76087 Le Havre, Cedex 4
Tel: +33(2) 32-92-59-99
Fax: +33(2) 35-42-11-16
EMail: info@em-normandie.fr
Website: http://www.ecole-management-normandie.fr

Director: Jean-Guy Bernard (2004-)
EMail: jg.bernard@em-normandie.fr

Administrative Manager: Daniel Choplet
Tel: +33(2) 32-92-59-95 EMail: d.choplet@em-normandie.fr

International Relations: Alain Ouvrieu
Tel: +33(2) 31-45-35-02 EMail: a.ouvrieu@em-normandie.fr

Programme

Graduate and Professional Studies *(IPER, Le Havre)*; **Graduate Studies in Management** (Management); **Undergraduate Studies** (Accountancy; International Business; Management; Marketing)

Further Information: campuses in: Caen, Deauville, Le Havre, Paris, Oxford

History: Founded 1871 as Ecole supérieure de Commerce du Havre. Became Ecole de Management de Normandie 2004 with campuses in Le Havre and Caen.

Admission Requirements: ESC Le Havre, competitive entrance examination following first university degree (DEUG); SUP EUROPE CESEC, Baccalauréat or equivalent; IPER, first university degree-postgraduate level and English test.

Fees: 7095 -7525 per annum (Euro)

Main Language(s) of Instruction: French, English

Accrediting Agency: Association to Advance Collegiate Schools of Business (AACSB)

Degrees and Diplomas: *Licence*; *Mastère spécialisé*: **Business Administration.** *Master*: **Management; Transport and Communications; Transport Management.**

Student Services: Academic Counselling, Canteen, Careers Guidance, Language Laboratory, Social Counselling, Sports Facilities

Publications: Cahiers de Recherche

Last Updated: 11/03/15

NOVANCIA BUSINESS SCHOOL

Novancia

8, avenue de la Porte de Champerret, 75017 Paris
Tel: +33(1) 55-65-53-55
EMail: information@novancia.fr
Website: http://www.novancia.fr

Director: Anne Stéfanini

Programme

Entrepreneurship (Business Administration; Business and Commerce; Economics; Finance; Human Resources; Management; Marketing)

Further Information: Two sites in Paris

History: Founded 2011 following merger of Advancia and Négocia.

Admission Requirements: National exam 'Atout +3' and secondary school certificate (Baccalauréat) or equivalent

Main Language(s) of Instruction: French

Degrees and Diplomas: *Mastère spécialisé*: **Business Administration; Finance.** *Master*: **Business Administration; Management.** Bachelor in Entrepreneurship and Management; Programmes are organised either as full-time studies or in alternating between studies and internships; MSc in International Business Development and Consulting

Last Updated: 09/04/15

PARIS COLLEGE OF ART

15 rue Fénelon, 75010 Paris
Tel: +33(1) 45-77-39-66
Fax: +33(1) 45-77-10-44
EMail: contact@paris.edu
Website: http://www.paris.edu

President: Reginald de Guillebon

Programme

Fine Arts (Art Criticism; Art History; Art Management; Design; Fashion Design; Fine Arts; Photography)

History: Founded 1921. Acquired present status and title 2010.

Main Language(s) of Instruction: French, English

Degrees and Diplomas: *Licence*; *Master*

Last Updated: 30/04/15

PARIS SCHOOL OF JOURNALISM

Ecole supérieure de Journalisme de Paris (ESJ-PARIS)

107 rue de Tolbiac, 75013 Paris
Tel: +33(1) 45 70 73 37
EMail: contact@esj-paris.com
Website: http://www.esj-paris.com

President: Guillaume Jobin EMail: guillaume.jobin@esj-paris.com

Director: Frédéric Dupuis EMail: frederic.dupuis@esj-paris.com

Programme

Journalism (Journalism)

History: Founded 1899.

Admission Requirements: Baccalauréat and Entrance examination.

Fees: 6,000; Mastère: 6,600-8,000 per annum (Euro)

Main Language(s) of Instruction: French

Degrees and Diplomas: *Mastère spécialisé*: **Journalism; Mass Communication.** Diplômes d'école

Last Updated: 18/03/15

PRIVATE FACULTY OF LAW, ECONOMICS AND MANAGEMENT

Faculté libre de Droit, d'Economie et de Gestion

115-117 rue Notre Dame des Champs, 75006 Paris
Tel: +33(1) 53 10 24 70
EMail: info@facoparis.org
Website: http://www.facoparis.com/

Dean: Marie-Christine Cauchy-Psaume

Programme

Economics and Management (Chinese; Economics; English; German; Italian; Management; Spanish); **Law and Political Science** (Law; Political Sciences)

History: Created 1967.

Academic Year: September to July (September-December; January-May)

Admission Requirements: Baccalauréat or equivalent

Fees: 5,900 per annum (Euro)

Main Language(s) of Instruction: French

Degrees and Diplomas: *Licence*: **Economics; Law; Management.** *Master*: **Law.**

Last Updated: 23/03/15

PSB PARIS BUSINESS SCHOOL

59 rue Nationale, 75013 Paris
Tel: +33(1) 53-36-44-19
EMail: hsmullen@psbedu.com
Website: http://www.psbedu.paris/

Director: Armand Derhy

Programme

Commerce and Management (Business Administration; Business and Commerce; International Business; Management); **Winter and Summer short programme** (Art Management; Finance; International Business; Management; Sports Management)

History: Founded 1974, acquired present status 1984. Become PSB Paris School of Business in 2015.

Admission Requirements: Competitive entrance examination. Secondary school Certificate (Baccalauréat) or foreign equivalent or after following 2 years further study after secondary school certificate (baccalauréat) or 2-3 year university degree

Main Language(s) of Instruction: French, English

Accrediting Agency: Ministry of Education

Degrees and Diplomas: *Licence*: **Accountancy; Business Administration; Finance; Human Resources; Information Technology; International Business; Management; Sports Management.** *Master*: **Accountancy; Advertising and Publicity; Art Management; Finance; Human Resources; Information Technology; International Business; Management; Marketing; Sports Management.**

Student Numbers *2014-2015*: Total 3,000

Last Updated: 24/03/15

RENNES SCHOOL OF NOTARY STUDIES

Institut des Métiers de Notariat de Rennes

2 mail Anne-Catherine, 35000 Rennes
Tel: +33(2) 99-65-50-60
Fax: +33(2) 99-65-53-65
EMail: contact@imnrennes.fr
Website: http://www.imnrennes.fr

Director: Anne-Sophie Lamé

Programme

Notary Studies (Justice Administration; Law; Notary Studies)

History: Founded 1892.

Admission Requirements: Secondary school certificate (baccalauréat) and jury selection; university degree in Law or in Notary studies and jury seclection

Main Language(s) of Instruction: French

Accrediting Agency: Ministry of Justice

Degrees and Diplomas: *Brevet de Technicien supérieur*: **Notary Studies.** Licence professionnelle (Université de Droit de Rennes); DIMN - Diplôme de l'institut des métiers du notariat (1 years following licence professionnelle with internship).

Last Updated: 26/03/15

SCHOOL OF ADVANCED ENGINEERING STUDIES

HEI - Hautes Etudes d'Ingénieur (HEI)

13, rue de Toul, 59046 Lille Cedex
Tel: +33(3) 28-38-48-58
Fax: +33(3) 28-38-48-04
EMail: contact@hei.fr
Website: http://www.hei.fr

Directeur: Vincent Six EMail: vincent.six@hei.fr

International Relations: David Perry, Head of International Relations Tel: +33(3) 28-38-46-60 EMail: david.perry@hei.fr

Department

Chemistry, textiles and innovative process (Chemical Engineering; Chemistry; Materials Engineering; Textile Technology); **Civil and mechanical construction** (Architecture and Planning; Civil Engineering; Construction Engineering; Mechanical Engineering); **Energy Engineering, Electrical Engineering and Automation** (Automation and Control Engineering; Biomedical Engineering; Electrical Engineering; Energy Engineering); **Organization, management and computer science** (Banking; Computer Science; Finance; Information Technology; Insurance; Management; Systems Analysis)

Further Information: Also campus in Châteauroux

History: Founded 1885. Acquired present title 2004.

Admission Requirements: Secondary school certificate (baccalauréat) or equivalent and competitive entrance examination

Fees: Engineering programme: 2,860-6,850 per annum; Master: 7,000 per annum (Euro)

Main Language(s) of Instruction: French

Accrediting Agency: Commission des Titres d'Ingénieur, Conférence des Grandes Ecoles

Degrees and Diplomas: *Licence professionnelle*: **Textile Technology.** *Diplôme d'Ingénieur*: **Chemistry; Civil Engineering; Computer Science; Electrical Engineering; Engineering; Industrial Management; Mechanics.** *Master*: **Energy Engineering; Environmental Studies.**

Student Services: Academic Counselling, Canteen, Careers Guidance, Cultural Activities, Language Laboratory, Sports Facilities

Last Updated: 25/03/15

SCHOOL OF ELECTRICAL ENGINEERING

Ecole supérieure d'Ingénieurs en Génie électrique (ESIGELEC)

B.P. 10024 Technopôle du Madrillet, 76801 St Etienne du Rouvray, Cedex
Tel: +33(2) 32-91-58-58
Fax: +33(2) 32-91-58-59
EMail: international@esigelec.fr
Website: http://www.esigelec.fr

Director General: Etienne Craye (2014-)

International Relations: Cecilia Brunel
EMail: cecilia.brunel@esigelec.fr

Department

Communication and Information Technologies (Information Technology); **Electrical Engineering and Energies** (Electrical Engineering; Energy Engineering); **Electronics and Telecommunications** (Electronic Engineering; Telecommunications Engineering); **Embedded System and Instrumentation** (Computer Science; Electronic Engineering; Instrument Making); **Humanities, Languages and Management** (Accountancy; Economics; Ethics; Law; Management; Modern Languages; Music)

Laboratory

Data Processing (Computer Engineering; Data Processing); **Industrial Automation** (Automation and Control Engineering; Electrical Engineering; Industrial Engineering); **Networks**

Architecture (Computer Networks); **Optical Telecommunications** (Telecommunications Engineering)

Graduate School

Electrical Engineering (Electrical Engineering)

History: Founded 1901 as Ecole Pratique d'Electricité Industrielle. Acquired present status and title 1980.

Academic Year: September to June (September-January; February-June)

Admission Requirements: Competitive entrance examination following 2-3 yrs further study after secondary school certificate (baccalauréat) or following first university qualification (DEUG, DUT or BTS), or equivalent

Fees: Engineering course: 6,450 per annum; Master: 11,100 (Euro)

Main Language(s) of Instruction: French, English

Degrees and Diplomas: *Diplôme d'Ingénieur*: **Engineering.** *Master*: **Computer Science; Electronic Engineering.** *Doctorat*: **Automation and Control Engineering; Computer Science; Electronic Engineering.**

Student Services: Canteen, Careers Guidance, Facilities for disabled people, Library

Last Updated: 19/03/15

SCHOOL OF ELECTRONICS - PARIS

Institut Supérieur d'Electronique de Paris

28, rue Notre Dame des Champs, 75006 Paris
Tel: +33(1) 49-54-52-43
Fax: +33(1) 49-54-52-01
EMail: info@isep.fr
Website: http://www.isep.fr/

Director General: Michel Ciazynski
EMail: michel.ciazynski@isep.fr

Programme

Engineering (Computer Engineering; Engineering; Information Technology; Software Engineering; Telecommunications Engineering)

History: Founded 1955. Affiliated to the Institut catholique de Paris.

Admission Requirements: Competitive entrance examination, secondary school certificate in Science (Baccalauréat S)

Fees: 3,100 - 7,900 per annum (Euro)

Main Language(s) of Instruction: French

Accrediting Agency: Commission des Titres d'ingénieur (CTI)

Degrees and Diplomas: *Diplôme d'Ingénieur*: **Computer Engineering; Engineering.** *Mastère spécialisé*: **Computer Engineering; Electronic Engineering; Information Technology; Telecommunications Engineering.**

Last Updated: 08/04/15

SCHOOL OF ENGINEERS IN ELECTRICAL ENGINEERING, PRODUCTION AND INDUSTRIAL MANAGEMENT

Ecole supérieure d'Ingénieurs en Génie Electrique, Productique et Management Industriel

13 Boulevard de l'Hautil, 95092 Cergy-Pontoise, Cedex
Tel: +33(1) 30-75-60-40
Fax: +33(1) 30-75-60-41
EMail: contact@epmi.fr
Website: http://www.epmi.fr

Directeur général: Moumen Darchérif

International Relations: Ursula Arnold
Tel: +33(1) 30-75-69-48 EMail: u.arnold@ecam-epmi.fr

Programme

Engineering (Electrical Engineering; Engineering; Production Engineering); **Industrial Management** (Industrial Management)

History: Founded 1992. Associated with the Institut catholique de Paris.

Admission Requirements: Secondary school certificate (Baccalauréat) in sciences or equivalent

Fees: 4,670-6,850 per annum (Euro)

Main Language(s) of Instruction: French

Accrediting Agency: Commission des titres d'ingénieur (CTI)

Degrees and Diplomas: *Diplôme d'Ingénieur*: **Energy Engineering; Engineering.** *Mastère spécialisé*: **Technology.**

Last Updated: 20/03/15

SCHOOL OF ENTREPRENEURS AND BUSINESS EXECUTIVES

Ecole des Dirigeants et des Créateurs d'Entreprise (EDC PARIS)

70, galerie des Damiers, La Défense 1, 92415 Courbevoie
Tel: +33(1) 46-93-02-70
Fax: +33(1) 46-93-02-74
EMail: informations@edcparis.edu
Website: http://www.edcparis.edu

Managing Director: Jean-Marcel Jammet

International Relations: Cécile Chiaramonti
Tel: +33(1) 46-93-02-85 EMail: cecile.chiaramonti@edcparis.edu

Programme

Management (Business and Commerce; Finance; International Business; Management; Marketing)

Institute

Luxury Brand Marketing (Marketing)

Further Information: Also Observatory and Research Entrepreneurship Centre (OCRE)

History: Founded 1950. Recognized by the State 1967. In 1995, it was bought by the EDC Alumni and transformed into a specialized business school.

Academic Year: September to April (September-December; January-April)

Admission Requirements: Baccalauréat or equivalent Secondary School degree, entrance exam

Main Language(s) of Instruction: French, English

Accrediting Agency: Ministère de l'Enseignement supérieur et de la Recherche, Conférence des Grandes Ecoles

Degrees and Diplomas: *Master*: **E- Business/Commerce; Finance; International Business; Management; Marketing.** Bachelor, MBA specialised in Luxury Brand Marketing

Student Services: Canteen, Library

Last Updated: 11/03/15

SCHOOL OF INFORMATION AND COMMUNICATIONS ENGINEERING TECHNOLOGIES

Ecole d'Ingénieur des Technologies de l'Information et de la Communication (EFREI)

30-32, av. de la République, 94800 Villejuif
Tel: +33(1) 46-77-46-77
Fax: +33(1) 43-37-65-77
EMail: informations@efrei.fr
Website: http://www.efrei.fr

Director: Frédéric Meunier (2009-) EMail: frederic.meunier@efrei.fr

Programme

General training (Business Administration; Chinese; Commercial Law; Communication Studies; English; French; Japanese; Modern Languages; Spanish); **Scientific and technical Engineering** (Electronic Engineering; Information Technology; Mathematics and Computer Science; Physics)

History: Founded 1936. Acquired present status 1956.

Academic Year: September to May (September-January; January-May)

Admission Requirements: Secondary school certificate (Baccalauréat) and competitive oral examination

Fees: 7,500 per annum (Euro)

Main Language(s) of Instruction: French

Accrediting Agency: CTI (Ministry of Education)

Degrees and Diplomas: *Licence*: **Engineering.** *Diplôme d'Ingénieur*: **Engineering; Information Technology.** *Master*: **Engineering.**

Student Services: Canteen, Residential Facilities

Student Numbers *2013*: Total 1,100

Last Updated: 11/03/15

SCHOOL OF INTERNATIONAL AND POLITICAL STUDIES

Ecole des hautes études internationales et politiques (HEI-HEP)

37-39 boulevard Murat, 75016 Paris
Tel: +33(1) 47-20-57-47
EMail: contact@hei-hep.com
Website: http://www.hei-hep.com

Vice-President: Odile Launay

School

International Studies (Communication Studies; Economics; English; International Relations; Law; Political Sciences); **Political Sciences** (Communication Studies; Economics; English; Law; Political Sciences; Social Sciences)

History: Founded 1899.

Admission Requirements: Secondary school certificate (baccalauréat) or foreign equivalent, jury selection and entrance examination.

Fees: Bachelor: 6,500; Master: 7,500 (Euro)

Main Language(s) of Instruction: French

Degrees and Diplomas: Bachelor; Mastère

Last Updated: 25/03/15

SCHOOL OF REAL ESTATE PROFESSIONS

Ecole supérieure des Professions immobilières (ESPI)

20-22 rue du Théâtre, 75015 Paris
Tel: +33(1) 45-67-20-82
Fax: +33(1) 42-73-19-85
EMail: accueil@espi.asso.fr
Website: http://www.espi.asso.fr

Director: Isabelle Favre

Programme

Real Estate (Real Estate)

Further Information: Also site in Nantes.

History: Founded 1972.

Admission Requirements: Baccalauréat or equivalent Secondary School degree

Fees: Undergraduate studies, 6,990 per annum; Mastère,7,990 per annum (Euro)

Main Language(s) of Instruction: French

Accrediting Agency: Ministry of Education

Degrees and Diplomas: *Master*: **Real Estate.** Diploma ESPI (undergraduate studies in 3 yrs).

Last Updated: 20/03/15

SCHOOL OF WELDING AND ITS APPLICATIONS

Ecole supérieure du Soudage et de ses Applications (ESSA)

Espace Cormontaigne, 4, Bd Henri Becquerel, 57970 Yutz
Tel: +33(1) 82-59-86-35
Fax: +33(1) 82-59-86-40
Website: www.essa-eaps.isgroupe.com

Director of Studies: Philippe Roguin
Tel: +33(3) 82-59-86-35 EMail: p.roguin@institutdesoudure.com

Programme

Welding (Construction Engineering; Materials Engineering; Metal Techniques)

History: Founded 1930, acquired present status and title 1931.

Academic Year: September to June

Admission Requirements: Diplôme d'Ingénieur or equivalent

Main Language(s) of Instruction: French

Accrediting Agency: Ministry of Education. Industries

Degrees and Diplomas: *Diplôme d'Ingénieur*: **Metal Techniques.**

Publications: Soudage et techniques connexes; Souder

Publishing House: PSA (Publications du Soudage et de ses Applications)

Last Updated: 23/03/15

SPECIAL SCHOOL OF ARCHITECTURE

Ecole spéciale d'Architecture

254 boulevard Raspail, 75014 Paris
Tel: +33(1) 40-47-40-47
Fax: +33(1) 40-47-40-30
EMail: info@esa-paris.fr
Website: http://www.esa-paris.fr

Director: François Bouvard EMail: francois_bouvard@esa-paris.net

International Relations: Marie-Hélène Amiot
EMail: mhamiot@esa-paris.net

Programme

Architecture (Architecture)

Admission Requirements: Entrance examination and jury selection

Fees: First cycle: 8 000 per annum; Second Cycle: 8 400 per annum (Euro)

Main Language(s) of Instruction: French

Degrees and Diplomas: 1er cycle (3 ans) : Diplôme de l'ESA Grade 1, valant grade de Licence. 2ème cycle (2 ans) : Diplôme de l'ESA Grade 2, valant grade de Master. Habilitation à exercer la maîtrise d'oeuvre en son nom propre : Architecte DESA (hmonp). 3ème cycle : Environnementaliste DESA, Urbaniste DESA

Last Updated: 17/03/15

SUPÉLEC

Ecole supérieure d'Electricité (SUPELEC)

Plateau de Moulon, 3 rue Joliot-Curie, 91192 Gif-sur-Yvette, Cedex
Tel: +33(1) 69-85-12-12
Fax: +33(1) 69-85-12-34
Website: http://www.supelec.fr

Director General: Hervé Biausser
EMail: catherine.luce@supelec.fr

Secretary General: Nadine Brière
Tel: +33(1) 69-85-12-71 EMail: nadine.briere@supelec.fr

International Relations: Claude Lhermitte, Head of International Relations
Tel: +33(1) 69-85-12-43 EMail: claude.lhermitte@supelec.fr

Department

Automatic Control Systems (Automation and Control Engineering); **Computer Science** (Artificial Intelligence; Computer Engineering; Computer Science); **Electromagnetism** (Applied Physics; Telecommunications Engineering); **Electronics and Signal Processing** (Electronic Engineering); **Languages and Culture** (Cultural Studies; Modern Languages); **Power Systems and Power Electronics** (Electrical Engineering; Power Engineering); **Telecommunications** (Radio and Television Broadcasting; Telecommunications Engineering)

Laboratory

Electrical Engineering *(LGEP)* (Electrical Engineering); **Electromagnetism and Radars** *(SONDRA: Singapore cooperation project)* (Applied Physics); **Optics and Solids Electronics** *(LMOPS)* (Optics; Solid State Physics); **Signals and Systems** *(L2S)* (Automation and Control Engineering; Statistics; Systems Analysis; Telecommunications Engineering)

Further Information: Also campuses in Metz and Rennes

History: Founded 1894. Managed by the Société des Electriciens et des Electroniciens (SEE); Electricité de France; Fédération des Industries électriques, électroniques et de Communication.

Academic Year: September to June

Admission Requirements: Competitive entrance examination following secondary school certificate (baccalauréat) or equivalent

Fees: Engineering course and specialization: 1320-5900; Master: 256; PhD: 391 (Euro)

Main Language(s) of Instruction: French

Accrediting Agency: Commission du Titre d'Ingénieur

Degrees and Diplomas: *Diplôme d'Ingénieur*: **Automation and Control Engineering; Computer Engineering; Electronic Engineering; Energy Engineering; Engineering; Telecommunications Engineering.** *Mastère spécialisé*: **Computer Science; Energy Engineering; Information Sciences.** *Doctorat*: **Automation and Control Engineering; Computer Science; Electrical and Electronic Engineering; Energy Engineering; Information Sciences; Telecommunications Engineering.** Also Masters Recherche

Student Services: Academic Counselling, Canteen, Cultural Activities, Facilities for disabled people, Language Laboratory, Sports Facilities

Last Updated: 30/03/15

THE ISG INTERNATIONAL BUSINESS SCHOOL

Institut supérieur de Gestion (ISG)
8, rue de Lota, 75116 Paris
Tel: +33(1) 56-26-26-26
Fax: +33(1) 56-26-26-00
EMail: isg@isg.fr
Website: http://www.isg.fr

President: Marc Sellam

International Relations: Juliette Leroy, Head of International Relations Tel: +33(1)56-26-26-28 EMail: international@isg.fr

Programme

Management (Business Administration; Finance; International Business; Management; Marketing; Sports Management)

Research Centre

Applied Research in Management *(IRSAM in collaboration with Paris XII)*

Further Information: Has schools in New York and Tokyo.

History: Founded in 1967.

Admission Requirements: Baccalaureate or equivalent high school diploma for Preparatory Classes; 2 years undergraduate studies and entrance exam

Main Language(s) of Instruction: French, English

Accrediting Agency: Association of Collegiate Business Schools and Programs, International Assembly for Collegiate Business Education, Conférence des Grandes Ecoles (CGE)

Degrees and Diplomas: *Master*: **Business Administration.** Bachelors in Business Administration, International MBA in English (offered in French or English), MBA spécialisé.

Last Updated: 09/04/15

TOULOUSE BUSINESS SCHOOL

Groupe ESC Toulouse (ESCT)
20, boulevard Lascrosses, 31068 Toulouse, Cedex 7
Tel: +33(5) 61-29-49-49
Fax: +33(5) 61-29-49-94
EMail: info@esc-toulouse.fr
Website: http://www.esc-toulouse.fr

Director: Jacques Igalens (2013-)

Programme

European MBA (Business Administration)

School

Business Administration and Management (Business Administration; Management)

Institute

European Negotiation (Business Administration)

Centre

Business Studies (Business and Commerce); **Research and Engineering** (Engineering)

Further Information: Also campuses in Barcelona and Casablanca

History: Founded 1903 by the Chambre de Commerce et d'Industrie de Toulouse.

Academic Year: September to June (September-December; January-March; April-June)

Admission Requirements: Competitive entrance examination following 2 yrs further study after secondary school certificate (baccalauréat) or equivalent

Fees: Commercial diploma course, 6,022 per annum; Master, 9,200 (Euro)

Main Language(s) of Instruction: French

Accrediting Agency: Association des Chambres Française de Commerce et d'Industrie (ACFCI), Répertoire Nationale des Certifications Professionnelles (RNCP), Ministry of Education

Degrees and Diplomas: *Licence professionnelle*; *Diplôme d'Etudes d'Ecole de Commerce et Gestion*; *Mastère spécialisé*. Also MBA, DBA

Publications: Les Cahiers de Recherche

Last Updated: 10/04/15

TRAINING CENTRE FOR BANKING

Centre de formation de la profession bancaire (CFPB)
Immeuble le Carillon, 5 esplanade Charles de Gaulle, 92739 Nanterre
Tel: +33(1) 41-02-55-00
Fax: +33(1) 41-02-55-55
EMail: international@cfpb.fr
Website: http://www.cfpb.fr

Managing Director: Michel Piano (2012-)

International Relations: Lionel Martin
EMail: international@cfpb.fr

Institute

Banking *(ITB)* (Banking; Management); **Markets** *(ITM)* (Banking; Finance; Management)

History: Founded in 1926.

Main Language(s) of Instruction: French

Degrees and Diplomas: *Brevet de Technicien supérieur*: **Banking.** *Licence professionnelle*: **Banking.** *Mastère spécialisé*: **Banking; Finance.** *Master*: **Banking; Business Administration; Finance.** Also: Masters professionnel, Certificate, Vocational Diploma

Last Updated: 11/03/15

France - French Guyana

INSTITUTION

PUBLIC INSTITUTION

UNIVERSITY OF THE FRENCH ANTILLES AND GUYANA - FRENCH GUYANA

Université des Antilles et de la Guyane
Avenue Bois Chaudat, BP 725, 97157 Kourou
Tel: +594-32-12-40
Fax: +594 32-10-64
EMail: charge.communication@guyane.univ-ag.fr
Website: http://www.univ-ag.fr

President: Corinne Mence-Caster (2013-)
Tel: +590 48-31-89 EMail: dina.saintau@univ-ag.fr

Administrative Officer: Christophe Audebert
Tel: +590 48-30-30 EMail: christophe.audebert@univ-ag.fr

International Relations: Maryvonne Charlery, Programme Coordinator
Tel: +590 48-32-21
EMail: bri@univ-ag.fr; maryvonne.charlery@univ-ag.fr

Faculty

Exact Sciences and Natural Sciences *(based in Guadeloupe and Martinique)* (Biological and Life Sciences; Chemistry; Engineering; Geology; Mathematics and Computer Science; Physics); **Law and Economics** *(based in Martinique and Guadeloupe)* (Economics; Law; Political Sciences); **Literature and Human Sciences** *(based in Martinique)* (Arts and Humanities; Educational Sciences; History; Information Sciences); **Medicine** (Medicine); **Sports Sciences** (Sports)

School

Teacher Training *(ESPE - based in French Guyana, Guadeloupe and Martinique)* (Teacher Training)

Institute

Higher Education *(Guyane-IESG)* (Arts and Humanities; Biochemistry; Biological and Life Sciences; Economics; English; Geology; Health Sciences; Law; Literature; Mathematics and Computer Science; Musicology; Portuguese; Waste Management; Water Management); **Law** *(IEJ - based in Martinique)* (Law); **Public Administration** *(IPAG)* (Public Administration); **Technology** *(IUT de Kourou, some departments are based in Guadeloupe and Martinique)* (Bioengineering; Biotechnology; Business Administration; Business Computing; Electrical Engineering; Hygiene; Management; Safety Engineering; Sales Techniques; Technology; Telecommunications Engineering; Transport Engineering)

Higher Institute

French Studies *(ISEF)* (French Studies)

Research Institute

Mathematics Education *(IREM)* (Mathematics Education)

Further Information: The University of the French Antilles and Guyana has campuses in Martinique, Guadeloupe and French Guyana along with Research Units

History: Established by the Bordeaux Law Faculty in 1883 as a Centre of Law Studies in Antilles-Guyane. It was expanded to include a Literature and Science Unit in 1963 and by 1971, it had gained its independent status with the addition of the Basic and Natural Science Unit. In 1982, the Ministry of Education awarded its full title of University.

Admission Requirements: Baccalauréat or equivalent Secondary School Diploma

Main Language(s) of Instruction: French

Accrediting Agency: Ministry of Education

Degrees and Diplomas: *Capacité en Droit*: **Law.** *Diplôme d'Accès aux Etudes universitaires*; *Diplôme universitaire de Technologie*; *Licence*: **Economics; Educational Sciences; Engineering; Health Sciences; Mathematics; Modern Languages; Physical Education; Social Sciences; Sports.** *Licence professionnelle*; *Diplôme d'Etat*: **Medicine.** *Diplôme d'Ingénieur*: **Energy Engineering; Environmental Engineering.** *Master*: **Biological and Life Sciences; Ecology; Economics; Education; Educational Sciences; French; Geography; History; Information Sciences; Law; Materials Engineering; Mathematics and Computer Science; Modern Languages; Natural Sciences; Political Sciences; Teacher Training.** *Doctorat*: **Agronomy; Applied Mathematics; Astronomy and Space Science; Biological and Life Sciences; Chemistry; Civil Engineering; Electrical Engineering; Mathematics and Computer Science; Mechanical Engineering; Physics; Public Health; Sports; Technology.** Prepares for Teaching Certificate

Last Updated: 08/04/15

France - French Polynesia

INSTITUTION

PUBLIC INSTITUTION

UNIVERSITY OF FRENCH POLYNESIA

Université de la Polynésie française

BP 6570-98 702 FAA'A Tahiti, 98702 Papeete, Tahiti
Tel: +689 40 803 894
Fax: +689 40 803 804
EMail: courrier@upf.pf
Website: http://www.upf.pf

Président: Eric Conte (2011-)
Tel: +689 80-38-14 EMail: president@upf.pf

Services Director: Alexandre Hourcade
Tel: +689 40 803 838 EMail: dgs@upf.pf

International Relations: Léopold Musiyan
EMail: relations-internationales@upf.pf

School

Teacher Training *(ESPE)* (Teacher Trainers Education; Teacher Training)

Department

Arts, Languages and Humanities (Arts and Humanities; Communication Studies; Development Studies; English; French; Geography; History; Island Studies; Literature; Spanish; Translation and Interpretation); **Law, Economics and Accountancy** (Accountancy; Economics; Law); **Sciences, Technology and Health** (Biological and Life Sciences; Biology; Cell Biology; Chemistry; Computer Science; Earth Sciences; Health Sciences; Marine Science and Oceanography; Mathematics; Mathematics and Computer Science; Natural Sciences; Physical Engineering; Physics; Technology)

History: Founded 1987. Acquired present status 1999.

Academic Year: September to June (September-December; January-June)

Admission Requirements: Secondary school certificate (baccalauréat) and entrance examination

Main Language(s) of Instruction: French

Degrees and Diplomas: *Capacité en Droit*: **Law.** *Diplôme d'Accès aux Etudes universitaires*; *Licence*: **Arts and Humanities; Biological and Life Sciences; Chemistry; Earth Sciences; Economics; Environmental Studies; Geography; Health Sciences; History; Law; Literature; Management; Mathematics and Computer Science; Medical Technology; Medicine; Modern Languages; Natural Sciences; Physics; Public Administration; Regional Studies; Social Sciences.** *Licence professionnelle*: **Computer Science; Electrical Engineering; Hotel and Restaurant.** *Master*: **Arts and Humanities; Educational Sciences; Environmental Studies; Law; Management; Regional Studies; Social Sciences; Teacher Training.** Also Continuing Education Degrees; Diplôme d'Université

Student Services: Academic Counselling, Canteen, Facilities for disabled people, Health Services, Library, Residential Facilities, Social Counselling, Sports Facilities

Publications: Revue juridique polynésienne

Student Numbers *2013-2014*: Total 3,390
Last Updated: 13/02/15

France - Guadeloupe

INSTITUTION

PUBLIC INSTITUTION

UNIVERSITY OF THE ANTILLES AND GUYANA - GUADELOUPE

Université des Antilles et de la Guyane - Guadeloupe (UAG)

BP 250, Campus de Fouillole, 97157 Pointe-à-Pitre, Cedex
Tel: +590-48-90-00
Fax: +590-91-06-57
Website: http://www.univ-ag.fr

President: Corinne Mence-Caster (2013 -)
EMail: dina.saintau@univ-ag.fr

Administrative Manager: Christophe Audebert
EMail: christophe.audebert@univ-ag.fr

Programme Coordinator: Maryvonne Charlery Maryvonne Charlery EMail: bri@univag.fr

Faculty
Exact Sciences and Natural Sciences *(Based in Guadeloupe and Martinique)* (Biological and Life Sciences; Chemistry; Engineering; Geology; Mathematics and Computer Science; Physics); **Law and Economics** *(based in Martinique and Guadeloupe)* (Economics; Law); **Literature and Human Sciences** *(Based in Martinique)* (Arts and Humanities; Education; History; Information Sciences); **Medical Sciences** (Medicine); **Sports** (Physical Education; Sports; Sports Management)

Institute
Law *(IEJ, based in Martinique)* (Law); **Public Administration** *(IPAG)* (Administration; Public Administration); **Teacher Training** *(ESPE - based in Guadeloupe, French Guyana and Martinique)* (Teacher Trainers Education; Teacher Training); **Technology** *(IUT de Kourou, some departments are based in Guadeloupe and Martinique)* (Biotechnology; Business Administration; Business Computing; Electrical Engineering; Management; Technology; Transport Management)

Research Institute
Mathematics Education (Mathematics Education)

Further Information: The University of the French Antilles and Guyana has campuses in Martinique, Guadeloupe and French Guyana along with Research Units

History: Founded 1970 as Centre Universitaire, incorporating previously existing University centres in Guadeloupe and Martinique. Became University 1982. Attached to the Académie de Bordeaux. Financially supported by the Ministry of Education.

Admission Requirements: Secondary school certificate (baccalauréat) or foreign equivalent or special entrance examination

Main Language(s) of Instruction: French

Accrediting Agency: Ministry of Education

Degrees and Diplomas: *Capacité en Droit*: **Law.** *Diplôme universitaire de Technologie*; *Licence*: **Economics; Educational Sciences; Engineering; Health Sciences; Mathematics; Modern Languages; Physical Education; Social Sciences; Sports.** *Licence professionnelle*; *Diplôme d'Ingénieur*: **Engineering.** *Master*: **Biological and Life Sciences; Ecology; Economics; Education; Educational Sciences; Geography; History; Information Sciences; Law; Materials Engineering; Mathematics and Computer Science; Modern Languages; Natural Sciences; Political Sciences; Teacher Training.** *Doctorat*: **Agronomy; Applied Mathematics; Astronomy and Space Science; Biological and Life Sciences; Chemistry; Civil Engineering; Electrical Engineering; Engineering; Mechanical Engineering; Physics; Public Health; Sports; Technology.** Also prepares for Teaching Certificate

Publications: Bulletin de liaison des chercheurs

Last Updated: 08/04/15

France - Martinique

PUBLIC INSTITUTIONS

ARTS CAMPUS OF MARTINIQUE

Campus caribéen des arts - Martinique (CCA)
rue Carlos -Finlais, 97200 Fort-de-France
Tel: +596 596 60-65-29
Fax: +596 596 63-74-09
EMail: contact@campuscaraibeendesarts.com

President: Daniel Robin (2014-)

Department

Arts *(Métiers des Arts)* (Fine Arts; Visual Arts); **Cinema and Communication** (Cinema and Television); **Performing Arts** (Dance; Music; Performing Arts; Theatre); **Research**; **Visual Arts** (Visual Arts)

History: Founded 2011

Main Language(s) of Instruction: French

Degrees and Diplomas: *Master*. Diplôme national d'arts plastiques (DNAP) 3 years; Diplôme national supérieur d'expression plastique (DNSEP) 5 years; Also Master in Arts with the University of the Antilles and Guyana

Last Updated: 07/04/15

UNIVERSITY OF THE ANTILLES AND GUYANA - MARTINIQUE

Université des Antilles et de la Guyane - Martinique
Campus de Schoelcher, 97200 Fort-de-France, Cedex
Website: http://www.univ-ag.fr/

President: Corinne Mence-Caster (2013-)
EMail: dina.saintau@univ-ag.fr

Administrative Officer: Christophe Audebert
EMail: christophe.audebert@univ-ag.fr

International Relations: Maryvonne Charlery, Programme Coordinator EMail: bri@univ-ag.fr

Faculty

Exact Sciences and Natural Sciences *(based in Martinique and Guadeloupe)* (Biological and Life Sciences; Chemistry; Engineering; Geology; Mathematics and Computer Science; Physics); **Law and Economics** (Economics; Law; Political Sciences); **Literature and Human Sciences** *(based in Martinique)* (Arts and Humanities; Educational Sciences; History; Information Sciences); **Medicine** (Medicine); **Sports sciences** (Sports)

School

Teacher training *(ESPE - based in Martinique, Guadeloupe and French Guyana)* (Teacher Training)

Institute

Higher Education *(French Guyana - IESG)* (Arts and Humanities; Civil Engineering; Computer Science; Economics; English; Law; Literature; Materials Engineering; Mathematics; Musicology; Portuguese); **Law** *(IEJ- based in Martinique)* (Law); **Public Administration** *(IPAG)* (Administration; Public Administration); **Technology** *(IUT de Kourou, some departments are based in Martinique and Guadeloupe)* (Bioengineering; Biotechnology; Business Administration; Business Computing; Electrical Engineering; Hygiene; Management; Safety Engineering; Sales Techniques; Technology; Telecommunications Engineering; Transport Engineering)

Higher Institute

French studies *(ISEF)* (French)

Research Institute

Mathematics Education *(IREM)* (Mathematics Education)

Further Information: The University of the French Antilles and Guyana has campuses in: Martinique, Guadeloupe and French Guyana along with Research Units

History: Founded 1850 as School of Law, became Centre universitaire des Antilles-Guyane 1949 and Université 1982. Attached to the Académie de Bordeaux. Financially supported by the Ministry of Education.

Admission Requirements: Secondary school certificate (baccalauréat) or foreign equivalent, or special entrance examination

Main Language(s) of Instruction: French

Accrediting Agency: Ministry of Education

Degrees and Diplomas: *Capacité en Droit*: **Law.** *Diplôme universitaire de Technologie*; *Licence*: **Arts and Humanities; Economics; Educational Sciences; Engineering; Health Sciences; Mathematics; Modern Languages; Physical Education; Social Sciences; Sports.** *Licence professionnelle*; *Diplôme d'Ingénieur*: **Engineering.** *Master*: **Biological and Life Sciences; Ecology; Economics; Education; Educational Sciences; Geography; History; Information Sciences; Law; Materials Engineering; Mathematics and Computer Science; Modern Languages; Natural Sciences; Political Sciences; Teacher Training.** *Doctorat*: **Agronomy; Applied Mathematics; Astronomy and Space Science; Biological and Life Sciences; Chemistry; Civil Engineering; Electrical Engineering; Mathematics and Computer Science; Mechanical Engineering; Physics; Public Health; Sports; Technology.**

Student Services: Academic Counselling, Canteen, Facilities for disabled people, Foreign Studies Centre, Health Services, Language Laboratory, Social Counselling, Sports Facilities

Last Updated: 08/04/15

France - New Caledonia

INSTITUTION

PUBLIC INSTITUTION

UNIVERSITY OF NEW CALEDONIA

Université de la Nouvelle Calédonie
BPR4, 98851 Nouméa, CEDEX
Tel: +687 29-02-90
Fax: +687 25-48-29
EMail: international@univ-nc.nc
Website: http://www.univ-nc.nc

Président: Gäel Lagadec
Tel: +687 29.00.01 EMail: gael.lagadec@univ-nc.nc

Directrice générale des Services: Odile Boyer
Tel: +687 29 02 90 EMail: sg@univ-nc.nc

International Relations: Joana Belo
Tel: +687 29 04 44 EMail: international@univ-nc.nc

Department

Continuing Education (Continuing Education); **Law, Economics and Management** (Business Administration; Economics; Law; Private Law; Public Law); **Literature, Languages and Humanities** *(Magenta)* (Ancient Civilizations; Comparative Literature; English; French; Geography (Human); History; Literature; Medieval Studies; Modern Languages; Pacific Area Studies); **Science and Technology** *(Nouville)* (Biochemistry; Biology; Cell Biology; Chemistry; Computer Science; Geology; Marine Biology; Mathematics; Metallurgical Engineering; Microbiology; Molecular Biology; Physics; Physiology)

Institute

Teacher Training *(IUFM)* (Teacher Training)

Graduate School

Multidisciplinary *(in cooperation with the University of French Polynesia)*

History: Founded 1987. A Centre of the Université française du Pacifique.

Academic Year: February to November

Admission Requirements: Secondary school certificate (baccalauréat) and entrance examination

Main Language(s) of Instruction: French

Accrediting Agency: Ministry of Education

Degrees and Diplomas: *Capacité en Droit*: **Law.** *Licence*: **Accountancy; Austronesian and Oceanic Languages; Biological and Life Sciences; Business Administration; Chemistry; Computer Engineering; Earth Sciences; English Studies; Geography; History; Law; Literature; Mathematics; Metallurgical Engineering; Physics.** *Master*: **Arts and Humanities; Law; Teacher Training.** *Doctorat*: **Arts and Humanities; Biological and Life Sciences; Environmental Studies; Law; Marine Science and Oceanography; Mathematics and Computer Science.**

Student Services: Canteen, Cultural Activities, Health Services, Library, Residential Facilities, Social Counselling, Sports Facilities

Last Updated: 13/02/15

France - Réunion

PUBLIC INSTITUTIONS

LA RÉUNION SCHOOL OF ARTS

École supérieure d'art de la Réunion (ESA)
102 avenue du 20 décembre 1848, B.P. 246, 97826 Le Port, Cedex
Tel: +262 262-43-08-01
Fax: +262 262-43-08-02
EMail: contact@esareunion.com
Website: http://www.esareunion.com/

Director: Patricia de Bollivier
EMail: patricia.debollivier@esareunion.com

Secretary General: Fabien Morin
EMail: fabien.morin@esareunion.com

International Relations: Markus Arnold, In charge of International Relations EMail: markus.arnold@esareunion.com

Programme

Arts and Design (Art History; Design; Furniture Design; Graphic Design; Multimedia; Visual Arts)

History: Founded 1991

Admission Requirements: Entrance examination. Secondary school certificate (Baccalauréat) or equivalent

Main Language(s) of Instruction: French

Accrediting Agency: Ministry of Culture; Ministry of Higher Education and Research

Degrees and Diplomas: Diplôme national d'arts Plastiques (DNAP) 3 years; Diplôme national supérieur d'expression plastique (DNSEP) 5 years

Last Updated: 07/04/15

UNIVERSITY OF LA RÉUNION

Université de La Réunion
15, avenue René Cassin, BP 7151, 97715 Saint-Denis Messag, Cedex 9
Tel: +262(93) 80-80
Fax: +262(93) 81-34
EMail: cabinet@univ-reunion.fr
Website: http://www.univ-reunion.fr

Président: Mohamed Rochdi (2008-)
EMail: cabinet@univ-reunion.fr

International Relations: Nicolas Moreau, Directeur
Tel: +262(2) 62-93-83-43 EMail: international@univ-reunion.fr

Faculty

Arts and Humanities (Arts and Humanities; Communication Studies; Educational Sciences; English; Ethnology; Geography; Germanic Studies; History; Literature); **Environment and Social Sciences** *(Campus SUD)* (Cultural Studies; French; Sports; Town Planning); **Health** (Dentistry; Medicine; Midwifery; Occupational Therapy; Pharmacy); **Law, Economics, and Political Science** (Economics; Law; Political Sciences); **Science and Technology** (Biochemistry; Biology; Chemistry; Computer Science; Earth Sciences; Food Technology; Mathematics; Molecular Biology; Natural Sciences; Physics; Technology)

School

Engineering (Engineering; Food Technology; Information Technology); **Teacher Training** *(ESPE, at both campuses)* (Educational Research; Educational Sciences; Teacher Trainers Education; Teacher Training)

Institute

Business Administration *(IAE)* (Business Administration); **Technology** *(IUT Saint-Pierre)* (Banking; Business Administration; Civil Engineering; E- Business/Commerce; Management; Technology; Telecommunications Engineering)

Further Information: Has a second campus at Le Tampon

History: Founded 1982 as Ecole de Jurisprudence, became Ecole de Droit 1926, Institut d'Etudes juridiques, politiques et économiques1950, and Centre Universitaire 1971. Acquired present status and title as a full-functioning French University and title 1982.

Academic Year: September to June (September-December; February-June)

Admission Requirements: Secondary school certificate (Baccalauréat) or equivalent and entrance examination

Main Language(s) of Instruction: French

Degrees and Diplomas: *Licence*: **Arts and Humanities; Business Administration; Economics; Health Sciences; Law; Natural Sciences; Social Sciences; Technology.** *Diplôme d'Ingénieur*: **Engineering.** *Master*: **Anthropology; Arts and Humanities; Biological and Life Sciences; Business Administration; Civil Engineering; Earth Sciences; Economics; Geography; Health Sciences; History; Information Sciences; Law; Mathematics and Computer Science; Modern Languages; Natural Sciences; Social Sciences; Sports; Teacher Training; Technology.** *Doctorat*: **Arts and Humanities; Economics; Law; Management.** Masters recherche, Masters professionnel. Also prepares for Teaching Certificate and French as a Foreign Language Certificates (DELF, DALF).

Student Services: Canteen, Cultural Activities, Facilities for disabled people, Health Services, Library, Residential Facilities, Sports Facilities

Student Numbers *2014-2015*: Total 14,264
Last Updated: 16/02/15

Gabon

STRUCTURE OF HIGHER EDUCATION SYSTEM

Description:

Higher education is provided by public universities as well as by various higher institutes, both public and private.

Stages of studies:

University level first stage: *Premier cycle*
The first stage leads after three years' study to the Licence.

University level second stage: *Deuxième cycle*
A further year of study leads to the Maîtrise. The Ecole nationale de la Magistrature trains Magistrates in four years after the Baccalauréat and in two years for holders of the Licence in Law. The title of Ingénieur is awarded on completion of five years' study. This stage is progressively being replaced by the Master as part of the implementation of the three-tier (LMD) reform in the country.

University level third stage: *Troisième cycle*
Doctorates are awarded after a minimum of three years' study and research after the Maitrise or Master. The Doctorat d'Etat in Medicine is awarded after six years' study.

ADMISSION TO HIGHER EDUCATION

Admission to university-level studies:
Name of secondary school credential required: Baccalauréat

For entry to: University

Foreign students admission:
Admission requirements: For access to university-level studies, foreign students must hold a secondary school leaving Certificate (Baccalauréat) or its equivalent and/or obtain the approval of the teachers' Commission of the department where they wish to be admitted. For access to postgraduate study and research, they must hold a Maîtrise or its equivalent.

Entry regulations: Foreign students must hold a visa and have financial guarantees.

Language proficiency: Students must have a good command of French.

NATIONAL BODIES

Ministère de l'Education nationale, de l'Enseignement supérieur et technique
Minister: Florentin MOUSSAVOU Moussavou
PO Box 06
Libreville
Tel: +241 764265
WWW: http://www.education-nationale.gouv.ga

Data for academic year: 2012-2013
Source: IAU from World Data on Education 2010/2011, UNESCO-IBE, 2012. Bodies 2016.

INSTITUTIONS

PUBLIC INSTITUTIONS

AFRICAN INSTITUTE OF COMPUTER SCIENCE

Institut africain d'Informatique (IAI)
BP 2263, Libreville
Tel: +241 72-00-05
Fax: +241 72-00-11
EMail: contact@iaisiege.com
Website: http://iai-siege.com

Directeur Général: Souleymane Koussoube (2007-)
EMail: skoussoube@yahoo.fr

Directeur de l'Enseignement: Jérome Avom
Tel: +241 07 19 68 65 EMail: avomj2011@yahoo.com

International Relations: Jocelyn Nembe, Directeur de la Recherche et du Développement

Department

Computer Networks (Computer Networks); **Economics/Management and Communication** (Communication Studies; Economics; Management); **Information Systems Engineering** (Information Technology); **Mathematics** (Mathematics); **Software Engineering** (Software Engineering)

Further Information: Also branches in Cameroon, Niger and Togo

History: Inter-states school founded in 1971.

Academic Year: From October to July

Admission Requirements: Baccalauréat (GCE A Level)

Fees: (FCFA) 2,500,000 per year

Main Language(s) of Instruction: French

Degrees and Diplomas: *Diplôme d'Ingénieur*: **Computer Science.** *Maîtrise*: **Computer Science; Management.**

Student Services: Health Services, Sports Facilities

Academic Staff *2010-2011*	MEN	WOMEN	TOTAL
FULL-TIME	10	–	**10**
PART-TIME	38	2	**40**
STAFF WITH DOCTORATE			
FULL-TIME	6	–	**6**
Student Numbers *2010-2011*			
All (Foreign included)	189	31	**220**
FOREIGN ONLY	138	20	**158**

NATIONAL SCHOOL OF FORESTRY AND WATER MANAGEMENT

Ecole nationale des Eaux et Forêts (ENEF)
BP 3960, Libreville
Tel: +241 48-02-12
Fax: +241 48-02-11
Website: http://www.labogabon.net/enef/index.html

Directeur général: Marcellin Nziengui EMail: bousseng1@yahoo.fr

Director of studies: Jean Paul Obame Engone
EMail: jpobame@hotmail.com

Department

Basic Sciences (Natural Sciences); **Continuing and Distance Education** (Civil Security; Environmental Studies; Hygiene); **Fauna and Hunting**; **Fishing and Aquaculture** (Aquaculture; Fishery); **Forest and Environmental Management** (Environmental Management; Forest Management); **Forest Exploitation and Wood Technology** (Forest Products; Wood Technology)

History: Founded 1959. Acquired present status 1975.

Academic Year: September to July: (September-April; April-July)

Main Language(s) of Instruction: French

Degrees and Diplomas: *Diplôme d'Ingénieur*. Also Diplôme d'Etudes Supérieures Spécialisées

Student Services: Academic Counselling, Canteen, Health Services, Sports Facilities

Last Updated: 24/08/12

NATIONAL SCHOOL OF MAGISTRACY

Ecole nationale de la Magistrature (ENM)
BP 46, Libreville
Tel: +241 72-00-06

Directeur des Etudes: Alphonse Nkorouma
EMail: alnko2000@yahoo.fr

Department

Administrative Law (Administrative Law); **Civil Law** (Civil Law); **Commercial Law**; **Justice**; **Law** (Law); **Magistracy** (Justice Administration); **Penal Law** (Criminal Law)

History: Founded 1971.

NATIONAL SCHOOL OF PUBLIC ADMINISTRATION

Ecole nationale d'Administration (ENA)
BP 86, Libreville
Tel: +241 74 56 37
Fax: +241 72 49 89
EMail: enagabon@yahoo.fr
Website: http://www.enagabon.com/

Directeur Général: Anatole Tsioukacka (2009-)

Secrétaire Général: Anny Carole Lembeme Dicka

Department

Administration (Administration); **Diplomacy** (International Relations); **Health and Hospital Administration** (Health Administration); **Labour Inspection** (Labour and Industrial Relations); **Local Authorities Administration** (Administration); **School and University Administration** (Educational Administration)

History: Founded 1962.

Academic Year: November-July (November-April; May-July)

Accrediting Agency: Ministère de la fonction publique et de la réforme administrative

Degrees and Diplomas: *Master*

Last Updated: 24/08/12

OMAR BONGO UNIVERSITY

Université Omar Bongo (UOB)
BP 13131, Libreville, Estuaire
Tel: +241 173-20-33
Fax: +241 173-20-45
EMail: rectorat2010@gmail.com
Website: http://www.uob.ga

Recteur: Pierre Dominique Nzinzi
Tel: +241 173-20-33 EMail: pierre.nzinzi@gmail.com

Secrétaire Général: Charles Mba Ovono Tel: +241 173-01-42

International Relations: Lucie Mba
Tel: +241 640-07-86 EMail: relations.internationales@yahoo.fr

Faculty

Arts and Humanities (African American Studies; African Studies; American Studies; Anthropology; Archaeology; Clinical Psychology; Communication Arts; Cultural Studies; Developmental Psychology; Educational Psychology; English; English Studies; French; French Studies; Geography (Human); German; Germanic Studies; Hispanic American Studies; History; Journalism; Linguistics; Literature; Mass Communication; Modern Languages; Philosophy; Portuguese; Psychology; Social Psychology; Sociology; Spanish); **Law and Economics** (Administration; Business Administration; Economics; Finance; Management; Private Law; Public Administration; Public Law; Social Sciences)

History: Founded 1970 incorporating institutions which were previously part of the Fondation de l'Enseignement supérieur en Afrique Centrale (FESAC) as Université nationale du Gabon (UNG). Renamed 1978 as Université Omar Bongo (UOB). Acquired present status 2002.

Academic Year: October to July (October-March; April-July)

Admission Requirements: Secondary school certificate (baccalauréat) or equivalent or entrance examination

Fees: (FCFA) 1rst cycle: 9,000 (189,000 for foreign students); 2nd and 3rd cycles: 20,000 (189,000 for foreign students)

Main Language(s) of Instruction: French

Accrediting Agency: Ministère de l'Enseignement Supérieur, de la Recherche Scientifique et du Développement Technologique

Degrees and Diplomas: *Licence*: **Arts and Humanities; Business Administration; Social Sciences.** *Master*: **Arts and Humanities; Business Administration; Information Sciences; Social Sciences.**

Student Services: Academic Counselling, Canteen, Cultural Activities, Foreign Studies Centre, Health Services, Social Counselling, Sports Facilities

Publications: Annales de l'Université Omar Bongo

Publishing House: Presse Universitaire du Gabon (PUG)

UNIVERSITY OF HEALTH SCIENCES

Université des Sciences de la Santé (USS)
BP 18 231, Owendo, Libreville
Tel: +241 70 28 20
Fax: +241 70 28 19
Website: http://www.labogabon.net/uss/index.html; http://www.uss-univ.com/

Recteur: André Moussavou-Mouyama
EMail: moussavoua@yahoo.fr

Secrétaire général: Lucien Nzong

Faculty

Medicine (Medicine)

History: Founded 2002.

Main Language(s) of Instruction: French

Accrediting Agency: Ministère de l'Enseignement Supérieur, de la Recherche Scientifique et du Développement Technologique

Degrees and Diplomas: *Docteur en Médecine*: **Medicine.** Also Certificat d'Etudes Spécialisées, Diplôme d'Etat de Sage-Femme, Diplôme d'Etat de Technicien Supérieur de Biologie Médicale

Last Updated: 23/08/12

UNIVERSITY OF SCIENCE AND TECHNIQUES OF MASUKU

Université des Sciences et Techniques de Masuku (USTM)
BP 901, Franceville
Tel: +241 67 74 49
Fax: +241 67 74 49
Website: http://www.labogabon.net/ustm

Recteur: Isaac Mouaragadja
Tel: +241 27 80 86 EMail: rectorat@masuku.net

Secrétaire général: Léon Ngadi Tel: +241 67 77 35

Faculty

Science (Biology; Chemistry; Geology; Mathematics; Physics)

School

Polytechnic *(EPM)*

Institute

Agronomy and Biotechnology *(INSAB)*

History: Founded 1986, incorporating Faculty of sciences of Université Omar Bongo (UOB) and Ecole Nationale Supérieure d'Ingénieurs de Libreville (ENSIL).

Main Language(s) of Instruction: French

Accrediting Agency: Ministère de l'Enseignement Supérieur, de la Recherche Scientifique et du Développement Technologique

Degrees and Diplomas: *Licence*; *Diplôme d'Ingénieur*: **Engineering.** *Maîtrise*

Last Updated: 23/08/12

PRIVATE INSTITUTION

INTERNATIONAL CENTRE FOR MEDICAL RESEARCH OF FRANCEVILLE

Centre international de Recherches médicales de Franceville (CIRMF)
BP 769, Franceville
Tel: +241 67 70 92
Fax: +241 67 72 95
EMail: faxcirmf@yahoo.com
Website: http://www.cirmf.org

Directeur général: Jean-Paul Gonzalez
Tel: +241 67 71 06 EMail: jeanpaul.gonzalez@ird.fr

Centre

Primatology (Veterinary Science)

Research Unit

Ecology of Health (Ecology; Health Sciences); **Hemopathy** (Haematology); **Parasitology** (Parasitology); **Tropical Ecosystems** (Tropical Agriculture); **Virology** (Virology)

Further Information: Also in Libreville.

History: Founded 1979.

Admission Requirements: Master's Degree

Main Language(s) of Instruction: French

Degrees and Diplomas: Postgraduate training at MSc and PhD levels.

Last Updated: 23/08/12

Gambia (The)

STRUCTURE OF HIGHER EDUCATION SYSTEM

Description:

Tertiary education in The Gambia covers all post-secondary programmes and includes technical, teacher, university education and research.

Stages of studies:

University level first stage: Bachelor's degree

The first stage of university education leads to a Bachelor's degree after four years of study in Humanities and Social Studies, Economics and Management Science and Nursing and Public Health and six years in Medicine and Surgery.

University level second stage: Master's degree

The second stage of university education leads to a Master's degree after one to two years of study.

ADMISSION TO HIGHER EDUCATION

Admission to university-level studies:

Name of secondary school credential required: West African Senior Secondary Certificate

Minimum score/requirement: Five credits

Foreign students admission:

Entry regulations: A visa is required for non-Commonwealth citizens as well as study or residential permits for all non-Gambians.

Language proficiency: Proficiency in English is required.

NATIONAL BODIES

Ministry of Higher Education, Research, Science and Technology

Minister: Aboubacar Senghore
Bertil Hardway
Kotu
Tel: +220 446 5752
Fax: +220 446 5408
EMail: info@moherst.gov.gm
WWW: http://www.moherst.gov.gm

National Training Authority - NTA

Director General: Ousman G.M. Nyang
PO Box 1087
Banjul
Tel: +220 437 0518
Fax: +220 437 0548
EMail: info@nta.gm; nta@nta.gm
WWW: http://www.nta.gm

Data for academic year: 2012-2013

Source: IAU from World Data on Education 2010/2011, IBE-UNESCO and the US Embassy in The Gambia website, 2012. Bodies 2016.

INSTITUTION

PUBLIC INSTITUTION

UNIVERSITY OF THE GAMBIA (UTG)

PO Box 3530, Administrative Building, Kanifing,
Serrekunda, Greater Banjul
Tel: +220 4372-213
Fax: +220 4395-064
EMail: info@utg.edu.gm
Website: http://www.utg.edu.gm/

Vice-Chancellor: Muhammadou M.O. Kah (2009-)
EMail: mkah@utg.edu.gm

Registrar: Lamin S. Jaiteh Tel: +220 4393-291

School

Agriculture and Environment Sciences (Agriculture; Biology; Environmental Studies); **Arts and Sciences** (Arabic; Arts and Humanities; Chemistry; Development Studies; English; French; Geography; History; Islamic Studies; Literature; Mathematics; Physics; Political Sciences; Psychology; Sociology); **Business and Public Administration** (Accountancy; Economics; Finance; Management; Marketing; Tourism); **Education** (Agricultural Education; Art Education; Science Education; Social Sciences); **Engineering and Architecture** *(in partnership with the University of Dalhousie)* (Architecture; Engineering); **Graduate Studies and Research** (African Studies; French Studies; History; Nursing; Public Health); **Information Technology and Communications** (Communication Studies; Computer Science; Information Technology; Media Studies; Software Engineering; Telecommunications Engineering); **Law** (Law); **Medicine and Allied Health Sciences** (Medicine; Midwifery; Nursing; Public Health; Surgery)

Department

Social Sciences (Development Studies; History; Social Sciences)

History: Founded 1999. Established by an Act of the National Assembly. Introduction of a 2-year Higher National Diploma (HND) programme in Construction Management in the Gambia Technical Training Institute, GTTI, under a franchise from South Bank University, London. With assistance from the Ministry of Health of Cuba, the pre-medical programme began September 1999.

Academic Year: October to July (October-February; March-July)

Admission Requirements: West African Senior School Certificate with five credits; General Certificate of Education with five credits

Fees: (Dalasis): Other than Science, c. 14,000; Science, c. 16,000; Medicine, c. 18,000; (US Dollars): Foreign Student, Humanities, 2,000; Science and Agriculture, 2,500; Medicine, 3,000

Main Language(s) of Instruction: English

Degrees and Diplomas: *Bachelor's Degree*: **Accountancy; Agriculture; Arabic; Banking; Biology; Chemistry; Christian Religious Studies; Computer Science; Design; Development Studies; Economics; English; Environmental Studies; Film; Finance; French; Geography; History; Hotel and Restaurant; Information Technology; Islamic Studies; Journalism; Management; Marketing; Mathematics; Medicine; Multimedia; Nursing; Physics; Public Administration; Radio and Television Broadcasting; Surgery; Tourism.** *Master's Degree*: **French; History; Mathematics; Nursing; Public Health.**

Student Services: Academic Counselling, Health Services, Social Counselling, Sports Facilities

Last Updated: 25/11/13

Georgia

STRUCTURE OF HIGHER EDUCATION SYSTEM

Description:

The three-cycle higher education system (Bachelor-Master-Doctorate) has been implemented. The higher education sector is composed of both public and private institutions. It is supervised by the Ministry of Education and Science. Higher education institutions are autonomous. They can be legal entities of public law, legal entities of private law, and non-profit legal entities. Rectors of public higher education institutions are elected by the Academic Council (composed of Professors). The majority of HEIs are funded through tuition fees. Grants are given to the students according to their performance in the national admission exam that takes place at the end of secondary education and their field of study. Loans schemes are also available.

Stages of studies:

University level first stage: *First cycle – Bachelor's degree (240 credits)*
Within the first cycle programme, the degree of Certified Specialist exists (120-180 credits).

University level second stage: *Second cycle – Master's degree (120 credits)*
The second stage leads to the award of a Magistris Xarisxi (Master's degree) after two years' study. Medicine, dental medicine and veterinary medicine (300-360 credits) are taught in integrated education programmes that equal Master's degrees.

University level third stage: *Third cycle – Doctor's degree (180 credits)*
Doctorandura comprises three years' study and ends with the presentation and defence of a dissertation.

ADMISSION TO HIGHER EDUCATION

Admission to university-level studies:

Name of secondary school credential required: Attestati

For entry to: All institutions

Admission requirements: Yes

Foreign students admission:

Definition of foreign student: Foreign students are those who are not citizens of Georgia.

Admission requirements: See: http://studyingeorgia.eu/

Health requirements: Medical certificate

RECOGNITION OF STUDIES

Quality assurance system:

Quality assurance (QA) system in Georgia consists of internal and external QA mechanisms. Internal self-evaluation is carried out by educational institutions commensurate with the procedure of evaluation of own performance and shall be summarised in an annual self-evaluation report. External QA is implemented through authorization and accreditation. Authorization grants a right to educational institutions to operate and is based on similar criteria as institutional accreditation. Accreditation looks more at the programme level and is linked with the state funding. All programmes in regulated professions have to pass accreditation. The national agency implementing external QA is the National Centre for Educational Quality Enhancement (EQE). Authorisation and accreditation have to be renewed in every 5 years.

Bodies dealing with recognition:

National Center for Educational Quality Enhancement (EQE)
1 Aleksidze st
Tbilisi 0193

Tel: +995(32) 2 200 220
EMail: info@eqe.ge
WWW: http://www.eqe.ge

NATIONAL BODIES

Ministry of Education and Science
Minister: Tamar Sanikidze
Dimitri Uznadze N 52
Tbilisi 0102
Tel: +995(32) 2 200 220
EMail: pr@mes.gov.ge
WWW: http://www.mes.gov.ge

National Center for Educational Quality Enhancement (EQE)
1 Aleksidze st
Tbilisi 0193
Tel: +995(32) 2 200 220
EMail: info@eqe.ge
WWW: http://www.eqe.ge

Role of national body: The National Center for Educational Quality Enhancement was founded on 1 September, 2010 under the Law of Georgia on Educational Quality Enhancement. The EQE is the legal successor of the LEPL - National Center for Educational Accreditation. Its main goal is to promote the formation of internal mechanisms of educational quality assurance and the implementation of external mechanisms in cooperation with educational institutions and other stakeholders.

Data for academic year: 2015-2016
Source: IAU from the website of the Ministry of Education and Science of Georgia; Higher Education in Georgia, 2012 (EACEA); Fiche Géorgie, Base Curie, 2014 (Ministère des Affaires étrangères, France); and World Data on Education 2010/11 (UNESCO-IBE), 2015.

INSTITUTIONS

PUBLIC INSTITUTIONS

AGRICULTURAL UNIVERSITY OF GEORGIA

Saqartvelos Sakhelmtsipo Agraruli Universiteti
13km, David Agmašenebeli Alley, 0131 Tbilisi
Tel: +995(32) 533-806
Fax: +995(32) 534-395
EMail: inter@agruni.edu.ge
Website: http://www.agruni.edu.ge/en

Rector: Lasha Gotsiridze Javakhishvili

School
Agricultural and Natural Sciences (Agronomy; Animal Husbandry; Biology; Chemistry; Food Technology; Forestry; Oenology); **Business Administration** (Business Administration); **Engineering and Technology** (Agricultural Engineering; Automation and Control Engineering; Civil Engineering; Electrical Engineering; Mechanical Engineering)

Further Information: Also branches in Batumi, Telavi and Marneuli

History: Founded 1919 as faculty of Tbilisi State University, became Georgian Agricultural Institute 1929, and acquired present status and title 1991.

Academic Year: September to June (September-January; February-June)

Main Language(s) of Instruction: Georgian

Degrees and Diplomas: *Bakalavriati*; *Magistratura*; *Doktorantura*: **Animal Husbandry; Crop Production; Food Science; Forestry; Veterinary Science.**

Publications: Annals of Agrarian Sciences; Practical Veterinary Medicine; Scientific Works

Last Updated: 30/01/15

AKAKI TSERETELI STATE UNIVERSITY

Akaki Ceretlis Sakhelobis Sakhelmtsipo Universiteti (KSU)
55 Tamar Mepe Street, 4600 Kutaisi, Imereti
Tel: +995(331) 45784
Fax: +995(331) 43833
EMail: atsu@atsu.edu.ge
Website: http://www.atsu.edu.ge/index_eng.php

Rector: Georgi Gavtadze EMail: rector@atsu.edu.ge

Faculty
Arts (Archaeology; English; French; German; Modern Languages; Native Language; Oriental Studies; Philology; Slavic Languages; Western European Studies); **Exact and Natural Sciences** (Biology; Chemistry; Computer Science; Geography; Mathematics; Physics); **Maritime Transport** (Marine Transport); **Medicine** (Medicine); **Pedagogy** (Pedagogy); **Social Sciences** (Business Administration; Economics; History; Journalism; Law; Philosophy; Political Sciences; Psychology); **Technical Engineering** (Civil Engineering;

Electrical Engineering; Engineering; Machine Building; Mechanical Engineering; Mechanics; Safety Engineering; Transport Engineering); **Technological Engineering** (Chemical Engineering; Food Technology; Industrial Engineering; Textile Design; Textile Technology)

History: Founded 1933 as State Pedagogical Institute, Tbilisi. Acquired present status and title 2006 following merger of Kutiasi Akaki Tsereteli State University and Kutaisi N. Muskhelishvili State Technical University..

Academic Year: September to June

Admission Requirements: Secondary school certificate (Sashualo Skolis Atestati)

Main Language(s) of Instruction: Georgian

Degrees and Diplomas: *Bakalavriati*; *Magistratura*; *Doktorantura*: **Arts and Humanities; Engineering; Natural Sciences; Social Sciences.**

Student Services: Academic Counselling, Canteen, Cultural Activities, Foreign Studies Centre, Health Services, Language Laboratory, Social Counselling, Sports Facilities

Publications: Kutaisi University Moambe; Kutaisi University Papers

Last Updated: 28/01/15

BATUMI ART TEACHING UNIVERSITY

Batumis Khelovnebis Sastsavlo Universiteti

L. Asatiani Street ° 37, Batumi

Tel: +995(422) 27-98-95

EMail: gelodi26@mail.ru

Website: http://www.batu.edu.ge

Rector: Ermile Meskhia EMail: ermile_mesxia@mail.ru

Head of Administration: Gela Beridze

Faculty

Education, Humanities and Social Sciences (Art Criticism; Art History; Art Management; Cultural Studies; Journalism; Mass Communication; Radio and Television Broadcasting); **Music** (Conducting; Musical Instruments; Singing); **Visual, Theatre and Film-TV Arts** (Acting; Architecture; Cinema and Television; Fashion Design; Fine Arts; Interior Design; Painting and Drawing; Textile Design)

History: Founded 1995 as State Institute of Art. Acquired present status 2009.

Main Language(s) of Instruction: Georgian

Degrees and Diplomas: *Bakalavriati*; *Magistratura*

Last Updated: 28/01/15

BATUMI STATE MARITIME ACADEMY

Batumis Sakhelmtsipo Sazghvao Akademia

53, Rustaveli Street, 6010 Batumi, Adjara

Tel: +995(222) 75388 +995(222) 74957

Fax: +995(222) 74850

EMail: info@bsma.edu.ge

Website: http://www.bsma.edu.ge/index.php?lang=en

Rector: Irakli Sharabidze EMail: i.sharabidze@bsma.edu.ge

Faculty

Business and Management (Banking; Business Administration; International Business; Marine Transport); **Maritime** (Marine Science and Oceanography)

History: Founded 1992.

Main Language(s) of Instruction: Georgian, Russian

Degrees and Diplomas: *Bakalavriati*; *Magistratura*

Last Updated: 30/01/15

GEORGIAN TECHNICAL UNIVERSITY

Saqartvelos Teqnikuri Universiteti (STU)

77, Kostava Street, 0175 Tbilisi

Tel: +995(32) 365-429 +995(32) 365-173

Fax: +995(32) 987-027

EMail: pr@gtu.ge; kanc@gtu.ge

Website: http://www.gtu.ge/

Rector: Archil Prangishvili (2009-)
Tel: +995(32) 441-161 EMail: rectoroffice@gtu.ge

Deputy-Rector for Education: Levan Klimiashvili
Tel: +995(32) 365-152

Deputy-Rector for Research: Zurab Gasitashvili

International Relations: Otar Zumburidze
EMail: o_zumburidze@gtu.ge

Faculty

Architecture, Urban Planning and Design (Architecture; Town Planning); **Business-Engineering** (Business Administration; Communication Studies; Economics; German; Law; Modern Languages); **Chemical Technology and Metallurgy** (Biotechnology; Chemical Engineering; Metal Techniques; Metallurgical Engineering); **Civil Engineering** (Civil Engineering; Hydraulic Engineering; Industrial Engineering; Mechanical Engineering); **Computer and Control Systems** (Computer Engineering; Instrument Making; Mathematics; Physics); **Mining and Geology** (Geological Engineering; Geology; Mining Engineering; Petroleum and Gas Engineering); **Power Engineering and Telecommunications** (Electrical and Electronic Engineering; Hydraulic Engineering; Mechanical Engineering; Power Engineering; Telecommunications Engineering; Thermal Engineering); **Transportation and Machine Building** (Machine Building; Road Engineering; Transport and Communications; Transport Engineering)

School

Architecture (Architecture; Landscape Architecture; Town Planning); **Aviation** (Air Transport); **Polytechnic** *(Batumi)*

Institute

Construction, Special Systems and Engineering Maintenance (Construction Engineering)

Research Centre

Technical Diagnosis and Expertise (Technology)

Further Information: Also Health Care Polyclinic.

History: Founded 1922 as Polytechnic Faculty of Tbilisi State University. Became Polytechnic Institute 1936 and acquired present title 2007.

Academic Year: September to June (September-January; February-June)

Admission Requirements: Competitive entrance examination following general or special secondary school certificate

Fees: Foreign students, c. 1,000-3,000 per annum (US Dollar)

Main Language(s) of Instruction: Georgian, Russian, English, French, German

Degrees and Diplomas: *Bakalavriati*; *Magistratura*

Student Services: Canteen, Cultural Activities, Foreign Studies Centre, Health Services, Sports Facilities

Publications: Technical Essays

Publishing House: GTU Publishing House

Last Updated: 10/04/15

IAKOB GOGEBASHVILI TELAVI STATE UNIVERSITY

Telavis Iakob Gogebashvilis' Sakhelobis Sakhelmtsipo Universiteti (TESAU)

1, Kartuli Universiteti Street, 2200 Telavi, Kakheti

Tel: +995(350) 72401

Fax: +995(350) 73264

EMail: info@tesau.edu.ge

Website: http://www.tesau.edu.ge

Rector: Tinatin Javakhishvili
Tel: +995(350) 73264 EMail: rectortesau@gmail.com

Vice-Rector: Davit Makhashvili
Tel: +995(350) 73551 EMail: davit_makhashvili@posta.ge

International Relations: Marina Javakhishvili
Tel: +995(350) 71533 EMail: office@tesau.edu.ge

Faculty

Agriculture and Food Production (Agriculture; Chemistry; Food Technology); **Exact and Natural Sciences** (Biology; Data Processing; Ecology; Geography; Information Technology; Mathematics; Natural Sciences; Physics); **Humanities** (English; French; German; History; International Relations; Law; Literature; Native Language;

Russian); **Medicine** (Dentistry; Genetics; Medicine; Pharmacology; Pharmacy; Physical Therapy; Rehabilitation and Therapy); **Pedagogy** (Pedagogy; Physical Education; Primary Education; Sports); **Social Sciences, Business and Law** (Accountancy; Business Administration; Journalism; Law; Social Sciences; Sociology; Taxation)

History: Founded 1939 as Pedagogical Institute, acquired present status2001.

Academic Year: September to July

Admission Requirements: Secondary school certificate (Atestati) and national examination

Fees: c. 200-1,500 per annum (Lari)

Main Language(s) of Instruction: Georgian

Accrediting Agency: Ministry of Education and Science

Degrees and Diplomas: *Bakalavriati*; *Magistratura*

Student Services: Academic Counselling, Canteen, Cultural Activities, Health Services, Language Laboratory, Nursery Care, Sports Facilities

Publications: University Scientific Works

Last Updated: 10/04/15

ILIA STATE UNIVERSITY

Ilia Sakhelmtsipo Universiteti

3/5, Kakutsa Cholokashvili Avenue, 0162 Tbilisi

Tel: +995(32) 294-197

EMail: uni@iliauni.edu.ge

Website: http://www.iliauni.edu.ge

Rector: Giga Zedania EMail: giga_zedania@iliauni.edu.ge

School

Arts and Science (Arts and Humanities; History; Modern Languages; Music; Natural Sciences; Political Sciences; Social Sciences; Theatre); **Business** (Banking; Business Administration; Finance; Management; Sports Management; Tourism); **Law** (Law); **Natural Sciences and Engineering** (Architecture; Computer Science; Construction Engineering)

Further Information: Also Tsageri and Marneuli branches

History: Created 2006 following the merger between 'Tbilisi 'Ilia Čavčavadze' State University of Languages and Culture' (Tbilisis 'Ilia Čavčavadzis' Sakhelobis Enata da Kulturata Sakhelmtsipo Universiteti, founded 1948) and Tbilisi Sulkhan-Saba Orbeliani State Pedagogical University (Tbilisis Sulkhan-Saba Orbelianis Sakhelobis Sakhelmtsipo Pedagogiuri Universiteti, founded 1935). Previously known as Ilia Čavčavadze Sakhelmtsipo Universiteti (Ilia Čavčavadze State University). Acquired present title 2010.

Academic Year: September to June

Admission Requirements: Unified National Exam

Fees: c. 500-2,000 per annum, depending on entrance examination (c. 50% study free) (Lari)

Main Language(s) of Instruction: Georgian

Degrees and Diplomas: *Bakalavriati*; *Magistratura*; *Doktorantura*: **Law; Music; Philology; Psychology; Sociology.**

Student Services: Academic Counselling, Canteen, Health Services, Language Laboratory, Sports Facilities

Last Updated: 30/01/15

IVANE JAVAHIŠVILI TBILISI STATE UNIVERSITY

Ivane Javahišvilis Sakhelobis Tbilisis Sakhelmtsipo Universiteti (TSU)

1, Čavčavadze Avenue, 0128 Tbilisi

Tel: +995(32) 221-103

Fax: +995(32) 221-103

EMail: tea.gergedava@tsu.ge

Website: http://www.tsu.edu.ge/

Rector: Vladimer Papava (2013-) EMail: vladimer.papava@tsu.ge

International Relations: Tea Gergedava, Head, Department of Foreign Relations EMail: tea.gergedava@tsu.ge

Department

Applied Mathematics and Computer Science (Applied Mathematics; Computer Science); **Biology** (Biology); **Business Administration** (Business Administration); **Chemistry** (Chemistry); **Commerce and Marketing** (Business and Commerce; Marketing); **Economics** (Economics); **Fine and Liberal Arts** (Fine Arts); **Geography** (Geography); **Geology** (Geology); **History** (History); **International Law and International Relations** (International Law; International Relations); **Journalism** (Journalism); **Law** (International Relations; Law); **Management and Micro Economics** (Business Administration; Management); **Mathematics** (Mathematics); **Medicine** (Medicine); **Oriental Studies** (Asian Studies; Middle Eastern Studies; Oriental Languages); **Philology** (Philology); **Philosophy and Sociology** (Philosophy; Sociology); **Physics** (Physics); **Psychology** (Psychology); **Western European Languages and Literature** (European Languages)

Institute

European Studies (European Studies)

Research Institute

Applied Mathematics (Applied Mathematics); **High Energy Physics** (Physics)

Further Information: Also 6 Research and Educational Centres. 80 Research Laboratories. Branches in Akhaltsine, Ozurgeti, Signani, Sokhumi and Zugdidi

History: Founded 1918.

Academic Year: September to June (September-February; February-June)

Admission Requirements: Competitive entrance examination following general or special secondary school certificate

Fees: c. 1,000-1,500 per annum (US Dollar)

Main Language(s) of Instruction: Georgian, Russian, English, French

Degrees and Diplomas: *Bakalavriati*; *Magistratura*

Student Services: Sports Facilities

Publications: Proceedings of Tbilisi University

Last Updated: 03/02/15

'SHOTA RUSTAVELI' STATE UNIVERSITY

Šota Rustavelis Sakhelobis Sakhelmtsipo Universiteti (BSU)

35, Ninošvili Street, 6010 Batumi, Adjara

Tel: +995(222) 71780

Fax: +995(222) 71787

EMail: info@bsu.edu.ge

Website: http://www.bsu.ge

Rector: Aliosha Bakuridze (2008-) Tel: +995(222) 71780

Head of Administration: Edisher Chavleishvili EMail: e.chavleishvili@bsu.edu.ge

Faculty

Agrarian Technologies and Ecology (Agricultural Business; Agricultural Engineering; Agriculture; Ecology; Forestry); **Education and Sciences** (Education; Natural Sciences; Pedagogy); **Engineering and Technology** (Civil Engineering; Industrial Engineering; Mining Engineering; Petroleum and Gas Engineering; Technology; Telecommunications Engineering; Transport and Communications); **Social Sciences, Business and Law** (Accountancy; Banking; Business Administration; European Studies; Finance; Law; Management; Marketing; Psychology); **Tourism** (Tourism)

History: Founded 1935. Acquired present status 2010.

Admission Requirements: Secondary school certificate, entrance examination

Fees: c. 350 per annum for local students; c. 1,000 for foreign students (US Dollar)

Main Language(s) of Instruction: Georgian

Degrees and Diplomas: *Bakalavriati*; *Magistratura*

Student Services: Academic Counselling, Canteen, Cultural Activities, Health Services, Language Laboratory, Social Counselling, Sports Facilities

Publications: "Collection of works"; "Historical Herald" Scientific Works of Shota Rustaveli Batumi State University; Series of Natural Sciences; The Humanities

Publishing House: University Publishing House
Last Updated: 10/04/15

SHOTA RUSTAVELI THEATRE AND FILM GEORGIA STATE UNIVERSITY

Saqartvelos 'Šota Rustavelis' Sakhelobis Teatrisa da Kinos Sakhelmtsipo Universiteti
19, Rustavili Avenue, 0118 Tbilisi
Tel: +995(32) 999-411
Fax: +995(32) 983-075
EMail: info@tafu.edu.ge
Website: http://www.tafu.edu.ge

Rector: Giorgi Margvelashvili

Faculty

Drama (Acting; Dance; Display and Stage Design; Film; Music; Theatre); **Film and TV Media** (Cinema and Television; Film); **Georgian Folk Music and Choreography** (Dance; Jazz and Popular Music; Music); **Humanities, Social Sciences, Business and Management** (Art Education; Journalism; Management; Mass Communication; Media Studies; Radio and Television Broadcasting; Theatre; Tourism)

History: Founded 1923, acquired present status 1992.

Main Language(s) of Instruction: Georgian

Degrees and Diplomas: *Bakalavriati*; *Magistratura*; *Doktorantura*: **Art History; Art Management; Film; Media Studies; Music; Theatre.**

Last Updated: 30/01/15

SOKHUMI STATE UNIVERSITY

Sokhumis Sakhelmtsipo Universiteti
9, Jikia Street, Sukhumi, Abkhazeti
Tel: +995(32) 541-406
EMail: info@sou.edu.ge
Website: http://www.sou.edu.ge

Rector: J. Apakidze (2009-)

Faculty

Economics and Business (Business Administration; Business and Commerce; Economics; Management); **Education** (Education); **Humanities** (Arts and Humanities; English; German; History; Law; Literature; Native Language; Oriental Languages; Philology; Turkish); **Law** (Law); **Mathematics and Computer Science** (Mathematics and Computer Science; Statistics); **Natural Sciences and Health Care** (Health Education; Natural Sciences); **Social and Political Sciences** (International Relations; Oriental Studies; Political Sciences; Psychology; Social Sciences; Sociology)

History: Founded 1932 as Sokhumi Pedagogical Institute. Reorganized 1979 into Abkhazian State University. Acquired present status and title 2008. Under the jurisdiction of the Ministry of People's Education of Georgia.

Academic Year: September to July (September-December; February-July)

Admission Requirements: Competitive entrance examination following general or special secondary school certificate

Main Language(s) of Instruction: Abkhazian, Georgian, Russian

Degrees and Diplomas: *Bakalavriati*; *Magistratura*

Student Services: Health Services

Publications: Staff Research Works

Last Updated: 10/04/15

SULKHAN SABA ORBELIANI TEACHING UNIVERSITY

4a Gia Abesadze, 0105 Tbilisi
Tel: +995(32) 2 98-95-16
EMail: info@sabauni.edu.ge
Website: http://www.sabauni.edu.ge

Rector: Vaja Vardidze EMail: v.vardidze@sabauni.edu.ge

Pro-rector: Nukri Gelashvili EMail: n.gelashvili@sabauni.edu.ge

Faculty

Humanities (Bible; Ethics; Modern Languages; Religious Art; Religious Practice; Theology); **Law** (Law)

History: Founded 2002 as Sulkhan Saba Orbeliani Institute of Philosophy, Theology, History and Culture. Acquired present title and status 2009.

Degrees and Diplomas: *Bakalavriati*; *Magistratura*
Last Updated: 10/04/15

TBILISI STATE ACADEMY OF ARTS

Tbilisis Apolon Qutateladzis Sakhelobis Sakhelmtsipo Samkhatvro Akademia
22, Griboedov Street, 0108 Tbilisi
Tel: +995(32) 932-972 +995(32) 995-425
Fax: +995(32) 920-164
EMail: info@art.edu.ge
Website: http://www.art.edu.ge

Rector: Giorgi Bugadze Tel: +995(32) 963-959

Faculty

Architecture (Architectural and Environmental Design; Architecture; Civil Engineering; Interior Design; Landscape Architecture); **Design** (Ceramic Art; Design; Fashion Design; Glass Art; Industrial Design; Interior Design; Jewellery Art; Textile Design); **Media Arts** (Media Studies); **Restoration and Art History** (Architecture; Art History; Cultural Studies; Fine Arts; Heritage Preservation; Restoration of Works of Art); **Visual Arts** (Visual Arts)

History: Founded 1922 as Georgian Academy of Arts.

Admission Requirements: Secondary School Certificate

Main Language(s) of Instruction: Georgian

Degrees and Diplomas: *Bakalavriati*; *Magistratura*

Student Services: Academic Counselling, Canteen, Facilities for disabled people, Health Services, Language Laboratory, Sports Facilities

Last Updated: 10/04/15

TBILISI STATE MEDICAL UNIVERSITY

Tbilisis Sakhelmtsipo Samedicino Universiteti (TSMU)
33, Vazha-Pšavela Avenue, 0177 Tbilisi
Tel: +995(32) 391-567 +995(32) 392-613
Fax: +995(32) 942-519
EMail: info@tsmu.edu; iad@tsmu.edu
Website: http://www.tsmu.edu

Rector: Zurab Vadachkoria Tel: +995(32) 395-432

Vice-Rector: Davit Chavchanidze

Deputy-Rector: Rima Beriashvili

Faculty

Dentistry (Dental Technology; Dentistry; Orthodontics; Stomatology; Surgery); **Medicine** (Anatomy; Biology; Biophysics; Cell Biology; Embryology and Reproduction Biology; Genetics; Histology; Immunology; Medicine; Microbiology; Molecular Biology; Parasitology; Pathology; Physics; Physiology; Surgery); **Pharmacy** (Applied Chemistry; Cosmetology; Pharmacy; Toxicology); **Physical Medicine and Rehabilitation** (Biological and Life Sciences; Biology; Cardiology; Gerontology; Neurosciences; Oncology; Pathology; Physical Therapy; Rehabilitation and Therapy; Respiratory Therapy; Sports Medicine; Urology); **Public Health** (Anatomy; Behavioural Sciences; Biochemistry; Biology; Biophysics; Cell Biology; Chemistry; Community Health; Dermatology; Embryology and Reproduction Biology; Epidemiology; Forensic Medicine and Dentistry; Genetics; Health Administration; Histology; Hygiene; Immunology; Mathematics; Modern Languages; Nutrition; Ophthalmology; Otorhinolaryngology; Parasitology; Pathology; Pharmacology; Philosophy; Physical Education; Physics; Physiology; Public Health; Radiology; Rehabilitation and Therapy; Social and Preventive Medicine; Sociology; Sports Medicine; Surgery; Toxicology; Venereology)

Higher School

Nursing (Nursing)

Institute

Postgraduate Medical Studies and Continuous Medical Education (Anaesthesiology; Anatomy; Cardiology; Forensic Medicine and Dentistry; Gynaecology and Obstetrics; Medicine; Neurology; Oncology; Ophthalmology; Orthopaedics; Otorhinolaryngology; Paediatrics; Parasitology; Pathology; Psychiatry and Mental Health; Radiology; Stomatology; Surgery; Urology)

Centre

Clinical Anatomy and Skills (Anatomy); **Family Medicine** (Medicine); **Interventional Radiology** (Radiology); **Language Teaching** (Modern Languages); **Strategic Development and Research in Medical Education**

Further Information: Also preparatory courses for foreign students

History: Founded 1918, acquired present status 1992.

Academic Year: September to July

Main Language(s) of Instruction: Georgian, Russian, English, French

Degrees and Diplomas: *Magistratura*

Student Services: Sports Facilities

Publications: Georgian Medical News; Proceedings of Scientific Societies

Last Updated: 10/04/15

TBILISI VANO SARAJIŠVILI STATE CONSERVATORY

Tbilisis Vano Sarajišvilis Sakhelobis Sakhelmtsipo Konservatoria

8-10, Griboedov Street, 0108 Tbilisi
Tel: +995(32) 987-186
Fax: +995(32) 987-187
EMail: info@conservatoire.edu.ge
Website: http://www.conservatoire.edu.ge

Rector: Rezo Kiknadze
Tel: +995(32) 987-187 EMail: rector@conservatoire.edu.ge

Head of Administration: Tamar Djandieri
Tel: +995(32) 999-147 EMail: admin@conservatoire.edu.ge

Faculty

Composition and Music Theory (Folklore; Music Theory and Composition; Religious Music); **Performing** (Conducting; Musical Instruments; Opera; Singing)

History: Founded 1917.

Main Language(s) of Instruction: Georgian

Degrees and Diplomas: *Bakalavriati*; *Magistratura*

Last Updated: 10/04/15

PRIVATE INSTITUTIONS

AMERICAN UNIVERSITY FOR HUMANITIES - TBILISI CAMPUS

Amerikuli Humanitaruli Universiteti Tbilisis Filiali Koleji

2 Tornike Eristavi Str., 0192 Tbilisi
Tel: +995(32) 660-091
Fax: +995(32) 660-094
EMail: info@auhtc.edu
Website: http://www.auhtc.edu/

Rector: Alexander Rondeli EMail: arondeli@gfsis.org

Director: Zurab Abashidze EMail: zabashidze@auhtc.edu

International Relations: Bawerjan Bakr, Head of International Relations Department EMail: bawerjan@auhtc.edu

Division

Business Administration (Business Administration; Management); **International Relations** (International Relations; International Studies; Law)

History: Created 2004. Acquired status 2007

Academic Year: October to January; February to May

Admission Requirements: School leaving certificate, English language proficiency

Fees: 6,400 per annum (Lari)

Main Language(s) of Instruction: English

Accrediting Agency: Ministry of Education and Science

Degrees and Diplomas: *Bakalavriati*: **Business Administration; International Law; International Relations.** *Magistratura*: **International Business.**

Student Services: Academic Counselling, Canteen, Careers Guidance, Health Services, Language Laboratory, Social Counselling, Sports Facilities

Last Updated: 28/01/15

BATUMI NAVIGATION TEACHING UNIVERSITY

Batumis Navigaciis Sastsavlo Universiteti

26, Tbilisi Avenue, Batumi, Adjara
Tel: +995(222) 92525
Fax: +995(222) 74840
EMail: info@bntu.edu.ge
Website: http://www.bntu.edu.ge/

Rector: Parmen Khvedelidze EMail: p.khvedelidze@gmail.com

Faculty

Logistic (Management); **Maritime Engineering** (Electrical Engineering; Marine Engineering; Transport Engineering; Transport Management)

Centre

International Maritime Training (Marine Engineering; Marine Science and Oceanography)

History: Founded 1999 as Batumi Maritime College. Acquired present status and title 2009.

Main Language(s) of Instruction: Georgian

Degrees and Diplomas: *Bakalavriati*; *Magistratura*

Last Updated: 30/01/15

CAUCASUS INTERNATIONAL UNIVERSITY

Kavkasiis Saertašoriso Universiteti

73, Chargali street, Tbilisi
Tel: +995(32) 308-641 +995(32) 105-203
Fax: +995(32) 611-298
EMail: ciu@caucasus.net
Website: http://www.ciu.edu.ge

Rector: Kakhaber Kordzaia EMail: rector@ciu.edu.ge

Faculty

Business (Business Administration; Finance; International Business; Management; Marketing; Tourism); **Law** (Commercial Law; Law); **Medicine** (Dentistry; Medicine; Pharmacy; Rehabilitation and Therapy); **Social Sciences** (International Relations; Journalism; Social Sciences)

History: Founded 1995.

Main Language(s) of Instruction: Georgian, Russian

Degrees and Diplomas: *Bakalavriati*; *Magistratura*; *Doktorantura*: **Business Administration; Law.**

Last Updated: 06/02/15

CAUCASUS UNIVERSITY

Kavkasiis Universiteti (CU)

77, Kostava Street, 0175 Tbilisi
Tel: +995(32) 237-77-77
Fax: +995(32) 231-32-26
EMail: info@cu.edu.ge
Website: http://www.cu.edu.ge/

President: Kakha Shengelia (2004-)
Tel: +995(32) 237-77-77 Ext. 101 EMail: president@cu.edu.ge

International Relations: Mariam Sutidze, Director, International Relations Department
Tel: +995(32) 237-77-77 Ext. 140 EMail: msutidze@cu.edu.ge

School

Business (Accountancy; Business Administration; Finance; Health Administration; Management; Marketing); **Cinema** (Cinema and Television); **Economics and Health Care** (Business Administration; Economics; Health Sciences); **Governance** (International Relations; Public Administration); **Humanities and Social Sciences** (Archaeology; Arts and Humanities; History; Philology; Psychology; Regional Studies; Sociology); **Law** (Law); **Media Studies**

(Journalism; Media Studies); **Safety and Security** (Civil Security); **Technology** (Computer Science; Information Technology); **Tourism** (International Business; Tourism)

History: Created in 1998 as Caucasus School of Business in partnership with Georgia State University, USA. Acquired current title and status 2004.

Admission Requirements: High School Certifiate; sufficient scores in the Unified National Exam.

Fees: Bachelor's programme, 3,000 per annum; Master's programme, (US Dollars): 5,580-7,500 (Euro)

Main Language(s) of Instruction: Georgian, English

Accrediting Agency: Ministry of Education and Science

Degrees and Diplomas: *Bakalavriati*: **Business Administration; Communication Studies; Law; Media Studies; Technology.** *Magistratura*: **Business and Commerce; Finance; Health Administration; Hotel Management; Management; Marketing.** *Doktorantura*: **Business Administration; Economics; Law.** Also double degrees with overseas institutions.

Student Services: Academic Counselling, Canteen, Careers Guidance, Foreign Studies Centre, Language Laboratory, Social Counselling

Student Numbers *2012-2013*: Total 2,685
Last Updated: 16/12/15

DAVID TVILDIANI MEDICAL UNIVERSITY

Umaghlesi Sameditsino Skola AIETI (AIETI)
2/6 Lubliana Street, 0159 Tbilisi
Tel: +995(32) 516-898
Fax: +995(32) 527-196
EMail: aieti@aieti.edu.ge
Website: http://www.aieti.edu.ge

President: Levan Tvildiani (2010-2020) EMail: rector@dtmu.edu.ge

International Relations: David Tvildiani (Jr), Head
EMail: pr@aieti.edu.ge

Faculty
Medicine (Medicine)

School
Public Health (Public Health)

History: Founded 1991 as AIETI Medical School, acquired present title 2011.

Academic Year: September to July

Admission Requirements: Sašualo Skolis Atestati. Unified Entrance Examinations. For foreign citizens: permission of Ministry of Education and Science of Georgia

Fees: 2,450 per annum (Lari)

Main Language(s) of Instruction: Georgian, English

Accrediting Agency: Ministry of Education and Science; National Centre for Educational Quality Enhancement of Georgia

Degrees and Diplomas: *Magistratura*; *Doktorantura*: **Biomedicine; Health Sciences; Medicine.**

Student Services: Careers Guidance, Health Services, Language Laboratory, Library

Publications: Transactions of Scientific Conference
Last Updated: 20/02/15

EKVTIME TAKAISHVILI TEACHING UNIVERSITY

3, Bostanqalaqi Str., 3700 Rustavi, Kvemo Kartli
Tel: +995(341) 24-18-98
EMail: rvaliuni@gmail.com
Website: http://www.rvali.edu.ge/

Rector: Gulkan Tsitskhvaia

Faculty
Social Sciences (Arts and Humanities; Banking; Business Administration; Economics; Education; Finance; Insurance; Law; Primary Education; Tourism)

History: Founded 1995 as Teaching University "Rvali".Acquired present status and title 2014.

Main Language(s) of Instruction: Georgian

Degrees and Diplomas: *Bakalavriati*; *Magistratura*
Last Updated: 03/02/15

EUROPEAN TEACHING UNIVERSITY

95 Agmashenibeli Ave, 380178 Tbilisi
Tel: +995(32) 308-661
EMail: rector@esu.edu.ge
Website: http://www.esu.edu.ge

Rector: Lasha Kandelakishvili

Faculty
Business and Technology (Banking; Business Administration; Computer Networks; Finance; Software Engineering); **Law, Humanities and Social Sciences** (English Studies; International Law; International Relations; Law; Psychology); **Medicine** (Medicine; Nursing; Pharmacy)

History: Founded 1992.

Main Language(s) of Instruction: Georgian and English

Degrees and Diplomas: *Bakalavriati*; *Magistratura*
Last Updated: 30/01/15

FREE UNIVERSITY OF TBILISI

Tbilisis Tavisufali Universiteti
University Campus of Dighomi, David Aghmashenebeli Alley/13 km, 0159 Tbilisi
Tel: +995(32) 220-0901
Fax: +995(32) 220-0902
EMail: info@freeuni.edu.ge
Website: http://www.freeuni.edu.ge/

Rector: Guram Chikovani (2009-)
Tel: +995(599) 55-32-23
EMail: g.chikovani@freeuni.edu.ge

Chancellor: George Meladze
Tel: +995(577) 20-10-22
EMail: g.meladze@freeuni.edu.ge

International Relations: Douglas Osborne, Head of International Programs
Tel: +995(595) 33-50-04 EMail: d.osborne@freeuni.edu.ge

School
Business *(ESM)* (Business Administration); **Computer Science and Mathematics** (Applied Mathematics; Mathematics and Computer Science; Software Engineering); **Governance and Social Sciences** (Government; Social Sciences); **Law** (Law); **Physics** (Physics)

Institute
Asia and Africa (African Studies; Asian Studies; East Asian Studies; International Relations; Middle Eastern Studies; Oriental Languages; Oriental Studies; South Asian Studies)

History: Established 2007 through the merger of two higher education schools, the European School of Management (ESM-Tbilisi) and the Tbilisi Institute of Asia and Africa (TIAA).

Academic Year: September-January; March -June

Admission Requirements: Unifies State Exam

Fees: 6900.00 per annum (Lari)

Main Language(s) of Instruction: Georgian

Degrees and Diplomas: *Bakalavriati*; *Magistratura*

Student Services: Academic Counselling, Canteen, Careers Guidance, Facilities for disabled people, Foreign Studies Centre, Language Laboratory, Nursery Care, Sports Facilities

Academic Staff *2011-2012*	MEN	WOMEN	**TOTAL**
FULL-TIME	51	35	**86**
STAFF WITH DOCTORATE			
FULL-TIME	30	10	**40**
Student Numbers *2011-2012*			
All (Foreign included)	452	301	**753**

Last Updated: 10/04/15

GEORGIAN-AMERICAN UNIVERSITY

SH.P.S. Qartul-Amerikuli Universiteti (GAU)
Chavchavadze ave. 2nd cul de sac, 5, 0179 Tbilisi
Tel: +995(32) 915-003 +995(32) 915-004
Fax: +995(32) 915-044
EMail: info@gau.ge
Website: http://www.gau.ge

President: R. Michael Cowgill
EMail: rmichaelcowgill@yahoo.com

Chancellor: Nino Toronjadze
EMail: ntoronjadze@taobamk.ge

International Relations: Kenneth A. Cutshaw, Vice-President, Global Affairs EMail: kcutshaw@churchs.com

School

Business (Business Administration; English; Finance; Management; Marketing); **Law** (Administrative Law; Civics; Constitutional Law; Criminal Law; International Law; Law)

Department

Languages (English; French; German; Native Language)

History: Created 2005. Western-style education system designed for the Georgian environment.

Academic Year: September to February; February to June; June to August

Admission Requirements: Secondary school certificate; UNE exam for Georgian students; university entrance exam for non-Georgian and transfer students.

Fees: Undergraduate, 7,500 per annum; Master and PhD programmes, 5,000 (Lari)

Main Language(s) of Instruction: Georgian, English

Accrediting Agency: Ministry of Education and Science

Degrees and Diplomas: *Bakalavriati*: **Administrative Law; Business Administration; Civil Law; Constitutional Law; Criminal Law; Law.** *Magistratura*: **Administrative Law; Business Administration; Civil Law; Constitutional Law; Criminal Law; Law.**

Student Services: Academic Counselling, Canteen, Careers Guidance, Facilities for disabled people, Health Services, Language Laboratory, Social Counselling, Sports Facilities

Last Updated: 10/04/15

GEORGIAN AVIATION UNIVERSITY

Saqartvelos Saaviatsio Universiteti
16, Ketevan Tsamebuli Street, 0103 Tbilisi
Tel: +995(32) 776-571
Fax: +995(32) 776-572
EMail: rector.gau@gmail.com; mail@ssu.edu.ge
Website: http://www.ssu.edu.ge/

Rector: Sergo Tepnadz

Faculty

Air Transport Flight Exploitation (Transport Management); **Business Administration and Management** (Air Transport; Business Administration; International Economics; Management; Transport Management); **Engineering** (Aeronautical and Aerospace Engineering); **Law** (International Law; Law)

History: Founded 1992 as Aviation Institute of Georgian Technical University (GTU).

Main Language(s) of Instruction: Georgian

Degrees and Diplomas: *Bakalavriati*; *Magistratura*; *Doktorantura*: **Aeronautical and Aerospace Engineering; Air Transport.**

Last Updated: 30/01/15

GEORGIAN INSTITUTE OF PUBLIC AFFAIRS

Saqartvelos Sazogadoebriv Sakmeta Instituti (GIPA)
2, Maria Brosset Street, 0108 Tbilisi
Tel: +995(32) 931-466 +995(32) 932-201
Fax: +995(32) 931-466
EMail: admin@gipa.ge
Website: http://www.gipa.ge

Rector: Giorgi Margvelashvili EMail: margvel@gipa.ge

School

Government (Government; International Relations; Law; Public Administration); **Journalism and Media Management** *(Caucasus)* (Journalism; Media Studies); **Law and Politics** (International Relations; Law; Political Sciences)

History: Founded 1994 as Institute of Public Administration. Acquired present title 2001.

Main Language(s) of Instruction: Georgian and English

Degrees and Diplomas: *Bakalavriati*; *Magistratura*

Last Updated: 10/04/15

GORGASALI - TBILISI INDEPENDENT UNIVERSITY

Tbilisis Damoukidebeli Universiteti 'Gorgasali'
64, Guramishvili Avenue, 0104 Tbilisi
Tel: +995(32) 453-865
EMail: Gorgasali1@rambler.ru
Website: http://www.gorgasali.edu.ge

Faculty

Health Care (Health Education); **Humanities and Social Sciences** (Arts and Humanities; Civil Law; Criminal Law; Economics; English; Finance; German; International Economics; International Relations; Law; Social Sciences)

Degrees and Diplomas: *Bakalavriati*; *Magistratura*

Last Updated: 10/04/15

GORI STATE TEACHING UNIVERSITY

53, Chavchavadze Street, Gori, Shida Kartli
Tel: +995(270) 72413
Fax: +995(270) 73554
EMail: contact@gu.edu.ge
Website: http://www.gu.edu.ge/en

Rector: Giorgi Sosiashvili EMail: giorgisosiashvili@gmail.com

Faculty

Education, Exact and Natural Sciences (Biology; Chemistry; Computer Science; Education; Geography; Mathematics; Natural Sciences); **Humanities** (English; German; History; Literature; Philology; Russian); **Social Sciences, Business and Law** (Business Administration; Business and Commerce; Law; Social Sciences)

History: Established 2007 following merger of Gori State University and Tskhinvali State University. Acquired present title 2012.

Main Language(s) of Instruction: Georgian

Degrees and Diplomas: *Bakalavriati*; *Magistratura*

Last Updated: 30/01/15

GRIGOL ROBAKIDZE UNIVERSITY

Grigol Robakidzis Sakhelobis Universiteti 'Alma Mater' (GRU)
6, Jano Bagrationi Street, 0160 Tbilisi
Tel: +995(32) 385-849 +995(32) 384-406
Fax: +995(32) 252-981
EMail: info@gruni.edu.ge
Website: http://www.gruni.edu.ge

Rector: Mamuka Tavkelidze (1992-)
EMail: m.tavkhelidze@gruni.edu.ge

Vice-Rector: Nino Kemertelidze

School

Business and Management (Business Administration; Management); **Criminology** (Criminal Law); **Humanities and Social Sciences** (Arts and Humanities; Journalism; Mass Communication; Philology; Philosophy; Psychology; Social Sciences; Sociology); **Law** (Civil Law; European Union Law; Government; Labour Law; Law); **Medicine** (Dentistry; Medicine); **Public Administration and Politics** (Political Sciences; Public Administration)

Further Information: Also 3 Dentistry clinics; Centre of Thrombosis Research; Institute of Clinical Psychology; Anti-terrorism Research Centre; Linguaphone Centre; Computer Centre; Different Laboratories

History: Founded 1992.

Academic Year: September to July

Admission Requirements: Secondary school certificate
Main Language(s) of Instruction: Georgian, English, German
Degrees and Diplomas: *Bakalavriati*; *Magistratura*; *Doktorantura*: **Business Administration; Law; Philosophy; Political Sciences.**
Student Services: Academic Counselling, Canteen, Careers Guidance, Cultural Activities, Foreign Studies Centre, Health Services, Language Laboratory, Social Counselling, Sports Facilities
Publications: Collective Works of Lecturers of the University
Last Updated: 30/01/15

INTERNATIONAL BLACK SEA UNIVERSITY

Šavi Zgvis Saertašoriso Universiteti (IBSU)
David Agmashenebeli Alley 13km, 2, 0131 Tbilisi
Tel: +995(32) 595-005
Fax: +995(32) 595-008
EMail: contact@ibsu.edu.ge
Website: http://www.ibsu.edu.ge

Rector: Ş Ercan Tunç EMail: rector@ibsu.edu.ge

Faculty

Business Administration (Accountancy; Business Administration; Finance; Management; Marketing); **Computer Technologies and Engineering** (Computer Engineering; Computer Graphics; Computer Networks; Industrial Engineering; Software Engineering; Technology); **Education** (Education; Educational Administration; Pedagogy; Philology); **Humanities** (American Studies; Literature; Turkish); **Social Sciences** (Economics; International Relations; Law; Social Sciences)

School

Languages (English; French; Russian; Spanish; Turkish)
History: Founded 1995. A joint Georgian-Turkish Educational Establishment.
Academic Year: September to July
Admission Requirements: Competitive entrance examination following general or special secondary school certificate
Main Language(s) of Instruction: English
Accrediting Agency: Ministry of Education and Science
Degrees and Diplomas: *Bakalavriati*; *Magistratura*
Student Services: Academic Counselling, Canteen, Careers Guidance, Cultural Activities, Health Services, Language Laboratory, Nursery Care, Social Counselling, Sports Facilities
Publications: Academic Journal of IBSU
Last Updated: 10/04/15

KUTAISI UNIVERSITY

Kutaisis Universiteti
13, Tsereteli Street, 4601 Kutaisi, Imereti
Tel: +995(331) 45297
Fax: +995(331) 45772
EMail: info@unik.edu.ge
Website: http://www.unik.edu.ge/

Rector: Lela Kelbakiani (2002-) EMail: rector@unik.edu.ge

Faculty

Humanities (Arts and Humanities; English; French; German; History; Modern Languages; Philosophy; Religious Studies)

Department

Mathematics and Information Technology (Information Technology; Mathematics); **Economics** (Banking; Business Administration; Economics; Finance; Management; Taxation; Tourism)
History: Founded 1991 as Kutaisi Institute of Law and Economics. Acquired present title 2010.
Academic Year: September to June
Admission Requirements: Examination held by National Assessment and Examination Centre
Main Language(s) of Instruction: Georgian
Accrediting Agency: Ministry of Education and Science
Degrees and Diplomas: *Bakalavriati*; *Magistratura*; *Doktorantura*: **Business Administration; Economics; Finance.**
Student Services: Academic Counselling, Canteen, Careers Guidance, Cultural Activities, Health Services, Language Laboratory, Sports Facilities
Publications: Economic Profile
Last Updated: 30/01/15

NEW VISION UNIVERSITY

1a Evgeni Mikeladze Street, 0159 Tbilisi
Tel: +995(32) 242-4440
EMail: info@newvision.ge
Website: http://www.newvision.ge/

Head of Academic Council: David Kereselidze (2013-)
EMail: kereselidze@newvision.ge

Head of Representative Council: Karlo Matitaishvili
EMail: kmatitaishvili@newvision.ge

School

Business Administration and Information Technology (Accountancy; Administration; Business Administration; Business and Commerce; Finance; Information Technology; Management; Marketing); **Law** (Comparative Law; Criminal Law; European Union Law; History of Law; Human Rights; International Law; Labour Law; Private Law; Public Law); **Medicine** (Medicine; Surgery; Treatment Techniques); **Politics and International Relations** (International Relations; Political Sciences)
History: Created 2013
Academic Year: Two semesters of 6 months - autumn and spring 6-month semesters. The autumn semester begins on the second Monday of September and spring semester – on the second Monday of March.
Admission Requirements: School Leaving Certificate or equivalent; Proof of Proficiency in English at B2 Level. Master programs: Bachelor degree or equivalent (Bachelor degree in Law for Master's program in Law), Proof of Proficiency in English at a level B2. PhD programs: Master's degree, Proof of Proficiency in English or other European (German, French) language at least Level B2.
Fees: Bachelor in Law (in Georgian), 2250 GEL; all other courses, 3,500 to 5,000 USD per annum
Main Language(s) of Instruction: English
Accrediting Agency: National Center for Educational Quality Enhancement
Degrees and Diplomas: *Bakalavriati*: **Business Administration; Information Technology; International Relations; Law; Medicine; Political Sciences.** *Magistratura*: **Business Administration; International Law; Law.** *Doktorantura*: **Law; Medicine.**

Academic Staff *2014-2015*	**TOTAL**
FULL-TIME	**20**
PART-TIME	**100**
STAFF WITH DOCTORATE	
FULL-TIME	**7**
Student Numbers *2014-2015*	
All (Foreign included)	**200**
FOREIGN ONLY	**135**

Last Updated: 21/08/15

PETRE SHOTADZE TBILISI MEDICAL ACADEMY

Petre Šotadzis Sakhelobis Tbilisis Samedicino Akademia (TMA)
Ketevan Tsamebuli Ave., 51/2, 0179 Tbilisi
Tel: +995(32) 291-2484
Fax: +995(32) 274-7134
EMail: tmac@caucasus.net
Website: http://www.tma.edu.ge

Rector: Kakha Kuntelia

Faculty

Medicine (Anatomy; Cardiology; Dermatology; Ethics; Gynaecology and Obstetrics; Medicine; Physiology; Radiology; Rehabilitation and Therapy; Sports Medicine; Surgery; Virology); **Stomatology** (Dentistry; Stomatology)
History: Founded 1992. Acquired present title 1999.

Main Language(s) of Instruction: Georgian

Degrees and Diplomas: *Bakalavriati*; *Magistratura*; *Doktorantura*
Last Updated: 30/01/15

SHOTA MESKHIA ZUGDIDI STATE TEACHING UNIVERSITY

Šota Meskia Zugdidis Sakhelmtsipo Sastsavlo Universiteti
Janašia 14, Zugdidi
Tel: +995(415) 25 62 17
EMail: zssuedu@gmail.com
Website: http://www.zssu.ge

Faculty
Health (Health Sciences; Pharmacy); **Humanitarian** (Arts and Humanities)

Programme
Business Administration and Law (Business Administration; Law)

Main Language(s) of Instruction: Georgian

Degrees and Diplomas: *Bakalavriati*; *Magistratura*
Last Updated: 07/05/15

ST ANDREW THE FIRST-CALLED OF THE PATRIARCHATE OF GEORGIA GEORGIAN UNIVERSITY

Saqartvelos Sapatriarqos Tsmida Andria Pirveltsodebulis Sakhelobis Qartuli Universiteti
53a, Chavchavadze Avenue, 0162 Tbilisi
Tel: +995(32) 258-246
Fax: +995(32) 258-247
EMail: contactinfo@sangu.edu.ge
Website: http://www.sangu.ge/

Rector: Sergo Vardosanidze

School
Economics and Business Administration (Business Administration; Economics; Finance; Management); **Humanities and Law** (Ethnology; History; International Relations; Linguistics; Philology; Translation and Interpretation); **Informatics, Mathematics and Natural Sciences** (Biology; Biotechnology; Computer Science; Geophysics; Information Technology; Mathematics; Physics); **Social Sciences** (Law; Psychology; Social Work)

History: Founded 2008.

Main Language(s) of Instruction: Georgian

Degrees and Diplomas: *Bakalavriati*; *Magistratura*; *Doktorantura*: **Business Administration; Computer Science; Economics; Environmental Studies; Ethnology; Geophysics; History; Linguistics; Literature; Psychology; Translation and Interpretation.**
Last Updated: 03/02/15

ST. GRIGOL PERADZE TBILISI UNIVERSITY

Tsminda Grigol Peradzis Sakhelobis Tbilisis Universiteti
4, Jikia Street, Tbilisi
Tel: +995(321) 87107
EMail: p-tato@mail.ru
Website: http://www.gpstu.com

Programme
Banking and Finance (Banking; Finance; Insurance); **Business and Management** (Business Administration; Business and Commerce; Management); **Journalism** (Journalism; Radio and Television Broadcasting); **Law**; **Modern Languages** (English; German; Modern Languages; Native Language); **Pedagogy**; **Pharmacy** (Pharmacy)

History: Founded 1991. Acquired present status 2002.

Degrees and Diplomas: *Bakalavriati*; *Magistratura*
Last Updated: 10/04/15

SUKHISHVILI TEACHING UNIVERSITY

Sukhishvilis Universiteti
9, Tskinvali Highway, 1400 Gori, Shida Kartli
Tel: +995(270) 70557
Fax: +995(270) 72408
EMail: info@sukhishvilebi.edu.ge; sukhishvilebi@mail.ru
Website: http://www.sukhishvilebi.edu.ge

Rector: Valeri Z. Sukhishvili EMail: sukhishvilebi@mail.ru

International Relations: Zurab Chkhikvadze

Faculty
Business Administration and Management (Accountancy; Administration; Banking; Business Administration; Economics; Finance; Hotel Management; Information Technology; Insurance; Management; Marketing; Taxation; Tourism); **Law** (Law); **Public Health Care** (Agricultural Engineering; Analytical Chemistry; Biochemistry; Ecology; Forestry; Medicine; Oncology; Pathology; Pharmacology; Pharmacy; Physiology; Public Health; Toxicology)

History: Founded 1995 as a branch of the Georgian Agrarian Science Academy. Acquired present status and title 2003.

Main Language(s) of Instruction: Georgian

Degrees and Diplomas: *Bakalavriati*; *Magistratura*
Last Updated: 10/04/15

TBILISI HUMANITARIAN TEACHING UNIVERSITY

Tbilisis Humanitaruli Universiteti (THU)
3, Sandro Euli Street, 0186 Tbilisi
Tel: +995(32) 545-908
EMail: rector@thu.edu.ge
Website: http://www.thu.edu.ge

Rector: Valentina Sakvarlize

Faculty
Economics, Business and Administration (Business Administration; Economics; Management; Marketing); **Health Care** (Dentistry); **Humanities** (European Studies; History; Literature; Modern Languages; Philology; Slavic Languages); **Law** (Law; Private Law; Public Law)

History: Founded 1992.

Main Language(s) of Instruction: Georgian, Russian

Degrees and Diplomas: *Bakalavriati*; *Magistratura*
Last Updated: 10/04/15

TBILISI MEDICAL TEACHING UNIVERSITY HIPPOCRATES

Tbilisis Samedicino Instituti 'Hipokrate'
Tamarashvili str. 4, (G. Svanidze 8), 0164 Tbilisi
Tel: +995(32) 229-3492
EMail: medicina@hippokrates.edu.ge
Website: http://www.hippocrates.edu.ge

Rector: David Kiteishvili EMail: davitkiteishvi@gmail.com

International Relations: Nino Tsasidze, Head of International Relations EMail: n.admission@hippocrates.edu.ge

Faculty
Dentistry (Dentistry); **Medicine** (Medicine); **Pharmacy** (Pharmacy); **Public Health** (Public Health)

History: Founded 2003.

Admission Requirements: Secondary school certificate

Main Language(s) of Instruction: Georgian, Russian, English

Accrediting Agency: Ministry of Education and Science

Degrees and Diplomas: *Bakalavriati*: **Medicine; Pharmacy; Stomatology.** *Magistratura*

Student Services: Academic Counselling, Canteen, Health Services, Language Laboratory, Social Counselling, Sports Facilities
Last Updated: 10/04/15

TBILISI TEACHING UNIVERSITY

Tbilisis Universiteti
10, Jikia Street, 0156 Tbilisi
Tel: +995(32) 188-134
Fax: +995(32) 186-792
EMail: info@tbuniver.edu.ge
Website: http://www.tbuniver.edu.ge

Faculty
Economics and Law (Banking; Economics; Finance; Insurance; Law); **Health Care** (Public Health; Stomatology); **Humanities**

Main Language(s) of Instruction: Georgian

Degrees and Diplomas: *Bakalavriati*; *Magistratura*
Last Updated: 10/04/15

TBILISI TEACHING UNIVERSITY OF INTERNATIONAL RELATIONS

Tbilisis Saertašoriso Urtiertobebis Universiteti
4, Jikia Street, 0177 Tbilisi
Tel: +995(32) 369-160
Fax: +995(32) 366-165
EMail: contact@tsuu.edu.ge
Website: http://tsuu.edu.ge

Faculty
Business and Management (Banking; Business Administration; Business and Commerce; Finance; Insurance; Management); **Humanities** (English; Literature); **Law** (Criminal Law; Law; Private Law)

History: Founded 19911 from the Academy of Science of Georgia and the Institute of Law Psychology. Acquired present title 1999.

Main Language(s) of Instruction: Georgian

Degrees and Diplomas: *Bakalavriati*; *Magistratura*
Last Updated: 10/04/15

THE UNIVERSITY OF GEORGIA

M. Kostava str. 77, 0171 Tbilisi
Tel: +995(32) 252-22-22
EMail: ug@ug.edu.ge
Website: http://www.ug.edu.ge

President: Giuli Alasania

School
Business, Economics and Management (Banking; Business Administration; Economics; Management; Marketing; Public Administration; Tourism); **Health Sciences and Public Health** *(Dental programme in English)* (Dentistry; Health Administration; Nursing; Pharmacy; Public Health); **Humanities** (Anthropology; Art History; English; German; History; Italian); **Information Technology, Engineering, and Mathematics** (Computer Engineering; Computer Science; Electrical Engineering; Information Technology; Mathematics); **Law** (Law); **Social Sciences** (International Relations; Journalism; Mass Communication; Political Sciences; Psychology; Public Relations)

History: Founded 2004 as Georgian University of Social Sciences.

Main Language(s) of Instruction: Georgian

Degrees and Diplomas: *Bakalavriati*: **Accountancy; Archaeology; Banking; Business Administration; Computer Engineering; Computer Science; Dentistry; Economics; Electrical Engineering; English; Fine Arts; Health Administration; International Relations; Journalism; Law; Management; Marketing; Mathematics; Native Language; Nursing; Oriental Studies; Pharmacy; Philology; Political Sciences; Psychology; Public Administration; Public Relations; Tourism.** *Magistratura*: **Advertising and Publicity; Anthropology; Business Administration; English; Health Administration; History; Information Technology; International Relations; Law; Public Health; Public Relations.** *Doktorantura*: **Anthropology; Business Administration; Computer Science; English; Law; Mass Communication; Political Sciences.**
Last Updated: 24/03/16

UNIVERSITY GEOMEDI

3 Krtsanisi Street, Tbilisi
Tel: +995(32) 293-789
Fax: +995(32) 292-306
EMail: info@geosis.edu.ge
Website: http://geosis.edu.ge/cms/en/

Rector: Marina Pirtskhalava EMail: m.pirtskhalava@geosis.edu.ge

Faculty
Dentistry (Dentistry); **Health Care Economics and Management** (Economics; Health Administration); **Medicine** (Medicine); **Physical Medicine and Rehabilitation** (Physical Therapy; Rehabilitation and Therapy)

History: Founded 1998.

Degrees and Diplomas: *Bakalavriati*; *Magistratura*

Student Services: Library
Last Updated: 07/05/15

ZUGDIDI TEACHING UNIVERSITY

Zugdidis Damoukidebeli Universiteti
1, University Street, 2100 Zugdidi
Tel: +995(821) 552-012
Fax: +995(821) 552-011
EMail: zdu@gol.ge
Website: http://www.zdu.edu.ge

Faculty
Business Administration (Business Administration); **Dentistry** (Dentistry); **Tourism** (Tourism)

Main Language(s) of Instruction: Georgian, German

Degrees and Diplomas: *Bakalavriati*; *Magistratura*
Last Updated: 10/04/15

Germany

STRUCTURE OF HIGHER EDUCATION SYSTEM

Description:

There are public and private state-recognized institutions of higher education categorized as: 1. universities (Universitäten) and equivalent higher education institutions (Technische Hochschulen/Technische Universitäten, Pädagogische Hochschulen); 2. colleges of art and music (Kunsthochschulen and Musikhochschulen); 3. Fachhochschulen (universities of applied sciences) and Verwaltungsfachhochschulen.

Stages of studies:

University level first stage: Bachelor's level

Degrees at Bachelor's level qualify graduates to apply for Master's degrees. They are awarded in 3, 3 1/2, or 4 years' full time study or 180, 210 or 240 ECTS credits.

University level second stage: Master's level

Degrees at Master's level are of several types: practice-oriented, research-oriented, artistic profile, and teaching career profile. They lasts between 1 and 2 years' study or 60, 90, or 120 ECTS credits. All degrees quality graduates to apply for a Doctorate.

University level third stage: Doctoral level

Degrees generally built on a Master's level degree.

ADMISSION TO HIGHER EDUCATION

Admission to university-level studies:

Name of secondary school credential required: Allgemeine Hochschulreife

For entry to: Subject-restricted programmes.

Name of secondary school credential required: Fachgebundene Hochschulreife

For entry to: All programmes.

Name of secondary school credential required: Fachhochschulreife

For entry to: All types of programmes at Fachhochschulen.

Alternatives to credentials: Interview, test grades, aptitude test, temporary registration for a trial study period. Completion of evening courses by employed adults or day school courses for pupils with work experience at Kollegs who hold a Nichtschülerprüfung (school examination for external candidates) or a Begabtenprüfung (examination for gifted working applicants).

Numerus clausus: There is a numerus clausus in certain subjects: e.g. Medicine, Veterinary Medicine, Dentistry, Business Administration, Biology, Psychology and Pharmacy (2004/2005). Such courses may differ from one semester to the nExt. Places for these courses are allocated through a central selection procedure (see www.zvs.de). Courses outside the national selection procedure may be subject to local selection procedures at certain higher education institutions on criteria such as average mark in the higher education entrance examination, the waiting period and social criteria.

Foreign students admission:

Admission requirements: Applicants who do not have German higher education entrance qualifications have to submit a secondary school certificate that qualifies them to attend higher education in their country of origin. If necessary, they also have to provide proof that they have passed an entrance examination at a university in their native country or proof of enrolment at the university. Applicants from some countries of origin must, moreover, provide proof that they have successfully completed some course modules at a higher education institution in the country of origin or, following attendance at a one-year core course, must take an assessment test at a Studienkolleg.

Entry regulations: Residence permits are obtained at German diplomatic missions.

Language proficiency: Foreign applicants for study places must prove that they have a sufficient command of the German language. This can be done, for example, by taking the German Language Diploma of the

Standing Conference – Level II (Deutsches Sprachdiplom der Kultusministerkonferenz – Zweite Stufe – DSD II), the German Language Proficiency Examination for Admission to Higher Education for Foreign Applicants (Deutsche Sprachprüfung für den Hochschulzugang ausländischer Studienbewerber – DSH), which is taken at the institution of higher education in Germany itself, the Test of German as a Foreign Language for foreign applicants (Test Deutsch als Fremdsprache für ausländische Studienbewerber – TestDaF) or by taking the German language examination as part of the Feststellungsprüfung (assessment test) at a Studienkolleg.

RECOGNITION OF STUDIES

Quality assurance system:
In order to guarantee the equivalence of academic degrees and enable students to move freely between higher education institutions, the Association of Universities and other Higher Education Institutions in Germany and the Standing Conference of Ministers of Education and Cultural Affairs of the Länder agree on general conditions for academic examinations (Diplom exams at universities and Fachhochschulen and Magister exams). For individual courses these are then complemented by framework examination regulations (Diplom exams) or by conditions specific to the subject (Magister exams).
Courses leading to Bachelor's or Master's degrees are regulated by the Standing Conference's agreement on Structural Requirements. Depending on the Land law, these courses may be or have to be accredited by an accreditation agency that must be accredited by the national accreditation council (Akkreditierungsrat) founded in 1998. The objective of the accreditation is to guarantee minimum standards in terms of academic content and to check the vocational relevance of the degrees.

Bodies dealing with recognition:

Deutscher Akademischer Austauschdienst - DAAD (German Academic Exchange Service)

Kennedyallee 50
Bonn D-53175
Tel: +49(228) 88200
Fax: +49(228) 882-444
EMail: postmaster@daad.de
WWW: http://www.daad.de

Zentralstelle für ausländisches Bildungswesen im Sekretariat der Ständigen Konferenz der Kultusminister der Länder in der Bundesrepublik Deutschland -ENIC-NARIC (Central Office for Foreign Education in the Secretariat of the Standing Conference of the Ministers of Education and Cultural Affairs in the Federal Republic of)

Head of Centre: Simone El Bahi
P.O. Box 2240
Bonn 53012
Tel: +49(228) 501-352
Fax: +49(228) 501-229
EMail: zab@kmk.org
WWW: http://www.kmk.org/zab/home.htm

NATIONAL BODIES

Bundesministerium für Bildung und Forschung - Bonn (Federal Ministry of Education and Research - Bonn Office)

Minister: Johanna Wanka
Parliamentary State Secretary: Thomas Rachel
Heinemannstrasse 2
Bonn 53175
Tel: +49(1888) 570
Fax: +49(1888) 5783601
EMail: bmbf@bmbf.bund.de
WWW: http://www.bmbf.de

Bundesministerium für Bildung und Forschung - Berlin (Federal Ministry of Education and Research - Berlin Office)

Hannoversche Strasse 30
Berlin 10115
Tel: +49(1888) 570
Fax: +49(1888) 5783601
EMail: bmbf@bmbf.bund.de
WWW: http://www.bmbf.de

Akkreditierungsrat (Accreditation Council)

Chair: Reinhold R. Grimm
Managing Director: Olaf Bartz
Adenauerallee 73
Bonn 53113
Tel: +49(228) 338 306-0
Fax: +49(228) 338 306-79
EMail: akr@akkreditierungsrat.de
WWW: http://www.akkreditierungsrat.de

Role of national body: The Association of Universities and other Higher Education Institutions in Germany (HRK) and the Standing Conference of Ministers of Education and Cultural Affairs of the Länder in the Federal Republic of Germany (KMK) established the Akkreditierungsrat for the purpose of providing accreditation services. The Akkreditierungsrat is responsible for the establishment of comparable quality standards for Bachelor's and Master's degree courses in an essential decentralised accreditation process which will be carried out by accreditation agencies. The Akkreditierungsrat performs these responsibilities by accrediting, coordinating and monitoring these agencies.

Deutsche Hochschulverband - DHV (German Association of University Professors and Lecturers)

President: Bernhard Kempen
Rheinallee 18
Bonn 53173
Tel: +49(228) 902-6666
Fax: +49(228) 902-6680
EMail: dhv@hochschulverband.de
WWW: http://www.hochschulverband.de/cms

Deutscher Akademischer Austauschdienst - DAAD (German Academic Exchange Service)

President: Margret Wintermantel
Vice President: Joybrato Mukherjee
Kennedyallee 50
Bonn D-53175
Tel: +49(228) 88200
Fax: +49(228) 882-444
EMail: postmaster@daad.de
WWW: http://www.daad.de

Role of national body: Funding organisation, supporting and promoting international exchange of students and scholars, as well as promoting German language, literature and cultural studies at foreign universities.

Gemeinsame Wissenschaftskonferenz - GWK (Joint Science Conference)

President; Federal Minister of Education and Research: Johanna Wanka
Friedrich-Ebert-Allee 38
Bonn 53113
Tel: +49(228) 5402-0
Fax: +49(228) 5402-150
EMail: gwk@gwk-bonn.de
WWW: http://www.gwk-bonn.de

Role of national body: Deals with questions of research funding, science and research policy strategies and the science system which jointly affect the Federal Government and the Länder with the aim of strengthening Germany's position as a location for science and research in the international field.

Hochschulrektorenkonferenz - HRK (Association of Universities and other Higher Education Institutions in Germany)

President: Horst Hippler
Secretary-General: Jens-Peter Gaul
Ahrstrasse 39
Bonn D-53175
Tel: +49(228) 8870
Fax: +49(228) 887110
EMail: post@hrk.de
WWW: http://www.hrk.de

Role of national body: To deal with questions relating to research, teaching and extension; to represent public and private state-recognized higher education institutions in Germany.

Kultusministerkonferenz - Berlin (Secretariat of the Standing Conference of Ministers of Education and Cultural Affairs of the Länder - Berlin Office)

Taubenstraße 10
Postfach 11342
Berlin 10117
Tel: +49(30) 25418-499
Fax: +49(30) 25418-450
EMail: internationales@berlin.kmk.org

Kultusministerkonferenz - Bonn (Secretariat of the Standing Conference of Ministers of Education and Cultural Affairs of the Länder - Bonn Office)

Secretary-General: Udo Michallik
Deputy Secretary-General: Heidi Weidenbach-Mattar
Graurheindorfer Str. 157
Postfach 2240
Bonn 53117
Tel: +49(228) 501-0
Fax: +49(228) 501-777
EMail: europa@kmk.org
WWW: http://www.kmk.org

Role of national body: To unite the ministers and senators of the Länder responsible for school education, higher education, research and cultural affairs in order to present a common viewpoint and a common will as representing common interests. It is based on an agreement between the Länder. A list of the addresses of the ministries of the 16 Länder is available on the Website of the Kultusministerkonferenz at http://www.kmk.org/auf-org/home.htm?adress

IAU Universität Bayern e.V. (Bavarian University Alliance - BUA)

Chair: Udo Hebel
CEO: Ines Jung
Seitzstrasse 5
München 80538
Tel: +49 89 2101 9940
Fax: +49 89 2101 9941
EMail: info@unibayern.de
WWW: http://www.unibayern.de

Role of national body: Regional association of HE institutions

Data for academic year: 2014-2015
Source: IAU from German ENIC-NARIC Centre, 2014. Bodies 2016.

INSTITUTIONS

PUBLIC INSTITUTIONS

AACHEN UNIVERSITY OF APPLIED SCIENCES

Fachhochschule Aachen (FH AACHEN)
Postfach 100 560, Kalverbenden 6, 52005 Aachen
Tel: +49(241) 6009-0
Fax: +49(241) 6009-51090
EMail: info@fh-aachen.de
Website: http://www.fh-aachen.de

Rektor: Marcus Baumann
Tel: +49(241) 6009-51000 EMail: rektor@fh-aachen.de

Kanzler: Volker Stempel
Tel: +49(241) 6009-51010 EMail: kanzler@fh-aachen.de

Faculty

Aerospace Technology (Aeronautical and Aerospace Engineering; Astronomy and Space Science; Automotive Engineering; Electronic Engineering; Mechanical Engineering); **Architecture** (Architecture; Regional Planning; Town Planning); **Business Studies** (Business and Commerce; International Business); **Chemistry and Biotechnology** (Applied Chemistry; Biotechnology; Chemistry; Polymer and Plastics Technology); **Civil Engineering** (Civil Engineering; Construction Engineering; Structural Architecture; Transport Engineering; Waste Management; Water Management); **Design** (Communication Arts; Design; Industrial Design; Interior Design; Media Studies; Visual Arts); **Electrical Engineering and Information Technology** (Computer Science; Electrical Engineering; Electronic Engineering; Information Technology; Multimedia; Telecommunications Engineering); **Energy Technology** (Electrical Engineering; Energy Engineering; Environmental Engineering; Mechanical Engineering; Physical Engineering); **Mechanical Engineering and Mechatronics** (Business Administration; Electronic Engineering; Machine Building; Mechanical Engineering); **Medical Engineering and Technomathematics** (Biomedical Engineering; Computer Science; Mathematics and Computer Science; Medical Technology)

History: Founded as University of Applied Science in 1971 out of four colleges dating back to the beginning of the 20th century. Acquired university status in 1976.

Academic Year: September-February; March-July

Admission Requirements: Allgemeine Hochschulreife (Abitur), Fachhochschulreife (Fachabitur). Basic three-month internship for most courses. Language certificate for international degree courses and artistic qualification for Design

Fees: None for first degree courses

Main Language(s) of Instruction: German, English

Accrediting Agency: Ministry of Science and Research North-Rhine Westphalia. Special accreditation agencies for the BEng and MSc courses

Degrees and Diplomas: *Bachelor's Degree*: **Aeronautical and Aerospace Engineering; Architecture; Biomedical Engineering; Biotechnology; Business Administration; Chemistry; Civil Engineering; Design; Electrical Engineering; Electronic Engineering; Energy Engineering; Information Technology; Mathematics; Mechanical Engineering; Technology.** *Master*: **Accountancy; Aeronautical and Aerospace Engineering; Architecture; Automation and Control Engineering; Automotive Engineering; Biomedical Engineering; Biotechnology; Business Computing; Civil Engineering; Electrical Engineering; Electronic Engineering; Energy Engineering; Finance; Graphic Design; Industrial Design; Industrial Engineering; Information Technology; International Business; Management; Mathematics; Nuclear Engineering; Polymer and Plastics Technology; Service Trades; Taxation; Technology.** Also Dual Study Programmes

Student Services: Academic Counselling, Canteen, Careers Guidance, Facilities for disabled people, Foreign Studies Centre, Language Laboratory, Library, Social Counselling, Sports Facilities

Student Numbers *2013-2014*: Total 12,701
Last Updated: 27/01/15

AALEN UNIVERSITY

Hochschule Aalen
PO Box 1728, Beethovenstrasse 1, 73430 Aalen
Tel: +49(7361) 576-0
Fax: +49(7361) 576-2250
EMail: info@htw-aalen.de
Website: http://www.fh-aalen.de

Rector: Gerhard Schneider
Tel: +49(7361) 576-2101 EMail: Gerhard.Schneider@htw-aalen.de

Chancellor: Claudia Uhrmann
Tel: +49(7361) 576-2120 EMail: Kanzlerin@htw-aalen.de

International Relations: Pascal Cromm, Head, Office of International Affairs
Tel: +49(7361) 9733-01 EMail: Pascal.Cromm@htw-aalen.de

Faculty

Chemistry (Analytical Chemistry; Chemistry; Molecular Biology); **Electronics and Computer Science** (Automation and Control Engineering; Computer Science; Electronic Engineering; Information Technology); **Management and Business Sciences** (Business Administration; Engineering; Health Administration; Industrial Management; International Business; Management; Small Business; Taxation); **Mechanical Engineering and Materials Sciences** (Machine Building; Materials Engineering; Mechanical Engineering); **Optics and Mechatronics** (Optics)

History: Founded 1962.

Main Language(s) of Instruction: German

Degrees and Diplomas: *Bachelor's Degree*; *Master*: **Analytical Chemistry; Computer Science; Information Technology; International Business; Leadership; Management; Marketing; Mechanical Engineering; Physics; Polymer and Plastics Technology; Production Engineering; Sales Techniques; Small Business; Taxation; Technology Education.** Also online distance-learning Master's degree Digital Forensics programm

Student Numbers *2013-2014*: Total 5,392
Last Updated: 03/03/15

ACADEMY OF FINE ARTS DRESDEN

Hochschule für Bildende Künste Dresden (HFBK DRESDEN)
Postfach 160 153, 01287 Dresden
Tel: +49(351) 440-20
Fax: +49(351) 459-0025
EMail: post@serv1.hfbk-dresden.de
Website: http://www.hfbk-dresden.de

Rector: Matthias Flügge
Tel: +49(351) 492-6715 EMail: rektor@hfbk-dresden.de

Chancellor: Jochen Beissert
Tel: +49(351) 4402-2146 EMail: kanzler@hfbk-dresden.de

Faculty

Fine Arts (Art History; Ceramic Art; Fine Arts; Handicrafts; Painting and Drawing; Photography; Sculpture; Video; Visual Arts; Weaving); **Restoration** (Art Therapy; Display and Stage Design; Restoration of Works of Art; Textile Design)

History: Founded 1764.

Academic Year: October to April; April to September

Admission Requirements: Portfolio and entrance examination

Main Language(s) of Instruction: German

Degrees and Diplomas: *Diplom (FH)*: **Display and Stage Design; Theatre.** *Künstlerische Abschlussprüfung*: **Display and Stage Design; Fine Arts.** *Diplom (Univ)*: **Art Therapy; Display and Stage Design; Fine Arts; Restoration of Works of Art; Textile Design.** *PhD*: **Art History; Fine Arts; Restoration of Works of Art.**

Student Services: Canteen, Careers Guidance, Library

Student Numbers *2013-2014*: Total 611
Last Updated: 29/01/15

ACADEMY OF FINE ARTS MUNICH

Akademie der Bildenden Künste München (ADBK)
Akademiestrasse 2, 80799 München
Tel: +49(89) 3852-0
Fax: +49(89) 3852-252
EMail: post@adbk.mhn.de; sekretariat@adbk.mhn.de
Website: http://www.adbk.de/

Präsident: Dieter Rehm
Tel: +49(89) 3852-104 EMail: praesidium@adbk.mhn.de

Kanzlerin: Corinna Deschauer
Tel: +49(89) 3852-102 EMail: sekretariat@adbk.mhn.de

International Relations: Herta Grill

Course

Architecture *(Postgraduate)* (Architecture); **Art Education** (Art Education); **Fine Arts** (Ceramic Art; Display and Stage Design; Fine Arts; Painting and Drawing; Photography; Printing and Printmaking; Sculpture; Textile Design; Visual Arts; Weaving); **Interior Design** (Industrial Design; Interior Design); **Interior Design (Graduate)** (Interior Design); **Visual Arts and Therapy** *(Postgraduate)* (Art Therapy; Visual Arts)

History: Founded 1808.

Fees: 111 per semester (Euro)

Main Language(s) of Instruction: German

Degrees and Diplomas: *Bachelor's Degree*: **Interior Design.** *Künstlerische Abschlussprüfung*: **Art Therapy.** *Master*: **Architecture; Fine Arts.** *PhD*: **Art Education.** Also Staatsexam in Art Education

Student Numbers *2014-2015*: Total: c. 700
Last Updated: 20/01/15

ACADEMY OF FINE ARTS MÜNSTER

Kunstakademie Münster - Hochschule für Bildende Künste
Leonardo-Campus 2, 48149 Münster
Tel: +49(251) 83-61330
EMail: kunstakademie@muenster.de
Website: http://www.kunstakademie-muenster.de

Rektor: Maik Löbbert (2005-)
Tel: +49(251) 8361-330
EMail: rektorat@kunstakademie-muenster.de

Kanzler: Frank Bartsch
EMail: bartsch@kunstakademie-muenster.de

International Relations: Sandra Musholt, Director, International Office
Tel: +49(251) 8361-205
EMail: musholt@kunstakademie-muenster.de

Programme

Fine Arts (Art Education; Fine Arts; Media Studies; Painting and Drawing; Performing Arts; Photography; Sculpture; Video); **Teachers Training** (Art Education; Teacher Training)

History: Founded 1972. Acquired present status 1987.

Admission Requirements: Abitur and artistic aptitude test

Main Language(s) of Instruction: German

Degrees and Diplomas: *Bachelor's Degree*: **Fine Arts.** *Künstlerische Abschlussprüfung*: **Fine Arts.** *Master*: **Fine Arts.** *PhD*: **Fine Arts.** State Examination in Art Education (Lehramt)

Student Services: Academic Counselling, Canteen, Cultural Activities, Language Laboratory, Social Counselling, Sports Facilities

Student Numbers *2013-2014*: Total 333
Last Updated: 19/03/15

ACADEMY OF FINE ARTS, NUREMBERG

Akademie der Bildenden Künste in Nürnberg
Bingstrasse 60, 90480 Nürnberg
Tel: +49(911) 9404-0
Fax: +49(911) 9404-150
EMail: info@adbk-nuernberg.de
Website: http://www.adbk-nuernberg.de

Präsident: Ottmar Hörl
Tel: +49(911) 9404-113 EMail: praesident@adbk-nuernberg.de

Kanzler: Peter Ochs
Tel: +49(911) 9404-112 EMail: ochs@adbk-nuernberg.de

Programme

Artistic Concepts (Fine Arts); **Artistry** (Film; Fine Arts; Video); **Fine Art and Art Pedagogy** (Art Education; Fine Arts); **General Principles of Creativity and Visual Arts** (Visual Arts); **Gold and Silversmith** (Weaving); **Graphic Design (Visual Communication)** (Graphic Design); **Painting** (Painting and Drawing); **Painting and Art Education** (Art Education; Painting and Drawing); **Sculpture** (Sculpture); **Visual Arts (Sculpture)** (Sculpture; Visual Arts)

Course

Architecture/Architecture and Urban Studies *(Post-graduate)* (Architecture; Interior Design); **Art and Public Places** *(Post-graduate)* (Fine Arts)

History: Founded 1662.

Main Language(s) of Instruction: German

Degrees and Diplomas: *Diplom (Univ)*: **Fine Arts.** *Master*: **Architecture; Urban Studies.** Also Staatsexamen in Art Education

Student Services: Library

Student Numbers *2014-2015*: Total: c. 300
Last Updated: 15/01/15

ACADEMY OF MEDIA ARTS COLOGNE

Kunsthochschule für Medien Köln
Peter-Welter-Platz 2, 50676 Köln, Nordrhein-Westfalen
Tel: +49(221) 20189-0
Fax: +49(221) 20189-17
EMail: studoffice@khm.de
Website: http://www.khm.de

Rektor: Hans Ulrich Reck (2014-)
Tel: +49(221) 20189-111 EMail: rektor@khm.de

Chancellor: Sabine Schulz
Tel: +49(221) 20189-212 EMail: kanzlerin@khm.de

International Relations: Andreas Altenhoff
Tel: +49(221) 20189-126 EMail: andreas@khm.de

Division

Art (Design; Fine Arts; Photography; Visual Arts); **Art and Media Studies** (Aesthetics; Art Education; Art History; Computer Science; Cultural Studies; Design; Gender Studies; Information Sciences; Mass Communication; Media Studies; Music; Natural Sciences); **Film and Television** (Cinema and Television; Film)

History: Founded 1990.

Main Language(s) of Instruction: German

Degrees and Diplomas: *Diplom (Univ)*: **Cinema and Television; Film; Fine Arts; Media Studies; Performing Arts; Photography; Visual Arts; Writing.** *PhD*: **Computer Science; Design; Film; Mass Communication.**

Student Services: IT Centre, Library

Academic Staff *2014-2015*	**TOTAL**
FULL-TIME	c. 60

Student Numbers *2014-2015*	
All (Foreign included)	**337**
FOREIGN ONLY	**98**

Last Updated: 10/03/15

ACADEMY OF MUSIC HANNS EISLER BERLIN

Hochschule für Musik Hanns Eisler Berlin
Charlottenstrasse 55, 10117 Berlin
Tel: +49(30) 688305-700
Fax: +49(30) 688305-701
EMail: rektorat.hfm@berlin.de
Website: http://www.hfm-berlin.de

Rector: Birgitta Wollenweber
Tel: +49(30) 688305-817 EMail: rektorat@hfm-berlin.de

Kanzler: Hans-Joachim Völz
Tel: +49(30) 688305-818
EMail: hans-joachim.voelz@hfm-berlin.de

International Relations: Ute Schmidt, International Affairs Officer
Tel: +49(30) 688305-831 EMail: schmidt_ute@hfm.in-berlin.de

Department

Piano, Composition, Theoretical Studies (Music Theory and Composition; Musical Instruments; Musicology); **Strings, Harp and Guitar** *(B)* (Musical Instruments); **Voice, Music Theatre and Stage Direction** *(A)* (Music; Singing; Theatre); **Wind, Percussion, Conducting** (Conducting; Musical Instruments)

Institute

Jazz *(Berlin)* (Jazz and Popular Music); **Musicians' Health** *(Kurt Singer)* (Health Sciences; Music; Physiology); **New Music** *(klangzeitort)* (Music)

Centre

Continuing Education

History: Founded 1950. Acquired present title 1964.

Academic Year: October to July (October-February; April-July)

Admission Requirements: Entrance examination and special entrance qualification for each course

Fees: c.90 per semester (Euro)

Main Language(s) of Instruction: German

Degrees and Diplomas: *Bachelor's Degree*; *Konzertexamen*; *Master*: **Conducting; Music Theory and Composition; Musical Instruments; Singing.**

Student Services: Academic Counselling, Canteen, Careers Guidance, Language Laboratory, Library, Social Counselling, Sports Facilities

Student Numbers *2013-2014*: Total 487
Last Updated: 09/03/15

ACADEMY OF VISUAL ARTS LEIPZIG

Hochschule für Grafik und Buchkunst Leipzig

Postfach 10 08 05, Wächerstrasse 11, 04008 Leipzig
Tel: +49(341) 2135-0
Fax: +49(341) 2135-166
EMail: hgb@hgb-leipzig.de
Website: http://www.hgb-leipzig.de

Rector: Ana Dimke
Tel: +49(341) 2135-159 EMail: rektorin@hgb-leipzig.de

Chancellor: Maria-Cornelia Ziesch
Tel: +49(341) 2135-105 EMail: kanzler@hgb-leipzig.de

International Relations: Frances Kind, International Relations Officer
Tel: +49(341) 2135-155
EMail: kind@hgb-leipzig.de; aaa@hgb-leipzig.de

Programme

Book Design/Graphic Design (Graphic Design; Printing and Printmaking); **Cultures of the Curatorial** *(Graduate)* (Cultural Studies; Dance; Film; Fine Arts; Music; Natural Sciences; Social Sciences; Theatre); **Media Art** (Media Studies); **Meisterschüler** (Fine Arts); **Painting/Graphics** (Graphic Arts; Painting and Drawing); **Photography** (Photography)

Institute

Theory (Aesthetics; Art History; Fine Arts)

History: Founded 1763.

Main Language(s) of Instruction: German

Degrees and Diplomas: *Künstlerische Abschlussprüfung*: **Communication Arts; Graphic Arts; Graphic Design; Painting and Drawing; Photography; Printing and Printmaking.** *Master*: **Cultural Studies; Natural Sciences; Performing Arts; Social Sciences.** *PhD*: **Aesthetics; Art History; Fine Arts.**

Student Services: Academic Counselling, Library, Residential Facilities

Student Numbers *2013-2014*: Total 548
Last Updated: 04/03/15

ACCADIS UNIVERSITY OF APPLIED SCIENCES BAD HOMBURG

Accadis Hochschule Bad Homburg

Du Pont-Straße 4, 61352 Bad Homburg, Hesse
Tel: +49(6172) 9842 +49(6172) 984-235
Fax: +49(6172) 9842-20
EMail: info@accadis.com
Website: http://www.accadis.com

President: Werner Meissner (2004-)
EMail: w.meissner@accadis.com

Managing Partner: Gerda Meinl-Kexel
EMail: g.meinl@accadis.com

International Relations: Britta Laudon-Reece, Head of International Programmes

Department

Health Care Management (Health Administration); **Management and Strategy** (Management); **Marketing and Communication** (Communication Studies; Marketing); **Media Management** (Management; Media Studies); **Sports Management** (Sports Management); **Tourism Management** (Tourism)

History: Created 1990 as International Business School Bad Homburg; 2001 added cooperative programmes with local businesses. Acquired current title and status 2004.

Academic Year: October to August

Admission Requirements: Abitur or equivalent university entry qualification; proficiency in German and English; personality and intelligence structure test.

Fees: National: Undergraduate, 695 per month; Postgraduate, 900 per month (c. 14,400-21,600 per programme) (Euro), International: Undergraduate, 640-725 per month; Graduate, 580 per month (Euro)

Main Language(s) of Instruction: German, English

Accrediting Agency: Wissenschaftsrat; Foundation for International Business Administration Accreditation, Germany (FIBAA)

Degrees and Diplomas: *Bachelor's Degree*: **Communication Studies; International Business; Management; Marketing; Media Studies; Sports Management; Tourism.** *Master*: **Business Administration; Health Administration; International Business; Leadership; Management; Marketing; Sports Management.** Also Dual Degrees

Student Services: Academic Counselling, Careers Guidance, Language Laboratory, Social Counselling

Last Updated: 20/01/15

ALBSTADT-SIGMARINGEN UNIVERSITY

Hochschule Albstadt-Sigmaringen

PO Box 1254, Anton-Günther-Straße 51, 72488 Sigmaringen
Tel: +49(7571) 732-0
Fax: +49(7571) 732-8229
EMail: info@hs-albsig.de
Website: http://www.hs-albsig.de

Rector: Ingeborg Mühldorfer
Tel: +49(7571) 732-8221 EMail: muehldorfer@hs-albsig.de

Chancellor: Bernadette Boden
Tel: +49(7571) 732-8400 EMail: boden@hs-albsig.de

Faculty

Business and Computer Science (Business Administration; Business Computing; Computer Science; Management); **Computer Science/Informatics** (Business Computing; Computer Engineering; Computer Science); **Engineering** (Business Administration; Clothing and Sewing; Communication Studies; Industrial Engineering; Machine Building; Mechanical Engineering; Software Engineering; Textile Technology); **Life Sciences** (Biological and Life Sciences; Biomedical Engineering; Food Technology; Hygiene; Management; Nutrition; Pharmacology)

Further Information: Also campus in Albstadt.

History: Founded 1971.

Main Language(s) of Instruction: German

Degrees and Diplomas: *Bachelor's Degree*; *Master*: **Biomedicine; Business Administration; Business Computing; Computer Engineering; Computer Science; Design; Industrial**

Engineering; Industrial Management; Information Technology; Management; Mechanical Engineering; Production Engineering; Textile Technology.
Student Services: Careers Guidance, Library

Student Numbers *2013-2014*: Total 3,135
Last Updated: 02/03/15

ALICE-SALOMON UNIVERSITY OF APPLIED SCIENCES BERLIN

Alice-Salomon Hochschule Berlin (ASH)

Alice-Salomon-Platz 5, 12627 Berlin
Tel: +49(30) 99245-0
Fax: +49(30) 99245-245
EMail: ash@ash-berlin.eu
Website: http://www.ash-berlin.eu/

Rektorin: Uwe Bettig
Tel: +49(30) 99245-400 EMail: rektorat@ash-berlin.eu
Kanzler: Andreas Flegl
Tel: +49(30) 99245-305
EMail: Flegl@verwaltung.asfh-berlin.de; kanzler@ash-berlin.eu
International Relations: Irene Gropp, Director, International Office
Tel: +49(30) 99245-304
EMail: ausland@asfh-berlin.de; gropp@ash-berlin.eu

Programme
Biographical and Creative Writing (Writing); **Child Protection - Quality Development Dialogue in Early Help and Child Protection** *(Postgraduate)* (Child Care and Development); **Clinical Social Work** *(Postgraduate)* (Social Work); **Early Childhood Education** (Education); **Health and Social Care Management** (Health Administration; Welfare and Protective Services); **Intercultural Conflict Management** *(Postgraduate)* (Peace and Disarmament); **Intercultural Conflict Management (Spanish)** *(Postgraduate)* (Peace and Disarmament); **Management and Quality Development in the Health Sector** *(Consecutive Master)* (Health Administration); **Physiotherapy/Occupational Therapy** (Occupational Therapy; Physical Therapy); **Research in Social Work and Pedagogy** *(Consecutive Master)* (Pedagogy; Social Work); **Russian-German Double-Master Intercultural Social Work** *(Postgraduate)* (Social Work); **Social Management** *(Postgraduate)* (Social Work); **Social Work** *(Sozialarbeit/Sozialpädagogik)* (Social Work); **Social Work (Online)** (Social Work); **Social Work as a Human Rights Profession** *(Postgraduate)* (Human Rights; Social Work); **Sustainable Development and Early Childhood Education** *(Postgraduate)* (Child Care and Development; Development Studies)
History: Founded 1908 as Women School of Social Work. Acquired present status and title 1971.
Academic Year: April to February (April-July; October-February)
Admission Requirements: Final secondary school examination
Main Language(s) of Instruction: German, English
Accrediting Agency: AQAS e.V. (Agentur für Qualitätssicherung durch Akkreditierung von Studiengängen)

Degrees and Diplomas: *Bachelor's Degree*: **Education; Health Sciences; Occupational Therapy; Physical Therapy; Preschool Education; Social Work.** *Master*: **Child Care and Development; Peace and Disarmament; Pedagogy; Preschool Education; Social Work; Welfare and Protective Services; Writing.**

Student Services: Academic Counselling, Canteen, Careers Guidance, Facilities for disabled people, Foreign Studies Centre, IT Centre, Language Laboratory, Library, Nursery Care, Social Counselling, Sports Facilities
Publications: Alice-Wissenschaft

Student Numbers *2013-2014*: Total 3,201
Last Updated: 20/01/15

ANHALT UNIVERSITY OF APPLIED SCIENCES

Hochschule Anhalt

PO Box 1458, Bernburger Strasse 55, 06354 Köthen
Tel: +49(3496) 67-1000
Fax: +49(3496) 67-1099
EMail: praesident@hs-anhalt.de
Website: http://www.hs-anhalt.de

President: Dieter Orzessek (1996-)
Tel: +49(3471) 355-1179
EMail: praesident@hs-anhalt.de; d.orzessek@loel.hs-anhalt.de
Manager, Administration: Sabine Thalmann
Tel: +49(3496) 67-4007 EMail: s.thalmann@verw.hs-anhalt.de
International Relations: Anne Beer, Head, International Office
Tel: +49 (3496) 67-5112
EMail: a.beeraaa.hs-anhalt.de; internationalhs-anhalt.de

Department
Agriculture, Ecotrophology and Landscape Development *(Bernburg)* (Agronomy; Environmental Studies; Landscape Architecture; Rural Planning); **Applied Biosciences and Process Engineering** *(Köthen)* (Biophysics; Food Technology; Pharmacology); **Architecture, Facility Management and Geoinformation** *(Dessau)* (Architecture; Construction Engineering; Management; Surveying and Mapping); **Computer Science and Language** *(Köthen)* (Computer Networks; Computer Science; Information Management; Media Studies; Software Engineering); **Design** *(Deassau)* (Design; Graphic Arts; Industrial Design); **Economics** *(Bernburg)* (Business Administration; Commercial Law; Economics; International Business; Real Estate); **Electrical and Electronic Engineering, Mechanical Engineering and Industrial Engineering** *(Köthen)* (Electrical Engineering; Industrial Engineering; Mechanical Engineering)
Further Information: Also campuses in Dieter and Orzessek
History: Founded 1991.
Main Language(s) of Instruction: German
Degrees and Diplomas: *Bachelor's Degree*; *Master*: **Agricultural Business; Agricultural Management; Air Transport; Architecture; Automotive Engineering; Biomedical Engineering; Biotechnology; Business Administration; Commercial Law; Computer Engineering; Design; Electrical Engineering; Environmental Management; Food Science; Food Technology; Human Resources; Industrial Engineering; Information Management; International Business; Landscape Architecture; Law; Mechanical Engineering; Surveying and Mapping; Transport Management.** Some Master's programmes taught in English.
Student Services: IT Centre, Library

Student Numbers *2014-2015*: Total: c. 7,900
Last Updated: 03/03/15

ANSBACH UNIVERSITY OF APPLIED SCIENCES

Hochschule für angewandte Wissenschaften Ansbach (HS ANSBACH)

Postfach 1963, Residenzstrasse 8, 91510 Ansbach, Bavaria
Tel: +49(981) 4877-0
Fax: +49(981) 4877-188
EMail: info@hs-ansbach.de
Website: http://www.hs-ansbach.de

Präsidentin: Ute Ambrosius (2012-)
Tel: +49(981) 4877-101 EMail: ute.ambrosius@fh-ansbach.de
Chancellor: Hans-Peter Smolka
Tel: +49(981) 4877-150 EMail: hsmolka@hs-ansbach.de

Faculty
Economic and General Sciences (Business Administration; Business Computing; Communication Studies; International Business; Journalism; Management; Multimedia); **Engineering** (Biomedical Engineering; Biotechnology; Energy Engineering; Engineering; Environmental Engineering; Industrial Engineering)
History: Founded 1996 as Fachhochschule Ansbach. Renamed Hochschule für angewandte Wissenschaften - Fachhochschule Ansbach 2009. Acquired present tile 2013.
Admission Requirements: Secondary school certificate
Fees: (Euros): 28 per semester
Main Language(s) of Instruction: German
Degrees and Diplomas: *Bachelor's Degree*: **Biomedical Engineering; Biotechnology; Business Administration; Business Computing; Energy Engineering; Environmental Engineering; Industrial Engineering; International Business; Journalism; Management; Mass Communication; Multimedia; Polymer and**

Plastics Technology. *Master*: **Energy Engineering; International Business; Management; Service Trades.** Also Continuing Education and Dual Studies Programmes.

Student Services: Academic Counselling, Canteen, Careers Guidance, Facilities for disabled people, Health Services, Language Laboratory, Library, Social Counselling

Publications: Wirtschaft und Technik für die Praxis

Student Numbers *2013-2014*: Total 2,757
Last Updated: 27/01/15

ART ACADEMY OF KARLSRUHE

Staatliche Akademie der Bildenden Künste Karlsruhe
PO Box 111209, Reinhold-Frank-Str. 67, 76133 Karlsruhe
Tel: +49(721) 926-0
Fax: +49(721) 926-5206
EMail: rektorat@kunstakademie-karlsruhe.de; mail@kunstakademie-karlsruhe.de
Website: http://www.kunstakademie-karlsruhe.de

Rector: Ernst Caramelle
Tel: +49(721) 926-5210
EMail: rektorat@kunstakademie-karlsruhe.de

Chancellor: Rüdiger Weis
Tel: +49(721) 926-5211
EMail: ruediger.weis@kunstakademie-karlsruhe.de

International Relations: Ilona Günthner

Division

Art education (Art Education); **Fine Arts** (Art History; Fine Arts; Painting and Drawing)

History: Founded 1854.

Main Language(s) of Instruction: German

Degrees and Diplomas: *Künstlerische Abschlussprüfung*: **Graphic Arts; Painting and Drawing; Sculpture.** Also Teacher Training Diploma (Staatsexam) in Art Education

Student Services: Library

Student Numbers *2013-2014*: Total: c. 319
Last Updated: 25/03/15

AUGSBURG UNIVERSITY OF APPLIED SCIENCES

Hochschule für angewandte Wissenschaften Augsburg (HS AUGSBURG)
Postfach 110605, An der Hochschule 1, 86031 Augsburg
Tel: +49(821) 5586-0
Fax: +49(821) 5586-3222
EMail: info@hs-augsburg.de
Website: http://www.hs-augsburg.de

President: Hans-Eberhard Schurk
Tel: +49(821) 5586-3213 EMail: hans.e.schurk@hs-augsburg.de

Chancellor: Tatjana Dörfler
Tel: +49(821) 5586-3217 EMail: kanzlerin@hs-augsburg.de

International Relations: Ingrid Hahn-Eisenhardt, Head, International Office
Tel: +49(821) 5586-3205
EMail: ingrid.hahn-eisenhardt@hs-augsburg.de; ausland@hs-augsburg.de

Faculty

Architecture and Civil Engineering (Architecture; Civil Engineering); **Business Administration** (Accountancy; Business Administration; Finance; International Business; Management; Taxation); **Computer Science** (Computer Science; Information Technology); **Design** (Communication Arts; Design; Media Studies; Multimedia); **Electrical Engineering** (Computer Engineering; Electrical and Electronic Engineering; Electronic Engineering; Mechanical Engineering); **Liberal Arts and Sciences** (Mathematics; Natural Sciences); **Mechanical and Process Engineering** (Mechanical Engineering; Production Engineering)

History: Founded 1971.

Main Language(s) of Instruction: German

Degrees and Diplomas: *Bachelor's Degree*; *Master*: **Accountancy; Architecture; Building Technologies; Business Computing; Civil Engineering; Computer Science; Design; Electronic Engineering; Energy Engineering; Engineering; Environmental Engineering; Finance; Human Resources; International Business; Marketing; Mass Communication; Media Studies; Production Engineering; Sales Techniques; Taxation.**

Student Services: Careers Guidance, IT Centre, Library

Academic Staff *2014-2015*: Total: c. 740
Student Numbers *2014-2015*: Total: c. 6,000
Last Updated: 05/03/15

BERLIN SCHOOL OF ECONOMICS AND LAW

Hochschule für Wirtschaft und Recht Berlin
Alt-Friedrichsfelde 60, 10315 Berlin
Tel: +49(30) 9021-4005
Fax: +49(30) 9021-4013
EMail: info@fhv-berlin.de
Website: http://www.hwr-berlin.de/

President: Bernd Reissert
Tel: +49(30) 30877-1001 EMail: praesident@hwr-berlin.de

Chancellor: Sandra Westerburg
Tel: +49(30) 30877-1201 EMail: kanzler@hwr-berlin.de

Department

Business and Economics (Business Administration; Economics); **Cooperative Studies** (Banking; Civil Engineering; Computer Science; Insurance; Mechanical Engineering; Real Estate; Retailing and Wholesaling; Taxation; Tourism); **Legal Studies** (Law); **Police and Security Management** (Police Studies); **Public Administration** (Public Administration)

History: Founded 2009 following merger of University of Applied Sciences for Administration and Law (FHVR) and Berlin School of Economics

Admission Requirements: Abitur, Fachgebundene Hoschschulreife, Fachhochschulereife, pre-study internship

Fees: None

Main Language(s) of Instruction: German

Degrees and Diplomas: *Bachelor's Degree*; *Diplom (FH)*; *Master*: **Accountancy; Administration; Business Administration; Commercial Law; Finance; Health Administration; Human Resources; Industrial Engineering; International Business; International Economics; Law; Management; Marketing; Political Sciences; Protective Services; Public Administration.** Also certificates and higher professional qualification (Fachwirt) in Notary Studies and Law.

Student Services: Academic Counselling, Canteen, Careers Guidance, Facilities for disabled people, Library, Sports Facilities

Academic Staff *2014-2015*: Total: c. 200
Student Numbers *2014-2015*: Total: c. 9,700
Last Updated: 10/03/15

BERLIN UNIVERSITY OF THE ARTS

Universität der Künste Berlin
PO Box 120544, 10595 Berlin
Tel: +49(30) 3185-0
Fax: +49(30) 3185-2758
EMail: beratung@udk-berlin.de
Website: http://www.udk-berlin.de

Präsident: Martin Rennert
Tel: +49(30) 3185-2447 EMail: p1@intra.udk-berlin.de

Kanzler: Wolfgang Abramowski
Tel: +49(30) 3185-2445
EMail: wolfgang.abramowski@intra.udk-berlin.de

College

Architecture, Media and Design (Architecture; Design; E- Business/Commerce; Industrial Design; Visual Arts); **Fine Arts** (Fine Arts); **Music** (Art Education; Art Therapy; Conducting; Instrument Making; Music; Music Education; Music Theory and Composition;

Religious Music; Sound Engineering (Acoustics)); **Performing Arts** (Performing Arts)

History: Founded 1975. Consists of the Hochschule für Bildende Künste, dating back to the Prussian Academy of Fine Arts, founded in 1696, and the Hochschule für Musik, established in 1869.

Main Language(s) of Instruction: German

Degrees and Diplomas: *Bachelor's Degree*; *Master*: **Art Education; Art Therapy; Fine Arts; Journalism; Mass Communication; Sound Engineering (Acoustics); Theatre.** *PhD*: **Architecture; Design; Fine Arts; Media Studies; Music; Performing Arts.**

Student Services: Library

Student Numbers *2013-2014*: Total 3,427
Last Updated: 27/03/15

BERLIN-WEISSENSEE SCHOOL OF ART

Kunsthochschule Berlin-Weissensee
Bühringstraße 20, 13086 Berlin
Tel: +49(30) 47705-0
Fax: +49(30) 47705-290
EMail: sekretariat.rektorin@kh-berlin.de
Website: http://www.kh-berlin.de

Rector: Leonie Baumann
Tel: +49(30) 4770-5220 EMail: rektorin@kh-berlin.de

Chancellor: Silvia Durin
Tel: +49(30) 47705-316 EMail: kanzlerin@kh-berlin.de

International Relations: Leoni Adams, Head of the International Office Tel: +49(30) +47705-232
EMail: international@kh-berlin.de

Department

Art Theory and History (Art History); **Art Therapy** (Art Therapy); **Fashion Design** (Fashion Design); **Fine Arts/Painting** (Fine Arts; Painting and Drawing); **Fine Arts/Sculpture** (Fine Arts; Sculpture); **Fine Arts/Stage and Costume Design** (Clothing and Sewing; Display and Stage Design; Fine Arts); **Product Design** (Industrial Design); **Space Strategy** (Display and Stage Design); **Textile and Surface Design** (Design; Textile Design); **Visual Communication** (Advertising and Publicity)

Course

Foundation (Design; Fine Arts)

History: Founded 1946.

Main Language(s) of Instruction: German

Degrees and Diplomas: *Bachelor's Degree*; *Master*: **Art Education; Art Therapy; Display and Stage Design; Fashion Design; Graphic Design; Industrial Design; Textile Design.**

Student Services: IT Centre, Library

Student Numbers *2013-2014*: Total: c. 800
Last Updated: 25/03/15

BEUTH UNIVERSITY OF APPLIED SCIENCES BERLIN

Beuth Hochschule für Technik Berlin (BEUTH HS)
Luxemburger Strasse 10, 13353 Berlin
Tel: +49(30) 4504-1
Fax: +49(30) 4504-2705
EMail: praesidentin@beuth-hochschule.de
Website: http://www.beuth-hochschule.de

Präsident: Monika Gross (2011-)
Tel: +49(30) 4504-2335 EMail: praesident@tfh-berlin.de

International Relations: Michael Kramp
Tel: +49(30) 4504-2950 EMail: ausland@tfh-berlin.de

Department

Architecture (Architecture); **Civil Engineering** (Civil Engineering); **Computer Science and Media** (Computer Science; Media Studies); **Economics and Business Administration** (Business Administration; Economics); **Electronic Engineering** (Automation and Control Engineering; Electronic Engineering; Telecommunications Engineering); **Life Sciences and Technology** (Biological and Life Sciences; Biotechnology; Landscape Architecture); **Mathematics, Physics and Chemistry** (Chemistry; Mathematics; Physics); **Mechanical Engineering** (Environmental Management; Mechanical Engineering)

History: Founded 1971 as Technische Fachhochschule Berlin.

Academic Year: October to July (October-February; April-July)

Admission Requirements: Secondary school certificate

Fees: National: Registration fee, 295 EUR per semester (including public transportation) (Euro), International: Registration fee, 295 EUR per semester (Euro)

Main Language(s) of Instruction: German

Accrediting Agency: ACQUIN; ASIIN; ZeVAA; FiBAA

Degrees and Diplomas: *Bachelor's Degree*; *Master*: **Applied Physics; Architecture; Biotechnology; Building Technologies; Business Administration; Chemical Engineering; Civil Engineering; Computer Engineering; Computer Science; Construction Engineering; Electronic Engineering; Energy Engineering; Food Technology; Industrial Engineering; Information Technology; Management; Mathematics and Computer Science; Mechanical Engineering; Optics; Optometry; Packaging Technology; Printing and Printmaking; Production Engineering; Real Estate; Structural Architecture; Surveying and Mapping; Town Planning.**

Student Services: Academic Counselling, Canteen, Health Services, Language Laboratory, Library, Sports Facilities

Academic Staff *2014-2015*	**TOTAL**
FULL-TIME	**334**
PART-TIME	**499**
Student Numbers *2014-2015*	
All (Foreign included)	**12,519**

Last Updated: 15/01/15

BIBERACH UNIVERSITY OF APPLIED SCIENCES

Hochschule Biberach
Karlstraße 11, 88400 Biberach
Tel: +49(7351) 582-0
Fax: +49(7351) 582-119
EMail: info@hochschule-bc.de
Website: http://www.hochschule-biberach.de

Rektor: Thomas Vogel (2003-)
Tel: +49(7351) 582-100 EMail: Rektor@hochschule-bc.de

Chancellor: Thomas Schwäble
Tel: +49(7351) 582-110 EMail: schwaeble@hochschule-bc.de

International Relations: Sinje Miebach
Tel: +49(7351) 582-103 EMail: miebach@hochschule-bc.de

Faculty

Architecture, Building Heating and Refrigeration (Architecture; Heating and Refrigeration); **Biotechnology** (Biotechnology; Pharmacy); **Business Administration** (Business Administration); **Civil Engineering and Project Management** (Civil Engineering; Engineering Management; Management)

Department

Contiunuing Education (Business Administration; Real Estate); **General Studies** (English; French; Italian; Japanese; Modern Languages; Spanish; Writing)

History: Founded 1964.

Main Language(s) of Instruction: German

Degrees and Diplomas: *Bachelor's Degree*; *Master*: **Architecture; Biotechnology; Business Administration; Civil Engineering; Engineering Management; Heating and Refrigeration; Management; Real Estate.**

Student Services: Canteen, Library

Academic Staff *2014-2015*: Total: c. 255
Student Numbers *2013-2014*: Total 2,339
Last Updated: 03/03/15

BIELEFELD UNIVERSITY OF APPLIED SCIENCES

Fachhochschule Bielefeld (FH BIELEFELD)
Postfach 10 11 13, Kurt-Schumacher-Straße 6, 33511 Bielefeld
Tel: +49(521) 106-01
Fax: +49(521) 106-7790
EMail: info@fh-bielefeld.de
Website: http://www.fh-bielefeld.de

President: Beate Rennen-Allhoff (2001-)
Tel: +49(521) 106-7738 EMail: praesidentin@fh-bielefeld.de

Vice President for Business and Staff Administration: Gehsa Schnier
Tel: +49(521) 106-7736/37 EMail: gehsa.schnier@fh-bielefeld.de

International Relations: Grit Dörfel, Head, International Office
Tel: +49(521) 106-7710
EMail: aaa@fh-bielefeld.de; grit.doerfel@fh-bielefeld.de

Department
Architecture and Civil Engineering (Architecture; Civil Engineering); **Business Administration and Health Sciences** (Business Administration; Business Computing; Commercial Law; Health Sciences; Industrial and Organizational Psychology; International Studies; Law; Management; Nursing); **Design** (Design; Fashion Design; Graphic Design; Media Studies; Multimedia; Photography); **Engineering** *(Minden Campus)* (Computer Science; Electrical Engineering; Industrial Engineering; Mechanical Engineering); **Engineering and Mathematics** (Applied Mathematics; Biotechnology; Business Administration; Computer Engineering; Electronic Engineering; Energy Engineering; Engineering; Machine Building; Mathematics; Mechanical Engineering; Production Engineering); **Social Studies** (Management; Pedagogy; Social Sciences; Social Studies; Social Work)

Campus
Gütersloh (Automation and Control Engineering; Business Administration; Electronic Engineering; Engineering); **Minden** (Architecture; Civil Engineering; Health Sciences; Nursing)

History: Founded 1971.

Admission Requirements: Fachhochschulreife

Main Language(s) of Instruction: German

Degrees and Diplomas: *Bachelor's Degree*: **Architecture and Planning; Business Administration; Design; Education; Engineering; Law; Mathematics and Computer Science; Social Sciences; Social Work.** *Master*: **Building Technologies; Business Administration; Commercial Law; Computer Science; Design; Electrical Engineering; Industrial Management; Mathematics and Computer Science; Mechanical Engineering; Rehabilitation and Therapy; Social Sciences; Vocational Education.** Also Certificate (Zertifikat)

Student Services: Academic Counselling, Canteen, Careers Guidance, Facilities for disabled people, Foreign Studies Centre, Language Laboratory, Library, Nursery Care, Social Counselling, Sports Facilities

Academic Staff *2014-2015*: Total 244
Student Numbers *2014-2015*: Total 9,691
Last Updated: 27/01/15

BOCHUM UNIVERSITY OF APPLIED SCIENCES

Hochschule Bochum
Postfach 100741, Lennershofstr. 140, 44707 Bochum
Tel: +49(234) 32-202
Fax: +49(234) 32-14312
EMail: hochschulverwaltung@fh-bochum.de
Website: http://www.hochschule-bochum.de

Rektor: Martin Sternberg
Tel: +49(234) 32-10000 EMail: martin.sternberg@hs-bochum.de

Vizepräsident Wirtschafts- und Personalverwaltung: Christina Reinhardt
Tel: +49(234) 32-10001 EMail: christina.reinhardt@hs-bochum.de

International Relations: Siegfried Engesser-Paris, Head, International Office
Tel: +49(234) 321-0002
EMail: siegfried.engesser-paris@hs-bochum.de

School
Geothermal Technology (Thermal Engineering)

Department
Architecture (Architecture; Media Studies); **Business Administration** (Accountancy; Business Administration; Business Computing; Economics; Finance; Human Resources; International Economics; Marketing; Taxation); **Civil Engineering** (Civil Engineering); **Electrical Engineering and Computer Science** (Computer Science; Electrical Engineering); **Geodesy** (Computer Science; Surveying and Mapping); **Mechatronics and Mechanical Engineering** (Electronic Engineering; Mechanical Engineering)

Institute
Education, Culture and Sustainable Development (Cultural Studies; Education; Environmental Studies); **Mathematics and Teaching Technology** (Educational Technology; Mathematics)

Centre
Mechatronics (Electronic Engineering)

History: Founded 1972. Formerly known as Fachhoschschule-Bochum.

Main Language(s) of Instruction: German

Degrees and Diplomas: *Bachelor's Degree*; *Master*: **Accountancy; Architecture; Business Administration; Civil Engineering; Electronic Engineering; Information Technology; International Business; Management; Mechanical Engineering; Taxation; Town Planning.**

Student Services: Academic Counselling, Canteen, Careers Guidance, Cultural Activities, Language Laboratory, Library, Sports Facilities

Publications: FHBO Journal

Student Numbers *2013-2014*: Total 6,588
Last Updated: 03/03/15

BONN-RHEIN-SIEG UNIVERSITY OF APPLIED SCIENCES

Hochschule Bonn-Rhein-Sieg
Grantham-Allee 20, 53757 Sankt Augustin
Tel: +49(2241) 865-0
Fax: +49(2241) 865-609
Website: http://www.fh-bonn-rhein-sieg.de

President: Hartmut Ihne
Tel: +49(2241) 865-600 EMail: praesident@h-brs.de

Chancellor: Michaela Schuhmann
Tel: +49(2241) 865-606
EMail: michaela.schuhmann@h-brs.de; vp5@h-brs.de

International Relations: Roland Weiss, Director
Tel: +49(2241) 865-711
EMail: roland.weiss@h-brs.de; international.office@h-brs.de

Department
Business Administration (Business Administration); **Computer Science** (Computer Science); **Electrical Engineering, Mechanical Engineering and Technical Journalism** (Electrical Engineering; Journalism; Mechanical Engineering); **Management Sciences** (Management); **Natural Sciences** *(Rheinbach)* (Applied Chemistry; Applied Physics; Biology; Chemistry; Natural Sciences); **Social Security Studies** (Welfare and Protective Services)

History: Founded 1995, acquired present status 2006.

Admission Requirements: Secondary school certificate or equivalent

Fees: 500 per semester (Euro)

Main Language(s) of Instruction: German

Accrediting Agency: FIBAA; ASIIN

Degrees and Diplomas: *Bachelor's Degree*; *Master*: **Analytical Chemistry; Biomedicine; Computer Science; Electronic Engineering; Engineering Management; Information Management; Management; Media Studies; Safety Engineering; Welfare and Protective Services.**

Student Services: Academic Counselling, Canteen, Facilities for disabled people, IT Centre, Language Laboratory, Library, Nursery Care, Social Counselling, Sports Facilities

Student Numbers *2013-2014*: Total 7,035
Last Updated: 04/03/15

BRANDENBURG UNIVERSITY OF APPLIED SCIENCES

Fachhochschule Brandenburg

Postfach 2132, Magdeburger Str. 50, 14737 Brandenburg
Tel: +49(3381) 355-0
Fax: +49(3381) 355-199
EMail: info@fh-brandenburg.de
Website: http://www.fh-brandenburg.de

President: Burghilde Wieneke-Toutaoui
Tel: +49(3381) 355-101 EMail: praesidentin@fh-brandenburg.de

Chancellor: Steffen Kissinger
Tel: +49(3381) 355-150 EMail: kanzler@fh-brandenburg.de

International Relations: Annett Kitsche, Head, International Studies Centre
Tel: +49(3381) 355-217 EMail: auslandsamt@fh-brandenburg.de; kitsche@fh-brandenburg.de

Department

Business and Management (Business Administration; Business Computing; Information Management; International Business; Management; Safety Engineering; Technology); **Engineering** (Automation and Control Engineering; Electronic Engineering; Information Technology; Machine Building; Mechanical Engineering; Optical Technology; Physical Engineering); **Informatics and Media** (Computer Science; Media Studies)

History: Founded 1992.

Main Language(s) of Instruction: German

Degrees and Diplomas: *Bachelor's Degree*: **Automation and Control Engineering; Business Administration; Business Computing; Computer Science; Electronic Engineering; Engineering; Machine Building.** *Master*: **Business Administration; Business Computing; Computer Engineering; Computer Science; Energy Engineering; Engineering Management; Multimedia; Safety Engineering.**

Student Services: Careers Guidance, Library

Student Numbers *2013-2014*: Total 2,780
Last Updated: 27/01/15

BRANDENBURG UNIVERSITY OF TECHNOLOGY COTTBUS-SENFTENBERG

Brandenburgische Technische Universität Cottbus-Senftenberg (BTU)

PO Box 101344, Konrad-Wachsmann-Allee 1, 03046 Cottbus
Tel: +49(355) 69-0
Fax: +49(355) 69-2721
EMail: webmaster@tu-cottbus.de
Website: http://www.tu-cottbus.de

Präsident: Jörg Steinbach
Tel: +49(355) 69-2283 EMail: praesident@b-tu.de

Chief Executive Officer: Wolfgang Schröder
Tel: +49(355) 69-3311 EMail: kanzler@b-tu.de

Faculty

Architecture, Civil Engineering and Urban Planning (Architecture; Civil Engineering; Structural Architecture; Town Planning); **Business Administration and Social Sciences, Music Education** (Business Administration; Music Education; Social Sciences); **Construction** (Construction Engineering); **Engineering and Computer Science** (Computer Science; Engineering); **Environmental Sciences and Process Engineering** (Automation and Control Engineering; Environmental Engineering); **Mathematics, Natural Sciences and Computer Science** (Applied Mathematics; Chemistry; Computer Science; Information Technology; Mathematics; Media Studies; Natural Sciences; Physics; Technology); **Mechanical, Electrical and Industrial Engineering** (Electrical Engineering; Electronic Engineering; Industrial Engineering; Mechanical Engineering); **Natural Sciences** (Applied Chemistry; Biotechnology; Natural Sciences)

Research Centre

Energy Technology *(Brandenburg)* (Energy Engineering); **Flow and Transport Modelling and Measurement** (Transport and Communications); **Human Ecology** (Ecology); **Landscape Development and Mining Landscapes** (Landscape Architecture); **Law and Administration** (Administration; Law); **Public Law and Environmental Network** *(German-Polish Centre; joint Scientific Institute of Brandenburg University of Technology Cottbus and University Wroclaw)* (Environmental Studies; Public Law); **Student Acquisition and University Preparation (College)** (Higher Education)

Research Institute

Teaching, Research and Communication in Civil Engineering *(David-Gilly)* (Civil Engineering; Communication Studies; Teacher Training)

History: Founded 1991.

Academic Year: October to July (October-February; April-July)

Admission Requirements: Secondary school certificate (Abitur) or equivalent. German Language Admission Test (DSH or TestDaF min. 16 points), and for programmes taught in English TOEFL 550, 213 Computer based or IELTS 6,5

Fees: None

Main Language(s) of Instruction: German (several degree programmes taught in English)

Degrees and Diplomas: *Bachelor's Degree*; *Master*: **Applied Chemistry; Applied Mathematics; Architectural Restoration; Architecture; Biotechnology; Building Technologies; Business Administration; Civil Engineering; Commercial Law; Computer Science; Construction Engineering; Cultural Studies; E- Business/Commerce; Electrical Engineering; Energy Engineering; Engineering; Environmental Engineering; Environmental Management; Heritage Preservation; Information Technology; Materials Engineering; Mechanical Engineering; Media Studies; Natural Resources; Physics; Power Engineering; Regional Planning; Social Work; Soil Management; Technology; Town Planning; Water Management.** *PhD*: **Environmental Management; Heritage Preservation; Mathematics and Computer Science; Natural Resources.**

Student Services: Academic Counselling, Canteen, Cultural Activities, Health Services, Language Laboratory, Residential Facilities, Social Counselling, Sports Facilities

Publications: Forum der Forschung

Student Numbers *2014-2015*: Total: c. 10,000
Last Updated: 23/01/15

BRAUNSCHWEIG UNIVERSITY OF ART

Hochschule für Bildende Künste Braunschweig (HBK BRAUNSCHWEIG)

PO Box 2538, Johannes-Selenka-Platz 1, 38118 Braunschweig, Lower Saxony
Tel: +49(531) 3919-122
Fax: +49(531) 3919-307
EMail: studienberatung@hbk-bs.de
Website: http://www.hbk-bs.de

President: Nikolas Lange
Tel: +49(531) 391-9162 EMail: hvp@hbk-bs.de

Vice President for Teaching, Study and Training: Annette Tietenberg Tel: +49(531) 391-9097
EMail: a.tietenberg@hbk-bs.de

International Relations: Susanne Fleischhacker, Head, International Office
Tel: +49(531) 391-9141 EMail: s.fleischhacker@hbk-bs.de

Course

Art Education (Art Education); **Art History** (Aesthetics; Art History); **Design in the Digital Society** (Communication Arts; Graphic Design); **Fine Arts** (Art Education; Fine Arts; Performing Arts; Visual Arts); **Media Studies** (Media Studies); **Performing Arts** (Performing Arts); **Secondary School Art Teaching** (Art Education; Secondary Education); **Secondary School Performing Arts Teaching** (Art Education; Secondary Education); **Transformation Design** (Industrial Design); **Visual Communication** (Communication Arts)

History: Founded 1963.

Academic Year: October to September

Admission Requirements: School leaving certificate or equivalent and entrance examination

Fees: According to programme

Main Language(s) of Instruction: German

Accrediting Agency: ZEVA

Degrees and Diplomas: *Bachelor's Degree*; *Künstlerische Abschlussprüfung*: **Fine Arts.** *Diplom (Univ)*: **Fine Arts.** *Master*: **Aesthetics; Art Education; Art History; Media Studies; Performing Arts.** *PhD*: **Fine Arts.**

Student Services: Academic Counselling, Canteen, Cultural Activities, Foreign Studies Centre, Library

Student Numbers *2013-2014*: Total 1,126
Last Updated: 05/03/15

BREMEN UNIVERSITY OF APPLIED SCIENCES

Hochschule Bremen
Neustadtswall 30, 28199 Bremen
Tel: +49(421) 5905-0
Fax: +49(421) 5905-2292
EMail: info@hs-bremen.de
Website: http://www.hs-bremen.de

Rector: Karin Luckey
Tel: +49(421) 5905-2221 EMail: Karin.Luckey@hs-bremen.de

Chancellor: Christiane Claus
Tel: +49(421) 5905-2224 EMail: Christiane.Claus@hs-bremen.de

International Relations: Heike Tauerschmidt, Head of International Office
Tel: +49(421) 5905-2640
EMail: Heike.Tauerschmidt@hs-bremen.de

Faculty

Architecture, Civil and Environmental Engineering (Architectural Restoration; Civil Engineering; Environmental Engineering); **Electrical Engineering and Computer Science** (Computer Science; Electrical Engineering); **Natural Sciences and Engineering** (Aeronautical and Aerospace Engineering; Architecture; Biology; Civil Engineering; Computer Engineering; Electrical Engineering; Electronic Engineering; Energy Engineering; Engineering; Environmental Engineering; Industrial Engineering; Marine Engineering; Mechanical Engineering; Media Studies; Natural Sciences; Physics); **Social Sciences and Media Studies** (Communication Studies; European Studies; Health Administration; Health Sciences; International Studies; Journalism; Leisure Studies; Management; Political Sciences; Social Sciences; Social Work; Tourism)

School

International Business (Business Administration; International Business; Management)

History: Founded 1982.

Main Language(s) of Instruction: German

Degrees and Diplomas: *Bachelor's Degree*; *Master*: **Aeronautical and Aerospace Engineering; Architectural and Environmental Design; Art Management; Business Administration; Civil Engineering; Computer Science; Electronic Engineering; Energy Engineering; Environmental Engineering; European Studies; Government; Management; Mechanical Engineering; Tourism.** International Master Degree Programmes in: Industrial and Environmental Biology; Health Administration; Business Administration (taught in English); Economics and Business Administration; Leisure Studies and Tourism

Student Services: Careers Guidance, IT Centre

Student Numbers *2013-2014*: Total 8,577
Last Updated: 04/03/15

BREMERHAVEN UNIVERSITY OF APPLIED SCIENCES

Hochschule Bremerhaven
An der Karlstadt 8, 27568 Bremerhaven
Tel: +49(471) 4823-0
Fax: +49(471) 4823-555
EMail: info@hs-bremerhaven.de
Website: http://www.hs-bremerhaven.de

Rektor: Josef Stockemer (2001-)
Tel: +49(471) 4823-100 EMail: rektor@hs-bremerhaven.de

Chancellor: Helga Schiwek
Tel: +49(471) 4823-121 EMail: kanzlerin@hs-bremerhaven.de

International Relations: Aleksandra Rupietta, Head, International Office
Tel: +49(471) 4823-118 EMail: arupietta@hs-bremerhaven.de

Faculty

Faculty 1 (Energy Engineering; Food Technology; Industrial Engineering; Marine Engineering; Medical Technology; Nautical Science; Production Engineering); **Faculty 2** (Business Administration; Computer Science; Management; Media Studies; Multimedia; Tourism; Transport and Communications; Transport Engineering; Transport Management)

History: Founded 1975.

Admission Requirements: University Entry Qualification or equivalent

Fees: None

Main Language(s) of Instruction: German

Degrees and Diplomas: *Bachelor's Degree*; *Master*: **Automation and Control Engineering; Biotechnology; Computer Engineering; Computer Science; Energy Engineering; Industrial Engineering; Medical Technology; Production Engineering; Safety Engineering; Small Business; Transport Engineering; Transport Management.** Some Programmes conducted in English

Student Services: Careers Guidance, Health Services, Library

Academic Staff *2014-2015*: Total: c. 150
Student Numbers *2014-2015*: Total 3,169
Last Updated: 04/03/15

BURG GIEBICHENSTEIN UNIVERSITY OF ART AND DESIGN HALLE

Burg Giebichenstein Kunsthochschule Halle
PO Box 200252, 06003 Halle
Tel: +49(345) 7751-50
Fax: +49(345) 7751-569
EMail: burgpost@halle.de
Website: http://www.burg-halle.de

Rector: Dieter Hofmann
Tel: +49(345) 7751-930
EMail: rektorat@burg-halle.de; hofmann@burg-halle.de

Chancellor: Wolfgang Stockert
Tel: +49(345) 7751-520
EMail: stockert@burg-halle.de; kanzler@burg-halle.de

International Relations: Marc Felfe
Tel: +49(345) 7751-555 EMail: international@burg-halle.de

Department

Design (Communication Studies; Design; Fashion Design; Industrial Design; Interior Design; Multimedia; Textile Design); **Fine Arts** (Ceramic Art; Fine Arts; Glass Art; Graphic Arts; Jewellery Art; Metal Techniques; Painting and Drawing; Printing and Printmaking; Sculpture; Textile Design)

History: Founded 1915. Acquired present status 1958.

Academic Year: October to March; April to September

Admission Requirements: Allgemeine Hochschulreife and entrance examination (artistic abilities)

Fees: 70 per semester (Euro)

Main Language(s) of Instruction: German

Degrees and Diplomas: *Bachelor's Degree*: **Design; Fine Arts.** *Diplom (Univ)*: **Ceramic Art; Film; Fine Arts; Glass Art; Graphic Design; Interior Design; Painting and Drawing; Textile Design; Video.** *Master*: **Ceramic Art; Design; Fashion Design; Furniture Design; Glass Art; Handicrafts; Industrial Design; Interior Design; Multimedia; Photography; Textile Design.** *PhD*: **Design.** Staatsexam in Art Education

Student Services: Academic Counselling, Canteen, Language Laboratory, Sports Facilities

Student Numbers *2013-2014*: Total 1,039
Last Updated: 02/03/15

CARL MARIA VON WEBER UNIVERSITY OF MUSIC, DRESDEN

Hochschule für Musik Carl Maria von Weber Dresden (HFMDD)

PO Box 120039, Wettiner Platz 13, 01067 Dresden
Tel: +49(351) 4923-600
Fax: +49(351) 4923-657
EMail: rektorat@hfmdd.de
Website: http://www.hfmdd.de

Rector: Ekkehard Klemm
Tel: +49(351) 4923-641 EMail: rektorat@hfmdd.de

Chancellor: Christian Krentel-Seremet
Tel: +49(351) 4923-627 EMail: kanzler@hfmdd.de

International Relations: Gerda Werner
Tel: +49(351) 4923-638 EMail: ausland@hfmdd.de

Department

Department 1 (Conducting; Music; Musical Instruments; Singing); **Department 2** (Jazz and Popular Music; Music Education; Music Theory and Composition; Pedagogy)

History: Founded 1856.

Main Language(s) of Instruction: German

Degrees and Diplomas: *Bachelor's Degree*: **Conducting; Jazz and Popular Music; Music; Music Education; Music Theory and Composition; Musical Instruments; Singing.** *Künstlerische Abschlussprüfung*: **Conducting; Jazz and Popular Music; Music Theory and Composition; Musical Instruments; Singing.** *Diplom (Univ)*: **Conducting; Music Education; Music Theory and Composition; Musical Instruments; Singing.** *Master*: **Conducting; Dance; Jazz and Popular Music; Music; Music Theory and Composition; Musical Instruments; Singing.** *PhD*: **Music Education; Music Theory and Composition; Musicology.** *Habilitation*: **Music Education; Music Theory and Composition; Musicology.** Diplom Degree is being phase out, enrollment no longer possible; Staatsexam (Lehramt) in Primary Education and Seconday Education

Student Services: Library, Residential Facilities

Student Numbers *2013-2014*: Total 576
Last Updated: 10/03/15

CARL VON OSSIETZKY UNIVERSITY OLDENBURG

Carl von Ossietzky Universität Oldenburg

Ammerländer Heerstr. 114-118, 26129 Oldenburg
Tel: +49(441) 798-0
Fax: +49(441) 798-3000
EMail: praesidium@uni-oldenburg.de
Website: http://www.uni-oldenburg.de

Präsidentin: Katharina Al-Shamery (2014-)
Tel: +49(441) 798-5450 EMail: praesidentin@uni-oldenburg.de

Vice President for Administration and Finance: Jörg Stahlmann
Tel: +49(441) 798-5460 EMail: vp.v@uni-oldenburg.de

Faculty

Computer Science, Business and Law (Business Administration; Computer Science; Economics; Education; Law); **Educational and Social Sciences** (Education; Rehabilitation and Therapy; Social Sciences; Special Education); **Humanities and Social Sciences** (History; Philosophy; Protestant Theology; Sports; Theology); **Language and Cultural Studies** (American Studies; Cultural Studies; Dutch; English Studies; Fine Arts; German; Germanic Studies; Media Studies; Music; Slavic Languages; Visual Arts); **Mathematics and Natural Sciences** (Biology; Chemistry; Environmental Studies; Marine Biology; Marine Science and Oceanography; Mathematics; Physics); **Medical and Health Sciences/European Medical School** (Applied Physics; Health Sciences; Medicine; Neurosciences; Psychology)

Further Information: Also Special Research Field 517 of the German Research Authority 'Human Brain's Cognitive Processes'

History: Founded 1973. Teaching started 1974 with incorporation of the Oldenburg branch of the College of Education, Niedersachsen. An autonomous institution financially supported by the State of Lower Saxony and under the jurisdiction of its Ministry of Education.

Academic Year: October to September (October-March; April-September)

Admission Requirements: Secondary school certificate (Abitur) or recognized equivalent. Technical secondary education (Fachhochschulreife) for certain courses. Examination for Master craftman's diploma (Meisterprüfung); and special course of studies (Zalassungsprüfung)

Fees: c. 315-815 per semester (Euro)

Main Language(s) of Instruction: German, English

Degrees and Diplomas: *Bachelor's Degree*: **Biology; Business Administration; Chemistry; Communication Arts; Comparative Law; Computer Science; Dutch; Economics; Education; English Studies; Environmental Studies; European Union Law; French; Gender Studies; Geography (Human); Germanic Studies; History; Humanities and Social Science Education; Law; Mathematics; Media Studies; Music; Philosophy; Physics; Political Sciences; Religious Studies; Slavic Languages; Social Sciences; Spanish; Special Education; Sports; Sports Management; Technology; Textile Design; Theology.** *Master*: **Biology; Business Administration; Business Computing; Business Education; Chemistry; Coastal Studies; Cognitive Sciences; Communication Arts; Computer Science; Cultural Studies; Demography and Population; Dutch; Ecology; Economics; Educational Administration; Educational Sciences; Energy Engineering; Engineering Management; English Studies; Environmental Studies; Finance; Foreign Languages Education; Germanic Studies; History; Insurance; International Law; Law; Management; Marine Science and Oceanography; Mathematics; Media Studies; Microbiology; Museum Studies; Musicology; Philosophy; Physics; Primary Education; Psychology; Religion; Robotics; Secondary Education; Slavic Languages; Social Sciences; Special Education; Speech Therapy and Audiology; Sports; Teacher Training; Water Management.** *PhD*: **Chemistry; Environmental Studies; Gender Studies; Neurosciences; Physics.** *Habilitation*. Also Staatsexam in Medicine; Two-subject Bachelor's Degree Programmes; Fast track Master and Ph.D. programmes; Some Master and Ph.D. courses are taught in English.

Student Services: Academic Counselling, Canteen, Careers Guidance, Cultural Activities, Facilities for disabled people, Foreign Studies Centre, Health Services, Language Laboratory, Nursery Care, Social Counselling, Sports Facilities

Publications: Einblicke

Academic Staff *2014-2015*	MEN	WOMEN	**TOTAL**
FULL-TIME	–	–	**1,299**
STAFF WITH DOCTORATE FULL-TIME	–	–	**203**
Student Numbers *2014-2015*			
All (Foreign included)	6,067	7,679	**13,746**

Last Updated: 23/01/15

CENTRAL HESSE TECHNICAL UNIVERSITY OF APPLIED SCIENCES

Technische Hochschule Mittelhessen

Wiesenstrasse 14, 35390 Giessen, Hessen
Tel: +49(641) 309-0
Fax: +49(641) 309-2901
EMail: info@thm.de
Website: http://www.thm.de

President: Günther Grabatin (2006-)
Tel: +49(641) 309-1000 EMail: praesident@thm.de

Faculty

Scientific Centre for Dual University Studies, Studium Plus *(Wetzlar)* (Business Administration; Engineering; Engineering Management)

Department

Construction *(Gießen)* (Construction Engineering); **Economics** *(Gießen)* (Economics); **Electrical and Computer Engineering** *(Gießen)* (Computer Engineering; Electrical Engineering); **Health** (Health Administration; Health Sciences; Medical Technology); **Hospital and Medical Technology, Environmental and Biotechnology** *(Gießen)* (Biotechnology; Environmental Engineering;

Health Sciences; Medical Technology); **Industrial Engineering** *(Friedberg)* (Engineering); **Information Technology, Electrical Engineering and Mechatronics** *(Friedberg)* (Electronic Engineering; Information Technology; Mechanical Engineering); **Mathematics, Natural Sciences and Computer Science** *(Gießen)* (Computer Science; Mathematics; Natural Sciences); **Mathematics, Natural Sciences and Data Processing** *(Friedberg)* (Data Processing; Mathematics; Natural Sciences); **Mechanical Engineering and Energy Technology** *(Gießen)* (Energy Engineering; Machine Building; Mechanical Engineering); **Mechanical Engineering, Mechatronics, Materials Technology** *(Friedberg)* (Electronic Engineering; Machine Building; Materials Engineering); **Social and Cultural Studies** *(Gießen, Friedberg)* (Cultural Studies; Social Sciences; Social Studies; Transport Management)

History: Founded 1971. Previously known as Fachhochschule Giessen-Friedberg (University of Applied Sciences Giessen-Friedberg).

Academic Year: October to July

Admission Requirements: Secondary School Certificate (Fachhochschulreife or Abitur)

Fees: None

Main Language(s) of Instruction: German

Accrediting Agency: ZEVA; ASIIN; AQUIN

Degrees and Diplomas: *Bachelor's Degree*: **Architecture; Business Administration; Computer Engineering; Computer Science; Engineering; Health Sciences; Multimedia.** *Master*: **Applied Mathematics; Architecture; Biological and Life Sciences; Biology; Biotechnology; Business Administration; Business Computing; Civil Engineering; Computer Science; Documentation Techniques; Electronic Engineering; Engineering; Environmental Studies; Health Administration; Hygiene; Industrial Engineering; Industrial Management; Management; Marketing; Mechanical Engineering; Media Studies; Multimedia; Optical Technology; Real Estate; Safety Engineering; Telecommunications Engineering; Transport Management.**

Student Services: Academic Counselling, Canteen, Facilities for disabled people, IT Centre, Language Laboratory, Library, Social Counselling, Sports Facilities

Student Numbers *2013-2014*: Total 14,289

Last Updated: 26/03/15

CHEMNITZ UNIVERSITY OF TECHNOLOGY

Technische Universität Chemnitz (TU)
Straße der Nationen 62, 09111 Chemnitz
Tel: +49(371) 531-0
EMail: iuz@tu-chemnitz.de; info@tu-chemnitz.de
Website: http://www.tu-chemnitz.de

Rektor: Arnold van Zyl (2011-)
Tel: +49(371) 531-10000 EMail: rektor@tu-chemnitz.de

Kanzler: Eberhard Alles
Tel: +49(371) 531-12000 EMail: kanzler@tu-chemnitz.de

International Relations: Wolfgang Lambrecht
Tel: +49(371) 531-13500

Faculty

Computer Science (Computer Science); **Economics and Business Administration** (Business Administration; Economics; Finance; Management; Marketing); **Electrical Engineering and Information Technology** (Electrical Engineering; Information Technology; Microelectronics); **Humanities and Social Sciences** (Adult Education; American Studies; Arts and Humanities; Communication Studies; Economics; Educational Sciences; English Studies; European Studies; Geography; Germanic Studies; History; International Studies; Linguistics; Literature; Media Studies; Philosophy; Political Sciences; Psychology; Romance Languages; Sociology; Sports); **Mathematics** (Finance; Mathematics); **Mechanical Engineering** (Construction Engineering; Industrial Engineering; Mechanical Engineering; Natural Sciences; Production Engineering); **Natural Sciences** (Chemistry; Computer Science; Materials Engineering; Natural Sciences; Physics)

History: Founded 1836 as Royal Trade School of Chemnitz, became College of Mechanical Engineering 1953, and College of Technology 1963. Acquired present title 1986. Responsible to the Ministry of Science and Culture.

Academic Year: October to September (October-March; April-September)

Admission Requirements: Secondary school certificate (Reifezeugnis) or equivalent

Fees: None

Main Language(s) of Instruction: German

Degrees and Diplomas: *Bachelor's Degree*; *Master*; *PhD*: **Arts and Humanities; Computer Science; Economics; Electrical and Electronic Engineering; European Studies; German; History; Linguistics; Literature; Mathematics; Mechanical Engineering; Modern Languages; Natural Sciences; Philosophy; Political Sciences; Social Sciences; Telecommunications Services.** *Habilitation*. Also Combined Degrees; Teacher Training State Examination Certificate (Lehramt)

Student Services: Academic Counselling, Canteen, Careers Guidance, Facilities for disabled people, Health Services, Library, Nursery Care, Social Counselling, Sports Facilities

Academic Staff *2014-2015*: Total 161

Student Numbers *2014-2015*: Total 11,652

Last Updated: 07/04/15

CHRISTIAN ALBRECHT UNIVERSITY OF KIEL

Christian-Albrechts-Universität zu Kiel
Christian-Albrechts-Platz 4, 24118 Kiel
Tel: +49(431) 880-00
Fax: +49(431) 880-2072
EMail: mail@uni-kiel.de
Website: http://www.uni-kiel.de

Präsident: Lutz Kipp (2013-)
Tel: +49(431) 880-3000 EMail: praesident@praesidium.uni-kiel.de

Kanzler: Oliver Herrmann
Tel: +49(431) 880-3003 EMail: kanzler@praesidium.uni-kiel.de

International Relations: Martina Schmode, Director
Tel: +49(431) 880-3719 EMail: mschmode@uv.uni-kiel.de

Faculty

Agriculture and Nutritional Sciences (Agricultural Economics; Agricultural Engineering; Agriculture; Animal Husbandry; Crop Production; Food Science; Nutrition; Soil Science); **Arts and Humanities** (Archaeology; Art History; Arts and Humanities; History; Linguistics; Musicology; Pedagogy; Philology; Philosophy; Phonetics; Psychology); **Business, Economics and Social Sciences** (Business Administration; Economics; Social Sciences; Statistics); **Engineering** (Computer Science; Electronic Engineering; Materials Engineering; Technology); **Law** (Criminology; European Union Law; Law); **Mathematics and Natural Sciences** (Biology; Chemistry; Marine Science and Oceanography; Mathematics; Natural Sciences; Pharmacy; Physics); **Medicine** (Health Sciences; Medicine); **Theology** (Theology)

History: Founded 1665 by Christian Albrecht, Duke of Holstein-Gottorf. Became Landes-Universität (provincial University) for the State of Schleswig-Holstein 1773. Incorporated as Prussian University 1867 and re-established as Landes-Universität 1945. Autonomous institution financially supported by the State of Schleswig-Holstein.

Academic Year: October to September (October-March; April-September)

Admission Requirements: Secondary school certificate (Abitur) or equivalent

Fees: None

Main Language(s) of Instruction: German

Degrees and Diplomas: *Bachelor's Degree*: **Agriculture; American Studies; Archaeology; Art History; Biochemistry; Biology; Business Administration; Business Computing; Computer Science; Czech; Danish; Earth Sciences; Economics; Educational Sciences; Electrical Engineering; English Studies; Ethnology; Fine Arts; Folklore; French; Geography (Human); German; Greek (Classical); History; Home Economics; Industrial Chemistry; Industrial Engineering; Information Technology; Islamic Studies; Italian; Latin; Law; Linguistics; Materials**

Engineering; Mathematics; Medicine; Molecular Biology; Musicology; Nutrition; Pharmacy; Philology; Philosophy; Physics; Polish; Political Sciences; Portuguese; Prehistory; Protestant Theology; Psychology; Religious Studies; Russian; Scandinavian Languages; Slavic Languages; Sociology; Spanish; Sports. *Kirchliche Abschlussprüfung*: **Theology.** *Diplom (Univ)*: **Pedagogy; Psychology; Theology.** *Master*: **Agriculture; American Studies; Archaeology; Art History; Biochemistry; Biology; Biomedicine; Business Administration; Chemistry; Computer Science; Consumer Studies; Cultural Studies; Danish; Demography and Population; Dentistry; Earth Sciences; Ecology; Economics; Educational Administration; Educational Sciences; Electrical Engineering; English; English Studies; Environmental Management; Environmental Studies; Ethnology; Finance; Fine Arts; Folklore; Food Science; French Studies; Geography; Geophysics; German; Germanic Studies; Greek (Classical); Health Administration; History; Industrial Chemistry; Information Technology; International Law; International Relations; Islamic Studies; Italian; Latin; Linguistics; Literature; Marine Biology; Marine Science and Oceanography; Materials Engineering; Mathematics and Computer Science; Media Studies; Meteorology; Molecular Biology; Musicology; Natural Resources; Nutrition; Pharmacology; Philology; Philosophy; Physics; Political Sciences; Prehistory; Protestant Theology; Regional Planning; Religious Studies; Romance Languages; Russian; Scandinavian Languages; Sociology; Spanish; Sports; Telecommunications Engineering; Town Planning; Water Science.** *PhD*: **Agriculture; Economics; Engineering; Food Science; Law; Mathematics; Medicine; Natural Sciences; Philosophy; Social Sciences; Theology.** *Habilitation*: **Agriculture; Economics; Food Science; Law; Mathematics; Medicine; Natural Sciences; Philosophy; Social Sciences; Theology.** One- or Two-subjects Bachelor and Master's Degree Porgrammes available; Staastexam in Dentistry, Medicine, Pharmacy, Law.

Student Services: Academic Counselling, Canteen, Careers Guidance, Cultural Activities, Facilities for disabled people, Foreign Studies Centre, Health Services, IT Centre, Language Laboratory, Library, Nursery Care, Residential Facilities, Social Counselling, Sports Facilities

Publications: Forschungsbericht Christiana Albertina; Vorlesungsverzeichnis

Student Numbers *2013-2014*: Total 24,396

Last Updated: 23/01/15

CLAUSTHAL UNIVERSITY OF TECHNOLOGY

Technische Universität Clausthal (TU CLAUSTHAL)

Adolph-Roemer-Strasse 2A, 38678 Clausthal-Zellerfeld

Tel: +49(5323) 72-0

Fax: +49(5323) 72-3500

EMail: info@tu-clausthal.de; international@tu-clausthal.de; presse@tu-clausthal.de

Website: http://www.tu-clausthal.de

President: Thomas Hanschke
Tel: +49(5323) 72-3018 EMail: Praesident@tu-clausthal.de

First Vice-President: Georg Frischmann
Tel: +49(5323) 72-3015 EMail: Vizepraesident.V@tu-clausthal.de

International Relations: Susanne Romanowski, Head of International Office
Tel: +49(5323) 72-2621
EMail: susanne.romanowski@tu-clausthal.de; international@tu-clausthal.de

Faculty

Energy and Management (Chemistry; Economics; Electrical Engineering; Energy Engineering; Environmental Studies; Geology; Management; Mechanical Engineering; Mineralogy; Paleontology); **Mathematics, Computer Science and Mechanical Engineering** (Computer Science; Machine Building; Mathematics; Mechanical Engineering; Production Engineering; Thermal Engineering); **Natural and Material Sciences** (Inorganic Chemistry; Laser Engineering; Metallurgical Engineering; Organic Chemistry; Physical Chemistry; Physics; Polymer and Plastics Technology)

History: Founded 1775, became 'Bergakademie Clausthal' 1864, acquired University status 1920. Present title conferred 1968. An autonomous institution under the jurisdiction of and financially supported by the State of Lower Saxony.

Academic Year: October to September (October-March; April-September)

Admission Requirements: Secondary school certificate (Reifezeugnis/Abitur) or equivalent

Main Language(s) of Instruction: German

Degrees and Diplomas: *Bachelor's Degree*; *Diplom (Univ)*: **Chemical Engineering; Electronic Engineering; Energy Engineering; Environmental Engineering; Industrial Engineering; Information Technology; Mechanical Engineering; Production Engineering.** *Master*: **Automation and Control Engineering; Business Administration; Business Computing; Chemical Engineering; Chemistry; Computer Science; Earth Sciences; Economics; Electronic Engineering; Energy Engineering; Environmental Engineering; Geological Engineering; Industrial Engineering; Industrial Management; Information Technology; Materials Engineering; Mathematics; Mechanical Engineering; Mining Engineering; Petroleum and Gas Engineering; Production Engineering; Thermal Engineering.** *PhD*: **Analytical Chemistry; Applied Mathematics; Automation and Control Engineering; Chemical Engineering; Chemistry; Computer Science; Economics; Electrical Engineering; Energy Engineering; Environmental Studies; Geological Engineering; Geology; Geophysics; Industrial Engineering; Information Technology; Inorganic Chemistry; Law; Materials Engineering; Mathematics; Mechanical Engineering; Mechanics; Metal Techniques; Metallurgical Engineering; Mining Engineering; Operations Research; Organic Chemistry; Paleontology; Petroleum and Gas Engineering; Physical Chemistry; Physics; Polymer and Plastics Technology; Production Engineering; Waste Management.** Also Master's Degree in Continuing Education in Engineering; No more intake allowed in Diplom (Univ) programmes, and in the Master's degree programmes in the field of Applied Mathematics, Energy Engineering, Materials Engineering, Operations Research, Physical Technologies, Waste Management, which are all being phased out.

Student Services: Academic Counselling, Canteen, Health Services, IT Centre, Language Laboratory, Library, Social Counselling, Sports Facilities

Academic Staff *2014-2015*: Total 85

Student Numbers *2014-2015*: Total 4,877

Last Updated: 09/02/15

COBURG UNIVERSITY OF APPLIED SCIENCES

Hochschule Coburg (FH COBURG)

Friedrich-Streib-Str. 2, 96450 Coburg

Tel: +49(9561) 317-0

Fax: +49(9561) 317-275

EMail: poststelle@hs-coburg.de

Website: http://www.fh-coburg.de

Präsident: Michael Pötzl
Tel: +49(9561) 317-112 EMail: michael.poetzl@hs-coburg.de

Kanzlerin: Maria Knott-Lutze
Tel: +49(9561) 317-140 EMail: maria.knott-lutze@hs-coburg.de

International Relations: Annette Stegemann, Head, International Office
Tel: +49(9561) 317-319
EMail: annette.stegemann@hs-coburg.de; international@hs-coburg.de

Faculty

Applied Natural Sciences (Biological and Life Sciences; Measurement and Precision Engineering; Natural Sciences; Physics); **Business Administration** (Accountancy; Banking; Data Processing; Human Resources; Insurance; International Business; Management; Marketing; Sales Techniques); **Design** (Architecture; Civil Engineering; Industrial Design; Interior Design); **Electrical Engineering and Computer Science** (Civil Engineering; Computer Engineering; Construction Engineering; Electrical and Electronic Engineering; Information Sciences; Information Technology; Machine Building; Mechanical Engineering; Physical Engineering); **Mechanical and Automotive Engineering** (Automotive

Engineering; Mechanical Engineering); **Social Work and Health Sciences** (Health Sciences; Social Work)

History: Founded 1971.

Academic Year: October to September (October-March; March-September)

Admission Requirements: Secondary school certificate (Fachhochschulreife)

Fees: None

Main Language(s) of Instruction: German

Degrees and Diplomas: *Bachelor's Degree*; *Master*: **Architectural Restoration; Automotive Engineering; Biological and Life Sciences; Business Administration; Business Computing; Civil Engineering; Computer Engineering; Design; Electrical Engineering; Finance; Health Sciences; Insurance; Management; Measurement and Precision Engineering; Mechanical Engineering; Social Work.**

Student Services: Academic Counselling, Canteen, Facilities for disabled people, Foreign Studies Centre, Language Laboratory, Social Counselling

Academic Staff *2014-2015*: Total: c. 110

Student Numbers *2014-2015*: Total: c. 4,800

Last Updated: 04/03/15

COLLEGE OF DESIGN, KARLSRUHE

Staatliche Hochschule für Gestaltung Karlsruhe

Lorenzstr. 15, 76135 Karlsruhe
Tel: +49(721) 8203-0
Fax: +49(721) 8203-2159
EMail: hochschule@hfg-karlsruhe.de
Website: http://www.hfg-karlsruhe.de

Rektor: Peter Sloterdijk (2001-)
Tel: +49(721) 8203-2306
EMail: r.nolte@mh-freiburg.de; rektorat@hfg-karlsruhe.de

Chancellor: Kathrin Schwalb
Tel: +49(721) 8203-0
EMail: astrid.lindner-maier@hfg-karlsruhe.de

International Relations: Lena Baunacke
Tel: +49(721) 8203-2371
EMail: international-office@hfg-karlsruhe.de

Department

Graphic Design (Graphic Design); **Media Arts** (Media Studies); **Philosophy and Aesthetics** (Aesthetics; Philosophy); **Production Design** (Design); **Scenography** (Display and Stage Design)

History: Founded 1992.

Main Language(s) of Instruction: German

Degrees and Diplomas: *Künstlerische Abschlussprüfung*: **Communication Arts; Display and Stage Design; Graphic Design; Industrial Design.** *Magister*: **Aesthetics; Philosophy.** *PhD*: **Aesthetics; Media Studies.**

Student Numbers *2013-2014*: Total 434

Last Updated: 25/03/15

COLOGNE UNIVERSITY OF APPLIED SCIENCES

Fachhochschule Köln (FH KOELN/CUAS)

Claudiusstrasse 1, 50678 Köln, Nordrhein-Westfalen
Tel: +49(221) 8275-1
Fax: +49(221) 8275-3131
EMail: kerstin.keller@fh-koeln.de
Website: http://www.fh-koeln.de

President: Christoph Seesselberg
Tel: +49(221) 8275-3100
EMail: christoph.seesselberg@fh-koeln.de

Vice President for Teaching and Learning: Sylvia Heuchemer
Tel: +49(221) 8275-3431 EMail: sylvia.heuchemer@fh-koeln.de

International Relations: Elisabeth Holuscha, Head, International Office
Tel: +49(221) 8275-3110 EMail: elisabeth.holuscha@fh-koeln.de

Faculty

Applied Natural Sciences (Chemistry; Natural Sciences; Pharmacology); **Applied Social Sciences** (Child Care and Development; Family Studies; Gender Studies; Media Studies; Social Sciences; Social Work); **Architecture** (Architecture; Architecture and Planning); **Automotive Systems and Production Engineering** (Automotive Engineering; Production Engineering); **Business, Economics and Law** (Banking; Business Administration; Commercial Law; Economics; Finance); **Civil Engineering and Environmental Technology** (Construction Engineering; Hydraulic Engineering; Transport Engineering); **Computer Science and Engineering** (Business Computing; Computer Science; Engineering; Information Technology); **Cultural Sciences** (Cultural Studies); **Information Science and Communication Studies** (Information Sciences; Telecommunications Services); **Information, Media and Electrical Engineering** (Automation and Control Engineering; Electrical Engineering; Information Technology; Telecommunications Engineering); **Process Engineering, Energy and Mechanical Systems** (Energy Engineering; Industrial Engineering; Mechanical Engineering)

Institute

Technology and Resources Management in the Tropics and Subtropics (Natural Resources; Technology; Tropical Agriculture)

History: Founded 1971.

Fees: 110-750 (Euro)

Main Language(s) of Instruction: German

Degrees and Diplomas: *Bachelor's Degree*; *Master*: **Accountancy; Actuarial Science; Architecture; Automation and Control Engineering; Automotive Engineering; Behavioural Sciences; Business Computing; Civil Engineering; Communication Studies; Computer Engineering; Computer Science; Design; Economics; Electrical Engineering; Electronic Engineering; Energy Engineering; Finance; Industrial Design; Information Management; Information Sciences; Information Technology; Insurance; International Business; Labour Law; Law; Library Science; Management; Marketing; Mechanical Engineering; Media Studies; Museum Studies; Natural Resources; Production Engineering; Psychology; Restoration of Works of Art; Safety Engineering; Social Work; Software Engineering; Taxation; Telecommunications Engineering; Terminology; Town Planning; Translation and Interpretation; Water Management.**

Student Services: Academic Counselling, Canteen, Careers Guidance, Facilities for disabled people, Foreign Studies Centre, IT Centre, Language Laboratory, Library, Sports Facilities

Academic Staff *2013-2014*: Total 414

Student Numbers *2013-2014*: Total 22,264

Last Updated: 28/01/15

CONSTANCE UNIVERSITY OF APPLIED SCIENCES

Hochschule Konstanz Technik, Wirtschaft und Gestaltung (HTWG)

Postfach 100 543, Brauneggerstr. 55, 78462 Konstanz, Baden-Württemberg
Tel: +49(7531) 206-0
Fax: +49(7531) 206-400
EMail: kontakt@htwg-konstanz.de
Website: http://www.fh-konstanz.de

President: Carsten Manz
Tel: +49(7531) 206-111 EMail: manz@htwg-konstanz.de

Chancellor: Margit Plahl
Tel: +49(7531) 206-118
EMail: plahl@htwg-konstanz.de; kanzlerin@htwg-konstanz.de

International Relations: Klemens Blass, Head, Office of International Affairs
Tel: +49(7531) 206-297 EMail: blass@htwg-konstanz.de

Department

Architecture and Design (Architecture; Graphic Design); **Civil Engineering** (Civil Engineering; Industrial Engineering); **Computer Science** (Business Computing; Computer Science; Information Technology; Software Engineering; Systems Analysis); **Economics**

and Social Sciences (Accountancy; Business Administration; Economics; Finance; Human Resources; International Business); **Electrical Engineering and Computer Engineering** (Automation and Control Engineering; Communication Studies; Electrical Engineering; Information Technology; Power Engineering); **Mechanical Engineering** (Environmental Engineering; Industrial Engineering; Industrial Management; Mechanical Engineering; Sales Techniques)

History: Founded 1906 as Higher Technical Training Institute for Mechanical, Electrical and Civil Engineering. Acquired present status 1971.

Academic Year: October to July (October-February; March-July)

Admission Requirements: Abitur or equivalent qualification

Main Language(s) of Instruction: German

Degrees and Diplomas: *Bachelor's Degree*; *Master*: **Architecture; Automotive Engineering; Business Administration; Business Computing; Civil Engineering; Computer Science; Construction Engineering; Electrical Engineering; Electronic Engineering; Environmental Engineering; Graphic Design; Industrial Engineering; International Business; Management; Mechanical Engineering; Packaging Technology; Sales Techniques.** Cooperative Doctoral Degree with other Universities

Student Services: Academic Counselling, Canteen, Careers Guidance, Cultural Activities, Facilities for disabled people, Foreign Studies Centre, IT Centre, Language Laboratory, Library, Nursery Care, Social Counselling, Sports Facilities

Publications: FHK - Forum

Academic Staff *2014-2015*: Total: c. 250

Student Numbers *2014-2015*: Total: c. 4,400

Last Updated: 11/03/15

DARMSTADT UNIVERSITY OF APPLIED SCIENCES

Hochschule Darmstadt (H_DA)

Haardtring 100, D-64295 Darmstadt, Hessen
Tel: +49(6151) 16-0
Fax: +49(6151) 16-8949
EMail: info@h-da.de
Website: http://www.h-da.de

Präsident: Ralph Stengler
Tel: +49(6151) 16-8002 EMail: praesident@h-da.de

Kanzler: N. N. Tel: +49(6151) 16-8006 EMail: Kanzler@h-da.de

International Relations: Lucia Koch, Director International Relations (17) Tel: +49(6151) 16-8016 EMail: lucia.koch@h-da.de

Department

Architecture (Architecture; Interior Design); **Business Administration** (Business Administration; Engineering Management); **Chemical Engineering and Biotechnology** (Biotechnology; Chemical Engineering); **Civil Engineering** (Civil Engineering; Environmental Engineering); **Computer Science** (Computer Science); **Design** (Graphic Design; Industrial Design); **Electrical Engineering and Information Technology** (Automation and Control Engineering; Electrical Engineering; Electronic Engineering; Engineering Management; Microelectronics); **Mathematics and Science** (Mathematics; Optical Technology); **Mechanical Engineering** (Automotive Engineering; Mechanical Engineering; Polymer and Plastics Technology); **Media** (Information Sciences; Journalism; Mass Communication; Media Studies; Multimedia); **Social and Cultural Studies** (Commercial Law; Cultural Studies; Law; Psychology; Social Studies; Social Work)

Further Information: Also Campus in Dieburg

History: Founded as Fachhochschule Darmstadt 1971. Merged with the formerly private Telekom FH Dieburg 2000. Acquired present title 2006.

Academic Year: September to August (September-February; March-August)

Admission Requirements: Secondary school certificate (Abitur; Fachabitur) or equivalent

Fees: National: c. 200 Euro per semester (social fees) (Euro), International: c. 200 Euro per semester (social fees) (Euro)

Main Language(s) of Instruction: German, English

Accrediting Agency: ASIIN; AQUIN; AQUAS

Degrees and Diplomas: *Bachelor's Degree*; *Diplom (FH)*: **Graphic Design; Industrial Design.** *Master*: **Architecture; Automotive Engineering; Biotechnology; Business Administration; Chemistry; Civil Engineering; Computer Science; Electrical Engineering; Energy Engineering; Finance; Industrial Engineering; Industrial Management; Information Sciences; Information Technology; Insurance; Interior Design; International Business; International Law; Leadership; Management; Mathematics; Mechanical Engineering; Media Studies; Optical Technology; Social Work.**

Student Services: Academic Counselling, Canteen, Careers Guidance, Facilities for disabled people, Foreign Studies Centre, IT Centre, Language Laboratory, Library, Nursery Care, Residential Facilities, Social Counselling, Sports Facilities

Academic Staff *2014-2015*	MEN	WOMEN	TOTAL
FULL-TIME	512	196	**708**
PART-TIME	101	167	**268**
STAFF WITH DOCTORATE			
FULL-TIME	230	43	c. **273**
Student Numbers *2014-2015*			
All (Foreign included)	–	–	c. **15,115**
FOREIGN ONLY	1,862	1,019	**2,881**

Part-time students, 285. **Distance students,** 156.

Last Updated: 03/02/15

DARMSTADT UNIVERSITY OF TECHNOLOGY

Technische Universität Darmstadt (TUD)

Karolinenplatz 5, 64289 Darmstadt, Hessen
Tel: +49(6151) 16-1
Fax: +49(6151) 16-5489
EMail: presse@tu-darmstadt.de; praesident@tu-darmstadt.de; woerner@pvw.tu-darmstadt.de
Website: http://www.tu-darmstadt.de

President: Hans Jürgen Prömel
Tel: +49(615)116-2120 EMail: praesident@tu-darmstadt.de

Chancellor: Manfred Efinger
Tel: +49(6151) 16-2128 EMail: kanzler@tu-darmstadt.de

International Relations: Marlis Tewes, Senior Manager, Department of International Affairs
Tel: +49(6151) 16-5320
EMail: tewes@pvw.tu-darmstadt.de; auslandsamt@pvw.tu-darmstadt.de

Department

Architecture (Architecture); **Biology** (Biology); **Chemistry** (Chemistry); **Civil and Enviromental Engineering** (Civil Engineering; Environmental Engineering); **Computer Science** (Computer Science); **Electrical Engineering and Information Technology** (Electrical Engineering; Energy Engineering; Information Technology); **History and Social Sciences** (History; Social Sciences); **Humanities** (Educational Sciences; Psychology; Sports); **Law and Economics** (Economics; Law); **Material and Earth Sciences** (Geography; Geology; Materials Engineering); **Mathematics** (Mathematics); **Mechanical Engineering** (Mechanical Engineering); **Physics** (Physics)

History: Founded 1836 as Höhere Gewerbeschule, became Technische Hochschule in 1877 and acquired University status in 1895. Faculties replaced by departments 1971. An autonomous institution under the jurisdiction of the State of Hesse.

Academic Year: October to July (November-February; April-July)

Admission Requirements: Secondary school certificate (Reifezeugnis) or equivalent

Fees: 50 per semester (Euro)

Main Language(s) of Instruction: German

Accrediting Agency: AVI e.U.

Degrees and Diplomas: *Bachelor's Degree*; *Master*: **Architecture; Biology; Catholic Theology; Chemistry; Civil Engineering; Computer Engineering; Computer Science; Economics; Education; Electronic Engineering; Energy Engineering; Environmental Studies; Ethics; German; History; Industrial Engineering; Information Technology; International Studies; Materials Engineering; Mathematics; Mechanical Engineering;**

Mechanics; Paper Technology; Philosophy; Physics; Political Sciences; Protestant Theology; Psychology; Sociology; Software Engineering; Sports; Sports Management; Telecommunications Engineering. *PhD*: **Architecture; Arts and Humanities; Automation and Control Engineering; Biology; Business Administration; Chemistry; Computer Science; Economics; Electrical Engineering; Electronic Engineering; English; Geology; German; History; Information Technology; Law; Materials Engineering; Mathematics; Mechanical Engineering; Physics; Social Sciences; Telecommunications Engineering.** *Habilitation*: **Architecture; Arts and Humanities; Business Administration; Economics; History; Law; Physics; Social Sciences.** Also Secondary Education Teacher Triaining (Lehramt).

Student Services: Academic Counselling, Canteen, Careers Guidance, Cultural Activities, Facilities for disabled people, Foreign Studies Centre, Language Laboratory, Social Counselling, Sports Facilities

Publications: Thema Forschung

Student Numbers *2013-2014*: Total 24,969

Last Updated: 27/03/15

DEGGENDORF INSTITUTE OF TECHNOLOGY

Technische Hochschule Deggendorf (THD/DIT)

Postfach 1320, Edlmairstrasse 6+8, 94469 Deggendorf, Bavaria

Tel: +49(991) 3615-0

Fax: +49(991) 3615-297

EMail: info@th-deg.de; info@dit.edu

Website: https://www.th-deg.de

President: Peter Sperber
Tel: +49(991) 3615-200 EMail: peter.sperber@th-deg.de

Kanzler: Gregor Biletzki
Tel: +49(991) 3615-210 EMail: gregor.biletzki@th-deg.de

International Relations: Elise von Randow, Director, Institute for International and Academic Affairs
Tel: +49(991) 3615-202 EMail: evr@th-deg.de

Faculty

Business Administration and Business Informatics (Business Administration; Business and Commerce; Business Computing; Management; Tourism); **Civil and Construction Engineering** (Civil Engineering; Construction Engineering; Environmental Management); **Electrical Engineering and Media Technology** (Electrical Engineering; Electronic Engineering; Information Technology; Media Studies); **Mechanical Engineering and Mechatronics** (Business Administration; Electronic Engineering; Engineering; Machine Building; Mechanical Engineering); **Natural Sciences and Industrial Engineering** (Industrial Engineering; Natural Sciences; Physical Engineering)

Institute

Applied Health Sciences (Business Computing; Health Sciences; Tourism)

History: Founded 1994

Academic Year: October to July (October-February; March-July)

Admission Requirements: Abitur or equivalent qualification

Fees: National: No tuition fee (Euro), International: No tuition fee (Euro)

Main Language(s) of Instruction: German

Accrediting Agency: FIBAA, ASIIN

Degrees and Diplomas: *Bachelor's Degree*; *Master*: **Business Computing; Civil Engineering; Computer Science; Construction Engineering; Electrical Engineering; Human Resources; Information Technology; Management; Mechanical Engineering; Media Studies; Tourism.** Also Combined Dual Course of Study with intensified practical experience; MBA; Master of Applied Research in Engineering; Agreements to offere other universities' Doctoral Porgrammes in Business Administration and Philosophy as of March 2015.

Student Services: Academic Counselling, Canteen, Careers Guidance, Facilities for disabled people, Foreign Studies Centre, IT Centre, Language Laboratory, Library, Sports Facilities

Student Numbers *2013-2014*: Total 5,044

Last Updated: 09/02/15

DORTMUND UNIVERSITY OF APPLIED SCIENCES AND ARTS

Fachhochschule Dortmund

PO Box 105018, Sonnenstrasse 96, 44047 Dortmund

Tel: +49(231) 9112-0

Fax: +49(231) 9112-313

EMail: pressestelle@fh-dortmund.de; rektor@fh-dortmund.de

Website: http://www.fh-dortmund.de

Rektor: Wilhelm Schwick Tel: +49(231) 9112-100

Kanzler: Rolf Pohlhausen
Tel: +49(231) 9112-104 EMail: rolf.pohlhausen@h-dortmund.de

International Relations: Gisela Moser
Tel: +49(231) 9112-345 EMail: moser@fh-dortmund.de

Faculty

Applied Social Studies (Social Studies; Social Work); **Architecture** (Architecture); **Business Studies** (Business Education; International Business); **Computer Science** (Computer Engineering; Computer Science; Medical Technology); **Design** (Communication Arts; Design; Display and Stage Design; Film; Graphic Design; Photography; Sound Engineering (Acoustics)); **Information Technology and Electronics** (Communication Studies; Electronic Engineering; Information Technology; Multimedia; Telecommunications Engineering); **Mechanical Engineering** (Energy Engineering; Environmental Engineering; Mechanical Engineering; Production Engineering)

History: Founded 1971.

Academic Year: September to August

Admission Requirements: Secondary school certificate (Abitur, Fachhochschulreife)

Fees: 110 per semester (Euro)

Main Language(s) of Instruction: German

Degrees and Diplomas: *Bachelor's Degree*: **Accountancy; Architecture; Automotive Engineering; Business Administration; Business Computing; Computer Science; Demography and Population; Electrical Engineering; Engineering; Film; Finance; Graphic Design; Industrial Engineering; Information Technology; Insurance; Interior Design; International Business; Management; Mechanical Engineering; Photography; Production Engineering; Social Work; Sound Engineering (Acoustics); Transport Management.** *Master*: **Architecture; Building Technologies; Business Administration; Business Computing; Computer Science; Demography and Population; Display and Stage Design; Electrical Engineering; Film; Finance; Information Technology; Insurance; International Business; Management; Photography; Public Administration; Social Work; Sound Engineering (Acoustics); Town Planning.**

Student Services: Academic Counselling, Canteen, Careers Guidance, Foreign Studies Centre, IT Centre, Language Laboratory, Library, Social Counselling, Sports Facilities

Student Numbers *2013-2014*: Total 12,268

Last Updated: 27/01/15

DRESDEN UNIVERSITY OF APPLIED SCIENCES

Hochschule für Technik und Wirtschaft Dresden (FH)

PF 120701, Friedrich-List-Platz 1, 01008 Dresden

Tel: +57(351) 462-0

Fax: +57(351) 462-2185

EMail: info@htw-dresden.de

Website: http://www.htw-dresden.de

Rector: Roland Stenzel (2010-)
Tel: +49(351) 462-3101 EMail: rektor@htw-dresden.de

Chancellor: Monika Niehues
Tel: +57(351) 462-3103 EMail: kanzler@htw-dresden.de

International Relations: Juliane Terpe, Head, International Office
Tel: +49(351) 462 33 77 EMail: auslandsamt@htw-dresden.de

Faculty

Agriculture/Landscape Management (Agricultural Economics; Horticulture; Landscape Architecture); **Business Administration** (Business Administration; Modern Languages); **Civil Engineering/ Architecture** (Architecture; Civil Engineering); **Design** (Design);

Electrical Engineering (Electrical Engineering); **Informatics/ Mathematics** (Computer Science; Mathematics); **Mechanical Engineering/Process Engineering** (Chemical Engineering; Mechanical Engineering; Physics); **Spatial Information** (Real Estate; Surveying and Mapping)

History: Founded 1992.

Main Language(s) of Instruction: German

Degrees and Diplomas: *Bachelor's Degree*; *Diplom (FH)*: **Automation and Control Engineering; Automotive Engineering; Business Computing; Civil Engineering; Computer Science; Electrical Engineering; Electronic Engineering; Engineering; Mechanical Engineering; Production Engineering; Telecommunications Engineering.** *Master*: **Agricultural Management; Agriculture; Architecture; Chemical Engineering; Electrical Engineering; Horticulture; Industrial Design; Information Technology; International Business; Management; Small Business; Surveying and Mapping.** Collaborative Phd programmes available in collaboration with other universities

Student Services: Canteen, Careers Guidance, IT Centre, Library

Student Numbers *2013-2014*: Total 5,189

Last Updated: 11/03/15

DRESDEN UNIVERSITY OF TECHNOLOGY

Technische Universität Dresden

Mommsenstrasse 7, 01069 Dresden

Tel: +49(351) 463-0

Fax: +49(351) 463-37165

EMail: pressestelle@tu-dresden.de

Website: http://www.tu-dresden.de

Rektor: Hans Müller-Steinhagen (2010-)
Tel: +49(351) 463-34312 EMail: rektor@tu-dresden.de

Chancellor: Undine Krätzig
Tel: +49(351) 463-34717 EMail: kanzler@tu-dresden.de

International Relations: Marion Helemann, Director, International Office
Tel: +49(351) 463-35358
EMail: auslandsamt@mailbox.tu-dresden.de; auslandsamt@tu-dresden.de

School

Civil and Environmental Engineering (Architecture; Civil Engineering; Environmental Studies; Transport and Communications); **Engineering Sciences** (Computer Engineering; Computer Science; Electrical Engineering; Engineering; Mechanical Engineering; Mechanics); **Humanities and Social Sciences** (Arts and Humanities; Business Administration; Cultural Studies; Economics; Education; Law; Linguistics; Literature; Social Sciences); **Medicine** (Medicine); **Science** (Biology; Chemistry; Mathematics; Natural Sciences; Physics; Psychology)

Further Information: Also Teaching Hospital. 50 European Mobility Programmes. German language courses (in August and September)

History: Founded 1828 as a technical college and renamed Polytechnische Schule in 1851. Became Technische Hochschule 1890, renamed Technische Universität 1961. Responsible to the Ministry of Science and Art.

Academic Year: October to September (October-March; April-September)

Admission Requirements: Secondary school certificate (Reifezeugnis) or equivalent

Fees: None

Main Language(s) of Instruction: German

Accrediting Agency: Saxon Ministry of Science and Art

Degrees and Diplomas: *Bachelor's Degree*; *Magister*; *Diplom (Univ)*: **Architecture; Business Computing; Civil Engineering; Computer Science; Economics; Electrical Engineering; Energy Engineering; Engineering; Engineering Management; Information Technology; Materials Engineering; Mechanical Engineering; Sociology; Transport Engineering.** *Master*: **Ancient Civilizations; Art History; Bioengineering; Biology; Biotechnology; Business Computing; Chemistry; Clinical Psychology; Clothing and Sewing; Computer Engineering; Computer Science; Cultural Studies; Economics; Electrical Engineering; Electronic Engineering; Engineering; Environmental Studies; Ethics; European Languages; Forestry; Geology; History; Humanities and Social Science Education; Information Technology; International Relations; International Studies; Landscape Architecture; Linguistics; Literature; Management; Mathematics; Media Studies; Medicine; Musicology; Nanotechnology; Natural Resources; Neurosciences; Philosophy; Physics; Political Sciences; Psychology; Psychotherapy; Public Health; Radiology; Railway Transport; Secondary Education; Sociology; Surveying and Mapping; Textile Technology; Transport Economics; Vocational Education; Waste Management; Water Science; Wood Technology.** *PhD*: **Architecture; Arts and Humanities; Business Administration; Civil Engineering; Computer Science; Cultural Studies; Economics; Education; Electrical Engineering; Environmental Studies; Information Technology; Law; Literature; Mathematics; Mechanical Engineering; Medicine; Modern Languages; Natural Sciences; Transport and Communications.** *Habilitation*: **Architecture; Arts and Humanities; Business Administration; Civil Engineering; Computer Science; Cultural Studies; Economics; Education; Electrical Engineering; Environmental Studies; Information Technology; Law; Literature; Mathematics; Mechanical Engineering; Medicine; Modern Languages; Natural Sciences; Psychology; Transport and Communications.** Also State Examination for Teacher Training (Lehramt) in Primary and Secondary Education and Vocational Educaiton; Staatsexam in Dentistry, Medicine and Food Technology.

Student Services: Health Services, Language Laboratory, Library, Residential Facilities, Sports Facilities

Publications: Vorlesungsverzeichnis der TUD; Wissenschaftliche Zeitschrift der Technischen Universität Dresden

Academic Staff *2014-2015*	**TOTAL**
PART-TIME	c. **4,400**
Student Numbers *2014-2015*	
All (Foreign included)	c. **37,000**

Last Updated: 27/03/15

DÜSSELDORF ART ACADEMY

Kunstakademie Düsseldorf

Eiskellerstraße 1, 40213 Düsseldorf

Tel: +49(211) 1396-0

Fax: +49(211) 1396-225

EMail: postmaster@kunstakademie-duesseldorf.de

Website: http://www.kunstakademie-duesseldorf.de

Rector: Rita McBride Tel: +1(211) 1396-217

Chancellor: Dietrich Koska
Tel: +49(211) 1396-220
EMail: dietrich.koska@kunstakademie-duesseldorf.de

Department

Art-related Sciences (Aesthetics; Art Education; Art History; Education; Fine Arts; Philosophy; Sociology); **Fine Arts** (Architecture; Display and Stage Design; Film; Fine Arts; Painting and Drawing; Photography; Sculpture; Video; Visual Arts)

History: Founded 1773.

Main Language(s) of Instruction: German

Degrees and Diplomas: *Bachelor's Degree*: **Art Education; Secondary Education.** *Künstlerische Abschlussprüfung*: **Architecture.** *Master*: **Education; Teacher Training.** *PhD*: **Fine Arts.** Lehramt

Student Services: Library

Student Numbers *2013-2014*: Total 631

Last Updated: 10/03/15

ERFURT UNIVERSITY OF APPLIED SCIENCES

Fachhochschule Erfurt

Postfach 45 01 55, Altonaer Strasse 25, 99051 Erfurt

Tel: +49(361) 6700-0

Fax: +49(361) 6700-703

EMail: information@fh-erfurt.de; praesidialamt@fh-erfurt.de

Website: http://www.fh-erfurt.de

Head: Volker Zerbe (2014-)
Tel: +49(361) 6700-701 EMail: praesidialamt@fh-erfurt.de

Chancellor: Claudia Rütten
Tel: +49(361) 6700-120 EMail: kanzleramt@fh-erfurt.de

International Relations: Cornelia Witter
Tel: 49(361) 6700-707 EMail: witter@fh-erfurt.de

Faculty

Applied Social Sciences (Preschool Education; Social Welfare); **Architecture and Urban Planning** (Architecture; Town Planning); **Business, Logistics and Transport** (Business Administration; Transport and Communications); **Civil Engineering and Conservation/Restoration** (Archaeology; Civil Engineering); **Engineering in Building and Computer Science** (Computer Science; Construction Engineering; Energy Engineering); **Landscape Architecture, Horticulture and Forestry** (Forestry; Horticulture; Landscape Architecture)

History: Founded 1991.

Academic Year: September to August

Admission Requirements: Abitur or Fachhochschulreife or Fachgebundene

Fees: None

Main Language(s) of Instruction: German

Degrees and Diplomas: *Bachelor's Degree*: **Agriculture; Architecture and Planning; Business Administration; Education; Engineering; Fine Arts; Mathematics and Computer Science; Welfare and Protective Services.** *Master*: **Accountancy; Architecture; Botany; Building Technologies; Business Administration; Civil Engineering; Computer Science; Energy Engineering; Finance; Forest Products; Landscape Architecture; Railway Transport; Regional Planning; Restoration of Works of Art; Social Work; Structural Architecture; Town Planning; Transport Engineering; Transport Management.** Part-time study mode available for some programmes; Dual degree programmes in: Industrial Engineerind and Railway Transport; Building Technology and Energy Engineering; Also Certificate programmes offered through Continuing Education Centre.

Student Services: Academic Counselling, Canteen, Careers Guidance, Cultural Activities, Facilities for disabled people, Foreign Studies Centre, Language Laboratory, Library, Nursery Care, Social Counselling, Sports Facilities

Academic Staff *2014-2015*: Total 133
Student Numbers *2014-2015*: Total 4,437
Last Updated: 27/01/15

ERNST-ABBE-HOCHSCHULE JENA UNIVERSITY OF APPLIED SCIENCES

Fachhochschule Jena Ernst-Abbe-Hochschule Jena (EAH JENA)

PO Box 100314, Carl-Zeiss-Promenade 2, 07745 Jena
Tel: +49(3641) 205-100
Fax: +49(3641) 205-101
EMail: info@fh-jena.de
Website: http://www.eah-jena.de/

Rector: Gabriele Beibst (2011-)
Tel: +49(3641) 205-100
EMail: rektor@fh-jena.de; rektorat@fh-jena.de; gabriele.beibst@fh-jena.de

Kanzler: Thoralf Held
Tel: +49(3641) 205-200 EMail: Kanzler@fh-jena.de

International Relations: Angelika Förster, Leiterin Akademisches Auslandsamt
Tel: +49(3641) 205-135 EMail: auslandsamt@fh-jena.de

Faculty

SciTec (Environmental Engineering; Laser Engineering; Materials Engineering; Natural Sciences; Optical Technology; Physical Engineering; Technology)

Department

Business Administration (Business Administration; Management); **Electrical Engineering and Information Technology** (Automation and Control Engineering; Computer Engineering; Design; Electrical Engineering; Electronic Engineering; Information Technology; Mechanical Engineering; Media Studies; Telecommunications Engineering); **Fundamental Sciences** (Computer Science; Mathematics; Natural Sciences; Physics); **Health and Care** (Gynaecology and Obstetrics; Health Sciences; Midwifery; Nursing); **Industrial Engineering** (E- Business/Commerce; Environmental Engineering; Industrial Engineering; Information Technology); **Mechanical Engineering** (Mechanical Engineering); **Medical Technology and Biotechnology** (Biomedical Engineering; Biotechnology; Medical Technology; Pharmacology); **Social Work** (Social Work)

History: Founded 1991 as Fachhochschule Jena. Acquired present title 2012.

Main Language(s) of Instruction: German

Degrees and Diplomas: *Bachelor's Degree*; *Master*: **Aeronautical and Aerospace Engineering; Biotechnology; Business Administration; Computer Engineering; Electronic Engineering; Health Administration; Industrial Engineering; Instrument Making; Laser Engineering; Management; Materials Engineering; Mechanical Engineering; Medicine; Optical Technology; Optometry; Pharmacology; Social Work.** Also Dual Bachelor's Degree Programmes in Engineering and Health Sciences; Distance Learning Master's degree programme in Nursing and Bachelor's degree in Nursing and Health Administration.

Student Services: Library

Student Numbers *2014-2015*: Total 4,742
Last Updated: 28/01/15

ERNST BUSCH ACADEMY OF DRAMATIC ART

Hochschule für Schauspielkunst 'Ernst Busch' Berlin

Schnellerstrasse 104, 12439 Berlin
Tel: +49(30) 639975-0
Fax: +49(30) 639975-75
EMail: rektorat@hfs-berlin.de
Website: http://www.hfs-berlin.de

Rector: Wolfgang Engler (2005-)
Tel: +49(30) 755417-112 EMail: rektorat@hfs-berlin.de

Chancellor: Kai Schlegel
Tel: +1(30) 755417-121 EMail: kanzler@hfs-berlin.de

Programme

Theatre (Theatre)

Department

Dance (Dance); **Directing** (Theatre); **Dramaturgy** (Theatre); **Puppetry** (Theatre)

History: Founded 1905, acquired present status and title 1981.

Academic Year: September to August (September-February; February-August)

Admission Requirements: Secondary school certificate (Reifezeugnis) or equivalent

Fees: None

Main Language(s) of Instruction: Russian, French, German

Degrees and Diplomas: *Bachelor's Degree*; *Diplom (Univ)*; *Master*: **Dance; Theatre.**

Student Services: Library

Student Numbers *2013-2014*: Total 224
Last Updated: 03/04/15

ERNST-MORITZ-ARNDT UNIVERSITY GREIFSWALD

Ernst-Moritz-Arndt-Universität Greifswald

Domstraße 11, 17487 Greifswald
Tel: +49(3834) 86-0
Fax: +49(3834) 86-1248
EMail: rektor@uni-greifswald.de; pressestelle@uni-greifswald.de
Website: http://www.uni-greifswald.de

Rektor: Johanna Eleonore Weber
Tel: +49(3834) 86-1100 EMail: rektorin@uni-greifswald.de

Chancellor: Wolfgang Flieger
Tel: +49(3834) 86-1111 EMail: kanzler@uni-greifswald.de

International Relations: Katharina Schmitt, Head of the International Office
Tel: +49(3834) 86-1117 EMail: schmittk@uni-greifswald.de

Faculty

Law and Economics (Economics; Law); **Mathematics and Natural Sciences** (Biochemistry; Biology; Chemistry; Computer Science; Genetics; Geography; Geology; Mathematics; Microbiology; Natural Sciences; Pharmacy; Physics); **Medicine** (Dentistry; Medicine); **Philosophy** (American Studies; Baltic Languages; English Studies; Music; Philology; Philosophy; Religious Music); **Theology** (Theology)

Academy

Graduate Studies (Communication Studies; Leadership; Management; Natural Sciences)

History: Founded 1456 and confirmed by Papal Bull of Calixtus III. The University came under the control of Sweden in 1648, becoming a Prussian University in 1815. Reorganized 1946 and 1990.

Academic Year: October to July

Admission Requirements: Secondary school certificate (Reifezeugnis) or equivalent

Fees: None

Main Language(s) of Instruction: German

Degrees and Diplomas: *Bachelor's Degree*: **Arts and Humanities; Fine Arts; Law; Natural Sciences; Social Sciences.** *Diplom (Univ)*: **Business Administration; Religious Music; Theology.** *Master*: **American Studies; Art History; Biochemistry; Biological and Life Sciences; Communication Studies; Comparative Literature; Cultural Studies; Development Studies; Earth Sciences; Ecology; English Studies; Environmental Management; Environmental Studies; Fine Arts; Fiscal Law; Geography; German; Germanic Studies; History; Linguistics; Literature; Mathematics; Molecular Biology; Philology; Philosophy; Physics; Physiology; Political Sciences; Regional Studies; Scandinavian Languages; Slavic Languages; Speech Studies; Tourism.** *PhD*: **Law; Mathematics; Medicine; Natural Sciences; Philosophy; Political Sciences; Theology.** Also Staatsexam in Medicine, Pharmacy, Law, Dentistry; Lehramt in Secondary Education, Foreign Languages Education, Humanities and Social Sciences Education.

Student Services: Academic Counselling, Canteen, Facilities for disabled people, Health Services, IT Centre, Library, Social Counselling, Sports Facilities

Publications: Greifswalder Universitätsreden

Publishing House: University Press

Student Numbers *2013-2014*: Total 11,477
Last Updated: 25/01/15

ESSLINGEN UNIVERSITY OF APPLIED SCIENCES

Hochschule Esslingen (HE)
Kanalstrasse 33, 73728 Esslingen
Tel: +49(711) 397-49
Fax: +49(711) 397-3100
EMail: info@hs-esslingen.de
Website: http://www.hs-esslingen.de

Rector: Christian Maercker
Tel: +49(711) 397-3000
EMail: Christian.Maercker@hs-esslingen.de

Chancellor: Heike Lindenschmid
Tel: +49(711) 397-3010
EMail: Heike.Lindenschmid@hs-esslingen.de

International Relations: Beate Maleska, Head, International Office
Tel: +49(711) 397-3082 EMail: Beate.Maleska@hs-esslingen.de

Faculty

Automotive Engineering (Automotive Engineering; Engineering; Engineering Drawing and Design); **Basic Sciences** (Automation and Control Engineering; Building Technologies; Electrical Engineering; Information Technology; Mechanical Engineering); **Building Services, Energy and Environmental Engineering** (Building Technologies; Energy Engineering; Environmental Engineering); **Industrial Engineering** (Business Computing; Engineering Management; Industrial Engineering; Industrial Management); **Information Technology** (Automotive Engineering; Computer Engineering; Information Technology; Media Studies; Software Engineering; Telecommunications Engineering); **Management** (Engineering Management; Industrial Management); **Mechanical Engineering** (Mechanical Engineering; Production Engineering); **Mechatronics and Elecrical Engineering** (Automation and Control Engineering; Electrical Engineering; Mechanical Engineering); **Natural Sciences** (Biotechnology; Chemical Engineering; Environmental Studies; Materials Engineering; Natural Sciences); **Social Work, Health Care and Nursing Sciences** (Health Sciences; Nursing; Social Work)

Graduate School

Graduate Studies (Automotive Engineering; Design; Industrial Management; Mechanical Engineering)

Further Information: Also Flandernstraße and Göppingen Campuses

History: Founded 1971. Acquired present status through merger between Fachhochschulen in Esslingen - Hochschule für Technik (FHTE) and Hochschule für Sozialwesen (HfS) 2006.

Academic Year: September to July (September-February; March-July)

Admission Requirements: Abitur and German Language Test for International Applicants (DSH or Test DGF)

Fees: None

Main Language(s) of Instruction: German, English

Accrediting Agency: FIBAA, DQS

Degrees and Diplomas: *Bachelor's Degree*; *Master*: **Automotive Engineering; Electronic Engineering; Engineering Management; Environmental Management; Industrial Management; Materials Engineering; Mechanical Engineering; Nursing; Social Work.** Also cooperative Master's degree programmes: Network Engineering and Grid Operation Gas/Water (in cooperation with Stuttgart Technical University and the EnBW Academy); Social Economics (in cooperation with the Paritätischen Bundesakademie and the Paritätischen Akademie Süd).

Student Services: Academic Counselling, Canteen, Careers Guidance, Foreign Studies Centre, Language Laboratory, Library, Sports Facilities

Publications: Spektrum

Academic Staff *2014-2015*: Total 666
Student Numbers *2014-2015*: Total 6,122
Last Updated: 04/03/15

EUROPA-UNIVERSITÄT FLENSBURG (EUF)

Auf dem Campus 1, 24943 Flensburg
Tel: +49(461) 805-02
Fax: +49(461) 805-2144
EMail: rektorat@uni-flensburg.de
Website: http://www.uni-flensburg.de

President: Werner Reinhart
Tel: +49(461) 805-2801 EMail: reinhart@uni-flensburg.de

Chancellor: Frank Kupfer
Tel: +49(461) 805-2804 EMail: frank.kupfer@uni-flensburg.de

International Relations: Ulrike Bischoff-Parker, Head, International Office
Tel: +49(461) 805-2774 EMail: bischoff@uni-flensburg.de

Institute

Aesthetical and Cultural Education (Aesthetics; Communication Arts; Cultural Studies; Fashion Design; Fine Arts; Media Studies; Music; Textile Design); **Educational Sciences** (Educational Sciences; Primary Education; Psychology); **Environmental, Social and Human Sciences** *(Interdisciplinary)* (Ecology; Environmental Management; Environmental Studies; Geography; Philosophy); **Health, Nutrition and Sport Sciences** (Consumer Studies; Health Education; Health Sciences; Nutrition; Psychology; Sports); **Language, Literature and Media** (Danish; English; German; Germanic

Studies; Literature; Media Studies; Romance Languages); **Management and Economic Education** *(International)* (Economics; Education; Educational Administration; European Union Law; Finance; Higher Education; Human Resources; Humanities and Social Science Education; Industrial and Organizational Psychology; International Economics; International Law; Management; Marketing; Media Studies; Public Law); **Mathematical, Scientific and Technical Education** (Biology; Chemistry; Mathematics; Physics; Secondary Education; Technology; Technology Education); **Social Sciences and Theology** (Catholic Theology; History; Humanities and Social Science Education; Political Sciences; Protestant Theology; Sociology); **Special Education** (Psychology; Special Education; Teacher Training); **Work and Technology** *(Professional Educational)* (Technology)

History: Founded 1946. Reorganized 1973 and acquired present status 2000. Financially supported by the State of Schleswig-Holstein.

Academic Year: October to September (October-March; April-September)

Admission Requirements: Secondary school certificate (Reifezeugnis) or equivalent

Fees: None

Main Language(s) of Instruction: German, English, Danish, Spanish

Degrees and Diplomas: *Bachelor's Degree*: **Educational Sciences; International Business.** *Master*: **Cultural Studies; Education; Environmental Management; European Studies; International Business; Media Studies; Modern Languages; Nursing; Primary Education; Secondary Education; Social and Preventive Medicine; Teacher Training; Vocational Education.** *PhD*: **Economics; Philosophy.**

Student Services: Academic Counselling, Canteen, IT Centre, Library, Nursery Care, Social Counselling, Sports Facilities

Student Numbers *2014-2015*: Total 4,810

Last Updated: 31/03/15

EUROPEAN UNIVERSITY OF APPLIED SCIENCES

Europäische Fachhochschule (EUFH)

Kaiserstraße 6, 50321 Brühl
Tel: +49(2232) 5673-0
Fax: +49(2232) 5673-219
EMail: info@eufh.de
Website: http://www.eufh.de

Präsident: Birger Lang
Tel: +49(2232) 5673-120 EMail: b.lang@eufh.de

Course

Business Computing (Business Computing); **Finance and Investment Management** (Finance; Management); **General Management** (Management); **Human Resources Management** (Human Resources); **Industrial Engineering** (Industrial Engineering); **Industrial Management** (Industrial Management); **IT Audit and Assurance** (Information Technology); **Logistics Management** (Transport Management); **Management in Dynamic Markets** (Management); **Marketing Management** (Management; Marketing); **Retail Management** (Management; Retailing and Wholesaling)

Further Information: Also Köln, Neuss and Aachen Campuses

History: Founded 2001.

Main Language(s) of Instruction: German

Accrediting Agency: Wissenschaftsrat (WR); FIBAA

Degrees and Diplomas: *Bachelor's Degree*: **Business Administration; Business Computing; Engineering; Finance; Industrial Management; Management; Retailing and Wholesaling; Transport Management.** *Master*: **Business Computing; Human Resources; Information Technology; International Business; Management; Marketing; Media Studies; Tourism; Transport Management.** Dual Bachelor's degree porgrammes; Programmes offered in full- and part-time modes.

Student Services: Canteen, IT Centre, Library

Student Numbers *2013-2014*: Total 1,833

Last Updated: 26/01/15

EUROPEAN UNIVERSITY VIADRINA FRANKFURT (ODER)

Europa-Universität Viadrina Frankfurt (Oder)

PO Box 1786, Grosse Scharrnstrasse 59, 15207 Frankfurt (Oder), Brandenburg
Tel: +49(335) 5534-0
Fax: +49(335) 5534-4305
EMail: presidents.office@euv-frankfurt-o.de
Website: http://www.europa-uni.de/de/studium/index.html

Präsident: Alexander Wöll (2014-)
Tel: +49(335) 5534-4274 EMail: president@europa-uni.de

Kanzler: Christian Zens
Tel: +49(335) 5534-4334 EMail: kanzler@euv-frankfurt-o.de

International Relations: Petra Weber, Head, Department of International Affairs
Tel: +49(335) 5534-2486 EMail: head-office@europa-uni.de

Faculty

Business Administration and Economics (Accountancy; Business Administration; Finance; Information Management; International Economics; Management; Marketing; Taxation); **Law** (Civil Law; Criminal Law; International Law; Law; Public Law); **Social and Cultural Sciences** *(Interdisciplinary)* (Cultural Studies; Linguistics; Literature; Social Sciences)

Centre

Language (Foreign Languages Education; Linguistics; Modern Languages)

Research Institute

Ethics *(Interdisciplinary, for graduates)* (Ethics); **Literature and Politics** *(Heinrich von Kleist for Graduate)* (Literature; Political Sciences); **Transformation Studies** *(Interdisciplinary, for graduates)* (Econometrics)

History: Founded 1991. Reviving the tradition of the first Brandenburg University, the Alma Mater Viadrina (1506-1811), the new Viadrina is an international and innovative University, bridging the gap between Eastern and Western Europe. The Collegium Polonicum, a teaching and research centre, is jointly managed by the Viadrina and the University of Poznan.

Academic Year: October to September (October-March; April-September)

Admission Requirements: Secondary school certificate (Reifezeugnis)

Main Language(s) of Instruction: German, English, Polish

Degrees and Diplomas: *Bachelor's Degree*: **Business Administration; Cultural Studies; Economics; Law; Social Sciences.** *Master*: **Aesthetics; Central European Studies; Communication Studies; Cultural Studies; Eastern European Studies; European Studies; European Union Law; Health Sciences; Human Rights; International Business; International Law; Jewish Studies; Law; Literature; Media Studies; Philosophy; Public Administration; Social Sciences; Tourism.** *PhD*: **Business Administration; Cultural Studies; Law.** Also Bachelor and Master's Degree Multilingual Programmes (German, English, French or Polish) in Cultural and Social Studies, Business Administration and Economics, Law.

Student Services: Academic Counselling, Canteen, Facilities for disabled people, Foreign Studies Centre, Language Laboratory, Library, Sports Facilities

Academic Staff *2013-2014*: Total 443

STAFF WITH DOCTORATE: Total 67

Student Numbers *2013-2014*: Total 6,645

Last Updated: 25/01/15

FEDERAL UNIVERSITY OF APPLIED ADMINISTRATIVE SCIENCES

Hochschule des Bundes für Öffentliche Verwaltung (HS BUND)

Willy-Brandt-Strasse 1, 50321 Brühl
Tel: +49(228) 99-629-0
Fax: +49(228) 99-629-5100
EMail: postzb@fhbund.de
Website: http://www.fhbund.de/

President: Thomas Bönders
Tel: +49(228) 99629-6100 EMail: Thomas.Boenders@hsbund.de

Department

Agricultural Social Insurance (Agriculture; Welfare and Protective Services); **Criminal Investigation** (Criminology); **Defense Administration** (Administration; Military Science); **Federal Police** (Police Studies); **Finance** (Finance); **Foreign Affairs** (International Relations); **General Internal Administration** (Administration); **Intelligence Services** (Protective Services); **Meteorological Service** (Meteorology); **Social Security** (Social Welfare)

Further Information: Also Departmental Branches in: Berlin, Lübeck, Mannheim, Münster, Wiesbaden, Kassel, Haar, Offenbach am Main.

History: An internal, interministerial university for public service at the federal level in Germany. It trains new personnel for the higher non-technical federal administrative service. Students already hold the legal status of temporary civil servants and become permanent civil servants once they have finished their studies.

Admission Requirements: Candidates should apply to the competent recruiting authority for the career of their choice within the civil service.

Main Language(s) of Instruction: German

Degrees and Diplomas: *Bachelor's Degree*: **Criminology; Social Welfare.** *Diplom (FH)*: **Administration; Agriculture; Computer Science; International Relations; Meteorology; Military Science; Police Studies; Protective Services; Public Administration; Social Welfare; Taxation.** *Master*: **Public Administration.**

Student Services: Library

Academic Staff *2014-2015*: Total: c. 200
Student Numbers *2014-2015*: Total: c. 3,300
Last Updated: 27/01/15

FELIX MENDELSSOHN BARTHOLDY UNIVERSITY OF MUSIC AND THEATRE OF LEIPZIG

Hochschule für Musik und Theater 'Felix Mendelssohn Bartholdy' Leipzig

Postfach 10 08 09, Grassistraße 8, 04008 Leipzig
Tel: +49(341) 2144-55
Fax: +49(341) 2144-503
EMail: studienangelegenheiten@hmt-leipzig.de; kbb@hmt-leipzig.de
Website: http://www.hmt-leipzig.de

Rector: Robert Ehrlich
Tel: +49(341) 2144-502 EMail: rektor@hmt-leipzig.de
Chancellor: Oliver Grimm
Tel: +49(341) 2144-601 EMail: kanzler@hmt-leipzig.de
Administrative Officer: Birgit Reichelt
Tel: +49(341) 2144-501 EMail: birgit.reichelt@hmt-leipzig.de

Department

Early Music (Music); **Brass and Woodwind, Drums and Percussion** (Musical Instruments); **Church Music** (Religious Music); **Composition and Harmony, Counterpoint** (Music Theory and Composition); **Conducting and Instrument Accompaniment** (Conducting); **Dramaturgy** (Theatre); **Jazz, Popular Music** (Jazz and Popular Music); **Music Pedagogy** (Music Education); **Musicology** (Musicology); **Piano** (Musical Instruments); **Strings/Harp** (Musical Instruments); **Voice Music Theatre** (Opera; Singing)

Institute

Drama *(Hans Otto)* (Acting)

History: Founded 1843.

Fees: 111,50 per semester (Euro)

Main Language(s) of Instruction: German

Degrees and Diplomas: *Bachelor's Degree*; *Konzertexamen*; *Master*: **Acting; Music; Music Education; Musicology; Theatre.** *PhD*: **Music Education; Musicology; Theatre.** *Habilitation*: **Music Education; Musicology; Theatre.** Staatsexam (Lehramt) in Music Education.

Student Services: Library

Student Numbers *2013-2014*: Total 955
Last Updated: 11/03/15

FLENSBURG UNIVERSITY OF APPLIED SCIENCES

Fachhochschule Flensburg

P.O. Box 1561, Kanzleistrasse 91-93, 24943 Flensburg
Tel: +49(461) 805-01
Fax: +49(461) 805-1300
EMail: presse@fh-flensburg.de
Website: http://www.fh-flensburg.de

President: Holger Watter (2014-)
Tel: +49(461) 805-1200 EMail: praesidium@fh-flensburg.de

Kanzlerin: Sabine Christiansen Tel: +49(461) 805-1202

Faculty

Business Administration (Business Administration); **Energy and Biotechnology** (Biotechnology; Energy Engineering); **Engineering, Process Engineering and Maritime Technologies** (Engineering; Marine Engineering; Production Engineering); **Information and Communication** (Communication Studies; Information Technology)

History: Founded 1886.

Main Language(s) of Instruction: German

Degrees and Diplomas: *Bachelor's Degree*: **Applied Mathematics; Biotechnology; Business Administration; Business Computing; Communication Studies; Electrical Engineering; Energy Engineering; Engineering; Environmental Studies; Information Technology; Machine Building; Marine Engineering; Marine Transport; Nautical Science.** *Master*: **Bioengineering; Biotechnology; Business Administration; Energy Engineering; Engineering; Health Sciences; Production Engineering.**

Student Services: Academic Counselling, IT Centre

Student Numbers *2013-2014*: Total 4,114
Last Updated: 27/01/15

FOLKWANG UNIVERSITY OF THE ARTS

Folkwang Universität der Künste

PO Box 164428, Klemensborn 39, 45224 Essen
Tel: +49(201) 4903-0
Fax: +49(201) 4903-288
EMail: info@folkwang-uni.de
Website: http://www.folkwang-uni.de

Rector: Kurt Mehnert
Tel: +49(201) 4903-100 EMail: kurt.mehnert@folkwang-uni.de

Chancellor: Michael Fricke
Tel: +49(201) 4903-200 EMail: fricke@folkwang-uni.de

International Relations: Hanns-Dietrich Schmidt, Prorector For International Affairs and Events
Tel: +49(201) 4903-101 EMail: hd.schmidt@folkwang-uni.de

Faculty

Faculty 1 (Conducting; Jazz and Popular Music; Music; Music Theory and Composition; Musical Instruments); **Faculty 2** (Music; Music Education; Music Theory and Composition; Musicology; Singing); **Faculty 3** (Acting; Art Education; Dance; Music; Music Theory and Composition; Singing; Theatre); **Faculty 4** (Communication Arts; Design; Fine Arts; Graphic Design; Industrial Design; Photography)

Further Information: In Duisburg, Bochum und Dortmund

History: Founded 1927 as Folkwang Hochschule. Acquired present status and title 2010.

Academic Year: October to September (October-February; April-September)

Admission Requirements: Secondary school certificate (Abitur); aptitude test

Fees: 650 per semester (Euro)

Degrees and Diplomas: *Bachelor's Degree*; *Künstlerische Abschlussprüfung*: **Theatre.** *Master*: **Art Education; Conducting; Dance; Design; Fine Arts; Jazz and Popular Music; Music Education; Music Theory and Composition; Musical Instruments; Musicology; Photography; Singing.** *PhD*: **Art History; Design; Educational Sciences; Industrial Design; Music Education; Musicology.** *Habilitation*: **Art History; Design;**

Educational Sciences; Industrial Design; Music Education; Musicology. Graduate Certificate (Zertifikatsabschluss) in Religious Music; Certificate of completion (Exzellenzstudiengang mit Zertifikatsabschluss) in Music; Brief in Design

Student Services: Library

Student Numbers *2013-2014*: Total 1,522
Last Updated: 29/01/15

FRANKFURT AM MAIN COLLEGE OF FINE ARTS

Staatliche Hochschule für Bildende Künste - Städelschule Frankfurt

Dürerstrasse 10, 60596 Frankfurt am Main
Tel: +49(69) 605008-0
Fax: +49(69) 605008-66
Website: http://www.staedelschule.de

Rector: Philippe Pirotte
Tel: +49(69) 605008-29 EMail: rektor@staedelschule.de

Programme

Architecture (Architecture); **Curatorial and Critical Studies** (Art Criticism; Art History; Museum Studies); **Fine Arts** (Art History; Fine Arts; Handicrafts)

Institute

Art Criticism (Art Criticism)

History: Founded 1942.

Main Language(s) of Instruction: German

Degrees and Diplomas: *Master*: **Architecture; Art Criticism; Museum Studies.** No degree is awarded for Fine Arts Programme

Student Services: IT Centre, Library

Student Numbers *2013-2014*: Total 174
Last Updated: 30/01/15

FRANKFURT UNIVERSITY OF APPLIED SCIENCES (FRA-UAS)

Nibelungenplatz 1, 60318 Frankfurt am Main
Tel: +49(69) 1533-0
Fax: +49(69) 1533-2400
EMail: post@fra-uas.de
Website: http://www.fh-frankfurt.de

Präsident: Frank E.P. Dievernich
Tel: +49(69) 1533-2415 EMail: praesident@fra-uas.de

Kanzler: Reiner Frey
Tel: +49(69) 1533-2412 EMail: kanzler@fra-uas.de

International Relations: Andrea Janssen, Head, International Affairs
Tel: +49(69) 1533-2735 EMail: andrea.janssen@io.fra-uas.de

Faculty

Architecture (Architecture; Civil Engineering; Construction Engineering; Geological Engineering; Information Technology; Surveying and Mapping; Town Planning); **Computer Science and Engineering** (Automation and Control Engineering; Automotive Engineering; Bioengineering; Business Computing; Computer Engineering; Computer Science; Electronic Engineering; Energy Engineering; Engineering; Machine Building; Materials Engineering; Mechanical Engineering); **Economics and Law** (Air Transport; Business Administration; Commercial Law; Economics; Engineering; Finance; Information Management; International Business; Law; Leadership; Management; Public Administration); **Social Work and Health** (Health Sciences; Nursing; Pedagogy; Rehabilitation and Therapy; Social Work; Welfare and Protective Services)

History: Founded 1971 as Fachhochschule Frankfurt am Main. Acquired present title 2014.

Main Language(s) of Instruction: German

Degrees and Diplomas: *Bachelor's Degree*; *Master*: **Accountancy; Air Transport; Architecture; Artificial Intelligence; Automotive Engineering; Business Administration; Civil Engineering; Commercial Law; Computer Engineering; Construction Engineering; Engineering; Finance; Health Administration; Health Sciences; Information Management; Information Technology; Labour Law; Leadership; Machine Building; Management; Nursing; Production Engineering; Psychology; Social Work; Surveying and Mapping; Transport Management; Urban Studies.**

Student Services: Academic Counselling, Careers Guidance, Facilities for disabled people, IT Centre, Library, Social Counselling, Sports Facilities

Student Numbers *2013-2014*: Total 11,556
Last Updated: 27/01/15

FRANKFURT UNIVERSITY OF MUSIC AND PERFORMING ARTS

Hochschule für Musik und Darstellende Kunst Frankfurt am Main

Eschersheimer Landstraße 29-39, 60322 Frankfurt am Main
Tel: +49(69) 154007-0
Fax: +49(69) 154007-108
EMail: praesident@hfmdk-frankfurt.de
Website: http://www.hfmdk-frankfurt.de

President: Thomas Rietschel
Tel: +49(69) 154007-311 EMail: praesident@hfmdk-frankfurt.de

Chancellor: Angelika Gartner
Tel: +49(69) 154007-321
EMail: angelika.gartner@hfmdk-frankfurt.de

Department

I - Artistic Instrumental Training and Conducting, Music Education, Church Music and Historically Informed Performance (Conducting; Music; Music Education; Musical Instruments; Musicology; Religious Music; Singing); **II - Teaching Careers, Science and Composition** (Music; Music Education; Music Theory and Composition; Secondary Education; Teacher Training); **III - Performing Arts** (Dance; Opera; Theatre)

History: Founded 1878.

Main Language(s) of Instruction: German

Degrees and Diplomas: *Bachelor's Degree*; *Konzertexamen*: **Musical Instruments.** *Diplom (Univ)*: **Theatre.** *Master*: **Art Management; Dance; Music; Music Education; Music Theory and Composition; Musical Instruments; Performing Arts; Religious Music; Singing.** *PhD*: **Music Education; Musicology.**

Student Services: Canteen, Library

Student Numbers *2013-2014*: Total 913
Last Updated: 11/03/15

FREE UNIVERSITY OF BERLIN

Freie Universität Berlin (FUB)

Kaiserswerther Str. 16-18, 14195 Berlin
Tel: +49(30) 838-1
Fax: +49(30) 838-73187
EMail: info-service@fu-berlin.de
Website: http://www.fu-berlin.de

President: Peter-André Alt
Tel: +49(30) 838-73100 +49(30) 838-73104
EMail: praesident@fu-berlin.de

Kanzler: Peter Lange
Tel: +49(30) 838-73211 EMail: kanzler@fu-berlin.de

International Relations: Elke Löschhorn, Director, Office of International Affairs
Tel: +49(30) 838-73400 EMail: international-office@fu-berlin.de

Faculty

Medicine *(Charité-Universitätsmedizin Berlin)* (Medicine)

Department

Biology, Chemistry and Pharmacy (Biology; Chemistry; Pharmacy); **Earth Sciences** (Earth Sciences; Geology; Meteorology); **Economics** (Business Administration; Economics); **Education and Psychology** (Educational Sciences; Primary Education; Psychology; Sports); **History and Cultural Studies** (History; Philosophy; Social Sciences); **Law** (Law); **Mathematics and Computer Science** (Mathematics and Computer Science); **Philosophy and**

Humanities (Film; German; Music; Philosophy; Theatre); **Physics** (Physics); **Political and Social Sciences** (Advertising and Publicity; Communication Studies; Ethnology; Political Sciences; Sociology); **Veterinary Science** (Veterinary Science)

Institute

Eastern Europe Studies (Eastern European Studies); **Latin American Studies** (Latin American Studies); **North American Studies** *(John F. Kennedy)* (American Studies)

Centre

Area Studies *(Interdisciplinary)* (Regional Studies); **Complex Quantum Systems (DCCQS)** *(Dahlem - Interdisciplinary)* (Physics); **French Studies** *(Interdisciplinary)* (French); **Humanities** *(Dahlem)* (Arts and Humanities); **Italian Studies** *(Interdisciplinary)* (Italian); **Modern Greece (CeMoG)** *(Interdisciplinary)* (Central European Studies)

Graduate School

Literary Studies *(Friedrich Schlegel)* (Literature); **Mathematics** *(Berlin)* (Mathematics); **Muslim Cultures and Societies** *(Berlin)* (Islamic Studies); **North American Studies** (American Studies); **Regenerative Therapies** *(Berlin-Brandenburg)* (Rehabilitation and Therapy)

Research Centre

Languages â of Emotion *(Interdisciplinary)* (Arts and Humanities)

History: Founded 1948 in response to the demand for the creation of a University in West Berlin. Reorganized and faculty structure replaced 1970. An independent body financially supported by the State of Berlin.

Academic Year: October to July (October-February; April-July)

Admission Requirements: Secondary school certificate (Reifezeugnis). Certificate of excellent knowledge of German

Fees: None

Main Language(s) of Instruction: German

Degrees and Diplomas: *Bachelor's Degree*; *Master*: **Accountancy; Administrative Law; American Studies; Ancient Civilizations; Anthropology; Arabic; Archaeology; Art History; Art Management; Biochemistry; Biology; Business Administration; Business Computing; Chemistry; Child Care and Development; Classical Languages; Clinical Psychology; Cognitive Sciences; Commercial Law; Comparative Literature; Computer Education; Computer Science; Contemporary History; Dance; Dutch; Earth Sciences; East Asian Studies; Eastern European Studies; Ecology; Economics; Educational Sciences; English; English Studies; Environmental Management; Environmental Studies; European Languages; European Studies; European Union Law; Film; Finance; Foreign Languages Education; Gender Studies; Geography; Geology; German; Germanic Studies; Greek; History; Humanities and Social Science Education; Industrial and Organizational Psychology; International Business; International Relations; Islamic Studies; Japanese; Jewish Studies; Korean; Latin American Studies; Law; Literature; Management; Marketing; Mass Communication; Mathematics; Mathematics Education; Media Studies; Medieval Studies; Meteorology; Modern History; Musicology; Native Language Education; Neurosciences; Persian; Philosophy; Physics; Political Sciences; Prehistory; Preschool Education; Primary Education; Psychology; Public Health; Publishing and Book Trade; Religion; Religious Education; Romance Languages; Science Education; Social and Preventive Medicine; Social Sciences; Sociology; Taxation; Theatre; Turkish; Veterinary Science.** *PhD*: **African Studies; American Studies; Ancient Civilizations; Ancient Languages; Anthropology; Applied Mathematics; Arabic; Archaeology; Art History; Arts and Humanities; Asian Studies; Biochemistry; Biology; Biomedicine; Botany; Business Administration; Business Computing; Cardiology; Catholic Theology; Cell Biology; Chemistry; Comparative Literature; Crystallography; Cultural Studies; Dutch; Earth Sciences; East Asian Studies; Ecology; Econometrics; Economics; Education; Engineering; English; Ethics; Ethnology; Film; Finance; Genetics; Geography (Human); German; Greek (Classical); History; Immunology; International Relations; Islamic Studies; Japanese; Jewish Studies; Latin; Latin American Studies; Law; Linguistics; Literature; Management; Marketing; Materials Engineering; Mathematics; Mathematics and Computer Science; Medicine; Molecular Biology; Musicology; Neurology; Neurosciences; Oncology; Oriental Languages; Oriental Studies; Paediatrics; Persian; Pharmacology; Pharmacy; Philosophy; Physics; Plant Pathology; Political Sciences; Protestant Theology; Psychiatry and Mental Health; Psychology; Regional Studies; Religion; Religious Studies; Romance Languages; Social Sciences; Sociology; Solid State Physics; Southeast Asian Studies; Statistics; Theatre; Turkish; Veterinary Science.** *Habilitation*: **Arts and Humanities; Biology; Chemistry; Cultural Studies; Earth Sciences; Economics; History; Law; Mathematics and Computer Science; Medicine; Pharmacy; Philosophy; Physics; Political Sciences; Social Sciences; Veterinary Science.** Also Double Bachelor and Master's Degrees with other international universities (in France, China, Romania, South Korea, Japan, United Kingdom, Netherlands, Belgium, Sweden, Portugal, Spain, Lithuania, Switzerland, Greece, Thailand). Combined Bachelor's Degree Programmes; Combined Bachelor's Degree Programmes with Teacher Training Option (Lehramt); Staatsexam in Medicine, Pharmacy, Veterinary Science, Dentistry; First Exam (Erste juristische Prüfung) in Law. English-language Master's Degree Programmes in areas such as: Natural Sciences, Social Sciences, Health Sciences, Mathematics and Computer sciences, Arts and Humanities, Business Administration.

Student Services: Academic Counselling, Canteen, Language Laboratory, Library, Social Counselling, Sports Facilities

Student Numbers *2013-2014*: Total 32,742

Last Updated: 29/01/15

FREIBERG UNIVERSITY OF MINING AND TECHNOLOGY

Technische Universität Bergakademie Freiberg

Akademiestrasse 6, 09596 Freiberg

Tel: +49(3731) 39-0

Fax: +49(3731) 22195

EMail: postmaster@tu-freiberg.de

Website: http://www.tu-freiberg.de

Rector: Bernd Meyer
Tel: +49(3731) 39-2550 EMail: Rektor@zuv.tu-freiberg.de

Chancellor: Andreas Handschuh
Tel: +49(3731) 39-2700 EMail: Kanzler@zuv.tu-freiberg.de

International Relations: Ingrid Lange, Head, International Office
Tel: +49(3731) 39-2625
EMail: ingrid.lange@iuz.tu-freiberg.de;
brigitta.boehland@iuz.tu-freiberg.de

Faculty

Business Administration and the International Ressource Industry (Business Administration; Engineering; Industrial Engineering; Natural Resources); **Chemistry and Physics** (Analytical Chemistry; Chemical Engineering; Chemistry; Inorganic Chemistry; Natural Sciences; Physical Chemistry; Physics); **Geosciences, Geo-Engineering and Mining** (Earth Sciences; Geochemistry; Geology; Geophysics; Mineralogy; Mining Engineering; Petroleum and Gas Engineering; Surveying and Mapping); **Materials Science and Technology** (Materials Engineering; Metallurgical Engineering; Physical Engineering); **Mathematics and Computer Science** (Computer Science; Mathematics); **Mechanical, Process and Energy Engineering** (Chemical Engineering; Energy Engineering; Engineering Management; Environmental Engineering; Mechanical Engineering)

Further Information: Also preparatory courses and German language courses

History: Founded 1765, acquired University status 1905. Became Technical University 1991.

Academic Year: October to July (October-February; April-July)

Admission Requirements: Secondary school certificate (Reifezeugnis) or equivalent, and German language certificate (DSH) for international students

Fees: None

Main Language(s) of Instruction: German, English

Degrees and Diplomas: *Bachelor's Degree*: **Archaeology; Business Administration; Chemistry; Computer Science; Energy Engineering; Engineering Management; Environmental Engineering; Geology; Geophysics; Industrial Engineering; Law;**

Mathematics; Mechanical Engineering; Metallurgical Engineering; Mineralogy; Natural Sciences. *Diplom (Univ)*: **Applied Mathematics; Automotive Engineering; Business Administration; Ceramics and Glass Technology; Economics; Environmental Engineering; Geological Engineering; Materials Engineering; Mechanical Engineering; Mining Engineering; Nanotechnology; Natural Resources; Surveying and Mapping.** *Master*: **Archaeology; Automotive Engineering; Business Administration; Ceramics and Glass Technology; Chemistry; Computer Engineering; Computer Science; Earth Sciences; Ecology; Economics; Electronic Engineering; Energy Engineering; Engineering; Engineering Management; Environmental Engineering; Geological Engineering; Geology; Heritage Preservation; Industrial Engineering; International Business; Law; Management; Materials Engineering; Mathematics; Mechanical Engineering; Mineralogy; Mining Engineering; Natural Resources; Natural Sciences; Physics; Water Science.** *PhD*: **Business Administration; Chemistry; Energy Engineering; Geological Engineering; Geology; Materials Engineering; Mathematics and Computer Science; Mechanical Engineering; Mining Engineering; Physics.** *Habilitation*: **Business Administration; Chemistry; Energy Engineering; Engineering Management; Geological Engineering; Geology; Materials Engineering; Mathematics and Computer Science; Mechanical Engineering; Mining Engineering; Physics.** Also Dual Degree Programmes.

Student Services: Academic Counselling, Canteen, Careers Guidance, Cultural Activities, Facilities for disabled people, Foreign Studies Centre, Health Services, Language Laboratory, Nursery Care, Social Counselling, Sports Facilities

Publications: Freiberger Forschungshefte; Report

Student Numbers *2013-2014*: Total 5,380
Last Updated: 27/03/15

FREIBURG UNIVERSITY OF MUSIC

Hochschule für Musik Freiburg

Schwarzwaldstraße 141, 79095 Freiburg
Tel: +49(761) 31915-0
Fax: +49(761) 31915-42
EMail: info@mh-freiburg.de
Website: http://www.mh-freiburg.de

Rector: Rüdiger Nolte
Tel: +49(761) 31915-49 EMail: rektor@mh-freiburg.de

Chancellor: Bernd Probst
Tel: +49(761) 31915-43 EMail: kanzler@mh-freiburg.de

International Relations: Jacqueline Pfann
Tel: +4(761) 31915-33 EMail: international@mh-freiburg.de

Programme

Music (Conducting; Music; Music Education; Music Theory and Composition; Musical Instruments; Musicology; Opera; Religious Music; Singing)

History: Founded 1946.

Main Language(s) of Instruction: German

Degrees and Diplomas: *Bachelor's Degree*; *Konzertexamen*: **Musical Instruments.** *Master*: **Conducting; Music; Music Education; Music Theory and Composition; Musical Instruments; Religious Music; Singing.** *PhD*: **Music Education; Musicology.** Also Teacher Training State Examination (Lehramt) in Music Education and a 2-semestrer Post-Master Advanced Diploma in Musical Instruments.

Student Services: Careers Guidance, Library

Student Numbers *2013-2014*: Total 520
Last Updated: 26/03/15

FRIEDRICH-ALEXANDER UNIVERSITY OF ERLANGEN-NUREMBERG

Friedrich-Alexander-Universität Erlangen-Nürnberg (FAU)

PO Box 3520, Schlossplatz 4, 91023 Erlangen, Bavaria
Tel: +49(9131) 85-0
Fax: +49(9131) 852-2131
EMail: praesident@fau.de
Website: http://www.fau.de

Präsident: Karl-Dieter Grüske
Tel: +49 9131 852-6605 EMail: president@fau.de

Kanzler: Sybille Reichert
Tel: +49 9131 852-6603 EMail: kanzlerin@fau.de

International Relations: Christoph Korbmacher
Tel: +49 9131 852-4801 EMail: Christoph.Korbmacher@fau.de

Faculty

Business, Economics and Law (Business Administration; Business Computing; Civil Law; Criminal Law; Criminology; Economics; International Law; Labour Law; Law; Private Law); **Engineering** (Bioengineering; Chemical Engineering; Computer Science; Electrical Engineering; Engineering; Information Technology; Machine Building; Materials Engineering; Mechanical Engineering; Production Engineering; Technology); **Humanities, Social Sciences and Theology** (American Studies; Archaeology; Art History; Chinese; Cultural Studies; Economics; Education; English Studies; Germanic Languages; Gerontology; History; History of Religion; Japanese; Media Studies; Modern Languages; Music; Musicology; Oriental Languages; Pedagogy; Philosophy; Political Sciences; Psychology; Romance Languages; Social Sciences; Sociology; Sports; Teacher Training; Theology); **Medicine** (Anatomy; Biochemistry; Biomedicine; Computer Science; Dentistry; Epidemiology; Medical Technology; Medicine; Molecular Biology; Occupational Health; Orthodontics; Orthopaedics; Pathology; Periodontics; Pharmacology; Physiology; Social and Preventive Medicine; Toxicology); **Sciences** (Astronomy and Space Science; Biochemistry; Biological and Life Sciences; Biology; Biotechnology; Chemistry; Genetics; Geography; Geology; Information Technology; Mathematics; Microbiology; Optics; Pharmacy; Physics; Physiology; Plant Pathology)

Centre

Bavaria California Technology Centre (BaCaTeC); Bavarian University Centre for Latin America (BAYLAT); Central Institute for Anthropology of Religion(s) (ZAR); Central Institute for Research on Teaching and Learning (ZiLL); Central Institute of Healthcare Engineering (ZiMT); Centre for Applied Ethics and Science Communication (ZIEW); Centre for Area Studies; Centre for Scientific Computing (ZISC); Centre for Teacher Education (ZfL); Cluster of Excellence 'Engineering of Advanced Materials' (EAM); Embedded Systems Institute (ESI); Emil Fischer Centre; Emmy Noether Centre for Algebra with a special focus on Representation Theory; Erlangen Catalysis Resource Centre (ECRC); Erlangen Centre for Infection Research (ECI); Erlangen Graduate School in Advanced Optical Technologies; Erlangen-Center of Plant Science (ERCOPS); FAU Graduate School; Institute of Advanced Materials and Processes (ZMP); Interdisciplinary Centre for Aesthetic Education (IZÄB); Interdisciplinary Centre for Clinical Research (IZKF); Interdisciplinary Centre for Contemporary Literature and Culture (IZG); Interdisciplinary Centre for Dialect Studies and Language Variation (IZD); Interdisciplinary Centre for Digital Humanities and Social Sciences (IZ Digital); Interdisciplinary Centre for Edition Philology; Interdisciplinary Centre for European Medieval and Renaissance Studies (IZEMIR); Interdisciplinary Centre for Gerontology (ICA); Interdisciplinary Centre for Islamic Religious Studies (IZIR); Interdisciplinary Centre for Lexicography, Valency and Collocation (IZLVK); Interdisciplinary Centre for Media Studies (IMZ); Interdisciplinary Centre for Molecular Materials (ICMM); Interdisciplinary Centre for Public Health (IZPH); Interdisciplinary Centre for the Study of the Ancient World; Interdisciplinary Centre of Interface-controlled Processes (IZICP); Interdisciplinary Centre of Neuroscience (IZN); Interdisciplinary Centre of Ophthalmic Preventive Medicine and Imaging (IZPI); Labour and Socio-Economic Research Centre (LASER); Medical Immunology Campus Erlangen (MICE)

Campus Abroad

FAU Campus Busan

History: Founded 1743, a research university with an international perspective.

Academic Year: October to September (October-March; April-September)

Admission Requirements: Secondary school certificate (Reifezeugnis) or equivalent

Fees: none

Main Language(s) of Instruction: German

Degrees and Diplomas: *Bachelor's Degree*: **Arts and Humanities; Business Administration; Education; Engineering; Fine Arts; Health Sciences; Information Sciences; Law; Mathematics and Computer Science; Natural Sciences; Performing Arts; Social Sciences; Technology.** *Kirchliche Abschlussprüfung*: **Religion.** *Diplom (Univ)*: **Pharmacy.** *Master*: **Arts and Humanities; Business Administration; Education; Engineering; Health Sciences; Information Sciences; Law; Mathematics and Computer Science; Natural Sciences; Social Sciences; Technology.** Also Teacher Training Diplom (Lehramt) in Primary Education and Secondary Education; Staatsexam in European Union Law, Law, Applied Chemistry, Medicine, Pharmacy and Dentistry.

Student Services: Academic Counselling, Canteen, Careers Guidance, Cultural Activities, Facilities for disabled people, Foreign Studies Centre, Health Services, IT Centre, Language Laboratory, Library, Nursery Care, Residential Facilities, Social Counselling, Sports Facilities, eLibrary

Publications: alexander - Aktuelles aus der FAU; Atzelsberger Gespräche; Ausgezeichnete Abschlussarbeiten der Erlanger Geisteswissenschaft; Erlangen Universitätsreden; Erlanger Universitätstage; FAU Forschungen, Reihe A, Geisteswissenschaften; FAU Forschungen, Reihe B, Medizin, Naturwissenschaft, Technik; FAU Kunst und Bildung; FAU Studien aus der Philosophischen Fakultät; FAU Studien Materialwissenschaft und Werkstofftechnik; FAU Studies Mathematics & Physics; Forschungsbericht; friedrich - Forschungsmagazin der FAU; frisch! an der FAU - Informationen zum Studienstart; Jahrbuch der Fränkischen Landesforschung; Kleine Schriften zu Kultur und Geschichte der Friedrich-Alexander-Universität; Münzkataloge; Schriften der Universitätsbibliothek Erlangen-Nürnberg

Academic Staff *2013-2014*	MEN	WOMEN	TOTAL
FULL-TIME	2,803	1,311	**4,114**
PART-TIME	1,260	1,674	**2,934**
STAFF WITH DOCTORATE			
FULL-TIME	1,034	362	**1,396**
Student Numbers *2014-2015*			
All (Foreign included)	19,943	19,685	**39,628**
FOREIGN ONLY	1,701	2,045	**3,746**

Part-time students, 260.

Last Updated: 29/01/15

FRIEDRICH SCHILLER UNIVERSITY JENA

Friedrich-Schiller-Universität Jena

Fürstengraben 1, 07743 Jena
Tel: +49(3641) 93-00
Fax: +49(3641) 93-1682
Website: http://www.uni-jena.de

President: Walter Rosenthal
Tel: +49(3641) 93-1000
EMail: walter.rosenthal@uni-jena.de; praesident@uni-jena.de

Kanzler: Klaus Bartholmé
Tel: +49(3641) 93-1050 EMail: kanzler@uni-jena.de

International Relations: Claudia Hillinger, Head, International Office
EMail: claudia.hillinger@uni-jena.de; international@uni-jena.de

Faculty

Biology and Pharmacy (Biology; Pharmacy); **Chemistry and Earth Sciences** (Chemistry; Earth Sciences; Geography; Geology; Geophysics; Mineralogy); **Economics** (Business Administration; Economics); **Law** (Law); **Mathematics and Computer Science** (Computer Science; Mathematics); **Medicine** (Dentistry; Medicine); **Philosophy** (Archaeology; Art History; Classical Languages; History; Linguistics; Literature; Modern Languages; Musicology; Philosophy); **Physics and Astronomy** (Astronomy and Space Science; Physics); **Social and Behavioural Sciences** (Behavioural Sciences; Educational Sciences; Political Sciences; Psychology; Social Sciences; Sociology; Sports); **Theology** (Protestant Theology)

History: Founded 1548 as academy by Kurfürst Johann Friedrich von Sachsen, became University 1558. Recognized after German unification, the University is under the jurisdiction of the Thuringian Ministry of Science and Arts.

Academic Year: October to September (October-March; April-September)

Admission Requirements: Secondary school certificate (Reifezeugnis) or equivalent

Fees: None

Main Language(s) of Instruction: German

Accrediting Agency: Ministry of Science, Research and Arts, State of Thuringia

Degrees and Diplomas: *Bachelor's Degree*; *Kirchliche Abschlussprüfung*: **Protestant Theology.** *Magister*: **Law; Theology.** *Diplom (Univ)*: **Pharmacy; Protestant Theology.** *Master*: **American Studies; Ancient Civilizations; Anthropology; Applied Chemistry; Arabic; Archaeology; Art History; Arts and Humanities; Biochemistry; Business Administration; Business Computing; Business Education; Chemistry; Christian Religious Studies; Communication Studies; Computer Science; Contemporary History; Cultural Studies; Earth Sciences; Ecology; Economics; Education; English; Ethics; European Studies; Film; Folklore; Foreign Languages Education; Geography; Geology; German; Greek (Classical); History; Human Resources; Latin; Linguistics; Literature; Mass Communication; Materials Engineering; Mathematics; Medicine; Medieval Studies; Microbiology; Middle Eastern Studies; Modern History; Molecular Biology; Natural Sciences; Philosophy; Physics; Polish; Political Sciences; Prehistory; Private Law; Psychology; Public Law; Social Work; Sociology; Sports; Sports Management; Surveying and Mapping; Western European Studies.** *PhD*: **Astronomy and Space Science; Behavioural Sciences; Biology; Business Administration; Chemistry; Cultural Studies; Dentistry; Economics; Education; Geology; Law; Mathematics and Computer Science; Medicine; Pharmacy; Philosophy; Physics; Social Sciences; Theology.** *Habilitation*: **Astronomy and Space Science; Behavioural Sciences; Biology; Business Administration; Chemistry; Economics; Geology; Law; Medicine; Pharmacy; Philosophy; Physics; Social Sciences; Theology.** Also Staatsexam in Psychotherapy, Behavioral Sciences, Pharmacy, Medicine, Dentistry; Secondary School Teacher Training state examination in Science Education, Humanities and Social Sciences Education, Religious Education, Computer Education, Art Education, Music Education, Mathematics Education, Physical Education.

Student Services: Canteen, Cultural Activities, IT Centre, Library, Social Counselling, Sports Facilities

Publications: Bibliographische Mitteilungen der Universitätsbibliothek, Jena; Forschungsmagazin; Jenaer Reden und Schriften; Jenaer Universitätsreden

Publishing House: Uni-Journal

Academic Staff *2014-2015*	TOTAL
FULL-TIME	**2,413**
Student Numbers *2013-2014*	
All (Foreign included)	**19,000**
FOREIGN ONLY	**2218**

Last Updated: 04/03/15

FULDA UNIVERSITY OF APPLIED SCIENCES

Hochschule Fulda

Leipziger Straße 123, 36037 Fulda
Tel: +49(661) 9640-0
Fax: +49(661) 9640-199
EMail: info@verw.hs-fulda.de
Website: http://www.fh-fulda.de

President: Karim Khakzar
Tel: +49(661) 9640-111 EMail: praesident@hs-fulda.de

Chancellor: Ralf Alberding
Tel: +49(661) 9640-115 EMail: kanzler@hs-fulda.de

International Relations: Winnie Rosatis, Head, International Office
Tel: +49(661) 9640-147 EMail: rosatis@hs-fulda.de

Faculty

Applied Computer Science (Business Computing; Computer Science); **Business Administration** (Business Administration; Management); **Electrical Engineering and Information Technology** (Electrical Engineering; Information Technology); **Food**

Technology (Food Technology); **Nursing and Health Sciences** (Health Administration; Nursing; Physical Therapy); **Nutritional, Food and Consumer Sciences** (Food Science; Food Technology; Nutrition); **Social and Cultural Sciences** (Cultural Studies; European Studies; International Relations; Social Sciences; Social Studies); **Social Work** (Social Work)

History: Founded 1974 as Fachhochschule Fulda. Acquired present title 2006.

Admission Requirements: General higher education entrance qualification (HEEQ)

Fees: 120 per semester; Master, 500 (Euro)

Main Language(s) of Instruction: German

Degrees and Diplomas: *Bachelor's Degree*: **Business Administration; Business Computing; Computer Science; Cooking and Catering; Cultural Studies; Dietetics; Electrical Engineering; Engineering; Food Technology; Health Administration; Health Sciences; Information Technology; International Business; Labour Law; Management; Media Studies; Midwifery; Nursing; Nutrition; Physical Therapy; Preschool Education; Social Sciences; Social Welfare; Social Work; Transport Management.** *Master*: **Communication Studies; Computer Science; Consumer Studies; Cultural Studies; Design; European Studies; Food Technology; Health Education; Industrial Management; International Business; Labour Law; Management; Nutrition; Psychology; Public Health; Social Work.** Also Distance Learning Bachelor in Social Work, 4 yrs; Distance Learning Master; 21/2 yrs

Student Services: Academic Counselling, Canteen, Facilities for disabled people, Foreign Studies Centre, IT Centre, Language Laboratory, Library, Residential Facilities, Social Counselling, Sports Facilities

Publications: Thema

Student Numbers *2013-2014*: Total 7,168
Last Updated: 05/03/15

FURTWANGEN UNIVERSITY

Hochschule Furtwangen - Informatik, Technik, Wirtschaft, Medien (HFU)

Robert-Gerwig-Platz 1, 78120 Furtwangen
Tel: +49(7723) 920-0
Fax: +49(7723) 920-1109
EMail: info@hs-furtwangen.de
Website: http://www.hs-furtwangen.de

Rector: Rolf Schofer
Tel: +49(7723) 920-1110 EMail: rk@hs-furtwangen.de

Chancellor: Birgit Rimpo-Repp
Tel: +49(7723) 920-2282 EMail: kanzlerin@hs-furtwangen.de

International Relations: Brigitte Minderlein, Head, International Office
Tel: +49(7723) 920-1310
EMail: international@hs-furtwangen.de; min@hs-furtwangen.de

Faculty

Health, Safety, Society (Health Sciences; Safety Engineering); **Medical and Life Sciences** (Bioengineering; Biotechnology; Medical Technology; Molecular Biology)

School

Business (Business Administration; Engineering; Health Administration; International Business; Management)

Department

Business Administration and Engineering (Business Administration; International Business; Management; Marketing; Production Engineering; Sales Techniques); **Business Computing** (Business Administration; Business Computing; E- Business/Commerce); **Computer Science** (Computer Engineering; Computer Science; Electrical Engineering; Safety Engineering; Software Engineering); **Digital Media** (Computer Science; Media Studies); **Industrial Technologies** (Industrial Engineering); **Mechanical and Medical Engineering** (Bioengineering; Biomedical Engineering; Biotechnology; Machine Building; Mechanical Engineering; Medical Technology; Production Engineering)

Further Information: Also campuses in Villingen-Schwenningen and Tuttlingen

History: Founded 1971. Formerly known as Fachhochschule Furtwangen - Hochschule für Technik und Wirtschaft.

Admission Requirements: Secondary school certificate (Fachhochschulreife)

Fees: None for undergaduate courses

Main Language(s) of Instruction: German

Degrees and Diplomas: *Bachelor's Degree*; *Master*. **Bioengineering; Biomedical Engineering; Business Administration; Business Computing; Computer Engineering; Computer Science; Data Processing; Design; Electronic Engineering; Health Administration; Industrial Engineering; Information Technology; International Business; Management; Measurement and Precision Engineering; Media Studies; Medical Technology; Safety Engineering; Sales Techniques.** Cooperatives HFU-doctoral programmes; Some Programmes offered in English

Student Services: Academic Counselling, Canteen, Language Laboratory, Library, Social Counselling

Academic Staff *2014-2015*: Total: c. 450
Student Numbers *2014-2015*: Total 6,409
Last Updated: 11/03/15

GEORG AUGUST UNIVERSITY GÖTTINGEN

Georg-August-Universität Göttingen

Postfach 3744, Gosslerstr. 5-7, 37027 Göttingen
Tel: +49(551) 39-0
Fax: +49(551) 39-9612
EMail: poststelle@uni-goettingen.de
Website: http://www.uni-goettingen.de

President: Ulrike Beisiegel (2011-)
Tel: +49(551) 39-4311 EMail: praesidentin@uni-goettingen.de

Vice President, Academic Affairs: Ruth Florack
Tel: +49(551) 39-12185 EMail: ruth.florack@zvw.uni-goettingen.de

International Relations: Hiltraud Casper-Hehne, Vice-President, International Affairs
Tel: +49(551) 39-12184
EMail: hiltraud.casper-hehne@zvw.uni-goettingen.de

International Relations: Uwe Muuss, Head, International Office
Tel: +49(551) 39-21343
EMail: uwe.muuss@zvw.uni-goettingen.de; international@uni-goettingen.de

Faculty

Agricultural Sciences (Agriculture); **Biology and Pschology** (Biology; Psychology); **Chemistry** (Chemistry); **Economic Sciences** (Accountancy; Business Administration; Economics; Finance; Human Resources; Management; Marketing; Taxation); **Forest Sciences and Forest Ecology** (Ecology; Forestry); **Geoscience and Geography** (Environmental Management; Geography; Geology); **Humanities** (Ancient Civilizations; Arabic; Archaeology; Art History; Arts and Humanities; Classical Languages; East Asian Studies; Finnish; History; Musicology; Philology; Philosophy; Romance Languages; Scandinavian Languages; Slavic Languages); **Law** (Law); **Mathematics and Computer Science** (Mathematics); **Physics** (Physics); **Social Sciences** (Ethnology; Gender Studies; Indic Languages; Political Sciences; Social Sciences; Sociology); **Theology** (Bible; Ethics; Jewish Studies; New Testament; Religious Studies; Theology)

Centre

Medicine (Dentistry; Medicine)

History: Founded 1737 by George II, Prince Elector of Hanover and King of England, the first modern University founded in Germany. Measures to guarantee quality and to promote excellence in research and teaching, reforms to strengthen autonomy and responsibility at all levels of the University, and the internationalization of the University have been implemented within the past few years. 2003, the University of Göttingen was the first full university in Germany to be converted into a publicly endowed university.

Academic Year: April to March (April-September; October-March)

Admission Requirements: Secondary school certificate (Reifezeugnis) or equivalent

Fees: 165.70 per semester (Euro)

Main Language(s) of Instruction: German, English

Accrediting Agency: Zentrale Evaluations und Akkreditierungsagentur (ZevA)

Degrees and Diplomas: *Bachelor's Degree*; *Kirchliche Abschlussprüfung*: **Protestant Theology.** *Magister*: **Protestant Theology; Theology.** *Diplom (Univ)*: **Protestant Theology.** *Master*: **Accountancy; Agriculture; American Studies; Ancient Civilizations; Animal Husbandry; Anthropology; Arabic; Archaeology; Art History; Biochemistry; Biology; Business Administration; Business Computing; Cardiology; Central European Studies; Chemistry; Comparative Literature; Computer Education; Computer Science; Earth Sciences; East Asian Studies; Ecology; Economics; Education; Educational Research; Educational Sciences; English; Environmental Management; Ethnology; European Studies; European Union Law; Finance; Finnish; Foreign Languages Education; Forestry; French; French Studies; Gender Studies; Geography; Geology; German; Germanic Studies; Greek (Classical); Hispanic American Studies; History; Human Resources; Humanities and Social Science Education; Information Technology; International Economics; International Studies; Islamic Studies; Italian; Latin; Law; Linguistics; Management; Marketing; Materials Engineering; Mathematics; Mathematics Education; Medicine; Medieval Studies; Microbiology; Modern History; Molecular Biology; Musicology; Native Language Education; Neurosciences; Pedagogy; Persian; Philosophy; Physical Education; Physics; Political Sciences; Portuguese; Prehistory; Psychology; Religious Education; Religious Studies; Romance Languages; Scandinavian Languages; Science Education; Slavic Languages; Sociology; South Asian Studies; Spanish; Sports; Statistics; Taxation; Theology; Tropical Agriculture; Turkish.** *PhD*: **Agriculture; Behavioural Sciences; Biochemistry; Biological and Life Sciences; Biology; Cell Biology; Chemistry; Cognitive Sciences; Earth Sciences; Ecology; Economics; Forest Biology; Forestry; Genetics; Geography; Mathematics; Medicine; Microbiology; Molecular Biology; Neurosciences; Social Sciences; Theology; Wood Technology.** *Habilitation*: **Agriculture; Biological and Life Sciences; Chemistry; Earth Sciences; Economics; Forestry; Geography; Law; Mathematics and Computer Science; Medicine; Philosophy; Physics; Social Sciences; Theology.** Also Also Certificate in Psychotherapie; Dual Bachelor's degree programmes; Teacher Training Diplom (Lehramt) and Bachelor's degree programmes with Teacher Training option (Lehramt); Staatsexam in Dentistry, Medicine, Law.

Student Services: Academic Counselling, Canteen, Careers Guidance, Cultural Activities, Facilities for disabled people, Health Services, IT Centre, Language Laboratory, Library, Social Counselling, Sports Facilities

Publications: Georgia Augusta Wissenschaftmagazin der Georg-August-Universität Göttingen

Academic Staff *2013-2014*: Total 4,365
Student Numbers *2014-2015*: Total 27,556
Last Updated: 30/01/15

GEORG-SIMON-OHM UNIVERSITY OF APPLIED SCIENCES NUREMBERG

Technische Hochschule Nürnberg Georg Simon Ohm (GSO-FHN)

Kesslerplatz 12, 90121 Nürnberg
Tel: +49(911) 5880-0
Fax: +49(911) 5880-8309
EMail: info@th-nuernberg.de
Website: http://www.fh-nuernberg.de

President: Michael Braun (2006-)
Tel: +49(911) 5880-4226
EMail: marion.ewald@th-nuernberg.de; monika.hegner@th-nuernberg.de

Kanzler: Achim Hoffmann
Tel: +49(911) 5880-4241 EMail: kanzler@th-nuernberg.de

International Relations: Nikolaus Hackl, Head of International Office
Tel: +49(911) 5880-4298
EMail: International.Office@th-nuernberg.de; nikolaus.hackl@th-nuernberg.de

Department

Applied Chemistry (Applied Chemistry); **Applied Mathematics, Physics and Humanities** (Applied Mathematics; Journalism; Physics); **Architecture** (Architecture); **Business Administration** (Business Administration); **Civil Engineering** (Civil Engineering); **Computer Science** (Business Computing; Computer Science); **Design** (Design); **Electrical Engineering, Precision Engineering and Information Technology** (Electrical Engineering; Information Technology); **Materials Engineering** (Materials Engineering); **Mechanical Engineering and Building Services Engineering** (Engineering; Mechanical Engineering); **Process Engineering** (Engineering Management); **Social Sciences** (Continuing Education; Social Work)

History: Founded 1823. Acquired present status 1971.

Academic Year: October to September

Admission Requirements: German Abitur or equivalent (plus language test for foreign students), pre-practicals

Main Language(s) of Instruction: German, English

Accrediting Agency: ACQUIN (Accreditation, Certification and Quality Assurance Institute); European Association for Quality Assurance in Higher Education (ENQA).

Degrees and Diplomas: *Bachelor's Degree*: **Applied Chemistry; Applied Mathematics; Applied Physics; Architecture; Business Administration; Business Computing; Civil Engineering; Computer Engineering; Computer Science; Construction Engineering; Design; Electrical Engineering; Electronic Engineering; Energy Engineering; International Business; Journalism; Materials Engineering; Measurement and Precision Engineering; Mechanical Engineering; Media Studies; Medicine; Production Engineering; Public Relations; Social Work.** *Master*: **Applied Chemistry; Architecture; Business Administration; Business Computing; Chemical Engineering; Commercial Law; Computer Science; Construction Engineering; Electronic Engineering; Energy Engineering; Engineering; Finance; International Business; International Economics; Marketing; Materials Engineering; Mechanical Engineering; Production Engineering; Social Work; Taxation; Transport Engineering.** Bachelor's degree and Master's degree programmes in International Business are conducted in English.

Student Services: Academic Counselling, Canteen, Careers Guidance, Facilities for disabled people, Foreign Studies Centre, Language Laboratory, Library, Nursery Care, Social Counselling, Sports Facilities

Publications: Schriftenreihe

Student Numbers *2014-2015*: Total 13,027
Last Updated: 29/01/15

GERMAN SPORT UNIVERSITY COLOGNE

Deutsche Sporthochschule Köln (DSHS-KOELN)

Am Sportpark Müngersdorf 6, NRW 50933 Köln, Nordrhein-Westfalen
Tel: +49(221) 4982-0
Fax: +49(221) 4982-8330
EMail: info@dshs-koeln.de
Website: http://www.dshs-koeln.de

Rektor: Heiko Strüder (2014-)
Tel: +49(221) 4982-2000 EMail: Strüder@dshs-koeln.de

Chancellor: Angelika Classen
Tel: +49(221) 4982-3000 EMail: Classen@dshs-koeln.de

International Relations: Werner Sonnenschein
Tel: +49(221) 4982-2160 EMail: auslandsamt@dshs-koeln.de

Faculty

Applied Movement Sciences (Pedagogy; Sports); **Education, Humanities and Social Sciences** (Arts and Humanities; Education; Social Sciences); **Medicine and Natural Sciences** (Medicine; Natural Sciences)

Division

Basketball and Handball (Sports)

Institute
Biochemistry (Biochemistry); **Biomechanics and Orthopedics** (Biotechnology; Orthopaedics); **Cardiology and Sports Medicine** (Cardiology; Sports Medicine); **Coaching Science and Sport Informatics** (Sports); **Communication and Media Research** (Communication Studies; Media Studies; Sports); **Dance and Movement Culture** (Dance); **Environmental Sport and Ecology** (Ecology; Sports); **European Sport Development and Leisure Studies** (Leisure Studies); **Motor Control and Movement Techniques** (Sports); **Movement and Sport Gerontology** (Gerontology; Sports); **Movement Science in Sport Games** (Sports); **Pedagogy and Philosophy** (Pedagogy; Philosophy); **Physiology and Anatomy** (Anatomy; Physiology); **Psychology** (Psychology); **Rehabilitation and Sports for the Disabled** (Rehabilitation and Therapy); **School Sport and School Development** (Pedagogy; Sports); **Sport Economy and Management** (Economics; Sports Management); **Sport History** (Sports); **Sport Sociology** (Sports)

Chair
Professorship of Music and Dance Education (Art Education; Dance; Music; Music Education)

History: Founded 1947 and tracing its origins to the former Berliner Hochschule für Leibesübungen, founded 1920. Acquired University status 1970. Under the jurisdiction of and financially supported by the State of North Rhine-Westphalia.

Academic Year: April to March (April-September; October-March)

Admission Requirements: Secondary school certificate (Abitur) and Physical Aptitude Test. German Language Proficiency Certificate (DSH level 2 or TESTDAF level 4)

Main Language(s) of Instruction: German

Degrees and Diplomas: *Bachelor's Degree*: **Journalism; Rehabilitation and Therapy; Sports; Sports Management.** *Master*: **Dance; Gerontology; Mass Communication; Medical Technology; Parks and Recreation; Physical Therapy; Rehabilitation and Therapy; Sports; Sports Management; Tourism.** *PhD*: **Natural Sciences; Social Sciences; Sports.** Master's degrees in Sports Management and MedicalTechnology are taught in English

Student Services: Academic Counselling, Canteen, Facilities for disabled people, Foreign Studies Centre, Health Services, Language Laboratory, Sports Facilities

Publications: F.I.T. - Das Wissenschaftsmagazin der DSHS Köln

Student Numbers *2014-2015*: Total: c. 5,300
Last Updated: 16/01/15

GERMAN UNIVERSITY OF ADMINISTRATIVE SCIENCES, SPEYER

Deutsche Hochschule für Verwaltungswissenschaften
Freiherr-vom-Stein-Strasse 2, Post Box 1409, 67346 Speyer
Tel: +49(6232) 654-0
Fax: +49(6232) 654-208
EMail: info@uni-speyer.de
Website: http://www.uni-speyer.de/

Rektor: Joachim Wieland
Tel: +49(6232) 654-212 EMail: rektor@uni-speyer.de

International Relations: Kirstin Reinke
Tel: +49(6232) 654-253 EMail: reinke@uni-speyer.de

Programme
Administrative Sciences (Administration); **Administrative Sciences Postgraduate Studies** (Administration); **E-learning** (Administrative Law; Media Studies; Public Law); **European Governance and Administration (MEGA)** (Administration; Government); **European Masters of Public Administration** (Public Administration); **Foreign-Graduate studies** (Administration); **Knowledge Management** (Management); **Law, State and Government in Europe** (Administration; Law); **Public Economics** (Economics)

Further Information: Also International Studies Programme and Continuing education programme in Knowledge Management

History: Founded 1947 as Staatliche Akademie, acquired present status and title 1997.

Academic Year: October to September

Admission Requirements: Staatsexamen, Diplom, or Magister Artium (corresponding to University degree of Master in Law, Economics, Political or Social Sciences). Certified knowledge of the German language (PNDS or DSH of a German University or Zentrale Mittelstufenprüfung (ZMP) of the Goethe Institute)

Fees: None

Main Language(s) of Instruction: German

Degrees and Diplomas: *Master*: **Administration; Economics; Law; Public Administration.** *PhD*: **Administration; Economics; Law.** *Habilitation*: **Public Administration.**

Student Services: Academic Counselling, Canteen, Facilities for disabled people, Foreign Studies Centre, Language Laboratory, Social Counselling, Sports Facilities

Publications: Schriftenreihe der Hochschule Speyer; Speyer Forschungsberichte; Speyerer Arbeitshefte

Student Numbers *2013-2014*: Total 382
Last Updated: 02/03/15

GOETHE UNIVERSITY FRANKFURT AM MAIN

Goethe-Universität Frankfurt am Main (GU)
Theodor-W.-Adorno-Platz 1, 60629 Frankfurt am Main
Tel: +49(69) 798-0
Fax: +49(69) 798-18383
EMail: international@uni-frankfurt.de
Website: http://www.uni-frankfurt.de

President: Birgitta Wolff
Tel: +49(69) 798-11101 EMail: praesidentin@uni-frankfurt.de

Chancellor: Holger Gottschalk
Tel: +49(69) 798-12240 EMail: kanzler@uni-frankfurt.de

International Relations: Martin Bickl, Head, International Office
Tel: +49(69) 798-13729
EMail: Bickl@em.uni-frankfurt.de; international@uni-frankfurt.de

Faculty
Biochemistry, Chemistry and Pharmacy (Biochemistry; Chemistry; Food Technology; Inorganic Chemistry; Organic Chemistry; Pharmacy; Physical Chemistry); **Biological Sciences** (Apiculture; Biology; Botany; Computer Science; Genetics; Microbiology; Zoology); **Computer Sciences and Mathematics** (Mathematics and Computer Science); **Economics and Business Administration** (Accountancy; Business Administration; Development Studies; Economics; Finance; Marketing; Statistics); **Educational Sciences** (Adult Education; Educational Sciences; International and Comparative Education; Primary Education; Special Education); **Geosciencs and Geography** (Earth Sciences; Economics; Geochemistry; Geography; Geography (Human); Geology; Geophysics; Meteorology; Mineralogy; Petrology); **Law** (Commercial Law; Criminal Law; History of Law; International Law; Labour Law; Law; Public Law); **Linguistics, Culture and Arts** (African Languages; Anthropology; Archaeology; Art Education; Art History; Chinese; Classical Languages; Cultural Studies; Ethnology; Fine Arts; Japanese; Latin; Music; Music Education; Oriental Languages; Philology; Phonetics; Slavic Languages; South and Southeast Asian Languages); **Medical Science** (Dentistry; Medicine); **Modern Languages** (English; French; German; Italian; Modern History; Philology; Portuguese; Scandinavian Languages; Spanish; Theatre); **Philosophy and History** (History; Philosophy); **Physics** (Applied Physics; Biophysics; History; Nuclear Physics; Physics); **Protestant Theology** (Protestant Theology); **Psychology and Sports Sciences** (Educational Psychology; Labour and Industrial Relations; Physical Education; Psychoanalysis; Psychology; Sports); **Roman Catholic Theology** (Catholic Theology); **Social Sciences** (Political Sciences; Social Sciences; Sociology)

Further Information: Also German language courses for advanced students

History: Founded 1914 by public subscription and with the support of the City of Frankfurt. As a result of the Krach in the 1920s the University lost most of its capital. Financial responsibility accepted by the Prussian State and City of Frankfurt 1923. Title of Johann Wolfgang Goethe adopted 1932. An autonomous institution financed by the State of Hesse.

Academic Year: October to September (October-March; April-September)

Admission Requirements: Secondary school certificate (Reifezeugnis) or equivalent

Fees: None for basic study programmes

Main Language(s) of Instruction: German

Accrediting Agency: ZEVA

Degrees and Diplomas: *Bachelor's Degree*: **Anthropology; Archaeology; Art Education; Art History; Biochemistry; Biological and Life Sciences; Biology; Biophysics; Business Administration; Business Education; Catholic Theology; Chemistry; Chinese; Computer Science; Cultural Studies; Earth Sciences; Economics; Education; English; English Studies; Ethnology; Film; Fine Arts; French; Geography; German; Germanic Studies; Greek (Classical); History; Islamic Studies; Italian; Japanese; Jewish Studies; Latin; Law; Linguistics; Mathematics; Media Studies; Medicine; Meteorology; Musicology; Pharmacy; Philology; Philosophy; Physics; Political Sciences; Protestant Theology; Psychology; Religion; Romance Languages; Scandinavian Languages; Sociology; South and Southeast Asian Languages; Southeast Asian Studies; Spanish; Sports; Teacher Training; Theatre; Theology.** *Kirchliche Abschlussprüfung*: **Religion.** *Magister*: **Theology.** *Master*: **African Studies; American Studies; Anthropology; Archiving; Art History; Biochemistry; Biophysics; Biotechnology; Business Administration; Business Computing; Business Education; Cell Biology; Chemistry; Chinese; Comparative Literature; Comparative Religion; Computer Science; Earth Sciences; East Asian Studies; Ecology; Economic and Finance Policy; Economics; Educational Sciences; Environmental Studies; Ethnology; Film; Finance; Geography; Geography (Human); History; International Economics; International Studies; Islamic Studies; Islamic Theology; Jewish Studies; Linguistics; Literature; Management; Marketing; Mathematics; Media Studies; Medicine; Meteorology; Molecular Biology; Neurosciences; Peace and Disarmament; Performing Arts; Philosophy; Physics; Physiology; Political Sciences; Psychology; Religious Studies; Romance Languages; Scandinavian Languages; Social Sciences; Sociology; Southeast Asian Studies; Sports Medicine; Theatre.** *PhD*: **Biochemistry; Biology; Business Administration; Catholic Theology; Chemistry; Computer Science; Cultural Studies; Dentistry; Earth Sciences; Economics; Educational Sciences; Geography; History; Law; Mathematics; Medicine; Modern Languages; Pharmacy; Philosophy; Physics; Protestant Theology; Psychology; Sociology; Sports.** *Habilitation*: **Business Administration; Cultural Studies; History; Modern Languages; Philosophy; Protestant Theology; Sociology.** Staatsexam in Law, Medicine, Dentistry, Pharmacy; Teacher Training Examination (Lehramt)

Student Services: Academic Counselling, Canteen, Careers Guidance, Cultural Activities, Facilities for disabled people, Health Services, Language Laboratory, Nursery Care, Social Counselling, Sports Facilities

Publications: Forschungsbericht; Jahresbibliographie; Rechenschaftsbericht; Vorlesungsverzeichnis

Student Numbers *2013-2014*: Total: c. 45,000
Last Updated: 10/03/15

GOTTFRIED WILHELM LEIBNIZ UNIVERSITY OF HANOVER

Gottfried Wilhelm Leibniz Universität Hannover
Postfach 6009, Welfengarten 1, 30060 Hannover
Tel: +49(511) 762-0
Fax: +49(511) 762-3456
EMail: kommunikation@uni-hannover.de
Website: http://www.uni-hannover.de

President: Volker Epping (2015-)
Tel: +49(511) 762-5110 EMail: praesident@uni-hannover.de

Vice President for Academic Affairs: Elfriede Billmann-Mahecha
Tel: +49(511) 762-5110 EMail: vpl@uni-hannover.de

International Relations: Birgit Barden, Head, International Office
Tel: +49(511) 762-2548
EMail: birgit.barden@zuv.uni-hannover.de; internationaloffice@uni-hannover.de

International Relations: Monika Sester, Vice Provost for International Affairs Tel: +49(511) 762-3588 EMail: vpi@uni-hannover.de

Faculty

Architecture and Landscape Sciences (Architectural and Environmental Design; Architecture; Architecture and Planning; Biology; Chemistry; Geology; Horticulture; Plant and Crop Protection); **Civil Engineering and Geodetic Science** (Civil Engineering; Surveying and Mapping); **Economics and Management** (Business Administration; Economics; Management); **Electrical Engineering and Computer Science** (Computer Science; Electrical Engineering; Electronic Engineering; Information Technology); **Humanities** (Adult Education; American Studies; Educational Sciences; English Studies; French Studies; Germanic Studies; History; Italian; Linguistics; Literature; Philosophy; Political Sciences; Psychology; Religious Education; Religious Studies; Social Sciences; Sociology; Special Education; Teacher Training; Theology; Vocational Education); **Law** (European Union Law; Law); **Mathematics and Physics** (Mathematics; Mathematics and Computer Science; Physics); **Mechanical Engineering** (Electronic Engineering; Mechanical Engineering; Metal Techniques; Production Engineering; Transport Management); **Natural Sciences** (Biology; Chemistry; Geography; Geology; Horticulture; Surveying and Mapping)

Laboratory

Nano and Quantum Engineering

Research Centre

Biomolecular Drug; **Garden Art and Landscape Architecture**; **L3S**; **Mechatronics**; **Optical Technologies**; **Solid State Chemistry and New Materials**

Research School

QUEST Leibniz (Geology; Mathematics; Mathematics and Computer Science; Meteorology; Nanotechnology; Optical Technology; Physics; Surveying and Mapping)

Further Information: Also Collaborative Research Centres

History: Founded 1831 as Höhere Gewerbeschule (secondary vocational school), became "Königliche Technische Hochschule" 1879. Reorganized 1921 and became "Technische Universität" 1968 and "Universität" 1978. Acquired present title 2006. An autonomous institution under the jurisdiction of and financed by the State of Lower Saxony.

Academic Year: October to September (October-March; April-September)

Admission Requirements: Secondary school certificate (Reifezeugnis) or foreign equivalent

Fees: None for regular students. Fees for Continuing Education

Main Language(s) of Instruction: German, English

Degrees and Diplomas: *Bachelor's Degree*: **Applied Linguistics; Architectural and Environmental Design; Architecture; Biochemistry; Biological and Life Sciences; Biology; Biotechnology; Catholic Theology; Chemistry; Civil Engineering; Computer Engineering; Computer Science; Development Studies; Earth Sciences; Economics; Education; Electrical Engineering; Electronic Engineering; Engineering; English; English Studies; Environmental Engineering; Ethics; Fine Arts; Food Science; Forest Products; Geography; Geology; German; Germanic Studies; History; Horticulture; Industrial Engineering; Information Technology; Interior Design; Landscape Architecture; Law; Management; Mathematics; Mechanical Engineering; Metal Techniques; Meteorology; Music; Nanotechnology; Philosophy; Political Sciences; Power Engineering; Private Law; Production Engineering; Protestant Theology; Religion; Religious Studies; Social Sciences; Social Studies; Spanish; Special Education; Sports; Surveying and Mapping; Technology Education; Transport Management.** *Master*: **Agricultural Education; Analytical Chemistry; Applied Chemistry; Applied Linguistics; Architectural and Environmental Design; Architecture; Art Education; Biochemistry; Biological and Life Sciences; Biomedical Engineering; Biotechnology; Botany; Business Administration; Coastal Studies; Computer Engineering; Computer Science; Cultural Studies; Development Studies; Earth Sciences; Economics; Education; Educational Sciences; Electrical Engineering; Electronic Engineering; Energy Engineering; Engineering; English Studies; Environmental Engineering; Environmental**

Management; European Union Law; Food Science; Foreign Languages Education; Geography (Human); Geology; History; Horticulture; Humanities and Social Science Education; Industrial Engineering; Information Technology; Landscape Architecture; Literature; Management; Mathematics; Mathematics Education; Mechanical Engineering; Meteorology; Music Education; Nanotechnology; Native Language Education; Natural Sciences; Optical Technology; Philosophy; Physical Education; Political Sciences; Power Engineering; Private Law; Production Engineering; Regional Planning; Rehabilitation and Therapy; Religion; Religious Education; Robotics; Science Education; Social Studies; Special Education; Structural Architecture; Surveying and Mapping; Technology; Technology Education; Town Planning; Transport Management; Water Management. *PhD*: **Astronomy and Space Science; Biological and Life Sciences; Biomedicine; Development Studies; Earth Sciences; Environmental Engineering; Information Technology; International Studies; Laser Engineering; Mathematics; Mechanical Engineering; Nanotechnology; Natural Sciences; Operations Research; Optics; Physics; Physiology.** *Habilitation*: **Arts and Humanities; Civil Engineering; Computer Engineering; Economics; Electrical Engineering; Law; Management; Mathematics; Mechanical Engineering; Natural Sciences; Physics.** Also Postgraduate Course in Industrial Management, Structural Architecture; Staatsexam in Law; Certificatum Legum Europae in European Union Law.

Student Services: Academic Counselling, Careers Guidance, Cultural Activities, Facilities for disabled people, Health Services, Language Laboratory, Library, Nursery Care, Social Counselling, Sports Facilities

Publications: Research Report (Forschungsbericht)

Academic Staff *2014-2015*	MEN	WOMEN	TOTAL
FULL-TIME	–	–	**2,930**
STAFF WITH DOCTORATE			
FULL-TIME	–	–	c. **321**

Student Numbers *2014-2015*			
All (Foreign included)	15,200	10,500	c. **25,700**
FOREIGN ONLY	–	–	**2,100**

Last Updated: 30/01/15

HAFENCITY UNIVERSITY HAMBURG

HafenCity Universität Hamburg (HCU)

Überseeallee 16, 20457 Hamburg
Tel: +49(40) 42827-5355 +49(40) 42827-5065
Fax: +49(40) 42827-2728
EMail: info@hcu-hamburg.de
Website: http://www.hcu-hamburg.de

President: Walter Pelka (2010-) Tel: +49(40) 42827-2726

Chancellor: Stephanie Egerland-Rau Tel: +49(40) 42827-2732

International Relations: Christiane Brück, Head, International Office
Tel: +49(40) 42827-4306
EMail: christiane.brueck@hcu-hamburg.de

Department

Architecture (Architecture; Architecture and Planning; Structural Architecture); **Civil Engineering** (Civil Engineering); **Geomatics** (Geology; Surveying and Mapping); **Metropolitan Culture** (Urban Studies); **Town Planning** (Town Planning)

History: Founded 2006 as "HafenCity Universität Hamburg – Universität für Baukunst und Raumentwicklung" through unification of four Departments from three Colleges in Hamburg. Reorganised 2008.

Main Language(s) of Instruction: German

Degrees and Diplomas: *Bachelor's Degree*; *Master*: **Architecture; Architecture and Planning; Geology; Structural Architecture; Surveying and Mapping; Town Planning.** *PhD*: **Architecture and Planning; Civil Engineering; Geology; Surveying and Mapping; Town Planning.** *Habilitation*: **Architecture and Planning; Civil Engineering; Geology; Surveying and Mapping; Town Planning.**

Academic Staff *2013-2014*: Total 190

Student Numbers *2013-2014*: Total 2,432

Last Updated: 03/02/15

HAMBURG UNIVERSITY OF APPLIED SCIENCES

Hochschule für Angewandte Wissenschaften Hamburg (HAW Hamburg)

Berliner Tor 5, 20099 Hamburg
Tel: +49(40) 42875-0
Fax: +49(40) 42875-9149
EMail: info@haw-hamburg.de
Website: http://www.haw-hamburg.de

President: Jacqueline Otten
Tel: +49(40) 42875-9000
EMail: praesident@haw-hamburg.de; jacqueline.otten@haw-hamburg.de

Chancellor: Bernd Klöver
Tel: +49(40) 42875-9003
EMail: kanzler@haw-hamburg.de; Bernd.Kloever@hv.haw-hamburg.de

International Relations: Ralf Behrens, Head, International Office
Tel: +49(40) 42875-9180
EMail: international@haw-hamburg.de; ralf.behrens@haw-hamburg.de

Faculty

Business and Social Sciences (Business Administration; Economics; Health Administration; Nursing; Public Administration; Social Sciences; Social Work); **Design, Media and Information** (Design; Information Sciences; Information Technology; Media Studies); **Engineering and Computer Science** (Aeronautical and Aerospace Engineering; Automotive Engineering; Computer Science; Electrical Engineering; Mechanical Engineering; Production Engineering); **Life Sciences** (Biological and Life Sciences; Biomedical Engineering; Biotechnology; Environmental Engineering; Health Sciences; Home Economics; Industrial Engineering; Nutrition)

History: Founded 1970. Acquired present status 2001.

Fees: None, excepted for professional Master programmes: Master of Public Health (2,400 per semester; MBA in Social and Health Management, 1,180 per semester) (Euro)

Main Language(s) of Instruction: German

Degrees and Diplomas: *Bachelor's Degree*; *Master*: **Aeronautical and Aerospace Engineering; Automation and Control Engineering; Automotive Engineering; Biomedical Engineering; Biotechnology; Business Administration; Computer Engineering; Computer Science; Design; Energy Engineering; Environmental Engineering; Family Studies; Food Science; Health Administration; Health Sciences; Information Sciences; Information Technology; International Business; Journalism; Library Science; Marketing; Media Studies; Microelectronics; Multimedia; Production Engineering; Public Administration; Public Health; Social Work; Telecommunications Engineering; Transport Management.**

Student Services: Canteen, Careers Guidance, Library, Residential Facilities

Academic Staff *2014-2015*	TOTAL
FULL-TIME	c. **800**
Student Numbers *2014-2015*	
All (Foreign included)	c. **16,300**
FOREIGN ONLY	**2200**

Last Updated: 03/03/15

HAMBURG UNIVERSITY OF MUSIC AND THEATRE

Hochschule für Musik und Theater Hamburg (HFMT)

Harvestehuder Weg 12, 20148 Hamburg
Tel: +49(40) 428482-586
Fax: +49(40) 428482-666
EMail: info@hfmt.hamburg.de
Website: http://www.hfmt-hamburg.de

President: Elmar Lampson
Tel: +49(40) 428482-582 EMail: elmar.lampson@hfmt.hamburg.de

Chancellor: Jörg Maaß
Tel: +49(40) 428482-581 EMail: joerg.maass@hfmt.hamburg.de

International Relations: Catherine Strauer, International Coordinator
Tel: +49(40) 428482-415 EMail: International@hfmt.hamburg.de

Department

"Zwoelf" (Arts and Humanities; Music); **I - Artistic Courses of Study** (Conducting; Jazz and Popular Music; Music Theory and Composition; Musical Instruments; Religious Music); **II - Theatre Academy** (Opera; Singing; Theatre); **III - Scientific and Educational Courses of Study** (Art Management; Art Therapy; Cultural Studies; Management; Media Studies; Music Education; Musicology)

History: Founded 1950.

Main Language(s) of Instruction: German

Degrees and Diplomas: *Bachelor's Degree*; *Konzertexamen*: **Musical Instruments.** *Master*: **Art Therapy; Conducting; Jazz and Popular Music; Media Studies; Multimedia; Music; Music Education; Music Theory and Composition; Musical Instruments; Opera; Religious Music; Singing; Theatre.** *PhD*: **Art Management; Art Therapy; Music; Music Education; Music Theory and Composition; Musicology.** Also Certificate programmes; Distance Programme in Cultural and Media Management

Student Services: Academic Counselling, Careers Guidance, IT Centre, Library

Student Numbers *2013-2014*: Total 1,272
Last Updated: 11/03/15

HAMBURG UNIVERSITY OF TECHNOLOGY

Technische Universität Hamburg-Harburg (TUHH)
Schwarzenbergstrasse 95, 21071 Hamburg
Tel: +49(40) 42878-0
Fax: +49(40) 42878-2040
EMail: praesident@tuhh.de
Website: http://www.tu-harburg.de

President: Garabed Antranikian
Tel: +49(40) 42878-3201 EMail: praesident@tuhh.de

Chancellor: Klaus-Joachim Scheunert
Tel: +49(40) 42878-3202 EMail: scheunert@tuhh.de

International Relations: Elvira Wilberg, Head, International Office
Tel: +49(40) 42878-3158 EMail: wilberg@tuhh.de

Department

Building (Civil Engineering); **Commercial and Technical Sciences** (Business and Commerce; Technology); **Electrical Engineering, Computer Science and Mathematics** (Computer Science; Electrical Engineering; Mathematics); **Management Sciences and Technology** (Management; Technology); **Mechanical Engineering** (Industrial Engineering; Industrial Management; Mechanical Engineering; Naval Architecture); **Processing Engineering** (Biotechnology; Engineering; Engineering Management; Environmental Engineering; Technology)

Research Department

Aeronautics; **Climate Protecting Energy- and Environmental Engineering**; **Integrated Biotechnology and Process Engineering**; **Logistics and Mobility for Sustainable Value Creation**; **Maritime Systems**; **On- and Offshore Civil Engineering Structures**; **Product-Oriented Materials Development**; **Regeneration, Implants, Medical Technology**; **Self-Organizing Wireless Sensor Networks and Data**

History: Founded 1978. Admitted first students 1982. Under the jurisdiction of the State of Hamburg.

Academic Year: October to September (October-March; April-September)

Admission Requirements: Secondary school certificate (Abitur) or equivalent. Sufficient knowledge of German

Fees: 500; social/administrative fees: 242 (Euro)

Main Language(s) of Instruction: German, English

Degrees and Diplomas: *Bachelor's Degree*; *Master*: **Aeronautical and Aerospace Engineering; Bioengineering; Chemical Engineering; Civil Engineering; Computer Engineering; Computer Science; Electrical Engineering; Electronic Engineering; Energy Engineering; Engineering; Engineering Management; Environmental Engineering; Environmental Studies; Hydraulic Engineering; Industrial Management; International Business; Marine Engineering; Materials Engineering; Mechanical Engineering; Medical Technology; Naval Architecture; Production Engineering; Transport Management.** *PhD*: **Economics; Engineering; Natural Sciences; Social Sciences.** *Habilitation*: **Engineering.** Some Master's taught in English.

Student Services: Academic Counselling, Canteen, Careers Guidance, Library, Social Counselling, Sports Facilities

Student Numbers *2013-2014*: Total 6,584
Last Updated: 27/03/15

HAMM-LIPPSTADT UNIVERSITY OF APPLIED SCIENCES

Hochschule Hamm-Lippstadt (HSHL)
Marker Allee 76-78, 59063 Hamm
Tel: +49(2381) 8789-234
EMail: info@hshl.de
Website: http://www.hshl.de/

President: Klaus Zeppenfeld
Tel: +49(2381) 8789-100 EMail: praesident@hshl.de

Vice-President: Karl-Heinz Sandknop
Tel: +49(2381) 8789-200 EMail: vize@hshl.de

International Relations: Johannes Zenke
Tel: +49(2381) 8789-142 EMail: johannes.zenke@hshl.de

Campus

Hamm (Automation and Control Engineering; Biomedical Engineering; Chemistry; Energy Engineering; Engineering Management; Environmental Studies; Health Sciences; Industrial and Organizational Psychology; Marketing; Sports); **Lippstadt** (Business Administration; Computer Science; Design; Electronic Engineering; Industrial Engineering; Mass Communication; Media Studies; Physics; Technology)

Further Information: Also Campus Lippstadt

Main Language(s) of Instruction: German

Degrees and Diplomas: *Bachelor's Degree*; *Master*: **Biomedicine; Business Administration; Engineering; Management; Marketing.**

Student Services: Careers Guidance, Sports Facilities

Student Numbers *2013-2014*: Total 2,336
Last Updated: 08/04/15

HANOVER MEDICAL SCHOOL

Medizinische Hochschule Hannover
Carl-Neuberg-Straße 1, 30625 Hannover
Tel: +49(511) 532-0
Fax: +49(511) 532-5550
Website: http://www.mh-hannover.de

President: Christopher Baum (2013-)
Tel: +49(511) 532-6000
EMail: Baum.Christopher@mh-hannover.de

Vice President for Business and Adminsitration: Andrea Aulkemeyer
Tel: +49(511) 532-6034
EMail: Aulkemeyer.Andrea@mh-hannover.de

International Relations: Hermann Haller, Dean for International Affairs EMail: auslandsamt@mh-hannover.de

Programme

Biochemistry *(Graduate)* (Biochemistry; Biophysics; Cell Biology; Chemistry; Physiology); **Biomedicine** *(Graduate)* (Biomedicine); **Dentistry** (Dentistry); **Ergo- and Physiotherapy** *(Graduate)* (Occupational Therapy; Physical Therapy); **Function and Pathophysiology of the Auditorial Systems** (Pathology; Physiology); **Lingual Orthodontics** *(Graduate)* (Orthodontics); **Medicine (HannibaL)** (Medicine); **Midwifery** *(European Masters)* (Midwifery); **Public Health** (Epidemiology; Ethics; Health Sciences; History; Medicine; Philosophy; Psychology; Public Health; Rehabilitation and Therapy; Social and Preventive Medicine; Sociology)

School
Medical Technology and Radiology Assistant (Medical Auxiliaries; Medical Technology; Radiology)

Institute
Psychotherapy (IPAW) (Psychotherapy)

Research School
Biomedicine *(Hannover)* (Biomedicine)

History: Founded 1963. Admitted first students 1965. An autonomous institution under the jurisdiction of and financially supported by the State of Lower Saxony.

Academic Year: October to September (October-March; April-September)

Admission Requirements: Secondary school certificate (Allgemeine Hochschulreife) or equivalent

Fees: 500 per semester (Euro)

Main Language(s) of Instruction: German, English

Degrees and Diplomas: *Bachelor's Degree*: **Biochemistry.** *Master*: **Biochemistry; Biomedicine; Midwifery; Occupational Therapy; Orthodontics; Physical Therapy; Public Health.** *PhD*: **Biochemistry; Biology; Dentistry; Medicine; Microbiology; Public Health; Speech Therapy and Audiology.** *Habilitation*: **Medicine.** The Diplom (Univ) is being phased out; The Master's Degree in Midwifery is a European degree programme. Also Medical Training Progamme (Approbationsordnung für Ärzte (ÄAppO)); State Examination Certificate (Staatsexam) in Medicine and Dentistry; Continuing Education Programmes for Psychotherapists.

Student Services: Academic Counselling, Canteen, Careers Guidance, Facilities for disabled people, Foreign Studies Centre, Health Services, Language Laboratory, Nursery Care, Social Counselling, Sports Facilities

Student Numbers *2013-2014*: Total 3,212
Last Updated: 25/03/15

HANOVER UNIVERSITY OF MUSIC, DRAMA AND MEDIA

Hochschule für Musik, Theater und Medien Hannover (HMTMH)
Emmichplatz 1, 30175 Hannover
Tel: +49(511) 3100-200
Fax: +49(511) 3100-200
EMail: hmtm@hmtm-hannover.de
Website: http://www.hmtm-hannover.de/

President: Susanne Rode-Breymann
Tel: +49(511) 3100-230 EMail: praesidentin@hmtm-hannover.de

Vice President: Jann Bruns
Tel: +49(511) 3100-7220 EMail: Jann.Bruns@hmtm-hannover.de

International Relations: Meike Marten, International Affairs Officer
EMail: internationaloffice@hmtm-hannover.de

Department
Drama (Acting); **Music Theory** (Music Theory and Composition); **Opera** (Opera)

Institute
Chamber Music (Music); **Early Music** (Music); **Journalism and Communication Research** (Communication Studies; Journalism); **Music Physiology and Music Medicine** (Art Therapy; Music); **Musical Education Research** (Music Education); **Musicology** (Musicology); **New Music** (Music)

Centre
Jewish Music *(European)* (Music); **World Music** (Music)

Research Centre
Music and Gender (Gender Studies; Music)

History: Founded 1950.

Main Language(s) of Instruction: German

Degrees and Diplomas: *Bachelor's Degree*; *Diplom (Univ)*: **Theatre.** *Master*: **Conducting; Jazz and Popular Music; Media Studies; Music; Music Education; Music Theory and Composition; Musical Instruments; Opera; Singing; Special Education.** *PhD*: **Mass Communication; Music Education; Musicology.** *Habilitation*: **Music; Theatre.**

Student Services: Library

Student Numbers *2013-2014*: Total 1,340
Last Updated: 11/03/15

HARZ UNIVERSITY OF APPLIED SCIENCES

Hochschule Harz
Friedrichstrasse 57-59, 38855 Wernigerode
Tel: +49(3943) 659-0
Fax: +49(3943) 659-109
EMail: info@hs-harz.de
Website: http://www.hs-harz.de/

Rector: Armin Willingman (2003-)
Tel: +49(3943) 659-100
EMail: rektor@hs-harz.de; awillingmann@hs-harz.de

Chancellor: Michael Schilling
Tel: +49(3943) 659-102
EMail: kanzler@hs-harz.de; mschilling@hs-harz.de

International Relations: Katja Betker, Head of International Office
Tel: +49(3943) 659-150
EMail: kbetker@hs-harz.de; international@hs-harz.de

Department
Automation and Computer Science (Automation and Control Engineering; Business Administration; Business Computing; Computer Science; Industrial Engineering; Information Technology); **Business Studies** (Business Administration; International Business; Management; Tourism); **Public Administration** (Administration; Economics; Government; Public Administration)

History: Founded 1991.

Admission Requirements: Abitur or equivalent

Main Language(s) of Instruction: German, English

Accrediting Agency: ASIIN, AQUIN

Degrees and Diplomas: *Bachelor's Degree*; *Master*: **Business Administration; Computer Science; Public Administration; Tourism.** Also MBA Degree

Student Services: Academic Counselling, Canteen, Facilities for disabled people, Language Laboratory, Library, Social Counselling, Sports Facilities

Publications: Forschungsbericht

Student Numbers *2013-2014*: Total 3,086
Last Updated: 11/03/15

HAWK UNIVERSITY OF APPLIED SCIENCES AND ARTS

Hochschule für Angewandte Wissenschaft und Kunst, Hildesheim/Holzminden/Göttingen
Hohnsen 4, 31134 Hildesheim
Tel: +49(5121) 881-0
Fax: +49(5121) 200-132
Website: http://www.hawk-hhg.de

President: Christiane Dienel (2011-)
Tel: +49(5121) 881-100 EMail: praesident@fh-hildesheim.de

Chancellor: Marc Hudy
Tel: +49(5121) 881-101 EMail: iris.linke@fh-hildesheim.de

International Relations: Sylvia Korz, Director, International Office
Tel: +49(5121) 881-143
EMail: korz@hawk-hhg.de; international@hawk-hhg.de

Faculty
Architecture, Engineering and Conservation (Architectural Restoration; Architecture; Architecture and Planning; Construction Engineering); **Design** (Advertising and Publicity; Design; Graphic Design; Interior Design); **Management, Social Work, Construction** (Social Work); **Natural Sciences and Technology** (Electrical Engineering; Information Technology; Mechanical Engineering; Optical Technology); **Resource Management** (Computer Science; Environmental Management; Forestry; Regional Planning); **Social Work and Health Sciences** (Health Administration; Health Sciences; Preschool Education; Social Work)

History: Founded 1971 as Fachhochschule Hildesheim. Became Fachhochschule Hildesheim/Holzminden/Göttingen 2000. Acquired present title 2003.

Main Language(s) of Instruction: German

Degrees and Diplomas: *Bachelor's Degree*; *Master*: **Architectural Restoration; Computer Science; Design; Electrical Engineering; Information Technology; Measurement and Precision Engineering; Mechanical Engineering; Optical Technology; Social Work.**

Student Services: IT Centre, Library

Student Numbers *2013-2014*: Total 5,317
Last Updated: 05/03/15

HEIDELBERG UNIVERSITY

Universität Heidelberg
PO Box 105760, Grabengasse 1, 69047 Heidelberg
Tel: +49(6221) 54-0
Fax: +49(6221) 54-2147
EMail: rektor@rektorat.uni-heidelberg.de
Website: http://www.uni-heidelberg.de

Rector: Bernhard Eitel (2013-)
Tel: +49(6221) 54-2147 EMail: rektor@rektorat.uni-heidelberg.de

Chancellor: Angela Kalous
Tel: +49(6221) 54-2100 EMail: kanzlerin@uni-heidelberg.de

International Relations: H. Joachim Gerke, Head of International Relations (1998-)
Tel: +49(6221) 54-2335 EMail: gerke@zuv.uni-heidelberg.de

Faculty

Law, Economics and Social Sciences (Behavioural Sciences; Cultural Studies; Economics; Law; Social Sciences); **Liberal Arts and Theology** (German; Modern Languages; Philosophy; Slavic Languages; Theology); **Medicine** *(Mannheim)* (Medicine); **Medicine** *(Heidelberg)* (Medicine); **Natural Sciences, Mathematics, and Computer Sciences** (Astronomy and Space Science; Biological and Life Sciences; Chemistry; Computer Science; Earth Sciences; Mathematics; Physics)

Centre

Biochemistry (Biochemistry); **East Asian Studies** (East Asian Studies); **Molecular Biology** (Molecular Biology); **Scientific Computing** *(Interdisciplinary)* (Computer Science)

History: Founded 1386 by Rupert I, Elector of the Palatinate. The character of the University was profoundly affected by the Renaissance and the Reformation. It was reorganized as an independent institution by the Grand Duke Charles Frederick of Baden in 1803 and is now an autonomous University financially supported by the State of Baden-Württemberg, and under the jurisdiction of its Ministry of Science and Art.

Academic Year: October to September (October-March; April-September)

Admission Requirements: Secondary school certificate (Reifezeugnis) or equivalent

Fees: None

Main Language(s) of Instruction: German. English in selected programmes.

Degrees and Diplomas: *Bachelor's Degree*; *Master*: **Ancient Civilizations; Anthropology; Archaeology; Art Criticism; Art History; Asian Religious Studies; Biotechnology; Chemistry; Chinese; Classical Languages; Computer Engineering; Computer Science; Cultural Studies; Earth Sciences; East Asian Studies; Economics; Educational Sciences; English Studies; Ethnology; Foreign Languages Education; French; Geography; German; Germanic Studies; Greek (Classical); Health Sciences; Hebrew; History; Italian; Japanese; Jewish Studies; Latin; Linguistics; Literature; Mathematics; Medical Technology; Medieval Studies; Middle Eastern Studies; Molecular Biology; Museum Studies; Music; Philosophy; Physics; Political Sciences; Prehistory; Primary Education; Psychology; Religious Studies; Romance Languages; Secondary Education; Slavic Languages; Sociology; South and Southeast Asian Languages; South Asian Studies; Spanish; Sports; Theology; Translation and Interpretation.** *PhD*: **Arts and Humanities; Dentistry; Economics; Law; Medicine; Natural Sciences; Philosophy; Protestant Theology.** *Habilitation*: **Arts and Humanities; Computer Science; Economics; Law; Mathematics; Medicine; Natural Sciences; Social Sciences; Theology.** Also State Examination Certificate (Staatsexam) in Medicine, Pharmacy, Law and Dentistry; Teacher Training State Certificate (Lehramt).

Student Services: Academic Counselling, Canteen, Careers Guidance, Facilities for disabled people, Foreign Studies Centre, Language Laboratory, Nursery Care, Social Counselling, Sports Facilities

Publications: Ruperto Carola Forschungsmagazin

Student Numbers *2013-2014*: Total 30,334
Last Updated: 31/03/15

COLLEGE OF JEWISH STUDIES, HEIDELBERG

HOCHSCHULE FÜR JÜDISCHE STUDIEN HEIDELBERG (HJS)
Landfriedstr. 12, 69117 Heidelberg
Tel: +49(6221) 5419-200
Fax: +49(6221) 5419-209
EMail: info@hfjs.eu
Website: http://www.hfjs.eu

Rector: Johannes Heil (2008-)
Tel: +49(6221) 54192-11 EMail: rektor@hfjs.eu

Head of Administration: Caroline Kiss
Tel: +49(6221) 54192-40 EMail: verwaltungsleitung@hfjs.eu

International Relations: Irene Kaufmann
Tel: +49(6221) 54192-50
EMail: aaa@zuv.uni-heidelberg.de; irene.kaufmann@hfjs.eu

Programme

Community Work (Social Work); **Jewish Studies** (Jewish Studies); **Medieval Studies** (Medieval Studies); **Rabbinics** (Jewish Studies)

History: Founded 1979, recognized by the State of Baden-Württemberg 1981. An institution of the Zentralrat der Juden in Deutschland and associated with the University of Heidelberg.

Academic Year: October to July (October-February; April-July)

Admission Requirements: Secondary school certificate (Abitur)

Main Language(s) of Instruction: German, English

Degrees and Diplomas: *Bachelor's Degree*: **Jewish Studies.** *Magister*, *Master*: **History; Jewish Studies; Judaic Religious Studies; Medieval Studies; Museum Studies.** *PhD*: **Jewish Studies.** Also Staatsexam in Religious Education.

Student Services: Canteen, Cultural Activities, Facilities for disabled people, Library, Residential Facilities

Publications: Trumah

Student Numbers *2013-2014*: Total 100

HEIDELBERG UNIVERSITY OF EDUCATION

Pädagogische Hochschule Heidelberg
Keplerstraße 87, 69120 Heidelberg
Tel: +49(6221) 477-0
Fax: +49(6221) 477-432
EMail: ph@vw.ph-heidelberg.de
Website: http://www.ph-heidelberg.de

Rector: Hans-Werner Huneke (2015-)
Tel: +49(6221) 477-112 EMail: rektorat@vw.ph-heidelberg.de

Kanzler: Christoph Glaser
Tel: +49(6221) 477-113 EMail: kanzler@vw.ph-heidelberg.de

International Relations: Henrike Schön, Head of International Office
Tel: +49(6221) 477-544
EMail: akad@vw.ph-heidelberg.de; hschoen@vw.ph-heidelberg.de

Faculty

Cultural Studies (Catholic Theology; Cultural Studies; English; Ethics; Fine Arts; Foreign Languages Education; French; German; Media Studies; Music; Native Language Education; Philosophy; Religious Education; Social Sciences; Theatre; Theology); **Education and Social Sciences** (Education; Social Sciences); **Natural and Social Sciences** (Natural Sciences; Social Sciences)

History: Founded 1904, acquired present status 1971.
Academic Year: October to September (October-March; April-September)
Admission Requirements: Secondary school certificate (Reifezeugnis)
Fees: 500 per semester (Euro)
Main Language(s) of Instruction: German
Degrees and Diplomas: *Bachelor's Degree*; *Master*: **Distance Education; Educational Sciences; Humanities and Social Science Education; Technology Education.** *PhD*: **Education.**
Student Services: Library
Publications: Schriftenreihe

Student Numbers *2014-2015*: Total: c. 4,700
Last Updated: 22/03/15

HEILBRONN UNIVERSITY

Hochschule Heilbronn

Max-Planck-Strasse 39, 74081 Heilbronn
Tel: +49(7131) 504-0
Fax: +49(7131) 252-470
EMail: info@hs-heilbronn.de; poststelle@hs-heilbronn.de
Website: http://www.hs-heilbronn.de

Rector: Jürgen Schröder
Tel: +49(7131) 504-200 EMail: rektor@hs-heilbronn.de

Chancellor: Lars Kulke
Tel: +49(7131) 504-202 EMail: kanzler@hs-heilbronn.de

International Relations: Gudrun Heller, Head, International Office
Tel: +49(7131) 504-262 EMail: gudrun.heller@hs-heilbronn.de

Faculty
Computer Science *(IT)* (Computer Science; Management; Medical Technology; Software Engineering); **Economics and Transport** (Business Administration; Management; Transport and Communications; Transport Management); **Engineering and Economics** *(Campus Künzelsau - Reinhold-Würth-Hochschule)* (Art Management; Business Administration; Electrical Engineering; Electronic Engineering; Energy Engineering; Engineering; Engineering Management; Industrial Engineering; International Business; Leisure Studies; Marketing; Mass Communication; Mechanical Engineering; Sports Management); **International Business** (Business Administration; Business and Commerce; Hotel and Restaurant; Hotel Management; International Business; Management; Oenology; Tourism); **Management and Distribution** *(Campus Schwäbisch Hall)* (Accountancy; Business Administration; Finance; Human Resources; Industrial Management; Management; Sales Techniques); **Mechanical and Electronical Engineering** *(T1)* (Automation and Control Engineering; Automotive Engineering; Electronic Engineering; Engineering; Information Technology; Machine Building; Mechanical Engineering; Robotics); **Technical Processes** (Engineering; Engineering Management; Environmental Engineering; Production Engineering; Transport Management)
Further Information: Also Schwäbisch Hall and Künzelsau Campuses.
History: Founded 1961 as a School of Engineering. Acquired present status 1971.
Main Language(s) of Instruction: German
Degrees and Diplomas: *Bachelor's Degree*; *Master*: **Art Management; Business Administration; Electrical Engineering; Electronic Engineering; Engineering Management; International Business; Leisure Studies; Management; Marketing; Mass Communication; Mechanical Engineering; Medical Technology; Production Engineering; Software Engineering; Sports Management; Tourism; Transport Management.**
Student Services: Canteen, Careers Guidance, IT Centre, Library

Student Numbers *2014-2015*: Total: c. 8,200
Last Updated: 03/02/15

HEINRICH HEINE UNIVERSITY DÜSSELDORF

Heinrich-Heine-Universität Düsseldorf (HHU)

Universitätsstr. 1, 40204 Duesseldorf, North Rhine-Westfalia
Tel: +49(211) 81-00
EMail: sos@verwaltung.uni-duesseldorf.de; international-office@uni-duesseldorf.de
Website: http://www.uni-duesseldorf.de

Rector: Anja Steinbeck (2014-)
Tel: +49(211) 81-10000 EMail: rektorin@hhu.de

Director, Communication office: Joachim Tomesch
Tel: +49(211) 81-10898 EMail: Joachim.Tomesch@hhu.de

Chancellor: Martin Goch
Tel: +49(211) 81-11000 EMail: Kanzler@hhu.de

International Relations: Anne Gellert, Director, International Office
Tel: +49(211) 81-14107 EMail: gellert@hhu.de

International Relations: Andrea von Hülsen-Esch, Prorector for International Affairs
EMail: Prorektorin.Internationales@hhu.de

Faculty
Arts and Humanities (Arts and Humanities; Cultural Studies; History; Linguistics; Literature; Philosophy; Social Sciences); **Business Administration and Economics** (Business Administration; Economics); **Law** (Law); **Mathematics and Natural Sciences** (Mathematics; Natural Sciences); **Medicine** (Medicine)
History: Founded 1907 as an Academy for practical medicine. Became a university 1965 and acquired present title 1988. Under the jurisdiction of and financially supported by the State of North Rhine-Westphalia
Academic Year: October to September (Oct - Mar; Apr - Sept).
Admission Requirements: School leaving certificate (Hochschulzugangsberechtigung) or equivalent
Fees: 246,61 per semester (Euro)
Main Language(s) of Instruction: German
Degrees and Diplomas: *Bachelor's Degree*; *Master*: **American Studies; Applied Physics; Art History; Biochemistry; Biology; Business Administration; Chemistry; Communication Studies; Comparative Literature; Computer Science; Cultural Studies; East Asian Studies; Economics; English; English Studies; European Studies; Germanic Studies; History; Information Sciences; Italian; Jewish Studies; Linguistics; Literature; Mathematics; Media Studies; Philosophy; Physics; Political Sciences; Psychology; Sociology; Toxicology; Translation and Interpretation.** *PhD*: **Business Administration; Economics; Mathematics; Natural Sciences.** Also Staatsexam in Dentistry, Medicine, Pharmacy and Law. Some programmes are taught in English: Matser's degrees in Comparative Literaure, English Studies, American Studies, European Studies, Biology, Physics; Bachelor's degree in English Studies (B.A.). Also Doctoral Programmes in Law, Natural Sciences, Medicine, Dentistry, Social and Preventive Medicine, Business Administration, Econonomics.
Student Services: Academic Counselling, Canteen, Careers Guidance, Facilities for disabled people, Health Services, Language Laboratory, Library, Nursery Care, Social Counselling, Sports Facilities

Academic Staff *2013-2014*	MEN	WOMEN	**TOTAL**
FULL-TIME	–	–	**3,000**
STAFF WITH DOCTORATE			
FULL-TIME	–	–	c. **314**

Student Numbers *2013-2014*			
All (Foreign included)	11,404	16,245	**27,649**
FOREIGN ONLY	–	–	**3,265**

Last Updated: 20/01/15

HELMUT SCHMIDT UNIVERSITY - UNIVERSITY OF THE FEDERAL ARMED FORCES OF HAMBURG

Helmut Schmidt Universität - Universität der Bundeswehr Hamburg

PO Box 700822, Holstenhofweg 85, 22043 Hamburg
Tel: +49(40) 6541-1
Fax: +49(40) 6541-2869
EMail: pressestelle@hsu-hh.de
Website: http://www.hsu-hh.de

Präsident: Wilfried Seidel
Tel: +49(40) 6541-2700 EMail: praesident@hsu-hh.de

Chancellor: Axel Puckhaber
Tel: +49(40) 6541-2701 EMail: kanzler@hsu-hh.de

International Relations: Martin Nassua, Head, International Office
Tel: +49(40) 6541-2711
EMail: nassua@hsu-hh.de; auslandsamt@hsu-hh.de

Department

Economics and Social Sciences (Administration; Economics; Social Sciences); **Electrical Engineering** (Electrical Engineering); **Humanities and Social Sciences** (History; Pedagogy; Psychology; Social Sciences; Sociology; Theology); **Mechanical Engineering** (Mechanical Engineering)

Centre

Language (Linguistics; Modern Languages)

History: Founded 1972. Teaching started 1973. Under the authority of the Hamburg Ministry of Science and Research and the Ministry of Defence.

Academic Year: October to September (October-December; January-March; April-September)

Admission Requirements: Secondary school certificate (Abitur). Students must have passed the Armed Forces Officer examination

Main Language(s) of Instruction: German

Degrees and Diplomas: *Bachelor's Degree*; *Master*: **Automotive Engineering; Business Administration; Computer Engineering; Economics; Education; Electronic Engineering; Energy Engineering; Environmental Engineering; History; Industrial Engineering; International Relations; Political Sciences; Psychology; Telecommunications Engineering.** *PhD*: **Business Administration; Economics; Education; Electronic Engineering; History; Mechanical Engineering; Political Sciences; Psychology; Sociology.** *Habilitation*

Student Services: Canteen, Facilities for disabled people, Health Services, IT Centre, Language Laboratory, Library, Sports Facilities

Publications: Uniforschung

Student Numbers *2013-2014*: Total 2,224
Last Updated: 03/03/15

HOF UNIVERSITY OF APPLIED SCIENCES

Hochschule für Angewandte Wissenschaften - Fachhochschule Hof
Alfons-Goppel-Platz 1, 95028 Hof
Tel: +49(9281) 409-300
Fax: +49(9281) 409-400
EMail: mail@fh-hof.de
Website: http://www.fh-hof.de

President: Jürgen Lehmann (2002-)
Tel: +49(9281) 409-3002
EMail: praesident@hof-university.de; juergen.lehmann@fh-hof.de

Head of Administration: Dagmar Pechstein
Tel: +49(9281) 409-3101 EMail: kanzler@hof-university.de

International Relations: Susanne Krause, Head, International Office
Tel: +49(9281) 409-3311
EMail: susanne.krause@hof-university.de; international@hof-university.de

Department

Business (Business Administration; Commercial Law; Human Resources; International Business; Management; Marketing; Media Studies; Transport Management); **Computer Science** (Business and Commerce; Business Computing; Computer Science; Media Studies); **Engineering** (Environmental Engineering; Industrial Engineering; Management; Materials Engineering; Mechanical Engineering; Textile Design)

History: Founded 1994.

Academic Year: October to September (October-March; March-September)

Admission Requirements: Secondary school certificate (Hochschulreife) together with a placement of 6 weeks related to study programme, entrance examination

Fees: Administration fee, 50 per semester; Master of Engineering, 2,000 per semester (Euro)

Main Language(s) of Instruction: German

Degrees and Diplomas: *Bachelor's Degree*; *Master*: **Human Resources; Industrial Management; Information Technology; International Business; Management; Marketing; Materials Engineering; Mechanical Engineering; Software Engineering.** Some Master's programmes taught in English

Student Services: Academic Counselling, Canteen, Careers Guidance, Facilities for disabled people, Foreign Studies Centre, IT Centre, Language Laboratory, Library, Residential Facilities, Social Counselling, Sports Facilities

Student Numbers *2013-2014*: Total 3,335
Last Updated: 05/03/15

HUMBOLDT UNIVERSITY BERLIN

Humboldt-Universität zu Berlin
Unter den Linden 6, 10099 Berlin
Tel: +49(30) 2093-0
Fax: +49(30) 2093-2770
EMail: pr@hu-berlin.de
Website: http://www.hu-berlin.de

Präsident: Jan-Hendrik Olbertz (2010-)
Tel: +49(30) 2093-2100 EMail: praesident@uv.hu-berlin.de

Vice President for Academic and International Affairs: Michael Kämper-van den Boogaart
Tel: +49(30) 2093-2102 EMail: vpsi@uv.hu-berlin.de

International Relations: Ursula Hans, Director, International Office
Tel: +49(30) 2093-46701
EMail: vpsi@uv.hu-berlin.de; ursula.hans@hu-berlin.de

Faculty

Agriculture and Horticulture (Agriculture; Horticulture); **Arts and Humanities I** (Ethnology; European Studies; History; Library Science; Philosophy); **Arts and Humanities II** (American Studies; English Studies; Linguistics; Philology; Romance Languages; Slavic Languages); **Arts and Humanities III** (African Studies; Archaeology; Art History; Asian Studies; Cultural Studies; Gender Studies; Media Studies; Musicology; Social Sciences); **Arts and Humanities IV** (Educational Sciences; Rehabilitation and Therapy; Sports); **Economics and Business Administration** (Business Administration; Economics); **Law** (Law); **Mathematics and Natural Sciences I** (Biology; Chemistry; Mathematics; Natural Sciences; Physics); **Mathematics and Natural Sciences II** (Computer Science; Geography; Mathematics; Natural Sciences; Psychology); **Theology** (Theology)

Graduate School

Humboldt (Safety Engineering; Service Trades); **International Humboldt** (Electronic Engineering; Materials Engineering; Mathematics; Natural Sciences); **Mathematics** *(Berlin)*; **Mind and Brain** *(Berlin)* (Behavioural Sciences; Neurosciences); **Social Sciences** *(Berlin)*

Further Information: Also German language courses for foreign students; Natural History Museum; Great Britain Central Institute - Centre.

History: Founded 1810 as Friedrich-Wilhelms-Universität. Reorganized 1946 and renamed 1948 Humboldt-Universität zu Berlin. Faculty structure replaced under 1968 reform by series of subject sections, and replaced following reunification 1990. An independent institution financially supported by the 'Land' of Berlin.

Academic Year: October to September (October-March; April-September)

Admission Requirements: Secondary school certificate (Abitur)

Fees: None

Main Language(s) of Instruction: German

Degrees and Diplomas: *Bachelor's Degree*; *Diplom (Univ)*: **Theology.** *Master*; *PhD*: **African Studies; Agriculture; Archaeology; Asian Studies; Biological and Life Sciences; Chemistry; Computer Science; Cultural Studies; Dentistry; East Asian Studies; Economics; Educational Sciences; English; Ethnology; Gender Studies; Geography; German; History; Horticulture; Information Sciences; Law; Linguistics; Literature; Mathematics; Mathematics Education; Media Studies; Medicine; Natural Sciences; Philosophy; Physics; Political Sciences; Psychology; Public Health; Rehabilitation and Therapy; Romance Languages; Science Education; Slavic Languages;**

Sociology; Southeast Asian Studies; Sports; Theology. *Habilitation.* Also Combined Bachelor's degrees; Also State Examination Certificate (Staatsexam) in Law and Psychotherapy. Certificates (Zertifikat) in German Law and International Development Studies.

Student Services: Academic Counselling, Canteen, Careers Guidance, Facilities for disabled people, Foreign Studies Centre, IT Centre, Language Laboratory, Library, Nursery Care, Social Counselling, Sports Facilities

Publications: Humboldt spektrum

Student Numbers *2012-2013*: Total 39,511
Last Updated: 07/04/15

ILMENAU UNIVERSITY OF TECHNOLOGY

Technische Universität Ilmenau
Postfach 10 05 65, 98684 Ilmenau
Tel: +49(3677) 69-0
Fax: +49(3677) 69-1701
EMail: rektor@tu-ilmenau.de
Website: http://www.tu-ilmenau.de

Rector: Peter Scharff (2004-)
Tel: +49(3677) 69-5001 EMail: rektor@tu-ilmenau.de

Chancellor: Margot Bock
Tel: +49(3677) 69-5031 EMail: kanzler@tu-ilmenau.de

Faculty

Computer Science and Automation (Automation and Control Engineering; Biotechnology; Computer Engineering; Computer Science; Electronic Engineering; Mathematics; Mechanical Engineering; Telecommunications Engineering); **Economics and Media Studies** (Automation and Control Engineering; Data Processing; Economics; Electrical Engineering; Information Management; Mechanical Engineering; Media Studies); **Electrical Engineering and Information Technology** (Automation and Control Engineering; Biotechnology; Computer Science; Electrical Engineering; Electronic Engineering; Information Technology; Materials Engineering; Microelectronics); **Mathematics and Natural Sciences** (Mathematics; Natural Sciences; Physical Engineering); **Mechanical Engineering** (Electronic Engineering; Materials Engineering; Measurement and Precision Engineering; Mechanical Engineering)

History: Founded 1884 as a private school. Became Hochschule für Elektrotechnik 1953. Became Technische Hochschule 1963. Acquired present status 1992.

Academic Year: October to September (October-March; April-September)

Admission Requirements: Secondary school certificate (Reifezeugnis) or equivalent

Fees: c. 65 per semester (Euro)

Main Language(s) of Instruction: German

Degrees and Diplomas: *Bachelor's Degree*; *Master*: **Automotive Engineering; Biomedical Engineering; Biotechnology; Business Computing; Computer Engineering; Computer Science; Econometrics; Electrical Engineering; Electronic Engineering; Energy Engineering; Industrial Engineering; Information Technology; Mass Communication; Materials Engineering; Mathematics; Mechanical Engineering; Media Studies; Nanotechnology; Optical Technology; Physics; Power Engineering; Robotics; Telecommunications Engineering.** *PhD*: **Automation and Control Engineering; Computer Engineering; Computer Science; Electronic Engineering; Mathematics; Mechanical Engineering; Natural Sciences.** *Habilitation*: **Automation and Control Engineering; Computer Engineering; Computer Science; Electronic Engineering; Mathematics; Mechanical Engineering; Natural Sciences.** Some Programmes conducted in English; Also Certificates.

Student Services: Academic Counselling, Canteen, Careers Guidance, Cultural Activities, Facilities for disabled people, Foreign Studies Centre, Language Laboratory, Nursery Care, Social Counselling, Sports Facilities

Publications: Summaries of the International Scientific Colloquium; Wissenschaftlicher Veranstaltungskalender

Academic Staff *2014-2015*: Total: c. 120
Student Numbers *2014-2015*: Total 6,639
Last Updated: 28/03/15

INGOLSTADT UNIVERSITY OF APPLIED SCIENCES

Technische Hochschule Ingolstadt (THI)
PO Box 21 04 54, Esplanade 10, 85019 Ingolstadt
Tel: +49(841) 9348-0
Fax: +49(841) 9348-200
EMail: info@thi.de
Website: http://www.thi.de/

Präsident: Walter Schober (2012-)
Tel: +49(841) 9348-1000 EMail: praesident@thi.de

Chancellor: Barbara Rehr
Tel: +49(841) 9348-1200 EMail: kanzler@thi.de

International Relations: Sonja Bedington, Birgit Mölder
Tel: +49(841) 9348-2110 EMail: Sonja.Bedington@thi.de

Faculty

Electrical Engineering and Computer Science (Automotive Engineering; Computer Engineering; Computer Science; Electrical Engineering; Electronic Engineering; Information Technology; Mechanical Engineering); **Mechanical Engineering** (Automotive Engineering; Construction Engineering; Electronic Engineering; Environmental Engineering; Geological Engineering; Industrial Engineering; Machine Building; Materials Engineering; Mathematics and Computer Science; Mechanical Engineering; Operations Research; Production Engineering; Safety Engineering; Thermal Engineering)

School

Business Administration (Accountancy; Business Administration; Business Computing; Commercial Law; Data Processing; E- Business/Commerce; International Business; Management; Marketing; Taxation; Transport Management)

History: Founded 1994. Acquired current title 2013, formerly known as Hochschule für Angewandte Wissenschaften FH Ingolstadt.

Admission Requirements: Secondary school certificate

Fees: None

Main Language(s) of Instruction: German

Degrees and Diplomas: *Bachelor's Degree*: **Aeronautical and Aerospace Engineering; Automotive Engineering; Business Administration; Business Computing; Computer Engineering; Computer Science; Electrical Engineering; Energy Engineering; Industrial Engineering; International Business; Management; Mechanical Engineering.** *Master*: **Accountancy; Automotive Engineering; Computer Science; Electrical Engineering; Engineering Management; Finance; Management; Marketing; Mass Communication; Production Engineering; Sales Techniques; Taxation.** Also MBA

Student Services: Academic Counselling, Canteen, Careers Guidance, Facilities for disabled people, IT Centre, Language Laboratory, Library, Social Counselling, Sports Facilities

Academic Staff *2014-2015*: Total 225
Student Numbers *2014-2015*: Total 5,151
Last Updated: 05/03/15

JADE UNIVERSITY OF APPLIED SCIENCES

Jade Hochschule
Fachhochschule Wilhelmshaven/Oldenburg/Elsfleth, Friedrich-Paffrath-Straße 101, 26389 Wilhelmshaven
Tel: +49(4421) 985-0
Fax: +49(4421) 985-2304
EMail: info@jade-hs.de
Website: http://www.jade-hs.de

President: Elmar Schreiber
Tel: +49(4421) 985-2200 EMail: praesident@jade-hs.de

International Relations: Andrea Menn, Head of International Office
Tel: +49(4421) 985-2386 EMail: menn@jade-hs.de

Department

Architecture *(Oldenburg, Elsfleth)* (Architecture); **Construction and Geo-information Engineering** *(Oldenburg, Elsfleth)* (Civil Engineering; Construction Engineering; Engineering; Rehabilitation and Therapy; Speech Therapy and Audiology; Surveying and Mapping); **Economics** *(Wilhelmshaven)* (Economics; Tourism);

Engineering *(Wilhelmshaven)* (Computer Science; Electronic Engineering; Engineering; Machine Building; Mechanical Engineering; Medical Technology; Multimedia); **Management, Information, Technology** *(Wilhelmshaven)* (Business Computing; Economics; Engineering; Journalism; Media Studies); **Maritime Studies** *(Elsfleth)* (Marine Transport; Transport and Communications)

Further Information: A traditional and distance learning institution.

History: Founded 2009 through the splitting of the Fachhochschule Oldenburg/Ostfriesland/Wilhelmshaven into Fachhochschule Emden/Leer and Jade Hochschule.

Main Language(s) of Instruction: German

Degrees and Diplomas: *Bachelor's Degree*; *Master*: **Architecture; Business Administration; Construction Engineering; Electrical Engineering; Industrial Engineering; Marine Engineering; Marine Transport; Mechanical Engineering; Media Studies; Public Health; Speech Therapy and Audiology; Surveying and Mapping.**

Student Services: IT Centre, Library

Student Numbers *2013-2014*: Total 6,701
Last Updated: 19/03/15

JOHANNES GUTENBERG UNIVERSITY MAINZ

Johannes Gutenberg-Universität Mainz (JGU)

Saarstr. 21, 55099 Mainz
Tel: +49(6131) 39-0
Fax: +49(6131) 39-22919
EMail: postmaster@verwaltung.uni-mainz.de
Website: http://www.uni-mainz.de

President: Georg Krausch (2007-)
Tel: +49(6131) 39-22301 EMail: praesident@uni-mainz.de

Chancellor: Waltraud Kreutz-Gers
Tel: +49(6131) 39-22202 EMail: fieker@uni-mainz.de

International Relations: Rainer Henkel-von Klaß, Head, International Office
Tel: +49(6131) 39-20038
EMail: international@international.uni-mainz.de

Faculty

Biology (Biology); **Catholic Theology** (Catholic Theology); **Chemistry, Pharmacy and Geoscience** (Chemistry; Crystallography; Earth Sciences; Geography; Geology; Mineralogy; Paleontology; Pharmacy); **History and Cultural Studies** (Cultural Studies; History); **Law, Management and Economics** (Economics; Law; Management); **Medicine** (Medicine); **Philosophy and Philology** (American Studies; Ancient Civilizations; Archaeology; Art History; Asian Studies; Classical Languages; English; German; Indic Languages; Linguistics; Literature; Middle Eastern Studies; Oriental Languages; Philology; Philosophy; Romance Languages; Slavic Languages); **Physics, Mathematics and Computer Science** (Computer Science; Mathematics; Physics); **Protestant Theology** (Protestant Theology); **Social Sciences, Media and Sports** (African Studies; Communication Studies; Ethnology; Journalism; Political Sciences; Psychology; Social Sciences; Sociology; Sports); **Translation Studies, Linguistics and Cultural Studies** *(Germersheim)* (Cultural Studies; English; French; Italian; Linguistics; Polish; Russian; Spanish; Translation and Interpretation)

School

Music (Jazz and Popular Music; Music; Musical Instruments; Religious Music; Singing)

Academy

Arts *(Mainz)* (Film; Media Studies; Metal Techniques; Painting and Drawing; Photography)

Research Centre

Innovative and Emerging Materials *(CINEMA)* (Materials Engineering); **Translational Medicine** (Medicine)

Further Information: Also integrated Master's Programme (leading to a German-French academic double degree Magister/Maîtrise). International Summer School 'The Federal Republic of Germany': Language, Literature, Economy, 'Politics and Art' (end of July to end of August of each year) designed for advanced students and teachers of German to improve their knowledge of German and Germany

History: Founded 1477 by the Archbishop of Mainz. Closed 1816 although the Faculty of Catholic Theology continued as a seminary. Re-established 1946. An autonomous institution financially supported by the State of Rhineland-Palatinate, and under the jurisdiction of its Ministry of Education, Science and Continuing Education.

Academic Year: October to September (October-March; April-September)

Admission Requirements: Secondary school certificate (Reifezeugnis) or equivalent

Main Language(s) of Instruction: German

Degrees and Diplomas: *Bachelor's Degree*; *Magister*: **Theology.** *Diplom (Univ)*: **Fine Arts; Religious Music.** *Master*: **American Studies; Ancient Civilizations; Anthropology; Archaeology; Art History; Biochemistry; Biology; Biomedicine; Business Education; Catholic Theology; Chemistry; Communication Studies; Comparative Literature; Computer Science; Earth Sciences; Economics; Education; Educational Sciences; English; English Studies; Epidemiology; Ethnology; European Studies; Fine Arts; Foreign Languages Education; French; Geography; Geography (Human); German; Germanic Studies; Greek (Classical); History; International Economics; Italian; Journalism; Latin; Linguistics; Literature; Management; Mathematics; Media Studies; Meteorology; Molecular Biology; Music; Musicology; Philosophy; Physics; Political Sciences; Private Law; Protestant Theology; Publishing and Book Trade; Religious Studies; Romance Languages; Russian; Slavic Languages; Social Studies; Sociology; Spanish; Sports; Translation and Interpretation.** *PhD*: **Advertising and Publicity; American Studies; Ancient Civilizations; Anthropology; Arabic; Archaeology; Art Education; Art History; Biology; Business Administration; Business Computing; Business Education; Catholic Theology; Chemistry; Computer Education; Computer Science; Cultural Studies; Dentistry; Earth Sciences; Economics; English; English Studies; Film; Fine Arts; French; Geography; German; Greek (Classical); History; Islamic Studies; Italian; Journalism; Latin; Law; Linguistics; Literature; Mathematics; Mathematics Education; Media Studies; Medicine; Meteorology; Music; Music Education; Musicology; Pharmacy; Philosophy; Physics; Polish; Political Sciences; Portuguese; Protestant Theology; Psychology; Publishing and Book Trade; Romance Languages; Russian; Science Education; Slavic Languages; Sociology; Spanish; Sports; Translation and Interpretation; Turkish.** *Habilitation*: **Fine Arts; Medicine; Music.** Also Dual Degrees; State Examination Certificate (Staatsexam) in Medicine, Pharmacy, Law, Dentistry; MBA.

Student Services: Academic Counselling, Canteen, Careers Guidance, Facilities for disabled people, Health Services, Library, Nursery Care, Social Counselling, Sports Facilities

Publications: Scientific Reports

Academic Staff *2014-2015*: Total: c. 4,150
Student Numbers *2013-2014*: Total 35,759
Last Updated: 11/03/15

JULIUS MAXIMILIAN UNIVERSITY OF WÜRZBURG

Julius-Maximilians-Universität Würzburg (JMU)

Sanderring 2, D 97070 Würzburg
Tel: +49(931) 31-0
Fax: +49(931) 31-82600
EMail: studienberatung@uni-wuerzburg.de; international@uni-wuerzburg.de
Website: http://www.uni-wuerzburg.de

President: Alfred Forchel
Tel: +49(931) 31-82241 EMail: praesident@uni-wuerzburg.de

Chancellor: Uwe Klug
Tel: +49(931) 31-82254 EMail: kanzler@uni-wuerzburg.de

Strategic Advisor to the President: Lennart Nooij
Tel: +49(931) 31-84573 EMail: lennart.nooij@uni-wuerzburg.de

International Relations: Thomas Berndt, Head International Officer
Tel: +49 931 31-84053

EMail: international@uni-wuerzburg.de; florian.evenbye@uni-wuerzburg.de

Faculty

Biology (Biology; Biotechnology; Botany; Genetics; Microbiology; Pharmacology; Zoology); **Catholic Theology** (Catholic Theology); **Chemistry and Pharmacy** (Biochemistry; Food Technology; Inorganic Chemistry; Organic Chemistry; Pharmacy; Physical Chemistry); **Economics** (Business Administration; Economics); **Human Sciences** (Arts and Humanities; Pedagogy; Philosophy; Political Sciences; Psychology; Religion; Social Studies; Sports; Theology); **Law** (Law); **Liberal Arts** (American Studies; Ancient Civilizations; Archaeology; Art History; Arts and Humanities; Asian Studies; Cultural Studies; East Asian Studies; Ethnology; French; Geography; German; Germanic Languages; Greek (Classical); History; Indic Languages; Japanese; Latin; Literature; Modern Languages; Music Education; Musicology; Philology; Slavic Languages); **Mathematics and Computer Science** (Computer Science; Mathematics; Statistics); **Medicine** (Anaesthesiology; Dentistry; Hygiene; Immunology; Medicine; Nursing; Otorhinolaryngology; Pharmacology; Surgery; Toxicology; Virology); **Physics and Astronomy** (Astronomy and Space Science; Astrophysics; Physics)

Centre

Adolf-Würth-Center for the history of Psychology; **Center for Continuing Education**; **Center for Media Didactics**; **Center for Teacher Training and Research on Education**; **M!ND-Center** *(Center for didactic in mathematics, information technology and sciences)*; **Rudolf-Virchow-Center for Experimental Biomedicine** *(Center for Experimental Biomedicine)*; **Young Africa Center**; **ZINF Research Center for Infectious Diseases** *(Research Center for Infectious Diseases)*

Graduate School

JMU Graduate School of Law, Economics, and Society (Economics; Law; Social Studies); **JMU Graduate School of Life Sciences** (Biological and Life Sciences); **JMU Graduate School of Science & Technology** (Natural Sciences; Technology); **JMU Graduate School of the Humanities** (Arts and Humanities)

History: Founded 1402 by the Prince Bishop Johann von Egloffstein, refounded 1582 by Julius Echter von Mespelbrunn, Duke of Franconia, the University is an autonomous institution financially supported by the State of Bavaria and under the jurisdiction of its Ministry of Science, Research and Art.

Academic Year: October to July (October-February; April-July)

Admission Requirements: Secondary school certificate (Reifezeugnis) or equivalent

Fees: National: None (Euro), International: None (Euro)

Main Language(s) of Instruction: German, English

Degrees and Diplomas: *Bachelor's Degree*: **Arts and Humanities; Business Administration; Education; Engineering; Fine Arts; Health Sciences; Home Economics; Information Sciences; Law; Mathematics and Computer Science; Natural Sciences; Religion; Service Trades; Social Sciences; Technology; Transport and Communications; Welfare and Protective Services.** *Magister*: **Arts and Humanities; Business Administration; Education; Engineering; Fine Arts; Health Sciences; Home Economics; Information Sciences; Law; Mathematics and Computer Science; Natural Sciences; Religion; Social Sciences; Technology; Theology; Transport and Communications; Welfare and Protective Services.** *Master*: **Arts and Humanities; Business Administration; Education; Engineering; Fine Arts; Health Sciences; Home Economics; Information Sciences; Law; Mathematics and Computer Science; Natural Sciences; Religion; Service Trades; Social Sciences; Technology; Transport and Communications; Welfare and Protective Services.** *PhD*: **Arts and Humanities; Astronomy and Space Science; Biological and Life Sciences; Biology; Business Administration; Chemistry; Computer Science; Economics; Education; Engineering; Fine Arts; Geography; Geology; Health Sciences; Home Economics; Information Sciences; Law; Mathematics; Mathematics and Computer Science; Natural Sciences; Pharmacy; Philosophy; Physics; Religion; Service Trades; Social Sciences; Social Studies; Technology; Transport and Communications; Welfare and Protective Services.** *Habilitation*: **Arts and Humanities; Business Administration; Education; Engineering; Fine Arts; Health Sciences; Home Economics; Information Sciences; Law; Mathematics and Computer Science; Natural Sciences; Religion; Service Trades; Social Sciences; Technology; Transport and Communications; Welfare and Protective Services.** Also State Examination Certificate (Staatsexam) in Food Chemistry, Medicine, Pharmacy, Law, Dentistry; Teacher Training Certificate (Lehramt) in Primary Education, Secondary Education, Special Education; MBA.

Student Services: Academic Counselling, Canteen, Careers Guidance, Cultural Activities, Facilities for disabled people, Foreign Studies Centre, IT Centre, Language Laboratory, Library, Nursery Care, Residential Facilities, Sports Facilities

Publications: Blick; DeuCze. Korpuslinguistik Deutsch-Tschechisch kontrastiv; FinDe. Arbeiten mit dem finnisch-deutschen Kontrastkorpus; Jahresberichte; Jean Paul im Netz; Schriften und Materialien der Würzburger Museologie; Schriftenreihe Junges Afrikazentrum; Schriftenreihen Empirische Bildungsforschung; Working Paper Series of the Institute of Business Management; Würzburger Arbeiten zum Wirtschaftsrecht; Würzburger Arbeitspapiere zur Politikwissenschaft und Sozialforschung; Würzburger Beiträge zur Leistungsbewertung Verteilter Systeme; Würzburger elektronische sprachwissenschaftliche Arbeiten; Würzburger Forschungsberichte in Robotik und Telematik; Würzburger Geographische Arbeiten; Würzburger Online-Schriften zum Europarecht

Academic Staff *2014-2015*	**TOTAL**
FULL-TIME	c. **2,880**

Student Numbers *2014-2015*	
All (Foreign included)	**27,955**
FOREIGN ONLY	**2304**

Last Updated: 11/03/15

JUSTUS LIEBIG UNIVERSITY GIESSEN

Justus-Liebig-Universität Giessen (JLU)
Ludwigstrasse 23, D-35390 Giessen, Hessen
Tel: +49(641) 99-0
Fax: +49(641) 99-12259
EMail: poststelle@admin.uni-giessen.de
Website: http://www.uni-giessen.de

President: Joybrato Mukherjee (2009-)
Tel: +49(641) 99-12000
EMail: joybrato.mukherjee@uni-giessen.de

Chancellor: Susanne Kraus
Tel: +49(641) 99-12030
EMail: Susanne.Kraus@admin.uni-giessen.de

International Relations: Julia Voltz, Head, International Office
Tel: +49(641) 99-12130 EMail: Julia.Volz@admin.uni-giessen.de

Faculty

Agricultural Sciences, Nutritional Sciences and Environmental Management (Agriculture; Environmental Management; Nutrition); **Biology and Chemistry** (Biology; Chemistry); **Economics and Business Studies** (Business Administration; Economics); **History and Cultural Studies** (Catholic Theology; Classical Languages; History; Philology; Protestant Theology; Theology); **Language, Literature, and Culture** (English; German; Philology; Romance Languages; Slavic Languages; Theatre); **Law** (Law); **Mathematics and Computer Science, Physics, Geography** (Computer Science; Geography; Mathematics; Physics); **Medicine** (Medicine); **Psychology and Sports Science** (Psychology; Sports); **Social Sciences and Cultural Studies** (Art Education; Music; Music Education; Pedagogy; Social Sciences); **Veterinary Medicine** (Veterinary Science)

History: Founded 1607 as University. Became the Justus Liebig-Hochschule (academy) in 1946. Full University status restored 1957. An autonomous institution financially supported by the State of Hesse, and under the jurisdiction of its Ministry of Education.

Academic Year: October to July (October-February; April-July)

Admission Requirements: Secondary school certificate (Reifezeugnis) or equivalent

Fees: None

Main Language(s) of Instruction: German

Accrediting Agency: Federal Government State of Hesse; AQAS

Degrees and Diplomas: *Bachelor's Degree*; *Magister*: **Comparative Law; European Union Law; International Law; Law.** *Master*: **Adult Education; Agricultural Economics; Animal Husbandry;**

Art Education; Biology; Biotechnology; Business Administration; Chemistry; Computer Science; Continuing Education; Cultural Studies; Dance; Development Studies; Eastern European Studies; Economics; English Studies; Environmental Management; Food Technology; Foreign Languages Education; Government; History; Home Economics; Horticulture; Linguistics; Literature; Materials Engineering; Mathematics; Media Studies; Modern Languages; Musicology; Natural Resources; Nutrition; Oenology; Performing Arts; Physical Therapy; Physics; Political Sciences; Primary Education; Psychology; Religion; Social Studies; Sports Management; Theatre; Vocational Education. *PhD*: **Agriculture; Arts and Humanities; Dentistry; Economics; Home Economics; Law; Medicine; Natural Sciences; Nutrition; Social Sciences; Veterinary Science.** *Habilitation*: **Agriculture; Ecology; Economics; Environmental Management; Medicine.** Also State Examination Certificate (Staatsexam) in Law, Medicine, Veterinary Science and Dentistry; Teacher Training Certificate (Lehramt) in Primary Education, Secondary Education, Special Education, Islamic Religion, Grammar School Education and Vocational Education. Some Master's degree programmes conducted in English.

Student Services: Academic Counselling, Canteen, Cultural Activities, Facilities for disabled people, Foreign Studies Centre, IT Centre, Language Laboratory, Library, Social Counselling, Sports Facilities

Publications: Spiegel der Forschung

Academic Staff *2014-2015*: Total 2,040

Student Numbers *2013-2014*: Total 26,780

Last Updated: 13/03/15

KAISERSLAUTERN UNIVERSITY OF APPLIED SCIENCES

Hochschule Kaiserslautern

Morlauterer Str. 31, 67657 Kaiserslautern, Rheinland-Pfaltz
Tel: +49(631) 3724-0
Fax: +49(631) 3724-105
EMail: presse@fh-kl.de
Website: http://www.fh-kl.de

President: Konrad Wolf
Tel: +49(631) 3724-2100 EMail: praesident@hs-kl.de

Chancellor: Rudolf Becker
Tel: +49(631) 3724-2110 EMail: kanzler@hs-kl.de

International Relations: Silvia Czerwinski
Tel: +49(631) 3724-2133
EMail: auslandsamt@verw-kl.fh-kl.de; silvia.czerwinski@fh-kl.de

Faculty

Applied Engineering (Business Administration; Computer Engineering; Electronic Engineering; Engineering; Information Technology; Machine Building; Mechanical Engineering); **Applied Logistics and Polymer Science** (Polymer and Plastics Technology; Transport Management); **Business Administration** (Business Administration; Business Computing; Engineering; Finance; Information Management; Small Business); **Construction and Design** (Architecture; Construction Engineering; Design; Interior Design); **Informatics and Microsystem Engineering** (Automation and Control Engineering; Computer Engineering; Electrical Engineering; Electronic Engineering; Information Technology; Systems Analysis; Telecommunications Engineering)

Further Information: Also branches in Pirmasens and Zweibrücken

History: Founded 1959. Acquired present status 1996.

Admission Requirements: Fachhochschulreife, allgemeine Hochschulreife

Fees: 55-110 with term ticket (Euro)

Main Language(s) of Instruction: German

Degrees and Diplomas: *Bachelor's Degree*; *Master*. **Architecture; Biological and Life Sciences; Civil Engineering; Computer Engineering; Computer Science; Construction Engineering; Electrical Engineering; Finance; Industrial Management; Information Management; Interior Design; Maintenance Technology; Management; Mechanical Engineering; Microelectronics; Nanotechnology; Polymer and Plastics Technology; Small Business; Transport Management.**

Student Services: Academic Counselling, Canteen, Facilities for disabled people, Foreign Studies Centre, Language Laboratory, Library, Sports Facilities

Publications: Forschungsbericht; Rundschau

Student Numbers *2013-2014*: Total 5,807

Last Updated: 02/03/15

KARLSRUHE INSTITUTE OF TECHNOLOGY

Karlsruher Institut für Technologie (KIT)

Kaiserstrasse 12, D-76131 Karlsruhe
Tel: +49(721) 6080
Fax: +49(721) 608-4290
Website: http://www.kit.edu

Rector: Holger Hanselka
Tel: +49(721) 608-22000 EMail: president@kit.edu

Vice-President, Higher Education and Academic Affairs: Alexander Wanner
Tel: +49(721) 608-41070 EMail: alexander.wanner@kit.edu

International Relations: Hana Fehrenbach, Director International Students Office
Tel: +49(721) 608-44916
EMail: hana.fehrenbach@kit.edu; student@intl.kit.edu

School

Engineering and Management *(Hector)* (Business Administration; Computer Science; Engineering)

Department

Architecture (Architecture); **Chemical and Process Engineering** (Chemical Engineering; Engineering Management); **Chemistry and Bio-Sciences** (Biology; Botany; Chemistry; Genetics; Inorganic Chemistry; Microbiology; Organic Chemistry; Physical Chemistry; Polymer and Plastics Technology; Toxicology; Zoology); **Civil Engineering, Geo- and Environmental Sciences** (Civil Engineering; Environmental Engineering; Geography; Mechanical Engineering; Mineralogy; Regional Planning); **Economics and Management** (Economics; Management); **Electrical Engineering and Information Technology** (Electrical Engineering; Information Technology); **Humanities and Social Sciences** (Arts and Humanities; Philosophy; Social Sciences; Sports); **Informatics** (Computer Science); **Mathematics** (Mathematics); **Mechanical Engineering** (Mechanical Engineering); **Physics** (Meteorology; Physics)

Further Information: Also International Seminar for Science and Teaching in Chemical Engineering, Technical and Physical Chemistry

History: Founded 1825 as Polytechnische Schule on the model of the Ecole polytechnique, Paris. Acquired University status 1865. Became Technische Hochschule Fridericiana 1885, acquired present title 2009 following merger with merged with the Forschungszentrum Karlsruhe. An autonomous institution under the jurisdiction of and financed by the State of Baden-Württemberg.

Academic Year: October to September (October-February; April-July)

Admission Requirements: Secondary school certificate (Abitur) or equivalent

Fees: Tuition, none

Main Language(s) of Instruction: German

Degrees and Diplomas: *Bachelor's Degree*; *Master*. **Applied Mathematics; Architectural Restoration; Architecture; Art History; Biology; Building Technologies; Chemical Engineering; Chemistry; Civil Engineering; Computer Science; Cultural Studies; Earth Sciences; Ecology; Economics; Education; Electrical Engineering; Electronic Engineering; Energy Engineering; Engineering; Engineering Management; Finance; Geology; Geophysics; Germanic Studies; Industrial Engineering; Industrial Management; Information Technology; Management; Materials Engineering; Mathematics; Mechanical Engineering; Metal Techniques; Meteorology; Natural Resources; Optics; Physics; Psychology; Regional Planning; Sports; Structural Architecture; Surveying and Mapping; Technology Education; Transport Engineering.** *PhD*: **Architecture; Arts and**

Humanities; Biological and Life Sciences; Chemical Engineering; Chemistry; Civil Engineering; Computer Science; Earth Sciences; Economics; Electrical Engineering; Engineering; Environmental Studies; Information Technology; Mathematics; Physics; Social Sciences. *Habilitation*: **Teacher Training.** Also Teacher State Examination in Secondary Education (Lehramt an Gymnasien); Post-doctorate Qualification.

Student Services: Academic Counselling, Canteen, Cultural Activities, Facilities for disabled people, Foreign Studies Centre, Language Laboratory, Nursery Care, Social Counselling, Sports Facilities

Academic Staff *2014-2015*: Total 6,021

Student Numbers *2013-2014*: Total 24,778
Last Updated: 19/03/15

KARLSRUHE UNIVERSITY OF APPLIED SCIENCES

Hochschule Karlsruhe -Technik und Wirtschaft
PO Box 2440, Moltkestr. 30, 76133 Karlsruhe
Tel: +49(721) 925-0
Fax: +49(721) 925-2000
EMail: mailbox@hs-karlsruhe.de
Website: http://www.hs-karlsruhe.de

Rector: Karl-Heinz Meisel
Tel: 49(721) 925-1000 EMail: rektor@hs-karlsruhe.de

Chancellor: Daniela Schweitzer
Tel: 49(721) 925-1020 EMail: daniela.schweitzer@fh-karlsruhe.de

International Relations: Joachim Lembach, Director of International Office
Tel: +49(721) 925-1084
EMail: joachim.lembach@hs-karlsruhe.de; aaa@hs-karlsruhe.de

Faculty

Architecture and Construction Engineering (Architecture; Civil Engineering; Construction Engineering); **Computer Science and Business Information Systems** (Business Computing; Computer Science; Multimedia); **Electrical Engineering and Information Technology** (Automation and Control Engineering; Electrical Engineering; Electronic Engineering; Information Technology; Telecommunications Engineering); **Information Management and Media** (Information Management; Mass Communication; Media Studies; Surveying and Mapping; Transport Management); **Management and Engineering** (Business Administration; Communication Studies; Engineering; Management; Sales Techniques); **Mechanical Engineering and Mechatronics** (Electronic Engineering; Machine Building; Mechanical Engineering)

History: Founded 1878. Acquired present status 2005.

Main Language(s) of Instruction: German

Degrees and Diplomas: *Bachelor's Degree*; *Master*: **Architecture; Automotive Engineering; Business Administration; Business Computing; Civil Engineering; Computer Science; Construction Engineering; Electrical Engineering; Electronic Engineering; Industrial Engineering; Information Management; Information Technology; International Business; Mechanical Engineering; Surveying and Mapping; Transport Management.** Some Master's degree programmes have an international aspects and are conducted in English.

Student Services: Library

Student Numbers *2013-2014*: Total 8,052
Last Updated: 11/03/15

KARLSRUHE UNIVERSITY OF EDUCATION

Pädagogische Hochschule Karlsruhe (PH KARLSRUHE)
Postfach 11 10 62, Bismarckstraße 10, 76060 Karlsruhe, Baden-Württemberg
Tel: +49(721) 925-3
Fax: +49(721) 925-4000
EMail: poststelle@ph-karlsruhe.de
Website: http://www.ph-karlsruhe.de/cms/

Rector: Christine Böckelmann
Tel: +49(721) 925-4011
EMail: christine.boeckelmann@ph-karlsruhe.de

Chancellor: Ursula Wöll
Tel: +49(721) 925-4018 EMail: ursula.woell@vw.ph-karlsruhe.de

International Relations: Simone Brandt, Head, International Office
Tel: +49(721) 925-4222 EMail: brandt@vw.ph-karlsruhe.de

Faculty

Faculty I: Humanities (Catholic Theology; Curriculum; Education; Educational Sciences; Islamic Theology; Philosophy; Preschool Education; Primary Education; Protestant Theology; Psychology; Secondary Education); **Faculty II: Languages and Literature Studies and Social Sciences** (Economics; English; French; German; Humanities and Social Science Education; Literature; Political Sciences; Social Sciences); **Faculty III: Natural Sciences, Cultural Studies, Mathematics and Sports** (Biology; Chemistry; Fine Arts; Health Sciences; Mathematics and Computer Science; Music; Physical Education; Physics; Sports; Technology Education)

History: Founded 1768 as Schul-Seminarium. Acquired present status 1962.

Academic Year: October to July

Admission Requirements: Secondary school certificate (Reifezeugnis)

Main Language(s) of Instruction: German, English

Accrediting Agency: -

Degrees and Diplomas: *Bachelor's Degree*; *Master*: **Adult Education; Educational Sciences; Environmental Studies; Linguistics; Modern Languages; Teacher Training.** *PhD*: **Educational Sciences; Teacher Training.** *Habilitation*: **Educational Sciences.** Also Undergraduate Certificates (Zertifikatsstudien); Teacher Training Programmes (Lehramt) for Primary Schools, Secondary Schools and European Teacher Training Courses for Secondary Schools.

Student Services: Canteen, IT Centre, Library, Sports Facilities

Publications: Karlsruher Pädagogische Beiträge

Academic Staff *2014-2015*: Total: c. 180

Student Numbers *2013-2014*: Total 3,849
Last Updated: 25/03/15

KARLSRUHE UNIVERSITY OF MUSIC

Hochschule für Musik Karlsruhe
Postfach 6040, Am Schloss Gottesaue 7, 76040 Karlsruhe
Tel: +49(721) 6629-0
Fax: +49(721) 6629-266
EMail: international.office@hfm-karlsruhe.de
Website: http://www.hfm-karlsruhe.de/

Rector: Hartmut Höll
Tel: +49(721) 6629-270
EMail: josefine.beinhauer@hfm-karlsruhe.de

Chancellor: Wolfram Scherer
Tel: +49(721) 6629-260
EMail: ulrike.demmak@hfm-karlsruhe.de

International Relations: Mattis Dänhardt, International Relations Coordinator
Tel: +49(721) 6629-272
EMail: international.office@hfm-karlsruhe.de

Faculty

Chamber Music (Piano) (Musical Instruments); **Chamber Music (String Instruments)** (Musical Instruments); **Chamber Music (Wind Instruments)** (Musical Instruments); **Composition** (Music Theory and Composition); **Direction** (Music); **Musical Instruments** (Musical Instruments); **Singing/Opera** (Opera; Singing); **Song Design** (Music Theory and Composition)

Institute

LernRadio (Journalism; Media Studies; Multimedia; Radio and Television Broadcasting); **Musical Theatre** (Music; Theatre); **Musicology/Music Informatics** (Computer Science; Music; Musicology); **New Music and Media** (Media Studies; Music)

History: Founded 1929.

Admission Requirements: Entrance Examination

Fees: Summer semester, 1,600; Winter semester, 2,000 (Euro)

Main Language(s) of Instruction: German, English

Accrediting Agency: Zentrale Evaluations- und Akkreditierungsagentur Hannover (ZEvA)

Degrees and Diplomas: *Bachelor's Degree*: **Computer Science; Journalism; Multimedia; Music; Musical Instruments; Musicology; Opera; Radio and Television Broadcasting.** *Master*: **Computer Science; Journalism; Multimedia; Music; Music Education; Musical Instruments; Musicology; Opera; Radio and Television Broadcasting; Singing; Theatre.** *PhD*: **Computer Science; Journalism; Media Studies; Music Education; Musicology.** Staatsexam in Secondary Education

Student Services: Canteen, Cultural Activities, Language Laboratory, Library

Student Numbers *2013-2014*: Total 1,812
Last Updated: 09/03/15

KEMPTEN UNIVERSITY OF APPLIED SCIENCES

Hochschule für Angewandte Wissenschaften Kempten

Postfach 1680, Bahnhofstrasse 61, 87406 Kempten
Tel: +49(831) 2523-0
Fax: +49(831) 2523-104
EMail: post@hs-kempten.de
Website: http://www.hs-kempten.de

President: Robert F. Schmidt
Tel: +49(831) 2523-102 EMail: praesident@hs-kempten.de

Chancellor: Christian Herrmann
Tel: +49(831) 2523-110 EMail: kanzler@hs-kempten.de

International Relations: Donata Santüns, International Programmes Director
Tel: +49(831) 2523-117
EMail: international@hs-kempten.de; Donata.Santuens@hs-kempten.de

Faculty

Business Administration (Business Administration; Management); **Computer Science** (Computer Science); **Electrical Engineering** (Electrical Engineering); **Mechanical Engineering** (Mechanical Engineering); **Social and Health Sciences** (Economics; Health Administration; Social Sciences); **Tourism** (Tourism)

History: Founded 1977.

Fees: 400 euros per semester (Euro)

Main Language(s) of Instruction: German

Accrediting Agency: Wissenschatsrat, ASIIN, ACQUIN

Degrees and Diplomas: *Bachelor's Degree*; *Master*: **Electrical Engineering; Energy Engineering; International Business; Leadership; Management; Mechanical Engineering; Production Engineering; Tourism; Transport Management.**

Student Services: IT Centre

Academic Staff *2014-2015*: Total: c. 300

Student Numbers *2014-2015*: Total: c. 4,500
Last Updated: 05/03/15

KIEL UNIVERSITY OF APPLIED SCIENCES

Fachhochschule Kiel

Sokratesplatz 1, 24149 Kiel
Tel: +49(431) 210-0
Fax: +49(431) 210-1900
EMail: info@fh-kiel.de; presse@fh-kiel.de
Website: http://www.fh-kiel.de

Rektor: Udo Beer
Tel: +49(431) 210-1000 EMail: udo.beer@fh-kiel.de

Kanzler: Klaus-Michael Heinze
Tel: +49(431) 210-1300 EMail: klaus.heinze@fh-kiel.de

International Relations: Christine Boudin, Head, International Office
Tel: +49(431) 210-1803
EMail: christine.boudin@fh-kiel.de; international@fh-kiel.de

Faculty

Agriculture (Agriculture); **Business Administration** (Business Administration); **Computer Science and Electrical Engineering** (Computer Science; Electrical and Electronic Engineering; Energy Engineering; Information Technology; Mechanical Engineering); **Media** (Media Studies; Multimedia); **Social Work and Health** (Physical Therapy; Social Work)

Department

Mechanical Engineering (Mechanical Engineering)

History: Founded 1969.

Main Language(s) of Instruction: German

Degrees and Diplomas: *Bachelor's Degree*; *Master*: **Agricultural Management; Business Administration; Business Computing; E- Business/Commerce; Electrical Engineering; Health Education; Industrial Engineering; Industrial Management; Information Technology; Journalism; Marine Engineering; Mass Communication; Mechanical Engineering; Media Studies; Naval Architecture; Preschool Education; Rehabilitation and Therapy; Social Work.**

Student Services: Library

Student Numbers *2013-2014*: Total 6,852
Last Updated: 28/01/15

'KONRAD WOLF' FILM UNIVERSITY BABELSBERG

Filmuniversität Babelsberg 'Konrad Wolf' (HFF)

Marlene-Dietrich-Allee 11, 14482 Potsdam-Babelsberg
Tel: +49(331) 6202-0
Fax: +49(331) 6202-199
EMail: info@filmuniversitaet.de; studium@filmuniversitaet.de; auslandsamt@filmunviersitaet.de
Website: http://www.filmuniversitaet.de/

President: Susanne Stürmer (2013-)
Tel: +49(331) 6202-100 EMail: praesidentin@filmuniversitaet.de

International Relations: Martin Steyer, Vizepräsident für künstlerische Praxis und internationale Beziehungen
Tel: +49(331) 6202-385 EMail: m.steyer@filmuniversitaet.de

Faculty

Fakultät I (Cinema and Television; Film; Media Studies; Multimedia; Music; Theatre; Writing); **Fakultät II** (Cinema and Television; Display and Stage Design; Film; Music; Sound Engineering (Acoustics); Visual Arts)

History: Founded 1954. Acquired university status and current title 2014. Formerly known as Hochschule für Film und Fernsehen 'Konrad Wolf' Potsdam-Babelsberg.

Main Language(s) of Instruction: German

Degrees and Diplomas: *Bachelor's Degree*; *Master*: **Acting; Cinema and Television; Display and Stage Design; Film; Media Studies; Music; Sound Engineering (Acoustics); Theatre; Visual Arts; Writing.** *PhD*: **Media Studies.**

Student Services: Library

Academic Staff *2014-2015*: Total: c. 110

Student Numbers *2014-2015*: Total: c. 600
Last Updated: 09/03/15

LANDSHUT UNIVERSITY OF APPLIED SCIENCES

Hochschule Landshut

Am Lurzenhof 1, 84036 Landshut
Tel: +49(871) 506-0
Fax: +49(871) 506-506
EMail: info@haw-landshut.de
Website: https://www.haw-landshut.de

Präsident: Karl Stoffel
Tel: +49(871) 506-101 EMail: praesident@fh-landshut.de

Kanzler: Johann Rist

Department

Computer Science (Business Computing; Computer Science); **Economics** (Banking; Business Computing; Economics; Finance; Marketing); **Electrical and Commercial Engineering** (Automation and Control Engineering; Electrical Engineering; Industrial Engineering; Microelectronics); **Mechanical Engineering** (Automotive

Engineering; Mechanical Engineering; Production Engineering); **Social Work** (Social Work)

History: Founded 1978. Formerly Fachhochschule Landshut.

Academic Year: October to September

Admission Requirements: Secondary school leaving certificates (Abitur), A-level or equivalent; German language level: advanced/ C1 (Common European Frame of Reference - Languages)

Fees: National: None (student union fees: 72 per semester, including local public transportation) (Euro), International: None (student union fees: 72 per semester, including local public transportation) (Euro)

Main Language(s) of Instruction: German, English

Accrediting Agency: AQAS (Faculty of Business Administration); ASIIN (Faculties of Computer Science, Electrical and Industrial Engineering, Mechanical Engineering); AHPGS (Faculty of Social Work)

Degrees and Diplomas: *Bachelor's Degree*: **Automotive Engineering; Business Administration; Business Computing; Computer Science; Electrical and Electronic Engineering; Energy Engineering; Industrial Engineering; International Business; Mechanical Engineering; Social Work.** *Master*: **Automotive Engineering; Computer Science; Electrical Engineering; Human Resources; Industrial Engineering; International Business; Marketing; Social Work.** Also MBA Degree

Student Services: Academic Counselling, Canteen, Careers Guidance, Cultural Activities, Facilities for disabled people, Foreign Studies Centre, IT Centre, Language Laboratory, Library, Residential Facilities, Social Counselling, Sports Facilities, eLibrary

Academic Staff *2014-2015*	MEN	WOMEN	**TOTAL**
FULL-TIME	154	67	**221**
PART-TIME	14	41	**55**
STAFF WITH DOCTORATE			
FULL-TIME	86	23	c. **109**
Student Numbers *2014-2015*			
All (Foreign included)	3,390	1,930	c. **5,320**
FOREIGN ONLY	240	175	**415**

Part-time students, 120. **Distance students,** 0.

Last Updated: 03/02/15

LEIPZIG UNIVERSITY OF APPLIED SCIENCES

Hochschule für Technik, Wirtschaft und Kultur Leipzig (FH) (HTWK)

Postfach 30 11 66, 04251 Leipzig
Tel: +49(341) 3076-0
Fax: +49(341) 3076-6456
EMail: poststelle@htwk-leipzig.de
Website: http://www.htwk-leipzig.de

Rector: Gesine Grande (2014-)
Tel: +49(341) 3076-6305
EMail: rektorin@htwk-leipzig.de; gesine.grande@htwk-leipzig.de

Chancellor: Swantje Heischkel
Tel: +49(341) 3076-6307 EMail: kanzlerin@htwk-leipzig.de

International Relations: Silke Mühl, Head, International Office
Tel: +49(341) 3076-6637
EMail: silke.muehl@htwk-leipzig.de; internationales@htwk-leipzig.de

Faculty

Architecture and Social Sciences (Architecture; Social Sciences); **Business Administration** (Business Administration; Management); **Civil Engineering** (Civil Engineering); **Computer Science, Mathematics and Natural Sciences** (Computer Science; Mathematics; Natural Sciences); **Electrical Engineering and Information Technology** (Electrical Engineering; Information Technology; Management); **Mechanical and Energy Engineering** (Energy Engineering; Mechanical Engineering); **Media** (Multimedia; Packaging Technology; Printing and Printmaking)

History: Founded 1992 in succession to Technische Hochschule Leipzig, Fachschule für wissenschaftliches Bibliothekswesen and Institute für Museologie. Under the jurisdiction of and financially supported by the State of Saxony.

Academic Year: September to August (September-February; March-August)

Admission Requirements: Secondary school certificate (Abitur) and certificate of German language proficiency

Fees: None

Main Language(s) of Instruction: German

Degrees and Diplomas: *Bachelor's Degree*; *Master*: **Applied Mathematics; Architecture; Business Administration; Civil Engineering; Computer Science; Electrical Engineering; Energy Engineering; Environmental Engineering; Information Sciences; Information Technology; Library Science; Management; Mechanical Engineering; Media Studies; Packaging Technology; Printing and Printmaking; Publishing and Book Trade; Social Work.**

Student Services: Academic Counselling, Canteen, Careers Guidance, Foreign Studies Centre, IT Centre, Language Laboratory, Library, Nursery Care, Social Counselling, Sports Facilities

Academic Staff *2014-2015*	**TOTAL**
FULL-TIME	**180**
Student Numbers *2014-2015*	
All (Foreign included)	c. **5,900**
FOREIGN ONLY	**742**

Last Updated: 10/03/15

LEUPHANA UNIVERSITY OF LÜNEBURG

Leuphana Universität Lüneburg (LU)

Scharnhorststrasse 1, 21335 Lüneburg, Lower Saxony
Tel: +49(4131) 677-1000
Fax: +49(4131) 677-1090
EMail: info@leuphana.de; international@leuphana.de
Website: http://www.leuphana.de/

Präsident: Sascha Spoun (2006-)
Tel: +49(4131) 677-1000 EMail: sascha.spoun@leuphana.de

Vice-President: Holm Keller
Tel: +49(4131) 677-1005 EMail: holm.keller@leuphana.de

International Relations: Sabine Busse, Director, International Office Tel: +49(4131) 677-1071 EMail: sbusse@uni.leuphana.de

Faculty

Business and Economics (Accountancy; Automation and Control Engineering; Business and Commerce; Commercial Law; Economics; Finance; Human Resources; Industrial Engineering; International Law; Management; Marketing; Production Engineering); **Education** (Educational Sciences; English Studies; Mathematics Education; Music Education; Native Language Education; Physical Education; Primary Education; Psychology; Religious Education; Secondary Education; Social Studies; Vocational Education); **Faculty of Humanities and Social Sciences** (Art History; Art Management; Communication Studies; Geography (Human); Literature; Media Studies; Modern History; Multimedia; Music; Philosophy; Political Sciences; Sociology; Urban Studies; Visual Arts); **Sustainability** (Biological and Life Sciences; Chemistry; Ecology; Environmental Management; Humanities and Social Science Education)

History: Founded 1946 as a teacher training college, acquired university status in the late 1970s. Today integrates two formerly independent institutions of higher education – the University of Lüneburg and the University of Applied Sciences. Became a foundation under public law – the highest degree of autonomy awarded to public universities - 2003.

Academic Year: October to July (October-February; April-July)

Admission Requirements: Secondary school leaving certificate (Abitur) or equivalent.

Fees: National: none, International: none

Main Language(s) of Instruction: German, English

Accrediting Agency: N/A (Leuphana University was established by the Federal State of Lower Saxony/Germany under the Higher Education Act)

Degrees and Diplomas: *Bachelor's Degree*: **Arts and Humanities; Business Administration; Commercial Law; Economics; Environmental Studies; Human Resources; Industrial Engineering; Information Management; Media Studies; Political Sciences; Primary Education; Secondary Education; Vocational Education.** *Master*: **Arts and Humanities; Business and Commerce; Educational Sciences; Engineering Management;**

Environmental Studies; Finance; Human Resources; Information Management; International Law; Management; Marketing; Primary Education; Secondary Education; Social Sciences; Vocational Education. *PhD*: **Arts and Humanities; Business Administration; Economics; Education; Engineering Management; Environmental Engineering; Environmental Studies; Human Resources; Industrial Engineering; Law; Media Studies; Political Sciences; Sociology; Urban Studies.**

Student Services: Academic Counselling, Canteen, Careers Guidance, Cultural Activities, Facilities for disabled people, Foreign Studies Centre, IT Centre, Language Laboratory, Library, Residential Facilities, Social Counselling, Sports Facilities, eLibrary

Publishing house: Leuphana University Press

Student Numbers *2014-2015*	MEN	WOMEN	**TOTAL**
All (Foreign included)	3,631	5,445	**9,076**
FOREIGN ONLY	237	350	**587**

Last Updated: 04/02/15

LÜBECK UNIVERSITY OF APPLIED SCIENCES

Fachhochschule Lübeck (FH LÜBECK/LUAS)

Mönkhofer Weg 239, 23562 Lübeck
Tel: +49(451) 300-6
Fax: +49(451) 300-5100
EMail: kontakt@fh-luebeck.de; studieninfo@fh-luebeck.de; praesidium@fh-luebeck.de
Website: http://www.fh-luebeck.de

President: Muriel Helbig
Tel: +49(451) 300-5300
EMail: bartels@fh-luebeck.de; praesidentin@fh-luebeck.de

Chancellor: Irene Strebl
Tel: +49(451) 300-5002 EMail: kanzlerin@fh-luebeck.de

International Relations: Dagmar Diehl, Head, Office of International Affairs
Tel: +49(451) 300-5098 EMail: dagmar.diehl@fh-luebeck.de

Department

Applied Natural Sciences (Biomedical Engineering; Chemical Engineering; Environmental Engineering; Physical Engineering); **Construction Engineering** (Construction Engineering); **Electronic Engineering and Computer Science** (Automation and Control Engineering; Energy Engineering; Information Technology; Media Studies); **Machine Building and Business Administration** (Business Administration; Machine Building)

History: Founded 1969.

Main Language(s) of Instruction: German

Degrees and Diplomas: *Bachelor's Degree*; *Master*: **Architecture; Biochemistry; Biomedical Engineering; Business Administration; Civil Engineering; Computer Science; Environmental Engineering; Industrial Engineering; Information Technology; Mechanical Engineering; Media Studies; Regional Planning; Town Planning.** Also Dual Degrees; International Programmes taught in English: Master's Programmes in Biomedical Engineering, Mechanical Engineering, Environmental Engineering; Bachelor's degree in Electrical Engineering, Mechanical Engineering, Engineering and Business Administration jointly offered with Milwaukee School of Engineering (MSOE); Bachelor's degree in Environmental Engineering/ Chemical Engineering and Technology, Information Technology/Electrical Engineering and Automation jointly offered with East China University of Science and Technology (ECUST).

Student Numbers *2013-2014*	MEN	WOMEN	**TOTAL**
All (Foreign included)	3,042	1,249	**4,291**
FOREIGN ONLY	269	113	**382**

Last Updated: 28/01/15

LUDWIG MAXIMILIAN UNIVERSITY OF MUNICH

Ludwig-Maximilians-Universität München (LMU MUNICH)

Geschwister-Scholl-Platz 1, 80539 München
Tel: +49(89) 2180-0
Fax: +49(89) 2180-2322
Website: http://www.lmu.de

President: Bernd Huber (2002-)
Tel: +49(89) 2180-2412 EMail: praesidium@lmu.de

Vice President for Finance and Administration: Christoph Mülke
Tel: +49(89) 2180-3269 EMail: vp-v@lmu.de

International Relations: Stefan Lauterbach
Tel: +49 (0) 89/2180 - 2823 EMail: international@lmu.de

Faculty

Biology (Biology; Botany; Genetics; Zoology); **Business Administration** (Business Administration); **Catholic Theology** (Catholic Theology); **Chemistry and Pharmacy** (Biochemistry; Chemistry; Nutrition; Pharmacy); **Economics** (Economics); **Geosciences** (Earth Sciences); **History and the Arts** (Art History; History); **Languages and Literatures** (Classical Languages; Comparative Literature; English; German; Indic Languages; Nordic Studies; Phonetics; Romance Languages; Slavic Languages); **Law** (Law); **Mathematics, Computer Science and Statistics** (Computer Science; Mathematics; Science Education; Statistics); **Medicine** (Dentistry; Medicine); **Philosophy, Philosophy of Science and Religious Science** (Philosophy; Religious Studies); **Physics** (Astronomy and Space Science; Meteorology; Physics); **Protestant Theology** (Protestant Theology); **Psychology and Educational Sciences** (Educational Sciences; Pedagogy; Psychology); **Social Sciences** (American Studies; Behavioural Sciences; Mass Communication; Media Studies; Political Sciences; Social Sciences; Sociology); **Study of Culture** (Cultural Studies); **Veterinary Science** (Veterinary Science)

History: Founded 1472 at Ingolstadt by Duke Ludwig, the Wealthy, transferred to Landshut 1800 by Elector Max IV Joseph, later King Maximilian I, and to Munich 1826 by King Ludwig I. An autonomous institution financially supported by the State of Bavaria, and under the jurisdiction of its Ministry for Education, Science and the Arts.

Academic Year: October to July (October to February; April to July)

Admission Requirements: Secondary school certificate (Reifezeugnis) or equivalent

Fees: National: None, except for summer programmes and some English-taught Master's programmes. Administrative fee, 111 per annum (including Student Services Organization fee/social activities fee and access to public transportation) (Euro), International: None, except for summer programmes and some English-taught Master's programmes. Administrative fee, 111 per annum (including Student Services Organization fee/social activities fee and access to public transportation) (Euro)

Main Language(s) of Instruction: German, English

Degrees and Diplomas: *Bachelor's Degree*; *Kirchliche Abschlussprüfung*: **Protestant Theology.** *Lizentiat*: **Canon Law; Catholic Theology.** *Master*: **American Studies; Ancient Civilizations; Anthropology; Applied Mathematics; Archaeology; Art History; Asian Religious Studies; Astrophysics; Biochemistry; Biological and Life Sciences; Biology; Business Administration; Business Education; Central European Studies; Chemistry; Chinese; Clinical Psychology; Cognitive Sciences; Communication Studies; Comparative Literature; Computer Science; Cultural Studies; Earth Sciences; Eastern European Studies; Ecology; Economics; Educational Administration; Educational Research; English; Environmental Engineering; Environmental Management; Environmental Studies; Epidemiology; Ethnology; European Languages; European Studies; Finnish; Folklore; Foreign Languages Education; Gender Studies; Geochemistry; Geography (Human); Geological Engineering; Geology; Geophysics; German; Germanic Studies; Greek; Greek (Classical); History; Human Resources; Industrial and Organizational Psychology; Insurance; Italian; Japanese; Journalism; Latin; Law; Linguistics; Literature; Logic; Management; Mathematical Physics; Mathematics; Media Studies; Meteorology; Middle Eastern Studies; Multimedia; Music Education; Musicology; Neurosciences; Occupational Health; Pharmacy; Philology; Philosophical Schools; Philosophy; Phonetics; Physics; Political Sciences; Psychology; Public Health; Public Relations; Publishing and Book Trade; Religious Studies; Romance Languages; Scandinavian Languages; Slavic Languages; Social Psychology; Sociology; Software Engineering; Speech Studies; Speech Therapy and Audiology; Statistics; Theatre; Translation and Interpretation.** *PhD*: **Albanian; American Studies; Ancient Civilizations; Anthropology; Applied Linguistics; Arabic; Archaeology; Art**

Education; Art History; Asian Religious Studies; Astronomy and Space Science; Biological and Life Sciences; Biology; Business Administration; Business Education; Canon Law; Catholic Theology; Chemistry; Chinese; Classical Languages; Communication Studies; Comparative Literature; Computer Education; Computer Science; Contemporary History; Cultural Studies; Dentistry; Earth Sciences; Economic History; Economics; Education; Educational Psychology; English; English Studies; Ethnology; European Languages; European Studies; Finnish; Folklore; Foreign Languages Education; Geography; Geography (Human); German; Germanic Studies; Greek; Greek (Classical); History; Humanities and Social Science Education; Islamic Studies; Italian; Japanese; Jewish Studies; Latin; Law; Linguistics; Literature; Mathematics; Mathematics Education; Media Studies; Medicine; Medieval Studies; Meteorology; Middle Eastern Studies; Modern History; Mongolian; Multimedia; Music Education; Musicology; Natural Sciences; Neurosciences; Nordic Studies; Orthodox Theology; Persian; Pharmacy; Philology; Philosophy; Phonetics; Physics; Political Sciences; Prehistory; Protestant Theology; Psychology; Religious Studies; Romance Languages; Scandinavian Languages; Slavic Languages; Social Sciences; Sociology; South Asian Studies; Spanish; Special Education; Speech Studies; Statistics; Technology; Theatre; Tibetan; Turkish; Veterinary Science. *Habilitation*: **Art History; Biology; Business Administration; Catholic Theology; Chemistry; Computer Science; Cultural Studies; Earth Sciences; History; Law; Literature; Mathematics; Medicine; Modern Languages; Natural Sciences; Pedagogy; Pharmacy; Philosophy; Physics; Psychology; Religion; Statistics; Theology; Veterinary Science.** Also State Examination Certificate (Staatsexam) in Dentistry, Medicine, Pharmacy, Veterinary Science and Law; Teacher Training Certificate (Lehramt).

Student Services: Academic Counselling, Canteen, Careers Guidance, Cultural Activities, Facilities for disabled people, Foreign Studies Centre, Health Services, IT Centre, Language Laboratory, Library, Nursery Care, Residential Facilities, Social Counselling, Sports Facilities, eLibrary

Publications: Münchener Universitätsschriften (Monograph Series)

Publishing House: Communications & Media Relations

Academic Staff *2013-2014*	MEN	WOMEN	**TOTAL**
FULL-TIME	601	146	**747**
Student Numbers *2014-2015*			
All (Foreign included)	20,462	31,544	**52,006**
FOREIGN ONLY	2,705	5,013	**7,718**

Last Updated: 05/02/15

LUDWIGSBURG UNIVERSITY OF EDUCATION

Pädagogische Hochschule Ludwigsburg (LUE)

Reuteallee 46, 71634 Ludwigsburg
Tel: +49(7141) 1400
Fax: +49(7141) 140-434
EMail: rektorat@ph-ludwigsburg.de
Website: http://www.ph-ludwigsburg.de

Rector: Martin Fix
Tel: +49(7141) 140-201 EMail: fix@ph-ludwigsburg.de

Chancellor: Vera Brüggemann
Tel: +49(7141) 140-204
EMail: vera.brueggemann@ph-ludwigsburg.de

Vice Rector for Research and the Support of Young Researchers: Christine Bescherer
Tel: +49(7141) 140-301 EMail: bescherer@ph-ludwigsburg.de

Vice Rector for Academic and International Affairs: Jörg-Ulrich Keßler Tel: +49(7141) 140-202 EMail: kessler@ph-ludwigsburg.de

International Relations: Peter Dines, Director of International Affairs
Tel: +49(7141) 140-432
EMail: dines@ph-ludwigsburg.de; international@ph-ludwigsburg.de

Faculty

Cultural and Natural Sciences (Biological and Life Sciences; Chemistry; Computer Science; Cultural Studies; English; Fine Arts; French; German; Handicrafts; Linguistics; Literature; Mathematics; Music; Physics; Sports; Technology); **Education and Social Sciences** (Economics; Educational Sciences; Geography; History; Philosophy; Political Sciences; Psychology; Sociology; Theology); **Special Education** *(Reutlingen)* (Special Education)

Centre

Language Studies *(Extra-curricular language courses)* (Greek; Italian; Spanish; Turkish)

History: Founded in 1962 in Stuttgart, transferred to present site in 1966. Acquired present status 1971. External Department Reutlingen (Special Education) founded 1987. Under the jurisdiction of and financially supported by the State of Baden-Württemberg.

Academic Year: October to September (October-March; April-September)

Admission Requirements: Secondary school certificate (Reifezeugnis)

Fees: None

Main Language(s) of Instruction: German, English, French

Accrediting Agency: Ministerium für Wissenschaft, Forschung und Kunst Baden-Württemberg; Kultusministerium Baden-Württemberg

Degrees and Diplomas: *Bachelor's Degree*: **Adult Education; Education; Preschool Education; Primary Education; Secondary Education; Special Education.** *Master*: **Adult Education; Cultural Studies; Educational Administration; Educational Research; Preschool Education; Primary Education; Religious Education; Secondary Education; Special Education; Teacher Training; Vocational Education.** *PhD*: **Education; Educational Sciences; Mathematics; Natural Sciences.** *Habilitation*: **Education.** Also State Exams: The University offers primarily Teacher Training Programmes (Lehramt), equivalent to a Master's degree for Primary and Secondary Education; Master's degrees in: Cultural Admin., International Education Management, Religious Education; Bachelor degree in: Culture and Media Education

Student Services: Academic Counselling, Canteen, Careers Guidance, Cultural Activities, Facilities for disabled people, Foreign Studies Centre, IT Centre, Language Laboratory, Library, Nursery Care, Residential Facilities, Social Counselling, Sports Facilities, eLibrary

Publications: Hochschulschriften

Academic Staff *2014-2015*: Total 100
STAFF WITH DOCTORATE: Total 200
Student Numbers *2014-2015*: Total: c. 5,400
Last Updated: 25/03/15

LUDWIGSHAFEN UNIVERSITY OF APPLIED SCIENCES

Hochschule Ludwigshafen am Rhein (HS LU)

Ernst-Boehe-Str. 4, 67059 Ludwigshafen am Rhein
Tel: +49(621) 5203-0
Fax: +49(621) 5203-105
EMail: info@hs-lu.de
Website: http://www.hs-lu.de/

President: Peter Mudra
Tel: +49(621) 5203-101 EMail: praesident@hs-lu.de

Chancellor: Klaus Eisold
Tel: +49(621) 5203-142 EMail: kanzler@hs-lu.de

International Relations: Kerstin Gallenstein
Tel: +49(621) 5203-119 EMail: international@hs-lu.de

Faculty

Management, Controlling and Health Care *(Fachbereich I)* (Business Computing; Health Sciences; Information Technology; Management); **Marketing and Human Resources Management** *(Fachbereich II)* (Human Resources; International Business; Marketing); **Services and Consulting** *(Fachbereich III)* (Service Trades); **Social Work and Health Care** *(Fachbereich IV)* (Health Sciences; Nursing; Social Work)

History: Founded 1996. Integrated the Ludwigshafen Protestant University of Applied Sciences (Evangelische Fachhochschule Ludwigshafen) as Faculty of Social work and Social Welfare 2008.

Main Language(s) of Instruction: German

Degrees and Diplomas: *Bachelor's Degree*; *Master*: **Accountancy; Business Computing; Engineering Management;**

Finance; Health Administration; Human Resources; Information Technology; International Business; Management; Marketing; Social Work; Transport Management. Distance-Learning MBA Programmes in: Business Administration, Transport Management and Business Administration, Management. Continuing education Programmes in: Business Administration, Human Resources, Management and International Business, Information Management and Management; Engineering Management, Management.

Student Services: IT Centre, Library

Student Numbers *2013-2014*: Total 4,299

Last Updated: 28/01/15

MAGDEBURG-STENDAL UNIVERSITY OF APPLIED SCIENCES

Hochschule Magdeburg-Stendal

Postfach 36 55, Breitscheidstr. 2, 39011 Magdeburg, Sachsen-Anhalt

Tel: +49(391) 886-30

Fax: +49(391) 886-4104

EMail: poststelle@hs-magdeburg.de

Website: http://www.hs-magdeburg.de

Rector: Anne Lequy

Tel: +49(391) 886-4100 EMail: rektorin@hs-magdeburg.de

Chancellor: Frank Richter

Tel: +49(391) 886-4102 EMail: kanzler@hs-magdeburg.de

International Relations: Nancy Brosig, ERASMUS University Coordinator

Tel: +49(391) 886-4229 EMail: nancy.brosig@hs-magdeburg.de

Department

Engineering and Industrial Design *(Magdeburg)* (Design; Engineering; Industrial Design); **Applied Human Sciences** *(Stendal)* (Child Care and Development; Psychology; Rehabilitation and Therapy); **Civil Engineering** *(Magdeburg)* (Civil Engineering); **Communications and Media** *(Magdeburg)* (Communication Studies; Media Studies; Translation and Interpretation); **Economics** *(Stendal)* (Business Administration; Economics; Health Administration); **Social and Health Studies** *(Magdeburg)* (Public Health; Rehabilitation and Therapy; Social Sciences; Social Work; Special Education); **Water and Waste Management** *(Magdeburg)* (Waste Management; Water Management)

History: Founded 1991. Fachhoschule Magdeburg unites different schools of former GDR in Magdeburg. Renamed Hochschule Magdeburg-Stendal 2000.

Academic Year: October to July

Admission Requirements: Secondary school certificate (Abitur) or equivalent.

Main Language(s) of Instruction: German

Degrees and Diplomas: *Bachelor's Degree*; *Master*: **Art Therapy; Civil Engineering; Construction Engineering; Electrical Engineering; Energy Engineering; Engineering Management; Environmental Engineering; Health Administration; Health Sciences; Hydraulic Engineering; Insurance; Journalism; Mechanical Engineering; Media Studies; Psychology; Rehabilitation and Therapy; Safety Engineering; Social Work; Water Management; Welfare and Protective Services.** European Master of Sign Language Interpreting

Student Services: Academic Counselling, Canteen, Facilities for disabled people, Foreign Studies Centre, Language Laboratory, Library, Social Counselling, Sports Facilities

Publications: Treffpunkt Campus

Student Numbers *2013-2014*: Total 6,619

Last Updated: 11/03/15

MAINZ UNIVERSITY OF APPLIED SCIENCES

Hochschule Mainz - University of Applied Sciences

PO Box 1967, Lucy Hillebrand-Str. 2, 55128 Mainz

Tel: +49(6131) 628-0

Fax: +49(6131) 628-7777

EMail: zentrale@hs-mainz.de

Website: http://www.hs-mainz.de

Präsident: Gerhard Muth (2007-2016)

Tel: +49(6131) 628-7010

EMail: praesident@hs-mainz.de; muth@hs-mainz

Kanzler: Leo Theisen

Tel: +49(6131) 628-7210 EMail: kanzler@hs-mainz.de

International Relations: Ursula Plate, Director, International Office

Tel: +49(6131) 628-7360 EMail: ulla.plate@hs-mainz.de

School

Business Studies *(Main Campus)* (Business Administration; Commercial Law; Economics; Health Administration; Information Sciences; International Business); **Design** *(Holzstraße)* (Communication Arts; Design; Interior Design; Media Studies); **Technology** *(Holzstraße)* (Architecture and Planning; Civil Engineering; Information Sciences; Surveying and Mapping)

Further Information: Also 7 Research Institutes

History: Founded 1996.

Academic Year: October to July (October-February; March-July)

Admission Requirements: Secondary school certificate (Abitur or Fachhochschulreife)

Fees: None (Euro)

Main Language(s) of Instruction: German, English

Accrediting Agency: German Accreditation Agency

Degrees and Diplomas: *Bachelor's Degree*: **Architecture; Business Administration; Civil Engineering; Communication Arts; Computer Science; Design; Interior Design; Media Studies; Real Estate; Surveying and Mapping.** *Master*: **Architecture; Business Administration; Civil Engineering; Commercial Law; Communication Arts; Computer Science; Construction Engineering; Design; Finance; Information Technology; Interior Design; International Business; Management; Media Studies; Surveying and Mapping; Taxation.**

Student Services: Academic Counselling, Canteen, Careers Guidance, Cultural Activities, Facilities for disabled people, IT Centre, Library, Social Counselling, Sports Facilities

Publications: Hochschule Mainz - Forum

Student Numbers *2014-2015*	MEN	WOMEN	**TOTAL**
All (Foreign included)	2,719	2,515	**5,234**
FOREIGN ONLY	–	–	**631**

Last Updated: 03/02/15

MANNHEIM UNIVERSITY OF APPLIED SCIENCES

Hochschule Mannheim

Paul-Wittsack-Str. 10, 68163 Mannheim, Baden-Württemberg

Tel: +49(621) 2926-111

Fax: +49(621) 2926-420

EMail: info@hs-mannheim.de

Website: http://www.hs-mannheim.de

Rector: Dieter Leonhard

Tel: +49(621) 2926-401 EMail: rektor@hs-mannheim.de

Chancellor: Birgitt Schulz

Tel: +49(621) 292-6378 EMail: kanzlerin@hs-mannheim.de

International Relations: Annette Flach, Head Internatinal Office

Tel: +49(621) 2926-6447 EMail: a.flach@hs-mannheim.de

Department

Biotechnology (Biotechnology); **Computer Science** (Computer Science); **Design** (Design); **Electrical Engineering** (Automation and Control Engineering; Electrical Engineering; Electronic Engineering; Energy Engineering); **Engineering Management** (Engineering; Management); **Information Technology** (Computer Engineering; Electrical and Electronic Engineering; Information Technology; Medical Technology); **Mechanical Engineering** (Mechanical Engineering; Production Engineering); **Process and Chemical Engineering** (Chemical Engineering); **Social Work** (Social Work)

History: Founded 1898. Merged with the Mannheim University of Applied Sciences for Social Studies (Fachhochschule Mannheim - Hochschule für Sozialwesen) 2006.

Academic Year: September to August

Main Language(s) of Instruction: German

Degrees and Diplomas: *Bachelor's Degree*; *Master*: **Automation and Control Engineering; Biotechnology; Chemical Engineering; Communication Arts; Computer Science; Electronic Engineering; Energy Engineering; Graphic Design; Industrial Engineering; Information Technology; Mechanical Engineering; Medical Technology; Social Work; Technology Education.** Also German-French Bi-national Master's degree Programmes in Chemical Engineering and Mechanical Engineering

Student Services: Canteen, Careers Guidance, IT Centre, Library

Student Numbers *2014-2015*	MEN	WOMEN	TOTAL
All (Foreign included)	3,637	1,716	**5,353**

Last Updated: 03/02/15

MANNHEIM UNIVERSITY OF MUSIC AND PERFORMING ARTS

Staatliche Hochschule für Musik und Darstellende Kunst Mannheim

N 7,18, 68161 Mannheim, Baden-Württemberg
Tel: +49(621) 292-3512
Fax: +49(621) 292-2072
EMail: rektorat@muho-mannheim.de
Website: http://www.muho-mannheim.de

Rector: Rudolf Meister (1997-)
Tel: +49(621) 292-3505 EMail: praesidium@muho-mannheim.de

Chancellor: Thilo Fischer
Tel: +49(621) 292-3510
EMail: fischer@muho-mannheim.de; kanzler@muho-mannheim.de

Division

Music and Dance (Conducting; Dance; Jazz and Popular Music; Music; Music Education; Music Theory and Composition; Musical Instruments; Musicology; Opera; Singing; Teacher Training)

History: Founded 1762. Acquired present status 1971

Academic Year: October to July

Admission Requirements: Secondary school certificate (Abitur) and entrance examination

Fees: 84 per semester (Euro)

Main Language(s) of Instruction: German

Degrees and Diplomas: *Bachelor's Degree*; *Master*: **Dance; Jazz and Popular Music; Music Education; Music Theory and Composition; Musical Instruments; Singing.** *PhD*: **Music Education; Musicology.** *Habilitation*: **Music Education; Musicology.** Also Diplom Aufbaustudiengang in Music and Dance, 1/2 yrs

Student Services: Academic Counselling, Canteen, Cultural Activities, Foreign Studies Centre, Library, Nursery Care, Social Counselling, Sports Facilities

Publications: Mannheim Hochschulschriften

Publishing House: Palatium Verlag

Student Numbers *2013-2014*: Total 638

Last Updated: 26/03/15

MARTIN LUTHER UNIVERSITY HALLE-WITTENBERG

Martin-Luther-Universität Halle-Wittenberg

Universitätsplatz 10, 06099 Halle, Saale
Tel: +49(345) 552-0
Fax: +49(345) 552-7077
EMail: rektor@uni-halle.de; pr@uni-halle.de
Website: http://www.uni-halle.de

Rector: Udo Sträter (2010-)
Tel: +49(345) 552-1000 EMail: rektor@uni-halle.de

Chancellor: Horst-Dieter Foerster
Tel: +49(345) 552-1010 EMail: kanzler@uni-halle.de

International Relations: Manja Hussner, Head, International Office
Tel: +49(345) 5521-590
EMail: manja.hussner@international.uni-halle.de; info@international.uni-hall.de

Faculty

Law, Economics and Business (Business Administration; Business Computing; Economics; Law); **Medicine** (Anatomy; Dentistry; Genetics; Hygiene; Medicine; Occupational Therapy; Pathology; Pharmacology; Physiology; Toxicology); **Natural Sciences I** (Biochemistry; Biology; Biotechnology; Natural Sciences; Pharmacy); **Natural Sciences II** (Chemistry; Mathematics; Physics); **Natural Sciences III** (Agriculture; Computer Science; Food Science; Geology; Mathematics; Natural Sciences); **Philosophy I** (Ethnology; Japanese; Oriental Studies; Philosophy; Political Sciences; Psychology; Sociology); **Philosophy II** (American Studies; Arts and Humanities; Communication Studies; English; English Studies; Media Studies; Music; Philology; Phonetics; Romance Languages; Slavic Languages; Sports); **Philosophy III** (Arts and Humanities; Education; Educational Sciences; Pedagogy; Teacher Training); **Theology** (Archaeology; Bible; Religious Art; Religious Studies; Theology)

Centre

Engineering Sciences (Engineering)

Further Information: Also International College Summer Course: Institute of German Language and Culture

History: Universität Wittenberg founded 1502, Universität Halle founded 1694. Merged 1817. Title changed to Martin-Luther-Universität 1933. Responsible to the Ministry of Education and Culture of the Federal State of Saxony-Anhalt.

Academic Year: October to September (October-March; April-September)

Admission Requirements: Secondary school certificate (Reifezeugnis) or equivalent

Fees: None

Main Language(s) of Instruction: German

Degrees and Diplomas: *Bachelor's Degree*; *Konzertexamen*: **Musical Instruments; Singing.** *Kirchliche Abschlussprüfung*: **Protestant Theology.** *Master*: **Accountancy; Agriculture; American Studies; Anthropology; Applied Mathematics; Arabic; Archaeology; Art History; Biochemistry; Biology; Biomedical Engineering; Biotechnology; Business Administration; Business Computing; Chemistry; Christian Religious Studies; Classical Languages; Commercial Law; Comparative Literature; Computer Science; East Asian Studies; Eastern European Studies; Educational Sciences; English; English Studies; Ethics; Ethnology; Finance; Foreign Languages Education; French; Geology; Germanic Studies; Health Sciences; Heritage Preservation; History; Human Resources; Indic Languages; International Business; International Studies; Islamic Studies; Italian; Japanese; Jewish Studies; Latin; Law; Literature; Mathematics; Media Studies; Medicine; Multimedia; Music Education; Musicology; Natural Sciences; Nutrition; Philosophy; Physics; Political Sciences; Polymer and Plastics Technology; Prehistory; Protestant Theology; Psychology; Radio and Television Broadcasting; Romance Languages; Romanian; Singing; Slavic Languages; Sociology; South Asian Studies; Spanish; Speech Studies; Sports; Taxation.** *PhD*: **Asian Studies; European Studies; Health Sciences; Literature; Modern Languages; Philosophy; Rehabilitation and Therapy; Social Studies.** *Habilitation*. Also Dual Degrees; State Examination Certificate (Staatsexam) in Dentistry, Medicine, Pharmacy, Food Technology, Law; Teacher Training Certificate (Lehramt) in Primary Education, Secondary Education.

Student Services: Academic Counselling, Canteen, Facilities for disabled people, Language Laboratory, Social Counselling, Sports Facilities

Student Numbers *2013-2014*: Total 19,711

Last Updated: 25/03/15

MERSEBURG UNIVERSITY OF APPLIED SCIENCES

Hochschule Merseburg

Eberhard-Leibnitz-Str. 2, 06217 Merseburg
Tel: +49(3461) 46-0
Fax: +49(3461) 46-2906
EMail: rektorat@hs-merseburg.de
Website: http://www.hs-merseburg.de

Rector: Jörg Kirbs
Tel: +49(3461) 46-2902 EMail: rektorat@hs-merseburg.de
Chancellor: Ulrich Müller
Tel: +49(3461) 46-2901 EMail: kanzler@hs-merseburg.de
International Relations: Gabi Meister, Head, International Office
Tel: +49(3461) 46-2307 EMail: gabi.meister@hs-merseburg.de

Department

Business Sciences (Business Administration; Economics; Management); **Computer Science and Communications Systems** (Automation and Control Engineering; Communication Studies; Computer Networks; Computer Science; Media Studies); **Engineering and Natural Sciences** (Business Administration; Chemical Engineering; Electronic Engineering; Engineering; Environmental Engineering; Industrial Engineering; Mechanical Engineering; Physics); **Social Work, Media and Culture** (Cultural Studies; Media Studies; Social Work)

History: Founded 1992.

Admission Requirements: Secondary school certificate (Fachhochschulreifezeugnis)

Fees: None

Main Language(s) of Instruction: German

Degrees and Diplomas: *Bachelor's Degree*; *Master*. **Accountancy; Art Management; Chemical Engineering; Computer Science; Cultural Studies; Electronic Engineering; Environmental Engineering; Gender Studies; Information Management; Information Technology; Management; Marketing; Mechanical Engineering; Media Studies; Physics; Social Work; Taxation.**

Student Services: Academic Counselling, Canteen, Careers Guidance, Cultural Activities, Facilities for disabled people, Foreign Studies Centre, Language Laboratory, Library, Social Counselling, Sports Facilities

Academic Staff *2014-2015*: Total 306
Student Numbers *2014-2015*: Total 2,986
Last Updated: 12/03/15

MITTWEIDA UNIVERSITY OF APPLIED SCIENCES

Hochschule Mittweida
Technikumplatz 17, 09648 Mittweida
Tel: +49(3727) 58-0
Fax: +49(3727) 58-1379
EMail: kontakt@hs-mittweida.de; studium@hs-mittweida.de
Website: http://www.htwm.de

Rector: Ludwig Hilmer
Tel: +49(3727) 58-1202 EMail: rektor@hs-mittweida.de
Chancellor: Sylvia Bässler
Tel: +49(3727) 58-1206 EMail: kanzler@hs-mittweida.de
International Relations: Saskia Langhammer, Head, International Office
Tel: +49(3727) 58-1737
EMail: langhamm@hs-mittweida.de; international@hs-mittweida.de

Faculty

Economics (Business Administration; Economics); **Electrical Engineering and Information Technology** (Automation and Control Engineering; Electrical Engineering; Electronic Engineering; Energy Engineering; Industrial Engineering; Information Technology; Microelectronics; Multimedia; Power Engineering; Telecommunications Engineering); **Mathematics, Natural Sciences and Computer Science** (Applied Mathematics; Biomedical Engineering; Computer Engineering; Computer Networks; Environmental Engineering; Laser Engineering; Mathematics; Physics; Software Engineering; Sound Engineering (Acoustics)); **Mechanical Engineering** (Mechanical Engineering); **Media Studies** (Media Studies); **Social Work** (Social Work)

History: Founded 1867.

Academic Year: September to July (September-January; March-July)

Admission Requirements: Secondary school certificate (Reifezeugnis)

Fees: None

Main Language(s) of Instruction: German

Degrees and Diplomas: *Bachelor's Degree*; *Diplom (FH)*: **Economics; Information Technology; Mechanical Engineering.** *Master*: **Applied Mathematics; Biological and Life Sciences; Business Administration; Computer Science; Electrical Engineering; Electronic Engineering; Industrial Management; Information Sciences; Laser Engineering; Mass Communication; Mechanical Engineering; Molecular Biology; Multimedia; Social Work.** Also Children and Youth Psychotherapy (Certificate/Approbation)

Student Services: Canteen, Careers Guidance, Language Laboratory, Library, Sports Facilities

Student Numbers *2013-2014*: Total 6,211
Last Updated: 12/03/15

MUNICH UNIVERSITY OF APPLIED SCIENCES

Hochschule München
Lothstr. 34, 80335 München
Tel: +49(89) 1265-0
Fax: +49(89) 1265-3000
EMail: verw@hm.edu
Website: http://www.fh-muenchen.de

President: Michael Kortstock (2006-)
Tel: +49(89) 1265-1312
EMail: michael.kortstock@hm.edu; praesident@hm.edu; monika.wildenhain@hm.edu
Chancellor: Kai Wülbern
Tel: +49(89) 1265-1294 EMail: kanzler@hm.edu
International Relations: Christian Rode
Tel: +49(89) 1265-1414 EMail: christian.rode@hm.edu

Department

Applied Sciences and Mechatronics (Automation and Control Engineering; Biological and Life Sciences; Chemistry; Measurement and Precision Engineering; Natural Sciences; Ophthalmology; Optometry; Production Engineering); **Applied Social Sciences** (Educational and Student Counselling; Management; Nursing; Social Sciences; Social Work); **Architecture** (Architecture); **Building Services Engineering, Paper and Packaging Technology and Print and Media Technology** (Construction Engineering; Media Studies; Packaging Technology; Paper Technology; Printing and Printmaking; Waste Management); **Business Administration** (Business Administration; Engineering Management); **Civil Engineering** (Civil Engineering; Construction Engineering; Structural Architecture); **Computer Science and Mathematics** (Business Computing; Computer Science; Mathematics and Computer Science); **Design** (Communication Arts; Industrial Design; Photography); **Electrical Engineering and Information Technology** (Electrical Engineering; Information Technology; Systems Analysis); **Engineering and Management** (Automotive Engineering; Business Administration; Engineering; Management; Transport Engineering; Transport Management); **General and Interdisciplinary Studies** (English; Foreign Languages Education; German; Modern Languages; Music); **Geoinformatics** (Surveying and Mapping); **Mechanical, Automotive and Aeronautical Engineering** (Aeronautical and Aerospace Engineering; Automation and Control Engineering; Mechanical Engineering); **Tourism** (Hotel Management; Tourism)

History: Founded 1971.

Main Language(s) of Instruction: German

Degrees and Diplomas: *Bachelor's Degree*; *Master*. **Architecture; Automation and Control Engineering; Automotive Engineering; Bioengineering; Biotechnology; Business Administration; Civil Engineering; Communication Studies; Computer Engineering; Computer Science; Construction Engineering; Cultural Studies; Design; Electrical Engineering; Electronic Engineering; Engineering; Finance; Hotel and Restaurant; Human Resources; Information Management; Information Technology; Management; Measurement and Precision Engineering; Mechanical Engineering; Media Studies; Nanotechnology; Packaging Technology; Paper Technology; Physics; Production Engineering; Psychiatry and Mental Health; Psychology; Publishing and Book Trade; Real Estate;**

Social and Community Services; Social Work; Surveying and Mapping; Taxation; Tourism.
Student Services: Canteen, Careers Guidance, IT Centre, Library, Sports Facilities

Academic Staff *2014-2015*: Total: c. 1,250
Student Numbers *2014-2015*: Total: c. 17,800
Last Updated: 12/03/15

MÜNSTER UNIVERSITY OF APPLIED SCIENCES

Fachhochschule Münster (FH-MUENSTER/MUAS)
Hüfferstrasse 27, 48149 Münster
Tel: +49(251) 83-64700 +49(251) 83-64054
Fax: +49(251) 83-64707 +49(251) 83-64060
EMail: serviceoffice@fh-muenster.de; praesidium@fh-muenster.de
Website: http://www.fh-muenster.de

President: Ute von Lojewski (2008-)
Tel: +49(251) 83-64050 EMail: praesidentin@fh-muenster.de
Vice-President for Economic and Personnel Administration: Jens Andreas Meinen
Tel: +49(251) 83-64000 EMail: vp1@fh-muenster.de
International Relations: Ines Roman, Head of International Office
Tel: +49(251) 83-64102
EMail: internationaloffice@fh-muenster.de; i.romanfh-muenster.de

Faculty
Architecture (Architecture); **Business Administration** (Business Administration); **Chemical Engineering** (Chemical Engineering; Industrial Engineering); **Civil Engineering** (Civil Engineering); **Design** (Design); **Electrical Engineering and Computer Science** (Computer Science; Electrical Engineering); **Energy, Building and Environmental Engineering** (Building Technologies; Energy Engineering; Environmental Engineering); **Engineering Physics** (Physical Engineering); **Home Economics and Nutrition, Facility Management** (Home Economics; Nutrition); **Mechanical Engineering** (Mechanical Engineering); **Nursing and Health** (Health Sciences; Nursing); **Social Studies** (Social Studies)

Institute
Business Administration in Technology (Business Administration); **Professional Teacher Training for Vocational Education (IBL)** (Vocational Education)
Further Information: Also Campus in Steinfurt
History: Founded 1971.
Admission Requirements: Fachhochschulreife, Abitur
Main Language(s) of Instruction: German, English
Degrees and Diplomas: *Bachelor's Degree*; *Master*: **Accountancy; Architecture; Biomedical Engineering; Building Technologies; Business Administration; Chemical Engineering; Civil Engineering; Computer Science; Design; Education; Electrical Engineering; Electronic Engineering; Energy Engineering; Engineering Management; Environmental Engineering; Finance; Food Technology; Health Administration; Health Education; Health Sciences; Industrial Chemistry; Industrial Engineering; International Business; Marketing; Mechanical Engineering; Nursing; Nutrition; Physical Engineering; Physics; Real Estate; Retailing and Wholesaling; Social Work; Taxation; Transport Management; Vocational Education; Welfare and Protective Services.**
Student Services: Academic Counselling, Canteen, Careers Guidance, Cultural Activities, Foreign Studies Centre, IT Centre, Language Laboratory, Library, Nursery Care, Sports Facilities
Publications: F(h)orum

Student Numbers *2013-2014*: Total 12,488
Last Updated: 28/01/15

MUTHESIUS ACADEMY OF FINE ARTS AND DESIGN

Muthesius Kunsthochschule
Lorentzendamm 6-8, 24103 Kiel
Tel: +49(431) 5198-400
Fax: +49(431) 5198-408
EMail: presse@muthesius.de
Website: http://www.muthesius.de

President: Arne Zerbst
Tel: +49(431) 5198-411 EMail: zerbst@muthesius.de
Chancellor: Dirk Mirow
Tel: +49(431) 5198-409 EMail: mirow@muthesius.de
International Relations: Maud Zieschang, International Relations Officer Tel: +49(431) 5198-501 EMail: fernweh@muthesius.de

Programme
Art Education (Art Education); **Communications Design** (Graphic Design); **Fine Arts** (Ceramic Art; Fine Arts; Graphic Arts; Painting and Drawing; Sculpture); **Industrial Design** (Industrial Design); **Spatial Strategies** (Architecture; Display and Stage Design; Fine Arts; Interior Design; Media Studies)

Department
Art and Media Studies (Fine Arts; Media Studies)

Centre
Media (Media Studies)
History: Founded 1907 as Werkkunsschule. Acquired present status 2005.
Main Language(s) of Instruction: German
Degrees and Diplomas: *Bachelor's Degree*; *Master*: **Display and Stage Design; Fine Arts; Graphic Design; Industrial Design.** *PhD*: **Aesthetics; Cultural Studies; Design; Display and Stage Design; Fine Arts; Media Studies.**
Student Services: Academic Counselling, Canteen, Foreign Studies Centre, Library
Publications: A Magazine about Fashion and Identity; Magazin zur Kunst am Bau; mash UP

Student Numbers *2013-2014*: Total 575
Last Updated: 25/03/15

NEUBRANDENBURG UNIVERSITY OF APPLIED SCIENCES

Hochschule Neubrandenburg
Postfach 11 01 21, 17041 Neubrandenburg
Tel: +49(395) 5693-0
Fax: +49(395) 5693-9999
EMail: presse@hs-nb.de; webmaster@hs-nb.de
Website: https://www.hs-nb.de/

Rector: Micha Teuscher
Tel: +49(395) 5693-1000 EMail: rektor@hs-nb.de
Chancellor: Reinhard Eckstein
Tel: +49(395) 5693-1005 EMail: kanzler@hs-nb.de
International Relations: Dorina Mackedanz, Head, International Office Tel: +49(395) 5693-1110 EMail: mackedanz@hs-nb.de

Department
Agricultural and Food Sciences (Agriculture; Food Technology); **Health, Nursing, Administration** (Health Administration; Health Sciences; Nursing); **Landscape Sciences and Geomatics** (Building Technologies; Civil Engineering; Construction Engineering; Environmental Management; Landscape Architecture; Surveying and Mapping); **Social Work and Education** (Preschool Education; Social Work)
History: Founded 1991. Acquired present status 2005.
Admission Requirements: High school diploma or equivalent, knowledge of German (DSH, Test Daf)
Fees: 3,850 per semester (Euro)
Main Language(s) of Instruction: German
Accrediting Agency: Ministry of Education, Sciences and Culture, Mecklenburg-West Pomerania
Degrees and Diplomas: *Bachelor's Degree*; *Master*: **Agriculture; Architectural and Environmental Design; Food Technology; Health Administration; Health Sciences; Landscape Architecture; Psychology; Social Work; Soil Science; Surveying and Mapping.**
Student Services: Academic Counselling, Canteen, Careers Guidance, Facilities for disabled people, Foreign Studies Centre, Health Services, Library, Social Counselling, Sports Facilities

Student Numbers *2013-2014*: Total 2,074
Last Updated: 12/03/15

NEU-ULM UNIVERSITY OF APPLIED SCIENCES

Hochschule für angewandte Wissenschaften Neu-Ulm (HNU)

Wileystraße 1, 89231 Neu-Ulm, Bavaria
Tel: +49(731) 9762-0
Fax: +49(731) 9762-299
EMail: info@hs-neu-ulm.de
Website: http://www.hs-neu-ulm.de

Präsidentin: Uta M. Feser
Tel: +49(731) 9762-1001
EMail: uta.feser@hs-neu-ulm.de; Praesidentin@hs-neu-ulm.de

Head of Administration: Marcus Dingel
Tel: +49(731) 9762-1300 EMail: Marcus.Dingel@hs-neu-ulm.de

International Relations: Verena Seitz, Head of the International Office
Tel: +49(731) 9762-2100 EMail: Verena.Seitz@hs-neu-ulm.de

Department

Business Administration and Economics (Business Administration; Industrial Engineering; Management; Transport Management); **Health Management** (Business Administration; Health Administration; Information Management); **Information Management** (Automotive Engineering; Business Computing; Communication Studies; Information Management)

Centre

Professional and Postgraduate Studies (Business Administration; Health Administration; Information Management; Information Technology; Management)

History: Founded 1994. Acquired present status 1998.

Academic Year: October to September (October-March; March-September)

Main Language(s) of Instruction: German

Accrediting Agency: FIBAA

Degrees and Diplomas: *Bachelor's Degree*; *Master*: **Business Administration; Health Administration; Information Management; Information Technology; Management.**

Student Services: Canteen, Careers Guidance, Library, Residential Facilities, Sports Facilities

Student Numbers *2014-2015*: Total: c. 3,700
Last Updated: 05/03/15

NIEDERRHEIN UNIVERSITY OF APPLIED SCIENCES

Hochschule Niederrhein (HN)

PO Box 100762, Reinarzstrasse 49, 47707 Krefeld
Tel: +49(2151) 822-0
Fax: +49(2151) 822-555
EMail: rektor@hs-niederrhein.de
Website: http://www.hs-niederrhein.de

President: Hans-Hennig von Grünberg
Tel: +49(2151) 822-1500 EMail: praesident@hs-niederrhein.de

Vice-President, Financial and Human Resources: Kurt Kühr
Tel: +49(2151) 822-2110 EMail: vpwp@hs-niederrhein.de

International Relations: Margot Timmer, Head of the International Office
Tel: +49(2151) 822-2710 EMail: margot.timmer@hs-niederrhein.de

Faculty

Applied Social Sciences (Cultural Studies; Education; Management; Social Work); **Business Administration and Economics** (Business Administration; Commercial Law; Economics; Management; Taxation); **Chemistry** (Biotechnology; Chemical Engineering; Chemistry); **Design** (Design); **Electrical Engineering and Computer Science** (Computer Science; Electrical Engineering; Information Technology); **Food, Nutrition and Hospitality Sciences** (Cooking and Catering; Food Science; Nutrition); **Health Care Management** (Health Administration); **Industrial Engineering** (Industrial Engineering); **Mechanical and Process Engineering** (Electronic Engineering; Mechanical Engineering); **Textile and Clothing Technology** (Textile Technology)

History: Founded 1971.

Academic Year: September to August (September-February; March-August)

Admission Requirements: Secondary school certificate (Fachhochschulreife) and 3 months practical in subject of study

Fees: 105,11 per semester (Euro)

Main Language(s) of Instruction: German

Degrees and Diplomas: *Bachelor's Degree*: **Biotechnology; Business Administration; Business Computing; Chemical Engineering; Chemistry; Clothing and Sewing; Commercial Law; Computer Science; Cooking and Catering; Cultural Studies; Design; Electrical Engineering; Health Administration; Health Sciences; Hotel and Restaurant; Industrial Engineering; Mechanical Engineering; Primary Education; Production Engineering; Social Work; Taxation; Textile Technology.** *Master*: **Applied Chemistry; Art Management; Business Administration; Business Computing; Chemical Engineering; Commercial Law; Computer Engineering; Computer Science; Cultural Studies; Design; E- Business/Commerce; Electrical Engineering; Food Science; Health Administration; Industrial Engineering; Management; Mechanical Engineering; Nutrition; Production Engineering; Psychology; Sales Techniques; Social Work; Taxation; Textile Technology; Transport Management.** Also Double Degree Programmes with The Netherlands and France; MBA; Some Programmes conducted in English (Textile and Clothing Technology).

Student Services: Academic Counselling, Canteen, Careers Guidance, Facilities for disabled people, IT Centre, Language Laboratory, Library, Social Counselling, Sports Facilities

Publications: Report Research and Development

Student Numbers *2014-2015*: Total: c. 14,200
Last Updated: 12/03/15

NORDHAUSEN UNIVERSITY OF APPLIED SCIENCES

Hochschule Nordhausen (HSN)

Weinberghof 4, 99734 Nordhausen
Tel: +49(3631) 420-0
Fax: +49(3631) 420-810
EMail: info@fh-nordhausen.de
Website: http://www.fh-nordhausen.de

Präsident: Jörg Wagner
Tel: +49(3631) 420-100 EMail: praesident@fh-nordhausen.de

Kanzler: Hans-Wolfgang Köllmann
Tel: +49(3631) 420-200 EMail: kanzler@fh-nordhausen.de

International Relations: Thomas Hoffmann, Secretary for International
Tel: +49(3631) 420-135 EMail: international@fh-nordhausen.de

Department

Business and Social Sciences (Business Administration; Engineering Management; Government; Health Sciences; Human Resources; International Business; Preschool Education; Public Administration; Social Sciences; Social Work; Special Education; Welfare and Protective Services); **Engineering** (Automation and Control Engineering; Computer Science; Ecology; Electrical and Electronic Engineering; Energy Engineering; Engineering; Environmental Engineering; Geological Engineering; Industrial Engineering; Industrial Management; Information Technology; Power Engineering)

History: Founded 1997, acquired present status 1998.

Academic Year: September to August

Admission Requirements: Secondary school certificate (Abitur)

Fees: None

Main Language(s) of Instruction: German

Degrees and Diplomas: *Bachelor's Degree*; *Master*: **Automation and Control Engineering; Business Administration; Electrical Engineering; Energy Engineering; Engineering Management; Government; Industrial Engineering; Preschool Education; Public Administration; Social Sciences; Social Work; Special Education; Town Planning.**

Student Services: Academic Counselling, Canteen, Cultural Activities, Foreign Studies Centre, Language Laboratory, Library, Sports Facilities

Student Numbers *2013-2014*: Total 2,364
Last Updated: 28/01/15

NUREMBERG SCHOOL OF MUSIC

Hochschule für Musik Nürnberg
Veilhofstraße 34, 90489 Nürnberg
Tel: +49(911) 231-14428
Fax: +49(911) 231-7697
EMail: info@hfm-nuernberg.de
Website: http://www.hfm-nuernberg.de

Präsident: Martin Ullrich (2009-)
EMail: hfm-praesidium@hfm-nuernberg.de

Kanzler: Hans-Werner Ittmann Tel: +49(911) 231-8442

International Relations: Dorothea Erdei, International Officer
Tel: +49(911) 231-8982 EMail: dorothea.erdei@hfm-nuernberg.de

Course

Artistic and Educational Training (Jazz and Popular Music; Music Education; Musical Instruments; Singing); **Artistic Education** (Conducting; Jazz and Popular Music; Musical Instruments; Singing)

History: Founded 1999 following merging of the Meistersinger-Konservatoriums in Nuremberg and the Leopold-Mozart-Konservatorium in Augsburg

Main Language(s) of Instruction: German

Degrees and Diplomas: *Bachelor's Degree*; *Master*: **Conducting; Jazz and Popular Music; Music Education; Music Theory and Composition; Musical Instruments; Opera; Singing.**

Student Services: Library

Student Numbers *2013-2014*: Total 409
Last Updated: 05/03/15

NÜRTINGEN-GEISLINGEN UNIVERSITY

Hochschule für Wirtschaft und Umwelt Nürtingen-Geislingen
Neckarsteige 6-10, 72603 Nürtingen
Tel: +49(7022) 201-0
Fax: +49(7022) 201-303
EMail: info@hfwu.de
Website: http://www.hfwu.de

Rector: Andreas Frey
Tel: +49(7022) 201-364 EMail: andreas.frey@hfwu.de

Chancellor: Alexander Leisner
Tel: +49(7022) 201-362 EMail: alexander.leisner@hfwu.de

International Relations: Iris Ramme, Director of International Affairs Tel: +49(7022) 201-304 EMail: iris.ramme@hfwu.de

Faculty

Agriculture, Economics and Management *(Nürtingen)* (Agriculture; Animal Husbandry; Economics; International Business; Management); **Business Administration and International Finance** *(Nürtingen)* (Accountancy; Business Administration; Finance; International Business; Management; Real Estate; Taxation); **Business and Law** *(Geislingen)* (Automotive Engineering; Commercial Law; Health Administration; Leadership; Management; Natural Resources; Real Estate; Tourism); **Landscape Architecture, Environmental and Urban Planning** (Environmental Management; Environmental Studies; Landscape Architecture; Regional Planning; Town Planning)

History: Founded 1949 as Institute of Higher Education in Agriculture. Acquired present status 1971.

Academic Year: October to August (October to February; March to August)

Admission Requirements: Fachhochschulreife

Main Language(s) of Instruction: German

Degrees and Diplomas: *Bachelor's Degree*; *Master*: **Accountancy; Automotive Engineering; Business Administration; Environmental Management; Finance; International Business; Landscape Architecture; Leadership; Management; Real Estate; Regional Planning; Taxation; Town Planning.**

Student Services: Academic Counselling, Canteen, Careers Guidance, Cultural Activities, Facilities for disabled people, IT Centre, Language Laboratory, Library, Residential Facilities, Social Counselling, Sports Facilities

Publications: FH Journal

Academic Staff *2014-2015*: Total 120
Student Numbers *2014-2015*: Total 5,089
Last Updated: 10/03/15

OFFENBACH UNIVERSITY OF ART AND DESIGN

Hochschule für Gestaltung Offenbach am Main (HFG)
PO Box 100823, Schlossstrasse 31, 63008 Offenbach
Tel: +49(69) 80059-0
Fax: +49(69) 80059-109
EMail: praesidium@hfg-offenbach.de
Website: http://www.hfg-offenbach.de

President: Bernd Kracke
Tel: +49(69) 80059-102
EMail: kracke@hfg-offenbach.de; praesidium@hfg-offenbach.de

Chancellor: Susanne Eickemeier
Tel: +49(69) 80059-104 EMail: eickemeier@hfg-offenbach.de

Department

Product Design (Aesthetics; Art History; Design; Industrial Design; Materials Engineering); **Visual Communication** (Aesthetics; Art History; Communication Arts; Display and Stage Design; Fine Arts; Graphic Design; Media Studies; Philosophy; Sociology; Theatre)

History: Founded 1970.

Main Language(s) of Instruction: German

Degrees and Diplomas: *Diplom (Univ)*: **Communication Arts; Graphic Design; Industrial Design.** *PhD*: **Communication Arts; Design; Graphic Design.**

Student Services: Careers Guidance, IT Centre, Library

Student Numbers *2013-2014*: Total 670
Last Updated: 03/02/15

OSNABRÜCK UNIVERSITY OF APPLIED SCIENCES

Hochschule Osnabrück
PO Box 1940, D-49009 Osnabrück
Tel: +49(541) 969-0
Fax: +49(541) 969-2066
EMail: pressestelle@fh-osnabrueck.de
Website: http://www.hs-osnabrueck.de

President: Andreas Bertram
Tel: +49(541) 969-2100 EMail: praesident@hs-osnabrueck.de

Vice President for Learning and Teaching: Alexander Schmehmann
Tel: +1(541) 969-3710 EMail: a.schmehmann@hs-osnabrueck.de

Faculty

Agricultural Sciences and Landscape Architecture (Agriculture; Landscape Architecture); **Business Management and Social Sciences** (Business Administration; Commercial Law; International Studies; Management; Public Administration; Social Sciences); **Engineering and Computer Science** (Chemical Engineering; Computer Science; Electrical Engineering; Materials Engineering; Mechanical Engineering); **Management, Culture and Technology** *(Lingen/Ems Campus)* (Business Administration; Business Computing; Engineering; Machine Building; Management; Technology)

Institute

Music (Music)

History: Founded 1971. Acquired present status 2003.

Admission Requirements: Higher education entry qualification, knowledge of German

Fees: 500 per semester plus approximately 170 per semester (Euro)

Main Language(s) of Instruction: German

Degrees and Diplomas: *Bachelor's Degree*; *Master*: **Accountancy; Agriculture; Automation and Control Engineering; Automotive Engineering; Business Administration; Commercial Law; Communication Studies; Computer Science; Educational Administration; Electrical Engineering; Electronic**

Engineering; Energy Engineering; Finance; Food Science; Health Administration; Home Economics Education; Industrial Engineering; Industrial Management; Landscape Architecture; Management; Nutrition; Physical Therapy; Production Engineering; Soil Science; Taxation; Teacher Training; Technology Education; Vocational Education; Water Science. Also Dual Degree Programmes; MBA.

Student Services: Academic Counselling, Canteen, Careers Guidance, Facilities for disabled people, Foreign Studies Centre, IT Centre, Language Laboratory, Library, Nursery Care, Social Counselling, Sports Facilities

Student Numbers *2013-2014*: Total 12,217
Last Updated: 10/03/15

OSNABRUECK UNIVERSITY

Universität Osnabrück

Postfach 44 69, Neuer Graben/Schloss, 49069 Osnabrueck
Tel: +49(541) 969-0
Fax: +49(541) 969-4570 +49(541) 969-14111
EMail: pressestelle@uni-osnabrueck.de
Website: http://www.uni-osnabrueck.de

President: Wolfgang Lücke (2013-)
Tel: +49(541) 969-4100 EMail: praesident@uni-osnabrueck.de

Vice-President for Academic Affairs: Joachim W. Härtling
Tel: +49(541) 969-4795 EMail: vp.sl@uni-osnabrueck.de

International Relations: Stephanie Schroeder, Head of International Office
Tel: +49(541) 969-4106
EMail: stephanie.schroeder@uni-osnabrueck.de

Department

Biology and Chemistry (Biochemistry; Biology; Biophysics; Botany; Chemistry; Genetics; Inorganic Chemistry; Microbiology; Organic Chemistry; Physical Chemistry; Zoology); **Business and Economics** (Business and Commerce; Economics; Information Management; Information Sciences); **Cultural Studies and Geosciences** (Art History; Fine Arts; Geography; History; Textile Design); **Education and Cultural Studies** (Catholic Theology; Education; Educational Research; Educational Sciences; Music; Primary Education; Protestant Theology; Sports; Theology); **Human Sciences** (Cognitive Sciences; Health Sciences; Psychology); **Language and Literature** (Artificial Intelligence; Cinema and Television; Computer Science; English; Film; French; German; Italian; Latin; Linguistics; Literature; Media Studies; Modern Languages; Romance Languages); **Law** (Commercial Law; European Union Law; Law); **Mathematics and Computer Sciences** (Computer Science; Information Technology; Mathematics; Mathematics Education); **Physics** (Computer Science; Physics); **Social Sciences** (European Studies; Political Sciences; Social Sciences; Sociology)

Institute

Cognitive Sciences (Cognitive Sciences); **Early Modern Intercultural Studies** (Cultural Studies); **Environmental Systems Research** (Environmental Engineering); **European Legal Studies** (Comparative Law; European Union Law); **Migration Research and Intercultural Studies** (Cultural Studies; Demography and Population)

Centre

Collaborative Research 431 *(Membrane proteins: functional dynamics and coupling to signal networks)*

Research Centre

Artificial Intelligence (Artificial Intelligence); **Early Childhood Education and Development** (Child Care and Development; Preschool Education); **Physiology and Dynamics of Cellular Microcompartments (CRC 944)** (Cell Biology; Physiology); **Prevention of Occupational Skin Diseases** (Dermatology; Occupational Health)

Research Group

E-learning and Knowledge Communication and Data Processing *(Fraunhofer)* (Data Processing; Distance Education; Educational Technology)

History: Founded in 1974.

Academic Year: October to September (October-March; April-September)

Admission Requirements: University entrance certificate (Reifezeugnis)

Fees: None

Main Language(s) of Instruction: German, English

Degrees and Diplomas: *Bachelor's Degree*; *Master*: **American Studies; Applied Mathematics; Architecture; Art Education; Art History; Biological and Life Sciences; Business Administration; Business Computing; Clinical Psychology; Cognitive Sciences; Commercial Law; Computer Education; Computer Science; Cultural Studies; Demography and Population; Economics; Educational Sciences; English Studies; Environmental Studies; European Languages; European Studies; Fiscal Law; Foreign Languages Education; Geography (Human); Geology; Germanic Studies; Government; Health Education; History; Home Economics Education; Humanities and Social Science Education; Law; Literature; Materials Engineering; Mathematics Education; Music Education; Musicology; Native Language Education; Natural Resources; Physical Education; Physics; Political Sciences; Primary Education; Psychology; Religious Education; Romance Languages; Science Education; Sociology; Soil Science; Technology Education; Theology; Water Science.** *PhD*: **Biological and Life Sciences; Cognitive Sciences; Computer Science; Demography and Population; Materials Engineering; Mathematics; Psychology.** Also Dual Bachelor's Degree; Staatsexam in Law

Student Services: Academic Counselling, Canteen, Facilities for disabled people, Language Laboratory, Nursery Care, Social Counselling, Sports Facilities

Publishing house: Press Office of the Universität Osnabrück

Academic Staff *2014-2015*: Total 472
Student Numbers *2014-2015*: Total 12,726
Last Updated: 12/02/15

OSTFALIA UNIVERSITY OF APPLIED SCIENCES

Ostfalia Hochschule für angewandte Wissenschaften (FH BS/WF)

Salzdahlumer Strasse 46-48, 38302 Wolfenbüttel, Lower Saxony
Tel: +49(5331) 939-0
Fax: +49(5331) 939-14624
EMail: info@ostfalia.de
Website: http://www.ostfalia.de/cms/de

President: Rosemarie Karger
Tel: +49(5331) 939-1000 EMail: praesidentin@ostfalia.de

Vice President: Volker Küch
Tel: +49(5331) 939-1010 EMail: hvp@ostfalia.de

International Relations: Holger Zimpel
Tel: +49(5331) 939-1750 EMail: h.zimpel@ostfalia.de

Faculty

Automotive Engineering *(Wolfsburg Campus)* (Automotive Engineering; Machine Building; Materials Engineering; Polymer and Plastics Technology; Production Engineering); **Business Administration** *(Wolfsburg Campus)* (Banking; Business Computing; Industrial Management; Insurance); **Civil and Enviromental Engineering** *(Suderburg Campus)* (Civil Engineering; Environmental Engineering); **Computer Science/IT** *(Wolfenbüttel Campus)* (Computer Engineering; Computer Networks; Computer Science; Information Technology; Media Studies; Software Engineering); **Electrical Engineering** *(Wolfenbüttel Campus)* (Electrical and Electronic Engineering; Microelectronics; Power Engineering; Telecommunications Engineering); **Law** *(Wolfenbüttel Campus)* (Commercial Law; Law; Private Law); **Mechanical Engineering** *(Wolfenbüttel Campus)* (Automation and Control Engineering; Mechanical Engineering; Production Engineering); **Public Health Services** *(Wolfsburg Campus)* (Health Administration; Health Sciences; Optometry; Public Health); **Social Work** *(Wolfenbüttel Campus)* (Social and Community Services; Social Welfare; Social Work); **Supply Engineering - Energy, Environment, Facility Management** *(Wolfenbüttel Campus)* (Energy Engineering; Engineering; Environmental Engineering); **Trade and Social Work** *(Suderburg Campus)* (Business and Commerce; Social Work;

Transport Management); **Transport, Sports, Tourism, Sports, Media** *(Salzgitter Campus - Karl-Scharfenberg-Fakultät)* (Leisure Studies; Media Studies; Sports; Sports Management; Tourism)

History: Founded 1928. Acquired present status 1971.

Academic Year: September to August (September-February; March-August)

Admission Requirements: Secondary school certificate (Abitur, Fachhochschulreife)

Fees: None

Main Language(s) of Instruction: German

Degrees and Diplomas: *Bachelor's Degree*; *Master*. **Automotive Engineering; Computer Science; Construction Engineering; Electrical Engineering; Information Technology; Law; Management; Mechanical Engineering; Power Engineering; Service Trades; Social Work; Soil Science; Transport Management; Water Science.**

Student Services: Academic Counselling, Careers Guidance, Cultural Activities, Facilities for disabled people, Language Laboratory, Library, Nursery Care, Social Counselling, Sports Facilities

Student Numbers *2013-2014*: Total 11,673
Last Updated: 25/03/15

OSTWESTFALEN-LIPPE UNIVERSITY OF APPLIED SCIENCES

Hochschule Ostwestfalen-Lippe (FH LUH)

Liebigstrasse 87, 32657 Lemgo, Northrhine-Westphalia
Tel: +49(5261) 702-0
Fax: +49(5261) 702-1711
EMail: pressestelle@hs-owl.de
Website: http://www.hs-owl.de

Rektor: Oliver Herrmann
Tel: +49(5261) 702-211
EMail: tilmann.fischer@fh-luh.de; praesident@hs-owl.de

Vice-Chancellor for Business and Personnel Management: Astrid Waldt
Tel: +49(5261) 702-200 EMail: astrid.waldt@hs-owl.de

International Relations: Kerstin Rosemann, International Student Advisor and Coordinator
Tel: +49(5261) 702-5836 EMail: kerstin.rosemann@hs-owl.de

School
Architecture and Interior Design *(Detmold)* (Architecture; Interior Design)

Department
Civil Engineering *(Detmold Campus)* (Civil Engineering; Construction Engineering); **Electrical Engineering and Computer Science** *(Lemgo Campus)* (Computer Science; Electrical Engineering); **Environmental Engineering and Applied Computer Science** *(Höxter Campus)* (Computer Science; Environmental Engineering); **Landscape Architecture and Environment Planning** *(Höxter Campus)* (Environmental Management; Landscape Architecture); **Life Science Technologies** *(Lemgo Campus)* (Biological and Life Sciences; Biotechnology; Cosmetology; Food Technology; Pharmacology); **Mechanical Engineering and Mechatronics** *(Lemgo Campus)* (Electronic Engineering; Mechanical Engineering); **Media Production** *(Lemgo Campus)* (Media Studies); **Production and Economics** *(Lemgo Campus)* (Economics; Production Engineering)

Further Information: Also campuses in Detmold and Höxter.

History: Founded 1971, acquired present name and status 2002. Formerly known as Fachhochschule Lippe und Höxter (University of Applied Sciences of Lippe and Höxter).

Academic Year: September to July (September-February; March-July)

Admission Requirements: Secondary school certificate (Abitur) or equivalent; German language test for foreign students

Fees: 60 per semester (Euro)

Main Language(s) of Instruction: German

Degrees and Diplomas: *Bachelor's Degree*; *Master*. **Architecture; Biological and Life Sciences; Building Technologies; Construction Engineering; Design; Electrical Engineering; Electronic Engineering; Environmental Engineering; Industrial Management; Information Technology; Interior Design; Landscape Architecture; Management; Mechanical Engineering; Media Studies; Production Engineering; Town Planning; Wood Technology.** Also cooperative doctoral programme with other universities; Dual Degree Programmes; MBA (General Management and Leadership); Some degree programmes are conducted in English.

Student Services: Academic Counselling, Canteen, Foreign Studies Centre, IT Centre, Language Laboratory, Library, Nursery Care, Residential Facilities, Social Counselling

Academic Staff *2014-2015*: Total: c. 620
Student Numbers *2014-2015*: Total: c. 6,600
Last Updated: 13/03/15

OTH AMBERG-WEIDEN UNIVERSITY OF APPLIED SCIENCES

Ostbayerische Technische Hochschule Amberg Weiden (OTH AW)

Kaiser-Wilhelm-Ring 23, 92224 Amberg
Tel: +49(9621) 482-0
Fax: +49(9621) 482-4991
EMail: amberg@oth-aw.de
Website: http://www.oth-aw.de

President: Andrea Klug (2016-) EMail: praesidentin@oth-aw.de

Chancellor: Ludwig von Stern
Tel: +49(9621) 482-1101 EMail: l.vstern@oth-aw.de

International Relations: Christian Erkenbrecher, Head, International Relations
Tel: +49(9621) 482-3136 EMail: c.erkenbrecher@oth-aw.de

Faculty
Business Administration *(Weiden)* (Business Administration; Commercial Law; Human Resources; Marketing; Retailing and Wholesaling); **Electrical Engineering and Information Technology** *(Amberg)* (Computer Engineering; Electronic Engineering; Information Technology; Media Studies); **Industrial Engineering** *(Weiden)* (Biomedical Engineering; Industrial Engineering); **Mechanical Engineering and Environmental Engineering** *(Amberg)* (Energy Engineering; Engineering; Environmental Engineering; Management; Mechanical Engineering; Polymer and Plastics Technology)

Further Information: Also Campus in Weiden

History: Founded 1994 and started first academic year October 1995 as Hochschule Amberg Weiden. Acquired present title 2013.

Academic Year: October to September.

Main Language(s) of Instruction: German, English

Accrediting Agency: Bavarian Ministry of Education, Science and Arts

Degrees and Diplomas: *Bachelor's Degree*; *Master*. **Automation and Control Engineering; Business Administration; Engineering; Engineering Management; Environmental Engineering; Human Resources; Industrial Engineering; Information Technology; Law; Management; Marketing; Media Studies.**

Student Services: Academic Counselling, Canteen, Careers Guidance, Facilities for disabled people, Language Laboratory, Social Counselling, Sports Facilities

Academic Staff *2014-2015*: Total: c. 84
Student Numbers *2014-2015*: Total: c. 3,500
Last Updated: 05/02/15

OTH REGENSBURG

Ostbayerischen Technischen Hochschule Regensburg (OTH REGENSBURG)

PO Box 120327, Prüfeningerstrasse 58, 93025 Regensburg, Bayern
Tel: +49(941) 943-02
Fax: +49(941) 943-1422
EMail: poststelle@oth-regensburg.de
Website: www.oth-regensburg.de

President: Wolfgang Baier
Tel: +49(941) 943-1001
EMail: wolfgang.baier@oth-regensburg.de; praesident@hs-regensburg.de

Chancellor: Peter Endres
Tel: +49(941) 943-1005 EMail: kanzler@fh-regensburg.de

Administrative Officer: Sarah Ruppert
EMail: sarah.ruppert@st.oth-regensburg.de

International Relations: Wilhelm Bomke
Tel: +49(941) 943-1068 EMail: auslandsamt@fh-regensburg.de

Department

Architecture (Architecture); **Business Administration** (Business Administration); **Civil Engineering** (Civil Engineering); **Computer Science and Mathematics** (Mathematics and Computer Science); **Electrical Engineering and Information Technology** (Electrical Engineering; Information Technology); **General Sciences and Microsystem Engineering** (Computer Engineering; Electronic Engineering; Engineering; Measurement and Precision Engineering; Natural Sciences); **Mechanical Engineering** (Mechanical Engineering); **Social and Health Care Sciences** (Health Sciences; Social Sciences; Social Work)

History: Founded 1971.

Academic Year: October to July (October-February; March- July)

Admission Requirements: Secondary school certificate (Abitur, Fachhochschulreife)

Main Language(s) of Instruction: German

Degrees and Diplomas: *Bachelor's Degree*; *Master*: **Architectural Restoration; Architecture; Automotive Engineering; Building Technologies; Business Administration; Computer Science; Electrical Engineering; Energy Engineering; Engineering; Human Resources; Industrial Engineering; Mathematics; Mechanical Engineering; Medical Technology; Microelectronics; Social Work; Transport Management.** Also Dual Bachelor's degree in Nursing; MBA.

Student Services: Academic Counselling, Canteen, Careers Guidance, Facilities for disabled people, Foreign Studies Centre, Language Laboratory, Library, Sports Facilities

Publications: Spectrum

Academic Staff *2014-2015*: Total: c. 220
Student Numbers *2014-2015*: Total: c. 1,050
Last Updated: 06/02/15

OTTO-FRIEDRICH UNIVERSITY BAMBERG

Otto-Friedrich-Universität Bamberg
Kapuzinerstraße 16, 96045 Bamberg
Tel: +49(951) 863-0
Fax: +49(951) 863-1005
EMail: post@uni-bamberg.de; kommunikation@uni-bamberg.de
Website: http://www.uni-bamberg.de;http://www.uni-bamberg.de/en/

President: Godehard Ruppert (since 2000)
Tel: +49(951) 863-1001 EMail: president@uni-bamberg.de

Chancellor: Dagmar Steuer-Flieser (since 2008)
Tel: +49(951) 863-1011 EMail: kanzlerin@uni-bamberg.de

International Relations: Andreas Weihe
Tel: +49(951) 863-1048 EMail: international@uni.bamberg.de

Faculty

Human Sciences and Education (Art Education; Education; Mathematics Education; Music Education; Protestant Theology; Psychology; Science Education; Teacher Training); **Humanities** (Archaeology; Art History; Catholic Theology; Classical Languages; Communication Studies; English; Ethnology; Geography; German; History; Literature; Oriental Studies; Philosophy; Romance Languages; Slavic Languages); **Information Systems and Applied Computer Sciences** (Business Computing; Computer Science); **Social Sciences, Economics and Business Administration** (Business Administration; Business Education; Econometrics; Economics; Political Sciences; Social Sciences; Sociology; Statistics)

Intermediate Institute

Applied Personality Psychology and Psychological Assessment (Psychology); **Applied small firms and traders Research** (Business Administration)

Academy

Trimberg Research *(TRAc)* (Cultural Studies; Education; Social Sciences)

Centre

Empirical Studies (Social Studies); **Innovative Applications of Computing** (Computer Science); **Interreligious Studies** *(ZIS)* (Religious Studies); **Medieval Studies** *(ZEMAS)* (Medieval Studies)

Graduate Division

Biopsychology of Pain and Emotions (Clinical Psychology); **Education as Landscape** (Education); **Professional Sciences** (Educational Administration)

Graduate School

Affective and Cognitive Sciences *(BaGrACS)* (Cognitive Sciences); **Business Administration** *(BaGSB)* (Business Administration); **Historical Studies** *(BaGraHist)* (Art History; History); **Linguistics** *(BaGL)* (Linguistics); **Literary, Cultural and Media Studies** *(BaGraLCM)* (Comparative Literature; Cultural Studies; Literature); **Medieval Studies** *(BaGraMS)* (Medieval Studies); **Near and Middle Eastern Studies** *(BaGOS)* (Middle Eastern Studies); **Social Sciences** *(BAGSS)* (Social Sciences)

Research Institute

European Forum for migration studies *(efms)* (Social Studies); **Leibniz Institute for Educational Trajectories (LIfBi)** *(The Leibniz Institute for Educational Trajectories specifically carries out the National Educational Panel Study (NEPS).)* (Education); **State Institute for Family Research** (Family Studies)

Further Information: Also Language Courses for foreign students

History: Founded 1647. Incorporated School of Theology, formerly part of 18th century University of Bamberg, and a College of Education established in 1958. An autonomous institution under the jurisdiction of and financially supported by the State of Bavaria. Acquired present title 1979.

Academic Year: October to September (October-February; April-July)

Admission Requirements: Secondary school certificate (Reifezeugnis)

Main Language(s) of Instruction: German

Degrees and Diplomas: *Bachelor's Degree*: **American Studies; Applied Linguistics; Archaeology; Architectural Restoration; Art History; Business Administration; Business Computing; Central European Studies; Communication Studies; Computer Science; Educational Sciences; English; English Studies; Folklore; French Studies; Geography (Human); German; Greek (Classical); History; International Economics; Jewish Studies; Latin; Medieval Studies; Music Education; Oriental Studies; Philosophy; Political Sciences; Protestant Theology; Psychology; Religious Studies; Slavic Languages; Sociology; Software Engineering; Sports; Vocational Education.** *Master*: **Adult Education; American Studies; Applied Linguistics; Arabic; Archaeology; Art History; Bulgarian; Business Administration; Business Computing; Business Education; Classical Languages; Communication Studies; Comparative Literature; Computer Science; Czech; Economics; Educational Administration; Educational Research; Educational Sciences; English; English Studies; Ethics; Folklore; Foreign Languages Education; French; Geography (Human); German; Heritage Preservation; History; Information Management; International Business; International Economics; Irish; Islamic Studies; Italian; Linguistics; Literature; Media Studies; Medieval Studies; Middle Eastern Studies; Oriental Languages; Persian; Philosophy; Polish; Political Sciences; Prehistory; Psychology; Religious Studies; Romance Languages; Russian; Serbocroatian; Slavic Languages; Sociology; Software Engineering; Spanish; Statistics; Theology; Turkish; Urdu; Vocational Education.** *PhD*: **Arts and Humanities; Business Administration; Business Computing; Computer Science; Cultural Studies; Economics; Education; Political Sciences; Psychology; Social Sciences; Sociology; Theology.** *Habilitation*: **Arts and Humanities; Business Administration; Business Computing;**

Computer Science; Cultural Studies; Economics; Education; Political Sciences; Psychology; Social Sciences; Sociology; Theology. Some Master's Degree Porgrammes are taught in English; also State Examination in Teacher Training (Lehramt) in Primary Education and Secondary Education; Double Degrees: Master in Business Administration in conjunction with the ESC Montpellier and in conjunction with the Université Jean Moulin Lyon; Double Masters Degree in Governance and International Politics, in conjunction with Aston University; Double Master's Degree in Political Science and Politics and Economics of Contemporary Eastern and Southeastern Europe in cooperation with University of Macedonia, Thessaloniki; Bachelor in European Economic Studies in cooperation with the Corvinus University of Budapest, Budapest University of Technology, the University of Sarajevo and the University of Tirana.

Student Services: Academic Counselling, Canteen, Careers Guidance, Cultural Activities, Facilities for disabled people, Foreign Studies Centre, IT Centre, Language Laboratory, Library, Residential Facilities, Social Counselling, Sports Facilities, eLibrary

Publications: uni.kat (German only) – News Magazine; uni.vers Forschung (partly in English) – Research Magazine; uni.vers Studium (German only) – Study Magazine

Academic Staff *2015-2016*	MEN	WOMEN	**TOTAL**
FULL-TIME	436	263	**699**
PART-TIME	181	441	**622**
STAFF WITH DOCTORATE			
FULL-TIME	178	83	**261**
Student Numbers *2015-2016*			
All (Foreign included)	5,090	8,286	**13,376**
FOREIGN ONLY	371	696	**1,067**

Part-time students, 445.

Last Updated: 30/11/15

OTTO-VON-GUERICKE UNIVERSITY MAGDEBURG

Otto-von-Guericke-Universität Magdeburg

Universitätsplatz 2, 39016 Magdeburg, Sachsen-Anhalt

Tel: +49(391) 67-01

Fax: +49(391) 671-1156

EMail: rektor@ovgu.de

Website: http://www.ovgu.de

Rector: Jens Strackeljan
Tel: +49(391) 67-58543 EMail: rektor@ovgu.de

Chancellor: Volker Zehle
Tel: +49(391) 671-8503 EMail: kanzler@uni-magdeburg.de

International Relations: Uwe Genetzke
Tel: +49(391) 67-18514 EMail: Uwe.Genetzke@ovgu.de

Faculty

Computer Science (Computer Science; Information Management; Systems Analysis; Telecommunications Engineering); **Economics and Management** (Accountancy; Economic and Finance Policy; Economics; Finance; International Economics; Management; Marketing; Operations Research; Taxation); **Electrical Engineering and Information Technology** (Automation and Control Engineering; Electrical Engineering; Energy Engineering); **Humanities, Social Sciences and Education** (Business Education; Educational Sciences; Germanic Studies; History; History of Societies; Literature; Philology; Political Sciences; Psychology; Sociology; Sports; Vocational Education); **Mathematics** (Applied Mathematics; Mathematics; Statistics); **Mechanical Engineering** (Artificial Intelligence; Automation and Control Engineering; Building Technologies; Materials Engineering; Measurement and Precision Engineering; Mechanical Engineering); **Medicine** (Medicine); **Natural Sciences** (Biology; Experimental Psychology; Natural Sciences; Physics); **Process and Systems Engineering** (Chemical Engineering; Chemistry; Environmental Engineering; Thermal Engineering)

Centre

Audiovisual Media (Media Studies); **Computer** (Computer Science); **Languages** *(Multimedia and Methods in Teaching a Foreign Language)* (English; French; German; Italian; Latin; Modern Languages; Phonetics; Russian; Spanish)

Further Information: Also Hospitals (Krankenhaus Altstadt Magdeburg, Krankenhaus Olvenstedt Magdeburg, Krankenhaus Halberstadt). German language courses for foreign students

History: Founded 1953 as College of Heavy Mechanical Engineering, became Technical University (Technische Hochschule) 1961. Renamed Technische Universität 1987. Acquired present status and title 1993 after the merging of 3 Universities of Magdeburg (Technische Universität Otto von Guericke, Pädagogische Hochschule, Medizinische Akademie Magdeburg).

Academic Year: October to September (October-March; April-September)

Admission Requirements: Secondary school certificate (Reifezeugnis)

Fees: None

Main Language(s) of Instruction: German

Degrees and Diplomas: *Bachelor's Degree*; *Diplom (Univ)*; *Master*: **Applied Mathematics; Bioengineering; Business Administration; Business Computing; Chemical Engineering; Cognitive Sciences; Computer Engineering; Computer Science; Data Processing; Economics; Electrical Engineering; Electronic Engineering; Energy Engineering; Engineering; English Studies; Environmental Engineering; European Studies; Finance; Germanic Studies; History; Industrial Engineering; Information Technology; International Economics; Management; Mathematics; Mathematics and Computer Science; Mechanical Engineering; Media Studies; Medical Technology; Neurosciences; Peace and Disarmament; Philosophy; Physics; Power Engineering; Psychology; Robotics; Safety Engineering; Science Education; Secondary Education; Social Studies; Sports; Statistics; Transport Management; Vocational Education.** *PhD*: **Arts and Humanities; Economics; Educational Research; Electrical Engineering; Engineering Management; Information Technology; Management; Mathematics; Mechanical Engineering; Medicine; Natural Sciences; Production Engineering; Social Studies; Vocational Education.** *Habilitation*: **Arts and Humanities; Engineering; Medicine; Natural Sciences; Social Sciences.** Programmes of the Faculty of Economics and some Master's degrees are conducted in English. Also MBA; State Diploma (Staatsexamen) in Medicine, 12 Sem. and 3 months; Teacher Training Certificate (Lehramt)

Student Services: Academic Counselling, Canteen, Careers Guidance, Cultural Activities, Facilities for disabled people, Health Services, Language Laboratory, Library, Social Counselling, Sports Facilities

Publications: Umweltbericht; Universitätsschriften und Preprint

Student Numbers *2013-2014*: Total 14,104

Last Updated: 25/03/15

PALUCCA UNIVERSITY OF DANCE DRESDEN

Palucca Hochschule für Tanz Dresden

Basteiplatz 4, 01277 Dresden

Tel: +49(351) 25906-0

Fax: +49(351) 25906-11

EMail: Info@palucca.eu; J.Reh@palucca.eu

Website: http://www.palucca-schule-dresden.de

Rector: Jason Beechey
Tel: +49(351) 25906-40
EMail: Rektor@palucca.eu; j.beechey@palucca.eu

Chancellor: Markus Strothteicher

International Relations: Martina Preissler
Tel: +49(351) 25906-21
EMail: martina.preissler@palucca.smwk.sachsen.de

Programme

Choreography (Dance); **Dance** (Dance; Theatre); **Elevenprogramm** *(with the Dresden SemperOper Ballett)*; **Teaching of Dancing (extension course)** (Dance); **Teaching of Dancing (foundation course)** (Dance)

Department

Palucca Tanz Studio (Dance)

History: Founded 1925. Acquired present status 1999.

Admission Requirements: School-leaving certificate qualifying for university entrance, aptitude tests and entrance examination

Fees: 206.90 per semester (Euro)

Main Language(s) of Instruction: German

Degrees and Diplomas: *Bachelor's Degree*; *Künstlerische Abschlussprüfung*: **Dance.** *Master*: **Art Education; Dance.**

Student Services: Academic Counselling, Canteen, Foreign Studies Centre, Health Services, Library, Residential Facilities, Social Counselling, Sports Facilities

Student Numbers *2013-2014*: Total 158
Last Updated: 24/03/15

PFORZHEIM UNIVERSITY

Hochschule Pforzheim
Tiefenbronner Strasse 65, 75175 Pforzheim
Tel: +49(7231) 28-5
Fax: +49(7231) 28-6666
EMail: info@hs-pforzheim.de; aaa@hs-pforzheim.de
Website: http://www.hochschule-pforzheim.de

Rector: Ulrich Jautz
Tel: +49(7231) 28-6000 EMail: ulrich.jautz@hs-pforzheim.de

Head of Administration: Wolfgang Hohl
Tel: +49(7231) 28-6021 EMail: wolfgang.hohl@hs-pforzheim.de

International Relations: Wolfgang Schöllhammer, Director of International Programmes, Institutional Coordinator Mobility Programmes
Tel: +49(7231) 28-6141
EMail: aaa@hs-pforzheim.de; schoellhammer@hs-pforzheim.de

School

Business (Accountancy; Advertising and Publicity; Business Administration; Commercial Law; Economics; Finance; Human Resources; International Business; Marketing; Taxation); **Design** (Design; Fashion Design; Jewellery Art); **Engineering** (Engineering; Industrial Engineering; Machine Building; Mechanical Engineering)

History: Design School founded 1877, Business School founded 1966, Engineering School founded 1992. Acquired present status 1992.

Academic Year: October to July (October-February; March-July)

Admission Requirements: Abitur or Fachhochschulreife

Main Language(s) of Instruction: German, English

Accrediting Agency: Department of Education and Science of the Land of Baden-Wuerttemberg

Degrees and Diplomas: *Bachelor's Degree*; *Master*: **Accountancy; Advertising and Publicity; Business Administration; Business Computing; Commercial Law; Engineering; Finance; Fine Arts; Human Resources; Information Sciences; Information Technology; International Business; Law; Marketing; Mass Communication; Media Studies; Production Engineering; Psychology; Taxation; Transport Engineering; Transport Management.** Also MBA (Human Resources Management and Consulting).

Student Services: Academic Counselling, Canteen, Careers Guidance, Cultural Activities, Facilities for disabled people, Foreign Studies Centre, Language Laboratory, Social Counselling, Sports Facilities

Publications: Konturen

Student Numbers *2013-2014*: Total 5,849
Last Updated: 19/03/15

PHILIPPS-UNIVERSITY OF MARBURG

Philipps-Universität Marburg
Biegenstrasse 10/12, 35037 Marburg/Lahn
Tel: +49(6421) 28-20
Fax: +49(6421) 28-22500
EMail: info@uni-marburg.de
Website: http://www.uni-marburg.de

President: Katharina Krause
Tel: +49(6421) 282-6000 EMail: praesidentin@uni-marburg.de

Chancellor: Friedhelm Nonne
Tel: +49(6421) 28-26100
EMail: kanzler@verwaltung.uni-marburg.de

International Relations: Petra Kienle
Tel: +49(6421) 28-26120
EMail: petra.kienle@verwaltung.uni-marburg.de

Faculty

Biology (Biology; Cell Biology; Ecology; Genetics; Microbiology; Molecular Biology; Parasitology; Plant Pathology); **Business Administration and Economics** (Business Administration; Economics); **Chemistry** (Analytical Chemistry; Biochemistry; Chemistry; Inorganic Chemistry; Organic Chemistry); **Education** (Education; Pedagogy; Sports); **Foreign Languages and Cultures** (Classical Languages; English; Latin; Oriental Languages; Romance Languages; Slavic Languages); **Geography** (Geography; Geology); **German Studies and History of the Arts** (Art History; German; Germanic Studies; Graphic Arts; Media Studies; Musicology; Painting and Drawing; Phonetics); **History and Cultural Studies** (Ancient Civilizations; Archaeology; Chinese; History; Japanese; Modern History; Prehistory); **Law** (Law); **Mathematics and Computer Science** (Computer Science; Mathematics); **Medicine** (Anatomy; Cell Biology; Dentistry; Dermatology; Genetics; Gynaecology and Obstetrics; Haematology; Hygiene; Medicine; Neurosciences; Ophthalmology; Otorhinolaryngology; Pathology; Surgery); **Pharmacy** (Pharmacology; Pharmacy; Toxicology); **Physics** (Physics); **Protestant Theology** (Archaeology; Bible; Ethics; Protestant Theology); **Psychology** (Clinical Psychology; Psychology); **Social Sciences and Philosophy** (Anthropology; Ethnology; Peace and Disarmament; Political Sciences; Sociology)

Centre

Canadian Studies (Canadian Studies)

History: Founded 1527 by Philip the Generous of Hesse as a Protestant State University. An autonomous institution financially supported by the State of Hesse under the jurisdiction of its Ministry of Science and Art.

Academic Year: October to July (October-February; April-July)

Admission Requirements: Secondary school certificate (Reifezeugnis) or equivalent

Fees: None

Main Language(s) of Instruction: German

Degrees and Diplomas: *Bachelor's Degree*; *Kirchliche Abschlussprüfung*: **Protestant Theology.** *Magister*: **Theology.** *Master*: **Aesthetics; Ancient Civilizations; Anthropology; Arabic; Archaeology; Art History; Biology; Business Administration; Cell Biology; Chemistry; Computer Science; Cultural Studies; Development Studies; Economics; Education; Educational Sciences; Ethnology; European Studies; Fine Arts; Foreign Languages Education; German; History; International Business; International Studies; Law; Linguistics; Literature; Mathematics; Media Studies; Molecular Biology; Musicology; Peace and Disarmament; Persian; Philosophy; Physical Therapy; Physics; Political Sciences; Protestant Theology; Religious Studies; Sociology; Speech Studies.** *PhD*: **Biology; Chemistry; Computer Science; Economics; Educational Sciences; Geography; Law; Mathematics; Medicine; Pharmacy; Philosophy; Physics; Psychology; Sociology.** *Habilitation*: **Cultural Studies; Educational Sciences; Geography; History; Law.** Also Teacher Training First State Examination (Lehramt); State Examination (Staatsexam) in Medicine, Pharmacy, Dentistry and Law.

Student Services: Library

Publications: Forschungsbericht; Vorlesungsverzeichnis

Student Numbers *2013-2014*: Total 24,978
Last Updated: 26/03/15

RAVENSBURG-WEINGARTEN UNIVERSITY OF APPLIED SCIENCES

Hochschule Ravensburg-Weingarten - Technik, Wirtschaft, Sozialwesen
Main Building H, Room H022, Doggenriedstr., 88250 Weingarten
Tel: +49(751) 501-9344
Fax: +49(751) 501-9876
EMail: info@hs-weingarten.de
Website: http://www.hs-weingarten.de

Rector: Thomas Spägele
Tel: +49(751) 501-9540
EMail: thomas.spaegele@fh-weingarten.de

Chancellor: Henning Rudewig
Tel: +49(751) 501-9543
EMail: henning.rudewig@hs-weingarten.de

International Relations: Christine Lauer, Head of International Office
Tel: +49(751) 501-4659 EMail: christine.lauer@hs-weingarten.de

Faculty
Electrical Engineering and Computer Science (Business Computing; Computer Science; E- Business/Commerce; Electrical Engineering; Electronic Engineering; Engineering; Information Technology; Mechanical Engineering); **Mechanical Engineering** (Mechanical Engineering); **Social Work, Health and Management** (Health Administration; Nursing; Social Work); **Technology and Management** (Management; Technology)

History: Founded 1964. Acquired present status 1971.

Academic Year: September to August (September-February; March-August)

Fees: 500 per semester (Euro)

Main Language(s) of Instruction: German, English

Accrediting Agency: ASIIN

Degrees and Diplomas: *Bachelor's Degree*; *Master*: **Business Administration; Business Computing; Computer Science; Electrical Engineering; Electronic Engineering; Environmental Engineering; Health Administration; Health Sciences; International Business; Mechanical Engineering; Optical Technology; Welfare and Protective Services.**

Student Services: Academic Counselling, Canteen, Careers Guidance, IT Centre, Language Laboratory, Library, Sports Facilities

Student Numbers *2013-2014*: Total 3,465
Last Updated: 19/03/15

REUTLINGEN UNIVERSITY

Hochschule Reutlingen
Alteburgstrasse 150, 72762 Reutlingen, Baden-Württemberg
Tel: +49(7121) 271-457
Fax: +49(7121) 271-688
EMail: vorzimmer.praesidium@reutlingen-university.de
Website: http://www.reutlingen-university.de/

Rector: Hendrick Brumme
Tel: +49(7121) 271-1001
EMail: hendrik.brumme@reutlingen-university.de

Chancellor: Paula Mattes
Tel: +49(7121) 271-1011 EMail: Paula.Mattes@fh-reutlingen.de

International Relations: Baldur Veit, Director, International Office
Tel: +49(7121) 271-1004 EMail: Baldur.Veit@fh-reutlingen.de

Faculty
Applied Chemistry (Applied Chemistry); **Informatics** (Computer Science); **Technology** (Electronic Engineering; Engineering; Machine Building; Mechanical Engineering); **Textile and Design** (Design; Textile Design)

School
Business (Business Administration; Business and Commerce)

History: Founded 1971.

Admission Requirements: Secondary school certificate (Abitur, Fachhochschulreifezeugnis)

Main Language(s) of Instruction: German

Degrees and Diplomas: *Bachelor's Degree*; *Master*: **Accountancy; Applied Chemistry; Biomedicine; Business Computing; Clothing and Sewing; Computer Science; Design; Electronic Engineering; Energy Engineering; Engineering Management; Environmental Management; International Business; Management; Mechanical Engineering; Microelectronics; Power Engineering; Taxation; Textile Design.** Also International Management (MBA), (full-time or part-time).

Student Services: Academic Counselling, Canteen, Facilities for disabled people, Foreign Studies Centre, Language Laboratory, Social Counselling, Sports Facilities

Student Numbers *2013-2014*: Total 5,480
Last Updated: 19/03/15

RHEIN-MAIN UNIVERSITY OF APPLIED SCIENCES

Hochschule Rhein-Main
Kurt-Schumacher-Ring 18, 65197 Wiesbaden
Tel: +49(611) 9495-01
Fax: +49(611) 4446-96
EMail: ipunkt@hs-rm.de
Website: https://www.hs-rm.de/

President: Detlev Reymann (2009-)
Tel: +49(611) 9495-1100 EMail: praesident@hs-rm.de

Chancellor: Wilfried Friedl
Tel: +49(611) 9495-1102 EMail: kanzler@hs-rm.de

International Relations: Birgit Klose, Director, International Office
EMail: birgit.klose@hs-rm.de

Faculty
Applied Social Sciences *(Wiesbaden)* (Social Work); **Architecture and Civil Engineering** *(Wiesbaden)* (Architecture; Civil Engineering); **Design, Computer Science and Media** *(Wiesbaden)* (Computer Science; Design; Interior Design; Media Studies); **Engineering** *(Rüsselsheim)* (Electrical Engineering; Engineering; Environmental Engineering; Industrial Engineering; Information Technology; Management); **Geisenheim** (Horticulture; Landscape Architecture; Oenology; Viticulture)

School
Business Studies *(Wiesbaden)* (Business Administration; Economics)

Further Information: A traditional and distance learning institution.

History: Founded 1971 as Fachhochschule Wiesbaden. Acquired present title 2009.

Main Language(s) of Instruction: German

Degrees and Diplomas: *Bachelor's Degree*; *Diplom (FH)*: **Electrical Engineering.** *Master*: **Applied Physics; Architecture; Automotive Engineering; Bioengineering; Business Administration; Civil Engineering; Computer Science; Construction Engineering; Environmental Engineering; Environmental Management; Finance; Information Technology; Interior Design; International Business; Law; Marketing; Media Studies; Production Engineering; Sales Techniques; Town Planning.** Cooperative Degree Programmes in: Electrical Engineering, Engineering, Industrial Engineering and International Business, Insurance and Finance; Part-time Degree Programmes for Professionals in: Electrical Engineering, Mechanical Engineering; Distance Learning Programmes: Social Work (Master of Arts); Social Work (Bachelor of Arts).

Student Services: Canteen, IT Centre, Library

Student Numbers *2013-2014*: Total 10,207
Last Updated: 19/03/15

RHENISH FRIEDRICH-WILHELM UNIVERSITY BONN

Rheinische Friedrich-Wilhelms-Universität Bonn
Regina-Pacis-Weg 3, 53012 Bonn
Tel: +49(228) 73-0
Fax: +49(228) 73-1780
EMail: kommunikation@uni-bonn.de
Website: http://www.uni-bonn.de

Rector: Jürgen Fohrmann
Tel: +49(228) 73-7297 EMail: rektor@uni-bonn.de

Kanzler: Reinhard Lutz
Tel: +49(228) 73-7636 EMail: kanzler@uni-bonn.de

International Relations: Lieselotte Krickau-Richter

Faculty
Agriculture (Agriculture; Economics; Food Science; Food Technology; Nutrition; Surveying and Mapping); **Arts** (Archaeology; Art History; Classical Languages; Comparative Religion; Educational Sciences; History; Linguistics; Literature; Modern Languages; Musicology; Philosophy; Political Sciences; Psychology; Sociology; Sports); **Catholic Theology** (Catholic Theology; Pastoral Studies; Religious Studies); **Law and Economics** (Economics; Law); **Mathematics and Natural Sciences** (Astronomy and Space

Science; Biology; Chemistry; Computer Science; Geography; Geology; Meteorology; Mineralogy; Physics); **Medicine** (Dentistry; Medicine); **Protestant Theology** (Protestant Theology)

Institute

Old Catholic Theology Seminary (Theology)

Centre

Development Research (Development Studies); **European Integration** (European Studies); **Teacher Training** *(Bonner Ausbildungszentrum für Lehrerinnen und Lehrer)*

Research Institute

Discrete Mathematics (Mathematics); **Late Classical Antiquity** *(Franz Joseph Dölger)*

History: Founded 1777 by the Electoral Archbishop of Cologne, raised to University rank 1786, dissolved 1794. Refounded 1818 by William III of Prussia. Academy of Agriculture incorporated 1934. An autonomous institution financially supported by the State of North Rhine-Westphalia, and under the jurisdiction of its Ministry of Education.

Academic Year: October to September (October-February; April-July)

Admission Requirements: Secondary school certificate (Reifezeugnis) or equivalent

Fees: None

Main Language(s) of Instruction: German

Degrees and Diplomas: *Bachelor's Degree*; *Kirchliche Abschlussprüfung*: **Catholic Theology; Protestant Theology.** *Magister*: **Catholic Theology; Protestant Theology.** *Master*: **Agricultural Economics; Agriculture; Agronomy; American Studies; Ancient Civilizations; Animal Husbandry; Anthropology; Applied Linguistics; Archaeology; Art History; Asian Studies; Astrophysics; Biological and Life Sciences; Biology; Biotechnology; Botany; Catholic Theology; Chemistry; Comparative Literature; Computer Science; Consumer Studies; Crop Production; Earth Sciences; Economics; Education; English; English Studies; Environmental Management; Ethnology; European Studies; Food Science; Food Technology; French; French Studies; Geography; German; Germanic Studies; Greek (Classical); History; Home Economics; Italian; Landscape Architecture; Latin; Latin American Studies; Law; Literature; Mathematics; Media Studies; Medicine; Medieval Studies; Mediterranean Studies; Microbiology; Modern History; Molecular Biology; Museum Studies; Neurosciences; Nutrition; Pharmacology; Philosophy; Physics; Political Sciences; Prehistory; Protective Services; Protestant Theology; Psychology; Religion; Romance Languages; Scandinavian Languages; Social Studies; Spanish; Surveying and Mapping; Theology; Tropical Agriculture; Zoology.** *PhD*: **Agriculture; Arts and Humanities; Catholic Theology; Law; Mathematics; Medicine; Natural Sciences; Protestant Theology.** *Habilitation*: **Agriculture; Arts and Humanities; Law; Mathematics; Medicine; Natural Sciences.** Also State Examination (Staatsexam) in Food Technology, Medicine, Dentistry, Pharmacy and Law; Teacher Training Examination (Lehramt).

Student Services: Academic Counselling, Canteen, Careers Guidance, Facilities for disabled people, Health Services, Nursery Care, Social Counselling, Sports Facilities

Publications: Bonner Akademische Reden

Student Numbers *2013-2014*: Total 31,878
Last Updated: 26/03/15

RHINE-WAAL UNIVERSITY OF APPLIED SCIENCES

Hochschule Rhein-Waal (HSRW)

Marie-Curie-Str. 1, D-47533 Kleve, North Rhine-Westphalia
Tel: +49 2821 806 73-0
Fax: +49 2821 806 73-160
EMail: info@hochschule-rhein-waal.de
Website: http://www.hochschule-rhein-waal.de

President: Marie Louise Klotz (2009 -)
Tel: +49 (2821) 80673-100
EMail: präsidentin@hochschule-rhein-waal.de

Vice-President for Research and Development: Peter Scholz
Tel: +49(2821) 80673-202
EMail: peter.scholz@hochschule-rhein-waal.de

Vice-President for Finance and Human Resources: Bibiana Kemner
Tel: +49(2821) 80673-102
EMail: bibiana.kemner@hochschule-rhein-waal.de

Vice-President for Studies, Teaching and Further Education: Anja von Richthofen
Tel: +49(2842) 90825-232
EMail: anja.von-richthofen@hochschule-rhein-waal.de

International Relations: Joost Kleuters, Director of the International Office
Tel: +49(2821) 80673-140
EMail: joost.kleuters@hochschule-rhein-waal.de

Department

Communication and Environmental Studies (Communication Studies; Computer Science; Energy Engineering; Environmental Studies; Industrial Engineering; International Business; Media Studies; Psychology; Social Sciences); **Life Sciences** (Agricultural Business; Agriculture; Bioengineering; Biological and Life Sciences; Food Science; Health Sciences); **Society and Economics** (Economics; Finance; Gender Studies; International Business; International Relations; Preschool Education; Social Sciences; Taxation; Tourism); **Technology and Bionics** (Biotechnology; Electronic Engineering; Industrial Engineering; Materials Engineering; Mechanical Engineering)

Further Information: Campus in Kamp-Lintfort

History: Founded 2009 by the federal state of North Rhine-Westphalia and overseen by the NRW Ministry of Education and Research.

Academic Year: September to August (September-February; March-August)

Fees: National: None. Students are required to pay a semester fee (251.46 as of Summer Semester 2015), which includes free access to buses and trains throughout the federal state of North Rhine-Westphalia for the duration of the semester (Euro), International: None

Main Language(s) of Instruction: English, German

Accrediting Agency: ASIIN; AQAS

Degrees and Diplomas: *Bachelor's Degree*: **Agricultural Business; Agriculture; Bioengineering; Biological and Life Sciences; Biotechnology; Communication Studies; Computer Science; Economics; Electronic Engineering; Energy Engineering; Environmental Studies; Finance; Gender Studies; Health Sciences; Industrial Engineering; International Business; International Relations; Materials Engineering; Mechanical Engineering; Media Studies; Preschool Education; Psychology; Social Sciences; Taxation; Tourism.** *Master*: **Computer Science; Economics; Food Science; Industrial and Organizational Psychology; Materials Engineering; Mechanical Engineering; Media Studies.** *PhD*. A doctorate can be earned in co-operation with a fully fledged research university.

Student Services: Academic Counselling, Canteen, Careers Guidance, Cultural Activities, Facilities for disabled people, Foreign Studies Centre, IT Centre, Language Laboratory, Library, Nursery Care, Residential Facilities, Social Counselling

Student Numbers *2014-2015*: Total: c. 5,300
Last Updated: 03/02/15

ROBERT SCHUMANN SCHOOL OF MUSIC AND MEDIA

Robert-Schumann-Hochschule Düsseldorf

Fischerstrasse 110, 40476 Düsseldorf
Tel: +49(211) 4918-0
Fax: +49(211) 4911-618
EMail: kontakt@rsh-duesseldorf.de
Website: http://www.rsh-duesseldorf.de/de/index.php

Rektor: Raimund Wippermann (2004-) Tel: +49(211) 4918-109
Chancellor: Cathrin Müller-Brosch Tel: +49(211) 4918-108

Institute
Church Music (Religious Music); **Composition and Music Theory** (Music Theory and Composition); **Music and Media** (Media Studies; Music); **Musicology** (Musicology)

History: Founded 1935.

Main Language(s) of Instruction: German

Degrees and Diplomas: *Bachelor's Degree*; *Konzertexamen*: **Music Theory and Composition; Musical Instruments; Singing.** *Master*: **Conducting; Musical Instruments; Musicology; Religious Music; Singing.** *PhD*: **Musicology.**

Student Services: Library

Student Numbers *2013-2014*: Total 804
Last Updated: 22/03/15

ROSENHEIM UNIVERSITY OF APPLIED SCIENCES

Hochschule Rosenheim
Hochschulstraße 1, 83024 Rosenheim
Tel: +49(8031) 805-0
Fax: +49(8031) 805-2105
EMail: info@fh-rosenheim.de
Website: http://www.fh-rosenheim.de/

President: Heinrich Köster
Tel: +49(8031) 805-2110
EMail: koester@fh-rosenheim.de; praesident@fh-rosenheim.de

Chancellor: Oliver Heller
Tel: +49(8031) 805-2130
EMail: heller@fh-rosenheim.de; kanzler@fh-rosenheim.de

International Relations: Sibylle Möbius, Head, International Office
Tel: +49(8031) 805-118
EMail: sibylle.moebius@fh-rosenheim.de; international@fh-rosenheim.de

Faculty
Applied Natural and Social Sciences (Chemistry; Computer Science; Cultural Studies; Data Processing; Economics; Environmental Studies; Industrial Management; Mathematics; Modern Languages; Natural Sciences; Operations Research; Physics; Public Administration; Safety Engineering; Social Sciences; Statistics; Transport Management); **Business Administration** (Business Administration; Business and Commerce; Business Computing); **Business Administration and Engineering** *(KPE)* (Electronic Engineering; Information Technology; Management; Materials Engineering; Production Engineering); **Computer Science** (Business Computing; Computer Science); **Engineering** (Business Administration; Engineering); **Interior Architecture** (Interior Design); **Wood Technology and Construction** (Industrial Engineering; Wood Technology)

Institute
Healthcare (Health Sciences; Physical Therapy)

Academy
Study for the Professional (Business Administration; Construction Engineering; Energy Engineering; Engineering; Information Technology; Machine Building)

History: Founded 1971. Formerly known as Fachhochschule Rosenheim - Hochschule für Technik und Wirtschaft.

Academic Year: October to July (October- February; March-July)

Admission Requirements: Secondary school certificate

Main Language(s) of Instruction: German

Degrees and Diplomas: *Bachelor's Degree*: **Actuarial Science; Business Administration; Business Computing; Computer Science; Electrical Engineering; Electronic Engineering; Energy Engineering; Engineering; Health Administration; Information Technology; Interior Design; Mechanical Engineering; Physical Therapy; Polymer and Plastics Technology; Production Engineering; Wood Technology.** *Master*: **Business Administration; Computer Science; Construction Engineering; Electrical Engineering; Electronic Engineering; Energy Engineering; Engineering; Information Technology; Interior Design; International Business; Management; Mechanical Engineering; Wood Technology.** Also Continuing Education Masters courses in Window and Façade; Wood Construction Architecture. MBA (Management and Leadership skills); Some Master's Degree programmes conducted in English.

Student Services: Academic Counselling, Canteen, Language Laboratory, Library, Social Counselling, Sports Facilities

Student Numbers *2013-2014*: Total 5,505
Last Updated: 13/03/15

ROSTOCK UNIVERSITY OF MUSIC AND DRAMA

Hochschule für Musik und Theater Rostock (HMT)
Beim St.-Katharinenstift 8, 18055 Rostock
Tel: +49(381) 5108-0
Fax: +49(381) 5108-101
EMail: hmt@hmt-rostock.de
Website: http://www.hmt-rostock.de

Rector: Susanne Winnacker (2012-)
Tel: +49(381) 5108-100 EMail: rektor@hmt-rostock.de

Chancellor: Frank Ivemeyer
Tel: +49 (381) 5108-200 EMail: Kanzler@hmt-rostock.de

International Relations: Philippe Olivier, international Relations
Tel: +33(1) 429-33958 EMail: philippe.olivier@berlin.de

Institute
Drama (Acting; Theatre); **Music** (Music); **Musicology and Music Education** (Music Education; Musicology)

History: Founded 1994.

Admission Requirements: Aptitude test

Main Language(s) of Instruction: German

Accrediting Agency: ACQUIN Accreditation Agency

Degrees and Diplomas: *Bachelor's Degree*: **Conducting; Jazz and Popular Music; Music Theory and Composition; Musical Instruments; Singing; Theatre.** *Konzertexamen*: **Conducting; Music Theory and Composition; Musical Instruments; Singing.** *Diplom (Univ)*: **Art Education; Conducting; Music Education; Music Theory and Composition; Musical Instruments; Musicology; Singing; Theatre.** *Master*: **Art Education.** *PhD*: **Music Education; Musicology.**

Student Services: Canteen, Library

Student Numbers *2013-2014*: Total 541
Last Updated: 03/02/15

ROTTENBURG UNIVERSITY OF APPLIED FOREST SCIENCES

Hochschule für Forstwirtschaft Rottenburg (HFR)
Schadenweilerhof, 72108 Rottenburg am Neckar
Tel: +49(7472) 951-0
Fax: +49(7472) 951-200
EMail: hfr@hs-rottenburg.de
Website: http://www.fh-rottenburg.de

Rector: Bastian Kaiser
Tel: +49(7472) 951-204 EMail: BKaiser@hs-rottenburg.de

Chancellor: Gerhard Weik
Tel: +49(7472) 951-201 EMail: weik@hs-rottenburg.de

International Relations: Stefan Ruge, Head, International Office
Tel: +49(7472) 951-233 EMail: ruge@hs-rottenburg.de

Programme
Forestry (Forestry); **Renewable Energy** (Energy Engineering); **Resource Efficient Building** *(Graduate)* (Building Technologies); **Sustainable Energy Competence** *(SENCE - Graduate)* (Energy Engineering); **Sustainable Regional Management** (Environmental Management); **Timber Industry** (Forest Products); **Water Management** (Water Management)

History: Founded 1954, acquired present status 1979. Formerly known as Fachhochschule Rottenburg - Hochschule für Fortswirtschaft.

Academic Year: October to July

Admission Requirements: Secondary school certificate (Hochschulreife) or equivalent

Fees: None

Main Language(s) of Instruction: German, English

Degrees and Diplomas: *Bachelor's Degree*: **Environmental Management; Environmental Studies; Forest Products; Forestry; Natural Resources.** *Master*: **Building Technologies; Energy Engineering; Environmental Engineering.**

Student Services: Academic Counselling, Canteen, Language Laboratory, Library, Social Counselling, Sports Facilities

Student Numbers *2013-2014*: Total 942

Last Updated: 05/03/15

RUHR-WEST UNIVERSITY OF APPLIED SCIENCES

Hochschule Ruhr-West

Brunshofstraße 12, 45470 Mülheim an der Ruhr
Tel: +49(208) 302 46-0
Fax: +49(208) 302 46-102
EMail: info@hs-ruhrwest.de
Website: http://www.hochschule-ruhr-west.de

President: Eberhard Menzel
Tel: +49(208) 88254-115 EMail: menzel.eberhard@hs-ruhrwest.de

Faculty

Business Administration *(II)* (Business Administration; International Business; Management; Water Management); **Computer Science** *(I)* (Computer Science; Engineering); **Electrical Engineering** *(IV)* (Electrical Engineering; Electronic Engineering); **Mechanical Engineering** *(III)* (Civil Engineering; Industrial Engineering; Mechanical Engineering)

History: Founded 2009.

Main Language(s) of Instruction: German

Degrees and Diplomas: *Bachelor's Degree*; *Master*: **Business Administration; Computer Science; Energy Engineering; Engineering; Industrial Engineering; Information Technology; Production Engineering.** Also Dual Degree Programmes; Bachelor Plus Progamme in International Economics - Emerging Markets (focused on China).

Student Services: Careers Guidance, IT Centre, Library

Student Numbers *2013-2014*: Total 852

Last Updated: 19/03/15

RWTH - AACHEN UNIVERSITY

Rheinisch-Westfälische Technische Hochschule Aachen

Templergraben 55, 52056 Aachen
Tel: +49(241) 80-1 +49(241) 80-13
Fax: +49(241) 80-92312
EMail: info@rwth-aachen.de
Website: http://www.rwth-aachen.de

Rector: Ernst M. Schmachtenberg (2008-)
Tel: +49(241) 80-94000 EMail: rektor@rwth-aachen.de

Chancellor: Manfred Nettekoven
Tel: +49(241) 80-94010 EMail: kanzler@zhv.rwth-aachen.de

International Relations: Henriette Finsterbusch, Head, International Office
Tel: +49(241) 80-90663
EMail: international@rwth-aachen.de; henriette.finsterbusch@zhv.rwth-aachen.de

Faculty

Architecture (Architectural and Environmental Design; Architecture; Art History; Design; Fine Arts; Landscape Architecture; Painting and Drawing; Regional Planning; Structural Architecture; Town Planning); **Arts and Humanities** (Educational Sciences; English; German; History; Linguistics; Literature; Philosophy; Political Sciences; Psychology; Romance Languages; Sociology; Theology); **Business and Economics** (Accountancy; Banking; Business Administration; Commercial Law; E- Business/Commerce; Economics; Finance; Industrial Management; Information Sciences; International Business; Management; Operations Research; Taxation; Technology; Transport Management); **Civil Engineering** (Business Administration; Civil Engineering; Construction Engineering; Environmental Engineering; Geological Engineering; Hydraulic Engineering; Management; Mechanical Engineering; Town Planning; Transport Engineering; Waste Management; Water Management); **Electrical Engineering and Information Technology** (Biomedical Engineering; Computer Science; Electrical Engineering; Electronic Engineering; Engineering; Information Technology; Measurement and Precision Engineering; Petroleum and Gas Engineering; Power Engineering; Sound Engineering (Acoustics); Telecommunications Engineering); **Georesources and Materials Engineering** (Geology; Materials Engineering; Metallurgical Engineering; Mining Engineering; Waste Management); **Mathematics, Computer Science and Natural Sciences** (Biology; Chemistry; Computer Science; Mathematics; Natural Sciences; Physics); **Mechanical Engineering** (Aeronautical and Aerospace Engineering; Automation and Control Engineering; Automotive Engineering; Biochemistry; Ceramics and Glass Technology; Chemical Engineering; Computer Engineering; Computer Science; Heating and Refrigeration; Industrial Engineering; Laser Engineering; Materials Engineering; Mechanical Engineering; Mechanics; Medical Technology; Metal Techniques; Nuclear Engineering; Operations Research; Optical Technology; Physical Engineering; Polymer and Plastics Technology; Power Engineering; Production Engineering; Railway Engineering; Textile Technology; Thermal Engineering); **Medicine** (Anaesthesiology; Cardiology; Dentistry; Gynaecology and Obstetrics; Medicine; Neurology; Ophthalmology; Orthodontics; Orthopaedics; Plastic Surgery; Psychiatry and Mental Health; Radiology; Surgery; Urology)

Further Information: Language courses and MSc programmes for international students. International Study programmes

History: Founded 1870 as Polytechnikum, became Technische Hochschule in 1880 and acquired present title 1948, reorganized 1970. Under the jurisdiction of and financed by the State of North Rhine-Westphalia.

Academic Year: October to September (October-March; April-September)

Admission Requirements: Secondary school certificate (Reifezeugnis) or equivalent

Fees: c. 1,300 per annum (Euro)

Main Language(s) of Instruction: German

Degrees and Diplomas: *Bachelor's Degree*; *Master*: **Aeronautical and Aerospace Engineering; Architecture; Automation and Control Engineering; Automotive Engineering; Biology; Biomedical Engineering; Biotechnology; Business Administration; Chemistry; Civil Engineering; Communication Studies; Computer Engineering; Computer Science; Dental Technology; Earth Sciences; Ecology; Economics; Educational Administration; Educational Research; Electrical Engineering; Electronic Engineering; Energy Engineering; Engineering; English; English Studies; Environmental Engineering; European Studies; Foreign Languages Education; Geography; Geography (Human); Geophysics; German; History; Humanities and Social Science Education; Industrial Engineering; Information Technology; Laboratory Techniques; Linguistics; Literature; Materials Engineering; Mathematics; Mechanical Engineering; Media Studies; Metallurgical Engineering; Molecular Biology; Natural Resources; Philosophy; Physics; Political Sciences; Power Engineering; Production Engineering; Psychology; Science Education; Secondary Education; Sociology; Software Engineering; Speech Studies; Technology Education; Telecommunications Engineering; Textile Technology; Town Planning; Transport and Communications; Transport Management.** *PhD*: **Architecture; Civil Engineering; Computer Engineering; Computer Science; Economics; Electrical Engineering; Materials Engineering; Mathematics; Mechanical Engineering; Medicine; Natural Resources; Natural Sciences; Philosophy.** *Habilitation*: **Architecture; Civil Engineering; Computer Engineering; Computer Science; Electronic Engineering; Materials Engineering; Mathematics; Mechanical Engineering; Medicine; Natural Resources; Natural Sciences; Philosophy.** Final State Examination (Staatsexam) in Medicine and Dentistry; Teacher Training State Examination (Lehrmat); Master's Degree Programmes are taught in English in: Geophysics, Automotive Engineering, Biomedical Engineering, Electrical Engineering, Information Technology and Computer Engineering, Media Studies, Metallurgical Engineering, Physics, Software Engineering.

Student Services: Canteen, IT Centre, Library, Social Counselling, Sports Facilities

Publications: Alma Mater Aquensis; RWTH-Themen

Academic Staff *2013-2014*: Total 5,257
Student Numbers *2014-2015*: Total 42,298
Last Updated: 25/03/15

SAAR COLLEGE OF FINE ARTS

Hochschule der Bildenden Künste Saar

Keplerstraße 3-5, 66117 Saarbrücken
Tel: +49(681) 92652-101
Fax: +49(681) 92652-149
EMail: info@hbks.uni-sb.de; presse@hbksaar.de
Website: http://www.hbks.uni-sb.de

Rektor: Gabriele Langendorf
Tel: +49(681) 92652-126 EMail: g.Langendorf@hbksaar.de

Chancellor: Heinrich Scherber EMail: h.Scherber@hbksaar.de

International Relations: Sabine Rauber, Officer, International Academic Affairs
Tel: +49(681) 92652-115 EMail: s.rauber@hbksaar.de

Programme

Communication Design (Communication Arts; Design); **Fine Arts** (Fine Arts); **Master Study** (Design; Fine Arts; Museum Studies); **Media Art and Design** (Communication Arts; Design); **Product Design** (Industrial Design); **Teacher Training in Art Education** (Art Education; Teacher Training)

History: Founded 1989.

Degrees and Diplomas: *Bachelor's Degree*: **Communication Arts; Design; Fine Arts; Graphic Design; Industrial Design.** *Künstlerische Abschlussprüfung*: **Communication Arts; Design; Fine Arts; Graphic Design; Industrial Design.** *Master*: **Design; Fine Arts; Museum Studies.** *PhD*: **Fine Arts.**

Student Services: Library

Student Numbers *2013-2014*: Total 398
Last Updated: 22/01/15

SAARLAND UNIVERSITY

Universität des Saarlandes

PO Box 151150, Im Stadtwald, 66041 Saarbrücken
Tel: +49(681) 302-0
Fax: +49(681) 302-2609
EMail: postzentrale@univw.uni-saarland.de
Website: http://www.uni-saarland.de

President: Volker Linneweber (2006-)
Tel: +49(681) 302-2000
EMail: praesident@uni-saarland.de; prbuero@univw.uni-saarland.de

Vice President for administrative and financial Management: Roland Rolles
Tel: +1(681) 302-2002 EMail: vpvw@uni-saarland.de

International Relations: Johannes Abele, Head, International Office Tel: +49(681) 302-71104 EMail: j.abele@io.uni-saarland.de

Faculty

Humanities I (Art History; Catholic Theology; History; Music; Theology); **Humanities II** (American Studies; English; German; Linguistics; Modern Languages; Romance Languages; Slavic Languages); **Humanities III** (Geography; Psychology; Sociology; Sports); **Law and Economics** (Business Administration; Economics; Law; Statistics); **Medicine** *(Homburg Campus)* (Health Sciences; Medicine); **Natural Sciences and Technology I** (Mathematics and Computer Science); **Natural Sciences and Technology II** (Mechanical Engineering; Physics); **Natural Sciences and Technology III** (Biotechnology; Chemistry; Materials Engineering; Pharmacy)

History: Founded 1948 with the help of France, the University became a member of the Western German Rectors' Conference (WRK; today Hochschulrektorenkonferenz-HRK) 1957. Financially supported by the State of the Saar, and under the jurisdiction of its Ministry of Education and Science.

Academic Year: October to September (October-March; April-September)

Admission Requirements: Secondary school certificate (Abitur) or equivalent

Fees: In some postgraduate programmes; normal course per semester 300 first year, 1,000 each following year (Euro)

Main Language(s) of Instruction: German, English

Degrees and Diplomas: *Bachelor's Degree*; *Master*: **American Studies; Ancient Civilizations; Applied Mathematics; Archaeology; Art History; Biological and Life Sciences; Biology; Biophysics; Biotechnology; Business Administration; Business Computing; Business Education; Chemistry; Classical Languages; Commercial Law; Communication Studies; Comparative Literature; Computer Engineering; Computer Graphics; Computer Science; Cultural Studies; Economics; Educational Technology; Engineering; English; English Studies; European Union Law; Finance; Foreign Languages Education; French Studies; German; Germanic Studies; Health Administration; History; International Law; Law; Linguistics; Literature; Management; Materials Engineering; Mathematics; Mechanical Engineering; Media Studies; Modern Languages; Molecular Biology; Musicology; Nanotechnology; Philosophy; Physics; Prehistory; Protective Services; Psychology; Religious Studies; Romance Languages; Slavic Languages; Speech Studies; Sports; Sports Management; Telecommunications Engineering; Translation and Interpretation.** *PhD*: **Cultural Studies; Economics; History; Law; Literature; Medicine; Modern Languages; Natural Sciences; Social Sciences; Technology.** *Habilitation*: **Law; Medicine; Natural Sciences; Social Sciences; Technology.** Some Programmes taught in French; Also Certificates (Zertifikate); State Examination Certificate (Staatsexam) in Medicine, Pharmacy, Law and Dentistry; Teacher Training State Certificate (Lehramt).

Student Services: Academic Counselling, Canteen, Careers Guidance, Facilities for disabled people, IT Centre, Language Laboratory, Library, Nursery Care, Social Counselling, Sports Facilities

Academic Staff *2014-2015*: Total 1,311
Student Numbers *2013-2014*: Total: c. 17,800
Last Updated: 30/03/15

SAARLAND UNIVERSITY OF APPLIED SCIENCES

Hochschule für Technik und Wirtschaft des Saarlandes (HTW SAAR)

Goebenstrasse 40, 66117 Saarbrücken
Tel: +49(681) 5867-0
Fax: +49(681) 5867-122
EMail: info@htwsaar.de
Website: http://www.htwsaar.de

Rektor: Wolrad Rommel (2013-)
Tel: +49(681) 5867-100 EMail: rektor@htwsaar.de

Head of Administration: Norbert Hudlet
Tel: +49(681) 5867-110 EMail: norbert.hudlet@htwsaar.de

International Relations: Doris Kollmann
Tel: +49(681) 5867-609
EMail: io@htwsaar.de; doris.kollmann@htwsaar.de

Faculty

Architecture and Civil Engineering *(Waldhausweg)* (Architecture; Civil Engineering); **Business Administration** *(Waldhausweg)* (Accountancy; Aeronautical and Aerospace Engineering; Business Administration; Industrial Engineering; International Business; Management); **Engineering** (Biomedical Engineering; Computer Engineering; Electrical and Electronic Engineering; Mechanical Engineering); **Social Science** (Health Sciences; Social Work)

History: Founded 1971.

Academic Year: October to September (October-March; April-September)

Admission Requirements: General or subject-specific university entrance qualification (e.g. A-Levels, High School Diploma) is required

Fees: 177,50 per semester (Euro)

Main Language(s) of Instruction: German, English, French

Accrediting Agency: ASIIN (Institutional Accreditation of Degree Programmes in Engineering, Computer Science, Natural Sciences, Mathematics and Teaching Qualification); FIBAA (Foundation for International Business Administration Accreditation); ZEvA (Central Evaluation and Accreditation Agency)

Degrees and Diplomas: *Bachelor's Degree*; *Master*: **Accountancy; Architecture; Art Management; Biomedical Engineering; Civil Engineering; Computer Science; Electrical Engineering; Electronic Engineering; Finance; Industrial Engineering; Leisure Studies; Management; Marketing; Mechanical Engineering; Sports; Tourism.**

Student Services: Academic Counselling, Canteen, Careers Guidance, Cultural Activities, Facilities for disabled people, Foreign Studies Centre, IT Centre, Language Laboratory, Library, Residential Facilities, Social Counselling, Sports Facilities, eLibrary

Academic Staff *2014-2015*: Total 450

STAFF WITH DOCTORATE: Total 140

Student Numbers *2014-2015*: Total: c. 5,800

Last Updated: 03/02/15

SCHWÄBISCH GMÜND UNIVERSITY OF APPLIED SCIENCES FOR DESIGN

Hochschule für Gestaltung Schwäbisch Gmünd

Postfach 1308, Rektor-Klaus-Straße 100, 73525 Schwäbisch Gmünd
Tel: +49(7171) 602 600
Fax: +49(7171) 692-59
EMail: info@hfg-gmuend.de
Website: http://www.hfg-gmuend.de

Rector: Ralf Dringenberg (2015-)
Tel: +49(7171) 602-601 EMail: ralf.dringenberg@hfg-gmuend.de

Programme

Communication Design (Graphic Design); **Foundations of Design** (Design); **Interaction Design** (Design); **Product Design** (Industrial Design); **Strategic Design** *(Master)* (Design)

History: Founded 1907. Acquired present status 1971.

Admission Requirements: Fachhochschulreife and entrance examination

Fees: None

Main Language(s) of Instruction: German, English

Degrees and Diplomas: *Bachelor's Degree*: **Design; Graphic Design; Industrial Design.** *Master*: **Design.**

Student Services: Academic Counselling, Canteen

Student Numbers *2013-2014*: Total 622

Last Updated: 05/03/15

SOUTH WESTPHALIA UNIVERSITY OF APPLIED SCIENCES

Fachhochschule Südwestfalen (FH-SWF)

PO Box 2061, Frauenstuhlweg 31, 58644 Iserlohn
Tel: +49(2371) 566-0
Fax: +49(2371) 566-274
EMail: aaa@fh-swf.de
Website: http://www.fh-swf.de

Rector: Claus Schuster (2008-)
Tel: +49(2371) 566-110
EMail: schuster@fh-swf.de; rektor@fh-swf.de

Vizepräsident für Wirtschafts- und Personalverwaltung: Heinz-Joachim Henkemeier
Tel: +49(2371) 566-121 EMail: henkemeier.heinz@fh-swf.de

International Relations: Dagmar Perizonius
Tel: +49(2371) 566-513
EMail: aaa@fh-swf.de; perizonius.dagmar@fh-swf.de

Department

Agriculture *(Soest)* (Agriculture); **Computer Science and Natural Sciences** *(Iserlohn)* (Computer Science; Natural Sciences); **Electrical and Computer Engineering** *(Hagen)* (Computer Engineering; Electrical Engineering); **Electrical Power Engineering** *(Soest)* (Electrical Engineering; Power Engineering); **Engineering and Economics** *(Meschede)* (Economics; Engineering); **Industrial Management** *(Hagen)* (Industrial Management); **Machine Building and Automation Engineering** *(Soest)* (Automation and Control Engineering; Machine Building); **Mechanical Engineering** *(Iserlohn)* (Mechanical Engineering)

Centre

Early Childhood Education *(Soest)* (Preschool Education)

Further Information: Campuses in Hagen, Iserlohn, Meschede, Soest, Lüdenscheid

History: Founded 2002, after merger with Märkischen Fachhochschulen Hagen and Iserlohn and Fachhochschulabteilungen Meschede and Soest of the Gesamthochschule-Universität Paderborn.

Main Language(s) of Instruction: German

Degrees and Diplomas: *Bachelor's Degree*; *Master*: **Agricultural Economics; Biotechnology; Business Administration; Commercial Law; Computer Science; Economics; Electronic Engineering; Engineering; Engineering Management; Industrial Engineering; Industrial Management; Information Management; Information Technology; International Business; Mechanical Engineering; Nanotechnology; Telecommunications Engineering.** Some programmes are offered in English: Bachelor's degree in Business Administration and Computer Science; Master's degree in International Business and Information Technoogy; Master's degree in Engineering and Engineering Management.

Student Services: Canteen, IT Centre, Library

Student Numbers *2013-2014*: Total 12,319

Last Updated: 28/01/15

STATE UNIVERSITY OF MUSIC AND PERFORMING ARTS STUTTGART

Staatliche Hochschule für Musik und Darstellende Kunst Stuttgart

Urbanstrasse 25, 70182 Stuttgart
Tel: +49(711) 212-0
Fax: +49(711) 21246-39
EMail: post@mh-stuttgart.de
Website: http://www.mh-stuttgart.de

Rector: Regula Rapp
Tel: +49(711) 212-4631 EMail: rektorin@mh-stuttgart.de

Chancellor: Albrecht Lang
Tel: +49(711) 21246-37 EMail: albrecht.lang@mh-stuttgart.de

International Relations: Katja Fisch
Tel: +49(711) 21246-60 EMail: katja.fisch@mh-stuttgart.de

Faculty

I (Music; Music Education; Music Theory and Composition; Musicology); **II** (Jazz and Popular Music; Music; Musical Instruments); **III** (Conducting; Music; Musical Instruments); **IV** (Communication Arts; Opera; Pedagogy; Singing; Speech Studies; Theatre)

History: Founded 1857 as Stuttgarter Musikschule.

Academic Year: October to March; April to September

Admission Requirements: Graduation diploma, entrance examination, language examination

Main Language(s) of Instruction: German

Degrees and Diplomas: *Bachelor's Degree*; *Konzertexamen*: **Music; Performing Arts.** *Master*: **Conducting; Jazz and Popular Music; Media Studies; Music; Music Education; Music Theory and Composition; Musical Instruments; Musicology; Opera; Religious Music; Speech Studies.** *PhD*: **Music Education; Musicology.** *Habilitation*: **Music Education; Musicology.** Also State Examination in Secondary School Music Education (Lehramt); Postgraduate Diploma/Third Cycle Examination (Konzertexam/Bühnenexam) in Music and Theatre.

Student Services: Canteen, Careers Guidance, Library

Publications: Vorlesungsverzeichnis

Student Numbers *2013-2014*: Total 748

Last Updated: 25/03/15

STRALSUND UNIVERSITY OF APPLIED SCIENCES

Fachhochschule Stralsund
Zur Schwedenschanze 15, 18435 Stralsund
Tel: +49(3831) 45-5
Fax: +49(3831) 456-680
EMail: Pressestelle@fh-stralsund.de
Website: http://www.fh-stralsund.de

Rector: Falk Höhn
Tel: +49(3831) 456-500 EMail: rektor@fh-stralsund.de

Chancellor: Susanne Bowen
Tel: +49(3831) 456-503 EMail: kanzler@fh-stralsund.de

School

Business Administration (Business Administration; Business Computing; Management; Tourism); **Electrical Engineering and Computer Science** (Biomedical Engineering; Computer Engineering; Electrical Engineering; Medical Technology); **Mechanical Engineering** (Mechanical Engineering)

History: Founded 1991.

Academic Year: September to August (September-February; March-August)

Admission Requirements: Secondary school certificate (Abitur) or foreign equivalent

Fees: None

Main Language(s) of Instruction: German

Accrediting Agency: Foundation for International Business Administration Accreditation (FIBAA) - Stiftung der Deutschen, Österreichischen und Schweizerischen Wirtschaft; Akkreditierungsagentur für Studiengänge der Ingenieurswissenschaften, der Informatik, der Naturwissenschaften und der Mathematik (ASIIN)

Degrees and Diplomas: *Bachelor's Degree*; *Diplom (FH)*: **Industrial Engineering.** *Master*: **Business Computing; Computer Science; Electrical Engineering; Industrial Engineering; Mechanical Engineering; Small Business; Tourism.** 2 programmes are conducted in English.

Student Services: Academic Counselling, Canteen, Careers Guidance, Facilities for disabled people, Language Laboratory, Library, Social Counselling, Sports Facilities

Publications: Wissenschaftliche Schriftenreihe

Student Numbers *2013-2014*: Total 2,398
Last Updated: 02/03/15

STUTTGART MEDIA UNIVERSITY

Hochschule der Medien (HDM)
Nobelstrasse 10, 70569 Stuttgart
Tel: +49(711) 8923-10
Fax: +49(711) 8923-11
EMail: info@hdm-stuttgart.de
Website: http://www.hdm-stuttgart.de

Rector: Alexander W. Roos (2006-)
Tel: +49(711) 8923-2004 EMail: roos@hdm-stuttgart.de

Chancellor: Peter Marquardt
Tel: +49(711) 8923-2077 EMail: marquardt@hdm-stuttgart.de

International Relations: Gottfried Ohnmacht-Neugebauer, Head, International Office
Tel: +49(711) 8923-2031 EMail: ohnmacht@hdm-stuttgart.de

Faculty

Electronic Media (Advertising and Publicity; Media Studies); **Information and Communication** (Information Management; Library Science); **Print and Media** (Media Studies; Packaging Technology; Printing and Printmaking)

History: Founded 2001 through the merger of the Fachhochschule Stuttgart – Hochschule fuer Bibliotheks- und Informationswesen (HBI) University of Applied Sciences and the Fachhochschule Stuttgart – Hochschule fuer Druck und Medien (HDM) University of Applied Sciences.

Main Language(s) of Instruction: German

Degrees and Diplomas: *Bachelor's Degree*; *Master*: **Computer Science; Design; Information Management; International Business; Marketing; Mass Communication; Media Studies; Packaging Technology; Printing and Printmaking; Publishing and Book Trade.** Also part time MBA; Copperation agreement with University of the West of Scotland (UWS) to offer Ph.D. (Promotion).

Student Services: IT Centre, Library

Student Numbers *2013-2014*: Total 4,199
Last Updated: 04/03/15

STUTTGART STATE ACADEMY OF ART AND DESIGN

Staatliche Akademie der Bildenden Künste Stuttgart
Am Weissenhof 1, 70191 Stuttgart
Tel: +49(711) 28440-0
Fax: +49(711) 28440-225
EMail: info@abk-stuttgart.de
Website: http://www.abk-stuttgart.de

Rector: Petra von Olschowski
Tel: +49(711) 28440-101
EMail: rektorat@abk-stuttgart.de; petra.olschowski@abk-stuttgart.de

Chancellor: Martin Böhnke
Tel: +49(711) 28440-114 EMail: martin.boehnke@abk-stuttgart.de

International Relations: Sonja Fendel, Head, International Relations
Tel: +49(711) 28440-103
EMail: auslandsberatung@abk-stuttgart.de

Department

Architecture (Architecture; Design; Textile Design); **Art Theory** (Aesthetics); **Communication Design** (Graphic Design); **Conservation and Restoration** (Museum Studies; Restoration of Works of Art); **Fine Arts** (Ceramic Art; Glass Art; Graphic Arts; Painting and Drawing; Sculpture); **Industrial Design** (Industrial Design); **Stage and Costume Design** (Clothing and Sewing; Display and Stage Design); **Textile Design** (Textile Design)

History: Founded 1902 from the Académie des Arts founded in 1761 and the Württemberg State School of Arts and Crafts founded in 1869 which were both amalgamated with the Royal teaching and Experimental Workshops in 1902.

Main Language(s) of Instruction: German

Degrees and Diplomas: *Bachelor's Degree*; *Künstlerische Abschlussprüfung*: **Display and Stage Design; Fine Arts; Graphic Design; Industrial Design; Textile Design.** *Master*: **Architecture; Information Technology; Museum Studies; Restoration of Works of Art.** *PhD*: **Aesthetics; Architecture; Restoration of Works of Art.** *Habilitation*: **Aesthetics; Architecture; Restoration of Works of Art.** Also State Examination (Staatsexam) for Secondary School Art Education.

Student Services: Library

Student Numbers *2013-2014*: Total 803
Last Updated: 25/03/15

STUTTGART UNIVERSITY OF APPLIED SCIENCES

Hochschule für Technik Stuttgart (HFT STUTTGART)
PO Box 101452, Schellingstrasse 24, 70013 Stuttgart, Baden-Württemberg
Tel: +49(711) 8926-2660
Fax: +49(711) 8926-2666
EMail: rektorat@hft-stuttgart.de
Website: http://www.fht-stuttgart.de

Rector: Rainer Franke
Tel: +49(711) 8926-2664 EMail: rainer.franke@hft-stuttgart.de

Chancellor: Ulrike Messerschmidt
Tel: +49(711) 8926-2661
EMail: ulrike.messerschmidt@hft-stuttgart.de

Press and Marketing Officer: Celia Eisele
Tel: +49(711) 8926-2344 EMail: celia.eisele@hft-stuttgart.de

International Relations: Michael Geiger
Tel: +49(711) 8926-2868 EMail: michael.geiger@hft-stuttgart.de

Faculty

Architecture and Design (Architecture; Environmental Engineering; Interior Design; Town Planning); **Building Physics** (Construction Engineering; Physical Engineering); **Civil Engineering** (Bridge Engineering; Civil Engineering; Engineering Management; Environmental Management; Real Estate; Structural Architecture; Town Planning; Transport Engineering); **Computer Science** (Computer Science; Software Engineering; Surveying and Mapping); **Economics** (Business Administration; Economics; Industrial and Organizational Psychology; Management); **Mathematics** (Mathematics); **Surveying** (Surveying and Mapping; Town Planning)

History: Founded as Winter School for Building Craftsmen 1832.

Academic Year: September to August

Main Language(s) of Instruction: German, English

Accrediting Agency: ASIIN (Akkreditierungsagentur für Studiengänge der Ingenieurwissenschaften, der Informatik, der Naturwissenschaften und der Mathematik e.V.)

Degrees and Diplomas: *Bachelor's Degree*; *Master*: **Architecture; Civil Engineering; Computer Science; Energy Engineering; Environmental Management; Interior Design; Management; Mathematics; Software Engineering; Structural Architecture; Surveying and Mapping; Town Planning; Transport Management.**

Student Services: Academic Counselling, Canteen, Cultural Activities, Facilities for disabled people, Foreign Studies Centre, IT Centre, Language Laboratory, Library, Nursery Care, Residential Facilities, Sports Facilities

Student Numbers *2014-2015*: Total: c. 3,700

Last Updated: 03/02/15

TECHNICAL UNIVERSITY OF BRAUNSCHWEIG

Technische Universität Carolo-Wilhelmina zu Braunschweig (TU BS)

PO Box 3329, Pockelsstrasse 14, 38023 Braunschweig, Lower Saxony

Tel: +49(531) 391-4331

Fax: +49(531) 391-4332

EMail: international@tu-braunschweig.de

Website: http://www.tu-braunschweig.de

Präsident: Jürgen Hesselbach (1999-)

Tel: +49(531) 391-4111 EMail: president@tu-braunschweig.de

International Relations: Astrid Sebastian, Head, International Office

Tel: +49(531) 391-4330 EMail: a.sebastian@tu-braunschweig.de

Unit

Instructional Development in Higher Education (Higher Education)

Department

Architecture, Civil Engineering and Environmental Sciences (Architecture; Civil Engineering; Environmental Studies; Geophysics; Industrial Engineering; Water Management); **Carl-Friedrich-Gauß** (Business Administration; Computer Science; Mathematics; Social Sciences); **Electrical Engineering, Information Technology and Physics** (Electrical and Electronic Engineering; Industrial Engineering; Information Technology; Physics); **Humanities and Educational Sciences** (Educational Sciences; English; German; History; Literature; Philosophy; Primary Education; Protestant Theology; Religious Education; Secondary Education); **Life Sciences** (Bioengineering; Biology; Biotechnology; Chemical Engineering; Chemistry; Food Science; Pharmacy; Psychology); **Mechanical Engineering** (Mechanical Engineering)

Centre

Languages (Modern Languages)

History: Founded 1745 as Collegium Carolinum and divided into Faculties of Arts, Commerce, and Technology 1835. Reorganized 1862, became Technische Hochschule 1877, and Technische Universität 1968. The Braunschweig branch of the College of Education, Lower Saxony, incorporated 1978. An autonomous institution under the jurisdiction of and financed by the State of Lower Saxony.

Academic Year: October to September (October-March; April-September)

Admission Requirements: Secondary school certificate (Abitur) or equivalent

Fees: 500 per semester (Euro)

Main Language(s) of Instruction: German

Degrees and Diplomas: *Bachelor's Degree*; *Master*: **Aeronautical and Aerospace Engineering; Architecture; Automotive Engineering; Biochemistry; Bioengineering; Biology; Biotechnology; Business Computing; Chemical Engineering; Chemistry; Civil Engineering; Computer Engineering; Computer Science; Design; Developmental Psychology; Ecology; Education; Electrical Engineering; Electronic Engineering; Engineering; Environmental Engineering; Industrial Engineering; Information Technology; Management; Mass Communication; Mathematics; Measurement and Precision Engineering; Mechanical Engineering; Media Studies; Physics; Primary Education; Psychology; Psychotherapy; Secondary Education; Transport and Communications; Water Science.** *PhD*: **Architecture; Arts and Humanities; Biological and Life Sciences; Business Administration; Civil Engineering; Economics; Educational Sciences; Electrical Engineering; Engineering; Environmental Studies; Information Technology; Mechanical Engineering; Media Studies; Philosophy; Physics; Social Sciences.** *Habilitation*: **Architecture; Arts and Humanities; Biological and Life Sciences; Civil Engineering; Computer Science; Economics; Educational Sciences; Electrical Engineering; Environmental Studies; Information Technology; Mathematics; Physics; Social Sciences.** Also Dual Bachelor's degrees; State Examination (Staatsexamen) in Pharmacy and Food Technology; Undergraduate Certificate in Personnel Development.

Student Services: Academic Counselling, Canteen, Careers Guidance, Cultural Activities, Facilities for disabled people, Foreign Studies Centre, IT Centre, Language Laboratory, Library, Nursery Care, Social Counselling, Sports Facilities

Academic Staff *2014-2015*: Total: c. 3,500

Student Numbers *2014-2015*: Total: c. 18,500

Last Updated: 26/03/15

TECHNICAL UNIVERSITY OF KAISERSLAUTERN

Technische Universität Kaiserslautern

Postfach 3049, Gottlieb-Daimler-Strasse 47, 67653 Kaiserslautern, Rheinland-Pfaltz

Tel: +49(631) 205-0

Fax: +49(631) 205-3200

EMail: info@uni-kl.de

Website: http://www.uni-kl.de

President: Helmut J. Schmidt (2002-)

Tel: +49(631) 205-2201 EMail: president@uni.kl.de

Chancellor: Stefan Lorenz

Tel: +49(631) 205-2204 EMail: kanzler@verw.uni-kl.de

International Relations: Parya Memar, Head, International Office

Tel: +49(631) 205-4002

EMail: memar@isgs.uni-kl.de; auslandsamt@uni-kl.de

Faculty

Architecture (Architecture); **Biology** (Biology); **Business Studies and Economics** (Business Administration; Economics; Industrial Management); **Chemistry** (Biochemistry; Chemistry; Organic Chemistry; Toxicology); **Civil Engineering** (Civil Engineering); **Computer Science** (Computer Science); **Electrical and Computer Engineering** (Computer Engineering; Electrical Engineering; Information Technology); **Mathematics** (Mathematics); **Mechanical and Process Engineering** (Mechanical Engineering; Production Engineering); **Physics** (Physics); **Social Sciences** (Social Sciences); **Spatial and Environmental Planning** (Environmental Management; Town Planning)

Institute

Biotechnology and Drug Research *(ibwf)* (Biotechnology); **Composite Materials** (Materials Engineering); **Experimental Software Engineering** *(Frauenhofer, IESE)* (Software Engineering); **Max Planck** (Software Engineering); **Physical Measurement**

(Fraunhofer) (Measurement and Precision Engineering); **Technical and Industrial Mathematics** *(Fraunhofer, ITWM)* (Mathematics)

Centre
Analysis of Materials and Surfaces *(IFOS)* (Physics); **Nano Structuring** (Nanotechnology)

Research Centre
Artificial Intelligence *(DFKI)* (Artificial Intelligence)

Research Institute
Technology and Work (Technology)

Further Information: Also courses in "German as a Foreign Language" and in technical English, French and Spanish. Regional Computing Centre (RHRK)

History: Founded 1970 with divisions in Kaiserslautern and Trier which were detached 1975 to form separate Universities. An autonomous institution under the jurisdiction of and financially supported by the State of Rheinland-Pfalz.

Academic Year: October to September (October-March; April-September)

Admission Requirements: Secondary school certificate (Reifezeugnis)

Fees: None

Main Language(s) of Instruction: German

Degrees and Diplomas: *Bachelor's Degree*; *Diplom (Univ)*: **Architecture; Biophysics; Chemistry; Computer Engineering; Economics; Electrical Engineering; Environmental Engineering; Mechanical Engineering; Physics.** *Master*: **Adult Education; Applied Mathematics; Automotive Engineering; Bioengineering; Biological and Life Sciences; Biology; Biotechnology; Business Administration; Cell Biology; Chemical Engineering; Chemistry; Communication Studies; Computer Engineering; Computer Science; Construction Engineering; Education of the Handicapped; Educational Administration; Electrical Engineering; Electronic Engineering; Energy Engineering; Engineering; Engineering Management; Environmental Engineering; Environmental Management; Food Technology; Geography; Health Administration; Human Resources; Management; Materials Engineering; Mathematics; Mechanical Engineering; Media Studies; Molecular Biology; Nanotechnology; Neurosciences; Physics; Primary Education; Production Engineering; Real Estate; Regional Planning; Safety Engineering; Social Sciences; Social Studies; Software Engineering; Sports; Telecommunications Engineering; Town Planning; Toxicology; Wood Technology.** *PhD*: **Architecture; Biology; Civil Engineering; Computer Engineering; Computer Science; Economics; Electronic Engineering; Engineering Management; Mechanical Engineering; Social Sciences.** *Habilitation*: **Biology; Civil Engineering; Engineering Management; Mechanical Engineering; Social Sciences.** Some Master's degree programmes conducted in English; Also Certificates and Teachher Training State Exam (Lehramt).

Student Services: Academic Counselling, Canteen, Careers Guidance, Cultural Activities, Foreign Studies Centre, Health Services, Language Laboratory, Library, Nursery Care, Social Counselling, Sports Facilities

Student Numbers *2013-2014*: Total 14,003
Last Updated: 30/03/15

TECHNISCHE UNIVERSITAET MUENCHEN
Technische Universität München (TUM)

Arcisstrasse 21, 80333 München
Tel: +49(89) 289-01
Fax: +49(89) 2892-2000
EMail: postmaster@tu-muenchen.de
Website: http://www.tum.de

President: Wolfgang A. Herrmann
Tel: +49(89) 2892-2200 EMail: Praesident@tum.de

Chancellor: Albert Berger
Tel: +49(89) 2892-2203 EMail: kanzler@tum.de

International Relations: Ana Santos-Kühn, Direktor
Tel: +49(89) 289 22393 EMail: santos-kuehn@zv.tum.de

Faculty
Architecture (Architecture); **Chemistry** *(Garching)* (Biochemistry; Chemistry); **Civil, Geo, and Environmental Engineering** (Civil Engineering; Surveying and Mapping); **Electrical, Electronic and Computer Engineering** (Automation and Control Engineering; Electrical Engineering; Information Technology; Power Engineering); **Informatics** (Computer Science); **Mathematics** (Mathematical Physics; Mathematics; Mathematics and Computer Science; Statistics); **Mechanical Engineering** (Mechanical Engineering); **Physics** *(Garching)* (Biophysics; Physics); **Sports and Health Sciences** (Sports); **TUM School of Education** (Education); **TUM School of Life Sciences Weihenstephan** (Biological and Life Sciences; Food Science); **TUM School of Management** (Business Administration); **TUM School of Medicine** (Medicine)

Further Information: Also Teaching Hospital

History: Founded 1827 as Polytechnische Zentralschule, became Polytechnische Schule 1868, Technische Hochschule 1877 and University 1970. An autonomous institution under the jurisdiction of the State of Bavaria.

Academic Year: October to September (October-March; April-September)

Admission Requirements: Secondary school certificate (Reifezeugnis) or equivalent

Fees: None

Main Language(s) of Instruction: German, English

Accrediting Agency: Organ für Akkreditierung und Qualitätssicherung OAQ

Degrees and Diplomas: *Bachelor's Degree*; *Master*: **Actuarial Science; Aeronautical and Aerospace Engineering; Agricultural Education; Agricultural Management; Agriculture; Applied Mathematics; Applied Physics; Architectural and Environmental Design; Architecture; Astrophysics; Atomic and Molecular Physics; Automotive Engineering; Biochemistry; Biological and Life Sciences; Biology; Biomedicine; Biotechnology; Building Technologies; Business Administration; Chemical Engineering; Chemistry; Civil Engineering; Computer Engineering; Computer Science; Construction Engineering; Consumer Studies; Design; Ecology; Electrical Engineering; Electronic Engineering; Energy Engineering; Engineering; Environmental Engineering; Finance; Food Technology; Forestry; Geological Engineering; Geology; Health Education; Health Sciences; Home Economics Education; Horticulture; Industrial Chemistry; Industrial Design; Information Management; Information Technology; Landscape Architecture; Management; Materials Engineering; Mathematics; Mechanical Engineering; Mechanics; Medical Technology; Microelectronics; Molecular Biology; Museum Studies; Nanotechnology; Natural Resources; Natural Sciences; Nuclear Engineering; Nutrition; Operations Research; Pharmacology; Philosophy; Physics; Power Engineering; Private Law; Real Estate; Restoration of Works of Art; Robotics; Safety Engineering; Secondary Education; Software Engineering; Soil Conservation; Solid State Physics; Sports; Surveying and Mapping; Technology; Technology Education; Telecommunications Engineering; Traditional Eastern Medicine; Transport and Communications; Transport Management; Urban Studies; Vocational Education; Wood Technology.** *PhD*: **Agriculture; Architectural Restoration; Architecture; Art Criticism; Art History; Building Technologies; Chemistry; Civil Engineering; Computer Engineering; Computer Science; Education; Electronic Engineering; Environmental Studies; Food Science; Geological Engineering; Health Sciences; Landscape Architecture; Machine Building; Mathematics; Medical Technology; Medicine; Physics; Sports.** *Habilitation*: **Agriculture; Communication Studies; Computer Education; Educational Research; Environmental Studies; Food Science; Humanities and Social Science Education; Mathematics Education; Pedagogy; Science Education; Secondary Education; Sociology; Technology; Technology Education.** Also Certificate (Zertifikat) in Computer Science; State Examination Certificate (Staatsexam) in Medicine and Physical Education for Secondary Schools (Lehramt); Alternatively to the individual Doctoral programmes offered, students can also engage in Collective PhD projects in a Cluster of Excellence or in a Collaborative/Transregional Research Centre focused on areas such as: Natural Sciences, Engineering, Biological and Life Sciences, Health Sciences and Interdisciplinary Research Areas.

Student Services: Academic Counselling, Canteen, Careers Guidance, Cultural Activities, Facilities for disabled people, Foreign Studies Centre, Health Services, IT Centre, Language Laboratory, Library, Nursery Care, Social Counselling, Sports Facilities, eLibrary

Academic Staff *2014-2015*	MEN	WOMEN	TOTAL
FULL-TIME	5,300	3,124	**8,424**
STAFF WITH DOCTORATE			
FULL-TIME	4,000	1,634	**5,634**
Student Numbers *2014-2015*			
All (Foreign included)	24,853	12,490	**37,343**
FOREIGN ONLY	5,291	2,717	**8,008**

Part-time students, 63.

Last Updated: 09/02/15

THE COLOGNE UNIVERSITY OF MUSIC AND DANCE

Hochschule für Musik und Tanz Köln (HFMT)
Unter Krahnenbäumen 87, 50668 Köln, Nordrhein-Westfalen
Tel: +49(221) 912818-0
Fax: +49(221) 131-204
EMail: kanzler@hfm-koeln.de
Website: http://www.mhs-koeln.de

Rector: Heinz Geuen
Tel: +49(221) 912818-100 EMail: rektor@hfmt-koeln.de

Chancellor: Marion Steffen
Tel: 49(221) 912818-111 EMail: kanzler@hfmt-koeln.de

International Relations: Heike Gecks, International Affairs Officer
EMail: heike.gecks@hfmt-koeln.de

Department

1 - Composition, Keyboard, Music Theory, Ear Training, Plucked Instruments, Institute for New Music, Electronic Composition (Jazz and Popular Music; Music Theory and Composition; Musical Instruments); **2 - Strings, Orchestral Conducting, Institute for Early Music** (Conducting; Music; Musical Instruments); **3 - Wind Instruments, Percussion, Harp** (Musical Instruments); **4 - Singing, Musical Theater** (Music; Singing; Theatre); **5 - Musicology, Music Education, Church Music, Choral Conducting** (Conducting; Music Education; Musicology; Religious Music); **6 - Jazz/Pop** (Jazz and Popular Music)

Further Information: Also campuses in Aachen and Wuppertal

History: Founded 1925. Acquired present title 2009.

Main Language(s) of Instruction: German

Degrees and Diplomas: *Bachelor's Degree*; *Konzertexamen*: **Musical Instruments.** *Diplom (Univ)*; *Master*: **Dance; Jazz and Popular Music; Music; Music Education; Music Theory and Composition; Musical Instruments; Opera; Singing.** *PhD*: **Art Therapy; Dance; Music Education; Musicology.** Staatsexam in Music Education (Lehramt); Diplom is being phased out.

Student Services: Library

Student Numbers *2013-2014*: Total 1,554

Last Updated: 11/03/15

THE LISZT SCHOOL OF MUSIC WEIMAR

Hochschule für Musik Franz Liszt Weimar
Postfach 2552, 99406 Weimar
Tel: +49(3643) 555-0
Fax: +49(3643) 555-188
EMail: presse@hfm-weimar.de
Website: http://www.hfm-weimar.de

President: Christoph Stölzl
Tel: +49(3643) 555-115 EMail: praesident@hfm-weimar.de

Chancellor: Christine Gurk
Tel: +49(3643) 555-151 EMail: kanzlerin@hfm-weimar.de

International Relations: Hans-Peter Hoffmann, Director of International Relations
Tel: +49(3643) 555-156
EMail: hans-peter.hoffmann@hfm-weimar.de

Faculty

I (Conducting; Musical Instruments; Opera; Singing; Theatre); **II** (Jazz and Popular Music; Music; Music Education; Musical Instruments; Pedagogy); **III** *(Church Music; School Music)* (Music Education; Musicology)

Centre

Chamber Music (Music); **Franz-Liszt** (Music); **Music Theory** (Music Theory and Composition)

History: Founded 1872 as one of the first German Orchestra Schools. Acquired present status 1930. Named after Franz Liszt 1956.

Academic Year: October to July

Admission Requirements: Successful audition; German Language Proficiency Test (proof); A-level for Musicology and School Music

Fees: None

Main Language(s) of Instruction: German

Degrees and Diplomas: *Bachelor's Degree*; *Konzertexamen*: **Music.** *Master*: **Art Management; Music Education; Music Theory and Composition; Musical Instruments; Musicology; Singing.** *PhD*: **Music; Music Education.** *Habilitation*: **Music.** Staatsexam in Music Education.

Student Services: Academic Counselling, Canteen, Facilities for disabled people, Foreign Studies Centre, Health Services, Language Laboratory, Nursery Care, Social Counselling, Sports Facilities

Publications: Resonanz

Student Numbers *2013-2014*: Total 792

Last Updated: 09/03/15

TRIER UNIVERSITY OF APPLIED SCIENCES

Hochschule Trier - Hochschule für Wirtschaft, Technik und Gestaltung
Postfach 1826, D-54208 Trier, Rhineland Palatinate
Tel: +49(651) 8103-0
Fax: +49(651) 8103-333
EMail: info@hochschule-trier.de
Website: http://www.hochschule-trier.de/

President: Jörg Wallmeier
Tel: +49(651) 8103-445 EMail: Praesident@hochschule-trier.de

Chancellor: Detlef Jahn
Tel: +49(651) 8103-492 EMail: kanzler@fh-trier.de

International Relations: Georg Schneider, Head, International Office Tel: +49(651) 8103-378 EMail: aaa@fh-trier.de

Department

Civil Engineering, Food Technology, Supply Technology (Civil Engineering; Energy Engineering; Food Technology); **Computer Science** (Computer Science); **Design** (Architecture; Design; Fashion Design; Jewellery Art); **Economics** (Business Administration; Business Computing; Information Management; Management); **Environmental Planning/Environmental Technology** *(Birkenfeld Campus)* (Bioengineering; Business Administration; Commercial Law; Computer Science; Energy Engineering; Engineering; Environmental Engineering; Environmental Management; Environmental Studies; European Union Law; Mechanical Engineering; Media Studies; Physical Engineering; Transport Management); **Technology** (Automation and Control Engineering; Electrical Engineering; Energy Engineering; Engineering; Industrial Engineering; Machine Building; Mechanical Engineering)

Further Information: Also Campus in Birkenfeld

History: Founded 1971, acquired present status 1996.

Academic Year: September to August

Admission Requirements: Upper Secondary school certificate (Allgemeine Hochschul- or Fachhochschulreife)

Fees: National: None, International: None

Main Language(s) of Instruction: German

Accrediting Agency: Agentur für Qualitätssicherung durch Akkreditierung von Studiengängen (AQAS) and others for the accreditation of individual courses

Degrees and Diplomas: *Bachelor's Degree*; *Master*: **Architecture; Automation and Control Engineering; Automotive Engineering; Bioengineering; Business Administration; Business Computing; Civil Engineering; Commercial Law; Communication Arts; Computer Science; Distance Education; Economics; Electrical Engineering; Energy Engineering; Engineering; Environmental Engineering; Environmental Management; Fashion Design; Food Technology; Graphic Design; Industrial Engineering; Information Management; Interior Design; Jewellery Art; Mechanical Engineering; Multimedia; Private Law; Production Engineering.**

Student Services: Academic Counselling, Canteen, Careers Guidance, Language Laboratory, Library, Social Counselling, Sports Facilities

Student Numbers *2013-2014*: Total 8,025
Last Updated: 03/02/15

TROSSINGEN UNIVERSITY OF MUSIC

Staatliche Hochschule für Musik Trossingen
Schultheiss-Koch-Platz 3, 78647 Trossingen
Tel: +49(7425) 9491-0
Fax: +49(7425) 9491-48
EMail: info@mh-trossingen.de; rektorat@mh-trossingen.de
Website: http://www.mh-trossingen.de

Rektorin: Elisabeth Gutjahr
Tel: +49(7425) 9491-12 EMail: rektorat@mh-trossingen.de
Kanzlerin: Margit Mosbacher
Tel: +49(7425) 9491-13 EMail: mosbacher@mh-trossingen.de
International Relations: Peter Nelson, Head, International Office
Tel: +49(7425) 9491-17 EMail: nelson@mh-trossingen.de

Programme

Church Music (Music Theory and Composition; Musical Instruments; Religious Music); **Music** (Conducting; Music; Music Theory and Composition; Musical Instruments; Singing); **Music Education** (Conducting; Music Education; Music Theory and Composition; Musical Instruments; Singing); **Music Education (Secondary School)** *(Lehramt)* (Jazz and Popular Music; Music; Music Education); **Musicology and Music Education** *(Promotion)* (Music Education; Musicology)

Main Language(s) of Instruction: German

Degrees and Diplomas: *Bachelor's Degree*; *Konzertexamen*: **Musical Instruments.** *Künstlerische Abschlussprüfung*: **Musical Instruments.** *Master*: **Music; Music Education; Musical Instruments.** *PhD*: **Music Education; Musicology.** Also Solist Diploma (Konzertexamen) and Diploma in Church Music. Diplomas are being phased down or transformed into Bachelor's degrees. State Examination in Secondary School Music Education (Lehramt).

Student Numbers *2013-2014*: Total 488
Last Updated: 27/03/15

TU DORTMUND UNIVERSITY

Technische Universität Dortmund
August-Schmidt-Strasse 4, 44227 Dortmund,
North Rhine-Westphalia
Tel: +49(231) 755-1
EMail: presse@tu-dortmund.de
Website: http://www.tu-dortmund.de

Rector: Ursula Gather (since 2008)
Tel: +49 (0)231-755 7551 EMail: rektorin@tu-dortmund.de

Chancellor: Albrecht Ehlers (since 2010)
Tel: +49 (0)231-755 7561 EMail: kanzler@tu-dortmund.de

International Relations: Barbara Schneider, Director International Office
Tel: +49 (0)231-755 6350
EMail: barbara.schneider@tu-dortmund.de

Faculty

Architecture and Civil Engineering (Architecture; Civil Engineering); **Art and Sport** (Art Education; Music Education; Sports; Teacher Training; Textile Design); **Biochemical and Chemical Engineering** (Bioengineering; Chemical Engineering); **Chemistry and Chemical Biology** (Biochemistry; Chemistry; Teacher Training); **Computer Science** (Computer Science; Teacher Training); **Culture Studies** (American Studies; Cultural Studies; English Studies; Foreign Languages Education; Germanic Studies; Journalism; Linguistics; Literature; Teacher Training); **Economics and Social Sciences** (Business Administration; Economics; Social Sciences; Teacher Training); **Education, Psychology and Sociology** (Education; Educational Research; Psychology; Social Sciences; Teacher Training); **Electrical Engineering and Information Technology** (Electrical and Electronic Engineering; Electrical Engineering; Industrial Engineering; Information Technology; Robotics; Teacher Training; Telecommunications Engineering); **Human Sciences and Theology** (Catholic Theology; Philosophy; Political Sciences; Protestant Theology; Religious Education; Teacher Training; Theology); **Mathematics** (Applied Mathematics; Mathematics; Teacher Training); **Mechanical Engineering** (Automation and Control Engineering; Industrial Engineering; Mechanical Engineering; Production Engineering; Teacher Training; Transport Engineering); **Physics** (Physics; Teacher Training); **Rehabilitation Sciences** (Education of the Handicapped; Rehabilitation and Therapy; Teacher Training); **Spatial Planning** (Regional Planning; Rural Planning; Town Planning); **Statistics** (Statistics)

Centre

Center for Higher Education (zhb) (Continuing Education; Education; Education of the Handicapped; Higher Education Teacher Training; Modern Languages); **Centre for Synchrotron Radiation (DELTA)** (Physics); **Dortmund Research and Development Center for Training, Learning and Professional Development (DoKoLL)** (Education; Teacher Training); **Social Research Centre Dortmund (sfs)** (Social Sciences)

History: Founded in 1968, TU Dortmund University is dedicated to a unique cross-weaving of natural sciences and engineering as well as social sciences and cultural studies. With its focus on interdisciplinary cooperation, the university has created a distinctive profile which fosters progressive research and facilitates innovative teaching. TU Dortmund University is a leading player in the fields of production engineering, electrical engineering and educational research. Its faculty has received numerous prestigious grants and distinctions.

Academic Year: October to September (October-March; April-September)

Admission Requirements: Secondary school certificate (Reifezeugnis) or equivalent

Fees: National: none, International: none

Main Language(s) of Instruction: German, English

Accrediting Agency: AQAS; ASIIN; ZEvA

Degrees and Diplomas: *Bachelor's Degree*; *Master*: **Applied Linguistics; Applied Mathematics; Architecture; Automation and Control Engineering; Bioengineering; Biology; Chemical Engineering; Chemistry; Computer Engineering; Computer Science; Cultural Studies; Data Processing; Economics; Education; Electrical Engineering; Industrial Engineering; Journalism; Literature; Mathematics; Mechanical Engineering; Philosophy; Physics; Political Sciences; Primary Education; Production Engineering; Real Estate; Regional Planning; Rehabilitation and Therapy; Robotics; Secondary Education; Social Studies; Special Education; Statistics; Structural Architecture; Town Planning; Transport Management; Vocational Education.** *PhD*: **American Studies; Architecture; Art Education; Art History; Automation and Control Engineering; Bioengineering; Business Administration; Catholic Theology; Chemical Engineering; Chemistry; Civil Engineering; Computer Engineering; Computer Science; Economics; Education; Electronic Engineering; English Studies; Fine Arts; Germanic Studies; History; Industrial Engineering; Journalism; Mathematics; Mechanical Engineering; Music Education; Musicology; Philosophy; Physics; Political Sciences; Protestant Theology; Psychology; Regional Planning; Rehabilitation and Therapy; Robotics; Science Education; Social Sciences; Sports; Statistics; Town Planning; Transport Management.** *Habilitation*: **Arts and Humanities; Cultural Studies; Education; Mathematics; Psychology; Regional Planning; Rehabilitation and Therapy; Sociology; Theology.**

Student Services: Academic Counselling, Canteen, Careers Guidance, Cultural Activities, Facilities for disabled people, Foreign

Studies Centre, IT Centre, Language Laboratory, Library, Residential Facilities, Social Counselling, Sports Facilities, eLibrary

Publications: mundo; unizet

Academic Staff *2013-14*	MEN	WOMEN	**TOTAL**
FULL-TIME	1,779	975	**2,754**
PART-TIME	507	725	**1,232**
Student Numbers *2013-14*			
All (Foreign included)	17,085	14,498	**31,583**
FOREIGN ONLY	–	–	**3,445**

Last Updated: 09/02/15

ULM UNIVERSITY

Universität Ulm (UULM)
Albert-Einstein-Allee, 89069 Ulm
Tel: +49(731) 50-22001
Fax: +49(731) 50-22200
EMail: praesident@uni-ulm.de
Website: http://www.uni-ulm.de

Rector: Karl Joachim Ebeling (2003-)
Tel: +49(731) 50-22000 EMail: praesident@uni-ulm.de

Chancellor: Dieter Kaufmann
Tel: +49(731) 50-25000 EMail: kanzler@uni-ulm.de

International Relations: Reinhold Lücker, Head, International Office Tel: +49(731) 50-22014 EMail: reinhold.luecker@uni-ulm.de

Faculty

Engineering and Computer Science (Automation and Control Engineering; Biomedical Engineering; Communication Arts; Computer Science; Electrical Engineering; Energy Engineering; Engineering; Information Technology; Materials Engineering; Microelectronics; Psychology; Telecommunications Engineering); **Mathematics and Economics** (Accountancy; Actuarial Science; Business Administration; Economics; Finance; Management; Mathematics; Operations Research); **Medicine** (Biomedicine; Dentistry; Medicine); **Natural Sciences** (Biology; Chemical Engineering; Chemistry; Economics; Materials Engineering; Natural Sciences; Physics)

Further Information: Also Teaching Hospitals: Rehabilitationskrankenhaus Ulm (RKU); Psychiatrisches Landeskrankenhaus Weissenau; Bezirkskrankenhaus Günzburg; Bundeswehrkrankenhaus Ulm. Language Courses, German for Foreign Students

History: Founded 1967. Financially supported by the State of Baden-Württemberg.

Academic Year: October to July (October-February; April-July)

Admission Requirements: Secondary school certificate (Reifezeugnis)

Fees: None (except for Master's degree programmes in Oncology, Engineering Management and Surveying and Mapping); Administrative fee, 156 per semester (Euro)

Main Language(s) of Instruction: German

Degrees and Diplomas: *Bachelor's Degree*; *Master*: **Applied Mathematics; Biochemistry; Biology; Biomedicine; Biophysics; Biotechnology; Business Administration; Chemistry; Cognitive Sciences; Computer Engineering; Computer Science; Economics; Electronic Engineering; Energy Engineering; Engineering Management; Environmental Studies; Finance; Industrial Chemistry; Information Technology; Materials Engineering; Mathematics; Multimedia; Nanotechnology; Oncology; Optical Technology; Physics; Psychology; Software Engineering; Surveying and Mapping; Telecommunications Engineering.** *PhD*: **Biomedicine; Biotechnology; Mathematics; Pharmacy.** *Habilitation*: **Natural Sciences.** Staatsexam in Medicine, Dentistry; Teacher Training Programmes (Lehramt)

Student Services: Academic Counselling, Canteen, Careers Guidance, Cultural Activities, Health Services, IT Centre, Language Laboratory, Library, Residential Facilities, Sports Facilities

Publications: Forschungsbericht

Publishing House: Universitätsverlag Ulm

Student Numbers *2013-2014*: Total 9,846
Last Updated: 12/02/15

ULM UNIVERSITY OF APPLIED SCIENCES

Hochschule Ulm Technik, Informatik und Medien (FHU)
Prittwitzstrasse 10, 89075 Ulm
Tel: +49(731) 50-208
Fax: +49(731) 50-28270
EMail: info@hs-ulm.de
Website: http://www.hs-ulm.de

Rector/President: Achim Bubenzer (2001-)
Tel: +49(731) 50-28104 EMail: bubenzer@hs-ulm.de

Chancellor: Iris Teicher
Tel: +49(731) 50-28108 EMail: teicher@hs-ulm.de

International Relations: Stephanie Wagner, Head, International Office
Tel: +49(731) 50-28272
EMail: wagner@hs-ulm.de; aaa@hs-ulm.de

Faculty

Computer Science (Business Computing; Computer Science); **Electrical Engineering and Information Technology** (Electrical Engineering; Information Technology); **Mathematics, Natural Sciences and Economics** (Chemistry; Economics; Mathematics; Modern Languages; Physics; Social Sciences); **Mechanical and Automotive Engineering** (Automotive Engineering; Mechanical Engineering); **Mechatronics and Medical Engineering** (Biomedical Engineering; Mechanical Engineering); **Production Engineering and Production Economics** (Economics; Production Engineering)

History: Founded 1960. Formerly known as Fachhochschule Ulm - Hochschule für Technik.

Admission Requirements: Secondary school certificate (Abitur, Fachhochschulreife)

Main Language(s) of Instruction: German

Degrees and Diplomas: *Bachelor's Degree*; *Master*: **Automotive Engineering; Biomedical Engineering; Computer Engineering; Computer Science; Electronic Engineering; Energy Engineering; Engineering; Information Technology; Management.** Also Dual Degree Programmes

Student Services: Academic Counselling, Canteen, Careers Guidance, Cultural Activities, Facilities for disabled people, Foreign Studies Centre, Health Services, IT Centre, Language Laboratory, Nursery Care, Social Counselling, Sports Facilities

Student Numbers *2013-2014*: Total 4,156
Last Updated: 19/03/15

UNIVERSITÄT REGENSBURG

Universitätsstrasse 31, 93053 Regensburg, Bayern
Tel: +49(941) 943-01
Fax: +49(941) 943-2305
EMail: praesident@ur.de
Website: http://www.uni-regensburg.de

Präsident: Udo Hebel
Tel: 49(941) 1943-2301 EMail: praesident@ur.de

Kanzler: Christian Blomeyer
Tel: +49(941) 943-2310
EMail: christian.blomeyer@verwaltung.uni-regensburg.de

International Relations: Marianne Sedlmeier, International Office
Tel: +49(941) 943-2373
EMail: marianne.sedlmeier@verwaltung.uni-regensburg.de

Faculty

Biologie and Pre-Clinical Medicine (Biology; Medicine); **Business, Economics, and Management Information Systems** (Business Administration; Econometrics; Economics; Management Systems; Real Estate); **Catholic Theology** (Catholic Theology); **Chemistry and Pharmacy** (Chemistry; Pharmacy); **Languages, Literature, and Culture** (Classical Languages; Cultural Studies; Linguistics; Literature; Modern Languages); **Law** (Law); **Mathematics** (Mathematics); **Medicine** (Dentistry; Medicine); **Philosophy, Art History, History and Humanities** (Archaeology; Fine Arts; History; Performing Arts; Philosophy); **Physics** (Physics); **Psychology, Education, and Sport Science** (Education; Pedagogy; Psychology; Sports)

Centre

East-West (Europaeum) (European Studies); **Hochschul- und Wissenschaftsdidaktik (ZHW)**; **Languages and Communication (ZSK)** (Communication Studies; Modern Languages); **Regensburger Universitätszentrum für Lehrerbildung (RUL)** (Teacher Training); **Sports** (Sports)

Further Information: Also Teaching Hospital

History: Founded 1962. Admitted first students 1967. An autonomous institution financially supported by the State of Bavaria.

Academic Year: October to September

Admission Requirements: Secondary school certificate (Allgemeine Hochschulreife)

Fees: None

Main Language(s) of Instruction: German, English

Degrees and Diplomas: *Bachelor's Degree*; *Lizentiat*: **Theology.** *Magister*: **Catholic Theology; Law.** *Master*: **American Studies; Archaeology; Art History; Arts and Humanities; Biochemistry; Biology; Business Administration; Business Computing; Chemistry; Communication Studies; Comparative Literature; Computer Science; Criminology; Eastern European Studies; Economics; Education; English; English Studies; European Studies; Fine Arts; Germanic Studies; Government; Greek (Classical); History; Information Sciences; International Economics; Latin; Linguistics; Literature; Mathematics; Media Studies; Medieval Studies; Molecular Biology; Multimedia; Musicology; Nanotechnology; Natural Sciences; Neurosciences; Philosophy; Physics; Prehistory; Protestant Theology; Psychology; Real Estate; Religious Education; Romance Languages; Slavic Languages; Speech Studies; Western European Studies.** *PhD*: **Arts and Humanities; Biomedicine; Business Administration; Chemistry; Classical Languages; Cultural Studies; Dentistry; Economics; Fine Arts; History; Law; Literature; Mathematics Education; Medicine; Modern Languages; Natural Sciences; Pedagogy; Pharmacy; Philosophy; Psychology; Science Education; Social Sciences; Sports; Theology.** *Habilitation*: **Biological and Life Sciences; Catholic Theology; Economics; Law; Medicine; Natural Sciences; Philosophy.** Also Staatsexam in Medicine, Pharmacy, Dentistry and Law; Teacher training Programmes (Lehramt).

Student Services: Academic Counselling, Canteen, Careers Guidance, Cultural Activities, Facilities for disabled people, Foreign Studies Centre, IT Centre, Language Laboratory, Library, Nursery Care, Residential Facilities, Social Counselling, Sports Facilities, eLibrary

Publications: Forschungsmagazin "Blick in die Wissenschaft"; Jahresbericht

Academic Staff *2014-2015*	MEN	WOMEN	**TOTAL**
FULL-TIME	1,115	731	**1,846**
PART-TIME	479	895	**1,374**
Student Numbers *2013-2014*			
All (Foreign included)	8,504	12,670	**21,174**
FOREIGN ONLY	488	1,005	**1,493**

Last Updated: 12/02/15

UNIVERSITY OF APPLIED SCIENCES AND ARTS HANOVER

Hochschule Hannover (HS HANNOVER)

PO Box 721154, Expo Plaza 4, 30531 Hannover
Tel: +49(511) 9296-0
Fax: +49(511) 9296-1010
EMail: poststelle@hs-hannover.de
Website: http://www.hs-hannover.de/

President: Josef von Helde (2014-)
Tel: +49(511) 9296-1001 EMail: praesident@hs-hannover.de

Vice-President: Thorsten Schumacher
Tel: +49(511) 9296-1000 EMail: hvp@hs-hannover.de

International Relations: Beate Blümel, Head of International Office
Tel: +49(511) 9296-2150 EMail: beate.bluemel@hs-hannover.de

Faculty

Business and Computer Science *(Fakultät IV)* (Banking; Business Administration; Business and Commerce; Business Computing; Industrial Management; Information Management; Insurance; Marketing); **Electrical Engineering and Information Engineering** *(Fakultät I)* (Automation and Control Engineering; Computer Science; Data Processing; Electrical Engineering; Energy Engineering; Information Technology; Mechanical Engineering; Microwaves; Power Engineering; Telecommunications Engineering); **Mechanical and Bio-engineering** *(Fakultät II)* (Bioengineering; Construction Engineering; Data Processing; Electronic Engineering; Energy Engineering; Environmental Engineering; Machine Building; Mechanical Engineering; Packaging Technology; Production Engineering; Technology); **Media, Information and Design** *(Fakultät III)* (Communication Arts; Communication Studies; Design; Documentation Techniques; Fashion Design; Industrial Design; Information Management; Interior Design; Journalism; Media Studies; Public Relations); **Social Welfare, Health and Social Sciences** *(Fakultät V)* (Health Administration; Health Education; Health Sciences; Psychotherapy; Religious Education; Social Sciences; Social Work)

History: Founded 1971. Integrated the Hanover Protestant University of Applied Sciences (Evangelische Fachhochschule Hannover), which was renamed as Fakultät V – Diakonie, Gesundheit und Soziales 2007.

Academic Year: March to February (March-August; September-February)

Admission Requirements: Secondary school certificate (Abitur, Fachhochschulreife), Vorpraktikum

Fees: 7.50-90 per semester (Euro)

Main Language(s) of Instruction: German

Degrees and Diplomas: *Bachelor's Degree*; *Master*: **Automation and Control Engineering; Business Administration; Communication Studies; Dairy; Design; Energy Engineering; Engineering; Health Administration; Industrial Management; Information Management; Journalism; Management; Media Studies; Nursing; Packaging Technology; Production Engineering; Radio and Television Broadcasting; Rehabilitation and Therapy; Social Work.** Also Dual Bachelor's Degree Programmes and Dual Master's Degree in Mechanical Engineering; Cooperative Doctorate Programmes with Leibniz Universität Hannover, Hochschule Hannover, Universität Vechta; Doctorate at other Universties.

Student Services: Academic Counselling, Canteen, Facilities for disabled people, Language Laboratory, Social Counselling, Sports Facilities

Academic Staff *2014-2015*: Total 227
Student Numbers *2014-2015*: Total: c. 9,630
Last Updated: 28/01/15

UNIVERSITY OF APPLIED SCIENCES ASCHAFFENBURG

Hochschule Aschaffenburg

Würzburger Strasse 45, 63743 Aschaffenburg, Bavaria
Tel: +49(6021) 4206-0
Fax: +49(6021) 4206-600
EMail: info@h-ab.de
Website: www.h-ab.de/

Präsident: Wilfried Diwischek (2001-)
Tel: +49(6021) 314-602
EMail: wilfried.diwischek@fh-aschaffenburg.de

Kanzler: Gerhard Sarich
Tel: +49(6021) 314-605
EMail: gerhard.sarich@fh-aschaffenburg.de

International Relations: Sabine Hock
Tel: +49(6021) 4206-623 EMail: sabine.hock@h-ab.de

Faculty

Business and Law (Business Administration; Finance; Insurance; Law; Management; Real Estate); **Engineering** (Electrical and Electronic Engineering; Electronic Engineering; Energy Engineering; Industrial Engineering; Mechanical Engineering)

History: Founded 1995, acquired present status 2000.

Fees: None

Main Language(s) of Instruction: German, English

Degrees and Diplomas: *Bachelor's Degree*; *Master*: **Business Administration; Electrical Engineering; Information Technology; International Business; Law; Management; Real Estate.** Also double degree programmes

Student Services: Academic Counselling, Canteen, Careers Guidance, Facilities for disabled people, Language Laboratory, Library, Residential Facilities, Sports Facilities

Student Numbers *2013-2014*: Total 3,141

Last Updated: 31/01/15

UNIVERSITY OF APPLIED SCIENCES BINGEN

Fachhochschule Bingen

Berlinstrasse 109, 55411 Bingen am Rhein

Tel: +49(6721) 409-0

Fax: +49(6721) 409-100

EMail: poststelle@fh-bingen.de; info@fh-bingen.de

Website: http://www.fh-bingen.de

President: Klaus Becker (2003-)

Tel: +49(6721) 409-400 EMail: praesident@fh-bingen.de

Chancellor: Astrid Clesius

Tel: +49(6721) 409-404

EMail: clesius@fh-bingen.de; kanzlerin@fh-bingen.de

Faculty

Engineering, Computer Science and Business Administration (Automotive Engineering; Computer Engineering; Computer Science; Electrical Engineering; Electronic Engineering; Industrial Engineering; Information Technology; Mechanical Engineering; Physical Engineering; Production Engineering); **Life Sciences and Engineering** (Agriculture; Biotechnology; Energy Engineering; Environmental Studies; Oenology; Power Engineering; Production Engineering; Viticulture)

History: Founded 1897.

Admission Requirements: Fachhochschulreife or equivalent diploma

Main Language(s) of Instruction: German

Accrediting Agency: AQAs

Degrees and Diplomas: *Bachelor's Degree*: **Agriculture; Biotechnology; Computer Engineering; Computer Science; Electrical Engineering; Energy Engineering; Environmental Engineering; Environmental Management; Industrial Engineering; Mechanical Engineering; Oenology; Physical Engineering; Production Engineering; Viticulture.** *Master*: **Agriculture; Automotive Engineering; Civil Engineering; Electrical Engineering; Electronic Engineering; Energy Engineering; Environmental Studies; Industrial Engineering; Information Technology; Production Engineering.**

Student Services: Canteen, Cultural Activities, Library, Social Counselling, Sports Facilities

Academic Staff *2014-2015*	**TOTAL**
FULL-TIME	**139**
STAFF WITH DOCTORATE FULL-TIME	**66**

Student Numbers *2014-2015*	
All (Foreign included)	**2,628**
FOREIGN ONLY	**253**

Last Updated: 27/01/15

UNIVERSITY OF APPLIED SCIENCES DÜSSELDORF

Fachhochschule Düsseldorf (FH D)

Universitaetsstrasse, Gebaeude 23.31/32, D-40225 Düsseldorf, Nordrhein Westfalen

Tel: +49(211) 4351-9018

Fax: +49(211) 81-14916

EMail: praesidium@fh-duesseldorf.de

Website: http://www.fh-duesseldorf.de

President: Brigitte Grass EMail: brigitte.grass@fh-duesseldorf.de

Vice President, Administration: Loretta Salvagno

EMail: vizepraesidentin@fh-duesseldorf.de

International Relations: Monika Katz, Head of International Office

EMail: monika.katz@fh-duesseldorf.de

Faculty

Architecture *(In the faculty of architecture Peter Behrens School of Architecture (PBSA) is located.)* (Architecture); **Business Studies** (Business Administration); **Design** (Design); **Electrical Engineering** (Electrical Engineering); **Mechanical Engineering** (Mechanical Engineering; Production Engineering); **Media Studies** (Media Studies); **Social Science and Cultural Studies** (Cultural Studies; Pedagogy; Social Sciences; Social Studies)

History: Founded 1971.

Academic Year: September to August

Admission Requirements: general qualification for university entrance (Abitur); advanced technical college entrance qualification (Fachhochschulreife); practical training (Praktikum); selection process (Auswahlverfahren)

Fees: 252,58 per semester (Euro)

Main Language(s) of Instruction: German

Degrees and Diplomas: *Bachelor's Degree*: **Architecture; Business and Commerce; Communication Arts; Design; Electronic Engineering; Information Technology; Mechanical Engineering; Media Studies.** *Master*: **Architecture; Business and Commerce; Communication Arts; Design; Electronic Engineering; Information Technology; Mechanical Engineering; Media Studies.**

Student Services: Academic Counselling, Canteen, Cultural Activities, Language Laboratory, Library, Sports Facilities

Academic Staff *2013-2014*	MEN	WOMEN	**TOTAL**
FULL-TIME	340	209	**549**
Student Numbers *2013-2014*			
All (Foreign included)	5,021	3,822	**8,843**
FOREIGN ONLY	–	–	**1,122**

Last Updated: 29/01/15

UNIVERSITY OF APPLIED SCIENCES EMDEN/LEER

Fachhochschule Emden/Leer

Constantiaplatz 4, 26723 Emden

Tel: +49(4921) 807-0

Fax: +49(4921) 807-1000

EMail: info@hs-emden-leer.de

Website: http://www.hs-emden-leer.de

President: Gerhard Kreutz

Tel: +49(4921) 807-1001 EMail: praesident@hs-emden-leer.de

International Relations: Andrea Meyenburg, Head of International Office

EMail: andrea.meyenburg@hs-emden-leer.de; international.office@hs-emden-leer.de

Faculty

Economics (Business Administration; Business and Commerce; Economics; International Business; Management); **Social Work and Health Sciences** (Health Sciences; Social Work); **Technology** (Automation and Control Engineering; Biological and Life Sciences; Biotechnology; Chemical Engineering; Computer Science; Electronic Engineering; Energy Engineering; Engineering; Engineering Management; Environmental Engineering; Environmental Management; Industrial Design; Information Technology; Machine Building; Physical Engineering; Physics; Technology)

Institute

Maritime Transport *(Leer)* (Transport and Communications)

Further Information: See also: www.fho-emden.de and www.fh-wilhelmshaven.de

History: Founded 1971. Oldenburg, Ostfriesland and Wilhelmshaven merged in 2000. Splitted into Fachhochschule Emden/Leer and Jade Hochschule 2009.

Academic Year: September to July

Admission Requirements: Secondary school certificate or equivalent. DaF or DSH Test for foreign students

Fees: (Euros): 106,32 per semester

Main Language(s) of Instruction: German

Accrediting Agency: ZEVA; ASII

Degrees and Diplomas: *Bachelor's Degree*: **Biotechnology; Business Administration; Chemical Engineering; Computer Science; Electronic Engineering; Energy Engineering; Environmental Engineering; Health Sciences; International Business; Marine Transport; Mechanical Engineering; Nautical Science; Physical Engineering; Social Work; Teacher Training.** *Master*: **Biological and Life Sciences; Business Administration; Computer Science; Engineering Management; Health Sciences; Management; Media Studies; Physical Engineering; Social Work.** *PhD*: **Energy Engineering; Social Work.** Medieninformatik (Online-Studiengang); The Doctoral Degree Programme in Energy Engineering is offered jointly with Universität Oldenburg; The Doctoral Degree Programme in Energy Engineering is offered jointly with Universität Vechta, Fachhochschule Oldenburg/Ostfriesland/Wilhelmshaven

Student Services: Academic Counselling, Canteen, Facilities for disabled people, Foreign Studies Centre, IT Centre, Language Laboratory, Library, Social Counselling, Sports Facilities

Publications: Blickpunkt

Academic Staff *2013-2014*: Total 396

STAFF WITH DOCTORATE: Total 107

Student Numbers *2014-2015*: Total 4,626

Last Updated: 27/01/15

UNIVERSITY OF APPLIED SCIENCES FOR POLICE AND ADMINISTRATION

Hessische Hochschule für Polizei und Verwaltung

Schönbergstr. 100, 65199 Wiesbaden
Tel: +49(611) 5829-0
Fax: +49(611) 5829-444
EMail: rektorat@hfpv-hessen.de
Website: http://www.hfpv.hessen.de/

Rector: Björn Gutzeit
Tel: +49(611) 5829-101 EMail: bjoern.gutzeit@hfpv-hessen.de

Chancellor: Manuela Sykstus
Tel: +49(611) 5829-102 EMail: manuela.sykstus@hfpv-hessen.de

Department

Police Studies (Police Studies); **Public Administration** (Public Administration)

Main Language(s) of Instruction: German

Degrees and Diplomas: *Master*: **Public Administration.**

Student Numbers *2013-2014*: Total 2,036

Last Updated: 07/04/15

UNIVERSITY OF APPLIED SCIENCES FOR TECHNOLOGY AND ECONOMICS BERLIN

Hochschule für Technik und Wirtschaft Berlin (HTW BERLIN)

Treskowallee 8, 10313 Berlin
Tel: +49(30) 5019-0
Fax: +49(30) 5090-134
EMail: fhtw@fhtw-berlin.de
Website: http://www.htw-berlin.de

President: Klaus Semlinger
Tel: +49(30) 5019-2800 EMail: Praesident@HTW-Berlin.de

Chancellor: Rainer Ziesener
Tel: +49(30) 5019-2466 EMail: Rainer.Ziesener@HTW-Berlin.de

International Relations: Daniela Englisch, Head, International Affairs
Tel: +49(30) 5019-2622 EMail: Daniela.Englisch@HTW-Berlin.de

Division

Business and Law *(III)* (Accountancy; Business Administration; Commercial Law; Economics; International Business; Law; Leadership; Management; Political Sciences; Public Administration; Real Estate; Retailing and Wholesaling); **Computer Science, Communication and Business** *(IV)* (Business Administration; Business Computing; Communication Studies; Computer Science; Finance; Industrial Engineering; Insurance); **Design and Cultural Studies** *(V)* (Archaeology; Communication Arts; Fashion Design; Graphic Design; Industrial Design; Museum Management; Museum Studies; Restoration of Works of Art; Textile Technology); **Engineering - Energy and Information Sciences** *(I)* (Automation and Control Engineering; Computer Engineering; Electrical Engineering; Energy Engineering; Engineering; Environmental Engineering; Information Sciences; Information Technology; Telecommunications Engineering); **Engineering Science - Technology and Life** *(II)* (Automotive Engineering; Bioengineering; Civil Engineering; Computer Engineering; Computer Science; Mechanical Engineering; Real Estate)

History: Founded 1991.

Main Language(s) of Instruction: German

Degrees and Diplomas: *Bachelor's Degree*: **Business Administration; Computer Science; Design; Engineering; Museum Studies.** *Master*: **Accountancy; Archaeology; Automation and Control Engineering; Automotive Engineering; Bioengineering; Business Administration; Business Computing; Civil Engineering; Commercial Law; Communication Studies; Computer Science; Electrical Engineering; Energy Engineering; Engineering; Fashion Design; Finance; Industrial Engineering; Information Technology; Insurance; International Business; Management; Mechanical Engineering; Museum Management; Public Administration; Real Estate; Restoration of Works of Art; Retailing and Wholesaling; Taxation; Telecommunications Engineering; Textile Technology.** Cooperative agreements for Doctoral Degree Programes ("Promotion") with other Universities.

Student Services: Academic Counselling, Canteen, Library, Sports Facilities

Student Numbers *2014-2015*: Total: c. 1,100

Last Updated: 27/01/15

UNIVERSITY OF APPLIED SCIENCES GEISENHEIM

Hochschule Geisenheim

Von-Lade-Straße 1, D-65366 Geisenheim
Tel: +49(6722) 502-0
Fax: +49(6722) 502-212
EMail: Info@hs-gm.de
Website: http://www.hs-geisenheim.de/

President: Hans Reiner Schultz
Tel: + 49(6722) 502-201 EMail: Praesidium@hs-gm.de

Chancellor: Marion Waldeck
Tel: +49(6722) 502-221 EMail: Kanzlerin@hs-gm.de

International Relations: Sonja Thielemann, Head of International Office
Tel: +49(6722) 502-718 EMail: Sonja.Thielemann@hs-gm.de

Programme

Beverage Technology (Food Technology); **Horticulture** (Horticulture); **International Wine Business (in English)** (Agricultural Business; International Business); **International Wine Economy** (Agricultural Economics); **Viticulture and Oenology** (Oenology; Viticulture)

Main Language(s) of Instruction: German

Degrees and Diplomas: *Bachelor's Degree*; *Master*: **Agricultural Business; Environmental Management; Food Technology; Horticulture; Oenology; Viticulture.**

Student Services: Careers Guidance, IT Centre, Library

Student Numbers *2013-2014*: Total 1,144

Last Updated: 08/04/15

UNIVERSITY OF APPLIED SCIENCES IN EBERSWALDE

Hochschule für nachhaltige Entwicklung Eberswalde

Schicklerstraße 5, 16225 Eberswalde
Tel: +49(3334) 657-0
Fax: +49(3334) 657-300
EMail: praesident@hnee.de
Website: http://www.hnee.de/

Rector: Wilhelm-Günther Vahrson
Tel: +49(3334) 657-151 EMail: buero.praesident@hnee.de

Chancellor: Jana Einsporn
Tel: +49(3334) 657-152 EMail: Jana.Einsporn@hnee.de

International Relations: Yvonne Blotny, Head, International Office
Tel: +49(3334) 657-137 EMail: Yvonne.Blotny@hnee.de

Faculty

Business (Business Administration; Finance; Management; Marketing; Tourism); **Forest and Environment** (Ecology; Environmental Studies; Forest Management; Forestry; Information Technology); **Landscape Management and Nature Conservation** (Ecology; Environmental Management; Landscape Architecture; Regional Planning; Tourism); **Wood Science and Technology** (Engineering; Wood Technology)

History: Founded 1992.

Admission Requirements: Hochschulzugangsberechtigung, DSH

Fees: 106 per semester (Euro)

Main Language(s) of Instruction: German, English

Degrees and Diplomas: *Bachelor's Degree*; *Master*. **Agricultural Management; Development Studies; Environmental Management; Environmental Studies; Information Technology; Tourism; Wood Technology.**

Student Services: Academic Counselling, Canteen, Careers Guidance, IT Centre, Language Laboratory, Library, Social Counselling

Student Numbers *2013-2014*: Total 2,026
Last Updated: 10/03/15

UNIVERSITY OF APPLIED SCIENCES OF ZWICKAU

Westsächsische Hochschule Zwickau

PO Box 201037, Dr.-Friedrichs-Ring 2a, 08056 Zwickau
Tel: +49(375) 536-0
Fax: +49(375) 536-1127
EMail: Pressestelle@fh-zwickau.de
Website: http://www.fh-zwickau.de/

Rector: Gunter Krautheim
Tel: +49(375) 536-1000 EMail: gunter.krautheim@fh-zwickau.de

Chancellor: Ralf Steiner
Tel: +49(375) 536-1100 EMail: kanzler@fh-zwickau.de

International Relations: Adriana Slavcheva, Head of International Office
Tel: +49(375) 536-1060
EMail: akademisches.auslandsamt@fh-zwickau.de

Faculty

Applied Arts *(Schneeberg)* (Fine Arts); **Applied Languages and Intercultural Commmunication** (Chinese; English; French; Modern Languages; Spanish); **Architecture** (Architecture; Landscape Architecture; Town Planning); **Automotive and Mechanical Engineering** (Automotive Engineering; Mechanical Engineering); **Automotive Engineering** (Automotive Engineering); **Economics** (Economics); **Electrical Engineering** (Electrical Engineering); **Health and Care Sciences** (Health Administration; Health Sciences); **Physical Engineering and Computer Science** (Computer Science; Physical Engineering)

History: Founded 1969.

Academic Year: September to July (September-January; February-July)

Admission Requirements: Technical training and secondary school certificate (Reifezeugnis)

Fees: None

Main Language(s) of Instruction: German

Degrees and Diplomas: *Bachelor's Degree*; *Diplom (FH)*; *Master*. **Automotive Engineering; Business Administration; Chinese; Computer Science; Design; Electrical and Electronic Engineering; German; Health Sciences; International Business; Management; Medical Technology; Nanotechnology; Textile Technology; Transport Management.**

Student Services: IT Centre, Library, Sports Facilities

Student Numbers *2013-2014*: Total 4,750
Last Updated: 28/03/15

UNIVERSITY OF APPLIED SCIENCES OFFENBURG

Hochschule Offenburg

Badstrasse 24, 77652 Offenburg
Tel: +49(781) 205-0
Fax: +49(781) 205-214
EMail: info@hs-offenburg.de
Website: http://www.fh-offenburg.de

Rector: Winfried Lieber (1997-)
Tel: +49(781) 205-201 EMail: lieber@hs-offenburg.de

Chancellor: Thomas Wiedemer
Tel: +49(781) 205-211 EMail: wiedemer@hs-offenburg.de

International Relations: Birgit Teubner-Jatzlau, Head of the International Office
Tel: +49(781) 205-218
EMail: birgit.teubner@hs-offenburg.de; io@hs-offenburg.de

Faculty

Business Administration and Industrial Engineering *(Gengenbach)* (Business and Commerce; Industrial Engineering; Industrial Management; International Business); **Electrical Engineering and Information Technology** (Automation and Control Engineering; Telecommunications Engineering); **Mechanical and Process Engineering** (Automotive Engineering; Biotechnology; Computer Engineering; Energy Engineering; Engineering Management; Environmental Engineering; Mechanical Engineering); **Media and Information** (Information Technology; Media Studies)

Further Information: Also Campus Gengenbach; CME and IBC entirely taught in English, ECM taught partly in English, partly in German. Systems Engineering (Génie des Systèmes), German-French bilingual study programme at University of Applied Sciences Offenburg and Université Louis Pasteur, Strasbourg

History: Founded 1964, acquired present status 1971. Formerly known as Fachhochschule Offenburg - Hochschule für Technik, Wirtschaft und Medien.

Academic Year: September to August

Admission Requirements: Secondary school certificate (Hochschulreife) or equivalent

Fees: None, except 'International Business Consulting': 5,300 for 3 semesters (Euro)

Main Language(s) of Instruction: German

Accrediting Agency: Akkreditierungsagentur für Studiengänge der Ingenieurwissenschaften und Informatik (ASII); Foundation of International Business Administration Accreditation (FIBAA)

Degrees and Diplomas: *Bachelor's Degree*; *Master*. **Business Administration; Business Computing; Computer Science; Electrical Engineering; Electronic Engineering; Energy Engineering; Industrial Engineering; Information Sciences; Information Technology; International Business; Management; Mass Communication; Mechanical Engineering; Media Studies; Medical Technology; Production Engineering.** Also MBA; Some programmes conducted in English.

Student Services: Academic Counselling, Canteen, Careers Guidance, Foreign Studies Centre, IT Centre, Language Laboratory, Social Counselling, Sports Facilities

Publications: IAF-Bericht

Student Numbers *2013-2014*: Total 4,332
Last Updated: 12/03/15

UNIVERSITY OF APPLIED SCIENCES POTSDAM

Fachhochschule Potsdam

PO Box 600608, 14406 Potsdam
Tel: +49(331) 580-00
Fax: +49(331) 580-2999
EMail: rektor@fh-potsdam.de
Website: http://www.fh-potsdam.de

President: Eckehard Binas
Tel: +49(331) 580-1000 EMail: praesident@fh-potsdam.de

Chancellor: Gerlinde Reich
Tel: +49(331) 580-1040 EMail: kanzlerin@fh-potsdam.de

International Relations: Uta Kotulla, Head, International Office
Tel: +49(331) 580-2010 EMail: kotulla@fh-potsdam.de

Faculty

Architecture and Town Planning (Architectural Restoration; Architecture; Town Planning); **Civil Engineering** (Civil Engineering; Construction Engineering); **Design** (Design; Graphic Design; Industrial Design); **Information Sciences** (Archiving; Documentation Techniques; Library Science); **Social Work** (Social Work)

Further Information: Also European Media Studies programme jointly offered with the Potsdam University.

History: Founded 1992.

Admission Requirements: Abitur; Fachabitur

Fees: c. 200 (Euro)

Main Language(s) of Instruction: German

Degrees and Diplomas: *Bachelor's Degree*; *Diplom (FH)*: **Civil Engineering.** *Master*: **Architectural Restoration; Architecture; Archiving; Construction Engineering; Design; Heritage Preservation; Information Sciences; Media Studies; Restoration of Works of Art; Social Work; Town Planning.**

Student Services: Academic Counselling, Library

Academic Staff *2014-2015*: Total: c. 200
Student Numbers *2014-2015*: Total 3,770
Last Updated: 28/01/15

UNIVERSITY OF APPLIED SCIENCES SCHMALKALDEN

Fachhochschule Schmalkalden - Hochschule für Angewandte Wissenschaften (FH SCHMALKALDEN)

Postfach 10 04 52, Blechhammer 9, 98564 Schmalkalden
Tel: +49(3683) 688-0
Fax: +49(3683) 688-1920
EMail: info@fh-schmalkalden.de
Website: http://www.fh-schmalkalden.de

Rector: Elmar Heinemann (2007-)
Tel: +49(3683) 688-1001 EMail: rektor@fh-schmalkalden.de

Kanzler: Thomas Losse
Tel: +49(3683) 688-1002 EMail: kanzler@fh-schmalkalden.de

Faculty

Business and Economics (Business Administration; Economics); **Business Law** (Commercial Law; Law); **Computer Science** (Computer Science); **Electrical Engineering** (Electrical Engineering; Information Technology); **Mechanical Engineering** (Machine Building; Mechanical Engineering)

History: Founded 1992.

Main Language(s) of Instruction: German

Degrees and Diplomas: *Bachelor's Degree*; *Master*: **Business Administration; Commercial Law; Computer Science; Electrical Engineering; Information Technology; International Business; International Economics; Management; Mechanical Engineering; Multimedia; Polymer and Plastics Technology; Public Law; Sports Management.**

Student Services: Library

Student Numbers *2014-2015*: Total: c. 3,000
Last Updated: 28/01/15

UNIVERSITY OF AUGSBURG

Universität Augsburg

Universitätsstr. 2, 86159 Augsburg
Tel: +49(821) 598-0
Fax: +49(821) 598-5505
EMail: wwwadm@uni-augsburg.de
Website: http://www.uni-augsburg.de

Präsidentin: Sabine Doering-Manteuffel (2011-)
Tel: +49(821) 598-5100
EMail: praesident@praesidium.uni-augsburg.de; rektor@rektorat.uni-augsburg.de

Chancellor: Alois Zimmermann
Tel: +49(821) 598-5200 EMail: kanzler@zv.uni-augsburg.de

International Relations: Sabine Tamm
Tel: +49(821) 598-5135
EMail: sabine.tamm@aaa.uni-augsburg.de

Faculty

Applied Computer Science (Computer Engineering; Computer Science; Geography; Software Engineering); **Business Administration and Economics** (Business Administration; Economics; International Relations; Marketing); **Catholic Theology** (Catholic Theology); **Law** (Law); **Mathematics, Natural Sciences and Materials Engineering** (Materials Engineering; Mathematics; Natural Sciences; Physics); **Philology and History** (Arts and Humanities; History; Modern Languages; Philology; Philosophy); **Philosophy and Social Sciences** (Catholic Theology; Education; Mass Communication; Media Studies; Philosophy; Social Sciences)

Centre

Continuing Education and Knowledge Transfer (ZWW) (Continuing Education); **Environmental Sciences (WZU)** (Environmental Studies); **Language** (Modern Languages)

History: Founded 1970. An autonomous institution financially supported by the State of Bavaria.

Academic Year: October to September (October-March; April-September)

Admission Requirements: Secondary school certificate (Reifezeugnis) or equivalent

Fees: None

Main Language(s) of Instruction: German

Degrees and Diplomas: *Bachelor's Degree*; *Magister*: **Arts and Humanities; Catholic Theology; Ethics; Literature.** *Master*: **American Studies; Applied Linguistics; Applied Mathematics; Art History; Art Therapy; Arts and Humanities; Business Administration; Computer Science; Cultural Studies; Economic and Finance Policy; Economics; Educational Sciences; English Studies; Environmental Studies; European Studies; Finance; French; Geography; German; History; Industrial Engineering; Information Management; Information Technology; Law; Literature; Management; Mass Communication; Materials Engineering; Mathematics; Media Studies; Meteorology; Multimedia; Music; Music Education; Physics; Political Sciences; Primary Education; Secondary Education; Social Sciences; Software Engineering.** *PhD*: **American Studies; Art History; Arts and Humanities; Catholic Theology; Cultural Studies; Educational Research; Educational Sciences; English; English Studies; Ethics; German; History; Humanities and Social Science Education; International Studies; Linguistics; Literature; Mathematics; Philology; Social Sciences.** *Habilitation*: **Catholic Theology; Physics; Social Sciences.** Some Master's Degree Programmes taught in English; Also State Examination Certificate (Staatsexam) in Law; Teacher Training State Certificate (Lehramt).

Student Services: Academic Counselling, Canteen, Careers Guidance, Facilities for disabled people, Foreign Studies Centre, Language Laboratory, Library, Nursery Care, Social Counselling, Sports Facilities

Publications: Forschungsbericht

Student Numbers *2013-2014*: Total 19,006
Last Updated: 30/03/15

UNIVERSITY OF BAYREUTH

Universität Bayreuth (UBT)

Universitätsstraße 30, 95440 Bayreuth, Bavaria
Tel: +49(921) 55-0
Fax: +49(921) 55-5290
EMail: international@uni-bayreuth.de
Website: http://www.uni-bayreuth.de

President: Stefan Leible (2013-)
Tel: +49(921) 55-5200 EMail: praesident@uni-bayreuth.de

Chancellor: Markus Zanner
Tel: +49(921) 55-5210 EMail: kanzler@uvw.uni-bayreuth.de

International Relations: Arnim Heinemann, Director of the International Office EMail: international@uni-bayreuth.de

Faculty

Applied Sciences (Applied Chemistry; Applied Mathematics; Applied Physics; Bioengineering; Engineering; Environmental Engineering; Materials Engineering; Natural Sciences); **Biology, Chemistry and Earth Sciences** (Biochemistry; Biology; Chemistry; Geography; Regional Planning; Soil Science; Town Planning; Water Science); **Cultural Studies** (Cultural Studies; Economics; Education; Ethnology; History; Modern History; Music; Philosophy; Political Sciences; Religious Studies; Sociology; Sports; Theology); **Languages and Literature** (African Languages; Arabic; English; English Studies; French Studies; German; Islamic Studies; Literature; Modern Languages; Romance Languages; Slavic Languages; Swahili; Theatre); **Law, Business and Economics** (Banking; Business Administration; Business and Commerce; Civil Law; Economics; Finance; Health Administration; International Law; Labour Law; Law; Management; Public Law); **Mathematics, Physics and Computer Science** (Applied Mathematics; Applied Physics; Atomic and Molecular Physics; Computer Science; Mathematics; Physics; Statistics; Systems Analysis; Thermal Physics)

Institute

African Studies (African Studies); **Earth Eco-Systems Research** *(Bayreuther Institut für Terrestrische Ökosystemforschung BITÖK)* (Earth Sciences; Forest Biology; Forestry; Soil Science; Water Science); **Experimental Geochemistry and Geophysics Research** *(Bayerisches Forschungsinstitut für experimentelle Geochemie und Geophysik BGI)* (Crystallography; Geochemistry; Geology; Geophysics; Mineralogy; Petrology; Seismology); **Macromolecular Research** (Molecular Biology); **Music Theatre Research** (Music; Theatre)

Centre

Colloids and Interfaces *(Bayreuther Zentrum für Kolloide und Grenzflächen BZKG)* (Physical Chemistry); **Ecology and Environmental Research** (Ecology; Environmental Studies); **Languages** (Linguistics; Modern Languages); **Materials Science and Engineering** (Materials Engineering); **Molecular Life Sciences** *(Bayreuther Zentrum für Molekulare Biowissenschaften BZMB)* (Biochemistry; Biomedicine; Biophysics; Cell Biology; Molecular Biology)

Research Centre

Bio-Macromolecules (Molecular Biology)

History: Founded 1972. Formally opened 1975. An autonomous institution financially supported by the State of Bavaria, and under the jurisdiction of its Ministry of Science, Research and Arts.

Academic Year: October to September (October-March; April-September)

Admission Requirements: Secondary school certificate (Reifezeugnis)

Fees: None for initial studies; additional study, 500 per semester (Euro)

Main Language(s) of Instruction: German, English

Accrediting Agency: ACQUIN

Degrees and Diplomas: *Bachelor's Degree*; *Master*: **African Languages; African Studies; Anthropology; Applied Mathematics; Automotive Engineering; Biochemistry; Biology; Biotechnology; Business Administration; Central European Studies; Chemistry; Computer Science; Cultural Studies; Earth Sciences; Ecology; Economics; Electronic Engineering; Energy Engineering; Engineering; English; English Studies; Environmental Studies; Ethnology; Food Science; French Studies; Geography; Geography (Human); German; Germanic Studies; Government; Health Administration; Health Sciences; History; Industrial Engineering; Information Management; International Economics; Law; Literature; Materials Engineering; Mathematics; Mechanics; Media Studies; Molecular Biology; Music; Performing Arts; Philosophy; Physics; Polymer and Plastics Technology; Religion; Romance Languages; Sports; Sports Management; Theatre.** *PhD*: **African Studies; Biology; Business Administration; Chemistry; Computer Science; Cultural Studies; Earth Sciences; Economics; Engineering; Law; Literature; Mathematics; Media Studies; Modern Languages; Music; Natural Sciences; Performing Arts; Physics.** *Habilitation*: **Computer Science; Economics; Engineering; Law; Literature; Mathematics; Modern Languages; Natural Sciences; Physics.** Also Dual Degrees; State Examination Certificate (Staatsexam) in Law; Teacher Training State Certificate (Lehramt).

Student Services: Academic Counselling, Canteen, Careers Guidance, Facilities for disabled people, IT Centre, Language Laboratory, Library, Social Counselling, Sports Facilities

Publications: Arbeitsmaterialien zur Raumordnung und Raumplanung; Bayreuther African Studies Series; Bayreuther Beiträge zur Dialektologie; Bayreuther Beiträge zur Literaturwissenschaft; Bayreuther Bodenkundliche Berichte; Bayreuther Forum Ökologie; Bayreuther Frankofonie Studien; Bayreuther Geowissenschaftliche Arbeiten; Bayreuther Historische Kolloquien; Bayreuther Mathematische Schriften; Beiträge zur Stadt- und Regionalplanung; Betriebswirtschaftliche Forschungsbeiträge; Forschungsbericht; Kolloquium Mathematik-Didaktik; Materialien zur Stadt- und Regionalplanung; Schriften zur Gesundheitsökonomie; Thurnauer Schriften zum Musiktheater; Universität Bayreuth: Fachgruppe Geowissenschaften: Forschungsmaterialien

Student Numbers *2013-2014*: Total 12,520
Last Updated: 30/03/15

UNIVERSITY OF BIELEFELD

Universität Bielefeld

PO Box 100131, Universitätsstrasse 25, 33501 Bielefeld
Tel: +49(521) 106-00
EMail: post@uni-bielefeld.de
Website: http://www.uni-bielefeld.de

Rector: Gerhard Sagerer
Tel: +49(521) 106-2000 EMail: rektor@uni-bielefeld.de

Chancellor: Stephan Becker
Tel: +49(521) 106-3000 EMail: kanzler@uni-bielefeld.de

International Relations: Thomas Lüttenberg, Head, International Office
Tel: +49(521) 106-4088
EMail: thomas.luettenberg@uni-bielefeld.de

Faculty

Biology (Biology); **Business Administration and Economics** (Business Administration; Economics); **Chemistry** (Chemistry); **Educational Sciences** (Educational Sciences); **Health Science** (Health Sciences; Public Health); **History, Philosophy and Theology** (History; Philosophy; Theology); **Law** (Law); **Linguistics and Literary Studies** (Linguistics; Literature); **Mathematics** (Mathematics); **Physics** (Physics); **Psychology and Sport Sciences** (Psychology; Sports); **Sociology** (Sociology); **Technology** (Biological and Life Sciences; Information Technology; Technology)

School

Education (Education)

Institute

Conflict and Violence Research *(Interdisciplinary)* (Peace and Disarmament); **Didactics of Mathematics** (Mathematics Education); **Mathematical Economics (IMW)** (Economics); **Simulation of Complex Systems** (Systems Analysis)

Centre

Biotechnology (Biophysics; Biotechnology; Genetics; Nanotechnology); **Cognitive Interaction Technology (Center of Excellence)** (Technology); **Interdisciplinary Research**; **Interdisciplinary Women's and Gender Studies** (Women's Studies)

Graduate School

History and Sociology (History; Sociology); **Theoretical Sciences** (Business Administration; Economics; Mathematics; Physics)

Research Centre

Mathematical Modelling (RCM) (Mathematics)

Research Institute

Cognition and Robotics (CoR-Lab) (Robotics)

History: Founded in 1969 in response to the demand for the creation of a University in East Westphalia. An autonomous institution financially supported by the State of North Rhine-Westphalia and under the jurisdiction of its Ministry of Science and Research.

Academic Year: October to September (October-March; April-September)

Admission Requirements: Secondary school certificate (Reifezeugnis) or equivalent

Fees: 100-500 plus 150,60 social fees (Euro)

Main Language(s) of Instruction: German

Degrees and Diplomas: *Bachelor's Degree*; *Master*: **American Studies; Artificial Intelligence; Behavioural Sciences; Biochemistry; Biology; Biophysics; Biotechnology; Business Administration; Cell Biology; Chemistry; Communication Studies; Ecology; Economics; Educational Sciences; English Studies; Foreign Languages Education; Gender Studies; Genetics; German; History; Linguistics; Literature; Mathematics; Media Studies; Molecular Biology; Nanotechnology; Natural Sciences; Philosophy; Physics; Political Sciences; Psychology; Public Health; Sociology; Special Education; Sports; Teacher Training.** *PhD*: **American Studies; Artificial Intelligence; Biological and Life Sciences; Biology; Biotechnology; Business Administration; Chemistry; Computer Science; Economics; English Studies; Fine Arts; Foreign Languages Education; German; Health Sciences; History; Law; Linguistics; Literature; Mathematics; Music; Philosophy; Physics; Psychology; Sociology; Sports; Theology.** *Habilitation*: **Biophysics; Computer Science; Economics; Education; History; Linguistics; Literature; Mathematics; Nanotechnology; Sociology; Technology.** Also State Examination Certificate (Staatsexam) in Law

Student Services: Academic Counselling, Canteen, Careers Guidance, Cultural Activities, Facilities for disabled people, Foreign Studies Centre, Health Services, Language Laboratory, Library, Nursery Care, Social Counselling, Sports Facilities

Publications: Bielefelder Forschungsmagazin; Vorlesungsverzeichnis

Student Numbers *2013-2014*: Total 21,552

Last Updated: 30/03/15

UNIVERSITY OF BREMEN

Universität Bremen

PO Box 330440, Bibliotheksstrasse 1, 28359 Bremen

Tel: +49(421) 218-1

Fax: +49(421) 218-4259

EMail: info@uni-bremen.de

Website: http://www.uni-bremen.de

Rector: Bernd Scholz-Reiter
Tel: +49(421) 218-60011 EMail: rektor@uni-bremen.de

Chancellor: Martin Mehrtens
Tel: +49(421) 218-60101 EMail: sekrkanz@uni-bremen.de

International Relations: Annette Lang, Head, International Office
Tel: +49(421) 218-60361 EMail: lang@uni-bremen.de

Faculty

Biology and Chemistry (Aquaculture; Biology; Chemistry); **Cultural Studies** (Art Education; Cultural Studies; Music; Philosophy; Religious Studies; Sports); **Economics** (Economics; International Relations; Management); **Geosciences** (Geology; Geophysics; Mineralogy; Paleontology); **Human and Health Sciences** (Nursing; Psychology; Public Health; Social Sciences; Social Studies); **Law** (European Union Law; International Law; Law); **Linguistics and Literature** (American Studies; English; English Studies; French; Germanic Studies; Linguistics; Romance Languages; Spanish); **Mathematics and Computer Science** (Mathematics and Computer Science); **Pedagogy and Educational Sciences** (Education; Education of the Handicapped; Educational Sciences); **Physical and Electrical Engineering** (Electrical Engineering; Physical Engineering); **Production Technology, Mechanical and Process Engineering** (Engineering Management; Mechanical Engineering; Production Engineering); **Social Sciences** (Eastern European Studies; Geography; History; Polish; Political Sciences; Social Studies; Sociology)

Area

Health Sciences; **Information, Cognition, and Communication Sciences**; **Logistics**; **Marine, Arctic and Climate Research**; **Materials Science and Production Engineering**; **Social Change, Social Policy, and the State**

Institute

Applied Materials Research *(Fraunhofer IFAM)* (Materials Engineering); **Marine Microbiology** *(Max Planck)* (Marine Biology; Microbiology)

Centre

Medical Diagnosis Systems and Visualization *(MeVis)*

Research Group

(Post) Cold War Europe; **Communicative Figurations of Mediatized Worlds**; **Decision Processes in Political Committees: Interests heterogeneity, power distribution, building majorities and commitment**; **Governance of Transnational Enterprises**; **Homo debilis: The Social Integration and Life Coping Strategies of Disabled Persons in Historical Perspective**; **Language Contact and Language Comparison**; **Migration, Integration and Regional Differentiation**; **Neurotechnology**

History: Founded 1971 as an autonomous institution under the jurisdiction of and financed by the State of Bremen. Previously existing College of Education (1947) incorporated 1973.

Academic Year: October to September (October-March; April-September)

Admission Requirements: Secondary school certificate (Reifezeugnis) or equivalent

Fees: None

Main Language(s) of Instruction: German

Degrees and Diplomas: *Bachelor's Degree*; *Diplom (Univ)*; *Master*: **Applied Chemistry; Applied Mathematics; Applied Physics; Automation and Control Engineering; Biochemistry; Biological and Life Sciences; Business Administration; Chemistry; Clinical Psychology; Community Health; Computer Engineering; Computer Science; Cultural Studies; Earth Sciences; Ecology; Educational Sciences; Electrical Engineering; English; Epidemiology; German; Health Sciences; History; Industrial and Organizational Psychology; Industrial Engineering; Information Technology; International Law; International Relations; Literature; Marine Biology; Marine Science and Oceanography; Mathematics; Media Studies; Microbiology; Mineralogy; Molecular Biology; Musicology; Neurosciences; Nursing; Pedagogy; Physics; Political Sciences; Primary Education; Production Engineering; Public Health; Regional Planning; Religious Studies; Secondary Education; Social Policy; Sociology; Special Education; Town Planning; Vocational Education.** *PhD*: **Arts and Humanities; Biology; Business Administration; Chemistry; Computer Science; Cultural Studies; Earth Sciences; Economics; Educational Sciences; Electrical Engineering; Health Sciences; Law; Linguistics; Mathematics; Pedagogy; Physics; Production Engineering; Social Sciences.** No more intakes allowed for Diplom (Univ) programmes, which are being phased down; Also offered: State Examination Certificate (Staatsexam) in Law; Teacher Training State Certificate (Lehramt).

Student Services: Academic Counselling, Careers Guidance, Facilities for disabled people, Health Services, Library, Social Counselling, Sports Facilities

Publications: Impulse aus der Forschung; Research Reports and Papers

Student Numbers *2013-2014*: Total 18,504

Last Updated: 01/04/15

UNIVERSITY OF COLOGNE

Universität zu Köln

Albertus-Magnus-Platz, 50923 Köln, Nordrhein-Westfalen

Tel: +49(221) 470-0

Fax: +49(221) 470-5151

EMail: pressestelle@uni-koeln.de

Website: http://www.uni-koeln.de

Rector: Axel Freimuth
Tel: +49(221) 470-2201 EMail: rektor@uni-koeln.de

Chancellor: Michael Stückradt
Tel: +49(221) 470-2236 EMail: kanzler@verw.uni-koeln.de

International Relations: Stefan Bildhauer, Head of International Office
Tel: +49(221) 470-2382
EMail: s.bildhauer@verw.uni-koeln.de; aaa@verw.uni-koeln.de

Faculty

Arts and Humanities (Ethnology; History; Media Studies; Modern Languages; Musicology; Philosophy; Psychology; Theology); **Human Sciences** (Education; Fine Arts; Music; Psychology; Rehabilitation and Therapy; Social Sciences; Special Education; Textile Design); **Law** (Law); **Management, Economics, and Social Sciences** (Business Administration; Economics; Management; Social Sciences); **Mathematics and Natural Sciences** (Biology; Chemistry; Earth Sciences; Mathematics; Natural Sciences; Physics); **Medicine** (Dentistry; Medicine; Neurosciences; Surgery)

History: Founded 1388 as a Municipal University. Closed 1798. At the beginning of the 20th century a College of Commerce, a Medical Academy and a College of Social Administration were estabished. These formed the basis for the re-establishment of the University 1919. Rheinland College of Education incorporated 1980. An autonomous institution financially supported by the State of North Rhine-Westphalia and under the jurisdiction of its Ministry of Education since 1953. Since 1970 under the jurisdiction of its Ministry of Science and Research.

Academic Year: October to September (October-March; April-September)

Admission Requirements: Secondary school certificate (Reifezeugnis) or equivalent

Fees: None

Main Language(s) of Instruction: German

Degrees and Diplomas: *Bachelor's Degree*; *Master*: **African Languages; African Studies; American Studies; Ancient Languages; Arabic; Archaeology; Art Education; Art History; Arts and Humanities; Asian Studies; Biological and Life Sciences; Biology; Business Administration; Catholic Theology; Chemistry; Chinese; Classical Languages; Commercial Law; Communication Studies; Cultural Studies; Data Processing; Dutch; Earth Sciences; East Asian Studies; Eastern European Studies; Economics; Education; Educational Sciences; English; English Studies; Environmental Studies; Ethnology; European Union Law; Fine Arts; French; German; Greek; Greek (Classical); Hindi; History; Humanities and Social Science Education; Information Technology; Islamic Studies; Italian; Japanese; Latin; Latin American Studies; Law; Linguistics; Literature; Management; Mathematics; Mathematics Education; Media Studies; Medieval Studies; Music; Musicology; Neurosciences; Pedagogy; Philosophy; Phonetics; Physics; Political Sciences; Protestant Theology; Psychology; Regional Studies; Rehabilitation and Therapy; Religion; Religious Education; Russian; Scandinavian Languages; Science Education; Slavic Languages; Sociology; Spanish; Western European Studies.** *PhD*: **Dentistry; Economics; Educational Sciences; Fine Arts; Health Education; Health Sciences; Law; Mathematics; Media Studies; Medicine; Music; Natural Sciences; Philosophy; Psychology; Public Health; Rehabilitation and Therapy; Social Sciences.** *Habilitation*: **Mathematics; Medicine; Natural Sciences; Social Sciences.** Also Staatsexamen.

Student Services: Library

Publications: Research Report; Universitätsreden; Veröffentlichungen einzelner Institute; Vorlesungsverzeichnis

Academic Staff *2013-2014*: Total 576

Student Numbers *2014-2015*: Total 48,179

Last Updated: 28/03/15

UNIVERSITY OF COOPERATIVE EDUCATION-BADEN WÜRTTEMBERG

Duale Hochschule Baden-Württemberg (DHBW)
Friedrichstrasse 14, 70174 Stuttgart, Baden-Württemberg
Tel: +49(711) 320-0660-0
Fax: +49(711) 320-660-66
EMail: info@cas.dhbw.de; poststelle@dhbw.de
Website: http://www.dhbw.de

President: Reinhold R. Geilsdörfer

International Relations: Axel Gerloff, Head of Foreign Relations
EMail: gerloff@dhbw.de

Campus

Heidenheim (Banking; Business Administration; Business Computing; Finance; Industrial Engineering; Information Technology; Insurance; International and Comparative Education; Management; Marketing; Mechanical Engineering; Social Sciences; Social Work); **Karlsruhe** (Accountancy; Banking; Business Administration; Business Computing; Computer Science; Electrical Engineering; Information Technology; Insurance; International Business; Management; Mechanical Engineering; Medical Auxiliaries; Safety Engineering); **Lörrach** (Automation and Control Engineering; Business Administration; Business Computing; Computer Science; Electrical Engineering; Finance; Health Administration; Information Technology; International Business; Management; Tourism; Transport Management); **Mannheim** (Accountancy; Administration; Banking; Business Administration; Health Administration; Information Technology; Management; Real Estate; Taxation; Transport Management); **Mosbach** (Business Administration); **Ravensburg** (Banking; Business Administration; Communication Studies; Computer Science; Economics; Finance; Hotel Management; Industrial Engineering; Media Studies; Tourism); **Stuttgart** (Accountancy; Business Administration; Computer Science; Electrical and Electronic Equipment and Maintenance; Health Administration; International Business; Management; Mechanical Engineering; Midwifery; Nursing; Real Estate; Social Work; Taxation); **Villingen-Schwenningen** (Accountancy; Banking; Engineering; Family Studies; Human Resources; Industrial Management; International Business; Management; Public Administration; Public Health; Small Business; Social Policy; Social Work; Taxation)

History: Created 1974 as Berufsakademie Baden-Württemberg, Acquired current title and status 2009. Based on the US state university model with campuses throughout the state of Baden-Württemberg.

Main Language(s) of Instruction: German

Accrediting Agency: Central Agency for Evaluation and Accreditation (CAEA/ZEvA)

Degrees and Diplomas: *Bachelor's Degree*: **Business Administration; Engineering; Social Work.** *Master*: **Accountancy; Automotive Engineering; Business Administration; Computer Engineering; Electronic Engineering; Engineering; Industrial Engineering; Machine Building; Paper Technology; Social Work; Taxation.**

Academic Staff *2014-2015*: Total: c. 650

Student Numbers *2014-2015*: Total: c. 34,000

Last Updated: 16/01/15

UNIVERSITY OF DUISBURG-ESSEN

Universität Duisburg-Essen
Universitätsstraße 2, 45141 Essen
Tel: +49(201) 183-0
Fax: +49(201) 183-3536
EMail: duisburg-io@uni-due.de; essen-io@uni-due.de
Website: http://www.uni-duisburg-essen.de/

Rector: Ulrich Radtke
Tel: +49(203) 183-2000 EMail: rektor@uni-duisburg-essen.de

Chancellor: Rainer Ambrosy
Tel: +49(201) 183-3000 EMail: kanzler@uni-due.de

International Relations: Petra Günther, Head, International Office
Tel: +49(201) 183-2068
EMail: petra.guenther@uni-due.de; essen-io@uni-due.de

Faculty

Biology (Biology); **Chemistry** (Chemistry); **Economics and Business Administration** (Accountancy; Banking; Business Administration; Civil Law; Economics; Finance; Information Management; International Relations; Management; Marketing; Taxation); **Educational Sciences** (Educational Sciences); **Engineering** (Computer Science; Electrical Engineering; Engineering; Information Technology; Materials Engineering; Mechanical Engineering; Multimedia; Software Engineering); **Humanities** (American Studies; Cultural Studies; English; Germanic Studies; Greek; History; Japanese; Latin; Linguistics; Literature; Philology; Philosophy; Theology; Turkish); **Mathematics** (Mathematics); **Medicine** (Medicine);

Physics (Applied Physics; Physics); **Social Sciences** (Cognitive Sciences; Communication Studies; Development Studies; Education; Geography; Peace and Disarmament; Political Sciences; Social Sciences; Sociology)

School

Management *(Mercator)* (Management)

Institute

East Asian Studies *(INEAST)* (East Asian Studies)

Centre

Logistics and Traffic *(ZLV)* (Transport and Communications; Transport Management)

Further Information: Also Duisburg Campus

History: Founded 2003 following merger between the University of Duisburg and the University of Essen (independent universities founded 1972).

Academic Year: October to September (October-March; April-September)

Admission Requirements: Secondary school certificate (Reifezeugnis)

Fees: None

Main Language(s) of Instruction: German

Accrediting Agency: AQAS; ASIIN; ZEvA

Degrees and Diplomas: *Bachelor's Degree*; *Master*: **Art History; Automation and Control Engineering; Automotive Engineering; Biological and Life Sciences; Biology; Business Administration; Chemistry; Christian Religious Studies; Civil Engineering; Communication Studies; Computer Engineering; Computer Science; Development Studies; Dutch; East Asian Studies; Economics; Education; Educational Administration; Educational Technology; Electronic Engineering; English Studies; Finance; French Studies; German; Germanic Studies; Government; Health Administration; History; Industrial Engineering; Information Technology; International Relations; Literature; Management; Mass Communication; Mathematics; Mechanical Engineering; Mechanics; Media Studies; Metallurgical Engineering; Nanotechnology; Pharmacy; Philosophy; Physics; Political Sciences; Power Engineering; Primary Education; Public Administration; Secondary Education; Social Work; Sociology; Spanish; Surveying and Mapping; Telecommunications Engineering; Toxicology; Transport Management; Urban Studies; Vocational Education; Water Management; Water Science.** *PhD*: **Arts and Humanities; Biology; Business Administration; Chemistry; Economics; Education; Engineering; Management; Mathematics; Medicine; Physics; Social Sciences.** *Habilitation*: **Arts and Humanities; Economics; Mathematics; Medicine; Physics; Social Sciences.** Some Programmes taught in English; Also State Examination in Medicine; Dual Degrees.

Student Services: Academic Counselling, Canteen, Careers Guidance, Cultural Activities, Facilities for disabled people, Language Laboratory, Nursery Care, Social Counselling, Sports Facilities

Publications: Forum Forschung; Universitätsreden

Publishing House: Pressestelle der Universität Duisburg-Essen

Student Numbers *2013-2014*: Total 39,184

Last Updated: 30/03/15

UNIVERSITY OF EDUCATION OF FREIBURG

Pädagogische Hochschule Freiburg
Kunzenweg 21, 79117 Freiburg
Tel: +49(761) 682-0
Fax: +49(761) 682-402
EMail: rektor@ph-freiburg.de
Website: http://www.ph-freiburg.de

Rector: Ulrich Druwe
Tel: +49(761) 682-261 EMail: ulrich.druwe@ph-freiburg.de

Chancellor: Hendrik Büggeln
Tel: +49(761) 682-263 EMail: kanzler@ph-freiburg.de

International Relations: Verena Bodenbender, Head of International Office
Tel: +49(761) 682-565
EMail: verena.bodenbender@ph-freiburg.de

Faculty

Educational Studies (Education; Educational Sciences; Psychology; Sociology); **Mathematics, Natural Sciences and Technology** (Biology; Chemistry; Geography; Health Sciences; Mathematics and Computer Science; Mathematics Education; Natural Sciences; Physics; Science Education; Technology; Technology Education; Vocational Education); **Social Sciences** (Education; English; French; German; History; Modern Languages; Music; Political Sciences; Theology)

History: Founded 1962. Acquired present status 1971. Under the jurisdiction of and financially supported by the State of Baden-Württemberg.

Academic Year: April to March (April-September; October-March)

Admission Requirements: Secondary school certificate (Reifezeugnis) or equivalent

Fees: None

Main Language(s) of Instruction: German, English, French

Degrees and Diplomas: *Bachelor's Degree*; *Master*: **Educational Psychology; Educational Sciences; Foreign Languages Education; Health Education; Science Education; Teacher Training.** *PhD*: **Cultural Studies; Educational Sciences; Mathematics; Natural Sciences; Social Sciences; Teacher Training; Technology.** *Habilitation*: **Educational Sciences.** Also State examination in Teacher Training (Lehramt)

Student Services: Library

Publications: PH-FR, Zeitschrift der Pädagogischen Hochschule Freiburg

Student Numbers *2013-2014*: Total 4,973

Last Updated: 24/03/15

UNIVERSITY OF EDUCATION OF SCHWÄBISCH GMÜND

Pädagogische Hochschule Schwäbisch Gmünd
Oberbettringer Straße 200, 73525 Schwäbisch Gmünd
Tel: +49(7171) 983-0
Fax: +49(7171) 983-212
EMail: info@ph-gmuend.de
Website: http://www.ph-gmuend.de

Rector: Astrid Beckmann
Tel: +49(7171) 983-346 EMail: rektorin@ph-gmuend.de

Chancellor: Edgar Buhl
Tel: +49(7171) 983-237 EMail: kanzler@ph-gmuend.de

International Relations: Monika Becker, Institutional Coordinator
Tel: +49(7171) 983-225 EMail: monika.becker@ph-gmuend.de

Faculty

Faculty II *(Fakultät II)* (Biology; Chemistry; Civics; Computer Science; Economics; English; Fine Arts; Geography; German; History; Household Management; Literature; Mathematics; Music; Natural Sciences; Physics; Political Sciences; Preschool Education; Social Studies; Sports; Technology; Textile Technology); **I** (Arts and Humanities; Educational Sciences; Health Sciences; Pedagogy; Philosophy; Political Sciences; Psychology; Religion; Religious Education; Sociology; Theology)

Institute

Education Development *(Fakultätsübergreifendes)* (Continuing Education; Educational Research; Media Studies)

Further Information: Continuing Education for Senior Citizens

History: Founded 1825 as University College with the right to award Doctorates since 1977. Became institute 1947 and college 1962. Under the jurisdiction of and financially supported by the State of Baden-Württemberg.

Academic Year: October to September (October-March; April-September)

Admission Requirements: Secondary school certificate (Allgemeine Hochschulsreife) or foreign equivalent

Fees: None; Administration fee, 75 per term (Euro)

Main Language(s) of Instruction: German

Accrediting Agency: EVALAG

Degrees and Diplomas: *Bachelor's Degree*; *Master*: **Cultural Studies; Education; Health Sciences; Preschool Education; Vocational Education.** *PhD*: **Arts and Humanities; Education; Mathematics; Natural Sciences; Philosophy.** *Habilitation*: **Education.** Also Teacher Training First State Examination (Lehramt) for Primary, Secondary and High School Education, 8 Semesters; Extension studies programme for those who have passed the above mentionned Teacher Training First State Examination.

Student Services: Academic Counselling, Canteen, Foreign Studies Centre, Library, Social Counselling, Sports Facilities

Publishing house: Gmünder Press

Academic Staff *2014-2015*: Total: c. 100

Student Numbers *2013-2014*: Total 2,659

Last Updated: 25/03/15

UNIVERSITY OF EDUCATION OF WEINGARTEN

Pädagogische Hochschule Weingarten
Kirchplatz 2, 88250 Weingarten
Tel: +49(751) 501-0
Fax: +49(751) 501-8200
EMail: info@ph-weingarten.de
Website: http://www.ph-weingarten.de

Rector: Werner Knapp (2011-)
Tel: +49(751) 501-8241 EMail: rektor@ph-weingarten.de

Chancellor: Gregor Kutsch
Tel: +49(751) 501-8244 EMail: kanzler@vw.ph-weingarten.de

Faculty

I (Catholic Theology; Economics; Educational Psychology; Educational Sciences; Ethics; Geography; Health Sciences; History; Home Economics; Islamic Theology; Philosophy; Political Sciences; Protestant Theology; Religious Education; Sociology; Sports); **II** (Biology; Chemistry; Computer Science; English; Fine Arts; German; Mathematics; Media Studies; Music; Physics; Technology)

History: Founded 1949 as institute, became college 1962. Acquired present status 1971. Under the jurisdiction of and financially supported by the State of Baden-Württemberg.

Academic Year: April to February (April-July; October-February)

Admission Requirements: Secondary school certificate (Reifezeugnis) or aptitude test

Fees: None

Main Language(s) of Instruction: German

Degrees and Diplomas: *Bachelor's Degree*: **Automotive Engineering; Business Computing; Computer Education; Education; Educational Administration; Educational Sciences; Electrical Engineering; Environmental Studies; Media Studies; Nutrition; Primary Education; Science Education; Speech Therapy and Audiology; Sports.** *Master*: **Business Education; Computer Education; Education; Educational Administration; Educational Sciences; Foreign Languages Education; Literacy Education; Media Studies; Music; Preschool Education; Science Education; Technology Education; Vocational Education.** *PhD*: **Education; Philosophy.** *Habilitation*: **Education.** Also Teacher Training First State Examination (Lehramt) for Primary, Secondary, High School Education and Vocational Education, 8 Semesters; Extension studies programme for those who have passed the above mentioned Teacher Training First State Examination; Continuing Education and Training Certificates.

Student Services: Academic Counselling, Canteen, Library, Sports Facilities

Student Numbers *2013-2014*: Total 3,281

Last Updated: 25/03/15

UNIVERSITY OF ERFURT

Universität Erfurt
PO Box 900221, Nordhäuser Strasse 63, 99105 Erfurt
Tel: +49(361) 737-0
Fax: +49(361) 737-5009
EMail: poststelle@uni-erfurt.de
Website: http://www.uni-erfurt.de

President: Walter Bauer-Wabnegg
Tel: +49(361) 737-5000 EMail: praesident@uni-erfurt.de

Chancellor: Jan Gerken
Tel: +49(361) 737-5010 EMail: kanzler@uni-erfurt.de

International Relations: Manuela Linde, Head of International Office Tel: +49(361) 737-5031 EMail: manuela.linde@uni-erfurt.de

Faculty

Catholic Theology (Catholic Theology; Theology); **Education** (Business Education; Education; Physical Education; Psychology; Special Education); **Law and Economics** (Economics; Law); **Philosophy** (Communication Studies; Geography; History; Literature; Modern Languages; Philosophy; Religion)

College

Cultural and Social Sciences *(Max Weber)* (Fine Arts; Geography; History; Music; Philosophy; Political Sciences; Sociology; Theology)

Centre

Language (Linguistics; Modern Languages)

History: First founded 1372. Closed 1816. Acquired present status and title 1994. Incorporated the Katholisch-Theologische Fakultät 2001. Responsible to the Ministry of Science and Culture of Thuringia.

Academic Year: October to July (October-February; April-July)

Admission Requirements: Secondary school certificate (Abitur)

Main Language(s) of Instruction: German

Degrees and Diplomas: *Bachelor's Degree*; *Magister*: **Catholic Theology.** *Master*: **Anthropology; Applied Linguistics; Communication Studies; Cultural Studies; Economics; Education; History; Law; Literature; Media Studies; Philosophy; Political Sciences; Primary Education; Psychology; Religious Studies; Secondary Education; Sociology; Special Education; Theology; Vocational Education.** *PhD*: **Catholic Theology; Cultural Studies; Education; Law; Philosophy; Political Sciences; Social Sciences.** *Habilitation*

Student Services: Library

Publishing house: Druckerei Jaecklein, Erfurt

Student Numbers *2013-2014*: Total 5,732

Last Updated: 27/03/15

UNIVERSITY OF FINE ARTS OF HAMBURG

Hochschule für Bildende Künste Hamburg (HFBK)
Lerchenfeld 2, 22081 Hamburg
Tel: +49(40) 428989-0
Fax: +49(40) 428989-271
EMail: presse@hfbk.hamburg.de
Website: http://www.hfbk-hamburg.de

Präsident: Martin Köttering
Tel: +49(40) 428989-201/202
EMail: martin.koettering@hfbk.hamburg.de

Chancellor: Anna Neubauer
Tel: +49(40) 428989-203 EMail: kanzlerin@hfbk.hamburg.de

International Relations: Andrea Klier
Tel: +49(40) 428989-207
EMail: andrea.klier@hfbk.hamburg.de; internationaloffice@hfbk.hamburg.de

Programme

Theory and History (Art History; Fine Arts)

Department

Design (Design); **Film** (Film); **Graphic Art, Typography, Photography** (Graphic Arts; Graphic Design; Photography); **Painting and Drawing** (Painting and Drawing); **Sculpture** (Sculpture); **Stage Design** (Fine Arts; Theatre); **Time-based Media** (Media Studies)

History: Founded 1972.

Main Language(s) of Instruction: German

Degrees and Diplomas: *Bachelor's Degree*: **Art Education; Fine Arts.** *Master*: **Art Education; Fine Arts.** *PhD*: **Fine Arts.**

Student Services: Library

Student Numbers *2013-2014*: Total 870

Last Updated: 05/03/15

UNIVERSITY OF FREIBURG

Albert-Ludwigs-Universität Freiburg im Breisgau
Fahnenbergplatz, 79085 Freiburg im Breisgau
Tel: +49(761) 203-0
Fax: +49(761) 203-4369 +49(761) 203-8866
EMail: info@verwaltung.uni-freiburg.de
Website: http://www.uni-freiburg.de

Rektor: Hans-Jochen Schiewer (2008-)
Tel: +49(761) 203-4315 EMail: rektor@uni-freiburg.de

Kanzler: Matthias Schenek
Tel: +49(761) 203-4321 EMail: kanzler@uni-freiburg.de

International Relations: Katharina Aly, Director, International Office
Tel: +49(761) 203-4376
EMail: katharina.aly@io.uni-freiburg.de; io@uni-freiburg.de

Faculty

Biology (Biology); **Chemistry and Pharmacy** (Analytical Chemistry; Biochemistry; Chemical Engineering; Chemistry; Inorganic Chemistry; Organic Chemistry; Pharmacy); **Economics and Behavioural Sciences** (Business Administration; Cognitive Sciences; Economics; Education; Finance; Psychology; Sports); **Engineering** (Engineering); **Environment and Natural Resources** (Botany; Crystallography; Earth Sciences; Environmental Studies; Forest Biology; Forest Economics; Forest Management; Forest Products; Forestry; Geography; Hydraulic Engineering; Landscape Architecture; Meteorology; Soil Science); **Humanities** (Anthropology; Archaeology; Art History; Asian Studies; Ethnology; History; Musicology; Philosophy; Political Sciences; Prehistory; Sociology); **Law** (Civil Law; Commercial Law; Criminal Law; Criminology; International Law; Law; Private Law); **Mathematics and Physics** (Mathematics; Physics); **Medicine** (Biochemistry; Dentistry; Forensic Medicine and Dentistry; Gynaecology and Obstetrics; Medicine; Molecular Biology; Ophthalmology; Paediatrics; Pathology); **Philology** (English; Linguistics; Modern Languages; Philology; Romance Languages; Slavic Languages); **Theology** (Bible; Theology)

Research Centre

Anthropology and Gender Studies *(ZAG)* (Anthropology; Gender Studies); **Biological Signalling Studies** *(Bioss)* (Biological and Life Sciences); **Business and Law** (Business Administration; Law); **Chronical Immunodeficiency** (Immunology); **Computational Neuroscience and Neurotechnology** *(Bernstein Center Freiburg)* (Computer Science; Neurosciences); **Data Analysis and Modelling** *(Freiburg - FDM)* (Data Processing); **French Studies**; **Interdisciplinary Ethics** *(Freiburg)* (Ethics); **Linguistics** *(Hermann Paul)* (Linguistics); **Materials** *(Freiburg - FMF)* (Materials Engineering); **Medieval Studies** (Medieval Studies); **Neurosciences** *(ZfN)* (Neurosciences); **Renewable Energy** *(ZEE)* (Energy Engineering); **Security and Society** (Protective Services); **Systems Biology** (Biology); **Transcultural Asian Studies** (Asian Studies)

Research Institute

Computer Science and Social Studies (Computer Science; Social Studies)

History: Founded 1457 by Archduke Albrecht of Austria and confirmed by the Emperor and the Pope. Now academically autonomous whilest financially supported by the State of Baden-Württemberg and under the jurisdiction of its Ministry of Science and Research. Teaching staff employed by the State (Land), independent in teaching and research, responsible to the above mentioned Ministry. The status of the University is guaranteed by the Constitution of the State (Land).

Academic Year: October to July (October-February; April-July)

Admission Requirements: Secondary school certificate (Reifezeugnis) or equivalent. For international students, good command of the German language

Main Language(s) of Instruction: German, English

Degrees and Diplomas: *Bachelor's Degree*; *Kirchliche Abschlussprüfung*: **Theology.** *Magister*: **Catholic Theology; Law; Theology.** *Diplom (Univ)*: **French Studies.** *Master*: **American Studies; Ancient Civilizations; Anthropology; Archaeology; Art History; Biochemistry; Biology; Biophysics; Business Administration; Chemistry; Classical Languages; Clinical Psychology; Cognitive Sciences; Computer Science; Cultural Studies; East Asian Studies; Ecology; Economics; Educational Sciences; Electronic Engineering; Energy Engineering; Engineering; English; English Studies; Environmental Management; European Languages; European Studies; Foreign Languages Education; Forest Management; Forestry; French; French Studies; Gender Studies; Geography; Geology; German; Germanic Studies; Health Sciences; History; International Economics; Islamic Studies; Jewish Studies; Journalism; Latin; Law; Linguistics; Literature; Materials Engineering; Mathematics; Media Studies; Medical Technology; Medicine; Medieval Studies; Middle Eastern Studies; Modern History; Molecular Biology; Musicology; Neurosciences; Nordic Studies; Periodontics; Pharmacy; Philology; Philosophy; Physics; Political Sciences; Psychology; Rehabilitation and Therapy; Romance Languages; Scandinavian Languages; Slavic Languages; Social Sciences; Social Studies; Sociology; Sports; Taxation; Water Science; Welfare and Protective Services.** *PhD*: **Behavioural Sciences; Biology; Chemistry; Economics; Engineering; Environmental Management; Mathematics; Medicine; Natural Resources; Pharmacy; Philology; Philosophy; Physics; Theology.** Also Statsexam in Dentistry, Medicine, Law, Pharmacy, Secondary Education (Biology, Catholic Theology, Chemistry, Computer Science, Danish, Educational Science, English, French, Geography, Geology, German, Archaeology, Greek, History, Italian, Latin, Mathematics, Norwegian, Philospohy, Ethics, Physical Education, Physics, Political Sciences, Economics, Spanish, Swedish).

Student Services: Canteen, Cultural Activities, Facilities for disabled people, IT Centre, Library, Nursery Care, Social Counselling, Sports Facilities

Student Numbers *2013-2014*: Total 24,157
Last Updated: 22/01/15

UNIVERSITY OF HAGEN

FernUniversität in Hagen
Universitätsstraße 11, 58084 Hagen
Tel: +49(2331) 987-2444
Fax: +49(2331) 987-2460
EMail: info@fernuni-hagen.de
Website: http://www.fernuni-hagen.de/

Rektor: Helmut Hoyer (1997-)
Tel: +49(2331) 987-2400 EMail: rektorbuero@fernuni-hagen.de

Kanzlerin: Regina Zdebel
Tel: +49(2331) 987-2414 EMail: kanzlerin@fernuni-hagen.de

International Relations: Irmgard Broekmann, Head, Office of International Affairs
Tel: +49(2331) 987-2454
EMail: Irmgard.Broekmann@FernUni-Hagen.de

Faculty

Cultural and Social Sciences (Arts and Humanities; Education; Social Sciences); **Economics** (Business Administration; Economics); **Law** (Law); **Mathematics and Computer Science** (Computer Engineering; Computer Science; Electrical Engineering; Mathematics)

Institute

Education and Media (Education; Media Studies); **History** (History); **Modern German Literature and Media Studies** (Literature; Media Studies); **Philosophy** (Philosophy); **Political Science** (Political Sciences); **Psychology** (Psychology); **Sociology** (Sociology)

Research Institute

European Constitutional Sciences *(Dimitris Tsatsos - Interdisciplinary)* (Constitutional Law); **History and Biography** *(Interdisciplinary)* (History; Literature)

Further Information: Study centres (information, counselling and student support services) in: Germany (45), Austria (7), Hungary (1), Latvia (1), Russian Federation (1), Switzerland (2).

History: Founded 1974, opened 1975. The FernUniversität in Hagen is the only single-mode distance teaching university in Germany.

Academic Year: October to September (October-March; April-September)

Admission Requirements: Secondary school certificate (Hochschulreife - Abitur - Fachhochschulreife) or recognized equivalent (for access to degree programmes)

Fees: Bachelor, 1,500-2,400 per programme; Master, 700-1,200 per programme (Euro)

Main Language(s) of Instruction: German

Accrediting Agency: Agency for quality assurance by accreditation of study progammes (AQAS)

Degrees and Diplomas: *Bachelor's Degree*; *Master*: **Business Administration; Computer Science; Distance Education; Economics; Education; Electrical Engineering; Government; History; Law; Literature; Mathematics; Media Studies; Philosophy.** *PhD*: **Business Administration; Computer Science; Cultural Studies; Economics; Electrical Engineering; Law; Mathematics; Social Sciences.** *Habilitation*: **Business Administration; Computer Science; Cultural Studies; Economics; Law; Mathematics; Social Sciences.** Also offered by all faculties/subject areas: further academic education (structured study offers - certificates, special degree programmes - Bachelor or Master); open access studies (Akademiestudien).

Student Services: Academic Counselling, Canteen, Facilities for disabled people, IT Centre, Library, Social Counselling

Publications: Forschungsbericht (Research Report); Reports and Papers from Faculties; Veröffentlichungen der Universitätsbibliothek

Academic Staff *2014-2015*: Total: c. 1,100

Student Numbers *2014-2015*: Total 77,395

Last Updated: 04/03/15

UNIVERSITY OF HAMBURG

Universität Hamburg
Mittelweg 177, 20148 Hamburg
Tel: +49(40) 42838-0
Fax: +49(40) 42838-6594
EMail: medien@uni-hamburg.de
Website: http://www.uni-hamburg.de

President: Dieter Lentzen (2010-)
Tel: +49(40) 42838-1807 EMail: praesident@uni-hamburg.de

Chancellor: Martin Hecht
Tel: +49(40) 42838-4423 EMail: kanzler@verw.uni-hamburg.de

International Relations: Courtney Peltzer-Hönicke, Head, International Office
Tel: +49(40) 42838-9261 EMail: courtney.peltzer@uni-hamburg.de

Faculty

Business Administration *(Hamburg Business School)* (Business Administration); **Business, Economics and Social Sciences** (Economics; Social Sciences); **Education** (Education); **Humanities** (African Studies; Arts and Humanities; Asian Studies; Catholic Theology; Cultural Studies; History; Literature; Media Studies; Modern Languages; Philosophy; Protestant Theology); **Law** (Civil Engineering; Commercial Law; Criminal Law; Labour Law; Law; Private Law; Public Law); **Mathematics, Informatics and Natural Sciences** (Biology; Chemistry; Computer Science; Earth Sciences; Mathematics; Physics); **Medicine** (Dentistry; Medicine); **Psychology and Human Movement** (Psychology; Sports)

Institute

International Tax (Taxation); **Peace Research and Security Policy** (Peace and Disarmament)

Centre

Marine and Atmospheric Sciences (ZMAW) (Marine Science and Oceanography; Meteorology); **Teaching and Learning in Higher Education (IZuLL)** *(Interdisciplinary)* (Higher Education)

Research Centre

Biotechnology, Society and the Environment (Biotechnology; Environmental Studies; Social Studies)

History: Founded 1919 with four faculties created through the incorporation of a number of existing institutions. Reorganized under a presidential constitution 1969 and faculties replaced by 19 Fachbereiche (departments) and several central institutes. An autonomous institution in which all academic staff and students take part in the tasks of self-government. Financially supported by the State of Hamburg and under the jurisdiction of its Ministry of Science and Research.

Academic Year: October to September

Admission Requirements: Secondary school certificate (Reifezeugnis) or equivalent

Fees: None

Main Language(s) of Instruction: German

Accrediting Agency: AQUIN

Degrees and Diplomas: *Bachelor's Degree*; *Kirchliche Abschlussprüfung*: **Protestant Theology.** *Magister*: **International Law; Protestant Theology.** *Diplom (Univ)*: **Protestant Theology.** *Master*: **African Languages; African Studies; American Studies; Ancient Civilizations; Anthropology; Applied Mathematics; Archaeology; Art History; Artificial Intelligence; Asian Religious Studies; Biological and Life Sciences; Biology; Business Administration; Business Computing; Chemistry; Chinese; Commercial Law; Computer Science; Cosmetology; Criminology; Cultural Studies; Economics; Education; Educational Sciences; Engineering; English; English Studies; European Studies; European Union Law; Fishery; Forest Economics; Geography; Geology; Geophysics; German; Greek; Greek (Classical); Health Administration; Higher Education; History; Human Resources; Industrial Engineering; Information Technology; Insurance; International Business; International Law; Islamic Studies; Japanese; Journalism; Korean; Latin; Latin American Studies; Law; Linguistics; Literature; Management; Marine Science and Oceanography; Mass Communication; Mathematics; Media Studies; Medieval Studies; Meteorology; Molecular Biology; Musicology; Nanotechnology; Peace and Disarmament; Performing Arts; Persian; Philosophy; Physics; Political Sciences; Primary Education; Protective Services; Psychology; Psychotherapy; Religion; Romance Languages; Secondary Education; Slavic Languages; Social Sciences; Sociology; South and Southeast Asian Languages; South Asian Studies; Southeast Asian Studies; Special Education; Sports; Taxation; Tibetan; Turkish; Vocational Education.** *PhD*: **African Studies; Asian Studies; Biology; Business Administration; Catholic Theology; Chemistry; Computer Science; Cultural Studies; Earth Sciences; Economics; Education; European Languages; History; Law; Literature; Mathematics; Media Studies; Medicine; Philosophy; Physics; Political Sciences; Protestant Theology; Psychology; Social Sciences; Sports.** *Habilitation*: **Arts and Humanities; Asian Studies; Business Administration; Computer Science; Economics; Education; Law; Mathematics; Medicine; Natural Sciences; Philosophy; Psychology; Social Sciences; Sports.** Some Master's Programmes taught in English; Also State Examination Certificate (Staatsexam) in Food Technology, Medicine, Pharmacy, Law and Dentistry; Teacher State Certificate of Teacher Training (Lehramt).

Student Services: Careers Guidance, Facilities for disabled people, Health Services, Nursery Care, Social Counselling, Sports Facilities

Publications: Forschungsbericht der Universität; uni hh Berichte und Meinungen

Academic Staff *2013-2014*: Total: c. 4,340

Student Numbers *2013-2014*: Total 41,019

Last Updated: 31/03/15

UNIVERSITY OF HILDESHEIM

Universität Hildesheim
Universitätsplatz 1, 31141 Hildesheim
Tel: +49(5121) 883-0
Fax: +49(5121) 883-91427
EMail: presse@rz.uni-hildesheim.de
Website: http://www.uni-hildesheim.de

President: Wolfgang-Uwe Friedrich
Tel: +49(5121) 883-90000 EMail: praesident@rz.uni-hildesheim.de

Head of Administration: Matthias Kreysing
Tel: +49(5121) 883-90006

International Relations: Elke Sasse-Fleige, Head of International Office Tel: +49(5121) 883-92000 EMail: aaa@rz.uni-hildesheim.de

Faculty

Cultural Studies and Aesthetics Communication (Aesthetics; Communication Studies; Cultural Studies; Media Studies; Music; Theatre; Writing); **Educational and Social Sciences** (Administration; Education; History; Philosophy; Primary Education; Psychology; Secondary Education; Social Sciences; Social Work; Sports; Theology); **Information and Communication Sciences** (Information Management; Linguistics; Mass Communication; Teacher Training); **Mathematics, Natural Sciences, Economics and Computer Science** (Computer Science; Economics; Mathematics; Natural Sciences)

Centre

Computer-Network (Computer Science); **Lifelong Education and Distance Study** (Distance Education; Education)

Research Centre

Education and Training; **Interdisciplinary Gender Studies**

History: Founded 1978, acquired present status 1990. An autonomous institution financially supported by the State of Lower Saxony, and under the jurisdiction of its Ministry of Science.

Academic Year: October to September (October-March; April-September)

Admission Requirements: Secondary school certificate (Reifezeugnis) or equivalent

Fees: None

Main Language(s) of Instruction: German

Degrees and Diplomas: *Bachelor's Degree*; *Master*: **Arts and Humanities; Business Computing; Communication Studies; Cultural Studies; Education; Educational Psychology; Educational Sciences; Environmental Management; Environmental Studies; Industrial and Organizational Psychology; Information Management; Information Technology; Linguistics; Management; Media Studies; Music Education; Philosophy; Preschool Education; Primary Education; Secondary Education; Social Psychology; Translation and Interpretation; Writing.** *PhD*: **Aesthetics; Communication Studies; Computer Science; Cultural Studies; Economics; Education; Information Sciences; Linguistics; Mathematics; Natural Sciences; Social Sciences.** *Habilitation*: **Aesthetics; Communication Studies; Cultural Studies.** State examination in Religious Educatio, Catholic Theology and Protestant Theology.

Student Services: Academic Counselling, Canteen, Cultural Activities, Facilities for disabled people, Foreign Studies Centre, Language Laboratory, Nursery Care, Social Counselling, Sports Facilities

Academic Staff *2013-2014*: Total: c. 540

Student Numbers *2013-2014*: Total 6,385

Last Updated: 28/03/15

UNIVERSITY OF HOHENHEIM

Universität Hohenheim

Schloss Hohenheim 1, 70593 Stuttgart
Tel: +49(711) 459-0
Fax: +49(711) 459-3960
EMail: post@uni-hohenheim.de
Website: https://www.uni-hohenheim.de

Rector: Stephan Dabbert
Tel: +49(711) 459-22000 EMail: rektor@uni-hohenheim.de

Chancellor: Julia Henke
Tel: +49(711) 459-23000 EMail: kanzler@uni-hohenheim.de

International Relations: Franziska Schenk
Tel: +49(711) 459-22020 EMail: aaa@uni-hohenheim.de

Faculty

Agricultural Sciences (Agriculture; Botany; Crop Production; Ecology; Horticulture; Soil Science; Tropical Agriculture); **Business, Economics and Social Sciences** (Business Administration; Business Education; Communication Studies; Cultural Studies; Economics; Journalism; Law; Social Sciences; Theology); **Natural Sciences** (Biochemistry; Botany; Chemistry; Food Technology; Genetics; Mathematics; Meteorology; Microbiology; Nutrition; Physics; Physiology; Zoology)

History: Founded 1818, became Hochschule 1904 and acquired University status 1919. Acquired present title 1967. An autonomous institution under the jurisdiction of and financed by the State of Baden-Württemberg.

Academic Year: October to July (October-February; April-July)

Admission Requirements: Secondary school certificate (Abitur) or equivalent

Fees: None

Main Language(s) of Instruction: German, English

Accrediting Agency: ACQUIN

Degrees and Diplomas: *Bachelor's Degree*: **Agriculture; Biological and Life Sciences; Business Administration; Information Sciences; Natural Sciences.** *Master*: **Agricultural Business; Agricultural Economics; Agriculture; Biological and Life Sciences; Biology; Biotechnology; Business Education; Chemistry; Communication Studies; Crop Production; Earth Sciences; Ecology; Economics; Environmental Management; Environmental Studies; Food Science; Food Technology; Information Sciences; Information Technology; International Business; International Economics; Management; Nutrition; Tropical Agriculture.** *PhD*: **Agriculture; Economics; Finance; Management; Natural Sciences; Social Sciences.** *Habilitation*: **Agriculture; Economics; Natural Sciences; Social Sciences.** Also State Examination Certificate (Staatsexam) in Food Chemistry; Secondary Teacher Training Certificate (Lehramt) in Biology.

Student Services: Academic Counselling, Canteen, Careers Guidance, Cultural Activities, Facilities for disabled people, Foreign Studies Centre, Health Services, IT Centre, Language Laboratory, Library, Nursery Care, Residential Facilities, Social Counselling, Sports Facilities, eLibrary

Publications: Jahresbericht

Publishing House: https://www.uni-hohenheim.de/presse

Academic Staff *2014-2015*	MEN	WOMEN	TOTAL
FULL-TIME	934	1,169	**2,103**
PART-TIME	310	354	**664**
Student Numbers *2014-2015*			
All (Foreign included)	4,329	5,589	**9,918**
FOREIGN ONLY	654	626	**1,280**

Last Updated: 10/02/15

UNIVERSITY OF KASSEL

Universität Kassel

Mönchebergstraße 19, 34109 Kassel
Tel: +49(561) 804-0
Fax: +49(561) 804-2330
EMail: poststelle@uni-kassel.de
Website: http://www.uni-kassel.de

President: Reiner Finkeldey (2015-)
EMail: praesident@uni-kassel.de

International Relations: Katharina Linke, Director, International Relations Tel: +49(561) 804-3039 EMail: linke@uni-kassel.de

Faculty

Architecture, Urban and Regional Planning (Architecture; Landscape Architecture; Regional Planning; Town Planning); **Civil and Environmental Engineering** (Civil Engineering; Construction Engineering; Environmental Studies; Geological Engineering; Mechanics; Structural Architecture; Transport and Communications; Water Management; Water Science); **Economics and Business** (Business Administration; Economics); **Electrical Engineering and Computer Science** (Computer Science; Electrical Engineering); **Humanities** (Education; Music; Psychology; Social Studies; Social Work); **Humanities and Cultural Studies** (American Studies; Catholic Theology; English; English Studies; Foreign Languages Education; German; Germanic Studies; Philosophy; Protestant Theology; Romance Languages); **Mathematics and Natural Science** (Biology; Chemistry; Mathematics; Physics); **Mechanical Engineering** (Automation and Control Engineering; Automotive Engineering; Engineering Management; Industrial Engineering; Materials Engineering; Measurement and Precision Engineering; Mechanical Engineering; Mechanics; Production Engineering; Thermal Engineering; Transport Management); **Organic Agricultural Sciences** (Agriculture; Animal Husbandry; Ecology; Rural

Planning); **Social Sciences** (Geography (Human); History; Physical Education; Political Sciences; Social Sciences; Sociology; Sports)

School

Art (Art Education; Design; Fine Arts; Natural Sciences; Visual Arts)

Department

Natural Sciences

Centre

Environmental Systems Research *(CESR)* (Environmental Studies); **Information System Design (ITeG)** (Information Technology); **Interdisciplinary Nanostructure Science and Technology** *(CINSaT)* (Nanotechnology); **International Higher Education Research Kassel** *(INCHER-Kassel)* (Higher Education; Labour and Industrial Relations)

History: Founded 1971 as a Gesamthochschule. An autonomous institution financially supported by the State of Hesse and under the jurisdiction of its Ministry of Education.

Academic Year: October to September

Admission Requirements: Secondary school certificate (Reifezeugnis). Fachhochschulreife (technical secondary education) for certain courses

Fees: None

Main Language(s) of Instruction: German

Degrees and Diplomas: *Bachelor's Degree*; *Künstlerische Abschlussprüfung*: **Fine Arts; Graphic Design.** *Diplom (Univ)*: **Industrial Design.** *Master*: **Agriculture; American Studies; Architecture; Biology; Business Administration; Civil Engineering; Clinical Psychology; Commercial Law; Computer Science; Consumer Studies; Continuing Education; Economics; Educational Administration; Educational Research; Electrical Engineering; Electronic Engineering; Energy Engineering; English; English Studies; Environmental Engineering; Fine Arts; Food Science; Foreign Languages Education; French; German; Health Education; Health Sciences; History; Humanities and Social Science Education; Industrial Engineering; Industrial Management; Labour and Industrial Relations; Labour Law; Landscape Architecture; Management; Marketing; Mathematics; Mechanical Engineering; Nanotechnology; Optical Technology; Physics; Political Sciences; Psychology; Psychotherapy; Public Administration; Regional Planning; Rural Planning; Social Work; Sociology; Spanish; Telecommunications Engineering; Town Planning; Vocational Education.** *PhD*: **Agriculture; Economics; Engineering; Law; Natural Sciences; Philosophy; Social Studies.** *Habilitation*. Some Master's degree programmes taught in English; Also Teacher Training State Certificate (Lehramt).

Student Services: Academic Counselling, Canteen, Facilities for disabled people, Library, Nursery Care, Social Counselling, Sports Facilities

Publications: Bericht zu Forschung und künstlerischen Entwicklung; Spektrum der Wissenschaft

Student Numbers *2013-2014*: Total 22,876
Last Updated: 31/03/15

UNIVERSITY OF KOBLENZ-LANDAU

Universität Koblenz-Landau
Postfach 1864, Rhabanusstraße 3, 55008 Mainz
Tel: +49(6131) 37460-0
Fax: +49(6131) 37460-40
EMail: service@uni-koblenz-landau.de
Website: http://www.uni-koblenz-landau.de/

President: Roman Heiligenthal (2005-)
Tel: +49(6131) 37460-14
EMail: praesident@uni-koblenz-landau.de

Interim Chancellor: Michael Ludewig
Tel: +49(6131) 37460-24 EMail: kanzler@uni-koblenz-landau.de

International Relations: Jutta Bohn, International Officer, Campus Landau
Tel: +49(6341) 280-3716 EMail: bohn@uni-koblenz-landau.de

International Relations: Bettina Holstein-Alter, International Officer, Campus Koblenz
Tel: +49(261) 287-1764 EMail: holstein@uni-koblenz-landau.de

Faculty

Computer Sciences *(Campus Koblenz)* (Business Computing; Computer Science; Information Technology; Management; Software Engineering); **Education** *(Campus Koblenz)* (Education; Educational Sciences; Pedagogy; Political Sciences; Primary Education; Psychology; Sociology); **Education** *(Campus Landau)* (Education; Philosophy; Primary Education; Secondary Education; Special Education); **Humanities and Social Sciences** *(Campus Landau)* (Art History; Catholic Theology; German; Modern Languages; Music; Musicology; Protestant Theology; Social Sciences; Visual Arts); **Mathematics and Natural Sciences** *(Campus Koblenz)* (Mathematics; Natural Sciences; Sports); **Natural and Environmental Sciences** *(Campus Landau)* (Environmental Studies; Mathematics; Natural Sciences; Science Education; Sports); **Philology and Cultural Studies** *(Campus Koblenz)* (Catholic Theology; English; Fine Arts; German; History; Music; Music Education; Philology; Protestant Theology; Romance Languages); **Psychology** *(Campus Landau)* (Clinical Psychology; Cognitive Sciences; Education; Educational Psychology; Industrial and Organizational Psychology; Mass Communication; Media Studies; Psychology; Psychotherapy; Social Psychology)

Further Information: Campus Koblenz and Landau

History: Founded 1949 as academy, became college 1964 and University of Educational Sciences 1969. Acquired present status and title 1990. Under the jurisdiction of and financially supported by the state of Rheinland-Pfalz.

Academic Year: October to September (October-March; April-September)

Admission Requirements: Secondary school certificate (Reifezeugnis) or recognized equivalent and knowledge of German language (TestDaF)

Fees: None

Main Language(s) of Instruction: German

Degrees and Diplomas: *Bachelor's Degree*; *Diplom (Univ)*: **Environmental Studies.** *Master*: **Biological and Life Sciences; Business Computing; Ceramics and Glass Technology; Communication Studies; Computer Graphics; Computer Science; Cultural Studies; Earth Sciences; Ecology; Education; Environmental Studies; Government; Information Management; Psychology; Social Sciences; Teacher Training; Toxicology.** *PhD*: **Art History; Biology; Catholic Theology; Chemistry; Computer Science; Cultural Studies; Economics; Education; English; Environmental Studies; Geography; German; Germanic Studies; History; Literature; Mathematics; Musicology; Philosophy; Physics; Political Sciences; Protestant Theology; Psychology; Sociology; Speech Studies; Sports.** *Habilitation*: **Computer Science; Cultural Studies; Mathematics; Natural Sciences; Philology; Psychology.** Also Staatsexam in Psychology and Psychotherapy; Teacher Training State Certificate (Lehramt).

Student Services: Academic Counselling, Canteen, Social Counselling, Sports Facilities

Publications: Forschungs- und Veröffentlichungsdokumentation

Academic Staff *2012-2013*	MEN	WOMEN	**TOTAL**
FULL-TIME	–	–	**497**
Student Numbers *2013-2014*			
All (Foreign included)	5,448	9,600	**15,048**

Last Updated: 31/03/15

UNIVERSITY OF KONSTANZ

Universität Konstanz
78457 Konstanz, Baden-Württemberg
Tel: +49(7531) 88-0
Fax: +49(7531) 88-3688
EMail: Posteingang@uni-konstanz.de
Website: http://www.uni-konstanz.de

Rector: Ulrich Rüdiger (2009-)
Tel: +49(7531) 88-2270 EMail: ulrich.ruediger@uni-konstanz.de

Chancellor: Jens Apitz
Tel: +49(7531) 88-2294 EMail: Jens.Apitz@Uni-Konstanz.de

International Relations: Maren Rühmann, Academic and International Affairs Officer

Tel: +49(7531) 88-2777
EMail: Maren.Ruehmann@uni-konstanz.de

Faculty

Humanities (Arts and Humanities; Educational Research; Fine Arts; History; Linguistics; Literature; Media Studies; Philosophy; Sociology; Sports); **Politics, Law and Economics** (Economics; Law; Political Sciences; Public Administration); **Sciences** (Biology; Chemistry; Computer Science; Information Sciences; Mathematics; Natural Sciences; Physics; Psychology; Statistics)

Further Information: Also 5 Collaborative Research Centres (Sonderforschungsbereiche), and 3 special Research Units

History: Founded 1966. An autonomous State institution financially supported by the State of Baden-Württemberg.

Academic Year: October to September (October-February; April-July)

Admission Requirements: Secondary school certificate (Reifezeugnis) or equivalent

Fees: None

Main Language(s) of Instruction: German

Degrees and Diplomas: *Bachelor's Degree*; *Magister*: **Law.** *Master*: **Ancient Civilizations; Anthropology; Biological and Life Sciences; Chemistry; Child Care and Development; Computer Science; Data Processing; Eastern European Studies; Economics; English; European Studies; Finance; German; Government; History; Humanities and Social Science Education; Information Sciences; Law; Linguistics; Literature; Mathematics; Media Studies; Modern Languages; Nanotechnology; Philosophy; Physics; Political Sciences; Psychology; Public Administration; Romance Languages; Slavic Languages; Social Sciences; Sociology; Speech Studies; Sports.** *PhD*: **Biology; Chemistry; Clinical Psychology; History; Linguistics; Literature; Neurology; Philosophy; Political Sciences; Psychology; Psychotherapy; Public Administration; Sociology.** *Habilitation*: **Arts and Humanities; Economics; Law; Mathematics; Natural Sciences; Political Sciences.** State Examination in Law; Teacher Training State Examination (Lehramt)

Student Services: Academic Counselling, Canteen, Cultural Activities, Facilities for disabled people, Health Services, Library, Nursery Care, Social Counselling, Sports Facilities

Student Numbers *2013-2014*: Total 11,410
Last Updated: 31/03/15

UNIVERSITY OF LEIPZIG

Universität Leipzig
PO Box 100920, Ritterstrasse 26, 04009 Leipzig, Saxony
Tel: +49(341) 971-08
Fax: +49(341) 973-0099
EMail: aaa@uni-leipzig.de
Website: http://www.uni-leipzig.de

Rector: Beate A. Schücking (2011-)
Tel: +49(341) 973-0000 EMail: rektorin@uni-leipzig.de

Chancellor: Birgit Dräger
Tel: +49(341) 97-30100 EMail: kanzler@uni-leipzig.de

International Relations: Svend Poller, Director, International Centre Tel: +49(341) 973-2020 EMail: aaa@uni-leipzig.de

Faculty

Biology, Pharmacy and Psychology (Biochemistry; Biological and Life Sciences; Biology; Pharmacology; Pharmacy; Psychology); **Chemistry and Mineralogy** (Chemistry; Crystallography; Mineralogy); **Economics and Management (including Civil Engineering)** (Accountancy; Building Technologies; Business Administration; Business and Commerce; Business Computing; Civil Engineering; Construction Engineering; Economics; Finance; Industrial Engineering; Management; Real Estate; Statistics); **Education** (Adult Education; Curriculum; Education; Education of the Handicapped; Educational Psychology; Educational Sciences; Primary Education; Secondary Education; Special Education); **History, Art and Oriental Studies** (African Studies; Arabic; Archaeology; Art History; Asian Studies; Cultural Studies; Ethnology; Fine Arts; History; Music; Musicology; Oriental Studies; Religious Studies; Theatre); **Law** (Law); **Mathematics and Computer Science** (Computer Science; Mathematics); **Medicine** (Biochemistry; Epidemiology; Forensic Medicine and Dentistry; Genetics; Medicine; Occupational Health; Physiology; Virology); **Philology** (American Studies; Classical Languages; Comparative Literature; English Studies; German; Germanic Studies; Linguistics; Modern Languages; Philology; Romance Languages; Slavic Languages; Translation and Interpretation); **Physics and Earth Sciences** (Earth Sciences; Geography; Geology; Geophysics; Meteorology; Paleontology; Physics); **Social Sciences and Philosophy** (Ethics; Journalism; Logic; Media Studies; Philosophy; Political Sciences; Social Sciences; Sociology); **Sports Science** (Physical Education; Rehabilitation and Therapy; Sports); **Theology** (Religious Education; Theology); **Veterinary Science** (Veterinary Science)

History: Founded 1409 when German scholars withdrew from the University of Prague. The establishment of the University was confirmed by Papal Bull. Reorganized 1946. The University has always adhered to the model of the Universitas Literarum.

Academic Year: October to September (October-March; April-September)

Admission Requirements: Secondary school certificate (Reifezeugnis) or equivalent

Fees: None. Some courses charge tuition

Main Language(s) of Instruction: German. English in some courses

Degrees and Diplomas: *Bachelor's Degree*; *Diplom (Univ)*: **Business and Commerce; Mathematics; Theology.** *Master*; *PhD*: **Arts and Humanities; Biological and Life Sciences; Chemistry; Earth Sciences; Economics; Education; Educational Sciences; History; Law; Mathematics and Computer Science; Medicine; Mineralogy; Oriental Studies; Pharmacy; Philology; Philosophy; Physics; Psychology; Social Sciences; Sports; Theology; Veterinary Science.** *Habilitation*

Student Services: Academic Counselling, Canteen, Cultural Activities, Facilities for disabled people, Foreign Studies Centre, Language Laboratory, Nursery Care, Social Counselling, Sports Facilities

Publishing house: Universitätsverlag

Student Numbers *2013*: Total 23,812
Last Updated: 07/04/15

UNIVERSITY OF LÜBECK

Universität zu Lübeck
Ratzeburger Allee 160, 23562 Lübeck
Tel: +49(451) 500-0
Fax: +49(451) 500-3016
EMail: presse@uni-luebeck.de
Website: http://www.uni-luebeck.de

President: Hendrik Lehnert
Tel: +49(451) 500-3000 EMail: praesidium@zuv.uni-luebeck.de

Chancellor: Oliver Grundei
Tel: +49(451) 500-3003 EMail: kanzler@zuv.uni-luebeck.de

Area

Computer Science and Technology (Cognitive Sciences; Computer Science; Mathematics; Medical Technology; Multimedia; Robotics; Software Engineering)

Department

Medicine (Anatomy; Dermatology; Medicine; Otorhinolaryngology; Psychiatry and Mental Health; Rheumatology; Surgery); **Natural Sciences** (Biochemistry; Biology; Chemistry; Mathematics; Medical Technology; Molecular Biology; Physics)

History: Founded 1964 as academy and faculty of Christian Albrecht University of Kiel. Became independent 1973 and acquired present status 1985.

Academic Year: October to September (October-March; April-September)

Admission Requirements: Secondary school certificate (Reifezeugnis) or equivalent

Fees: None

Main Language(s) of Instruction: German

Accrediting Agency: ANSII

Degrees and Diplomas: *Bachelor's Degree*; *Master*: **Biological and Life Sciences; Biomedical Engineering; Computer Science; Education; Engineering; Medical Technology; Molecular Biology; Psychology.** *PhD*: **Biomedicine; Computer Engineering; Computer Science; Medical Technology; Medicine; Natural Sciences.** *Habilitation*: **Computer Science; Medical Technology; Medicine; Natural Sciences.** Master's degree in Biomedical Engineering and Infection Biology taught in English.

Student Services: Academic Counselling, Canteen, Cultural Activities, Facilities for disabled people, Foreign Studies Centre, IT Centre, Library, Social Counselling, Sports Facilities

Publications: FOCUS MUL; Sonderheft Forschung

Student Numbers *2013-2014*: Total 3,471
Last Updated: 28/03/15

UNIVERSITY OF MANNHEIM

Universität Mannheim

Schloss, 68131 Mannheim, Baden-Württemberg
Tel: +49(621) 181-2222
Fax: +49(621) 181-1010
EMail: studium@verwaltung.uni-mannheim.de
Website: http://www.uni-mannheim.de

Rector: Ernst-Ludwig von Thadden (2012-)
Tel: +49(621) 181-1000 EMail: rektor@uni-mannheim.de

Chancellor: Susann-Annette Storm
Tel: +49(621) 181-1020
EMail: kanzlerin@verwaltung.uni-mannheim.de

International Relations: Jessica Gödert, Head, International Office
Tel: +49(621) 181-1154
EMail: jessica.goedert@verwaltung.uni-mannheim.de

School

Business (Business Administration; Business Computing; Business Education); **Business Computing and Mathematics** (Business Computing; Mathematics); **Humanities** (Arts and Humanities; History; Literature; Modern Languages; Philosophy); **Law and Economics** (Economics; Law); **Social Sciences** (Political Sciences; Psychology; Social Sciences; Sociology)

History: Founded 1907 as Städtische Handelshochschule, attached to University of Heidelberg 1933, became Wirtschaftshochschule 1946. Title of University conferred 1967.

Academic Year: October to September

Admission Requirements: Secondary school certificate (Reifezeugnis) or recognized equivalent

Fees: None; Administrative fee, 60 per semester (Euro)

Main Language(s) of Instruction: German

Degrees and Diplomas: *Bachelor's Degree*; *Master*: **Accountancy; Applied Mathematics; Business Administration; Business Education; Clinical Psychology; Cognitive Sciences; Commercial Law; Communication Studies; Comparative Law; Economics; English; French; German; Germanic Studies; History; Italian; Law; Literature; Management; Media Studies; Modern Languages; Philosophy; Political Sciences; Psychology; Sociology; Spanish; Taxation.** *PhD*: **Arts and Humanities; Business Administration; Business Computing; Economics; Law; Mathematics; Social Sciences.** *Habilitation*: **Arts and Humanities; Business Computing; Mathematics; Social Sciences.** Some Master's degree programmes taught in English.

Student Services: Careers Guidance, Library, Sports Facilities

Publications: Amtliche Mitteilungen; Forum

Student Numbers *2013-2014*: Total 11,735
Last Updated: 31/03/15

UNIVERSITY OF MUSIC AND PERFORMING ARTS MUNICH

Hochschule für Musik und Theater München

Arcisstrasse 12, 80333 München
Tel: +49(89) 289-03 +49(89) 289-27450
Fax: +49(89) 289-27419
EMail: verwaltung@musikhochschule-muenchen.de
Website: http://www.musikhochschule-muenchen.de

President: Bernd Redmann
Tel: +49(89) 289-27403 EMail: praesident@hmtm.de

Chancellor: Alexander Krause
Tel: +49(89) 289-27410
EMail: kanzler@musikhochschule-muenchen.de; kanzler@hmtm.de

International Relations: Edgar Krapp
Tel: +49(89) 289-27402/27437
EMail: edgar.krapp@musikhochschule-muenchen.de

Department

Church Music/ Organ (Music; Musical Instruments; Religious Music); **Folk Music** (Folklore); **Historical Performance Practice** (Dance; Music; Musical Instruments); **Instrumental and Vocal Pedagogy** (Music Education; Musical Instruments; Singing)

Institute

Cultural Management (Art Management); **Jazz** (Jazz and Popular Music); **Music Educational Institute of Teacher Training and Education Research (MILU)** (Teacher Training); **Musicology** (Musicology)

Academy

Ballet Academy (Dance); **Youth Academy for Gifted** (Education of the Gifted; Music)

History: Founded 1867.

Main Language(s) of Instruction: German

Degrees and Diplomas: *Bachelor's Degree*; *Master*: **Art Management; Jazz and Popular Music; Journalism; Music; Musical Instruments; Opera; Singing; Theatre.** *PhD*: **Music Education; Musicology.** Teaching Certificate (Lehramt) in Primary Education, Secondary Education; Post Master Certificate

Student Services: Library

Student Numbers *2013-2014*: Total 1,084
Last Updated: 09/03/15

UNIVERSITY OF MUSIC DETMOLD

Hochschule für Musik Detmold

Neustadt 22, 32756 Detmold
Tel: +49(5231) 975-5
Fax: +49(5231) 975-972
EMail: info@hfm-detmold.de
Website: http://www.hfm-detmold.de

Rektor: Thomas Grosse
Tel: +49(5231) 975-601 EMail: rektor@hfm-detmold.de

Kanzler: Hans Bertels
Tel: +49(5231) 975-700 EMail: kanzler@hfm-detmold.de

International Relations: Vanessa Aldemir, Head, International Office Tel: +49(5231) 975-773 EMail: aldemir@hfm-detmold.de

Programme

Chamber Music (Music); **Choir and Orchestra Conducting** (Conducting; Singing); **Church Music** (Religious Music); **Composition** (Music Theory and Composition); **Conducting** (Conducting); **Free-Lance Musician** (Music; Musical Instruments); **Music** (Music); **Music and Sound Recording** (Music; Sound Engineering (Acoustics)); **Music Education** (Music Education); **Music Teaching** *(Lehramt)* (Music Education); **Music Teaching and Musical Instruments and Singing** (Music Education; Musical Instruments; Singing); **Musical Instruments and Singing** (Musical Instruments; Singing); **Musical Instruments and Singing Education** (Music Education; Musical Instruments; Singing); **Musical Mediation/ Concert Pedagogy** (Conducting; Music; Music Theory and Composition); **Musical Theater and Opera** (Music; Opera; Theatre); **Musical Theory** (Music Theory and Composition); **New Music** (Music); **Opera/Concert** (Music; Opera); **Orchestra** (Conducting; Music); **Orchestral Musician** (Music); **Piano Chamber Music and Accompanying** (Music)

History: Founded 1947.

Admission Requirements: Secondary school certificate and qualification examination

Main Language(s) of Instruction: German

Degrees and Diplomas: *Bachelor's Degree*; *Konzertexamen*: **Musical Instruments; Singing.** *Master*: **Art Management; Conducting; Music Education; Music Theory and Composition;**

Musical Instruments; Musicology; Opera; Primary Education; Religious Music; Secondary Education; Singing; Sound Engineering (Acoustics). *PhD*: **Sound Engineering (Acoustics).**

Student Services: Academic Counselling, Canteen, Careers Guidance, Cultural Activities, Facilities for disabled people, Foreign Studies Centre, Health Services, IT Centre, Library, Nursery Care, eLibrary

Student Numbers *2014-2015*: Total: c. 750
Last Updated: 03/02/15

UNIVERSITY OF MUSIC LÜBECK

Musikhochschule Lübeck
Grosse Petersgrube 17-29, 23552 Lübeck
Tel: +49(451) 1505-0
Fax: +49(451) 1505-300
EMail: info@mh-luebeck.de
Website: http://www.mh-luebeck.de

President: Rico Gubler (2014-)

Chancellor: Jürgen Claussen
Tel: +49(451) 1505-151 EMail: Kanzler@mh-luebeck.de

Programme

Arts (Music Education); **Education** (Music Education); **Music** (Music; Musical Instruments; Religious Music)

History: Founded 1933 and acquired present status and title 1973.

Academic Year: October to September (October-March; April-September)

Admission Requirements: Entrance Audition

Fees: (Euros): 171 per annum

Main Language(s) of Instruction: German

Degrees and Diplomas: *Bachelor's Degree*: **Music; Music Education.** *Master*: **Music; Music Education.** *PhD*: **Music Education; Music Theory and Composition; Musicology.**

Student Services: Academic Counselling, Canteen, Language Laboratory, Library, Sports Facilities

Student Numbers *2013-2014*: Total 411
Last Updated: 22/03/15

UNIVERSITY OF MUSIC WUERZBURG

Hochschule für Musik Würzburg
Hofstallstrasse 6-8, 97070 Würzburg
Tel: +49(931) 32187-0
Fax: +49(931) 32187-2800
EMail: hochschule@hfm-wuerzburg.de
Website: http://www.hfm-wuerzburg.de

President: Bernd Clausen
Tel: +49(931) 32187-21 EMail: praesident@hfm-wuerzburg.de

Chancellor: Eva Stumpf-Wirths
Tel: +49(931) 32187-30 EMail: kanzlerin@hfm-wuerzburg.de

International Relations: Dirk Bräuer, Head, International Office
EMail: international.office@hfm-wuerzburg.de

Department

I - Voice/Opera; Conducting (Conducting; Singing); **II - Piano** (Musical Instruments); **III - Strings** (Musical Instruments); **IV - Woodwinds/Brass** (Musical Instruments); **V - Jazz/Guitar/Accordion/Percussion/Harp** (Musical Instruments); **VI - Organ/Sacred Music; Historical Instruments; Composition/Music Theory** (Music Theory and Composition; Musical Instruments; Religious Music); **VII - Musicology/Music Pedagogy** (Music; Music Education)

History: Founded 1973.

Main Language(s) of Instruction: German

Degrees and Diplomas: *Bachelor's Degree*; *Konzertexamen*: **Music Theory and Composition.** *Master*: **Conducting; Jazz and Popular Music; Music; Musical Instruments; Singing.** *PhD*: **Music Education; Music Theory and Composition; Musicology.** Also State Examination/Teaching Certificates (Lehramt Musik) in Primary Education, Secondary Education, Music Education; Advanced performance training classe (Fortbildungsklasse) in Music Theory and Composition.

Student Services: IT Centre, Library

Student Numbers *2014-2015*: Total: c. 670
Last Updated: 09/03/15

UNIVERSITY OF PADERBORN

Universität Paderborn
Warburger Strasse 100, 33098 Paderborn
Tel: +49(5251) 60-0
Fax: +49(5251) 60-2519
Website: http://www.upb.de

President: Wilhelm Schäfer (2015-)
Tel: +49(5251) 60-2559 EMail: praesident@uni-paderborn.de

Vice President for Operations: Simone Probst
Tel: +49(5251) 60-2557 EMail: probst@zv.uni-paderborn.de

Faculty

Arts and Humanities (American Studies; Catholic Theology; Comparative Literature; Education; English; Fine Arts; History; Media Studies; Music; Musicology; Philosophy; Political Sciences; Protestant Theology; Psychology; Romance Languages; Sociology; Textile Design); **Business Administration and Economics** (Accountancy; Business Administration; Economics; Finance; Human Resources; Management; Taxation); **Computer Science, Electrical Engineering and Mathematics** (Computer Science; Electrical Engineering; Information Technology; Mathematics); **Mechanical Engineering** (Mechanical Engineering); **Science** (Chemistry; Health Education; Physics; Sports)

History: Founded 1972. An autonomous institution financially supported by the State of North Rhine-Westphalia.

Academic Year: October to September (October-March; April-September)

Admission Requirements: Secondary school certificate (Reifezeugnis) or equivalent

Fees: 122 per semester (Euro)

Main Language(s) of Instruction: German

Degrees and Diplomas: *Bachelor's Degree*; *Master*: **American Studies; Art Education; Art History; Business Administration; Business Computing; Business Education; Chemical Engineering; Chemistry; Comparative Literature; Computer Education; Computer Engineering; Computer Science; Consumer Studies; Cultural Studies; Educational Sciences; Electrical and Electronic Engineering; Electrical Engineering; Electronic Engineering; English; English Studies; European Studies; Fine Arts; Foreign Languages Education; French; Gender Studies; German; Health Sciences; History; Home Economics; Humanities and Social Science Education; Industrial Engineering; Information Management; International Business; International Economics; Jazz and Popular Music; Linguistics; Literature; Management; Mathematics; Mathematics Education; Mechanical Engineering; Media Studies; Music Education; Musicology; Native Language Education; Nutrition; Pedagogy; Philosophy; Physics; Religious Education; Romance Languages; Science Education; Sociology; Spanish; Sports; Theology.** *PhD*: **Chemistry; Computer Science; Cultural Studies; Economics; Electrical and Electronic Engineering; Health Sciences; Home Economics; Mathematics; Mechanical Engineering; Natural Sciences; Nutrition; Physics; Sports; Sports Medicine.** *Habilitation*: **Analytical Chemistry; Applied Physics; Automation and Control Engineering; Chemical Engineering; Chemistry; Computer Education; Computer Science; Construction Engineering; Cultural Studies; Electrical and Electronic Engineering; Electronic Engineering; Health Sciences; Home Economics; Materials Engineering; Mathematics; Mathematics Education; Mechanical Engineering; Natural Sciences; Nutrition; Organic Chemistry; Physical Chemistry; Physics; Science Education; Sports; Sports Medicine.**

Student Services: Academic Counselling, Canteen, Careers Guidance, Cultural Activities, Facilities for disabled people, Foreign Studies Centre, Health Services, Language Laboratory, Library, Nursery Care, Social Counselling, Sports Facilities

Academic Staff *2013-2014*: Total: c. 1,320
Student Numbers *2013-2014*: Total 19,312
Last Updated: 31/03/15

UNIVERSITY OF PASSAU

Universität Passau

Innstrasse 41, 94030 Passau
Tel: +49(851) 509-0
Fax: +49(851) 509-1005
EMail: info@uni-passau.de
Website: http://www.uni-passau.de

Rector: Burkhard Freitag
Tel: +49(851) 509-1000 EMail: president@uni-passau.de

Chancellor: Andrea Bör
Tel: +49(851) 509-1010 EMail: kanzlerin@uni-passau.de

International Relations: Barbara Zacharias, Head of International Office
Tel: +49(851) 509-1160
EMail: barbara.zacharias@uni-passau.de; international@uni-passau.de

International Relations: Ursula Reutner, Vice President for International Relations
Tel: +49(851) 509-2888 EMail: ursula.reutner@uni-passau.de

Faculty

Arts and Humanities (Arts and Humanities; Catholic Theology; Cultural Studies; Government; History; Linguistics; Media Studies; Philosophy); **Business Administration and Economics** (Accountancy; Business Computing; Economics; Finance; Information Technology; Management; Marketing; Taxation); **Computer Science and Mathematics** (Computer Science; Data Processing; Mathematics); **Law** (European Union Law; Law)

History: Founded 1973. Teaching started 1978. An autonomous institution financially supported by the State of Bavaria.

Academic Year: October to September (October-March; April-September)

Admission Requirements: Abitur

Fees: National: None, International: None

Main Language(s) of Instruction: German, English

Degrees and Diplomas: *Bachelor's Degree*; *Master*: **Business Administration; Business Computing; Central European Studies; Communication Studies; Computer Science; Cultural Studies; Eastern European Studies; European Studies; Geography (Human); Government; History; International Business; International Economics; Law; Mass Communication; Media Studies; Russian; Southeast Asian Studies; Teacher Training; Tourism.** *PhD*: **American Studies; Art Education; Art History; Business Administration; Business Computing; Catholic Theology; Computer Science; Cultural Studies; Economics; English; Ethnology; European Studies; Foreign Languages Education; Geography (Human); German; History; International Business; Law; Linguistics; Literature; Mathematics; Media Studies; Medieval Studies; Modern History; Music Education; Pedagogy; Philology; Philosophy; Primary Education; Psychology; Romance Languages; Science Education; Sociology; Southeast Asian Studies; Speech Studies.** *Habilitation*: **Arts and Humanities.** Some courses taught in English; Also Double Master's degrees in International Business and Business Administration with foreign universities (in France and Hungary); Staatsexam in Law; Teacher Training Certificates (Lehramt).

Student Services: Academic Counselling, Canteen, Careers Guidance, Cultural Activities, Facilities for disabled people, Foreign Studies Centre, Health Services, IT Centre, Language Laboratory, Library, Nursery Care, Social Counselling, Sports Facilities

Publications: Vorlesungsverzeichnis

Student Numbers *2013-2014*: Total 11,294
Last Updated: 10/02/15

UNIVERSITY OF POTSDAM

Universität Potsdam (UP)

Am Neuen Palais 10, 14469 Potsdam
Tel: +49(331) 977-0
Fax: +49(331) 977-1089
EMail: presse@uni-potsdam.de
Website: http://www.uni-potsdam.de

Präsident: Oliver Günther (2012-2017)
Tel: +49(331) 977-1790 EMail: praesident@uni-potsdam.de

Chancellor/Registrar: Karsten Gerlof
Tel: +49(331) 977-1785 EMail: kanzler@uni-potsdam.de

International Relations: Regina Neum-Flux, Director of the International Relations Office, International Cooperation, Projects, and Partnership
Tel: +49(331) 977-1533
EMail: regina.neum-flux@uni-potsdam.de; infoaaa@uni-potsdam.de

Faculty

Arts (American Studies; Arts and Humanities; Classical Languages; English Studies; Germanic Studies; History; Jewish Studies; Media Studies; Philology; Philosophy; Religious Studies; Romance Languages; Slavic Languages); **Economics and Social Sciences** (Administration; Business Administration; Economics; Political Sciences; Social Sciences; Sociology); **Human Sciences** (Arts and Humanities; Linguistics; Music; Pedagogy; Primary Education; Psychology; Sports; Sports Management); **Law** (Civil Law; Criminal Law; Public Law); **Science** (Biochemistry; Biology; Chemistry; Computer Science; Earth Sciences; Mathematics; Natural Sciences; Nutrition; Physics)

History: Founded 1991. The University has branches in Potsdam-Babelsberg, Golm and Am Neuen Palais

Academic Year: October to September (October-March; April-September)

Admission Requirements: Secondary school certificate (Abitur), or equivalent.

Fees: None

Main Language(s) of Instruction: German, English

Degrees and Diplomas: *Bachelor's Degree*: **Biological and Life Sciences; Business Administration; Chemistry; Computer Science; Cultural Studies; Earth Sciences; Economics; Educational Sciences; English; French; History; Judaic Religious Studies; Latin; Law; Linguistics; Mathematics; Nutrition; Philosophy; Physics; Polish; Political Sciences; Psychology; Religious Studies; Russian; Social Sciences; Sociology; Sports; Sports Management; Teacher Training.** *Master*: **Administration; Biochemistry; Biology; Biotechnology; Business Administration; Chemistry; Cognitive Sciences; Commercial Law; Comparative Literature; Computer Science; Contemporary History; Cultural Studies; Earth Sciences; Eastern European Studies; Ecology; Economics; Educational Sciences; English Studies; Environmental Management; Fine Arts; Fiscal Law; Geology; Health Administration; Judaic Religious Studies; Law; Leadership; Linguistics; Literature; Management; Mathematics; Media Studies; Medical Technology; Military Science; Nutrition; Philosophy; Physics; Political Sciences; Polymer and Plastics Technology; Psychology; Public Administration; Sociology; Sports Management; Teacher Training; Technology.** *PhD*: **Administration; Biological and Life Sciences; Business Administration; Chemistry; Computer Science; Cultural Studies; Earth Sciences; Economics; Educational Sciences; History; Judaic Religious Studies; Law; Linguistics; Management; Marketing; Mathematics; Media Studies; Modern Languages; Nutrition; Philosophy; Physics; Political Sciences; Psychology; Religious Studies; Sociology; Sports.** Also Teacher Training Programmes (Lehramt); Dual Degree Programmes: European Master in Clinical Linguistics (EMCL) offered in cooperation between the University of Potsdam, the University of Groningen in the Netherlands, and the University of Eastern Finland in Joensuu; German-Frensh Jurisprudence programme offered by University of Potsdam and the Université Paris Ouest Nanterre La Défense (formerly: Paris X – Nanterre) in cooperation with the German-French University (DFH); German-Russian Master of Administration; Master of Arts International Relations (MAIB) awarded by the German Academic Exchange Service (DAAD) and the Stifterverband für die Deutsche Wissenschaft.

Student Services: Academic Counselling, Canteen, Cultural Activities, Facilities for disabled people, Foreign Studies Centre, Language Laboratory, Library, Nursery Care, Residential Facilities, Social Counselling, Sports Facilities

Academic Staff *2014-2015*	**TOTAL**
FULL-TIME	**632**
STAFF WITH DOCTORATE	
FULL-TIME	**220**

Student Numbers *2014-2015*	
All (Foreign included)	**19,972**
FOREIGN ONLY	**2139**

Last Updated: 12/02/15

UNIVERSITY OF ROSTOCK

Universität Rostock

Universitätsplatz 1, 18051 Rostock
Tel: +49(381) 498-0
Fax: +49(381) 498-1006
EMail: rektor@uni-rostock.de; pressestelle@uni-rostock.de
Website: http://www.uni-rostock.de

Rector: Wolfgang Schareck
Tel: +49(381) 498-1000 EMail: rektor@uni-rostock.de

Acting Chancellor: Jan Tamm
Tel: +49(381) 498-1014 EMail: kanzler@uni-rostock.de

Quality Assurance Officer: Antje Mayer
Tel: +49(381) 498-1243 EMail: antje.mayer@uni-rostock.de

International Relations: Bettina Eichler-Löbermann, Vice-Rector for International Affairs, Equality and Diversity Management
Tel: +49(381) 498-1008 EMail: pi@uni-rostock.de

Faculty

Agriculture and Environmental Sciences (Agriculture; Environmental Engineering); **Computer Science and Electronic Engineering** (Business Computing; Computer Engineering; Computer Science; Electrical and Electronic Engineering; Teacher Training); **Economics and Social Sciences** (Business Administration; Business Education; Political Sciences; Social Sciences; Sociology; Teacher Training); **Humanities** (Archaeology; Arts and Humanities; Classical Languages; Education; Educational Research; History; Mass Communication; Modern Languages; Pedagogy; Philosophy; Sports; Teacher Training); **Law** (Law); **Mathematics and Natural Sciences** (Biology; Chemistry; Mathematics; Physics; Teacher Training); **Mechanical Engineering and Marine Technology** (Automation and Control Engineering; Biomedical Engineering; Engineering Management; Marine Engineering; Mechanical Engineering; Teacher Training); **Medicine** (Biomedical Engineering; Biomedicine; Dentistry; Medicine); **Theology** (Protestant Theology; Religious Studies)

Further Information: Also 12 Clinics, 1 Radiology Centre and 1 Neurology Centre

History: Founded 1419 with faculties of Arts, Medicine and Law. The oldest University in the Baltic Sea area, reorganized and reopened 1946. Following reunification in 1989, the University experienced significant changes, such as an increase of 75% of the number of students.

Academic Year: October to September (October-March; April-September)

Admission Requirements: Secondary school certificate and, depending on State of origin, language requirements (DSH, Test DaF)

Fees: None, excluding courses in continuing and distance education

Main Language(s) of Instruction: German

Degrees and Diplomas: *Bachelor's Degree*: **Agriculture; Arts and Humanities; Business Administration; Education; Engineering; Health Sciences; Information Sciences; Law; Mathematics and Computer Science; Natural Sciences; Religion; Social Sciences.** *Kirchliche Abschlussprüfung*: **Theology.** *Master*: **Agriculture; Arts and Humanities; Business Administration; Education; Engineering; Health Sciences; Information Sciences; Law; Mathematics and Computer Science; Natural Sciences; Social Sciences.** *PhD*: **Agriculture; Arts and Humanities; Business Administration; Education; Engineering; Health Sciences; Information Sciences; Law; Mathematics and Computer Science; Natural Sciences; Religion; Social Sciences.** *Habilitation*: **Agriculture; Arts and Humanities; Business Administration; Education; Engineering; Health Sciences; Information Sciences; Law; Mathematics and Computer Science; Natural Sciences; Religion; Social Sciences.** Also Staatsexamen in Medicine and Teacher Training.

Student Services: Academic Counselling, Canteen, Careers Guidance, Cultural Activities, Facilities for disabled people, IT Centre, Language Laboratory, Library, Residential Facilities, Social Counselling, Sports Facilities, eLibrary

Student Numbers *2013-2014*: Total: c. 14,420
Last Updated: 12/02/15

UNIVERSITY OF SIEGEN

Universität Siegen

Postfach, 57068 Siegen
Tel: +49(271) 740-0
Fax: +49(271) 4899
EMail: info.studienberatung@zv.uni-siegen.de
Website: http://www.uni-siegen.de

Rector: Holger Burckhart
Tel: +49(271) 740-4858 EMail: rektor@uni-siegen.de

Chancellor: Ulf Richter
Tel: +49(271) 740-4856 EMail: kanzler@zv.uni-siegen.de

Faculty

Arts (Catholic Theology; English; German; History; Media Studies; Philosophy; Romance Languages; Sociology; Theology); **Economics, Computer Science and Economics, Business Law** (Business Administration; Business Computing; Economics; Law); **Education, Architecture and Arts** (Architecture; Cultural Studies; Education; Fine Arts; Music; Psychology); **Natural Science and Technology** (Biology; Chemistry; Civil Engineering; Computer Science; Electronic Engineering; Machine Building; Mathematics; Physics)

Further Information: Also German Language Courses for beginners and advanced students

History: Founded 1972 as Gesamthochschule, incorporating former Technical College, Siegen-Gummersbach and branch of College of Education, Westfalen-Lippe. Became University 1980. An autonomous institution under the jurisdiction of and financially supported by the State of North Rhine-Westphalia.

Academic Year: October to July

Admission Requirements: Secondary school certificate (Reifezeugnis) or international equivalent. Technical secondary education (Fachhochschulreife) for certain courses

Fees: 500 per semester (Euro)

Main Language(s) of Instruction: German

Degrees and Diplomas: *Bachelor's Degree*; *Master*: **Accountancy; Applied Linguistics; Architecture; Automation and Control Engineering; Business Computing; Chemistry; Civil Engineering; Computer Engineering; Computer Science; Cultural Studies; Economic and Finance Policy; Education; Electronic Engineering; English; Finance; German; Industrial Engineering; Industrial Management; International Studies; Linguistics; Literature; Management; Materials Engineering; Mathematics; Mechanical Engineering; Media Studies; Physics; Political Sciences; Romance Languages; Small Business; Social Sciences; Social Work; Taxation; Telecommunications Engineering; Urban Studies.** *PhD*: **Architecture; Business Administration; Business Computing; Chemistry; Civil Engineering; Commercial Law; Computer Science; Education; Fine Arts; Mathematics; Mechanical Engineering; Music; Philosophy; Physics; Psychology.** *Habilitation*: **Architecture; Business Administration; Business and Commerce; Commercial Law; Economics; Education; Engineering; Fine Arts; Music; Natural Sciences; Philosophy; Psychology.** Also State Certificate in Teacher Training (Lehramt)

Student Services: Academic Counselling, Canteen, Careers Guidance, Facilities for disabled people, Foreign Studies Centre, Language Laboratory, Nursery Care, Social Counselling, Sports Facilities

Publications: Forschungsbericht (Research Report); Lili - Zeitschrift für Literaturwissenschaft und Linguistik; Muk (Massenmedien und Kommunikation); Navigationen; Reihe Medienwissenschaften; Reihe Siegen; Siegen: Social; SPIEL (Siegener Periodicum zur International Empirischen Literaturwissenschaften)

Student Numbers *2013-2014*: Total 18,760
Last Updated: 28/03/15

UNIVERSITY OF STUTTGART

Universität Stuttgart

Postfach 10 60 37, Keplerstrasse 7, 70049 Stuttgart
Tel: +49(711) 685-0
Fax: +49(711) 685-82271
EMail: poststelle@uni-stuttgart.de
Website: http://www.uni-stuttgart.de

Rector: Wolfram Ressel (2006-)
Tel: +49(711) 685-82201 EMail: rektor@uni-stuttgart.de

Chancellor: Bettina Buhlmann
Tel: +49(711) 685-82204 EMail: kanzlerin@uni-stuttgart.de

International Relations: Bernadette Burger, Manager of the Dept. of International Education Services
Tel: +49(711) 685-68547
EMail: burger@ia.uni-stuttgart.de; auslandsstudium@ia.uni-stuttgart.de

Faculty

Aerospace Engineering and Geodesy (Aeronautical and Aerospace Engineering; Geological Engineering; Surveying and Mapping); **Architecture and Urban Planning** (Architecture; Design; Landscape Architecture; Town Planning); **Chemistry** (Chemistry; Food Science; Materials Engineering); **Civil and Environmental Engineering** (Civil Engineering; Environmental Engineering; Hydraulic Engineering; Railway Engineering; Regional Planning; Road Engineering; Surveying and Mapping; Water Management); **Computer Science, Electrical Engineering and Information Technology** (Computer Science; Electrical Engineering; Information Technology; Software Engineering); **Energy Technology, Process Engineering and Biological Engineering** (Biomedical Engineering; Cell Biology; Chemical Engineering; Energy Engineering; Immunology; Industrial Engineering; Microbiology; Polymer and Plastics Technology); **Engineering Design, Production Engineering and Automotive Engineering** (Automotive Engineering; Engineering Drawing and Design; Engineering Management; Mechanical Engineering; Production Engineering; Road Engineering; Water Management); **Humanities** (Art History; English; German; History; Linguistics; Philosophy; Romance Languages); **Management, Economics and Social Sciences** (Educational Sciences; Information Sciences; Management; Social Sciences; Sports; Technology Education; Vocational Education); **Mathematics and Physics** (Mathematics; Physics)

History: Founded 1829 as a grammar and vocational school, became Polytechnische Schule 1840, Technische Hochschule 1890. Present title conferred 1967. An autonomous institution under the jurisdiction of and financed by the State of Baden-Württemberg.

Academic Year: October to September (October-March; April-September)

Admission Requirements: Secondary school certificate (Reifezeugnis) or equivalent

Fees: 500 per semester (Euro)

Main Language(s) of Instruction: German

Degrees and Diplomas: *Bachelor's Degree*: **Aeronautical and Aerospace Engineering; Architecture; Art History; Automotive Engineering; Business Administration; Chemistry; Civil Engineering; Computer Science; Economics; Electrical Engineering; Energy Engineering; Engineering Management; English; Environmental Engineering; Food Technology; German; History; Information Technology; Linguistics; Materials Engineering; Mechanical Engineering; Medical Technology; Natural Sciences; Philosophy; Physics; Political Sciences; Real Estate; Romance Languages; Social Sciences; Sociology; Software Engineering; Sports; Surveying and Mapping; Technology; Technology Education; Transport Engineering; Vocational Education.** *Master*: **Aeronautical and Aerospace Engineering; Architectural and Environmental Design; Architecture; Art History; Automation and Control Engineering; Automotive Engineering; Biology; Business Administration; Chemistry; Civil Engineering; Comparative Literature; Computer Science; Electrical Engineering; Electronic Engineering; Energy Engineering; Engineering Management; English; Environmental Engineering; Fine Arts; Food Technology; Geological Engineering; Health Sciences; History; Hydraulic Engineering; Information Technology; Linguistics; Literature; Materials Engineering; Mathematics; Mechanical Engineering; Medical Technology; Philosophy; Physics; Political Sciences; Power Engineering; Public Administration; Real Estate; Romance Languages; Social Sciences; Software Engineering; Sports; Surveying and Mapping; Technology Education; Town Planning; Transport Engineering; Transport Management; Waste Management; Water Management.** *PhD*: **Aeronautical and Aerospace Engineering; Architecture and Planning; Arts and Humanities; Automotive Engineering; Bioengineering; Chemistry; Civil Engineering; Computer Science; Design; Economics; Electrical Engineering; Electronic Engineering; Environmental Engineering; Geological Engineering; Information Technology; Management; Physics; Production Engineering; Social Sciences; Town Planning.** *Habilitation*: **Automotive Engineering; Biotechnology; Civil Engineering; Computer Science; Construction Engineering; Electronic Engineering; Energy Engineering; Environmental Engineering; Information Technology; Production Engineering.** Also TeacherTraining State Examination; German-French Master of Arts' Study Programmes; International English Master of Science Study Programmes; Study Programs taught in English.

Student Services: Academic Counselling, Canteen, Careers Guidance, Facilities for disabled people, Foreign Studies Centre, Language Laboratory, Library, Nursery Care, Social Counselling, Sports Facilities

Publications: Research; Research Development Consulting

Student Numbers *2013-2014*: Total 26,052
Last Updated: 01/04/15

UNIVERSITY OF TELEVISION AND FILM MUNICH

Hochschule für Fernsehen und Film München (HFF MÜNCHEN)

Bernd-Eichinger-Platz 1, 80333 München
Tel: +49(89) 68957-0
Fax: +49(89) 68957-9900
EMail: info@hff-muc.de
Website: http://www.hff-muenchen.de/

President: Gerhard Fuchs
Tel: +49(89) 68957-8000 EMail: d.brennstuhl@hff-muc.de

Chancellor: Ingrid Baumgartner-Schmidt
Tel: +49(89) 68957-801 EMail: kanzlerin@hff-muc.de

Department

Cinematography (Cinema and Television; Visual Arts); **Feature Film and Television Feature** (Cinema and Television; Film); **Film and Television Documentary** (Cinema and Television; Journalism; Radio and Television Broadcasting); **Media Studies** (Media Studies); **Production and Media Business** (Advertising and Publicity; Business Administration; Media Studies); **Screenplay** (Writing); **Technology** (Technology)

History: Founded 1966.

Academic Year: October to July (October-February; May-July)

Admission Requirements: Secondary school certificate (Abitur)

Main Language(s) of Instruction: German

Degrees and Diplomas: *Künstlerische Abschlussprüfung*: **Art Criticism.** *Diplom (Univ)*: **Cinema and Television; Film; Media Studies; Writing.** *PhD*: **Media Studies.** Künstlerische Abschlussprüfung in Art Critism is offered joinlty with Bayerischen Theaterakademie "August Everding".

Student Services: Library

Student Numbers *2013-2014*: Total 391
Last Updated: 29/01/15

UNIVERSITY OF THE ARTS BREMEN

Hochschule für Künste Bremen

Am Speicher XI Nr. 8, 28217 Bremen
Tel: +49(421) 9595-1000
Fax: +49(421) 9595-200
EMail: pressestelle@hfk-bremen.de
Website: http://www.hfk-bremen.de

Rector: Herbert Grüner (2012-)
Tel: +49(421) 9595-1017 EMail: rektor@hfk-bremen.de

Chancellor: Markus Wortmann
Tel: +49(421) 9595-1025
EMail: kanzler@hfk-bremen.de; m.wortmann@hfk-bremen.de

International Relations: Birgit Harte
Tel: +49(421) 9595-1040 EMail: b.harte@hfk-bremen.de

Faculty
Art and Design (Art Education; Design; Fine Arts; Interior Design; Media Studies); **Music** (Art Education; Music; Music Education; Musical Instruments; Religious Music)

History: Founded 1922.

Main Language(s) of Instruction: German

Degrees and Diplomas: *Bachelor's Degree*: **Design; Media Studies; Music; Music Education.** *Diplom (Univ)*: **Fine Arts.** *Master*: **Design; Media Studies; Music; Music Education.** Also Konzertexam

Student Numbers *2014-2015*: Total: c. 900
Last Updated: 09/03/15

UNIVERSITY OF THE FEDERAL ARMED FORCES MUNICH

Universität der Bundeswehr München
Werner-Heisenberg-Weg 39, 85577 Neubiberg
Tel: +49(89) 6004-0
Fax: +49(89) 6004-3560
EMail: info@unibw.de
Website: http://www.unibw-muenchen.de

President: Merith Niehuss (2005-)
Tel: +49(89) 6004-2001 EMail: vorzimmer.praesidentin@unibw.de

Chancellor: Siegfried Rapp
Tel: +49(89) 6004-4000 EMail: kanzler@unibw-muenchen.de

International Relations: Alexandra Bettag, Head, International Office Tel: +49(89) 6004-4683 EMail: alexandra.bettag@unibw.de

Faculty
Aviation and Aerospace Engineering (Aeronautical and Aerospace Engineering); **Business Administration** (Business Administration); **Civil Engineering and Enviromental Studies** (Civil Engineering; Environmental Studies); **Computer Science** (Computer Science); **Economics and Organizational Sciences** (Business Administration; Economics); **Electrical and Computer Engineering** (Computer Engineering; Electrical Engineering); **Electrical Engineering and Computer Science** (Business Administration; Computer Science; Electrical Engineering; Mechanical Engineering); **Human Sciences** (Education; Psychology; Sports); **Mechanical Engineering** (Mechanical Engineering); **State and Social Sciences** (Social Sciences)

History: Founded 1973 by decision of the Federal Government. Authorized 1973 by the Bavarian Ministry for Education, Culture, Science and Arts. Responsible to the Bavarian Ministry of Education, Culture, Science and Arts, and to the Federal Ministry of Defence.

Academic Year: October to June (October-December; January-March; April-June)

Admission Requirements: Secondary school certificate (Reifezeugnis) or equivalent. Students must have passed the Armed Forces officers examination and have accepted a 12-yr engagement

Fees: None

Main Language(s) of Instruction: German

Degrees and Diplomas: *Bachelor's Degree*; *Master*: **Adult Education; Aeronautical and Aerospace Engineering; Business Administration; Business Computing; Civil Engineering; Computer Engineering; Economics; Educational Sciences; Electrical Engineering; Engineering; Engineering Management; Environmental Engineering; International Business; Management; Mathematics; Media Studies; Psychology; Social Sciences; Sports.** *PhD*: **Aeronautical and Aerospace Engineering; Business Administration; Civil Engineering; Computer Engineering; Computer Science; Electrical Engineering; Environmental Engineering; Law; Mechanical Engineering; Pedagogy; Social Sciences.** *Habilitation*: **Aeronautical and Aerospace Engineering; Business Administration; Civil Engineering; Computer Engineering; Computer Science; Electrical Engineering; Environmental Studies; Mechanical Engineering; Social Sciences.**

Student Services: Careers Guidance

Student Numbers *2013-2014*: Total 2,806
Last Updated: 30/03/15

UNIVERSITY OF THE RUHR, BOCHUM

Ruhr-Universität Bochum (RUB)
Universitätsstrasse 150, 44801 Bochum, North Rhine-Westphalia
Tel: +49(234) 32-22926 +49(234) 32-22927
Fax: +49(234) 32-14131
EMail: info@uv.ruhr-uni-bochum.de
Website: http://www.ruhr-uni-bochum.de

Rector: Elmar Weiler
Tel: +49(234) 32-22 EMail: rektor@ruhr-uni-bochum.de

Chancellor: Karl-Heinz Schloßer
Tel: +49(234) 32-22921 EMail: kanzler@ruhr-uni-bochum.de

International Relations: Monika Sprung
Tel: +49(234) 32-23024
EMail: monika.sprung@uv.ruhr-uni-bochum.de

Faculty
Biology and Biotechnology (Biology; Biotechnology); **Catholic Theology** (Catholic Theology; Theology); **Chemistry and Biochemistry** (Biochemistry; Chemistry); **Civil and Environmental Engineering** (Civil Engineering; Environmental Engineering); **East Asian Studies** (Chinese; East Asian Studies; Japanese; Korean; Literature); **Economics** (Economics); **Electrical Engineering and Information Technology** (Electrical Engineering; Information Sciences; Information Technology); **Geoscience** (Earth Sciences; Geography; Geology; Geophysics); **History** (Archaeology; Art History; History; Musicology); **Law** (Law); **Mathematics** (Mathematics); **Mechanical Engineering** (Automation and Control Engineering; Automotive Engineering; Energy Engineering; Engineering Drawing and Design; Engineering Management; Materials Engineering; Mechanical Engineering); **Medicine** (Medicine); **Philology** (Classical Languages; Comparative Literature; English Studies; Film; Germanic Studies; Linguistics; Media Studies; Oriental Studies; Philology; Romance Languages; Slavic Languages; Theatre); **Philosophy and Educational Research** (Education; Educational Research; Philosophy); **Physics and Astronomy** (Astronomy and Space Science; Physics); **Protestant Theology** (Protestant Theology); **Psychology** (Psychology); **Social Sciences** (Political Sciences; Social Sciences; Sociology); **Sports Science** (Sports)

Centre
Continuing Education; **Interdisciplinary Research of the Ruhr Area** (Regional Studies); **Teacher Training** (Teacher Training)

History: Formally opened June 1965. An autonomous institution financially supported by the State of North Rhine-Westphalia, and under the jurisdiction of its Ministry of Education.

Academic Year: October to July (October-February; April-July)

Admission Requirements: Secondary school certificate (Reifezeugnis) or equivalent

Main Language(s) of Instruction: German, English

Accrediting Agency: Accreditation Council, Bonn

Degrees and Diplomas: *Bachelor's Degree*: **Archaeology; Art History; Asian Studies; Behavioural Sciences; Biochemistry; Biology; Catholic Theology; Chemistry; Chinese; Civil Engineering; Computer Science; East Asian Studies; Economics; Educational Sciences; Electrical and Electronic Engineering; English; Environmental Engineering; French; Geography; Geology; Geophysics; German; Greek (Classical); History; Industrial and Organizational Psychology; International Law; Islamic Studies; Italian; Japanese; Korean; Latin; Linguistics; Literature; Management; Mathematics; Mechanical Engineering; Media Studies; Mineralogy; Oriental Languages; Oriental Studies; Philosophy; Physics; Political Sciences; Production Engineering; Protestant Theology; Psychology; Religious Studies; Romance Languages; Russian; Social Studies; Spanish; Systems Analysis.** *Magister*: **Catholic Theology; Protestant Theology.** *Master*: **Accountancy; American Studies; Ancient Civilizations; Archaeology; Art History; Asian Studies; Biochemistry; Biology; Business Administration; Catholic Theology; Cell Biology; Chemistry; Cinema and Television; Civil Engineering; Clinical Psychology; Cognitive Sciences; Comparative Literature; Computer Engineering; Computer Science; Criminal Law; Development Studies; East Asian Studies; Eastern European Studies; Economics; Education; Educational Sciences; Electrical Engineering; English; English Studies; Environmental Engineering; Ethics; European Studies; Film; Fine Arts; Fiscal Law; French; Gender Studies;**

Genetics; Geography; Geography (Human); Geology; Geophysics; German; Germanic Studies; Greek; Greek (Classical); History; Human Resources; Industrial and Organizational Psychology; International Law; Islamic Law; Islamic Studies; Italian; Justice Administration; Laser Engineering; Latin; Linguistics; Management; Materials Engineering; Mathematics; Mechanical Engineering; Media Studies; Medical Technology; Medieval Studies; Mineralogy; Molecular Biology; Neurology; Neurosciences; Oriental Studies; Philosophy; Physics; Prehistory; Protestant Theology; Religious Studies; Russian; Social Sciences; Spanish; Systems Analysis; Telecommunications Engineering; Theatre; Town Planning; Video. *PhD*: **American Studies; Ancient Civilizations; Applied Linguistics; Archaeology; Art History; Asian Studies; Astronomy and Space Science; Biochemistry; Biology; Catholic Theology; Chemistry; Civil Engineering; Comparative Literature; Computer Engineering; Dentistry; Development Studies; East Asian Studies; Educational Sciences; Electrical Engineering; English Studies; Environmental Engineering; French; Gender Studies; Geography; Geology; Geophysics; German; Germanic Studies; Greek; Greek (Classical); History; Italian; Latin; Law; Linguistics; Materials Engineering; Mathematics; Mechanical Engineering; Media Studies; Medicine; Mineralogy; Neurosciences; Oriental Studies; Philosophy; Physics; Prehistory; Protestant Theology; Psychology; Religious Studies; Romance Languages; Russian; Slavic Languages; Social Sciences; Spanish; Theatre.** *Habilitation*: **Accountancy; Administrative Law; Advertising and Publicity; American Studies; Anaesthesiology; Analytical Chemistry; Anatomy; Ancient Civilizations; Applied Chemistry; Applied Linguistics; Applied Mathematics; Applied Physics; Archaeology; Art History; Artificial Intelligence; Asian Religious Studies; Asian Studies; Astronomy and Space Science; Astrophysics; Atomic and Molecular Physics; Automation and Control Engineering; Banking; Behavioural Sciences; Bible; Bilingual and Bicultural Education; Biochemistry; Bioengineering; Biology; Biomedical Engineering; Biomedicine; Biophysics; Biotechnology; Botany; Bridge Engineering; Canon Law; Cardiology; Catholic Theology; Cell Biology; Central European Studies; Ceramics and Glass Technology; Chemical Engineering; Chemistry; Chinese; Christian Religious Studies; Cinema and Television; Civil Engineering; Civil Law; Clinical Psychology; Cognitive Sciences; Commercial Law; Communication Studies; Comparative Law; Comparative Literature; Comparative Politics; Comparative Religion; Comparative Sociology; Computer Engineering; Computer Science; Constitutional Law; Construction Engineering; Criminal Law; Crystallography; Demography and Population; Dentistry; Dermatology; Development Studies; Developmental Psychology; Diabetology; Distance Education; E- Business/Commerce; East Asian Studies; Eastern European Studies; Econometrics; Economic and Finance Policy; Economic History; Education; Education of the Handicapped; Education of the Socially Disadvantaged; Educational and Student Counselling; Educational Psychology; Educational Research; Educational Technology; Educational Testing and Evaluation; Electrical Engineering; Electronic Engineering; Embryology and Reproduction Biology; Endocrinology; Energy Engineering; Engineering Management; English; English Studies; Environmental Engineering; Epidemiology; Ethics; Ethnology; European Studies; European Union Law; Experimental Psychology; Explosive Engineering; Family Studies; Finance; Fiscal Law; Foreign Languages Education; French; French Studies; Futurology; Gastroenterology; Gender Studies; Genetics; Geochemistry; Geography; Geography (Human); Geological Engineering; Geology; Geophysics; German; Gerontology; Government; Greek (Classical); Gynaecology and Obstetrics; Haematology; Hepatology; Higher Education; Histology; History; History of Law; History of Religion; History of Societies; Holy Writings; Human Resources; Human Rights; Humanities and Social Science Education; Hydraulic Engineering; Immunology; Industrial and Organizational Psychology; Industrial and Production Economics; Industrial Chemistry; Industrial Engineering; Industrial Management; Information Management; Information Technology; Inorganic Chemistry; Insurance; International and Comparative Education; International Business; International Economics; International Law; International Relations; Islamic Law; Islamic Studies; Islamic Theology; Italian; Japanese; Journalism; Judaic Religious Studies; Justice Administration; Koran; Korean; Labour and Industrial Relations; Labour Law; Laser Engineering; Latin; Law; Leadership; Linguistics; Literature; Logic; Machine Building; Management Systems; Marketing; Materials Engineering; Mathematical Physics; Mathematics; Mathematics and Computer Science; Mathematics Education; Mechanical Engineering; Mechanics; Media Studies; Medical Parasitology; Medical Technology; Medicine; Medieval Studies; Metal Techniques; Metallurgical Engineering; Microbiology; Microelectronics; Microwaves; Mineralogy; Modern History; Molecular Biology; Multimedia; Nanotechnology; Native Language Education; Nephrology; Neurology; Neurosciences; New Testament; Nuclear Physics; Oncology; Operations Research; Ophthalmology; Optical Technology; Optics; Organic Chemistry; Oriental Languages; Oriental Studies; Orthodox Theology; Orthopaedics; Otorhinolaryngology; Paediatrics; Paleontology; Pastoral Studies; Pathology; Petrology; Philosophical Schools; Philosophy; Philosophy of Education; Physical Chemistry; Physical Education; Physical Engineering; Physics; Physiology; Plant Pathology; Plastic Surgery; Pneumology; Podiatry; Political Sciences; Polymer and Plastics Technology; Power Engineering; Prehistory; Private Law; Production Engineering; Protestant Theology; Psychiatry and Mental Health; Psychoanalysis; Psychology; Psychometrics; Psychotherapy; Public Administration; Public Law; Public Relations; Radio and Television Broadcasting; Radiology; Radiophysics; Railway Engineering; Religious Education; Religious Practice; Rheumatology; Road Engineering; Romance Languages; Rubber Technology; Russian; Safety Engineering; Secondary Education; Seismology; Small Business; Social Policy; Social Problems; Social Psychology; Social Studies; Sociology; Solid State Physics; Sound Engineering (Acoustics); Spanish; Speech Studies; Sports Medicine; Statistics; Systems Analysis; Taxation; Theatre; Thermal Physics; Toxicology; Transport Engineering; Urban Studies; Urology; Venereology; Virology; Western European Studies; Zoology.** Also State Examintation (Staatsexam) in Medicine and Law; Teaching Degree Programme (Lehramt) in secondary and comprehensive school education. Also Sports (Bachelor/Master/PhD/Habilitation)

Student Services: Academic Counselling, Canteen, Careers Guidance, Cultural Activities, Facilities for disabled people, Foreign Studies Centre, Health Services, IT Centre, Language Laboratory, Library, Nursery Care, Residential Facilities, Social Counselling, Sports Facilities, eLibrary

Publications: Forschungsbericht; Wissenschaftsmagazin rubin

Academic Staff *2014-2015*	MEN	WOMEN	**TOTAL**
FULL-TIME	1,061	632	**1,693**
STAFF WITH DOCTORATE			
FULL-TIME	806	480	c. **1,286**
Student Numbers *2014-2015*			
All (Foreign included)	21,892	20,826	**42,718**
FOREIGN ONLY	2,648	2,990	**5,638**

Part-time students, –

Last Updated: 06/02/15

UNIVERSITY OF TRIER

Universität Trier

Universitätsring 15, 54286 Trier, Rhineland Palatinate

Tel: +49(651) 201-0

Fax: +49(651) 201-4299

Website: http://www.uni-trier.de

President: Michael Jäckel (2011-)

Tel: +49(651) 201-4241 EMail: praesident@uni-trier.de

Chancellor: Ulrike Graßnick

Tel: +49(651) 201-4233 EMail: kanzlerin@uni-trier.de

International Relations: Birgit Roser, Head, International Office

Tel: +49(651) 201-2807

EMail: roser@uni-trier.de; aaa@uni-trier.de

Faculty

I (Educational Sciences; Nursing; Pedagogy; Philosophy); **II** (Chinese; Classical Languages; English Studies; Germanic Studies; Greek (Classical); Japanese; Latin; Linguistics; Media Studies; Phonetics; Romance Languages; Slavic Languages); **III** (Ancient Civilizations; Archaeology; Art History; History; Political Sciences);

IV (Business Administration; Computer Science; Economics; Ethnology; Mathematics; Sociology); **Theology** (Theology); **V** (Law); **VI** (Earth Sciences; Geography)

Institute

BioGeoAnalytik, Umweltproben- biobanks - IBU; **History of the Jews - AMIGJ** *(Arye Maimon)*; **Labour Law and Industrial Relations in the European Union - IAAEU**

Centre

Competence Center E-Business - ceb; **Digital Humanities/ Competence Centre for Electronic Processing and Publication in the Humanities**; **Research network Interactive Science - Internal Science Communication through digital media**

Research Centre

America Romana Centrum - ARC; **American Studies - TCAS**; **Ancient Studies at the University of Trier - ZAT**; **Canadian Studies - ZKS**; **East Asian and Pacific Studies - Zops**; **Environment and Regional Statistics - forumstat** (Statistics); **Europa - FZE** (Arts and Humanities; Social Sciences); **European Centre for Psychotherapy and Psychotherapy Research - EZPP**; **European Studies - ZES**; **Greco-Roman Egypt**; **Health Economics - ZfG**; **Historical and Cultural Sciences**; **Kant**; **Languages ã *and* Literatures Luxembourg - FSL**; **Medieval Studies - TZM**; **Poli Clinical Psychotherapy Clinic for Training, Education and Research - PALF**; **Postcolonial and Gender Studies - CePoG**; **Psychological Assessment and Evaluation - ZDiag**; **Service Center for Applied Mathematics - ZAM**; **Teacher Education - ZfL**

Research Institute

Cusanus; **Environmental and Technology Law at the University of Trier - IUTR**; **European Constitutional Law - IETL**; **German and European Criminal Law and Police Law - ISP**; **German and European Water Management Law - IDEW**; **Health Care Management - IHCI** *(International)*; **Media and Culture**; **Psychobiology**; **Research and Training Profession - IPW** *(Interregional)*

History: Founded 1473 and closed in Napoleonic era. Re-established 1970 as a modern campus University. Incorporated the Theologische Fakultät Trier (founded 1950).

Academic Year: October to September (October-March; April-September)

Admission Requirements: Secondary school certificate (Reifezeugnis)

Fees: (Euros): Tuition, none; social fees: 145.50 per semester

Main Language(s) of Instruction: German

Degrees and Diplomas: *Bachelor's Degree*; *Lizentiat*: **Catholic Theology.** *Master*: **Ancient Civilizations; Archaeology; Art History; Arts and Humanities; Business Administration; Business Computing; Catholic Theology; Chinese; Classical Languages; Computer Science; Earth Sciences; Economics; English; French; Gender Studies; Geography; Geography (Human); German; History; Italian; Japanese; Mathematics; Media Studies; Paper Technology; Pedagogy; Philosophy; Phonetics; Political Sciences; Psychology; Public Law; Romance Languages; Russian; Slavic Languages; Sociology; Spanish; Teacher Training.** *PhD*: **Archaeology; Art History; Business Administration; Business Computing; Chinese; Computer Science; Earth Sciences; Economics; Education; English; Environmental Studies; French; Geography; Geology; German; Greek (Classical); Health Administration; History; Italian; Japanese; Latin; Law; Linguistics; Literature; Mathematics; Media Studies; Medieval Studies; Meteorology; Modern History; Modern Languages; Natural Sciences; Philosophy; Phonetics; Political Sciences; Psychology; Romance Languages; Slavic Languages; Social Sciences; Soil Science; Spanish; Statistics; Surveying and Mapping; Theology; Water Science.** *Habilitation*: **Ancient Civilizations; Archaeology; Art History; Business Administration; Economics; Ethnology; Geography; Geology; History; Law; Linguistics; Literature; Mathematics; Pedagogy; Philosophy; Political Sciences; Psychology; Sociology; Theology.** Also Teacher Training State Examination in Teacher Training (Lehramt) and Law.

Student Services: Academic Counselling, Canteen, Careers Guidance, Cultural Activities, Facilities for disabled people, Foreign Studies Centre, Health Services, IT Centre, Language Laboratory, Library, Nursery Care, Social Counselling, Sports Facilities

Publications: Trierer Beiträge

Student Numbers *2013-2014*: Total 14,668

Last Updated: 01/04/15

UNIVERSITY OF TÜBINGEN

Eberhard Karls Universität Tübingen

Geschwister-Scholl-Platz, 72074 Tübingen

Tel: +49(7071) 29-0

Fax: +49(7071) 29-5990

EMail: info@uni-tuebingen.de

Website: http://www.uni-tuebingen.de

Rektor: Bernd Engler (2006-)
Tel: +49(7071) 29-72512 EMail: bernd.engler@uni-tuebingen.de

Kanzler: Andreas Rothfuss
Tel: +49(7071) 29-72515
EMail: andreas.rothfuss@kanzler.uni-tuebingen.de

International Relations: Wolfgang Mekle, Vice-Provost
Tel: +49(7071) 29-72938
EMail: international.office@uni-tuebingen.de

Faculty

Catholic Theology (Catholic Theology); **Cultural Studies** (Ancient Civilizations; Ancient Languages; Archaeology; Art History; Asian Studies; Chinese; Cultural Studies; Ethnology; Greek (Classical); Japanese; Korean; Latin; Music; Musicology; Oriental Studies; Philology; Prehistory; Religion; South Asian Studies); **Economics and Social Sciences** (Accountancy; Business Administration; Econometrics; Economics; Finance; International Business; International Economics; Management; Statistics); **Humanities** (American Studies; Archaeology; Art History; Chinese; English; Ethnology; German; Greek; History; Japanese; Jewish Studies; Korean; Latin; Linguistics; Literature; Media Studies; Middle Eastern Studies; Music; Oriental Studies; Philology; Romance Languages; Russian; Scandinavian Languages; Slavic Languages); **Law** (Law); **Medicine** (Behavioural Sciences; Cell Biology; Dentistry; Medicine; Molecular Biology; Neurology; Neurosciences); **Protestant Theology** (Judaic Religious Studies; Protestant Theology); **Science** (Biochemistry; Biology; Chemistry; Computer Science; Earth Sciences; Mathematics; Pharmacy; Physics; Psychology)

Further Information: 17 Teaching Hospitals

History: Founded 1477 by Count Eberhard the Bearded, 1863 the first German University to establish a faculty of Natural Sciences. An autonomous institution financially supported by the State of Baden-Württemberg and under the jurisdiction of its Ministry of Arts and Sciences.

Academic Year: October to September (October-March; April-September); two semesters

Admission Requirements: Secondary school certificate (Reifezeugnis) or equivalent

Fees: National: None, International: None

Main Language(s) of Instruction: German, English

Accrediting Agency: Accreditation, Certification and Quality Assurance Institute (ACQUIN)

Degrees and Diplomas: *Bachelor's Degree*; *Kirchliche Abschlussprüfung*: **Protestant Theology.** *Lizentiat*: **Catholic Theology.** *Magister*: **Catholic Theology; Protestant Theology.** *Diplom (Univ)*: **Catholic Theology; Protestant Theology.** *Master*: **Accountancy; Adult Education; American Studies; Anthropology; Archaeology; Art History; Asian Studies; Behavioural Sciences; Biochemistry; Biological and Life Sciences; Biology; Biomedical Engineering; Cell Biology; Chemistry; Chinese; Classical Languages; Cognitive Sciences; Comparative Politics; Computer Science; Continuing Education; Cultural Studies; Earth Sciences; East Asian Studies; Eastern European Studies; Ecology; Economics; Educational Psychology; Educational Research; English; English Studies; Environmental Studies; Ethnology; European Studies; Finance; Foreign Languages Education; French Studies; Geography; Geography (Human); German; Germanic Studies; Greek (Classical); History; International Business; International Economics; International Studies; Islamic Theology; Japanese; Jewish Studies; Korean; Latin; Law; Linguistics; Literature; Management; Mathematics; Media Studies; Medical Technology; Medieval Studies; Middle Eastern Studies; Molecular Biology; Multimedia; Music; Nanotechnology; Natural Sciences; Neurosciences; Nordic Studies; Peace and Disarmament; Pharmacy; Philology; Philosophy; Physics; Political Sciences; Psychology; Radiology; Romance Languages; Scandinavian Languages; Slavic Languages; Social Sciences; Social Work;**

Sociology; Speech Studies; Sports; Sports Management. *PhD*: **Archaeology; Behavioural Sciences; Biochemistry; Biological and Life Sciences; Biology; Business Administration; Catholic Theology; Chemistry; Cognitive Sciences; Computer Science; Cultural Studies; Ecology; Education; Environmental Studies; Geography; Geology; History; Law; Mathematics; Medicine; Pharmacy; Philosophy; Physics; Political Sciences; Prehistory; Protestant Theology; Psychology; Sociology; Sports.** *Habilitation*: **Behavioural Sciences; Business Administration; Catholic Theology; Mathematics; Natural Sciences; Philosophy; Protestant Theology; Social Sciences.** Also Teacher Training Degree (Lehramt); Staatsexam in Medicine, Pharmacy, Law, Dentistry; Theologische Hauptprüfung in Catholic Theology

Student Services: Academic Counselling, Canteen, Careers Guidance, Cultural Activities, Facilities for disabled people, Foreign Studies Centre, Health Services, IT Centre, Language Laboratory, Library, Nursery Care, Residential Facilities, Social Counselling, Sports Facilities, eLibrary

Academic Staff *2014-2015*: Total 4,000

STAFF WITH DOCTORATE: Total 450

Student Numbers *2014-2015*: Total: c. 28,500

Last Updated: 29/01/15

UNIVERSITY OF VECHTA

Universität Vechta

Postfach 15 53, Driverstraße 22, 49364 Vechta

Tel: +49(4441) 15-0

Fax: +49(4441) 15-444

EMail: info@uni-vechta.de

Website: http://www.uni-vechta.de

President: Marianne Assenmacher

Tel: +49(4441) 15-270 EMail: praesidentin@uni-vechta.de

Vice-President for Teaching and Academic Programmes: Marion Rieken

International Relations: Judith Peltz, Head, International Office

Tel: +49(4441) 15-613 EMail: judith.peltz@uni-vechta.de

Programme

Art (Fine Arts); **Biology/Chemistry** (Biology; Chemistry); **Design** (Design); **Ecology** (Ecology); **Geography** (Geography); **Landscape Ecology** (Ecology; Landscape Architecture); **Music** (Music)

Institute

Catholic Theology *(IKT)* (Catholic Theology); **Didactics for Mathematics and Applied Sciences** *(IfD)* (Biology; Chemistry; Earth Sciences; Mathematics; Physics); **Gerontology** *(IfG)* (Gerontology; Health Sciences); **Humanities and Cultural Sciences** (English; German; History; Literature); **Social Sciences and Philosophy** *(ISP)* (Cultural Studies; Ethics; Philosophy; Political Sciences; Social Sciences; Sociology); **Social Work, Education and Sports Science** *(ISBS)* (Educational Sciences; Pedagogy; Psychology; Social Work; Sports); **Spatial Analysis and Planning in Areas of Intensive Agriculture** *(ISPA)* (Agriculture; Geography; Rural Planning)

History: Founded 1830 as a School for Teacher Training, became a College after World War II, and branch of the University of Osnabrück 1973. Acquired present status and title 2010.

Academic Year: October to July (October-February; April-July)

Admission Requirements: Secondary school certificate (Reifezeugnis) or equivalent

Fees: None

Main Language(s) of Instruction: German

Accrediting Agency: Zentrale Evaluations- und Akkreditierungsagentur (ZEvA)

Degrees and Diplomas: *Bachelor's Degree*; *Master*: **Art Education; Cultural Studies; Education; Educational Sciences; Foreign Languages Education; Geography; Gerontology; Humanities and Social Science Education; Mathematics Education; Music; Native Language Education; Physical Education; Primary Education; Religious Education; Science Education; Secondary Education; Social Work.** *PhD*: **Art Education; Biology; Catholic Theology; Design; Education; Educational Psychology; English; Geography; German; Gerontology; History; Mathematics Education; Philosophy; Physical Education; Political Sciences; Psychology; Social Work; Sociology.** *Habilitation*: **Art Education; Design; Educational Psychology; Educational Sciences; English; Geography; German; Gerontology; Mathematics Education; Music Education; Philosophy; Physical Education; Political Sciences; Psychology; Science Education; Sociology.**

Student Services: Academic Counselling, Canteen, Cultural Activities, Facilities for disabled people, Foreign Studies Centre, Library, Social Counselling, Sports Facilities

Student Numbers *2013-2014*: Total 4,047

Last Updated: 01/04/15

UNIVERSITY OF VETERINARY MEDICINE HANOVER

Stiftung Tierärztliche Hochschule Hannover, Foundation

PO Box 711180, Bünteweg 2, 30545 Hannover

Tel: +49(511) 953-6

Fax: +49(511) 953-8050

EMail: info@tiho-hannover.de

Website: http://www.tiho-hannover.de

President: Gerhard Greif (2002-)

Tel: +49(511) 953-8000 EMail: praesident@tiho-hannover.de

Administrative Officer: Maritta Ledwoch

Tel: +49(511) 953-8092 EMail: maritta.ledwoch@tiho-hannover.de

Department

Cell Biology (Cell Biology); **Fish Pathology and Farming** (Fishery; Veterinary Science); **General Radiology and Medical Physics** (Applied Physics; Radiology); **History of Veterinary Medicine and Domestic Animals** (History; Veterinary Science); **Immunology** (Immunology; Veterinary Science)

Institute

Biometry, Epidemiology and Information Processing *(Field Station, Bakum)* (Animal Husbandry; Data Processing; Epidemiology); **Anatomy** (Anatomy); **Animal Breeding and Genetics** (Animal Husbandry; Cattle Breeding; Genetics); **Animal Ecology and Cell Biology** (Cell Biology); **Animal Hygiene, Animal Welfare and Ethology** (Animal Husbandry; Zoology); **Animal Nutrition** (Food Science); **Animal Welfare and Behaviour** (Welfare and Protective Services); **Food Quality and Safety** (Food Technology); **Food Toxicology and Chemical Analysis** (Chemistry; Food Science; Toxicology); **Microbiology** (Microbiology); **Parasitology** (Parasitology); **Pathology** (Pathology); **Pharmacology, Toxicology and Pharmacy** (Pharmacology; Pharmacy; Toxicology); **Physiological Chemistry** (Chemistry; Physiology); **Physiology** (Physiology); **Reproductive Biology** (Embryology and Reproduction Biology); **Terrestrial and Aquatic Wildlife Research** (Wildlife; Zoology); **Virology** (Virology); **Zoology** (Zoology)

Research Centre

Emerging Infections and Zoonoses (Epidemiology; Veterinary Science; Zoology)

Further Information: Affiliated organizations: WHO-Centre, EU-Reference Laboratory for Classical Swine Fever (CSF), Unit for Wildlife Research, Company for Innovative Veterinary Diagnostics (IVD). Animal clinics

History: Founded 1778 as Royal School of Equine Medicine, acquired University status 1887.

Academic Year: October to July (October-February; April-July)

Admission Requirements: Secondary school certificate (Abitur) or equivalent

Fees: 138,90 per semester (Euro)

Main Language(s) of Instruction: German

Accrediting Agency: European Association of Establishments for Veterinary Education (EAEVE)

Degrees and Diplomas: *Bachelor's Degree*; *Master*: **Biology; Biomedicine.** *PhD*: **Biology; Natural Sciences; Neurosciences; Veterinary Science.** Also Staatsexam in Veterinary Science.

Student Services: Academic Counselling, Canteen, Careers Guidance, Cultural Activities, Foreign Studies Centre, Language Laboratory, Library, Social Counselling, Sports Facilities

Publications: TiHo-Gazette

Student Numbers *2013-2014*: Total 2,412
Last Updated: 26/03/15

UNIVERSITY OF WISMAR

Hochschule Wismar

PO Box 1210, Philipp-Müller-Strasse 14, 23952 Wismar
Tel: +49(3841) 753-0
Fax: +49(3841) 753-7383
EMail: rektor@hs-wismar.de
Website: http://www.hs-wismar.de

Rector: Bodo Wiegand-Hoffmeister
Tel: +49(3841) 753-7216 EMail: rektor@hs-wismar.de

Chancellor: Meike Quaas
Tel: +49(3841) 753-7269 EMail: kanzlerin@hs-wismar.de

International Relations: Korinna Stubbe, Head, International Office
Tel: +49(3841) 753-240 EMail: korinna.stubbe@hs-wismar.de

Faculty

Architecture and Design (Architecture; Communication Arts; Design; Industrial Design; Interior Design; Jewellery Art; Regional Planning; Town Planning; Visual Arts); **Business** *(Wismar)* (Business Administration; Business Computing; Commercial Law; Information Technology; Management; Taxation; Transport Management); **Engineering** (Civil Engineering; Computer Science; Electrical Engineering; Environmental Engineering; Marine Engineering; Mechanical Engineering; Multimedia; Production Engineering)

Further Information: Also Malchow and Rostock-Warnemünde campuses

History: Founded 1992.

Academic Year: September to June

Admission Requirements: Abitur, Practical Training

Fees: 50 per semester (Euro)

Main Language(s) of Instruction: German

Degrees and Diplomas: *Bachelor's Degree*; *Diplom (FH)*: **Business Administration; Business Computing; Communication Arts; Design; Management; Media Studies.** *Master*: **Architecture; Building Technologies; Business Administration; Business Computing; Civil Engineering; Commercial Law; Design; Electrical Engineering; Electronic Engineering; Energy Engineering; Environmental Engineering; Health Administration; Information Management; Information Technology; Interior Design; Marine Engineering; Marketing; Mechanical Engineering; Multimedia; Real Estate; Safety Engineering; Sales Techniques; Taxation; Town Planning; Transport Management.**

Student Services: Canteen, Foreign Studies Centre, IT Centre, Language Laboratory, Library, Social Counselling, Sports Facilities

Publications: HS-Magazine

Academic Staff *2014-2015*	**TOTAL**
FULL-TIME	c. **140**
Student Numbers *2014-2015*	
All (Foreign included)	**8,542**
FOREIGN ONLY	**748**

Last Updated: 13/03/15

UNIVERSITY OF WUPPERTAL

Bergische Universität Wuppertal (UW)

Gaussstrasse 20, 42119 Wuppertal
Tel: +49(202) 439-1
Fax: +49(202) 439-2904
EMail: rektor@uni-wuppertal.de; a.kluge@uni-wuppertal.de
Website: http://www.uni-wuppertal.de

Rektor: Lambert T. Koch (2008-)
Tel: +49(202) 439-2223 EMail: rektor@uni-wuppertal.de

Kanzler: Roland Kischkel EMail: kanzler@uni-wuppertal.de

International Relations: Andrea Bieck, Head, International Department
Tel: +49(202) 439-2181 EMail: bieck@uni-wuppertal.de

Faculty

Architecture, Civil Engineering, Mechanical Engineering and Safety Engineering (Architecture; Civil Engineering; Machine Building; Mechanical Engineering; Real Estate; Safety Engineering); **Art and Design** (Fine Arts; Industrial Design); **Business and Economics** *(Schumpeter)* (Business Administration; Commercial Law; Economics); **Electrical, Information and Media Engineering** (Electrical Engineering; Information Technology; Media Studies; Technology); **Human and Social Sciences** (Geochemistry; Pedagogy; Political Sciences; Psychology; Social Sciences; Sociology; Sports; Technology Education); **Humanities** (Catholic Theology; Comparative Literature; English; History; Linguistics; Literature; Music; Music Education; Philology; Philosophy; Protestant Theology); **Mathematics and Natural Sciences** (Biological and Life Sciences; Chemistry; Computer Science; Mathematics; Physics)

School

Education (Education)

History: Founded 1972. Incorporated a branch of Rheinland College of Education, Köln, and Technical College. Acquired present title 1975. An autonomous institution under the jurisdiction of and financially supported by the State of North Rhine-Westphalia.

Academic Year: October to September (October-March; April-September)

Admission Requirements: Secondary school certificate (Reifezeugnis).

Main Language(s) of Instruction: German

Degrees and Diplomas: *Bachelor's Degree*: **Architecture; Biology; Building Technologies; Business and Commerce; Catholic Theology; Chemistry; Civil Engineering; Computer Science; Design; Educational Sciences; Electrical and Electronic Engineering; English; Fine Arts; French; Geography; German; Health Administration; History; Industrial Design; Information Technology; Latin; Linguistics; Mathematics; Music; Painting and Drawing; Philosophy; Physics; Political Sciences; Protestant Theology; Psychology; Safety Engineering; Sociology; Spanish; Sports; Transport Economics.** *Diplom (Univ)*: **Food Technology.** *Master*: **Architecture; Bilingual and Bicultural Education; Building Technologies; Business and Commerce; Chemistry; Comparative Literature; Computer Science; Economic and Finance Policy; Economics; Education; Educational Sciences; Electrical and Electronic Engineering; Energy Engineering; English; Family Studies; Finance; Fire Science; German; History; Industrial and Organizational Psychology; Industrial and Production Economics; Industrial Management; Information Technology; International Economics; Management; Marketing; Mathematics; Mechanical Engineering; Philosophy; Physics; Printing and Printmaking; Psychology; Real Estate; Safety Engineering; Social Studies; Sociology; Special Education; Teacher Training.** *PhD*: **Administration; Architecture; Art History; Business and Commerce; Chemistry; Civil Engineering; Classical Languages; Comparative Literature; Computer Engineering; Computer Science; Design; Economics; Educational Sciences; Electrical and Electronic Engineering; Energy Engineering; Finance; Fine Arts; Graphic Arts; Health Administration; History; Information Management; Information Technology; Linguistics; Management; Marketing; Materials Engineering; Mathematics; Mechanical Engineering; Modern Languages; Philosophy; Physics; Political Sciences; Production Engineering; Psychology; Railway Transport; Safety Engineering; Social Sciences; Social Work; Sociology; Sports; Statistics; Technology; Theology; Transport Economics; Transport Management.** *Habilitation*: **Architecture and Planning; Arts and Humanities; Business Administration; Education; Engineering; Fine Arts; Mathematics and Computer Science; Natural Sciences; Religion; Social Sciences; Social Work; Sports; Technology; Transport Economics.**

Student Services: Academic Counselling, Canteen, Careers Guidance, Cultural Activities, Facilities for disabled people, Foreign Studies Centre, IT Centre, Language Laboratory, Library, Nursery Care, Residential Facilities, Social Counselling, Sports Facilities

Publications: BUW OUTPUT; MagazIn

Academic Staff *2014-2015*	MEN	WOMEN	TOTAL
FULL-TIME	–	–	**935**
STAFF WITH DOCTORATE			
FULL-TIME	–	–	c. **251**
Student Numbers *2014-2015*			
All (Foreign included)	9,700	10,450	c. **20,150**
FOREIGN ONLY	–	–	**2,300**

Last Updated: 15/01/15

VALLENDAR UNIVERSITY OF PHILOSOPHY AND THEOLOGY

Philosophisch-Theologische Hochschule Vallendar

Pallottistrasse 3, 56179 Vallendar
Tel: +49(261) 6402-0
Fax: +49(261) 6402-300
EMail: info@pthv.de
Website: http://www.pthv.de

Rector: Paul Rheinbay
Tel: +49(261) 6402-600 EMail: prheinbay@pthv.de

Head of Administration: Michael Zimmermann
Tel: +49(261) 6402-330 EMail: mzimmermann@pthv.de

Faculty

Nursing (Gerontology; Nursing); **Theology** (Ancient Languages; Catholic Theology; Greek (Classical); Latin; Religion; Religious Education; Theology)

History: Founded 1979.

Main Language(s) of Instruction: German

Degrees and Diplomas: *Bachelor's Degree*; *Lizentiat*; *Magister*: **Theology.** *Master*: **Health Education; Nursing.** *PhD*: **Nursing; Theology.** *Habilitation*: **Theology.**

Student Services: Library

Student Numbers *2013-2014*: Total 4,527
Last Updated: 22/03/15

WEIHENSTEPHAN TRIESDORF UNIVERSITY OF APPLIED SCIENCES

Hochschule Weihenstephan-Triesdorf

Am Hofgarten 4, 85354 Freising
Tel: +49(8161) 71-0
Fax: +49(8161) 71-4207
EMail: info@fh-weihenstephan.de
Website: http://www.hswt.de

President: Hermann Heiler
Tel: +49(8161) 71-3339 EMail: praesident@hswt.de

Head of Administration: Johann Schelle
Tel: +49(8161) 71-3341 EMail: kanzler@hswt.de

International Relations: Michaela Ring, Head, International Office
Tel: +49(8161) 71-5778
EMail: michaela.ring@hswt.de; auslandsamt.weihenstephan@hswt.de

Department

Agriculture *(Triesdorf)* (Agriculture; Animal Husbandry; Business Administration; Meat and Poultry; Nutrition); **Agriculture and Food Economy** (Agricultural Economics); **Biotechnology and Bioinformatics** *(Weihenstephan)* (Biotechnology; Computer Science); **Environmental Engineering** *(Triesdorf)* (Environmental Engineering); **Forestry** *(Weihenstephan)* (Forestry); **Horticulture and Food Technology** *(Weihenstephan)* (Food Technology; Horticulture); **Landscape Architecture** *(Weihenstephan)* (Landscape Architecture)

Further Information: Also Triesdorf Campus

History: Founded 1804, acquired present status 1971.

Academic Year: October to September (October-March; March-September)

Admission Requirements: Secondary school certificate, six weeks of relevant practical experience, German language test for foreign students

Fees: 50 per semester (Euro)

Main Language(s) of Instruction: German

Accrediting Agency: Akkreditierungsagentur ACQUIN

Degrees and Diplomas: *Bachelor's Degree*; *Master*: **Agricultural Management; Bioengineering; Biotechnology; Business Administration; Energy Engineering; Forestry; Horticulture; Landscape Architecture; Management; Natural Resources; Regional Planning.** Also MBA in Regional planning and International MBA in Agricultural Management

Student Services: Academic Counselling, Canteen, Careers Guidance, IT Centre, Language Laboratory, Library, Sports Facilities

Student Numbers *2013-2014*: Total 5,928
Last Updated: 19/03/15

WEIMAR BAUHAUS UNIVERSITY

Bauhaus-Universität Weimar

Geschwister-Scholl-Strasse 8, 99421 Weimar
Tel: +49(3643) 58-0
Fax: +49(3643) 58-1120
EMail: info@uni-weimar.de
Website: http://www.uni-weimar.de

Rector: Karl Beucke (2011-)
Tel: +49(3643) 58-1111 EMail: rektor@uni-weimar.de

Chancellor: Horst Henrici
Tel: +49(3643) 58-1211 EMail: kanzler@uni-weimar.de

International Relations: Christian Kästner, Head, International Office
Tel: +49(3643) 58-2364 EMail: christian.kaestner@uni-weimar.de

Faculty

Architecture and Urbanism (Architecture; Town Planning; Urban Studies); **Art and Design** (Art Education; Fine Arts; Graphic Design; Industrial Design; Visual Arts); **Civil Engineering** (Business Administration; Civil Engineering; Computer Engineering; Computer Science; Construction Engineering; Environmental Studies; Management; Materials Engineering; Real Estate; Structural Architecture; Water Science); **Media** (Computer Science; Cultural Studies; Design; Economics; Film; Fine Arts; Information Management; Media Studies)

Institute

Bauhaus Further Education Academy *(WBA)* (Construction Engineering; Management; Town Planning); **International Transfer Centre Environmental Technology** *(KNOTEN WEIMAR)* (Construction Engineering; Environmental Engineering); **Materials Research and Testing** *(MFPA)* (Construction Engineering; Environmental Engineering; Geological Engineering; Materials Engineering)

History: Founded 1860 as Academy of Fine Arts, Applied Arts added 1907, became 'Staatliches Bauhaus Weimar' 1919 and college 1926. Applied Arts detached 1950. Reorganized 1954 and granted full University status. Faculty structure replaced under 1968 reform by series of subject sections. Reorganized 1991/92. Under the jurisdiction of the Ministry of Science and Art. Acquired present name 1995.

Academic Year: October to July (October-March; April-July)

Admission Requirements: Secondary school certificate (Reifezeugnis) or equivalent, and German Language test (DSH)

Fees: None

Main Language(s) of Instruction: German

Degrees and Diplomas: *Bachelor's Degree*: **Architecture; Civil Engineering; Computer Science; Design; Media Studies; Urban Studies.** *Diplom (Univ)*: **Fine Arts.** *Master*: **Architecture; Civil Engineering; Communication Arts; Computer Science; Design; Environmental Engineering; Environmental Management; Environmental Studies; Fine Arts; Industrial Design; Information Management; Mass Communication; Media Studies; Structural Architecture; Urban Studies; Visual Arts; Water Science.** *PhD*: **Communication Arts; Design; Fine Arts; Heritage Preservation; Urban Studies.** *Habilitation*: **Architecture; Civil Engineering; Design; Media Studies.** Also Staastsexam in Art Education

Student Services: Academic Counselling, Canteen, Careers Guidance, Facilities for disabled people, Language Laboratory, Library, Social Counselling, Sports Facilities

Publications: Thesis.Wissenschaftliche Zeitschrift: Architecture, Engineering Design; Verso (International Architectural Theories); Vorlesungsverzeichnis; Zeitung 'Bogen'

Academic Staff *2013-2014*: Total: c. 100

Student Numbers *2013-2014*: Total 4,373

Last Updated: 02/03/15

WESTCOAST UNIVERSITY OF APPLIED SCIENCES

Fachhochschule Westküste (FHW)

Fritz-Thiedemann-Ring 20, 25746 Heide
Tel: +49(481) 8555-0
Fax: +49(481) 8555-101
EMail: info@fh-westkueste.de; poststelle@fh-westkueste.de
Website: http://www.fh-westkueste.de

Präsident: Hanno Kirsch (2003-)
Tel: +49(481) 8555-105
EMail: kirsch@fh-westkueste.de; praesidium@fh-westkueste.de

Chancellor: Rüdiger Günther
Tel: +49(481) 8555-115 EMail: guenther@fh-westkueste.de

International Relations: Michael Engelbrecht
Tel: +49(481) 8555-120 EMail: aaa@fh-westkueste.de

Faculty

Engineering (Automation and Control Engineering; Electrical and Electronic Engineering; Information Technology)

Department

Economics (Accountancy; Business Administration; Business Education; Economics; Finance; Human Resources; Law; Management; Marketing; Taxation; Tourism)

History: Founded 1994.

Admission Requirements: Fachhochschulreife

Main Language(s) of Instruction: German

Degrees and Diplomas: *Bachelor's Degree*: **Business Administration; Commercial Law; Electronic Engineering; Engineering; Environmental Engineering; Industrial and Organizational Psychology; Management; Tourism.** *Master*: **Energy Engineering; Microelectronics; Tourism.**

Student Services: Academic Counselling, Canteen, Foreign Studies Centre, Language Laboratory, Library, Social Counselling, Sports Facilities

Student Numbers *2013-2014*: Total 1,440

Last Updated: 28/01/15

WESTPHALIAN UNIVERSITY OF APPLIED SCIENCES

Westfälische Hochschule (WH)

Neidenburger Strasse 43, 45877 Gelsenkirchen
Tel: +49(209) 9596-0
Fax: +49(209) 9596-445
EMail: info@w-hs.de
Website: http://www.w-hs.de/

Präsident: Bernd Kriegesmann (2008-)
Tel: +49(209) 9596-461 EMail: praesident@w-hs.de

Department

Business Administration (Business Administration); **Business Administration and Computer Engineering** (Business Administration; Business Computing; International Business; Service Trades; Software Engineering); **Commercial Law** (Business Administration; Commercial Law; International Law); **Computer Science and Communication** (Computer Science; Information Technology; Mass Communication); **Electronic Engineering and Applied Natural Sciences** (Electrical Engineering; Energy Engineering; Molecular Biology; Physical Engineering); **Industrial Engineering** (Chemistry; Industrial Engineering); **Machine Building** (Bioengineering; Electronic Engineering; Industrial Engineering); **Machine Building and Facilities Management** (Energy Engineering; Machine Building)

Further Information: Also branches in Bocholt, Recklinghausen, Ahaus

History: Founded 1992 as Fachhochschule Gelsenkirchen. Acquired present title 2012.

Main Language(s) of Instruction: German

Degrees and Diplomas: *Bachelor's Degree*; *Master*. **Business Administration; Business Computing; Commercial Law; Computer Engineering; Computer Science; Electronic Engineering; Energy Engineering; Industrial Engineering; Machine Building; Management; Media Studies; Medical Technology; Molecular Biology; Service Trades.** Also Dual Bachelor's Degree Programmes; Cooperative Degree Programmes: Bachelor in Journalism and Public Relations with the Technical Academy Wuppertal; Master of Business Administration with the Academy of Economic Studies Bucharest (ASE, University of Bucharest); Bachelor in Radiology with the Haus der Technik, Essen.

Student Numbers *2013-2014*: Total 8,263

Last Updated: 28/01/15

WESTPHALIAN WILHELMS UNIVERSITY MÜNSTER

Westfälische Wilhelms-Universität Münster

Schlossplatz 2, 48149 Münster
Tel: +49(251) 83-0
Fax: +49(251) 83-24831
EMail: verwaltung@uni-muenster.de
Website: http://www.uni-muenster.de

Rector: Ursula Nelles
Tel: +49(251) 83-22210 EMail: Rektorin@uni-muenster.de

Chancellor: Matthias Schwarte
Tel: +49(251) 83-22111 EMail: kanzler@uni-muenster.de

International Relations: Anke Kohl, Head, International Office
Tel: +49(251) 83-22227
EMail: anke.kohl@uni-muenster.de;
international.office@uni-muenster.de

Department

Biology (Biology; Biomedicine; Biotechnology); **Chemistry and Pharmacy** (Chemistry; Pharmacy); **Economics** *(Munster)* (Business Administration; Economics); **Education and Social Studies** (Communication Studies; Education; Political Sciences; Sociology); **Geosciences** (Earth Sciences; Ecology; Geography; Geology; Mineralogy; Paleontology); **History/Philosophy** (History; Philosophy); **Law** (Law); **Mathematics and Computer Science** (Mathematics and Computer Science); **Medicine** (Medicine); **Music** (Music); **Philologies** (Philology); **Physics** (Physics); **Protestant Theology** (Protestant Theology); **Psychology, Sport and Exercise Sciences** (Psychology; Sports); **Roman Catholic Theology** (Canon Law; Catholic Theology)

History: Founded 1780 as a University. Became an Academy of Philosophy and Theology 1818. The institution was restored to University status 1902 and received its present title 1907. An autonomous institution financially supported by the State of North Rhine-Westphalia, and under the jurisdiction of its Ministry of Education.

Academic Year: October to September (October-March; April-September)

Admission Requirements: Secondary school certificate (Reifezeugnis) or equivalent

Fees: Tuition, none

Main Language(s) of Instruction: German

Degrees and Diplomas: *Bachelor's Degree*; *Kirchliche Abschlussprüfung*: **Catholic Theology; Protestant Theology.** *Magister*: **Catholic Theology; Protestant Theology.** *Master*: **American Studies; Ancient Civilizations; Ancient Languages; Anthropology; Applied Linguistics; Arabic; Archaeology; Art History; Art Therapy; Biological and Life Sciences; Biology; Biomedicine; Biotechnology; Business Administration; Chemistry; Chinese; Communication Studies; Computer Science; Cultural Studies; Dutch; Earth Sciences; Ecology; Economics; Education; Educational Sciences; English; English Studies; European Studies; Fine Arts; Food Technology; Foreign Languages Education; French; Geography; Geography (Human); Geophysics; German; Germanic Studies; Government; History; Humanities and Social Science Education;**

Industrial Chemistry; Information Technology; Islamic Studies; Islamic Theology; Italian; Latin; Law; Linguistics; Literature; Mathematics; Mathematics Education; Medieval Studies; Modern Languages; Music; Musicology; Pedagogy; Pharmacology; Philosophy; Physics; Political Sciences; Prehistory; Psychology; Religious Education; Romance Languages; Scandinavian Languages; Science Education; Social Sciences; Sociology; Spanish; Sports; Surveying and Mapping. *PhD*: **American Studies; Ancient Civilizations; Ancient Languages; Anthropology; Applied Linguistics; Arabic; Archaeology; Art History; Astronomy and Space Science; Baltic Languages; Biology; Biotechnology; Business Administration; Business Computing; Catholic Theology; Chemistry; Chinese; Classical Languages; Communication Studies; Comparative Literature; Computer Education; Computer Science; Dentistry; Dutch; Earth Sciences; Ecology; Economics; Education; Educational Research; Educational Technology; English; English Studies; Ethnology; European Languages; European Studies; Fine Arts; Folklore; Food Technology; Foreign Languages Education; French; Geography; Geography (Human); Geology; Geophysics; German; Greek (Classical); Hebrew; History; Home Economics; Humanities and Social Science Education; Industrial Chemistry; Islamic Studies; Islamic Theology; Latin; Latin American Studies; Law; Linguistics; Literature; Mathematics; Mathematics Education; Medicine; Mineralogy; Music; Music Education; Musicology; Native Language Education; Orthodox Theology; Paleontology; Pedagogy; Pharmacology; Pharmacy; Philology; Philosophy; Physical Education; Physics; Political Sciences; Portuguese; Prehistory; Protestant Theology; Psychology; Religious Education; Religious Studies; Romance Languages; Russian; Scandinavian Languages; Science Education; Slavic Languages; Social Studies; Sociology; South Asian Studies; Spanish; Sports; Technology; Technology Education; Textile Design.** *Habilitation*: **Biology; Catholic Theology; Chemistry; Earth Sciences; Economics; Education; History; Law; Mathematics and Computer Science; Medicine; Pharmacy; Philology; Philosophy; Physics; Protestant Theology; Psychology; Social Sciences; Sports.** Also Staatsexamen in Medicine, Pharmacy, Law, Dentistry.

Student Services: Academic Counselling, Canteen, Foreign Studies Centre, Language Laboratory, Social Counselling, Sports Facilities

Publications: Forschungsjournal

Academic Staff *2014-2015*	**TOTAL**
FULL-TIME	c. **6,850**
Student Numbers *2013-2014*	
All (Foreign included)	**42,592**
FOREIGN ONLY	**3403**

Last Updated: 26/03/15

WILDAU TECHNICAL UNIVERSITY OF APPLIED SCIENCES

Technische Hochschule Wildau

Hochschulring 1, 15745 Wildau
Tel: +49(3375) 508-300
Fax: +49(3375) 500-324
EMail: ungvari@wi-bw.tfh-wildau.de
Website: http://www.tfh-wildau.de

President: Lászlo Ungvári (1999-)
Tel: +49(3375) 508-101 EMail: laszlo.ungvari@th-wildau.de

Chancellor: Thomas Lehne
Tel: +49(3375) 508-900 EMail: thomas.lehne@th-wildau.de

International Relations: Angelika Schubert, Head of International Office
Tel: +49(3375) 508-197 EMail: angelika.schubert@th-wildau.de

Faculty

Economics, Computer Science and Law (Administration; Business Administration; Business Computing; Law; Management; Marketing); **Engineering and Natural Sciences** (Aeronautical and Aerospace Engineering; Air Transport; Automation and Control Engineering; Bioengineering; Computer Science; Engineering; Industrial Engineering; Industrial Management; Mechanical Engineering; Transport Engineering)

History: Founded 1991.

Main Language(s) of Instruction: German

Degrees and Diplomas: *Bachelor's Degree*; *Master*: **Aeronautical and Aerospace Engineering; Air Transport; Bioengineering; Business Administration; Business Computing; Computer Science; Law; Management; Mechanical Engineering; Physics; Transport Management.**

Student Services: Academic Counselling, Canteen, Careers Guidance, Facilities for disabled people, Social Counselling, Sports Facilities

Publications: Wissenschaftlich Beiträge der TFH Wildau

Student Numbers *2013-2014*: Total 4,209
Last Updated: 26/03/15

WORMS UNIVERSITY OF APPLIED SCIENCES

Hochschule Worms (UAS)

Erenburger Strasse 19, 67549 Worms
Tel: +49(6241) 509-0
Fax: +49(6241) 509-280
EMail: kontakt@hs-worms.de
Website: http://www.fh-worms.de

President: Jens Hermsdorf (2009-)
EMail: praesident@hs-worms.de

Chancellor: Christiane Müller EMail: chmueller@hs-worms.de

International Relations: Joachim Mayer, Director International Center Tel: +49(6241) 509-266 EMail: mayer@hs-worms.de

Faculty

Business Administration (Business Administration; International Business; Management; Taxation; Transport Management); **Computer Science** (Business Computing; Computer Science); **Tourism and Travel Management** (Air Transport; International Business; Management; Tourism)

History: Created 1977 as Division Ludwigshafen/Worms of the University of Applied Sciences Rhineland-Palatinate from former Teacher Training College of Worms. Acquired current title and status 1996.

Academic Year: March to September

Admission Requirements: Secondary school certificate.

Fees: None

Main Language(s) of Instruction: German, English

Degrees and Diplomas: *Bachelor's Degree*: **Air Transport; Business Administration; Business Computing; Computer Science; International Business; Management; Retailing and Wholesaling; Taxation.** *Master*: **Business Computing; Computer Science; International Business; Management; Taxation; Tourism.**

Student Services: Academic Counselling, Canteen, Careers Guidance, Cultural Activities, Facilities for disabled people, Foreign Studies Centre, Language Laboratory, Library, Social Counselling, Sports Facilities

Academic Staff *2013-2014*: Total: c. 100
Student Numbers *2013-2014*: Total 3,186
Last Updated: 28/01/15

WÜRZBURG-SCHWEINFURT UNIVERSITY OF APPLIED SCIENCES

Fachhochschule Würzburg-Schweinfurt (FHWS)

Münzstrasse 12, 97070 Würzburg
Tel: +49(931) 3511-0
Fax: +49(931) 3511-6994
EMail: praesidialamt-wue@fhws.de
Website: http://www.fh-wuerzburg.de

President: Robert Grebner (2012-)
Tel: +49(931) 3511-102 EMail: praesident@fhws.de

Chancellor: Andra Wunder
Tel: +49(931) 3511-104
EMail: kanzlerin@fh-wuerzburg.de; andra.wunder@fhws.de

International Relations: Daniel Wimmer, Head, International Services Tel: +49(931) 3511-8173 EMail: daniel.wimmer@fhws.de

Faculty

Applied Natural Sciences and Humanities (Journalism; Mass Communication; Mathematics; Natural Sciences; Translation and Interpretation); **Applied Social Sciences** *(Würzburg)* (Art Therapy; Health Administration; Health Sciences; Media Studies; Social Work); **Architecture and Civil Engineering** *(Würzburg)* (Architecture; Civil Engineering); **Business Administration** (Business Administration; Management; Media Studies); **Computer Science and Business Computing** *(Würzburg)* (Business Computing; Computer Science; Information Technology); **Design** (Design); **Electrical Engineering** *(Schweinfurt)* (Electrical Engineering); **Industrial Engineering** *(Schweinfurt)* (Industrial Engineering); **Mechanical Engineering** *(Schweinfurt)* (Mechanical Engineering); **Plastic Technology, Surveying and Mapping** *(Würzburg)* (Polymer and Plastics Technology; Surveying and Mapping)

Further Information: Also Campus in Schweinfurt

History: Founded 1971.

Main Language(s) of Instruction: German

Degrees and Diplomas: *Bachelor's Degree*; *Master*: **Architecture and Planning; Art Therapy; Communication Studies; Computer Engineering; Construction Engineering; Design; Electrical Engineering; Electronic Engineering; Engineering Management; Health Administration; Industrial Engineering; Information Sciences; Information Technology; International Business; Journalism; Marketing; Mass Communication; Media Studies; Social Work; Translation and Interpretation.** Some programmes are offered in English: Dual Bachelor's Degree Porgrammes in Business Administration and Engineering, Transport Management, International Business; Master's Degree in International Business.

Student Services: Careers Guidance, IT Centre, Library, Residential Facilities

Academic Staff *2014-2015*: Total: c. 190

Student Numbers *2014-2015*: Total: c. 9,000

Last Updated: 28/01/15

ZITTAU/GÖRLICH UNIVERSITY OF APPLIED SCIENCES

Hochschule Zittau/Görlitz (FH)

Theodor-Körner-Allee 16, 02763 Zittau

Tel: +49(3583) 61-0

Fax: +49(3583) 510626

EMail: info@hszg.de

Website: http://www.hszg.de/

Rector: Friedrich Albrecht
Tel: +49(3583) 61-1400 EMail: rektor@hszg.de

Chancellor: Karin Hollstein
Tel: +49(3583) 61-1405
EMail: kanzlerin@hszg.de

International Relations: Stefan Kühne, Head, International Office
Tel: +49(3583) 61-1511
EMail: s.kuehne@hszg.de

Faculty

Economics, Business Studies and Industrial Engineering (Business Administration; Economics; Industrial Engineering; International Business; Management; Real Estate); **Electrical Engineering and Computer Sciences** (Automation and Control Engineering; Business Administration; Business Computing; Computer Science; Electrical Engineering; Electronic Engineering; Energy Engineering; Information Management; Mechanical Engineering); **Managemental and Cultural Studies** (Cultural Studies; Czech; English; French; German; Health Administration; Management; Polish; Russian; Spanish; Tourism; Translation and Interpretation); **Mathematics and Natural Sciences** (Biotechnology; Chemistry; Ecology; Energy Engineering; Environmental Management; Mathematics; Molecular Biology); **Mechanical Engineering** (Energy Engineering; Environmental Engineering; Machine Building; Mechanical Engineering; Production Engineering); **Social Sciences** (Gerontology; Pedagogy; Preschool Education; Psychology; Social Sciences; Social Studies; Social Work; Special Education)

Further Information: Also Görlitz campus

History: Founded 1992.

Main Language(s) of Instruction: German

Degrees and Diplomas: *Bachelor's Degree*; *Diplom (FH)*: **Automation and Control Engineering; Business Administration; Business Computing; Construction Engineering; Electrical Engineering; Electronic Engineering; Energy Engineering; Engineering; Environmental Engineering; Mechanical Engineering; Nuclear Engineering; Production Engineering; Real Estate; Telecommunications Engineering.** *Master*: **Biotechnology; Business Administration; Chemistry; Cultural Studies; Ecology; Electrical Engineering; Electronic Engineering; Energy Engineering; Gerontology; Health Administration; International Business; Management; Mechanical Engineering; Social Work; Tourism; Translation and Interpretation.** Also Dual Degrees.

Student Services: IT Centre, Residential Facilities, Sports Facilities

Student Numbers *2013-2014*: Total 3,374

Last Updated: 13/03/15

PRIVATE INSTITUTIONS

AKAD UNIVERSITY OF APPLIED SCIENCES

AKAD University (AKAD)

Maybachstraße 18-20, 70469 Stuttgart

Tel: +49(711) 81495-0

Fax: +49(711) 81495-999

EMail: beratung@akad.de

Website: https://www.akad.de/

Chief Executive Officer: Ronny Fürst

Programme

Business Administration (Business Administration); **Business Computing** (Business Computing); **Business Engineering** (Business Administration; Engineering); **Engineering** (Electronic Engineering; Engineering; Industrial Engineering; Machine Building); **Financial Services Management** (Finance; Management); **International Business Communication** (Communication Studies; International Business)

Further Information: 32 examination centers accross the country

History: Founded 1959. Acquired present title 2014 after regrouping the activities of the former AKAD Hochschule Stuttgart, AKAD Hochschule Pinneberg and AKAD Hochschule Leipzig to become fully Integrated distance education institution with headquarters in Stuttgart.

Main Language(s) of Instruction: German

Accrediting Agency: Wissenschaftsrat; ACQUIN; ZeVA; Zentralstelle für Fernunterricht (ZFU)

Degrees and Diplomas: *Bachelor's Degree*; *Master*: **Engineering Management; Industrial Engineering; Information Technology; Management.** Also Hochschulzertifikate in Economics, Engineering and Management

Academic Staff *2014-2015*: Total: c. 400

Student Numbers *2014-2015*: Total: c. 6,000

Distance students, 8800.

Last Updated: 20/01/15

AKAD UNIVERSITY OF APPLIED SCIENCES LAHR

Wissenschaftliche Hochschule Lahr (WHL)

Hohbergweg 15-17, 77933 Lahr

Tel: +49(7821) 9238-50

Fax: +49(7821) 9238-52

EMail: info@whl-lahr.de

Website: http://www.whl-lahr.de

Rektor: Martin Reckenfelderbäumer
EMail: martin.reckenfelderbaeumer@whl-lahr.de

Graduate School
Business and Economics (Banking; Behavioural Sciences; Business Administration; Business Computing; Economics; Engineering; Finance; Health Administration; Industrial Engineering; Insurance; International Business; Management; Marketing)

History: Founded 1996.

Main Language(s) of Instruction: German

Degrees and Diplomas: *Bachelor's Degree*; *Master*: **Industrial Engineering; Information Technology; Management.**

Student Numbers *2013-2014*: Total 367
Last Updated: 09/03/15

ALANUS UNIVERSITY OF ARTS AND SOCIAL SCIENCES

Alanus Hochschule für Kunst und Gesellschaft
Villestraße 3, 53347 Alfter bei Bonn
Tel: +49(2222) 9321-0
Fax: +49(2222) 9321-21
EMail: info@alanus.edu
Website: http://www.alanus.edu

Rektor: Marcelo da Veiga
Tel: +49(2222) 9321-28
EMail: marcelo.daveiga@alanus.edu; rektor@alanus.edu

Kanzler: Dirk Vianden
Tel: +49(2222) 9321-1911 EMail: dirk.vianden@alanus.edu

Programme
Architecture (Architecture); **Art in Dialogue** (Fine Arts; Performing Arts; Visual Arts); **Art Teacher Training/Education** (Art Education; Teacher Training); **Art Therapy** (Art Therapy); **Business Administration** (Business Administration); **Chilhood Education** (Preschool Education); **Curative Education** (Health Education; Rehabilitation and Therapy; Social Work); **Eurythmics** (Dance; Performing Arts); **Painting** (Painting and Drawing); **Sculpture** (Sculpture); **Voice/Drama** (Singing; Theatre)

Institute
Studium Generale (Aesthetics; Anthropology; Art History; Ethics; Natural Sciences; Philosophy)

History: Founded 1973. Acquired present status 2002.

Admission Requirements: Allgemeine Hochschulreife (Abitur)

Fees: (Euros): 260 per month

Main Language(s) of Instruction: German

Degrees and Diplomas: *Bachelor's Degree*: **Architecture; Art Education; Art Therapy; Business Administration; Dance; Painting and Drawing; Preschool Education; Sculpture.** *Diplom (FH)*: **Theatre.** *Master*: **Architecture; Art Education; Art Therapy; Business Administration; Dance; Educational Research; Health Education; Painting and Drawing; Sculpture.** *PhD*: **Education.**

Student Numbers *2013-2014*: Total 993
Last Updated: 22/01/15

APOLLON UNIVERSITY OF HEALTH MANAGEMENT

APOLLON Hochschule der Gesundheitswirtschaft
Universitätsallee 18, 28359 Bremen
Tel: +49(421) 378266-0
Fax: +49(421) 378266-190
EMail: info@apollon-hochschule.de
Website: http://www.apollon-hochschule.de

Präsident: Bernd Kümmel

Kanzler: Michael Timm

Division
Health Economics (Economics; Health Administration; Health Sciences); **Prevention and Health Promotion** (Health Sciences; Information Technology; Marketing; Social and Preventive Medicine); **Technology and Logistics** (Health Administration; Health Sciences; Information Technology)

History: Founded 2005. A distance education institution.

Main Language(s) of Instruction: German

Accrediting Agency: FIBAA (Foundation for International Business Administration Accreditation)

Degrees and Diplomas: *Bachelor's Degree*; *Master*: **Economics; Health Administration; Management.** Bachelor and Master's Degrees are Distance Education Programmes; Also Hochschulzertifikatskurse (university certificate courses), 1 week-8 months depending on field of studies.

Student Numbers *2013-2014*: Total 1,690
Last Updated: 23/01/15

BBW UNIVERSITY

bbw Hochschule
Leibnizstraße 11-13, 10625 Berlin-Karlshorst
Tel: +49(30) 31990-950
Fax: +49(30) 31990-9555
EMail: info@bbw-hochschule.de
Website: http://www.bbw-hochschule.de

Rector: Gerhard Hörber

Chancellor: Jürgen Weiss

Programme
Business Administration (MBA) *(Graduate)* (Business Administration); **Business Communication** (Communication Studies); **Business Computing** (Business Computing); **Economics** *(Graduate)* (Economics); **Economics** (Economics); **Engineering** (Automation and Control Engineering; Electrical Engineering; Engineering; Mechanical Engineering); **Industrial Engineering** (Industrial Engineering); **Industrial Engineering** (Industrial Engineering); **Mechanical Engineering** (Mechanical Engineering)

History: Founded 2007.

Main Language(s) of Instruction: German

Degrees and Diplomas: *Bachelor's Degree*; *Master*: **Business Administration; Health Administration; Management; Tourism; Transport Management.**

Student Services: Careers Guidance

Student Numbers *2014-2015*: Total: c. 1,200
Last Updated: 01/04/15

BERLIN PROTESTANT UNIVERSITY OF APPLIED SCIENCES

Evangelische Hochschule Berlin (EHB)
Postfach 37 02 55, Teltower Damm 118-122, 14167 Berlin
Tel: +49(30) 84582-0
Fax: +49(30) 84582-450
EMail: info@evfh-berlin.de
Website: http://www.evfh-berlin.de

Rector: Angelika Thol-Hauke (2007-)
Tel: +49(30) 84582-100 EMail: thol-hauke@eh-berlin.de

Chancellor: Helmut Sankowski
Tel: +49(30) 84582-400 EMail: sankowsky@eh-berlin.de

International Relations: Dagmar Preiss-Allesch, International Officer Tel: +49(30) 84582-135 EMail: preiss-allesch@eh-berlin.de

Programme
Childhood Education and Elementary Education (Preschool Education; Primary Education); **Health Care and Care Management** (Health Administration; Health Sciences); **Management, Education and Diversity** *(Master)* (Education; Management); **Midwifery** (Midwifery); **Nursing** (Nursing); **Protestant Religion Education** (Protestant Theology; Religious Education); **Social Work** (Social Work); **Social Work** *(Master)* (Social Work)

History: Founded 1971. Acquired present title 2010.

Main Language(s) of Instruction: German

Degrees and Diplomas: *Bachelor's Degree*: **Health Administration; Midwifery; Nursing; Preschool Education; Primary Education; Religious Education; Social Work.** *Master*: **Education; Management; Social Work.**

Student Services: IT Centre, Library

Student Numbers *2013-2014*: Total 1,323
Last Updated: 26/01/15

BERLIN TECHNICAL UNIVERSITY OF ARTS

Berliner Technische Kunsthochschule - Hochschule für Gestaltung (FH)

Bernburger Str. 24-25, 10963 Berlin
Tel: +49(30) 2535-8698
Fax: +49(30) 2694-9605
EMail: info@btk-fh.de; berlin@btk-fh.de
Website: http://www.btk-fh.de

Bergmoser: Walter Leupold EMail: w.bergmoser@btk-fh.de

Vice-rector studies: Thomas Noller EMail: t.noller@btk-fh.de

International Relations: Johanna Kunze
Tel: +49(30) 338-539-532 EMail: international@btk-fh.de

Programme

Basics of Communication Design; **Information and Interface Design** (Computer Science; Design; Graphic Design; Information Sciences); **Visual and Motion Design** (Communication Arts; Design; Film; Photography; Visual Arts)

History: Founded 2006.

Main Language(s) of Instruction: German

Degrees and Diplomas: *Bachelor's Degree*; *Master*: **Design; Media Studies.**

Student Numbers *2013-2014*: Total 416
Last Updated: 03/04/15

BERLIN UNIVERSITY OF TECHNOLOGY

Technische Universität Berlin

Strasse des 17. Juni 135, 10623 Berlin
Tel: +49(30) 3140
Fax: +49(30) 3142-3222
EMail: k@tu-berlin.de; pressestelle@tu-berlin.de
Website: http://www.tu-berlin.de

President: Christian Thomsen (2014-)
Tel: +49(30) 314-0

Chancellor: Ulrike Gutheil Tel: +49(30) 3142-2500

International Relations: Carola Beckmeier, Head, International Office Tel: +49(30) 314-24799
EMail: auslandsamt@tu-berlin.de

Faculty

Economics and Management (Business Administration; Economics; Energy Engineering; Health Sciences; Law; Management; Technology; Transport Management); **Electrical Engineering and Computer Science** (Automation and Control Engineering; Computer Engineering; Computer Science; Electrical Engineering; Energy Engineering; Microelectronics; Software Engineering; Telecommunications Engineering); **Humanities** (Communication Arts; French; Gender Studies; History; Literature; Pedagogy; Philosophy; Social Sciences; Vocational Education); **Mathematics and Natural Sciences** (Astronomy and Space Science; Chemistry; Mathematics and Computer Science; Optics; Physics; Solid State Physics); **Mechanical Engineering and Transport System** (Aeronautical and Aerospace Engineering; Astronomy and Space Science; Engineering Drawing and Design; Management; Mechanics; Psychology; Transport and Communications); **Planning, Building, Environment** (Architectural and Environmental Design; Ecology; Environmental Management; Heritage Preservation; Landscape Architecture; Regional Planning; Sociology; Town Planning; Urban Studies); **Process Sciences** (Biotechnology; Energy Engineering; Environmental Engineering; Food Science; Food Technology; Materials Engineering; Sound Engineering (Acoustics))

History: Founded 1799 as Bauakademie (Building Academy), became Technische Hoschschule 1879. The Bergakademie (Mining Academy), founded 1770, was incorporated in 1916. Reopened as Technische Universität in 1946. Reorganized 1969 and faculties replaced by series of Fachbereiche (departments). The structural reform decided by the Berlin University of Technology came into force officially in October 1993. As part of this reform, the number of departments was reduced from 22 to 15, and again reformed, reducing the number of faculties to 8.

Academic Year: October to September (October-March; April-September)

Admission Requirements: Secondary school certificate (Reifezeugnis) or equivalent

Fees: None

Main Language(s) of Instruction: German

Degrees and Diplomas: *Bachelor's Degree*; *Master*: **Aeronautical and Aerospace Engineering; Architectural Restoration; Architecture; Art History; Automotive Engineering; Biomedical Engineering; Biotechnology; Brewing; Chemical Engineering; Chemistry; Civil Engineering; Communication Studies; Computer Engineering; Computer Science; Construction Engineering; Design; Educational Sciences; Electrical Engineering; Energy Engineering; Engineering; Engineering Management; Environmental Engineering; Environmental Management; Environmental Studies; Food Science; Food Technology; Foreign Languages Education; Geological Engineering; Geology; Industrial and Production Economics; Industrial Engineering; Industrial Management; Information Management; Information Technology; Landscape Architecture; Management; Marine Engineering; Materials Engineering; Mathematics; Mechanical Engineering; Media Studies; Modern Languages; Naval Architecture; Neurosciences; Nutrition; Philosophy; Physics; Polymer and Plastics Technology; Production Engineering; Regional Planning; Sociology; Statistics; Technology; Telecommunications Engineering; Town Planning; Transport and Communications; Urban Studies; Vocational Education.** *PhD*: **Architecture and Planning; Arts and Humanities; Business Administration; Civil Engineering; Computer Science; Ecology; Economics; Education; Electronic Engineering; Engineering; Engineering Management; Landscape Architecture; Mathematics; Measurement and Precision Engineering; Mechanical Engineering; Natural Sciences; Regional Planning; Sociology; Town Planning; Transport Engineering.** *Habilitation*: **Architecture and Planning; Arts and Humanities; Business Administration; Chemistry; Civil Engineering; Computer Science; Ecology; Economics; Education; Electronic Engineering; Engineering; Engineering Management; Geology; Landscape Architecture; Mathematics; Measurement and Precision Engineering; Mechanical Engineering; Natural Sciences; Physics; Regional Studies; Sociology; Town Planning; Transport Engineering.** Also Staatsexam in Food Technology

Student Services: Academic Counselling, Canteen, Cultural Activities, Facilities for disabled people, Health Services, Nursery Care, Social Counselling, Sports Facilities

Publications: Vorlesungsverzeichnis der Technischen Universität Berlin

Student Numbers *2013-2014*: Total 31,013
Last Updated: 27/03/15

BRAND ACADEMY - UNIVERSITY OF APPLIED ARTS

Brand Academy - Hochschule für Design und Kommunikation (BA)

Rainvilleterrasse 4, 22765 Hamburg
Tel: +49(40) 380-893-56-0
Fax: +49(40) 380-893-56-20
EMail: info@brand-acad.com
Website: http://www.brand-acad.com/

President: Shan Fan

Chancellor: Stefan Haarhaus

International Relations: Katja Reinhardt, Head of BA International College
Tel: +49(40) 380-893-56-11
EMail: katja.reinhardt@brand-acad.com

Programme

Brand Design - Communications Design (Communication Arts); **Brand Design - Digital Design** (Design); **Brand Management** (Management); **International Brand Communication** *(Graduate)* (Mass Communication); **International Brand Management** *(Graduate)* (Management)

History: Founded 2010-

Main Language(s) of Instruction: German

Degrees and Diplomas: *Bachelor's Degree*; *Master*: **Management; Mass Communication.**

Student Numbers *2013-2014*: Total 102
Last Updated: 07/04/15

BSP BUSINESS SCHOOL BERLIN POTSDAM

BSP Business School Berlin - Hochschule für Management (BSP)
Calandrellistraße 1-9, D-12247 Berlin
Tel: +49(30) 7668- 3753-10
Fax: +49(30) 7668- 3753-19
EMail: info@businessschool-berlin.de
Website: http://www.businessschool-berlin-potsdam.de/

Rector: Thomas Thiessen
Tel: +49(30) 7668-3753-10
EMail: thomas.thiessen@businessschool-berlin.de

International Relations: Alexander Trefz, Head of International Office
Tel: +49(40) 3612-26-464
EMail: alexander.trefz@businessschool-berlin.de

Faculty

Business and Management (Business Administration; Industrial and Organizational Psychology; Management; Mass Communication)

History: Founded 2009.

Main Language(s) of Instruction: German

Degrees and Diplomas: *Bachelor's Degree*; *Master*: **Business Administration; Industrial and Organizational Psychology; Psychology.**

Student Services: Careers Guidance, IT Centre, Library

Student Numbers *2013-2014*: Total 383
Last Updated: 07/04/15

BUCERIUS LAW SCHOOL

Bucerius Law School, Hochschule für Rechtswissenschaft (BLS)
Jungiusstrasse 6, 20355 Hamburg
Tel: +49(40) 30706-0
Fax: +49(40) 30706-145
EMail: info@law-school.de
Website: http://www.law-school.de

Präsident: Karsten Thorn (2014-)
Tel: +49(40) 30706-100 EMail: praesident@law-school.de

CEO: Hariolf Wenzler
Tel: +49(40) 30706-100 EMail: hariolf.wenzler@law-school.de

International Relations: Kasia Kwietniewska, Director, International Exchange
Tel: +49(40) 30706-109 EMail: kasia.kwietniewska@law-school.de

Area

Civil Law (Civil Law); **Criminal Law** (Criminal Law); **Fundamentals of Law** (Law); **Law and Business** *(Graduate)* (Business Administration; Law); **Public Law** (Public Law); **Tax Law** (Fiscal Law)

Institute

Corporate Law (Commercial Law; Law); **Foundation Law** (Law)

Centre

Transnational IP, Media and Technology Law and Policy (Information Technology; Law; Media Studies)

History: Founded 2000.

Academic Year: End of Sept. to mid-July. Only the Fall semester is open for international students (September - December).

Admission Requirements: Secondary school certificate (Abitur)

Fees: 12,000 per annum (only for LLB students) (Euro)

Main Language(s) of Instruction: German

Accrediting Agency: German Council of Science and Humanties

Degrees and Diplomas: *Bachelor's Degree*: **Law.** *Master*: **Business Administration; Law.** *PhD*: **Law.** *Habilitation*: **Law.** Also State Examination (Bar exam) in Law

Student Services: Academic Counselling, Canteen, Careers Guidance, Facilities for disabled people, Foreign Studies Centre, IT Centre, Language Laboratory, Library, Sports Facilities

Publications: Schriftenreihe der Bucerius Law School; Schriftenreihe des Instituts für Stiftungsrechts; Schriftenreihe zu Kunst und Recht

Academic Staff *2014-2015*: Total: c. 170
Student Numbers *2014-2015*: Total 645
Last Updated: 07/07/15

BUSINESS AND INFORMATION TECHNOLOGY SCHOOL ISERLOHN (BITS)

Reiterweg 26b, 58636 Iserlohn
Tel: +49(2371) 776-500
Fax: +49(2371) 776-503
EMail: info@bits-iserlohn.de
Website: http://www.bits-iserlohn.de

Rector: Stefan Stein
Tel: +49(2371) 776-554 EMail: stefan.stein@bits-iserlohn.de

Director and CEO: Carlos Bertrán
Tel: +49(2371) 776-140
EMail: carlos.bertran@laureate-germany.de

International Relations: Heike Ramin, Head, International Office
Tel: +49(2371) 776-571
EMail: heike.ramin@bits-iserlohn.de; studyabroad@bits-iserlohn.de

Faculty

Business and Management (Business Administration; Finance; Management; Marketing); **Business Psychology** (Business Administration; Human Resources; Management; Marketing; Psychology; Staff Development); **International Service Industries** (Management; Sports Management); **Media and Communication** (Communication Studies; Journalism; Management; Media Studies)

Further Information: Also offices in Berlin and Hamburg

History: Founded 2000.

Academic Year: March to July; October to February

Admission Requirements: Abitur, Fachabitur

Fees: 3,600 per semester; Business Journalism: 3,900 (Euro)

Main Language(s) of Instruction: German, English

Accrediting Agency: Wissenschaftsrat; Foundation for International Business Administration Accreditation (FIBAA)

Degrees and Diplomas: *Bachelor's Degree*: **Business Administration; Communication Studies; Industrial and Organizational Psychology; Industrial Management; Journalism; Management; Mass Communication; Media Studies; Sports Management.** *Master*: **Finance; Industrial and Organizational Psychology; Management; Marketing; Mass Communication; Public Relations; Sports Management.**

Student Services: Academic Counselling, Canteen, Careers Guidance, Facilities for disabled people, Language Laboratory, Library, Sports Facilities

Student Numbers *2013-2014*: Total 1,614
Last Updated: 23/01/15

CATHOLIC UNIVERSITY FOR APPLIED SCIENCES BERLIN (KHSB)

Katholischen Hochschule für Sozialwesen Berlin
Köpenicker Allee 39-57, 10318 Berlin
Tel: +49(30) 5010100
Fax: +49(30) 501010-88
EMail: sekretariat-praesident@KHSB-Berlin.de
Website: http://www.khsb-berlin.de

Präsident: Ralf-Bruno Zimmermann
Tel: +49(30) 501010-13
EMail: Ralf-Bruno.Zimmermann@KHSB-Berlin.de

Kanzler: Martin Wrzesinski
Tel: +49(30) 501010-14
EMail: verwaltung@khsb-berlin.de; wrzesinski@khsb-berlin.de

Programme
Clinical Social Work *(Postgraduate)* (Public Health; Social Work); **Education** *(Bildung und Erziehung)* (Education; Pedagogy; Preschool Education); **Religious Education** (Religious Education); **Social Gerontology** *(Soziale Gerontologie)* (Gerontology; Public Health; Social Work); **Social Work** (Social Work); **Social Work as a Human Rights Profession** *(Postgraduate)* (Human Rights; Social Work); **Special Education** *(Heilpädagogik)* (Education of the Handicapped; Social Work)

History: Founded 1991.

Main Language(s) of Instruction: German

Degrees and Diplomas: *Bachelor's Degree*: **Education of the Handicapped; Preschool Education; Religious Education; Social Work.** *Master*: **Education of the Handicapped; Social Work.**

Student Services: Canteen, Facilities for disabled people, Library

Publications: Einblicke

Student Numbers *2013-2014*: Total 1,436
Last Updated: 04/02/15

CATHOLIC UNIVERSITY OF APPLIED SCIENCES IN FREIBURG

Katholische Hochschule Freiburg
Karlstrasse 63, 79104 Freiburg
Tel: +49(761) 200-476
Fax: +49(761) 200-444
EMail: rektorat@kfh-freiburg.de
Website: http://www.kh-freiburg.de

Rector: Edgar Kösler
Tel: +49(761) 200-1502 EMail: rektorat@kh-freiburg.de

Kanzler: Martin Kraft
Tel: +49(761) 200-1504 EMail: kanzler@kh-freiburg.de

International Relations: Naomi Hiroe-Helbing
Tel: +49(761) 200-1506 EMail: international@kh-freiburg.de

Programme
Clinical Curative Education *(Graduate)* (Health Sciences); **Management of Education Institutions** (Educational Administration); **Nursing** (Nursing); **Nursing Education** (Health Education; Nursing); **Service Development/Development of social and health services** *(Graduate)* (Health Administration; Welfare and Protective Services); **Social Work** *(Master)* (Social Work); **Special/ Inclusive Education** (Special Education); **Vocational Education in Health Care** (Health Sciences)

History: Founded 1918, acquired present status 1971.

Academic Year: September to August

Admission Requirements: Academic Standard required for University Entrance

Fees: 280 per semester (Euro)

Main Language(s) of Instruction: German

Degrees and Diplomas: *Bachelor's Degree*; *Master*: **Ethics; Health Administration; Health Education; Health Sciences; Leadership; Management; Social Sciences; Welfare and Protective Services.**

Student Services: IT Centre, Library, Nursery Care

Student Numbers *2013-2014*: Total 1,797
Last Updated: 19/03/15

CATHOLIC UNIVERSITY OF APPLIED SCIENCES IN MAINZ

Katholische Hochschule Mainz (KH MAINZ)
PO Box 2340, 55013 Mainz
Tel: +49(6131) 28944-0
Fax: +49(6131) 28944-50
EMail: e-mail@kh-mz.de
Website: http://www.kh-mz.de

Rector: Martin Klose
Tel: +49(6131) 289-44450
EMail: rektorat@kfh-mainz.de; martin.klose@kh-mz.de

Vice Rector: Susanne Schewior-Popp
Tel: +49(6131) 289-44290
EMail: susanne.schewior-popp@kh-mz.de

International Relations: Thomas Hermsen, Manager and Coordinator, Institute for Research and International Affairs
Tel: +49(6131) 289-44170 EMail: thomas.hermsen@kh-mz.de

Department
Health Sciences and Nursing (Gerontology; Health Administration; Health Sciences; Nursing); **Practical Theology** (Theology); **Social Work** (Social Work)

Institute
Continuing Education (Health Sciences; Social Work); **Research and International Affairs**

History: Founded 1972.

Main Language(s) of Instruction: German

Degrees and Diplomas: *Bachelor's Degree*: **Health Sciences; Social Work; Theology.** *Master*: **Health Administration; Health Education; Social Work.**

Student Numbers *2013-2014*: Total 1,205
Last Updated: 04/02/15

CATHOLIC UNIVERSITY OF APPLIED SCIENCES MUNICH

Katholische Stiftungsfachhochschule München
Preysingstrasse 83, 81667 München
Tel: +49(89) 480-92271
Fax: +49(89) 480-1907
EMail: ksfh.muc@ksfh.de
Website: http://www.ksfh.de

President: Hermann Sollfrank
Tel: +49(89) 48092-1272
EMail: praesident@ksfh.de; egon.endres@ksfh.de

Verwaltungsleiterin: Cordula Schön
Tel: +49(89) 48092-1277 EMail: verwaltungsleitung@ksfh.de

International Relations: Andrea Gavrilina, International Officer
Tel: +1(89) 48092-1403 EMail: andrea.gavrilina@ksfh.de

Programme
Nursing *(Dual)* (Nursing); **Social Work** *(Munich)* (Social Work)

Department
Social Work *(Benediktbeuern)* (Social Work)

Further Information: Also Theology Additional Programme in Munich and Benediktbeuern; E-Learning programme offered by the KSFH München and the Virtuellen Hochschule Bayern.

History: Founded 1971.

Main Language(s) of Instruction: German

Degrees and Diplomas: *Bachelor's Degree*; *Master*: **Education; Health Administration; Rehabilitation and Therapy; Social Sciences; Social Work; Welfare and Protective Services.** Cooperative PhD (Promotion) with the Ludwig-Maximilians-Universität (LMU).

Student Services: Library

Student Numbers *2013-2014*: Total 2,152
Last Updated: 19/03/15

CATHOLIC UNIVERSITY OF APPLIED SCIENCES NORTH RHINE-WESTPHALIA

Katholische Hochschule Nordrhein-Westfalen (KFH NW)
Robert-Schuman Str. 25, 52066 Aachen
Tel: +49(241) 600 03-0
Fax: +49(241) 600 03-88
EMail: postmaster@kfhnw.de
Website: http://www.katho-nrw.de

Rector: Peter Berker
Tel: +49(221) 7757-601 EMail: rektor@kfhnw.de

Head of Administration: Bernward Robrecht (2009-)
Tel: +49(221) 7757-612 EMail: kanzler@katho-nrw.de

International Relations: Helene Hofmann, Helene Hofmann (+149(221) 7757-313) EMail: h.hofmann@katho-nrw.de

Department

Health Science (Health Administration; Health Sciences; Nursing); **Social Sciences** (Social Work; Special Education); **Theology** (Theology)

Further Information: Campuses in Köln, Münster and Paderborn

History: Founded 1971.

Main Language(s) of Instruction: German

Degrees and Diplomas: *Bachelor's Degree*; *Master*. **Education; Educational Administration; Family Studies; Health Administration; Health Education; Health Sciences; Management; Psychology; Rehabilitation and Therapy; Social Work; Special Education.**

Student Services: Library

Student Numbers *2013-2014*: Total 4,400
Last Updated: 19/03/15

COLLEGE OF APPLIED LANGUAGES MUNICH

Hochschule für Angewandte Sprachen München - Fachhochschule des SDI (SDI MÜNCHEN)

Baierbrunner Straße 28, 81379 München
Tel: +49(89) 288102-0
Fax: +49(89) 288440
EMail: kontakt@sdi-muenchen.de; studienberatung@sdi-muenchen.de
Website: http://www.sdi-muenchen.de/hochschule/

President: Felix Mayer
Tel: +49(89) 288102-16 EMail: Felix.Mayer@sdi-muenchen.de

Vice President: Florian Feuser
Tel: +49(89) 288102-14 EMail: Florian.Feuser@sdi-muenchen.de

International Relations: Antonia Happ, International Officer
Tel: +49(89) 288102-33 EMail: Auslandsamt@sdi-muenchen.de

Department

International Business Communication (Chinese; Communication Studies; Cultural Studies; International Business); **International Media Communication** (Communication Studies; Information Technology; Mass Communication; Media Studies); **Translation** (Chinese; Translation and Interpretation)

History: Founded 2007.

Main Language(s) of Instruction: German

Accrediting Agency: Wissenschaftsrat; ACQUIN

Degrees and Diplomas: *Bachelor's Degree*; *Master*. **Communication Studies; Media Studies; Translation and Interpretation.**

Student Services: IT Centre

Student Numbers *2013-2014*: Total 370
Last Updated: 05/03/15

COLLEGE OF THE SPARKASSEN-FINANCIAL GROUP - UNIVERSITY OF APPLIED SCIENCES BONN

Hochschule der Sparkassen-Finanzgruppe, University of Applied Sciences, Bonn GmbH

Simrockstraße 4, 53113 Bonn
Tel: +49(228) 204-9901
Fax: +49(228) 204-9903
EMail: info@s-hochschule.de
Website: http://www.s-hochschule.de

Rector: Bernd Heitzer
Tel: +49(228) 204-9900 EMail: bernd.heitzer@s-hochschule.de

Programme

Banking and Sales (Banking; Business Administration; Economics; Finance; Law; Mathematics; Sales Techniques); **Banking Industry** (Banking); **Finance** (Banking; Business Administration; Economics; Finance; Law; Mathematics); **Financial Information Systems** *(Bachelor programme)* (Banking; Business Administration; Communication Studies; Computer Science; E- Business/Commerce; Finance; Law; Management; Mathematics; Software Engineering)

History: Founded 2003.

Academic Year: September to August (September-January; February-August)

Admission Requirements: Applicants must hold a Secondary School Leaving Certificate or equivalent or have a working/training contract with a finance service company or have had one year of relevant work experience; additionally, applicants to the "Corporate Banking" programme must pass TOEFL exam (with at least 250 points for the computerised version and 600 points for the paper version)

Fees: 12,600-13,100; Registation fee, 600-1,100 (Euro)

Main Language(s) of Instruction: German

Degrees and Diplomas: *Bachelor's Degree*; *Master*. **Finance; Management.**

Student Numbers *2013-2014*: Total 974
Last Updated: 04/03/15

COLOGNE BUSINESS SCHOOL (CBS) - EUROPEAN UNIVERSITY OF APPLIED SCIENCES (CBS)

Hardefuststr. 1, D-50677 Köln
Tel: +49(221) 9318-0931
Fax: +49(221) 9318-0930
EMail: study@cbs.de
Website: http://www.cbs.de/

President: Elisabeth Fröhlich
Tel: +49(221) 931809-81 EMail: e.froehlich@cbs.de

Vice-President for Economy and Administration: Jürgen Weischer Tel: +49(221) 931809-24 EMail: j.weischer@cbs.de

International Relations: Markus Raueiser, Vice-President for International Relations
Tel: +49(221) 931809-49 EMail: m.raueiser@cbs.de

Programme

Business Psychology (Industrial and Organizational Psychology); **General Management** (Management); **International Business** (International Business); **International Culture and Management** (Cultural Studies); **International Media Management** (Media Studies); **International Tourism Management** (Tourism); **MBA/ Executive Education** (Business Administration)

Main Language(s) of Instruction: German

Accrediting Agency: FIBAA (Foundation for International Business Administration Accreditation)

Degrees and Diplomas: *Bachelor's Degree*; *Master*. **Business Administration; Cultural Studies; International Business; Management; Media Studies; Tourism.**

Student Services: Canteen, Sports Facilities

Student Numbers *2013-2014*: Total 1,368
Last Updated: 07/04/15

DESIGN ACADEMY - UNIVERSITY OF COMMUNICATION AND DESIGN, BERLIN

Design Akademie Berlin - SRH Hochschule für Kommunikation und Design

Paul-Lincke-Ufer 8e, 10999 Berlin
Tel: +49 (30) 6165-480
Fax: +49 (30) 6165-4819
EMail: info@design-akademie-berlin.de
Website: http://www.design-akademie-berlin.de

Rector: Dörte Schultze-Seehof
EMail: Schultze-seehof@design-akademie-berlin.de

Public Relations and Communication Officer: Angela Bittner
EMail: bittner@design-akademie-berlin.de

Department

Design (Design); **Marketing Communication** (Marketing; Mass Communication)

History: Founded 2007 from the Design Akademie Berlin (created in 1995).

Main Language(s) of Instruction: German

Degrees and Diplomas: *Bachelor's Degree*: **Computer Graphics; Design; Film; Graphic Design; Marketing; Mass Communication; Painting and Drawing; Photography; Visual Arts.** *Master*: **Design; Marketing; Mass Communication.**

Student Numbers *2013-2014*: Total 290
Last Updated: 23/01/15

DEUTSCHE TELEKOM UNIVERSITY OF APPLIED SCIENCES LEIPZIG

Hochschule für Telekommunikation Leipzig (HTFL)

Gustav-Freytag-Str. 43-45, 04277 Leipzig
Tel: +49(341) 3062-100
Fax: +49(341) 3015-069
EMail: pr@hft-leipzig.de
Website: http://www.hft-leipzig.de

Rector: Volker Saupe
Tel: +49(341) 3062-100 EMail: saupe@hft-leipzig.de

Chancellor: Oliver Lange
Tel: +49(341) 3062-236 EMail: edith.pohling@telekom.de

International Relations: Birgit Graf
Tel: +49(341) 3062-250 EMail: graf.b@hft-leipzig.de

Department

Communication and Information Technology (Information Technology; Telecommunications Engineering); **Communication Technology** (Information Technology; Telecommunications Engineering); **Economics (German)** (Economics); **Fundamentals of Telecommunications (German)** (Telecommunications Engineering)

History: Founded 1991. Previously known as Deutsche Telekom Fachhochschule Leipzig.

Main Language(s) of Instruction: German

Accrediting Agency: Akkreditierungsagentur für Studiengänge der Ingenieurwissenschaften, der Informatik, der Naturwissenschaften und der Mathematik e.V. (ASIIN); Akkreditierungs-, Certifizierungs- und Qualitätssicherungs-Institut ACQUIN

Degrees and Diplomas: *Bachelor's Degree*; *Master*: **Business Computing; Information Technology.**

Student Services: IT Centre, Library

Student Numbers *2013-2014*: Total 1,131
Last Updated: 10/03/15

DIACONIA - UNIVERSITY OF APPLIED SCIENCES

Fachhochschule der Diakonie

Grete-Reich-Weg 9, 33617 Bielefeld
Tel: +49(521) 144-2700
Fax: +49(521) 144-3032
EMail: info@fh-diakonie.de
Website: http://www.fhdd.de

Rector: Hilke Bertelsmann
Tel: +49(521) 144-2702 EMail: hilke.bertelsmann@fhdd.de

Head of Administration: Alexa von Hören
Tel: +49(521) 144-2701 EMail: alexa.vonhoeren@fhdd.de

Programme

Diaconia (Bible; Health Sciences; History of Religion; Religion; Social Work; Theology); **Management in Social and Health Services** (Business Administration; Health Administration; Management; Social Work; Welfare and Protective Services); **Mentoring in Social and Health Services** (Management; Social Work; Welfare and Protective Services)

History: Founded 2006.

Main Language(s) of Instruction: German

Degrees and Diplomas: *Bachelor's Degree*; *Master*: **Management.**

Student Services: IT Centre

Student Numbers *2013-2014*: Total 682
Last Updated: 03/04/15

DIPLOMA UNIVERSITY OF APPLIED SCIENCES

DIPLOMA Hochschule - Private Fachhochschule Nordhessen

Am Hegeberg 2, 37242 Bad Sooden-Allendorf
Tel: +49(5652) 58777-0
Fax: +49(5652) 58777-29
EMail: info@diploma.de; sg@diploma.de
Website: http://diploma.de

Präsident: Hans F.W. Hübner (1997-) Tel: +49(5722) 950-526

Kanzler: Bernd Blindow
Tel: +49(5722) 950-50 EMail: drg@diploma.de

International Relations: Stefan Siehl, Head, International Office

Department

Business Administration (Business Administration; Management; Media Studies; Tourism); **Business Administration (Distance)** (Business Administration; Economics; Law; Management; Media Studies; Tourism); **Engineering** (Electronic Engineering; Engineering; Industrial Engineering); **Engineering (Distance)** (Electronic Engineering; Engineering; Industrial Engineering); **Graphic Design** (Graphic Design); **Graphic Design (Distance)** (Graphic Design); **Health and Social Sciences (Distance)** (Educational Administration; Ergotherapy; Gerontology; Health Sciences; Occupational Therapy; Physical Therapy; Preschool Education; Social Sciences; Speech Therapy and Audiology); **Law** (Commercial Law; Law); **Law (Distance)** (Commercial Law; International Law; Law)

Further Information: Also campsuses in Berlin-Treptow, Bonn, Friedrichshafen, Heilbronn, Kassel, Mannheim, Nürnberg, Plauen, Schwentinental, Baden-Baden, Bochum, Bückeburg, Hannover, Kaiserslautern, Leipzig, München, Oldenburg, Regenstauf.

History: Founded 1997. Formerly known as DIPLOMA Hochschule - Private Fachhochschule Nordhessen.

Main Language(s) of Instruction: German

Accrediting Agency: AHPGS; FIIBA; ACQUIN; AQAS

Degrees and Diplomas: *Bachelor's Degree*: **Business Administration; Business Computing; Commercial Law; Educational Administration; Electronic Engineering; Graphic Design; Health Sciences; Industrial Engineering; Management; Mechanical Engineering; Media Studies; Medicine; Preschool Education; Tourism.** *Master*: **Business Administration; Commercial Law; Economics; Health Sciences; Industrial Engineering; Law; Management; Media Studies; Tourism.** *PhD*: **Business Administration; Commercial Law; Economics; Health Sciences; Industrial Engineering; Law; Management; Media Studies; Tourism.** Masters' and Doctoral Degree Programmes are only offered through Distance Mode

Student Services: Residential Facilities

Student Numbers *2013-2014*: Total 4,107
Last Updated: 23/01/15

DIU - DRESDEN INTERNATIONAL UNIVERSITY (DIU)

Freiberger Str. 37, 01067 Dresden
Tel: +49(351) 40470-0
Fax: +49(351) 40470-110
EMail: info@di-uni.de
Website: http://www.di-uni.de

President: Irene Schneider-Böttcher Tel: +49(351) 40470-102

Director: Reinhard Kretzschmar Tel: +49(351) 40470-102

Centre

Environment and Energy Management (Environmental Management); **Health Science and Medicine** (Chiropractic; Health Administration; Health Sciences; Law; Management; Medical Auxiliaries; Medicine; Midwifery; Osteopathy; Periodontics; Pharmacy; Physical Therapy; Rehabilitation and Therapy; Social and Preventive Medicine; Sports Medicine); **Humanities and Social Sciences** (Arts and Humanities; Behavioural Sciences; Communication Studies; Cultural Studies; Management; Social Sciences); **Law in an Interndisciplinary Context** (Business Administration; Commercial Law; Criminal Law; Economics; Law); **Logistics and Management** (Business Administration; Leadership; Management; Transport Management); **Natural Sciences and Engineering**

(Business Administration; Engineering; Engineering Drawing and Design; Fire Science; Natural Sciences; Occupational Health; Railway Engineering; Real Estate; Safety Engineering)

History: Founded 2003.

Main Language(s) of Instruction: German

Degrees and Diplomas: *Bachelor's Degree*; *Master*: **Business Administration; Chiropractic; Communication Studies; Cultural Studies; Economics; Fire Science; Health Sciences; Law; Management; Occupational Health; Osteopathy; Periodontics; Pharmacy; Real Estate; Safety Engineering; Social and Preventive Medicine; Transport Management.** Also Certificates Courses (Zertifikatskurse)

Student Numbers *2013-2014*: Total 1,585
Last Updated: 25/01/15

EBS UNIVERSITY OF BUSINESS AND LAW

EBS Universität für Wirtschaft und Recht (EBS)
Gustav-Stresemann-Ring 3, 65189 Wiesbaden
Tel: +49(611) 7102-00
Fax: +49(6723) 69-133
EMail: info@ebs.de
Website: http://www.ebs.de

President and Director: Rolf Wolff (2013-)

Programme

Executive Education (Business Administration; English; Finance; French; German; Health Administration; Management; Real Estate; Sales Techniques)

School

Business (Accountancy; Business Administration; Economics; Finance; Management; Marketing); **Law** (Law)

History: Founded 1971 as European Business School Oestrich-Winkel. A private institution authorized by the government to award degrees. Acquired present title and status 2010 following the seting up of the EBS Law School.

Academic Year: September to April

Admission Requirements: Secondary school certificate (Abitur) and entrance examination

Fees: 4,950 per semester (Euro)

Main Language(s) of Instruction: English

Accrediting Agency: Wissenschaftsrat (WR); European Quality Improvement System (EQUIS); Foundation for International Business Administration Accreditation (FIBAA)

Degrees and Diplomas: *Bachelor's Degree*: **Air Transport; International Business; Management.** *Master*: **Automotive Engineering; Business Administration; Finance; Management; Marketing; Real Estate.** *PhD*: **Economics; Finance; Law; Management.** *Habilitation*: **Economics; Finance; Law; Management.** Degree programmes offered in full-time and part-time mode; Also Staatsexam in Law; Executive MBA in: Business Administration, Health Administration; Certificate programmes and Corporate programmes.

Student Services: Careers Guidance

Academic Staff *2014-2015*: Total: c. 70
Student Numbers *2014-2015*: Total: c. 2,000
Last Updated: 26/01/15

EBZ BUSINESS SCHOOL - UNIVERSITY OF APPLIED SCIENCES

Springorumallee 20, 44795 Bochum
Tel: +49(234) 9447-704
Fax: +49(234) 9447-777
EMail: a.unkhoff@ebz-bs.de
Website: http://www.ebz-business-school.de

Interim Rector: Sigrid Schaefer

Chancellor: Klaus Leuchtmann

Programme

Project Development (Management); **Real Estate** (Real Estate)

Main Language(s) of Instruction: German

Degrees and Diplomas: *Bachelor's Degree*; *Master*: **Business Administration; Management; Real Estate.**

Student Services: Library

Student Numbers *2013-2014*: Total 775
Last Updated: 07/04/15

EICHSTÄTT CATHOLIC UNIVERSITY

Katholische Universität Eichstätt-Ingolstadt
Ostenstrasse 26, 85071 Eichstätt
Tel: +49(8421) 93-0
Fax: +49(8421) 93-1796
EMail: info@ku.de
Website: http://www.ku.de/

President: Gabriele Gien
Tel: +49(8421) 93-21230
EMail: praesidentin@ku.de

Chancellor: Thomas Kleinert
Tel: +49(8421) 93-21229
EMail: kanzler@ku.de

International Relations: Martin Groos, Head, International Office
Tel: +49(8421) 93-21207
EMail: international@ku.de

Faculty

Business Administration (Business Administration; Economics; Ethics; Law; Statistics); **History and Social Sciences** (Folklore; History; Political Sciences; Social Sciences; Sociology); **Languages and Literatures** (American Studies; Archaeology; English; German; Journalism; Latin; Philosophy; Romance Languages); **Mathematics and Geography** (Biology; Chemistry; Computer Science; Geography; Mathematics; Pedagogy); **Philosophy and Education** (Art History; Education; Fine Arts; Labour and Industrial Relations; Music; Philosophy; Psychology; Sports); **Religious Education and Ecclesiastical Educational Work** (Ethics; Religious Education); **Social Work** (Social Work); **Theology** (Bible; Catholic Theology; Philosophy)

Institute

Entrepreneursh!p; Latin American Studies (Latin American Studies); **Marriage and Family in Society** *(The Central)* (Family Studies)

Further Information: Also Ingolstadt Campus.

History: Founded 1972 as Gesamthochschule, incorporating College of Education, founded 1958 and College of Philosophy and Theology, established 1924 and tracing its origins to the Collegium Willibaldinum, founded 1564. Became University 1980. An autonomous institution financially supported by the State of Bavaria 80% and the seven Bavarian Dioceses (20%).

Academic Year: October to September

Admission Requirements: Secondary school certificate (Reifezeugnis)

Fees: None for most degrees

Main Language(s) of Instruction: German

Degrees and Diplomas: *Bachelor's Degree*; *Diplom (FH)*: **Nursing; Primary Education; Religious Education; Secondary Education; Social Work; Technology Education.** *Lizentiat*: **Theology.** *Master*: **Advertising and Publicity; Aesthetics; Ancient Civilizations; Archaeology; Art History; Business Administration; Business Computing; Contemporary History; Education; English; Environmental Studies; Ethnology; European Studies; Folklore; Foreign Languages Education; Geography; History; Humanities and Social Science Education; International Relations; Italian; Journalism; Latin; Literature; Mathematics; Medieval Studies; Modern History; Philosophy; Political Sciences; Psychology; Regional Planning; Romance Languages; Social Work; Sociology; Spanish; Technology Education; Tourism; Visual Arts; Vocational Education.** *PhD*: **American Studies; Art History; Catholic Theology; Communication Studies; Economics; English Studies; Ethnology; European Studies; Germanic Studies; History; Latin; Literature; Mathematics; Pedagogy; Philosophy; Political Sciences; Psychology; Romance Languages; Sociology.** *Habilitation*:

Economics; History; Literature; Pedagogy; Philosophy; Sociology; Speech Studies; Theology. Also Teacher Training Certificate (Lehramt) in Primary Education and Scondary Education, 2-3 sem.; Dual Degrees

Student Services: Canteen, IT Centre, Library, Sports Facilities

Publications: Eichstätter Beiträge; Eichstätter Hochschulreden; Eichstätter Materialien; Eichstätter Theologische Studien; Forum für osteuropäische Ideen- und Zeitgeschichte; Mesa Redonda

Student Numbers *2013-2014*: Total 5,171
Last Updated: 19/03/15

ESCP-EUROPE BUSINESS SCHOOL - BERLIN

ESCP Europe Wirtschaftshochschule Berlin

Heubnerweg 8-10, 14059 Berlin
Tel: +49(30) 32007-0
Fax: +49(30) 32007-111
EMail: info.de@escpeurope.eu
Website: http://www.escp-eap.de

Dean: Frank Bournois

Campus Director: Marion Festing
Tel: +49(30) 32007-153
EMail: mfesting@escpeurope.eu

Dean for Academic Affairs: Ulrich Pape
Tel: +49(30) 32007-134
EMail: ulrich.pape@escpeurope.de

Department

Economics, Law and Social Sciences (Economics; Law; Social Sciences); **Finance** (Finance); **Financial Reporting and Audit** (Finance); **Information and Operations Management** (Information Management; Management); **Language and Culture** (Cultural Studies; Modern Languages); **Management Control** (Management); **Marketing** (Marketing); **Strategy, Organizational Behavior and Human Resources** (Behavioural Sciences; Business Administration; Human Resources)

Further Information: Also Campuses in Paris, London, Madrid and Torino

History: Founded 1819 by Parisian entrepreneurs and scientists, the ESCP is one of the oldest Business Schools in Europe. In 1973 the Chambre de Commerce et d'Industrie de Paris decided to set up the first European Business School (EAP) in four countries. Both French Grandes Ecoles merged in 1999 to form ESCP-EAP European School of Management. Previously known as ESCP-EAP Europäische Wirtschaftshochschule Acquired current name 2009.

Academic Year: Starts September (two and three terms)

Admission Requirements: At least 2 years' university studies in business administration or work experience

Fees: 3,900-32,000 per annum, depending on the programme (Euro)

Main Language(s) of Instruction: German, English

Accrediting Agency: AACSB; EFMD (EQUIS); AMBA

Degrees and Diplomas: *Bachelor's Degree*: **Management.** *Master*: **Art Management; Business Administration; Commercial Law; Communication Studies; Finance; Health Administration; International Business; International Law; Leisure Studies; Management; Marketing; Media Studies; Tourism.** *PhD*: **International Business.** Also Diplôme de Grande Ecole; Executive MBA

Student Services: Academic Counselling, Careers Guidance, Cultural Activities, Facilities for disabled people, Foreign Studies Centre, IT Centre, Language Laboratory, Library, Nursery Care, Social Counselling, Sports Facilities

Publications: European Management Journal (EMJ)

Student Numbers *2013-2014*: Total 179
Last Updated: 25/01/15

ESMOD BERLIN INTERNATIONAL UNIVERSITY OF ART FOR FASHION

ESMOD Berlin Internationale Hochschule für Mode

Görlitzer Str. 51, 10997 Berlin
Tel: +49(30) 6112214
Fax: +49(30) 6112187
EMail: info@esmod.de
Website: http://www.esmod.de/de/berlin/

Programme

Fashion Design - Stylist/Modelist (Fashion Design); **Sustainability in Fashion** *(Graduate)* (Fashion Design)

Further Information: Camuses in Beijing, Beirut, Bordeaux, Damas, Dubai, Genf, Istanbul, Jakarta, Lyon, Moskau, München, Osaka, Oslo, Paris, Rennes, Roubaix, Sao Paulo, Séoul, Sousse, Tokyo andnd Tunis

Main Language(s) of Instruction: German

Degrees and Diplomas: *Bachelor's Degree*: **Fashion Design.** *Master*: **Fashion Design.**

Student Numbers *2013-2014*: Total 226
Last Updated: 08/04/15

ESMT - EUROPEAN SCHOOL OF MANAGEMENT AND TECHNOLOGY - BERLIN

Schlossplatz 1, 10178 Berlin
Tel: +49(30) 21231-0
EMail: info@esmt.org
Website: http://www.esmt.org

Präsident: Jörg Rocholl
Tel: +49(30) 21231-1010 EMail: joerg.rocholl@esmt.org

Associate Dean of Academic Affairs: Valentina Werner

Area

European Competitiveness (Business Administration; Psychology); **Leadership and Social Responsibility** (Leadership; Management); **Management of Technology** (Business Administration; Management; Sociology; Technology)

Further Information: Also Campus in Schloss Gracht

History: Founded 2002.

Main Language(s) of Instruction: German, English

Accrediting Agency: AACSB; AMBA; FIBAA

Degrees and Diplomas: *Master*: **Business Administration; Management.** *PhD*: **Business Administration; Management.** Also Executive MBA

Academic Staff *2014-2015*: Total: c. 30
Student Numbers *2013-2014*: Total 233
Last Updated: 25/01/15

EUROPEAN DISTANCE EDUCATION UNIVERSITY OF APPLIED SCIENCES HAMBURG

Europäische Fernhochschule Hamburg (EURO-FH)

Doberaner Weg 20, 22143 Hamburg
Tel: +49(40) 6757-0700
Fax: +49(40) 6757-0710
EMail: Information@euro-fh.com; studienberatung@Euro-FH.de
Website: http://www.euro-fh.com

President: Thomas Tegen EMail: thomas.tegen@euro-fh.de

Chancellor: Catherine Möhring
EMail: catherine.moehring@euro-fh.de

Programme

Continuing Education (Business Administration; Commercial Law; English; Finance; Fiscal Law; Industrial and Organizational Psychology; Insurance; International Law; Labour Law; Management; Marketing; Sales Techniques; Spanish; Transport and Communications; Transport Management); **Graduate Studies** (Accountancy; Business Administration; Finance; Industrial and Organizational Psychology; Management; Marketing; Taxation); **Undergraduate Studies** (Art Management; Business

Administration; Business Education; Commercial Law; Finance; Industrial and Organizational Psychology; Information Technology; International Business; Management; Retailing and Wholesaling; Transport Management)

History: Founded 2003.

Fees: Undergraduate, 280 per month; postgraduate, 11,760 (24 months at 490 per month); the monthly rate for a reduced period of study is 590 (18 months)/ 690 (14 months), i.e a minimum fee of 9,660 (Euro)

Main Language(s) of Instruction: German, English

Accrediting Agency: Wissenschaftsrat (WR); Foundation for International Business Administration Accreditation (FIBAA); Staatliche Zentralstelle für Fernunterricht, Köln (ZFU)

Degrees and Diplomas: *Bachelor's Degree*: **Business Administration; Commercial Law; Finance; Information Technology; International Business; Management; Real Estate; Retailing and Wholesaling; Transport Management.** *Master*: **Accountancy; Business Administration; Finance; Industrial and Organizational Psychology; Management; Marketing; Psychology; Taxation.** Aslo Hochschulzertifikat (Continuing Studies Certificates)

Academic Staff *2014-2015*: Total 300

Student Numbers *2014-2015*: Total: c. 6,500

Last Updated: 26/01/15

EVANGELICAL UNIVERSITY OF APPLIED SCIENCES FOR CHURCH MUSIC

Evangelische Hochschule für Kirchenmusik Halle an der Saale (EHK)

Kleine Ulrichstrasse 35, 06108 Halle
Tel: +49(345) 21969-0
Fax: +49(345) 21969-29
EMail: sekretariat@ehk-halle.de
Website: http://www.ehk-halle.de

Rektor: Wolfgang Kupke (2000-)
Tel: +49(345) 21969-19 EMail: kupke@ehk-halle.de

Prorektorin: Franziska Seils
Tel: +49(345) 21969-30 EMail: seils@ehk-halle.de

Programme

Choir and Conducting (Conducting); **Music Education** (Music Education); **Organ Performance** (Musical Instruments); **Religious Music** (Religious Music); **Religious Music/Music Education** *(Combined Studies)* (Music Education; Religious Music); **Singing** (Singing)

History: Founded 1926.

Main Language(s) of Instruction: German

Degrees and Diplomas: *Bachelor's Degree*: **Music Education; Religious Music.** *Diplom (FH)*: **Religious Music.** *Master*: **Conducting; Musical Instruments; Religious Music; Singing.**

Student Services: Library

Student Numbers *2013-2014*: Total 48

Last Updated: 26/01/15

EVANGELICAL UNIVERSITY OF APPLIED SCIENCES FOR SOCIAL WORK, EDUCATION AND NURSING

Evangelische Hochschule für Dresden (EHS)

PO Box 200143, Semperstrasse 2A, 01191 Dresden
Tel: +49(351) 46902-0
Fax: +49(351) 4715-993
EMail: info@ehs-dresden.de; rektorat@ehs-dresden.de
Website: http://www.ehs-dresden.de

Rector: Holger Brandes (2013-)
Tel: +49(351) 46902-10
EMail: rektorat@ehs-dresden.de; holger.brandes@ehs-dresden.de

Head of Administration: Peter Schiller
Tel: +49(351) 46902-18 EMail: peter.schiller@ehs-dresden.de

International Relations: Uta Heinrich-Barth
Tel: +49(351) 4690233
EMail: auslandsamt@ehs-dresden.de; heinrich-barth@ehs-dresden.de

Programme

Counseling *(Postgraduate)* (Psychology); **Education** (Teacher Training); **Health and Care** (Health Administration; Nursing); **Social Management (MBA) - Distance Learning** (Management; Social Work); **Social Work** (Social Work)

History: Founded 1991.

Main Language(s) of Instruction: German

Degrees and Diplomas: *Bachelor's Degree*: **Health Administration; Health Education; Health Sciences; Nursing; Preschool Education; Social Work.** *Master*: **Management; Psychology; Social Work.** *PhD*: **Theology.**

Student Numbers *2013-2014*: Total 701

Last Updated: 26/01/15

FACULTY OF THEOLOGY IN PADERBORN

Theologische Fakultät Paderborn

Kamp 6, 33098 Paderborn
Tel: +49(5251) 121-6
Fax: +49(5251) 121-700
EMail: theol-fakultaet-paderborn@t-online.de; rektorat@thf-paderborn.de
Website: http://www.theol-fakultaet-pb.de

Rektorin: Josef Meyer zu Schlochtern
Tel: +49(5251) 121-701
EMail: sekretariat@thf-paderborn.de

Quästor: Anton Schäfers Tel: +49(5251) 121-704

Programme

Philosophy (Philosophy); **Theology** (Theology)

History: Founded 1614.

Main Language(s) of Instruction: German

Degrees and Diplomas: *Lizentiat*: **Theology.** *Magister*: **Theology.** *PhD*: **Philosophy; Theology.** *Habilitation*: **Theology.**

Student Services: Library

Student Numbers *2013-2014*: Total 94

Last Updated: 24/01/15

FHDW - UNIVERSITY OF APPLIED SCIENCES

Fachhochschule der Wirtschaft (FHDW)

Fürstenalle 3-5, 33102 Paderborn
Tel: +49(5251) 301-02
Fax: +49(5251) 301-188
EMail: info-pb@fhdw.de
Website: http://www.fhdw.de

President: Stefan Nieland
Tel: +49(5251) 301-180 EMail: stefan.nieland@fhdw.de

Director and Chancellor: Georg Herrmann
Tel: +49(5251) 301-100 EMail: georg.herrmann@fhdw.de

International Relations: Karin Carroll-Scott
Tel: +49(5251) 301-183
EMail: karin.carroll-scott@fhdw.de; international.office@fhdw.de

Programme

Dual Bachelor's degree (Business Administration; Business Computing; Commercial Law; Computer Science; International Business); **Part-time Master's studies** (Automotive Engineering; Business Administration; Finance; Information Management; Information Technology; Management; Marketing; Retailing and Wholesaling; Transport Management); **Part-time Undergraduate Studies** (Business Administration; Business Computing)

Further Information: Campuses in Bergisch Gladbach, Bielefeld, Marburg, Mettmann, Sister university: FHDW Hannover

History: Founded 1993.

Main Language(s) of Instruction: German

Accrediting Agency: Wissenschaftsrat (WR); FIBAA

Degrees and Diplomas: *Bachelor's Degree*; *Master*: **Automotive Engineering; Finance; Information Management; Information**

Technology; Management; Marketing; Retailing and Wholesaling; Transport Management.

Student Services: Careers Guidance

Student Numbers *2014-2015*: Total: c. 2,050

Last Updated: 27/01/15

FLIEDNER UNIVERSITY DÜSSELDORF

Fliedner Fachhochschule Düsseldorf

Alte Landstraße 179, Geschwister-Aufricht-Straße 9, 40489 Düsseldorf

Tel: +49(211) 409- 3224

EMail: info@fliedner-fachhochschule.de

Website: http://www.fliedner-fachhochschule.de/

Rector: Marianne Dierks
Tel: +49(211) 409-3220 EMail: dierks@fliedner-fachhochschule.de

Head of Administration: Thore Eggert
Tel: +49(211) 409-3230 EMail: eggert@fliedner-fachhochschule.de

Programme

Care Management and Organizational Knowledge (Health Administration); **Counseling in Health, Education and Social Services** (Education; Health Sciences; Social Work); **Education and Education in Childhood** (Education); **Education for Emergency Medical Services** (Education); **Education in Childhood** (Education); **Education Management** *(Graduate)* (Educational Administration); **Intensive Pedagogy** *(Graduate)* (Pedagogy); **Medical Assistant - Surgery** (Medical Auxiliaries); **Nursing and Health (dual)** (Health Sciences; Nursing); **Nursing Education** (Health Education); **Social Work - Focus on Children and Youth Services** *(Graduate)* (Social Work); **Vocational Education and Health Care** *(Graduate)* (Health Sciences; Vocational Education)

Main Language(s) of Instruction: German

Degrees and Diplomas: *Bachelor's Degree*; *Master*: **Educational Administration; Health Sciences; Pedagogy; Social Work; Vocational Education.**

Student Services: Library

Student Numbers *2013-2014*: Total 513

Last Updated: 07/04/15

FRANKFURT SCHOOL OF FINANCE AND MANAGEMENT

PO Box 100341, Sonnemannstraße 9-11, 60314 Frankfurt am Main

Tel: +49(69) 154008-0

Fax: +49(69) 154008-728

EMail: info@frankfurt-school.de

Website: http://www.frankfurt-school.de

President and CEO: Udo Steffens (1996-)
Tel: +49(69) 154008-136 EMail: u.steffens@fs.de

Vice President Academic Affairs: Michael H. Grote
Tel: +49(69) 154008-716 EMail: a.schilling@fs.de

Vice President, Managing Director: Ingolf Jungmann
Tel: +49(69) 154008-250 EMail: i.jungmann@fs.de

International Relations: Joana Rosenkranz, Head of International Student Recruitment
Tel: +49(69) 154008-578 EMail: j.rosenkranz@fs.de

Department

Accountancy (Accountancy); **Economics** (Economics); **Finance** (Banking; Finance; Insurance; Management); **Languages** (Modern Languages); **Legal Studies and Ethics** (Ethics; Law); **Management** (Management)

Further Information: Study centresin Hamburg and Munich; External offices in Nairobi, Beijing, Pune, Istanbul; 80 regional study centres in Germany

History: Founded 1957 as Bankakademi. Hochschule für Bankwirtschaft Frankfurt am Main (HfB) (Business School of Finance and Management, Frankfurt am Main) added 1990. All activities regrouped under current title 2007.

Admission Requirements: Graduation from high school and selection process

Fees: 4,700 per semester (Euro)

Main Language(s) of Instruction: German, English

Accrediting Agency: AACSB International; EQUIS; Wirtschaftsrat (WR); Programmes accredited by the Foundation for International Business Administration Accreditation (FIBAA) and AQAS.

Degrees and Diplomas: *Bachelor's Degree*: **Business Administration; Business Computing; Chinese; Economics; English; French; German; International Business; Management; Philosophy; Spanish.** *Master*: **Business Administration; Commercial Law; Finance; Health Administration; Insurance; International Business; Management.** *PhD*: **Accountancy; Finance; Management.** Some Bachelor's and Master's Degrees are conducted in English; Certificates (in German) in Banking, Business Administration, Finance, Teacher Training, Management, Leadership; Frankfurt Evening MBA, 1-2 yrs; Executive MBA; Executive Education

Student Services: Canteen, Careers Guidance, Foreign Studies Centre, IT Centre, Language Laboratory, Library, Residential Facilities

Publishing house: Bankakademie Verloj

Academic Staff *2013-2014*: Total 67

Student Numbers *2013-2014*: Total 1,376

Last Updated: 29/01/15

FREE UNIVERSITY STUTTGART - WALDORF TEACHERS COLLEGE

Freie Hochschule Stuttgart - Seminar für Waldorfpädagogik

Haußmannstr. 44a, 70188 Stuttgart

Tel: +49(711) 21094-0

Fax: +49(711) 23489-13

EMail: info@freie-hochschule-stuttgart.de

Website: http://www.freie-hochschule-stuttgart.de/

Programme

Eurythmy Pedadogy *(Graduate)* (Teacher Training); **Eurythmy Pedagogical Basic Qualification** (Teacher Training); **Teacher Training** (Teacher Training)

Main Language(s) of Instruction: German

Degrees and Diplomas: *Bachelor's Degree*; *Master*: **Performing Arts; Secondary Education; Teacher Training.**

Student Services: Library

Student Numbers *2013-2014*: Total 228

Last Updated: 07/04/15

FRESENIUS UNIVERSITY OF APPLIED SCIENCES

Hochschule Fresenius (HSF)

Limburger Strasse 2, 65510 Idstein

Tel: +49(6126) 9352-0

Fax: +49(6126) 9352-10

EMail: idstein@hs-fresenius.de

Website: http://www.hs-fresenius.de

Präsident: Botho von Portatius EMail: service@fh-fresenius.de

Managing Director: Hermann Kögler

International Relations: Leo Gros, Vizepräsident (International Relations) EMail: auslandsamt@fh-fresenius.de

School

AMD Design (Design); **AMD Fashion** (Fashion Design; Management; Mass Communication); **Business Administration** (Business Administration); **Chemistry, Biology and Pharmacy** (Biology; Chemistry; Pharmacy); **International Business** (International Business); **Media Studies** (Media Studies; Psychology); **Medicine** (Health Sciences; Occupational Therapy; Osteopathy; Physical Therapy; Speech Therapy and Audiology); **Psychology** (Psychology)

Further Information: Also branches in Cologne, Hamburg, Darmstadt, Munich, Zwickau and Vienna.

History: Founded 1848.

Main Language(s) of Instruction: German

Accrediting Agency: ASIIN, ACQAS, FIBAA, AHPGS

Degrees and Diplomas: *Bachelor's Degree*; *Master*: **Alternative Medicine; Biology; Business Administration; Health Administration; Industrial and Organizational Psychology; Industrial Chemistry; Information Management; International Economics; Leadership; Management; Marketing; Mass Communication; Media Studies; Pharmacy; Rehabilitation and Therapy; Taxation; Transport Management; Welfare and Protective Services.**

Student Numbers *2013-2014*: Total 8,193

Last Updated: 04/03/15

FRIEDENSAU ADVENTIST UNIVERSITY

Theologische Hochschule Friedensau
An der Ihle 19, 39291 Friedensau
Tel: +49(3921) 916-0
Fax: +49(3921) 916-120
EMail: hochschule@thh-friedensau.de
Website: http://www.thh-friedensau.de/

Rector: Friedbert Ninow Tel: +49(3921) 916-131

Chancellor: Tobias H. Koch
Tel: +49(3921) 916-100 EMail: tobias.koch@thh-friedensau.de

International Relations: Lilli Unrau
Tel: +49(3921) 916-134 EMail: zulassung@thh-friedensau.de

School

Social Sciences (Social Sciences; Social Work)

Department

German as a Foreign Language (German); **Theology** (Hebrew; Missionary Studies; Music; Pastoral Studies; Theology)

History: Founded 1899.

Fees: 1.765-2.468 per semester (Euro)

Main Language(s) of Instruction: German

Degrees and Diplomas: *Bachelor's Degree*; *Master*: **Art Therapy; Health Administration; Psychology; Social Sciences; Theology.**

Student Services: Canteen, IT Centre, Library, Residential Facilities

Student Numbers *2013-2014*: Total 179

Last Updated: 22/03/15

GEORG AGRICOLA UNIVERSITY OF APPLIED SCIENCES OF BOCHUM

Technische Fachhochschule 'Georg Agricola' zu Bochum
Postfach 10 27 49, Herner Str. 45, 44782 Bochum
Tel: +49(234) 968-02
Fax: +49(234) 968-3417
EMail: info@tfh-bochum.de
Website: http://www.tfh-bochum.de

Rector: Jürgen Kretschmann
Tel: +49(234) 968-02 EMail: kretschmann@tfh-bochum.de

Vice President for Budget and Administration:
Susanne-Christiane Buchbinder
Tel: +49(234) 968-3411 EMail: buchbinder@tfh-bochum.de

International Relations: Daniela Naumann-El Kady
Tel: +49(234) 968 3266 EMail: naumann@tfh-bochum.de

Faculty

Electronical Engineering and Information Technology (Electronic Engineering; Information Technology); **Geotechnical Engineering, Mining and Technical Business Management** (Geological Engineering; Mining Engineering); **Machine Building and Process Engineering** (Engineering Management; Machine Building)

History: Founded 1816 as Bochumer Bergschule. Acquired present name 1995. Acquired present title 1998.

Academic Year: March to February (March-August; September-February)

Admission Requirements: Secondary school certificate (Abitur) or recognized equivalent

Fees: c. 80 per semester (Euro)

Main Language(s) of Instruction: German

Degrees and Diplomas: *Bachelor's Degree*: **Business Administration; Electrical Engineering; Environmental Engineering; Geological Engineering; Geology; Information Technology; Materials Engineering; Mechanical Engineering; Mining Engineering; Surveying and Mapping.** *Master*: **Business Administration; Electrical Engineering; Geological Engineering; Information Technology; Mechanical Engineering; Mining Engineering; Safety Engineering.**

Student Services: Careers Guidance

Academic Staff *2014-2015*	**TOTAL**
FULL-TIME	50
PART-TIME	c. 120
Student Numbers *2014-2015*	
All (Foreign included)	2,383
FOREIGN ONLY	188

Last Updated: 27/03/15

GERMAN GRADUATE SCHOOL OF MANAGEMENT AND LAW, HEILBRONN (GGS)

Bildungscampus 2, 74076 Heilbronn
Tel: +49(7131) 6456-36-0
EMail: info@ggs.de
Website: http://www.ggs.de

Präsident: Dirk Zupancic
Tel: +49(7131) 645636-74 EMail: dirk.zupancic@ggs.de

Academic Dean: Tomás Bayón
Tel: +49(7131) 645636-31 EMail: tomas.bayon@ggs.de

International Relations: Constanze Wagenblast, International Projects and Programmes Coordinator
Tel: +49(7131) 645636-38 EMail: constanze.wagenblast@ggs.de

Programme

Business Administration *(MBA)* (Business Administration); **Business Law** (Commercial Law); **Legal Management** (Management; Private Law); **Management - Services Management or Retail Logistics** (Retailing and Wholesaling; Service Trades; Transport Management); **UK's Leeds University Business** (Management)

History: Founded 2005 as Heilbronn Business School. Acquired present status and title 2009.

Fees: 18,000-24,000 (Euro)

Main Language(s) of Instruction: German

Degrees and Diplomas: *Master*: **Business Administration; Commercial Law; Management; Private Law; Retailing and Wholesaling; Service Trades; Transport Management.** Leeds University Business School (UK) Master's degree in Management also offered.

Student Services: Library

Student Numbers *2013-2014*: Total 148

Last Updated: 30/01/15

GERMAN UNIVERSITY OF APPLIED SCIENCES FOR PREVENTION AND HEALTH MANAGEMENT

Deutsche Hochschule für Prävention und Gesundheitsmanagement
Hermann Neuberger Sportschule 3, 66123 Saarbrücken
Tel: +49(681) 6855-150
Fax: +49(681) 6855-190
EMail: info@dhfpg.de
Website: http://www.dhfpg.de

Rektor: D. Luppa

Programme

Fitness and Economics (Business Administration; Economics; Marketing; Medicine; Nutrition; Pedagogy; Psychology; Sports); **Fitness Training** (Business Administration; Marketing; Medicine; Nutrition; Pedagogy; Psychology; Service Trades; Sports); **Health Care Management** (Health Administration); **Nutritional**

Consulting (Nutrition); **Prevention and Health Management** *(Postgraduate)* (Health Administration; Sports); **Sports and Economics** (Economics; Sports); **Sports and Health Management** *(Postgraduate)* (Health Administration; Sports)
Further Information: Campuses in Switzerland and Austria

History: Founded 2001 Occupational Academy (Berufsakademie). Acquired present status and title 2008.

Main Language(s) of Instruction: German

Accrediting Agency: Wissenschaftsrat; AHPGS

Degrees and Diplomas: *Bachelor's Degree*: **Health Administration; Nutrition; Sports; Sports Management.** *Master*: **Health Administration; Social and Preventive Medicine; Sports Management.**

Student Numbers *2013-2014*: Total: c. 4,084
Last Updated: 23/01/15

GUSTAV-SIEWERTH ACADEMY

Gustav-Siewerth-Akademie (GSA)

Oberbierbronnen 1, 79809 Weilheim-Bierbronnen
Tel: +49(7755) 364
Fax: +49(7755) 80109
EMail: sekretariat@siewerth-akademie.de
Website: http://www.siewerth-akademie.de

Rektor: Albrecht Graf von Brandenstein-Zeppelin (1999-)
Tel: +49(7755) 6616

Kanzler: August Weh Tel: +49(7755) 3081

International Relations: Alma von Stockhausen

Programme
Philosophy (Philosophy); **Philosophy of Science** (Philosophy)
Course
Catholic Theology (Catholic Theology); **General Studies** (Arts and Humanities; Economics; Journalism; Law; Medicine; Social Sciences)

History: Founded 1985, acquired present status 1993.

Admission Requirements: Abitur

Fees: 900 per semester (Euro)

Main Language(s) of Instruction: German

Accrediting Agency: Volksbank Hochrhein Waldshut

Degrees and Diplomas: *Magister*: **Catholic Theology; Journalism; Pedagogy; Philosophy; Sociology.**

Student Services: Academic Counselling, Careers Guidance, Social Counselling

Student Numbers *2012-2013*: Total 13
Last Updated: 30/01/15

HAMBURG DISTANCE TEACHING UNIVERSITY OF APPLIED SCIENCES

Hamburger Fern-Hochschule (HFH)

Alter Teichweg 19-23a, 22081 Hamburg
Tel: +49(40) 35094-360
Fax: +49(40) 35094-310
EMail: info@hamburger-fh.de
Website: http://www.hamburger-fh.de

President: Peter François (2010-)
Tel: +49(40) 35094-333 EMail: peter.francois@hamburger-fh.de

Chancellor: Johannes Wolf
Tel: +49(40) 35094-3452 EMail: johannes.wolf@hamburger-fh.de

Department
Business Adminstration and Law (Business Administration; Commercial Law); **Engineering** (Industrial Engineering; Mechanical Engineering); **Health Sciences** (Health Administration; Health Sciences)

Further Information: 50 study centers in Germany, Austria and Switzerland.

History: Founded 1997.

Main Language(s) of Instruction: German

Accrediting Agency: ACQUIN; FIBAA; ZEvA

Degrees and Diplomas: *Bachelor's Degree*: **Business Administration; Commercial Law; Health Administration; Health Sciences; Industrial Engineering; Law; Nursing; Occupational Therapy; Physical Therapy.** *Master*: **Business Administration; Commercial Law; Health Administration; Management; Mechanical Engineering.** The Master's Degree in Commercial Law is offered online; Also Certificates; Cooperative programmes with other Universities (Dual degrees) in Business Administration and Law; Health Sciences (Occupational Therapy, Speech Therapy, Nursing and Physical Therapy).

Academic Staff *2014-2015*: Total 1,200
Student Numbers *2014-2015*: Total 10,000
Last Updated: 04/02/15

HAMBURG PROTESTANT UNIVERSITY OF APPLIED SCIENCES FOR SOCIAL AND COMMUNITY WORK

Evangelische Hochschule für Soziale Arbeit und Diakonie

Horner Weg 170, 2111 Hamburg
Tel: +49(40) 65591-238
Fax: +49(40) 65591-228
EMail: ev-fhs-hh@rauheshaus.de
Website: http://www.ev-hochschule-hh.de

Rektor: Andreas Theurich (2011-)
Tel: +49(40) 65591-381 EMail: atheurich@rauheshaus.de

Head of Administration: Herta Klett
Tel: +49(40) 65591-180 EMail: hklett@rauheshaus.de

International Relations: Timm Kunstreich
Tel: +49(40) 65591-186 EMail: timmkunstreich@aol.com

Programme
Social Work *(Part-time)* (Social Work); **Social Work and Deaconry** (Law; Protestant Theology; Social Sciences; Social Studies; Social Work)
Centre
Deaconry Education (Theology)

History: Founded 1834, acquired present status 1971. Formerly known as Evangelische Fachhochschule für Sozialpädagogik - Diakonenanstalt des Rauhen Hauses Hamburg.

Admission Requirements: Secondary school certificate (Abitur) or equivalent

Fees: (Euros): 93 per semester

Main Language(s) of Instruction: German

Degrees and Diplomas: *Bachelor's Degree*: **Health Sciences; Social Welfare; Social Work.** *Master*: **Social Work.** *PhD*: **Social Work.**

Student Services: Academic Counselling, Canteen, Library, Social Counselling

Student Numbers *2013-2014*: Total 473
Last Updated: 26/01/15

HAMBURG SCHOOL OF BUSINESS ADMINISTRATION (HSBA)

Adolphsplatz 1, 20457 Hamburg
Tel: +49(40) 36138-700
Fax: +49(40) 36138-751
EMail: info@hsba.de
Website: http://www.hsba.de

President: Hans-Jörg Schmidt-Trenz
Tel: +49(40) 36138-731 EMail: hansjoerg.schmidttrenz@hk24.de

Managing Director: Uve Samuels
Tel: +49(40) 36138-736 EMail: uve.samuels@hsba.de

International Relations: Yvonne Ewen, Senior International Officer
Tel: +49(40) 36138-716 EMail: yvonne.ewen@hsba.de

School
MBS Maritime Business (Business Administration; Marine Transport)

Department
Applied Economics (Economics); **Finance and Accounting** (Accountancy; Finance); **Marketing and Sales** (Marketing; Sales Techniques); **Media and IT** (Information Technology; Media Studies); **Strategy and Leadership** (Business Administration; Leadership)

History: Founded 2004.

Main Language(s) of Instruction: German

Degrees and Diplomas: *Bachelor's Degree*; *Master*: **International Business; Leadership; Management; Marine Transport.** *PhD*: **Business Administration.** The Doctor of Business Administration (DBA) is awarded by the Napier University Edinburgh through part-time programme offered jointly with Claussen-Simon Graduate Centre at HSBA.

Student Services: Library, Social Counselling, Sports Facilities

Academic Staff *2014-2015*: Total 100

STAFF WITH DOCTORATE: Total 27

Student Numbers *2014-2015*: Total: c. 840

Last Updated: 04/02/15

HANNOVER UNIVERSITY OF APPLIED SCIENCES FOR ECONOMICS

Fachhochschule für die Wirtschaft Hannover (FHDW)

Freundallee 15, 30173 Hannover
Tel: +49(511) 28483-70
Fax: +49(511) 28483-72
EMail: info-ha@fhdw.de
Website: http://www.fhdw-hannover.de

Präsident: Karl-Wilhelm Müller-Siebers (1999-)
Tel: +49(511) 284-8371 EMail: mueller-siebers@ha.bib.de

Programme
Business Administration (Business Administration); **Business Administration (part-time)** (Business Administration); **Business Computing** (Business Computing); **Business Process Engineering** (Business Administration; Engineering); **Computer Science** (Computer Science)

History: Founded 1996.

Main Language(s) of Instruction: German

Degrees and Diplomas: *Bachelor's Degree*: **Business Administration; Business Computing; Computer Science.** *Master*: **Business Administration; Engineering; Insurance; Management; Marketing; Sales Techniques.**

Student Services: Sports Facilities

Student Numbers *2013-2014*: Total 533

Last Updated: 27/01/15

HERTIE SCHOOL OF GOVERNANCE

Quartier 110 - Friedrichstrasse 180, 10117 Berlin
Tel: +49 (30) 259-219-0
Fax: +49 (30) 259-219-111
EMail: info@hertie-school.org; grad-admissions@hertie-school.org
Website: http://hertie-school.org

Dean: Helmut K. Anheier (2009-) EMail: anheier@hertie-school.org

Managing Director: Anna Sophie Herken
EMail: herken@hertie-school.org

International Relations: Judith Zylla-Wöllner, Manager Student Affairs and Study Abroad
Tel: +49(30) 259-219-116 EMail: zylla-woellner@hertie-school.org

Programme
Governance *(PhD)* (Government); **Public Administration (Executive MPA)** (Public Administration); **Public Policy** *(Master)* (Government; Public Administration)

Graduate School
Transnational Studies (BTS) (International Studies)

History: Founded 2003.

Main Language(s) of Instruction: English

Accrediting Agency: Berlin Senate Department for Education, Youth and Science (Senatsverwaltung für Wissenschaft, Forschung und Kultur)

Degrees and Diplomas: *Master*: **Economic and Finance Policy; Government; International Relations; Public Administration; Social Policy.** *PhD*: **Government; International Studies.** Also Executive Master of Public Administration (Executive MPA)

Academic Staff *2014-2015*: Total 21

Student Numbers *2014-2015*: Total 432

Last Updated: 02/03/15

INTERNATIONAL PSYCHOANALYTIC UNIVERSITY BERLIN

Stromstr. 1, 10555 Berlin
Tel: +49(30) 300-117
EMail: info@ipu-berlin.de
Website: http://www.ipu-berlin.de

President: Martin Teising
Tel: +49(30) 300-117-520 EMail: martin.teising@ipu-berlin.de

Chancellor: Rainer Kleinholz
Tel: +49(30) 300-117-511 EMail: rainer.kleinholz@ipu-berlin.de

International Relations: Carmen Scher, Director, International Office
Tel: +49(30) 300-117-722 EMail: carmen.scher@ipu-berlin.de

Programme
Educational Studies (Child Care and Development); **Integrated Care/Psychosis** (Psychology); **Organisational Studies** (Management); **Psychoanalysis** (Psychoanalysis); **Psychology** (Psychology)

History: Founded 2009.

Main Language(s) of Instruction: German

Degrees and Diplomas: *Bachelor's Degree*; *Master*: **Educational Sciences; Management; Psychoanalysis; Psychology.** *PhD*: **Psychoanalysis.**

Student Services: IT Centre, Library

Student Numbers *2013-2014*: Total 485

Last Updated: 19/03/15

INTERNATIONAL SCHOOL OF MANAGEMENT (ISM)

Otto-Hahn-Straße 19, 44227 Dortmund
Tel: +49(231) 9751-390
Fax: +49(231) 9751-3939
EMail: ism.dortmund@ism.de
Website: http://www.ism.de

President: Ingo Böckenholt
Tel: +49(231) 9751-3948 EMail: ingo.boeckenholt@ism.de

Vice-President for Business and Personnel: Anke Czyborra
Tel: +49(231) 9751-3912 EMail: anke.czyborra@ism.de

International Relations: Gertrud Schink, Head, International Office
Tel: +49(231) 9751-3933 EMail: gertrud.schink@ism.de

Programme
Communication and Media Management (Global Track) (Mass Communication); **Energy Management** *(MBA)* (Management); **Finance** *(Graduate)* (Finance); **Finance and Management (Global Track)** (Finance; Management); **General Management** *(MBA)* (Management); **German Business Certificate** *(For Exchange Students)* (Business Administration); **Global Brand and Fashion Management (Global Track)** (International Business; Management); **International Business Certificate** *(For Exchange Students)* (International Business); **International Management** *(Graduate)* (International Business; Management); **International Management (Global)** (International Business; Management); **International Management English Trail (Global Track)** (International Business; Management); **International Transport and Logistics** (Transport and Communications; Transport

Management); **Psychology and Management** *(Graduate)* (Management; Psychology); **Psychology and Management (Global Track)** (Management; Psychology); **Strategic Marketing Management** *(Graduate)* (Management; Marketing); **Tourism and Event Management (Global Track)** (Hotel Management; Tourism)

Further Information: Also campuses in Frankfurt and München

History: Founded 1991.

Fees: 3,500 per semester (Euro)

Main Language(s) of Instruction: German, English

Degrees and Diplomas: *Bachelor's Degree*; *Master*. **Finance; International Business; Management; Marketing; Psychology; Sales Techniques; Tourism; Transport and Communications; Transport Management.** Also Certificates and MBA (General Management, Energy Management, Facility Management).

Student Services: Careers Guidance, Library

Student Numbers *2013-2014*: Total 2,273
Last Updated: 13/03/15

INTERNATIONAL UNIVERSITY HEIDELBERG

Hochschule für Internationales Management Heidelberg (HIMH)

Sickingenstraße 63-65, 69126 Heidelberg
Tel: +49(6221) 6442-0
Fax: +49(6221) 6442-42
EMail: info@himh.de
Website: http://www.himh.de/

President: Matthew Kershaw

Programme

Business Psychology (Industrial and Organizational Psychology); **Event Management** (Management); **International Leadership** *(Graduate)* (Leadership); **International Management** (Management); **Marketing and Corporate Communications** (Communication Studies; Marketing); **Sustainable Management** (Management); **Tourism Management** (Tourism)

Main Language(s) of Instruction: German

Accrediting Agency: FIIBA

Degrees and Diplomas: *Bachelor's Degree*; *Master*. **Leadership.**

Student Numbers *2013-2014*: Total 159
Last Updated: 08/04/15

INTERNATIONAL UNIVERSITY OF APPLIED SCIENCES BAD HONNEF - BONN

Internationale Hochschule Bad Honnef - Bonn (IUBH)

Mühlheimer Strasse 38, 53604 Bad Honnef
Tel: +49(2224) 9605-108
Fax: +49(2224) 9605-115
EMail: info@iubh.de
Website: http://www.iubh.de

Rector and Dean: Ingo Dahm (2014-)
Tel: +49(2224) 9605-200 EMail: i.dahm@iubh.de

Chancellor: Georg Ummenhofer
Tel: +49(2224) 9605-222 EMail: g.ummenhofer@iubh.de

International Relations: Ulrike von Aswegen, Head, International Office Tel: +49(2224) 9605-114 EMail: u.von-aswegen@iubh.de

Programme

Aviation Management (Air Transport); **Hospitality Management** (Hotel Management); **Hospitality Real Estate Certificate** (Hotel and Restaurant; Real Estate); **International Aviation Management** (Air Transport; International Business); **International Event Management** (Management); **International Hospitality Management** (Hotel and Restaurant; International Business); **International Management** (International Business; Management); **International Management (Graduate)** (International Business; Management); **International Management - Aviation (Graduate)** (Air Transport; International Business); **International Management - Finance and Accounting (Graduate)** (Accountancy; Finance; International Business); **International Management - for Non-Business Graduates (Graduate)** (Business Administration; International Business); **International Management - Health Care (Graduate)** (Health Administration; International Business); **International Management - Hospitality (Graduate)** (Hotel and Restaurant; International Business); **International Management - Human Resources (Graduate)** (Human Resources; International Business); **International Management - IT Management (Graduate)** (Information Technology; International Business); **International Management - Marketing (Graduate)** (International Business; Marketing); **International Marketing Management** (International Business; Marketing); **International Tourism Management** (International Business; Tourism); **MBA International Business (Graduate)** (International Business); **Tourism Management** (Tourism); **Transport and Logistics Management (Graduate)** (Management; Transport and Communications)

Further Information: Campuses in Salzburg and Berlin

History: Founded 1999.

Admission Requirements: Secondary school certificate (Abitur, Fachhochschulreife) and entrance examination, TOEFL (minimum score 80) or IELTS (minimum score 6.0)

Fees: c. 8,200 per annum (Euro)

Main Language(s) of Instruction: English

Degrees and Diplomas: *Bachelor's Degree*; *Master*. **International Business; Management; Transport Management.** Also Fast-track Bachelor's degree in Hospitality Management; Certificates in Hospitality Real Estate, Aviation, Quality Management in Hospitality.

Student Services: Academic Counselling, Canteen, Careers Guidance, Foreign Studies Centre, Language Laboratory, Social Counselling, Sports Facilities

Student Numbers *2014-2015*: Total: c. 1,800
Last Updated: 04/02/15

INTERNATIONAL YMCA UNIVERSITY OF APPLIED SCIENCES

CVJM-Hochschule

Hugo-Preuß-Straße 40, 34131 Kassel-Bad Wilhelmshöhe, Hessen
Tel: +49(561) 3087-530
Fax: +49(561) 3087-501
EMail: info@cvjm-hochschule.de
Website: http://www.cvjm-hochschule.de/

Rector: Rüdiger Gebhardt
Tel: +49(561) 3087-503
EMail: gebhardt@cvjm-hochschule.de

Chancellor: Stefan Jung
Tel: +49(561) 3087-530
EMail: jung@cvjm-hochschule.de

Programme

Management (Management); **Social Work** (Social Work); **Theology** (Theology)

Main Language(s) of Instruction: German

Degrees and Diplomas: *Bachelor's Degree*; *Master*. **Ethics; Management.** Some Programmes taught in English

Student Numbers *2013-2014*: Total 321
Last Updated: 07/04/15

JACOBS UNIVERSITY

PO Box 750561, 28725 Bremen
Tel: +49(421) 2004-0
Fax: +49(421) 2004-113
EMail: info@jacobs-university.de
Website: http://www.jacobs-university.de/

President: Katja Windt (2014-)
Tel: +49(421) 200-4100 EMail: a.muhs@jacobs-university.de

Managing Director: Michael Hülsmann
Tel: +49(421) 200-4100 EMail: a.muhs@jacobs-university.de

International Relations: Yuliya Salauyova, International Programs Coordinator
Tel: +49(421) 200-4315
EMail: y.salauyova@jacobs-university.de

School

Engineering and Science (Astronomy and Space Science; Biochemistry; Biological and Life Sciences; Biology; Biotechnology; Chemistry; Computer Science; Earth Sciences; Electrical Engineering; Environmental Studies; Mathematics; Natural Resources; Natural Sciences; Neurosciences; Physics; Transport Management); **Humanities and Social Sciences** (Arts and Humanities; Economics; Law; Management; Psychology; Social Sciences; Statistics)

Centre

Lifelong Learning and Institutional Development

Course

Foundation Year (Economics; Mathematics; Natural Sciences; Political Sciences); **Language** (Chinese; French; German; Spanish); **University Studies** (Environmental Studies; Heritage Preservation; Sculpture; Town Planning; Water Science)

Graduate School

Social Sciences (BIGSSS) *(Bremen International)* (Social Sciences; Statistics)

History: Founded 1999. Acquired present title 2007. Formerly known as International University Bremen.

Academic Year: September to May

Admission Requirements: Secondary school certificate (Reifezeugniss) or equivalent. SAT and TOEFL test

Fees: 20,000 per annum (Euro)

Main Language(s) of Instruction: English

Accrediting Agency: City-State of Bremen, Wissenschaftsrat

Degrees and Diplomas: *Bachelor's Degree*; *Master*: **Arts and Humanities; Cognitive Sciences; Communication Arts; Computer Science; Electronic Engineering; International Relations; Mathematics; Molecular Biology; Petroleum and Gas Engineering; Physics; Telecommunications Engineering; Transport Management; Visual Arts.** *PhD*: **Arts and Humanities; Biological and Life Sciences; Cultural Studies; Engineering; Social Sciences; Welfare and Protective Services.** Executive Master in Basin and Petroleum System Dynamics (MSc)

Student Services: Academic Counselling, Canteen, Careers Guidance, Foreign Studies Centre, Language Laboratory, Library, Residential Facilities, Social Counselling, Sports Facilities

Student Numbers *2014-2015*: Total 1,253

Last Updated: 11/03/15

KARLSHOCHSCHULE INTERNATIONAL UNIVERSITY

Karlstraße 36-38, 76133 Karlsruhe

Tel: +49(721) 1303-500

Fax: +49(721) 1303-300

EMail: info@karlshochschule.de

Website: http://www.karlshochschule.de

President: Michael Zerr EMail: mzerr@karlshochschule.de

Head of Administration: Gérard Massé
Tel: +49(721) 1303-337 EMail: gmasse@karlshochschule.de

International Relations: Jutta Walz
Tel: +49(721) 1303-555 EMail: jwalz@karlshochschule.de

Faculty

I (Communication Studies; International Business; Management; Marketing); **II** (Art Management; International Business; Management; Media Studies; Tourism)

History: Founded as Merkur Internationale FH Karlsruhe.

Fees: Bachelor, 650,00 per month (Euro)

Main Language(s) of Instruction: German

Accrediting Agency: FIBAA

Degrees and Diplomas: *Bachelor's Degree*; *Master*: **Management.**

Student Services: Careers Guidance, Facilities for disabled people, IT Centre, Library

Student Numbers *2013-2014*: Total 664

Last Updated: 19/03/15

KOBLENZ UNIVERSITY OF APPLIED SCIENCES

Hochschule Koblenz (FH KOBLENZ)

Konrad-Zuse-Strasse 1, 56075 Koblenz

Tel: +49(261) 9528-0

Fax: +49(261) 9528-567

EMail: infos@hs-koblenz.de

Website: http://www.hs-koblenz.de

Präsident: Kristian Bosselmann-Cyran
Tel: +49(261) 9528-101 EMail: bosselmann@hs-koblenz.de

Chancellor: Heidi Mikoteit-Olsen
Tel: +49(261) 9528-102 EMail: kanzlerin@hs-koblenz.de

International Relations: Anne Dommershausen
Tel: +49(261) 9528-243
EMail: dommersh@fh-koblenz.de; international@fh-koblenz.de

Department

Business Administration (Business Administration); **Business Administration and Social Management** *(Remagen)* (Business Administration; Child Care and Development; E- Business/Commerce; Educational Administration; Health Administration; Management; Marketing; Social and Community Services; Social Sciences; Sports Management; Tourism; Transport Management); **Civil Engineering** (Architecture; Civil Engineering; Town Planning); **Engineering** (Ceramic Art; Ceramics and Glass Technology; Computer Engineering; Design; Electrical Engineering; Electronic Engineering; Information Technology; Machine Building; Materials Engineering; Mechanical Engineering; Production Engineering); **Mathematics and Technology** *(Remagen)* (Mathematics; Technology); **Social Sciences** (European Union Law; Social Sciences; Social Work)

Further Information: Also Rhein Ahr Campus in Remagen and Wester Wald Campus in Höhr-Grenzhausen

History: Founded 1996

Academic Year: October to July (October-January; March-July)

Admission Requirements: Hochschulreife, Practical Training, Language Competence

Fees: 101,20 per semester (social contribution) (Euro)

Main Language(s) of Instruction: German

Degrees and Diplomas: *Bachelor's Degree*; *Master*: **Applied Mathematics; Applied Physics; Architecture; Business Administration; Business Education; Ceramic Art; Ceramics and Glass Technology; Child Care and Development; Civil Engineering; Economics; Electronic Engineering; Finance; Fine Arts; Health Administration; Human Resources; Industrial Engineering; Leadership; Machine Building; Management; Marketing; Social Sciences; Sports Management; Tourism; Transport Management; Vocational Education.** Master's degree in Business (MBA) offered through continuing/distance education mode

Student Services: Academic Counselling, Canteen, Foreign Studies Centre, Language Laboratory, Library, Social Counselling

Student Numbers *2013-2014*: Total 8,463

Last Updated: 28/01/15

KÜHNE LOGISTICS UNIVERSITY

Kühne Logistics University - Wissenschaftliche Hochschule für Logistik und Unternehmensführung (KLU)

Großer Grasbrook 17, 20457 Hamburg

Tel: +49(40) 328707-0

Fax: +49(40) 328707-109

EMail: info@the-klu.org; study@the-klu.org

Website: https://www.the-klu.org/

President: Thomas Strothotte
Tel: +49(40) 328707-110 EMail: president@the-klu.org

Managing Director: Fabian Berger
Tel: +49(40) 328707-141 EMail: fabian.berger@the-klu.org

International Relations: Ulrike Schneider, Head, International Office Tel: +49(40) 328707-142 EMail: exchange@the-klu.org

Programme
Executive MBA (Business Administration); **Global Logistics** *(Graduate)* (Transport Management); **International Logistics** *(Doctoral)* (Transport Management); **Management** (Management); **Management** *(Graduate)* (Management)

Main Language(s) of Instruction: German

Degrees and Diplomas: *Bachelor's Degree*; *Master*: **Transport Management.** *PhD*: **Transport Management.** PhD offered in English

Student Numbers *2014-2015*: Total 170
Last Updated: 09/04/15

LEIBNIZ-FH SCHHOL OF BUSINESS

Leibniz-Fachhochschule Hannover

Expo Plaza 11, 30539 Hannover
Tel: +49(511) 95784-12
Fax: +49(511) 95784-13
EMail: info@leibniz-fh.de
Website: http://www.leibniz-fh.de

President: Heiner Feldhaus EMail: feldhaus@leibniz-fh.de

Vice President for Administration: Matthias Ritter
Tel: +49(511) 95784-18 EMail: ritter@leibniz-fh.de

International Relations: Anna Kanalieva-Vacheva
Tel: +49(511) 95784-21 EMail: kanalieva@leibniz-fh.de

Programme
Business Administration (Business Administration); **Business Computing** (Business Computing); **Health Management** (Health Administration); **Integrated Management** *(Graduate)* (Management)

History: Founded as Leibniz-Akademie 1920. Acquired present status and title 2011.

Main Language(s) of Instruction: German

Degrees and Diplomas: *Bachelor's Degree*; *Master*: **Business Administration.**

Student Numbers *2013-2014*: Total 443
Last Updated: 09/04/15

LEIPZIG GRADUATE SCHOOL OF MANAGEMENT

Handelshochschule Leipzig (HHL)

Jahnallee 59, 04109 Leipzig
Tel: +49(341) 985-160
Fax: +49(341) 9851-679
EMail: info@hhl.de
Website: http://www.hhl.de

Dean: Andreas Pinkwart
Tel: +49(341) 9851-721 EMail: rektor@hhl.de

Chancellor: Axel Baisch
Tel: +49(341) 9851-726 EMail: kanzler@hhl.de

International Relations: Frank Hoffmann, Director, International Relations Tel: +49(341) 9851-745 EMail: frank.hoffmann@hhl.de

Group
Economics and Regulation (Economics; Health Administration; Information Technology; Law); **Finance, Accounting and Corporate Governance** (Accountancy; Finance; Management); **Innovation and Entrepreneurship** (Management; Technology); **Strategic and International Management** (Business Administration; International Business; Management; Small Business); **Sustainability and Competitiveness** (Business Administration; Economics; Ethics; Information Technology; Marketing; Transport Management)

Further Information: Also preparatory courses for foreign students; one semester abroad compulsory for all students

History: Founded 1898, acquired present status 1996.

Academic Year: September to August (September-December; January-March; April-June; July-August)

Admission Requirements: Equivalence to BA; practical experience; TOEFL; GMAT; entrance examination

Fees: 8,000-15,000 per semester depending on programme (Euro)

Main Language(s) of Instruction: English

Accrediting Agency: AACSB; ACQUIN

Degrees and Diplomas: *Master*: **Management.** *PhD*: **Economic and Finance Policy; Economics; Management.** Also Global Executive MBA and Euro MBA in Management

Student Services: Academic Counselling, Canteen, Careers Guidance, Foreign Studies Centre, Language Laboratory, Library, Social Counselling, Sports Facilities

Academic Staff *2014-2015*	**TOTAL**
FULL-TIME	c. **20**
Student Numbers *2014-2015*	
All (Foreign included)	c. **550**
FOREIGN ONLY	**160**

Last Updated: 03/03/15

LUTHERAN UNIVERSITY OF APPLIED SCIENCES IN NUREMBERG

Evangelische Hochschule Nürnberg (EVHN)

Bärenschanzstraße 4, 90429 Nürnberg
Tel: +49(911) 27253-6
Fax: +49(911) 27253-799
EMail: zentrale@evhn.de
Website: http://www.evfh-nuernberg.de/

Präsident: Barbara Städtler-Mach
Tel: +49(911) 27253-890 EMail: barbara.staedtler-mach@evhn.de

Kanzler: Kurt Füglein
Tel: +49(911) 27253-777 EMail: kurt.fueglein@evhn.de

International Relations: Márta Turcsányi, International Officer
Tel: +49(911) 27253-730 EMail: marta.turcsanyi@evhn.de

Faculty
Health and Care (Health Administration; Health Education; Nursing; Rehabilitation and Therapy); **Religious Education, Adult Education and Diakonik (Christian Social Work)** (Adult Education; Religious Education; Social Work); **Social Sciences** (Business Administration; Social Work; Special Education)

History: Founded 1971.

Main Language(s) of Instruction: German

Degrees and Diplomas: *Bachelor's Degree*: **Child Care and Development; Education; Health Administration; Health Education; Health Sciences; Religious Education; Social Sciences; Social Work; Special Education.** *Master*: **Adult Education; Health Sciences; Social Sciences; Social Work.** *PhD*: **Education.**

Student Services: Library

Student Numbers *2013-2014*: Total 1,271
Last Updated: 26/01/15

MACROMEDIA UNIVERSITY FOR MEDIA AND COMMUNICATION

Macromedia Hochschule für Medien und Kommunikation (MHMK)

Gollierstraße 4, 80339 München
Tel: +49(89) 544-151-0
Fax: +49(89) 544-151-15
EMail: info.muc@macromedia.de
Website: http://www.macromedia.de

President: Jürgen Faust
Tel: +49(89) 544-151-0 EMail: j.faust@macromedia.de

Vice President for Academic Affairs and Research: Castulus Kolo

International Relations: Florence Kanngiesser, International Officer
Tel: +49(40) 300-3089-48 EMail: f.kanngiesser@macromedia.de

Programme
Film and Television (Film; Radio and Television Broadcasting); **Journalism** (Cultural Studies; Economics; Journalism; Sports); **Management** (Management); **Media and Communication Design** (Computer Science; Design; Information Technology; Media Studies; Software Engineering); **Media and Communication Management**

(Communication Studies; Media Studies); **Media Management** (Communication Studies; Management; Media Studies; Music; Radio and Television Broadcasting; Sports Management)

Graduate School

Graduate Studies (Design; Journalism; Mass Communication; Media Studies)

Further Information: Also campuses in Stuttgart, Cologne, Hamburg, Berlin, Osnabruck.

History: Founded 2006.

Main Language(s) of Instruction: German, English

Accrediting Agency: FIBAA

Degrees and Diplomas: *Bachelor's Degree*; *Master*. **Communication Studies; Design; Journalism; Media Studies.**

Student Services: Careers Guidance, Library

Student Numbers *2014-2015*: Total: c. 2,000

Last Updated: 20/03/15

MEDIADESIGN UNIVERSITY OF APPLIED SCIENCES

Mediadesign Hochschule für Design und Informatik (MD.H)

Lindenstrasse 20-25, 10969 Berlin

Tel: +49(30) 399-266-0

Fax: +49(30) 399-26615

EMail: info-ber@mediadesign.de

Website: http://www.mediadesign.de

Rector: Hartmut Bode

Chancellor: Arnim Zubke

Programme

Digital Film Design - Animation (Film; Visual Arts); **Fashion Design** (Fashion Design); **Gamedesign** (Computer Graphics; Mathematics); **Media Design** (Communication Arts; Design; Visual Arts); **Media Management** (Communication Studies; Journalism; Marketing; Mathematics; Media Studies)

Further Information: Also sites in München und Düsseldorf.

Fees: 349-799 per month; registration fee, 350 (Euro)

Main Language(s) of Instruction: German

Degrees and Diplomas: *Bachelor's Degree*: **Computer Engineering; Computer Science; Design; Fashion Design; Media Studies.** *Master*. **Computer Engineering; Design; Media Studies.**

Student Services: Careers Guidance

Student Numbers *2013-2014*: Total 1,268

Last Updated: 20/03/15

MERZ ACADEMY - UNIVERSITY OF APPLIED ARTS STUTTGART

Merz Akademie

Teckstraße 58, 70190 Stuttgart

Tel: +49(771) 26866-0

Fax: +49(771) 26866-21

EMail: info@merz-akademie.de

Website: http://www.merz-akademie.de

Rector: Markus Merz (1981-)
Tel: +49(771) 26866-20 EMail: markus.merz@merz-akademie.de

Verwaltungsleiter: Stefan Grünenwald
Tel: +49(771) 26866-28
EMail: stefan.gruenenwald@merz-akademie.de

Programme

Design, Art and Media (Design; Film; Graphic Design; Media Studies; Video)

History: Founded 1918. Acquired present status 1985.

Academic Year: October to February; March to July

Admission Requirements: Fachhochschulreife

Fees: 330 per semester (Euro)

Main Language(s) of Instruction: German

Degrees and Diplomas: *Bachelor's Degree*; *Master*. **Design; Fine Arts; Media Studies.**

Student Services: Academic Counselling, Canteen, Social Counselling

Student Numbers *2013-2014*: Total 270

Last Updated: 19/03/15

MSB MEDICAL SCHOOL BERLIN

Medical School Berlin - Hochschule für Gesundheit und Medizin (MSB)

Calandrellistraße 1-9, D-12247 Berlin

Tel: +49(30) 7668-3753-60

Fax: +49(30) 7668-3753-69

EMail: info@medicalschool-berlin.de

Website: http://www.medicalschool-berlin.de/

Director: Ilona Renken-Olthoff
Tel: +49(30) 7668-3753-20
EMail: ilona.renken-olthoff@medicalschool-berlin.de

International Relations: Alexander Trefz, Head, International Office
Tel: +49(40) 361226-464
EMail: alexander.trefz@medicalschool-berlin.de

Faculty

Health Sciences (Health Sciences); **Natural Sciences** (Natural Sciences)

Main Language(s) of Instruction: German

Accrediting Agency: Akkreditierungsagentur im Bereich Gesundheit und Soziales (AHPGS)

Degrees and Diplomas: *Bachelor's Degree*; *Master*. **Clinical Psychology; Health Education; Psychotherapy.** No Numerus clausus for Master's degree programmes.

Student Services: Careers Guidance

Student Numbers *2013-2014*: Total 415

Last Updated: 09/04/15

MSH MEDICAL SCHOOL HAMBURG UNIVERSITY OF APPLIED SCIENCE AND MEDICAL UNIVERSITY

Am Kaiserkai 1, 20457 Hamburg

Tel: +49(40) 361-226-40

Fax: +49(40) 361-226-430

EMail: info@medicalschool-hamburg.de

Website: http://www.medicalschool-hamburg.de/

Director: Ilona Renken-Olthoff
EMail: info@medicalschool-hamburg.de

International Relations: Alexander Trefz, Head, International Office
Tel: +49(40) 361226-464
EMail: Alexander.Trefz@medicalschool-hamburg.de

Faculty

Health Sciences (Health Education; Health Sciences; Nursing; Psychology; Rehabilitation and Therapy); **Human Sciences** (Psychology)

Main Language(s) of Instruction: German

Degrees and Diplomas: *Bachelor's Degree*; *Master*. **Art Therapy; Clinical Psychology; Health Education; Psychology; Psychotherapy.**

Student Services: Careers Guidance

Student Numbers *2013-2014*: Total 1,078

Last Updated: 09/04/15

MUNICH BUSINESS SCHOOL

Elsenheimerstrasse 61, 80687 München

Tel: +49(89) 547678-0

Fax: +49(89) 547678-26

EMail: info@munich-business-school.de

Website: http://www.munich-business-school.de

President: Rudolf Gröger

Administrative Officer: Nadine Westphal

International Relations: Elvira Stephenson, Head of the International Center
Tel: +49(89) 547678-11
EMail: international@munich-business-school.de

Programme

Business Administration (Business Administration); **International Business** (International Business); **International Management** (Management); **Management** (Management); **Sports Business and Communication** (Business Administration; Communication Studies)

History: Founded 1991.

Main Language(s) of Instruction: German

Degrees and Diplomas: *Bachelor's Degree*; *Master*: **Business Administration; International Business; Management.** *PhD*: **Business Administration.** Also MBA; Executive MBA.

Student Services: Careers Guidance

Student Numbers *2013-2014*: Total 573
Last Updated: 20/03/15

MUNICH SCHOOL OF PHILOSOPHY

Hochschule für Philosophie München

Philosophische Fakultät S.J., Kaulbachstraße 31a, 80539 München
Tel: +49(89) 2386-2300
Fax: +49(89) 2386-2302
EMail: info@hfph.de
Website: http://www.hfph.de/

President: Johannes Wallacher
Tel: +49(89) 2386-2301 EMail: johannes.wallacher@hfph.de

Chancellor: Dina Brandt
Tel: +49(89) 2386-2301 EMail: dina.brandt@hfph.de

Institute

Philosophy and Leadership *(IPL)* (Leadership; Philosophy); **Philosophy of Religion** *(IRP)* (Philosophy; Religion); **Scientific Issues related to Philosophy and Theology** *(ING)* (Philosophy; Theology); **Social and Development Studies** *(IGP)* (Development Studies; Social Studies)

History: Founded 1925. Acquired present status 1971.

Main Language(s) of Instruction: German

Accrediting Agency: ACQUIN; AKAST

Degrees and Diplomas: *Bachelor's Degree*; *Master*: **Cultural Studies; Ethics; Philosophy.** *PhD*: **Philosophy.** *Habilitation*: **Philosophy.** Also Undergraduate Certificate

Student Services: Library

Publications: Theologie und Philosophie

Academic Staff *2014-2015*: Total: c. 30
Student Numbers *2014-2015*: Total: c. 570
Last Updated: 10/03/15

NÜRTINGEN UNIVERSITY OF APPLIED SCIENCES FOR ART THERAPY

Hochschule für Kunsttherapie Nürtingen (HKT)

Sigmaringer Strasse 15, 72622 Nürtingen
Tel: +49(7022) 93336-0
Fax: +49(7022) 93336-23
EMail: info@hkt-nuertingen.de
Website: http://www.hkt-nuertingen.de

Rektor: Johannes Junker
Tel: +49(7022) 93336-13 EMail: j.junker@hkt-nuertingen.de

Chancellor: Roswitha Bader
Tel: +49(7022) 93336-12 EMail: r.bader@hkt-nuertingen.de

International Relations: Heike Maher, Erasmus Coordinator
Tel: +49(49) 7022-933360 EMail: h.maher@hkt-nuertingen.de

Programme

Art Therapy (Art Therapy; Fine Arts; Psychotherapy; Rehabilitation and Therapy)

History: Founded 1987. Formerly known as Fachhochschule für Kunsttherapie Nürtingen.

Main Language(s) of Instruction: German

Degrees and Diplomas: *Bachelor's Degree*: **Art Therapy.** *Master*: **Art Therapy.**

Student Services: Cultural Activities, Health Services

Student Numbers *2013-2014*: Total 291
Last Updated: 09/03/15

PRIVATE UNIVERSITY OF APPLIED SCIENCES FOR ECONOMIC AND TECHNICAL STUDIES VECHTA/DIEPHOLZ/OLDENBURG

Private Fachhochschule für Wirtschaft und Technik Vechta-Diepholz-Oldenburg

Rombergstrasse 40, 49377 Vechta
Tel: +49(4441) 915-0
Fax: +49(4441) 915-109
EMail: info@fhwt.de
Website: http://www.fhwt.de

Rector: Ludger Bölke
Tel: +49(4441) 915-0 EMail: boelke@phwt.de

Full time Vice-President and Head of Administration:
Anne-Katrin Reich Tel: +49(4441) 915-101 EMail: reich@fhwt.de

Department

Business Administration (Accountancy; Agricultural Business; Business Administration; Finance; Human Resources; Information Technology; Marketing; Transport and Communications); **Electronic Engineering and Mechatronics** (Business Administration; Communication Studies; Electronic Engineering; English; Information Technology; Mathematics; Mechanical Engineering; Software Engineering); **Engineering** *(Dr. Jürgen Ulderup)* (Accountancy; Business Administration; English; Finance; Marketing; Mechanical Engineering; Production Engineering; Safety Engineering; Transport Management)

History: Founded 1998.

Main Language(s) of Instruction: German

Degrees and Diplomas: *Bachelor's Degree*; *Master*: **Small Business.**

Student Services: Library

Student Numbers *2013-2014*: Total 703
Last Updated: 24/03/15

PRIVATE UNIVERSITY OF APPLIED SCIENCES GÖTTINGEN

Private Fachhochschule Göttingen

Weender Landstrasse 3-7, 37073 Göttingen
Tel: +49(551) 54700-100
Fax: +49(551) 54700-190
EMail: info@pfh.de
Website: https://www.pfh.de/

President: Frank Albe (2014-)
Tel: +49(551) 54700-103 EMail: praesidialbuero@pfh.de

Chancellor: Benno Fleer

International Relations: Joachim Ahrens, Head of International Affairs Tel: +49(551) 54700-100 EMail: ahrens@pfh.de

Programme

Healthcare Technology (Health Sciences; Technology); **Management** (Management); **Technology** (Engineering)

History: Founded 1995.

Main Language(s) of Instruction: German

Degrees and Diplomas: *Bachelor's Degree*; *Master*: **Business Administration; Engineering; Industrial and Organizational Psychology; Management; Materials Engineering; Orthopaedics; Psychology; Rehabilitation and Therapy.**

Student Numbers *2014-2015*: Total 2,200
Last Updated: 22/03/15

PROTESTANT UNIVERSITY OF APPLIED SCIENCES DARMSTAD

Evangelische Hochschule Darmstadt (EHD)

Zweifalltorweg 12, 64293 Darmstadt, Hessen
Tel: +49(6151) 8798-0
Fax: +49(6151) 8798-58
EMail: info@eh-darmstadt.de
Website: http://www.efh-darmstadt.de

Präsidentin: Marion Gross Klaus Seidel
Tel: +49(6151) 8798-11
EMail: grossklaus-seidel@efh-darmstadt.de

Chancellor: Arne Lankenau

Programme

Basic Studies Religious Education (Religious Studies); **Care and Health Promotion** (Health Sciences); **Child Education and Development** (Child Care and Development); **Inclusive Education/Integrative Special Education** (Education; Special Education); **Postgraduate Studies** (Ethics; Leadership; Management; Nursing; Psychology; Religious Studies; Social Work); **Social Work** (Social Work)

Further Information: Also Campus in Hephata

History: Founded 1971.

Academic Year: September to August

Admission Requirements: Fachhochschulreife/Abitur

Fees: None

Main Language(s) of Instruction: German

Accrediting Agency: Akkreditierungsagentur für Studiengänge im Bereich Heilpädagogik, Pflege, Gesundheit und Soziale Arbeit

Degrees and Diplomas: *Bachelor's Degree*: **Child Care and Development; Education; Health Sciences; Social Work.** *Master*: **Education; Management; Nursing; Psychology; Social Work; Special Education.**

Student Services: Academic Counselling, Careers Guidance, Language Laboratory, Library, Social Counselling

Academic Staff *2013-2014*: Total: c. 40

Student Numbers *2013-2014*: Total: c. 1,700

Last Updated: 26/01/15

PROTESTANT UNIVERSITY OF APPLIED SCIENCES FREIBURG

Evangelische Hochschule Freiburg (EH FREIBURG)

Bugginger Strasse 38, 79114 Freiburg
Tel: +49(761) 47812-0
Fax: +49(761) 47812-30
EMail: mail@eh-freiburg.de
Website: http://www.efh-freiburg.de

Rektor: Renate Kirchhoff (2013-)
Tel: +49(761) 47812-20
EMail: rektorin@eh-freiburg.de; rektorat@eh-freiburg.de

Prorector: Björn Kraus
Tel: +49(761) 47812-41 EMail: bkraus@eh-freiburg.de

Verwaltungsdirektor: Ulrich Rolf
Tel: +49(761) 47812-15
EMail: verwaltungsdirektor@eh-freiburg.de

Chancellor: Ulrich Rolf
Tel: +49(761) 47812-15 EMail: rolf@eh-freiburg.de

International Relations: Markus Breuer
Tel: +49(761) 47812-433
EMail: breuer@eh-freiburg.de; internationaloffice@eh-freiburg.de

Department

Pedagogy and Supervision (Pedagogy); **Social Work** (Social Work); **Theological Education and Diaconia Studies** *(Protestant)* (Religious Education; Theology)

History: Founded 1972

Main Language(s) of Instruction: German

Accrediting Agency: Wissenschaftsrat (WR)

Degrees and Diplomas: *Bachelor's Degree*: **Child Care and Development; Religious Education; Social Work.** *Master*: **Child Care and Development; Ethics; Management; Pastoral Studies; Psychology; Religious Education; Social Work.** *PhD*: **Social Work.**

Student Services: Academic Counselling, Library

Student Numbers *2014-2015*: Total: c. 1,000

Last Updated: 26/01/15

PROTESTANT UNIVERSITY OF APPLIED SCIENCES OF LUDWIGSBURG

Evangelische Fachhochschule Ludwigsburg

Paulusweg 6, 71638 Ludwigsburg
Tel: +49(7141) 9745-200
Fax: +49(7141) 9745-400
EMail: rektorat@eh-ludwigsburg.de; m.quattlender@eh-ludwigsburg.de
Website: http://www.eh-ludwigsburg.de

Rector: Norbert Collmar
Tel: +49(7141) 9745-201 EMail: n.collmar@eh-ludwigsburg.de

Head of Administration: Beate Käser
Tel: +49(7141) 9745-205 EMail: b.kaeser@eh-ludwigsburg.de

International Relations: Melinda Madew, Head, International Office
Tel: +49(7141) 9745-280 EMail: m.madew@eh-ludwigsburg.de

Programme

Christian Education/Social Work (Christian Religious Studies; Social Work); **Diaconal Studies (Graduate)** (Religion); **Diaconal Studies and International Social Work** (Religion; Social Work); **Diaconal Studies and Social Work** (Religion; Social Work); **Early Childhood Education (Graduate)** (Preschool Education); **Early Childhood Education and Teaching** (Preschool Education; Teacher Training); **Inclusive Education and Special Education** (Education; Special Education); **International Social Work** (Social Work); **Nursing** (Nursing); **Organizational Development** (Management); **Religious Education** (Religious Education); **Religious Education and Social Work** (Bible; Humanities and Social Science Education; Religion; Religious Education; Social Work; Theology); **Social Work** (Social Work); **Social Work (Graduate)** (Social Work)

History: Founded 1954.

Main Language(s) of Instruction: German

Degrees and Diplomas: *Bachelor's Degree*: **Nursing; Preschool Education; Religious Education; Social Work; Special Education; Teacher Training.** *Master*: **Management; Preschool Education; Religion; Religious Education; Social Work.** No more enrollment allowed for the Master's Degree in Religious Education.

Student Services: Library

Student Numbers *2013-2014*: Total 1,123

Last Updated: 02/03/15

PROTESTANT UNIVERSITY OF APPLIED SCIENCES RHINELAND-WESTPHALIA-LIPPE IN BOCHUM

Evangelische Fachhochschule Rheinland-Westfalen-Lippe Bochum (EFH FWD)

Immanuel-Kantstr. 18-20, 44803 Bochum
Tel: +49(234) 36901-0
Fax: +49(234) 36901-100
EMail: efh@efh-bochum.de
Website: http://www.efh-bochum.de

Rektor: Gerhard K. Schäfer
Tel: +49(234) 36901-133 EMail: rektor@efh-bochum.de

Kanzlerin: Heike Schmidtchen
Tel: +49(234) 36901-131 EMail: rektorat@efh-bochum.de

International Relations: Karen Bossow, International Officer
Tel: +49(234) 36901-215 EMail: bossow@efh-bochum.de

Division

Social Work, Education and Social Welfare (Education; Social Welfare; Social Work); **Special Education and Care** (Health Sciences; Special Education)

History: Founded 1971.

Main Language(s) of Instruction: German

Degrees and Diplomas: *Bachelor's Degree*: **Christian Religious Studies; Health Administration; Nursing; Primary Education; Social Work; Special Education.** *Master*: **Education; Health Sciences; Management; Social Work.** *PhD*: **Social Work.**

Student Services: Academic Counselling, Canteen, Facilities for disabled people, Library, Social Counselling

Publications: Bochumer Beiträge zur Pflege; EFH International; Hochschulzeitung: EFH-Aktuell; Rektoratsbericht: Jahresringe; Schriftenreihe: Denken und Handeln

Student Numbers *2013-2014*: Total: c. 2,200
Last Updated: 26/01/15

PROTESTANT UNIVERSITY OF APPLIED SCIENCES TABOR

Evangelische Hochschule Tabor
Dürerstraße 43, Marburg, 35039
Tel: +49(6421) 967-3
Fax: +49(6421) 967-411
EMail: info@eh-tabor.de
Website: http://www.eh-tabor.de/

Rector: Norbert Schmidt Tel: +49(6421) 967 431

Chancellor: Benjamin Wenzel EMail: rektor@eh-tabor.de

Programme

Protestant Community Practice (Religion); **Protestant Theology** (Protestant Theology); **Religion and Psychotherapy** (Psychotherapy; Religion)

Main Language(s) of Instruction: German

Degrees and Diplomas: *Bachelor's Degree*; *Master*: **Psychotherapy; Religion.**

Student Services: Library
Last Updated: 03/04/15

PROVADIS SCHOOL OF INTERNATIONAL MANAGEMENT AND TECHNOLOGY

Industriepark Höchst, Geb. B845, 65926 Frankfurt am Main
Tel: +49(69) 305-81051
Fax: +49(69) 305-16277
EMail: info@provadis-hochschule.de
Website: http://www.provadis-hochschule.de

President: Eva Schwinghammer
Tel: +49(69) 305-5160
EMail: eva.schwinghammer@provadis-hochschule.de

Programme

Biopharmaceutical Science (Pharmacology); **Business Administration** (Business Administration; Industrial Management); **Business Information Management** (Business Computing; Information Management); **Chemical Engineering** *(Graduate)* (Chemical Engineering); **Chemical Engineering** (Chemical Engineering); **Technologie and Management** *(Graduate)* (Engineering; Management)

History: Founded 2003.

Main Language(s) of Instruction: German

Degrees and Diplomas: *Bachelor's Degree*; *Master*: **Chemical Engineering; Engineering; Management.** Also dual Bachelors programme in Business Administration in cooperation with Deutsche Telekom

Student Numbers *2013-2014*: Total 793
Last Updated: 24/03/15

PSYCHOLOGICAL UNIVERSITY BERLIN

Psychologische Hochschule Berlin (PHB)
Am Köllnischen Park 2, 10179 Berlin
Tel: +49(30) 209166-201
EMail: kontakt@psychologische-hochschule.de
Website: http://www.psychologische-hochschule.de/

Rector: Siegfried Preiser
Tel: +49(30) 209-166-210
EMail: rektor@psychologische-hochschule.de

Director: Günter Koch
Tel: +49(30) 209-166-201
EMail: g.koch@psychologische-hochschule.de

Programme

Behavior Therapy (Psychotherapy); **Child and Adolescent Psychotherapy** (Psychotherapy); **Depth psychology-based Psychotherapy** (Psychotherapy); **Forensic Psychology** (Psychology); **Psychology** *(Graduate)* (Psychology); **Psychology and Psychotherapy of the Family** (Psychology; Psychotherapy)

Main Language(s) of Instruction: German

Degrees and Diplomas: *Master*: **Psychology.**

Student Numbers *2013-2014*: Total 75
Last Updated: 09/04/15

QUADRIGA UNIVERSITY BERLIN

Quadriga Hochschule Berlin
Werderscher Markt 13, D-10117 Berlin
Tel: +49(30) 447-294-00
Fax: +49(30) 447-293-00
EMail: info@quadriga.eu
Website: http://www.quadriga.eu/

President: Peter Voß

Vice-President: René Seidenglanz
EMail: rene.seidenglanz@quadriga.eu

Programme

Communication and Leadership (Communication Studies; Leadership); **Leadership and Human Resources** (Human Resources; Leadership); **Public Affairs and Leadership** (Leadership; Public Administration)

Main Language(s) of Instruction: German

Accrediting Agency: Zentrale Evaluations- und Akkreditierungsagentur Hannover (ZEvA)

Degrees and Diplomas: *Master*: **Communication Studies; Leadership; Public Administration.**

Student Services: Library

Student Numbers *2013-2014*: Total 105
Last Updated: 09/04/15

RHENISH UNIVERSITY OF APPLIED SCIENCES, COLOGNE

Rheinische Fachhochschule Köln
Schaevenstraße 1 a-b, 50676 Köln, Nordrhein-Westfalen
Tel: +49(221) 20302-0
Fax: +49(221) 20302-49
EMail: verw@rfh-koeln.de
Website: http://www.rfh-koeln.de

President: Wilfried Saxler
Tel: +49(221) 20302-20 EMail: praesident@rfh-koeln.de

Faculty

Business and Law (Business Administration; Business Computing; Law; Taxation); **Engineering** (Electronic Engineering; Engineering; Industrial Engineering; Mathematics; Mechanical Engineering); **Media Studies** (Business Administration; E- Business/Commerce; Marketing; Media Studies); **Medicine Economics** (Health Administration)

History: Founded 1958. Acquired present status 1971.

Main Language(s) of Instruction: German

Degrees and Diplomas: *Bachelor's Degree*; *Master*: **Business Administration; Commercial Law; E- Business/Commerce; Engineering; Health Administration; Marketing; Media Studies; Taxation.** Also MBA. PhD-Programme is offered jointly with the Loughborough University (UK).

Student Services: Academic Counselling, Careers Guidance, Foreign Studies Centre, Language Laboratory, Library, Social Counselling, Sports Facilities

Student Numbers *2013-2014*: Total 5,303
Last Updated: 24/03/15

RIEDLINGEN UNIVERSITY

SRH FernHochschule Riedlingen

Lange Str. 19, 88499 Riedlingen
Tel: +49(7371) 9315-0
Fax: +49(7371) 9315-15
EMail: info@fh-riedlingen.srh.de
Website: http://www.fh-riedlingen.de/

Rector: Julia S. Sander
Tel: +49(7371) 9315-33 EMail: julia.sander@fh-riedlingen.srh.de

Head of Administration: Tobias Heilig
Tel: +49(7371) 9315-0 EMail: tobias.heilig@fh-riedlingen.srh.de

International Relations: Christian Beditsch
Tel: +49(7371) 9315-20
EMail: christian.beditsch@fh-riedlingen.srh.de

Programme

Business Administration (Business Administration); **Business Administration** *(Continuing Education)* (Business Administration); **Business Psychology** (Psychology); **Business Psychology and Change Management** (Industrial and Organizational Psychology; Management); **Business Psychology, Leadership and Management** (Industrial and Organizational Psychology; Leadership; Management); **Corporate Management and Governance** (Management); **Food Management and Technology** (Food Technology; Management); **Health Administration** (Health Administration); **Health Care Management** (Health Administration); **Health Economics for Physicians** *(Continuing Education)* (Health Administration); **Management Assistant** *(Continuing Education)* (Management); **Master of Business Administration** (Business Administration); **Media and Communications Management** (Mass Communication; Media Studies); **Pharmaceutical Management and Technology** (Health Administration); **Prevention and Health Psychology** (Psychology; Social and Preventive Medicine); **Social Management** (Social Work)

History: Founded 1996.

Main Language(s) of Instruction: German

Degrees and Diplomas: *Bachelor's Degree*; *Master*: **Finance; Health Administration; Human Resources; Industrial and Organizational Psychology; Leadership; Management; Marketing.** Also MBA; Double Degree-Programmes; Further Education Certificates.

Student Numbers *2013-2014*: Total 2,405
Last Updated: 24/03/15

SANKT GEORGEN GRADUATE SCHOOL OF PHILOSOPHY AND THEOLOGY, FRANKFURT AM MAIN

Philosophisch-Theologische Hochschule Sankt Georgen Frankfurt am Main

Offenbacher Landstrasse 224, D-60599 Frankfurt am Main
Tel: +49(69) 6061-0
Fax: +49(69) 6061-307
EMail: rektorat@sankt-georgen.de
Website: http://www.sankt-georgen.de

Rektor: Ansgar Wucherpfennig
Tel: +49(69) 6061-219 EMail: rektorat@sankt-georgen.de

Programme

Philosophy (Philosophy); **Theology** (Catholic Theology; Theology)

Institute

Economic and Societal Ethics *(Oswald von Nell-Breuning)* (Ethics); **History of Dogma and Liturgy** (Religious Studies); **Pastoral Psychology and Spirituality** (Psychology); **Study of the Middle Ages** *(Hugo von Sankt Viktor)* (Medieval Studies); **World Church and Mission** (Missionary Studies)

History: Founded 1926.

Academic Year: October to September

Admission Requirements: Hochschulzugangsberechtigung, Abitur, Matura

Fees: 90 per semester (Euro)

Main Language(s) of Instruction: German

Accrediting Agency: AKAST

Degrees and Diplomas: *Bachelor's Degree*: **Philosophy.** *Lizentiat*: **Catholic Theology.** *Magister*: **Catholic Theology.** *PhD*: **Catholic Theology.** *Habilitation*: **Catholic Theology.**

Student Services: Academic Counselling, Canteen, Cultural Activities, Facilities for disabled people, Foreign Studies Centre, IT Centre, Library, Social Counselling, Sports Facilities

Publications: Theologie und Philosophie

Academic Staff *2014-2015*	**TOTAL**
FULL-TIME	**30**
PART-TIME	**20**
Student Numbers *2013-2014*	
All (Foreign included)	**383**

Last Updated: 06/02/15

SCHOOL OF ECONOMICS FOR MANAGEMENT

Hochschule der Wirtschaft für Management (HDWM)

Neckarauer Straße 200, 68163 Mannheim
Tel: +49(621) 490712-0
Fax: +49(621) 490712-88
EMail: info@hdwm.de
Website: http://www.hdwm.eu/

President: Franz Egle
Tel: +49(621) 490712-10 EMail: franz.egle@hdwm.de

Programme

Consulting and Sales Management (Management); **IT Management** (Information Technology); **Management and Corporate Governance** (Management); **Management in International Business** (International Business; Management); **MBA Sales Management** (Sales Techniques); **MBA Sustainable Management** (Management)

Main Language(s) of Instruction: German

Degrees and Diplomas: *Bachelor's Degree*; *Master*: **Management; Sales Techniques.**

Student Services: Careers Guidance

Student Numbers *2013-2014*: Total 368
Last Updated: 07/04/15

SCHOOL OF HEALTH AND SPORTS, TECHNOLOGY AND ART

Hochschule für Gesundheit und Sport, Technik und Kunst (H:G)

Vulkanstraße 1, 10367 Berlin
Tel: +49 (030) 577 97 37 0
Fax: +49 (030) 577 97 37 999
EMail: info@my-campus-berlin.com
Website: http://www.my-campus-berlin.com

President: Christian Werner
Tel: +49(30) 577-9737-0
EMail: christian.werner@my-campus-berlin.com

Chancellor: Andreas Mues
Tel: +49(30) 577-9737-0
EMail: andreas.mues@my-campus-berlin.com

International Relations: Tanja Brosch
Tel: +49(30) 577-9737-100
EMail: tanja.brosch@my-campus-berlin.com

Faculty

Art (Architecture; Design; Jazz and Popular Music; Mass Communication; Music); **Engineering** (Biotechnology; Electronic Engineering; Environmental Engineering; Industrial Engineering); **Health Sciences** (Alternative Medicine; Clinical Psychology; Health Administration; Health Sciences; Medicine; Nursing; Psychology); **Sports** (Sports; Sports Management)

History: Founded 2007.

Main Language(s) of Instruction: German

Degrees and Diplomas: *Bachelor's Degree*: **Alternative Medicine; Architecture; Biotechnology; Design; Electronic Engineering; Environmental Engineering; Fine Arts; Health Sciences; Industrial Engineering; Jazz and Popular Music;**

Media Studies; Medicine; Music; Psychiatry and Mental Health; Psychology; Sports. *Master*: **Design; Health Sciences; Psychiatry and Mental Health; Psychology; Sports.**

Student Services: Careers Guidance, Library

Student Numbers *2013-2014*: Total 541
Last Updated: 05/03/15

SRH UNIVERSITY BERLIN

SRH Hochschule Berlin
Ernst-Reuter-Platz 10, 10587 Berlin
Tel: +49(30) 374-374-0
Fax: +49(30) 374-374-375
EMail: info@srh-hochschule-berlin.de
Website: http://www.srh-hochschule-berlin.de/

President: Victoria Büsch
EMail: victoria.buesch@srh-hochschule-berlin.de

International Relations: Ulrike Scharmann
Tel: +49(30) 374-374-150
EMail: ulrike.scharmann@srh-hochschule-berlin.de

Programme

Entrepreneurship *(Graduate)* (Management); **International Business Administration** (Environmental Management; International Business); **International Business Administration** (International Business); **International Healthcare Management** *(MBA)* (Health Administration); **International Hospitality Management** (Hotel and Restaurant; International Business); **International Management** *(Tripartite/Transatlantic)* (Management); **International Management** *(Berlin)* (Management); **Renewable Energy and Environmental Management** *(MBA)* (Environmental Management)

History: Founded 2002 as OTA Hochschule (OTA Private University of Applied Sciences). Acquired current title 2008.

Academic Year: October to August

Admission Requirements: For Bachelor programs: Abitur/Fachabitur (University entrance diploma) or equivalent; TOEFL iBT score of 79 to 80 required for programmes in English. For Master's programme: Bachelor's or advanced academic degree (Diploma) in the related subject.

Fees: 700 per month for Bachelor's and Master's Programmes (Euro)

Main Language(s) of Instruction: German, English

Accrediting Agency: FIBAA; AHPGS

Degrees and Diplomas: *Bachelor's Degree*; *Master*: **Environmental Management; Health Administration; Hotel Management; Industrial and Organizational Psychology; International Business; Management.** Also Executive MBA; Further Education Certificates.

Student Services: Academic Counselling, Canteen, Careers Guidance, Facilities for disabled people, Language Laboratory, Library, Social Counselling, Sports Facilities

Student Numbers *2013-2014*: Total 707
Last Updated: 24/03/15

SRH UNIVERSITY HEIDELBERG

SRH Hochschule Heidelberg
Ludwig-Guttmann-Straße 6, 69123 Heidelberg
Tel: +49(6221) 88-1000
Fax: +49(6221) 88-4122
EMail: info@hochschule-heidelberg.de
Website: http://www.fh-heidelberg.de

Rektor: Jörg M. Winterberg Tel: +49(6221) 88-2258

Faculty

Applied Psychology (Psychology); **Computer Science** (Business Computing; Computer Science; Health Administration; Multimedia); **Economics** (Business Administration; Sports Management); **Engineering and Architecture** (Architecture; Construction Engineering; Electrical Engineering; Engineering; Industrial Engineering; Information Technology; Mechanical Engineering; Production Engineering); **Social and Legal Sciences** (Law; Leadership; Management; Social Sciences); **Therapy** (Art Therapy; Music; Physical Therapy)

History: Founded 1969. Formerly known as Fachhochschule Heidelberg.

Main Language(s) of Instruction: German

Degrees and Diplomas: *Bachelor's Degree*; *Master*: **Architecture; Commercial Law; Computer Science; Construction Engineering; Dance; Engineering; Industrial and Organizational Psychology; Information Technology; International Business; Labour Law; Leadership; Management; Psychology; Real Estate; Rehabilitation and Therapy; Small Business; Social Work; Sports Management.**

Student Services: Residential Facilities

Student Numbers *2013-2014*: Total 2,941
Last Updated: 25/03/15

SRH UNIVERSITY OF APPLIED SCIENCES CALW

SRH Hochschule Calw
Lederstr. 1, 75365 Calw
Tel: +49(7051) 9203-0
Fax: +49(7051) 9203-59
EMail: info@hs-calw.de
Website: http://www.hochschule-calw.de

Rector: Peter J. Weber
Tel: +49(7051) 9203-0 EMail: info@hochschule-calw.de

International Relations: Loreto Aravena
Tel: +49(7051) 9203-41
EMail: loreto.aravena-martinez@hs-calw.de

Programme

Business Administration (Business Administration); **Controlling** (Finance; Taxation); **Media and Communications Management** (Mass Communication; Media Studies); **Media Management and Mass Communication** *(Graduate)* (Communication Studies; Media Studies)

Main Language(s) of Instruction: German

Degrees and Diplomas: *Bachelor's Degree*; *Master*: **Mass Communication; Media Studies.**

Student Services: Careers Guidance, Library

Student Numbers *2013-2014*: Total 322
Last Updated: 24/03/15

SRH UNIVERSITY OF APPLIED SCIENCES FOR LOGISTICS AND ECONOMICS

SRH Hochschule für Logistik und Wirtschaft
Platz der Deutschen Einheit 1, 59065 Hamm
Tel: +49(2381) 9291-121
Fax: +49(2381) 9291-199
EMail: info@fh-hamm.srh.de
Website: http://www.fh-hamm.srh.de

Rector: Heinz Joachim Opitz (2012-)
Tel: +49(2381) 9291-140 EMail: joachim.opitz@fh-hamm.srh.de

Programme

Business Administration (Business Administration); **Energy and Industrial Engineering** (Energy Engineering; Industrial Engineering); **Energy Management** (Energy Engineering); **Industrial Engineering Logistics** (Industrial Engineering; Transport Management); **Logistic Management** *(Postgraduate)* (Transport Management); **Logistics and Industrial Engineering** (Industrial Engineering; Transport Management); **Social Work** (Social Work); **Supply Chain Management** (Management)

Main Language(s) of Instruction: German

Degrees and Diplomas: *Bachelor's Degree*; *Master*: **Business Administration; Energy Engineering; Management; Transport Management.** Also Dual Degree Programmes; Further Education Certificates.

Student Services: Sports Facilities

Student Numbers *2013-2014*: Total 561
Last Updated: 25/03/15

SRH UNIVERSITY OF APPLIED SCIENCES GERA

SRH Fachhochschule für Gesundheit Gera

Neue Straße 28-30, 07548 Gera
Tel: +49(365) 773-407-0
Fax: +49(365) 773-407-77
EMail: info@srh-gesundheitshochschule.de
Website: http://www.gesundheitshochschule.de/

President: Johannes Schaller (2012-)

Head of Administration: Kai Metzner

International Relations: Julia König
Tel: +49(6221) 882873
EMail: julia.koenig@srh-gesundheitshochschule.de

Programme

Health Psychology (Psychology); **Logopedics** *(Karlsruhe, Stuttgart)* (Speech Therapy and Audiology); **Logopedics** *(Düsseldorf, Bonn, Heidelberg)* (Speech Therapy and Audiology); **Mental Health and Psychotherapy** (Psychiatry and Mental Health; Psychotherapy); **Neurorehabilitation** (Neurological Therapy); **Nursing** (Nursing); **Occupational Therapy** (Occupational Therapy); **Physiotherapy** *(Leverkusen)* (Physical Therapy); **Physiotherapy** (Physical Therapy); **Physiotherapy** *(Karlsruhe, Stuttgart)* (Physical Therapy); **Theory and Practice of Medical Teaching** (Health Education)

Course

Cross-Discipline Early Intervention Degree (Law; Medicine; Pedagogy; Psychology)

History: Founded 2007.

Main Language(s) of Instruction: German

Degrees and Diplomas: *Bachelor's Degree*; *Master*: **Neurological Therapy; Psychiatry and Mental Health; Psychotherapy.**

Student Numbers *2013-2014*: Total 667
Last Updated: 24/03/15

STEINBEIS UNIVERSITY BERLIN

Steinbeis-Hochschule-Berlin

Gürtelstrasse 29A/30, 10247 Berlin
Tel: +49(30) 293309-0
Fax: +49(30) 293309-20
EMail: shb@stw.de
Website: http://www.steinbeis-hochschule.de

Präsident: Johann Löhn (1998-)
EMail: loehn@stw.de

School

Business *(Alb-Schwarzwald)* (Business Administration); **Business** *(ADG)* (Business Administration); **Dental and Oral Medicine Alliance** (Dentistry); **Executive Management** *(IBR)* (Management); **Governance, Risk and Compliance** (Government; Insurance); **International Business and Entrepreneurship** (Business Administration); **Management and Innovation** (Management); **Management and Technology** (Management; Technology)

Academy

Business (Business Administration)

Group

Technology (Technology)

History: Founded 1998.

Main Language(s) of Instruction: German

Degrees and Diplomas: *Bachelor's Degree*; *Master*: **Arts and Humanities; Business Administration; Computer Science; Dental Technology; Engineering; Finance; Health Administration; Insurance; Law; Management; Natural Sciences; Real Estate.** *PhD*: **Business Administration; Engineering.**

Student Services: eLibrary

Academic Staff *2014-2015*: Total: c. 1,800

Student Numbers *2013-2014*: Total 6,202
Last Updated: 26/03/15

BERLIN UNIVERSITY FOR PROFESSIONAL STUDIES

DEUTSCHE UNIVERSITÄT FÜR WEITERBILDUNG (DUW)

Katharinenstraße 17-18, 10711 Berlin
Tel: +49(30) 2000-306-211
Fax: +49(30) 2000-306-296
EMail: info@duw-berlin.de; izabela.ahmad@duw-berlin.de
Website: http://www.duw-berlin.com

Präsidentin: Ada Pellert EMail: ada.pellert@duw-berlin.de

Chancellor: Julian Bomert EMail: julian.bomert@duw-berlin.de

Programme

Corporate Master's Studies (Business Administration); **General Management (MBA)** (Management); **International Media Innovation Management (M.A.)** (Management)

Academy

Management (Management)

History: Founded 2008 as Germany's first state-approved continuing education university.

Admission Requirements: For Master programmes: an undergraduate degree; 2 years of work experience; sufficient English language proficiency (at least level B2/C1 in the Common European Framework of Reference for Languages). For Master programmes: an undergraduate degree or an equivalent qualification in the form of a qualification for admission to higher education and several years' work experience, or completed vocational training and several years' work experience.

Fees: National: Master programme, 15,600; Certificate programme, 1,900-7,600 (Euro), International: Master programme, 15,600; Certificate programme, 1,900-7,600 (Euro)

Main Language(s) of Instruction: German

Accrediting Agency: ACQUIN

Degrees and Diplomas: *Master*: **Accountancy; Administration; Business Administration; Business and Commerce; Education; Educational Sciences; Finance; Human Resources; Management; Marketing.** Also certificate programs: 2, 4, 5 and 8 months.

Student Services: Academic Counselling, Careers Guidance, Cultural Activities, Library, eLibrary

Student Numbers *2013-2014*: Total 230

THE NORDAKADEMIE

NORDAKADEMIE - Hochschule der Wirtschaft

Köllner Chaussee 11, 25337 Elmshorn
Tel: +49(4121) 4090-0
Fax: +49(4121) 4090-40
EMail: info@nordakademie.de
Website: http://www.nordakademie.de

President: Stefan Behringer
Tel: +49(4121) 4090-15
EMail: stefan.behringer@nordakademie.de

Chancellor: Jörg Meier
Tel: +49(4121) 4090-13 EMail: j.meier@nordakademie.de

International Relations: Kirsten Andersen, Head, International Office
Tel: +49(4121) 4090-63
EMail: auslandsamt@nordakademie.de; kirsten.andersen@nordakademie.de

Department

Applied Computer Science (Business Computing); **Business Administration** (Business Administration); **Computer Science and Business Administration** (Business Administration; Business Computing; Computer Science); **Industrial Engineering and Business Administration** (Business Administration; Industrial Engineering)

History: Founded 1992.

Admission Requirements: Secondary school certificate (Abitur or Fachhochschulreife)

Fees: c. 2,040-2,180 per semester; MBA, 3,750 per semester (Euro)

Main Language(s) of Instruction: German

Accrediting Agency: FIBAA

Degrees and Diplomas: *Bachelor's Degree*; *Master*: **Accountancy; Business Administration; Business Computing; Finance; Industrial Engineering; Information Technology; Management; Marketing; Sales Techniques.**

Student Services: Academic Counselling, Canteen, Careers Guidance, Language Laboratory, Sports Facilities

Student Numbers *2013-2014*: Total 1,456

Last Updated: 22/03/15

TOURO COLLEGE BERLIN

Am Rupenhorn 5, 14055 Berlin
Tel: +49(30) 3006-860
Fax: +49(30) 3006-8639
EMail: info@touroberlin.de
Website: http://www.touroberlin.de

Vice President/Director: Sara Nachama
EMail: sara.nachama@touroberlin.de

Programme

Business Administration (Business Administration); **Holocaust Studies** (Jewish Studies); **Management** (Management); **Psychology** (Psychology)

History: Founded 2003.

Main Language(s) of Instruction: German

Degrees and Diplomas: *Bachelor's Degree*: **Business Administration; Management; Psychology.** *Master*: **Business Administration; Communication Studies; History; Jewish Studies.**

Student Services: Library

Student Numbers *2013-2014*: Total 133

Last Updated: 26/03/15

UNIVERSITY FOR CHURCH MUSIC OF THE DIOCESE OF ROTTENBURG-STUTTGART

Hochschule für Kirchenmusik Rottenburg

Diözese Rottenburg-Stuttgart, St.-Meinrad-Weg 6, 72108 Rottenburg am Neckar
Tel: +49(7472) 9363-0
Fax: +49(7472) 936363
EMail: hfk-rottenburg@bo.drs.de
Website: http://www.hfk-rottenburg.de

Rector: Inga Behrendt

Pro-rector: Jan Schumacher

Programme

Church Music (Religious Music); **Postgraduate Studies** (Music Education; Musical Instruments; Singing)

History: Founded 1949. Acquired present status 1997.

Main Language(s) of Instruction: German

Degrees and Diplomas: *Bachelor's Degree*; *Master*: **Conducting; Music Education; Musical Instruments; Singing.**

Student Services: Library

Last Updated: 09/03/15

UNIVERSITY FOR PROTESTANT CHURCH MUSIC BAYREUTH

Hochschule für Evangelische Kirchenmusik Bayreuth

Wilhelminenstrasse 9, 95444 Bayreuth, Bavaria
Tel: +49(921) 75934-17
Fax: +49(921) 75934-36
EMail: info@hfk-bayreuth.de; verwaltung@hfk-bayreuth.de
Website: http://www.hfk-bayreuth.de

Rector: Thomas Albus
Tel: +49(921) 759-3417 EMail: rektor@hfk-bayreuth.de

Prorektor: Wolfgang Doeberlein
EMail: doeberlein@hfk-bayreuth.de

Programme

Church Music (Conducting; Musical Instruments; Religious Music)

History: Founded 2000.

Main Language(s) of Instruction: German

Degrees and Diplomas: *Bachelor's Degree*: **Conducting; Musical Instruments; Religious Music.** *Diplom (Univ)*: **Conducting; Jazz and Popular Music; Musical Instruments; Religious Music.** Diplom (Univ) replace by Bachelor since summer 2013. A Postgraduate Degree (Aufbaustudiengang) will continue being offered until the Master's Degree is introduced.

Student Services: Library

Student Numbers *2013-2014*: Total 31

Last Updated: 02/03/15

UNIVERSITY OF APPLIED MANAGEMENT

Hochschule für Angewandtes Management

Am Bahnhof 2, 85435 Erding
Tel: +49 (8122) 955-948-0
Fax: +49 (8122) 955-948-49
EMail: info@my-fham.de
Website: http://www.myfham.de

Pesident: Claudius Schikora EMail: claudius.schikora@fham.de

Kanzlerin: Frank Heinrich
Tel: +49 (8122) 955-948-22 EMail: frank.heinrich@fham.de

Faculty

Business Administration (Business Administration; Health Administration; Media Studies; Real Estate); **Industrial Psychology** (Accountancy; Business Administration; Communication Studies; Data Processing; English; Management; Marketing; Psychology; Statistics); **Key Qualifications** (Commercial Law; Education; Educational Administration); **Sports Management** (Business Administration; Law; Psychology; Sociology; Sports Management)

History: Founded 2004.

Main Language(s) of Instruction: German

Accrediting Agency: Wissenschaftsrat (WR); Foundation for International Business Administration Accreditation (FIBAA)

Degrees and Diplomas: *Bachelor's Degree*: **Advertising and Publicity; Art Management; Business Administration; Commercial Law; E- Business/Commerce; Hotel Management; Industrial and Organizational Psychology; Management; Marketing; Mass Communication; Media Studies; Public Administration; Real Estate; Retailing and Wholesaling; Sports Management; Taxation; Tourism.** *Master*: **Business Administration; Commercial Law; Educational Administration; Industrial and Organizational Psychology; Sports Management.** Also Dual Study Programmes; Master's degree programmes in Educational Management and Sports Management are offered in English Languages.

Student Numbers *2013-2014*: Total 2,156

Last Updated: 27/01/15

UNIVERSITY OF APPLIED SCIENCES (HWTK)

Hochschule für Wirtschaft, Technik und Kultur (HWTK) (HWTK)

Friedrichstraße 189, 10117 Berlin
Tel: +49(30) 2061-7685
EMail: info@hwtk.de
Website: http://www.hwtk.de/

President: Hartmut Sangmeister
EMail: hartmut.sangmeister@hwtk.de

Chancellor: Suzan Edebali
Tel: +49(30) 206176-81 EMail: suzan.edebali@hwtk.de

Programme

Business Administration (Business Administration); **Business Administration (English)** (Business Administration); **Business and Organisation** *(Graduate)* (Business Administration); **Business Informatics (dual study, full-time study)** (Business Computing)

Further Information: Also campus in Baden-Baden

Main Language(s) of Instruction: German

Degrees and Diplomas: *Bachelor's Degree*; *Master*: **Business Administration.**

Student Services: Library

Student Numbers *2013-2014*: Total 252
Last Updated: 08/04/15

UNIVERSITY OF APPLIED SCIENCES AND ARTS IN OTTERSBERG

Hochschule für Künste im Sozialen, Ottersberg

Am Wiestebruch 68, 28870 Ottersberg
Tel: +49(4205) 3949-0
Fax: +49(4205) 3949-79
EMail: info@hks-ottersberg.de
Website: http://www.hks-ottersberg.de

Rector: Ralf Rummel-Suhrcke EMail: rus@hks-ottersberg.de

Managing Director: Andreas Möhle
Tel: +49(4205) 3949-10
EMail: andreas.moehle@hks-ottersberg.de

International Relations: Gabriele Schmid, Prorector and Academic Executive Director, Internationalization
EMail: gs@hks-ottersberg.de

Programme

Art Therapy and Pedagogy (Art Education; Art Therapy); **Drama** (Art Therapy; Pedagogy; Theatre); **Fine Arts** (Fine Arts); **Fine Arts and Performing Arts in Society** (Fine Arts; Performing Arts); **Performing Arts Pedagogy** (Art Education)

Research Institute

Arts Therapy and Research in Arts and Performing Arts (Art Therapy; Performing Arts)

History: Founded 1967. Acquired present status 1984. Formerly known as 'Freie Kunst-Studienstätte Ottersberg - Fachhochschule für Kunsttherapie und Kunst' and 'Fachhochschule Ottersberg' (until 2012).

Admission Requirements: Secondary school certificate (Fachhochschulreife)

Fees: National: Bachelor's degree, 3,484 per annum; Master's degree, 4,440 per annum (Euro), International: Bachelor's degree, 7,500 per annum; Master's degree, 8,800 per annum

Main Language(s) of Instruction: German

Degrees and Diplomas: *Bachelor's Degree*; *Master*: **Fine Arts; Performing Arts.**

Student Services: Academic Counselling, Canteen, Careers Guidance, Cultural Activities, Library, Social Counselling

Student Numbers *2013-2014*: Total 456
Last Updated: 09/03/15

UNIVERSITY OF APPLIED SCIENCES FOR ECONOMICS AND MANAGEMENT ESSEN

Hochschule für Oekonomie und Management Essen (FOM)

Leimkugelstrasse 6, 45141 Essen
Tel: +49(201) 81004-0
Fax: +49(201) 81004-180
EMail: info@fom.de
Website: http://www.fom.de

Rector: Burghard Hermeier (2000-)
Tel: +49(201) 81004-350
EMail: burghard.hermeier@bildungscentrum.de

Chancellor: Harald Beschorner
Tel: +49(201) 81004-27
EMail: harald.beschorner@bildungscentrum.de

International Relations: Clemens Jäger, Head, International Office
EMail: international@fom.de

School

Open Businesss (Business Administration; Business and Commerce; Finance; Health Administration; Information Technology; Management; Marketing; Mass Communication; Real Estate; Sales Techniques; Transport Management)

Department

Business and Law (Business Administration; Commercial Law; Taxation); **Business and Management** (Banking; Business Administration; Finance; International Business; Management); **Business and Psychology** (Business Administration; Industrial and Organizational Psychology); **Dual Studies** (Banking; Business Administration; Civil Engineering; Electronic Engineering; Engineering; Finance; Health Administration; International Business; Machine Building; Mechanical Engineering); **Engineering** (Electronic Engineering; Engineering; Machine Building; Mechanical Engineering); **Health and Social Sciences** (Health Administration; Social Work); **Information Technology Management** (Business Computing; Information Technology)

Further Information: Campuses in Aachen, Berlin, Bochum, Bonn, Bremen, Cologne, Dortmund, Duisburg, Düsseldorf, Essen, Frankfurt a. M., Gütersloh, Hamburg, Kassel, Leipzig, Marl, Munich, Neuss, Nürnberg, Siegen, Stuttgart and Luxemburg.

History: Founded 1993.

Fees: c.1,620-1,800 per semester (Euro)

Main Language(s) of Instruction: German, English

Degrees and Diplomas: *Bachelor's Degree*: **Banking; Business Administration; Business Computing; Commercial Law; Electronic Engineering; Engineering; Finance; Health Administration; Health Sciences; Industrial and Organizational Psychology; Information Management; International Business; Machine Building; Management; Mechanical Engineering; Psychology; Social Work; Taxation.** *Master*: **Accountancy; Business Administration; Commercial Law; Electronic Engineering; Engineering; Finance; Human Resources; Industrial and Organizational Psychology; Machine Building; Management; Marketing; Mass Communication; Mechanical Engineering; Public Health; Sales Techniques; Transport Management.**

Student Services: Academic Counselling, Canteen

Student Numbers *2014-2015*: Total: c. 31,000
Last Updated: 02/03/15

UNIVERSITY OF APPLIED SCIENCES OF THE SMALL AND MEDIUM-SIZED ENTERPRISES BIELEFELD

Fachhochschule des Mittelstandes (FHM) Bielefeld (FHM)

Ravensberger Strasse 10 G, 33602 Bielefeld
Tel: +49(521) 96655-10
Fax: +49(521) 96655-11
EMail: info@hm-mittelstand.de
Website: http://www.fhm-mittelstand.de/

Rector: Anne Dreier EMail: dreier@fh-mittelstand.de

Director: Richard Merk EMail: merk@fh-mittelstand.de

International Relations: Heike Kollmeier, International Officer
Tel: +49(521) 96655-248 EMail: kollmeier@fh-mittelstand.de

Faculty

Economics (Banking; Business Administration; Economics; Finance; Management); **Human Resource, Health and Social Affairs** (Education; Health Administration; Health Sciences; Hotel and Restaurant; Marketing; Rehabilitation and Therapy; Service Trades; Social Work; Tourism); **Media Studies** (Communication Arts; Communication Studies; Design; Journalism; Media Studies)

Further Information: Also Campuses in Köln, Pulheim, Hannover, Rostock, Bamberg und Schwerin.

History: Founded 2000.

Main Language(s) of Instruction: German

Accrediting Agency: Wissenschaftsrat (WR); Foundation for International Business Administration Accreditation FIBAA); Evaluationsagentur Baden-Württemberg (Evalag)

Degrees and Diplomas: *Bachelor's Degree*: **Business Administration; Construction Engineering; Educational Sciences; Engineering Management; Finance; Health Administration; Health Sciences; Hotel and Restaurant; Industrial Engineering; International Business; Marketing; Physical Therapy; Social Work; Special Education; Sports Management; Teacher**

Training; Tourism; Welfare and Protective Services. *Master*: **International Business; Management; Marketing; Tourism.** *PhD*: **Business Administration.**

Student Services: Careers Guidance

Student Numbers *2013-2014*: Total: c. 2,420
Last Updated: 27/01/15

UNIVERSITY OF APPLIED SCIENCES WESERBERGLAND

Hochschule Weserbergland
Am Stockhof 2, 31785 Hameln
Tel: +49(5151) 95590
Fax: +49(5151) 45271
EMail: info@hsw-hameln.de
Website: http://www.hsw-hameln.de/

President: Volkmar Langer
Tel: +49(5151) 9559-0 EMail: langer@hsw-hameln.de

Department
Business Administration (Business Administration); **Computer Science** (Business Computing; Computer Science); **Engineering** (Electronic Engineering; Energy Engineering; Industrial Engineering); **Health Sciences** (Health Administration; Health Sciences)

Main Language(s) of Instruction: German

Degrees and Diplomas: *Bachelor's Degree*; *Master*: **Management.**

Student Services: Library

Student Numbers *2013-2014*: Total 457
Last Updated: 08/04/15

UNIVERSITY OF CATHOLIC CHURCH MUSIC AND MUSIC EDUCATION

Hochschule für Katholische Kirchenmusik und Musikpädagogik Regensburg (HFKM)
Andreasstraße 9, 93059 Regensburg
Tel: +49(941) 83009-0
Fax: +49(941) 83009-46
EMail: info@hfkm-regensburg.de
Website: http://www.hfkm-regensburg.de

Rektor: Stefan Baier
Tel: +49(941) 83009-10 EMail: s.baier@hfkm-regensburg.de

Head of Administration: Johannes Lederer
Tel: +49(941) 83009-13 EMail: j.lederer@hfkm-regensburg.de

Programme
Church Music (Conducting; Music Education; Musical Instruments; Religious Music; Singing)

School
Music (Music)

History: Founded 1874 as the "Kirchenmusikschule Regensburg" - Church Music School of Regensburg. Accredited in 2001.

Main Language(s) of Instruction: German

Degrees and Diplomas: *Bachelor's Degree*; *Master*: **Conducting; Music Education; Music Theory and Composition; Musical Instruments; Musicology; Religious Music.**

Student Services: Library, Residential Facilities

Student Numbers *2013-2014*: Total 99
Last Updated: 05/03/15

UNIVERSITY OF CHURCH MUSIC OF DRESDEN

Hochschule für Kirchenmusik Dresden
Käthe-Kollwitz-Ufer 97, 01309 Dresden
Tel: +49(351) 31864-0
Fax: +49(351) 31864-22
EMail: info@kirchenmusik-dresden.de
Website: http://www.kirchenmusik-dresden.de/

Rektor: Stephan Lennig (2013-)
Tel: +49(351) 31864-0 EMail: lennig@kirchenmusik-dresden.de

Prorektor: Martin Strohhäcker
EMail: strohhaecker@kirchenmusik-dresden.de

Programme
Church Music (Conducting; Jazz and Popular Music; Music Education; Musical Instruments; Religious Music)

History: Founded 1949.

Degrees and Diplomas: *Bachelor's Degree*; *Künstlerische Abschlussprüfung*; *Diplom (Univ)*

Student Services: Library

Student Numbers *2014-2015*: Total 35
Last Updated: 09/03/15

UNIVERSITY OF CHURCH MUSIC OF THE PROTESTANT CHURCH OF WESTPHALIA

Hochschule für Kirchenmusik der Evangelischen Kirche von Westfalen
Parkstrasse 6, 32049 Herford
Tel: +49(5221) 991-450
Fax: +49(5221) 830-809
EMail: info@hochschule-herford.de
Website: http://www.hochschule-herford.de

Rector: Helmut Fleinghaus
Tel: +49(5221) 5731-94720
EMail: Helmut.Fleinghaus@hochschule-herford.de

Department
Choral and Orchestral Conducting (Conducting; Religious Music); **Popular Music** (Jazz and Popular Music; Religious Music); **Winds Instruments** (Musical Instruments; Religious Music)

History: Founded 1947.

Main Language(s) of Instruction: German

Degrees and Diplomas: *Bachelor's Degree*: **Religious Music.** *Künstlerische Abschlussprüfung*: **Religious Music.** *Master*: **Religious Music.** Also Konzertexam in Religious Music.

Student Services: Library

Student Numbers *2013-2014*: Total 42
Last Updated: 05/03/15

UNIVERSITY OF CHURCH MUSIC OF THE PROTESTANT REGIONAL CHURCH IN BADEN

Hochschule für Kirchenmusik der Evangelischen Landeskirche in Baden - Heidelberg
Hildastrasse 8, 69115 Heidelberg
Tel: +49(6221) 270-62
Fax: +49(6221) 218-76
EMail: sekretariat@hfk-heidelberg.de
Website: http://www.hfk-heidelberg.de

Rektor: Bernd Stegmann
Tel: +1(6221) 27062
EMail: rektor@hfk-heidelberg.de

Programme
Artistic Education (Musical Instruments; Religious Music; Singing); **Church Music** (Religious Music; Singing)

History: Founded 1931.

Main Language(s) of Instruction: German

Degrees and Diplomas: *Bachelor's Degree*; *Künstlerische Abschlussprüfung*: **Conducting; Music Education; Musical Instruments; Religious Music; Singing.**
Last Updated: 05/03/15

UNIVERSITY OF CHURCH MUSIC OF THE PROTESTANT REGIONAL CHURCH IN WÜRTTEMBERG

Hochschule für Kirchenmusik der Evangelischen Landeskirche in Württemberg - Tübingen

Gartenstrasse 12, 72074 Tübingen
Tel: +49(7071) 925-997
Fax: +49(7071) 925-998
EMail: info@kirchenmusikhochschule.de
Website: http://www.kirchenmusikhochschule.de

Rector: Christian Fischer
Tel: +49(711) 925-997
EMail: rektorat@kirchenmusikhochschule.de

Vice Rector: Patrick Bebelaar
EMail: prorektor@kirchenmusikhochschule.de

Programme

Religious Music (Musical Instruments; Religious Music; Singing)

History: Founded 1945 in Esslingen. Acquired university status 1989. Moved to Tübingen 1998.

Admission Requirements: Abitur and entrance examination

Main Language(s) of Instruction: German

Degrees and Diplomas: *Bachelor's Degree*; *Künstlerische Abschlussprüfung*; *Kirchliche Abschlussprüfung*; *Diplom (Univ)*; *Master*: **Religious Music.** Diploma programmes are being phased out, No more enrolment accepted.

Last Updated: 09/03/15

UNIVERSITY OF MUSIC SAARLAND

Hochschule für Musik Saar (HFM)

Bismarckstraße 1, 66111 Saarbrücken
Tel: +49(681) 96731-0
Fax: +49(681) 96731-30
EMail: presse@hfm.saarland.de
Website: http://www.hfm.saarland.de

Rector: Wolfgang Mayer
Tel: +49(681) 96731-14 EMail: rektor@hfm.saarland.de

Chancellor: Alfred Jost (Alfred Jost)
Tel: +49(681) 96731-13 EMail: a.jost@hfm.saarland.de

International Relations: Jörg Nonnweiler, Head, International Office

Division

Reflection and Mediation (Art Management; Conducting; Education; Fine Arts; Music Education; Music Theory and Composition; Musicology; Religious Music); **Stage and concert** (Music; Musical Instruments; Opera; Singing)

History: Founded 1947.

Main Language(s) of Instruction: German, English

Degrees and Diplomas: *Bachelor's Degree*; *Konzertexamen*: **Conducting.** *Master*: **Conducting; Jazz and Popular Music; Music; Music Education; Music Theory and Composition; Religious Music; Singing; Teacher Training; Theatre.** Statsexam in Music Education and Teacher Training

Student Services: Library

Student Numbers *2013-2014*: Total: c. 450
Last Updated: 09/03/15

WEDEL UNIVERSITY OF APPLIED SCIENCES

Fachhochschule Wedel

Feldstrasse 143, 22880 Wedel, Holstein
Tel: +49(4103) 8048-0
Fax: +49(4103) 8048-39
EMail: sekretariat@fh-wedel.de
Website: http://www.fh-wedel.de

Rektor: Dirk Harms (1975-)
Tel: +49(4103) 8048-0 EMail: ha@fh-wedel.de

International Relations: Nicole Limberg, Head, International Office
Tel: +49(4103) 8048-47 EMail: lim@fh-wedel.de

Programme

Business Administration (Business Administration); **Business Computing** (Business Computing; Software Engineering); **Computer Games Technology** (Computer Engineering); **Computer Science** (Computer Engineering; Computer Science; Software Engineering); **E-Business/Commerce** (E- Business/Commerce); **Industrial Engineering** (Business Administration; Electronic Engineering; Engineering; Industrial Engineering; Industrial Management; Management; Natural Sciences; Production Engineering; Transport Management); **IT Engineering** (Computer Engineering; Information Technology); **IT Security** (Information Management; Information Technology); **Media Information Science** (Information Technology; Media Studies); **Technical informatics** (Automation and Control Engineering; Computer Science; Electronic Engineering; Information Technology; Software Engineering; Technology)

History: Founded 1945.

Academic Year: October to July (October-January; April-July)

Admission Requirements: Fachhochschulreife or Abitur

Fees: c. 800-1,200 per semester (Euro)

Main Language(s) of Instruction: German

Accrediting Agency: ASIIN; FIBAA

Degrees and Diplomas: *Bachelor's Degree*: **Business Administration; Business Computing; Computer Engineering; Computer Science; Engineering; Industrial Engineering; Information Technology; Multimedia.** *Master*: **Business Administration; Business Computing; Computer Science; Engineering; Industrial Engineering; Information Technology.** Also Dual Bachelor's Degrees; the Master's Degree programme in Information Technology and Engineering is conducted in English.

Student Services: Academic Counselling, Canteen, Facilities for disabled people, Foreign Studies Centre, Library

Publications: Auditorium

Student Numbers *2013-2014*: Total 981
Last Updated: 28/01/15

WHU - OTTO BEISHEIM SCHOOL OF MANAGEMENT (WHU)

Burgplatz 2, 56179 Vallendar
Tel: +49(261) 650-90
Fax: +49(261) 650-9509
EMail: whu@whu.edu
Website: http://www.whu.edu/

Rector/Dean: Markus Rudolf
Tel: +49(261) 650-9150
EMail: rektorat@whu.edu; markus.rudolf@whu.edu

Programme

Business Administration/Management (Business Administration; Commercial Law; Economics; Management)

Institute

Management, Accounting and Control (Accountancy; Management)

Centre

Asia (International Business); **Collaborative Commerce**; **Consumer Goods** *(Henkel)*; **European Studies**; **Logistics Management** *(Kuehne)*; **Management** *(Biopharma)*; **Market-oriented Corporate Management** (Business Administration); **Private Banking** (Banking)

Further Information: Campus in Düsseldorf

History: Founded 1984.

Main Language(s) of Instruction: German, English

Accrediting Agency: FIBAA; EQUIS; AACSB

Degrees and Diplomas: *Bachelor's Degree*: **International Business; Management.** *Master*: **Business Administration; Finance; Management.** *PhD*: **Economics.** Master's Degree Programmes are available in part-time mode; Also Kellogg-WHU Global EMBA Programme in Management jointly offerd with the Kellogg School of Management at Northwestern University (USA; Chicago and Miami campuses), in partnership with Hong Kong University of Science and Technology (Hong Kong), Guanghua School of Management at

Peking University (China), Tel Aviv University (Israel) and York University (Canada).

Student Services: Academic Counselling, Canteen, Careers Guidance, Facilities for disabled people, Language Laboratory, Library, Sports Facilities

Student Numbers *2013-2014*: Total 990
Last Updated: 30/01/15

WILHELM BÜCHNER UNIVERSITY OF APPLIED SCIENCE DARMSTADT

Wilhelm Büchner Hochschule - Private Fernhochschule Darmstadt
Ostendstraße 3, 64319 Pfungstadt bei Darmstadt
Tel: +49(6157) 806-404
Fax: +49(6157) 806-401
EMail: info@wb-fernstudium.de
Website: http://www.wb-fernstudium.de

Präsident: Joachim Loeper Tel: +49(6157) 806-401

Kanzler: Thomas Kirchenkamp
Tel: +49(6157) 806-408
EMail: thomas.kirchenkamp@privatfh-da.de

Programme

Computer Science (Computer Science); **Electrical Engineering and Information Technology** (Electrical Engineering; Information Technology); **Energy, Environment and Process Engineering** (Energy Engineering; Engineering Management; Environmental Engineering); **Industrial Engineering** (Industrial Engineering); **Mechanical Engineering** (Machine Building); **Mechatronics** (Electronic Engineering; Mechanical Engineering); **Technology Management** (Industrial Management)

History: Founded 1996. Acquired present status 2001.

Main Language(s) of Instruction: German

Degrees and Diplomas: *Bachelor's Degree*; *Master*: **Business Computing; Computer Science; Electronic Engineering; Engineering Management; Industrial Engineering; Information Technology; Media Studies.**

Student Services: Academic Counselling, Canteen, Careers Guidance, Social Counselling

Student Numbers *2013-2014*: Total 6,203
Last Updated: 27/03/15

WILHELM LÖHE UNIVERSITY OF APPLIED SCIENCES

Wilhelm Löhe Hochschule für angewandte Wissenschaften (WLH)
Merkurstraße 41/Südstadtpark, 90763 Fürth
Tel: +49(911) 766069-0
Fax: +49(911) 766069-29
EMail: info@wlh-fuerth.de
Website: http://www.wlh-fuerth.de/

Chancellor: Sabine König EMail: kanzler@wlh-fuerth.de

Vice-President: Jürgen Zerth EMail: info@wlh-fuerth.de

Department

Continuing Education; **Economics and Management** (Economics; Management); **Ethics and Philosophy** (Ethics; Philosophy); **Research firm IDC**; **Social Infrastructure and Health** (Health Sciences; Welfare and Protective Services)

Main Language(s) of Instruction: German

Degrees and Diplomas: *Bachelor's Degree*; *Master*: **Health Administration; Welfare and Protective Services.**

Student Numbers *2013-2014*: Total 39
Last Updated: 09/04/15

WITTEN/HERDECKE UNIVERSITY

Universität Witten/Herdecke
Alfred-Herrhausen-Straße 50, 58448 Witten
Tel: +49(2302) 926-0
Fax: +49(2302) 926-407
EMail: public@uni-wh.de
Website: http://www.uni-wh.de

Präsident: Martin Butzlaff
Tel: +49(2302) 926-928 EMail: Martin.Butzlaff@uni-wh.de

Chancellor: Jan Peter Nonnenkamp
Tel: +49(2302) 926-932 EMail: Jan.Nonnenkamp@uni-wh.de

International Relations: Dagmar Koch
Tel: +49(2302) 926-563 EMail: Dagmar.Koch@uni-wh.de

Faculty

Culture (Cultural Studies; Economics; Philosophy; Political Sciences); **Foundation Studies** (Communication Studies; Fine Arts; Performing Arts); **Health** (Alternative Medicine; Dentistry; Medicine; Nursing; Oral Pathology; Pharmacy; Traditional Eastern Medicine); **Management and Economics** (Business Administration; Economics; Management)

Further Information: Also 18 Affiliated Hospitals

History: Founded 1980 as the first private University in the Federal Republic of Germany. Financed by donations and grants stipulated for specific research programmes as well as tuition fees paid by students.

Academic Year: April to March (April-July; October-March)

Admission Requirements: Secondary school certificate (Abitur) or work experience according to Faculty

Main Language(s) of Instruction: German

Degrees and Diplomas: *Bachelor's Degree*; *Master*: **Business Administration; Clinical Psychology; Cultural Studies; Economics; Management; Nursing; Philosophy; Political Sciences; Psychotherapy.** *PhD*: **Cultural Studies; Dentistry; Economics; Health Sciences; Medicine; Natural Sciences; Nursing.** *Habilitation*: **Arts and Humanities; Business Administration; Nursing; Psychology; Psychotherapy.** Pharmacy Degree Programme taught in English; Also Staatsexamen in Dentistry and Medicine.

Student Services: Academic Counselling, Canteen, Cultural Activities, Facilities for disabled people, Foreign Studies Centre, Language Laboratory, Library, Nursery Care, Social Counselling

Publications: Perspektiven

Publishing House: Universität Witten/Herdecke Verlagsgesellschaft mbH

Student Numbers *2013-2014*: Total 1,688
Last Updated: 28/03/15

ZEPPELIN UNIVERSITY, FRIEDRICHSHAFEN (ZU)

Am Seemooser Horn 20, 88045 Friedrichshafen
Tel: +49(7541) 6009-0
Fax: +49(7541) 6009-1199
EMail: ZUmaster@zu.de
Website: http://www.zeppelin-university.de

President: Alfred Kieser
Tel: +49(7541) 6009-1122 EMail: alfred.kieser@zu.de

Chancellor: Alexander Kübler-Kreß
Tel: +49(7541) 6009-2121 EMail: alexander.kuebler-kress@zu.de

International Relations: Silke Pfaller, Head, International Office
Tel: +49(7541) 6009-2040 EMail: silke.pfaller@zu.de

Department

Cultural Studies (Cultural Studies; Fine Arts; Mass Communication; Media Studies; Sociology); **Economics** (Business and Commerce; Economics; Finance; Leadership; Management; Political Sciences; Transport and Communications; Transport Management); **State and Social Sciences** (Administration; Business Computing; Communication Studies; Cultural Studies; European Union Law; Fiscal Law; Government; Industrial and Organizational Psychology; International Relations; Law; Leadership; Political

Sciences; Public Administration; Public Law; Secondary Education; Social Psychology)

History: Founded 2003.

Fees: 3,700 per semester (Euro)

Main Language(s) of Instruction: German, English

Degrees and Diplomas: *Bachelor's Degree*; *Master*: **Administration; Communication Studies; Cultural Studies; Economics; International Relations; Management; Political Sciences.** *PhD*: **Communication Studies; Cultural Studies; Economics; Management; Media Studies; Political Sciences; Social Sciences; Sociology.** *Habilitation*: **Communication Studies; Cultural Studies; Economics; Management; Media Studies; Political Sciences; Social Sciences; Sociology.** Also Executive Masters Programmes

Student Services: Library

Student Numbers *2013-2014*: Total 919

Last Updated: 30/03/15

Ghana

STRUCTURE OF HIGHER EDUCATION SYSTEM

Description:

The system of higher education includes universities and university colleges; professional institutes and pre-service training institutes.

Stages of studies:

University level first stage: *Bachelor's degree*

The first degree is conferred after four to seven years of study depending on the subject.

University level second stage: *Master's degree*

Degree awarded after two years' study following upon a Bachelor's degree.

University level third stage: *Doctorate*

The Doctorate degree is open to graduates who hold a Master's degree.

ADMISSION TO HIGHER EDUCATION

Admission to university-level studies:

Name of secondary school credential required: West African Senior School Certificate Examination

Foreign students admission:

Definition of foreign student: Any student who is not a Ghanaian.

Admission requirements: Foreign students should have good CGE "O" level passes (or their equivalent) in English language and four other subjects plus three "A" level passes (required subjects vary according to degree course).

Entry regulations: Foreign students with the exception of ECOWAS citizens need visas to enter Ghana. All foreign students, including ECOWAS citizens, are required to secure resident permits for the period of their study. Foreign students are required to pay their fees in convertible currency to be drawn on a American or British bank.

Health requirements: Health certificate required.

Language proficiency: Good knowledge of English required for all regular university courses. English-language proficiency courses are offered as well as general orientation programmes for all freshmen.

RECOGNITION OF STUDIES

Quality assurance system:

The National Accreditation Board (NAB) reviews study programmes.

Special provisions for recognition:

Recognition for university level studies: Foreign credentials in the form of certificates should be sent to the Academic Registrar of the University. This applies to both nationals with foreign credentials and foreigners.

For access to advanced studies and research: Foreign credentials in the form of certificates, transcripts and Referee's report of two or three people should be sent to the office of the Dean of Graduate Studies of the University. This applies to both nationals and foreigners.

For exercising a profession: Access to the professions is subject to the recognition of credentials by the professional associations and to passing professional qualifying examinations. Foreign credentials should be sent to the Board or Institute of the individual professions. In addition, candidates should pass the professional examination conducted by the professional body.

NATIONAL BODIES

Ministry of Education

Minister: Naana Jane Opoku-Agyemang
PO Box M45
Accra
Tel: +233(21) 302 683627
EMail: pro@moe.gov.gh
WWW: http://www.moe.gov.gh
Role of national body: Authority responsible for policy formulation, the administration and financing of education at the national level.

National Accreditation Board - NAB

Chairman: Joseph Ghartey Ampiah
Executive Secretary: Kwame Dattey
East Legon
PO Box CT 3256 - Cantonments
Accra
EMail: nabsec@nab.gov.gh
WWW: http://www.nab.gov.gh
Role of national body: Accredits both public and private higher education institutions' programmes and determines the equivalences of diplomas, certificates and other qualifications awarded by institutions in Ghana or elsewhere.

Ghana Association of University Administrators - GAUA

Accra

Vice Chancellors Ghana - VCG

Accra

Data for academic year: 2012-2013
Source: IAU from World Data on Education 2010/2011, UNESCO-IBE and documentation, 2012. Bodies 2016.

INSTITUTIONS

PUBLIC INSTITUTIONS

GHANA INSTITUTE OF JOURNALISM (GIJ)

PO Box 667 Gamel Abdul Nasser Road, Accra
Tel: +233(232) 228-336
Fax: +233(232) 221-750
EMail: info@gij.edu.gh; gijacademic@gmail.com
Website: http://www.gij.edu.gh

Rector: David Newton

Vice-Rector: K. A. Batse

Faculty
Social Studies (Social Studies); **Journalism** (Journalism); **Public Relations** (Public Relations)

Degrees and Diplomas: *Bachelor's Degree*: **Communication Studies; Journalism; Public Relations.**
Last Updated: 25/07/12

GHANA INSTITUTE OF MANAGEMENT AND PUBLIC ADMINISTRATION (GIMPA)

PO Box AH 50, Achimota, Accra
Tel: +233(302) 401681/2/3 +233(302) 412337
Fax: +233(302) 405805
EMail: info@gimpa.edu.gh
Website: http://www.gimpa.edu.gh/

Rector: Yaw Agyeman Badu (2012-)
Tel: +233(302) 405-801 EMail: ybadu@gimpa.edu.gh

Division
Consultancy Services (Management)

School
Business *(Greenhill College (Undergraduate Programmes and Graduate School))* (Business Administration); **Governance, Leadership and Public Management** *(Graduate Programmes)* (Government; Leadership; Management; Public Administration); **Law** (Law); **Public Service** *(Undergraduate Programme)* (Public Administration); **Technology** *(Undergraduate and Graduate Programmes)* (Technology)

Centre
Distance Learning

History: Founded 1961 as a joint Ghana government/United Nations special Fund Project. Relocated in Legon 1966. Acquired present title and status 1969.

Academic Year: September to August

Fees: Vary according to Programmes

Main Language(s) of Instruction: English

Accrediting Agency: National Accreditation Board (NAB), Ghana

Degrees and Diplomas: *Certificate*: **Administration; Management; Town Planning.** *Bachelor's Degree*: **Accountancy; Banking; Business Administration; Computer Science; Economics;**

Finance; Hotel Management; Human Resources; Information Technology; Law; Management; Marketing; Public Administration; Tourism. *Graduate Diploma*; *Master's Degree*: **Business Administration; Leadership; Public Administration.** *Doctorate*: **Leadership.** Master's Degree Programmes both Executive and Regular (equivalent to M.Phil). Competency-based short courses, and In-plant courses.

Student Services: Canteen, Health Services, Sports Facilities

Publications: GIMPA Journal of Leadership, Management and Public Administration; GIMPA Occasional Papers

Publishing House: GIMPA Press

Last Updated: 26/06/12

INSTITUTE OF LOCAL GOVERNMENT STUDIES

PO Box LG 549, Legon, Accra
Tel: +233(302) 508817
Fax: +233(302) 508818
EMail: ilgs@ilgs-edu.org; info@ilgs-edu.org
Website: http://www.ilgs-edu.org

Director: Esther Ofei-Aboagye

Programme

Environmental Science, Policy and Management (Environmental Management; Environmental Studies); **Local Economic Development** (Development Studies; Economics); **Local Government Administration and Organisation** (Administration; Government); **Local Government Financial Management** (Finance; Human Resources; Management)

Further Information: Also a campus in Tamale

Admission Requirements: Bachelor's Degree

Fees: (US Dollars): 7500 for non Ghanaians

Degrees and Diplomas: *Master's Degree*

Last Updated: 24/10/12

KOFI ANNAN INTERNATIONAL PEACEKEEPING TRAINING CENTER

PMB CT 210, Cantonments, Accra
Tel: +233 (302) 718200-2000
Fax: +233 (302) 718201
EMail: info@kaiptc.org
Website: http://www.kaiptc.org/

Programme

Development Diplomacy; **Peace and Security**

Degrees and Diplomas: *Graduate Diploma*

Last Updated: 26/04/12

KWAME NKRUMAH UNIVERSITY OF SCIENCE AND TECHNOLOGY, KUMASI (KNUST)

Private Mail Bag, University Post Office, Kumasi
Tel: +233(32) 206-0334
Fax: +233(32) 206-0137
EMail: info@knust.edu.gh; vc@knust.edu.gh; admissions@knust.edu.gh
Website: http://www.knust.edu.gh

Vice-Chancellor: William Otoo Ellis (2010-)
Tel: +233(32) 206-0334
EMail: vc@knust.edu.gh; elliswo@yahoo.com

Registrar: Kobby Yebo-Okrah
Tel: +233(51) 60331 EMail: registrar@knust.edu.gh

International Relations: William Oduro, Dean, International Programmes Officer Tel: +233(32) 206-3944 EMail: ipo@knust.edu.gh

College

Agriculture and Natural Resources (Agricultural Business; Agricultural Economics; Agriculture; Animal Husbandry; Cattle Breeding; Crop Production; Dairy; Fishery; Forest Management; Forest Products; Forestry; Horticulture; Rural Planning; Soil Science; Water Management; Wildlife; Wood Technology; Zoology); **Architecture and Planning** (Architecture; Architecture and Planning); **Art and Social Sciences** (African Studies; Commercial Law; Cultural Studies; Design; Economics; English; Fine Arts; Industrial Design; Industrial Management; Modern Languages; Painting and Drawing; Private Law; Public Law; Publishing and Book Trade; Sculpture; Social Studies); **Engineering** (Aeronautical and Aerospace Engineering; Agricultural Engineering; Chemical Engineering; Civil Engineering; Computer Engineering; Electrical Engineering; Energy Engineering; Engineering; Geological Engineering; Materials Engineering; Mechanical Engineering; Petroleum and Gas Engineering; Technology); **Health Sciences** (Biology; Dentistry; Health Administration; Health Education; Health Sciences; Medicine; Pharmacology; Pharmacy; Veterinary Science); **Science** (Biochemistry; Biotechnology; Chemistry; Computer Science; Distance Education; Environmental Studies; Food Science; Food Technology; Information Technology; Mathematics; Mathematics and Computer Science; Natural Sciences; Ophthalmology; Optometry; Physics; Technology)

School

Graduate Studies (Agriculture; Architecture and Planning; Arts and Humanities; Engineering; Health Sciences; Natural Sciences; Social Sciences)

Further Information: Also 10 research centres

History: Founded 1951 as Kumasi College of Technology, acquired present status and title 1998.

Academic Year: September to June (September-January; March-June)

Admission Requirements: General Certificate of Education (GCE), Ordinary ('O') level, with 5 credits, including English, and General Certificate of Education Advanced ('A') level, with 2 passes. Senior Secondary School Certificate (SSCE) with passes in core English and Mathematics and three elective subjects relevant to chosen programme with a total aggregate of 24

Fees: (Cedi): Foreign students, undergraduate, 14m.-26m. per annum; postgraduate, 16m.-28m

Main Language(s) of Instruction: English

Degrees and Diplomas: *Bachelor's Degree*; *Master's Degree*; *Master of Philosophy*; *Doctorate*

Student Services: Academic Counselling, Canteen, Cultural Activities, Health Services, Nursery Care, Sports Facilities

Publications: Journal of the University of Science and Technology

Publishing House: University Printing Press. Design Press (College of Art)

Student Numbers *2010-2011*: Total 28,964

Last Updated: 14/03/13

NATIONAL FILM AND TELEVISION INSTITUTE (NAFTI)

Private Mail Bag, General Post Office, Accra
Tel: +233(302) 777610 +233(302) 777159
Fax: +233(302) 774522
EMail: info@nafti.edu.gh
Website: http://www.nafti.edu.gh

Director: Linus Abraham

Registrar: Godfried Narter-Olaga

Department

Design (Design); **Directing**; **Editing**; **Film and Television Sound Production** (Film; Radio and Television Broadcasting); **Motion Picture Photography** (Film; Photography; Video); **Production Management** (Film; Radio and Television Broadcasting); **Technical** (Cinema and Television; Film; Sound Engineering (Acoustics))

History: Founded 1978. Acquired present status 1998.

Admission Requirements: General Certificate of Education: 'O' Level Passes with credits in 5 subjects (including English Language, Mathematics, an Arts subject and a Science subject) and 3 passes at 'A' Level. At least one of the 'A' Level passes should be a grade D or better. A pass in General Paper is necessary. Senior Secondary Certificate: Passes in four core subjects, namely English, Mathematics, Science or Integrated Science and Social Studies or Life Skills and any three relevant elective subjects, with an aggregate score of not more than 24 in the WAEC Senior Secondary School Certificate Examinations. Entrance Examination

Main Language(s) of Instruction: English

Accrediting Agency: Ghana National Accreditation Board

Degrees and Diplomas: *Certificate*; *Bachelor's Degree*: **Fine Arts.** *Graduate Diploma*

Student Services: Academic Counselling, Canteen, Health Services, Language Laboratory, Sports Facilities

Academic Staff *2011-2012*	**TOTAL**
FULL-TIME	**120**
PART-TIME	c. **30**
Student Numbers *2011-2012*	
All (Foreign included)	c. **150**

Last Updated: 06/08/12

REGIONAL MARITIME UNIVERSITY (RMU)

PO Box GP 1115, Accra
Tel: +233(302) 714070 +233(302)712343
Fax: +233(302) 712047
EMail: registrar@rmu.edu.gh
Website: http://www.rmu.edu.gh

Rector: Alock Kwadwo Asamoah EMail: rector@rmu.edu.gh

Department

Electrical & Electronic Engineering (Electrical and Electronic Engineering); **Information Communication Technology** (Computer Engineering; Computer Science; Telecommunications Engineering); **Marine Engineering** (Marine Engineering); **Maritime Safety** (Environmental Management; Marine Transport); **Nautical Studies** (Nautical Science); **Ports and Shipping** (Marine Transport; Transport Management)

Further Information: Also Professional/Upgrading and Short Courses.

History: Founded as Ghana Nautical College 1958, became Regional Maritime Academy (RMA) 1982, comprising five West African States (Cameroon, Gambia, Ghana, Liberia and Sierra Leone). Acquired present status 2007.

Academic Year: August to June

Admission Requirements: West African School Certificate Examination; Senior Secondary School Certificate of Education; General Certificate of Education 'O' and 'A' levels; International Baccalaureate; IGCSE; American Grades 12 and 13; Advanced Technician Diploma; Higher National Diploma (HND)

Fees: (US Dollars): 1st semester fee: 1,682.36 for member states students; 2,889,36 for non member states students, or 9,22.36 for member states students; 2,125.36 for non member states students, depending on Departments or programme

Main Language(s) of Instruction: English

Accrediting Agency: National Accreditation Boards of Ghana, The Gambia and Liberia; ISO 9001: 2008 certified; European Union Certified (EMSA)

Degrees and Diplomas: *Certificate*: **Marine Transport.** *Bachelor's Degree*: **Computer Engineering; Electrical Engineering; Marine Engineering; Marine Transport; Nautical Science; Transport Management.** *Master's Degree*: **Marine Transport.** The Master of Arts in Ports and Shipping Administration is organized in collaboration with the School of Research and Graduate Studies, University of Ghana

Student Services: Academic Counselling, Canteen, Careers Guidance, Health Services, Language Laboratory, Social Counselling, Sports Facilities

Academic Staff *2011-2012*	MEN	WOMEN	**TOTAL**
FULL-TIME	71	11	**82**
PART-TIME	29	3	**32**
STAFF WITH DOCTORATE			
FULL-TIME	–	–	**4**
Student Numbers *2011-2012*			
All (Foreign included)	1,006	111	**1,117**
FOREIGN ONLY	288	23	**311**

Last Updated: 31/05/12

UNIVERSITY FOR DEVELOPMENT STUDIES (UDS)

PO Box TL 1350, Tamale
Tel: +233(71) 22078
Fax: +233(71) 23957
EMail: registrar@uds.edu.gh
Website: http://www.uds.edu.gh

Vice-Chancellor: Haruna Yakubu
Tel: +233(71) 22369 EMail: vc@uds.edu.gh; yakubuh@uds.edu.gh

Pro-Vice Chancellor: David Millar
Tel: +233(71) 23617 EMail: provc@uds.edu.gh

Faculty

Agriculture *(Nyankpala)* (Agriculture; Agronomy; Animal Husbandry; Environmental Studies; Horticulture; Irrigation; Natural Resources; Rural Planning); **Applied Sciences** *(Navrongo)* (Biochemistry; Biological and Life Sciences; Botany; Chemistry; Computer Science; Mathematics; Physical Engineering); **Integrated Development Studies** *(Wa)* (Development Studies; Economics; History; Management; Political Sciences; Social Studies); **Planning and Land Management** (Accountancy; Business Administration; Economics; Geography; Rural Planning); **Renewable Natural Resources** (Aquaculture; Ecology; Environmental Studies; Fishery; Forestry; Natural Resources; Tourism; Wildlife)

School

Graduate Studies *(Navrongo)*; **Medicine and Health Sciences** (Community Health; Health Sciences; Medicine; Nutrition)

History: Founded 1992. First students admitted September 1993.

Academic Year: September to July (September-December; January-April; May-July)

Admission Requirements: Senior Secondary School Certificate; State Registered Nurses Certificate; Higher National Diploma/ Diploma holders; West Africa Senior Secondary School Certificate; Mature Applicants and Entrance examination

Fees: (Cedi): Tuition, 318,50-688,50 per annum

Main Language(s) of Instruction: English

Accrediting Agency: National Accreditation Board; Ghana Medical and Dental Council; Nurses and Midwives Council of Ghana

Degrees and Diplomas: *Bachelor of Medicine and Surgery*: **Medicine.** *Bachelor's Degree*: **Agriculture; Architecture and Planning; Community Health; Fine Arts; Nursing; Nutrition.**

Student Services: Academic Counselling, Canteen, Health Services, Language Laboratory, Social Counselling, Sports Facilities

Publications: Ghana Journal of Development Studies

Last Updated: 09/03/11

IAU UNIVERSITY OF CAPE COAST (UCC)

University Post Office, Cape Coast
Tel: +233(3321) 32378
Fax: +233(3321) 32485
EMail: registrar@ucc.edu.gh
Website: http://www.ucc.edu.gh/

Vice-Chancellor: Domwini Dabire Kuupole (2012-)
Tel: +233(3321) 32378 EMail: vc@ucc.edu.gh

Registrar: J. K. Nyan

Faculty

Arts (African Languages; African Studies; Arts and Humanities; Classical Languages; Communication Studies; English; French; History; Modern Languages; Music; Native Language; Philosophy; Religion; Religious Studies; Theatre); **Education** (Continuing Education; Education; Educational Administration; Educational Sciences; Health Sciences; Humanities and Social Science Education; Mathematics Education; Parks and Recreation; Physical Education; Primary Education; Science Education; Social Sciences; Technology Education; Vocational Education); **Social Sciences** (Development Studies; Economics; Family Studies; Geography (Human); Regional Planning; Social Sciences; Sociology; Tourism)

School

Agriculture (Agricultural Economics; Agricultural Engineering; Agriculture; Animal Husbandry; Crop Production; Meat and Poultry; Soil Science); **Biological Sciences** (Biochemistry; Biological and

Life Sciences; Biology; Biotechnology; Entomology; Environmental Studies; Fishery; Molecular Biology; Nursing; Wildlife); **Business** (Accountancy; Business Administration; Finance; Management); **Medical Sciences** (Anatomy; Biochemistry; Food Science; Gynaecology and Obstetrics; Medicine; Nutrition; Physiology; Psychology; Surgery); **Physical Sciences** (Chemistry; Computer Science; Environmental Studies; Laboratory Techniques; Mathematics; Physics)

Institute

Development Studies *(CDS)* (Development Studies; Economics; Environmental Studies; Rural Planning; Social Studies; Town Planning); **Education** (Education); **Educational Planning and Administration** *(IEPA)* (Educational Administration; Educational Research)

Centre

Continuing Education (Continuing Education); **International Education** (International and Comparative Education); **Research on Improving Quality of Primary Education in Ghana** *(CRIQPEG)* (Educational Research; Primary Education)

History: Founded 1962 as University College of Cape Coast, acquired present status and title 1971.

Academic Year: October to July (October-February; March-July)

Admission Requirements: General Certificate of Education/ advanced level or recognized foreign equivalent, or senior secondary school certificate and entrance examination

Fees: (US Dollars): Foreign Students, 600-1,500 per semester

Main Language(s) of Instruction: English

Degrees and Diplomas: *Certificate*: **Business and Commerce; Computer Science; Education; Health Education; Health Sciences.** *Bachelor's Degree*: **Agriculture; Education; Fine Arts; Nursing; Social Sciences.** *Graduate Diploma*: **Education.** *Master's Degree*: **Education; Fine Arts; Management; Philosophy.** *Doctorate*: **Social Sciences.**

Student Services: Academic Counselling, Canteen, Careers Guidance, Cultural Activities, Facilities for disabled people, Health Services, Language Laboratory, Nursery Care, Social Counselling, Sports Facilities

Publishing house: University Printing Press

Last Updated: 03/08/12

UNIVERSITY OF EDUCATION, WINNEBA (UEW)

PO Box 25, Winneba
Tel: +233(3323) 22361
EMail: registrar@uew.edu.gh
Website: http://www.uew.edu.gh

Vice-Chancellor: Mawutor Avoke (2015-) EMail: vc@uew.edu.gh

Registrar: C.Y. Akwaa-Mensah
Tel: +233(3323) 21036 EMail: cymensah@uew.edu.gh

Faculty

Agriculture Education *(Mampong Campus)* (Agricultural Education); **Business Education** *(Kumasi Campus)* (Business Education; Management); **Language Education** (African Languages; Communication Studies; English; French; Modern Languages); **Science Education** (Biological and Life Sciences; Chemistry; Health Sciences; Home Economics; Leisure Studies; Mathematics; Natural Sciences; Physical Education; Science Education; Sports); **Social Sciences** *(Mampong Campus)* (African Studies; Human Rights; Social Sciences; Social Studies); **Technical and Vocational Education** *(Kumasi Campus)* (Information Technology; Technology; Vocational Education)

School

Creative Arts (Art Education; Cultural Studies; Music Education)

Institute

Educational Development and Extension *((IEDE) Distance and continuing education)* (Continuing Education; Distance Education)

Centre

School and Community Science and Technology Studies *(SACOST)* (Educational Sciences; Educational Technology; Social and Community Services)

Further Information: Also campuses in Kumasi and Mampong

History: Founded 1992, merging seven diploma-awarding colleges.

Academic Year: August-May (August-December; January-May)

Admission Requirements: Entrance examination

Fees: (US Dollars): 2,218 for undergraduate Foreign Students (Sandwich) Certificate, Diploma and Post Diploma Programme. 3,801 for MA/M.ED Programmes (Foreign Students)

Main Language(s) of Instruction: English

Degrees and Diplomas: *Certificate*: **Education.** *Bachelor's Degree*: **Education.** *Master's Degree*: **Arts and Humanities; Education.** *Doctorate*: **Arts and Humanities.**

Student Services: Canteen, Facilities for disabled people, Health Services, Social Counselling, Sports Facilities

Publications: Journal of Special Education

Last Updated: 03/08/12

IAU UNIVERSITY OF GHANA (UG)

PO Box LG 25, Legon, Accra
Tel: +233(302) 500381
Fax: +233(302) 514745
EMail: pad@ug.edu.gh; vcoffice@ug.edu.gh
Website: http://www.ug.edu.gh

Vice-Chancellor: Ernest Aryeetey (2010-)
EMail: vcoffice@ug.edu.gh

Registrar: Joseph Maafo Budu
Tel: +233(302) 500383 EMail: registrar@ug.edu.gh

International Relations: Naa Ayikailey Adamafio, Dean, International Programmes
Tel: +233(302) 507147 EMail: inep@ug.edu.gh; dp@ug.edu.gh

Faculty

Arts (Arabic; Arts and Humanities; Classical Languages; Dance; English; French; Linguistics; Modern Languages; Music; Philosophy; Russian; Spanish; Swahili; Theatre); **Engineering Sciences** (Agricultural Engineering; Biomedical Engineering; Computer Engineering; Engineering; Food Technology; Materials Engineering); **Law** (Constitutional Law; Environmental Studies; Family Studies; Human Rights; International Business; International Law; Law); **Science** (Biochemistry; Botany; Chemistry; Computer Science; Environmental Studies; Fishery; Food Science; Geography; Geology; Marine Science and Oceanography; Mathematics; Natural Resources; Natural Sciences; Nursing; Nutrition; Physics; Psychology; Statistics; Zoology); **Social Sciences** (Archaeology; Computer Science; Economics; Geography; History; Information Sciences; Mathematics; Nursing; Political Sciences; Psychology; Social Work; Sociology; Statistics)

College

Agriculture and Consumer Sciences (Agriculture; Consumer Studies); **Health Sciences** (Dentistry; Health Sciences; Medicine; Nursing; Public Health)

Programme

Entomology (Entomology); **Environmental Sciences** (Environmental Studies)

School

Agriculture (Agricultural Business; Agricultural Economics; Agriculture; Animal Husbandry; Crop Production; Soil Science); **Allied Health Sciences** (Health Sciences; Laboratory Techniques; Physical Therapy; Radiology); **Business** (Accountancy; Administration; Banking; Finance; Health Administration; Human Resources; Information Management; Information Sciences; Management; Marketing; Public Administration); **Communication Studies** (Advertising and Publicity; Communication Studies; Public Relations; Social Psychology); **Dentistry** (Dental Hygiene; Dental Technology; Dentistry; Orthodontics; Social and Preventive Medicine; Surgery); **Graduate Studies** (Arts and Humanities; Business Administration; Fine Arts; Health Administration; Law; Medicine; Natural Sciences; Public Health); **Medicine** (Anaesthesiology; Anatomy; Gynaecology and Obstetrics; Haematology; Medicine; Microbiology; Pathology; Pharmacology; Physiology; Psychiatry and Mental Health; Radiology; Surgery); **Nursing** (Child Care and Development; Community Health; Health Sciences; Nursing; Psychiatry and Mental Health); **Performing Arts** (Dance; Music; Performing Arts; Theatre); **Public Health** (Public Health)

Department
Modern Languages (Modern Languages); **Rehabilitation Medicine and Therapy** (Medicine; Rehabilitation and Therapy)

Institute
Adult Education (Adult Education); **African Studies** (African Studies); **Medical Research** *(Noguchi Memorial, NMIMR)* (Medicine); **Population Studies** (Demography and Population); **Statistical, Social and Economic Research** (Economics; Social Studies; Statistics)

Centre
African Music and Dance (Dance; Music); **African Wetlands**; **Biotechnology** (Biotechnology); **International Affairs** (International Relations; International Studies); **Languages** (African Languages; English; Modern Languages; Social Policy; Writing); **Tropical Clinical Pharmacology and Therapeutics** (Pharmacology; Physical Therapy)

Further Information: Also United Nations University Institute for Natural Resources in Africa (UNU/INRA); Volta Basin Research Project; Agricultural Research Centres (Legon, Kade, Kpong). English proficiency course for foreign students

History: Founded 1948 as University College of Gold Coast, became University College of Ghana 1957, and acquired present status and title 1961. Methodist University College Ghana affiliated 2002.

Academic Year: August to July (August-December; January-July)

Admission Requirements: General Certificate of Education (GCE) with 5 credits including English, Mathematics, Arts and Science or West Africa School Certificate (WASC) Ordinary ('O') level and three passes at Advanced ('A') level, with a minimum grade D for one. Senior Secondary School Certificate with passes in core English, Mathematics and any 3 elective subjects, with aggregate score of 24 in the WAEC entrance examination

Fees: (US Dollars): Foreign students, 2,475-3,500 per semester

Main Language(s) of Instruction: English

Degrees and Diplomas: *Bachelor of Dental Surgery*: **Dentistry.** *Bachelor of Medicine and Surgery*: **Medicine; Surgery.** *Bachelor's Degree*: **Administration; Agriculture; Fine Arts; Home Economics; Law; Music; Natural Sciences; Nursing.** *Graduate Diploma*; *Master's Degree*: **African Studies; Agriculture; Archiving; Business Administration; Communication Studies; Demography and Population; Entomology; Environmental Studies; Fine Arts; Law; Linguistics; Philosophy; Public Administration; Public Health; Theatre.** *Master of Philosophy*; *Doctorate*

Student Services: Academic Counselling, Canteen, Careers Guidance, Cultural Activities, Facilities for disabled people, Foreign Studies Centre, Health Services, Language Laboratory, Social Counselling, Sports Facilities

Publications: Journal of Faculty of Science; Legon Journal of Humanities; Legon Journal of International Affairs (LEJIA); Management and Organisations; Social Studies Journal; Universitas

Publishing House: School of Communication Studies Printing Press; Institute of Adult Education Printing Press; Institute of African Studies Printing Press

Student Numbers *2011-2012*: Total 42,629
Last Updated: 26/03/12

UNIVERSITY OF MINES AND TECHNOLOGY (UMAT)

PO Box 237, Tarkwa
Tel: +233(362) 20324
Fax: +233(362) 20306
EMail: vc@umat.edu.gh
Website: http://www.umat.edu.gh

Vice-Chancellor: Jerry S.Y. Kuma (2012-) EMail: vc@umat.edu.gh
Registrar: Emmanuel K. Bedai EMail: registrar@umat.edu.gh

International Relations: Elias Asiam, Dean
Tel: +233(244) 593-689 EMail: ekasiam@yahoo.com

Faculty
Engineering (Computer Engineering; Electrical and Electronic Engineering; Engineering; Information Technology; Mathematics; Mechanical Engineering); **Mineral Resources Technology** (Engineering; Geological Engineering; Mineralogy; Mining Engineering; Petroleum and Gas Engineering; Surveying and Mapping)

School
Postgraduate Studies (Electrical and Electronic Engineering; Geological Engineering; Mathematics; Mechanical Engineering; Mineralogy; Mining Engineering)

Centre
Communication and Entrepreneurship Skills (Communication Studies; Economics; English; Ethics; French)

History: Founded 1952 as Tarkwa Technical Institute. Acquired present status and title 2004.

Academic Year: August to May (August-December; February-May)

Admission Requirements: Passes in core: English language, Mathematics, Integrated Science ans also passes in elective Physics, Chemistry and Mathematics. A pass in Technical Drawing or Metal Work is also accepted for Mechanical Engineering while Applied Electricity or Electronic for Electrical and Electronic Engineering in lieu of elective in Chemistry.

Fees: (Cedi): Ghanaian regular students, 252.36 for undergraduate fresh students; 227.36 for undergraduate continuing students and 324.92 for postgraduate students. Ghanaian fee paying students, Ghanaian regular students, 2918.40 for undergraduate fresh students; 2,893.40 for foreign students; 6,403 for undergraduate fresh students; 7,003 for postgraduate fresh students; 6,253 for continuing undergraduate students; 6,903 for continuing postgraduate students

Main Language(s) of Instruction: English

Accrediting Agency: National Accreditation Board

Degrees and Diplomas: *Bachelor's Degree*; *Graduate Diploma*; *Master's Degree*: **Electrical and Electronic Engineering; Geological Engineering; Mechanical Engineering; Mining Engineering.** *Master of Philosophy*: **Electrical and Electronic Engineering; Geological Engineering; Mechanical Engineering; Mining Engineering.** *Doctorate*: **Geological Engineering; Mining Engineering.**

Student Services: Academic Counselling, Social Counselling

Academic Staff *2011-2012*: Total 60
STAFF WITH DOCTORATE: Total 20
Student Numbers *2011-2012*: Total: c. 1,800
Last Updated: 03/08/12

UNIVERSITY OF PROFESSIONAL STUDIES (UPSA)

PO Box LG 149, Legon, Greater Accra
Tel: +233(302) 500 171 +233(302) 500 722
Fax: +233(302) 501 174
EMail: info@upsa.edu.gh; admin@upsa.edu.gh
Website: http://upsa.edu.gh/

Vice-Chancellor: Joshua Alabi (2009-)
Tel: +233(28) 910-6786
EMail: alabij@ips.edu.gh; jalabius@yahoo.com

Registrar: Seidu Mustapha
Tel: +233(302) 500-725 EMail: mmustapha@ips.edu.gh

International Relations: Arkoful Helen, Dean
Tel: +233(24) 253-5747 EMail: harkoful@ips.edu.gh

Faculty
Accounting (Accountancy; Banking; Finance); **Communication Studies** (Communication Studies; Information Technology; Public Relations); **Management** (Business Administration; Management; Marketing)

School
Research and Graduate Studies (Accountancy; Banking; Business Administration; Finance; Management; Marketing; Public Relations)

History: Founded 1965 as Institute of Professional Studies. Previously affiliated to the University of Ghana. Acquired present title and status 2012.

Academic Year: August to December; January to May

Admission Requirements: Senior Secondary School Certificate Examination (SSSCE)/West African Senior School Examination (WASSCE) of the West African Examinations Council with Passes in English Language (Core), Mathematics (Core), Integrated Science (Core) and any other three subjects with an aggregate score of 24 or better.

Fees: (Cedi): Undergraduate, 1,265 per annum; postgraduate, 3,950 per annum

Main Language(s) of Instruction: English

Accrediting Agency: National Accreditation Board

Degrees and Diplomas: *Certificate*: **Business Administration.** *Bachelor's Degree*: **Accountancy; Banking; Business Administration; Finance; Marketing.** *Master's Degree*: **Accountancy; Leadership; Management; Marketing.** Also Professional Programmes

Student Services: Academic Counselling, Canteen, Foreign Studies Centre, Health Services, Social Counselling, Sports Facilities

Publications: Journal of Business Research

Publishing House: INSTI (CSIR) Ghana

Academic Staff *2010-2011*	MEN	WOMEN	**TOTAL**
FULL-TIME	54	19	**73**
PART-TIME	29	11	**40**
STAFF WITH DOCTORATE			
FULL-TIME	4	1	**5**
Student Numbers *2010-2011*			
All (Foreign included)	4,191	3,010	**7,201**
FOREIGN ONLY	12	15	**27**

Part-time students, 1,961.

Last Updated: 26/03/12

PRIVATE INSTITUTIONS

ACCRA INSTITUTE OF TECHNOLOGY

PO Box AN-19782, Accra-North
Tel: +233(302) 913227 +233(28) 8181817
Fax: +233(302) 913227
EMail: ait@ait.edu.gh
Website: http://www.ait.edu.gh

President: Clement Dzidonu

School

Advanced Systems and Data Studies *(ASSDAS)* (Computer Networks; Computer Science; E- Business/Commerce; Electronic Engineering; Information Technology; Mathematics; Multimedia; Software Engineering); **Advanced Technology and Engineering Sciences** *(SATES)* (Civil Engineering; Electrical and Electronic Engineering; Engineering; Industrial Engineering; Production Engineering; Telecommunications Engineering); **Business** *(AIT Business School (ABS))* (Accountancy; Banking; Business Administration; Business and Commerce; Cooking and Catering; E-Business/Commerce; Finance; Information Management; Information Technology; Management; Marketing; Public Administration; Secretarial Studies; Tourism)

Further Information: Also AIT Virtual University (the AIT Virtual Campus) and the AIT Online- Your e-University

Degrees and Diplomas: *Certificate*; *Bachelor's Degree*; *Graduate Diploma*; *Master's Degree*

Last Updated: 25/07/12

AFRICAN UNIVERSITY COLLEGE OF COMMUNICATIONS (AUCC)

PO Box LG 510, Legon, Accra
Tel: +233(302) 258584/6
Fax: +233(302) 237671
EMail: info@aucc.edu.gh
Website: http://www.aucc.edu.gh

President: Kojo Yankah

Programme

Business Administration (Banking; Business Administration; Finance; Human Resources; Marketing); **Communication Studies** (Communication Studies)

History: Founded 2001 as the Africa Institute of Journalism and Communications (AIJC). Acquired present status and title 2007.

Degrees and Diplomas: *Bachelor's Degree*

Last Updated: 06/08/12

ALL NATIONS UNIVERSITY COLLEGE

PO Box KF 1908, Koforidua
Tel: +233(34) 202-1587-8
Fax: +233(34) 202-6526
EMail: registrar@allnationsuniversity.org
Website: http://www.anuc.edu.gh/home/

President: Samuel Donkor (2002-)
Tel: +233(34) 202-1587-8
EMail: president@anuc.edu.gh; drsdonkor@anfgc.org

Registrar: Lynn Kisembe Darkwah
Tel: +233 20-8088119 EMail: lkisembe@anuc.edu.gh

International Relations: Carlene Kyeremeh, Head of International Relations
Tel: +233 240-641627 EMail: drckyeremeh@anuc.edu.gh

School

Business Administration (Accountancy; Banking; Business Administration; Finance; Human Resources; Marketing); **Engineering** (Biomedical Engineering; Computer Engineering; Computer Science; Electronic Engineering; Petroleum and Gas Engineering; Telecommunications Engineering); **Humanities and Social Studies** (Arts and Humanities; Bible; Social Sciences)

History: Founded 1996.

Academic Year: August to December; January to April; May to July

Admission Requirements: Secondary school certificate or equivalent

Main Language(s) of Instruction: English

Accrediting Agency: National Accreditation Board (NAB)

Degrees and Diplomas: *Bachelor's Degree*: **Bible; Biomedical Engineering; Business Administration; Computer Engineering; Computer Science; Electronic Engineering; Petroleum and Gas Engineering; Telecommunications Engineering.**

Student Services: Academic Counselling, Canteen, Careers Guidance, Facilities for disabled people, Foreign Studies Centre, Health Services, Language Laboratory, Social Counselling, Sports Facilities

Publications: All Nations University Journal of Applied Thought

Academic Staff *2010-2011*	MEN	WOMEN	**TOTAL**
FULL-TIME	101	12	**113**
PART-TIME	2	–	**2**
STAFF WITH DOCTORATE			
FULL-TIME	5	–	**5**
Student Numbers *2012-2013*			
All (Foreign included)	1,597	512	**2,109**
FOREIGN ONLY	689	42	**731**

Last Updated: 14/03/13

ASHESI UNIVERSITY COLLEGE

PMB CT3 Cantonments, 1 University Avenue, Berekuso, Accra
Tel: +233(302) 610330
Fax: +233(302) 610340
EMail: admissions@ashesi.edu.gh; info@ashesi.edu.gh
Website: http://www.ashesi.edu.gh

President: Patrick G. Awuah

Registrar: Carol Williams

International Relations: Matthew Taggart, Director of Development

Department

Arts and Sciences (African Studies; Arts and Humanities; Leadership; Mathematics; Social Sciences); **Business Administration** (Accountancy; Business Administration; Finance; Human

Resources; Leadership; Management; Marketing); **Computer Science** (Computer Science)

History: Founded 2002.

Degrees and Diplomas: *Bachelor's Degree*

Last Updated: 21/06/12

CATHOLIC UNIVERSITY COLLEGE OF GHANA

PO Box 363, Sunyani, Brong Ahafo Region
Tel: +233(352) 26751 +233(302) 512208
EMail: cugadmin@cug.edu.gh
Website: http://www.cug.edu.gh

Vice-Chancellor: James Hawkins Ephraim

Registrar: Ernest K. Odoom

Faculty

Economics and Business Administration (Business Administration; Economics); **Education** (Computer Education; Education; Mathematics Education); **Information and Communication Science and Technology** (Communication Studies; Information Sciences; Information Technology); **Public Health and Allied Sciences** (Health Administration; Health Education; Public Health); **Religious Studies** (Religious Studies)

History: Founded 1998.

Fees: (Cedi): 1,360 per annum; foreign students, (US Dollars), 2,000 per annum

Main Language(s) of Instruction: English

Accrediting Agency: National Accreditation Board

Degrees and Diplomas: *Bachelor's Degree*: **Business Administration; Economics; Education; Information Technology.** *Graduate Diploma*: **Education.** *Master's Degree*

Last Updated: 25/07/12

CENTRAL UNIVERSITY COLLEGE (CUC)

Mahateko, PO Box DS 2310, Dansoman, Accra, Greater Accra
Tel: +233(302) 311040
Fax: +233(302) 311042
EMail: admissions@central.edu.gh
Website: http://central.edu.gh/

President: Victor Patrick Gadzekpo (2004-)
EMail: vgadzekpo@yahoo.com

Faculty

Arts and Social Sciences (Development Studies; Economics; English; Environmental Studies; French; Social Sciences)

School

Applied Sciences (Architecture; Civil Engineering; Medical Auxiliaries; Nursing; Pharmacy); **Business** (Accountancy; Administration; Agricultural Business; Banking; Finance; Human Resources; Management; Marketing); **Theology and Missions** (Bible; Christian Religious Studies; Family Studies; Hebrew; Theology)

History: Founded 1988. Became Bible College 1991. Acquired present status 1997 and converted to tertiary institution 1998.

Academic Year: October to July (October-February; March-July)

Admission Requirements: Senior secondary school certificate, advanced level

Fees: Fixed on a semester basis

Main Language(s) of Instruction: English

Accrediting Agency: Ghana National Accreditation Board; International Central Gospel Church-Ghana (ICGC); Council for Christian Colleges and Universities, USA

Degrees and Diplomas: *Bachelor's Degree*: **Accountancy; Administration; Agricultural Business; Banking; Christian Religious Studies; Development Studies; Economics; Environmental Studies; Family Studies; Finance; Human Resources; Management; Marketing; Theology.** *Master's Degree*: **Administration; Human Resources; Management; Marketing; Theology.**

Student Services: Academic Counselling, Canteen, Careers Guidance, Facilities for disabled people, Health Services, Language Laboratory, Social Counselling, Sports Facilities

Publishing house: Central University Press

Last Updated: 02/08/12

CHRISTIAN SERVICE UNIVERSITY COLLEGE

PO Box 3110, Kumasi
Tel: +233(322) 28781
Fax: +233(322) 28780
EMail: info@csuc.edu.gh
Website: http://www.csuc.edu.gh/csuc/

President: Emmanuel Frempong

Registrar: Kwame Oti Duah

Department

Business Administration (Accountancy; Banking; Business Administration; Finance; Human Resources; Marketing); **Communication Studies** (Communication Studies); **Computer Science** (Computer Networks; Computer Science); **Theology** (Bible; Theology)

History: Founded 1974.

Degrees and Diplomas: *Certificate*; *Bachelor's Degree*

Last Updated: 25/10/12

DATA LINK INSTITUTE

PO Box 2481, Along the Community, 10 New Road, Tema
Tel: +233(303) 307080
EMail: info@datalinkuniversity.com
Website: http://www.datalinkuniversity.com/

President: Seth Abang Laryea

Vice-President of Academic Affair: Ingrid Ansah

Programme

Business Administration (Accountancy; Banking; Finance; Human Resources; Insurance; Marketing); **Computer Science and Information System** (Computer Science; Information Technology)

History: Founded 2006 as Data Link University College.

Admission Requirements: Two levels of admissions to the undergraduate degree programmes:General Certificate of Education (GCE) Ordinary and Advanced Levels. Senior Secondary School Certificate Examinations (SSSCE)

Degrees and Diplomas: *Certificate*; *Bachelor's Degree*

Last Updated: 01/08/12

EVANGELICAL PRESBYTERIAN UNIVERSITY COLLEGE (EPUC)

PO Box HP 678, Ho-Volta Region
Tel: +233(362) 26724
Website: http://www.epuc.edu.gh

President: Ciryl G.K. Fayose

Registrar: S.W.K. Buami

School

Business Administration (Agricultural Business; Finance; Human Resources; Management; Marketing; Secretarial Studies); **Theology** (Pastoral Studies; Theology)

Accrediting Agency: National Accreditation Board

Degrees and Diplomas: *Bachelor's Degree*

Last Updated: 13/06/12

GARDEN CITY UNIVERSITY COLLEGE

PO Box KS 12755, Kumasi
Tel: +233 2673-85354
EMail: info@gcuc.edu.gh; registrar@gcuc.edu.gh
Website: http://www.gcuc.edu.gh

President: Steve Sobotie

School

Business (Accountancy; Banking; Business Administration; Business Computing; Economics; Finance; Management; Marketing); **Information and Communication Technology** (Accountancy; Communication Studies; Computer Science; Information Technology); **Nursing** (Nursing)

History: Founded 2001. Acquired present status 2004.

Degrees and Diplomas: *Certificate*; *Bachelor's Degree*

Last Updated: 24/10/12

GHANA BAPTIST UNIVERSITY COLLEGE (GBUC)

PMB, Kumasi
Tel: +233(302) 2080195
Fax: +233(302) 2028592
EMail: prof.buatsi@gbuc.edu.gh
Website: http://gbuc.edu.gh/

President: Kojo Osei-Wusuh

School
Business Administration (Accountancy; Banking; Business Administration; Finance; Human Resources; Management; Marketing); **Theology and Ministry** (Pastoral Studies; Theology)

History: Affiliated with University of Cape Coast, Ghana.

Admission Requirements: Senior Secondary School Certificate (SSSC); Senior High School Certificate (SHSC); West African School Certificate (WASC)

Fees: (Cedi): 750,00 per semester

Main Language(s) of Instruction: English

Accrediting Agency: National Accreditations Board (NAB), Ghana

Degrees and Diplomas: *Certificate*: **Religious Music; Theology.** *Bachelor's Degree*: **Business Administration; Theology.** *Master's Degree*: **Missionary Studies.**

Student Services: Academic Counselling, Canteen, Health Services, Social Counselling, Sports Facilities

Publications: Journal of Excellence in Leadership and Stewardship

Publishing House: Ghana Baptist University College Press

Last Updated: 13/06/12

GHANA CHRISTIAN UNIVERSITY COLLEGE (GHANACU)

PO Box AF 919, Adenta-Accra
Tel: +233 5732-32966
EMail: international@ghanacu.org; info@ghanacu.org
Website: http://www.ghanacu.org

President: Manuel Budu-Adjei

School
Development Management (Accountancy; Development Studies; Finance; Human Resources; Management; Marketing; Public Health); **Theology** (Bible; Christian Religious Studies; Missionary Studies; Theology)

History: Founded 1966 as Ghana Christian College and Seminary.

Accrediting Agency: National Accreditation Board

Degrees and Diplomas: *Bachelor's Degree*

Last Updated: 02/08/12

GHANA SCHOOL OF MARKETING

PO Box 18235, Accra
Tel: +233(302) 211156
Fax: +233(302) 241160
EMail: info@cimghana.org
Website: http://www.cimghana.org

Head: Kwabena Agyekum

Programme
Marketing (Marketing)

Degrees and Diplomas: *Certificate*; *Diploma*; *Graduate Diploma*: **Marketing.**

Last Updated: 18/06/12

GHANA TELECOM UNIVERSITY COLLEGE (GTUC)

Private Mail Bag 100, Tesano, Accra-North
Tel: +233(302) 221412
Fax: +233(302) 223531
EMail: info@gtuc.edu.gh
Website: http://www.gtuc.edu.gh/

President: Osei K. Darkwa (2005-)
Tel: +233(302) 226-766
EMail: odarkwa@ghanatel.net; president@gtuc.edu.gh

Faculty
Informatics (Computer Engineering; Information Technology); **Telecommunications Engineering** (Computer Engineering; Telecommunications Engineering)

School
IT Business (Accountancy; Banking; Business Administration; Economics; Finance; Human Resources; Management; Marketing)

History: Founded 2005.

Degrees and Diplomas: *Certificate*; *Bachelor's Degree*; *Master's Degree*; *Doctorate*

Last Updated: 02/08/12

ISLAMIC UNIVERSITY GHANA (IUCG)

PO Box CT 3221, Cantonments, Accra
Tel: +233(30) 7012770 +233(20) 2112267
Fax: +233(30) 778930
EMail: info@islamicug.com
Website: http://www.islamicug.com

President: Ahmad Ali Ghane

Department
Business Administration (Accountancy; Banking; Business Administration; Finance; Marketing); **Computing** (Computer Engineering); **Languages** (Communication Studies); **Religious Studies** (Islamic Studies; Religious Studies)

History: Founded 1986. Acquired present status 2002.

Degrees and Diplomas: *Bachelor's Degree*

JAYEE UNIVERSITY COLLEGE

PO Box OS 672, Osu, Acrra
Tel: + 233(302) 335057
EMail: info@juc.edu.gh
Website: http://juc.edu.gh/

President: John Emmanuel Donkoh

Vice President: Stephen Nibebale Bemile

Programme
Business Administration (Business Administration; Human Resources; Management; Marketing; Public Relations; Secretarial Studies); **Communication Science** (Communication Studies; Journalism)

Degrees and Diplomas: *Certificate*; *Bachelor's Degree*

Last Updated: 25/10/12

KNUTSFORD UNIVERSITY COLLEGE

PO Box AN 19480, 10 Bamako Road, East Legon, Accra-North
Tel: +233(302) 521610/11
Fax: +233(302) 544022
EMail: info@knutsford.edu.gh
Website: http://www.knutsford.edu.gh

Chancellor: Douglas Akuamoah Boateng

School
Business Administration (Accountancy; Business Administration; Finance; Human Resources; Information Management; Marketing); **Nursing** (Nursing); **Science and Technology** (Computer Science; Information Technology)

History: Founded 2007.

Academic Year: January to September

Admission Requirements: General Certificate of Education (Ordinary and Advanced Levels) or Senior Secondary School Certificate (SSSC) with good passes.

Accrediting Agency: National Accreditation Board

Degrees and Diplomas: *Bachelor's Degree*

Last Updated: 24/10/12

METHODIST UNIVERSITY COLLEGE GHANA (MUCG)

PO Box DC 940, Dansoman, Accra
Tel: +233(302) 312980 +233(302) 314542
Fax: +233(302) 312989
EMail: mucg2001@yahoo.co.uk
Website: http://www.mucg.edu.gh

Principal: Samuel Kwesi Adjepong (2004-)

Registrar: J. N. Aryeetay

Vice-Principal: J. N. Kudadjie

International Relations: Kwesi A. Adjepong

Faculty

Agriculture (Agricultural Business; Agriculture; Horticulture); **Arts and General Studies** (English; Ethics; French; Music; Psychology; Religion); **Business Administration** (Accountancy; Banking; Business Administration; Finance; Human Resources; Management; Marketing); **Social Studies** (Applied Mathematics; Economics; Information Technology; Psychology; Social Studies; Statistics)

History: Founded 2000.

Admission Requirements: GCE A level; Higher National Diploma

Fees: (Cedi): 90,000 per semester

Main Language(s) of Instruction: English

Accrediting Agency: National Accreditation Board, Ghana

Degrees and Diplomas: *Certificate*: **Agriculture; Horticulture; Information Technology; Music.** *Bachelor's Degree*; *Master's Degree*: **Accountancy; Business Administration; Finance; Human Resources; Marketing; Psychology.**

Student Services: Academic Counselling, Canteen, Health Services, Sports Facilities

Academic Staff *2010-2011*	MEN	WOMEN	TOTAL
FULL-TIME	–	–	**111**
PART-TIME	-2	81	**79**
Student Numbers *2010-2011*			
All (Foreign included)	2,766	2,881	**5,647**
FOREIGN ONLY	37	27	**64**

Last Updated: 05/07/12

OSEI TUTU II INSTITUTE FOR ADVANCED ICT STUDIES

PMB, Kumasi
Tel: +233(322) 83275

Rector: Martin Looijen

Programme

Business and ICT Strategy (Accountancy; E- Business/Commerce; Information Technology; Management); **ICT Management and Security** (Computer Engineering); **Mathematics and Industry** (Applied Mathematics; Automation and Control Engineering); **Project Management**; **Technology** (Computer Networks; Information Technology)

History: Affiliated to Kwame Nkrumah University of Science and Technology, Kumasi 2009.

Degrees and Diplomas: *Master's Degree*

PENTECOST UNIVERSITY COLLEGE

PO Box KN 1739, Kaneshie, Accra KN 1736
Tel: +233(302) 417057/8
Fax: +233(302) 417064
EMail: iarm@pentvars.edu.gh
Website: http://www.pentvars.edu.gh

Rector: Peter Ohene Kyei (2008-) EMail: kyeipk@yahoo.com

Registrar: Gibson Annor-Antwi EMail: info@pentvars.edu.gh

Faculty

Business Administration (Accountancy; Banking; Business Administration; Finance; Human Resources; Insurance; Marketing); **Health, Engineering and Computing** (Computer Engineering; Information Technology); **Theology and Mission** (Missionary Studies; Theology)

History: Founded 1954 as Pentecost Bible College. Acquired present title 2003. Acquired present status 2004. Affiliated to University of Ghana.

Academic Year: August to June

Admission Requirements: Three core and three elective passes in WASSCE/SSSCE with aggregate 6-24

Main Language(s) of Instruction: English

Accrediting Agency: National Accreditation Board

Degrees and Diplomas: *Bachelor's Degree*

Student Services: Academic Counselling, Canteen, Careers Guidance, Facilities for disabled people, Health Services, Language Laboratory, Social Counselling, Sports Facilities

Publications: Pentvars Business Journal

Last Updated: 25/10/12

PRESBYTERIAN UNIVERSITY COLLEGE

PO Box 59, Abetifi-Kwahu, Eastern Region
Tel: +233(342) 30037
Fax: +233(342) 30038
EMail: info@presbyuniversity.edu.gh
Website: http://www.presbyuniversity.edu.gh

Principal: Kofi Sraku-Lartey (2002-)
Tel: +233(342) 30033
EMail: ksrakulartey@presbyuniversity.edu.gh

Registrar: Kwadwo Amo Osei
Tel: +233(201) 741784 EMail: kamosei@presbyuniversity.edu.gh

Campus

Akuapem (Business Administration; Development Studies; English; Environmental Studies; French; Natural Resources; Rural Planning; Rural Studies); **Asante-Akyem** (Community Health; Health Sciences; Nursing); **Okwahu** (Communication Studies; Computer Networks; Information Management; Information Sciences; Information Technology; Mathematics; Mathematics and Computer Science; Software Engineering); **Tema** (Business Administration; Economics)

History: Founded 2003.

Academic Year: September to May (September-December; February-May)

Admission Requirements: SSSCE/WASSCE/GBEC applicants must have passed in three core subjets including English, Mathematics and Integrated Science (with grade D/C4 or better in each core subject) and three relevant elective subjects with a total aggragate of 24 or better. Three GCE Advanced Level Passes (including General Paper) at Grade D or better in Accounting, Economics, Business Management, Mathematics, or any other three Arts subjets or any three science subjets, plus five GCE "O" Level passes including English and Mathematics at grade 6 or better. (Canditate with two A level subjets of an average of 'c' may be considered.

Fees: BSc. Nursing: 2200, GH Cedi (Local Students), 3000 Dollars (Foreign Students); BSc. ICT 1750, GH Cedi (Local Students), 3000 Dollars; All other programmes 1620GH Cedi (Local Students), 3000 Foreign Students

Main Language(s) of Instruction: English

Degrees and Diplomas: *Bachelor's Degree*: **Accountancy; Business Administration; Environmental Studies; Finance; Information Technology; Mathematics; Nursing.**

Student Services: Academic Counselling, Canteen, Careers Guidance, Health Services, Language Laboratory, Social Counselling, Sports Facilities

Last Updated: 25/10/12

REGENT UNIVERSITY COLLEGE OF SCIENCE AND TECHNOLOGY (RUCST)

PO Box DS 1636, Dansoman, Accra
Tel: +233(302) 662885
Fax: +233(302) 662531
EMail: info@regentghana.net
Website: http://www.regentghana.net/

President and Chief Executive Officer: E. Kingsley Larbi (2005-)
EMail: president@regentghana.net

Vice-President, Administration and Development: Albert Amonoo Tel: +233(21) 662-440 EMail: vicepresident@regentghana.net

International Relations: Nancy Ansah, Public Affairs Officer Tel: +233(21) 324-541 EMail: nancy.ansah@regentghana.net

School
Business and Economics (Accountancy; Banking; Business Administration; E- Business/Commerce; Economics; Finance); **Informatics and Engineering** *(King's Campus)* (Computer Science; Electrical Engineering; Information Technology; Statistics); **Theology, Ministry and Human Development** (Development Studies; Missionary Studies; Psychology; Theology)

Institute
Modern Languages and General Studies (Chinese; English; French; German)

History: Founded 2005.

Academic Year: January to August

Admission Requirements: Minimum of aggregate 24 including Mathematics and English. Some courses have prerequisites

Main Language(s) of Instruction: English

Accrediting Agency: National Accreditation Board

Degrees and Diplomas: *Bachelor's Degree*: **Business Administration; Statistics.** *Master's Degree*: **Business Administration; Electrical Engineering; Information Technology; Religious Studies; Theology.**

Student Services: Academic Counselling, Canteen, Careers Guidance, Health Services, Language Laboratory, Social Counselling

Publications: Voice of Regent

Last Updated: 02/08/12

SIKKIM MANIPAL UNIVERSITY

PO Box AD 421, Adabraka, Accra
Tel: +230(30) 2253630
Fax: +230(30) 2250649
EMail: info@smughana.com
Website: http://www.smughana.com/

Dean: Abhishek Tyagi

Programme
Postgraduate (Business Administration; Information Technology; Journalism; Mass Communication); **Undergraduate** (Business Administration; Information Technology; Journalism; Mass Communication)

History: Created 2008 and first accredited 2012. An overseas branch of Sikkim Manipal University in India recognized in Ghana.

Accrediting Agency: National Accreditation Board (NAB)

Degrees and Diplomas: *Bachelor's Degree*: **Business Administration; Information Technology; Journalism; Mass Communication.** *Master's Degree*: **Business Administration; Information Technology; Journalism; Mass Communication.**

Last Updated: 17/04/14

SPIRITAN UNIVERSITY COLLEGE

PO Box 111, Ejisu-Ashanti
Tel: +233(322) 94456-60
EMail: ejisusip@yahoo.com
Website: http://www.spiritanuc.edu.gh

Rector: Francis Ato Jackson-Donkoh
EMail: atojackson2002@yahoo.com

Vice-Rector: Adrian Edwards EMail: ejisusip@yahoo.com

Programme
Philosophy and Social Sciences (Philosophy; Religious Studies; Social Sciences; Sociology)

School
Business (Banking; Business Administration; Economics; Finance; Human Resources; Management; Marketing)

History: Founded 1990 as Spiritan Institute of Philosophy, acquired present title and status 2005.

Accrediting Agency: National Accreditation Board

Degrees and Diplomas: *Certificate*; *Bachelor's Degree*

Last Updated: 25/10/12

UNIVERSITY COLLEGE OF MANAGEMENT STUDIES

PO Box GP 482, Accra
Tel: +233(302) 853304
Fax: +233(302) 853304
EMail: imscolle@yahoo.co.uk
Website: http://www.ucoms.edu.gh/

Director: Sazrar Opata

Department
Accounting, Finance and Marketing (Accountancy; Banking; Finance; Marketing); **Human Resource Management** (Human Resources); **Procurement and Supply Chain Management.** (Management; Marketing; Transport Management)

Further Information: Also campus in Kumasi

History: Founded 1974. Acquired present status and title 2006. In affiliation with the School of Business of Kwame Nkrumah University of Science and Technology, Kumasi and the University of Education Winneba, Kumasi Campus.

Fees: US Dollars: 2000 for foreign students

Degrees and Diplomas: *Bachelor's Degree*. Professional Degree Programmes in Business Administration - Marketing; Accounting; Banking and Finance; Human Resource Management; Procurement and Supply Chain Management - 4 yrs

Last Updated: 03/08/12

UNIVERSITY OF APPLIED MANAGEMENT

PO Box KN 2560, House No. 129, 18th Avenue, McCarthy Hill, Accra
Tel: +233(27) 2007121
EMail: info@ghana.my-university.com; Kojogyambrah@yahoo.com
Website: http://www.ghana.my-university.com

President: Christian Werner

Vice-President for University Development: Florian Kainz

Programme
Business Administration (Business Administration; Business Computing; Marketing); **Business Psychology** (Advertising and Publicity; Business Administration; Psychology); **Sport Management** (Sports Management)

Degrees and Diplomas: *Bachelor's Degree*; *Master's Degree*

Last Updated: 03/08/12

VALLEY VIEW UNIVERSITY (VVU)

PO Box AF 595, Adentan, Accra GH100
Tel: +233(307) 11832
EMail: info@vvu.edu.gh
Website: http://www.vvu.edu.gh/

Vice-Chancellor: Daniel Buor
Tel: +233(307) 011844 EMail: vc@vvu.edu.gh

Pro-Vice Chancellor: Philip Maiyo
Tel: +233(307) 011837 EMail: provc@vvu.edu.gh

School
Business Studies (Accountancy; Banking; Business Administration; Finance; Human Resources; Management; Marketing); **Development Studies, Education, Health Sciences** (Biomedicine; Development Studies; Education; Nursing; Secondary Education); **Theology and Mission** (Religious Studies; Theology)

Institute
Computer Science (Computer Science; Information Technology)

History: Created 1979 by West African Union Mission of Seventh-day Adventists as Adventist Missionary School College. In 1995 was affiliated to Griggs University, USA in order to offer Bachelor degrees. Accredited by NAB, Ghana in 1997 to award own degrees. Obtained current status 2006.

Academic Year: August to December; January to May.

Admission Requirements: Secondary School Certificate equivalent.

Fees: (US Dollar): 25-50 per credit depending on programme. MBA Programme: 6,400

Main Language(s) of Instruction: English

Accrediting Agency: National Accreditation Board (NAB); Adventist Accrediting Association

Degrees and Diplomas: *Certificate*: **Biomedical Engineering.** *Bachelor's Degree*: **Accountancy; Banking; Computer Science; Development Studies; Finance; Human Resources; Information Technology; Marketing; Nursing; Religion; Secondary Education; Theology.**

Student Services: Academic Counselling, Canteen, Careers Guidance, Health Services, Language Laboratory, Social Counselling, Sports Facilities

Publications: The Integrator

Publishing House: Advent Press

Last Updated: 06/08/12

WISCONSIN INTERNATIONAL UNIVERSITY COLLEGE

PO Box LG 751, Legon, Accra
Tel: +233(302) 501449
Fax: +233(302) 501491
EMail: info@wiuc-ghana.edu.gh
Website: http://www.wiuc-ghana.edu.gh

Vice-Chancellor: Kaku Sagary Nokoe (2010-)
EMail: sagary.nokoe@wiuc-ghana.edu.gh

Registar: Akosua Eghan EMail: info@wiuc-ghana.edu.gh

Programme

Business Administration (Accountancy; Business Administration; Computer Science; Finance; Human Resources; Information Technology; Management; Marketing); **Information Technology** (Computer Science; Information Technology; Management)

Department

Adult Education (Adult Education)

History: Founded 2000.

Admission Requirements: 3 A-Level passes with aggregate not more than 14 or 6 SSS passes with aggregate not more than 24 including English, Mathematics and Integrated Science

Degrees and Diplomas: *Bachelor's Degree*; *Master's Degree*

Last Updated: 06/08/12

ZENITH UNIVERSITY COLLEGE

PO Box TF 511, La Education Centre, Trade Fair Centre, Accra
Tel: +233(302) 784849
Fax: +233(302) 779099
EMail: mails@zenithcollegeghana.org; info@zenithcollegeghana.org
Website: http://www.zenithcollegeghana.org

President: Gibrine Adam

School

Business (Accountancy; Business and Commerce; Finance; Human Resources; Information Technology; Management; Tourism); **Law** (Law)

Graduate School

Business *(Accra International Graduate School)* (Business Administration; Business and Commerce)

History: Founded 2001. Acquired present status 2005.

Degrees and Diplomas: *Certificate*; *Bachelor's Degree*; *Master's Degree*

Last Updated: 03/08/12

Greece

STRUCTURE OF HIGHER EDUCATION SYSTEM

Description:

Higher education in Greece is public and provided free of charge. It is composed of institutions of two different levels: universities and technological education institutes. They are under the supervision of the Ministry of National Education, Lifelong Learning and Religious Affairs which supports them financially. Admission is based on performance in nation-wide exams which take place at the end of the upper secondary level. There are no private universities. The diplomas awarded by some private post-secondary education institutions are not recognized by the State.

Stages of studies:

University level first stage: *Ptychio*

Undergraduate degree programmes at universities normally last for four years (eight semesters) and lead to the Ptychio in the relevant field. In Veterinary Science, Dentistry, Engineering and Agriculture, studies last for ten semesters. In Medicine, they last for twelve. The study programme comprises compulsory and elective courses. Each semester, students are required to follow a number of compulsory courses consisting of the core programme and a number of elective courses. The total number of courses to be taken is decided by the respective course programme of the department. In some departments, the submission of a dissertation describing the final (graduation) project is required. For example, the 10th semester of all Engineering departments is devoted to the preparation of a final year project and the submission of a dissertation. The entrance requirements for technological institutions (TEI) are the same as for universities. Studies at TEI last for eight semesters, including the compulsory professional placement and the completion of a graduation project and lead to a Ptychio. Subjects include general compulsory subjects, mandatory elective subjects and optional subjects. The Ptychio qualifies holders for immediate employment. It also allows them to continue their studies in a related university undergraduate course and, at postgraduate level, in a Greek or a foreign university.

University level second stage: *Metaptychiako Díploma Exidíkefsis*

The first level of postgraduate studies, which takes at least four semesters to complete, leads to the Metaptychiako Díploma Exidíkefsis (Postgraduate Diploma of Specialization).

University level third stage: *Didaktoriko*

The Doctoral Degree (Didaktoriko) is conferred after the public defence of a thesis. The research must be original and show advances in research and science. A doctoral thesis requires at least three years' study since the student was admitted to doctoral studies.

ADMISSION TO HIGHER EDUCATION

Admission to university-level studies:

Name of secondary school credential required: Apolytirio Lykeiou

For entry to: Universities and TEIs

Numerus clausus: Entrance is restricted and dependent on candidates' grades and preferences.

Foreign students admission:

Definition of foreign student: Foreign students are defined as those who either do not possess Greek nationality or whose parents, whether Greek public servants on duty abroad or permanent residents in a foreign country, have raised their children abroad.

Admission requirements: Secondary School-leaving Certificate equivalent to the Apolytirio Lykeiou or confirmation of the number of completed years of secondary schooling in Greece or abroad. They must have a recommendation.

Entry regulations: Residence permits are to be obtained from the Foreigners Services Department of the Greek Department.

Health requirements: A medical check-up is required before registration.

Language proficiency: Students must hold a certificate which proves their knowledge of the Greek language.

RECOGNITION OF STUDIES

Quality assurance system:

The external evaluation procedures of higher education institutes are coordinated and supported at national level by an independent administrative authority named "Quality Assurance Authority in Higher Education" which has administrative independence and is supervised by the Minister. The process of internal evaluation of higher education institutes is under the responsibility of each academic unit.

Bodies dealing with recognition:

DOATAP (Hellenic NARIC)

Director, Information Department:Bessy Athanasopoulou
54 Ag. Konstantinou Str.
Athens 10 437
Tel: +30(210) 5281000
Fax: +30(210) 5239525
EMail: information_dep@doatap.gr
WWW: http://www.doatap.gr/

Special provisions for recognition:

Recognition for university level studies: A number of foreign degrees and diplomas are recognized (consult the above bodies or the Unesco Study Abroad volume for details)

For access to advanced studies and research: Foreign students are invited to address themselves to the administrative office of the respective school or institution of higher education.

NATIONAL BODIES

Ministry of Culture, Education and Religious Affairs

Minister: Aristides Baltas
Alternate Minister, Research and Innovation: Kostas Fotakis
37, Andrea Papandreou Str.
Marousi 151 80
Tel: +30 210 3443163
Fax: +30 210 3442485
EMail: eurydice@minedu.gov.gr
WWW: http://www.minedu.gov.gr

Hellenic Quality Assurance Agency for Higher Education

56, Sygrou Avenue
Athens 117 42
Tel: +30 210 922 0944
Fax: +30 210 922 0143
EMail: adipsecretariat@hqaa.gr
WWW: http://www.adip.gr

Synodos Ellinikon Pritaneon (Greek Rectors' Conference)

30 Panepistimiou Street
Athens 106 79
Tel: +30(210) 3689719
Fax: +30(210) 3689691
EMail: lilnikol@interel.uoa.gr
WWW: http://www.synodos-aei.gr/

Data for academic year: 2011-2012

Source: IAU from the Hellenic Eurydice Unit, Directorate for European Union Affairs, Ministry of Education, Lifelong Learning and Religious Affairs, Greece, 2011. Bodies 2015.

INSTITUTIONS

PUBLIC INSTITUTIONS

AGRICULTURAL UNIVERSITY OF ATHENS

Georgikon Panepistimion Athinon
Iera odos 75, 11855 Athinai
Tel: +30(210) 549-4893
Fax: +30(210) 346-0885
EMail: vr1@aua.gr
Website: http://www.aua.gr

Rector: George Papadoulis EMail: r@aua.gr

Faculty
Agricultural Biotechnology *(AB)* (Agriculture; Biological and Life Sciences; Biology; Biotechnology; Botany; Genetics; Microbiology; Molecular Biology; Natural Sciences; Plant Pathology); **Animal Science and Aquaculture** *(AS)* (Agriculture; Anatomy; Animal Husbandry; Aquaculture; Biology; Nutrition; Physiology); **Crop Science** *(CP)* (Agriculture; Agronomy; Animal Husbandry; Apiculture; Biological and Life Sciences; Crop Production; Ecology; Entomology; Environmental Studies; Floriculture; Horticulture; Landscape Architecture; Natural Sciences; Plant and Crop Protection; Plant Pathology; Sericulture; Vegetable Production; Viticulture; Zoology); **Science** *(S)* (Chemistry; Computer Science; Earth Sciences; Geology; Information Sciences; Mathematics; Mechanics; Meteorology; Natural Sciences; Physics; Statistics)

Department
Agricultural Economics and Rural Development (Agricultural Business; Agricultural Economics; Agricultural Management; Agriculture; Development Studies; Rural Planning; Rural Studies; Social Policy; Social Sciences; Sociology); **Food Science and Technology** *(FS&T)* (Agriculture; Biological and Life Sciences; Biotechnology; Chemistry; Dairy; Food Science; Food Technology; Hygiene; Microbiology; Natural Sciences; Safety Engineering); **Natural Resources Management and Agricultural Engineering** *(NRM&AE)* (Agricultural Engineering; Agricultural Equipment; Agriculture; Chemistry; Natural Resources; Soil Science; Water Management; Water Science)

History: Founded 1920, acquired present status 1989. Under the jurisdiction of the Ministry of Education.

Academic Year: September to August (October-January; February-June)

Admission Requirements: Secondary school certificate (Apolytirion Lykiou) and entrance examination

Fees: None

Main Language(s) of Instruction: Greek

Degrees and Diplomas: *Ptychio*; *Metaptychiako Diploma Eidikefsis*: **Agricultural Management; Agriculture; Animal Husbandry; Biotechnology; Food Science; Horticulture; Marine Science and Oceanography; Oenology; Technology; Viticulture.** *Didaktoriko Diploma*: **Agricultural Management; Agriculture; Animal Husbandry; Biotechnology; Food Science; Horticulture; Marine Science and Oceanography; Oenology; Technology; Viticulture.**

Last Updated: 21/04/15

ALEXANDER TECHNOLOGICAL EDUCATIONAL INSTITUTE OF THESSALONIKI

Technologiko Ekpaideutiko Idrima, Thessalonikis (ATEI OF THESSALONIKI)
P.O. Box 141, 574 00 Sindos, Thessaloniki
Tel: +30(2310) 791-100 +30(2310) 791-111
Fax: +30(2310) 799-152
EMail: pubrel@admin.teithe.gr
Website: http://www.teithe.gr/

President: Karakoltsisdi Pavlos

International Relations: Despina Dimaki-Gouita

School
Agricultural Technology *(HOME)* (Animal Husbandry; Crop Production; Farm Management); **Business Administration and Economics** *(SDO)* (Accountancy; Advertising and Publicity; Information Sciences; Library Science; Marketing; Tourism); **Geoponics, Food Technology and Nutrition** *(STET-D)* (Agricultural Economics; Animal Husbandry; Crop Production; Food Technology; Nutrition); **Health and Medical Care** *(SEYP)* (Aesthetics; Child Care and Development; Gynaecology and Obstetrics; Laboratory Techniques; Midwifery; Nursing; Physical Therapy); **Technological Applications** *(STEF)* (Automation and Control Engineering; Civil Engineering; Computer Science; Electronic Engineering; Transport Engineering)

Department
Clothing Design and Production *(Kilkis Branch)* (Business Administration; Fashion Design; Management; Marketing); **Fisheries Technology - Aquaculture** *(Moudania Branch)* (Aquaculture; Fishery); **Standardization and Transfer Products (Logistics)** *(Katerini Branch)* (Transport Management)

Centre
Foreign Languages and Physical Education *(Thessaloniki Branch)* (English; French; German; Greek; Italian; Modern Languages; Physical Education; Russian)

History: Founded 1974. An autonomous institution under the supervision of the Institute of Technological Education (Ministry of National Education and Religious Affairs).

Academic Year: September to August

Main Language(s) of Instruction: Greek

Degrees and Diplomas: *Ptychio*

Student Services: Academic Counselling, Canteen, Careers Guidance, Facilities for disabled people, Foreign Studies Centre, Health Services, Language Laboratory, Nursery Care, Sports Facilities

Publications: Technologia and Ekpedefsi

Publishing House: University Press

Last Updated: 24/04/15

ARISTOTLE UNIVERSITY OF THESSALONIKI

Aristoteleion Panepistimion Thessalonikis (AUTH)
University Campus, 54124 Thessaloniki
Tel: +30(2310) 996-000
Fax: +30(2310) 991621
EMail: internat-rel@auth.gr
Website: http://www.auth.gr

Rector: Pericles A. Mitkas (2014-)
EMail: rector@auth.gr; rector-secretary@auth.gr

International Relations: Helen Bahtsavanopoulou-Kotsaki, Head, International Relations Department
EMail: helenko@auth.gr; internat-rel@auth.gr

Faculty
Agriculture, Forestry and Natural Environment (Agriculture; Fishery; Forestry; Harvest Technology; Water Science; Wildlife); **Economics and Political Science** (Economics; Journalism; Mass Communication; Political Sciences); **Education** (Preschool Education; Primary Education); **Engineering** (Architecture; Chemical Engineering; Civil Engineering; Computer Engineering; Electrical Engineering; Engineering; Mechanical Engineering; Regional Planning; Surveying and Mapping); **Fine Arts** (Film; Music; Theatre; Visual Arts); **Health Sciences** (Anatomy; Biological and Life Sciences; Dentistry; Medicine; Neurosciences; Pathology; Pharmacology; Physiology; Radiology; Social and Preventive Medicine; Surgery; Veterinary Science); **Law** (Law); **Philosophy** (Archaeology; Education; English; French; German; History; Italian; Philology; Philosophy; Psychology); **Physical Education and Sport Sciences** (Physical Education; Sports); **Science** (Biology; Chemistry; Computer Science; Geology; Mathematics; Physics); **Theology** (Theology)

Institute
Modern Greek Studies *(Manolis Triantafillidis)* (Greek)

Foundation
Art *(Telloglion)* (Fine Arts)

Chair
UNESCO (Human Rights; Peace and Disarmament)

Further Information: Also 4 Teaching Hospitals

History: Founded 1925. An autonomous institution under the supervision of the Ministry of Education. Financed by the State.

Academic Year: September to June (September-January; February-June)

Admission Requirements: Secondary school certificate (Apolytirion Lykiou) or recognized foreign equivalent and entrance examination

Fees: None

Main Language(s) of Instruction: Greek

Degrees and Diplomas: *Ptychio*; *Metaptychiako Diploma Eidikefsis*; *Didaktoriko Diploma*: **Archaeology; Biology; Chemistry; Geology; History; Italian; Law; Mathematics; Pharmacy; Philology; Physics; Psychology; Theology; Veterinary Science.**

Student Services: Academic Counselling, Canteen, Careers Guidance, Cultural Activities, Facilities for disabled people, Health Services, Language Laboratory, Nursery Care, Social Counselling, Sports Facilities

Publications: Periodicals published by the various Schools; The Aristotle University Today

Publishing House: Aristotle University Publication Office

Last Updated: 21/04/15

ATHENS SCHOOL OF FINE ARTS

Anotati Scholi Kalon Technon (ASFA)

42, Patission Str, 10682 Athinai
Tel: +30(210) 381-6930
Fax: +30(210) 382-8028
EMail: info@asfa.gr
Website: http://www.asfa.gr

Rector: Panagiotis Xaralambos EMail: elerzi@asfa.gr

Secretary-General: Rolanda Tzianalou EMail: rolanda@asfa.gr

International Relations: Maria Felidou EMail: mfelidou@asfa.gr

Section
Ceramic (Ceramic Art; Fine Arts; Handicrafts); **Fresco and Icon Painting** (Fine Arts; Painting and Drawing; Visual Arts); **Graphic Design** (Design; Fine Arts; Graphic Design); **Marble**; **Materials and Material Technology**; **Metal** (Fine Arts; Handicrafts; Sculpture; Visual Arts); **Mosaic** (Fine Arts; Handicrafts); **Multimedia** (Multimedia); **Painting** (Fine Arts; Painting and Drawing; Visual Arts); **Photography** (Fine Arts; Photography; Visual Arts); **Plaster** (Fine Arts; Handicrafts; Sculpture; Visual Arts); **Postgraduate Studies** (Fine Arts); **Printmaking** (Printing and Printmaking); **Sculpture**; **Stage Design**; **Woodcarving** (Handicrafts)

Further Information: Also Rentis Site.

History: Founded 1837.

Academic Year: October to June

Admission Requirements: Secondary school certificate or recognized foreign equivalent

Fees: Foreign students, 391 per annum (Euro)

Main Language(s) of Instruction: Greek

Degrees and Diplomas: *Ptychio*: **Fine Arts.** *Metaptychiako Diploma Eidikefsis*: **Fine Arts; Graphic Design.**

Student Services: Academic Counselling, Canteen, Cultural Activities, Facilities for disabled people, Health Services, Language Laboratory

Last Updated: 21/04/15

ATHENS UNIVERSITY OF ECONOMICS AND BUSINESS

Ikonomikon Panepistimion Athinon

Patission 76, 10434 Athinai
Tel: +30(210) 820-3911
Fax: +30(210) 822-6204
EMail: registrar@aueb.gr
Website: http://www.aueb.gr

Rector: Konstantine Gatsios (2011-2015) EMail: rector@aueb.gr

Vice-Rector for Academic Affairs: Emmanouil Giakoumakis

Department
Accountancy and Finance (Accountancy; Business Administration; Finance; International Business); **Business Administration** (Business Administration; Communication Studies; International Business; Management; Marketing); **Economics** (Banking; Economics; Finance; International Economics); **Informatics** (Business Computing; Computer Science; Information Management; Information Sciences; Management); **International and European Economic Studies** (Economics; European Studies; International Economics); **Management Science and Technology** (Business Administration; Human Resources; International Business; Management; Technology); **Marketing and Communication** (Business Administration; Communication Studies; Human Resources; International Business; Management; Marketing; Operations Research; Public Relations); **Statistics** (Statistics)

History: Founded 1920. A State University under the supervision of the Ministry of Education.

Academic Year: September to June (September-January; February-June including the exams)

Admission Requirements: National Entrance Examination

Fees: None

Main Language(s) of Instruction: Greek

Degrees and Diplomas: *Ptychio*; *Metaptychiako Diploma Eidikefsis*: **Accountancy; Business Administration; Business and Commerce; Communication Arts; Computer Science; Economics; European Studies; Finance; Human Resources; Information Technology; International Business; Mathematics; Statistics.** *Didaktoriko Diploma*: **Accountancy; Banking; Business Administration; Computer Science; Economics; Finance; International Business; Statistics.** Also MBA International programme (in English); MBA Program in Greek; Executive MBA

Student Services: Academic Counselling, Canteen, Careers Guidance, Cultural Activities, Facilities for disabled people, Foreign Studies Centre, Health Services, Language Laboratory, Social Counselling, Sports Facilities

Last Updated: 21/04/15

DEMOCRITUS UNIVERSITY OF THRACE

Dimokrition Panepistimion Thrakis (DUTH)

University Campus, 69100 Komotini, Rhodopi
Tel: +30(25310) 39000
EMail: intrela@duth.gr
Website: http://duth.gr/index.en.shtml

Rector: Athanasios I. Karabinis EMail: rector@duth.gr

Deputy Rector for Academic Affairs and Personnel: Charitomeni Piperidou

Faculty
Educational Sciences *(Alexandroupolis)* (Education; Educational Sciences; Preschool Education; Primary Education); **Engineering** *(Xanthi)* (Architecture; Civil Engineering; Computer Engineering; Electrical Engineering; Engineering; Engineering Management; Environmental Engineering; Environmental Studies; Production Engineering)

School
Agricultural Sciences and Forestry (Agriculture; Forestry); **Health Sciences** *(Alexandroupolis)* (Gynaecology and Obstetrics; Medicine; Pathology; Psychiatry and Mental Health; Surgery); **Physical Education and Sports** *(Komotini)* (Leisure Studies; Physical Education; Sports; Sports Management; Sports Medicine)

Department

Agricultural Development *(Orestiada)* (Agriculture); **Architectural Engineering** (Architecture); **Business Administration** *(Komotini)* (Business Administration; Management); **Forestry, Environmental and Natural Resources Management** *(Orestiada)* (Environmental Management; Forestry; Natural Resources); **Greek Literature** *(Komotini)* (Arts and Humanities; Greek; Literature); **History and Ethnology** *(Komotini)* (Ancient Civilizations; Anthropology; Archaeology; Ethnology; Folklore; History; Modern History); **International Economic Relations and Development** *(Komotini)* (International Economics; International Relations); **Languages, Literature and Culture of Black Sea Countries** *(Komotini)* (Cultural Studies; Literature; Modern Languages); **Law** *(Komotini)* (Civil Law; European Union Law; International Law; Labour Law; Law; Private Law; Public Law); **Molecular Biology and Genetics** *(Alexandroupolis)* (Genetics; Molecular Biology); **Political Science** *(Komotini)* (Political Sciences; Social Sciences); **Social Administration** *(Komotini)* (Public Administration; Social Policy; Social Work)

Further Information: Also campuses in Xanthi, Alexandroupoli and Orestiada. (General Hospital in Alexandroupolis)

History: Founded 1973. An autonomous institution under the supervision of the Ministry of Education.

Academic Year: September to August

Admission Requirements: Secondary school certificate (Apolytirion Lykiou) and entrance examination

Main Language(s) of Instruction: Greek

Degrees and Diplomas: *Ptychio*: **Medicine.** *Metaptychiako Diploma Eidikefsis*: **Civil Engineering; Computer Engineering; Electrical Engineering; Hydraulic Engineering; Law; Physical Education.** *Didaktoriko Diploma*: **Civil Engineering; Computer Engineering; Electrical Engineering; Law; Physical Education; Sports.**

Student Services: Canteen, Sports Facilities

Publishing house: Printing Office of the University

Last Updated: 08/02/12

HAROKOPIO UNIVERSITY

Harokopio Panepistimio

El. Venizelou 70, Kallithea, 176 71 Athinai
Tel: +30(210) 9549-100
Fax: +30(210) 9577-050
EMail: haruniv@hua.gr
Website: http://www.hua.gr

Rector: Andreas Kyriakousis EMail: rector@hua.gr

Department

Dietetics and Nutrition (Dietetics; Nutrition); **Geography** (Computer Science; Demography and Population; Economics; Geography; Marine Science and Oceanography; Mathematics and Computer Science; Natural Sciences; Regional Planning; Social Sciences; Surveying and Mapping; Town Planning); **Home Economics and Ecology** (Child Care and Development; Ecology; Home Economics; House Arts and Environment; Household Management; Nutrition); **Informatics and Telematics** (Artificial Intelligence; Automation and Control Engineering; Computer Engineering; Computer Networks; Computer Science; Data Processing; Electronic Engineering; Information Technology; Logic; Mathematics; Mathematics and Computer Science; Operations Research; Software Engineering; Statistics; Systems Analysis; Telecommunications Engineering)

History: Founded 1990.

Academic Year: September to June (September-February; February-June)

Admission Requirements: Secondary school certificate (Apolytirion Lykiou) and entrance examination

Fees: None

Main Language(s) of Instruction: Greek

Degrees and Diplomas: *Ptychio*; *Metaptychiako Diploma Eidikefsis*; *Didaktoriko Diploma*: **Computer Science; Food Science; Geography.**

Student Services: Academic Counselling, Canteen, Careers Guidance, Facilities for disabled people, Health Services, Social Counselling

Last Updated: 21/04/15

HELLENIC OPEN UNIVERSITY

Elliniko Anoikto Panepistimio (EAP)

18, Parodos Aristotelous, 26335 Patra,
Achaïa
Tel: +31(2610) 367-300 +31(2610) 367-400
Fax: +31(2610) 367-650 +31(2610) 367-321
EMail: info@eap.gr
Website: http://www.eap.gr

President: Haralambos Coccossis (2004-)
EMail: president@eap.gr

Vice-President: Panayiotis Giannopoulos

School

Applied Arts (Design; Graphic Arts; Multimedia); **Humanities** (Adult Education; Arts and Humanities; Cultural Studies; Education; English; European Studies; Foreign Languages Education; French; German; Greek; Modern Languages; Orthodox Theology; Spanish); **Science and Technology** (Computer Science; Environmental Engineering; Environmental Studies; Information Sciences; Mathematics; Mathematics and Computer Science; Natural Sciences; Physics; Safety Engineering; Scandinavian Languages; Technology; Waste Management; Welfare and Protective Services); **Social Sciences** (Banking; Business Administration; Health Administration; Social Sciences; Tourism)

History: Founded 1992. ISO 9001:2000.

Admission Requirements: 'Geniko apolytirio' or equivalent for undergraduate studies

Fees: (Euros): 600 per module (12 modules required for undergraduate degree and 4 for postgraduate)

Main Language(s) of Instruction: Greek

Degrees and Diplomas: *Ptychio*; *Metaptychiako Diploma Eidikefsis*

Last Updated: 21/04/15

INTERNATIONAL HELLENIC UNIVERSITY

4th km Thessaloniki - Moudania,
57001 Thermi
EMail: pr@ihu.edu.gr
Website: http://www.ihu.edu.gr

President: Costas Th. Grammenos

School

Economics, Business Administration and Legal Studies (Banking; Business Administration; Commercial Law; Economics; Finance; Law; Management); **Humanities** (Ancient Civilizations; Archaeology; Arts and Humanities; Cultural Studies); **Science and Technology** (Computer Science; Energy Engineering; Natural Sciences; Software Engineering; Technology)

History: Founded 2005.

Degrees and Diplomas: *Metaptychiako Diploma Eidikefsis*

Last Updated: 21/04/15

IONIAN UNIVERSITY

Ionian Panepistimion

7, Rizospaston Voulefton str., 49100 Corfu
Tel: +30(266) 1087-609
Fax: +30(266) 1022-549
EMail: publicrelations@ionio.gr
Website: http://www.ionio.gr

Rector: Anastasia Sali-Papasali EMail: rosa@ionio.gr

Vice Rector of Academic Affairs and Human Resources: Miranda Kaldi EMail: alexia@ionio.gr

International Relations: Dionisia Karvouni
EMail: intl_rel@ionio.gr

Faculty

History and Translation-Interpreting (Ancient Books; Anthropology; Archaeology; Art History; English; Ethnology; French; German; Greek (Classical); History; Latin; Modern Languages; Philology; Philosophy; Translation and Interpretation); **Information Science and Informatics** (Archiving; Computer Science; Library Science; Museum Studies); **Music and Audio-visual Arts** (Art Therapy; Conducting; Jazz and Popular Music; Multimedia; Music;

Music Education; Music Theory and Composition; Musical Instruments; Musicology; Singing; Visual Arts)

History: Founded 1984. A State institution under the jurisdiction of the Ministry of Education.

Academic Year: October to June (October-February; February-June)

Admission Requirements: Secondary school certificate (Apolytirio Lykiou)

Fees: None

Main Language(s) of Instruction: Greek

Degrees and Diplomas: *Ptychio*; *Metaptychiako Diploma Eidikefsis*; *Didaktoriko Diploma*: **Archiving; History; Library Science; Museum Studies; Music; Visual Arts.**

Last Updated: 21/04/15

NATIONAL AND KAPODISTRIAN UNIVERSITY OF ATHENS

Ethniko kai Kapodistriako Panepistimio Athinon (NKUA)

30 Panepistimiou street, 10679 Athinai
Tel: +30(210) 368-9771 +30(210) 368-9684
Fax: +30(210) 368-9717
EMail: rector@uoa.gr
Website: http://www.uoa.gr

Rector: Meletios-Athanasios C. Dimopoulos (2015-)
EMail: rector@uoa.gr

International Relations: Fotini Fryda, Head, Department of European and International Relations
Tel: +30(210) 368-9713 EMail: ffryda@uoa.gr

International Relations: Konstantinos Buraselis, Vice-Rector of Academic Affairs and International Relations
EMail: vrec-acafir@uoa.gr

School

Economics and Political Science (Asian Studies; Communication Studies; Economics; Media Studies; Political Sciences; Public Administration; Turkish); **Education** (Preschool Education; Primary Education); **Health Sciences** (Dentistry; Medicine; Nursing; Pharmacy); **Law** (Law); **Philosophy** (Archaeology; English; French; German; History; Italian; Literature; Music; Pedagogy; Philology; Philosophy; Psychology; Slavic Languages; Spanish; Theatre); **Physical Education and Sport Science** (Physical Education; Sports); **Science** (Biology; Chemistry; Computer Science; Geology; History; Mathematics; Philosophy; Physics; Telecommunications Engineering); **Theology** (Theology)

Further Information: Also 2 University Hospitals

History: Founded in 1837. The first university after the foundation of the Greek state. Autonomous institution under the jurisdiction of the Ministry of Education

Academic Year: September to July

Admission Requirements: Secondary school certificate (Apolytirion Lykiou) or foreign equivalent and entrance examination

Fees: None

Main Language(s) of Instruction: Greek

Degrees and Diplomas: *Ptychio*: **Dentistry; Medicine; Music; Pharmacy.** *Metaptychiako Diploma Eidikefsis*; *Didaktoriko Diploma*: **Archaeology; Asian Studies; Dentistry; Economics; Education; English; French; German; History; Law; Music; Pedagogy; Pharmacy; Philology; Philosophy; Political Sciences; Psychology; Turkish.**

Student Services: Academic Counselling, Canteen, Careers Guidance, Cultural Activities, Facilities for disabled people, Foreign Studies Centre, Health Services, Language Laboratory, Nursery Care, Social Counselling, Sports Facilities

Last Updated: 16/12/15

NATIONAL TECHNICAL UNIVERSITY OF ATHENS

Ethniko Metsovio Polytechnico (NTUA)

28 Oktovriou (Patision) 42, 10682 Athinai
Tel: +30(210) 7722-017 +30(210) 7722-006
Fax: +30(210) 7722-028
EMail: rector@mail.ntua.gr
Website: http://www.ntua.gr

Rector: Ioannis Golias

Vice Rector for Academic Affairs: Dimitrios Papantonis
EMail: papan@fluid.mech.ntua.gr

School

Applied Mathematics and Physics *(Zografou)* (Applied Mathematics; Applied Physics; Arts and Humanities; Law; Mathematics; Physics; Social Sciences); **Architecture** (Architecture); **Chemical Engineering** *(Zografou)* (Chemical Engineering; Chemistry; Computer Science; Engineering; Industrial Engineering; Systems Analysis); **Civil Engineering** (Civil Engineering; Construction Engineering; Engineering; Engineering Management; Geological Engineering; Marine Engineering; Transport Engineering); **Electrical and Computer Engineering** *(Zografou)* (Computer Engineering; Computer Science; Electrical and Electronic Engineering; Electrical Engineering; Engineering; Power Engineering); **Mechanical Engineeering** *(Zografou)* (Automation and Control Engineering; Engineering; Industrial Engineering; Mathematics; Mathematics and Computer Science; Mechanical Engineering; Nuclear Engineering; Operations Research; Thermal Engineering); **Mining and Metallurgical Engineering** *(Zografou)* (Civil Engineering; Engineering; Geological Engineering; Materials Engineering; Metallurgical Engineering; Mining Engineering); **Naval Architecture and Marine Engineering** *(Zografou)* (Engineering; Marine Engineering; Naval Architecture); **Rural Surveying and Engineering** *(Zografou)* (Development Studies; Earth Sciences; Engineering; Geography; Natural Sciences; Rural Studies; Social Sciences; Surveying and Mapping)

Further Information: Also Zografou Campus

History: Founded 1836 by decree as technical school, became technical college 1887 and acquired present status 1929. Reorganized 1982. An autonomous institution under the supervision of the Ministry of Education.

Academic Year: September to July

Admission Requirements: Secondary school certificate (Apolytirion Lykiou) or foreign equivalent and entrance examination

Fees: None

Main Language(s) of Instruction: Greek

Degrees and Diplomas: *Ptychio*: **Engineering.** *Metaptychiako Diploma Eidikefsis*; *Didaktoriko Diploma*: **Architecture; Chemical Engineering; Computer Engineering; Electrical Engineering; Mechanical Engineering; Metallurgical Engineering; Mining Engineering.**

Student Services: Academic Counselling, Canteen, Careers Guidance, Health Services, Language Laboratory, Nursery Care, Sports Facilities

Publications: Pyrphoros

Last Updated: 21/04/15

PANTEION UNIVERSITY OF ECONOMICS AND POLITICAL SCIENCE

Panteion Panepestimion Ikonomikon kai Politicon Epistimon

136 Sygrou Ave., Kallithea, 17671 Athinai
Tel: +30(210) 922-0100
Fax: +30(210) 922-3690
EMail: thesak@panteion.gr
Website: http://www.panteion.gr

Rector: Smini Kriari-Katrani EMail: rector@panteion.gr

Faculty

Economics and Public Administration (Economics; Public Administration; Regional Planning); **International Studies, Communication and Culture** (Communication Studies; Cultural Studies; European Studies; International Studies; Media Studies);

Political Science (History; Political Sciences; Social Policy); **Social Sciences and Psychology** (Anthropology; Psychology; Sociology)

History: Founded 1930 as private school, acquired present status 1937 as a State institution. Reorganized 1983 and acquired 5 new departments and present title 1989.

Academic Year: September to June (September-January; February-June)

Admission Requirements: Secondary school certificate (Apolytirion Lykiou) and entrance examination

Main Language(s) of Instruction: Greek

Degrees and Diplomas: *Ptychio*; *Metaptychiako Diploma Eidikefsis*: **Criminology; Cultural Studies; European Studies; History; International Studies; Social Policy; Sociology.** *Didaktoriko Diploma*: **Communication Studies; Cultural Studies; Economics; European Studies; International Studies; Media Studies; Psychology; Public Administration; Sociology.**

Last Updated: 22/04/15

SCHOOL OF PEDAGOGICAL AND TECHNOLOGICAL EDUCATION (ASPETE)

141 21 N. Heraklion, Athens
Tel: +30(210) 289-6700
Fax: +30(210) 282-3247
EMail: gdaspete@aspete.gr
Website: http://www.aspete.gr/

President: Sarantos I. Psycharis

Department

Civil Engineering Educators (Civil Engineering; Construction Engineering; Teacher Training; Technology Education); **Education** (Education; Teacher Training); **Electrical and Electronic Engineering Educators** (Electrical and Electronic Engineering); **Mechanical Engineering Educators** (Mechanical Engineering)

Further Information: Also campuses in Thessaloniki, Patra, Volos, Ioannina, Heraklion-Crete, and Sapes.

History: Founded 2002.

Main Language(s) of Instruction: Greek

Degrees and Diplomas: *Ptychio*. Also 'Certificate of Further Training' or Specialization Training'; Joint postgraduate programmes (M.A.) in cooperation with Higher Education Institutions in Greece or abroad.

Last Updated: 23/04/15

TECHNICAL UNIVERSITY OF CRETE

Polytechnion Kritis

Agiou Markou, 73132 Chania, Chania
Tel: +30(28210) 28404
Fax: +30(28210) 28418
EMail: intoffice@isc.tuc.gr
Website: http://www.tuc.gr

Rector: Vassilios V. Digilakis EMail: rector@central.tuc.gr

Vice-Rector of Academic Affairs and Research: Elia Psillakis EMail: vice-rector-aca@central.tuc.gr

School

Architectural Engineering (Architecture; Architecture and Planning; Landscape Architecture; Town Planning; Visual Arts); **Electronic and Computer Engineering** (Computer Engineering; Electronic Engineering; Telecommunications Engineering); **Environmental Engineering** (Environmental Engineering; Environmental Management; Environmental Studies); **Mineral Resources Engineering** (Geological Engineering; Mineralogy); **Production Engineering and Management** (Engineering Management; Industrial and Production Economics; Operations Research; Production Engineering)

History: Founded 1977. Admitted first students 1984. An autonomous institution under the supervision of the Ministry of Education.

Academic Year: September to August

Admission Requirements: Secondary school certificate (Apolytirion Lykiou) or foreign equivalent and entrance examination

Fees: None

Main Language(s) of Instruction: Greek

Degrees and Diplomas: *Ptychio*: **Engineering.** *Metaptychiako Diploma Eidikefsis*; *Didaktoriko Diploma*: **Architecture; Computer Engineering; Electronic Engineering; Engineering; Environmental Engineering; Production Engineering.** Also Postgraduate Diploma of Specialization

Student Services: Academic Counselling, Canteen, Careers Guidance, Cultural Activities, Facilities for disabled people, Language Laboratory, Sports Facilities

Publications: News of the Technical University of Crete

Last Updated: 22/04/15

TECHNOLOGICAL EDUCATIONAL INSTITUTE OF ATHENS

Technologiko Ekpaideutiko Idrima, Athinas (TEI OF ATHENS)

Ag. Spyridonos Str, Egaleo, 12210 Athens
Tel: +30(210) 538-5100
Fax: +30(210) 591-1590
EMail: info@teiath.gr; publirela@teiath.gr
Website: http://www.teiath.gr

President: Michael Bratakos EMail: antipro@teiath.gr

International Relations: Dia Roufani, Head of Public and International Relations Office

Faculty

Fine Arts and Design (Cinema and Television; Design; Fine Arts; Graphic Arts; Graphic Design; Interior Design; Photography; Restoration of Works of Art; Visual Arts); **Food Technology and Nutrition** (Food Technology; Nutrition; Oenology); **Health Care Sciences** (Aesthetics; Child Care and Development; Cosmetology; Dental Hygiene; Dental Technology; Dentistry; Laboratory Techniques; Medical Technology; Midwifery; Nursing; Occupational Therapy; Optics; Physical Therapy; Public Health; Radiology; Social Work); **Management and Economics** (Administration; Advertising and Publicity; Business Administration; Health Administration; Information Management; Information Sciences; Library Science; Management; Marketing; Tourism); **Technological Applications** (Biomedical Engineering; Civil Engineering; Computer Science; Electronic Engineering; Energy Engineering; Marine Engineering; Medical Technology; Naval Architecture; Surveying and Mapping; Technology)

History: Founded 1974. Acquired present status 2001.

Academic Year: September to June (September-January; February-June)

Admission Requirements: Secondary school certificate (Apolitirio Likiou) and central selection by Ministry of Education

Fees: None

Main Language(s) of Instruction: Greek

Degrees and Diplomas: *Ptychio*

Student Services: Academic Counselling, Canteen, Careers Guidance, Cultural Activities, Health Services, Language Laboratory, Nursery Care, Social Counselling, Sports Facilities

Last Updated: 23/04/15

TECHNOLOGICAL EDUCATIONAL INSTITUTE OF CENTRAL GREECE

Technologiko Ekpaideutiko Idrima, Lamia

3rd km of Old National Road Lamia-Athens, Lamia
EMail: tei@teihal.gr
Website: http://www.teihal.gr/

President: Anastasios Konstantinos

Faculty

Business and Economics (Accountancy; Advertising and Publicity; Business Administration; Finance; Marketing)

School

Agricultural Technology, Food Technology and Nutrition (Agriculture; Food Science; Forestry); **Health and Welfare** (Nursing; Physical Therapy); **Technological Appliance** (Aeronautical and Aerospace Engineering; Automation and Control Engineering; Computer Engineering; Electrical and Electronic Engineering; Mechanical Engineering)

History: Founded 1983. Acquired present status and title 2013 following the merger of TEI of Lamia and TEI of Chalkida.An autonomous institution under the supervision of the Institute of Technological Education.

Academic Year: September to August

Main Language(s) of Instruction: Greek

Degrees and Diplomas: *Ptychio*

Last Updated: 22/04/15

TECHNOLOGICAL EDUCATIONAL INSTITUTE OF CRETE

Technologiko Ekpaideutiko Idrima, Kritis (TEI OF CRETE)

Stauromenos, 71004 Heraklion, Crete
Tel: +30(2810) 379317
Fax: +30(2810) 379328
EMail: info@staff.teicrete.gr
Website: http://www.teicrete.gr

President: Evangelos Kapetanakis EMail: ekap@staff.teicrete.gr

Vice President: Manolis Antonidakis
EMail: antonidakis@staff.teicrete.gr

School

Agricultural and Food Technology (Agriculture; Crop Production; Dietetics; Floriculture; Food Technology; Nutrition); **Applied Sciences** (Electronic Engineering; Environmental Engineering; Music; Natural Resources; Sound Engineering (Acoustics)); **Engineering** (Civil Engineering; Computer Engineering; Electrical Engineering; Mechanical Engineering); **Health and Welfare Services** (Health Sciences; Nursing; Social Work); **Management and Economics** (Accountancy; Administration; Advertising and Publicity; Business Administration; Business and Commerce; Finance; Insurance; Management; Marketing)

Further Information: Also campuses in Chania,Rethymnon, Agios Nikolaos, Ierapetra, and Sitia

History: Founded 1983.

Academic Year: September to August

Main Language(s) of Instruction: Greek

Degrees and Diplomas: *Ptychio*

Last Updated: 24/04/15

TECHNOLOGICAL EDUCATIONAL INSTITUTE OF EASTERN MACEDONIA AND THRACE

Technologiko Ekpaideutiko Idrima, Kavalas

Agios Lukas, 65404 Kavala
Tel: +30(2510) 462-177
EMail: tei@teikav.edu.gr
Website: http://www.teikav.edu.gr/teikav/index.php?lang=en

President: Athanasios Mitropoulos

Vice-President of Academic Affairs:: Dimitrios Bandekas

School

Agricultural Technology *(Drama)* (Agricultural Engineering; Environmental Management; Forestry; Landscape Architecture; Oenology); **Management and Economics** (Accountancy; Administration; Business Administration; Economics); **Technological Engineering** *(Kavala)* (Computer Engineering; Electrical Engineering; Mechanical Engineering; Petroleum and Gas Engineering)

Further Information: Also campuses in Drama and Didymoteicho.

History: Founded 1976. Acquired present status 2007.

Academic Year: September to August

Main Language(s) of Instruction: Greek

Degrees and Diplomas: *Ptychio*; *Metaptychiako Diploma Eidikefsis*

Student Services: Academic Counselling, Canteen, Careers Guidance, Cultural Activities, Facilities for disabled people, Foreign Studies Centre, Health Services, Language Laboratory, Nursery Care, Social Counselling, Sports Facilities

Last Updated: 22/04/15

TECHNOLOGICAL EDUCATIONAL INSTITUTE OF EPIRUS

Technologiko Ekpaideutiko Idrima, Epirou (TEI OF EPIRUS)

Gefira Arachthou, 47100 Arta, Epirus
Tel: +30(26810) 50001
Fax: +30(26810) 76405
EMail: pubrel@teiep.gr
Website: http://www.teiep.gr

President: Sotirios Kandrelis
Tel: +30(26810) 21164 EMail: sotkan@teiep.gr

Vice-President: Athina Tzora-Skoufa Tel: +30(26810) 21417

International Relations: George Papadopoulos, Vice-President
Tel: +30(26810) 21158 EMail: pubrel@teiep.gr

Faculty

Agricultural Technology, Food Technology and Nutrition (Animal Husbandry; Crop Production; Floriculture; Landscape Architecture); **Applied Technology** (Computer Engineering; Computer Networks; Software Engineering); **Arts** (Music); **Health and Welfare Professions** *(Ioannina Branch)* (Nursing; Preschool Education; Speech Therapy and Audiology); **Management and Economics** *(Preveza Branch)* (Accountancy; Economics; Finance; Hotel Management; Modern Languages; Tourism)

Further Information: Also campuses in Preveza; Ioannina and Igoumenitsa

History: Founded 1994.

Academic Year: September to August

Main Language(s) of Instruction: Greek

Degrees and Diplomas: *Ptychio*

Last Updated: 23/04/15

TECHNOLOGICAL EDUCATIONAL INSTITUTE OF PELEPONNESE

Technologiko Ekpaideutiko Idrima, Kalamata (TEI OF KALAMATA)

Antikalamos, 24100 Kalamata, Messina
Tel: +30(27210) 45100
Fax: +30(27210) 45200
EMail: lib@teikal.gr
Website: http://www.teikal.gr

President: Dimitrios Velissariou EMail: management@teikal.gr

School

Agricultural Technology, Food Technology and Nutrition (Agricultural Engineering; Crop Production; Floriculture; Food Technology); **Health and Welfare Professions** (Health Sciences; Radiology; Speech Therapy and Audiology; Welfare and Protective Services); **Management and Economics** (Accountancy; Economics; Finance; Government; Management)

History: Founded 1986. Acquired present status 1990.

Academic Year: September to June

Admission Requirements: Apolitirio Lykeloy (High School Certificate) and entrance examination

Fees: None

Main Language(s) of Instruction: Greek

Degrees and Diplomas: *Ptychio*: **Accountancy; Administration; Agricultural Engineering; Agriculture; Crop Production; Economics; Finance; Floriculture; Health Sciences; Public Administration; Social Welfare.**

Student Services: Academic Counselling, Canteen, Careers Guidance, Cultural Activities, Facilities for disabled people, Foreign Studies Centre, Health Services, Language Laboratory, Sports Facilities

Last Updated: 22/04/15

TECHNOLOGICAL EDUCATIONAL INSTITUTE OF PIRAEUS

Technologiko Ekpaideutiko Idrima, Piraea (TEI OF PIRAEUS)

Peter Ralli and Thebes 250, 12244 Aigaleo
Tel: +30(210) 538-1100
Fax: +30(210) 545-0962
EMail: lvryz@teipir.gr
Website: http://www.teipir.gr

President: Lazaros Vryzidis

Vice-President: Antoniou Antonis Tel: +30(210) 538-1425

Vice-President: Kantzos Constantinos
Tel: +30(210) 569-0768 EMail: ckantzos@teipir.gr

International Relations: Ouranos Dimitrios
Tel: +30(210) 538-1356 EMail: eu@teipir.gr

School

Business and Economics (Accountancy; Business Administration; Economics; Management; Tourism); **Engineering** *(S.T.Ef.)* (Automation and Control Engineering; Civil Engineering; Computer Science; Electrical Engineering; Electronic Engineering; Mechanical Engineering; Textile Technology)

Centre

Foreign Languages and Physical Education (English; French; German; Italian; Modern Languages)

History: Founded 1983.

Academic Year: October to July (October-January; February-July)

Admission Requirements: Entrance examination

Main Language(s) of Instruction: Greek

Degrees and Diplomas: *Ptychio*; *Metaptychiako Diploma Eidikefsis*. Also Postgraduate programmes in partnership with foreign universities

Student Services: Canteen, Careers Guidance, Cultural Activities, Facilities for disabled people, Health Services, Language Laboratory, Social Counselling, Sports Facilities

Publications: Applied Research Review

Last Updated: 24/04/15

TECHNOLOGICAL EDUCATIONAL INSTITUTE OF THE IONIAN ISLANDS

Technologiko Ekpaideutiko Idrima, Ionion Nison (TEI OF IONIAN ISLANDS)

Iosif Momferatou & Ilia Miniati, 28100 Argostoli, Kefallonia Island
Tel: +30(26710) 25820 +30(26710) 25922
Fax: +30(26710) 25923
EMail: dioikisi@teiion.gr
Website: http://www.teiion.gr

President: Napoleon Maravegias

School

Management and Economics *(Lefkada)* (Business Administration; Business Computing; Economics; Hotel Management; Tourism); **Musical Technology** (Musical Instruments; Sound Engineering (Acoustics)); **Technological Applications** *(Cephalonia, Zante)* (Communication Studies; Environmental Engineering; Heritage Preservation; Media Studies)

History: Founded 2003.

Degrees and Diplomas: *Ptychio*

Last Updated: 24/04/15

TECHNOLOGICAL EDUCATIONAL INSTITUTE OF THESSALY

Technologiko Ekpaideutiko Idrima, Larissas (TEI OF LARISSA)

41110 Larissa
Tel: +30(2410) 684-200
Fax: +30(2410) 610-803
EMail: pr@teilar.gr
Website: http://www.teilar.gr

President: Panagiotis Goulas

Vice-President: Argiris Noulas EMail: noulas@teilar.gr

School

Agricultural Technology (Agricultural Engineering; Agricultural Equipment; Animal Husbandry; Crop Production; Food Technology; Nutrition); **Business and Economics** (Accountancy; Business Administration; Economics; Management; Tourism); **Health and Welfare Professions** (Health Administration; Laboratory Techniques; Medical Technology; Nursing; Public Health); **Technological Applications** (Civil Engineering; Computer Science; Electrical and Electronic Engineering; Electrical Engineering; Engineering; Mathematics and Computer Science; Mechanical Engineering; Telecommunications Engineering)

Centre

Foreign Languages and Physical Education (English; Modern Languages; Physical Education)

History: Founded 1974. Acquired present status 1983. An autonomous institution under the supervision of the Institute of Technological Education.

Academic Year: September to August

Main Language(s) of Instruction: Greek

Degrees and Diplomas: *Ptychio*

Student Services: Canteen, Language Laboratory, Sports Facilities

Last Updated: 23/04/15

TECHNOLOGICAL EDUCATIONAL INSTITUTE OF WESTERN GREECE

Technologiko Ekpaideutiko Idrima, Patras (TEI OF MESOLONGHI)

1 Megalou Alexandrou Str., Patras
Tel: +30(26310) 58200
Fax: +30(26310) 25183
EMail: relation@teimes.gr
Website: http://www.teiwest.gr/index.php/en/

President: Vangelis Politis Stergiou
Tel: +30(26310) 58361 EMail: prsdnt@teimes.gr

Vice-President: George Hotos

Faculty

Agricultural Technology (Agricultural Engineering; Agricultural Equipment; Aquaculture; Crop Production; Fishery; Floriculture; Irrigation); **Health** (Health Sciences); **Management and Economics** (Accountancy; Administration; Business Administration; Business Computing; Economics; Finance; Management)

History: Founded 1983. An autonomous institution under the supervision of the Institute of Technological Education.

Academic Year: September to August

Main Language(s) of Instruction: Greek

Degrees and Diplomas: *Ptychio*

Last Updated: 24/04/15

TECHNOLOGICAL EDUCATIONAL INSTITUTE OF WESTERN MACEDONIA

Technologiko Ekpaideutiko Idrima, Dytikis Makedonias (TEI OF WEST MACEDONIA)

Kila, 50100 Kozani
Tel: +30(24610) 40161
Fax: +30(24610) 39682
Website: http://www.teiwm.gr

President: Nikolaos Asimopoulos EMail: vpres1@teikoz.gr

School

Agricultural Technology, Food Technology and Nutrition *(Florina Branch)* (Agricultural Business; Agricultural Engineering; Agriculture; Animal Husbandry; Crop Production; Food Technology; Nutrition); **Applied Sciences** *(Kozani)* (Electrical Engineering; Environmental Engineering; Environmental Management; Environmental Studies; Industrial Design; Mechanical Engineering; Natural Sciences; Sanitary Engineering; Technology); **Business and Finance** (Accountancy; Administration; Business Administration; Economics; Finance; Management); **Health and Welfare** *(Ptolemaida)* (Midwifery)

Campus
Grevena Branch (Administration; Business Administration; Business Computing; Computer Science; Economics; Finance; Management); **Kastoria Branch** (Communication Studies; Computer Engineering; Computer Science; Information Technology; International Business; Marketing; Public Relations)

History: Founded 1976 as Higher Technological Education Centre of Kozani. Acquired present title 1999. An autonomous institution under the supervision of the Institute of Technological Education.

Academic Year: September to August

Main Language(s) of Instruction: Greek

Degrees and Diplomas: *Ptychio*. Also Master in Applied Informatics offered in cooperation with University of Macedonia and Master in Mechatronics offered in cooperation with University of Catalonia UPC (Universitat Politecnica de Catalunya).

Last Updated: 23/04/15

TECHNOLOGICAL EDUCATIONAL OF CENTRAL MACEDONIA

Technologiko Ekpaideutiko Idrima, Serron (TEI OF SERRES)
Terma Magnesias Str., 62124 Serres
Tel: +30(23210) 49101
Fax: +30(23210) 46556
EMail: pr@teiser.gr
Website: http://www.teicm.gr/index.php?lang=en

President: Dimirios Paschaloudis

Faculty
Administration and Economics (Accountancy; Administration; Business Administration); **Applied Technology** (Civil Engineering; Computer Science; Fashion Design; Mechanical Engineering; Surveying and Mapping; Telecommunications Engineering)

Department
Interior Architecture, Decoration & Design (Interior Design)

History: Founded 1974. Acquired present status and title 2013. An autonomous institution under the supervision of the Ministry of National Education.

Academic Year: September to August

Main Language(s) of Instruction: Greek

Degrees and Diplomas: *Ptychio*: **Accountancy; Business Administration; Civil Engineering; Computer Engineering; Computer Science; Mechanical Engineering; Surveying and Mapping.** *Metaptychiako Diploma Eidikefsis*. Also Master degree (MSc) in Natural Disaster Prevention and Management, in collaboration with the National Kapodistrian University of Athens

Last Updated: 22/04/15

UNIVERSITY OF CRETE

Panepistimio Kritis
Gallos University Campus, 74100 Rethymnon
Tel: +30(28310) 77900
Fax: +30(28310) 77909
EMail: secretary@rector.uoc.gr
Website: http://www.uoc.gr

Rector: Evripides Stefanou EMail: pallikaris@rector.uoc.gr

School
Education (Education; Preschool Education; Primary Education); **Medicine** *(Heraklion Vassilika-Voutes)* (Anatomy; Behavioural Sciences; Child Care and Development; Health Sciences; Laboratory Techniques; Medicine; Neurology; Psychiatry and Mental Health; Radiology; Social and Preventive Medicine; Surgery); **Philosophy** (Archaeology; History; Philology; Philosophy; Social Studies); **Sciences and Engineering** *(Heraklion)* (Applied Mathematics; Biology; Chemistry; Computer Science; Engineering; Materials Engineering; Mathematics; Physics; Technology); **Social,Economic and Political Sciences** (Economics; Political Sciences; Psychology; Social Sciences; Sociology)

Further Information: Also Heraklion campus.

History: Founded 1973. A State institution under the jurisdiction of the Ministry of National Education and Religious Affairs.

Academic Year: September to June

Admission Requirements: Secondary school certificate and Panhellenic entrance examination

Fees: None

Main Language(s) of Instruction: Greek

Accrediting Agency: Ministry of National Education and Religious Affairs

Degrees and Diplomas: *Ptychio*; *Metaptychiako Diploma Eidikefsis*; *Didaktoriko Diploma*: **Ancient Civilizations; Archaeology; Art History; Biology; Chemistry; Computer Science; Economics; Materials Engineering; Mathematics; Philology; Philosophy; Physics; Political Sciences; Social Sciences.**

Student Services: Academic Counselling, Canteen, Careers Guidance, Cultural Activities, Facilities for disabled people, Health Services, Language Laboratory, Nursery Care, Social Counselling, Sports Facilities

Last Updated: 21/04/15

UNIVERSITY OF IOANNINA

Panepistimion Ioanninon (UOI)
P.O. Box 1186, 45110 Ioannina
Tel: +30(26510) 07105
Fax: +30(26510) 07024
EMail: piro@cc.uoi.gr
Website: http://www.uoi.gr

Rector: George D. Kapsalis

Principal University Officer: Loukas-Nikitas Papaloukas
Tel: +30(26510) 07104

International Relations: Vasiliki Katsadima, Head, International and Public Relations Directorate
EMail: intlrel@cc.uoi.gr; vkatsad@cc.uoi.gr

School
Education (Education; Educational Sciences; Preschool Education; Primary Education); **Fine Arts** *(Independent)* (Art History; Fine Arts; Graphic Design; Multimedia; Painting and Drawing; Photography; Sculpture; Visual Arts); **Health Sciences** (Medicine); **Natural Resources and Enterprise Management** *(Agrinio)* (Agricultural Economics; Animal Husbandry; Biochemistry; Biology; Business Administration; Computer Science; Ecology; Environmental Studies; Molecular Biology; Natural Resources; Physical Chemistry); **Philosophy** (Archaeology; Arts and Humanities; Education; History; Literature; Philology; Philosophy; Psychology); **Science and Technology** (Biochemistry; Biological and Life Sciences; Biology; Biotechnology; Botany; Chemistry; Ecology; Engineering; Genetics; Materials Engineering; Microbiology; Molecular Biology; Physical Chemistry; Plant Pathology; Polymer and Plastics Technology; Technology; Zoology); **Sciences** (Chemistry; Computer Science; Mathematics; Natural Sciences; Physics)

Department
Cultural Heritage Management and New Technologies *(Independent, Agrinio)* (Cultural Studies; Heritage Preservation; Technology)

Further Information: Also University Hospital. Centre for the Teaching of Greek Language and Culture. Vocational Training Centre. Career Office. Technological Educational Park

History: Founded 1964 as a Department of the Aristoteleion University of Thessaloniki, acquired present status and title 1970. Reorganized 1982. A State institution of the Epirus Region.

Academic Year: September to June (September-January; February-June)

Admission Requirements: Secondary school certificate (Apolytirion Lykiou) and entrance examination

Fees: None

Main Language(s) of Instruction: Greek

Degrees and Diplomas: *Ptychio*; *Metaptychiako Diploma Eidikefsis*; *Didaktoriko Diploma*: **Biology; Business Administration; Computer Science; Education; Engineering; Environmental Studies; Fine Arts; Management; Materials Engineering; Mathematics; Nursing; Philology; Physics.**

Student Services: Academic Counselling, Canteen, Careers Guidance, Cultural Activities, Facilities for disabled people, Foreign Studies Centre, Health Services, Language Laboratory, Nursery Care, Social Counselling, Sports Facilities

Publications: Epitris (Prospectus, Education); Epitris Dodoni I (History and Archaeology); Epitris Dodoni II (Literature and Philology); Epitris Dodoni III (Philosophy, Education and Psychology)

Publishing House: University of Ioannina Press

Last Updated: 21/04/15

UNIVERSITY OF MACEDONIA

Panepistimion Makedonias
Odos Egnatia 156, 54006 Thessaloniki
Tel: +30(2310) 891-101
Fax: +30(2310) 844-536
EMail: pubrel@uom.gr
Website: http://www.uom.gr

Rector: Achilleas Zapranis

International Relations: Mariet Vainas

Programme
Postgraduate Studies (Accountancy; Business Administration; Computer Science; Economics; European Studies; Finance; Information Sciences)

Department
Accountancy and Finance (Accountancy; Finance); **Applied Informatics** (Computer Science); **Balkan, Slavic and Oriental Studies** (Baltic Languages; Oriental Studies; Slavic Languages); **Business Administration** (Business Administration; Computer Science; Political Sciences); **Economics** (Economics); **Educational and Social Policy** (Educational Sciences; Social Sciences); **International and European Economic Studies** (Economics; European Studies; International Studies); **Marketing and Operations Management** (Marketing; Operations Research); **Music Science and Art** (Music; Music Theory and Composition); **Technology Management** (Management; Technology)

Research Institute
Applied Economic and Social Sciences *(URI)* (Economics; Social Sciences)

History: Founded 1948, reorganized 1958. Previously the Graduate Industrial School of Thessaloniki. Acquired present status and title 1990.

Academic Year: September to August

Admission Requirements: Secondary school certificate (Apolytirion Lykiou) and entrance examination

Fees: None

Main Language(s) of Instruction: Greek

Degrees and Diplomas: *Ptychio*; *Metaptychiako Diploma Eidikefsis*: **Accountancy; Business Administration; Computer Engineering; Economics; Finance; Information Technology.**

Student Services: Academic Counselling, Canteen, Careers Guidance, Facilities for disabled people, Health Services, Nursery Care, Sports Facilities

Last Updated: 21/04/15

UNIVERSITY OF PATRAS

Panepistimion Patron
University Campus, 26504 Rio Patras
Tel: +30(2610) 991-822 +30(2610) 991-040
Fax: +30(2610) 991-711
EMail: rectorate@upatras.gr
Website: http://www.upatras.gr

Rector: Venetsana E. Kyriazopoulou EMail: rector@upatras.gr

Vice-Rector for Research and Development: Demosthenes Polyzos

International Relations: Nikos Karamanos, Vice rector of Academic and International affairs

School
Business Administration *(Independent)* (Economics; Finance; Human Resources; Information Technology; Management; Marketing); **Engineering** (Aeronautical and Aerospace Engineering; Architecture; Chemical Engineering; Civil Engineering; Computer Engineering; Computer Science; Electrical Engineering; Engineering; Information Technology; Mechanical Engineering); **Health Sciences** (Medicine; Pharmacy); **Humanities and Social Sciences** (Child Care and Development; Educational Sciences; Philology; Philosophy; Preschool Education; Primary Education; Theatre); **Natural Sciences** (Biology; Chemistry; Geology; Materials Engineering; Mathematics; Physics)

Further Information: Also University Hospital at Rion. Greek Language Programme for foreign students

History: Founded 1964. Acquired present status 1966. In June 2013 the University of Western Greece was incorporated in the University of Patras. An autonomous institution under the supervision of the Ministry of Education.

Academic Year: September to August (September-February; February-August)

Admission Requirements: Secondary school certificate (Apolytirion Lykiou) and national entrance examination

Fees: None

Main Language(s) of Instruction: Greek

Degrees and Diplomas: *Ptychio*: **Arts and Humanities; Business Administration; Economics; Medicine; Natural Sciences; Pharmacy.** *Metaptychiako Diploma Eidikefsis*; *Didaktoriko Diploma*: **Aeronautical and Aerospace Engineering; Biology; Business Administration; Chemical Engineering; Chemistry; Computer Engineering; Computer Science; Education; Electrical Engineering; Electronic Engineering; Engineering; Environmental Studies; Geology; Linguistics; Materials Engineering; Mathematics; Mechanical Engineering; Medical Technology; Pharmacy; Philosophy; Physics; Polymer and Plastics Technology; Theatre.**

Student Services: Academic Counselling, Canteen, Careers Guidance, Cultural Activities, Health Services, Language Laboratory, Nursery Care, Social Counselling, Sports Facilities

Last Updated: 21/04/15

UNIVERSITY OF PIRAEUS

Panepistimion Pireos
Karaoli M. and A.Dimitriou 80, 18534 Piraeus
Tel: +30(210) 414-2000
EMail: publ@unipi.gr
Website: http://www.unipi.gr

Rector: Nikolaos Georgopoulos EMail: rector@unipi.gr

International Relations: Christina Kontogoulidou, International Relations Officer Tel: +30(210) 414-2245 EMail: ckonto@unipi.gr

School
Economics, Business and International Studies (Business Administration; Economics; European Studies; Industrial and Production Economics; International Economics; International Relations); **Finance and Statistics** (Banking; Finance; Insurance; Statistics); **Information and Communication Technologies** (Computer Science); **Maritime and Industrial Studies** (Industrial Management; Marine Science and Oceanography; Marine Transport; Transport and Communications; Transport Management)

Centre
Research (Information Management; Information Technology)

History: Founded 1938 as Graduate School of Industrial Studies. Acquired present status and title 1989.

Academic Year: September to July (September-January; February-July)

Admission Requirements: Secondary school certificate (Apolytrion Lykiou) and entrance examination

Fees: (Euros): Foreign students, c. 735 per annum

Main Language(s) of Instruction: Greek. Also English for Erasmus students.

Degrees and Diplomas: *Ptychio*: **Banking; Business Administration; Computer Science; Economics; European Studies; Finance; Industrial Management; International Studies.** *Metaptychiako Diploma Eidikefsis*: **Banking; Business Administration; Computer Science; Economics; European Studies; Finance; Industrial Management; International Studies.** *Didaktoriko Diploma*: **Banking; Business Administration; Computer Science; Economics; European Studies; Finance; Industrial Management; International Studies.**

Student Services: Academic Counselling, Canteen, Careers Guidance, Cultural Activities, Facilities for disabled people, Foreign Studies Centre, Health Services, Social Counselling, Sports Facilities

Publications: Spoudai (studies)

Last Updated: 22/04/15

UNIVERSITY OF THE AEGEAN

Panepistimion Aegaeou

University Hill, Administration Bldg., 81100 Mytilene, Lesvos
Tel: +30(22510) 36000
Fax: +30(22510) 36009
EMail: secr@aegean.gr
Website: http://www.aegean.gr

Rector: Stefanos Gritzalis EMail: rector@aegean.gr

Vice Rector of Academic Affairs and Quality Assurance:: Alexandra Bounia EMail: vice-rector-aaqa@aegean.gr

School

Business Studies *(Chios, CHIOS)* (Business Administration; Finance; Management; Marine Transport; Tourism; Transport Management); **Environment** *(Mytilene, LEVSOS)* (Environmental Studies; Food Science; Marine Science and Oceanography; Nutrition); **Humanities** *(Rhodes, RHODES)* (Mediterranean Studies; Preschool Education; Primary Education); **Science** *(Karlovasi, SAMOS)* (Actuarial Science; Communication Studies; Information Management; Information Technology; Mathematics; Natural Sciences; Statistics; Telecommunications Engineering); **Social Sciences** *(Mytilene, LESVOS)* (Anthropology; Communication Studies; Cultural Studies; Geography; Information Sciences; Mass Communication; Museum Studies; Social Sciences; Sociology; Technology)

Department

Product and Systems Design Engineering *(Ermoupolis, SYROS)* (Art Management; Design; Engineering Drawing and Design)

Further Information: Akso campuses in Chios, Samos, Syros and Rhodes

History: Founded 1984. A State institution under the jurisdiction of the Ministry of Education.

Academic Year: October to June (October-February; February-June)

Admission Requirements: Secondary school certificate (Apolytirion Lykiou)

Fees: None

Main Language(s) of Instruction: Greek

Degrees and Diplomas: *Ptychio*; *Metaptychiako Diploma Eidikefsis*; *Didaktoriko Diploma*: **Anthropology; Environmental Studies; Geography; History; Marine Science and Oceanography; Mediterranean Studies; Sociology.**

Student Services: Academic Counselling, Canteen, Careers Guidance, Health Services, Language Laboratory, Social Counselling

Last Updated: 21/04/15

UNIVERSITY OF THE PELOPONNESE

Red Cross 28, Karyotakis, 22100 Tripoli
Tel: +30(2710) 230-000
Fax: +30(2710) 230-005
EMail: secr-rector@uop.gr
Website: http://www.uop.gr

President: Theodoros Papatheodorou

Faculty

Economics, Management and Informatics *(Tripoli)* (Computer Science; Economics; Information Technology; Management); **Fine Arts** *(Nafplio)* (Fine Arts; Theatre); **Human Movement and Quality of Life** *(Sparta)* (Nursing; Sports; Sports Management); **Humanities and Cultural Studies** *(Kalamata)* (Archaeology; Arts and Humanities; Cultural Studies; History; Philology); **Social Sciences** *(Corinth)* (Education; International Relations; Political Sciences; Social Policy; Social Sciences)

Further Information: Also campuses in Tripoli, Korinthos, Kalamata, Nafplio and Sparti

History: Founded 2000.

Main Language(s) of Instruction: Greek

Degrees and Diplomas: *Ptychio*; *Metaptychiako Diploma Eidikefsis*: **Business Administration; Computer Science; Finance; Management; Public Administration; Sports Management.** *Didaktoriko Diploma*: **Computer Science; Economics.**

Last Updated: 24/04/15

UNIVERSITY OF THESSALY

Panepistimio Thesalias (UTH)

Argonafton and Filellinon, 38221 Volos, Magnesia
Tel: +30(24210) 74000
Fax: +30(24210) 74614
EMail: chkostop@adm.uth.gr
Website: http://www.uth.gr

Rector: Ioannis E. Messinis

Programme

Postgraduate Studies (Agriculture; Anthropology; Aquaculture; Archaeology; Architecture; Architecture and Planning; Biochemistry; Biotechnology; Civil Engineering; Computer Engineering; Crop Production; Economics; History; Mechanical Engineering; Medicine; Physical Education; Preschool Education; Primary Education; Regional Planning; Rural Studies; Special Education; Sports; Telecommunications Engineering; Veterinary Science)

School

Agricultural Sciences (Agriculture; Animal Husbandry; Crop Production; Fishery; Rural Planning; Water Science); **Engineering** (Architecture; Civil Engineering; Computer Engineering; Industrial Engineering; Mechanical Engineering; Regional Planning; Structural Architecture; Telecommunications Engineering; Town Planning); **Health Sciences** (Biochemistry; Biotechnology; Medicine; Veterinary Science); **Humanities and Social Sciences** (Anthropology; Archaeology; Economics; History; Preschool Education; Primary Education; Special Education); **Physical Education and Sport Science** (Physical Education; Sports); **Science** (Computer Science)

Further Information: Also University Hospital.

History: Founded 1984. A State institution under the jurisdiction of the Ministry of Education.

Academic Year: September to August (September-February; February-August)

Admission Requirements: Secondary school certificate (Apolytirion Lykiou) and entrance examination

Fees: None

Main Language(s) of Instruction: Greek

Degrees and Diplomas: *Ptychio*; *Metaptychiako Diploma Eidikefsis*; *Didaktoriko Diploma*: **Aquaculture; Architecture; Biochemistry; Biotechnology; Computer Engineering; Computer Science; Electrical Engineering; Mechanical Engineering; Physical Education; Psychology; Regional Planning; Sports; Veterinary Science.** Also joint Greek-French Master Programme; International Master In Sports Tourism Engineering (Imiste)

Student Services: Academic Counselling, Canteen, Careers Guidance, Facilities for disabled people, Health Services, Language Laboratory, Sports Facilities

Publications: Social Science Tribune

Last Updated: 21/04/15

UNIVERSITY OF WESTERN MACEDONIA (UOWM)

Parko Agiou Dimitriou, GR 50100 Kozani
Tel: + (30) 24610 56200
EMail: info@uowm.gr
Website: http://www.uowm.gr

President: Theodoros Xatzipantelis

Faculty

Education (Education; Preschool Education; Primary Education; Teacher Training); **Engineering** *(Kozani)* (Computer Engineering; Engineering; Environmental Engineering; Mechanical Engineering; Telecommunications Engineering); **Fine Arts** *(Florina)* (Fine Arts; Visual Arts)

History: Founded 2003.

Degrees and Diplomas: *Ptychio*; *Metaptychiako Diploma Eidikefsis*; *Didaktoriko Diploma*: **Preschool Education; Primary Education.**

Last Updated: 24/04/15

Guatemala

STRUCTURE OF HIGHER EDUCATION SYSTEM

Description:

Higher education is provided by one State and several private universities. There are also higher institutes and schools. The State university is autonomous. Its main authority is the Higher University Council. The private universities are under the authority of a Consejo de la Enseñanza Privada Superior which accredits them. The qualifications they award are officially recognized.

Stages of studies:

University level first stage: *Licenciatura*
The Licenciatura is awarded after five to six years' study and the defense of a thesis.

University level second stage: *Maestría, Doctorado*
The Maestria is conferred after 2 1/2 further years of study and the submission of a thesis. The Doctorado is awarded after 3 years of study following upon the Maestria.

ADMISSION TO HIGHER EDUCATION

Admission to university-level studies:

Name of secondary school credential required: Bachillerato

Foreign students admission:

Admission requirements: Foreign students must hold the Bachillerato or a diploma of an official secondary study programme recognized by the government.

Language proficiency: Knowledge of Spanish is essential.

NATIONAL BODIES

Ministerio de Educación (Ministry of Education)

Minister: Rubén Alfonso Ramírez
6a Calle 1-87 zona 10
Guatemala 01010
Tel: +502 2411-9595
EMail: info@mineduc.gob.gt
WWW: http://www.mineduc.gob.gt

Consejo de la Enseñanza Privada Superior - CEPS (Private Higher Education Council)

Edificio Colegios Profesionales, calle 15-46 zona 15
Colonia El Maestro
Guatemala
Tel: +502 2369-6344
WWW: http://www.ceps.edu.gt
Role of national body: To coordinate and assess private universities.

Consejo Nacional de Ciencia y Tecnología - CONCYT (Secretariat for Science and Technology)

3av. 13-28 Zona 1
Guatelamala 01000
Tel: +502 2317-2600
EMail: infosenacyt@concyt.gob.gt
WWW: http://www.concyt.gob.gt/

Data for academic year: 2015-2016
Source: IAU from CEPS and MINEDUC websites, 2015.

INSTITUTIONS

PUBLIC INSTITUTION

UNIVERSITY OF SAN CARLOS OF GUATEMALA

Universidad de San Carlos de Guatemala
Ciudad Universitaria, Zona 12, Guatemala City 01012
Tel: +502(2) 443-9500
Fax: +502(2) 443-9500
EMail: usacdiga@usac.edu.gt
Website: http://www.usac.edu.gt

Rector: Carlos Alvarado Cerezo EMail: rector@usac.edu.gt

Faculty
Agronomy (Agronomy; Environmental Management; Forestry; Natural Resources); **Architecture** (Architecture; Graphic Design); **Chemistry and Pharmacy** (Chemistry; Nutrition; Pharmacy); **Dentistry** (Dentistry; Surgery); **Economics** (Accountancy; Business Administration; Economics); **Engineering** (Applied Mathematics; Applied Physics; Chemical Engineering; Civil Engineering; Computer Engineering; Electrical Engineering; Electronic Engineering; Engineering; Industrial Engineering; Mechanical Engineering); **Humanities** (Art History; Curriculum; Educational Administration; Educational Research; English; Fine Arts; Human Rights; Library Science; Literature; Pedagogy; Philosophy); **Law and Social Sciences** (Law; Social Sciences); **Medical Sciences** (Medicine; Nursing; Surgery); **Veterinary Science and Zoology** (Veterinary Science; Zoology)

School
Art (Dance; Music; Theatre; Visual Arts); **Communication Studies** (Communication Studies); **History** (History); **Linguistics** (Linguistics; Translation and Interpretation); **Political Science** (International Relations; Political Sciences; Sociology); **Psychology** (Physical Education; Psychology; Sports); **Social Work** (Social Work); **Teacher Training** (Teacher Training)

History: Founded 1676 by royal decree of Charles II of Spain. Became an autonomous institution 1945.

Academic Year: January to December (January-June; July-December)

Admission Requirements: Secondary school certificate (bachillerato) or recognized foreign equivalent

Main Language(s) of Instruction: Spanish

Degrees and Diplomas: *Técnico*: **Nutrition; Social Work.** *Licenciatura*: **Accountancy; Anthropology; Applied Mathematics; Archaeology; Architecture; Biochemistry; Biology; Business Administration; Chemistry; Classical Languages; Economics; Education; History; International Relations; Journalism; Law; Library Science; Literature; Medicine; Pharmacology; Philosophy; Physics; Psychology; Social Sciences; Sociology; Spanish.** *Maestría*: **Anaesthesiology; Animal Husbandry; Architecture; Art History; Business Administration; Communication Studies; Curriculum; Dermatology; Educational Research; Energy Engineering; Environmental Engineering; Environmental Management; Gynaecology and Obstetrics; Health Sciences; Information Technology; Law; Microbiology; Neurology; Nutrition; Ophthalmology; Orthodontics; Orthopaedics; Otorhinolaryngology; Paediatrics; Political Sciences; Psychiatry and Mental Health; Radiology; Rural Planning; Social Work; Teacher Training.** *Doctorado*: **Agriculture; Architecture; Education; Environmental Studies; Law; Philosophy; Public Health.**

Last Updated: 01/03/16

SAN MARCOS UNIVERSITY CENTRE

CENTRO UNIVERSITARIO SAN MARCOS
13 avenida "A" 7-42 zona 3, San Marcos
Tel: +502 7957-3300
Website: http://www.cusam.edu.gt

Directora: Eugenia Elizabeth Makepeace Alfaro

Programme
Agronomy (Agronomy); **Business Administration** (Business Administration); **Law and Social Sciences** (Law; Social Sciences); **Medicine** (Medicine); **Pedagogy and Educational Sciences** (Educational Sciences; Pedagogy); **Social Work** (Social Work)

History: Founded 1987.

Main Language(s) of Instruction: Spanish

Degrees and Diplomas: *Licenciatura*; *Maestría*

UNIVERSITY CENTRE OF BAJA VERAPAZ

CENTRO UNIVERSITARIO DE BAJA VERAPAZ
Baja Verapaz
Website: http://sitios.usac.edu.gt/cunbav

Director: Edgar Guillermo Ruiz Recinos

Programme
Agronomy (Agricultural Engineering; Agronomy); **Business Administration** (Business Administration); **Law** (Law); **Pedagogy** (Pedagogy)

History: Founded 2008.

Main Language(s) of Instruction: Spanish

Degrees and Diplomas: *Licenciatura*

UNIVERSITY CENTRE OF CHIMALTENANGO

CENTRO UNIVERSITARIO DE CHIMALTENANGO
2° Av. 5-080 Zona 1. Quinta Los Aposentos II, Chimaltenango
Tel: +502 7839-6582
Website: http://sitios.usac.edu.gt/cundech

Director: Rudy Cheguen

Programme
Accountancy and Auditing (Accountancy); **Business Administration** (Business Administration); **Law and Social Sciences** (Law; Social Sciences); **Pedagogy and Educational Management** (Educational Administration; Pedagogy); **Tourism** (Tourism)

History: Founded 2007.

Main Language(s) of Instruction: Spanish

Degrees and Diplomas: *Licenciatura*

UNIVERSITY CENTRE OF EL PROGRESO

CENTRO UNIVERSITARIO DE EL PROGRESO
Barrio El porvenir, Guastatoya
Website: http://www.cunprogreso.edu.gt/carreras

Director: Edwin Emili García

Programme
Agronomy (Agronomy); **Business Administration** (Business Administration); **Industrial Engineering** (Industrial Engineering); **Law** (Law); **Pedagogy and Educational Management** (Educational Administration; Pedagogy); **Teacher Training** (Teacher Training)

History: Founded 2002.

Main Language(s) of Instruction: Spanish

Degrees and Diplomas: *Licenciatura*

UNIVERSITY CENTRE OF IZABAL

CENTRO UNIVERSITARIO DE IZABAL
Entrada al Hospital Nacional Amistad Japón-Guatemala, Calle Karen Lee, Colonia San Manuel, Santo Tomás de Castilla
Tel: +502 7947-5792
EMail: cunizab@hotmail.com
Website: http://cunizab.blogspot.fr

Directora: Juana Isabel Galdámez Mendoza

Programme

Accountancy and Auditing (Accountancy); **Business Administration** (Business Administration); **Environmental Management** (Environmental Management); **Law and Social Sciences** (Law; Social Sciences); **Social Work** (Social Work)

Degrees and Diplomas: *Licenciatura*

UNIVERSITY CENTRE OF JUTIAPA

CENTRO UNIVERSITARIO DE JUTIAPA

5a Avenida 2-03, Calzada Los Almendros, Barrio La Federal, Jutiapa
Tel: +502 7844-6284
Website: http://jusac.usac.edu.gt

Director: Walter Reyes Sanabria

Programme

Accountancy and Auditing (Accountancy); **Business Administration** (Business Administration); **Law and Social Sciences** (Law; Social Sciences); **Pedagogy and Educational Management** (Educational Administration; Pedagogy)

History: Founded 2007.

Main Language(s) of Instruction: Spanish

Degrees and Diplomas: *Licenciatura*

UNIVERSITY CENTRE OF PETEN

CENTRO UNIVERSITARIO DE PETÉN

Calzada Rodríguez Macal y 4a calle, Zona 2, Santa Elena, Petén
Tel: +502 7873-0505
Website: https://www.usac.edu.gt/catalogo/cudep.pdf

Director: Byron Agusto Milian

Programme

Agronomy (Agronomy); **Archaeology** (Archaeology); **Communication Sciences** (Communication Studies); **Environmental Education** (Environmental Studies); **Forestry** (Forestry); **Land Management** (Regional Planning); **Law and Social Sciences** (Law; Social Sciences); **Pedagogy and Educational Sciences** (Educational Sciences; Pedagogy); **Social Work** (Social Work); **Tourism Administration** (Tourism)

History: Founded 1987.

Main Language(s) of Instruction: Spanish

Degrees and Diplomas: *Licenciatura*; *Maestría*: **Education; Regional Planning.**

UNIVERSITY CENTRE OF QUICHE

CENTRO UNIVERSITARIO DE QUICHÉ

3ra Av 0-14, zona 5, Santa Cruz del Quiché.
Tel: +502 7755-1273
EMail: cusacq@usac.edu
Website: http://sitios.usac.edu.gt/wp_cusacq/

Director: Marco de la Rosa

Programme

Agronomy (Agronomy); **Business Administration** (Business Administration); **Law and Social Sciences** (Law; Social Sciences)

History: Founded 2008.

Main Language(s) of Instruction: Spanish

Degrees and Diplomas: *Licenciatura*

UNIVERSITY CENTRE OF SANTA ROSA

CENTRO UNIVERSITARIO SANTA ROSA

Barrio Santiago, Calzada de entra Chiquimulilla, Santa Rosa
Website: http://usac.edu.gt/catalogo/cunsaro.pdf

Director: Élmer Álvarez

Programme

Business Administration (Business Administration); **Law and Social Sciences** (Law; Social Sciences); **Pedagogy and Educational Management** (Educational Administration; Pedagogy); **Tourism** (Tourism)

History: Founded 2006.

Degrees and Diplomas: *Licenciatura*

UNIVERSITY CENTRE OF SOLALA

CENTRO UNIVERSITARIO SOLALÁ

8a. calle 4-27 zona 1, Barrio San Antonio., Sololá
Tel: +502 7762-3480
EMail: USAC_SOLOLA@yahoo.com
Website: http://www.actiweb.es/usac_solola/contacto.html

Director: Hector Fernandez

Programme

Bilingual Primary Education (Bilingual and Bicultural Education); **Law and Social Sciences** (Law; Social Sciences); **Physical Education** (Physical Education); **Public Accountancy and Auditing** (Accountancy)

Main Language(s) of Instruction: Spanish

Degrees and Diplomas: *Licenciatura*

UNIVERSITY CENTRE OF TOTONICAPÁN

CENTRO UNIVERSITARIO DE TOTONICAPÁN

Website: http://sitios.usac.edu.gt/wp_cuntoto

Director: Eduardo. Abril Gálvez

Programme

Forestry (Forestry); **Law and Social Sciences** (Law; Social Sciences); **Pedagogy and Educational Management** (Educational Administration; Pedagogy)

History: Founded 2008.

Main Language(s) of Instruction: Spanish

Degrees and Diplomas: *Licenciatura*

UNIVERSITY CENTRE OF THE EAST

CENTRO UNIVERSITARIO DE ORIENTE

Finca El Zapotillo Zona 5, CA-10, Chiquimula
Tel: +502 5155-3025
Website: http://cunori.edu.gt

Director: Nery Galdámez

Programme

Agronomy (Agronomy); **Business Administration** (Business Administration); **Communication Studies** (Communication Studies); **Economics** (Economics); **Engineering** (Civil Engineering; Computer Engineering; Environmental Engineering; Industrial Engineering); **Law and Notary Studies** (Law); **Medicine and Surgery** (Medicine; Surgery); **Teacher Training** (Teacher Training); **Zoology** (Zoology)

History: Founded 1977.

Main Language(s) of Instruction: Spanish

Degrees and Diplomas: *Licenciatura*; *Maestría*: **Civil Law; Constitutional Law; Criminal Law; Education; Health Administration; Human Resources.** *Doctorado*: **Law.**

UNIVERSITY CENTRE OF THE NORTH

CENTRO UNIVERSITARIO DEL NORTE

Cobán, Alta Verapaz 1601
Tel: +502 7566600
EMail: coordinacion@cunor.usac.edu.gt
Website: http://cunor.usac.edu.gt/cms

Director: Fredy Giovani Macz Choc

Programme

Agronomy (Agronomy; Soil Science); **Geology** (Geology); **Social Work** (Social Work); **Zoology** (Zoology)

History: Founded 1975.

Main Language(s) of Instruction: Spanish

Degrees and Diplomas: *Licenciatura*; *Maestría*: **Agronomy.**

UNIVERSITY CENTRE OF THE NORTH-WEST

CENTRO UNIVERSITARIO DE NOR-OCCIDENTE

Carretera Interamericana, Km. 262, Huehuetenango
Tel: +502 7764-2359
EMail: info@cunoroc.edu.gt
Website: http://www.cunoroc.edu.gt/website/index.php?option=com_content&view=article&id=7&Itemid=3

Director: Otto Gabriel Salguero Vásquez

Programme

Agronomy (Agronomy); **Forestry** (Forestry); **Law and Social Sciences** (Law; Social Sciences); **Pedagogy and Educational Management** (Educational Administration; Pedagogy); **Social Work** (Social Work); **Teacher Training** (Teacher Training); **Zoology** (Zoology)

History: Founded 1976.

Main Language(s) of Instruction: Spanish

Degrees and Diplomas: *Licenciatura*

UNIVERSITY CENTRE OF THE SOUTH

CENTRO UNIVERSITARIO DEL SUR

Calz. Manuel Cordón Argueta 2-75 Z.2, Escuintla
Website: http://cunsur.atwebpages.com

Programme

Accountancy and Auditing (Accountancy); **Agro-industrial Engineering** (Agricultural Engineering; Industrial Engineering); **Business Administration** (Business Administration); **Law and Social Sciences** (Law; Social Sciences)

History: Founded 1977.

Main Language(s) of Instruction: Spanish

Degrees and Diplomas: *Licenciatura*

UNIVERSITY CENTRE OF THE SOUTH-EAST

CENTRO UNIVERSITARIO DE SUR ORIENTE

3ra. Calle Final 1-69, Zona 5 Barrio Chipilapa, Jalapa
Tel: +502 7922-4273
EMail: cunsurori@usac.edu.gt
Website: http://sitios.usac.edu.gt/wp_cunsurori

Director: Otto René Solís Méndez

Programme

Agronomy (Agronomy); **Business Administration** (Business Administration); **Law and Social Sciences** (Law; Social Sciences); **Pedagogy** (Pedagogy); **Social Work** (Social Work); **Zoology** (Zoology)

History: Founded 1977.

Degrees and Diplomas: *Licenciatura*

UNIVERSITY CENTRE OF THE SOUTH-WEST

CENTRO UNIVERSITARIO DEL SUR OCCIDENTE

Final Colonia Los Almendros, Zona 2. Mazatenango, Suchitepéquez.
Tel: +502 7872-2422

Website: http://informacioncunsuroc.blogspot.fr/p/carreras_31.html

Directora: Alba Ruth Maldonado

Programme

Business Administration (Business Administration); **Food Technology** (Food Technology); **Law and Social Sciences** (Law; Social Sciences); **Local Environmental Management** (Environmental Management); **Pedagogy and Educational Management** (Educational Administration; Pedagogy); **Social Work** (Social Work); **Tropical Agronomy** (Agronomy; Tropical Agriculture)

History: Founded 1997.

Degrees and Diplomas: *Licenciatura*

UNIVERSITY CENTRE OF THE WEST

CENTRO UNIVERSITARIO DE OCCIDENTE

Calle Rodolfo Robles 29-99 Zona 1, Quetzaltenango
Tel: +502 7873-0000
Website: http://www.cunoc.edu.gt

Directora: María del Rosario Paz Cabrera

Division

Architecture (Architecture); **Dentistry** (Dentistry; Surgery); **Economics** (Accountancy; Business Administration; Economics); **Engineering** (Civil Engineering; Industrial Engineering; Mechanical Engineering); **Health Sciences** (Medicine; Surgery); **Humanities** (Pedagogy; Psychology; Social Work); **Law and Social Sciences** (Law; Social Sciences); **Science and Technology** (Agronomy; Environmental Management; Surveying and Mapping)

History: Founded 1970.

Main Language(s) of Instruction: Spanish

Degrees and Diplomas: *Licenciatura*; *Maestría*: **Administration; Anthropology; Education; Hydraulic Engineering; Law.**

UNIVERSITY CENTRE OF ZACAPA

CENTRO UNIVERSITARIO DE ZACAPA

3a. Calle 16-19 Barrio las Flores, Zacapa
Tel: +502 5787-3388

Programme

Accountancy and Auditing (Accountancy); **Agro-Industry and Forestry** (Agricultural Business; Forestry); **Agronomy** (Agronomy); **Law and Social Sciences** (Law; Social Sciences); **Psychology** (Psychology)

Degrees and Diplomas: *Licenciatura*

PRIVATE INSTITUTIONS

DA VINCI UNIVERSITY OF GUATEMALA

Universidad Da Vinci de Guatemala

7ª. Calle 13-70, El Terrero, Zona 4, Huehuetenango
Tel: +502 7728-0777
EMail: infohuehue@udv.edu.gt
Website: http://udv.edu.gt

Rector: José Cyrano Ruiz Cabarrús

Faculty

Administration and Commerce (Administration; Business Administration; International Business; Marketing); **Auditing and Finance** (Accountancy; Finance); **Educational Sciences** (Curriculum; Educational Administration; Pedagogy); **Engineering** (Civil Engineering; Electrical Engineering; Graphic Design; Industrial Engineering); **Health Sciences** (Health Administration; Nursing; Nutrition; Physical Therapy; Respiratory Therapy); **Humanities** (Communication Studies; Cultural Studies; Educational Administration; Pedagogy; Psychology; Social Work); **Law, Social Sciences and International Relations** (International Relations; Law; Social Sciences)

Further Information: Also campus in Guatemala City

History: Founded 2008.

Main Language(s) of Instruction: Spanish

Degrees and Diplomas: *Licenciatura*; *Maestría*: **Business Administration; Criminal Law; Educational Administration; Finance; Health Administration; International Business; Management; Nutrition.** *Doctorado*: **Administration; Criminal Law.**

Last Updated: 02/03/16

FRANCISCO MARROQUÍN UNIVERSITY

Universidad Francisco Marroquín (UFM)
Calle Manuel F. Ayau (6 Calle Final), Zona 10,
Guatemala City 01010
Tel: +502(2) 338-7700
Fax: +502(2) 334-6896
EMail: inf@ufm.edu.gt
Website: http://www.ufm.edu.gt

Rector: Gabriel Calzada (2013-) EMail: rectoria@ufm.edu.gt

Secretario General: Ricardo Castillo
EMail: rca@ufm.edu.gt; secretariageneral@ufm.edu

Faculty
Architecture (Architecture; Design; Furniture Design; Town Planning); **Dentistry** (Dentistry); **Economics** (Business Administration; Computer Science; Economics; Finance; Marketing); **Law** (Law); **Medicine** (Medicine)

School
Business (Business Administration; Economics; Finance; Real Estate); **Cinema and Visual Arts** (Cinema and Television; Visual Arts); **Nutrition** (Nutrition)

Institute
Political Science and International Relations (International Relations; Political Sciences)

Further Information: Also Teaching Hospital

History: Founded 1971. A private institution financed by tuition fees and donations.

Academic Year: January to November (January-May; July-November)

Admission Requirements: Secondary school certificate (bachillerato) or foreign equivalent and entrance examination

Main Language(s) of Instruction: Spanish

Degrees and Diplomas: *Licenciatura*: **Accountancy; Advertising and Publicity; Architecture; Business Administration; Clinical Psychology; Computer Science; Dentistry; Economics; Education; Finance; Human Resources; International Business; International Relations; Law; Literature; Marketing; Medicine; Native Language; Nutrition; Political Sciences; Psychology.** *Maestría*: **Business Administration; Dentistry; Economics; Finance; Social Sciences.** *Doctorado*: **Economics; History; Law.**

Student Services: Canteen, Facilities for disabled people

Publications: Laissez-faire; Revista de la Facultad de Derecho

Publishing House: Editorial Universidad Francisco Marroquín
Last Updated: 25/02/16

GALILEO UNIVERSITY

Universidad Galileo
7a Avenida, Calle Dr. Eduardo Suger Cofiño, Zona 10,
Guatemala City 01010
Tel: +502(2) 423-8000
Fax: +502(2) 423-8000
EMail: info@galileo.edu
Website: http://www.galileo.edu

Rector: José Eduardo Suger Cofiño

Vicerrectora: Mayra Roldán de Ramírez

Faculty
Administration (Business Administration; Marketing); **Biology, Chemistry and Pharmacy** (Biology; Chemistry; Food Science; Nutrition); **Communication Studies** (Communication Studies; Design); **Construction Engineering** (Building Technologies); **Education** *(FACED)* (Biology; Chemistry; Computer Science; Educational Administration; History; Mathematics and Computer Science; Social Sciences; Teacher Training); **Health Sciences** (Business Administration; Health Administration; Nursing; Optometry; Physical Therapy); **Science, Technology and Industry** (Administration; Industrial Engineering; International Business; Management; Public Administration); **Sports** (Sports; Sports Management); **Systems Engineering, Informatics and Computer Science** *(FISICC)* (Computer Networks; Computer Science; Electronic Engineering; Systems Analysis; Telecommunications Engineering)

School
Arts (Fine Arts; Music; Sound Engineering (Acoustics)); **Continuing Education** (Administration; Finance); **Diplomacy and International Relations** (International Relations); **Professional Development** (Business Administration; International Business; Management); **Technical** *(ESTEC)* (Aeronautical and Aerospace Engineering; Automation and Control Engineering; Electrical Engineering; Industrial Management; Telecommunications Engineering)

Institute
Earth Sciences and Astrology Research (Astronomy and Space Science; Earth Sciences); **Energy Resources** (Energy Engineering); **Family Studies** (Family Studies); **Open Education** (Administration; Business Administration; Hotel Management; Human Resources; Marketing; Telecommunications Engineering); **Security Studies** (Criminal Law; Criminology; Protective Services); **Sustainable Development** (Development Studies); **Von Neumann** (Distance Education)

History: Founded 1977 as Instituto de Informática y Ciencias de la Computación (IICC), part of the Universidad Francisco Marroquín. Acquired present status and title 2000.

Main Language(s) of Instruction: Spanish

Degrees and Diplomas: *Licenciatura*; *Maestría*: **Development Studies; Educational Administration; Educational Psychology; Electronic Engineering; Energy Engineering; Family Studies; Finance; Gerontology; Health Administration; Hotel Management; Human Resources; Information Technology; International Business; International Relations; Law; Medicine; Ophthalmology; Oral Pathology; Public Administration.** *Doctorado*: **Administration; Industrial Engineering; Public Administration.**
Last Updated: 26/02/16

MARIANO GÁLVEZ UNIVERSITY OF GUATEMALA

Universidad Mariano Gálvez de Guatemala
3a. Avenida 9-00 Zona 2, Interior Finca El Zapote,
Apartado Postal 1811, Guatemala City 01002
Tel: +502(2) 288-7592
Fax: +502(2) 288-4040
EMail: informacionumg@umg.edu.gt
Website: http://www.umg.edu.gt/

Rector: Alvaro R. Torres Moss

Faculty
Administration (Administration); **Architecture** (Architecture); **Civil Engineering** (Civil Engineering); **Economics** (Economics); **Law and Social Sciences** (Law; Social Sciences); **Odontology** (Dentistry)

History: Founded 1966. A private institution recognized by the State.

Academic Year: February to November (February-June; July-November)

Admission Requirements: Secondary school certificate (bachillerato) or foreign equivalent

Main Language(s) of Instruction: Spanish

Degrees and Diplomas: *Licenciatura*: **Business Administration; Civil Engineering; Economics; Law; Social Sciences.** *Maestría*: **Accountancy; Administration; Communication Studies; Computer Science; Dentistry; Economics; Education; Higher Education; International Business; Law; Theology.** *Doctorado*: **Education; Law.**

Publications: Winak
Last Updated: 18/03/16

ALTA VERAPAZ BRANCH
SEDE ALTA VERAPAZ
6a Avenida 2-33, zona 1, Cobán, Alta Verapaz
Tel: +502 7952-1041

Programme
Architecture (Architecture); **Business Administration** (Business Administration); **Clinical Psychology** (Clinical Psychology);

Computer Engineering (Computer Engineering); **Hotel Management, Tourism and Gastronomy** (Cooking and Catering; Hotel Management; Tourism); **Law and Social Sciences** (Law; Social Sciences); **Medicine and Health Sciences** (Health Sciences; Medicine); **Nursing** (Nursing); **Pedagogy and Educational Sciences** (Educational Sciences; Pedagogy); **Primary Education** (Primary Education); **Public Accountancy and Auditing** (Accountancy); **Public Administration** (Public Administration); **Social Work** (Social Work)

Main Language(s) of Instruction: Spanish

Degrees and Diplomas: *Licenciatura*; *Maestría*: **Administration; Nursing; Public Administration.**

ANTIGUA GUATEMALA BRANCH

SEDE ANTIGUA GUATEMALA

6a. Ave. Norte 31, Antigua Guatemala, Sacatepéquez
Tel: +502 7832-0972
EMail: antigua@umg.edu.gt

Programme

Administration (Administration); **Architecture** (Architecture); **Computer Engineering** (Computer Engineering); **Education** (Education); **Hotel Management, Tourism and Gastronomy** (Cooking and Catering; Hotel Management; Tourism); **Interior Design** (Interior Design); **Law and Social Sciences** (Law; Social Sciences); **Public Accountancy and Auditing** (Accountancy); **Social Work** (Social Work)

Main Language(s) of Instruction: Spanish

Degrees and Diplomas: *Licenciatura*; *Maestría*: **Education; Human Resources.**

BAJA VERAPAZ BRANCH

SEDE BAJA VERAPAZ

4ta Calle 9-51, zona 1 Barrio El Centro, Salama, Baja Verapaz
Tel: +502 4823-9180
EMail: salama@umg.edu.gt

Area

Social Sciences and Administration (Accountancy; Business Administration; Clinical Psychology; Law; Social Sciences; Social Work)

Degrees and Diplomas: *Licenciatura*

CHIMALTENANGO BRANCH

SEDE CHIMALTENANGO

2a Calle 1-49, zona 4, Chimaltenango
Tel: +502 7839-2213

Directora: Julieta de Obregón

Programme

Business Administration (Business Administration); **Clinical Psychology** (Clinical Psychology); **Computer Engineering** (Computer Engineering); **Educational Management** (Educational Administration); **Gynaecology and Obstetrics** (Gynaecology and Obstetrics); **Law and Social Sciences** (Law; Social Sciences); **Public Accountancy and Auditing** (Accountancy); **Social Work** (Social Work)

Degrees and Diplomas: *Licenciatura*; *Maestría*: **Gynaecology and Obstetrics.**

CHINAUTLA BRANCH

SEDE CHINAUTLA

2a Calle F-2 Colonia Sausalito Edificio Municipal 2do Nivel, Chinautla
Tel: +502 2245-9800
Website: http://umg-chinautla.es.tl/Home.htm

Programme

Business Administration (Business Administration); **Computer Engineering** (Computer Engineering); **Education** (Education); **Law and Social Sciences** (Law; Social Sciences); **Public Accountancy and Auditing** (Accountancy)

Further Information: Also Tierra Nueva campus

Main Language(s) of Instruction: Spanish

Degrees and Diplomas: *Licenciatura*

CHIQUIMULA BRANCH

SEDE CHIQUIMULA

5ta Calle 6-31, zona 1, Chiquimula

Programme

Business Administration (Business Administration); **Clinical Psychology** (Clinical Psychology); **Computer Engineering** (Computer Engineering); **Human Resource Management** (Human Resources; Management); **Law and Social Sciences** (Law; Social Sciences); **Marketing** (Marketing); **Pre-school Education** (Pre-school Education); **Social Work** (Social Work); **Teacher Training** (Educational Administration; Pedagogy; Teacher Training)

Further Information: Also campuses in Concepción Las Minas and Quetzaltepeque

Degrees and Diplomas: *Licenciatura*; *Maestría*: **Human Resources.**

CHIQUIMULILLA BRANCH

SEDE CHIQUIMULILLA

4ta Calle Barrio Santiago a un costado del Beneficio Vásquez, Chiquimulilla, Santa Rosa
Tel: +502 7884-9219

Programme

Administration (Administration); **Computer Engineering** (Computer Engineering); **Law and Social Sciences** (Law; Social Sciences)

Degrees and Diplomas: *Licenciatura*

COATEPEQUE BRANCH

SEDE COATEPEQUE

2a calle 1-95, zona 3, Barrio San Francisco, Coatepeque, Quetzaltenango
Tel: +502 7775-7048

Programme

Business Administration (Business Administration); **Clinical Psychology** (Clinical Psychology); **Computer Engineering** (Computer Engineering); **Educational Management** (Educational Administration); **Law and Social Sciences** (Law; Social Sciences); **Nursing** (Nursing); **Public Accountancy and Auditing** (Accountancy); **Social Work** (Social Work)

Main Language(s) of Instruction: Spanish

Degrees and Diplomas: *Licenciatura*

CUILAPA BRANCH

SEDE CUILAPA

2a. Av. 1-51, zona 4 Barrio El Llanito, Cuilapa, Santa Rosa
Tel: +502 7888-9100

Programme

Administration (Administration); **Business Administration** (Business Administration); **Clinical Psychology** (Clinical Psychology); **Computer Engineering** (Computer Engineering); **Education** (Education); **Law and Social Sciences** (Law; Social Sciences); **Public Accountancy and Auditing** (Accountancy); **Social Work** (Social Work)

Main Language(s) of Instruction: Spanish

Degrees and Diplomas: *Licenciatura*; *Maestría*: **Education; Human Resources.**

EL PROGRESO BRANCH

SEDE EL PROGRESO

2a Calle 3-21 zona 5, Barrio El Porvenir, Guastatoya
Tel: +502 7945-2482

Programme
Administration (Administration); **Computer Engineering** (Computer Engineering); **Law and Social Sciences** (Law; Social Sciences); **Pedagogy and Educational Management** (Educational Administration; Pedagogy); **Public Accountancy and Auditing** (Accountancy); **Social Work** (Social Work)

History: Founded 2010.

Main Language(s) of Instruction: Spanish

Degrees and Diplomas: *Licenciatura*

ESCUINTLA BRANCH

SEDE ESCUINTLA

1a Av. 6-65, zona 1, Escuintla
Tel: +502 7889-7383
EMail: escuintla@umg.edu.gt

Programme
Business Administration (Business Administration); **Clinical Psychology** (Clinical Psychology); **Computer Engineering** (Computer Engineering); **Education** (Education); **Educational Management** (Educational Administration); **Industrial Engineering** (Industrial Engineering); **Law and Social Sciences** (Law; Social Sciences); **Public Accountancy and Auditing** (Accountancy); **Social Work** (Social Work); **Teacher Training** (Teacher Training)

Further Information: Also campuses in Santa Lucía Cotzumalguapa and Nueva Concepción

Degrees and Diplomas: *Licenciatura*; *Maestría*: **Education.**

HUEHUETENANGO BRANCH

SEDE HUEHUETENANGO

6a Av. 1-197, zona 8, Proyecto San José, Huehuetenango
Tel: +502 7768-1706

Programme
Administration (Administration); **Architecture** (Architecture); **Computer Engineering** (Computer Engineering); **Criminology** (Criminal Law); **Education** (Education; Educational Administration); **Hotel Management, Tourism and Gastronomy** (Cooking and Catering; Hotel Management; Tourism); **Law and Social Sciences** (Law; Social Sciences); **Medicine and Health Sciences** (Clinical Psychology; Gynaecology and Obstetrics; Health Sciences; Medicine; Paediatrics); **Public Accountancy and Auditing** (Accountancy); **Social Work** (Social Work)

History: Founded 2011.

Main Language(s) of Instruction: Spanish

Degrees and Diplomas: *Licenciatura*; *Maestría*: **Gynaecology and Obstetrics; Human Resources; Paediatrics.**

JALAPA BRANCH

SEDE JALAPA

Calle Transito Rojas 0-60, zona 6, Jalapa
Tel: +502 7922-3665

Programme
Business Administration (Business Administration); **Clinical Psychology** (Clinical Psychology); **Computer Engineering** (Computer Engineering); **Education** (Education); **Human Resource Management** (Human Resources; Management); **Law and Social Sciences** (Law; Social Sciences); **Public Accountancy and Auditing** (Accountancy)

Main Language(s) of Instruction: Spanish

Degrees and Diplomas: *Licenciatura*; *Maestría*: **Clinical Psychology; Education; Psychiatry and Mental Health; Public Administration.**

JUTIAPA BRANCH

SEDE JUTIAPA

0 Av., 2-54 zona 3, Barrio Allegre, Jutiapa
Tel: +502 7844-1018

Programme
Architecture (Architecture); **Business Administration** (Business Administration); **Clinical Psychology** (Clinical Psychology); **Computer Engineering** (Computer Engineering); **Education** (Education); **Educational Management** (Educational Administration); **Industrial Engineering** (Industrial Engineering); **Law and Social Sciences** (Law; Social Sciences); **Medicine and Health Sciences** (Health Sciences; Medical Auxiliaries; Medicine; Nursing); **Public Accountancy and Auditing** (Accountancy); **Social Work** (Social Work)

Further Information: Also campuses in Jalpatagua, Santa Catarina Mita and Yupiltepeque

Main Language(s) of Instruction: Spanish

Degrees and Diplomas: *Licenciatura*; *Maestría*: **Computer Science; Education; Human Resources.**

MAZATENANGO BRANCH

SEDE MAZATENANGO

2a. avenida 4-44 zona 1, 2a Nivel, Mazatenango, Suchitepéquez
Tel: +502 7867-9295
Website: http://umgmazate.com/

Programme
Business Administration (Business Administration); **Computer Engineering** (Computer Engineering); **Industrial Engineering** (Industrial Engineering); **Law and Social Sciences** (Law; Social Sciences); **Pedagogy and Educational Management** (Educational Administration; Pedagogy); **Public Accountancy and Auditing** (Accountancy)

History: Founded 1996.

Main Language(s) of Instruction: Spanish

Degrees and Diplomas: *Licenciatura*

PETÉN BRANCH

SEDE PETÉN

2a. Av. 4-30, zona 1 Santa Elena, Flores, Petén
Tel: +502 7926-2303
EMail: peten@umg.edu.gt

Programme
Business Administration (Business Administration); **Clinical Psychology** (Clinical Psychology); **Computer Engineering** (Computer Engineering); **Law and Social Sciences** (Law; Social Sciences); **Nursing** (Nursing); **Public Accountancy and Auditing** (Accountancy); **Social Work** (Social Work)

Degrees and Diplomas: *Licenciatura*; *Maestría*: **Human Resources; Law.**

PUERTO BARRIOS BRANCH

SEDE PUERTO BARRIOS

20 Calle y 9a Avenida Esquina, Puerto Barrios, Izabal
Tel: +502 7948-5070

Programme
Administration (Administration); **Clinical Psychology** (Clinical Psychology); **Computer Engineering** (Computer Engineering); **Education** (Education); **Educational Management** (Educational Administration); **Industrial Engineering** (Industrial Engineering); **Law and Social Sciences** (Law; Social Sciences); **Public Accountancy and Auditing** (Accountancy); **Public Administration** (Public Administration); **Social Work** (Social Work)

Further Information: Also campuses in El Estor and Morales

Main Language(s) of Instruction: Spanish

Degrees and Diplomas: *Licenciatura*; *Maestría*: **Human Resources.**

QUICHÉ BRANCH

SEDE QUICHÉ

4ta. Calle 6-12, zona 5, Santa Cruz del Quiché, Quiché
Tel: +502 7755-2895

Programme
Business Administration (Business Administration); **Clinical Psychology** (Clinical Psychology); **Computer Engineering** (Computer Engineering); **Education** (Education); **Law and Social Sciences** (Law; Social Sciences); **Public Accountancy and Auditing** (Accountancy); **Social Work** (Social Work)

Main Language(s) of Instruction: Spanish

Degrees and Diplomas: *Licenciatura*; *Maestría*: **Education; Law.**

SEDE QUETZALTENANGO BRANCH

SEDE QUETZALTENANGO

6a. Calle 22-39, zona 3, Quetzaltenango
Tel: +502 7736-8580
EMail: quetzaltenango@umg.edu.gt

Programme
Architecture (Architecture); **Business Administration** (Business Administration); **Civil Engineering** (Civil Engineering); **Clinical Psychology** (Clinical Psychology); **Computer Engineering** (Computer Engineering); **Education** (Education; Pedagogy); **Educational Management** (Educational Administration); **Industrial Engineering** (Industrial Engineering); **Law and Social Sciences** (Law; Social Sciences); **Medical and Health Sciences** (Health Sciences; Medicine); **Nursing** (Nursing); **Psychology** (Psychology); **Public Accountancy and Auditing** (Accountancy); **Radiology** (Radiology); **Social Work** (Social Work); **Stomatology** (Stomatology)

Main Language(s) of Instruction: Spanish

Degrees and Diplomas: *Licenciatura*; *Maestría*: **Law; Nursing; Radiology.**

SOLOLA BRANCH

SEDE SOLOLÁ

13 Calle, 8-24, zona 2, Barrio San Bartolo, Sololá
Tel: +502 7762-4687

Programme
Business Administration (Business Administration); **Clinical Psychology** (Clinical Psychology); **Computer Engineering** (Computer Engineering); **Education** (Education); **Law and Social Sciences** (Law; Social Sciences); **Public Accountancy and Auditing** (Accountancy); **Social Work** (Social Work)

Degrees and Diplomas: *Licenciatura*

VILLA NUEVA BRANCH

SEDE VILLA NUEVA

7a. calle 6-37, zona 1 de Villa Nueva, Villa Nueva
Tel: +502(66)367-760
EMail: villanueva@umg.edu.gt
Website: http://umgvillanueva.info

Faculty
Architecture (Architecture); **Business Administration** (Business Administration); **Engineering** (Civil Engineering; Computer Engineering; Industrial Engineering); **Law and Social Sciences** (Law; Social Sciences); **Psychology** (Clinical Psychology; Industrial and Organizational Psychology); **Public Accountancy** (Accountancy); **Teacher Training** (Teacher Training)

School
Languages (English)

History: Founded 2013.

Main Language(s) of Instruction: Spanish

Degrees and Diplomas: *Licenciatura*

ZACAPA BRANCH

SEDE ZACAPA

4ta calle 2-31, zona 2, Colegio Luterano, Zacapa
Tel: +502 7941-2000

Programme
Architecture (Architecture); **Business Administration** (Business Administration); **Clinical Psychology** (Clinical Psychology); **Computer Engineering** (Computer Engineering); **Law and Social Sciences** (Law; Social Sciences); **Nursing** (Nursing); **Physical Education, Sports and Recreation** (Physical Education; Sports)

Main Language(s) of Instruction: Spanish

Degrees and Diplomas: *Licenciatura*; *Maestría*: **Clinical Psychology; Nursing; Psychiatry and Mental Health.**

MESOAMERICAN UNIVERSITY

Universidad Mesoaméricana

40 Calle 10-01, Zona 8, Guatemala City
Tel: +502 2413-8000
EMail: umesecgen@umes.edu.gt
Website: http://www.umes.edu.gt

Rector: Félix Javier Serrano Ursúa EMail: secrec@umes.edu.gt

Vicerrectora: Ana Cristina Estrada Quintero

Faculty
Humanities and Social Sciences (Educational Administration; Educational Sciences; Pedagogy; Philosophy; Theology); **Social Communication** (Advertising and Publicity; Cinema and Television; Graphic Design; Radio and Television Broadcasting)

Department
Economics (Accountancy; Business Administration); **Engineering** (Computer Engineering); **Law and Social Sciences** (Law; Social Sciences)

History: Founded 2000.

Academic Year: January to December

Admission Requirements: Secondary school certificate, entrance examination

Main Language(s) of Instruction: Spanish

Degrees and Diplomas: *Licenciatura*; *Maestría*: **Business Administration; Finance; Marketing; Production Engineering.**

Last Updated: 09/03/16

AMATITLÁN BRANCH

SEDE AMATITLÁN

Calle "C", No.106 Colonia Lupita, Amatitlán
Website: http://umes.escuelaupa.edu.gt/carreras-2015/

Programme
Business Administration (Business Administration); **Educational Management** (Educational Administration); **Pedagogy and Educational Sciences** (Educational Sciences; Pedagogy); **Public Accountancy** (Accountancy)

History: Founded 2010.

Main Language(s) of Instruction: Spanish

Degrees and Diplomas: *Licenciatura*

QUEZALTENANGO BRANCH

SEDE QUEZALTENANGO

3a Calle, Quezaltenango
Website: http://www.mesoamericana.edu.gt/?post_type=team

Faculty
Architecture (Advertising and Publicity; Architecture; Graphic Design); **Economics** (Advertising and Publicity; Business Administration; International Business; Marketing); **Engineering** (Civil Engineering; Computer Engineering; Electronic Engineering; Telecommunications Engineering); **Law** (Law); **Medicine** (Medicine; Surgery); **Odontology** (Dentistry)

Department
Pedagogy (Educational Psychology; Teacher Training); **Social Communication** (Cinema and Television; Communication Studies)

History: Founded 2006.

Main Language(s) of Instruction: Spanish

Degrees and Diplomas: *Licenciatura*; *Maestría*: **Economics; Pedagogy.**

PANAMERICAN UNIVERSITY

Universidad Panamericana

Diagonal 34, 31-43 zona 16, Ciudad de Guatemala

EMail: info@upana.edu.gt

Website: http://www.upana.edu.gt

Rector: Mynor Augusto Herrera Lemus

Vicerrectora: Alba Aracely Rodríguez de González

Faculty

Applied Sciences (Engineering); **Communication Studies** (Communication Studies); **Economics** (Accountancy; Business Administration; Business and Commerce; Economics; Marketing); **Education** (Education; Educational Administration; Educational and Student Counselling; Social Work; Teacher Training); **Law and Justice** (Law; Social Sciences); **Medicine and Health Sciences** (Nursing); **Psychology** (Clinical Psychology; Educational Psychology; Industrial and Organizational Psychology); **Social Sciences** (Social Sciences); **Theology** (Pastoral Studies; Theology)

Further Information: Also 106 branches nationwide

History: Founded 1998.

Main Language(s) of Instruction: Spanish

Degrees and Diplomas: *Licenciatura*; *Maestría*: **Business Administration; Communication Studies; Educational Administration; Finance; Law; Management; Psychology; Theology.** *Doctorado*: **Law.**

Student Services: Library

Last Updated: 18/03/16

RAFAEL LANDÍVAR UNIVERSITY

Universidad Rafael Landívar

Vista Hermosa 111, Zona 16, Apartado Postal 39 C, Guatemala City 01016

Tel: +502(2) 426-2626

EMail: info@url.edu.gt

Website: http://principal.url.edu.gt/

Rector: Eduardo Valdés Barría

Faculty

Agricultural and Environmental Sciences (Agricultural Engineering; Agriculture; Environmental Engineering; Environmental Studies); **Architecture and Design** (Architecture; Design; Graphic Design; Industrial Design); **Economics and Business Administration** (Business Administration; Economics; Hotel Management; Marketing; Tourism); **Engineering** (Chemical Engineering; Civil Engineering; Computer Engineering; Engineering; Mechanical Engineering); **Health Sciences** (Medicine; Nutrition; Respiratory Therapy); **Humanities** (Arts and Humanities; Education; Literature; Philosophy; Psychology); **Law and Social Sciences** (Law; Social Sciences); **Political and Social Sciences** (International Relations; Political Sciences; Social Sciences); **Theology** (Theology)

Campus

Huehuetenango *(San Roque González de Santa Cruz)* (Accountancy; Business Administration; Pedagogy; Psychology); **La Verapaz** *(San Pedro Claver)* (Bilingual and Bicultural Education; Business Administration; Civil Engineering; Law; Nursing; Social Sciences); **Quetzaltenango** (Accountancy; Agronomy; Architecture; Business Administration; Hotel Management); **Quiché** *(P. Cesar Augusto Jerez García)* (Business Administration; Mathematics Education); **Zacapa** *(San Luis Gonzaga)* (Business Administration; Horticulture)

History: Founded 1961, a private Catholic institution recognized by the State. Acquired status of independent University 1966.

Main Language(s) of Instruction: Spanish

Degrees and Diplomas: *Licenciatura*; *Maestría*: **Administration; Architecture; Business Administration; Commercial Law; Constitutional Law; Criminal Law; Design; Forestry; International Relations; Literature; Marketing; Philosophy; Public Health; Tropical Agriculture.**

Publications: Boletín de Lingüística; Revista Cultura de Guatemala; Revista Estudios Sociales

Last Updated: 11/03/16

ESCUINTLA BRANCH

SEDE ESCUINTLA

Escuela Nacional para Niñas 15 de septiembre, Escuintla 05001, Escuintla

Tel: +(502)7889-2429

Website: http://principal.url.edu.gt/index.php/2014-02-26-10-03-40/escuintla

Director: Rodolfo Rubio Pérez

Faculty

Agriculture and Environmental Studies (Agriculture; Tropical Agriculture); **Economics and Business Studies** (Business Administration); **Health Sciences** (Nursing); **Humanities** (Industrial and Organizational Psychology); **Political and Social Sciences** (Social Work)

History: Founded 1990.

Main Language(s) of Instruction: Spanish

Degrees and Diplomas: *Licenciatura*

JUTIAPA BRANCH

SEDE JUTIAPA

1a. Ave. 5-35 zona 1, barrio central Frente al Restaurante la fonda, 1 ave. 7, Jutiapa

Website: http://principal.url.edu.gt/index.php/campusysedes/jutiapa

Director: Juan Carlos Pereira Quan

Faculty

Agriculture and Environmental Studies (Agriculture); **Economics and Business Administration** (Business Administration); **Health Sciences** (Nursing); **Humanities** (Teacher Training); **Political and Social Sciences** (Social Work)

History: Founded 1997.

Main Language(s) of Instruction: Spanish

Degrees and Diplomas: *Licenciatura*

LA ANTIGUA GUATEMALA BRANCH

SEDE LA ANTIGUA GUATEMALA

Pasaje Rubio No. 1 Carretera a San Bartolomé Becerra, Antigua Guatemala

EMail: antiguasede@url.edu.gt

Website: http://principal.url.edu.gt/index.php/2014-02-26-10-03-40/antiguaguatemala

Director: Jorge Mario Carranza Corzo

Programme

Business Administration (Business Administration); **Clinical Psychology** (Clinical Psychology); **Teacher Training** (Teacher Training)

History: Founded 1968.

Main Language(s) of Instruction: Spanish

Degrees and Diplomas: *Licenciatura*

RURAL UNIVERSITY OF GUATEMALA

Universidad Rural de Guatemala

7 Calle 6-49 Zona 2, Guatemala City

Tel: +502 2254-7311

Fax: +502 2254-1215

EMail: info_urural@gua.net

Website: http://www.urural.edu.gt

Rector: Fidel Reyes Lee EMail: rector@urural.edu.gt

Faculty

Economics (Accountancy; Administration; Economics; Political Sciences); **Educational Sciences** (Educational Administration;

Physical Education; Preschool Education; Primary Education; Psychology; Special Education; Teacher Training); **Law and Social Sciences** (Law; Notary Studies; Social Sciences); **Natural and Environmental Sciences** (Agricultural Engineering; Environmental Engineering; Forestry; Industrial Engineering; Natural Resources)

History: Founded 1995.

Main Language(s) of Instruction: Spanish

Degrees and Diplomas: *Licenciatura*; *Maestría*: **Economics; Human Rights; Law; Political Sciences; Social Sciences.** *Doctorado*: **Human Rights.**

Last Updated: 02/03/16

SAN PABLO OF GUATEMALA UNIVERSITY

Universidad San Pablo de Guatemala

4ta. Calle. 23-03 zona 14, Ciudad de Guatemala

Tel: +502 4769-1181

EMail: info@uspg.edu.gt

Website: https://uspg.edu.gt

Rector: Harold Caballeros L

Faculty

Business Studies (Architecture; Business Administration; Computer Science; Graphic Design; Industrial and Organizational Psychology; Industrial Engineering; Marketing; Photography); **Humanities** (Education; Theology); **Law and Justice** (Law)

Campus

Escuintla (Architecture; Business Administration; Computer Science; Graphic Design; Industrial and Organizational Psychology; Law; Marketing; Photography)

History: Founded 2006.

Main Language(s) of Instruction: Spanish

Degrees and Diplomas: *Licenciatura*; *Maestría*: **Business Administration; Civil Law; Fiscal Law; Justice Administration; Leadership.** *Doctorado*: **Leadership.**

Last Updated: 18/03/16

UNIVERSITY OF THE ISTHMUS

Universidad del Istmo (UNIS)

7a. Avenida 3-67, Zona 13, Guatemala City 01013

Tel: +502 2429-1400

Fax: +502 2475-3526

EMail: unis@unis.edu.gt

Website: http://www.unis.edu.gt

Rector: Manuel Angel Pérez Lara

Vicerrectora Académica: Linda Yolanda Paz Quezada

Faculty

Architecture and Design (Architecture; Fashion Design; Graphic Design; Interior Design); **Communication** (Communication Studies; Journalism); **Economics and Business Administration** (Administration; Business Administration; Economics); **Education** (Clinical Psychology; Educational Psychology); **Engineering** (Computer Engineering; Engineering; Industrial Engineering; Telecommunications Engineering); **Law** (Law)

School

Business (Business Administration)

History: Founded 1997.

Academic Year: January to November

Main Language(s) of Instruction: Spanish

Degrees and Diplomas: *Licenciatura*; *Maestría*: **Architecture; Biology; Education; Ethics; Graphic Design.**

Student Services: Academic Counselling, Facilities for disabled people, Social Counselling

Publications: News Bulletin

Last Updated: 25/02/16

UNIVERSITY OF THE VALLEY OF GUATEMALA

Universidad del Valle de Guatemala

18 Avenida 11-95, Zona 15, Vista Hermosa III, Guatemala City 01015

Tel: +502 (2) 364-0336

EMail: info@uvg.edu.gt; info1@uvg.gt

Website: http://www.uvg.edu.gt

Rector: Roberto Moreno Godoy (2001-)
EMail: rmoreno@uvg.edu.gt

Secretaria General: Victoria Eugenia Rosales
Tel: +502(2) 364-0336, Ext. 458 EMail: erosales@uvg.edu.gt

International Relations: Mónica de Andrade
Tel: +502(2) 364-0340 EMail: mandrade@uvg.edu.gt

Faculty

Education (Education; Educational Psychology; Health Education; Music Education; Teacher Training); **Engineering** (Agricultural Engineering; Chemical Engineering; Civil Engineering; Computer Engineering; Electronic Engineering; Food Technology; Forestry; Industrial Engineering; Mechanical Engineering); **Science and Humanities** (Arts and Humanities; Biochemistry; Biology; Biotechnology; Chemistry; Environmental Studies; Literature; Mathematics; Microbiology; Natural Sciences; Nutrition; Physics); **Social Sciences** (Anthropology; Archaeology; History; Psychology; Social Sciences; Sociology)

Campus

Altiplano (Agriculture; Business Administration; Computer Science; Education; Educational Psychology; Forestry); **Sur** (Agricultural Engineering; Education; Industrial Engineering)

History: Founded 1961 as a private institution under the patronage of the Asociación del Colegio Americano de Guatemala. Formally recognized 1966.

Academic Year: January to November (January-May; June-July; August-November)

Admission Requirements: Secondary school certificate (bachillerato) or foreign equivalent, and entrance examination

Main Language(s) of Instruction: Spanish

Degrees and Diplomas: *Licenciatura*; *Maestría*: **Business Administration; Cosmetology; Curriculum; Economics; Educational Administration; Educational Technology; Environmental Engineering; Epidemiology; Finance; Food Technology; Management; Neurological Therapy; Pharmacy; Psychiatry and Mental Health.** *Doctorado*: **Psychology.** Also, Teaching qualifications, 4 yrs

Student Services: Library

Publications: Revista Universidad del Valle de Guatemala

Last Updated: 23/03/16

UNIVERSITY OF THE WEST

Universidad de Occidente

Avenida Las Américas 10a calle 9-84 Z. 9, Quetzaltenango

Tel: +502 7763-0983

EMail: info@udeo.edu.gt

Website: http://udeo.edu.gt

Rector: Ottavio Benfatto Buggin

Faculty

Architecture (Architecture; Graphic Design); **Economics** (Accountancy; Business Administration); **Educational Sciences** (Educational Sciences; Pedagogy); **Engineering** (Computer Engineering; Electronic Engineering; Industrial Engineering; Telecommunications Engineering); **Law and Social Sciences** (Law; Social Sciences)

History: Founded 2010.

Main Language(s) of Instruction: Spanish

Degrees and Diplomas: *Licenciatura*; *Maestría*: **Criminal Law.** *Doctorado*: **Economics; Law; Political Sciences; Social Sciences.**

Last Updated: 03/03/16

Guinea

STRUCTURE OF HIGHER EDUCATION SYSTEM

Description:

Higher education is provided by public and private universities and institutes. Higher education institutions are under the responsibility of the Ministère de l'Enseignement supérieur et de la Recherche scientifique.

Stages of studies:

University level first stage: *Licence*
The Licence is awarded after three years' study.

University level second stage: *Master*
A further two years beyond the Licence lead to the Master.

University level third stage: *DEA*
This is the third cycle of higher education. Entry to the course is based on the Master. Students must submit a thesis.

ADMISSION TO HIGHER EDUCATION

Admission to university-level studies:

Name of secondary school credential required: Baccalauréat

For entry to: Universities
Admission requirements: Concours d'Entrée for universities

NATIONAL BODIES

Ministère de l'Enseignement supérieur et de la Recherche scientifique (Ministry of Higher Education and Scientific Research)
Minister: Abdoulaye Balde Yero
Conakry

Data for academic year: 2012-2013
Source: IAU from Base Curie, Ministère des Affaires étrangères et européennes, France, and documentation, 2012. Bodies 2016.

INSTITUTIONS

PUBLIC INSTITUTIONS

GAMAL ABDEL NASSER UNIVERSITY OF CONAKRY

Université Gamal Abdel Nasser de Conakry (UGANC)
BP 1147, Conakry
Tel: +224 46-46-89
Fax: +224 46-48-08

Recteur: Doussou Lansana Traoré (2012-)

Secrétaire Général: Mamady Kéita

Vice-recteur chargé des Etudes: Boubacar Sylla

Vice-recteur chargé de la Recherche: Youssouf Bah

Faculty
Medicine, Pharmacy, Dentistry and Stomatology (Biochemistry; Dentistry; Medicine; Paediatrics; Pharmacy; Public Health; Stomatology); **Science** (Biochemistry; Biology; Chemistry; Energy Engineering; Mathematics; Microbiology; Natural Sciences; Physics; Physiology; Zoology)

Institute
Polytechnic (Chemical Engineering; Civil Engineering; Electrical Engineering; Engineering; Food Technology; Technology; Telecommunications Engineering; Telecommunications Services)

Centre
Applied Technology (Technology); **Computer Science** (Computer Science); **Economics** (Economics); **Environmental Studies and Research** (Environmental Studies)

Further Information: Also 2 University Hospitals

History: Founded 1962 as Institut Polytechnique, became University 1984. Acquired present status 1989. Previously known as Université de Conakry. A State institution under the supervision of the Ministry of Education.

Academic Year: September to June (September-January; February-June)

Admission Requirements: Secondary school certificate (baccalauréat) and competitive entrance examination

Main Language(s) of Instruction: French

Accrediting Agency: Ministère de l'Enseignement Supérieur et de la Recherche Scientifique

Degrees and Diplomas: *Licence*; *Master*; *Doctorat*: **Medicine; Pharmacy.**

Publications: Annales de l'Université; Bulletin de la Recherche; Guinée Médicale

Publishing House: Service des Editions Universitaires

Last Updated: 31/08/12

GÉNÉRAL LANSANA CONTÉ UNIVERSITY OF SONFONIA

Université Général Lansana Conté de Sonfonia (UGLC-SC)

030 BP 970, Sonfonia, Ratoma, Conakry
Tel: +224 21-83-09
EMail: scolarite@uglc-sonfonia.org
Website: http://www.uglc-sonfonia.org/web/

Recteur: Mamadi Kourouma (2008-) EMail: k.mamadi@yahoo.fr

Vice-recteur chargé des Etudes: Aboubacar Touré (2011-)

Secrétaire général: Foromo Listher Haba (2011-)

Vice-recteur chargé de la Recherche: Magan Kéita (2011-)

Faculty

Arts and Linguistics *(FLSL)* (Arts and Humanities; Linguistics); **Economics and Management** *(FSEG)* (Economics; Management); **Law and Political Sciences** *(FSJP)* (Law; Political Sciences); **Social Sciences** (Social Sciences)

School

Tourism and Hotel Management (Hotel and Restaurant; Hotel Management; Tourism)

History: Founded 2005 as Université des Sciences Humaines, Juridiques et Economiques de Sonfonia–Conakry. Acquired present title 2006.

Main Language(s) of Instruction: French

Accrediting Agency: Ministère de l'Enseignement Supérieur et de la Recherche Scientifique

Degrees and Diplomas: *Licence*; *Master*. Also Diplôme d'Etudes Approfondies (DEA) and Diplôme d'Etudes Supérieures Spécialisées (DESS).

Student Services: Cultural Activities, Social Counselling, Sports Facilities

Last Updated: 30/08/12

HIGHER INSTITUTE FOR DISTANCE EDUCATION

Institut supérieur de Formation à Distance (ISFAD)

BP 1961, Conakry
Tel: +224 60 28 13 96 +224 64 37 30 32
EMail: isfad_gn-dgae@yahoo.fr
Website: http://www.isfadguinee.org/

Directeur général: Mamadou Dian Gongörè Diallo
Tel: +224 62 90 65 18
EMail: madiangongore@isfadguinee.org; madiangongore@yahoo.fr

Sécrétaire Générale: Marie Rose Bangoura

Directeur général adjoint des Etudes: N'Famara Camara
Tel: +224 67 59 47 59

Department

Economics and Management (Economics; Management); **Higher Officers in Community Development** (Development Studies; Social and Community Services; Social Sciences; Urban Studies); **Law** (Law)

History: Founded 2003.

Admission Requirements: School leaving certificate

Fees: (GNF): 200,000.00 per year (c. 25 Euros)

Main Language(s) of Instruction: French

Accrediting Agency: Ministère de ÍEnseignement supérieur et de la Recherche scientifique

Degrees and Diplomas: *Licence*: **Development Studies; Economics; Law.**

Academic Staff *2011-2012*	MEN	WOMEN	TOTAL
FULL-TIME	19	3	**22**
PART-TIME	10	–	**10**
STAFF WITH DOCTORATE			
FULL-TIME	3	–	**3**
Student Numbers *2011-2012*			
All (Foreign included)	4,938	986	**5,924**
FOREIGN ONLY	251	107	**358**

Distance students, 5,924.

Last Updated: 26/04/12

HIGHER INSTITUTE OF ARCHITECTURE AND TOWN PLANNING OF CONAKRY

Institut supérieur d'Architecture et d'Urbanisme de Conakry (ISAU)

BP 2201, Conakry

Directeur général: Mamady Touré

Secrétaire général: Gonona Traoré

Directeur Général adjoint chargé de la Recherche: Mamadou Djouldé Sow

Directeur général adjoint chargé des Etudes: Benoit Curtis

Department

Architecture (Architecture); **Town Planning** (Town Planning)

History: Founded 2004.

Main Language(s) of Instruction: French

Last Updated: 30/08/12

HIGHER INSTITUTE OF EDUCATIONAL SCIENCES OF GUINEA/LAMBANDJI

Institut supérieur des Sciences de l'Education de Guinée/Lambandji (ISSEG)

BP 795, Conakry
Tel: +224 60 25 61 31
EMail: info@isseg-gn.org
Website: http://www.isseg-gn.org/index.php

Directeur général: Mohamed Lamine Bayo

Secrétaire Général: Faya Traoré

Directeur Général adjoint chargé de la Recherche: Albert Balamou

Directeur Général adjoint chargé des Etudes: Djemba Barry

Department

Educational Administration (Educational Administration); **Pedagogy and Educational Sciences** *(DEPSE)* (Educational Sciences; Pedagogy); **Teacher Training I** *(DFPEN/CPMF/IEE)* (Educational Research; Primary Education; Teacher Training); **Teacher Training II** *(DFPCL/APES/IES)* (Educational Sciences; Secondary Education; Teacher Training)

History: Founded 1991. Formerly Ecole Normale Supérieure de Manéah. Acquired present status and title 2003.

Academic Year: October to July

Admission Requirements: University degree (Maîtrise) and entrance examination. Professional experience may also be required in some sections.

Main Language(s) of Instruction: French

Degrees and Diplomas: *Master*. Certificate in Teacher Training

Student Services: Canteen, Health Services, Sports Facilities
Publications: Faisceau
Last Updated: 31/08/12

HIGHER INSTITUTE OF FINE ARTS OF GUINEA

Institut supérieur des Arts de Guinée (ISAG)
Dubréka
Tel: +224 65 53 20 11

Directeur général: Aly Badara Sylla (2011-)

Directeur Général adjoint chargé des Etudes: Edouard Binet Bangoura (2011-)

Secrétaire Général: Souleymane Kéita

Directeur Général adjoint chargé de la Recherche: Siba Alain Koukémou

Department
Cinema and Audio-Visual Arts (Cinema and Television); **Drama** (Theatre); **Fine Arts** (Fine Arts); **Music and Musicology** (Music; Musicology)

History: Founded 2004.

Main Language(s) of Instruction: French

Degrees and Diplomas: *Licence*; *Master*
Last Updated: 31/08/12

HIGHER INSTITUTE OF INFORMATION AND COMMUNICATION OF KOUNTIA

Institut supérieur de l'Information et de la Communication de Kountia (ISIC)
BP 954, Kountia, Conakry
Tel: +224 60 52 69 20

Directeur général: Bangaly Camara

Directeur Général adjoint chargé de la Recherche: Augustin Gnimassou

Secrétaire général: Saâ Leno

Directeur général adjoint chargé des Etudes: Faya Pascal Ifono

Department
Audio Visual Communication (Media Studies); **Communication and Information Technology** (Communication Studies; Information Technology); **Journalism** (Journalism)

History: Founded 2006.

Main Language(s) of Instruction: French

Degrees and Diplomas: *Licence*. Also Maîtrise.
Last Updated: 30/08/12

HIGHER INSTITUTE OF MINING AND GEOLOGY OF BOKÉ

Institut supérieur des Mines et Géologie de Boké (ISMGB)
BP 84, Boké
Tel: +224 30 21 83 09

Directeur général: Karinka Diawara (2011-)

Directeur Général adjoint chargé des Etudes: Hassane Thioye

Secrétaire Général: Jean Delacroix Camara

Directeur Général adjoint chargé de la Recherche: Lansana Katia Camara

Department
Geology (Geology); **Metallurgical Engineering** (Metallurgical Engineering); **Mining Engineering** (Mining Engineering); **Technology** (Technology)

History: Founded 1991.

Academic Year: October to June

Main Language(s) of Instruction: French

Degrees and Diplomas: *Master*
Last Updated: 31/08/12

HIGHER INSTITUTE OF SCIENCE AND VETERINARY MEDICINE OF DALABA

Institut supérieur des Sciences et de Médecine vétérinaire de Dalaba (ISSMV)
BP 2201, Dalaba

Directeur Général: Youssouf Sidimé

Directeur Général adjoint chargé des Etudes: Morlaye Kindia Sylla

Directeur Général adjoint chargé de la Recherche: Souleymane Sy Savané

Secrétaire Général: Mohamed Keira

Department
Animal Husbandry and Veterinary Science Production Control (Animal Husbandry; Veterinary Science); **Basic Sciences** (Veterinary Science); **Epidemiology, Infectious Diseases and Parasitology** (Epidemiology; Parasitology); **Therapeutic Sciences** (Veterinary Science)

History: Founded 2004.

Main Language(s) of Instruction: French

Degrees and Diplomas: *Licence*; *Master*
Last Updated: 31/08/12

HIGHER INSTITUTE OF TECHNOLOGY OF MAMOU

Institut supérieur de Technologie de Mamou (IST)
BP 84, Mamou

Directeur général: Cellou Kanté

Secrétaire général: Mafory Bangoura

Directeur Général adjoint chargé de la Recherche: Mamadou Foulah Barry

Directeur général adjoint chargé des Etudes: Saâ Poindo Tonguino

Department
Basic Sciences (Mathematics and Computer Science; Natural Sciences); **Energy Engineering** (Energy Engineering); **Instrumentation** (Instrument Making); **Technology** (Technology)

History: Founded 2004.

Main Language(s) of Instruction: French
Last Updated: 30/08/12

KANKAN UNIVERSITY

Université Julius Nyerere de Kankan (UJNK)
BP 209, Kankan
Tel: +224 68-22-09
EMail: administrateur@ujnk.org; recust_universitekankan@yahoo.fr
Website: http://www.ujnk.org/

Recteur: Idrissa Magassouba (2011-)
Tel: +224 68-22-73-09 EMail: administrateur@ujnk.org

Secrétaire Général: Kaba Sidibe
Tel: +224 62-47-79-13; +224 67-70-41-81
EMail: sidibakaba2004@yahoo.fr

Chef de service Relations Extérieures: Mamoudou Dioubate
Tel: +224 65-89-23-51
EMail: dioubatemamoudou@yahoo.fr; recust_universitekankan@yahoo.fr

Vice-Recteur chargé des Etudes: Kabinè Oulare
Tel: +224 64-51-63-95 EMail: koulare2001@yahoo.fr

Vice Director of External Relations in charge of Cooperation: Idrissa Feindouno
Tel: +224 62-43-20-45; +224 65-59-16-18
EMail: feindriss@gmail.com

Vice-Recteur chargé de la Recherche: Mamadou Samba Barry
Tel: +224 68-22-73-09 EMail: barry_mamadous@yahoo.fr

Secrétaire Général: Kaba Sidibe
Tel: +224 62-47-79-13; +224 67-70-41-81
EMail: sidibekaba2004@yahoo.fr

Faculty
Language Sciences (Arabic; English; French; Linguistics; Literature); **Management and Economics** (Administration; Business Administration; Economics; Finance; Management); **Natural Sciences** (Biology; Chemistry; Geology; Mathematics; Physics); **Social Sciences** (Geography; History; Philosophy; Sociology)

School
Information Sciences (Archiving; Documentation Techniques; Library Science); **Medicine, Pharmacy, Odonto-Stomatology** (Biomedicine; Dentistry; Forensic Medicine and Dentistry; Health Sciences; Medical Parasitology; Medicine; Ophthalmology; Optometry; Pharmacology; Rheumatology; Stomatology; Tropical Medicine)

History: Founded 1963 as school, became Institut polytechnique 1967 and acquired present status and title 1989. A State institution under the supervision of the Ministry of Education.

Academic Year: October to June (October-December; January-March; April-June)

Admission Requirements: Secondary School Certificate (baccalauréat) and competitive entrance examination

Fees: (GNF): 1,500,000 (3,000,000 for non-Guineans)

Main Language(s) of Instruction: French

Degrees and Diplomas: *Licence*: **Biology; Chemistry; Geography; History; Philosophy; Physics; Sociology.** *Master*: **Agronomy; Biology; Chemistry; Geography; History; Philosophy; Physics; Sociology.**

Student Services: Academic Counselling, Careers Guidance, Cultural Activities, Health Services, Language Laboratory, Social Counselling, Sports Facilities

Publications: Revue Scientifique de l'Université Julius Nyéréré de Kankan (RESUK)

Academic Staff *2012*	MEN	WOMEN	**TOTAL**
FULL-TIME	264	17	**281**
PART-TIME	33	4	**37**
STAFF WITH DOCTORATE			
FULL-TIME	27	–	**27**
Student Numbers *2012*			
All (Foreign included)	6,319	1,205	**7,524**

UNIVERSITY CENTRE OF LABÉ

Centre Universitaire de Labé (CULBE)
BP 210-Labe, Labe
Tel: +224 622 90 65 18
EMail: driculbe@gmail.com

Directeur général: Mamadou Dian Gongore Diallo (2013-)
EMail: mdgongore@gmail.com

Secrétaire général: Momoyah Sylla
EMail: syllamomoyah@yahoo.fr

International Relations: Fatoumata Diallo, Head of External Relations and Cooperation EMail: malickdiao.912@gmail.com

Faculty
Administration and Management (Business and Commerce; Economics; Management; Public Administration); **Languages and Humanities** (Arabic; English; Fine Arts; Sociology); **Science** (Biology; Computer Science; Mathematics)

History: Founded in 2000 under a decentralized policy of the government in order to supplement the two largest universities in the country. First students accepted in 2001. This policy was supposed to help students access to universities close to their hometowns. The University Centre of Labe was part of Gamal Abdel Nasser University of Conakry. Gained Independence in 2008. Located about 400km from Conakry.

Academic Year: October to June

Admission Requirements: Attestation d'admission au Baccalauréat unique

Fees: 95,000, 1st year; 100,000, 2nd year; 105,000, 3rd year (Guinea Franc)

Main Language(s) of Instruction: French

Accrediting Agency: Ministère de l'Enseignement Supérieur et de la Recherche Scientifique

Degrees and Diplomas: *Licence*: **Arabic; Computer Science; Economics; English; Fine Arts; Management; Mathematics; Public Administration; Sociology.** Licence professionnelle in 4 years in Biology.

Student Services: Cultural Activities, Sports Facilities

Academic Staff *2014-2015*	**TOTAL**
FULL-TIME	**146**
PART-TIME	**62**
STAFF WITH DOCTORATE	
FULL-TIME	**8**
Student Numbers *2014-2015*	
All (Foreign included)	**2,500**

Last Updated: 12/02/15

UNIVERSITY CENTRE OF N'ZÉRÉKORÉ

Centre Universitaire de N'Zérékoré
N'Zérékoré
Tel: +224 60 36 58 73

Directeur général: Binko Mamady Touré (2011-)

Secrétaire général: Ousmane Wouro Diallo

Directeur adjoint chargé de la Recherche: Siba Alain Koulémou

Directeur général adjoint chargé des Etudes: Namory Bérété

Faculty
Environmental Sciences (Environmental Studies; Forestry); **Science and Technology** (Natural Sciences; Technology)

History: Founded 2001.

Main Language(s) of Instruction: French

Accrediting Agency: Ministère de l'Enseignement Supérieur et de la Recherche Scientifique

Degrees and Diplomas: *Licence*

Last Updated: 29/08/12

VALÉRY GISCARD D'ESTAING HIGHER INSTITUTE OF AGRONOMY AND VETERINARY MEDICINE OF FARANAH

Institut supérieur agronomique et vétérinaire Valéry Giscard d'Estaing de Faranah (ISAV)
BP 131, Faranah
Tel: +224(60) 58-15-00

Directeur général: Sara Baïlo Diallo (2007-)
Tel: +224(64) 65-25-94 +224(60) 58-15-00
EMail: diallosbailo@yahoo.fr

Directeur Général adjoint chargé de la Recherche: Adrien Faya Ouendouno

Directeur général adjoint chargé des Etudes: Gadapaye Kalivogui Tel: +224(62) 13-78-86 +224(66) 25-75-12

Secrétaire Général: Joseph Béavogui

International Relations: Mamadou Dian Diallo, Chef du Service des Relations extérieures et de la Coopération
Tel: +224(62) 02-60-58 EMail: mdiandiallo@yahoo.fr

Department
Agricultural Economics (Agricultural Economics); **Agricultural Engineering** (Agricultural Engineering); **Agriculture** (Agricultural Economics; Agriculture); **Agriculture Extension** (Agricultural Economics; Agriculture); **Agroforestry** (Agriculture; Forestry); **Animal Sciences** (Animal Husbandry; Cattle Breeding; Veterinary Science); **Forestry Environment** (Forestry; Water Science)

History: Founded 1978. Acquired present status and title 1991.

Academic Year: April to December.

Admission Requirements: Undergraduate: Baccalauréat or equivalent; Postgraduate: Licence.

Main Language(s) of Instruction: French

Accrediting Agency: Ministère de l'Agriculture; Ministère de l'Enseignement Supérieur et de la Recherche Scientifique

Degrees and Diplomas: *Licence*; *Master*

Student Services: Academic Counselling, Cultural Activities, Foreign Studies Centre, Health Services, Language Laboratory, Social Counselling, Sports Facilities

Publications: Agrovision

Publishing House: Imprimerie de l'Education nationale, Conakry (IDEC)

Academic Staff *2011-2012*	MEN	WOMEN	**TOTAL**
FULL-TIME	121	5	**126**
PART-TIME	3	–	**3**
STAFF WITH DOCTORATE			
FULL-TIME	16	–	**16**
Student Numbers *2011-2012*			
All (Foreign included)	3,303	721	**4,024**
FOREIGN ONLY	55	3	**58**

Part-time students, 50.
Last Updated: 23/05/12

PRIVATE INSTITUTIONS

KOFI ANNAN UNIVERSITY OF GUINEA

Université Kofi Annan de Guinée (UKAG)
BP 1367, Conakry
Tel: +224 60 21 42 18
Website: http://www.univ-kag.org

Fondateur, Promoteur et PDG: Ousmane Kaba (1999-)

Recteur: Jean-Pierre Colin

Faculty
Computer Science (Computer Science); **Economics and Management** (Economics; Management); **Humanities** (Humanities and Social Science Education); **Law** (Law); **Medicine** (Medicine)

School
Engineering *(Polytechnique)* (Engineering)

Institute
Kofi Annan (Accountancy; Banking; Building Technologies; Business Administration; Civil Engineering; Communication Studies; Electrical and Electronic Engineering; Electrical Engineering; Insurance; Journalism; Management; Marketing; Mechanical Engineering; Mining Engineering; Secretarial Studies; Software Engineering; Transport and Communications)

History: Founded 1999.

Main Language(s) of Instruction: French

Accrediting Agency: Ministère de l'Enseignement Supérieur et de la Recherche Scientifique

Degrees and Diplomas: *Master*; *Doctorat*
Last Updated: 24/09/12

LA SOURCE UNIVERSITY

Université La Source (US)
BP 105, Conakry
Tel: +224 64 26 63 28
Fax: +224 62 09 77 98
EMail: info@universitelasource.org
Website: http://www.universitelasource.org

Fondateur: Sanoussy Kaba

Faculty
Economics and Management (Business Administration; Computer Science; Economics); **Law, Politics and Social Science** (International Relations; Law; Sociology); **Medical Science** (Medicine; Pharmacy)

History: Founded 2004. Acquired present status and title 2007.

Main Language(s) of Instruction: French

Accrediting Agency: Ministère de l'Enseignement Supérieur et de la Recherche Scientifique

Degrees and Diplomas: *Licence*; *Doctorat*
Last Updated: 25/09/12

MERCURE INTERNATIONAL UNIVERSITY

Université Mercure International (UMI)
BP 2838, Complexe Scolaire St. Georges, Taouyah, Conakry
Tel: +224 42 13 81
Fax: +224 41 38 11
EMail: secretariat@post-graduate-institute.com
Website: http://conakry.mercure-international.org/

Fondateur et Admistrateur Général: Georges Gandhi Faraguet Tounkara

Institute
Post Graduate (Economics; Management)

History: Founded 2005.

Main Language(s) of Instruction: French

Accrediting Agency: Ministère de l'Enseignement Supérieur et de la Recherche Scientifique

Degrees and Diplomas: *Master*; *Doctorat*
Last Updated: 25/09/12

Guinea-Bissau

STRUCTURE OF HIGHER EDUCATION SYSTEM

Description:

Guinea-Bissau opened its first public university in November 2003. Created by government decree in 1999, the Amilcar Cabral University admitted its first students in January 2004. The University, due to financial problems, had to come back under the tutoring of the Grupo Lusófona and became the Universidade lusófona de Guiné (ULG) in 2008. The Universidade Colinas de Boé, a private institution, opened in 2003.

Stages of studies:

University level first stage: *Licenciatura*

The first cycle of university studies leads to a Licenciatura awarded after four or five years' study (Medicine, Law).

ADMISSION TO HIGHER EDUCATION

Admission to university-level studies:

Name of secondary school credential required: High School Diploma

NATIONAL BODIES

Ministry of National Education

Minister: Odete Semedo
Bissau

Data for academic year: 2012-2013

Source: IAU from Guinea-Bissau EFA Profile 2012, UNESCO-Dakar, and UIS ISCED Mapping, 2012. Bodies 2016.

INSTITUTIONS

PRIVATE INSTITUTIONS

COLINAS UNIVERSITY OF BOÉ

Universidade Colinas de Boé (UCB)
CP 1340, Avenida 14 de Novembro, Entrada do Bairro de Hafia, Bissau
Tel: +245 677-2339
EMail: uco@rocketmail.com

Reitor: Fafali Koudawo EMail: fafali@eguitel.com

Programme
Accountancy and Management (Accountancy; Management); **Computer Engineering** (Computer Engineering); **Law** (Law); **Public Administration and Social Economy** (Economics; Public Administration); **Social Communication and Marketing** (Communication Studies; Marketing)

History: Founded 2003.

Academic Year: October to June

Accrediting Agency: Ministério da Educação (Ministry of Education)

Degrees and Diplomas: *Licenciatura*
Last Updated: 25/07/12

LUSOPHONE UNIVERSITY OF GUINEA

Universidade Lusófona da Guiné (ULG)
Caixia postal 659, Bairro D' Ajuda (2ª Fase), Bissau
Tel: +245 3256-066
Website: http://ulg.grupolusofona.pt

Reitor: Rui Jandi

Administrador Executivo: Montenegro Fiúza Tel: +245 20-59-70

Programme
Business Administration and Management (Accountancy; African Studies; Applied Mathematics; Business Administration; Commercial Law; Computer Science; Economics; English; French; Human Resources; Industrial and Organizational Psychology; International Business; Law; Leadership; Management; Marketing; Social Sciences; Statistics; Taxation); **Computer Engineering** (Computer Engineering); **Economics** (Accountancy; Applied Mathematics; Business Administration; Computer Science; Econometrics; Economic and Finance Policy; Economics; English; French; Human Resources; Industrial and Production Economics; International Business; Law; Management; Public Administration; Social Sciences; Statistics; Taxation); **Education** (Curriculum; Distance Education; Education; Educational Administration; Educational and Student Counselling; Educational Psychology; Educational Research; Educational Sciences; Educational Technology; International and Comparative Education; Pedagogy; Social Sciences;

Statistics; Teacher Trainers Education; Writing); **Human Resources** (Business Administration; Economics; Human Resources; Labour Law; Occupational Health; Social Sciences; Social Welfare); **Law** (Law); **Medicine** (Epidemiology; Hygiene; Laboratory Techniques; Medicine); **Organizational Communication and Journalism** (Advertising and Publicity; Business Administration; Communication Studies; Cultural Studies; English; French; Human Resources; Information Technology; Journalism; Linguistics; Marketing; Media Studies; Multimedia; Portuguese; Public Administration; Public Relations; Radio and Television Broadcasting; Writing); **Social Services** (Social and Community Services); **Sociology** (African Studies; Anthropology; Applied Mathematics; Computer Science; Demography and Population; Development Studies; Economic History; Educational Sciences; English; French; Geography (Human); Industrial and Organizational Psychology; Law; Linguistics; Rural Studies; Social and Preventive Medicine; Social Psychology; Social Sciences; Social Studies; Sociology; Statistics; Urban Studies)

History: Founded 1999. Former public institution, under the administration of the Universidade Lusófona de Humanidades e Tecnologias (Lisboa, Portugal) since 2008.

Academic Year: October to June

Main Language(s) of Instruction: Portuguese

Accrediting Agency: Ministério da Educação (Ministry of Education)

Degrees and Diplomas: *Licenciatura*

Last Updated: 25/07/12

Guyana

STRUCTURE OF HIGHER EDUCATION SYSTEM

Description:

Higher education in Guyana is provided by the University of Guyana and by specialized institutions of higher education: Technical Institutes, a College of Education, a School of Agriculture and a Management Training Institute. Resources come from government grants. The University is governed by the University Council and the Academic Board.

Stages of studies:

University level first stage: *Undergraduate studies*
The minimum entrance requirement for a Bachelor's degree is the Caribbean Examinations Council Secondary Education Certificate (general proficiency) or the General Certificate of Education 'O' level. Courses last three to four years depending on the subject.

University level second stage: *Graduate studies*
Graduate studies lead to the award of a Master's degree in Arts, Science or Social Sciences, following a minimum of one year of study, more often two. The University of Guyana also confers Graduate Diplomas in Education and Development Studies after two years' study.

ADMISSION TO HIGHER EDUCATION

Admission to university-level studies:

Name of secondary school credential required: Caribbean Secondary Education Certificate

Minimum score/requirement: Five CSEC Grades 1 to 3 at no more than 2 sittings; English and Mathematics are major subjects for entry to School of Education and Humanities, faculties of Health Sciences, Natural Sciences, Social Sciences and Technology.

For entry to: All institutions and programmes

RECOGNITION OF STUDIES

Quality assurance system:

NAC is the principal body in Guyana for conducting and advising on the accreditation and recognition of educational and training institutions, providers, programmes and awards, whether foreign or national and for the promotion of the quality and standards of education and training in Guyana.

Bodies dealing with recognition:

National Accreditation Council - NAC

109 Barima Avenue, Bel Air Park
Georgetown
Tel: +592 225-9526
EMail: info@nac.gov.gy
WWW: http://nac.gov.gy/

NATIONAL BODIES

Ministry of Education

Minister: Rupert Roopnaraine
21 Brickdam
Georgetown
Tel: +592 225-4422
WWW: http://www.education.gov.gy/

Role of national body: Education delivery; Development of policies for all levels of the education system in Guyana; Implementation of plans to achieve objectives affecting education delivery.

National Accreditation Council - NAC

Chairman: Vincent Alexander
109 Barima Avenue, Bel Air Park
Georgetown
Tel: +592 225-9526
EMail: info@nac.gov.gy
WWW: http://nac.gov.gy/

Role of national body: Responsible for conducting and advising on the accreditation and recognition of educational and training institutions, providers, programmes and awards, whether foreign or national and for the promotion of the quality and standards of education and training in Guyana.

Data for academic year: 2016-2017
Source: IAU from the websites of the Ministry of Education and NAC, 2016.

INSTITUTIONS

PUBLIC INSTITUTIONS

AMERICAN UNIVERSITY OF PEACE STUDIES

135 Sheriff & Fourth Sts., Campbellville, Georgetown
Tel: +592 231 1284
EMail: ceo@auops.org
Website: http://auops.org

Chief Executive Officer: Eton Simon

Programme

Human Resource Management (Human Resources; Management); **Peace and Conflict Studies** (Peace and Disarmament); **Professional Counselling** (Psychology); **Psychology** (Psychology); **Public Communication** (Communication Studies); **Strategic Project Management** (Management)

History: Founded 2002.

Main Language(s) of Instruction: English

Degrees and Diplomas: *Bachelor's Degree*; *Master's Degree*: **Clinical Psychology; Management; Peace and Disarmament; Psychology.**

Last Updated: 07/04/16

RAJIV GANDHI UNIVERSITY OF SCIENCE AND TECHNOLOGY

Sheriff Street Campus: 135 Sheriff Street, Campbellville, Georgetown
Tel: +592 227-1027
EMail: info@rgust.org
Website: http://rgust.org

Vice-Chancellor: Sherlock Peter Rawana

School

Arts and Sciences (Arts and Humanities; Natural Sciences); **Management Studies** (Management); **Medicine** (Medicine); **Nursing** (Nursing); **Pharmacy** (Pharmacy)

History: Founded 2004.

Main Language(s) of Instruction: English

Accrediting Agency: National Accreditation Council of Guyana

Degrees and Diplomas: *Bachelor's Degree*; *Master's Degree*

Last Updated: 08/04/16

TEXILA AMERICAN UNIVERSITY

Lot A, Goedverwagting, Sparendaam, East Coast Demerara
Tel: (+592) 2225224
EMail: enquiry@tauedu.org
Website: http://www.tauedu.org

President: S.P Saju Bhaskar

College

Medicine (Medicine); **Nursing** (Nursing)

School

Alternative Medicine (Alternative Medicine); **Behavioural Science** (Clinical Psychology; Psychology; Social Work); **Clinical Research** (Medicine); **Education** (Education); **Information Technology** (Information Technology); **Management** (Management); **Public Health** (Public Health)

History: Founded 2010.

Accrediting Agency: National Accreditation Council of Guyana

Degrees and Diplomas: *Bachelor's Degree*; *Master's Degree*: **Medicine.**

Last Updated: 07/04/16

UNIVERSITY OF GUYANA (UG)

PO Box 10-1110, Turkeyen, Greater Georgetown
Tel: +592 222-4184
Fax: +592 222-3596
EMail: registrar_ug@yahoo.com
Website: http://www.uog.edu.gy

Vice-Chancellor: Jacob Opadeyi EMail: vc@uog.edu.gy

Deputy Vice-Chancellor for Academic Affairs: Barbara Reynolds:

Faculty

Agriculture and Forestry (Agriculture; Animal Husbandry; Crop Production; Forestry; Soil Science); **Health Sciences** (Dentistry; Environmental Studies; Health Sciences; Medical Technology; Medicine; Nursing; Pharmacy; Radiology; Surgery); **Natural Sciences** (Biology; Chemistry; Computer Science; Environmental Studies; Mathematics; Physics; Statistics); **Social Sciences** (Accountancy; Banking; Communication Studies; Finance; Government; International Relations; Law; Management; Marketing; Public Administration; Social Sciences; Social Work; Sociology); **Technology** (Aeronautical and Aerospace Engineering; Agricultural Engineering; Architecture; Civil Engineering; Electrical Engineering; Engineering Management; Geological Engineering; Mechanical Engineering; Technology)

School
Earth and Environmental Sciences (Environmental Studies; Geography); **Education and Humanities** (Administration; Agriculture; Business Education; Economics; English; Fine Arts; French; Geography; History; Home Economics; Literacy Education; Literature; Mathematics; Modern Languages; Music; Preschool Education; Primary Education; Science Education; Social Studies; Spanish; Teacher Training; Technology Education; Theatre; Tourism; Writing); **Professional Development**

Institute
Distance and Continuing Education (Communication Studies; Criminology; Developmental Psychology; English; Hygiene; Industrial Management; International Relations; Management; Marketing; Mathematics; Nutrition; Occupational Health; Preschool Education; Primary Education; Public Relations; Secretarial Studies; Social Work; Sociology; Spanish)

Research Unit
Amerindian Studies (Amerindian Languages)

History: Founded and acquired present status 1963.

Academic Year: September to May (September-December; February-May)

Admission Requirements: Three subjects at the GCE Advanced Level plus two subjects at CXC General Proficiency/GCE Ordinary Level or two subjects at the GCE Advanced Level plus three subject at the CXC/CSEC General Proficiency/ GCE Ordinary Level in both case English and in some case Mathematics must be among the subjects obtained. A minimum of five CXC/CSEC General Proficiency (Grades I, II or III)/ five passes at GCE 'O' Level at ONE sitting, including English Language, the subject(s) required for the pursuit of the major, where applicable, and Mathematics for designated programmes. Or a minimum of 6 CXC/CSEC General Proficiency(Grades I, II or III)/ six passes at the GCE 'O' Level AT NOT MORE THAN TWO SITTINGS, including English Language, the subject(s) required for the pursuit of the major, where applicable, and Mathematics for designated programmes.

Fees: (Guyana Dollars): Local students: 127,000-500,000; Foreign students: 4,000-10,000 US$

Main Language(s) of Instruction: English

Degrees and Diplomas: *Bachelor's Degree*: **Agriculture; Architecture; Biology; Chemistry; Civil Engineering; Communication Arts; Computer Science; Economics; Education; Electrical Engineering; Environmental Studies; Fine Arts; Forestry; Geology; History; International Studies; Law; Management; Mathematics; Mechanical Engineering; Medicine; Mining Engineering; Nursing; Physics; Social Work; Sociology; Statistics; Surgery.** *Master's Degree*: **Biology; Chemistry; Economics; Education; Forestry; Geography; Gynaecology and Obstetrics; History; Paediatrics; Political Sciences.** *Graduate Diploma*: **Development Studies; Education; International Studies.**

Student Services: Academic Counselling, Canteen, Facilities for disabled people, Health Services, Social Counselling, Sports Facilities

Publications: Guyana Health Information Digest; Transition
Last Updated: 07/04/16

Haiti

STRUCTURE OF HIGHER EDUCATION SYSTEM

Description:

Higher education is provided by universities and other public and private institutions. Higher education institutions do not always fall under the responsibility of the MENPF: the University of Haiti is autonomous, some institutions fall under the responsibility of the Ministry of their field of activity, and other institutions are from foreign countries or international organisations. A bill on the modernisation of higher education was introduced in 2013 but was not adopted.

Stages of studies:

University level first stage:
First degree courses normally last for four to five years and lead to the award of the Licence or a professional title.
University level second stage:
A Maîtrise is conferred after two years' study beyond the Licence. In Medicine, the Diplôme de Docteur en Médecine is conferred after seven years' study, including periods of internship and practical training.

ADMISSION TO HIGHER EDUCATION

Admission to university-level studies:

Name of secondary school credential required: Baccalauréat

For entry to: All institutions/programmes

Admission requirements: Competitive entrance examination.

Foreign students admission:

Admission requirements: Foreign students must have completed secondary education and passed the competitive entrance examination.

Entry regulations: Residence permit.

RECOGNITION OF STUDIES

Bodies dealing with recognition:

Ministère de l'Education nationale et de la Formation professionnelle - MENFP (Ministry of National Education and Vocational Training)

5, Ave Jn-Paul
Port-au-Prince
Tel: +509 2913-0273
WWW: http://www.menfp.gouv.ht/

NATIONAL BODIES

Ministère de l'Education nationale et de la Formation professionnelle - MENFP (Ministry of National Education and Vocational Training)

Minister: Nesmy Manigat
5, Ave Jn-Paul
Port-au-Prince
Tel: +509 2913-0273
WWW: http://www.menfp.gouv.ht/

Data for academic year: 2015-2016
Source: IAU from the website of the Ministry of Education (MENPF), 2015.

INSTITUTIONS

PUBLIC INSTITUTIONS

INUKA UNIVERSITY

Université INUKA
Tabarre 43, Blvd 15 Octobre, Port-au-prince
Tel: +509 2944-0109
EMail: decanat@inuka.edu.ht
Website: http://www.inuka.edu.ht

Recteur: Antenor Gabaud

Faculty
Administration and Economics (Accountancy; Economics; Management); **Engineering and New Technologies** (Architecture; Civil Engineering; Computer Science; Electronic Engineering); **Religious Studies, Educational Sciences and Psychology** (Christian Religious Studies; Educational Sciences; Psychology; Religious Studies; Theology)

History: Founded 1988 as Institut universitaire Quisqueya-Amérique. Acquired present status and title 2015.

Degrees and Diplomas: *Licence*; *Maîtrise*: **Business Computing; Finance; Management.**
Last Updated: 23/03/16

PUBLIC UNIVERSITY OF THE ARTIBONITE

Université Publique de l'Artibonite
45 rue Chrysostome Humbert, Les Gonaïves
Tel: +509 4789-2929
EMail: upag2007@yahoo.fr

Recteur: Wildanaud Auguste

Programme
Accountancy (Accountancy); **Educational Sciences** (Educational Sciences); **Management** (Management); **Nursing** (Nursing)

History: Founded 2007.

Degrees and Diplomas: *Licence*
Last Updated: 25/03/16

STATE UNIVERSITY OF HAÏTI

Université d'Etat d'Haïti (UEH)
BP 2279, 21, Rue Rivière, Port-au-Prince HT 6115
Tel: +509 244-2942 +509 244-2943
Fax: +509 244-2910
EMail: recteur@ueh.edu.ht
Website: http://www.ueh.edu.ht

Recteur: Jean Vernet Henry
Tel: +509 244-2944 EMail: recteur@ueh.edu.ht

Faculty
Agronomy and Veterinary Science (Agriculture; Animal Husbandry; Environmental Studies; Food Science; Rural Planning; Veterinary Science); **Applied Linguistics** (Applied Linguistics); **Dentistry** (Dentistry); **Ethnology** (Anthropology; Ethnology; Psychology; Sociology); **Humanities** (Arts and Humanities; Communication Studies; Psychology; Social Work; Sociology); **Law and Economics** (Economics; Law); **Medicine and Pharmacy** (Medical Technology; Medicine; Pharmacy); **Science** (Civil Engineering; Electrical Engineering; Electronic Engineering; Hydraulic Engineering; Mechanical Engineering; Natural Sciences; Surveying and Mapping)

School
Arts *(ENARTS)* (Arts and Humanities); **Law** *(Cayes, Fort-Liberté, Gonaives, Saint-Marc)* (Law); **Law, Economics and Management** *(Cap-Haïtien)* (Economics; Law; Management); **Teacher Training** (Teacher Training)

Institute
Administration, Management and International Studies (Business Administration; International Studies; Management); **African Research and Studies** (African Studies)

Centre
Technical Studies, Planning, Applied Economics *(CTPEA)* (Architecture and Planning; Economics; Technology)

Further Information: Also University Hospital

History: Founded 1944 by decree incorporating or affiliating existing institutions of higher education. Individual Faculties and Schools are responsible to the relevant Ministries and Government Departments. Confirmed as State institution by decree 1960. Financed by the State.

Academic Year: October to July

Admission Requirements: Secondary school certificate (baccalauréat) and competitive entrance examination

Main Language(s) of Instruction: French

Degrees and Diplomas: *Licence*: **Accountancy; African American Studies; African Studies; Anthropology; Arts and Humanities; Caribbean Studies; Geography; History; Law; Linguistics; Management; Mathematics; Natural Sciences.** *Maîtrise*: **Anthropology; Communication Arts; Psychology; Sociology.**
Last Updated: 23/03/16

PRIVATE INSTITUTIONS

ADVENTIST UNIVERSITY OF HAITI

Université Adventiste d'Haïti (UNAH)
63, Route de la Mairie de Carrefour, Diquini, Port-au-Prince
Tel: +509 234-9210
Fax: +509 234-0562
EMail: universiteadventistehaiti@hotmail.com
Website: http://www.unah.edu.ht

Recteur: Jean Josué Pierre (2005-) EMail: jjpierre28@hotmail.com

Vice-recteur: José Dorismar EMail: josedorismar@yahoo.fr

International Relations: Charles Fresnel

Faculty
Administration (Accountancy; Business Administration; Business and Commerce; Computer Science); **Educational Sciences** (Biology; Chemistry; Educational Sciences; Mathematics; Physics; Social Sciences); **Nursing** (Nursing); **Theology** (Ancient Languages; Bible; Religion; Religious Studies; Theology)

History: Founded 1921 in Cap-Haiti. Transferred to Port-au-Prince 1934 and Diquini Campus 1947. Acquired present status and title 1989.

Admission Requirements: Secondary school certificate (baccalauréat) and entrance examination

Fees: (Gourdes): 6,000 for general fees (800 gourdes per credit)

Main Language(s) of Instruction: French

Accrediting Agency: Association of Seventh-day Adventist Schools, Colleges and Universities

Degrees and Diplomas: *Licence*; *Maîtrise*: **Educational Sciences; Religion.** Also other degrees in Computer Sciences, Modern Languages, Accountancy, Typing

Student Services: Academic Counselling, Careers Guidance, Health Services, Language Laboratory, Nursery Care, Sports Facilities

Publishing house: University Press
Last Updated: 24/03/16

CARIBBEAN UNIVERSITY

Université Caraïbe (CUC)
Delmas 29, No. 7, Port-au-Prince
Tel: +506 3946-8232
EMail: rectorat@universitecaraibe.com
Website: http://www.universitecaraibe.com/

Recteur: Jocelyne Trouillot (2005-)
EMail: rectorat@universitecaraibe.com; jotrouillot@yahoo.com

Vice-Rectrice: Marjoto Mathurin
EMail: marjoto@universitecaraibe.com

International Relations: François Lherisson, Director, International Relations EMail: lherissonfils@yahoo.fr

Faculty
Agronomy (Agronomy; Animal Husbandry; Crop Production); **Computer Science** (Computer Engineering; Computer Science); **Education** (Bilingual and Bicultural Education; Educational Administration; Native Language Education; Pedagogy; Preschool Education; Primary Education; Secondary Education; Special Education; Teacher Training); **Engineering** (Architecture; Civil Engineering; Electronic Engineering; Mechanical Engineering); **Management and Accounting** (Accountancy; Business Administration; Business Computing; Management)

History: Created 1988. The University has developed some programmes in Haitian Creole. Publishing house, Editions CUC Université Caraïbe specialises in educational and youth literature. Acquired status 1990.

Academic Year: October to January; February to June

Admission Requirements: Baccalaureat - deuxième partie.

Fees: (US Dollar): 700 per annum

Main Language(s) of Instruction: Haitian Creole, French

Degrees and Diplomas: *Licence*: **Administration; Agriculture; Civil Engineering; Computer Science; Education.**

Student Services: Academic Counselling, Canteen, Careers Guidance, Cultural Activities, Health Services, Language Laboratory, Sports Facilities

Publications: L'Université en bref

Publishing House: Editions CUC Université Caraïbe
Last Updated: 23/03/16

CHRISTIAN UNIVERSITY OF THE NORTH

Université Chrétienne du Nord d'Haïti
BP 40, Cap-Haïtien, Nord
EMail: info@ucnh.info
Website: http://www.ucnh.org

Recteur: Jules Casseus EMail: jcasseus@ucnh.info

Secrétaire général: Jean-Louis Gineville EMail: ucnh@ucnh.info

International Relations: Laurel Casseus
EMail: lcasseus@ucnh.info

Faculty
Administration (Administration); **Agronomy** (Agronomy); **Fine Arts** (Music; Painting and Drawing; Theatre); **Theology** (Theology)

Department
English (English)

History: Founded 1947 as Séminaire Théologique Baptiste d'Haïti. Acquired present status 1994.

Academic Year: September to May

Admission Requirements: Baccalauréat II

Main Language(s) of Instruction: French

Accrediting Agency: Enseignement supérieur d'Haiti

Degrees and Diplomas: *Licence*; *Maîtrise*: **Theology.** Also Diplôme and Certificat

Student Services: Academic Counselling, Careers Guidance, Cultural Activities, Health Services, Language Laboratory, Sports Facilities

Publications: Shalom; Theologia
Last Updated: 23/03/16

EPISCOPAL UNIVERSITY OF HAITI

Université épiscopal d'Haïti
14,Rue Légitime Champs-de-Mars, Port-au-Prince
Tel: +509 221-2191
EMail: secretariat@uneph.edu.ht,
Website: http://www.uneph.edu.ht

Recteur: Lucien Jean Bernard

Faculty
Administration (Administration); **Agronomy** (Agronomy); **Communication and Public Relations** (Communication Studies; International Relations); **Computer Science** (Computer Science); **Educational Sciences** (Educational Sciences); **Medicine** (Medicine); **Nursing** (Nursing); **Rehabilitation Sciences** (Rehabilitation and Therapy); **Religious Studies** (Religious Studies)

History: Founded 1995.
Degrees and Diplomas: *Licence*
Last Updated: 24/03/16

HAITI HIGHER SCHOOL OF INFOTRONICS

Ecole Supérieure d'Infotronique d'Haïti (ESIH)
29, Deuxième Ruelle Nazon, Port-au-Prince
Tel: +509 3859-3885
Fax: +509 2245-5091
EMail: informations@esih.edu
Website: http://esih.edu/

Director: Mackenson Doucet EMail: mackenson.doucet@esih.edu

International Relations: Marlène Sam, International Relations Officer Tel: +509 3446-7383 EMail: marlene.sam@esih.edu

School
Business Administration (Business Administration); **Computer Engineering** (Computer Engineering); **Vocational Training in Information Technology** (Information Technology)

History: Created 1995.

Degrees and Diplomas: *Licence*

Last Updated: 23/03/16

INSTITUTE OF ADVANCED STUDIES IN BUSINESS AND ECONOMICS

Institut des Hautes Etudes commerciales et économiques (IHECE)
PO Box 436, 275, avenue John Brown, Port-au-Prince
Tel: +509 245-6133 +509 245-3572
Website: http://ihece.org/pres.htm

Directeur-Général: Raoul Berret

Department
Accountancy (Accountancy; Commercial Law; Marketing); **Economics** (Accountancy; Commercial Law; Economics; Marketing; Sociology; Statistics); **Management**

Degrees and Diplomas: *Licence*
Last Updated: 10/04/16

JEAN-PRICE MARS UNIVERSITY

Université Jean-Price Mars (UJPM HINCHE)
174 Rue Toussaint Louverture, Hinche, Province du Centre
Website: http://ujpm-hinche.org

Recteur: Jean Claude François EMail: jcfrancois@bluewin.ch

Executive director: Joseph Walner EMail: walnerjoseph@yahoo.fr

Course
Accountancy (Accountancy); **Business Administration** (Business Administration); **Civil Engineering** (Civil Engineering); **Law** (Law); **Nursing** (Nursing)

History: Since the earthquake in 2010, courses are given by a subsidiary of the University Jean Price-Mars in Hinche.

Degrees and Diplomas: *Licence*: **Accountancy; Business Administration; Civil Engineering; Nursing.** *Maîtrise*: **Law.**
Last Updated: 10/04/16

QUISQUEYA UNIVERSITY

Université Quisqueya (UNIQ)
218 Ave Jean-Paul II, Haut de Turgeau, Port-au-Prince
Tel: +509 221-4516 +509 221-4330 +509 222-9103
Fax: +509 223-7430 +509 221-4211
EMail: vraac@uniq.edu.ht
Website: http://uniq.edu.ht

Recteur: Jacky Lumarque (2007-) EMail: recteur@uniq.edu

Vice-Rectrice (Affaires académiques): Marie-Gisèle Pierre

Faculty

Agriculture and Environmental Sciences (Agricultural Economics; Agriculture; Environmental Studies); **Economics and Administration** (Accountancy; Administration; Economics); **Educational Sciences** (Biology; Chemistry; Education; Geography; History; Literature; Modern Languages; Physics; Preschool Education; Primary Education); **Health** (Health Sciences; Medicine; Public Health); **Law and Political Science** (Law; Political Sciences); **Science, Engineering and Architecture** (Architecture; Civil Engineering; Computer Engineering; Electrical Engineering; Engineering; Environmental Studies; Industrial Engineering; Telecommunications Engineering)

History: Founded 1988.

Academic Year: October to July (October-February; March-July)

Admission Requirements: Secondary school certificate (baccalauréat)

Main Language(s) of Instruction: French

Degrees and Diplomas: *Docteur en Médecine*: **Medicine.** *Licence*; *Professional Title*: **Architecture; Engineering.** *Maîtrise*: **Educational Sciences; Environmental Studies; Management; Public Health; Toxicology.** Also Postgraduate Programmes in Social Sciences, Economics and Project Management

Student Services: Academic Counselling, Careers Guidance, Social Counselling, Sports Facilities

Publications: Revue Juridique de l'UniQ

Last Updated: 23/03/16

UNIVERSITY NOTRE-DAME OF HAITI

Université Notre-Dame d'Haïti (UNDH)

6, rue Sapotille, Pacot, Port-au-Prince

Tel: +509 245-9522 +509 244-4694 +509 244 -4616

Fax: +509 245-3295 +509 244-4674

EMail: infos@undh.org

Recteur: Mgr André-Pierre EMail: mgrandrepierre@undh.org

Vice-Recteur aux Affaires académiques et scientifiques: Jean-Elie Larrieux Tel: +509 245-8121 EMail: jeanelielarrieux@undh.org

International Relations: Joseph Hilaire, Secrétaire Général EMail: smmbr@yahoo.com

Faculty

Administration *(Cap Haïtien, Jacmel)* (Administration); **Agriculture** *(Cayes)* (Agriculture; Agronomy); **Arts and Humaities** (Arts and Humanities; Literature; Modern Languages; Philosophy; Religious Studies; Theology); **Economics, Social and Political Sciences** (Accountancy; Business Administration; Criminology; Economics; Government; International Studies; Political Sciences; Public Administration; Sociology); **Educational Sciences** (Educational Sciences); **Medicine and Health Sciences** (Health Sciences; Medicine)

Further Information: Also campuses in Cap-Haitien and Cayes

History: Founded 1995 by the Conference of Bishops of Haiti.

Academic Year: October to July

Admission Requirements: Secondary school certificate (baccalaureat II)

Main Language(s) of Instruction: French

Accrediting Agency: Association of Caribbean Universities and Research Institutes; International Federation of Catholic Universities

Degrees and Diplomas: *Docteur en Médecine*: **Medicine.** *Licence*: **Business Administration; Education; Nursing.** *Maîtrise*. Also Certificate and DES: in Psychopedagogy (3 yrs), Pedagogy (2 yrs); Educational Administration (2 yrs)

Student Services: Canteen, Health Services, Language Laboratory

Publications: Bulletin de l'UNDH

Last Updated: 25/03/16

UNIVERSITY OF KING HENRI CHRISTOPHE

Université du Roi Henri Christophe

45 Rue 17-18, H-1, Cap-Haïtien

Tel: +509-2260-4826

EMail: rectorat@urhc.edu.ht

Website: http://www.urhc.edu.ht

Academic Vice-President: Nelson Gesner

Faculty

Administration (Accountancy; Economics; Management); **Agriculture and Ecology** (Agronomy; Ecology; Fishery; Marine Biology); **Applied Sciences** (Civil Engineering; Computer Science; Mining Engineering; Surveying and Mapping); **Computer Science** (Software Engineering; Telecommunications Engineering); **Nursing** (Nursing)

History: Founded 1980.

Main Language(s) of Instruction: French

Degrees and Diplomas: *Licence*

Student Services: Academic Counselling, Nursery Care

Last Updated: 23/03/16

Holy See

STRUCTURE OF HIGHER EDUCATION SYSTEM

Description:

Ecclesiastical universities, faculties and other academic institutions carry out teaching and research in disciplines related to the Christian revelation and are therefore involved in the Church's mission of evangelization. They grant academic qualifications under the authority of the Holy See.
The Congregation for Catholic Education (Congregatio de Institutione Catholica) has administrative oversight of these institutions and oversight of Catholic education.
The Congregation for the Clergy is in charge of seminaries.
Institutions listed in the WHED are limited to those offering more than just studies in Theology and which are located in Italy.

Stages of studies:

University level first stage: *First stage*
The first stage takes usually three years and leads to the Baccalaureatus.

University level second stage: *Second stage*
Two more years of study following upon the first stage lead to the Licentia.
University level third stage: *Third stage*
This stage leads to the Doctorate, which is usually awarded three years after the Licentia, on submission and defence of a thesis.

ADMISSION TO HIGHER EDUCATION

Admission to university-level studies:

Name of secondary school credential required: Secondary School Leaving Certificate
For entry to: All institutions and programmes
Alternatives to credentials: No
Other requirements: A suitable knowledge of Latin is required for enrolment in the Faculties of Sacred Sciences.

Foreign students admission:

Admission requirements: Foreign students applying to an Ecclesiastical university or faculty must hold a pre-university diploma or an academic title and their candidacy must be submitted by the competent authorities.
Language proficiency: Candidates, in addition to their mother tongue, must have a good knowledge of Latin and, depending on the course they wish to follow, of Greek or Hebrew. For the doctoral level, they should be able to do research in the principal modern languages.

NATIONAL BODIES

Congregazione per l'Educazione Cattolica (CEC) (Congregation for Catholic Education)
Piazza Pio XII, 3
Città del Vaticano, Roma 00120
Tel: +39 06 69 88 41 67
Fax: +39 06 69 88 41 72
WWW: http://www.educatio.va/content/cec/it.html

Agenzia della Santa Sede per la Valutazione e la Promozione della Qualità delle Università e Facoltà Ecclesiastiche (AVEPRO) (Agency for the Evaluation and Promotion of Quality in Ecclesiastical Universities and Faculties)

Director: Franco Imoda
Via della Conciliazione, 5
Roma 00193
Tel: +39 06 6988 4034
Fax: +39 06 6988 5211
EMail: segreteria@avepro.va
WWW: http://www.avepro.va/

Role of national body: The mission of AVEPRO, established on 19 September 2007, is to promote and develop a culture of quality within the academic institutions that depend directly on the Holy See and ensure they possess internationally valid quality criteria, as established by the Bologna Process.

Data for academic year: 2015-2016
Source: IAU from CEC and AVEPRO websites, 2015.

INSTITUTIONS

PUBLIC INSTITUTIONS

PONTIFICAL GREGORIAN UNIVERSITY

Pontificia Università Gregoriana (PUG)
Piazza della Pilotta 4, 00187 Roma
Tel: +39(06) 6701-1
Fax: +39(06) 6701-5419
EMail: segreteria@unigre.it
Website: http://www.unigre.it

Rettore Magnifico: François-Xavier Dumortier, S.J.
EMail: rettore@unigre.it

Faculty
Canon Law (Canon Law); **History and Cultural Heritage of the Church** (Art History; Heritage Preservation; Museum Studies; Religious Studies); **Missiology** (Pastoral Studies); **Philosophy** (Philosophy); **Social Sciences** (Anthropology; Economics; Journalism; Media Studies; Political Sciences; Social Sciences; Sociology); **Theology** (Theology)

Institute
Psychology (Psychology); **Spirituality** (Religion)

Centre
Cardinal Bea Centre for Judaic Studies (Judaic Religious Studies); **Child Protection; Faith and Culture** *(Alberto Hurtado)* (Cultural Studies; Religious Studies)

Further Information: Also Italian Language course for foreign students

History: Founded 1551 as 'Collegium Romanum' by Ignatius of Loyola and Francis Borgia. Constituted as University by Pope Julius III, 1553. The Institution developed considerably under Pope Gregory XIII, who is considered to be 'founder and father' of the University which now bears his name. Depends directly on the Holy See and administration is entrusted to the Society of Jesus. The Grand Chancellor is the Cardinal Prefect of the Congregation of Studies and the Vice-Grand Chancellor the Superior-General of the Society of Jesus. Juridical recognition is granted to the University by the government of Italy.

Academic Year: October to May (October-January; February-May)

Admission Requirements: Completed classical secondary education and, where necessary, additional preparatory studies to meet Faculty requirements

Fees: 1,620 per annum (Euro)

Main Language(s) of Instruction: Italian, English, French, German, Spanish

Degrees and Diplomas: *Baccalaureatus*: **Missionary Studies; Philosophy; Psychology; Social Sciences; Theology.** *Licentia*: **Canon Law; Christian Religious Studies; Missionary Studies; Philosophy; Psychology; Social Sciences; Theology.** *Doctoratus*: **Canon Law; Christian Religious Studies; Missionary Studies; Philosophy; Psychology; Social Sciences; Theology.**

Student Services: Academic Counselling, Canteen, Cultural Activities, Health Services, Language Laboratory, Social Counselling

Publications: Acta Nuntiaturae Gallicae; Analecta Gregoriana; Archivum Historiae Pontificiae; Documenta Missionalia; Gregorianum; Interreligious and Cultural Investigation; Miscellanea Historiae Pontificiae; Periodica de re morali, canonica, liturgica; Studia Missionalia; Studia Sociala; Tesi Gregoriana

Publishing House: Editrice della Pontificia Universitas Gregoriana

Last Updated: 13/03/15

PONTIFICAL LATERAN UNIVERSITY

Pontificia Università Lateranense (PUL)
Piazza S. Giovanni in Laterano 4,
00120 Città del Vaticano
Tel: +39 06 6988 6401
Fax: +39 06 6988 6508
EMail: info@pul.it
Website: http://www.pul.it

Rettore Magnifico: Enrico dal Covolo
Tel: +39(06) 6989-5632 EMail: segretario@pul.it
Segretario Generale: Roberto De Odorico De Odorico
EMail: segretario.generale@pul.it

Faculty
Canon Law (Canon Law); **Civil Law** (Civil Law; Public Law); **Philosophy** (Philosophy); **Sacred Theology** (Theology)

Institute
Pastoral Studies *(Redemptor Hominis)* (Catholic Theology; Pastoral Studies); **Utriusque Iuris** (Canon Law; Comparative Law)

Centre
Advanced Studies *(Lateran)* (Classical Languages; Economics; Italian; Journalism; Law; Modern Languages)

History: Founded 1773 by Pope Clement XIV as "Collegio Romano". Moved to the Lateran hill 1937 and became Pontificio

Ateneo Lateranense and Pontificia Universitas Lateranensis 1959. Directly dependent on the Holy See, legally established in the Vatican City State. Under the jurisdiction of the Congregation for Catholic Education.

Academic Year: October to June (October-January; February-June)

Admission Requirements: Secondary school certificate or high school graduation certificate (level of study required for access to university in student's home country)

Fees: 600-2,500 per annum (Euro)

Main Language(s) of Instruction: Italian

Degrees and Diplomas: *Baccalaureatus*: **Canon Law; Philosophy; Theology.** *Licentia*: **Canon Law; Civil Law.** *Doctoratus*: **Canon Law; Civil Law; Modern Languages; Philosophy; Theology.** Also Master

Student Services: Academic Counselling, Canteen, Social Counselling, Sports Facilities

Publications: Anthropotes; Apollinaris; Aquinas; Civitas et Iustitia; CVII; Latenarum; Nuntium; Studia et Documenta Historiae et Iuris

Publishing House: Lateran University Press

Last Updated: 13/03/15

PONTIFICAL URBANIANA UNIVERSITY

Pontificia Università Urbaniana (PUU)

Via Urbano VIII 16, 00165 Roma

Tel: +39 06 6988 9611

Fax: +39 06 6988 1871

EMail: segretaria@urbaniana.edu

Website: http://www.urbaniana.edu

Rettore Magnifico: Alberto Trevisiol
EMail: rettore@urbaniana.edu

Vice-rettore: Godfrey Igwebuike Onah

Faculty

Canon Law (Canon Law); **Missiology** (Missionary Studies); **Philosophy** (Philosophy); **Theology** (Theology)

Institute

Catechism and Missionary Spirituality (Christian Religious Studies); **Non-Belief, Religion and Culture Studies** (Agnosticism and Atheism; Cultural Studies)

Further Information: Also branch in Castel Gandolfo

History: Founded 1627 as college by Pope Urban VIII, became Pontifical University 1962. Directed by the Pontifical Congregation for the Propagation of the Faith (Holy See).

Academic Year: September to June (September-February; February-June)

Admission Requirements: Secondary school certificate

Main Language(s) of Instruction: Italian

Degrees and Diplomas: *Baccalaureatus*; *Licentia*; *Doctoratus*: **Canon Law; Philosophy; Theology.**

Publications: Annales; Bibliographia Missionalia; Euntes Docete; Redemptoris Missio

Publishing House: Urbaniana University Press

Last Updated: 13/03/15

PRIVATE INSTITUTIONS

AUXILIUM PONTIFICAL FACULTY OF EDUCATION

Pontificia Facoltà di Scienze dell'Educazione "Auxilium"

Via Cremolino, 141, 00166 Roma

Tel: +39 (0)6 6156 4226

Fax: +39 (0)6 6156 4640

EMail: segreteria@pfse-auxilium.net

Website: http://www.pfse-auxilium.org

Preside: Giuseppina del Core
Tel: +39 (0)6 6157 2029 EMail: preside@pfse.auxilium.org

Institute

Catechist Methodology (Christian Religious Studies); **Pedagogical Methodology** (Pedagogy); **Psychological Research in the Field of Education** (Educational Psychology); **Sociological Research in the Field of Education** (Education; Sociology)

History: Founded 1954 in Turin (Italy) as the International Institute of Higher Education for Educational Sciences in 1970 and transferred to Rome in 1978. Acquired present status 1999.

Academic Year: October to September

Admission Requirements: High School Diploma

Fees: 1,000 per annum (paid in two installments) (Euro)

Main Language(s) of Instruction: Italian

Accrediting Agency: Holy See

Degrees and Diplomas: *Doctoratus*: **Educational Sciences.** Laurea, Laurea magistrale, Master

Student Services: Academic Counselling, Canteen, Cultural Activities, Foreign Studies Centre, Language Laboratory, Sports Facilities

Publications: Rivista di Scienze dell' Educazione

Last Updated: 13/03/15

JOHN PAUL II PONTIFICAL INSTITUTE FOR STUDIES ON MARRIAGE AND FAMILY

Pontificio Istituto Giovanni Paolo II per Studi su Matrimonio e Famiglia

Piazza San Giovanni in Laterano, 4, 00120 Città del Vaticano

Tel: +39(6) 698-86113

Fax: +39(6) 698-86103

EMail: segretario@istitutogp2.it

Website: http://www.istitutogp2.it

Preside: Livio Melina EMail: segpreside@istitutogp2.it

Programme

Family Studies (Family Studies)

History: Founded 1981.

Degrees and Diplomas: *Licentia*; *Doctoratus*: **Family Studies; Home Economics.** Also Master

Last Updated: 13/03/15

PONTIFICAL AMBROSIAN INSTITUTE OF SACRED MUSIC

Pontificio Istituto Ambrosiano di Musica Sacra

Viale Gorizia, 5, 20144 Milano

Tel: +39 02.8940 6400

Fax: +39 02.8940 6400

EMail: istituto@unipiams.org

Website: http://www.unipiams.org/

Preside: Gianluigi Rusconi

Programme

Sacred Music (Religious Music)

History: Founded 1931.

Degrees and Diplomas: *Baccalaureatus*; *Licentia*; *Doctoratus*: **Religious Music.**

Last Updated: 13/03/15

PONTIFICAL ATHENAEUM REGINA APOSTOLORUM

Ateneo Pontificio Regina Apostolorum

Via degli Aldobrandeschi 190, 00163 Roma

Tel: +39 06 665 431

EMail: info@upra.org

Website: http://www.uprait.org/

Rettore: Pedro Barrajón

Faculty

Bioethics (Biology; Ethics); **Philosophy** (Philosophy); **Theology** (Theology)

Institute

Bioethics and Human Rights (Ethics; Human Rights); **Economics Ethics** *(Fidelis)* (Economics; Ethics); **Religion** (Religious Studies);

Sacerdos (Pastoral Studies; Theology); **Science and Faith** (Natural Sciences; Philosophy; Religion); **Women's Studies** (Women's Studies)

History: Founded 1993. Acquired present status 1998.

Admission Requirements: Secondary school certificate

Main Language(s) of Instruction: Italian

Degrees and Diplomas: *Baccalaureatus*; *Licentia*; *Doctoratus*: **Biological and Life Sciences; Philosophy; Theology.** Also Masters

Last Updated: 12/03/15

PONTIFICAL BIBLICAL INSTITUTE

Pontificio Istituto Biblico
Via della Pilotta 25, 00187 Roma
Tel: +39 06 695 2611
Fax: +39 06 6952 6211
Website: http://www.biblico.it

Rettore: Michael Francis Kolarcik

Segretario Generale: Carlo Valentino

Faculty

Biblical Studies (Archaeology; Bible; Geography; Greek; Hebrew; Latin; Philology); **Oriental Studies** (Ancient Civilizations; History; Middle Eastern Studies; Philology; Religion)

Further Information: Branch in Jerusalem

History: Founded 1909. Acquired present status 1932.

Main Language(s) of Instruction: Italian

Degrees and Diplomas: *Licentia*; *Doctoratus*: **Ancient Civilizations; Bible.**

Publications: Biblica; Orientalia

Last Updated: 13/03/15

PONTIFICAL INSTITUTE FOR ARABIC AND ISLAMIC STUDIES

Pontificio Istituto di Studi Arabi e d'Islamistica (PISAI)
Viale di Trastevere 89, 00153 Roma
Tel: +39(06) 583-92611
Fax: +39(06) 588-2595
EMail: info@pisai.it
Website: http://www.pisai.it

Preside: Valentino Cottini

Programme

Arabic (Arabic); **Islamic Studies** (Islamic Studies)

History: Founded 1926 in Tunis. Moved to Rome 1964. Acquired present title and status 1979.

Main Language(s) of Instruction: Italian

Degrees and Diplomas: *Licentia*: **Islamic Studies.** *Doctoratus*: **Islamic Studies.**

Publications: Encounter; Etudes arabes; Islamochristiana

Last Updated: 13/03/15

PONTIFICAL INSTITUTE OF CHRISTIAN ARCHAEOLOGY

Pontificio Istituto di Archeologia Cristiana
Via Napoleone III,1, 00185 Roma
Tel: +39 06 446 5574
Fax: +39 06 446 9197
EMail: segreteria@piac.it
Website: http://www.piac.it

Rettore: Danilo Mazzoleni EMail: piac.rettore@piac.it

Segretario: Carlo Dell'Osso EMail: piac.segretario@piac.it

Division

Archaeology (Ancient Civilizations; Archaeology; Architecture; Art Education)

History: Founded 1925 by a Motu Propio of Pope Pius XI as a research centre.

Academic Year: November to May

Fees: 850 per annum (Euro)

Main Language(s) of Instruction: Italian

Degrees and Diplomas: *Baccalaureatus*; *Licentia*; *Doctoratus*: **Archaeology.** Also specialization course

Publications: Rivista di Archeologia Cristiana

Last Updated: 13/03/15

PONTIFICAL INSTITUTE OF SACRED MUSIC

Pontificio Istituto di Musica Sacra
Via di Torre Rossa 21, 00165 Roma
Tel: +39(06) 663-8792
Fax: +39(06) 662-2453
EMail: pims@musica-sacra.va
Website: http://www.musicasacra.va

Preside: Vincenzo De Gregorio EMail: preside@musicasacra.va

Segretario: Giuseppe Moretti

Course

Sacred Music (Music Theory and Composition; Musical Instruments; Musicology; Religious Music; Singing)

History: Founded 1910 as Scuola Superiore di Musica Sacra. Acquired present status 1931.

Main Language(s) of Instruction: Italian

Degrees and Diplomas: *Baccalaureatus*; *Licentia*; *Doctoratus*: **Religious Music.**

Last Updated: 13/03/15

PONTIFICAL ORIENTAL INSTITUTE

Pontificio Istituto Orientale
Piazza di Santa Maria Maggiore, 7, 00185 Roma
Tel: +39 06 447 4170
EMail: urp@pontificio-orientale.it
Website: http://www.unipio.org/

Rettore: James McCann EMail: rettore@pontificio-orientale.com

Faculty

Eastern Canon Law (Canon Law); **Eastern Church Studies** (Religious Studies; Theology)

History: Founded 1917. Acquired present status 1920.

Academic Year: October to June

Admission Requirements: Bachelor Degree in Theology (or equivalent completed in a major seminary)

Main Language(s) of Instruction: Italian

Degrees and Diplomas: *Licentia*; *Doctoratus*: **Canon Law; Religious Studies.**

Last Updated: 13/03/15

PONTIFICAL UNIVERSITY ANTONIANUM

Pontificia Università Antonianum
Via Merulana, 124, 00185 Roma
Tel: +39 (0)6 7037 3502
EMail: segreteria@antonianum.eu
Website: http://www.antonianum.eu/

Rettore Magnifico: Mary Melone (2011-)
EMail: rettorato@antonianum.eu

Faculty

Biblical Studies and Archaeology (Archaeology; History of Religion); **Canon Law** (Canon Law); **Philosophy** (Philosophy); **Theology** (Theology)

School

Medieval and Franciscan Studies (Christian Religious Studies; Medieval Studies)

Institute

Ecumenical Studies *(San Bernardino di Venezia)* (Christian Religious Studies); **Religious Studies** (Religious Studies); **Spirituality** *(Franciscan)* (Religious Studies); **Theological** *(Murcia)* (Theology)

History: Founded 1887 as Studium Generale. Became Athenaeum Antonianum de Urbe 1933. Acquired present status and title 2005.

Main Language(s) of Instruction: Italian

Degrees and Diplomas: *Baccalaureatus*; *Licentia*; *Doctoratus*: **Canon Law; Philosophy; Theology.**

Student Services: Academic Counselling, Cultural Activities

Publications: Revista Antonianum
Last Updated: 12/03/15

PONTIFICAL UNIVERSITY OF ST. THOMAS AQUINAS

Angelicum Pontificia Università S. Tommaso d'Aquino (PUST)
Largo Angelicum 1, 00184 Roma
Tel: +39(06) 670-21
Fax: +39(06) 679-0407
EMail: segreteria@pust.urbe.it
Website: http://www.pust.it

Rettore Magnifico: Miroslav Adam Konštanc

Segretario Generale: Glenn Morris EMail: segreteria@pust.urbe.it

Faculty
Canon Law (Canon Law); **Philosophy** (Philosophy); **Social Sciences** (Social Sciences); **Theology** (Theology)

Institute
Religious Sciences *(Mater Ecclesiae)* (Religion)

History: Founded 1580 as College of St. Thomas for students of the Dominican Order. Faculty of Philosophy added 1882 by Apostolic Decree of Pope Leo XIII, Faculty of Canon Law added 1896. Became Pontifical University 1906. Acquired present title 1963.

Academic Year: October to June (October-February; February-June)

Admission Requirements: Secondary school certificate

Main Language(s) of Instruction: Italian, English

Degrees and Diplomas: *Baccalaureatus*: **Philosophy; Social Sciences; Theology.** *Licentia*: **Canon Law; Philosophy; Social Sciences; Theology.** *Doctoratus*: **Canon Law; Philosophy; Social Sciences; Theology.**

Publishing house: Angelicum University Press
Last Updated: 12/03/15

PONTIFICAL UNIVERSITY OF THE HOLY CROSS

Pontificia Università della Santa Croce
Piazza S. Apollinare, 49, 00186 Roma
Tel: +39 (0)6 681 641
Fax: +39 (0)6 6816 4400
EMail: santacroce@pusc.it
Website: http://www.pusc.it

Rettore Magnifico: Luis Romera

Faculty
Canon Law (Canon Law); **Facoltà di Teologia** (Theology); **Institutional Social Communication** (Communication Studies; Information Sciences); **Philosophy** (Philosophy)

Institute
Religious Studies *(all'Apollinare)* (Religious Studies)

Centre
Languages (Modern Languages)

History: Founded 1985. Acquired present status 1998.

Academic Year: October to June

Admission Requirements: Diploma di Scuola Secondaria Superiore

Fees: 1,300-2,000 per annum (Euro)

Main Language(s) of Instruction: Italian

Degrees and Diplomas: *Baccalaureatus*: **Philosophy; Theology.** *Licentia*: **Canon Law; Philosophy; Theology.** *Doctoratus*: **Canon Law; Philosophy; Theology.**

Student Services: Academic Counselling, Library

Publications: Acta Philosophica; Annales Theologici; Ius Ecclesiae

Distance students, 537.
Last Updated: 12/03/15

SALESIAN PONTIFICAL UNIVERSITY

Università Pontificia Salesiana (UPS)
Piazza dell' Ateneo Salesiano, 1,
00139 Roma
Tel: +39 06 872 901
Fax: +39 06 872-90-318
EMail: segreteria@unisal.it
Website: http://www.unisal.it

Rettore Magnifico: Mauro Mantovani (2015-)
EMail: rettore@unisal.it

Faculty
Canon Law (Canon Law); **Christian and Classical Letters** (Literature); **Education** (Education; Pedagogy); **Philosophy** (Philosophy); **Social Communication Sciences** (Communication Studies; Welfare and Protective Services); **Theology** (Theology)

History: Founded 1904 as institute, became athenaeum 1940 and University 1973. Under the jurisdiction of the Congregation for Catholic Education and of the Salesian Order.

Academic Year: October to June (October-January; February-June)

Admission Requirements: Secondary school certificate acceptable for University admission in the country of award

Fees: 1200 per annum (Euro)

Main Language(s) of Instruction: Italian

Degrees and Diplomas: *Baccalaureatus*; *Licentia*; *Doctoratus*: **Canon Law; Communication Studies; Philosophy; Theology; Welfare and Protective Services.**

Student Services: Academic Counselling, Cultural Activities, Health Services, Language Laboratory, Nursery Care, Sports Facilities

Publications: Orientamenti Pedagogici; Salesianum
Last Updated: 13/03/15

SOPHIA UNIVERSITY INSTITUTE

Istituto Universitario Sophia (IUS)
Via San Vito 28, Loppiano, 50064
Tel: +39 (0)55 905 1500
Fax: +39 (0)55 905 1599
EMail: info@iu-sophia.org
Website: http://www.iu-sophia.org

Preside: Piero Coda.

Area
Music and Aesthetics (Aesthetics); **Social Sciences and Communication** (Economics; Management; Political Sciences; Religion)

Department
Economics and Management (Economics; Management); **Political Studies** (Political Sciences); **Theology and Philosophy** (Philosophy; Theology)

Degrees and Diplomas: *Doctoratus*: **Economics; Logic; Philosophy; Political Sciences; Social Sciences; Theology.** Master's degree (Economics, Political Science)
Last Updated: 12/03/15

ST ANSELM'S PONTIFICAL ATHENAEUM

Pontificio Ateneo S. Anselmo
Piazza dei Cavalieri di Malta, 5, 00153 Roma
Tel: +39 06 579 1401
Fax: +33 06 579 1402
EMail: segretaria@santanselmo.org
Website: http://www.santanselmo.org

Rettore Magnifico: Juan Javier Flores Arcas

Segretario Generale: Pachomius Okogie
EMail: segretariogenerale@santanselmo.org

Faculty
Philosophy (Philosophy); **Theology** (Theology)

Institute
Liturgical Studies (Religion)

History: Founded 1687. Acquired present status 1867.

Admission Requirements: Secondary school certificate

Fees: 800-1,200 (Euro)

Main Language(s) of Instruction: Italian

Degrees and Diplomas: *Baccalaureatus*; *Licentia*; *Doctoratus*: **Philosophy; Theology.**

Student Services: Academic Counselling, Language Laboratory

Publications: Ecclesia Orans; Studia Anselmiana

Last Updated: 13/03/15

ST. PIUS X FACULTY OF CANON LAW OF VENICE

Facoltà di Diritto Canonico S. Pio X di Venezia

Dorsoduro 1, 30123 Venezia
Tel: +39 (0)41 274 3911
Fax: +39 (0)41 274 3998
EMail: info@marcianum.it
Website: http://fdc.marcianum.it/

Preside: Giuliano Brugnotto

Main Language(s) of Instruction: Italian

Degrees and Diplomas: *Licentia*; *Doctoratus*: **Canon Law.**

Last Updated: 12/03/15

Honduras

STRUCTURE OF HIGHER EDUCATION SYSTEM

Description:

Higher education is provided by public and private universities and specialized institutes and schools. The Universidad Nacional Autónoma de Honduras is autonomous and draws its funds from government grants, fees and gifts. It is responsible for higher education.

Stages of studies:

University level first stage:

The first stage of higher education leads after four years' study to the degree of Licenciatura or to a Doctorado in Medicina after a minimum of 6 years' study.

University level second stage:

The Maestría is conferred after two to three years' study. A Doctorado is conferred after two years' study.

ADMISSION TO HIGHER EDUCATION

Admission to university-level studies:

Name of secondary school credential required: Bachillerato

Foreign students admission:

Admission requirements: Students must hold the Bachiller, Perito or Maestro de Educacion primaria and must follow a general orientation course

Entry regulations: Foreign students must hold a visa.

Language proficiency: Students must have a good knowledge of Spanish. Students who need to upgrade their Spanish can follow a course.

RECOGNITION OF STUDIES

Bodies dealing with recognition:

Universidad Nacional Autónoma de Honduras - UNAH (National Autonomous University of Honduras)

Bulevar Suyapa, Ciudad Universitaria, Francisco Morazán

Tegucigalpa

EMail: info@unah.edu.hn

WWW: https://www.unah.edu.hn/

NATIONAL BODIES

Universidad Nacional Autónoma de Honduras - UNAH (National Autonomous University of Honduras)

Bulevar Suyapa, Ciudad Universitaria, Francisco Morazán

Tegucigalpa

EMail: info@unah.edu.hn

WWW: https://www.unah.edu.hn/

Role of national body: Supervises and manages the higher education system of the country.

Data for academic year: 2015-2016

Source: IAU from Ley fundamental de educación (2012) and Ley de educación superior (1989), 2015.

INSTITUTIONS

PUBLIC INSTITUTIONS

FRANCISCO MORAZÁN NATIONAL PEDAGOGICAL UNIVERSITY, TEGUCIGALPA

Universidad Pedagógica Nacional Francisco Morazán (UPNFM)
Colonia el Dorado, Frente a Plaza Miraflores, Tegucigalpa
Tel: +504 2239-8842 +504 2235-8349 +504 2239-8002
Fax: +504 2231-1257
EMail: info@upnfm.edu.hn
Website: http://www.upnfm.edu.hn

Rector: David Orlando Marín López
Tel: +504 2232-5386
EMail: dmarin@upnfm.edu.hn; dmarin1956@gmail.com

Secretaría General: Celfa Idalisis Bueso
Tel: +504 2235-3224
EMail: celfa7@yahoo.com; registro@upnfm.edu.hn

Vicerrector Administrativo: Jorge Alberto Alvarez Flores
Tel: +504 2235-3206 EMail: jalvarez@upnfm.edu.hn

Faculty
Humanities (FAHU) (Educational Administration; Educational and Student Counselling; Educational Sciences; Foreign Languages Education; Humanities and Social Science Education; Literature; Modern Languages; Music; Native Language Education; Physical Education; Preschool Education; Social Sciences; Special Education; Sports; Theatre; Visual Arts); **Sciences and Technology (FACYT)** (Business and Commerce; Food Technology; Hotel Management; Industrial Engineering; Mathematics; Natural Sciences; Textile Technology; Tourism)

Institute
Cooperation and Development (INCODER); **Research (INIEES)**

Centre
Distance Education (CUED) (Business Administration; Educational Sciences; Food Technology; Industrial Engineering; Literature; Mathematics; Modern Languages; Natural Sciences; Social Sciences; Textile Technology); **Educational Research and Innovation (CIIE)** (Educational Sciences)

Further Information: Also San Pedro Sula Regional Centre

History: Founded 1989 in co-operation with UNESCO, on the basis of Escuela Superior del Profesorado Francisco Morazán, an institution founded 1956. Financed by the central Government. Under the jurisdiction of the Consejo de Educación Superior and the Government.

Academic Year: February to November (February-May; June-July; August-November)

Admission Requirements: Secondary school certificate (Título de Educación Secundaria de Bachillerato en Ciencias y Letras)

Main Language(s) of Instruction: Spanish

Degrees and Diplomas: *Técnico*; *Licenciatura*; *Maestría*: **Administration; Curriculum; Education; Educational Administration; Educational Research; Educational Sciences; Finance; Foreign Languages Education; Gender Studies; Human Rights; Humanities and Social Science Education; Mathematics Education; Native Language Education; Physical Education; Primary Education; Science Education; Teacher Trainers Education; Technology Education.** *Doctorado*: **Education.**

Student Services: Academic Counselling, Health Services, Library, Social Counselling, Sports Facilities

Publications: Paradigma

Publishing House: UPNFM University Editorial

Student Numbers *2014-2015*: Total 25,383
Last Updated: 03/03/16

HONDURAS NATIONAL POLICE UNIVERSITY

Universidad Nacional de la Policia de Honduras (UNPH)
Apartado Aéreo 2163, El Ocotal, Francisco Morazán
Tel: +504 229-0463 +504 229-0462 +504 229-0424 +504 229-0448
Fax: +504 229-0456
EMail: unph@ymail.com
Website: http://unph.es.tl/UNPH.htm

Rector: Osman Javier Diaz Santos

Secretario General: Reydilio Reyes Sorto

Unit
Postgraduate Studies (Criminology; Protective Services)

Area
Administration (Administration); **General Studies** (Arts and Humanities); **Law** (Law); **Police Studies** (Police Studies); **Social Studies** (Social Studies)

History: Founded 1996 as Instituto Superior de Educación Policial (ISEP). Acquired current status and title 2009.

Main Language(s) of Instruction: Spanish

Degrees and Diplomas: *Licenciatura*; *Maestría*: **Criminology; Protective Services.** Also Diplomados
Last Updated: 02/03/16

NATIONAL AUTONOMOUS UNIVERSITY OF HONDURAS

Universidad Nacional Autónoma de Honduras (UNAH)
Boulevard Suyapa, Ciudad Universitaria, Tegucigalpa
Tel: +504 232-2110
Fax: +504 235-3361
EMail: rectoria@unah.edu.hn
Website: https://www.unah.edu.hn

Rectora: Julieta Gonzalina Castellanos Ruiz (2009-)
Tel: +504 2239-1194 +504 2232-5163
EMail: rectoria@unah.edu.hn

Secretaria General: Emma Virginia Rivera
Tel: +504 2232-5776 EMail: sgeneral@unah.edu.hn

International Relations: Julio Cesar Raudales, Vicerrector de Relaciones Internacionales
Tel: +504 2232-2110
EMail: julio.raudales@unah.edu.hn; vri@unah.edu.hn

Faculty
Arts and Humanities (Architecture; Educational Sciences; English; Foreign Languages Education; French; Native Language Education; Pedagogy; Philosophy; Physical Education; Spanish); **Chemistry and Pharmacy** (Chemistry; Pharmacy); **Dentistry** (Dentistry); **Economics** (Accountancy; Banking; Business Administration; Business Computing; Economics; Finance; Food Science; Marketing; Public Administration; Taxation); **Engineering** (Chemical Engineering; Civil Engineering; Computer Engineering; Electrical Engineering; Engineering; Industrial Engineering; Mechanical Engineering); **Law** (Law); **Medicine** (Medicine; Nursing; Radiology; Rehabilitation and Therapy); **Science** (Biology; Mathematics; Metallurgical Engineering; Microbiology; Physics); **Social Sciences** (Development Studies; History; Journalism; Psychology; Social Work; Sociology); **Space Science** (Astronomy and Space Science)

Institute
Economics and Social Research (Economics; Social Studies); **Law Research** (Law)

Research Department
Science (Natural Sciences)

Further Information: Also 10 Regional University Centres

History: Founded 1847 as Academy. Acquired present status and title 1957.

Academic Year: February to December (February-June; June-October; October-December)

Admission Requirements: Secondary school certificate (bachillerato) or equivalent

Main Language(s) of Instruction: Spanish

Degrees and Diplomas: *Técnico*; *Licenciatura*; *Maestría*: **Animal Husbandry; Astronomy and Space Science; Astrophysics; Business Administration; Business Computing; Clinical Psychology; Commercial Law; Construction Engineering; Demography and Population; Development Studies; Economics; Epidemiology; Human Rights; Industrial and Organizational Psychology; International Business; Management; Marine Transport; Maritime Law; Marketing; Pharmacy; Physics; Political Sciences; Public Administration; Public Health; Regional Planning; Safety Engineering; Social Studies; Social Work; Telecommunications Services.** *Especialidad*: **Anaesthesiology; Anatomy; Community Health; Criminal Law; Dermatology; Gynaecology and Obstetrics; Medicine; Neurology; Nursing; Oncology; Ophthalmology; Otorhinolaryngology; Paediatrics; Pathology; Plastic Surgery; Psychiatry and Mental Health; Rehabilitation and Therapy; Surgery.** *Doctorado*: **Business Administration; Development Studies; Social Sciences.**

Student Services: Academic Counselling, Facilities for disabled people, Health Services, Language Laboratory, Library, Nursery Care, Sports Facilities

Publications: Boletín del Instituto de Ciencias Económicas; Ciencia y Tecnología; Revista de la Universidad; Revista Economía Política

Publishing House: Editorial Universitaria

Last Updated: 03/03/16

NATIONAL SCHOOL OF FORESTRY

Escuela Nacional de Ciencias Forestales (ESNACIFOR)

Carretera del Norte, Colonia Las Américas, Apartado Postal # 2, Siguatepeque, Comayagua
Tel: +504 2773-0011 +504 2773-0018
Fax: +504 2773-0023 +504 2773-0698
EMail: esna_info@gmail.com; relacionesexternas@esnacifor.edu.hn
Website: http://www.esnacifor.hn

Director Ejecutivo: Emilio Esbeih
EMail: e.esbeih@esnacifor.edu.hn

Secretario General: Gerardo Tomé
EMail: gerardotome4@yahoo.com; gerardotome2@yahoo.com

Diretor, Administração e Finanças: Daniel Villatoro
EMail: d.villatoro@esnacifor.edu.hn

International Relations: Dora Valdivieso, Directora de Relaciones Externas

Programme

Forestry (Agricultural Business; English; Forest Management; Forestry; Social Sciences); **Forestry Engineering** (Agricultural Engineering; Forestry)

History: Founded 1969. Acquired present status 1993.

Fees: National: 45,000 per annum (Lempira), International: 5,000 per annum (US Dollar)

Main Language(s) of Instruction: Spanish

Degrees and Diplomas: *Licenciatura*; *Maestría*: **Forestry.**

Student Services: Careers Guidance, Cultural Activities, Health Services, IT Centre, Library, Social Counselling, Sports Facilities

Last Updated: 02/03/16

NATIONAL UNIVERSITY OF AGRICULTURE

Universidad Nacional de Agricultura (UNA)

Olancho, Carretera a Dulce Nombre de Culmi, Kilometro 215, Barrio El Espino, Catacamas, Olancho
Tel: +504 2799-4901 +504 2799-4135
Fax: +504 2799-4900
EMail: infomacion@unag.edu.hn; rrhhuna35@yahoo.com
Website: http://www.unag.edu.hn

Rector: Oscar Ovidio Redondo Flores
EMail: rectoria@unag.edu.hn; redondouna@yahoo.com; rectoriaunag@gmail.com

Vicerrector Administrativo: Marlon Oniel Escoto Valerio
EMail: moescoto@uc.cl

Secretario General: Carlos Manuel Ulloa
Tel: +504 2799-4902 EMail: secretariageneral@unag.edu.hn

Programme

Agricultural Engineering (Agricultural Engineering); **Business Administration** (Business Administration); **Food Technology** (Food Technology); **Natural Resources and Environmental Studies** (Environmental Studies; Natural Resources); **Veterinary Medicine** (Animal Husbandry; Veterinary Science)

History: Founded 1950 as Escuela Granja Demostrativa. Renamed Escuela Nacional de Agricultura (ENA) 1968. Acquired university status 1978 and current title 2002.

Main Language(s) of Instruction: Spanish

Degrees and Diplomas: *Licenciatura*

Student Services: Library

Last Updated: 03/03/16

PRIVATE INSTITUTIONS

CATHOLIC UNIVERSITY OF HONDURAS OUR LADY QUEEN OF PEACE

Universidad Católica de Honduras Nuestra Señora Reina de la Paz (UNICAH)

Barrio Casamata, Calle el seminario No 1501, Tegucigalpa 4473
Tel: +504 238-6795
Fax: +504 238-6794
EMail: rector@unicah.edu
Website: http://www.unicah.edu

Rector: Elio David Alvarenga

Programme

Administration (Business Administration; Finance; Marketing); **Engineering** (Architecture; Civil Engineering; Computer Science; Environmental Engineering; Industrial Engineering); **Health Sciences** (Dentistry; Medicine; Nursing; Psychology); **Social Sciences** (Communication Studies; International Relations; Law); **Theology** (Theology)

Further Information: Also following Campuses: Santiago Apóstol (Danlí), San Pedro y San Pablo (San Pedro Sula), Dios Espíritu Santo (Choluteca), Santa Rosa de Lima (Santa Rosa de Copán), Santa Clara (Juticalpa), San Isidro (La Ceiba), Jesús Sacramentado (Siguatepeque), San Jorge (Olanchito)

History: Founded 1992.

Academic Year: January to December (January-April; May-August; September-December)

Admission Requirements: Secondary School Certificate

Main Language(s) of Instruction: Spanish

Degrees and Diplomas: *Licenciatura*; *Maestría*: **Business Administration; Business and Commerce; Economics; Finance; Health Administration; International Relations; Management; Psychology; Religious Studies; Theology.** *Especialidad*: **Dentistry; Orthodontics; Periodontics.** *Doctorado*: **Administration; Bible; Pastoral Studies; Theology.**

Student Services: Academic Counselling, Health Services, Nursery Care, Sports Facilities

Last Updated: 02/03/16

CENTRAL AMERICAN TECHNOLOGICAL UNIVERSITY

Universidad Tecnológica Centroamericana (UNITEC)

Apartado Aéreo 3530, Zona Jacaleapa, Tegucigalpa
Tel: +504 2268-1000 +504 2202-4400
Fax: +504 230-4008
EMail: viestcom@unitec.edu; admisionesteg@unitec.edu; programagraduados@unitec.edu
Website: http://www.unitec.edu

Rector: Luis Orlando Zelaya Medrano

Faculty

Health Sciences (Architecture; Biomedical Engineering; Civil Engineering; Computer Engineering; Computer Science; Dentistry;

Electronic Engineering; Industrial Engineering; Mechanical Engineering; Medicine; Nutrition; Surgery; Telecommunications Engineering)

Programme

Engineering (Architecture; Biomedical Engineering; Civil Engineering; Computer Engineering; Computer Science; Electronic Engineering; Industrial Engineering; Telecommunications Engineering); **Postgraduate Studies** (Commercial Law; Development Studies; Energy Engineering; Finance; Human Resources; Information Technology; Management; Marketing; Safety Engineering; Structural Architecture; Tourism; Transport Management); **Undergraduate Studies** (Advertising and Publicity; Banking; Business Administration; Finance; Graphic Design; Industrial Management; International Business; International Relations; Law; Management; Marketing; Mass Communication; Psychology; Tourism)

Further Information: Also San Pedro Sula, Sede La Ceiba, Sede Los Próceres and Sede El Prado Campuses

History: Founded 1987.

Admission Requirements: Diploma de Bachiller en Ciencias y Letras, Perito Mercantil, Maestro, Bachiller en Computación

Main Language(s) of Instruction: Spanish

Accrediting Agency: Asociación de Universidades Privadas de Centroamérica (AUPRICA); Red Latinoamericana de Cooperación universitaria (RLCU)

Degrees and Diplomas: *Doctorado en Medicina*: **Dentistry; Medicine; Surgery.** *Licenciatura*; *Maestría*: **Business Administration; Civil Engineering; Commercial Law; Development Studies; Energy Engineering; Finance; Human Resources; Information Technology; International Business; Management; Marketing; Safety Engineering; Tourism; Transport Management.** *Doctorado*: **Business Administration; Economics.** Also Título de Ingeniero, 5 yrs

Student Services: Academic Counselling, Canteen, Careers Guidance, Health Services, Language Laboratory, Social Counselling, Sports Facilities

Last Updated: 03/03/16

CENTRE FOR DESIGN, ARCHITECTURE AND CONSTRUCTION

Centro de Diseño, Arquitectura y Construcción (CEDAC)

Col. Palmira, Ave. Rep. de Chile, Torre 214, Tegucigalpa
Tel: +504 2220-0480 +504 2220-0872 +504 2220-0874
EMail: info@cedac.edu.hn; registro@cedac.edu.hn
Website: http://www.cedac.edu.hn

Rector: Mario E. Martín EMail: rector@cedac.edu.hn

Programme

Architecture (Architecture); **Graphic Design** (Graphic Design); **Interior Design** (Interior Design)

Further Information: Also San Pedro Sula Campus

History: Founded 1996.

Main Language(s) of Instruction: Spanish

Degrees and Diplomas: *Licenciatura*: **Architecture; Graphic Design; Interior Design.**

Last Updated: 02/03/16

CHRISTIAN UNIVERSITY OF HONDURAS

Universidad Cristiana de Honduras (UCRISH)

Col. Satelite 5 etapa, Instalaciones del Ministerio Internacional La Cosecha, Salida a la Lima, San Pedro Sula
Tel: +504 2559-1132 +504 2559-1203
EMail: ucrish@hotmail.com; universidad@ucrishedu.org
Website: http://www.ucrishedu.org

Presidente: Misael Argeñal

Secretarío General: Guillermo Rivera

Programme

Business Administration (Business Administration); **Clinical Laboratory Technician** (Laboratory Techniques); **Computer Engineering** (Computer Engineering); **Industrial Engineering** (Industrial Engineering); **Law (Lawyer Professional Title)** (Law); **Marketing** (Marketing); **Psychology** (Psychology); **Theology** (Theology)

History: Founded 2004.

Main Language(s) of Instruction: Spanish

Degrees and Diplomas: *Técnico*; *Licenciatura*. Also Titulo de Ingeniero

Last Updated: 02/03/16

JESUS OF NAZARETH INSTITUTE OF TECHNOLOGY

Instituto Superior Tecnológico Jesús de Nazareth (UJN)

Boulevard Las Torres, Colonia Villas del Sol, San Pedro Sula
Tel: +504 2566-0005 +504 2566-0024
Fax: +504 2566-2312
EMail: ldchacon@ujn.edu.hn; l.chacon@jesusdenazareth.org
Website: http://www.ujn.edu.hn

Rector: José María Sánchez Alvarado

Programme

Business Administration (Business Administration); **Computer Engineering** (Computer Engineering); **Electronic Engineering** (Electronic Engineering); **Industrial and Systems Engineering** (Industrial Engineering); **Public Accounting and Finance** (Accountancy; Finance)

History: Founded 2004. Formerly known as Instituto Superior Tecnológico Jesús de Nazareth.

Main Language(s) of Instruction: Spanish

Degrees and Diplomas: *Licenciatura*. Also Título de Ingeniero

Last Updated: 02/03/16

JOSÉ CECILIO DEL VALLE UNIVERSITY, TEGUCIGALPA

Universidad José Cecilio del Valle (UJCV)

Colonia Humuya, Avenida Altiplano, Calle Poseidón, Apartado Postal 917, Tegucigalpa
Tel: +504 2280-8528
Fax: +504 2239-8448
EMail: info@ujcv.edu.hn; admisiones@ujcv.edu.hn
Website: http://www.ujcv.edu.hn

Rector: Francisco José Rosa
Tel: +504 2280-8528 Ext. 116
EMail: francisco.rosa@ujcv.edu.hn; rectoria@ujcv.edu.hn

Secretaría General: Sayra Vargas Tel: +504 2280-8528 Ext.121
EMail: sayra.vargas@ujcv.edu.hn;
secretaria.general@ujcv.edu.hn

Faculty

Economics and Social Sciences (Accountancy; Administration; Advertising and Publicity; Business Administration; Communication Arts; Finance; Graphic Design; Interior Design; International Business; Journalism; Law; Management; Marketing; Tourism); **Engineering and Architecture** (Agricultural Engineering; Architecture; Civil Engineering; Computer Science; Construction Engineering; Forestry; Industrial Engineering; Information Technology)

Further Information: Also Comayagua Campus

History: Founded 1978. A private autonomous institution financially supported by tuition fees and donations.

Academic Year: January to December (January-March; April-June; July-September; October-December)

Admission Requirements: Secondary school certificate (bachillerato)

Main Language(s) of Instruction: Spanish

Accrediting Agency: Asociacíon de Universidades Privadas de Centroamérica (AUPRICA)

Degrees and Diplomas: *Técnico*; *Licenciatura*; *Maestría*: **Management.**

Student Services: Academic Counselling

Last Updated: 03/03/16

METROPOLITAN UNIVERSITY OF HONDURAS

Universidad Metropolitana de Honduras (UMH)

Edificio, 1 Plaza COLPROSUMAH, Cruce del Blvd. Centro América y Suyapa, Contiguo a casa presidencial, lado posterior, Tegucigalpa
Tel: +504 280-1111 Ext.116/189/118
EMail: info_umh@unimetro.edu.hn; admisiones@umh.edu.hn
Website: http://www.unimetro.edu.hn

Rectora: Rosario Duarte Galeas

Vicerrectora Académica: Alma Mejía Banegas
EMail: amejia@unimetro.edu.hn

Programme

Business Engineering (Business Administration; Engineering); **Business Management and Accountancy** (Accountancy; Business Administration; Management); **Ecotourism** (Ecology; Environmental Management; Tourism); **Graduate Studies** (Business Administration; Economics; Engineering; Environmental Management; Finance; Marketing; Tourism); **Management and Social Development** (Administration; Development Studies; Social Studies); **Marketing and International Business** (International Business; Marketing); **Social and Public Communication** (Communication Studies; Mass Communication)

History: Founded 2002.

Main Language(s) of Instruction: Spanish

Degrees and Diplomas: *Licenciatura*; *Maestría*: **Business Administration; Economics; Engineering; Environmental Management; Finance; Marketing; Tourism.**

Last Updated: 03/03/16

NEW MILLENNIUM CHRISTIAN EVANGELICAL UNIVERSITY

Universidad Cristiana Evangélica Nuevo Milenio (UCENM)

Residencial Llanos del Potrero, carretera al batallon, calle Los Alcandes, Tegucigalpa
Tel: +504 2291-0026 +504 3337-0546 +504 2557-0607
Fax: +504 2557-0728 +504 2557-0732
EMail: info@ucenm.net
Website: http://www.ucenm.net

Rectora: María Antonia de Suazo EMail: rectora@ucenm.net

Vicerrector Académico: Rosel Faustino Cerrato Juárez
EMail: vicerrector@ucenm.net

Secretario General: Luis Galeano EMail: lgaleano@ucenm.net

Director Administrativo: Roldan Suazo EMail: rsuazo@ucenm.net

Programme

Business Administration (Business Administration); **Community Health** (Community Health); **Computer Systems** (Computer Engineering); **Laboratory Techniques** (Laboratory Techniques; Medical Technology); **Marketing** (Marketing); **Theology** (Theology)

Further Information: Also Peña Blanca and Catacamas Regional Campuses

History: Founded 2001.

Main Language(s) of Instruction: Spanish

Degrees and Diplomas: *Técnico*; *Licenciatura*; *Maestría*: **Business Administration.** Also título de Ingeniero

Student Services: Library

Last Updated: 02/03/16

PAN-AMERICAN ZAMORANO SCHOOL OF AGRICULTURE

Escuela Agrícola Panamericana Zamorano (EAP ZAMORANO)

Apartado Postal 93, Km 30 carretera de Tegucigalpa a Danlí, Valle del Yeguare, San Antonio de Oriente, Francisco Morazán
Tel: +504 2287-2000
Fax: +504 2776-6240 +504 2776-6113
EMail: zamorano@zamorano.edu; admisiones@zamorano.edu
Website: http://www.zamorano.edu

Rector: Jeffrey Lansdale EMail: zamonoticias@zamorano.edu

Decano Académico: Raúl Zelaya EMail: rzelaya@zamorano.edu

Department

Agricultural Business and Management (Accountancy; Agricultural Business; Economics; Finance; Marketing; Statistics); **Agricultural Science and Production** (Agricultural Economics; Agricultural Engineering; Agriculture; Food Science); **Environmental Studies and Development** (Environmental Studies); **Food Technology** (Agricultural Business; Agriculture; Food Technology; Industrial Engineering; Natural Sciences); **General Curriculum** (Agricultural Business; Agriculture; Animal Husbandry; English; Environmental Studies; Natural Sciences)

History: Founded 1942.

Fees: 18,900 per annum (US Dollar)

Main Language(s) of Instruction: Spanish

Degrees and Diplomas: Professional title, 4 yrs (Licenciatura Level)

Student Services: Careers Guidance, Health Services, IT Centre, Library, Sports Facilities

Student Numbers *2016-2017*: Total: c. 1,300

Last Updated: 02/03/16

POLYTECHNIC UNIVERSITY OF ENGINEERING

Universidad Politécnica de Ingeniería (UPI)

Residencial La Granja, Bloque F, calle de acceso al Club Social del BCIE, Apartado Postal 30617, Comayagüela
Tel: +504 2225-7455 +504 2225-7456
EMail: info@upi.edu.hn
Website: http://www.upi.edu.hn

Rectora: Jance Carolina Funes de Eveline
Tel: +504 2225-7454 +504 2225-7455 +504 2225-2888
EMail: jcfunes@upi.edu.hn

Vice-Rectora Académica: Rina Enamorado
EMail: rwenamorado@upi.edu.hn

Secretario General: Luis Eveline EMail: leveline@upi.edu.hn

Programme

Civil Engineering (Civil Engineering; Construction Engineering; Hydraulic Engineering; Road Engineering); **Environmental Engineering** (Environmental Engineering); **Finance Engineering** (Accountancy; Banking; Finance; Information Technology; Insurance; International Business; Management); **Geology** (Geology); **Industrial Design** (Industrial Design); **Information and Communication Technology** (Information Technology); **Topography and Cadastre** (Surveying and Mapping)

History: Founded 2007.

Main Language(s) of Instruction: Spanish

Degrees and Diplomas: *Técnico*; *Licenciatura*. Also Diplomados Universitarios, título de Ingeniero, 5 yrs

Student Services: Cultural Activities, Sports Facilities

Last Updated: 03/03/16

POLYTECHNIC UNIVERSITY OF HONDURAS

Universidad Politécnica de Honduras

Barrio San Rafael, Avenida Cervantes, 50, metros del Hotel Excelsior, Tegucigalpa
Tel: +504 238-3804 +504 238-3812
Website: http://www.lapolitecnicahn.org

Rector: José Cárleton Corrales

Secretaria General: Marta Julia Valle Aguilar

Programme

Business and Commerce (Business and Commerce); **Computer Systems Engineering** (Computer Engineering); **Electronic Engineering** (Electronic Engineering); **Industrial Production Engineering** (Industrial Engineering; Production Engineering); **Law** (Law); **Tourism** (Tourism)

Further Information: Also Comayagua, Choluteca, Danli, Progreso and Lima Campuses

History: Founded 2005.

Main Language(s) of Instruction: Spanish

Degrees and Diplomas: *Licenciatura*. Also título de Ingeniero

Student Services: Library, eLibrary

Last Updated: 03/03/16

TECHNOLOGICAL UNIVERSITY OF HONDURAS

Universidad Tecnológica de Honduras (UTH)

3 cuadras al oeste del puente rio blanco, bulevar del norte, San Pedro Sula, Cortés 2508-2600
Tel: +504 2508-2600/1/2
Fax: +504 2551-6108
EMail: info@uth.hn; alejandra.parada@uth.hn
Website: http://www.uth.hn

Vicerrector General: Javier Mejía
Tel: +504 2508-2600 Ext.1003 EMail: javier.mejia@uth.hn

Director Académico General: José Jesús Mora García
EMail: jose.mora@uth.hn

Secretario General: Romell Galo
Tel: +504 2508-2600 Ext.1004 EMail: javier.mejia@uth.hn

Programme

Engineering (Computer Engineering; Electronic Engineering; Finance; Industrial Engineering; Production Engineering); **Graduate Studies** (Civil Law; Criminal Law; Finance; Human Resources; International Business; Marketing; Sales Techniques); **Undergraduate Studies** (Accountancy; Business Administration; Business and Commerce; Finance; International Business; Labour and Industrial Relations; Law; Marketing; Tourism)

Further Information: Also Tegucigalpa, La Ceiba, El Progreso, Puerto Cortés, Santa Bárbara, Siguatepeque, Roatán Campuses

History: Founded 1992. Acquired present status and title 1996.

Fees: 850-3,400 per month (Lempira)

Main Language(s) of Instruction: Spanish

Degrees and Diplomas: *Licenciatura*; *Maestría*: **Civil Law; Criminal Law; Finance; Human Resources; International Business; Marketing; Sales Techniques.** *Doctorado*: **Administration.** Also titulo de Ingenierías; The Doctorado in Administration is a double degree offered with the Universidad Internacional, UNINTER, de Cuernavaca, Morelos, México

Student Services: eLibrary

Last Updated: 03/03/16

UNIVERSITY OF SAN PEDRO SULA

Universidad de San Pedro Sula (USAP)

Campus Universitario, Avenida Circunvalación, San Pedro Sula, Cortés 1064
Tel: +504 2561-8727
Fax: +504 2561-8787
EMail: info@usap.edu
Website: http://www.usap.edu

Rector: Roberto Martínez Arias (1984-)
EMail: roberto.martinez@usap.edu

Vicerrector: Senén Villanueva Henderson
EMail: svillanueva@usap.edu

Secretario General: Osvaldo Valladares
EMail: osvaldo.valladares@usap.edu

Faculty

Economics and Administration (Advertising and Publicity; Banking; Business Administration; Business Computing; Finance; Industrial Management; Law; Marketing; Mass Communication; Retailing and Wholesaling; Tourism); **Technology** (Agricultural Engineering; Agricultural Management; Architecture; Computer Engineering; Graphic Design; Industrial Engineering)

Department

Postgraduate Studies (Business Administration; Civil Law; Industrial Management)

History: Founded 1978.

Academic Year: January to December (January-April; May-August; September-December)

Admission Requirements: High school diploma

Main Language(s) of Instruction: Spanish

Degrees and Diplomas: *Bachillerato*; *Técnico*; *Licenciatura*; *Maestría*: **Business Administration; Civil Law; Industrial Management.**

Student Services: Academic Counselling, Canteen, Cultural Activities, Health Services, Library, Social Counselling, Sports Facilities

Publications: El Comunicador; Revista Perspectiva

Last Updated: 03/03/16

Hungary

STRUCTURE OF HIGHER EDUCATION SYSTEM

Description:

Higher education can be provided by the Hungarian state, the national minority government, ecclesiatical and business organisations, or foundations. All higher education institutions must obtain an operating license and their recognition must be endorsed by the National Assembly. The Senate is the supreme body of higher education institutions.

Stages of studies:

University level first stage: *Undergraduate studies*

The Alapfokozat (Bachelor degree) is a first cycle degree. Courses leading to Alapfokozat (Bachelor degree) require the taking of a minimum of 180 and a maximum of 240 credits. The length of the programme extends to a minimum of 6 and a maximum of 8 semesters. Students complete their studies with a final examination. The final examination may consist of several parts – the defence of the degree thesis, and an additional oral, written or practical examinations – as defined in the curriculum. The degree give access to the labour market as well as to second cycle degree programmes.

University level second stage: *Postgraduate studies*

The Mesterfokozat (Master degree) is a second cycle degree. Courses leading to the Mesterfokozat require at least 60 credits but such courses may not exceed 120 credits. The length of the programme extends to a minimum of 2 and a maximum of 4 semesters. In a few fields (e.g. Medicine, Law, Arts), the Mesterfokozat (Master degree) can be obtained in a one-tier undivided programme of 10 to 12 semesters requiring the completion of at least 300 credits and a maximum of 360 credits. Students complete their studies with a final examination. The final examination may consist of several parts – the defence of the degree thesis, and additional oral, written or practical examinations – as defined in the curriculum. Both degrees give access to the labour market as well as to doctoral degree programmes. The Szakirányú továbbképzés (postgraduate specialist training) following upon a Alapfokozat (Bachelor degree) or a Mesterfokozat (Master degree) is a non-degree programme leading to the Szakirányú továbbképzési oklevél (Further specialization diploma). Courses require at least 60 credits and a maximum of 120 credits. The length of the programme can extend to a minimum of 2 and a maximum of 4 semesters. The Szakirányú továbbképzési oklevél (Further specialization diploma) does not give access to doctorate courses.

University level third stage: *Doctorate studies*

In the higher education system, doktori képzés (doctorate course) constitutes the third training cycle. The doctorate courses prepare students for taking a doktori fokozat (doctoral degree) following the conferral of the Mesterfokozat (Master degree). Doctorate courses require at least 180 credits. The length of the programme extends to 6 semesters. Following a doctorate course, in a separate degree awarding procedure, the scientific degree 'Doctor of Philosophy' (abbreviation: PhD), or in art education 'Doctor of Liberal Arts' (abbreviation: DLA) may be awarded.

ADMISSION TO HIGHER EDUCATION

Admission to university-level studies:

Name of secondary school credential required: Érettségi Bizonyítvány

For entry to: Alapfokozat (Bachelor degree), Mesterfokozat (Master degree in one tier long cycle, undivided programme)

Admission requirements: The number of students who can be admitted to higher education is limited. From the academic year 2004/2005 onwards, there are no more entrance examinations. Applicants are admitted based on final grades obtained at secondary school and their secondary school leaving examination results or based solely on the latter, considering the interest of the applicant. The admission to some programmes could be based on additional aptitude test or practical examination.

Numerus clausus: Restrictions in some cases depending on places available

Other requirements: An aptitude test (e.g. teacher training) or practical examinations (e.g. in arts, sports, etc) is required for some study programmes.

Foreign students admission:

Definition of foreign student: Students who are not Hungarian citizens and have not settled in Hungary.

Admission requirements: The prerequisite of admission to any study programme in a higher education institution is either (a) the Hungarian secondary school leaving certificate, or (b) its foreign equivalent, or (c) a degree obtained in higher education accredited or recognized in Hungary. There are a few exceptions where practical examinations or aptitude tests are also required. Study programmes in the fields of music and arts require applicants to demonstrate their particular artistic abilities. The basic requirement of admission to PhD degrees is to hold a university degree which is equivalent to an MA/MSc degree.

Entry regulations: Foreign students from outside the European Union and students who are not citizens of countries listed in the 539/2001/EC council regulation Annex II. are required to apply for a visa.

Language proficiency: Knowledge of the Hungarian language is a requirement in courses conducted in Hungarian. Hungarian higher education institutions also offer higher education programmes in foreign languages. In this case, the knowledge of the given language is a prerequisite.

RECOGNITION OF STUDIES

Quality assurance system:

The Hungarian Accreditation Committee (HAC) (http://www.mab.hu/english/index.html) continuously monitors the standard of training and scientific activity in higher education institutions. All programmes have to be approved by the HAC.

Bodies dealing with recognition:

Magyar Felsőktatási Akkreditációs Bizottság - MAB (Hungarian Accreditation Committee - HAC)

Krisztina krt. 39/B 4. em.
Budapest 1013
Tel: +36(1) 344 0314
Fax: +36(1) 344 0313
EMail: titkarsag@mab.hu
WWW: http://www.mab.hu/web/index.php?lang=en

Magyar Ekvivalencia és Információs Központ, Oktatási Hivatal (Hungarian Equivalence and Information Centre, Educational Authority - ENIC-NARIC)

Head of the ENIC-NARIC: Gábor Mészáros
Szalay u. 10-14
Budapest 1055
Tel: +36(1) 374-2212
Fax: +36(1) 374-2492
EMail: recognition@oh.gov.hu
WWW: http://www.naric.hu

Special provisions for recognition:

Recognition for university level studies: Act C of 2001 on the recognition of foreign certificates and degrees. It also applies to foreigners.

For access to advanced studies and research: Act C of 2001 on the recognition of foreign certificates and degrees. It also applies to foreigners.

For exercising a profession: Act C of 2001 on the recognition of foreign certificates and degrees. It also applies to foreigners.

NATIONAL BODIES

Ministry of Human Capacities

Minister: Zoltán Balog
Akadémia u. 3
Budapest 1054
Tel: +36 1 795 1200
EMail: ugyfelszolgalat@emmi.gov.hu
WWW: http://www.kormany.hu/en/ministry-of-human-resources

Oktatási Hivatal (Educational Authority)

President (Acting): Emese Pupek
Szalay utca 10-14.
Budapest 1055
Tel: +36(1) 374 2100
Fax: +36(1) 374 2499
EMail: info@oh.gov.hu
WWW: http://www.oktatas.hu

Role of national body: The Educational Authority embodies all organizations performing educational administrative tasks. At the higher education level, the Educational Authority administers the application system to higher education and operates the Hungarian Equivalence and Information Centre.

Magyar Felsőoktatási Akkreditációs Bizottság - MAB (Hungarian Accreditation Committee - HAC)

President: Ervin Balázs
Krisztina krt. 39/B 4. em.
Budapest 1013
Tel: +36(1) 344 0314
Fax: +36(1) 344 0313
EMail: titkarsag@mab.hu
WWW: http://www.mab.hu/web/index.php?lang=en

Role of national body: The Hungarian Accreditation Committee is, according to the 2005 Higher Education Act, "an independent national body of experts assessing quality in education, research and artistic activities in higher education, and examining the operation of the institutional quality development scheme."

IAU Magyar Rektori Konferencia (Hungarian Rectors' Conference)

President: József Bódis
Secretary-General: Zoltán Dubéczi
Benczúr u. 43. IV/3
Budapest 1068
Tel: +36(70) 932 4203
Fax: +36(1) 322 9679
EMail: mrk@mrk.hu
WWW: http://www.mrk.hu

Role of national body: The Hungarian Rectors' Conference is an independent public corporation entitled to represent higher education institutions and to protect their interests.

Data for academic year: 2015-2016

Source: IAU from the Hungarian Equivalence and Information Centre, 2012, updated from the websites of the Ministry, Tempus Public Foundation, and Hungarian Rectors Conference, 2015

INSTITUTIONS

PUBLIC INSTITUTIONS

BUDAPEST BUSINESS SCHOOL

Budapesti Gazdasági Főiskola (BGF)
Buzogány utca 11-13., 1149 Budapest
Tel: +36(1) 383-4799
Fax: +36(1) 469-6636
EMail: bgf@bgf.hu
Website: http://www.bgf.hu

Rector: Éva Sándorné Kriszt EMail: kriszt.eva@bgf.hu

Secretary-General: Szilvia Ács EMail: acs.szilvia@bgf.hu

International Relations: Judit Hidasi, Head of International Relations EMail: hidasi.judit@kkfk.bgf.hu

College
Business Administration *(Zalaegerszeg)* (Business Administration); **Commerce, Catering and Tourism** (Advertising and Publicity; Business and Commerce; Cooking and Catering; European Studies; Finance; Hotel Management; International Business; Management; Marketing; Tourism); **Finance and Accountancy** (Accountancy; Banking; Finance; Human Resources; Insurance; Taxation); **International Management and Business** (International Business; Management)

Institute
Business Teacher Training and Pedagogy *(Professional Academic)* (Business Education); **Commerce and Marketing** *(Professional Academic)* (Business and Commerce; Marketing); **Economics and Methodology** (Economics); **Finance and Accountancy** *(Professional Academic)* (Accountancy; Finance); **International Business Economics** *(Professional Academic)* (International Business; International Economics); **Language and Communication** (Communication Studies); **Management and Human Resources** *(Professional Academic)* (Human Resources; Management); **Social Sciences** *(Professional Academic)* (Social Sciences); **Tourism and Catering** *(Professional Academic)* (Cooking and Catering; Tourism)

History: Founded 2000.

Main Language(s) of Instruction: Hungarian

Degrees and Diplomas: *Alapfokozat megszerzését tanúsító oklevél*; *Mesterfokozat megszerzését tanúsító oklevél*; *Doktori oklevél*: **Business Administration.**
Last Updated: 13/01/15

BUDAPEST UNIVERSITY OF TECHNOLOGY AND ECONOMICS

Budapesti Műszaki és Gazdaságtudományi Egyetem (BME)
Műegyetem rakpart 3., H-1111 Budapest
Tel: +36(1) 463-1111
Fax: +36(1) 463-1110
EMail: info@mail.bme.hu; nki@mail.bme.hu
Website: http://www.bme.hu

Rector: Gábor Péceli EMail: rektor@mail.bme.hu

Secretary-General: Tibor Szabó EMail: tiborszabo@mail.bme.hu

International Relations: László Dvorszki, Head, Department of International Affairs EMail: dvorszkil@mail.bme.hu

Faculty
Architecture (Architecture; Town Planning); **Chemical Technology and Biotechnology** (Biotechnology; Chemical Engineering; Chemistry); **Civil Engineering** (Civil Engineering); **Economic and Social Sciences** (Business Administration; Economics; Management; Social Sciences); **Electrical Engineering and Informatics** (Automation and Control Engineering; Computer Engineering; Electrical Engineering; Power Engineering); **Mechanical Engineering** (Mechanical Engineering); **Natural Sciences** (Cognitive Sciences; Mathematics; Nuclear Engineering; Physics); **Transportation Engineering and Vehicle Engineering** (Civil Engineering; Road Transport; Transport Engineering)

Centre
International Education *(IEC)* (International and Comparative Education)

History: Founded 1782 as Institutum Geometricum Hydrotechnicum, acquired University status 1871. Reorganized 1949 as Technical University of Budapest incorporating former Technical University of Building and Transport Engineering, founded 1952. Acquired present title 2000. Under the jurisdiction of the Ministry of Culture and Education and financed by the State.

Academic Year: September to June (September-January; February-June)

Admission Requirements: Secondary school certificate (érettségi bizonyítvány) and entrance examination

Fees: None for Hungarian citizens. Foreign students: 3,200 (Euro)

Main Language(s) of Instruction: Hungarian, English, French, German

Degrees and Diplomas: *Alapfokozat megszerzését tanúsító oklevél*; *Mesterfokozat megszerzését tanúsító oklevél*; *Doktori oklevél*: **Architecture; Economics; Electrical Engineering; Mathematics; Psychology; Social Sciences.**

Student Services: Academic Counselling, Canteen, Careers Guidance, Cultural Activities, Health Services, Nursery Care, Sports Facilities

Publications: Periodica Polytechnica (8 series); Research News

Publishing House: Publishing House
Last Updated: 14/01/15

COLLEGE OF DUNAÚJVÁROS

Dunaújvárosi Főiskola (DF)
Táncsics Mihály utca 1/a., 2400 Dunaújváros
Tel: +36(25) 551-100
Fax: +36(25) 551-231
EMail: international@mail.duf.hu
Website: http://portal.duf.hu

Rektor: István András

Programme
Andragogy (Adult Education); **Business Administration** (Business Administration); **Communication and Media Sciences** (Communication Studies; Media Studies); **Computer Engineering** (Computer Engineering); **Engineering Business Management** (Business Administration; Engineering; Management); **Engineering Teacher** *(Master Degree Programs)* (Engineering; Teacher Trainers Education); **Materials Engineering** (Materials Engineering); **Mechanical Engineering** (Mechanical Engineering); **Technology Education** (Technology Education); **Vocational Education** (Vocational Education)

History: Founded 1969. Acquired present status 2000.

Degrees and Diplomas: *Alapfokozat megszerzését tanúsító oklevél*; *Szakirányú továbbképzési oklevél*; *Mesterfokozat megszerzését tanúsító oklevél*
Last Updated: 14/01/15

COLLEGE OF NYIREGYHÁZA

Nyíreghyházi Főiskola (NYF)
Sóstói út. 31/b, 4401 Nyíregyháza
Tel: +36(42) 599-400
Fax: +36(42) 404-092 +36(42) 402-485
EMail: international.center@nyf.hu
Website: http://www.nyf.hu

Rector: Zoltán Jánosi

Faculty
Agriculture and Engineering (Agricultural Engineering; Agriculture); **Arts** (Arts and Humanities; English; Literature; Management; Music; Russian); **Economics and Social Studies**

(Communication Studies; Economics; International Studies; Media Studies; Social Sciences); **Science and Information Technology** (Biology; Chemistry; Environmental Studies; Geography; Information Technology; Library Science; Mathematics; Physical Education); **Teacher Training** (Psychology; Teacher Training)

History: Founded 2000 as a result of the integration of György Bessenyei Teachers Training College (1962) and the Nyíregyháza Agricultural College Faculty of the Agricultural University of Gödöllő (1961).

Degrees and Diplomas: *Alapfokozat megszerzését tanúsító oklevél*; *Szakirányú továbbképzési oklevél*; *Mesterfokozat megszerzését tanúsító oklevél*. Also Postgraduate courses

Last Updated: 21/01/15

COLLEGE OF SZOLNOK

Szolnoki Főiskola (SZF)
Tiszaligeti sétány 14, 5000 Szolnok
Tel: +36(56) 510-300
Fax: +36(56) 426-719
EMail: szolf@szolf.hu
Website: http://www.szolf.hu/Lapok/default.aspx

Rektor: Imre Túróczi

Faculty

Business (Accountancy; Business and Commerce; Communication Studies; Finance; International Business; Tourism); **Technical and Agricultural** (Agricultural Engineering; Cooking and Catering; Food Science; Mechanical Engineering; Rural Planning)

Institute

Foreign Language (Foreign Languages Education)

History: Founded 1993 when the Szolnok branches of the Budapest based College of Commerce and Catering and the College of Foreign Trade merged.

Degrees and Diplomas: *Alapfokozat megszerzését tanúsító oklevél*; *Mesterfokozat megszerzését tanúsító oklevél*

Last Updated: 22/01/15

IAU CORVINUS UNIVERSITY OF BUDAPEST

Budapesti Corvinus Egyetem
Fővám tér 8, 1093 Budapest
Tel: +36(1) 482-5000
Fax: +36(1) 482-5023
EMail: intoffice@uni-corvinus.hu
Website: http://www.uni-corvinus.hu

Rector: Zsolt Rostovanyi (2012-) EMail: rektor@uni-corvinus.hu

Faculty

Business Administration (Accountancy; Business Administration; Business and Commerce; Commercial Law; Computer Science; Economics; Environmental Studies; Ethics; Finance; Fiscal Law; Human Resources; Management; Marketing; Media Studies; Rural Planning; Transport Management); **Economics** (Actuarial Science; Economic and Finance Policy; Economic History; Economics; European Studies; Finance; Human Resources; Management; Mathematics; Operations Research; Public Administration; Statistics); **Food Science** (Applied Chemistry; Biotechnology; Brewing; Crop Production; Food Science; Food Technology; Harvest Technology; Microbiology; Nutrition; Oenology; Viticulture); **Horticultural Science** (Biochemistry; Biotechnology; Botany; Chemistry; Ecology; Entomology; Environmental Studies; Farm Management; Floriculture; Fruit Production; Horticulture; Information Management; Management; Marketing; Mathematics; Nursing; Physiology; Plant and Crop Protection; Soil Science; Vegetable Production; Viticulture; Water Management); **Landscape Architecture** (Architectural and Environmental Design; Architecture; Development Studies; Heritage Preservation; Landscape Architecture; Regional Planning; Rural Planning; Town Planning); **Social Sciences** (Behavioural Sciences; Central European Studies; Communication Studies; Development Studies; Eastern European Studies; Economics; Educational Sciences; European Languages; European Studies; Foreign Languages Education; Government; History of Societies; International Relations; International Studies; Philosophy; Political Sciences; Psychology; Regional Studies; Social Policy; Sociology; Teacher Training)

History: Founded 1920 as Faculty of Economics of the Royal Hungarian University of Budapest. Became part of the Hungarian University of Economics 1948. Academic programme divided into three faculties 1952. Reorganized as Budapest University of Economic Sciences 1990. Became Budapest University of Economic Sciences and Public Administration (BUESPA) 2000. The former University of Horticulture and Food Industry (3 faculties of Szent István University) joined BUESPA 2003. Acquired present status and title 2004.

Academic Year: September to June (September-December; February-June)

Admission Requirements: Secondary school certificate (érettségi bizonyítvány)

Main Language(s) of Instruction: Hungarian

Degrees and Diplomas: *Alapfokozat megszerzését tanúsító oklevél*; *Mesterfokozat megszerzését tanúsító oklevél*; *Doktori oklevél*: **Agriculture; Business Administration; Economics; Food Science; International Relations; Landscape Architecture; Management; Political Sciences; Sociology.**

Student Services: Academic Counselling, Canteen, Health Services, Sports Facilities

Publications: Hungarian Bibliography of Economics and Statistics; Management Science; Társadalom és Gazdaság

Last Updated: 13/01/15

EÖTVÖS JÓZSEF COLLEGE

Eötvös József Főiskola (EJF)
Szegedi út. 2, 6500 Baja
Tel: +36(79) 524-624 +36(79) 524-641
Fax: +36(79) 524-630
EMail: rektor@ejf.hu
Website: http://www.ejf.hu

Rektor: Zoltán Melicz

Faculty

Pedagogy (Arts and Humanities; Cultural Studies; Fine Arts; Foreign Languages Education; Hungarian; Pedagogy; Physical Education; Social Studies); **Technology** (Computer Science; Construction Engineering; Mathematics; Technology; Water Management)

History: Founded 1870, acquired present status and title 1996.

Degrees and Diplomas: *Alapfokozat megszerzését tanúsító oklevél*

Last Updated: 14/01/15

EÖTVÖS LORÁND UNIVERSITY

Eötvös Loránd Tudományegyetem (ELTE)
Egyetem tér 1-3., 1053 Budapest
Tel: +36(1) 411-6500
Fax: +36(1) 411-6546
EMail: is@rekthiv.elte.hu
Website: http://www.elte.hu

Rector: Mezey Barna EMail: rektor@elte.hu

Secretary-General: András Kisfaludi EMail: fotitkar@ludens.elte.hu

Faculty

Education and Psychology (Educational Psychology); **Humanities** (American Studies; Ancient Languages; Arts and Humanities; Communication Studies; English Studies; Germanic Studies; History; Information Sciences; Library Science; Media Studies; Oriental Languages; Romance Languages; Slavic Languages); **Informatics** (Computer Engineering); **Law and Political Science** (Civil Law; Commercial Law; Constitutional Law; Criminal Law; Criminology; International Law; Law; Philosophy; Political Sciences); **Primary and Pre-school Education** (Preschool Education; Primary Education); **Science** (Biology; Chemistry; Geography; Geology; Mathematics; Multimedia; Natural Sciences; Physics); **Social Sciences** (Cultural Studies; International Studies; Political Sciences; Social Sciences; Sociology); **Special Education** *(Bárczi Gusztáv)* (Phonetics; Rehabilitation and Therapy; Sociology; Special Education; Speech Therapy and Audiology)

History: Founded 1561 as Jesuit college and established as University at Nagyszombat 1635 by Archbishop Péter Pázmány. Became secular institution 1773. Transferred to Buda 1777, and to

Pest 1784. Acquired present title 1950. Faculty of Medicine detached and re-established as Medical University 1949. Under the jurisdiction of the Ministry of Culture and Education and financed by the State.

Academic Year: September to July (September-January; February-July)

Admission Requirements: Secondary school certificate (érettségi bizonyítvány) and entrance examination

Fees: 2,000-5,500 per semester (Euro)

Main Language(s) of Instruction: Hungarian, English, German

Degrees and Diplomas: *Alapfokozat megszerzését tanúsító oklevél*; *Mesterfokozat megszerzését tanúsító oklevél*; *Doktori oklevél*: **Art History; Biology; Chemistry; Computer Science; Criminal Law; Earth Sciences; Environmental Studies; History; Law; Linguistics; Literature; Mathematics; Philosophy; Physics; Political Sciences; Psychology; Social Sciences.**

Student Services: Academic Counselling, Canteen, Cultural Activities, Health Services, Nursery Care, Sports Facilities

Publications: Acta Facultatis Politico-Juridicae; Annales Universitatis de Rolando Eötvös nominatae (15 sections); Bulletin of the Eötvös Loránd University

Publishing House: Eötvös University Press

Last Updated: 14/01/15

ESZTERHÁZY KÁROLY COLLEGE

Eszterházy Károly Főiskola (EKF)

Eszterházy tér 1., 3300 Eger

Tel: +36(36) 520-400

Fax: +36(36) 520-440

EMail: dir@ektf.hu

Website: http://old.ektf.hu/ujweb/index_en.php

Rector: Kálmán Csaba Liptai

Faculty

Economics and Social Sciences (Commercial Law; Communication Studies; Computer Science; Economics; Educational Psychology; Marketing; Pedagogy; Psychology; Social Sciences; Sociology); **Humanities** (American Studies; Arts and Humanities; Cultural Studies; Economics; English; French; German; Graphic Arts; History; Hungarian; Linguistics; Literature; Modern Languages; Music; Philosophy; Russian); **Natural Sciences** (Biology; Botany; Chemistry; Computer Science; Environmental Studies; Geography; Information Technology; Mathematics; Natural Sciences; Physical Education; Physics; Zoology); **Teacher Training and Knowledge Technology** (Computer Science; Education; Information Technology; Pedagogy; Psychology; Teacher Training)

History: Founded 1948. Formerly known as Eszterházy Károly Tanárképzô Fõiskola.

Degrees and Diplomas: *Alapfokozat megszerzését tanúsító oklevél*; *Szakirányú továbbképzési oklevél*; *Mesterfokozat megszerzését tanúsító oklevél.* Also Bachelor and Master degrees

Last Updated: 21/01/15

HUNGARIAN DANCE ACADEMY

Magyar Táncmüvészeti Főiskola (MTF)

Columbus utca 87-89., 1145 Budapest

Tel: +36(1) 273-3434

Fax: +36(1) 273-3433

EMail: info@mtf.hu

Website: http://www.mtf.hu

Rector: György Szakály (2011-)

International Relations: Béláné Melis EMail: melish@mtf.hu

Department

Choreography and Dance Theory (Dance); **Classical Ballet** (Dance); **Dance Pedagogy** (Dance); **Folk Dance** (Dance); **Theoretical** (Dance; Modern Languages; Theatre); **Training Choreographers** (Dance); **Training Pedagogues** (Teacher Training)

Further Information: Also primary and secondary schools

History: Founded 1950 as State Institute of Ballet. Acquired present status and title 1990. Under the jurisdiction of the Ministry of Culture and Education.

Academic Year: September to June (September-January; February-June)

Admission Requirements: Dance teacher training. Secondary school certificate. Folk dancing: elementary education. Ballet: no preliminary training needed, general education given at the Academy. Students over the age of 10 accepted

Fees: 250 a month (US Dollar)

Main Language(s) of Instruction: Hungarian, English

Degrees and Diplomas: *Alapfokozat megszerzését tanúsító oklevél*; *Szakirányú továbbképzési oklevél*: **Dance.** *Mesterfokozat megszerzését tanúsító oklevél.* Also Bachelor and Master degrees

Last Updated: 20/01/15

KAPOSVÁR UNIVERSITY

Kaposvári Egyetem (KE)

Guba Sándor út. 40, 7401 Kaposvár

Tel: +36(82) 505-800

Fax: +36(82) 505-986

EMail: rektor@ke.hu

Website: http://www.ke.hu/

Rector: Ferenc Szávai

International Relations: Zoltán Gál, Director
EMail: gal.zoltan@ke.hu

Faculty

Agricultural and Environmental Sciences (Animal Husbandry; Biochemistry; Botany; Chemistry; Environmental Studies; Hygiene; Nutrition); **Arts** (Art History; Communication Studies; Film; Fine Arts; Media Studies; Photography); **Economics** (Agricultural Economics; Agricultural Engineering; Computer Science; Economics; Finance; Food Science; Marketing; Rural Planning); **Pedagogy** *(Csokonai Vitéz Mihály)* (Pedagogy)

Research Institute

Forage Science *(Iregszemce)*

History: Founded 2000 due to changes in the Hungarian higher education system. The Faculty of Animal Husbandry of the Pannon University of Agricultural Sciences, the Csokonai Vitéz Mihály Teacher Training College of Kaposvár, the Research Institute of Forage Science of Iregszemce and the Research Institute of Chemical and Process Engineering of Veszprém merged as University of Kaposvár and acquired present status and title.

Academic Year: September to June (September-January; February-June)

Admission Requirements: Secondary school certificate (érettségi bizonyÍtvány) and entrance examination

Main Language(s) of Instruction: Hungarian

Accrediting Agency: Hungarian Accreditation Committee (MAB)

Degrees and Diplomas: *Alapfokozat megszerzését tanúsító oklevél*: **Animal Husbandry; Communication Arts; Cultural Studies; Education of the Handicapped; Preschool Education; Primary Education.** *Mesterfokozat megszerzését tanúsító oklevél*: **Agricultural Education; Agricultural Engineering; Economics.** *Doktori oklevél*: **Economics; Veterinary Science.**

Student Services: Canteen, Health Services, Language Laboratory, Sports Facilities

Publications: Acta Agrarie Kasposvariensis; Reports, Articles and Scientific Memoirs for Agriculture

Last Updated: 15/01/15

KÁROLY RÓBERT UNIVERSITY COLLEGE

Károly Róbert Föiskola (KRF)

Mátrai utca 36., 3201 Gyöngyös

Tel: +36(37) 518-300 +36(37) 518-305

Fax: +36(37) 313-170

EMail: rektor@karolyrobert.hu

Website: http://honlap.karolyrobert.hu/h_en/index.html

Rector: Ilona Eszter Helgertné Szabó

Programme

Business and Management (Business Administration; Management); **Business Development** (Business and Commerce;

Marketing); **Finance and Accounting** (Accountancy; Finance); **Management and Leadership** (Management); **Tourism-Management** (Management; Tourism)

History: Founded 1961.

Degrees and Diplomas: *Alapfokozat megszerzését tanúsító oklevél; Szakirányú továbbképzési oklevél*: **Agriculture.** *Mesterfokozat megszerzését tanúsító oklevél*

Last Updated: 15/01/15

KECSKEMÉT COLLEGE

Kecskeméti Főiskola (KF)
Izsáki út 10, 6000 Kecskemét
Tel: +36(76) 501-960
Fax: +36(76) 501-979
EMail: rh@kefo.hu
Website: http://www.kefo.hu

Rector: Ailer Piroska EMail: rector@kefo.hu

Faculty

Horticulture (Horticulture); **Mechanical Engineering and Automation** *(GAMF)* (Engineering; Information Technology; Management; Mechanical Engineering; Technology); **Teacher Training** *(Kindergarten, Primary level)* (Teacher Training)

History: Founded 2000 through the merger of 3 Kecskemét-based tertiary colleges (Faculty of Mechanical Engineering and Automation, the Teacher Training Faculty and the Horticultural Faculty).

Degrees and Diplomas: *Alapfokozat megszerzését tanúsító oklevél; Szakirányú továbbképzési oklevél*: **Horticulture.** Also Vocational Training Programme.

Last Updated: 16/01/15

LISZT FERENC ACADEMY OF MUSIC IN BUDAPEST

Liszt Ferenc Zeneművészeti Egyetem (LFZE)
Liszt Ferenc tér 8, 1061 Budapest
Tel: +36(1) 462-4616
Fax: +36(1) 462-4615
EMail: international@lfze.hu
Website: http://www.liszt.hu/

President: Andrea Vigh
EMail: rektor@lisztacademy.hu

School

Young Talents (Education of the Gifted; Music Education)

Department

Chamber Music (Music); **Church Music** (Religious Music); **Composition** (Music; Music Theory and Composition); **Conducting** (Conducting); **Folk Music** (Jazz and Popular Music); **Jazz** (Jazz and Popular Music; Music); **Keyboard and Harp** (Musical Instruments); **Musicology and Music Theory** (Music Theory and Composition; Musicology); **Strings** (Musical Instruments); **Vocal and Opera Studies** (Opera; Singing); **Woodwinds and Brass** (Musical Instruments)

Institute

Pedagogical *(Kodály)* (Music Education; Teacher Training)

Further Information: Also Music Teachers' Training Institute in Budapest, Pécs and Szeged

History: Founded 1875 by Franz Liszt. Reorganized 1971. Due to changes in the Hungarian higher education system, acquired present status and title 2000. Under the jurisdiction of the Ministry of Culture and Education.

Academic Year: September to June (September-January; February-June)

Admission Requirements: Secondary school certificate and adequate musical knowledge

Main Language(s) of Instruction: Hungarian

Degrees and Diplomas: *Alapfokozat megszerzését tanúsító oklevél; Szakirányú továbbképzési oklevél; Mesterfokozat megszerzését tanúsító oklevél; Doktori oklevél*: **Music.**

Student Services: Social Counselling, Sports Facilities

Last Updated: 20/01/15

MOHOLY-NAGY UNIVERSITY OF ARTS AND DESIGN, BUDAPEST

Moholy-Nagy Művészeti Egyetem (MOME)
Zugligeti út. 9/25, 1121 Budapest
Tel: +36(1) 392-1193
Fax: +36(1) 392-1190
EMail: international@mome.hu
Website: http://www.mome.hu

Rector: József Fülöp EMail: rektor@mome.hu

Chancellor: Zsombor Nagy EMail: kancellaria@mome.hu

International Relations: Zsolt Petri EMail: petri@mome.hu

Institute

Architecture (Architecture; Design; Furniture Design; Interior Design); **Design** (Ceramic Art; Ceramics and Glass Technology; Design; Fashion Design; Industrial Design; Jewellery Art; Metal Techniques; Textile Design); **Media** (Graphic Design; Media Studies; Photography); **Theoretical Studies** (Aesthetics; Art Education; Arts and Humanities; Ethics; Social Sciences)

Graduate School

Liberal Arts *(Doctoral school)*

History: Founded 1880 as Hungarian Royal Institute of Arts and Crafts, acquired present status 1971 and title 2006. Under the jurisdiction of the Ministry of Culture and Education and financed by the State.

Academic Year: September to June (September-January; February-June)

Admission Requirements: Secondary school certificate (érettségi bizonyítvány) and entrance examination

Main Language(s) of Instruction: Hungarian

Accrediting Agency: Magyar Akkreditációs Bizottság

Degrees and Diplomas: *Alapfokozat megszerzését tanúsító oklevél; Szakirányú továbbképzési oklevél; Mesterfokozat megszerzését tanúsító oklevél*: **Architecture; Arts and Humanities; Communication Arts; Design; Education; Fine Arts; Textile Design; Visual Arts.** *Doktori oklevél*: **Architecture; Design; Fine Arts; Multimedia.**

Student Services: Canteen, Foreign Studies Centre, Health Services, Sports Facilities

Last Updated: 21/01/15

NATIONAL UNIVERSITY OF PUBLIC SERVICE

Nemzeti Közszolgálati Egyetem
Ludovika tér 2, 1083 Budapest
Tel: +36(1)432-9000
EMail: nke@uni-nke.hu
Website: http://uni-nke.hu/

Rector: András Patyi (2012-) EMail: rektor@uni-nke.hu

International Relations: Norbert Kis, Vice-Rector for Continuing Education and International Affairs
EMail: Kis.Norbert@vtki.uni-nke.hu

Faculty

International and European Studies (Cultural Studies; European Studies; International Studies); **Law Enforcement** (Law); **Military Sciences and Officer Training** (Military Science; Police Studies); **Public Administration** (Administration; Public Administration)

Institute

Disaster Management (Management); **Executive Training and Continuing Education** (Continuing Education); **International Studies** (International Studies); **National Security** (Civil Security)

History: Created 2012 following merger between Zrínyi Miklós National Defence University (created 2009), the Police College of Hungary (created 2009), and Faculty of Public Administration of Corvinus University of Budapest (created 2008).

Academic Year: September to June

Main Language(s) of Instruction: Hungarian, English

Accrediting Agency: Hungarian Accreditation Committee

Degrees and Diplomas: *Alapfokozat megszerzését tanúsító oklevél; Szakirányú továbbképzési oklevél; Mesterfokozat*

megszerzését tanúsító oklevél; *Doktori oklevél*: **Military Science; Public Administration.**
Last Updated: 21/01/15

OBUDA UNIVERSITY

Óbudai Egyetem
Bécsi út 96/B, 1034 Budapest
Tel: +36(1) 666-5500
Fax: +36(1) 666-5621
EMail: kancellar@uni-obuda.hu
Website: http://www.uni-obuda.hu/

Rector: János Fodor

Faculty

Business and Management *(Keleti)* (Business Administration; Business and Commerce; Management; Marketing); **Electrical Engineering** *(Kandó Kálmán)* (Electrical Engineering); **Informatics** *(John von Neumann)* (Computer Science; Information Technology); **Light Industry and Environmental Protection Engineering** *(Sándor Rejtő)* (Environmental Engineering; Industrial Engineering); **Mechanical and Safety Engineering** *(Bánki Donát)* (Mechanical Engineering; Safety Engineering); **Technical** *(Alba Regia)* (Computer Science; Engineering)

Centre

Engineering Education *(Ágoston Trefort)* (Engineering)

History: Founded 1395. Óbuda University is the legal successor of the Public Secondary Industrial School of Budapest, established in 1879 and the Hungarian Royal Public Training School of Mechanics and Watchmaking, established in 1889. Óbuda University's direct predecessor is Budapest Tech, 2000. Acquired present title 2010.

Degrees and Diplomas: *Alapfokozat megszerzését tanúsító oklevél*; *Mesterfokozat megszerzését tanúsító oklevél*; *Doktori oklevél*: **Applied Mathematics; Computer Science; Materials Engineering; Safety Engineering.** Also Bachelor degrees, Master degrees and Doctorates
Last Updated: 21/01/15

POLICE OFFICER TRAINING COLLEGE

Rendőrtiszti Főiskola (RTF)
Farkasvölgyi út 12., 1121 Budapest
Tel: +36(1) 392-3500
Fax: +36(1) 392-3501
EMail: nki@rtf.hu

Major-General, Rector: István Sárkány
Tel: +36(1) 392-3504 EMail: rector@rtf.hu

Programme

Police Studies (Law; Police Studies)

History: Fouinded 1971.

Degrees and Diplomas: *Alapfokozat megszerzését tanúsító oklevél*; *Mesterfokozat megszerzését tanúsító oklevél*
Last Updated: 21/01/15

IAU SEMMELWEIS UNIVERSITY

Semmelweis Egyetem (SE)
Üllői út. 26, 1085 Budapest
Tel: +36(1) 459-1500
Fax: +36(1) 317-2220
EMail: international@semmelweis-univ.hu
Website: http://www.semmelweis-univ.hu

Rector: Agoston Szél (2012-)
EMail: titkarsag.rektor@semmelweis-univ.hu

Vice-Rector for Scientific Affairs: Mária Judit Molnár
EMail: rektorhelyettes@semmelweis-univ.hu

Faculty

Dentistry (Dentistry); **Health and Public Services** (Health Administration; Social Work); **Health Sciences** (Health Sciences); **Medicine** (Medicine); **Pharmacy** (Pharmacy)

School

Doctoral Studies

Further Information: Also Teaching Hospital. University degree programmes for foreign students in English and German. The university's Health Services Management Training Centre provides post-graduate courses in health management.

History: Founded 1769 as Faculty of Medicine of the Pázmány Péter University, now Eötvös Lóránd, detached and re-established as separate Institution 1951. Due to changes in the Hungarian higher education system, Semmelweis University of Medicine, The College of Health Care of Haynal Imre University and the Hungarian University of Physical Education and Sport Sciences merged as Semmelweis University and acquired present status and title 2000. Under the jurisdiction of the Ministry of Culture and Education.

Academic Year: September to June (September-January; February-June)

Admission Requirements: Secondary school certificate (érettségi bizonyítvány) and entrance examination

Fees: Foreign students, c. 10,000 per annum according to course (US Dollar)

Main Language(s) of Instruction: Hungarian, German, English

Accrediting Agency: Hungarian Accreditation Committee (MAB)

Degrees and Diplomas: *Alapfokozat megszerzését tanúsító oklevél*: **Medical Technology; Nursing; Physical Education; Physical Therapy; Sports; Sports Management.** *Mesterfokozat megszerzését tanúsító oklevél*: **Dentistry; Human Resources; Medicine; Pharmacy; Physical Education; Physical Therapy; Sports Management.** *Doktori oklevél*: **Health Sciences; Medicine; Microbiology; Neurosciences; Pathology; Pharmacy; Psychiatry and Mental Health.**

Student Services: Academic Counselling, Canteen, Cultural Activities, Foreign Studies Centre, Health Services, Language Laboratory, Nursery Care, Social Counselling, Sports Facilities

Publications: Semmelweis Egyetem; Szinapszis

Publishing House: Semmelweis Publishing and Multimedia Studio Ltd
Last Updated: 21/01/15

SZÉCHENYI ISTVÁN UNIVERSITY

Széchenyi István Egyetem (SZE)
Egyetem ter 1, 9026 Győr
Tel: +36(96) 503-400
Fax: +36(96) 503-406
EMail: information@sze.hu
Website: http://www.sze.hu

Rector: Péter Földesi EMail: foldesi@sze.hu

Faculty

Economics *(Kautz Gyula)* (Accountancy; Economics; Finance; International Studies; Management; Marketing; Regional Studies; Social Sciences); **Engineering Sciences** (Architectural and Environmental Design; Architecture; Automation and Control Engineering; Automotive Engineering; Computer Science; Construction Engineering; Electrical Engineering; Engineering; Environmental Engineering; Materials Engineering; Mathematics; Mechanical Engineering; Railway Engineering; Technology Education; Telecommunications Engineering; Town Planning; Transport and Communications; Transport Management); **Law and Political Sciences** *(Deak Ferenc)* (Administrative Law; Civil Law; Commercial Law; Constitutional Law; Criminal Law; European Union Law; International Law; Labour Law; Private Law; Public Law)

Institute

Health and Social Sciences *(Petz Lajos)* (Health Sciences; Social Psychology; Social Work); **Musical Art** *(Vagar Tibor)* (Music; Music Theory and Composition; Musical Instruments)

History: Founded 1968 as Széchényi István College. Acquired present status and title 2002.

Main Language(s) of Instruction: Hungarian

Accrediting Agency: Hungarian Accreditation Committee

Degrees and Diplomas: *Alapfokozat megszerzését tanúsító oklevél*; *Mesterfokozat megszerzését tanúsító oklevél*; *Doktori oklevél*: **Economics; Engineering; Law; Political Sciences.** Also Bachelor and Master degrees

Student Services: Careers Guidance, Facilities for disabled people, Health Services, Language Laboratory, Sports Facilities
Last Updated: 21/01/15

SZENT ISTVÁN UNIVERSITY

Szent István Egyetem (SZIE)
Páter Károly utca 1., 2103 Gödöllö
Tel: +36(28) 522-000
Fax: +36(28) 410-804
EMail: info@szie.hu
Website: http://www.szie.hu

Rector: János Tőzsér EMail: rector@szie.hu

International Relations: István Szabó, Director
EMail: international@szie.hu

Faculty

Agricultural and Environmental Studies (Agriculture; Animal Husbandry; Biotechnology; Botany; Crop Production; Environmental Management; Environmental Studies; Genetics; Horticulture; Landscape Architecture; Plant and Crop Protection; Wildlife; Zoology); **Applied Arts and Pedagogy** *(Jászberény)* (Pedagogy; Primary Education; Teacher Training); **Architecture and Civil Engineering** *(YBL Miklós)* (Architecture; Civil Engineering; Construction Engineering); **Economics and Social Sciences** (Accountancy; Economic and Finance Policy; Economics; Finance; Human Resources; Management; Marketing; Public Administration; Rural Studies; Social Sciences); **Economics, Agriculture and Health Studies** *(Békéscsaba)* (Accountancy; Adult Education; Agriculture; Business Administration; Cooking and Catering; Economics; Finance; Health Sciences; Management; Tourism); **Mechanical Engineering** (Computer Science; Mathematics; Mechanical Engineering; Mechanics); **Veterinary Science** (Anatomy; Animal Husbandry; Biochemistry; Botany; Chemistry; Computer Science; Ecology; Microbiology; Ophthalmology; Parasitology; Pharmacology; Physiology; Surgery; Toxicology; Veterinary Science; Zoology); **Water and Environmental Management** *(Szarvas)* (Agricultural Engineering; Agricultural Management; Environmental Management; Mechanical Engineering; Waste Management)

Institute

Health Care and Environmental Sanitation Studies (Environmental Studies; Health Sciences)

Further Information: Branches in Békéscaba; Budapest, Jászberény.

History: Founded 1787 as Veterinary Institute of the University of Pest, became independent 1851, incorporated in University of Engineering and Economics 1934 and in University of Agriculture 1945. Became University of Veterinary Science, 1952. Due to changes in the Hungarian higher education system, University of Veterinary Science, Gödöllö University of Agricultural Sciences, University of Horticultural and Food Sciences, Miklós YBL Polytechnical College and Teacher Training College of Jászberény, Szent István University, one of Hungary's largest institutions of higher education merged. Later on, in 2009, Tessedik Sámuel College merged with SZIE as well. Acquired present status and title 2000 as Szent István University. Under the jurisdiction of the Ministry of Education and Culture.

Academic Year: September to May (September-December; February-May)

Admission Requirements: Secondary school certificate (érettségi bizonyÍtvány) and entrance examination

Fees: Application fees, 50; Bachelor Studies, c. 2,200-4,600 per annum; Master studies, c. 2,800-10,980 per annum; Postgraduate, c. 3,000-5,000; Short courses, c. 950 per semester (US Dollar)

Main Language(s) of Instruction: Hungarian, German, English

Accrediting Agency: Hungarian Accreditation Committee (MAB)

Degrees and Diplomas: *Alapfokozat megszerzését tanúsító oklevél; Mesterfokozat megszerzését tanúsító oklevél; Doktori oklevél*: **Animal Husbandry; Biology; Business Administration; Environmental Studies; Horticulture; Management; Mechanical Engineering; Regional Studies; Veterinary Science.** Also Special Degree: Veterinary Medicine (DVM): 5 yrs

Student Services: Academic Counselling, Canteen, Cultural Activities, Foreign Studies Centre, Health Services, Language Laboratory, Library, Social Counselling, Sports Facilities

Last Updated: 22/01/15

THE ANDRÁS PETŐ COLLEGE

Pető András Foïskola (MPANNI)
Kútvölgyi út. 6, 1125 Budapest
Tel: +36(1) 224-1500
Fax: +36(1) 355-6649
EMail: info@peto.hu
Website: http://www.peto.hu

Rector: Franz Schaffhauser

Department

Conductive Education (Education); **Conductive Teaching and Education for Children** (Pedagogy; Primary Education); **Education and Social Sciences** (Education; Social Sciences); **Foreign Languages** (Modern Languages); **Medical Biology** (Biomedicine)

History: Founded 1963, acquired present status and title 1995.

Degrees and Diplomas: *Alapfokozat megszerzését tanúsító oklevél; Mesterfokozat megszerzését tanúsító oklevél*

Last Updated: 21/01/15

THE HUNGARIAN UNIVERSITY OF FINE ARTS, BUDAPEST

Magyar Képzőművészeti Egyetem (MKE)
Andrássy út. 69/71, 1062 Budapest
Tel: +36(1) 342-1738 +36(1) 342-8556
Fax: +36(1) 342-1563
EMail: rektor@mke.hu
Website: http://www.mke.hu

Rector: Tibor Somorjai-Kiss

Department

Art History (Art History); **Art Restoration** (Restoration of Works of Art); **Art Theory** *(Artist Colony, Tihany)* (Fine Arts); **Artistic Anatomy and Geometry and Projection** (Painting and Drawing); **Conservation** (Architectural Restoration); **Graphic Design** (Graphic Design); **Graphics** (Graphic Arts); **Intermedia** (Communication Studies; Media Studies; Multimedia); **Painting** (Painting and Drawing); **Printmaking** (Printing and Printmaking); **Scenography** (Display and Stage Design); **Sculpture** (Sculpture); **Visual Education** (Education; Visual Arts)

History: Founded 1871 as School, reorganized 1949. Acquired present status and title 1971.

Academic Year: October to June (October-January; February-June)

Admission Requirements: Secondary school certificate (érettségi bizonyÍtvány) and presentation of original work

Fees: 510 per month (Euro)

Main Language(s) of Instruction: Hungarian

Degrees and Diplomas: *Alapfokozat megszerzését tanúsító oklevél*: **Fine Arts.** *Mesterfokozat megszerzését tanúsító oklevél; Doktori oklevél*: **Arts and Humanities; Fine Arts.**

Student Services: Canteen, Foreign Studies Centre, Health Services, Sports Facilities

Last Updated: 20/01/15

UNIVERSITY OF DEBRECEN

Debreceni Egyetem (DE)
Egyetem tér. 1, 4010 Debrecen, Hajdú-Bihar
Tel: +36(52) 512-900/23054
Fax: +36(52) 416-490
EMail: internationaloffice@admin.unideb.hu
Website: http://www.unideb.hu

Rector: Zoltán Szilvássy EMail: rector@admin.unideb.hu

Registrar: József Mészáros EMail: fotitkar@unideb.hu

Faculty

Agricultural and Food Sciences and Environmental Management (Agriculture; Environmental Management; Food Science); **Applied Economics and Rural Development** (Accountancy; Administration; Agricultural Business; Agricultural Economics; Agricultural Management; Business and Commerce; Economics; English; Farm Management; Finance; Forestry; Human Resources; Management; Marketing); **Arts and Humanities** (Arts and Humanities); **Child and Adult Education** (Adult Education; Child Care and Development); **Dentistry** (Dental Hygiene; Dental Technology; Dentistry; Oral Pathology; Orthodontics; Periodontics; Stomatology); **Economics and Business Administration** (Business Administration; Economics); **Engineering** (Engineering); **Health** *(Nyíregyháza)* (Health Sciences); **Informatics** (Computer Engineering); **Law** (Law); **Medicine** (Medicine); **Music** (Music); **Pharmacy** (Endocrinology; Organic Chemistry; Pharmacy); **Public Health** (Public Health); **Science and Technology** (Natural Sciences; Technology)

College

Education *(Hajdúböszörmény)*

Institute

Research *(Karcag)* (Animal Husbandry; Crop Production; Soil Management; Soil Science); **Research** *(Nyíregyháza)*; **Research and Experiment**

Conservatory

Music

History: Founded 1912 as Royal Hungarian University of Debrecen, renamed Count István Tisza University, University of Debrecen and Kossuth Lajos University, opened 1914-15 with Faculties of Law, Arts and Humanities, Language and History and Reformed Theology. Faculties of Medicine and Science established 1918 and 1949. Faculty of Law suspended by Government decree 1949 and reorganized 1996 and Faculty of Theology separated from the University 1950 (as Debrecen Academy of Reformed Theology). Faculty of Medicine reorganized separately as Medical University of Debrecen and Faculties of Arts and Humanities and Natural Sciences reorganized as Kossuth Lajos University Debrecen 1952. Due to changes in the Hungarian higher education system, universities of Debrecen (Debrecen University of Medicine, Debrecen Agricultural University, Kossuth Lajos University Debrecen) and Hajdúböszörményi Wargha István College of Education merged and acquired present status and title 2000 as University of Debrecen.

Academic Year: September to June

Admission Requirements: Secondary school certificate (érettségi bizonyÍtvány) or foreign equivalent and entrance examination

Main Language(s) of Instruction: Hungarian

Accrediting Agency: Hungarian Accreditation Committee (MAB)

Degrees and Diplomas: *Alapfokozat megszerzését tanúsító oklevél*: **Agricultural Economics; Agriculture; Education; Engineering; Health Sciences; Music; Natural Sciences; Social Work.** *Szakirányú továbbképzési oklevél*: **Agricultural Economics; Agriculture; Arts and Humanities; Economics; Education; Engineering; Health Sciences; Medicine; Natural Sciences.** *Mesterfokozat megszerzését tanúsító oklevél*: **Agricultural Economics; Agriculture; Arts and Humanities; Dentistry; Economics; Law; Medicine; Music; Natural Sciences; Pharmacy.** *Doktori oklevél*: **Agriculture; Animal Husbandry; Arts and Humanities; Biology; Chemistry; Earth Sciences; Economics; Environmental Studies; Health Sciences; History; Horticulture; Information Technology; Linguistics; Literature; Mathematics; Medicine; Pharmacy; Philology; Physics.**

Student Services: Academic Counselling, Canteen, Careers Guidance, Cultural Activities, Facilities for disabled people, Foreign Studies Centre, Health Services, Language Laboratory, Nursery Care, Social Counselling, Sports Facilities

Publications: A Debreceni Egyetem Magyar Nyelvtudományi Intézetének kiadványai; Acta Andragogiaie; Acta Classica; Acta Debrecina; Acta geographica ac geologica et meteorologica Debrecina; Acta Neerlandica; Acta pericemonologica rerum ambietum Debrecina; Acta Physica et Chimica; Agrártudományi közlemények; Beiträge zur Methodik und Fachdidaktik, Deutsch als Fremdsprache; Collectio iuridica Universitatis Debreceniensis; Competitio; Debreceni szemle; Ethnica; Ethnographica Folcloristica Carpatica; Folia Uralica Debreceneniensia; Gond; Hungarian Journal of English and American Studies; Italianistica Debreceniensis; Journal of Agricultural Sciences; Kitaibelia; Könyv és könyvtár; Magyar Nyelvjárások; Módszerek és eljárások; Német filológiai tanulmányok; Ókortudományi Értesitő; Posztbizánci Közlemények; Publ. Mathematicae; Slavica; Sprachteorie und Germanistiche Linguistik; Studia Letteraria; Studia Romanica; Studies in Linguistics; Teaching Mathematics and Computer Science; Történeti Tanulmányok; Werkstatt Arbeitspapiere

Academic Staff *2011*	**TOTAL**
FULL-TIME	**1,425**
Student Numbers *2011*	
All (Foreign included)	**30,418**
FOREIGN ONLY	**2390**

Last Updated: 14/01/15

UNIVERSITY OF MISKOLC

Miskolci Egyetem (UM)

3515 Miskolc - Egyetemvaros, Borsod-Abaúj-Zemplén
Tel: +36(46) 565-111 +36(46) 565-034
Fax: +36(46) 565-014 +36(46) 565-423
EMail: info@uni-miskolc.hu
Website: http://www.uni-miskolc.hu

Rector: András Torma

Pro-Rector: Viktor Kovács
Tel: +36(46) 563-423 EMail: rektno@gold.uni-miskolc.hu

International Relations: Edit Szőke, Secretary-General
Tel: +36(46) 565-111/Ext. 22-76 EMail: rekszoke@uni-miskolc.hu

Faculty

Arts (Anthropology; Arts and Humanities; Comparative Literature; Cultural Studies; Education; History; Linguistics; Modern Languages; Philosophy; Political Sciences; Psychology; Sociology; Translation and Interpretation); **Earth Sciences and Engineering** (Earth Sciences; Environmental Engineering; Geological Engineering; Mining Engineering; Petroleum and Gas Engineering; Surveying and Mapping); **Economics** (Accountancy; Business Administration; Business and Commerce; Economics; Finance; Human Resources; Management; Marketing; Regional Studies); **Health Care** (Health Sciences; Medical Technology; Nursing; Radiology); **Law** (Law; Political Sciences); **Materials Science and Engineering** (Materials Engineering; Metallurgical Engineering); **Mechanical Engineering and Informatics** (Automation and Control Engineering; Civil Engineering; Computer Engineering; Electrical and Electronic Engineering; Information Sciences; Information Technology; Mathematics; Mechanical Engineering; Production Engineering; Statistics)

Institute

Confucius (Chinese); **Music** *(Béla Bartók)* (Music; Musical Instruments; Musicology)

History: Founded 1735 as School of Mining, became Academy 1770. German replaced by Hungarian as language of instruction 1867. Reorganized at Sopron 1919, became Technical University of Heavy Industry and transferred to Miskolc 1949. Acquired present status and title 1990. Under the jurisdiction of the Ministry of Culture and Education and financed by the State.

Academic Year: September to May (September-December; February-May)

Admission Requirements: Secondary school certificate (érettségi bizonyítvány) or foreign equivalent and entrance examination

Fees: Foreign students, 6,000 per annum; preparatory year, 2,000 per annum (US Dollar)

Main Language(s) of Instruction: Hungarian, English

Accrediting Agency: Hungarian Accreditation Committee (Ministry of Education)

Degrees and Diplomas: *Alapfokozat megszerzését tanúsító oklevél*: **Electrical Engineering; English; German; Mechanical Engineering; Musicology; Nursing; Production Engineering; Teacher Training.** *Szakirányú továbbképzési oklevél*; *Mesterfokozat megszerzését tanúsító oklevél*: **Arts and Humanities; Business Administration; Earth Sciences; Economics; Engineering Management; Environmental Engineering; Information Technology; Law; Materials Engineering; Mechanical Engineering; Metallurgical Engineering; Mining Engineering; Petroleum and Gas Engineering.** *Doktori oklevél*: **Administration; Earth Sciences; Information Sciences; Law; Literature; Materials Engineering; Mechanical Engineering.**

Student Services: Academic Counselling, Canteen, Careers Guidance, Cultural Activities, Facilities for disabled people, Foreign Studies Centre, Health Services, Language Laboratory, Social Counselling, Sports Facilities

Publications: K+F Kiadvány; MERT A Miskolci Egyetem közéleti és kulturális lapja; Miskolci Egyetem Idegennyelvű Közleményei; Miskolci Egyetem Közleményei

Last Updated: 21/01/15

UNIVERSITY OF PANNONIA

Pannon Egyetem (PE)

PO Box 158, Egyetem út. 10, 8201 Veszprém
Tel: +36(88) 624-000
Fax: +36(88) 624-529
EMail: pr@uni-pannon.hu
Website: http://www.uni-pannon.hu

Rector: Andras Gelencser EMail: rektor@uni-pannon.hu

Secretary-General: Angéla Bognár Sabjanics
EMail: fotitkar@uni-pannon.hu

Faculty

Economics (Economics); **Engineering** (Analytical Chemistry; Automation and Control Engineering; Chemical Engineering; Chemistry; Computer Science; Earth Sciences; Economics; Electrical Engineering; Engineering; Engineering Management; Environmental Engineering; Environmental Studies; Information Technology; Management; Materials Engineering; Mechanical Engineering; Mechanics; Organic Chemistry; Physical Chemistry; Physics; Radiophysics; Tourism); **Georgikon** *(Georgikon, Keszthely)* (Agricultural Economics; Agricultural Equipment; Agriculture; Agronomy; Animal Husbandry; Chemistry; Crop Production; Farm Management; Horticulture; Microbiology; Oenology; Plant and Crop Protection; Soil Science; Viticulture; Waste Management; Water Management; Zoology); **Information Technology** (Computer Science; Electrical Engineering; Information Sciences; Nanotechnology; Software Engineering); **Modern Philology and Social Sciences** (Anthropology; Applied Linguistics; Educational Psychology; Ethics; European Studies; French; German; Hungarian; International Studies; Native Language; Pedagogy; Political Sciences; Social Sciences; Social Studies; Theatre)

Further Information: Also evening and correspondence courses, distance education and continuing education

History: Founded 1949 as Faculty of the Technical University of Budapest, became Veszprém University of Chemical Engineering 1951. The Georgikon Faculty of Agriculture of the Pannon University of Agricultural Sciences attached to the University 1989. Faculty of Teacher Training started 1990. Due to changes to the Hungarian higher education system, the Georgikon Faculty of Agriculture of the Pannon University of Agricultural Sciences, Keszthely and the Faculty of Agriculture of Mosonmagyaróvár became part of Veszprémi University 2000. Under the jurisdiction of the Ministry of Culture and Education. Known as Veszprémi Egyetem (University of Veszprém) until March 2006, when obtained current title and status.

Academic Year: September to June (September-January; February-June)

Admission Requirements: Secondary school certificate (érettségi bizonyitvány) and entrance examination

Main Language(s) of Instruction: Hungarian, English

Degrees and Diplomas: *Alapfokozat megszerzését tanúsító oklevél*: **Agricultural Engineering; Agricultural Management; Biotechnology; Business Administration; Chemical Engineering; Chemistry; Computer Engineering; Economics; Education; Electrical Engineering; English; Environmental Engineering; Fine Arts; French; German; Horticulture; Hotel and Restaurant; Hotel Management; Hungarian; Information Technology; International Relations; Materials Engineering; Mechanical Engineering; Natural Sciences; Political Sciences; Tourism; Transport Management.** *Mesterfokozat megszerzését tanúsító oklevél*: **Agricultural Engineering; Applied Linguistics; Art History; Business Administration; Chemical Engineering; Computer Engineering; Economics; Educational Sciences; English; Environmental Engineering; Fine Arts; German; Hungarian; International Relations; Materials Engineering; Natural Sciences; Pedagogy; Political Sciences; Teacher Training; Translation and Interpretation.** *Doktori oklevél*: **Chemistry; Computer Science; Economics; Education; Environmental Studies; Horticulture; Management; Zoology.**

Student Services: Academic Counselling, Canteen, Careers Guidance, Cultural Activities, Foreign Studies Centre, Health Services, Language Laboratory, Social Counselling, Sports Facilities

Publications: Georgikon for Agriculture; Hungarian Journal of Industrial Chemistry

Publishing House: Veszprémi Egyetemi Kiadó

Last Updated: 10/04/15

UNIVERSITY OF PÉCS

Pécsi Tudományegyetem (PTE)

Vasvári Pál utca 4., 7622 Pécs
Tel: +36(72) 501-500
Fax: +36(72) 501-508
EMail: info@pte.hu
Website: http://www.pte.hu

Rector: József Bódis EMail: rector@rektori.pte.hu

International Relations: Gyöngyi Komlódiné Pozsgai
EMail: gyongyi.pozsgai@iro.pte.hu

Faculty

Adult Education and Human Resources Development (Adult Education; Human Resources); **Business and Economics** (Business Administration; Business and Commerce; Economics; Management; Marketing); **Engineering and Information Technology** *(Mihály Pollack)* (Civil Engineering; Electrical and Electronic Engineering; Engineering; Environmental Engineering; Information Technology; Mechanical Engineering); **Health Sciences** (Health Administration; Health Sciences; Public Health); **Humanities** (Arts and Humanities; Communication Studies; Education; English; Ethnology; History; Linguistics; Literature; Psychology; Slavic Languages); **Law** (Civil Law; European Union Law; International Law; Labour Law; Law; Public Law); **Music and Visual Arts** (Fine Arts; Music; Musical Instruments; Painting and Drawing; Performing Arts; Sculpture; Singing); **Sciences** (Botany; Chemistry; Genetics; Geography; Mathematics; Natural Sciences; Physical Education; Physics; Sports Medicine; Zoology)

School

Medicine (Dentistry; Medicine; Pharmacy)

Institute

Teacher Training (Educational Sciences; Teacher Training)

Centre

Asia (Asian Studies); **Balkan Studies** (Eastern European Studies); **European Studies** (European Studies; Social Sciences); **Francophone** (French Studies); **Latin American** (Latin American Studies)

Further Information: Also courses in foreign languages, and programmes in English

History: Founded 1921, formerly Academy of Law established 1785, and succeeding University of Pécs founded 1367 by King Louis I. Faculties of Theology and Medicine detached and re-established as separate Institutions 1949 and 1951. Faculty of Teacher Training incorporated and acquired present title 1982. Due to changes in the Hungarian higher education system, Janus Pannonius University Pécs, Pécs University Medical School and Illyés Gyula College of Education, Szekszárd merged as University of Pécs and acquired present status and title 2000. A State institution under the jurisdiction of the Ministry of Culture and Education and part of the Ministry of Health and financed by the State.

Academic Year: September to May (September-December; February-May)

Admission Requirements: Secondary school certificate (érettségi bizonyítvány) or equivalent and entrance examination

Fees: Tuition, c. 2,000-8600 per semester (US Dollar)

Main Language(s) of Instruction: Hungarian, English, German

Accrediting Agency: Hungarian Accreditation Committee (MAB)

Degrees and Diplomas: *Alapfokozat megszerzését tanúsító oklevél; Mesterfokozat megszerzését tanúsító oklevél; Doktori oklevél*: **Architecture; Biology; Business Administration; Chemistry; Earth Sciences; English; Health Sciences; Law; Linguistics; Physics; Regional Planning.**

Student Services: Academic Counselling, Canteen, Careers Guidance, Cultural Activities, Facilities for disabled people, Foreign Studies Centre, Health Services, Language Laboratory, Nursery Care, Social Counselling, Sports Facilities

Publishing house: Univ Pécs

Last Updated: 21/01/15

UNIVERSITY OF SZEGED

Szegedi Tudományegyetem (SZTE)

Dugonics tér 13, 6720 Szeged
Tel: +36(62) 544-000
Fax: +36(62) 546-371
EMail: rektor@rekt.szte.hu
Website: http://www.u-szeged.hu

Rector: Gabor Szabo (2006-)

International Relations: György Pálfi
EMail: palfi.gyorgy@rekt.u-szeged.hu

Faculty

Agriculture *(Hódmezővásárhely)* (Agricultural Engineering; Agriculture); **Arts** (American Studies; Archaeology; Arts and Humanities; Classical Languages; Contemporary History; Education; English Studies; Ethnology; European Studies; French Studies; Germanic Studies; Hungarian; Modern History; Oriental Studies; Psychology; Slavic Languages; Social Sciences); **Dentistry** (Dentistry); **Economics and Business Administration** (Business Administration; Economics); **Engineering** (Engineering); **Health Sciences and Social Studies** (Health Sciences; Social Studies); **Law and Political Sciences** (Administrative Law; Civil Law; Commercial Law; Comparative Law; Constitutional Law; Criminal Law; Demography and Population; European Union Law; International Law; Labour Law; Law; Political Sciences; Statistics); **Medicine** (Medicine); **Music** (Music; Music Theory and Composition; Musical Instruments; Opera; Singing); **Pharmacy** (Pharmacy); **Science and Informatics** (Biology; Chemistry; Computer Science; Environmental Engineering; Geography; Geology; Materials Engineering; Mathematics; Natural Sciences; Physics; Software Engineering); **Teacher Training** *(Juhász Gyula)* (Teacher Training)

History: Founded 1872 as Hungarian Royal University of Kolozsvar. Renamed Ferencz-Joseph University of Kolozvar 1881, moved to Szeged, 1921. In 1940 the university was divided into two institutions, one in Kolozsvar and one remained in Szeged, they were reorganized and became Szeged University 1945, named after József Attila 1962. Due to changes in the Hungarian higher education system, 'József Attila' University Szeged, 'Albert Szent-Györgyi Medical University Szeged, and 'Juhász Gyula' Teacher's Training College, Szeged merged as University of Szeged 2000.

Academic Year: September to June (September-December; February-June)

Admission Requirements: Secondary school certificate (érettségi bizonyitvány) and entrance examination

Main Language(s) of Instruction: Hungarian, English, German

Accrediting Agency: Ministry of Culture and Education

Degrees and Diplomas: *Alapfokozat megszerzését tanúsító oklevél*; *Mesterfokozat megszerzését tanúsító oklevél*; *Doktori oklevél*: **Biology; Chemistry; Computer Science; Economics; Educational Sciences; Environmental Studies; Geology; History; Law; Literature; Mathematics; Medicine; Pharmacy; Physics; Political Sciences.**

Student Services: Academic Counselling, Canteen, Careers Guidance, Cultural Activities, Foreign Studies Centre, Health Services, Language Laboratory, Nursery Care, Social Counselling, Sports Facilities

Publications: Acta Biologica Szegdiensis; Acta Climatologica; Acta Cybernetica; Acta Scientiarum Mathematicarum; Aetas; Analysis Mathematica; Belvedere; Bolcso; Egyetem; Electronic Journal of Qualitative Theory of Differential Equations; Eleszto; Fosszilla; Informatikalap; Jogelméleti Szemle; Kari Kurir; Kozgazolo; Linklap; Magyar Kozony; Newtone; Polygon; Tiscia; Ujsagvari

Publishing House: JATE Press (József Attila University Press)

Last Updated: 21/01/15

UNIVERSITY OF THEATRE AND FILM ARTS BUDAPEST

Szinház-és Filmművészeti Egyetem (SZFE)
Vas út. 2/c, 1088 Budapest
Tel: +36(1) 318-8111
Fax: +36(1) 338-4749
EMail: rektorihivatal@szfe.hu
Website: http://www.filmacademy.hu

Rector: Tamás Ascher

International Relations: Sylvia Huszár
EMail: huszar.sylvia@szfe.hu

Faculty

Film and Television (Cinema and Television; Film; Video); **Theatre** (Acting; Theatre)

History: Founded 1865, acquired present status and title 2000.

Academic Year: September to June

Main Language(s) of Instruction: Hungarian

Degrees and Diplomas: *Alapfokozat megszerzését tanúsító oklevél*; *Mesterfokozat megszerzését tanúsító oklevél*; *Doktori oklevél*: **Film; Theatre.** Also Bachelor and Master degrees

Last Updated: 22/01/15

UNIVERSITY OF WEST HUNGARY

Nyugat-Magyarországi Egyetem (NYME)
Bajcsy-Zsilinszki utca 4., 9400 Sopron
Tel: +36(99) 518-100 +36(99) 518-142
Fax: +36(99) 312-240
EMail: rectoro@nyme.hu
Website: http://www.uniwest.hu

Rector: Sándor Faragó (1998-)

Secretary-General: Mária Merényi
Tel: +36(99) 311-104 EMail: merenyim@nyme.hu

International Relations: Judit Engelmann-Kékesi
Tel: +36(99) 518-210 EMail: tudrh@nyme.hu

Faculty

Agriculture and Food Science *(Mosonmagyaróvár)* (Agricultural Economics; Agricultural Equipment; Agriculture; Agronomy; Animal Husbandry; Crop Production; Food Science; Food Technology; Horticulture); **Arts** (Arts and Humanities; Modern Languages; Social Sciences); **Economics** (Accountancy; Business and Commerce; Economics; Finance; Human Resources; Management; Marketing); **Forestry** (Environmental Engineering; Forestry; Surveying and Mapping; Wildlife); **Geoinformatics** *(Székesfehérvár)* (Geophysics; Natural Sciences; Surveying and Mapping); **Natural Sciences** *(Savaria Campus)* (Natural Sciences); **Pedagogy** *(Benedek Elek)* (Pedagogy); **Teacher Training** *(Apáczai Csere János)* (Education; Linguistics; Literature; Natural Sciences; Social Sciences; Teacher Training; Tourism); **Visual Arts and Music, Education and Sport** *(Savaria Campus)* (Education; Music; Sports; Visual Arts); **Wood Sciences** (Architecture; Forest Products; Industrial Design; Paper Technology; Wood Technology)

History: Founded 1808 as a School of Forestry, became an academy 1846. Moved to Sopron 1919 and reorganized 1962. Due to changes in the Hungarian higher education system, the University of Agricultural Sciences, Pannon and the University of Sopron merged and acquired present status and title as University of West Hungary. Under the jurisdiction of the Ministry of Agriculture.

Academic Year: September to July

Admission Requirements: Secondary school certificate and/or entrance examination

Fees: 100,000-125,000 per semester (Forint)

Main Language(s) of Instruction: Hungarian

Degrees and Diplomas: *Alapfokozat megszerzését tanúsító oklevél*: **Pedagogy; Wildlife; Wood Technology.** *Szakirányú továbbképzési oklevél*; *Mesterfokozat megszerzését tanúsító oklevél*: **Forestry; Pedagogy; Wildlife; Wood Technology.** *Doktori oklevél*: **Wood Technology.**

Student Services: Canteen, Careers Guidance, Cultural Activities, Health Services, Social Counselling, Sports Facilities

Publications: Acta Agronomica Ováriensis; Acta Facultatis Forestalis; Acta Facultatis Ligniensis; Apáczai Csere János Tanítóképzö Föiskolai Kar Tanulmánykötet; Benedek Elek Pedagógiai Föiskolai Kar Tudomány napja; Erdészeti Tallózó; Magyar Apróvad Közlemények; Magyar Visidad Közlemények; Tilia

Last Updated: 21/01/15

PRIVATE INSTITUTIONS

ANDRÁSSY UNIVERSITY BUDAPEST

Andrássy Universität Budapest
Pollack Mihály tér 3., 1088 Budapest
Tel: +36(1) 266-3101
Fax: +36(1) 266-3099
EMail: uni@andrassyuni.hu
Website: http://www.andrassyuni.hu

Rector: András Masát
Tel: +36(1) 266-4408 EMail: andras.masat@andrassyuni.hu

Faculty

Central European Studies (Central European Studies); **Comparative Law and Governance** (Law; Political Sciences); **International Relations** (International Business; International Economics; International Relations)

History: Founded 2001.

Main Language(s) of Instruction: German

Degrees and Diplomas: *Szakirányú továbbképzési oklevél*; *Doktori oklevél*: **Comparative Law; Economics; History; Political Sciences.**

Last Updated: 13/01/15

APOR VILMOS CATHOLIC COLLEGE

Apor Vilmos Katolikus Főiskola (AVKF)
Konstantin tér 1-5., 2600 Vác
Tel: +36(27) 511-151
Fax: +36(27) 511-141
EMail: avkf@avkf.hu
Website: http://www.avkf.hu

Rector: Mary Woods

Department

Arts and Physical Education (Physical Education; Visual Arts); **Church Music and Music** (Music; Religious Music); **Educational Sciences and Psychology** (Educational Sciences; Psychology); **Languages and Literature** (Linguistics; Literature; Modern Languages)

History: Founded 1993.

Degrees and Diplomas: *Alapfokozat megszerzését tanúsító oklevél*; *Szakirányú továbbképzési oklevél*; *Mesterfokozat megszerzését tanúsító oklevél*

Last Updated: 21/01/15

BUDAPEST CONTEMPORARY DANCE ACADEMY

Budapest Kortárstánc Főiskola (BKTF)
Perc utca 2, 1036 Budapest
Tel: +36(1) 250-3046
Fax: +36(1) 250-3056
EMail: budapest@tanc.sulinet.hu
Website: http://tanc.org.hu/wp/bcda/

General Director: Iván Angelus

Programme

Dance (Dance)

Degrees and Diplomas: *Alapfokozat megszerzését tanúsító oklevél*; *Mesterfokozat megszerzését tanúsító oklevél*

Last Updated: 13/01/15

BUDAPEST METROPOLITAN UNIVERSITY OF APPLIED SCIENCES

Budapesti Metropolitan Főiskola (MET)
Nagy Lajos Király út 1-9, 1148 Budapest
Tel: +36(1) 766-5397
EMail: international@metropolitan.hu
Website: http://www.metropolitan.hu

Rektor: László Vass (2001-) EMail: l.vass@bkf.hu

International Relations: Jolán Róka, Vice-Rector for International Relations EMail: j.roka@bkf.hu

International Relations: Denissza Blanár, International Director EMail: dblanar@metropolitan.hu

Programme

Arts (Architectural and Environmental Design; Art History; Design; Fashion Design; Film; Furniture Design; Graphic Design; Handicrafts; Interior Design; Media Studies; Painting and Drawing; Photography; Textile Design); **Business** (Business Administration; International Business; Management; Marketing; Public Relations; Tourism); **Communication Studies** (Advertising and Publicity; American Studies; Journalism; Media Studies; Public Relations); **Tourism** (Cooking and Catering; Hotel and Restaurant; Tourism; Treatment Techniques)

History: Founded 2000. Previously known as Budapesti Kommunikációs és Üzleti Főiskola (University of Applied Sciences, Budapest). Acquired current name 2015.

Admission Requirements: Please see website

Main Language(s) of Instruction: Hungarian

Degrees and Diplomas: *Alapfokozat megszerzését tanúsító oklevél*; *Szakirányú továbbképzési oklevél*; *Mesterfokozat megszerzését tanúsító oklevél*

Student Services: Academic Counselling, Canteen, Careers Guidance, Cultural Activities, Facilities for disabled people, Foreign Studies Centre, Health Services, IT Centre, Language Laboratory, Library, Nursery Care, Social Counselling, Sports Facilities, eLibrary

Last Updated: 09/10/15

CENTRAL EUROPEAN UNIVERSITY

Kozep-Europai Egyetem (CEU)
Nador ut. 9, 1051 Budapest
Tel: +36(1) 327-3000
Fax: +36(1) 327-3005
EMail: public@ceu.hu; kakucsn@ceu.hu
Website: http://www.ceu.hu

Rector and President: John Shattuck (2009-)
Tel: +36(1) 327-3004 EMail: KakucsN@ceu.hu

Provost: Liviu Matei

International Relations: Ildikó Moran, Vice President for External Relations Tel: +36(1) 327-3821 EMail: morani@ceu.hu

Programme

Nationalism Studies (Central European Studies; Government; Political Sciences)

Department

Cognitive Science (Cognitive Sciences); **Economics** (Commercial Law; Economic and Finance Policy; Economics); **Environmental Sciences and Policy** (Environmental Management; Environmental Studies); **Gender Studies** (Gender Studies; Women's Studies); **History** (Central European Studies; Eastern European Studies; European Studies; History; Medieval Studies); **International Relations and European Studies** (European Studies; International Relations; Law; Political Sciences; Public Administration); **Legal Studies** (Commercial Law; Comparative Law; Constitutional Law; Economics; European Studies; Human Rights; International Law; International Relations; Law; Political Sciences); **Mathematics and its Applications** (Applied Mathematics; Mathematics); **Medieval Studies** (History; Medieval Studies); **Philosophy** (Philosophy); **Political Science** (European Studies; International Relations; Law; Political Sciences); **Sociology and Social Anthropology** (Anthropology; Sociology; Urban Studies)

Graduate School

Business (Business Administration; Business and Commerce; Information Management; International Business; Management); **Public Policy** (European Studies; International Relations; Law; Political Sciences)

Further Information: Also Joint Programme With Bard College, USA: Study Abroad In Budapest. 19 Research Centres: see http://www.ceu.hu/researchcenters

History: Founded 1991 as Central European University Foundation, acquired present title 1995. National accreditation acquired 2005. CEU is also accredited by the Middle States Association of Schools and Colleges, USA.

Academic Year: August to July

Admission Requirements: First (undergraduate) Degree, English proficiency (TOEFL test), and professional interview

Fees: 12,000 per annum (US Dollar)

Main Language(s) of Instruction: English

Accrediting Agency: Accredited both in the United States and in Hungary

Degrees and Diplomas: *Alapfokozat megszerzését tanúsító oklevél*; *Szakirányú továbbképzési oklevél*: **Business Administration; Central European Studies; Comparative Law; Economics; Environmental Management; Environmental Studies;**

European Studies; Gender Studies; History; Human Rights; Information Technology; International Relations; Management; Medieval Studies; Social Sciences; Sociology. *Mesterfokozat megszerzését tanúsító oklevél*; *Doktori oklevél*: **Economics; History.** Also Joint International Master of Business Administration (MBA)

Student Services: Academic Counselling, Canteen, Careers Guidance, Cultural Activities, Facilities for disabled people, Health Services, IT Centre, Language Laboratory, Library, Residential Facilities, Social Counselling, Sports Facilities

Publications: East European Constitutional Review

Publishing House: Central European University Press

Academic Staff *2012-2013*: Total 308

Student Numbers *2012-2013*: Total 1,283

Last Updated: 24/11/14

DENNIS GABOR COLLEGE

Gábor Dénes Főiskola (GDF)
Mérnok u. 39., 1119 Budapest
Tel: +36(1) 203-0283
Fax: +36(1) 883-3636
EMail: info@gdf.hu
Website: http://www.gdf.hu

Rector: Sarolta Zárda EMail: zarda@gdf.hu

Institute

Basic Science and Technology (Computer Engineering; Engineering Management); **Economics and Social Sciences** (Business Administration; Economics; Management); **Information Technology** (Information Technology)

History: Founded 1992.

Degrees and Diplomas: *Alapfokozat megszerzését tanúsító oklevél*. Also Bachelor degrees

Last Updated: 15/01/15

DHARMA GATE BUDAPEST BUDDHIST UNIVERSITY

A Tan Kapuya Buddhista Főiskola (TKBF)
Börzsöny u. 11, 1098 Budapest
Tel: +36(1) 280-6712 +36(70) 339-9905
Fax: +36(1) 280-6714
EMail: tankapu@tkbf.hu
Website: http://www.tkbf.eu

Rector: Janos Jelen EMail: rektor@tkbf.hu

Administrative Officer: Attiláné Kovács

International Relations: Tamás Agócs, Vice-Rector for International Relations EMail: agocsster@gmail.com

Programme

Buddhist Studies (Asian Religious Studies); **Chinese and Japanese** (Chinese; Japanese); **Classical Tibetan** (Tibetan); **Oriental Studies and Philosophy** (Oriental Studies; Philosophical Schools); **Pali** (Ancient Languages; Indic Languages); **Sanskrit** (Sanskrit)

History: Founded 1991, acquired present status and title 1999.

Accrediting Agency: State

Degrees and Diplomas: *Alapfokozat megszerzését tanúsító oklevél*: **Asian Religious Studies.** *Mesterfokozat megszerzését tanúsító oklevél*: **Asian Religious Studies.** Also Bachelor and Master programmes

Last Updated: 13/01/15

EDUTUS COLLEGE

Edutus Foiskola
Bécsi út 324., 1137 Budapest
Tel: +36(1) 883-6437
Fax: +36(1) 883-6438
EMail: info@hjf.hu
Website: http://www.edutus.hu

Rector: Jandala Csilla EMail: rektorihivatal@hjf.hu

Programme

Business and Management (Business Administration; Management); **Crafts and Trades** (Crafts and Trades); **Electronic Imaging** (Communication Arts; Graphic Design; Visual Arts); **Tourism** (Hotel Management; Tourism)

History: Formerly known as JánosHarsányi College.

Degrees and Diplomas: *Alapfokozat megszerzését tanúsító oklevél*; *Mesterfokozat megszerzését tanúsító oklevél*: **Marketing.**

Last Updated: 15/01/15

GÁL FERENC COLLEGE OF SZEGED

Gál Ferenc Főiskola (GFHF)
Dóm tér 6, 6720 Szeged
Tel: +36(62) 425-738
Fax: +36(62) 425-738
EMail: gfhf@gfhf.hu
Website: http://www.gfhf.hu

Rektor: Kozma Gábor EMail: rektor@gfhf.hu

Department

Cultural Studies (Cultural Studies); **Foreign Languages** (Modern Languages); **Hungarian Language and Literature** (Hungarian); **Mathematics and Sciences** (Mathematics; Natural Sciences); **Physical Education** (Physical Education); **Slovak** (Slavic Languages); **Social and Religious Studies** (Religious Studies; Social Sciences); **Sociology and Pedagogy** (Pedagogy; Sociology); **Visual Education** (Education)

Institute

Music and Ethics *(Saint Gerard)* (Ethics; Music; Physical Education)

History: Founded 1930. Became Szegedi Hittudományi Főikola 1997.

Degrees and Diplomas: *Alapfokozat megszerzését tanúsító oklevél*; *Szakirányú továbbképzési oklevél*; *Mesterfokozat megszerzését tanúsító oklevél*

Last Updated: 15/01/15

INTERNATIONAL BUSINESS SCHOOL

IBS Nemzetkozi Uzleti Főiskola (IBS)
Tárogató út 2-4., 1021 Budapest
Tel: +36(1) 391-2574
Fax: +36(1) 391-2550
EMail: info@ibs-b.hu
Website: http://www.ibs-b.hu

Chancellor: Istvánedek Tamás

Vice-Chancellor: László Lang
Tel: +36(1) 391-25-20 EMail: llang@ibs-b.hu

International Relations: László Lendvai, Chief International Recruitment Officer EMail: llendvai@ibs-b.hu

Department

Arts Management (Art Management); **Business Administration** (Business Administration); **Economics** (Economics); **Finance** (Accountancy; Finance); **Foreign Languages** (Foreign Languages Education); **Human Resources** (Human Resources); **International Relations** (International Relations); **Management** (Management); **Marketing** (Marketing); **Quantitative Methodology and IT** (Information Technology); **Tourism** (Tourism)

History: Founded 1991, acquired present status and title 1997.

Academic Year: September-July

Admission Requirements: High School Diploma or College/University degree, sufficient level of English

Fees: 900 registration fee for non-EU citizens; BA: 1,900-2,900/sem; MSc: 4,500/sem (Euro)

Main Language(s) of Instruction: English with some programmes in Hungarian

Accrediting Agency: Hungarian Accreditation Committee (Hungary); QAA (UK)

Degrees and Diplomas: *Alapfokozat megszerzését tanúsító oklevél*: **Accountancy; Art Management; Business and Commerce; Finance; International Business; Tourism; Transport**

Management. *Mesterfokozat megszerzését tanúsító oklevél*: **Finance; Human Resources; International Business; Management.**

Student Services: Academic Counselling, Canteen, Careers Guidance, Cultural Activities, Facilities for disabled people, Foreign Studies Centre, Language Laboratory, Social Counselling, Sports Facilities

Last Updated: 15/01/15

KÁROLI GÁSPÁR UNIVERSITY OF THE HUNGARIAN REFORMED CHURCH, BUDAPEST

Károli Gáspár Református Egyetem (KRE)
Kálvin tér 9, 1091 Budapest
Tel: +36(1) 455-9060
Fax: +36(1) 455-9061
EMail: internationall@kre.hu
Website: http://www.kre.hu

Rector: Péter Balla EMail: balla.peter@kre.hu

Chief Secretary: Niké Szkárosi EMail: szkarosi.nike@kre.hu

Faculty

Humanities (Arts and Humanities; Dutch; English; History; Hungarian; Japanese; Modern Languages; Pedagogy; Philology); **Law** (Law; Political Sciences); **Teacher Training** (Primary Education; Religious Education; Social Work); **Theology** (Bible; Canon Law; History of Religion; New Testament; Pastoral Studies; Protestant Theology; Religious Education; Religious Studies; Sociology; Theology)

History: Founded 1855, acquired present status and title 1990.

Main Language(s) of Instruction: Hungarian

Degrees and Diplomas: *Alapfokozat megszerzését tanúsító oklevél*; *Mesterfokozat megszerzését tanúsító oklevél*; *Doktori oklevél*

Last Updated: 15/01/15

KING SIGISMUND BUSINESS SCHOOL

Zsigmond Király Főiskola (ZSKF)
Kelta utca 2., 1032 Budapest
Tel: +36(1) 454-7600 +36(1) 454-7620
Fax: +36(1) 454-7623
EMail: mail@zskf.hu; fh@zskf.hu
Website: http://www.zskf.hu

Rector: József Bayer (2001-)

Institute

Business and Management Studies (Accountancy; Business Administration; Finance; Human Resources; International Business; Management); **Communication and Media Studies** (Communication Studies; Media Studies); **Foreign Languages** (English; French; German; Italian; Russian; Spanish); **International and Political Studies** (International Studies; Political Sciences)

History: Founded 2000.

Main Language(s) of Instruction: English, Hungarian

Degrees and Diplomas: *Alapfokozat megszerzését tanúsító oklevél*; *Szakirányú továbbképzési oklevél*; *Mesterfokozat megszerzését tanúsító oklevél*

Last Updated: 22/01/15

KODOLÁNYI JÁNOS UNIVERSITY OF APPLIED SCIENCES

Kodolányi János Főiskola (KJF)
Fürdö u. 1, 8000 Székesfehérvár
Tel: +36(22) 543-400
Fax: +36(22) 312-288
EMail: international@kjf.hu
Website: http://www.kodolanyi.hu

Rector: Péter Szabó EMail: kjfhivatal@mail.kodolanyi.hu

International Relations: Éva Horvati
Tel: +36(22) 543-391 EMail: horvatieva@mail.kodolanyi.hu

Institute

Cultural, Communication and Media Studies (Communication Studies; Fine Arts; Jazz and Popular Music; Media Studies; Musical Instruments; Singing); **Social Sciences and Liberal Arts** (Arts and Humanities; Education; English; European Studies; History; International Relations; Literature; Psychology; Social Studies); **Tourism and Business Studies** (Hotel Management; Management; Tourism)

Further Information: Also on-line programmes

History: Founded 1992.

Degrees and Diplomas: *Alapfokozat megszerzését tanúsító oklevél*; *Mesterfokozat megszerzését tanúsító oklevél*. Also Bachelor's degree (Alapképzések); Vocational Degree Programmes.

Last Updated: 16/01/15

KÖLCSEY FERENC TEACHER TRAINING COLLEGE OF THE REFORMED CHURCH

Kölcsey Ferenc Református Tanítóképző Főiskola (KTIF)
Péterfia utca 1-7., 4026 Debrecen
Tel: +36(52) 518-500
Fax: +36(52) 518-556
EMail: info@kfrtkf.hu
Website: http://www.kfrtkf.hu

Rector: Zoltán Völgyesi
Tel: +36(52) 412-980 EMail: rektor@kfrtkf.hu

Programme

Christian Education (Christian Religious Studies); **Communication and Media Sciences** (Communication Studies; Media Studies); **Library and Computer Science** (Computer Science; Library Science); **Liturgical Music** (Religious Music); **Teacher Training** *(Primary level)* (Teacher Training); **Youth Assistance** (Social Work)

History: Founded 1855, acquired present status and title 1996.

Degrees and Diplomas: *Alapfokozat megszerzését tanúsító oklevél*. Higher professional training programme, 2 yrs. Also Bachelor degrees

Last Updated: 21/01/15

PÁZMÁNY PÉTER CATHOLIC UNIVERSITY, BUDAPEST

Pázmány Péter Katolikus Egyetem (PPKE/PPCU)
Szentkirályi útca 28, H-1088 Budapest
Tel: +36(1) 429-7211
Fax: +36(1) 318-0507
EMail: rektor@ppke.hu
Website: http://www.ppke.hu

Rector: Szabolcs Anzelm Szuromi

Faculty

Humanities (Art History; Arts and Humanities; Communication Studies; History; Linguistics; Literature; Medieval Studies; Philosophy; Sociology; Teacher Training); **Information Technology** (Biotechnology; Information Technology); **Law and Political Science** (Civil Law; Ethics; European Union Law; History of Law; International Law; Law; Political Sciences); **Teacher Training** *(Vitez Janos)* (Teacher Training); **Theology** (Ancient Languages; Bible; Catholic Theology; Christian Religious Studies; Theology)

Institute

Canon Law *(Postgraduate)* (Canon Law)

Centre

Italian Interuniversity (European Studies; International Business)

History: Founded 1635 as Department of Theology of the University founded by Péter Pázmány, Cardinal, Primate, and Archbishop of Esztergom in Nagyszombat. Acquired present status and title 1993. An ecclesiastic institution recognized by the State under the supervision of the Holy See.

Academic Year: September to June

Admission Requirements: Secondary school certificate (érettségi bizonyítvány) and entrance examination

Main Language(s) of Instruction: Hungarian

Accrediting Agency: Hungarian Accreditation Committee (MAB)

Degrees and Diplomas: *Alapfokozat megszerzését tanúsító oklevél*: **French; Theology.** *Mesterfokozat megszerzését tanúsító oklevél*: **Arts and Humanities; Communication Arts; European**

Studies; Information Technology; Law; Political Sciences; Theology. *Doktori oklevél*: **Canon Law; Law; Political Sciences; Technology; Theology.**

Student Services: Academic Counselling, Canteen, Careers Guidance, Cultural Activities, Facilities for disabled people, Foreign Studies Centre, Health Services, Language Laboratory, Nursery Care, Social Counselling, Sports Facilities

Publications: Folia Canonica; Folia Theologica; Kánonjog; Mester és Tanítvány; Teologia; VERBUM Analecta Neolatina

Last Updated: 22/01/15

TOMORI PÁL COLLEGE

Tomori Pál Főiskola (TPF)

Szent István király utca 2-4., 6300 Kalocsa

Tel: +36(78) 564-600

Fax: +36(78) 464-445

EMail: info@tpfk.hu

Website: http://www.tpfk.hu

Rector: Rózsa Meszlényi EMail: meselenyi.rozsa@tpfk.hu

Programme

Business and Economics (Business Administration; Economics); **Finance and Accountancy** (Accountancy; Finance); **Management** (Management); **Regional Economy** (Economics)

History: Founded 2004.

Degrees and Diplomas: *Alapfokozat megszerzését tanúsító oklevél; Mesterfokozat megszerzését tanúsító oklevél*

Last Updated: 22/01/15

WEKERLE BUSINESS SCHOOL

Wekerle Sándor Üzleti Főiskola

Jázmin u. 10., 1083 Budapest

Tel: +36(1) 323-1070

EMail: info@wbsc-h.eu

Website: http://wbsc-h.eu

Rector: Attila Borbély

Programme

Business Administration (Business Administration; Business and Commerce; Marketing)

History: Founded 2008.

Degrees and Diplomas: *Alapfokozat megszerzését tanúsító oklevél.* Also Post-graduate Specialist Diploma

Last Updated: 22/01/15

Iceland

STRUCTURE OF HIGHER EDUCATION SYSTEM

Description:
While pre-primary and compulsory education is the responsibility of municipalities, central government is responsible for the operation of upper secondary schools and higher education institutions. Although education in Iceland has traditionally been provided by the public sector, a certain number of private institutions are in operation today, primarily at the pre-primary, upper-secondary and higher education levels.

Stages of studies:

University level first stage: *Diploma/Bachelor's degree*
The first cycle of higher education includes 2 stages leading to (1) the Diploma (1 semester to 2 years' study) and (2) the Bachelor's degree (3 to 4 years' study).

University level second stage: *Qualification at Master level/Master's degree*
The second cycle of higher education includes two stages leading to a qualification at Master level (1 semester to 2 years' study) and the Masteŕs degree (1 1/2 to 2 years' study).

University level third stage: *Doctoral degree*
The third cycle of higher education cycle has one stage leading to the Doctoral degree.

ADMISSION TO HIGHER EDUCATION

Admission to university-level studies:

Name of secondary school credential required: Stúdentspróf

For entry to: all higher education institutions

Alternatives to credentials: A foreign equivalent of a secondary-school-leaving Certificate can be accepted as an entrance requirement.

Other requirements: In addition to the general admission requirements (stúdentspróf), individual universities or faculties may have specific requirements.

Foreign students admission:

Definition of foreign student: Foreign students are persons enrolled at a higher education institution in Iceland but not permanent residents in Iceland.

Quotas: With the exception of the University of Iceland and the University at Akureyri, Icelandic higher education institutions limit their intake of students each year.

Admission requirements: The minimum qualification required of foreign students is a pass in the final examination of a Scandinavian or European type of upper secondary education. In general, students must possess the necessary qualifications to enter a university in their respective countries.

Entry regulations: Foreign students entering Iceland from non-Nordic and non-EU countries must submit documents proving that they have been admitted to an Icelandic higher education institution and evidence that they are financially self-sufficient. They must also register with the Immigration Office.

Health requirements: Students from non-Nordic and non-EU countries should make arrangements for health insurance before they leave their home countries.

Language proficiency: Students must have a good knowledge of Icelandic. Courses are arranged for foreign students at the University of Iceland.

RECOGNITION OF STUDIES

Quality assurance system:

The Minister of Education, Science and Culture grants accreditation to higher education institutions (HEIs) that fulfil the criteria laid down in national legislation as well as internationally accepted criteria. The Quality Board for Icelandic Higher Education has issued a Quality Enhancement Framework (QEF) that includes various elements of quality assurance and enhancement such as reviews at institutional and subject levels as well as continuing and additional accreditation of HEIs.
Recognition of studies completed and credentials awarded in Iceland is the responsibility of the higher education authority concerned. In 2003, the five Nordic ENIC/NARIC offices (Denmark, Finland, Iceland, Norway and Sweden) established a regional network named Nordic National Recognition Information Centres (NORRIC) to initiate joint Nordic projects to learn from each other and reduce barriers to the recognition of foreign qualifications in the Nordic region (http://www.norric.org).

Bodies dealing with recognition:

ENIC/NARIC Islands (ENIC/NARIc Iceland)
Director, Academic Affairs:Thordur Kristinsson
University of Iceland
Saemundargata 4
Reykjavík 101
Tel: +354 525 4360
Fax: +354 525 4317
EMail: enicnaric@hi.is
WWW: http://www.enic-naric.hi.is/

NATIONAL BODIES

Mennta- og menningarmálaráðuneytið (Ministry of Education, Science and Culture)
Minister: Illugi Gunnarsson
Director, Department of Education and Science: Hellen Gunnarsdóttir
Sölvhólsgötu 4
Reykjavik 101
Tel: +354 545 9500
Fax: +354 562 3068
EMail: postur@mrn.stjr.is
WWW: http://www.menntamalaraduneyti.is/
Role of national body: The main areas of responsibility of the Ministry of Education, Science and Culture are education, science, culture, media, sports and youth.

Data for academic year: 2015-2016
Source: IAU from the websites of the Ministry of Education, Science and Culture and ENIC/NARIC Iceland, 2015.

INSTITUTIONS

PUBLIC INSTITUTIONS

AGRICULTURAL UNIVERSITY OF ICELAND

Landbúnaðarháskóli Íslands
Hvanneyri, 311 Borgarnes
Tel: +354 433-5000
Fax: +354 433-5001
EMail: lbhi@lbhi.is
Website: http://www.lbhi.is/

Rector: Ágúst Sigurðsson EMail: agust@lbhi.is

International Relations: Björn Thorsteinsson

Faculty
Environmental Sciences (Environmental Management; Forestry; Natural Resources); **Land and Animal Resources** (Animal Husbandry; Earth Sciences)
History: Founded 2005.
Admission Requirements: Secondary school certificate (stúdentsprof) or equivalent
Main Language(s) of Instruction: Icelandic
Degrees and Diplomas: *Bakkalárpróf*: **Agricultural Engineering; Landscape Architecture; Natural Resources.** *Meistarapróf*:

Agricultural Engineering; Natural Resources. *Doktorspróf*: **Agriculture.** Also Diploma in Basic Agricultural Education
Last Updated: 14/04/15

HÓLAR UNIVERSITY COLLEGE

Hólaskóli - Háskólinn á Hólum
Sauðárkrókur 551
Tel: +354 455-6300
Fax: +354 455-6301
EMail: holaskoli@holar.is
Website: http://www.holar.is

Rector: Erla Björk Örnólfsdóttir EMail: erlabjork@holar.is

Department

Aquaculture and Fish Biology (Aquaculture; Zoology); **Equine Science** (Animal Husbandry; Zoology); **Rural Tourism** (Tourism)
History: Founded 1882. Acquired present status 2003.
Admission Requirements: Islandic "Stúdentspróf" certificate (high school matriculation) or equivalent secondary school certificate. Mature students (over 25 yrs) are required to have finished 60 credits at secondary school level and have appropriate work experience. Applicants not satifying the requirements can pass an examination after attending a one year preliminary studies program. For equine Science program, applicants need at least 65 credits (130 ECTS) from a secondary school, sufficient riding experience and they must have reached 18 years of age and good understanding of the Icelandic language.
Fees: (Iceland Krona): administration fee, 50,000 per annum; total cost (including books, transport, housing,...) c. 150,000 per annum, except third year of Equine Studies, 320,000
Degrees and Diplomas: *Diplómapróf*, *Bakkalárpróf*, *Meistarapróf*. Also vocational study programme in Rural Tourism and Aquaculture and Fish Biology, 1yr; Programme in Equine Studies and Riding, 3 yrs (the second and third years are at university levels).
Last Updated: 14/04/15

UNIVERSITY OF AKUREYRI

Háskólinn á Akureyri
Nordurslod 2, 600 Akureyri
Tel: +354 460-8000
EMail: international@unak.is
Website: http://www.unak.is

Rector: Eyjólfur Guðmundsson EMail: rektor@unak.is

School

Business and Science (Aquaculture; Biotechnology; Business Administration; Environmental Studies; Fishery; Information Technology; Management; Marketing; Natural Sciences; Tourism); **Health Sciences** (Health Sciences; Nursing; Occupational Therapy); **Humanities and Social Sciences** (Education; Law; Media Studies; Psychology; Social Sciences)

Institute

Research (Education; Fishery; Management; Nursing)
History: Founded 1987. A State Institution.
Academic Year: August to June (August-December; January-June)
Admission Requirements: Secondary school certificate (stúdentsprof) or equivalent
Fees: (Iceland Krona): 45,000 per annum
Main Language(s) of Instruction: Icelandic
Degrees and Diplomas: *Bakkalárpróf*, *Meistarapróf*
Student Services: Academic Counselling, Canteen, Social Counselling, Sports Facilities
Last Updated: 14/04/15

UNIVERSITY OF ICELAND

Háskóli Íslands
Sæmundargötu 2, 101 Reykjavík
Tel: +354 525-4000
Fax: +354 552-1331
EMail: hi@hi.is
Website: http://www.hi.is

Rector: Kristín Ingólfsdóttir (2005-) EMail: kring@hi.is
Head of Academic Affairs: Thórdur Kristinsson EMail: thordkri@hi.is
International Relations: Karitas Kvaran EMail: karitask@hi.is

School

Education (Education; Leisure Studies; Social Studies; Sports; Teacher Training); **Engineering and Natural Sciences** (Chemical Engineering; Civil Engineering; Computer Engineering; Computer Science; Earth Sciences; Electrical Engineering; Engineering; Environmental Engineering; Industrial Engineering; Mechanical Engineering; Software Engineering); **Health Sciences** (Dentistry; Food Science; Medicine; Nursing; Nutrition; Pharmacy; Psychology); **Humanities** (Archaeology; Arts and Humanities; Comparative Literature; Cultural Studies; Danish; English; Finnish; German; Greek; History; Icelandic; Italian; Latin; Linguistics; Native Language Education; Norwegian; Philosophy; Religious Studies; Russian; Spanish; Swedish; Theology); **Social Sciences** (Anthropology; Business Administration; Economics; Education; Ethnology; Information Sciences; Law; Library Science; Media Studies; Political Sciences; Psychology; Social Sciences; Social Work; Sociology)
History: Founded 1911 by merging Theological seminary, Medical College, and School of Law, and adding Faculty of Philosophy. Merged with the Iceland University of Education 2008.
Academic Year: September to May (September-December; January-May)
Admission Requirements: Upper secondary school certificate (stúdentsprof) or equivalent
Main Language(s) of Instruction: Icelandic
Degrees and Diplomas: *Bakkalárpróf*: **Anthropology; Applied Physics; Archaeology; Biochemistry; Biology; Business Administration; Chemical Engineering; Chemistry; Civil Engineering; Comparative Literature; Computer Engineering; Computer Science; Danish; Economics; Education; Electrical Engineering; English; Environmental Engineering; Ethnology; Finnish; Food Science; French; Geography; Geology; Geophysics; German; Greek; History; Icelandic; Industrial Engineering; Information Sciences; Latin; Library Science; Linguistics; Mathematics; Norwegian; Nursing; Philosophy; Physical Therapy; Physics; Psychology; Religious Studies; Social Work; Sociology; Software Engineering; Spanish; Swedish; Theology; Tourism.** *Viðbótarpróf á meistarastigi*: **Business Administration; Dentistry; Law; Medicine; Midwifery; Pharmacy; Psychology; Theology.** *Meistarapróf*: **Anthropology; Astrophysics; Biochemistry; Biology; Business Administration; Chemistry; Civil Engineering; Comparative Literature; Computer Engineering; Computer Science; Danish; Dentistry; Economics; Education; Electrical Engineering; English; Environmental Engineering; Environmental Studies; Ethnology; Fishery; Food Science; Geography; Geology; Geophysics; German; Health Sciences; History; Icelandic; Industrial Engineering; Information Sciences; Library Science; Literature; Mathematics; Mechanical Engineering; Natural Sciences; Nursing; Nutrition; Pharmacy; Philosophy; Physics; Psychology; Sociology; Theology.** *Doktorspróf*: **Anthropology; Astrophysics; Biochemistry; Biology; Business Administration; Chemistry; Civil Engineering; Computer Engineering; Computer Science; Dentistry; Economics; Education; Electrical Engineering; Environmental Engineering; Food Science; Geography; Geology; Geophysics; History; Icelandic; Industrial Engineering; Information Sciences; Library Science; Literature; Mathematics; Mechanical Engineering; Medicine; Natural Sciences; Nutrition; Pharmacy; Physics; Psychology; Sociology; Theology.**
Student Services: Academic Counselling, Facilities for disabled people, Language Laboratory, Library, Nursery Care, Social Counselling, Sports Facilities
Publications: Ársskýrla Háskóla Íslands
Publishing House: University Press (Háskólaútgáfan)
Last Updated: 14/04/15

PRIVATE INSTITUTIONS

BIFRÖST UNIVERSITY

Háskólinn á Bifröst
Nordurárdalur, 311 Borgarnes
Tel: +354 433-3000
Fax: +354 433-3001
EMail: bifrost@bifrost.is
Website: http://www.bifrost.is

Rector: Ágúst Einarsson EMail: agust@bifrost.is

Department

Business (Banking; Business Administration; Finance; International Business; Management); **Law** (Commercial Law; International Law); **Social Sciences** (Economics; European Studies; Management; Philosophy; Political Sciences)

History: Founded 1918 as Samvinnuskólinn á Bifröst (Co-operative College of Iceland). Became Bifröst Business School in 1988. Acquired present status 1989 and present title 2006

Academic Year: September to May (September-December; January-May)

Admission Requirements: Upper secondary school leaving examination (stúdentspróf) or equivalent for undergraduate studies and first cycle degree (Bachelor's degree) for graduate studies

Fees: Undergraduate, 189,000-205,000 per term; graduate, 310,000 per term (Iceland Krona)

Main Language(s) of Instruction: Icelandic, English (in international exchange programme)

Degrees and Diplomas: *Bakkalárpróf*: **Business Administration; Commercial Law.** *Meistarapróf*: **Business Administration; Law; Social Sciences.** Also Diploma in Management (2 yrs) and lifelong learning programmes

Student Services: Academic Counselling, Facilities for disabled people, Nursery Care, Sports Facilities

Publications: Bifröst School of Business Research Paper Series

Last Updated: 14/04/15

ICELAND ACADEMY OF THE ARTS

Listaháskóli Íslands (LHI)

Skipholt 1, 105 Reykjavík

Tel: +354 552-4000

Fax: +354 562-3629

EMail: lhi@lhi.is

Website: http://www.lhi.is

Rector: Hjálmar H. Ragnarsson (1999-) EMail: hjalmar@lhi.is

Director of Academic Affairs: Anna Kristín Ólafsdóttir EMail: annakristin@lhi.is

International Relations: Anna Kristín Ólafsdóttir Tel: +354 545 2205 EMail: hannba@lhi.is

Department

Art Education (Art Education); **Design and Architecture** (Architecture; Design; Fashion Design; Graphic Design; Industrial Design; Textile Design); **Fine Arts** (Fine Arts; Visual Arts); **Music** (Music; Music Theory and Composition; Performing Arts; Religious Music); **Theatre and Dance** (Acting; Dance; Theatre)

Course

Post-Baccalaureate Teacher Training (Teacher Training)

History: Founded 1998 following the merger of Leiklistarskóli Íslands (Icelandic Drama School), Myndlista-og Handíðskóli Íslands (Icelandic College of Arts and Crafts).

Academic Year: August to July

Admission Requirements: Secondary school certificate (stúdentspróf), entrance examination and Portfolio

Fees: 160,000 per annum (Iceland Krona)

Main Language(s) of Instruction: Icelandic

Degrees and Diplomas: *Bakkalárpróf*; *Meistarapróf*

Last Updated: 14/04/15

REYKJAVÍK UNIVERSITY

Háskólinn í Reykjavík (RU)

Ofanleiti 2, 103 Reykjavík

Tel: +354 510-6200

Fax: +354 510-6201

EMail: ru@ru.is

Website: http://www.ru.is

Rector: Ari Kristinn Jónsson

School

Business (Business Administration; Business and Commerce; Finance; Human Resources; Management); **Computer Science** (Computer Science; Mathematics; Software Engineering); **Energy** *(Icelandic)* (Energy Engineering); **Law** (Law); **Science and Engineering** (Biomedical Engineering; Civil Engineering; Electrical Engineering; Mechanical Engineering)

History: Founded 1998 as Icelandic School of Business, acquired present status and title 2001.

Admission Requirements: Secondary school certificate (stúdentsprof) or equivalent

Main Language(s) of Instruction: Icelandic

Degrees and Diplomas: *Bakkalárpróf*: **Business Administration; Computer Science; Law.** *Meistarapróf*: **Computer Science; Human Resources; Law; Management.** *Doktorspróf*: **Business Administration; Computer Science; Engineering; Law.**

Student Services: Academic Counselling, Canteen, Foreign Studies Centre, Language Laboratory, Sports Facilities

Last Updated: 14/04/15

India

STRUCTURE OF HIGHER EDUCATION SYSTEM

Description:

Higher education is provided by: 1) Universities - including agricultural universities and medical universities- divided into Central Universities, funded directly by the Ministry of Human Resources Development, and State Universities, set up and funded by various states. 2) "Deemed to be universities", single-faculty, multi subjects institutions which enjoy the same academic status and privileges of a university; and 3) Institutions of National Importance, university-level institutions funded by the central government. These include the Indian Institutes of Technology. Most universities belong to the affiliating and teaching type in which departments impart instruction at the postgraduate level and undertake research. Finally, there are open universities and research institutions, as well as more than 15,000 colleges, most of which are affiliated to universities. Universities are governed by statutory bodies such as the Academic Council, the Senate/Court and the Executive Council/ Syndicate. Funding for public universities largely comes from State governments and the University Grants Commission. Higher education falls mainly under its jurisdiction. The Association of Indian Universities (AIU) represents universities and has the responsibility for all matters within the higher education sector other than funding. Professional institutions are coordinated by different bodies. The All-India Council for Technical Education (AICTE) is responsible for the coordination of technical and management education institutions.

Stages of studies:

University level first stage: *Undergraduate*

First degrees generally require three years' full-time study leading to Bachelor's degrees. In professional subjects, courses last for 4 to 5 1/2 years.

University level second stage: *Postgraduate*

A Master's degree generally requires two years of study after a first degree.

University level third stage: *Pre-Doctoral*

One-year MPhil programmes are open to those who have completed their second stage postgraduate degree. It is a preparatory programme for doctoral level studies.

University level fourth stage: *Doctoral education*

The PhD programme involves five years' study beyond the Master's degree.

ADMISSION TO HIGHER EDUCATION

Admission to university-level studies:

Name of secondary school credential required: Higher Secondary School Certificate

Foreign students admission:

Admission requirements: A minimum of twelve years' secondary education with English as one of the subjects. Science stream subjects are required for professional courses.

Entry regulations: A visa is needed to study in India.

Language proficiency: Students must have a good knowledge of English. Where necessary, special English language courses are organized prior to university entrance.

RECOGNITION OF STUDIES

Quality assurance system:

Once recognized by the UGC (NACC) or the AICTE or a similar body, institutions of higher education are expected to maintain a good standard and quality of education and their degrees and diplomas are recognized throughout the country. There are provisions for penal action or withdrawal of recognition if reasonable quality and standards are not maintained and/or if an institution is found involved in serious malpractice.

NATIONAL BODIES

Department of Higher Education, Ministry of Human Resources Development

Minister: Smriti Irani
Minister of State for HRD (Higher Education): Ram Shankar Katheria
Shastri Bhawan
New Delhi 110001
Tel: +91(11) 2338 3936
Fax: +91(11) 2338 1355
EMail: dhe-mhrd@nic.in
WWW: http://mhrd.gov.in/higher_education

Role of national body: The Department of Higher Education, MHRD, is responsible for the overall development of the basic infrastructure of the higher education sector, both in terms of policy and planning.

University Grants Commission - UGC

Chairman: Ved Prakash
Secretary: Jaspal Singh Sandhu
Bahadur Shah Zafar Marg
New Delhi 110 002
Tel: +91(11) 2323 2701
Fax: +91(11) 2323 1797
EMail: webmaster@ugc.ac.in
WWW: http://www.ugc.ac.in

Role of national body: Responsible for providing funds and for the coordination, determination and maintenance of standards in institutions of higher education.

National Assessment and Accreditation Council - NAAC

President: Ved Prakash
Director: Dhirendra Pal Singh
PO Box 1075, Nagarbhavi
Bangalore, Karnataka 560072
Tel: +91(80) 2321 0261
Fax: +91(80) 2321 0270
WWW: http://www.naac.gov.in

Role of national body: Autonomous institution established by the University Grant Commission to assess and accredit higher education institutions.

Distance Education Bureau

Secretary: Renu Batra
University Grants Commission (UGC)
Bahadur Shah Zafar Marg
New Delhi 110 002
EMail: vikramsahay.edu@nic.in
WWW: http://www.ugc.ac.in/deb/index.html

Role of national body: Since 2012, the regulatory functions with regard to distance education programmes in higher education have been vested with the University Grants Commission. The Distance Education Council which was the regulator of distance education programmes, has been dissolved and all regulatory functions are being undertaken by the Distance Education Bureau at UGC.

Association of Indian Universities - AIU

President: Ranbir Singh
Secretary-General: Furqan Qamar
Joint Secretary, International and Student Information Services: Veena Bhalla
AIU House
16 Comrade Indrajit Gupta Marg (Kotla Marg)
New Delhi 110002
Tel: +91(11) 2323 0059
Fax: +91(11) 2323 2131

EMail: info@aiuweb.org; administration@aiuweb.org
WWW: http://www.aiuweb.org
Role of national body: Serves as an inter-university organization and acts as a liaison between universities and the Government.

All India Council for Technical Education
Chairman: Anil D. Sahasrabudhe
Chanderlok Building, 7th Floor, Janpath
New Delhi 110001
Tel: +91(11) 2372-4151
Fax: +91(11) 2372-4183
WWW: http://www.aicte-india.org
Role of national body: Promotes quality in technical tducation, plans and coordinates the development of the technical education system, and sets out regulations for the maintenance of norms and standards.

Data for academic year: 2013-2014
Source: IAU from Department of Higher Education and University Grants Commission websites, 2014. Bodies 2016.

INSTITUTIONS

ACHARYA NAGARJUNA UNIVERSITY

Acharya Nagarjuna Vishwavidhyalayamu
Nagarjuna Nagar, Andhra Pradesh 522510
Tel: +91(863) 229-3189
Fax: +91(863) 229-3378
Website: http://www.nagarjunauniversity.ac.in

Vice-Chancellor: K.Viyyanna Rao
Tel: +91(863) 234-6182 EMail: nu_vc@yahoo.co.in

Rector: Y. P. Rama Subbaiah

College
Architecture & Planning (Architecture and Planning); **Arts Commerce and Law** (Arts and Humanities; Business and Commerce; Law); **Engineering and Technology**; **Ongole (Postgraduate Centre)** (Business Administration; Communication Studies; Economics; History; Mathematics); **Pharmaceutical Sciences** (Pharmacology); **Physical Education and Sports Sciences** (Physical Education); **Sciences**

Centre
Aquaculture and Research Education (Aquaculture; Educational Research); **Biotechnology** (Biotechnology); **Science Instrumentation** (Instrument Making; Science Education)

Research Centre
Afro-Asian Philosophies (Prof. K.S. Murthi Centre); **Disaster Mitigation Studies** (Safety Engineering); **Mahayana Buddhist Studies** (Asian Religious Studies); **Scientific Socialism**; **Social Policy (Ambedkar)**; **Women's Studies** (Women's Studies)

Further Information: Also 271 Affiliated Colleges

History: Founded 1976 as Nagarjuna University. Also P.G. Centres at Nuzvid and Ongole.

Academic Year: July to April (July-November; January-April)

Admission Requirements: 12th year senior secondary/intermediate examination or recognized foreign equivalent for undergraduate courses. 3 years Bachelor's Degree for admission to Postgraduate courses

Fees: 6,000-50,000 per annum (Indian Rupee)

Main Language(s) of Instruction: English

Accrediting Agency: National Assessment and Accreditation Council, Bangalore

Degrees and Diplomas: *Post Diploma*; *Bachelor's Degree*; *Master's Degree*

Student Services: Academic Counselling, Canteen, Cultural Activities, Health Services, Sports Facilities

Last Updated: 13/05/11

ACHARYA N.G. RANGA AGRICULTURAL UNIVERSITY (ANGRAU)

Rajendranagar, Hyderabad, Andhra Pradesh 500030
Tel: +91(40) 2401-5011
Fax: +91(40) 2401-5031
EMail: angrau@ap.nic.in
Website: http://www.angrau.ac.in

Vice-Chancellor: A. Padma Raju
Tel: +91(40) 2401-5035 EMail: angrau_vc@yahoo.com

Registrar: V. Praveen Rao
Tel: +91(40) 2401-5122 EMail: registrarangrau@rediffmail.com

College
Agricultural Engineering *(Bapatla; Madkasira)* (Agricultural Engineering; Food Technology; Soil Science; Water Management; Water Science); **Agricultural Polytechnic** *(Palerm; Jagtial; Maruteru; Anakapalle; Podalakur; Reddipalle; Utukuru; Rudrur; Garikapadu; Kampasagar; Madakasira)* (Agriculture; Animal Husbandry); **Agriculture** (Agriculture; Biotechnology; Fishery; Food Science; Food Technology; Horticulture; Veterinary Science); **Food Science & Technology** (Food Science; Food Technology); **Home Science** *(Saifabad)* (Home Economics)

History: Founded 1964. A State University.

Academic Year: June to May (June-December; January-May)

Admission Requirements: 12th year senior secondary/intermediate examination or recognized foreign equivalent

Main Language(s) of Instruction: English

Accrediting Agency: Indian Council of Agricultural Accreditation, New Delhi

Degrees and Diplomas: *Post Diploma*; *Bachelor's Degree*; *Master's Degree*; *Doctor of Philosophy*: **Agriculture; Home Economics.**

Student Services: Canteen, Cultural Activities, Health Services, Language Laboratory, Sports Facilities

Publications: Journal of Research ANGRAU

Last Updated: 08/08/13

ADIKAVI NANNAYA UNIVERSITY

25-07-9/1, Jayakrishnapuram,
Rajahmundry, Andhra Pradesh 533 105
Tel: +91-883-2472617,
Fax: +91-883-2472615
EMail: registrar_aknu@rediffmail.com
Website: http://www.nannayauniversity.info

Vice-Chancellor: Allam Apparao

Registrar: N. Bhargavaram

School
Chemical Sciences (Chemistry); **Cultural Studies and Communication** (Communication Studies; Cultural Studies); **Earth and Atmospheric Science** (Earth Sciences; Meteorology); **Life and Health Sciences** (Biological and Life Sciences; Health Sciences); **Management Studies** (Management); **Mathematics and Information Sciences** (Information Sciences; Mathematics)

Department
Computer Science (Computer Science); **Mathematics** (Mathematics)

History: Founded 2006.

Degrees and Diplomas: *Master's Degree*

Student Services: Health Services, Sports Facilities

Last Updated: 21/07/11

A. D. PATEL INSTITUTE OF TECHNOLOGY (ADIT)

New Vallabh Vidyanagar, Post Box No - 52, Dist. Anand,
Vitthal Udyognagar, Gujarat 388 121
Tel: +91(2692) 233-680
Fax: +91(2692) 238-180
EMail: principal@adit.ac.in
Website: http://www.adit.ac.in

Principal: R. K. Jain

Department
Automobile Engineering (Automotive Engineering; Energy Engineering); **Civil Engineering** (Civil Engineering); **Computer Engineering** (Computer Engineering; Software Engineering); **Electrical Engineering** (Automation and Control Engineering; Computer Engineering; Electrical Engineering; Electronic Engineering; Information Technology; Telecommunications Engineering); **Electronics and Communication Engineering** (Computer Engineering; Computer Networks; Electronic Engineering; Microwaves; Power Engineering; Telecommunications Engineering); **Food Processing Technology** (Engineering; Food Technology); **Information Technology** (Computer Science; Information Technology); **Mechanical Engineering** (Design; Industrial Engineering; Mechanical Engineering; Thermal Engineering)

History: Founded 2000 in accreditation with Sardar Patel University.

Accrediting Agency: National Board of Accreditation (NBA); All India Council for Technical Education (AICTE)

Degrees and Diplomas: *Bachelor's Degree (professional)*; *Postgraduate Diploma*: **Communication Arts; Electronic Engineering; Mechanical Engineering.**

Student Services: Careers Guidance

Last Updated: 08/08/13

AHMEDABAD UNIVERSITY

AES Bungalow, 2, Navrangpura, Ahmedabad,
Gujarat 380009
Tel: +91(79) 4004-4161
Fax: +91(79) 2656-0359
EMail: info@ahduni.edu.in
Website: http://www.ahduni.edu.in

President: Sanjay Lalbhai

Provost: Amarlal H. Kalro

Chairman: Prafull Anubhai

School
Computer Studies (Computer Engineering; Software Engineering); **Management** *(Amrut Mody)* (Business Administration; Business and Commerce; Management)

History: Founded 2009.

Degrees and Diplomas: *Bachelor's Degree*; *Postgraduate Diploma*; *Master's Degree*; *Doctor of Philosophy*. Also Certificate Programs

Last Updated: 18/10/11

ALAGAPPA UNIVERSITY

Alagappa Nagar, Karaikudi, Tamil Nadu 630 003
Tel: +91(4565) 228-080
Fax: +91(4565) 225-202
EMail: alagappauniversity@gmail.com
Website: http://www.alagappauniversity.ac.in

Vice-Chancellor: S. Sudalaimuthu

Registrar: K. Manimekalai
EMail: registraralagappauniv@gmail.com

Faculty
Arts (English; Indic Languages; Women's Studies); **Education** (Education; Physical Education); **Management** (Banking; Business and Commerce; International Business; International Economics; Management; Secretarial Studies); **Science** (Bioengineering; Biotechnology; Coastal Studies; Computer Engineering; Computer Science; Engineering; Industrial Chemistry; Information Sciences; Library Science; Marine Science and Oceanography; Mathematics; Nanotechnology; Physics; Veterinary Science)

Centre
Computer; **Gandhian Studies** (History); **Nehru Studies** (Political Sciences; Social Sciences); **Rural Development** (Agriculture)

Further Information: Also 2 Constituent Colleges

History: Founded 1985. A postgraduate Institution of the unitary type.

Academic Year: July to April (July-December; January-April)

Admission Requirements: Minimum requirement for admission to postgraduate courses

Main Language(s) of Instruction: English

Accrediting Agency: University Grants Commission

Degrees and Diplomas: *Post Diploma*; *Postgraduate Diploma*; *Master's Degree*; *Master of Philosophy*; *Doctor of Philosophy*

Publications: Monographs; Research Papers

Last Updated: 08/04/11

ALIAH UNIVERSITY

21, Haji Md. Mohsin Square, Kolkata, West Bengal 700016
Tel: +91(33) 2706-2124
EMail: infodesk@aliah.ac.in
Website: http://www.aliah.ac.in

Vice-Chancellor: Syed Samsul Alam
Tel: +91(33) 2706-2269 EMail: vcau@aliah.ac.in

Registrar: Anwar Hussain Dafadar EMail: registrar@aliah.ac.in

Department
Commerce and Business (Business and Commerce; Finance; Insurance); **Engineering** (Civil Engineering; Computer Engineering; Electrical Engineering; Electronic Engineering; Mechanical Engineering; Telecommunications Engineering; Vocational Education); **Humanities and Social Sciences** (Arts and Humanities; Economics; Education; Islamic Studies; Journalism; Mass Communication; Media Studies; Social Sciences); **Languages** (Arabic; English; Indic Languages); **Management Sciences** (Finance; Management; Retailing and Wholesaling); **Medical Sciences** (Nursing); **Natural Sciences** (Biological and Life Sciences; Chemistry; Computer Science; Geography; Mathematics; Natural Sciences; Physics; Statistics); **Theology** (Islamic Law; Islamic Theology)

History: Founded 2007.

Degrees and Diplomas: *Bachelor's Degree*; *Master's Degree*

Last Updated: 05/01/12

ALIGARH MUSLIM UNIVERSITY

Aligarh, Uttar Pradesh 202002
Tel: +91(571) 270-0220
Fax: +91(571) 270-0087
EMail: vcamu@amu.ac.in; vcamu@sancharnet.in
Website: http://www.amu.ac.in

Vice-Chancellor: Zameeruddin Shah (2012-)

Registrar: V.K. Abdul Jaleel

Faculty

Agricultural Sciences (Agricultural Business; Agricultural Economics; Agriculture; Harvest Technology; Home Economics; Microbiology; Plant and Crop Protection); **Arts** (Arabic; English; Fine Arts; Hindi; Indic Languages; Linguistics; Persian; Philosophy; Sanskrit; Urdu); **Commerce** (Business and Commerce); **Engineering and Technology** *(Zakir Hussain College)* (Applied Chemistry; Applied Mathematics; Applied Physics; Architecture; Chemical Engineering; Civil Engineering; Computer Engineering; Electrical Engineering; Electronic Engineering; Engineering; Mechanical Engineering; Petroleum and Gas Engineering; Technology); **Law** (Law); **Life Sciences** (Biochemistry; Biological and Life Sciences; Botany; Museum Studies; Wildlife; Zoology); **Management Studies and Research** (Management); **Medicine** *(Jawahar Lal Nehru Medical College)* (Anaesthesiology; Anatomy; Biochemistry; Community Health; Dentistry; Dermatology; Forensic Medicine and Dentistry; Gynaecology and Obstetrics; Medicine; Microbiology; Ophthalmology; Orthodontics; Orthopaedics; Otorhinolaryngology; Paediatrics; Pathology; Periodontics; Pharmacology; Physiology; Plastic Surgery; Psychiatry and Mental Health; Radiology; Surgery); **Science** (Chemistry; Computer Science; Geology; Mathematics; Natural Sciences; Operations Research; Physics; Statistics); **Social Sciences** (Economics; Education; History; Information Sciences; Islamic Studies; Library Science; Mass Communication; Political Sciences; Psychology; Social Sciences; Social Work; Sociology; Sports); **Theology** (Theology); **Unani Medicine** (Alternative Medicine)

Centre

Advanced Studies in History (History); **Brain Research** (Neurology); **Cardiology and Vascular Research** (Cardiology); **Career Planning** *(Women's College)*; **Coaching and Guidance** (Educational and Student Counselling); **Comparative Study of Indian Languages and Culture** (Cultural Studies; Indic Languages; South Asian Studies); **Computer Science** (Computer Science); **Continuing and Adult Education and Extension**; **Diabetes and Endocrinology** (Diabetology; Endocrinology); **Distance Education**; **General Education** (Education); **Interdisciplinary Development Studies** (Development Studies); **Koranic Studies** *(Prof. K.A. Nizami Centre)* (Koran); **Professional Courses**; **Promotion of Educational and Cultural Advancement of Muslims of India**; **Promotion of Science**; **Telematics Centre** (Electronic Engineering); **Theoretical Physics** (Physics); **Women's Studies** (Social Sciences; Women's Studies)

History: Founded 1920.

Academic Year: July to May

Admission Requirements: Senior Secondary School Certificate or Intermediate or equivalent.

Fees: (Rupees): 15-500 per month, Tuition fee is charged except for Faculty of Theology

Main Language(s) of Instruction: English

Degrees and Diplomas: *Bachelor's Degree*: **Architecture; Arts and Humanities; Biological and Life Sciences; Business and Commerce; Education; Engineering; Home Economics; Islamic Theology; Law; Library Science; Social Sciences.** *Master's Degree*; *Doctor of Philosophy*

Publishing house: A.M.U. Press
Last Updated: 13/09/12

ALL INDIA INSTITUTE OF MEDICAL SCIENCES (AIIMS)

Ansari Nagar, New Delhi 110029
Tel: +91(11) 2658-8851
Fax: +91(11) 2658-8663
EMail: director@aiims.ac.in
Website: http://www.aiims.edu

Director: Ramesh Deka Tel: +91(11) 2685-7639

Registrar: Ved Prakash Gupta
Tel: +91(11) 2696-4796 EMail: reg@aiims.ac.in

International Relations: Shakti Gupta Tel: +91(11) 2685-1929

College

Nursing (Nursing)

Department

Medicine (Anaesthesiology; Anatomy; Biochemistry; Biomedical Engineering; Biophysics; Biotechnology; Dermatology; Endocrinology; Gastroenterology; Gynaecology and Obstetrics; Haematology; Health Administration; Medicine; Microbiology; Nephrology; Nutrition; Orthopaedics; Osteopathy; Paediatrics; Pathology; Pharmacology; Physiology; Psychiatry and Mental Health; Rehabilitation and Therapy; Surgery; Urology; Venereology)

Institute

Rotary-Cancer Hospital (Oncology)

Centre

Cardiothoracic (Cardiology); **Community Medicine** (Community Health); **Dental Education and Research** (Dentistry); **Drug Dependence Treatment** (Psychiatry and Mental Health; Toxicology); **Neurosciences** (Neurosciences); **Ophthalmic Sciences** (Ophthalmology); **Trauma Specialty Centers** *(Jai Prakash Narayan Apex)* (Anaesthesiology; Forensic Medicine and Dentistry; Laboratory Techniques; Medicine; Neurology; Orthopaedics; Radiology; Surgery)

History: Founded 1956 as an autonomous Institution of national importance, awarding degrees recognized by the Medical Council of India.

Academic Year: July to June

Admission Requirements: 12th year senior secondary/intermediate examination

Main Language(s) of Instruction: English

Degrees and Diplomas: *Bachelor's Degree*: **Medicine; Surgery.** *Master's Degree*: **Surgery.** *Doctor of Philosophy*: **Medicine; Surgery.**
Last Updated: 16/05/11

ALLIANCE UNIVERSITY

Chikkahagade Cross, Chandapura - Anekal Main Road,
Bangalore, Karnataka 562106
Tel: +91(80) 3093-8000/1
Fax: +91(80) 2784-1600
EMail: enquiry@alliance.edu.in
Website: http://www.alliance.edu.in

Vice-Chancellor: D. Ayyappa

College

Arts and the Humanities (Arts and Humanities); **Commerce** (Business and Commerce); **Education and Human Services** (Education); **Engineering and Design** (Design; Engineering); **Law and International Affairs** (International Business; International Law; Law); **Media and Communications** (Communication Studies; Media Studies); **Medicine and Dentistry** (Dentistry; Medicine); **Science** (Natural Sciences)

School

Business (Business Administration); **Health Professions and Studies** (Health Sciences)

History: Founded 1996 as Alliance Business Academy (ABA). Acquired present status and title 2010.

Degrees and Diplomas: *Bachelor's Degree*; *Master's Degree*; *Doctor of Philosophy*
Last Updated: 27/12/11

AMBEDKAR UNIVERSITY

Sector-9, Plot No. 13, Dwarka, New Delhi, 110077
Tel: +91(11) 2507-4052 +91(11) 2507-4061
Fax: +91(11) 2507-4056
EMail: vc@aud.ac.in
Website: http://www.aud.ac.in/

Vice-Chancellor: Shyam Menon EMail: vc@aud.ac.in

International Relations: Vijaya S. Varma, Advisor (Planning)
EMail: vsvarma@aud.ac.in

School

Business, Public Policy and Social Entrepreneurship (Business Administration); **Culture and Creative Expressions** (Art Education; Cinema and Television; Cultural Studies; Performing Arts; Visual Arts); **Design** (Design); **Educational Studies** (Education; Educational Sciences); **Human Ecology** (Development Studies; Environmental Management; Environmental Studies); **Human Studies** (Gender Studies; Psychology); **Law, Governance and Citizenship** (Government; Social Sciences); **Liberal Studies** (Economics; English; History; Sociology); **Under-graduate Studies** (Arts and Humanities; Economics; English; History; Mathematics; Social Sciences; Sociology)

Centre

Community Knowledge; **Early Childhood Education and Development**; **Engaged Spiritualities and Peace Building**; **Equality and Social Justice**; **Leadership and Change**; **Social Applications of Mathematics**

History: Created 2008.

Degrees and Diplomas: *Bachelor's Degree*: **Arts and Humanities; Economics; English; History; Mathematics; Psychology; Social Sciences; Sociology.** *Master's Degree*: **Business Administration; Development Studies; Economics; Education; English; Environmental Studies; Gender Studies; History; Psychology; Sociology.**

Academic Staff *2011-2012*	**TOTAL**
FULL-TIME	**88**
PART-TIME	**6**
Student Numbers *2011-2012*	
All (Foreign included)	**536**

Last Updated: 01/10/12

AMET UNIVERSITY

135, East Coast Road, Kanathur, Tamil Nadu 603112
Tel: +91(44) 274-72155
EMail: amet@vsnl.com
Website: http://www.ametuniv.ac.in

Vice-Chancellor: S. Bhardwaj

Faculty

Applied Marine I.T. (Information Technology); **Harbour and Offshore Technology** (Marine Engineering); **Management Studies** (Management); **Marine Electrical and Electronic Engineering** (Marine Science and Oceanography); **Marine Engineering** (Marine Engineering); **Marine Life Sciences** (Biological and Life Sciences; Marine Biology; Marine Science and Oceanography); **Nautical Sciences**; **Naval Architecture and Offshore Engineering** (Naval Architecture)

History: Founded 1993 as Academy of Marine Education and Training. Acquired present status 2007.

Degrees and Diplomas: *Post Diploma*; *Bachelor's Degree*; *Master's Degree*

Last Updated: 16/05/11

AMITY UNIVERSITY, HARYANA

Amity Education Valley, Gurgaon, Haryana 122413
Tel: +91(124) 233-7015
EMail: info@ggn.amity.edu
Website: http://www.amity.edu/gurgaon/

Programme

Architecture (Architecture); **Biotechnology** (Biotechnology); **Commerce** (Business and Commerce); **Communication** (Communication Studies; Graphic Arts; Visual Arts); **Computer Science/Information Technology** (Computer Science; Information Technology); **Economics** (Economics); **Engineering** (Aeronautical and Aerospace Engineering; Automation and Control Engineering; Civil Engineering; Computer Engineering; Computer Science; Electronic Engineering; Mechanical Engineering; Telecommunications Engineering); **English literature** (English; Literature); **Fashion** (Fashion Design); **Fine Arts** (Fine Arts); **Liberal Arts**; **Management** (Business Administration; Management); **Medicine** (Medicine); **Nursing** (Nursing); **Pharmacy** (Pharmacy); **Physical Education** (Physical Education)

History: Founded 2010.

Degrees and Diplomas: *Bachelor's Degree*; *Master's Degree*

Last Updated: 27/12/11

AMITY UNIVERSITY, MADHYA PRADESH

Maharajpura, Gwalior, Madhya Pradesh 474005
Tel: +91(751) 3290-666
EMail: info@gwa.amity.edu
Website: http://www.amity.edu/gwalior/

Programme

Biotechnology (Biotechnology); **Commerce** (Business and Commerce); **Communication** (Communication Studies); **Computer Science/Information Technology** (Computer Engineering; Computer Science; Information Technology); **Engineering** (Engineering); **Fashion** (Fashion Design); **Management** (Management)

Degrees and Diplomas: *Bachelor's Degree*; *Master's Degree*

Last Updated: 03/01/12

AMITY UNIVERSITY, RAJASTHAN (AUR)

NH-11C, Kant Kalwar, Jaipur, Rajasthan 303002
Tel: +91(141) 237-2489
EMail: info@jpr.amity.edu
Website: http://www.amity.edu/jaipur/

Vice-Chancellor: Raj Singh

Programme

Architecture (Architecture); **Biotechnology** (Bioengineering; Biotechnology; Microbiology); **Commerce** (Business and Commerce); **Communication** (Communication Studies; Journalism); **Computer Science and Information Technology** (Computer Science; Information Technology); **Economics** (Economics); **Engineering** (Automation and Control Engineering; Computer Engineering; Electronic Engineering; Engineering; Information Technology; Mechanical Engineering); **Fashion** (Fashion Design); **Fine Arts** (Fine Arts); **Hotel Management Hospitality** (Hotel and Restaurant; Hotel Management); **Law** (Law); **Liberal Arts** (Arts and Humanities); **Management** (International Relations; Management); **Nanotechnology** (Nanotechnology); **Performing Arts** (Music; Performing Arts); **Physical Education** (Physical Education); **Psychology and Behavioural Science** (Behavioural Sciences; Psychology)

History: Founded 2008.

Degrees and Diplomas: *Bachelor's Degree*; *Master's Degree*

Student Services: Sports Facilities

Last Updated: 16/12/11

AMITY UNIVERSITY, UTTAR PRADESH

Sector-125, Noida, Uttar Pradesh 201303
Tel: +91(120) 243-1845
Fax: +91(120) 243-1870
EMail: registrar@amity.edu
Website: http://www.amity.edu/

Vice-Chancellor: K. Jai Singh (2005-)
EMail: vcau@amityuniversity.ac.in

Registrar: Anil Singh Mathur
Tel: +91(120) 243-1859 EMail: registrar@amity.edu

International Relations: R. K. Dhawan, Sr. Vice President
Tel: +91(120) 439-2570 EMail: iad@amity.edu

Programme

Anthropology; **Applied Sciences** (Applied Chemistry; Applied Mathematics; Applied Physics); **Architecture**; **Biotechnology** (Biotechnology; Medical Technology); **Commerce**; **Communication** (Journalism; Mass Communication); **Computer Science and Information Technology**; **Design** (Design); **Education** (Preschool Education; Primary Education); **Engineering** (Aeronautical and Aerospace Engineering; Automotive Engineering; Computer Science; Electronic Engineering; Engineering; Information Technology; Mechanical Engineering; Telecommunications Engineering); **Fashion**; **Finance** (Finance); **Fine Arts**; **Food Technology** (Food Technology); **Forensic Science**; **Hospitality** (Hotel Management);

Insurance and Actuarial Science (Actuarial Science; Insurance); **Languages** (English; French; Spanish); **Law** (Commercial Law; International Law; Law); **Management** (Accountancy; Business Administration; Finance; International Business; Management; Marketing; Sales Techniques); **Microbial Sciences** (Microbiology); **Nanotechnology** (Nanotechnology); **NGO Management and Development Studies** (Administration; Development Studies); **Organic Agriculture** (Agriculture); **Performing Arts** (Dance; Music; Musical Instruments; Performing Arts; Singing); **Pharmacy** (Pharmacy); **Physical Education** (Physical Education); **Physiotherapy** (Physical Therapy); **Psychology and Behavioural Science** (Behavioural Sciences; Clinical Psychology; Industrial and Organizational Psychology; Psychology); **Rural and Urban Management** (Rural Studies; Urban Studies); **Social Work** (Social Work); **Telecommunications** (Telecommunications Engineering); **Travel and Tourism** (Tourism)

History: Created 1986.

Academic Year: July - June

Admission Requirements: Relevant Secondary School certificate with satisfactory pass marks; Interview; Essay

Fees: 21,500 - 237,000 per annum (Indian Rupee)

Main Language(s) of Instruction: English

Accrediting Agency: University Grants Commission (UGC), India

Degrees and Diplomas: *Post Diploma*: **Health Education; Nursing; Primary Education.** *Bachelor's Degree*: **Accountancy; Administration; Aeronautical and Aerospace Engineering; Anthropology; Architecture; Banking; Biological and Life Sciences; Biotechnology; Business Administration; Business and Commerce; Communication Arts; Computer Engineering; Computer Science; Dance; Electronic Engineering; English; Fashion Design; Film; Finance; Fine Arts; Food Technology; Forensic Medicine and Dentistry; French; Hotel Management; Information Technology; Interior Design; Journalism; Law; Mass Communication; Medicine; Microbiology; Music; Pharmacy; Physical Education; Physical Therapy; Primary Education; Psychology; Social Work; Spanish; Technology; Telecommunications Engineering; Tourism.** *Postgraduate Diploma*: **Data Processing; Health Sciences; Insurance; Management; Microbiology; Physical Education.** *Master's Degree*: **Actuarial Science; Administration; Advertising and Publicity; Agricultural Business; Agriculture; Anthropology; Architecture; Biological and Life Sciences; Biotechnology; Business Administration; Chemistry; Cinema and Television; Computer Engineering; Computer Networks; Computer Science; Development Studies; Education; English; Film; Finance; Fine Arts; Food Science; Forensic Medicine and Dentistry; Hotel Management; Human Resources; Information Management; Interior Design; Journalism; Law; Management; Marketing; Mass Communication; Mathematics; Microbiology; Nanotechnology; Physical Therapy; Physics; Tourism.** *Doctor of Philosophy*: **Biotechnology; Business Administration; Forensic Medicine and Dentistry; Hotel Management; Information Technology; Law; Microbiology; Nanotechnology; Psychology.** Also: Integrated Master (4-5$\frac{1}{2}$ yrs) in: Biotechnology; Business Administration; Microbial Sciences; Nanotechnology; Psychology

Student Services: Academic Counselling, Canteen, Careers Guidance, Cultural Activities, Facilities for disabled people, Foreign Studies Centre, Health Services, Language Laboratory, Nursery Care, Social Counselling, Sports Facilities

Publications: Amity Business Review; Amity Global Business Review; Amity Global HR Review; Amity Global Strategic Management Review; Amity Law Watch; International Business Horizon; International Business Review

Publishing House: Amity University Press

AMRITA UNIVERSITY

Amrita Vishwa Vidyapeetham

Amritanagar Post, Ettimadai, Coimbatore, Tamil Nadu 641 112
Tel: 91(422) 2685000
Fax: 91(422) 2652125
EMail: univhq@amrita.edu
Website: http://www.amrita.edu

Vice-Chancellor: Venkat Rangan
Tel: 91(422) 2685000 EMail: vcoffice@amrita.edu

Registrar: Krishnamorthy S
Tel: 91(422) 2685000 EMail: univhq@amrita.edu

International Relations: Maneesha Ramesh, Director - ACIP
Tel: 91(476) 2801280 EMail: maneesha@am.amrita.edu

School

Arts and Sciences *(Mysore, Kochi and Amritapuri campuses)* (Arts and Humanities; Biochemistry; Botany; Business and Commerce; Chemistry; Computer Science; English; Fine Arts; Health Administration; Management; Mathematics; Media Studies; Microbiology; Natural Sciences; Physics); **Ayurveda** *(Amritapuri Campus)* (Ayurveda); **Biotechnology** *(Amritapuri Campus)* (Biotechnology; Medical Technology; Microbiology); **Business** *(Coimbatore campus)* (Business Administration; Business and Commerce); **Dentistry** *(Kochi campus)* (Dentistry); **Education** *(Mysore Campus)* (Education); **Engineering** *(Amritapuri, Bangalore and Coimbatore campuses)* (Aeronautical and Aerospace Engineering; Automotive Engineering; Biomedical Engineering; Chemical Engineering; Civil Engineering; Computer Engineering; Computer Networks; Computer Science; Electrical and Electronic Engineering; Engineering; Engineering Drawing and Design; Materials Engineering; Mechanical Engineering); **Management** *(Coimbatore campus)* (Management); **Medicine** *(Kochi campus)* (Medicine); **Nursing** *(Kochi campus)* (Nursing); **Pharmacy** *(Kochi campus)* (Pharmacy)

Department

Communication *(Coimbatore campus)* (Communication Studies); **Management** *(Amritapuri, Bangalore and Kochi campuses)* (Management); **Social Work** *(Coimbatore campus)* (Social Work)

Further Information: Campuses in Amritapuri, Bangalore, Coimbatore, Kochi, Mysore.

History: Created 1994. Acquired university status 2003.

Academic Year: July/August to April/May

Admission Requirements: Secondary or High School certificate for undergraduate programmes; undergraduate degree in related area for postgraduate programmes; postgraduate degree for Ph.D.

Fees: Vary according to programme of study

Main Language(s) of Instruction: English

Accrediting Agency: National Assessment and Accreditation Council (NAAC); National Board of Accreditation (NBA)

Degrees and Diplomas: *Bachelor's Degree*: **Arts and Humanities; Dentistry; Engineering; Health Sciences; Medicine; Nursing; Pharmacy.** *Master's Degree*: **Arts and Humanities; Business and Commerce; Engineering; Management; Medicine; Nursing; Pharmacy; Radiology; Social Work.** *Doctor of Philosophy*: **Arts and Humanities; Biotechnology; Engineering; Management; Medicine; Pharmacy.**

Student Services: Academic Counselling, Canteen, Careers Guidance, Cultural Activities, Facilities for disabled people, Health Services, Language Laboratory, Nursery Care, Social Counselling, Sports Facilities

Publications: Amrita Journal of Medicine; Journal of the Indian Society of Toxicology

Publishing House: Amrita Press, Amaritapuri

Academic Staff *2012-2013*	MEN	WOMEN	**TOTAL**
FULL-TIME	966	783	**1,749**
PART-TIME	–	–	**42**
STAFF WITH DOCTORATE			
FULL-TIME	–	–	**245**
Student Numbers *2012-2013*			
All (Foreign included)	8,746	7,752	**16,498**
FOREIGN ONLY	5	3	**8**

Part-time students, 442.

Last Updated: 02/05/13

ANAND AGRICULTURAL UNIVERSITY

Anand, Gujarat
Tel: +91 (2692) 225-800

Vice-Chancellor: A.M. Shekh
Tel: +91(2692) 261-273 EMail: vc@aau.in

Registrar: P.R. Vaishnav
Tel: +91(2692) 261-310 EMail: registrar@aau.in

Faculty

Agricultural Engineering and Technology (Agricultural Engineering; Technology); **Agricultural Information Technology** (Agricultural Engineering; Information Technology); **Agriculture** (Agricultural Economics; Agriculture; Agronomy; Horticulture; Plant and Crop Protection; Plant Pathology; Soil Science); **Dairy Science** (Dairy); **Food Processing Technology and Bio-Energy** (Food Science; Food Technology); **Post Graduate**; **Veterinary Science and Animal Husbandry** (Animal Husbandry; Epidemiology; Parasitology; Veterinary Science)

History: Founded 2004.

Degrees and Diplomas: *Bachelor's Degree*; *Postgraduate Diploma*

Last Updated: 01/08/11

ANDHRA PRADESH UNIVERSITY OF LAW

Palace Layout, Pedawaltair,
Visakhapatnam, Andhra Pradesh 530017
Tel: +91(891) 252-9952
Fax: +91(891) 304-0170
EMail: apuniversityoflaw@gmail.com
Website: http://www.apulvisakha.org

Vice-Chancellor: Y. Satyanarayana

Registrar: Amancherla Subrahmanyam

Programme

Law (Law)

Further Information: Also branches in Kadapa and Nizamabad

History: Founded 2008.

Degrees and Diplomas: *Bachelor's Degree*; *Postgraduate Diploma*; *Doctor of Philosophy*

Last Updated: 16/05/11

ANDHRA UNIVERSITY

Waltair, Visakhapatnam, Andhra Pradesh 530003
Tel: +91(891) 275-5324
Fax: +91(891) 275-5547
EMail: vicechancellor@andhrauniversity.info
Website: http://www.andhrauniversity.info

Vice-Chancellor: Beela Satyanarayana (2008-)

Registrar: Prasad Reddy EMail: prof.prasadreddy@gmail.com

College

Arts and Commerce (Adult Education; Anthropology; Archaeology; Arts and Humanities; Business and Commerce; Distance Education; Economics; Education; English; Fine Arts; History; Indic Languages; Information Sciences; Journalism; Labour and Industrial Relations; Library Science; Linguistics; Management; Mass Communication; Modern Languages; Philosophy; Political Sciences; Public Administration; Sanskrit; Social Work; Sociology; Special Education; Theatre; Urdu; Yoga); **Engineering** *(Autonomous)* (Chemical Engineering; Civil Engineering; Computer Engineering; Electrical Engineering; Electronic Engineering; Engineering; Marine Engineering; Mechanical Engineering; Metallurgical Engineering; Social Sciences; Systems Analysis; Telecommunications Engineering); **Law** (Law); **Pharmacy**; **Science and Technology** (Analytical Chemistry; Anthropology; Applied Mathematics; Biochemistry; Botany; Environmental Studies; Genetics; Geography; Geology; Geophysics; Inorganic Chemistry; Instrument Making; Marine Biology; Marine Science and Oceanography; Mathematics; Meteorology; Natural Sciences; Nuclear Physics; Organic Chemistry; Pharmacy; Physics; Statistics; Zoology)

Centre

Postgraduate *(Srikakulam)*; **Postgraduate** *(Kakinada)*; **Science and Instrumentation** (Instrument Making; Natural Sciences)

Further Information: Also campuses in Kakinada, Vizianagaram, and Tadepalligudem

History: Founded 1926.

Academic Year: July to June.

Admission Requirements: Entrance examination.

Main Language(s) of Instruction: English

Degrees and Diplomas: *Bachelor's Degree*; *Master's Degree*; *Doctor of Philosophy*

Publishing house: Andhra University Press and Publications

Last Updated: 17/05/11

ANNA UNIVERSITY

Sardar Patel Road, Guindy, Chennai, Tamil Nadu 600025
Tel: +91(44) 2235-2161
Fax: +91(44) 2235-0397
EMail: registrar@annauniv.edu
Website: http://www.annauniv.edu/

Vice-Chancellor: P. Mannar Jawahar (2008-)
EMail: vc@annauniv.edu

Deputy Registrar: Thiru.K. Gopinathan
EMail: registrar@annauniv.edu

Faculty

Architecture and Planning (Architecture and Planning); **Civil Engineering** (Civil Engineering); **Electrical and Electronics Engineering** (Electrical Engineering; Electronic Engineering; Power Engineering); **Information and Communication Engineering** (Information Technology; Telecommunications Engineering); **Management Sciences** (Management); **Mechanical Engineering** (Mechanical Engineering); **Science and Humanities** (Arts and Humanities; Geology; Media Studies; Natural Sciences; Social Sciences); **Technology** (Biotechnology; Ceramics and Glass Technology; Chemical Engineering; Polymer and Plastics Technology; Technology; Textile Technology)

College

Engineering *(Guindy)* (Arts and Humanities; Chemistry; Civil Engineering; Electrical and Electronic Engineering; Engineering; Geology; Geophysics; Management; Mathematics; Mechanical Engineering; Mining Engineering; Physics; Printing and Printmaking; Social Sciences; Telecommunications Engineering); **Technology** *(Alagappa, Guindy)*

Institute

Ocean Management (Marine Science and Oceanography); **Remote Sensing** (Surveying and Mapping); **Technology** *(Madras, Chromepet)* (Aeronautical and Aerospace Engineering; Automotive Engineering; Electronic Engineering; Instrument Making; Production Engineering; Rubber Technology; Technology)

Centre

Biotechnology (Biotechnology); **Building Technology** (Building Technologies); **Computer Science** *(Ramajuan)* (Computer Science); **Computer Science** (Computer Science); **Crystal Growth** (Crystallography); **Curriculum Development**; **Environmental Studies** (Environmental Studies); **Human Settlements** (Social Studies); **New and Renewable Sources of Energy** (Natural Resources); **Water Resources** (Water Management)

History: Founded as Perarignar Anna University of Technology 1978, acquired present title 1982. Merger of 5 regional Anna Universities of Technologies 2012.

Academic Year: July to April (July-October; December-April)

Admission Requirements: 12th year senior secondary/intermediate examination or recognized foreign equivalent, and entrance examination.

Main Language(s) of Instruction: English

Degrees and Diplomas: *Post Diploma*; *Bachelor's Degree*; *Master's Degree*; *Doctor of Philosophy*

Student Services: Sports Facilities

Last Updated: 17/05/11

ANNA UNIVERSITY OF TECHNOLOGY CHENNAI (AUT)

CPT Campus, Tharamani, Chennai, Tamilnadu 600113
EMail: registrar@annatech.ac.in
Website: http://www.annatech.ac.in

Vice-Chancellor: C. Thangaraj
Tel: +91(442) 254-1777 EMail: vc@annatech.ac.in

Registrar: S. Gowri

Department

Civil Engineering (Civil Engineering; Construction Engineering); **Computer Science and Engineering** (Architecture); **Management Studies** (Business Administration; Management)

History: Founded 2007. Merged with Anna University (Chennai) 2012.

Degrees and Diplomas: *Master's Degree*; *Doctor of Philosophy*

ANNA UNIVERSITY OF TECHNOLOGY COIMBATORE (AUT)

Academic Campus, Jothipuram, Coimbatore, Tamilnadu 641 047
Tel: +91(422) 654-5566
Fax: +91(422) 269-4400
EMail: registrar@annauniv.ac.in
Website: http://www.autcbe.ac.in

Vice-Chancellor: K. Karunakaran

Registrar: S. Premchand

School
Management Studies (Management)

Department
Civil Engineering (Civil Engineering; Computer Engineering; Engineering; Materials Engineering; Mechanical Engineering; Mineralogy; Printing and Printmaking); **Computer Applications** (Computer Engineering; Software Engineering); **Computer Science and Engineering** (Computer Engineering; Computer Science); **Electrical and Electronics Engineering** (Electrical and Electronic Engineering); **Information Technology** (Information Technology); **Mechanical Engineering** (Mechanical Engineering); **Science and Humanities** (Arts and Humanities; Natural Sciences)

Centre
Biotechnology

Further Information: Also distance education

History: Founded 2006. Merged with Anna University (Chennai) 2012.

Degrees and Diplomas: *Bachelor's Degree*; *Master's Degree*

ANNA UNIVERSITY OF TECHNOLOGY MADURAI (AUT)

Alagar Koil Road, Madurai, Tamilnadu 625 002
Tel: +91(452) 252-0111
Fax: +91(452) 255-5577
EMail: info@autmdu.ac.in
Website: http://autmdu.ac.in

Vice-Chancellor: R. Murugesan
Tel: +91(452) 255-5554 EMail: vc@autmdu.ac.in

Registrar: E.B. Perumal Pillai EMail: registrar@autmdu.ac.in

Programme
Architecture (Architecture); **Business Administration** (Business Administration); **Engineering** (Aeronautical and Aerospace Engineering; Biomedical Engineering; Biotechnology; Chemical Engineering; Civil Engineering; Computer Science; Construction Engineering; Electrical and Electronic Engineering; Heating and Refrigeration; Industrial Design; Marine Engineering; Mechanical Engineering; Power Engineering; Software Engineering; Telecommunications Engineering; Textile Technology)

Further Information: Also university Campuses located at Ramanathapuram, Dindigul and Distance Education

History: Founded 2010. Merged with Anna University (Chennai) 2012.

Degrees and Diplomas: *Bachelor's Degree*; *Master's Degree*

ANNA UNIVERSITY OF TECHNOLOGY TIRUCHIRAPPALLI (AUT)

Tiruchirappalli, Tamilnadu 620024
Website: http://www.tau.edu.in/

Vice-Chancellor: Devadas Manoharan
Tel: +91(431) 240-7095 EMail: vc@tau.edu.in

Registrar: J. Raja
Tel: +91(431) 240-7946 EMail: registrar@tau.edu.in

Department
Biotechnology (Biotechnology); **Chemistry** (Chemistry); **Civil Engineering** (Civil Engineering); **Computer Application** (Computer Engineering); **Computer Science and Engineering** (Computer Engineering; Computer Science); **Electrical and Electronics Engineering** (Electrical and Electronic Engineering); **Electronics and Communication Engineering** (Electronic Engineering; Telecommunications Engineering); **English** (English); **Management** (Management); **Mathematics**; **Mechanical Engineering** (Mechanical Engineering); **Petrochemical Technology** (Petroleum and Gas Engineering); **Pharmaceutical Technology** (Pharmacy); **Physics** (Physics)

History: Founded 2006. Merged with Anna University (Chennai) 2012.

Degrees and Diplomas: *Bachelor's Degree*; *Master's Degree*; *Doctor of Philosophy*

ANNA UNIVERSITY OF TECHNOLOGY TIRUNELVELI (AUT)

Tirunelveli, 627007
Tel: +91(462) 255-4255
Fax: +91(462) 255-2877

Vice-Chancellor: M. Rajaram

Faculty
Civil Engineering (Civil Engineering); **Electrical Engineering** (Electrical and Electronic Engineering); **Information and Communication Engineering** (Information Technology; Telecommunications Engineering); **Management Sciences** (Human Resources; Marketing); **Mechanical Engineering** (Mechanical Engineering)

Further Information: Also 65 affiliated colleges and 2 University Colleges of Engineering, at Thoothukudi and Nagercoil

History: Founded 2006. Merged with Anna University (Chennai) 2012.

Degrees and Diplomas: *Bachelor's Degree*; *Master's Degree*

ANNAMALAI UNIVERSITY

Annamalainagar, Tamil Nadu 608002
Tel: +91(4144) 238-248
Fax: +91(4144) 238-080
EMail: info@annamalaiuniversity.ac.in
Website: http://www.annamalaiuniversity.ac.in

Vice-Chancellor: M. Ramanathan
Tel: +91(4144) 238-283 EMail: vc_lbv@hotmail.com

Registrar: M. Rathinasabapathi
Tel: +91(4144) 238-259 EMail: aumrsl@hotmail.com

Faculty
Agriculture (Agricultural Economics; Agriculture; Agronomy; Entomology; Horticulture; Microbiology; Plant Pathology; Soil Science); **Arts** (Arts and Humanities; Business Administration; Business and Commerce; Demography and Population; Economics; English; History; Information Sciences; Library Science; Philosophy; Political Sciences; Rural Studies; Sociology); **Dentistry** (Dentistry); **Distance Education**; **Education** (Adult Education; Education; Educational Psychology; Physical Education; Sports); **Engineering and Technology** (Chemical Engineering; Civil Engineering; Computer Science; Electrical Engineering; Engineering; Environmental Engineering; Mechanical Engineering; Pharmacy; Technology); **Fine Arts** (Fine Arts; Music); **Indian Languages** (Indic Languages); **Medicine** (Medicine; Nursing); **Science** (Biochemistry; Biotechnology; Botany; Chemistry; Earth Sciences; Mathematics; Natural Sciences; Physics; Statistics; Zoology)

Further Information: Also 2 Teaching Hospitals

History: Founded 1929. A Unitary teaching University with no Affiliated Colleges, and with all Faculties on a single campus.

Academic Year: July to April (July-November; January-April)

Admission Requirements: 12th year senior secondary/intermediate examination or recognized foreign equivalent

Main Language(s) of Instruction: English, Tamil

Accrediting Agency: National Assessment and Accreditation Council; National Board of Accreditation, ICAR, MCI

Degrees and Diplomas: *Bachelor's Degree*; *Master's Degree*; *Doctor of Philosophy*

Student Services: Academic Counselling, Canteen, Careers Guidance, Cultural Activities, Facilities for disabled people, Health Services, Language Laboratory, Nursery Care, Social Counselling, Sports Facilities

Publications: University Journal

Publishing House: Annamalai University Publication Division.
Last Updated: 18/05/11

APEEJAY SCHOOL OF MANAGEMENT (ASM)

Sector VIII, Institutional Area, Dwarka, Gujarat 110 077
Tel: +91(11) 2536-3979 +91(11) 2536-3980
Fax: +91(11) 2536-3985
EMail: asm.dwk.del@apeejay.edu
Website: http://apeejay.edu/

Director: Alok Saklani

Programme

International Business (International Business); **Management** (Accountancy; Advertising and Publicity; Finance; Human Resources; Information Technology; Management; Marketing; Media Studies; Public Relations)

History: Founded 1993.

Accrediting Agency: All India Council for Technical Education (AICTE); Ministry of Human Resource Development

Degrees and Diplomas: *Postgraduate Diploma*

Student Services: Canteen

Last Updated: 23/01/12

APEEJAY STYA UNIVERSITY (ASU)

Palwal Road, Sohna, Gurgaon, Haryana 122103
EMail: asu.admissions@apeejay.edu
Website: http://university.apeejay.edu

Vice-Chancellor: Kamal Kant Dwivedi

School

Bio-Sciences and Pharmaceutical Sciences (Biological and Life Sciences; Pharmacy); **Computational Sciences** (Computer Science); **Education** (Education); **Engineering and Technology** (Electrical and Electronic Engineering; Electronic Engineering; Engineering; Mechanical Engineering; Technology); **Journalism and Mass Communication** (Journalism; Mass Communication); **Management Sciences** (Business Administration; Management); **Visual Arts and Design**

History: Founded 2010.

Degrees and Diplomas: *Bachelor's Degree*; *Master's Degree*; *Doctor of Philosophy*

Last Updated: 27/12/11

APG (ALAKH PRAKASH GOYAL) SHIMLA UNIVERSITY

Shoghi – Mehli by-pass Road, Near Panthaghati,
Shimla, Himachal Pradesh 171009
Tel: +91(177) 2620074
Fax: +91(177) 2006000
EMail: dr@apg.edu.in
Website: http://apg.edu.in/

Vice-Chancellor: Devendra Pathak (2012-) EMail: vc@apg.edu.in

International Relations: Ajit Nedungadi, Director, Admission and Marketing EMail: da@apg.edu.in

School

Architecture and Planning (Architecture; Building Technologies; Town Planning); **Engineering** (Civil Engineering; Computer Engineering; Electrical and Electronic Engineering; Mechanical Engineering; Telecommunications Engineering); **Fashion and Textile Design** (Fashion Design; Textile Design); **Hotel Management** (Hotel and Restaurant; Hotel Management); **Journalism and Mass Communication** (Journalism; Mass Communication); **Legal Studies** (Law); **Management** (Business Administration)

History: Created 2012.

Academic Year: August to June

Accrediting Agency: UGC

Degrees and Diplomas: *Bachelor's Degree*: **Architecture; Business Administration; Engineering; Fashion Design; Hotel Management; Law; Mass Communication.** *Master's Degree*: **Business Administration; Engineering; Law; Mass Communication.**

Student Numbers *2013-2014*: Total 429

Last Updated: 17/02/14

ARNI UNIVERSITY

Kathgarh, Distt Kangra, Himachal Pardesh
Tel: +91(11) 434-000-00
Fax: +91(11) 434-000-34
EMail: info@arni.in
Website: http://arni.in

Vice-Chancellor: R. Bhardwaj

School

Arts and Commerce and Humanities (Arts and Humanities; Business and Commerce; Economics; English; Public Administration); **Basic Sciences** (Biology; Biotechnology; Chemistry; Physics); **Business Management** (Business Administration); **Computer Science** (Computer Engineering; Computer Science); **Hospitality Management** (Cooking and Catering; Hotel Management); **Polytechnic** (Civil Engineering; Computer Engineering; Electrical Engineering; Mechanical Engineering); **Technology** (Biotechnology; Civil Engineering; Computer Engineering; Computer Science; Electrical and Electronic Engineering; Mechanical Engineering)

Degrees and Diplomas: *Bachelor's Degree*; *Master's Degree*; *Doctor of Philosophy*

Student Services: Academic Counselling, Sports Facilities

Last Updated: 27/12/11

ASSAM AGRICULTURAL UNIVERSITY (AAU)

Jorhat, Assam 785013
Tel: +91(376) 234-0008
Fax: +91(376) 234-0001
EMail: info@aau.ac.in
Website: http://www.aau.ac.in

Vice-Chancellor: K. M. Bujarbaruah

Registrar: Krishna Gohain

Faculty

Agriculture (Agriculture; Fishery); **Home Science** (Home Economics); **Veterinary Science** (Veterinary Science)

History: Founded 1969.

Academic Year: July to June (July/August-November/December; January/February-May/June)

Admission Requirements: 12th year senior secondary/intermediate examination or recognized foreign equivalent

Main Language(s) of Instruction: English

Accrediting Agency: ICAR

Degrees and Diplomas: *Bachelor's Degree*; *Master's Degree*; *Doctor of Philosophy*

Publications: AAU Bulletin; Ghare Pathare

Last Updated: 18/05/11

ASSAM DON BOSCO UNIVERSITY (ADBU)

Airport Road, Azara, Gunawati, Assam 781017
Tel: +91(361) 213-9291 +91(361) 213-9292
Fax: +61(361) 284-1949
EMail: contact@dbuniversity.ac.in;
vicechancellor@dbuniversity.ac.in
Website: http://www.dbuniversity.ac.in

Rector and Vice-Chancellor: Stephen Mavely (2009-)
EMail: mavely@dbuniversity.ac.in; mavely@outlook.com

Pro-Vice Chancellor: Joseph Nellanat EMail: nellanatt@gmail.com

International Relations: Kashi Nath Hazarika, Advisor and Head, Training and Placement
EMail: hazarika.k@dbuniversity.ac.in; hazarika.k@gmail.com

School

Applied Sciences *(DBCET)* (Chemistry; Physics); **Commerce and Management** *(DBIM, Kharguli)* (Business and Commerce; Management); **Health Sciences** (Health Sciences; Nursing; Paramedical Sciences; Pharmacy); **Religion and Culture** (Asian Studies; Christian Religious Studies; Cultural Studies; Ethics; Religion; Social Studies); **Social Sciences** *(DBCET)* (Social Work); **Technology** (Biotechnology; Civil Engineering; Computer Science; Electrical and Electronic Engineering; Electronic Engineering;

Information Technology; Mechanical Engineering; Technology; Telecommunications Engineering)

Centre

Distance Education; **Social Sciences** *(Paltan Bazaar)* (Child Care and Development; Social Work)

Further Information: Also Global online programmes (DBU Global Centre for Online & Distance Education): www.dbuglobal.com and two constituent Colleges (Engineering Technology and Management)

History: Founded 2008.

Academic Year: July to June

Admission Requirements: For B. Tech: Higher Secondary School Leaving Certificate Examination (or equivalent) with at least 50% in the aggregate, 50% in the aggregate of Physics, Chemistry and Mathematics and 45% separately in Physics, Chemistry and Mathematics. Entrance examination - AIEEE (All India) or CE (Assam) or DBU-GET (ADBU)

Fees: 20,000-50,000 per semester depending on programmes. PhD: 20,000 per annum (for Humanities); Rs 25,000 (for Science and Technology) (Indian Rupee)

Main Language(s) of Instruction: English

Accrediting Agency: National Accreditation and Assessment Council (NAAC)

Degrees and Diplomas: *Post Diploma*: **Law; Social Work.** *Bachelor's Degree*: **Engineering.** *Postgraduate Diploma*; *Master's Degree*: **Engineering; Management; Social Sciences.** *Doctor of Philosophy*: **Arts and Humanities; Cultural Studies; Engineering; Social Sciences.** Also Certificate and Diploma Course

Student Services: Academic Counselling, Canteen, Careers Guidance, Cultural Activities, Facilities for disabled people, Health Services, Language Laboratory, Social Counselling, Sports Facilities

Publications: Kultura

Academic Staff *2011-2012*	**TOTAL**
FULL-TIME	**68**
PART-TIME	**4**
STAFF WITH DOCTORATE	
FULL-TIME	**7**

Student Numbers *2012-2013*	
All (Foreign included)	**1,607**

Distance students, 1221.

Last Updated: 27/10/11

ASSAM UNIVERSITY

Assam University Post Office, Silchar, Assam 788011
Tel: +91(3842) 270-806
Fax: +91(3842) 270-806
EMail: vc@aus.ac.in
Website: http://www.aus.ac.in/

Vice-Chancellor: Tapodhir Bhattacharjee
Tel: +91(3842) 270-801

Registrar: Debabrata Deb Tel: +91(3842) 270-368

School

Creative Arts and Communication Studies *(Abanindranath Tagore)* (Mass Communication; Visual Arts); **Earth Sciences** *(Aryabhatta)* (Earth Sciences); **Economics and Commerce** *(Mahatma Gandhi)* (Business and Commerce; Economics); **Education** *(Ashutosh Mukhopadhyay)* (Education); **English and Foreign Language Studies** *(Suniti Kumar Chattopadhyay)* (Arabic; English; Foreign Languages Education; French); **Environmental Sciences** *(E. P Odam)* (Ecology; Environmental Studies); **Indian Languages and Cultural Studies** *(Rabindranath Tagore)* (Arabic; Cultural Studies; English; Hindi; Linguistics; Modern Languages; Sanskrit); **Legal Studies** *(Deshabandhu Chittaranjan)* (Law); **Library Sciences** *(Swami Vivekananda)* (Information Sciences; Library Science); **Life Sciences** *(Hargobind Khurana)* (Biological and Life Sciences; Biotechnology; Microbiology); **Management Studies** *(Jawarharlal Nehru)* (Business Administration); **Medical and Paramedical Sciences** *(Susruta)* (Pharmacy); **Philosophy** *(Sarvepalli Radhakrishnan)* (Philosophy); **Physical Sciences** *(Albert Einstein)* (Chemistry; Computer Science; Mathematics; Physics); **Social Sciences** *(Jadunath Sarkar)* (History; Political Sciences; Social Sciences; Social Work; Sociology); **Technology** *(Triguna Sen)* (Agricultural Engineering; Electronic Engineering; Information Technology; Technology; Telecommunications Engineering)

Further Information: Also campuses in Silchar and Diphu

History: Founded 1994.

Academic Year: July to July (July-December; January-July)

Admission Requirements: 12th standard senior secondary/intermediate examination or recognized foreign equivalent. Selection is on a competitive basis

Main Language(s) of Instruction: English

Accrediting Agency: National Assessment and Accreditation Council (NAAC)

Degrees and Diplomas: *Bachelor's Degree*: **Business and Commerce; Computer Science; Education; Fine Arts; Law; Medicine; Social Work; Surgery.** *Master's Degree*: **Arts and Humanities; Business and Commerce; Fine Arts; Mass Communication; Social Work.** *Master of Philosophy*: **Biotechnology; Business Administration; Computer Science.** *Doctor of Philosophy*

Student Services: Academic Counselling, Canteen, Health Services, Sports Facilities

Publications: University Journal

Last Updated: 18/05/11

ATAL BIRAHI VAJPAYEE - INDIAN INSTITUTE OF INFORMATION TECHNOLOGY AND MANAGEMENT (IIITM)

Morena Link Road, Gwalior, Madhya Pradesh 474010
Tel: +91(751) 246-0315 +91(751) 244-9704
Fax: +91(751) 244-9813
Website: http://www.iiitm.ac.in

Director: S. G. Deshmukh
Tel: +91(751) 244-9702 EMail: director@iiitm.ac.in

Registrar: Deleep Kumar Tel: +91(751) 243-8408

Programme

Business Administration (Business Administration; Management); **Information Technology** (Computer Engineering; Information Technology; Software Engineering)

History: Founded 2001.

Degrees and Diplomas: *Postgraduate Diploma*; *Master's Degree*; *Doctor of Philosophy*

Last Updated: 18/05/11

AVINASHILINGAM DEEMED UNIVERSITY FOR WOMEN

Mettupalayam Road, Coimbatore,
Tamil Nadu 641043
Tel: +91(422) 244-0241
Fax: +91(422) 243-8786
EMail: pro@avinuty.ac.in; info_adu@avinuty.ac.in
Website: http://www.avinashilingam.edu

Vice-Chancellor: Sheela Ramachandran
EMail: vc@avinuty.ac.in

Registrar: Gowri Ramakrishnan
EMail: registrar@avinuty.ac.in

Faculty

Business Administration (Business Administration; Business and Commerce; Business Computing; Tourism); **Community Education and Entrepreneurship Development** (Communication Arts; Communication Studies; Information Technology; Medical Auxiliaries; Multimedia); **Education** (Education; Physical Education; Special Education); **Engineering** (Civil Engineering; Computer Engineering; Electrical Engineering; Electronic Engineering; Engineering; Telecommunications Engineering); **Home Science** (Clothing and Sewing; Food Science; Home Economics; Nutrition; Textile Design); **Humanities** (Economics; English; French; Hindi; Music; Psychology; South and Southeast Asian Languages);

Science (Biochemistry; Biotechnology; Botany; Chemistry; Computer Science; Mathematics; Physics; Zoology)

History: Founded 1957 as Sri Avinashilingam Home Science College for Women. Also known as Avinashilingam Institute for Home Science and Higher Education for Women. Acquired present status as 'Deemed University' and title 1988.

Academic Year: July to April (July-November; December-April)

Admission Requirements: 12th year senior secondary/intermediate examination or recognized foreign equivalent

Fees: (Rupees): 490-3,000 per semester; Engineering, 39,000 per annum

Main Language(s) of Instruction: English

Accrediting Agency: National Council of Assessment and Accreditation, Bangalore

Degrees and Diplomas: *Bachelor's Degree*; *Postgraduate Diploma*; *Master's Degree*; *Master of Philosophy*; *Doctor of Philosophy*

Student Services: Academic Counselling, Canteen, Careers Guidance, Cultural Activities, Facilities for disabled people, Health Services, Language Laboratory, Nursery Care, Social Counselling, Sports Facilities

Publications: Indian Journal of Nutrition and Dietetics; Journal of Research Highlights; Vignana Chudar (Science Digest in Tamil)

Publishing House: Saradalaya Press

Last Updated: 17/06/11

AWADHESH PRATAP SINGH UNIVERSITY

Awadhesh Pratap Singh Vishwavidyalaya

Rewa, Madhya Pradesh 486003
Tel: +91(7662) 230-050
Fax: +91(7662) 230-819
EMail: ccapsu@gmail.com
Website: http://apsurewa.nic.in/

Vice-Chancellor: Shivnarayan Yadav

Registrar: Magan Singh Awasya

Faculty

Arts (Arts and Humanities; Hindi; History); **Commerce and Management** (Business and Commerce; Management); **Education** (Education); **Home Science** (Home Economics); **Law** (Law); **Life Sciences** (Biological and Life Sciences); **Medicine** (Medicine); **Prachya Sanskrit** (Sanskrit); **Science** (Natural Sciences); **Social Sciences** (Social Sciences); **Technology** (Engineering)

Further Information: Also 83 Affiliated Colleges, 21 Prachya Sanskrit Colleges and Teaching Hospitals

History: Founded 1968.

Academic Year: July to June (July-October-November; November-June)

Admission Requirements: 12th year senior secondary/intermediate examination or recognized foreign equivalent

Main Language(s) of Instruction: Hindi, English

Degrees and Diplomas: *Post Diploma*; *Bachelor's Degree*; *Master's Degree*; *Doctor of Philosophy*

Publications: Annual Research Journal; Vindhya Bharati

Last Updated: 17/06/11

AYUSH AND HEALTH SCIENCE UNIVERSITY CHHATTISGARH

G. E. Roas, Raipur, Chhattisgarh 429001
Website: http://cghealthuniv.com/

Vice-Chancellor: G B Gupta

Course

Ayurved (Ayurveda); **Dentistry** (Dentistry); **Homeopathic Medicine**; **Medicine** (Medical Technology; Medicine; Radiology); **Nursing** (Nursing); **Physiotherapy** (Physical Therapy); **Unani Chikitsa**; **Yoga and Prakritic Chikitsa** (Yoga)

Degrees and Diplomas: *Bachelor's Degree*; *Master's Degree*; *Doctor of Philosophy*

Last Updated: 28/07/11

AZIM PREMJI UNIVERSITY

Pixel Park, B Block, Electronics City, Hosur Road (Beside NICE Road), Bangalore, Karnataka 560100
Fax: +91(80) 6614-5145
EMail: info@azimpremjifoundation.org
Website: http://www.azimpremjiuniversity.edu.in/

Vice-Chancellor: Anurag Behar

Registrar: S. Giridhar

Programme

Development Studies (Development Studies); **Education** (Education); **Teacher Education** (Teacher Trainers Education)

History: Founded 2010.

Degrees and Diplomas: *Master's Degree*

Last Updated: 27/12/11

BABA FARID UNIVERSITY OF HEALTH SCIENCES

Kotkapura Road, Faridkot, Punjab 151203
Tel: +91(1639) 256-232
Fax: +91(1639) 256-234
EMail: generalinfo@bfuhs.ac.in
Website: http://www.bfuhs.ac.in

Vice-Chancellor: S.S. Gill

Faculty

Dentistry (Anatomy; Biochemistry; Dental Hygiene; Dentistry; Medicine; Microbiology; Oral Pathology; Orthodontics; Periodontics; Physiology; Radiology; Surgery); **Homeopathy** (Biochemistry; Haematology; Histology; Medical Technology; Microbiology; Pathology); **Medicine** (Anatomy; Biophysics; Cardiology; Dentistry; Dermatology; Gastroenterology; Gynaecology and Obstetrics; Medicine; Ophthalmology; Orthopaedics; Otorhinolaryngology; Paediatrics; Physiology; Plastic Surgery; Psychiatry and Mental Health; Radiology; Toxicology; Venereology); **Nursing** (Anatomy; Biochemistry; Community Health; Gynaecology and Obstetrics; Microbiology; Midwifery; Nursing; Nutrition; Physiology; Psychiatry and Mental Health; Psychology; Sociology; Surgery; Welfare and Protective Services); **Physiotherapy** (Physical Therapy)

College

Ayurveda (Ayurveda); **Homeopathy** (Anatomy; Biochemistry; Forensic Medicine and Dentistry; Gynaecology and Obstetrics; Homeopathy; Medicine; Microbiology; Pathology; Philosophy; Physiology; Psychology)

History: Founded 1998.

Academic Year: August to July (August-January, February-July)

Admission Requirements: 12th year senior secondary/intermediate examination or recognized foreign equivalent and entrance examination

Fees: (Rupees): 35,000-75,000 per annum

Main Language(s) of Instruction: English

Degrees and Diplomas: *Bachelor's Degree*: **Ayurveda; Dentistry; Homeopathy; Medicine; Nursing; Physical Therapy; Surgery.** *Postgraduate Diploma*: **Anaesthesiology; Child Care and Development; Gynaecology and Obstetrics; Ophthalmology; Otorhinolaryngology; Radiology; Sports Medicine; Surgery.** *Master's Degree*: **Homeopathy; Medicine; Nursing; Surgery.** *Doctor of Philosophy*

Last Updated: 17/06/11

BABA GHULAM SHAH BADSHAH UNIVERSITY

Rajouri Camp Office, Bye Pass Road, Opp. Channi Himmat, Jammu, Jammu and Kashmir 185131
Tel: +91(1962) 241001
EMail: vc_bgsbu@rediffmail.com
Website: http://www.bgsbuniversity.org/admissions.htm

Vice-Chancellor: I. A. Hamal

College

Engineering and Technology (Civil Engineering; Computer Networks; Electrical Engineering; Electronic Engineering; Energy Engineering; Engineering; Information Sciences; Technology; Telecommunications Engineering)

School
Biosciences and Biotechnology (Biological and Life Sciences; Biotechnology); **Healthcare and Pharmacy** (Health Sciences; Pharmacy); **Islamic Studies** (Arabic; Island Studies); **Management** (Business Administration; Finance; Management); **Material Sciences and Nanotechnology** (Materials Engineering; Nanotechnology); **Mathematical Sciences and Engineering** (Engineering; Mathematics)

History: Founded 2005.

Degrees and Diplomas: *Bachelor's Degree*; *Master's Degree*

Last Updated: 14/11/11

BABASAHEB BHIMRAO AMBEDKAR BIHAR UNIVERSITY

Muzaffarpur, Bihar 842001
Tel: +91(621) 224-3071
Fax: +91(621) 224-2495
EMail: vcbrabu@yahoo.com
Website: http://www.brabu.net

Vice-Chancellor: Rajdeo Singh

Registrar: Mohd A.A. Khan

Faculty
Commerce (Business and Commerce); **Education** (Education); **Engineering** (Engineering); **Homeopathy**; **Humanities** (Arts and Humanities); **Law** (Law); **Medicine** (Medicine); **Science** (Natural Sciences)

Further Information: Also 38 Affiliated Colleges

History: Founded 1952. Acquired present status 1960.

Academic Year: June to May

Admission Requirements: 12th year senior secondary/intermediate examination or recognized foreign equivalent

Fees: (Rupees): 120-240 per annum

Main Language(s) of Instruction: English, Hindi

Degrees and Diplomas: *Bachelor's Degree*; *Master's Degree*; *Doctor of Philosophy*

IAU BABASAHEB BHIMRAO AMBEDKAR UNIVERSITY

Vidya Vihar, Rai Bareilly Road, Lucknow,
Uttar Pradesh 226025
Tel: +91(522) 244-1515
Fax: +91(522) 244-0821
EMail: info@bbauindia.org
Website: http://www.bbauindia.org

Vice-Chancellor: R.C. Sobti (2013-)
Tel: +91(522) 244-0820 EMail: vcbbaulucknow@yahoo.co.in

Registrar: P.Hanmaiya Naik Tel: +91(522) 244-0822

School
Ambedkar Studies (Economics; History; Political Sciences; Sociology); **Bio-Science and Bio-Technology** (Animal Husbandry; Biotechnology; Botany; Fruit Production; Horticulture; Pharmacology; Sericulture; Zoology); **Environmental Science** (Biological and Life Sciences; Biotechnology; Development Studies; Environmental Studies; Microbiology; Toxicology); **Home Sciences** (Environmental Studies; Human Rights; Indigenous Studies; Political Sciences; Women's Studies); **Information Science and Technology** (Computer Science; Information Sciences; Information Technology; Library Science; Mass Communication); **Legal Studies** (Law); **Management** (Economics; Management); **Physical Sciences** (Applied Chemistry; Applied Mathematics; Applied Physics)

History: Founded 1989, acquired present status and title 1996. A Central University.

Academic Year: July to June

Admission Requirements: Bachelor Degree of the revelant course with minimum 50% (40% for SC/ST) marks and entrance examination

Main Language(s) of Instruction: English

Degrees and Diplomas: *Postgraduate Diploma*; *Master's Degree*; *Master of Philosophy*. Also Post-Doctoral Degrees

Student Services: Academic Counselling, Canteen, Careers Guidance, Cultural Activities, Facilities for disabled people, Foreign Studies Centre, Health Services, Language Laboratory, Nursery Care, Social Counselling, Sports Facilities

Last Updated: 15/04/13

BABU BANARASI DAS UNIVERSITY

BBD City, Faizabad Road, Lucknow, Uttar Pradesh 227015
Tel: +91(522) 3911-000
Website: http://bbdu.org/

Vice-Chancellor: Arun Kumar Mittal

Faculty
Applied Sciences (Chemistry; Mathematics; Natural Sciences; Physics); **Hotel Management** (Hotel Management)

College
Dentistry (Dentistry)

School
Architecture (Architecture); **Computer Applications** (Computer Engineering; Computer Science); **Engineering** (Civil Engineering; Electrical Engineering; Engineering; Mechanical Engineering); **Management** (Business Administration; Management); **Pharmacy** (Pharmacy)

History: Founded 2010.

Degrees and Diplomas: *Bachelor's Degree*; *Master's Degree*; *Doctor of Philosophy*

Student Services: Health Services, Sports Facilities

Last Updated: 02/01/12

BADDI UNIVERSITY OF EMERGING SCIENCES AND TECHNOLOGY

Makhnumajra, Baddi, Pradesh 173 205
Tel: +91(1795) 247353
Fax: +91(1795) 247352
Website: http://www.baddiuniv.ac.in

Vice-Chancellor: S.S Dasaka

School
Engineering and Emerging Technologies (Chemistry; Civil Engineering; Computer Engineering; Computer Networks; Electrical and Electronic Engineering; Information Technology; Mathematics; Mechanical Engineering; Physics); **Management Studies** (Business Administration; Finance; Human Resources; Information Technology; Management; Marketing); **Pharmacy and Emerging Sciences** (Pharmacy)

History: Founded 2009.

Degrees and Diplomas: *Bachelor's Degree*; *Master's Degree*; *Doctor of Philosophy*

Last Updated: 16/11/11

BAHRA UNIVERSITY

Waknaghat, Distt. Solan, Himachal Pradesh 160022
Tel: +91(981) 6014-412
Fax: +91(980) 5092-446
EMail: bahrauniversity@rayatbahra.com
Website: http://www.bahrauniversity.edu.in

Vice-Chancellor: R.K. Gupta

Registrar: C.R.B. Lalit

School
Basic Sciences (Chemistry; Mathematics; Natural Sciences; Physics); **Engineering and Technology** (Civil Engineering; Computer Engineering; Electronic Engineering; Engineering; Materials Engineering; Technology; Telecommunications Engineering); **Hospitality and Tourisme** (Tourism); **Management** (Business Administration; Management); **Pharmaceutical Sciences** (Pharmacy)

History: Founded 2011.

Degrees and Diplomas: *Bachelor's Degree*; *Master's Degree*; *Doctor of Philosophy*

Last Updated: 16/01/12

BANARAS HINDU UNIVERSITY

Kashi Hindu Vishwavidyalaya

Varanasi, Uttar Pradesh 221005
Tel: +91(542) 236-8938
Fax: +91(542) 236-8174
EMail: vc_bhu@sify.com; vcbhu1@gmail.com
Website: http://www.bhu.ac.in

Vice-Chancellor: Lalji Singh (2011-)
Tel: +91(542) 236-8938
EMail: vc_bhu@bhu.ac.in; vc_bhu@sify.com

Registrar: Natarajan Sundaram

Public Relations Officer: Viswanath Pandey
Tel: +91(542) 236-8598

International Relations: Mallickarjun Joshi, Chairman, International Centre
Tel: +91(542) 236-8130
EMail: intcent@bhu.ac.in

Faculty

Agriculture (Agriculture); **Arts** (Ancient Civilizations; Arabic; Archaeology; Art History; Arts and Humanities; Asian Religious Studies; Chinese; Cultural Studies; English; French; German; Hindi; Indic Languages; Journalism; Library Science; Linguistics; Mass Communication; Modern Languages; Music; Musical Instruments; Painting and Drawing; Philosophy; Physical Education; Singing; Urdu); **Ayurveda** (Ayurveda); **Commerce** (Business and Commerce); **Dental Sciences** (Dentistry); **Education** (Education); **Engineering and Technology** (Engineering; Technology); **Law** (Law); **Management** (Management); **Medicine** (Medicine); **Performing Arts** (Performing Arts); **Sanskrit Vidya Dharm Vigyan** (Sanskrit); **Science** (Biochemistry; Chemistry; Geology; Geophysics; Natural Sciences); **Social Sciences** (Economics; History; Political Sciences; Social Sciences; Sociology); **Visual Arts** (Visual Arts)

School

Biotechnology (Biotechnology)

Institute

Agricultural Sciences (Agricultural Economics; Agriculture; Agronomy; Botany; Distance Education; Entomology; Horticulture; Plant Pathology; Soil Science; Zoology); **Environment and Sustainable Development** (Development Studies; Environmental Studies); **Medical Sciences** (Anaesthesiology; Anatomy; Ayurveda; Biochemistry; Biophysics; Dentistry; Dermatology; Forensic Medicine and Dentistry; Gynaecology and Obstetrics; Medicine; Microbiology; Ophthalmology; Orthopaedics; Otorhinolaryngology; Paediatrics; Pathology; Pharmacology; Physiology; Psychiatry and Mental Health; Radiology; Social and Preventive Medicine; Surgery; Venereology); **Technology** (Applied Chemistry; Applied Mathematics; Applied Physics; Biochemistry; Biomedical Engineering; Ceramics and Glass Technology; Civil Engineering; Computer Engineering; Electrical Engineering; Electronic Engineering; Materials Engineering; Mechanical Engineering; Metallurgical Engineering; Mining Engineering; Pharmacology; Technology)

Further Information: Also affiliated schools and colleges, 4 Constituent Colleges. Teaching Hospital (Sir Sundeslal Hospital). Research centers and interdisciplinary schools

History: Founded 1915.

Academic Year: July to May (July-October; November-December; January-May)

Admission Requirements: 12th year senior secondary/intermediate examination or recognized foreign equivalent

Fees: (Rupees): 120-260

Main Language(s) of Instruction: English, Hindi

Degrees and Diplomas: *Bachelor's Degree*; *Master's Degree*; *Doctor of Philosophy*

Publications: Journal of Research in Indian Systems of Medicine; Scientific Research Journal

Publishing House: University Press

Student Numbers *2011-2012*: Total 30,698

Last Updated: 08/09/11

BANASTHALI UNIVERSITY

Banasthali Vidyapith

P.O. Banasthali Vidyapith, Banasthali Vidyapith, Rajasthan 304022
Tel: +91(1438) 228787 +91(1438) 228373
Fax: +91(1438) 228365
EMail: vc@banasthali.ac.in
Website: http://www.banasthali.org

Vice-Chancellor: Aditya Shastri
Tel: +91(1438) 228787
EMail: adityashastri@banasthali.in; vc@banasthali.ac.in

International Relations: Shalini Chandra, Coordinator, International Relations
Tel: +91(1438) 228787 EMail: chandrshalini@gmail.com

International Relations: Tripti Sharma, Coordinator, International Relations Tel: +91(1438) 228787 EMail: triptish03@gmail.com

Faculty

Design *(Banasthali Institute of Design)* (Fashion Design; Textile Design); **Education** (Education; Physical Education); **Fine Arts** (Dance; Journalism; Mass Communication; Music; Theatre; Visual Arts); **Home Science** (Child Care and Development; Clothing and Sewing; Home Economics; Nutrition); **Humanities** (English; European Languages; Hindi; Sanskrit); **Management** (Finance; Human Resources; Information Technology; Marketing); **Mathematical Sciences** (Computer Science; Electronic Engineering; Mathematics; Physics; Statistics); **Science and Technology** (Biological and Life Sciences; Biophysics; Chemical Engineering; Chemistry; Pharmacy); **Social Sciences** (Economics; History; Political Sciences; Psychology; Public Administration; Sociology; Women's Studies)

School

Earth Sciences (Geography; Geology; Surveying and Mapping); **Legal Studies** (Law)

Further Information: https://www.facebook.com/banasthali.org

History: Banasthali University was founded in 1935 and became an 'Institution Deemed to be University' in the year 1983. It is one of the largest residential university for women's education in the world.

Academic Year: July to April

Admission Requirements: XII/senior secondary/intermediate examination or recognized foreign equivalent

Fees: National: MBA, MCA, PGDCA, M.Tech., M.Des., B.Tech., BBA, BCA, LLB (Integrated), B. Design: 1700 M.Sc., M. Pharma, Master in Social Work, B.Pharma, B.Sc., B.Sc. (Aviation Science), Bachelor of Journalism and Mass Communication, B.Com., B.Ed., B.P.Ed., M.Ed.: 1400 B.A., M.A., M.Phil., B.Sc. (Home Science), M.Sc. (Home Science): 1100 (US Dollar), International: MBA, MCA, PGDCA, M.Tech., M.Des., B.Tech., BBA, BCA, LLB (Integrated), B. Design: 3200 M.Sc., M. Pharma, Master in Social Work, B.Pharma, B.Sc., B.Sc. (Aviation Science), Bachelor of Journalism and Mass Communication, B.Com., B.Ed., B.P.Ed., M.Ed.: 2400 B.A., M.A., M.Phil., B.Sc. (Home Science), M.Sc. (Home Science): 1600 (US Dollar)

Main Language(s) of Instruction: Hindi, English

Accrediting Agency: National Assessment and Accreditation Council (NAAC)

Degrees and Diplomas: *Bachelor's Degree*: **Arts and Humanities; Bioengineering; Business Administration; Chemical Engineering; Computer Engineering; Design; Education; Electrical and Electronic Engineering; Journalism; Law; Mass Communication; Mathematics and Computer Science; Natural Sciences; Pharmacy.** *Postgraduate Diploma*: **Computer Science; Human Rights; Information Technology; Women's Studies.** *Master's Degree*: **Bioengineering; Biotechnology; Business Administration; Chemical Engineering; Chemistry; Clothing and Sewing; Computer Engineering; Computer Science; Design; Economics; Education; Electronic Engineering; English; Food Science; Geography; Hindi; History; Information Technology; Mathematics; Microbiology; Music; Nutrition; Operations Research; Painting and Drawing; Pharmacology; Pharmacy; Physics; Plant Pathology; Political Sciences; Psychology; Sanskrit; Social Work; Sociology; Statistics; Surveying and Mapping; Textile Design; Zoology.** *Master of Philosophy*: **Economics; English; Foreign Languages Education; Hindi; History; Mathematics; Music; Painting and**

Drawing; Political Sciences; Sanskrit; Sociology. *Doctor of Philosophy*: **Biotechnology; Chemistry; Child Care and Development; Computer Science; Design; Economics; Education; Electronic Engineering; English; Geography; Hindi; History; Management; Mathematics; Music; Nutrition; Painting and Drawing; Pharmacy; Physical Education; Physics; Political Sciences; Psychology; Public Administration; Sanskrit; Sociology; Statistics; Textile Technology.**

Student Services: Academic Counselling, Canteen, Careers Guidance, Cultural Activities, Facilities for disabled people, Foreign Studies Centre, Health Services, IT Centre, Language Laboratory, Library, Nursery Care, Residential Facilities, Social Counselling, Sports Facilities, eLibrary

Academic Staff *2015-2016*	MEN	WOMEN	TOTAL
FULL-TIME	196	408	**604**
STAFF WITH DOCTORATE			
FULL-TIME	95	280	**375**
Student Numbers *2015-2016*			
All (Foreign included)	–	10,973	**10,973**
FOREIGN ONLY	–	275	**275**

Last Updated: 19/10/15

BANGALORE UNIVERSITY

Jnana Bharathi Campus, Bangalore, Karnataka 560056
Tel: +91(80) 2321-3172
Fax: +91(80) 2321-9295
Website: http://www.bangaloreuniversity.ac.in

Vice-Chancellor: A.N Prabhu Deva

Registrar: Sanjay Veer Singh
Tel: +91(80) 2321-3023 EMail: buregistrar@vsnl.in

International Relations: H.M. Revanasiddaiah, Director, Student's Welfare Tel: +91(80) 2296-1096

Faculty

Arts (Dance; Development Studies; Economics; English; French; German; Hindi; Indic Languages; Italian; Japanese; Music; Performing Arts; Philosophy; Political Sciences; Psychology; Rural Studies; Social Work; Sociology; South and Southeast Asian Languages; Spanish; Theatre; Urdu; Visual Arts; Women's Studies); **Commerce and Management** (Accountancy; Administration; Business Administration; Finance; Health Administration; International Business; Management; Tourism); **Education** (Education); **Science** (Biotechnology; Botany; Chemistry; Computer Engineering; Electronic Engineering; Environmental Studies; Geology; Information Sciences; Library Science; Mathematics; Media Studies; Microbiology; Physics; Sericulture; Statistics; Zoology)

College

Engineering (Civil Engineering; Computer Engineering; Electrical Engineering; Electronic Engineering; Information Sciences; Information Technology; Mechanical Engineering; Structural Architecture; Telecommunications Engineering); **Law** (Law); **Physical Education**

Further Information: Also 387 Affiliated Colleges. Study Abroad Programme with North Essex Community College, Massachusetts

History: Founded 1964. Acquired present status 1976.

Academic Year: July to April (July-November; December-April)

Admission Requirements: 12th year senior secondary/intermediate examination or recognized foreign equivalent

Fees: (Rupees): 150 to 3,000

Main Language(s) of Instruction: English, Kannada

Accrediting Agency: National Assessment and Accreditation Council

Degrees and Diplomas: *Post Diploma*: **Fine Arts.** *Bachelor's Degree*: **Fine Arts.** *Postgraduate Diploma*: **Fine Arts.** *Master's Degree*; *Doctor of Philosophy*

Student Services: Academic Counselling, Canteen, Careers Guidance, Cultural Activities, Health Services, Language Laboratory, Nursery Care, Social Counselling, Sports Facilities

Publications: Janapriya Vignana (Kannada); Sadane (Kannada); Vidya Bharathi (English); Vignana Bharathi (English)

Publishing House: Bangalore University Press

BARKATULLAH UNIVERSITY

Barkatullah Vishwavidyalaya
Hoshangabad Road, Bhopal, Madhya Pradesh 462026
Tel: +91(755) 258-7257
Fax: +91(755) 267-7703
EMail: buvc_office@yahoo.com
Website: http://www.bubhopal.nic.in

Vice-Chancellor: Nisha Dube

Registrar: Sanjay Prakesh Tiwari
Tel: +91(755) 249-1706+91(755) 249-1701
EMail: buregistrar@yahoo.co.in

Faculty

Arts (Arabic; Arts and Humanities; Cultural Studies; Persian); **Commerce** (Business and Commerce); **Education** (Consumer Studies; Education; Physical Education; Yoga); **Engineering** (Engineering; Information Technology; Materials Engineering; Pharmacy; Technology); **Law** (Law); **Life Sciences** (Aquaculture; Biological and Life Sciences; Biotechnology; Environmental Studies; Genetics; Limnology; Microbiology; Zoology); **Natural Sciences** (Natural Sciences; Physics); **Science** (Computer Science; Electronic Engineering; Geology; Home Economics; Physics); **Social Sciences** (Economics; Political Sciences; Psychology; Social Sciences; Social Work; Sociology)

Institute

Distance Education

Further Information: Also 16 Affiliated Colleges

History: Founded 1970 as Bhopal University, acquired present title 1988.

Academic Year: July to June

Admission Requirements: Higher Secondary Certificate or equivalent.

Main Language(s) of Instruction: Hindi and English

Accrediting Agency: University Grants Commission

Degrees and Diplomas: *Bachelor's Degree*: **Arts and Humanities; Business and Commerce; English; Fine Arts; Health Sciences; Law; Management; Mass Communication; Mathematics and Computer Science; Microbiology; Pharmacy; Photography; Social Sciences.** *Postgraduate Diploma*; *Master's Degree*: **Arts and Humanities; Business and Commerce; English; Fine Arts; Library Science; Management; Medicine; Natural Sciences; Photography; Public Administration; Social Sciences; Sports.** *Master of Philosophy*; *Doctor of Philosophy*

Student Services: Academic Counselling, Canteen, Careers Guidance, Cultural Activities, Facilities for disabled people, Health Services, Language Laboratory, Social Counselling, Sports Facilities

Publishing house: University Press B.U. Bhopal

Last Updated: 20/06/11

BASTAR VISHWAVIDYALAYA

Dharampura-II, Jagdalpur, Chhattisgarh 494005
Tel: +91(77) 8223-9039
EMail: info@bvvjdp.ac.in
Website: http://bvvjdp.ac.in/

Vice-Chancellor: Jaylaxmi Thakur EMail: vc@bvvjdp.ac.in

Registrar: J.K. Jain EMail: registrar@bvvjdp.ac.in

School

Biotechnology (Biotechnology); **Computer Application** (Computer Engineering); **Forest and Wild Life** (Forestry; Wildlife); **Rural Technology and Management** (Rural Planning); **Science and Social Studies** (Anthropology; Social Sciences; Social Work)

History: Founded 2008

Degrees and Diplomas: *Post Diploma*; *Postgraduate Diploma*; *Master's Degree*

Last Updated: 28/07/11

BENGAL ENGINEERING AND SCIENCE UNIVERSITY, SHIBPUR (BESU)

PO Botanic Garden, Howrah, West Bengal 711103
Tel: +91(33) 2668-4561 +91(33) 2668-4563
Fax: +91(33) 2668-2916
EMail: vc@becs.ac.in
Website: http://www.becs.ac.in

Vice-Chancellor: Ajoy Kumar Ray EMail: vc@becs.ac.in

Registrar: Biman Bondopadhyay EMail: regis@becs.ac.in

Department

Applied Mechanics and Drawing (Mechanical Engineering; Painting and Drawing); **Architecture** (Architecture; Regional Planning; Town Planning); **Chemistry** (Chemistry); **Civil Engineering** (Civil Engineering); **Computer Science and Technology** (Computer Science; Technology); **Electrical Engineering** (Electrical Engineering); **Electronics and Telecommunication** (Electronic Engineering; Telecommunications Engineering); **Geology** (Geology); **Human Resource Management** (Human Resources; Management); **Humanities and Social Sciences** (Arts and Humanities; Social Sciences); **Information Technology** (Information Technology); **Mathematics** (Mathematics); **Mechanical Engineering** (Mechanical Engineering); **Metallurgy and Materials Engineering** (Materials Engineering; Metallurgical Engineering); **Mining Engineering** (Mining Engineering); **Physics** (Physics)

History: Founded 1856. Acquired present status and title 2004.

Degrees and Diplomas: *Bachelor's Degree*; *Master's Degree*; *Doctor of Philosophy*. Also DSc (Honorary)

Last Updated: 20/06/11

BERHAMPUR UNIVERSITY

Bhanja Bihar, District Ganjam, Berhampur, Orissa 760007
Tel: +91(680) 224-3615 +91(680) 224-3404 +91(680) 224-2172
Fax: +91(680) 224-3322
EMail: registrarbuorissa@gmail.com
Website: http://www.bamu.nic.in

Vice-Chancellor: J. K. Mohapatra
Tel: +91(680) 224-2233 EMail: vcbuorissa@gmail.com

Registrar: B. P. Rath Tel: +91(680) 224-2234

Faculty

Arts (Arts and Humanities; Economics; English; History; Indic Languages; Linguistics; Mass Communication; Police Studies); **Business** (Business Administration; Business and Commerce); **Education** (Education); **Law** (Law); **Science** (Botany; Chemistry; Electronic Engineering; Marine Science and Oceanography; Mathematics; Mathematics and Computer Science; Natural Sciences; Physics; Zoology)

Further Information: Also 118 Affiliated Colleges

History: Founded 1967.

Academic Year: June to May (June-December; January-May)

Admission Requirements: 12th year senior secondary/intermediate examination or recognized foreign equivalent

Fees: (Rupees): 1,200-1,800 per annum; Free for women

Main Language(s) of Instruction: English

Accrediting Agency: NAAC, Bangalore

Degrees and Diplomas: *Bachelor's Degree*: **Ayurveda; Business Administration; Business and Commerce; Computer Engineering; Electronic Engineering; Fine Arts; Homeopathy; Medicine; Nursing; Surgery.** *Master's Degree*: **Accountancy; Business Administration; Business and Commerce; Finance; Fine Arts; Law.** *Doctor of Philosophy*

Student Services: Canteen, Careers Guidance, Cultural Activities, Health Services, Language Laboratory, Sports Facilities

Publications: One

Last Updated: 21/06/11

BHAGAT PHOOL SIGN MAHILA VISHWAVIDYALA

Khanpur Kalan, Sonipat, Haryana 131305
EMail: enquiry@bpswomenuniversity.ac.in
Website: http://www.bpswomenuniversity.ac.in

Vice-Chancellor: Asha Kadyan
EMail: vc@bpswomenuniversity.ac.in

Registrar: Kavita Chakravarty
EMail: Registrar@bpswomenuniversity.ac.in

School

Engineering and Sciences (Engineering; Natural Sciences); **Pharmaceutical Education and Research** (Pharmacology)

Department

English (English); **Foreign Languages** (Foreign Languages Education); **Law** (Law); **Management Studies** (Management); **Social Work and Economics** (Economics; Social Work)

Institute

Ayurveda (Ayurveda); **Polytechnic** (Computer Engineering; Electronic Engineering; Information Technology; Library Science; Medical Technology)

History: Founded 2006. First all-women university in the region.

Degrees and Diplomas: *Bachelor's Degree*; *Master's Degree*

Last Updated: 12/08/11

BHAGWANT UNIVERSITY

Sikar Road, Ajmer, 305001 Rajasthan
EMail: unibhagwant@rediffmail.com
Website: http://www.bhagwantuniversity.com/

Vice-Chancellor: Virendra Kumar Sharma

College

Education (Education); **Para Medical Science** (Orthopaedics; Rehabilitation and Therapy)

Institute

Computer Application (Computer Engineering); **Engineering and Technology** (Aeronautical and Aerospace Engineering; Agricultural Engineering; Civil Engineering; Electronic Engineering; Engineering; Information Sciences; Mechanical Engineering; Nanotechnology; Petroleum and Gas Engineering; Technology); **Hospitality and Aviation** (Food Technology; Hotel and Restaurant; Household Management; Tourism); **Humanities and Applied Sciences** (Applied Chemistry; Applied Mathematics; Applied Physics; Arts and Humanities); **Management** (Management); **Media and Mass Communication** (Mass Communication; Media Studies); **Pharmaceutical Science and Research Center** (Pharmacy)

History: Founded 2008,

Degrees and Diplomas: *Bachelor's Degree*; *Master's Degree*; *Doctor of Philosophy*

Last Updated: 16/12/11

BHARAT RATNA DR B.R. AMBEDKAR UNIVERSITY

Bharat Ratna Dr B.R. Ambedkar Vishwavidyalaya (AUD)
IIT Campus, plot n° 13, Sector 9, Dwarka, New Delhi 110 077
Tel: +91(11) 2507-4875
EMail: info@aud.ac.in
Website: http://www.aud.ac.in/

Vice-Chancellor: Shyam B. Menon

Registrar: Chandan Mukherjee

School

Business, Public Policy and Social Entrepreneurship (Business Administration; Public Administration; Social Policy); **Culture and Creative Expressions** (Cultural Studies); **Design** (Design); **Development Studies** (Development Studies; Gender Studies); **Educational Studies** (Education); **Human Ecology** (Ecology); **Law, Governance and Citizenship** (Civics; Government; Law); **Liberal Studies** (History; Labour and Industrial Relations; Modern Languages; Social Sciences; Translation and Interpretation); **Undergraduate Studies** (Arts and Humanities; Mathematics; Social Sciences)

History: Founded 2007.

Degrees and Diplomas: *Bachelor's Degree*; *Master's Degree*

Last Updated: 05/01/12

BHARATH UNIVERSITY

173 Agharam Road, Selaiyur, Chennai, Tamil Nadu 600073
Tel: + 91(44) 2229-0742
Fax: + 91(44) 2229-3886
EMail: admission@bharathuniv.ac.in
Website: http://www.bharathuniv.com

Vice-Chancellor: M Ponnavaikko EMail: vc@bharathuniv.ac.in

Registrar: V. Kanagasabai EMail: reg@bharathuniv.ac.in

College

Dentistry *(Sree Balaji Dental College and Hospital)* (Dentistry); **Medicine** *(Sree Balaji Medical College and Hospital)* (Medicine); **Nursing** *(Sree Balaji)* (Nursing); **Physiotherapy** *(Sree Balaji)* (Physical Therapy)

Institute

Medical Sciences *(Sri Lakshmi Narayana)* (Medicine; Surgery); **Science and Technology** (Architecture; Chemistry; Computer Science; Engineering; Hotel Management; Information Technology; Mathematics; Physics; Tourism)

History: Founded 1984 as Bharath Institute of Science and Technology (BIST). Acquired present status 2003.

Degrees and Diplomas: *Bachelor's Degree*; *Master's Degree*; *Doctor of Philosophy*

Academic Staff *2015-2016*	**TOTAL**
FULL-TIME	**1,050**
PART-TIME	**120**
STAFF WITH DOCTORATE	
FULL-TIME	**335**

Student Numbers *2015-2016*	
All (Foreign included)	**12,190**

Last Updated: 21/06/11

BHARATHIAR UNIVERSITY

Coimbatore, Tamil Nadu 641046
Tel: +91(422) 2428-100
Fax: +91(422) 2422-387
EMail: regr@buc.edu.in
Website: http://www.b-u.ac.in/

Vice-Chancellor: G. James Pitchai (2012-) EMail: vc@buc.edu.in

Registrar: P. Thirumalvalavan

School

Biotechnology and Genetic Engineering (Biotechnology; Genetics); **Chemical Sciences** (Chemistry); **Commerce** (Accountancy; Business and Commerce; Finance); **Computer Science and Engineering** (Computer Engineering; Computer Science; Information Technology); **Economics** (Economics); **Educational Studies** (Communication Studies; Education; Mass Communication; Media Studies; Physical Education); **English and Other Foreign Languages** (English; Foreign Languages Education; French; German; Linguistics); **Life Sciences** (Biological and Life Sciences; Botany; Environmental Studies; Zoology); **Management and Entrepreneur Development** (Business Administration; Management); **Mathematics and Statistics** (Mathematics; Mathematics and Computer Science; Statistics); **Physical Sciences** (Electronic Engineering; Nanotechnology; Physics); **Social Sciences** (Demography and Population; Psychology; Social Sciences; Social Work; Sociology; Women's Studies); **Tamil and Other Indian Languages** (Indic Languages)

Department

Textiles and Apparel Design (Textile Design)

Further Information: Also 47 Affiliated Colleges

History: Founded 1982.

Academic Year: June to May (June-November; December-May). MBA, June to May (June-September; October-January; February-May).

Admission Requirements: Higher Secondary Certificate (HSC)

Main Language(s) of Instruction: English

Degrees and Diplomas: *Bachelor's Degree*; *Master's Degree*; *Doctor of Philosophy*. Also postgraduate Diplomas

Student Services: Academic Counselling, Canteen, Health Services, Social Counselling

Last Updated: 23/06/11

BHARATHIDASAN UNIVERSITY

Palkalaiperur, Tiruchirappalli, Tamil Nadu 620024
Tel: +91(431) 240-7071
Fax: +91(431) 240-7045
EMail: info@bdu.ac.in
Website: http://www.bdu.ac.in

Vice-Chancellor: K. Meena (2010-)
Tel: +91(431) 240-7048 EMail: vc@bdu.ac.in

Registrar: T. Ramaswamy
Tel: +91(431) 240-7092 EMail: reg@bdu.ac.in

Faculty

Arts (Arts and Humanities; Business and Commerce; Economics; Education; Educational Technology; Finance; History; Physical Education; Social Work; Sociology; Women's Studies; Yoga); **Indian and Other Languages** (English; Foreign Languages Education; Indic Languages; Modern Languages; Performing Arts); **Management** *(Bharathidasan)* (Management); **Science, Engineering and Technology** (Biochemistry; Biological and Life Sciences; Biomedicine; Biotechnology; Botany; Chemistry; Computer Engineering; Computer Science; Engineering; Environmental Management; Environmental Studies; Geography; Geology; Information Sciences; Library Science; Marine Biology; Marine Science and Oceanography; Mathematics; Medicine; Microbiology; Physics; Surveying and Mapping; Technology; Zoology)

School

Basic Medical Sciences (Medicine); **Chemistry** (Chemistry); **Computer Science, Engineering and Applications** (Computer Engineering; Computer Science); **Earth Sciences** (Earth Sciences); **Economics, Commerce and Financial Studies** (Business and Commerce; Economics; Finance); **Education** (Adult Education; Distance Education; Economics; Engineering; Journalism; Mathematics; Physics; Preschool Education; Primary Education; Social Work); **Energy** (Energy Engineering); **Engineering and Technology** (Engineering; Technology); **English and Other Foreign Languages** (English; Modern Languages); **Environmental Studies** (Environmental Management; Environmental Studies); **Geosciences** (Geography; Geology; Surveying and Mapping); **Library and Information Sciences** (Information Sciences; Library Science); **Life Sciences** (Biochemistry; Biological and Life Sciences; Biotechnology; Botany; Microbiology; Zoology); **Marine Sciences** (Biotechnology; Marine Science and Oceanography); **Mathematics** (Mathematics); **Performing Arts** (Performing Arts); **Physics** (Physics); **Social Sciences** (History; Social Sciences; Social Work; Sociology; Women's Studies); **Tamil and Indian Languages** (Indic Languages)

Centre

Alternatives to the Use of Animals in Life Science Education *(Mahatma Gandhi Dorenkamp Center)*; **Bharathidasan Studies** (Cultural Studies); **Bio-Informatics**; **Bio-Inorganic Chemistry** (Inorganic Chemistry); **Business Development Cell**; **Canadian Studies** (Canadian Studies); **Geographic Information Technology**; **Herbal Drug and Discovery**; **Human Conciousness Yogic Studies** (Yoga); **Jawaharlal Nehru Studies**; **Kalaigner Studies**; **Nano-Science and Nanotechnology** (Nanotechnology); **National Facility for Marine Cyanobacteria**; **Non-Linear Dynamics**; **Periyar Studies**

Further Information: University Colleges: Bharathidasan, Orathanadu; Bharathidasan, Perambalur; Dr. Kalaignar College of Arts and Science, Lalgudi. Also 104 Affiliated Colleges and 13 Approved Institutions

History: Founded 1982 by the Barathidasan University Act 1981 (Act 2 of 1982), and named after the Tamil poet Bharathidasan (1891-1964). Includes Madras University's former Postgraduate Centre at Tiruchirappalli.

Academic Year: July to April (July-November; December-April)

Admission Requirements: 12th year senior secondary/intermediate examination or recognized foreign equivalent

Fees: (Rupees): Postgraduate, 1,000-20,000 per semester

Main Language(s) of Instruction: Tamil and English

Degrees and Diplomas: *Bachelor's Degree*; *Postgraduate Diploma*: **Biological and Life Sciences; Biomedical Engineering; Biotechnology; Computer Engineering; Computer Science; Earth Sciences; Film; History; Physics; Surveying and Mapping.** *Master's Degree*: **Biochemistry; Biological and Life Sciences; Biotechnology; Botany; Chemistry; Computer Engineering; Economics; Education; English; Environmental Management; Finance; Geography; History; Information Technology; Management; Mathematics; Physical Therapy; Physics; Social Work; Sociology; Surveying and Mapping; Veterinary Science; Women's Studies.** *Master of Philosophy*; *Doctor of Philosophy*

Student Services: Health Services

Publications: Journal of Science and Technology

Last Updated: 23/06/11

BHARATI UNIVERSITY

Bharati Vidyapeeth
Lal Bahadur Shastri Marg, Pune, Maharashtra 411030
Tel: +91(20) 2433-1317 +91(20) 2433-5701
Fax: +91(20) 2433-9121
EMail: bharati@vsnl.com
Website: http://www.bharatividyapeeth.edu

Vice-Chancellor: Shivajirao Kadam Tel: +91(20) 2433-1317

Secretary: Vishwajeet Kadam

College

Arts, Sciences and Commerce *(Yashwantrao Mohite)* (Arts and Humanities; Business and Commerce; Natural Sciences); **Ayurveda** (Ayurveda); **Dentistry** *(Hospital)* (Dentistry); **Engineering** (Engineering; Information Sciences; Information Technology; Technology); **Homeopathy**; **Law** (Law); **Medicine** (Medicine; Surgery); **Nursing** (Nursing); **Pharmacy** *(Poona)* (Pharmacy); **Physical Education** (Physical Education)

School

Health Affairs *(Interactive Research)* (Health Sciences)

Institute

Environment Education and Research (Environmental Studies); **Information Technology** *(Rajiv Gandhi)* (Biotechnology; Information Technology); **Management and Entrepreneurship Development** (Management); **Social Sciences Studies and Research** *(Yashwantrao Chavan)* (Social Sciences)

Centre

Social Sciences (Social Sciences)

Research Centre

Pharmacy and Applied Chemistry (Applied Chemistry; Pharmacy)

History: Founded 1964. Acquired present status and title 1996.

Academic Year: June to May

Admission Requirements: 12th year senior secondary/intermediate examination or recognized foreign equivalent and entrance test

Main Language(s) of Instruction: English, Marathi

Accrediting Agency: National Assessment and Accreditation Council (NAAC) of the University Grants Commission (UGC)

Degrees and Diplomas: *Post Diploma*: **Ayurveda; Business and Commerce; Environmental Studies; Law; Management; Medicine; Nursing.** *Bachelor's Degree*: **Ayurveda; Business and Commerce; Dentistry; Engineering; Environmental Studies; Fine Arts; Homeopathy; Information Sciences; Law; Library Science; Management; Medicine; Nursing; Pharmacy; Physical Education; Social Sciences.** *Master's Degree*: **Ayurveda; Business and Commerce; Dentistry; Engineering; Environmental Studies; Fine Arts; Homeopathy; Information Sciences; Law; Library Science; Management; Medicine; Nursing; Pharmacy; Physical Education; Social Sciences.**

Student Services: Academic Counselling, Canteen, Careers Guidance, Cultural Activities, Facilities for disabled people, Foreign Studies Centre, Health Services, Language Laboratory, Nursery Care, Social Counselling, Sports Facilities

Publications: Bharati Vidyapeeth Research Bulletin

Last Updated: 24/06/11

BHARATI VIDYAPEETH UNIVERSITY

Bharati Vidyapeeth Bhavan, Lal Bahadur Shastri Marg, Pune, Maharashtra 411030
EMail: info@bharatividyapeeth.edu
Website: http://www.bharatividyapeeth.edu/

Vice-Chancellor: Shivajirao Kadam
EMail: sskadam.vc@gmail.com

Faculty

Agriculture (Agriculture); **Architecture** (Architecture; Interior Design); **Arts, Science and Commerce** (Analytical Chemistry; Computer Science; Economics; English; Microbiology); **Biotechnology** (Biotechnology); **Engineering** (Biomedical Engineering; Chemical Engineering; Civil Engineering; Electrical Engineering; Electronic Engineering; Engineering; Information Technology; Telecommunications Engineering); **Environmental Science** (Environmental Management; Environmental Studies); **Fine Arts** (Fine Arts; Photography); **Geo Informatics** (Surveying and Mapping); **Health Sciences** (Ayurveda; Dentistry; Health Administration; Homeopathy; Medicine; Nursing; Optometry); **Hotel Management** (Cooking and Catering; Hotel and Restaurant; Hotel Management); **Law** (Law); **Management** (Business Administration; Human Resources; Management; Marketing); **Pharmaceutical Science** (Pharmacy); **Physical Education** (Physical Education; Sports); **Social Science** (Business and Commerce; Social Work)

History: Created 1964, acquired 'Deemed University' status 1996.

Accrediting Agency: UGC, India

Degrees and Diplomas: *Bachelor's Degree*; *Postgraduate Diploma*; *Master's Degree*; *Doctor of Philosophy*
Last Updated: 01/04/14

BHATKHANDE MUSIC INSTITUTE DEEMED UNIVERSITY

Bhatkhande Sangeet Sansthan
1, Kaiserbagh, Lucknow, Uttar Pradesh 226001
Tel: +91(522) 261-0318
Fax: +91(522) 262-2926
EMail: info@bhatkhandemusic.edu.in
Website: http://www.bhatkhandemusic.edu.in

Vice-Chancellor: VyasShruti Sadolikar
Tel: +91(522) 261-0248 EMail: vc@bhatkhandemusic.edu.in

Faculty

Applied Music (Music); **Dance** (Dance; Folklore); **Musical Instruments** (Music; Musical Instruments); **Musicology and Research** (Musicology); **Percussion Instruments** (Musical Instruments); **Vocal Music** (Singing)

History: Founded 1926 as Marris College. Acquired present status 2000 and title 2001

Academic Year: July to June

Admission Requirements: School certificate and music exam certificate

Main Language(s) of Instruction: Hindi

Accrediting Agency: University Grants Commission, New Delhi

Degrees and Diplomas: *Bachelor's Degree*: **Music.** *Master's Degree*: **Music.** *Doctor of Philosophy*: **Music.** Also Sangeet praveshika, Parichaya-Certificate Course; Sangeet Prabuddha, Parangt-Diploma course

Student Services: Cultural Activities

BHAVNAGAR UNIVERSITY

Gaurishanker Lake Road, Bhavnagar, Gujarat 364002
Tel: +91(278) 242-8014
Fax: +91(278) 242-6706
EMail: registrar@bhavuni.edu
Website: http://www.bhavuni.edu

Vice-Chancellor: J. P. Maiyanil Tel: +91(278) 242-6519

Registrar: Kaushik L. Bhatt

Faculty

Engineering and Technology (Automation and Control Engineering; Civil Engineering; Electronic Engineering; Engineering; Mechanical Engineering; Production Engineering;

Telecommunications Engineering); **Law** (Law); **Management** (Management); **Medicine** (Medicine); **Rural Studies** (Rural Studies)

Department

Bioinformatics (Computer Engineering); **Business Adminintration** (Business Administration); **Chemistry** (Chemistry); **Commerce** (Business and Commerce); **Computer Science and Application** (Computer Science); **Economics** (Economics); **Education** (Education); **English** (English); **Gujarati** (Indic Languages); **Hindi** (Hindi); **History** (History); **Library and Information Sciences** (Information Sciences; Library Science); **Life Science** (Biological and Life Sciences); **Marine Science** (Marine Science and Oceanography); **Mathematics** (Mathematics); **Physics** (Physics); **Psychology** (Psychology); **Sanskrit** (Sanskrit); **Social Work** (Social Work); **Sociology** (Sociology); **Statistics** (Statistics)

Further Information: Also 16 Affiliated Colleges and 1 Recognized Institution

History: Founded 1978 to impart knowledge on various aspects of rural life, including cultural and rural developments.

Academic Year: June to March (June-October; November-March)

Admission Requirements: 12th year senior secondary/intermediate examination or recognized foreign equivalent

Fees: (Rupees): Postgraduates 600-1,200 per annum; PhD, 3,800

Main Language(s) of Instruction: English

Degrees and Diplomas: *Bachelor's Degree*: **Arts and Humanities; Business and Commerce; Education; Engineering; Information Sciences; Law; Library Science; Medicine; Rural Studies.** *Postgraduate Diploma*; *Master's Degree*: **Business and Commerce; Education; Fine Arts; Information Sciences; Library Science; Medicine.** *Doctor of Philosophy*. Also Postgraduate Diploma courses

Publications: Bhavrup

Last Updated: 24/06/11

BHUPENDRA NARAYAN MANDAL UNIVERSITY

Madhepura, Bihar 852113
Tel: +91(6476) 222-779
Fax: +91(6476) 222-068
EMail: registrar@bnmu.in

Vice-Chancellor: Qamar Ahsan EMail: vc@bnmu.in

Faculty

Commerce (Business and Commerce); **Humanities** (Arts and Humanities); **Medicine** (Medicine); **Science** (Natural Sciences); **Social Sciences** (Social Sciences)

History: Founded 1992.

Degrees and Diplomas: *Bachelor's Degree*; *Master's Degree*

Last Updated: 17/06/11

BIDHAN CHANDRA AGRICULTURAL UNIVERSITY

Bidhan Chandra Krishi Viswavidyalaya

PO Krishi Vishnavidyalaya, District Nadia,
Mohanpur, West Bengal 741252
Tel: +91(3473) 587-8163
Fax: +91(3473) 22-275
EMail: vcbckv@vsnl.net
Website: http://www.bckv.edu.in

Vice-Chancellor: Chittaranjan Kole
EMail: bckvvc@gmail.com; ckole2012@gmail.com; vice-chacellor@bckv.edu.in

Registrar: Hemanta Banerjee
EMail: hembckv@rediffmail.com; banerjee.hemanta@gmail.com

Faculty

Agricultural Engineering (Agricultural Engineering); **Agriculture** (Agricultural Economics; Agriculture; Biotechnology; Environmental Studies; Plant and Crop Protection; Zoology); **Horticulture** (Horticulture); **Postgraduate Studies**

History: Founded 1974 by an Act, amended 1981. The only Agricultural University in the State of West Bengal, is primarily responsible for generating technical manpower and providing research and extension support for the development of Agriculture in the State.

Admission Requirements: 12th year senior secondary/intermediate examination or recognized foreign equivalent

Main Language(s) of Instruction: English

Degrees and Diplomas: *Bachelor's Degree*; *Master's Degree*; *Doctor of Philosophy*

Last Updated: 24/06/11

BIJU PATNAIK UNIVERSITY OF TECHNOLOGY

Jail Road, Chhend Colony, Rourkela, Orissa
Tel: +91(661) 240-2560
Fax: +91(661) 240-2556
EMail: bput@bput.ac.in; students@bput.ac.in
Website: http://www.bput.ac.in

Vice-Chancellor: Jitendriya Kumar Satapathy

Programme

Architecture (Architecture); **Business Administration** (Business Administration); **Engineering** (Computer Engineering; Engineering; Mining Engineering); **Information Technology** (Computer Engineering; Information Technology)

History: Founded 2002.

Degrees and Diplomas: *Bachelor's Degree*; *Postgraduate Diploma*; *Master's Degree*; *Doctor of Philosophy*

Last Updated: 06/12/11

BIRLA INSTITUTE OF MANAGEMENT TECHNOLOGY

Plot No. 5, Knowledge Park II, Greater Noida, Uttar Pradesh 201306
Tel: +91(120) 2323-001/10
Fax: +91(120) 2323-001/22
EMail: director@bimtech.ac.in
Website: http://www.bimtech.ac.in

Director: H. Chaturvedi

Programme

Management (Insurance; International Business; Management; Retailing and Wholesaling)

History: Founded 1988.

Accrediting Agency: All India Council for Technical Education (AICTE)

Degrees and Diplomas: *Postgraduate Diploma*

Last Updated: 02/02/12

BIRLA INSTITUTE OF TECHNOLOGY

Mesra, Ranchi, Bihar 835215
Tel: +91(651) 227-6052
Fax: +91(651) 227-5401
EMail: pkbarhai@bitmesra.ac.in
Website: http://www.bitmesra.ac.in/

Vice-Chancellor: Ajay Chakrabarty EMail: vc@bitmesra.ac.in

Registrar: R.K. Verma EMail: registrar@bitmesra.ac.in

Department

Applied Mechanics (Mechanical Engineering); **Applied Sciences** (Applied Chemistry; Applied Mathematics; Applied Physics); **Architecture** (Architecture); **Bio-Medical Instrumentation** (Medical Technology); **Biotechnology** (Biotechnology); **Civil Engineering** (Civil Engineering; Geology); **Computer Engineering** (Computer Engineering); **Electrical and Electronic Engineering** (Electrical and Electronic Engineering); **Electronics and Communication Engineering** (Electrical Engineering; Telecommunications Engineering); **Environmental Science and Engineering** (Environmental Engineering; Environmental Studies); **Food Processing Technology** (Food Technology); **Hotel Management and Catering Technology** (Cooking and Catering; Hotel Management); **Information Technology** (Information Technology); **Management and Humanities** (Arts and Humanities; Economics; Industrial Engineering; Law; Management; Statistics); **Mechanical Engineering** (Mechanical Engineering); **Pharmaceutical Sciences** (Pharmacy); **Physical Education and Training** (Physical

Education; Sports); **Polymer Engineering** (Polymer and Plastics Technology); **Production Engineering** (Mineralogy; Physics; Production Engineering); **Remote Sensing** (Software Engineering; Surveying and Mapping); **Space Engineering and Rocketry** (Aeronautical and Aerospace Engineering)

Centre

Continuing Education *(Lalpur, Ranchi)* (Engineering; Management; Technology)

History: Founded 1955 as an all-India Institution for Technical Education Research and Training by the Hindustan Charity Trust. Initially an affiliated College of Bihar University, became autonomous 1972, and acquired present status as 'Deemed University' 1986.

Academic Year: July to June (July-December; January-June)

Admission Requirements: 12th year senior secondary/intermediate examination or recognized foreign equivalent

Main Language(s) of Instruction: English

Degrees and Diplomas: *Post Diploma*; *Bachelor's Degree*: **Architecture; Engineering; Pharmacy; Polymer and Plastics Technology.** *Master's Degree*; *Doctor of Philosophy*

Publications: Annual Report and Research Compendium

Last Updated: 24/06/11

BIRLA INSTITUTE OF TECHNOLOGY AND SCIENCE (BITS)

PO Box 12, Vidya Vihar, Pilani, Rajasthan 333031
Tel: +91(1596) 242-192
Fax: +91(1596) 244-183
EMail: mmsanand@bits-pilani.ac.in
Website: http://www.bits-pilani.ac.in

Acting Vice-Chancellor: V.S. Rao (2015-)
EMail: vsr@hyderabad.bits-pilani.ac.in

Registrar: M.M.S. Anand
Tel: +91(1596) 242-192 EMail: mmsanand@pilani.bits-pilani.ac.in

International Relations: Suman Kapur, Dean, International Programmes and Collaboration
Tel: +91(40) 6630-3563 EMail: skapur@hyderabad.bits-pilani.ac.in

Department

Biological Sciences (Biological and Life Sciences); **Chemical Engineering** (Chemical Engineering); **Chemistry** (Chemistry); **Civil Engineering** (Civil Engineering); **Computer Science and Information Systems** (Computer Science; Information Technology); **Economics and Finance** (Economics; Finance); **Electrical and Electronic Engineering** (Electrical and Electronic Engineering); **Engineering Technology** (Engineering; Technology); **Humanistic Studies** (Arts and Humanities); **Instrumentation** (Instrument Making); **Languages** (Modern Languages); **Management** (Management); **Mathematics** (Mathematics); **Mechanical Engineering** (Mechanical Engineering); **Pharmacy** (Pharmacy); **Physics** (Physics)

Further Information: Also campuses in Goa, Hyderabad, Pilani (India) and Dubai (UAE).

History: Founded 1964, incorporating 3 existing Colleges affiliated to the University of Rajasthan. A 'Deemed University'.

Academic Year: August to July (August-December; January-May; May-July)

Admission Requirements: 12th year senior secondary/intermediate examination or equivalent with Physics, Chemistry, Mathematics with minimum aggregate 75% and at least 60% in each discipline; admission on merit level determined by a computer based online entry test (BITSAT)

Fees: 70,000 per semester (Indian Rupee)

Main Language(s) of Instruction: English

Accrediting Agency: National Assessment and Accreditation Council (NAAC)

Degrees and Diplomas: *Bachelor's Degree*: **Biotechnology; Chemical Engineering; Civil Engineering; Communication Arts; Computer Science; Electrical and Electronic Engineering; Engineering; Information Technology; Marine Engineering; Medical Auxiliaries; Nautical Science; Ophthalmology; Optometry; Pharmacy; Power Engineering; Technology.** *Master's Degree*: **Chemical Engineering; Civil Engineering; Communication Arts; Computer Engineering; Computer Science; Design; Electrical Engineering; Engineering; Engineering Management; Information Technology; Management; Mechanical Engineering; Medical Technology; Metaphysics; Microelectronics; Petroleum and Gas Engineering; Pharmacy; Public Health; Software Engineering; Transport Engineering.** *Master of Philosophy*: **Biological and Life Sciences; Chemistry; Economics; English; Health Administration; Management; Mathematics; Medical Auxiliaries; Optometry; Physics.** *Doctor of Philosophy*

Student Services: Academic Counselling, Canteen, Careers Guidance, Cultural Activities, Facilities for disabled people, Health Services, Language Laboratory, Social Counselling, Sports Facilities

Publications: BITS in the News; BITSCAN; Bulletin; Research at BITS

Academic Staff *2010-2011*: Total 617
STAFF WITH DOCTORATE: Total 550

Student Numbers *2012-2012*: Total: c. 10,000

Last Updated: 04/04/13

BIRSA AGRICULTURAL UNIVERSITY (BAU)

Kanke, Ranchi, Jharkhand 834006
Tel: +91(651) 245-015 +91(651) 245-0500
Fax: +91(651) 245-0850
EMail: vc_bau@rediffmail.com
Website: http://www.baujharkhand.org/

Vice-Chancellor: N.N. Singh Tel: +91(651) 245-0500

Registrar: N. Kudada Tel: +91(651) 245-0832

Faculty

Agriculture (Agriculture); **Forestry** (Forestry); **Veterinary Science** (Animal Husbandry; Veterinary Science)

College

Biotechnology (Biotechnology)

History: Founded 1980.

Academic Year: July to June

Admission Requirements: 12th year senior secondary/intermediate examination or recognized foreign equivalent

Fees: (Rupees): Undergraduate, 2,500 per semester, postgraduate, 3,450; PhD, 4,200

Main Language(s) of Instruction: English

Accrediting Agency: Indian Council of Agricultural Research

Degrees and Diplomas: *Bachelor's Degree*: **Agriculture; Animal Husbandry; Forestry; Veterinary Science.** *Master's Degree*: **Agriculture; Animal Husbandry; Biotechnology; Forestry; Veterinary Science.** *Doctor of Philosophy*: **Agriculture; Animal Husbandry; Veterinary Science.**

Student Services: Academic Counselling, Canteen, Careers Guidance, Cultural Activities, Facilities for disabled people, Foreign Studies Centre, Health Services, Language Laboratory, Nursery Care, Social Counselling, Sports Facilities

Publications: BAU Journal of Research; Pathari Krishi

Academic Staff *2010-2011*: Total 200
STAFF WITH DOCTORATE: Total 150

Student Numbers *2010-2011*: Total: c. 700

Last Updated: 28/06/11

BLDE UNIVERSITY

Bangaramma Sajjan Campus, Sholapur Road,
Bijapur, Karnakata 586103
Tel: +91(8352) 262770
Fax: +91(8352) 263303
EMail: office@bldeuniversity.org
Website: http://www.bldeuniversity.org

Vice-Chancellor: B. G. Mulimani EMail: vcbldeu@gmail.com

Registrar: J. G. Ambekar EMail: registrarbldeu@gmail.com

Programme

Medicine (Anatomy; Community Health; Forensic Medicine and Dentistry; Gynaecology and Obstetrics; Medicine; Microbiology; Ophthalmology; Otorhinolaryngology; Paediatrics; Pathology; Pharmacology; Physiology; Surgery)

Degrees and Diplomas: *Bachelor's Degree*; *Postgraduate Diploma*; *Master's Degree*
Last Updated: 10/01/12

B.S. ABDUR RAHMAN UNIVERSITY (BSAUNIV)

Seethakathi Estate, Vandalur, Chennai, Tamil Nadu 600 048
Tel: +91(44) 227-50005
Fax: +91(44) 227-50405
EMail: bsar@bsauniv.ac.in
Website: http://www.bsauniv.ac.in/

Vice-Chancellor: Jalees A. K. Tareen (2013-)
EMail: vc@bsauniv.ac.in

Registrar: V.M. Periasamy EMail: registrar@bsauniv.ac.in

International Relations: S. Prince Arockia Doss, Director, International Collaboration

School

Architecture *(Crescent)* (Architecture); **Business** *(Crescent)* (Business Administration); **Computer, Information and Mathematical Sciences** (Computer Engineering; Computer Science; Information Sciences; Information Technology; Mathematics); **Electrical and Communication Sciences** (Electrical Engineering; Electronic Engineering; Measurement and Precision Engineering; Telecommunications Engineering); **Infrastructure** (Civil Engineering); **Islamic Studies** (Islamic Studies); **Life Sciences** (Biochemistry; Biotechnology; Genetics; Microbiology; Molecular Biology); **Mechanical Sciences** (Aeronautical and Aerospace Engineering; Automotive Engineering; Mechanical Engineering; Polymer and Plastics Technology); **Physical and Chemical Sciences** (Chemistry; Physics); **Social Sciences and Humanities** (Economics; English; French; Law; Psychology; Sociology)

History: Founded 1984 as B.S. Abdur Rahman Crescent Engineering College. Acquired 'Deemed University' status 2008 and present title 2009.

Degrees and Diplomas: *Bachelor's Degree*; *Bachelor's Degree (professional)*; *Master's Degree*; *Master of Philosophy*; *Doctor of Philosophy*. Also MBA

Student Services: Canteen, Health Services

Academic Staff *2012-2013*: Total 347
STAFF WITH DOCTORATE: Total 92
Student Numbers *2012-2013*: Total 5,646
Last Updated: 25/04/13

BUNDELKHAND UNIVERSITY

Kanpur Road, Jhansi, Uttar Pradesh 284128
Tel: +91(517) 232-0496
Fax: +91(517) 232-0761
EMail: registrar@bujhansi.org
Website: http://www.bujhansi.org/

Vice-Chancellor: S. V. S. Rana (2010-)

Faculty

Agriculture (Agriculture); **Arts** (Arts and Humanities); **Commerce** (Business and Commerce); **Education** (Education); **Engineering**; **Law** (Law); **Medicine** (Medicine); **Science** (Natural Sciences)

College

Medicine *(Maharani Laxmi Bai)* (Medicine)

Institute

Engineering and Technology (Engineering; Technology)

Further Information: Also 15 Affiliated Colleges
History: Founded 1975.
Degrees and Diplomas: *Post Diploma*; *Bachelor's Degree*; *Master's Degree*; *Doctor of Philosophy*
Last Updated: 28/06/11

CALORX TEACHERS' UNIVERSITY (CTU)

Opp. Sun Rise Park, Between Sanjivani Hospital & Advait Complex, Ahmedabad, Gujerat 380054
Tel: +91(271) 7242-328/29
EMail: registrarctu@calorx.org
Website: http://www.ctu.org.in/

President: M. P. Chhaya

Programme

Education (Education; Educational Administration; Primary Education; Special Education)

Degrees and Diplomas: *Bachelor's Degree*; *Master's Degree*; *Master of Philosophy*; *Doctor of Philosophy*
Student Services: Sports Facilities
Last Updated: 19/10/11

CENTER FOR ENVIRONMENTAL PLANNING AND TECHNOLOGY UNIVERSITY

Kasturbhai Lalbhai Campus, University Road, Ahmedabad, Gujarat 380009
Website: http://www.cept.ac.in/

President: R.N. Vakil

Registrar: Anita Hiranandani EMail: registrar@cept.ac.in

International Relations: Rema Haridasan EMail: sa@cept.ac.in

Faculty

Arts and Humanities (Arts and Humanities); **Architecture** (Architecture); **Design** (Design); **Environmental and Climate Change Studies** (Environmental Studies; Meteorology); **Geomatics and Space Applications**; **Infrastructure Systems**; **Landscape Studies** (Landscape Architecture); **Planning and Public Policy** (Social and Community Services); **Rural and Development Studies** (Development Studies; Rural Studies); **Technology** (Technology); **Technology Management** (Technology)

History: Founded 2005.
Accrediting Agency: All India Council for Technical Education (AICTE)
Degrees and Diplomas: *Bachelor's Degree*; *Master's Degree*
Last Updated: 05/08/11

CENTRAL AGRICULTURAL UNIVERSITY

Iroisemba, Imphal, Manipur 795004
Tel: +91(385) 241-5933 +91(385) 241-0644
Fax: +91(385) 241-5196 +91(385) 241-0414
EMail: snpuri@rediffmail.com
Website: http://dare.nic.in/cau.htm

Vice-Chancellor: S.N. Puri EMail: snpuri04@yahoo.co.in
Registrar: M. Premjit Singh

College

Agricultural Engineering and Post Harvest Technology *(Gangtok; Sikkim)*; **Agriculture** (Agriculture); **Fisheries** *(Lembucherra, Agartala, Tripura)*; **Home Science** *(Tura, Meghalaya)* (Home Economics); **Horticulture and Forestry** *(Pasighat, Arunachal Pradesh)* (Forestry; Horticulture); **Veterinary Science and Animal Husbandry** *(Selesih, Aizawl, Mizoram)*

History: Founded 1993, acquired present status and title 1993.
Academic Year: August to July
Admission Requirements: 12th year senior secondary/intermediate examination or recognized foreign equivalent
Main Language(s) of Instruction: English
Accrediting Agency: Indian Council of Agricultural Research, New Delhi
Degrees and Diplomas: *Bachelor's Degree*: **Agricultural Engineering; Agriculture; Animal Husbandry; Fishery; Harvest Technology; Home Economics; Horticulture; Veterinary Science.** *Master's Degree*: **Agriculture; Veterinary Science; Zoology.**
Student Services: Academic Counselling, Canteen, Careers Guidance, Health Services, Social Counselling, Sports Facilities
Publications: Central Agricultural University Newsletter
Last Updated: 28/06/11

CENTRAL INSTITUTE OF FISHERIES EDUCATION (CIFE)

Fisheries University Road, Seven Bungalows, Andheri, Mumbai, Maharashtra 400061
Tel: +91(22) 2636-1446
Fax: +91(22) 2636-1573
EMail: contact@cife.edu.in
Website: http://www.cife.edu.in

Director: W. S. Lakra Tel: +91(22) 2636-3404

Chief Administrative Officer: Suresh Kumar
EMail: sureshkumar@cife.edu.in

Division

Aquaculture (Aquaculture); **Aquatic Environmental Management** (Environmental Management; Marine Biology); **Fish Genetics and Biotechnology** (Biotechnology; Fishery; Genetics); **Fish Nutrition and Biochemistry**; **Fisherie Economics, Extension ans Statistics** (Economics; Fishery; Statistics); **Fishery Resource, Harvest and Post-harvest Management** (Harvest Technology; Management)

History: Founded 1961.

Academic Year: September to August (September-February; March-August)

Admission Requirements: Bachelor's degree with at least 60% mark or OGPA of 6.50 out of 10

Fees: (Rupees): 4,000 per annum

Main Language(s) of Instruction: English

Accrediting Agency: National Agricultural Accreditation Board

Degrees and Diplomas: *Post Diploma*; *Master's Degree*; *Doctor of Philosophy*. Also Postgraduate Certificate in Inland Fisheries Development and Administration, 1 yr

Student Services: Academic Counselling, Canteen, Careers Guidance, Cultural Activities, Foreign Studies Centre, Health Services, Social Counselling, Sports Facilities

Publications: Journal of the Indian Fisheries Association

Last Updated: 28/06/11

CENTRAL UNIVERSITY OF BIHAR (CUB)

BIT Campus, P.O. B.V. College, Patna 800 014
Website: http://www.cub.ac.in/

Vice-Chancellor: Janak Pandey
Tel: +91(612) 222-6535 EMail: vc@cub.ac.in

Registrar: Mohammad Nehal EMail: registrar@cub.ac.in

School

Earth, Biological and Environmental Sciences (Biological and Life Sciences; Biotechnology; Earth Sciences; Environmental Studies); **Human Sciences** (Psychology); **Mathematics, Statistics and Computer Science** (Computer Science; Mathematics; Statistics); **Media, Arts and Aesthetics** (Aesthetics; Fine Arts; Mass Communication; Media Studies); **Social Sciences and Policy** (Development Studies; Social Policy; Social Sciences)

History: Founded 2009.

Degrees and Diplomas: *Master's Degree*

Last Updated: 08/12/11

CENTRAL UNIVERSITY OF GUJARAT (CUG)

Sector-30, Gandhinagar 382 030
Tel: +91(79) 292-8905
Fax: +91(79) 232-60076
Website: http://www.cug.ac.in/

Vice-Chancellor: R. K. Kale
Tel: +91(79) 2326-0076 EMail: vc@cug.ac.in

Registrar: Gitesh Joshi
Tel: +91(79) 2928-8401
EMail: registrar@cug.ac.in; cug2009registrar@gmail.com

School

Chemical Sciences (Chemistry; Industrial Chemistry); **Environment and Sustainable Development** (Environmental Studies); **International Studies** (Government; International Studies; Political Sciences); **Language, Literature and Cultural Studies** (Asian Studies; Chinese; Comparative Literature; Cultural Studies; English; German; Hindi; Literature; Modern Languages); **Life Sciences** (Biological and Life Sciences); **Social Sciences** (Demography and Population; Development Studies; Economics; Management; Peace and Disarmament; Social Sciences; Social Studies)

History: Founded 2009.

Degrees and Diplomas: *Master's Degree*. Also Certificates and integrated M.Phil/Ph.D.

Last Updated: 08/12/11

CENTRAL UNIVERSITY OF HARYANA

Temporary Campus:, Govt. B.Ed. College Building,
Distt. Mahendergarh, Narnaul, Haryana 122010
Tel: +91(1282) 255-002 +91(1282) 255-003
EMail: contact@cuharyana.org
Website: http://www.cuharyana.org/

Vice-Chancellor (Acting): U. P. Sinha

School

Agriculture and Allied (Agro based technological) Sciences (Agricultural Business; Agricultural Economics; Agriculture; Food Science; Harvest Technology; Horticulture; Plant Pathology); **Arts, Humanities and Social Sciences** (Anthropology; Archaeology; Arts and Humanities; Asian Religious Studies; Business and Commerce; Comparative Literature; Economics; Education; Geography; History; Philosophy; Physical Education; Psychology; Social Sciences; Sociology; Sports; Tourism; Translation and Interpretation; Urdu; Women's Studies); **Chemical Sciences** (Chemistry); **Computer Science and Informatics** (Computer Science; Information Technology; Statistics); **Earth, Environment and Space Studies** (Astronomy and Space Science; Astrophysics; Earth Sciences; Environmental Studies; Surveying and Mapping); **Engineering and Technology** (Electronic Engineering; Engineering; Food Technology; Geological Engineering; Nanotechnology; Technology); **Journalism, Mass Communication and Media** (Information Sciences; Journalism; Library Science; Mass Communication; Media Studies); **Language, Linguistics, Culture and Heritage** (Cultural Studies; English; Heritage Preservation; Hindi; Indic Languages; Linguistics; Modern Languages); **Law, Governance, Public Policy and Management** (Government; Law; Political Sciences; Public Administration; Social Policy); **Life Sciences** (Biological and Life Sciences; Biotechnology; Botany; Chemistry; Genetics; Microbiology; Molecular Biology; Zoology); **Life-long Learning**; **Medical Sciences** (Medicine; Virology); **Physical and Mathematical Sciences** (Mathematics; Physics)

History: Founded 2009.

Degrees and Diplomas: *Master of Philosophy*; *Doctor of Philosophy*. Also MBA

Last Updated: 07/12/11

CENTRAL UNIVERSITY OF HIMACHAL PRADESH

PO Box 21, Dist. Kangra, Dharamshala, Himachal Pradesh 176 215
Tel: +91(1892) 229-330
Fax: +91(1892) 229-331
EMail: vc@cuhimachal.ac.in; contact@cuhimachal.ac.in
Website: http://www.cuhimachal.ac.in/

Vice-Chancellor: Yoginder Singh Verma
EMail: vc@cuhimachal.ac.in; vc.cuhimachal@gmail.com

Registrar: Jagdish Chand Rangra
EMail: registrar.cuhimachal@gmail.com

School

Business and Management Science (Accountancy; Behavioural Sciences; Business Administration; Finance; Management; Marketing); **Earth and Environmental Sciences** (Earth Sciences; Environmental Studies); **Education** (Education; Teacher Training); **Fine Arts and Art Education** (Art Education; Fine Arts; Visual Arts); **Humanities and Languages** (Arts and Humanities; English; Hindi; Indic Languages; Modern Languages); **Journalism, Mass Communication and New Media** (Journalism; Mass Communication; Media Studies; Writing); **Life Sciences** (Biological and Life Sciences); **Mathematics, Computers and Information Science** (Computer Science; Information Sciences; Library Science; Mathematics); **Physical and Material Sciences** (Astronomy and Space Science; Materials Engineering; Physics); **Social Sciences** (Economics; Social Policy; Social Sciences; Social Work); **Tourism, Travel and Hospitality Management** (Hotel Management; Tourism)

Further Information: Also Dhauladhar and Beas campuses.

History: Founded 2009.

Degrees and Diplomas: *Master's Degree*. Also integrated M.Phil/Ph.D.; MBA

Last Updated: 07/12/11

CENTRAL UNIVERSITY OF JHARKHAND (CUJ)

Ratu Lohardaga Road, Brambe, Ranchi, Jharkhand 835 205
Tel: +91(6531) 294-163
EMail: pio@cuj.ac.in
Website: http://www.cuj.ac.in/

Vice-Chancellor: Darlando T. Khathing Tel: +91(6531) 294-160

Registrar: Shyam Narain Tel: +91(6531) 294-182

School

Cultural Studies (Cultural Studies; Indigenous Studies); **Engineering and Technologies** (Engineering; Nanotechnology; Technology); **Languages** (English; Modern Languages); **Management Sciences** (Business Administration; Management); **Mass Communication and Media Technology** (Mass Communication; Media Studies); **Natural Resource and Management** (Hydraulic Engineering; Management; Natural Resources; Water Management); **Natural Sciences** (Applied Chemistry; Applied Mathematics; Applied Physics; Biological and Life Sciences; Natural Sciences)

History: Founded 2009.

Accrediting Agency: University Grants Commission (UGC); Ministry of Human Resource Development (MHRD)

Degrees and Diplomas: Integrated Master's degree programme, 5 yrs

Last Updated: 07/12/11

CENTRAL UNIVERSITY OF KARNATAKA (CUK)

II Floor, Karya Soudha, Gulbarga University, Gulbarga 585 106
Website: http://www.cuk.ac.in/

Vice-Chancellor: M.N. Sudheendra Rao
Tel: +91(8472) 27206 EMail: mns_rao@yahoo.com

Registrar & Controller of Examinations: Ali Raza Moosvi
Tel: +91(8472) 272057 EMail: moosvi1@gmail.com

School

Business Studies (Business Administration; Business and Commerce; Economics); **Earth Sciences** (Earth Sciences; Geography; Regional Planning; Surveying and Mapping); **Humanities and Languages** (Arts and Humanities; English; Modern Languages; South and Southeast Asian Languages); **Social and Behavioral Sciences** (Behavioural Sciences; History; Psychology; Social Sciences); **Undergraduate Studies** (Economics; English; Geography; History; Psychology)

History: Founded 2009.

Degrees and Diplomas: *Bachelor's Degree*; *Master's Degree*; *Master of Philosophy*; *Doctor of Philosophy*. Also integrated M.A, M.Phil and Ph.D Courses, 5 yrs.

Last Updated: 06/09/12

CENTRAL UNIVERSITY OF KASHMIR

Transit Campus, Sonwar (Near G.B.Pant Hospital),
Srinagar, Jammu and Kashmir 190-004
Tel: +91(194) 246-8357 +91(194) 246-8346
Fax: +91(194) 246-8351 +91(194) 246-8354
EMail: mail@cukashmir.ac.in
Website: http://www.cukashmir.ac.in/

Vice-Chancellor: Abdul Wahid

School

Business and Economic Studies *(SOBES)* (Business Administration; Economics); **Computer Science and Information Technology** *(SOCScIT)* (Computer Science; Information Technology; Mathematics); **Languages** *(SOL)* (English; Modern Languages); **Legal Studies** (Civil Law; Criminal Law; Law); **Media Studies** (Journalism; Media Studies); **Social Sciences** (Economics; Social Sciences)

History: Founded 2009. Formerly known as the Central University of Jammu and Kashmir.

Degrees and Diplomas: *Bachelor's Degree (professional)*: **Law.** *Master's Degree.* Also MBA

Last Updated: 07/12/11

CENTRAL UNIVERSITY OF KERALA

Vidyanagar, Kasaragod, Kerala 671 123
Tel: +91(4994) 256-420
EMail: registrarcuk@gmail.com
Website: http://www.cukerala.ac.in/

Vice-Chancellor: Jancy James (2010-)

Registrar: N.N. Sampathkumar

School

Biological Sciences (Biochemistry; Biological and Life Sciences; Botany; Genetics; Molecular Biology; Zoology); **Computer Science** (Computer Science); **Global Studies** (Economics); **Languages and Comparative Literature** (Comparative Literature; English; Hindi; Modern Languages); **Mathematical and Physical Science** (Mathematics; Physics); **Mathematics** (Mathematics)

History: Founded 2009.

Fees: (Indian Rupee): 600-1,000 per semester

Degrees and Diplomas: *Master's Degree*. Also integrated MPhil/PhD

Last Updated: 07/12/11

CENTRAL UNIVERSITY OF ORISSA

Central Silk Board Building Landiguda, Koraput
Tel: +90 6852-251288
Fax: +90 6852-251244
EMail: info@centraluniversityorissa.ac.in
Website: http://centraluniversityorissa.ac.in/

Vice-Chancellor: Surabhi Banerjee
Tel: +90(674) 274-8094
EMail: vccu-or@nic.in; vc@cuorissa.org; vc@centraluniversityorissa.ac.in

School

Basic Sciences and Information Sciences (Chemistry; Computer Science; Information Sciences; Mathematics; Natural Sciences; Physics; Statistics); **Biodiversity and Conservation of Natural Resources** (Aquaculture; Biotechnology; Natural Resources); **Development Studies** (Development Studies; Economics; Peace and Disarmament); **Education and Education Technology** (Education; Educational Technology; Teacher Training); **Health Sciences** (Community Health; Health Sciences; Nursing; Public Health); **Languages** (English; Indic Languages; Literature; Modern Languages); **Legal Studies** (Human Rights; Law); **Social Sciences** (Anthropology; Development Studies; Journalism; Mass Communication; Philosophy; Social Sciences; Sociology; Welfare and Protective Services)

Further Information: Also Campus in Bhubaneswar.

History: Founded 2009.

Degrees and Diplomas: *Master's Degree*

Last Updated: 07/12/11

CENTRAL UNIVERSITY OF PUNJAB (CUP)

P.O. Box-55, Bathinda 151 001
Tel: +91(164) 224-0555 +91(164) 243-0586
Fax: +91(164) 224-0555
EMail: cu.punjab.info@gmail.com
Website: http://www.centralunipunjab.com/

Vice-Chancellor: Jai Rup Singh

Registrar: Jagdev Kartar Singh

School

Basic and Applied Sciences (Biological and Life Sciences; Chemistry; Natural Sciences; Pharmacy); **Design and Planning** (Architecture and Planning; Design); **Emerging Life Science Technologies** (Biological and Life Sciences); **Engineering and Technology** (Engineering; Technology); **Environment and Earth Sciences** (Earth Sciences; Environmental Studies); **Global Relations** (Asian Studies; International Relations; South Asian Studies); **Health Sciences** (Health Sciences); **Information and Communicative Sciences** (Information Sciences; Mass Communication); **Languages, Literature and Culture** (Comparative Literature; Cultural Studies; Literature; Modern Languages); **Legal Studies and Governance** (Government; Law); **Management** (Management); **Social Sciences** (Social Sciences)

History: Founded 2009.

Degrees and Diplomas: *Master's Degree*. Also integrated postgraduate programmes (M.Phil. - Ph.D.; LL.M. - Ph.D.; M.Pharm. - Ph.D.).

Student Services: Health Services, Sports Facilities
Last Updated: 06/12/11

CENTRAL UNIVERSITY OF RAJASTHAN (CURAJ)

City Road, Distt. Ajmer, Kishangarh, Rajasthan 305 802
Tel: +91(1463) 246-735
Fax: +91(1463) 246-735
EMail: info.curaj@gmail.com
Website: http://www.curaj.ac.in/

Vice-Chancellor: M.M. Salunkhe

School

Architecture (Architecture); **Chemical Sciences and Pharmacy** (Chemistry; Pharmacy); **Commerce and Management** (Business Administration; Business and Commerce; Management); **Engineering and Technology** (Engineering; Technology); **Humanities** (Arts and Humanities; English; Hindi; Modern Languages); **Life Sciences** (Biotechnology; Environmental Studies); **Mathematics, Statistics and Computational Sciences** (Actuarial Science; Computer Science; Mathematics and Computer Science; Statistics); **Physical Sciences** (Physics); **Social Sciences** (Cultural Studies; Economics; Media Studies; Social Sciences)

History: Founded 2009.

Fees: (Indian Rupees): 2,600-7,250 per semester

Degrees and Diplomas: *Master's Degree*. Also MBA

Student Services: Canteen, Health Services, Sports Facilities

Student Numbers *2011-2012*: Total: c. 460
Last Updated: 06/12/11

CENTRAL UNIVERSITY OF TAMIL NADU (CUTN)

Collectorate Annexe, Thanjavur Road,
Thiruvarur, Tamil Nadu State 610-00
Tel: +91(4366) 220-311 +91(4366) 225-205
Fax: +91(4366) 225-312
EMail: vccutn@gmail.com; psvccutn@gmail.com
Website: http://www.cutn.ac.in/

Vice-Chancellor: B. P. Sanjay
Tel: +91(4366) 220-311 EMail: psvccutn@gmail.com

Registrar: V. K. Sridhar
Tel: +91(4366) 220-023 EMail: registrar.cutn@gmail.com

School

Basic and Applied Sciences (Chemistry; Physics); **Mathematics and Computer Sciences** (Computer Science; Mathematics); **Social Sciences and Humanities** (Arts and Humanities; Economics; English; Finance; Social Sciences)

History: Founded 2009. A 'Central University'.

Degrees and Diplomas: *Master's Degree*. Also integrated Master's degree, 5 yrs.

Student Services: Canteen

Academic Staff *2011-2012*: Total: c. 11
Student Numbers *2011-2012*: Total: c. 200
Last Updated: 06/12/11

IAU CENTRAL UNIVERSITY OF TIBETAN STUDIES (CIHTS)

Sarnath, Varanasi, Uttar Pradesh 221007
Tel: +91(542) 258-5148
Fax: +91(542) 258-5150
EMail: registrar@in.com
Website: http://www.cuts.ac.in/

Vice-Chancellor: Lobsang Norbu Shastri
EMail: vcoffice.cuts@gmail.com

Faculty

Arts and Crafts (Fine Arts; Handicrafts); **Languages and Literature** (English; Hindi; Literature; Sanskrit; Tibetan); **Logic and Spirituality** (Asian Religious Studies; Logic); **Medical Sciences** (Medicine; Traditional Eastern Medicine); **Modern Studies** (Ancient Languages; Asian Studies; Cultural Studies; Economics; History; Political Sciences)

Research Unit

Dictionary; Publication; Rare Buddhist Texts; Restoration; Translation

History: Founded 1967 as envisioned by H.H. the Dalai Lama in consultation with Pandit Jawarhalal Nehru for the preservation and promotion of Tibetan Culture and Buddhist Studies. Fully funded by the Central Government of India through the Ministry of Culture, Youth and Sports. Declared as 'Deemed University' 1988. Acquired present title 2009. Formerly known as the Central Institute of Higher Tibetan Studies.

Academic Year: July to May (July-December; January-May)

Admission Requirements: Standard IX with Tibetan Language or knowledge of Tibetan Language, plus minimum 35% marks in qualifying entrance examination

Fees: None

Main Language(s) of Instruction: Tibetan

Accrediting Agency: University Grants Commission

Degrees and Diplomas: *Bachelor's Degree*; *Master's Degree*; *Master of Philosophy*; *Doctor of Philosophy*

Student Services: Academic Counselling, Careers Guidance, Cultural Activities, Facilities for disabled people, Health Services, Nursery Care, Social Counselling, Sports Facilities

Publications: 'Dhih' Research Journal; Biblioteca Indo-Tibetica Series; Miscellaneous Series; Prof. L.M. Joshi Commemorative Lecture Series; Rare Buddhist Text Series; Samyak Vak Series; The Dalai Lama Tibetico-Indological Series

Publishing House: Publication Unit

CENTRE FOR MANAGEMENT DEVELOPMENT, MODINAGAR

NH-58, Opp-ESI Hospital, Modinagar, Uttar Pradesh 201204
EMail: director@cmd.edu; admissions@cmd.edu
Website: http://www.cmd.edu/

President: Devendra K. Modi

Programme

Management (Business Administration; Management)

History: Founded 1983.

Accrediting Agency: All India Council for Technical Education (AICTE)

Degrees and Diplomas: *Postgraduate Diploma*: **Management.**
Last Updated: 02/02/12

CENTURION UNIVERSITY OF TECHNOLOGY AND MANAGEMENT (CUTM)

HIG – 5, Phase -1, BDA Duplex, Pokhariput,
Bhubaneswar, Orrisa 751020
Tel: +91(674) 2352-667
Fax: +91(674) 2352-433
EMail: admissions@cutm.ac.in
Website: http://www.cutm.ac.in

Vice-Chancellor: D. Nageswar Rao

Registrar: Ashok Mishra

School

Rural Enterprise Management (CSREM) *(Centurion)*

Institute

Technology and Management (JITM) *(Jagannath)*

Further Information: Also Parlakhemundi and Bhubaneswar Campuses

History: Founded 2005.

Degrees and Diplomas: *Bachelor's Degree*; *Master's Degree*; *Doctor of Philosophy*
Last Updated: 03/01/12

CHANAKYA NATIONAL LAW UNIVERSITY

Gandhi Maidan, Patna, Assam 800 001
Website: http://www.cnlu.ac.in

Vice-Chancellor: A. Lakshminath EMail: alakshminath@gmail.com

Registrar: S. P. Singh

Programme

Law (Law)

History: Founded 2006.

Degrees and Diplomas: *Bachelor's Degree*; *Postgraduate Diploma*; *Doctor of Philosophy*

Last Updated: 22/07/11

CHANDIGARH UNIVERSITY

Gharuan, Mohali, Chandigarh, Punjab
Tel: +91(160) 301-4444
Fax: +91(160) 301-4402
EMail: info@chandigarhuniversity.ac.in
Website: http://www.chandigarhuniversity.ac.in/

Vice-Chancellor: R.S. Bawa (2012-)
Tel: +91(160) 301-4448 EMail: vicechancellor.cu@gmail.com

Registrar: D.S. Cheema
Tel: +91(160) 301-417 EMail: registrar@chandigarhuniversity.ac.in

International Relations: Rajan Sharma, Deputy Director (L & IR)

School

Business (Business Administration; Business and Commerce; Hotel Management; International Business; Tourism)

Institute

Animation and Multimedia (Computer Graphics; Multimedia); **Architecture** (Architecture); **Computing** (Computer Science); **Engineering** (Automotive Engineering; Chemical Engineering; Computer Engineering; Computer Science; Electrical Engineering; Electronic Engineering; Information Technology; Mechanical Engineering; Petroleum and Gas Engineering; Telecommunications Engineering); **Hotel Management** (Hotel Management; Tourism); **Languages, Literature and Culture** (English; Indic Languages; Native Language); **Pharmacy** (Pharmacy)

History: Created 2009. Acquired current status 2012.

Academic Year: July-May (July-November; January-May)

Fees: (Indian Rupee): 22,000-54,000

Main Language(s) of Instruction: English

Accrediting Agency: National Assessment and Accreditation Council (NAAC)

Degrees and Diplomas: *Bachelor's Degree*; *Master's Degree*: **Biotechnology; Business Administration; Computer Engineering; Multimedia.**

Academic Staff *2013-2014*	TOTAL
FULL-TIME	542
STAFF WITH DOCTORATE	
FULL-TIME	65

Student Numbers *2013-2014*	
All (Foreign included)	3,611
FOREIGN ONLY	6

Last Updated: 10/12/13

CHANDRA SHEKHAR AZAD UNIVERSITY OF AGRICULTURE AND TECHNOLOGY

Nawabganj, Kanpur, Uttar Pradesh 208002
Tel: +91(512) 253-4155
Fax: +91(512) 253-3808 +91(512) 243-4113
EMail: info@csauk.ac.in
Website: http://www.csauk.ac.in/

Vice-Chancellor: G.C. Tewari Tel:: EMail: vc@csauk.ac.in

Registrar: V.P. Kanaujia

Faculty

Agriculture (Agricultural Business; Agricultural Economics; Agriculture; Forestry; Horticulture; Plant and Crop Protection; Plant Pathology; Soil Science; Water Management); **Agriculture Engineering and Technology** (Agricultural Engineering; Agricultural Equipment; Civil Engineering; Computer Science; Electrical and Electronic Engineering; Farm Management; Food Technology; Irrigation; Mechanical Engineering; Power Engineering; Soil Conservation; Technology; Telecommunications Engineering; Water Management); **Veterinary Science** (Animal Husbandry; Veterinary Science)

Department

Home Science (Child Care and Development; Clothing and Sewing; Food Science; Home Economics; Human Resources; Nutrition)

History: Founded 1975.

Academic Year: July to May (July-December; January-May)

Admission Requirements: 12th year senior secondary/intermediate examination or recognized foreign equivalent

Main Language(s) of Instruction: Hindi, English

Degrees and Diplomas: *Bachelor's Degree*: **Agriculture; Veterinary Science.** *Master's Degree*; *Doctor of Philosophy*

Publications: Farm Science Journal

Last Updated: 29/06/11

CHAROTAR UNIVERSITY OF SCIENCE AND TECHNOLOGY (CHARUSAT)

Changa, Anand District, Gujarat 388 421
Tel: +91(2697) 247-500
Fax: +91(2697) 247-100
EMail: info@charusat.ac.in
Website: http://www.charusat.ac.in

President: Surendra M. Patel

Provost: M. C. Patel

Institute

Applied Sciences *(P. D. Patel)* (Biochemistry; Biotechnology; Mathematical Physics; Microbiology; Nanotechnology; Natural Sciences; Physics); **Computer Application** *(Charotar)* (Computer Engineering); **Management** *(Indukaka Ipcowala)* (Business Administration; Management); **Nursing** *(Charotar)* (Nursing); **Pharmacy** *(Ramanbhai Patel)* (Pharmacy); **Physiotherapy** *(Charotar)* (Physical Therapy); **Technology** *(Chandubhai Patel)* (Civil Engineering; Computer Engineering; Electrical Engineering; Information Technology; Mechanical Engineering; Telecommunications Engineering)

History: Founded 2000. Acquired present status 2009.

Degrees and Diplomas: *Bachelor's Degree*; *Master's Degree*

Student Numbers *2010-2011*: Total 3,300

Last Updated: 18/10/11

CHAUDHARY CHARAN SINGH HARYANA AGRICULTURAL UNIVERSITY (CCSHAU)

Hisar, Haryana 125004
Tel: +91(1662) 234-613
Fax: +91(1662) 234-952
EMail: reg@hau.nic.in
Website: http://www.hau.ernet.in

Vice-Chancellor: K. Singh Khokhar
Tel: +91(1662) 231-640 EMail: vc@hau.ernet.in

Registrar: Surat Singh Dahiya

International Relations: S.S. Bisla, Director, Students Welfare
Tel: +91(1662) 231-171/73; +91(1662) 284-315
EMail: faculty@hau.nic.in

College

Agricultural Engineering and Technology (Agricultural Engineering; Agricultural Equipment; Food Science; Soil Science; Technology; Water Science); **Agriculture** (Agricultural Economics; Agriculture; Agronomy; Business Administration; Cattle Breeding; Entomology; Forestry; Horticulture; Meteorology; Plant and Crop Protection; Plant Pathology; Soil Science; Vegetable Production); **Agriculture** *(Agri. Kaul, Kaithal)* (Agricultural Economics; Agriculture; Crop Production; Farm Management; Forestry; Horticulture; Soil Science); **Animal Sciences** (Animal Husbandry; Cattle Breeding; Food Technology; Physiology); **Basic Sciences**

(Biochemistry; Biology; Biotechnology; Botany; Chemistry; Fishery; Food Science; Genetics; Mathematics; Microbiology; Molecular Biology; Sociology; Statistics; Zoology); **Home Sciences** (Child Care and Development; Clothing and Sewing; Family Studies; Home Economics; Nutrition); **Veterinary Science** (Anatomy; Biochemistry; Embryology and Reproduction Biology; Medicine; Microbiology; Parasitology; Pharmacology; Physiology; Surgery; Toxicology; Veterinary Science)

History: Founded 1970. Modelled on the Land Grant Institutions of USA.

Academic Year: July to June

Admission Requirements: 12th year senior secondary/intermediate examination or recognized foreign equivalent

Main Language(s) of Instruction: English, Hindi

Accrediting Agency: Indian Council of Agricultural Research

Degrees and Diplomas: *Post Diploma*: **Medicine; Surgery; Veterinary Science.** *Bachelor's Degree*: **Agricultural Engineering; Agriculture; Home Economics; Veterinary Science.** *Master's Degree*: **Agricultural Business; Agricultural Engineering; Agriculture; Home Economics; Technology; Veterinary Science; Zoology.** *Doctor of Philosophy*: **Agriculture; Home Economics; Veterinary Science; Zoology.**

Student Services: Academic Counselling, Canteen, Careers Guidance, Cultural Activities, Health Services, Social Counselling, Sports Facilities

Publications: Haryana Farming/Haryana Kheti; Journal of Research; Thesis Abstract

Publishing House: HAU Press

Last Updated: 29/06/11

CHAUDHARY CHARAN SINGH UNIVERSITY

Meerut, Uttar Pradesh 250005
Tel: +91(121) 276-3539
Fax: +91(121) 276-0577
EMail: registrar@ccsuniversity.ac.in
Website: http://www.ccsuniversity.ac.in

Vice-Chancellor: A.K. Bakhshi
EMail: vicechancellor@ccsuniversity.ac.in

Registrar: V.K. Sinha

Faculty

Agriculture (Agriculture; Botany; Food Science; Horticulture; Plant and Crop Protection; Plant Pathology; Technology); **Arts** (Arts and Humanities; Economics; Education; English; Geography; Hindi; History; Indic Languages; Journalism; Library Science; Mass Communication; Mathematics; Music; Philosophy; Political Sciences; Psychology; Russian; Sanskrit; Social Work; Sociology; Statistics; Urdu); **Commerce and Management** (Accountancy; Business and Commerce; Economics; Management); **Education** (Education); **Engineering and Technology** (Engineering; Technology); **Law** (Law); **Medicine** (Medicine); **Science** (Biotechnology; Botany; Computer Science; Environmental Management; Mathematics; Microbiology; Natural Sciences; Physics; Statistics; Toxicology; Zoology)

Further Information: Also 1 Constituent and 65 Affiliated Colleges

History: Founded 1965 as University of Meerut. Acquired present title 1994.

Academic Year: July to June

Admission Requirements: 12th year senior secondary/intermediate examination or recognized foreign equivalent

Main Language(s) of Instruction: Hindi, English

Degrees and Diplomas: *Bachelor's Degree*; *Master's Degree*; *Doctor of Philosophy*

Last Updated: 29/06/11

CHAUDHARY DEVI LAL UNIVERSITY (CDLU)

Sirsa, Haryana 125055
Website: http://www.cdlu.in/

Vice-Chancellor: K.C. Bhardwaj

Registrar: Manoj Siwach

Department

Biotechnology (Biotechnology); **Business Administration** (Business Administration); **Chemistry** (Chemistry); **Commerce** (Business and Commerce); **Computer Science and Applications** (Computer Science; Software Engineering); **Economics** (Economics); **Education** (Education); **Energy and Environmental Science** (Energy Engineering; Environmental Studies); **English** (English); **Food Science and Technology** (Food Science; Food Technology); **Journalism and Mass Communication** (Journalism; Mass Communication); **Law** (Law); **Mathematics** (Mathematics); **Physical Education** (Physical Education); **Physics** (Physics); **Public Administration** (Public Administration)

History: Founded 2003.

Degrees and Diplomas: *Bachelor's Degree*; *Master's Degree*; *Doctor of Philosophy*

Student Services: Health Services

Last Updated: 18/10/11

CHAUDHARY SARWAN KUMAR HIMACHAL PRADESH AGRICULTURAL UNIVERSITY

Chaudhary Sarwan Kumar Himachal Pradesh Krishi Vishwavidyalaya

Palampur, Himachal Pradesh 176062
Tel: +91(1894) 230-521
Fax: +91(1894) 230-465
EMail: vc@hillagric.ernet.in
Website: http://hillagric.ernet.in

Vice-Chancellor: Shyam Kumar Sharma
Tel: +91(1894) 230-521 EMail: vc@hillagric.ernet.in

Registrar: Rupali Thakur
Tel: +91(1894) 230-383 EMail: registrar@hillagric.ernet.in

College

Agriculture (Agricultural Economics; Agricultural Engineering; Agriculture; Agronomy; Crop Production; Entomology; Floriculture; Forestry; Genetics; Horticulture; Plant Pathology; Soil Science; Vegetable Production); **Basic Sciences** (Biochemistry; Botany; Chemistry; Mathematical Physics; Microbiology; Modern Languages; Natural Sciences; Statistics; Zoology); **Home Science** (Clothing and Sewing; Family Studies; Food Science; Home Economics; Home Economics Education; Nutrition; Textile Design); **Veterinary and Animal Sciences** (Anatomy; Animal Husbandry; Cattle Breeding; Fishery; Genetics; Histology; Immunology; Microbiology; Parasitology; Toxicology; Veterinary Science)

Further Information: Also Directorate of Research and Directorate of Extension

History: Founded 1978 as Himachal Pradesh Krishi Vishvavidyalaya. Acquired present status and title 2001.

Academic Year: July - June; Doctoral Programmes, January - December

Admission Requirements: 12th year senior secondary/intermediate examination or recognized foreign equivalent

Fees: (Rupees): Undergraduate, 9,711-15,211 per semester; postgraduate, 7,146-11,356 per semester. Free tuition for women students

Main Language(s) of Instruction: English

Accrediting Agency: Indian Council of Agricultural Research (ICAR)

Degrees and Diplomas: *Bachelor's Degree*: **Agriculture; Animal Husbandry; Chemistry; Home Economics; Mathematics; Physics; Veterinary Science.** *Master's Degree*: **Agriculture; Animal Husbandry; Chemistry; Home Economics; Mathematics; Physics; Veterinary Science.** *Doctor of Philosophy*: **Agriculture; Home Economics; Veterinary Science.**

Student Services: Academic Counselling, Canteen, Careers Guidance, Cultural Activities, Health Services, Nursery Care, Social Counselling, Sports Facilities

Publications: Himachal Journal of Agriculture Research; Journal of Research; Newsletter; Parvatiya Khetibari

Publishing House: Printing Press

Last Updated: 04/07/11

CHENNAI MATHEMATICAL INSTITUTE

Plot H1, SIPCOT IT Park, Padur PO, Siruseri 603103
Tel: +91(44) 2747-0226
Fax: +91(44) 2747-0225.
EMail: office@cmi.ac.in
Website: http://www.cmi.ac.in

Director: R.L. Karandikar

Faculty
Computer Science (Computer Science); **Humanities** (Arts and Humanities); **Mathematics** (Mathematics); **Physics** (Physics)

History: Founded 1989. Acquired present status as Deemed University 2007.
Admission Requirements: 12th year senior secondary school and entrance examination
Degrees and Diplomas: *Bachelor's Degree*; *Master's Degree*; *Doctor of Philosophy*
Last Updated: 04/07/11

CHETTINAD UNIVERSITY

Rajiv Gandhi Salai, Kelambakkam, Kanchipuram Dist, Chennai, Tamil Nadu 603103
Tel: +91(44) 4741-1000
Fax: +91(44) 4741-1011
Website: http://www.chettinadhealthcity.com

Vice-Chancellor: V. Raji EMail: drvraji@chettinadhealthcity.com

Registrar: SPK. Chidambaram
EMail: spk.chidambaram@chettinadhealthcity.com

College
Dentistry (Dentistry)

Department
Medicine (Cardiology; Dermatology; Endocrinology; Gastroenterology; Gerontology; Gynaecology and Obstetrics; Medicine; Nephrology; Orthopaedics; Paediatrics; Psychiatry and Mental Health; Surgery; Urology)

History: Founded 2005.
Degrees and Diplomas: *Bachelor's Degree*; *Master's Degree*
Last Updated: 10/01/12

CHHATRAPATI SHAHU INSTITUTE OF BUSINESS EDUCATION AND RESEARCH (SIBER)

University Road, Kolhapur, Maharashtra 416004
EMail: director@siberindia.co.in
Website: http://www.siberindia.edu.in/

Director: M.M. Ali EMail: director@siberindia.co.in

Programme
Business Administration (Business Administration); **Computer Application** (Computer Science; Information Technology); **Environmental Management** (Environmental Management); **Social Work** (Social Work)

History: Founded 1976. Status acquired 1995.
Accrediting Agency: National Board of Accreditation (NBA) of All India Council for Technical Education (AICTE); National Assessment and Accreditation Council (NAAC)
Degrees and Diplomas: *Master's Degree*: **Business Administration; Computer Science; Social Work.** *Master of Philosophy*: **Business Administration.**
Student Services: Canteen, Sports Facilities
Last Updated: 26/01/12

CHHATRAPATI SHAHU JI MAHARAJ UNIVERSITY

Kalyanpur, Kanpur, Uttar Pradesh 208024
Tel: +91(512) 257-0301
Fax: +91(512) 257-0006
EMail: csjmu@kanpuruniversity.org
Website: http://www.kanpuruniversity.org

Vice-Chancellor: Ashok Kumar (2011-) Tel: +91(512) 257-0450

Registrar: Syed Waqar Hussain Tel: +91(512) 257-0301

Faculty
Agriculture (Agriculture); **Arts** (Arts and Humanities; Social Sciences); **Ayurvedic and Unani** (Ayurveda; Traditional Eastern Medicine); **Commerce** (Business and Commerce); **Education** (Education); **Engineering** (Engineering); **Law** (Law); **Life Sciences** (Biological and Life Sciences); **Management** (Business Administration; Management); **Medicine** (Medicine); **Science** (Natural Sciences)

Department
Adult and Continuing Education; **Education** (Education); **English** (English); **Fine Arts and Painting** (Fine Arts; Painting and Drawing); **Journalism and Mass Communication** (Journalism; Mass Communication); **Library and Information Sciences** (Information Management; Library Science); **Music** (Music); **Physical Education** (Physical Education); **Social Work** (Social Work)

Institute
Bio-Sciences and Bio-Technology (Biochemistry; Biotechnology; Environmental Engineering; Microbiology); **Business Management** (Business Administration; Economics; Finance; Management; Tourism); **Engineering and Technology** (Biology; Chemical Engineering; Computer Science; Electronic Engineering; Engineering; Information Technology; Materials Engineering; Mechanical Engineering; Technology; Telecommunications Engineering); **Life Sciences** (Biological and Life Sciences); **Paramedical Sciences**; **Pharmacy** (Pharmacy)

Centre
Computer Science (Computer Science)

Research Unit
College Development Council

Further Information: Also 1 Constituent College and 355 affiliated colleges

History: Founded 1966 as Kanpur University. Acquired present title 1997.

Academic Year: July to June

Admission Requirements: 12th year senior secondary/intermediate examination or recognized foreign equivalent

Fees: (Rupees): 1,000-45,000 per annum

Main Language(s) of Instruction: English, Hindi

Accrediting Agency: National Assessment and Accreditation Council

Degrees and Diplomas: *Post Diploma*; *Bachelor's Degree*; *Postgraduate Diploma*; *Master's Degree*; *Master of Philosophy*; *Doctor of Philosophy*

Student Services: Academic Counselling, Canteen, Careers Guidance, Cultural Activities, Health Services, Nursery Care, Social Counselling, Sports Facilities
Last Updated: 04/07/11

CHHATTISGARH SWAMI VIVEKANAND TECHNICAL UNIVERSITY

North Park Avenue, Sector-8, Bhilai, Chhattisgarh
Tel: +91(788) 226-1311
Fax: +91(788) 226-1411
EMail: vc_csvtu@csvtu.ac.in
Website: http://csvtu.ac.in/

Rector: Bimal Chandra

Registrar: Ashok Kumar Dubey

Faculty
Applied Science (Geology); **Architecture** (Architecture; Interior Design); **Ecology and Environment** (Ecology; Environmental Engineering; Environmental Studies); **Engineering and Technology** (Bioengineering; Chemical Engineering; Civil Engineering; Computer Science; Electronic Engineering; Engineering; Industrial Engineering; Information Technology; Mechanical Engineering; Metallurgical Engineering; Mining Engineering; Production Engineering; Water Science); **Humanities** (Arts and Humanities); **Management and Entrepreneurship** (Business Administration; Management); **Pharmacy** (Pharmacy)

History: Founded 2004.

Degrees and Diplomas: *Post Diploma*; *Bachelor's Degree*; *Postgraduate Diploma*; *Master's Degree*
Last Updated: 29/07/11

CHITKARA UNIVERSITY

Saraswati Kendra, SCO 160-161, Sector 9 C,
Chandigarh, Himachal Pradesh 160 009
Tel: +91(172) 4090-900
Fax: +91(172) 4691-800
EMail: admissions@chitkara.edu.in
Website: http://www.chitkara.edu.in

Vice-Chancellor: Madhu Chitkara

College
Education for Women (Education); **Pharmacy** (Medicine; Pharmacy)

School
Business Administration (Business Administration; Management); **Engineering and Technology** (Engineering; Technology); **Health Sciences** (Health Sciences); **Hospitality** (Cooking and Catering; Hotel Management; Tourism); **Mass Communication** (Mass Communication); **Planning and Architecture** (Architecture and Planning)

Institute
Engineering and Technology (Engineering; Technology)

Further Information: Also campuses in Himachal Pradesh and in Punjab

Accrediting Agency: University Grants Commission

Degrees and Diplomas: *Bachelor's Degree*; *Postgraduate Diploma*; *Master's Degree*; *Doctor of Philosophy*
Last Updated: 06/07/11

CHRIST UNIVERSITY

Hosur Road, Bangalore, Karnataka 560029
Tel: +91(80) 4012-9100
Fax: +91(80) 4012-9000
EMail: mail@christuniversity.in
Website: http://www.christuniversity.in/

Vice-Chancellor: Thomas C. Mathew EMail: vc@christuniversity.in

Registrar: J. Subramanian EMail: registrar@christuniversity.in

Faculty
Engineering (Civil Engineering; Electrical and Electronic Engineering; Engineering; Information Technology; Mechanical Engineering; Natural Sciences; Telecommunications Engineering)

School
Law (Law)

Department
Biotechnology (Biotechnology); **Botany** (Botany); **Chemistry** (Chemistry); **Commerce** (Business and Commerce); **Computer Science and Applications** (Computer Science); **Economics** (Economics); **Electronics** (Electronic Engineering); **English** (English); **Foreign Language** (Foreign Languages Education); **History** (History); **Journalism** (Journalism); **Mathematics**; **Media Studies** (Media Studies); **Performing Arts** (Performing Arts); **Philosophy and Theology** (Philosophy; Theology); **Physics** (Physics); **Political Sciences** (Political Sciences); **Psychology** (Psycholinguistics); **Social Work** (Social Work); **Sociology** (Sociology); **Statistics** (Statistics); **Tourism Studies** (Tourism); **Zoology** (Zoology)

Institute
Management (MBA) *(CUIM)* (Business Administration; Management)

Centre
Professional Studies

History: Founded as Christ College 1969. Acquired present name and status 2007.

Degrees and Diplomas: *Master's Degree*; *Master of Philosophy*; *Doctor of Philosophy*
Last Updated: 09/01/12

CMJ UNIVERSITY

Mondrina Mansion, Laitumkhrah, Shillong, Maghalaya 793003
Tel: +91(364) 2500-631
Fax: +91(364) 2500-632
EMail: ccii@cmjuniversity.edu.in
Website: http://www.cmju.in/

Chancellor: C. M. Jha

Programme
Computer Science and Information Technology (Computer Science; Information Technology); **Design and planning** (Architecture; Design; Textile Design); **Engineering** (Chemical Engineering; Electrical Engineering; Engineering; Mechanical Engineering; Metallurgical Engineering; Nanotechnology); **Health and Paramedicals** (Communication Studies; Health Sciences; Medical Auxiliaries; Medical Technology; Optometry; Paramedical Sciences; Physical Therapy); **Humanities and Education and Juridical Science** (Advertising and Publicity; Arts and Humanities; Commercial Law; Education; Human Rights; Journalism; Law; Preschool Education; Primary Education; Public Relations); **Management and Commerce** (Business and Commerce; Criminology; Finance; Human Resources; Information Technology; Management; Marketing; Retailing and Wholesaling; Sports); **Science and Technology** (Information Sciences; Library Science; Natural Sciences; Technology)

History: Founded 2009.

Degrees and Diplomas: *Bachelor's Degree*; *Master's Degree*; *Doctor of Philosophy*
Last Updated: 03/01/12

COCHIN UNIVERSITY OF SCIENCE AND TECHNOLOGY (CUSAT)

PO Cochin University, Kochi, Kerala 682022
Tel: +91(484) 257-5396
Fax: +91(484) 257-7595
EMail: registrar@cusat.ac.in
Website: http://www.cusat.ac.in

Vice-Chancellor: Ramachandran Thekkedath
Tel: +91(484) 257-7619 EMail: rector@cusat.ac.in

Registrar: N. Chandramohanakumar

Faculty
Engineering (Civil Engineering; Computer Engineering; Computer Science; Electrical and Electronic Engineering; Electronic Engineering; Engineering; Fire Science; Marine Engineering; Mechanical Engineering; Safety Engineering; Software Engineering; Telecommunications Engineering); **Humanities and Foreign Languages** (Arabic; Arts and Humanities; French; German; Hindi; Japanese; Modern Languages; Russian; Translation and Interpretation); **Law** (Law); **Marine Sciences** (Marine Science and Oceanography); **Medical Sciences and Technology** (Health Sciences; Technology)

School
Computer Science; **Environmental Studies** (Biotechnology; Environmental Engineering; Environmental Studies); **Management**; **Photonics**

Department
Applied Chemistry (Chemistry); **Applied Economics**; **Atmospheric Sciences** (Meteorology); **Biotechnology** (Biotechnology); **Chemical Oceanography** (Marine Science and Oceanography); **Industrial Fishery** (Fishery); **Instrumentation**; **Marine Biology** (Marine Biology); **Marine Geology** (Marine Science and Oceanography); **Mathematics**; **Oceanography**; **Physics**; **Polymer Science and Technology** (Polymer and Plastics Technology; Technology); **Ship Technology** (Naval Architecture); **Statistics**

Centre
Computer (Computer Science); **Creative Writing** (Writing); **Interdisciplinary Studies**; **Rural Development and Appropriate Technology** (Rural Planning; Technology); **Science in Society**

History: Founded 1971 as Cochin University, acquired present title 1986.

Academic Year: July to April (July-November; December-April).

Admission Requirements: Common Admission Test (CAT). Foreign students admitted through Indian Council for Cultural Relations (ICCR)

Fees: (Rupees): Undergraduate, 3,000-17,500; postgraduate, 750-6,000. Foreign students, undergraduate, (US Dollars): 7,000, postgraduate, 5,000

Main Language(s) of Instruction: English

Accrediting Agency: National Accreditation Council; University Grants Commission

Degrees and Diplomas: *Bachelor's Degree*; *Master's Degree*; *Doctor of Philosophy*

Student Services: Academic Counselling, Canteen, Careers Guidance, Cultural Activities, Foreign Studies Centre, Health Services, Language Laboratory, Nursery Care, Sports Facilities

Publications: Cochin University Law Review; CUSAT News

Last Updated: 06/07/11

COLLEGE OF ENGINEERING TRIVANDRUM

Thiruvananthapuram, Kerala 695016
Tel: +91(471) 251-5556
Fax: +91(471) 259-8370
EMail: principal@cet.ac.in
Website: http://www.cet.ac.in

Principal: V. Gopa Kumar EMail: gopa1959@yahoo.com

Deanery

Mechanical Engineering (Industrial Engineering; Mechanical Engineering)

Department

Architecture (Architecture); **Civil Engineering** (Civil Engineering); **Computer Science and Engineering** (Computer Engineering; Computer Science); **Electrical and Electronics Engineering** (Electrical and Electronic Engineering; Electronic Engineering; Measurement and Precision Engineering; Telecommunications Engineering)

History: Created 1939.

Accrediting Agency: UGC; National Board of Accreditation (NBA)

Degrees and Diplomas: *Bachelor's Degree*; *Master's Degree*

Last Updated: 05/02/13

DATTA MEGHE INSTITUTE OF MEDICAL SCIENCES, DEEMED UNIVERSITY (DMIMSU)

Atrey Layout, Pratapnagar, Nagpur, Maharashtra 440020
Tel: +91(712) 329-5207
Fax: +91(712) 224-5318
EMail: info@dmims.org
Website: http://www.dmimsu.edu.in/

Vice-Chancellor: Vedprakash Mishra
Tel: +91(712) 224-5314 EMail: info@dmims.org

Registrar: R.M. Borle Tel: +91(712) 224-9163

Faculty

Ayurveda *(Mahatma Gandhi College of Ayurveda and Research)* (Ayurveda); **Dentistry** *(Sharad Pawar Dental College)* (Dentistry); **Medicine** *(Jawaharlal Nehru Medical College)*; **Nursing** (Nursing); **Paramedical Sciences** (Paramedical Sciences)

History: Created in 1990. Acquired current status and name 2005. Made up of three constituent colleges.

Academic Year: July to May.

Admission Requirements: Secondary School Certificate.

Fees: (Rupees): 85,000 to 428,000 depending on year and degree

Main Language(s) of Instruction: English.

Accrediting Agency: National Assessment and Accreditation Council (NAAC), India

Degrees and Diplomas: *Bachelor's Degree*: **Ayurveda; Dentistry; Medicine; Surgery.** *Postgraduate Diploma*: **Dentistry.** *Master's Degree*: **Dentistry; Medicine; Public Health; Surgery.** *Doctor of Philosophy*. Also: Certificate Courses in Dental Mechanics and Dental Hygiene

Student Services: Academic Counselling, Canteen, Careers Guidance, Cultural Activities, Facilities for disabled people, Foreign Studies Centre, Health Services, Language Laboratory, Nursery Care, Social Counselling, Sports Facilities

Publications: Journal of Datta Meghe Institute of Medical Sciences University

Academic Staff *2010-2011*	**TOTAL**
FULL-TIME	**500**
STAFF WITH DOCTORATE	
FULL-TIME	c. **5**
Student Numbers *2010-2011*	
All (Foreign included)	c. **1,500**
FOREIGN ONLY	**5**

Last Updated: 06/07/11

DAVANGERE UNIVERSITY

Shivagangothri, Davangere, Karnataka 577002
Tel: +91(8192) 208029
Fax: +91(8192) 208008
EMail: info@davangereuniversity.ac.in
Website: http://davangereuniversity.ac.in

Vice-Chancellor: S. Indumati

Registrar: D.S. Prakash

Department

Arts (Arts and Humanities; Economics; English; Indic Languages; Political Sciences; Social Work; Sociology); **Commerce** (Accountancy; Business and Commerce; Finance; Management); **Education** (Education); **Fine Arts** (Fine Arts; Painting and Drawing; Sculpture); **Science** (Analytical Chemistry; Biochemistry; Botany; Computer Science; Food Technology; Mathematics; Microbiology; Natural Sciences; Physics)

History: Founded as a post-graduate centre of the University of Mysore from 1979 to 1987, and later functioned as P.G Centre of Kuvempu University from 1987 to 2009. Acquired present status 2009.

Degrees and Diplomas: *Bachelor's Degree*; *Master's Degree*; *Master of Philosophy*; *Doctor of Philosophy*

Student Services: Canteen, Sports Facilities

Last Updated: 18/01/12

DAYALBAGH EDUCATIONAL INSTITUTE (DEI)

PO Dayalbagh, Agra, Uttar Pradesh 282005
Tel: +91(562) 280-545
Fax: +91(562) 280-226
EMail: admin@dei.ac.in
Website: http://www.dei.ac.in

Director: V. Gurusaran Das (2005-) Tel: +91(562) 280-1545

Registrar: Anand Mohan

Faculty

Arts (Arts and Humanities; Cultural Studies; English; Hindi; Home Economics; Literature; Music; Musical Instruments; Painting and Drawing; Sanskrit; Singing); **Commerce** (Accountancy; Business Administration; Business and Commerce; Commercial Law; Economics); **Education** (Education; Pedagogy); **Engineering** (Electrical Engineering; Engineering; Mechanical Engineering); **Science** (Botany; Chemistry; Computer Science; Mathematics; Physics; Zoology); **Social Sciences** (Economics; Management; Political Sciences; Psychology; Sociology)

College

Prem Vidyalaya Girls Intermediate Studies (Arts and Humanities; Fine Arts; Natural Sciences); **Technical** (Engineering)

History: Founded 1981.

Academic Year: July to June (July-December; January-May; May-June)

Admission Requirements: 12th year senior secondary/intermediate examination or recognized foreign equivalent

Main Language(s) of Instruction: English, Hindi

Accrediting Agency: University Grants Commission; All India Council of Technical Education; National Council for Teacher Education; National Assessment and Accreditation Council (NAAC)

Degrees and Diplomas: *Post Diploma*: **Engineering; Technology.** *Bachelor's Degree*: **Business and Commerce; Education; Engineering; Fine Arts; Social Sciences.** *Postgraduate Diploma*: **Business and Commerce; Computer Science; Economics; Mathematics; Religion.** *Master's Degree*; *Master of Philosophy*: **Education.** *Doctor of Philosophy*: **Business and Commerce; Education; Engineering; Fine Arts; Management; Psychology; Social Sciences.** Mtech

Student Services: Academic Counselling, Canteen, Careers Guidance, Cultural Activities, Health Services, Sports Facilities

Publications: DEI Journal of Science and Engineering Research

Last Updated: 11/07/11

DECCAN COLLEGE POST-GRADUATE AND RESEARCH INSTITUTE (DCPRI)

Deccan College Road, Yerwada, Pune, Maharashtra 411006
Tel: +91(20) 2651-3204
Fax: +91(20) 2669-2104
EMail: info@deccancollegepune.ac.in
Website: http://www.deccancollegepune.ac.in

Director: V.P. Bhatta Tel: +91(20) 2669-2982

Registrar: N.S. Gaware Tel: +91(20) 2661-5232

Department

Archaeology (Arts and Humanities); **Linguistics** (Arts and Humanities); **Sanskrit and Lexicography** (Sanskrit)

Further Information: Also Sanskrit Dictionary Project

History: Founded 1821 as Sanskrit School; became Poona College 1851; Became Deccan College 1864; Acquired present title 1939; Acquired present status 1994.

Academic Year: July to June (July-November; January-June)

Admission Requirements: A graduate degree in Humanities or Science

Main Language(s) of Instruction: English

Accrediting Agency: NAAC

Degrees and Diplomas: *Postgraduate Diploma*: **Archaeology.** *Master's Degree*: **Archaeology; Linguistics.** *Doctor of Philosophy*: **Archaeology; Linguistics.**

Student Services: Academic Counselling, Canteen, Sports Facilities

Publications: Bulletin of the Deccan College Post-graduate and Research Institute; Monograph Series

Last Updated: 11/07/11

DEENBANDHU CHHOTU RAM UNIVERSITY OF SCIENCE AND TECHNOLOGY

50th K.M. Stone, N.H. 1, Murthal (Sonepat), Haryana 131039
Tel: +91(130) 2484-005
EMail: info@dcrustm.org
Website: http://www.dcrustm.ac.in

Vice-Chancellor: Er. Har Sarup Chahal (2008-)
EMail: vc@dcrustm.org

Registrar: R. K. Arora EMail: registrar@dcrustm.org

Faculty

Architecture, Urban and Town Planning (Architecture; Town Planning); **Engineering and Technology** (Biomedical Engineering; Civil Engineering; Electrical and Electronic Engineering; Electronic Engineering; Mechanical Engineering; Telecommunications Engineering); **Information Technology and Communication Sciences** (Communication Studies; Information Technology); **Management Studies** (Management); **Non Conventional Source of Energy and Environment Science** (Biotechnology; Chemical Engineering; Energy Engineering); **Science and Technology Interface** (Chemistry; Communication Studies; English; Nanotechnology; Physics; Technology)

History: Founded 2006.

Admission Requirements: Should be a pass in 10+2 examination from recognised Board/University with Physics and Mathematics or Chemistry/Biology as compulsory subjects or International Baccalaureate Diploma, admission will be made on the basis of Entrance Test

Degrees and Diplomas: *Bachelor's Degree*; *Master's Degree*; *Doctor of Philosophy*

Student Services: Health Services, Sports Facilities

Last Updated: 18/10/11

DEFENCE INSTITUTE OF ADVANCED TECHNOLOGY (DIAT)

Girinagar, Pune, Maharashtra 411025
Tel: +91(20) 2430-4021
Fax: +91(20) 2438-9318
EMail: registrar@diat.ac.in
Website: http://www.diat.ac.in/

Vice-Chancellor: Prahlada EMail: vc@diat.ac.in

Registrar: R. Premkumar EMail: registrar@diat.ac.in

Department

Aerospace Engineering (Aeronautical and Aerospace Engineering); **Air Force** (Aeronautical and Aerospace Engineering); **Applied Chemistry** (Applied Chemistry); **Applied Mathematics** (Applied Mathematics); **Applied Physics** (Applied Physics); **Armament Engineering** (Engineering); **Army** (Civil Security); **Computer Engineering** (Computer Engineering; Computer Networks); **Electronics Engineering** (Electronic Engineering); **Materials Engineering** (Materials Engineering); **Mechanical Engineering** (Mechanical Engineering); **Navy** (Marine Engineering; Naval Architecture)

History: Founded 1952 as Institute of Armament Studies, became Institute of Armament Technology 1967. Acquired present title and status 2006.

Degrees and Diplomas: *Master's Degree*; *Doctor of Philosophy*

Last Updated: 21/11/11

DELHI TECHNOLOGICAL UNIVERSITY

Shahbad Daulatpur, Main Bawana Road 42,
Delhi, NCT of Delhi 110042
Tel: +91(11) 2787-1018
Fax: +91(11) 2787-1023
EMail: mail@dce.edu
Website: http://www.dce.edu

Vice-Chancellor: P.B. Sharma
Tel: +91(11) 2787-1018 EMail: pbsharma48@yahoo.co.in

International Relations: R.C. Sharma, International Affairs
EMail: rcsharma_263@yahoo.co.in

School

Management (Business Administration; Management)

Department

Applied Chemistry (Applied Chemistry); **Applied Mathematics** (Applied Mathematics); **Applied Physics** (Applied Physics); **Biotechnology** (Biotechnology); **Civil and Environmental** (Civil Engineering; Environmental Engineering); **Computer Engineering** (Computer Engineering); **Electrical** (Electrical Engineering); **Electronics and Communication** (Electronic Engineering; Telecommunications Engineering); **Humanities** (Accountancy; Arts and Humanities; Economics; English); **Information Technology** (Information Technology); **Mechanical and Production** (Mechanical Engineering; Production Engineering)

History: Founded 1941 as Delhi College of Engineering. Acquired present title and status 2009.

Degrees and Diplomas: *Bachelor's Degree*; *Master's Degree*; *Doctor of Philosophy*

Last Updated: 05/01/12

DEV SANSKRITI VISHWAVIDYALAYA

Gayatrikunj-Shantikunj, Hardwar, Uttarakhand 249411
Tel: +91(1334) 261-367 +91(1334) 262-094
Fax: +91(1334) 260-723
EMail: vc@dsvv.org
Website: http://www.dsvv.ac.in/

Vice-Chancellor: S.P. Mishra

Registrar: R.P. Karmyogi

Department

Clinical Psychology (Clinical Psychology); **Computer Science** (Computer Science); **English**; **Holistic Health and Management** (Health Administration); **Human Consciousness and Yogic Sciences** (Yoga); **Indian Culture and Tourism Studies** (Indigenous Studies; Tourism); **Journalism Mass Communication** (Journalism; Mass Communication); **Life Management**; **Rural Management** (Rural Studies); **Sanskrit** (Sanskrit); **Scientific Spirituality**; **Sports** (Sports); **Theology** (Theology)

History: Founded 2002.

Academic Year: July to May (July-December; January-May)

Degrees and Diplomas: *Bachelor's Degree*; *Postgraduate Diploma*: **English.** *Master's Degree*: **Clinical Psychology; South Asian Studies; Tourism; Yoga.** Also Certificate Courses in Yoga, English Proficiency; Theology; Holistic Health Management (6 months)

Student Services: Health Services, Sports Facilities

Last Updated: 11/07/11

DEVI AHILYA VISHWAVIDYALAYA

University House, 235 RNT Marg, Indore, Madhya Pradesh 452001
Tel: +91(731) 252-7532
Fax: +91(731) 252-9540
EMail: registrar.davv@dauniv.ac.in
Website: http://www.dauniv.ac.in/

Vice-Chancellor: P.K. Mishra Tel: +91(731) 252-1887

Registrar: R.D. Musalgoankar

Faculty

Medicine (Medicine)

School

Biochemistry (Biochemistry); **Biotechnology** (Biotechnology); **Chemical Sciences** (Chemistry); **Commerce** (Business and Commerce); **Computer Science and Information Technology** (Computer Science; Information Technology); **Economics** (Economics); **Education** (Education); **Electronics** (Electronic Engineering; Engineering); **Energy and Environmental Studies** (Energy Engineering; Environmental Studies); **Future Studies and Planning**; **Instrumentation**; **Journalism and Mass Communication** (Journalism; Mass Communication); **Language** (Modern Languages); **Law** (Law); **Life Sciences** (Biological and Life Sciences); **Mathematics** (Mathematics); **Pharmacy** (Pharmacy); **Physical Education**; **Physics** (Physics); **Social Science**; **Statistics** (Statistics)

Institute

Engineering and Technology (Management); **Management Studies** (Management); **Professional Studies**

Centre

Science Communication

Further Information: Also 29 Affiliated Colleges, and Teaching Hospitals

History: Founded 1963.

Academic Year: July to April

Admission Requirements: 12th year senior secondary/intermediate examination or recognized foreign equivalent

Main Language(s) of Instruction: English

Degrees and Diplomas: *Bachelor's Degree*; *Master's Degree*; *Doctor of Philosophy*

Publishing house: University Press

Last Updated: 11/07/11

DHARMSINH DESAI UNIVERSITY (DDU)

College Road, Nadiad, Gujarat 387001
Tel: +91(268) 252-0502
Fax: +91(268) 252-0501
EMail: vcddit@yahoo.co.in
Website: http://www.ddu.ac.in

Vice-Chancellor: H.M. Desai
Tel: +91(268) 252-0503 EMail: vc@ddu.ac.in

registrar@ddu.ac.in: M. R. Bhavsar

Faculty

Commerce (Business and Commerce); **Dental Science** (Dentistry); **Management and Information Sciences** (Information Sciences; Management); **Pharmacy** (Pharmacy); **Technology** (Chemical Engineering; Civil Engineering; Computer Engineering; Electronic Engineering; Mathematics; Mechanical Engineering; Telecommunications Engineering)

History: Founded 1968. Acquired present status 2005.

Academic Year: July to April

Admission Requirements: 12th year senior secondary/intermediate examination or recognized foreign equivalent

Main Language(s) of Instruction: English

Accrediting Agency: National Assessment and Accreditation Council (NAAC); All India Council for Technical Education (AICTE)

Degrees and Diplomas: *Bachelor's Degree*: **Business Administration; Engineering.** *Master's Degree*: **Engineering; Management; Technology.** *Doctor of Philosophy*: **Engineering; Management.**

Student Services: Academic Counselling, Canteen, Careers Guidance, Cultural Activities, Health Services, Social Counselling, Sports Facilities

Publications: DDU Newsletter

Last Updated: 12/07/11

DHIRUBHAI AMBANI INSTITUTE OF INFORMATION AND COMMUNICATION TECHNOLOGY

Near Indroda Circle, Gandhinagar, Gujarat 382007
Tel: +91(79) 3052-0000
Fax: +91(79) 3052-0010
EMail: info@daiict.ac.in
Website: http://www.daiict.ac.in

Director: S.C. Sahasrabudhe

Programme

Agriculture and Rural Development (Agriculture; Rural Planning; Rural Studies); **Design** (Design); **Information and Communication Technology** (Computer Engineering; Computer Science; Electronic Engineering; Information Technology; Software Engineering)

History: Founded 2001. Acquired present status 2003.

Degrees and Diplomas: *Bachelor's Degree*; *Master's Degree*; *Doctor of Philosophy*

Last Updated: 12/07/11

DIBRUGARH UNIVERSITY

Dibrugarh, Assam 786004
Tel: +91(373) 237-0231
Fax: +91(373) 237-0323
EMail: info@dibru.ac.in
Website: http://www.dibru.ac.in

Vice-Chancellor: Kandarpa K. Deka EMail: vc@dibru.ac.in

Department

Anthropology (Anthropology); **Applied Geology** (Geology); **Assamese** (Indic Languages); **Chemistry** (Chemistry); **Commerce** (Business and Commerce); **Economics** (Economics); **Education**; **English** (English); **History** (History); **Life Sciences** (Biological and Life Sciences); **Mathematics** (Mathematics); **Petroleum Technology** (Petroleum and Gas Engineering); **Pharmaceutical Sciences** (Pharmacy); **Physics** (Physics); **Political Science** (Political Sciences); **Sociology** (Sociology); **Statistics** (Statistics)

Further Information: Also Affiliated Colleges. Assam Medical College Teaching Hospital Dibrugarh

History: Founded 1965.

Academic Year: January to March (January-December; April-March).

Admission Requirements: Higher Secondary Certificate (HSC), standard 12, or equivalent.

Main Language(s) of Instruction: English, Assamese

Accrediting Agency: NAAC

Degrees and Diplomas: *Bachelor's Degree*; *Master's Degree*; *Doctor of Philosophy*

Student Services: Academic Counselling, Canteen, Health Services, Social Counselling, Sports Facilities

Publications: Assam Economic Journal; Bulletin of Department of Anthropology; Journal of Department of Assamese; Journal of Historical Research; Journal of Politics; North East Research Bulletin; Padartha Vigyan Patrika; Pharmray; Vanijya - Journal of Commerce

Last Updated: 12/07/11

DOCTOR BABASAHEB AMBEDKAR MARATHWADA UNIVERSITY

University Campus, Aurangabad, Maharashtra 431004
Tel: +91(240) 240-0104
Fax: +91(240) 240-0291
EMail: vc@bamu.net
Website: http://www.bamu.net/

Vice-Chancellor: V.M. Pandharipande Tel: +91(240) 240-0069

Registrar: Manvendra Kachole EMail: registrar@bamu.net

Department

Biochemistry (Biochemistry); **Botany** (Botany); **Chemical Technology** (Chemical Engineering); **Chemistry** (Chemistry); **Commerce** (Business and Commerce); **Computer Science and IT** (Computer Engineering; Computer Science; Telecommunications Engineering); **Dance**; **Dramatics** (Theatre); **Economics** (Economics); **Education** (Education); **English** (English); **Environmental Science**; **Fine Arts** (Fine Arts); **Foreign Language** (Foreign Languages Education); **Geography** (Geography); **Hindi** (Hindi); **History and Ancient Indian Culture** (Ancient Civilizations; History); **Journalism** (Journalism); **Law** (Law); **Library and Information Sciences** (Information Sciences; Library Science); **Management Science** (Management); **Marathi Language and Literature** (Indic Languages; Literature); **Mathematics** (Mathematics); **Nanotechnology** (Nanotechnology); **Pali and Buddhism** (Asian Religious Studies; Indic Languages); **Physical Education** (Physical Education); **Physics** (Physics); **Political Science** (Political Sciences); **Printing Technology** (Printing and Printmaking); **Psychology** (Psychology); **Public Administration** (Public Administration); **Sanskrit** (Sanskrit); **Sociology** (Sociology); **Statistics** (Statistics); **Tourism Administration and Management** (Management; Tourism); **Urdu** (Urdu); **Zoology** (Zoology)

Further Information: Also 227 Affiliated Colleges

History: Founded 1958 as Marathwada University. Acquired present title 1994.

Academic Year: June to April (June-October; November-April)

Admission Requirements: 12th year senior secondary/intermediate examination or recognized foreign equivalent

Main Language(s) of Instruction: English, Marathi

Degrees and Diplomas: *Bachelor's Degree*: **Ayurveda; Business and Commerce; Dentistry; Education; Engineering; Fine Arts; Homeopathy; Journalism; Law; Library Science; Medicine; Pharmacy; Physical Education; Social Work; Surgery; Technology; Theatre.** *Master's Degree*: **Business Administration; Business and Commerce; Education; Engineering; Fine Arts; Law; Library Science; Mass Communication; Philosophy; Physical Education; Surgery.** *Doctor of Philosophy*: **Medicine.** Also undergraduate and postgraduate Diplomas

Publications: University Journal

Publishing House: University Press

Last Updated: 13/07/11

DOCTOR BABASAHEB AMBEDKAR OPEN UNIVERSITY

9 Government Bungalow, Near Dafnala, Shahibaug, Ahmedabad, Gujarat 380003
Tel: +91(79) 2285-0184
Fax: +91(79) 2286-9691
EMail: baouvc@yahoo.com
Website: http://www.baou.org

Vice-Chancellor: Manoj Soni EMail: amerchantvc@rediffmail.com

Registrar: Piyushbhai Shah EMail: shbarotreg@rediffmail.com

School

Commerce and Management (Business and Commerce; Management); **Computer Science** (Computer Science); **Education; Distance Education and Education Technology** (Distance Education; Education; Educational Technology); **Humanities and Social Sciences** (Arts and Humanities; Social Sciences)

History: Founded 1994.

Academic Year: August to July

Main Language(s) of Instruction: Gujarati

Degrees and Diplomas: *Post Diploma*; *Bachelor's Degree*; *Postgraduate Diploma*

Last Updated: 13/07/11

DOCTOR BABASAHEB AMBEDKAR TECHNOLOGICAL UNIVERSITY

Vidyavihar, District Raigad, Lonere, Maharashtra 402103
Tel: +91(2140) 275-103
Fax: +91(2140) 275-040
EMail: admin@dbatu.ac.in
Website: http://www.dbatu.ac.in/

Vice-Chancellor: R.B. Mankar EMail: vc@dbatu.ac.in

Registrar: Madhukar S. Tandale EMail: registrar@dbatu.ac.in

Department

Chemical Engineering (Chemical Engineering); **Chemistry** (Chemistry); **Civil Engineering** (Civil Engineering); **Computer Engineering** (Computer Engineering); **Electrical Engineering** (Electrical Engineering); **Electronics and Telecommunications Engineering** (Electronic Engineering; Telecommunications Engineering); **English** (English); **Information Technology** (Information Technology); **Mathematics** (Mathematics); **Mechanical Engineering** (Mechanical Engineering); **Petrochemical Engineering** (Petroleum and Gas Engineering); **Physics** (Physics)

History: Founded 1989.

Academic Year: August to June (August-January; February-June)

Admission Requirements: 12th year senior secondary/intermediate examination or recognized foreign equivalent

Main Language(s) of Instruction: English

Degrees and Diplomas: *Post Diploma*: **Engineering.** *Bachelor's Degree*: **Technology.** *Master's Degree*

Student Services: Academic Counselling, Canteen, Careers Guidance, Health Services, Social Counselling, Sports Facilities

Last Updated: 13/07/11

DOCTOR B.R. AMBEDKAR OPEN UNIVERSITY (BRAOU)

Prof. G. Ram Reddy Marg., Road No 46, Jubilee Hills, Hyderabad, Andhra Pradesh 500033
Tel: +91(40) 2354-4910
Fax: +91(40) 2354-4830
EMail: info@braou.ac.in
Website: http://www.braou.ac.in

Vice-Chancellor: P. Prakash (2012-) EMail: vc@braou.ac.in

Registrar: C. Venkataiah EMail: registrar@braou.ac.in

Faculty

Arts (Arts and Humanities; English; Hindi; Indic Languages; Urdu); **Commerce** (Business and Commerce; Management); **Education** (Education); **Science** (Botany; Chemistry; Computer Science; Geology; Mathematics; Natural Sciences; Physics; Zoology); **Social Sciences** (Computer Science; Economics; Educational Technology; History; Library Science; Political Sciences; Public Administration; Public Relations; Social Sciences; Sociology)

Centre

Economic and Social Studies *(CESS)* (Economics; Social Studies)

History: Founded 1982 as Andhra Pradesh Open University, renamed 1991, and has the same legal and academic status as any other University in India. It is designed to enable persons who do not have any formal educational qualification to pursue courses leading to a first degree as well as a Postgraduate degree. The aim of the University is to provide equality of opportunity for as large a segment of the population as possible, through use of print, audio-visual media, teleconferencing and contact, and counselling programmes at 131 study centres.

Academic Year: August to July

Admission Requirements: Applicants who have passed the Intermediate examination conducted by the Board of Intermediate Education, or equivalent. Applicants without any qualifications have to pass the Eligibility test conducted by the University

Main Language(s) of Instruction: English, Telugu, Urdu

Degrees and Diplomas: *Bachelor's Degree*; *Postgraduate Diploma*; *Master's Degree*; *Master of Philosophy*; *Doctor of Philosophy*. Also Certificate courses

Student Services: Academic Counselling, Canteen, Careers Guidance, Cultural Activities, Facilities for disabled people, Foreign Studies Centre, Health Services, Language Laboratory, Nursery Care, Social Counselling, Sports Facilities

Last Updated: 23/04/12

DOCTOR HARISINGH GOUR UNIVERSITY

Doctor Harisingh Gour Vishwavidyalaya

Gour Nagar, Sagar, Madhya Pradesh 470003

Tel: +91(7582) 265-228

Fax: +91(7582) 264-163

EMail: sagaruniversity@mp.nic.in

Website: http://www.sagaruniversity.nic.in/

Vice-Chancellor: N. S. Gajbhiye Tel: +91(7582) 223-199

Department

Applied Microbiology and Biotechnology (Biotechnology; Microbiology); **Arts** *(Graduate, Sagar)* (Arts and Humanities; English; Hindi; Indic Languages; Linguistics; Music; Persian; Philosophy; Sanskrit; Urdu); **Commerce** (Business and Commerce); **Computer Science and Application**; **Criminology and Forensic Science**; **Distance Education**; **Education** *(Graduate)* (Education; Yoga); **Engineering** *(Graduate)* (Engineering); **Law** *(Graduate)* (Law); **Life Sciences** (Biological and Life Sciences; Biophysics; Botany; Microbiology; Zoology); **Management Studies** *(Graduate)* (Management); **Pharmaceutical Sciences** (Pharmacy); **Science** (Anthropology; Chemistry; Criminology; Electronic Engineering; Forensic Medicine and Dentistry; Geography; Instrument Making; Mathematics; Measurement and Precision Engineering; Natural Sciences; Physics; Statistics); **Social Sciences** (Economics; History; Social Sciences); **Technology** (Geology; Technology)

Further Information: Also 69 Affiliated Colleges

History: Founded 1946 as University of Sagar, acquired present title 1983. An autonomous Institution.

Academic Year: July to April

Admission Requirements: 12th year senior secondary/intermediate examination or recognized foreign equivalent

Main Language(s) of Instruction: English, Hindi

Degrees and Diplomas: *Post Diploma*; *Bachelor's Degree*: **Education; Engineering; Law; Library Science; Pharmacy.** *Master's Degree*; *Master of Philosophy*; *Doctor of Philosophy*

Publications: Madhya Bharti (Research Journals)

Publishing House: University Printing Press

Last Updated: 13/07/11

DOCTOR PANJABRAO DESHMUKH AGRICULTURE UNIVERSITY

Doctor Panjabrao Deshmukh Krishi Vidyapeeth

PO Krishi Nagar, Akola, Maharashtra 444104

Tel: +91(724) 225-8372

Fax: +91(724) 225-8219

EMail: tsvc@pdkv.ac.in

Website: http://pdkv.ac.in/

Vice-Chancellor: V. M. Mayande (2007-)
Tel: +91(722) 225-8365 EMail: vc@pdkv.ac.in

Registrar: V.M. Bhale
Tel: +91 (724) 225-8372 EMail: registrar@pdkv.ac.in

International Relations: P.G. Ingole, Public Relations Officer
Tel: +91 (724) 225-8365 EMail: tsvc@pdkv.ac.in

Faculty

Agricultural Engineering (Agricultural Engineering; Agricultural Equipment; Agricultural Management; Energy Engineering; Farm Management; Irrigation; Soil Conservation; Water Management); **Agriculture** (Agricultural Economics; Agriculture; Agronomy; Animal Husbandry; Applied Chemistry; Botany; Crop Production; Dairy; Entomology; Forestry; Horticulture; Plant Pathology; Soil Science)

Further Information: Also 17 Constituent and 2 Affiliated Colleges

History: Founded 1969.

Academic Year: July to June (July-December; January-June)

Admission Requirements: 12th year senior secondary/intermediate examination or recognized foreign equivalent

Fees: (Rupees): Undergraduate, 9,000 per annum; postgraduate, 19,476; PhD, 23,776

Main Language(s) of Instruction: English

Degrees and Diplomas: *Bachelor's Degree*: **Agricultural Engineering; Agriculture; Forestry; Horticulture.** *Master's Degree*; *Doctor of Philosophy*: **Agricultural Engineering; Agriculture; Horticulture.**

Student Services: Academic Counselling, Canteen, Careers Guidance, Health Services, Social Counselling, Sports Facilities

Publications: PVK Research Journal

Publishing House: Printing Press Dr. P.D.K.V., Akola

Last Updated: 18/07/11

DOCTOR RAM MANOHAR LOHIA AWADH UNIVERSITY

Dr. R. M. L. Avadh University Campus,
Faizabad, Uttar Pradesh 224001

Tel: +91(5278) 245-957

Fax: +91(5278) 246-330

EMail: registrar@rmlau.ac.in

Website: http://www.rmlau.ac.in

Vice-Chancellor: Arun Kumar Mittal
Tel: +91(5278) 246-223 EMail: vc@rmlau.ac.in

Registrar: K.N Pandey EMail: registrar@rmlau.ac.in

Faculty

Arts (Archaeology; Arts and Humanities; Cultural Studies; Development Studies; Economics; History); **Commerce** (Business and Commerce); **Education** (Education); **Engineering and Technology** (Electronic Engineering; Engineering; Technology); **Law** (Law); **Science** (Natural Sciences)

Department

Biochemistry (Biochemistry); **Business Management and Entrepreneurship** (Business Administration; Management); **Economics and Rural Development** (Economics; Rural Planning); **Environmental Science**; **History, Culture and Archaeology** (Archaeology; Cultural Studies; History); **Mathematics and Statistics** (Mathematics; Statistics); **Microbiology** (Microbiology); **Solid State Physics and Electronics** (Electronic Engineering; Solid State Physics)

Centre

Adult and Continuing Education

Further Information: Also 287 Affiliated Colleges

History: Founded 1975 as Avadh University an autonomous institution.

Academic Year: July to April (both annual and semester system)

Admission Requirements: For Bachelor's Degree: 12th year senior secondary/intermediate examination or recognized foreign equivalent. For Master's Degree - Graduation in relevant discipline

Fees: (Rupees): 4000-50,000 per annum varying with the courses of study in annual and semester system

Main Language(s) of Instruction: Hindi, English

Accrediting Agency: National Assessment and Accreditation Council (NAAC) Bangalore

Degrees and Diplomas: *Post Diploma*: **Fashion Design.** *Bachelor's Degree*: **Business Administration; Computer Science; Electronic Engineering; Information Sciences; Information Technology; Library Science; Mechanical Engineering;**

Physical Education. *Master's Degree*: **Biotechnology; Computer Science; Education; Physical Education; Social Work; Tourism.** *Doctor of Philosophy*: **Business and Commerce; Fine Arts; Management.**

Student Services: Academic Counselling, Careers Guidance, Health Services, Language Laboratory, Sports Facilities

DOCTOR YASHWANT SINGH PARMAR UNIVERSITY OF HORTICULTURE AND FORESTRY

District Solan, Nauni, Himachal Pradesh 173230
Tel: +91(1792) 252-363
Fax: +91(1792) 252-242
Website: http://www.yspuniversity.ac.in

Vice-Chancellor: K. R. Dhiman EMail: vc@yspuniversity.ac.in

Registrar: B. R. Kamal EMail: registrar@yspuniversity.ac.in

College

Forestry (Environmental Studies; Forest Biology; Forest Products; Forestry; Natural Sciences; Social Sciences; Soil Science; Water Management); **Horticulture** (Agricultural Business; Apiculture; Biotechnology; Entomology; Food Science; Fruit Production; Horticulture; Vegetable Production)

Centre

Computer Science and Instrumentation (Computer Science; Instrument Making); **Regional Horticultural Research** *(Jachh, Sharbo, Bajaura, Dhaulakuar, Kandaghat, Tabo, Nagrota Bhagwan, Seobagh, Manala)* (Horticulture); **Seed Production** (Agriculture)

Further Information: Also 14 Departments of the Colleges

History: Founded 1985.

Academic Year: July to June

Admission Requirements: 12th year senior secondary/intermediate examination or recognized foreign equivalent

Main Language(s) of Instruction: English

Degrees and Diplomas: *Bachelor's Degree*: **Forestry; Horticulture.** *Master's Degree*; *Doctor of Philosophy*

Last Updated: 18/07/11

DOON UNIVERSITY

Motharawala Road, Kedarpur, PO Ajabpur, Dehradun, Uttarkhand
EMail: doonvc@gmail.com
Website: http://doonuniversity.ac.in/

Vice-Chancellor: Girijesh Pant Tel: +91(135) 2532-012

School

Communication (Communication Studies; Media Studies); **Environment and Natural Resources** (Environmental Studies; Natural Resources); **Languages** (Modern Languages); **Management** (Business Administration; Management); **Social Sciences** (Social Sciences)

History: Founded 2005.

Degrees and Diplomas: *Bachelor's Degree*; *Master's Degree*

Last Updated: 04/01/12

DRAVIDIAN UNIVERSITY

District Chitoor, Kuppam, Andhra Pradesh 517425
Tel: +91(8570) 278-220
Fax: +91(8570) 278-230
Website: http://www.dravidianuniversity.ac.in/

Vice-Chancellor: K, Rathnaiah (2012-)
Tel: +91(8570) 278-236 EMail: kankanalarathnaiah@gmail.com

Registrar: C.Varadarajulu Naidu

School

Commerce and Management (Business and Commerce; Management); **Comparative Literature and Translation Studies** (Communication Studies; English; Indic Languages; Literature; Philosophy; Religion; South and Southeast Asian Languages; Translation and Interpretation); **Education and Human Resources Development** (Education; Human Resources; Indic Languages; Physical Education); **Herbal Studies and Natural Sciences** (Biotechnology; Chemistry; Environmental Studies; Molecular Biology; Traditional Eastern Medicine); **Human and Social Sciences** (Archaeology; History; Indigenous Studies; Philosophy; Religion); **Information Sciences and Technology** (Computer Science; Information Sciences; Library Science; Technology)

History: Founded 1997.

Academic Year: July to June.

Main Language(s) of Instruction: English. Telugu, Tamil, Kannada and Malayalam.

Degrees and Diplomas: *Bachelor's Degree*; *Master's Degree*; *Master of Philosophy*

Publications: Dravidian Studies

Last Updated: 13/09/12

DR. B. R. AMBEDKAR NATIONAL INSTITUTE OF TECHNOLOGY JALANDHAR

Jalandhar, Punjab 144011
Tel: +91(181) 269-0301 +91(181) 269-0302
Fax: +91(181) 269-0320 +91(181) 269-0932
EMail: admin@nitj.ac.in
Website: http://www.nitj.ac.in/

Director: S. B. Mishra EMail: director@nitj.ac.in

Registrar: A. L. Sangal

Department

Mathematics (Mathematics); **Biotechnology** (Biotechnology); **Chemical Engineering** (Chemical Engineering); **Chemistry** (Applied Chemistry; Chemistry); **Civil Engineering** (Civil Engineering); **Computer Science and Engineering** (Computer Engineering; Computer Science; Engineering); **Electronics and Communication Engineering** (Electronic Engineering; Telecommunications Engineering); **Humanities and Management** (Communication Studies; Economics; Human Resources; Industrial and Organizational Psychology; Management; Marketing; Psychology); **Industrial and Production Engineering**; **Instrumentation and Control Engineering** (Automation and Control Engineering); **Mechanical Engineering**; **Physics**; **Textile Technology** (Textile Technology)

History: Created 1986 as Dr B R Ambedkar Regional Engineering College. Acquired current title and status 2002.

Degrees and Diplomas: *Bachelor's Degree*: **Automation and Control Engineering; Chemical Engineering; Civil Engineering; Communication Arts; Computer Science; Electronic Engineering; Industrial Engineering; Instrument Making; Mechanical Engineering; Production Engineering; Textile Technology.** *Postgraduate Diploma*: **Textile Technology.** *Master's Degree*: **Chemical Engineering; Computer Science; Industrial Engineering; Mathematics; Production Engineering.** *Doctor of Philosophy*

Last Updated: 18/07/11

DR. B. R. AMBEDKAR UNIVERSITY

Paliwal Park, Agra, Uttar Pradesh 282004
Tel: +91(562) 215-2118
Fax: +91(562) 252-0051
EMail: info@dbrau.ac.in
Website: http://www.dbrau.ac.in/

Vice-Chancellor: D.N. Jauhar EMail: vc@dbrau.ac.in

Registrar: Shri A. K. Arvind EMail: registrar@dbrau.ac.in

Faculty

Arts (Arts and Humanities); **Commerce** (Business and Commerce); **Education** (Fine Arts); **Engineering** (Engineering); **Home Science** (Home Economics); **Law** (Law); **Management** (Management); **Medical Science** (Homeopathy; Medicine); **Science** (Natural Sciences)

School

Life Sciences (Biological and Life Sciences)

Institute

Basic Sciences (Botany; Chemistry; Mathematics; Natural Sciences; Physics; Zoology); **Hindi Studies and Linguistics** *(K.M.)* (Hindi; Linguistics; Russian); **Home Science** (Child Care and Development; Clothing and Sewing; Dietetics; Family Studies;

Home Economics; House Arts and Environment; Nutrition; Textile Technology); **Social Sciences** (Social Sciences; Social Work; Sociology; Statistics)

Further Information: Also Khandari campus, Chalesar Campus and Khandelwal Kothi. University has approx 500 affiliated Institutes/Colleges

History: Founded 1927 as Agra University by Act of the United Provinces legislature. Acquired current title 1996.

Academic Year: July to May

Admission Requirements: 12th year senior secondary/intermediate examination or recognized foreign equivalent

Main Language(s) of Instruction: Hindi, English

Degrees and Diplomas: *Bachelor's Degree*; *Master's Degree*; *Doctor of Philosophy*

Last Updated: 18/07/11

DR. BALASAHEB SAWANT KONKAN KRISHI VIDYPEETH

Dapoli, Maharashtra 415712
Tel: +91(2358) 282064
Fax: +91(2358) 282074
EMail: root@kkv.ren.nic.in
Website: http://www.dbskkv.org

Vice-Chancellor: Kisan E. Lawande EMail: vcbskkv@yahoo.co.in

Faculty

Agricultural Engineering (Agricultural Engineering; Agricultural Equipment; Computer Science; Soil Conservation; Water Management); **Agriculture** (Agricultural Business; Agricultural Economics; Agricultural Engineering; Agriculture; Agronomy; Animal Husbandry; Entomology; Food Science; Forestry; Horticulture; Plant Pathology); **Forestry** (Forest Biology; Forest Management; Forestry); **Horticulture** (Arts and Humanities; Floriculture; Fruit Production; Harvest Technology; Landscape Architecture; Natural Resources; Plant and Crop Protection; Vegetable Production)

College

Fisheries (Fishery)

Research Centre

Agricultural *(Regional)* (Agriculture); **Fruit** *(Regional)* (Agricultural Economics; Entomology; Fruit Production; Horticulture; Plant Pathology; Soil Science)

Further Information: Also 10 constituent Agricultural Colleges

History: Founded 1972 as Konkan Krishi Vidyapeeth. Acquired present status and title 2001.

Academic Year: July to June

Admission Requirements: Higher secondary certificate or recognized equivalent

Fees: (Rupees): 13,876-19,776

Main Language(s) of Instruction: English

Accrediting Agency: ICAR

Degrees and Diplomas: *Bachelor's Degree*; *Master's Degree*; *Doctor of Philosophy*

Student Services: Academic Counselling, Canteen, Cultural Activities, Facilities for disabled people, Health Services, Sports Facilities

Academic Staff *2010-2011*: Total 260

STAFF WITH DOCTORATE: Total 120

Student Numbers *2010-2011*: Total: c. 680

Last Updated: 18/07/11

DR. C.V. RAMAN UNIVERSITY

Kargi Road, Kota, Bilaspur, Chhattisgarh
Tel: +91(7753) 253736
Fax: +91(7753) 253728
EMail: cvruraipur@yahoo.co.in
Website: http://www.cvru.ac.in

Vice-Chancellor: A.S. Zadgaonkar

Registrar: Shailesh Pandey

Faculty

Commerce (Business and Commerce); **Education** (Education); **Engineering** (Civil Engineering; Electronic Engineering; Engineering; Information Technology; Mechanical Engineering; Telecommunications Engineering); **Information Technology and Computer ScienceComputer Science &Computer Science and Information Technology** (Computer Science; Information Technology); **Management** (Agricultural Management; Finance; Human Resources; Insurance; Management; Marketing; Retailing and Wholesaling); **Science** (Biology; Biotechnology; Botany; Chemistry; Information Sciences; Library Science; Mathematics; Microbiology; Physics; Zoology)

Degrees and Diplomas: *Bachelor's Degree*; *Master's Degree*; *Master of Philosophy*

Last Updated: 18/07/11

DR. D. Y. PATIL VIDYAPEETH

Sant Tukaram Naga, Pimpri, Pune, Maharashtra 411018
Tel: +91(20) 2742-0069
Fax: +91(20) 2742-0010
EMail: info@dpu.edu.in
Website: http://www.dpu.edu.in

Vice-Chancellor: Pushpati Nath Razdan EMail: vc@dpu.edu.in

College

Dentistry (Dentistry); **Medicine** (Medicine); **Nursing** (Nursing); **Physiotherapy** (Physical Therapy)

School

Business *(Global)* (Business Administration)

Institute

Biotechnology and Bioinformatics (Biotechnology); **Distance Learning**; **Optometry and Visual Sciences** (Optometry)

Degrees and Diplomas: *Bachelor's Degree*; *Master's Degree*; *Doctor of Philosophy*

Last Updated: 09/01/12

DR. K. N. MODI UNIVERSITY

Plot No. INS-1, RIICO Industrial Area Ph-II, Newai, Newai, Rajasthan 304021
Tel: +91(11) 2683-7275
Fax: +91(11) 4162-7930
EMail: info@dknmu.org
Website: http://www.dknmu.org

President: Francis C. Peter

Faculty

Management and Business Studies (Accountancy; Business Administration; Finance; International Business; Management; Retailing and Wholesaling); **Science, Engineering and Technology** (Automotive Engineering; Civil Engineering; Computer Science; Electrical and Electronic Engineering; Electronic Engineering; Engineering; Mechanical Engineering; Natural Sciences; Technology)

Degrees and Diplomas: *Bachelor's Degree*; *Master's Degree*; *Doctor of Philosophy*

Last Updated: 02/01/12

DR. M.G.R. EDUCATIONAL AND RESEARCH INSTITUTE (UNIVERSITY)

E.V.R. High Road (NH4 Highway), Maduravoyal, Chennai, Tamil Nadu 600095
EMail: registrar@drmgrdu.ac.in
Website: http://www.drmgrdu.ac.in

Vice-Chancellor: P. Aravindan EMail: vc@drmgrdu.ac.in

Registrar: C. B. Palanivelu

Faculty

Engineering and Technology (Automation and Control Engineering; Biotechnology; Business Administration; Chemical Engineering; Civil Engineering; Computer Engineering; Computer Science; Electrical and Electronic Engineering; Information Technology; Management; Mechanical Engineering; Production Engineering; Telecommunications Engineering); **Medicine and Dental Science**

(Dentistry; Medicine; Nursing; Physical Therapy); **Science and Humanities** (Arts and Humanities; Cooking and Catering; Food Technology; Hotel Management)

History: Founded 1988 as Dr.M.G.R. Engineering College. Acquired present status and title 2003.

Accrediting Agency: UGC, India

Degrees and Diplomas: *Post Diploma*; *Bachelor's Degree*; *Postgraduate Diploma*; *Master's Degree*; *Doctor of Philosophy*

Last Updated: 20/07/11

DR. RAM MANOHAR LOHIYA NATIONAL LAW UNIVERSITY

Sec- D1, LDA Colony, Kanpur Road Scheme,
Lucknow, Uttar Pradesh 226012
Tel: +91(522) 2425- 902
Fax: +91(522) 2422- 841
EMail: registrar@rmlnlu.ac.in
Website: http://www.rmlnlu.ac.in/

Vice-Chancellor: Balraj Chauhan

Programme

Law (Law)

History: Founded 2005.

Fees: 40,000 per annum (Indian Rupee)

Degrees and Diplomas: *Bachelor's Degree*; *Master's Degree*; *Doctor of Philosophy*

Last Updated: 04/01/12

DR. SHAKUNTALA MISRA REHABILITATION UNIVERSITY

Lucknow, Uttar Pradesh 226017
EMail: vc.dsmru@gmail.com
Website: http://dsmru.up.nic.in/

Vice-Chancellor: Nishith Rai

Registrar: SK Srivastava EMail: registrarofdsmru@gmail.com

Faculty

Arts and Music (Economics; English; Hindi; History; Political Sciences; Social Work; Sociology); **Commerce and Management** (Business Administration; Business and Commerce; Finance; Human Resources; Marketing); **Special Education** (Special Education; Speech Therapy and Audiology)

Degrees and Diplomas: *Bachelor's Degree*; *Master's Degree*

Last Updated: 04/01/12

D.Y. PATIL MEDICAL COLLEGE

Kasba Bawda, Kolhapur, Maharastra 416006
Tel: +91(231) 2601-235
Fax: +91(231) 2601-238
EMail: info@dypatilkolhapur.org
Website: http://www.dypatilunikop.org/

Vice-Chancellor: S.H. Pawar EMail: vc@dypatilunikop.org

Registrar: V. V. Bhosale
Tel: +91(231) 2601-595 EMail: registrar@dypatilunikop.org

College

Medicine (Anaesthesiology; Cell Biology; Dermatology; Gynaecology and Obstetrics; Health Sciences; Medicine; Microbiology; Ophthalmology; Orthopaedics; Paediatrics; Psychiatry and Mental Health; Radiology; Surgery); **Nursing** (Nursing); **Physiotherapy** (Physical Therapy)

Institute

Hospital Research *(Padmashree Dr. D.Y. Patil)*

History: Founded 2009.

Degrees and Diplomas: *Bachelor's Degree*; *Master's Degree*; *Doctor of Philosophy*

Last Updated: 10/01/12

EASTERN INSTITUTE FOR INTEGRATED LEARNING IN MANAGEMENT (EIILM)

District Namchi, Jorethang, Sikkim 737121
EMail: info@eiilmuniversity.ac.in
Website: http://www.eiilmuniversity.ac.in/

Vice-Chancellor: A. Sankara Reddy

Department

Arts and Commerce (Arts and Humanities; Business and Commerce); **Biotechnology and Environmental Science** (Biotechnology; Ecology; Environmental Studies); **Computer Science and Information Technology** (Computer Science; Information Technology); **Engineering** (Civil Engineering; Electronic Engineering; Engineering; Mechanical Engineering; Telecommunications Engineering); **Fashion** (Fashion Design); **Hospitality and Tourism** (Tourism); **Library Science** (Library Science); **Management** (Business Administration; Finance; Human Resources; Insurance; International Business; Management; Marketing; Retailing and Wholesaling); **Media and Communication** (Communication Studies; Media Studies)

Further Information: Also Malabassey Campus

History: Founded 2006.

Degrees and Diplomas: *Post Diploma*; *Bachelor's Degree*; *Postgraduate Diploma*; *Master's Degree*

Last Updated: 28/12/11

ETERNAL UNIVERSITY

Baru Sahib, Via Rajgarh, Distt. Sirmour,
Himachal Pradesh, Himachal Pradesh 173101
Tel: +91(1799) 276002
Fax: +91(1799) 276006
EMail: contact@eternaluniversity.org
Website: http://www.eternaluniversity.edu.in/

Vice-Chancellor: Manmohan Singh Atwal

Registrar: Davinder Singh

College

Arts and Sciences (Arts and Humanities; Natural Sciences); **Divine Music and Spiritualism** (Religious Music); **Engineering and Technology** (Engineering; Technology); **Nursing** (Nursing); **Post Graduate Studies**

School

Biotechnology (Biotechnology); **Business Administration** (Business Administration); **Chemistry** (Chemistry); **Economics** (Economics); **Nutrition and Food Technology** (Food Technology; Nutrition); **Physics** (Physics); **Public Health** (Public Health)

Institute

Applied Sciences (Natural Sciences); **Renewable Energy Research** (Energy Engineering)

Degrees and Diplomas: *Bachelor's Degree*; *Master's Degree*; *Doctor of Philosophy*

Last Updated: 14/11/11

FORE SCHOOL OF MANAGEMENT (FSM)

B-18, Qutub Institutional Area, New Delhi 110 016
Tel: +91(11) 4124-2424
Fax: +91(11) 2696-4229
EMail: admissions@fsm.ac.in; asif@fsm.ac.in
Website: http://fsm.ac.in/

Director: Jitendra K. Das EMail: fore@fsm.ac.in

Programme

International Business (International Business); **Management** (Management)

History: Founded 1981.

Accrediting Agency: All India Council for Technical Education (AICTE)

Degrees and Diplomas: *Postgraduate Diploma*

Student Services: Canteen, Sports Facilities

Last Updated: 23/01/12

FAKIR MOHAN UNIVERSITY

Vyasa Vihar, Near Remuna Golei, Balasore,
Orissa 756019
Tel: +91(6782) 261-711
Fax: +91(6782) 264-244
EMail: fmuniversity@rediffmail.com
Website: http://www.fmuniversity.nic.in

Vice-Chancellor: Kumar Bar Das (2011-)

Registrar: Sridhar Behera

Department

Applied Physics and Ballistics (Applied Physics); **Biotechnology** (Biotechnology); **Business Administration** (Business Administration); **Environmental Studies** (Environmental Studies); **Information and Communication Technology** (Information Technology); **Population Studies** (Demography and Population); **Social Science** (Social Sciences)

History: Founded 1999.

Degrees and Diplomas: *Bachelor's Degree*; *Master's Degree*
Last Updated: 20/07/11

FOREST RESEARCH INSTITUTE - DEEMED UNIVERSITY

PO New Forest, Dehradun
Uttarakhand 248006
Tel: +91(135) 275-5277
Fax: +91(135) 275-6865
EMail: negiss@icfre.org
Website: http://fri.icfre.gov.in/

Director: S.S Negi EMail: dg@icfre.org

Secretary: Sh. Piarchand EMail: sudhanshu@icfre.org

Programme

Forestry (Botany; Chemistry; Ecology; Environmental Studies; Forestry; Paper Technology; Wood Technology)

History: Founded 1906. Acquired present status and title 1991.

Fees: 5,000 per annum (Indian Rupee)

Degrees and Diplomas: *Bachelor's Degree*; *Postgraduate Diploma*; *Master's Degree*; *Doctor of Philosophy*
Last Updated: 20/07/11

FORTUNE INSTITUTE OF INTERNATIONAL BUSINESS (FIIB)

Plot 5, Rao Tula Ram Marg, Vasant Vihar,
New Delhi 110 057
Tel: +91(11) 4728-5000
Fax: +91(11) 2614-4279
EMail: fiib@fiib.edu.in
Website: http://fiib.edu.in/

Executive Director: Radhika Shrivastava

Programme

International Business (Accountancy; Business Administration; Communication Studies; Economics; Finance; Human Resources; Industrial and Organizational Psychology; Information Management; Information Technology; International Business; Management; Marketing; Operations Research)

History: Founded 1995.

Accrediting Agency: National Board of Accreditation (NBA); All India Council of Technical Education (AICTE)

Degrees and Diplomas: *Postgraduate Diploma*. Equivalence of the PGDM to a MBA

Academic Staff *2011-2012*: Total: c. 20

Student Numbers *2011-2012*: Total: c. 240
Last Updated: 09/01/12

GALGOTIAS UNIVERSITY

1, Institutional Area, Knowledge Park - 2,
Greater Noida, Uttar Pradesh 201306
EMail: info@galgotiasuniversity.edu.in
Website: http://www.galgotiasuniversity.edu.in/

Vice-Chancellor: K.N. Tripathi

School

Business (Business Administration); **Arts and Social Sciences** (Arts and Humanities; Economics; English; Fashion Design; French; Library Science; Psychology; Social Sciences; Social Work; Sociology); **Basic and Applied Sciences** (Biomedical Engineering; Chemistry; Mathematics; Natural Sciences; Physics); **Computer and Information Sciences** (Computer Science; Information Sciences); **Engineering and Technology** (Civil Engineering; Computer Engineering; Computer Science; Electrical Engineering; Electronic Engineering; Mechanical Engineering; Telecommunications Engineering); **Finance and Commerce** (Business and Commerce; Finance); **Hospitality and Tourism** (Hotel Management; Tourism); **Journalism and Mass Communication** (Journalism; Mass Communication); **Law** (Law)

History: Founded 2011.

Fees: (Indian Rupees): 52,000-128,000 per annum depending on programmes

Degrees and Diplomas: *Bachelor's Degree*; *Master's Degree*; *Doctor of Philosophy*
Last Updated: 28/12/11

GANDHIGRAM RURAL INSTITUTE - DEEMED UNIVERSITY

Dindigul District, Gandhigram, Tamil Nadu 624302
Tel: +91(451) 245-2371
Fax: +91(451) 245-3071
EMail: grucc@ruraluniv.ac.in
Website: http://www.ruraluniv.ac.in/

Vice-Chancellor: S.M. Ramasamy

Registrar: N. Narayanasamy

Faculty

Agriculture and Animal Husbandry (Agriculture; Animal Husbandry); **English and Foreign Languages** (English; Modern Languages); **Rural Development** (Adult Education; Continuing Education; Rural Studies); **Rural Health and Sanitation** (Health Sciences; Sanitary Engineering); **Rural Oriented Sciences** (Biology; Chemistry; Mathematics; Natural Sciences; Physics; Rural Studies); **Rural Social Sciences** (Administration; Economics; Peace and Disarmament; Political Sciences; Rural Planning; Rural Studies; Social Sciences; Sociology); **Tamil and Indian Languages and Rural Arts** (Indic Languages)

Centre

Computer (Computer Science); **Rural Energy Centre** (Rural Studies); **Rural Technology** (Agricultural Engineering)

History: Founded 1956. Of the 14 Rural Institutes of Higher Education started in India, this is the only one to be declared as 'Deemed University' in 1976.

Academic Year: July to April (July-November; December-April)

Admission Requirements: 12th year senior secondary/intermediate examination or recognized foreign equivalent

Main Language(s) of Instruction: English

Degrees and Diplomas: *Bachelor's Degree*; *Postgraduate Diploma*; *Master's Degree*; *Master of Philosophy*; *Doctor of Philosophy*
Last Updated: 08/08/11

GANPAT UNIVERSITY

Ganpat Vidyanagar, Goazaria Highway,
Meshana, North Gujarat 382711
Tel: +91(2762) 286-080
EMail: info@ganpatuniversity.ac.in
Website: http://www.ganpatuniversity.ac.in

President: Anilbhai T. Patel

Registrar: Amit Patel

College

Engineering (Computer Engineering; Engineering; Mechanical Engineering); **Management Studies** *(V.M.Patel)* (Management); **Pharmacy** (Pharmacy)

Department
Education (Education)

Institute
Bioscience *(Mehsana)* (Biotechnology; Microbiology); **Computer Science** (Computer Science); **Management** *(V.M.Patel)* (Business Administration; Management)

Centre
Management Studies (Management)

History: Founded 2005.

Degrees and Diplomas: *Bachelor's Degree*; *Master's Degree*; *Master of Philosophy*

Student Services: Canteen

Last Updated: 08/08/11

GAUHATI UNIVERSITY

Gopinath Bardoloi Nagar, Quarter No. 39, Guwahati, Assam 781014
Tel: +91(361) 257-0415
Fax: +91(361) 257-0311
EMail: vc@gauhati.ac.in
Website: http://www.gauhati.ac.in

Vice-Chancellor: Okhil Kumar Mehdi Tel: +91(361) 257-0412

Registrar: Uttam Chandra Das EMail: registrar@gauhati.ac.in

Faculty
Arts (Arabic; Arts and Humanities; Communication Studies; English; Foreign Languages Education; French; Hindi; History; Indic Languages; Information Sciences; Journalism; Library Science; Linguistics; Mass Communication; Modern Languages; Persian; Psychology; Sanskrit; Women's Studies); **Business Administration** (Business Administration); **Commerce** (Business and Commerce); **Engineering** (Engineering); **Fine Arts** (Fine Arts); **Law** (Law); **Management** (Economics; Management); **Medicine** *(Regional Dental College, Guwahati)* (Medicine); **Science** (Anthropology; Biotechnology; Botany; Computer Science; Electronic Engineering; Environmental Studies; Geography; Mathematics; Natural Sciences; Physics; Telecommunications Engineering; Zoology); **Technology** (Technology)

College
Law (Law)

Centre
Women's Study Research

Further Information: Also 1 Constituent and 201 Affiliated Colleges

History: Founded 1948.

Academic Year: June to May

Admission Requirements: 12th year senior secondary/intermediate examination or recognized foreign equivalent

Main Language(s) of Instruction: English

Degrees and Diplomas: *Post Diploma*; *Bachelor's Degree*: **Business and Commerce; Engineering; Fine Arts; Law.** *Master's Degree*; *Master of Philosophy*; *Doctor of Philosophy*

Publications: Arts and Science

Publishing House: University Press

Last Updated: 25/07/11

GAUTAM BUDDH TECHNICAL UNIVERSITY (GBTU)

Institute of Engineering and Technology Campus, Sitapur Road, Lucknow, Uttar Pradesh 226 021
Tel: +91(522) 273-2376 +91(522) 273-2193
Fax: +91(522) 273-2185
EMail: registrar@uptu.ac.in
Website: http://www.uptu.ac.in/

Vice-Chancellor: Kripa Shanker
Tel: +91(522) 273-2194 EMail: vc@uptu.ac.in

Registrar: U.S. Tomer
Tel: +91(522) 2732193 EMail: ustomer@uptu.nic.in

Faculty
Architecture (Architecture; Architecture and Planning; Building Technologies; Construction Engineering; Interior Design)

Programme
Agricultural Engineering (Agricultural Engineering); **Hotel Management and Catering Technology** (Cooking and Catering; Hotel and Restaurant; Hotel Management); **Pharmacology** (Pharmacology)

Institute
Engineering and Technology *(Lucknow, IET)* (Applied Chemistry; Arts and Humanities; Biotechnology; Business Administration; Chemical Engineering; Civil Engineering; Computer Engineering; Computer Science; Electrical Engineering; Electronic Engineering; Engineering; Mechanical Engineering; Technology)

Further Information: Also 238 affiliated colleges/institutions

History: Founded 2000 as Uttar Pradesh Technical University. Acquired present title 2010.

Academic Year: July to June

Admission Requirements: undergraduate programs, 10+2; graduate programs, graduation in relevant field; State entrance examination test

Fees: (Rupees): maximum of 50,000 per annum

Main Language(s) of Instruction: English

Accrediting Agency: All India Council for Technical Education (AICTE)

Degrees and Diplomas: *Bachelor's Degree*; *Bachelor's Degree (professional)*; *Master's Degree*; *Doctor of Philosophy*. Also MBA

Student Services: Academic Counselling, Careers Guidance

Publications: Technical Tribune

Last Updated: 29/11/11

GAUTAM BUDDHA UNIVERSITY

Yammuna Expressway, Greater Noida,
Gautam Budh Nagar, Uttar Pradesh 201308
Tel: +91(120) 2344-200
Website: http://www.gbu.ac.in/

Vice-Chancellor: S.R. Lakha

School
Biotechnology (Biotechnology); **Buddhist Studies and Civilization** (Asian Religious Studies); **Engineering** (Civil Engineering; Electrical Engineering; Mechanical Engineering); **Humanities and Social Sciences** (Arts and Humanities; Development Studies; Education; Social Sciences; Social Work); **Information and Communication Technology** (Information Technology; Telecommunications Engineering); **Law, Justice and Governance** (Government; Law); **Management** (Business Administration; Management)

Degrees and Diplomas: *Bachelor's Degree*; *Master's Degree*; *Doctor of Philosophy*

Last Updated: 18/01/12

GITAM UNIVERSITY

Gandhi Nagar, Rushikonda,
Visakhapatnam, Andhra Pradesh 530 045
Tel: +91(891) 279-0101
EMail: gitam@gitam.edu
Website: http://www.gitam.edu

Vice-Chancellor: G. Subrahmanyam

Registrar: Potharaju

College
Dental Sciences (Dentistry)

School
Architecture (Architecture); **Business** *(Hyderabad)* (Business Administration)

Institute
International Business (International Business); **Management** (Business Administration; Human Resources; Management); **Pharmacy** (Pharmacy); **Science** (Applied Mathematics; Biochemistry; Biotechnology; Chemistry; Computer Science; Electronic Engineering; Environmental Studies; Microbiology; Physics); **Technology** (Biotechnology; Chemistry; Civil Engineering; Computer Science; Construction Engineering; Electrical and Electronic

Engineering; English; Industrial Engineering; Information Technology; Mechanical Engineering; Physics; Technology)

History: Founded 1980 as Gandhi Institute of Technology and Management (GITAM). Acquired present status 2007.

Degrees and Diplomas: *Bachelor's Degree*; *Postgraduate Diploma*; *Master's Degree*; *Doctor of Philosophy*
Last Updated: 25/07/11

GLA UNIVERSITY

17km Stone, NH-2, Mathura-Delhi Road,
P.O. Chaumuhan, Mathura, Uttar Pradesh 281406
Tel: +91(5662) 250900
Fax: +91(5662) 241687
EMail: glauniversity@gla.ac.in
Website: http://www.gla.ac.in/

Vice-Chancellor: Jai Prakash

Institute

Applied Science and Humanities (Arts and Humanities; Natural Sciences); **Business Management** (Business Administration; Management); **Engineering and Technology** (Civil Engineering; Computer Engineering; Electrical Engineering; Engineering; Mechanical Engineering; Technology); **Pharmaceutical Research** (Pharmacy)

History: Founded 2010.

Fees: (Indian Rupees): 62,000-126,000 per annum depending on programmes

Degrees and Diplomas: *Bachelor's Degree*; *Master's Degree*; *Doctor of Philosophy*
Last Updated: 28/12/11

GOA INSTITUTE OF MANAGEMENT (GIM)

Ribandar, Goa 403 006
Tel: +91(832) 249-0300
Fax: +91(832) 244-4136
EMail: admin@gim.ac.in; director@gim.ac.in
Website: http://www.gim.ac.in/

Director: P.F.X D'Lima EMail: director@gim.ac.in

Administrator: Steve Fernandes EMail: steve@gim.ac.in

Programme

Corporate Studies; **Management** (Management); **Management Development** (Management)

Accrediting Agency: All India Council of Technical Education of the Government of India (AICTE); National Board of Accreditation (NBA)

Degrees and Diplomas: *Postgraduate Diploma*. Also Part-time Executive MBA
Last Updated: 23/01/12

GOA UNIVERSITY

Taleigao Plateau, Goa 403206
Tel: +91(832) 245-1345 +91(832) 245-6480
Fax: +91(832) 245-1184 +91(832) 245-2889
EMail: registrar@unigoa.ac.in
Website: http://www.unigoa.ac.in/

Vice-Chancellor: Dileep N. Deobagkar
Tel: +91(832) 245-1576 EMail: vc@unigoa.ac.in

Registrar: Vijayendra P. Kamat
Tel: +91(832) 651-9005 EMail: registrar@unigoa.ac.in

Faculty

Commerce (Business and Commerce); **Design** (Design); **Education** (Education); **Engineering** (Architecture; Civil Engineering; Computer Engineering; Electrical Engineering; Electronic Engineering; Engineering; Industrial Engineering; Mechanical Engineering; Technology; Telecommunications Engineering); **Languages and Literature** (English; French; Indic Languages; Literature; Modern Languages; Portuguese); **Law** (Law); **Life Sciences and Environment** (Biological and Life Sciences; Biotechnology; Botany; Marine Science and Oceanography; Microbiology; Zoology); **Management Studies** (Management); **Medicine, Dentistry, Pharmacy and Ayurvedic Medicine** (Ayurveda; Dentistry; Homeopathy; Medicine; Pharmacy); **Natural Sciences** (Chemistry; Computer Science; Earth Sciences; Electronic Engineering; Mathematics; Natural Sciences; Physics; Technology); **Performing, Fine Arts and Music** (Aesthetics; Fine Arts; Music; Painting and Drawing; Performing Arts); **Social Sciences** (Economics; History; Latin American Studies; Philosophy; Political Sciences; Social Sciences; Sociology; Women's Studies)

Institute

Antarctic and Ocean Research *(National Centre, NCAOR)* (Marine Science and Oceanography); **Archives** (Archiving); **Konkani Kendra** *(Thomas Stephens)* (Environmental Studies; Occupational Health); **Local Self Government** *(All India)*; **Oceanography** *(National Institute)* (Marine Science and Oceanography); **Psychiatry and Human Behaviour** (Behavioural Sciences; Psychiatry and Mental Health)

Centre

Historical Research (History); **Latin American Studies** (Caribbean Studies; Latin American Studies); **Malaria Research**

Further Information: Also 46 Affiliated Colleges and 8 Recognized Postgraduate Institutions

History: Founded 1985. All Colleges in Goa (previously affiliated to Bombay) were affiliated with the University 1986.

Academic Year: June to March/April (June-October; November-March/April)

Admission Requirements: 12th year senior secondary/intermediate examination or recognized foreign equivalent

Main Language(s) of Instruction: English

Accrediting Agency: University Grants Commission; National Assessment and Accreditation Council

Degrees and Diplomas: *Bachelor's Degree*: **Architecture; Ayurveda; Business Administration; Business and Commerce; Dentistry; Education; Engineering; Fine Arts; Homeopathy; Law; Medicine; Music; Naval Architecture; Pharmacy; Surgery.** *Postgraduate Diploma*: **Computer Engineering; Management.** *Master's Degree*: **Business Administration; Business and Commerce; Computer Engineering; Dentistry; Education; Fine Arts; Industrial Engineering; Marine Science and Oceanography; Pharmacy; Philosophy; Surgery.** *Doctor of Philosophy*: **Medicine.**

Student Services: Academic Counselling, Canteen, Careers Guidance, Health Services, Language Laboratory, Social Counselling, Sports Facilities
Last Updated: 25/07/11

GOKHALE INSTITUTE OF POLITICS AND ECONOMICS

BMCC Road, DECCAN Gymkhana, Pune,
Maharashtra 411004
Tel: +91(20) 2565-0287
Fax: +91(20) 2565-2579
EMail: gokhaleinstitute@gipe.ac.in
Website: http://www.gipe.ac.in/

Director: Rajas Parchure

Programme

Economics (Economics); **Political Sciences** (Political Sciences)

History: Founded 1930. Acquired 'Deemed University' status 1993.

Main Language(s) of Instruction: English

Accrediting Agency: National Assessment and Accreditation Council (NAAC)

Degrees and Diplomas: *Master's Degree*; *Doctor of Philosophy*

Student Services: Academic Counselling, Careers Guidance, Facilities for disabled people, Health Services

Publications: Arth Vijnana
Last Updated: 08/08/11

GOVIND BALLABH PANT UNIVERSITY OF AGRICULTURE AND TECHNOLOGY

Govind Ballabh Pant Krishi Evam Praudyogik Vishwavidyalaya

District Udham Singh Nagar, Pantnagar, Uttarakhand 263145
Tel: +91(5944) 233-333 +91(5944) 233-663
Fax: +91(5944) 233-500
EMail: mail@gbpuat.ac.in
Website: http://www.gbpuat.ac.in

Vice-Chancellor: B.S. Bisht EMail: vcgbpuat@gmail.com

Registrar: J. Kumar
Tel: +91(5944) 233-640
EMail: registrar_pantversity@rediffmail.com

Faculty

Agribusiness Management (Agricultural Business; Agricultural Management; Finance; Human Resources; Marketing); **Agriculture** (Agricultural Economics; Agriculture; Agronomy; Entomology; Food Science; Food Technology; Horticulture; Meteorology; Plant Pathology; Soil Science); **Basic Sciences and Humanities** (Arts and Humanities; Biochemistry; Biological and Life Sciences; Chemistry; Computer Science; Environmental Studies; Genetics; Mathematics; Microbiology; Molecular Biology; Physics; Social Sciences; Statistics); **Fisheries** (Aquaculture; Fishery; Food Science; Food Technology); **Forestry and Hill Agriculture** (Agriculture; Biological and Life Sciences; Crop Production; Forestry; Horticulture; Social Sciences; Water Management); **Home Science** (Child Care and Development; Clothing and Sewing; Family Studies; Home Economics; Nutrition; Textile Technology); **Horticulture** *(VSCG College - Bharsar)* (Horticulture; Natural Resources); **Postgraguate Studies**; **Technology** (Agricultural Engineering; Agricultural Equipment; Civil Engineering; Computer Engineering; Electrical Engineering; Electronic Engineering; Mechanical Engineering; Power Engineering; Production Engineering; Soil Conservation; Technology; Telecommunications Engineering; Water Science); **Veterinary and Animal Sciences** (Animal Husbandry; Veterinary Science)

History: Founded 1960 as Uttar Pradesh Agricultural University, acquired present title 1974. The University, based on the pattern of the Land Grant Colleges of the USA and set up in collaboration with Illinois University, aims to bring the results of science nearer to the farmer and to stimulate the adoption of new methods and techniques as a means of achieving greater prosperity for the rural population and the country as a whole.

Academic Year: July to June

Admission Requirements: 12th year senior secondary/intermediate examination or recognized foreign equivalent

Main Language(s) of Instruction: English, Hindi

Degrees and Diplomas: *Post Diploma*; *Bachelor's Degree*; *Master's Degree*; *Doctor of Philosophy*

Student Services: Academic Counselling, Canteen, Careers Guidance, Cultural Activities, Facilities for disabled people, Foreign Studies Centre, Health Services, Language Laboratory, Nursery Care, Social Counselling, Sports Facilities

Publications: Indian Farmers Digest (English); Kisan Bharàti (Hindi)

Publishing House: University Press

GRAPHIC ERA UNIVERSITY

600, Bell Road, Clement Town, Dehradun, Uttarakhand 248002
EMail: enquiry@geu.ac.in
Website: http://www.geu.ac.in/

Vice-Chancellor (Acting): V.K. Tewari

Faculty

Applied Sciences (Biochemistry; Biotechnology; Computer Science; Forensic Medicine and Dentistry; Information Technology; Microbiology); **Computer Application** (Computer Engineering; Computer Science); **Engineering** (Civil Engineering; Computer Science; Electrical and Electronic Engineering; Engineering; Information Technology; Mechanical Engineering; Telecommunications Engineering); **Hospitality Management** (Hotel Management; Tourism); **Humanities and Social Science** (Arts and Humanities; Graphic Design; Journalism; Mass Communication; Social Sciences); **Management** (Business Administration; Management)

Further Information: Also campus at Garhwal Region

History: Founded 2008.

Last Updated: 02/01/12

GUJARAT AYURVED UNIVERSITY

Chanakya Bhavan, Irwin Hospital Road, Jamnagar, Gujarat 361008
Tel: +91(288) 267-6854
Fax: +91(288) 255-5966
EMail: info@ayurveduniversity.com
Website: http://www.ayurveduniversity.com

Vice-Chancellor: Medhavi Lal Sharma Tel: +91(288) 267-7324

Registrar: Rajendrasinh N. Jhala
EMail: registrar@ayurveduniversity.com

Faculty

Ayurved (Ayurveda); **Medicinal Plants** (Traditional Eastern Medicine); **Pharmaceutical Sciences** (Pharmacology)

College

Ayurved *(Shri Gulabkunverba)* (Ayurveda)

Programme

Rural Health (Health Sciences)

Institute

Ayurvedic Pharmaceutical Sciences (Ayurveda); **Medicinal Plant Sciences** (Alternative Medicine); **Naturopathy, Yoga Education and Research** *(Maharishi Patanjali)* (Alternative Medicine; Yoga); **Post-Graduate Teaching and Research in Ayurveda** (Ayurveda)

Centre

Ayurvedic Studies *(International)* (Ayurveda)

Further Information: Also 2 Constituent and 8 Affiliated Colleges, and 2 Teaching Hospitals

History: Founded 1965.

Academic Year: July to June

Admission Requirements: 12th year senior secondary/intermediate examination or recognized foreign equivalent

Fees: (Rupees): 250 per annum; foreign students, (US Dollars): 3,600

Main Language(s) of Instruction: English, Sanskrit, Hindi, Gujarati

Degrees and Diplomas: *Bachelor's Degree*; *Master's Degree*; *Doctor of Philosophy*. Also Diploma and Certificate courses

Student Services: Academic Counselling, Canteen, Cultural Activities, Facilities for disabled people, Health Services, Language Laboratory, Nursery Care, Social Counselling, Sports Facilities

Publications: GAU News Monthly

Last Updated: 09/08/11

GUJARAT FORENSIC SCIENCES UNIVERSITY

DFS Head Quarters, Sector 18-A, Near Police Bhavan, Gandhinagar, Gujarat 382007
Tel: +91(79) 6573-5502
Fax: +91(79) 2325-6251
EMail: pro@gfsu.edu.in
Website: http://www.gfsu.edu.in/

Director-General: J. M. Vyas EMail: dg@gfsu.edu.in

Institute

Behavioural Science (Clinical Psychology; Law; Neurosciences); **Forensic Sciences** (Forensic Medicine and Dentistry); **Research and Development** (Computer Engineering)

History: Founded 2008.

Degrees and Diplomas: *Post Diploma*; *Bachelor's Degree*; *Master's Degree*; *Doctor of Philosophy*

Last Updated: 05/08/11

GUJARAT NATIONAL LAW UNIVERSITY (GNLU)

E-4, GIDC Electronics Estate, Sector 26,
Gandhinagar, Gujarat 382 028
Tel: +91(79) 2328-7157
Fax: +91(79) 2328-7156
EMail: contact@gnlu.ac.in
Website: http://www.gnlu.ac.in/

Director: Bimal Patel EMail: vc@gnlu.ac.in

Registrar: Jabbal Dolly

Programme

Law (Accountancy; Banking; Biotechnology; Business Administration; Economics; Environmental Studies; Finance; Forensic Medicine and Dentistry; Law; Management; Natural Sciences; Political Sciences; Social Work; Taxation)

History: Founded 2003.

Degrees and Diplomas: *Bachelor's Degree*: **Law.** *Master's Degree*: **Law.** *Doctor of Philosophy*: **Law.**

Last Updated: 05/08/11

GUJARAT TECHNOLOGICAL UNIVERSITY

JACPC Building, Navranpura, Ahmedabad, Gujarat
Tel: +91(79) 2630-0499
Fax: +91(79) 2630-1500
EMail: info@gtu.ac.in
Website: http://www.gtu.ac.in

Vice-Chancellor: Akshai Aggarwal

Programme

Business Administration (Business Administration); **Engineering** (Engineering); **Hotel Management** (Hotel Management); **Pharmacy** (Pharmacy)

History: Founded 2007.

Degrees and Diplomas: *Post Diploma*; *Bachelor's Degree*; *Master's Degree*; *Doctor of Philosophy*

Last Updated: 05/08/11

GUJARAT UNIVERSITY

Navrangpura, Ahmedabad, Gujarat 380009
Tel: +91(79) 2630-1341 +91(79) 2630-1342
Fax: +91(79) 2630-2654
Website: http://www.gujaratuniversity.org.in

Vice-Chancellor: Parimal H. Trivedi

Registrar: M.S. Shah

Faculty

Arts (Computer Science); **Commerce** (Business and Commerce); **Dentistry** (Dentistry); **Education** (Education); **Engineering and Technology** (Engineering; Technology); **Law**; **Medicine** (Medicine; Surgery); **Nursing and Physiotherapy** (Nursing); **Pharmacy** (Pharmacy); **Science**

School

Business Management *(Dr Biharlal Kanaiyalal)* (Business Administration; Management); **Commerce** *(Sheth Damodardas)* (Business and Commerce); **Languages** (English; Indic Languages; Linguistics; Sanskrit; Urdu); **Law** (Law); **Philosophy, Education and Psychology** (Education; Philosophy; Psychology); **Sciences** (Biochemistry; Biological and Life Sciences; Biomedicine; Botany; Chemistry; Computer Science; Environmental Studies; Geography; Geology; Mathematics; Microbiology; Natural Sciences; Physics; Statistics; Zoology); **Social Sciences** (Economics; History; Political Sciences; Social Sciences; Sociology)

Department

Library and Information Science (Information Sciences; Library Science)

Centre

Computer Studies *(Rollwala)*

Further Information: Also 151 Affiliated Colleges and 10 Recognized Institutes. Student Exchange Programme with Japan

History: Founded 1949.

Academic Year: June to April (June-October; November-April)

Admission Requirements: Higher Secondary Certificate (HSC) or equivalent.

Fees: (Rupees): 465-6,000 per annum

Main Language(s) of Instruction: Gujarati, English and/or Hindi

Degrees and Diplomas: *Bachelor's Degree*: **Business Administration; Business and Commerce; Education; Engineering; Fine Arts; Law; Medicine; Nursing; Pharmacy; Surgery.** *Master's Degree*; *Doctor of Philosophy*. Also undergraduate and postgraduate Diplomas.

Student Services: Canteen, Careers Guidance, Cultural Activities, Health Services, Nursery Care, Social Counselling, Sports Facilities

Publishing house: Gujarat University Press

Last Updated: 09/08/11

GUJARAT VIDYAPITH

Near Income Tax Office, Ashram Road,
Ahmedabad, Gujarat 380014
Tel: +91(79) 2754-1148 +91(79) 2754-0746
Fax: +91(79) 2754-2547
EMail: registrar@gujaratvidyapith.org
Website: http://www.gujaratvidyapith.org

Vice-Chancellor: Sudarshan Iyengar
Tel: +91(79) 2754-1392 EMail: vc@gujaratvidyapith.org

Registrar: Rajendra Khimani Tel: +91(79) 754-6767

International Relations: Rajendra Khimani

Faculty

Social Sciences, Arts and Humanities *(Mahadev Desai Samajseva Mahavidyalaya)* (Anthropology; Archiving; Arts and Humanities; Computer Science; Journalism; Library Science; Mass Communication; Peace and Disarmament; Philosophy; Rural Studies; Social Sciences; Social Work)

College

Biogas Research and Microbiology (Microbiology); **Education** *(Shikshan Mahavidyalaya)* (Education); **Hindi Teacher's Training** *(Hindi Shikshak Mahavidyalaya)* (Hindi; Teacher Training); **Physical Education** (Physical Education); **Social Sciences** (Anthropology; Computer Science; Cultural Studies; Ethnology; History; Indic Languages; Journalism; Library Science; Mass Communication; Philosophy; Rural Studies; Social Work); **Teacher Training** (Teacher Training)

Centre

Adult Education *(State Resource)* (Education); **Adult Education, Continuing Education and Extension Work**; **Computer Science** *(Postgraduate)* (Computer Science); **Rural Management Studies** *(Postgraduate, Randheja)* (Rural Studies); **Studies in Peace Research** *(Ahimsa)* (Peace and Disarmament; Philosophy); **Tribal Research and Training** (Indigenous Studies)

Further Information: Also Centre on Indian Culture and Gandhian Thought for foreign students (October to December)

History: Founded 1920 by Mahatma Gandhi.

Academic Year: June to April

Admission Requirements: 12th year senior secondary/intermediate examination or recognized foreign equivalent

Fees: (Rupees): 3,000-5,000 per annum

Main Language(s) of Instruction: Gujarati, Hindi

Degrees and Diplomas: *Bachelor's Degree*: **Education; Library Science.** *Master's Degree*: **Business Computing; Education; Fine Arts; Journalism; Library Science; Mass Communication; Rural Studies; Social Work.** *Master of Philosophy*; *Doctor of Philosophy*

Student Services: Academic Counselling, Canteen, Careers Guidance, Cultural Activities, Foreign Studies Centre, Health Services, Language Laboratory, Nursery Care, Social Counselling, Sports Facilities

Publications: Vidyapith

Publishing House: Navjivan Publishing House

Last Updated: 10/08/11

GULBARGA UNIVERSITY

Jnana Ganga, Gulbarga, Karnataka 585106
Tel: +91(8472) 245-446
Fax: +91(8472) 245-632
Website: http://www.gulbargauniversity.kar.nic.in

Vice-Chancellor: E.T. Puttaiah
Tel: +91(8472) 245-447 EMail: vcgug@rediffmail.com

Registrar: S. Rajanna

Faculty

Arts (Arts and Humanities; English; Fine Arts; Indic Languages; Persian; Sanskrit; Urdu); **Commerce and Management** (Business Administration; Business and Commerce; Management); **Education** (Education; Educational Administration; Educational Psychology; Educational Sciences; Educational Technology; Physical Education; Teacher Training); **Law** (Commercial Law; Human Rights; Law); **Science and Technology** (Biochemistry; Biological and Life Sciences; Biotechnology; Botany; Chemistry; Earth Sciences; Environmental Engineering; Industrial Chemistry; Instrument Making; Materials Engineering; Mathematics and Computer Science; Natural Sciences; Physics; Statistics; Technology; Zoology); **Social Sciences** (Communication Studies; Demography and Population; Economics; History; Information Sciences; International Studies; Library Science; Political Sciences; Psychology; Social Sciences; Sociology; Women's Studies)

Further Information: Also 200 Affiliated Colleges

History: Founded 1980.

Academic Year: June to May

Admission Requirements: 12th year senior secondary/intermediate examination or recognized foreign equivalent for undergraduate courses. Graduation for Master programs. Postgraduation PhD courses.

Main Language(s) of Instruction: English, Kannada

Accrediting Agency: National Assessment and Accreditation Council, Bangalore

Degrees and Diplomas: *Bachelor's Degree*; *Master's Degree*; *Master of Philosophy*; *Doctor of Philosophy*

Student Services: Academic Counselling, Canteen, Careers Guidance, Cultural Activities, Health Services, Language Laboratory, Sports Facilities

Publications: Kalaganga, Jnanaganga, Vijnanaganga

Last Updated: 10/08/11

GURU ANGAD DEV VETERINARY AND ANIMAL SCIENCES UNIVERSITY

Ludhiana, Punjab 141004
Tel: +91(161) 255-3342
EMail: registrar@gadvasu.in
Website: http://www.gadvasu.in/

Vice-Chancellor: Vijay Kumar Taneja (2006-)

Registrar: Prayag Dutt Juyal

College

Dairy Science and Technology (Dairy; Food Technology); **Fisheries** (Fishery); **Veterinary Science** (Veterinary Science)

Programme

Veterinary Polytechnic *(Kaljharani)* (Veterinary Science)

School

Animal Biothechnology *(Post-Graduate Institute of Veterinary Educatioan and Research (PGIVER))* (Veterinary Science)

History: Founded 2005.

Degrees and Diplomas: *Bachelor's Degree*; *Master's Degree*; *Doctor of Philosophy*

Student Services: Canteen, Nursery Care, Sports Facilities

Last Updated: 06/12/11

GURU GHASIDAS VISHWAVIDYALAYA

Bilaspur, Chhattisgarh 495009
Tel: +91(7752) 260-209
Fax: +91(7752) 260-148
EMail: registrarggu@gmail.com
Website: http://www.ggu.ac.in/

Vice-Chancellor: Lakshman Chaturvedi (2009-)
Tel: +91(7752) 260-283 EMail: laksh44@rediffmail.com

Registrar: M.S.K. Khokhar

Department

Adult and Continuing Education; **Anthropology and Tribal Development** (Anthropology; Development Studies; Indigenous Studies); **Biotechnology** (Biotechnology); **Botany** (Botany); **Chemistry** (Chemistry); **Commerce** (Business and Commerce); **Computer Science and IT** (Computer Science; Information Technology); **Distance Education**; **Economics** (Economics); **Education** (Education); **English** (English); **Forestry, Wildlife, Environmental Science** (Environmental Studies; Forest Products; Wildlife); **Hindi** (Hindi); **History** (History); **Information Technology** (Information Technology); **Journalism and Mass Communication** (Journalism; Mass Communication); **Library and Information Sciences** (Information Sciences; Library Science); **Management Studies** (Business and Commerce; Management); **Pharmacy** (Pharmacy); **Physical Education** (Physical Education); **Political Science and Public Administration** (Political Sciences; Public Administration); **Pure and Applied Mathematics** (Applied Mathematics; Mathematics); **Pure and Applied Physics** (Applied Physics; Physics); **Rural Technology** (Forestry; Rural Studies); **Social Work** (Social Work)

Institute

Technology (Technology)

Further Information: Also 154 Affiliated Colleges

History: Founded 1983 as Guru Ghasidas University (State University), acquired present title and status (Central University) 2009.

Academic Year: July to June

Admission Requirements: 12th year senior secondary/intermediate examination or recognized foreign equivalent

Main Language(s) of Instruction: Hindi, English

Accrediting Agency: National Assessment and Accreditation Council (NAAC)

Degrees and Diplomas: *Bachelor's Degree*; *Postgraduate Diploma*; *Master's Degree*; *Doctor of Philosophy*

Student Services: Academic Counselling, Canteen, Careers Guidance, Cultural Activities, Facilities for disabled people, Health Services, Language Laboratory, Social Counselling, Sports Facilities

Publications: Chhattisgarh Journal of Science and Technology; Focus; GGU Journal of Business

Academic Staff *2010-2011*	**TOTAL**
FULL-TIME	**90**
PART-TIME	**75**
STAFF WITH DOCTORATE	
FULL-TIME	c. **60**
Student Numbers *2010-2011*	
All (Foreign included)	c. **13,510**

Last Updated: 11/08/11

GURU GOBIND SINGH INDRAPRASTHA UNIVERSITY

Old Delhi College of Engineering Campus, Kashmere Gate, New Delhi 110006
Tel: +91(11) 2386-9313
Fax: +91(11) 2386-5941
EMail: mail@ipu.edu
Website: http://www.ipu.ac.in

Vice-Chancellor: Dilip K. Bandyopadhyay (2008-)

Registrar: B. P. Joshi

School
Architecture and Planning (Architecture; Architecture and Planning); **Basic and Applied Sciences** (Natural Sciences); **Biotechnology** (Biotechnology); **Chemical Technology**; **Education** (Education); **Engineering and Technology** (Engineering; Technology); **Environmental Management** (Environmental Management); **Humanities and Social Sciences** (Arts and Humanities; Social Sciences); **Information Technology** (Information Technology); **Law and Legal Studies** (Law); **Management Studies** (Management); **Mass Communication** (Mass Communication); **Medicine and Paramedical Health Sciences** (Health Sciences; Medicine; Paramedical Sciences)

Institute
Technology (Technology)

Centre
Disaster Management Studies; **IT Services and Infrastructure Management** (Information Technology)

History: Founded 1998.

Fees: (Rupees): 2,400 per annum

Degrees and Diplomas: *Bachelor's Degree*; *Master's Degree*
Last Updated: 11/08/11

GURU JAMBESHWAR UNIVERSITY (GJUST)

Hisar, Haryana 125001
Tel: +91(1622) 276-025
Fax: +91(1662) 276-240
EMail: gju_tech@yahoo.com
Website: http://www.gjust.ac.in/

Vice-Chancellor: M.L. Ranga
EMail: vc_gju@yahoo.co.in

Registrar: R. S. Jaglan
EMail: registrar_gju@rediffmail.com

International Relations: H. L. Verma
Tel: +9(11662) 263-101
EMail: verma_hl@yahoo.com

Faculty
Engineering and Technology (Biomedical Engineering; Computer Engineering; Computer Science; Electrical and Electronic Engineering; Engineering; Mechanical Engineering; Printing and Printmaking; Telecommunications Engineering); **Environmental and Bio Sciences and Technology** (Biological and Life Sciences; Environmental Engineering; Environmental Studies; Food Technology; Nanotechnology; Technology); **Media Studies** (Advertising and Publicity; Communication Studies; Media Studies; Public Relations); **Medicall Sciences** (Pharmacology; Physical Therapy; Psychology); **Physical Sciences** (Applied Physics; Chemistry; Mathematics)

School
Business *(Haryana)* (Business Administration)

Institute
Religious Studies *(Guru Jambheshwar)* (Asian Religious Studies)

History: Founded 1995.

Fees: (Rupees): 1,800-3,000 per annum

Accrediting Agency: National Assessment and Accreditation Council (NAAC)

Degrees and Diplomas: *Bachelor's Degree*; *Postgraduate Diploma*; *Master's Degree*. Also Diploma and Certificate courses; MBA
Last Updated: 14/11/11

GURU NANAK DEV UNIVERSITY (GNDU)

Amritsar, Punjab 143005
Tel: +91(183) 225-8855
Fax: +91(183) 225-8819
Website: http://www.gndu.ac.in

Vice-Chancellor: Ajaib Singh Brar (2009-)
Tel: +91(183) 225-8811 EMail: vc@gndu.ac.in

Registrar: Inderjit Singh
Tel: +91(183) 225-8855 EMail: reg_gndu@yahoo.com

International Relations: K.S. Kahlon Tel: +91(183) 225-8831

Faculty
Applied Sciences (Applied Chemistry; Food Science; Pharmacy; Textile Technology); **Arts and Social Sciences** (Arts and Humanities; History; Information Sciences; Library Science; Political Sciences; Psychology; Social Sciences); **Economics and Business** (Business Administration; Business and Commerce; Economics); **Engineering and Technology** (Computer Engineering; Electronic Engineering; Engineering; Technology); **Humanities and Religious Studies** (Arts and Humanities; Religious Studies); **Languages** (English; Foreign Languages Education; Indic Languages; Modern Languages; Sanskrit; Urdu); **Law** (Law); **Life Sciences** (Biochemistry; Biological and Life Sciences; Biotechnology; Botany; Microbiology; Molecular Biology; Zoology); **Physical Education** (Physical Education); **Physical Planning and Architecture** (Architecture; Town Planning); **Science** (Chemistry; Mathematics; Natural Sciences; Physics); **Sports Medicine and Physiotherapy** (Physical Therapy; Sports Medicine); **Visual and Performing Arts** (Music; Performing Arts; Visual Arts)

Campus
Gurdaspur *(Regional)* (Business Administration; Business and Commerce; Computer Science; Electronic Engineering; Engineering; Management); **Jalahandar** *(Regional)* (Computer Engineering; Computer Science; Electronic Engineering)

Further Information: Also 150 affiliated colleges, 3 constituent colleges, 2 regional campuses and 42 postgraduate teaching departments

History: Founded 1969 on the 500th anniversary of the birth of Guru Nanak Dev, founder of the Sikh Religion. Acquired present status 1970.

Academic Year: July to June

Admission Requirements: 12th year senior secondary/intermediate examination or recognized foreign equivalent, and entrance test

Fees: National: Undergraduate, Indian students,11,445-14,000 per annum; Postgraduate, Indian students,13,425-36,500 per annum (Indian Rupee), International: Undergraduate, foreign students, 1,000-15,000 per annum; Postgraduate, foreign students 1,000-18,000 per annum (US Dollar)

Main Language(s) of Instruction: English, Hindi, Punjabi for all courses, Urdu only for Diploma/Certificate

Accrediting Agency: National Assessment and Accreditation Council; University Grants Commission

Degrees and Diplomas: *Post Diploma*: **Business and Commerce; Computer Science; Economics; Fine Arts; Journalism; Law; Mass Communication.** *Bachelor's Degree*: **Agriculture; Arts and Humanities; Biological and Life Sciences; Business and Commerce; Education; Fine Arts; Law; Modern Languages; Music; Physical Education; Religion; Social Sciences.** *Bachelor's Degree (professional)*: **Architecture and Planning; Engineering; Technology.** *Master's Degree*: **Agriculture; Architecture and Planning; Arts and Humanities; Biological and Life Sciences; Business and Commerce; Economics; Education; Engineering; Fine Arts; Law; Modern Languages; Music; Physical Education; Religion; Social Sciences; Technology.** *Master of Philosophy*: **Hindi; History; Musical Instruments; Psychology; Religious Studies; Singing; Sociology.**

Student Services: Academic Counselling, Canteen, Careers Guidance, Cultural Activities, Facilities for disabled people, Foreign Studies Centre, Health Services, Language Laboratory, Nursery Care, Sports Facilities

Publications: Amritsar Law Journal; Guru Nanak Journal of Sociology; Indian Journal of Quantitative Economics; Journal of Management Studies; Journal of Regional History; Journal of Sikh Studies; Journal of Sports Traumatology and Allied Sports Sciences; Khoj Darpan; Personality Study and Group Behaviour; Pradhikrit; PSE Economic Analyst; Punjab Journal of English Studies; Punjab Journal of Politics; University Samachar
Last Updated: 14/11/11

GURUKUL KANGRI UNIVERSITY

Gurukula Kangri Vishwavidyalaya

PO Gurukul Kangri, Uttaranchal, Haridwar, Uttar Pradesh 249404
Tel: +91(1334) 249-013
EMail: registrargkv@yahoo.co.in
Website: http://gkvharidwar.org/

Vice-Chancellor: Swatantra Kumar
EMail: swantantrak56@yahoo.com

Registrar: A.K. Chopra

Faculty

Ayurved and Medical Science (Pharmacy); **Distance Education** (Arts and Humanities; Natural Sciences; Yoga); **Engineering and Technology** (Electrical and Electronic Engineering; Engineering; Mechanical Engineering; Technology); **Humanities** (Arts and Humanities; English); **Life Sciences** (Biological and Life Sciences; Botany; Environmental Studies; Microbiology; Zoology); **Management** (Business Administration; Economics; Finance; Management); **Oriental Studies** (Archaeology; Oriental Studies; Philosophy; Physical Education); **Science** (Natural Sciences); **Technology**

Centre

Vedic Studies (Asian Religious Studies)

Further Information: Also 2 Constituent Colleges

History: Founded 1900 to educate, through the medium of Hindi, young people of all classes, castes and creeds according to the ideals of Vedic ancient Indian culture. Modern Science subjects were added later.

Academic Year: July to June (July-November; January-May)

Admission Requirements: 12th year senior secondary/intermediate examination or recognized foreign equivalent

Fees: (Rupees): 450-13,800 per annum

Main Language(s) of Instruction: Hindi, English

Degrees and Diplomas: *Post Diploma*; *Bachelor's Degree*; *Master's Degree*; *Doctor of Philosophy*

Publications: Arya Bhatt; The Vedic Path

Last Updated: 14/11/11

HAMDARD UNIVERSITY

Jamia Hamdard

Hamdard Nagar, New Delhi 110062
Tel: +91(11) 2605-9688
Fax: +91(11) 2605-9663
EMail: inquiry@jamiahamdard.edu
Website: http://www.jamiahamdard.edu

Vice-Chancellor: G.N. Qazi (2008-)
Tel: +91(11) 2605-9688
EMail: vice-chancellor@jamiahamdard.ac.in

Registrar: Firdous Ahmad Wani
Tel: +91(11) 2605-9664 EMail: firdouswani@jamiahamdard.ac.in

Faculty

Allied Health Sciences (Occupational Therapy; Physical Therapy); **Islamic Studies and Social Sciences** (International Relations; Islamic Studies; Islamic Theology; Political Sciences; Social Sciences; Social Studies); **Management Studies and Information Technology** (Computer Science; Information Technology; Management); **Medicine (Unani)** (Alternative Medicine; Biochemistry; Hygiene; Physical Therapy; Social and Preventive Medicine; Surgery); **Nursing** (Midwifery; Nursing); **Pharmacy** (Chemistry; Pharmacology; Pharmacy); **Science** (Biochemistry; Biotechnology; Botany; Health Sciences; Natural Sciences; Toxicology)

Further Information: Also Majeedia Hospital

History: Founded 1989. An Institution with 'Deemed University' status.

Academic Year: July to May

Admission Requirements: 12th year senior secondary/intermediate examination or recognized equivalent with 50% marks in Physics, Chemistry, Biology and Mathematics

Main Language(s) of Instruction: English, Urdu

Accrediting Agency: National Assessment and Accreditation Council

Degrees and Diplomas: *Post Diploma*: **Medical Technology; Radiology; Technology; Urology.** *Bachelor's Degree*: **Computer Engineering; Occupational Therapy; Optometry; Physical Therapy.** *Master of Philosophy*: **Biochemistry; Biotechnology; Botany; Cardiology; Chemistry; Computer Engineering; Islamic Studies; Management; Medicine; Neurology; Orthopaedics; Osteopathy; Paediatrics; Pharmacology; Pharmacy; Toxicology; Traditional Eastern Medicine.** *Doctor of Philosophy*: **Biochemistry; Biotechnology; Botany; Chemistry; Computer Science; Islamic Studies; Management; Medicine; Pharmacology; Pharmacy; Toxicology.**

Student Services: Academic Counselling, Canteen, Careers Guidance, Cultural Activities, Health Services, Language Laboratory, Sports Facilities

Publications: Indian Journal for Federal Studies; Studies on History of Medicine and Science; Studies on Islam

Publishing House: Jamia Hamdard Printing Press

Last Updated: 22/11/11

HEMCHANDRACHARYA NORTH GUJARAT UNIVERSITY

PO Box 21, University Road, Patan, North Gujarat 384265
Tel: +91(2766) 230-427
Fax: +91(2766) 231-917
Website: http://www.ngu.ac.in

Vice-Chancellor: Hemixaben Rao
Tel: +91(2766) 230-456 EMail: vc@ngu.ac.in

Registrar: B. J. Rathore EMail: regi@ngu.ac.in

Faculty

Arts (Arabic; Arts and Humanities; Economics; English; History; Home Economics; Indic Languages; Information Sciences; Library Science; Military Science; Persian; Political Sciences; Psychology; Sanskrit; Sociology); **Commerce** (Accountancy; Business and Commerce; Computer Science; Economics; Secretarial Studies; Statistics); **Education** (Education); **Engineering** (Civil Engineering; Electrical Engineering; Electronic Engineering; Engineering; Mechanical Engineering; Transport and Communications); **Law** (Law); **Management** (Management); **Medicine** (Homeopathy); **Pharmacy** (Pharmacy); **Rural Studies** (Rural Studies); **Science** (Botany; Chemistry; Mathematics; Natural Sciences; Physics; Zoology)

Further Information: Also 91 Affiliated Colleges

History: Founded 1986.

Academic Year: June to May

Admission Requirements: 12th year senior secondary/intermediate examination or recognized foreign equivalent

Fees: (Rupees): 400-3,000 per annum

Main Language(s) of Instruction: English

Degrees and Diplomas: *Bachelor's Degree*: **Business and Commerce; Education; Engineering; Fine Arts; Homeopathy.** *Master's Degree*: **Business and Commerce; Education; Fine Arts.** *Doctor of Philosophy*: **Business and Commerce; Education; Fine Arts; Law; Pharmacy.** Also Diploma and Postgraduate Diploma courses

Publications: Anarta; Udeechya; Uttara

Last Updated: 09/03/11

HEMWATI NANDAN BAHUGUNA GARHWAL UNIVERSITY

District Pauri Garhwal, Srinagar, Uttarakhand 246174
Tel: +91(1346) 252-143
Fax: +91(1346) 252-247
EMail: registrar.hnbgu@gmail.com
Website: http://hnbgu.ac.in/

Vice-Chancellor: S.K. Singh EMail: vc@hnbgugrw.ren.nic.in

Registrar: U.S. Rawat

School

Agriculture and Allied Science (Agriculture; Crop Production; Forestry; Horticulture; Rural Studies); **Arts, Communication and Languages** (Arts and Humanities; English; Hindi; Information Sciences; Library Science; Mass Communication; Modern Languages; Music; Painting and Drawing; Performing Arts; Sanskrit); **Ayurveda**

and Unani System (Ayurveda); **Commerce** (Administration; Business and Commerce); **Dental Science** (Dentistry); **Earth Science** (Geography; Geology); **Education** (Adult Education; Education; Physical Education; Yoga); **Engineering and Technology** (Computer Science; Engineering; Technology); **Humanities and Social Sciences** (Anthropology; Economics; History; Philosophy; Psychology; Sociology); **Law** (Law); **Life Sciences** (Natural Sciences); **Management** (Business Administration; Tourism); **Medicine** (Medicine); **Sciences** (Mathematics; Natural Sciences; Pharmacy; Physics; Statistics)

Further Information: Also 22 Affiliated Colleges

History: Founded 1973 as University of Garhwal, acquired present title 1989.

Academic Year: July to May

Admission Requirements: 12th year and senior secondary/intermediate examination

Main Language(s) of Instruction: Hindi, English

Degrees and Diplomas: *Bachelor's Degree*; *Master's Degree*; *Doctor of Philosophy*. Also Postgraduate Diploma courses

Student Services: Academic Counselling, Canteen, Careers Guidance, Social Counselling, Sports Facilities

Last Updated: 15/11/11

HIDAYATULLAH NATIONAL LAW UNIVERSITY

Uparwara Post, Abhanpur, New Raipur, Chhattisgarth
EMail: registrar@hnlu.ac.in
Website: http://hnlu.ac.in

Vice-Chancellor: Sukhpal Singh

Registrar: Anand Pawar

School

Administration of Justice, Continuing and Clinical Legal Education (Administrative Law; Law); **Business and Global Trade Laws Development** (Business Administration; Commercial Law); **Constitutional and Administrative Governance** (Administrative Law; Constitutional Law); **International Legal Studies** (International Law); **Juridical and Social Sciences** (Law; Social Sciences); **Science, Technology and Sustainable Development** (Development Studies; Technology)

History: Founded 2003.

Degrees and Diplomas: *Bachelor's Degree*; *Master's Degree*; *Doctor of Philosophy*

Last Updated: 01/08/11

HIHT UNIVERSITY

Swami Ram Nagar, P.O. Doiwala, Dehradun, Uttarakhand 248 140
Tel: +91(135) 247-1151
EMail: info@hihtuniversity.edu.in
Website: http://www.hihtuniversity.edu.in/

Vice-Chancellor: S.P. Singh
Tel: +91(135) 247-1152 EMail: vc@hihtuniversity.edu.in

Registrar: A.R. Nautiyal
Tel: +91(135) 247-1151 EMail: reg@hihtuniversity.edu.in

Department

Anaesthesiology (Anaesthesiology); **Anatomy** (Anatomy); **Biochemistry** (Biochemistry); **Community Medicine** (Community Health); **ENT** (Otorhinolaryngology); **Forensic Medicine** (Forensic Medicine and Dentistry); **Medicine and Allied Branches** (Medical Auxiliaries; Medicine); **Microbiology** (Microbiology); **Obstetrics and Gynaecology** (Gynaecology and Obstetrics); **Ophthalmology** (Ophthalmology); **Orthopaedics** (Orthopaedics); **Paediatrics** (Paediatrics); **Pathology** (Pathology); **Pharmacology** (Pharmacology); **Physiology** (Physiology); **Radiology** (Radiology); **Surgery and Allied Branches** (Cardiology; Neurological Therapy; Paediatrics; Plastic Surgery; Surgery; Urology)

Further Information: 750 bed multi specialty hospital

History: Founded 1995 as Swami Ram Vidhyapeeth. Acquired 'Deemed University' status 2007. Acquired present title 2008.

Degrees and Diplomas: *Post Diploma*; *Bachelor's Degree*; *Bachelor's Degree (professional)*; *Postgraduate Diploma*; *Master's Degree*; *Doctor of Philosophy*. Also Certificate courses

Student Services: Sports Facilities

Last Updated: 16/12/11

HIMACHAL PRADESH TECHNICAL UNIVERSITY

Hamirpur, Himachal Pradesh 177030
Tel: +91(98171) 09004
Website: http://himtu.ac.in/

Vice-Chancellor: Shashi Kumar Dhiman
EMail: shashikdhiman@gmail,com

Registrar: Rakhil Kahlon

Programme

Engineering (Civil Engineering; Computer Engineering; Computer Science; Electrical and Electronic Engineering; Electrical Engineering; Electronic Engineering; Engineering; Mechanical Engineering; Telecommunications Engineering; Textile Technology); **Pharmacy** (Pharmacy)

Degrees and Diplomas: *Bachelor's Degree*; *Master's Degree*. Also MBA

Last Updated: 18/01/12

HIMACHAL PRADESH UNIVERSITY

Summer Hill, Shimla, Himachal Pradesh 171005
Tel: +91(177) 283-0912
Fax: +91(177) 283-0775
EMail: webhpu@hp.nic.in; gad.hpu@gmail.com
Website: http://www.hpuniv.nic.in

Vice-Chancellor: Arun Diwakar Nath Bajpai
EMail: vc_hpu@hotmail.com

Faculty

Commerce and Management Studies (Business and Commerce; Management); **Education** (Education); **Engineering and Technology** *(Hamirpur)* (Engineering; Technology); **Languages** (English; Indic Languages; Modern Languages; Sanskrit); **Law** (Law); **Medical Sciences and Ayurvedic** (Ayurveda; Medicine); **Performing and Visual Arts** (Performing Arts; Visual Arts); **Physical Science** (Biology; Biotechnology; Chemistry; Computer Science; Mathematics; Natural Sciences; Physics); **Social Sciences** (Economics; Geography; History; Political Sciences; Psychology; Public Administration; Social Sciences; Sociology)

College

Ayurveda (Ayurveda)

Department

Mathematics (Mathematics)

Institute

Environment Studies (Environmental Studies); **Himalayan Studies** (Asian Studies); **Management Studies** *(International)* (Management)

Centre

Distance Education and Open Learning *(International)*

Research Centre

Agro-Economic (Agricultural Business)

Further Information: Also 54 Affiliated Colleges, and 2 Teaching Hospitals, total, 65,000 students

History: Founded 1970.

Academic Year: March to November (March-May; September-November).

Admission Requirements: 12th year senior secondary/intermediate examination or recognized foreign equivalent

Main Language(s) of Instruction: English, Hindi

Degrees and Diplomas: *Post Diploma*; *Bachelor's Degree*; *Master of Philosophy*; *Doctor of Philosophy*: **Law.**

Last Updated: 19/09/11

HIMGIRI ZEE UNIVERSITY

Sheeshambada, P.O. Sherpur, Via-Sahaspur,
Dehradun, Uttarakhand 248 197
Tel: +91(135) 2102-676
Fax: +91(135) 2760-464
EMail: himgirizeeuniversity@gmail.com; hnvddn@yahoo.com
Website: http://www.hnv.edu.in

Head: Binod C. Agrawal

Registrar: Dalip Kumar S. Bora

Faculty

Architecture, Design and Planning (Architecture and Planning; Design); **Computer Science and Information Technology** (Computer Engineering; Computer Science; Information Technology); **Education** (Education); **Expressive Cultures, Media and Communications** (Communication Studies; Cultural Studies; Media Studies); **Human Sciences** (Social Sciences); **Naturopathy and Yogic Sciences** (Yoga); **Population Sciences** (Demography and Population)

Department

Distance Education; **Library and Information Science** (Information Sciences; Library Science)

History: Founded 2003.

Degrees and Diplomas: *Bachelor's Degree*; *Master's Degree*; *Doctor of Philosophy*

Last Updated: 04/01/12

HINDUSTAN UNIVERSITY

P.O. Box No.1, Rajiv Gandhi Salai (OMR), via Kelambakkam, Padur, Chennai 603103
Tel: +91(44) 2747-4262
Fax: +91(44) 2747-4208
EMail: hetc@vsnl.com
Website: http://www.hindustanuniv.ac.in/

Vice-Chancellor: K. Sarukesi

Programme

Architecture (Architecture); **Computer Application** (Computer Science; Software Engineering); **Engineering** (Aeronautical and Aerospace Engineering; Automotive Engineering; Civil Engineering; Computer Engineering; Electrical and Electronic Engineering; Heating and Refrigeration; Mechanical Engineering; Polymer and Plastics Technology; Rubber Technology); **Information Technology** (Information Technology); **Management** (Business Administration; Management)

History: Founded 1956 as Hindustan College of Engineering. Acquired present status 2008.

Degrees and Diplomas: *Post Diploma*; *Bachelor's Degree*; *Master's Degree*; *Doctor of Philosophy*

Last Updated: 16/11/11

HOMEOPATHY UNIVERSITY SAIPURA

Saipura, Sanganer, Jaipur, Rajastan 302029
EMail: info@homoeopathyuniversity.org
Website: http://www.homoeopathyuniversity.org

President: K. C. Bhinda

Programme

Homeopathy (Homeopathy)

History: Founded 2010,

Admission Requirements: A 10+2 pass-out with PCB but not less than 17 years of age can apply for the bachelors' course. Eligibility for PG course will be a BHMS degree.

Degrees and Diplomas: *Bachelor's Degree*; *Master's Degree*

Last Updated: 28/12/11

HOMI BHABHA NATIONAL INSTITUTE

2nd Floor, Training School Complex, Anushaktinagar, Mumbai, Maharashtra 400 094
Website: http://www.hbni.ac.in/

Director: Ravi Grover

Administrative Officer: Lata B.

Department

Chemical Sciences (Chemistry); **Engineering Sciences** (Engineering); **Health Sciences** (Anaesthesiology; Health Sciences; Oncology; Pathology; Radiology); **Life Sciences** (Biological and Life Sciences); **Mathematical Sciences** (Mathematics); **Physical Sciences** (Physics); **Strategic Studies**

Further Information: With also Constituent Institutions across the country

Degrees and Diplomas: *Postgraduate Diploma*; *Master's Degree*; *Doctor of Philosophy*

Last Updated: 10/01/12

IFHE, HYDERABAD

Donthanapally, Shankarapalli Road, Hyderabad, Andhra Pradesh 501504
EMail: vrs@ibsindia.org
Website: http://www.ifheindia.org/

Vice-Chancellor: J. Mahender Reddy
EMail: jmreddy@icfaiuniversity.in

Registrar: V. R. Shankara

Faculty

Law (Law); **Management Studies** *(IBS)* (Business Administration; Management); **Science and Technology** (Engineering; Technology); **Social Sciences** (Economics; Social Sciences)

Degrees and Diplomas: *Bachelor's Degree*; *Master's Degree*; *Doctor of Philosophy*

Student Services: Academic Counselling

Last Updated: 12/01/12

IFIM BUSINESS SCHOOL, BANGALORE (THE INSTITUTE OF FINANCE AND INTERNATIONAL MANAGEMENT)

Opp. Infosys Campus Gate # 4), # 8P & 9P, KIADB Industrial Area, Electronics City 1st Phase, Bangalore 560-100
Tel: +91(80) 4143-2800 +91(80) 4143-2888
Fax: +91(80) 4143-2844
EMail: ifimblr@ifimbschool.com
Website: http://www.ifimbschool.com/

Director: Bramh Prakash Pethiya

Programme

Finance (Finance); **International Business** (International Business); **Management** (Management)

History: Founded 1995.

Fees: (Indian Rupees): c. 500,000 per annum

Degrees and Diplomas: *Postgraduate Diploma*; *Doctor of Philosophy*. The Ph.D. programmes is offered in affiliation with the Visvesvaraya Technological University (VTU), Belgaum

Student Services: Health Services

Last Updated: 24/01/12

IFTM UNIVERSITY

Lodhipur Rajput, Delhi Road (NH-24), Moradabad, Uttar Pradesh 244102
Tel: +91(591) 2360-817
Fax: +91(591) 2360-818
EMail: info@iftmuniversity.ac.in
Website: http://www.iftmuniversity.ac.in/

Vice-Chancellor: R.M. Dubey

School

Biotechnology (Biotechnology); **Business Management** (Business Administration; Management); **Computer Engineering and Applications** (Computer Engineering; Software Engineering); **Engineering and Technology** (Civil Engineering; Electrical Engineering; Electronic Engineering; Engineering; Mechanical Engineering; Technology; Telecommunications Engineering); **Pharmaceutical Sciences** (Pharmacy); **Science** (Botany; Chemistry; Mathematics; Physical Therapy; Zoology); **Social Sciences** (Arts and Humanities; Business and Commerce; Economics; Engineering Management; Social Sciences; Social Work)

History: Founded 1996. Acquired present status 2010.

Degrees and Diplomas: *Bachelor's Degree*; *Master's Degree*; *Doctor of Philosophy*

Last Updated: 16/01/12

IIS UNIVERSITY

ICG Campus, Gurukul Marg, SFS, Mansarovar,
Jaipur, Rajastan 302020
Tel: +91(141) 2400-160
Fax: +91(141) 2395-494
EMail: icg@iisuniv.ac.in
Website: http://www.iisuniv.ac.in/

Vice-Chancellor: Ashok Gupta

Director and Registrar: Raakhi Gupta

Department

Advertising (Advertising and Publicity); **Biotechnology** (Biotechnology); **Botany** (Botany); **Chemistry** (Chemistry); **Commerce** (Business and Commerce); **Computer Science** (Computer Science); **Drawing and Paintings** (Painting and Drawing); **Economics/Business Economics** (Economics); **English** (English); **Environment Science** (Environmental Studies); **Fine Arts** (Fine Arts); **French** (French); **Garment Production and Export Management, Fashion Designing, Textiles** (Fashion Design; Textile Design); **Geography** (Geography); **Hindi** (Hindi); **History** (History); **Home Science**; **Management Studies** (Management); **Mass Communication** (Mass Communication); **Mathematics and Statistics** (Mathematics; Statistics); **Modern European Languages** (French; German); **Physical Education**; **Physics** (Physics); **Political Science** (Political Sciences); **Psychology** (Psychology); **Public Administration** (Public Administration); **Sociology** (Social Work); **Tourism and Travel Management** (Tourism); **Zoology** (Zoology)

History: Founded 1995 as International College for Girls.

Degrees and Diplomas: *Bachelor's Degree*; *Master's Degree*; *Doctor of Philosophy*
Last Updated: 12/01/12

INDIAN AGRICULTURAL RESEARCH INSTITUTE (PG SCHOOL, IARI)

Pusa Campus, New Delhi 110012
Tel: +91(11) 2573-3367
Fax: +91(11) 2584-6420
EMail: director@iari.res.in
Website: http://www.iari.res.in

Director: H.S. Gupta Tel: +91(11) 2584-3375

Director of Education & Dean: H.S. Gaur
Tel: +91(11) 2573-3382 EMail: dean@iari.res.in

Programme

Agriculture (Agricultural Economics; Agricultural Engineering; Agriculture; Agronomy; Biochemistry; Biotechnology; Crop Production; Entomology; Environmental Studies; Floriculture; Fruit Production; Genetics; Horticulture; Microbiology; Plant Pathology; Soil Science; Vegetable Production; Water Science)

History: Founded 1905. A postgraduate Institution.

Academic Year: August to July

Admission Requirements: University degree at Bachelor level for MSc, and Masters degree for PhD

Main Language(s) of Instruction: English

Accrediting Agency: Indian Council of Agricultural Research (ICAR)

Degrees and Diplomas: *Master's Degree*; *Doctor of Philosophy*

Student Services: Academic Counselling, Canteen, Careers Guidance, Health Services, Sports Facilities
Last Updated: 16/11/11

INDIAN INSTITUTE OF FOREIGN TRADE (IIFT)

IIFT Bhawan, B-21, Qutab Institutional Area, New Delhi 110 016
Tel: +91(11) 2685-3055
Fax: +91(11) 2685-3956
Website: http://www.iift.edu/

Director: Sh. K. T. Chacko

Registrar: L. D. Mago EMail: ldmago@iift.ac.in

Programme

Management (Business Administration; Finance; Information Technology; International Business; Marketing)

Further Information: Campus in Kolkata

History: Founded 1963. Declared Deemed University, 2008.

Admission Requirements: Recognized Bachelor's degree of minimum 3 years' duration in any discipline for MBA programmes. Written test and interview

Degrees and Diplomas: *Master's Degree*: **Business Administration.**
Last Updated: 16/11/11

INDIAN INSTITUTE OF FOREST MANAGEMENT

Po Box 357, Nehru Nagar, Bhopal, Madhya Pradesh 462003
EMail: director@iifm.ac.in
Website: http://www.iifm.ac.in/

Director: Giridhar A Kinhal EMail: director@iifm.ac.in

International Relations: Subodh Shukla, Chief Administrative Officer EMail: cao@iifm.ac.in

Programme

Forestry Management (Forest Management)

History: Created 1982.

Fees: 400,000 for two-year programme (Indian Rupee)

Accrediting Agency: Association of Indian Universities; All India Council for Technical Education

Degrees and Diplomas: *Postgraduate Diploma*: **Forest Management.** The instute also prepares MPhils for Saurashtra University and PhDs for the Forest Research Institute.
Last Updated: 26/06/14

INDIAN INSTITUTE OF INFORMATION TECHNOLOGY (IIIT-A)

Deoghat Jhalwa, Allahabad, Uttar Pradesh 211002
Tel: +91(532) 243-1684 +91(532) 292-2000
Fax: +91(532) 243-0006 +91(532) 243-1689
EMail: contact@iiita.ac.in; mdt@iiita.ac.in
Website: http://www.iiita.ac.in

Director: Somenath Biswas EMail: director@iiita.ac.in

International Relations: Ran Bahadur Singh, Administrative Officer Tel: +91(532) 292-2007 EMail: dfo@iiita.ac.in

Division

Applied Science; **Electronics and Communications Engineering** (Electronic Engineering; Telecommunications Engineering); **Management and Cyber Laws** (Law; Management); **Postgraduate** (Artificial Intelligence; Business Administration; Information Technology; Robotics; Software Engineering; Telecommunications Engineering); **Undergraduate** (Electronic Engineering; Information Technology; Telecommunications Engineering)

Further Information: Campuses in Saltanpur, Raibareli, Unchahar, Lalganj, Jagdishpur, Jayas, Gauriganj and Amethi

History: Founded as a Centre of Excellence in Information Technology in 1999. Granted "Deemed University" status in 2000.

Academic Year: July to June

Admission Requirements: 12th year senior secondary/intermediate examination or recognized foreign equivalent

Fees: (Rupees): 73,000- 102,000 per annum depending on programmes

Main Language(s) of Instruction: English

Accrediting Agency: UGC/MHRD

Degrees and Diplomas: *Bachelor's Degree*: **Communication Arts; Electronic Engineering; Information Technology.** *Master's Degree*: **Biological and Life Sciences; Business Administration; Computer Engineering; Computer Science; Information Technology; Law; Software Engineering; Telecommunications Services.** *Doctor of Philosophy*: **Information Technology.**

Student Services: Academic Counselling, Canteen, Careers Guidance, Cultural Activities, Facilities for disabled people, Health Services, Nursery Care, Social Counselling, Sports Facilities

Publications: Annual Audited Accounts Report; Annual Report; Convocation Report and other periodic publications

INDIAN INSTITUTE OF INFORMATION TECHNOLOGY AND MANAGEMENT, GWALIOR

Morena Link Road, Gwalior,
Madhya Pradesh 474010
Tel: +91(751) 2449-704
Fax: +91(751) 2449-813
EMail: director@iiitm.ac.in
Website: http://www.iiitm.ac.in

Director: S.G. Deshmukh

Programme
Information Technology (Computer Engineering; Computer Networks; Information Technology); **Management** (Business Administration)

Fees: (Indian Rupees): 25,000-31,000 depending on programmes

Degrees and Diplomas: *Master's Degree*; *Doctor of Philosophy*
Last Updated: 09/01/12

INDIAN INSTITUTE OF MANAGEMENT AHMEDABAD (IIMA)

Vastrapur, Ahmedabad,
Gujarat 380015
Tel: +91(79) 6632-4631
EMail: admission@iimahd.ernet.in; cao@iimahd.ernet.in
Website: http://www.iimahd.ernet.in

Director: S. K. Barua EMail: director@iimahd.ernet.in

Programme
Agribusiness Management (Agricultural Business; Agricultural Management); **Management** (Management); **Public Management and Policy** (Management; Public Administration)

History: Created 1960.

Degrees and Diplomas: *Postgraduate Diploma*
Last Updated: 11/10/12

INDIAN INSTITUTE OF MANAGEMENT BANGALORE (IIMB)

Bannerghatta Road, Bangalore,
Karnataka 560076
Tel: +91(80) 2658-2450
Fax: +91(80) 2658-4050
EMail: info@iimb.ernet.in
Website: http://www.iimb.ernet.in/

Director: Pankaj Chandra

Programme
Management (Management); **Public Policy and Management** (Management; Public Administration); **Software Enterprise Management** (Business Computing; Management; Management Systems)

History: Created 1973.

Degrees and Diplomas: *Postgraduate Diploma*
Last Updated: 11/10/12

INDIAN INSTITUTE OF MANAGEMENT CALCUTTA (IIMC)

Diamond Harbour Road, Calcutta,
West Bengal 700104
Tel: +91(33) 2467-8300
Website: http://www.iimcal.ac.in/

Director: Shekhar Chaudhuri

Programme
Management (Management)

History: Created 1961

Degrees and Diplomas: *Postgraduate Diploma*; *Doctor of Philosophy*
Last Updated: 11/10/12

INDIAN INSTITUTE OF MANAGEMENT INDORE (IIMI)

Prabandh Shikhar Rau - Pithampur Road,
Indore, Madhya Pradesh 453556
Tel: +91(731) 2439-666
Fax: +91(731) 2439-800
EMail: webman@iimidr.ac.in
Website: http://www.iimidr.ac.in/iimi/

Director: N. Ravichandran

Programme
Management (Management)

History: Created 1996.

Degrees and Diplomas: *Postgraduate Diploma*
Last Updated: 11/10/12

INDIAN INSTITUTE OF MANAGEMENT KOZHIKODE (IIMK)

IIMK Campus PO, Kozhikode, Kerala 673570
Tel: +91(495) 2809-100
Fax: +91(495) 2803-010
Website: http://www.iimk.ac.in/

Director: Debashis Chatterjee

Programme
Management (Finance; Human Resources; Management; Marketing)

History: Created 1997.

Degrees and Diplomas: *Postgraduate Diploma*; *Doctor of Philosophy*
Last Updated: 17/10/12

INDIAN INSTITUTE OF MANAGEMENT LUCKNOW (IIML)

Prabandh Nagar, off Sitapur Road, Lucknow, Uttar Pradesh 226013
Tel: +91(522) 2734-101
Fax: +91(522) 2734-025
EMail: admission@iiml.ac.in; ccmr@iiml.ac.in
Website: http://www.iiml.ac.in

Director: Devi Singh EMail: diroffice@iiml.ac.in

Programme
Management (Agricultural Business; Agricultural Management; Management)

History: Created 1984.

Degrees and Diplomas: *Postgraduate Diploma*
Last Updated: 17/10/12

INDIAN INSTITUTE OF MANAGEMENT RANCHI (IIMR)

Suchana Bhawan, 5th Floor, Audrey House Campus, Meur's Road, Ranchi, Jharkhand 834008
Tel: +91(651) 2280-113
Fax: +91(651) 2280-940
Website: http://www.iimranchi.ac.in/

Director: M.J. Xavier

Programme
Human Resource Management (Human Resources); **Management**

History: Created 2010.

Degrees and Diplomas: *Postgraduate Diploma*; *Doctor of Philosophy*
Last Updated: 17/10/12

INDIAN INSTITUTE OF SCIENCE (IISC)

Bangalore, Karnataka 560012
Tel: +91(80) 2293-2001
Fax: +91(80) 2360-0085
EMail: regr@admin.iisc.ernet.in
Website: http://www.iisc.ernet.in

Director: P. Balaram
Tel: +91(80) 2360-0690
EMail: diroff@admin.iisc.ernet.in
Associate Director: N. Balakrishnan
Tel: +91(80) 2360-0129
EMail: ad@admin.iisc.ernet.in
International Relations: Rahul Pandit, Chairman
Tel: +91(80) 2239-2560
EMail: rahul@physics.iisc.ernet.in

Division

Biological Sciences (Biochemistry; Biological and Life Sciences; Ecology; Microbiology; Molecular Biology; Neurosciences); **Chemical Sciences** (Chemistry; Inorganic Chemistry; Organic Chemistry; Physical Chemistry); **Earth and Environmental Sciences** (Development Studies; Earth Sciences; Environmental Studies; Foreign Languages Education; Management; Marine Science and Oceanography); **Electrical Sciences** (Automation and Control Engineering; Computer Education; Electrical Engineering; Engineering; Mechanical Engineering; Metallurgical Engineering); **Mechanical Engineering** (Aeronautical and Aerospace Engineering; Chemical Engineering; Industrial Design; Materials Engineering; Mechanical Engineering); **Physical and Mathematical Sciences** (Applied Physics; Astronomy and Space Science; Astrophysics; Mathematics; Physics)

Research Centre

Super Computer Education (Computer Education)

History: Founded 1909. An autonomous body, funded by Central Government through the Ministry of Human Resources Development.

Academic Year: August to July

Admission Requirements: University degree in Science or Engineering at Bachelor level

Fees: (Rupees): 5,000-15,000 per annum

Main Language(s) of Instruction: English

Degrees and Diplomas: *Master's Degree*: **Engineering; Technology.** *Doctor of Philosophy*

Student Services: Academic Counselling, Canteen, Careers Guidance, Cultural Activities, Foreign Studies Centre, Health Services, Nursery Care, Social Counselling, Sports Facilities

Publications: IISc Journal
Last Updated: 16/11/11

INDIAN INSTITUTE OF SCIENCE EDUCATION AND RESEARCH BHOPAL (IISER BHOPAL)

Indore By-pass Road, Bhauri, Bhopal, Madhya Pradesh 462066
Website: https://www.iiserbhopal.ac.in

Director: Vinod K. Singh
EMail: rmishra@iiserb.ac.in; director@iiserb.ac.in
Registrar: Satya Murty K V EMail: registrar@iiserb.ac.in

Department

Biological Sciences (Biological and Life Sciences); **Chemistry** (Chemistry); **Earth and Environmental Sciences** (Earth Sciences; Environmental Studies); **Mathematics** (Mathematics); **Physics** (Physics)

History: Created 2008 by the Government of India, through the Ministry of Human Resource Development (MHRD), to carry out research in frontier areas of science and to provide quality science education at the undergraduate and postgraduate level.

Accrediting Agency: Department of Higher Education, Ministry of Human Resources Development

Degrees and Diplomas: *Bachelor's Degree*: **Biological and Life Sciences; Chemistry; Earth Sciences; Environmental Studies; Mathematics; Physics.** *Master's Degree*: **Biological and Life Sciences; Chemistry; Earth Sciences; Environmental Studies; Mathematics; Physics.** *Doctor of Philosophy*: **Biological and Life Sciences; Chemistry; Earth Sciences; Environmental Studies; Mathematics; Physics.**
Last Updated: 18/09/14

INDIAN INSTITUTE OF SCIENCE EDUCATION AND RESEARCH KOLKATA (IISER KOLKATA)

Main Campus, Mohanpur, West Bengal 741246
Tel: +91(33) 2587-3017
Website: http://www.iiserkol.ac.in/

Director: R. N. Mukherjee EMail: director@iiserkol.ac.in

Registrar: Joydeep Sil EMail: registrar@iiserkol.ac.in

Department

Biological Sciences (Biological and Life Sciences); **Chemical Sciences** (Chemistry); **Earth Sciences** (Earth Sciences); **Mathematics and Statistics** (Mathematics; Statistics); **Physical Sciences** (Physics)

History: Created 2006 by the Government of India, through the Ministry of Human Resource Development (MHRD), to carry out research in frontier areas of science and to provide quality science education at the undergraduate and postgraduate level.

Accrediting Agency: Department of Higher Education, Ministry of Human Resources Development

Degrees and Diplomas: *Bachelor's Degree*: **Biological and Life Sciences; Chemistry; Geography; Mathematics; Physics.** *Master's Degree*: **Astronomy and Space Science; Astrophysics; Biological and Life Sciences; Chemistry; Geography; Mathematics; Optics; Physics.** *Doctor of Philosophy*: **Biological and Life Sciences; Chemistry; Geography; Mathematics; Physics.**
Last Updated: 18/09/14

INDIAN INSTITUTE OF SCIENCE EDUCATION AND RESEARCH MOHALI (IISER)

Manauli PO 140306, Knowledge City, Sector 81, SAS Nagar, Mohali, Punjab
Website: http://www.iisermohali.ac.in

Director: N. Sathyamurthy EMail: nsath@iisermohali.ac.in

Department

Biological Sciences (Biological and Life Sciences; Biology); **Chemical Sciences** (Chemistry); **Mathematical Sciences** (Mathematics); **Physical Sciences** (Physics)

History: Created 2007 by the Government of India, through the Ministry of Human Resource Development (MHRD), to carry out research in frontier areas of science and to provide quality science education at the undergraduate and postgraduate level.

Accrediting Agency: Department of Higher Education, Ministry of Human Resources Development

Degrees and Diplomas: *Bachelor's Degree*: **Mathematics; Natural Sciences.** *Master's Degree*: **Mathematics; Natural Sciences.** *Doctor of Philosophy*: **Earth Sciences; Mathematics; Natural Sciences.**
Last Updated: 28/01/14

INDIAN INSTITUTE OF SCIENCE EDUCATION AND RESEARCH PUNE (IISER PUNE)

Dr. Homi Bhabha Road, Pashan, Pune, Maharashtra 411 008
Tel: +91(20) 2590-8001
Fax: +91(20) 2590-8186
Website: http://www.iiserpune.ac.in/

Director: Krishna N. Ganesh

Registrar: G. Raja Sekhar EMail: registrar@iiserpune.ac.in

Programme

Biology (Biological and Life Sciences; Biology); **Chemistry** (Chemistry); **Mathematics** (Mathematics); **Physics** (Physics)

History: Created 2006 by the Government of India, through the Ministry of Human Resource Development (MHRD), to carry out research in frontier areas of science and to provide quality science education at the undergraduate and postgraduate level.

Accrediting Agency: Department of Higher Education, Ministry of Human Resources Development

Degrees and Diplomas: *Bachelor's Degree*: **Biological and Life Sciences; Chemistry; Mathematics; Physics.** *Master's Degree*: **Biological and Life Sciences; Chemistry; Mathematics; Physics.** *Doctor of Philosophy*: **Biological and Life Sciences; Chemistry; Mathematics; Physics.**
Last Updated: 17/09/14

INDIAN INSTITUTE OF SCIENCE EDUCATION AND RESEARCH THIRUVANANTHAPURAM (IISER-TVM)

Computer Science Building, College of Engineering, Trivandrum Campus, Thiruvananthapuram, Kerala 695016
Tel: +91(471) 259-7459
EMail: registrar@iisertvm.ac.in
Website: http://www.iisertvm.ac.in/

Director: Veerabahu Ramakrishnan
EMail: director@iisertvm.ac.in

Registrar: Shri M. Radhakrishnan
EMail: registrar@iisertvm.ac.in

Programme
Biological Sciences (Biological and Life Sciences); **Chemistry** (Chemistry); **Mathematics** (Mathematics); **Physics** (Physics)

History: Created 2008 by the Government of India, through the Ministry of Human Resource Development (MHRD), to carry out research in frontier areas of science and to provide quality science education at the undergraduate and postgraduate level.

Accrediting Agency: Department of Higher Education, Ministry of Human Resources Development

Degrees and Diplomas: *Bachelor's Degree*: **Biological and Life Sciences; Chemistry; Mathematics; Physics.** *Master's Degree*: **Biological and Life Sciences; Chemistry; Mathematics; Physics.** *Doctor of Philosophy*: **Biological and Life Sciences; Chemistry; Mathematics; Physics.**

Last Updated: 18/09/14

INDIAN INSTITUTE OF SPACE SCIENCE AND TECHNOLOGY (IIST)

Valiamala P.O., Thiruvananthapuram, Kerala 695 547
Tel: +91(471) 256-8462
Fax: +91(471) 256-8406
EMail: ao@iist.ac.in
Website: http://www.iist.ac.in/

Director: K.S. Dasgupta EMail: ksd@iist.ac.in

Registrar: K. Sasikumar
Tel: +91(471) 2568-403 EMail: registrar@iist.ac.in

Department
Aerospace Engineering (Aeronautical and Aerospace Engineering); **Avionics** (Computer Science; Electrical and Electronic Engineering; Electronic Engineering); **Chemistry** (Chemistry); **Earth and Space Sciences** (Earth Sciences); **Humanities** (Economics; English; Management; Social Sciences; Sociology); **Mathematics** (Mathematics); **Physics** (Physics)

INDIAN INSTITUTE OF TECHNOLOGY, BHUBANESWAR

Bhubaneswar 751013
Tel: +91(674) 2301-292
EMail: director.office@iitbbs.ac.in
Website: http://www.iitbbs.ac.in/

Director: Madhusudan Chakraborty

Registrar: Bata Kishore Ray

School
Basic Sciences (Chemistry; Mathematics; Physics); **Earth, Ocean and Climate Sciences** (Earth Sciences; Marine Science and Oceanography; Meteorology); **Electrical Sciences** (Electrical Engineering); **Humanities, Social Sciences and Management** (Arts and Humanities; Literature; Management; Modern Languages; Social Sciences); **Infrastructure** (Civil Engineering; Town Planning; Transport Engineering; Urban Studies); **Mechanical Sciences** (Mechanical Engineering)

Degrees and Diplomas: *Bachelor's Degree*; *Master's Degree*; *Doctor of Philosophy*

Student Services: Careers Guidance

Last Updated: 06/01/12

INDIAN INSTITUTE OF TECHNOLOGY, BOMBAY

Powai, Mumbai, Maharashtra 400076
Tel: +91(22) 2572-2545
Fax: +91(22) 2572-3480
EMail: dean.ir.office@iitb.ac.in
Website: http://www.iitb.ac.in

Director: Devang Khakhar (2009-)
Tel: +91(22) 2576-7001 +91(22) 2576-7002
EMail: director@iitb.ac.in

Registrar: Shri B. S. Punalkar
Tel: +91(22) 2576-7020 EMail: registrar@iitb.ac.in

School
Information Technology *(Kanwal Rekki)*; **Management** *(Shailesh J. Mehta)* (Management; Technology)

Department
Aerospace Engineering (Aeronautical and Aerospace Engineering); **Chemical Engineering** (Chemical Engineering); **Chemistry** (Chemistry); **Civil Engineering** (Civil Engineering); **Computer Science and Engineering** (Computer Science; Engineering); **Earth Sciences** (Earth Sciences); **Electrical Engineering** (Electrical Engineering); **Energy Science and Engineering** (Energy Engineering); **Humanities and Social Sciences** (Arts and Humanities; Social Sciences); **Mathematics** (Mathematics); **Mechanical Engineering** (Mechanical Engineering); **Metallurgical Engineering and Materials Sciences** (Materials Engineering; Metallurgical Engineering); **Physics** (Physics)

Centre
Aerospace Systems, Design and Engineering (Aeronautical and Aerospace Engineering; Design); **Alternative Technology for Rural Areas** (Technology); **Computer** (Computer Science); **Distance Engineering Education Programme** (Engineering); **Environmental Science and Engineering** (Engineering; Environmental Engineering); **Formal Design and Verification of Software** (Design; Software Engineering); **Nanotechnology and Sciences** (Nanotechnology); **Sophisticated Analytical Instrument Facility** *(Regional)* (Measurement and Precision Engineering); **Studies in Resources Engineering** (Natural Resources)

History: Founded 1958, and declared to be an autonomous body empowered to confer all academic distinctions.

Academic Year: July to April (July-November; January-April)

Admission Requirements: 12th year senior secondary/intermediate examination or recognized foreign equivalent, and all Indian competitive joint entrance examinations (JEE) conducted by the 7 Institutes of Technology (IITs)

Main Language(s) of Instruction: English

Degrees and Diplomas: *Bachelor's Degree*: **Technology.** *Master's Degree*: **Design; Management; Technology.** *Doctor of Philosophy*. Also Dual degree in Technology (Bachelor and Master), 4 yrs, extended to 6 yrs

Student Services: Academic Counselling, Canteen, Careers Guidance, Cultural Activities, Facilities for disabled people, Health Services, Language Laboratory, Social Counselling, Sports Facilities

Last Updated: 16/11/11

INDIAN INSTITUTE OF TECHNOLOGY, DELHI

Hauz Khas, New Delhi 110016
Tel: +91(11) 2658-1988
Fax: +91(11) 2658-2659
EMail: webmaster@admin.iitd.ac.in
Website: http://www.iitd.ac.in

Director: R.K. Shevgaonkar (2011-) Tel: +91(11) 2659-1701

Registrar: Kumar Rakesh
Tel: +91(11) 2659-1710 EMail: registrar@admin.iitd.ac.in

Department
Applied Mechanics (Mechanical Engineering); **Biochemical Engineering and Biotechnology** (Biochemistry; Biotechnology); **Chemistry** (Chemistry); **Civil Engineering** (Civil Engineering); **Computer Science and Engineering** (Computer Science; Engineering); **Electrical Engineering** (Electrical Engineering);

Humanities and Social Sciences (Arts and Humanities; Social Sciences); **Management Studies** (Management); **Mathematics** (Mathematics); **Mechanical Engineering** (Mechanical Engineering); **Physics** (Physics); **Textile Technology** (Textile Technology)

Centre

Applied Research in Electronics (Electronic Engineering); **Atmospheric Sciences** (Meteorology); **Biomedical Engineering** (Biomedical Engineering); **Computer Service** (Computer Science); **Educational Technology** (Educational Technology); **Energy Studies** (Energy Engineering); **Industrial Tribology** (Mechanical Engineering; Mechanical Equipment and Maintenance); **Instrument Design** (Industrial Design); **National Resource**; **Polymer Science and Engineering** (Engineering; Polymer and Plastics Technology); **Rural Development and Technology** (Rural Planning; Technology)

History: Founded 1961 as College of Engineering and Technology, declared to be an autonomous body empowered to confer all academic distinctions, and acquired present title 1963.

Academic Year: July to June (July-December; January-June)

Admission Requirements: Competitive joint entrance examination conducted by the 6 Institutes of Technology (IITs), Banaras Hindu University Institute of Technology, and the Indian Institute of Mines

Main Language(s) of Instruction: English

Degrees and Diplomas: *Post Diploma*; *Bachelor's Degree*; *Postgraduate Diploma*; *Master's Degree*; *Doctor of Philosophy*

Student Services: Academic Counselling, Canteen, Careers Guidance, Cultural Activities, Health Services, Social Counselling, Sports Facilities

Publishing house: Publication Cell

Last Updated: 16/11/11

INDIAN INSTITUTE OF TECHNOLOGY, GANDHINAGAR (IIT GANDHINAGAR)

Vishwakarma Government Engineering College Complex,
Chandkheda, Visat-Gandhinagar Highway,
Ahmedabad, Gujarat 382424
Tel: +91 93284 74222
Fax: +91(79) 2397-2324
EMail: office@iitgn.ac.in
Website: http://www.iitgn.ac.in

Director: Sudhir K. Jain
Tel: +91(79) 2397-2574 EMail: director@iitgn.ac.in

Registrar: B. S. Punalkar

Programme

Engineering (Chemical Engineering; Civil Engineering; Electrical and Electronic Equipment and Maintenance; Mechanical Engineering); **Humanities and Social Sciences** (Cognitive Sciences; Economics; English; Human Resources; Philosophy; Social Sciences; Sociology); **Science** (Chemistry; Mathematics; Physics)

Degrees and Diplomas: *Bachelor's Degree*; *Master's Degree*; *Doctor of Philosophy*

Last Updated: 06/01/12

INDIAN INSTITUTE OF TECHNOLOGY, GUWAHATI

Guwahati, Assam 781039
Tel: +91(361) 269-0401
Fax: +91(361) 269-2321
EMail: root@iitg.ernet.in
Website: http://www.iitg.ernet.in

Director: Gautam Barua EMail: director@iitg.ernet.in

Registrar: Brajendra Nath Raychoudhury
EMail: registrar@iitg.ernet.in

Department

Biotechnology (Biotechnology); **Chemical Engineering** (Chemical Engineering); **Chemistry** (Chemistry); **Civil Engineering** (Civil Engineering); **Computer Science and Engineering** (Computer Science; Engineering); **Design** (Design); **Electronics and Electrical Engineering** (Computer Networks; Electronic Engineering); **Humanities and Social Sciences** (Archaeology; Arts and Humanities; Economics; English; History; Linguistics; Philosophy; Psychology; Social Sciences; Sociology); **Mathematics** (Mathematics); **Mechanical Engineering** (Mechanical Engineering); **Physics** (Physics)

History: Founded 1994.

Academic Year: July to May (July-November; December-May).

Degrees and Diplomas: *Bachelor's Degree*: **Technology.** *Master's Degree*; *Doctor of Philosophy*

Last Updated: 17/11/11

INDIAN INSTITUTE OF TECHNOLOGY, HYDERABAD

Ordnance Factory Estate, Yeddumailaram, Andhra Pradesh 502205
Tel: +91(40) 2301-6033
Fax: +91(40) 2301-6032
EMail: info@iith.ac.in
Website: http://www.iith.ac.in

Director: Uday B. Desai (2009-) EMail: director@iith.ac.in

Department

Engineering (Biomedicine; Biotechnology; Civil Engineering; Computer Engineering; Computer Science; Electrical Engineering; Materials Engineering; Mechanical Engineering); **Liberal Arts** (Cultural Studies; English; Literature; Psychology); **Sciences** (Chemistry; Mathematics; Physics)

History: Founded 2008.

Degrees and Diplomas: *Bachelor's Degree*; *Master's Degree*; *Doctor of Philosophy*

Student Services: Sports Facilities

Publications: Reverb

Last Updated: 05/01/12

INDIAN INSTITUTE OF TECHNOLOGY, INDORE (IIT INDORE)

M-Block, Institute of Engineering and Technology, Devi Ahilya
Vishwavidyalaya Campus, Khandwa Road,
Indore, Madhya Pradesh 452017
Tel: +91(731) 2364-182
Fax: +91(731) 2431-482
EMail: contactus@iiti.ac.in
Website: http://www.iiti.ac.in

Director: Pradeep Mathur
Tel: +91(731) 236-4182 EMail: director@iiti.ac.in

Registrar: G. Raja Sekhar
Tel: +91(731) 2438-718 EMail: registrar@iiti.ac.in

School

Basic Science (Chemistry; Mathematics; Physics); **Engineering** (Computer Engineering; Computer Science; Electrical Engineering; Engineering; Mechanical Engineering); **Humanities and Social Science** (Arts and Humanities; Economics; Literature; Philosophy; Social Sciences)

Degrees and Diplomas: *Bachelor's Degree*; *Master's Degree*; *Doctor of Philosophy*

Last Updated: 06/01/12

INDIAN INSTITUTE OF TECHNOLOGY, KANPUR (PO IIT)

PO IIT, Kanpur, Uttar Pradesh 208016
Tel: +91(512) 259-7808
Fax: +91(512) 259-0465
EMail: registrar@iitk.ac.in
Website: http://www.iitk.ac.in

Director: Sanjay Gobind Dhande (2001-) EMail: sgd@iitk.ac.in

Registrar: Sanjeev Kashalkar

Department

Aerospace Engineering (Aeronautical and Aerospace Engineering); **Biological Sciences and Bioengineering**; **Chemical Engineering** (Chemical Engineering); **Chemistry** (Biochemistry; Chemistry; Physical Chemistry); **Civil Engineering** (Civil Engineering; Environmental Engineering; Geology); **Computer Science and Engineering** (Computer Science; Engineering); **Design**;

Electrical Engineering (Electrical Engineering); **Environmental Science and Management** (Environmental Management; Environmental Studies); **Humanities and Social Sciences** (Arts and Humanities; Social Sciences); **Industrial and Management Engineering** (Engineering Management; Industrial Engineering; Management); **Laser Technology**; **Materials Engineering and Metallurgical Engineering** (Materials Engineering; Metallurgical Engineering); **Materials Science** (Materials Engineering); **Mathematics ans Statistics** (Mathematics; Statistics); **Mechanical Engineering** (Design; Mechanical Engineering; Production Engineering; Robotics); **Nuclear Engineering and Technology** (Nuclear Engineering); **Physics** (Laser Engineering; Nuclear Physics; Physics)

History: Founded 1959 as a College of Engineering and Technology, declared to be an autonomous body empowered to confer all academic distinctions, and acquired its present title 1962.

Academic Year: July to April (July-November; January-April)

Admission Requirements: 12th year senior secondary/intermediate examination or recognized foreign equivalent, and all Indian competitive joint entrance examination (JEE) conducted by the Institutes of Technology (IITs)

Fees: (Rupees): 25,000 per semester

Main Language(s) of Instruction: English

Degrees and Diplomas: *Bachelor's Degree*; *Master's Degree*; *Doctor of Philosophy*

Last Updated: 17/11/11

INDIAN INSTITUTE OF TECHNOLOGY, KHARAGPUR

PO Kharagpur Technology, Kharagpur,
West Bengal 721302
Tel: +91(3222) 255-221
Fax: +91(3222) 255-303
EMail: registrar@hijli.iitkgp.ernet.in
Website: http://www.iitkgp.ernet.in

Director: K. Damodar Acharya Tel: +91(3222) 282-002

Registrar: Dharmalingam Gunasekaran

School

Engineering Entrepreneurship *(Rajendra Mishra)* (Engineering Management); **Information Technology** (Information Technology); **Infrastructure Design and Management** *(Ranbir and Chitra Gupta)* (Design; Management); **Intellectual Property Law** *(Rajiv Gandhi)*; **Management** *(Vinod Gupta)* (Accountancy; Administration; Business and Commerce; Finance; Human Resources; Industrial Management; Institutional Administration; Insurance; International Business; Labour and Industrial Relations; Management; Marketing; Public Administration; Systems Analysis); **Medical Science and Technology** (Automation and Control Engineering; Biomedicine; Biophysics; Electronic Engineering; Information Technology); **Telecommunications** *(G.S. Sanyal)* (Information Technology; Telecommunications Engineering); **Water Resources** (Water Management; Water Science)

Department

Aerospace Engineering (Aeronautical and Aerospace Engineering); **Agriculture and Food Engineering** (Agriculture; Agronomy; Aquaculture; Crop Production; Dairy; Farm Management; Fishery; Food Technology; Forest Biology; Harvest Technology; Horticulture; Irrigation; Meat and Poultry; Soil Conservation; Soil Science; Tropical Agriculture; Water Management; Water Science); **Architecture and Regional Planning** (Architectural Restoration; Architecture; Landscape Architecture; Regional Planning; Structural Architecture; Town Planning); **Biotechnology** (Biochemistry; Biotechnology; Cell Biology; Genetics; Immunology; Microbiology; Molecular Biology; Physiology; Toxicology); **Chemical Engineering** (Chemical Engineering; Industrial Design; Petroleum and Gas Engineering); **Chemistry** (Chemistry; Industrial Chemistry; Inorganic Chemistry; Organic Chemistry; Physical Chemistry); **Civil Engineering** (Civil Engineering; Construction Engineering; Environmental Engineering; Hydraulic Engineering; Transport Engineering); **Computer Science and Engineering** (Computer Engineering; Information Sciences; Software Engineering; Technology); **Electrical Engineering** (Automation and Control Engineering; Electrical Engineering; Energy Engineering; Instrument Making; Power Engineering); **Electronics and Electrical Communication Engineering** (Computer Science; Electrical and Electronic Engineering; Microelectronics; Telecommunications Engineering); **Geology and Geophysics** (Crystallography; Earth Sciences; Geochemistry; Geology; Geophysics; Mineralogy; Paleontology; Petroleum and Gas Engineering; Seismology); **Humanities and Social Sciences** (Arts and Humanities; Communication Studies; Comparative Literature; Economics; English; Ethics; French; German; International Studies; Literature; Logic; Modern Languages; Philosophy; Psychology; Social Sciences; Sociology); **Industrial Engineering and Management** (Industrial Engineering; Management; Management Systems; Systems Analysis); **Mathematics** (Applied Mathematics; Computer Science; Mathematics; Software Engineering; Statistics); **Mechanical Engineering** (Automotive Engineering; Heating and Refrigeration; Hydraulic Engineering; Mechanical Engineering; Power Engineering; Production Engineering; Sound Engineering (Acoustics)); **Metallurgical and Materials Engineering** (Materials Engineering; Metallurgical Engineering); **Mining Engineering** (Mining Engineering); **Ocean Engineering and Naval Architecture** (Marine Engineering; Naval Architecture); **Physics and Meteorology** (Meteorology; Physics; Solid State Physics)

Centre

Cryogenic Engineering (Heating and Refrigeration); **Educational Technology** (Distance Education; Educational Research; Educational Sciences; Educational Technology; Educational Testing and Evaluation; Pedagogy); **Materials Science** (Ceramics and Glass Technology; Materials Engineering; Polymer and Plastics Technology); **Oceans, Rivers, Atmosphere and Land Sciences** (Earth Sciences; Meteorology; Soil Science; Water Science); **Reliability Engineering** (Safety Engineering); **Rubber Technology** (Rubber Technology); **Rural Development** (Development Studies)

History: Founded 1951 as Indian Institute of Technology, declared an autonomous body empowered to confer all Academic distinctions, and acquired its present title 1956.

Academic Year: July to May (July-December; December-May). Also Summer Term (May to July) for special courses

Admission Requirements: 12th year senior secondary/intermediate examination or recognized foreign equivalent, and all Indian competitive joint entrance examination (JEE) conducted by 7 Indian Institutes of Technology (IITs)

Fees: (Rupees): 15,000 per semester; foreign students (US Dollars), 5,000

Main Language(s) of Instruction: English

Degrees and Diplomas: *Bachelor's Degree*: **Architecture; Technology.** *Postgraduate Diploma*: **Information Technology.** *Master's Degree*: **Architecture; Business and Commerce; Management; Medical Technology; Regional Planning; Technology.** *Doctor of Philosophy*. Also Dual Degree, BTech/MTech, 5 yrs in Technology

Student Services: Academic Counselling, Canteen, Careers Guidance, Cultural Activities, Foreign Studies Centre, Health Services, Language Laboratory, Nursery Care, Social Counselling, Sports Facilities

Publications: Electronic Journal of Indian Culture and Society; Research and Innovation

Publishing House: Institute Press

Last Updated: 17/11/11

INDIAN INSTITUTE OF TECHNOLOGY, MADRAS (IITM)

IIT Post Office, Chennai, Chennai, Tamil Nadu 600036
Tel: +91(44) 2257-8001
Fax: +91(44) 2257-0509
EMail: ananth@iitm.ac.in
Website: http://www.iitm.ac.in

Director: Bhaskar Ramamurthi EMail: director@iitm.ac.in

Registrar: A. Thirunavukkarasu
Tel: +91(44) 2257-8100 EMail: registrar@iitm.ac.in

International Relations: K. Ramamurthy, Dean, Academic Courses Tel: +91(44) 2257-8030 EMail: deanac@iitm.ac.in

Department

Aerospace Engineering; **Applied Mechanics**; **Biotechnology** (Agricultural Engineering; Biology; Biomedical Engineering;

Biotechnology; Cell Biology; Chemistry; Computer Science; Engineering; Genetics; Molecular Biology; Neurosciences; Organic Chemistry; Pharmacy); **Chemical Engineering**; **Chemistry**; **Civil Engineering**; **Computer Science and Engineering**; **Electrical Engineering**; **Humanities and Social Sciences**; **Management Studies** (Finance; Human Resources; Labour and Industrial Relations; Management; Marketing; Public Administration; Transport Management); **Mathematics**; **Mechanical Engineering**; **Metallurgical and Materials Engineering**; **Ocean Engineering**; **Physics**

Research Centre

Central Electronics (Electronic Engineering); **Composites Technology** (Aeronautical and Aerospace Engineering; Ceramics and Glass Technology; Chemical Engineering; Civil Engineering; Mechanical Engineering; Metallurgical Engineering; Polymer and Plastics Technology; Technology); **Continuing Education** (Systems Analysis); **Materials Science** (Chemical Engineering; Chemistry; Civil Engineering; Electrical Engineering; Engineering; Inorganic Chemistry; Materials Engineering; Metallurgical Engineering; Physics; Technology); **Sophisticated Analysis Instrumentation Facilities** (Chemistry; Instrument Making; Materials Engineering; Metallurgical Engineering; Physics)

Further Information: Also Research Laboratories attached to each Department

History: Founded 1959, acquired present status 1962.

Academic Year: July to May (July-November; January-May)

Admission Requirements: BTech: 12th year senior secondary/intermediate examination or recognized foreign equivalent, and all Indian Competitive Joint Entrance Examination (JEE) conducted by the 6 Institutes of Technology (IITs). MTech/MS: BE/BTech with GATE. PhD: ME/MTech/MSc with a National level test

Main Language(s) of Instruction: English

Degrees and Diplomas: *Bachelor's Degree*: **Engineering.** *Master's Degree*: **Chemistry; Engineering; Management; Mathematics; Physics.** *Doctor of Philosophy*: **Engineering; Natural Sciences.** Also Dual degree (5 yrs) in Engineering, B.Tech. and M.Tech.; Master of Science by Research (a further 2 yrs) in Engineering

Student Services: Academic Counselling, Canteen, Careers Guidance, Cultural Activities, Facilities for disabled people, Health Services, Language Laboratory, Nursery Care, Social Counselling, Sports Facilities

Publications: Abstracts of MS and PhD Theses; Research, Consultancy, Expertise and Facilities

Publishing House: IIT Madras

Last Updated: 17/11/11

INDIAN INSTITUTE OF TECHNOLOGY, MANDI (IIT MANDI)

PWD Rest House, Mandi, Himachal Pradesh 175001
Tel: +91(1905) 237943
Fax: +91(1905) 237945
EMail: regis@iitmandi.ac.in
Website: http://www.iitmandi.ac.in/

Director: Timothy A. Gonsalves
Tel: +91(1905) 237731 EMail: diroffice@iitmandi.ac.in

Registrar: R.C. Sawhney

School

Basic Sciences (Biological and Life Sciences; Chemistry; Mathematics; Physics); **Computing and Electrical Engineering** (Computer Engineering; Electrical Engineering); **Engineering** (Civil Engineering; Engineering; Mechanical Engineering); **Humanities and Social Sciences** (Arts and Humanities; Cultural Studies; Economics; Management; Modern Languages; Social Psychology; Social Work)

History: Founded 2009.

Fees: Foreign students - US $ 2000 + other charges in Indian Rupees (for SAARC countries); US $ 4000 + other charges in Indian Rupees (for other countries)

Degrees and Diplomas: *Bachelor's Degree*; *Master's Degree*; *Doctor of Philosophy*

Last Updated: 06/01/12

INDIAN INSTITUTE OF TECHNOLOGY, PATNA

Navin Government Polytechnic Campus, Patliputra Colony, Patna, Bihar 800 013
Tel: +91(612) 2552-067
Fax: +91(612) 2277-383
EMail: iitpatnaoff@iitp.ac.in
Website: http://www.iitp.ac.in/

Director: Anil K. Bhowmick

School

Engineering (Computer Engineering; Computer Science; Electrical Engineering; Engineering; Mechanical Engineering); **Humanities and Social Science** (Arts and Humanities; Social Sciences); **Sciences** (Chemistry; Mathematics; Physics)

History: Founded 2008.

Degrees and Diplomas: *Bachelor's Degree*; *Doctor of Philosophy*

Last Updated: 06/01/12

INDIAN INSTITUTE OF TECHNOLOGY, RAJASTHAN

Old Residency Road, Ratanada, Jodhpur, Rajasthan 342011
Tel: +91(291) 244-9024
Fax: +91(291) 251-6823
EMail: dir@iitj.ac.in
Website: http://www.iitj.ac.in/

Director: Prem K. Kalra
Tel: +91(291) 251-2141 EMail: pkk@iitj.ac.in

Department

Postgraduate Programmes (Energy Engineering; Information Technology; Systems Analysis; Telecommunications Engineering); **Undergraduate Programmes** (Computer Engineering; Computer Science; Electrical and Electronic Engineering; Mechanical Engineering; Systems Analysis)

History: Founded 2008.

Degrees and Diplomas: *Bachelor's Degree*; *Master's Degree*; *Doctor of Philosophy*

Last Updated: 05/01/12

INDIAN INSTITUTE OF TECHNOLOGY, ROORKEE (IITR)

Roorkee, Uttarakhand 247667
Tel: +91(1332) 285-311
Fax: +91(1332) 285-310
EMail: regis@iitr.ernet.in
Website: http://www.iitr.ac.in

Director: Pradipta Banerji
Tel: +91(1332) 285-500 EMail: director@iitr.ernet.in

Registrar: A.K. Srivastava

Department

Architecture and Planning (Architecture and Planning); **Biotechnology** (Biological and Life Sciences; Biotechnology); **Chemical Engineering** (Chemical Engineering); **Chemistry** (Chemistry); **Civil Engineering** (Civil Engineering); **Earth Sciences** (Earth Sciences; Geology; Geophysics); **Earthquake Engineering** (Seismology); **Electrical Engineering** (Electrical Engineering); **Electronics and Computer Engineering** (Computer Engineering; Electronic Engineering); **Humanities and Social Sciences** (Arts and Humanities; English; Psychology; Social Sciences); **Hydrology** (Hydraulic Engineering); **Management Studies** (Management); **Mathematics** (Mathematics); **Mechanical and Industrial Engineering** (Industrial Engineering; Mechanical Engineering; Production Engineering); **Metallurgical and Materials Sciences** (Materials Engineering; Metallurgical Engineering); **Paper Technology** (Paper Technology); **Physics** (Physics); **Water Resources Development and Management** (Water Management)

History: Founded 1847 as Thomason College of Civil Engineering, the oldest Engineering College in India, became University of Roorkee 1949. Acquired present status 1949 and title 2001.

Academic Year: July to May (July-December; January-May)

Admission Requirements: 12th year senior secondary/intermediate examination or recognized foreign equivalent

Main Language(s) of Instruction: English

Degrees and Diplomas: *Bachelor's Degree*; *Postgraduate Diploma*; *Master's Degree*; *Doctor of Philosophy*

Student Services: Academic Counselling, Canteen, Careers Guidance, Cultural Activities, Facilities for disabled people, Foreign Studies Centre, Health Services, Language Laboratory, Nursery Care, Social Counselling, Sports Facilities

Last Updated: 18/11/11

INDIAN INSTITUTE OF TECHNOLOGY, ROPAR

Nangal Road, Rupnagar, Punjab 140001
Tel: +91(1881) 227078
Fax: +91(1881) 223395
Website: http://www.iitrpr.ac.in/

Director: M.K. Surappa EMail: director@iitrpr.ac.in

Registrar: A. Palanivel

Programme

Engineering (Computer Education; Computer Science; Electrical Engineering; Mechanical Engineering); **Humanities and Social Science** (Arts and Humanities; Social Sciences); **Sciences** (Chemistry; Mathematics; Physics)

History: Founded 2008.

Degrees and Diplomas: *Bachelor's Degree*; *Master's Degree*; *Doctor of Philosophy*

Last Updated: 06/01/12

INDIAN LAW INSTITUTE

Bhagwandas Road, New Delhi 110001
Tel: +91(11) 2338-7526
Fax: +91(11) 2378-2140
EMail: ili@ili.ac.in
Website: http://www.ili.ac.in

Director: S. Sivakumar EMail: director@ili.ac.in

Registrar: Dalip Kumar

Programme

Law (Commercial Law; Labour Law; Law; Taxation)

History: Founded 1956. Acquired Deemed University status 2004.

Degrees and Diplomas: *Bachelor's Degree*; *Postgraduate Diploma*; *Doctor of Philosophy*

Last Updated: 18/11/11

INDIAN MARITIME UNIVERSITY (IMU)

East Coast Road, Uthandi, Chennai 600 119
Tel: +91(44) 2453-0343 +91(44) 2453-0345
Fax: +91(44) 2453-0342
Website: http://www.imu.edu.in/

Vice-Chancellor: P. Vijayan

Programme

Marine Engineering (Marine Engineering); **Nautical** (Nautical Science); **Port and Shipping Management** (Computer Science; Finance; Human Resources; Management; Marine Transport; Transport Engineering; Transport Management)

School

Business (Business Administration; International Business; Marine Transport; Transport and Communications; Transport Management)

Further Information: Regional Campuses in Mumbai, Kolkata, Visakhapatnam, Cochin.

History: Founded 2008. A 'Central University'.

Degrees and Diplomas: *Post Diploma*; *Bachelor's Degree*; *Postgraduate Diploma*; *Master's Degree*; *Doctor of Philosophy*

Last Updated: 08/12/11

INDIAN SCHOOL OF MINES

Jharkand, Dhanbad, Bihar 826004
Tel: +91(326) 229-6559
Fax: +91(326) 229-6563
EMail: rg@ismdhanbad.ac.in
Website: http://www.ismdhanbad.ac.in/

Director: D.C. Panigrahi EMail: dt@ismdhanbad.ac.in

Registrar: M.K. Singh Tel: +91(326) 223-5202

Department

Applied Chemistry (Applied Chemistry); **Applied Geology** (Geology); **Applied Geophysics** (Geophysics); **Applied Mathematics** (Applied Mathematics); **Applied Physics** (Applied Physics); **Chemical Engineering** (Chemical Engineering); **Computer Science and Engineering** (Computer Science; Engineering); **Electrical Engineering** (Electrical Engineering); **Electronics Engineering** (Electronic Engineering; Measurement and Precision Engineering); **Engineering and Mining Machinery** (Engineering; Mechanical Equipment and Maintenance); **Environmental Science and Engineering** (Environmental Engineering); **Fuel and Mineral Engineering** (Mineralogy; Petroleum and Gas Engineering); **Humanities and Social Sciences** (Arts and Humanities; English; Social Sciences); **Management** (Management); **Mechanical Engineering and Mining Machinery Engineering** (Mechanical Engineering; Mining Engineering); **Mining Engineering** (Mining Engineering); **Petroleum Engineering** (Petroleum and Gas Engineering)

Research Centre

Biotechnology; **Materials Science**

History: Founded 1926 following the pattern of Royal School of Mines, London, and Mining Colleges of Japan. Declared an autonomous body with a 'Deemed University' status granted 1967.

Academic Year: July to June

Admission Requirements: 12th year senior secondary/intermediate examination or recognized foreign equivalent

Main Language(s) of Instruction: English

Accrediting Agency: University Grants Commission

Degrees and Diplomas: *Bachelor's Degree*; *Master's Degree*; *Doctor of Philosophy*

Last Updated: 18/11/11

INDIAN STATISTICAL INSTITUTE

203 Barrackpore Trunk Road, Kolkata, West Bengal 700108
Tel: +91(33) 2577-6037
Fax: +91(33) 2577-6680
EMail: director@isical.ac.in
Website: http://www.isical.ac.in

Director: Bimal K. Roy
Tel: +91(33) 2577-3084 EMail: sanka@isical.ac.in

Dean of Studies: G.M. Saha

Division

Applied Statistics (Statistics); **Biological Sciences** (Agriculture; Biological and Life Sciences; Ecology; Genetics); **Computer and Communication Sciences** (Computer Engineering; Computer Networks; Telecommunications Engineering); **Library, Documentation and Information Sciences** (Documentation Techniques; Information Sciences; Library Science; Photography); **Physics and Earth Sciences** (Earth Sciences; Physics); **Social Sciences** (Linguistics; Psychology; Social Sciences; Sociology); **Statistical Quality Control** (Statistics); **Teaching and Training** (Teacher Training); **Theoretical Statistics and Mathematics** (Mathematics; Statistics)

Further Information: Calcutta, New Delhi, Bangalore and Hyderabad

History: Founded 1932, recognized as an Institution of national importance and empowered to confer degrees in Statistics 1959.

Academic Year: July-June

Admission Requirements: 12th year senior secondary/intermediate examination or recognized foreign equivalent

Main Language(s) of Instruction: English

Accrediting Agency: Ministry of Statistics and Programme Implementation

Degrees and Diplomas: *Bachelor's Degree*: **Mathematics; Statistics.** *Master's Degree*: **Computer Science; Statistics.** *Doctor of Philosophy*: **Computer Science; Economics; Mathematics; Statistics.** Also Associateship in Library Documentation and Information Sciences 2 yrs

Student Services: Academic Counselling, Canteen, Careers Guidance, Cultural Activities, Facilities for disabled people, Foreign Studies Centre, Health Services, Sports Facilities

Publications: Sankhya - the Indian Journal of Statistics

Last Updated: 18/11/11

INDIAN VETERINARY RESEARCH INSTITUTE

Bhartiya Pashu-Chikitsa Anusandhan Sansthan

Izatnagar, Uttar Pradesh 243122
Tel: +91(581) 230-0096
Fax: +91(581) 230-3284
EMail: dirivri@ivri.res.in; directoriivri@gmail.com
Website: http://ivri.nic.in

Director: M.C. Sharma
EMail: dirivri@ivri.res.in

International Relations: Shri U.C. Prasad, Registrar
EMail: registrar@ivri.res.in

Division
Animal Biotechnology (Biotechnology; Zoology); **Animal Genetics**; **Animal Nutrition**; **Animal Reproduction** (Animal Husbandry); **Avian Diseases** (Veterinary Science); **Bacterilogy and Mycology**; **Biochemistry and Food Science** (Biochemistry; Food Science; Veterinary Science; Zoology); **Biological Products** (Biology); **Biological Products**; **Epidemiology**; **Extension Education** (Education; Veterinary Science); **Livestock Economics and Statistics** (Animal Husbandry; Statistics); **Medicine** (Medicine; Veterinary Science); **P. and T.** (Pharmacology; Veterinary Science); **Parasitology** (Parasitology; Veterinary Science); **Pathology** (Pathology; Veterinary Science); **Physiology and Climatology** (Physiology; Zoology); **Standardisation**; **Surgery** (Surgery); **Veterinary Public Health** (Public Health; Veterinary Science); **Virology** (Veterinary Science; Virology)

Institute
Central Avian Research

Section
Immunology (Immunology); **Livestock Production and Management** (Animal Husbandry); **Livestock Production and Management**

History: Founded 1889. Acquired present status as 'Deemed to be University' 1983.

Academic Year: September to August

Admission Requirements: 12th year senior secondary/intermediate examination or recognized foreign equivalent; Bachelor of Veterinary Sciences and Animal Husbandry for Master of Vet. Sc.(M.V.SC.); M.V.Sc. for PhD

Main Language(s) of Instruction: English

Accrediting Agency: Indian Council of Agricultural Research

Degrees and Diplomas: *Postgraduate Diploma*: **Animal Husbandry; Food Technology; Medicine; Surgery; Veterinary Science; Wildlife; Zoology.** *Master's Degree*: **Animal Husbandry; Biochemistry; Biological and Life Sciences; Epidemiology; Gynaecology and Obstetrics; Immunology; Microbiology; Parasitology; Pathology; Pharmacology; Public Health; Statistics; Surgery; Veterinary Science; Virology.** *Doctor of Philosophy*: **Animal Husbandry; Biochemistry; Gynaecology and Obstetrics; Immunology; Microbiology; Parasitology; Pathology; Pharmacology; Public Health; Surgery; Veterinary Science; Virology.** Also Short term training Courses and International Short Term Training for Foreign Nationals

Student Numbers *2011-2012*: Total 641

Last Updated: 24/06/11

INDIRA GANDHI AGRICULTURAL UNIVERSITY

Indira Gandhi Krishi Vishwavidyalaya

Krishak Nagar, Raipur, Madhya Pradesh 492006
Tel: +91(771) 244-2537
Fax: +91(771) 244-2131
EMail: matappandey@yahoo.in
Website: http://igau.edu.in

Vice-Chancellor: M.P. Pandey EMail: matappandey@yahoo.in

Registrar: S.R. Ratre

Faculty
Agriculture (Agriculture); **Agriculture Engineering** (Agricultural Engineering); **Dairy Technology** (Dairy); **Veterinary Science and Animal Husbandry** (Animal Husbandry; Veterinary Science)

Further Information: Also 9 constituent colleges

History: Founded 1987.

Degrees and Diplomas: *Bachelor's Degree*; *Master's Degree*; *Doctor of Philosophy*. Also Undergraduate and Postgraduate Diplomas

Last Updated: 18/11/11

INDIRA GANDHI INSTITUTE OF DEVELOPMENT RESEARCH (IGIDR)

Gen. A.K.Vaidya Marg, Goregaon (E),
Mumbai, Maharashtra 400065
Tel: +91(22) 2840-0919 +91(22) 2840-0920
Fax: +91(22) 2840-2752
EMail: director@igidr.ac.in
Website: http://www.igidr.ac.in

Director: S. Mahendra Dev
Tel: +91(22) 2841-6501 EMail: profmahendra@igidr.ac.in

Registrar and Chief Administrative Officer: Pandit Jai Mohan

Programme
Development Studies (Development Studies; Economics)

History: Founded 1987 by the Reserve Bank of India. Granted 'Deemed University' status. A postgraduate Institution.

Academic Year: August to July (August-December; January to July)

Admission Requirements: For admission to BA, BSc in Economics, B.Com, B.Stat, BSc (Mathematics or Physics), B.tech, BE, M.Sc. in Economics, MScBTech/BE, MSc. in Economics, MBA/ M.Tech/ME/B.Tech/BE, MPhil/PhD, 55% to 60%

Fees: (Rupees): 8,000 per semester

Main Language(s) of Instruction: English

Accrediting Agency: National Assessment and Accreditation Council

Degrees and Diplomas: *Master's Degree*: **Economics.** *Master of Philosophy*: **Development Studies.** *Doctor of Philosophy*: **Development Studies.**

Student Services: Academic Counselling, Canteen, Cultural Activities, Health Services, Nursery Care, Sports Facilities

Publications: India Development Report (IDR)

Publishing House: Oxford University Press, New Dehli

Last Updated: 18/11/11

INDIRA GANDHI NATIONAL OPEN UNIVERSITY

Indira Gandhi Rashtriya Mukta Vishwavidyalaya (IGNOU)

Maidan Garhi, New Delhi 110068
Tel: +91(11) 2953-5924-32
Fax: +91(11) 2953-2312
Website: http://www.ignou.ac.in

Vice-Chancellor: Gopinath Pradhan (2012-)
Tel: +91(11) 2953-2484 EMail: vc@ignou.ac.in

Registrar: Udai Singh Tolia EMail: ustolia@ignou.ac.in

School
Agriculture (Agriculture); **Computer and Information Sciences** (Computer Engineering; Information Sciences); **Continuing**

Education (Child Care and Development; Food Science; Rural Planning; Women's Studies); **Education** (Education); **Engineering and Technology** (Civil Engineering; Electrical Engineering; Mechanical Engineering; Technology); **Extension and Development Studies** (Development Studies); **Foreign Languages** (Foreign Languages Education); **Gender and Development Studies** (Development Studies; Gender Studies); **Health Sciences** (Health Sciences; Medical Auxiliaries; Nursing; Paramedical Sciences); **Humanities** (Arts and Humanities; English; Hindi; Indic Languages; Writing); **Inter-Disciplinary and Trans-Disciplinary Studies** (Astrophysics; Folklore); **Journalism and New Media Studies** (Journalism; Media Studies); **Law** (Law); **Management Studies** (Management); **Performing and Visual Arts** (Performing Arts; Visual Arts); **Science** (Biological and Life Sciences; Physics); **Social Sciences** (Economics; History; Library Science; Political Sciences; Public Administration; Social Sciences; Sociology; Tourism); **Social Work** (Social Work); **Tourism and Hospitality** (Tourism); **Translation Studies and Training** (Translation and Interpretation); **Vocational Education and Training** (Vocational Education)

Further Information: Also 30 Regional Centres and 17 Special Regional Centres for the Armed Forces

History: Founded 1985.

Academic Year: January to December

Admission Requirements: 12th year senior secondary/intermediate examination or recognized foreign equivalent

Main Language(s) of Instruction: English, Hindi

Degrees and Diplomas: *Post Diploma*: **Business and Commerce; Child Care and Development; Civil Engineering; Computer Science; Distance Education; Environmental Studies; Food Science; Forest Management; Health Education; Human Rights; Information Technology; Journalism; Management; Mass Communication; Nutrition; Tourism; Town Planning; Welfare and Protective Services; Women's Studies; Writing.** *Bachelor's Degree*: **Botany; Business and Commerce; Chemistry; Computer Science; Economics; Education; Engineering; English; Hindi; History; Information Sciences; Information Technology; Library Science; Mathematics; Nursing; Physics; Public Administration; Sociology; Technology; Tourism; Zoology.** *Postgraduate Diploma*: **Business and Commerce; Child Care and Development; Civil Engineering; Computer Science; Distance Education; Environmental Studies; Food Science; Forest Management; Health Education; Human Rights; Information Technology; Journalism; Management; Mass Communication; Nutrition; Tourism; Town Planning; Welfare and Protective Services; Women's Studies; Writing.** *Master's Degree*: **Banking; Business Administration; Computer Science; Distance Education; English; Finance; Hindi; Library Science; Public Administration.** *Doctor of Philosophy*: **Economics; Education; History; Library Science; Public Administration; Sociology; Tourism.** Also 2-year Certificate programmes

Student Services: Academic Counselling, Canteen, Careers Guidance, Cultural Activities, Facilities for disabled people, Health Services, Nursery Care, Social Counselling, Sports Facilities

Publications: Indian Journal of Open Learning

Last Updated: 18/11/11

INDIRA GANDHI NATIONAL TRIBAL UNIVERSITY, AMARKANTAK (IGNTU)

Kapil Dhara Road, Mekal Sadan, Dist-Anuppur,
Amarkantak, Madhya Pradesh 484 886
Tel: +90 7629-269640
Fax: +90 7629-269432
EMail: igntribaluniv@gmail.com
Website: http://igntu.nic.in/theuniversity.htm

Vice-Chancellor: C.D. Singh
Tel: +90 7629-269544 EMail: vcigntu@gmail.com

Registrar: Ashok Singh
Tel: +90 7629-269617 EMail: registrarigntua@gmail.com

Faculty

Commerce and Management (Business and Commerce; Forest Management; Hotel Management; Management; Tourism); **Computronics** (Computer Science; Information Technology); **Education** (Education; Physical Education); **Humanities and Philology** (Arts and Humanities; English; Hindi; Modern Languages; Philology; Philosophy; Psychology); **Journalism and Mass Communication** (Journalism; Mass Communication); **Law** (Law); **Pharmacy** (Pharmacy); **Science** (Biotechnology; Botany; Chemistry; Environmental Studies; Geology; Home Economics; Mathematics; Meteorology; Mineralogy; Nutrition; Physics; Statistics; Zoology); **Social Science** (Anthropology; Archaeology; Cultural Studies; Economics; Geography; History; Human Rights; Political Sciences; Rural Studies; Social Sciences; Social Work; Sociology); **Tribal Studies** (Folklore; History; Linguistics; Literature; Museum Studies; Traditional Eastern Medicine)

History: Founded 2007. A 'Central University'.

Fees: 1,000-3,000 per term (Indian Rupee)

Degrees and Diplomas: *Bachelor's Degree*; *Master's Degree*; *Master of Philosophy*

Last Updated: 06/12/11

INDRAPRASTHA INSTITUTE OF INFORMATION TECHNOLOGY

3rd Floor, Library Building, NSIT Campus, Sector 3,
Dwarka, New Delhi 110073
Tel: +91(11) 2509-9177
Fax: +91(11) 2509-9176
EMail: registrar@iiitd.ac.in
Website: http://www.iiitd.ac.in

Director: Pankaj Jalote

Programme

Computer Science (Computer Engineering; Computer Science; Information Technology)

History: Founded 2008.

Degrees and Diplomas: *Bachelor's Degree*; *Master's Degree*; *Doctor of Philosophy*

Last Updated: 05/01/12

INDUS INTERNATIONAL UNIVERSITY

VPO Bathu, Tehsil Haroli, District UNA, Himachal Pradesh
EMail: info@iiuedu.in
Website: http://www.iiuedu.in

Vice-Chancellor: Raman Kr. Jha

School

Arts, Media and Education (Advertising and Publicity; Arts and Humanities; Education; English; Journalism; Media Studies); **Business and Management** (Business Administration; Management); **Science, Engineering and Technology** (Biotechnology; Civil Engineering; Computer Science; Electrical Engineering; Engineering; Mathematics; Mechanical Engineering; Physics; Technology; Telecommunications Engineering)

History: Created 2010.

Degrees and Diplomas: *Bachelor's Degree*; *Master's Degree*; *Master of Philosophy*

Last Updated: 16/11/11

INSTITUTE OF ADVANCED STUDIES IN EDUCATION

Ghandi Vidya Mandir, Sardarshahr, Rajasthan 331401
Tel: +91(1564) 220-025 +91(1564) 220-056
Fax: +91(1564) 223-682
EMail: info@iaseuniversity.org.in
Website: http://www.iaseuniversity.org.in/

Vice-Chancellor: Milap Dugar EMail: vc@iaseuniversity.org.in

Registrar: R.S. Tripathi

Faculty

Engineering (Biotechnology; Computer Science; Electrical Engineering; Engineering; Mechanical Engineering; Telecommunications Engineering); **Management** (Banking; Business Administration; Computer Education; Computer Networks; Computer Science; E- Business/Commerce; Education; Electronic Engineering; Finance; Health Administration; Human Resources; Information Technology; Insurance; International Business; Laboratory Techniques; Management; Marketing; Midwifery;

Multimedia; Nursing; Physical Therapy; Public Relations; Radiology; Telecommunications Engineering; Vocational Counselling)

Programme

Para-medical Allied Health Science (Health Administration; Laboratory Techniques; Medicine; Nursing; Occupational Therapy; Physical Therapy)

Department

Education (Accountancy; Business Administration; Civics; Computer Education; Economics; Education; Educational Administration; Educational Psychology; Educational Technology; English; Environmental Studies; Geography; Hindi; History; Library Science; Natural Sciences; Painting and Drawing; Physical Education; Preschool Education; Public Administration; Sanskrit; Social Sciences; Social Studies; Yoga)

Further Information: Also constituent College including Institute of Advanced Studies in Education (Sardarshahr), Distance Education Academic Centre, Distance Education Study Centres, Institute of Ayurved (Sardarshahr), Homeopathic College and Hospital and Nursing College

History: Founded 1953 as Basic Teachers Training College. Acquired present title 1993 and present status 2002.

Academic Year: July to June

Admission Requirements: 12th year senior secondary/intermediate examination or recognized foreign equivalent

Degrees and Diplomas: *Post Diploma*; *Bachelor's Degree*; *Postgraduate Diploma*; *Doctor of Philosophy*
Last Updated: 18/11/11

INSTITUTE OF CHARTERED FINANCIAL ANALYSTS OF INDIA UNIVERSITY, DEHRADUN

Rajawala Road, Central Hope Town, Selaqui,
Dehradun, Uttrakhand 248197
Tel: +91(135) 324-6450
EMail: registrar@iuuttarakhand.edu.in
Website: http://www.iudehradun.edu.in/

Vice-Chancellor: G.P. Srivastava Tel: +91(135) 325-4612

Registrar: P.K. Dash Tel: +91(135) 300-3009

Faculty

Education (Education); **Law** (Law); **Science and Technology** (Biotechnology; Computer Science; Electrical Engineering; Electronic Engineering; Engineering; Mechanical Engineering; Technology; Telecommunications Engineering)

Programme

Business Administration (Business Administration; Management)

Further Information: Tripura, Sikkim, Meghalaya, Mizoram, Nagaland, and Jharkhand

History: ICFAI University refers to the Universities sponsored by the Institute of Chartered Financial Analysts of India.

Admission Requirements: Students who pass with 50% and above in graduation or its equivalent and admission test

Accrediting Agency: University Grants Commission (UGC)

Degrees and Diplomas: *Bachelor's Degree*; *Master's Degree*; *Doctor of Philosophy*
Last Updated: 21/11/11

INSTITUTE OF CHARTERED FINANCIAL ANALYSTS OF INDIA UNIVERSITY, JHARKHAND

Between Road No.1 & 2, Ashok Nagar, Ranchi, Jharkhand 834002
Tel: +91(651) 2243-255
Fax: +91(651) 2245-178
EMail: registrar@iujharkhand.edu.in
Website: http://www.iujharkhand.edu.in

Vice-Chancellor: O.R.S. Rao Tel: +91(651) 2245-178

Faculty

Management Studies (Business Administration; Hotel Management; Tourism); **Science and Technology** (Computer Engineering; Computer Networks; Software Engineering)

History: Founded 2008.

Degrees and Diplomas: *Bachelor's Degree*; *Master's Degree*; *Doctor of Philosophy*
Last Updated: 12/01/12

INSTITUTE OF CHARTERED FINANCIAL ANALYSTS OF INDIA UNIVERSITY, MEGHALAYA

4th Floor, Near Sundari Complex, Circular Road, West Garo Hils, Tura, Meghalaya 794001
EMail: registrar@iumeghalaya.edu.in
Website: http://www.iumeghalaya.edu.in

Vice-Chancellor: Y.K. Bhushan Tel: +91(3651) 224683

Registrar: Biplab Halder Tel: +91(3651) 224683

Programme

Computer Application (Computer Networks; Software Engineering); **Management** (Business Administration; Tourism)

Degrees and Diplomas: *Bachelor's Degree*; *Master's Degree*
Last Updated: 13/01/12

INSTITUTE OF CHARTERED FINANCIAL ANALYSTS OF INDIA UNIVERSITY, MIZORAM

Dawrkawn, Chaltlang, Aizawl, Mizoram 796012
Tel: +91(389) 2344-917
Fax: +91(389) 2306-568
Website: http://www.iumizoram.edu.in

Vice-Chancellor: J.P. Ramappa

Registrar: C. Lalkima

Programme

Computer Application (Computer Networks; Construction Engineering; Software Engineering); **Management Studies** (Accountancy; Business Administration; Finance; Human Resources; Marketing; Tourism)

Degrees and Diplomas: *Bachelor's Degree*; *Master's Degree*
Last Updated: 13/01/12

INSTITUTE OF CHARTERED FINANCIAL ANALYSTS OF INDIA UNIVERSITY, NAGALAND

Nepali Basti, Behind Nepali Mandir, Dimapur, Nagaland 797112
Tel: +91(3862) 234816
Fax: +91(3862) 234815
EMail: registrar@iunagaland.edu.in
Website: http://www.iunagaland.edu.in

Vice-Chancellor: O.P. Gupta

Faculty

Management Studies (Business Administration; Management)

History: Founded 2006. Acquired present status 2008.

Degrees and Diplomas: *Bachelor's Degree*; *Master's Degree*
Last Updated: 13/01/12

INSTITUTE OF CHARTERED FINANCIAL ANALYSTS OF INDIA UNIVERSITY, SIKKIM

Nam Nang Commercial Complex, Nam Nang, Deorali,
Gangtok, Sikkim 737101
Tel: +91(3592) 202065
Fax: +91(3592) 201466
EMail: registrar@iusikkim.edu.in
Website: http://www.iusikkim.edu.in

Vice-Chancellor: M. Raja Tel: +91(3592) 202065

Faculty

Law (Law); **Management Studies** (Management); **Science and Technology** (Natural Sciences; Technology)

History: Founded 2004.

Degrees and Diplomas: *Bachelor's Degree*; *Master's Degree*
Last Updated: 04/01/12

INSTITUTE OF CHARTERED FINANCIAL ANALYSTS OF INDIA UNIVERSITY, TRIPURA

Agartala, Kamalghat Sadar, West Tripura 799210
Tel: +91(381) 2865-752
Fax: +91(381) 2865-754
EMail: registrar@iutripura.edu.in
Website: http://www.iutripura.edu.in

Vice-Chancellor: R.K. Patnaik

Registrar: Snehalata Behura

Faculty

Education (Education); **Law** (Law); **Management Studies** (Business Administration; Management); **Science and Technology** (Civil Engineering; Computer Engineering; Computer Science; Electronic Engineering; Mechanical Engineering; Technology; Telecommunications Engineering)

History: Founded 2004.

Degrees and Diplomas: *Bachelor's Degree*; *Master's Degree*; *Doctor of Philosophy*
Last Updated: 12/01/12

INSTITUTE OF CHEMICAL TECHNOLOGY

Nathalal Parekh Marg, Matunga, Mumbai 400019
Tel: +91(22) 3361-1111
Fax: +91(22) 3361-1020
EMail: admission@ictmumbai.edu.in
Website: http://www.ictmumbai.edu.in/

Vice-Chancellor: G. D. Yadav

Department

Chemical Engineering (Chemical Engineering); **Chemistry** (Chemistry); **Dyestuff Technology** (Chemical Engineering); **Fibers and Textile Processing** (Textile Technology); **Food Engineering and Technology** (Food Science; Food Technology); **General Engineering** (Engineering); **Mathematics** (Mathematics); **Oils, Oleochemicals and Surfactants Technology** (Chemical Engineering); **Pharmaceutical Sciences and Technology** (Pharmacology; Pharmacy); **Physics** (Physics); **Polymer and Surface Engineering** (Polymer and Plastics Technology)

History: Founded 1933, as Department of Chemical Technology of the University of Mumbai. Converted in to an Institute, 1922. Acquired the status of deemed university 2009.

Degrees and Diplomas: *Bachelor's Degree*; *Master's Degree*; *Doctor of Philosophy*
Last Updated: 11/01/12

INSTITUTE OF HEALTH MANAGEMENT RESEARCH JAIPUR (IIHMR)

Prabhu Dayal Marg, Sanganer Airport, Jaipur, Rajastan 302011
Tel: +91(141) 2791-431/32
Fax: +91(141) 3924-738
EMail: iihmr@iihmr.org
Website: http://www.jaipur.iihmr.org

Director: S. D. Gupta

Programme

Health Management (Health Administration; Pharmacy; Public Health); **Rural Management** (Management; Rural Studies)

Further Information: Also campuses in Dehli and Bangalore

History: Founded 1984. Formerly known as Indian Institute of Health Management Research.

Accrediting Agency: All India Council for Technical Education (AICTE)

Degrees and Diplomas: *Postgraduate Diploma*
Last Updated: 27/01/12

INSTITUTE OF INTEGRATED LEARNING IN MANAGEMENT (IILM)

Lodhi Institutional Area, Lodhi Road, New Delhi 110 003
Tel: +91(11) 4093-4318
EMail: deanubs@iilm.edu
Website: http://www.iilm.edu/

Trustee: Anil Kanodia EMail: anil.kanodia@iilm.edu

International Relations: Rakesh Chaudhry, Senior Director EMail: rakesh.chaudhry@iilm.edu

Programme

Management (Management)

Further Information: Also Gurgaon Campus

History: Founded 1993.

Accrediting Agency: All India Council for Technical Education (AICTE)

Degrees and Diplomas: *Postgraduate Diploma*: **Management.** Bachelor's degree also offered by Bradford University

Academic Staff *2014-2015*: Total 34

STAFF WITH DOCTORATE: Total 12

Student Numbers *2014-2015*: Total 259
Last Updated: 09/01/12

INSTITUTE OF LIVER AND BILIARY SCIENCES

D-1, Vasant Kunj, New Delhi 110070
Tel: +91(11) 4630-0000
EMail: info@ilbs.in
Website: http://www.ilbs.in/

Director: S.K. Sarin

Programme

Medicine (Anaesthesiology; Biomedicine; Hepatology; Medicine; Pathology; Radiology; Surgery)

Degrees and Diplomas: *Postgraduate Diploma*; *Master's Degree*; *Doctor of Philosophy*
Last Updated: 12/01/12

INSTITUTE OF MANAGEMENT TECHNOLOGY

Raj Nagar, Ghaziabad, Uttar Pradesh 201 001
Tel: +91(120) 3002-200
Fax: +91(120) 3002-300
EMail: info@imt.edu
Website: http://www.imt.edu

Director: Bibek Banerjee EMail: director@imt.edu

Academic Administration: Amarendra Sahoo

Programme

Management (Finance; Human Resources; Information Technology; International Business; Management; Marketing)

Further Information: Also campuses in Nagpur (2004) in Dubai (2006), and in Hyderabad (2011)

Accrediting Agency: All India Council for Technical Education (AICTE)

Degrees and Diplomas: *Postgraduate Diploma*; *Doctor of Philosophy*
Last Updated: 02/02/12

INSTITUTE OF PROFESSIONAL EDUCATION AND RESEARCH (IPER)

Bhojpur Road, Misrod, Bhopal, Madhya Pradesh 462 026
Tel: +91(755) 302-4821 +91(755) 302-4800
Fax: +91(755) 302-4818
EMail: soni.mahesh@iper.ac.in
Website: http://www.iper.ac.in/

Director: A. S. Khalsa EMail: khalsa.amarjeet@iper.ac.in

Head, Administration: Abhishek Jain EMail: jain.abhishek@iper.ac.in

Programme

Business Administration (Business Administration); **Business Administration** *(Part-time)* (Business Administration); **Management** (Management)

History: Founded 1996.

Accrediting Agency: All India Council for Technical Education (AICTE)

Degrees and Diplomas: *Postgraduate Diploma.* PGDM programme is equivalent to a University MBA Degree
Last Updated: 25/01/12

INTEGRAL UNIVERSITY

P.O. Bas-ha Kursi Road, Lucknow, Uttar Pradesh 226026
Tel: +91 2890730
Fax: +91 2890809
EMail: info@integraluniversity.ac.in
Website: http://www.integraluniversity.ac.in

Vice-Chancellor: S.W. Akhtar EMail: vc@integraluniversity.ac.in
Registrar: Irfan Ali Khan

Faculty
Applied Sciences (Biotechnology; Chemistry; English; Environmental Studies; Mathematics; Physics); **Architecture and Fine Arts** (Architecture; Fine Arts); **Computer Apllication** (Computer Engineering; Computer Science); **Education** (Education); **Engineering** (Biophysics; Civil Engineering; Computer Engineering; Electrical and Electronic Engineering; Engineering; Information Sciences; Mechanical Engineering; Telecommunications Engineering); **Management** (Business Administration); **Medicine** (Medicine); **Pharmacy** (Pharmacy)

Programme
Polytechnic (Engineering)

History: Founded 2004.

Degrees and Diplomas: *Post Diploma*; *Bachelor's Degree*; *Master's Degree*; *Doctor of Philosophy*
Last Updated: 28/12/11

INTERNATIONAL INSTITUTE FOR POPULATION SCIENCES

Govandi Station Road, Deonar, Mumbai, Maharashtra 400088
Tel: +91(22) 2556-3254
Fax: +91(22) 2556-3257
EMail: director@iipsindia.org
Website: http://www.iipsindia.org

Director: Faujdar Ram Tel: +91(22) 2556-3254

Registrar: M.K. Kulkarini
Tel: +91(22) 2556-3485 EMail: registrar@iips.net

Department
Development Studies (Anthropology; Development Studies); **Extra Mural Studies and Distance Education (Project Basis)** *(Project Basis)* (Demography and Population); **Fertility Studies** (Demography and Population); **Mathematical Demography and Statistics** (Demography and Population; Statistics); **Migration and Urban Studies** (Geography (Human); Urban Studies); **Population Policies and Programmes** (Demography and Population); **Public Health and Mortality Studies** (Public Health)

History: Founded 1956. Declared to be an Institution 'deemed to be a University' 1985. A Regional Institute for Training and Research in Population Studies for the countries of Asia and Pacific regions of the United Nations.

Academic Year: July to May

Admission Requirements: Bachelor Degree

Fees: (Rupees): MA Studies for Indian Students: 1,000 per annum; Foreign students: 3000 (US Dollars)

Main Language(s) of Instruction: English

Accrediting Agency: Government of India; UN Population Fund; Sir Dorabji Tata Trust; University Grants Commission

Degrees and Diplomas: *Post Diploma*; *Master's Degree*; *Master of Philosophy*; *Doctor of Philosophy*. Also Diploma course in Population Studies for UN students under UNFPA fellowship programme

Student Services: Canteen, Sports Facilities

Publications: IIPS Newsletter
Last Updated: 21/11/11

INTERNATIONAL INSTITUTE OF INFORMATION TECHNOLOGY, BANGALORE (IIIT-B)

26/C, Electronics City, Hosur Road, Bangalore, Karnakata 560100
Tel: +91(80) 4140-7777
Fax: +91(80) 4140-7704
EMail: info@iiitb.ac.in
Website: http://www.iiitb.ac.in/

Director: S. Sadagopan

Registrar: A.N. Ramachandra

Programme
Information Technology (Computer Networks; Computer Science; Information Technology; Software Engineering)

History: Founded 1999.

Degrees and Diplomas: *Master's Degree*; *Doctor of Philosophy*
Last Updated: 09/01/12

INTERNATIONAL INSTITUTE OF INFORMATION TECHNOLOGY, HYDERABAD (IIIT-H)

Gachibowli, Hyderabad, Andhra Pradesh 500032
Tel: +91(40) 6653-1000
Fax: +91(40) 6653-1413
EMail: query@iiit.ac.in
Website: http://www.iiit.ac.in

Director: Rajeev Sangal EMail: sangal@iiit.net

Registrar: R. Govindarajulu EMail: gregeti@iiit.ac.in

Programme
Engineering (Building Technologies; Cognitive Sciences; Computer Engineering; Construction Engineering; Electrical Engineering; Information Technology; Software Engineering; Telecommunications Engineering)

History: Founded 1998 as Indian Institute of Technology. Acquired present status and title 2001.

Degrees and Diplomas: *Post Diploma*; *Bachelor's Degree*; *Postgraduate Diploma*; *Master's Degree*; *Doctor of Philosophy*
Last Updated: 22/11/11

INTERNATIONAL MANAGEMENT INSTITUTE (IMI)

B-10, Qutab Institutional Area, Tara Crescent, New Delhi 110 016
Tel: +91(11) 719-4100 +91(11) 719-4200
Fax: +91(11) 2686-7539
EMail: imiinfo@imi.edu
Website: http://www.imi.edu/

Director General: Pritam Singh

Programme
Human Resources *(Postgraduate)* (Human Resources); **Management** *(Executive Post Graduate)* (Management); **Management** *(Postgraduate)* (Management); **Management** *(Fellow Programme)* (Management); **Management** *(Doctoral Studies)* (Management)
Further Information: Also Bhubaneswar and Kolkata campuses
History: Founded 1981.

Accrediting Agency: All India Council for Technical Education (AICTE); Ministry of Human Resource Development, Govt. of India

Degrees and Diplomas: *Postgraduate Diploma*; *Doctor of Philosophy*. PGDM equivalence to a MBA; Also Executive Post Graduate Diploma, 15 months
Last Updated: 09/01/12

INVERTIS UNIVERSITY

Invertis village, Bareilly, Lucknow National Highway - 24,
Bareilly, Uttar Pradesh 243123
Tel: +91(581) 2460-442
Fax: +91(581) 2460-454
EMail: admissions@invertis.org
Website: http://www.invertisuniversity.ac.in

Vice-Chancellor: Shripad Ganap Bhat

Registrar: Narendra Singh

Institute
Architecture (Architecture); **Biotechnology** (Biotechnology); **Computer Application** (Computer Science); **Engineering and Technology** (Engineering; Technology); **Journalism and Mass Communication** (Journalism; Mass Communication); **Law** (Law); **Management Studies** (Business Administration; Management); **Pharmacy** (Pharmacy)

History: Founded 2010.
Last Updated: 04/01/12

ITM UNIVERSITY - GURGAON

HUDA Sector 23-A, Gurgaon, Gujarat 122017
Tel: +91(124) 236-5811
Fax: +91(124) 236-7488
EMail: itm1@vsnl.com; itm@itmindia.edu
Website: http://www.itmindia.edu

Vice-ChancellorVice-Chancellor: Prem Vrat

Registrar: S.K. Sharma

School

Engineering and Technology (Civil Engineering; Computer Engineering; Computer Science; Electrical and Electronic Engineering; Engineering; Information Technology; Mechanical Engineering; Technology; Telecommunications Engineering); **Law** (Law); **Management** (Business and Commerce; Management)

History: Founded 1996. Acquired present status 2009.

Degrees and Diplomas: *Bachelor's Degree*; *Master's Degree*; *Doctor of Philosophy*

Last Updated: 19/10/11

ITM UNIVERSITY - GWALIOR

Opp. Sithouli Railway Station, NH-75, Jhansi Road, Gwalior, Madhya Padesh 474001
Tel: +91(751) 243-2977
Fax: +91(751) 243-2988
EMail: vc@itmuniversity.ac.in
Website: http://www.itmuniversity.ac.in

Vice-Chancellor: R. K. Pandey

School

Computer Applications (Computer Science; Construction Engineering); **Engineering and Technology** (Engineering; Technology); **Languages and Literary Studies** (Literature; Modern Languages); **Management and Commerce** (Business and Commerce; Management); **Nursing Sciences** (Nursing); **Sciences** (Natural Sciences); **Teachers Training (Education)** (Teacher Trainers Education); **Technology Management** (Management)

Degrees and Diplomas: *Post Diploma*; *Bachelor's Degree*; *Master's Degree*; *Doctor of Philosophy*

Last Updated: 03/01/12

JADAVPUR UNIVERSITY (JU)

188 Raja S.C. Mallik Road, Kolkata, West Bengal 700032
Tel: +91(33) 2414-6414
Fax: +91(33) 2413-7121
EMail: registrar@admin.jdvu.ac.in
Website: http://www.jaduniv.edu.in/

Vice-Chancellor: Pradip Narayan Ghosh
Tel: +91(33) 2414-6000 EMail: vc@admin.jdvu.ac.in

Registrar: Pradip Kumar Ghosh EMail: pradip_12@vsnl.net

Faculty

Arts (Comparative Literature; Economics; English; Film; History; Indic Languages; Information Sciences; International Relations; Library Science; Philosophy; Physical Education; Sanskrit; Sociology); **Engineering and Technology** (Adult Education; Architecture; Biomedical Engineering; Chemical Engineering; Civil Engineering; Computer Science; Construction Engineering; Electrical Engineering; Electronic Engineering; Engineering; Food Technology; Information Technology; Instrument Making; Materials Engineering; Mechanical Engineering; Metallurgical Engineering; Pharmacy; Power Engineering; Printing and Printmaking; Production Engineering; Telecommunications Engineering); **Science** (Biological and Life Sciences; Chemistry; Geology; Instrument Making; Mathematics; Physics)

Further Information: Also a campus in Salt Lake City (Kolkata) and 2 Affiliated Institutes: Institute of Business Management and J. D. Birla Institute

History: Founded 1955.

Academic Year: July to July

Admission Requirements: 12th year senior secondary/intermediate examination or recognized foreign equivalent

Main Language(s) of Instruction: English, Bengali

Accrediting Agency: NAAC

Degrees and Diplomas: *Bachelor's Degree*: **Chemical Engineering; Chemistry; Civil Engineering; Comparative Literature; Computer Science; Construction Engineering; Economics; Electrical Engineering; English; Environmental Engineering; Geology; Indic Languages; Information Sciences; Information Technology; Instrument Making; International Relations; Library Science; Mathematics; Mechanical Engineering; Metallurgical Engineering; Pharmacy; Philosophy; Physical Education; Physics; Power Engineering; Production Engineering; Sanskrit; Sociology; Structural Architecture; Women's Studies.** *Master's Degree*: **Chemical Engineering; Chemistry; Civil Engineering; Comparative Literature; Computer Science; Construction Engineering; Economics; Electrical Engineering; English; Environmental Engineering; Geology; Indic Languages; Information Sciences; Information Technology; Instrument Making; International Relations; Library Science; Mathematics; Mechanical Engineering; Metallurgical Engineering; Pharmacy; Philosophy; Physical Education; Physics; Power Engineering; Production Engineering; Sanskrit; Sociology; Structural Architecture; Women's Studies.** *Doctor of Philosophy*: **Chemical Engineering; Chemistry; Civil Engineering; Comparative Literature; Computer Science; Construction Engineering; Economics; Electrical Engineering; English; Environmental Engineering; Geology; Indic Languages; Information Sciences; Information Technology; Instrument Making; International Relations; Library Science; Mathematics; Mechanical Engineering; Metallurgical Engineering; Pharmacy; Philosophy; Physical Education; Physics; Power Engineering; Production Engineering; Sanskrit; Sociology; Structural Architecture; Women's Studies.** Also Diploma and Certificate courses

Student Services: Academic Counselling, Canteen, Careers Guidance, Cultural Activities, Facilities for disabled people, Foreign Studies Centre, Health Services, Language Laboratory, Social Counselling, Sports Facilities

Publishing house: University Press

Last Updated: 22/11/11

JAGADGURU RAMANANDACHARYA RAJASTHAN SANSKRIT UNIVERSITY

Village-Madau, Post-Bhonkrota, Jaipur, Rajasthan 302026
Tel: +91(141) 513-2021
EMail: jrrsu@yahoo.com
Website: http://www.jrrsanskrituniversity.ac.in

Vice-Chancellor: R. Devnathan Tel: +91(141) 513-2001

Registrar: Parmeshwari Choudhary Tel: +91(941) 401-2366

Programme

Business Administration, Arts and Humanities (English; Hindi; History; Political Sciences; Public Administration; Sanskrit); **Education, Social Sciences and Home Economics** (Economics; Education; Educational Administration; Home Economics; Physical Education; Political Sciences; Sociology)

History: Founded 2001.

Academic Year: July to April

Main Language(s) of Instruction: Sanskrit

Degrees and Diplomas: *Bachelor's Degree*; *Master's Degree*

Student Services: Academic Counselling, Canteen, Health Services, Sports Facilities

Publications: Pravarti

Publishing House: University Publishing House

JAGADGURU RAMBHADRACHARYA HANDICAPPED UNIVERSITY

Chitrakoot, Karwi, Uttar Pradesh 210204
Tel: +91(5198) 224481
Fax: +91(5198) 224293
EMail: jrhuniversity@yahoo.com
Website: http://www.jrhu.com/

Vice-Chancellor: B. Pandey

Registrar: Kamlesh Kumar

Faculty

Commerce and Management (Business and Commerce; Management); **Computer and Information Sciences** (Computer Engineering; Information Sciences); **Education** (Education; Special Education); **Fine Arts** (Fine Arts; Painting and Drawing); **Humanities** (Economics; English; Hindi; Psychology; Sanskrit); **Music** (Music); **Prosthetics and Orthotics** (Orthodontics); **Social Sciences** (Archaeology; Cultural Studies; History; Social Sciences; Social Work; Sociology); **Vocational Studies** (Vocational Education)

History: Founded 2001.

Student Services: Sports Facilities

Last Updated: 02/01/12

JAGADGURU SRI SHIVARATHREESHWARA UNIVERSITY

JSS Medical Institutions Campus, Sri Shivarathreeshwara Nagara, Mysore, Karnataka 570 015
Tel: +91(821) 2548400
Fax: +91(821) 2548394
EMail: vc@jssuni.edu.in
Website: http://www.jssuni.edu.in/

Vice-Chancellor: B. Suresh

Registrar: Mruthyunjaya P. Kulenur EMail: registrar@jssuni.edu.in

Department

Anatomy (Anatomy); **Dentistry** (Dentistry); **Medicine** (Medicine); **Orthopaedics** (Orthopaedics); **Pharmacology** (Pharmacology); **Surgery** (Surgery)

Degrees and Diplomas: *Bachelor's Degree*; *Master's Degree*; *Doctor of Philosophy*

Last Updated: 10/01/12

JAGAN INSTITUTE OF MANAGEMENT STUDIES (JIMS)

3, Institutional Area, Sector - 5, Rohini, Delhi 110 085
Tel: +91(11) 4518-4000
Fax: +91(11) 4518-4032
Website: http://www.jimsindia.org/

Director-General: R. P. Maheshwari

Programme

Information Technology (Information Technology); **Management** (International Business; Management; Marketing)

History: Founded 1993.

Fees: (Indian Rupee): 415,000-520,000

Accrediting Agency: All India Council for Technical Education (AICTE); Ministry of HRD, Government of India; National Board of Accreditation (NBA)

Degrees and Diplomas: *Bachelor's Degree*; *Postgraduate Diploma*; *Master's Degree*. The Bachelor's degree and Master's degree are affiliated to the Guru Gobind Singh Indraprastha University.

Last Updated: 09/01/12

JAGAN NATH UNIVERSITY

Village Rampura, Teshil-Chaksu, Jaipur, Rajasthan 303901
Tel: +91(141) 302-0500
Fax: +91(141) 302-0538
EMail: admission@jagannathuniversity.org
Website: http://www.jagannathuniversity.org/

Vice-Chancellor: M.K. Bhargava

Faculty

Architecture (Architecture); **Commerce** (Business and Commerce); **Engineering and Technology** (Engineering; Technology); **Information Technology** (Information Technology); **Law** (Law); **Management** (Management); **Mass Communication** (Mass Communication)

History: Founded 2008.

Fees: (Rupiah): 22500-75000 depending on programmes

Degrees and Diplomas: *Bachelor's Degree*; *Master's Degree*; *Doctor of Philosophy*

Last Updated: 16/12/11

JAGDISHPRASAD JHABARMAL TIBREWALA UNIVERSITY (JJTU)

Churu - Bishau Road Chudella, Jhunjhunu, Rajasthan 333 001
Tel: +91(1595) 513-007 +91(1595) 513-006
EMail: jjtu@jjtu.ac.in
Website: http://jjtu.ac.in/

Head: Vinod Tibrewala

Department

Administration (Administration); **Chemistry** (Chemistry); **Computer Science Engineering** (Computer Engineering; Computer Science); **Electronic Engineering** (Electronic Engineering); **Management** (Management); **Mathematics** (Mathematics); **Mechanical Engineering** (Mechanical Engineering); **Mechanical Engineering** (Mechanical Engineering)

History: Founded 2008.

Fees: (Indian Rupee): Undergraduate programmes, 5,000-30,000 per annum; Graduate programmes 15,000-60,000 per annum

Degrees and Diplomas: *Post Diploma*; *Bachelor's Degree*; *Bachelor's Degree (professional)*; *Postgraduate Diploma*; *Master's Degree*; *Doctor of Philosophy*. Also Certificate; MBA

Student Services: Canteen, Sports Facilities

Last Updated: 21/12/11

JAI NARAIN VYAS UNIVERSITY

Bhagat ki Kothi, Pali Road, Jodhpur, Rajasthan 342011
Tel: +91(291) 264-9733
Fax: +91(291) 264-9465
EMail: info@jnvu.edu.in
Website: http://www.jnvu.edu.in/

Vice-Chancellor: B.S. Rajpurohit
Tel: +91(291) 243-2947 EMail: vcjnvu@gmail.com

Registrar: Nirmala Meena Tel: +91(291) 264-9733

Faculty

Arts (Arts and Humanities; Economics; Education; English; Geography; Hindi; History; Home Economics; Indic Languages; Music; Painting and Drawing; Philosophy; Physical Education; Political Sciences; Psychology; Public Administration; Sanskrit; Social Sciences; Sociology); **Commerce and Management Studies** (Accountancy; Business Administration; Business and Commerce; Economics; Finance; Management); **Engineering** (Architecture; Civil Engineering; Computer Science; Construction Engineering; Electrical Engineering; Electronic Engineering; Engineering; Industrial Engineering; Mechanical Engineering; Mining Engineering; Production Engineering; Telecommunications Engineering; Town Planning); **Law** (Law); **Science** (Botany; Chemistry; Geology; Mathematics; Natural Sciences; Physics; Zoology)

Further Information: Colleges situated within the municipal limits of Jodhpur are affiliated to the University

History: Founded 1962.

Academic Year: July to April (July-September; October-December; January-April)

Admission Requirements: 12th year senior secondary/intermediate examination or recognized foreign equivalent

Main Language(s) of Instruction: English, Hindi

Degrees and Diplomas: *Post Diploma*; *Bachelor's Degree*; *Master's Degree*; *Master of Philosophy*; *Doctor of Philosophy*

Publishing house: University Press

Last Updated: 22/11/11

JAI PRAKASH UNIVERSITY

Jai Prakash Vishwavidyalaya

Rahul Sankrityan Nagar, Near Parwati Ashram (Chota Telpa), Chapra, Bihar 841301
Tel: +91(6152) 233-121
Fax: +91(6152) 232-607
Website: http://jpv.bih.nic.in/

Vice-Chancellor: Ram Vinod Sinha Tel: +91(6152) 243-898

Registrar: Bijay Pratap Kumar Tel: +91(6152) 233-507

Faculty

Commerce (Business and Commerce; Economics); **Engineering** (Engineering); **Humanities** (Arts and Humanities; English; Hindi; Philosophy; Sanskrit; Social Sciences); **Science** (Chemistry; Mathematics; Physics; Zoology); **Social Sciences** (Economics; Geography; History; Political Sciences; Psychology; Social Sciences)

Further Information: Also 21 constituent Colleges, 2 affiliated deficit grant colleges (including one Minority College), and 12 affiliated Colleges.

History: Founded 1990 through separation with Bihar University Muzaffarpur. A state Institution.

Academic Year: July to June

Admission Requirements: Senior school certificate (10+2)

Main Language(s) of Instruction: English, Hindi

Degrees and Diplomas: *Bachelor's Degree*: **Arts and Humanities; Business and Commerce; Law; Technology.** *Master's Degree*: **Arts and Humanities; Business and Commerce.** *Doctor of Philosophy*

Student Services: Language Laboratory

Last Updated: 22/11/11

JAIN UNIVERSITY

91/2, Dr A N Krishna Rao Road, V V Puram, Bangalore 560004
Tel: +91(80) 4343-1000
Fax: +91(80) 4343-1010
EMail: admissions@jainuniversity.ac.in
Website: http://www.jainuniversity.ac.in

Vice-Chancellor: N. Sundararajan

Registrar: N.V.H. Krishnan

School

Engineering and Technology (Engineering; Technology); **Graduate Studies** *(J C Road)* (Arts and Humanities; Business and Commerce; Computer Engineering; Natural Sciences; Social Sciences)

Institute

Aerospace Engineering and Management *(International)* (Aeronautical and Aerospace Engineering; Transport Management)

Centre

Ancient Indian History and Culture (Ancient Civilizations; Ayurveda; Cultural Studies; History); **Disaster Mitigation** (Earth Sciences; Fire Science); **Emerging Technologies** (Engineering); **Entrepreneurship** *(RCJ)* (Business Administration); **Management Studies** (Business Administration; Management); **Post Graduate Studies** (Biochemistry; Biotechnology; Electronic Engineering; Microbiology; Physics); **Research in Pure and Applied Sciences** (Natural Sciences); **Research in Social Sciences and Education** (Education; Social Sciences)

History: Founded as Sri Bhagawan Mahaveer Jain College, (SBMJC). Acquired the status of deemed university 2008.

Degrees and Diplomas: *Bachelor's Degree*; *Master's Degree*; *Doctor of Philosophy*

Last Updated: 11/01/12

JAIN VISHVA BHARATI UNIVERSITY (JVBU)

PO Box 6, District Nagaur, Ladnun, Rajasthan 34306
Tel: +91(1581) 222-110 +91(1581) 223-316
Fax: +91(1581) 223-472
EMail: registrar@jvbi.ac.in
Website: http://www.jvbi.ac.in

Vice-Chancellor: Samani Charitra Prajna
Tel: +91(1581) 222-116 EMail: vicechancellor@jvbi.ac.in

Registrar: J.P.N Mishra

College

Acharya Kalu Kanya Mahavidyalay *(Girls only)*; **Education** *(Girls Only)* (Education); **English** (English); **Jainology, Comparative Religion and Philosophy** (Asian Religious Studies; Comparative Religion; Esoteric Practices; Ethics; Metaphysics); **Mahadevlal Saraogi Anekant Shodhpeeth**; **Non-Violence and Peace and Relative Economics** (Asian Religious Studies; Economics; Ethics; Human Rights; International Relations; Peace and Disarmament; Philosophy); **Sanskrit and Prakrit** (Indic Languages; Linguistics; Literature; Sanskrit); **Science of Living, Preshka Meditation and Yoga** (Alternative Medicine; Esoteric Practices; Physiology; Psychotherapy; Yoga); **Social Work** (Social Work)

Further Information: Also Directorate of Distance Education

History: Founded 1970 as Institute. Granted 'Deemed University' status by the University Grants Commission 1991.

Academic Year: July to June

Admission Requirements: University degree at Bachelor level (12th year senior secondary examination with 50% marks).

Fees: (Rupees): Undergraduate, 6,300; postgraduate, 2,987-25,775 per annum (depends on courses)

Main Language(s) of Instruction: Hindi, English

Accrediting Agency: National Assessment and Accreditation Council (NAAC)

Degrees and Diplomas: *Bachelor's Degree*; *Postgraduate Diploma*; *Master's Degree*; *Doctor of Philosophy*. Also Certificate Courses

Student Services: Academic Counselling, Canteen, Language Laboratory, Sports Facilities

Publications: Samvahini; Tulsi Prajna

Last Updated: 22/11/11

JAIPUR NATIONAL UNIVERSITY

Jaipur-Agra Bypass, Near New RTO office,
Jagatpura, Jaipur 302025
Tel: +91(141) 275-3377
Fax: +91(141) 275-2418
EMail: info@jnujaipur.ac.in
Website: http://www.jnujaipur.ac.in

Vice-Chancellor: K.L. Sharma

School

Business and Management (Business Administration; Management); **Computer And Systems Sciences** (Computer Science); **Distance Education and Learning** (Distance Education); **Education** (Education); **Engineering and Technology** (Engineering; Technology); **Hotel Management and Catering Technology** (Cooking and Catering; Hotel Management); **Languages, Literature And Society** (Literature; Modern Languages; Social Studies); **Law and Governance** *(Seedling)* (Government; Law); **Life and Basic Sciences** (Biological and Life Sciences; Natural Sciences); **Nursing** (Nursing); **Pharmaceutical Sciences** (Pharmacy)

Institute

Media Studies *(Seedling (SIMS))* (Media Studies); **Social Sciences** (Social Sciences)

History: Founded 2007.

Degrees and Diplomas: *Bachelor's Degree*; *Master's Degree*

Last Updated: 26/12/11

JAMIA MILLIA ISLAMIA UNIVERSITY

Jamia Millia Islamia

Maulana Mohammed Ali Jauhar Marg, Jamia Nagar,
New Delhi 110025
Tel: +91(11) 2698-1717
Fax: +91(11) 2698-1232
EMail: registrr@jmi.ernet.in
Website: http://jmi.ac.in/

Vice-Chancellor: Najeeb Jung Tel: +91(11) 2698-4650

Registrar: S. M. Sajid
Tel: +91(11) 2698-0337 EMail: ssajid@jmi.ac.in

Faculty

Architecture and Ekistics (Architecture); **Dentistry** (Dentistry); **Education** (Art Education; Computer Education; Education; Educational Sciences; Fine Arts); **Engineering and Technology** (Applied Chemistry; Applied Mathematics; Applied Physics; Architecture; Civil Engineering; Computer Engineering; Electrical

Engineering; Electronic Engineering; Engineering; Environmental Engineering; Humanities and Social Science Education; Mechanical Engineering; Technology); **Humanities and Languages** (Arabic; Cultural Studies; English; Hindi; History; Islamic Studies; Modern Languages; Persian; Urdu); **Law** (Law); **Natural Sciences** (Biological and Life Sciences; Chemistry; Computer Science; Geography; Mathematics; Physics); **Social Sciences** (Adult Education; Business and Commerce; Economics; Education; Human Rights; Political Sciences; Psychology; Public Administration; Social Sciences; Social Work; Sociology)

Research Centre

Academy of Third World Studies; **Mass Communication**

History: Founded 1920, acquired present status 1988.

Academic Year: July to May

Admission Requirements: 12th year senior secondary/intermediate examination or recognized foreign equivalent

Main Language(s) of Instruction: Urdu, Hindi, English

Accrediting Agency: Universities Grants Commission

Degrees and Diplomas: *Bachelor's Degree*; *Postgraduate Diploma*; *Master's Degree*; *Doctor of Philosophy*

Student Services: Academic Counselling, Canteen, Careers Guidance, Health Services, Language Laboratory, Nursery Care, Social Counselling, Sports Facilities

Publications: Islam and the Modern Age (English); Islam Aur Asr-i-Jadeed (Urdu); Jamia Monthly

Last Updated: 22/11/11

JANARDAN RAI NAGAR RAJASTHAN VIDYAPEETH (DEEMED TO BE) UNIVERSITY

Janardan Rai Nagar Rajasthan Vidyapeeth University

93 Parshwanath Colony, Ajmer Road, Jaipur, Rajasthan 313001

Tel: +91(141) 281-1581

Fax: +91(141) 281-0467

EMail: info@jrnrvu.edu.in

Website: http://www.jrnrvu.edu.in/index.php

Vice-Chancellor: Divya Prabha Naga

Registrar: Vijay Singh Panwar

Faculty

Arts and Commerce (Arts and Humanities; Business and Commerce; Economics; Education; English; History; Political Sciences; Social Work; Sociology); **Computer Science** (Computer Engineering; Computer Science; Information Technology; Software Engineering); **Management** (Business Administration; Finance; Fire Science; Human Resources; Management; Marketing); **Medical Science** (Medical Technology; Medicine; Optometry; Radiology); **Science** (Biology; Fashion Design; Interior Design; Jewellery Art; Mathematics; Physics)

Further Information: Distance Education

History: Founded 1937. Granted 'Deemed University' status 1987.

Admission Requirements: 12th year senior secondary/intermediate examination or recognized foreign equivalent

Main Language(s) of Instruction: English

Accrediting Agency: Distance Education Council

Degrees and Diplomas: *Post Diploma*; *Bachelor's Degree*; *Master's Degree*

Last Updated: 22/11/11

JAWAHARLAL NEHRU AGRICULTURAL UNIVERSITY

Jawaharlal Nehru Krishi Vishwavidyalaya

PO Adhartal, Krishinigar, Jabalpur, Madhya Pradesh 482004

Tel: +91(761) 234-3778

Fax: +91(761) 234-2719

EMail: registrarjnkvv@yahoo.com

Website: http://www.jnkvv.nic.in

Vice-Chancellor: Gautam Kalloo

Tel: +91(761) 268-1706 EMail: gkalloo_jnkvv@yahoo.co.in

Registrar: B.B. Mishra EMail: registrarjnkvv@yahoo.com

College

Agricultural Engineering (Agricultural Engineering; Applied Physics; Engineering; Environmental Engineering; Farm Management; Food Technology; Harvest Technology; Mathematics; Meteorology; Soil Conservation; Soil Management; Soil Science; Statistics; Water Science); **Agriculture** (Agricultural Economics; Agriculture; Agronomy; Animal Husbandry; Entomology; Food Science; Forestry; Genetics; Plant and Crop Protection; Plant Pathology; Soil Science; Veterinary Science)

Further Information: Campuses of Agricultural Studies at Rewa, Tikamgah, Ganjbasoda

History: Founded 1964.

Academic Year: July to June (July-November; December-June)

Admission Requirements: 12th year senior secondary/intermediate examination or recognized foreign equivalent

Main Language(s) of Instruction: English

Degrees and Diplomas: *Post Diploma*; *Bachelor's Degree*; *Master's Degree*; *Doctor of Philosophy*

Student Services: Academic Counselling, Canteen, Cultural Activities, Health Services, Sports Facilities

Publications: Krishni Vishwa

Last Updated: 23/11/11

JAWAHARLAL NEHRU ARCHITECTURE AND FINE ARTS UNIVERSITY

Masab Tank, Hyderabad, Andhra Pradesh 500028

Tel: +91(40) 2332-1226

EMail: registrar@jnafau.ac.in

Website: http://www.jnafau.ac.in/

Vice-Chancellor: P. Padmavathi

Registrar: Shaik Khaleel-ur-Rahman

College

Fine Arts (Fine Arts); **Planning and Architecture** (Architectural and Environmental Design; Architecture and Planning; Building Technologies; Interior Design; Town Planning)

History: Founded 2008.

Degrees and Diplomas: *Bachelor's Degree*; *Master's Degree*; *Doctor of Philosophy*

Last Updated: 22/07/11

JAWAHARLAL NEHRU CENTRE FOR ADVANCED SCIENTIFIC RESEARCH (JNCASR)

Jakkur, Bangalore, Karnakata 560064

Tel: +91(80) 2208-2750

EMail: admin@jncasr.ac.in

Website: http://www.jncasr.ac.in

President: M.R.S. Rao

Dean, Academic Affairs: Hemalatha Balaram

Unit

Chemistry and Physics of Materials (Chemistry; Mathematics; Physical Chemistry; Physics); **Engineering Mechanics** (Mathematics; Mechanical Engineering); **Evolutionary and Organismal Biology** (Biology); **Molecular Biology and Genetics** (Biochemistry; Genetics; Immunology; Molecular Biology); **New Chemistry** (Chemistry; Inorganic Chemistry; Organic Chemistry); **Theoretical Sciences** (Mathematics; Mechanical Engineering)

Centre

Materials Science *(International)* (Materials Engineering)

History: Founded 1989. Acquired Deemed University status 2002.

Degrees and Diplomas: *Master's Degree*; *Doctor of Philosophy*

Last Updated: 23/11/11

JAWAHARLAL NEHRU TECHNOLOGICAL UNIVERSITY

Kukatpally, Hyderabad, Andhra Pradesh 500085

Tel: +91(40) 2315-8661

Fax: +91(40) 2315-6184

EMail: director.ufr@jntuh.ac.in

Website: http://www.jntu.ac.in

Vice-Chancellor: Rameshwar Rao
Tel: +91(40) 2315-6109 EMail: vcjntu@yahoo.com

Registrar: K. Lal Kishore Tel: +91(40) 3242-2253

International Relations: Anji Reddy, Director

College

Engineering *(Karimnagar)* (Arts and Humanities; Computer Engineering; Computer Science; Electrical and Electronic Engineering; Electronic Engineering; Engineering; Information Technology; Mechanical Engineering; Nautical Science; Telecommunications Engineering); **Engineering** *(Hyderabad)* (Electrical Engineering; Engineering; Surveying and Mapping); **Engineering** *(Manthani)* (Civil Engineering; Computer Science; Electrical and Electronic Engineering; Engineering; Mechanical Engineering; Mining Engineering; Telecommunications Engineering)

School

Continuing and Distance Education (Civil Engineering; Computer Engineering; Computer Science; Electrical and Electronic Engineering; Electrical Engineering; Electronic Engineering; Mechanical Engineering; Telecommunications Engineering); **Information Technology** *(SIT, Hyderabad)* (Information Technology); **Management Studies** (Management)

Institute

Science and Technology *(IST, Hyderabad)* (Biotechnology; Chemistry; Environmental Engineering; Nanotechnology; Pharmacology; Water Science)

History: Founded 1972.

Academic Year: June/July to April (June/July-November; December/January-April)

Admission Requirements: 12th year senior secondary/intermediate examination or recognized foreign equivalent

Main Language(s) of Instruction: English

Accrediting Agency: National Assessment and Accreditation Council (N.A.A.C.).

Degrees and Diplomas: *Bachelor's Degree*; *Master's Degree*; *Doctor of Philosophy*

Student Services: Academic Counselling, Canteen, Careers Guidance, Cultural Activities, Health Services, Language Laboratory, Sports Facilities

Last Updated: 23/11/11

JAWAHARLAL NEHRU TECHNOLOGICAL UNIVERSITY, KAKINADA

Kakinada, Andhra Pradesh 533 003
EMail: registrar@jntuk.edu.in
Website: http://www.jntuk.edu.in/

Vice-Chancellor: G. Tulasi Ram Das EMail: vc_das@jntuk.edu.in

College

Engineering *(Kakinada)* (Aeronautical and Aerospace Engineering; Chemical Engineering; Civil Engineering; Computer Engineering; Computer Science; Electrical Engineering; Telecommunications Engineering); **Engineering** *(Vijayanagaram)* (Biotechnology; Business Administration; Computer Science; Electrical and Electronic Engineering; Engineering; Information Technology; Mathematics; Mechanical Engineering; Physical Education; Physics)

History: Founded 2008.

Degrees and Diplomas: *Bachelor's Degree*; *Master's Degree*; *Doctor of Philosophy*

Last Updated: 22/07/11

JAWAHARLAL NEHRU UNIVERSITY

Jawaharlal Nehru Vishvavidyalaya (JNU)
New Mehrauli Road, New Delhi 110067
Tel: +91(11) 2674-2676
Fax: +91(11) 2674-2580
EMail: vc@mail.jnu.ac.in
Website: http://www.jnu.ac.in

Vice-Chancellor: S.K. Sopory
Tel: +91(11) 2674-1500 EMail: sopory@mail.jnu.ac.in

Registrar: Sandeep Chatterjee
Tel: +91(11) 2670-4005
EMail: registrar@mail.jnu.ac.in; s_chatterjee@mail.jnu.ac.in

Unit

Archives of Contemporary History (Contemporary History); **Educational Research Record** (Educational Research)

Programme

Postgraduate Studies (M.A.); **Study of Discrimination and Exclusion** (Social Sciences); **Women's Studies** (Women's Studies)

School

Arts and Aesthetics (Aesthetics; Arts and Humanities; Cinema and Television; Theatre; Visual Arts); **Biotechnology** (Biotechnology); **Computational and Integrative Sciences** (Construction Engineering; Information Technology); **Computer and Systems Sciences** (Computer Science); **Environmental Sciences** (Environmental Studies); **International Studies** (International Relations); **Language, Literature and Cultural Studies** (Cultural Studies; Literature; Modern Languages); **Life Sciences** (Biological and Life Sciences); **Physical Sciences** (Physics); **Social Sciences** (Social Sciences)

Centre

Law and Governance (Government; Law); **Molecular Medicine** (Medical Technology; Medicine); **Nano Sciences** (Nanotechnology); **Sanskrit Studies** (Sanskrit)

Group

Adult Education (Adult Education)

Further Information: Also 11 recognized Institutions awarding up to postgraduate degrees

History: Founded 1969. The basic academic units are not single-discipline departments but multidisciplinary Schools of study, the School being visualized as a body of scholars and disciplines linked with each other in terms of their subject matter and methodology, as well as in terms of problem areas.

Academic Year: July to May (July-December; January-May)

Admission Requirements: Senior school certificate (10+2) or recognized foreign equivalent

Fees: (US Dollars): Humanities and Social Sciences, 600 per semester; Science disciplines, 850

Main Language(s) of Instruction: English

Accrediting Agency: University Grants Commission

Degrees and Diplomas: *Post Diploma*; *Bachelor's Degree*; *Master's Degree*: **Computer Engineering; Public Health; Technology.** *Master of Philosophy*; *Doctor of Philosophy*. Also Certificate of Proficiency and Advanced (postgraduate) Diploma, 2 sem.

Student Services: Academic Counselling, Canteen, Careers Guidance, Cultural Activities, Facilities for disabled people, Foreign Studies Centre, Health Services, Language Laboratory, Nursery Care, Social Counselling, Sports Facilities

Publications: Hispanic Horizon; International Studies; JNU Annual Report; Journal of the School of Language, Literature and Culture Studies; Studies in History

Last Updated: 23/11/11

JAYOTI VIDYAPEETH WOMEN'S UNIVERSITY

Vedant Gyan Valley, Village Jharna, Mahala-Jobner,
Jaipur, Rajasthan 303007
Tel: +91(1428) 287427
Fax: +91(1428) 287428
EMail: info@jvwomensuniv.com
Website: http://www.jvwomensuniv.com/

President: S.K. Vashistha

Registrar: Meghna Singhal

Faculty

Architecture and Applied Arts (Architecture); **Diagnosis and Allied Health Science** (Health Sciences); **Distance Education** (Distance Education); **Education** (Education); **Engineering and Technology** (Engineering; Technology); **Homoeopathic Science** (Homeopathy); **Hotel Management and Catering Technology** (Cooking and Catering; Hotel Management); **Law and Governance**

(Government; Law); **Management and Humanities** (Arts and Humanities; Management); **Pharmaceutical Science** (Pharmacy)

Further Information: Also distance education

History: Founded 2008.

Degrees and Diplomas: *Post Diploma*; *Bachelor's Degree*; *Master's Degree*; *Doctor of Philosophy*

Student Services: Sports Facilities

Last Updated: 26/12/11

JAYPEE INSTITUTE OF INFORMATION TECHNOLOGY (JIIT)

A-10,Sector-62, Noida, Uttar Pradesh 201307
Tel: +91(120) 2400-973
Fax: +91(120) 2400-986
EMail: webadmin@jiit.ac.in
Website: http://www.jiit.ac.in/

Vice-Chancellor (Acting): S.C. Saxena EMail: sc.saxena@jiit.ac.in

Dean Students Affairs and Head: K.K. Rohatgi
EMail: kk.rohatgi@jiit.ac.in

School

Business *(Jaypee)* (Business Administration)

Department

Biotechnology (Biotechnology); **Computer Science and Information Technology** (Computer Engineering; Computer Science; Information Technology); **Electronics and Communication** (Electronic Engineering; Telecommunications Engineering); **Humanities and Social Sciences** (Arts and Humanities; Social Sciences); **Mathematics** (Mathematics); **Physics and Material Science** (Materials Engineering; Physics)

Degrees and Diplomas: *Bachelor's Degree*; *Master's Degree*; *Doctor of Philosophy*

Last Updated: 11/01/12

JAYPEE UNIVERSITY OF ENGINEERING AND TECHNOLOGY (JUET)

AB Road, Raghogarh, Guna, Madhya Pradesh 473226
EMail: vc@juet.ac.in
Website: http://www.juet.ac.in/

Vice-Chancellor: N.J. Rao

Registrar: S.K.S. Negi

Academic Dean: K.K. Jain

Programme

Engineering (Building Technologies; Chemical Engineering; Civil Engineering; Computer Engineering; Computer Science; Construction Engineering; Electronic Engineering; Environmental Engineering; Mechanical Engineering; Telecommunications Engineering)

Department

Physics; **Humanities and Social Sciences** (Arts and Humanities; Social Sciences); **Mathematics** (Mathematics)

JAYPEE UNIVERSITY OF INFORMATION TECHNOLOGY

P.O. Waknaghat, Distt Solan,
Kandaghat, Himachal Pradesh 173 234
Tel: +91(1792) 257-999 +91(1792) 245-371
Fax: +91(1792) 245-362
EMail: yaj.medury@juit.ac.in
Website: http://www.juit.ac.in

Vice-Chancellor: Ravi Prakash
Tel: +91(1792) 239-390 EMail: ravi.prakash@juit.ac.in

Registrar: Balbir Singh
Tel: +91(1792) 239-203 EMail: balbir.singh@juit.ac.in

Department

Biotechnology and Bio-Informatics (Biotechnology; Pharmacy); **Civil Engineering** (Civil Engineering); **Computer Science and Information Technology** (Computer Engineering; Computer Science; Information Technology); **Electronics and Communication Engineering** (Electronic Engineering; Telecommunications Engineering); **Humanities and Social Sciences** (Arts and Humanities; Social Sciences); **Mathematics** (Mathematics); **Physics** (Physics)

History: Founded 2002.

Academic Year: July to June

Admission Requirements: Higher secondary school certificate and entrance examination

Main Language(s) of Instruction: English

Degrees and Diplomas: *Bachelor's Degree*; *Master's Degree*; *Doctor of Philosophy*

Student Services: Academic Counselling, Canteen, Health Services, Language Laboratory, Social Counselling, Sports Facilities

Last Updated: 24/11/11

JIWAJI UNIVERSITY

Vidya Vihar, Gwalior, Madhya Pradesh 474011
Tel: +91(751) 244-2712
Fax: +91(751) 234-1768
Website: http://www.jiwaji.edu

Vice-Chancellor: Mazaahir Kidwai Tel: +91(751) 244-2701

Registrar: Anand Mishra Tel: +91(751) 234-1896

Faculty

Arts (Arts and Humanities; Information Sciences; Journalism; Library Science; Mass Communication; Modern Languages); **Commerce** (Business and Commerce); **Education** (Education); **Engineering** (Engineering; Technology); **Engineering Sciences** (Computer Science; Electronic Engineering; Engineering); **Law** (Law); **Life Sciences** (Biochemistry; Biological and Life Sciences; Botany; Environmental Studies; Microbiology; Neurosciences; Zoology); **Management** (Management); **Physical Education** (Physical Education; Yoga); **Physical Sciences** (Chemistry; Earth Sciences; Mathematics; Physics); **Social Sciences** (Archaeology; Cultural Studies; History; Political Sciences; Public Administration); **Technology** (Biomedical Engineering; Biotechnology; Food Technology; Pharmacy)

School

Distance Education

History: Founded 1964.

Admission Requirements: 12th year senior secondary/intermediate examination or recognized foreign equivalent

Main Language(s) of Instruction: English, Hindi

Degrees and Diplomas: *Post Diploma*; *Bachelor's Degree*; *Master's Degree*; *Doctor of Philosophy*

Last Updated: 24/11/11

JODHPUR NATIONAL UNIVERSITY

Jodhpur Rastriya Vishvavidyalaya
Narnadi, Jhanwar Road, Jodhpur, Rajasthan 342001
Tel: +91(2931) 281-551
Fax: +91(2931) 281-416
EMail: info@jodhpurnationaluniversity.com
Website: http://jodhpurnationaluniversity.com/

Chancellor: C. A. Kamal Mehta
EMail: cmo@jodhpurnationaluniversity.com

Registrar: Pradeep Kumar Dey
EMail: registrar@jodhpurnationaluniversity.com

International Relations: Joe Thomas, Vice-President
EMail: vp@jodhpurnationaluniversity.com

Faculty

Applied Science (Applied Chemistry; Applied Mathematics; Applied Physics; Natural Sciences); **Computer Applications** (Computer Networks; Computer Science); **Dentistry and Health** (Dentistry; Medicine; Oral Pathology; Orthodontics; Periodontics; Physical Therapy; Public Health); **Education** (Education); **Engineering and Technology** (Civil Engineering; Computer Engineering; Electrical Engineering; Electronic Engineering; Engineering; Information Technology; Mechanical Engineering; Telecommunications Engineering); **Law** (Law); **Management** (Banking; Finance; Human Resources; Information Technology; International Business;

Management; Marketing); **Pharmaceutical Sciences** (Pharmacology; Pharmacy)

History: Founded 2008.

Academic Year: July to December; January to June

Admission Requirements: Secondary school certificate or equivalent.

Fees: (Rupees): 10,000 to 160,000 per annum

Main Language(s) of Instruction: English

Accrediting Agency: University Grants Commission; Government of Rajasthan

Degrees and Diplomas: *Bachelor's Degree*; *Master's Degree*; *Doctor of Philosophy*

Student Services: Academic Counselling, Canteen, Careers Guidance, Cultural Activities, Facilities for disabled people, Health Services, Language Laboratory, Social Counselling, Sports Facilities

Last Updated: 24/11/11

KADI SARVA VISHWAVIDYALAYA

Sector - 15, Near KH - 5, Gandhinagar, Gujarat 382015
Tel: +91(79) 2324-4690
EMail: info@ksvuniversity.org.in
Website: http://ksvuniversity.org.in

President: M. M. Patel

Registrar: S.K. Mantrala EMail: registrar@ksvuniversity.org.in

Faculty

Biotechnology (Biotechnology); **Commerce** (Business and Commerce); **Computer** (Computer Engineering); **Education** (Education); **English** (English); **Management** (Management); **Nursing** (Nursing); **Pharmacy** (Pharmacy); **Physical Education** (Physical Education)

History: Founded 2007.

Degrees and Diplomas: *Bachelor's Degree*; *Master's Degree*; *Doctor of Philosophy*

Last Updated: 24/11/11

KAKATIYA UNIVERSITY

Vidyaranyapuri, Warangal, Andhra Pradesh 506009
Tel: +91(8712) 438-866
Fax: +91(8712) 439-600
EMail: registrar@kakatiya.ac.in
Website: http://www.kuwarangal.com

Vice-Chancellor: Boda Venkat Ratnam (2011-)
EMail: vc@kakatiya.ac.in

Registrar: T.S. Jagannatha Swamy EMail: registrar@kakatiya.ac.in

Faculty

Arts (Arts and Humanities; English; Hindi; Indic Languages; Sanskrit; Urdu); **Commerce and Business Management** (Business Administration; Business and Commerce); **Education** (Education); **Engineering** (Civil Engineering; Computer Science; Engineering; Mechanical Engineering; Mining Engineering); **Law** (Law); **Pharmacy** (Pharmacy); **Sciences** (Botany; Chemistry; Geology; Mathematics; Natural Sciences; Physics; Zoology); **Social Sciences** (Economics; History; Political Sciences; Public Administration; Social Sciences; Sociology; Tourism)

History: Founded 1976.

Academic Year: July to April (July-December; January-April)

Admission Requirements: 12th year senior secondary/intermediate examination or recognized foreign equivalent

Main Language(s) of Instruction: English, Telugu, Urdu

Degrees and Diplomas: *Bachelor's Degree*: **Business and Commerce; Education; Fine Arts; Information Sciences; Law; Library Science; Management; Oriental Studies; Pharmacy; Technology.** *Master's Degree*: **Accountancy; Business Administration; Business and Commerce; Education; Finance; Fine Arts; Law; Pharmacy; Technology.** *Master of Philosophy*; *Doctor of Philosophy*. Also Postgraduate Diplomas

Last Updated: 02/11/11

KALASALINGAM UNIVERSITY

Anand Nagar, Krishnankoil, Tamil Nadu 626126
Tel: +91(4563) 289-042
Fax: +91(4563) 289-322
EMail: info@kalasalingam.ac.in
Website: http://www.kalasalingam.ac.in

Vice-Chancellor: S. Radhakrishnan

Registrar: T. Vasudevan

Department

Biotechnology (Biotechnology; Chemical Engineering); **Business Administration** (Business Administration); **Chemistry** (Chemistry; English; Mathematics; Physics); **Civil Engineering** (Civil Engineering; Environmental Engineering); **Computer Applications** (Computer Science); **Computer Science and Engineering** (Computer Engineering; Computer Networks; Computer Science); **Electrical and Electronics Engineering** (Electrical and Electronic Engineering; Power Engineering); **Electronics and Communication Engineering** (Electronic Engineering; Telecommunications Engineering); **English** (English); **Information Technology** (Information Technology); **Instrumentation and Control Engineering** (Automation and Control Engineering; Instrument Making); **Mathematics** (Mathematics); **Mechanical Engineering** (Mechanical Engineering); **Physics** (Physics)

History: Founded 1984 as Arulmigu Kalasalingam College of Engineering. Acquired present status and title 2006.

Degrees and Diplomas: *Bachelor's Degree*; *Bachelor's Degree (professional)*; *Master's Degree*; *Doctor of Philosophy*

Last Updated: 24/11/11

KAMESHWAR SINGH DARBHANGA SANSKRIT UNIVERSITY

Kameshwara Nagar, Darbhanga, Bihar 846004
Tel: +91(6272) 222-178
Fax: +91(6272) 222-217
EMail: info@ksdsu.edu.in
Website: http://www.ksdsu.edu.in

Vice-Chancellor: Arvindh Pandey (2011-)
Tel: +91(6272) 248-067 EMail: vc@ksdsu.edu.in

Registrar: Sudhir Kumar Choudhary

Faculty

Astrology and Jyotish (Asian Religious Studies; Esoteric Practices); **Ayurvedic Medicine** (Ayurveda); **Darshan** (Asian Religious Studies); **Dharmashastra and Puranas** (Asian Religious Studies); **Fine Arts** (Fine Arts); **Sahitya** (Asian Religious Studies); **Sociology** (Sociology); **Vedas** (Asian Religious Studies); **Vyakarana and Linguistics** (Asian Religious Studies; Linguistics)

History: Founded 1961. A multi-faculty University specializing in the teaching of Indian Culture along both traditional and modern lines.

Academic Year: July to June

Admission Requirements: Upshastri/intermediate

Fees: None

Main Language(s) of Instruction: Sanskrit, Hindi

Accrediting Agency: NAAC

Degrees and Diplomas: *Bachelor's Degree*; *Master's Degree*; *Doctor of Philosophy*

Student Services: Careers Guidance, Cultural Activities, Social Counselling, Sports Facilities

Last Updated: 25/11/11

KANNADA UNIVERSITY

Vidyaranya, Hospet, Bellary district,
Kamalapura, Karnataka 583276
Tel: +91(8394) 241-337 +91(8394) 241-335
Fax: +91(8394) 241-334
EMail: mail@kannadauniversity.org
Website: http://www.kannadauniversity.org

Vice-Chancellor: A. Murigeppa EMail: vc@kannadauniversity.org

Registrar: H.C. Boralingaiah
EMail: registrar@kannadauniversity.org

Faculty

Fine Arts (Architectural Restoration; Dance; Museum Studies; Music; Sculpture); **Language and Literature** (Ancient Books; Indic Languages; Literature; Modern Languages; Translation and Interpretation; Women's Studies); **Sciences** (Natural Sciences); **Social Sciences** (Anthropology; Archaeology; Development Studies; Folklore; History; Social Problems; Women's Studies)

Further Information: Also Distance Education Courses

History: Founded 1991.

Fees: (Rupees): PhD, 1,000 per annum

Degrees and Diplomas: *Post Diploma*; *Bachelor's Degree*; *Master's Degree*; *Master of Philosophy*; *Doctor of Philosophy*

Last Updated: 25/11/11

KANNUR UNIVERSITY

Mangattuparamba, Kannur University Campus P.O.,
Kannur, Kerala 670567
Tel: +91(497) 278-2330
Fax: +91(497) 278-2190
EMail: registrar@kannuruniversity.ac.in
Website: http://www.kannuruniversity.ac.in

Vice-Chancellor: P.K Michael Tharakan (2009-)
Tel: +91(497) 278-2310 EMail: vc@kannuruniversity.ac.in

Registrar: A. Ashokan
Tel: +91(497) 278-2330 EMail: registrar@kannuruniversity.ac.in

Faculty

Ayurveda (Ayurveda); **Commerce and Management** (Business and Commerce; Management); **Communication** (Cognitive Sciences; Information Sciences; Information Technology; Journalism; Speech Studies); **Education** (Educational Sciences; Pedagogy; Physical Education; Teacher Training); **Engineering** (Computer Science; Electrical Engineering; Engineering; Information Technology); **Humanities** (Arts and Humanities; Fine Arts; Music; Singing; Visual Arts); **Languages and Literature** (Canadian Studies; Communication Studies; English; Foreign Languages Education; Indic Languages; Literature; Multimedia; Psycholinguistics); **Law** (Law); **Modern Medicine** (Biochemistry; Laboratory Techniques; Medical Technology; Medicine; Microbiology; Physical Therapy); **Sciences** (Applied Physics; Botany; Chemistry; Natural Sciences; Physics); **Social Sciences** (Behavioural Sciences; Clinical Psychology; Psychology)

College

Fashion Design *(Community)* (Fashion Design); **Printing Technology** *(Community)* (Printing and Printmaking); **Yogic Science and Indigeneous Health Care** *(Community)* (Traditional Eastern Medicine; Yoga)

School

Distance Education (Economics; English; Finance; History; Mathematics)

Further Information: Several campuses; Affiliated Colleges and Education Centres

History: Founded 1995 as Malabar University. Acquired present name 1996.

Academic Year: June to March

Admission Requirements: For graduate courses, higher Secondary course certificate. For postgraduate courses, Graduate diploma. For Ph.D. programme, 55% marks in Post-graduation.

Main Language(s) of Instruction: English

Accrediting Agency: University Grants Commission (U.G.C.)

Degrees and Diplomas: *Bachelor's Degree*; *Master's Degree*; *Master of Philosophy*; *Doctor of Philosophy*. Also Certificate courses

Student Services: Academic Counselling, Canteen, Facilities for disabled people, Health Services, Language Laboratory, Sports Facilities

Publications: University News

Publishing House: Co-operative Press

Last Updated: 28/11/11

KARNATAK UNIVERSITY (KUD)

Pavate Nagar, Dharwad, Karnataka 580003
Tel: +91(836) 244-8600
Fax: +91(836) 274-7884
EMail: vc@kud.ac.in
Website: http://www.kud.ac.in/

Vice-Chancellor: H. B. Walikar Tel: +91(836) 244-8600

Registrar: S.B. Hinchigeri
Tel: +91(836) 244-7750 EMail: registrar@kud.ac.in

Faculty

Arts (Arabic; Dance; English; Folklore; French; German; Hindi; History; Linguistics; Music; Painting and Drawing; Persian; Philosophy; Russian; Sanskrit; Urdu); **Commerce** (Business and Commerce; Marketing; Secretarial Studies); **Education** (Education; Physical Education); **Law** (Law); **Management** (Management); **Science and Technology** (Biochemistry; Biotechnology; Botany; Chemistry; Computer Science; Electronic Engineering; Genetics; Geography; Geology; Marine Biology; Mathematics; Microbiology; Physics; Polymer and Plastics Technology; Sericulture; Statistics; Zoology); **Social Sciences** (Anthropology; Economics; Information Sciences; Journalism; Library Science; Mass Communication; Political Sciences; Psychology; Social Studies; Social Work; Sociology; Yoga)

Campus

Belgaum; **Bijapur** *(Postgraduate courses)* (Arabic; Archaeology; Art History; Food Science; History; Social Work; Tourism); **Gadag**; **Haveri**; **Karwar** *(Postgraduate courses)* (Marine Biology; Zoology)

Further Information: Also 48 Postgraduate Departments; 314 Affiliated Colleges and University; Primary and Public School

History: Founded 1949.

Academic Year: June to March (June-October; November-March)

Admission Requirements: 12th year senior secondary/intermediate examination or recognized foreign equivalent

Main Language(s) of Instruction: English, Kannada

Accrediting Agency: National Assessment and Accreditation Council (NAAC)

Degrees and Diplomas: *Bachelor's Degree*: **Business and Commerce; Fine Arts.** *Master's Degree*: **Business and Commerce; Education; Fine Arts; Law; Technology.** *Doctor of Philosophy*: **Business and Commerce; Education; Fine Arts; Law; Management; Technology.**

Student Services: Canteen, Careers Guidance, Cultural Activities, Facilities for disabled people, Foreign Studies Centre, Health Services, Language Laboratory, Social Counselling, Sports Facilities

Last Updated: 28/11/11

KARNATAKA STATE LAW UNIVERSITY

Navanagar, Hubli, Karnataka 580025
Tel: +91(836) 222-2079
Fax: +91(836) 222-2261
EMail: vcsksl u@gmail.com
Website: http://www.kslu.ac.in/

Vice-Chancellor: Jaiprakashreddy Sannabasanagouda Patil
EMail: vcskslu@gmail.com

Registrar: K.S. Bagale
Tel: +91(836) 2222-392 EMail: regkslu@gmail.com

Programme

Law (Criminal Law; International Law; Labour Law; Law)

History: Founded 2009.

Degrees and Diplomas: *Bachelor's Degree*; *Postgraduate Diploma*; *Master's Degree*

Last Updated: 06/12/11

KARNATAKA STATE OPEN UNIVERSITY (KSOU)

Manasagangotri, Mysore, Karnataka 570006
Tel: +91(821) 251-5149
Fax: +91(821) 250-0846
EMail: vc@ksouedu.com
Website: http://www.ksouedu.com/

Vice-Chancellor: K.S. Rangappa EMail: vc@ksouedu.com

Registrar: Sri K. R. Jayaprakash Rao
EMail: registrar@ksouedu.com

Programme

Engineering (Chemical Engineering; Civil Engineering; Computer Science; Electrical Engineering; Fire Science; Mechanical

Engineering; Multimedia; Telecommunications Engineering; Textile Technology); **Information Technology** (Information Technology); **Management** (Banking; Business Administration; Finance; Hotel Management; Human Resources; Information Technology; International Business; Management; Marketing; Transport Management); **Multimedia Studies** (Communication Studies; Multimedia); **Postgraduate Studies** (Communication Studies; Multimedia); **Undergraduate Studies** (Communication Studies; Economics; English; History; Medical Technology; Multimedia; Political Sciences; Public Administration)

Further Information: Also Barath Postgraduate College (a partner of KSOU)

History: Founded 1996.

Academic Year: August to June.

Degrees and Diplomas: *Bachelor's Degree*; *Master's Degree*; *Doctor of Philosophy*. Also Diploma and Certificate courses

Last Updated: 28/11/11

KARNATAKA STATE WOMEN'S UNIVERSITY (KSWU)

Station Road, Near Dr. B.R. Ambedkar Circle,
Bijapur, Karnataka 586101
Tel: +91(8352) 240-023
Fax: +91(8352) 240-024
Website: http://www.kswubij.ac.in/

Vice-Chancellor: Geetha Bali

Registrar: G.V. Sugur Tel: +91(8352) 240-025

Faculty

Arts (Arts and Humanities); **Commerce** (Business and Commerce); **Education** (Education); **Science and Technology** (Natural Sciences; Technology); **Social Sciences** (Social Sciences)

History: Founded 2003.

Degrees and Diplomas: *Bachelor's Degree*; *Master's Degree*; *Master of Philosophy*; *Doctor of Philosophy*

Student Services: Sports Facilities

Last Updated: 06/12/11

KARPAGAM UNIVERSITY

Karpagam Academy of Higher Education,
Coimbatore, Tamil Nadu 641021
Tel: +91(422) 6471-113
Fax: +91(422) 2611-043
EMail: info@karpagamuniversity.ac.in
Website: http://www.karpagamuniv.com/

Vice-Chancellor: K. Ramasamy

Faculty

Architecture (Architecture); **Arts** (English; Indic Languages); **Commerce** (Business and Commerce); **Engineering** (Aeronautical and Aerospace Engineering; Automation and Control Engineering; Civil Engineering; Computer Engineering; Computer Science; Electrical and Electronic Engineering; Electronic Engineering; Information Technology; Mechanical Engineering; Software Engineering; Telecommunications Engineering); **Humanities** (Social Sciences); **Management** (Business Administration; Cooking and Catering; Hotel Management); **Sciences** (Biochemistry; Biotechnology; Chemistry; Mathematics; Microbiology; Physics)

Degrees and Diplomas: *Bachelor's Degree*; *Master's Degree*; *Doctor of Philosophy*

Last Updated: 11/01/12

KARUNYA UNIVERSITY

Karunya Nagar, Coimbatore, Tamil Nadu 641114
Tel: +91(422) 261-4300
Fax: +91(422) 261-5615
EMail: info@karunya.edu
Website: http://karunya.edu

Vice-Chancellor: Paul P. Appasamy

Registrar: Anne Mary Fernandez

Dean - Academic Affairs i/c: C. Joseph Kennady
EMail: deanaa@karunya.edu

School

Biotechnology and Health Sciences (Biotechnology; Health Sciences); **Civil Engineering** (Civil Engineering); **Computer Science and Technology** (Computer Networks; Technology); **Electrical Sciences** (Electrical and Electronic Engineering); **Food Sciences and Technology** (Food Science; Food Technology); **Management** (Management); **Mechanical Sciences** (Mechanical Engineering); **Media** (Media Studies); **Science and Humanities** (Chemistry; Education; English; Mathematics; Nanotechnology; Physics)

Department

Physical Education (Physical Education); **Value Education**

History: Founded 1986 as Karunya Institute of Technology. Acquired present title and status 2004.

Degrees and Diplomas: *Bachelor's Degree*; *Master's Degree*

Last Updated: 28/11/11

KAVIKULGURU KALIDAS SANSKRIT UNIVERSITY

Kavikulguru Kalidas Sanskrit Vishwavidyalaya
Pradishskiya Bahwan, Ramtek Mouda Road, District Nagpur,
Ramtek, Maharashtra 441106
Tel: +91(7114) 255-549 +91(7114) 256-476
Fax: +91(7114) 255-549
EMail: admin@sanskrituni.net
Website: http://www.sanskrituni.net/

Vice-Chancellor: Pankaj T. Chande (1998-)

Librarian and Registrar: Harshda H. Dave
EMail: registrarkk@bsnl.in; admin@sanskrituni.net

Programme

Computer Application (Computer Science); **Education** (Education); **Fine Arts** (Fine Arts); **Music** (Music); **Religion Culture and Philosophy** (Philosophy; Religious Studies); **Sanskrit** (Sanskrit); **Vedic Studies and Avestan Studies**; **Yoga, Naturopathy and Dietetics** (Dietetics; Yoga)

History: Founded 1997.

Academic Year: July to June.

Admission Requirements: Matriculate pass for 'AGAM'

Main Language(s) of Instruction: Marathi, Sanskrit, English

Accrediting Agency: National Assessment; Accreditation Council

Degrees and Diplomas: *Post Diploma*; *Bachelor's Degree*; *Postgraduate Diploma*; *Master's Degree*

Last Updated: 01/12/11

KERALA AGRICULTURAL UNIVERSITY

Vellanikkara, Thrissur, Kerala 680656
Tel: +91(487) 237-0432
Fax: +91(487) 237-0019
EMail: registrar@kau.in
Website: http://www.kau.edu

Vice-Chancellor: K. R. Viswambharan EMail: vc@kau.in

Registrar: P.B. Pushpalatha Tel: +91(487) 237-1619

Faculty

Agricultural Engineering (Agricultural Engineering); **Agriculture** (Agricultural Business; Agricultural Management; Agriculture; Food Science; Forestry; Horticulture; Nutrition); **Fisheries** (Fishery); **Veterinary and Animal Sciences** (Animal Husbandry; Veterinary Science)

Further Information: Also10 Constituent Colleges, and 21 Research Stations

History: Founded 1971.

Admission Requirements: 12th year senior secondary/intermediate examination or recognized foreign equivalent

Main Language(s) of Instruction: English

Degrees and Diplomas: *Post Diploma*; *Bachelor's Degree*; *Master's Degree*; *Doctor of Philosophy*

Last Updated: 01/12/11

KERALA KALAMANDALAM DEEMED UNIVERSITY FOR ART AND CULTURE

Cheruthuruthy, Thrissur, Kerala 679 531
Tel: +91(4884) 262-418
Fax: +91(4884) 262-019
EMail: info@kalamandalam.org
Website: http://www.kalamandalam.org

Vice-Chancellor: P.N. Suresh
Tel: +91(4884) 263-440 EMail: vicechancellor@kalamandalam.org

Registrar: K.K. Sundaresan Tel: +91(4884) 262-418

Programme

Cultural Studies (Cultural Studies); **Performing Arts** (Dance; Music; Performing Arts; Theatre)

History: Founded 1930

Degrees and Diplomas: *Bachelor's Degree*; *Master's Degree*; *Master of Philosophy*; *Doctor of Philosophy*
Last Updated: 01/12/11

KHWAJA MOINUDDIN CHISHTI URDU, ARABI˜FARSI UNIVERSITY

Sitapur-Hardoi Bypass Road, Lucknow, Uttar Pradesh 226013
Tel: +91(522) 277-4042
Fax: +91(522) 277-4046
EMail: upuafulucknow@gmail.com
Website: http://uafulucknow.ac.in/

Vice-Chancellor: Khan Masood Ahmad

Institute

Mass Communication in Science and Technology (Mass Communication)

Course

Ancient Indian History and Archaeology (Ancient Civilizations; Archaeology); **Business and Commerce** (Business and Commerce); **Education** (Education); **English** (English); **Geography** (Geography); **Hindi** (Hindi); **Home Science** (Home Economics); **Persian** (Persian); **Physical Education** (Physical Education); **Political Science** (Political Sciences); **Tourism and Travel Management** (Tourism; Transport Management)

History: Created 2009 as Uttar Pradesh Urdu, Arabi-Farsi University. Changed name to Shri Kanshiramji Urdu, Arabi-Farsi University in 2011. Acquired current title 2012.

Degrees and Diplomas: *Bachelor's Degree*; *Master's Degree*
Last Updated: 05/01/12

KIIT UNIVERSITY (KIIT)

PO-KIIT, Bhubaneswar, Orissa 751024
Tel: +91(674) 274-2103
Fax: +91(674) 274-1465
EMail: kiit@kiit.ac.in
Website: http://www.kiit.ac.in/

Founder: Achyuta Samanta (1997-)
Tel: +91(674) 274-0326 EMail: achyuta@kiit.ac.in

Vice-Chancellor: Ashok S. Kolaskar
Tel: +91(674) 272-5171 EMail: vc@kiit.ac.in

Registrar and Director, Admissions: Sasmita Samanta
Tel: +91(674) 274-1747
EMail: sasmitasr@kiit.ac.in; director_admission@kiit.ac.in

International Relations: Dwiti Vikramaditya, Advisor
EMail: dwiti.vikramaditya@gmail.com

School

Biotechnology (Biotechnology; Microbiology); **Computer Applications** (Computer Science); **Dental Sciences** (Dentistry; Orthodontics); **Engineering and Technology** *(Programmes imparted by six constituent schools)* (Civil Engineering; Computer Engineering; Electrical Engineering; Electronic Engineering; Mechanical Engineering; Metallurgical Engineering; Telecommunications Engineering); **Film and Media Sciences and Fashion Technology** (Cinema and Television; Fashion Design; Film; Media Studies; Textile Design; Theatre); **Languages** (English; Modern Languages); **Law** (Law); **Management** (Business Administration; Management); **Mass Communication** (Journalism; Mass Communication); **Medical Sciences** (Medicine; Nephrology); **Medicine** (Anatomy; Biochemistry; Dentistry; Forensic Medicine and Dentistry; Gynaecology and Obstetrics; Medicine; Microbiology; Ophthalmology; Orthopaedics; Paediatrics; Pathology; Pharmacology; Physiology; Psychiatry and Mental Health; Radiology; Surgery); **Nursing** (Midwifery; Nursing); **Rural Management** (Rural Planning); **Sciences** (Natural Sciences); **Sculpture** (Sculpture); **Technology** (Information Technology; Technology); **Tourism and Hospitality Management** (Hotel Management; Tourism)

History: Created 1992. Acquired present status and title 2004.

Academic Year: July to June

Admission Requirements: Secondary School Certificate (+10) for Diploma and Intermediate Courses; Higher Secondary School Certificate (+12) for Bachelor courses; Bachelor degree or equivalent for Master courses

Fees: (Rupees): 150,000 per annum; MBA, 275,000; Medicine, 375,000

Main Language(s) of Instruction: English

Accrediting Agency: UGC/NAAC

Degrees and Diplomas: *Post Diploma*: **Engineering.** *Bachelor's Degree*: **Business Administration; Civil Engineering; Computer Science; Dentistry; Electrical and Electronic Engineering; Electrical Engineering; Electronic Engineering; Information Technology; Law; Mechanical Engineering; Medicine; Surgery; Telecommunications Engineering.** *Master's Degree*: **Biotechnology; Business Administration; Computer Science; Technology.**

Student Services: Academic Counselling, Canteen, Careers Guidance, Cultural Activities, Facilities for disabled people, Foreign Studies Centre, Health Services, Language Laboratory, Nursery Care, Social Counselling, Sports Facilities

Publications: KIIT Review

Last Updated: 25/11/11

KING GEORGE MEDICAL UNIVERSITY

Chowk, Lucknow, Uttar Pradesh 226003
Tel: +91(522) 2257-450
Fax: +91(522) 2257-539
EMail: info@kgmcindia.edu
Website: http://www.kgmu.org

Vice-Chancellor: Ravi Kant EMail: vc@kgmcindia.edu

Faculty

Dental Sciences (Dentistry; Orthodontics; Periodontics); **Medical Sciences** (Community Health; Health Administration; Medicine)

History: Founded 1906 as King George Medical College, an affiliated college of Allahabad University. In 2002 became Chhatrapati Shahuji Maharaj Medical University. Acquired current title 2003.

Degrees and Diplomas: *Bachelor's Degree*: **Dentistry; Medicine; Surgery.** *Master's Degree*: **Anatomy; Medicine; Ophthalmology; Orthopaedics; Otorhinolaryngology; Surgery.** *Master of Philosophy*: **Clinical Psychology; Health Sciences.** *Doctor of Philosophy*: **Medicine; Surgery.**
Last Updated: 24/04/15

KL UNIVERSITY

Green Fields, Vaddeswaram,
Guntur District, Andhra Pradesh 522502
Tel: +91(8645) - 246948
EMail: registraroffice@kluniversity.in
Website: http://www.kluniversity.in

Vice-Chancellor: G.L. Datta EMail: vc@kluniversity.in

School

Bio Sciences and Engineering (Bioengineering; Biotechnology); **Computing** (Computer Engineering; Computer Science; Electronic Engineering); **Electrical Sciences** (Electrical and Electronic Engineering; Electronic Engineering; Telecommunications Engineering); **Management Sciences** (Accountancy; Business Administration; Business and Commerce; Finance; Hotel Management); **Mechanical and Civil Sciences** (Civil Engineering; Mechanical Engineering); **Sciences and Humanities** (Arts and Humanities; Chemistry; Communication Studies; English; Fine Arts; Mathematics; Natural Sciences; Physical Education; Physics; Social Work)

History: Founded 1980 as Koneru Lakshmaiah College of Engineering, became Koneru Lakshmaiah Education Foundation 2006. Acquired status of deemed university 2009.

Degrees and Diplomas: *Bachelor's Degree*; *Master's Degree*; *Doctor of Philosophy*

Student Services: Sports Facilities

Last Updated: 13/01/12

KLE UNIVERSITY

JNMC Campus, Nehru Nagar, Belgaum, Karnataka 590010
Tel: +91(831) 2444-444
Fax: +91(831) 2493-777
EMail: info@kleuniversity.edu.in
Website: http://www.kleuniversity.edu.in

Head: Chandrakant Kokate

Registrar: P.F. Kotur

Faculty

Ayurveda (Ayurveda); **Dentistry** (Dentistry); **Medicine** (Cardiology; Medicine; Neurological Therapy; Urology); **Nursing** (Nursing); **Pharmacy** (Pharmacy); **Physiotherapy** (Physical Engineering)

Department

Public Health (Public Health)

History: Founded as KLE Academy of Higher Education and Research). Acquired present title and status 2006.

Degrees and Diplomas: *Postgraduate Diploma*

Last Updated: 09/01/12

KOLHAN UNIVERSITY

NH 75, Chaibasa, Jharkhand, Jammu Kashimir
EMail: vc@kolhanuniversity.org
Website: http://www.kolhanuniversity.org/

Vice-Chancellor: Salil Kumar Roy EMail: saliroy29@gmail.com

Department

Anthropology (Anthropology); **Botany** (Botany); **Chemistry** (Chemistry); **Commerce** (Business and Commerce); **Economics** (Economics); **English** (English); **Geography** (Geography); **Geology** (Geology); **Hindi** (Hindi); **History** (History); **Mathematics** (Mathematics); **Philosophy** (Philosophy); **Physics** (Physics); **Political Sciences** (Political Sciences); **Zoology** (Zoology)

Degrees and Diplomas: *Bachelor's Degree*; *Postgraduate Diploma*; *Master's Degree*

Last Updated: 18/11/11

KRANTIGURU SHYAMJI KRISHNA VERMA KACHCHH UNIVERSITY

Mundra Road, Bhuj-Kachchh, Gujarat 370001
EMail: info@kskvkachchhuniversity.org
Website: http://kskvku.digitaluniversity.ac/

Vice-Chancellor: Shashiranjan Yadav

Registrar: Kashyap Trivedi

Department

Chemistry (Chemistry); **Commerce and Management** (Business and Commerce; Management); **Computer Science** (Computer Science); **Earth and Environment Science** (Earth Sciences; Environmental Studies); **Economics** (Economics); **Education** (Education); **English** (English); **Gujarati** (Indic Languages); **Public Administration** (Public Administration); **Sanskrit** (Sanskrit); **Social Work** (Social Work)

Degrees and Diplomas: *Bachelor's Degree*; *Master's Degree*

Last Updated: 12/08/11

KRISHNA INSTITUTE OF MEDICAL SCIENCES UNIVERSITY

Malkapur, Karad, Dist.Satara, Maharashtra 415110
Tel: +91(2164) 241555
Fax: +91(2164) 241410
EMail: contact@kimsuniversity.in
Website: http://www.kimsuniversity.in

Vice-Chancellor: Arvind V. Nadkkarni
EMail: thevc@kimsuniversity.in

Registrar: Ajit Palekar

School

Dental (Dentistry)

Department

Science (Biotechnology)

Institute

Medical Sciences (Medicine); **Nursing Sciences** (Nursing); **Physiotherapy** (Physical Therapy)

Degrees and Diplomas: *Bachelor's Degree*; *Postgraduate Diploma*; *Master's Degree*; *Doctor of Philosophy*

Last Updated: 09/01/12

KRISHNA KANTA HANDIQUE STATE OPEN UNIVERSITY (KKHSOU)

Housefed Complex, Dispur, Guwahati, Assam 781006
EMail: kkh_sou@yahoo.com
Website: http://www.kkhsou.in/

Vice-Chancellor: Srinath Baruah

Programme

Arts and Humanities (Education; English; Hindi; History; Indic Languages; Philosophy; Political Sciences; Sociology); **Business Administration** (Business Administration; Economics; Finance; Human Resources; Insurance; Management; Marketing); **Mass Communication** (Mass Communication); **Political Sciences** (Political Sciences)

History: Founded 2007.

Degrees and Diplomas: *Post Diploma*; *Bachelor's Degree*; *Master's Degree*; *Doctor of Philosophy*

Last Updated: 22/07/11

KRISHNA UNIVERSITY

Andhra Jateeya Kalasala Campus, Rajupeta,
Machipatnam, Andhra Pradesh 521 001
Tel: +91 8672 – 226969
EMail: registrar@krishnauniversity.ac.in
Website: http://krishnauniversity.net/

Vice-Chancellor: M. K. Durga Prasad

Administrative Officer: D. Surya Chandra Rao

Department

Biotechnology (Biotechnology); **Chemistry** (Chemistry); **Computer Science** (Computer Science); **Electronics** (Electronic Engineering); **English** (English); **Journalism and Mass Communications** (Journalism; Mass Communication); **Management** (Management); **Pharmacy** (Pharmacy); **Telugu** (Indic Languages)

History: Founded 2008.

Degrees and Diplomas: *Bachelor's Degree*; *Master's Degree*

Last Updated: 22/07/11

KUMAUN UNIVERSITY

Nainital, Uttar Pradesh 263001
Tel: +91(5942) 235-563 +91(5942) 235-068
Fax: +91(5942) 235-576
EMail: vicechancellor@kuntl.in
Website: http://www.kuntl.in/

Vice-Chancellor: V.P.S. Arora Tel: +91(5942) 235-068

Registrar: Kamal K. Pande

Faculty

Arts (Arts and Humanities; English); **Commerce and Management** (Business and Commerce; Economics); **Education** (Education); **Law** (Law); **Medical Education** (Pharmacy); **Science** (Biotechnology; Botany; Geography; Mathematics; Natural Sciences; Physics; Zoology); **Technology** (Information Sciences; Technology)

Further Information: Also Almora and Nainital campuses. 62 affiliated colleges

History: Founded 1973.

Admission Requirements: 12th year senior secondary/intermediate examination or recognized foreign equivalent

Main Language(s) of Instruction: Hindi, English

Degrees and Diplomas: *Post Diploma*: **Tourism.** *Bachelor's Degree*; *Master's Degree*; *Doctor of Philosophy*

Last Updated: 01/12/11

KURUKSHETRA UNIVERSITY

Kurukshetra, Haryana 136119
Tel: +91(1744) 238-039
Fax: +91(1744) 238-277
EMail: kuru@doe.ernet.in
Website: http://kuk.ac.in/

Vice-Chancellor: Devinder Dayal Singh Sandhu
Tel: +91(1744) 238-039 EMail: vc.kuk@rediffmail.com

Registrar: Surinder Deswal EMail: regskuk@gmail.com

Faculty

Arts and Languages (Arts and Humanities; English; Foreign Languages Education; Hindi; Indic Languages; Information Sciences; Journalism; Library Science); **Commerce and Management** (Business and Commerce; Hotel Management; Management; Mass Communication; Media Studies; Tourism); **Education** (Education; Physical Education; Special Education); **Engineering and Technology** (Civil Engineering; Communication Studies; Computer Engineering; Electrical Engineering; Electronic Engineering; Engineering; Mechanical Engineering; Technology); **Indic Studies** (Ancient Civilizations; Archaeology; Cultural Studies; Fine Arts; Music; Philosophy; Sanskrit); **Law** (Law); **Life Sciences** (Biochemistry; Biotechnology; Botany; Chemistry; Environmental Studies; Microbiology; Natural Sciences; Pharmacy; Zoology); **Science** (Chemistry; Computer Science; Electronic Engineering; Geography; Geology; Geophysics; Mathematics; Physics; Statistics); **Social Sciences** (Economics; History; Political Sciences; Psychology; Public Administration; Social Sciences; Social Work; Sociology)

Further Information: Also 105 Affiliated Colleges

History: Founded 1956.

Academic Year: June to May

Admission Requirements: 12th year senior secondary/intermediate examination or recognized foreign equivalent

Main Language(s) of Instruction: Hindi, English

Degrees and Diplomas: *Post Diploma*; *Bachelor's Degree*; *Postgraduate Diploma*; *Master's Degree*; *Master of Philosophy*; *Doctor of Philosophy*

Publications: Journal of Arts and Humanities; Journal of Human Studies (Praci Jyoti); Journal of Law; Sambhawana (Hindi, Kalanidhi, Jeevanti)

Publishing House: University Press

Last Updated: 01/12/11

KUSHABHAU THAKRE PATRAKARITA AVAM JANSANCHAR VISHWAVIDYALAYA

Post Office-Sunder Nagar, Raipur, Chhattisgarh 492 013
Tel: +91(771) 649-9184
Fax: +91(771) 257-5217
EMail: kulsachiv@ktujm.ac.in
Website: http://www.ktujm.ac.in

Vice-Chancellor: Shri Sachchidanand Joshi

Registrar: D. N. Varma EMail: kulsachiv@ktujm.ac.in

Department

Advertising and Public Relations (Advertising and Publicity; Public Relations); **Electronic Media** (Media Studies; Radio and Television Broadcasting; Video); **Journalism** (Journalism); **Management** (Management); **Mass Communications** (Mass Communication); **Social Works** (Social Work)

History: Founded 2004

Degrees and Diplomas: *Bachelor's Degree*; *Master's Degree*; *Doctor of Philosophy*

Last Updated: 01/08/11

KUVEMPU UNIVERSITY

Kuvempu Vishwavidyanilaya

Jnana Sahyadri, Shimoga Dist., Shankaraghatta, Karnataka 577451
Tel: +91(8282) 256-301 +91(8282) 256-302
Fax: +91(8282) 256-255
EMail: reg_admn@kuvempu.ac.in
Website: http://www.kuvempu.ac.in

Vice-Chancellor: S.A. Bari
Tel: +91(8282) 656-222 EMail: vc@kuvempu.ac.in

Registrar: T.R, Manjunath Tel: +91(8282) 256-221

Programme

Nanoscience and Technology (Nanotechnology; Technology)

School

Bio Science (Biotechnology; Botany; Clinical Psychology; Microbiology; Wildlife; Zoology); **Chemical Sciences** (Biochemistry; Chemistry; Industrial Chemistry; Inorganic Chemistry; Organic Chemistry); **Earth Sciences and Environmental Science** (Environmental Engineering; Geology; Surveying and Mapping; Water Management); **Economics and Business Studies** (Accountancy; Banking; Business Administration; Business and Commerce; Economics; Finance; Insurance; Tourism); **Education** (Education; Physical Education); **Languages, Literature and Fine Arts** (English; Indic Languages; Sanskrit; Urdu); **Law** (Law); **Physical Sciences** (Computer Engineering; Computer Science; Electronic Engineering; Information Sciences; Library Science; Mathematics; Natural Sciences; Physics); **Social Sciences** (Adult Education; Archaeology; Cultural Studies; History; Journalism; Political Sciences; Social Sciences; Social Work)

Further Information: 120 affiliated colleges and 4 constituent colleges

History: Founded 1973 as Postgraduate Centre of University of Mysore, acquired present status and title 1987.

Academic Year: June to March (June-October; December-March)

Admission Requirements: 12th year senior secondary/intermediate examination or recognized foreign equivalent

Main Language(s) of Instruction: English, Kannada

Accrediting Agency: National Assessment and Accreditation Council (NAAC)

Degrees and Diplomas: *Bachelor's Degree*: **Arts and Humanities; Business and Commerce; Business Computing; Engineering; Fine Arts; Law; Management; Physical Education.** *Postgraduate Diploma*; *Master's Degree*: **Arts and Humanities; Business and Commerce; Business Computing; Engineering; Fine Arts; Law; Management; Physical Education; Technology.** *Doctor of Philosophy*

Student Services: Academic Counselling, Canteen, Careers Guidance, Cultural Activities, Facilities for disabled people, Health Services, Language Laboratory, Social Counselling, Sports Facilities

Publications: University Newsletter

Publishing House: Prasaranga

Last Updated: 01/12/11

LAKSHMIBAI NATIONAL INSTITUTE OF PHYSICAL EDUCATION

Race Course Road, Shaktinagar, Gwalior, Madhya Pradesh 474002
Tel: +91(751) 400-0902
Fax: +91(751) 400-0995
EMail: registrar@lnipe.gov.in
Website: http://www.lnipe.gov.in

Vice-Chancellor: Sarbjit Singh Pawar EMail: vc@lnipe.gov.in

Registrar: L.N. Sarkar

Department

Exercise Physiology (Physiology); **Health Sciences and Yoga** (Health Sciences; Yoga); **Management and Mass Communication** (Mass Communication; Sports Management); **Physical Education Pedagogy** (Physical Education); **Research Development and Advanced Studies**; **Sports Biomechanics** (Sports); **Sports Coaching** (Sports); **Sports Psychology** (Psychology; Sports)

History: Founded 1957 as Lakshmibai National College of Education. Acquired present status 1995.

Accrediting Agency: National Assessment and Accreditation Council (NAAC)

Degrees and Diplomas: *Bachelor's Degree*; *Postgraduate Diploma*; *Master's Degree*; *Master of Philosophy*

Publications: Indian Journal of Physical Education, Sports Medicine and Exercise Science

Last Updated: 02/12/11

LAL BAHADUR SHASTRI INSTITUTE OF MANAGEMENT (LBSIM)

Plot No. 11/7, Sector 11, (Near Metro Station), Dwarka, New Delhi 110 075
Tel: +91(11) 2530-7700
Fax: +91(11) 2530-7799
Website: http://www.lbsim.ac.in

Director: Gautam Sinha

Programme

Computer Applications (Computer Science); **Finance** (Finance; Management); **Management** (Management)

Centre

Entrepreneurship *(LBSIM Business Incubation)* (Management)

History: Founded 1995.

Accrediting Agency: All India Council for Technical Education (AICTE), Ministry of Human Resource Development, Government of India;

Degrees and Diplomas: *Postgraduate Diploma*; *Master's Degree*. Postgraduate diploma are equivalent to a university MBA; Master's Degree is offered through the Guru Gobind Singh Indraprastha University, Delhi

Student Services: Sports Facilities

Last Updated: 23/01/12

LALA LAJPAT RAI UNIVERSITY OF VETERINARY AND ANIMAL SCIENCES

Hisar, Haryana 121006
Tel: +91(166) 227-0164
EMail: vc@llruvas.edu.in
Website: http://llruvas.edu.in

Vice-Chancellor: Hardeep Kumar

Programme

Veterinary and Animal Sciences (Animal Husbandry; Veterinary Science)

Admission Requirements: Merit in Entrance Test provided the candidates have passed 10+2 with Physics, Chemistry, Biology and English and or equivalent from recognized Board/University with atleast 50% marks in aggregate in these four subjects (40% in aggregate for SC/BC candidates).

Main Language(s) of Instruction: English

Degrees and Diplomas: *Bachelor's Degree*; *Master's Degree*; *Doctor of Philosophy*

Last Updated: 19/10/11

LALIT NARAYAN MITHILA UNIVERSITY

Kameshwarnagar, Darbhanga, Bihar 846008
Tel: +91(6272) 222-428
Fax: +91(6272) 222-598
EMail: vc_lnmu@indiatimes.com
Website: http://www.lnmu.edu.in/

Vice-Chancellor: Samrendra Pratap Singh
Tel: +91(6272) 222-463 EMail: vc@lnmu.edu.in

Registrar: Bimal Kumar EMail: registrar@lnmu.edu.in

Faculty

Arts (Arts and Humanities; English; Hindi; History; Music; Philosophy; Political Sciences; Psychology; Sanskrit; Sociology; Theatre; Urdu); **Commerce** (Business Administration; Business and Commerce; Economics); **Education** (Education); **Law** (Law); **Medicine** (Medicine); **Science** (Biotechnology; Botany; Chemistry; Geography; Mathematics; Natural Sciences; Physics; Zoology)

Further Information: Also 67 Constituent and 14 Affiliated Colleges

History: Founded 1972.

Admission Requirements: 12th year senior secondary/intermediate examination or recognized foreign equivalent

Main Language(s) of Instruction: Hindi, English

Degrees and Diplomas: *Post Diploma*; *Bachelor's Degree*; *Master's Degree*; *Doctor of Philosophy*

Last Updated: 02/12/11

LINGAYA'S UNIVERSITY

Nachauli, Jasana Road, Faridabad, Haryana 121002
Tel: +91(129) 2598-200
EMail: lu@lingayasuniversity.edu.in
Website: http://lingayasuniversity.edu.in/

Vice-President: K. Jayarama Rao

School

Built Environment and Design (Building Technologies; Design)

Department

Automobile Engineering (Automotive Engineering); **Business Administration** (Business Administration; Management); **Civil Engineering** (Civil Engineering); **Computer Applications** (Computer Networks; Software Engineering); **Computer Science and Engineering** (Computer Engineering; Computer Science); **Education** (Education); **Electrical and Electronics Engineering** (Electrical and Electronic Engineering); **Electrical Engineering** (Electrical Engineering); **Electronics and Communication Engineering** (Electronic Engineering; Telecommunications Engineering); **Information Technology** (Information Technology); **Mechanical Engineering** (Mechanical Engineering)

History: Founded as Lingaya's Institute of Management and Technology (LIMAT). Acquired the status of deemed university 2009.

Degrees and Diplomas: *Bachelor's Degree*; *Master's Degree*; *Doctor of Philosophy*

Student Services: Sports Facilities

Last Updated: 11/01/12

LOVELY PROFESSIONAL UNIVERSITY (LPU)

Jalandhar - Delhi G.T. Road (NH-1), Phagwada, Punjab 144402
Tel: +91(1824) 510-274
Fax: +91(1824) 509-425
EMail: dll@lpu.co.in; info@lpu.co.in
Website: http://www.lpu.in

Chancellor: Ashok Mittal
Tel: +91(1824) 501-201
EMail: chancellor@lpu.co.in; ashok.mittal@lpu.co.in

Registrar: Monica Gulati EMail: dll@lpu.co.in

International Relations: Aman Mittal, Deputy Director
EMail: aman.mittal@lpu.co.in

Faculty

Applied Medical Sciences (Ayurveda; Biochemistry; Gerontology; Gynaecology and Obstetrics; Haematology; Immunology; Microbiology; Molecular Biology; Neurology; Paediatrics; Paramedical Sciences; Pharmacology; Pharmacy; Physical Therapy; Sports Medicine; Surgery; Virology); **Business and Arts** (Accountancy; Architecture; Banking; Business and Commerce; Cinema and Television; Clothing and Sewing; Commercial Law; Econometrics; Economics; English; Fashion Design; Film; Finance; Fine Arts; Food Technology; Furniture Design; Health Administration; Hotel Management; Human Resources; Indic Languages; Insurance; Interior Design; International Business; Journalism; Landscape Architecture; Linguistics; Literature; Management; Marketing; Modern Languages; Multimedia; Music; Musical Instruments; Nutrition; Painting and Drawing; Performing Arts; Radio and Television Broadcasting; Retailing and Wholesaling; Sculpture; Small Business; Social Sciences; Textile Technology; Theatre; Tourism; Transport Management; Visual Arts; Writing); **Education** (Education; Educational Technology; Library Science; Physical Education; Rehabilitation and Therapy; Sports Medicine); **Technology and Sciences** (Agriculture; Applied Chemistry; Artificial Intelligence; Biochemistry; Biology; Biotechnology; Botany; Chemistry; Civil Engineering; Computer

Graphics; Computer Networks; Computer Science; E- Business/ Commerce; Electronic Engineering; Engineering; Mathematical Physics; Mathematics; Mechanical Engineering; Microbiology; Organic Chemistry; Physical Chemistry; Physics; Software Engineering; Solid State Physics; Telecommunications Engineering; Zoology)

Department

Open and Distance Learning (Accountancy; Business Administration; Business and Commerce; Commercial Law; Computer Science; Economics; Education; English; Finance; Hindi; History; Human Resources; Information Sciences; Library Science; Management; Marketing; Political Sciences; Retailing and Wholesaling; Sociology; Software Engineering)

History: Created 2001. Acquired status 2005.

Academic Year: August to December; January to May

Admission Requirements: Secondary School Certificate for undergraduate programmes; Recognized undergraduate degree for Master's programmes. See website for individual course requirements.

Fees: (INR): 14,500 to 89,000 per semester. See website for more details

Main Language(s) of Instruction: English

Accrediting Agency: Recognized by the University Grants Commission(UGC), the Distance Education Council (DEC). Porgrammes regonized by the National Council for Teacher Education (NCTE), the Pharmacy Council of India (PCI), the Indian Association of Physiotherapists (IAP), the Council of Architecture (COA), the Bar Council of India (BCI).

Degrees and Diplomas: *Post Diploma*; *Bachelor's Degree*; *Bachelor's Degree (professional)*; *Postgraduate Diploma*; *Master's Degree*; *Master of Philosophy*. Also undergraduate certificate in Food Production, 6 months; Honours degrees: B.Tech (Hons.), 4-5 yrs and Master, 2-4 yrs; MBA, 2 yrs; Advance Diploma, 1yr.

Student Services: Academic Counselling, Canteen, Careers Guidance, Cultural Activities, Facilities for disabled people, Foreign Studies Centre, Health Services, Language Laboratory, Nursery Care, Social Counselling, Sports Facilities

Publications: Biobuzz; JOHAR; Lovely Journal of International Business

Academic Staff *2010-2011*	MEN	WOMEN	**TOTAL**
FULL-TIME	1,256	731	**1,987**
STAFF WITH DOCTORATE			
FULL-TIME	79	39	**118**
Student Numbers *2010-2011*			
All (Foreign included)	20,134	6,436	**26,570**
FOREIGN ONLY	137	32	**169**

Part-time students, 281. **Distance students,** 444.

Last Updated: 21/06/11

MADHAV INSTITUTE OF TECHNOLOGY AND SCIENCE, GWALIOR (MITS-GWALIOR)

91, Laxmi Bai Colony, Padav, Gwalior, Madhya Pradesh 474 002
Tel: +91(751) 240-9382
Fax: +91(751) 240-9382
Website: http://www.mitsgwl.ac.in/

Director: Sanjeev Jain

Registrar: O.P. Paliwal

Department

Applied Science (Applied Physics; Chemistry); **Architecture** (Architecture); **Biotechnology** (Biotechnology); **Chemical Engineering** (Chemical Engineering); **Civil Engineering** (Civil Engineering); **Computer Applications** (Computer Engineering); **Computer Science and Information Technology** (Computer Science; Information Technology); **Electrical Engineering** (Electrical Engineering); **Electronic Engineering** (Electronic Engineering); **Mechanical Engineering** (Mechanical Engineering)

History: Founded 1957.

Fees: (Indian Rupees): Undergraduate tuition fee, 22,300 per annum

Accrediting Agency: All India Council for Technical Education (AICTE)

Degrees and Diplomas: *Bachelor's Degree (professional)*; *Master's Degree*; *Doctor of Philosophy*

Last Updated: 25/01/12

MADHYA PRADESH BHOJ (OPEN) UNIVERSITY (MPBOU)

Kolar Road (Raja Bhoj Marg), Bhopal, Madhya Pradesh 462016
Tel: +91(755) 249-2090 +91(755) 249-2091
Fax: +91(755) 260-0669
EMail: registraroffice.mpbou@gmail.com
Website: http://www.bhojvirtualuniversity.com

Vice-Chancellor: Tariq Zafar (2009-)
Tel: +91(755) 249-4185; +91(755) 249-4094
EMail: vcoffice.mpbou@gmail.com

Registrar: Anand Kamble
Tel: +91(755) 249-2093 EMail: registrar@bhojvirtualuniversity.com

Programme

Master of Laws *(L.L.M.)* (Law)

School

Basic Science (Biology; Botany; Chemistry; Mathematics; Physics; Zoology); **Health Science** (Dietetics; Health Administration; Health Education; Health Sciences; Nursing; Nutrition; Physical Therapy); **Management** (Business Administration; Business and Commerce; Economics; Heritage Preservation; Hotel Management; International Business; Management; Safety Engineering; Secretarial Studies; Tourism)

Department

History, Archaeology, Culture and Tourism *(HACT)* (Archaeology; Cultural Studies; Economics; English; Hindi; History; Hotel Management; Political Sciences; Sanskrit; Social Work; Sociology; Tourism); **Multimedia Education** (Education); **Special Education** (Special Education)

Institute

Information Technology *(IT)* (Computer Science; Educational Technology; Information Technology; Multimedia)

Research Centre

Electronic Media Production *(EMPRC)*

Further Information: Also 11 regional centres and one sub-Regional Centre located in Bhopal, Bilaspur, Durg, Gwalior, Indore, Jabalpur, Jagdalpur (Bastar), Raipur, Sagar, Ujjain, Rewa, and Satna.

History: Founded 1991 as Madhya Pradesh Bhoj University. Acquired present status and title 1997.

Academic Year: July to June

Admission Requirements: 12th year senior secondary/intermediate examination or recognized foreign equivalent

Fees: (Rupees): undergradaute programmes, 1,500-18,000 per annum; graduate programmes, 4,200-24,000 per annum

Main Language(s) of Instruction: English, Hindi

Degrees and Diplomas: *Bachelor's Degree*: **Business Administration; Business and Commerce; Computer Engineering; Education; Fine Arts; Nursing.** *Postgraduate Diploma*; *Master's Degree*: **Business Administration; Computer Engineering; Fine Arts; Mathematics.** *Doctor of Philosophy*

Student Services: Academic Counselling, Careers Guidance, Language Laboratory, Social Counselling

Publishing house: In House Publishing

Last Updated: 22/06/11

MADHYA PRADESH PASHU CHIKITSA VIGYAN VISHWAVIDYALAYA (MPPCVV)

South Civil Lines, Jabalpur, Madhya Pradesh 482 001
Tel: +91(761) 262-0783 +91(761) 267-8007
Fax: +91(761) 262-0783
EMail: vcmppcvv@yahoo.in
Website: http://www.mppcvv.org/

Vice Chancellor: Govind Prasad Mishra
Tel: +91(761) 267-8007 EMail: vcmppcvv@yahoo.co.in

Registrar: R. P. Pandey Tel: +91(942) 547-6189

College

Veterinary Science and Animal Husbandry *(Mhow)* (Agricultural Economics; Agronomy; Animal Husbandry; Biochemistry; Genetics;

Immunology; Meat and Poultry; Microbiology; Nutrition; Pathology; Pharmacology; Physiology; Radiology; Surgery; Toxicology; Veterinary Science); **Veterinary Science and Animal Husbandry** *(Jabalpur)* (Anatomy; Animal Husbandry; Biochemistry; Fishery; Genetics; Gynaecology and Obstetrics; Histology; Meat and Poultry; Microbiology; Nutrition; Parasitology; Pathology; Pharmacology; Physiology; Public Health; Radiology; Surgery; Toxicology; Veterinary Science; Wildlife); **Veterinary Science and Animal Husbandry** *(Rewa)* (Anatomy; Animal Husbandry; Biochemistry; Genetics; Microbiology; Nutrition; Parasitology; Pathology; Pharmacology; Toxicology; Veterinary Science)

Centre

Animal Biotechnology (Biotechnology; Embryology and Reproduction Biology; Genetics; Molecular Biology); **Wildlife Forensic and Health** (Health Sciences; Pathology; Veterinary Science; Wildlife)

History: Founded 2009.

Degrees and Diplomas: *Bachelor's Degree*; *Master's Degree*; *Doctor of Philosophy*

Last Updated: 04/01/12

MADURAI KAMARAJ UNIVERSITY

Palkalai Nagar, Madurai, Tamil Nadu 625021
Tel: +91(452) 245-9455
Fax: +91(452) 245-9181
EMail: mkuregistrar@rediffmail.com
Website: http://www.mkuniversity.org

Vice-Chancellor: Kalyani Mathivanan (2012-)
Tel: +91(452) 245-9166 EMail: vcmku@mkuniversity.org

Registrar: V. Alagappan
Tel: +91(452) 245-9181 EMail: mkuregistrar@rediffmail.com

School

Biological Sciences (Anatomy; Animal Husbandry; Biochemistry; Biological and Life Sciences; Biology; Botany; Genetics; Immunology; Microbiology; Molecular Biology; Physiology); **Biotechnology** (Biotechnology; Engineering; Genetics; Microbiology; Molecular Biology); **Business Studies** (Accountancy; Business Administration; Business and Commerce; Finance; Management); **Chemistry** (Chemistry; Inorganic Chemistry; Materials Engineering; Organic Chemistry; Physical Chemistry); **Earth and Atmospheric Sciences** (Earth Sciences; Geography; Surveying and Mapping); **Economics** (Agricultural Economics; Development Studies; Econometrics; Economics; Human Resources; Rural Studies); **Education** (Education; Physical Education); **Energy Environment and Natural Resources** (Energy Engineering; Environmental Studies; Futurology; Natural Resources; Waste Management); **English and Foreign Languages** (Comparative Literature; English; French; Modern Languages); **Historical Studies** (Ancient Civilizations; History; Medieval Studies; Modern History); **Indian Languages** (Comparative Literature; Indic Languages; Sanskrit); **Information and Communication Sciences** (Communication Studies; Information Sciences; Journalism; Library Science; Media Studies); **Mathematics** (Applied Mathematics; Mathematics; Statistics); **Performing Arts** (Aesthetics; Art History; Fine Arts; Folklore; Performing Arts); **Physics** (Computer Engineering; Computer Science; Laser Engineering; Physics); **Religions Philosophy and Humanist Thought** (Christian Religious Studies; Islamic Studies; Islamic Theology; Philosophy; Religious Studies); **Social Sciences** (Political Sciences; Social Sciences; Sociology); **Tamil Studies** (Ancient Books; Comparative Literature; Grammar; Linguistics; Literature; South and Southeast Asian Languages)

Department

Adult Education (Adult Education); **Youth Welfare**

Centre

Computer (Computer Science); **University Science Instrumentation** (Instrument Making)

Research Centre

Educational Media (Cinema and Television; Film; Mass Communication; Media Studies; Video)

Further Information: Also 116 affiliated colleges.

History: Founded 1966 as Madurai University. Acquired present title 1978. A 'University with Potential for Excellence'.

Academic Year: July to March (July-October; December-March)

Admission Requirements: 12th year senior secondary/intermediate examination or recognized foreign equivalent

Main Language(s) of Instruction: English, Tamil

Accrediting Agency: National Assessment and Accreditation Council (NAAC)

Degrees and Diplomas: *Bachelor's Degree*; *Postgraduate Diploma*; *Master's Degree*; *Master of Philosophy*; *Doctor of Philosophy*. Also undergraduate certificates and diplomas.

Student Services: Canteen, Careers Guidance, Health Services, Sports Facilities

Publishing house: University Printing Press

Student Numbers *2010-2011*	MEN	WOMEN	TOTAL
All (Foreign included)	60,000	60,000	c. **120,000**

Last Updated: 13/09/12

MAGADH UNIVERSITY

Bodh-Gaya, Bihar 824234
Tel: +91(631) 220-0572
Fax: +91(631) 220-0572
EMail: info@magadhuniversity.org
Website: http://www.magadhuniversity.org

Vice-Chancellor: Arvind Kumar Tel: +91(631) 220-0493

Registrar: D.K. Yadav Tel: +91(631) 220-0490

Faculty

Commerce (Business and Commerce; Economics); **Humanities** (Arts and Humanities; Asian Religious Studies; Child Care and Development; English; Geography; Hindi; History; Music; Persian; Philosophy; Political Sciences; Psychology; Sanskrit; Sociology; Urdu); **Management** (Business Administration; Home Economics; Management); **Science** (Applied Physics; Botany; Chemistry; Computer Science; Electronic Engineering; Mathematics; Microbiology; Physics; Zoology); **Vocational Studies** (Agriculture; Air Transport; Biochemistry; Biotechnology; Communication Studies; Dietetics; Education; Food Science; Hotel Management; Information Technology; Journalism; Laboratory Techniques; Mass Communication; Nursing; Nutrition; Physical Therapy; Rural Studies; Tourism; Transport and Communications; Vocational Education; Women's Studies; Yoga)

Further Information: Also 44 constituent and 105 affiliated colleges. A traditional and distance education institution.

History: Founded 1962.

Academic Year: June to May

Admission Requirements: 12th year senior secondary/intermediate examination or recognized foreign equivalent

Fees: (Rupees): 240-400 per annum

Main Language(s) of Instruction: English, Hindi

Degrees and Diplomas: *Bachelor's Degree*; *Master's Degree*; *Doctor of Philosophy*. Also Honours Bachelor's degree.

Student Services: Language Laboratory

Last Updated: 05/12/11

MAHAMAYA TECHNICAL UNIVERSITY (MTU)

C-22, Sector-62, Noida, Uttar Pradesh 201 301
Tel: +91(120) 240-0416
EMail: info@mtu.ac.in
Website: http://www.mtu.ac.in/

Vice-Chancellor: S. K. Kak
Tel: +91(120) 240-0416 EMail: vc@mtu.ac.in

Registrar: Pushyapati Saxena
Tel: +91(120) 240-0417 EMail: registrar@mtu.ac.in

Programme

Agriculture (Agriculture); **Architecture** (Architecture); **Biotechnology** (Biotechnology); **Business Administration** *(Postgraduate)* (Business Administration); **Computer Applications** *(Postgraduate)* (Computer Engineering); **Fashion and Apparel Design** (Fashion Design); **Hotel Management and Catering Technology** (Cooking and Catering; Food Technology; Hotel Management); **Pharmacy** (Pharmacy); **Pharmacy** *(Postgraduate)*

(Pharmacy); **Technology** *(Postgraduate)* (Technology); **Technology** (Technology)

Further Information: Also 385 affiliated colleges and institutions

History: Founded 2010.

Degrees and Diplomas: *Bachelor's Degree (professional)*; *Master's Degree*. Also MBA

Last Updated: 05/01/12

MAHARAJA GANGA SINGH UNIVERSITY (MGSU)

National Highway, 15, Jaisalmer Road, Bikaner, Rajasthan
Tel: +91(151) 221-2041
Fax: +91(151) 221-2042
EMail: info@mgsubikaner.ac.in
Website: http://www.mgsubikaner.ac.in

Vice-Chancellor: Ganga Ram Jakher
Tel: +91(151) 221-2041 EMail: grjvcmgsub@rediffmail.com

Registrar: Sh. Dinesh Chandra Gupta Tel: +91(151) 221-2044

Faculty

Arts (English; Fine Arts; Hindi; Indic Languages; Music; Painting and Drawing; Philosophy; Physical Education; Sanskrit; Urdu); **Commerce** (Administration; Business Administration; Economics; Finance); **Law** (Labour Law; Law); **Science** (Biochemistry; Biotechnology; Botany; Chemistry; Computer Science; Food Science; Forensic Medicine and Dentistry; Geology; Information Technology; Mathematics; Microbiology; Nutrition; Physics; Zoology); **Social Science** (Criminology; Economics; Environmental Management; Geography; History; Political Sciences; Public Administration; Social Sciences; Sociology)

Further Information: Also 297 affiliated colleges in Bikaner, Churu, Hanumangarh and Sriganganagar districts of Rajasthan.

History: Founded 2003 as Bikaner University. Acquired present title 2008.

Degrees and Diplomas: *Bachelor's Degree*; *Bachelor's Degree (professional)*; *Postgraduate Diploma*; *Master's Degree*; *Master of Philosophy*

Last Updated: 23/06/11

MAHARANA PRATAP UNIVERSITY OF AGRICULTURE AND TECHNOLOGY (MPUAT)

PO Box 171, New Campus, Udaipur, Rajasthan 313001
Tel: +91(294) 247-1101 +91(294) 247-0682
Fax: +91(294) 247-0682
Website: http://www.mpuat.ac.in

Vice-Chancellor: Sarabjit Singh Chahal (2009-)
EMail: vc@mpuat.ac.in; vc_mpuat@yahoo.co.in

Registrar: Shri L.N. Mantri EMail: registrar@mpuat.ac.in

College

Agriculture *(Rajasthan)* (Agricultural Business; Agricultural Economics; Agricultural Management; Agriculture; Agronomy; Animal Husbandry; Biotechnology; Chemistry; Computer Science; Education; Entomology; Genetics; Horticulture; Molecular Biology; Physiology; Plant and Crop Protection; Soil Science; Statistics; Zoology); **Dairy and Food Science Technology** *(CDFST)* (Biotechnology; Chemistry; Dairy; Economics; Food Science; Food Technology; Microbiology); **Fisheries** (Aquaculture; Fishery); **Home Science** (Communication Studies; Development Studies; Family Studies; Food Science; Home Economics; Nutrition; Textile Design); **Horticulture and Forestry** (Forestry; Horticulture); **Technology and Engineering** *(CTAE)* (Agricultural Engineering; Agricultural Equipment; Automation and Control Engineering; Civil Engineering; Computer Science; Electrical Engineering; Electronic Engineering; Energy Engineering; Engineering; Information Technology; Irrigation; Mechanical Engineering; Mining Engineering; Power Engineering; Water Management)

Further Information: Also constituent colleges, Agricultural Research Stations (ARSs), Agricultural Research Sub Stations (ARSSs), Livestock Research Station (LRS), Dryland Farming Research Station (DFRS), and Krishi Vigyan Kendras (KVKs) spread over 12 districts of the south and south eastern part of the state of Rajasthan (Banswara, Baran, Bhilwara, Bundi, Chittorgarh, Dungarpur, Jhalawar, Kota, Pratapgarh, Rajsamand, Sirohi and Udaipur).

History: Founded 1999 as Agricultural University, Udaipur. Acquired present status and title 2000.

Fees: (Indian Rupee): Tuition fee for undergraduate programmes, 500-950 per semester; For graduate programmes, 600-1,900 per semester; For Ph.D programmes., 3,200 per semester. Excepted for Technology and Engineering Programmes, 9,000-10,000 per annum. For International students, 4,000 Dollar per annum

Accrediting Agency: All India Council For Technical Education (AICTE); Indian Council of Agricultural Research (ICAR).

Degrees and Diplomas: *Bachelor's Degree*; *Bachelor's Degree (professional)*; *Postgraduate Diploma*; *Master's Degree*; *Doctor of Philosophy*

Last Updated: 23/06/11

MAHARASHTRA ANIMAL AND FISHERY SCIENCES UNIVERSITY

High Land Drive road, Seminary Hills, Nagpur, Maharashtra 440006
Tel: +91(712) 251-1282
Fax: +91(712) 251-1273
Website: http://www.mafsu.in

Vice-Chancellor: C. S. Prasad
Tel: +91(712) 251-1282 EMail: vc@mafsu.in

Registrar: L. B. Sarkate
Tel: +91(712) 251-1273 EMail: registrar@mafsu.in

College

Dairy Technology *(DTC, Warud)* (Chemistry; Computer Science; Dairy; Economics; Engineering; Food Science; Food Technology; Microbiology); **Fishery** *(COFS, Udgir)* (Fishery); **Fishery** *(COFS, Nagpur)* (Fishery); **Veterinary** *(NVC - Nagpur)* (Anatomy; Animal Husbandry; Epidemiology; Genetics; Gynaecology and Obstetrics; Meat and Poultry; Microbiology; Nutrition; Parasitology; Pathology; Public Health; Surgery; Veterinary Science); **Veterinary** *(BVC - Bombay)* (Anatomy; Animal Husbandry; Biochemistry; Embryology and Reproduction Biology; Genetics; Gynaecology and Obstetrics; Histology; Meat and Poultry; Medicine; Microbiology; Nutrition; Parasitology; Pathology; Pharmacology; Physiology; Public Health; Surgery; Veterinary Science); **Veterinary and Animal Sciences** *(COVAS - Udgir)* (Anatomy; Animal Husbandry; Biochemistry; Genetics; Medicine; Microbiology; Nutrition; Pathology; Physiology; Surgery; Veterinary Science); **Veterinary and Animal Sciences** *(COVAS - Parbhani)* (Animal Husbandry; Biochemistry; Genetics; Gynaecology and Obstetrics; Medicine; Microbiology; Nutrition; Pathology; Pharmacology; Physiology; Surgery; Veterinary Science); **Veterinary Science** *(KNP COVS - Krantisinh Nana Patil, Shirval)* (Agriculture; Animal Husbandry; Veterinary Science)

Institute

Veterinary and Animal Sciences *(PGIVAS - Postgraduate, Akola)* (Animal Husbandry; Biochemistry; Dairy; Genetics; Gynaecology and Obstetrics; Meat and Poultry; Nutrition; Pathology; Physiology; Radiology; Surgery; Veterinary Science)

History: Founded 2000.

Degrees and Diplomas: *Bachelor's Degree*; *Bachelor's Degree (professional)*; *Postgraduate Diploma*; *Master's Degree*; *Doctor of Philosophy*

Last Updated: 23/06/11

MAHARASHTRA UNIVERSITY OF HEALTH SCIENCES (MUHS)

Vani Road, Mhasrul, Nashik, Maharashtra 422 004
Tel: +91(253) 253-9191 +91(253) 253-9190
Fax: +91(253) 253-9195
EMail: academic@muhsnashik.com; computer@muhsnashik.com
Website: http://www.muhsnashik.com

Vice-Chancellor: Arun V. Jamkar
Tel: +91(253) 253-1835
EMail: vc@muhsnashik.com; vcoffice@muhsnashik.com

Registrar: Adinath N. Suryakar
Tel: +91(253) 253-9292
EMail: registrar@muhsnashik.com; registraroffice@muhsnashik.com

Faculty
Allied Health Sciences (Community Health; Dental Technology; Health Sciences; Nursing; Occupational Therapy; Physical Therapy; Respiratory Therapy); **Ayurveda and Unani** (Alternative Medicine; Ayurveda); **Dentistry** (Dentistry); **Homeopathy** (Homeopathy); **Medicine** (Anaesthesiology; Anatomy; Biochemistry; Cardiology; Dermatology; Diabetology; Endocrinology; Forensic Medicine and Dentistry; Gastroenterology; Gynaecology and Obstetrics; Haematology; Health Administration; Immunology; Medicine; Microbiology; Nephrology; Neurological Therapy; Neurology; Oncology; Ophthalmology; Paediatrics; Pathology; Pharmacology; Physiology; Plastic Surgery; Psychiatry and Mental Health; Public Health; Radiology; Social and Preventive Medicine; Surgery; Toxicology; Urology)

History: Founded 1998.

Academic Year: August to July (August-January; February-July)

Degrees and Diplomas: *Bachelor's Degree*; *Postgraduate Diploma*; *Master's Degree*
Last Updated: 23/06/11

MAHARISHI MAHESH YOGI VEDIC UNIVERSITY

Maharishi Mahesh Yogi Vedic Vishwavidyalaya (MMYVV)

H.O. Village Karondi, District Katni,
Umariapan, Madhya Pradesh 483332
Tel: +91(7625) 220-345
Fax: +91(7625) 220-285
EMail: registrarmmyvv@gmail.com; mmyvvarpr@yahoo.co.in
Website: http://www.mmyvv.com

Vice-Chancellor: Bhuvnesh Sharma
EMail: vc_mmyvv@rediffmail.com

Registrar: Arvind Singh Rajput

Programme
Arts (Arts and Humanities); **Astrology** (Esoteric Practices); **Audio Programme Production** (Mass Communication); **Commerce** (Business and Commerce); **Computer Science** (Computer Science); **Education** (Education); **Educational Administration** (Educational Administration); **Finance** (Finance); **Healt Care and Beauty Culture** (Cosmetology; Health Sciences); **Human Resources** (Human Resources); **Management** (Management); **Marketing** (Marketing); **Vedic Medicine** (Ayurveda); **Yoga** (Yoga)

Further Information: Also campuses in Bhopal, Indore and Jabalpur.

History: Founded 1995.

Fees: (Rupees): Tuition fees for undergraduate programmes, per annum, 2,285-27,000 per annum; Graduate programmes, 4,550-16,500 per annum; Ph.D., 10,000 per annum

Main Language(s) of Instruction: English and Hindi.

Degrees and Diplomas: *Post Diploma*; *Bachelor's Degree*; *Postgraduate Diploma*; *Master's Degree*; *Doctor of Philosophy*. Also undergraduate certificates.
Last Updated: 24/06/11

IAU MAHARISHI MARKANDESHWAR UNIVERSITY (MMU)

Mullana-Ambala, Haryana 133207
Tel: +91(1731) 304-100
Fax: +91(1731) 274-375
EMail: info@mmumullana.org
Website: http://www.mmumullana.org

Vice-Chancellor: Satyawan G. Damle
Tel: +91(1731) 301-525 EMail: vice-chancellor@mmumullana.org

International Relations: Harish K. Sharma, Registrar; Director, International Affairs
Tel: +91(1731) 304-440 EMail: registrarmmu@mmumullana.org

College
Dental Sciences and Research (Dental Hygiene; Dental Technology; Dentistry; Oral Pathology; Orthodontics; Periodontics; Radiology; Surgery); **Education** (Education); **Engineering** (Arts and Humanities; Biotechnology; Chemistry; Civil Engineering; Computer Engineering; Electrical Engineering; Electronic Engineering; Engineering; Information Technology; Mathematics; Measurement and Precision Engineering; Mechanical Engineering; Physics; Social Sciences; Telecommunications Engineering); **Nursing** (Community Health; Gynaecology and Obstetrics; Nursing; Paediatrics; Psychiatry and Mental Health); **Pharmacy** (Pharmacology; Pharmacy)

Programme
General Nursing and Midwifery (Midwifery; Nursing)

Department
Law (Law)

Institute
Computer Technology and Business Management *(Hotel Management)* (Business Administration; Cooking and Catering; Dietetics; Hotel and Restaurant; Hotel Management); **Computer Technology and Business Management** *(MCA)* (Business Computing; Computer Science); **Management** (Business Administration; Business and Commerce; Management); **Medical Sciences and Research** (Anaesthesiology; Anatomy; Biochemistry; Community Health; Dermatology; Forensic Medicine and Dentistry; Gynaecology and Obstetrics; Medicine; Microbiology; Ophthalmology; Orthopaedics; Otorhinolaryngology; Paediatrics; Pathology; Pharmacology; Physiology; Radiology; Respiratory Therapy; Surgery; Venereology); **Nursing** (Midwifery; Nursing); **Physiotherapy and Rehabilitation** (Cardiology; Paediatrics; Physical Therapy; Rehabilitation and Therapy; Sports)

History: Founded 1993. Acquired present status of Deemed University 2007.

Fees: (Indian Rupee): Tuition Fee, undergraduate programmes, 25,000-56,000 per annum; Graduate programmes, 25,000-180,000 per annum

Accrediting Agency: National Assessment and Accreditation Council (NAAC); Accreditation Service for International Colleges (ASIC).

Degrees and Diplomas: *Post Diploma*; *Bachelor's Degree*; *Bachelor's Degree (professional)*; *Postgraduate Diploma*; *Master's Degree*; *Master of Philosophy*; *Doctor of Philosophy*. Also MBA; Undergraduate certificates.

Student Services: Sports Facilities

Academic Staff *2010-2011*: Total 1,300

STAFF WITH DOCTORATE: Total 80

Student Numbers *2010-2011*: Total 10,250
Last Updated: 24/06/11

MAHARISHI MARKANDESHWAR UNIVERSITY, SADOPUR

V.P.O. Sadhopur, Chandigarh Road, Ambala, Haryana 134007
Tel: +91(94176) 25153
EMail: info@mmambala.org
Website: http://www.mmambala.org/

Director: Ashok K. Goel

Programme
Architecture (Architecture); **Engineering** (Civil Engineering; Computer Engineering; Electronic Engineering; Mechanical Engineering); **Fashion Design** (Fashion Design; Interior Design); **Management Studies** (Business Administration; Finance; Information Technology; Management; Marketing); **Sciences** (Chemistry; Mathematics; Physics); **Social Sciences** (Business and Commerce; English)

History: Founded 2010.

Fees: (Rupees): 15000-50000 per annum depending on programmes

Degrees and Diplomas: *Bachelor's Degree*; *Master's Degree*; *Doctor of Philosophy*

Student Services: Academic Counselling, Sports Facilities
Last Updated: 17/01/12

MAHARISHI MARKANDESHWAR UNIVERSITY, SOLAN (MMU SOLAN)

Solan, Himachal Pradesh 173 229
Tel: +91(1792) 268-224
Fax: +91(1792) 268-221
EMail: info@mmusolan.org
Website: http://mmusolan.org

Chancellor: Tarsem Garg

Registrar: Ajay Singal

School

Business Management (Business Administration; Management); **Computer Technology** (Computer Engineering; Computer Science); **Engineering and Technology** (Civil Engineering; Electrical Engineering; Engineering; Mechanical Engineering; Structural Architecture; Technology; Telecommunications Engineering)

Degrees and Diplomas: *Bachelor's Degree (professional)*; *Master's Degree*. Also MBA

Last Updated: 29/08/11

MAHARISHI UNIVERSITY OF MANAGEMENT AND TECHNOLOGY (MUMT)

Maharishi Vidya Mandir Campus, Mangla,
Bilaspur, Chhattisgarh 495 001
Tel: 07752-518424
Fax: 07752-518390
EMail: mumtho@mahaemail.com
Website: http://www.mumt.com/

Pro-Vice Chancellor: B. S. Mehta

Faculty

Education (Education); **Health Sciences** (Health Sciences); **Maharishi Vedic Science** (Esoteric Practices); **Management Studies** (Business Administration; Business and Commerce; Finance; Human Resources; Information Sciences; Labour and Industrial Relations; Management; Marketing); **Technology** (Computer Science; Technology)

Further Information: Also campuses in Raipur, Durg and Raigarh.

History: Founded 2002.

Fees: (Indian Rupee): Certificate, 3,000; Bachelor's degree, 6,000-17,000; Postgraduate diploma, 9,000

Accrediting Agency: University Grants Commission (UGC)

Degrees and Diplomas: *Post Diploma*; *Bachelor's Degree*; *Postgraduate Diploma*. Also Professional Certificate and Advanced Diploma, 1 yr.

Last Updated: 25/08/11

MAHARSHI DAYANAND SARASWATI UNIVERSITY

Pushkar By-pass, Ghooghara, Ajmer, Rajasthan 305009
Tel: +91(145) 278-7056 +91(145) 278-7058
Fax: +91(145) 278-7049 +91(145) 278-7055
Website: http://www.mdsuajmer.ac.in

Vice-Chancellor: Sh. Atul Sharma
Tel: +91(145) 278-7055 +91(145) 278-7051

Registrar: B. L. Sunaria

Department

Botany (Biotechnology; Botany); **Commerce** (Business and Commerce; Tourism); **Computer Science** (Computer Science; Data Processing; Information Management; Information Technology); **Economics** (Agricultural Economics; Banking; Economics); **Environmental Studies** (Environmental Studies); **Food and Nutrition** (Dietetics; Food Science; Management; Nutrition); **History** (Archiving; History); **Management Studies** (Business Administration; Management); **Microbiology** (Biology; Biotechnology; Microbiology); **Political Science** (Political Sciences; Public Administration); **Population Studies** (Demography and Population); **Pure and Applied Chemistry** (Applied Chemistry; Chemistry); **Remote Sensing** (Surveying and Mapping); **Zoology** (Biology; Laboratory Techniques; Molecular Biology; Zoology)

Centre

Yoga (Yoga)

Further Information: Also 214 government and private affiliated colleges.

History: Founded as University of Ajmer 1987 by an Act of State Legislature. Acquired present title 1992.

Admission Requirements: 12th year senior secondary/intermediate examination or recognized foreign equivalent

Fees: (Rupees): 250-1,500 per annum

Main Language(s) of Instruction: Hindi, English

Accrediting Agency: National Assessment and Accreditation Council, Bangalore

Degrees and Diplomas: *Postgraduate Diploma*; *Master's Degree*; *Master of Philosophy*; *Doctor of Philosophy*. Also undergraduate diploma and certificate programmes in yoga.

Student Services: Academic Counselling, Canteen, Foreign Studies Centre, Health Services, Language Laboratory, Sports Facilities

Last Updated: 24/06/11

MAHARSHI DAYANAND UNIVERSITY

Rohtak, Haryana 124001
Tel: +91(1262) 294-327
Fax: +91(1262) 294-133
Website: http://www.mdurohtak.ac.in

Vice-Chancellor: R.P. Hooda (2010-)
Tel: +91(1262) 274-327 +91(1262) 292-431
EMail: vcmdu@hotmail.com

Registrar: Sat Pal Vats Tel: +91(1262) 274-640

International Relations: S.K. Gakhar, Lecturer

Faculty

Commerce (Business and Commerce; Management; Retailing and Wholesaling); **Education** (Education; Physical Education); **Engineering and Technology** (Automation and Control Engineering; Biotechnology; Computer Engineering; Computer Science; Electronic Engineering; Engineering; Mechanical Engineering; Production Engineering; Software Engineering; Technology; Telecommunications Engineering); **Humanities** (Arts and Humanities; English; French; Hindi; Journalism; Mass Communication; Media Studies; Modern Languages; Sanskrit; Spanish; Translation and Interpretation); **Law** (Law); **Life Sciences** (Biochemistry; Biotechnology; Botany; Environmental Studies; Food Technology; Forensic Medicine and Dentistry; Genetics; Microbiology; Zoology); **Management Sciences** (Business Administration; Economics; Hotel and Restaurant; Hotel Management; Management; Tourism); **Performing and Visual Arts** (Fine Arts; Music; Musical Instruments; Painting and Drawing; Performing Arts; Singing; Visual Arts); **Pharmaceutical Sciences** (Pharmacology; Pharmacy); **Physical Sciences** (Chemistry; Computer Science; Mathematics; Physics; Statistics); **Social Sciences** (Economics; Geography; History; Library Science; Military Science; Political Sciences; Psychology; Public Administration; Social Sciences; Sociology)

Institute

Law and Management Studies *(ILMS - Gurgaon)* (International Business; Law)

Centre

Haryana Studies (Regional Studies); **Indira Gandhi PG Regional** *(Rewari)* (Business and Commerce; English; History; Mathematics); **Women Studies** (Women's Studies)

Further Information: Over 490 affiliated Institutions/Colleges.

History: Founded as Rohtak University 1976. Acquired present title 1977 and present status 1978.

Academic Year: July to March (July-September; October-December; January-March)

Admission Requirements: 12th year senior secondary/intermediate examination or recognized foreign equivalent

Fees: (Rupees): Undergraduate programmes, 2,200-62,315 per annum; Graduate programmes, 1,610-72,315 per annum; MBA, 36,295-48,815 per annum

Main Language(s) of Instruction: Hindi. English

Accrediting Agency: National Assessment and Accreditation Council (NAAC)

Degrees and Diplomas: *Post Diploma*; *Bachelor's Degree*; *Bachelor's Degree (professional)*; *Postgraduate Diploma*; *Master's Degree*; *Doctor of Philosophy*. Also Honours Bachelor and Master's degree; Professional Master degree; MBA; Undergraduate certificate.

Student Services: Academic Counselling, Canteen, Careers Guidance, Health Services, Sports Facilities

Publishing house: Maharshi Dayanand University Press

Last Updated: 24/06/11

MAHARSHI PANINI SANSKRIT UNIVERSITY

Maharshi Panini Sanskrit Vishwavidyalaya (MPSVVUJJAIN)
B.M. Birla Shodh Sansthan, Parisar Dewas Road,
Ujjain, Madhya Pradesh 456 010
Tel: +91(734) 252-6044
Fax: +91(734) 252-4845
Website: http://mpsvvujjain.org/

Vice-Chancellor: Mithla Prasad Tripathi

Programme

Sanskrit (Administration; Astronomy and Space Science; Ayurveda; Environmental Studies; Esoteric Practices; History; Literature; Mathematics; Military Science; Philosophy; Sanskrit; Sculpture; Zoology)

Further Information: Also 17 Affiliated Colleges.

History: Founded 2008.

Degrees and Diplomas: *Bachelor's Degree*; *Master's Degree*. Also Shastri, 7 years; Asharya, (Post Graduate Degree).

Last Updated: 04/01/12

MAHATMA GANDHI CHITRAKOOT GRAMODAYA UNIVERSITY

Mahatma Gandhi Chitrakoot Gramodaya Vishwavidyalaya (MGCGV)
District Satna, Chitrakoot, Madhya Pradesh 485331
Tel: +91(7670) 265-411
Fax: +91(7670) 265-413
EMail: mgcgv@rediffmail.com
Website: http://www.ruraluniversity-chitrakoot.org

Vice-Chancellor: Krishna B. Pandeya
Tel: +91(7670) 265-413 EMail: kbpandeya@yahoo.com

Registrar: Rama Shankar Tripathi

Faculty

Agriculture (Agriculture; Agronomy; Biochemistry; Botany; Crop Production; Genetics; Home Economics; Horticulture; Soil Science; Technology; Zoology); **Education, Fine Arts, Humanities and Social Sciences** (Ancient Civilizations; Arts and Humanities; Cultural Studies; Education; Fine Arts; Hindi; History; Information Sciences; Journalism; Library Science; Mass Communication; Music; Painting and Drawing; Political Sciences; Public Administration; Sanskrit; Sculpture; Social Sciences; Women's Studies; Yoga); **Engineering and Technology** (Agricultural Engineering; Civil Engineering; Electronic Engineering; Engineering; Food Technology; Information Technology; Mechanical Engineering; Technology); **Rural Development and Business Management** (Administration; Agricultural Business; Business Administration; Development Studies; Management; Small Business); **Science and Environment** (Biochemistry; Biological and Life Sciences; Biology; Chemistry; Environmental Studies; Forestry; Geology; Information Technology; Mathematics; Surveying and Mapping; Wildlife; Zoology)

History: Founded 1991 as Chitrakoot Gramodaya Vishwavidyalaya. Renamed Mahatma Gandhi Gramodaya Vishwavidyalaya. Acquired present title 1997.

Fees: Tuition fees, 9,000-19,800 per annum for undergraduate programmes and 10,000-24,300 per annum for graduate programmes. MBA, 41,400 per annum (Indian Rupee)

Main Language(s) of Instruction: English, Hindi

Accrediting Agency: Government Agencies (UGC; AICTE; ICAR; NCTE)

Degrees and Diplomas: *Post Diploma*; *Bachelor's Degree*; *Bachelor's Degree (professional)*; *Postgraduate Diploma*; *Master's Degree*; *Doctor of Philosophy*. Also MBA.

Student Services: Academic Counselling, Canteen, Cultural Activities, Health Services, Nursery Care, Social Counselling

Last Updated: 27/06/11

MAHATMA GANDHI INTERNATIONAL HINDI UNIVERSITY

Mahatma Gandhi Antarrashtriya Hindi Vishwavidyalaya
Post - Manas Temple, Gandhi Hill, Wardha, Maharashtra 442001
Tel: +91(7152) 230-905
Fax: +91(7152) 240-760
EMail: hindiunv@vsnl.net.in
Website: http://www.hindivishwa.org

Vice-Chancellor: Vibhuti Narain Rai
Tel: +91(7152) 230-907 EMail: vc@hindivishwa.org

Registrar: A. Biswdvidyaly Arvindakshn
Tel: +91(7152) 230-902 EMail: registrar@hindivishwa.org

School

Culture *(Mganahiv)* (Cultural Studies; Peace and Disarmament; Social Sciences; Women's Studies); **Language** (Chinese; Engineering; French; Hindi; Linguistics; Modern Languages; South and Southeast Asian Languages; Spanish; Urdu); **Literature** (Comparative Literature; Film; Literature; Theatre); **Translation and Interpretation** (Translation and Interpretation)

Centre

Buddhist Learning *(Dr. Bdnt fun Kauslyayn)* (Asian Religious Studies); **Communication and Media Studies** (Advertising and Publicity; Communication Studies; Journalism; Mass Communication; Media Studies; Public Relations; Radio and Television Broadcasting; Video); **Dalit and Tribal Studies** *(Dr. Babasaheb Ambedkar)* (Social Studies); **Indian and foreign languages** *(Advanced Studies)* (Computer Science; Sanskrit); **Master Peace Studies** *(Mahatma Gandhi Fuji)* (Peace and Disarmament; Social Work); **Technology Learning** (Computer Science; Information Technology; Modern Languages); **Zakir Husain Studies** (Educational Sciences)

Further Information: Also Distance Education programme.

History: Founded 1997. A 'Central University'.

Degrees and Diplomas: *Post Diploma*; *Postgraduate Diploma*; *Master's Degree*; *Master of Philosophy*; *Doctor of Philosophy*. Also undergraduate certificate.

Student Services: Health Services, Sports Facilities

Last Updated: 24/06/11

MAHATMA GANDHI KASHI UNIVERSITY

Mahatma Gandhi Kashi Vidyapeeth (MGKV)
Varanasi, Uttar Pradesh 221 002
Tel: +91(542) 222-2689
Fax: +91(542) 222-5472
EMail: mgkv@rediffmail.com
Website: http://www.mgkvp.ac.in

Vice-Chancellor: Avadh Ram (2008-)
Tel: +91(542) 222-5472
EMail: vcmgkvp@sancharnet.in; profavadhram@yahoo.com; profavadhram@gmail.com

Registrar (Acting): Indupati Jha Tel: +91(542) 222-2689

Faculty

Commerce and Management (Accountancy; Business Administration; Business and Commerce; Finance; Management); **Education** (Education); **Humanities** (Ancient Languages; Arts and Humanities; English; Fine Arts; Hindi; History; Information Sciences; Journalism; Library Science; Literature; Modern Languages; Philosophy; Physical Education; Russian; Sanskrit; South and Southeast Asian Languages; Tourism; Urdu); **Law** (Law); **Science and Technology** (Botany; Chemistry; Computer Science; Home Economics; Mathematics; Physics; Statistics; Technology; Zoology); **Social Sciences** (Economics; Political Sciences; Psychology; Social Sciences; Sociology; Women's Studies); **Social Work** (Development Studies; Human Rights; Labour and Industrial Relations; Social Work; Welfare and Protective Services); **Student Welfare**

Institute

Hindi Journalism *(Madan Mohan Malviya)* (Information Sciences; Journalism)

Further Information: Also Sonebhadra campus and Dr. Vibhuti Narayan Singh Rural Medical Institute Gangapur Campus,

Varanasi. 229 affiliated colleges located in Varanasi, Chandauli, Sant Ravidas Nagar (Bhadohi), Mirzapur, Sonebhadra and Ballia.

History: Founded 1921 by Mahatma Gandhi. Acquired present status 1974.

Academic Year: July to June

Admission Requirements: 12th year senior secondary/intermediate examination or recognized foreign equivalent

Fees: (Rupees): 10-100

Main Language(s) of Instruction: English and Hindi

Accrediting Agency: UGC; NAAC

Degrees and Diplomas: *Post Diploma*; *Bachelor's Degree*; *Postgraduate Diploma*; *Master's Degree*; *Master of Philosophy*; *Doctor of Philosophy*. Also undergraduate certificates and advance diploma Courses.

Student Services: Academic Counselling, Canteen, Careers Guidance, Cultural Activities, Health Services, Sports Facilities

Last Updated: 27/06/11

MAHATMA GANDHI UNIVERSITY (KHANAPARA) (MGU)

13th Mile, G.S.Road, PO&OP - Byrnihat, PS- Nongpoh, District- Ri-Bhoi, Khanapara, Meghalaya 793101
Tel: +91 8800697050/+91 880069705
EMail: info@mgu.edu.in
Website: http://www.mgu.edu.in/

Faculty

Applied Technology (Biotechnology; Laboratory Techniques; Medical Parasitology); **Arts** (Air Transport; Arts and Humanities; English; Hotel Management; Mass Communication; Multimedia; Tourism); **Management and Commerce** (Business and Commerce; Economic History; Finance; Management); **Sciences and Technology** (Computer Engineering; Engineering; Information Technology)

Further Information: Also Tura Campus

History: Founded 2010.

Fees: (Indian Rupee): Tuition fee for Indian students, 4,000-7,000; 10,000-30,000 for International students

Accrediting Agency: University Grants Commission (UGC); Distance Education Council (DEC)

Degrees and Diplomas: *Post Diploma*; *Bachelor's Degree*; *Postgraduate Diploma*; *Master's Degree*; *Master of Philosophy*; *Doctor of Philosophy*. Also certificate; MBA

Last Updated: 30/08/11

MAHATMA GANDHI UNIVERSITY (KOTTAYAM) (M.G. UNIVERSITY)

Priyadarsini Hills P.O., Kottayam, Kerala 686 560
Tel: +91(481) 273-1050
Fax: +91(481) 273-1002 +91(481) 273-1009
EMail: mgu@mgu.ac.in
Website: http://www.mguniversity.edu

Vice-Chancellor: Rajan Gurukkal
Tel: +91(481) 273-1001 EMail: rgurukkal@gmail.com

Registrar: Sri. M.R. Unni
Tel: +91(481) 273-1007 EMail: registrar@mgu.ac.in

School

Behavioural Sciences (Behavioural Sciences; Nursing; Psychology; Rehabilitation and Therapy; Special Education); **Biosciences** *(SBS)* (Biochemistry; Biophysics; Biotechnology; Microbiology); **Chemical Sciences** (Chemistry; Inorganic Chemistry; Organic Chemistry; Physical Chemistry; Polymer and Plastics Technology); **Computer Sciences** (Computer Science); **Distance Education** *(SDE)* (Business Administration; Computer Engineering; Computer Science; English; Fashion Design; Information Technology; Law; Library Science; Literature; Management; Mathematics; Multimedia; Sociology; Software Engineering; Tourism); **Environmental Sciences** (Environmental Management; Environmental Studies; Surveying and Mapping; Tourism; Waste Management; Water Management); **Gandhian Thought and Development Studies** (Development Studies; Peace and Disarmament); **Indian Legal Thought** (Administrative Law; Civil Law; Constitutional Law; Human Rights; Law); **International Relations and Politics** *(SIRP)* (Government; Human Rights; International Relations; Political Sciences); **Letters** (Cinema and Television; Comparative Literature; Literature; Modern Languages; Performing Arts; Theatre; Translation and Interpretation; Writing); **Management and Business Studies** (Business Administration; Finance; Human Resources; Information Technology; Management; Marketing); **Pedagogical Sciences** (Arabic; Business Education; Computer Education; Curriculum; Education; Educational Administration; Educational and Student Counselling; Educational Psychology; Educational Technology; English; Foreign Languages Education; Higher Education; Hindi; Humanities and Social Science Education; Mathematics Education; Pedagogy; Primary Education; Sanskrit; Science Education; Secondary Education; South and Southeast Asian Languages; Special Education; Statistics; Teacher Training); **Physical Education and Sports Sciences** (Physical Education; Sports); **Pure and Applied Physics** (Applied Physics; Astrophysics; Electronic Engineering; Materials Engineering; Physics); **Social Sciences** (Anthropology; Ecology; Economics; History; Social Sciences; Sociology); **Tourism** (Tourism)

Department

Lifelong Learning and Extension (Alternative Medicine; Farm Management; Gerontology; Health Sciences; Psychiatry and Mental Health; Psychology; Yoga)

Institute

Intensive Research in Basic Sciences (Human Resources; Laboratory Techniques; Natural Sciences)

Centre

Disability Studies *(Inter University)* (Health Sciences; Rehabilitation and Therapy; Special Education); **English Language and Communication Skills** *(CELCS)* (English); **Environmental Studies and Sustainable Development** *(Advanced - ACESSD)* (Development Studies; Environmental Studies); **High Performance Computing** *(CHPC)* (Computer Science; Software Engineering); **Nanoscience and Nanotechnology** (Nanotechnology); **Social Sciences Research and Extension** *(Inter-University)* (Archaeology; Cultural Studies; Development Studies; Gender Studies; Social Sciences; Social Welfare)

Further Information: Also 8 satellite campuses at Pullarikkunnu, Soorya Kaladi Hills, Nattassery, Puthuppally, Gandhi Nagar and Cheruvandoor in Kottayam, Thodupuzha and Nedumkandam in Idukki Districts and Chuttippara in Pathanamthitta District. 245 affiliated colleges. 7 constitutent colleges.

History: Founded 1983 as Gandhiji University, acquired present title 1988.

Academic Year: June to March (June-September; October-December; January-March)

Admission Requirements: 12th year senior secondary/intermediate examination or recognized foreign equivalent

Fees: (Rupees): 300-600 per term for Indian students and 600-1,200 per term for international students. Ph.D., 3,000 for Indian students and 5,000 for international students

Main Language(s) of Instruction: English

Degrees and Diplomas: *Bachelor's Degree*; *Postgraduate Diploma*; *Master's Degree*; *Master of Philosophy*; *Doctor of Philosophy*. Also undergraduate certificates, 6 months-1 year.

Student Services: Canteen, Careers Guidance, Cultural Activities, Health Services, Nursery Care, Social Counselling, Sports Facilities

Last Updated: 27/06/11

MAHATMA GANDHI UNIVERSITY (NALGONDA)

Nalgonda, Andhra Pradesh 508001
Tel: +91(863) 2230927
Fax: +91(863) 2237923
EMail: info@mahatmagandhicollege.com
Website: http://www.mguniversity.ac.in

Vice-Chancellor: K. Narasimha Reddy

Programme

Applied Economics (Economics); **Business Administration** (Business Administration; Finance); **Commerce** (Business and Commerce); **English Literature** (English; Literature); **Sciences**

(Biochemistry; Biotechnology; Mathematics; Organic Chemistry; Pharmacology)

History: Founded 2008.

Degrees and Diplomas: *Bachelor's Degree*; *Master's Degree*

Student Services: Health Services, Sports Facilities

Last Updated: 22/07/11

MAHATMA JYOTI RAO PHOOLE UNIVERSITY

Ram Nagar Ext., New Sanganer Road, Sodala,
Jaipur, Rajasthan 302019
Tel: +91(141) 229-4680 +91(141) 229-5101
Fax: +91(141) 229-4947
EMail: info@mjrpuniversity.com
Website: http://www.mjrpuniversity.com

Vice-Chancellor: Nirmal Panwar

Faculty

Agriculture (Agricultural Business; Agricultural Management; Agriculture; Crop Production; Farm Management; Food Technology; Horticulture; Landscape Architecture; Safety Engineering; Water Management); **Allied Health Sciences** (Health Sciences; Laboratory Techniques; Medical Technology; Public Health); **Arts** (Arts and Humanities; Economics; English; Fine Arts; History; Home Economics; Hotel and Restaurant; Political Sciences; Psychology; Public Administration; Social Sciences; Social Work; Sociology; Surveying and Mapping; Visual Arts); **Bio-Technology and Microbiology** (Biological and Life Sciences; Biotechnology; Computer Science; Microbiology); **Business and Management** (Business Administration; Economics; Health Administration; Hotel Management; Human Resources; Information Technology; International Business; Management; Marketing); **Commerce** (Business Administration; Business and Commerce; E- Business/Commerce; Economics; Finance; International Business); **Education** (Education; Educational Psychology; Special Education); **Engineering** (Agricultural Engineering; Architecture; Automotive Engineering; Biotechnology; Chemical Engineering; Civil Engineering; Computer Science; Electrical Engineering; Electronic Engineering; Engineering; Information Technology; Mechanical Engineering; Nuclear Engineering; Telecommunications Engineering); **Fashion Design Technology** (Fashion Design; Jewellery Art; Textile Design); **Film Technology** (Acting; Computer Graphics; Dance; Film; Multimedia; Photography; Radio and Television Broadcasting; Video); **Information Science and Technology** (Computer Science; Information Sciences; Information Technology); **Law** (Commercial Law; Law; Private Law); **Media** (Advertising and Publicity; Journalism; Marketing; Mass Communication; Media Studies; Printing and Printmaking; Public Relations); **Pharmacy** (Chemistry; Management; Pharmacology; Pharmacy; Safety Engineering); **Polytechnic and ITI** (Civil Engineering; Computer Science; Electrical Engineering; Engineering; Fashion Design; Information Technology; Mechanical Engineering; Mechanics; Metal Techniques); **Science** (Biochemistry; Biotechnology; Botany; Chemistry; Clinical Psychology; Computer Science; Development Studies; Dietetics; Economics; English; Environmental Studies; Geography; Home Economics; Interior Design; Mathematics; Microbiology; Nutrition; Physics; Psychology; Safety Engineering; Social Work; Statistics; Surveying and Mapping; Textile Design; Zoology); **Vedic Science and Yoga** (Alternative Medicine; Ayurveda; Esoteric Practices; Health Sciences; Yoga)

History: Founded 2009.

Accrediting Agency: University Grants Commission (UGC)

Degrees and Diplomas: *Post Diploma*; *Bachelor's Degree*; *Bachelor's Degree (professional)*; *Postgraduate Diploma*; *Master's Degree*; *Master of Philosophy*; *Doctor of Philosophy*. Also Certificate; Honours Bachelor's and Master's degree; MBA and Executive MBA; Dual degrees (Bachelor/Master or MBA).

Last Updated: 02/09/11

MAHATMA JYOTIBA PHULE (MJP) ROHILKHAND UNIVERSITY

Pilibhit By Pass Road, Bareilly, Uttar Pradesh 243 006
Tel: +91(581) 252-7263
Fax: +91(581) 252-4232
EMail: info@mjpru.ac.in;
Website: http://www.mjpru.ac.in

Vice-Chancellor: Satya P. Gautam
Tel: +91(581) 252-7282 EMail: vcoffice@mjpru.ac.in

Registrar: Bal Krishna Pandey
Tel: +91(581) 252-7263 +91(581) 252-1122
EMail: registrar@mjpru.ac.in

Faculty

Advanced Social Sciences (Ancient Civilizations; Development Studies; Economics; History; Social Sciences; Women's Studies); **Agriculture** (Agriculture); **Applied Science** (Aquaculture; Biochemistry; Biotechnology; Botany; Cell Biology; Embryology and Reproduction Biology; Endocrinology; Entomology; Environmental Studies; Fishery; Genetics; Immunology; Microbiology; Molecular Biology; Parasitology; Physiology; Zoology); **Arts** (Arts and Humanities; Fine Arts); **Commerce** (Business Administration; Business and Commerce); **Dental Sciences** (Dentistry); **Education** (Education); **Education and Allied Sciences** (Clinical Psychology; Computer Science; Education; English; Journalism; Mass Communication; Philosophy; Social Sciences); **Engineering and Technology** (Arts and Humanities; Chemical Engineering; Chemistry; Computer Networks; Computer Science; Data Processing; Economics; Electrical Engineering; Electronic Engineering; Engineering; English; Information Technology; Management; Mathematics; Measurement and Precision Engineering; Mechanical Engineering; Microwaves; Pharmacy; Physics; Software Engineering; Technology); **Law** (Civil Law; Comparative Law; Human Rights; International Law; Labour and Industrial Relations; Law); **Management Studies** (Business Administration; Cooking and Catering; Hotel Management; International Business; Management; Marketing; Tourism); **Sciences** (Natural Sciences)

Department

Training and Placement Cell

Further Information: Also 154 affiliated colleges.

History: Founded as M.J.P. Rohilkhand University 1975. Acquired present status and title 1997.

Academic Year: July to June

Admission Requirements: 12th year senior secondary/intermediate examination or recognized foreign equivalent

Main Language(s) of Instruction: Hindi, English

Degrees and Diplomas: *Post Diploma*; *Bachelor's Degree*; *Bachelor's Degree (professional)*; *Postgraduate Diploma*; *Master's Degree*; *Master of Philosophy*; *Doctor of Philosophy*. Also undergraduate certificates; MBA and Professional Postgraduate Courses.

Student Services: Health Services, Sports Facilities

Publications: I.A.S.E.; Journal of Education and Allied Sciences; Prospectus; Seminar Abstracts and Proceedings; University Magazine; University Yearbook

Last Updated: 27/06/11

MAHATMA PHULE AGRICULTURAL UNIVERSITY

Mahatma Phule Krishi Vidyapeeth (MPKV)
Ahmednagar District, Rahuri, Maharashtra 413722
Tel: +91(2426) 243-216
Fax: +91(2426) 243-302
EMail: vc.mpkv@nic.in
Website: http://mpkv.mah.nic.in

Vice-Chancellor: Tukaram A. More (2010-) EMail: vc.mpkv@nic.in

Registrar: Shri. B.H. Palwe
Tel: +91(2426) 243-216 EMail: registrar.mpkv@nic.in

College

Agricultural Engineering *(Rahuri)* (Agricultural Engineering; Agricultural Equipment; Automation and Control Engineering; Electrical Engineering; Electronic Engineering; Energy Engineering; Engineering Drawing and Design; Farm Management; Irrigation; Physics; Soil Conservation; Water Management); **Agriculture** *(Pune)* (Agriculture; Horticulture); **Agriculture** *(Dhule)* (Agriculture); **Agriculture** *(Kolhapur)* (Agriculture); **Horticulture** *(Pune)* (Horticulture)

Institute

Post-Graduate Studies *(Rahuri)* (Agriculture); **Post-Graduate Studies** *(Pune)* (Agriculture)

History: Founded 1968. An 'Agricultural University'.

Admission Requirements: 12th year senior secondary/intermediate examination or recognized foreign equivalent
Fees: (Rupees): 10,000-20,000 per annum
Main Language(s) of Instruction: English
Accrediting Agency: Indian Council of Agricultural Research
Degrees and Diplomas: *Post Diploma*; *Bachelor's Degree*; *Bachelor's Degree (professional)*; *Postgraduate Diploma*; *Master's Degree*; *Doctor of Philosophy*
Student Services: Academic Counselling, Canteen, Careers Guidance, Cultural Activities, Health Services, Social Counselling, Sports Facilities
Publications: Krishidarshani Diairy; Shri Sugi
Publishing House: University Printing Press
Last Updated: 28/06/11

MAKHANLAL CHATURVEDI NATIONAL UNIVERSITY OF JOURNALISM AND COMMUNICATION

Makhanlal Chaturvedi Rashtriya Patrakarita Vishwavidyalaya
P.O. Box No. RSN/560, Trilochan Singh Nagar, Bhopal, Madhya Pradesh 462016
Tel: +91(755) 272-5307 +91(755) 272-5559
Fax: +91(755) 256-1970
EMail: mcu.pravesh@gmail.com
Website: http://www.mcu.ac.in

Vice-Chancellor: B.K. Kuthiala
Tel: +91(755) 255-1531
EMail: vc@mcu.ac.in; kuthialavc@gmail.com

Registrar: Chander Sonane
Tel: +91(755) 272-5307 EMail: registrar@mcu.ac.in

Department

Computer Science and Applications (Computer Science); **Electronic Media** (Media Studies); **Journalism** (Journalism); **Management** (Management); **Mass Communication** (Mass Communication); **Public Relations and Advertising Studies** (Advertising and Publicity; Public Relations); **Publications** (Information Sciences; Library Science); **Research**; **Short Term Training Programmes**; **Text Book Writing** (Writing)
Further Information: Also Noida and Khandwa (Karmveer Vidhyapeeth) campuses. An Open University providing Distance Education.
History: Founded 1990.
Academic Year: August to June (August-December; January-June)
Admission Requirements: 12th year senior secondary/intermediate examination
Fees: (Rupees): 3,000-16,000 per annum
Main Language(s) of Instruction: Hindi, English
Degrees and Diplomas: *Bachelor's Degree*; *Postgraduate Diploma*; *Master's Degree*; *Doctor of Philosophy*. Also MBA in Media Management.
Student Services: Cultural Activities, Sports Facilities
Publications: Vidura
Last Updated: 28/06/11

MALAVIYA NATIONAL INSTITUTE OF TECHNOLOGY (MNIT)

Jawahar Lal Nehru Marg, Jaipur, Rajasthan 302017
Tel: +91(141) 252-9087
Fax: +91(141) 252-9029
EMail: info@mnit.ac.in
Website: http://www.mnit.ac.in

Director: I.K. Bhat
Tel: +91(141) 252-9087 EMail: director@mnit.ac.in

Registrar: P.S. Dhaka
Tel: +91(141) 252-9078; +91(141) 271-3204
EMail: registrar@mnit.ac.in

Department

Architecture (Architecture); **Chemical Engineering** (Biotechnology; Chemical Engineering; Petroleum and Gas Engineering); **Chemistry** (Chemistry); **Civil Engineering** (Civil Engineering; Environmental Engineering; Hydraulic Engineering; Transport Engineering); **Computer Engineering** (Computer Engineering; Information Technology); **Electrical Engineering** (Electrical Engineering; Power Engineering); **Electronics and Communication Engineering** (Electronic Engineering; Telecommunications Engineering); **Humanities** (Arts and Humanities; Communication Studies; Economics; English; Industrial Management; Management; Social Sciences); **Management Studies** (Management); **Mathematics** (Mathematics; Statistics); **Mechanical Engineering** (Mechanical Engineering); **Metallurgical and Materials Engineering** (Materials Engineering; Metallurgical Engineering); **Physics** (Laser Engineering; Mathematical Physics; Mechanics; Nanotechnology; Nuclear Physics; Physics; Solid State Physics); **Structural Engineering** (Building Technologies; Civil Engineering; Engineering; Geological Engineering; Seismology; Structural Architecture)
History: Founded 1963 as Malaviya Regional Engineering College. Acquired present title and status 2002 (Deemed University). An 'Institute of National Importance'.
Academic Year: July to August
Fees: (Rupees): tuition fee 17,500 per annum
Degrees and Diplomas: *Bachelor's Degree (professional)*; *Postgraduate Diploma*; *Master's Degree*; *Doctor of Philosophy*. Also Professional Master's degree programmes and MBA.
Student Services: Canteen, Health Services, Sports Facilities
Last Updated: 28/06/11

MANAGEMENT DEVELOPMENT INSTITUTE (MDI)

Mehrauli Road, Sukhrali, GurgaonSukhrali,Gurgaon, Haryana 122 007
Website: http://www.mdi.ac.in/

Director: Mukul P. Gupta

Programme

Energy Management (Energy Engineering; Management); **Human Resources** (Human Resources); **International Management** (International Business; Management); **Management** (Management); **Public Policy and Management** (Management; Public Administration)
History: Founded 1973.
Degrees and Diplomas: *Postgraduate Diploma*. Also Part-time Postgraduate programmes; Executive Fellow Programmes
Last Updated: 23/01/12

MANAV BHARTI UNIVERSITY (MBU)

Village - Laddo, Sultanpur (Kumhar Hatti), Tehsil & Distt. Solan, Solan, Himachal Pardesh 173229
Tel: +91(1792) 268-279 +91(1792) 268-280
EMail: manavbhartiuniversity@gmail.com
Website: http://manavbhartiuniversity.edu.in/

Vice-Chancellor: S. P. Bhardwaj

Registrar: Roshan Lal

Programme

Arts, Commerce and Science (Biochemistry; Biotechnology; Business and Commerce; Chemistry; Foreign Languages Education; Microbiology); **Ayurveda** (Ayurveda); **Computer Science** (Computer Engineering; Computer Networks; Computer Science); **Doctoral Studies** (Alternative Medicine; Ayurveda; Business and Commerce; Chemistry; Computer Science; Cooking and Catering; Engineering; Fire Science; Food Science; Hotel Management; Information Sciences; Information Technology; Library Science; Management; Medical Auxiliaries; Medical Technology; Microbiology; Nutrition; Pharmacy; Physical Therapy; Safety Engineering; Veterinary Science; Yoga); **Engineering and IT** (Biotechnology; Civil Engineering; Computer Engineering; Computer Networks; Computer Science; Construction Engineering; Electrical Engineering; Electronic Engineering; Engineering; Information Technology; Mechanical Engineering; Microelectronics; Nanotechnology; Power

Engineering; Software Engineering; Structural Architecture; Telecommunications Engineering; Water Management); **Fire Safety Management** (Fire Science; Safety Engineering); **Food and Nutrition** (Food Science; Nutrition); **Hotel Management and Catering Technology** (Cooking and Catering; Food Technology; Hotel Management); **Library and Information Science** (Information Sciences; Library Science); **Management** (Business Administration; Finance; Health Administration; Hotel and Restaurant; Human Resources; Information Technology; Management; Marketing; Retailing and Wholesaling; Tourism); **Paramedical Science** (Laboratory Techniques; Medical Auxiliaries; Medical Technology); **Pharmacy** (Pharmacy); **Physiotherapy** (Neurological Therapy; Orthopaedics; Physical Therapy); **Ultrasonography** (Medical Technology); **Veterinary Science** (Animal Husbandry; Pharmacy; Veterinary Science); **Yoga and Naturopathy** (Alternative Medicine; Yoga)

History: Founded 2009.

Fees: Undergraduate programmes, 20,000-30,000 per semester; Postgraduate programmes, 15,000-60,000 per semester (Indian Rupee)

Accrediting Agency: University Grants Commission (UGC)

Degrees and Diplomas: *Post Diploma*; *Bachelor's Degree*; *Bachelor's Degree (professional)*; *Postgraduate Diploma*; *Master's Degree*; *Doctor of Philosophy*. Also MBA

Student Services: Sports Facilities

Last Updated: 29/08/11

MANAV RACHNA INTERNATIONAL UNIVERSITY (MRIU)

MRIU Aravalli Campus Sector, 43, Delhi Surajkund Road,
Faridabad, Haryana 121-004
Tel: +91(129) 4259-000
EMail: manager.admissions@mriu.edu.in
Website: http://info.mriu.edu.in/

Vice-Chancellor: N.C. Wadhwa

Registrar: K.C. Dadhwal

Faculty

Applied Science (Dietetics; Hotel Management; Nutrition; Physical Therapy); **Business Administration and Computer Applications** *(FBC)* (Business Administration; Computer Science); **Engineering and Technology** *(FET)* (Aeronautical and Aerospace Engineering; Automotive Engineering; Biotechnology; Civil Engineering; Computer Engineering; Computer Science; Electrical Engineering; Electronic Engineering; Engineering; Information Technology; Mechanical Engineering; Technology; Telecommunications Engineering); **International Programmes** *(FIP)* (Information Technology; Interior Design; International Business); **Management Studies** *(FMS)* (Agricultural Business; Business Administration; Finance; Human Resources; Information Sciences; International Business; Management; Marketing; Real Estate; Sports); **Media Studies** (Journalism; Mass Communication; Media Studies)

Further Information: A traditional and distance education institution.

History: Founded 2008 as Career Institute of Technology and Management (CITM). Acquired 'Deemed University' status 2008.

Accrediting Agency: All India Council for Technical Education (AICTE)

Degrees and Diplomas: *Bachelor's Degree*; *Bachelor's Degree (professional)*; *Master's Degree*; *Doctor of Philosophy*. Also Integrated B.Tech, 6 yrs; MBA

Student Services: Canteen, Health Services, Sports Facilities

Last Updated: 20/12/11

MANGALAYATAN UNIVERSITY (MU)

Extended NCR, Mathura-Aligarh Highway, 33rd Milestone,
Aligarh, Uttar Pradesh 202 145
Tel: +91(5722) 272-100
Fax: +91(5722) 254-220
EMail: admissions@mangalayatan.edu.in;
info@mangalayatan.edu.in
Website: http://mangalayatan.in

Vice-Chancellor: S. C. Jain

Registrar: Manjeet Singh

Institute

BioMedical Education and Research (Biomedicine; Biotechnology; Pharmacy); **Business Management** (Banking; Business Administration; Economics; Finance; Insurance; International Business; Management); **Computer Applications** (Computer Science); **Education and Research** (Education); **Engineering and Technology** (Chemistry; Computer Science; Electrical Engineering; Electronic Engineering; Engineering; Information Technology; Mathematics; Mechanical Engineering; Physics; Technology; Telecommunications Engineering); **Journalism and Mass Communication** (Journalism; Mass Communication); **Legal Studies and Research** (Commercial Law; Law); **Tourism and Hospitality Management** (Air Transport; Hotel Management; Tourism); **Visual and Performing Arts** (Performing Arts; Visual Arts)

History: Founded 2006.

Fees: (Indian Rupee): Undergraduate tuition, 25,000-115,000 per annum; Graduate tuition, 40,000-200,000 per annum

Degrees and Diplomas: *Post Diploma*; *Bachelor's Degree*; *Bachelor's Degree (professional)*; *Postgraduate Diploma*; *Master's Degree*; *Master of Philosophy*; *Doctor of Philosophy*. Also MBA; Dual Degree Programme: Bachelor's degree + MBA/Master's degree.

Last Updated: 22/12/11

MANGALORE UNIVERSITY

New Administrative Building, Mangalagangothri,
Mangalore, Karnataka 574 199
Tel: +91(824) 228-7276 +91(824) 228-7347
Fax: +91(824) 228-7367 +91(824) 228-7424
EMail: info@mangaloreuniversity.ac.in
Website: http://www.mangaloreuniversity.ac.in

Vice-Chancellor: T. C. Shivashankara Murthy
Tel: +91(824) 228-7347 EMail: vc@mangaloreuniversity.ac.in

Registrar: Chinnappa Gowda
Tel: +91(824) 228-7276
EMail: registrar@mangaloreuniversity.ac.in

Department

Applied Botany (Biotechnology; Botany; Ecology; Microbiology; Plant and Crop Protection; Plant Pathology); **Applied Zoology** (Animal Husbandry; Biology; Cell Biology; Genetics; Molecular Biology; Nutrition; Oncology; Physiology; Toxicology; Wildlife; Zoology); **Bio-Sciences** (Biochemistry; Biological and Life Sciences; Biophysics; Biotechnology; Cell Biology; Genetics; Immunology; Microbiology; Molecular Biology; Physiology); **Biochemistry** (Biochemistry; Biophysics; Biotechnology; Cell Biology; Chemistry; Microbiology; Nutrition; Physiology); **Business Administration** (Accountancy; Behavioural Sciences; Business Administration; Economics; French; Human Resources; International Business; Management; Marketing; Tourism); **Chemistry** (Applied Chemistry; Chemistry; Inorganic Chemistry; Organic Chemistry); **Commerce** (Banking; Business and Commerce; Finance; Human Resources; Insurance; Labour Law; Marketing; Sales Techniques; Taxation); **Computer Science** (Business Computing; Computer Networks; Computer Science; Data Processing; Mathematics; Software Engineering); **Economics** (Agricultural Economics; Econometrics; Economics; International Economics); **Electronics** (Electronic Engineering); **English** (English; Literature); **Geoinformatics** (Computer Science; Data Processing; Earth Sciences; Geological Engineering; Geology; Information Sciences; Surveying and Mapping); **History** (Ancient Civilizations; Contemporary History; History; Medieval Studies; Modern History); **Human Consciousness and Yogic Sciences** (Alternative Medicine; Esoteric Practices; Health Sciences; Yoga); **Kannada** (Linguistics; Literature; South and Southeast Asian Languages); **Library Information Science** (Information Sciences; Information Technology; Library Science); **Marine Geology** (Earth Sciences; Geochemistry; Geology; Geophysics; Information Sciences; Marine Science and Oceanography; Mineralogy; Natural Resources; Paleontology; Surveying and Mapping); **Mass Communication and Journalism** (Advertising and Publicity; Communication Studies; Film; Journalism; Marketing; Mass Communication; Media Studies; Printing and Printmaking; Radio and Television Broadcasting; Writing); **Materials Science** (Materials Engineering; Physical Chemistry; Polymer and Plastics Technology; Solid State Physics); **Mathematics** (Mathematics); **Microbiology** (Biochemistry; Biophysics; Biotechnology; Genetics; Microbiology; Molecular Biology);

Physical Education (Physical Education; Physical Therapy; Physiology; Psychology; Rehabilitation and Therapy; Sports; Sports Management); **Physics** (Electronic Engineering; Mechanics; Nuclear Engineering; Nuclear Physics; Physics; Solid State Physics); **Political Science** (Comparative Politics; International Relations; Political Sciences; Regional Studies; Sociology); **Social Work** (Human Resources; Social and Community Services; Social Work; Welfare and Protective Services); **Sociology** (Development Studies; Labour and Industrial Relations; Social Studies; Sociology; Statistics; Women's Studies); **Statistics** (Statistics)

Centre

Study of Social Exclusion and Inclusive Policy *(CSEIP)* (Economics; Labour and Industrial Relations; Social Policy; Social Problems; Sociology)

Further Information: Also 187 affiliated colleges/institutions (including 2 constituent colleges, 4 law colleges, 18 education colleges and 5 autonomous colleges).

History: Founded 1980.

Academic Year: June to March (June-September; November-March)

Admission Requirements: 12th year senior secondary/intermediate examination or recognized foreign equivalent

Fees: (Rupees): Postgraduate tuition fee, 3,400 per annum; MBA, 30,000-80,000 per annum; Ph.D., 2,600 per term (6 months)

Main Language(s) of Instruction: English

Accrediting Agency: National Assessment and Accreditation Council

Degrees and Diplomas: *Bachelor's Degree*; *Postgraduate Diploma*; *Master's Degree*; *Master of Philosophy*; *Doctor of Philosophy*. Also undergraduate certificate.

Student Services: Academic Counselling, Canteen, Careers Guidance, Cultural Activities, Facilities for disabled people, Health Services, Nursery Care, Sports Facilities

Last Updated: 28/06/11

MANIPAL UNIVERSITY

Madhav Nagar, Udupi District, Manipal, Karnataka 576119
Tel: +91(820) 257-1201
Fax: +91(825) 257-0062
EMail: office.mahe@manipal.edu; vc.mahe@manipal.edu
Website: http://www.manipal.edu

Chancellor: Ramdas M. Pai
Tel: +91(820) 292-2463; +91(820) 292-2350
EMail: chancellor@manipal.edu

Vice-Chancellor: K. Ramnarayan (2010-)
Tel: +91(820) 292-2615; +91(820) 257-1975
EMail: vicechancellor@manipal.edu

Registrar: G. K. Prabhu
Tel: +91(820) 292-2323; +91(820) 257-1300
EMail: reg.mahe@manipal.edu

College

Allied Health Sciences *(Manipal - MCOAHS)* (Cardiology; Clinical Psychology; Health Administration; Health Sciences; Laboratory Techniques; Medical Technology; Medicine; Occupational Therapy; Oncology; Optometry; Physical Therapy; Radiology; Rehabilitation and Therapy; Respiratory Therapy; Speech Therapy and Audiology); **Allied Health Sciences** *(AHS, Mangalore)* (Health Sciences; Physical Therapy; Rehabilitation and Therapy; Speech Therapy and Audiology); **Allied Health Sciences** *(AHS, Bangalore)* (Health Sciences; Physical Therapy; Rehabilitation and Therapy); **Dental Sciences** *(Manipal - MCODS)* (Dental Hygiene; Dental Technology; Dentistry; Oral Pathology; Orthodontics; Periodontics; Social and Preventive Medicine; Surgery); **Dental Sciences, Mangalore** *(MCODS Mangalore)* (Dental Technology; Dentistry; Oral Pathology; Orthodontics; Periodontics; Public Health; Radiology; Surgery); **Medicine** *(Kasturba - KMC Manipal)* (Alternative Medicine; Anaesthesiology; Anatomy; Ayurveda; Biochemistry; Cardiology; Clinical Psychology; Community Health; Dermatology; Embryology and Reproduction Biology; Forensic Medicine and Dentistry; Gastroenterology; Gynaecology and Obstetrics; Health Administration; Health Education; Medicine; Microbiology; Nephrology; Neurological Therapy; Neurology; Oncology; Ophthalmology; Orthopaedics; Otorhinolaryngology; Paediatrics; Pathology; Pharmacology; Physical Therapy; Physiology; Plant Pathology; Pneumology; Psychiatry and Mental Health; Radiology; Surgery; Urology; Yoga); **Medicine** *(Melaka - MMMC Manipal)* (Anatomy; Biochemistry; Medicine; Microbiology; Pathology; Pharmacy; Physiology); **Medicine** *(Manipal - MMMC Melaka)* (Anatomy; Biochemistry; Community Health; Dentistry; Medicine; Microbiology; Paediatrics; Pathology; Pharmacy; Physiology); **Medicine** *(Kasturba - KMC Mangalore)* (Anaesthesiology; Anatomy; Biochemistry; Community Health; Dermatology; Forensic Medicine and Dentistry; Gynaecology and Obstetrics; Medicine; Microbiology; Oncology; Ophthalmology; Otorhinolaryngology; Paediatrics; Pathology; Pharmacology; Physical Education; Physical Engineering; Physiology; Pneumology; Psychiatry and Mental Health; Radiology; Surgery); **Nursing** *(MCON Manipal)* (Child Care and Development; Gynaecology and Obstetrics; Health Sciences; Midwifery; Nursing; Psychiatry and Mental Health; Surgery); **Nursing** *(MCON Bangalore)* (Nursing); **Nursing** *(MCON Mangalore)* (Nursing); **Pharmaceutical Sciences** *(MCOPS)* (Biotechnology; Management; Pharmacology; Pharmacy; Safety Engineering)

Programme

Animation (Visual Arts); **Corporate Studies** (Automation and Control Engineering; Automotive Engineering; Business Administration; Computer Graphics; Computer Networks; Computer Science; Electronic Engineering; Engineering Drawing and Design; Finance; Human Resources; Information Sciences; Management; Marketing; Software Engineering; Telecommunications Engineering); **Media and Entertainment** (Computer Graphics; Media Studies; Public Relations; Radio and Television Broadcasting; Visual Arts)

School

Architecture and Planning *(Manipal - MSAP)* (Architecture; Architecture and Planning; Fashion Design; Interior Design; Safety Engineering)

Department

Advanced Pharmaceutical Sciences (Pharmacy); **Commerce** (Banking; Business and Commerce; Finance); **Geopolitics and International Relations** (International Relations); **Public Health** (Epidemiology; Health Administration; Public Health; Social Work); **Sciences** (Applied Mathematics; Mathematics and Computer Science; Organic Chemistry; Physics); **Statistics** (Statistics)

Institute

Advertising and Communication (Advertising and Publicity; Communication Studies; Marketing); **Communication** *(Manipal - MIC)* (Communication Studies; Journalism); **Jewellery Management** *(MIJM Manipal)* (Jewellery Art; Management); **Management** *(MIM Manipal)* (Business Administration; Management); **Regenerative Medicine** *(MIRM Bangalore)* (Medicine; Rehabilitation and Therapy); **Technology** *(MIT Manipal)* (Aeronautical and Aerospace Engineering; Automation and Control Engineering; Automotive Engineering; Biomedical Engineering; Biotechnology; Civil Engineering; Computer Engineering; Computer Graphics; Computer Networks; Computer Science; Electrical and Electronic Engineering; Electronic Engineering; Engineering; Information Technology; Measurement and Precision Engineering; Mechanical Engineering; Media Studies; Printing and Printmaking; Production Engineering; Software Engineering; Telecommunications Engineering)

Academy

Banking and Insurance *(ICICI Manipal - IMA)* (Banking; Business Administration; Finance; Insurance)

Centre

Applied Sciences *(International - ICAS)* (Aeronautical and Aerospace Engineering; Architecture; Biomedical Engineering; Biotechnology; Chemical Engineering; Civil Engineering; Computer Engineering; Electrical and Electronic Engineering; Electrical Engineering; Electronic Engineering; Industrial Engineering; Mechanical Engineering; Telecommunications Engineering); **Atomic and Molecular Physics** *(CAMP)* (Atomic and Molecular Physics; Physics); **European Studies** *(MCES)* (European Studies; Management; Peace and Disarmament; Public Health); **Information Science** *(MCIS Manipal)* (Information Management; Information Sciences; Information Technology; Software Engineering); **KMC International** *(KMCIC)* (Health Sciences); **Life Sciences** *(MLSC Manipal)* (Biological and Life Sciences; Biotechnology; Genetics; Medical Technology; Molecular Biology); **Philosophy and Humanities** *(MCPH Manipal)* (Arts and Humanities; Philosophy); **Virus Research** (Virology)

Graduate School

Hotel Administration *(Welcomgroup - WGSHA Manipal)* (Cooking and Catering; Dietetics; Hotel and Restaurant; Hotel Management; Nutrition; Tourism)

Campus

Bangalore *(MU Bangalore)* (Advertising and Publicity; Communication Arts; Communication Studies; Graphic Design; Journalism; Management; Media Studies; Visual Arts); **Dubai** *(MU Dubai)* (Automation and Control Engineering; Biotechnology; Business Administration; Civil Engineering; Communication Studies; Computer Engineering; Computer Science; Electronic Engineering; Fashion Design; Forensic Medicine and Dentistry; Genetics; Graphic Design; Information Management; Information Sciences; Information Technology; Interior Design; Management; Marketing; Measurement and Precision Engineering; Mechanical Engineering; Media Studies; Multimedia)

Further Information: Also branch campuses in Bangalore, Malaysia, Dubai and Antigua in the Caribbean Island. Campus in Mangalore. 20 constituent institutions and 4 teaching hospitals.

History: First College founded 1953. Acquired 'Deemed University' status 1993. Previously known as Manipal Academy of Higher Education (MAFE).

Academic Year: August to July

Admission Requirements: 12th year senior secondary intermediate examination

Fees: (Rupees): Certificate courses, 15,000-375,000 for Indian students and 3,900-36,150 per annum for foreign students; Undergraduate fees, 25,000-562,000 per annum; Graduate fees, 29,000-930,000 per annum for Indian students and 700-43,650 per annum for foreign/NRI students; PG Diploma, 26,000-676,000 per annum

Main Language(s) of Instruction: English

Accrediting Agency: Medical Council of India; Dental Council of India; Pharmacy Council of India; All India Council for Technical Education; National Assessment and Accreditation Council

Degrees and Diplomas: *Bachelor's Degree*; *Bachelor's Degree (professional)*; *Postgraduate Diploma*; *Master's Degree*; *Master of Philosophy*; *Doctor of Philosophy*. Also undergraduate certificates; MBA.

Student Services: Academic Counselling, Canteen, Cultural Activities, Health Services, Nursery Care, Sports Facilities

Publications: British Journal of Ophthalmology; British Medical Journal; Paediatrics

Publishing House: Manipal Press Ltd

Last Updated: 29/06/11

MANIPUR UNIVERSITY

Canchipur, Imphal, Manipur 795003
Tel: +91(385) 243-5276 +91(385) 243-55055
Fax: +91(385) 243-5145
EMail: vcmu@sancharnet.in
Website: http://manipuruniv.ac.in

Acting Vice-Chancellor: Hidangmayum Nandakumar Sarma
Tel: +91(385) 243-5878 EMail: vcmu@sancharnet.in

Registrar: N. Lokendra Singh
Tel: +91(385) 243-5125 +91(385) 243-5831
EMail: lokendra_n@rediffmail.com

School

Human and Environmental Science (Anthropology; Archaeology; Earth Sciences; Environmental Studies; Geochemistry; Geography; Geography (Human); Geology; Paleontology; Petroleum and Gas Engineering; Physical Education; Sports; Surveying and Mapping); **Humanities** (Applied Linguistics; Arts and Humanities; Cultural Studies; Dance; English; Folklore; Hindi; Linguistics; Literature; Musical Instruments; Philosophy); **Life Sciences** (Biochemistry; Biological and Life Sciences; Biotechnology); **Mathematical and Physical Sciences** (Artificial Intelligence; Astrophysics; Chemistry; Computer Graphics; Computer Networks; Computer Science; Data Processing; Demography and Population; Inorganic Chemistry; Materials Engineering; Mathematics; Mechanics; Nuclear Engineering; Nuclear Physics; Organic Chemistry; Physical Chemistry; Physics; Software Engineering; Solid State Physics; Statistics); **Medical Sciences** (Medicine); **Social Sciences** (Accountancy; Adult Education; Agricultural Economics; Ancient Civilizations; Archaeology; Business and Commerce; Business Computing; Continuing Education; Econometrics; Economics; Education; Educational Administration; Finance; History; Human Resources; Information Management; Information Sciences; Insurance; International Economics; International Relations; Library Science; Management; Marketing; Mass Communication; Medieval Studies; Modern History; Political Sciences; Public Administration; Regional Studies; Social Sciences; Sociology)

Centre

Computer Science (Computer Science); **Gandhian Studies** (Philosophy; Political Sciences); **Manipur Studies** (Cultural Studies; Regional Studies); **Myanmar Studies** (South and Southeast Asian Languages); **Social Exclusion and Inclusive Policy** (Social Policy; Social Problems)

Research Centre

Educational Multimedia (Educational Technology; Multimedia)

Further Information: Also 72 affiliated colleges and one constituent college i.e. Manipur Institute of Technology (MIT).

History: Founded 1980 under Act of Manipur State Legislative Assembly. Acquired present title 2005. Formerly Jawaharlal Nehru University Centre of Postgraduate Studies at Imphal, the University is today an Affiliating University.

Academic Year: September to August

Admission Requirements: Graduate degree or recognized foreign equivalent

Fees: (Rupees): 1,890 per annum

Main Language(s) of Instruction: English

Accrediting Agency: National Assessment and Accreditation Council

Degrees and Diplomas: *Bachelor's Degree*; *Bachelor's Degree (professional)*; *Postgraduate Diploma*; *Master's Degree*; *Master of Philosophy*; *Doctor of Philosophy*. Also Also Bachelor's degree Honours; Undegraduate certificate.

Student Services: Academic Counselling, Canteen, Careers Guidance, Cultural Activities, Health Services, Sports Facilities

Last Updated: 29/06/11

MANONMANIAM SUNDARANAR UNIVERSITY (MSU)

University Building, Abishekapatti, Tirunelveli, Tamil Nadu 627012
Tel: +91 9487999687 +91 9487999688
EMail: info@msuniv.ac.in
Website: http://www.msuniv.ac.in

Vice-Chancellor: R.T. Sabapathy Mohan
Tel: +91 9487999651 EMail: vc@msuniv.ac.in

Registrar: S. Manickam
Tel: +91 9487999602 EMail: registrar@msuniv.ac.in

Department

Biotechnology (Biotechnology); **Chemistry** (Chemistry); **Commerce** (Business and Commerce); **Communication** (Advertising and Publicity; Communication Studies; Film; Journalism; Media Studies; Radio and Television Broadcasting); **Computer Science and Engineering** (Computer Engineering; Computer Science); **Criminology and Criminal Justice** (Criminal Law; Criminology); **Economics** (Business Administration; Economics); **Education** (Education); **English** (Comparative Literature; Cultural Studies; English; Literature; Media Studies; Theatre; Translation and Interpretation); **Environmental Science** (Biotechnology; Environmental Studies); **Geotechnology** (Geology; Geophysics; Marine Science and Oceanography); **Hindi** (Hindi); **History** (History); **Information Technology and Engineering** (Computer Engineering; Computer Networks; Computer Science; E- Business/Commerce; Information Technology; Mathematics and Computer Science); **Management Studies** (Finance; Human Resources; Management; Marketing); **Mathematics** (Mathematics); **Nanobiotechnology** (Biotechnology; Nanotechnology); **Pharmaceutical Chemistry** (Biochemistry; Chemistry; Molecular Biology; Organic Chemistry; Pharmacology; Pharmacy; Physical Chemistry; Statistics); **Physical Education and Sports** (Physical Education; Sports); **Physics** (Physics); **Psychology** (Psychology); **Social Exclusion and Inclusive Policy** (Social Policy; Social Problems); **Sociology** (Sociology); **Statistics** (Computer Science; Data Processing; Statistics); **Tamil** (South and Southeast Asian Languages)

Centre

Marine Science and Technology (Aquaculture; Biological and Life Sciences; Biotechnology; Marine Engineering; Marine Science and Oceanography; Microbiology)

Further Information: Also 61 affiliated colleges, 5 Mano colleges and 1 constituent college. Also distance education.

History: Founded 1990.

Academic Year: July to April (July-November; December-April)

Admission Requirements: Secondary school certificate

Fees: (Rupees): 1,000-20,000 per semester; MBA, 12,500 per semester

Main Language(s) of Instruction: Tamil, English

Accrediting Agency: University Grants Commission; Association of Indian Universities

Degrees and Diplomas: *Bachelor's Degree*; *Postgraduate Diploma*; *Master's Degree*; *Master of Philosophy*; *Doctor of Philosophy*. Also MBA; Undergraduate certificate

Student Services: Academic Counselling, Canteen, Sports Facilities

Publications: Mano International Journal of Mathematical Sciences

Last Updated: 29/06/11

MARATHWADA AGRICULTURAL UNIVERSITY

Marathwada Krishi Vidyapeeth (MAU)

PO Krishinagar, Parbhani, Maharashtra 431402
Tel: +91(2452) 223-801
Fax: +91(2452) 223-582
EMail: vcmau@rediffmail.com
Website: http://mkv2.mah.nic.in

Vice-Chancellor: K.P. Gore

Registrar: B.B. Bhosale

College

Agricultural Biotechnology *(Latur)* (Agriculture; Agrobiology; Biotechnology); **Agricultural Engineering** *(Parbhani)* (Agricultural Engineering); **Agriculture** *(Badnapur)* (Agriculture); **Agriculture** *(Parbhani)* (Agriculture); **Agriculture** *(Osmanabad)* (Agriculture); **Agriculture** *(Ambajogai)* (Agriculture); **Agriculture** *(Latur)* (Agriculture); **Food Technology** *(Parbhani)* (Food Technology); **Home Science** *(Parbhani)* (Home Economics); **Horticulture** (Horticulture)

Further Information: Also 8 Constituent Colleges

History: Founded 1972.

Academic Year: July to May (July-December; January-May)

Admission Requirements: 12th year senior secondary/intermediate examination or recognized foreign equivalent

Fees: (Rupees): 2,600-6,000 per annum

Main Language(s) of Instruction: English

Degrees and Diplomas: *Bachelor's Degree*; *Bachelor's Degree (professional)*; *Master's Degree*; *Doctor of Philosophy*

Publishing house: Marathwada Agriculture University Printing Press

Last Updated: 29/06/11

MARTIN LUTHER CHRISTIAN UNIVERSITY (MLCU)

KJPA Conference Centre, Central Ward,
Shillong, Meghalya 793001
Tel: 9206040427
Fax: +91(364) 250-64890
EMail: admin@mlcuniv.in; registrar@mlcuniv.in
Website: http://www.mlcuniv.in

Vice-Chancellor: G.C. Kharkongor EMail: vc@mlcuniv.in

Registrar: E.H. Kharkongor EMail: registrar@mlcuniv.in

Campus

Nongtalang (Computer Science; Information Sciences); **Rymbai** (Computer Science); **Shillong** (Business Administration; Community Health; Dietetics; Fine Arts; Health Sciences; Information Technology; Medical Technology; Microbiology; Music; Nutrition; Optometry; Peace and Disarmament; Psychology; Social Work; Tourism); **Tura** (Business Administration; Computer Science; Information Sciences; Management; Social Work)

History: Founded 2005.

Fees: Tuition fees for undergraduate tuition fees, 6,000-15,000 per semester; For postgraduate programmes, 10,000-30,000 per semester; Ph.D. 7,500-15,000 over three years (Indian Rupee)

Accrediting Agency: University Grants Commission (UGC)

Degrees and Diplomas: *Bachelor's Degree*; *Postgraduate Diploma*; *Master's Degree*; *Doctor of Philosophy*

Last Updated: 30/06/11

MATS UNIVERSITY

Aarang Kharora Highway, Aarang, Raipur 493 441
Tel: +91(771) 407-8994 +91(771) 407-8995
Fax: +91(771) 407-8997
EMail: info@matsuniversity.ac.in
Website: http://www.matsuniversity.ac.in

Vice-Chancellor: Kanwal Singh

Registrar: A.K. Shukla

School

Basic Sciences (Botany; Chemistry; Energy Engineering; Environmental Engineering; Materials Engineering; Mathematics; Mathematics and Computer Science; Nanotechnology; Physics; Software Engineering); **Business Studies** (Accountancy; Banking; Business Administration; Business and Commerce; Business Computing; Finance; Insurance); **Education** (Education; Educational and Student Counselling; Educational Psychology); **Engineering and Technology** (Aeronautical and Aerospace Engineering; Civil Engineering; Computer Engineering; Computer Science; Electronic Engineering; Engineering; Information Technology; Technology; Telecommunications Engineering); **Fashion Designing** (Fashion Design; Textile Technology); **Humanities and Social Sciences** (Arts and Humanities; English; Hindi; Social Sciences); **Information Technology** (Computer Science; Information Technology); **Law** (Arabic; Chinese; English; European Union Law; French; Law; Russian); **Life Sciences** (Biochemistry; Biological and Life Sciences; Biotechnology; Microbiology); **Management Studies and Research** (Business Administration; Finance; Human Resources; Information Technology; Management; Marketing)

Research Centre

Research and Development Cell (Analytical Chemistry; Biological and Life Sciences; Biotechnology; Data Processing; Genetics; Molecular Biology; Organic Chemistry)

Further Information: Also distance education.

History: Founded 2006.

Admission Requirements: 10+2 or any equivalent examination from a recognized board for undergraduate programmes; Graduate or equivalent examination from a recognized university for graduate programmes.

Accrediting Agency: University Grants Commission (UGC); All India Council for Technical Education (AICTE); National Council fro Teacher Education (NCTE); Bar Council of India (BCI); American University Accreditation Council (AUAC).

Degrees and Diplomas: *Bachelor's Degree*; *Postgraduate Diploma*; *Master's Degree*; *Master of Philosophy*; *Doctor of Philosophy*. Also MBA and undergraduate certificate.

Student Services: Sports Facilities

Last Updated: 30/06/11

MAULANA AZAD NATIONAL INSTITUTE OF TECHNOLOGY (MANIT)

Bhopal, Madhya Pradesh 462051
Tel: +91(755) 405-1000 +91(755) 405-2000 +91(755) 520-6006
Fax: +91(755) 267-0562 +91(755) 267-0802
EMail: info@manit.ac.in
Website: http://www.manit.ac.in

Director: R.P. Singh
Tel: +91(755) 405-1001
EMail: prof.rpsingh@gmail.com; singhrp@manit.ac.in; director@manit.ac.in

Registrar: Savita Raje
Tel: +91(755) 267-0416 EMail: savita_raje@manit.ac.in

Department

Applied Mechanics (Materials Engineering; Mechanics); **Architecture and Planning** (Architecture and Planning); **Bio-Informatics** (Computer Science; Molecular Biology; Statistics); **Chemical Engineering** (Chemical Engineering); **Chemistry** (Analytical Chemistry; Chemistry); **Civil Engineering** (Civil Engineering; Construction Engineering; Environmental Engineering; Geological Engineering; Hydraulic Engineering); **Computer Applications** (Computer Science; Information Technology); **Computer Science and Engineering** (Computer Engineering; Computer Science); **Electrical Engineering** (Electrical Engineering; Power Engineering); **Electronics and Communication Engineering** (Electronic Engineering; Microwaves; Telecommunications Engineering); **Energy** (Energy Engineering); **Humanities** (Arts and Humanities; Social Sciences); **Information Technology** (Information Technology); **Management Studies** (Advertising and Publicity; Business Administration; International Business; Management; Marketing); **Material Science and Metallurgical Engineering** (Materials Engineering; Metallurgical Engineering); **Mathematics** (Mathematics; Mathematics and Computer Science); **Mechanical Engineering** (Industrial Design; Maintenance Technology; Mechanical Engineering; Thermal Engineering); **Physical Education** (Physical Education; Sports); **Physics** (Nanotechnology; Physics); **Production and Industrial Engineering** (Industrial Engineering; Production Engineering)

History: Founded 1960 as Maulana Azad College of Technology (MACT). Acquired present status and title 2002. An 'Institute of National Importance'.

Admission Requirements: Secondary school certificate and entrance examination

Fees: (Rupees): Tuition fee, 25,500-35,500 per annum; Ph.D., 15,000 per annum

Degrees and Diplomas: *Bachelor's Degree*; *Bachelor's Degree (professional)*; *Master's Degree*; *Doctor of Philosophy*

Student Services: Canteen, Careers Guidance, Sports Facilities

Academic Staff *2010-2011*: Total: c. 200

Student Numbers *2010-2011*: Total: c. 4,000

Last Updated: 30/06/11

MAULANA AZAD NATIONAL URDU UNIVERSITY

Gachibowli, Hyderabad, Andhra Pradesh 500032
Tel: +91(40) 2300-6602
Fax: +91(40) 2300-6603
EMail: registrar@manuu.ac.in
Website: http://www.manuu.ac.in

Vice-Chancellor: Mohammad Miyan (2010-)
Tel: +91(40) 2300-6612 EMail: secretarytovc@manuu.ac.in

Registrar: H. Khatija Begum
Tel: +91(40) 2300-6121 EMail: registrar@manuu.ac.in

College

Academic Staff; Teacher Education (Education; Teacher Training)

School

Arts and Social Sciences (Arts and Humanities; Political Sciences; Public Administration; Social Sciences; Social Work; Sociology); **Commerce and Business Management** (Business Administration; Business and Commerce; Management); **Education and Training** (Education); **Languages, Linguistics and Indology** (Arabic; Comparative Literature; English; Hindi; Linguistics; Literature; Modern Languages; Persian; Translation and Interpretation; Urdu); **Mass Communication and Journalism** (Advertising and Publicity; Film; Journalism; Mass Communication; Media Studies; Public Relations); **Sciences** (Computer Science; Data Processing; Information Technology; Multimedia; Software Engineering)

Department

Distance Education (Business and Commerce; Education; English; Food Science; Hindi; History; Journalism; Mass Communication; Museum Studies; Nutrition; Tourism; Urdu); **Women's Education** (Women's Studies)

Centre

Instructional Media *(IMC)* (Journalism; Mass Communication; Video); **Professional Development of Urdu Medium Teachers** (Native Language Education; Teacher Training); **Study of Social Exclusion and Inclusive Policy** *(CSSEIP)* (Social Policy; Social Problems); **Urdu Language, Literature and Culture** (Cultural Studies; Literature; Urdu); **Women's Studies** (Women's Studies)

Course

Polytechnic *(Darbhanga)* (Civil Engineering; Computer Engineering; Electrical Engineering; Telecommunications Engineering); **Polytechnic** *(Hyderabad)* (Civil Engineering; Computer Engineering; Computer Science; Electronic Engineering; Information Technology; Telecommunications Engineering); **Polytechnic** *(Bangalore)* (Civil Engineering; Computer Engineering; Electronic Engineering; Telecommunications Engineering)

Further Information: Education under distance and campus modes; Model schools in Hyderabad and Darbhanga.

History: Founded 1998. A 'Central University'.

Admission Requirements: 12th year senior secondary/intermediate examination or recognized equivalent and entrance examination

Fees: (Rupees): tuition fee, 300-900 per semester; MBA, 4,500-8,300 per semester

Main Language(s) of Instruction: Urdu

Accrediting Agency: National Assessment and Accreditation Council (NAAC).

Degrees and Diplomas: *Post Diploma*; *Bachelor's Degree*; *Postgraduate Diploma*; *Master's Degree*; *Master of Philosophy*; *Doctor of Philosophy*. Also MBA and undergraduate certificate.

Last Updated: 30/06/11

MAULANA MAZHARUL HAQUE ARABIC AND PERSIAN UNIVERSITY (MMHAPU)

5, Bailey Road, Patna 800 001
Tel: +91(612) 645-6010
Fax: +91(612) 250-5040 +91(612) 250-4357
EMail: mmhapupatna@yahoo.in
Website: http://mmhapu.bih.nic.in/

Vice-Chancellor: Md. Shamsuzzoha (2011-)
EMail: vc-mmhu-bih@nic.in

Registrar: M. G. Mustafa EMail: registrar-mmhu-bih@nic.in

School

Knowledge Management and Media Studies *(Abudul Qayum Ansari)* (Journalism; Library Science; Mass Communication; Media Studies); **Management and Information** *(Justice Sarwar Ali)* (Business Administration; Information Sciences; Management); **Social Works and Rural Development** *(Prof. Abdul Bari)* (Accountancy; Social Work); **Sufism Oriental Languages History and Culture** *(Makhdoom Sharfuddin Yahya Maneri)* (Ancient Books; Arabic; Cultural Studies; History; Library Science; Oriental Languages; Persian)

History: Founded 1998. Started its first academic session 2008.

Fees: (Indian Rupees): Undergraduate Certificate and Diplomas, 2,500-6,500 per course; Undergraduate Degree Courses, 5,500-8,500 per annum; M.B.A., 1,7500-2,350 per semester

Degrees and Diplomas: *Post Diploma*; *Bachelor's Degree*. Also Certificate Courses; MBA

Student Numbers *2010-2011*: Total: c. 14,000

Last Updated: 03/01/12

MEENAKSHI ACADEMY OF HIGHER EDUCATION AND RESEARCH (MEENAKSHI UNIVERSITY) (MAHER)

No. 12, Vembuli Amman Koil Street, West K.K. Nagar,
Chennai, Tamil Nadu 600 078
Tel: +91(44) 236-43955 +91(44) 23643956
Fax: +91(44) 236-43958
EMail: info@maher.ac.in
Website: http://www.maher.ac.in

Vice-Chancellor: P. Jayakumar

Registrar: A.N. Santhanam

Faculty

Engineering and Technology (Business Administration; Business Computing; Computer Engineering; Computer Science; Electrical and Electronic Engineering; Electronic Engineering; Engineering; Information Technology; Measurement and Precision Engineering; Technology; Telecommunications Engineering); **Health Sciences** (Anaesthesiology; Cardiology; Dietetics; Health Administration; Health Sciences; Laboratory Techniques; Medical Technology; Microbiology; Pneumology); **Hotel Management and Catering Technology** (Cooking and Catering; Hotel Management); **Humanities and Sciences** (Administration; Arts and Humanities; Biotechnology; Business Administration; Business and Commerce; Computer Science; Electronic Engineering; Health Administration; Information Management; Microbiology; Molecular Biology; Social Work; Statistics; Telecommunications Engineering; Visual Arts)

College

Dental Studies *(Meenakshi Ammal)* (Dental Technology; Dentistry; Oral Pathology; Periodontics; Radiology; Surgery); **Medicine** *(Meenakshi Ammal)* (Anaesthesiology; Anatomy; Biochemistry; Community Health; Dermatology; Forensic Medicine and Dentistry; Gastroenterology; Gynaecology and Obstetrics; Medicine; Microbiology; Ophthalmology; Orthopaedics; Paediatrics; Pathology; Pharmacology; Physiology; Psychiatry and Mental Health; Radiology; Respiratory Therapy; Surgery; Urology; Venereology); **Nursing** *(Arulmigu Meenakshi)* (Nursing); **Nursing** *(Meenakshi)* (Community Health; Gynaecology and Obstetrics; Nursing; Paediatrics; Psychiatry and Mental Health); **Physiotherapy** *(Meenakshi)* (Cardiology; Dietetics; Gerontology; Health Sciences; Neurological Therapy; Neurology; Nutrition; Orthopaedics; Paediatrics; Physical Therapy; Respiratory Therapy; Speech Therapy and Audiology; Sports Medicine)

Programme

Medicine, Dentistry, Nursing, Physiotheraphy and Engineering *(Ph.D.)* (Dentistry; Engineering; Medicine; Nursing; Physical Therapy)

Institute

Distance Education (Administration; Business Administration; Business and Commerce; Computer Science; Economics; English; Food Science; History; Hotel Management; Information Technology; Marketing; Mathematics; Nursing; Nutrition; Philosophy; Public Administration; Sociology; Software Engineering; South and Southeast Asian Languages)

Further Information: Also Distance Education. Meenakshi Ammal Dental Hospital, Meenakshi Medical Research Institute

History: Founded 2004 as Meenakshi Academy of Higher Education and Research. A 'Deemed University'.

Admission Requirements: Common Entrance Test conducted on All India level

Fees: (Ruppes): 35,000-350,000 per annum; Distance education programmes, 2,500-25,000 per annum

Degrees and Diplomas: *Post Diploma*; *Bachelor's Degree*; *Bachelor's Degree (professional)*; *Postgraduate Diploma*; *Master's Degree*; *Doctor of Philosophy*

Student Services: Canteen, Health Services, Sports Facilities
Last Updated: 30/06/11

MEWAR UNIVERSITY (MU)

NH - 79 Gangrar, Chittorgarh, Rajasthan 312901
Tel: +91(1471) 220-881 +91(1471) 291-148
EMail: info@mewaruniversity.org; admission@mewaruniversity.org
Website: http://www.mewaruniversity.org

President: Ramesh Chandra (2009-)
EMail: vc@mewaruniversity.org

Registrar: S. Sengupta EMail: registrar@mewaruniversity.org

Faculty

Arts and Humanities (Anthropology; Arts and Humanities; Child Care and Development; Clinical Psychology; Development Studies; Economics; English; Family Studies; Geography; Hindi; History; Labour and Industrial Relations; Management; Philosophy; Political Sciences; Psychology; Public Administration; Sociology); **Computer Science and System Studies** (Computer Science; Information Technology); **Education** (Art Education; Business Education; Education; Science Education); **Engineering and Technology** (Ceramics and Glass Technology; Chemical Engineering; Civil Engineering; Computer Science; Electrical and Electronic Engineering; Electrical Engineering; Electronic Engineering; Engineering; Engineering Drawing and Design; Industrial Chemistry; Materials Engineering; Measurement and Precision Engineering; Mechanical Engineering; Nanotechnology; Power Engineering; Production Engineering; Structural Architecture; Telecommunications Engineering; Transport Engineering); **Journalism and Mass Communication** (Journalism; Mass Communication); **Legal Studies** (Commercial Law; Criminology; Law; Private Law; Taxation); **Management and Commerce** (Business Administration; Business and Commerce; Civil Engineering; Computer Science; Electrical and Electronic Engineering; Electrical Engineering; Electronic Engineering; Finance; Human Resources; Information Technology; International Business; Management; Marketing; Mechanical Engineering; Telecommunications Engineering); **Science** (Biotechnology; Botany; Chemistry; Electronic Engineering; Environmental Studies; Histology; Mathematics; Pathology; Physics; Zoology)

History: Founded 2009.

Fees: Undergraduate fees, 10,000-65,000 per annum; Graduate programme, 12,000-50,000 per annum; MBA, 47,000-65,000 per annum (Indian Rupee)

Accrediting Agency: University Grants Commission (UGC); All India Council for Technical Education (AICTE); Ministry of Human Resources Development

Degrees and Diplomas: *Post Diploma*; *Bachelor's Degree*; *Bachelor's Degree (professional)*; *Master's Degree*; *Master of Philosophy*; *Doctor of Philosophy*. Also Integrated Diploma and Dual Degree Programmes; Bachelor's Degree Honours, 3 yrs; MBA 2 yrs.

Student Services: Academic Counselling, Canteen, Cultural Activities, Health Services, Sports Facilities
Last Updated: 30/06/11

MGM INSTITUTE OF HEALTH SCIENCES (MGMUHS)

Post Box -06, MGM Educational campus, Sector -18 Kamothe, Navi MumbaiNavi Mumbai, Maharashtra 410 209
Tel: +91(22) 274-22471 +91(22) 274-21995 +91(22) 651-68127
Fax: +91(22) 274-20320
EMail: mgmuniversity@mgmuhs.com; mgmuniversity@yahoo.co.in
Website: http://www.mgmuhs.com/

Vice-Chancellor: R.D. Bapat EMail: vc@mgmuhs.com

Registrar: R.C. Sharma EMail: registrar@mgmuhs.com

College

Medicine *(Navi Mumbai)* (Medicine; Surgery); **Medicine** *(Aurangabad)* (Anaesthesiology; Anatomy; Biochemistry; Biotechnology; Genetics; Gynaecology and Obstetrics; Health Administration; Medicine; Microbiology; Nursing; Ophthalmology; Orthopaedics; Paediatrics; Pathology; Pharmacology; Physical Therapy; Physiology; Psychiatry and Mental Health; Radiology; Surgery)

History: Founded 2006. A 'Deemed University'.

Degrees and Diplomas: *Post Diploma*; *Bachelor's Degree*; *Bachelor's Degree (professional)*; *Master's Degree*; *Doctor of Philosophy*. Also MBA
Last Updated: 16/12/11

MIZORAM UNIVERSITY (MZU)

P.O.Box No. 190, Tanhril, Aizawl, Mizoram 796 004
Tel: +91(389) 233-0654
Fax: +91(389) 233-0642
EMail: vc@mzu.edu.in
Website: http://www.mzu.edu.in

Vice-Chancellor: R. Lalthantluanga (2011-)
Tel: +91(389) 233-0650 +91(389) 233-0651
EMail: vc@mzu.edu.in

Acting Registrar: Thangchungnunga
Tel: +91(389) 233-0654 +91(389) 231-9367
EMail: registrar@mzu.edu.in

School
Earth Sciences and Natural Resources Management (Botany; Development Studies; Earth Sciences; Education; Environmental Studies; Forestry; Geology; Horticulture; Natural Resources; Rural Studies); **Economics Management and Information Sciences** (Business and Commerce; Economics; Information Sciences; Library Science; Management); **Education and Humanities** (Arts and Humanities; Education; English; Hindi; Literature; South and Southeast Asian Languages); **Engineering and Technology** (Electronic Engineering; Engineering; Information Technology); **Life Sciences** (Biological and Life Sciences; Biotechnology; Botany; Zoology); **Physical Sciences** (Chemistry; Mathematics and Computer Science; Physics); **Social Sciences** (Ethnology; History; Political Sciences; Psychology; Public Administration; Social Sciences; Social Work)

Further Information: Also 27 Affiliated Colleges and 1 Constituent College.

History: Founded 2001. A 'Central University'.

Academic Year: Post-Graduate, August to June (August-November; February-June); Under-Graduate, April to November for first and then February to November.

Fees: (Rupees): Fee for undergraduate programmes, 12,000 per semester; Tuition fee for postgraduate programmes, 120-185 per months; MBA, 10,000 per semester; Ph.D., 250 per month

Degrees and Diplomas: *Bachelor's Degree (professional)*; *Master's Degree*; *Master of Philosophy*; *Doctor of Philosophy*

Student Services: Canteen, Health Services, Sports Facilities

Last Updated: 01/07/11

MODY INSTITUTE OF TECHNOLOGY AND SCIENCE (MITS)

Jaipur-Bikaner highway (NH-11), Lakshmangarh, Rajasthan 332311
Tel: +91(1573) 225-001
Fax: +91(1573) 225-041
EMail: contact@mitsuniversity.ac.in
Website: http://www.mitsuniversity.ac.in

Vice-Chancellor: N.V. Subba Reddy
EMail: vc@mitsuniversity.ac.in

Registrar: J. L. Arora EMail: registrar@mitsuniversity.ac.in

Faculty
Arts, Science and Commerce (Biotechnology; Business Administration; Business and Commerce; Chemistry; Computer Science; Economics; English; Esoteric Practices; French; Information Technology; International Business; Literature; Microbiology; Political Sciences; Psychology; Sociology; Zoology); **Engineering and Technology** (Computer Engineering; Computer Graphics; Computer Science; Electrical Engineering; Electronic Engineering; Energy Engineering; Engineering; Information Technology; Mechanical Engineering; Nanotechnology; Nuclear Engineering; Technology; Telecommunications Engineering); **Law** (Commercial Law; Criminal Law; Human Rights; Justice Administration; Law); **Management Studies** (Business Administration; Management)

History: A 'Deemed University'.

Fees: (Ruppes): Tuition fee for undergraduate programmes, 40,000-105,000 per annum; Postgraduate programmes, 50,000-55,000 per annum. Foreign students, 3,000-5,500 per annum; Nepalese students, 1,600-3,200 per annum

Degrees and Diplomas: *Bachelor's Degree*; *Bachelor's Degree (professional)*; *Master's Degree*; *Doctor of Philosophy*. Also Bachelor's degree Honours, 3 yrs; MBA, yrs.

Last Updated: 01/07/11

MOHAN LAL SUKHADIA UNIVERSITY (MLSU)

Pratapnagar, Udaipur, Rajasthan 313001
Tel: +91(294) 247-1035
Fax: +91(294) 247-1150
EMail: registrar@mlsu.ac.in
Website: http://www.mlsu.ac.in

Vice-Chancellor: I. V. Trivedi
Tel: +91(294) 247-0597 EMail: vcmlsu@mlsu.ac.in

Registrar: Shri M.L. Sharma
Tel: +91(294) 247-0166 EMail: registrar@mlsu.ac.in

Faculty
Commerce (Accountancy; Banking; Business Administration; Business and Commerce; Economic History; Economics; Statistics); **Humanities** (English; Hindi; History; Literature; Music; Painting and Drawing; Philosophy; Sanskrit; South and Southeast Asian Languages; Visual Arts); **Management** (Business Administration; Hotel Management; Management; Marketing; Tourism); **Science** (Biotechnology; Botany; Chemistry; Computer Engineering; Computer Networks; Computer Science; Environmental Studies; Geology; Information Technology; Mathematics; Nanotechnology; Pharmacy; Physics; Polymer and Plastics Technology; Statistics; Zoology); **Social Sciences** (Economics; Geography; Journalism; Library Science; Political Sciences; Psychology; Public Administration; Social Sciences; Sociology)

College
Commerce and Management Studies *(University)* (Accountancy; Banking; Business and Commerce; Economics; Management; Statistics); **Law** *(University)* (Law); **Science** *(University)* (Biotechnology; Botany; Chemistry; Environmental Studies; Geology; Mathematics; Physics; Statistics; Zoology); **Social Sciences and Humanities** *(University)* (Arts and Humanities; Economics; English; Geography; Hindi; History; Library Science; Music; Philosophy; Political Sciences; Psychology; Public Administration; Sanskrit; Social Sciences; Sociology; South and Southeast Asian Languages; Urdu; Visual Arts)

Centre
Women Studies (Women's Studies)

Research Centre
Population (Demography and Population)

Further Information: Also 180 affiliated colleges in the districts of Udaipur, Banswara, Dungarpur, Sirohi, Rajasmand, Chittorgarh, Pratapgarh.

History: Founded 1962 as Rajasthan Agricultural University. Named as University of Udaipur 1964. Acquired present title 1984 and status 1987.

Academic Year: July to June

Admission Requirements: 12th year senior secondary/intermediate examination or recognized foreign equivalent

Fees: (Rupees): Undergraduate, 600-900 per annum; postgraduate, 1,200-1,500

Main Language(s) of Instruction: Hindi, English

Accrediting Agency: NAAC (U.G.C.)

Degrees and Diplomas: *Bachelor's Degree*; *Postgraduate Diploma*; *Master's Degree*; *Master of Philosophy*; *Doctor of Philosophy*. Also Baclerор's degree honours; Undergraduate certificate courses; Professional courses (M.H.R.M., M.I.B., D.I.B.); MBA.

Student Services: Academic Counselling, Canteen, Careers Guidance, Cultural Activities, Facilities for disabled people, Foreign Studies Centre, Health Services, Language Laboratory, Nursery Care, Social Counselling, Sports Facilities

Last Updated: 01/07/11

MONAD UNIVERSITY

N.H. 24, Delhi Hapur Road, PO - Pilkhua,
Kasmabad, Uttar Pradesh 245101
EMail: admissions@monad.edu.in
Website: http://www.monad.edu.in/

Vice-Chancellor: Mian Jan

Programme
Architecture (Architecture); **Biotechnology** (Biotechnology); **Computer Science** (Computer Science); **Engineering and Information Technology** (Agricultural Engineering; Chemical Engineering; Civil Engineering; Computer Engineering; Electrical Engineering; Electronic Engineering; Information Technology; Mechanical Engineering; Telecommunications Engineering); **Home Science** (Clothing and Sewing; Dietetics; Home Economics; Nutrition; Public Health; Textile Design); **Islamic Finance** (Banking; Finance); **Law** (Law); **Management** (Business Administration; Health Administration; Hotel Management; Human Resources; Management; Marketing); **Mass Communication and Journalism** (Journalism; Mass Communication); **Pharmacy** (Pharmacy); **Science** (Biochemistry; Chemistry; Microbiology)

History: Created 2010.

Accrediting Agency: UGC

Degrees and Diplomas: *Bachelor's Degree*; *Postgraduate Diploma*; *Master's Degree*; *Doctor of Philosophy*

Last Updated: 08/10/13

MOTHER TERESA WOMEN'S UNIVERSITY

Annai Teresa Magalir Palkalaikazhgam

Kodaikanal, Tamilnadu 624101

Tel: +91(4542) 241-021 +91(4542) 241-122

Fax: +91(4542) 245-314 +91(4542) 241-122

EMail: atwunivc@yahoo.co.in

Vice-Chancellor: D. Janakii Dhanapal

Registrar: S. Sundari

School

Distance Education

Department

Biotechnology (Biotechnology); **Computer Science** (Mathematics and Computer Science); **Economics**; **Education** (Education; Educational and Student Counselling); **English** (English); **Family Life Management** (Family Studies; Home Economics); **Historical Studies and Tourism** (History; Tourism); **Management**; **Music** (Fine Arts; Music); **Physics** (Physics); **Sociology** (Sociology); **Tamil** (Indic Languages); **Visual Communication** (Visual Arts); **Women's Studies** (Women's Studies)

History: Founded 1984. A Research Institution solely for women. Through teaching, training, and extension services, the University seeks to promote the welfare of rural and urban disadvantaged women at all levels.

Academic Year: July to April (July-November; December-April)

Admission Requirements: Minimum Bachelor's Degree

Fees: (Rupees): 3,900-35,000 per annum

Main Language(s) of Instruction: English

Accrediting Agency: National Assessment and Accreditation Council, Bangalore

Degrees and Diplomas: *Postgraduate Diploma*; *Master's Degree*; *Master of Philosophy*; *Doctor of Philosophy*

Student Services: Academic Counselling, Canteen, Cultural Activities, Health Services, Language Laboratory, Nursery Care, Social Counselling, Sports Facilities

Publications: Gender and Progress

MOTILAL NEHRU NATIONAL INSTITUTE OF TECHNOLOGY ALLAHABAD (MNNIT)

Allahabad, Uttar Pradesh 211004

Tel: +91(532) 227-1104

Fax: +91(532) 254-5341 +91(532) 254-5677

EMail: director@mnnit.ac.in

Website: http://www.mnnit.ac.in/

Director: P. Chakrabarti (2011-)
Tel: +91(532) 254-5190 +91(532) 227-1101
EMail: director@mnnit.ac.in

Registrar: Sri Sarvesh Kumar Tiwari

School

Management Studies (Business Administration; Finance; Human Resources; International Business; Management; Marketing; Operations Research)

Department

Applied Mechanics (Biomedical Engineering; Biotechnology; Engineering; Hydraulic Engineering; Materials Engineering; Mechanical Engineering; Mechanics; Nanotechnology; Power Engineering; Solid State Physics); **Chemistry** (Chemical Engineering; Chemistry; Materials Engineering); **Civil Engineering** (Civil Engineering; Computer Graphics; Construction Engineering; Environmental Engineering; Geological Engineering; Irrigation; Transport Engineering); **Computer Science and Engineering** (Computer Engineering; Computer Science; Information Technology; Software Engineering); **Electrical Engineering** (Automation and Control Engineering; Electrical Engineering; Measurement and Precision Engineering; Power Engineering); **Electronics and Communication Engineering** (Computer Graphics; Electronic Engineering; Microelectronics; Telecommunications Engineering); **Geographic Information System** *(GIS)* (Information Sciences; Surveying and Mapping); **Humanities and Social Sciences** (Accountancy; Arts and Humanities; English; Finance; Human Resources; Industrial and Organizational Psychology; Management; Social Psychology; Social Sciences; Social Studies); **Mathematics** (Mathematics; Mathematics and Computer Science); **Mechanical Engineering** (Chemical Engineering; Computer Graphics; Engineering Drawing and Design; Industrial Engineering; Mechanical Engineering; Production Engineering; Thermal Engineering); **Physics** (Physics)

History: Created 1961 as Motilal Nehru Regional Engineering College, Allahabad. Acquired current title and status 2002. An 'Institute of National Importance".

Academic Year: July to April (July-November; January-April) Summer semester May to July.

Admission Requirements: For undergraduate degrees, All India Engineering Entrance Examination (A.I.E.E.E) conducted by C.B.S.E.; candidates who have passed 10+2 or an equivalent. For graduate degrees, an aggregate of 60% marks or equivalent grade in a Bachelor's degree in Science or Engineering or equivalent; For MBA, a bachelor's degree in engineering/technology/science or an equivalent degree with mathematics/economics as one of the subjects in qualifying examination. Candidates appearing in their final year of bachelor's degree may also apply.

Fees: (Rupees): Undergraduate fee, 10,301-25,401 per semester; Graduate semester, 8,826-31,776 per semester. MBA, 25,375-27,750 per semester. Ph.D., 4,775-8,550 (full time) and 2,750-6,525 (part time)

Degrees and Diplomas: *Bachelor's Degree (professional)*; *Master's Degree*

Last Updated: 01/07/11

NAGALAND UNIVERSITY (NU)

Dist. – Zunheboto, Lumami, Nagaland 798627

Tel: +91(370) 229-0488 +91(370) 229-0808

Fax: +91(307) 229-0246

EMail: nagalanduniversity@yahoo.co.in

Website: http://www.nagauniv.org.in/

Vice-Chancellor: Bolin Kumar Konwar
Tel: +91(369) 226-8268 EMail: vicechancellornu@yahoo.com

Registrar: Shri. D.K. Mohanty
Tel: +91(369) 226-8270 EMail: nuregistrar@yahoo.in

School

Agriculture Sciences and Rural Development *(SASRD)* (Agricultural Economics; Agricultural Education; Agricultural Engineering; Agriculture; Agronomy; Animal Husbandry; Biochemistry; Biotechnology; Botany; Chemistry; Crop Production; Ecology; Entomology; Environmental Studies; Genetics; Horticulture; Plant Pathology; Rural Planning; Soil Conservation; Soil Science); **Engineering and Technology** (Biotechnology; Business Administration; Computer Engineering; Computer Networks; Computer Science; Electronic Engineering; Engineering; Information Technology; Management; Software Engineering; Telecommunications Engineering); **Humanities and Education** (Arts and Humanities; Cultural Studies; Education; English; Linguistics; Literature); **Sciences** (Botany; Chemistry; Geography; Geology; Inorganic Chemistry; Natural Resources; Natural Sciences; Organic Chemistry; Physical Chemistry; Surveying and Mapping; Zoology); **Social Science** (Archaeology; Business and Commerce; Comparative Politics; Economics; Government; History; International Relations; Political Sciences; Public Administration; Social Sciences; Sociology)

Further Information: Also campuses in Kohima and Medziphema. 48 affiliated colleges.

History: Founded 1994. A 'Central University'.

Academic Year: July to June

Admission Requirements: Pre-University for degree courses in Agriculture and graduate with 50% marks for Postgraduate courses; Postgraduate with 55% marks for PhD admission

Fees: (Rupees): 990 per annum

Main Language(s) of Instruction: English

Accrediting Agency: National Assessment and Accreditation Council

Degrees and Diplomas: *Bachelor's Degree*; *Bachelor's Degree (professional)*; *Master's Degree*; *Doctor of Philosophy*. Also MBA, 2 yrs.

Student Services: Academic Counselling, Canteen, Cultural Activities, Health Services, Sports Facilities

Publications: Research Journal of Nagaland University

Last Updated: 15/06/12

NALANDA OPEN UNIVERSITY

Nalanda Khula Vishwavidyalaya

2nd/3rd Floor, Biscomaun Bhawan, Gandhi Maidan, Patna, Bihar 800001

Tel: +91(612) 220-1013 +91(612) 220-6916

Fax: +91(612) 220-1001

EMail: nalopuni@sancharnet.in

Website: http://www.nalandaopenuniversity.com

Vice-Chancellor: Jitendra Singh

Registrar: Sidheshwar Prasad Sinha

School

Computer and Information Sciences (Computer Science; Information Sciences); **Economics, Commerce and Management** (Business and Commerce; Economics; Finance; Insurance; Management; Marketing; Safety Engineering); **Health and Environmental Sciences** (Alternative Medicine; Child Care and Development; Dental Hygiene; Dental Technology; Environmental Studies; Epidemiology; Family Studies; Food Science; Health Sciences; Laboratory Techniques; Medical Technology; Nursing; Nutrition; Ophthalmology; Optometry; Physical Therapy; Psychology; Radiology; Rehabilitation and Therapy; Yoga); **Indian and Foreign Languages** (Hindi; Modern Languages; Sanskrit; South and Southeast Asian Languages; Urdu); **Indology** (Ancient Civilizations; Archaeology; Asian Religious Studies; Christian Religious Studies; Cultural Studies; History; Islamic Studies; Literature; Philosophy; Tourism); **Journalism and Mass Communication** (Journalism; Mass Communication); **Library and Information Science** (Information Sciences; Library Science); **Pure and Agricultural Sciences** (Agriculture; Biology; Botany; Chemistry; Floriculture; Geography; Home Economics; Mathematics; Physics; Soil Conservation; Zoology); **Social Sciences** (Constitutional Law; Geography; Home Economics; Human Rights; Political Sciences; Psychology; Public Administration; Rural Planning; Social Sciences; Social Work; Sociology; Women's Studies); **Teacher's Education** (Education; Higher Education; Primary Education; Secondary Education; Teacher Training)

History: Founded 1987.

Academic Year: July to June

Admission Requirements: School or College Certificate according to courses

Fees: (Rupees): Certificate, 500-1,000 per annum; Intermediate degree, 1,500-11,500 per annum; Bachelor's degree, 1,800-8,000 per annum; Postgraduate degree, 3,000 per annum; Master's degree, 2,700-7,000 per annum; Ph.D., 10,000 per annum

Main Language(s) of Instruction: Hindi, English

Accrediting Agency: Distance Education Council (DEC), University Grants Commission (UGC), and Ministry of HRD, Government of India.

Degrees and Diplomas: *Bachelor's Degree*; *Bachelor's Degree (professional)*; *Postgraduate Diploma*; *Master's Degree*; *Doctor of Philosophy*. Also undergraduate certificates, 6-9 months; Short certificate courses, 4 weeks; Bachelor's degrees Honours, 3 yrs; Intermediate degree, 2 yrs.

Student Services: Academic Counselling, Social Counselling

Last Updated: 04/07/11

NARENDRA DEVA UNIVERSITY OF AGRICULTURE AND TECHNOLOGY (NDUAT)

Narendranagar, Kumarganj, Faizabad, Uttar Pradesh 224229

Tel: +91(5270) 262-161

Fax: +91(5270) 262-097

EMail: nduat@up.nic.in

Website: http://www.nduat.ernet.in

Vice-Chancellor: R.S. Kureel (2010-)
Tel: +91(5270) 262-097 +91(5270) 262-161
EMail: vc_nduat2010@yaho.co.in; vc@mail.nduat.ernet.in

Registrar: Padmaker Tripathi
Tel: +91(5270) 262-035 EMail: hpt@india.com

College

Agricultural Engineering and Technology *(Mahamaya - MCAET)* (Agricultural Engineering; Agricultural Equipment; Irrigation; Power Engineering; Soil Conservation; Water Management); **Agriculture** (Agricultural Economics; Agricultural Education; Agricultural Engineering; Agriculture; Agronomy; Biochemistry; Botany; Entomology; Fishery; Food Technology; Forestry; Genetics; Horticulture; Meteorology; Microbiology; Plant and Crop Protection; Plant Pathology; Soil Science; Statistics; Zoology); **Fishery** (Agricultural Economics; Aquaculture; Biology; Biotechnology; Fishery; Genetics; Microbiology; Natural Resources; Pathology; Statistics; Water Science); **Home Science** (Development Studies; Family Studies; Food Science; Home Economics; Nutrition; Textile Design; Textile Technology); **Horticulture** (Horticulture); **Veterinary Science and Animal Husbandry** (Anatomy; Animal Husbandry; Biochemistry; Epidemiology; Ethics; Farm Management; Genetics; Gynaecology and Obstetrics; Microbiology; Nutrition; Parasitology; Pharmacology; Physiology; Public Health; Radiology; Social and Preventive Medicine; Surgery; Toxicology; Veterinary Science)

Further Information: Also University Hospital.

History: Founded 1975. Based on the model of the Land Grant Colleges of the USA and undertaking teaching research and extension education in an integrated manner. Responsible for all round development of rural communities in 15 districts of the Faizabad, Gorakhpur and Varanasi regions.

Admission Requirements: 12th year senior secondary/intermediate examination or recognized foreign equivalent

Fees: (Rupees): Undergraduate, 2,400; postgraduate, 4,000 per annum

Main Language(s) of Instruction: Hindi, English

Degrees and Diplomas: *Bachelor's Degree*; *Bachelor's Degree (professional)*; *Postgraduate Diploma*; *Master's Degree*; *Doctor of Philosophy*

Student Services: Sports Facilities

Student Numbers *2010-2011*: Total 642

Last Updated: 04/07/11

NATIONAL ACADEMY OF LEGAL STUDIES AND RESEARCH UNIVERSITY (NALSAR UNIVERSITY OF LAW)

Justice City, Shameerpet, R.R.Dist., Hyderabad, Andhra Pradesh 500 078

Tel: +91(40) 2349-8105 +91(40) 2349-8108

Fax: +91(8418) 245-161 +91(8418) 245-174

EMail: admissions@nalsar.ac.in

Website: http://www.nalsar.ac.in

Vice-Chancellor: Veer Singh
Tel: +91(40) 2349-8102 EMail: vc@nalsarlawuniv.org

Registrar: K. V. S. Sarma
Tel: +91(40) 2349-8104 EMail: registrar@nalsarlawuniv.org

Programme

Law (Commercial Law; Comparative Law; Constitutional Law; Criminal Law; Environmental Studies; Human Rights; International Law; Law; Private Law; Public Law); **Other Studies** (Air and Space Law; Air Transport; Finance; Fiscal Law; Law)

History: Founded 1998.

Academic Year: June to April (June-November; December-April)

Admission Requirements: 12th year senior secondary/intermediate examination or recognized foreign equivalent

Fees: Indian Students (Rupees): Bachelor, 85,000 per annum; Master, 65,000 per annum; Postgraduate Programs, 5,000. Non-locals/Foreign (US Dollars):, Bachelor's degree, 5,000-10,000 per annum; Master, 2,000 per annum; Postgraduate Programs, 750-1,000 per annum

Main Language(s) of Instruction: English

Degrees and Diplomas: *Bachelor's Degree*; *Postgraduate Diploma*; *Master's Degree*; *Master of Philosophy*; *Doctor of Philosophy*. Also Bachelor's degree Honours; Undergraduate certificate.

Student Services: Academic Counselling, Canteen, Foreign Studies Centre, Health Services, Language Laboratory, Sports Facilities

Publications: Green News; IP Law Newsletter; NALSAR Law Review; NALSAR Newsletter

Last Updated: 04/07/11

NATIONAL BRAIN RESEARCH CENTRE (NBRC)

NH-8, Manesar, Gurgaon, Haryana 122 050
Tel: +91(124) 2845-200
Fax: +91(124) 2338-910 +91(124) 2338-928
EMail: info@nbrc.ac.in
Website: http://www.nbrc.ac.in/

Director: Subrata Sinha (2010-)

Programme

Neurosciences (Neurosciences)

History: Founded 1997. Acquired 'Deemed University' status 2002.

Degrees and Diplomas: *Doctor of Philosophy*. Also integrated Ph.D.; Summer Training and Short-term Programmes.

Last Updated: 13/12/11

NATIONAL DAIRY RESEARCH INSTITUTE (NDRI)

Karnal, Haryana 132001
Tel: +91(184) 225-9008
Fax: +91(184) 225-0042
EMail: registrar.ndri@gmail.com
Website: http://karnal.nic.in/res_ndri.asp

Director: A.K. Srivastava
Tel: +91(184) 225-2800 +91(184) 225-9002
EMail: dir@ndri.res.in

Joint Director (Administration) and Registrar: J. Kewalramani
Tel: +91(184) 225-9023 +91(184) 227-2392
EMail: cao@ndri.res.in

Division

Animal Biochemistry (Biochemistry; Biotechnology; Food Technology); **Dairy Cattle Breeding** (Animal Husbandry; Dairy; Genetics); **Dairy Cattle Nutrition** (Animal Husbandry; Dairy; Nutrition); **Dairy Cattle Physiology** (Animal Husbandry; Dairy; Physiology); **Dairy Chemistry** (Chemistry; Dairy; Physical Chemistry); **Dairy Economics, Statistics and Management** (Computer Science; Dairy; Economics; Management; Statistics); **Dairy Engineering** (Dairy; Engineering; Food Technology); **Dairy Extension** (Agricultural Education; Behavioural Sciences; Dairy; Hindi; Leadership; Management; Psychology; Sociology); **Dairy Microbiology** (Biotechnology; Dairy; Food Technology; Microbiology; Physiology); **Dairy Technology** (Dairy; Food Technology); **Live Stock Production and Management** (Agricultural Business; Animal Husbandry; Environmental Management; Meat and Poultry; Waste Management)

Centre

Animal Biotechnology (Biotechnology; Embryology and Reproduction Biology; Genetics; Molecular Biology)

Research Centre

Artificial Breeding (Animal Husbandry; Embryology and Reproduction Biology)

History: Founded 1923 as as Imperial Institute of Animal Husbandry and Dairying. Expanded and renamed as Imperial Dairy Institute 1936. Headquarter shifted to Karnal 1955. Acquired present title 1947. Granted 'Deemed University' status 1989.

Academic Year: August to July (August-December; January-July)

Admission Requirements: 12th year senior secondary/intermediate examination or recognized foreign equivalent

Fees: (Rupees): 2,000 per semester

Main Language(s) of Instruction: English

Accrediting Agency: Indian Council of Agricultural Research (ICAR)

Degrees and Diplomas: *Bachelor's Degree (professional)*; *Master's Degree*; *Doctor of Philosophy*

Student Services: Academic Counselling, Canteen, Careers Guidance, Health Services, Sports Facilities

Publications: Annual Report; Quarterly Report

Publishing House: NDRI Printing Press

Last Updated: 04/07/11

NATIONAL INSTITUTE OF AGRICULTURAL EXTENSION MANAGEMENT (MANAGE)

Rajendranagar, Hyderabad, Andhra Pradesh 500 030
Tel: +91(40) 2401-6702 +91(40) 2401-6709
Fax: +91(40) 2401-5388
EMail: helpline@manage.gov.in; anandreddy@manage.gov.in
Website: http://www.manage.gov.in/

Director-General: Sanjeev Gupta
EMail: dgmanage@manage.gov.in

Programme

Agri Business Management (Agricultural Business; Management); **Agricultural Extension Management** (Agriculture; Management); **Agricultural Extension Services for Input Dealers** (Agriculture)

History: Founded 1987 by the Ministry of Agriculture, Government of India as an autonomous institute.

Main Language(s) of Instruction: Hindi

Accrediting Agency: All India Council for Technical Education (AICTE); National Board of Accreditation (NBA)

Degrees and Diplomas: *Post Diploma*; *Postgraduate Diploma*

Last Updated: 05/12/11

NATIONAL INSTITUTE OF FOUNDRY AND FORGE TECHNOLOGY (NIFFT)

Hatia, Ranchi, Jharkhand 834 003
Tel: +91(651) 229-0859
Fax: +91(651) 229-0860
EMail: nifftranchi@gmail.com
Website: http://www.nifft.ernet.in/

Department

Applied Science and Humanities (Arts and Humanities; Computer Engineering; Environmental Engineering; Environmental Studies; Natural Sciences); **Forge Technology** (Metallurgical Engineering); **Foundry Technology** (Metallurgical Engineering); **Manufacturing Engineering** (Industrial Engineering); **Materials and Metallurgical Engineering** (Materials Engineering; Metallurgical Engineering)

History: Founded 1966.

Accrediting Agency: All India Council for Technical Education (AICTE)

Degrees and Diplomas: *Bachelor's Degree (professional)*; *Master's Degree*; *Doctor of Philosophy*. Also Advanced Diploma Course, 18 Months.

Student Services: Sports Facilities

Last Updated: 24/01/12

NATIONAL INSTITUTE OF INDUSTRIAL ENGINEERING (NITIE)

Vihar Lake, Mumbai, Maharashtra 400 087
Tel: +91(22) 2803 5317
Fax: +91(22) 2857-3251
EMail: admissions@nitie.edu
Website: http://www.nitie.edu/

Director: De Amitabha

Registrar: U. K. Debnath
Tel: +91(22) 2857-3371 EMail: registrar@nitie.edu

Programme
Doctoral Level Fellowship (Business Administration; Environmental Management; Industrial Engineering; Management; Safety Engineering; Social Studies); **Industrial Engineering** (Finance; Human Resources; Industrial Engineering; Management; Marketing); **Industrial Management** (Industrial Management); **Industrial Safety and Environmental Management** (Environmental Management; Safety Engineering); **Information Technology Management** (Information Management; Information Technology)

History: Founded 1963.

Degrees and Diplomas: *Postgraduate Diploma*

Student Services: Sports Facilities
Last Updated: 27/01/12

NATIONAL INSTITUTE OF MENTAL HEALTH AND NEURO SCIENCES (NIMHANS)

PO Box 2900, Hosur Road, Bangalore, Karnataka 560029
Tel: +91(80) 2699-5005
Fax: +91(80) 2656-6811
EMail: info@nimhans.kar.nic.in
Website: http://www.nimhans.kar.nic.in

Vice-Chancellor and Director: P. Satishchandra (2011-)
Tel: +91(80) 269-95001 +91(80) 269-95002
EMail: vc@nimhans.kar.nic.in; psatish@nimhans.kar.nic.in

Registrar: V. Ravi
Tel: +91(80) 269-95005
EMail: regt@nimhans.kar.nic.in; vravi@nimhans.kar.nic.in

Department
Biophysics (Biophysics); **Biostatistics** (Biological and Life Sciences; Statistics); **Child and Adolescent Psychiatry** (Child Care and Development; Psychiatry and Mental Health); **Clinical Psychology** (Behavioural Sciences; Child Care and Development; Clinical Psychology; Psychology; Rehabilitation and Therapy; Social Problems); **Epidemiology** (Epidemiology; Psychiatry and Mental Health; Public Health); **Human Genetics** (Genetics; Neurology; Psychiatry and Mental Health); **Mental Health Education** (Health Education; Psychiatry and Mental Health); **Neuroanaesthesia** (Anaesthesiology; Neurosciences; Radiology); **Neurochemistry** (Chemistry; Neurosciences); **Neuroimaging and Interventional Radiology** (Neurological Therapy; Neurology; Neurosciences; Radiology; Surgery); **Neurology** (Medicine; Neurological Therapy; Neurology; Paediatrics; Psychiatry and Mental Health; Surgery); **Neuromicrobiology** (Microbiology; Neurology; Nursing; Psychiatry and Mental Health; Surgery); **Neuropathology** (Neurology; Pathology; Surgery); **Neurophysiology** (Neurology; Physiology; Psychiatry and Mental Health; Surgery); **Neurosurgery** (Neurology; Nursing; Psychiatry and Mental Health; Surgery); **Neurovirology** (Neurology; Virology); **Nursing** (Nursing; Psychiatry and Mental Health); **Psychiatric and Neurological Rehabilitation** (Neurological Therapy; Psychiatry and Mental Health; Rehabilitation and Therapy); **Psychiatric Social Work** (Child Care and Development; Psychiatry and Mental Health; Social Work); **Psychiatry** (Forensic Medicine and Dentistry; Gerontology; Neurological Therapy; Pharmacology; Psychiatry and Mental Health; Rehabilitation and Therapy); **Psychopharmacology** (Neurosciences; Pharmacology; Psychiatry and Mental Health); **Speech Pathology and Audiology** (Speech Therapy and Audiology)

History: Founded 1974 as autonomous National Institute of Mental Health and Neuro Sciences (NIMHANS) through amalgamation of the Mental Hospital and the All India Institute of Mental Health. Acquired present status and title 1994. A 'Deemed University'.

Fees: (Rupees): Tuition fee for Indian students, undergraduate programmes, 10,000-35,000 per annum; Postgraduate programmes, 10,000-50,000 per annum; Ph.D., 18,000 per annum. Foreign students (US Dollars), undergraduate programmes, 20,000 per annum; postgraduate programmes, 15,000-60,000 per annum; Ph.D., 30,000 per annum

Degrees and Diplomas: *Post Diploma*; *Postgraduate Diploma*; *Master's Degree*; *Master of Philosophy*; *Doctor of Philosophy*

Student Services: Canteen, Language Laboratory, Sports Facilities
Last Updated: 04/07/11

NATIONAL INSTITUTE OF PHARMACEUTICAL EDUCATION AND RESEARCH (NIPER)

Sector 67, S.A.S. Nagar, Mohali, Punjab 160062
Tel: +91(172) 221-4682 +91(172) 221-4687
Fax: +91(172) 221-4692
EMail: registrar@niper.ac.in
Website: http://www.niper.nic.in

Director: K. K. Bhutani
Tel: +91(172) 221-4690 EMail: director@niper.ac.in

Acting Registrar: Sh. Rajesh Moza
Tel: +91(172) 223-0068 EMail: registrar@niper.ac.in

Programme
Training and Continuing Education (Pharmacy)

Department
Biotechnology (Biotechnology); **Medicinal Chemistry** (Chemistry); **Natural Products** (Chemistry); **Pharmaceutical Analysis** (Pharmacy); **Pharmaceutical Management** (Management; Pharmacy); **Pharmaceutical Technology** (Biotechnology; Pharmacy; Technology); **Pharmaceutics** (Pharmacy); **Pharmacoinformatics** (Computer Science; Pharmacy); **Pharmacology and Toxicology** (Pharmacology; Toxicology); **Pharmacy Practice** (Pharmacy)

History: Founded 1991. An 'Institute of National Importance'

Academic Year: July-June (July-December; January-June)

Fees: (Rupees): Master's degree,14,404 per semester (25,696-118,042 per semester for government- and industry sponsored students); Non-Resident Indians,. MBA, 57,739 per semester (103,003 per semester for sponsored students. Non-resident Indian students (US Dollars), 6,100 per semester. Ph.D. 14,404 per semester (26,428 per semester for sponsored students)

Degrees and Diplomas: *Master's Degree*; *Doctor of Philosophy*. Also MBA
Last Updated: 05/07/11

NATIONAL INSTITUTE OF TECHNOLOGY AGARTALA

Jirania, Tripura 799055
Tel: +91(381) 2346-360 +91(381) 2346-630
Fax: +91(381) 2346-360 +91(381) 2346-630
EMail: nitaedc@gmail.com
Website: http://www.nitagartala.in/

Director: Probir Kumar Bose
Tel: +91(381) 234-6630
EMail: pkbdirector@gmail.com; pkb32@yahoo.com

Registrar: D. Bhattacharjee Tel: +91(381) 234-6629

Department
Chemical Engineering (Chemical Engineering); **Chemistry** (Biochemistry; Chemistry; Inorganic Chemistry; Nanotechnology; Organic Chemistry); **Civil Engineering** (Civil Engineering; Construction Engineering; Geological Engineering; Transport Engineering); **Computer Science and Engineering** (Computer Engineering; Computer Science); **Electrical Engineering** (Electrical Engineering; Measurement and Precision Engineering; Power Engineering); **Electronics and Communication Engineering** (Computer Graphics; Electronic Engineering; Microelectronics; Telecommunications Engineering); **Electronics and Instrumentation Engineering** (Electronic Engineering; Measurement and Precision Engineering); **Humanities and Social Sciences** (Arts and Humanities; Communication Studies; Economics; Management; Social Sciences); **Mathematics** (Mathematics); **Mechanical Engineering** (Mechanical Engineering; Thermal Engineering); **Physics** (Nanotechnology; Optics; Physics); **Production Engineering** (Production Engineering)

History: Created in 1965 as Tripura Engineering College, Agartala. Acquired current title and status 2006. An 'Institute of National Importance'.

Academic Year: July to June (July-December; January-June).

Degrees and Diplomas: *Bachelor's Degree (professional)*; *Postgraduate Diploma*; *Master's Degree*; *Doctor of Philosophy*. Also MBA

Student Services: Health Services
Last Updated: 05/07/11

NATIONAL INSTITUTE OF TECHNOLOGY CALICUT (NITC)

Calicut, Kerala 673601
Tel: +91(495) 228-6106
Fax: +91(495) 228-7250
EMail: director@nitc.ac.in
Website: http://www.nitc.ac.in

Director: T. L. Jose EMail: director@nitc.ac.in

Registrar: Abraham T. Mathew
Tel: +91(495) 228-6314 EMail: atm@nitc.ac.in

School

Biotechnology (Biotechnology); **Management Studies** (Business Administration; Finance; Human Resources; Management; Marketing; Operations Research); **Nano Science and Technology** (Nanotechnology)

Department

Architecture (Architecture); **Chemical Engineering** (Bioengineering; Chemical Engineering; Computer Science); **Chemistry** (Analytical Chemistry; Chemistry; Inorganic Chemistry; Organic Chemistry; Physical Chemistry; Polymer and Plastics Technology); **Civil Engineering** (Civil Engineering; Construction Engineering; Environmental Engineering; Geological Engineering; Transport Engineering); **Computer Science and Engineering** (Computer Engineering; Computer Science); **Electrical Engineering** (Automation and Control Engineering; Electrical and Electronic Engineering; Electrical Engineering; Energy Engineering; Measurement and Precision Engineering; Power Engineering); **Electronics and Communication Engineering** (Computer Graphics; Electronic Engineering; Microelectronics; Telecommunications Engineering); **Mathematics** (Applied Mathematics; Mathematics; Statistics); **Mechanical Engineering** (Mechanical Engineering); **Physical Education** (Physical Education); **Physics** (Engineering; Materials Engineering; Nanotechnology; Physics)

Centre

Continuing Education (Computer Networks; Electronic Engineering; Engineering; Environmental Studies; Heritage Preservation; Medical Technology; Physics; Power Engineering; Structural Architecture; Surveying and Mapping; Thermal Engineering)

History: Founded 1960 as Calicut Regional Engineering College. Acquired present title and academic and administrative autonomy 2002. Acquired status of 'Institute of National Importance' 2007.

Fees: (Rupees): BTech, 12,000; MTech, 13,000; EDT, 24,000; MCA, 13,000

Degrees and Diplomas: *Bachelor's Degree (professional)*; *Postgraduate Diploma*; *Master's Degree*; *Doctor of Philosophy*. Also MBA

Student Services: Canteen, Cultural Activities, Health Services, Social Counselling, Sports Facilities
Last Updated: 05/07/11

NATIONAL INSTITUTE OF TECHNOLOGY DURGAPUR (NITDGP)

Mahatma Gandhi Avenue, Durgapur, West Bengal 713209
Tel: +91(343) 254-6397
Fax: +91(343) 254-7375
EMail: director@admin.nitdgp.ac.in
Website: http://www.nitdgp.ac.in/

Director: Tarkeshwar Kumar (2011-)
Tel: +91 943478-8001
EMail: profdg@yahoo.com; debidas.ghosh@cse.nitdgp.ac.in; director@admin.nitdgp.ac.in

Dean (Administration): P. P. Sengupta
Tel: +91 9434788002 EMail: deanadmin@admin.nitdgp.ac.in

Registrar: A. Gangopadhyay
Tel: +91(343) 275-5240 EMail: registrar@admin.nitdgp.ac.in

Department

Biotechnology (Biotechnology); **Chemical Engineering** (Chemical Engineering); **Chemistry** (Chemistry); **Civil Engineering** (Civil Engineering); **Computer Application** *(MCA)* (Computer Networks; Computer Science); **Computer Centre** (Computer Science); **Computer Science and Engineering** (Computer Engineering; Computer Science); **Electrical Engineering** (Electrical Engineering); **Electronics and Communication Engineering** (Electronic Engineering; Telecommunications Engineering); **Geology** (Geology); **Humanities** (Arts and Humanities; English; Literature); **Information Technology** (Information Technology); **Management Studies** (Management); **Mathematics** (Mathematics); **Mechanical Engineering** (Mechanical Engineering); **Metallurgical and Materials Engineering** (Materials Engineering; Metallurgical Engineering); **Physics** (Physics)

History: Founded 1960 as Regional Engineering College. Acquired current status and title 2003. An 'Institute of National Importance'.

Admission Requirements: For undergraduate programmes: "pass" in the qualifying examination (10+2 or its equivalent) with Physics, Chemistry, Mathematics and English, having secured pass marks in each subject. For graduate programmes: B.E. or B.Tech in an appropriate subject.

Accrediting Agency: National Board of Accreditation (NBA)

Degrees and Diplomas: *Bachelor's Degree (professional)*; *Master's Degree*; *Doctor of Philosophy*. Also MBA

Student Services: Canteen, Health Services

Student Numbers *2010-2011*	MEN	WOMEN	**TOTAL**
All (Foreign included)	2,500	500	c. **3,000**

Last Updated: 05/07/11

NATIONAL INSTITUTE OF TECHNOLOGY HAMIRPUR

Toni Devi Road, Hamirpur, Himachal Pradesh 177 005
Tel: +91(1972) 254-001
Fax: +91(1972) 223-834
EMail: registrar@nitham.ac.in
Website: http://www.nith.ac.in/

Director: R. L. Sharma
Tel: +91(1972) 222-308 EMail: director@nitham.ac.in

Registrar: A.S. Singha
Tel: +91(1972) 224-390 EMail: registrar@nitham.ac.in

Department

Architecture (Architecture); **Chemistry** (Chemical Engineering; Chemistry); **Civil Engineering** (Civil Engineering; Construction Engineering; Environmental Engineering; Geological Engineering; Geology; Hydraulic Engineering; Transport Engineering); **Computer Science and Engineering** (Computer Engineering; Computer Graphics; Computer Science); **Electrical Engineering** (Electrical Engineering; Power Engineering); **Electronics and Communication Engineering** *(E&CE)* (Computer Graphics; Computer Networks; Electronic Engineering; Telecommunications Engineering); **Humanities and Social Science** (Accountancy; Arts and Humanities; Behavioural Sciences; Business Administration; Communication Studies; Economics; Finance; Human Resources; International Economics; Labour and Industrial Relations; Management; Marketing; Social Sciences; Social Studies; Sociology); **Mathematics** (Mathematical Physics; Mathematics; Mathematics and Computer Science; Operations Research; Statistics; Thermal Engineering); **Mechanical Engineering** (Mechanical Engineering); **Physics** (Applied Physics; Physics)

History: Created in 1986 as Regional Engineering College. Acquired current title and status 2002. An 'Institute of National Importance'.

Fees: (Rupees): Tuition fee for Bachelor and Master's degree, 17,500 per semester (4,000-6,000 per semester for slow pace Master's degree programme). MBA, 45,000 per semester. Ph.D., 2,500-5,000 per semester

Degrees and Diplomas: *Bachelor's Degree (professional)*; *Master's Degree*; *Doctor of Philosophy*
Last Updated: 05/07/11

NATIONAL INSTITUTE OF TECHNOLOGY JAMSHEDPUR (NITJSR)

NIT Campus, P.O. RIT, Jamshedpur, Jharkhand 831014
Tel: +91(657) 240-7614 +91(657) 240-7642
Fax: +91(657) 238-2246 +91(657) 240-8811
EMail: director@nitjsr.ac.in
Website: http://www.nitjsr.ac.in/

Director: Rajnish Shrivastava
Tel: +91(657) 237-3407 EMail: director@nitjsr.ac.in

Registrar: S.B.L Saksena EMail: subodhseksena_03@yahoo.co.in

Department

Chemistry (Chemistry); **Civil Engineering** (Civil Engineering); **Computer Applications** (Computer Science); **Computer Science and Engineering** (Computer Engineering; Computer Science); **Electrical and Electronics Engineering** (Electrical and Electronic Engineering; Electrical Engineering; Electronic Engineering; Power Engineering); **Electronics and Communications Engineering** (Computer Graphics; Electronic Engineering; Telecommunications Engineering); **Maths and Humanities** (Arts and Humanities; Mathematics; Operations Research; Statistics); **Mechanical Engineering** (Mechanical Engineering; Thermal Engineering); **Metallurgical and Materials Engineering** (Materials Engineering; Metallurgical Engineering); **Physics** (Physics); **Production and Industrial Engineering** (Engineering Management; Industrial Engineering; Production Engineering)

History: Created 1960 as Regional Institute of Technology Jamshedpur. Upgraded to a National Institute of Technology 2002. Became an 'Institute of National Importance' 2007.

Degrees and Diplomas: *Bachelor's Degree (professional)*; *Master's Degree*; *Doctor of Philosophy*. Also Non-Formal Bachelor of Science in Engineering; Bachelor's degree honours.

Student Services: Health Services, Sports Facilities
Last Updated: 05/07/11

NATIONAL INSTITUTE OF TECHNOLOGY KARNATAKA (NITK)

Surathkal, PO Srinivasnagar, Dashina Kannada District, Karnataka 575025
Tel: +91(824) 247-4000
Fax: +91(824) 247-4033
Website: http://www.nitk.ac.in

Director: Sandeep Sancheti
Tel: +91(824) 247-4000, Ext. 3006 EMail: director@nitk.ac.in

Registrar: M. Govindaraj
Tel: +91(824) 247-4000, Ext. 3006 EMail: registrar@nitk.ac.in

Division

Basic Science, Humanities, Social Sciences and Management Systems (Arts and Humanities; Business Administration; Chemistry; Management; Mathematics and Computer Science; Natural Sciences; Physics; Social Sciences); **Civil Engineering Systems** (Civil Engineering; Hydraulic Engineering; Mechanics; Mining Engineering); **Electrical, Electronics and Computing Systems** (Computer Engineering; Electrical and Electronic Engineering; Electrical Engineering; Electronic Engineering; Information Technology; Telecommunications Engineering); **Mechanical and Chemical Systems** (Chemical Engineering; Materials Engineering; Mechanical Engineering; Metallurgical Engineering)

History: Founded 1960 as Karnataka Regional Engineering College, Surathkal. Became a 'Deemed Unviersity' and upgraded to National Institute of Technology 2002. Declared as 'Institute of National Importance' 2007.

Academic Year: July to May (July-December; January-May); also winter and summer sessions

Admission Requirements: Higher secondary school certificate

Fees: (Rupees): Tuition fee for undergraduate programmes, 6,000-17,500 per semester; Postgraduate programmes, 15,000 per semester

Degrees and Diplomas: *Bachelor's Degree (professional)*; *Master's Degree*; *Doctor of Philosophy*. Also MBA

Student Services: Canteen, Careers Guidance, Health Services, Sports Facilities

Last Updated: 05/07/11

NATIONAL INSTITUTE OF TECHNOLOGY KURUKSHETRA (NITKKR)

Kurukshetra, Haryana 136119
Tel: +91(1744) 238-122
Fax: +91(1744) 238-494
EMail: mbandyopadhyay@yahoo.com
Website: http://www.nitkkr.ac.in

Director: Anand Mohan Tel: +91(1744) 238-083

Registrar: G. R. Samantray
Tel: +91(1744) 233-212 EMail: registrarnitk@rediffmail.com

Department

Business Administration (Business Administration; Finance; Human Resources; Information Technology; International Business; Marketing); **Chemistry** (Chemistry; Materials Engineering; Polymer and Plastics Technology); **Civil Engineering** (Civil Engineering; Construction Engineering; Environmental Engineering; Hydraulic Engineering; Mechanics; Seismology; Surveying and Mapping; Transport Engineering); **Computer Applications** (Computer Science); **Computer Engineering** (Computer Engineering; Computer Networks; Software Engineering); **Electrical Engineering** (Artificial Intelligence; Automation and Control Engineering; Computer Engineering; Electrical Engineering; Electronic Engineering; Power Engineering; Robotics); **Electronics and Communication Engineering** *(ECE)* (Computer Graphics; Electronic Engineering; Telecommunications Engineering); **Humanities and Social Sciences** (Arts and Humanities; Business Administration; Communication Studies; Economics; Industrial and Organizational Psychology; Management; Social Sciences); **Mathematics** (Applied Mathematics; Mathematics); **Mechanical Engineering** (Mechanical Engineering); **Physics** (Measurement and Precision Engineering; Nanotechnology; Physics)

History: Founded 1963. Upgraded to Kurukshetra to National Institute of Technology, Kurukshetra with the status of Deemed University 2002. An 'Institution of National Importance'.

Admission Requirements: Higher secondary school certificate

Fees: (Rupees): BTech, 6,000 per semester; MTech, 7,500 pers semester; MCA and MBA, 50,000 per semester; MBA. Ph.D., 6,000 per semester for full time, 1,000-5,000 for part-time and (US Dollars) 2,000 per sesmester for foreign students

Degrees and Diplomas: *Bachelor's Degree (professional)*; *Master's Degree*; *Doctor of Philosophy*. Also MBA

Student Services: Health Services, Sports Facilities
Last Updated: 06/07/11

NATIONAL INSTITUTE OF TECHNOLOGY PATNA (NITP)

Ashok Rajpath, Patna, Bihar 800005
Tel: +91(612) 237-1715
EMail: info@nitp.ac.in
Website: http://www.nitp.ac.in

Director: U. C. Ray
Tel: +91(612) 237-1715 Ext. 221 EMail: director@nitp.ac.in

Registrar: Sagar Vidya
Tel: +91(612) 266-0480 EMail: registrar@nitp.ac.in

Department

Architecture (Architectural and Environmental Design; Architecture; Design; Graphic Design; Sound Engineering (Acoustics); Visual Arts); **Civil Engineering** (Civil Engineering; Construction Engineering; Hydraulic Engineering; Surveying and Mapping; Transport Engineering); **Computer Science and Engineering** (Artificial Intelligence; Computer Engineering; Computer Networks; Computer Science; Data Processing); **Electrical Engineering** (Automation and Control Engineering; Electrical Engineering; Machine Building; Measurement and Precision Engineering; Power Engineering); **Electronics and Communication Engineering** (Computer Graphics; Electronic Engineering; Instrument Making; Optical Technology; Solid State Physics; Telecommunications Engineering); **Information Technology** (Data Processing; Information Technology; Multimedia; Software Engineering; Technology); **Mechanical Engineering** (Heating and Refrigeration; Machine Building; Mechanical Engineering; Mechanics; Thermal Physics)

History: Created in 1924 as Bihar College of Engineering Patna. Upgraded into a National Institute of Technology 2004. An 'Institution of National Importance'.

Fees: (Rupees): Tuition fee, 17,500 per semester

Degrees and Diplomas: *Bachelor's Degree (professional)*; *Master's Degree*; *Doctor of Philosophy*

Student Services: Health Services
Last Updated: 06/07/11

NATIONAL INSTITUTE OF TECHNOLOGY RAIPUR (NITRR)

G.E. Road, Raipur, Chhattisgarh 492010
Tel: +91(771) 225-4200
Fax: +91(771) 225-4600
Website: http://www.nitrr.ac.in/

Director: S. K. Pandey EMail: director@nitrr.ac.in

Department

Applied Geology (Geology); **Applied Mechanics** (Mechanical Engineering; Mechanics); **Architecture** (Architecture); **Bio Technology** (Biotechnology); **Biomedical Engineering** (Biomedical Engineering; Medical Technology); **Chemical Engineering** (Chemical Engineering); **Chemistry** (Chemistry); **Civil Engineering** (Civil Engineering; Irrigation); **Computer Science and Engineering** (Computer Engineering; Computer Science); **Electrical Engineering** (Electrical Engineering); **Electronics and Telecommunication Engineering** (Electronic Engineering; Telecommunications Engineering); **English** (English); **Information Technology** (Information Technology); **Master In Computer Application** *(MCA)* (Computer Science); **Mathematics** (Mathematics); **Mechanical Engineering** (Mechanical Engineering); **Metallurgical Engineering** (Metallurgical Engineering); **Mining Engineering** (Mining Engineering); **Physics** (Physics); **Workshop**

History: Created in 1956 as Government College of Mining and Metallurgy. Acquired current title and status of National Institute of Technology (NIT) 2005. An 'Institution of National Importance'.

Admission Requirements: Secondary School Certificate

Fees: (Rupees): 35,000 per annum (except fourth and fifth year of Bachelor's degree, 18,000 per annum)

Degrees and Diplomas: *Bachelor's Degree (professional)*; *Master's Degree*. Also undergraduate certificate.

Student Services: Sports Facilities
Last Updated: 06/07/11

NATIONAL INSTITUTE OF TECHNOLOGY ROURKELA (NITRKL)

PO Rourkela, Distt. Sundargarh, Rourkela, Orissa 769008
Tel: +91(661) 247-6773
Fax: +91(661) 247-2926
EMail: info@nitrkl.ac.in
Website: http://www.nitrkl.ac.in

Director: Prafulla Chandra Panda
Tel: +91(661) 247-2050 EMail: director@nitrkl.ac.in

Registrar: Santosh Kumar Upadhyay
Tel: +91(661) 246-2021 EMail: registrar@nitrkl.ac.in

School

Business Management (Accountancy; Business Administration; Economics; Finance; Human Resources; Industrial and Organizational Psychology; Information Management; Information Technology; Management; Marketing; Operations Research)

Department

Applied Mathematics (Applied Mathematics; Mathematics; Mechanics; Operations Research); **Biotechnology and Medical Engineering** (Biology; Biomedical Engineering; Biotechnology; Cell Biology; Computer Science; Genetics; Immunology; Medical Technology; Microbiology; Molecular Biology); **Ceramic Engineering** (Ceramics and Glass Technology); **Chemical Engineering** (Chemical Engineering; Energy Engineering; Nanotechnology; Thermal Engineering); **Chemistry** (Chemistry; Inorganic Chemistry; Organic Chemistry; Physical Chemistry); **Civil Engineering** (Arts and Humanities; Civil Engineering; Construction Engineering; Engineering Drawing and Design; Environmental Engineering; Geological Engineering; Irrigation; Mathematics; Physics; Surveying and Mapping; Transport Engineering); **Computer Science and Engineering** (Computer Engineering; Computer Science; Information Technology; Software Engineering); **Electrical Engineering** (Artificial Intelligence; Automation and Control Engineering; Computer Engineering; Electrical Engineering; Electronic Engineering; Power Engineering; Robotics); **Electronics and Communication Engineering** (Computer Engineering; Computer Graphics; Electronic Engineering; Measurement and Precision Engineering; Telecommunications Engineering); **Humanities and Social Sciences** (Arts and Humanities; Economics; English; Psychology; Social Sciences; Sociology); **Life Science** (Agriculture; Biochemistry; Biological and Life Sciences; Biophysics; Biotechnology; Botany; Chemistry; Mathematics; Microbiology; Molecular Biology; Pharmacology; Physics; Physiology; Zoology); **Mechanical Engineering** (Automation and Control Engineering; Energy Engineering; Engineering Drawing and Design; Industrial Engineering; Mechanical Engineering; Mechanics; Power Engineering; Robotics; Thermal Engineering); **Metallurgical and Materials Engineering** (Ceramics and Glass Technology; Computer Engineering; Heating and Refrigeration; Management; Materials Engineering; Mechanical Engineering; Metallurgical Engineering; Operations Research; Polymer and Plastics Technology; Thermal Engineering); **Mining Engineering** (Computer Science; Economics; Environmental Engineering; Geology; Geophysics; Law; Machine Building; Mechanics; Mining Engineering; Safety Engineering; Surveying and Mapping); **Physics** (Physics)

Centre

Computer (Computer Science)

History: Founded 1961 as Regional Engineering College, Rourkela. Acquired present status and title 2002. An 'Institution of National Importance'.

Academic Year: July to May (July -December; January-May)

Fees: (Rupees): Tuition fees for M.Tech., 17,500 per semester. Other Graduate programmes, 60,000 per semester

Degrees and Diplomas: *Bachelor's Degree (professional)*; *Master's Degree*; *Doctor of Philosophy*. Also MBA

Student Services: Health Services, Sports Facilities
Last Updated: 06/07/11

NATIONAL INSTITUTE OF TECHNOLOGY SILCHAR (NITS)

Silchar, Assam 788010
Tel: +91(3842) 224-879
Fax: +91(3842) 224-797
Website: http://www.nits.ac.in

Director: P.K. Bose EMail: director@nits.ac.in

Registrar: Fazal A. Talukdar EMail: registrar@nits.ac.in

Department

Chemistry (Chemistry); **Civil Engineering** (Civil Engineering); **Computer Science and Engineering** (Computer Engineering; Computer Science); **Electrical Engineering** (Electrical Engineering); **Electronics and Communication Engineering** (Electronic Engineering; Telecommunications Engineering); **Electronics and Instrumentation Engineering** (Electronic Engineering; Measurement and Precision Engineering); **Humanities and Social Sciences** (Arts and Humanities; Social Sciences); **Mathematics** (Mathematics); **Mechanical Engineering** (Mechanical Engineering); **Physics** (Physics)

History: Founded 1967 as as a Regional Engineering College (REC), Silchar. Acquired status of National Institute Of Technology and title 2002. An 'Institution of National Importance'.

Degrees and Diplomas: *Bachelor's Degree*; *Bachelor's Degree (professional)*; *Master's Degree*; *Doctor of Philosophy*

Academic Staff *2010-2011*: Total: c. 200

Last Updated: 06/07/11

NATIONAL INSTITUTE OF TECHNOLOGY SRINAGAR (NITSRI)

Hazratbal, Srinagar, Jammu and Kashmir 190006
Tel: +91(194) 242-4792
EMail: director@nitsri.net
Website: http://www.nitsri.net/

Director: U.C. Ray EMail: director@nitsri.net

Registrar: Shri. F. A. Wani Tel: +91(194) 242-1347

Department

Chemical Engineering (Biochemistry; Chemical Engineering; Electrical Engineering; Electronic Engineering; Energy Engineering; Heating and Refrigeration; Industrial Management; Management;

Mechanical Engineering; Organic Chemistry; Power Engineering; Statistics); **Chemistry** (Chemistry); **Civil Engineering** (Civil Engineering; Construction Engineering; Geological Engineering; Hydraulic Engineering; Irrigation; Water Science); **Computer Science and Engineering** (Artificial Intelligence; Computer Engineering; Computer Graphics; Computer Networks; Computer Science; Data Processing; Software Engineering); **Electrical Engineering** (Automation and Control Engineering; Electrical Engineering; Electronic Engineering; Mathematics; Power Engineering); **Electronics and Communication Engineering** (Automation and Control Engineering; Computer Graphics; Electronic Engineering; Industrial Management; Mathematics; Microelectronics; Microwaves; Multimedia; Power Engineering; Telecommunications Engineering); **Humanities and Social Sciences** (Arts and Humanities; Social Sciences); **Information Technology** (Computer Engineering; Computer Graphics; Computer Networks; Data Processing; Information Management; Information Technology; Software Engineering); **Mathematics** (Mathematics); **Mechanical Engineering** (Artificial Intelligence; Automation and Control Engineering; Computer Engineering; Computer Graphics; Machine Building; Mathematics; Mechanical Engineering; Mechanics; Power Engineering); **Mechanical Engineering** (Hydraulic Engineering; Measurement and Precision Engineering; Mechanical Engineering); **Mechanical Engineering** (Automation and Control Engineering; Computer Engineering; Computer Graphics; Economics; Electrical Engineering; Electronic Engineering; Engineering Drawing and Design; Heating and Refrigeration; Industrial Engineering; Industrial Management; Machine Building; Materials Engineering; Mathematics; Measurement and Precision Engineering; Mechanical Engineering; Mechanics; Operations Research; Power Engineering; Production Engineering; Thermal Engineering); **Metallurgical and Materials Engineering** (Computer Engineering; Electronic Engineering; Geology; Heating and Refrigeration; Information Management; Machine Building; Materials Engineering; Mathematics; Mechanics; Metal Techniques; Metallurgical Engineering; Mineralogy); **Physics** (Atomic and Molecular Physics; Energy Engineering; Nanotechnology; Nuclear Physics; Physics; Solid State Physics)

History: Created in 1960 as Regional Engineering College. Acquired current title and status 2003. An 'Institution of National Importance'.

Fees: (Rupees): Tuition fee for B.Tech., 17,500 per semester

Degrees and Diplomas: *Bachelor's Degree (professional)*; *Master's Degree*; *Doctor of Philosophy*

Student Services: Health Services, Sports Facilities
Last Updated: 06/07/11

NATIONAL INSTITUTE OF TECHNOLOGY TIRUCHIRAPPALLI (NITT)

Tanjore Main Road., National Highway 47,
Tiruchirappalli, Tamil Nadu 620015
Tel: +91(431) 250-3000 +91(431) 250-4000
Fax: +91(431) 250-0133
EMail: deanac@nitt.edu
Website: http://www.nitt.edu

Director: Srinivasan Sundarrajan
Tel: +91(431) 250-0370 EMail: sundar@nitt.edu

Registrar: A. K. Banerjee
Tel: +91(431) 250-3051
EMail: banerjee@nitt.edu; registrar@nitt.edu

Department

Architecture (Architecture); **Chemical Engineering** (Agricultural Engineering; Automation and Control Engineering; Chemical Engineering; Energy Engineering); **Chemistry** (Chemical Engineering; Chemistry); **Civil Engineering** (Civil Engineering; Construction Engineering; Environmental Engineering; Transport Engineering; Transport Management); **Computer Applications** (Computer Science; Operations Research); **Computer Science and Engineering** (Artificial Intelligence; Computer Engineering; Computer Networks; Computer Science; Software Engineering); **Electrical and Electronics Engineering** (Electrical and Electronic Engineering; Electrical Engineering; Electronic Engineering; Power Engineering); **Electronics and Communication Engineering** (Computer Engineering; Computer Graphics; Computer Networks; Electronic Engineering; Microwaves; Telecommunications Engineering); **Humanities** (Arts and Humanities; Business Administration; Communication Studies; English; Industrial and Organizational Psychology; Industrial Management; Labour Law; Psychology); **Instrumentation and Control Engineering** (Automation and Control Engineering; Engineering Management; Measurement and Precision Engineering); **Management Studies** (Business Administration; Commercial Law; Economics; Finance; Human Resources; Information Management; Management; Marketing; Operations Research); **Mathematics** (Mathematics); **Mechanical Engineering** (Industrial Engineering; Mechanical Engineering; Power Engineering; Safety Engineering; Thermal Engineering); **Metallurgical and Materials Engineering** (Materials Engineering; Metal Techniques; Metallurgical Engineering); **Physics** (Applied Physics; Environmental Engineering; Physics); **Production Engineering** (Industrial Engineering; Production Engineering)

History: Created in 1964 as Regional Engineering College. Acquired 'Deemed University' Status with the approval of the UGC/ AICTE and Govt. of India and renamed as National Institute of Technology 2003. An 'Institution of National Importance'.

Fees: (Rupees): Tuition for undergraduate programmes, 17,500 per semester (except in 4th and 5th year, 6,000 per semester); Postgraduate programmes, 10,000-17,500 per semester; MBA, 25,000 per semester

Degrees and Diplomas: *Bachelor's Degree (professional)*; *Master's Degree*; *Doctor of Philosophy*. Also M.S. (by Research), MCA and MBA

Student Services: Health Services, Sports Facilities
Last Updated: 06/07/11

NATIONAL INSTITUTE OF TECHNOLOGY WARANGAL (NITW)

Warangal, Andhra Pradesh 506004
Tel: +91(870) 245-9191
Fax: +91(870) 245-9547
EMail: registrar@nitw.ac.in
Website: http://www.nitw.ac.in/

Director: T. Srinivasa Rao
Tel: +91(870) 245-9216
EMail: director@nitw.ac.in; tsrao@nitw.ac.in; tsrao60@gmail.com

Registrar: K. Madhu Murthy

School

Management (Business Administration; Finance; Human Resources; Information Management; Information Technology; Management; Marketing; Operations Research)

Department

Biotechnology (Biotechnology); **Chemical Engineering** (Chemical Engineering; Engineering Management); **Chemistry** (Chemistry; Industrial Chemistry); **Civil Engineering** (Civil Engineering; Construction Engineering; Environmental Engineering; Geological Engineering; Hydraulic Engineering; Surveying and Mapping; Transport Engineering); **Computer Science and Engineering** (Computer Engineering; Computer Science); **Electrical and Electronics Engineering** (Electrical Engineering; Electronic Engineering); **Electronics and Communications Engineering** (Computer Engineering; Electrical and Electronic Engineering; Electronic Engineering; Information Technology; Power Engineering; Telecommunications Engineering); **Humanities** (Arts and Humanities); **Mathematics** (Applied Mathematics; Mathematics; Mathematics and Computer Science); **Mechanical Engineering** (Automotive Engineering; Industrial Design; Materials Engineering; Mechanical Engineering; Production Engineering; Thermal Engineering); **Metallurgical and Materials Engineering** (Materials Engineering; Metallurgical Engineering); **Physical Education** (Physical Education); **Physics** (Electronic Engineering; Physical Engineering; Physics)

Centre

Educational Technology (Educational Technology); **Value Education** (Peace and Disarmament)

History: Founded 1959 as Regional Engineering College, Warangal. Acquired present title and status of Deemed University 2002. An 'Institution of National Importance'.

Degrees and Diplomas: *Bachelor's Degree (professional)*; *Master's Degree*; *Doctor of Philosophy*. Also MBA

Student Services: Sports Facilities
Last Updated: 07/07/11

NATIONAL LAW INSTITUTE UNIVERSITY

PB N° 369, Bhopal Bhadbhada Road, Barkheri Kalan,
Bhopal, Madhya Pradesh 462003
Tel: +91(755) 269-6717
Fax: +91(755) 269-6965
EMail: info@nliu.com
Website: http://www.nliu.com

Director: S.S. Singh
Tel: +91(755) 269-6965 EMail: director@nliu.com

Registrar: Chandrakanta Garg EMail: registrar@nliu.com

Programme

Law (Accountancy; Administrative Law; Civil Law; Commercial Law; Computer Science; Constitutional Law; Criminal Law; Criminology; Economics; Finance; History; Human Rights; International Business; International Law; Labour Law; Law; Political Sciences; Sociology)

History: Founded 1997.

Fees: (Rupees): Undergraduate tuition, 49,500 per annum; Graduate, 35,000 per annum

Degrees and Diplomas: *Bachelor's Degree*; *Bachelor's Degree (professional)*; *Master's Degree*. Also Bachelor's degree Honours.

Student Services: Canteen, Health Services, Sports Facilities
Last Updated: 07/07/11

NATIONAL LAW SCHOOL OF INDIA UNIVERSITY (NLS)

P.O. Bag 7201, Nagarbhavi, Bangalore, Karnataka 560 072
Tel: +91(80) 2321-3160 +91(80) 2316-0532
Fax: +91(80) 2316-0534
EMail: registrar@nls.ac.in
Website: http://www.nls.ac.in

Director: R. Venkata Rao
EMail: vice-chancellor@nls.ac.in; vc@nls.ac.in; venkatarao@nls.ac.in; profrao@yahoo.com

Registrar: V. Nagara EMail: registrar@nls.ac.in

Programme

Distance Education (Commercial Law; Consumer Studies; Environmental Studies; Ethics; Human Rights; Law); **Law** *(Undergraduate)* (Administrative Law; Civil Law; Constitutional Law; Criminal Law; Economics; English; Fiscal Law; History; Human Rights; International Law; Labour Law; Law; Political Sciences; Sociology); **Law** *(Postgraduate)* (Commercial Law; Constitutional Law; Human Rights; Law; Social Studies); **Research Degrees** (Law)

History: Founded 1987 by an Act of the Karnataka State Legislature, sponsored by the Bar Council of India.

Academic Year: July to May (July-September; November-January; March-May)

Admission Requirements: 12th year senior secondary/intermediate examination with aggregate marks of not less than 50%, or foreign equivalent

Fees: (Rupees): 80,000 per annum; Postgraduate programmes, 30,000 per annum; Foreign students, (US Dollars), 5,000 per annum. Registration fees for research degrees, 10,000-15,000 for indian students and 35,000-52,000 for foreign students. Distance education programmes, 10,150-11,100 per annum for Indian students and 35,000-43,000 per annum for foreign students

Main Language(s) of Instruction: English

Degrees and Diplomas: *Bachelor's Degree*; *Bachelor's Degree (professional)*; *Postgraduate Diploma*; *Master's Degree*; *Master of Philosophy*; *Doctor of Philosophy*. Also Bachelor's degree Honours.

Student Services: Canteen, Health Services, Sports Facilities

Publications: March of the Law; National Law School Journal
Last Updated: 07/07/11

NATIONAL LAW UNIVERSITY - JODHPUR (NLU)

NH-65, Nagour Road, Mandore, Jodhpur, Rajasthan 342304
Tel: +91(291) 257-7530 +91(291) 257-7526
Fax: +91(291) 257-7540
EMail: nlu-jod-rj@nic.in
Website: http://www.nlujodhpur.ac.in

Vice-Chancellor: N.N. Mathur (2007-)
Tel: +91 9829027701 EMail: nnmathurj@gmail.com

Registrar: Ratan Lahoti

Programme

Business Administration and Law *(Undergraduate)* (Business Administration; Finance; Human Resources; Law; Management; Marketing; Mathematics; Statistics); **Corporate Laws** *(Postgraduate)* (Commercial Law; International Law; Law; Taxation); **Distance Education** (Commercial Law; Criminal Law; Criminology; Forensic Medicine and Dentistry; International Business); **Insurance** *(Postgraduate - MBA)* (Accountancy; Commercial Law; Communication Studies; Finance; Insurance; Management; Marketing); **Insurance** *(Postgraduate - Master of Science)* (Actuarial Science; Communication Studies; Insurance); **Intellectual Property Rights (IPR) and Technology Law** *(Postgraduate)* (Biotechnology; Chemistry; Commercial Law; Economics; Law; Management; Physics; Private Law); **Political Sciences and Law** *(Undergraduate)* (Economics; History; Law; Philosophy; Political Sciences; Psychology; Sociology); **Research Degree** *(In collaboration with National Law University (NLU))* (Administrative Law; Analytical Chemistry; Banking; Biological and Life Sciences; Chemistry; Commercial Law; Constitutional Law; Criminal Law; Economics; Environmental Studies; Finance; Human Resources; Law; Literature; Marketing; Natural Sciences; Philosophy; Physics; Political Sciences; Psychology); **Research Degree** *(In collaboration with National Law University (NLU))* (Law); **Technology and Law** *(Undergraduate)* (Applied Chemistry; Biotechnology; Electronic Engineering; Industrial Chemistry; Information Technology; Law; Nanotechnology; Pharmacology; Polymer and Plastics Technology; Technology; Telecommunications Engineering)

School

Insurance *(SIS-NLU)* (Business Administration; Insurance; Management)
History: Founded 1999.
Academic Year: July to April
Admission Requirements: Admissions are conducted strictly on the basis of National Entrance Test and minimum eligibility criteria is 50% marks aggregate in 10+2 for Undergraduate Courses and 55% marks aggregate in Undergraduate for Postgraduate Courses
Fees: (Rupees): Fee, 42,500 per semester for Indian students and (US Dollars): 1,800 per semester for Foreign students
Main Language(s) of Instruction: English
Accrediting Agency: National Assessment and Accreditation Council
Degrees and Diplomas: *Bachelor's Degree*; *Bachelor's Degree (professional)*; *Master's Degree*; *Doctor of Philosophy*: **Law; Public Administration; Social Sciences.** Also Bachelor's degree honours and MBA
Student Services: Academic Counselling, Canteen, Careers Guidance, Cultural Activities, Health Services, Language Laboratory, Social Counselling, Sports Facilities
Publications: 'Scholasticus' Journal
Publishing House: Vijay Printers, Johdpur, Rajasthan, India
Last Updated: 07/07/11

NATIONAL LAW UNIVERSITY - NEW DELHI (NLU DELHI)

Sector 14, Dwarka, New Delhi 110 078
Tel: +91(11) 2803-4993 +91(11) 2803-4257
EMail: info@nludelhi.ac.in
Website: http://nludelhi.ac.in

Vice-Chancellor: Ranbir Singh

Registrar: Srikrishna Deva Rao

Programme

Law (Law)
History: Founded 2008.
Fees: Undergraduate tuition fee, 35,000 per semester; Graduate tuition fee, 65,000 per semester (Indian Rupee)
Degrees and Diplomas: *Postgraduate Diploma*; *Master's Degree*; *Doctor of Philosophy*. Also Honours Bachelor's degree (B.A., LL.B. (Hons.)), 5yrs
Student Services: Health Services, Sports Facilities
Last Updated: 06/01/12

NATIONAL LAW UNIVERSITY - ORISSA (NLUO)

Chahata Ghat, Mahanadi Ring Road, Tulasipur, Cuttack, Orissa 753 008
Tel: +91(671) 250-6516
Fax: +91(671) 250-6516
EMail: registrar@nluo.ac.in
Website: http://www.nluo.ac.in/

Vice-Chancellor: V. Nagaraj

Registrar: Pabitra Mohan Samal Tel: +91(671) 250-6516

School
Liberal Arts (Arts and Humanities; Comparative Politics; Development Studies; Economics; Film; Finance; Gender Studies; Government; International Economics; Law; Literature; Mass Communication; Political Sciences; Public Administration; Religion; Social Studies; Sociology; Urban Studies); **Managerial Excellence** (Accountancy; Behavioural Sciences; Economics; Ethics; Finance; Human Resources; Industrial and Organizational Psychology; Leadership; Management; Marketing); **Private Law** (Civil Law; Commercial Law; International Law; Labour Law; Law; Private Law); **Public Law** (Administrative Law; Constitutional Law; Criminal Law; Environmental Studies; Fiscal Law; Human Rights; Law; Public Law; Taxation)

History: Founded 2008.

Degrees and Diplomas: *Bachelor's Degree*; *Master's Degree*; *Doctor of Philosophy*. Also Conjoint Undergraduate and Postgraduate Programmes (B.A.LL.B; B.B.A.LL.B; LL.M-PhD)

Last Updated: 04/01/12

NATIONAL MUSEUM INSTITUTE OF HISTORY OF ART, CONSERVATION AND MUSEOLOGY (NMI)

National Museum, Janpath, New Delhi 110011
Tel: +91(11) 2301-1901
Fax: +91(11) 2301-1921
EMail: dgnationalmuseum@gmail.com
Website: http://nmi.gov.in

Vice-Chancellor: C.V. Ananda Bose
Tel: +91(11) 230-18159 EMail: dgnationalmuseum@gmail.com

Registrar: K.K. Kulshreshtha
Tel: +91(11) 230-11901 EMail: kkshreshtha@indiatimes.com

Programme
Conservation (Fine Arts; Heritage Preservation; Museum Studies); **History of Art** (Aesthetics; Architecture; Art History; Heritage Preservation; Museum Studies); **Museology** (Art History; Art Management; Heritage Preservation; Marketing; Museum Management; Museum Studies; Public Relations)

History: Founded 1989. A postgraduate Institution with 'deemed University' status.

Admission Requirements: University degree at Master level and examination. Interview for Doctorate

Fees: (Rupees): For Indian students, Master's degree, 1,200 per semester; Ph.D. 3,000 per annum; For Foreign students, Master's degree, 100 per semester, PhD per annum and certificates (Rupees) 3,000 per course

Degrees and Diplomas: *Master's Degree*; *Doctor of Philosophy*. Also short-term undergraduate certificate courses.

Last Updated: 08/07/11

NATIONAL SANSKRIT UNIVERSITY

Rashtriya Sanskrit Vidyapeetha
Tirupati, Andhra Pradesh 517064
Tel: +91(877) 228-7649 +91(877) 228-6799
Fax: +91(877) 228-7809
EMail: registrar_rsvp@yahoo.co.in
Website: http://rsvidyapeetha.ac.in

Vice-Chancellor: Harekrishna Satapathy (2006-)
Tel: +91(877) 228-7838 EMail: hks_vc@yahoo.co.in

Registrar: A. Gurumurthi
Tel: +91(877) 223-0840
EMail: registrar_rsvp@yahoo.co.in; agmurti@gmail.com

Faculty
Darshanas (Holy Writings; Philosophical Schools; Philosophy; Sanskrit; Yoga); **Pedagogy** (Education; Educational Research; Pedagogy; Physical Education); **Sahitya and Samskriti** (Arts and Humanities; Asian Religious Studies; English; Hindi; Indic Languages; Literature; Sanskrit); **Veda Vedangas** (Computer Science; Esoteric Practices; Grammar; Linguistics; Mathematics; Sanskrit)

History: Founded 1962. Acquired 'Deemed University' status 1987.

Academic Year: July to April/May

Admission Requirements: 12th year senior secondary/intermediate examination or recognized foreign equivalent

Fees: (Rupees): Tuition fee for undegraduate programmes, 250-380 per annum; Graduate programmes, 450-5,000 per annum

Main Language(s) of Instruction: Sanskrit, English, Hindi, Telugu

Degrees and Diplomas: *Post Diploma*; *Bachelor's Degree*; *Bachelor's Degree (professional)*; *Postgraduate Diploma*; *Master's Degree*; *Master of Philosophy*; *Doctor of Philosophy*. Also Intermediate courses; Career Oriented Programmes

Student Services: Health Services, Language Laboratory, Sports Facilities

Last Updated: 19/07/11

NATIONAL UNIVERSITY OF ADVANCED LEGAL STUDIES (NUALS)

Kinfra Salut-Tech Park, HMT Colony, PO Kalamassery, Ernakulam, Kochi, Kerala 683 503
EMail: vc@nuals.ac.in
Website: http://www.nuals.ac.in/

Vice-Chancellor: Rose Varghese EMail: vc@nuals.ac.in

Registrar: V. Narayana Swami
Tel: +91(484) 255-5990 EMail: registrar@nuals.ac.in

Programme
Law (Ethics; Fiscal Law; Law)

History: Founded 2005 through merger with National Institute for Advanced Legal Studies (NIALS).

Accrediting Agency: University Grants Commission (UGC)

Degrees and Diplomas: *Bachelor's Degree (professional)*; *Postgraduate Diploma*; *Master's Degree*; *Doctor of Philosophy*. Also Certificate

Student Numbers *2010-2011*: Total: c. 310

Last Updated: 04/01/12

NATIONAL UNIVERSITY OF EDUCATIONAL PLANNING AND ADMINISTRATION (NUEPA)

17-B, Sri Aurobindo Marg, New Delhi 110 016
Tel: +91(11) 268-63562 +91(11) 269-62335
Fax: +91(11) 268-53041 +91(11) 268-65180
EMail: nuepa@nuepa.org
Website: http://www.nuepa.org/

Vice-Chancellor: R. Govinda
EMail: vc@nuepa.org; rgovinda@nuepa.org

Registrar: B.K. Singh EMail: registrar@nuepa.org

Department
Comparative Education and International Cooperation (Education; Educational Sciences; International Relations); **Educational Administration** (Educational Administration); **Educational Finance** (Educational Sciences; Finance); **Educational Management Information System** (Educational Administration; Educational Technology); **Educational Planning** (Educational Sciences); **Educational Policy** (Educational Sciences); **Foundations of Education** (Education); **Higher and Professional Education** (Higher Education; Vocational Education); **Inclusive Education** (Education; Educational Sciences); **School and Non-Formal Education** (Education)

History: A 'Deemed University'.

Degrees and Diplomas: *Master of Philosophy*; *Doctor of Philosophy*. Also Post-Doctoral Programmes and award degrees.

Last Updated: 19/12/11

NATIONAL UNIVERSITY OF STUDY AND RESEARCH IN LAW, RANCHI (NUSRL)

Polytechnic Campus, BIT Mesra, Ranchi, Jharkhand 835217
Tel: +91(651) 2275-250 +91(651) 6570-860
Fax: +91(651) 2275-028
EMail: info@nusrlranchi.com; nusrlranchi@gmail.com
Website: http://nusrlranchi.com/

Vice-Chancellor: A.K. Koul

Registrar: Aloke Kumar Sengupta

Programme

Law (Agricultural Economics; Arts and Humanities; Constitutional Law; Criminal Law; Economics; Environmental Studies; Family Studies; History of Law; Human Rights; International Relations; Law; Philosophy; Political Sciences; Social Sciences)

History: Founded 2010.

Fees: (Indian Rupee): Undergraduate tuition, 50,000 per semester; Ph.D., 25,000 per semestrer

Accrediting Agency: University Grants Commission (UGC)

Degrees and Diplomas: *Bachelor's Degree (professional)*; *Master's Degree*; *Doctor of Philosophy*. The Bachelor's degree offered is a combined BA(Hons.) LLB(Hons); Also integrated Doctor of Juridical Sciences(JSD)/LLM and PhD programmes.

Last Updated: 30/08/11

NAVA NALANDA MAHAVIHARA

Nalanda, Bihar 803-111
Tel: +91(611) 228-1672
Fax: +91(611) 228-1505
EMail: nnmdirector@sify.com
Website: http://navanalandamahavihara.org/

Vice-Chancellor: Ravindra Panth

Registrar: S.P. Sinha
Tel: +91(611) 228-1672 EMail: spsinhanalanda@gmail.com

Course

Ancient History, Culture and Archaeology *(Postgraduate)* (Ancient Civilizations; Archaeology; Cultural Studies); **Buddhism and Languages** *(Postgraduate)* (Asian Religious Studies; Modern Languages); **Buddhist Studies** *(Postgraduate)* (Asian Religious Studies); **Chinese and Japanese** *(Postgraduate)* (Chinese; Japanese); **English** *(Postgraduate)* (English); **Hindi** *(Postgraduate)* (Hindi); **Pali** *(Postgraduate)* (Indic Languages); **Pali** (Indic Languages); **Philosophy** *(Postgraduate)* (Philosophy); **Sanskrit** *(Postgraduate)* (Sanskrit); **Tibetan Studies** *(Postgraduate)* (Tibetan); **Tibetan Studies** (Tibetan)

History: Founded 1951. A 'Deemed University'.

Degrees and Diplomas: *Post Diploma*; *Bachelor's Degree*; *Master's Degree*. Also Certificates and Preparatory Course.

Last Updated: 08/12/11

NAVRACHNA UNIVERSITY

Vasna Road, Vadodara, Gujarat 391 140
Tel: +91(265) 2254-392 +91(265) 2250-705
EMail: university@navrachana.edu.in
Website: http://university.navrachana.edu.in

President: Rahul Amin

Provost: Veena Mistry

School

Business and Law (Business Administration; Finance; International Business; Management; Marketing); **Engineering and Technology** (Computer Engineering; Computer Science); **Environmental Design and Architecture** (Architecture; Arts and Humanities; Communication Arts; Environmental Studies); **Science and Education** (Biochemistry; Biology; Botany; Chemistry; Ecology; Education; Electronic Engineering; English; Genetics; Mathematics; Molecular Biology; Natural Sciences; Nuclear Physics; Optics; Physics; Physiology; Special Education; Statistics; Thermal Physics)

History: Founded 2009.

Fees: (Indian Rupee): 20,000-38,000 per semester for Indian students; 30,000-55,000 per semester for international students

Accrediting Agency: University Grants Commission (UGC)

Degrees and Diplomas: *Bachelor's Degree*; *Bachelor's Degree (professional)*; *Postgraduate Diploma*; *Master's Degree*; *Doctor of Philosophy*. Also Short-term programmes; Dual BCA+MCA Programme.

Student Services: Canteen, Sports Facilities

Last Updated: 25/08/11

NEHRU GRAM BHARTI UNIVERSITY

Nehru Gram Bharati Vishwavidyalaya

Hanumanganj Campus, G.T. Road, Hanumanganj, Allahabad, Uttar Pradesh
EMail: info@ngbu.edu.in
Website: http://www.ngbu.edu.in

Vice-Chancellor: K.B. Pandeya EMail: kbpandeya@yahoo.com

Course

Computer Application *(Vocational)* (Computer Science); **Education** *(Vocational)* (Education); **Journalism** *(Vocational)* (Journalism); **Law** *(Vocational)* (Law); **Management** *(Vocational)* (Management); **Others** *(Vocational)* (Rural Studies; Social Work); **Special Education** *(Vocational)* (Special Education)

Group

Commerce (Business and Commerce); **Humanities** (Ancient Civilizations; Arts and Humanities; Economics; Education; English; Hindi; Home Economics; Music; Philosophy; Political Sciences; Sanskrit; Sociology); **Science** (Botany; Chemistry; Home Economics; Mathematics; Natural Sciences; Physics; Zoology)

Further Information: Also Hanumanganj campus

History: Founded 2008. A 'Deemed University'.

Accrediting Agency: National Assessment and Accreditation Council (NAAC); University Grants Commission (UGC)

Degrees and Diplomas: *Bachelor's Degree*; *Bachelor's Degree (professional)*; *Postgraduate Diploma*; *Master's Degree*; *Doctor of Philosophy*

Last Updated: 19/12/11

NETAJI SUBHAS OPEN UNIVERSITY (NSOU)

1, Woodburn Park, Kolkata, West Bengal 700 020
Tel: +91(33) 2283-5157
Fax: +91(33) 2283-5082
EMail: registrar@wbnsou.com
Website: http://www.wbnsou.ac.in

Vice-Chancellor: Manimala Das (2008-)
Tel: +91(33) 2283-5157 EMail: manimala.das@gmail.com

Registrar: Bikas Ghosh Tel: +91(33) 2283-5157 Ext. 13

Programme

Postgraduate Studies (Advertising and Publicity; Education; English; Foreign Languages Education; Geography; History; Information Sciences; Journalism; Library Science; Mass Communication; Mathematics; Political Sciences; Public Administration; Public Relations; Radio and Television Broadcasting; Social Work; South and Southeast Asian Languages; Zoology); **Undergraduate Studies** (Botany; Business and Commerce; Chemistry; Economics; English; Geography; History; Human Rights; Information Sciences; Library Science; Mathematics; Physics; Political Sciences; Public Administration; Social Sciences; Sociology; South and Southeast Asian Languages; Special Education; Zoology)

Course

Innovative Studies *(Non-conventional)* (Business Computing; Cardiology; Clothing and Sewing; Computer Engineering; Computer Networks; Fashion Design; Health Administration; Management; Medical Auxiliaries; Multimedia; Nursing; Physical Therapy; Preschool Education; Psychology; Retailing and Wholesaling; Small Business; Social Work; Women's Studies); **Professional Studies** (Computer Science; Health Administration; Nursing); **Vocational Studies** *(Job oriented)* (Business Computing; Computer Engineeering; Computer Networks; Fashion Design; Fishery; Horticulture; Information Technology; Laboratory Techniques; Medical Technology; Physical Therapy; Tourism; Yoga)

Further Information: 191 Study Centres; 6 campuses in Kolkata, Salt Lake City and Kalyani.

History: Founded 1997.

Fees: (Rupees): Undegraduate programmes,9,990-19,990 per semester; Postgraduate degree programmes, 10,000-16,000; Vocational diploma courses, 1,200-12,000 per annum; Professional degree programmes, 10,000-28,000 per annum

Accrediting Agency: University Grants Commission (UGC); Distance Education Council (DEC); Govt. of West Bengal; Dept. of Education, Ministry of Human Resources Development, Govt. of India;

Degrees and Diplomas: *Post Diploma*; *Bachelor's Degree*; *Bachelor's Degree (professional)*; *Postgraduate Diploma*; *Master's Degree*; *Master of Philosophy*. Also Bachelor's degree Honours; Certificate courses in Computer Science; Vocational programmes.

Last Updated: 08/07/11

NEW DELHI INSTITUTE OF MANAGEMENT (NDIM)

60 & 50(B&C), Behind Batra Hospital, Tughlakabad Institutional Area, New Delhi 110 062
Tel: +91(11) 2995-6566 +91(11) 2995-67
Fax: +91(11) 2996-5136
EMail: info@ndimdelhi.org
Website: http://www.ndimdelhi.org/

Director: Sudhiranjan Dey

Programme

Management (Finance; Human Resources; Information Technology; International Business; Management; Marketing; Operations Research); **Management** *(Part-time)* (Economics; Finance; Information Technology; International Business; Management; Marketing; Statistics); **Management (Marketing)** (Management; Marketing)

History: Founded 1996.

Accrediting Agency: All India Council for Technical Education (AICTE), Ministry of HRD, Government of India; National Board of Accreditation (NBA)

Degrees and Diplomas: *Postgraduate Diploma*. Postgraduate Degree equivalent to a university MBA degree.

Student Services: Canteen, Health Services, Sports Facilities
Last Updated: 23/01/12

NILAMBER-PITAMBER UNIVERSITY (NPU)

Palamu district, Medininagar, Jharkhand
Tel: +91(6562) 231-580
EMail: vc@npu.ac.in
Website: http://www.npu.ac.in/

Vice-Chancellor: Firoz Ahmad Tel: +91(6562) 231-580

Registrar: P. K. Verma
Tel: +91(94311) 55-097 EMail: pkv_ru@yahoo.com

College

G.L.A. *(Medininagar, Palamau)* (Botany; Chemistry; English; Geography; Geology; Hindi; History; Mathematics; Physics; Political Sciences; Psychology; Urdu; Zoology); **S.S.J.S.N.** *(Garhwa)* (Anthropology; Botany; Business and Commerce; Chemistry; Economics; English; Geography; Geology; Hindi; History; Mathematics; Philosophy; Physics; Political Sciences; Psychology; Sanskrit; Sociology; Urdu; Zoology); **Y.S.N.M.** *(Medininagar)* (Botany; Chemistry; Economics; English; Hindi; History; Home Economics; Mathematics; Philosophy; Physics; Political Sciences; Psychology; Zoology)

Further Information: Also 4 Constituent Colleges; 8 Affiliated Colleges; 5 Professional/Technical Colleges

History: Founded 2009.

Degrees and Diplomas: *Bachelor's Degree*; *Bachelor's Degree (professional)*; *Master's Degree*; *Doctor of Philosophy*
Last Updated: 03/01/12

NIMS UNIVERSITY

Shobha Nagar, Delhi Highway, Jaipur, Rajasthan 303 121
Tel: +91(1426) 513-102 +91(1426) 513-103
Fax: +91(141) 2605-050 +91(1426) 213-909
EMail: info@nimsuniversity.org; chairman@nimsuniversity.org
Website: http://nimsuniversity.org

Vice-Chancellor: K.C. Singhal

Registrar: K. P. Singh

College

Dentistry (Dentistry; Medical Auxiliaries); **Nursing** (Nursing; Surgery)

Programme

Distance Education (Accountancy; Air Transport; Banking; Communication Arts; Computer Networks; Dental Technology; Diabetology; Environmental Management; Environmental Studies; Health Administration; Heritage Preservation; Insurance; International Business; Jewellery Art; Journalism; Laboratory Techniques; Management; Mass Communication; Medical Technology; Microbiology; Musical Instruments; Nursing; Ophthalmology; Optics; Orthodox Theology; Pharmacy; Photography; Physical Therapy; Psychology; Radiology; Sports; Taxation; Tourism; Treatment Techniques; Venereology; Video)

School

Architecture and Planning (Architecture and Planning); **Law** (Law)

Institute

Advance Sciences (Biochemistry; Biotechnology; Microbiology; Natural Sciences); **Advanced Engineering** (Aeronautical and Aerospace Engineering; Biotechnology; Chemical Engineering; Civil Engineering; Computer Science; Electrical Engineering; Electronic Engineering; Energy Engineering; Engineering; Geology; Industrial Engineering; Information Technology; Nuclear Engineering; Petroleum and Gas Engineering; Power Engineering; Structural Architecture; Telecommunications Engineering; Thermal Engineering); **Air Hostess and Aviation** (Air Transport); **Applied Arts** (Fine Arts; Performing Arts; Visual Arts); **Basic Sciences** (Botany; Chemistry; Environmental Studies; Geography; Geology; Home Economics; Mathematics; Physics; Psychology; Statistics; Zoology); **Commerce** (Business and Commerce); **Computer Science** (Computer Science; Electronic Engineering; Information Technology); **Education and Physical Education** (Health Education; Physical Education; Sports); **Engineering and Technology** (Agricultural Engineering; Automotive Engineering; Biotechnology; Chemical Engineering; Civil Engineering; Computer Engineering; Computer Science; Electrical Engineering; Electronic Engineering; Engineering; Information Technology; Mechanical Engineering; Technology; Telecommunications Engineering); **Hotel Management and Tourism** (Cooking and Catering; Food Technology; Hotel Management; Tourism); **Humanities and Social Sciences** (Anthropology; Arts and Humanities; Economics; English; Geography; Hindi; History; Philosophy; Political Sciences; Psychology; Public Administration; Rural Studies; Sanskrit; Social Sciences; Social Welfare; Sociology); **Journalism and Mass Communication** (Journalism; Mass Communication); **Library Science** (Information Sciences; Library Science); **Management** (Banking; Business Administration; Finance; Health Administration; Human Resources; Information Sciences; Information Technology; International Business; Management; Marketing; Pharmacy; Retailing and Wholesaling); **Medical Sciences and Research and Hospital** *(NIMS Medical College)* (Anaesthesiology; Anatomy; Biochemistry; Community Health; Dermatology; Forensic Medicine and Dentistry; Genetics; Gynaecology and Obstetrics; Health Administration; Immunology; Medicine; Microbiology; Ophthalmology; Orthopaedics; Otorhinolaryngology; Paediatrics; Pathology; Pharmacology; Physiology; Pneumology; Radiophysics; Surgery; Venereology); **Paramedical Technology** (Laboratory Techniques; Medical Auxiliaries; Medical Technology; Ophthalmology; Optometry; Radiology; Treatment Techniques); **Pharmacy** (Chemistry; Marketing; Pharmacology; Pharmacy; Safety Engineering); **Physiotheraphy** (Cardiology; Gynaecology and Obstetrics; Neurology; Neurosciences; Occupational Therapy; Orthopaedics; Paediatrics; Physical Therapy; Respiratory Therapy); **Textile and Fashion Design** (Fashion Design; Journalism; Marketing; Textile Design; Textile Technology); **Theatre, Film and Television Technology** (Acting; Film; Graphic Arts; Radio and Television Broadcasting; Theatre; Visual Arts)

History: Founded 2008.

Fees: (Indian Rupee): Undergraduate programmes, 15,000-295,000 per annum; Postgraduate programmes, 17,000-600,000 per annum; Ph.D., 55,000-150,000 per annum

Degrees and Diplomas: *Post Diploma*; *Bachelor's Degree*; *Bachelor's Degree (professional)*; *Postgraduate Diploma*; *Master's Degree*; *Master of Philosophy*; *Doctor of Philosophy*. Also Certificates; Honours Bachelor's degrees; Dual Specialization (B.Tech/B.Tech); M. Tech. Integrated with B.Tech; MBA and integrated MBA

Student Services: Canteen, Cultural Activities, Sports Facilities

Last Updated: 05/09/11

NIRMA UNIVERSITY

Sarkhej-Gandhinagar Highway, Post: Chandlodia, Via: Gota, Ahmedabad, Gujarat 382 481
Tel: +91 (2717) 241-900 +91 (2717) 241-911
Fax: +91 (2717) 241-916 +91 (2717) 241-917
EMail: asst_registrar@nirmauni.ac.in
Website: http://www.nirmauni.ac.in/

Vice-Chancellor/Director General: N. V. Vasani
Tel: +91(2717) 241-230 EMail: vc@nirmauni.ac.in

Executive Registrar: Shri D.P. Chhaya
Tel: +91(2717) 241-168 EMail: registrar@nirmauni.ac.in

Faculty

Law (Commercial Law; Law); **Management** (Business Administration; Finance; Human Resources; International Business; Management; Operations Research); **Pharmacy** (Biotechnology; Chemistry; Pharmacology; Pharmacy); **Science** (Biochemistry; Biotechnology; Microbiology); **Technology and Engineering** (Automation and Control Engineering; Chemical Engineering; Civil Engineering; Computer Engineering; Computer Science; Electrical Engineering; Electronic Engineering; Engineering; Information Technology; Measurement and Precision Engineering; Mechanical Engineering; Polymer and Plastics Technology; Technology; Telecommunications Engineering)

History: Founded 1994, as Nirma Education and Research Foundation. Acquired present status and name 2003 through the merger of the Foundation's various institutes.

Accrediting Agency: University Grants Commission (UGC)

Degrees and Diplomas: *Post Diploma*; *Bachelor's Degree*; *Bachelor's Degree (professional)*; *Postgraduate Diploma*; *Master's Degree*; *Doctor of Philosophy*. Also Bachelor's degree Honours and MBA

Student Services: Canteen, Sports Facilities

Last Updated: 08/07/11

NITTE UNIVERSITY

6th Flr, University Enclave, Medical Sciences Complex, Deralakatte, Mangalore, Karnataka 575018
Tel: +91(824) 220-4300 +91(824) 220-4301
Fax: +91(824) 220-4305
EMail: info@nitte.edu.in; admissions@nitte.edu.in
Website: http://nitte.edu.in/

Vice-Chancellor: M. Shantharam Shetty

Registrar: H.V. Sudhaker Nayak

Institute

Dental Sciences *(A. B. Shetty Memorial)* (Dentistry; Microbiology; Oral Pathology; Orthodontics; Periodontics; Radiology; Surgery); **Nursing Sciences** *(Nitte Usha)* (Child Care and Development; Community Health; Midwifery; Nursing; Psychiatry and Mental Health; Surgery); **Pharmaceutical Sciences** *(Nitte Gulabi Shetty Memorial)* (Biotechnology; Chemistry; Microbiology; Pharmacology; Pharmacy); **Physiotherapy** (Physical Therapy)

Academy

Medicine *(K. S. Hegde)* (Anatomy; Biochemistry; Biophysics; Community Health; Forensic Medicine and Dentistry; Gynaecology and Obstetrics; Medicine; Microbiology; Pathology; Pharmacology; Physiology; Surgery; Toxicology)

History: Founded 1979 as the Nitte Education Trust. Acquired 'Deemeed University' status 2008.

Degrees and Diplomas: *Bachelor's Degree (professional)*; *Postgraduate Diploma*; *Master's Degree*; *Doctor of Philosophy*

Last Updated: 14/12/11

NIZAM'S INSTITUTE OF MEDICAL SCIENCES (NIMS)

Punjagutta, Hyderabad, Andhra Pradesh 500 082
Tel: +91(40) 2348-9000
Fax: +91(40) 2331-0076
EMail: nims@ap.nic.in
Website: http://nims.ap.nic.in/

Director: Prasanta Mahapatra
Tel: +91(40) 2339-0933 +91(40)2348-9999
EMail: Director.nims@ap.nic.in

Executive Registrar: M. Sudershanam
Tel: +91(40) 2339-9690 +91(40) 2348-9130
EMail: er.nims@ap.nic.in

Division

Computer (Computer Science)

College

Nursing (Gynaecology and Obstetrics; Midwifery; Nursing; Paediatrics; Psychiatry and Mental Health; Surgery)

Department

Anaesthesiology and Intensive Care (Anaesthesiology; Respiratory Therapy); **Biochemistry** (Biochemistry); **Biomedical Engineering** (Biomedical Engineering); **Cardiology** (Cardiology); **Cardiothoracic Surgery** (Cardiology; Surgery); **Chest Clinic** (Pneumology); **Civil** (Civil Security); **Clinical Pharmacology and Therapeutics** (Pharmacology; Pharmacy); **Dental Studies** (Dental Hygiene; Dentistry); **Dermatology** (Dermatology); **Electrical** (Electrical Engineering); **Endocrinology and Metabolism** (Endocrinology); **Gastroenterology** (Gastroenterology); **General Medicine** (Medicine); **Gynaecology** (Gynaecology and Obstetrics); **Hospital Administration** (Health Administration); **Medical Oncology** (Oncology); **Medical Records**; **Microbiology** (Biotechnology; Laboratory Techniques; Medical Technology; Medicine; Microbiology; Nephrology; Nursing; Pathology; Physical Therapy); **Nephrology** (Nephrology); **Neuro Surgery** (Neurological Therapy; Surgery); **Neurology** (Biomedicine; Neurology; Physical Therapy; Psychiatry and Mental Health); **Nuclear Medicine** (Medical Technology); **Orthopaedics** (Orthopaedics); **Paediatrics** (Paediatrics); **Pathology** (Pathology); **Physio Therapy** (Physical Therapy); **Plastic Surgery** (Plastic Surgery); **Radiation Oncology** (Medicine; Nursing; Oncology; Radiology); **Radiology and Imageology** (Radiology); **Rheumatology** (Rheumatology); **Surgical Gastroenterology** (Gastroenterology; Surgery); **Surgical Oncology** (Oncology; Rehabilitation and Therapy; Surgery); **Transfusion Medicine** (Medicine); **Urology** (Urology); **Vascular Surgery** (Cardiology; Surgery)

Further Information: 985 beds hospital.

History: Founded 1980 as Institute of Medical Sciences (IMS). Acquired present title 1986 with the tranfer of the Nizam's Institute of Orthopaedics and Specialities (NIOS), inaugurated 1964. Acquired university status and title 1989.

Accrediting Agency: University Grants Commission (UGC) and Medical Council of India (MCI).

Degrees and Diplomas: *Post Diploma*; *Bachelor's Degree*; *Postgraduate Diploma*; *Master's Degree*; *Doctor of Philosophy*

Academic Staff *2010-2011*: Total: c. 140

Last Updated: 08/07/11

NMIMS UNIVERSITY (NMIMS)

V. L. Mehta Road, Vile Parle (W), Mumbai, Maharashtra 400 056
Tel: +91(22) 2613-4577
EMail: enquiry@nmims.edu; anjali.barmukh@nmims.edu
Website: http://www.nmims.edu

Vice-Chancellor: Rajan Saxena
EMail: vc@nmims.edu; rajan.saxena@nmims.edu

Director (Admin.) and Incharge Registrar: Varsha Parab

School

Architecture *(Balwant Sheth)* (Architecture); **Business Management** (Actuarial Science; Banking; Business Administration; Human Resources; Management); **Commerce** *(Anil Surendra Modi)*

(Accountancy; Business Administration; Business and Commerce; Finance; Taxation); **Distance Learning** *(SDL)* (Management); **Pharmacy and Technology Management** (Biotechnology; Business Administration; Chemistry; Health Administration; Pharmacology; Pharmacy; Safety Engineering)); **Science** (Biological and Life Sciences; Chemistry; Statistics); **Technology Management and Engineering** *(Mukesh Patel)* (Chemical Engineering; Civil Engineering; Computer Engineering; Electronic Engineering; Engineering; Engineering Management; Information Technology; Management; Mechanical Engineering; Production Engineering; Telecommunications Engineering)

Further Information: Also campuses in Bengaluru, Shirpur and Hyderabad.

History: Founded 1981 as Narsee Monjee Institute of Management Studies (NMIMS). Acquired present status of 'Deemed University' 2003 and present title 2006.

Fees: (Rupees): Undergraduate programmes, 15,000-130,000; Postgraduate programmes, 30,000-170,000; MBA, 60,000-250,000; PhD, 30,000-45,000

Degrees and Diplomas: *Post Diploma*; *Bachelor's Degree*; *Bachelor's Degree (professional)*; *Postgraduate Diploma*; *Master's Degree*; *Doctor of Philosophy*. Also Bachelor's degree honours; M.B.A; Integrated Master of Science – Doctor of Philosophy Programme.

Academic Staff *2010-2011*: Total: c. 200

Student Numbers *2010-2011*: Total: c. 5,000

Last Updated: 08/07/11

NOIDA INTERNATIONAL UNIVERSITY (NIU)

309, Jaipuria Plaza, Sector - 26, Noida, Uttar Pradesh 201 301
Tel: +91(120) 455-6360
Fax: +91(120) 416-7418
EMail: info@niu.ac.in
Website: http://www.niu.ac.in/

Vice-Chancellor: Vikram Singh EMail: vc@niu.ac.in

Dean, Administration: Mian Jan

School

Architecture (Architecture); **Business Management** (Air Transport; Business Administration; Finance; Human Resources; International Business; Labour and Industrial Relations; Management; Marketing; Transport Management); **Education** (Education); **Engineering and Technology** (Aeronautical and Aerospace Engineering; Automation and Control Engineering; Biotechnology; Civil Engineering; Computer Engineering; Computer Science; Electrical Engineering; Electronic Engineering; Energy Engineering; Engineering; Information Technology; Mechanical Engineering; Nanotechnology; Technology; Telecommunications Engineering); **Fashion** (Fashion Design; Jewellery Art; Textile Design; Textile Technology); **Fine Arts** (Fashion Design; Fine Arts; Painting and Drawing; Sculpture; Textile Design); **Home Economics** (Development Studies; Home Economics; Interior Design; Nutrition; Textile Technology); **Hotel Management** (Hotel Management); **Journalism and Mass Communication** (Advertising and Publicity; Journalism; Marketing; Mass Communication; Media Studies; Multimedia; Public Relations; Radio and Television Broadcasting; Sound Engineering (Acoustics)); **Legal Studies and Research** (Law); **Liberal Arts** (Arts and Humanities; English; French; Geography; German; Hindi; History; Home Economics; Modern Languages; Painting and Drawing; Political Sciences; Psychology; Sanskrit; Sociology; Spanish); **Library Science** (Library Science); **Nursing** (Midwifery; Nursing); **Physical Education and Sports Science** (Physical Education; Sports); **Sciences** (Biochemistry; Biotechnology; Industrial Chemistry; Microbiology)

History: Founded 2010.

Fees: (Indian Rupees): undergraduate fee, 10,000-100,000 per semester; graduate fee, 11,250-142,500 per semester

Accrediting Agency: University Grants Commission (UGC)

Degrees and Diplomas: *Post Diploma*; *Bachelor's Degree*; *Bachelor's Degree (professional)*; *Postgraduate Diploma*; *Master's Degree*; *Doctor of Philosophy*. Also Honours Bachelor's degrees, 3 yrs; Dual degrees (B.Tech+ M.Tech), 5 yrs; MBA

Last Updated: 02/01/12

NOORUL ISLAM CENTRE FOR HIGHER EDUCATION (NICHE)

Kumaracoil, Thuckalay, Kanyakumari District,
Thuckalay, Tamilnadu 629 180
Tel: +91(4651) 250-566
Fax: +91(4651) 250-266
EMail: info@niuniv.com
Website: http://www.niuniv.com/

Chancellor: A.P. Majeed Khan
Tel: +91(4651) 252-366 EMail: info@niceindia.com

Vice-Chancellor: R. Perumalsamy EMail: vc@niuniv.com

Director, Human Resources: K.A. Janardhanan
Tel: +91(4651) 252-966 EMail: kajanardhanan@yahoo.com

International Relations: A. Shajin Nargunam, Director, Academic Affairs Tel: +91(4651) 252-440 EMail: shajin@niuniv.com

Faculty

Civil Engineering (Civil Engineering); **Computer and Information Engineering** (Computer Engineering; Computer Science; Information Technology); **Electrical and Electronics Engineering** (Electrical and Electronic Engineering; Electronic Engineering; Telecommunications Engineering); **Interdiscilinary Studies** (Biomedical Engineering; Marine Engineering; Nanotechnology); **Management Studies** (Business Administration); **Mechanical Engineering** (Aeronautical and Aerospace Engineering; Automotive Engineering; Mechanical Engineering); **Science and Humanities** (Chemistry; English; Mathematics; Physics)

History: Founded 1988 as a constituent College of the Noorul Islam University. Acquired 'Deemed University' status 2008.

Academic Year: July to May

Admission Requirements: High School Diploma or equivalent.

Fees: (INR): 107,000 per annum

Main Language(s) of Instruction: English

Accrediting Agency: National Board of Accreditation (NBA); All India Council for Technical Education (AICTE)

Degrees and Diplomas: *Bachelor's Degree (professional)*; *Postgraduate Diploma*; *Master's Degree*; *Master of Philosophy*; *Doctor of Philosophy*. Also MBA

Student Services: Academic Counselling, Canteen, Careers Guidance, Cultural Activities, Facilities for disabled people, Foreign Studies Centre, Health Services, Language Laboratory, Social Counselling, Sports Facilities

Publications: Abstracts of Research Publications; Journal of Emerging Technology; Journal of Emerging Technology in Mechanical Science and Engineering; Noorul Islam Strategic Management

Academic Staff *2012-2013*	MEN	WOMEN	TOTAL
FULL-TIME	189	120	**309**
STAFF WITH DOCTORATE FULL-TIME	54	19	**73**
Student Numbers *2012-2013*			
All (Foreign included)	2,156	795	**2,951**

Last Updated: 15/03/13

NORTH BENGAL AGRICULTURAL UNIVERSITY

Uttar Banga Krishi Vishwavidyalaya (UBKV)
PO Pundibari, Koch Bihar, West Bengal 736165
Tel: +91(3582) 270249
Fax: +91(3582) 270249
EMail: vcubkvv@gmail.com
Website: http://www.ubkv.ac.in

Vice-Chancellor: Biswanath Bandyopadhyay

Faculty

Agricultural Engineering (Agricultural Engineering); **Agriculture** (Agricultural Business; Agriculture; Animal Husbandry; Dairy; Forestry; Home Economics; Veterinary Science); **Horticulture** (Horticulture)

History: Founded 2001. Formerly part of Bidhan Chandra Krishi Viswadidyalaya.

Main Language(s) of Instruction: Hindi

Accrediting Agency: University Grants Commission (UGC); All India Council for Technical Education (AICTE)

Degrees and Diplomas: *Bachelor's Degree*; *Bachelor's Degree (professional)*; *Master's Degree*; *Doctor of Philosophy*. Also MBA

Last Updated: 29/11/11

NORTH-EASTERN HILL UNIVERSITY (NEHU)

Umshing Mawkynroh Shillong, Shillong, Meghalaya 793022
Tel: +91(364) 255-0067
Fax: +91(364) 255-0076
Website: http://www.nehu.ac.in

Vice-Chancellor: A.N. Rai (2010-)
Tel: +91(364) 272-1001 +91(364) 255-0101
EMail: vcnehu@nehu.ac.in

Registrar: Shri Lambha Roy
Tel: +91(364) 272-1012 +91(364) 255-0067
EMail: regtroffice@nehu.ac.in

School

Economics, Management and Information Sciences (Agricultural Business; Business Administration; Business and Commerce; Economics; Finance; Human Resources; Information Sciences; Library Science; Management; Marketing); **Education** (Adult Education; Continuing Education; Distance Education; Education; Floriculture; Management; Mathematics Education; Safety Engineering; Science Education; Special Education); **Human and Environmental Sciences** (Agricultural Economics; Anthropology; Environmental Studies; Geography); **Humanities** (Arts and Humanities; English; Hindi; Linguistics; Literature; Philosophy; South and Southeast Asian Languages; Translation and Interpretation; Writing); **Life Sciences** (Biochemistry; Biological and Life Sciences; Biotechnology; Botany; Cell Biology; Computer Science; Genetics; Microbiology; Molecular Biology; Zoology); **Physical Sciences** (Chemistry; Mathematics; Organic Chemistry; Physics; Statistics); **Social Sciences** (Cultural Studies; Fine Arts; Folklore; History; Law; Music; Musicology; Painting and Drawing; Political Sciences; Prehistory; Social Sciences; Sociology; Visual Arts); **Technology** (Accountancy; Biotechnology; Chemistry; Economics; Electrical and Electronic Engineering; Electrical Engineering; Electronic Engineering; Engineering; Environmental Studies; Finance; Industrial Management; Information Technology; Marketing; Mathematics; Mechanics; Natural Sciences; Physics; Social Sciences; Statistics; Technology; Telecommunications Engineering)

Further Information: The University has two campuses: Shillong Campus (main) and Tura Campus. Also 54 undergraduate colleges affiliated to the University, including eight professional colleges.

History: Founded 1973. A 'Central University'.

Admission Requirements: 12th year senior secondary/intermediate examination or recognized foreign equivalent

Fees: 2,250 - 5,515 per annum (Indian Rupee)

Main Language(s) of Instruction: English

Degrees and Diplomas: *Bachelor's Degree (professional)*; *Postgraduate Diploma*; *Master's Degree*; *Master of Philosophy*; *Doctor of Philosophy*. Also Bachelor's degree honours; Undergraduate Certificates/Diplomas.

Student Services: Canteen, Cultural Activities, Facilities for disabled people, Health Services, Sports Facilities

Publications: N.-E Hill University Journal of Social Sciences and Humanities

Publishing House: Publication Cell

Last Updated: 11/07/11

NORTH EASTERN REGIONAL INSTITUTE OF SCIENCE AND TECHNOLOGY (NERIST)

Nirjuli, Itanagar, Arunachal Pradesh 791 109
Website: http://www.nerist.ac.in

Director: P. K. Das Tel: +91(360) 224-5094 +91(360) 225-7584

Registrar: R. P. Bhattacharjee
Tel: +91(360) 225-7401 EMail: registrar@nerist.ernet.in

Department

Agricultural Engineering (Agricultural Engineering; Agricultural Equipment; Agriculture; Dairy; Energy Engineering; Food Technology; Harvest Technology; Irrigation; Power Engineering; Soil Conservation; Water Science); **Chemistry** (Chemistry; Engineering; Forestry; Technology); **Civil Engineering** (Civil Engineering; Construction Engineering; Engineering; Environmental Engineering; Geological Engineering; Geology; Hydraulic Engineering; Road Engineering; Safety Engineering; Surveying and Mapping); **Computer Science and Engineering** (Artificial Intelligence; Computer Engineering; Computer Graphics; Computer Networks; Computer Science; Data Processing; Electronic Engineering; Information Technology; Mathematics; Software Engineering); **Electrical Engineering** (Automation and Control Engineering; Electrical Engineering; Energy Engineering; Maintenance Technology; Measurement and Precision Engineering; Power Engineering); **Electronics and Communication Engineering** (Electronic Engineering; Telecommunications Engineering); **Forestry** (Forestry); **Humanities and Social Science** (Agricultural Business; Arts and Humanities; Business Administration; Economics; English; Management; Mass Communication; Psychology; Social Sciences; Sociology); **Mathematics** (Applied Mathematics; Mathematics; Statistics); **Mechanical Engineering** (Heating and Refrigeration; Maintenance Technology; Mechanical Engineering); **Physics** (Applied Physics; Engineering; Materials Engineering; Physics)

History: Founded 1984. A 'Deemed University'.

Fees: (Rupees): Tuition fee for undegraduate programmes, 1,450-1,700 per semester; Postgraduate programmes, 2,500-3,000 per semester; MBA, 10,000 per semester; Ph.D., 3,000 per semester

Degrees and Diplomas: *Post Diploma*; *Bachelor's Degree*; *Bachelor's Degree (professional)*; *Postgraduate Diploma*; *Master's Degree*; *Doctor of Philosophy*. Also undergraduate certificates and MBA.

Student Services: Health Services, Sports Facilities

Last Updated: 08/07/11

NORTH MAHARASHTRA UNIVERSITY

Uttar Maharashtra Vidyapeeth (NMU)
PO Box 80, Umavinagar, Jalgaon, Maharashtra 425001
Tel: +91(257) 225-8428
Fax: +91(257) 225-8403
EMail: registrar@nmu.ac.in
Website: http://www.nmu.ac.in

Vice-Chancellor: Sudhir. U. Meshram (2011-)

Registrar: A. B. Chaudhari

School

Chemical Sciences (Analytical Chemistry; Chemistry; Industrial Chemistry; Physical Chemistry; Polymer and Plastics Technology); **Environmental Sciences** (Environmental Studies; Geochemistry; Geology); **Life Sciences** (Biochemistry; Biological and Life Sciences; Biotechnology; Microbiology); **Mathematical Sciences** (Actuarial Science; Computer Science; Mathematics; Mathematics and Computer Science; Statistics); **Physical Sciences** (Electronic Engineering; Energy Engineering; Materials Engineering; Physics; Telecommunications Engineering); **Social Sciences** (Economics; Journalism; Mass Communication; Military Science; Political Sciences; Psychology; Social Sciences; Sociology)

Department

Chemical Technology (Chemical Engineering; Food Technology; Nanotechnology; Petroleum and Gas Engineering; Pharmacy; Polymer and Plastics Technology; Technology); **Comparative Languages and Literature** (Comparative Literature; Cultural Studies; English; Hindi; Indic Languages; Translation and Interpretation); **Computer Science** (Computer Science; Information Technology); **Education** (Education; Physical Education); **Law** (Law); **Library and Information Science** (Information Sciences; Library Science); **Management Studies** (Banking; Business Administration; Management); **Organic Chemistry** (Chemistry; Organic Chemistry); **Performing Arts** (Music; Performing Arts; Theatre)

Centre

Pratap Philosophy *(Amalner)* (Philosophy)

Further Information: Also 119 Affiliated Colleges and 21 Recognized Institutions. A traditional and distance education institution.

History: Founded 1990, by Act passed by the legislature of the State of Maharashtra.

Academic Year: June to April (June-October; November-April)

Admission Requirements: 12th year senior secondary/intermediate examination

Fees: (Rupees): 800-18,000 per annum

Main Language(s) of Instruction: Marathi, English

Accrediting Agency: University Grants Commission; National Accreditation and Assessment Council (NAAC)

Degrees and Diplomas: *Post Diploma*; *Bachelor's Degree*; *Bachelor's Degree (professional)*; *Postgraduate Diploma*; *Master's Degree*; *Master of Philosophy*; *Doctor of Philosophy*. Also Vocational Certificate, Diploma and Advanced Diploma Courses.

Student Services: Health Services, Social Counselling, Sports Facilities

Publications: Philosophical Quarterly; Sane Guruji Sanskav Vartapatra; Tatwadnyan Mandir

Last Updated: 29/11/11

NORTH ORISSA UNIVERSITY (NOU)

Sriram Chandra Vihar, Takatpur, Baripada,
Mayurbhanj, Orissa 757003
Tel: +91(6792) 256-906
Fax: +91(6792) 255-127
EMail: directoriconou@gmail.com
Website: http://nou.nic.in

Vice-Chancellor: Shiba Prasad Rath (2008-)
Tel: +91(6792) 255-127

Registrar: Upendra Nath Sahoo Tel: +91(6792) 256-906

Programme

Distance Education (Advertising and Publicity; Anthropology; Business Administration; Business and Commerce; Computer Science; Education; English; History; Information Sciences; Information Technology; Journalism; Library Science; Management; Mass Communication; Molecular Biology; Philosophy; Political Sciences; Public Administration; Public Relations; Sanskrit; Sociology; South and Southeast Asian Languages; Surveying and Mapping; Tourism; Wildlife)

Department

Anthropology and Tribal Studies (Anthropology; Archaeology; Cultural Studies; Museum Studies); **Bioinformatics** (Biochemistry; Cell Biology; Genetics; Mathematics; Mathematics and Computer Science; Statistics); **Biotechnology** (Biochemistry; Biology; Biotechnology; Genetics; Molecular Biology; Physiology; Statistics); **Botany** (Biology; Biotechnology; Botany; Cell Biology; Ecology; Genetics; Molecular Biology; Statistics); **Business Administration** (Accountancy; Advertising and Publicity; Business Administration; Business Computing; Commercial Law; Communication Studies; Computer Networks; E-Business/Commerce; Economics; Finance; Human Resources; Information Management; Information Sciences; International Business; Management; Marketing; Software Engineering); **Chemistry** (Analytical Chemistry; Chemistry; Inorganic Chemistry; Organic Chemistry; Physical Chemistry; Polymer and Plastics Technology); **Computer Science and Applications** (Computer Science; Data Processing; E- Business/Commerce; Mathematics; Mathematics and Computer Science; Multimedia; Operations Research; Robotics; Software Engineering); **Economics** (Agricultural Economics; Business Computing; Econometrics; Economics; Finance; International Business); **Law** (Commercial Law; Law); **Library and Information Sciences** (Information Management; Information Sciences; Information Technology; Library Science); **Mathematics and Computer Science** (Computer Science; Mathematics; Mathematics and Computer Science); **Physics** (Electronic Engineering; Mathematical Physics; Mechanics; Nuclear Physics; Physics); **Remote Sensing and Geographic Information System** (Geological Engineering; Surveying and Mapping); **Wildlife** (Ecology; Forest Management; Wildlife); **Zoology** (Anatomy; Biochemistry; Biology; Cell Biology; Endocrinology; Genetics; Immunology; Microbiology; Molecular Biology; Physiology; Statistics; Toxicology; Zoology)

Further Information: Also 80 affiliated colleges.

History: Founded 1998.

Fees: (Rupees): Distance education, 5,000-15,000 per annum

Accrediting Agency: University Grants Commission (University Grants Commission (UGC).

Degrees and Diplomas: *Bachelor's Degree*; *Postgraduate Diploma*; *Master's Degree*; *Master of Philosophy*; *Doctor of Philosophy*. Also Bachelor's degree honours; MBA; MCA.

Student Services: Academic Counselling, Canteen, Health Services, Sports Facilities

Publications: Tathya; Tattva; The Banani; Vision

Last Updated: 08/07/11

NTR UNIVERSITY OF HEALTH SCIENCES ANDHRA PRADESH (NTRUHS)

Vijayawada, Andhra Pradesh 520008
Tel: +91(866) 245-1206
Fax: +91(866) 245-0463
EMail: ntruhs@hotmail.com; drntruhs@gmail.com
Website: http://ntruhs.ap.nic.in/

Vice-Chancellor: I. Venkateswara Rao (2010-)

Registrar: Jayakar Babu

College

Allopathy (Medicine); **Applied Nutrition** (Nutrition); **Ayurveda** (Ayurveda); **Dentistry** (Dentistry); **Homeopathy** (Homeopathy); **Medical Laboratory Technology** *(MLT)* (Laboratory Techniques; Medical Technology); **Naturopathy and Yoga** (Alternative Medicine; Yoga); **Nursing** (Nursing); **Physiotherapy** (Physical Therapy); **Unani** (Indic Languages)

History: Founded 1986 as University of Health Sciences. Acquired present title 1998.

Academic Year: June to May (June-November; December-May)

Admission Requirements: 12th year senior secondary/intermediate examination or recognized foreign equivalent

Fees: (Rupees): 2,800-12,000 per annum

Main Language(s) of Instruction: English

Degrees and Diplomas: *Bachelor's Degree*; *Postgraduate Diploma*; *Master's Degree*

Publications: Journal of UHS

Last Updated: 11/07/11

O.P. JINDAL GLOBAL UNIVERSITY (JGU)

Sonipat Narela Road, Near Jagdishpur Village,
Sonipat, Haryana 131 001
Tel: +91(130) 3057-800 +91(130) 3057-801
Fax: +91(130) 3057-888
EMail: info@jgu.edu.in
Website: http://www.jgu.edu.in

Vice-Chancellor: C. Raj Kumar
Tel: +91(130) 3057-899; +91(130) 3057-900
EMail: crk@jgu.edu.in; crajkumar4@yahoo.com

Registrar: Aman Shah

School

Business *(JGBS)* (Accountancy; Banking; Business Administration; Commercial Law; Economics; Ethics; Finance; Information Management; International Law; Law; Management; Marketing; Political Sciences; Social Sciences); **Government and Public Policy** *(JGLS)* (Government; Public Administration); **International Affairs** *(JSIA)* (Business Administration; Government; International Law; International Relations; Law); **Law** (Civil Law; Commercial Law; Fiscal Law; International Law; Law)

History: Founded 2009. A non-profit university.

Accrediting Agency: University Grants Commission (UGC)

Degrees and Diplomas: *Bachelor's Degree (professional)*; *Master's Degree*. Also Honours Bachelor's degree; MBA and Corporate MBA.

Student Services: Canteen, Health Services

Last Updated: 26/08/11

ORISSA UNIVERSITY OF AGRICULTURE AND TECHNOLOGY (OUAT)

Bhubaneswar, Orissa 751003
Tel: +91(674) 239-7818 +91(674) 239-7868
Fax: +91(674) 239-7780
EMail: ouatmain@hotmail.com
Website: http://www.ouat.ac.in

Vice-Chancellor: D.P. Ray (2006-) Tel: +91(674) 239-7700

Registrar: Shri Sangram Keshari Ray Tel: +91(674) 239-7424

College

Agricultural Engineering and Technology (Agricultural Business; Agricultural Engineering; Agricultural Equipment; Aquaculture; Civil Engineering; Computer Science; Dairy; Electrical Engineering; Energy Engineering; Engineering; Engineering Drawing and Design; Environmental Engineering; Farm Management; Food Technology; Harvest Technology; Heating and Refrigeration; Irrigation; Machine Building; Mathematics; Mechanical Engineering; Mechanics; Power Engineering; Soil Conservation; Surveying and Mapping; Water Management; Water Science); **Agriculture** *(Chiplima)* (Agriculture); **Agriculture** *(Bhubaneswar)* (Agricultural Economics; Agricultural Education; Agriculture; Agronomy; Biotechnology; Chemistry; Computer Science; Crop Production; English; Entomology; Forestry; Genetics; Harvest Technology; Horticulture; Physiology; Plant Pathology; Soil Science; Statistics; Zoology); **Agriculture** *(Bhawanipatna)* (Agriculture); **Basic Science and Humanities** (Botany; Chemistry; English; Information Technology; Mathematics; Physics; South and Southeast Asian Languages; Zoology); **Fisheries** *(Rangeilunda, Berhampur)* (Aquaculture; Biology; Fishery; Food Science); **Home Science** (Child Care and Development; Clothing and Sewing; Food Science; Home Economics; Nutrition; Textile Technology); **Horticulture** *(Chiplima)* (Horticulture); **Postgraduate Studies** (Biology; Computer Engineering; Computer Science; Information Technology; Microbiology); **Veterinary Science and Animal Husbandry** *(Bhubaneswar)* (Anatomy; Animal Husbandry; Genetics; Gynaecology and Obstetrics; Meat and Poultry; Medicine; Microbiology; Nutrition; Parasitology; Pathology; Pharmacology; Physiology; Public Health; Surgery; Veterinary Science; Virology)

History: Founded 1962.

Admission Requirements: 12th year senior secondary/intermediate examination or recognized foreign equivalent

Fees: 2,000-4,000 per annum (Indian Rupee)

Main Language(s) of Instruction: English

Degrees and Diplomas: *Bachelor's Degree*; *Bachelor's Degree (professional)*; *Master's Degree*; *Doctor of Philosophy*. Also Bachelor's degree honours.

Student Services: Careers Guidance

Publications: Journal of Research

Last Updated: 11/07/11

OSMANIA UNIVERSITY

Hyderabad, Andhra Pradesh 500007
Tel: +91(40) 2709-8043
Fax: +91(40) 2709-8704
EMail: osmanian@hdl.vsnl.net.in
Website: http://www.osmania.ac.in

Vice-Chancellor: D. N. Reddy
Tel: +91(40) 270-98048 EMail: vc@osmania.ac.in

Registrar: V. Kishan Rao
Tel: +91(40) 270-98043 EMail: registrar@osmania.ac.in

College

Arts and Social Sciences (Ancient Civilizations; Applied Linguistics; Arabic; Archaeology; Archiving; Arts and Humanities; Classical Languages; Economics; English; Foreign Languages Education; French; German; Hindi; History; Indic Languages; Information Sciences; Islamic Studies; Journalism; Library Science; Linguistics; Literature; Mass Communication; Military Science; Modern Languages; Museum Studies; Persian; Philosophy; Political Sciences; Psychology; Public Administration; Rehabilitation and Therapy; Russian; Sanskrit; Social Sciences; Social Work; Sociology; South and Southeast Asian Languages; Theatre; Translation and Interpretation; Urdu); **Commerce and Business Management** (Business Administration; Business and Commerce; E- Business/Commerce; Engineering Management; Taxation); **Engineering** (Biomedical Engineering; Civil Engineering; Computer Engineering; Computer Science; Electrical and Electronic Engineering; Electrical Engineering; Engineering; Information Technology; Measurement and Precision Engineering; Mechanical Engineering; Production Engineering; Telecommunications Engineering); **Law** (Commercial Law; Constitutional Law; Criminal Law; International Law; Labour Law; Law; Public Law); **Law Basheerbagh** *(Postgraduate)* (Law); **Nizam** (Arabic; Botany; Business Administration; Business and Commerce; Chemistry; Economics; English; Genetics; Geography; Hindi; History; Indic Languages; Mathematics; Microbiology; Persian; Philosophy; Physics; Political Sciences; Psychology; Public Administration; Sanskrit; Sociology; Statistics; Theatre; Urdu; Zoology); **Physical Education** (Journalism; Physical Education; Rehabilitation and Therapy; Sports; Sports Management; Sports Medicine; Yoga); **Science** *(Postgraduate - Saifabad)* (Applied Mathematics; Arabic; Biotechnology; Botany; Chemistry; Computer Science; Cultural Studies; English; Foreign Languages Education; Geology; Hindi; Mathematics; Modern Languages; Physical Education; Physics; Sanskrit; Zoology); **Science** (Applied Mathematics; Astronomy and Space Science; Astrophysics; Biochemistry; Biotechnology; Botany; Chemistry; Computer Science; Dietetics; Electronic Engineering; Environmental Studies; Forensic Medicine and Dentistry; Genetics; Geography; Geology; Geophysics; Health Administration; Mathematics; Microbiology; Nutrition; Physics; Statistics; Surveying and Mapping; Zoology); **Secunderabad** *(Postgraduate - Sec'bad)* (Computer Science; Economics; English; Hindi; History; Political Sciences; Public Administration; Social Work); **Technology** (Biotechnology; Chemical Engineering; Chemistry; English; Food Technology; Mathematics; Mechanical Engineering; Pharmacy; Physical Education; Physics; Technology; Textile Technology); **Women** *(OUCWKOTI)* (Accountancy; Arabic; Botany; Business Administration; Business and Commerce; Chemistry; Communication Studies; Computer Science; Dietetics; Economics; English; Food Science; French; Genetics; Geography; Hindi; History; Inorganic Chemistry; Laboratory Techniques; Management; Mathematics; Medical Technology; Nutrition; Persian; Philosophy; Physics; Political Sciences; Psychology; Public Administration; Sanskrit; Sociology; South and Southeast Asian Languages; Urdu; Zoology)

Institute

Advanced Study in Education (Education; Special Education)

Further Information: Also Postgraduate Centres and Colleges; 5 Constituent and 12 Affiliated Colleges

History: Founded 1918.

Academic Year: July to March (July-November; December-March)

Admission Requirements: 12th year senior secondary/intermediate examination or recognized foreign equivalent

Fees: (Rupees): Undegraduate programmes, 4,600-4,710 per annum; Postgraduate programmes, 930-5,710 per annum

Main Language(s) of Instruction: English, Hindi, Telugu, Urdu, Marathi

Accrediting Agency: National Accreditation and Assessment Council (NAAC); University Grants Commission (UGC)

Degrees and Diplomas: *Post Diploma*; *Bachelor's Degree*; *Bachelor's Degree (professional)*; *Postgraduate Diploma*; *Master's Degree*; *Master of Philosophy*; *Doctor of Philosophy*. Also Advanced, Junior and Senior Diploma; MBA

Student Services: Careers Guidance, Health Services

Publishing house: University Press

Last Updated: 11/07/11

PACIFIC ACADEMY OF HIGHER EDUCATION & RESEARCH UNIVERSITY (PAHER)

Airport Road, Pratap Nagar Extension, Debari,
Udaipur, Rajasthan 313001
Tel: +91(97724-22999 +91-97725-22999
EMail: admission@pahersociety.org
Website: http://www.pacific-university.ac.in/

President: Bhagvan Das Rai

Faculty

Arts (Humanities and Social Sciences) (Arts and Humanities; Economics; English; Fashion Design; Fine Arts; Geography; Hindi; History; Interior Design; International Relations; Literature;

Musicology; Painting and Drawing; Philosophy; Political Sciences; Psychology; Public Administration; Sanskrit; Sculpture; Social Sciences; Sociology; Textile Design); **Computer Application** (Computer Science); **Education** (Education; Educational Technology); **Engineering** (Aeronautical and Aerospace Engineering; Automotive Engineering; Biotechnology; Chemical Engineering; Civil Engineering; Computer Science; Energy Engineering; Engineering; Industrial Engineering; Information Technology; Measurement and Precision Engineering; Mechanical Engineering; Power Engineering; Production Engineering; Software Engineering); **Management Studies** (Actuarial Science; Business Administration; Business and Commerce; Finance; Health Administration; Hotel Management; Human Resources; Insurance; International Business; Management; Marketing; Real Estate; Social Work; Tourism); **Science** (Chemistry; Industrial Chemistry; Mathematics; Natural Sciences)

College

Dental Studies (Dental Hygiene; Dentistry; Oral Pathology; Orthodontics; Periodontics; Surgery); **Pharmacy** (Chemistry; Pharmacology; Pharmacy; Safety Engineering)

Institute

Fashion Technology (Fashion Design; Fine Arts; Graphic Design; Interior Design; Jewellery Art; Management; Textile Design; Textile Technology); **Hotel Management** (Cooking and Catering; Food Technology; Hotel Management; Tourism); **Media and Mass Communication** (Journalism; Mass Communication; Media Studies; Radio and Television Broadcasting; Video)

History: Founded 1997 as Pacific Institute of Management and Pacific Commerce College.

Degrees and Diplomas: *Post Diploma*; *Bachelor's Degree*; *Bachelor's Degree (professional)*; *Postgraduate Diploma*; *Master's Degree*; *Master of Philosophy*; *Doctor of Philosophy*. Also Advance Diploma; MBA; integrated Bachelor's degree-MBA

Student Services: Canteen

Student Numbers *2010-2011*: Total: c. 12,000
Last Updated: 21/12/11

PADMASHREE DR. D. Y. PATIL VIDYAPEETH

Sector 15, Plot no 50, CBD Belapur,
Navi Mumbai, Maharashtra 400 614
Tel: +91(22) 392-85999
Fax: +91(22) 392-86197
EMail: dypuniversity_1@yahoo.co.in; dypuniversity@gmail.com
Website: http://www.dypatil.ac.in

Vice-Chancellor: James Thomas
EMail: vicechancellor@dypatil.edu

Registrar: F.A. Fernandes

College

Ayurved *(Dr. D.Y. Patil - and Research Institute)* (Ayurveda); **Dentistry** *(Dr. D.Y. Patil - and Hospital)* (Community Health; Dental Hygiene; Dental Technology; Dentistry; Microbiology; Oral Pathology; Orthodontics; Periodontics; Radiology; Surgery); **Medicine** *(Dr. D.Y. Patil)* (Anaesthesiology; Anatomy; Biochemistry; Community Health; Dermatology; Forensic Medicine and Dentistry; Gynaecology and Obstetrics; Medicine; Microbiology; Ophthalmology; Orthopaedics; Paediatrics; Pathology; Pharmacology; Physiology; Pneumology; Surgery; Toxicology; Venereology); **Nursing** *(Dr. D.Y. Patil)* (Anatomy; Biochemistry; Community Health; Educational Technology; English; Genetics; Gynaecology and Obstetrics; Health Sciences; Microbiology; Midwifery; Nursing; Nutrition; Pathology; Pharmacology; Physiology; Psychiatry and Mental Health; Psychology; Sociology; Statistics)

Department

Biotechnology and Bioinformatics (Biological and Life Sciences; Biology; Biomedical Engineering; Biotechnology; Computer Science); **Business Management** (Banking; Business Administration; Finance; Health Administration; Human Resources; International Business; Management; Marketing; Retailing and Wholesaling; Sports Management); **Education** (Education; Educational Psychology; Educational Technology); **Hospitality and Tourism Studies** (Cooking and Catering; Hotel and Restaurant; Tourism); **Physiotherapy** (Administration; Anatomy; Biochemistry; Cardiology; Communication Studies; Dermatology; Gynaecology and Obstetrics; Management; Marketing; Medicine; Microbiology; Neurological Therapy; Orthopaedics; Paediatrics; Pathology; Pharmacology; Physical Therapy; Physiology; Pneumology; Psychology; Rehabilitation and Therapy; Surgery)

Further Information: Also College of Engineering and Technology, College of Architecture, College of Hotel Management and Catering Technology, College of Ayurveda, College of Law affiliated to the University of Mumbai

History: Founded 2002. A 'Deemed University'.

Academic Year: July to June

Admission Requirements: Higher secondary school certificate and entrance examination

Fees: (Rupees): Undergraduate programmes, 25,000-350,000 per annum; Postgraduate programmes, 10,000-100,000 per annum; 60,000-322,000 MBA, per annum; Ph.D., 30,000 per annum

Accrediting Agency: National Assessment and Accreditation Council (NAAC)

Degrees and Diplomas: *Post Diploma*; *Bachelor's Degree*; *Bachelor's Degree (professional)*; *Postgraduate Diploma*; *Master's Degree*; *Master of Philosophy*; *Doctor of Philosophy*. Also undergraduate certificates; MBA

Student Services: Health Services, Sports Facilities

Last Updated: 11/07/11

PALAMURU UNIVERSITY

Near Bandamedi Palli, Raichur Road,
Mahboobnagar, Andhra Pradesh 509 001
Tel: +91(8542) 275-006
Fax: +91(8542) 275-088
EMail: registrar@palamuruuniversity.ac.in
Website: http://www.palamuruuniversity.ac.in/

Vice-Chancellor: V. Gopal Reddy Tel: +91(8542) 221-011

Registrar: K. Venkatachalam
Tel: +91(8542) 221-020 EMail: drkv.chalam@yahoo.co.in

Department

Business Administration (Business Administration); **Business and Commerce** (Business and Commerce); **Chemistry** (Chemistry); **Computer Science** (Computer Science); **English** (English); **Mathematics** (Mathematics); **Microbiology** (Microbiology); **Organic Chemistry** (Organic Chemistry); **Pharmacy** (Pharmacy); **Political Sciences** (Political Sciences); **Social Work** (Social Work)

History: Founded 2008.

Degrees and Diplomas: *Master's Degree*. Also MBA

Student Numbers *2010-2011*: Total: c. 440
Last Updated: 02/01/12

PANDIT BHAGWAT DAYAL SHARMA UNIVERSITY OF HEALTH SCIENCES, ROHTAK (UHSR)

Rohtak, Haryana 124 001
Tel: +91(1262) 212-812
Fax: +91(1262) 212-812
EMail: vicechancellor.uhsr@gmail.com
Website: http://www.uhsr.ac.in/

Vice-Chancellor: S.S. Sangwan Tel: +91(1262) 212-812

Registrar: Rajeev Sen Tel: +91(1262) 211-109

College

Medicine (Anaesthesiology; Anatomy; Biochemistry; Cardiology; Community Health; Dermatology; Forensic Medicine and Dentistry; Laboratory Techniques; Medicine; Microbiology; Orthopaedics; Otorhinolaryngology; Paediatrics; Pathology; Pharmacology; Pharmacy; Physiology; Plastic Surgery; Pneumology; Venereology); **Nursing** (Nursing; Psychiatry and Mental Health; Social Work); **Ophthalmology** (Dental Hygiene; Dental Technology; Dentistry; Oral Pathology; Orthodontics; Surgery)

Centre

Cancer *(Regional)* (Biotechnology; Molecular Biology; Oncology; Radiology; Surgery)

Degrees and Diplomas: *Post Diploma*; *Bachelor's Degree*; *Bachelor's Degree (professional)*; *Postgraduate Diploma*; *Master's Degree*; *Master of Philosophy*

Last Updated: 03/01/12

PANDIT DEENDAYAL PETROLEUM UNIVERSITY (PDPU)

Raisan Village, Gandhinagar, Gujarat 382 007
Tel: +91(79) 2327-5020
Fax: +91(79) 2327-5030
EMail: info@pdpu.ac.in
Website: http://www.pdpu.ac.in

President: Mukesh Ambani

Registrar: N. Sundaram

School

Liberal Studies (Accountancy; Arts and Humanities; Business Administration; Dance; Economics; English; Environmental Studies; Finance; Geography; Government; History; International Relations; Law; Literature; Management; Marketing; Mathematics; Modern Languages; Music; Operations Research; Philosophy; Political Sciences; Psychology; Public Administration; Social Sciences; Spanish; Theatre); **Nuclear Energy** (Laboratory Techniques; Maintenance Technology; Nuclear Engineering; Nuclear Physics); **Petroleum Management** (Accountancy; Economics; Finance; International Business; Law; Management; Petroleum and Gas Engineering); **Petroleum Technology** (Automation and Control Engineering; Engineering; Measurement and Precision Engineering; Petroleum and Gas Engineering; Technology); **Solar Energy** (Energy Engineering; Mechanics; Nuclear Physics; Physics; Solid State Physics); **Technology** (Civil Engineering; Electrical Engineering; Engineering; Mechanical Engineering; Technology)

History: Founded 2007.

Accrediting Agency: University Grants Commission (UGC); All India Council for Technical Education (AICTE).

Degrees and Diplomas: *Bachelor's Degree*; *Bachelor's Degree (professional)*; *Master's Degree*; *Doctor of Philosophy*. Also MBA

Student Services: Health Services, Sports Facilities

Academic Staff *2010-2011*: Total: c. 110

Student Numbers *2010-2011*: Total: c. 1,450

Last Updated: 11/07/11

PANDIT DWARKA PRASAD MISHRA INDIAN INSTITUTE OF INFORMATION TECHNOLOGY, DESIGN AND MANUFACTURING, JABALPUR (IIITDMJ)

Dumna Airport Road, Khamaria,
Jabalpur, Madhya Pradesh 482 005
Tel: +91(761) 263-2273
Fax: +91(761) 263-2524
EMail: query@iiitdmj.ac.in
Website: http://www.iiitdmj.ac.in

Director: Aparajita Ojha
Tel: +91(761) 263-2615 EMail: director@iiitdmj.ac.in

Registrar: P. S. Sandhu
Tel: +91(761) 263-2068 EMail: rg@iiitdmj.ac.in

Programme

Postgraduate Studies (Computer Engineering; Computer Science; Design; Electronic Engineering; Mechanical Engineering; Telecommunications Engineering); **Undergraduate Studies** (Computer Engineering; Computer Science; Electronic Engineering; Mechanical Engineering; Telecommunications Engineering)

History: Created 2005. A 'Deemed University'.

Fees: 44,165 per annum. Postgraduate programmes, 2,500 per semester

Accrediting Agency: University Grants Commission (UGC)

Degrees and Diplomas: *Bachelor's Degree (professional)*; *Master's Degree*; *Doctor of Philosophy*

Last Updated: 11/07/11

PANJAB UNIVERSITY (PU)

Chandigarh, Union Territory 160014
Tel: +91(172) 254-1716 +91(172) 254-1441
Fax: +91(172) 278-335 +91(172) 254-1022
Website: http://www.puchd.ac.in

Vice-Chancellor: Arun Kumar Grover (2012-)
Tel: +91(172) 254-1945 EMail: vc@pu.ac.in

Registrar: A. K. Bhandari
Tel: +91(172) 253-4867 +91(172) 253-4868 EMail: regr@pu.ac.in

International Relations: Naval Kishore, Dean of International Students
Tel: +91(172) 254-1873 +91(172) 253-4574 EMail: dis@pu.ac.in

Unit

Panjabi Lexicography (Indic Languages; Linguistics)

School

Business *(University - Ludhiana)* (Business Administration; Finance; Human Resources; Management; Marketing; Operations Research); **Business** *(University)* (Biotechnology; Business Administration; Business and Commerce; E- Business/Commerce; Human Resources; International Business); **Communication Studies** (Advertising and Publicity; Communication Studies; Journalism; Mass Communication; Media Studies; Public Relations); **Open Learning** *(Ludhiana)* (Alternative Medicine; Human Rights; Statistics; Yoga)

Department

Ancient Indian History, Culture and Archaeology (Archaeology; Cultural Studies; History; Tourism); **Anthropology** (Anthropology; Criminology; Forensic Medicine and Dentistry); **Arts History and Visual Arts** (Art History; Visual Arts); **Biochemistry** (Biochemistry); **Biophysics** (Biophysics); **Biotechnology** (Biotechnology); **Botany** (Botany); **Chemistry** (Chemistry); **Chinese and Tibetan Languages** (Asian Studies; Chinese; Tibetan); **Community Education and Disability Studies** (Education; Rehabilitation and Therapy); **Computer Science and Applications** (Computer Science); **Defence and National Security Studies** (Military Science; Protective Services; Safety Engineering); **Economics** (Agricultural Economics; Development Studies; Economics; Finance; Industrial and Production Economics); **Education** (Education; Educational and Student Counselling; Educational Technology); **English and Cultural Studies** (English; English Studies; Literature); **Environment and Vocational Studies** (Agriculture; Environmental Studies; Vocational Education; Waste Management); **Evening Studies** (Arts and Humanities; Business and Commerce; Economics; English; History; Indic Languages; Political Sciences); **French and Francophone Studies** (French; French Studies); **Gandhian Studies** (Peace and Disarmament; Philosophy); **Geography** (Geography; Safety Engineering; Surveying and Mapping); **Geology** (Geology; Petrology); **German** (German); **Guru Nanak Sikh Studies** (Asian Religious Studies; Cultural Studies; History; Literature; Philosophy); **Hindi** (Hindi; Translation and Interpretation); **History** (Ancient Civilizations; Contemporary History; History; Medieval Studies; Modern History); **Indian Theatre** (Acting; Singing; Speech Studies; Theatre; Yoga); **Laws** (Law); **Library and Information Science** (Information Sciences; Library Science); **Life Long Learning and Extension** (Continuing Education; Education; Educational and Student Counselling; Gender Studies; Literacy Education; Nutrition; Vocational Education); **Mathematics** (Mathematics; Mathematics and Computer Science); **Microbiology** (Microbiology); **Music** (Music; Musical Instruments; Singing); **Philosophy** (Aesthetics; Ethics; Philosophy; Religion); **Physical Education** (Physical Education); **Physics** (Electronic Engineering; Physics); **Political Science** (International Relations; Political Sciences); **Psychology** (Psychology); **Public Administration** (Administration; Economics; Human Resources; Management; Public Administration); **Punjabi** (Cultural Studies; Indic Languages; Translation and Interpretation); **Russian** (Literature; Russian; Slavic Languages); **Sanskrit** (Grammar; Literature; Philology; Philosophy; Sanskrit); **Sociology** (Demography and Population; Development Studies; Family Studies; Gender Studies; Social Studies; Sociology; Urban Studies); **Statistics** (Statistics); **Urdu** (Persian; Urdu); **Women's Studies and Development** *(cum Center)* (Women's Studies); **Zoology** (Zoology)

Institute

Applied Management Sciences *(University)* (Business Administration; Business and Commerce; Finance; Human Resources; Management; Marketing; Operations Research); **Chemical Engineering and Technology** *(University)* (Business Administration; Chemical Engineering; Engineering; Food Technology; Industrial Chemistry; Polymer and Plastics Technology; Technology); **Dental Sciences and Hospital** *(Dr. Harvansh Singh Judge)* (Dentistry; Surgery); **Educational Technology and Vocational Education** (Educational Technology; Primary Education; Secondary Education;

Vocational Education); **Engineering and Technology** *(University)* (Biotechnology; Business Administration; Computer Engineering; Computer Science; Electrical and Electronic Engineering; Electronic Engineering; Engineering; Information Technology; Mechanical Engineering; Technology; Telecommunications Engineering); **Fashion Technology and Vocational Development** *(University)* (Fashion Design; Journalism; Management; Photography; Textile Design; Textile Technology); **Forensic Science and Criminology** (Criminology; Forensic Medicine and Dentistry); **Hotel Management and Tourism** *(University)* (Hotel Management; Tourism); **Laws** *(University - Ludhiana)* (Law); **Legal Studies** *(University)* (Law); **Pharmaceutical Sciences** *(University)* (Pharmacy); **Sanskrit and Indological Studies** *(Vishveshvaranand Vishwa Bandhu)* (Sanskrit; South Asian Studies)

Centre

Ambedkar (Philosophy; Social Sciences; Sociology); **Human Genome Studies and Research** *(National - NCHGSR)* (Biotechnology; Genetics; Molecular Biology); **Human Rights and Duties** *(U.I.E.A.S.S)* (Human Rights); **IAS and Other Competitive Examinations** (Justice Administration; Public Administration); **Medical Physics** *(U.I.E.A.S.T.)* (Nuclear Physics; Oncology; Physics; Radiology; Radiophysics); **Microbial Biotechnology** *(U.I.E.A.S.T.)* (Biotechnology; Microbiology); **Nanoscience and Nanotechnology** *(U.I.E.A.S.T.)* (Nanotechnology); **Nuclear Medicine** *(U.I.E.A.S.T.)* (Medical Technology; Radiology); **Petroleum and Applied Geology** *(U.I.E.A.S.T.)* (Geochemistry; Geology; Geophysics; Petroleum and Gas Engineering); **Police Administration** *(U.I.E.A.S.S)* (Administration; Police Studies); **Public Health** *(U.I.E.A.S.T.)* (Health Sciences; Public Health); **Social Work** *(U.I.E.A.S.S)* (Social Work); **Sophisticated Analytical Instrumentation Facility, CIL and UCIM** (Instrument Making); **Stem Cell and Tissue Engineering** (Bioengineering; Cell Biology; Embryology and Reproduction Biology); **Study of Geopolitics** (International Relations; Natural Resources; Political Sciences; Regional Studies); **Study of Mid-West and Central Asia** (Asian Studies); **Study of Social Exclusion and Inclusive Policy** (Social Policy; Social Problems); **System Biology and Bioinformatics** *(U.I.E.A.S.T.)* (Biology; Computer Science; Genetics; Measurement and Precision Engineering; Molecular Biology)

Research Centre

Energy (Energy Engineering; Environmental Management); **Population** (Demography and Population; Family Studies; Health Sciences)

Chair

Bhai Vir Singh (Comparative Literature; Writing); **Medieval Indian Literature** *(Sheikh Baba Farid)* (Hindi; Literature; Medieval Studies; Urdu); **Sant Sahitya Studies** *(Guru Ravi Das)* (Ancient Books; Hindi; Indic Languages; Medieval Studies); **Vedic Studies** *(Dayanand)* (Ayurveda; Esoteric Practices)

Further Information: 185 affiliated colleges spread over Punjab and Chandigarh, Regional Centres at Muktsar, Ludhiana, Hoshiarpur (Swami Sarvanand Giri), Kauni. A traditional, open and distance education institution.

History: Founded 1882 as University of the Punjab at Lahore, acquired present title 1947. Relocated in Chandigarh 1956. Recognized as the 'University with Potential for Excellence in Bio-Medical Sciences' by the University Grants Commission (UGC).

Academic Year: July to April (July-October; October-December; January-April)

Admission Requirements: 12th year senior secondary/intermediate examination or recognized foreign equivalent

Fees: (Rupees): Undergraduate programmes, 5,500-100,690 per annum; Postgraduate programmes, 3,370-69,367 per annum); Ph.D., 1,150-1,500 per annum

Main Language(s) of Instruction: English, Hindi, Panjabi, Urdu

Degrees and Diplomas: *Post Diploma*; *Bachelor's Degree*; *Bachelor's Degree (professional)*; *Postgraduate Diploma*; *Master's Degree*; *Master of Philosophy*; *Doctor of Philosophy*. Also certificate and advanced diploma courses; Bachelor's and Master's degree Honours; MBA

Student Services: Academic Counselling, Canteen, Careers Guidance, Cultural Activities, Health Services, Nursery Care, Social Counselling, Sports Facilities

Publications: Arts and Science and Social Sciences Journals

Publishing House: University Press

Last Updated: 12/07/11

PATNA UNIVERSITY (PU)

Ashok Rajpath, Patna, Bihar 800005
Tel: +91(612) 267-0531 +91(612) 267-0852
Fax: +91(612) 267-0877 +91(612) 268-8872
EMail: contact@puccmail.ac.in
Website: http://pucc.bih.nic.in/

Vice-Chancellor: Shambhu Nath Singh (2011-)
Tel: +91(612) 267-0352

Registrar: Manoj Kumar
Tel: +91(612) 267-0531 EMail: registrar_pu@hotmail.com

Faculty

Commerce (Business and Commerce; Human Resources; Labour and Industrial Relations); **Education** (Education); **Humanities** (Arabic; Archaeology; Arts and Humanities; English; Hindi; History; Indic Languages; Persian; Philosophy; Sanskrit; Urdu); **Law** (Law); **Medicine** *(Under state government management and control)* (Dentistry; Medicine); **Science** (Biochemistry; Botany; Chemistry; Geography; Geology; Mathematics; Natural Sciences; Physics; Statistics; Zoology); **Social Sciences** (Ancient Civilizations; Economics; Political Sciences; Psychology; Social Sciences; Sociology)

College

Arts and Crafts (Crafts and Trades; Fine Arts; Painting and Drawing; Sculpture; Visual Arts); **Bihar National** (Arts and Humanities; Business and Commerce; Natural Sciences); **Magadha Mahila**; **Patna**; **Patna Law** (Law); **Patna Science** (Botany; Chemistry; Geology; Mathematics; Natural Sciences; Physics; Statistics; Zoology); **Patna Training**; **Patna Women's** (Women's Studies); **Vanijya Mahavidyalaya** (Business and Commerce); **Women's Training** (Women's Studies)

Programme

Distance Education *(Offered through the Directorate of Distance Education)* (Communication Studies; Journalism; Library Science)

Institute

Library and Information Science (Information Sciences; Library Science); **Music** (Music); **Psychological Research and Services** (Psychology); **Public Administration** (Public Administration)

Centre

Computer (Biology; Business Computing; Computer Science)

Research Centre

Population (Demography and Population)

Further Information: Also 12 Constituent Colleges. A traditional and distance education institution.

History: Founded 1917, acquired present status and title 1951.

Academic Year: July to May (July-October; November-December; January-May)

Admission Requirements: 12th year senior secondary/intermediate examination or recognized foreign equivalent

Fees: (Rupees): 150-200 per annum

Main Language(s) of Instruction: Hindi, English

Accrediting Agency: NAAC (UGC); MCI; DCI; NCTE; AICTE

Degrees and Diplomas: *Post Diploma*; *Bachelor's Degree*; *Postgraduate Diploma*; *Master's Degree*; *Doctor of Philosophy*. Also MBA and MCA

Student Services: Academic Counselling, Cultural Activities, Facilities for disabled people, Health Services, Language Laboratory, Social Counselling, Sports Facilities

Publications: Patna University Journal

Academic Staff *2010-2011*: Total 448

Student Numbers *2010-2011*: Total 18,741

Last Updated: 02/11/11

PEC UNIVERSITY OF TECHNOLOGY (PEC)

Sector-12, Chandigarh, Union Territory 160012
Tel: +91(172) 275-3055 +91(172) 275-3051
Fax: +91(172) 274-8197 +91(172) 274-5175
EMail: admissionug@pec.ac.in
Website: http://www.pec.ac.in

Director: Manoj Datta
Tel: 274-6074 275-3051 EMail: director@pec.ac.in

Registrar: Ashwani Prashar
Tel: 274-8197 275-3055 EMail: registrar@pec.ac.in

Department

Aerospace Engineering (Aeronautical and Aerospace Engineering; Chemistry; Maintenance Technology; Mechanics; Physics; Solid State Physics); **Applied Sciences** (Arts and Humanities; Chemistry; Engineering; Environmental Engineering; Geological Engineering; Mathematics; Physics; Statistics); **Civil Engineering** (Civil Engineering; Construction Engineering; Environmental Engineering; Geological Engineering; Hydraulic Engineering; Irrigation; Road Engineering; Transport Engineering); **Computer Science and Engineering** (Artificial Intelligence; Computer Engineering; Computer Graphics; Computer Networks; Computer Science; Data Processing; Multimedia; Software Engineering); **Electrical Engineering** (Automation and Control Engineering; Biomedical Engineering; Economics; Electrical Engineering; Measurement and Precision Engineering; Operations Research; Power Engineering; Telecommunications Engineering); **Electronics and Electrical Communication** (Computer Engineering; Electrical and Electronic Engineering; Electronic Engineering; Materials Engineering; Microwaves; Telecommunications Engineering); **Information Technology** (Arts and Humanities; Behavioural Sciences; Economics; Information Technology; Management; Women's Studies); **Materials and Metallurgical Engineering** (Ceramics and Glass Technology; Computer Engineering; Computer Graphics; Engineering Drawing and Design; Heating and Refrigeration; Materials Engineering; Mechanical Engineering; Metal Techniques; Metallurgical Engineering; Production Engineering); **Mechanical Engineering** (Computer Engineering; Engineering Drawing and Design; Heating and Refrigeration; Industrial Engineering; Machine Building; Management; Materials Engineering; Mathematics; Mechanical Engineering; Mechanics; Production Engineering; Safety Engineering; Thermal Engineering; Transport Engineering); **Production Engineering** (Mathematics; Metal Techniques; Production Engineering; Robotics)

History: Founded as Mugalpura Engineering College at Lahore (now in Pakistan) 1921. Changed name to Maclagan Engineering College 1924. Affiliated to Punjab University, Lahore 1931. Parted and moved to Roorkee (India), it was renamed as East Punjab College of Engineering 1947. Renamed Punjab Engineering College 1950. Moved to Chandigarh 1953. Acquired present status of 'Deemed University' 2003, it became known as became known as Punjab Engineering College (Deemed University). Acquired present title 2009.

Fees: (Rupees): Bachelor's and Master's degree programmes, 32,500 per semester; Ph.D. programmes, 5,000 per annum

Degrees and Diplomas: *Bachelor's Degree (professional)*; *Master's Degree*; *Doctor of Philosophy*

Student Services: Sports Facilities

Last Updated: 12/07/11

PERIYAR MANIAMMAI UNIVERSITY (PMU)

Periyar Nagar Vallam, Thanjavur 613403
EMail: registrar@pmu.edu
Website: http://www.pmu.edu/

Vice-Chancellor: N. Ramachandran

Registrar: M. Ayyavoo

School

Architecture, Engineering and Technology *(SAET)* (Aeronautical and Aerospace Engineering; Architecture; Biotechnology; Chemical Engineering; Civil Engineering; Electrical Engineering; Electronic Engineering; Engineering; Mechanical Engineering; Technology; Telecommunications Engineering); **Computer Science and Engineering** *(SCSE)* (Computer Engineering; Computer Science); **Humanities, Sciences and Management** *(Chemistry)* (Arts and Humanities; Chemistry; Education; English; Information Sciences; Library Science; Management; Mathematics; Natural Sciences; Physical Education; Physics)

Further Information: Campuses in Thanjavur, Tiruchirapalli, Chennai and New Delhi.

History: Founded as Periyar Maniammai College of Technology for Women 1988. Started functioning as an affiliated college to Anna University, Chennai 2001. Acquire university status 2007. A 'Deemed University'.

Accrediting Agency: National Assessment and Accreditation Council (NAAC); National Board of Accreditation (NBA); All India Council for Technical Education (AICTE).

Degrees and Diplomas: *Bachelor's Degree*; *Bachelor's Degree (professional)*; *Master's Degree*; *Master of Philosophy*; *Doctor of Philosophy*. Also M.B.A.; Lateral and integrated Master's course, 2-5 yrs.

Last Updated: 16/12/11

PERIYAR UNIVERSITY

Bangalore main road, Salem, Tamil Nadu 636 011
Tel: +91(427) 234-5766 +91(427) 234-5220
Fax: +91(427) 234-5565
EMail: info@periyaruniversity.ac.in
Website: http://periyaruniversity.ac.in

Vice-Chancellor: K. Muthuchelian
Tel: +91(427) 234-5565
EMail: vc@periyaruniversity.ac.in; drchelian1960@yahoo.co.in

Registrar: S. Gunasekaran
Tel: +91(427) 234-5778
EMail: registrar@periyaruniversity.ac.in;
sethugunasekaran@rediffmail.com

Department

Biochemistry (Biochemistry); **Biotechnology** (Biological and Life Sciences; Biotechnology; Computer Science; Energy Engineering; Engineering; Nanotechnology); **Chemistry** (Chemistry); **Commerce** (Accountancy; Business Administration; Business and Commerce; Finance; Human Resources; International Business; Management; Marketing; Taxation); **Computer Science** (Computer Science; Data Processing; Software Engineering; Telecommunications Engineering); **Economics** (Economics); **Education** (Education); **English** (English; Human Rights; Journalism; Literature; Translation and Interpretation; Writing); **Food Science** (Cooking and Catering; Food Science; Food Technology; Nutrition); **Geology** (Earth Sciences; Geology; Surveying and Mapping); **Journalism and Mass Communication** (Communication Arts; Journalism; Mass Communication); **Mathematics** (Applied Mathematics; Mathematics); **Microbiology** (Microbiology); **Physics** (Physics); **Psychology** (Industrial and Organizational Psychology; Psychology); **Sociology** (Management; Sociology); **Tamil** (South and Southeast Asian Languages)

Institute

Distance Education *(Periyar)* (Banking; Biotechnology; Botany; Business Administration; Chemistry; Child Care and Development; Computer Engineering; Computer Graphics; Computer Networks; Computer Science; Crafts and Trades; Dental Technology; Economics; Education; Electronic Engineering; English; Environmental Studies; Geology; Health Administration; History; Home Economics; Hotel Management; Human Resources; Human Rights; Indic Languages; Information Sciences; Information Technology; International Business; Journalism; Laboratory Techniques; Library Science; Management; Marketing; Mass Communication; Mathematics; Medical Technology; Microbiology; Optics; Physics; Political Sciences; Public Administration; Radiology; Sanskrit; Social Work; Sociology; South and Southeast Asian Languages; Telecommunications Engineering; Tourism; Yoga; Zoology); **Management Studies** *(Periyar - PRIMS)* (Management)

Further Information: Also 66 affiliated and 11 constituent colleges. A traditional and distance education institution.

History: Founded 1997. Acquired present status 2007.

Academic Year: July to June

Admission Requirements: 12th year senior secondary/intermediate examination or recognized foreign equivalent

Fees: (Rupees): Postgraduate programmes, 6,500-8,500 per annum

Main Language(s) of Instruction: English

Accrediting Agency: University Grants Commission (UGC); National Assessment and Accreditation Council (NAAC)

Degrees and Diplomas: *Post Diploma*; *Bachelor's Degree*; *Bachelor's Degree (professional)*; *Postgraduate Diploma*; *Master's*

Degree; *Master of Philosophy*; *Doctor of Philosophy*. Also undergraduate certificates, MBA, executive MBA, MCA

Student Services: Health Services

Last Updated: 12/07/11

PES UNIVERSITY

100 Feet Ring Road, BSK III Stage, Bangalore, Karnataka 560085

Tel: +91(80) 26721983

Fax: +91(80) 26720886

EMail: admissions@pes.edu

Website: http://www.pes.edu/

Vice-Chancellor: K N Balasubramanya Murthy EMail: vice.chancellor@pes.edu

Registrar: V. Krishnamurthy EMail: registrar@pes.edu

International Relations: Kavi Mahesh, Dean, Research EMail: kavi.mahesh@pes.edu

Programme

Business Administration (Advertising and Publicity; Banking; Business Administration; Finance; Human Resources; Marketing; Public Relations; Taxation); **Engineering** (Automotive Engineering; Bioengineering; Biotechnology; Bridge Engineering; Civil Engineering; Computer Engineering; Computer Networks; Computer Science; Construction Engineering; Electrical Engineering; Electronic Engineering; Geological Engineering; Mathematics; Mechanical Engineering; Microelectronics; Power Engineering; Road Engineering; Software Engineering; Telecommunications Engineering)

History: Created 1988 as PES Institute of Technology.

Academic Year: Jan - May; June – August; August – December

Admission Requirements: For undergraduate degrees, secondary school certificate. For postgraduate degrees, a recognized undergraduate degree.

Fees: Bachelor degrees, 120,000 to 240,000 per annum; Masters degrees, 180,00 to 360,000 per annum (Indian Rupee)

Main Language(s) of Instruction: English

Accrediting Agency: UGC; NAAC

Degrees and Diplomas: *Bachelor's Degree*: **Biotechnology; Business Administration; Civil Engineering; Computer Science; Electrical and Electronic Engineering; Hotel Management; Management; Mechanical Engineering; Telecommunications Engineering.** *Master's Degree*: **Aeronautical and Aerospace Engineering; Automotive Engineering; Business Administration; Computer Engineering; Computer Science; Electrical and Electronic Engineering; Human Resources; Information Sciences; Management; Marketing; Mechanical Engineering; Production Engineering; Software Engineering; Telecommunications Engineering.** *Doctor of Philosophy*: **Engineering; Management; Natural Sciences.**

Academic Staff *2013-2014*	**TOTAL**
FULL-TIME	**289**
PART-TIME	**22**
STAFF WITH DOCTORATE	
FULL-TIME	**72**

Student Numbers *2013-2014*	
All (Foreign included)	**1,639**
FOREIGN ONLY	**28**

Last Updated: 13/05/14

PONDICHERRY UNIVERSITY (PONDIUNI)

Bharat Ratna Dr. B.R.Ambedkar Administrative Building, R.V.Nagar, Kalapet, Kalapet, Pondicherry 605014

Tel: +91(413) 265-5179

Fax: +91(413) 265-5734

EMail: registrar@pondiuni.edu.in

Website: http://www.pondiuni.org

Vice-Chancellor: J.A.K. Tareen (2007-) Tel: +91(413) 265-5175 EMail: vc@pondiuni.edu.in

Registrar: Shri. S. Loganathan Tel: +91(413) 265-5261 EMail: registrar@pondiuni.edu.in

International Relations: M. Vallathan, Assistant Registrar (Public Relations) EMail: arprs@pondiuni.edu.in

School

Education (Education; Educational Administration; Educational Psychology; Educational Technology; Preschool Education; Teacher Training); **Engineering and Technology** (Computer Engineering; Computer Networks; Computer Science; Electronic Engineering; Engineering; Environmental Engineering; Environmental Management; Information Technology; Technology); **Green Energy Technologies** *(Madanjeet)* (Chemistry; Energy Engineering; Environmental Engineering; Nanotechnology); **Humanities** (Arts and Humanities; Chinese; Christian Religious Studies; Comparative Literature; English; French; German; Hindi; Italian; Japanese; Korean; Modern Languages; Philosophy; Physical Education; Russian; Sanskrit; Spanish; Sports; Translation and Interpretation); **Life Sciences** (Biochemistry; Biological and Life Sciences; Biology; Biotechnology; Coastal Studies; Computer Science; Ecology; Environmental Studies; Food Science; Food Technology; Marine Biology; Marine Science and Oceanography; Microbiology; Molecular Biology; Nutrition; Safety Engineering); **Management** (Banking; Business Administration; Business and Commerce; Economics; Finance; Insurance; International Business; Management; Tourism); **Mathematical Sciences** *(Ramanujan)* (Mathematics; Mathematics and Computer Science; Statistics); **Media and Communication** (Film; Information Sciences; Library Science; Mass Communication; Media Studies; Radio and Television Broadcasting); **Medical Sciences** (Medicine); **Performing Arts** (Performing Arts; Theatre); **Physical, Chemical and Applied Sciences** (Chemistry; Clinical Psychology; Earth Sciences; Geology; Industrial and Organizational Psychology; Information Sciences; Laser Engineering; Library Science; Media Studies; Physics; Psychology); **Social Sciences and International Studies** (Anthropology; History; Human Rights; International Studies; Labour and Industrial Relations; Political Sciences; Rural Studies; Social Problems; Social Sciences; Social Work; Sociology; South Asian Studies; Women's Studies); **Tamil Language and Literature** *(Subramania Bharathi)* (Literature; South and Southeast Asian Languages)

Further Information: Also Port Blair, Karaikal and Community college campuses; 87 Affiliated Colleges. A traditional and distance education institution. Distance education programmes launched in the United Arab Emirates, Qatar and Kuwait with centres at Dubai, Abu Dhabi, Doha and Kuwait

History: Founded 1985. A 'Central University'.

Academic Year: July to April (July-December; January-April)

Admission Requirements: 12th year senior secondary/intermediate examination or recognized foreign equivalent

Fees: (Rupees): Tuition fee: P.G. Diploma Programmes, 50 per semester and credit for Indian students and (US Dollars) 250-500 per semester for international students; M.Sc. In Bioinformatics, Computational Biology, Food Science and Technology, 100 per credit and semester for Indian students and (US Dollars) 500-750 per semester for international students; M.Sc Microbiology/M.Tech (Nano Sciences and Technology, Green Energy Technology, Exploration Geosciences, Electronics), 3,500 per annum for Indian students and 50,000-100,000 per annum for international students; M.B.A., 3,000 per semester for Indian students and 20,000-26,500 per semester for international students; M.Tech./M.Sc. (Computer Science)/M.C.A., 100 per credit (US Dollars, 500-750 per semester for international students); M.Phil. and Post-graduate programmes, 30-50 per credit and per semester (US Dollars, 250-500 for international students); Ph.D. programmes, 1,000 (full-time) or 2,000 (part-time) per semester for Indian students and 1,200 (full-time) or 2,400 (part-time) per semester for international students

Main Language(s) of Instruction: English, Tamil, Malayalam, Hindi, Bengali

Accrediting Agency: National Assessment and Accreditation Council (NAAC)

Degrees and Diplomas: *Bachelor's Degree*; *Postgraduate Diploma*; *Master's Degree*; *Master of Philosophy*; *Doctor of Philosophy*. Also undergraduate certificates; MBA; MCA

Student Services: Academic Counselling, Canteen, Cultural Activities, Facilities for disabled people, Health Services, Sports Facilities

Publications: Push

Academic Staff *2010-2011*	MEN	WOMEN	**TOTAL**
FULL-TIME	271	85	**356**

Student Numbers *2010-2011*			
All (Foreign included)	2,881	1,766	c. **4,647**

Distance students, 10,755.

Last Updated: 13/07/11

POSTGRADUATE INSTITUTE OF MEDICAL EDUCATION AND RESEARCH (PGIMER)

Sector 12, Chandigarh, Union Territory 160012
Tel: +91(172) 274-6018 +91(172) 275-6565
Fax: +91(172) 274-4401 +91(172) 274-5078
EMail: pgimer-chd@nic.in
Website: http://www.pgimer.nic.in

Acting Director: Vinay Sakhuja Tel: +91(172) 274-8363
Registrar: Naresh Virdi

Programme

Elective Training; **Short Term Training** (Medicine)

Course

Medicine (Anaesthesiology; Biochemistry; Biotechnology; Cardiology; Community Health; Dental Technology; Dermatology; Endocrinology; Forensic Medicine and Dentistry; Gastroenterology; Gynaecology and Obstetrics; Health Administration; Hepatology; Immunology; Medical Technology; Medicine; Microbiology; Nephrology; Neurological Therapy; Neurology; Ophthalmology; Orthodontics; Orthopaedics; Otorhinolaryngology; Paediatrics; Pathology; Pharmacology; Plastic Surgery; Pneumology; Psychiatry and Mental Health; Public Health; Radiology; Rehabilitation and Therapy; Social and Preventive Medicine; Surgery; Urology; Venereology); **Nursing** (Community Health; Medicine; Nursing; Surgery); **Paramedical** (Biochemistry; Biotechnology; Laboratory Techniques; Medical Technology; Microbiology; Pathology; Pharmacology; Physiology; Radiology; Speech Therapy and Audiology; Treatment Techniques)

Further Information: Also Nehru Hospital (1,400 beds).

History: Founded 1962, its objectives being to train in all branches of Medicine, conduct research and provide patient care of the highest standard. Declared an Institute of 'national importance' and became an autonomous body 1966.

Admission Requirements: 12th year senior secondary/intermediate examination or recognized foreign equivalent

Main Language(s) of Instruction: English

Degrees and Diplomas: *Bachelor's Degree*; *Bachelor's Degree (professional)*; *Postgraduate Diploma*; *Master's Degree*; *Doctor of Philosophy*. Also Diploma and Certificate courses.

Student Services: Cultural Activities, Health Services, Sports Facilities

Last Updated: 13/07/11

POTTI SREERAMULU TELUGU UNIVERSITY

Lalitha Kala Kshetram, Public Gardens,
Hyderabad, Andhra Pradesh 500 004
Tel: +91(40) 2323-0435
Fax: +91(40) 2323-6045
EMail: info@teluguuniversity.ac.in
Website: http://www.teluguuniversity.ac.in

Vice-Chancellor: Elluri Siva Reddy (2012-)
Tel: +91(40) 2323-4815 EMail: vc@teluguuniversity.ac.in

Registrar: Battu Ramesh
Tel: +91(40) 2323-0435 EMail: registrar@teluguuniversity.ac.in

College

Sri Siddhendra Yogi Kala Pitham *(Kuchipudi Campus)* (Dance; Music; Singing; Theatre)

School

Comparative Studies (Aesthetics; Comparative Literature; Comparative Religion; English; European Languages; Indic Languages; Philosophy; Sanskrit; Translation and Interpretation); **Fine Arts** (Cultural Studies; Dance; Fine Arts; Folklore; Music; Musical Instruments; Painting and Drawing; Performing Arts; Psychology; Sculpture; Singing; Theatre; Tourism); **Folk and Tribal Lore** *(Warangal Campus)* (Folklore; Social Studies); **History, Culture and Archaeology** *(Sri Sailam Campus)* (Anthropology; Archaeology; Architecture; Art History; Cultural Studies; History; Prehistory); **Language Development** (Applied Linguistics; Indic Languages; Linguistics; Native Language Education; Terminology); **Social and other Sciences** (Architecture; Esoteric Practices; Journalism; Mass Communication; Social Sciences); **Telugu Literature** *(Rajahamundry Campus)* (Indic Languages; Literature)

Centre

Distance Education (Esoteric Practices; Film; Folklore; Foreign Languages Education; Indic Languages; Linguistics; Media Studies; Music; Native Language Education; Performing Arts; Sanskrit; Singing; Tourism); **International Telugu** (Dance; Indic Languages; Music); **Preparation of Encyclopedia** (Indic Languages)

Course

Computer Science (Computer Science; Multimedia)

Further Information: Campuses in Rajahmundry, Sri Sailam, Warangal and Kuchipudi. Also 14 Affiliated Colleges. A traditional and distance education institution.

History: Founded 1985.

Academic Year: July to April (July-December; December-April)

Fees: (Rupees): Undergraduate diploma, 450-10,200; Bachelor's degree, 2,400; Postgraduate diploma,1,900-10,200; Master, 2,000-3,000; M.Phil., 3,400; Ph.D., 3,900

Accrediting Agency: University Grants Commission (UGC).

Degrees and Diplomas: *Bachelor's Degree*; *Postgraduate Diploma*; *Master's Degree*; *Master of Philosophy*; *Doctor of Philosophy*. Also undergraduate certificate and diploma.

Publications: Telugu Vaani

Last Updated: 13/09/12

PRAVARA INSTITUTE OF MEDICAL SCIENCES (PIMS)

Rahata, Loni, Ahmednagar (Maharashtra) 413736
Tel: +91(2422) 273-600 +91(2422) 273-486
Fax: +91(2422) 273-442
EMail: contact@pmtpims.org; admission@pmtpims.org
Website: http://www.pravara.com

Vice-Chancellor: M.G. Takwale
Tel: +91(2422) 271-211 EMail: vcpims@pmtpims.org

Registrar: A.L. Bhosale EMail: registrar@pmtpims.org

College

Biotechnology (Biotechnology; Medical Technology); **Nursing** (Communication Studies; Midwifery; Nursing; Paediatrics; Surgery); **Physiotherapy and Rehabilitation Center** (Cardiology; Community Health; Neurosciences; Paediatrics; Physical Therapy; Rehabilitation and Therapy; Respiratory Therapy); **Rural Dental** *(and Hospital)* (Dental Technology; Dentistry; Medicine; Microbiology; Oral Pathology; Orthodontics; Periodontics; Radiology; Social and Preventive Medicine; Surgery); **Rural Medical** *(and Hospital)* (Anaesthesiology; Anatomy; Forensic Medicine and Dentistry; Gynaecology and Obstetrics; Medicine; Microbiology; Ophthalmology; Orthopaedics; Otorhinolaryngology; Paediatrics; Pathology; Pharmacology; Physiology; Radiology; Social and Preventive Medicine; Surgery; Toxicology; Treatment Techniques)

School

Bioscience Management *(Sinnar)* (Biological and Life Sciences; Business Administration; Marketing; Pharmacy)

Centre

Social Medicine (Epidemiology; Health Administration; Health Sciences; Social and Preventive Medicine)

Further Information: 800 hospital beds

History: Founded 2003. A 'Deemed University'.

Fees: (Rupees): Undergraduate programmes, 65,000-4,50,000 per annum for Indian students and (US Dollars) 5,000-40,000 per annum for international students. Graduate programmes, 50,000-525,000 per annum for Indian students and 80,000-650,000 per annum for international students

Accrediting Agency: Government of India; University Grants commission (UGC); Medical Council of India (MCI); Dental Council of India (DCI); All India Physiotherapists Association (AIPA) Rehabilitation Council of India (RCI); Nursing Council of India (INC).

Degrees and Diplomas: *Bachelor's Degree*; *Bachelor's Degree (professional)*; *Postgraduate Diploma*; *Master's Degree*; *Doctor of Philosophy*. Also undergraduate diploma and certificate programmes; MBA

Student Services: Canteen

Last Updated: 13/07/11

PRESIDENCY UNIVERSITY, KOLKATA (PRESIUNIV)

86/1 College Street, Kolkata, West Bengal 700 073
EMail: registrar@presiuniv.ac.in
Website: http://www.presiuniv.ac.in/

Vice-Chancellor: Malabika Sarkar

Faculty

Arts (Arts and Humanities; English; Hindi; History; Indic Languages; Philosophy; Political Sciences; Sociology); **Science** (Biotechnology; Botany; Chemistry; Economic and Finance Policy; Geography; Geology; Mathematics; Physics; Physiology; Statistics; Zoology)

Centre

Bioinformatics *(DBT)* (Biological and Life Sciences; Computer Science); **North-Eastern Languages, Bengali, Santali and Hindi** *(Ghandi)* (Hindi; Modern Languages)

History: Founded 1817 as Hindoo College. Renamed Presidency College 1855. Acquired university status 2010.

Degrees and Diplomas: *Bachelor's Degree*; *Master's Degree*; *Master of Philosophy*; *Doctor of Philosophy*

Student Services: Canteen, Sports Facilities

Last Updated: 06/01/12

PRIN. L. N. WELINGKAR INSTITUTE OF MANAGEMENT DEVELOPMENT AND RESEARCH

Lakhamshi Napoo Road, Near Matunga,
Mumbai, Maharashtra 400 019
Tel: +91(22) 2417-8300
Fax: +91(22) 2410-5585
Website: http://welingkar.org

Director: Uday Salunkhe

Programme

Management (Business Administration; Finance; Health Administration; Human Resources; Marketing; Retailing and Wholesaling)

Further Information: Also Bengaluru Campus

Degrees and Diplomas: *Post Diploma*; *Postgraduate Diploma*; *Master's Degree*

Last Updated: 23/01/12

PRIST UNIVERSITY (PRIST)

Trichy – Thanjavur Highway, Vallam,
Thanjavur, Tamil Nadu 613403
Tel: +91(4362) 265-021 +91(4362) 265-022
Fax: +91(4362) 265-150
EMail: contact@prist.ac.in
Website: http://www.prist.ac.in

Vice-Chancellor: N. Ethirajalu

Registrar: K. V. Balasubrmanian
EMail: registrar@prist.ac.in; bsubramanian43@yahoo.com

Faculty

Arts and Science (Biochemistry; Biotechnology; Chemistry; Computer Science; English; Information Technology; Mathematics; Microbiology; Physics; Social Work; South and Southeast Asian Languages); **Catering and Hotel Management** (Cooking and Catering; Hotel Management; Management); **Commerce and Management** (Business Administration; Business and Commerce; Economics; Health Administration; Insurance; Management); **Education** (Business Education; Computer Education; Education; Foreign Languages Education; Humanities and Social Science Education; Mathematics Education; Native Language Education; Science Education); **Engineering and Technology** (Biotechnology; Civil Engineering; Computer Engineering; Computer Networks; Computer Science; Data Processing; Electrical and Electronic Engineering; Electronic Engineering; Engineering; Information Technology; Mechanical Engineering; Mechanical Equipment and Maintenance; Pharmacology; Pharmacy; Software Engineering; Technology; Telecommunications Engineering)

Further Information: Two campuses in Thanjavur (East and West) and other sites in Kumbakonam, Chennai, Tiruchirappalli, Puducherry

History: Founded 1994 as Ponnaiyah Ramajayam College. Acquired present status 2008. A 'Deemed University'.

Accrediting Agency: All India Council of Technical Education (AICTE); University Grants Commission (UGC)/National Assessment and Accreditation Council (NAAC); Directorate of Employment and Training (DET); National council for Teachers Education (NCTE); Distance Education Council (DEC)

Degrees and Diplomas: *Post Diploma*; *Bachelor's Degree*; *Bachelor's Degree (professional)*; *Postgraduate Diploma*; *Master's Degree*; *Master of Philosophy*; *Doctor of Philosophy*. Also MBA

Student Services: Health Services, Sports Facilities

Last Updated: 18/07/11

PT. RAVISHANKAR SHUKLA UNIVERSITY

Pandit Ravishankar Shukla Vishwavidyalaya (PT. R.S.U)

Amanaka G.E. Road,
Raipur, Madhya Pradesh (Chhattisgarh) 492010
Tel: +91(771) 226-2540
Fax: +91(771) 226-2818
EMail: drianant@gmail.com
Website: http://www.prsu.ac.in

Vice-Chancellor: Shiv Kumar Pandey
Tel: +91 (771) 2262540
EMail: skp@iucaa.ernet.in; proskp@gmail.com

Registrar: K. K. Chandrakar Tel: +91 (771) 2262540

School

Studies in Adult, Continuing Education and Extension (Adult Education; Education); **Studies in Ancient Indian History, Culture and Archaeology** (Archaeology; Architecture; Art History; Cultural Studies; History; Museum Studies; Political Sciences; Regional Studies; Tourism); **Studies in Anthropology** (Anthropology; Criminology; Forensic Medicine and Dentistry); **Studies in Bio-Technology** (Biotechnology); **Studies in Chemistry** (Analytical Chemistry; Chemistry; Organic Chemistry; Physical Chemistry); **Studies in Comparative Religion and Philosophy** (Comparative Religion; Philosophy; Philosophy of Education; Yoga); **Studies in Computer Science** (Computer Networks; Computer Science; Data Processing; Information Technology); **Studies in Economics** (Agricultural Economics; Economics); **Studies in Electronics** (Automation and Control Engineering; Electronic Engineering; Information Technology; Laser Engineering; Measurement and Precision Engineering; Nanotechnology; Optical Technology; Optics; Solid State Physics); **Studies in Geography** (Geography; Geography (Human); Marine Science and Oceanography; Meteorology; Natural Resources; Regional Planning; Surveying and Mapping); **Studies in Geology and Water Resource Management** (Geology; Mineralogy; Petrology; Surveying and Mapping; Water Management; Water Science); **Studies in History** (History; Philosophy); **Studies in Law** (Administrative Law; Commercial Law; Constitutional Law; Criminal Law; Criminology; International Law; Law); **Studies in Library and Information Science** (Computer Science; Documentation Techniques; Information Management; Information Sciences; Information Technology; Library Science); **Studies in Life Sciences** (Biochemistry; Biological and Life Sciences; Microbiology); **Studies in Literature and Languages** (English; French; German; Hindi; Linguistics; Literature; Modern Languages; Russian; Translation and Interpretation); **Studies in Mathematics** (Mathematics); **Studies in Physical Education** (Physical Education); **Studies in Physics and Astrophysics** (Astrophysics; Physics; Solid State Physics); **Studies in Psychology** (Clinical Psychology; Labour and Industrial Relations; Psychology); **Studies in Sociology** (Sociology); **Studies in Statistics** (Applied Mathematics; Operations Research; Statistics)

Institute

Management (Business Administration; Finance; Human Resources; Management; Marketing); **Pharmacy** (Pharmacy); **Teachers Education** (Teacher Training); **Technology** (Technology); **Tourism and Hotel Management** (Hotel and Restaurant; Tourism)

Centre

Regional Studies and Research (Development Studies; Regional Planning; Regional Studies); **Women's Studies** (Women's Studies)

Further Information: Also 261 Affiliated Colleges.

History: Founded 1964.

Academic Year: July to April

Admission Requirements: 12th year senior secondary/intermediate examination or recognized foreign equivalent

Fees: Varies from course to course

Main Language(s) of Instruction: English

Accrediting Agency: UGC, AICTE, NCTE, NAAC etc.

Degrees and Diplomas: *Post Diploma*; *Bachelor's Degree*; *Bachelor's Degree (professional)*; *Postgraduate Diploma*; *Master's Degree*; *Master of Philosophy*; *Doctor of Philosophy*. Also undergraduate certificates; Bachelor's degree honours; MBA and MCA

Student Services: Academic Counselling, Canteen, Careers Guidance, Cultural Activities, Facilities for disabled people, Health Services, Language Laboratory, Sports Facilities

Publications: Ravishankar University Journal

Last Updated: 11/07/11

PT. SUNDERLAL SHARMA (OPEN) UNIVERSITY (PSSOU)

Vyapar Vihar, Near Deen Dayal Upadhyay Park,
Bilaspur, Chattisgarh 495 001
Tel: +91(7752) 414-225 +91(7752) 261-051
Fax: +91(7752) 414-245
EMail: vc@pssou.ac.in; registrar@pssou.ac.in; info@pssou.ac.in
Website: http://www.pssou.ac.in/

Vice-Chancellor: A. R. Chandraker Tel: +91(7752) 414-255

Registrar: Smt. Indu Anant Tel: +91(94255) 33-303

Faculty

Commerce (Business and Commerce; E- Business/Commerce); **Continuing Education** (Continuing Education); **Education** (Education); **Health Sciences** (Alternative Medicine; Ayurveda; Health Sciences; Yoga); **Humanities** (Arts and Humanities; English; Hindi; History; Sanskrit); **Management** (Management); **Science and Technology** (Computer Science; Information Technology; Mathematics; Technology); **Social Sciences** (Economics; Political Sciences; Social Sciences; Sociology)

History: Founded 2005.

Degrees and Diplomas: *Post Diploma*; *Bachelor's Degree*; *Postgraduate Diploma*; *Master's Degree*
Last Updated: 03/01/12

PUNJAB AGRICULTURAL UNIVERSITY (PAU)

Ludhiana, Punjab 141004
Tel: +91(161) 240-1960 +91(161) 240-1979
Fax: +91(161) 240-0945
EMail: registrar@pau.edu
Website: http://www.pau.edu/

Vice-Chancellor: Baldev Singh Dhillon (2011-)
Tel: +91(161) 240-1794 EMail: vc@pau.edu

Registrar: Raj kumar Mahey
Tel: +91(161) 240-1960 EMail: registrar@pau.edu

College

Agricultural Engineering (Agricultural Engineering; Agricultural Equipment; Civil Engineering; Computer Engineering; Computer Science; Electrical Engineering; Energy Engineering; Environmental Engineering; Food Technology; Information Technology; Irrigation; Machine Building; Mechanical Engineering; Power Engineering; Production Engineering; Soil Science; Thermal Engineering; Water Management; Water Science); **Agriculture** (Agricultural Education; Agricultural Engineering; Agriculture; Agronomy; Biotechnology; Crop Production; Ecology; Entomology; Floriculture; Food Science; Food Technology; Forestry; Genetics; Home Economics; Horticulture; Landscape Architecture; Meteorology; Natural Resources; Physiology; Plant Pathology; Soil Science; Toxicology; Vegetable Production); **Basic Sciences and Humanities** (Agricultural Business; Agricultural Economics; Agricultural Management; Arts and Humanities; Biochemistry; Botany; Business Administration; Chemistry; Cultural Studies; Economics; Embryology and Reproduction Biology; Finance; Fishery; Inorganic Chemistry; Journalism; Management; Marketing; Mass Communication; Mathematics; Microbiology; Modern Languages; Nuclear Physics; Organic Chemistry; Parasitology; Physical Chemistry; Physics; Physiology; Sociology; Solid State Physics; Statistics; Zoology); **Home Sciences** (Child Care and Development; Clothing and Sewing; Cooking and Catering; Development Studies; Dietetics; Fashion Design; Food Science; Handicrafts; Home Economics; Interior Design; Nutrition; Textile Technology)

Course

Post Graduate Studies (Actuarial Science; Agricultural Economics; Agricultural Education; Agricultural Equipment; Agriculture; Agronomy; Animal Husbandry; Biochemistry; Biotechnology; Botany; Business Administration; Cell Biology; Chemistry; Civil Engineering; Clothing and Sewing; Communication Studies; Computer Engineering; Computer Graphics; Computer Networks; Computer Science; Crop Production; Cultural Studies; E- Business/Commerce; Economics; Electrical Engineering; Embryology and Reproduction Biology; Endocrinology; Energy Engineering; Entomology; Finance; Floriculture; Food Science; Food Technology; Forestry; Genetics; Gerontology; Home Economics; Horticulture; Human Resources; Human Rights; Information Management; Information Sciences; Inorganic Chemistry; International Business; Journalism; Labour and Industrial Relations; Labour Law; Landscape Architecture; Library Science; Literature; Management; Marketing; Mathematics; Measurement and Precision Engineering; Mechanical Engineering; Mechanics; Meteorology; Microbiology; Molecular Biology; Natural Resources; Nuclear Physics; Nutrition; Parasitology; Physical Chemistry; Physics; Plant Pathology; Power Engineering; Production Engineering; Retailing and Wholesaling; Social Problems; Sociology; Software Engineering; Soil Science; Solid State Physics; Statistics; Textile Technology; Thermal Engineering; Water Management; Water Science; Wildlife; Writing; Zoology)

Further Information: Also University Farm. 16 Regional Research Stations

History: Founded 1962. The University is modelled on the United States Land Grant Institutions, has a semester system of education, and aims to integrate the threefold functions of teaching, research and extension education by linking them with the needs of Agricultural Production and Livestock Development.

Academic Year: August to July

Admission Requirements: 12th year senior secondary/intermediate examination or recognized foreign equivalent

Fees: (Rupees):Tuition fees for undergraduate programmes, 4,100-38,500 per semester; For postgraduate programmes, 6,710-49,500 per semester

Main Language(s) of Instruction: English

Accrediting Agency: ICAR

Degrees and Diplomas: *Post Diploma*; *Bachelor's Degree*; *Bachelor's Degree (professional)*; *Postgraduate Diploma*; *Master's Degree*; *Doctor of Philosophy*. Also undergraduate certificate; Bachelor's degree Honours, 3-6 yrs.

Student Services: Academic Counselling, Canteen, Careers Guidance, Cultural Activities, Health Services, Language Laboratory, Nursery Care, Social Counselling, Sports Facilities

Publications: Journal of Research; Package of Practices for Rabi and Kharif Crops; Progressive Farming

Publishing House: University Press

Academic Staff *2010-2011*: Total 866

Last Updated: 18/07/11

PUNJAB TECHNICAL UNIVERSITY (PTU)

Jalandhar-Kapurthala Highway, Near Pushpa Gujral Science City,
Kapurthala, Punjab 144061
Tel: +91(1822) 662-501
Fax: +91(1822) 662-500
EMail: rajneesh.ptu@gmail.com
Website: http://ptu.ac.in

Vice-Chancellor: Sh. Rakesh Kumar Verma EMail: vc@ptu.ac.in

Registrar: H.S. Bains
Tel: +91(1822) 662-521
EMail: registrar@ptu.ac.in; bains.ptu2010@gmail.com

International Relations: Buta Singh Sidhu, Dean (Academics)
Tel: +91(1822) 662-562

EMail: deanacad@ptu.ac; deanacad.ptu@gmail.com; butasidhu@yahoo.com

Programme

Biotechnology (Biotechnology); **Engineering** (Architecture; Automotive Engineering; Biomedical Engineering; Biotechnology; Chemical Engineering; Civil Engineering; Computer Engineering; Computer Science; Electrical Engineering; Electronic Engineering; Engineering; Information Technology; Measurement and Precision Engineering; Mechanical Engineering; Production Engineering; Telecommunications Engineering; Textile Design); **Hotel Management and Air Lines** (Air Transport; Cooking and Catering; Hotel Management; Management; Service Trades; Tourism); **Management** (Business Administration; Business Computing; Management); **Others** (Computer Science; Fashion Design; Laboratory Techniques; Medical Technology; Multimedia; Pharmacy; Visual Arts); **Pharmacy** (Pharmacy); **Technology** *(M-Tech)* (Automation and Control Engineering; Biotechnology; Chemical Engineering; Computer Engineering; Computer Graphics; Computer Science; Construction Engineering; Electrical Engineering; Electronic Engineering; Environmental Studies; Industrial Engineering; Information Technology; Machine Building; Measurement and Precision Engineering; Mechanical Engineering; Nanotechnology; Power Engineering; Production Engineering; Technology; Telecommunications Engineering; Thermal Engineering)

Further Information: Also over 300 affiliated institutions: 40 Engineering colleges, 56 Management colleges, 17 Pharmacy colleges, 6 Architecture colleges, 2 Hotel Management colleges and 13 colleges offering programmes in Medical Lab Technology and IT disciplines. A traditional and distance education institution.

History: Founded 1997.

Academic Year: July to December; January to May

Admission Requirements: Secondary School Education (10+2 yrs)

Fees: (Rupees): Tuition fee, 15,000 to 25,000 per semester

Main Language(s) of Instruction: English

Accrediting Agency: University Grants Commission (UGC); All India Council for Technical Education (AICTE)

Degrees and Diplomas: *Bachelor's Degree*; *Bachelor's Degree (professional)*; *Postgraduate Diploma*; *Master's Degree*. Also MBA and MCA

Student Services: Academic Counselling, Canteen, Careers Guidance, Cultural Activities, Facilities for disabled people, Foreign Studies Centre, Health Services, Language Laboratory, Social Counselling, Sports Facilities

Publications: International Journals of Surface Engineering and Material Technology

Academic Staff *2011-2012*: Total 147

STAFF WITH DOCTORATE: Total 56

Student Numbers *2011-2012*: Total 40,000

Last Updated: 16/04/12

PUNJABI UNIVERSITY

Patiala, Punjab 147002
Tel: +91(175) 304-6366
Fax: +91(175) 228-3073
EMail: dpm@pbi.ac.in
Website: http://punjabiuniversity.ac.in/

Vice-Chancellor: Jaspal Singh
Tel: +91(175) 228-6418 EMail: vc@pbi.ac.in

Director, Planning and Monitoring: A.S. Chawla
Tel: +91(175) 228-6416
EMail: regpup@pbi.ac.in; registrar@pbi.ac.in

Faculty

Arts and Culture (Cultural Studies; Dance; Fine Arts; Music; Musical Instruments; Performing Arts; Radio and Television Broadcasting; Theatre); **Business Studies** (Accountancy; Banking; Business Administration; Business and Commerce; Business Computing; Economics; Finance; Insurance; Management; Marketing); **Education and Information Sciences** (Education; Film; Information Sciences; Journalism; Mass Communication; Media Studies; Physical Education; Radio and Television Broadcasting; Yoga); **Engineering and Technology** (Computer Engineering; Electronic Engineering; Engineering; Mechanical Engineering; Technology; Telecommunications Engineering); **Languages** (Arabic; Chinese; English; French; German; Hindi; Indic Languages; Linguistics; Literature; Persian; Russian; Sanskrit; South and Southeast Asian Languages; Terminology); **Law** (Administrative Law; Civil Law; Commercial Law; Constitutional Law; Criminal Law; Environmental Studies; International Law; Labour Law; Law; Public Law); **Life Sciences** (Biological and Life Sciences; Biotechnology; Botany; Food Technology; Genetics; Zoology); **Medicine** (Nutrition; Pharmacology; Pharmacy; Physical Therapy; Sports; Sports Management); **Physical Sciences** (Applied Physics; Astrophysics; Chemistry; Computer Engineering; Computer Science; Electronic Engineering; Forensic Medicine and Dentistry; Information Technology; Inorganic Chemistry; Maintenance Technology; Mathematics; Meteorology; Operations Research; Organic Chemistry; Physical Chemistry; Physics; Statistics); **Social Sciences** (Anthropology; Asian Religious Studies; Clinical Psychology; Comparative Religion; Economics; Educational Psychology; Ethics; Geography; History; Human Rights; Industrial and Organizational Psychology; International Law; International Relations; Medieval Studies; Military Science; Modern History; Peace and Disarmament; Philosophy; Political Sciences; Protective Services; Psychology; Public Administration; Religious Studies; Social Psychology; Social Sciences; Social Work; Sociology; Women's Studies)

Department

Development of Punjabi Language (South and Southeast Asian Languages); **Punjab Historical Studies** (History); **Punjabi Literary Studies** (Literature; Performing Arts; Theatre); **Sri Guru Granth Sahib Studies** (Religion; Religious Studies); **Tourism, Hospitality and Hotel Management** (Hotel and Restaurant; Hotel Management; Tourism)

Centre

Advanced Media Studies (Media Studies); **Computer** *(University)* (Computer Science); **Dr. Balbir Singh Sahitya Kendra Panchbati** (Comparative Religion; Cultural Studies; History); **I.A.S. and Allied Services Training**; **Prof. Harban Singh Encyclopaedia of Sikhism** (Religion); **Research in Economic Change** (Economics); **Sufi Studies** *(Baba Farid)* (Arts and Humanities; Business and Commerce; Fine Arts; History; Linguistics; Medieval Studies); **Technical Development of Punjabi language, Literature and Culture** *(Advanced)* (Cultural Studies; Literature; South and Southeast Asian Languages)

Research Department

Maharishi Valmiki Chair (Literature); **Text Book Cell**; **Translation Cell** (Translation and Interpretation)

Chair

Gurmat Sangeet (Cultural Studies; Literature; Music); **Sri Guru Tegh Bahadur National Integration** (Religious Studies)

Further Information: Also 166 Colleges Affiliated Colleges and 65 Teaching/Research Departments; Campuses in Rampura Phul, Jhunir, Karandi, Sardulgarh, Rallah and Delha Sihan, Bathinda, Mansa and Sangrur. Regional Centres: Guru Kashi Campus, Talwandi Sabo, Guru Kashi Regional Centre, Bathinda, Nawab Sher Mohammed Khan Institute of Advanced Studies, Malerkotla, Regional Centre for Information Technology and Management, Mohali, and Dr Balbir Singh Sahitya Kendra, Dehradun.

History: Founded 1962. A Government aided institution under the jurisdiction of the Patiala, Ropar, Sangrur, Bhatinda and Faridkot Districts of Punjab.

Academic Year: July to June (July-December; January-June)

Admission Requirements: 12th year senior secondary/intermediate examination or recognized foreign equivalent

Fees: (Rupees): 1,920-12,000 per annum

Main Language(s) of Instruction: English, Punjabi, Hindi, Urdu

Degrees and Diplomas: *Post Diploma*; *Bachelor's Degree*; *Bachelor's Degree (professional)*; *Postgraduate Diploma*; *Master's Degree*; *Master of Philosophy*; *Doctor of Philosophy*. Also Advanced Diploma and Certificate courses; MBA

Student Services: Health Services, Sports Facilities

Publications: Bakha Sanjam Khoj, Patrika; Nanak Prakash Patrika; Punjab Past and Present; Sahitya Marg

Publishing House: University Press

Last Updated: 18/07/11

RABINDRA BHARATI UNIVERSITY

Rabindra Bharati Viswavidyaiaya (RBU)
Emerald Bower, 56-A Barrackpore Trunk Road,
Kolkata, West Bengal 700050
Tel: +91(33) 556-8079 5573028
Fax: +91(33) 2556-8079
EMail: rbreg@cal13.vsnl.net.in
Website: http://www.rbu.ac.in

Vice-Chancellor: Karuna Sindhu Das Tel: +91(33) 2556-8019

Registrar: Tapati Mukherjee EMail: registrar@rbu.ac.in

Faculty

Arts (Arts and Humanities; Economics; Education; English; History; Indic Languages; Information Sciences; Library Science; Mathematics; Philosophy; Political Sciences; Sanskrit; Social Sciences); **Fine Arts** (Dance; Fine Arts; Mass Communication; Musical Instruments; Performing Arts; Singing; Theatre; Video); **Visual Arts** (Art History; Fine Arts; Graphic Arts; Museum Studies; Painting and Drawing; Sculpture; Visual Arts)

Programme

Adult and Continuing Education (Adult Education; Management; Media Studies; Social Work)

School

Language and Culture (French; Hindi; Indic Languages; Italian; Japanese); **Vedic Studies** (Ayurveda)

Centre

Dr. Sarvepalli Radhakrishnan Study; **Gandhian Studies** (History; Political Sciences); **Studies and Research on Tagore** (Literature)

Further Information: Also one Affiliated College

History: Founded 1954 as West Bengal State Academy of Dance, Drama, Music and Visual Arts. Acquired present status and title 1962.

Academic Year: June to June

Admission Requirements: Graduate courses, 12th year senior secondary/intermediate examination or recognized foreign equivalent. P.G. courses, Hons. Graduate with higher percentage of marks; M.Phil and Ph.D. courses, Post graduate with higher percentage of marks.

Fees: (Rupees): Bachelor, 1,169 per annum; Master, 2,104 per annum

Main Language(s) of Instruction: Bengali, English

Accrediting Agency: National Assessment and Accreditation Council (NAAC)

Degrees and Diplomas: *Post Diploma*; *Bachelor's Degree*; *Bachelor's Degree (professional)*; *Master's Degree*; *Master of Philosophy*; *Doctor of Philosophy*. Also Certificate courses in Foreign languages (French, Spanish, Japanese, Italian), Hindi, in NGO Management and in Rabindra Sangeet; Bachelor's degree honours, 3-5 yrs.

Student Services: Academic Counselling, Canteen, Careers Guidance, Cultural Activities, Facilities for disabled people, Health Services, Language Laboratory, Nursery Care, Social Counselling, Sports Facilities

Publications: Rabindra Bharati Patrika (Bilingual)

Publishing House: Rabindra Bharati University
Last Updated: 18/07/11

RAFFLES UNIVERSITY

Japanese Zone, National Highway-8, Neemrana, Rajasthan 301705
Tel: +91(9928) 777777
EMail: admission@rafflesuniversity.edu.in
Website: http://www.rafflesuniversity.edu.in

President: Kanta Ahuja

School

Behavioural Sciences (Behavioural Sciences); **Engineering** (Civil Engineering; Electrical Engineering; Engineering; Mechanical Engineering); **Law** (Law); **Liberal Studies** (Behavioural Sciences; Psychology); **Life Long Learning**; **Management** *(Alabbar)* (Business Administration; Management); **Sciences** (Natural Sciences)

History: Founded 2011.

Degrees and Diplomas: *Bachelor's Degree*; *Master's Degree*
Last Updated: 17/01/12

RAJASTHAN AYURVED UNIVERSITY, JODHPUR

Kadwad, Jodhpur–Nagaur Highway Road,
Jodhpur, Rajasthan 342 037
Tel: +91(291) 515-3721
Fax: +91(291) 515-3700
EMail: rau_jodhpur@yahoo.co.in
Website: http://www.raujodhpur.org/

Vice-Chancellor: Radhey Shyam Sharma Tel: +91(291) 515-3711

Registrar: Veena Lahoti Tel: +91(291) 515-3702

College

Ayurveda (Anatomy; Ayurveda; Forensic Medicine and Dentistry; Gynaecology and Obstetrics; Hygiene; Medicine; Paediatrics; Pathology; Pharmacy; Surgery; Toxicology)

Further Information: Also 44 affiliated colleges/institutions

History: Founded 2002.

Fees: (Indian Rupee): 30,000-120,000 per annum

Degrees and Diplomas: *Post Diploma*; *Bachelor's Degree (professional)*; *Master's Degree*; *Doctor of Philosophy*. Also Certificate Course

Student Numbers *2010-2011*: Total: c. 7,000
Last Updated: 04/01/12

RAJASTHAN TECHNICAL UNIVERSITY (RTU)

Rawatbhata Road, Kota, Rajasthan 324 010
Tel: +91(744) 247-3861
EMail: rtuweb@gmail.com
Website: http://www.rtu.ac.in/

Vice-Chancellor: R.P. Yadav
Tel: +91(744) 247-3001 EMail: vcofficertu@yahoo.co.in

Registrar: Ambrish Mehta
Tel: +91(744) 247-3003 EMail: registrar_rtu@yahoo.co.in

College

Engineering (Arts and Humanities; Chemistry; Civil Engineering; Computer Engineering; Electrical Engineering; Electronic Engineering; Engineering; English; Mathematics; Mechanical Engineering; Physics; Telecommunications Engineering)

Further Information: Also affiliates about 135 Engineering Colleges, 35 MCA Colleges, 142 MBA Colleges, 8 M.Tech Colleges and 3 Hotel Management and Catering Institutes

History: Founded 2006.

Degrees and Diplomas: *Bachelor's Degree (professional)*; *Master's Degree*. Also MBA
Last Updated: 05/01/12

RAJASTHAN UNIVERSITY OF HEALTH SCIENCES (RUHSRAJ)

Sector-18, Kumbha Marg, Pratap Nagar, Tonk Road,
Jaipur, Rajasthan
Tel: +91(141) 279-5501
EMail: rajmed_university@rediffmail.com
Website: http://www.ruhsraj.org/

Vice-Chancellor: Raja Babu Panwar Tel: +91(141) 279-0481

Registrar: Anuprerna Kuntal Tel: +91(141) 279-1928

Course

Dentistry (Dentistry); **Medicine** (Medicine); **Nursing** (Nursing); **Paramedical Sciences** (Medical Auxiliaries); **Pharmacy** (Pharmacy); **Physiotherapy and Occupational Therapy** (Occupational Therapy; Physical Therapy)

Further Information: Also 14 Affilated Colleges

History: Founded 2005.

Degrees and Diplomas: *Post Diploma*; *Bachelor's Degree*; *Bachelor's Degree (professional)*; *Master's Degree*
Last Updated: 05/01/12

RAJENDRA AGRICULTURAL UNIVERSITY (RAU)

Pusa, Samastipur, Bihar 848125
Tel: +91(6274) 240-239
Fax: +91(6274) 240-277
EMail: info@pusavarsity.org.in
Website: http://www.pusavarsity.org.in/pusa1.htm

Vice-Chancellor: M.L. Choudhary
Tel: +91(6274) 240-226 EMail: vcrau@sify.com

Registrar: R. C. Rai Tel: +91(6274) 240-239

College

Agricultural Engineering (Agricultural Engineering; Agricultural Equipment; Energy Engineering; Harvest Technology; Irrigation; Power Engineering; Soil Conservation; Soil Science; Water Management; Water Science); **Agriculture** *(Tirhut - Dholi, Muzaffarpur)* (Agriculture); **Agriculture** *(Bhola Paswan Shastry - Dumraon (Buxar))* (Agriculture); **Agriculture** *(Mandan Bharti - Agwanpur, (Saharsa))* (Agriculture); **Basic Sciences and Humanities** (Agriculture; Biochemistry; Biotechnology; Botany; Chemistry; Computer Science; Mathematics; Microbiology; Modern Languages; Molecular Biology; Physics; Statistics); **Fisheries** *(Dholi)* (Agricultural Economics; Agricultural Engineering; Aquaculture; Biochemistry; Biology; Fishery; Food Technology; Marine Science and Oceanography; Microbiology; Statistics); **Home Science** (Child Care and Development; Clothing and Sewing; Food Science; Home Economics; Home Economics Education; Nutrition); **Horticulture** *(Noorsarai, (Nalanda))* (Horticulture); **Veterinary** *(Bihar)* (Anatomy; Animal Husbandry; Biochemistry; Biological and Life Sciences; Embryology and Reproduction Biology; Epidemiology; Ethics; Genetics; Gynaecology and Obstetrics; Histology; Microbiology; Parasitology; Pathology; Pharmacology; Physiology; Public Health; Radiology; Social and Preventive Medicine; Surgery; Toxicology; Veterinary Science)

Institute

Dairy ScienceTechnology *(Sanjay Gandhi - Patna)* (Agricultural Economics; Animal Husbandry; Chemistry; Dairy; Embryology and Reproduction Biology; Engineering; Food Technology; Microbiology)

Further Information: Also 7 Constituent Colleges and 10 Research Institutes

History: Founded 1970.

Admission Requirements: 12th year senior secondary/intermediate examination or recognized foreign equivalent

Fees: (Rupees): 500-700 per semester

Main Language(s) of Instruction: Hindi, English

Degrees and Diplomas: *Bachelor's Degree*; *Bachelor's Degree (professional)*; *Postgraduate Diploma*; *Master's Degree*; *Doctor of Philosophy*. Also Certificate Courses; Bachelor's degree honours; MBA.

Last Updated: 19/07/11

RAJIV GANDHI INDIAN INSTITUTE OF MANAGEMENT SHILLONG

Mayurbhanj Complex, Nongthymmai, Shillong, Meghalaya 793014
Tel: +91(364) 2308-000
EMail: admissions@iimshillong.in; pr@iimshillong.in
Website: http://www.iimshillong.in/

Director: Keya Sengupta EMail: director@iimshillong.in

Programme

Management (Management)

History: Created 2004.

Degrees and Diplomas: *Postgraduate Diploma*; *Doctor of Philosophy*

Last Updated: 17/10/12

RAJIV GANDHI NATIONAL INSTITUTE OF YOUTH DEVELOPMENT (RGNIYD)

Bangalore Highway, Beemanthangal, Sriperumbudur, Chennai, Tamil Nadu 602 105
Tel: +91(44) 2716-2741 +91(44) 2716-2705
Fax: +91(44) 2716-3227
EMail: info@rgniyd.gov.in
Website: http://www.rgniyd.gov.in

Director: Michael Vetha Siromony
Tel: +91(44) 2716-2705 EMail: dir@rgniyd.gov.in

Registrar: D. Jayalakshmi
Tel: +91(44) 2716-3942 EMail: registrar@rgniyd.gov.in

School

Counseling (Psychology); **Gender Studies** (Gender Studies); **Governance and Public Policy** (Government; Public Administration); **Life Skills Education and Social Harmony**; **Youth Studies and Extension** (Information Technology; Management; Psychology)

History: A 'Deemed University'.

Degrees and Diplomas: *Master's Degree*

Last Updated: 20/12/11

RAJIV GANDHI NATIONAL UNIVERSITY OF LAW (RGNUL)

Mohindra Kothi, Mall Road, Patiala, Punjab 147 001
Tel: +91(175) 230-4188 +91(175) 230-4491
Fax: +91(175) 230-4189
EMail: info@rgnul.ac.in
Website: http://rgnul.ac.in/

Vice-Chancellor: Paramjit S. Jaswal

Registrar: G.I.S. Sandhu

School

Law (Administrative Law; Banking; Commercial Law; Constitutional Law; Environmental Studies; Family Studies; Human Rights; Insurance; International Law; Labour Law; Law; Public Law; Taxation)

History: Founded 2006.

Fees: (Indian Rupee): Undergraduate tuition, 7,500 per annum; Graduate tuition, 43,000 per annum

Accrediting Agency: Bar Council of India (BCI); University Grants Commission (UGC)

Degrees and Diplomas: *Master's Degree*; *Master of Philosophy*; *Doctor of Philosophy*. Also Honours undergraduate integrated programme: B.A., LL.B. (HONS.), 5 yrs;

Student Services: Canteen, Health Services, Sports Facilities

Last Updated: 04/01/12

RAJIV GANDHI UNIVERSITY (RGU)

Rono Hills, Itanagar, Arunachal Pradesh 791112
Tel: +91(360) 277-253
Fax: +91(360) 277-317
EMail: rikamnt@yahoo.com
Website: http://www.rgu.ac.in

Vice-Chancellor: David R, Syiemlieh (2011-)
Tel: +91(360) 227-7252 EMail: vcrguniv@gmail.com

Registrar: Amitav Mitra
Tel: +91(360) 227-7253 EMail: registrar@rgu.ac.in

Faculty

Basic Sciences (Mathematics; Mathematics and Computer Science; Statistics); **Commerce and Management** (Accountancy; Advertising and Publicity; Business Administration; Business and Commerce; Business Computing; Commercial Law; Cooking and Catering; E- Business/Commerce; Finance; Hotel and Restaurant; Human Resources; Industrial and Organizational Psychology; Information Technology; International Business; Labour and Industrial Relations; Management; Marketing; Statistics; Taxation; Tourism); **Education** (Adult Education; Continuing Education; Education; Educational Administration; Educational Psychology; Educational Technology; Preschool Education; Special Education; Teacher Training); **Engineering and Information Technology** (Advertising and Publicity; Computer Engineering; Computer Graphics; Computer Networks; Computer Science; Data Processing; E-Business/Commerce; Electronic Engineering; Engineering; Information Technology; Mass Communication; Mathematics; Media Studies; Photography; Radio and Television Broadcasting; Software Engineering; Video; Visual Arts); **Environmental Sciences** (Demography and Population; Environmental Studies; Geography; Geography (Human); Safety Engineering; Surveying and Mapping); **Languages** (English; Hindi; Literature; Modern Languages); **Life**

Sciences (Biochemistry; Biotechnology; Botany; Cell Biology; Ecology; Endocrinology; Entomology; Environmental Studies; Genetics; Horticulture; Immunology; Microbiology; Molecular Biology; Natural Resources; Plant Pathology; Statistics; Wildlife; Zoology); **Social Sciences** (Agricultural Economics; Archaeology; Economics; History; International Economics; Mathematics; Political Sciences; Social Sciences; Sociology; Statistics)

Institute

Biodiversity; **Distance Education**; **Tribal Studies** *(Arunachal - AITS)* (Anthropology; Folklore; Linguistics; Native Language; Social Studies)

Further Information: Also 15 Affiliated Colleges. A traditional and distance education institution.

History: Founded 1984 as Arunachal University. Turned into a 'Central University' 2007.

Academic Year: July to June (July-December; January-June)

Admission Requirements: 12th year senior secondary/intermediate examination or recognized foreign equivalent. For Graduate admission, applicants must normally hold a First Degree with Honours or 50% marks

Fees: (Rupees): Undergraduate, 1,550 per annum; graduate, 1,275-2,490; postgraduate, 3,000

Main Language(s) of Instruction: English

Accrediting Agency: University Grants Commission (UGC)

Degrees and Diplomas: *Bachelor's Degree*; *Bachelor's Degree (professional)*; *Postgraduate Diploma*; *Master's Degree*; *Master of Philosophy*; *Doctor of Philosophy*. Also Certificate Courses; MBA

Student Services: Canteen, Cultural Activities, Sports Facilities

Last Updated: 19/07/11

RAJIV GANDHI UNIVERSITY OF HEALTH SCIENCES (RGUHS)

4th 'T' Block, Jayanagar, Bangalore, Karnataka 560 041
Tel: +91(80) 2696-1933 +91(80) 2696-1935
Fax: +91(80) 2665-8569
EMail: info@rguhs.ac.in
Website: http://www.rguhs.ac.in

Vice-Chancellor: K.S. Sriprakash (2011-)
Tel: +91(80) 2696-1926 EMail: vc@rguhs.ac.in

Registrar: Kumar Prem
Tel: +91(80) 2696-1928 EMail: registrar@rguhs.ac.in

Faculty

Anaesthesia Technology (Anaesthesiology; Cardiology; Oncology); **Ayurveda** (Ayurveda); **Cardiac Care Technology** (Cardiology; Medical Technology; Medicine); **Clinical Psychology** (Clinical Psychology); **Clinical Research** (Medicine); **Dentistry** (Dentistry); **Echo Cardiography** (Cardiology; Medical Technology); **Homeopathy** (Homeopathy); **Hospital Administration** (Health Administration); **Imaging Technology** (Medical Technology; Oncology); **Medical Laboratory Technology** (Laboratory Techniques; Medical Technology); **Medicine** (Cardiology; Medicine); **Naturopathy and Yogic Sciences** (Alternative Medicine; Yoga); **Neuro Science Technology** (Medical Technology; Neurosciences); **Nursing** (Nursing); **Operation Theater Technology** (Cardiology; Health Sciences; Medical Technology; Medicine; Oncology; Paramedical Sciences); **Optometry** (Optometry); **Perfusion Technology** (Medical Technology; Medicine); **Pharmacy** (Pharmacy); **Physiotherapy** (Physical Therapy); **Prosthetics and Orthotics** (Dental Technology; Orthodontics); **Psychol Social Rehabilitation** (Psychology; Rehabilitation and Therapy; Social Problems); **Public Health** (Public Health); **Radiography** (Radiology); **Renal Dialysis Technology** (Medical Technology); **Respiratory Care Technology** (Cardiology; Respiratory Therapy); **Unani** (Traditional Eastern Medicine)

Department

Health Science Library and Information System (Health Sciences; Information Sciences; Library Science)

History: Founded 1996.

Degrees and Diplomas: *Post Diploma*; *Bachelor's Degree*; *Bachelor's Degree (professional)*; *Postgraduate Diploma*; *Master's Degree*; *Doctor of Philosophy*

Last Updated: 19/07/11

RAMAKRISHNA MISSION VIVEKANANDA UNIVERSITY (RKMVU)

PO Belur Math, Howrah, West Bengal 711202
Tel: +91(33) 2654-9999
Fax: +91(33) 2654-4640
EMail: vivekananda.university@gmail.com
Website: http://www.rkmvu.ac.in/

Vice-Chancellor: Swami Atmapriyananda

Registrar: Swami Durgananda

School

Agriculture and Rural Development *(Off-Campus)* (Agricultural Management; Agriculture; Rural Studies); **Humanities and Social Sciences** (Arts and Humanities; Economics; Philosophy; Social Sciences; South and Southeast Asian Languages); **Indian Heritage** (Cultural Studies; Sanskrit); **Mathematical Sciences** (Computer Science; Mathematics; Mathematics and Computer Science; Physics)

History: Founded 2005 as Ramakrishna Mission Vivekananda Educational and Research Institute (RKMVERI). A 'Deemed University'.

Accrediting Agency: University Grants Commission (UGC); Ministry of Human Resource Development

Degrees and Diplomas: *Post Diploma*; *Bachelor's Degree*; *Master's Degree*; *Master of Philosophy*; *Doctor of Philosophy*. Also Certificate Courses.

Last Updated: 19/12/11

RANCHI UNIVERSITY

Shaheed Chowk, Ranchi, Bihar 834001
Tel: +91(651) 220-8553
Fax: +91(651) 230-1051
EMail: admin@ranchiuniversity.org.in
Website: http://ranchiuniversity.org.in/

Vice-Chancellor: A.A. Khan (2006-) Tel: +91(651) 220-5177

Registrar: Jyoti Kumar Tel: +91(651) 220-8553

Faculty

Commerce (Accountancy; Administration; Advertising and Publicity; Business Administration; Business and Commerce; Business Computing; Insurance; Management; Mass Communication; Secretarial Studies; Tourism); **Education** (Education; Physical Education); **Engineering** (Engineering); **Humanities** (English; Hindi; Indic Languages; Journalism; Mass Communication; Native Language; Sanskrit; Urdu); **Law** (Law); **Medicine** (Medicine); **Science** (Botany; Chemistry; Computer Science; Geology; Mathematics; Physics; Statistics; Zoology); **Social Science** (Anthropology; Economics; Esoteric Practices; Geography (Human); History; Home Economics; Philosophy; Political Sciences; Social Sciences; Sociology)

Further Information: Also 15 Consituent College and 24 affiliated colleges/institutions.

History: Founded 1960.

Fees: (Rupees): 180-240 per annum

Accrediting Agency: National Assessment and Accreditation Council (NAAC)

Degrees and Diplomas: *Bachelor's Degree*; *Bachelor's Degree (professional)*; *Postgraduate Diploma*; *Master's Degree*; *Doctor of Philosophy*. Also Certificate, Diploma and Advanced Diploma; M.B.A; Undergraduate and postgraduate vocational courses.

Student Services: Social Counselling

Last Updated: 19/07/11

RANI CHANNAMMA UNIVERSITY (RCUB)

Vidya Sangama, PBRH-4, Belagavi, Karnataka 591 156
EMail: rcuregistrar@gmail.com
Website: http://www.rcub.ac.in/

Vice-Chancellor: B.R. Ananthan

Registrar: S.S. Patagundi

Department

Geography (Geography); **Mathematics** (Mathematics); **Media** (Indic Languages; Media Studies); **National Service Scheme** (Physical Education); **Studies in Economics** (Economics)

Further Information: Also 333 affiliated College; 63 Postgraduate Colleges

History: Founded 1982 as Karnatak University PG Centre. Acquired present title and university status 2010.
Degrees and Diplomas: *Post Diploma*; *Postgraduate Diploma*; *Master's Degree*; *Master of Philosophy*; *Doctor of Philosophy*. Also Certificate Courses; MBA
Student Services: Canteen, Health Services

Student Numbers *2010-2011*: Total: c. 500
Last Updated: 03/01/12

RANI DURGAVATI UNIVERSITY

Rani Durgavati Vishwavidyalaya, Jabalpur
Saraswati Vihar, Pachpedi, Jabalpur, Madhya Pradesh 482 001
Tel: +91(761) 260-0567 +91(761) 260-0568
Fax: +91(761) 260-3752
EMail: rdvvcc1@rediffmail.com
Website: http://www.rdunijbpin.org/

Vice-Chancellor: Ram Rajesh Mishra Tel: +91(761) 260-1452
Registrar: U.N. Shukla Tel: +91(761) 260-0785

Faculty
Arts (English; Hindi; Indic Languages; Information Sciences; Journalism; Library Science; Linguistics; Literature; Mass Communication; Philosophy; Sanskrit); **Education** (Development Studies; Education; Physical Education; Rural Studies); **Law** (Administrative Law; Labour Law; Law; Taxation); **Life Science** (Biochemistry; Biological and Life Sciences; Biotechnology; Botany; Microbiology); **Management** (Management); **Mathematical Science** (Computer Engineering; Computer Graphics; Computer Science; Mathematics; Mathematics and Computer Science; Software Engineering); **Science** (Chemistry; Electronic Engineering; Physics); **Social Sciences** (Ancient Civilizations; Archaeology; Cultural Studies; Economics; Geography; History; Political Sciences; Public Administration; Social Sciences; Social Studies; Social Work; Sociology)

Division
Mahatmah Gandhi Srijan Peet

Programme
Dentistry (*Hitkarini Dental College and Hospital, Jabalpur*) (Dentistry)

Centre
Ambedakar Studies; **Gandhian Studies** (Peace and Disarmament; Political Sciences); **Science Instrumentation** (Instrument Making); **University Study**; **Yoga** (Yoga)

Research Centre
Macromolecular (Molecular Biology); **Women's Studies Development** (Women's Studies)

Further Information: Also 151 Affiliated Colleges. A traditional and distance education institution.
History: Founded 1956 as University of Jabalpur, acquired present title 1983.
Academic Year: July to April
Admission Requirements: 12th year senior secondary/intermediate examination or recognized foreign equivalent
Main Language(s) of Instruction: English, Hindi
Accrediting Agency: National Assessment and Accreditation Council (NAAC)
Degrees and Diplomas: *Post Diploma*; *Bachelor's Degree*; *Bachelor's Degree (professional)*: **Dentistry.** *Postgraduate Diploma*; *Master's Degree*; *Master of Philosophy*; *Doctor of Philosophy*. Also Certificate courses; Bachelor's degree honours, 5 yrs; MBA
Student Services: Careers Guidance, Health Services
Last Updated: 19/07/11

RASHTRASANT TUKADOJI MAHARAJ NAGPUR UNIVERSITY

Chhatrapati Shivaji Maharaj Administrative Premises, Ravindranath Tagore Marg, Nagpur, Maharashtra 440001
Tel: +91(712) 252-5417
Fax: +91(712) 253-2841 +91(712) 250-0736
EMail: vcnaguni@hotmail.com; vc.rtmnu@nagpuruniversity.org
Website: http://www.nagpuruniversity.org

Vice-Chancellor: Vilas S. Sapkal EMail: vc@nagpuruniversity.org
Registrar: Maheshkumar Yenkie
EMail: registrar.rtmnu@nagpuruniversity.org

Faculty
Arts (Arabic; Dance; English; Fine Arts; French; German; Indic Languages; Linguistics; Literature; Modern Languages; Music; Musical Instruments; Painting and Drawing; Persian; Russian; Sanskrit; Sculpture; Singing; Theatre; Urdu); **Ayurveda** (Ayurveda); **Commerce** (Banking; Business Administration; Business and Commerce; Farm Management; Human Resources; Labour and Industrial Relations; Management; Marketing; Taxation); **Education** (Education; Educational Psychology; Physical Education; Sports); **Engineering and Technology** (Architecture; Chemical Engineering; Civil Engineering; Computer Engineering; Computer Science; Construction Engineering; Electrical Engineering; Electronic Engineering; Engineering; Fire Science; Food Technology; Industrial Engineering; Information Technology; Interior Design; Measurement and Precision Engineering; Mechanical Engineering; Metallurgical Engineering; Mining Engineering; Paper Technology; Petroleum and Gas Engineering; Polymer and Plastics Technology; Power Engineering; Production Engineering; Telecommunications Engineering); **Home Science** (Clothing and Sewing; Cooking and Catering; Cosmetology; Dietetics; Fashion Design; Food Science; Home Economics; Interior Design; Nutrition; Printing and Printmaking; Psychology; Textile Design); **Law** (Administrative Law; Commercial Law; Constitutional Law; Criminal Law; Environmental Studies; Human Rights; International Law; Labour Law; Law); **Medicine** (Anaesthesiology; Anatomy; Biochemistry; Community Health; Dentistry; Dermatology; Forensic Medicine and Dentistry; Gynaecology and Obstetrics; Laboratory Techniques; Medical Technology; Medicine; Microbiology; Occupational Health; Ophthalmology; Oral Pathology; Orthodontics; Orthopaedics; Otorhinolaryngology; Paediatrics; Pathology; Periodontics; Pharmacology; Pharmacy; Physiology; Plastic Surgery; Pneumology; Public Health; Radiology; Social and Preventive Medicine; Surgery; Venereology); **Science** (Analytical Chemistry; Aquaculture; Biochemistry; Botany; Chemistry; Computer Science; Electronic Engineering; Embryology and Reproduction Biology; Entomology; Environmental Studies; Geology; Information Technology; Inorganic Chemistry; Mathematics; Microbiology; Molecular Biology; Operations Research; Organic Chemistry; Physical Chemistry; Physics; Physiology; Statistics; Zoology); **Social Science** (Administration; Ancient Civilizations; Archaeology; Cultural Studies; Economics; Government; History; Information Sciences; Journalism; Library Science; Mass Communication; Media Studies; Peace and Disarmament; Philosophy; Political Sciences; Psychology; Public Administration; Social Sciences; Tourism; Video)

Further Information: Also 3 Constituent Colleges/Institutions (Law college, Laxminarayan Institute of Technology, and College of Education) and 439 Affiliated Colleges. 7 campuses.
History: Founded 1923 as Nagpur University.
Academic Year: June to May
Admission Requirements: 12th year senior secondary/intermediate examination or recognized foreign equivalent
Main Language(s) of Instruction: English, Hindi, Marathi
Accrediting Agency: National Assessment and Accreditation Council
Degrees and Diplomas: *Post Diploma*; *Bachelor's Degree*; *Bachelor's Degree (professional)*; *Postgraduate Diploma*; *Master's Degree*; *Master of Philosophy*; *Doctor of Philosophy*. Also undegraduate certificates, 1-2 yrs; Higher Diplomas, 1 yr; Bachelor's degree honours, 5 yrs; MBA, 2 yrs.
Student Services: Academic Counselling, Canteen, Careers Guidance, Cultural Activities, Facilities for disabled people, Foreign Studies Centre, Health Services, Language Laboratory, Nursery Care, Social Counselling, Sports Facilities
Publications: NU Humanities Journal; NU Science Journal
Publishing House: NU Printing Press
Last Updated: 19/07/11

RASHTRIYA SANSKRIT SANSTHAN

56-57 Institutional Area, Janakpuri, New Delhi 110-058
Tel: +91(11) 285-24993 +91(11) 285-24995
Fax: +91(11) 285-21948
EMail: rsks@nda.vsnl.net.in
Website: http://www.sanskrit.nic.in/

Vice-Chancellor: Radhavallabh Tripathi (2008-)
EMail: rskspvc@yahoo.com

Registrar: K.B. Subbarayudu EMail: registrar.rsks@gmail.com

Programme

Sanskrit (Sanskrit)

Further Information: Also campuses in Allahabad, Puri, Jammu, Trichur, Jaipur, Lucknow, Sringeri, Kangra, Bhopal, Mumbai; 23 Adarsh Sanskrit Mahavidyalayas, Shodh-Sansthans and about 84 Affiliated Sanskrit Institutions.

History: Founded 1970. Acquired 'Deemed University' status 2002.

Degrees and Diplomas: *Post Diploma*; *Bachelor's Degree*; *Master's Degree*; *Doctor of Philosophy*
Last Updated: 19/12/11

RAVENSHAW UNIVERSITY

Cuttack, Orissa 753003
Tel: +91(671) 260-7710
Fax: +91(671) 261-0060
EMail: ravenshawuniversity@yahoo.co.in; ravenshaw@sify.com
Website: http://www.ravenshawuniversity.ac.in/

Vice-Chancellor: Devdas Chhotray (2006-)
Tel: +61(671) 261-0060
EMail: devdas_chhotray@hotmail.com; devdaschhotray@gmail.com

Registrar: Smarapriya Mishra
Tel: +61(671) 263-2690 EMail: smarapriyamishra57@gmail.com

Department

Applied Geography (Geography); **Bengali** (Indic Languages); **Biotechnology** (Biotechnology); **Botany** (Botany); **Chemistry** (Chemistry); **Commerce and Business Management** (Accountancy; Business Administration; Business and Commerce; Business Computing; Economics; Finance; Management; Marketing; Statistics); **Economics** (Economics); **Education** (Education); **English** (English); **Geology** (Geology); **Hindi** (Hindi); **History** (History); **Mathematics** (Mathematics); **Oriya** (Indic Languages); **Philosophy** (Philosophy); **Physics** (Physics); **Political Science** (Political Sciences); **Psychology** (Psychology); **Sanskrit** (Sanskrit); **Sociology** (Sociology); **Statistics** (Statistics); **Urdu and Persian Languages** (Persian; Urdu); **Zoology** (Zoology)

Course

Self-financing Studies (Biotechnology; Business Administration; Computer Engineering; Computer Networks; Computer Science; Data Processing; Information Technology; Journalism; Mass Communication; Software Engineering; Telecommunications Engineering)

History: Founded in 1868 as Ravenshaw College. Successively affiliated to Calcutta University, Patna University (1917) and Utkal University (1943). Acquired current status and title 2006.

Academic Year: January to December
Admission Requirements: High School Certificate
Main Language(s) of Instruction: English
Accrediting Agency: National Assessment and Accreditation Council (NAAC)

Degrees and Diplomas: *Post Diploma*; *Bachelor's Degree*; *Master's Degree*; *Master of Philosophy*; *Doctor of Philosophy*. Also Bachelor's degree honours; MBA
Last Updated: 19/07/11

RAYALASEEMA UNIVERSITY

Kurnool, Andhra Pradesh 518 002
Tel: +91(8518) 271-183
Website: http://www.rayalaseemauniversity.ac.in/

Vice- Chancellor: K. Krishna Naik

Programme

Biotechnology (Biotechnology); **Business Administration** *(Distance Education)* (Business Administration); **Business and Commerce** *(Distance Education)* (Business and Commerce); **Computers and Business Management** *(Distance Education)* (Business Computing; Management); **Education** (Education); **Organic Chemistry** *(Distance Education)* (Organic Chemistry); **Psychology** *(Distance Education)* (Psychology)

Further Information: A traditional and distance education institution.

History: Founded 2008.

Degrees and Diplomas: *Bachelor's Degree*; *Master's Degree*; *Master of Philosophy*. Also MBA; Pre-Ph.D. research programme.
Last Updated: 02/01/12

SAM HIGGINBOTTOM INSTITUTE OF AGRICULTURE, TECHNOLOGY AND SCIENCES (SHIATS)

PO Allahabad Agricultural Institute,
Allahabad, Uttar Pradesh 211007
Tel: +91(532) 268-4281
Fax: +91(532) 268-4394
EMail: registrar@shiats.edu.in
Website: http://www.aaidu.org

Chief Executive and Vice-Chancellor: Rajendra B. Lal (2000-)
Tel: +91(532) 268-4284 EMail: vc@shiats.edu.in

Registrar: A.K.A. Lawrence
Tel: +91(532) 268-4781 EMail: registrar@shiats.edu.in

Faculty

Agriculture (Agricultural Business; Agricultural Economics; Agriculture; Agronomy; Biochemistry; Biology; Biotechnology; Clothing and Sewing; Community Health; Development Studies; Dietetics; Environmental Studies; Family Studies; Food Science; Forest Biology; Forest Management; Forest Products; Forestry; Genetics; Health Sciences; Home Economics; Horticulture; Microbiology; Nutrition; Plant and Crop Protection; Rural Studies; Soil Science; Textile Technology; Wildlife); **Animal Husbandry and Dairying** (Animal Husbandry; Dairy; Embryology and Reproduction Biology; Genetics; Meat and Poultry; Nutrition); **Business Studies** (Accountancy; Agricultural Business; Banking; Business Administration; Environmental Management; Finance; Forest Management; Human Resources; Information Technology; International Business; Management; Marketing; Retailing and Wholesaling); **Engineering and Technology** (Agricultural Engineering; Agricultural Equipment; Animal Husbandry; Automation and Control Engineering; Bioengineering; Biotechnology; Civil Engineering; Computer Engineering; Computer Science; Construction Engineering; Dairy; Electrical and Electronic Engineering; Electronic Engineering; Engineering; Food Science; Food Technology; Heating and Refrigeration; Hydraulic Engineering; Industrial Engineering; Information Technology; Mechanical Engineering; Mechanics; Microbiology; Microwaves; Molecular Biology; Power Engineering; Production Engineering; Soil Management; Soil Science; Technology; Telecommunications Engineering; Water Management; Water Science); **Film, Media Studies and Technology** (Advertising and Publicity; Communication Studies; Film; Journalism; Mass Communication; Media Studies; Music; Performing Arts; Radio and Television Broadcasting; Singing; Visual Arts); **Health, Medical Sciences, Indigenous and Alternative Systems of Medicine** (Alternative Medicine; Biochemistry; Health Sciences; Immunology; Laboratory Techniques; Medical Technology; Medicine; Microbiology; Pharmacy; Public Health); **Humanities, Social Sciences and Education** (Accountancy; Anthropology; Arabic; Arts and Humanities; Business Administration; Economics; Education; English; French; Information Sciences; Japanese; Law; Library Science; Literature; Modern Languages; Physical Education; Portuguese; Psychology; Social Sciences; Social Work; Teacher Training); **Science** (Biological and Life Sciences; Botany; Chemistry; Computer Science; Forensic Medicine and Dentistry; Mathematics; Physics; Statistics; Zoology); **Theology** (Bible; Ethics; History of Religion; Missionary Studies; Religion; Religious Studies; Theology)

Further Information: A traditional and distance education institution.

History: Founded in 1910. Formerly known as Allahabad Agricultural Institute - Deemed University. Acquired current title 2009.

Fees: (Rupees): Undergraduate programmes, 5,000-76,000 per semester (except Diploma, 1,000-4,000 per annum, B.Ed., 90,000 per annum and B.P.Ed., 60,000 per annum) for Indian students; Postgraduate programmes, 6,000-70,000 per semester (except B.Ed., and) for Indian students; MBA, 60,000-98,000 per semester for Indian students; Ph.D., 35,000 per semester for Indian students; Fee for international students, 5,000 per semester irrespective of programme level and field of study

Main Language(s) of Instruction: English

Accrediting Agency: National Assessment and Accreditation Council (NAAC)

Degrees and Diplomas: *Post Diploma*; *Bachelor's Degree*; *Bachelor's Degree (professional)*; *Postgraduate Diploma*; *Master's Degree*; *Master of Philosophy*; *Doctor of Philosophy*. Alos undergraduate certificates, 2 sem.; Bachelor's degree honours, 8 sem.; MBA, 4 sem.

Student Services: Academic Counselling, Canteen, Cultural Activities, Foreign Studies Centre, Health Services, Social Counselling, Sports Facilities

Publications: Allahabad Farmer; Hamar Gaon (Our Village)

Publishing House: University Publication Division (UPD)

Last Updated: 20/07/11

SAMBALPUR UNIVERSITY (SUNIV)

Jyoti Vihar, Sambalpur, Orissa 768019
Tel: +91(663) 243-0157
Fax: +91(663) 243-0158
EMail: registrar@suniv.ac.in
Website: http://www.suniv.ac.in/

Vice-Chancellor: Arun Kumar Pujari
Tel: +91(663) 243-0158 EMail: vc@suniv.ac.in

Registrar: Sudhanshu Sekhar Rath
Tel: +91(663) 243-0157 EMail: registrar@suniv.ac.in

School

Chemistry (Applied Chemistry; Chemistry; Industrial Chemistry; Inorganic Chemistry; Organic Chemistry; Physical Chemistry); **Life Sciences** (Biochemistry; Biological and Life Sciences; Biotechnology; Ecology; Microbiology; Molecular Biology; Physiology); **Physics** (Electronic Engineering; Nuclear Physics; Physics; Solid State Physics)

Department

Anthropology (Anthropology); **Business Administration** *(Postgraduate)* (Business Administration; Finance; Human Resources; Industrial Management; Insurance; Marketing); **Computer Science and Application** (Computer Science; Electronic Engineering; Information Technology; Mathematics; Physics; Statistics; Telecommunications Engineering); **Earth Science** (Computer Science; Earth Sciences; Environmental Studies; Geology; Natural Resources; Surveying and Mapping; Water Management); **Economics** (Agricultural Economics; Econometrics; Economics; Finance); **English** (Comparative Literature; English; Linguistics; Translation and Interpretation); **Environmental Science** (Biotechnology; Ecology; Environmental Management; Environmental Studies; Geology; Safety Engineering; Soil Conservation; Surveying and Mapping; Water Science); **History** (History); **Home Science** (Dietetics; Education; Family Studies; Food Science; Home Economics; Nutrition; Women's Studies); **Law** (Commercial Law; Criminal Law; Environmental Studies; Law; Private Law); **Library and Information Science** *(Postgraduate)* (Educational Research; Educational Technology; Information Sciences; Library Science); **Mathematics** (Mathematics; Operations Research); **Oriya** (Comparative Literature; Folklore; Literature); **Political Science and Public Administration** (Development Studies; Journalism; Political Sciences; Public Administration); **Region Art and Culture Studies** (Cultural Studies; Fine Arts; Regional Studies); **Sociology** *(Postgraduate)* (Criminology; Gerontology; Rural Studies; Sociology); **Statistics** (Demography and Population; Operations Research; Statistics)

Further Information: Also 92 Affiliated Colleges. A traditional and distance education institution.

History: Founded 1967.

Academic Year: June to May

Admission Requirements: 12th year senior secondary/intermediate examination or recognized foreign equivalent

Fees: (Rupees): 144-12,000 per annum

Main Language(s) of Instruction: English

Accrediting Agency: National Assessment and Accreditation Council (NAAC)

Degrees and Diplomas: *Post Diploma*; *Bachelor's Degree*; *Bachelor's Degree (professional)*; *Postgraduate Diploma*; *Master's Degree*; *Master of Philosophy*; *Doctor of Philosophy*. Also Bachelor's degree honours; M.C.A., Executive MBA, 3 yrs and MBA, 2-3 yrs.

Student Services: Academic Counselling, Canteen, Careers Guidance, Cultural Activities, Facilities for disabled people, Health Services, Sports Facilities

Publications: Sambalpur University Journal of Humanities; Sambalpur University Journal of Science and Technology; Septarshi

Last Updated: 20/07/11

SAMPURNANAND SANSKRIT UNIVERSITY

Sampurnanand Sanskrit Vishwavidyalaya (SSVV)
Varanasi, Uttar Pradesh 221002
Tel: +91(542) 203-911
Fax: +91(542) 206-617
EMail: vsssvv_vns@satyam.net.in
Website: http://ssvv.up.nic.in

Vice-Chancellor: Binda Prasad Mishra Tel: +91(542) 220-4089

Registrar: Rajneesh Kumar Shukla Tel: +91(542) 220-3911

Faculty

Adhunika Gyan Vijyana (Archaeology; Economics; Education; Geography; History; Home Economics; Library Science; Linguistics; Modern Languages; Political Sciences; Social Sciences; Sociology); **Philosophy** (Comparative Religion; Ethics; Philosophical Schools; Philosophy; Yoga); **Sahitya Sanskriti** (Holy Writings; Literature); **Sramana Vidya** (Asian Religious Studies; Grammar; Indic Languages; Literature; Philosophical Schools; Philosophy; Religious Studies; Theatre); **Veda-Vedanga** (Asian Religious Studies; Ayurveda; Cultural Studies; Esoteric Practices; Grammar; Sanskrit)

Programme

Sports Education (Sports)

Further Information: Also 1441 Affiliated Colleges.

History: Founded 1958 as Varanaseya Sanskrit Vishwavidyalaya. Acquired present title 1974.

Admission Requirements: 12th year senior secondary/intermediate examination or recognized foreign equivalent. Good command of Hindi and Sanskrit required

Fees: (Rupees): 171-245

Main Language(s) of Instruction: Hindi, Sanskrit

Degrees and Diplomas: *Post Diploma*; *Bachelor's Degree*; *Bachelor's Degree (professional)*; *Master's Degree*; *Doctor of Philosophy*

Last Updated: 20/07/11

SANJAY GANDHI POSTGRADUATE INSTITUTE OF MEDICAL SCIENCES (SGPGIMS)

Raebareli Road, Lucknow, Uttar Pradesh 226014
Tel: +91(522) 266-8008
Fax: +91(522) 266-8017
EMail: root@sgpgi.ac.in
Website: http://www.sgpgi.ac.in

Director: R.K. Sharma Tel: +91(522) 266-8800

Executive Registrar: Sita Naik
Tel: +91(522) 266-8700 EMail: registrar@sgpgi.ac.in

International Relations: Usha Kant Misra

Department

Anaesthesiology (Anaesthesiology); **Biostatistics and Health Informatics** (Computer Science; Statistics); **Cardiology** (Cardiology); **Cardiovascular and Thoracic Surgery** (Cardiology; Surgery); **Critical Care Medicine** (Medicine; Nursing); **Endocrine Surgery** (Endocrinology; Oncology; Surgery); **Endocrinology** (Endocrinology); **Gastroenterology** (Gastroenterology); **Hematology** (Haematology); **Immunology** (Immunology); **Medical Genetics** (Biotechnology; Genetics); **Microbiology** (Biotechnology; Epidemiology; Medical Auxiliaries; Microbiology); **Nephrology** (Nephrology); **Neurology** (Neurology); **Neurosurgery**

(Neurological Therapy; Surgery); **Nuclear Medicine** (Medical Technology); **Paediatric Gastroenterology** (Gastroenterology; Paediatrics); **Pathology** (Pathology); **Radiodiagnosis** (Radiology); **Radiotherapy** (Oncology; Radiology; Treatment Techniques); **Surgical Gastroenterology** (Gastroenterology; Surgery); **Transfusion Medicine** (Haematology; Immunology; Medical Technology; Medicine); **Urology** (Urology)

Further Information: Also 600-bed hospital.

History: Founded 1983.

Academic Year: January to December

Admission Requirements: 12th year senior secondary/intermediate examination or recognized foreign equivalent

Fees: (Rupees): 5,000-100,000 per annum

Main Language(s) of Instruction: English

Accrediting Agency: Medical Council of India

Degrees and Diplomas: *Bachelor's Degree (professional)*; *Postgraduate Diploma*; *Master's Degree*; *Doctor of Philosophy*

Student Services: Academic Counselling, Canteen, Cultural Activities, Health Services, Nursery Care

Publications: SGPGI Newsletter

Last Updated: 20/07/11

SANT GADGE BABA AMRAVATI UNIVERSITY (SGBAU)

Amravati, Maharashtra 444602
Tel: +91(721) 266-2108
Fax: +91(721) 266-2135
EMail: reg@sgbau.ac.in
Website: http://www.sgbau.ac.in

Vice-Chancellor: Mohan Krishnarao Khedar
Tel: +91(721) 266-2093 EMail: vc@sgbau.ac.in

Registrar: Shri Dineshkumar Joshi
Tel: +91(721) 266-2173 EMail: reg@sgbau.ac.in

Faculty

Arts (Arts and Humanities; Hindi; Literature; Native Language; Translation and Interpretation); **Ayurved** (Ayurveda); **Commerce** (Business and Commerce; Finance; Human Resources; Labour and Industrial Relations; Management; Marketing; Operations Research; Transport Management); **Education** (Education; Physical Education; Sports; Sports Medicine; Yoga); **Engineering and Technology** (Chemical Engineering; Computer Engineering; Computer Science; Data Processing; Electronic Engineering; Engineering; Software Engineering; Technology); **Home Science** (Communication Studies; Food Science; Home Economics; Nutrition); **Law** (Administrative Law; Constitutional Law; Criminal Law; Human Rights; Law); **Medicine** (Medicine); **Sciences** (Biological and Life Sciences; Botany; Chemistry; Geology; Mathematics; Microbiology; Natural Sciences; Physics; Statistics; Zoology); **Social Science** (Biotechnology; Information Sciences; Library Science; Social Sciences; Sociology)

Department

Adult Continuing Education Extension and Field Outreach *(DACEEFO)* (Business Administration; Dietetics; Food Science; Geology; Harvest Technology; Home Economics; Information Technology; Library Science; Nutrition; Sales Techniques)

Further Information: Also 181 Affiliated Colleges

History: Founded 1983 as Amravati University.

Academic Year: June to April (June-October; November-April).

Admission Requirements: Higher Secondary School Certificate (HSSC) grade 12, or equivalent. International students should apply through the Ministry of Foreign Affairs.

Fees: (Rupees): 1,000-6,000 per annum

Main Language(s) of Instruction: English, Marathi, Hindi

Accrediting Agency: NAAC (B+)

Degrees and Diplomas: *Bachelor's Degree*; *Bachelor's Degree (professional)*; *Postgraduate Diploma*; *Master's Degree*; *Master of Philosophy*; *Doctor of Philosophy*. Also Certificate Courses; MCA and MBA.

Last Updated: 20/07/11

SANT LONGOWAL INSTITUTE OF ENGINEERING AND TECHNOLOGY (SLIET)

Longowal, Distt. Sangrur (Punjab) 148106
Tel: +91(1672) 253-151
EMail: director@sliet.ac.in
Website: http://www.sliet.ac.in

Director: V. Sahni
Tel: +91(1672) 253-100 EMail: vsahni_2002@yahoo.co.in

Registrar: S.S. Dhaliwal
Tel: +91(1672) 253-180 EMail: sukhjit_d@yahoo.com

Department

Chemical Technology (Chemical Engineering; Paper Technology; Polymer and Plastics Technology; Printing and Printmaking; Technology); **Chemistry** (Chemistry); **Computer Science and Engineering** (Computer Engineering; Computer Science); **Electrical and Instrumentation Engineering** (Automation and Control Engineering; Electrical Engineering; Maintenance Technology; Measurement and Precision Engineering); **Electronics and Communication Engineering** (Electronic Engineering; Maintenance Technology; Telecommunications Engineering); **Entrepreneurship Development Programme (EDP) and Humanities** (Arts and Humanities; English; Labour and Industrial Relations; Management); **Food Engineering and Technology** (Food Science); **Mathematics** (Mathematics; Operations Research; Statistics); **Mechanical Engineering** (Heating and Refrigeration; Industrial Engineering; Maintenance Technology; Mechanical Engineering; Metal Techniques; Metallurgical Engineering; Production Engineering); **Persons with Disability Scheme** (Special Education); **Physics** (Physics)

History: Founded 1991. Received AICTE accreditation 2003. Acquired 'Deemed University' status 2006.

Fees: (Rupees): Tuition fees for Indian students for Certificates, 1,500 per semester; Diplomas, 3,000 per semester; Undegraduate Degree, 15,000 per semester; Postgraduate degree, 8,000 per semester. For international students (US Dollars): Diplomas, 500-800 per annum; Other programmes, 1,000-5,000 per annum

Accrediting Agency: All India Council for Technical Education (AICTE)

Degrees and Diplomas: *Post Diploma*; *Master's Degree*; *Doctor of Philosophy*. Also Certificate Programmes, 2 yrs; Undergraduate degree in Engineering; MBA

Student Services: Health Services, Sports Facilities

Last Updated: 20/07/11

SANTOSH UNIVERSITY

No.1, Santosh Nagar, Ghaziabad, Uttar Pradesh 201 009
Tel: +91(120) 274-1141 +91(120) 274-1143 +91(120) 274-1777
Fax: +91(120) 274-1140
EMail: santosh@santoshuniversity.com
Website: http://santoshuniversity.com/

Vice-Chancellor: V.K. Arora

Registrar: V. Dos

Course

Basic Medical Sciences *(Postgraduate Diploma)* (Forensic Medicine and Dentistry; Pathology; Public Health); **Basic Medical Sciences** *(Postgraduate Degree)* (Biochemistry; Community Health; Forensic Medicine and Dentistry; Medicine; Microbiology; Pathology; Pharmacology; Physiology); **Clinical Studies** *(Postgraduate Diploma)* (Anaesthesiology; Child Care and Development; Gynaecology and Obstetrics; Health Sciences; Ophthalmology; Orthopaedics; Pneumology; Psychology); **Clinical Studies** *(Postgraduate Degree)* (Anaesthesiology; Gynaecology and Obstetrics; Medicine; Ophthalmology; Orthopaedics; Otorhinolaryngology; Paediatrics; Pneumology; Psychiatry and Mental Health; Surgery); **Dentistry** *(Postgraduate)* (Dental Technology; Dentistry; Orthodontics; Periodontics; Surgery); **Undergraduate Studies** (Dentistry; Medicine; Surgery)

History: Founded as Santosh Medical and Dental College Hospitals 1995. Acquired 'Deemed University' status 2007.

Degrees and Diplomas: *Bachelor's Degree (professional)*; *Postgraduate Diploma*; *Master's Degree*

Last Updated: 19/12/11

SARDAR PATEL UNIVERSITY (SPU)

University Road, Via Anand, Dist. Anand,
Vallabh Vidyanagar, Gujarat 388120
Tel: +91(2692) 236-545 +91(2692) 226-6801
Fax: +91(2692) 236-475
EMail: registrar_spu@spuvvn.edu
Website: http://www.spuvvn.edu

Vice-Chancellor: Harish Padh Tel: +91(2692) 230-009
EMail: vc_spu@spuvvn.edu

Registrar: Tushar Majmudar Tel: +91(2692) 226-801

Faculty

Arts (Arts and Humanities; Communication Studies; Dance; Economics; English; Environmental Management; Geography; Hindi; History; Indic Languages; Information Sciences; Interior Design; Library Science; Linguistics; Logic; Media Studies; Music; Philosophy; Political Sciences; Psychology; Sanskrit; Social Work; Sociology; Theatre); **Business Studies and Commerce** (Accountancy; Banking; Business Administration; Business and Commerce; English; Finance; Human Resources; Management; Marketing); **Education** (Education; Educational Administration; Foreign Languages Education; Humanities and Social Science Education; Native Language Education; Physical Education); **Engineering and Technology** (Architecture; Civil Engineering; Computer Engineering; Construction Engineering; Electronic Engineering; Engineering; Environmental Engineering; Food Technology; Hygiene; Industrial Engineering; Information Technology; Machine Building; Mechanical Engineering; Power Engineering; Production Engineering; Technology; Telecommunications Engineering; Town Planning); **Home Science** (Biotechnology; Child Care and Development; Clothing and Sewing; Family Studies; Fashion Design; Food Science; Home Economics; Nutrition; Textile Technology); **Homeopathy** (Homeopathy); **Law** (Labour and Industrial Relations; Law; Taxation); **Management** (Accountancy; Administration; Business Administration; Finance; Hotel Management; Human Resources; Information Technology; International Business; Management; Marketing; Operations Research; Tourism); **Medicine** (Anaesthesiology; Anatomy; Biochemistry; Laboratory Techniques; Medical Technology; Medicine; Microbiology; Midwifery; Nursing; Otorhinolaryngology; Pharmacology; Physical Therapy; Physiology; Public Health; Radiology; Surgery); **Pharmaceutical Sciences** (Pharmacy); **Science** (Analytical Chemistry; Applied Chemistry; Biochemistry; Biotechnology; Botany; Chemistry; Computer Science; Electronic Engineering; Environmental Studies; Genetics; Home Economics; Industrial Chemistry; Information Sciences; Instrument Making; Materials Engineering; Mathematics; Microbiology; Physics; Polymer and Plastics Technology; Safety Engineering; Statistics; Zoology)

Further Information: Also 3 satellite campuses; 80 Affiliated Colleges; 25 Postgraduate Departments

History: Founded 1955 as Sardar Vallabhbhai Vidyapeeth. Recognized by UGC 1968.

Academic Year: June to May (June-October/November; December-April/May)

Admission Requirements: 12th year senior secondary/intermediate examination or recognized foreign equivalent

Fees: (Rupees): Professional courses, 25,000; Non-professional courses, 15,000

Main Language(s) of Instruction: Gujarati, English, Hindi

Degrees and Diplomas: *Post Diploma*; *Bachelor's Degree*; *Bachelor's Degree (professional)*; *Postgraduate Diploma*; *Master's Degree*; *Master of Philosophy*; *Doctor of Philosophy*. Also Advanced Diploma, Advanced Certificate and Certificate Courses; MBA

Student Services: Canteen, Careers Guidance, Health Services

Publications: Artha Vikas; Journal of Education and Psychology; Journal of Engineering and Technology; Mimansa; Prajna; Sheel Shrutum; Synergie; Vocational Guide

Publishing House: University Press

Academic Staff *2010-2011*: Total 191

Last Updated: 20/07/11

SARDAR VALLABHBHAI NATIONAL INSTITUTE OF TECHNOLOGY (SVNIT)

Ichchhanath, Surat, Gujarat 395 007
Tel: +91(261) 225-9571 +91(261) 225-9582
Fax: +91(261) 222-7334 +91(261) 222-8394
Website: http://www.svnit.ac.in/

Director: P. D. Porey
Tel: +91(261) 220-1505
EMail: director@svnit.ac.in; pdporey@svnit.ac.in

Registrar: H. A. Parmar
Tel: +91(261)220-1509 EMail: registrar@svnit.ac.in

Department

Applied Chemistry (Applied Chemistry; Chemistry; Inorganic Chemistry; Nanotechnology; Organic Chemistry; Polymer and Plastics Technology); **Applied Mathematics and Humanities** (Applied Mathematics; Arts and Humanities; English; Management; Mathematics); **Applied Mechanics** (Civil Engineering; Construction Engineering; Engineering; Geological Engineering; Mechanics; Soil Science); **Applied Physics** (Applied Physics; Physics); **Chemical Engineering** (Chemical Engineering); **Civil Engineering** (Civil Engineering; Environmental Engineering; Rural Planning; Town Planning; Transport Engineering; Transport Management; Water Science); **Computer Engineering** (Computer Engineering); **Electrical Engineering** (Computer Engineering; Electrical Engineering; Software Engineering); **Electronics Engineering** (Computer Engineering; Electronic Engineering; Software Engineering; Telecommunications Engineering); **Mechanical Engineering** (Industrial Management; Mechanical Engineering; Production Engineering)

History: Created in 1961 as Sardar Vallabhbhai Regional Engineering College. Acquired current title and status 2001. An 'Institution of National Importance.

Fees: (Rupees): Tuition fees, 17,500 per semester (as of 7th semester, 6,000 for B.Tech and 7,500 for M.Sc. And Ph.D.)

Degrees and Diplomas: *Bachelor's Degree (professional)*; *Master's Degree*; *Doctor of Philosophy*

Student Services: Canteen, Sports Facilities

Student Numbers *2010-2011*: Total 426

Last Updated: 21/07/11

SARDAR VALLABHBHAI PATEL UNIVERSITY OF AGRICULTURE AND TECHNOLOGY (SVPUAT)

Modipuram, Meerut, Uttar Pradesh 250110
Tel: +91(121) 288-8503
Fax: +91(121) 288-8505
EMail: vc@svbpuniversitymerrut.org
Website: http://www.svbpmeerut.ac.in

Vice-Chancellor: A. K. Bakshi Tel: +91 (121) 241-1522

Registrar: Narendra Sharma Tel: +91(121) 288-8502

Faculty

Agriculture (Agricultural Economics; Agricultural Engineering; Agricultural Equipment; Agricultural Management; Agronomy; Animal Husbandry; Biology; Crop Production; English; Entomology; Farm Management; Floriculture; Food Science; Food Technology; Horticulture; Industrial and Production Economics; Mathematics; Physics; Plant and Crop Protection; Plant Pathology; Rural Planning; Soil Science; Statistics; Water Management); **Biotechnology** (Biochemistry; Biotechnology; Cell Biology; Genetics; Immunology; Microbiology; Molecular Biology; Pathology; Physiology)

Further Information: College of Veterinary and Animal Science under development

History: Founded 2000 as India's first agricultural university

Academic Year: July to June

Fees: (Indian Rupee): Undergraduate, 16,150 per annum; Postgraduate, 25,085 per annum

Main Language(s) of Instruction: Undergraduate: English, Hindi. Postgraduate: English

Degrees and Diplomas: *Bachelor's Degree*; *Bachelor's Degree (professional)*; *Master's Degree*; *Doctor of Philosophy*

Student Services: Academic Counselling, Canteen, Careers Guidance, Cultural Activities, Facilities for disabled people, Health Services, Social Counselling, Sports Facilities

Publications: Krishi Darshika; Vallabh Krishi Darpan

Last Updated: 21/07/11

SARDARKRUSHINAGAR DANTIWADA AGRICULTURAL UNIVERSITY (SDAU)

Dantiwada Campus, District Banaskantha,
Sardar Krushinagar, North Gujarat 385506
Tel: +91(2748) 278-226
Fax: +91(2748) 278-261
EMail: vc@sdau.edu.in
Website: http://www.sdau.edu.in/

Vice-Chancellor: R. C. Maheshwari
Tel: +91(2748) 278-222 EMail: vc@sdau.edu.in

Registrar: H.N. Kher
Tel: +91(2748) 278-226 EMail: registrar@sdau.edu.in

College

Agri Business Management (Accountancy; Agricultural Business; Development Studies; Economics; Finance; Human Resources; Information Management; Information Technology; Management; Marketing; Rural Studies; Statistics); **Agriculture** *(Chimanbhai Patel)* (Agricultural Economics; Agricultural Education; Agriculture; Agronomy; Chemistry; Entomology; Genetics; Horticulture; Plant Pathology; Soil Science; Statistics); **Basic Science and Humanities** (Arts and Humanities; Biochemistry; Biological and Life Sciences; Chemistry; Computer Science; Environmental Studies; Genetics; Mathematics; Microbiology; Molecular Biology; Natural Sciences; Physics; Physiology; Social Sciences; Statistics); **Dairy Science and Food Technology** (Business Administration; Dairy; Engineering; Food Science; Food Technology; Microbiology; Safety Engineering); **Home Science and Nutrition** (Child Care and Development; Communication Studies; Cooking and Catering; Dietetics; Distance Education; Family Studies; Food Science; Harvest Technology; Home Economics; Information Technology; Interior Design; Journalism; Mass Communication; Nutrition; Special Education; Textile Design); **Horticulture** (Agriculture; Horticulture; Vegetable Production); **Renewable Energy and Environmental Engineering** (Agriculture; Energy Engineering; Engineering; Environmental Engineering; Environmental Management; Forestry; Harvest Technology; Natural Resources; Public Health; Thermal Engineering; Waste Management); **Veterinary Science and Animal Husbandary** (Animal Husbandry; Gynaecology and Obstetrics; Surgery; Veterinary Science)

Further Information: Also 10 Constituent Colleges

History: Founded 1972 as Gujarat Agricultural University whose Act, No. 5 of 2004 was repealed on May 1, 2004. Sardarkrushinagar Dantiwada Agricultural University elevated as individual university for precise consideration of need based location specific agricultural research.

Admission Requirements: 12th year senior secondary/intermediate examination or recognized foreign equivalent

Fees: (Rupees): 200 per semester

Main Language(s) of Instruction: English

Degrees and Diplomas: *Post Diploma*; *Bachelor's Degree*; *Bachelor's Degree (professional)*; *Postgraduate Diploma*; *Master's Degree*; *Doctor of Philosophy*. Also undegraduate Certificate; Bachelor's degree honours.

Last Updated: 21/07/11

SARGUJA VISHWAVIDYALAYA

Sarguja University (SUA)

Near Govt. Hospital Road, Sarguja District,
Ambikapur, Chhattigarh 497 001
Tel: +91(7774) 222-789 +91(7774) 222-790
Fax: +91(7774) 222-791
EMail: registrarsua@yaho.co.in
Website: http://www.sua.nic.in/

Vice-Chancellor: S. K. Verma Tel: +91(7774) 222-788

Registrar: R. D. Sharma Tel: +91(7774) 222-790

Faculty

Engineering (Civil Engineering; Computer Engineering; Computer Science; Electrical Engineering; Engineering; Mechanical Engineering)

Programme

Biotechnology *(Postgraduate)* (Biotechnology); **Business and Commerce** (Business and Commerce; Economics); **Farm Forestry** *(Postgraduate)* (Forestry)

Department

Arts and Humanities (Arts and Humanities; English; Hindi; History; Sanskrit); **Computer Science** (Computer Science); **Health Sciences** (Health Sciences); **Pharmacy** (Pharmacy); **Sciences** (Botany; Chemistry; Geography; Mathematics; Microbiology; Physics; Zoology); **Social Sciences** (Political Sciences; Psychology; Sociology)

Further Information: Also 42 affiliated colleges

History: Founded 2008.

Degrees and Diplomas: *Bachelor's Degree*; *Postgraduate Diploma*; *Master's Degree*

Last Updated: 03/01/12

SASTRA UNIVERSITY (SASTRA)

Shanmugha Campus, Tirumalaisamaduram,
Thanjavur, Tamil Nadu 613401
Tel: +91(4362) 264-101 +91(4362) 266-502
Fax: +91(4362) 264-120
EMail: admissions@sastra.edu
Website: http://www.sastra.edu

Vice-Chancellor: R. Sethuraman Tel: +91(4362) 304-101

Registrar: S.N.S. Srivastava
Tel: +91(4362) 304-106 EMail: registrar@sastra.edu

School

Chemical and Biotechnology (Bioengineering; Biological and Life Sciences; Biotechnology; Chemical Engineering; Computer Science; Medical Technology; Nanotechnology; Nuclear Engineering; Pharmacy); **Civil Engineering** (Civil Engineering; Construction Engineering; Safety Engineering); **Computing** (Computer Engineering; Computer Graphics; Computer Science; Information Technology; Law; Multimedia; Telecommunications Engineering); **Education** (Distance Education; Education; Mathematics Education); **Electrical and Electronics Engineering** (Automation and Control Engineering; Electrical Engineering; Electronic Engineering; Measurement and Precision Engineering; Power Engineering; Telecommunications Engineering); **Humanities and Sciences** (Arts and Humanities; Communication Studies; Cultural Studies; English; Ethics; Mathematics); **Law** (Accountancy; Administrative Law; Business Administration; Civil Law; Commercial Law; Constitutional Law; Criminal Law; Criminology; Economics; English; History; International Law; Labour Law; Law; Management; Marketing; Political Sciences; Private Law; Public Law; Sociology; Statistics); **Management** (Accountancy; Business Administration; Commercial Law; Economics; Ethics; Finance; Information Management; Information Technology; International Business; Management; Marketing; Operations Research; Statistics); **Mechanical Engineering** (Automotive Engineering; Electronic Engineering; Mechanical Engineering; Production Engineering)

Department

Directorate of Distance Education - SASTRA (Dance; Education; Esoteric Practices; Fine Arts; Music)

Centre

Advanced Research in Indian System of Medicine *(CARISM)* (Ayurveda; Laboratory Techniques; Pharmacy; Safety Engineering; Toxicology); **Nanotechnology and Advanced Biomaterials** *(CeNTAB)* (Nanotechnology)

Further Information: A traditional and distance education institution.

History: Founded 1984 as Shanmugha College of Engineering. Renamed Shanmugha Arts, Science, Technology and Research Academy (SASTRA). Acquired present status 2001.

Fees: (Rupees): Tuition fees, undegraduate programmes, 5,000-40,000 per semester; Postgraduate programmes, 5,000-60,000 per semester

Accrediting Agency: National Assessment and Accreditation Council (NAAC) (Grade 'A'); The Institution of Engineering; Tata Consultancy Services Ltd. (TCS)

Degrees and Diplomas: *Bachelor's Degree*; *Bachelor's Degree (professional)*; *Postgraduate Diploma*; *Master's Degree*; *Doctor of Philosophy*. Also Certificate courses; Bachelor's degree honours; Integrated M.Tech. Programmes, 5 yrs; MCA.; MBA

Academic Staff *2010-2011*: Total: c. 700

Student Numbers *2010-2011*: Total: c. 9,000

Last Updated: 21/07/11

SATAVAHANA UNIVERSITY

Jyothinagar, Karimnagar, Andhra Pradesh 505 001
Tel: +91(878) 225-5800
Website: http://www.satavahana.ac.in/

Vice-Chancellor: B. Venkat Rathnam Tel: +91(878) 225-5800

Registrar: G. Laxmaiah EMail: prof_gklh@yahoo.co.in

Faculty

Arts (Arts and Humanities; English; Indic Languages; Urdu); **Business Administration and Commerce** (Business Administration; Business and Commerce; Management); **Pharmacy** (Pharmacy); **Sciences** (Chemistry; Information Sciences); **Social Sciences** (Economics; Social Sciences; Sociology)

History: Founded as a college 1956. Became a College of the Osmania University Hyderabad 1989. Acquired university status 2008.

Accrediting Agency: University Grants Commission (UGC)

Degrees and Diplomas: *Bachelor's Degree*; *Bachelor's Degree (professional)*; *Master's Degree*. Also MBA

Student Services: Health Services, Sports Facilities

Last Updated: 02/01/12

SATHYABAMA UNIVERSITY

Jeppiaar Nagar, Rajiv Gandhi Road, Chennai, Tamil Nadu 600 119
Tel: +91(44) 2450-150 +91(44) 2450-151
Fax: +91(44) 2450-2344
EMail: registrar@sathyabamauniversity.ac.in
Website: http://www.sathyabamauniversity.ac.in/

Vice-Chancellor: B. Sheela Rani
EMail: vc@sathyabamauniversity.ac.in

Registrar: S.S. Rau

Faculty

Architecture (Architecture; Building Technologies); **BioEngineering** (Biomedical Engineering; Biotechnology; Computer Science); **Chemical Engineering** (Chemical Engineering; Environmental Engineering); **Civil Engineering** (Civil Engineering; Construction Engineering); **Computer Science and Engineering** (Computer Engineering; Computer Science; Information Technology); **Education** (Education); **Electrical Engineering** (Electrical and Electronic Engineering; Electrical Engineering; Power Engineering); **Electronics Engineering** (Automation and Control Engineering; Computer Graphics; Electronic Engineering; Measurement and Precision Engineering; Nanotechnology; Telecommunications Engineering); **Management Studies** (Business Administration; Management); **Mechanical Engineering** (Aeronautical and Aerospace Engineering; Automotive Engineering; Computer Graphics; Mechanical Engineering; Production Engineering; Thermal Engineering); **Medicine** (Dentistry; Surgery); **Science and Humanities** (Biological and Life Sciences; Biotechnology; Business and Commerce; Communication Arts; Computer Engineering; Computer Science; Cooking and Catering; Economics; Electronic Engineering; Hotel Management; Microbiology; Secretarial Studies; Software Engineering)

History: Founded 1988 as Sathyabama Engineering College. Previously known as Sathyabama Institute of Science and Technology (SIST). Acquired "Deemed University" status 2001 and University status 2006.

Accrediting Agency: National Assessment and Accreditation Council (NAAC) (B++ Grade)

Degrees and Diplomas: *Bachelor's Degree*; *Bachelor's Degree (professional)*; *Master's Degree*; *Master of Philosophy*; *Doctor of Philosophy*. Also Dual Degree Courses, 5 yrs; MCA; MBA

Student Services: Canteen, Careers Guidance, Health Services, Sports Facilities

Last Updated: 21/07/11

SAURASHTRA UNIVERSITY

University Campus, University Road, Rajkot, Gujarat 360005
Tel: +91(281) 257-6347
Fax: +91(281) 257-7633
EMail: registrar@sauuni.ernet.in
Website: http://www.saurashtrauniversity.edu/

Vice-Chancellor: Kamlesh P. Joshipura (2005-)
Tel: +91(281) 257-7633
EMail: kpjoshipura@yahoo.com; vc@sauuni.ernet.in

Registrar: Shri Gajendra Jani
Tel: +91(281) 257-6347 EMail: registrar@sauuni.ernet.in

International Relations: K.H. Metha, Head, Department of English

Department

Biochemistry (Biochemistry); **Biosciences** (Biochemistry; Biological and Life Sciences; Biology; Biotechnology; Botany; Microbiology; Molecular Biology; Zoology); **Business Management** (Business Administration; Management); **Chemistry** (Chemistry); **Commerce** (Accountancy; Business and Commerce; Finance); **Computer Science** (Computer Science; Information Technology); **Economics** (Economics); **Education** (Education; Educational Technology); **Electronics** (Computer Engineering; Electronic Engineering; Software Engineering); **English and Comparative Literary Studies** (Comparative Literature; Cultural Studies; English; Literature); **Gujarati** (Indic Languages; Literature); **Hindi** (Hindi; Literature; Translation and Interpretation); **History** (History); **Home Science** (Home Economics; Nutrition); **Human Rights and I. H. L.** (Human Rights; International Law); **Journalism** *(Amrutlal Dalpatbhai Sheth)* (Journalism; Mass Communication); **Law** (Banking; Forensic Medicine and Dentistry; International Law; Law); **Library and Information Science** (Information Sciences; Library Science); **Mathematics** (Mathematics); **Pharmaceutical Science** (Biotechnology; Pharmacology; Pharmacy; Safety Engineering); **Philosophy** (Philosophy); **Physical Education** (Physical Education); **Physics** (Physics); **Psychology** (Psychology); **Sanskrit** (Sanskrit); **Social Work** (Labour and Industrial Relations; Social Work; Welfare and Protective Services); **Sociology** (Sociology); **Statistics** (Econometrics; Mathematics; Mathematics and Computer Science; Operations Research; Statistics)

Further Information: Also 28 Postgraduate Departments, 348 Affiliated Colleges and 4 Recognized Institutions

History: Founded 1967.

Academic Year: June to May

Admission Requirements: 12th year senior secondary/intermediate examination or recognized foreign equivalent (10+2+3 pattern)

Fees: (Rupees): 1,100-1,500

Main Language(s) of Instruction: Gujarati, Hindi, English

Accrediting Agency: National Assessment Accreditation Council, Bangalore

Degrees and Diplomas: *Post Diploma*; *Bachelor's Degree (professional)*; *Postgraduate Diploma*; *Master's Degree*; *Master of Philosophy*; *Doctor of Philosophy*. Also Certificate Courses; MBA and MCA

Student Services: Academic Counselling, Canteen, Careers Guidance, Cultural Activities, Facilities for disabled people, Foreign Studies Centre, Health Services, Language Laboratory, Nursery Care, Social Counselling, Sports Facilities

Publications: Sayujva; Vak

Publishing House: Saurashtra University Press

Last Updated: 21/07/11

SAVEETHA UNIVERSITY

No. 162 Poonamalle High Road, Chennai, Tamil Nadu 600 077
Tel: +91(44) 2680-1580 +91(44) 2680-1585
Fax: +91(44) 2680-0892
EMail: registrar@saveetha.com
Website: http://www.saveetha.com

Vice-Chancellor: R. Rajagopal
EMail: vicechancellor@saveetha.com

College

Dentistry (Dental Hygiene; Dental Technology; Dentistry; Forensic Medicine and Dentistry; Oncology; Oral Pathology; Orthodontics; Periodontics; Public Health; Radiology; Surgery); **Engineering** (Civil Engineering; Communication Studies; Computer Engineering; Computer Graphics; Computer Science; Electrical Engineering; Electronic Engineering; Engineering; Information Technology; Mechanical Engineering; Medical Technology; Nanotechnology; Power Engineering; Robotics; Telecommunications Engineering); **Medicine** (Anatomy; Biochemistry; Community Health; Gynaecology and Obstetrics; Medicine; Microbiology; Ophthalmology; Orthopaedics; Otorhinolaryngology; Paediatrics; Pathology; Pharmacology; Physiology; Radiology; Surgery; Treatment Techniques); **Nursing** (Community Health; Nursing; Psychiatry and Mental Health); **Physiotherapy** (Cardiology; Gynaecology and Obstetrics; Neurosciences; Orthopaedics; Paediatrics; Physical Therapy; Respiratory Therapy; Sports; Sports Medicine; Urology)

School

Law (Law); **Management** (Health Administration; Human Resources; Management)

Further Information: Also Saveetha Nagar Campus.

History: Founded 1988 as Saveetha Institute of Medical and Technical Sciences. Acquired present status and title of 'Deemed University' 2005.

Accrediting Agency: National Assessment and Accreditation Council (NAAC)

Degrees and Diplomas: *Post Diploma*; *Bachelor's Degree*; *Bachelor's Degree (professional)*; *Postgraduate Diploma*; *Master's Degree*; *Doctor of Philosophy*. Alos Certificate Courses; Bachelor's degree honours; Integrated M.E/M.Tech, 5 Yrs; MCA; MBA

Student Services: Sports Facilities

Last Updated: 21/07/11

SAVITRIBAI PHULE PUNE UNIVERSITY

Ganeshkhind, Pune, Maharashtra 411007
Tel: +91(20) 2560-1099 +91(20) 2569-6061
Fax: +91(20) 2569-3899
EMail: dyracademic@unipune.ac.in
Website: http://www.unipune.ac.in/

Vice-Chancellor: W. N. Gade EMail: puvc@unipune.ac.in

Registrar: N. M. Kadu EMail: regis@unipune.ac.in

Faculty

Commerce (Business and Commerce); **Education and Extension** (Education; Educational Technology); **Fine Arts** (English; Fine Arts; French; Geography; German; Hindi; Indic Languages; Japanese; Logic; Modern Languages; Performing Arts; Russian; Sanskrit; Spanish); **Law** (Law); **Management** *(PUMBA)* (Management); **Mental, Moral and Social Sciences** (Adult Education; Anthropology; Continuing Education; Economics; History; Information Sciences; Journalism; Library Science; Mass Communication; Military Science; Philosophy; Political Sciences; Protective Services; Psychology; Public Administration; Social Sciences; Sociology); **Physical Education** (Physical Education); **Science** (Biotechnology; Botany; Chemistry; Communication Studies; Computer Science; Electronic Engineering; Environmental Studies; Geography; Geology; Instrument Making; Mathematics; Meteorology; Microbiology; Natural Sciences; Physics; Statistics; Zoology)

College

Academic Staff (Teacher Training)

School

Basic Medical Sciences (Medicine); **Energy Studies** (Energy Engineering); **Health Sciences** (Health Sciences); **Interdisciplinary Studies** *(Humanities and Social Sciences)* (Arts and Humanities; Social Sciences); **Science** *(Interdisciplinary)* (Natural Sciences); **Scientific Computing** (Computer Science); **Scientific Computing** *(Interdisciplinary)* (Computer Science)

Department

Buddhist Studies and Dr. Ambedkar Thoughts (Asian Religious Studies; Economics; Literature; Political Sciences; Social Sciences)

Institute

Bioinformatics and Biotechnology (Biological and Life Sciences; Biotechnology; Computer Science)

Centre

Bioinformatics (Biological and Life Sciences; Computer Science); **Free Radical Research** *(National - NCFRR)* (Chemistry); **Information and Network Security** *(C.I.N.S.)* (Computer Networks; Information Management); **Modeling and Simulation** (Computer Science); **Network Computing** *(CNC)* (Computer Networks); **Philosophy and History of Science** (Natural Sciences; Philosophy); **Social Sciences and Humanities** *(CSSH)* (Arts and Humanities; Social Sciences); **Women's Studies** (Women's Studies)

Further Information: Also 307 recognized research institutes and 612 affiliated colleges.

History: Founded 1948 as University of Pune.

Academic Year: June to June

Admission Requirements: 12th year senior secondary/intermediate examination or recognized foreign equivalent

Main Language(s) of Instruction: English, Marathi

Degrees and Diplomas: *Bachelor's Degree*; *Postgraduate Diploma*; *Master's Degree*; *Master of Philosophy*; *Doctor of Philosophy*: **Arts and Humanities; Business and Commerce; Fine Arts; Law; Management; Natural Sciences; Performing Arts; Pharmacy; Physical Education.**

Student Services: Canteen, Cultural Activities, Facilities for disabled people, Foreign Studies Centre, Health Services, Language Laboratory, Social Counselling, Sports Facilities

Publications: Poona University (1949-1974) Silver Jubilee Commemoration Vol; Rabindranath Tagore; Vidyapeeth Varta

Last Updated: 28/11/11

SCHOOL OF COMMUNICATION AND MANAGEMENT STUDIES (SCMS-COCHIN)

Prathap Nagar, Muttom, Aluva, Cochin, Kerala 683 106
Tel: +91(484) 262-3803
EMail: info@scmsgroup.org
Website: http://scmsgroup.org/scms/

Director: V. Raman Nair

Programme

Management (Banking; Insurance; Management; Retailing and Wholesaling); **Management** *(Part-time)* (Management)

History: Founded 1976.

Accrediting Agency: All India Council for Technical Education (AICTE)

Degrees and Diplomas: *Postgraduate Diploma*. Postgraduate Diploma equivalent to a University MBA

Last Updated: 25/01/12

SCHOOL OF PLANNING AND ARCHITECTURE (SPA)

4-Block-B, Indraprastha Estate, New Delhi 110002
Tel: +91(11) 2370-2375 +91(11) 2370-2376
Fax: +91(11) 2370-2383
EMail: info@spa.ac.in; admission@spa.ac.in
Website: http://www.spa.ac.in/

Director: A.K. Sharma EMail: director@spa.ac.in

Registrar: D.R. Bains EMail: dr.bains@spa.ac.in

Department

Architectural Conservation (Architectural Restoration; Architecture); **Architecture** (Architecture; Architecture and Planning; Landscape Architecture); **Building Engineering and Management** (Construction Engineering); **Environment Planning** (Environmental Management; Environmental Studies; Landscape Architecture); **Housing** (Architectural and Environmental Design; Architecture; Finance; Real Estate; Safety Engineering); **Industrial Design** (Industrial Design); **Landscape Architecture** (Architectural and Environmental Design; Ecology; Landscape Architecture); **Physical Planning** (Architecture and Planning); **Regional Planning** (Rural Planning); **Transport Planning** (Architecture and Planning; Law; Management; Rural Planning; Transport and

Communications; Urban Studies); **Urban Design** (Architectural and Environmental Design; Town Planning); **Urban Planning** (Architectural and Environmental Design; Town Planning; Urban Studies)

History: Founded 1941 as a Department of Architecture of Delhi Polytechnic. Renamed School of Planning and Architecture 1959. Granted 'Deemed University' status 1979.

Academic Year: August to May (August-December; January-May)

Admission Requirements: 12th year senior secondary/intermediate examination or recognized foreign equivalent

Fees: (Rupees): Undergraduate programmes, 31,300 per annum; Postgraduate programmes, 39,100 per annum; Ph.D. programmes, 33,100 per annum

Main Language(s) of Instruction: English

Degrees and Diplomas: *Bachelor's Degree (professional)*; *Master's Degree*; *Doctor of Philosophy*

Publications: Space

Last Updated: 21/07/11

SHARDA UNIVERSITY

Plot No. 32-34, Knowledge Park III,
Greater Noida, Uttar Pradesh 201 306
Tel: +91(120) 312-1001
EMail: admission@sharda.ac.in
Website: http://www.sharda.ac.in/

Vice-Chancellor: J. Gupta EMail: Chancellor@sharda.ac.in

International Relations: Ashok Daryani, Principal Secretary to the Chancellor; President, Corporate and International Relations
EMail: ashok.daryani@sharda.ac.in

School

Allied Health Sciences (Health Sciences); **Allied Sciences and Creative Arts** (Mass Communication); **Architecture and Planning** (Architecture; Architecture and Planning); **Basic Sciences and Research** (Biological and Life Sciences; Chemistry; Mathematics; Physics); **Business Studies** (Business Administration); **Dental Sciences** (Dentistry); **Engineering and Technology** (Engineering; Technology); **Foreign Languages** (English; French; German; Modern Languages; Spanish); **Law** (Law); **Medical Sciences and Research** (Medicine); **Studies of Investigation, Intelligence and Security** (Protective Services)

Further Information: Also Patna, Guwahati, Lucknow, Kota, Dehradun, Gorakhpur.

History: Created 2009

Accrediting Agency: University Grants Commission (UGC)

Degrees and Diplomas: *Bachelor's Degree (professional)*; *Master's Degree*; *Doctor of Philosophy*. Also Honours Bachelor's degree.

Student Services: Sports Facilities

Academic Staff *2010-2011*: Total: c. 1,200
Student Numbers *2010-2011*: Total: c. 22,000
Last Updated: 23/12/11

SHER-E-KASHMIR UNIVERSITY OF AGRICULTURAL SCIENCES AND TECHNOLOGY-JAMMU (SKUAST-J)

Railway Road, Jammu, Jammu and Kashmir 180012
Tel: +91(191) 247-1745 +91(191) 247-3417
Fax: +91(191) 247-3883
EMail: vc@skuast.org
Website: http://www.skuast.org/

Vice-Chancellor: B. Mishra

Registrar: H.N. Khajuria Tel: +91(191) 247-5149

Faculty

Agriculture (Agricultural Engineering; Agronomy; Biochemistry; Economics; Entomology; Floriculture; Forestry; Genetics; Harvest Technology; Plant Pathology; Sericulture; Soil Science; Statistics); **Veterinary Science and Animal Husbandry** (Anatomy; Animal Husbandry; Biochemistry; Embryology and Reproduction Biology; Epidemiology; Genetics; Gynaecology and Obstetrics; Histology; Hygiene; Immunology; Law; Medicine; Parasitology; Pathology; Pharmacology; Physiology; Public Health; Radiology; Social and Preventive Medicine; Surgery; Toxicology; Veterinary Science; Zoology)

History: Founded 1999.

Academic Year: August to June

Admission Requirements: Undergraduate, 10 + 2 with English, Physics, Chemistry and Math/Biology; For Master's degree, Bachelor's degree in the related Field

Fees: (Rupees): Undergraduates, 9,000 + semester fee; Postgraduate, 11,000 + semester fee

Main Language(s) of Instruction: English

Accrediting Agency: Indian Council of Agricultural Research (ICAR)

Degrees and Diplomas: *Bachelor's Degree*; *Bachelor's Degree (professional)*; *Master's Degree*; *Doctor of Philosophy*. Also undergraduate basic courses.

Student Services: Academic Counselling, Canteen, Cultural Activities, Foreign Studies Centre, Health Services, Nursery Care, Social Counselling, Sports Facilities

Publications: Skuast - Jammu

Last Updated: 22/07/11

SHER-E-KASHMIR UNIVERSITY OF AGRICULTURAL SCIENCES AND TECHNOLOGY-SRINAGAR (SKUAST-K)

PO Box 262, GPO, Srinagar, Jammu and Kashmir 190001
Tel: +91(194) 246-1271
Fax: +91(191) 246-2160
EMail: skuast_k@rediffmail.com; skuast_k@yahoo.com; gora_manzoor@yahoo.com.in
Website: http://www.skuastkashmir.ac.in/

Vice-Chancellor: Tej Partap (2010-)
Tel: +91(194) 246-2159
EMail: vcskuastkashmir@skuastkashmir.ac.in

Registrar: F.A. Zaki
Tel: 91(194) 246-1271 EMail: farooqzaki@gmail.com

Faculty

Agriculture (Agricultural Economics; Agricultural Engineering; Agriculture; Agronomy; Animal Husbandry; Dairy; Entomology; Forestry; Genetics; Horticulture; Plant Pathology; Soil Science; Statistics); **Fisheries** (Agricultural Engineering; Aquaculture; Biochemistry; Biology; Biotechnology; Environmental Studies; Fishery; Genetics; Harvest Technology; Nutrition; Pathology; Social Sciences); **Postgraduate Studies** (Agriculture; Environmental Studies; Forestry; Sericulture; Statistics; Veterinary Science); **Veterinary Sciences and Animal Husbandry** (Agricultural Education; Anatomy; Animal Husbandry; Biochemistry; Embryology and Reproduction Biology; Epidemiology; Ethics; Genetics; Gynaecology and Obstetrics; Histology; Immunology; Microbiology; Nutrition; Parasitology; Pathology; Pharmacology; Physiology; Public Health; Radiology; Surgery; Toxicology; Veterinary Science)

History: Founded 1982. The University is based on the concept of the United States Land Grant Colleges. Has multidisciplinary regional sub-stations in various agro-climatic zones of the state for zone-specific programmes.

Admission Requirements: 12th year senior secondary/intermediate examination or recognized foreign equivalent

Fees: (Rupees): Fee for undergraduate programmes, 1,419 per semester; Postgraduate programmes, 1,889 per semester; Ph.D. programmes, 2,358 per semester

Main Language(s) of Instruction: English

Degrees and Diplomas: *Bachelor's Degree*; *Bachelor's Degree (professional)*; *Master's Degree*; *Doctor of Philosophy*

Last Updated: 22/07/11

SHIV NADAR UNIVERSITY

A-10-11, Sector-3, Noida, Uttar Pradesh 201301
EMail: registrar@snu.edu.in
Website: http://snu.edu.in/

Vice-Chancellor: Nikhil Sinha

Registrar: J. Ernest Samuel Ratnakumar

School

Business (Business Administration); **Communication** (Communication Studies); **Education** (Education); **Engineering** (Civil Engineering; Computer Engineering; Computer Science; Electrical Engineering; Mechanical Engineering; Telecommunications Engineering); **Natural Science** (Mathematics; Natural Sciences); **Social Sciences and Humanities** (Arts and Humanities; Social Sciences)

History: Founded 2011.

Degrees and Diplomas: *Bachelor's Degree*; *Master's Degree*; *Doctor of Philosophy*
Last Updated: 18/01/12

SHIVAJI UNIVERSITY

Vidyanagar, Kolhapur, Maharashtra 416 004
Tel: +91(231) 260-9000
Fax: +91(231) 269-2333
Website: http://www.unishivaji.ac.in

Vice-Chancellor: N. J. Pawar (2009-)
Tel: +91(231) 269-2122 EMail: vcoffice@unishivaji.ac.in

Registrar: D. V. Muley
Tel: +91(231) 260-9063 EMail: registrar@unishivaji.ac.in

International Relations: D.T. Shirke

Department

Adult and Continuing Education (Business Administration; Computer Science; Cooking and Catering; Cosmetology; English; Environmental Studies; Fashion Design; Folklore; Home Economics; Human Rights; Interior Design; Journalism; Library Science; Mass Communication; Medical Auxiliaries; Musical Instruments; Nursing; Public Relations; Social Work; Taxation; Teacher Training; Tourism); **Agrochemicals and Pest Management** (Biological and Life Sciences; Biotechnology; Chemistry; Entomology; Plant and Crop Protection; Toxicology); **Applied Chemistry** (Analytical Chemistry; Applied Chemistry; Chemistry; Industrial Chemistry; Inorganic Chemistry; Organic Chemistry; Pharmacy; Physical Chemistry; Technology); **Bio-Chemistry** (Biochemistry; Biological and Life Sciences; Biotechnology; Computer Science; Environmental Studies); **Bio-Technology** (Biotechnology; Cell Biology; Computer Science; Genetics; Industrial Management; Microbiology; Molecular Biology; Virology); **Botany** (Biotechnology; Botany; Ecology; Environmental Studies; Genetics; Physiology; Plant Pathology); **Chemistry** (Analytical Chemistry; Applied Chemistry; Chemistry; Industrial Chemistry; Inorganic Chemistry; Organic Chemistry; Physical Chemistry); **Commerce and Management** (Accountancy; Banking; Business and Commerce; Finance; Management); **Commerce and Management - MBA Unit** (Accountancy; Agricultural Management; Business Administration; Business and Commerce; Business Computing; Commercial Law; Communication Studies; Economics; Finance; Human Resources; Industrial and Organizational Psychology; Information Management; Information Technology; Management; Marketing; Mathematics; Operations Research; Statistics); **Computer Science** (Computer Science); **Economics** (Agricultural Economics; Economics; Finance); **Education** (Education; Educational Administration; Educational and Student Counselling; Educational Psychology; Educational Sciences; Educational Technology; Foreign Languages Education; Information Technology; Journalism; Mass Communication; Public Relations; Science Education; Special Education; Teacher Trainers Education; Teacher Training); **Electronics** (Electronic Engineering; Microwaves; Power Engineering); **English** (Comparative Literature; English; Linguistics; Literature); **Environmental Science** (Demography and Population; Environmental Management; Environmental Studies; Safety Engineering; Toxicology); **Food Science and Technology** (Biochemistry; Biotechnology; Chemistry; Food Science; Food Technology; Harvest Technology; Laboratory Techniques; Microbiology; Nutrition; Toxicology); **Foreign Languages** (French; German; Japanese; Modern Languages; Russian); **Geography** (Computer Science; Geography; Tourism); **Hindi** (Hindi; Translation and Interpretation); **History** (History; Medieval Studies; Museum Studies); **Journalism and Communication** (Journalism; Mass Communication); **Law** (Criminology; Law); **Library and Information Science** (Information Sciences; Library Science); **Marathi** (Indic Languages; Literature); **Mathematics** (Mathematics); **Micro-Biology** (Cell Biology; Computer Science; Genetics; Immunology; Laboratory Techniques; Microbiology; Statistics; Virology); **Music** (Dance; Music; Musical Instruments; Painting and Drawing; Singing; Theatre; Visual Arts); **Physics** (Astronomy and Space Science; Energy Engineering; Materials Engineering; Optics; Physics; Solid State Physics); **Political Science** (Comparative Politics; Government; Human Rights; International Relations; Political Sciences; Public Administration); **Sociology** (Development Studies; Human Resources; Social Work; Sociology); **Statistics** (Statistics); **Technology** (Chemical Engineering; Civil Engineering; Computer Engineering; Computer Science; Electronic Engineering; Engineering; Environmental Engineering; Environmental Studies; Food Technology; Telecommunications Engineering); **Zoology** (Aquaculture; Entomology; Fishery; Immunology; Technology; Zoology)

Centre

Community Development (Animal Husbandry; Child Care and Development; Clothing and Sewing; Computer Engineering; Dietetics; Electrical Engineering; English; Health Sciences; Heating and Refrigeration; Home Economics; Mechanical Equipment and Maintenance; Nutrition); **Distance Education** (Arts and Humanities; Business Administration; Business and Commerce; Mathematics; Real Estate); **Gandhian Studies** (Development Studies; Political Sciences; Rural Studies); **Women's Studies** (Women's Studies)

Course

Industrial Chemistry (Industrial Chemistry); **Sericulture** (Sericulture)

Research Centre

Shahu (Cultural Studies; History)

Further Information: Also 225 affiliated colleges. A traditional and distance education institution.

History: Founded 1962.

Academic Year: June to April (June-November; November-April) except for Engineering, Technology, Architecture, Pharmacy, Textile and Management studies: July to May (July-November; January-May)

Admission Requirements: 12th year senior secondary/intermediate examination or recognized foreign equivalent

Fees: (Rupees): Tuition fee for undergraduate programmes, from 400 per term to 800 per annum for Indian students and 2,000 per term for foreign students; Postgraduate programmes, from 1,250 per term to 11,000 per annum for Indian students and 2,500 per term for foreign students; M.Ed. Course, 2,000 per term

Main Language(s) of Instruction: English, Marathi

Accrediting Agency: National Assessment and Accreditation Council (NAAC)

Degrees and Diplomas: *Post Diploma*; *Bachelor's Degree*; *Bachelor's Degree (professional)*; *Postgraduate Diploma*; *Master's Degree*; *Master of Philosophy*; *Doctor of Philosophy*. Also Certificate Courses; Higher Diploma; MCA; MBA

Student Services: Health Services, Sports Facilities

Publications: Shivaji University Journal; Shivaji University Journal; Shivsandesh

Publishing House: Shivaji University Press

Student Numbers *2010-2011*: Total: c. 200,000
Last Updated: 22/07/11

SHOBHIT UNIVERSITY

NH-58, Modipuram, Meerut, Uttar Pradesh 250 110
Tel: +91(121) 257-5091 +91(121) 326-4004
Fax: +91(121) 257-5724
EMail: mail@shobhituniversity.ac.in
Website: http://www.shobhituniversity.ac.in

Vice-Chancellor: Anoop Swarup

Registrar: S.K. Sareen EMail: registrar@shobhituniversity.ac.in

School

Basic and Applied Sciences (Biotechnology; Chemical Engineering; Environmental Management; Information Technology; Mathematics; Software Engineering); **Biotechnology** (Biotechnology); **Business Studies** (Business Administration; Finance; Human Resources; Information Management; Information Technology; International Business; Management; Marketing; Operations Research); **Computer Engineering and Information Technology**

(Computer Engineering; Computer Science; Information Technology; Telecommunications Engineering); **Electronics Engineering** (Aeronautical and Aerospace Engineering; Electrical and Electronic Engineering; Electronic Engineering; Measurement and Precision Engineering; Microelectronics; Telecommunications Engineering); **Pharmaceutical Sciences** (Chemistry; Pharmacology; Pharmacy)

Centre

Agri-Informatics (Agricultural Engineering; Agriculture; Information Technology); **Bio-Informatics** (Agriculture; Biological and Life Sciences; Computer Science); **Biomedical Engineering** (Bioengineering; Biomedical Engineering; Medical Technology); **Media Research** (Journalism; Mass Communication; Media Studies); **Professional Development**

History: Founded 2000 as Shobhit Institute of Engineering and Technology. Acquired present status as Deemed University 2006.

Accrediting Agency: American University Accreditation Council (AUAC)

Degrees and Diplomas: *Bachelor's Degree (professional)*; *Master's Degree*; *Master of Philosophy*; *Doctor of Philosophy*. Also Dual Degree (B.Tech./M.Tech.); MBA; MCA.

Student Services: Canteen, Health Services, Sports Facilities

Last Updated: 22/07/11

SHOOLINI UNIVERSITY OF BIOTECHNOLOGY AND MANAGEMENT SCIENCES

SILB, The Mall, Solan, Himachal Pradesh 173212
EMail: info@shooliniuniversity.com
Website: http://www.shooliniuniversity.com/

Vice-Chancellor: Kumar Khosla
EMail: vicechancellor@shooliniuniversity.com

Registrar: Ramanand Chauhan

Faculty

Biotechnology (Biology; Biotechnology; Computer Science; Food Technology; Microbiology); **Engineering and Technology** (Biology; Biotechnology; Civil Engineering; Computer Science; Electronic Engineering; Food Technology; Mechanical Engineering; Telecommunications Engineering); **Management Sciences** (Biotechnology; Business Administration; Computer Science; Electronic Engineering; Esoteric Practices; Finance; Food Technology; Human Resources; Information Technology; Management; Marketing; Telecommunications Engineering; Yoga); **Pharmaceutical Sciences** (Biotechnology; Chemistry; Pharmacology; Pharmacy; Safety Engineering); **Science, Social Science and Languages** (Botany; Chemistry; Environmental Studies; Physics; Zoology)

History: Founded 2009.

Accrediting Agency: University Grants Commission (UGC); AICTE; DISR

Degrees and Diplomas: *Bachelor's Degree (professional)*; *Master's Degree*; *Master of Philosophy*; *Doctor of Philosophy*. Also Honours Bachelor's and Master's Degrees; Dual Bachelor's Degree Programmes with MBA or M.Tech.; MBA.

Student Services: Health Services, Sports Facilities

Last Updated: 26/08/11

SHREE SOMNATH SANSKIT UNIVERSITY

Somnath-VERAVA, District- Junagadh, Gujarat
Tel: +91(2876) 244-528
Website: http://shreesomnathsanskrituniversity.info

Vice-Chancellor: Pankaj L. Jani

Faculty

Darshan (Indian Philosophy) (Philosophy); **Indian culture and Fine Arts** (Fine Arts; South Asian Studies); **Modern Science and Ancient Shastras** (Astronomy and Space Science; Ayurveda; Chemistry; Natural Sciences; Physics); **Sahitya** (Literature; Sanskrit); **Teacher Training** *(Shikshak - Prashikshan)* (Teacher Training)

History: Founded 2005.

Admission Requirements: Higher Secondary School Certificate Examination i.e. twelfth standard examination or any equivalent examination approved by the UGC

Degrees and Diplomas: *Bachelor's Degree*; *Master's Degree*; *Doctor of Philosophy*

Student Services: Sports Facilities

Last Updated: 12/08/11

SHREEMATI NATHIBAI DAMODAR THACKERSEY WOMEN'S UNIVERSITY

1, Nathibai Thavkersey Road, New Marine Lines,
Mumbai, Maharashtra 400020
Tel: +91(22) 2203-1879 +91(22) 2203-2159
Fax: +91(22) 2201-8226
EMail: pvc@sndt.ac.in
Website: http://sndt.digitaluniversity.ac/

Vice-Chancellor: Vasudha Kamat (2011-)

Registrar: Madhu Madan

School

Law *(Juhu Campus)* (Business Administration; Law); **Library and Information Science** *(SHPT - Churchgate Campus)* (Information Sciences; Library Science)

Department

Actuarial Science *(Juhu Campus)* (Actuarial Science); **Adult and Continuing Education and Extension Work** *(Churchgate Campus)* (Adult Education; Continuing Education); **Computer Science** *(Postgraduate)* (Computer Science); **Education Management** *(Juhu Campus)* (Educational Administration); **Educational Technology** *(Juhu Campus)* (Educational Technology); **Jewellery Design and Manufacture** *(Juhu Campus)* (Jewellery Art); **Physical Education** *(Churchgate Campus)* (Physical Education); **Post Graduate Studies and Research** *(Pune Campus)* (Business and Commerce; Communication Studies; Economics; Fine Arts; Geography; Hindi; Music; Painting and Drawing; Psychology; Social Work); **Postgraduate Studies** *(Churchgate Campus)* (Business and Commerce; Economics; Education; English; Fine Arts; Foreign Languages Education; Hindi; History; Indic Languages; Music; Painting and Drawing; Political Sciences; Psychology; Sanskrit; Social Work; Sociology); **Postgraduate Studies in Home Science** *(Juhu Campus)* (Home Economics)

Centre

Distance Education *(Juhu Campus)* (Distance Education); **Special Education** *(Juhu Campus)* (Special Education)

Research Centre

Womens Studies *(Juhu Campus)* (Women's Studies)

Further Information: Also Churchgate Campus, JUHU Campus and Pune Campus; 11 University Colleges (including SNDT for Women); 233 Affiliated Colleges

History: Founded 1916 on the model of the Women's University of Tokyo.

Academic Year: June to April (June-November; November-April)

Admission Requirements: 12th year senior secondary/intermediate examination or recognized foreign equivalent

Fees: (Rupees): 400-15,000

Main Language(s) of Instruction: English, Gujarati, Marathi, Hindi

Accrediting Agency: Accreditation National assessment and accreditation council (NAAC)

Degrees and Diplomas: *Post Diploma*; *Bachelor's Degree*; *Bachelor's Degree (professional)*; *Postgraduate Diploma*; *Master's Degree*; *Master of Philosophy*; *Doctor of Philosophy*. Also Certificate courses

Last Updated: 23/08/11

SHRI JAGANNATH SANSKRIT UNIVERSITY

Shri Jagannath Sanskrit Vishwavidyalaya (SJSV)
Shri Vihar, Puri, Orissa 752003
Tel: +91(6752) 251-669
Fax: +91(6752) 251-073
EMail: sanskrit.university@yahoo.com;
sanskrit.university@yahoo.co.in
Website: http://sjsv.nic.in/

Vice-Chancellor: Nilakantha Pati Tel: +91(6752) 251-663

Registrar: R.C. Dash Tel: +91(6752) 251-669

Department

Advaita Vedanta (Philosophical Schools); **Computer Application** (Computer Science); **Dharmashastra** (Law); **Jyotirvigyan** (Astronomy and Space Science; Esoteric Practices); **Nyaya** (Logic; Philosophy); **Physical Education** (Physical Education); **Sahitya** (Literature); **Sarvadarshan** (Philosophy); **Veda** (Philosophy); **Vyakaran** (Linguistics; Literature)

Further Information: Also 142 Affiliated Colleges

History: Founded 1981. Acquired present status 1990.

Academic Year: June to May

Admission Requirements: 12th year senior secondary/intermediate examination or recognized foreign equivalent

Main Language(s) of Instruction: English

Degrees and Diplomas: *Post Diploma*; *Bachelor's Degree*; *Master's Degree*; *Doctor of Philosophy*

Student Services: Health Services

Last Updated: 23/08/11

SHRI LAL BAHADUR SHASTRI NATIONAL SANSKRIT UNIVERSITY

Shri Lal Bahadur Shastri Rashtriya Sanskrit Vidyapeeth (SLBSRSV)

Qutub Institutional Area, New Delhi 110016
Tel: +91(11) 46060-606
Fax: +91(11) 2653-3512 +91(11) 2652-0255
EMail: info@slbsrsv.ac.in
Website: http://www.slbsrsv.ac.in

Vice-Chancellor: Vachaspati Upadhyaya (1994-)
Tel: +91(11) 2685-1253 +91(11) 2656-4003
EMail: vc@slbsrsv.ac.in; vu_vidyapeetha@hotmail.com; vcslbsrsv@yahoo.co.in

Registrar: B.K. Mohapatra
Tel: +91(11) 26851251 +91(11) 4606-0555
EMail: registrar@slbsrsv.ac.in; reg_slbsrsv@yahoo.co.in

Faculty

Darshan Sankay (Law; Literature; Philosophical Schools; Philosophy; Yoga); **Sahitya Sanskriti** (Asian Religious Studies; Computer Science; English; Hindi; Literature; Philosophy; Political Sciences; Religious Studies; Sanskrit; Social Studies; Sociology; Tourism); **Ved Vedang** (Cultural Studies; Esoteric Practices; Heritage Preservation; Law; Linguistics; Literature; Philosophy)

Department

Adhunik Gyan-Vigyan Sankay (Education; Educational Technology; Environmental Studies; Foreign Languages Education; Psychology; Sanskrit); **Research and Publications**

History: Founded 1962. Acquired present status and title 1987. A deemed university.

Degrees and Diplomas: *Post Diploma*; *Bachelor's Degree*; *Master's Degree*; *Doctor of Philosophy*. Also certificates.

Last Updated: 23/08/11

SHRI MATA VAISHNO DEVI UNIVERSITY (SMVDU)

Sub-Post Office, Katra, Jammu and Kashmir 182320
Tel: +91(1991) 285-535 +91(1991) 285-524
Fax: +91(1991) 285-694
EMail: info@smvdu.ac.in
Website: http://www.smvdu.ac.in

Vice-Chancellor: Sudhir K. Jain (2012-)
Tel: +91(1991) 285-686 EMail: vc@smvdu.ac.in

Registrar: Roop Avtar Kaur Tel: +91(1991) 285-687

College

Engineering *(COE)* (Architecture; Biotechnology; Computer Engineering; Computer Science; Electronic Engineering; Energy Engineering; Engineering; Landscape Architecture; Mechanical Engineering; Natural Resources; Telecommunications Engineering); **Humanities and Social Sciences** (Arts and Humanities; Cultural Studies; English; French; Literature; Logic; Modern Languages; Philosophy; Social Sciences); **Management** *(COM)* (Business Administration; Economics; Management); **Sciences** *(COS)* (Biology; Biotechnology; Chemistry; Mathematics; Natural Sciences; Physics)

History: Founded 1999. Acquired present status 2004.

Academic Year: August to June (August-December; January-June)

Admission Requirements: Secondary School Certificate and All India Engineering Entrance Examination

Fees: (Rupees): Bachelor's degree, 60,000 per annum; Master's degree, 10,000-40,000 per annum; MBA, 14,000 per annum; Ph.D., 8,000-20,000 per annum

Main Language(s) of Instruction: English

Accrediting Agency: University Grants Commission; Association of Indian Universities; All India Council for Technical Education; Council of Architecture

Degrees and Diplomas: *Bachelor's Degree (professional)*; *Master's Degree*; *Doctor of Philosophy*. Also Certificate and MBA

Student Services: Academic Counselling, Canteen, Careers Guidance, Cultural Activities, Health Services, Language Laboratory, Sports Facilities

Last Updated: 23/08/11

SHRIDHAR UNIVERSITY (SU)

Pilani-Chirawa Road, Pilani, Rajasthan 333031
Tel: +91(1596) 510-000
Fax: +91(1596) 510-002
EMail: info@shridharuniversity.ac.in
Website: http://www.shridharuniversity.ac.in

Vice-Chancellor: P.S. Siwach

Programme

Business Administration *(Postgraduate)* (Business Administration; Finance; Human Resources; Information Technology; Marketing); **Civil Engineering** (Civil Engineering); **Computer Applications** *(Postgraduate)* (Computer Science); **Computer Science and Engineering** (Computer Engineering; Computer Science); **Computer Science and Engineering** *(Postgraduate)* (Software Engineering); **Electrical and Electronics** (Electrical Engineering; Electronic Engineering); **Electronics and Communication** (Electronic Engineering; Telecommunications Engineering); **Environmental Engineering** *(Postgraduate)* (Environmental Engineering); **Environmental Science** (Environmental Studies); **Geo Informatics** *(Postgraduate)* (Computer Science; Earth Sciences; Geology); **Geography** *(Postgraduate)* (Geography); **Mechanical Engineering** (Mechanical Engineering); **Mining Engineering** (Mining Engineering); **Pharmaceutics** *(Postgraduate)* (Pharmacology; Pharmacy); **Software Engineering** *(Postgraduate)* (Software Engineering)

History: Founded 2010.

Degrees and Diplomas: *Bachelor's Degree*; *Bachelor's Degree (professional)*; *Master's Degree*; *Doctor of Philosophy*

Last Updated: 22/12/11

SIDHO KANHO BIRSHA UNIVERSITY (SKBU)

North Bengal University, DD 27/C, Sector-I, Salt Lake, Kolkata, West Bengal 700 064
Tel: +91(3252) 224-438
EMail: vcskbuniversity@gmail.com
Website: http://skbu.ac.in/

Vice-Chancellor: Tapati Mukherjee

Registrar: Nachiketa Bandyopadhyay
EMail: registrarskbu@gmail.com

Programme

Bangladesh (South and Southeast Asian Languages); **Chemistry** (Chemistry); **Education** (Education); **English** (English); **Mathematics** (Mathematics); **Philosophy** (Philosophy); **Physics** (Physics); **Political Sciences** (Political Sciences); **Sanskrit** (Sanskrit)

Further Information: Also Purulia Campus; 24 affiliated colleges.

History: Founded 2010.

Accrediting Agency: University Grants Commission (UGC)

Degrees and Diplomas: *Bachelor's Degree*; *Master's Degree*

Last Updated: 06/01/12

SIDO KANHU MURMU UNIVERSITY (SKMU)

Santal Pargana, Dumka, Bihar 814101
Tel: +91(6434) 222-495
Fax: +91(6434) 222-415
Website: http://skmu.edu.in/

Vice-Chancellor: Basheer Ahmed Khan (2010-)
Tel: +91(6434) 223-006 EMail: vc@skmu.edu.in

Registrar: Md. Shamshadullah
Tel: +91(6434) 222-495 EMail: registrar@skmu.edu.in

Faculty

Commerce (Accountancy; Banking; Business and Commerce; Commercial Law; Development Studies; Economics; Finance; Statistics); **Humanities** (Anthropology; Arts and Humanities; English; Hindi; Indic Languages; Literature; Persian; Philosophy; Sanskrit; Urdu); **Science** (Botany; Chemistry; Geology; Mathematics; Natural Sciences; Physics; Statistics; Zoology); **Social Sciences** (Agricultural Economics; Anthropology; Economics; Geography; History; Labour and Industrial Relations; Music; Political Sciences; Psychology; Social Sciences; Social Welfare; Sociology; Statistics)

Course

Vocational Studies (Advertising and Publicity; Harvest Technology; Sales Techniques; Sericulture)

Further Information: 13 constituent colleges and 11 Affiliated colleges.

History: Founded 1991 by an Act of Bihar Legislative Assembly with a view to providing higher education to the people of tribal culture in the Santhal Parganas region of South Bihar. Acquired present title 2003. Formerly known as Siddhu Kanhu Murmu University.

Academic Year: June to May

Admission Requirements: 12th year senior/secondary intermediate examination or recognized foreign equivalent

Fees: (Rupees): 144-252 per annum

Main Language(s) of Instruction: English, Hindi, Bengali, Santhali

Accrediting Agency: University Grants Commission (UGC)

Degrees and Diplomas: *Bachelor's Degree*; *Bachelor's Degree (professional)*; *Master's Degree*; *Doctor of Philosophy*. Also MBA and MPA

Student Services: Sports Facilities

Last Updated: 23/08/11

SIKKIM MANIPAL UNIVERSITY OF HEALTH, MEDICAL AND TECHNOLOGY SCIENCE (SMU)

5th Mile, Tadong, Gangtok, East Sikkim 737102
Tel: +91(3592) 270-294
Fax: +91(3592) 231-47
EMail: info@smu.edu.in
Website: http://www.smu.edu.in/

Vice-Chancellor: Somnath Mishra
Tel: +91(3592) 03-592 EMail: vc@smu.edu.in

Registrar: Namrata Thapa

Division

Distance Education *(SMU DDE)* (Arts and Humanities; Biotechnology; Business Administration; Business and Commerce; Computer Networks; Computer Science; Cooking and Catering; Fashion Design; Health Administration; History; Information Sciences; Information Technology; International Business; Journalism; Laboratory Techniques; Mass Communication; Medical Technology; Political Sciences; Telecommunications Engineering; Tourism)

School

Architecture (Architecture); **Basic and Applied Sciences** (Chemistry; Computer Engineering; Computer Science; Engineering; Information Technology; Mathematics; Nanotechnology; Physics; Telecommunications Engineering); **Nursing** *(SMCON)* (Nursing); **Physiotherapy** *(SMCPT)* (Physical Therapy)

Institute

Medical Sciences *(SMIMS)* (Anatomy; Biochemistry; Biotechnology; Laboratory Techniques; Medical Technology; Medicine; Microbiology; Physiology; Surgery); **Skill Development**; **Technology** *(SMIT)* (Chemistry; Civil Engineering; Computer Engineering; Computer Science; Electrical and Electronic Engineering; Electrical Engineering; Electronic Engineering; Engineering; Information Technology; Management; Mathematics; Mechanical Engineering; Physics; Technology; Telecommunications Engineering)

Further Information: Also Majitar SMIT campus.

History: Founded 1995.

Academic Year: July to August

Admission Requirements: 12th year senior secondary examination

Fees: (Indian Rupees): Tuition fees for undergraduate programmes, 20,000-60,000 per annum; Professional undergraduate programmes, 90,000-360,000 per annum; Postgraduate programmes, 21,700-74,600 per annum; MBA, 123,000 per annum. For International students (US Dollars): 2,650-18,000 per annum

Main Language(s) of Instruction: English

Accrediting Agency: State Legislative; University Grants Commission; All India Council for Technical Education

Degrees and Diplomas: *Post Diploma*; *Bachelor's Degree*; *Bachelor's Degree (professional)*; *Postgraduate Diploma*; *Master's Degree*; *Doctor of Philosophy*. Also advanced diploma; Bachelor's degree honours; MBA and MCA

Student Services: Academic Counselling, Canteen, Careers Guidance, Cultural Activities, Health Services, Language Laboratory, Nursery Care, Social Counselling, Sports Facilities

Publications: Manipal Link

Publishing House: Manipal Power Press

Last Updated: 27/01/12

SIKKIM UNIVERSITY

6th mile Samdur, Tadong, Gangtok, Sikkim 737 102
Tel: +91(3592) 251-438
Fax: +91(3592) 251-438
EMail: sikkimuniversity@gmail.com; admin@sikkimunivesity.in
Website: http://www.sikkimuniversity.in/

Vice-Chancellor: Mahendra P. Lama

Registrar: P. V. Ravi

Department

Asian Languages (Chinese); **Chemical Sciences** (Chinese); **Economic studies and Planning** (Economics); **Geography and Natural Resource Management** (Geography; Natural Resources); **International Relations** (International Relations); **Journalism and Mass Communication** (Journalism; Mass Communication); **Management and Commerce** (Business Administration; Business and Commerce; Management); **Microbiology** (Microbiology); **Nepali Language and Literature** (Indic Languages; Linguistics; Literature); **Peace and Conflicts** (Peace and Disarmament); **Physical Sciences** (Physics); **Plantation Management and Studies** (Horticulture); **Psychology** (Psychology); **Social System and Anthropology** (Anthropology; Social Sciences)

Centre

Law and Legal Jurisprudence (Law)

Further Information: Also 10 affiliated colleges.

History: Founded 2007. A 'Central University'.

Degrees and Diplomas: *Bachelor's Degree*; *Postgraduate Diploma*; *Master's Degree*. Also integrated Bachelor-Master's degree.

Last Updated: 06/12/11

SIKSHA "O" ANUSANDHAN UNIVERSITY

Khandagiri Square, Bhubaneswar, Bhubaneswar, Orissa 751030
Tel: +91(674) 2350-635 +91(674) 2350-791
Fax: +91(674) 2350-642
EMail: info@soauniversity.ac.in
Website: http://www.soauniversity.ac.in/

Vice-Chancellor: Rajendra Prasad Mohanty
Tel: +91(22) 25811-506
EMail: rpmohanty@gmail.com; rajendramohanty@hotmail.com; mohantyrp@yahoo.com; vcsoa@soauniversity.ac.in

Registrar: Bibhuti Pradhan Bhusan
EMail: registrar@soauniversity.ac.in

College
SUM Nursing *(SNC)* (Nursing)

School
Pharmaceutical Sciences *(SPS)* (Anatomy; Biotechnology; Pharmacology; Pharmacy; Safety Engineering)

Institute
Business and Computer Studies *(IBCS)* (Business Administration; Computer Science; Finance; Human Resources; Information Technology; Marketing); **Dental Sciences** *(IDS)* (Dental Technology; Dentistry; Microbiology; Oral Pathology; Orthodontics; Periodontics; Radiology; Surgery); **Hotel Management** *(SHM)* (Cooking and Catering; Hotel Management); **Law** *(SOA National)* (Law); **Medical Sciences and SUM Hospital** *(IMS & SH)* (Anaesthesiology; Anatomy; Biochemistry; Dentistry; Dermatology; Endocrinology; Forensic Medicine and Dentistry; Gastroenterology; Gynaecology and Obstetrics; Medicine; Microbiology; Ophthalmology; Orthopaedics; Otorhinolaryngology; Paediatrics; Pathology; Pharmacology; Physiology; Plastic Surgery; Pneumology; Psychiatry and Mental Health; Radiology; Respiratory Therapy; Social and Preventive Medicine; Surgery; Venereology); **Technical Education and Research** *(ITER)* (Arts and Humanities; Automation and Control Engineering; Chemistry; Civil Engineering; Computer Engineering; Computer Science; Electrical and Electronic Engineering; Electrical Engineering; Electronic Engineering; English; Information Technology; Literature; Mathematics; Measurement and Precision Engineering; Mechanical Engineering; Physics; Telecommunications Engineering)

Centre
Biotechnology *(CBT)* (Biotechnology)

History: A deemed university.

Fees: (Indian Rupees): undergraduate programmes, 35,000-75,000 per annum; Undergraduate professional programmes, 150,000-195,000 per annum; Postgraduate programmes, 50,000-275,000 per annum; MBA, 230,000-250,000 per annum

Accrediting Agency: National Assessment and Accreditation Council (NAAC) of University Grants Commission (UGC) - Grade "A".

Degrees and Diplomas: *Bachelor's Degree*; *Bachelor's Degree (professional)*; *Master's Degree*; *Doctor of Philosophy*. Also MBA
Last Updated: 24/08/11

SINGHANIA UNIVERSITY

.P.O. - Pacheri Bari, Jhunjhunu, Rajasthan 333 515
Tel: +91(1593) 271299 +91(1593) 271300
Fax: +91(1593) 271003
EMail: info@singhaniauniversity.co.in
Website: http://www.singhaniauniversity.co.in/

Chancellor: D.C. Singhania

School
Applied Sciences and Social Sciences (Applied Mathematics; Chemistry; Mathematics; Physics; Social Sciences); **Computer Science and Information Technology** (Computer Engineering; Computer Networks; Computer Science; Information Technology); **Electronics and Electrical Engineering** (Electrical Engineering; Electronic Engineering; Telecommunications Engineering); **Humanities, Languages and Social Sciences** (Arts and Humanities; Business and Commerce; Economics; Education; English; Geography; Hindi; History; Indic Languages; Modern Languages; Physical Education; Political Sciences; Social Sciences; Social Work; Sociology); **Industrial Engineering** (Automotive Engineering; Civil Engineering; Industrial Engineering; Mechanical Engineering); **Law and Management** (Business Administration; Law; Management); **Life Sciences** (Agriculture; Biological and Life Sciences; Biotechnology; Botany; Computer Science; Microbiology; Zoology); **Pharmacy and Medical Sciences** (Alternative Medicine; Medicine; Pharmacology; Pharmacy; Physical Therapy; Yoga)

History: Created 2003 as Singhania Institute. Acquired current title and status 2007.

Accrediting Agency: University Grants Commission (UGC)

Degrees and Diplomas: *Post Diploma*; *Bachelor's Degree*; *Bachelor's Degree (professional)*; *Postgraduate Diploma*; *Master's Degree*; *Doctor of Philosophy*. Also MBA
Last Updated: 21/11/11

SIR PADAMPAT SINGHANIA UNIVERSITY (SPSU)

Bhatewar, Tehsil, Vallabhnagar District, Udaipur Rajasthan
Tel: +91(2957) 226-095 +91(294) 243-0102
Fax: +91(2957) 226-094
EMail: info@spsu.ac.in
Website: http://www.spsu.ac.in/

Vice-Chancellor: Pradip Chandra Deka

School
Engineering (Biotechnology; Civil Engineering; Computer Engineering; Computer Science; Electrical Engineering; Electronic Engineering; Engineering; Mechanical Engineering; Telecommunications Engineering); **Management** (Accountancy; Advertising and Publicity; Banking; Business Administration; E-Business/Commerce; Economics; Finance; Human Resources; Law; Management; Marketing; Operations Research; Safety Engineering; Small Business; Taxation)

History: Founded 2007.

Degrees and Diplomas: *Bachelor's Degree*; *Bachelor's Degree (professional)*; *Master's Degree*; *Doctor of Philosophy*. Also MBA; integrated Bachelor and Master's degrees (BTech + M.Tech.; BBM + MBA)

Student Services: Sports Facilities
Last Updated: 21/12/11

SOLAPUR UNIVERSITY (SU)

Dnyanteerth Nagar, Kegaon, Solapur-Pune National Highway, Solapur, Maharashtra 413 255
EMail: registrarsolapur@yahoo.in
Website: http://su.digitaluniversity.ac/

Vice-Chancellor: N. N. Maldar EMail: maldar_nn@rediffmail.com

School
Chemical Sciences (Chemistry; Industrial Chemistry; Organic Chemistry; Polymer and Plastics Technology); **Computational Sciences** (Computer Science; Mathematics; Statistics); **Earth Sciences** (Computer Science; Earth Sciences; Environmental Studies; Geology); **Physical Sciences** (Applied Physics; Chemistry; Electronic Engineering; Materials Engineering; Physics); **Social Sciences** (Agricultural Economics; Ancient Civilizations; Archaeology; Banking; Cultural Studies; Economics; International Economics; Journalism; Mass Communication; Museum Studies; Rural Studies; Social Sciences; Tourism)

Department
Educational Sciences (Education; Educational Sciences); **Management** (Business Administration; Business and Commerce; Finance; Human Resources; Industrial Management; International Business; Management; Marketing; Retailing and Wholesaling)

Further Information: Also 126 Affiliated Colleges.

History: Founded 2004.

Degrees and Diplomas: *Bachelor's Degree*; *Bachelor's Degree (professional)*; *Master's Degree*; *Master of Philosophy*; *Doctor of Philosophy*. Also MBA
Last Updated: 04/01/12

SOUTH ASIAN UNIVERSITY (SAU)

Akbar Bhawan, Chanakyapuri, New Delhi 110-021
Tel: +91(11) 2412-2512 +91(11) 2412-2514
Fax: +91(11) 2412-2511
EMail: sau@southasianuniversity.org
Website: http://www.southasianuniversity.org/

President: G.K. Chadha
Tel: +91(11) 2412-2507
EMail: gkchadha@mail.jnu.ac.in; gkchadha@southasianuniversity.org

Registrar: A. K. Malik
Tel: +91(11) 2412-2508 EMail: registrar@southasianuniversity.org

Faculty
Economics (Economics); **Legal Studies** (Criminal Law; International Law; Law; Maritime Law); **Life Sciences and Biotechnology** (Biological and Life Sciences; Biotechnology); **Mathematics and Computer Science** (Computer Science; Mathematics); **Social Sciences** (International Relations; Sociology)

Further Information: Also Akbar Bhawan Campus.

History: Founded 2010. A 'Central University'.

Fees: (US Dollar): South Asian Association for Regional Cooperation (SAARC) students, 440-500 per semester; non-SAARC students, 4,500-5,100 per semester

Degrees and Diplomas: *Master's Degree*; *Master of Philosophy*

Last Updated: 06/12/11

SOUTH INDIAN INSTITUTION FOR THE PROPAGATION OF HINDI

Dakshina Bharat Hindi Prachar Sabha
Thanikachalam Road, Chennai, Tamil Nadu 600017
Tel: +91(44) 2434-1824
Fax: +91(44) 2434-8420
EMail: info@dbhps-chennai.com
Website: http://www.dbhps-chennai.com

Vice-Chancellor: B.D. Jatti

Registrar: R.F. Neerlakatti

Faculty
Comparative Literature and Journalism *(Dharwad-Karnataka and Hyderabad Complexes)* (Comparative Literature; Journalism); **Education** *(Hyderabad Complex)* (Education); **Humanities** (Arts and Humanities); **Literature** *(Madras and Ernakulum Complexes)* (Literature)

History: Founded 1918 by Mahatma Gandhi, achieved degree-granting status 1964. A postgraduate institution.

Academic Year: July to June (July-December; January-June)

Admission Requirements: University degree

Fees: (Rupees): 1,050-2,800 per annum

Main Language(s) of Instruction: Hindi

Degrees and Diplomas: *Bachelor's Degree*: **Education.** *Master's Degree*; *Doctor of Philosophy*

S.P. JAIN INSTITUTE OF MANAGEMENT AND RESEARCH (SPJIMR)

Munshi Nagar, Dadabhai Road, Andheri West,
Mumbai, Maharashtra 400 058
Tel: +91(22) 2623-7454 +91(22) 2623-0396
Fax: +91(22) 2623-7042
EMail: spjicom@spjimr.org
Website: http://www.spjimr.org/

Director: Sesha Iyer (2007-)
Tel: +91(22) 6145-4202 EMail: seshaiyer@spjimr.org

Registrar: A.K. Singh Suryavanshi
Tel: +91(22) 6145-4261 EMail: surya@spjimr.org

International Relations: Suresh Advani, Chairperson, International Operations Tel: +91(22) 6145-4208 EMail: sadvani@spjimr.org

International Relations: Prem Chandrani, Chairperson, International Relations
Tel: +91(22) 6145-4209 EMail: pchandrani@spjimr.org

Centre
Continuing Management Education *(CME)* (Business Administration; International Business; Leadership; Management); **Development of Corporate Citizenship** *(DOCC)* (Government; Management); **Entrepreneurship Development** *(CED)* (Business Administration; Management); **Family Managed Business** *(FMB)* (Business Administration; Small Business); **Services Sciences, Management and Engineering** *(SSME)* (Business Administration; Engineering; Management; Social Studies)

History: Founded 1918. Started offering Postgraduate programmes 1992. A constituent unit of the Bharatiya Vidya Bhavan educational trust, founded 1938.

Academic Year: June to April

Admission Requirements: Minimum 3 yrs Bachelor's degree in any discipline from a recognized University in India or abroad; Contiuous Good Academic Records in SSC, HSC and Degree; The minimum score required to get the final offer is 85 percentile in CAT2010/XAT2011 or a score of 680 in GMAT taken in 2010.

Fees: (Indian Rupee): 87,000 for two years

Main Language(s) of Instruction: English

Accrediting Agency: All India Council for Technical Education (AICTE); National Board of Accreditation (NBA); Association of MBAs (AMBA); Credit Rating and Information Services of India Ltd. (CRISIL)

Degrees and Diplomas: *Postgraduate Diploma*: **Finance; Information Management; Management; Marketing.**

Student Services: Academic Counselling, Canteen, Careers Guidance, Cultural Activities, Facilities for disabled people, Health Services, Language Laboratory, Social Counselling, Sports Facilities

Academic Staff *2011-2012*	MEN	WOMEN	TOTAL
FULL-TIME	27	16	**43**
PART-TIME	14	2	**16**
STAFF WITH DOCTORATE			
FULL-TIME	11	6	**17**
Student Numbers *2011-2012*			
All (Foreign included)	105	72	**177**
FOREIGN ONLY	115	62	**177**

Last Updated: 09/01/12

SREE CHITRA TIRUNAL INSTITUTE FOR MEDICAL SCIENCES AND TECHNOLOGY (SCTIMST)

PO Medical College, Thiruvananthapuram, Kerala 695011
Tel: +91(471) 252-4150
Fax: +91(471) 244-6433
EMail: sct@sctimst.ker.nic.in
Website: http://www.sctimst.ac.in/

Director: K. Radhakrishnan

Registrar: A.V. George

Division
Biomedical Technology (Biomedical Engineering; Technology); **Patient Care** (Administration; Anaesthesiology; Biochemistry; Cardiology; Cell Biology; Microbiology; Molecular Biology; Neurological Therapy; Neurology; Nursing; Pathology; Radiology)

Centre
Health Science Studies *(Achutha Menon - AMCHSS)* (Health Sciences; Public Health)

Further Information: Also Teaching Hospital

History: Founded 1974 and declared Institution of national importance 1980. A postgraduate Institution.

Academic Year: January to December

Admission Requirements: University degree

Main Language(s) of Instruction: English

Degrees and Diplomas: *Post Diploma*; *Master's Degree*; *Doctor of Philosophy*. Also short courses.

Last Updated: 21/11/11

SREE SANKARACHARYA UNIVERSITY OF SANSKRIT (SSUS)

PO Box 14, Ernakulam District, Kalady, Kerala 683574
Tel: +91(484) 2463380
Fax: +91(484) 2463580
EMail: ssusvc@sancharnet.in
Website: http://www.ssus.ac.in

Vice-Chancellor: J. Prasad
Tel: +91(484) 2463580 EMail: ssuvc@sancharnet.in

Registrar: K. Ramachandran
Tel: +91(484) 2463480 EMail: sureg@sancharnet.in

School
Vedic Studies (Ayurveda; Esoteric Practices)

Department

Ayurveda (Ayurveda); **Dance** (Dance); **Economics** (Economics); **Education** (Education); **English** (English); **Geography** (Geography); **Hindi** (Hindi); **History** (History); **Malayalam** (Indic Languages); **Music** (Music); **Painting** (Painting and Drawing); **Philosophy** (Philosophy); **Political Science** (Political Sciences); **Sanskrit Nyaya** (Sanskrit); **Sanskrit Sahitya** (Sanskrit); **Sanskrit Vedanta** (Sanskrit); **Social Work** (Social Work); **Sociology** (Sociology); **Theatre** (Theatre); **Urdu** (Urdu); **Vastuvidya** (Esoteric Practices)

Further Information: Nine Regional Centres: Thiruvananthapuram, Panmana, Thuravoor, Ettumanoor, Kalady (Main Campus), Thrissur, Tirur, Koyilandy and Payyannur.

History: Founded 1993.

Fees: (Rupees): 400-4,500 per annum

Degrees and Diplomas: *Bachelor's Degree*; *Postgraduate Diploma*; *Master's Degree*; *Master of Philosophy*; *Doctor of Philosophy*. Also integrated M.Phil/Ph.D.

Last Updated: 21/11/11

SRI BALAJI VIDYAPEETH, MAHATMA GANDHI MEDICAL COLLEGE AND RESEARCH INSTITUTE (MGMCRI)

Pillaiyarkuppam, Pondicherry 607 402
Tel: +91(413) 261-5449 +91(413) 261-5458
Fax: +91(413) 261-5457
EMail: mgmcri@sify.com; info@mgmcri.ac.in
Website: http://www.mgmcri.ac.in/

Vice-Chancellor: D. R. Gunasekaran

Department

Anaesthesiology (Anaesthesiology); **Anatomy** (Anatomy); **Biochemistry** (Biochemistry); **Cardiology** (Cardiology); **Cardiothoracic Surgery** (Surgery); **Community Medicine** (Community Health); **Dermatology, Venereology and Leprology** (Dermatology; Venereology); **Emergency Services** (Medical Technology); **ENT** (Otorhinolaryngology); **Forensic Medicine** (Forensic Medicine and Dentistry); **General Medicine** (Medicine); **General Surgery** (Surgery); **Master Health Checkup** (Health Sciences); **Microbiology** (Microbiology); **Music Therapy** (Art Therapy); **Neuro Surgery** (Neurological Therapy; Surgery); **Neurology** (Urology); **Obstetrics and Gynaecology** (Gynaecology and Obstetrics); **Ophthalmology** (Ophthalmology); **Orthopaedics** (Orthopaedics); **Paediatric Surgery** (Surgery); **Pathology** (Pathology); **Pharmacology** (Pharmacology); **Physiology** (Physiology); **Plastic Surgery** (Plastic Surgery); **Psychiatry** (Psychiatry and Mental Health); **Radiology and Imageology** (Medical Technology; Radiology); **Surgical Gastroenterology** (Gastroenterology; Surgery); **TB and CD** (Medicine; Rehabilitation and Therapy); **Telemedicine** (Medicine); **Urology** (Urology); **Yoga Therapy** (Alternative Medicine; Yoga)

Laboratory

Skill (Medicine)

Research Laboratory

Medicine *(Central)* (Medicine)

History: A 'Deemed University'.

Degrees and Diplomas: *Bachelor's Degree*; *Bachelor's Degree (professional)*; *Postgraduate Diploma*; *Master's Degree*. Also Certificate Course

Last Updated: 16/12/11

SRI CHANDRASEKHARENDRA SARASWATHI VISWA MAHAVIDYALAYA (SCSVMV)

Sri Jayendra Saraswathi Street, Enathur,
Kanchipuram, Tamil Nadu 631 561
Tel: +91(44) 27264293 +91(44) 27264308
Fax: +91(44) 27264285
EMail: registrar@kanchiuniv.ac.in
Website: http://www.kanchiuniv.ac.in/

Vice-Chancellor: B. Vaidyanathan

Registrar: V.S. Vishnu Potty Tel: +91(44) 27264279

Faculty

Education (Education; Physical Education); **Engineering and Technology** (Civil Engineering; Computer Engineering; Computer Science; Electrical Engineering; Electronic Engineering; Engineering; Information Technology; Instrument Making; Mechanical Engineering; Structural Architecture; Technology; Telecommunications Engineering); **Health and Life Sciences** (Ayurveda; Biological and Life Sciences; Health Sciences); **Management** (Business and Commerce; Human Resources; Management); **Sanskrit and Languages** (English; Hindi; Sanskrit); **Sciences** (Chemistry; Computer Science; Mathematics; Physics); **Social Science and Humanities** (Arts and Humanities; Cultural Studies; History; Philosophy; Social Sciences)

Further Information: Also campus in Poonamalle, Chennai.

History: Founded 1993. A deemed university.

Academic Year: June-July to April-May

Admission Requirements: Pass in XII standard

Fees: (Rupees): 7,500-24,750 per semester

Main Language(s) of Instruction: English. Sanskrit

Degrees and Diplomas: *Bachelor's Degree*; *Bachelor's Degree (professional)*; *Postgraduate Diploma*; *Master's Degree*; *Master of Philosophy*; *Doctor of Philosophy*. Also certificates; MBA and Executive MBA

Student Services: Academic Counselling, Careers Guidance, Cultural Activities, Social Counselling, Sports Facilities

Last Updated: 21/11/11

SRI DEVARAJ URS UNIVERSITY (SDUU)

Tamaka, Kolar, Karnataka 563 101
Tel: +91(8152) 649-208 +91(8152) 649-209
Fax: +91(8152) 649-208 +91(8152) 243-008
EMail: registrar@sduu.ac.in
Website: http://www.sduu.ac.in/

Vice-Chancellor: S.Chandrashekar Shetty

Registrar: A.V. Moideen Kutty

Course

Medicine *(Post Graduate Diploma)* (Anaesthesiology; Gynaecology and Obstetrics; Medicine; Ophthalmology; Orthopaedics; Paediatrics; Radiology); **Medicine** *(Post Graduate)* (Anaesthesiology; Biochemistry; Dermatology; Gynaecology and Obstetrics; Medicine; Microbiology; Ophthalmology; Orthopaedics; Otorhinolaryngology; Paediatrics; Pathology; Pharmacology; Physiology; Radiology; Surgery); **Medicine** *(Undergraduate)* (Medicine; Surgery)

History: Founded 1986 as Sri Devaraj Urs Medical College. Acquired present title and deemed university status 2007.

Accrediting Agency: National Assessment and Accreditation Council (NAAC)

Degrees and Diplomas: *Bachelor's Degree (professional)*; *Postgraduate Diploma*; *Master's Degree*

Last Updated: 13/12/11

SRI GURU GRANTH SAHIB WORLD UNIVERSITY

University Campus, Fathegarh Sahib, Punjab 140406
Tel: +91(1763) 232300
EMail: info@sggswu.org
Website: http://sggswu.org

Vice-Chancellor: Jasbir Singh Ahluwalia

Course

Religious and Civilization Studies (History of Religion; History of Societies); **Science and Technologies** (Biotechnology; Computer Engineering; Computer Science; Food Technology; Instrument Making; Mathematics; Nanotechnology; Natural Sciences; Physical Engineering; Physics; Technology); **Social Sciences** (Management; Mass Communication; Social Sciences)

History: Founded 2008.

Degrees and Diplomas: *Bachelor's Degree*; *Master's Degree*. Also MBA

Last Updated: 18/01/12

SRI KRISHNADEVARAYA UNIVERSITY

Sri Venkateswarapuram, Anantapur, Andhra Pradesh 515003
Tel: +91(8554) 255-700
Fax: +91(8554) 255-244
EMail: vc@kanchiuniv.ac.in
Website: http://www.skuniversity.org/

Vice-Chancellor: K. Ramakrishna Reddy (2011-)
Tel: +91(8554) 255231 EMail: vicechancellor@skuniversity.org

Registrar: N. Ravindranath
Tel: +91(8554) 255700 EMail: registrar@skuniversity.org

Faculty

Languages and Literature (Comparative Literature; English; Indic Languages); **Law** (Law); **Life Sciences** (Biochemistry; Biological and Life Sciences; Biotechnology; Botany; Geography; Microbiology; Pharmacy; Sericulture; Zoology); **Management** (Business and Commerce; Management); **Physical Sciences** (Chemistry; Computer Science; Electronic Engineering; Instrument Making; Mathematics; Physical Education; Physics; Polymer and Plastics Technology; Sports; Statistics; Technology); **Social Sciences** (Adult Education; Continuing Education; Development Studies; Economics; Education; History; Information Sciences; Library Science; Political Sciences; Public Administration; Social Sciences; Social Work; Sociology)

Further Information: Also 109 Affiliated Colleges; A traditional and distance education institution.

History: Founded 1981.

Academic Year: July to June (July-December; January-June)

Admission Requirements: 12th year senior secondary/intermediate examination or recognized foreign equivalent

Fees: (Rupees): 283-332

Main Language(s) of Instruction: English, Telugu

Degrees and Diplomas: *Bachelor's Degree*; *Postgraduate Diploma*; *Master's Degree*; *Master of Philosophy*; *Doctor of Philosophy*. Also MBA

Last Updated: 21/11/11

SRI PADMAVATI WOMEN'S UNIVERSITY

Sri Padmavati Mahila Viswavidyalayam (SPMVV)

District Chittoor, Tirupati, Andhra Pradesh 517502
Tel: +91(877) 228-4538
Fax: +91(877) 224-8416
EMail: vcspmvv@yahoo.com
Website: http://www.spmvv.ac.in

Vice-Chancellor: N. Prabhakara Rao
Tel: +91(877) 2249727
EMail: vcsvutpt@yahoo.com; npr_nagineni@hotmail.com

Registrar: E. Manju Vani

School

Engineering and Technology (Biotechnology; Computer Engineering; Computer Science; Electrical and Electronic Engineering; Electrical Engineering; Electronic Engineering; Engineering; Industrial Engineering; Information Technology; Technology; Telecommunications Engineering); **Science** (Applied Mathematics; Biochemistry; Biological and Life Sciences; Biotechnology; Botany; Computer Science; Home Economics; Microbiology; Organic Chemistry; Pharmacy; Physics; Sericulture; Zoology); **Social Sciences, Humanities and Management** (Arts and Humanities; Business Administration; Communication Studies; Continuing Education; Education; English; Fine Arts; Indic Languages; Journalism; Literature; Management; Music; Physical Education; Social Sciences; Social Work; Women's Studies)

History: Founded 1983.

Academic Year: June to April (June-November-November-April)

Admission Requirements: 12th year senior secondary/intermediate examination or recognized foreign equivalent

Fees: (Rupees): 4,560-8,650 per term, according to courses

Main Language(s) of Instruction: English

Accrediting Agency: University Grants Commission and NAAC

Degrees and Diplomas: *Bachelor's Degree*; *Bachelor's Degree (professional)*; *Postgraduate Diploma*; *Master's Degree*; *Master of Philosophy*; *Doctor of Philosophy*

Student Services: Academic Counselling, Canteen, Careers Guidance, Health Services, Language Laboratory, Nursery Care, Social Counselling, Sports Facilities

Publications: Ph.D; Processing of National

Academic Staff *2010-2011*	MEN	WOMEN	**TOTAL**
FULL-TIME	82	222	**304**
PART-TIME	15	92	**107**
STAFF WITH DOCTORATE			
FULL-TIME	5	85	**90**
Student Numbers *2010-2011*			
All (Foreign included)	–	–	c. **2,700**

Part-time students, 280. **Distance students,** 1,030.

Last Updated: 21/11/11

SRI RAMACHANDRA UNIVERSITY

1 Ramachandra Nagar, Porur, Chennai, Tamil Nadu 600116
Tel: +91(44) 2476-8423
Fax: +91(44) 2476-5995 +91(44) 2476-7008
EMail: registrarsru@gmail.com
Website: http://www.sriramachandra.edu.in/new_university/index.html

Vice-Chancellor: J.S.N. Murthy (2012-)
Tel: +91(44) 2476-8431 EMail: vcsrmc@hotmail.com

Registrar: Thiru.N. Natarajan
Tel: +91(44) 2476-5512 Ext.203 EMail: registrarsru@gmail.com

International Relations: T.K. Partha Sarathy, Pro-Chancellor
Tel: +91(44) 2476-7770 EMail: pcsrmc@hotmail.com

Faculty

Allied Health Sciences (Anaesthesiology; Clinical Psychology; Gastroenterology; Genetics; Health Sciences; Laboratory Techniques; Medical Technology; Neurosciences; Nutrition; Optometry; Radiology; Respiratory Therapy; Secretarial Studies; Speech Therapy and Audiology; Urology); **Biomedical Sciences, Technology and Research** (Biological and Life Sciences; Biomedical Engineering; Biomedicine; Biotechnology; Chemistry; Computer Science; Genetics); **Dental Sciences** (Dental Technology; Dentistry; Oral Pathology; Orthodontics; Periodontics; Radiology; Social and Preventive Medicine; Surgery); **Management Sciences** (Health Administration; Management); **Nursing** (Community Health; Gynaecology and Obstetrics; Nursing; Paediatrics; Psychiatry and Mental Health); **Pharmacy** (Pharmacology; Pharmacy; Safety Engineering); **Physiotherapy** (Cardiology; Neurosciences; Orthopaedics; Physical Therapy; Pneumology)

College

Medical Studies and Research Institute *(Sri Ramachandra)* (Anaesthesiology; Anatomy; Biochemistry; Cardiology; Community Health; Dermatology; Gastroenterology; Gynaecology and Obstetrics; Medicine; Microbiology; Molecular Biology; Nephrology; Neurological Therapy; Neurology; Ophthalmology; Orthopaedics; Otorhinolaryngology; Paediatrics; Pathology; Pharmacology; Physiology; Plastic Surgery; Psychiatry and Mental Health; Radiology; Surgery; Urology; Venereology)

History: Founded 1985 as part of the Sri Ramachandra Education and Health Trust. An institution with a 'Deemed University' status since 1994.

Academic Year: July to April

Main Language(s) of Instruction: English

Accrediting Agency: University Grants Commission; Medical Council of India; Dental Council of India; Nursing Council of India; Pharmacy Council of India; All India Coucil for Technical Education; Rehabilitation Council of India; General Medical Council, UK; Ireland Medical Council; Srilankan Medical Council; Association of the Commonwealth Universities,UK; Association of Indian Univerisities; National Assessment and Accreditation (NAAC).

Degrees and Diplomas: *Post Diploma*; *Bachelor's Degree*; *Bachelor's Degree (professional)*; *Postgraduate Diploma*; *Master's Degree*; *Doctor of Philosophy*. Also Certificate Course; MBA

Student Services: Academic Counselling, Canteen, Cultural Activities, Health Services, Nursery Care, Sports Facilities

Last Updated: 13/09/12

SRI SAI UNIVERSITY

Palampur, Himachal Pradesh
Tel: +91(92184) 50302
EMail: contact@srisaiuniversity.com
Website: http://srisaiuniversity.com/

Vice-Chancellor: Balram Dogra

School

Engineering and Technology (Civil Engineering; Computer Engineering; Computer Networks; Electrical Engineering; Electronic Engineering; Engineering; Information Technology; Mechanical Engineering; Telecommunications Engineering); **Languages and Social Sciences** (Economics; English; Hindi; Social Sciences); **Management and Commerce Studies** (Business and Commerce; Management; Marketing; Tourism)

History: Founded 2011.

Degrees and Diplomas: *Bachelor's Degree*; *Master's Degree*

Last Updated: 17/01/12

SRI SATHYA SAI INSTITUTE OF HIGHER LEARNING (SSSIHL)

Vidyagiri, Anantapur District,
Prasanthi Nilayam, Andhra Pradesh 515 134
Tel: +91(8555) 287-239
Fax: +91(8555) 287-239
EMail: registrar@sssihl.edu.in
Website: http://sssu.edu.in

Vice-Chancellor: Shashidhara Prasad (2010-)

Registrar: Naren Ramji

Campus

Anantapur *(For Women)* (Biological and Life Sciences; Business and Commerce; Chemistry; Economics; Education; English; Hindi; History; Home Economics; Indic Languages; Mathematics; Philosophy; Physics; Political Sciences; Sanskrit); **Brindavan** *(For Men)* (Biological and Life Sciences; Business and Commerce; Chemistry; Mathematics; Physics); **Prasanthi Nilayam** *(For Men)* (Accountancy; Biological and Life Sciences; Business Administration; Chemistry; Economics; English; Finance; Hindi; History; Management; Mathematics and Computer Science; Physics; Political Sciences; Sanskrit)

Further Information: Also Sri Sathya Sai Institute of Higher Medical Sciences (Hospital).

History: Founded 1981 as Sri Sathya Sai Institute of Higher Learning based on Bhagawan Sri Sathya Sai Baba's Teaching emphasizing character building as much as academic excellence. Acquired present status 2006. Deemed to be University.

Academic Year: June to March

Admission Requirements: 12th year senior secondary/intermediate examination or recognized foreign equivalent with a minimum of 55% in General English and 60% in aggregate for undergraduate programmes

Fees: None. Scholarships are given to deserving students to meet hostel expenses

Main Language(s) of Instruction: English

Accrediting Agency: Ministry of Education; University Grants Commission; All India Council for Technical Education; National Assessment and Accreditation Council (NAAC); Association of Indian Universities

Degrees and Diplomas: *Bachelor's Degree*; *Master's Degree*; *Master of Philosophy*; *Doctor of Philosophy*. Also MBA

Student Services: Academic Counselling, Cultural Activities, Health Services, Language Laboratory, Social Counselling, Sports Facilities

Academic Staff *2010-2011*: Total 130

STAFF WITH DOCTORATE: Total 80

Student Numbers *2010-2011*: Total: c. 1,200

Last Updated: 21/11/11

SRI SIDDHARTHA ACADEMY OF HIGHER EDUCATION (SAHE)

Agalakote, B.H. Road, Tumkur, Karnataka 572 107
Tel: +91(816) 227-5516
EMail: info@sahe.in
Website: http://www.sahe.in/

Vice Chancellor: K. A. Krishnamurthy

Registrar: M.Z. Kurian

College

Dentistry (Dental Technology; Dentistry; Orthodontics; Periodontics; Surgery); **Engineering** (Biotechnology; Civil Engineering; Computer Engineering; Computer Graphics; Computer Science; Electrical Engineering; Electronic Engineering; Engineering; Industrial Engineering; Information Sciences; Mechanical Engineering; Medical Technology; Power Engineering; Telecommunications Engineering; Thermal Engineering); **Medicine** (Anaesthesiology; Anatomy; Medicine; Microbiology; Ophthalmology; Paediatrics; Pathology; Physiology; Radiology; Surgery)

History: Founded 2008. A 'Deemed University".

Fees: (Indian Rupees): Non-Karnataka Candidates, 2,000 per annum for undergraduate programmes and 3,000 per annum for postgraduate programmes; NRI/Foreign, 5,000 per annum

Degrees and Diplomas: *Bachelor's Degree (professional)*; *Postgraduate Diploma*; *Master's Degree*

Last Updated: 13/12/11

SRI VENKATESWARA INSTITUTE OF MEDICAL SCIENCES (SVIMS UNIVERSITY)

Alipiri Road, Chittoor District, Tirupati, Andhra Pradesh 517 507
Tel: +91(877) 2287152 +91(877) 2286131
Fax: +91(877) 2286803
EMail: svimshosp@yahoo.com
Website: http://svimstpt.ap.nic.in

Director: B. Vengamma EMail: bvengamma@yahoo.com

Registrar: P.V. Ramasubba Reddy

College

Nursing (Nursing); **Physiotherapy** (Physical Therapy)

Department

Diagnostic (Biochemistry; Medical Technology; Microbiology; Pathology; Radiology); **Interdisciplinary Studies** (Biotechnology; Computer Science); **Medicine** (Anaesthesiology; Anatomy; Cardiology; Endocrinology; Gastroenterology; Haematology; Medicine; Nephrology; Neurology; Oncology; Physiology; Treatment Techniques; Urology); **Surgery** (Gastroenterology; Neurological Therapy; Oncology; Plastic Surgery; Surgery)

History: Founded in 1986. Functional since 1992. Acquired University status 1995.

Academic Year: August to July

Admission Requirements: 12th year senior secondary/intermediate or equivalent.

Fees: (Rupees): Paramedical Technical courses, 4,200-12,800 per annum; B.Sc. 13,000-33,000 per annum; M.Sc.and DM/M.Ch. 50,000 per annum; MPT 100,000

Main Language(s) of Instruction: English

Accrediting Agency: Medical Council of India (MCI) University Grants Commission (UGC), Indian Nursing Council (INC); Indian Association of Physiotherapists (IAP); Department of Biotechnology

Degrees and Diplomas: *Bachelor's Degree*; *Bachelor's Degree (professional)*; *Postgraduate Diploma*; *Master's Degree*. Certificate Courses; Short Term Training Programmes; Post Doctoral Certificate Courses.

Student Services: Academic Counselling, Canteen, Careers Guidance, Cultural Activities, Health Services, Sports Facilities

Last Updated: 21/11/11

SRI VENKATESWARA UNIVERSITY

District Chittoor, Tirupati, Andhra Pradesh 517502
Tel: +91(877) 2249727
Fax: +91(877) 2289555
EMail: vc@svuniversity.ac.in
Website: http://www.svuniversity.ac.in

Vice-Chancellor: W. Rajendra

Registrar: K.Sathyavelu Reddy
Tel: +91(877) 2289414 EMail: registrar@svuniversity.ac.in

College

Arts (Adult Education; Ancient Civilizations; Archaeology; Continuing Education; Demography and Population; Development Studies; Econometrics; Economics; Education; English; Fine Arts; Hindi; History; Human Rights; Indic Languages; Information Sciences; Journalism; Law; Library Science; Linguistics; Mass Communication; Modern Languages; Pacific Area Studies; Peace and Disarmament; Philosophy; Physical Education; Political Sciences; Public Administration; Sanskrit; Sociology; Southeast Asian Studies; Urdu); **Commerce, Management and Computer Science** (Business and Commerce; Computer Science; Management); **Engineering** (Chemical Engineering; Civil Engineering; Computer Engineering; Computer Science; Electrical and Electronic Engineering; Electrical Engineering; Electronic Engineering; Engineering; Mechanical Engineering; Telecommunications Engineering); **Sciences** (Anthropology; Aquaculture; Biochemistry; Biotechnology; Botany; Chemistry; Environmental Studies; Fishery; Geography; Geology; Home Economics; Mathematics; Physics; Psychology; Statistics; Virology; Zoology)

Centre

Post-Graduate Studies (Business Administration; Business and Commerce; Computer Science; Economics; Mathematics; Physics; Zoology)

Further Information: Also 62 Affiliated and Oriental Colleges

History: Founded 1954.

Admission Requirements: 12th year senior secondary/intermediate examination or recognized foreign equivalent

Fees: (Rupees): Postgraduate programmes, 1,200-4,125 per semester (except MBA, 9,433-10,508 per semester); M. Phil. and PhD programmes, 1,325-3,336 per term

Main Language(s) of Instruction: Telugu, English

Degrees and Diplomas: *Post Diploma*; *Postgraduate Diploma*; *Master of Philosophy*; *Doctor of Philosophy*. Also Certificate courses; MBA

Student Services: Cultural Activities, Health Services, Sports Facilities

Publications: Oriental Journal

Publishing House: University Press

Academic Staff *2010-2011*: Total: c. 400

Student Numbers *2010-2011*: Total: c. 5,000

Last Updated: 21/11/11

SRI VENKATESWARA VEDIC UNIVERSITY

Alipiri-Chandragiri Bypass Road, Tirupati, Andhra Pradesh
Tel: +91(877) 222-2586
Fax: +91(877) 222-2587
EMail: vcvedicuniversity@yahoo.com
Website: http://www.svvedicuniversity.org/

Vice-Chancellor: Sannidhanam Sudarsana Sarma

Registrar: Manojkumar Mishra Tel: +91(877) 226-4404

Faculty

Agama Adhyayana (Esoteric Practices); **Modern Subjects** (Computer Science; English); **Paurohitya Adhyayana** (Esoteric Practices); **Research and Publication**; **Veda Adhyayana** (Esoteric Practices); **Vedabhashya** (Esoteric Practices; Yoga)

History: Founded 2006.

Degrees and Diplomas: Sastri Course (undergraduate programme), 3 yrs; Acharya Course (Postgraduate programme), 2 yrs.

Last Updated: 02/01/12

SRI VENKATESWARA VETERINARY UNIVERSITY (SVVU)

Administrative Office, Dr. Y.S. R. Bhawan, Chittoor District, Tirupati, Andhra Pradesh 517 502
Tel: +91(877) 224-8006 +91(877) 224-8068
Fax: +91(877) 224-9222
EMail: registrarsvvutpt@yahoo.in
Website: http://svvu.edu.in/

Vice-Chancellor: Manmohan Singh
Tel: +91(877) 224-8986 EMail: splcs_ahf@ap.gov.in

Registrar: P. Sudhakara Reddy Tel: +91(877) 224-8894

College

Animal Husbandry Polytechnic *(Madakasira, Dist: Anantpur)* (Animal Husbandry); **Animal Husbandry Polytechnic** *(Ramachandra Puram, Dist: East Godavari)* (Animal Husbandry); **Animal Husbandry Polytechnic** *(Garividi, Dist: Vizianagaram)* (Animal Husbandry); **Animal Husbandry Polytechnic** *(Mamnoor, Dist: Warangal)* (Animal Husbandry); **Animal Husbandry Polytechnic** *(Karimnagar, Dist: Karimnagar)* (Animal Husbandry); **Animal Husbandry Polytechnic** *(Rapur, Dist: Nellore)* (Animal Husbandry); **Animal Husbandry Polytechnic** *(Palamner, Dist: Chittoor)* (Animal Husbandry); **Animal Husbandry Polytechnic** *(Siddipet, Dist: Medak)* (Animal Husbandry); **Animal Husbandry Polytechnic** *(Venkataramana Gudem, Dist: West Godavari)* (Animal Husbandry); **Animal Husbandry Polytechnic** *(Mahaboob Nagar, Dist: Mahaboobnagar)* (Animal Husbandry); **Dairy Technology** *(Tirupati)* (Dairy; Microbiology; Technology); **Fisheries Polytechnic** *(Bhavadevarapalli, Avanigadda, Dist: Krishna)* (Fishery); **Fishery Science** *(Muthukur)* (Aquaculture; Engineering; Fishery); **Veterinary Science** *(Rajendranagar)* (Anatomy; Animal Husbandry; Biochemistry; Epidemiology; Genetics; Meat and Poultry; Medicine; Microbiology; Pharmacology; Physiology; Public Health; Veterinary Science); **Veterinary Science** *(NTR - Gannavaram)* (Animal Husbandry; Microbiology; Pathology; Pharmacology; Radiology; Surgery; Toxicology; Veterinary Science); **Veterinary Science** *(Korutla)* (Animal Husbandry; Genetics; Gynaecology and Obstetrics; Meat and Poultry; Parasitology; Veterinary Science); **Veterinary Science** *(Proddutur)* (Animal Husbandry; Biochemistry; Meat and Poultry; Microbiology; Parasitology; Pathology; Pharmacology; Physiology; Veterinary Science); **Veterinary Science** *(Tirupati)* (Animal Husbandry; Pathology; Veterinary Science)

Programme

Dairy Technology *(Kamareddy)* (Agricultural Education; Agricultural Engineering; Chemistry; Dairy; Engineering; Microbiology; Technology)

Further Information: Also Veterinary Hospital.

History: Founded 2005.

Fees: (Indian Rupees): Undegraduate tuition fee, 400-4,360 per semester

Degrees and Diplomas: *Post Diploma*; *Bachelor's Degree*; *Bachelor's Degree (professional)*; *Master's Degree*; *Doctor of Philosophy*

Student Services: Cultural Activities, Sports Facilities

Last Updated: 02/01/12

SRM UNIVERSITY

SRM Nagar, Kancheepuram District, Kattankulatthur, Tamil Nadu 603203
Tel: +91(44) 2745 5715 +91(44) 2745 3433
Fax: +94(44) 2745 3622
EMail: registrar@srmuniv.ac.in
Website: http://www.srmuniv.ac.in/

Vice-Chancellor: M. Ponnavaikko EMail: vc@srmuniv.ac.in

Registrar: N. Sethuraman EMail: registrar@srmuniv.ac.in

College

Humanities (Arts and Humanities; Business and Commerce; Communication Arts; Cooking and Catering; Education; English; Film; Fine Arts; Hotel and Restaurant; Indic Languages; Journalism; Mass Communication; Media Studies; Modern Languages; Visual Arts); **Medicine** (Anaesthesiology; Anatomy; Animal Husbandry; Biochemistry; Cardiology; Communication Studies; Dental Technology; Dentistry; Dermatology; Forensic Medicine and Dentistry; Gynaecology and Obstetrics; Medicine; Microbiology; Nephrology; Neurological Therapy; Neurology; Nursing; Occupational Therapy; Oral Pathology; Orthodontics; Orthopaedics; Osteopathy; Paediatrics; Pathology; Periodontics; Pharmacology; Pharmacy; Physical Therapy; Physiology; Plastic Surgery; Pneumology; Psychiatry and Mental Health; Public Health; Radiology; Surgery; Urology); **Sciences** (Biological and Life Sciences; Biotechnology; Computer Science; Mathematics)

School

Architecture and Interior Design (Architecture; Interior Design); **Basic Sciences** (Chemistry; Mathematics; Physics);

Bioengineering (Bioengineering; Biomedical Engineering; Biotechnology; Computer Science; Food Technology; Genetics); **Chemical and Material Technology** (Chemical Engineering; Materials Engineering; Nanotechnology; Nuclear Engineering); **Civil Engineering** (Civil Engineering); **Computing** (Computer Engineering; Computer Science; Information Technology); **Electrical and Electronics Engineering** (Automation and Control Engineering; Electrical and Electronic Engineering; Electronic Engineering; Measurement and Precision Engineering; Telecommunications Engineering); **Languages** (English; French; German; Japanese; Korean; Modern Languages); **Management** (Business Administration; Finance; Health Administration; Hotel and Restaurant; Human Resources; Management; Marketing; Operations Research; Pharmacy; Retailing and Wholesaling); **Mechanical Engineering** (Aeronautical and Aerospace Engineering; Automotive Engineering; Electronic Engineering; Mechanical Engineering)

Centre

Nanotechnology (Nanotechnology); **Total Quality Management** *(TQM)* (Safety Engineering)

Further Information: Also Ramapuram, Modi Nagar, Trichy Campuses.

History: Created in 1984 as Valliammai Polytechnic. Formerly known as SRM Institute of Science and Technology

Accrediting Agency: National Assessment and Accreditation Council (NAAC); Engineering Accreditation Commission of ABET (USA)

Degrees and Diplomas: *Post Diploma*; *Bachelor's Degree*; *Bachelor's Degree (professional)*; *Postgraduate Diploma*; *Master's Degree*; *Master of Philosophy*; *Doctor of Philosophy*. Also Certificate Courses; MBA

Academic Staff *2010-2011*: Total: c. 1,500

Student Numbers *2010-2011*: Total: c. 20,000

Last Updated: 21/11/11

ST PETER'S UNIVERSITY

College Road, Avadi, Chennai, Tamil Nadu 600054
Tel: +91(44) 2655-8080 +91(44) 2655-8085
EMail: spiher@stpetersuniversity.org
Website: http://www.stpetersuniversity.org

Vice-Chancellor: K. Balagurunathan

Registrar: M. Shanmugham

Department

Business Administration (Business Administration; Management); **Computer Application** (Computer Engineering; Computer Science; Information Technology); **Engineering** (Aeronautical and Aerospace Engineering; Automotive Engineering; Biomedical Engineering; Biotechnology; Chemical Engineering; Civil Engineering; Computer Science; Electrical Engineering; Electronic Engineering; Engineering; Information Technology; Mechanical Engineering; Production Engineering; Telecommunications Engineering); **Science and Humanities** (Arts and Humanities; Chemistry; English; Mathematics; Natural Sciences; Physics)

Further Information: A traditional and Distance Education Institution.

History: Founded 1956 as St Peter's Institute of Higher Education and Research. Acquired present status 2008. A Deemed-to-be University.

Accrediting Agency: University Grants Commission (UGC)

Degrees and Diplomas: *Bachelor's Degree*; *Master's Degree*. Also MBA

Student Services: Academic Counselling, Canteen, Sports Facilities

Last Updated: 21/11/11

SUMANDEEP VIDYAPEETH UNIVERSITY

At and Po Pipariya, Ta. Waghodia, Vadodara, Gujarat 391760
Tel: +91(2668) 245262 +91(2668) 245264
Fax: +91(2668) 245292
EMail: info@sumandeepuniversity.co.in
Website: http://www.sumandeepuniversity.co.in

Chancellor: Jayshree Mehta

Registrar: N. N. Shah

College

Dentistry *(K. M. Shah - and Hospital)* (Dental Technology; Dentistry; Microbiology; Oral Pathology; Orthodontics; Periodontics; Radiology; Social and Preventive Medicine; Surgery); **Nursing** *(Sumandeep)* (Community Health; Gynaecology and Obstetrics; Nursing; Paediatrics; Psychiatry and Mental Health; Surgery); **Physiotherapy** *(K. J. Pandya)* (Physical Therapy)

Department

Management (Health Administration; Management); **Pharmacy** (Management; Pharmacology; Pharmacy; Safety Engineering; Technology)

Institute

Medical Studies and Research Centre *(S.B.K.S.)* (Anaesthesiology; Anatomy; Biochemistry; Dermatology; Forensic Medicine and Dentistry; Gynaecology and Obstetrics; Laboratory Techniques; Medicine; Microbiology; Ophthalmology; Orthopaedics; Otorhinolaryngology; Paediatrics; Pathology; Pharmacology; Physiology; Psychiatry and Mental Health; Radiology; Respiratory Therapy; Social and Preventive Medicine; Surgery; Venereology)

History: A deemed university.

Degrees and Diplomas: *Post Diploma*; *Bachelor's Degree*; *Postgraduate Diploma*; *Master's Degree*; *Doctor of Philosophy*. Also MBA

Last Updated: 22/11/11

SURESH GYAN VIHAR UNIVERSITY (SGVU)

Mahal, Jagatpura, Jaipur, Rajasthan
Tel: +91(141) 645-0389 +91(141) 645-0390
Fax: +91(141) 279-6255
EMail: registrar@gyanvihar.org; admissions@gyanvihar.org
Website: http://www.gyanvihar.org/

Vice-Chancellor: B.V. Somasekhar

School

Business Management (Business Administration; Business Computing; Commercial Law; Economics; Finance; Human Resources; Management; Marketing); **Engineering and Technology** (Civil Engineering; Computer Engineering; Computer Science; Electrical Engineering; Electronic Engineering; Engineering; Information Technology; Mechanical Engineering; Technology; Telecommunications Engineering); **Hotel Management** (Finance; Food Technology; Hotel Management; Human Resources; Law; Management; Marketing; Real Estate; Sales Techniques); **Pharmacy** (Biotechnology; Chemistry; Pharmacology; Pharmacy; Safety Engineering); **Sciences** (Biochemistry; Biological and Life Sciences; Biotechnology; Microbiology; Natural Sciences); **Social Science** (Archaeology; Museum Studies; Social Sciences; Social Work)

History: Founded 2008.

Accrediting Agency: All India Council for Technical Education (AICTE); National Board of Accreditation (NBA)

Degrees and Diplomas: *Post Diploma*; *Bachelor's Degree*; *Bachelor's Degree (professional)*; *Postgraduate Diploma*; *Master's Degree*; *Doctor of Philosophy*. Also Dual Degrees (Bachelor+-Master's degrees); MBA

Last Updated: 21/12/11

SWAMI KESHWANAND RAJASTHAN AGRICULTURAL UNIVERSITY (SKRAU)

PO Box No 19, Bikaner, Rajasthan 334006
Tel: +91(151) 225-1083
Fax: +91(151) 225-1083
EMail: cimca@raubikaner.org
Website: http://www.raubikaner.org

Vice-Chancellor: A.K. Dahama (2011-)
Tel: +91(151) 225-0488 +91(151) 225-0443
EMail: vcrau@raubikaner.org

Registrar: Ramdev Goyal
Tel: +91(151) 225-0025 EMail: reg@raubikaner.org

College

Agriculture *(COA)* (Agricultural Economics; Agriculture; Agronomy; Biotechnology; Education; Entomology; Genetics; Horticulture; Plant

Pathology; Soil Science); **Agriculture** *(Lalsot)* (Agriculture); **Agriculture** *(Jobner)* (Agricultural Business; Agricultural Economics; Agriculture; Agronomy; Animal Husbandry; Biochemistry; Chemistry; Education; Entomology; Genetics; Horticulture; Physiology; Plant Pathology; Soil Science; Zoology); **Home Science** *(CHS)* (Clothing and Sewing; Communication Studies; Family Studies; Food Science; Home Economics; Nutrition; Textile Technology)

Institute

Agribusiness Management *(IABM)* (Agricultural Business; Agricultural Equipment; Agricultural Management; Animal Husbandry; Food Technology; Horticulture; Irrigation)

Centre

Academic Staff cum Distance Education *(ASC-DEC)*

Further Information: Also 8 Constituent Colleges. A traditional and distance education institution.

History: Founded 1987, an autonomous body receiving financial grants from State, Central Government and ICAR.

Academic Year: July to June

Admission Requirements: 12th year senior secondary/intermediate examination or recognized foreign equivalent

Fees: (Rupees): 200-1,600 per annum

Main Language(s) of Instruction: English

Degrees and Diplomas: *Post Diploma*; *Bachelor's Degree*; *Master's Degree*; *Doctor of Philosophy*. Also Bachelor's degree honours, 4 yrs.

Publications: Apna Patra; Research Journal

Publishing House: University Communication Centre

Last Updated: 18/07/11

SWAMI RAMANAND TEERTH MARATHWADA UNIVERSITY (SRTMUN)

Dnyanteerth Vishnupuri, Nanded, Maharashtra 431 606
Tel: +91(2462) 229-242 +91(2462) 229-243
Fax: +91(2462) 229-245
EMail: provc@srtmun.ac.in
Website: http://www.srtmun.org

Vice-Chancellor: S. B. Nimse Tel: +91(2462) 299-282

Registrar: P.D. Jadhav
Tel: +91(2462) 229-246 EMail: registrar@srtmun.ac.in

School

Chemical Sciences (Analytical Chemistry; Chemistry; Inorganic Chemistry; Organic Chemistry; Physical Chemistry; Polymer and Plastics Technology); **Commerce and Management Sciences** (Business Administration; Business and Commerce; Finance; Human Resources; Management; Marketing); **Computational Sciences** (Computer Networks; Computer Science); **Earth Sciences** (Environmental Studies; Geography; Geology; Geophysics); **Educational Sciences** (Educational Sciences); **Fine and Performing Arts** (Fine Arts; Performing Arts); **Languages and Literature** (English; Indic Languages; Literature); **Life Sciences** (Biological and Life Sciences; Biotechnology; Botany; Microbiology; Zoology); **Mathematical Sciences** (Mathematics; Statistics); **Media Studies** (Media Studies); **Pharmacy** (Pharmacology; Pharmacy; Safety Engineering); **Physical Sciences** (Applied Physics; Physics); **Social Sciences** (Economics; Social Sciences; Sociology)

Centre

Latur *(Sub-centre)* (Banking; Business Administration; Computer Science; Economics; Finance; Human Resources; Information Technology; Management; Marketing; Social Work)

Further Information: A traditional and distance education institution.

History: Founded 1994.

Academic Year: June to May

Fees: (Rupees): 4,000-25,000 per annum

Main Language(s) of Instruction: English

Accrediting Agency: National Assessment and Accreditation Committee (NAAC)

Degrees and Diplomas: *Post Diploma*; *Bachelor's Degree*; *Master's Degree*; *Master of Philosophy*; *Doctor of Philosophy*. Also certificate courses and MBA

Student Services: Canteen, Facilities for disabled people, Sports Facilities

Last Updated: 22/11/11

SWAMI VIVEKANAND SUBHARTI UNIVERSITY

Subhartipuram, NH-58, Delhi-Haridwar Bye Pass Road, Meerut 250 005
Tel: +91(121) 300-1058
Fax: +91(121) 243-9067
EMail: subharti.uni@gmail.com
Website: http://www.subharti.org/

Vice-Chancellor: Bhagirath Singh Rathore

College

Computer Application (Computer Science); **Dentistry** (Dental Technology; Dentistry); **Engineering** (Biotechnology; Engineering; Environmental Engineering; Industrial Engineering; Nanotechnology; Safety Engineering); **Higher Education** (Education; Higher Education; Information Sciences; Library Science); **Journalism and Mass Communication** (Journalism; Mass Communication); **Medicine** (Anatomy; Biochemistry; Health Administration; Medicine; Microbiology; Pharmacology; Physiology); **Nursing** (Midwifery; Nursing); **Pharmacy** (Biotechnology; Pharmacy); **Physiotherapy** (Physical Therapy)

Institute

Fine Arts and Fashion Design (Fashion Design; Fine Arts; Painting and Drawing; Sculpture; Textile Design); **Hotel Management** (Hotel Management); **Law** (Human Rights; Labour Law; Law); **Management and Information Technology** (Business Administration; Business and Commerce; Information Technology; Management; Protective Services); **Naturopathy and Yogic Sciences** (Alternative Medicine; Yoga)

Further Information: Also Chhatrapati Shivaji Subharti Hospital (800 beds). A traditional and distance education college.

History: Founded 2008.

Fees: (Indian Rupees): Undergraduate fee, 2,000-182,000 per annum; Graduate fee, 25,000-900,000 per annum

Accrediting Agency: University Grants Commission (U.G.C.)

Degrees and Diplomas: *Post Diploma*; *Bachelor's Degree*; *Bachelor's Degree (professional)*; *Postgraduate Diploma*; *Master's Degree*; *Master of Philosophy*; *Doctor of Philosophy*. Also Certificates; M.B.A.

Last Updated: 02/01/12

SWAMI VIVEKANANDA YOGA ANUSANDHANA SAMSTHANA (SVYASA)

19, Eknath Bhavan, Gavipuram Circle, Kempegowda Nagar, Bangalore, Karnataka 560 019
Tel: +91(80) 26608645
Fax: +91(80) 26612669
EMail: info@svyasa.org
Website: http://www.svyasa.org/

Vice-Chancellor: H. R. Nagendra (2002-) EMail: hrn@vyasa.org

Registrar: N.K Manjunath EMail: nkmsharma@gmail.com

International Relations: N. V. Raghuram, International Coordinator EMail: nv.raghuran@gmail.com

Division

Yoga and Humanities (Anthropology; Fine Arts; History; Linguistics; Literature; Social Sciences; Sociology); **Yoga and Life Sciences** (Agriculture; Biochemistry; Biological and Life Sciences; Biology; Biomedicine; Biophysics; Cardiology; Dairy; Diabetology; Esoteric Practices; Forestry; Gastroenterology; Gynaecology and Obstetrics; Health Sciences; Horticulture; Immunology; Medicine; Microbiology; Molecular Biology; Natural Sciences; Neurosciences; Oncology; Physiology; Psychology; Rheumatology; Soil Science; Urology; Virology; Water Management; Wildlife; Yoga); **Yoga and Management Studies** (Education; Management; Yoga); **Yoga and Physical Sciences** (Engineering; Mathematics; Physics; Yoga); **Yoga and Spirituality** (Ayurveda; Comparative Religion; Sanskrit; Yoga)

History: Founded in 1986 as Vivekananda Yoga Cikitsa Tatha Anusandhana Samiti. Acquired current status and title 2002.

Academic Year: August to May

Admission Requirements: Undergraduate: Secondary School Certificate; Master's degree: Bachelor's degree or equivalent; PhD: Master's degree or equivalent; MD: Medical degree

Fees: (Rupees): Indian nationals, 73,500-155,000; foreign students, US Dollars: 6,120-23,000, all prices approximate, per annum

Main Language(s) of Instruction: English

Accrediting Agency: National Assessment and Accreditation Council

Degrees and Diplomas: *Post Diploma*; *Bachelor's Degree*; *Postgraduate Diploma*; *Master's Degree*; *Master of Philosophy*; *Doctor of Philosophy*. Also Short Term courses

Student Services: Academic Counselling, Canteen, Careers Guidance, Cultural Activities, Facilities for disabled people, Foreign Studies Centre, Health Services, Language Laboratory, Nursery Care, Social Counselling, Sports Facilities

Publications: IJOY; Yoga Sudha

Last Updated: 22/11/11

SYMBIOSIS INTERNATIONAL UNIVERSITY

Gram-Lavale, Tal-Mulshi, Pune, Maharashtra 412115
Tel: +91(20) 3911-6200 +91(20) 3911-6202 +91(20) 3911-6208
Fax: +91(20) 3911-6206
EMail: registrar@siu.edu.in; dr_vidya@symbiosis.ac.in
Website: http://www.siu.edu.in

Vice-Chancellor: Rajani R. Gupte (2013-) EMail: vc@siu.edu.in

Registrar: Madhu Sharma
Tel: +91(20) 39116205 EMail: registrar@siu.edu.in

International Relations: Vidya Yeravdekar, Principal Director, Head of Centre for International Education
EMail: dr_vidya@symbiosis.ac.in

Faculty

Computer Studies (Computer Science; Information Technology); **Engineering** (Engineering; Technology); **Health Sciences** (Biomedicine; Health Sciences; Nursing); **Humanities and Social Sciences** (Arts and Humanities; Economic History; English; Social Sciences); **Law** (Commercial Law; Human Rights; Law; Taxation); **Management** (Business Administration; Human Resources; International Business; Management); **Media, Communication and Design** (Design; Mass Communication; Media Studies)

Further Information: Constituent institutes: Symbiosis Society's Law College (SSLC); Symbiosis Institute of Business Management (SIBM); Symbiosis Institute of Computer Studies and Research (SICSR). Pune, Bengaluru, Nashik, NOIDA campuses.

History: Founded 1971 as a Cultural and Educational Centre. Acquired present status and title 2006. A deemed university.

Degrees and Diplomas: *Post Diploma*; *Bachelor's Degree*; *Bachelor's Degree (professional)*; *Postgraduate Diploma*; *Master's Degree*; *Doctor of Philosophy*. Also certificate; advanced certificate; MBA and executive MBA

Student Services: Health Services, Sports Facilities

Last Updated: 22/11/11

T. A. PAI MANAGEMENT INSTITUTE (TAPMI)

Manipal, Karnataka 576 104
Tel: +91(820) 270-1000
Fax: +91(820) 257-0699
EMail: tapmi@tapmi.edu.in
Website: http://www.tapmi.edu.in/

Director: Vasudev Rao A. S.
Tel: +91(820) 270-1002 EMail: vasudevrao@tapmi.edu.in

Programme

E-Governance (Management); **European Studies and Management** (European Studies; Management); **Management** (Management); **Management - Healthcare** (Health Administration; Management)

History: Founded 1984.

Fees: (Indian Rupees): c. 400,000 per annum

Accrediting Agency: National Board of Accreditation (NBA); All India Council for Technical Education (AICTE)

Degrees and Diplomas: *Postgraduate Diploma*; *Master's Degree*

Last Updated: 25/01/12

TAMIL NADU AGRICULTURAL UNIVERSITY (TNAU)

Coimbatore, Tamil Nadu 641003
Tel: +91(422) 6611210
Fax: +91(422) 6611410
EMail: deanagri@tnau.ac.in
Website: http://www.tnau.ac.in

Vice-Chancellor: P. Murugesa Boopathi
Tel: +91(422) 6611251 EMail: vc@tnau.ac.in

Registrar: P. Subbian
Tel: +91(422) 6611200 EMail: registrar@tnau.ac.in

College

Agricultural Engineering and Research Institute *(Coimbatore)* (Agricultural Engineering; Agricultural Equipment; Energy Engineering; Environmental Engineering; Food Technology; Harvest Technology; Information Technology; Machine Building; Physics; Power Engineering; Soil Conservation; Water Management); **Agricultural Engineering and Research Institute, Kumulur** *(Trichy)* (Agricultural Engineering; Agricultural Equipment; Agriculture; Energy Engineering; Soil Conservation; Water Management); **Agriculture and Research Institute** *(Killikulam)* (Agricultural Economics; Agriculture; Agronomy; Biochemistry; Biotechnology; Computer Science; Crop Production; Entomology; Food Science; Genetics; Mathematics; Nutrition; Plant and Crop Protection; Plant Pathology; Social Sciences; Soil Science); **Agriculture and Research Institute** *(Coimbatore)* (Agricultural Business; Agriculture; Biotechnology; Computer Science; Information Technology); **Agriculture and Research Institute** *(Madurai)* (Agricultural Economics; Agricultural Engineering; Agriculture; Agronomy; Animal Husbandry; Crop Production; Entomology; Environmental Studies; Genetics; Horticulture; Microbiology; Plant and Crop Protection; Plant Pathology; Soil Science); **Anbil Dharmalingam Agricultural Studies and Research Institute** *(Trichy)* (Agriculture; Crop Production; Social Sciences); **Forestry and Research Institute** *(Mettupalayam)* (Forest Biology; Forest Products; Forestry; Wood Technology); **Home Science Studies and Research Institute** *(Madurai)* (Development Studies; Family Studies; Food Science; Food Technology; Home Economics; Human Resources; Nutrition; Psychology; Rural Studies; Textile Technology); **Horticulture and Research Institute** *(Coimbatore)* (Crop Production; Floriculture; Fruit Production; Horticulture; Vegetable Production); **Horticulture and Research Institute** *(Periyakulam)* (Computer Science; Crop Production; Economics; Floriculture; Fruit Production; Horticulture; Library Science; Physical Education; Social Sciences; Soil Science; Vegetable Production)

School

Post Graduate Studies *(Coimbatore)* (Agricultural Economics; Agricultural Engineering; Agriculture; Agronomy; Biochemistry; Biotechnology; Business Administration; Chemistry; Crop Production; Energy Engineering; Entomology; Environmental Studies; Floriculture; Food Science; Forestry; Fruit Production; Genetics; Meteorology; Microbiology; Nutrition; Physiology; Plant and Crop Protection; Power Engineering; Sociology; Soil Conservation; Soil Science; Vegetable Production; Water Management)

Further Information: Also 4 affiliated colleges: Adhiparasakthi Agricultural college, Kalavai, Vellore District; Vanavarayar Agricultural College, Pollachi; Thanthai Rover Institute of Agriculture and Rural Development, Perambalur; College of Agricultural Technology, Kullapuram, Theni.

History: Founded 1971.

Academic Year: July to April

Fees: (Rupees): 6,000 per semester for regular UG Courses; Technology courses, 31,000

Main Language(s) of Instruction: English

Accrediting Agency: Ministry of Human Resource Development

Degrees and Diplomas: *Bachelor's Degree*; *Bachelor's Degree (professional)*; *Master's Degree*; *Doctor of Philosophy*

Last Updated: 22/11/11

TAMIL NADU DOCTOR AMBEDKAR LAW UNIVERSITY

Poompozhil, 5, Dr. D.G.S. Dinakaran Salai,
Chennai, Tamil Nadu 600 028
Tel: +91(44) 2464-1212
Fax: +91(44) 2495-7414
Website: http://www.tndalu.org

Vice-Chancellor: V. Vijayakumar (2010-)
Tel: +91(44) 24611364 EMail: vc@tndalu.ac.in

Registrar: D. Gopal
Tel: +91(44) 24610813 EMail: registrar@tndalu.ac.in

School

Excellence in Law *(SOEL)* (Administrative Law; Arts and Humanities; Banking; Civil Law; Commercial Law; Constitutional Law; Criminal Law; Criminology; Economics; English; Environmental Studies; History; Human Rights; International Law; Labour Law; Law; Political Sciences; Social Sciences; Sociology; Taxation)

Department

Business Law *(Postgraduate)* (Commercial Law; Marketing); **Constitutional Law and Human Rights** *(Postgraduate)* (Constitutional Law; Human Rights); **Criminal Law** *(Postgraduate)* (Criminal Law); **Distance Education** (Commercial Law; Environmental Studies; Human Rights; Information Technology; Labour Law; Law); **Environmental Law** (Environmental Studies; Law); **Human Rights and Duties Education Center for Human Rights** *(Postgraduate)* (Human Rights); **Intellectual Property Rights** *(Postgraduate)* (Private Law); **International Law** *(Postgraduate)* (International Law)

Course

Post Graduate Diploma (Commercial Law; Environmental Studies; Information Technology; Law; Private Law)

Further Information: A traditional and distance education programme.

History: Founded 1997.

Fees: (Indian Rupee): Undergraduate programmes, 25,000 per annum; Postgraduate programmes, 10,000 per annum; Distance education programmes, 1,500-5,000 per annum

Main Language(s) of Instruction: Indian

Degrees and Diplomas: *Bachelor's Degree*; *Bachelor's Degree (professional)*; *Postgraduate Diploma*; *Master's Degree*. Also Certificate Course; Honours Bachelor's degree, 3-5 yrs.

Last Updated: 22/11/11

TAMIL NADU DOCTOR M.G.R. MEDICAL UNIVERSITY

PO Box 1200, 69 Anna Salai, Guindy, Chennai, Tamil Nadu 600032
Tel: +91(44) 22301760 +91(44) 22353093
Fax: +91(44) 22353698
EMail: mail@tnmgrmu.ac.in/
Website: http://www.tnmgrmu.ac.in/

Vice-Chancellor: D. Shantharam (2012-)
Tel: +91(44) 22353595 EMail: vc@tnmgrmu.ac.in

Registrar: Sudha Seshayyan
Tel: +91(44) 22353572 EMail: registrar@tnmgrmu.ac.in

International Relations: S. Jeevanandam, Academic Officer
EMail: ao@tnmgrmu.ac.in

Faculty

Allied Health Sciences (Anaesthesiology; Anatomy; Biochemistry; Business Administration; Cardiology; Community Health; Dental Hygiene; Dental Technology; Diabetology; Dietetics; Entomology; Epidemiology; Genetics; Gerontology; Gynaecology and Obstetrics; Health Administration; Health Education; Laboratory Techniques; Medical Technology; Medicine; Microbiology; Neurological Therapy; Neurology; Nursing; Nutrition; Occupational Therapy; Optometry; Orthopaedics; Paediatrics; Physiology; Pneumology; Podiatry; Public Health; Radiology; Respiratory Therapy; Social Work; Sociology; Speech Therapy and Audiology; Sports Medicine; Statistics; Surgery; Virology); **Ayurveda** (Ayurveda; Medicine; Surgery); **Basic Medical Sciences** (Anatomy; Biochemistry; Forensic Medicine and Dentistry; Medicine; Microbiology; Pathology; Pharmacology; Physiology); **Community Health** (Community Health; Medicine; Public Health); **Dentistry** (Dental Technology; Dentistry; Microbiology; Oral Pathology; Orthodontics; Orthopaedics; Periodontics; Public Health; Radiology; Surgery); **Homoeopathy** (Alternative Medicine; Medicine; Surgery); **Medical Specialities** (Anaesthesiology; Dermatology; Diabetology; Gerontology; Haematology; Immunology; Medical Technology; Medicine; Pneumology; Psychiatry and Mental Health; Radiology; Rehabilitation and Therapy; Toxicology; Treatment Techniques; Venereology); **Medical Super Specialities** (Cardiology; Epidemiology; Gastroenterology; Haematology; Hepatology; Medicine; Nephrology; Neurology; Oncology; Paediatrics; Psychiatry and Mental Health; Rheumatology); **Naturopathy and Yogic Science** (Alternative Medicine; Yoga); **Nursing** (Community Health; Gynaecology and Obstetrics; Nursing; Paediatrics; Psychiatry and Mental Health); **Obstetrics and Gynaecology** (Gynaecology and Obstetrics; Medicine); **Paediatrics** (Health Sciences; Medicine; Nephrology; Neurology; Paediatrics; Pneumology); **Pharmacy** (Alternative Medicine; Biotechnology; Chemistry; Pharmacology; Pharmacy); **Physiotherapy** (Gynaecology and Obstetrics; Neurology; Orthopaedics; Paediatrics; Physical Therapy); **Siddha** (Alternative Medicine; Medicine; Surgery); **Surgical Specialities** (Ophthalmology; Orthopaedics; Otorhinolaryngology; Podiatry; Sports Medicine; Surgery); **Surgical Super Specialities** (Cardiology; Endocrinology; Gastroenterology; Neurological Therapy; Oncology; Paediatrics; Plastic Surgery; Rehabilitation and Therapy; Surgery; Urology); **Unani** (Alternative Medicine; Medicine; Surgery); **Undergraduate Medicine and Surgery** (Medicine; Surgery)

Further Information: Also 223 Affiliated Colleges

History: Founded 1987, formerly affiliated to the University of Madras.

Main Language(s) of Instruction: English, Bachelor program of Unani Medicine and Surgery in Arabic

Degrees and Diplomas: *Post Diploma*; *Bachelor's Degree*; *Bachelor's Degree (professional)*; *Postgraduate Diploma*; *Master's Degree*; *Doctor of Philosophy*. Also Certificate Courses.

Student Services: Canteen

Publications: Medfocus

Last Updated: 26/03/13

TAMIL NADU OPEN UNIVERSITY (TNOU)

Chennai, Tamilnadu
EMail: contact@tnou.ac.in
Website: http://www.tnou.ac.in

Vice-Chancellor: A. Kalyani

Registrar: S. Shanmugiah

School

Computer Sciences (Computer Engineering; Computer Science; Data Processing; Information Management; Software Engineering); **Continuing Education** (Business Computing; Computer Engineering; Computer Science; Cooking and Catering; Cosmetology; Environmental Studies; Fashion Design; Food Science; Foreign Languages Education; Health Sciences; Heating and Refrigeration; Mathematics Education; Multimedia; Music; Nutrition; Preschool Education; Primary Education; Rural Studies; Technology; Women's Studies); **Criminology and Criminal Justice** (Criminal Law; Criminology; Justice Administration); **Education** (Education; Special Education); **Health Sciences** (Health Sciences; Speech Therapy and Audiology); **History and Tourism Studies** (Heritage Preservation; History; Tourism; Transport and Communications); **Humanities** (Arts and Humanities; Communication Studies; English); **Journalism and New Media Studies** (Journalism; Media Studies; Radio and Television Broadcasting); **Management Studies** (Business Administration; Finance; Human Resources; Information Technology; Insurance; Management; Marketing); **Politics and Public Administration** (Economics; Environmental Studies; Geography; Human Rights; Political Sciences; Public Administration; Public Relations; Safety Engineering); **Science** (Computer Science; Mathematics; Mathematics and Computer Science); **Social Sciences** (Accountancy; Banking; Business and Commerce; Finance; Psychoanalysis; Psychology; Social Sciences; Social Work; Sociology); **Special Education and Rehabilitation** (Rehabilitation and Therapy; Special Education); **Tamil and Cultural Studies** (Cultural Studies; Literature; Media Studies; South and Southeast Asian Languages)

History: Founded 2002.

Degrees and Diplomas: *Post Diploma*; *Bachelor's Degree*; *Postgraduate Diploma*; *Master's Degree*. Also Certificate Course; Advanced Diploma; MBA; Vocational Diploma Programmes.
Last Updated: 08/12/11

TAMIL NADU PHYSICAL EDUCATION AND SPORTS UNIVERSITY (TNPESU)

8th Floor, EVK Sampath Maaligai, College Road,
Chennai, Tamil Nadu 600 006
Tel: +91(44) 2825-2245 +91(44) 2825-2247
Fax: +91(44) 2825-2246
EMail: enquiry@tnpesu.org
Website: http://www.tnpesu.org/

Vice-Chancellor: K. Vaithianathan
Tel: +91(44) 2825-2244 EMail: dr.vaithianathan@yahoo.com

Registrar: J.P. Sukumar

Faculty
Health and Allied Sciences (Computer Science; Health Sciences; Journalism; Mass Communication; Nutrition; Physiology; Psychology; Sociology; Sports; Statistics); **Management** (Information Technology; Management; Marketing; Sports Management; Technology); **Teacher Education** (Physical Education; Teacher Training; Yoga); **Youth and Sports Affairs** (Sports)

Further Information: Also 13 affiliated colleges; a traditional and distance education institution

History: Founded 2005.

Degrees and Diplomas: *Post Diploma*; *Bachelor's Degree*; *Postgraduate Diploma*; *Master's Degree*; *Master of Philosophy*; *Doctor of Philosophy*. Also MBA
Last Updated: 06/01/12

TAMIL NADU TEACHERS EDUCATION UNIVERSITY (TNTEU)

Lady Willingdon College Campus, Kamarajar Salai,
Chennai, Tamil Nadu 600 005
Tel: +91(44) 2844-7300 +91(44) 2844-7304
Fax: +91(44) 2844-7303
EMail: admin@tnteu.in
Website: http://www.tnteu.in/

Vice-Chancellor: T. Padmanabhan

Registrar: A.R. Veeramani

Programme
Teacher Education (Teacher Training)

History: Founded 2008.

Degrees and Diplomas: *Bachelor's Degree (professional)*; *Master's Degree*; *Master of Philosophy*; *Doctor of Philosophy*
Last Updated: 05/01/12

TAMIL NADU VETERINARY AND ANIMAL SCIENCES UNIVERSITY (TANUVAS)

Madhavaram, Chennai, Tamil Nadu 600051
Tel: +91(44) 2555-1584
Fax: +91(44) 2555-1585
EMail: tanuvas@vsnl.com
Website: http://www.tanuvas.ac.in

Vice-Chancellor: R. Prabakaran
Tel: +91(44) 2555-1574 EMail: vc@tanuvas.org.in

Registrar: C. Balachandran

Faculty
Basic Sciences (Natural Sciences); **Fisheries Science** (Fishery); **Food Sciences** (Animal Husbandry; Dairy; Fishery; Food Science; Nutrition); **Veterinary and Animal Sciences** (Animal Husbandry; Veterinary Science)

College
Fisheries and Research Institute *(Thoothukkudi)* (Agricultural Economics; Aquaculture; Biology; Fishery; Food Technology; Natural Resources; Statistics); **Madras Veterinary** *(Chennai)* (Agricultural Economics; Agronomy; Animal Husbandry; Biochemistry; Biotechnology; Computer Science; Dairy; Epidemiology; Ethics; Genetics; Gynaecology and Obstetrics; Library Science; Meat and Poultry; Microbiology; Natural Sciences; Nutrition; Parasitology; Pathology; Pharmacology; Physiology; Surgery; Toxicology; Veterinary Science; Wildlife); **Veterinary Science and Research Institute** *(Tirunelveli)* (Animal Husbandry; Dairy; Fishery; Veterinary Science); **Veterinary Science and Research Institute** *(Namakkal)* (Agricultural Economics; Agronomy; Animal Husbandry; Biochemistry; Epidemiology; Ethics; Gynaecology and Obstetrics; Histology; Library Science; Meat and Poultry; Microbiology; Nutrition; Pharmacology; Physical Education; Physiology; Radiology; Safety Engineering; Surgery; Toxicology; Veterinary Science)

Institute
Food and Dairy Technology (Dairy; Food Technology)

Research Institute
Animal Sciences *(Postgraduate - Kattupakkam)* (Zoology)

Further Information: Also 3 Constituent Colleges; Veterinary Hospital and Clinics; Laboratories; Research Stations and Farms; 17 University Training and Research Centres. A traditional and distance education institution.

History: Founded 1989.

Academic Year: September to June (September-January; February-June)

Admission Requirements: 12th year senior secondary/higher examination or equivalent

Fees: (Rupees): Undergraduate, 5,380 per semester; postgraduate, 7,675

Main Language(s) of Instruction: English

Accrediting Agency: Indian Council of Agricultural Research

Degrees and Diplomas: *Bachelor's Degree*; *Bachelor's Degree (professional)*; *Postgraduate Diploma*; *Master's Degree*; *Master of Philosophy*; *Doctor of Philosophy*

Student Services: Academic Counselling, Canteen, Careers Guidance, Health Services, Sports Facilities

Publications: Kalnadai Kathir; Tamil Nadu Veterinary Journal

Last Updated: 22/11/11

TAMIL UNIVERSITY

Administrative Buildings, Trichy Road,
Thanjavur, Tamil Nadu 613005
Tel: +91(4362) 226-720
Fax: +91(4362) 226-159
EMail: contact@tamiluniversity.ac.in
Website: http://www.tamiluniversity.ac.in

Vice-Chancellor: M. Rajendran (2008-)
Tel: +91(4362) 222-7040

Registrar: G. Bhaskaran

International Relations: Thiru G. Panneer Selvam

Faculty
Arts (Fine Arts; Music; Performing Arts; Sculpture; Theatre); **Developing Tamil** (Economics; Education; Indic Languages; Linguistics; Native Language Education; Social Sciences; Translation and Interpretation); **Language** (Cultural Studies; Folklore; Indic Languages; Linguistics; Literature; Philosophy); **Manuscriptology** (Ancient Books; Archaeology); **Science** (Architecture; Computer Science; Earth Sciences; Environmental Studies; Industrial Engineering; Natural Sciences; Traditional Eastern Medicine)

Further Information: A traditional and distance education institution.

History: Founded 1981. A high level Research Institution.

Academic Year: July to June

Admission Requirements: University degree

Main Language(s) of Instruction: Tamil, English

Degrees and Diplomas: *Post Diploma*; *Bachelor's Degree*; *Postgraduate Diploma*; *Master's Degree*; *Master of Philosophy*; *Doctor of Philosophy*. Also Certificates

Publications: Tamil Kalai and Tamil Civilization

Publishing House: University Press
Last Updated: 23/11/11

TATA INSTITUTE OF FUNDAMENTAL RESEARCH (TIFR)

Homi Bhabha Road, Mumbai, Maharashtra 400 005
Tel: +91(22) 2278-2000
Fax: +91(22) 2280-4610
EMail: webmaster@tifr.res.in
Website: http://www.tifr.res.in/About_TIFR/

Director: Mustansir Barma
Tel: +91(22) 2278-2306 EMail: rvp@tifr.res.in

Registrar: Jayant N. Kayarkar
Tel: +91(22) 2278-2315 EMail: jnkayarkar@math.tifr.res.in

School

Mathematics (Mathematics); **Natural Sciences** (Astronomy and Space Science; Astrophysics; Atomic and Molecular Physics; Biology; Biophysics; Chemistry; Mathematical Physics; Nuclear Physics; Physics); **Technology and Computer Science** (Computer Science; Technology)

History: Founded 1945. Acquired Deemed University status 2002.

Degrees and Diplomas: *Master's Degree*; *Doctor of Philosophy*. Also integrated Ph.D.

Last Updated: 23/11/11

TATA INSTITUTE OF SOCIAL SCIENCES (TISS)

Po Box No 8313, Sion-Trombay Road, Deonar,
Mumbai, Maharashtra 400088
Tel: +91(22) 2556-7417
Fax: +91(22) 2556-2912
EMail: rrsingh@tiss.edu
Website: http://www.tiss.edu

Director: S. Parasuraman EMail: sparasuraman@tiss.edu

Registrar: Neela Dabir EMail: ndabir@tiss.edu

International Relations: Bipin Jojo, Chairperson, International Students Office Tel: +91(22) 2552-5427

School

Habitat Studies (Architecture; Economics; Engineering; Environmental Studies; Management; Social Sciences); **Health Systems Studies** (Economics; Finance; Health Administration; Health Sciences; Public Health; Social Sciences); **Management and Labour Studies** (Human Resources; Labour and Industrial Relations; Leadership; Management); **Rural Development** (Development Studies; Rural Studies; Social Work); **Social Sciences** (Adult Education; Development Studies; Ecology; Education; Health Education; Higher Education; Human Rights; Primary Education; Secondary Education; Social Problems; Social Sciences; Sociology; Women's Studies); **Social Work** (Child Care and Development; Criminology; Development Studies; Epidemiology; Family Studies; Health Sciences; Law; Peace and Disarmament; Protective Services; Psychiatry and Mental Health; Social Work; Women's Studies)

Further Information: Also Malti and Jal A.D. Naoroji Campus.

History: Founded 1936. Granted 'Deemed University' status 1964. A postgraduate institution.

Academic Year: June to April

Admission Requirements: University degree at Bachelor level

Fees: (Rupees): 3,000-4,500 per semester

Main Language(s) of Instruction: English

Degrees and Diplomas: *Bachelor's Degree*: **Social Work.** *Master's Degree*; *Master of Philosophy*; *Doctor of Philosophy*. Also Diploma and Certificate courses

Student Services: Academic Counselling, Canteen, Careers Guidance, Cultural Activities, Facilities for disabled people, Health Services, Nursery Care, Social Counselling, Sports Facilities

Publications: Indian Journal of Social Work

Last Updated: 23/11/11

TECHNO GLOBAL UNIVERSITY (TGU)

Anita Mension, Bishnupur, Shillong, Meghalaya 793 004
Website: http://technoindiagroup.com/academics/index.php?id1=1001

Programme

Civil Engineering (Civil Engineering); **Computer Science and Engineering** (Computer Engineering; Computer Science); **Electrical Engineering** (Electrical Engineering); **Electronics and Communications Engineering** (Electronic Engineering; Telecommunications Engineering); **Mechanical Engineering** (Mechanical Engineering)

History: Founded 2008.

Accrediting Agency: University Grants Commission (UGC)

Degrees and Diplomas: *Bachelor's Degree (professional)*. Dual Bachelor/Master's degrees (B.Tech-M.Tech and B.Tech-MBA).

Last Updated: 31/08/11

TEERTHANKER MAHAVEER UNIVERSITY (TMU)

Delhi Road, NH 24, Moradabad, Uttar Pradesh 244 001
Tel: +91(591) 236-0500 +91(591) 236-0077
Fax: +91(591) 236-0444 +91(591) 248-7444
EMail: admission@tmu.ac.in
Website: http://www.tmu.ac.in/

Vice-Chancellor: R. K. Mittal
Tel: +91(591) 236-0222 EMail: vicechancellor@tmu.ac.in

Registrar: Rakesh Kr. Mudgal
Tel: +91(591) 236-0006 EMail: registrar@tmu.ac.in

International Relations: K. K. Pande, Director, International Affairs
EMail: director.int@tmu.ac.in

College

Architecture (Architecture; Fine Arts); **Dentistry** *(and Research Centre)* (Dentistry; Surgery); **Education** (Education; Physical Education); **Engineering** (Chemical Engineering; Civil Engineering; Computer Engineering; Computer Science; Electrical Engineering; Electronic Engineering; Engineering; Mathematics; Mechanical Engineering); **Law and Legal Studies** (Criminology; Law); **Management and Computer Applications** (Accountancy; Business Administration; Business Computing; Computer Science; Management; Marine Transport; Transport Management); **Medicine** *(and Research Centre)* (Anaesthesiology; Anatomy; Biochemistry; Cardiology; Community Health; Dermatology; Forensic Medicine and Dentistry; Gynaecology and Obstetrics; Medicine; Microbiology; Ophthalmology; Orthopaedics; Otorhinolaryngology; Paediatrics; Pathology; Pharmacology; Physiology; Psychiatry and Mental Health; Radiology; Surgery; Urology; Venereology); **Nursing** (Midwifery; Nursing); **Pharmacy** (Chemistry; Pharmacology; Pharmacy; Safety Engineering); **Polytechnic** (Automotive Engineering; Civil Engineering; Computer Engineering; Computer Science; Electrical Engineering; Electronic Engineering; Engineering; Mechanical Engineering; Naval Architecture; Production Engineering)

Department

Hospital Administration (Health Administration; Health Sciences); **Social Work** (Social Work)

History: Founded 2008.

Degrees and Diplomas: *Bachelor's Degree*; *Bachelor's Degree (professional)*; *Master's Degree*; *Doctor of Philosophy*. Also Certificate; Bachelor's degree; Hons.; MBA

Student Numbers *2010-2011*: Total 7,800

Last Updated: 23/12/11

TELANGANA UNIVERSITY

Nizamabad, Andhra Pradesh 503 322
Tel: +91(8461) 222-220
Fax: +91(8461) 222-212
EMail: tu@telanganauniversity.ac.in
Website: http://www.telanganauniversity.ac.in/

Vice-Chancellor: Mohd. Akbar Ali Kha
Tel: +91(8461) 222-217 EMail: vc@telanganauniversity.ac.in

Registrar: M. Yadagiri
Tel: +91(8461) 222-211 EMail: registrar@telanganauniversity.ac.in

Faculty

Arts (Arts and Humanities; English; Hindi; Indic Languages; Mass Communication; Urdu); **Business Management** (Business

Administration; Management); **Commerce** (Business and Commerce; E- Business/Commerce); **Computer Science** (Computer Science); **Law** (Law); **Science** (Biotechnology; Botany; Chemistry; Computer Science; Electronic Engineering; Geology; Organic Chemistry; Pharmacy; Physics; Statistics); **Social Science** (Economics; Social Sciences; Social Work)

Further Information: Also South-Campus of Bhiknoor. A traditional and distance education institution.

History: Founded 2006.

Degrees and Diplomas: *Master's Degree*. Also MBA

Last Updated: 02/01/12

TERI UNIVERSITY

Plot No. 10 Institutional Area, Vasant Kunj, New Delhi 110 070
Tel: +91(11) 2612-2222
Fax: +91(11) 2612-2874
EMail: registrar@teri.res.in
Website: http://www.teriuniversity.ac.in

Vice-Chancellor: Bhavik R. Bakshi
EMail: bhavik.bakshi@teri.res.in

Registrar: Rajiv Seth EMail: rseth@teri.res.in

Faculty

Applied Sciences (Biotechnology; Computer Science; Energy Engineering; Environmental Engineering; Environmental Studies; Meteorology; Natural Resources; Water Management); **Policy and Planning** (Business Administration; Development Studies; Economics; Regional Planning)

History: Founded 1998 as TERI School of Advanced Studies. Acquired 'deemed university' status 1999.

Academic Year: July to June

Fees: (Rupees): 80,000-200,000 per annum

Main Language(s) of Instruction: English

Accrediting Agency: University Grants Commission

Degrees and Diplomas: *Postgraduate Diploma*; *Master's Degree*; *Doctor of Philosophy*. Also MBA

Student Services: Academic Counselling, Careers Guidance

Last Updated: 23/11/11

TEZPUR UNIVERSITY

Napaam, District Sonitpur, Tezpur, Assam 784 028
Tel: +91(3712) 267007 +91(3712) 267008 +91(3712) 267009
Fax: +91(3712) 267005 +91(3712) 267006
Website: http://www.tezu.ernet.in

Vice-Chancellor: Mihir Kanti Chaudhuri Tel: +91(3712) 267003

Registrar: Alak Kumar Buragohain
Tel: +91(3712) 267114 EMail: boral@tezu.ernet.in

School

Engineering (Civil Engineering; Computer Engineering; Computer Science; Electronic Engineering; Energy Engineering; Food Technology; Mechanical Engineering; Telecommunications Engineering); **Humanities and Social Sciences** (Chinese; Cultural Studies; English; Hindi; Journalism; Linguistics; Literature; Mass Communication; Modern Languages; Phonetics; Sociology); **Management Sciences** (Business Administration; Management; Tourism); **Science and Technology** (Applied Chemistry; Astrophysics; Biotechnology; Chemistry; Electronic Engineering; Environmental Studies; Inorganic Chemistry; Mathematics; Mathematics and Computer Science; Molecular Biology; Nanotechnology; Organic Chemistry; Physics; Polymer and Plastics Technology)

Further Information: A traditional and distance education institution.

History: Founded 1994. A Central University.

Academic Year: January to December (January-June; July-December)

Admission Requirements: Undergraduate programmes, 10+2 standard secondary studies; Graduate Programmes, University degree

Fees: (Rupees): 10,000-15,000 per semester

Main Language(s) of Instruction: English

Degrees and Diplomas: *Post Diploma*; *Bachelor's Degree (professional)*; *Postgraduate Diploma*; *Master's Degree*; *Doctor of Philosophy*. Also Certificate; integrated Bachelor's degree (B.Sc. B.Ed.) and Master's degree (M.Sc.; M.Tech), 4 yrs following Bachelor's degree; MBA

Student Services: Careers Guidance, Health Services, Sports Facilities

Last Updated: 23/11/11

THAPAR UNIVERSITY (TU)

P.O Box 32, Patiala, Punjab 147004
Tel: +91(175) 2393021
Fax: +91(175) 2364498 +91(175) 2393020
EMail: registrar@thapar.edu; webadmin@thapar.edu
Website: http://www.thapar.edu

Director: Abhijit Mukherjee
Tel: +91(175) 2393001 +91(175) 2363007
EMail: abhijit@thapar.edu

Registrar: J. E. Samuel Ratnakumar
Tel: +91(175) 2393021 EMail: registrar@thapar.edu

School

Chemistry and Biochemistry (Analytical Chemistry; Biochemistry; Chemistry; Inorganic Chemistry; Organic Chemistry; Physical Chemistry; Polymer and Plastics Technology); **Management** *(L. M. Thapar - LMTSOM)* (Business Administration; Data Processing; E-Business/Commerce; Finance; Human Resources; Information Sciences; International Business; Management; Marketing; Operations Research); **Management and Social Sciences** *(SMSS)* (E-Business/Commerce; Economics; Industrial Management; Management; Retailing and Wholesaling; Social Sciences); **Mathematics and Computer Applications** *(SMCA)* (Computer Networks; Computer Science; Data Processing; Mathematics; Mechanics; Statistics); **Physics and Materials Science** *(SPMS)* (Ceramics and Glass Technology; Materials Engineering; Metallurgical Engineering; Nanotechnology; Physics; Solid State Physics)

Department

Biotechnology and Environment Sciences *(BTESD)* (Biotechnology; Environmental Studies; Microbiology); **Chemical Engineering** *(CHED)* (Chemical Engineering); **Civil Engineering** *(CED)* (Civil Engineering; Structural Architecture); **Computer Science and Engineering** *(CSED)* (Computer Engineering; Computer Science; Software Engineering); **Distance Education** *(DDE)* (Civil Engineering; Computer Engineering; Computer Science; Electrical Engineering; Mechanical Engineering); **Electrical and Instrumentation Engineering** *(EIED)* (Electrical Engineering; Electronic Engineering; Measurement and Precision Engineering; Power Engineering); **Electronics and Communication Engineering** *(ECED)* (Design; Electronic Engineering; Telecommunications Engineering); **Mechanical Engineering** *(MED)* (Industrial Engineering; Mechanical Engineering; Production Engineering; Robotics; Thermal Engineering)

Centre

Central Workshop (Industrial Maintenance; Metal Techniques; Technology); **Information and Technology Management** *(CITM)* (Information Management; Information Technology); **Relevance and Excellence in Agro and Industrial Biotechnology** *(CORE)* (Biotechnology); **Science and Technology Entrepreneur's Park** *(STEP)* (Biotechnology; Business Administration; Food Technology; Management)

Further Information: A traditional and distance education institution.

History: Founded 1956 as Thapar Institute of Engineering and Technology. Granted 'Deemed University' status 1985.

Academic Year: July to June

Admission Requirements: 10+2 examination with Math, Physics, Chemistry/Biology/Biotechnology/Computer Science and also qualified All India Engineering Entrance Examination (AIEEE) conducted by CBSE, New Dehli

Fees: (Rupees): Bachelor of Engineering, 36,000; Master of Computer Applications, 36,000; ME/M. Tech./M.Sc., 16,000; PhD, 10,000

Main Language(s) of Instruction: English

Accrediting Agency: National Assessment and Accreditation Council (NAAC); All India Concil for Technical Education (CTE)

Degrees and Diplomas: *Bachelor's Degree*; *Bachelor's Degree (professional)*; *Master's Degree*; *Master of Philosophy*; *Doctor of Philosophy*. Also MBA

Student Services: Academic Counselling, Canteen, Careers Guidance, Health Services, Social Counselling, Sports Facilities

Last Updated: 23/11/11

THE ENGLISH AND FOREIGN LANGUAGES UNIVERSITY (EFL-U)

Osmania University Road, Hyderabad, Andhra Pradesh 500605
Tel: +91(40) 2709-8141
Fax: +91(40) 2707-0029
EMail: abhaimaurya@gmail.com
Website: http://www.efluniversity.ac.in

Vice-Chancellor: Sunaina Singh (2012-) Tel: +91(40) 2709-8141

Registrar: Lata Mallikarjuna
Tel: +91(40) 2709-8225 EMail: lmallikarjuna@yahoo.com

International Relations: Hemalatha Nagarajan, Dean, International Relations EMail: hemalatha@efluniversity.ac.in

School

Asian Studies (Asian Studies; Chinese; Japanese; Korean; Persian; Turkish); **Communication Studies** (Cinema and Television; Communication Studies; Journalism; Mass Communication; Media Studies); **Distance Education** (Distance Education; English; Foreign Languages Education; Linguistics; Literature; Phonetics); **English Language Education** (English; Foreign Languages Education; Literature); **English Literary Studies** (English; Literature); **Germanic Studies** (German; Germanic Languages; Literature); **Interdisciplinary Studies** (Arts and Humanities; Asian Studies; Comparative Literature; Cultural Studies; Esoteric Practices; Grammar; Hindi; History; Literature; Philosophy; Social Problems; Translation and Interpretation); **Language Sciences** (Computer Science; English; Linguistics; Phonetics); **Middle East and African Studies** (African Studies; Arabic; Literature; Middle Eastern Studies); **Romance Studies** (Cultural Studies; French; French Studies; Italian; Literature; Portuguese; Romance Languages; Spanish); **Russian Studies** (Linguistics; Literature; Russian)

Further Information: Also campuses in Lucknow and Shillong. A traditional and distance education institution.

History: Founded 1958 as Central Institute of English, known as Central Institute of English and Foreign Languages from 1972, and status as 'Deemed University' 1973. A postgraduate Institution with branches at Lucknow and Shillong. Acquired current title 2007. A Central University.

Academic Year: August to April

Admission Requirements: Postgraduate degree in the language concerned, with at least 55% pass marks

Fees: (Rupees): 200-300 per semester

Main Language(s) of Instruction: English

Accrediting Agency: NAAC, UGC

Degrees and Diplomas: *Bachelor's Degree*; *Postgraduate Diploma*; *Master's Degree*; *Master of Philosophy*; *Doctor of Philosophy*

Student Services: Academic Counselling, Canteen, Careers Guidance, Cultural Activities, Facilities for disabled people, Foreign Studies Centre, Health Services, Language Laboratory, Nursery Care, Social Counselling, Sports Facilities

Publishing house: EFL-U Publications Unit

Last Updated: 23/11/11

THE GLOBAL OPEN UNIVERSITY

Opposite Railway Station, Dimapur, Nagaland 797112
Tel: +91(3862) 231959
EMail: univ@nagaland.net.in
Website: http://nagaland.net.in/

Programme

Applied Science (Bioengineering; Biology; Biotechnology; Dairy; Nanotechnology); **Computers and Information Technology** (Computer Education; Computer Networks; Information Technology); **Ecology and Environment** (Ecology; Environmental Management); **Education** (Adult Education; Child Care and Development; Education; Educational Administration; Educational Technology; Health Education; Higher Education; Physical Education; Science Education; Vocational Education); **Health and Medical Sciences** (Health Administration; Medicine; Yoga); **Journalism and Mass Communication** (Journalism; Mass Communication); **Law and Juridical Science** (Criminology; Forensic Medicine and Dentistry; Law); **Library and Information Science** (Information Sciences; Library Science); **Management and Commerce** (Business Administration; Business and Commerce; Insurance); **Psychology and Counselling** (Psycholinguistics); **Social Sciences** (Economics; Ethics; Geography; Government; Peace and Disarmament; Social Sciences; Sociology; South Asian Studies); **Tourism, Travel and Hospitality Management** (Hotel Management; Tourism)

History: Founded 2006.

Degrees and Diplomas: *Bachelor's Degree*; *Postgraduate Diploma*; *Master's Degree*

Last Updated: 17/01/12

THE LNM INSTITUTE OF INFORMATION TECHNOLOGY (LNMIIT)

Rupa ki Nangal, Post-Sumel, Via-Jamdoli,
Jaipur, Rajasthan 302031
Tel: +91(141) 518-9211 +91(141) 268-9011
Fax: +91(141) 268-9014
EMail: info.lnmiit@lnmiit.ac.in
Website: http://www.lnmiit.ac.in

Director: Sudhir Raniwala EMail: director@lnmiit.ac.in

Programme

Communication and Computer Engineering *(Postgraduate)* (Computer Engineering; Telecommunications Engineering); **Communication and Computer Engineering** (Computer Engineering; Telecommunications Engineering); **Computer Science and Engineering** (Computer Engineering; Computer Science); **Computer Science and Engineering** *(Postgraduate)* (Computer Engineering; Computer Science); **Electronics and Communication Engineering** *(Postgraduate)* (Electronic Engineering; Telecommunications Engineering); **Electronics and Communication Engineering** (Electronic Engineering; Telecommunications Engineering); **Engineering Physics** (Engineering; Physics); **Mathematics and Information Technology** (Information Technology; Mathematics)

History: Founded 2002. A deemed university.

Main Language(s) of Instruction: Hindi

Degrees and Diplomas: *Bachelor's Degree (professional)*; *Master's Degree*; *Doctor of Philosophy*

Last Updated: 23/11/11

THE MAHARAJA SAYAJIRAO UNIVERSITY OF BARODA

Fatehgani, Vadodara, Gujarat 390002
Tel: +91(265) 279-5521
Fax: +91(265) 279-3693
EMail: registrar@msubaroda.ac.in
Website: http://www.msubaroda.ac.in

Vice-Chancellor: Yogesh Singh
Tel: +91(265) 2795600
EMail: ys66@rediffmail.com; vc@msubaroda.ac.in

Registrar: M. M. Beedkar
Tel: +91(265) 2795521 EMail: registrar@msubaroda.ac.in

Faculty

Arts (Ancient Civilizations; Arabic; Archaeology; Arts and Humanities; Canadian Studies; Economics; English; French; German; Hindi; History; Indic Languages; Information Sciences; Library Science; Linguistics; Persian; Philosophy; Political Sciences; Russian; Sanskrit; Sociology; Urdu); **Baroda Sanskrit Mahavidyalaya** (Esoteric Practices; Sanskrit); **Commerce** (Accountancy; Banking; Business Administration; Business and Commerce; Economics; Insurance; Management); **Education and Psychology** (Education; Educational Administration; Psychology); **Family and Community Science** (Child Care and Development; Clothing and Sewing; Communication Studies; Development Studies; Family Studies; Food Science; Home

Economics; Nutrition; Textile Technology; Women's Studies); **Fine Arts** (Aesthetics; Art History; Fine Arts; Graphic Arts; Museum Studies; Painting and Drawing; Sculpture); **Journalism and Communication** (Journalism; Mass Communication; Media Studies); **Law** (Commercial Law; Law); **Management Studies** (Business Administration; Management); **Medicine** (Anaesthesiology; Anatomy; Biochemistry; Dermatology; Forensic Medicine and Dentistry; Gynaecology and Obstetrics; Medicine; Microbiology; Ophthalmology; Orthopaedics; Otorhinolaryngology; Paediatrics; Pathology; Pharmacology; Physical Therapy; Physiology; Plastic Surgery; Psychiatry and Mental Health; Radiology; Social and Preventive Medicine; Surgery; Venereology); **Performing Arts** (Dance; Musical Instruments; Performing Arts; Singing; Theatre); **Polytechnics** (Applied Chemistry; Applied Mathematics; Applied Physics; Chemical Engineering; Civil Engineering; Electrical Engineering; Mechanical Engineering; Mechanics; Petroleum and Gas Engineering); **Science** (Biochemistry; Botany; Chemistry; Geography; Geology; Mathematics; Microbiology; Physics; Statistics; Zoology); **Social Work** (Social Work); **Technology and Engineering** (Applied Chemistry; Applied Mathematics; Applied Physics; Architecture; Chemical Engineering; Civil Engineering; Computer Science; Electrical Engineering; Engineering; Materials Engineering; Mechanical Engineering; Mechanics; Metallurgical Engineering; Pharmacy; Technology; Textile Design)

College

Science and Commerce *(M.K. Amin)* (Business and Commerce; Natural Sciences)

History: Founded 1949.

Academic Year: June to May (June-December; December-May).

Admission Requirements: 12th year senior secondary school/ intermediate examination or recognized foreign equivalent

Main Language(s) of Instruction: English

Degrees and Diplomas: *Post Diploma*; *Bachelor's Degree*; *Bachelor's Degree (professional)*; *Postgraduate Diploma*; *Master's Degree*; *Master of Philosophy*; *Doctor of Philosophy*. Also Certificate courses; MBA

Publications: Journal of Animal Morphology and Physiology; Oriental Institute Journal; PAVO and Baroda Reporter; Social Sciences and Technology; Swadhyay; University Journals

Publishing House: M.S. University of Baroda Press

Student Numbers *2010-2011*: Total: c. 3,700

Last Updated: 23/11/11

THE WEST BENGAL UNIVERSITY OF HEALTH SCIENCES (WBUHS)

DD - 36, Sector - 1, Salt Lake, Kolkata, West Bengal 700 064
Tel: +91(33) 2321-3461 +91(33) 2334-6602
EMail: vcwbunivhealthsciences@gmail.com
Website: http://www.wbuhs.ac.in/

Vice-Chancellor: Amit Banerjee

Department

Medicine and Surgery (Anaesthesiology; Anatomy; Community Health; Dermatology; Forensic Medicine and Dentistry; Gynaecology and Obstetrics; Medicine; Microbiology; Orthopaedics; Otorhinolaryngology; Paediatrics; Pathology; Pharmacology; Physiology; Pneumology; Psychiatry and Mental Health; Radiology; Rehabilitation and Therapy; Surgery; Tropical Medicine)

Course

Audiology and Speech Language Pathology (Speech Therapy and Audiology); **Dentistry** (Dentistry); **Health Administration** *(Postgraduate)* (Health Administration); **Nursing** (Nursing); **Physiotherapy** (Physical Therapy); **Prosthetics and Orthotics** (Dental Technology; Orthodontics)

History: Founded 2003.

Degrees and Diplomas: *Bachelor's Degree*; *Bachelor's Degree (professional)*; *Postgraduate Diploma*; *Master's Degree*; *Doctor of Philosophy*. Also Honours Bachelor's degree.

Last Updated: 06/01/12

THIRUVALLUVAR UNIVERSITY

Serkkadu, Vellore, Tamil Nadu 632 106
Tel: +91(416) 227-4755 +91(416) 227-4756
Fax: +91(416) 227-4748
EMail: registrartvu@gmail.com
Website: http://thiruvalluvaruniversity.ac.in/

Vice-Chancellor: A. Jothi Murugan

Department

Biotechnology (Biotechnology); **Chemistry** (Chemistry); **Economics** (Economics); **English** (English); **Mathematics** (Mathematics); **Tamil** (South and Southeast Asian Languages); **Zoology** (Zoology)

Further Information: Also 98 affiliated colleges. A traditional and distance education institution.

History: Founded 2002.

Degrees and Diplomas: *Master's Degree*; *Master of Philosophy*; *Doctor of Philosophy*

Student Services: Health Services, Sports Facilities

Last Updated: 05/01/12

TILAK MAHARASHTRA VIDYAPEETH (TMV)

Vidyapeeth Bhavan, Gultekadi, Pune, Maharashtra 411 037
Tel: +91(20) 24261856 +91(20) 24264699
Fax: +91(20) 24266068 +91(20) 24271695
EMail: tmvadmin@tmv.edu.in; kulguru@tmv.edu.in
Website: http://www.tmv.edu.in

Vice-Chancellor: Deepak Tilak (2007-)
Tel: +91(20) 2427-1695 +91(20) 2445-9250
EMail: d_tilak@hotmail.com; kulaguru@tmv.ernet.in

Registrar: Umesh Keskar
Tel: +91(20) 2426-1685; +91(20) 2426-3952
EMail: keskarumesh@yahoo.com; kulasachiv@tmv.ernet.in

Faculty

Arts and Fine Arts (Arts and Humanities; Asian Studies; Cultural Studies; Fine Arts; Indic Languages; Sanskrit); **Ayurveda** (Ayurveda; Dietetics; Pharmacy; Physical Therapy); **Distance Education** (Business Administration; Dance; Fine Arts; Hotel Management; Journalism; Social Work); **Education** (Education); **Engineering** (Engineering); **Health Sciences** (Dental Technology; Health Sciences; Medicine; Nursing; Optometry; Physical Therapy); **Modern Sciences and Professional Skills** (Biotechnology; Business Administration; Engineering; Fine Arts; Hotel Management; Mass Communication; Media Studies; Microbiology); **Moral and Social Sciences** (Economics; Geography; History; Library Science; Philosophy; Political Sciences; Social Sciences; Sociology)

Further Information: Also Mumbai, Aurangabad and Delhi campuses. A traditional and distance education institution.

History: Founded 1921. Acquired status of deemed university 1987.

Academic Year: July to May

Admission Requirements: 12th year senior secondary/intermediate examination or recognized foreign equivalent

Fees: (Rupees): 300-11,000 per annum

Main Language(s) of Instruction: English, Marathi

Accrediting Agency: National Assessment and Accreditation Council (an autonomous body of the University Grants Commission); Distance Education Council (Autonomous Body of IGNOU); National Council of Teacher Education

Degrees and Diplomas: *Post Diploma*; *Bachelor's Degree*; *Master's Degree*; *Master of Philosophy*; *Doctor of Philosophy*. Also Certificate and MBA

Student Services: Academic Counselling, Canteen, Facilities for disabled people, Health Services, Language Laboratory, Sports Facilities

Last Updated: 23/11/11

TILKA MANJHI BHAGALPUR UNIVERSITY (TMBU)

Tilka Manjhi, Bhagalpur, Bihar 812007
Tel: +91(641) 240-1001
Fax: +91(641) 242-2153
Website: http://www.tmbu.org/

Vice-Chancellor: K. N. Dubey
Tel: +91(641) 2620100 EMail: vc.drkndubey@gmail.com

Registrar: Chandra Mohan Das

Faculty

Commerce (Accountancy; Banking; Business Administration; Business and Commerce; Finance; Human Resources; Marketing); **Humanities** (Arts and Humanities; English; Hindi; Music; Persian; Philosophy; Sanskrit; Urdu); **Law** (Criminal Law; Environmental Studies; Human Rights; International Law; Law; Private Law); **Management Studies** (Business Administration; Management); **Science** (Biotechnology; Botany; Chemistry; Computer Science; Mathematics; Physics; Statistics; Zoology); **Social Sciences** (Agricultural Economics; Anthropology; Economics; Geography; History; Home Economics; Human Resources; Information Sciences; Labour and Industrial Relations; Peace and Disarmament; Political Sciences; Psychology; Rural Studies; Social Sciences; Sociology)

Centre

Bioinformatics (Biological and Life Sciences; Computer Science; Data Processing; Sericulture); **Computer Science** (Computer Science); **Regional Studies** (Regional Studies)

Research Centre

Agro-Economics (Agricultural Economics)

Further Information: Also 29 constituent colleges and 24 affiliated Colleges.

History: Founded 1960 as Bhagalpur University. Acquired present title 1991.

Admission Requirements: 12th year senior secondary/intermediate examination or recognized equivalent

Fees: (Rupees): 164-240 per annum

Degrees and Diplomas: *Post Diploma*; *Postgraduate Diploma*; *Master's Degree*; *Doctor of Philosophy*. Also Certificate Courses; M.B.A

Academic Staff *2010-2011*	MEN	WOMEN	**TOTAL**
FULL-TIME	–	–	**1,220**
Student Numbers *2010-2011*			
All (Foreign included)	43,884	16,943	**60,827**

Last Updated: 23/11/11

TRIPURA UNIVERSITY

Suryamaninagar, Tripura 799 022
Tel: +91(381) 237-4801
Fax: +91(381) 237-4802
EMail: tripurauniversity@rediffmail.com
Website: http://tripurauniv.in/

Vice-Chancellor: Arunoday Saha
Tel: +91(381) 2374801 EMail: arunodaysaha@rediffmail.com

Registrar: Kalyan Bijoy Jamatia
Tel: +91(381) 2374803 EMail: k_jamatia@yahoo.co.in

Faculty

Arts and Commerce *(Postgraduate)* (Arts and Humanities; Business and Commerce; Development Studies; Economics; English; Fine Arts; Hindi; Histology; Indic Languages; Journalism; Management; Mass Communication; Music; Philosophy; Political Sciences; Rural Studies; Sanskrit); **Science** *(Postgraduate)* (Botany; Chemistry; Computer Engineering; Computer Science; Electrical and Electronic Equipment and Maintenance; Geography; Information Technology; Mathematics; Physics; Physiology; Safety Engineering; Zoology)

Department

Distance Education (Arts and Humanities; Computer Science; Education; Indic Languages; Political Sciences)

Centre

Bamboo Cultivation and Resource Utilization (Agriculture); **Bioinformatics** (Biological and Life Sciences; Computer Science; Zoology); **Gandhian Studies** (Environmental Studies); **IGNOU Study**; **Manuscript Resource and Manuscript Conservation** (Ancient Books); **NET/SET Coaching** (Mathematics; Philosophy); **Rubber Technology** (Rubber Technology); **Rural Studies** (Rural Studies); **Study of Social Exclusion and Inclusive Policies** (Social Policy; Social Problems; Social Work); **Tribal Language** (Native Language); **Women's Studies** (Women's Studies)

Further Information: Also 24 affiliated colleges. A traditional and distance education institution.

History: Founded 1987, incorporating 10 departments which had previously formed the Calcutta University Postgraduate Centre at Agartala. Acquired Central University status 2007.

Academic Year: June to May

Admission Requirements: Undergraduate programs, 12th year senior secondary/intermediate examination or recognized foreign equivalent; graduate programs, Gradute with Hons

Fees: (Rupees): Arts and Commerce programs, 1,050 per annum; Science programs, 1,250 per annum

Main Language(s) of Instruction: English

Accrediting Agency: National assessment and Accreditation Council (NAAC)

Degrees and Diplomas: *Post Diploma*; *Bachelor's Degree*; *Postgraduate Diploma*; *Master's Degree*; *Master of Philosophy*; *Doctor of Philosophy*. Also Certificate course.

Student Services: Academic Counselling, Canteen, Careers Guidance, Cultural Activities, Facilities for disabled people, Health Services, Language Laboratory, Sports Facilities

Academic Staff *2010-2011*: Total: c. 120

Last Updated: 23/11/11

TUMKUR UNIVERSITY

Vishwavidyanilaya Karyalaya, University Constituent College Campus, B.H Road, Tumkur 572 103
Tel: +91(816) 225-4546 +91(816) 225-5596
Fax: +91(816) 227-0719

Vice-Chancellor: S.C. Sharma

Registrar: D. Shivalingaiah

Faculty

Arts (Archaeology; Arts and Humanities; Economics; English; History; Indic Languages; Journalism; Physical Education; Political Sciences; Social Work; Sociology); **Commerce and Management** (Business Administration; Business and Commerce; Management); **Science and Technology** (Biochemistry; Biotechnology; Botany; Chemistry; Computer Science; Electronic Engineering; Information Sciences; Library Science; Mathematics; Microbiology; Physics; Zoology)

Further Information: Also 2 constituent colleges: University College of Arts and University College of Science

History: Founded 2004.

Degrees and Diplomas: *Bachelor's Degree*; *Master's Degree*; *Doctor of Philosophy*

Last Updated: 03/01/12

UNIVERSITY OF AGRICULTURAL SCIENCES, BANGALORE (UASBNG)

GKVK Campus, Bangalore, Karnataka 560 065
Tel: +91(80) 2333-0153 +91(80) 2333-2442
Fax: +91(80) 2333-0277
EMail: registrar@uasbangalore.edu.in
Website: http://www.uasbng.kar.nic.in

Vice-Chancellor: Narayana Gowda
EMail: vc@uasbangalore.edu.in; knarayanagowda@yahoo.co.in

Registrar: Chikkadevaiah
Tel: +91(80) 2333-0984 EMail: registrar@uasbangalore.edu.in

International Relations: S. Suryaprakash

College

Agriculture *(Shimoga)* (Agriculture; Crop Production; Plant and Crop Protection; Social Sciences); **Agriculture** *(Mandya)* (Agriculture; Crop Production; Plant and Crop Protection; Social Sciences); **Agriculture** *(Bangalore)* (Agricultural Economics; Agricultural Engineering; Agriculture; Agronomy; Apiculture; Biotechnology; Chemistry; Crop Production; Entomology; Environmental Studies; Food Science; Forestry; Horticulture; Marketing; Microbiology; Nutrition; Physiology; Plant and Crop Protection; Sericulture; Soil Science; Statistics); **Agriculture** *(Hassan)* (Agricultural Economics; Agriculture; Agronomy; Crop Production;

Entomology; Forest Products; Forestry; Physiology); **Forestry** *(Ponnampet)* (Agriculture; Forestry; Natural Resources); **Sericulture** *(Chintamani)* (Agronomy; Crop Production; Genetics; Horticulture; Plant and Crop Protection; Sericulture)

Further Information: Two campuses in Bangalore and one in Hebbal.

History: Founded 1964. The University has 8 campuses, two at Bangalore and one at Mangalore, Mudigere, Ponnampet, Shimadya, Shimoga and Chintamani. It is modelled on the pattern of the Land Grant Institutions of the USA. It aims to integrate teaching, research and extension education in Agricultural Sciences.

Admission Requirements: 12th year senior secondary/intermediate examination or recognized foreign equivalent

Fees: (Rupees): Undergraduate, Agriculture and allied subjects 7,873, Veterinary Science, 12,528 per semester; postgraduate, 8,318

Main Language(s) of Instruction: English

Accrediting Agency: Indian Council of Agricultural Research (ICAR), Veterinary Council of India (VCI)

Degrees and Diplomas: *Bachelor's Degree*; *Bachelor's Degree (professional)*; *Master's Degree*. Also MBA; Partner of the International Academic Post Graduate Programme: International Masters in Rural Development (IMRD).

Student Services: Canteen, Careers Guidance, Cultural Activities, Foreign Studies Centre, Health Services, Sports Facilities

Publications: Current Science; Mysore Journal of Agricultural Sciences

Last Updated: 24/11/11

UNIVERSITY OF AGRICULTURAL SCIENCES, DHARWAD (USAD)

Krishinagar, Dharwad, Karnataka 580 005
Tel: +91(836) 2747-958
Fax: +91(836) 2745-276
EMail: registrar@uasd.edu; registraruasd@rediffmail.com; uasdregistrar@gmail.com
Website: http://www.uasd.edu

Vice-Chancellor: Rayappa Ramappa Hanchinal
EMail: vc@uasd.edu

Registrar: H.S. Vijayakumar
Tel: +91(836) 2747-958
EMail: registrar@uasd.edu; registraruasd@rediffmail.com

International Relations: M.B. Chetti, Registrar

College

Agriculture *(Bijapur)* (Agricultural Economics; Agricultural Engineering; Agriculture; Agronomy; Arts and Humanities; Chemistry; Crop Production; Dairy; Entomology; Fishery; Forestry; Genetics; Horticulture; Meat and Poultry; Meteorology; Microbiology; Natural Sciences; Plant and Crop Protection; Sericulture; Soil Science; Veterinary Science); **Agriculture** *(Dharwad)* (Agricultural Business; Agricultural Economics; Agricultural Education; Agricultural Engineering; Agricultural Management; Agriculture; Agronomy; Biochemistry; Biotechnology; Botany; Chemistry; Crop Production; Entomology; Environmental Studies; Genetics; Horticulture; Marketing; Microbiology; Physical Education; Plant and Crop Protection; Sericulture; Soil Science; Statistics; Veterinary Science; Zoology); **Agriculture** *(Hanumanmatti)* (Agriculture); **Forestry** *(Sirsi)* (Agricultural Engineering; Agriculture; Arts and Humanities; Forest Biology; Forest Management; Forestry; Natural Sciences); **Rural Home Science** *(Dharwad)* (Communication Studies; Development Studies; Family Studies; Food Science; Home Economics; Nutrition; Physical Education; Textile Design)

Further Information: 6 campuses offering programmes; 4 campuses offering postgraduate programmes

History: Founded 1986 under UAS Act 1963. The University is modelled on the pattern of the Land Grant Institutions of the USA.

Academic Year: September to August (September-February; March-August)

Admission Requirements: 12th year senior secondary/intermediate examination or recognized foreign equivalent with PCMB/PCB/PCM

Fees: (Rupees): undergraduate, 7,570 for first semester and 5,780 for second semester; graduate, 8,360 for first semester and 6,000 for second semester. (US Dollars): Foreign students, 4,000

Main Language(s) of Instruction: English

Accrediting Agency: Indian Council of Agricultural Research, New Delhi

Degrees and Diplomas: *Post Diploma*; *Bachelor's Degree*; *Master's Degree*; *Doctor of Philosophy*. Also Certificate Courses

Student Services: Academic Counselling, Canteen, Careers Guidance, Cultural Activities, Health Services, Social Counselling, Sports Facilities

Publications: Karnataka Journal of Agricultural Sciences; Krishi Munnade in Kannada; UAS Newsletter

Publishing House: Publication Centre, UAS, Dharwad

Last Updated: 24/11/11

UNIVERSITY OF ALLAHABAD (ALLDUNIV)

PO Allahabad, Agricultural Institute, Allahabad, Uttar Pradesh 211007
Tel: +91(532) 246-1083
Fax: +91(532) 254-5021
Website: http://www.allduniv.ac.in

Vice-Chancellor: Anil K. Singh

Faculty

Arts (Ancient Civilizations; Arabic; Archaeology; Arts and Humanities; Cultural Studies; Economics; Education; English; Fine Arts; Geography; Hindi; Journalism; Medicine; Modern History; Modern Languages; Music; Performing Arts; Persian; Philosophy; Physical Education; Political Sciences; Psychology; Sanskrit; Urdu); **Commerce** (Business and Commerce; Economics); **Law** (Law); **Science** (Applied Physics; Biochemistry; Botany; Chemistry; Earth Sciences; Mathematics; Natural Sciences; Photography; Physics; Statistics; Zoology)

Further Information: Also 7 Associated and Constituent Colleges

History: Founded 1887. A 'Central University'.

Academic Year: August to April (August-May; July-April)

Admission Requirements: 12th year senior secondary/intermediate examination or recognized foreign equivalent, and competitive entrance examination

Fees: (Rupees): 144-300 per annum

Main Language(s) of Instruction: English

Degrees and Diplomas: *Bachelor's Degree*; *Master's Degree*; *Doctor of Philosophy*. Also Diploma and Certificate courses

Publications: Indian Journal of Economics

Last Updated: 16/05/11

UNIVERSITY OF BURDWAN (BU)

Rajbati, Burdwan, West Bengal 713 104
Tel: +91(342) 263-4975
Fax: +91(342) 253-0452
EMail: pio@buruniv.ac.in
Website: http://www.buruniv.ac.in

Vice-Chancellor: Subrata Pal (2008-)
Tel: +91(342) 263-4900 EMail: vc@buruniv.ac.in

Registrar: Debidas Mondal EMail: dyregistrar@buruniv.ac.in

Faculty

Other (Animal Husbandry; Business Computing; Demography and Population; Family Studies; Health Administration; Laboratory Techniques; Maintenance Technology; Social and Community Services; Special Education; Welfare and Protective Services; Yoga); **Post-graduate Studies in Arts, Commerce, Law, Fine Arts and Music** (Arts and Humanities; Business Administration; Business and Commerce; Economics; Education; English; Fine Arts; French; German; Hindi; History; Human Resources; Indic Languages; Information Sciences; Law; Library Science; Mass Communication; Music; Philosophy; Political Sciences; Russian; Sanskrit; Sociology; Tourism); **Post-graduate Studies in Medicine** (Anatomy; Biochemistry; Gynaecology and Obstetrics; Medicine; Ophthalmology; Surgery); **Post-graduate Studies in Science** (Biochemistry; Biology; Biotechnology; Botany; Chemistry; Computer Engineering; Computer Science; Education; Electronic

Engineering; Environmental Studies; Geography; Geology; Mathematics; Microbiology; Physics; Physiology; Statistics; Surveying and Mapping; Telecommunications Engineering; Zoology); **Under-graduate Studies in Engineering** (Civil Engineering; Computer Engineering; Computer Science; Electrical Engineering; Electronic Engineering; Engineering; Information Technology; Measurement and Precision Engineering; Metallurgical Engineering; Telecommunications Engineering); **Under-graduate Studies in Medicine** (Homeopathy; Laboratory Techniques; Medical Technology; Medicine; Surgery); **Under-graduate Studies in Science, Arts, Commerce, Law, Fine Arts and Music** (Accountancy; Advertising and Publicity; Arabic; Arts and Humanities; Biochemistry; Biotechnology; Botany; Business and Commerce; Chemistry; Computer Science; Crop Production; E- Business/Commerce; Economics; Education; Electronic Engineering; English; Environmental Management; Environmental Studies; Fashion Design; Fine Arts; Fishery; French; Geography; Geology; Hindi; History; Information Technology; Interior Design; Law; Mathematics; Microbiology; Music; Natural Sciences; Nutrition; Persian; Philosophy; Physical Education; Physical Therapy; Physics; Physiology; Political Sciences; Sanskrit; Sericulture; Singing; Sociology; Statistics; Urdu; Water Management; Zoology)

Further Information: Also 6 Constituent and 110 Affiliated Colleges. A traditional and distance education institution.

History: Founded 1960.

Academic Year: June to May

Admission Requirements: 12th year senior secondary/intermediate examination or recognized foreign equivalent

Fees: (Rupees): 100-500 per month

Main Language(s) of Instruction: English, Bengali

Accrediting Agency: NAAC

Degrees and Diplomas: *Post Diploma*; *Bachelor's Degree*; *Bachelor's Degree (professional)*; *Postgraduate Diploma*; *Master's Degree*; *Master of Philosophy*. Also Certificate; Advance Diploma; Honours Bachelor; Integrated B.A. LL.B.(Hons.); MBA

Student Services: Academic Counselling, Canteen, Careers Guidance, Cultural Activities, Facilities for disabled people, Health Services, Language Laboratory, Sports Facilities

Publishing house: Burdwan University Press
Last Updated: 24/11/11

UNIVERSITY OF CALCUTTA

Kalikata Viswavidyalaya

Senate House, 87/1 College Street, Kolkata, West Bengal 700073
Tel: +91(33) 2241-0071
Fax: +91(33) 2241-3222
EMail: admin@caluniv.ac.in
Website: http://www.caluniv.ac.in/

Vice-Chancellor: Suranjan Das (2008-)
Tel: +91(33) 2241-3288 EMail: vc@caluniv.ac.in

Registrar: Basab Chaudhuri EMail: registrar@caluniv.ac.in

Faculty

Agriculture (Agriculture; Agronomy; Horticulture; Plant and Crop Protection; Soil Science; Veterinary Science); **Arts** (Ancient Civilizations; Ancient Languages; Arabic; Archaeology; Arts and Humanities; Asian Religious Studies; Economics; English; Heritage Preservation; Hindi; History; Indic Languages; Islamic Studies; Linguistics; Literature; Museum Studies; Persian; Philosophy; Political Sciences; Sanskrit; Sociology; South Asian Studies; Southeast Asian Studies; Urdu); **Commerce, Social Welfare and Business Management** (Business Administration; Business and Commerce); **Education, Journalism and Library Science** (Education; Educational Administration; Film; Journalism; Library Science; Mass Communication; Media Studies; Psychiatry and Mental Health; Radio and Television Broadcasting); **Engineering and Technology** (Applied Physics; Automation and Control Engineering; Bioengineering; Chemical Engineering; Computer Science; Electrical Engineering; Electronic Engineering; Engineering; Materials Engineering; Measurement and Precision Engineering; Meteorology; Optics; Petroleum and Gas Engineering; Pharmacology; Polymer and Plastics Technology; Power Engineering; Radiophysics; Rubber Technology; Technology); **Fine Arts, Music and Home Science** (Fine Arts; Home Economics; Music; Nutrition); **Law** (Civil Law; Criminal Law; Law); **Science** (Analytical Chemistry; Anthropology; Applied Mathematics; Archaeology; Biochemistry; Biophysics; Biotechnology; Botany; Chemistry; Clinical Psychology; Computer Science; Electronic Engineering; Genetics; Geography; Geology; Geophysics; Industrial and Organizational Psychology; Inorganic Chemistry; Instrument Making; Marine Science and Oceanography; Mathematics; Microbiology; Molecular Biology; Natural Sciences; Nuclear Physics; Optics; Organic Chemistry; Physical Chemistry; Physics; Physiology; Psychology; Solid State Physics; Statistics; Toxicology; Zoology)

Further Information: Also 18 research centres.

History: Founded 1857.

Academic Year: June to May

Admission Requirements: 12th year senior secondary/intermediate examination or recognized foreign equivalent, and competitive entrance examination

Main Language(s) of Instruction: English

Accrediting Agency: University Grants Commission

Degrees and Diplomas: *Post Diploma*; *Bachelor's Degree*; *Postgraduate Diploma*; *Master's Degree*; *Master of Philosophy*; *Doctor of Philosophy*

Student Services: Academic Counselling, Canteen, Careers Guidance, Cultural Activities, Facilities for disabled people, Foreign Studies Centre, Health Services, Language Laboratory, Nursery Care, Social Counselling, Sports Facilities

Publications: Calcutta Review; Journals

Publishing House: Calcutta University Press
Last Updated: 25/11/11

UNIVERSITY OF CALICUT (UNICAL)

PO Calicut University, Thenhipalam, Malappuram District, Kozhikode, Kerala 673635
Tel: +91(494) 240-1144 +91(494) 240-1152
Fax: +91(494) 240-0269
EMail: regcltuty@rediffmail.com
Website: http://www.unical.ac.in

Vice-Chancellor: M. Abdul Salam (2011-) Tel: +91(494) 240-0241

Registrar: P.P. Mohamed Tel: +91(494) 240-0252

School

Drama (Theatre)

Department

Arabic (Arabic); **Biotechnology** (Biotechnology); **Botany** (Botany); **Chemistry** (Applied Chemistry; Chemistry); **Commerce and Management Studies** (Business Administration; Business and Commerce; Management); **Computer Science** (Computer Science); **Economics** (Economics); **Education** (Education); **English** (English); **Folklore Studies** (Folklore); **Hindi** (Hindi); **History** (History); **Journalism and Mass Communication** (Journalism; Mass Communication); **Library and Information Sciences** (Information Sciences; Library Science); **Life Sciences** (Biochemistry; Biological and Life Sciences; Microbiology; Physiology); **Lifelong Learning and Extension** (Adult Education; Continuing Education; Educational and Student Counselling); **Malayam** (Indic Languages); **Mathematics** (Mathematics); **Philosophy** (Philosophy); **Physics** (Physics); **Psychology** (Psychology); **Russian** (Russian); **Sanskrit** (Sanskrit); **Statistics** (Statistics); **Zoology** (Entomology; Zoology)

Centre

Computer (Computer Science); **West Asian Studies** *(Kunhali Marakkar)* (Asian Studies; International Relations; Political Sciences); **Women's Studies** (Women's Studies)

Research Centre

Educational Multimedia (Educational Technology; Multimedia)

Further Information: Also 304 affiliated colleges (83 are located in Kozhikode district, 72 in Thrissur, 82 in Malappuram, 50 in Palakkad and 10 in Wayanad district). Extension centres at Thrissur, Calicut and Vatakara. A traditional and distance education institution.

History: Founded 1968. Main campus Thenhippalam.

Academic Year: June to March

Admission Requirements: 12th year senior secondary/intermediate examination or recognized foreign equivalent

Main Language(s) of Instruction: English, Malayaam

Degrees and Diplomas: *Post Diploma*; *Bachelor's Degree*; *Bachelor's Degree (professional)*; *Postgraduate Diploma*; *Master's Degree*; *Master of Philosophy*; *Doctor of Philosophy*. Also Certificate courses; integrated M.Phil/Ph.D; MBA

Student Services: Canteen, Careers Guidance, Health Services, Sports Facilities

Publishing house: Publication Division

Last Updated: 24/11/11

IAU UNIVERSITY OF DELHI

Delhi Vishwavidyalaya

University Road, Delhi 110007

Tel: +91(11) 2766-7725

Fax: +91(11) 2766-6350

EMail: registrar@du.ac.in

Website: http://www.du.ac.in

Vice-Chancellor: Dinesh Singh (2010-)
Tel: +91(11) 2766-7011 EMail: vc@du.ac.in

Registrar: Alka Sharma EMail: registrar@du.ac.in

International Relations: Anand Prakesh, Dean, International Relations Tel: +97(11) 2766-7011 EMail: dean_ir@du.ac.in

Faculty

Applied Social Sciences and Humanities (Arts and Humanities; Business and Commerce; Economics; Finnish; Hungarian; Slavic Languages; Social Sciences); **Arts** (Arabic; Asian Religious Studies; English; German; Hindi; Indic Languages; Information Sciences; Library Science; Linguistics; Literature; Modern Languages; Persian; Philosophy; Psychology; Romance Languages; Sanskrit; Urdu); **Ayurvedic and Unani Medicine** (Ayurveda; Traditional Eastern Medicine); **Commerce and Business** (Business and Commerce; Finance); **Education** (Education); **Homeopathic Medicine**; **Interdisciplinary and Applied Sciences** (Biochemistry; Biology; Biophysics; Electronic Engineering; Environmental Studies; Genetics; Microbiology; Molecular Biology); **Law** (Law); **Management Studies** (Business Administration; Industrial Management; Management); **Mathematical Sciences** (Computer Science; Mathematics; Operations Research; Statistics); **Medical Sciences** (Medicine); **Music and Fine Arts** (Fine Arts; Music); **Science** (Anthropology; Astrophysics; Botany; Chemistry; Geology; Home Economics; Nursing; Pharmacy; Physics; Zoology); **Social Sciences** (Adult Education; African Studies; Continuing Education; East Asian Studies; Economics; Geography; History; Political Sciences; Social Work; Sociology); **Technology** (Technology)

Centre

Agro-Chemicals and Pest Management (Agricultural Management; Pest Management); **Bio-Medical Research** *(Bhim Rao Ambedkar)*

Further Information: Also 79 Affiliated/Constituent Colleges. Teaching Hospitals and campus of open learning

History: Founded 1922. Acquired present status and title 1952. The University has two campuses: Main Campus (North Campus), and the South Delhi Campus, founded 1973 as first step towards a multi-campus system for the University, with more than 600 postgraduate students.

Academic Year: July to March (July-September; October-December; January-March)

Admission Requirements: 12th year senior secondary/intermediate examination or recognized foreign equivalent

Fees: (Rupees): 3,500-7,500 per annum

Main Language(s) of Instruction: English, Hindi

Degrees and Diplomas: *Bachelor's Degree*: **Anthropology; Arabic; Automation and Control Engineering; Ayurveda; Biochemistry; Biological and Life Sciences; Biomedical Engineering; Biotechnology; Botany; Business and Commerce; Chemical Engineering; Chemistry; Civil Engineering; Computer Engineering; Computer Science; Dentistry; Economics; Educational Sciences; Electrical Engineering; English; Environmental Engineering; Finance; Fine Arts; Food Technology; French; Geography; Geology; German; Health Education; Hindi; History; Home Economics; Homeopathy; Indic Languages; Information Technology; Instrument Making; Italian; Journalism; Law; Library Science; Mass Communication; Mathematics; Mechanical Engineering; Medical Technology; Medicine; Microbiology; Modern Languages; Music; Nursing; Occupational Therapy; Persian; Pharmacy; Philosophy; Physical Education; Physical Therapy; Physics; Polymer and Plastics Technology; Primary Education; Psychology; Sanskrit; Social Work; Sociology; Spanish; Sports; Statistics; Surgery; Telecommunications Engineering; Traditional Eastern Medicine; Urdu; Vocational Education; Zoology.** *Postgraduate Diploma*: **Medicine.** *Master's Degree*: **Accountancy; Agriculture; Anaesthesiology; Anatomy; Anthropology; Applied Physics; Arabic; Asian Religious Studies; Biochemistry; Biology; Biomedical Engineering; Botany; Business Administration; Business and Commerce; Cardiology; Chemical Engineering; Chemistry; Communication Arts; Community Health; Comparative Law; Comparative Literature; Computer Engineering; Computer Science; Dermatology; Economics; Education; Electronic Engineering; English; Environmental Engineering; Environmental Studies; Finance; Fine Arts; Forensic Medicine and Dentistry; French; Gastroenterology; Genetics; Geography; Geology; German; Gynaecology and Obstetrics; Hindi; History; Home Economics; Human Resources; Hydraulic Engineering; Indic Languages; Information Sciences; Information Technology; International Business; Italian; Japanese; Law; Library Science; Mathematics; Measurement and Precision Engineering; Medicine; Microbiology; Microwaves; Modern Languages; Molecular Biology; Music; Neurological Therapy; Nursing; Operations Research; Ophthalmology; Orthopaedics; Otorhinolaryngology; Paediatrics; Pathology; Persian; Pharmacology; Pharmacy; Philosophy; Physical Education; Physics; Physiology; Plastic Surgery; Pneumology; Polymer and Plastics Technology; Power Engineering; Production Engineering; Psychology; Radiology; Russian; Sanskrit; Social Work; Sociology; Spanish; Statistics; Surgery; Thermal Engineering; Urdu; Zoology.** *Master of Philosophy*; *Doctor of Philosophy*. Also Diploma and Certificate courses

Student Services: Academic Counselling, Canteen, Careers Guidance, Cultural Activities, Facilities for disabled people, Health Services, Language Laboratory, Nursery Care, Social Counselling, Sports Facilities

Publications: Old Question Papers

Publishing House: Delhi University Press

Student Numbers *2012-2013*: Total 184,668

Last Updated: 05/03/13

UNIVERSITY OF GORAKHPUR

Deen Dayal Upadhyay Gorakhpur University

Gorakhpur, Uttar Pradesh 273009

Tel: +91(551) 234-0363 +91(551) 233-0767

Fax: +91(551) 234-0458

EMail: registrarddugu@gmail.com

Website: http://www.ddugu.edu.in

Vice-Chancellor: P. C. Trivedi EMail: vc@ddugu.edu.in

Registrar: Ram Charan Lal EMail: registrar@ddugu.edu.in

Faculty

Agriculture (Agriculture); **Arts** (Arts and Humanities); **Commerce** (Business and Commerce); **Education** (Education); **Law** (Law); **Science** (Computer Science; Electronic Engineering; Natural Sciences; Physics)

Further Information: Also 36 Affiliated Colleges

History: Founded 1957. Acquired present title 1997.

Academic Year: July to April

Main Language(s) of Instruction: Hindi, English

Degrees and Diplomas: *Post Diploma*; *Bachelor's Degree*; *Master's Degree*; *Doctor of Philosophy*

Student Services: Health Services, Sports Facilities

Last Updated: 11/07/11

UNIVERSITY OF GOUR BANGA

N.H-34 (NEAR RABINDRA BHABAN), P.O.Mokdumpur, Malda, West Bengal 732103

Tel: +91(3512) 223666

EMail: registrar@ugb.ac.in

Website: http://www.ugb.ac.in/

Vice-Chancellor: Gopalchandra Misra

Registrar: Syam Sundar Bairagya Tel: +91(3512) 223664

Programme

Arts and Humanities (Arabic; Education; English; History; Sanskrit); **Hospitality Management** (Hotel Management); **Mathematics** (Mathematics)

Degrees and Diplomas: *Bachelor's Degree*; *Master's Degree*
Last Updated: 05/01/12

UNIVERSITY OF HYDERABAD (UOHYD)

Prof. C.R. Rao Road, PO Central University, Gachibowli,
Hyderabad, Andhra Pradesh 500046
Tel: +91(40) 2313-2100
Fax: +91(40) 2301-0145, +91(40) 2301-1089
EMail: acadinfo@uohyd.ernet.in
Website: http://www.uohyd.ernet.in

Vice-Chancellor: Ramakrishna Ramaswamy (2011-)
Tel: +91(40) 2313-2000
EMail: vc@uohyd.ernet.in; r.ramaswamy@gmail.com

Director, International Affairs: Vinod Pavarala
Tel: +91(40) 2313-4041 EMail: international@uohyd.ernet.in

Registrar: Mohan Kumar
Tel: +91(40) 2301-0245 EMail: registrar@uohyd.ernet.in

School

Arts and Communication *(Sarojini Naidu)* (Dance; Fine Arts; Journalism; Mass Communication; Media Studies; Performing Arts; Radio and Television Broadcasting; Theatre); **Chemistry** (Chemistry; Inorganic Chemistry; Organic Chemistry; Physical Chemistry); **Engineering Science and Technology** (Engineering; Materials Engineering; Nanotechnology; Technology); **Humanities** (Applied Linguistics; Arts and Humanities; Comparative Literature; English; French; Hindi; Indic Languages; Native Language; Philosophy; Sanskrit; Translation and Interpretation; Urdu); **Life Sciences** (Biochemistry; Biological and Life Sciences; Botany; Environmental Management; Zoology); **Management Studies** (Business Administration; Finance; Human Resources; Information Technology; Management; Marketing; Operations Research); **Mathematics and Computer/Information Sciences** (Computer Education; Computer Science; Information Sciences; Mathematics; Mathematics and Computer Science; Statistics); **Medical Sciences** (Health Sciences; Medicine; Nutrition); **Physics** (Computer Science; Electronic Engineering; Physics); **Social Sciences** (Anthropology; Cultural Studies; Economics; Folklore; History; Human Rights; Political Sciences; Regional Studies; Social Problems; Social Sciences; Sociology)

Centre

Advanced Research in High Energy Materials (Energy Engineering; Materials Engineering); **Buddhist Studies** (Asian Religious Studies); **Cognitive Science** (Cognitive Sciences); **Earth and Space Sciences** (Astronomy and Space Science; Earth Sciences); **Health Psychology** (Psychology); **Integrated Studies**; **Modelling Simulation and Design** (Design); **Nanotechnology** (Nanotechnology); **Women's Studies**

Research Institute

Animal Biotechnology (Animal Husbandry; Biotechnology); **Health Science Education and Research Translation** (Health Education; Translation and Interpretation)

Further Information: A traditional and distance education institution.

History: Founded 1974 as a unitary and teaching University destined to develop as one of the outstanding Centres of higher learning in the country. The University is open to persons of either sex and of any race, creed, caste or class and offers postgraduate and research courses. A Central University.

Academic Year: July to April (July-November; January-April)

Admission Requirements: University degree at Bachelor's level

Fees: Please visit out website http://www.uohyd.ernet.in/index.php/admissions/prospectus

Main Language(s) of Instruction: English

Degrees and Diplomas: *Post Diploma*; *Master's Degree*; *Master of Philosophy*; *Doctor of Philosophy*. Also Integrated Master's Degree, 5 yrs (Sciences; Humanities; Social Sciences); MBA

Student Services: Canteen, Foreign Studies Centre, Health Services, Sports Facilities

Last Updated: 24/11/11

UNIVERSITY OF JAMMU

Baba Saheb Ambedkar Road, New Campus,
Jammu, Jammu and Kashmir 180006
Tel: +91(191) 243-1365 +91(191) 243-5248
Fax: +91(191) 243-1365
EMail: daa@jammuuniversity.in; isp_ju@jammuuniversity.in
Website: http://jammuuniversity.in

Vice-Chancellor: Mohan Paul Singh Ishar (2012-)
Tel: +91(191) 245-0014
EMail: mpsishar@gmail.com; mpsishar@jammuuniversity.in

Registrar: Naresh Padha
Tel: +91(191) 243-1365 EMail: nareshpadha@jammuuniversity.in

Faculty

Arts/Oriental Languages (Arts and Humanities; English; Hindi; Indic Languages; Oriental Languages; Sanskrit; Urdu); **Business Studies** (Business Administration; Business and Commerce; Management; Tourism); **Education** (Education; Physical Education); **Engineering** (Engineering); **Law** (Criminology; Human Rights; Law; Police Studies); **Life Sciences** (Biological and Life Sciences; Biotechnology; Botany; Environmental Studies; Microbiology; Zoology); **Mathematical Science** (Computer Science; Information Technology; Mathematics; Statistics); **Medicine** (Alternative Medicine; Ayurveda; Medicine; Physical Education); **Music and Fine Arts** (Fine Arts; Music); **Sciences** (Chemistry; Child Care and Development; Electronic Engineering; Family Studies; Geography; Geology; Home Economics; Natural Resources; Physics; Surveying and Mapping; Women's Studies); **Social Science** (Computer Science; Design; Economics; English; French; History; Information Sciences; Library Science; Management; Political Sciences; Psychology; Regional Studies; Social Sciences; Sociology; Urdu)

Institute

Human Genetics (Genetics)

Centre

Computer (Computer Science); **Cross-Cultural Research And Human Resource Management** *(International)* (Cultural Studies; Human Resources; Management); **Disaster Management** (Safety Engineering); **Dr. Ambedkar Studies** (Philosophy); **Field Operations and Research on Himalayan Glaciology** *(Regional - RCFOR-HG)* (Earth Sciences; Geology; Surveying and Mapping; Water Science); **History and Culture of Jammu and Ladakh Regions** *(Jammu and Ladakh)* (Cultural Studies; History); **Nehru Studies** (Social Sciences); **New Literatures** (Literature); **Peace and Conflict Studies** *(Gandhian)* (Peace and Disarmament); **Professional Studies in Urdu** (Urdu); **Quality Assurance** *(Directorate of Quality Assurance)* (Safety Engineering); **Studies in Museology** (Museum Studies); **University Science Instrumentation** (Measurement and Precision Engineering); **Yoga** (Yoga)

Further Information: Also 5 Constituent, 52 Affiliated Colleges, and 113 Recognized Colleges. A traditional and distance education institution.

History: Founded 1948 as University of Jammu and Kashmir. Became separate University 1969. A Central University.

Academic Year: February to December (February-June; July-November; August-December)

Admission Requirements: 12th year senior secondary/intermediate examination or recognized equivalent

Fees: 3,300-10,000 per annum (Indian Rupee)

Main Language(s) of Instruction: English, Classical or Modern Indian

Accrediting Agency: National Assessment and Accreditation Council (NAAC)

Degrees and Diplomas: *Post Diploma*; *Bachelor's Degree*; *Postgraduate Diploma*; *Master's Degree*; *Master of Philosophy*; *Doctor of Philosophy*. Also B.A./B.Sc./B.Com./BBA

Student Services: Academic Counselling, Canteen, Careers Guidance, Cultural Activities, Facilities for disabled people, Foreign Studies Centre, Health Services, Language Laboratory, Nursery Care, Social Counselling, Sports Facilities

Publications: Review Journal (Languages, Sciences, Social Sciences)
Last Updated: 24/11/11

UNIVERSITY OF KALYANI (KU)

Kalyani, West Bengal 741235
Tel: +91(33) 2582-2505
Fax: +91(33) 2582-8282
EMail: vckalyani@yahoo.com
Website: http://www.klyuniv.ac.in/

Vice-Chancellor: Alok Kumar Banerjee (2009-)
Tel: +91(94) 2582-8282
EMail: vckalyani@yahoo.com; vckalyani@klyuniv.ac.in

Registrar: Utpal Bhattacharya
Tel: +91(33) 2582-2505
EMail: klyuniv_rgs@yahoo.co.in; ubku2001@yahoo.com

Faculty

Arts and Commerce (Arts and Humanities; Business and Commerce; Chinese; Economics; English; Folklore; History; Indic Languages; Information Sciences; Library Science; Modern Languages; Political Sciences; Russian; Sociology); **Education** (Education; Physical Education); **Engineering, Technology and Management** (Business Administration; Computer Engineering; Computer Science; Development Studies; Engineering; Management; Rural Studies; Technology); **Science** (Biochemistry; Biological and Life Sciences; Biophysics; Biotechnology; Botany; Chemistry; Environmental Studies; Geography; Mathematics; Microbiology; Molecular Biology; Physics; Physiology; Statistics; Zoology)

Further Information: Also 37 Affiliated Colleges. A traditional and distance education institution.

History: Founded 1960.

Academic Year: June to May (June-October; November-January; February-May)

Admission Requirements: 12th year senior secondary/intermediate examination or recognized foreign equivalent

Fees: (Rupees): 168-600 per annum (regular fee); 1,200-20,000 per annum (enhanced fee)

Main Language(s) of Instruction: English

Accrediting Agency: National Assessment and Accreditation Council (NAAC)

Degrees and Diplomas: *Bachelor's Degree*; *Bachelor's Degree (professional)*; *Postgraduate Diploma*; *Master's Degree*; *Master of Philosophy*; *Doctor of Philosophy*. Also Certificate Courses; MBA

Student Services: Academic Counselling, Canteen, Careers Guidance, Cultural Activities, Health Services, Language Laboratory, Sports Facilities

Publications: Loke Darpan

Publishing House: University Press
Last Updated: 24/11/11

UNIVERSITY OF KASHMIR

University Campus, Hazratbal,
Srinagar, Jammu and Kashmir 190006
Tel: +91(194) 242-0333
Fax: +91(194) 242-5195
EMail: info@uok.edu.in
Website: http://www.uok.edu.in

Vice-Chancellor: Khurshid I. Andrabi
EMail: vcoffice@kashmiruniversity.net

Registrar: Musadiq A. Sahaf
EMail: registrar@kashmiruniversity.ac.in

Faculty

Applied Sciences and Technology (Computer Science; Electronic Engineering; Food Science; Food Technology; Home Economics; Instrument Making; Pharmacy); **Arts** (Arabic; Arts and Humanities; English; Hindi; Indic Languages; Information Sciences; Library Science; Modern Languages; Native Language; Persian; Sanskrit; Urdu); **Biological Sciences** (Biochemistry; Biological and Life Sciences; Biotechnology; Botany; Zoology); **Business and Management** (Business Administration; Finance; Management); **Dentistry** (Dentistry); **Education** (Education; Physical Education); **Engineering** (Engineering); **Law** (Law); **Medicine** (Medicine); **Music and Fine Arts** (Fine Arts; Music); **Oriental Learning** (Oriental Studies); **Physical and Material Science** (Environmental Studies; Geography; Geology; Geophysics; Mathematics; Physics; Regional Studies; Statistics); **Social Sciences** (Economics; History; Islamic Studies; Media Studies; Political Sciences; Psychology; Social Sciences; Social Work; Sociology)

Institute

Culture and Philosophy *(Allama Iqbal)* (Cultural Studies; Philosophy)

Centre

Central Asian Studies *(CCAS)* (Asian Studies); **Energy Studies** (Energy Engineering); **Hygiene and Environment** (Environmental Studies; Hygiene); **Information Technology and Support System** *(IT & SS)* (Information Sciences; Information Technology); **Internal Quality Assurance** *(DIQA)* (Safety Engineering); **Music and Fine Arts** (Fine Arts; Music); **Physical Education and Sports** (Physical Education; Sports)

Research Centre

Educational Multimedia (Educational Technology; Multimedia); **Population** (Demography and Population)

Further Information: 39 affiliated colleges; 5 constituent colleges; 8 oriental colleges; 69 private colleges. South and North Satellite campuses. Sheikl-ul-Allam Chair. A traditional and distance education institution.

History: Founded 1969, replacing University of Jammu and Kashmir established 1948. A Central University.

Academic Year: March to December

Admission Requirements: 12th year senior secondary/intermediate examination or recognized foreign equivalent

Fees: (Rupees): 1,790-8,750 per annum

Main Language(s) of Instruction: English

Accrediting Agency: National Assessment and Accreditation Council (NAAC)

Degrees and Diplomas: *Bachelor's Degree*; *Postgraduate Diploma*; *Master's Degree*; *Master of Philosophy*; *Doctor of Philosophy*

Student Services: Health Services

Publications: Anhaar; Communications (in English) & Tarseel (in Urdu); Human Behaviour - Journal of Applied Psychology; Insight Journal of Applied Research in Education; Journal of Himalayan Ecology and Sustainable Development; Journal of Research and Development; Kashmir University Law Review (KULR); Majallah Al-Dirasat Al-Arabia; Media Times; The Business Review; The Journal of Central Asian Studies; The Journal of Kashmir Studies; Trends in Information Management (TRIM); Vitasta
Last Updated: 25/11/11

UNIVERSITY OF KERALA

University Buildings, Thiruvananthapuram, Kerala 695034
Tel: +91(471) 2305738 +91(471) 2305994
Fax: +91(471) 2307158
EMail: ku.release@gmail.com
Website: http://www.keralauniversity.edu

Vice-Chancellor: A. Jayakrishnan
Tel: +91(471) 230-6634 EMail: vc@keralauniversity.edu

Registrar: K. S. Chandrasekar
Tel: +91(471) 2305631 EMail: regrku@gmail.com

Faculty

Applied Sciences (Biotechnology; Computer Science; Electronic Engineering; Environmental Studies; Futurology; Optical Technology); **Arts** (Arts and Humanities; Communication Arts; English; German; Information Sciences; Journalism; Library Science; Philosophy; Russian); **Ayurvedic Medicine** (Ayurveda); **Commerce** (Business and Commerce); **Dentistry** (Dentistry); **Education** (Education); **Engineering and Technology** (Engineering; Technology); **Fine Arts** (Fine Arts; Music); **Homeopathy** (Homeopathy); **Law** (Law); **Management Studies** (Management); **Medicine** (Medicine; Nursing; Pharmacy); **Oriental Studies** (Arabic; Indic Languages; Linguistics; Oriental Languages; Oriental Studies; Sanskrit); **Physical Education** (Physical Education); **Science**

(Aquaculture; Biochemistry; Botany; Chemistry; Demography and Population; Fishery; Geography; Geology; Mathematics; Natural Sciences; Physics; Statistics; Zoology); **Social Sciences** (Archaeology; Economics; History; Islamic Studies; Political Sciences; Psychology; Social Sciences; Sociology)

Centre

Adult Continuing Education *(CACEE)*; **Arthropod Bio Resources and Biotechnology** (Biotechnology; Natural Resources); **Australian Studies** (Regional Studies); **Bioinformatics** (Biology; Computer Science); **Canadian Studies** (Canadian Studies; Literature); **Christian Studies for Cultural and Social Change** (Christian Religious Studies; Development Studies); **Convergence Media Studies** (Media Studies); **English Language Teaching** (Foreign Languages Education); **Enterpreneurship Development Cell** (Management); **Geo-Information Science and Technology** (Information Sciences; Information Technology); **Geomatics and Earth System Management** (Earth Sciences); **Ghandian Studies** (Philosophy); **International Relations** *(V.K. Krishna Menon)* (International Relations); **Kerala Studies** *(International - ICKS)* (Cultural Studies); **Management Education and Enterpreneurship Development** *(C-MEE)* (Management); **Marine Diversity** (Marine Biology); **Nanoscience and Nanotechnology** (Nanotechnology); **Performing and Visual Arts** (Performing Arts; Visual Arts); **Quantitative Analysis** (Mathematics); **Rural Studies** (Rural Studies); **Social Change** *(Sree Narayana)* (Social Studies); **Survey Research** (Operations Research); **Systems and Synthetic Biology** *(CSSB)* (Biology); **Technology and Resource for Malayalam** (Native Language); **Trivandrum Astronomical Observatory** (Astronomy and Space Science); **UGC Nehru Study** (Political Sciences); **Vedanta Studies** (Philosophy); **Women's Studies** (Women's Studies)

Research Centre

Population (Demography and Population); **Study on the Cost of Cultivation of Principal Crops in Kerala** *(Kariavattom)* (Agricultural Economics)

Chair

Dr B R Ambedkar (Human Rights; Social Sciences); **Parliamentary Affairs** *(V.K. Sukumaran Nayar)* (Government; Political Sciences)

Further Information: Also 187 Affiliated Colleges, 45 University Departments, and other Departments and Centres. A traditional and Distance Education.

History: Founded 1937 as University of Travancore. Acquired present title and status 1957. A Cetral University.

Academic Year: June to March

Admission Requirements: 12th year senior secondary/intermediate examination or recognized foreign equivalent

Fees: (Indian Rupees): Undergraduate programmes, 4,750-6,000 (except B. Ed. Course, 18,000); Postgraduate programmes, 270-1,000 per annum (except M.Tech., 3,340 per annum and MBA, 9,070 per annum)

Main Language(s) of Instruction: English

Accrediting Agency: National Assessment and Accreditation Council (NAAC)

Degrees and Diplomas: *Post Diploma*; *Bachelor's Degree*; *Bachelor's Degree (professional)*; *Postgraduate Diploma*; *Master's Degree*; *Master of Philosophy*; *Doctor of Philosophy*. Also MBA

Student Services: Canteen, Careers Guidance, Health Services, Sports Facilities

Publications: Bhasha Sahithi; Indian Unity Problems and Prospectus; Indo-German Journal; Janasankhya; Journal of Aquatic Biology and Fisheries; Journal of Indian History and Kerala Studies; Journal of Manuscript Studies; Kalari; Kerala Journal of Legal Studies; Kerala Journal of Social Sciences; Pracina Kairali

Publishing House: University Press

Last Updated: 25/11/11

UNIVERSITY OF KOTA (UOK)

Saraswati Bhawan, Near Kabir Circle, Swami Vivekanand Nagar, Kota, Rajasthan 324 010

EMail: info@uok.ac.in

Website: http://www.uok.ac.in/

Vice-Chancellor: Madhu Sudan Sharma Tel: +91(744) 247-2911

Registrar: Ram Niwas Tel: +91(744) 247-2934

Faculty

Arts (Arts and Humanities; Biological and Life Sciences); **Commerce and Management** (Business and Commerce; Finance; Management); **Education** (Physical Education); **Law** (Law); **Science** (Applied Chemistry; Applied Physics; Chemistry; Computer Science; Energy Engineering; Industrial Chemistry; Physics); **Social Sciences** (Geography; Heritage Preservation; History; Museum Management; Political Sciences; Social Sciences; Sociology; Surveying and Mapping; Tourism)

Further Information: 148 Affiliated Colleges

History: Founded 2003.

Degrees and Diplomas: *Bachelor's Degree*; *Bachelor's Degree (professional)*; *Master's Degree*; *Master of Philosophy*. Also MBA

Last Updated: 05/01/12

UNIVERSITY OF LUCKNOW

Badshahbagh, Lucknow, Uttar Pradesh 226 007

Tel: +91(522) 2740086

Fax: +91(522) 274-0412 +91(522) 385-592

EMail: info@lkouniv.ac.in

Website: http://www.lkouniv.ac.in

Vice-Chancellor: Manoj K. Mishra
Tel: +91(522) 2740467 EMail: vc@lkouniv.ac.in

Registrar (Acting): G. P. Tripathi
Tel: +91(522) 2740412 EMail: registrar@lkouniv.ac.in

Faculty

Arts (Ancient Civilizations; Anthropology; Arabic; Archaeology; Arts and Humanities; Economics; English; Esoteric Practices; European Languages; Geography; Hindi; History; Home Economics; Information Sciences; Journalism; Library Science; Linguistics; Mass Communication; Medieval Studies; Modern History; Modern Languages; Persian; Philosophy; Political Sciences; Protective Services; Psychology; Public Administration; Sanskrit; Social Work; Sociology; Urdu); **Ayurveda** (Anatomy; Ayurveda; Gynaecology and Obstetrics; Music; Paediatrics; Surgery); **Commerce** (Business Administration; Business and Commerce; Economics); **Education** (Education); **Fine Arts** (Fine Arts; Painting and Drawing; Photography; Sculpture; Visual Arts); **Law** (Law); **Mass Communication in Science and Technology** (Mass Communication); **Science** (Anthropology; Astronomy and Space Science; Biochemistry; Botany; Chemistry; Computer Science; Geology; Mathematics; Physics; Statistics; Zoology)

Institute

Development Studies (Development Studies); **Management Sciences** (Management); **Minorities Coaching** (Psychology); **Tourism Studies** (Tourism); **Women's Studies** (Women's Studies)

Centre

Sanskriti (Cultural Studies; Sanskrit)

Research Centre

Population (Demography and Population); **Urban and Environmental Studies** (Environmental Studies; Urban Studies)

Further Information: Also 5 Constituent and 20 Associated Colleges, and 5 Recognized Institutions

History: Founded 1921.

Academic Year: January to December (January-June; July-December).

Admission Requirements: 12th year senior secondary/intermediate examination or recognized foreign equivalent

Fees: (Rupees): 180-240 per annum

Main Language(s) of Instruction: English, Hindi

Degrees and Diplomas: *Post Diploma*; *Bachelor's Degree*; *Postgraduate Diploma*; *Master's Degree*; *Master of Philosophy*. Also Advance Diploma and MBA

Last Updated: 25/11/11

UNIVERSITY OF MADRAS (UNOM)

Chepauk, Triplicane (P.O.), Chennai, Tamil Nadu 600005

Tel: +91(44) 2536-8778

Fax: +91(44) 2536-6693 +91(44) 2536-7654

EMail: regmu@unimad.ernet.in

Website: http://www.unom.ac.in

Vice-Chancellor: R. Thandavan EMail: vcoffice@unom.ac.in

Registrar: Anne Mary Fernandez EMail: registrar@unom.ac.in

School

Basic Medical Science *(Taramani campus)* (Anatomy; Biochemistry; Endocrinology; Genetics; Pathology; Pharmacology; Physiology; Toxicology); **Business and Management** *(Chepauk campus)* (Business Administration; Management); **Chemical Sciences** *(Guindy campus)* (Chemistry); **Earth and Atmospheric Science** *(Chepauk campus)* (Earth Sciences; Meteorology); **Earth and Atmospheric Science** *(Guindy campus)* (Earth Sciences; Meteorology); **Economics** *(Chepauk campus)* (Econometrics; Economics); **English and Foreign Language** *(Chepauk campus)* (English; Modern Languages); **Fine and Performing Arts** *(Chepauk campus)* (Fine Arts; Performing Arts); **Historical Studies** *(Chepauk campus)* (History); **Information and Communication Studies** *(Chepauk campus)* (Communication Studies; Information Sciences; Mass Communication); **Life Sciences** *(Guindy campus)* (Biochemistry; Biotechnology; Botany; Zoology); **Mathematics, Statistics and Computer Science** *(Chepauk campus)* (Computer Science; Mathematics; Statistics); **Nanoscience and Photonics** *(Taramani campus)* (Nanotechnology; Physics); **Philosophy and Religious Thought** *(Chepauk campus)* (Philosophy; Religious Studies); **Physical Sciences** *(Guindy campus)* (Biophysics; Crystallography; Nuclear Physics; Physics); **Political and International Studies** *(Chepauk campus)* (Law; Military Science; Political Sciences; Public Administration; South and Southeast Asian Languages); **Sanskrit and other Indian Languages** *(Marina campus)* (Arabic; Hindi; Persian; Sanskrit; Urdu); **Social Sciences** *(Chepauk campus)* (Adult Education; Anthropology; Continuing Education; Criminology; Education; Psychology; Sociology); **Tamil and other Dravidian Languages** *(Marina campus)* (Indic Languages)

Further Information: Also 123 Affiliated and Approved Colleges and 45 Recognized Institutions. campuses in Chepauk, Marina, Guindy and Taramani.

History: Founded 1857. Campuses in Chepauk, Guindy, Marina and Taramani.

Academic Year: June to April

Admission Requirements: undergraduate programmes, 12 years of school education (senior secondary grade or higher secondary level); postgraduate programmes, completion of undergraduate programmes

Fees: (Rupees): 4,000-60,000 per annum

Main Language(s) of Instruction: English, Tamil

Accrediting Agency: National Assessment and Accreditation Council (NAAC)

Degrees and Diplomas: *Bachelor's Degree*; *Bachelor's Degree (professional)*; *Postgraduate Diploma*; *Master's Degree*; *Master of Philosophy*; *Doctor of Philosophy*. Also Certificate courses

Student Services: Sports Facilities

Publications: Annals of Oriental Research; Madras University Journal

Academic Staff *2010-2011*: Total: c. 300

Student Numbers *2010-2011*: Total: c. 8,000

Last Updated: 26/03/13

UNIVERSITY OF MUMBAI

Mahatma Gandhi Road, Fort Mumbai,
Mumbai, Maharashtra 400032
Tel: +91(22) 2265-6789
Fax: +91(22) 2267-3579
Website: http://www.mu.ac.in

Vice-Chancellor: Rajan Welukar (2010-) EMail: vc@fort.mu.ac.in

Registrar: Jayant P. Dighe
Tel: +91(22) 2265-6953 EMail: registrar@fort.mu.ac.in

International Relations: Anil K. Patil Tel: +91(22) 2204-6959

Faculty

Arts and Humanities (Arts and Humanities; Education; Library Science; Linguistics; Management; Modern Languages; Social Sciences); **Ayurvedic Medicine** (Ayurveda); **Commerce** (Business and Commerce); **Engineering and Technology** (Engineering; Technology); **Fine Arts** (Fine Arts); **Law** (Law); **Science** (Natural Sciences)

College

Architecture (Architecture)

Institute

Career Education and Development *(Garware)* (Development Studies; Education); **Financial and Management Studies** *(Alkesh Dinesh Mody)* (Finance; Management)

Centre

Advanced Study in Applied Chemistry (Applied Chemistry; Polymer and Plastics Technology; Textile Technology); **Advanced Study in Economics** (Finance; Industrial and Production Economics); **Advanced Study in Mathematics** (Mathematics); **African Studies** (African Studies); **Central Eurasian Studies** (Eurasian and North Asian Languages)

Further Information: Also 399 Constituent Colleges, and 90 recognized institutes. A traditional, distance and open learning institution.

History: Founded 1857, but until the passing of the Indian Universities Act of 1904 its function was limited to examining candidates and arranging for the courses of study which led to degrees. Acquired right to organize teaching, arrange for University extension lectures, and publish such works as necessary for the direct educational work it was to carry out 1904. Postgraduate instruction and research introduced 1928. Reconstituted 1953.

Academic Year: June to April (June-October; November-April)

Admission Requirements: 12th year senior secondary/intermediate examination or recognized foreign equivalent

Fees: (Rupees): 390-15,000 per annum

Main Language(s) of Instruction: English, Hindi, Marathi

Accrediting Agency: National Assessment and Accreditation Council (NAAC)

Degrees and Diplomas: *Post Diploma*; *Bachelor's Degree*; *Postgraduate Diploma*; *Doctor of Philosophy*. Also Certificate courses

Student Services: Academic Counselling, Canteen, Careers Guidance, Cultural Activities, Facilities for disabled people, Foreign Studies Centre, Health Services, Language Laboratory, Social Counselling, Sports Facilities

Publishing house: University Press

Last Updated: 28/11/11

UNIVERSITY OF MUSIC AND FINE ARTS

Indira Kala Sangit Vishwavidyalaya
Khairagarh District, Rajnandgaon, Chhattisgarh 491881
Tel: +91(7820) 234-534 +91(7820) 234-232
Fax: +91(7820) 234-108
EMail: reg@iksvv.com
Website: http://www.iksvv.com

Vice-Chancellor: Mandavi Singh EMail: vc@iksvv.com

Registrar: Shri P.S. Dhruv Tel: +91(7820) 234-232

Faculty

Arts (English; Hindi; Sanskrit; South Asian Studies; Theatre); **Dance** (Dance); **Folk Music and Arts** (Dance; Folklore; Music); **Music** (Music; Musical Instruments; Musicology; Singing); **Visual Arts** (Fine Arts; Graphic Arts; Painting and Drawing; Sculpture)

Further Information: Also 44 affiliated colleges and 34 recognized centers

History: Founded 1956. The aim of the University is to provide instruction in all branches of Music and Fine Arts and to make provision for Research, the advancement of studies and the dissemination of knowledge in these subjects.

Academic Year: July to april

Admission Requirements: 12th year senior secondary/intermediate examination or recognized foreign equivalent

Accrediting Agency: NAAC

Degrees and Diplomas: *Post Diploma*: **English; Multimedia; Music; Sanskrit; Visual Arts.** *Bachelor's Degree*: **Dance; Fine Arts; Multimedia; Music; Visual Arts.** *Postgraduate Diploma*: **Museum Studies.** *Master's Degree*: **Art History; Cultural Studies; Fine Arts; Graphic Design; Jazz and Popular Music; Musical Instruments; Musicology; Sculpture; Theatre.** *Master of Philosophy*: **Dance; Musical Instruments; Singing.** *Doctor of*

Philosophy: **Dance; Fine Arts; Jazz and Popular Music; Music; Visual Arts.**

Publications: Kala Saurabh; Kala Vaibhav

Last Updated: 18/11/11

UNIVERSITY OF MYSORE

Vishwavidyalaya Karyasoudha, Crawford Hall,
Mysore, Karnataka 570005
Tel: +91(821) 241-9361
Fax: +91(821) 242-1263
Website: http://www.uni-mysore.ac.in

Vice-Chancellor: K.S. Rangappa
Tel: +91(821) 241-9611 EMail: vc@uni-mysore.ac.in

Registrar: P.S. Naik
Tel: +91(821) 241-9361 EMail: registrar@uni-mysore.ac.in

College

Academic Staff (Distance Education; Educational and Student Counselling; Teacher Training)

School

Design (Design); **Foreign Languages** (French; German; Modern Languages; Russian; Translation and Interpretation); **Information Management** *(International - ISIM)* (Information Management)

Department

Ancient History and Archaeology (Ancient Civilizations; Archaeology); **Anthropology** (Anthropology); **Applied Botany and Biotechnology** (Biotechnology; Botany); **Biochemistry** (Biochemistry); **Botany** (Botany); **Chemistry** (Chemistry); **Christianity** (Christian Religious Studies); **Commerce** (Business and Commerce); **Communication and Journalism** (Journalism; Mass Communication); **Computer Science** (Computer Science); **Economics and Cooperation** (Economics); **Education** (Education); **English** (English); **Environmental Science** (Environmental Studies); **Food Science and Nutrition** (Food Science; Nutrition); **Geography** (Geography); **Geology** (Geology); **Hindi** (Hindi); **History** (History); **Jainology and Prakit** (Ancient Languages); **Law** (Commercial Law; Constitutional Law; International Law; Law); **Library and Information Science** (Information Sciences; Library Science); **Mathematics** (Mathematics); **Microbiology** (Mathematics); **Philosophy** (Philosophy); **Physical Education** (Physical Education); **Physics** (Physics); **Political Sciences** (Political Sciences); **Psychology** (Psychology); **Sanskrit** (Sanskrit); **Sericulture Science** (Sericulture); **Social Work** (Social Work); **Sociology** (Sociology); **Statistics** (Statistics); **Urdu** (Urdu); **Zoology** (Zoology)

Institute

Development Studies (Development Studies); **Kannada Studies** *(Kuvempu)* (Asian Studies); **Management Science** *(B.N.Bahadur)* (Management); **Oriental Research** (Oriental Studies)

Centre

Information Science and Technology (Information Management; Information Sciences; Information Technology; Software Engineering); **Study of Social Exclusion and Inclusive Policy** (Social Policy; Social Problems; Social Work); **Women's Studies** (Women's Studies)

Research Centre

Ambedkar; **Educational Multimedia** (Educational Technology; Multimedia); **Third Sector** (Management)

Further Information: Also 5 Constituent Colleges and 122 Affiliated Colleges. Postgraduate campuses in Manasagangotri, Hemagangotri and Sri Lanka.

History: Founded 1916.

Academic Year: July to April

Admission Requirements: 12th year senior secondary/intermediate examination or equivalent

Fees: 762 (Indian Rupee)

Main Language(s) of Instruction: English, Kannada

Degrees and Diplomas: *Post Diploma*; *Bachelor's Degree*; *Postgraduate Diploma*; *Master's Degree*; *Master of Philosophy*; *Doctor of Philosophy*. Also Advanced Diploma; Certificate courses; MBA

Last Updated: 26/03/13

UNIVERSITY OF NORTH BENGAL

PO North Bengal University, Darjeeling District,
Raja Rammohunpur, West Bengal 734430
Tel: +91(353) 269-9099
Fax: +91(353) 269-9001 +91(353) 258-1212
EMail: regnbu@sancharnet.in
Website: http://www.nbu.ac.in

Vice-Chancellor: Arunabha Basumajumdar (2008-)
Tel: +91(353) 277-6366
EMail: nbuvc@nbu.ac.in; a_basumajumdar@vsnl.net

Registrar: Dilip Kumar Sarkar
Tel: +91(353) 277-6331 EMail: regnbu@sancharnet.in

Faculty

Arts, Commerce and Law (Arts and Humanities; Business Administration; Business and Commerce; Economics; English; Environmental Studies; French; Hindi; History; Indic Languages; Information Sciences; Law; Library Science; Management; Mass Communication; Philosophy; Political Sciences; Sociology; Video); **Science** (Anthropology; Biological and Life Sciences; Biotechnology; Botany; Chemistry; Computer Science; Geography; Information Technology; Mathematics; Microbiology; Natural Sciences; Physics; Safety Engineering; Surveying and Mapping; Zoology); **Technology** (Technology)

Further Information: Also 8 Constituent and 87 Affiliated Colleges

History: Founded 1962.

Admission Requirements: 12th year senior secondary/intermediate examination or recognized foreign equivalent

Main Language(s) of Instruction: English

Accrediting Agency: National Assessment and Accreditation Council (NAAC)

Degrees and Diplomas: *Bachelor's Degree*; *Master's Degree*; *Master of Philosophy*; *Doctor of Philosophy*. Also MBA

Last Updated: 28/11/11

UNIVERSITY OF PATANJALI

Mahrish Dayanad Gram, Delhi Haridwar National Highway, Near Bahadrabad Haridwar, Haridwar, Uttarakhand 249 402
Tel: +91(1334) 242-526
EMail: admin@patanjaliuniversity.com
Website: http://patanjaliuniversity.com/

Vice-Chancellor: Acharya Balkrishana
Tel: +91(1334) 244-107 EMail: acharyaji@dicyayoga.com

Registrar: Ram Kumar Sharma
Tel: +91(1334) 242-526 EMail: uopyp2009@gmail.com

Area

Commerce (Business and Commerce); **Computer Science** (Computer Science); **Information Technology** (Information Technology); **Medical Sciences** (Acupuncture; Ayurveda; Medicine; Physical Therapy); **Natural Sciences** (Botany; Chemistry; Mathematics; Natural Sciences; Physics; Zoology); **Pharmacology** (Pharmacology); **Social Sciences** (Civics; Geography; History; Political Sciences; Social Sciences); **Yoga** (Yoga)

History: Founded 2006.

Degrees and Diplomas: *Post Diploma*; *Bachelor's Degree*; *Master's Degree*; *Doctor of Philosophy*. Also Certificate

Student Services: Canteen, Health Services

Student Numbers *2010-2011*: Total: c. 5,000

Last Updated: 02/01/12

UNIVERSITY OF PETROLEUM AND ENERGY STUDIES (UPES)

Bidholi Campus Office Energy Acres, P.O. Bidholi Via-Prem Nagar, Dehradun, Uttarakhand 248007
Tel: +91(135) 277-6201 +91(135) 277-6061
Fax: +91(135) 277-6090
EMail: enrollments@upes.ac.in
Website: http://www.upes.ac.in

Vice-Chancellor: Honwad Shrihari
EMail: vc@upes.ac.in; SHRIHARI@DDN.UPES.AC.IN

College

Engineering Studies (Aeronautical and Aerospace Engineering; Artificial Intelligence; Automotive Engineering; Business Computing; Chemical Engineering; Computer Engineering; Electronic Engineering; Engineering; Fire Science; Geological Engineering; Information Management; Information Technology; Materials Engineering; Mechanical Engineering; Petroleum and Gas Engineering; Power Engineering; Safety Engineering; Telecommunications Engineering); **Legal Studies** *(CoLS)* (Computer Science; Law); **Management Studies** *(CoMES)* (Air Transport; Business Administration; Economics; Energy Engineering; Information Technology; International Business; Management; Marine Transport; Petroleum and Gas Engineering; Power Engineering; Retailing and Wholesaling; Transport Management)

Further Information: Also Overseas Office in Canada.

History: Created 2003.

Accrediting Agency: National Assessment and Accreditation Council (NAAC); Distance Education Council; University Grants Commission (UGC)

Degrees and Diplomas: *Bachelor's Degree*; *Bachelor's Degree (professional)*; *Master's Degree*; *Doctor of Philosophy*. Also Integrated BBA - LL. B., 5 years; MBA and Executive MBA

Last Updated: 28/11/11

UNIVERSITY OF RAJASTHAN

JLN Marg, Jaipur, Rajasthan 302055
Tel: +91(141) 270-8824
Fax: +91(141) 271-1799
EMail: info@uniraj.ernet.in

Vice-Chancellor: B.L. Sharma EMail: vc@uniraj.ernet.in

Registrar: Nishkam Divakar Tel: +91(141) 270-6813

Faculty

Arts (Ancient Languages; Arts and Humanities; Cultural Studies; English; European Languages; Hindi; Journalism; Literature; Mass Communication; Philosophy; Sanskrit); **Commerce** (Accountancy; Business Administration; Business and Commerce; Economics; Finance; Management; Statistics); **Education** (Education; Library Science; Physical Education); **Engineering and Technology** (Engineering; Technology); **Fine Arts** (Fine Arts; Music; Painting and Drawing; Theatre); **Law** (Law); **Management** (Management); **Science** (Botany; Chemical Engineering; Computer Science; Energy Engineering; Geography; Geology; Home Economics; Information Technology; Mathematics; Natural Sciences; Physics; Psychology; Science Education; Statistics; Zoology); **Social Science** (Anthropology; Economics; Political Sciences; Public Administration; Social Sciences; Sociology; Women's Studies)

Further Information: Also 7 Constituent Colleges and 866 Affiliated Colleges spanning 7 districts.

History: Founded 1947.

Academic Year: July to May (July-January; January-May)

Admission Requirements: 12th year senior secondary/intermediate examination or recognized foreign equivalent

Fees: (Rupees): 100-2,000 per annum

Main Language(s) of Instruction: English, Hindi

Degrees and Diplomas: *Bachelor's Degree*; *Postgraduate Diploma*; *Master's Degree*; *Master of Philosophy*; *Doctor of Philosophy*. Also Certificate courses; Honours Bachelor's degree; Add-On Vocational programmes; MBA

Publications: University Studies and Extension Lectures

Publishing House: Rajasthan University Press

Last Updated: 28/11/11

UNIVERSITY OF SCIENCE AND TECHNOLOGY, MEGHALAYA (USTM)

Techno City, Killing Road, 9th mile, Ri-Bhoi, Meghalaya 793 101
EMail: ustm_erdf@rediffmail.com
Website: http://www.ustm.ac.in

Programme

Technology (Technology)

History: Founded 2008.

Last Updated: 01/09/11

UNIVERSITY OF TECHNOLOGY AND MANAGEMENT

Bijni Complex (Old NEHU Campus), Laitumkhrah, Shillong, Meghalaya 793 003
Tel: +91(364) 2500969
EMail: enrollements@utm.ac.in
Website: http://www.utm.ac.in/

Vice-Chancellor: S.J. Chopra

Registrar: Deepa Verma

School

Applied Sciences (Biological and Life Sciences; Biotechnology); **Design** (Design); **Media and Communication** (Journalism; Mass Communication; Media Studies); **Retail and Fashion** (Fashion Design; Retailing and Wholesaling); **Technology** (Computer Science; Electronic Engineering; Technology; Telecommunications Engineering); **Travel and Leisure** (Leisure Studies; Management; Sports Management; Tourism)

Degrees and Diplomas: *Bachelor's Degree*; *Postgraduate Diploma*; *Master's Degree*

Last Updated: 17/01/12

UNIVERSITY OF TECHNOLOGY OF MADHYA PRADESH

Rajiv Gandhi Proudyogiki Vishwavidyalaya (RGPV)

Gandhi Nagar, Bhopal, Madhya Pradesh 462036
Tel: +91(755) 2678-833
Fax: +91(755) 274-2002
EMail: rgtu@rgtu.net; egov@rgtu.net
Website: http://rgpv.ac.in/

Vice-Chancellor: Piyush Trivedi (2008-) Tel: +91(755) 267-8801

Registrar: A.K.S. Bhadoria
Tel: +91(755) 267-8899 EMail: registrar@rgtu.net

School

Biotechnology (Biotechnology); **Energy Technology** (Energy Engineering; Environmental Management); **Information Technology** (Computer Engineering; Computer Graphics; Data Processing; Information Technology; Software Engineering); **Nanotechnology** (Nanotechnology); **Pharmaceutical Science** (Pharmacy; Safety Engineering)

Institute

Technology *(UIT-RGPV)* (Civil Engineering; Computer Engineering; Computer Science; Construction Engineering; Electrical and Electronic Engineering; Electronic Engineering; Industrial Engineering; Information Technology; Mechanical Engineering; Power Engineering; Production Engineering; Telecommunications Engineering)

Further Information: Also 200 affiliated Engineering Colleges, 98 Pharmacy Colleges, 95 MCA Colleges, 4 Architecture Colleges and 85 Polytechnic institutions.

History: Founded 1998.

Degrees and Diplomas: *Bachelor's Degree (professional)*; *Master's Degree*; *Doctor of Philosophy*

Student Services: Canteen

Last Updated: 19/07/11

UTKAL UNIVERSITY

PO Vani Vihar, Bhubaneswar, Orissa 751004
Tel: +91(674) 258-1387
Fax: +91(674) 258-1850
EMail: vc@utkal-university.org
Website: http://www.utkal-university.org

Vice-Chancellor: Prasant Kumar Sahoo

Registrar: Gobinda Chandra Pradhan

College

Law (Law)

Department

Analytical and Applied Economics (Economics); **Ancient Indian History, Culture and Archaeology** (Ancient Civilizations; Archaeology; Cultural Studies; History); **Anthropology** (Anthropology);

Biotechnology (Biotechnology); **Botany** (Botany); **Business Administration** (Business Administration); **Chemistry** (Chemistry); **Commerce** (Business and Commerce); **Computer Science and Applications** (Computer Science); **English** (English); **Geography** (Geography); **Geology** (Geology); **History** (History); **Law** (Law); **Library and Information Science** (Information Sciences; Library Science); **Mathematics** (Mathematics); **Oriya** (Indic Languages); **Personnel Management and Industrial Relations** (Human Resources; Labour and Industrial Relations); **Philosophy** (Philosophy); **Physics** (Physics); **Political Science** (Political Sciences); **Psychology** (Psychology); **Public Administration** (Public Administration); **Sanskrit** (Sanskrit); **Sociology** (Sociology); **Statistics** (Statistics); **Zoology** (Zoology)

Further Information: Also 267 affiliated Colleges (219 Degree Colleges, 44 Professional College, 3 Other Constituent Colleges). A traditional, distance and continuing education institution.

History: Founded 1943.

Academic Year: June to May (June-December; January-May)

Admission Requirements: 12th year senior secondary/intermediate examination or recognized foreign equivalent

Fees: (Rupees): 108-360 per annum

Main Language(s) of Instruction: English

Degrees and Diplomas: *Post Diploma*; *Bachelor's Degree*; *Postgraduate Diploma*; *Master's Degree*; *Master of Philosophy*; *Doctor of Philosophy*. Also MBA

Publications: Prachi Publication

Publishing House: M.S.R.C. Utkal University Press, Vani Vihar, Bhubaneswar

Student Numbers *2010-2011*: Total: c. 3,000

Last Updated: 29/11/11

UTKAL UNIVERSITY OF CULTURE

Utkal Sanskruti Viswavidyalaya

Sardar Patel Hall Complex, Unit-II, Bhubaneswar, Orissa 751009
Tel: +91(674) 253-5484
Fax: +91(674) 253-5486
EMail: mail@uuc.ac.in
Website: http://www.uuc.ac.in/

Vice-Chancellor: Amiya Kumar Pattanayak
EMail: vice.chancellor@utkaluniversityculture.org

Registrar: Sachindra Raul

Faculty

Architecture and Archaeology (Archaeology; Architecture; Heritage Preservation); **Cultural Studies** (Asian Religious Studies; Classical Languages; Cultural Studies; Hotel and Restaurant; Sanskrit; Tourism); **Language and Literature** (Linguistics; Literature; Modern Languages; South and Southeast Asian Languages); **Orissan Studies** (Cultural Studies; South Asian Studies; Southeast Asian Studies); **Performing Arts** (Acting; Dance; Musical Instruments; Performing Arts; Singing; Theatre); **Visual Arts** (Art History; Design; Fine Arts; Painting and Drawing; Sculpture; Visual Arts)

Further Information: Also 12 affiliated colleges

History: Founded 1999.

Academic Year: June to May

Admission Requirements: 12th year senior secondary/intermediate examination or recognized foreign equivalent. University degree for Postgraduate programme.

Fees: (Rupees): Tourism and Hospitality, 20,000 per annum; Heritage and Conservation Technology, 3,050; others, 2,040

Main Language(s) of Instruction: English, Oriya, Hindi

Accrediting Agency: University Grants Commission (UGC), Association of Indian Universities (AIU), American Institute of Indian Studies

Degrees and Diplomas: *Postgraduate Diploma*; *Master's Degree*. Also Certificate courses.

Student Services: Academic Counselling, Canteen, Cultural Activities, Facilities for disabled people, Language Laboratory, Social Counselling, Sports Facilities

Publications: Sanskruti

Last Updated: 29/11/11

UTTAR PRADESH RAJARSHI TANDON OPEN UNIVERSITY (UPRTOU)

17 Maharshi Dayanand Marg, (Thornhill Road), Allahabad, Uttar Pradesh 211001
Tel: +91(532) 242-1284 +91(532) 262-3250 +91(532) 329-5300
Fax: +91(532) 262-3250
EMail: uprtou@yahoo.co.in
Website: http://www.uprtou.ac.in/

Vice-Chancellor: A. K. Bakhshi
Tel: +91(532) 242-1283; +91(532) 242-1624
EMail: vcuprtou@yahoo.co.in

Registrar: A. K. Singh

School

Agricultural Sciences (Agriculture; Animal Husbandry; Dairy; Environmental Studies; Farm Management; Fruit Production; Harvest Technology; Vegetable Production); **Computer and Information Sciences** (Computer Engineering; Computer Science; Information Sciences); **Education** (Distance Education; Education; Educational Administration; Environmental Studies; Law; Special Education; Vocational Counselling); **Health Sciences** (Child Care and Development; Community Health; Diabetology; Environmental Studies; Health Education; Health Sciences; Nutrition); **Humanities** (Arts and Humanities; Economics; English; Environmental Studies; Hindi; Information Sciences; Journalism; Library Science; Mass Communication; Native Language; Philosophy; Rural Studies; Sanskrit; Translation and Interpretation; Urdu; Writing); **Management Studies** (Business Administration; Business and Commerce; E- Business/Commerce; Environmental Studies; Finance; Human Resources; Industrial Management; Management; Marketing); **Science** (Biochemistry; Botany; Chemistry; Computer Science; Mathematics; Natural Sciences; Physics; Statistics; Zoology); **Social Sciences** (Development Studies; Environmental Studies; Family Studies; Health Education; History; Human Rights; Labour and Industrial Relations; Political Sciences; Protective Services; Public Administration; Social Sciences; Social Work; Sociology; Tourism; Women's Studies)

History: Founded 1998.

Academic Year: July to June

Admission Requirements: Undergraduate programmes, 12th year Intermediate examination; Postgraduate programmes, Bachelor degree.

Fees: (Rupees): 1,200-12,000 per annum

Main Language(s) of Instruction: Hindi and English

Accrediting Agency: Distance Education Council

Degrees and Diplomas: *Post Diploma*; *Bachelor's Degree*; *Postgraduate Diploma*; *Master's Degree*; *Master of Philosophy*. Also MBA; Certificate (6 months), vocational (2 yrs), professional (3 yrs), and awarness (2 months) programmes.

Student Services: Academic Counselling

Publications: The Journal of Research and ODL Studies

Publishing House: University Press

Last Updated: 29/11/11

UTTARAKHAND TECHNICAL UNIVERSITY

Goverment Girls Polytechnic Post Office, Chandanwadi, Prem Nagar Sudhowala, Dehradun, Uttarakhand 248007
EMail: vcutu@rediffmail.com
Website: http://uktech.ac.in/

Vice-Chancellor: Durg Singh Chauhan Tel: +91(135) 2770-128

Registrar: Shri C.S. Mehta Tel: +91(135) 2770-126

Programme

Architecture (Architecture); **Business Administration** (Business Administration); **Engineering** (Automation and Control Engineering; Biochemistry; Bioengineering; Civil Engineering; Computer Engineering; Computer Science; Electrical and Electronic Engineering; Electrical Engineering; Electronic Engineering; Industrial Engineering; Information Technology; Mechanical Engineering; Production Engineering; Telecommunications Engineering; Thermal Engineering); **Hotel Management, Catering Technology** (Cooking and Catering; Hotel Management); **Law** (Law); **Pharmacy** (Pharmacy)

History: Founded 2008.

Degrees and Diplomas: *Bachelor's Degree*; *Bachelor's Degree (professional)*; *Master's Degree*. Also MBA
Last Updated: 04/08/11

UTTARANCHAL SANSKRIT UNIVERSITY (USVV)

Haridwar Delhi National Highway, Haridwar, Uttarakhand 249 401
Tel: +91(1334) 251-720
Fax: +91(1334) 250-636
EMail: sanskrituniversity@yahoo.com
Website: http://usvv.org/

Vice-Chancellor: Sudha Pandey

Faculty

Literature - Culture (Cultural Studies; Literature); **Pedagogy** (Education); **Philosophy** (Philosophy); **Science** (Computer Science; Linguistics); **Veda - Vedanga** (Computer Science; Grammar; Sanskrit)

Further Information: Also 52 affiliated colleges.

History: Founded 2005.

Fees: (Indian Rupees): 600-10,000 per annum

Degrees and Diplomas: *Bachelor's Degree*; *Bachelor's Degree (professional)*; *Postgraduate Diploma*; *Master's Degree*. Also Certificate; Acharya and Shastri courses.

Student Services: Canteen
Last Updated: 06/01/12

VARDHAMAN MAHAVEER KOTA OPEN UNIVERSITY (VMOU)

Rawatbhata Road, Akelgarh, Kota, Rajasthan 324010
Tel: +91(744) 247-0971
Fax: +91(744) 247-2525
EMail: vc@vmou.ac.in
Website: http://www.vmou.ac.in

Vice-Chancellor: Naresh Dadhich (2006-)
Tel: +91(744) 2471-254 EMail: vc@vmou.ac.in

Registrar: Aradhana Saxena
Tel: +91(744) 247-0971 EMail: reg@vmou.ac.in

Department

Botany (Botany; Ecology; Plant and Crop Protection; Plant Pathology); **Commerce** (Accountancy; Business and Commerce; Economics; Finance; Statistics); **Computer Science** (Computer Science; Information Technology; Multimedia); **Economics** (Demography and Population; Economics; International Economics); **Education** (Education; Educational Administration; Educational and Student Counselling; Educational Technology); **English** (English; Literature; Translation and Interpretation); **Hindi** (Hindi); **History** (History; Modern History); **Law** (Law); **Library and Information Science** (Information Sciences; Information Technology; Library Science); **Management** (Finance; Human Resources; Insurance; International Business; Management; Marketing); **Political Sciences** (Political Sciences)

Further Information: Also regional centres at Ajmer, Bikaner, Jaipur, Jodhpur, Kota, Udaipur with 86 study centres, 12 information centres and 10 computer work centres

History: Founded 1987 as an Open University through amalgamation of Institute of Correspondence Studies and Continuing Education Jaipur and (College of Correspondence Studies) Udaipur. Previously known as Kota Open University.

Admission Requirements: 12th year senior secondary/intermediate examination or recognized foreign equivalent

Fees: (Rupees): 700-13,000 per annum depending on programmes

Main Language(s) of Instruction: English, Hindi

Accrediting Agency: Distance Education Council, New Delhi

Degrees and Diplomas: *Post Diploma*; *Bachelor's Degree*; *Postgraduate Diploma*; *Master's Degree*; *Master of Philosophy*; *Doctor of Philosophy*. Also Certificate Courses; Vocational Programmes; MBA

Student Services: Academic Counselling, Canteen, Careers Guidance, Language Laboratory, Sports Facilities

Publications: Gyan Vimarsh; MEERA Newsletter

Last Updated: 30/11/11

VEER BAHADUR SINGH PURVANCHAL UNIVERSITY (VBSPU)

Devkali Jasopur, Saraykhaja, Jaunpur, Uttar Pradesh 222002
Tel: +91(5452) 252-244
Fax: +91(5452) 252-222
EMail: vc@vbspu.ac.in
Website: http://www.vbspu.ac.in

Vice-Chancellor: Sunder Lal
Tel: +91(5452) 252-222 EMail: vicechancellor.vbspu@gmail.com

Registrar: B. L. Arya
Tel: +91(5452) 252-244 EMail: registrar.vbspu@gmail.com

Department

Applied Psychology (Psychology); **Biochemistry** (Biochemistry); **Biotechnology** (Biochemistry; Bioengineering; Biological and Life Sciences; Biophysics; Biotechnology; Computer Science; Genetics; Immunology; Microbiology; Molecular Biology; Statistics); **Business Economics** (Business Administration; Economics; Finance; Marketing); **Business Management** (Agricultural Business; Business Administration; E- Business/Commerce; Management); **Computer Applications** (Computer Engineering; Computer Science); **Environmental Science** (Biotechnology; Chemistry; Ecology; Environmental Management; Environmental Studies); **Financial Studies** (Finance); **Human Resources Development** (Human Resources); **Mass Communication** (Advertising and Publicity; Mass Communication; Media Studies; Public Relations; Radio and Television Broadcasting); **Microbiology** (Microbiology); **Pharmacy** (Pharmacy)

Institute

Engineering and Technology *(UNS)* (Computer Engineering; Computer Science; Electrical Engineering; Electronic Engineering; Engineering; Information Technology; Measurement and Precision Engineering; Mechanical Engineering; Technology; Telecommunications Engineering)

Further Information: Also 367 affiliated graduate and post-graduate colleges

History: Founded 1987 as Purvanchal University. Acquired present title 2000.

Fees: (Indian Rupee): 20,000-50,000 per annum

Main Language(s) of Instruction: Hindi

Accrediting Agency: National Assessment and Accreditation Council (NAAC)

Degrees and Diplomas: *Bachelor's Degree (professional)*; *Master's Degree*; *Doctor of Philosophy*. Also MBA
Last Updated: 29/11/11

VEER KUNWAR SINGH UNIVERSITY (VKSU)

Arrah, Bihar 802 301
Tel: +91(6182) 239-209
Fax: +91(6182) 239-369
EMail: registrar@vksu-ara.org
Website: http://www.vksu-ara.org

Vice-Chancellor: Deo Muni Prasad EMail: vc@vksu-ara.org

Registrar: Amjad Ali Khan EMail: registrar@vksu-ara.org

Department

Botany (Botany); **Chemistry** (Chemistry); **Commerce** (Business and Commerce); **Economics** (Economics); **Geography** (Geography); **Hindi** (Hindi); **History** (History); **Mathematics** (Mathematics); **Physics** (Physics); **Political Science** (Political Sciences); **Psychology** (Psychology); **Public Administration** (Public Administration); **Sociology** (Sociology); **Zoology** (Zoology)

Further Information: Also 17 Constituent Degree Colleges, 3 Law Colleges and 47 affiliated Degree Colleges.

History: Founded 1992.

Degrees and Diplomas: *Bachelor's Degree*; *Master's Degree*; *Doctor of Philosophy*. Also Certificate; Advanced Diploma; MBA
Last Updated: 30/11/11

VEER NARMAD SOUTH GUJARAT UNIVERSITY

PO Box 49, Udhna-Magdalla Road, Surat, Gujarat 395007
Tel: +91(261) 222-7141
Fax: +91(261) 222-7312
Website: http://www.vnsgu.ac.in

Vice-Chancellor: Dakshesh R. Thakar

Department

Aquatic Biology (Biology); **Bio Science** (Biological and Life Sciences); **Business and Industrial Management** (Business Administration; Industrial Management); **Chemistry** (Chemistry); **Comparative Literature** (Comparative Literature); **Computer Science** (Computer Science); **Economics** (Economics); **Education** (Education); **English** (English); **Information and Communication Technology** *(Postgraduate)* (Information Technology; Telecommunications Engineering); **Information Technology** *(Postgraduate)* (Information Technology); **Mathematics** (Mathematics); **Physics** (Physics); **Public Administration** (Public Administration); **Research Methodology**; **Rural Studies** (Rural Studies); **Sociology** (Sociology); **Statistics** (Statistics)

Further Information: Also 61 Affiliated Colleges, 1 Approved and 3 Recognized Institutions

History: Founded 1967 as South Gujarat University. Acquired present title 2004.

Academic Year: June to May (June-October; November-May)

Admission Requirements: 12th year senior secondary/intermediate examination or recognized foreign equivalent

Fees: (Rupees): 70,000-92,000 per annum

Main Language(s) of Instruction: English, Gujarati

Degrees and Diplomas: *Post Diploma*; *Bachelor's Degree*; *Master's Degree*; *Doctor of Philosophy*

Last Updated: 30/11/11

VEER SURENDRA SAI UNIVERSITY OF TECHNOLOGY (VSSUT)

Distr. Sambalpur, Burla, Orissa 768 018
Tel: +91(663) 243-0211
Fax: +91(663) 243-0204
EMail: info@uceburla.ac.in
Website: http://www.vssut.ac.in/

Vice-Chancellor: Bijay Kumar Nanda

Registrar: P.K. Pradhan

Programme

Computer Applications *(Postgraduate - MCA)* (Artificial Intelligence; Computer Engineering; Computer Graphics; Data Processing; Information Management; Information Technology; Software Engineering)

Department

Chemistry (Chemical Engineering; Chemistry; Industrial Chemistry; Inorganic Chemistry; Nanotechnology; Organic Chemistry; Physical Chemistry; Polymer and Plastics Technology; Solid State Physics); **Civil Engineering** (Civil Engineering; Environmental Engineering; Structural Architecture; Transport Engineering; Water Management); **Computer Science and Engineering** (Computer Engineering; Computer Science; Information Technology); **Electrical Engineering** (Electrical Engineering; Electronic Engineering; Power Engineering); **Electronics and Telecommunications Engineering** (Electronic Engineering; Telecommunications Engineering); **Humanities** (Arts and Humanities; Behavioural Sciences; Economics; English; Industrial and Organizational Psychology; Linguistics; Literature; Psychology); **Information Technology** (Information Technology); **Manufacturing Science and Engineering** (Automation and Control Engineering; Computer Engineering; Computer Science; Human Resources; Management; Production Engineering; Robotics); **Mathematics** (Computer Science; Data Processing; Mathematics; Mathematics and Computer Science); **Mechanical Engineering** (Heating and Refrigeration; Machine Building; Mechanical Engineering; Power Engineering; Production Engineering); **Physics** (Applied Physics; Physics)

History: Founded 1956 as University College of Engineering (UCE). Acquired present status and title 2009.

Fees: (Indian Rupee): Tuition fee, 5,000-17,000 per semester

Accrediting Agency: University Grants Commission (UGC)

Degrees and Diplomas: *Bachelor's Degree*; *Bachelor's Degree (professional)*; *Master's Degree*; *Master of Philosophy*; *Doctor of Philosophy*

Student Numbers *2010-2011*: Total: c. 580

Last Updated: 04/01/12

VEL TECH RANGARAJAN DR. SAGUNTHALA R&D INSTITUTE OF SCIENCE AND TECHNOLOGY (VEL-TECH)

42 Avadi-Vel Tech Road, Avadi, Chennai, Tamil Nadu 600 062
Tel: +91(44) 268-41601 +91(44) 268-40896
Fax: +91(44) 268-40262
EMail: admission@vel-tech.org
Website: http://www.vel-tech.org/

Vice-Chancellor: Mahalakshmi Rangarajan
EMail: vicechancellor@vel-tech.org

Registrar: E. Kannan EMail: registrar@vel-tech.org

Programme

Doctoral Studies (Computer Engineering; Computer Science; Electrical Engineering; Electronic Engineering; English; Management; Mathematics; Mechanical Engineering; Telecommunications Engineering)

School

Electrical Engineering (Automation and Control Engineering; Electrical Engineering; Electronic Engineering; Measurement and Precision Engineering; Power Engineering; Telecommunications Engineering); **Information and Computing Technology** (Artificial Intelligence; Computer Engineering; Computer Networks; Computer Science; Information Technology; Software Engineering); **Management** (Business Administration; Management); **Mechanical Engineering** (Aeronautical and Aerospace Engineering; Automotive Engineering; Mechanical Engineering; Metal Techniques; Metallurgical Engineering; Production Engineering; Robotics); **Science and Humanities** (Applied Mathematics; Arts and Humanities; Computer Science; Electronic Engineering; Hotel Management; Natural Sciences; Nuclear Physics); **Technology** (Civil Engineering; Structural Architecture; Technology)

History: Founded 1990. A 'Deemed University'.

Fees: (Indian Rupee): 70,000-120,000 per annum

Accrediting Agency: National Board of Accreditation (NBA)

Degrees and Diplomas: *Bachelor's Degree*; *Bachelor's Degree (professional)*; *Postgraduate Diploma*; *Master's Degree*; *Master of Philosophy*; *Doctor of Philosophy*. Also MBA

Student Numbers *2010-2011*: Total 12,028

Last Updated: 19/12/11

IAU VELLORE INSTITUTE OF TECHNOLOGY (VIT) UNIVERSITY

Katpadi, Thiruvalam Road, Vellore, Tamil Nadu 632014
Tel: +91(416) 224-3091
Fax: +91(416) 224-3092 +91(416) 224-0411
EMail: director_ir@vit.ac.in
Website: http://www.vit.ac.in/

Vice-Chancellor and Director, International Relations: V. Raju
EMail: vc@vit.ac.in; director.ir@vit.ac.in

Registrar: T.S. Thiagarajan EMail: registrar@vit.ac.in

Programme

Innovative Studies *(Postgraduate)* (Engineering; Technology)

School

Advanced Sciences *(SAS)* (Chemistry; Electronic Engineering; Inorganic Chemistry; Organic Chemistry; Pharmacy); **Bio Sciences and Technology** *(SBST)* (Biological and Life Sciences; Biomedical Engineering; Biotechnology; Computer Science; Genetics; Microbiology); **Computing Sciences and Engineering** *(SCSE)* (Computer Engineering; Computer Science); **Electrical Engineering** *(SELECT)* (Electrical Engineering; Electronic Engineering; Power Engineering); **Electronics Engineering** (Automotive Engineering;

Electronic Engineering; Measurement and Precision Engineering; Nanotechnology; Telecommunications Engineering); **Information Technology and Engineering** *(SITE)* (Computer Engineering; Computer Networks; Information Technology; Multimedia; Software Engineering); **Mechanical and Building Sciences** *(SMBS)* (Automotive Engineering; Building Technologies; Chemical Engineering; Civil Engineering; Electronic Engineering; Energy Engineering; Environmental Engineering; Industrial Engineering; Mechanical Engineering); **Social Sciences and Languages** *(SSL)* (Chinese; Computer Science; French; German; Japanese; Modern Languages; Social Sciences); **VIT Business** *(VIT BS)* (Business Administration; International Business)

History: Founded 1984 as Vellore Engineering College. Acquired present status and title 2001. A Deemed University.

Academic Year: June to May (June-November; December-May)

Admission Requirements: Undergraduate: A pass in 10+2 or its equivalent with a minimum average of 60% of marks. Admission is based on the marks secured in the Entrance Examination conducted by VIT (VITEE). A pass in Higher Secondary Examination conducted by the State/Central Board of Examination with relevant subjects (Science Courses). Postgraduate: BE/Btech Degree in relevant discipline with minimum of 50% aggregate marks is required.

Fees: (Rs): 55,000-100,000 per annum

Main Language(s) of Instruction: English

Accrediting Agency: National Board of Accreditation (All India Council for Technical Education); National Assessment and Accreditation Council (NAAC)

Degrees and Diplomas: *Bachelor's Degree*; *Bachelor's Degree (professional)*; *Master's Degree*; *Master of Philosophy*; *Doctor of Philosophy*. Also MBA; Integrated B. Tech-MBA degree, 5 yrs; Integrated Ph. D. Programme

Student Services: Academic Counselling, Canteen, Careers Guidance, Cultural Activities, Facilities for disabled people, Foreign Studies Centre, Health Services, Language Laboratory, Nursery Care, Social Counselling, Sports Facilities

Last Updated: 30/11/11

VELS UNIVERSITY (VISTAS)

Velan Nagar, P.V. Vaithiyalingam Road, Pallavaram,
Chennai, Tamil Nadu 600 117
Tel: + 91(44) 2266-2500 + 91(44) 2501-2502
Fax: + 91(44) 2266-2513
EMail: vistas@velsuniv.org; admission@velsuniv.org
Website: http://www.velsuniv.ac.in

President: Ishari K. Ganesh EMail: chancellor@velsuniv.org

International Relations: M. Chandra Sekaran, Head, International Relations EMail: director.semc@velsuniv.org

School

Basic Sciences (Biochemistry; Chemistry; Industrial Chemistry; Industrial Management); **Computing Sciences** (Computer Science); **Hotel and Catering Management** (Cooking and Catering; Hotel and Restaurant); **Languages** (English); **Life Sciences** (Biological and Life Sciences; Biotechnology; Computer Science; Microbiology); **Management Studies and Commerce** (Business Administration; Business and Commerce; Management); **Maritime Science and Engineering** (Engineering; Marine Engineering; Marine Science and Oceanography); **Mass Communication** (Mass Communication); **Pharmacy** (Pharmacy); **Physiotherapy** (Physical Therapy)

History: Founded 1992. Acquired present title 2008. A 'Deemed University'.

Degrees and Diplomas: *Bachelor's Degree*: **Automotive Engineering; Biochemistry; Biotechnology; Business Administration; Civil Engineering; Computer Engineering; Computer Graphics; Computer Science; Electrical Engineering; Hotel Management; Information Technology; Marine Engineering; Mass Communication; Mechanical Engineering; Microbiology; Nautical Science; Pharmacy; Physical Therapy; Telecommunications Engineering.** *Bachelor's Degree (professional)*: **Computer Science.** *Master's Degree*: **Automotive Engineering; Biochemistry; Biotechnology; Business Administration; Chemistry; Cinema and Television; Computer Engineering; Computer Science; Engineering Management; English; Film; Hotel Management; Immunology; Industrial Chemistry; Industrial Management; Information Technology; Microbiology; Organic Chemistry; Pharmacy; Physical Therapy; Power Engineering.** *Master of Philosophy*; *Doctor of Philosophy*

Academic Staff *2013-2014*	**TOTAL**
FULL-TIME	**393**
PART-TIME	**40**
STAFF WITH DOCTORATE	
FULL-TIME	**105**
Student Numbers *2013-2014*	
All (Foreign included)	**2,475**

Last Updated: 16/12/11

VIDYASAGAR UNIVERSITY

Vidyasagar Viswavidyalaya

Midnapore, West Bengal 721102
Tel: +91(3222) 275-329
Fax: +91(3222) 275-329
EMail: vidya295@sancharnet.in
Website: http://www.vidyasagar.ac.in

Vice-Chancellor: Ranjan Chakrabarti (2011-)
Tel: +91(3222) 275329
EMail: vc@mail.vidyasagar.ac.in; vuvc@rediffmail.com

Registrar: Ranjit Dhar
Tel: +91(3222) 275-297 EMail: registrar@mail.vidyasagar.ac.in

Faculty

Arts and Commerce (Administration; Agricultural Management; Arts and Humanities; Business Administration; Economics; English; Farm Management; History; Indic Languages; Information Sciences; Library Science; Mass Communication; Philosophy; Political Sciences; Rural Studies; Sanskrit; Sociology); **Science** (Anthropology; Applied Mathematics; Aquaculture; Biomedical Engineering; Botany; Chemical Engineering; Chemistry; Community Health; Computer Science; Electronic Engineering; Environmental Management; Forestry; Geography; Management; Marine Science and Oceanography; Microbiology; Physics; Physiology; Surveying and Mapping; Zoology)

Further Information: Also 54 Affiliated Colleges. Distance Education programmes in Bengali, English, History, Political Science, Sanskrit, Botanics, Zoology, Dietetics and Community Nutrition Management, Mathematics, Physics, Chemistry, Environmental Science.

History: Founded 1981. Acquired present status 1990.

Academic Year: July to June

Admission Requirements: 12th year senior secondary/intermediate examination or recognized foreign equivalent

Fees: (Rupees): Scientific studies, 1,320 per annum; Arts and Commerce Studies, 960 per annum

Main Language(s) of Instruction: English, Bengali

Accrediting Agency: University Grants Commission (UGC); National Assessment and Accreditation Council (NAAC)

Degrees and Diplomas: *Post Diploma*; *Bachelor's Degree*; *Postgraduate Diploma*; *Master's Degree*; *Doctor of Philosophy*. Also Certificate, Honours Bachelor's degree; MBA

Student Services: Academic Counselling, Canteen, Careers Guidance, Cultural Activities, Facilities for disabled people, Foreign Studies Centre, Health Services, Language Laboratory, Nursery Care, Social Counselling, Sports Facilities

Publications: Economics with Rural Development; Journal of Biological Science; Journal of Commerce with Farm Management; Journal of Department of Bengali; Journal of English; Journal of Geography and Environmental Management; Journal of History; Journal of Library and Information Science; Journal of Philosophy and Life-World; Journal of Physical Science; Journal of Politics and Societies; Vidyasagar University Journal

Last Updated: 30/11/11

VIGNAN UNIVERSITY

Vadlamudi, Guntur, Andhra Pradesh 522-213
Tel: +91(863) 253-4645
EMail: vnratnakaram@vignanuniversity.org
Website: http://www.vignanuniversity.org/

Vice-Chancellor: Govardhana Rao Vadlamudi
Tel: +91(863) 253-4645 EMail: vc@vignanuniversity.org

Registrar: A. Leela Mohana Rao Tel: +91(863) 211-8237

School

Biotechnology (Biological and Life Sciences; Biotechnology; Computer Science); **Chemical Engineering** (Chemical Engineering; Textile Technology); **Civil Engineering** (Civil Engineering); **Computing** (Computer Science; Information Technology); **Electrical Engineering** (Electrical Engineering; Electronic Engineering); **Electronics** (Electronic Engineering; Telecommunications Engineering); **Management, Humanities and Basic Sciences** (Arts and Humanities; Business Administration; Engineering; Management; Physics; Social Sciences); **Mechanical Engineering** (Electronic Engineering; Machine Building; Mechanical Engineering; Power Engineering)

History: Founded 1997. A 'Deemed University'.

Degrees and Diplomas: *Bachelor's Degree (professional)*; *Master's Degree*; *Doctor of Philosophy*. Also MBA

Student Services: Canteen

Last Updated: 20/12/11

VIJAYANAGARA SRI KRISHNADEVARAYA UNIVERSITY (VSKU)

Jnana Sagara Campus, Vinayaka Nagar, Cantonment,
Bellary, Karnataka 583 104
Tel: +91(8392) 242-703
Fax: +91(8392) 242-806
EMail: vc@uskub.ac.in
Website: http://www.vskub.ac.in

Vice-Chancellor: Manjappa D. Hosamane

Registrar: Yashavantha Dongre

School

Business (Business Administration; Business and Commerce; Management); **Chemical Sciences** (Chemistry; Industrial Chemistry); **Earth Sciences** (Earth Sciences; Geology; Mineralogy); **Humanities** (Arts and Humanities; English; Indic Languages); **Mathematics** (Computer Science; Mathematics); **Physical Sciences** (Physics); **Social Sciences** (Archaeology; Economics; History; Social Sciences; Social Work; Women's Studies)

Further Information: Also 100 affiliated colleges; Second Campus at Nandihalli in Sandur taluka (Bellary district)

History: Founded 2000.

Degrees and Diplomas: *Postgraduate Diploma*; *Master's Degree*. Also MBA

Student Services: Sports Facilities

Last Updated: 03/01/12

VIKRAM UNIVERSITY

University Road, Ujjain, Madhya Pradesh 456010
Tel: +91(734) 251-4270 +91(734) 251-4277
Fax: +91(734) 251-4276
EMail: vcvikramujn@gmail.com
Website: http://www.vikramuniv.net/

Vice-Chancellor: T. R. Thapak Tel: +91(734) 251-4270

Registrar: B.L. Bunkar Tel: +91(734) 251-4277

Faculty

Arts (Arts and Humanities; English; Hindi; Modern Languages; Philosophy; Sanskrit); **Commerce** (Business and Commerce); **Education** (Continuing Education; Education); **Information Technology** (Computer Science; Information Sciences; Information Technology; Library Science); **Life Science** (Biological and Life Sciences; Biotechnology; Botany; Environmental Management; Environmental Studies; Microbiology; Zoology); **Management** (Business Administration; Management); **Physical Science** (Biochemistry; Chemistry; Earth Sciences; Mathematics; Natural Sciences; Pharmacy; Physics; Statistics); **Social Sciences** (Ancient Civilizations; Archaeology; Cultural Studies; Economics; Political Sciences; Public Administration; Social Sciences; Sociology)

Further Information: Also 85 Affiliated Colleges; 2 Constituent Colleges

History: Founded 1957.

Academic Year: July to April (July-October; November-December; January-April)

Admission Requirements: 12th year senior secondary/intermediate examination or recognized foreign equivalent

Fees: (Rupees): 180-240 per annum

Main Language(s) of Instruction: English, Hindi

Accrediting Agency: National Assessment and Accreditition Council (NAAC)

Degrees and Diplomas: *Post Diploma*; *Bachelor's Degree*; *Postgraduate Diploma*; *Master's Degree*; *Master of Philosophy*; *Doctor of Philosophy*. Also Certificate courses; Honours Bachelor's degree; MBA

Student Services: Health Services, Sports Facilities

Publications: The Vikram

Publishing House: University Press

Last Updated: 01/12/11

VIKRAMA SIMHAPURI UNIVERSITY

Dargamitta, Sri Pottisriramulu Nellore District,
Nellore, Andhra Pradesh 524 003
Tel: +91(861) 235-2366 +91(861) 235-2377
Fax: +91(861) 235-2356
EMail: admin@simhapuriuniv.org
Website: http://www.simhapuriuniv.org/

Vice-Chancellor: G. Rajarami Reddy
Tel: +91(861) 235-2366 EMail: vc@simhapuriuniv.org

Registrar: V. Narayana Reddy
Tel: +91(861) 235-2377 EMail: registrar@simhapuriuniv.org

Course

Business Management (Business Administration; Management); **Computer Science** (Computer Science); **English** (English); **Marine Biology** (Marine Biology); **Organic Chemistry** (Organic Chemistry); **Social Work** (Social Work)

History: Founded 2008.

Degrees and Diplomas: *Master's Degree*. Also MBA

Student Numbers *2010-2011*: Total: c. 200

Last Updated: 02/01/12

VINAYAKA MISSION'S UNIVERSITY (VMU)

NH-47 Sankari Main Road, Ariyanoor, Salem, Tamil Nadu 636308
Tel: +91(427) 398-7000 +91(427) 247-7316
Fax: +91(427) 247-7903
EMail: vmu@vinayakamission.com
Website: http://www.vinayakamission.com

Vice-Chancellor: V.R. Rajendran

Registrar: Y. Abraham EMail: registrar@vinayakamission.com

International Relations: Anup K. Gogna, Director, Office of International Affairs
EMail: anup@vinayakamissions.com; akgogna@gmail.com

Faculty

Allied Health Sciences (Health Sciences; Occupational Therapy; Optometry; Speech Therapy and Audiology); **Architecture** (Architecture); **Arts and Science** (Arts and Humanities; Biochemistry; Business Administration; Computer Science; Cooking and Catering; Hotel and Restaurant; Microbiology; Natural Sciences); **Computer Applications** (Computer Science; Information Technology); **Dentistry** (Dental Hygiene; Dental Technology; Dentistry; Oral Pathology; Orthodontics; Periodontics; Radiology; Social and Preventive Medicine; Surgery); **Education** (Education); **Engineering and Technology** (Aeronautical and Aerospace Engineering; Automotive Engineering; Biomedical Engineering; Biotechnology; Civil Engineering; Computer Engineering; Computer Science; Construction Engineering; E- Business/Commerce; Electronic Engineering; Engineering; Environmental Engineering; Industrial Engineering; Information Management; Information Technology; Mechanical Engineering; Natural Resources; Power Engineering; Software Engineering; Structural Architecture; Technology; Telecommunications Engineering; Water Management; Water Science); **Homeopathy** (Homeopathy; Medicine; Paediatrics; Philosophy; Surgery);

Management (Air Transport; Business Administration; Environmental Management; Health Administration; International Business; Management); **Medicine** (Anaesthesiology; Anatomy; Biochemistry; Community Health; Dermatology; Gynaecology and Obstetrics; Medicine; Microbiology; Ophthalmology; Orthopaedics; Otorhinolaryngology; Paediatrics; Psychiatry and Mental Health; Radiology; Surgery; Venereology); **Nursing** (Community Health; Gynaecology and Obstetrics; Nursing; Paediatrics; Surgery); **Paramedical Sciences** (Medical Auxiliaries; Medical Technology); **Pharmacy** (Biotechnology; Chemistry; Pharmacology; Pharmacy); **Physical Education** (Physical Education; Sports; Sports Management); **Physiotherapy** (Cardiology; Gynaecology and Obstetrics; Physical Therapy; Rehabilitation and Therapy; Sports Medicine)

Further Information: Also Research programs in all specialitie; Penang Internatioanl Dental College, Malaysia; VMRDFU Off-shore Campus, Bangkok, Thailand. A traditional and distance higher education institution.

History: Founded 1981 as Vinayaka Mission's College of Pharmacy. Acquired present status 2001, incorporating three existing colleges. Formerly known as Vinayaka Mission's Research Foundation - University. A Deemed University.

Main Language(s) of Instruction: Hindi

Accrediting Agency: National Board of Accreditation (NBA); All India Council for Technical Education (AICTE)

Degrees and Diplomas: *Post Diploma*; *Bachelor's Degree*; *Bachelor's Degree (professional)*; *Postgraduate Diploma*; *Master's Degree*; *Master of Philosophy*; *Doctor of Philosophy*. Also Certificates; MBA

Academic Staff *2010-2011*: Total: c. 3,000

Student Numbers *2010-2011*: Total: c. 15,000

Last Updated: 01/12/11

VINAYAKA MISSIONS SIKKIM UNIVERSITY (VMSU)

(PO) NH 31-A Tadong, East Sikkim, Gangtok, Sikkim 737 102
Tel: +91(3592) 232-588
Fax: +91(3592) 232-417
EMail: contactus@vmsu.in
Website: http://www.vmsu.in/

Vice-Chancellor: N.S. Rame Gowda

Faculty

Arts and Science (Advertising and Publicity; Arts and Humanities; Business Administration; Business and Commerce; Computer Science; Economics; English; Geography; History; Information Sciences; Information Technology; Library Science; Marketing; Natural Sciences; Political Sciences; Public Relations; Sales Techniques; Sociology); **Education** (Education); **Nursing** (Midwifery; Nursing); **Pharmacy** (Pharmacy)

Further Information: A traditional and distance education institution.

History: Founded 2008.

Accrediting Agency: University Grants Commission (UGC); All India Council for Technical Education (AICTE); Bar Council of India (BCI); Distance Education Council (DEC); Dental Council of India (DCI); Indian Nursing Council (INC); Medical Council of India (MCI); National Council for Teacher Education (NCTE); Pharmacy Council of India (PCI)

Degrees and Diplomas: *Post Diploma*; *Bachelor's Degree*; *Bachelor's Degree (professional)*; *Postgraduate Diploma*; *Master's Degree*

Last Updated: 22/12/11

VINOBA BHAVE UNIVERSITY (VBU)

PO Box 31, Hazaribagh, Bihar 825301
Tel: +91(6546) 294-003
Fax: +91(6546) 270-982
EMail: info@vbuhazaribag.org
Website: http://vbu.co.in

Vice-Chancellor: Ravindra Nath Bhagat

Registrar: E.N. Siddiqui EMail: enamsiddiqui@yahoo.com

Department

Commerce (Business and Commerce); **Humanities** (Arts and Humanities; English; Hindi; Philology; Sanskrit; Urdu); **Management** (Business Administration; Management); **Professional Studies** (Computer Science; Nutrition); **Science** (Botany; Chemistry; Geology; Mathematics; Physics; Zoology); **Social Sciences** (Anthropology; Economics; Geography; History; Home Economics; Political Sciences; Psychology; Social Sciences)

Further Information: Also 26 constituent colleges/

History: Founded 1992.

Fees: (Rupees): 180-240 per annum

Main Language(s) of Instruction: Hindi

Accrediting Agency: All India Council for Technical Education (AICTE)

Degrees and Diplomas: *Post Diploma*; *Bachelor's Degree*; *Master's Degree*; *Master of Philosophy*; *Doctor of Philosophy*. Also MBA

Last Updated: 01/12/11

VISVA-BHARATI

PO Santiniketan, District Birbhum,
Santiniketan, West Bengal 731235
Tel: +91(3463) 261-531
Fax: +91(3463) 262-672
Website: http://www.visva-bharati.ac.in

Vice-Chancellor: Sushanta Dattagupta (2011-)

Registrar: M.M. Mitra

Department

Arabic, Persian, Urdu and Islamic Studies (Arabic; Islamic Studies; Persian; Urdu); **Assamese** (Indic Languages); **Bengali** (Indic Languages); **Chinese Language and Culture** (Asian Studies; Chinese); **English and OMEL** (English); **Hindi** (Hindi); **Indo-Tibetan Studies** (South Asian Studies; Tibetan); **Japanese** (Japanese); **Oriya** (Indic Languages); **Sanskrit, Pali and Prakrit** (Classical Languages; Sanskrit); **Santali** (South and Southeast Asian Languages); **Tamil** (South and Southeast Asian Languages)

Further Information: Also 1 Constituent Institute

History: Founded 1921. Incorporated as a Central University 1951. A Centre of Culture where research into and study of Religious Literature, History, Science and Art of Hindu, Buddhist, Jain, Islamic, Sikh, Christian and other civilizations may be pursued with the culture of the West.

Academic Year: June to May

Admission Requirements: 12th year senior secondary/intermediate examination or recognized foreign equivalent

Main Language(s) of Instruction: English, Bengali, Sanskrit

Degrees and Diplomas: *Post Diploma*; *Bachelor's Degree*; *Postgraduate Diploma*; *Master's Degree*; *Doctor of Philosophy*. Also Certificates, Advanced Diploma, Pre-degree Courses.

Student Services: Academic Counselling, Canteen, Careers Guidance, Cultural Activities, Facilities for disabled people, Health Services, Language Laboratory, Nursery Care, Sports Facilities

Publications: Journal of Philosophy; Rabindra Vishka; Visva-Bharati Annals; Visva-Bharati Patrika

Publishing House: University Press

Academic Staff *2010-2011*: Total: c. 520

Student Numbers *2010-2011*: Total: c. 6,500

Last Updated: 01/12/11

VISVESVARAYA NATIONAL INSTITUTE OF TECHNOLOGY (VNIT)

South Ambazari Road, Nagpur, Maharashtra 440010
Tel: +91(712) 222-2828 +91(712) 222-4123
Fax: +91(712) 222-3969 +91(712) 222-3230
EMail: dr_acd@vnit.ac.in
Website: http://www.vnit.ac.in

Director: S.S. Gokhale
Tel: +91(712) 222-3969 EMail: ssg1@vnit.ac.in

Registrar: B.M. Ganveer
Tel: +91 (712) 222-6240 EMail: registrar@vnit.ac.in

Department
Applied Chemistry (Applied Chemistry; Nanotechnology); **Applied Mechanics** (Construction Engineering; Mechanics; Structural Architecture); **Applied Physics** (Applied Physics); **Architecture and Planning** (Architecture; Architecture and Planning; Town Planning); **Chemical Engineering** (Chemical Engineering); **Civil Engineering** (Civil Engineering; Construction Engineering; Environmental Engineering); **Computer Science and Engineering** (Computer Engineering; Computer Science; Data Processing; Software Engineering; Telecommunications Engineering); **Electrical and Electronics Engineering** (Electrical and Electronic Engineering; Electrical Engineering; Electronic Engineering; Power Engineering); **Electronics and Communication Engineering** (Electronic Engineering; Telecommunications Engineering); **Mathematics** (Mathematics); **Mechanical Engineering** (Heating and Refrigeration; Industrial Engineering; Mechanical Engineering; Power Engineering); **Metallurgical and Materials Engineering** (Materials Engineering; Metallurgical Engineering); **Mining Engineering** (Mining Engineering)

Further Information: A traditional and distance education institution.

History: Founded 1960. Acquired present status of 'Institution of National Importance' 2007.

Admission Requirements: Not less than 50% marks in 10+2 Board examination, must qualify All India Engineering Entrance Examination (AIEEE)

Fees: (Indian Rupees): 35,000 per annum

Main Language(s) of Instruction: English

Accrediting Agency: National Board of Accreditation

Degrees and Diplomas: *Bachelor's Degree (professional)*; *Master's Degree*; *Doctor of Philosophy*. Also distance education programme programme administered by Kanwal Rekhi School of Information Technology and Continuing Education

Student Services: Academic Counselling, Canteen, Careers Guidance, Cultural Activities, Facilities for disabled people, Health Services, Language Laboratory, Nursery Care, Social Counselling, Sports Facilities

Last Updated: 02/12/11

VISVESVARAYA TECHNOLOGICAL UNIVERSITY (VTU)

"Jnana Sangama", Macche, Belgaum, Karnataka 590 018
Tel: +91(831) 249-8100
Fax: +91(831) 240-5467
EMail: registrar@vtu.ac.in
Website: http://www.vtu.ac.in

Vice-Chancellor: H. Maheshappa
Tel: +91(831) 240-5455 EMail: vc@vtu.ac.in

Registrar: S.A. Kori EMail: registrar@vtu.ac.in

Board of Study
Automobile Engineering (Automotive Engineering); **Biotechnology** (Biotechnology); **Business Administration** *(Postgraduate)* (Business Administration); **Chemical Engineering** *(Postgraduate)* (Chemical Engineering; Polymer and Plastics Technology); **Chemical Engineering** (Chemical Engineering; Polymer and Plastics Technology; Textile Technology); **Civil Engineering** (Ceramics and Glass Technology; Civil Engineering; Environmental Engineering); **Civil Engineering** *(Postgraduate)* (Civil Engineering; Computer Graphics; Computer Science; Design; Environmental Engineering; Geological Engineering; Hydraulic Engineering; Road Engineering; Structural Architecture; Transport Engineering); **Computer Science and Engineering** (Computer Engineering; Computer Science; Information Sciences); **Computer Science and Engineering** *(Postgraduate Studies)* (Computer Engineering; Computer Networks; Computer Science; Information Technology; Software Engineering); **Electronic and Communication Engineering** *(Postgraduate)* (Computer Engineering; Computer Networks; Electronic Engineering; Information Sciences; Telecommunications Engineering); **Electronic Engineering** (Electronic Engineering; Telecommunications Engineering); **Electronic Engineering** *(Postgraduate)* (Computer Science; Electrical Engineering; Electronic Engineering; Energy Engineering; Power Engineering); **Industrial and Production Engineering** (Industrial Engineering; Industrial Management; Production Engineering); **Industrial and Production Engineering** *(Postgraduate)* (Industrial Design; Industrial Engineering; Industrial Management; Production Engineering); **Instrumentation Technology** (Biomedical Engineering; Electronic Engineering; Medical Technology); **Mechanical Engineering** (Aeronautical and Aerospace Engineering; Electrical Engineering; Electronic Engineering; Mechanical Engineering; Mining Engineering); **Mechanical Engineering** *(Postgraduate)* (Aeronautical and Aerospace Engineering; Automation and Control Engineering; Design; Engineering; Industrial Engineering; Instrument Making; Machine Building; Mechanical Engineering; Power Engineering; Robotics; Thermal Engineering); **Textile Technology** *(Postgraduate)* (Textile Technology)

Further Information: Also regional centres in Belgaum, Bangalore, Mysore and Gulbarga; Affiliated Colleges in Bangalore (96), Belgaum (26), Gulbarga (14), Mysore (49); 17 extension centres.

History: Founded 1998.

Academic Year: Secondary school certificate with Physics, Chemistry and Mathematics as optional subjects and English as a field of study (with minimum 35% of marks scored in Physics; Mathematics; Chemistry; Biology; Biotechnoogy; Computer Science)

Main Language(s) of Instruction: English

Degrees and Diplomas: *Bachelor's Degree (professional)*; *Master's Degree*; *Doctor of Philosophy*. Also MBA

Publications: Annual Report; VTU Bulletin

Student Numbers *2010-2011*: Total: c. 79,800
Last Updated: 02/12/11

WEST BENGAL NATIONAL UNIVERSITY OF JURIDICAL SCIENCES (WBNUJS)

Dr. Ambedkar Bhavan 12, LB Block, Sector III, Salt Lake City, Kolkata, West Bengal 700098
Tel: +91(33) 2335-7379 +91(33) 2335-0765
Fax: +91(33) 2335-7422 +91(33) 2335-0511
EMail: nujs@vsnl.com; nujs@cal3.vsnl.net.in
Website: http://www.nujs.edu

Vice-Chancellor: M.P. Singh EMail: vc@nujs.edu

Registrar: Susil Kumar Pal

School
Criminal Justice and Administration *(SCJA)* (Criminal Law; Justice Administration); **Economic and Business Laws** *(SEBL)* (Commercial Law; Economics); **Legal Practice and Development** (Law); **Private Laws and Comparative Jurisprudence** *(SPLCJ)* (Comparative Law; Private Law); **Public Law and Governance** *(SPLG)* (Government; Public Law); **Social Sciences** *(SSS)* (Social Sciences); **Technology, Law and Development** (Development Studies; Law; Technology)

Centre
Consumer Protection and Welfare (Law; Welfare and Protective Services); **Human Rights and Citizenship Studies** (Civics; Human Rights); **Studies in WTO Laws** (Commercial Law; International Law); **Women and Law** (Law; Women's Studies)

Chair
Human Rights (Human Rights); **Intellectual Property Rights** (Law)

History: Founded 1999.

Academic Year: June to April

Admission Requirements: 12th year senior secondary/intermediate examination or recognized foreign equivalent

Fees: (Rupees): 64,000 per annum

Main Language(s) of Instruction: English

Degrees and Diplomas: *Bachelor's Degree*; *Postgraduate Diploma*; *Master's Degree*; *Master of Philosophy*; *Doctor of Philosophy*. Also Certificates.

Student Services: Academic Counselling, Canteen, Careers Guidance, Cultural Activities, Health Services, Language Laboratory, Social Counselling, Sports Facilities

Publications: Indian Journal of Juridical Science; Indian Juridical Review

Last Updated: 02/12/11

WEST BENGAL STATE UNIVERSITY

Barasat, North 24 Parganas, Berunanpukuria, P.O. Malikapur, North 24- Parganas, Kolkata, West Bengal 700 126
Tel: +91(33) 2524-1975 +91(33) 2524-1976
Fax: +91(33) 2524-1977
EMail: vc.wbsu@gmail.com
Website: http://www.wbsubregistration.org/

Vice-Chancellor: Kausik Gupta

Department

Anthropology (Anthropology); **Botany** (Botany); **Chemistry** (Chemistry); **Commerce and Management** (Business and Commerce; Management); **Comparative Literature** (Comparative Literature; Literature; Translation and Interpretation); **Computer Science** (Computer Science); **Economics** (Economics); **Education** (Education; Educational and Student Counselling; Educational Sciences); **Electronics** (Electronic Engineering); **English** (English; Literature; Writing); **Geography** (Geography); **Hindi** (Hindi; Literature); **History** (History); **Journalism and Mass Communication** (Journalism; Mass Communication); **Mathematics** (Mathematics); **Microbiology** (Biochemistry; Biology; Biophysics; Cell Biology; Microbiology); **Physics** (Astrophysics; Biophysics; Physics); **Physiology** (Physiology); **Political Science** (Political Sciences); **Psychology** (Industrial and Organizational Psychology; Psychology); **Sanskrit** (Sanskrit); **Sociology** (Sociology); **Statistics** (Statistics); **Zoology** (Zoology)

Degrees and Diplomas: *Master's Degree*; *Master of Philosophy*; *Doctor of Philosophy*

Last Updated: 06/01/12

WEST BENGAL UNIVERSITY OF ANIMAL AND FISHERY SCIENCES (WBUAFSCL)

68 Kshudiram Bose Sarani, Belgachia, Kolkata 700037
Tel: +91(33) 2556-3123
Fax: +91(33) 2557-1986
Website: http://wbuafscl.ac.in

Vice-Chancellor: C.S. Chakrabarti Tel: +91(33) 2556-3450

Registrar (Acting): Dipak.Kr. De Tel: +91(33) 2556-3123

Faculty

Dairy Technology (Dairy); **Fishery Sciences** (Aquaculture; Fishery); **Veterinary and Animal Sciences** (Animal Husbandry; Veterinary Science)

History: Founded as Bengal Veterinary College 1893. Acquired present status and title 1995.

Academic Year: July to June

Admission Requirements: Higher Secondary (Sc.)

Main Language(s) of Instruction: English

Accrediting Agency: Indian Council of Agricultural Research; Veterinary Council of India

Degrees and Diplomas: *Bachelor's Degree*; *Bachelor's Degree (professional)*; *Master's Degree*; *Doctor of Philosophy*

Student Services: Academic Counselling, Canteen, Careers Guidance, Health Services, Language Laboratory

Last Updated: 02/12/11

WEST BENGAL UNIVERSITY OF TECHNOLOGY (WBUTECH)

BF-142, Salt Lake, Sector 1, Kolkata, West Bengal 700064
Tel: +91(33) 2321-7578 +91(33) 2321-1327
Fax: +91(33) 2321-7578
EMail: registrar@wbut.ac.in
Website: http://www.wbut.net

Vice-Chancellor: Sabyasachi Sen Gupta
Tel: +91(33) 2321-7578 EMail: vcwbut@sify.com; vc@wbut.ac.in

Registrar: Syed Rafikul Islam
Tel: +91(33) 2321-8771
EMail: srislam56@yahoo.co.in; registrar@wbut.ac.in

School

Advance Interdisciplinary Study and Research; **Applied Sciences** (Biotechnology; Chemical Engineering; Computer Science; Electrical Engineering; Genetics; Mechanical Engineering; Media Studies; Microbiology; Molecular Biology; Nautical Science; Optometry; Pharmacology; Pharmacy; Physics; Production Engineering); **Engineering and Technology** (Agricultural Engineering; Automation and Control Engineering; Automotive Engineering; Bioengineering; Biological and Life Sciences; Biomedical Engineering; Biotechnology; Ceramics and Glass Technology; Chemical Engineering; Civil Engineering; Computer Engineering; Computer Networks; Computer Science; Construction Engineering; Electrical Engineering; Electronic Engineering; Food Technology; Industrial Engineering; Information Technology; Leather Techniques; Marine Engineering; Mechanical Engineering; Microbiology; Mining Engineering; Power Engineering; Production Engineering; Software Engineering; Structural Architecture; Telecommunications Engineering; Textile Technology); **Management** (Administration; Biotechnology; Business Administration; Business Computing; Health Administration; Hotel and Restaurant; Hotel Management; Industrial Management; Insurance; Sports Management)

History: Founded 2001.

Academic Year: June to May

Admission Requirements: Secondary school certificate

Fees: (Rupees) 30,000-45,000 per annum

Main Language(s) of Instruction: English

Accrediting Agency: University Grants Commission, All India Council of Technical Education

Degrees and Diplomas: *Bachelor's Degree*; *Bachelor's Degree (professional)*; *Postgraduate Diploma*; *Master's Degree*; *Master of Philosophy*; *Doctor of Philosophy*. Also MBA

Student Services: Academic Counselling, Canteen, Careers Guidance, Cultural Activities, Health Services, Language Laboratory, Social Counselling

Last Updated: 02/12/11

XAVIER INSTITUTE OF MANAGEMENT BHUBANESWAR (XIMB)

Xavier Square, Bhubaneswar, Orissa 751013
Tel: +91(674) 3012-345
Fax: +91(674) 2300-995
EMail: info@ximb.ac.in
Website: http://www.ximb.ac.in

Director: P. T. Joseph

Dean of Academic Studies: Subhajyoti Ray

Programme

Management (Accountancy; Economics; Finance; Human Resources; Management; Marketing); **Rural Management** (Agricultural Equipment)

History: Founded 1987.

Accrediting Agency: All India Council for Technical Education (AICTE)

Degrees and Diplomas: *Postgraduate Diploma*; *Doctor of Philosophy*. Also MBA, and Certificate Courses

Last Updated: 26/01/12

XAVIER INSTITUTE OF MANAGEMENT AND ENTREPRENEURSHIP (XIME)

Electronics City, Phase II, Hosur Road, Bangalore, Karnataka 560 100
Tel: + 91(80) 2852-8477 + 91(80) 2852-8597
Fax: + 91(80) 2852-0809
EMail: xime@xime.org
Website: http://www.xime.org/

Director: Stephan Mathews

Programme

Communications Management (Communication Studies; Management); **Management** (Accountancy; Business Administration; Commercial Law; Economics; Management; Marketing); **Management** *(Executive)* (Management)

History: Founded 1991. Acquired present status 2004. A 'B-School'.

Accrediting Agency: All India Council for Technical Education (AICTE)

Degrees and Diplomas: *Postgraduate Diploma*. Also Executive Postgraduate Diploma.
Last Updated: 25/01/12

YMCA UNIVERSITY OF SCIENCE AND TECHNOLOGY, FARIDABAD (YMCAUST)

NH-2, Sector-6, Mathura Road, Faridabad, Haryana 121 006
Tel: +91(129) 224-2142 +91(129) 224-2143
Fax: +91(129) 224-2143
EMail: contact@ymcaust.ac.in
Website: http://ymcaust.ac.in/

Vice-Chancellor: Mohinder Kumar

Faculty

Engineering and Technology (Computer Engineering; Computer Science; Electrical Engineering; Engineering; Information Technology; Mechanical Engineering; Technology; Telecommunications Engineering); **Humanities and Applied Sciences** (Mathematics; Physics); **Management Studies** (Business Administration; Management)

History: Founded 1969 as YMCA Institute of Engineering, Faridabad - a joint venture of the National Council Of YMCAs of India, Govt of Haryana, and the Central Agencies for Development Aid, Bonn, Germany. Acquired University status 2009.

Accrediting Agency: University Grants Commission (UGC)

Degrees and Diplomas: *Bachelor's Degree (professional)*; *Master's Degree*; *Doctor of Philosophy*. Also MBA
Last Updated: 03/01/12

YASHWANTRAO CHAVAN MAHARASHTRA OPEN UNIVERSITY (YCMOU)

Dnyangangotri, Near Gandapur Dam, Nashik, Maharashtra 422222
Tel: +91(253) 223-1714 +91(253) 223-1715
Fax: +91(253) 223-1716
EMail: vc@ycmou.com
Website: http://www.ycmou.com

Vice-Chancellor: R. Krishnakumar
Tel: +91(253) 223-0228 EMail: vc@ycmou.com

Registrar: N.R. Kapadnis
Tel: +91(253) 223-0470 EMail: registrar@ycmou.com

International Relations: Anuradha Deshmukh
Tel: +91(253) 223-0009 EMail: anuradhadeshmukh@hotmail.com

School

Agricultural Sciences (Agriculture); **Architecture, Science and Technology** (Actuarial Science; Architectural and Environmental Design; Architecture; Automotive Engineering; Biotechnology; Computer Science; Construction Engineering; Electronic Engineering; Industrial Engineering; Interior Design; Marine Engineering; Mechanical Engineering; Nautical Science; Production Engineering; Regional Planning; Thermal Engineering; Town Planning); **Commerce and Management** (Business Administration; Management); **Computer Science** (Computer Science); **Continuing Education** (Continuing Education); **Education** (Education); **Health Sciences** (Health Sciences); **Humanities and Social Sciences** (Arts and Humanities; Social Sciences)

Further Information: Also Regional Centres in Amravati, Aurangabad, Goa, Kolhapur, Mumbai, Nagpur, Nanded, Nashik, and Pune.

History: Founded 1989.

Academic Year: June to May

Admission Requirements: 12th year senior secondary/intermediate examination or recognized equivalent

Fees: (Rupees): Certificate level, 460 (3 months' programme) - 5,015 (6 months' programme); Diploma level, 1,550 (1 yr programme) - 20,060 (2 yrs programme); Undergraduate level, 3,590 (3 yrs programme) - 60,000 (per sem. in Marine Engineering programme); Postgraduate level, 2,860 (1 yr programme) - 12,500 (1-1 1/2 yrs programme); Research level, 4060 (1-1 1/2 yrs programme) - 21,000 (3 yrs programme)

Main Language(s) of Instruction: Marathi, English

Accrediting Agency: National Assessment and Accreditation Council (NAAC); Distance Education Council (DEC)

Degrees and Diplomas: *Post Diploma*; *Bachelor's Degree*; *Bachelor's Degree (professional)*; *Postgraduate Diploma*; *Master's Degree*; *Master of Philosophy*; *Doctor of Philosophy*. Also online Certificates

Student Services: Academic Counselling, Sports Facilities

Publications: Mukta Vidya

Academic Staff *2010-2011*: Total: c. 4,300
Student Numbers *2010-2011*: Total: c. 400,000
Last Updated: 02/12/11

YENEPOYA UNIVERSITY

University Road, Deralakatte,
Mangalore, Karnataka, IndeMangalore, Karnataka 575018
Tel: +91 824 2204668/69/70
Fax: +91 824 2204667
EMail: reachus@yenepoya.org
Website: http://www.yenepoya.edu.in/

Vice-Chancellor: P. Chandramohan
EMail: ViceChancellor@Yenepoya.edu.in

Registrar: Janardhana Konaje EMail: Registrar@Yenepoya.org

Faculty

Dentistry (Community Health; Dental Technology; Dentistry; Oral Pathology; Orthodontics; Periodontics; Surgery); **Medicine** (Anatomy; Biochemistry; Community Health; Forensic Medicine and Dentistry; Medicine; Microbiology; Pathology; Pharmacology; Physiology); **Nursing** (Gynaecology and Obstetrics; Nursing; Paediatrics; Psychiatry and Mental Health; Surgery); **Physiotherapy** (Cardiology; Health Sciences; Neurology; Orthopaedics; Physical Therapy)

Further Information: Also Yenepoya Medical College Hospital.

Accrediting Agency: University Grants Commission (UGC); Ministry of Human Resource Development

Degrees and Diplomas: *Bachelor's Degree (professional)*; *Postgraduate Diploma*; *Master's Degree*
Last Updated: 13/12/11

YOGI VEMANA UNIVERSITY

Kadapa, Andhra Pradesh 516 003
Tel: +91(8562) 225-446
Fax: +91(8562) 225-443
EMail: vc@yogivemanauniversity.ac.in
Website: http://www.yogivemanauniversity.ac.in/

Vice-Chancellor: B. Syama Sundar Tel: +91(8562) 225-400

Registrar: S. Ramanaiah
Tel: +91(8562) 225-429 EMail: registraryvu@gmail.com

School

Earth Sciences and Biotechnology/Bioinformatics (Biological and Life Sciences; Biotechnology; Computer Science; Earth Sciences); **Humanities** (Arts and Humanities; English; Fine Arts; Indic Languages; Journalism; Mass Communication; Theatre); **Life Sciences** (Biochemistry; Biological and Life Sciences; Biotechnology; Botany; Environmental Studies; Genetics; Microbiology; Psychology; Zoology); **Management** (Business and Commerce; Management); **Mathematics and Computer/Information Sciences** (Applied Mathematics; Information Sciences; Mathematics and Computer Science); **Physical Education and Sports** (Physical Education; Sports); **Physical Sciences** (Chemistry; Computer Science; Geology; Materials Engineering; Nanotechnology; Physics); **Social Sciences** (Archaeology; Economics; History; Political Sciences; Public Administration; Social Sciences)

Further Information: Also Prodatur Campus

History: Founded 2006.

Degrees and Diplomas: *Bachelor's Degree*; *Postgraduate Diploma*; *Master's Degree*. Also integrated Master's degree (M.Sc.), 5 yrs; MBA

Student Services: Canteen, Health Services, Sports Facilities
Last Updated: 02/01/12